TELEVISION & CABLE FACTBOOK
VOLUME 79

Albert Warren
Editor & Publisher 1961-2006

Publications & Services of Warren Communications News

TELEVISION & CABLE FACTBOOK: ONLINE

CABLE & STATION COVERAGE ATLAS ON CD-ROM
Published Annually

COMMUNICATIONS DAILY

CONSUMER ELECTRONICS DAILY

GREEN ELECTRONICS DAILY

PUBLIC BROADCASTING REPORT
Published Biweekly

SATELLITE WEEK

TELECOM A.M.
Daily News Service

WARREN'S WASHINGTON INTERNET DAILY

WASHINGTON TELECOM NEWSWIRE

Daily News Service

ISBN: 1-57696-063-3
ISSN: 0732-8648

Index to Sections
Television & Cable Factbook No. 79

TV STATIONS VOLUME

Section A

Section B

Section C – Charts

CABLE SYSTEMS VOLUME

Section D

Section E

Section F – Charts

Professional Cards

ENGINEERING & CONSULTING SERVICES ►

Index to Contents
Television & Cable Factbook No. 79

A

TELEVISION & CABLE
Factbook Online
continuous updates
fully searchable
easy to use

B

C

TELEVISION & CABLE
Factbook Online
continuous updates
fully searchable
easy to use

D

E

F

TELEVISION & CABLE
Factbook Online
continuous updates
fully searchable
easy to use

G

H

TELEVISION & CABLE
Factbook Online
continuous updates
fully searchable
easy to use

I

J

K

L

M

N

O

TELEVISION & CABLE
Factbook Online
continuous updates
fully searchable
easy to use
For more information call 800-771-9202 or visit www.warren-news.com

P

TELEVISION & CABLE
Factbook Online
continuous updates
fully searchable
easy to use

Q

R

S

T

For more information call **800-771-9202** or visit **www.warren-news.com**

TELEVISION & CABLE
Factbook Online
continuous updates
fully searchable
easy to use

U

V

W

X

Y

Z

U.S. Television Stations by Call Letters

As of October 1, 2010 with channel numbers in parentheses.

Operating stations only. Dagger(†) indicates Non-Commercial/Educational station.
Asterisk (*) indicates operating Construction Permit.
Please refer to the Online Factbook (http://www.tvcablefactbook.com) for the most current information.

K

W

ICARUS ™

Integrated Cable Areas – U.S.

Television & Cable Factbook's Database Cable Systems

Integrated Cable Area (ICA) Definition

Warren Communications News defines as one cable system a community or group of communities which receive essentially the same service at the same price from the same company, regardless of the number of headends or hubs used to deliver this service. *Television & Cable Factbook* has designated each system as an **I**ntegrated **C**able **A**rea and assigned it a unique identifier, the ICA. The ICA also is the unique record number used to relate data in clients' computerized applications that use the ICARUS ™ cable system database.

General Description

A cable television system is defined by the FCC (Sec. 76.5 of the Rules) as follows: "A facility consisting of a set of closed transmission paths and associated signal generation, reception, and control equipment that is designed to provide cable service which includes video programming and which is provided to multiple subscribers within a community, but such term does not include (1) a facility that serves only to retransmit the television signals of one or more television broadcast stations; (2) a facility that serves only subscribers in one or more multiple unit dwellings under common ownership, control or management, unless such facility or facilities uses any public right-of-way; (3) a facility of a common carrier which is subject, in whole or in part, to the provisions of Title II of the Communications Act of 1934, as amended, except that such facility shall be considered a cable system to the extent such facility is used in the transmission of video programming directly to subscribers; or (4) any facilities of any electric utility used solely for operating its electric utility systems."

*Indicates a franchise awarded but not yet operating.

†Indicates application for franchise is pending.

N.A. means information is not available.

All communities with cable service are listed in the index following the cable listings, with a reference to the appropriate cable system.

Information/Data

NOTE: All data is as reported by cable operators or individual cable systems. Not all cable systems report complete data.

Subscriber Counts

Subscriber count is as reported by cable operators or individual cable systems. Basic Subscribers, Expanded Basic Subscribers, and Pay Unit totals at the beginning of each state includes analog and digital subscribers. Not all cable systems report complete data.

NOTE: Reports from systems are of varying dates. The reporting dates for most systems are mid-year 2010 to year end 2010, and the total is an average of the various reporting dates. Total of basic subscribers listed in this edition of the Factbook is 77,732,882. Expanded basic subscribers total 23,898,344. Pay units total 10,302,872. Including subscribers not reported to the *Factbook* or to the government, we estimated total basic subscribers as of January 1, 2011 at 77,850,000.

TV Market Ranking

Indicates whether a system lies within 35-mile radius of commercial TV market as defined by FCC Rules & Regulations Governing Cable. If a system lies within the 35-mile radius of more than one Top-100 TV Market, both market numbers are shown. These market rankings are as of September 2010.

Began

Date service started.

Channel Capacity

Number of 6-MHz channels a system can carry.

Two-Way

Indicates whether a system has 2-way capability between subscribers and other points. If system is using its 2-way capability, that is also noted.

Signals

Call letters and affiliations are as of October 1, 2010.

A cable network program is any program furnished to the system by a cable network (national, regional or special) or by a series of interconnected cable systems. Delayed telecasts of programs originated by cable networks or by a series of interconnected cable systems are classified as a network.

Subscriber Fee

Charges for installation and monthly service are shown as well as converter charges when separately stated by the system operator.

Pay Service

A special program service, for which the subscriber pays an extra fee, is listed under "Pay Service" for each system providing such service. Data include number of units using the pay-cable service, programming, transmission method (via local tape, microwave or satellite) and charges to subscribers.

Pay-Per-View

The number of addressable homes; services offered; fee.

Interactive Services

Subscribers; services offered; fee.

Plant

Both coaxial and fiber-optic miles of plant in use are listed.

Homes passed indicates number of homes passed by cable and currently accessible to cable.

Homes in franchised area indicates number of housing units in area for which system holds franchise.

Personnel

The five types listed are: Manager; chief technician; program director; marketing director; customer service manager.

Franchise Fee

Amount paid by system operator to the franchising authority including percent of gross, flat fee, etc.

Ownership

Officers, titles and percentages listed are as reported by system operators to *Television & Cable Factbook* or to the FCC.

All cable system owners are listed in Ownership of Cable Systems in U.S. following the cable system listings.

Interests in broadcasting, manufacturing, microwave, telephone, publishing, etc., are noted.

Recent sales of systems are reported on individual systems as well as in ownership sections.

Information is obtained through system operators, the FCC, franchise holders, applicants, city officials and other sources. Though data may be incomplete, it is the best obtainable through diligent inquiry.

For statistical tables of cable industry development (1952-2009), largest systems, etc., consult Index at beginning of this Volume.

WARREN COMMUNICATIONS NEWS
2115 Ward Court NW
Washington, DC 20037
Phone: 202-872-9200
Fax: 202-318-8350
Email: info@warren-news.com
Web site: www.warren-news.com

Cable Systems State Index

ALABAMA

Total Systems: **149**
Total Communities Served: **630**
Franchises Not Yet Operating: **0**
Applications Pending: **0**
Communities with Applications: **0**
Number of Basic Subscribers: **1,149,987**
Number of Expanded Basic Subscribers: **303,124**
Number of Pay Units: **160,540**

Top 100 Markets Represented: Atlanta-Rome, GA (18); Birmingham (40); Mobile, AL-Pensacola, FL (59); Chattanooga, TN (78); Columbus, GA (94); Huntsville-Decatur, AL (96).

For a list of cable communities in this section, see the Cable Community Index located in the back of Cable Volume 2.
For explanation of terms used in cable system listings, see p. D-11.

ABBEVILLE—Comcast Cable, 1316 Harrison Ave, Ste 2, Panama City, FL 32401. Phone: 850-769-2929. Fax: 850-769-2988. Web Site: http://www.comcast.com. Also serves Henry County (portions). ICA: AL0161.
TV Market Ranking: Below 100 (ABBEVILLE, Henry County (portions)). Franchise award date: N.A. Franchise expiration date: N.A. Began: N.A.
Channel capacity: N.A. Channels available but not in use: N.A.

Basic Service
Subscribers: 1,038.
Programming (received off-air): WBIF (IND) Marianna [LICENSED & SILENT]; WDFX-TV (FOX) Ozark; WDHN (ABC) Dothan; WGIQ (PBS) Louisville; WIYC (IND) Troy; WSFA (NBC) Montgomery; WTVY (CBS, CW, MNT) Dothan.
Programming (via satellite): CTV Newsnet; QVC; TV Guide Network.
Fee: $43.30 installation.

Expanded Basic Service 1
Subscribers: N.A.
Programming (via satellite): ABC Family Channel; AMC; Animal Planet; Arts & Entertainment; BET Networks; Cartoon Network; CNBC; CNN; Comcast/Charter Sports Southeast (CSS); Comedy Central; Cooking Channel; Country Music TV; C-SPAN; C-SPAN 2; CW+; Discovery Channel; Disney Channel; Do-It-Yourself; E! Entertainment Television; ESPN; ESPN 2; ESPN Classic Sports; Eternal Word TV Network; Food Network; Fox News Channel; FX; Golf Channel; Great American Country; GSN; Headline News; HGTV; History Channel; Home Shopping Network; INSP; Lifetime; MTV; Nickelodeon; Speed Channel; Spike TV; SportSouth; Style Network; Syfy; TBS Superstation; The Learning Channel; Trinity Broadcasting Network; truTV; Turner Classic Movies; Turner Network TV; Turner South; TV Land; USA Network; Versus; VH1; Weather Channel.
Fee: $43.25 monthly.

Digital Basic Service
Subscribers: N.A.
Programming (received off-air): WDFX-TV (FOX) Ozark; WGIQ (PBS) Louisville; WSFA (NBC) Montgomery; WTVY (CBS, CW, MNT) Dothan.
Programming (via satellite): BBC America; Bio; C-SPAN 3; Discovery Digital Networks; Encore (multiplexed); ESPNews; Flix; GAS; History Channel International; MoviePlex; MTV Networks Digital Suite; Music Choice; Nick Jr.; Nick Too; SoapNet; Sundance Channel; Toon Disney.
Fee: $14.95 monthly.

Pay Service 1
Pay Units: N.A.
Programming (via satellite): Cinemax; HBO; Showtime.

Digital Pay Service 1
Pay Units: N.A.
Programming (via satellite): Cinemax (multiplexed); HBO (multiplexed); Showtime (multiplexed); Starz (multiplexed); The Movie Channel (multiplexed).
Fee: $8.50 monthly (each).
Video-On-Demand: No
Pay-Per-View
iN DEMAND (delivered digitally); Hot Choice (delivered digitally); Playboy TV (delivered digitally); Fresh (delivered digitally).
Internet Service
Operational: Yes.
Broadband Service: Comcast High Speed Internet.
Fee: $42.95 monthly.
Telephone Service
None
Homes passed: 1,544.
General Manager: Fritz Hoehne. Technical Operations Manager: Tim Denton. Marketing Manager: Kevin Canel.
Ownership: Comcast Cable Communications Inc. (MSO).

ABERNANT—Comcast Cable. Now served by TUSCALOOSA, AL [AL0230]. ICA: AL0113.

ADDISON—Alabama Broadband LLC, 3447A Parkwood Rd SE, Bessemer, AL 35022. Phones: 877-840-5040; 205-426-3432. E-mail: contact@alabamabroadband.net. Web Site: http://www.alabamabroadband.net. Also serves Winston County (eastern portion). ICA: AL0162.
TV Market Ranking: 96 (ADDISON, Winston County (eastern portion)). Franchise award date: January 1, 1988. Franchise expiration date: N.A. Began: February 1, 1990.
Channel capacity: 45 (not 2-way capable). Channels available but not in use: 15.

Basic Service
Subscribers: 122.
Programming (received off-air): WAAY-TV (ABC) Huntsville; WBIQ (PBS) Birmingham; WBRC (FOX) Birmingham; WCFT-TV (ABC) Tuscaloosa; WHNT-TV (CBS) Huntsville; WIAT (CBS) Birmingham; WTJP-TV (TBN) Gadsden; WTTO (CW) Homewood; WVTM-TV (NBC) Birmingham.
Programming (via satellite): ABC Family Channel; AMC; Animal Planet; CNBC; CNN; Comcast Sports Net Southeast; Discovery Channel; Disney Channel; ESPN; ESPN 2; Fox News Channel; HGTV; Lifetime; Spike TV; TBS Superstation; The Learning Channel; Turner Classic Movies; Turner Network TV; USA Network; Weather Channel; WGN America.
Fee: $29.95 installation; $30.20 monthly.

Pay Service 1
Pay Units: 46.
Programming (via satellite): Cinemax.
Fee: $10.00 installation; $9.00 monthly.
Video-On-Demand: No
Internet Service
Operational: No.
Telephone Service
None
Miles of Plant: 20.0 (coaxial); None (fiber optic).
President: Tom Early.
Ownership: Alabama Broadband LLC (MSO).

AKRON—Formerly served by CableSouth Inc. No longer in operation. ICA: AL0163.

ALBERTVILLE—Charter Communications, 2100 Columbiana Rd, Vestavia, AL 35216. Phone: 205-824-5400. Fax: 205-824-5490. Web Site: http://www.charter.com. Also serves Arab, Boaz, Crossville, DeKalb County (southwestern portion), Douglas, Etowah County (portions), Geraldine, Lakeview, Marshall County (portions), Mountainboro, Sardis City & Union Grove. ICA: AL0014.
TV Market Ranking: 96 (Arab, Union Grove); Below 100 (ALBERTVILLE, Boaz, Crossville, DeKalb County (southwestern portion), Douglas, Etowah County (portions), Geraldine, Lakeview, Marshall County (portions), Mountainboro, Sardis City). Franchise award date: N.A. Franchise expiration date: N.A. Began: November 1, 1964.
Channel capacity: N.A. Channels available but not in use: N.A.

Basic Service
Subscribers: 63,257.
Programming (received off-air): WAAY-TV (ABC) Huntsville; WAFF (NBC) Huntsville; WBRC (FOX) Birmingham; WHDF (CW) Florence; WHIQ (PBS) Huntsville; WHNT-TV (CBS) Huntsville; WIAT (CBS) Birmingham; WTJP-TV (TBN) Gadsden; WVTM-TV (NBC) Birmingham; WZDX (FOX, MNT) Huntsville.
Programming (via satellite): WGN America.
Current originations: Public Access.
Fee: $29.99 installation.

Expanded Basic Service 1
Subscribers: 15,568.
Programming (via satellite): ABC Family Channel; AMC; Animal Planet; Arts & Entertainment; Cartoon Network; CNBC; CNN; Comcast Sports Net Southeast; Comcast/Charter Sports Southeast (CSS); Comedy Central; Country Music TV; C-SPAN; Discovery Channel; Disney Channel; ESPN; ESPN 2; Fox News Channel; FX; G4; Headline News; HGTV; History Channel; Home Shopping Network; ION Television; Lifetime; MTV; Nickelodeon; Product Information Network; QVC; Speed Channel; Spike TV; SportSouth; Syfy; TBS Superstation; The Learning Channel; Turner Classic Movies; Turner Network TV; TV Guide Network; TV Land; Univision; USA Network; VH1; WE tv; Weather Channel.
Fee: $43.00 monthly.

Digital Basic Service
Subscribers: N.A.
Programming (via satellite): BBC America; Bio; Discovery Digital Networks; Do-It-Yourself; GalaVision; Great American Country; History Channel International; Independent Film Channel; Lifetime Movie Network; Music Choice; Sundance Channel; Versus.
Fee: $16.99 monthly; $8.95 converter.

Digital Pay Service 1
Pay Units: N.A.
Programming (via satellite): Cinemax (multiplexed); Encore (multiplexed); Flix; HBO (multiplexed); Showtime (multiplexed); Starz (multiplexed); The Movie Channel (multiplexed).
Fee: $11.95 monthly (Cinemax, HBO, Flix/Showtime/TMC, or Starz/Encore).
Video-On-Demand: Yes
Pay-Per-View
Addressable homes: 2,040.
iN DEMAND (delivered digitally); Playboy TV (delivered digitally); Pleasure (delivered digitally); Fresh (delivered digitally); Shorteez (delivered digitally).
Internet Service
Operational: Yes. Began: May 1, 1999.
Broadband Service: Charter Pipeline.
Fee: $29.99 monthly.
Telephone Service
Digital: Operational
Miles of Plant: 739.0 (coaxial); 155.0 (fiber optic). Total homes in franchised area: 102,824.
Vice President & General Manager: Don Karell. Technical Operations Director: Greg Prim. Marketing Director: David Redmond. Marketing Manager: Jeff Hatcher.
City fee: 4% of gross.
Ownership: Charter Communications Inc. (MSO).

ALEXANDER CITY—Charter Communications. Now served by LEEDS, AL [AL0192]. ICA: AL0164.

ALICEVILLE—Northland Cable Television, PO Box 1269, 307 1st St, Reform, AL 35481. Phones: 800-828-8019; 205-375-2275. Fax: 205-375-2298. E-mail: aliceville@northlandcabletv.com. Web Site: http://www.northlandcabletv.com. Also serves Carrollton, Gordo, Pickens County, Pickensville & Reform. ICA: AL0055.
TV Market Ranking: Below 100 (ALICEVILLE, Carrollton, Gordo, Pickens County (portions), Pickensville, Reform); Outside TV Markets (Pickens County (portions)). Franchise award date: N.A. Franchise expiration date: N.A. Began: May 1, 1971.
Channel capacity: 39 (operating 2-way). Channels available but not in use: N.A.

Basic Service
Subscribers: 4,214.
Programming (received off-air): WBIQ (PBS) Birmingham; WBRC (FOX) Birmingham; WCBI-TV (CBS, CW, MNT) Columbus; WCFT-TV (ABC) Tuscaloosa; WDBB (CW) Bessemer; WLOV-TV (FOX) West Point; WTVA (NBC) Tupelo; WVTM-TV (NBC) Birmingham.
Programming (via satellite): ABC Family Channel; AMC; Arts & Entertainment; BET Networks; Cartoon Network; CNN; Comcast Sports Net Southeast; C-SPAN; Discovery Channel; ESPN; ESPN 2; Great American Country; Headline News; HGTV; Nickelodeon; QVC; Spike TV; TBS Superstation; Trinity Broadcasting Network; Turner Classic Movies; Turner Network TV; USA Network; Weather Channel; WGN America.
Fee: $31.99 installation; $25.00 monthly.
Pay Service 1
Pay Units: 639.
Programming (via satellite): Cinemax; Encore; HBO; Showtime.
Fee: $20.95 monthly.
Video-On-Demand: Yes
Internet Service
Operational: Yes.
Broadband Service: Northland Express.
Telephone Service
None
Miles of Plant: 142.0 (coaxial); 36.0 (fiber optic). Homes passed: 5,500.
Regional Manager: Ricky Moneyham. Manager: Tom Earley. Chief Technician: Bart Hudgins. Marketing Director: Lee Beck.
Ownership: Northland Communications Corp. (MSO).

ALLGOOD—Formerly served by SouthTel Communications LP. No longer in operation. ICA: AL0165.

ALTOONA—Rapid Cable, 355 S Main St, Clinton, IN 47842. Phones: 866-301-5388; 765-832-3586. Fax: 765-832-3595. Also serves Walnut Grove. ICA: AL0231.
TV Market Ranking: Below 100 (ALTOONA, Walnut Grove). Franchise award date: N.A. Franchise expiration date: N.A. Began: N.A.
Channel capacity: N.A. Channels available but not in use: N.A.
Basic Service
Subscribers: 610.
Programming (received off-air): WAAY-TV (ABC) Huntsville; WABM (MNT) Birmingham; WAFF (NBC) Huntsville; WBIQ (PBS) Birmingham; WBRC (FOX) Birmingham; WCFT-TV (ABC) Tuscaloosa; WIAT (CBS) Birmingham; WPXH-TV (ION) Gadsden; WTJP-TV (TBN) Gadsden; WTTO (CW) Homewood; WVTM-TV (NBC) Birmingham.
Programming (via satellite): ABC Family Channel; AMC; Animal Planet; Arts & Entertainment; BET Networks; Bravo; Cartoon Network; CNBC; CNN; Comedy Central; Country Music TV; C-SPAN; Discovery Channel; Disney Channel; E! Entertainment Television; ESPN; ESPN 2; Food Network; FX; Golf Channel; Hallmark Channel; Headline News; HGTV; History Channel; Home Shopping Network; Lifetime; MSNBC; MTV; National Geographic Channel; Nickelodeon; Outdoor Channel; QVC; Speed Channel; Syfy; TBS Superstation; The Learning Channel; Toon Disney; Travel Channel; truTV; Turner Classic Movies; Turner Network TV; TV Land; Univision; USA Network; VH1; Weather Channel; WGN America.
Fee: $29.95 installation; $19.95 monthly.
Digital Basic Service
Subscribers: N.A.
Programming (via satellite): Music Choice.
Fee: $12.95 monthly.
Digital Pay Service 1
Pay Units: 98.
Programming (via satellite): HBO (multiplexed).
Fee: $11.95 monthly.
Digital Pay Service 2
Pay Units: 62.
Programming (via satellite): Cinemax (multiplexed); Encore; Flix; Showtime (multiplexed); Starz (multiplexed); The Movie Channel (multiplexed).
Video-On-Demand: No
Pay-Per-View
iN DEMAND (delivered digitally).
Internet Service
Operational: No.
Telephone Service
None
Miles of Plant: 33.0 (coaxial); None (fiber optic).
Regional Manager: Paul Broseman. Plant Manager: Ron Page.
Franchise fee: 3% of gross.
Ownership: Rapid Communications LLC (MSO).

ANDALUSIA—TV Cable Co. of Andalusia Inc., PO Box 34, 213 Dunson St, Andalusia, AL 36420-3705. Phone: 334-222-6464. Fax: 334-222-7226. E-mail: support@andycable.com. Web Site: http://www.andycable.com. ICA: AL0043.
TV Market Ranking: Outside TV Markets (ANDALUSIA). Franchise award date: January 1, 1963. Franchise expiration date: N.A. Began: March 1, 1965.
Channel capacity: 53 (operating 2-way). Channels available but not in use: 4.
Basic Service
Subscribers: 4,000.
Programming (received off-air): WAKA (CBS) Selma; WCOV-TV (FOX) Montgomery; WDIQ (PBS) Dozier; WEAR-TV (ABC) Pensacola; WIYC (IND) Troy; WKRG-TV (CBS) Mobile; WNCF (ABC) Montgomery; WPMI-TV (NBC) Mobile; WSFA (NBC) Montgomery; WTVY (CBS, CW, MNT) Dothan; 1 FM.
Programming (via satellite): ABC Family Channel; AMC; Animal Planet; Arts & Entertainment; BET Networks; CNBC; CNN; Comcast Sports Net Southeast; Country Music TV; C-SPAN; Discovery Channel; Disney Channel; ESPN; ESPN 2; Fox News Channel; FX; Golf Channel; Hallmark Channel; Headline News; HGTV; History Channel; Lifetime; MSNBC; MTV; Nickelodeon; Outdoor Channel; QVC; Speed Channel; Spike TV; Syfy; TBS Superstation; The Learning Channel; Toon Disney; Trinity Broadcasting Network; Turner Classic Movies; Turner Network TV; TV Guide Network; TV Land; USA Network; VH1; Weather Channel; WGN America.
Fee: $30.00 installation; $29.00 monthly.
Pay Service 1
Pay Units: 1,181.
Programming (via satellite): Cinemax; HBO; Showtime.
Fee: $15.00 installation; $10.00 monthly (Cinemax), $12.00 monthly (HBO or Showtime).
Video-On-Demand: No
Internet Service
Operational: Yes. Began: May 1, 2003.
Subscribers: 850.
Broadband Service: In-house.
Fee: $45.00 installation; $39.00 monthly.
Telephone Service
None
Miles of Plant: 125.0 (coaxial); None (fiber optic). Homes passed: 4,300. Total homes in franchised area: 4,400.
Manager: Ivan Bishop. Chief Technician: Darrell Mitchell. Senior Internet Administrator: Wayne E. Alday.
City fee: $125 annually.
Ownership: TV Cable Co. of Andalusia Inc.

ANNISTON—Cable One, 620 Noble St, Anniston, AL 36201-5622. Phone: 256-236-7034. Fax: 256-236-4475. E-mail: cptomlin@cableone.net. Web Site: http://www.cableone.net. Also serves Anniston Army Depot, Calhoun County (unincorporated areas), Fort McClellan, Hobson City, Jacksonville, Munford, Ohatchee, Oxford, Talladega County (unincorporated areas) & Weaver. ICA: AL0008.
TV Market Ranking: Below 100 (ANNISTON, Anniston Army Depot, Calhoun County (unincorporated areas), Fort McClellan, Hobson City, Jacksonville, Munford, Ohatchee, Oxford, Talladega County (unincorporated areas), Weaver). Franchise award date: May 5, 2009. Franchise expiration date: N.A. Began: May 2, 1961.
Channel capacity: 78 (operating 2-way). Channels available but not in use: 6.
Basic Service
Subscribers: 32,796.
Programming (received off-air): WABM (MNT) Birmingham; WBMA-LP (ABC) Birmingham; WBRC (FOX) Birmingham; WCIQ (PBS) Mount Cheaha State Park; WIAT (CBS) Birmingham; WJXS-CA Jacksonville; WPXH-TV (ION) Gadsden; WTJP-TV (TBN) Gadsden; WTTO (CW) Homewood; WVTM-TV (NBC) Birmingham.
Current originations: Public Access.
Fee: $46.00 monthly.
Expanded Basic Service 1
Subscribers: N.A.
Programming (via satellite): ABC Family Channel; AMC; Animal Planet; Arts & Entertainment; BET Networks; Cartoon Network; CNBC; CNN; Comcast Sports Net Southeast; Comedy Central; Country Music TV; C-SPAN; C-SPAN 2; Discovery Channel; Disney Channel; E! Entertainment Television; ESPN; ESPN 2; Food Network; Fox Movie Channel; Fox News Channel; FX; Headline News; HGTV; History Channel; Home Shopping Network; Lifetime; MSNBC; MTV; Nickelodeon; QVC; Spike TV; Syfy; TBS Superstation; The Learning Channel; Turner Classic Movies; Turner Network TV; TV Guide Network; TV Land; USA Network; VH1; Weather Channel.
Digital Basic Service
Subscribers: 13,744.
Programming (received off-air): WVTM-TV (NBC) Birmingham.
Programming (via satellite): 3 Angels Broadcasting Network; ABC Family HD; Arts & Entertainment HD; Bio; Boomerang; Boomerang en Espanol; BYU Television; Cine Mexicano; CNN en Espanol; Discovery Channel HD; Discovery HD Theater; Discovery Health Channel; Discovery Kids Channel; Discovery Military Channel; Disney Channel HD; ESPN 2 HD; ESPN Classic Sports; ESPN Deportes; ESPN HD; ESPNews; FamilyNet; Food Network HD; Fox College Sports Atlantic; Fox College Sports Central; Fox College Sports Pacific; Fox HD; Fox Soccer; Fox Sports en Espanol; Fuel TV; Golf Channel; Great American Country; GSN; Hallmark Channel; HGTV HD; History Channel HD; History Channel International; INSP; La Familia Network; Latele Novela Network; mun2 television; Music Choice; National Geographic Channel; National Geographic Channel HD Network; Outdoor Channel; PBS HD; Science Channel; SoapNet; Speed Channel; TBS in HD; Telemundo; TLC HD; Toon Disney; Toon Disney en Espanol; Trinity Broadcasting Network; Turner Network TV HD; TVG Network; Universal HD; WE tv.
Fee: $9.95 monthly.
Digital Pay Service 1
Pay Units: N.A.
Programming (via satellite): Cinemax (multiplexed); Encore (multiplexed); Flix; HBO (multiplexed); HBO HD; HBO Latino; Showtime (multiplexed); Showtime HD; Starz (multiplexed); Sundance Channel; The Movie Channel (multiplexed).
Fee: $15.00 monthly (each).
Video-On-Demand: No
Pay-Per-View
Movies (delivered digitally), Addressable: Yes; Pleasure (delivered digitally); Ten Clips (delivered digitally); Ten Blox (delivered digitally); Ten Blue (delivered digitally).
Internet Service
Operational: Yes. Began: July 1, 2000.
Subscribers: 11,000.
Broadband Service: CableONE.net.
Fee: $75.00 installation; $43.00 monthly; $5.00 modem lease.
Telephone Service
Analog: Not Operational
Digital: Operational
Fee: $75.00 installation; $39.95 monthly
Miles of Plant: 1,185.0 (coaxial); 200.0 (fiber optic). Homes passed: 46,304. Total homes in franchised area: 46,304.
Manager: Terry Womack. Plant Manager: Tim Thompson. Marketing Manager: Mike Huey.
Ownership: Cable One Inc. (MSO).

APPLETON—Formerly served by Trust Cable. No longer in operation. ICA: AL0166.

ARDMORE—Mediacom, 123 Ware Dr NE, Huntsville, AL 35811-1061. Phones: 850-934-7700 (Gulf Breeze regional office); 256-852-7427. Fax: 256-851-7708. Web Site: http://www.mediacomcable.com. Also serves Limestone County, AL; Ardmore, Elkton, Giles County, Lincoln County & Prospect, TN. ICA: AL0095.
TV Market Ranking: 96 (Ardmore, ARDMORE, Elkton, Giles County (portions), Limestone County, Lincoln County (portions), Prospect); Outside TV Markets (Giles County (portions), Lincoln County (portions)). Franchise award date: November 3, 1980. Franchise expiration date: N.A. Began: August 15, 1982.
Channel capacity: N.A. Channels available but not in use: N.A.
Basic Service
Subscribers: 7,342.
Programming (received off-air): WAAY-TV (ABC) Huntsville; WAFF (NBC) Huntsville; WHDF (CW) Florence; WHIQ (PBS) Huntsville; WHNT-TV (CBS) Huntsville; WSMV-TV (NBC, TMO) Nashville; WZDX (FOX, MNT) Huntsville.
Programming (via satellite): ABC Family Channel; AMC; AmericanLife TV Network; Animal Planet; Arts & Entertainment; BET Networks; Black Family Channel; Bravo; Cartoon Network; CNBC; CNN; Comcast Sports Net Southeast; Comedy Central; Country Music TV; C-SPAN; C-SPAN 2; Discovery Channel; Disney Channel; E! Entertainment Television; ESPN; ESPN 2; Eternal Word TV Network; FitTV; Food

Network; Fox Movie Channel; Fox News Channel; FX; Golf Channel; Hallmark Channel; Headline News; HGTV; History Channel; INSP; ION Television; Lifetime; MSNBC; MTV; NASA TV; Nickelodeon; Outdoor Channel; Oxygen; QVC; SoapNet; Speed Channel; Spike TV; SportSouth; Syfy; TBS Superstation; The Learning Channel; Toon Disney; Travel Channel; Trinity Broadcasting Network; truTV; Turner Classic Movies; Turner Network TV; TV Guide Network; TV Land; USA Network; VH1; WE tv; Weather Channel; WGN America.
Fee: $21.50 installation; $44.95 monthly; $1.00 converter; $32.00 additional installation.

Digital Basic Service
Subscribers: 2,344.
Programming (via satellite): BBC America; Bio; Bloomberg Television; Discovery Digital Networks; Fox Sports World; Fuse; G4; GSN; Halogen Network; History Channel International; Independent Film Channel; Lifetime Movie Network; Lime; Music Choice; National Geographic Channel; Style Network; Versus.
Fee: $9.95 monthly.

Digital Pay Service 1
Pay Units: N.A.
Programming (via satellite): Cinemax (multiplexed); Encore; Flix; HBO (multiplexed); Showtime (multiplexed); Starz (multiplexed); Sundance Channel; The Movie Channel (multiplexed).

Video-On-Demand: Yes

Pay-Per-View
Addressable homes: 7,342.
ESPN Now (delivered digitally), Addressable: Yes; Pleasure (delivered digitally); TVN Entertainment; TVN Entertainment (delivered digitally); sports (delivered digitally).

Internet Service
Operational: Yes. Began: September 1, 2002.
Broadband Service: Mediacom High Speed Internet.
Fee: $106.00 installation; $40.95 monthly.

Telephone Service
None

Miles of Plant: 1,200.0 (coaxial); None (fiber optic). Homes passed: 11,944. Miles of plant (coax) includes Huntsville, Big Cove, Huntland TN, and Louisville MS

Vice President: David Servies. Manager: Tommy Hill. Chief Technician: Harold Balch. Sales & Marketing Manager: Joey Nagem. Customer Service Supervisor: Sandy Acklin.

City fee: 3% of gross.

Ownership: Mediacom LLC (MSO).

ARLEY—Galaxy Cablevision, PO Box 879, 118 S Jackson St, Grove Hill, AL 36451-0879. Phone: 251-275-3118. Fax: 251-275-3120. Web Site: http://www.galaxycable.com. ICA: AL0128.

TV Market Ranking: Outside TV Markets (ARLEY). Franchise award date: N.A. Franchise expiration date: N.A. Began: November 1, 1990.

Channel capacity: 61 (not 2-way capable). Channels available but not in use: 23.

Basic Service
Subscribers: 103.
Programming (received off-air): W55BJ Jasper; WABM (MNT) Birmingham; WBIQ (PBS) Birmingham; WBRC (FOX) Birmingham; WCFT-TV (ABC) Tuscaloosa; WIAT (CBS) Birmingham; WTJP-TV (TBN) Gadsden; WTTO (CW) Homewood; WVTM-TV (NBC) Birmingham.
Programming (via satellite): ABC Family Channel; Animal Planet; Arts & Entertainment; CNBC; CNN; Comcast Sports Net Southeast; Discovery Channel; Disney Channel; ESPN; ESPN 2; Fox News Channel; FX; Great American Country; Headline News; History Channel; Lifetime; Outdoor Channel; QVC; TBS Superstation; The Learning Channel; Toon Disney; Travel Channel; Trinity Broadcasting Network; Turner Classic Movies; Turner Network TV; USA Network; Weather Channel; WGN America.
Fee: $40.10 monthly.

Pay Service 1
Pay Units: N.A.
Programming (via satellite): HBO.
Fee: $9.95 monthly.

Internet Service
Operational: No.

Telephone Service
None

Miles of Plant: 34.0 (coaxial); None (fiber optic). Homes passed: 664.

State Manager: Bill Flowers. Technical Manager & Engineer: Greg Berthaut. Customer Service Representative: Lisa Ray.

Ownership: Galaxy Cable Inc. (MSO).

ASHLAND—CommuniComm Services, 3164 Hwy 431, Ste 9, Roanoke, AL 36274-1702. Phone: 334-863-7080. Fax: 334-863-2027. Web Site: http://www.netcommander.com. Also serves Lineville. ICA: AL0096.

TV Market Ranking: Below 100 (ASHLAND, Lineville). Franchise award date: January 1, 1984. Franchise expiration date: N.A. Began: April 1, 1987.

Channel capacity: N.A. Channels available but not in use: N.A.

Basic Service
Subscribers: 644.
Programming (received off-air): WAXC-LP (IND) Alexander City; WBRC (FOX) Birmingham; WCIQ (PBS) Mount Cheaha State Park; WGCL-TV (CBS) Atlanta; WIAT (CBS) Birmingham; WJSU-TV (ABC) Anniston; WSFA (NBC) Montgomery; WTTO (CW) Homewood; WTVM (ABC) Columbus; WVTM-TV (NBC) Birmingham.
Programming (via satellite): TBS Superstation; WGN America.
Fee: $20.00 installation; $11.00 monthly; $12.50 additional installation.

Expanded Basic Service 1
Subscribers: N.A.
Programming (via satellite): ABC Family Channel; American Movie Classics; Animal Planet; Arts & Entertainment; BET Networks; Bravo; Cartoon Network; CNBC; CNN; Comcast/Charter Sports Southeast (CSS); Comedy Central; Country Music TV; C-SPAN; C-SPAN 2; Discovery Channel; Disney Channel; E! Entertainment Television; ESPN; ESPN 2; ESPN Classic Sports; Food Network; Fox Movie Channel; Fox News Channel; FX; Great American Country; Hallmark Channel; Headline News; HGTV; History Channel; Home Shopping Network; ION Television; Lifetime; Lifetime Movie Network; MSNBC; MTV; Nick Jr.; Outdoor Channel; QVC; ShopNBC; Spike TV; Syfy; The Learning Channel; The Sportsman Channel; Travel Channel; Trinity Broadcasting Network; truTV; Turner Network TV; Turner South; TV Land; USA Network; VH1; WE tv; Weather Channel.

Digital Basic Service
Subscribers: 96.
Programming (via satellite): BBC America; Bloomberg Television; Discovery Health Channel; Discovery Kids Channel; Discovery Military Channel; Discovery Planet Green; DMX Music; FitTV; Fox Soccer; G4; Golf Channel; GSN; Halogen Network; ID Investigation Discovery; Independent Film Channel; Science Channel; Sleuth; SoapNet; Speed Channel; Toon Disney; Turner Classic Movies; Versus.

Digital Pay Service 1
Pay Units: 137.
Programming (via satellite): Cinemax (multiplexed); Encore (multiplexed); HBO (multiplexed); Showtime (multiplexed); Starz (multiplexed).

Video-On-Demand: No

Pay-Per-View
iN DEMAND (delivered digitally); Hot Choice (delivered digitally); Playboy TV (delivered digitally); Fresh (delivered digitally).

Internet Service
Operational: No.

Telephone Service
None

Miles of Plant: 27.0 (coaxial); None (fiber optic). Homes passed: 2,086.

General Manager: Brian Chase. Chief Technician: William Boyd.

Ownership: James Cable LLC (MSO).

ASHVILLE—Alabama Broadband LLC, 3447A Parkwood Rd SE, Bessemer, AL 35022. Phones: 877-840-5040; 205-426-3432. E-mail: contact@alabamabroadband.com. Web Site: http://www.alabamabroadband.net. Also serves Springville, St. Clair County (portions) & Steele. ICA: AL0168.

TV Market Ranking: 40 (ASHVILLE, Springville, St. Clair County (portions)); Below 100 (Steele, St. Clair County (portions)). Franchise award date: N.A. Franchise expiration date: N.A. Began: January 1, 1988.

Channel capacity: 45 (not 2-way capable). Channels available but not in use: N.A.

Basic Service
Subscribers: 650.
Programming (received off-air): WABM (MNT) Birmingham; WBIQ (PBS) Birmingham; WBRC (FOX) Birmingham; WIAT (CBS) Birmingham; WJSU-TV (ABC) Anniston; WPXH-TV (ION) Gadsden; WTJP-TV (TBN) Gadsden; WTTO (CW) Homewood; WVTM-TV (NBC) Birmingham.
Programming (via satellite): ABC Family Channel; AMC; Animal Planet; Arts & Entertainment; CNN; Comcast Sports Net Southeast; Country Music TV; C-SPAN; C-SPAN 2; Discovery Channel; Disney Channel; ESPN; ESPN 2; Fox News Channel; FX; Headline News; HGTV; Home Shopping Network; MTV; National Geographic Channel; Nickelodeon; Outdoor Channel; QVC; Spike TV; TBS Superstation; The Learning Channel; truTV; Turner Network TV; TV Guide Network; USA Network; VH1; Weather Channel; WGN America.
Fee: $29.95 installation; $31.20 monthly.

Pay Service 1
Pay Units: 475.
Programming (via satellite): HBO.
Fee: $10.00 installation; $9.00 monthly (HBO), $8.00 monthly (Showtime).

Pay Service 2
Pay Units: 348.
Programming (via satellite): Showtime.
Fee: $40.00 installation; $8.00 monthly (Cinemax).

Video-On-Demand: No

Internet Service
Operational: Yes.
Fee: $29.95-$54.95 monthly.

Telephone Service
Digital: Operational
Fee: $34.95 monthly

Miles of Plant: 186.0 (coaxial); None (fiber optic).

President: Tom Early. Marketing Director: Bob Garner.

City fee: 3% of gross.

Ownership: Alabama Broadband LLC (MSO).

ATHENS—Charter Communications, 2100 Columbiana Rd, Vestavia, AL 35216. Phone: 205-824-5400. Fax: 205-824-5490. Web Site: http://www.charter.com. Also serves Elkmont & Limestone County (portions). ICA: AL0169.

TV Market Ranking: 96 (ATHENS, Elkmont, Limestone County (portions)). Franchise award date: N.A. Franchise expiration date: N.A. Began: October 24, 1966.

Channel capacity: N.A. Channels available but not in use: N.A.

Basic Service
Subscribers: 8,900.
Programming (received off-air): WAAY-TV (ABC) Huntsville; WAFF (NBC) Huntsville; WHDF (CW) Florence; WHIQ (PBS) Huntsville; WHNT-TV (CBS) Huntsville; WTZT-CA Athens; WYAM-LP (IND) Priceville; WZDX (FOX, MNT) Huntsville; allband FM.
Programming (via satellite): CNBC; C-SPAN; C-SPAN 2; Fox News Channel; Home Shopping Network; INSP; ION Television; NASA TV; QVC; Trinity Broadcasting Network; Weather Channel; WGN America.
Fee: $29.99 installation; $19.99 monthly.

Expanded Basic Service 1
Subscribers: 7,707.
Programming (via satellite): ABC Family Channel; AMC; AmericanLife TV Network; Animal Planet; Arts & Entertainment; BET Networks; Bravo; Cartoon Network; CNBC; CNN; Comcast Sports Net Southeast; Comedy Central; Country Music TV; Discovery Channel; Disney Channel; E! Entertainment Television; ESPN; ESPN 2; Eternal Word TV Network; Food Network; FX; G4; Golf Channel; GSN; Hallmark Channel; Headline News; HGTV; History Channel; Lifetime; MSNBC; MTV; National Geographic Channel; Nickelodeon; Outdoor Channel; Oxygen; Product Information Network; Shop at Home; SoapNet; Speed Channel; Spike TV; SportSouth; Syfy; Telemundo; The Learning Channel; Toon Disney; Travel Channel; truTV; Turner Classic Movies; Turner Network TV; TV Guide Network; TV Land; Univision; USA Network; Versus; VH1; WE tv.
Fee: $43.00 monthly.

Digital Basic Service
Subscribers: N.A.
Programming (via satellite): BBC America; Bio; Bloomberg Television; Discovery Digital Networks; Do-It-Yourself; ESPN Classic Sports; ESPNews; Fox College Sports Atlantic; Fox College Sports Central; Fox College Sports Pacific; Fox Movie Channel; Fox Sports en Espanol; Fox Sports World; GAS; Great American Country; History Channel International; Independent Film Channel; Lifetime Movie Network; MTV Networks Digital Suite; MuchMusic Network; Music Choice; Nick Jr.; Nick Too; NickToons TV; Style Network; Sundance Channel.
Fee: $16.99 monthly.

Digital Pay Service 1
Pay Units: 1,590.
Programming (via satellite): Cinemax (multiplexed); Starz (multiplexed).
Fee: $7.95 monthly.

Digital Pay Service 2
Pay Units: 1,810.
Programming (via satellite): HBO (multiplexed).
Fee: $9.95 monthly.
Digital Pay Service 3
Pay Units: 779.
Programming (via satellite): Flix; Showtime (multiplexed); The Movie Channel (multiplexed).
Fee: $9.95 monthly.
Digital Pay Service 4
Pay Units: N.A.
Programming (via satellite): Encore (multiplexed).
Video-On-Demand: Yes
Pay-Per-View
iN DEMAND (delivered digitally); NHL Center Ice/MLB Extra Innings (delivered digitally); Playboy (delivered digitally); The Pleasure Network (delivered digitally); Spice (delivered digitally); Spice 2 (delivered digitally).
Internet Service
Operational: Yes. Began: July 1, 2001.
Broadband Service: Charter Pipeline.
Fee: $29.99 monthly.
Telephone Service
Digital: Operational
Miles of Plant: 463.0 (coaxial); None (fiber optic). Homes passed: 12,441.
Vice President & General Manager: Don Karell. Technical Operations Director: Greg Prim. Marketing Director: David Redmond. Marketing Manager: Jeff Hatcher.
Ownership: Charter Communications Inc. (MSO).

ATHENS—Formerly served by Madison Communications. No longer in operation. ICA: AL0256.

ATHENS—Knology, 2401 10th St SW, Huntsville, AL 35805. Phones: 888-472-2311; 256-533-5353. Fax: 256-533-2353. Web Site: http://www.knology.com. Also serves Decatur. ICA: AL0257. **Note:** This system is an overbuild.
TV Market Ranking: 96 (ATHENS, Decatur). Franchise award date: N.A. Franchise expiration date: N.A. Began: January 1, 1995.
Channel capacity: N.A. Channels available but not in use: N.A.
Basic Service
Subscribers: N.A.
Programming (received off-air): WAAY-TV (ABC) Huntsville; WAFF (NBC) Huntsville; WHDF (CW) Florence; WHIQ (PBS) Huntsville; WHNT-TV (CBS) Huntsville; WMJN-LP Somerville; WZDX (FOX, MNT) Huntsville.
Programming (via satellite): ABC Family Channel; AMC; Animal Planet; Arts & Entertainment; BET Networks; Cartoon Network; CBS College Sports Network; CNBC; CNN; CNN International; Comcast Sports Net Southeast; Comedy Central; Country Music TV; C-SPAN; C-SPAN 2; Discovery Channel; Disney Channel; ESPN; ESPN 2; ESPN Classic Sports; Eternal Word TV Network; Food Network; Fox News Channel; FX; Golf Channel; GSN; Hallmark Channel; Headline News; Healthy Living Channel; HGTV; History Channel; Home Shopping Network; ION Television; Lifetime; Lifetime Movie Network; MTV; NASA TV; Nickelodeon; Outdoor Channel; QVC; SoapNet; Speed Channel; Spike TV; SportSouth; Syfy; TBS Superstation; The Learning Channel; The Sportsman Channel; Travel Channel; Trinity Broadcasting Network; truTV; Turner Classic Movies; Turner Network TV; TV Guide Network; TV Land; USA Network; VH1; WE tv; Weather Channel; WGN America.
Current originations: Educational Access.
Fee: $39.95 monthly.
Pay Service 1
Pay Units: N.A.
Programming (via satellite): Cinemax; HBO; Showtime; The Movie Channel.
Fee: $11.95 monthly (Cinemax, Showtime or TMC), $13.95 monthly (HBO).
Video-On-Demand: No
Pay-Per-View
iN DEMAND, Fee: $3.95, Addressable: Yes; special events.
Internet Service
Operational: Yes.
Broadband Service: In-house.
Fee: $39.95 monthly.
Telephone Service
Digital: Operational
Fee: $39.95 monthly
Miles of Plant: 350.0 (coaxial); None (fiber optic).
President & Chief Financial Officer: M. Todd Holt.
Ownership: Knology Inc. (MSO).

ATMORE—Mediacom. Now served by GULF BREEZE, FL [FL0070]. ICA: AL0064.

ATTALLA—Comcast Cable, 1131 Whigham Place, Tuscaloosa, AL 35405. Phone: 765-832-3586. Web Site: http://www.comcast.com. Also serves Etowah County, Reece City & Ridgeville. ICA: AL0170.
TV Market Ranking: Below 100 (ATTALLA, Etowah County, Reece City, Ridgeville). Franchise award date: July 1, 1966. Franchise expiration date: N.A. Began: August 1, 1968.
Channel capacity: N.A. Channels available but not in use: N.A.
Basic Service
Subscribers: 2,784.
Programming (received off-air): WAAY-TV (ABC) Huntsville; WABM (MNT) Birmingham; WAFF (NBC) Huntsville; WBIQ (PBS) Birmingham; WBRC (FOX) Birmingham; WCFT-TV (ABC) Tuscaloosa; WIAT (CBS) Birmingham; WPXH-TV (ION) Gadsden; WTJP-TV (TBN) Gadsden; WTTO (CW) Homewood; WVTM-TV (NBC) Birmingham; allband FM.
Programming (via satellite): Home Shopping Network; QVC; TBS Superstation; Weather Channel; WGN America.
Fee: $29.95 installation; $19.95 monthly.
Expanded Basic Service 1
Subscribers: N.A.
Programming (received off-air): WJXS-CA Jacksonville.
Programming (via satellite): ABC Family Channel; AMC; Animal Planet; Arts & Entertainment; BET Networks; Bravo; Cartoon Network; CNBC; CNN; Comcast Sports Net Southeast; Comedy Central; Country Music TV; C-SPAN; Discovery Channel; Disney Channel; E! Entertainment Television; ESPN; ESPN 2; Food Network; Fox News Channel; FX; Golf Channel; Hallmark Channel; Headline News; HGTV; History Channel; Lifetime; MSNBC; MTV; National Geographic Channel; Nickelodeon; Outdoor Channel; Speed Channel; Spike TV; SportSouth; Style Network; Syfy; The Learning Channel; Toon Disney; Travel Channel; truTV; Turner Classic Movies; Turner Network TV; TV Land; Univision; USA Network; VH1.
Fee: $20.00 monthly.
Digital Basic Service
Subscribers: N.A.
Programming (via satellite): BBC America; Bio; CMT Pure Country; Discovery Kids Channel; Discovery Military Channel; Discovery Planet Green; Do-It-Yourself; Fuse; History Channel International; ID Investigation Discovery; Independent Film Channel; Lifetime Movie Network; MTV Hits; MTV2; Music Choice; Nick Jr.; Nick Too; NickToons TV; Science Channel; Sundance Channel; VH1 Classic; VH1 Soul.
Fee: $12.95 monthly.
Digital Pay Service 1
Pay Units: 235.
Programming (via satellite): Cinemax (multiplexed).
Fee: $6.00 installation; $10.95 monthly.
Digital Pay Service 2
Pay Units: 340.
Programming (via satellite): HBO (multiplexed).
Fee: $11.95 monthly.
Digital Pay Service 3
Pay Units: 423.
Programming (via satellite): Showtime (multiplexed).
Fee: $10.95 monthly.
Digital Pay Service 4
Pay Units: 60.
Programming (via satellite): The Movie Channel (multiplexed).
Fee: $10.95 monthly.
Digital Pay Service 5
Pay Units: N.A.
Programming (via satellite): Encore (multiplexed); Starz (multiplexed).
Video-On-Demand: No
Pay-Per-View
iN DEMAND (delivered digitally); Playboy TV (delivered digitally); Fresh (delivered digitally); Shorteez (delivered digitally).
Internet Service
Operational: Yes.
Broadband Service: Rapid High Speed Internet.
Fee: $39.95 monthly.
Telephone Service
None
Miles of Plant: 122.0 (coaxial); None (fiber optic). Homes passed: 4,272.
Chief Technician: Johnny Mills.
Ownership: Comcast Cable Communications Inc. (MSO).

AUBURN—Charter Communications. Now served by LEEDS, AL [AL0192]. ICA: AL0009.

AUTAUGAVILLE—Formerly served by NewWave Communications. No longer in operation. ICA: AL0141.

BAILEYTON—Charter Communications, 2100 Columbiana Rd, Vestavia, AL 35216. Phone: 205-824-5400. Fax: 205-824-5490. Web Site: http://www.charter.com. Also serves Cullman County (portions), Hog Jaw, Hulaco, Joppa, Marshall County (unincorporated areas), Morgan County (portions) & Ruth. ICA: AL0053.
TV Market Ranking: 96 (BAILEYTON, Cullman County (portions), Hog Jaw, Hulaco, Joppa, Marshall County (unincorporated areas), Morgan County (portions), Ruth). Franchise award date: January 20, 1989. Franchise expiration date: N.A. Began: January 1, 1989.
Channel capacity: N.A. Channels available but not in use: N.A.
Basic Service
Subscribers: 1,506.
Programming (received off-air): WAAY-TV (ABC) Huntsville; WAFF (NBC) Huntsville; WBRC (FOX) Birmingham; WHDF (CW) Florence; WHIQ (PBS) Huntsville; WHNT-TV (CBS) Huntsville; WIAT (CBS) Birmingham; WTJP-TV (TBN) Gadsden; WTTO (CW) Homewood; WVTM-TV (NBC) Birmingham; WZDX (FOX, MNT) Huntsville.
Programming (via satellite): WGN America.
Fee: $29.99 installation.
Expanded Basic Service 1
Subscribers: 1,413.
Programming (via satellite): ABC Family Channel; AMC; Animal Planet; Arts & Entertainment; Cartoon Network; CNBC; CNN; Comcast Sports Net Southeast; Comcast/Charter Sports Southeast (CSS); Comedy Central; Country Music TV; C-SPAN; Discovery Channel; Disney Channel; ESPN; ESPN 2; Fox News Channel; FX; G4; Headline News; HGTV; History Channel; Home Shopping Network; ION Television; Lifetime; MTV; Nickelodeon; QVC; Speed Channel; Spike TV; SportSouth; Syfy; TBS Superstation; The Learning Channel; Turner Classic Movies; Turner Network TV; TV Guide Network; TV Land; Univision; USA Network; VH1; WE tv; Weather Channel.
Fee: $43.00 monthly.
Digital Basic Service
Subscribers: N.A.
Programming (via satellite): BBC America; Bio; Discovery Digital Networks; Do-It-Yourself; GalaVision; Great American Country; History Channel International; Independent Film Channel; Lifetime Movie Network; Music Choice; Science Television; Sundance Channel; Versus.
Fee: $16.99 monthly.
Digital Pay Service 1
Pay Units: N.A.
Programming (via satellite): Cinemax (multiplexed); HBO (multiplexed); Starz (multiplexed).
Fee: $4.95 installation; $11.45 monthly (each).
Video-On-Demand: No
Pay-Per-View
iN DEMAND (delivered digitally); Playboy TV (delivered digitally); Pleasure (delivered digitally); Fresh (delivered digitally); Shorteez (delivered digitally).
Internet Service
Operational: No.
Telephone Service
None
Miles of Plant: 217.0 (coaxial); None (fiber optic). Homes passed: 3,158.
Vice President & General Manager: Don Karell. Technical Operations Director: Greg Prim. Marketing Director: David Redmond. Marketing Manager: Jeff Hatcher.
Ownership: Charter Communications Inc. (MSO).

BALDWIN COUNTY (northwestern portion)—Formerly served by Baldwin County Cable. No longer in operation. ICA: AL0237.

BALDWIN COUNTY (portions)—Cable Options Inc., PO Box 1404, Fairhope, AL 36533-1404. Phone: 251-550-5796. E-mail: cabopt@webtv.net. ICA: AL0121.
TV Market Ranking: 59 (BALDWIN COUNTY (PORTIONS) (portions)); Outside TV Markets (BALDWIN COUNTY (PORTIONS) (portions)). Franchise award date: June 1, 1989. Franchise expiration date: N.A. Began: June 1, 1991.
Channel capacity: N.A. Channels available but not in use: N.A.

Basic Service
Subscribers: 245.
Programming (received off-air): WALA-TV (FOX) Mobile; WEAR-TV (ABC) Pensacola; WEIQ (PBS) Mobile; WFNA (CW) Gulf Shores; WHBR (IND) Pensacola; WJTC (IND) Pensacola; WKRG-TV (CBS) Mobile; WMPV-TV (TBN) Mobile; WPMI-TV (NBC) Mobile; WSRE (PBS) Pensacola.
Programming (via satellite): ABC Family Channel; AMC; Animal Planet; Arts & Entertainment; Cartoon Network; CNBC; CNN; Comcast Sports Net Southeast; Comedy Central; Country Music TV; C-SPAN; C-SPAN 2; Discovery Channel; Disney Channel; E! Entertainment Television; Encore (multiplexed); ESPN; ESPN 2; Eternal Word TV Network; Food Network; Fox News Channel; FX; G4; Headline News; HGTV; History Channel; Home Shopping Network; Lifetime; MTV; Nickelodeon; Outdoor Channel; QVC; Speed Channel; Spike TV; SportSouth; Syfy; TBS Superstation; The Learning Channel; Travel Channel; Turner Classic Movies; Turner Network TV; TV Land; USA Network; VH1; Weather Channel; WGN America.
Fee: $39.00 monthly.
Pay Service 1
Pay Units: N.A.
Programming (via satellite): Cinemax; HBO.
Fee: $9.00 monthly (Cinemax), $11.00 monthly (HBO).
Video-On-Demand: No
Internet Service
Operational: No.
Telephone Service
None
Miles of Plant: 12.0 (coaxial); None (fiber optic).
Manager & Chief Technician: J. Alex Bowab.
Ownership: Cable Options Inc.

BARNWELL—Mediacom. Now served by FAIRHOPE (formerly Daphne), AL [AL0124]. ICA: AL0234.

BAY MINETTE—Mediacom. Now served by FAIRHOPE (formerly Daphne), AL [AL0124]. ICA: AL0057.

BEATRICE—Clearview Cable, PO Box 7, 28795 Commerce St, Gantt, AL 36038-0001. Phone: 334-388-2716. Fax: 334-388-2718. E-mail: jmike@oppcatv.com. ICA: AL0156.
TV Market Ranking: Outside TV Markets (BEATRICE). Franchise award date: May 17, 1989. Franchise expiration date: N.A. Began: November 1, 1989.
Channel capacity: N.A. Channels available but not in use: N.A.
Basic Service
Subscribers: N.A. Included in Heath
Programming (received off-air): WAKA (CBS) Selma; WALA-TV (FOX) Mobile; WEAR-TV (ABC) Pensacola; WHBR (IND) Pensacola; WSFA (NBC) Montgomery.
Programming (via satellite): ABC Family Channel; AMC; Animal Planet; BET Networks; Cartoon Network; CNBC; CNN; Comcast Sports Net Southeast; Country Music TV; Discovery Channel; Disney Channel; ESPN; Fox News Channel; Lifetime; Nickelodeon; Spike TV; TBS Superstation; Travel Channel; Turner Network TV; USA Network; WGN America.
Fee: $29.95 installation; $28.45 monthly.
Pay Service 1
Pay Units: N.A. Included in Heath
Programming (via satellite): Cinemax; HBO.
Fee: $10.95 monthly.
Video-On-Demand: No
Internet Service
Operational: No.
Telephone Service
None
Miles of Plant: 11.0 (coaxial); None (fiber optic). Homes passed: 200. Total homes in franchised area: 200.
Manager: J Mike Russell.
Ownership: Clearview Cable Inc. (MSO).

BELLAMY—Sky Cablevision, PO Box 65, 1309 Roebuck Dr, Meridian, MS 39301. Phone: 601-485-6980. Fax: 601-483-0103. ICA: AL0157.
TV Market Ranking: Below 100 (BELLAMY). Franchise award date: N.A. Franchise expiration date: N.A. Began: September 1, 1990.
Channel capacity: 35 (not 2-way capable). Channels available but not in use: N.A.
Basic Service
Subscribers: N.A.
Programming (received off-air): WAKA (CBS) Selma; WDBB (CW) Bessemer; WIIQ (PBS) Demopolis; WSFA (NBC) Montgomery; WTOK-TV (ABC, CW, FOX, MNT) Meridian.
Programming (via satellite): ABC Family Channel; CNN; Discovery Channel; Disney Channel; ESPN; TBS Superstation; Turner Network TV; USA Network; WGN America.
Fee: $20.00 installation; $34.00 monthly.
Pay Service 1
Pay Units: N.A.
Programming (via satellite): HBO.
Fee: $11.00 monthly.
Internet Service
Operational: No.
Telephone Service
None
Miles of Plant: 6.0 (coaxial); None (fiber optic). Homes passed: 200.
Manager & Chief Technician: Berry Ward.
Ownership: Sky Cablevision Ltd. (MSO).

BERRY—Formerly served by Almega Cable. No longer in operation. ICA: AL0240.

BEULAH—Charter Communications, 401 S 6th St, Lanett, AL 36863-2673. Phones: 770-806-7060 (Duluth office); 334-644-2311. Fax: 334-644-2131. Web Site: http://www.charter.com. Also serves Lee County (northeastern portion). ICA: AL0171.
TV Market Ranking: 94 (BEULAH, Lee County (northeastern portion)). Franchise award date: N.A. Franchise expiration date: N.A. Began: November 1, 1990.
Channel capacity: 60 (not 2-way capable). Channels available but not in use: N.A.
Basic Service
Subscribers: 960.
Programming (received off-air): WJSP-TV (PBS) Columbus; WLTZ (CW, NBC) Columbus; WRBL (CBS) Columbus; WSFA (NBC) Montgomery; WTVM (ABC) Columbus; WXTX (FOX) Columbus.
Programming (via satellite): C-SPAN; C-SPAN 2; Turner Network TV; WGN America.
Fee: $29.99 installation.
Expanded Basic Service 1
Subscribers: N.A.
Programming (via satellite): ABC Family Channel; Animal Planet; Arts & Entertainment; Bravo; Cartoon Network; CNBC; CNN; Comcast Sports Net Southeast; Country Music TV; Discovery Channel; Disney Channel; E! Entertainment Television; ESPN; ESPN 2; Food Network; Fox News Channel; FX; Headline News; HGTV; History Channel; Lifetime; MSNBC; MTV; National Geographic Channel; Nickelodeon; SoapNet; Speed Channel; Spike TV; Syfy; TBS Superstation; The Learning Channel; Toon Disney; Travel Channel; truTV; TV Land; USA Network; VH1; Weather Channel.
Fee: $48.99 monthly.
Digital Basic Service
Subscribers: 266.
Programming (via satellite): BBC America; Discovery Digital Networks; GAS; MTV Networks Digital Suite; Music Choice; Nick Jr.; Nick Too; NickToons TV; SportSouth; Sundance Channel.
Digital Pay Service 1
Pay Units: N.A.
Programming (via satellite): Cinemax (multiplexed); Encore (multiplexed); Flix; HBO (multiplexed); Showtime (multiplexed); Starz (multiplexed); The Movie Channel (multiplexed).
Fee: $8.95 monthly (Cinemax), $9.95 monthly (HBO).
Video-On-Demand: No
Pay-Per-View
Addressable homes: 266.
iN DEMAND (delivered digitally); Shorteez (delivered digitally); Fresh (delivered digitally); Playboy TV (delivered digitally).
Internet Service
Operational: Yes.
Broadband Service: Charter Pipeline.
Telephone Service
Digital: Operational
Homes passed: 1,785.
Vice President & General Manager: Matt Favre. Operations Manager: David Spriggs. Sales & Marketing Director: Antoinette Carpenter.
Ownership: Charter Communications Inc. (MSO).

BIG COVE—Mediacom, 123 Ware Dr NE, Huntsville, AL 35811-1061. Phones: 850-934-7700 (Gulf Breeze regional office); 256-852-7427. Fax: 256-851-7708. Web Site: http://www.mediacomcable.com. ICA: AL0172.
TV Market Ranking: 96 (BIG COVE). Franchise award date: April 26, 1982. Franchise expiration date: N.A. Began: January 1, 1984.
Channel capacity: 36 (operating 2-way). Channels available but not in use: 4.
Basic Service
Subscribers: 478.
Programming (received off-air): WAAY-TV (ABC) Huntsville; WAFF (NBC) Huntsville; WHIQ (PBS) Huntsville; WHNT-TV (CBS) Huntsville; WZDX (FOX, MNT) Huntsville.
Programming (via satellite): ABC Family Channel; AMC; CNBC; CNN; Country Music TV; C-SPAN; Discovery Channel; Disney Channel; ESPN; Headline News; Lifetime; MTV; Nickelodeon; QVC; Spike TV; TBS Superstation; Turner Network TV; USA Network; VH1; Weather Channel; WGN America.
Fee: $21.50 installation; $15.74 monthly; $1.00 converter.
Pay Service 1
Pay Units: 129.
Programming (via satellite): Cinemax.
Fee: $9.95 monthly.
Pay Service 2
Pay Units: 118.
Programming (via satellite): Showtime.
Fee: $9.95 monthly.
Pay Service 3
Pay Units: 118.
Programming (via satellite): Flix.
Fee: $2.95 monthly.
Pay Service 4
Pay Units: 133.
Programming (via satellite): HBO.
Fee: $9.95 monthly.
Video-On-Demand: No
Internet Service
Operational: No.
Telephone Service
None
Miles of plant (coax) included in Ardmore
Vice President: David Servies. General Manager: Tommy Hill. Technical Operations Supervisor: Mark Darwin. Sales & Marketing Manager: Joey Nagem. Customer Service Supervisor: Sandy Acklin.
Ownership: Mediacom LLC (MSO).

BIRMINGHAM—Bright House Networks, 151 London Pkwy, Birmingham, AL 35211-4541. Phones: 205-591-6880 (Customer service); 205-290-1300. Fax: 205-941-1398. Web Site: http://www.birmingham.mybrighthouse.com. Also serves Bessemer (portions), Brighton, Brownville, Fairfield (portions), Hueytown (portions), Irondale, Jefferson County (portions), Lipscomb & Roosevelt City. ICA: AL0001.
TV Market Ranking: 40 (Bessemer (portions), BIRMINGHAM, Brighton, Brownville, Fairfield (portions), Hueytown (portions), Irondale, Jefferson County (portions), Lipscomb, Roosevelt City). Franchise award date: January 1, 1973. Franchise expiration date: N.A. Began: September 30, 1976.
Channel capacity: 61 (operating 2-way). Channels available but not in use: N.A.
Basic Service
Subscribers: 75,000.
Programming (received off-air): WABM (MNT) Birmingham; WBIQ (PBS) Birmingham; WBRC (FOX) Birmingham; WIAT (CBS) Birmingham; WJSU-TV (ABC) Anniston; WPXH-TV (ION) Gadsden; WTJP-TV (TBN) Gadsden; WTTO (CW) Homewood; WVTM-TV (NBC) Birmingham.
Programming (via satellite): C-SPAN; C-SPAN 2; QVC; TV Guide Network; WGN America.
Current originations: Leased Access; Religious Access; Government Access; Educational Access; Public Access.
Fee: $45.75 installation; $.55 converter; $23.95 additional installation.
Expanded Basic Service 1
Subscribers: N.A.
Programming (via satellite): ABC Family Channel; AMC; Animal Planet; Arts & Entertainment; BET Networks; Cartoon Network; CNBC; CNN; Comcast Sports Net Southeast; Comedy Central; Discovery Channel; Disney Channel; E! Entertainment Television; ESPN; ESPN 2; ESPN Classic Sports; Eternal Word TV Network; Food Network; Fox News Channel; Fuse; FX; Golf Channel; Great American Country; Hallmark Channel; Headline News; HGTV; History Channel; Home Shopping Network; Lifetime; Lifetime Movie Network; MoviePlex; MSNBC; MTV; National Geographic Channel; Nickelodeon; Oxygen; ShopNBC; SoapNet; Spike TV; SportSouth; Style Network; Syfy; TBS Superstation; The Learning Channel; Travel Channel; truTV; Turner Classic Movies; Turner Network TV; TV Land; Univision; USA Network; Versus; VH1; WE tv; Weather Channel.
Fee: $49.45 monthly.
Digital Basic Service
Subscribers: 22,000.
Programming (via satellite): AmericanLife TV Network; BBC America; Bio; Bloomberg Television; CBS College Sports Network; Church Channel; Daystar TV Network; Discovery Health Channel; Discovery Kids Channel; Discovery Military Channel; Dis-

covery Planet Green; Disney XD; ESPNews; FitTV; Fox Business Channel; Fox College Sports Atlantic; Fox College Sports Central; Fox College Sports Pacific; Fox Movie Channel; G4; Gospel Music Channel; GSN; Hallmark Movie Channel; Halogen Network; History Channel International; ID Investigation Discovery; Independent Film Channel; Lifetime Movie Network; Music Choice; Nick Jr.; NickToons TV; RFD-TV; Science Channel; Sleuth; Speed Channel; Style Network; TeenNick; WE tv.
Fee: $11.00 monthly.

Digital Expanded Basic Service
Subscribers: N.A.
Programming (received off-air): WLTZ (CW, NBC) Columbus; WRBL (CBS) Columbus; WTVM (ABC) Columbus; WXTX (FOX) Columbus.
Programming (via satellite): Arts & Entertainment HD; Discovery HD Theater; ESPN 2 HD; ESPN HD; National Geographic Channel HD Network; Turner Network TV HD; Universal HD.

Digital Expanded Basic Service 2
Subscribers: N.A.
Programming (via satellite): CMT Pure Country; Fuse; MTV Hits; MTV Jams; MTV Tres; MTV2; VH1 Classic; VH1 Soul.

Digital Expanded Basic Service 3
Subscribers: N.A.
Programming (via satellite): Canal 52MX; Cine Latino; CNN en Espanol; Discovery en Espanol; ESPN Deportes; Fuse; History Channel International; VeneMovies.

Digital Pay Service 1
Pay Units: 17,847.
Programming (via satellite): Cinemax (multiplexed); HBO (multiplexed); HBO HD; Showtime (multiplexed); Showtime HD; Starz (multiplexed); The Movie Channel (multiplexed).
Fee: $10.50 monthly (each).

Video-On-Demand: Yes

Pay-Per-View
iN DEMAND (delivered digitally); NBA League Pass (delivered digitally); Playboy TV (delivered digitally); Fresh (delivered digitally), Addressable: Yes; Pleasure (delivered digitally); Hot Choice (delivered digitally); ESPN (delivered digitally); MLB Extra Innings (delivered digitally); NHL Center Ice (delivered digitally).

Internet Service
Operational: Yes.
Subscribers: 8,000.
Broadband Service: Road Runner; AOL for Broadband; EarthLink.
Fee: $24.95 installation; $29.95 monthly.

Telephone Service
Digital: Operational
Fee: $29.95 monthly

Miles of Plant: 1,536.0 (coaxial); 300.0 (fiber optic). Additional miles planned: 15.0 (coaxial). Homes passed: 147,000. Total homes in franchised area: 158,000.

Division President: Karen Broach. Vice President, Engineering: Garland Thomas. Marketing Director: Tammy Strong. Program Director: Tim Stout. Customer Service Director: Jimmy Robinson.

City fee: 5% of gross.

Ownership: Bright House Networks LLC (MSO).

BLOUNT COUNTY—Alabama Broadband LLC, 3447A Parkwood Rd SE, Bessemer, AL 35022. Phones: 205-426-3432; 877-840-5040. E-mail: webmaster@southerncable.net. Web Site: http://www.alabamabroadband.net. Also serves Hayden & Jefferson County. ICA: AL0198.

TV Market Ranking: 40 (BLOUNT COUNTY, Hayden, Jefferson County). Franchise award date: N.A. Franchise expiration date: N.A. Began: January 1, 1989.

Channel capacity: 45 (not 2-way capable). Channels available but not in use: 2.

Basic Service
Subscribers: 1,566.
Programming (received off-air): WABM (MNT) Birmingham; WBIQ (PBS) Birmingham; WBRC (FOX) Birmingham; WCFT-TV (ABC) Tuscaloosa; WIAT (CBS) Birmingham; WPXH-TV (ION) Gadsden; WTJP-TV (TBN) Gadsden; WTTO (CW) Homewood; WVTM-TV (NBC) Birmingham.
Programming (via satellite): ABC Family Channel; AMC; Animal Planet; Arts & Entertainment; CNN; Comcast Sports Net Southeast; Country Music TV; C-SPAN; C-SPAN 2; Discovery Channel; Disney Channel; ESPN; ESPN 2; Fox News Channel; Headline News; HGTV; Home Shopping Network; MTV; National Geographic Channel; Nickelodeon; QVC; Spike TV; TBS Superstation; The Learning Channel; truTV; Turner Network TV; TV Guide Network; USA Network; VH1; Weather Channel; WGN America.
Current originations: Religious Access.
Fee: $29.95 installation; $34.80 monthly.

Pay Service 1
Pay Units: 533.
Programming (via satellite): HBO.
Fee: $10.00 installation; $9.00 monthly.

Pay Service 2
Pay Units: 365.
Programming (via satellite): Showtime.
Fee: $10.00 installation; $8.00 monthly.

Video-On-Demand: No

Internet Service
Operational: No.

Telephone Service
None

Miles of Plant: 153.0 (coaxial); None (fiber optic).

President: Tom Early. Marketing Director: Bob Garner.

Ownership: Alabama Broadband LLC (MSO).

BLOUNTSVILLE—Time Warner Cable. Now served by CULLMAN, AL [AL0034]. ICA: AL0142.

BOLIGEE—Sky Cablevision, PO Box 65, 1309 Roebuck Dr, Meridian, MS 39301. Phone: 601-485-6980. Fax: 601-483-0103. Web Site: http://skycablevision.com. ICA: AL0173.

TV Market Ranking: Outside TV Markets (BOLIGEE). Franchise award date: N.A. Franchise expiration date: N.A. Began: August 1, 1989.

Channel capacity: N.A. Channels available but not in use: N.A.

Basic Service
Subscribers: N.A.
Programming (received off-air): WGBC (NBC) Meridian; WIIQ (PBS) Demopolis; WMDN (CBS) Meridian; WTOK-TV (ABC, CW, FOX, MNT) Meridian.
Programming (via satellite): ABC Family Channel; Arts & Entertainment; CNN; Discovery Channel; Disney Channel; ESPN; TBS Superstation; Turner Network TV; USA Network; WGN America.
Fee: $34.00 monthly.

Pay Service 1
Pay Units: N.A.
Programming (via satellite): HBO.
Fee: $11.00 monthly.

Internet Service
Operational: No.

Telephone Service
None

Manager: Berry Ward.

Ownership: Sky Cablevision Ltd. (MSO).

BOOTH—Galaxy Cablevision, PO Box 879, 118 S Jackson St, Grove Hill, AL 36451. Phone: 251-275-3118. Fax: 251-275-3120. Web Site: http://www.galaxycable.com. ICA: AL0277.

TV Market Ranking: Below 100 (BOOTH).

Channel capacity: N.A. Channels available but not in use: N.A.

Internet Service
Operational: No.

Telephone Service
None

State Manager: Bill Flowers.

Ownership: Galaxy Cable Inc. (MSO).

BREWTON—Mediacom. Now served by GULF BREEZE, FL [FL0070]. ICA: AL0051.

BRIDGEPORT—Charter Communications, 1235 King St SE, Cleveland, TN 37323. Phones: 423-478-1934; 865-984-1400 (Maryville TN office). Fax: 423-476-1621. Web Site: http://www.charter.com. Also serves Stevenson. ICA: AL0266.

TV Market Ranking: 78 (BRIDGEPORT, Stevenson).

Channel capacity: N.A. Channels available but not in use: N.A.

Basic Service
Subscribers: N.A.
Programming (received off-air): WAAY-TV (ABC) Huntsville; WDEF-TV (CBS) Chattanooga; WDSI-TV (FOX, MNT) Chattanooga; WELF-TV (TBN) Dalton; WFLI-TV (CW) Cleveland; WNGH-TV (PBS) Chatsworth; WRCB (NBC) Chattanooga; WTCI (PBS) Chattanooga; WTVC (ABC) Chattanooga.
Programming (via satellite): C-SPAN; C-SPAN 2; Daystar TV Network; Home Shopping Network; ION Television; QVC; Shop at Home; TV Guide Network; WGN America.
Current originations: Leased Access.

Expanded Basic Service 1
Subscribers: N.A.
Programming (via satellite): ABC Family Channel; AMC; Animal Planet; Arts & Entertainment; BET Networks; Bravo; Cartoon Network; CNBC; CNN; Comcast Sports Net Southeast; Comcast/Charter Sports Southeast (CSS); Comedy Central; Country Music TV; Discovery Channel; Disney Channel; E! Entertainment Television; ESPN; ESPN 2; Food Network; Fox News Channel; FX; G4; Golf Channel; GSN; Hallmark Channel; Headline News; HGTV; History Channel; Lifetime; MSNBC; MTV; National Geographic Channel; Nickelodeon; Oxygen; SoapNet; Speed Channel; Spike TV; SportSouth; Style Network; Syfy; TBS Superstation; The Learning Channel; Toon Disney; Travel Channel; truTV; Turner Classic Movies; Turner Network TV; TV Land; USA Network; Versus; VH1; WE tv; Weather Channel.

Digital Basic Service
Subscribers: N.A.
Programming (via satellite): AmericanLife TV Network; BBC America; Bio; Bloomberg Television; CBS College Sports Network; Cine Mexicano; CMT Pure Country; CNN en Espanol; CNN International; Cooking Channel; Discovery en Espanol; Discovery Health Channel; Discovery Home Channel; Discovery Kids Channel; Discovery Military Channel; Discovery Times Channel; Do-It-Yourself; ESPN Classic Sports; ESPN Deportes; ESPN U; ESPNews; FitTV; Fox College Sports Atlantic; Fox College Sports Central; Fox College Sports Pacific; Fox Movie Channel; Fox Soccer; Fox Sports en Espanol; Fuel TV; Fuse; GAS; Gol TV; Gospel Music Channel; Great American Country; Halogen Network; History Channel en Espanol; History Channel International; Independent Film Channel; INSP; Jewelry Television; La Familia Network; Lifetime Movie Network; Lifetime Real Women; MTV Hits; MTV Jams; MTV Tres; MTV2; Music Choice; Nick Jr.; Nick Too; NickToons TV; Once Mexico; Science Channel; Sorpresa; Sundance Channel; Tennis Channel; The Sportsman Channel; VH1 Classic; VH1 Soul; Video Rola.

Digital Pay Service 1
Pay Units: N.A.
Programming (via satellite): Cinemax (multiplexed); Encore (multiplexed); Flix; HBO (multiplexed); LOGO; Showtime (multiplexed); Starz (multiplexed); The Movie Channel (multiplexed).

Video-On-Demand: No

Pay-Per-View
iN DEMAND (delivered digitally); Playboy en Espanol (delivered digitally); Ten Clips (delivered digitally); Ten Blue (delivered digitally).

Internet Service
Operational: Yes.
Broadband Service: Charter Pipeline.
Fee: $29.99 monthly.

Telephone Service
Digital: Operational

Operations Director: Mike Burns. Technical Operations Director: Grant Evans. Technical Operations Manager: David Ogle. Marketing Director: Pat Hollenbeck. Government Relations Director: Nick Parlis.

Ownership: Charter Communications Inc. (MSO).

BROOKWOOD—Charter Communications. Now served by LEEDS, AL [AL0192]. ICA: AL0059.

BUTLER—Galaxy Cablevision, PO Box 879, 118 S Jackson St, Grove Hill, AL 36451-0879. Phone: 251-275-3118. Fax: 251-275-3120. Web Site: http://www.galaxycable.com. Also serves Lisman. ICA: AL0174.

TV Market Ranking: Below 100 (BUTLER, Lisman). Franchise award date: January 1, 1968. Franchise expiration date: N.A. Began: December 12, 1968.

Channel capacity: N.A. Channels available but not in use: N.A.

Basic Service
Subscribers: 660.
Programming (received off-air): WAKA (CBS) Selma; WALA-TV (FOX) Mobile; WGBC (NBC) Meridian; WIIQ (PBS) Demopolis; WMDN (CBS) Meridian; WTOK-TV (ABC, CW, FOX, MNT) Meridian.
Programming (via satellite): ABC Family Channel; AMC; Arts & Entertainment; BET Networks; Cartoon Network; CNBC; CNN; Comcast Sports Net Southeast; Discovery Channel; Disney Channel; E! Entertainment Television; ESPN; ESPN 2; Fox News Channel; Fuse; FX; Great American Country; Hallmark Channel; Headline News; HGTV; History Channel; Lifetime; Outdoor Channel; QVC; Speed Channel; SportSouth; TBS Superstation; The Learning Channel; Toon Disney; Trinity Broadcasting Network; truTV; Turner Network TV; USA Network; Weather Channel; WGN America.
Fee: $25.00 installation; $43.50 monthly; $25.00 additional installation.

Digital Basic Service
Subscribers: 112.
Programming (via satellite): BBC America; Bio; Bloomberg Television; Discovery Health Channel; Discovery Kids Channel; Discovery Military Channel; Discovery Planet Green; ESPN Classic Sports; ESPNews; FitTV; Fox College Sports Atlantic; Fox College Sports Central; Fox College Sports Pacific; Fox Movie Channel; Fox Soccer; G4; Golf Channel; GSN; Halogen Network; History Channel International; ID Investigation Discovery; Independent Film Channel; Lifetime Movie Network; National Geographic Channel; PBS Kids Sprout; RFD-TV; Science Channel; Sleuth; Style Network; WE tv.
Pay Service 1
Pay Units: N.A.
Programming (via satellite): HBO; Showtime.
Fee: $25.00 installation; $11.00 monthly (HBO).
Digital Pay Service 1
Pay Units: N.A.
Programming (via satellite): Cinemax (multiplexed); Encore (multiplexed); Flix; HBO (multiplexed); Showtime (multiplexed); Starz (multiplexed); The Movie Channel (multiplexed).
Pay-Per-View
iN DEMAND (delivered digitally); Playboy TV (delivered digitally); Club Jenna (delivered digitally).
Internet Service
Operational: Yes.
Subscribers: 55.
Broadband Service: Galaxy Cable Internet.
Fee: $49.95 installation; $35.00 monthly.
Telephone Service
None
Miles of Plant: 55.0 (coaxial); None (fiber optic). Homes passed: 1,532.
State Manager: Bill Flowers. Technical Manager & Engineer: Greg Berthaut. Customer Service Representative: Lisa Ray.
City fee: 2% of gross.
Ownership: Galaxy Cable Inc. (MSO).

CAMDEN—Mediacom, 760 Middle St, PO Box 1009, Fairhope, AL 36532. Phones: 850-934-7700 (Gulf Breeze regional office); 251-928-0374. Fax: 251-928-3804. Web Site: http://www.mediacomcable.com. Also serves Conecuh County (portions), Evergreen, Excel, Frisco City, Monroe County (portions), Monroeville, Repton & Wilcox County (portions). ICA: AL0112.
TV Market Ranking: Below 100 (CAMDEN, Wilcox County (portions)); Outside TV Markets (Conecuh County (portions), Evergreen, Excel, Frisco City, Monroe County (portions), Monroeville, Repton). Franchise award date: December 9, 1975. Franchise expiration date: N.A. Began: July 1, 1970.
Channel capacity: N.A. Channels available but not in use: N.A.
Basic Service
Subscribers: 4,936.
Programming (received off-air): WAKA (CBS) Selma; WALA-TV (FOX) Mobile; WBIH (IND) Selma; WCOV-TV (FOX) Montgomery; WEAR-TV (ABC) Pensacola; WEIQ (PBS) Mobile; WKRG-TV (CBS) Mobile; WNCF (ABC) Montgomery; WPMI-TV (NBC) Mobile; WSFA (NBC) Montgomery.
Programming (via satellite): ABC Family Channel; AMC; Animal Planet; Arts & Entertainment; BET Networks; Bravo; Cartoon Network; CNBC; CNN; Comcast Sports Net Southeast; Comedy Central; Country Music TV; C-SPAN; C-SPAN 2; Discovery Channel; Disney Channel; E! Entertainment Television; ESPN; ESPN 2; Eternal Word TV Network; FitTV; Food Network; Fox News Channel; FX; Hallmark Channel; Headline News; HGTV; History Channel; Home Shopping Network; INSP; Lifetime; MSNBC; MTV; Nickelodeon; Outdoor Channel; QVC; Speed Channel; Spike TV; SportSouth; Syfy; TBS Superstation; The Learning Channel; Travel Channel; Trinity Broadcasting Network; truTV; Turner Classic Movies; Turner Network TV; TV Land; USA Network; VH1; WE tv; Weather Channel; WGN America.
Fee: $49.95 monthly.
Digital Basic Service
Subscribers: N.A.
Programming (via satellite): AmericanLife TV Network; BBC America; Bio; Bloomberg Television; Discovery Digital Networks; ESPNews; Fox Movie Channel; Fox Soccer; G4; Golf Channel; GSN; Halogen Network; History Channel International; Lifetime Movie Network; Lime; Music Choice; National Geographic Channel; Nick Jr.; NickToons TV; Sleuth; Style Network; TVG Network; Versus; Weatherscan.
Digital Pay Service 1
Pay Units: N.A.
Programming (via satellite): Cinemax (multiplexed); Encore (multiplexed); Flix (multiplexed); HBO (multiplexed); Starz (multiplexed); Sundance Channel (multiplexed); The Movie Channel (multiplexed).
Video-On-Demand: No
Internet Service
Operational: Yes.
Broadband Service: Mediacom High Speed Internet.
Fee: $45.95 monthly.
Telephone Service
Digital: Planned
Miles of Plant: 800.0 (coaxial); None (fiber optic). Miles of plant (coax & fiber combined) includes Greensboro, Linden, Livingston, Thomasville
Vice President: David Servies. Operations Director: Gene Wuchner. Technical Operations Manager: Mike Sneary. Sales & Marketing Manager: Joey Nagen.
City fee: 3% of gross.
Ownership: Mediacom LLC (MSO).

CASTLEBERRY—Clearview Cable, PO Box 7, 28795 Commerce St, Gantt, AL 36038-0001. Phone: 334-388-2716. Fax: 334-388-2718. E-mail: jmike@oppcatv.com. ICA: AL0149.
TV Market Ranking: Outside TV Markets (CASTLEBERRY). Franchise award date: N.A. Franchise expiration date: N.A. Began: January 1, 1989.
Channel capacity: 40 (not 2-way capable). Channels available but not in use: 14.
Basic Service
Subscribers: N.A. Included in Heath
Programming (received off-air): WALA-TV (FOX) Mobile; WDIQ (PBS) Dozier; WEAR-TV (ABC) Pensacola; WHBR (IND) Pensacola; WKRG-TV (CBS) Mobile; WMPV-TV (TBN) Mobile; WPMI-TV (NBC) Mobile; WSFA (NBC) Montgomery.
Programming (via satellite): ABC Family Channel; Arts & Entertainment; BET Networks; CNBC; CNN; Comcast Sports Net Southeast; Disney Channel; ESPN; Fox News Channel; Headline News; Spike TV; Syfy; TBS Superstation; Turner Network TV; USA Network; WGN America.
Fee: $29.95 installation; $30.00 monthly.
Pay Service 1
Pay Units: N.A. Included in Heath
Programming (via satellite): Cinemax; HBO.
Fee: $10.95 monthly (each).
Video-On-Demand: No
Internet Service
Operational: No.
Telephone Service
None
Miles of Plant: 10.0 (coaxial); None (fiber optic). Homes passed: 250. Total homes in franchised area: 250.
Manager: J Mike Russell.
Ownership: Clearview Cable Inc. (MSO).

CEDAR BLUFF—Envision Media Inc., 300 N 5th Ave, Rome, GA 30165. Phones: 800-653-3511; 256-779-8700. Fax: 706-295-1286. Also serves Cherokee County (portions). ICA: AL0175.
TV Market Ranking: 18 (CEDAR BLUFF, Cherokee County (portions)). Franchise award date: N.A. Franchise expiration date: N.A. Began: November 1, 1982.
Channel capacity: N.A. Channels available but not in use: N.A.
Basic Service
Subscribers: 800 Includes Leesburg.
Programming (received off-air): WAAY-TV (ABC) Huntsville; WBRC (FOX) Birmingham; WCIQ (PBS) Mount Cheaha State Park; WHNT-TV (CBS) Huntsville; WJSU-TV (ABC) Anniston; WPXH-TV (ION) Gadsden; WTJP-TV (TBN) Gadsden; WVTM-TV (NBC) Birmingham; WXIA-TV (NBC) Atlanta.
Programming (via satellite): ABC Family Channel; AMC; Bravo; CNBC; ESPN; Home Shopping Network; Nickelodeon; QVC; Syfy; Turner Network TV; Weather Channel.
Fee: $29.95 installation; $19.95 monthly.
Expanded Basic Service 1
Subscribers: 731.
Programming (via satellite): Animal Planet; Arts & Entertainment; Cartoon Network; CNN; Country Music TV; Discovery Channel; Disney Channel; Headline News; History Channel; Lifetime; MTV; Spike TV; TBS Superstation; The Learning Channel; USA Network; VH1; WE tv; WGN America.
Fee: $20.00 monthly.
Digital Basic Service
Subscribers: N.A.
Programming (via satellite): AmericanLife TV Network; BBC America; Bio; Bloomberg Television; Discovery Digital Networks; ESPN 2; ESPN Classic Sports; Fox Movie Channel; G4; GAS; Golf Channel; GSN; Halogen Network; HGTV; History Channel International; Independent Film Channel; Lifetime Movie Network; MTV Networks Digital Suite; MuchMusic Network; Music Choice; Nick Jr.; Outdoor Channel; ShopNBC; Speed Channel; Style Network; Toon Disney; Trinity Broadcasting Network; Turner Classic Movies; TV Guide Interactive Inc.; Versus.
Fee: $12.95 monthly.
Pay Service 1
Pay Units: 33.
Programming (via satellite): Showtime.
Fee: $9.95 monthly.
Digital Pay Service 1
Pay Units: N.A.
Programming (via satellite): Cinemax (multiplexed); Encore (multiplexed); Flix; HBO (multiplexed); Showtime (multiplexed); Starz (multiplexed); The Movie Channel (multiplexed).
Video-On-Demand: No
Pay-Per-View
ESPN Gameplan (delivered digitally); ESPN Now (delivered digitally); iN DEMAND (delivered digitally); Playboy TV (delivered digitally); Fresh (delivered digitally); Shorteez (delivered digitally).
Internet Service
Operational: No.
Telephone Service
None
Miles of Plant: 35.0 (coaxial); None (fiber optic). Homes passed: 1,032.
General Manager: Tom Holt.
Franchise fee: 3% of gross.
Ownership: Envision Media Inc. (MSO).

CENTER POINT—Charter Communications. Now served by LEEDS, AL [AL0192]. ICA: AL0029.

CENTRE—Charter Communications. Now served by PIEDMONT, AL [AL0065]. ICA: AL0085.

CENTREVILLE—Sky Cablevision, PO Box 65, 1309 Roebuck Dr, Meridian, MS 39301. Phone: 601-485-6980. Fax: 601-483-0103. Web Site: http://skycablevision.com. Also serves Bibb County (portions) & Brent. ICA: AL0069.
TV Market Ranking: 40 (Bibb County (portions)); Below 100 (Brent, CENTREVILLE, Bibb County (portions)). Franchise award date: January 10, 1980. Franchise expiration date: N.A. Began: December 1, 1980.
Channel capacity: N.A. Channels available but not in use: N.A.
Basic Service
Subscribers: 556.
Programming (received off-air): WBIQ (PBS) Birmingham; WBRC (FOX) Birmingham; WCFT-TV (ABC) Tuscaloosa; WIAT (CBS) Birmingham; WTTO (CW) Homewood; WVTM-TV (NBC) Birmingham.
Programming (via satellite): C-SPAN; Home Shopping Network; Trinity Broadcasting Network; WGN America.
Current originations: Religious Access; Government Access; Educational Access; Public Access.
Fee: $29.95 installation; $19.95 monthly.
Expanded Basic Service 1
Subscribers: N.A.
Programming (via satellite): ABC Family Channel; AMC; Animal Planet; Arts & Entertainment; Bravo; Cartoon Network; CNBC; CNN; Comedy Central; Country Music TV; Discovery Channel; Disney Channel; E! Entertainment Television; ESPN; ESPN 2; Fox News Channel; FX; G4; Golf Channel; Headline News; HGTV; History Channel; Lifetime; MSNBC; MTV; Nickelodeon; Oxygen; Speed Channel; Spike TV; Syfy; TBS Superstation; The Learning Channel; Toon Disney; Turner Classic Movies; Turner Network TV; TV Land; USA Network; VH1; Weather Channel.
Fee: $20.00 monthly.
Digital Basic Service
Subscribers: N.A.
Programming (via satellite): BBC America; Bio; Bloomberg Television; Discovery Digital Networks; ESPN Classic Sports; FitTV; Fox Movie Channel; Fox Soccer; Fuse; GAS; GSN; History Channel International; Independent Film Channel; Lifetime Movie Network; MTV Networks Digital Suite; Music Choice; Nick Jr.; Nick Too; NickToons TV; Science Television; Style Network; Sundance Channel; WE tv.
Fee: $12.95 monthly.
Digital Pay Service 1
Pay Units: 632.
Programming (via satellite): Cinemax (multiplexed); Encore (multiplexed); Flix; HBO

(multiplexed); Starz (multiplexed); The Movie Channel (multiplexed).
Video-On-Demand: No
Pay-Per-View
ESPN Extra (delivered digitally); ESPN Now (delivered digitally); iN DEMAND (delivered digitally); Playboy TV (delivered digitally); Fresh (delivered digitally).
Internet Service
Operational: No.
Telephone Service
None
Miles of Plant: 53.0 (coaxial); None (fiber optic). Homes passed: 2,682. Total homes in franchised area: 2,173.
Manager & Chief Technician: Berry Ward.
City fee: 2% of gross.
Ownership: Sky Cablevision Ltd. (MSO).

CHANCELLOR—Clearview Cable, PO Box 7, 28795 Commerce St, Gantt, AL 36038-0001. Phone: 334-388-2716. Fax: 334-388-2718. E-mail: jmike@oppcatv.com. Also serves Bellwood, Coffee Springs & Geneva County (portions). ICA: AL0105.
TV Market Ranking: Below 100 (Bellwood, CHANCELLOR, Coffee Springs, Geneva County (portions)). Franchise award date: September 1, 1989. Franchise expiration date: N.A. Began: March 1, 1990.
Channel capacity: N.A. Channels available but not in use: N.A.
Basic Service
Subscribers: N.A. Included in Heath
Programming (received off-air): WDFX-TV (FOX) Ozark; WDHN (ABC) Dothan; WJHG-TV (CW, MNT, NBC) Panama City; WMBB (ABC) Panama City; WPMI-TV (NBC) Mobile; WSFA (NBC) Montgomery; WTVY (CBS, CW, MNT) Dothan.
Programming (via satellite): ABC Family Channel; AMC; AmericanLife TV Network; Arts & Entertainment; CNN; Country Music TV; Discovery Channel; Disney Channel; ESPN; Hallmark Channel; Lifetime; MTV; Nickelodeon; Spike TV; TBS Superstation; Trinity Broadcasting Network; Turner Network TV; USA Network; Weather Channel; WGN America.
Fee: $29.95 installation; $29.45 monthly.
Pay Service 1
Pay Units: N.A. Included in Heath
Programming (via satellite): Encore; HBO; Showtime; The Movie Channel.
Fee: $10.95 monthly (each).
Video-On-Demand: No
Internet Service
Operational: No.
Telephone Service
None
Miles of Plant: 69.0 (coaxial); None (fiber optic). Homes passed: 935.
Manager: J Mike Russell.
Ownership: Clearview Cable Inc. (MSO).

CHATOM—Sky Cablevision, PO Box 65, 1309 Roebuck Dr, Meridian, MS 39301. Phone: 601-485-6980. Fax: 601-483-0103. Web Site: http://skycablevision.com. ICA: AL0176.
TV Market Ranking: Outside TV Markets (CHATOM). Franchise award date: N.A. Franchise expiration date: N.A. Began: N.A.
Channel capacity: N.A. Channels available but not in use: N.A.
Basic Service
Subscribers: 174.
Programming (received off-air): WALA-TV (FOX) Mobile; WEAR-TV (ABC) Pensacola; WKRG-TV (CBS) Mobile; WLOX (ABC) Biloxi; WPMI-TV (NBC) Mobile.
Programming (via satellite): ABC Family Channel; AMC; Animal Planet; BET Networks; Cartoon Network; CNN; Country Music TV; Discovery Channel; ESPN; ESPN 2; HGTV; Lifetime; Nickelodeon; QVC; Spike TV; Syfy; TBS Superstation; The Learning Channel; Trinity Broadcasting Network; Turner Network TV; TV Land; USA Network; Weather Channel; WGN America.
Current originations: Educational Access.
Fee: $11.95 monthly.
Pay Service 1
Pay Units: N.A.
Programming (via satellite): Cinemax; HBO (multiplexed).
Video-On-Demand: No
Internet Service
Operational: No.
Telephone Service
None
Manager & Chief Technician: Berry Ward.
Ownership: Sky Cablevision Ltd. (MSO).

CHEROKEE—Ramco Broadband Services, 726 Rt 202, Ste 320-119, Bridgewater, NJ 8807. Phone: 903-424-2015. E-mail: info@fmnj.net. Web Site: http://www.rmnj.net. Also serves Barton. ICA: AL0177.
TV Market Ranking: Below 100 (Barton, CHEROKEE). Franchise award date: N.A. Franchise expiration date: N.A. Began: December 18, 1968.
Channel capacity: N.A. Channels available but not in use: N.A.
Basic Service
Subscribers: 883.
Programming (received off-air): WAAY-TV (ABC) Huntsville; WAFF (NBC) Huntsville; WFIQ (PBS) Florence; WHDF (CW) Florence; WHNT-TV (CBS) Huntsville; WZDX (FOX, MNT) Huntsville.
Programming (via satellite): CNN; C-SPAN; Home Shopping Network; INSP; QVC; Trinity Broadcasting Network; Turner Network TV.
Fee: $29.95 installation; $19.95 monthly.
Expanded Basic Service 1
Subscribers: 855.
Programming (via satellite): ABC Family Channel; AMC; Animal Planet; Arts & Entertainment; Bravo; Cartoon Network; CNBC; Comcast Sports Net Southeast; Comcast/Charter Sports Southeast (CSS); Comedy Central; Country Music TV; Discovery Channel; Disney Channel; E! Entertainment Television; ESPN; ESPN 2; Fox News Channel; FX; G4; Golf Channel; Headline News; HGTV; History Channel; Lifetime; MSNBC; MTV; Nickelodeon; Oxygen; Speed Channel; Spike TV; Syfy; TBS Superstation; The Learning Channel; Travel Channel; Turner Classic Movies; TV Land; USA Network; VH1; Weather Channel; WGN America.
Fee: $20.00 monthly.
Digital Basic Service
Subscribers: N.A.
Programming (via satellite): BBC America; Bio; Bloomberg Television; Discovery Digital Networks; FitTV; Fox Movie Channel; Fox Soccer; Fuse; GAS; GSN; History Channel International; Independent Film Channel; Lifetime Movie Network; MTV Networks Digital Suite; Music Choice; Nick Jr.; Nick Too; NickToons TV; Science Television; SoapNet; Style Network; Sundance Channel; Toon Disney; WE tv.
Fee: $12.95 monthly.
Pay Service 1
Pay Units: N.A.
Programming (via satellite): Flix; Showtime (multiplexed); The Movie Channel (multiplexed).
Digital Pay Service 1
Pay Units: 128.
Programming (via satellite): Cinemax (multiplexed); HBO (multiplexed); Starz (multiplexed).
Fee: $7.95 monthly.
Video-On-Demand: No
Pay-Per-View
ESPN Gameplan (delivered digitally); ESPN Now (delivered digitally); iN DEMAND (delivered digitally); Playboy TV (delivered digitally); Fresh (delivered digitally); Shorteez (delivered digitally).
Internet Service
Operational: No.
Telephone Service
None
Miles of Plant: 46.0 (coaxial); None (fiber optic). Homes passed: 1,319.
President & General Manager: Robert Motyka.
Ownership: Ramco Broadband Services.

CLANTON—Charter Communications, 2100 Columbiana Rd, Vestavia, AL 35216. Phone: 205-824-5400. Fax: 205-824-5490. Web Site: http://www.charter.com. Also serves Chilton County. ICA: AL0056.
TV Market Ranking: Below 100 (Chilton County (portions)); Outside TV Markets (Chilton County (portions), CLANTON). Franchise award date: N.A. Franchise expiration date: N.A. Began: March 16, 1979.
Channel capacity: 50 (2-way capable). Channels available but not in use: N.A.
Basic Service
Subscribers: 2,825.
Programming (received off-air): WAKA (CBS) Selma; WBIQ (PBS) Birmingham; WBRC (FOX) Birmingham; WCFT-TV (ABC) Tuscaloosa; WIAT (CBS) Birmingham; WPXH-TV (ION) Gadsden; WSFA (NBC) Montgomery; WTTO (CW) Homewood; WVTM-TV (NBC) Birmingham; allband FM.
Programming (via satellite): C-SPAN; INSP; Trinity Broadcasting Network.
Fee: $29.99 installation.
Expanded Basic Service 1
Subscribers: 2,723.
Programming (via satellite): ABC Family Channel; AMC; Animal Planet; Arts & Entertainment; BET Networks; Cartoon Network; CNN; Comcast Sports Net Southeast; Country Music TV; C-SPAN 2; Discovery Channel; Disney Channel; ESPN; ESPN 2; Fox News Channel; FX; Headline News; HGTV; Home Shopping Network; Lifetime; MSNBC; MTV; Nickelodeon; Oxygen; QVC; Shop at Home; Speed Channel; Spike TV; SportSouth; TBS Superstation; The Learning Channel; truTV; Turner Network TV; TV Guide Network; TV Land; USA Network; Weather Channel.
Fee: $43.00 monthly.
Digital Basic Service
Subscribers: N.A.
Programming (via satellite): BBC America; Bio; Bloomberg Television; Bravo; Discovery Digital Networks; DMX Music; ESPN Classic Sports; ESPNews; FitTV; Fox Movie Channel; Fox Soccer; Fuse; G4; GAS; Golf Channel; Great American Country; GSN; Halogen Network; History Channel; History Channel International; Independent Film Channel; Lifetime Movie Network; MTV Networks Digital Suite; National Geographic Channel; Nick Jr.; Outdoor Channel; Science Television; Style Network; Sundance Channel; Syfy; Toon Disney; Turner Classic Movies; TV Guide Interactive Inc.; Versus; WE tv.
Fee: $16.99 monthly.
Pay Service 1
Pay Units: N.A.
Programming (via satellite): Encore; Showtime (multiplexed); The Movie Channel (multiplexed).
Fee: $12.20 monthly.
Digital Pay Service 1
Pay Units: N.A.
Programming (via satellite): Cinemax (multiplexed); HBO; Starz (multiplexed).
Video-On-Demand: No
Pay-Per-View
iN DEMAND (delivered digitally); Playboy TV (delivered digitally); Fresh (delivered digitally); Shorteez (delivered digitally).
Internet Service
Operational: No.
Telephone Service
None
Miles of Plant: 80.0 (coaxial); None (fiber optic). Homes passed: 2,946. Total homes in franchised area: 3,087.
Vice President & General Manager: Don Karell. Technical Operations Director: Greg Prim. Marketing Director: David Redmond. Marketing Manager: Jeff Hatcher.
City fee: 3% of gross.
Ownership: Charter Communications Inc. (MSO).

CLAYTON—Comcast Cable, 1316 Harrison Ave, Panama City, FL 32401. Phones: 850-769-0392; 850-769-2929. Fax: 850-769-2988. E-mail: frtiz_hoehne@cable.comcast.com. Web Site: http://www.comcast.com. ICA: AL0134.
TV Market Ranking: Below 100 (CLAYTON (VILLAGE)). Franchise award date: N.A. Franchise expiration date: N.A. Began: November 1, 1982.
Channel capacity: N.A. Channels available but not in use: N.A.
Basic Service
Subscribers: 346.
Programming (received off-air): WDHN (ABC) Dothan; WGIQ (PBS) Louisville; WLTZ (CW, NBC) Columbus; WRBL (CBS) Columbus; WSFA (NBC) Montgomery; WTVM (ABC) Columbus; WTVY (CBS, CW, MNT) Dothan.
Programming (via satellite): ABC Family Channel; AMC; Animal Planet; Arts & Entertainment; BET Networks; CNN; Comedy Central; Country Music TV; C-SPAN; Discovery Channel; Disney Channel; E! Entertainment Television; ESPN; ESPN 2; Food Network; Fox News Channel; FX; Golf Channel; Great American Country; Headline News; HGTV; Lifetime; MSNBC; MTV; Nickelodeon; QVC; Spike TV; TBS Superstation; TLC; Trinity Broadcasting Network; Turner Network TV; TV Land; USA Network; Weather Channel.
Fee: $43.30 installation; $38.95 monthly.
Pay Service 1
Pay Units: N.A.
Programming (via satellite): HBO; Showtime.
Video-On-Demand: No
Internet Service
Operational: Yes.
Telephone Service
Digital: Operational
Fee: $39.95 monthly
Homes passed: 736. Miles of plant included in Dothan
General Manager: Fritz Hoehne. Technical Operations Manager: Tim Denton. Marketing Manager: Kevin Canel.
Ownership: Comcast Cable Communications Inc. (MSO).

CLIO—Bright House Networks, 1394 N Eufaula Ave, Eufaula, AL 36027. Phone: 334-687-5555. Fax: 334-687-9049. Web Site: http://www.eufaula.mybrighthouse.com. Also serves Ariton & Louisville. ICA: AL0123.

TV Market Ranking: Below 100 (Ariton, CLIO, Louisville). Franchise award date: N.A. Franchise expiration date: N.A. Began: December 1, 1981.

Channel capacity: N.A. Channels available but not in use: N.A.

Basic Service

Subscribers: 1,423.

Programming (received off-air): WDFX-TV (FOX) Ozark; WDHN (ABC) Dothan; WGIQ (PBS) Louisville; WSFA (NBC) Montgomery; WTVM (ABC) Columbus; WTVY (CBS, CW, MNT) Dothan.

Programming (via satellite): CNN; TBS Superstation; WGN America.

Expanded Basic Service 1

Subscribers: N.A.

Programming (via satellite): ABC Family Channel; AMC; AmericanLife TV Network; Animal Planet; Arts & Entertainment; BET Networks; Bravo!; Cartoon Network; CNBC; Comcast Sports Net Southeast; Comedy Central; Country Music TV; C-SPAN; C-SPAN 2; Discovery Channel; Disney Channel; E! Entertainment Television; ESPN; ESPN 2; Food Network; Fox News Channel; Fuse; FX; Hallmark Channel; Headline News; HGTV; History Channel; Home Shopping Network; INSP; Lifetime; Lifetime Movie Network; MSNBC; MTV; National Geographic Channel; Nickelodeon; Oxygen; QVC; ShopNBC; Spike TV; SportSouth; Syfy; The Learning Channel; The Word Network; Travel Channel; Trinity Broadcasting Network; truTV; Turner Classic Movies; Turner Network TV; TV Land; USA Network; Versus; VH1; WE tv; Weather Channel.

Fee: $44.35 monthly.

Digital Basic Service

Subscribers: N.A.

Programming (via satellite): BBC America; Bloomberg Television; Current; Discovery Digital Networks; ESPN Classic Sports; ESPN Now; ESPNews; Fox Movie Channel; Fox Sports World; G4; GAS; Golf Channel; GSN; MTV Networks Digital Suite; Music Choice; Nick Jr.; Outdoor Channel; Ovation; Speed Channel; Toon Disney.

Fee: $13.00 monthly.

Digital Pay Service 1

Pay Units: N.A.

Programming (via satellite): Cinemax (multiplexed); Encore; HBO (multiplexed); Independent Film Channel; Showtime (multiplexed); Starz (multiplexed); Sundance Channel; The Movie Channel (multiplexed).

Fee: $10.50 monthly (each).

Video-On-Demand: No

Pay-Per-View

iN DEMAND (delivered digitally); Hot Choice (delivered digitally); Fresh (delivered digitally); Shorteez (delivered digitally); Sports PPV (delivered digitally).

Internet Service

Operational: Yes.

Broadband Service: Road Runner.

Fee: $32.95-$57.95 monthly.

Telephone Service

None

Miles of Plant: 51.0 (coaxial); None (fiber optic).

Manager: Jim Smith. Chief Technician: Jeff Clark. Office Manager: Lisa Taylor.

Ownership: Bright House Networks LLC (MSO).

CLOVERDALE—Comcast Cable. Now served by FLORENCE, AL [AL0187]. ICA: AL0178.

CODEN—Mediacom, 2320 E Second St, Gulf Shores, AL 36542. Phone: 800-239-8411. Web Site: http://www.mediacomcable.com. ICA: AL0179.

TV Market Ranking: 59 (CODEN). Franchise award date: N.A. Franchise expiration date: N.A. Began: N.A.

Channel capacity: N.A. Channels available but not in use: N.A.

Basic Service

Subscribers: 43.

Programming (received off-air): WALA-TV (FOX) Mobile; WEAR-TV (ABC) Pensacola; WJTC (IND) Pensacola; WKRG-TV (CBS) Mobile; WPMI-TV (NBC) Mobile; WSRE (PBS) Pensacola.

Programming (via satellite): TBS Superstation; WGN America.

Video-On-Demand: No

Internet Service

Operational: Yes.

Fee: $29.95 monthly.

Telephone Service

Digital: Operational

Fee: $29.95 monthly

Ownership: Mediacom LLC (MSO).

COFFEEVILLE—Sky Cablevision. No longer in operation. ICA: AL0265.

COLLINSVILLE—Collinsville TV Cable, PO Box 272, Collinsville, AL 35961-0272. Phone: 256-524-2267. ICA: AL0138.

TV Market Ranking: 18 (COLLINSVILLE). Franchise award date: N.A. Franchise expiration date: N.A. Began: N.A.

Channel capacity: 22 (not 2-way capable). Channels available but not in use: 3.

Basic Service

Subscribers: 236.

Programming (received off-air): WAAY-TV (ABC) Huntsville; WAFF (NBC) Huntsville; WAGA-TV (FOX) Atlanta; WBRC (FOX) Birmingham; WCIQ (PBS) Mount Cheaha State Park; WGCL-TV (CBS) Atlanta; WHNT-TV (CBS) Huntsville; WPCH-TV (IND) Atlanta; WPXH-TV (ION) Gadsden; WZDX (FOX, MNT) Huntsville.

Programming (via satellite): ABC Family Channel; Discovery Channel; ESPN; Spike TV; Turner Network TV; USA Network.

Fee: $40.00 installation; $29.00 monthly.

Pay Service 1

Pay Units: 3.

Programming (via satellite): Cinemax.

Fee: $12.00 monthly.

Pay Service 2

Pay Units: 23.

Programming (via satellite): HBO.

Fee: $12.00 monthly.

Video-On-Demand: No

Internet Service

Operational: No.

Telephone Service

None

Miles of Plant: 9.0 (coaxial); None (fiber optic). Homes passed: 430.

Manager: Mary Ann Pendergrass. Chief Technician: Jimmy Pendergrass.

Ownership: Collinsville TV Cable.

COLUMBIANA—Charter Communications, 2100 Columbiana Rd, Vestavia, AL 35216. Phones: 205-824-5400; 888-438-2427 (Customer service). Fax: 205-824-5490. Web Site: http://www.charter.com. Also serves Shelby County (portions) & Wilsonville. ICA: AL0180.

TV Market Ranking: 40 (COLUMBIANA, Shelby County (portions), Wilsonville). Franchise award date: January 1, 1981. Franchise expiration date: N.A. Began: January 1, 1982.

Channel capacity: N.A. Channels available but not in use: N.A.

Basic Service

Subscribers: 1,385.

Programming (received off-air): WABM (MNT) Birmingham; WBIQ (PBS) Birmingham; WBRC (FOX) Birmingham; WCFT-TV (ABC) Tuscaloosa; WIAT (CBS) Birmingham; WPXH-TV (ION) Gadsden; WTTO (CW) Homewood; WVTM-TV (NBC) Birmingham.

Programming (via satellite): C-SPAN; Home Shopping Network; Trinity Broadcasting Network; WGN America.

Fee: $29.99 installation.

Expanded Basic Service 1

Subscribers: N.A.

Programming (via satellite): ABC Family Channel; AMC; Arts & Entertainment; Bravo; Cartoon Network; CNBC; CNN; Comcast Sports Net Southeast; Comedy Central; Country Music TV; Discovery Channel; Disney Channel; E! Entertainment Television; ESPN; ESPN 2; Fox News Channel; FX; G4; Golf Channel; Headline News; HGTV; History Channel; Lifetime; MSNBC; MTV; Nickelodeon; Oxygen; Speed Channel; Spike TV; SportSouth; Syfy; TBS Superstation; The Learning Channel; Turner Classic Movies; Turner Network TV; TV Land; USA Network; VH1; WE tv; Weather Channel.

Fee: $43.00 monthly.

Digital Basic Service

Subscribers: N.A.

Programming (via satellite): BBC America; Bio; Bloomberg Television; Discovery Digital Networks; ESPN Classic Sports; FitTV; Fox Movie Channel; Fox Soccer; Fuse; GAS; GSN; History Channel International; Independent Film Channel; Lifetime Movie Network; MTV Networks Digital Suite; Music Choice; Nick Jr.; Nick Too; NickToons TV; Science Television; SoapNet; Style Network; Sundance Channel; Toon Disney.

Fee: $16.99 monthly.

Pay Service 1

Pay Units: N.A.

Programming (via satellite): Encore (multiplexed); Flix; Showtime (multiplexed); The Movie Channel (multiplexed).

Digital Pay Service 1

Pay Units: 578.

Programming (via satellite): Cinemax (multiplexed); HBO (multiplexed); Starz (multiplexed).

Fee: $9.95 monthly (each).

Video-On-Demand: No

Pay-Per-View

ESPN Extra (delivered digitally); ESPN Now (delivered digitally); iN DEMAND (delivered digitally); Playboy TV (delivered digitally); Fresh (delivered digitally).

Internet Service

Operational: No.

Telephone Service

None

Miles of Plant: 69.0 (coaxial); None (fiber optic). Homes passed: 2,133.

Vice President & General Manager: Don Karell. Technical Operations Director: Tommy Taylor. Marketing Director: David Redmond. Marketing Manager: Jeff Hatcher.

City fee: 3% of gross.

Ownership: Charter Communications Inc. (MSO).

CUBA—Galaxy Cablevision, PO Box 879, 118 S Jackson St, Grove Hill, AL 36451-0879. Phone: 251-275-3118. Fax: 251-275-3120. Web Site: http://www.galaxycable.com. ICA: AL0181.

TV Market Ranking: Below 100 (CUBA). Franchise award date: N.A. Franchise expiration date: N.A. Began: February 1, 1984.

Channel capacity: 36 (not 2-way capable). Channels available but not in use: 3.

Basic Service

Subscribers: 43.

Programming (received off-air): WGBC (NBC) Meridian; WIIQ (PBS) Demopolis; WMDN (CBS) Meridian; WTOK-TV (ABC, CW, FOX, MNT) Meridian.

Programming (via satellite): ABC Family Channel; Animal Planet; Arts & Entertainment; Cartoon Network; CNN; Discovery Channel; Disney Channel; ESPN; ESPN 2; Fox News Channel; Great American Country; HGTV; History Channel; Lifetime; Outdoor Channel; Speed Channel; SportSouth; Syfy; TBS Superstation; Turner Classic Movies; Turner Network TV; USA Network; Weather Channel; WGN America.

Fee: $25.00 installation; $39.60 monthly.

Pay Service 1

Pay Units: 50.

Programming (via satellite): HBO.

Fee: $25.00 installation; $10.00 monthly.

Internet Service

Operational: No.

Telephone Service

None

Miles of Plant: 8.0 (coaxial); None (fiber optic). Homes passed: 195.

State Manager: Bill Flowers. Technical Manager & Engineer: Greg Berthaut. Customer Service Representative: Lisa Ray.

Ownership: Galaxy Cable Inc. (MSO).

CULLMAN—Windjammer Cable, 4400 PGA Blvd, Ste 902, Palm Beach Gardens, FL 33410. Phones: 877-450-5558; 561-775-1208. Fax: 561-775-7811. Web Site: http://www.windjammercable.com. Also serves Blount County (northwestern portion), Blountsville, Cullman County (portions), Fairview, Garden City, Hanceville, Holly Pond, Jefferson County (portions), Kimberly, Vinemont, Warrior & West Point. ICA: AL0034.

TV Market Ranking: 40 (Jefferson County (portions), Kimberly, Warrior); 96 (CULLMAN, Cullman County (portions), Fairview, Garden City, Hanceville, Holly Pond, Vinemont, West Point); Below 100 (Blount County (northwestern portion), Blountsville). Franchise award date: May

1, 1967. Franchise expiration date: N.A. Began: May 1, 1967.
Channel capacity: N.A. Channels available but not in use: N.A.

Basic Service
Subscribers: N.A. Included in Fort Payne
Programming (received off-air): WAAY-TV (ABC) Huntsville; WAFF (NBC) Huntsville; WBIQ (PBS) Birmingham; WBRC (FOX) Birmingham; WCFT-TV (ABC) Tuscaloosa; WCQT-LP Cullman; WHNT-TV (CBS) Huntsville; WIAT (CBS) Birmingham; WTJP-TV (TBN) Gadsden; WTTO (CW) Homewood; WVTM-TV (NBC) Birmingham; WZDX (FOX, MNT) Huntsville.
Programming (via satellite): ABC Family Channel; AMC; Arts & Entertainment; CNBC; Comcast Sports Net Southeast; Country Music TV; C-SPAN; Discovery Channel; E! Entertainment Television; ESPN; Eternal Word TV Network; Food Network; Headline News; HGTV; Home Shopping Network; Lifetime; MSNBC; MTV; Nickelodeon; QVC; Spike TV; TBS Superstation; The Learning Channel; truTV; TV Guide Network; TV Land; USA Network; VH1; Weather Channel; WGN America.
Current originations: Public Access; Educational Access.
Fee: $49.95 installation; $37.36 monthly.

Expanded Basic Service 1
Subscribers: N.A. Included in Fort Payne
Programming (via satellite): Animal Planet; CNN; Disney Channel; ESPN 2; FX; History Channel; Syfy; Travel Channel; Turner Classic Movies; Turner Network TV.
Fee: $21.11 installation; $16.41 monthly.

Digital Basic Service
Subscribers: N.A. Included in Fort Payne
Programming (via satellite): BBC America; Bio; Bloomberg Television; Bravo; Discovery Digital Networks; ESPN Classic Sports; ESPNews; Fox Movie Channel; Fox Sports World; Fuse; G4; GAS; Golf Channel; GSN; History Channel International; Independent Film Channel; INSP; MTV Networks Digital Suite; Music Choice; National Geographic Channel; Nick Jr.; NickToons TV; Outdoor Channel; Sorpresa; Speed Channel; Style Network; Toon Disney; Trinity Broadcasting Network; Turner Classic Movies; Versus; WE tv.
Fee: $58.99 monthly.

Digital Pay Service 1
Pay Units: N.A.
Programming (via satellite): Cinemax (multiplexed); Encore (multiplexed); HBO (multiplexed); Showtime (multiplexed); Starz (multiplexed); The Movie Channel (multiplexed).
Fee: $12.00 monthly (each).

Video-On-Demand: Planned

Pay-Per-View
Fresh (delivered digitally); Playboy TV (delivered digitally); Movies (delivered digitally).

Internet Service
Operational: Yes.
Broadband Service: Road Runner.
Fee: $20.99-$49.99 installation; $44.95 monthly.

Telephone Service
Digital: Operational
Fee: $74.95 installation; $49.95 monthly
Miles of Plant: None (coaxial); 12.0 (fiber optic). Miles of plant (coax) & homes passed included in Fort Payne
General Manager: Timothy Evard. Operations Director: Belinda Graham. Engineering Director: Mike Earehart. Finance & Accounting Director: Cindy Johnson.
Cullman & Vinemont fee: 1.5% of gross.
Ownership: Windjammer Communications LLC (MSO).

CURRY—Charter Communications, 2100 Columbiana Rd, Vestavia, AL 35216. Phone: 205-824-5400. Fax: 205-824-5490. Web Site: http://www.charter.com. ICA: AL0182.
TV Market Ranking: Outside TV Markets (CURRY). Franchise award date: N.A. Franchise expiration date: N.A. Began: N.A.
Channel capacity: N.A. Channels available but not in use: N.A.

Basic Service
Subscribers: 651.
Programming (received off-air): W55BJ Jasper; WABM (MNT) Birmingham; WBIQ (PBS) Birmingham; WBRC (FOX) Birmingham; WCFT-TV (ABC) Tuscaloosa; WIAT (CBS) Birmingham; WPXH-TV (ION) Gadsden; WTTO (CW) Homewood; WVTM-TV (NBC) Birmingham.
Programming (via satellite): C-SPAN; WGN America.
Fee: $29.99 installation.

Expanded Basic Service 1
Subscribers: N.A.
Programming (via satellite): ABC Family Channel; AMC; Animal Planet; Arts & Entertainment; Bravo; Cartoon Network; CNBC; CNN; Comcast Sports Net Southeast; Comedy Central; Country Music TV; Discovery Channel; Disney Channel; E! Entertainment Television; ESPN; ESPN 2; Fox News Channel; FX; G4; Golf Channel; Headline News; HGTV; History Channel; MTV; Nickelodeon; Oxygen; Speed Channel; Spike TV; Syfy; TBS Superstation; The Learning Channel; Toon Disney; Turner Classic Movies; Turner Network TV; TV Land; USA Network; VH1; WE tv; Weather Channel.
Fee: $43.00 monthly.

Digital Basic Service
Subscribers: N.A.
Programming (via satellite): BBC America; Bio; Bloomberg Television; Discovery Digital Networks; DMX Music; ESPN Classic Sports; ESPNews; Fox Movie Channel; Fox Soccer; Fuse; GAS; GSN; History Channel International; Independent Film Channel; Lifetime Movie Network; MTV Networks Digital Suite; Nick Jr.; Nick Too; NickToons TV; Style Network; Sundance Channel.
Fee: $16.99 monthly.

Pay Service 1
Pay Units: 230.
Programming (via satellite): Flix; Showtime (multiplexed); The Movie Channel (multiplexed).
Fee: $9.95 monthly (each).

Digital Pay Service 1
Pay Units: N.A.
Programming (via satellite): Cinemax (multiplexed); Encore (multiplexed); HBO (multiplexed); Starz (multiplexed).

Video-On-Demand: No

Pay-Per-View
iN DEMAND (delivered digitally); ESPN Extra (delivered digitally); ESPN Now (delivered digitally); Hot Choice (delivered digitally); Urban Xtra (delivered digitally); Playboy TV (delivered digitally); Fresh (delivered digitally); Shorteez (delivered digitally).

Internet Service
Operational: No.

Telephone Service
None
Miles of Plant: 50.0 (coaxial); None (fiber optic). Homes passed: 1,498.
Vice President & General Manager: Don Karell. Technical Operations Manager: Greg Prim. Marketing Director: David Redmond. Marketing Manager: Jeff Hatcher.
Ownership: Charter Communications Inc. (MSO).

DADEVILLE—CommuniComm Services, 3164 Hwy 431, Ste 9, Roanoke, AL 36274-1702. Phone: 334-863-7080. Fax: 334-863-2027. Web Site: http://www.netcommander.com. ICA: AL0183.
TV Market Ranking: Below 100 (DADEVILLE). Franchise award date: N.A. Franchise expiration date: N.A. Began: December 1, 1982.
Channel capacity: N.A. Channels available but not in use: N.A.

Basic Service
Subscribers: N.A.
Programming (received off-air): WAKA (CBS) Selma; WAXC-LP (IND) Alexander City; WBRC (FOX) Birmingham; WCIQ (PBS) Mount Cheaha State Park; WCOV-TV (FOX) Montgomery; WJSU-TV (ABC) Anniston; WMCF-TV (TBN) Montgomery; WNCF (ABC) Montgomery; WSFA (NBC) Montgomery; WTTO (CW) Homewood.
Programming (via satellite): Superstation WGN; TBS Superstation.
Fee: $12.50 monthly.

Expanded Basic Service 1
Subscribers: N.A.
Programming (via satellite): ABC Family Channel; American Movie Classics; Animal Planet; Arts & Entertainment; BET Networks; Bravo; Cartoon Network; CNBC; CNN; Comcast/Charter Sports Southeast (CSS); Comedy Central; Country Music TV; C-SPAN; C-SPAN 2; Discovery Channel; Disney Channel; E! Entertainment Television; ESPN; ESPN 2; ESPN Classic Sports; Food Network; Fox Movie Channel; Fox News Channel; FX; Great American Country; Hallmark Channel; Headline News; HGTV; History Channel; Home Shopping Network; ION Television; Lifetime; Lifetime Movie Network; MSNBC; MTV; Nick Jr.; Nickelodeon; Outdoor Channel; QVC; ShopNBC; Spike TV; Syfy; The Learning Channel; The Sportsman Channel; Travel Channel; Trinity Broadcasting Network; truTV; Turner Network TV; Turner South; TV Land; USA Network; VH1; WE tv; Weather Channel.

Digital Basic Service
Subscribers: N.A.
Programming (via satellite): BBC America; Bloomberg Television; Discovery Health Channel; Discovery Home Channel; Discovery Kids Channel; Discovery Military Channel; DMX Music; FitTV; Fox Soccer; G4; Golf Channel; GSN; Halogen Network; ID Investigation Discovery; Independent Film Channel; Science Channel; Sleuth; SoapNet; Speed Channel; Toon Disney; Turner Classic Movies; Versus.

Digital Pay Service 1
Pay Units: 173.
Programming (via satellite): Cinemax (multiplexed); Encore (multiplexed); HBO (multiplexed); Showtime (multiplexed); Starz (multiplexed).

Video-On-Demand: No

Pay-Per-View
iN DEMAND (delivered digitally); Playboy TV (delivered digitally); Fresh (delivered digitally).

Internet Service
Operational: Yes.
Subscribers: 74.
Broadband Service: Net Commander.
Fee: $39.95 installation; $51.95 monthly.

Telephone Service
None
Miles of Plant: 27.0 (coaxial); None (fiber optic). Homes passed: 1,270.
General Manager: Brian Chase. Chief Technician: William Boyd.
Ownership: James Cable LLC (MSO).

DALEVILLE—Troy Cablevision, 740 S Daleville Ave, Daleville, AL 36322-2390. Phone: 334-598-1119. Fax: 334-598-1200. Web Site: http://www.troycable.net. ICA: AL0068. **Note:** This system is an overbuild.
TV Market Ranking: Below 100 (DALEVILLE). Franchise award date: N.A. Franchise expiration date: N.A. Began: February 1, 1993.
Channel capacity: 65 (not 2-way capable). Channels available but not in use: None.

Basic Service
Subscribers: 1,000.
Programming (received off-air): WDFX-TV (FOX) Ozark; WDHN (ABC) Dothan; WGIQ (PBS) Louisville; WJHG-TV (CW, MNT, NBC) Panama City; WSFA (NBC) Montgomery; WTVY (CBS, CW, MNT) Dothan.
Programming (via satellite): Animal Planet; INSP; QVC; TBS Superstation; WGN America.
Current originations: Public Access.
Fee: $25.00 installation; $11.45 monthly.

Expanded Basic Service 1
Subscribers: 850.
Programming (via satellite): ABC Family Channel; AMC; AmericanLife TV Network; Arts & Entertainment; BET Networks; Cartoon Network; CNBC; CNN; Comcast Sports Net Southeast; Comedy Central; Country Music TV; C-SPAN; C-SPAN 2; Discovery Channel; Disney Channel; E! Entertainment Television; ESPN; ESPN 2; Fox News Channel; FX; Headline News; HGTV; History Channel; Home Shopping Network; Lifetime; MTV; Nickelodeon; Spike TV; Syfy; The Learning Channel; Toon Disney; Travel Channel; Trinity Broadcasting Network; truTV; Turner Network TV; Univision; USA Network; VH1; Weather Channel.
Fee: $28.95 monthly.

Pay Service 1
Pay Units: 122.
Programming (via satellite): Cinemax (multiplexed).
Fee: $8.50 monthly.

Pay Service 2
Pay Units: 264.
Programming (via satellite): HBO (multiplexed).
Fee: $8.50 monthly.

Pay Service 3
Pay Units: 92.
Programming (via satellite): The Movie Channel.
Fee: $8.50 monthly.

Pay Service 4
Pay Units: 142.
Programming (via satellite): Showtime (multiplexed).
Fee: $8.50 monthly.

Video-On-Demand: No

Internet Service
Operational: No.

Telephone Service
None
Miles of Plant: 27.0 (coaxial); None (fiber optic). Homes passed: 2,700. Total homes in franchised area: 2,700.
General Manager: Roger Pritt. Office Manager: Beccie Grantham.
Ownership: Troy Cablevision (MSO).

DAPHNE—Mediacom, 7325 Theodore Dawes Rd, Ste 7, Theodore, AL 36582-4029. Phone: 800-239-8411. Fax: 850-932-9237. Web Site: http://www.mediacomcable.com. Also serves Baldwin County (portions), Belforest, Malbis & Plantation Hills. ICA: AL0148.

TV Market Ranking: 59 (Baldwin County (portions), Belforest, DAPHNE, Malbis, Plantation Hills). Franchise award date: January 1, 1983. Franchise expiration date: N.A. Began: January 1, 1989.

Channel capacity: N.A. Channels available but not in use: N.A.

Basic Service

Subscribers: 440.

Programming (received off-air): WALA-TV (FOX) Mobile; WEAR-TV (ABC) Pensacola; WEIQ (PBS) Mobile; WFNA (CW) Gulf Shores; WHBR (IND) Pensacola; WJTC (IND) Pensacola; WKRG-TV (CBS) Mobile; WMPV-TV (TBN) Mobile; WPAN (IND) Fort Walton Beach; WPMI-TV (NBC) Mobile.

Programming (via satellite): ABC Family Channel; AMC; Animal Planet; Arts & Entertainment; BET Networks; Bravo; Cartoon Network; CNBC; CNN; Comedy Central; Country Music TV; C-SPAN; C-SPAN 2; Discovery Channel; Disney Channel; E! Entertainment Television; ESPN; ESPN 2; Eternal Word TV Network; Food Network; Fox News Channel; Fox Sports Net; FX; Golf Channel; Hallmark Channel; Headline News; HGTV; History Channel; Home Shopping Network; INSP; ION Television; Lifetime; Lifetime Movie Network; MoviePlex; MSNBC; MTV; Nickelodeon; Outdoor Channel; Oxygen; QVC; Speed Channel; Spike TV; SportSouth; Syfy; TBS Superstation; The Learning Channel; Travel Channel; truTV; Turner Network TV; TV Guide Network; TV Land; USA Network; VH1; WE tv; Weather Channel; WGN America.

Fee: $29.95 installation; $30.45 monthly.

Digital Basic Service

Subscribers: N.A.

Programming (received off-air): WALA-TV (FOX) Mobile; WEAR-TV (ABC) Pensacola; WEIQ (PBS) Mobile; WPMI-TV (NBC) Mobile.

Programming (via satellite): ABC News Now; BBC America; Bio; Bloomberg Television; CNN HD; Discovery Health Channel; Discovery Home Channel; Discovery Kids Channel; Discovery Military Channel; Discovery Times Channel; DMX Music; ESPN HD; ESPNews; FitTV; Fox Movie Channel; Fox Soccer; FSN HD; Fuse; G4; Great American Country; GSN; Halogen Network; HDNet; HDNet Movies; History Channel International; Independent Film Channel; ION Life; Lifetime Movie Network; MTV Hits; MTV2; National Geographic Channel; Nick Jr.; NickToons TV; Qubo; ReelzChannel; Science Channel; Sleuth; Style Network; TBS in HD; TeenNick; Turner Classic Movies; Turner Network TV HD; TVG Network; Universal HD; Versus; VH1 Classic.

Digital Pay Service 1

Pay Units: N.A.

Programming (via satellite): Cinemax (multiplexed); Encore (multiplexed); Flix; HBO (multiplexed); HBO HD; Showtime (multiplexed); Showtime HD; Starz (multiplexed); Sundance Channel; The Movie Channel (multiplexed).

Video-On-Demand: Yes

Internet Service

Operational: Yes.

Fee: $29.95 monthly.

Telephone Service

Digital: Operational

Fee: $29.95 monthly

Miles of Plant: 10.0 (coaxial); None (fiber optic).

County fee: 3% of basic.

Ownership: Mediacom LLC.

DAUPHIN ISLAND—Comcast Cable, 3248 Springhill Ave, Mobile, AL 36607-1831. Phone: 251-476-2190. Fax: 251-665-6670. Web Site: http://www.comcast.com. ICA: AL0247.

TV Market Ranking: 59 (DAUPHIN ISLAND). Franchise award date: N.A. Franchise expiration date: N.A. Began: N.A.

Channel capacity: N.A. Channels available but not in use: N.A.

Basic Service

Subscribers: N.A. Included in Mobile

Programming (received off-air): WALA-TV (FOX) Mobile; WEAR-TV (ABC) Pensacola; WEIQ (PBS) Mobile; WHBR (IND) Pensacola; WJTC (IND) Pensacola; WKRG-TV (CBS) Mobile; WMPV-TV (TBN) Mobile; WPMI-TV (NBC) Mobile.

Programming (via satellite): ABC Family Channel; AMC; Animal Planet; Arts & Entertainment; BET Networks; Black Family Channel; Bravo; Cartoon Network; CNBC; CNN; Comcast/Charter Sports Southeast (CSS); Comedy Central; Country Music TV; C-SPAN; C-SPAN 2; Discovery Channel; Discovery Health Channel; Disney Channel; E! Entertainment Television; ESPN; ESPN 2; ESPN Classic Sports; Eternal Word TV Network; Food Network; Fox News Channel; Fox Sports Net; FX; G4; Golf Channel; Great American Country; GSN; Headline News; HGTV; History Channel; Home Shopping Network; Lifetime; MSNBC; MTV; MTV2; Nickelodeon; Outdoor Channel; QVC; Speed Channel; Spike TV; Syfy; TBS Superstation; The Learning Channel; truTV; Turner Classic Movies; Turner Network TV; TV Guide Network; TV Land; USA Network; Versus; VH1; Weather Channel; WGN America.

Fee: $43.94 installation; $13.65 monthly.

Digital Basic Service

Subscribers: N.A. Included in Mobile

Programming (received off-air): WEDU (PBS) Tampa; WTOG (CW) St. Petersburg; WTSP (CBS) St. Petersburg; WTTA (MNT) St. Petersburg; WTVT (FOX) Tampa; WWSB (ABC) Sarasota.

Programming (via satellite): ABC Family HD; Animal Planet HD; Arts & Entertainment HD; BBC America; Big Ten Network; Bio; Cartoon Network; CMT Pure Country; CNN HD; Cooking Channel; C-SPAN 3; Current; Discovery Channel HD; Discovery Kids Channel; Discovery Military Channel; Discovery Planet Green; Disney Channel; Disney Channel HD; DMX Music; Do-It-Yourself; Encore (multiplexed); ESPN 2 HD; ESPN HD; Eternal Word TV Network; Flix; Food Network HD; Fox Business Channel; Fox College Sports Atlantic; Fox College Sports Central; Fox College Sports Pacific; Fox News HD; Fox Reality Channel; Fox Soccer; Fuse; FX HD; G4; Gol TV; Golf Channel HD; Great American Country; GSN; Hallmark Movie Channel; HDNet; HGTV HD; History Channel; History Channel HD; History Channel International; ID Investigation Discovery; Independent Film Channel; Jewelry Television; Lifetime Movie Network; LOGO; MLB Network; MoviePlex; MTV Hits; MTV Tres; MTV2; National Geographic Channel; National Geographic Channel HD Network; NBA TV; NFL Network; NHL Network; Nick Jr.; Nick Too; NickToons TV; Outdoor Channel; Oxygen; PBS Kids Sprout; Retro Television Network; Science Channel; Science Channel HD; ShopNBC; SoapNet; Speed HD; Sundance Channel; Syfy HD; TBS in HD; TeenNick; Tennis Channel; The Sportsman Channel; TLC HD; Toon Disney; Turner Network TV HD; TV One; TVG Network; Universal HD; USA Network HD; Versus HD; VH1 Classic; VH1 Soul; WE tv; WFLA-TV (NBC) Tampa.

Digital Pay Service 1

Pay Units: N.A.

Programming (via satellite): Cinemax (multiplexed); Cinemax HD; HBO (multiplexed); HBO HD; Showtime (multiplexed); Showtime HD; Starz (multiplexed); Starz HDTV; The Movie Channel (multiplexed).

Video-On-Demand: No

Pay-Per-View

iN DEMAND; Playboy TV (delivered digitally); iN DEMAND (delivered digitally); Fresh (delivered digitally); Shorteez (delivered digitally); Penthouse TV (delivered digitally).

Internet Service

Operational: Yes.

Broadband Service: Comcast High Speed Internet.

Fee: $42.95 monthly.

Telephone Service

Digital: Operational

Homes passed & total homes in franchised area included in Mobile

General Manager: Ray Kistler. Technical Operations Manager: Jay Murray.

Ownership: Comcast Cable Communications Inc. (MSO).

DECATUR—Charter Communications, 2100 Columbiana Rd, Vestavia, AL 35216. Phone: 205-824-5400. Fax: 205-824-5490. Web Site: http://www.charter.com. Also serves Cotaco, Danville, Falkville, Flint, Hartselle, Laceys Spring, Morgan County, Morgan County (unincorporated areas), Oakville, Pence, Priceville (portions), Speake & Valhermoso Springs. ICA: AL0184.

TV Market Ranking: 96 (Cotaco, Danville, DECATUR (VILLAGE), Falkville, Flint, Hartselle, Laceys Spring, Morgan County, Morgan County (unincorporated areas), Oakville, Pence, Priceville (portions), Priceville (portions), Speake, Valhermoso Springs). Franchise award date: N.A. Franchise expiration date: N.A. Began: August 20, 1964.

Channel capacity: N.A. Channels available but not in use: N.A.

Basic Service

Subscribers: 18,277.

Programming (received off-air): WAAY-TV (ABC) Huntsville; WAFF (NBC) Huntsville; WHDF (CW) Florence; WHIQ (PBS) Huntsville; WHNT-TV (CBS) Huntsville; WMJN-LP Somerville; WTZT-CA Athens; WYAM-LP (IND) Priceville; WZDX (FOX, MNT) Huntsville; 5 FMs.

Programming (via satellite): C-SPAN; C-SPAN 2; Fox News Channel; Home Shopping Network; INSP; ION Television; MyNetworkTV Inc.; NASA TV; QVC; Trinity Broadcasting Network; Weather Channel; WGN America.

Current originations: Educational Access.

Fee: $29.99 installation.

Expanded Basic Service 1

Subscribers: 8,500.

Programming (via satellite): ABC Family Channel; AMC; Animal Planet; Arts & Entertainment; BET Networks; Bravo; Cartoon Network; CNBC; CNN; Comcast Sports Net Southeast; Comcast/Charter Sports Southeast (CSS); Comedy Central; Country Music TV; Discovery Channel; Disney Channel; E! Entertainment Television; ESPN; ESPN 2; Food Network; FX; G4; Golf Channel; GSN; Hallmark Channel; Headline News; HGTV; History Channel; Lifetime; MSNBC; MTV; National Geographic Channel; Nickelodeon; Outdoor Channel; Oxygen; Speed Channel; Spike TV; SportSouth; Style Network; Syfy; TBS Superstation; The Learning Channel; Toon Disney; Travel Channel; truTV; Turner Classic Movies; Turner Network TV; TV Guide Network; TV Land; Univision; USA Network; Versus; VH1.

Fee: $43.00 monthly.

Digital Basic Service

Subscribers: N.A.

Programming (received off-air): WAAY-TV (ABC) Huntsville; WAFF (NBC) Huntsville; WHIQ (PBS) Huntsville; WHNT-TV (CBS) Huntsville; WZDX (FOX, MNT) Huntsville.

Programming (via satellite): BBC America; Bio; Bloomberg Television; Canales N; CBS College Sports Network; CMT Pure Country; Discovery Digital Networks; Discovery HD Theater; Do-It-Yourself; Do-It-Yourself On Demand; ESPN 2 HD; ESPN Classic Sports; ESPN HD; ESPN U; ESPNews; Food Network On Demand; Fox College Sports Atlantic; Fox College Sports Central; Fox College Sports Pacific; Fox Movie Channel; Fox Soccer; Fuel TV; Fuse; GalaVision; GAS; Gospel Music Channel; Great American Country; HBO HD; HGTV On Demand; History Channel International; Howard TV; Independent Film Channel; Jewelry Television; Lifetime Movie Network; LOGO; MTV Networks Digital Suite; Music Choice; Nick Jr.; Nick Too; NickToons TV; SoapNet; Style Network; Sundance Channel; Telemundo; Tennis Channel; Turner Network TV HD; Universal HD; WE tv.

Fee: $16.99 monthly.

Digital Pay Service 1

Pay Units: N.A.

Programming (via satellite): Cinemax (multiplexed); Cinemax HD; Cinemax On Demand; Encore (multiplexed); Flix; HBO (multiplexed); HBO On Demand; Showtime (multiplexed); Showtime HD; Showtime On Demand; Starz (multiplexed); Starz HDTV; Starz On Demand; The Movie Channel (multiplexed).

Fee: $1.75 monthly (Encore), $6.75 monthly (Starz), $10.00 monthly (Cinemax, HBO or Showtime).

Video-On-Demand: Yes

Pay-Per-View

Addressable homes: 13,778.

iN DEMAND (delivered digitally); NHL Center Ice (delivered digitally); MLB Extra Innings (delivered digitally); Ten Blox (delivered digitally); Ten Clips (delivered digitally); Playboy TV (delivered digitally).

Internet Service

Operational: Yes.

Broadband Service: Charter Pipeline.

Fee: $29.99 monthly.

Telephone Service

Digital: Operational

Miles of Plant: 365.0 (coaxial); None (fiber optic). Additional miles planned: 9.0 (coaxial). Homes passed: 21,485. Total homes in franchised area: 21,863.

Vice President & General Manager: Don Karell. Technical Operations Director: Greg Prim. Marketing Director: David Redmond. Marketing Manager: Jeff Hatcher.

City fee: 3% of gross.

Ownership: Charter Communications Inc. (MSO).

DEMOPOLIS—Demopolis CATV Co., PO Box 477, 105 S Cedar Ave, Demopolis, AL 36732. Phone: 334-289-0727. Fax: 334-289-2707. Web Site: http://www.demopoliscatv.com. ICA: AL0071.

TV Market Ranking: Outside TV Markets (DEMOPOLIS). Franchise award date: N.A. Franchise expiration date: N.A. Began: October 1, 1963.

Channel capacity: 68 (operating 2-way). Channels available but not in use: None.

Basic Service

Subscribers: 1,725.

Programming (received off-air): WBIQ (PBS) Birmingham; WBRC (FOX) Birmingham; WCFT-TV (ABC) Tuscaloosa; WDBB (CW) Bessemer; WIIQ (PBS) Demopolis; WMAW-TV (PBS) Meridian; WNCF (ABC) Montgomery; WSFA (NBC) Montgomery; WTOK-TV (ABC, CW, FOX, MNT) Meridian; 1 FM.

Programming (via satellite): ABC Family Channel; AMC; Animal Planet; Arts & Entertainment; BET Networks; Cartoon Network; CNBC; CNN; Comcast Sports Net Southeast; Comcast/Charter Sports Southeast (CSS); Comedy Central; Country Music TV; C-SPAN; C-SPAN 2; Discovery Channel; Discovery Health Channel; Disney Channel; E! Entertainment Television; ESPN; ESPN 2; ESPN Classic Sports; Eternal Word TV Network; Food Network; Fox News Channel; FX; Golf Channel; Great American Country; Hallmark Channel; Headline News; HGTV; History Channel; Home Shopping Network; INSP; Lifetime; MTV; Nickelodeon; Outdoor Channel; QVC; ShopNBC; Speed Channel; Spike TV; SportSouth; Syfy; TBS Superstation; The Learning Channel; Travel Channel; Trinity Broadcasting Network; truTV; Turner Classic Movies; Turner Network TV; TV Guide Network; TV Land; USA Network; VH1; Weather Channel; WGN America.

Current originations: Religious Access.

Fee: $20.00 installation; $40.00 monthly.

Pay Service 1

Pay Units: 221.

Programming (via satellite): Cinemax; HBO; Showtime.

Fee: $20.00 installation; $9.00 monthly (each).

Video-On-Demand: No

Internet Service

Operational: Yes.

Subscribers: 291.

Broadband Service: In-house.

Fee: $30.00-$60.00 monthly.

Telephone Service

Analog: Not Operational

Digital: Operational

Subscribers: 13.

Fee: $40.00 monthly

Miles of Plant: 75.0 (coaxial); None (fiber optic).

Manager: Lynn Goldman. Chief Technician: David Johnson.

City fee: 3% of gross.

Ownership: Demopolis CATV Co.

DOTHAN—Comcast Cable, 1316 Harrison Ave, Panama City, FL 32401. Phone: 850-769-2929. Fax: 850-769-2988. Web Site: http://www.comcast.com. Also serves Ashford, Avon, Cottonwood, Cowarts, Headland, Henry County (southern portion), Houston County (portions), Kinsey, Newville & Webb, AL; Esto, Holmes County (northern portion), Jackson County & Noma, FL. ICA: AL0185.

TV Market Ranking: Below 100 (Ashford, Avon, Cottonwood, Cowarts, DOTHAN, Esto, Headland, Henry County (southern portion), Holmes County (northern portion), Houston County (portions), Jackson County, Kinsey, Newville, Noma, Webb). Franchise award date: January 1, 1963. Franchise expiration date: N.A. Began: January 1, 1963.

Channel capacity: N.A. Channels available but not in use: N.A.

Basic Service

Subscribers: 16,802.

Programming (received off-air): WDFX-TV (FOX) Ozark; WDHN (ABC) Dothan; WGIQ (PBS) Louisville; WJHG-TV (CW, MNT, NBC) Panama City; WSFA (NBC) Montgomery; WTVY (CBS, CW, MNT) Dothan.

Programming (via satellite): CTV News 1; CW+; ION Television; QVC; TV Guide Network.

Current originations: Public Access.

Fee: $43.30 installation; $6.50 monthly.

Expanded Basic Service 1

Subscribers: 12,939.

Programming (via satellite): ABC Family Channel; AMC; Animal Planet; Arts & Entertainment; BET Networks; Cartoon Network; CNBC; CNN; Comcast Sports Net Southeast; Comcast/Charter Sports Southeast (CSS); Comedy Central; Country Music TV; C-SPAN; Discovery Channel; Disney Channel; E! Entertainment Television; ESPN; ESPN 2; ESPN Classic Sports; Eternal Word TV Network; Food Network; Fox News Channel; FX; Golf Channel; Great American Country; GSN; Headline News; HGTV; History Channel; Home Shopping Network; INSP; Lifetime; MTV; Nickelodeon; Speed Channel; Spike TV; SportSouth; Style Network; Syfy; TBS Superstation; The Learning Channel; Travel Channel; Trinity Broadcasting Network; Turner Network TV; TV Land; USA Network; Versus; VH1; Weather Channel.

Fee: $36.75 monthly.

Digital Basic Service

Subscribers: N.A.

Programming (received off-air): WDFX-TV (FOX) Ozark; WGIQ (PBS) Louisville; WJHG-TV (CW, MNT, NBC) Panama City; WTVY (CBS, CW, MNT) Dothan.

Programming (via satellite): BBC America; Bio; CMT Pure Country; Cooking Channel; C-SPAN 2; C-SPAN 3; Discovery Digital Networks; Discovery HD Theater; Do-It-Yourself; Encore (multiplexed); ESPN 2 HD; ESPN HD; ESPNews; FearNet; Flix; GAS; History Channel International; MoviePlex; MTV Networks Digital Suite; Nick Jr.; Nick Too; SoapNet; Sundance Channel; Toon Disney; Turner Network TV HD.

Fee: $14.95 monthly.

Pay Service 1

Pay Units: N.A.

Programming (via satellite): HBO; Showtime.

Fee: $12.95 monthly (each).

Digital Pay Service 1

Pay Units: N.A.

Programming (via satellite): Cinemax (multiplexed); HBO (multiplexed); Showtime (multiplexed); Starz (multiplexed); The Movie Channel (multiplexed).

Fee: $8.50 monthly (each).

Video-On-Demand: Yes

Pay-Per-View

iN DEMAND (delivered digitally); Hot Choice (delivered digitally); Playboy TV (delivered digitally); Fresh (delivered digitally).

Internet Service

Operational: Yes.

Broadband Service: Comcast High Speed Internet.

Fee: $42.95 monthly.

Telephone Service

None

Miles of Plant: 600.0 (coaxial); None (fiber optic). Homes passed: 23,041. Total homes in franchised area: 30,541. Miles of plant (coax & fiber combined) includes Abbeville & Clayton

General Manager: Fritz Hoehne. Technical Operations Manager: Tim Denton. Marketing Manager: Keven Canel.

City fee: 3% of gross.

Ownership: Comcast Cable Communications Inc. (MSO).

DOTHAN—Knology, 2660 Montgomery Hwy, Dothan, AL 36303. Phones: 706-645-8553; 334-699-3333. Web Site: http://www.knology.com. Also serves Ashford. ICA: AL0267. **Note:** This system is an overbuild.

TV Market Ranking: Below 100 (Ashford, DOTHAN).

Channel capacity: N.A. Channels available but not in use: N.A.

Basic Service

Subscribers: N.A.

Programming (received off-air): WDFX-TV (FOX) Ozark; WDHN (ABC) Dothan; WGIQ (PBS) Louisville; WJHG-TV (CW, MNT, NBC) Panama City; WSFA (NBC) Montgomery; WTVY (CBS, CW, MNT) Dothan.

Programming (via satellite): CW+; Home Shopping Network; INSP; TV Guide Network; WGN America.

Expanded Basic Service 1

Subscribers: N.A.

Programming (via satellite): ABC Family Channel; American Movie Classics; Animal Planet; Arts & Entertainment; BET Networks; Cartoon Network; CNBC; CNN; Comcast Sports Net Southeast; Comedy Central; Country Music TV; C-SPAN; C-SPAN 2; Discovery Channel; Discovery Health Channel; Disney Channel; E! Entertainment Television; ESPN; ESPN 2; ESPN Classic Sports; ESPN U; Food Network; Fox News Channel; FX; Golf Channel; Gospel Music Channel; Hallmark Channel; Headline News; HGTV; History Channel; ION Television; Lifetime; MSNBC; MTV; MyNetworkTV Inc.; National Geographic Channel; Nickelodeon; Outdoor Channel; QVC; Speed Channel; Spike TV; SportSouth; Syfy; TBS Superstation; The Learning Channel; Travel Channel; Trinity Broadcasting Network; truTV; Turner Classic Movies; Turner Network TV; TV Land; USA Network; VH1; Weather Channel.

Digital Basic Service

Subscribers: N.A. Included in Valley

Programming (received off-air): WDFX-TV (FOX) Ozark; WJHG-TV (CW, MNT, NBC) Panama City; WTVY (CBS, CW, MNT) Dothan.

Programming (via satellite): ABC News Now; BBC America; Bio; Bloomberg Television; CMT Pure Country; Discovery Channel HD; Discovery Home Channel; Discovery Kids Channel; Discovery Military Channel; DMX Music; ESPN 2 HD; ESPN HD; ESPNews; Fox Movie Channel; Fox Soccer; G4; GSN; History Channel International; ID Investigation Discovery; Lifetime Movie Network; MTV Hits; MTV2; Nick Jr.; NickToons TV; PBS HD; Science Channel; SoapNet; Style Network; Teen-Nick; Toon Disney; Universal HD; Versus; VH1 Classic; VH1 Soul; WAM! America's Kidz Network; WE tv.

Digital Pay Service 1

Pay Units: N.A.

Programming (via satellite): Cinemax (multiplexed); Cinemax HD; Encore (multiplexed); HBO (multiplexed); HBO HD; Showtime (multiplexed); Starz (multiplexed); Sundance Channel; The Movie Channel (multiplexed).

Video-On-Demand: No

Pay-Per-View

iN DEMAND (delivered digitally); Spice (delivered digitally); Spice: Xcess (delivered digitally).

Internet Service

Operational: Yes.

Broadband Service: Knology.Net.

Fee: $57.95 monthly.

Telephone Service

Digital: Operational

General Manager: James Etheredge. Marketing Manager: Alicia Simms.

Ownership: Knology Inc. (MSO).

DOTHAN—Time Warner Cable, 104 S Woodburn Dr, Dothan, AL 36305-1020. Phones: 334-793-3383; 334-836-0680. Fax: 334-793-5667. Web Site: http://www.timewarnercable.com. Also serves Clayhatchee, Dale County, Daleville, Fort Rucker, Geneva County, Grimes, Houston County, Level Plains, Malvern, Midland City, Napier Field, Newton, Pinckard, Rehobeth & Taylor. ICA: AL0012.

TV Market Ranking: Below 100 (Clayhatchee, Dale County, Daleville, DOTHAN, Fort Rucker, Geneva County (portions), Grimes, Houston County, Level Plains, Malvern, Midland City, Napier Field, Newton, Pinckard, Rehobeth, Taylor); Outside TV Markets (Geneva County (portions)). Franchise award date: February 18, 1966. Franchise expiration date: N.A. Began: August 1, 1966.

Channel capacity: N.A. Channels available but not in use: N.A.

Basic Service

Subscribers: 27,400 Includes Enterprise & Fort Benning GA.

Programming (received off-air): WDFX-TV (FOX) Ozark; WDHN (ABC) Dothan; WGIQ (PBS) Louisville; WJHG-TV (CW, MNT, NBC) Panama City; WSFA (NBC) Montgomery; WTVY (CBS, CW, MNT) Dothan; 1 FM.

Programming (via satellite): C-SPAN; C-SPAN 2; Home Shopping Network; TV Guide Network.

Current originations: Public Access.

Fee: $19.95 installation; $19.95 monthly; $34.95 additional installation.

Expanded Basic Service 1
Subscribers: 10,425.
Programming (via satellite): ABC Family Channel; AMC; Animal Planet; Arts & Entertainment; BET Networks; Bravo; Cartoon Network; CNBC; CNN; Comcast Sports Net Southeast; Comedy Central; Country Music TV; Discovery Channel; Disney Channel; E! Entertainment Television; ESPN; ESPN 2; ESPN Classic Sports; Eternal Word TV Network; Food Network; Fox News Channel; FX; Golf Channel; Hallmark Channel; Headline News; HGTV; History Channel; ION Television; Lifetime; MSNBC; MTV; National Geographic Channel; Nickelodeon; Ovation; Oxygen; QVC; Speed Channel; Spike TV; SportSouth; Syfy; TBS Superstation; The Learning Channel; Travel Channel; Trinity Broadcasting Network; truTV; Turner Classic Movies; Turner Network TV; TV Land; Univision; USA Network; VH1; WE tv; Weather Channel.
Fee: $22.79 monthly.

Digital Basic Service
Subscribers: N.A.
Programming (via satellite): AmericanLife TV Network; BBC America; Bloomberg Television; Discovery Digital Networks; ESPNews; FitTV; Fox Sports World; Fuse; G4; GAS; GSN; Lifetime Movie Network; MTV2; Music Choice; Nick Jr.; Outdoor Channel; Style Network; Toon Disney; Versus.
Fee: $4.00 monthly (digital access), $6.00 monthly (each tier).

Digital Pay Service 1
Pay Units: N.A.
Programming (via satellite): Cinemax (multiplexed); Encore (multiplexed); HBO (multiplexed); Independent Film Channel; Showtime (multiplexed); Starz (multiplexed); Sundance Channel; The Movie Channel (multiplexed).
Fee: $12.00 monthly (each).

Video-On-Demand: Yes

Pay-Per-View
NBA TV (delivered digitally), Fee: $3.95-$7.95, Addressable: Yes; NHL (delivered digitally); Fresh (delivered digitally); Shorteez (delivered digitally); Hot Choice (delivered digitally); iN DEMAND (delivered digitally).

Internet Service
Operational: Yes.
Broadband Service: Road Runner.
Fee: $99.95 installation; $44.95 monthly.

Telephone Service
Digital: Operational
Fee: $74.95 installation; $44.95 monthly

Miles of Plant: 590.0 (coaxial); None (fiber optic). Homes passed: 57,500. Homes passed includes Enterprise & Fort Benning GA

General Manager: Ramona Byrd. Technical Operations Manager: Michael Tate. Marketing Manager: Judi Gates.

City fee: 3% of gross.

Ownership: Time Warner Cable (MSO).

DOUBLE SPRINGS—Charter Communications, 2100 Columbiana Rd, Vestavia, AL 35216. Phone: 205-824-5400. Fax: 205-824-5490. Web Site: http://www.charter.com. Also serves Winston County. ICA: AL0241.

TV Market Ranking: Outside TV Markets (DOUBLE SPRINGS, Winston County). Franchise award date: N.A. Franchise expiration date: N.A. Began: N.A.

Channel capacity: N.A. Channels available but not in use: N.A.

Basic Service
Subscribers: 216.
Programming (received off-air): WBIQ (PBS) Birmingham; WBRC (FOX) Birmingham; WCFT-TV (ABC) Tuscaloosa; WIAT (CBS) Birmingham; WTTO (CW) Homewood; WVTM-TV (NBC) Birmingham.
Programming (via satellite): C-SPAN; C-SPAN 2; Home Shopping Network; Weather Channel; WGN America.
Fee: $29.99 installation.

Expanded Basic Service 1
Subscribers: 210.
Programming (via satellite): ABC Family Channel; AMC; Animal Planet; Arts & Entertainment; Cartoon Network; CNN; Comcast Sports Net Southeast; Country Music TV; Discovery Channel; Disney Channel; ESPN; ESPN 2; Headline News; MTV; Nickelodeon; Spike TV; TBS Superstation; Toon Disney; Turner Network TV; USA Network; WE tv.
Fee: $43.00 monthly.

Digital Basic Service
Subscribers: N.A.
Programming (via satellite): AmericanLife TV Network; BBC America; Bio; Bloomberg Television; Bravo; Discovery Digital Networks; ESPN Classic Sports; ESPNews; Fox Movie Channel; G4; GAS; Golf Channel; GSN; Halogen Network; HGTV; History Channel; History Channel International; Independent Film Channel; Lifetime Movie Network; MTV Networks Digital Suite; MuchMusic Network; Music Choice; Nick Jr.; Outdoor Channel; ShopNBC; Speed Channel; Style Network; Syfy; Trinity Broadcasting Network; Turner Classic Movies; TV Guide Interactive Inc.; Versus.
Fee: $16.99 monthly.

Digital Pay Service 1
Pay Units: 39.
Programming (via satellite): HBO (multiplexed).

Digital Pay Service 2
Pay Units: 46.
Programming (via satellite): Flix; Showtime (multiplexed).

Digital Pay Service 3
Pay Units: N.A.
Programming (via satellite): Cinemax (multiplexed); Encore (multiplexed); Starz (multiplexed); The Movie Channel (multiplexed).

Video-On-Demand: No

Pay-Per-View
ESPN Extra (delivered digitally); ESPN Now (delivered digitally); Hot Choice (delivered digitally); iN DEMAND (delivered digitally); Playboy TV (delivered digitally); Fresh (delivered digitally).

Internet Service
Operational: No.

Telephone Service
None

Miles of Plant: 12.0 (coaxial); None (fiber optic). Homes passed: 435.

Vice President & General Manager: Don Karell. Technical Operations Director: Greg Prim. Marketing Director: David Redmond. Marketing Manager: Jeff Hatcher.

Ownership: Charter Communications Inc. (MSO).

ELBA—Charter Communications. Now served by TROY, AL [AL0027]. ICA: AL0086.

ELGIN—Charter Communications, 2100 Columbiana Rd, Vestavia, AL 35216. Phone: 205-824-5400. Fax: 205-824-5490. Web Site: http://www.charter.com. Also serves Anderson, Center Star, Killen, Lauderdale County (portions), Lexington, North Rogersville, Rogersville & West Killen. ICA: AL0039.

TV Market Ranking: 96 (Anderson, Center Star, ELGIN, Lauderdale County (portions) (portions), Rogersville); Below 100 (Killen, Lexington, North Rogersville, West Killen, Lauderdale County (portions) (portions)). Franchise award date: N.A. Franchise expiration date: N.A. Began: May 1, 1981.

Channel capacity: N.A. Channels available but not in use: N.A.

Basic Service
Subscribers: 3,704.
Programming (received off-air): WAAY-TV (ABC) Huntsville; WAFF (NBC) Huntsville; WFIQ (PBS) Florence; WHDF (CW) Florence; WHNT-TV (CBS) Huntsville; WZDX (FOX, MNT) Huntsville.
Programming (via satellite): AMC; Animal Planet; Arts & Entertainment; CNN; Comcast Sports Net Southeast; Country Music TV; C-SPAN; Discovery Channel; E! Entertainment Television; ESPN; ESPN 2; Headline News; MTV; QVC; Syfy; The Learning Channel; Turner Network TV; USA Network; VH1; Weather Channel.
Fee: $29.99 installation.

Expanded Basic Service 1
Subscribers: 3,158.
Programming (via satellite): ABC Family Channel; Comedy Central; Disney Channel; Fox News Channel; Golf Channel; HGTV; Lifetime; Nickelodeon; Spike TV; TBS Superstation; TV Land; WGN America.
Fee: $43.00 monthly.

Digital Basic Service
Subscribers: N.A.
Programming (via satellite): DMX Music.
Fee: $16.99 monthly.

Pay Service 1
Pay Units: 481.
Programming (via satellite): Cinemax; HBO; Showtime; The Movie Channel.
Fee: $7.95 monthly.

Digital Pay Service 1
Pay Units: N.A.
Programming (via satellite): Cinemax (multiplexed); Encore (multiplexed); HBO (multiplexed); Showtime (multiplexed); The Movie Channel (multiplexed).

Video-On-Demand: No

Pay-Per-View
ESPN sports (delivered digitally); ESPN Now (delivered digitally); Hot Choice (delivered digitally); iN DEMAND (delivered digitally); Playboy TV (delivered digitally); Spice (delivered digitally); Spice 2 (delivered digitally); Urban Xtra (delivered digitally).

Internet Service
Operational: No.

Telephone Service
None

Miles of Plant: 136.0 (coaxial); 19.0 (fiber optic). Homes passed: 6,077. Total homes in franchised area: 6,388.

Vice President & General Manager: Don Karell. Technical Operations Director: Greg Prim. Marketing Director: David Redmond. Marketing Manager: Jeff Hatcher.

Franchise fee: 3% of gross.

Ownership: Charter Communications Inc. (MSO).

ENTERPRISE—Time Warner Cable, 104 S Woodburn Dr, Dothan, AL 36305-1020. Phone: 334-793-3383. Fax: 334-793-5667. Web Site: http://www.timewarnercable.com. Also serves New Brockton. ICA: AL0022.

TV Market Ranking: Below 100 (ENTERPRISE, New Brockton). Franchise award date: N.A. Franchise expiration date: N.A. Began: September 1, 1966.

Channel capacity: N.A. Channels available but not in use: N.A.

Basic Service
Subscribers: N.A. Included in Dothan
Programming (received off-air): WDFX-TV (FOX) Ozark; WDHN (ABC) Dothan; WGIQ (PBS) Louisville; WIYC (IND) Troy; WSFA (NBC) Montgomery; WTVY (CBS, CW, MNT) Dothan.
Programming (via satellite): AMC; Bravo; C-SPAN; C-SPAN 2; Gospel Music TV; Home Shopping Network; INSP; ION Television; QVC; ShopNBC; Style Network; Trinity Broadcasting Network; TV Guide Network; WGN America.
Planned originations: Leased Access.
Fee: $35.80 installation; $8.00 monthly.

Expanded Basic Service 1
Subscribers: 8,608.
Programming (via satellite): ABC Family Channel; Animal Planet; Arts & Entertainment; BET Networks; Cartoon Network; CNBC; CNN; Comcast Sports Net Southeast; Comedy Central; Country Music TV; Discovery Channel; Disney Channel; E! Entertainment Television; ESPN; ESPN 2; Eternal Word TV Network; Food Network; Fox News Channel; FX; Golf Channel; Hallmark Channel; Headline News; HGTV; History Channel; Lifetime; MSNBC; MTV; Nickelodeon; Oxygen; Spike TV; Syfy; TBS Superstation; The Learning Channel; Travel Channel; truTV; Turner Classic Movies; Turner Network TV; Turner South; TV Land; Univision; USA Network; VH1; WE tv; Weather Channel.
Fee: $41.51 monthly.

Digital Basic Service
Subscribers: N.A.
Programming (via satellite): AmericanLife TV Network; BBC America; Bio; Black Family Channel; Bloomberg Television; Discovery Digital Networks; Do-It-Yourself; ESPN Classic Sports; ESPNews; Fox Movie Channel; Fox Sports World; Fuse; G4; GAS; Great American Country; Halogen Network; History Channel International; Independent Film Channel; MTV Networks Digital Suite; Music Choice; National Geographic Channel; Nick Jr.; Nick Too; Outdoor Channel; SoapNet; Speed Channel; Style Network; Sundance Channel; Toon Disney; Versus.

Digital Pay Service 1
Pay Units: N.A.
Programming (via satellite): Cinemax (multiplexed); Encore (multiplexed); HBO (multiplexed); Showtime (multiplexed); Starz (multiplexed); The Movie Channel (multiplexed).
Fee: $12.00 monthly (each).

Video-On-Demand: Yes

Pay-Per-View
Addressable homes: 2,270.
Urban American Television Network (delivered digitally); Hot Choice (delivered digitally); Fresh (delivered digitally); Shorteez (delivered digitally); Movies (delivered digitally), Addressable: Yes; Playboy TV (delivered digitally).
Internet Service
Operational: Yes.
Broadband Service: Road Runner.
Fee: $99.95 installation; $44.95 monthly.
Telephone Service
Digital: Operational
Fee: $74.95 installation; $44.95 monthly
Miles of Plant: 440.0 (coaxial); 180.0 (fiber optic). Homes passed included in Dothan
General Manager: Ramona Byrd. Technical Operations Manager: Michael Tate. Marketing Manager: Judi Gates.
City fee: 3% of basic.
Ownership: Time Warner Cable (MSO).

EUFAULA—Bright House Networks, 1394 N Eufaula Ave, Eufaula, AL 36027. Phone: 334-687-5555. Fax: 334-687-9049. Web Site: http://www.eufaula.mybrighthouse.com. Also serves Barbour County (unincorporated areas) & Henry County (unincorporated areas), AL; Georgetown & Quitman County, GA. ICA: AL0036.
TV Market Ranking: 94 (Barbour County (unincorporated areas) (portions)); Below 100 (Henry County (unincorporated areas), Barbour County (unincorporated areas) (portions)); Outside TV Markets (EUFAULA, Georgetown, Quitman County, Barbour County (unincorporated areas) (portions)). Franchise award date: January 1, 1970. Franchise expiration date: N.A. Began: October 2, 1971.
Channel capacity: N.A. Channels available but not in use: N.A.
Basic Service
Subscribers: 4,690.
Programming (received off-air): KHGI-CA North Platte; WACS-TV (PBS) Dawson; WGIQ (PBS) Louisville; WLTZ (CW, NBC) Columbus; WRBL (CBS) Columbus; WSFA (NBC) Montgomery; WTVM (ABC) Columbus; WXTX (FOX) Columbus.
Programming (via satellite): WGN America.
Current originations: Religious Access.
Expanded Basic Service 1
Subscribers: N.A.
Programming (via satellite): ABC Family Channel; AMC; AmericanLife TV Network; Animal Planet; Arts & Entertainment; BET Networks; Bravo; Cartoon Network; CNBC; CNN; Comcast Sports Net Southeast; Comedy Central; Country Music TV; C-SPAN; C-SPAN 2; Discovery Channel; Disney Channel; E! Entertainment Television; ESPN; ESPN 2; ESPN Classic Sports; ESPN Now; Food Network; Fox News Channel; Fuse; FX; Hallmark Channel; Headline News; HGTV; History Channel; Home Shopping Network; ION Television; Lifetime; Lifetime Movie Network; MSNBC; MTV; National Geographic Channel; Nickelodeon; Oxygen; QVC; ShopNBC; SoapNet; Spike TV; SportSouth; Style Network; Syfy; TBS Superstation; The Learning Channel; The Word Network; Travel Channel; Trinity Broadcasting Network; truTV; Turner Classic Movies; Turner Network TV; TV Land; USA Network; Versus; VH1; WE tv; Weather Channel.
Fee: $44.35 monthly.
Digital Basic Service
Subscribers: N.A.
Programming (via satellite): BBC America; Bloomberg Television; Current; Discovery Digital Networks; DMX Music; ESPNews; FitTV; Fox Movie Channel; Fox Sports World; G4; GAS; Golf Channel; GSN; MTV2; Nick Jr.; Outdoor Channel; Ovation; Speed Channel; Toon Disney; VH1 Classic.
Fee: $13.00 monthly.
Digital Pay Service 1
Pay Units: 593.
Programming (via satellite): Cinemax (multiplexed); HBO (multiplexed); Showtime (multiplexed); Starz (multiplexed); The Movie Channel (multiplexed).
Fee: $10.50 monthly (each).
Video-On-Demand: No
Pay-Per-View
Addressable homes: 190.
Addressable: Yes; iN DEMAND (delivered digitally), Fee: $3.95; ESPN Now (delivered digitally); Fresh (delivered digitally), Fee: $7.95; Shorteez (delivered digitally); Sports PPV (delivered digitally).
Internet Service
Operational: Yes. Began: June 1, 2003.
Subscribers: 650.
Broadband Service: RoadRunner.
Fee: $29.95 monthly.
Telephone Service
Digital: Operational
Fee: $19.95 installation; $39.95 monthly
Miles of Plant: 172.0 (coaxial); None (fiber optic). Homes passed: 6,320. Total homes in franchised area: 6,320.
Manager: Bruce Burgess. Chief Technician: Jeff Clark. Office Manager: Lisa Taylor.
Ownership: Bright House Networks LLC (MSO).

EUTAW—Sky Cablevision, PO Box 65, 1309 Roebuck Dr, Meridian, MS 39301. Phone: 601-485-6980. Fax: 601-483-0103. Web Site: http://skycablevision.com. Also serves Greene County (unincorporated areas). ICA: AL0186.
TV Market Ranking: Below 100 (EUTAW, Greene County (unincorporated areas)). Franchise award date: N.A. Franchise expiration date: N.A. Began: September 1, 1972.
Channel capacity: 38 (not 2-way capable). Channels available but not in use: 1.
Basic Service
Subscribers: 1,500 Included in Marion.
Programming (received off-air): WBIQ (PBS) Birmingham; WBRC (FOX) Birmingham; WCBI-TV (CBS, CW, MNT) Columbus; WCFT-TV (ABC) Tuscaloosa; WIAT (CBS) Birmingham; WTOK-TV (ABC, CW, FOX, MNT) Meridian; WTTO (CW) Homewood; WTVA (NBC) Tupelo; WVTM-TV (NBC) Birmingham; WVUA-CA Tuscaloosa.
Programming (via satellite): AMC; Animal Planet; Arts & Entertainment; BET Networks; Cartoon Network; CNN; Comcast Sports Net Southeast; Comedy Central; Country Music TV; C-SPAN; Discovery Channel; Disney Channel; E! Entertainment Television; ESPN; ESPN 2; ESPN Classic Sports; Flix; Food Network; Fox Movie Channel; Fox News Channel; FX; Golf Channel; Great American Country; Hallmark Channel; Headline News; HGTV; History Channel; Home Shopping Network; INSP; Lifetime; MTV; Nickelodeon; Outdoor Channel; QVC; Speed Channel; Spike TV; SportSouth; Syfy; TBS Superstation; The Learning Channel; The Sportsman Channel; Trinity Broadcasting Network; truTV; Turner Classic Movies; Turner Network TV; TV Guide Network; TV Land; USA Network; VH1; WE tv; Weather Channel; WGN America.
Fee: $25.00 installation; $31.99 monthly; $3.00 converter.
Pay Service 1
Pay Units: 188.
Programming (via satellite): Cinemax.
Fee: $7.00 monthly.
Pay Service 2
Pay Units: 198.
Programming (via satellite): HBO.
Fee: $7.00 monthly.
Pay Service 3
Pay Units: N.A.
Programming (via satellite): Encore (multiplexed); Showtime.
Internet Service
Operational: No.
Telephone Service
None
Miles of Plant: 20.0 (coaxial); None (fiber optic).
Manager & Chief Technician: Berry Ward.
Ownership: Sky Cablevision Ltd. (MSO).

FAIRFIELD—Charter Communications, 2100 Columbiana Rd, Vestavia, AL 35216. Phone: 205-824-5400. Fax: 205-824-5490. Web Site: http://www.charter.com. Also serves Hueytown, Midfield & Pleasant Grove. ICA: AL0013.
TV Market Ranking: 40 (FAIRFIELD, Hueytown, Midfield, Pleasant Grove). Franchise award date: N.A. Franchise expiration date: N.A. Began: December 1, 1970.
Channel capacity: N.A. Channels available but not in use: N.A.
Basic Service
Subscribers: 12,677.
Programming (received off-air): WABM (MNT) Birmingham; WBIQ (PBS) Birmingham; WBRC (FOX) Birmingham; WCFT-TV (ABC) Tuscaloosa; WIAT (CBS) Birmingham; WOTM-LP Montevallo; WPXH-TV (ION) Gadsden; WTTO (CW) Homewood; WVTM-TV (NBC) Birmingham.
Programming (via satellite): INSP; Trinity Broadcasting Network; WGN America.
Current originations: Leased Access.
Fee: $29.99 installation.
Expanded Basic Service 1
Subscribers: 11,464.
Programming (via satellite): ABC Family Channel; AMC; Animal Planet; Arts & Entertainment; BET Networks; Cartoon Network; CNBC; CNN; Comcast Sports Net Southeast; Comcast/Charter Sports Southeast (CSS); Comedy Central; Country Music TV; C-SPAN; C-SPAN 2; Discovery Channel; Disney Channel; E! Entertainment Television; ESPN; ESPN 2; ESPN Classic Sports; Eternal Word TV Network; Food Network; Fox News Channel; FX; G4; Golf Channel; Hallmark Channel; Headline News; HGTV; History Channel; Home Shopping Network; Lifetime; MSNBC; MTV; National Geographic Channel; Nickelodeon; Oxygen; QVC; Speed Channel; Spike TV; SportSouth; Syfy; TBS Superstation; The Learning Channel; Travel Channel; truTV; Turner Classic Movies; Turner Network TV; TV Land; USA Network; VH1; WE tv; Weather Channel.
Fee: $43.00 monthly.
Digital Basic Service
Subscribers: N.A.
Programming (via satellite): BBC America; Bio; Bloomberg Television; Bravo; Canales N; Discovery Digital Networks; Discovery Health Channel; DMX Music; ESPNews; Fox Movie Channel; Fox Sports World; GAS; Great American Country; GSN; Halogen Network; History Channel International; Independent Film Channel; Lifetime Movie Network; MTV Networks Digital Suite; MuchMusic Network; Nick Jr.; Outdoor Channel; Style Network; Sundance Channel; Toon Disney; TV Guide Interactive Inc.; Versus.
Fee: $16.99 monthly.
Digital Pay Service 1
Pay Units: N.A.
Programming (via satellite): Cinemax (multiplexed); Encore (multiplexed); HBO (multiplexed); Showtime (multiplexed); Starz (multiplexed); The Movie Channel (multiplexed).
Video-On-Demand: Yes
Pay-Per-View
iN DEMAND (delivered digitally); Playboy TV (delivered digitally); Fresh (delivered digitally); Shorteez (delivered digitally).
Internet Service
Operational: Yes.
Broadband Service: Charter Pipeline.
Fee: $29.99 monthly; $10.00 modem lease.
Telephone Service
Digital: Operational
Miles of Plant: 188.0 (coaxial); None (fiber optic). Homes passed: 16,460. Total homes in franchised area: 17,456.
Vice President & General Manager: Don Karell. Technical Operations Director: Greg Prim. Marketing Director: David Redmond. Marketing Manager: Jeff Hatcher.
City fee: 5% of gross.
Ownership: Charter Communications Inc. (MSO).

FAIRHOPE—Mediacom, 760 Middle St, PO Box 1009, Fairhope, AL 36532. Phone: 251-928-0374. Fax: 251-928-3804. Web Site: http://www.mediacomcable.com. Also serves Baldwin County (portions), Barnwell, Bay Minette, Daphne, Fish River, Lake Forest, Lillian, Marlow, Montrose, Point Clear, Spanish Cove, Spanish Fort, Stapleton & Whitehouse Forks. ICA: AL0124.
TV Market Ranking: 59 (Baldwin County (portions), Barnwell, Bay Minette, Daphne, FAIRHOPE, Fish River, Lake Forest, Lillian, Marlow, Montrose, Point Clear, Spanish Cove, Spanish Fort, Stapleton, Whitehouse Forks). Franchise award date: May 18, 1982. Franchise expiration date: N.A. Began: January 1, 1988.
Channel capacity: N.A. Channels available but not in use: N.A.
Basic Service
Subscribers: 18,504.
Programming (received off-air): WALA-TV (FOX) Mobile; WEAR-TV (ABC) Pensacola; WEIQ (PBS) Mobile; WFNA (CW) Gulf Shores; WHBR (IND) Pensacola; WJTC (IND) Pensacola; WKRG-TV (CBS) Mobile; WMPV-TV (TBN) Mobile; WPMI-TV (NBC) Mobile.
Programming (via satellite): ABC Family Channel; AMC; Animal Planet; Arts & Entertainment; BET Networks; Bravo; Cartoon Network; CNBC; CNN; Comcast Sports Net Southeast; Comedy Central; Country Music TV; C-SPAN; C-SPAN 2; Discovery Channel; Disney Channel; E! Entertainment Television; ESPN; ESPN 2; Eternal Word TV Network; Food Network; Fox News Channel; FX; Golf Channel; Hallmark Channel; Headline News; HGTV; History Channel; Home Shopping Network; INSP; ION Television; Lifetime; MoviePlex; MSNBC; MTV; Nickelodeon; Oxygen; QVC; Spike TV; SportSouth; Syfy; TBS Superstation; The Learning Channel; Travel Channel; truTV; Turner Network TV; TV Guide Network; TV Land; USA Network; VH1; WE tv; Weather Channel; WGN America.
Fee: $34.95 installation; $44.95 monthly.

Digital Basic Service

Subscribers: 4,741.

Programming (via satellite): AmericanLife TV Network; BBC America; Bio; Bloomberg Television; Discovery Digital Networks; ESPNews; Fox Movie Channel; Fox Sports World; Fuse; G4; GSN; Halogen Network; History Channel International; Independent Film Channel; Lifetime Movie Network; Music Choice; National Geographic Channel; Outdoor Channel; Speed Channel; Style Network; Trinity Broadcasting Network; Turner Classic Movies; Versus.

Fee: $12.00 monthly.

Digital Pay Service 1

Pay Units: 2,317.

Programming (via satellite): Cinemax (multiplexed); Encore (multiplexed); Flix; HBO (multiplexed); Showtime (multiplexed); Starz (multiplexed); Sundance Channel; The Movie Channel (multiplexed).

Fee: $10.95 monthly (Cinemax, HBO, Showtime, Flix/Sundance/TMC, or Starz/Encore).

Video-On-Demand: Yes

Pay-Per-View

Addressable homes: 3,994.

ESPN Now (delivered digitally); Playboy TV (delivered digitally); Pleasure (delivered digitally); Fresh (delivered digitally); TVN Entertainment (delivered digitally); sports (delivered digitally).

Internet Service

Operational: Yes.

Broadband Service: Mediacom High Speed Internet.

Telephone Service

Digital: Operational

Miles of Plant: 512.0 (coaxial); None (fiber optic). Homes passed: 26,301.

General Manager: Jeff Walker. Technical Operations Manager: Bobby Hollifield. Chief Technician: Billy Brooks.

Ownership: Mediacom LLC (MSO).

FAYETTE—West Alabama TV Cable Co. Inc., PO Box 930, 213 2nd Ave NE, Fayette, AL 35555-0930. Phone: 205-932-4700. Fax: 205-932-3585. E-mail: cable@watvc.com. Web Site: http://www.watvc.com. Also serves Belk. ICA: AL0072.

TV Market Ranking: Below 100 (Belk); Outside TV Markets (FAYETTE). Franchise award date: N.A. Franchise expiration date: N.A. Began: February 1, 1966.

Channel capacity: 60 (operating 2-way). Channels available but not in use: 4.

Basic Service

Subscribers: 2,348.

Programming (received off-air): WABM (MNT) Birmingham; WBIQ (PBS) Birmingham; WBRC (FOX) Birmingham; WCFT-TV (ABC) Tuscaloosa; WIAT (CBS) Birmingham; WTTO (CW) Homewood; WTVA (NBC) Tupelo; WVTM-TV (NBC) Birmingham; allband FM.

Programming (via satellite): ABC Family Channel; AMC; Arts & Entertainment; BET Networks; Cartoon Network; CNBC; CNN; Country Music TV; C-SPAN; Discovery Channel; Disney Channel; E! Entertainment Television; ESPN; ESPN 2; Food Network; Fox News Channel; FX; Golf Channel; Gospel Music TV; Hallmark Channel; Headline News; HGTV; History Channel; Home Shopping Network; Lifetime; MTV; Nickelodeon; QVC; SportSouth; TBS Superstation; The Learning Channel; Travel Channel; Trinity Broadcasting Network; Turner Classic Movies; Turner Network TV; TV Guide Network; TV Land; USA Network; VH1; Weather Channel; WGN America.

Current originations: Leased Access.

Fee: $35.00 installation; $37.25 monthly.

Digital Basic Service

Subscribers: N.A.

Programming (via satellite): BBC America; Bio; Bloomberg Television; Discovery Health Channel; Discovery Kids Channel; Discovery Military Channel; Discovery Planet Green; DMX Music; ESPN Classic Sports; ESPN Now; ESPNews; Fox Movie Channel; Fox Soccer; G4; History Channel International; ID Investigation Discovery; Independent Film Channel; INSP; Lifetime Movie Network; Lime; National Geographic Channel; Outdoor Channel; Science Channel; Sleuth; Speed Channel; Toon Disney; Versus; WE tv.

Fee: $14.00 monthly.

Pay Service 1

Pay Units: 540.

Programming (via satellite): Cinemax; HBO.

Fee: $15.00 installation; $10.95 (Cinemax), $11.95 monthly (HBO).

Digital Pay Service 1

Pay Units: N.A.

Programming (via satellite): Cinemax (multiplexed); Encore (multiplexed); HBO (multiplexed); Showtime (multiplexed); Starz (multiplexed); The Movie Channel (multiplexed).

Fee: $10.95 monthly (Cinemax or Starz/Encore/TMC), $12.95 monthly (HBO or Showtime).

Video-On-Demand: No

Pay-Per-View

iN DEMAND (delivered digitally); Hot Choice (delivered digitally); Spice (delivered digitally); ESPN Now (delivered digitally); Sports PPV (delivered digitally).

Internet Service

Operational: Yes.

Broadband Service: In-house.

Fee: $24.95 monthly.

Telephone Service

None

Miles of Plant: 150.0 (coaxial); None (fiber optic). Homes passed: 8,000. Total homes in franchised area: 10,000.

Manager: Kyle South.

City fee: $125 license fee annually.

Ownership: West Alabama TV Cable Co. Inc. (MSO).

FLORALA—Bright House Networks, 94 Walton Rd, DeFuniak Springs, FL 32433. Phones: 205-591-6880 (Customer service); 800-288-1664; 850-892-3155. Fax: 850-892-1315. Web Site: http://panhandle.brighthouse.com. Also serves Lockhart, AL; Paxton, FL. ICA: AL0092.

TV Market Ranking: Outside TV Markets (FLORALA, Lockhart, Paxton). Franchise award date: N.A. Franchise expiration date: N.A. Began: February 1, 1970.

Channel capacity: N.A. Channels available but not in use: N.A.

Basic Service

Subscribers: 971.

Programming (received off-air): WBIF (IND) Marianna [LICENSED & SILENT]; WDHN (ABC) Dothan; WGIQ (PBS) Louisville; WJHG-TV (CW, MNT, NBC) Panama City; WMBB (ABC) Panama City; WPGX (FOX) Panama City; WSFA (NBC) Montgomery; WTVY (CBS, CW, MNT) Dothan; WWEO-CA De Funiak Springs; 1 FM.

Programming (via satellite): BET Networks; CW+; Discovery Channel; Fox News Channel; Hallmark Channel; Home Shopping Network; TBS Superstation; The Learning Channel; WGN America.

Current originations: Government Access; Educational Access; Public Access.

Fee: $53.75 installation.

Expanded Basic Service 1

Subscribers: N.A.

Programming (via satellite): ABC Family Channel; AMC; Animal Planet; Arts & Entertainment; Bravo; Cartoon Network; CNBC; CNN; Comcast Sports Net Southeast; Comedy Central; Country Music TV; C-SPAN; Disney Channel; E! Entertainment Television; ESPN; ESPN 2; Food Network; Fuse; FX; Headline News; HGTV; History Channel; Jewelry Television; Lifetime; Lifetime Movie Network; MSNBC; MTV; National Geographic Channel; Nickelodeon; Oxygen; QVC; ShopNBC; Spike TV; Style Network; Syfy; Travel Channel; Trinity Broadcasting Network; truTV; Turner Network TV; USA Network; Versus; VH1; WE tv; Weather Channel.

Fee: $44.35 monthly.

Digital Basic Service

Subscribers: N.A.

Programming (via satellite): AmericanLife TV Network; Arts & Entertainment HD; BBC America; Bio; Bloomberg Television; Current; Discovery HD Theater; Discovery Health Channel; Discovery Home Channel; Discovery Kids Channel; Discovery Military Channel; Discovery Times Channel; ESPN 2 HD; ESPN Classic Sports; ESPN HD; ESPN U; ESPNews; Fox Business Channel; Fox Movie Channel; Fox Reality Channel; Fox Soccer; G4; GAS; Golf Channel; Great American Country; GSN; HDNet; HDNet Movies; History Channel HD; History Channel International; MTV Hits; MTV2; Music Choice; Nick Jr.; NickToons TV; Outdoor Channel; Ovation; Science Channel; Sleuth; Speed Channel; TBS in HD; Toon Disney; Turner Classic Movies; Turner Network TV HD; TV Land; Universal HD; VH1 Classic; WebMD Television.

Fee: $12.55 monthly.

Digital Pay Service 1

Pay Units: N.A.

Programming (via satellite): Cinemax (multiplexed); Encore (multiplexed); HBO (multiplexed); HBO HD; Independent Film Channel; Showtime (multiplexed); Showtime HD; Starz (multiplexed); The Movie Channel (multiplexed).

Fee: $10.50 monthly (each).

Video-On-Demand: Yes

Pay-Per-View

Pleasure (delivered digitally), Addressable: Yes; Hot Choice (delivered digitally); iN DEMAND (delivered digitally); Fresh (delivered digitally); Shorteez (delivered digitally); Ten Blue (delivered digitally); Ten Blox (delivered digitally).

Internet Service

Operational: Yes.

Broadband Service: Road Runner.

Fee: $32.95 monthly.

Telephone Service

Analog: Not Operational

Digital: Operational

Fee: $39.95 monthly

Miles of Plant: 37.0 (coaxial); None (fiber optic). Homes passed: 1,369. Total homes in franchised area: 1,480.

Marketing Director: Nicole Hardy. Technical Operations Manager: Lynn Miller. Chief Technician: Edward Harrison. Business Manager: Elaine West.

City fee: 3% of gross.

Ownership: Bright House Networks LLC (MSO).

FLORENCE—Comcast Cable, 2047 Max Luther Dr NW, Huntsville, AL 35810-3801. Phone: 256-859-7828. Web Site: http://www.comcast.com. Also serves Cloverdale, Colbert County, Hawk Pride Mountain, Lauderdale County, Muscle Shoals, Sheffield, St. Florian & Tuscumbia. ICA: AL0187.

TV Market Ranking: 96 (Lauderdale County); Below 100 (Cloverdale, Colbert County, FLORENCE, Hawk Pride Mountain, Muscle Shoals, Sheffield, St. Florian, Tuscumbia, Lauderdale County). Franchise award date: N.A. Franchise expiration date: N.A. Began: September 1, 1953.

Channel capacity: N.A. Channels available but not in use: N.A.

Basic Service

Subscribers: 30,828.

Programming (received off-air): WAAY-TV (ABC) Huntsville; WAFF (NBC) Huntsville; WBRC (FOX) Birmingham; WFIQ (PBS) Florence; WHDF (CW) Florence; WHNT-TV (CBS) Huntsville; WZDX (FOX, MNT) Huntsville.

Programming (via satellite): ION Television; QVC.

Current originations: Public Access.

Fee: $62.99 installation; $11.99 monthly; $2.43 converter.

Expanded Basic Service 1

Subscribers: 29,702.

Programming (via satellite): ABC Family Channel; AMC; Animal Planet; Arts & Entertainment; BET Networks; Cartoon Network; CNBC; CNN; Comcast Sports Net Southeast; Comcast/Charter Sports Southeast (CSS); Comedy Central; Country Music TV; C-SPAN; C-SPAN 2; Discovery Channel; Discovery Health Channel; E! Entertainment Television; ESPN; ESPN 2; Eternal Word TV Network; Food Network; Fox News Channel; FX; Golf Channel; Great American Country; GSN; Headline News; HGTV; History Channel; Home Shopping Network; Lifetime; MSNBC; MTV; Nickelodeon; Outdoor Channel; Speed Channel; Spike TV; Style Network; Syfy; TBS Superstation; The Learning Channel; Trinity Broadcasting Network; truTV; Turner Network TV; TV Guide Network; TV Land; USA Network; VH1; Weather Channel; Weatherscan.

Fee: $35.51 monthly.

Digital Basic Service

Subscribers: N.A.

Programming (via satellite): BBC America; C-SPAN 3; Discovery Digital Networks; Disney Channel; DMX Music; ESPN; ESPNews; G4; GAS; INHD; MTV Networks Digital Suite; Nick Jr.; Nick Too; SoapNet;

Toon Disney; WAM! America's Kidz Network; Weatherscan.
Fee: $14.95 monthly.
Digital Pay Service 1
Pay Units: N.A.
Programming (via satellite): Cinemax (multiplexed); Cinemax HD; Encore (multiplexed); Flix (multiplexed); HBO (multiplexed); HBO HD; Showtime (multiplexed); Showtime HD; Starz (multiplexed); Sundance Channel (multiplexed); The Movie Channel (multiplexed).
Fee: $14.70 monthly (each).
Video-On-Demand: Yes
Pay-Per-View
iN DEMAND (delivered digitally); Hot Choice (delivered digitally); Playboy TV (delivered digitally); Fresh (delivered digitally); Shorteez (delivered digitally); Pleasure (delivered digitally).
Internet Service
Operational: Yes.
Broadband Service: Comcast High Speed Internet.
Fee: $42.95 monthly.
Telephone Service
None
Miles of Plant: 930.0 (coaxial); None (fiber optic). Total homes in franchised area: 53,135.
Vice President & General Manager: Ellen Rosson. Technical Operations Director: Butch Jernigan. Government Affairs Manager: Patricia Collins.
City fee: 3% of gross.
Ownership: Comcast Cable Communications Inc. (MSO).

FOLEY—Riviera Utilities Cable TV, PO Box 2050, 413 E Laurel Ave, Foley, AL 36535-2619. Phone: 251-943-5001. Fax: 251-943-5275. E-mail: michaelr@riviera.com. Web Site: http://www.rivierautilities.com. Also serves Bon Secour, Elberta, Magnolia Springs, Miflin & Summerdale. ICA: AL0046.
TV Market Ranking: 59 (Bon Secour, Elberta, FOLEY, Magnolia Springs, Miflin, Summerdale). Franchise award date: June 2, 1980. Franchise expiration date: N.A. Began: March 2, 1982.
Channel capacity: 136 (operating 2-way). Channels available but not in use: N.A.
Basic Service
Subscribers: 6,085.
Programming (received off-air): WALA-TV (FOX) Mobile; WEAR-TV (ABC) Pensacola; WEIQ (PBS) Mobile; WHBR (IND) Pensacola; WJTC (IND) Pensacola; WKRG-TV (CBS) Mobile; WMPV-TV (TBN) Mobile; WPAN (IND) Fort Walton Beach; WPMI-TV (NBC) Mobile; WSRE (PBS) Pensacola.
Programming (via satellite): QVC; Weather Channel; WPIX (CW, IND) New York.
Fee: $20.00 installation; $22.95 monthly; $20.00 additional installation.
Expanded Basic Service 1
Subscribers: 5,942.
Programming (via satellite): ABC Family Channel; AMC; Animal Planet; Arts & Entertainment; BET Networks; Bravo; Cartoon Network; CNBC; CNN; Comcast Sports Net Southeast; Comedy Central; Country Music TV; C-SPAN; C-SPAN 2; Discovery Channel; Disney Channel; E! Entertainment Television; ESPN; ESPN 2; ESPN Classic Sports; Eternal Word TV Network; Food Network; Fox Movie Channel; FX; Great American Country; Hallmark Channel; Headline News; HGTV; History Channel; Lifetime; MSNBC; MTV; National Geographic Channel; Nickelodeon; Outdoor Channel; Oxygen; SoapNet; Spike TV; Syfy; TBS Superstation; The Learning Channel; Toon Disney; Travel Channel; truTV; Turner Network TV; Turner South; TV Land; USA Network; VH1; WGN America.
Digital Basic Service
Subscribers: 902.
Programming (received off-air): WALA-TV (FOX) Mobile; WEAR-TV (ABC) Pensacola; WEIQ (PBS) Mobile; WJTC (IND) Pensacola; WKRG-TV (CBS) Mobile; WPMI-TV (NBC) Mobile; WSRE (PBS) Pensacola.
Programming (via satellite): Arts & Entertainment HD; BBC America; Bio; Bloomberg Television; Discovery Health Channel; Discovery Home Channel; Discovery Kids Channel; Discovery Military Channel; Discovery Times Channel; DMX Music; ESPN 2 HD; ESPN HD; ESPNews; FitTV; Food Network HD; Fox Movie Channel; GAS; Golf Channel; GSN; HGTV HD; History Channel International; Lifetime; MTV2; National Geographic Channel HD Network; Nick Jr.; NickToons TV; Science Channel; Speed Channel; Style Network; Turner Classic Movies; Universal HD; Versus; VH1 Classic; VH1 Country; WE tv.
Fee: $35.00 installation; $11.00 monthly.
Pay Service 1
Pay Units: 383.
Programming (via satellite): Cinemax.
Fee: $13.95 monthly.
Pay Service 2
Pay Units: 866.
Programming (via satellite): HBO.
Fee: $13.95 monthly.
Digital Pay Service 1
Pay Units: N.A.
Programming (via satellite): Cinemax (multiplexed); Encore (multiplexed); Flix; HBO (multiplexed); Showtime (multiplexed); Starz (multiplexed); Starz HDTV; The Movie Channel (multiplexed).
Video-On-Demand: No
Pay-Per-View
iN DEMAND (delivered digitally); Fresh (delivered digitally); Playboy TV (delivered digitally).
Internet Service
Operational: No.
Telephone Service
None
Miles of Plant: 285.0 (coaxial); None (fiber optic). Homes passed: 10,000. Total homes in franchised area: 10,000.
Manager: Michael Dugger. Chief Technician: Robert Clark. Marketing Director & Customer Service Manager: Chris Bonner.
City fee: 5% of gross.
Ownership: Riviera Utilities Cable TV.

FORKLAND—Sky Cablevision, PO Box 65, 1309 Roebuck Dr, Meridian, MS 39301. Phone: 601-485-6980. Fax: 601-483-0103. Web Site: http://skycablevision.com. ICA: AL0189.
TV Market Ranking: Outside TV Markets (FORKLAND). Franchise award date: N.A. Franchise expiration date: N.A. Began: February 1, 1990.
Channel capacity: N.A. Channels available but not in use: N.A.
Basic Service
Subscribers: N.A.
Programming (received off-air): WGBC (NBC) Meridian; WIIQ (PBS) Demopolis; WMDN (CBS) Meridian; WTOK-TV (ABC, CW, FOX, MNT) Meridian.
Programming (via satellite): ABC Family Channel; Arts & Entertainment; CNN; Discovery Channel; Disney Channel; ESPN; TBS Superstation; Turner Network TV; USA Network; WGN America.
Fee: $34.00 monthly.
Pay Service 1
Pay Units: N.A.
Programming (via satellite): HBO.
Fee: $11.00 monthly.
Internet Service
Operational: No.
Telephone Service
None
Manager & Chief Technician: Berry Ward.
Ownership: Sky Cablevision Ltd. (MSO).

FORT PAYNE—Windjammer Cable, 4400 PGA Blvd, Ste 902, Palm Beach Gardens, FL 33410. Phones: 561-775-1208; 877-450-5558. Fax: 561-775-7811. Web Site: http://www.windjammercable.com. Also serves Adamsburg, Collbran, De Kalb County, Pine Ridge & Valley Head. ICA: AL0040.
TV Market Ranking: 18 (Adamsburg, Collbran, De Kalb County, FORT PAYNE, Pine Ridge, Valley Head). Franchise award date: N.A. Franchise expiration date: N.A. Began: August 19, 1968.
Channel capacity: N.A. Channels available but not in use: N.A.
Basic Service
Subscribers: 11,600 Includes Cullman.
Programming (received off-air): WAAY-TV (ABC) Huntsville; WAFF (NBC) Huntsville; WDEF-TV (CBS) Chattanooga; WHDF (CW) Florence; WHIQ (PBS) Huntsville; WHNT-TV (CBS) Huntsville; WRCB (NBC) Chattanooga; WTJP-TV (TBN) Gadsden; WTVC (ABC) Chattanooga; WVTM-TV (NBC) Birmingham; WZDX (FOX, MNT) Huntsville; allband FM.
Programming (via satellite): ABC Family Channel; AMC; Arts & Entertainment; Cartoon Network; CNBC; CNN; Comcast Sports Net Southeast; Comedy Central; Country Music TV; C-SPAN; C-SPAN 2; Discovery Channel; Disney Channel; E! Entertainment Television; ESPN; ESPN 2; ESPN Classic Sports; Food Network; FX; Hallmark Channel; Headline News; HGTV; History Channel; Home Shopping Network; Lifetime; MSNBC; MTV; Nickelodeon; Oxygen; Product Information Network; QVC; ShopNBC; Syfy; The Learning Channel; truTV; Turner Network TV; TV Guide Network; TV Land; Univision; USA Network; VH1; Weather Channel.
Current originations: Public Access; Leased Access.
Fee: $49.95 installation; $45.95 monthly.
Expanded Basic Service 1
Subscribers: 9,200 Includes Cullman.
Programming (via satellite): Animal Planet; BET Networks; Bravo; Eternal Word TV Network; Fox News Channel; GalaVision; INSP; Speed Channel; Spike TV; TBS Superstation; Travel Channel; WGN America.
Fee: $10.00 installation; $12.16 monthly.
Digital Basic Service
Subscribers: 2,900 Includes Cullman.
Programming (via satellite): AmericanLife TV Network; BBC America; Bio; Black Family Channel; Bloomberg Television; Canales N; Discovery Digital Networks; Do-It-Yourself; ESPNews; Fox College Sports Atlantic; Fox College Sports Central; Fox College Sports Pacific; Fox Movie Channel; Fox Sports World; Fuse; G4; GAS; Golf Channel; Great American Country; GSN; Halogen Network; History Channel International; Independent Film Channel; MTV Networks Digital Suite; Music Choice; National Geographic Channel; Nick Jr.; Nick Too; NickToons TV; Outdoor Channel; SoapNet; Style Network; Sundance Channel; Toon Disney; Trinity Broadcasting Network; Turner Classic Movies; Versus; WE tv.
Fee: $58.99 monthly.
Digital Pay Service 1
Pay Units: N.A.
Programming (via satellite): Cinemax (multiplexed); Encore (multiplexed); Flix; HBO (multiplexed); Showtime (multiplexed); Starz (multiplexed); The Movie Channel (multiplexed).
Fee: $12.00 monthly (HBO, Cinemax, Showtime/TMC or Starz), $19.95 monthly (Playboy).
Video-On-Demand: Planned
Pay-Per-View
Urban American Television Network (delivered digitally); Hot Choice (delivered digitally); Fresh (delivered digitally); Playboy TV (delivered digitally); Movies (delivered digitally).
Internet Service
Operational: Yes.
Subscribers: 2,900.
Broadband Service: Road Runner.
Fee: $20.99-$49.99 installation; $44.95 monthly.
Telephone Service
Digital: Operational
Fee: $74.95 installation; $49.95 monthly
Miles of Plant: 1,211.0 (coaxial); None (fiber optic). Homes passed: 36,500. Miles of plant (coax) & homes passed include Cullman
General Manager: Timothy Evard. Operations Director: Belinda Graham. Engineering Director: Mike Earehart. Finance & Accounting Director: Cindy Johnson.
Ownership: Windjammer Communications LLC (MSO).

FREEMANVILLE—Formerly served by CableSouth Inc. No longer in operation. ICA: AL0190.

GADSDEN—Comcast Cable, 1131 Whigham Place, Tuscaloosa, AL 35405-3669. Phone: 205-391-3677. Web Site: http://www.comcast.com. Also serves Etowah County, Glencoe & Rainbow City. ICA: AL0191.
TV Market Ranking: Below 100 (Etowah County, GADSDEN, Glencoe, Rainbow City). Franchise award date: March 14, 1961. Franchise expiration date: N.A. Began: June 1, 1962.
Channel capacity: 57 (operating 2-way). Channels available but not in use: None.
Basic Service
Subscribers: 19,389.
Programming (received off-air): WABM (MNT) Birmingham; WAFF (NBC) Huntsville; WBRC (FOX) Birmingham; WCIQ (PBS) Mount Cheaha State Park; WIAT (CBS) Birmingham; WJSU-TV (ABC) Anniston; WPXH-TV (ION) Gadsden; WSB-TV (ABC) Atlanta; WTJP-TV (TBN) Gadsden; WTTO (CW) Homewood; WVTM-TV (NBC) Birmingham.
Current originations: Government Access; Educational Access.
Fee: $62.99 installation; $9.75 monthly; $2.79 converter.
Expanded Basic Service 1
Subscribers: N.A.
Programming (via satellite): ABC Family Channel; AMC; Animal Planet; Arts & Entertainment; Cartoon Network; CNBC; CNN; Comcast Sports Net Southeast; Comedy Central; C-SPAN; C-SPAN 2; Discovery Channel; Disney Channel; E! Entertainment Television; ESPN; ESPN 2; Food Network; Fox News Channel; FX; Golf Channel; Great American Country;

Headline News; HGTV; History Channel; Lifetime; MTV; Nickelodeon; QVC; Spike TV; SportSouth; Style Network; Syfy; TBS Superstation; The Learning Channel; Turner Network TV; TV Land; USA Network; VH1; Weather Channel.
Fee: $38.24 monthly.

Digital Pay Service 1
Pay Units: N.A.
Programming (via satellite): Cinemax (multiplexed); DMX Music; Flix; HBO (multiplexed); Showtime (multiplexed); The Movie Channel (multiplexed).
Fee: $14.95 monthly (each).
Video-On-Demand: Planned

Pay-Per-View
Addressable homes: 5,000.
Hot Choice, Addressable: Yes; iN DEMAND; iN DEMAND (delivered digitally).

Internet Service
Operational: Yes.
Broadband Service: Comcast High Speed Internet.
Fee: $42.95 monthly.

Telephone Service
Digital: Operational
Miles of Plant: 700.0 (coaxial); 45.0 (fiber optic). Total homes in franchised area: 31,288.
Chief Technician: Johnny Mills.
City fee: 5% of gross.
Ownership: Comcast Cable Communications Inc. (MSO).

GENEVA—Bright House Networks, 94 Walton Rd, DeFuniak Springs, FL 32433. Phones: 850-892-3155; 800-288-1644; 205-290-1300. Fax: 850-892-1318. Web Site: http://panhandle.brighthouse.com. Also serves Geneva County. ICA: AL0081.
TV Market Ranking: Below 100 (GENEVA, Geneva County (portions)); Outside TV Markets (Geneva County (portions)). Franchise award date: N.A. Franchise expiration date: N.A. Began: July 1, 1966.
Channel capacity: 35 (operating 2-way). Channels available but not in use: 3.

Basic Service
Subscribers: 1,457.
Programming (received off-air): WDFX-TV (FOX) Ozark; WDHN (ABC) Dothan; WGIQ (PBS) Louisville; WJHG-TV (CW, MNT, NBC) Panama City; WMBB (ABC) Panama City; WSFA (NBC) Montgomery; WTVY (CBS, CW, MNT) Dothan; allband FM.
Programming (via satellite): BET Networks; C-SPAN; CW+; Discovery Channel; Fox News Channel; Home Shopping Network; TBS Superstation; The Learning Channel; WGN America.
Current originations: Public Access.
Fee: $30.00 installation; $2.00 converter.

Expanded Basic Service 1
Subscribers: 1,389.
Programming (via satellite): ABC Family Channel; AMC; Animal Planet; Arts & Entertainment; Bravo; Cartoon Network; CNBC; CNN; Comedy Central; Country Music TV; C-SPAN 2; Disney Channel; E! Entertainment Television; ESPN; ESPN 2; Food Network; Fuse; FX; Headline News; HGTV; History Channel; Lifetime; Lifetime Movie Network; MSNBC; MTV; National Geographic Channel; Nickelodeon; Oxygen; QVC; ShopNBC; Spike TV; Style Network; Syfy; Travel Channel; Trinity Broadcasting Network; truTV; Turner Network TV; USA Network; Versus; VH1; WE tv; Weather Channel.
Fee: $44.35 monthly.

Digital Basic Service
Subscribers: N.A.
Programming (received off-air): WGIQ (PBS) Louisville; WJHG-TV (CW, MNT, NBC) Panama City; WSFA (NBC) Montgomery; WTVY (CBS, CW, MNT) Dothan.
Programming (via satellite): AmericanLife TV Network; BBC America; Bio; Bloomberg Television; Bravo; Current; Discovery Digital Networks; Discovery HD Theater; ESPN 2 HD; ESPN Classic Sports; ESPN HD; ESPN Now; ESPN U; ESPNews; Fox Movie Channel; Fox Reality Channel; Fox Soccer; G4; GAS; Golf Channel; Great American Country; GSN; HDNet; HDNet Movies; History Channel International; INHD; MTV Networks Digital Suite; Music Choice; Nick Jr.; NickToons TV; Outdoor Channel; Ovation; Sleuth; Speed Channel; Toon Disney; Turner Classic Movies; TV Land; Universal HD; WebMD Television.
Fee: $12.45 monthly.

Digital Pay Service 1
Pay Units: N.A.
Programming (via satellite): Cinemax (multiplexed); Encore (multiplexed); HBO (multiplexed); HBO HD; Independent Film Channel; Showtime (multiplexed); Showtime HD; Starz (multiplexed); Sundance Channel; The Movie Channel (multiplexed).
Fee: $10.50 monthly (each).
Video-On-Demand: No

Pay-Per-View
iN DEMAND (delivered digitally); Fresh (delivered digitally); Hot Choice (delivered digitally); Ten Blue (delivered digitally); Ten Blox (delivered digitally); Shorteez (delivered digitally); Pleasure (delivered digitally).

Internet Service
Operational: Yes.
Broadband Service: Road Runner.
Fee: $49.95 installation; $29.95 monthly.

Telephone Service
Analog: Not Operational
Digital: Operational
Fee: $39.95 monthly
Miles of Plant: 47.0 (coaxial); None (fiber optic). Homes passed: 1,954. Total homes in franchised area: 2,636.
Manager: Bruce Burgess. Chief Technician: Edward Harrison.
City fee: 3% of gross.
Ownership: Bright House Networks LLC (MSO).

GOOD HOPE—Alabama Broadband LLC, 3447A Parkwood Rd SE, Bessemer, AL 35022. Phones: 877-840-5040; 205-426-3432. E-mail: contact@alabamabroadband.com. Web Site: http://www.alabamabroadband.net. Also serves Cullman County (portions) & Dodge City. ICA: AL0193.
TV Market Ranking: 96 (Cullman County (portions), Dodge City, GOOD HOPE). Franchise award date: N.A. Franchise expiration date: N.A. Began: January 1, 1988.
Channel capacity: 45 (not 2-way capable). Channels available but not in use: 1.

Basic Service
Subscribers: 982.
Programming (received off-air): WAAY-TV (ABC) Huntsville; WABM (MNT) Birmingham; WBIQ (PBS) Birmingham; WBRC (FOX) Birmingham; WCFT-TV (ABC) Tuscaloosa; WHNT-TV (CBS) Huntsville; WIAT (CBS) Birmingham; WTJP-TV (TBN) Gadsden; WTTO (CW) Homewood; WVTM-TV (NBC) Birmingham.
Programming (via satellite): ABC Family Channel; AMC; Animal Planet; CNN; Comcast Sports Net Southeast; Country Music TV; C-SPAN; C-SPAN 2; Discovery Channel; Disney Channel; ESPN; ESPN 2; Fox News Channel; Headline News; HGTV; Home Shopping Network; MTV; National Geographic Channel; Nickelodeon; QVC; Spike TV; TBS Superstation; The Learning Channel; truTV; Turner Network TV; TV Guide Network; USA Network; VH1; Weather Channel; WGN America.
Fee: $29.95 installation; $32.20 monthly.

Pay Service 1
Pay Units: 259.
Programming (via satellite): HBO.
Fee: $9.00 monthly.

Pay Service 2
Pay Units: 189.
Programming (via satellite): Showtime.
Fee: $8.00 monthly.
Video-On-Demand: No

Internet Service
Operational: No.

Telephone Service
None
Miles of Plant: 110.0 (coaxial); None (fiber optic).
President: Tom Early. Marketing Director: Bob Garner.
Ownership: Alabama Broadband LLC (MSO).

GORDON—Gordon Cable TV, PO Box 80, Siloam, NC 27047-0080. Phone: 334-522-3107. Fax: 334-374-5055. ICA: AL0242.
TV Market Ranking: Below 100 (GORDON). Franchise award date: November 11, 1991. Franchise expiration date: N.A. Began: February 1, 1992.
Channel capacity: 60 (not 2-way capable). Channels available but not in use: 43.

Basic Service
Subscribers: 75.
Programming (received off-air): WDFX-TV (FOX) Ozark; WDHN (ABC) Dothan; WJHG-TV (CW, MNT, NBC) Panama City; WTVY (CBS, CW, MNT) Dothan.
Programming (via satellite): ABC Family Channel; BET Networks; Cartoon Network; CNN; ESPN; Home Shopping Network; Syfy; TBS Superstation; Trinity Broadcasting Network; Turner Network TV; USA Network; WGN America.
Fee: $25.00 installation; $16.00 monthly.

Pay Service 1
Pay Units: 30.
Programming (via satellite): HBO.
Fee: $10.50 monthly.
Video-On-Demand: No

Internet Service
Operational: No.

Telephone Service
None
Miles of Plant: 3.0 (coaxial); None (fiber optic). Homes passed: 154. Total homes in franchised area: 214.
Manager: Dale Norman.
Ownership: Norman & Associates Inc. (MSO).

GRANT—New Hope Telephone Cooperative. Now served by NEW HOPE, AL [AL0070]. ICA: AL0195.

GREENSBORO—Mediacom, 760 Middle St, PO Box 1009, Fairhope, AL 36532. Phones: 850-934-7700 (Gulf Breeze regional office); 251-928-0374. Fax: 251-928-3804. Web Site: http://www.mediacomcable.com. Also serves Hale County (portions). ICA: AL0110.
TV Market Ranking: Below 100 (Hale County (portions) (portions)); Outside TV Markets (GREENSBORO, Hale County (portions) (portions)). Franchise award date: August 27, 1970. Franchise expiration date: N.A. Began: October 1, 1970.
Channel capacity: N.A. Channels available but not in use: N.A.

Basic Service
Subscribers: 1,183.
Programming (received off-air): WAKA (CBS) Selma; WBIH (IND) Selma; WBRC (FOX) Birmingham; WCFT-TV (ABC) Tuscaloosa; WDBB (CW) Bessemer; WDVZ-CA Greensboro; WIIQ (PBS) Demopolis; WNCF (ABC) Montgomery; WSFA (NBC) Montgomery; WTOK-TV (ABC, CW, FOX, MNT) Meridian; WVTM-TV (NBC) Birmingham.
Programming (via satellite): ABC Family Channel; AMC; Animal Planet; Arts & Entertainment; BET Networks; Bravo; Cartoon Network; CNBC; CNN; Comcast Sports Net Southeast; Comedy Central; Country Music TV; C-SPAN; C-SPAN 2; Discovery Channel; E! Entertainment Television; ESPN; ESPN 2; FitTV; Food Network; Fox News Channel; FX; Hallmark Channel; Headline News; HGTV; History Channel; Home Shopping Network; INSP; Lifetime; MSNBC; MTV; Nickelodeon; Outdoor Channel; QVC; Speed Channel; Spike TV; SportSouth; Syfy; TBS Superstation; The Learning Channel; Travel Channel; Trinity Broadcasting Network; truTV; Turner Classic Movies; Turner Network TV; TV Land; USA Network; VH1; WE tv; Weather Channel; WGN America.
Fee: $49.95 installation; $17.95 monthly; $2.95 converter.

Digital Basic Service
Subscribers: N.A.
Programming (via satellite): AmericanLife TV Network; BBC America; Bio; Bloomberg Television; Discovery Digital Networks; DMX Music; Fox Movie Channel; Fox Sports World; G4; GSN; History Channel International; Independent Film Channel; INSP; Lifetime Movie Network; MuchMusic Network; Outdoor Channel; Style Network.

Digital Pay Service 1
Pay Units: N.A.
Programming (via satellite): Cinemax (multiplexed); Encore (multiplexed); Flix (multiplexed); HBO (multiplexed); Showtime (multiplexed); Sundance Channel (multiplexed); The Movie Channel (multiplexed).
Video-On-Demand: No

Pay-Per-View
Special events (delivered digitally).

Internet Service
Operational: Yes.
Broadband Service: Mediacom High Speed Internet.
Fee: $45.95 monthly.

Telephone Service
Digital: Planned
Homes passed: 1,525. Total homes in franchised area: 5,020. Miles of plant (coax & fiber) included in Camden
Vice President: David Servies. Operations Director: Gene Wuchner. Technical Operations Manager: Mike Sneary. Sales & Marketing Manager: Joey Nagem.
Ownership: Mediacom LLC (MSO).

GREENVILLE—Bright House Networks, 3996 US Hwy 231, Wetumpka, AL 36093. Phones: 334-567-4344 (Office); 800-822-0060 (Customer service); 205-290-1300. Fax: 334-567-2123. Web Site: http://www.elmore.mybrighthouse.com. Also serves Butler County (portions), Fort Deposit & Georgiana. ICA: AL0058.
TV Market Ranking: Below 100 (Butler County (portions), Fort Deposit); Outside TV Markets (Butler County (portions), Georgiana, GREENVILLE). Franchise award date: January 1, 1965. Franchise expiration date: N.A. Began: February 1, 1965.
Channel capacity: 72 (operating 2-way). Channels available but not in use: N.A.
Basic Service
Subscribers: 3,554.
Programming (received off-air): WAIQ (PBS) Montgomery; WAKA (CBS) Selma; WBMM (CW) Tuskegee; WCOV-TV (FOX) Montgomery; WIYC (IND) Troy; WMCF-TV (TBN) Montgomery; WNCF (ABC) Montgomery; WSFA (NBC) Montgomery.
Programming (via satellite): TBS Superstation; TV Guide Network; WGN America.
Fee: $35.83 installation; $41.05 monthly; $23.00 additional installation.
Digital Basic Service
Subscribers: N.A.
Programming (received off-air): WAIQ (PBS) Montgomery; WBIH (IND) Selma; WNCF (ABC) Montgomery; WSFA (NBC) Montgomery.
Programming (via satellite): AmericanLife TV Network; BBC America; Bio; Bloomberg Television; Boomerang; CNN International; Cooking Channel; Current; Discovery Digital Networks; Discovery HD Theater; Do-It-Yourself; ESPN Classic Sports; ESPNews; Fox Movie Channel; Fox Sports World; G4; GAS; Great American Country; GSN; History Channel International; Lifetime Real Women; MTV Networks Digital Suite; Music Choice; Nick Jr.; NickToons TV; Ovation; SoapNet; Speed Channel; Toon Disney; Turner Network TV.
Fee: $8.00 monthly.
Digital Expanded Basic Service
Subscribers: N.A.
Programming (via satellite): CBS College Sports Network; Fox College Sports Atlantic; Fox College Sports Central; Fox College Sports Pacific; Fuel TV; NBA TV; Outdoor Channel; Tennis Channel; The Movie Channel (multiplexed); The Sportsman Channel.
Fee: $3.95 monthly.
Digital Expanded Basic Service 2
Subscribers: N.A.
Programming (via satellite): Encore (multiplexed); Independent Film Channel; Sundance Channel.
Fee: $4.95 monthly.
Digital Pay Service 1
Pay Units: 1,025.
Programming (via satellite): Cinemax (multiplexed); HBO (multiplexed); HBO HD; Showtime (multiplexed); Showtime HD; Starz (multiplexed).
Fee: $10.50 monthly (each).
Video-On-Demand: No
Pay-Per-View
Hot Choice (delivered digitally); iN DEMAND (delivered digitally); Shorteez (delivered digitally); Pleasure (delivered digitally); Fresh (delivered digitally); NBA TV (delivered digitally); NASCAR In Car (delivered digitally).
Internet Service
Operational: Yes.
Subscribers: 171.
Broadband Service: RoadRunner.
Fee: $29.95 monthly.
Telephone Service
Digital: Operational
Fee: $39.95 monthly
Miles of Plant: 52.0 (coaxial); None (fiber optic). Homes passed: 4,425.
Manager: Bruce Burgess. Marketing Director: Dennis Burns. Technical Operations Manager: Mike Truelove.
Ownership: Bright House Networks LLC (MSO).

GROVE HILL—Galaxy Cablevision, PO Box 879, 118 S Jackson St, Grove Hill, AL 36451-0879. Phone: 251-275-3118. Fax: 251-275-3120. Web Site: http://www.galaxycable.com. Also serves Clarke County (portions) & Whatley. ICA: AL0117.
TV Market Ranking: Outside TV Markets (Clarke County (portions), GROVE HILL, Whatley). Franchise award date: July 18, 1980. Franchise expiration date: N.A. Began: December 10, 1980.
Channel capacity: 116 (2-way capable). Channels available but not in use: None.
Basic Service
Subscribers: 523.
Programming (received off-air): WAKA (CBS) Selma; WALA-TV (FOX) Mobile; WEAR-TV (ABC) Pensacola; WIIQ (PBS) Demopolis; WJTC (IND) Pensacola; WKRG-TV (CBS) Mobile; WPMI-TV (NBC) Mobile; WSFA (NBC) Montgomery; WTOK-TV (ABC, CW, FOX, MNT) Meridian; allband FM.
Programming (via satellite): ABC Family Channel; Arts & Entertainment; BET Networks; Cartoon Network; CNBC; CNN; Comcast Sports Net Southeast; Comedy Central; Discovery Channel; Disney Channel; ESPN; ESPN 2; Fox News Channel; Great American Country; Hallmark Channel; Headline News; HGTV; Lifetime; Outdoor Channel; QVC; Syfy; TBS Superstation; Trinity Broadcasting Network; Turner Network TV; USA Network; Weather Channel; WGN America.
Current originations: Leased Access; Religious Access; Government Access; Educational Access; Public Access.
Fee: $35.00 installation; $44.43 monthly; $10.00 additional installation.
Digital Basic Service
Subscribers: 89.
Programming (via satellite): AmericanLife TV Network; BBC America; Bio; Bloomberg Television; Discovery Digital Networks; DMX Music; Encore; ESPN Classic Sports; ESPNews; FitTV; Fox College Sports Atlantic; Fox College Sports Central; Fox College Sports Pacific; Fox Movie Channel; Fox Sports World; G4; Golf Channel; GSN; History Channel International; INSP; Lifetime Movie Network; National Geographic Channel; Style Network; Toon Disney; Turner Classic Movies; WE tv.
Fee: $13.96 monthly.
Pay Service 1
Pay Units: 372.
Programming (via satellite): HBO; Showtime.
Fee: $10.00 monthly (each).
Digital Pay Service 1
Pay Units: 82.
Programming (via satellite): Cinemax (multiplexed); Flix; HBO (multiplexed); Showtime (multiplexed); The Movie Channel (multiplexed).
Fee: $10.00 monthly (each).
Pay-Per-View
Addressable homes: 19.
ESPN Now (delivered digitally), Addressable: Yes; Hot Choice (delivered digitally); Movies (delivered digitally); Playboy TV (delivered digitally); Fresh (delivered digitally); Shorteez (delivered digitally); Urban Xtra (delivered digitally).
Internet Service
Operational: No.
Subscribers: 216.
Broadband Service: Galaxy Cable Internet.
Fee: $49.95 installation; $44.95 monthly.
Telephone Service
None
Miles of Plant: 42.0 (coaxial); None (fiber optic). Homes passed: 1,147. Total homes in franchised area: 1,331.
State Manager: Bill Flowers. Technical Manager & Engineer: Greg Berthaut. Customer Service Representative: Lisa Ray.
City fee: 2% of gross. County fee: 2% of gross.
Ownership: Galaxy Cable Inc. (MSO).

GUIN—CommuniComm Services, 3164 Highway 431, Ste 9, Roanoke, AL 36274-1702. Phone: 334-863-7080. Fax: 334-863-2027. Web Site: http://www.netcommander.com. Also serves Marion County (portions). ICA: AL0109.
TV Market Ranking: Outside TV Markets (GUIN, Marion County (portions)). Franchise award date: N.A. Franchise expiration date: N.A. Began: October 24, 1966.
Channel capacity: N.A. Channels available but not in use: N.A.
Basic Service
Subscribers: 416.
Programming (received off-air): WBRC (FOX) Birmingham; WCBI-TV (CBS, CW, MNT) Columbus; WCFT-TV (ABC) Tuscaloosa; WFIQ (PBS) Florence; WIAT (CBS) Birmingham; WLOV-TV (FOX) West Point; WTTO (CW) Homewood; WTVA (NBC) Tupelo; WVTM-TV (NBC) Birmingham; allband FM.
Programming (via satellite): Superstation WGN.
Fee: $25.00 installation; $11.95 monthly; $10.00 additional installation.
Expanded Basic Service 1
Subscribers: N.A.
Programming (via satellite): ABC Family Channel; American Movie Classics; Animal Planet; Arts & Entertainment; BET Networks; Bravo; Cartoon Network; CNBC; CNN; Comcast/Charter Sports Southeast (CSS); Comedy Central; Country Music TV; C-SPAN; C-SPAN 2; Discovery Channel; Disney Channel; E! Entertainment Television; ESPN; ESPN 2; ESPN Classic Sports; ESPNews; Food Network; Fox News Channel; FX; Headline News; HGTV; History Channel; Home Shopping Network; Lifetime; MSNBC; MTV; Nick Jr.; Nickelodeon; Outdoor Channel; QVC; RFD-TV; ShopNBC; Speed Channel; Spike TV; Syfy; TBS Superstation; The Learning Channel; Travel Channel; Trinity Broadcasting Network; truTV; Turner Classic Movies; Turner Network TV; TV Land; USA Network; VH1; WE tv; Weather Channel.
Digital Basic Service
Subscribers: 42.
Programming (via satellite): AmericanLife TV Network; BBC America; Bio; Blackbelt TV; Bloomberg Television; Church Channel; CMT Pure Country; Current; Discovery Health Channel; Discovery Kids Channel; Discovery Military Channel; Discovery Planet Green; DMX Music; FitTV; Fox Movie Channel; Fox Soccer; Fuse; G4; Golf Channel; Gospel Music Channel; Great American Country; GSN; Halogen Network; Healthy Living Channel; History Channel International; ID Investigation Discovery; JCTV; Lifetime Movie Network; MTV Hits; MTV Jams; National Geographic Channel; Ovation; Science Channel; Sleuth; SoapNet; TeenNick; The Word Network; Toon Disney; Versus; VH1 Classic; VH1 Soul.
Digital Pay Service 1
Pay Units: 77.
Programming (via satellite): Cinemax (multiplexed); Encore (multiplexed); Flix; HBO (multiplexed); Showtime (multiplexed); Starz (multiplexed); The Movie Channel.
Video-On-Demand: No
Pay-Per-View
iN DEMAND (delivered digitally); Hot Choice (delivered digitally); Playboy TV (delivered digitally); Fresh (delivered digitally); Spice: Xcess (delivered digitally).
Internet Service
Operational: Yes.
Subscribers: 79.
Broadband Service: Net Commander.
Fee: $39.95 installation; $51.95 monthly.
Telephone Service
None
Miles of Plant: 48.0 (coaxial); None (fiber optic). Homes passed: 1,394.
General Manager: Brian Chase. Chief Technician: William Boyd.
City fee: $25 per subscriber annually.
Ownership: James Cable LLC (MSO).

GUNTERSVILLE—Charter Communications, 2100 Columbiana Rd, Vestavia, AL 35216. Phone: 205-824-5500. Fax: 205-824-5490. Web Site: http://www.charter.com. Also serves Grant, Hollywood, Horton, Jackson County (unincorporated portions), Marshall County (northwestern portion), Marshall County (portions), Morgan City (portions), Morgan County (eastern portion), Oleander, Rescue, Scottsboro & Union Hill. ICA: AL0033.
TV Market Ranking: 78 (Jackson County (unincorporated portions) (portions)); 96 (Grant, GUNTERSVILLE, Hollywood, Horton, Marshall County (northwestern portion), Marshall County (portions), Morgan City (portions), Morgan County (eastern portion), Oleander, Rescue, Scottsboro, Union Hill); Below 100 (Morgan City (portions)); Outside TV Markets (Jackson County (unincorporated portions) (portions)). Franchise award date: N.A. Franchise expiration date: N.A. Began: December 1, 1966.
Channel capacity: N.A. Channels available but not in use: N.A.
Basic Service
Subscribers: 6,612.
Programming (received off-air): WAAY-TV (ABC) Huntsville; WAFF (NBC) Huntsville; WHDF (CW) Florence; WHIQ (PBS) Huntsville; WHNT-TV (CBS) Huntsville; WIAT (CBS) Birmingham; WTJP-TV (TBN) Gadsden; WVTM-TV (NBC) Birmingham; WZDX (FOX, MNT) Huntsville.
Programming (via satellite): C-SPAN; WGN America.
Current originations: Leased Access.
Fee: $29.99 installation.

Expanded Basic Service 1
Subscribers: 6,210.
Programming (via satellite): ABC Family Channel; AMC; Animal Planet; Arts & Entertainment; BET Networks; Cartoon Network; CNBC; CNN; Comcast Sports Net Southeast; Comcast/Charter Sports Southeast (CSS); Comedy Central; Country Music TV; C-SPAN 2; Discovery Channel; Disney Channel; E! Entertainment Television; ESPN; ESPN 2; Food Network; Fox News Channel; FX; G4; Hallmark Channel; Headline News; HGTV; History Channel; Home Shopping Network; ION Television; Lifetime; MSNBC; MTV; National Geographic Channel; Nickelodeon; Oxygen; Product Information Network; QVC; Shop at Home; Speed Channel; Spike TV; SportSouth; Syfy; TBS Superstation; Telemundo; The Learning Channel; Travel Channel; truTV; Turner Classic Movies; Turner Network TV; TV Guide Network; TV Land; Univision; USA Network; VH1; WE tv; Weather Channel.
Fee: $43.00 monthly.

Digital Basic Service
Subscribers: N.A.
Programming (via satellite): BBC America; Bio; Discovery Digital Networks; Do-It-Yourself; GalaVision; Great American Country; History Channel International; Independent Film Channel; Lifetime Movie Network; Music Choice; Sundance Channel; Versus.
Fee: $16.99 monthly.

Digital Pay Service 1
Pay Units: 699.
Programming (via satellite): Cinemax (multiplexed).
Fee: $11.95 monthly.

Digital Pay Service 2
Pay Units: 893.
Programming (via satellite): HBO (multiplexed).
Fee: $11.95 monthly.

Digital Pay Service 3
Pay Units: 790.
Programming (via satellite): Flix; Showtime (multiplexed).
Fee: $11.95 monthly.

Digital Pay Service 4
Pay Units: 673.
Programming (via satellite): The Movie Channel (multiplexed).
Fee: $11.95 monthly.

Digital Pay Service 5
Pay Units: N.A.
Programming (via satellite): Encore (multiplexed); Starz (multiplexed).
Fee: $11.95 monthly.

Video-On-Demand: Yes

Pay-Per-View
Addressable homes: 821.
iN DEMAND (delivered digitally); Playboy TV (delivered digitally); Pleasure (delivered digitally); Fresh (delivered digitally); Shorteez (delivered digitally).

Internet Service
Operational: Yes.
Broadband Service: Charter Pipeline.
Fee: $29.99 monthly.

Telephone Service
Digital: Operational

Miles of Plant: 432.0 (coaxial); 651.0 (fiber optic). Homes passed: 10,785. Total homes in franchised area: 13,525.

Vice President & General Manager: Don Karell. Technical Operations Director: Greg Prim. Marketing Director: David Redmond. Marketing Manager: Jeff Hatcher.

Ownership: Charter Communications Inc. (MSO).

GURLEY—Charter Communications, 2100 Columbiana Rd, Vestavia, AL 35216. Phones: 888-438-2427; 205-884-5555. Fax: 205-824-5490. Web Site: http://www.charter.com. Also serves Jackson County & Paint Rock. ICA: AL0130.

TV Market Ranking: 96 (GURLEY, Jackson County (portions), Paint Rock); Outside TV Markets (Jackson County (portions)). Franchise award date: March 15, 1983. Franchise expiration date: N.A. Began: June 1, 1984.

Channel capacity: N.A. Channels available but not in use: N.A.

Basic Service
Subscribers: 387.
Programming (received off-air): WAAY-TV (ABC) Huntsville; WAFF (NBC) Huntsville; WHIQ (PBS) Huntsville; WHNT-TV (CBS) Huntsville; WZDX (FOX, MNT) Huntsville.
Programming (via satellite): AMC; Arts & Entertainment; C-SPAN; Discovery Channel; E! Entertainment Television; ESPN; ESPN 2; Home Shopping Network; QVC; Syfy; The Learning Channel; Trinity Broadcasting Network; Turner Network TV.
Fee: $29.99 installation.

Expanded Basic Service 1
Subscribers: 380.
Programming (via satellite): ABC Family Channel; Animal Planet; CNN; Country Music TV; Disney Channel; Headline News; Nickelodeon; Spike TV; SportSouth; TBS Superstation; Travel Channel; TV Land; USA Network; Weather Channel; WGN America.
Fee: $43.00 monthly.

Digital Basic Service
Subscribers: N.A.
Programming (via satellite): AmericanLife TV Network; BBC America; Bio; Bloomberg Television; Bravo; Discovery Digital Networks; ESPN Classic Sports; Fox Movie Channel; G4; GAS; Golf Channel; GSN; Halogen Network; HGTV; History Channel; History Channel International; Independent Film Channel; Lifetime Movie Network; MTV Networks Digital Suite; MuchMusic Network; Music Choice; Nick Jr.; Outdoor Channel; ShopNBC; Speed Channel; Style Network; Toon Disney; Turner Classic Movies; TV Guide Interactive Inc.; Versus; WE tv.
Fee: $16.99 monthly.

Pay Service 1
Pay Units: 18.
Programming (via satellite): Showtime.
Fee: $9.95 monthly.

Digital Pay Service 1
Pay Units: 73.
Programming (via satellite): Cinemax (multiplexed); Encore (multiplexed); Flix; HBO (multiplexed); Showtime (multiplexed); Starz (multiplexed); The Movie Channel (multiplexed).

Video-On-Demand: No

Pay-Per-View
ESPN Extra (delivered digitally); ESPN Now (delivered digitally); iN DEMAND (delivered digitally); Playboy TV (delivered digitally); Fresh (delivered digitally); Shorteez (delivered digitally).

Internet Service
Operational: Yes.
Broadband Service: Charter Pipeline.
Fee: $29.99 monthly.

Telephone Service
Digital: Operational

Miles of Plant: 19.0 (coaxial); None (fiber optic). Homes passed: 555.

Vice President & General Manager: Don Karell. Technical Operations Director: Greg Prim. Marketing Director: David Redmond. Marketing Manager: Jeff Hatcher.

Franchise fee: 3% of gross.

Ownership: Charter Communications Inc. (MSO).

HACKLEBURG—CommuniComm Services, 3164 Hwy 431, Ste 9, Roanoke, AL 36274-1702. Phone: 334-863-7080. Fax: 334-863-2027. Web Site: http://www.netcommander.com. ICA: AL0137.

TV Market Ranking: Outside TV Markets (HACKLEBURG). Franchise award date: N.A. Franchise expiration date: N.A. Began: August 1, 1984.

Channel capacity: N.A. Channels available but not in use: N.A.

Basic Service
Subscribers: 130.
Programming (received off-air): WAAY-TV (ABC) Huntsville; WBRC (FOX) Birmingham; WFIQ (PBS) Florence; WHDF (CW) Florence; WHNT-TV (CBS) Huntsville; WIAT (CBS) Birmingham; WTTO (CW) Homewood; WTVA (NBC) Tupelo; WVTM-TV (NBC) Birmingham.
Programming (via satellite): TBS Superstation; WCFT-TV (ABC) Tuscaloosa; WGN America.
Fee: $10.00 installation; $9.00 monthly.

Expanded Basic Service 1
Subscribers: N.A.
Programming (via satellite): ABC Family Channel; AMC; Animal Planet; Arts & Entertainment; Cartoon Network; CNN; Comcast/Charter Sports Southeast (CSS); Country Music TV; C-SPAN; Discovery Channel; ESPN; ESPN 2; Gospel Music Channel; Headline News; HGTV; History Channel; Lifetime; Nick Jr.; Nickelodeon; QVC; Spike TV; Syfy; The Learning Channel; Trinity Broadcasting Network; Turner Classic Movies; Turner Network TV; TV Land; USA Network; VH1; Weather Channel.

Digital Basic Service
Subscribers: N.A.
Programming (via satellite): AmericanLife TV Network; BBC America; Bio; Bloomberg Television; Bravo; CMT Pure Country; Current; Discovery Health Channel; Discovery Kids Channel; Discovery Military Channel; Discovery Planet Green; DMX Music; Encore (multiplexed); ESPN Classic Sports; ESPNews; FitTV; Fox Movie Channel; Fox Soccer; Fuse; G4; Golf Channel; GSN; Halogen Network; History Channel International; ID Investigation Discovery; Independent Film Channel; Lifetime Movie Network; MTV Hits; MTV2; Nick Jr.; Outdoor Channel; Ovation; Science Channel; Sleuth; Speed Channel; Style Network; TeenNick; Turner Classic Movies; Versus; VH1 Classic; VH1 Soul; WE tv.

Pay Service 1
Pay Units: 11.
Programming (via satellite): Cinemax; HBO.
Fee: $10.00 installation; $10.00 monthly.

Digital Pay Service 1
Pay Units: N.A.
Programming (via satellite): Cinemax (multiplexed); HBO (multiplexed); Starz (multiplexed).

Video-On-Demand: No

Internet Service
Operational: Yes.

Telephone Service
None

Miles of Plant: 16.0 (coaxial); None (fiber optic). Homes passed: 608.

General Manager: Brian Chase. Chief Technician: William Boyd.

Ownership: James Cable LLC (MSO).

HALEYVILLE—Charter Communications, 2100 Columbiana Rd, Vestavia, AL 35216. Phone: 205-824-5400. Fax: 205-824-5490. Web Site: http://www.charter.com. Also serves Bear Creek, Marion County (portions) & Winston County (portions). ICA: AL0047.

TV Market Ranking: Outside TV Markets (Bear Creek, HALEYVILLE, Marion County (portions), Winston County (portions)). Franchise award date: N.A. Franchise expiration date: N.A. Began: April 1, 1969.

Channel capacity: N.A. Channels available but not in use: N.A.

Basic Service
Subscribers: 2,379. Commercial subscribers: 4.
Programming (received off-air): WBIQ (PBS) Birmingham; WBRC (FOX) Birmingham; WCFT-TV (ABC) Tuscaloosa; WHNT-TV (CBS) Huntsville; WIAT (CBS) Birmingham; WPXH-TV (ION) Gadsden; WTTO (CW) Homewood; WVTM-TV (NBC) Birmingham.
Programming (via satellite): C-SPAN; Trinity Broadcasting Network; Weather Channel; WGN America.
Current originations: Leased Access.
Fee: $29.99 installation.

Expanded Basic Service 1
Subscribers: N.A.
Programming (via satellite): ABC Family Channel; AMC; Animal Planet; Arts & Entertainment; Bravo!; Cartoon Network; CNBC; CNN; Comcast Sports Net Southeast; Comedy Central; Country Music TV; Discovery Channel; Disney Channel; E! Entertainment Television; ESPN; ESPN 2; Fox News Channel; FX; G4; Headline News; HGTV; History Channel; Home Shopping Network; Lifetime; MTV; Nickelodeon; Oxygen; SoapNet; Speed Channel; Spike TV; SportSouth; Syfy; TBS Superstation; The Learning Channel; Travel Channel; Turner Network TV; TV Land; USA Network; VH1.
Fee: $43.00 monthly.

Digital Basic Service
Subscribers: N.A.
Programming (via satellite): BBC America; Bio; Bloomberg Television; Discovery Digital Networks; ESPN Classic Sports; ESPNews; FitTV; Fox Movie Channel; Fox Soccer; Fuse; GAS; GSN; History Channel International; Independent Film Channel; Lifetime Movie Network; MTV Networks Digital Suite; Music Choice; Nick Jr.; Nick Too; NickToons TV; Science Television; Style Network; Sundance Channel; Toon Disney; WE tv.
Fee: $16.99 monthly.

Pay Service 1
Pay Units: N.A.
Programming (via satellite): Flix; Showtime (multiplexed).
Digital Pay Service 1
Pay Units: 670.
Programming (via satellite): Cinemax (multiplexed); Encore (multiplexed); HBO (multiplexed); Starz (multiplexed); The Movie Channel (multiplexed).
Fee: $9.95 monthly (each).
Video-On-Demand: No
Pay-Per-View
ESPN Extra (delivered digitally); ESPN Now (delivered digitally); iN DEMAND (delivered digitally); Playboy TV (delivered digitally); Fresh (delivered digitally).
Internet Service
Operational: Yes.
Broadband Service: Charter Pipeline.
Fee: $29.99 monthly.
Telephone Service
Digital: Operational
Miles of Plant: 84.0 (coaxial); None (fiber optic). Homes passed: 4,305.
Vice President & General Manager: Don Karell. Technical Operations Director: Greg Prim. Marketing Director: David Redmond. Marketing Manager: Jeff Hatcher.
City fee: 1% of gross.
Ownership: Charter Communications Inc. (MSO).

HAMILTON—West Alabama TV Cable Co. Inc., PO Box 930, 213 2nd Ave NE, Fayette, AL 35555-0930. Phones: 205-921-3800; 205-932-4700 (Fayette office). Fax: 205-932-3585. E-mail: cable@watvc.com. Web Site: http://www.watvc.com. ICA: AL0073.
TV Market Ranking: Outside TV Markets (HAMILTON). Franchise award date: N.A. Franchise expiration date: N.A. Began: June 1, 1965.
Channel capacity: 60 (2-way capable). Channels available but not in use: 4.
Basic Service
Subscribers: 2,233.
Programming (received off-air): WABM (MNT) Birmingham; WBIQ (PBS) Birmingham; WBRC (FOX) Birmingham; WCFT-TV (ABC) Tuscaloosa; WIAT (CBS) Birmingham; WTTO (CW) Homewood; WTVA (NBC) Tupelo; WVTM-TV (NBC) Birmingham; allband FM.
Programming (via satellite): ABC Family Channel; AMC; Arts & Entertainment; BET Networks; Cartoon Network; CNBC; CNN; Country Music TV; C-SPAN; Discovery Channel; Disney Channel; E! Entertainment Television; ESPN; ESPN 2; Food Network; Fox News Channel; FX; Golf Channel; Gospel Music TV; Hallmark Channel; Headline News; HGTV; History Channel; Home Shopping Network; Lifetime; MTV; Nickelodeon; QVC; SportSouth; TBS Superstation; The Learning Channel; Travel Channel; Trinity Broadcasting Network; Turner Classic Movies; Turner Network TV; TV Guide Network; TV Land; USA Network; VH1; Weather Channel; WGN America.
Current originations: Leased Access.
Fee: $35.00 installation; $37.25 monthly.
Digital Basic Service
Subscribers: N.A.
Programming (via satellite): BBC America; Bio; Bloomberg Television; Discovery Health Channel; Discovery Kids Channel; Discovery Military Channel; Discovery Planet Green; DMX Music; ESPN Classic Sports; ESPNews; Fox Movie Channel; Fox Soccer; G4; History Channel International; ID Investigation Discovery; Independent Film Channel; INSP; Lifetime Movie Network; Lime; National Geographic Channel; Outdoor Channel; Science Channel; Sleuth; Speed Channel; Toon Disney; Versus; WE tv.
Fee: $14.00 monthly.
Pay Service 1
Pay Units: 540.
Programming (via satellite): Cinemax; HBO.
Fee: $15.00 installation; $10.95 monthly (Cinemax), $11.95 monthly (HBO).
Digital Pay Service 1
Pay Units: N.A.
Programming (via satellite): Cinemax (multiplexed); Encore (multiplexed); HBO (multiplexed); Showtime (multiplexed); Starz (multiplexed); The Movie Channel (multiplexed).
Fee: $10.95 monthly (Cinemax or Starz/Encore/TMC), $12.95 monthly (HBO or Showtime).
Video-On-Demand: No
Pay-Per-View
iN DEMAND (delivered digitally); Hot Choice (delivered digitally); Spice (delivered digitally); ESPN Now (delivered digitally); Sports PPV (delivered digitally).
Internet Service
Operational: Yes.
Broadband Service: In-house.
Fee: $24.95 monthly.
Telephone Service
None
Miles of Plant: 150.0 (coaxial); None (fiber optic). Homes passed: 8,000. Total homes in franchised area: 10,000.
Manager: Kyle South.
City fee: $100.50 flat fee.
Ownership: West Alabama TV Cable Co. Inc. (MSO).

HARTSELLE—Charter Communications. Now served by Decatur, AL [AL0184]. ICA: AL0020.

HAYNEVILLE—Alabama Broadband LLC, 3447A Parkwood Rd SE, Bessemer, AL 35022. Phones: 877-840-5040; 205-426-3432. E-mail: contact@alabamabroadband.com. Web Site: http://www.alabamabroadband.net. ICA: AL0143.
TV Market Ranking: Below 100 (HAYNEVILLE). Franchise award date: N.A. Franchise expiration date: N.A. Began: January 1, 1989.
Channel capacity: 40 (not 2-way capable). Channels available but not in use: 14.
Basic Service
Subscribers: 220.
Programming (received off-air): WAIQ (PBS) Montgomery; WAKA (CBS) Selma; WCOV-TV (FOX) Montgomery; WIYC (IND) Troy; WMCF-TV (TBN) Montgomery; WNCF (ABC) Montgomery; WSFA (NBC) Montgomery.
Programming (via satellite): ABC Family Channel; Arts & Entertainment; BET Networks; CNBC; CNN; Comcast Sports Net Southeast; Discovery Channel; Disney Channel; ESPN; Fox News Channel; Headline News; Spike TV; Syfy; TBS Superstation; Turner Network TV; USA Network; WGN America.
Fee: $29.95 installation; $35.15 monthly.
Pay Service 1
Pay Units: 63.
Programming (via satellite): Cinemax.
Fee: $10.00 monthly.
Pay Service 2
Pay Units: 56.
Programming (via satellite): HBO.
Fee: $11.00 monthly.
Video-On-Demand: No
Internet Service
Operational: No.
Telephone Service
None
Miles of Plant: 13.0 (coaxial); None (fiber optic). Homes passed: 300.
President: Tom Early.
Ownership: Alabama Broadband LLC (MSO).

HEATH—Clearview Cable, PO Box 7, 28795 Commerce St, Gantt, AL 36038-0001. Phone: 334-388-2716. Fax: 334-388-2718. E-mail: jmike@oppcatv.com. Also serves Antioch, Babbie, Dozier, Gantt, Harmony, Red Level, River Falls, Sanford & Straughn. ICA: AL0078.
TV Market Ranking: Below 100 (Dozier); Outside TV Markets (Antioch, Babbie, Gantt, Harmony, HEATH, Red Level, River Falls, Sanford, Straughn). Franchise award date: June 1, 1986. Franchise expiration date: N.A. Began: October 1, 1987.
Channel capacity: N.A. Channels available but not in use: N.A.
Basic Service
Subscribers: 2,056 Includes Beatrice, Castleberry, Chancellor & McKenzie.
Programming (received off-air): WAKA (CBS) Selma; WCOV-TV (FOX) Montgomery; WDIQ (PBS) Dozier; WIYC (IND) Troy; WNCF (ABC) Montgomery; WSFA (NBC) Montgomery.
Programming (via satellite): ABC Family Channel; AMC; Animal Planet; Arts & Entertainment; BET Networks; Cartoon Network; CNN; Country Music TV; Discovery Channel; Disney Channel; E! Entertainment Television; ESPN; ESPN 2; Fox News Channel; HGTV; Lifetime; National Geographic Channel; Nickelodeon; QVC; Spike TV; Syfy; TBS Superstation; The Learning Channel; Trinity Broadcasting Network; Turner Network TV; USA Network; Versus; Weather Channel; WGN America.
Fee: $29.95 installation; $29.45 monthly.
Pay Service 1
Pay Units: 235 Includes Beatrice, Castleberry, Chancellor, & McKenzie.
Programming (via satellite): Cinemax; HBO.
Fee: $10.00 installation; $10.95 monthly (each).
Video-On-Demand: No
Internet Service
Operational: Yes.
Broadband Service: In-house.
Fee: $45.00 installation; $19.00 monthly.
Telephone Service
None
Miles of Plant: 119.0 (coaxial); 52.0 (fiber optic). Homes passed: 3,000. Total homes in franchised area: 3,000.
Manager: J Mike Russel.
City fee: 3% of basic gross.
Ownership: Clearview Cable Inc. (MSO).

HEFLIN—Charter Communications, 2100 Columbiana Rd, Vestavia, AL 35216. Phone: 205-824-5400. Fax: 205-824-5490. Web Site: http://www.charter.com. Also serves Cleburne County (western portion), Edwardsville, Fruithurst & Muscadine. ICA: AL0087.
TV Market Ranking: Below 100 (Cleburne County (western portion), Edwardsville, Fruithurst, HEFLIN, Muscadine). Franchise award date: N.A. Franchise expiration date: N.A. Began: May 1, 1984.
Channel capacity: N.A. Channels available but not in use: N.A.
Basic Service
Subscribers: 1,241.
Programming (received off-air): WBRC (FOX) Birmingham; WCIQ (PBS) Mount Cheaha State Park; WGCL-TV (CBS) Atlanta; WJSU-TV (ABC) Anniston; WTJP-TV (TBN) Gadsden; WTTO (CW) Homewood; WVTM-TV (NBC) Birmingham; WXIA-TV (NBC) Atlanta.
Programming (via satellite): Home Shopping Network; ION Television; WGN America.
Fee: $40.00 installation; $11.45 monthly.
Expanded Basic Service 1
Subscribers: 1,005.
Programming (via satellite): ABC Family Channel; AMC; Animal Planet; Arts & Entertainment; Cartoon Network; CNBC; CNN; Comcast Sports Net Southeast; Comcast/Charter Sports Southeast (CSS); Comedy Central; Country Music TV; C-SPAN; C-SPAN 2; Discovery Channel; Disney Channel; E! Entertainment Television; ESPN; ESPN 2; Food Network; Fox News Channel; FX; Headline News; HGTV; History Channel; Lifetime; MSNBC; MTV; National Geographic Channel; Nickelodeon; SoapNet; Spike TV; SportSouth; Syfy; TBS Superstation; The Learning Channel; Toon Disney; Travel Channel; Turner Network TV; TV Guide Network; TV Land; USA Network; VH1; Weather Channel.
Fee: $22.95 monthly.
Digital Basic Service
Subscribers: N.A.
Programming (via satellite): AmericanLife TV Network; BBC America; Bio; Bloomberg Television; Bravo; Discovery Digital Networks; ESPN Classic Sports; Fox Movie Channel; G4; GAS; Golf Channel; GSN; Halogen Network; History Channel International; Independent Film Channel; Lifetime Movie Network; MTV Networks Digital Suite; MuchMusic Network; Music Choice; Nick Jr.; Outdoor Channel; ShopNBC; Speed Channel; Style Network; Turner Classic Movies; TV Guide Interactive Inc.; Versus; WE tv.
Digital Pay Service 1
Pay Units: 159.
Programming (via satellite): HBO (multiplexed).
Fee: $11.95 monthly.
Digital Pay Service 2
Pay Units: 221.
Programming (via satellite): Flix; Showtime (multiplexed).
Fee: $11.95 monthly.
Digital Pay Service 3
Pay Units: N.A.
Programming (via satellite): Cinemax (multiplexed); Encore (multiplexed); Starz (multiplexed); The Movie Channel (multiplexed).
Video-On-Demand: No
Pay-Per-View
Addressable homes: 87.
ESPN Extra (delivered digitally); ESPN Now (delivered digitally); Hot Choice (delivered digitally); iN DEMAND (delivered digitally); Playboy TV; Playboy TV (delivered digitally); Spice (delivered digitally); Spice 2 (delivered digitally).
Internet Service
Operational: Yes.
Broadband Service: Charter Pipeline.
Fee: $29.99 monthly.
Telephone Service
Digital: Operational
Miles of Plant: 214.0 (coaxial); 16.0 (fiber optic). Homes passed: 1,831. Total homes in franchised area: 4,598.

Vice President & General Manager: Don Karell. Technical Operations Director: Greg Prim. Marketing Director: David Redmond. Marketing Manager: Jeff Hatcher.
Ownership: Charter Communications Inc. (MSO).

HENAGAR—Charter Communications, 2100 Columbiana Rd, Vestavia, AL 35216. Phone: 205-824-5400. Fax: 205-824-5490. Web Site: http://www.charter.com. Also serves De Kalb County (portions), Hammondville, Higdon, Ider, Jackson County (portions), Pisgah & Sylvania. ICA: AL0045.
TV Market Ranking: 78 (DeKalb County (portions), Hammondville, Higdon, Ider); 78,96 (Jackson County (portions)); Below 100 (DeKalb County (portions)); Outside TV Markets (HENAGAR, Pisgah, Sylvania, DeKalb County (portions), Jackson County (portions)). Franchise award date: N.A. Franchise expiration date: N.A. Began: N.A.
Channel capacity: 37 (not 2-way capable). Channels available but not in use: 3.
Basic Service
Subscribers: 1,457.
Programming (received off-air): WAAY-TV (ABC) Huntsville; WAFF (NBC) Huntsville; WDEF-TV (CBS) Chattanooga; WHIQ (PBS) Huntsville; WHNT-TV (CBS) Huntsville; WRCB (NBC) Chattanooga; WTVC (ABC) Chattanooga; WZDX (FOX, MNT) Huntsville.
Programming (via satellite): Home Shopping Network; INSP; ION Television.
Fee: $29.99 installation.
Expanded Basic Service 1
Subscribers: N.A.
Programming (via satellite): ABC Family Channel; AMC; Animal Planet; Arts & Entertainment; Bravo; Cartoon Network; CNBC; CNN; Comcast Sports Net Southeast; Comedy Central; Country Music TV; C-SPAN; Discovery Channel; Disney Channel; E! Entertainment Television; ESPN; ESPN 2; Food Network; Fox News Channel; FX; G4; GalaVision; Golf Channel; Hallmark Channel; Headline News; HGTV; History Channel; Lifetime; MSNBC; MTV; Nickelodeon; Oxygen; SoapNet; Speed Channel; Spike TV; SportSouth; Syfy; TBS Superstation; Telemundo; The Learning Channel; Toon Disney; Travel Channel; truTV; Turner Classic Movies; Turner Network TV; TV Land; Univision; USA Network; VH1; WE tv; Weather Channel.
Fee: $43.00 monthly.
Digital Basic Service
Subscribers: N.A.
Programming (via satellite): BBC America; Bio; Discovery Digital Networks; Fox Movie Channel; Fox Soccer; Fuse; GAS; GSN; History Channel International; Independent Film Channel; Lifetime Movie Network; MTV Networks Digital Suite; Music Choice; Nick Jr.; Nick Too; NickToons TV; Style Network.
Fee: $16.99 monthly.
Digital Pay Service 1
Pay Units: N.A.
Programming (via satellite): Cinemax (multiplexed); Encore; Flix; HBO (multiplexed); Showtime; Starz; The Movie Channel.
Fee: $11.95 monthly (each).
Video-On-Demand: No
Pay-Per-View
Addressable homes: 989.
ESPN Extra (delivered digitally); ESPN Now (delivered digitally); iN DEMAND (delivered digitally); Playboy TV (delivered digitally); Fresh (delivered digitally); Shorteez (delivered digitally).
Internet Service
Operational: No.
Telephone Service
None
Miles of Plant: 232.0 (coaxial); None (fiber optic). Homes passed: 4,420. Total homes in franchised area: 15,507.
Vice President & General Manager: Don Karell. Technical Operations Director: Greg Prim. Marketing Director: David Redmond. Marketing Manager: Jeff Hatcher.
City fee: 3% of basic.
Ownership: Charter Communications Inc. (MSO).

HILLSBORO—Formerly served by Shoals Cable TV Inc. No longer in operation. ICA: AL0140.

HOLLIS CROSSROADS—Communi-Comm Services, 3164 Hwy 431, Ste 9, Roanoke, AL 36274-1702. Phone: 334-863-7080. Fax: 334-863-2027. Web Site: http://www.netcommander.com. ICA: AL0199.
TV Market Ranking: Below 100 (HOLLIS CROSSROADS). Franchise award date: N.A. Franchise expiration date: N.A. Began: April 1, 1990.
Channel capacity: N.A. Channels available but not in use: N.A.
Basic Service
Subscribers: 62.
Programming (received off-air): WAAY-TV (ABC) Huntsville; WBRC (FOX) Birmingham; WCFT-TV (ABC) Tuscaloosa; WCIQ (PBS) Mount Cheaha State Park; WIAT (CBS) Birmingham; WPXA-TV (ION) Rome; WPXH-TV (ION) Gadsden; WTJP-TV (TBN) Gadsden; WTTO (CW) Homewood; WVTM-TV (NBC) Birmingham.
Programming (via satellite): ABC Family Channel; Arts & Entertainment; CNN; Country Music TV; C-SPAN; Discovery Channel; Disney Channel; ESPN; ESPN 2; Headline News; History Channel; Lifetime; Nickelodeon; Spike TV; TBS Superstation; The Learning Channel; Turner Network TV; TV Land; USA Network; Weather Channel; WGN America.
Fee: $39.95 monthly.
Pay Service 1
Pay Units: 15.
Programming (via satellite): Cinemax; HBO.
Fee: $10.00 monthly (each).
Video-On-Demand: No
Internet Service
Operational: No.
Telephone Service
None
Miles of Plant: 18.0 (coaxial); None (fiber optic). Homes passed: 271.
General Manager: Brian Chase. Chief Technician: William Boyd.
Ownership: James Cable LLC (MSO).

HOOVER—Charter Communications. Now served by LEEDS, AL [AL0192]. ICA: AL0007.

HUNTSVILLE—Comcast Cable, 2047 Max Luther Dr NW, Huntsville, AL 35810-3801. Phone: 256-859-7828. Fax: 256-852-5599. Web Site: http://www.comcast.com. ICA: AL0004.
TV Market Ranking: 96 (HUNTSVILLE). Franchise award date: N.A. Franchise expiration date: N.A. Began: June 1, 1954.
Channel capacity: 72 (operating 2-way). Channels available but not in use: N.A.
Basic Service
Subscribers: 36,196.
Programming (received off-air): MyNetworkTV Inc.; WAAY-TV (ABC) Huntsville; WAFF (NBC) Huntsville; WHDF (CW) Florence; WHIQ (PBS) Huntsville; WHNT-TV (CBS) Huntsville; WZDX (FOX, MNT) Huntsville; allband FM.
Programming (via satellite): C-SPAN; C-SPAN 2; Disney Channel; Home Shopping Network; QVC; WGN America.
Current originations: Government Access; Educational Access.
Fee: $49.95 installation; $12.95 monthly.
Expanded Basic Service 1
Subscribers: N.A.
Programming (via satellite): ABC Family Channel; AMC; Animal Planet; Arts & Entertainment; BET Networks; Bravo; Cartoon Network; CBS College Sports Network; CNBC; CNN; Comcast Sports Net Southeast; Comcast/Charter Sports Southeast (CSS); Comedy Central; Country Music TV; Discovery Channel; Discovery Health Channel; E! Entertainment Television; ESPN; ESPN 2; Eternal Word TV Network; Food Network; Fox News Channel; FX; G4; GAS; Golf Channel; GSN; Hallmark Channel; Headline News; HGTV; History Channel; INSP; ION Television; Lifetime; MTV; NASA TV; Nick Jr.; Nickelodeon; Speed Channel; Spike TV; SportSouth; Style Network; Syfy; TBS Superstation; The Learning Channel; Travel Channel; Trinity Broadcasting Network; truTV; Turner Classic Movies; Turner Network TV; TV Guide Network; TV Land; USA Network; Versus; VH1; Weather Channel; WeatherVision.
Fee: $30.00 monthly.
Digital Basic Service
Subscribers: 6,512.
Programming (via satellite): BBC America; Bio; CMT Pure Country; Cooking Channel; C-SPAN 3; Current; Discovery Digital Networks; Do-It-Yourself; Encore; ESPNews; Fox Reality Channel; Great American Country; History Channel International; Lifetime Movie Network; Military History Channel; MTV Networks Digital Suite; National Geographic Channel; Nick Too; NickToons TV; PBS Kids Sprout; SoapNet; Toon Disney; Weatherscan.
Fee: $14.95 monthly.
Pay Service 1
Pay Units: 10,857.
Programming (via satellite): Cinemax; HBO; Showtime.
Fee: $10.95 monthly (each).
Digital Pay Service 1
Pay Units: N.A.
Programming (via satellite): Cinemax (multiplexed); Flix; HBO (multiplexed); Showtime (multiplexed); Starz (multiplexed); The Movie Channel.
Fee: $13.70 monthly (each).
Video-On-Demand: Yes
Pay-Per-View
ESPN Extra (delivered digitally); ESPN Now (delivered digitally); Hot Choice (delivered digitally); iN DEMAND (delivered digitally); Playboy TV (delivered digitally); Spice (delivered digitally); Spice2 (delivered digitally); Sports PPV (delivered digitally).
Internet Service
Operational: Yes.
Subscribers: 2,145.
Broadband Service: Comcast High Speed Internet.
Fee: $42.95 monthly; $7.00 modem lease.
Telephone Service
Digital: Operational
Miles of Plant: 741.0 (coaxial); None (fiber optic). Homes passed: 65,000.
Vice President & General Manager: Ellen Rosson. Technical Operations Director: Butch Jernigan. Government Affairs Manager: Patricia Collins.
City fee: 3% of gross.
Ownership: Comcast Cable Communications Inc. (MSO).

HUNTSVILLE—Knology, 2401 10th St SW, Huntsville, AL 35805-4057. Phones: 706-645-8553 (Corporate office); 256-533-5359; 256-533-5353 (Customer service). Fax: 256-533-2353. Web Site: http://www.knology.com. Also serves Limestone County (eastern portion), Madison, Madison County (portions) & Redstone Arsenal. ICA: AL0006.
Note: This system is an overbuild.
TV Market Ranking: 96 (HUNTSVILLE, Limestone County (eastern portion), Madison, Madison County (portions), Redstone Arsenal). Franchise award date: March 1, 1986. Franchise expiration date: N.A. Began: April 1, 1986.
Channel capacity: N.A. Channels available but not in use: N.A.
Basic Service
Subscribers: 35,269.
Programming (received off-air): WAAY-TV (ABC) Huntsville; WAFF (NBC) Huntsville; WHDF (CW) Florence; WHIQ (PBS) Huntsville; WHNT-TV (CBS) Huntsville; WZDX (FOX, MNT) Huntsville.
Programming (via satellite): ABC Family Channel; AMC; Animal Planet; Arts & Entertainment; BET Networks; Bravo; Cartoon Network; CNBC; CNN; Comcast Sports Net Southeast; Comedy Central; Country Music TV; C-SPAN; C-SPAN 2; Discovery Channel; Discovery Health Channel; Disney Channel; E! Entertainment Television; ESPN; ESPN 2; ESPN Classic Sports; Eternal Word TV Network; Food Network; Fox News Channel; FX; Golf Channel; Great American Country; Hallmark Channel; Headline News; HGTV; History Channel; Home Shopping Network; INSP; Lifetime; Lifetime Movie Network; MSNBC; MTV; MyNetworkTV Inc.; NASA TV; National Geographic Channel; Nick At Nite; Nickelodeon; Outdoor Channel; Oxygen; QVC; ShopNBC; Speed Channel; Spike TV; SportSouth; Syfy; TBS Superstation; The Learning Channel; Toon Disney; Travel Channel; Trinity Broadcasting Network; truTV; Turner Classic Movies; Turner Network TV; TV Guide Network; TV Land; Univision; USA Network; VH1; WE tv; Weather Channel; WGN America.
Current originations: Government Access; Educational Access.
Fee: $50.95 monthly; $1.45 converter.
Digital Basic Service
Subscribers: N.A. Included in Valley
Programming (received off-air): WAAY-TV (ABC) Huntsville; WAFF (NBC) Huntsville;

WHIQ (PBS) Huntsville; WHNT-TV (CBS) Huntsville; WZDX (FOX, MNT) Huntsville.
Programming (via satellite): BBC America; Bio; Bloomberg Television; Boomerang; CBS College Sports Network; Church Channel; CMT Pure Country; Cooking Channel; C-SPAN 3; Discovery HD Theater; Discovery Kids Channel; Discovery Military Channel; Discovery Planet Green; Do-It-Yourself; ESPN 2 HD; ESPN HD; ESPN U; ESPNews; Fox College Sports Atlantic; Fox College Sports Central; Fox College Sports Pacific; Fox Soccer; FSN HD; Fuel TV; Fuse; G4; Gospel Music Channel; GSN; Hallmark Movie Channel; HDNet; HDNet Movies; History Channel International; ID Investigation Discovery; Independent Film Channel; JCTV; Jewelry Television; Lifetime Real Women; MTV Hits; MTV Jams; MTV Tres; MTV2; mtvU; Music Choice; National Geographic Channel HD Network; NFL Network; Nick Jr.; NickToons TV; Pentagon Channel; QVC HD; Science Channel; SoapNet; Style Network; TBS in HD; TeenNick; Tennis Channel; The Sportsman Channel; Turner Network TV HD; Universal HD; Versus; Versus HD; VH1 Classic; VH1 Soul.

Pay Service 1
Pay Units: 6,678.
Programming (via satellite): Showtime.
Fee: $10.95 monthly.

Pay Service 2
Pay Units: 7,572.
Programming (via satellite): HBO.
Fee: $10.95 monthly.

Digital Pay Service 1
Pay Units: N.A.
Programming (via satellite): Cinemax (multiplexed); Cinemax HD; Cinemax On Demand; Encore (multiplexed); Flix; Flix On Demand; HBO (multiplexed); HBO HD; HBO On Demand; Showtime (multiplexed); Showtime HD; Showtime On Demand; Starz (multiplexed); Starz HDTV; Sundance Channel; The Movie Channel (multiplexed); The Movie Channel On Demand.

Video-On-Demand: Yes

Pay-Per-View
iN DEMAND (delivered digitally); Hot Choice (delivered digitally); Spice: Xcess (delivered digitally); Shorteez (delivered digitally); Playboy TV (delivered digitally); Fresh (delivered digitally); Club Jenna (delivered digitally); ESPN Now (delivered digitally); ESPN Extra (delivered digitally).

Internet Service
Operational: Yes.
Broadband Service: Knology.Net.
Fee: $29.95 installation; $57.95 monthly.

Telephone Service
Analog: Not Operational
Digital: Operational
Fee: $23.15 monthly

Miles of Plant: 1,330.0 (coaxial); 367.0 (fiber optic). Homes passed: 84,400.
General Manager: Jerry Strauser. Technical Operations Manager: Randy Grayson. Marketing Manager: Cotton DeMarcus.
Ownership: Knology Inc. (MSO).

HUNTSVILLE—Mediacom, 123 Ware Dr NE, Huntsville, AL 35811-1061. Phones: 256-852-7427; 850-934-7700 (Gulf Breeze regional office). Fax: 256-851-7708. Web Site: http://www.mediacomcable.com. Also serves Capshaw, Gurley (unincorporated areas), Harvest, Hazel Green, Madison County, Meridianville, New Market & Toney (portions). ICA: MS0102.
TV Market Ranking: 96 (Capshaw, Gurley (unincorporated areas), Harvest, Hazel Green, HUNTSVILLE, Madison County, Meridianville, New Market, Toney (portions)). Franchise award date: January 1, 1980. Franchise expiration date: N.A. Began: August 1, 1982.
Channel capacity: N.A. Channels available but not in use: N.A.

Basic Service
Subscribers: 8,000.
Programming (received off-air): WAAY-TV (ABC) Huntsville; WAFF (NBC) Huntsville; WHDF (CW) Florence; WHIQ (PBS) Huntsville; WHNT-TV (CBS) Huntsville; WTZT-CA Athens; WZDX (FOX, MNT) Huntsville.
Programming (via satellite): ABC Family Channel; AMC; AmericanLife TV Network; Animal Planet; Arts & Entertainment; BET Networks; Bravo; Cartoon Network; CNBC; CNN; Comcast Sports Net Southeast; Comedy Central; Country Music TV; C-SPAN; C-SPAN 2; Discovery Channel; E! Entertainment Television; ESPN; ESPN 2; Eternal Word TV Network; Food Network; Fox News Channel; FX; G4; Golf Channel; Hallmark Channel; Headline News; HGTV; History Channel; Home Shopping Network; INSP; Lifetime; MSNBC; MTV; NASA TV; Nickelodeon; Outdoor Channel; QVC; Speed Channel; Spike TV; SportSouth; Syfy; TBS Superstation; The Learning Channel; Toon Disney; Travel Channel; Trinity Broadcasting Network; truTV; Turner Classic Movies; Turner Network TV; TV Land; USA Network; VH1; WE tv; Weather Channel; WGN America.
Current originations: Public Access.
Fee: $21.50 installation; $17.57 monthly; $32.00 additional installation.

Digital Basic Service
Subscribers: N.A.
Programming (via satellite): BBC America; Discovery Digital Networks; Fox Sports World; GSN; Independent Film Channel; Music Choice.

Digital Pay Service 1
Pay Units: 1,189.
Programming (via satellite): Cinemax.
Fee: $9.95 monthly.

Digital Pay Service 2
Pay Units: 2,171.
Programming (via satellite): Flix.
Fee: $2.95 monthly.

Digital Pay Service 3
Pay Units: 2,370.
Programming (via satellite): HBO.
Fee: $9.95 monthly.

Digital Pay Service 4
Pay Units: 2,267.
Programming (via satellite): Showtime.
Fee: $9.95 monthly.

Digital Pay Service 5
Pay Units: 2,129.
Programming (via satellite): The Movie Channel.
Fee: $9.95 monthly.

Digital Pay Service 6
Pay Units: N.A.
Programming (via satellite): Encore (multiplexed); Starz (multiplexed); Sundance Channel.

Video-On-Demand: Yes

Pay-Per-View
ESPN Extra (delivered digitally); ESPN Now (delivered digitally); Hot Choice (delivered digitally); iN DEMAND (delivered digitally); Fresh (delivered digitally); Sports PPV (delivered digitally).

Internet Service
Operational: Yes.
Subscribers: 1,000.
Broadband Service: Mediacom High Speed Internet.
Fee: $29.95 monthly; $10.00 modem lease.

Telephone Service
Digital: Operational

Miles of Plant: None (coaxial); 25.0 (fiber optic). Homes passed: 10,567. Miles of plant (coax) included in Ardmore
Vice President: David Servies. Operations Manager: Tommy Hill. Chief Technician: Harold Balch. Technical Operations Supervisor: Mark Darwin. Sales & Marketing Manager: Joey Nagem. Customer Service Supervisor: Sandy Acklin.
City fee: 3% of gross.
Ownership: Mediacom LLC (MSO).

JACKSON—Mediacom. Now served by THOMASVILLE, AL [AL0080]. ICA: AL0083.

JASPER—Charter Communications, 2100 Columbiana Rd, Vestavia, AL 35216. Phone: 205-824-5400. Fax: 205-824-5490. Web Site: http://www.charter.com. Also serves Carbon Hill, Cordova, Dora, Eldridge, Kansas, Parish, Sipsey, Sumiton, Walker County (portions) & West Jefferson. ICA: AL0026.
TV Market Ranking: 40 (Cordova, Dora, Parish, Sipsey, Sumiton, Walker County (portions), West Jefferson); Below 100 (Walker County (portions)); Outside TV Markets (Carbon Hill, Eldridge, JASPER, Kansas, Walker County (portions)). Franchise award date: January 1, 1985. Franchise expiration date: N.A. Began: April 1, 1969.
Channel capacity: N.A. Channels available but not in use: N.A.

Basic Service
Subscribers: 11,237.
Programming (received off-air): W55BJ Jasper; WABM (MNT) Birmingham; WBIQ (PBS) Birmingham; WBRC (FOX) Birmingham; WCFT-TV (ABC) Tuscaloosa; WIAT (CBS) Birmingham; WPXH-TV (ION) Gadsden; WTJP-TV (TBN) Gadsden; WTTO (CW) Homewood; WVTM-TV (NBC) Birmingham; 1 FM.
Programming (via satellite): WGN America.
Fee: $29.99 installation.

Expanded Basic Service 1
Subscribers: N.A.
Programming (via satellite): ABC Family Channel; AMC; Animal Planet; Arts & Entertainment; BET Networks; Bravo; Cartoon Network; CNBC; CNN; Comcast Sports Net Southeast; Comcast/Charter Sports Southeast (CSS); Comedy Central; Country Music TV; C-SPAN; C-SPAN 2; Discovery Channel; Disney Channel; E! Entertainment Television; ESPN; ESPN 2; Eternal Word TV Network; Food Network; Fox News Channel; FX; G4; Golf Channel; GSN; Hallmark Channel; Headline News; HGTV; History Channel; Home Shopping Network; INSP; Lifetime; MSNBC; MTV; National Geographic Channel; Nickelodeon; Oxygen; Product Information Network; QVC; ShopNBC; SoapNet; Speed Channel; Spike TV; SportSouth; Syfy; TBS Superstation; Telemundo; The Learning Channel; Toon Disney; Travel Channel; truTV; Turner Classic Movies; Turner Network TV; TV Guide Network; TV Land; USA Network; Versus; VH1; WE tv; Weather Channel.
Fee: $43.00 monthly.

Digital Basic Service
Subscribers: N.A.
Programming (via satellite): BBC America; Bio; Bloomberg Television; Discovery Digital Networks; Do-It-Yourself; ESPNews; Fox College Sports Atlantic; Fox College Sports Central; Fox College Sports Pacific; Fox Movie Channel; Fox Sports en Espanol; Fox Sports World; GAS; Great American Country; History Channel International; Independent Film Channel; Lifetime Movie Network; MTV Networks Digital Suite; Music Choice; Nick Jr.; Nick Too; NickToons TV; Style Network; Sundance Channel.
Fee: $16.99 monthly.

Digital Pay Service 1
Pay Units: 4,942.
Programming (via satellite): Cinemax (multiplexed); Encore (multiplexed); Flix; HBO (multiplexed); Showtime (multiplexed); Starz (multiplexed); The Movie Channel (multiplexed).
Fee: $9.95 monthly (each).

Video-On-Demand: Yes

Pay-Per-View
iN DEMAND (delivered digitally); Playboy TV (delivered digitally); Pleasure (delivered digitally); Fresh (delivered digitally); Shorteez (delivered digitally); Sports PPV (delivered digitally); Video On Demand (delivered digitally).

Internet Service
Operational: Yes. Began: March 1, 2001.
Broadband Service: Charter Pipeline.
Fee: $29.99 monthly; $5.00 modem lease; $205.00 modem purchase.

Telephone Service
Digital: Operational

Miles of Plant: 464.0 (coaxial); None (fiber optic). Homes passed: 23,096.
Vice President & General Manager: Don Karell. Technical Operations Director: Tommy Taylor. Marketing Director: David Redmond. Marketing Manager: Jeff Hatcher.
City fee: 3% of basic.
Ownership: Charter Communications Inc. (MSO).

JASPER—Galaxy Cablevision, PO Box 879, 118 S Jackson St, Grove Hill, AL 36451-0879. Phone: 251-275-3118. Fax: 251-275-3120. Web Site: http://www.galaxycable.com. Also serves Piney Woods & Walker County. ICA: AL0262.
TV Market Ranking: 18 (Piney Woods); Outside TV Markets (JASPER, Walker County). Franchise award date: August 29, 1998. Franchise expiration date: N.A. Began: N.A.
Channel capacity: 54 (not 2-way capable). Channels available but not in use: 13.

Basic Service
Subscribers: 80.
Programming (received off-air): WABM (MNT) Birmingham; WBIQ (PBS) Birmingham; WBRC (FOX) Birmingham; WCFT-TV (ABC) Tuscaloosa; WIAT (CBS) Birmingham; WTTO (CW) Homewood; WVTM-TV (NBC) Birmingham.
Programming (via satellite): ABC Family Channel; AMC; Animal Planet; Arts & Entertainment; Cartoon Network; CNBC; CNN; Comcast Sports Net Southeast; Discovery Channel; Disney Channel; ESPN; ESPN 2; Fox News Channel; FX; Great American Country; Hallmark Channel; Headline News; HGTV; Lifetime; Outdoor Channel; QVC; Speed Channel; TBS Superstation; The Learning Channel; Toon Disney; Trinity Broadcasting Network; Turner Network TV; USA Network; Weather Channel; WGN America.
Fee: $36.55 monthly.

Pay Service 1
Pay Units: N.A.
Programming (via satellite): HBO.

Internet Service
Operational: No.

Telephone Service
None

Miles of Plant: 25.0 (coaxial); None (fiber optic). Homes passed: 571.

State Manager: Bill Flowers. Technical Manager & Engineer: Greg Berthaut. Customer Service Representative: Lisa Ray.
Ownership: Galaxy Cable Inc. (MSO).

LAFAYETTE—CommuniComm Services, 3164 Hwy 431, Ste 9, Roanoke, AL 36274-1702. Phone: 334-863-7080. Fax: 334-863-2027. Web Site: http://www.netcommander.com. ICA: AL0097.
TV Market Ranking: Outside TV Markets (LAFAYETTE). Franchise award date: N.A. Franchise expiration date: N.A. Began: July 1, 1981.
Channel capacity: N.A. Channels available but not in use: N.A.

Basic Service
Subscribers: 595.
Programming (received off-air): WAXC-LP (IND) Alexander City; WCAG-LP La Grange; WCIQ (PBS) Mount Cheaha State Park; WJSU-TV (ABC) Anniston; WLGA (CW) Opelika; WLTZ (CW, NBC) Columbus; WRBL (CBS) Columbus; WSFA (NBC) Montgomery; WTVM (ABC) Columbus; WXTX (FOX) Columbus.
Programming (via satellite): ABC Family Channel; AMC; Arts & Entertainment; BET Networks; Cartoon Network; CNBC; CNN; Comcast/Charter Sports Southeast (CSS); Comedy Central; Country Music TV; C-SPAN; C-SPAN 2; Discovery Channel; Disney Channel; E! Entertainment Television; ESPN; ESPN 2; Food Network; Fox News Channel; FX; Gospel Music Channel; Great American Country; Hallmark Channel; Headline News; HGTV; History Channel; Home Shopping Network; ION Television; Lifetime; MSNBC; MTV; Nick Jr.; Nickelodeon; Outdoor Channel; QVC; ShopNBC; Spike TV; SportSouth; Syfy; TBS Superstation; The Learning Channel; Trinity Broadcasting Network; truTV; Turner Network TV; Turner South; TV Land; USA Network; VH1; WE tv; Weather Channel; WGN America.
Fee: $39.95 installation; $29.99 monthly.

Digital Basic Service
Subscribers: 46.
Programming (via satellite): BBC America; Discovery Health Channel; Discovery Home Channel; Discovery Kids Channel; Discovery Military Channel; DMX Music; ESPN Classic Sports; Fox Soccer; Golf Channel; GSN; ID Investigation Discovery; Independent Film Channel; Science Channel; Speed Channel; Turner Classic Movies; Versus; WE tv.
Fee: $9.95 monthly.

Digital Pay Service 1
Pay Units: 80.
Programming (via satellite): Cinemax (multiplexed); Encore (multiplexed); HBO (multiplexed); Showtime; Starz (multiplexed).
Fee: $13.95 monthly (HBO, Cinemax, Showtime, Starz or Encore).

Video-On-Demand: No

Pay-Per-View
iN DEMAND (delivered digitally); Playboy TV (delivered digitally).

Internet Service
Operational: No.

Telephone Service
None
Miles of Plant: 45.0 (coaxial); None (fiber optic). Homes passed: 1,870.
General Manager: Brian Chase. Chief Technician: William Boyd.
City fee: 3% of gross.
Ownership: James Cable LLC (MSO).

LAKE MARTIN RESORT—Com-Link Inc., 206 Hardaway Ave E, Union Springs, AL 36089-1609. Phones: 800-722-2805; 334-738-2204. Fax: 334-738-5555. E-mail: ustc@ustconline.net. Web Site: http://www.ustconline.net. Also serves Coosa County (portions) & Tallapoosa County (portions). ICA: AL0090.
TV Market Ranking: Below 100 (Coosa County (portions), LAKE MARTIN RESORT, Tallapoosa County (portions)); Outside TV Markets (Coosa County (portions), Tallapoosa County (portions)). Franchise award date: November 13, 1989. Franchise expiration date: N.A. Began: January 17, 1990.
Channel capacity: 60 (not 2-way capable). Channels available but not in use: 18.

Basic Service
Subscribers: 1,400.
Programming (received off-air): WAIQ (PBS) Montgomery; WAKA (CBS) Selma; WAXC-LP (IND) Alexander City; WCOV-TV (FOX) Montgomery; WNCF (ABC) Montgomery; WSFA (NBC) Montgomery.
Programming (via satellite): ABC Family Channel; AMC; Arts & Entertainment; BET Networks; Cartoon Network; CNBC; CNN; Comcast Sports Net Southeast; Country Music TV; C-SPAN; C-SPAN 2; Discovery Channel; E! Entertainment Television; ESPN; Hallmark Channel; Headline News; Lifetime; MTV; Nickelodeon; QVC; Spike TV; Syfy; TBS Superstation; The Learning Channel; Travel Channel; truTV; Turner Classic Movies; Turner Network TV; USA Network; VH1; Weather Channel; WGN America.
Current originations: Public Access.
Fee: $35.00 installation; $41.70 monthly.

Pay Service 1
Pay Units: 112.
Programming (via satellite): Cinemax.
Fee: $8.50 monthly.

Pay Service 2
Pay Units: 58.
Programming (via satellite): The Movie Channel.
Fee: $8.50 monthly.

Pay Service 3
Pay Units: 251.
Programming (via satellite): HBO.
Fee: $8.50 monthly.

Pay Service 4
Pay Units: 74.
Programming (via satellite): Showtime.
Fee: $8.50 monthly.

Video-On-Demand: No

Pay-Per-View
Special events, Addressable: No.

Internet Service
Operational: Yes.
Broadband Service: In-house.
Fee: $42.50 installation; $34.95-$59.95 monthly.

Telephone Service
None
Miles of Plant: 165.0 (coaxial); None (fiber optic). Homes passed: 2,486.
Executive Vice President: Larry Grogan. Chief Technician: Lynn Rotton.
County fee: 3% of gross.
Ownership: Com-Link Inc. (MSO).

LEEDS—Charter Communications, 2100 Columbiana Rd, Vestavia, AL 35216. Phone: 205-824-5400. Fax: 205-824-5490. Web Site: http://www.charter.com. Also serves Adamsville, Alabaster, Alexander City, Auburn, Birmingham (portions), Bluff Park, Bon Air, Brockwood, Brookside, Buhl, Cahaba Heights, Calera, Camp Hill, Center Point, Chambers County (portions), Childersburg, Clay County (portions), Coaling, Coker, Coosa County (portions), Cottondale, Duncanville, Elrod, Five Points, Forestdale, Fultondale, Gardendale, Goodwater, Grayson Valley, Graysville, Helene, Homewood, Hoover, Indian Springs Village, Jacksons' Gap, Jefferson County, Lee County (portions), Maytown, Montevallo, Moody, Morris, Moundville, Mount Olive, Mountain Brook, Mulga, New Site, Northport, Oak Grove, Opelika, Pelham, Peterson, Pinson, Riverchase, Rockford, Shelby County (portions), St. Clair County (portions), Sycamore, Sylacauga, Sylvan Springs, Talladega, Talladega County (portions), Tallapoosa County (portions), Tarrant City, Taylorville, Trussville, Tuscaloosa, Tuscaloosa County, Tuscaloosa County (portions), Tuskegee, Vance, Vestavia Hills, West End, Westover, Whites Chapel & Wilton. ICA: AL0192.
TV Market Ranking: 40 (Adamsville, Alabaster, Birmingham (portions), Bluff Park, Bon Air, Brockwood, Brookside, Cahaba Heights, Calera, Center Point, Childersburg, Forestdale, Fultondale, Gardendale, Grayson Valley, Graysville, Helene, Homewood, Hoover, Indian Springs Village, Jefferson County, LEEDS, Maytown, Montevallo, Moody, Morris, Mount Olive, Mountain Brook, Mulga, Pelham, Pinson, Riverchase, Shelby County (portions), St. Clair County (portions), Sylvan Springs, Talladega County (portions), Tarrant City, Trussville, Tuscaloosa County (portions), Vance, Vestavia Hills, Westover, Whites Chapel, Wilton); 94 (Auburn, Chambers County (portions), Lee County (portions), Opelika); Below 100 (Buhl, Camp Hill, Clay County (portions), Coaling, Coker, Coosa County (portions), Cottondale, Duncanville, Elrod, Jacksons' Gap, Moundville, Northport, Peterson, Talladega, Tallapoosa County (portions), Taylorville, Tuscaloosa, Tuscaloosa County, Tuskegee, West End, Talladega County (portions), Tuscaloosa County (portions), Auburn, Chambers County (portions), Lee County (portions)); Outside TV Markets (Alexander City, Clay County (portions), Coosa County (portions), Five Points, Goodwater, New Site, Oak Grove, Rockford, Sycamore, Sylacauga, Tallapoosa County (portions), Birmingham (portions)). Franchise award date: N.A. Franchise expiration date: N.A. Began: October 1, 1979.
Channel capacity: N.A. Channels available but not in use: None.

Basic Service
Subscribers: 143,584.
Programming (received off-air): WABM (MNT) Birmingham; WBIQ (PBS) Birmingham; WBRC (FOX) Birmingham; WCFT-TV (ABC) Tuscaloosa; WIAT (CBS) Birmingham; WOTM-LP Montevallo; WPXH-TV (ION) Gadsden; WTJP-TV (TBN) Gadsden; WTTO (CW) Homewood; WVTM-TV (NBC) Birmingham.
Programming (via satellite): INSP; WGN America.
Current originations: Leased Access.
Fee: $29.99 installation; $9.54 monthly.

Expanded Basic Service 1
Subscribers: 29,751.
Programming (via satellite): ABC Family Channel; AMC; Animal Planet; Arts & Entertainment; BET Networks; Bravo; Cartoon Network; CNBC; CNN; Comcast Sports Net Southeast; Comcast/Charter Sports Southeast (CSS); Comedy Central; Country Music TV; C-SPAN; C-SPAN 2; Discovery Channel; Disney Channel; E! Entertainment Television; ESPN; ESPN 2; Eternal Word TV Network; Food Network; Fox News Channel; FX; G4; Golf Channel; GSN; Hallmark Channel; Headline News; HGTV; History Channel; Home Shopping Network; Lifetime; MSNBC; MTV; MTV2; National Geographic Channel; Nickelodeon; Oxygen; Product Information Network; QVC; Speed Channel; Spike TV; SportSouth; Style Network; Syfy; TBS Superstation; The Learning Channel; Toon Disney; Travel Channel; truTV; Turner Network TV; TV Guide Network; TV Land; Univision; USA Network; Versus; VH1; Weather Channel.
Fee: $43.00 monthly.

Digital Basic Service
Subscribers: N.A.
Programming (received off-air): WBIQ (PBS) Birmingham; WBRC (FOX) Birmingham; WCFT-TV (ABC) Tuscaloosa; WIAT (CBS) Birmingham; WVTM-TV (NBC) Birmingham.
Programming (via satellite): ABC News Now; AmericanLife TV Network; Arts & Entertainment HD; BabyFirst TV; BBC America; Bio; Bloomberg Television; CBS College Sports Network; Cine Latino; CMT Pure Country; Cooking Channel; C-SPAN 2; Discovery en Espanol; Discovery HD Theater; Discovery Health Channel; Discovery Home Channel; Discovery Kids Channel; Discovery Military Channel; Do-It-Yourself; ESPN 2 HD; ESPN Classic Sports; ESPN Deportes; ESPN HD; ESPN U; ESPNews; FitTV; Fox Business Channel; Fox College Sports Atlantic; Fox College Sports Central; Fox College Sports Pacific; Fox Movie Channel; Fox Soccer; Fox Sports en Espanol; Fuel TV; Fuse; Gospel Music Channel; Great American Country; History Channel HD; History Channel International; ID Investigation Discovery; Independent Film Channel; Jewelry Television; La Familia Network; Lifetime Movie Network; MTV Hits; MTV Jams; MTV Tres; Music Choice; NHL Network; Nick Jr.; Nick Too; NickToons TV; Outdoor Channel; Palladia; Science Channel; SoapNet; Sundance Channel; TeenNick; Telemundo; Tennis Channel; The Sportsman Channel; Turner Network TV HD; TV One; TVN Entertainment; Universal HD; VH1 Classic; VH1 Soul; VHUNO; WE tv.
Fee: $16.99 monthly.

Digital Pay Service 1
Pay Units: 23,890.
Programming (via satellite): Cinemax (multiplexed); Cinemax HD; Encore (multiplexed); Flix; HBO (multiplexed); HBO HD; Showtime (multiplexed); Showtime HD; Starz (multiplexed); Starz HDTV; The

Movie Channel (multiplexed); The Movie Channel HD.
Fee: $9.95 monthly (each).
Video-On-Demand: Yes
Pay-Per-View
iN DEMAND (delivered digitally); Playboy TV (delivered digitally); Pleasure (delivered digitally); Fresh (delivered digitally); Shorteez (delivered digitally); Video On Demand (delivered digitally).
Internet Service
Operational: Yes.
Broadband Service: Charter Pipeline.
Fee: $29.99 monthly.
Telephone Service
Analog: Not Operational
Digital: Operational
Fee: $29.99 monthly
Miles of Plant: 2,391.0 (coaxial); 25.0 (fiber optic). Homes passed: 152,126.
Vice President & General Manager: Don Karell. Technical Operations Director: Greg Prim. Marketing Director: David Redmond. Marketing Manager: Jeff Hatcher.
City fee: 3% of gross.
Ownership: Charter Communications Inc. (MSO).

LEESBURG—Envision Media Inc., 300 N 5th Ave, Rome, GA 30165. Phone: 601-957-7979. Fax: 706-295-1286. ICA: AL0264.
TV Market Ranking: 18 (LEESBURG).
Channel capacity: N.A. Channels available but not in use: N.A.
Basic Service
Subscribers: N.A. Included in Cedar Bluff
Programming (received off-air): WBRC (FOX) Birmingham; WCIQ (PBS) Mount Cheaha State Park; WIAT (CBS) Birmingham; WJSU-TV (ABC) Anniston; WJXS-CA Jacksonville; WTJP-TV (TBN) Gadsden; WTTO (CW) Homewood; WVTM-TV (NBC) Birmingham.
Programming (via satellite): ABC Family Channel; AMC; AmericanLife TV Network; Animal Planet; Arts & Entertainment; Cartoon Network; CNN; Country Music TV; Discovery Channel; ESPN; ESPN 2; Food Network; Fox News Channel; Fox Sports Net; FX; Hallmark Channel; Headline News; HGTV; History Channel; Lifetime; Nickelodeon; Pentagon Channel; QVC; Speed Channel; Spike TV; Syfy; TBS Superstation; The Learning Channel; The Sportsman Channel; truTV; Turner Classic Movies; Turner Network TV; Turner South; TV Land; USA Network; VH1; Weather Channel; WSBK-TV (IND) Boston.
Fee: $37.99 monthly.
Pay Service 1
Pay Units: N.A.
Programming (via satellite): Cinemax; HBO (multiplexed).
Fee: $19.95 monthly.
Internet Service
Operational: No.
Telephone Service
None
General Manager: Tom Holt.
Ownership: Envision Media Inc. (MSO).

LEIGHTON—Charter Communications, 2100 Columbiana Rd, Vestavia, AL 35216. Phone: 205-824-5400. Fax: 205-824-5490. Web Site: http://www.charter.com. Also serves Colbert County (unincorporated areas), Courtland, Lawrence County (portions), North Courtland, Spring Valley & Town Creek. ICA: AL0203.
TV Market Ranking: 96 (Colbert County (unincorporated areas) (portions), Courtland, Lawrence County (portions), LEIGHTON, North Courtland, Town Creek); Below 100 (Spring Valley, Colbert County (unincorporated areas) (portions)). Franchise award date: N.A. Franchise expiration date: N.A. Began: March 1, 1982.
Channel capacity: N.A. Channels available but not in use: N.A.
Basic Service
Subscribers: 2,567.
Programming (received off-air): WAAY-TV (ABC) Huntsville; WAFF (NBC) Huntsville; WFIQ (PBS) Florence; WHDF (CW) Florence; WHNT-TV (CBS) Huntsville; WZDX (FOX, MNT) Huntsville.
Programming (via satellite): BET Networks; Comcast Sports Net Southeast; C-SPAN; Home Shopping Network; INSP; QVC; Trinity Broadcasting Network; WGN America.
Fee: $29.99 installation.
Expanded Basic Service 1
Subscribers: 2,522.
Programming (via satellite): ABC Family Channel; AMC; Animal Planet; Arts & Entertainment; Bravo; Cartoon Network; CNBC; CNN; Comedy Central; Country Music TV; Discovery Channel; Disney Channel; E! Entertainment Television; ESPN; ESPN 2; Fox News Channel; FX; G4; Golf Channel; Headline News; HGTV; History Channel; Lifetime; MTV; Nickelodeon; Oxygen; Speed Channel; Spike TV; Syfy; TBS Superstation; The Learning Channel; Toon Disney; Turner Classic Movies; Turner Network TV; TV Land; USA Network; VH1; WE tv; Weather Channel.
Fee: $43.00 monthly.
Digital Basic Service
Subscribers: N.A.
Programming (via satellite): BBC America; Bio; Bloomberg Television; Discovery Digital Networks; ESPN Classic Sports; FitTV; Fox Movie Channel; Fuse; GAS; GSN; History Channel International; Independent Film Channel; Lifetime Movie Network; MTV Networks Digital Suite; Music Choice; Nick Jr.; Nick Too; NickToons TV; Science Television; SoapNet; Style Network; Sundance Channel.
Fee: $16.99 monthly.
Pay Service 1
Pay Units: 251.
Programming (via satellite): Encore (multiplexed); Flix; Showtime (multiplexed); The Movie Channel (multiplexed); The Movie Channel.
Fee: $9.00 monthly.
Digital Pay Service 1
Pay Units: N.A.
Programming (via satellite): Cinemax (multiplexed); HBO (multiplexed); Starz (multiplexed).
Video-On-Demand: No
Pay-Per-View
iN DEMAND (delivered digitally); Playboy TV (delivered digitally); Shorteez (delivered digitally); Shorteez (delivered digitally).
Internet Service
Operational: No.
Telephone Service
None
Miles of Plant: 116.0 (coaxial); None (fiber optic). Homes passed: 3,413.
Vice President & General Manager: Don Karell. Technical Operations Director: Greg Prim. Marketing Director: David Redmond. Marketing Manager: Jeff Hatcher.
Franchise fee: 3% of gross.
Ownership: Charter Communications Inc. (MSO).

LIMESTONE COUNTY (western portion)—Charter Communications. Now served by ATHENS, AL [AL0169]. ICA: AL0120.

LINCOLN—Coosa Cable. Now served by PELL CITY, AL [AL0212]. ICA: AL0098.

LINDEN—Mediacom, 760 Middle St, PO Box 1009, Fairhope, AL 36532. Phones: 251-928-0374; 850-934-7700 (Gulf Breeze regional office). Fax: 251-928-3804. Web Site: http://www.mediacomcable.com. ICA: AL0106.
TV Market Ranking: Outside TV Markets (LINDEN). Franchise award date: January 19, 1976. Franchise expiration date: N.A. Began: November 1, 1970.
Channel capacity: N.A. Channels available but not in use: N.A.
Basic Service
Subscribers: 691.
Programming (received off-air): WAKA (CBS) Selma; WBIH (IND) Selma; WBRC (FOX) Birmingham; WCFT-TV (ABC) Tuscaloosa; WDBB (CW) Bessemer; WIIQ (PBS) Demopolis; WNCF (ABC) Montgomery; WSFA (NBC) Montgomery; WTOK-TV (ABC, CW, FOX, MNT) Meridian; WVTM-TV (NBC) Birmingham.
Programming (via satellite): ABC Family Channel; AMC; Animal Planet; Arts & Entertainment; BET Networks; Bravo; Cartoon Network; CNBC; CNN; Comcast Sports Net Southeast; Comedy Central; Country Music TV; C-SPAN; C-SPAN 2; Discovery Channel; Disney Channel; E! Entertainment Television; ESPN; ESPN 2; FitTV; Food Network; Fox News Channel; FX; Hallmark Channel; Headline News; HGTV; History Channel; Home Shopping Network; INSP; Lifetime; MSNBC; MTV; Nickelodeon; Outdoor Channel; QVC; Speed Channel; Spike TV; SportSouth; Syfy; TBS Superstation; The Learning Channel; Travel Channel; Trinity Broadcasting Network; truTV; Turner Classic Movies; TV Land; USA Network; VH1; WE tv; Weather Channel; WGN America.
Fee: $49.95 monthly.
Digital Basic Service
Subscribers: N.A.
Programming (via satellite): AmericanLife TV Network; BBC America; Bio; Bloomberg Television; Discovery Digital Networks; DMX Music; Fox Movie Channel; Fox Sports World; G4; GSN; History Channel International; Independent Film Channel; INSP; Lifetime Movie Network; MuchMusic Network; Outdoor Channel; Style Network.
Digital Pay Service 1
Pay Units: N.A.
Programming (via satellite): Cinemax (multiplexed); Encore (multiplexed); Flix (multiplexed); HBO (multiplexed); Showtime (multiplexed); Sundance Channel (multiplexed); The Movie Channel (multiplexed).
Video-On-Demand: No
Internet Service
Operational: Yes.
Broadband Service: Mediacom High Speed Internet.
Fee: $45.95 monthly.
Telephone Service
Digital: Planned
Homes passed: 1,106. Total homes in franchised area: 1,150. Miles of plant (coax & fiber) included in Camden
Vice President: David Servies. Operations Director: Gene Wuchner. Technical Operations Manager: Mike Sneary. Sales & Marketing Manager: Joey Nagem.
City fee: 3% of gross.
Ownership: Mediacom LLC (MSO).

LIVINGSTON—Mediacom, 760 Middle St, PO Box 1009, Fairhope, AL 36532. Phone: 251-928-0374. Fax: 251-928-3804. Web Site: http://www.mediacomcable.com. Also serves York. ICA: AL0067.
TV Market Ranking: Below 100 (LIVINGSTON, York). Franchise award date: July 27, 1970. Franchise expiration date: N.A. Began: July 1, 1970.
Channel capacity: N.A. Channels available but not in use: N.A.
Basic Service
Subscribers: N.A.
Programming (received off-air): WBIH (IND) Selma; WCFT-TV (ABC) Tuscaloosa; WCOV-TV (FOX) Montgomery; WDBB (CW) Bessemer; WEIQ (PBS) Mobile; WGBC (NBC) Meridian; WMDN (CBS) Meridian; WTOK-TV (ABC, CW, FOX, MNT) Meridian; WVTM-TV (NBC) Birmingham.
Programming (via satellite): ABC Family Channel; AMC; Animal Planet; Arts & Entertainment; BET Networks; Bravo; Cartoon Network; CNBC; CNN; Comcast Sports Net Southeast; Comedy Central; Country Music TV; C-SPAN; C-SPAN 2; Discovery Channel; Disney Channel; E! Entertainment Television; ESPN; ESPN 2; Eternal Word TV Network; FitTV; Food Network; Fox News Channel; FX; Great American Country; Hallmark Channel; Headline News; HGTV; History Channel; Home Shopping Network; INSP; Lifetime; MSNBC; MTV; Nickelodeon; Outdoor Channel; QVC; ShopNBC; SoapNet; Speed Channel; Spike TV; SportSouth; Syfy; TBS Superstation; The Learning Channel; Travel Channel; Trinity Broadcasting Network; truTV; Turner Classic Movies; Turner Network TV; TV Land; USA Network; VH1; WE tv; Weather Channel; WGN America.
Fee: $49.95 installation; $19.22 monthly; $1.75 converter.
Digital Basic Service
Subscribers: N.A.
Programming (via satellite): AmericanLife TV Network; BBC America; Bio; Bloomberg Television; Discovery Digital Networks; ESPNews; Fox Movie Channel; Fox Soccer; Fuse; G4; Golf Channel; GSN; Halogen Network; History Channel International; Independent Film Channel; Lifetime Movie Network; Lime; National Geographic Channel; Nick Jr.; NickToons TV; Sleuth; Style Network; TVG Network; Versus; Weatherscan.
Digital Pay Service 1
Pay Units: N.A.
Programming (via satellite): Cinemax (multiplexed); Encore (multiplexed); Flix (multiplexed); HBO (multiplexed); Music Choice; Showtime (multiplexed); Starz (multiplexed); Sundance Channel (multiplexed); The Movie Channel (multiplexed).
Video-On-Demand: No
Internet Service
Operational: Yes.
Broadband Service: Mediacom High Speed Internet.
Fee: $45.95 monthly.
Telephone Service
None
Homes passed: 2,343. Total homes in franchised area: 2,383. Miles of plant (coax & fiber) included in Camden
Vice President: David Servies. Operations Director: Gene Wuchner. Technical Operations Manager: Mike Sneary. Sales & Marketing Manager: Joey Nagem.

City fee: 3% of gross.
Ownership: Mediacom LLC (MSO).

LOCUST FORK—Formerly served by Almega Cable. No longer in operation. ICA: AL0204.

LOWNDES COUNTY—Alabama Broadband LLC, 3447A Parkwood Rd SE, Bessemer, AL 35022. Phones: 877-840-5040; 205-426-3432. E-mail: contact@alabamabroadband.com. Web Site: http://www.alabamabroadband.net. Also serves Gordonsville, Mosses & White Hall. ICA: AL0102.
TV Market Ranking: Below 100 (Gordonsville, LOWNDES COUNTY, Mosses, White Hall). Franchise award date: September 1, 1989. Franchise expiration date: N.A. Began: July 1, 1990.
Channel capacity: 45 (not 2-way capable). Channels available but not in use: 20.
Basic Service
Subscribers: 303.
Programming (received off-air): WAIQ (PBS) Montgomery; WAKA (CBS) Selma; WCOV-TV (FOX) Montgomery; WNCF (ABC) Montgomery; WSFA (NBC) Montgomery.
Programming (via satellite): ABC Family Channel; Arts & Entertainment; BET Networks; CNN; Discovery Channel; Disney Channel; ESPN; Headline News; MTV; QVC; Spike TV; TBS Superstation; Trinity Broadcasting Network; Turner Network TV; USA Network; Weather Channel; WGN America.
Fee: $29.95 installation; $20.76 monthly.
Pay Service 1
Pay Units: N.A.
Programming (via satellite): Cinemax; HBO; Showtime.
Fee: $9.95 monthly (each).
Video-On-Demand: No
Internet Service
Operational: No.
Telephone Service
None
Miles of Plant: 37.0 (coaxial); None (fiber optic). Homes passed: 1,200.
President: Tom Early.
Ownership: Alabama Broadband LLC (MSO).

LUVERNE—Crenshaw Cable, 90 S Forest Ave, Luverne, AL 36049-1501. Phones: 800-735-9546; 334-335-3435. Fax: 334-335-3177. E-mail: support@troycable.net. Web Site: http://www.troycable.net. Also serves Brantley, Glenwood & Rutledge. ICA: AL0103.
TV Market Ranking: Below 100 (Brantley, Glenwood, LUVERNE, Rutledge). Franchise award date: January 1, 1965. Franchise expiration date: N.A. Began: December 1, 1967.
Channel capacity: 68 (operating 2-way). Channels available but not in use: N.A.
Basic Service
Subscribers: 1,550.
Programming (received off-air): WAKA (CBS) Selma; WBMM (CW) Tuskegee; WCIQ (PBS) Mount Cheaha State Park; WCOV-TV (FOX) Montgomery; WIYC (IND) Troy; WLTZ (CW, NBC) Columbus; WNCF (ABC) Montgomery; WSFA (NBC) Montgomery; WTVM (ABC) Columbus; WTVY (CBS, CW, MNT) Dothan.
Programming (via satellite): ABC Family Channel; AMC; Animal Planet; Arts & Entertainment; BET Networks; Bravo; Cartoon Network; CNBC; CNN; Comcast Sports Net Southeast; Comcast/Charter Sports Southeast (CSS); Comedy Central; Country Music TV; C-SPAN; C-SPAN 2; Discovery Channel; Disney Channel; E! Entertainment Television; ESPN; ESPN 2; ESPN Classic Sports; Food Network; Fox News Channel; FX; Golf Channel; GSN; Hallmark Channel; Headline News; HGTV; History Channel; Home Shopping Network; INSP; Lifetime; MSNBC; MTV; National Geographic Channel; Nickelodeon; QVC; Speed Channel; Spike TV; SportSouth; Syfy; TBS Superstation; The Learning Channel; Travel Channel; truTV; Turner Classic Movies; Turner Network TV; TV Guide Network; TV Land; USA Network; VH1; Weather Channel; WGN America.
Current originations: Educational Access; Public Access.
Fee: $29.95 installation; $35.95 monthly.
Digital Basic Service
Subscribers: N.A.
Programming (via satellite): AmericanLife TV Network; BBC America; Bio; Bloomberg Television; Discovery Digital Networks; Discovery HD Theater; ESPN; ESPNews; FitTV; Fox College Sports Atlantic; Fox College Sports Central; Fox College Sports Pacific; Fox Movie Channel; Fox Soccer; Fox Sports en Espanol; Fuse; G4; GAS; Halogen Network; HDNet; HDNet Movies; History Channel International; Lifetime Movie Network; MTV Networks Digital Suite; Music Choice; Nick Jr.; Nick Too; NickToons TV; Outdoor Channel; Sleuth; SoapNet; Style Network; Toon Disney; Trinity Broadcasting Network.
Fee: $15.95 monthly.
Digital Pay Service 1
Pay Units: N.A.
Programming (via satellite): Cinemax (multiplexed); Encore (multiplexed); Flix; HBO (multiplexed); Showtime (multiplexed); Starz (multiplexed); Sundance Channel; The Movie Channel (multiplexed).
Fee: $7.95 monthly (Cinemax or Starz), $8.95 monthly (Encore), $10.95 monthly (Showtime & TMC), $11.95 monthly (HBO).
Video-On-Demand: No
Pay-Per-View
iN DEMAND (delivered digitally); Hot Choice (delivered digitally); Pleasure (delivered digitally); College Football (delivered digitally).
Internet Service
Operational: Yes.
Broadband Service: In-house.
Fee: $39.95 monthly.
Telephone Service
Digital: Operational
Miles of Plant: 45.0 (coaxial); 9.0 (fiber optic).
Manager: William Freeman. Chief Technician: Ken Jordan.
City fee: 3% of gross.
Ownership: Troy Cablevision (MSO).

MARGARET—Alabama Broadband LLC, 3447A Parkwood Rd SE, Bessemer, AL 35022. Phones: 877-840-5040; 205-426-3432. E-mail: contact@alabamabroadband.com. Web Site: http://www.alabamabroadband.net. Also serves Argo, Jefferson County (eastern portion), St. Clair County & Trussville. ICA: AL0205.
TV Market Ranking: 40 (Argo, Jefferson County (eastern portion), MARGARET, St. Clair County (portions), Trussville); Below 100 (St. Clair County (portions)). Franchise award date: N.A. Franchise expiration date: N.A. Began: January 1, 1990.
Channel capacity: 45 (operating 2-way). Channels available but not in use: 3.
Basic Service
Subscribers: 443.
Programming (received off-air): WABM (MNT) Birmingham; WBIQ (PBS) Birmingham; WBRC (FOX) Birmingham; WIAT (CBS) Birmingham; WJSU-TV (ABC) Anniston; WPXH-TV (ION) Gadsden; WTJP-TV (TBN) Gadsden; WTTO (CW) Homewood; WVTM-TV (NBC) Birmingham.
Programming (via satellite): ABC Family Channel; AMC; Animal Planet; Arts & Entertainment; CNN; Comcast Sports Net Southeast; Country Music TV; C-SPAN; C-SPAN 2; Discovery Channel; Disney Channel; ESPN; ESPN 2; Fox News Channel; Headline News; HGTV; Home Shopping Network; MTV; National Geographic Channel; Nickelodeon; Outdoor Channel; QVC; Spike TV; TBS Superstation; The Learning Channel; truTV; Turner Network TV; TV Guide Network; USA Network; Weather Channel; WGN America.
Fee: $29.95 installation; $32.20 monthly.
Pay Service 1
Pay Units: 116.
Programming (via satellite): Cinemax; HBO.
Fee: $9.00 monthly (each).
Video-On-Demand: Yes
Internet Service
Operational: Yes.
Subscribers: 25.
Fee: $29.95-$54.95 monthly.
Telephone Service
None
Miles of Plant: 17.0 (coaxial); None (fiber optic).
President: Tom Early.
Ownership: Alabama Broadband LLC (MSO).

MARION—Sky Cablevision, PO Box 65, 1309 Roebuck Dr, Meridian, MS 39301. Phone: 601-485-6980. Fax: 601-483-0103. Web Site: http://skycablevision.com. Also serves Perry County (unincorporated areas). ICA: AL0091.
TV Market Ranking: Below 100 (MARION, Perry County (unincorporated areas)). Franchise award date: N.A. Franchise expiration date: N.A. Began: January 1, 1982.
Channel capacity: N.A. Channels available but not in use: N.A.
Basic Service
Subscribers: 1,500 Includes Eutaw.
Programming (received off-air): WAKA (CBS) Selma; WBIQ (PBS) Birmingham; WBRC (FOX) Birmingham; WCFT-TV (ABC) Tuscaloosa; WCOV-TV (FOX) Montgomery; WNCF (ABC) Montgomery; WSFA (NBC) Montgomery; WTTO (CW) Homewood; WVTM-TV (NBC) Birmingham.
Programming (via satellite): AMC; Animal Planet; Arts & Entertainment; BET Networks; Cartoon Network; CNN; Comcast Sports Net Southeast; Comedy Central; Country Music TV; C-SPAN; Discovery Channel; Disney Channel; E! Entertainment Television; ESPN; ESPN 2; ESPN Classic Sports; Flix; Food Network; Fox Movie Channel; Fox News Channel; FX; Golf Channel; Great American Country; Hallmark Channel; Headline News; HGTV; History Channel; Home Shopping Network; INSP; Lifetime; MTV; Nickelodeon; Outdoor Channel; QVC; SoapNet; Speed Channel; Spike TV; SportSouth; Syfy; TBS Superstation; The Learning Channel; The Sportsman Channel; Trinity Broadcasting Network; truTV; Turner Classic Movies; Turner Network TV; TV Guide Network; TV Land; USA Network; VH1; WE tv; Weather Channel; WGN America.
Fee: $25.00 installation; $31.99 monthly; $3.00 converter.
Pay Service 1
Pay Units: 268.
Programming (via satellite): Cinemax; HBO.
Fee: $7.00 monthly (each).
Pay Service 2
Pay Units: N.A.
Programming (via satellite): Encore (multiplexed); Showtime.
Internet Service
Operational: No.
Telephone Service
None
Miles of Plant: 20.0 (coaxial); None (fiber optic). Additional miles planned: 2.0 (coaxial). Homes passed: 1,384.
Manager & Chief Technician: Berry Ward.
Ownership: Sky Cablevision Ltd. (MSO).

MCKENZIE—Clearview Cable, PO Box 7, 28795 Commerce St, Gantt, AL 36038-0001. Phone: 334-388-2716. Fax: 334-388-2718. ICA: AL0144.
TV Market Ranking: Outside TV Markets (MCKENZIE). Franchise award date: June 1, 1986. Franchise expiration date: N.A. Began: December 23, 1987.
Channel capacity: N.A. Channels available but not in use: N.A.
Basic Service
Subscribers: N.A. Included in Heath
Programming (received off-air): WAKA (CBS) Selma; WCOV-TV (FOX) Montgomery; WDIQ (PBS) Dozier; WIYC (IND) Troy; WNCF (ABC) Montgomery; WSFA (NBC) Montgomery.
Programming (via satellite): ABC Family Channel; Animal Planet; BET Networks; CNBC; CNN; Comcast Sports Net Southeast; Country Music TV; Discovery Channel; ESPN; Fox News Channel; Lifetime; Nickelodeon; Spike TV; Syfy; TBS Superstation; Travel Channel; Turner Network TV; USA Network; WGN America.
Fee: $29.95 installation; $28.45 monthly.
Pay Service 1
Pay Units: N.A. Included in Heath
Programming (via satellite): Cinemax; HBO.
Fee: $10.00 installation; $10.95 monthly (each).
Video-On-Demand: No
Internet Service
Operational: No.
Telephone Service
None
Miles of Plant: 7.0 (coaxial); None (fiber optic). Homes passed: 300. Total homes in franchised area: 350.
Manager: J Mike Russell.
City fee: 3% of gross.
Ownership: Clearview Cable Inc. (MSO).

MENTONE—Charter Communications, 2100 Columbiana Rd, Vestavia, AL 35216. Phone: 205-824-5400. Fax: 706-824-5490. Web Site: http://www.charter.com. ICA: AL0243.
TV Market Ranking: 18 (MENTONE).
Channel capacity: N.A. Channels available but not in use: N.A.
Basic Service
Subscribers: N.A.
Programming (received off-air): WAAY-TV (ABC) Huntsville; WAFF (NBC) Huntsville; WDEF-TV (CBS) Chattanooga; WDSI-TV (FOX, MNT) Chattanooga; WHNT-TV (CBS) Huntsville; WNGH-TV (PBS) Chatsworth; WPXA-TV (ION) Rome; WRCB (NBC) Chattanooga; WTVC (ABC) Chattanooga;

WXIA-TV (NBC) Atlanta; WZDX (FOX, MNT) Huntsville.
Programming (via satellite): C-SPAN; C-SPAN 2; Home Shopping Network; INSP; QVC; Trinity Broadcasting Network; WGN America.
Fee: $29.99 installation.

Expanded Basic Service 1
Subscribers: N.A.
Programming (via satellite): ABC Family Channel; AMC; Animal Planet; Arts & Entertainment; BET Networks; Bravo; Cartoon Network; CNBC; CNN; Comcast Sports Net Southeast; Comcast/Charter Sports Southeast (CSS); Comedy Central; Country Music TV; Discovery Channel; Disney Channel; E! Entertainment Television; ESPN; ESPN 2; Eternal Word TV Network; Food Network; Fox News Channel; FX; G4; GalaVision; Golf Channel; Hallmark Channel; Headline News; HGTV; History Channel; Lifetime; MSNBC; MTV; National Geographic Channel; Nickelodeon; Oxygen; SoapNet; Speed Channel; Spike TV; SportSouth; Syfy; TBS Superstation; Telemundo; The Learning Channel; Toon Disney; Travel Channel; truTV; Turner Classic Movies; Turner Network TV; TV Guide Network; TV Land; USA Network; Versus; VH1; Weather Channel.
Fee: $43.00 monthly.

Digital Basic Service
Subscribers: N.A.
Programming (via satellite): BBC America; Bio; Discovery Digital Networks; Do-It-Yourself; Fox Movie Channel; GAS; Great American Country; History Channel International; Independent Film Channel; Jewelry Television; Lifetime Movie Network; Lifetime Real Women; MTV Networks Digital Suite; Music Choice; Nick Jr.; Nick Too; NickToons TV; Sundance Channel; WE tv.
Fee: $16.99 monthly.

Digital Expanded Basic Service
Subscribers: N.A.
Programming (via satellite): ESPN Classic Sports; ESPNews; Fox College Sports Atlantic; Fox College Sports Central; Fox College Sports Pacific; Fox Soccer; Fuel TV; Jewelry Television; NFL Network.

Digital Pay Service 1
Pay Units: N.A.
Programming (via satellite): Cinemax (multiplexed); HBO (multiplexed); Starz (multiplexed).

Video-On-Demand: No

Internet Service
Operational: Yes.
Broadband Service: Charter Pipeline.
Fee: $29.99 monthly.

Telephone Service
Digital: Operational

Vice President & General Manager: Don Karell. Technical Operations Director: Greg Prim. Marketing Director: David Redmond. Marketing Manager: Jeff Hatcher.
Ownership: Charter Communications Inc. (MSO).

MEXIA—Formerly served by Galaxy Cablevision. No longer in operation. ICA: AL0261.

MILLPORT—Northland Cable Television, PO Box 1269, 307 1st St, Reform, AL 35481. Phones: 800-828-8019; 662-323-1615. Fax: 205-373-8704. E-mail: aliceville@northlandcabletv.com. Web Site: http://www.northlandcabletv.com. Also serves Kennedy. ICA: AL0125.
TV Market Ranking: Below 100 (Kennedy, MILLPORT). Franchise award date: N.A. Franchise expiration date: N.A. Began: August 1, 1982.
Channel capacity: N.A. Channels available but not in use: N.A.

Basic Service
Subscribers: 663.
Programming (received off-air): WBIQ (PBS) Birmingham; WBRC (FOX) Birmingham; WCBI-TV (CBS, CW, MNT) Columbus; WCFT-TV (ABC) Tuscaloosa; WDBB (CW) Bessemer; WKDH (ABC) Houston; WLOV-TV (FOX) West Point; WTVA (NBC) Tupelo; WVTM-TV (NBC) Birmingham.
Programming (via satellite): ABC Family Channel; Arts & Entertainment; BET Networks; Bloomberg Television; Cartoon Network; CNN; Comcast Sports Net Southeast; Comedy Central; C-SPAN; Discovery Channel; ESPN; ESPN 2; Food Network; Fox Movie Channel; Fox News Channel; FX; Golf Channel; Great American Country; Hallmark Channel; Headline News; HGTV; History Channel; Lifetime; Nickelodeon; Outdoor Channel; QVC; Speed Channel; Spike TV; TBS Superstation; Trinity Broadcasting Network; Turner Classic Movies; Turner Network TV; Turner South; TV Land; USA Network; WE tv; Weather Channel; WGN America.
Fee: $25.00 installation; $54.99 monthly; $3.00 converter.

Digital Basic Service
Subscribers: N.A.
Programming (via satellite): BBC America; Discovery Health Channel; Discovery Home Channel; Discovery Kids Channel; Discovery Military Channel; Discovery Times Channel; DMX Music; ESPNews; Fox Soccer; National Geographic Channel; Science Channel; Versus.
Fee: $10.00 monthly.

Pay Service 1
Pay Units: 114.
Programming (via satellite): Cinemax.
Fee: $11.50 monthly.

Pay Service 2
Pay Units: 113.
Programming (via satellite): HBO.
Fee: $12.50 monthly.

Digital Pay Service 1
Pay Units: N.A.
Programming (via satellite): Cinemax (multiplexed); Encore (multiplexed); Flix; HBO (multiplexed); Showtime (multiplexed); Starz (multiplexed); The Movie Channel (multiplexed).
Fee: $14.75 monthly (HBO, Cinemax, Starz/Encore or Showtime/TMC/Flix).

Video-On-Demand: Planned

Pay-Per-View
iN DEMAND (delivered digitally); Playboy TV (delivered digitally); Fresh (delivered digitally); Hot Choice (delivered digitally).

Internet Service
Operational: Yes.
Fee: $42.99 monthly.

Telephone Service
None

Miles of Plant: 29.0 (coaxial); None (fiber optic). Homes passed: 733.
Chief Technician: Bart Hudgins. Regional Manager: Ricky Moneyham. Manager: Pam Parham. Marketing Director: Lee Beck.
Ownership: Northland Communications Corp. (MSO).

MILLRY—Sky Cablevision. No longer in operation. ICA: AL0207.

MOBILE—Comcast Cable, 3248 Springhill Ave, Mobile, AL 36607-1831. Phone: 251-476-2190. Fax: 251-665-6670. Web Site: http://www.comcast.com. Also serves Chickasaw, Mobile County, Prichard & Saraland. ICA: AL0002.
TV Market Ranking: 59 (Chickasaw, MOBILE, Mobile County, Prichard, Saraland). Franchise award date: N.A. Franchise expiration date: N.A. Began: July 1, 1971.
Channel capacity: N.A. Channels available but not in use: None.

Basic Service
Subscribers: 69,000 Includes Dauphin Island.
Programming (received off-air): WALA-TV (FOX) Mobile; WEAR-TV (ABC) Pensacola; WEIQ (PBS) Mobile; WHBR (IND) Pensacola; WJTC (IND) Pensacola; WKRG-TV (CBS) Mobile; WMPV-TV (TBN) Mobile; WPMI-TV (NBC) Mobile.
Programming (via satellite): Headline News.
Current originations: Religious Access; Government Access; Educational Access.
Fee: $62.99 installation; $9.10 monthly.

Expanded Basic Service 1
Subscribers: 65,116.
Programming (via satellite): ABC Family Channel; AMC; Animal Planet; Arts & Entertainment; BET Networks; Bravo; Cartoon Network; CNBC; CNN; Comcast Sports Net Southeast; Comcast/Charter Sports Southeast (CSS); Comedy Central; Country Music TV; C-SPAN; C-SPAN 2; Discovery Channel; Discovery Health Channel; E! Entertainment Television; ESPN; ESPN 2; ESPN Classic Sports; Eternal Word TV Network; Food Network; Fox News Channel; FX; G4; Golf Channel; Gospel Music Channel; Great American Country; GSN; Hallmark Channel; HGTV; History Channel; Home Shopping Network; MSNBC; MTV; Nickelodeon; Outdoor Channel; QVC; Speed Channel; Spike TV; SportSouth; Style Network; Syfy; TBS Superstation; The Learning Channel; Travel Channel; truTV; Turner Classic Movies; Turner Network TV; TV Guide Network; TV Land; TV One; USA Network; VH1; Weather Channel; WGN America.
Fee: $40.89 monthly.

Digital Basic Service
Subscribers: 16,375 Includes Dauphin Island.
Programming (received off-air): WEAR-TV (ABC) Pensacola; WEIQ (PBS) Mobile; WKRG-TV (CBS) Mobile; WPMI-TV (NBC) Mobile.
Programming (via satellite): BBC America; Bio; CMT Pure Country; Cooking Channel; C-SPAN 3; Current; Discovery Channel HD; Discovery Kids Channel; Discovery Military Channel; Discovery Planet Green; Disney Channel; DMX Music; Do-It-Yourself; Encore (multiplexed); ESPN HD; ESPNews; Flix; FSN HD; History Channel International; ID Investigation Discovery; Lifetime Movie Network; MoviePlex; MTV Hits; MTV Tres; MTV2; National Geographic Channel; NFL Network; Nick Jr.; Nick Too; NickToons TV; PBS Kids Sprout; Retro Television Network; Science Channel; SoapNet; Sundance Channel; TeenNick; Toon Disney; Turner Network TV HD; VH1 Classic; VH1 Soul.
Fee: $14.95 monthly.

Pay Service 1
Pay Units: 3,916.
Programming (via satellite): Cinemax; HBO (multiplexed); Showtime.
Fee: $10.95 monthly (each).

Digital Pay Service 1
Pay Units: N.A.
Programming (via satellite): Cinemax (multiplexed); Cinemax HD; HBO (multiplexed); HBO HD; Showtime (multiplexed); Showtime HD; Starz (multiplexed); Starz HDTV; The Movie Channel (multiplexed).
Fee: $14.05 monthly (each).

Video-On-Demand: Yes

Pay-Per-View
Addressable homes: 15,443.
iN DEMAND, Addressable: Yes; iN DEMAND (delivered digitally); Hot Choice (delivered digitally); Playboy TV (delivered digitally); Pleasure (delivered digitally).

Internet Service
Operational: Yes.
Broadband Service: Comcast High Speed Internet.
Fee: $42.95 monthly; $7.00 modem lease.

Telephone Service
Digital: Operational

Miles of Plant: 1,200.0 (coaxial); 100.0 (fiber optic). Additional miles planned: 20.0 (coaxial); 15.0 (fiber optic). Homes passed: 118,000. Total homes in franchised area: 126,000. Homes passed & total homes in franchised area include Dauphin Island
General Manager: Ray Kistler. Technical Operations Manager: Jan Murray.
City fee: 5% of gross.
Ownership: Comcast Cable Communications Inc. (MSO).

MOBILE COUNTY—Formerly served by Charter Communications. No longer in operation. ICA: AL0037.

MOBILE COUNTY—Mediacom, 7325 Theodore Dawes Rd, Ste 7, Theodore, AL 36582-4029. Phones: 800-239-8411 (Customer service); 850-934-7700. Fax: 850-932-9237. Web Site: http://www.mediacomcable.com. Also serves Bayou la Batre, Citronelle, Creola, Grand Bay, Irvington, McIntosh, Mount Vernon, Satsuma, Semmes, Theodore, Tillman's Corner, Washington County (unincorporated areas) & Wilmer. ICA: AL0017.
TV Market Ranking: 59 (Bayou la Batre, Citronelle, Creola, Grand Bay, Irvington, MOBILE COUNTY, Mount Vernon, Satsuma, Semmes, Theodore, Tillman's Corner, Wilmer); Outside TV Markets (McIntosh, Washington County (unincorporated areas)). Franchise award date: January 27, 1981. Franchise expiration date: N.A. Began: October 21, 1981.
Channel capacity: N.A. Channels available but not in use: N.A.

Basic Service
Subscribers: 11,254.
Programming (received off-air): WALA-TV (FOX) Mobile; WEAR-TV (ABC) Pensacola; WEIQ (PBS) Mobile; WFNA (CW) Gulf Shores; WHBR (IND) Pensacola; WJTC (IND) Pensacola; WKRG-TV (CBS) Mobile; WMPV-TV (TBN) Mobile; WPMI-TV (NBC) Mobile.
Programming (via satellite): ABC Family Channel; AMC; Animal Planet; Arts & Entertainment; BET Networks; Cartoon Network; CNBC; CNN; Comcast Sports Net Southeast; Comedy Central; Country Music TV; C-SPAN; Discovery Channel; Disney Channel; E! Entertainment Television; ESPN; ESPN 2; Eternal Word TV Network; Fox News Channel; FX; Golf Channel; Hallmark Channel; Headline News; HGTV; History Channel; Home Shopping Network; INSP; ION Television; Lifetime; Lifetime Movie Network; MSNBC; MTV; Nickelodeon;

Outdoor Channel; QVC; SoapNet; Speed Channel; Spike TV; SportSouth; Syfy; TBS Superstation; The Learning Channel; Toon Disney; Travel Channel; truTV; Turner Classic Movies; Turner Network TV; TV Guide Network; USA Network; VH1; WE tv; Weather Channel; WGN America.

Fee: $32.00 installation; $44.95 monthly.

Digital Basic Service

Subscribers: 3,132.

Programming (via satellite): ABC News Now; AmericanLife TV Network; BBC America; Bio; Bloomberg Television; CNN HD; Discovery HD Theater; Discovery Health Channel; Discovery Home Channel; Discovery Kids Channel; Discovery Military Channel; ESPN HD; ESPNews; Fox Movie Channel; Fox Soccer; Fuse; G4; Great American Country; GSN; Halogen Network; HDNet; HDNet Movies; History Channel International; ID Investigation Discovery; Independent Film Channel; ION Life; Lifetime Movie Network; MTV Hits; MTV2; Music Choice; National Geographic Channel; Nick Jr.; NickToons TV; Outdoor Channel; Qubo; ReelzChannel; Science Channel; Sleuth; Style Network; TBS in HD; TeenNick; Turner Network TV HD; TVG Network; Universal HD; VH1 Classic; Weatherscan.

Fee: $12.00 monthly.

Digital Pay Service 1

Pay Units: 2,371.

Programming (via satellite): Cinemax (multiplexed); HBO HD; Showtime HD.

Fee: $10.45 monthly.

Digital Pay Service 2

Pay Units: 4,411.

Programming (via satellite): HBO (multiplexed).

Digital Pay Service 3

Pay Units: 3,959.

Programming (via satellite): Showtime (multiplexed).

Fee: $10.45 monthly.

Digital Pay Service 4

Pay Units: 2,346.

Programming (via satellite): Flix; Sundance Channel; The Movie Channel (multiplexed).

Fee: $10.45 monthly.

Digital Pay Service 5

Pay Units: 4,909.

Programming (via satellite): Encore (multiplexed); Starz (multiplexed).

Fee: $10.45 monthly.

Video-On-Demand: Planned

Pay-Per-View

Addressable homes: 3,132.

ESPN Extra (delivered digitally), Addressable: Yes; ESPN Now (delivered digitally); Pleasure (delivered digitally); iN DEMAND (delivered digitally); Playboy TV (delivered digitally).

Internet Service

Operational: Yes.

Subscribers: 2,254.

Broadband Service: Mediacom High Speed Internet.

Fee: $40.95 monthly; $5.00 modem lease.

Telephone Service

Analog: Not Operational

Digital: Operational

Fee: $29.95 monthly

Miles of Plant: 532.0 (coaxial); None (fiber optic). Homes passed: 24,346.

Manager: David Fyffe. Marketing Director: Steve Purcell. Chief Technician: Garry Evans. Customer Service Manager: Judy Smythe.

City fee: 3% of gross.

Ownership: Mediacom LLC (MSO).

MONROEVILLE—Mediacom. Now served by CAMDEN, AL [AL0112]. ICA: AL0052.

MONTGOMERY—Charter Communications, 2100 Columbiana Rd, Vestavia, AL 35216. Phone: 205-824-5400. Fax: 205-824-5490. Web Site: http://www.charter.com. Also serves Autauga County, Elmore County, Montgomery County & Prattville. ICA: AL0003.

TV Market Ranking: Below 100 (Autauga County, Elmore County, MONTGOMERY, Montgomery County, Prattville). Franchise award date: January 1, 1969. Franchise expiration date: N.A. Began: July 1, 1977.

Channel capacity: N.A. Channels available but not in use: N.A.

Basic Service

Subscribers: 77,500.

Programming (received off-air): WAIQ (PBS) Montgomery; WAKA (CBS) Selma; WBIH (IND) Selma; WCOV-TV (FOX) Montgomery; WETU-LP Wetumpka; WIYC (IND) Troy; WMCF-TV (TBN) Montgomery; WNCF (ABC) Montgomery; WSFA (NBC) Montgomery; 30 FMs.

Programming (via satellite): Weather Channel; WGN America.

Current originations: Leased Access; Government Access; Educational Access; Public Access.

Fee: $29.99 installation.

Expanded Basic Service 1

Subscribers: 49,742.

Programming (via satellite): ABC Family Channel; AMC; Animal Planet; Arts & Entertainment; BET Networks; Bravo; Cartoon Network; CNBC; CNN; Comcast Sports Net Southeast; Comcast/Charter Sports Southeast (CSS); Comedy Central; Country Music TV; C-SPAN; C-SPAN 2; Discovery Channel; Disney Channel; E! Entertainment Television; ESPN; ESPN 2; Eternal Word TV Network; Food Network; Fox News Channel; FX; Golf Channel; Hallmark Channel; Headline News; HGTV; History Channel; Home Shopping Network; Lifetime; MSNBC; MTV; National Geographic Channel; Nickelodeon; Oxygen; QVC; Shop at Home; SoapNet; Speed Channel; Spike TV; SportSouth; Syfy; TBS Superstation; The Learning Channel; Travel Channel; truTV; Turner Network TV; TV Guide Network; TV Land; Univision; USA Network; VH1; WE tv.

Fee: $43.00 monthly.

Digital Basic Service

Subscribers: N.A.

Programming (via satellite): AmericanLife TV Network; BBC America; Bio; Bloomberg Television; Canales N; Discovery Digital Networks; DMX Music; ESPN Classic Sports; ESPNews; Fox Movie Channel; Fox Sports World; G4; GAS; Great American Country; GSN; Halogen Network; History Channel; History Channel International; Independent Film Channel; Lifetime Movie Network; MTV Networks Digital Suite; MuchMusic Network; Nick Jr.; Outdoor Channel; Style Network; Sundance Channel; Toon Disney; Trinity Broadcasting Network; Turner Classic Movies; TV Guide Interactive Inc.; Versus.

Fee: $16.99 monthly.

Digital Pay Service 1

Pay Units: N.A.

Programming (via satellite): Cinemax (multiplexed); HBO (multiplexed); Showtime (multiplexed); Starz (multiplexed); The Movie Channel (multiplexed).

Video-On-Demand: Yes

Pay-Per-View

iN DEMAND (delivered digitally); Playboy TV (delivered digitally); Fresh (delivered digitally); Shorteez (delivered digitally); Urban Xtra (delivered digitally).

Internet Service

Operational: Yes.

Subscribers: 6,000.

Broadband Service: Charter Pipeline.

Fee: $29.99 monthly; $10.00 modem lease.

Telephone Service

Digital: Operational

Miles of Plant: 970.0 (coaxial); 51.0 (fiber optic).

Vice President & General Manager: Don Karell. Technical Operations Director: Greg Prim. Marketing Director: David Redmond. Marketing Manager: Jeff Hatcher.

City fee: 3% of gross.

Ownership: Charter Communications Inc. (MSO).

MONTGOMERY—Knology, 1637 Eastern Blvd, Montgomery, AL 36117. Phones: 706-645-8553 (Corporate office); 334-356-1000 (Customer service). Fax: 334-356-1001. Web Site: http://www.knology.com. Also serves Maxwell AFB, Pike Road & Prattville. ICA: AL0015. **Note:** This system is an overbuild.

TV Market Ranking: Below 100 (Maxwell AFB, MONTGOMERY, Pike Road, Prattville). Franchise award date: April 5, 1990. Franchise expiration date: N.A. Began: September 28, 1990.

Channel capacity: N.A. Channels available but not in use: N.A.

Basic Service

Subscribers: 27,242.

Programming (received off-air): WAIQ (PBS) Montgomery; WAKA (CBS) Selma; WBIH (IND) Selma; WBMM (CW) Tuskegee; WCOV-TV (FOX) Montgomery; WIYC (IND) Troy; WMCF-TV (TBN) Montgomery; WNCF (ABC) Montgomery; WSFA (NBC) Montgomery.

Programming (via satellite): ABC Family Channel; AMC; Animal Planet; Arts & Entertainment; BET Networks; Bravo; Cartoon Network; CNBC; CNN; Comcast Sports Net Southeast; Comedy Central; Country Music TV; C-SPAN; C-SPAN 2; Discovery Channel; Discovery Health Channel; Disney Channel; E! Entertainment Television; ESPN; ESPN 2; ESPN Classic Sports; Food Network; Fox News Channel; FX; G4; Golf Channel; Hallmark Channel; Headline News; HGTV; History Channel; Home Shopping Network; Lifetime; Lifetime Movie Network; MSNBC; MTV; Nick At Nite; Nickelodeon; Outdoor Channel; Oxygen; QVC; ShopNBC; Spike TV; SportSouth; Syfy; TBS Superstation; The Learning Channel; Toon Disney; Travel Channel; truTV; Turner Classic Movies; Turner Network TV; TV Guide Network; TV Land; Univision; USA Network; VH1; Weather Channel; WGN America.

Current originations: Religious Access; Public Access.

Planned originations: Educational Access.

Fee: $44.95 monthly; $3.50 converter.

Digital Basic Service

Subscribers: N.A. Included in Valley

Programming (received off-air): ESPN 2 HD; QVC HD; WAKA (CBS) Selma; WCOV-TV (FOX) Montgomery; WNCF (ABC) Montgomery; WSFA (NBC) Montgomery.

Programming (via satellite): BBC America; Bloomberg Television; Boomerang; Church Channel; CMT Pure Country; C-SPAN 3; Discovery Channel HD; Discovery HD Theater; Discovery Kids Channel; Discovery Military Channel; Discovery Planet Green; ESPN HD; ESPN U; Eternal Word TV Network; FitTV; FSN HD; Gospel Music Channel; GSN; Hallmark Movie Channel; HDNet; HDNet Movies; ID Investigation Discovery; Independent Film Channel; INSP; JCTV; Jewelry Television; Lifetime Real Women; MBC America; MTV Hits; MTV Jams; MTV Tres; MTV2; mtvU; Music Choice; NASA TV; National Geographic Channel; National Geographic Channel HD Network; NFL Network; Nick Jr.; Nick Too; NickToons TV; PBS HD; Pentagon Channel; Retro Television Network; Science Channel; Science Channel HD; SoapNet; Speed Channel; TBS in HD; TeenNick; TLC HD; Turner Network TV HD; Universal HD; Versus; Versus HD; VH1 Classic; VH1 Soul; WE tv.

Digital Expanded Basic Service

Subscribers: N.A.

Programming (via satellite): CBS College Sports Network; ESPNews; Fox College Sports Atlantic; Fox College Sports Central; Fox College Sports Pacific; Fox Soccer; Fuel TV; Tennis Channel; The Sportsman Channel.

Pay Service 1

Pay Units: 2,800.

Programming (via satellite): Showtime.

Fee: $6.95 monthly.

Pay Service 2

Pay Units: 2,100.

Programming (via satellite): HBO.

Fee: $10.95 monthly.

Digital Pay Service 1

Pay Units: N.A.

Programming (via satellite): Cinemax (multiplexed); Cinemax HD; Encore (multiplexed); Flix; HBO (multiplexed); HBO HD; Showtime (multiplexed); Showtime HD; Starz (multiplexed); Starz HDTV; Sundance Channel; The Movie Channel (multiplexed).

Video-On-Demand: Yes

Pay-Per-View

Addressable homes: 4,151.

iN DEMAND (delivered digitally), Addressable: Yes; Hot Choice (delivered digitally); ESPN Extra (delivered digitally); Pleasure (delivered digitally); Playboy TV (delivered digitally); Fresh (delivered digitally); Shorteez (delivered digitally); Spice: Xcess (delivered digitally); Club Jenna (delivered digitally); ESPN Now (delivered digitally).

Internet Service

Operational: Yes.

Broadband Service: Knology.Net.

Fee: $29.95 installation; $59.95 monthly.

Telephone Service

Analog: Not Operational

Digital: Operational

Fee: $24.15 monthly

Miles of Plant: 270.0 (coaxial); 40.0 (fiber optic). Additional miles planned: 900.0 (coaxial); 900.0 (fiber optic). Homes passed: 90,800.

General Manager: Art Loescher. Technical Operations Manager: Toby Carroll. Marketing Manager: Richard Coats.

City fee: 5% of gross.

Ownership: Knology Inc. (MSO).

MORGAN CITY—Charter Communications. Now served by GUNTERSVILLE, AL [AL0033]. ICA: AL0093.

MOULTON—Charter Communications, 2100 Columbiana Rd, Vestavia, AL 35216. Phone: 205-824-5400. Fax: 205-824-5490. Web Site: http://www.charter.com. Also serves Lawrence County (portions). ICA: AL0252.

TV Market Ranking: 96 (Lawrence County (portions), MOULTON). Franchise award

date: N.A. Franchise expiration date: N.A. Began: N.A.
Channel capacity: N.A. Channels available but not in use: N.A.
Basic Service
Subscribers: 1,000.
Programming (received off-air): WAAY-TV (ABC) Huntsville; WAFF (NBC) Huntsville; WBRC (FOX) Birmingham; WHDF (CW) Florence; WHIQ (PBS) Huntsville; WHNT-TV (CBS) Huntsville; WZDX (FOX, MNT) Huntsville.
Programming (via satellite): C-SPAN; C-SPAN 2; TBS Superstation; The Learning Channel; WGN America.
Fee: $29.99 installation.
Expanded Basic Service 1
Subscribers: N.A.
Programming (via satellite): ABC Family Channel; AMC; Animal Planet; Arts & Entertainment; BET Networks; Cartoon Network; CNBC; CNN; Comcast Sports Net Southeast; Comcast/Charter Sports Southeast (CSS); Comedy Central; Country Music TV; Discovery Channel; Disney Channel; ESPN; ESPN 2; Food Network; Fox News Channel; Golf Channel; Hallmark Channel; HGTV; History Channel; Home Shopping Network; Lifetime; MTV; Nickelodeon; Product Information Network; Speed Channel; Spike TV; Syfy; Toon Disney; Trinity Broadcasting Network; Turner Classic Movies; Turner Network TV; TV Guide Network; TV Land; USA Network; VH1; WE tv; Weather Channel.
Fee: $43.00 monthly.
Digital Basic Service
Subscribers: N.A.
Programming (via satellite): BBC America; Discovery Digital Networks; GAS; MTV Networks Digital Suite; Music Choice; Nick Jr.; Nick Too; NickToons TV; Sundance Channel.
Fee: $16.99 monthly.
Digital Pay Service 1
Pay Units: N.A.
Programming (via satellite): Cinemax (multiplexed); Encore (multiplexed); Flix; HBO (multiplexed); Showtime (multiplexed); Starz (multiplexed); The Movie Channel (multiplexed).
Video-On-Demand: Yes
Pay-Per-View
iN DEMAND; iN DEMAND (delivered digitally).
Internet Service
Operational: Yes.
Broadband Service: Charter Pipeline.
Fee: $29.99 monthly.
Telephone Service
Digital: Operational
Vice President & General Manager: Don Karell. Technical Operations Director: Greg Prim. Marketing Director: David Redmond. Marketing Manager: Jeff Hatcher.
Ownership: Charter Communications Inc. (MSO).

NAUVOO—Formerly served by Galaxy Cablevision. No longer in operation. ICA: AL0210.

NEW HOPE—New Hope Telephone Cooperative, PO Box 452, 5415 Main Dr, New Hope, AL 35760. Phone: 256-723-4211. Fax: 256-723-2800. Web Site: http://www.nehp.net. Also serves Grant, Madison County (portions), Marshall County (portions) & Owens Cross Roads. ICA: AL0070.
TV Market Ranking: 96 (Grant, Madison County (portions), Marshall County (portions), NEW HOPE, Owens Cross Roads). Franchise award date: N.A. Franchise expiration date: N.A. Began: October 1, 1966.
Channel capacity: N.A. Channels available but not in use: N.A.
Basic Service
Subscribers: N.A.
Programming (received off-air): WAAY-TV (ABC) Huntsville; WAFF (NBC) Huntsville; WHIQ (PBS) Huntsville; WHNT-TV (CBS) Huntsville; WZDX (FOX, MNT) Huntsville.
Programming (via satellite): ABC Family Channel; AMC; Animal Planet; Arts & Entertainment; Bravo; Cartoon Network; CNN; Comcast Sports Net Southeast; Comedy Central; Country Music TV; C-SPAN; C-SPAN 2; Discovery Channel; Disney Channel; E! Entertainment Television; ESPN; ESPN 2; Food Network; Fox News Channel; Fox Sports World; FX; G4; Hallmark Channel; Headline News; HGTV; History Channel; Home Shopping Network; Lifetime; MTV; Nickelodeon; Outdoor Channel; Oxygen; Speed Channel; Spike TV; Syfy; TBS Superstation; The Learning Channel; Travel Channel; Trinity Broadcasting Network; truTV; Turner Classic Movies; Turner Network TV; Turner South; TV Guide Network; TV Land; USA Network; VH1; WE tv; Weather Channel; WGN America.
Fee: $30.00 installation; $44.00 monthly; $20.00 additional installation.
Video-On-Demand: No
Internet Service
Operational: No, DSL & dial-up.
Telephone Service
None
Miles of Plant: 68.0 (coaxial); None (fiber optic). Homes passed: 2,250. Total homes in franchised area: 4,500.
General Manager: Tom Wing. Outside Plant Manager: Tim Wright. Marketing Manager: Misty Williams. Office Manager: Tammy Weeks.
City fee: None.
Ownership: New Hope Telephone Cooperative.

NORTH BREWTON—Formerly served by CableSouth Inc. No longer in operation. ICA: AL0238.

NOTASULGA—Com-Link Inc., 206 Hardaway Ave E, Union Springs, AL 36089-1609. Phones: 800-722-2805; 334-738-2204. Fax: 334-738-5555. Web Site: http://www.ustconline.net. Also serves Lee County (portions), Loachapoka & Macon County (portions). ICA: AL0135.
TV Market Ranking: Below 100 (Lee County (portions), Loachapoka, Macon County (portions), NOTASULGA). Franchise award date: June 3, 1988. Franchise expiration date: N.A. Began: August 30, 1988.
Channel capacity: 35 (not 2-way capable). Channels available but not in use: 10.
Basic Service
Subscribers: 303.
Programming (received off-air): WAIQ (PBS) Montgomery; WAKA (CBS) Selma; WCOV-TV (FOX) Montgomery; WMCF-TV (TBN) Montgomery; WNCF (ABC) Montgomery; WSFA (NBC) Montgomery.
Programming (via satellite): CNN; ESPN; TBS Superstation; WGN America.
Fee: $35.00 installation; $19.94 monthly.
Expanded Basic Service 1
Subscribers: N.A.
Programming (via satellite): ABC Family Channel; Arts & Entertainment; Comcast Sports Net Southeast; Discovery Channel; ESPN 2; Headline News; Lifetime; MTV; Nickelodeon; Spike TV; Turner Network TV; USA Network.
Fee: $7.30 monthly.
Pay Service 1
Pay Units: 53.
Programming (via satellite): Cinemax.
Fee: $10.00 monthly.
Pay Service 2
Pay Units: 68.
Programming (via satellite): HBO.
Fee: $10.00 monthly.
Video-On-Demand: No
Internet Service
Operational: No, DSL only.
Telephone Service
None
Miles of Plant: 30.0 (coaxial); None (fiber optic). Homes passed: 700.
Executive Vice President: Larry Grogan. Chief Technician: Lynn Rotton.
City fee: 0% of gross.
Ownership: Com-Link Inc. (MSO).

OAKMAN—Formerly served by Almega Cable. No longer in operation. ICA: AL0239.

ODENVILLE—Coosa Cable. Now served by PELL CITY, AL [AL0212]. ICA: AL0104.

ONEONTA—Otelco Telephone Co., 505 3rd Ave E, Oneonta, AL 35121-1557. Phone: 205-625-3591. Fax: 205-625-3523. E-mail: info@otelco.net. Web Site: http://www.otelco.net. ICA: AL0049.
TV Market Ranking: 40 (ONEONTA). Franchise award date: January 1, 1972. Franchise expiration date: N.A. Began: January 1, 1975.
Channel capacity: 40 (operating 2-way). Channels available but not in use: 4.
Basic Service
Subscribers: 3,840.
Programming (received off-air): WABM (MNT) Birmingham; WBIQ (PBS) Birmingham; WBRC (FOX) Birmingham; WIAT (CBS) Birmingham; WTJP-TV (TBN) Gadsden; WTTO (CW) Homewood; WVTM-TV (NBC) Birmingham; WZDX (FOX, MNT) Huntsville; 1 FM.
Programming (via satellite): ABC Family Channel; Animal Planet; Arts & Entertainment; Bravo; Cartoon Network; CNBC; CNN; Comedy Central; Country Music TV; C-SPAN; C-SPAN 2; Discovery Channel; Discovery Health Channel; Disney Channel; Do-It-Yourself; E! Entertainment Television; ESPN; ESPN 2; ESPN Classic Sports; FitTV; Food Network; Fox News Channel; Fox Sports Net; FX; Golf Channel; GSN; Hallmark Channel; Headline News; HGTV; History Channel; Home Shopping Network; Lifetime; MSNBC; MTV; National Geographic Channel; Nickelodeon; Paxson Communications Corp.; QVC; Spike TV; SportSouth; Syfy; TBS Superstation; The Learning Channel; The Sportsman Channel; Toon Disney; Travel Channel; truTV; Turner Classic Movies; Turner Network TV; TV Land; Univision; USA Network; VH1; Weather Channel; WGN America.
Fee: $25.00 installation; $40.95 monthly.
Digital Basic Service
Subscribers: N.A.
Programming (via satellite): BBC America; Bio; Bloomberg Television; CBS College Sports Network; Discovery Digital Networks; DMX Music; ESPNews; Fox College Sports Atlantic; Fox College Sports Central; Fox College Sports Pacific; Fox Movie Channel; Fox Soccer; Fuse; G4; GAS; Great American Country; Halogen Network; History Channel International; Lifetime Movie Network; MTV Networks Digital Suite; Nick Jr.; NickToons TV; Outdoor Channel; Speed Channel; Sundance Channel; Versus; WE tv.
Fee: $11.95 monthly.
Digital Expanded Basic Service
Subscribers: N.A.
Programming (via satellite): Canales N.
Fee: $7.95 monthly.
Pay Service 1
Pay Units: N.A.
Programming (via satellite): HBO.
Fee: $13.95 monthly.
Digital Pay Service 1
Pay Units: 222.
Programming (via satellite): Cinemax (multiplexed); HBO (multiplexed).
Fee: $16.95 monthly.
Digital Pay Service 2
Pay Units: 243.
Programming (via satellite): Encore (multiplexed); Starz (multiplexed).
Fee: $10.00 monthly.
Digital Pay Service 3
Pay Units: N.A.
Programming (via satellite): Showtime (multiplexed); The Movie Channel (multiplexed).
Fee: $15.95 monthly.
Video-On-Demand: No
Pay-Per-View
iN DEMAND (delivered digitally).
Internet Service
Operational: Yes, Dial-up only.
Subscribers: 1,125.
Broadband Service: Otelco.
Fee: $39.95 monthly.
Telephone Service
None
Miles of Plant: 150.0 (coaxial); None (fiber optic). Homes passed: 8,227. Total homes in franchised area: 8,227.
President: Mike Weaver. Accounting: Stacey Willis.
Ownership: Oneonta Telephone Co. Inc.

OPP—Opp Cablevision, PO Box 610, Opp, AL 36467-0610. Phone: 334-493-4571. Fax: 334-493-6666. Web Site: http://www.oppcatv.com. Also serves Horn Hill, Kinston & Onycha. ICA: AL0050.
TV Market Ranking: Below 100 (Kinston); Outside TV Markets (Horn Hill, Onycha, OPP). Franchise award date: N.A. Franchise expiration date: N.A. Began: August 1, 1967.
Channel capacity: N.A. Channels available but not in use: N.A.
Basic Service
Subscribers: 3,434.
Programming (received off-air): WAKA (CBS) Selma; WDIQ (PBS) Dozier; WNCF (ABC) Montgomery; WSFA (NBC) Montgomery; WTVY (CBS, CW, MNT) Dothan.
Programming (via satellite): ABC Family Channel; AMC; Arts & Entertainment; BET Networks; CNBC; CNN; Comcast Sports Net Southeast; Country Music TV; C-SPAN; Discovery Channel; Disney Channel; ESPN; Headline News; HGTV; Home Shopping Network; Lifetime; MSNBC; MTV; Nickelodeon; Spike TV; Syfy; TBS Superstation; The Learning Channel; Travel Channel; Trinity Broadcasting Network; Turner Classic Movies; Turner Network TV; TV Guide Network; USA Network; VH1; Weather Channel; WGN America.
Fee: $15.00 installation; $20.00 monthly.
Pay Service 1
Pay Units: 231.
Programming (via satellite): HBO.
Fee: $10.00 installation; $10.00 monthly.

Pay Service 2
Pay Units: 55.
Programming (via satellite): Cinemax.
Fee: $9.00 monthly.
Pay Service 3
Pay Units: 21.
Programming (via satellite): Showtime; The Movie Channel.
Fee: $9.00 monthly.
Video-On-Demand: No
Pay-Per-View
Addressable homes: 120.
Addressable: Yes.
Internet Service
Operational: Yes. Began: January 1, 2000.
Subscribers: 507.
Broadband Service: Gill Blue.
Fee: $45.00 installation; $24.95 monthly; $125.00 modem purchase.
Telephone Service
None
Miles of Plant: 194.0 (coaxial); 12.0 (fiber optic). Homes passed: 3,600. Total homes in franchised area: 4,000.
Ownership: Opp Cablevision.

ORRVILLE—Galaxy Cablevision, PO Box 879, 118 S Jackson St, Grove Hill, AL 36451-0879. Phone: 251-275-3118. Fax: 251-275-3120. Web Site: http://www.galaxycable.com. ICA: AL0158.
TV Market Ranking: Below 100 (ORRVILLE). Franchise award date: December 6, 1988. Franchise expiration date: N.A. Began: November 1, 1989.
Channel capacity: 54 (not 2-way capable). Channels available but not in use: 25.
Basic Service
Subscribers: 39.
Programming (received off-air): WAKA (CBS) Selma; WCOV-TV (FOX) Montgomery; WIIQ (PBS) Demopolis; WMCF-TV (TBN) Montgomery; WNCF (ABC) Montgomery; WSFA (NBC) Montgomery.
Programming (via satellite): ABC Family Channel; AMC; Arts & Entertainment; BET Networks; Cartoon Network; CNN; Discovery Channel; Disney Channel; E! Entertainment Television; ESPN; ESPN 2; Great American Country; Headline News; Outdoor Channel; QVC; SportSouth; TBS Superstation; The Learning Channel; Trinity Broadcasting Network; Turner Network TV; USA Network; Weather Channel.
Fee: $25.00 installation; $39.60 monthly.
Pay Service 1
Pay Units: N.A.
Programming (via satellite): HBO.
Fee: $25.00 installation; $9.95 monthly.
Internet Service
Operational: No.
Telephone Service
None
Miles of Plant: 12.0 (coaxial); None (fiber optic). Homes passed: 289.
State Manager: Bill Flowers. Technical Manager & Engineer: Greg Berthaut. Customer Service Representative: Lisa Ray.
Ownership: Galaxy Cable Inc. (MSO).

OWENS CROSS ROADS—New Hope Telephone Cooperative. Now served by NEW HOPE, AL [AL0070]. ICA: AL0263.

OZARK—Charter Communications. Now served by TROY, AL [AL0027]. ICA: AL0211.

PELL CITY—Coosa Cable, 1701 Cogswell Ave, Pell City, AL 35125-1646. Phones: 800-560-7707 (Talladega office); 800-824-4773 (Ogenville office); 205-884-4545. Fax: 205-884-4510. E-mail: coosacable@coosahs.net. Web Site: http://www.coosahs.net. Also serves Alpine, Branchville, Brompton, LINCOLN, Odenville, Riverside, St. Clair County (portions) & Talladega County (portions). ICA: AL0212.
TV Market Ranking: 40 (Branchville, Brompton, Odenville, PELL CITY, Riverside, St. Clair County (portions)); Below 100 (Alpine, Lincoln, Talladega County (portions)). Franchise award date: October 1, 1968. Franchise expiration date: N.A. Began: September 11, 1971.
Channel capacity: 45 (operating 2-way). Channels available but not in use: 8.
Basic Service
Subscribers: 7,457.
Programming (received off-air): WABM (MNT) Birmingham; WBIQ (PBS) Birmingham; WBRC (FOX) Birmingham; WIAT (CBS) Birmingham; WJSU-TV (ABC) Anniston; WPXH-TV (ION) Gadsden; WTJP-TV (TBN) Gadsden; WTTO (CW) Homewood; WVTM-TV (NBC) Birmingham.
Programming (via satellite): ABC Family Channel; AMC; Animal Planet; Arts & Entertainment; BET Networks; Cartoon Network; CNBC; CNN; Comcast Sports Net Southeast; Comedy Central; Country Music TV; Discovery Channel; Disney Channel; E! Entertainment Television; ESPN; ESPN 2; FitTV; Fox News Channel; FX; Great American Country; Hallmark Channel; HGTV; History Channel; Home Shopping Network; Lifetime; MSNBC; MTV; National Geographic Channel; Nickelodeon; QVC; Spike TV; SportSouth; Syfy; TBS Superstation; The Learning Channel; Travel Channel; Turner Network TV; TV Guide Network; TV Land; USA Network; VH1; Weather Channel; WGN America.
Fee: $40.00 installation; $30.00 monthly; $1.80 converter; $10.00 additional installation.
Digital Basic Service
Subscribers: N.A.
Programming (via satellite): 3 Angels Broadcasting Network; BBC America; Bio; Bloomberg Television; BYU Television; Church Channel; Daystar TV Network; Discovery Health Channel; Discovery Home Channel; Discovery Kids Channel; Discovery Military Channel; Discovery Times Channel; Do-It-Yourself; Encore (multiplexed); Eternal Word TV Network; Familyland Television Network; FamilyNet; Food Network; Fox Movie Channel; G4; GAS; Golden Eagle Broadcasting; Gospel Music TV; GSN; Halogen Network; History Channel International; Independent Film Channel; JCTV; Lifetime Movie Network; Lime; MTV2; National Geographic Channel; Nick Jr.; Science Channel; Sleuth; SoapNet; Style Network; Trinity Broadcasting Network; truTV; Turner Classic Movies; VH1 Classic; VH1 Country; WE tv.
Fee: $11.95 monthly.
Digital Expanded Basic Service
Subscribers: N.A.
Programming (via satellite): CBS College Sports Network; ESPN Classic Sports; ESPNews; Fox College Sports Atlantic; Fox College Sports Central; Fox College Sports Pacific; Fox Soccer; Fuel TV; Golf Channel; Outdoor Channel; RFD-TV; Speed Channel; The Sportsman Channel; Versus.
Fee: $7.95 monthly.
Digital Pay Service 1
Pay Units: N.A.
Programming (via satellite): Cinemax (multiplexed); Flix; HBO (multiplexed); Showtime (multiplexed); Starz (multiplexed); The Movie Channel (multiplexed).
Fee: $5.95 monthly (Starz), $9.50 monthly (Cinemax), $12.00 monthly (HBO), $13.50 monthly (Showtime, TMC & Flix).
Video-On-Demand: No
Pay-Per-View
iN DEMAND (delivered digitally).
Internet Service
Operational: Yes.
Subscribers: 2,220.
Broadband Service: In-house.
Fee: $40.00 installation; $18.95 monthly; $5.00 modem lease; $65.40 modem purchase.
Telephone Service
Analog: Not Operational
Digital: Planned
Miles of Plant: 300.0 (coaxial); 17.0 (fiber optic). Additional miles planned: 10.0 (coaxial).
President & Chief Technician: Jeff Smith. Chief Executive Officer: Arthur M. Smith.
City fee: 3% of gross.
Ownership: Coosa Cable Co.

PENNINGTON—Galaxy Cablevision, PO Box 879, 118 S Jackson St, Grove Hill, AL 36451-0879. Phone: 251-275-3118. Fax: 251-275-3120. Web Site: http://www.galaxycable.com. ICA: AL0160.
TV Market Ranking: Outside TV Markets (PENNINGTON). Franchise award date: N.A. Franchise expiration date: N.A. Began: September 1, 1982.
Channel capacity: 41 (not 2-way capable). Channels available but not in use: 13.
Basic Service
Subscribers: 35.
Programming (received off-air): WAKA (CBS) Selma; WALA-TV (FOX) Mobile; WGBC (NBC) Meridian; WIIQ (PBS) Demopolis; WMDN (CBS) Meridian; WTOK-TV (ABC, CW, FOX, MNT) Meridian.
Programming (via satellite): ABC Family Channel; Arts & Entertainment; Cartoon Network; CNBC; CNN; Discovery Channel; Disney Channel; ESPN; Hallmark Channel; Headline News; Lifetime; Outdoor Channel; Speed Channel; SportSouth; Syfy; TBS Superstation; Trinity Broadcasting Network; Turner Network TV; USA Network; WGN America.
Fee: $25.00 installation; $35.60 monthly.
Pay Service 1
Pay Units: 63.
Programming (via satellite): HBO.
Fee: $25.00 installation; $11.00 monthly.
Internet Service
Operational: No.
Telephone Service
None
Miles of Plant: 7.0 (coaxial); None (fiber optic). Homes passed: 186.
State Manager: Bill Flowers. Technical Manager & Engineer: Greg Berthaut. Customer Service Representative: Lisa Ray.
Ownership: Galaxy Cable Inc. (MSO).

PERDIDO BEACH—Mediacom, 760 Middle St, PO Box 1009, Fairhope, AL 36532. Phones: 800-239-8411 (Customer service); 251-928-0374. Fax: 251-928-3804. E-mail: gene.wuchner@mediacomcc.com. Web Site: http://www.mediacomcable.com. ICA: AL0236.
TV Market Ranking: 59 (PERDIDO BEACH). Franchise award date: N.A. Franchise expiration date: N.A. Began: N.A.
Channel capacity: 45 (operating 2-way). Channels available but not in use: 3.
Basic Service
Subscribers: 411.
Programming (received off-air): WALA-TV (FOX) Mobile; WEAR-TV (ABC) Pensacola; WEIQ (PBS) Mobile; WHBR (IND) Pensacola; WJTC (IND) Pensacola; WKRG-TV (CBS) Mobile; WMPV-TV (TBN) Mobile; WPMI-TV (NBC) Mobile; WSRE (PBS) Pensacola.
Programming (via satellite): Comcast Sports Net Southeast; Travel Channel; Turner Network TV; TV Land.
Fee: $49.95 installation; $11.95 monthly.
Expanded Basic Service 1
Subscribers: N.A.
Programming (via satellite): ABC Family Channel; AMC; Animal Planet; Arts & Entertainment; CNBC; CNN; Country Music TV; C-SPAN; Discovery Channel; Disney Channel; ESPN; Fox News Channel; Headline News; History Channel; Lifetime; MTV; Nickelodeon; QVC; Spike TV; TBS Superstation; The Learning Channel; TV Guide Network; USA Network; VH1; Weather Channel; WGN America.
Fee: $18.50 monthly.
Pay Service 1
Pay Units: 64.
Programming (via satellite): HBO.
Fee: $10.95 monthly.
Pay Service 2
Pay Units: 27.
Programming (via satellite): Showtime.
Fee: $10.95 monthly.
Video-On-Demand: Yes
Internet Service
Operational: Yes.
Broadband Service: Mediacom High Speed Internet.
Fee: $45.95 monthly.
Telephone Service
Digital: Planned
Miles of Plant: 32.0 (coaxial); None (fiber optic). Homes passed: 782.
General Manager: Gene Wuchner. Technical Operations Manager: Bobby Hollifield. Chief Technician: Billy Brooks.
Ownership: Mediacom LLC (MSO).

PHENIX CITY—Cable TV of East Alabama, PO Box 130, 2400 Sportsman Dr, Phenix City, AL 35867. Phone: 334-298-7000. Fax: 334-298-0833. Web Site: http://www.ctvea.net. Also serves Fort Mitchell, Hatchechubbee, Hurtsboro, Lee County, Russell County, Salem, Seale & Smiths. ICA: AL0011.
TV Market Ranking: 94 (Fort Mitchell, Hatchechubbee, Hurtsboro, Lee County, PHENIX CITY, Russell County, Salem, Seale, Smiths). Franchise award date: N.A. Franchise expiration date: N.A. Began: May 1, 1965.
Channel capacity: 56 (operating 2-way). Channels available but not in use: None.
Basic Service
Subscribers: 18,154.
Programming (received off-air): WCIQ (PBS) Mount Cheaha State Park; WIYC (IND) Troy; WJSP-TV (PBS) Columbus; WLGA (CW) Opelika; WLTZ (CW, NBC) Columbus; WRBL (CBS) Columbus; WTVM (ABC) Columbus; WXTX (FOX) Columbus; WYBU-CD (IND) Columbus.
Programming (via satellite): ABC Family Channel; AMC; Animal Planet; Arts & Entertainment; BET Networks; Cartoon Network; CNBC; CNN; Comedy Central; Country Music TV; C-SPAN; C-SPAN 2; Discovery Channel; Disney Channel; E! Entertainment Television; ESPN; ESPN 2; ESPN Classic Sports; Food Network; Fox News Channel; Fox Sports Net; FX; Golf

Channel; Great American Country; Hallmark Channel; Halogen Network; Headline News; HGTV; History Channel; Home Shopping Network; INSP; ION Television; Lifetime; MSNBC; MTV; National Geographic Channel; Nickelodeon; Outdoor Channel; QVC; Radar Channel; SoapNet; Spike TV; SportSouth; Syfy; TBS Superstation; The Learning Channel; Travel Channel; Trinity Broadcasting Network; truTV; Turner Classic Movies; Turner Network TV; TV Guide Network; TV Land; USA Network; Versus; VH1; Weather Channel; WGN America.

Current originations: Public Access; Leased Access; Religious Access; Government Access; Educational Access.

Fee: $25.00 installation; $45.61 monthly; $3.00 converter.

Digital Basic Service

Subscribers: 3,218.

Programming (via satellite): BBC America; Bio; Bloomberg Television; Bravo; Discovery Digital Networks; ESPN Classic Sports; Fox Sports World; G4; GSN; Halogen Network; History Channel International; Independent Film Channel; Lifetime Movie Network; MTV Networks Digital Suite; Music Choice; Speed Channel; Sundance Channel; Toon Disney; VH1; WE tv.

Fee: $17.10 monthly.

Digital Pay Service 1

Pay Units: N.A.

Programming (via satellite): Cinemax (multiplexed); Encore (multiplexed); Flix; HBO (multiplexed); Showtime (multiplexed); Starz (multiplexed); Starz HDTV; Sundance Channel; The Movie Channel (multiplexed).

Fee: $4.00 monthly (Encore), $7.50 monthly (Starz), $12.95 monthly (Cinemax or Showtime/Sundance/TMC), $13.95 monthly (HBO).

Video-On-Demand: Yes

Pay-Per-View

Addressable homes: 8,077.

ESPN Extra (delivered digitally), Addressable: Yes; ESPN Now (delivered digitally); Hot Choice (delivered digitally); iN DEMAND; iN DEMAND (delivered digitally).

Internet Service

Operational: Yes. Began: March 1, 2000.

Subscribers: 6,000.

Broadband Service: In-house.

Fee: $80.00 installation; $29.95-$69.95 monthly.

Telephone Service

Digital: Operational

Subscribers: 120.

Fee: $34.95-$39.95 monthly

Miles of Plant: 585.0 (coaxial); 104.0 (fiber optic). Homes passed: 25,000. Total homes in franchised area: 40,000.

Manager: Lynne Frakes. Chief Technician: Jerry Burrell. Administration: Myra Boatwell.

Ownership: R. M. Greene Inc. (MSO).

PHIL CAMPBELL—CommuniComm Services, 3164 Hwy 431, Ste 9, Roanoke, AL 36274-1702. Phone: 334-863-7080. Fax: 334-863-2027. Web Site: http://www.netcommander.com. Also serves Franklin County (portions). ICA: AL0136.

TV Market Ranking: Below 100 (Franklin County (portions), PHIL CAMPBELL). Franchise award date: N.A. Franchise expiration date: N.A. Began: N.A.

Channel capacity: N.A. Channels available but not in use: N.A.

Basic Service

Subscribers: 223.

Programming (received off-air): WAAY-TV (ABC) Huntsville; WAFF (NBC) Huntsville; WBRC (FOX) Birmingham; WFIQ (PBS) Florence; WHDF (CW) Florence; WHNT-TV (CBS) Huntsville; WIAT (CBS) Birmingham; WTVA (NBC) Tupelo; WVTM-TV (NBC) Birmingham; WZDX (FOX, MNT) Huntsville.

Programming (via satellite): TBS Superstation; WGN America.

Fee: $30.00 installation; $9.95 monthly.

Expanded Basic Service 1

Subscribers: N.A.

Programming (via satellite): ABC Family Channel; AMC; Arts & Entertainment; Cartoon Network; CNN; Comcast/Charter Sports Southeast (CSS); Country Music TV; C-SPAN; Discovery Channel; ESPN; ESPN 2; Headline News; HGTV; History Channel; Lifetime; Nick Jr.; Nickelodeon; QVC; Spike TV; The Learning Channel; Trinity Broadcasting Network; Turner Classic Movies; Turner Network TV; USA Network; VH1; Weather Channel.

Digital Basic Service

Subscribers: N.A.

Programming (via satellite): AmericanLife TV Network; BBC America; Bio; Bloomberg Television; Bravo; CMT Pure Country; Current; Discovery Health Channel; Discovery Kids Channel; Discovery Military Channel; Discovery Planet Green; DMX Music; ESPN Classic Sports; ESPNews; FitTV; Fox Movie Channel; Fox Soccer; Fuse; G4; Golf Channel; GSN; Halogen Network; History Channel; History Channel International; ID Investigation Discovery; Independent Film Channel; Lifetime Movie Network; MTV Hits; MTV2; Nick Jr.; Outdoor Channel; Ovation; Science Channel; Sleuth; Speed Channel; Style Network; TeenNick; Turner Classic Movies; Versus; VH1 Classic; VH1 Soul; WE tv.

Pay Service 1

Pay Units: 20.

Programming (via satellite): Cinemax; HBO.

Fee: $9.95 monthly (Cinemax), $10.95 monthly (HBO).

Digital Pay Service 1

Pay Units: N.A.

Programming (via satellite): Cinemax (multiplexed); Encore (multiplexed); HBO (multiplexed); Starz (multiplexed).

Video-On-Demand: No

Pay-Per-View

iN DEMAND (delivered digitally); Club Jenna (delivered digitally); Playboy TV (delivered digitally); Fresh (delivered digitally).

Internet Service

Operational: No.

Telephone Service

None

Miles of Plant: 60.0 (coaxial); None (fiber optic). Homes passed: 1,233.

General Manager: Brian Chase. Chief Technician: William Boyd.

Ownership: James Cable LLC (MSO).

PIEDMONT—Charter Communications, 2100 Columbiana Rd, Vestavia, AL 35216. Phone: 205-824-5400. Fax: 208-824-5490. Web Site: http://www.charter.com. Also serves Centre & Cherokee County (portions). ICA: AL0065.

TV Market Ranking: 18 (Centre, Cherokee County (portions), PIEDMONT). Franchise award date: N.A. Franchise expiration date: N.A. Began: August 1, 1966.

Channel capacity: 42 (not 2-way capable). Channels available but not in use: N.A.

Basic Service

Subscribers: 3,682.

Programming (received off-air): WABM (MNT) Birmingham; WBRC (FOX) Birmingham; WCFT-TV (ABC) Tuscaloosa; WCIQ (PBS) Mount Cheaha State Park; WIAT (CBS) Birmingham; WJXS-CA Jacksonville; WPXH-TV (ION) Gadsden; WTTO (CW) Homewood; WVTM-TV (NBC) Birmingham; WXIA-TV (NBC) Atlanta.

Programming (via satellite): C-SPAN; Home Shopping Network; Home Shopping Network 2; INSP; QVC; Trinity Broadcasting Network; Weather Channel.

Current originations: Government Access.

Fee: $29.99 installation; $9.97 monthly.

Expanded Basic Service 1

Subscribers: 1,984.

Programming (via satellite): ABC Family Channel; AMC; Animal Planet; Arts & Entertainment; BET Networks; Bravo; Cartoon Network; CNBC; CNN; Comcast Sports Net Southeast; Comcast/Charter Sports Southeast (CSS); Comedy Central; Country Music TV; Discovery Channel; Disney Channel; E! Entertainment Television; ESPN; ESPN 2; ESPN Classic Sports; Food Network; Fox News Channel; FX; G4; Golf Channel; Hallmark Channel; Headline News; HGTV; History Channel; Lifetime; MSNBC; MTV; National Geographic Channel; Nickelodeon; Outdoor Channel; Oxygen; SoapNet; Speed Channel; Spike TV; SportSouth; Syfy; TBS Superstation; The Learning Channel; Toon Disney; Travel Channel; Turner Network TV; TV Land; Univision; USA Network; Versus; VH1; WE tv.

Fee: $43.00 monthly.

Digital Basic Service

Subscribers: N.A.

Programming (via satellite): BBC America; Bloomberg Television; Discovery Digital Networks; GSN; MTV Networks Digital Suite; Music Choice; Nick Jr.; Nick Too; NickToons TV; Science Television; Sundance Channel.

Digital Pay Service 1

Pay Units: 1,208.

Programming (via satellite): Cinemax (multiplexed); HBO (multiplexed); Starz (multiplexed).

Digital Pay Service 2

Pay Units: N.A.

Video-On-Demand: No

Pay-Per-View

iN DEMAND (delivered digitally); NASCAR In Car (delivered digitally); Playboy TV (delivered digitally); Fresh (delivered digitally); Shorteez (delivered digitally).

Internet Service

Operational: Yes.

Telephone Service

Digital: Operational

Fee: $29.99 monthly

Miles of Plant: 104.0 (coaxial); None (fiber optic). Total homes in franchised area: 4,852.

Vice President & General Manager: Don Karell. Technical Operations Director: Greg Prim. Marketing Director: David Redmond. Marketing Manager: Jeff Hatcher.

City fee: 3% of gross.

Ownership: Charter Communications Inc. (MSO).

PINE HILL—Galaxy Cablevision, PO Box 879, 118 S Jackson St, Grove Hill, AL 36451-0879. Phone: 251-275-3118. Fax: 251-275-3120. Web Site: http://www.galaxycable.com. Also serves Wilcox County. ICA: AL0145.

TV Market Ranking: Outside TV Markets (PINE HILL, Wilcox County). Franchise award date: October 24, 1988. Franchise expiration date: N.A. Began: November 1, 1989.

Channel capacity: 54 (not 2-way capable). Channels available but not in use: 20.

Basic Service

Subscribers: 133.

Programming (received off-air): WAKA (CBS) Selma; WCOV-TV (FOX) Montgomery; WIIQ (PBS) Demopolis; WNCF (ABC) Montgomery; WSFA (NBC) Montgomery.

Programming (via satellite): ABC Family Channel; AMC; Arts & Entertainment; Cartoon Network; CNN; Comcast Sports Net Southeast; Discovery Channel; Disney Channel; ESPN; ESPN 2; Fox News Channel; FX; Great American Country; Hallmark Channel; Headline News; Lifetime; Outdoor Channel; Speed Channel; TBS Superstation; Toon Disney; Trinity Broadcasting Network; Turner Network TV; USA Network; Weather Channel; WGN America.

Current originations: Public Access.

Fee: $25.00 installation; $39.85 monthly.

Pay Service 1

Pay Units: N.A.

Programming (via satellite): HBO.

Fee: $9.95 monthly.

Internet Service

Operational: No.

Telephone Service

None

Miles of Plant: 21.0 (coaxial); None (fiber optic). Homes passed: 378.

State Manager: Bill Flowers. Technical Manager & Engineer: Greg Berthaut. Customer Service Representative: Lisa Ray.

Ownership: Galaxy Cable Inc. (MSO).

POLLARD—Formerly served by CableSouth Inc. No longer in operation. ICA: AL0214.

PROVIDENCE—Sky Cablevision, PO Box 65, 1309 Roebuck Dr, Meridian, MS 39301. Phone: 601-485-6980. Fax: 601-483-0103. Web Site: http://skycablevision.com. ICA: AL0151.

TV Market Ranking: Outside TV Markets (PROVIDENCE). Franchise award date: N.A. Franchise expiration date: N.A. Began: July 1, 1990.

Channel capacity: 35 (not 2-way capable). Channels available but not in use: 20.

Basic Service

Subscribers: N.A.

Programming (received off-air): WAKA (CBS) Selma; WDBB (CW) Bessemer; WIIQ (PBS) Demopolis; WSFA (NBC) Montgomery; WTOK-TV (ABC, CW, FOX, MNT) Meridian.

Programming (via satellite): ABC Family Channel; CNN; Discovery Channel; Disney Channel; ESPN; TBS Superstation; Turner Network TV; USA Network; WGN America.

Fee: $20.00 installation; $34.00 monthly.

Pay Service 1

Pay Units: N.A.

Programming (via satellite): HBO.

Fee: $11.00 monthly.

Internet Service

Operational: No.

Telephone Service

None

Miles of Plant: 8.0 (coaxial); None (fiber optic). Homes passed: 230.

Manager & Chief Technician: Berry Ward.

Ownership: Sky Cablevision Ltd. (MSO).

RAGLAND—Ragland Telephone Co., PO Box 577, Ragland, AL 35131-0577. Phone: 205-472-2141. Fax: 205-472-2145.

E-mail: info@ragland.net. Web Site: http://www.ragland.net. ICA: AL0216.
TV Market Ranking: Below 100 (RAGLAND). Franchise award date: N.A. Franchise expiration date: N.A. Began: March 1, 1984.
Channel capacity: N.A. Channels available but not in use: N.A.

Basic Service
Subscribers: 584.
Programming (received off-air): WABM (MNT) Birmingham; WBIQ (PBS) Birmingham; WBMG-LP (IND) Moody; WBRC (FOX) Birmingham; WDBB (CW) Bessemer; WJSU-TV (ABC) Anniston; WTTO (CW) Homewood; WVTM-TV (NBC) Birmingham.
Programming (via satellite): ABC Family Channel; CNN; Discovery Channel; Disney Channel; ESPN; Spike TV; TBS Superstation; Trinity Broadcasting Network; Turner Network TV; USA Network; WGN America.
Fee: $30.00 installation; $25.00 monthly.

Pay Service 1
Pay Units: 195.
Programming (via satellite): HBO.
Fee: $10.00 monthly.

Video-On-Demand: No

Internet Service
Operational: Yes, Both DSL & dial-up.

Telephone Service
None
Miles of Plant: 47.0 (coaxial); None (fiber optic). Total homes in franchised area: 1,300.
Manager & Chief Technician: Stanley Bean. Customer Service Manager: Susan Williams.
City fee: 2% of gross.
Ownership: Cablestar Inc.

RAINSVILLE—Charter Communications, 2100 Columbiana Rd, Vestavia, AL 35216. Phone: 205-824-5400. Fax: 205-824-5490. Web Site: http://www.charter.com. Also serves DeKalb County, Dutton, Fyffe, Jackson County, Powell, Section & Shiloh. ICA: AL0220.
TV Market Ranking: 18 (Shiloh); 78,18 (DeKalb County (portions)); 78,96 (Jackson County (portions)); 96 (Dutton, RAINSVILLE); Below 100 (Fyffe, Section, Shiloh, DeKalb County (portions)); Outside TV Markets (Powell, DeKalb County (portions), Jackson County (portions), RAINSVILLE). Franchise award date: N.A. Franchise expiration date: N.A. Began: March 1, 1981.
Channel capacity: N.A. Channels available but not in use: N.A.

Basic Service
Subscribers: 2,039.
Programming (received off-air): WAAY-TV (ABC) Huntsville; WAFF (NBC) Huntsville; WDEF-TV (CBS) Chattanooga; WHIQ (PBS) Huntsville; WHNT-TV (CBS) Huntsville; WRCB (NBC) Chattanooga; WTVC (ABC) Chattanooga; WZDX (FOX, MNT) Huntsville.
Programming (via satellite): AMC; CNN; Comcast Sports Net Southeast; Country Music TV; ESPN; ESPN 2; Headline News; MTV; QVC; Syfy; The Learning Channel; Travel Channel; Trinity Broadcasting Network; Turner Network TV; TV Land; USA Network; Weather Channel.
Fee: $29.99 installation.

Expanded Basic Service 1
Subscribers: 1,963.
Programming (via satellite): ABC Family Channel; Animal Planet; Arts & Entertainment; CNBC; C-SPAN; Discovery Channel; Disney Channel; HGTV; Lifetime; Nickelodeon; Spike TV; TBS Superstation; WE tv; WGN America.
Fee: $43.00 monthly.

Digital Basic Service
Subscribers: N.A.
Programming (via satellite): AmericanLife TV Network; BBC America; Bio; Bloomberg Television; Bravo; Discovery Digital Networks; ESPN Classic Sports; Fox Movie Channel; G4; GAS; Golf Channel; GSN; Halogen Network; History Channel; History Channel International; Independent Film Channel; Lifetime Movie Network; MTV Networks Digital Suite; MuchMusic Network; Music Choice; Nick Jr.; Outdoor Channel; ShopNBC; Speed Channel; Style Network; Toon Disney; Turner Classic Movies; TV Guide Interactive Inc.; Versus.
Fee: $16.99 monthly.

Digital Pay Service 1
Pay Units: 290.
Programming (via satellite): Cinemax (multiplexed).
Fee: $8.95 monthly.

Digital Pay Service 2
Pay Units: 314.
Programming (via satellite): HBO (multiplexed).
Fee: $9.95 monthly.

Digital Pay Service 3
Pay Units: N.A.
Programming (via satellite): Encore (multiplexed); Flix; Showtime (multiplexed); Starz (multiplexed); The Movie Channel (multiplexed).

Video-On-Demand: No

Pay-Per-View
ESPN Extra (delivered digitally), Addressable: Yes; ESPN Now (delivered digitally); iN DEMAND (delivered digitally); Playboy TV (delivered digitally); Fresh (delivered digitally); Shorteez (delivered digitally).

Internet Service
Operational: Yes.
Broadband Service: Charter Pipeline.

Telephone Service
Digital: Operational
Miles of Plant: 125.0 (coaxial); None (fiber optic). Homes passed: 3,548.
Vice President & General Manager: Don Karell. Technical Operations Director: Greg Prim. Marketing Director: David Redmond. Marketing Manager: Jeff Hatcher.
Ownership: Charter Communications Inc. (MSO).

RANBURNE—Ranburne Cable, 21124 Main St, Ranburne, AL 36273. Fax: 866-810-4523. Web Site: http://www.ranburnecable.com. ICA: AL0217.
TV Market Ranking: Below 100 (RANBURNE). Franchise award date: April 1, 2007. Franchise expiration date: N.A. Began: December 1, 1988.
Channel capacity: 21 (not 2-way capable). Channels available but not in use: N.A.

Basic Service
Subscribers: 50.
Programming (received off-air): WAGA-TV (FOX) Atlanta; WATL (MNT) Atlanta; WBIQ (PBS) Birmingham; WBRC (FOX) Birmingham; WGCL-TV (CBS) Atlanta; WPCH-TV (IND) Atlanta; WXIA-TV (NBC) Atlanta.
Programming (via satellite): Arts & Entertainment; Discovery Channel; ESPN; Headline News; Turner Network TV; USA Network; WGN America.
Fee: $30.00 installation; $9.95 monthly.

Pay Service 1
Pay Units: 2.
Programming (via satellite): Cinemax.
Fee: $25.00 installation; $9.95 monthly.

Pay Service 2
Pay Units: 1.
Programming (via satellite): HBO.
Fee: $25.00 installation; $10.95 monthly.

Internet Service
Operational: No.

Telephone Service
None
Miles of Plant: 10.0 (coaxial); None (fiber optic).
General Manager: Gary Mayfield.
Ownership: Mayfield Communications LLC.

RED BAY—MetroCast Communications, 311 Heritage Dr, Oxford, MS 38852. Phones: 662-234-4711; 662-728-8111. Fax: 662-236-3593. Web Site: http://www.metrocastcommunications.com. ICA: AL0218.
TV Market Ranking: Outside TV Markets (RED BAY). Franchise award date: N.A. Franchise expiration date: N.A. Began: September 1, 1963.
Channel capacity: N.A. Channels available but not in use: N.A.

Basic Service
Subscribers: 1,033.
Programming (received off-air): W44CF Clarksburg; WCBI-TV (CBS, CW, MNT) Columbus; WCFT-TV (ABC) Tuscaloosa; WFIQ (PBS) Florence; WHDF (CW) Florence; WHNT-TV (CBS) Huntsville; WKDH (ABC) Houston; WLOV-TV (FOX) West Point; WTVA (NBC) Tupelo; allband FM.
Programming (via satellite): Home Shopping Network; QVC; WGN America.
Current originations: Public Access.
Fee: $49.95 installation; $17.95 monthly.

Expanded Basic Service 1
Subscribers: N.A.
Programming (via satellite): ABC Family Channel; AMC; Animal Planet; Arts & Entertainment; BET Networks; Cartoon Network; CNBC; CNN; Comcast Sports Net Southeast; Comedy Central; Cooking Channel; Country Music TV; C-SPAN; C-SPAN 2; CW+; Discovery Channel; Disney Channel; Do-It-Yourself; E! Entertainment Television; ESPN; ESPN 2; FitTV; Food Network; Fox News Channel; FX; Great American Country; Hallmark Channel; Headline News; HGTV; History Channel; INSP; Lifetime; MSNBC; MTV; National Geographic Channel; Nickelodeon; Outdoor Channel; SoapNet; Spike TV; Syfy; TBS Superstation; The Learning Channel; Travel Channel; Trinity Broadcasting Network; truTV; Turner Network TV; Turner South; TV Land; USA Network; Versus; VH1; WE tv; Weather Channel.
Fee: $33.00 monthly.

Digital Basic Service
Subscribers: 153.
Programming (via satellite): AmericanLife TV Network; BBC America; Bio; Bloomberg Television; Discovery Digital Networks; Discovery HD Theater; DMX Music; ESPN Classic Sports; ESPNews; Fox Movie Channel; Fox Soccer; Fuse; G4; GAS; Golf Channel; GSN; Halogen Network; History Channel International; Independent Film Channel; Lifetime Movie Network; Lime; MTV Networks Digital Suite; NFL Network; Nick Jr.; NickToons TV; Outdoor Channel; Sleuth; Speed Channel; Style Network; Toon Disney; Turner Classic Movies; Turner Network TV HD; Universal HD.
Fee: $10.00 monthly.

Digital Pay Service 1
Pay Units: N.A.
Programming (via satellite): Cinemax (multiplexed); Encore (multiplexed); Flix; HBO (multiplexed); Showtime (multiplexed); Starz (multiplexed); The Movie Channel (multiplexed).
Fee: $6.00 monthly (Encore), $13.00 monthly (HBO, Cinemax, Showtime/TMC or Starz).

Video-On-Demand: Yes

Pay-Per-View
Addressable homes: 135.
iN DEMAND (delivered digitally); ESPN (delivered digitally), Fee: $3.99, Addressable: Yes; Hot Choice (delivered digitally); MLB Extra Innings (delivered digitally); Playboy TV (delivered digitally); Fresh (delivered digitally).

Internet Service
Operational: Yes.
Subscribers: 23.
Broadband Service: MetroCast Internet.
Fee: $79.99 installation; $43.95 monthly.

Telephone Service
Digital: Operational
Fee: $24.95 installation; $29.95 monthly
Miles of Plant: 47.0 (coaxial); 5.0 (fiber optic). Homes passed: 1,729. Total homes in franchised area: 2,027.
General Manager: Rick Ferrell. Technical Operations Manager: Jerry Morris. Marketing Manager: Lee Beck.
Ownership: Harron Communications LP (MSO).

ROANOKE—CommuniComm Services, 3164 Hwy 431, Ste 9, Roanoke, AL 36274-1702. Phones: 800-239-5367; 334-863-7080. Fax: 334-863-2027. Web Site: http://www.netcommander.com. Also serves Randolph County & Rock Mills. ICA: AL0023.
TV Market Ranking: Outside TV Markets (Randolph County, ROANOKE, Rock Mills). Franchise award date: January 1, 1970. Franchise expiration date: N.A. Began: April 1, 1970.
Channel capacity: N.A. Channels available but not in use: N.A.

Basic Service
Subscribers: 1,888.
Programming (received off-air): WAGA-TV (FOX) Atlanta; WBRC (FOX) Birmingham; WCAG-LP La Grange; WCIQ (PBS) Mount Cheaha State Park; WGCL-TV (CBS) Atlanta; WJSU-TV (ABC) Anniston; WSB-TV (ABC) Atlanta; WSFA (NBC) Montgomery; WTTO (CW) Homewood; allband FM.
Programming (via satellite): TBS Superstation; WGN America.
Fee: $25.00 installation; $11.00 monthly; $15.00 additional installation.

Expanded Basic Service 1
Subscribers: 774.
Programming (via satellite): ABC Family Channel; American Movie Classics; Animal Planet; Arts & Entertainment; BET Networks; Bravo; Cartoon Network; CNBC; CNN; Comcast/Charter Sports Southeast (CSS); Comedy Central; Country Music TV; C-SPAN; C-SPAN 2; Discovery Channel; Disney Channel; E! Entertainment Television; ESPN; ESPN 2; ESPN Classic Sports; Food Network; Fox Movie Channel; Fox News Channel; FX; Great American Country; Hallmark Channel; Headline News; HGTV; History Channel; Home Shopping Network; ION Television; Lifetime; Lifetime Movie Network; MSNBC; MTV; Nick Jr.; Nickelodeon; Outdoor Channel; ShopNBC; Spike TV; Syfy; The Learning Channel; The Sportsman Channel; Travel Channel; Trinity Broadcasting Network; truTV; Turner Classic Movies; Turner Network TV; Turner South; TV Guide Network; TV Land; USA Network; VH1; WE tv; Weather Channel.
Fee: $15.00 installation; $5.00 monthly.

Digital Basic Service
Subscribers: N.A.
Programming (via satellite): BBC America; Bio; Bloomberg Television; Discovery Health Channel; Discovery Kids Channel; Discovery Military Channel; Discovery Planet Green; DMX Music; Fox Soccer; Fuse; Golf Channel; GSN; Halogen Network; History Channel International; ID Investigation Discovery; Independent Film Channel; National Geographic Channel; Science Channel; Sleuth; SoapNet; Speed Channel; Toon Disney; Versus.
Pay Service 1
Pay Units: 281.
Programming (via satellite): Cinemax (multiplexed); Encore; HBO (multiplexed); MoviePlex; Starz (multiplexed).
Fee: $15.00 installation; $10.00 monthly.
Digital Pay Service 1
Pay Units: N.A.
Programming (via satellite): Cinemax (multiplexed); Encore; HBO (multiplexed); Showtime (multiplexed); Starz (multiplexed).
Video-On-Demand: No
Pay-Per-View
iN DEMAND (delivered digitally); Hot Choice (delivered digitally); Playboy TV (delivered digitally); Fresh (delivered digitally).
Internet Service
Operational: Yes.
Subscribers: 648.
Broadband Service: Net Commander.
Fee: $39.95 installation; $51.95 monthly.
Telephone Service
None
Miles of Plant: 68.0 (coaxial); 15.0 (fiber optic). Total homes in franchised area: 3,685.
General Manager: Brian Chase. Chief Technician: William Boyd.
City fee: 3% of gross.
Ownership: James Cable LLC (MSO).

ROBERTSDALE—Mediacom, 760 Middle St, PO Box 1009, Fairhope, AL 36532. Phones: 800-239-8411 (Customer service); 251-928-3804. Fax: 251-928-3804. E-mail: gene.wuchner@mediacomcc.com. Web Site: http://www.mediacomcable.com. Also serves Baldwin County (portions), Fort Morgan, Gulf Shores, Loxley, Orange Beach, Romar Beach & Silver Hill. ICA: AL0019.
TV Market Ranking: 59 (Baldwin County (portions), Fort Morgan, Gulf Shores, Loxley, Orange Beach, ROBERTSDALE, Romar Beach, Silver Hill). Franchise award date: April 23, 1980. Franchise expiration date: N.A. Began: September 1, 1981.
Channel capacity: 71 (operating 2-way). Channels available but not in use: None.
Basic Service
Subscribers: 6,507.
Programming (received off-air): WALA-TV (FOX) Mobile; WEAR-TV (ABC) Pensacola; WEIQ (PBS) Mobile; WFNA (CW) Gulf Shores; WHBR (IND) Pensacola; WJTC (IND) Pensacola; WKRG-TV (CBS) Mobile; WMPV-TV (TBN) Mobile; WPAN (IND) Fort Walton Beach; WPMI-TV (NBC) Mobile; WSRE (PBS) Pensacola.
Programming (via satellite): ABC Family Channel; AMC; Animal Planet; Arts & Entertainment; BET Networks; Bravo; Cartoon Network; CNBC; CNN; Comcast Sports Net Southeast; Comedy Central; Country Music TV; C-SPAN; C-SPAN 2; Discovery Channel; Disney Channel; E! Entertainment Television; ESPN; ESPN 2; Eternal Word TV Network; Food Network; Fox News Channel; FX; Golf Channel; Hallmark Channel; Headline News; HGTV; History Channel; Home Shopping Network; INSP; ION Television; Lifetime; MSNBC; MTV; Nickelodeon; Outdoor Channel; Oxygen; QVC; Speed Channel; Spike TV; SportSouth; Syfy; TBS Superstation; The Learning Channel; Travel Channel; truTV; Turner Network TV; TV Guide Network; TV Land; USA Network; VH1; WE tv; Weather Channel; WGN America.
Fee: $21.50 installation; $45.95 monthly.
Digital Basic Service
Subscribers: 1,811.
Programming (via satellite): AmericanLife TV Network; BBC America; Bio; Bloomberg Television; Discovery Digital Networks; Fox Movie Channel; Fox Sports World; Fuse; G4; GSN; Halogen Network; History Channel International; Independent Film Channel; Lifetime Movie Network; Music Choice; Style Network; Trinity Broadcasting Network; Turner Classic Movies.
Fee: $12.00 monthly.
Pay Service 1
Pay Units: 1,117.
Programming (via satellite): Cinemax.
Fee: $10.45 monthly.
Pay Service 2
Pay Units: 1,828.
Programming (via satellite): HBO.
Fee: $10.45 monthly.
Pay Service 3
Pay Units: 1,764.
Programming (via satellite): Showtime.
Fee: $10.45 monthly.
Pay Service 4
Pay Units: 1,720.
Programming (via satellite): Flix.
Fee: $3.95 monthly.
Digital Pay Service 1
Pay Units: 2,914.
Programming (via satellite): Cinemax (multiplexed); Encore (multiplexed); Flix; HBO (multiplexed); Showtime (multiplexed); Starz (multiplexed); Sundance Channel; The Movie Channel (multiplexed).
Fee: $10.95 monthly (Cinemax, HBO, Showtime, Flix/Sundance/TMC, or Starz/Encore).
Video-On-Demand: Planned
Pay-Per-View
Addressable homes: 1,811.
ESPN Now (delivered digitally); Pleasure (delivered digitally); TVN Entertainment (delivered digitally); sports (delivered digitally).
Internet Service
Operational: Yes.
Broadband Service: Mediacom High Speed Internet.
Fee: $45.95 monthly.
Telephone Service
Analog: Not Operational
Digital: Planned
Miles of Plant: 305.0 (coaxial); None (fiber optic). Homes passed: 19,112.
General Manager: Gene Wuchner. Chief Technician: Billy Brooks. Technical Operations Manager: Bobby Hollifield.
City fee: 3% of gross.
Ownership: Mediacom LLC (MSO).

RUSSELLVILLE—Charter Communications, 2100 Columbiana Rd, Vestavia, AL 35216. Phone: 205-824-5400. Fax: 204-824-5490. Web Site: http://www.charter.com. Also serves Franklin County & Littleville. ICA: AL0028.
TV Market Ranking: Below 100 (Franklin County, Littleville, RUSSELLVILLE). Franchise award date: January 1, 1954. Franchise expiration date: N.A. Began: July 7, 1954.
Channel capacity: N.A. Channels available but not in use: N.A.
Basic Service
Subscribers: 5,921.
Programming (received off-air): W45CW Russellville; WAAY-TV (ABC) Huntsville; WAFF (NBC) Huntsville; WBRC (FOX) Birmingham; WFIQ (PBS) Florence; WHDF (CW) Florence; WHNT-TV (CBS) Huntsville; WZDX (FOX, MNT) Huntsville; allband FM.
Programming (via satellite): CNBC; C-SPAN; C-SPAN 2; Fox News Channel; Home Shopping Network; INSP; ION Television; NASA TV; QVC; Trinity Broadcasting Network; Weather Channel; WGN America.
Current originations: Religious Access; Government Access; Educational Access.
Fee: $29.99 installation.
Expanded Basic Service 1
Subscribers: N.A.
Programming (via satellite): ABC Family Channel; AMC; Animal Planet; Arts & Entertainment; BET Networks; Bravo; Cartoon Network; CNN; Comcast Sports Net Southeast; Comcast/Charter Sports Southeast (CSS); Comedy Central; Country Music TV; Discovery Channel; Disney Channel; E! Entertainment Television; ESPN; ESPN 2; Food Network; FX; G4; GalaVision; Golf Channel; GSN; Hallmark Channel; Headline News; HGTV; History Channel; Lifetime; MSNBC; MTV; National Geographic Channel; Nickelodeon; Outdoor Channel; Oxygen; Shop at Home; SoapNet; Speed Channel; Spike TV; SportSouth; Syfy; TBS Superstation; Telemundo; The Learning Channel; Toon Disney; Travel Channel; truTV; Turner Classic Movies; Turner Network TV; TV Guide Network; TV Land; Univision; USA Network; Versus; VH1; WE tv.
Fee: $43.00 monthly.
Digital Basic Service
Subscribers: N.A.
Programming (via satellite): BBC America; Bio; Bloomberg Television; Discovery Digital Networks; Do-It-Yourself; ESPN Classic Sports; ESPNews; Fox College Sports Atlantic; Fox College Sports Central; Fox College Sports Pacific; Fox Movie Channel; Fox Sports en Espanol; Fox Sports World; GAS; Great American Country; History Channel International; Independent Film Channel; Lifetime Movie Network; MTV Networks Digital Suite; MuchMusic Network; Music Choice; Nick Jr.; Nick Too; NickToons TV; Style Network; Sundance Channel.
Fee: $16.99 monthly.
Digital Pay Service 1
Pay Units: N.A.
Programming (via satellite): Cinemax (multiplexed); Encore (multiplexed); Flix; HBO (multiplexed); Showtime (multiplexed); Starz (multiplexed); The Movie Channel (multiplexed).
Video-On-Demand: Yes
Pay-Per-View
iN DEMAND (delivered digitally); NHL Center Ice/MLB Extra Innings (delivered digitally); Playboy TV (delivered digitally); Pleasure (delivered digitally); Fresh (delivered digitally); Shorteez (delivered digitally).
Internet Service
Operational: Yes.
Broadband Service: Charter Pipeline.
Fee: $29.99 monthly.
Telephone Service
Digital: Operational
Miles of Plant: 201.0 (coaxial); None (fiber optic). Additional miles planned: 4.0 (coaxial). Homes passed: 6,700. Total homes in franchised area: 8,500.
Vice President & General Manager: Don Karell. Technical Operations Director: Greg Prim. Marketing Director: David Redmond. Marketing Manager: Jeff Hatcher.
City fee: 5% of basic.
Ownership: Charter Communications Inc. (MSO).

SAMSON—Bright House Networks, 151 London Pkwy, Birmingham, AL 35211-4541. Phone: 205-290-1300. Fax: 850-892-1315. Web Site: http://panhandle.brighthouse.com. ICA: AL0115.
TV Market Ranking: Below 100 (SAMSON). Franchise award date: N.A. Franchise expiration date: N.A. Began: January 1, 1970.
Channel capacity: 35 (operating 2-way). Channels available but not in use: 3.
Basic Service
Subscribers: 593.
Programming (received off-air): WDFX-TV (FOX) Ozark; WDHN (ABC) Dothan; WGIQ (PBS) Louisville; WJHG-TV (CW, MNT, NBC) Panama City; WMBB (ABC) Panama City; WSFA (NBC) Montgomery; WTVY (CBS, CW, MNT) Dothan.
Programming (via satellite): BET Networks; C-SPAN; CW+; Discovery Channel; Fox News Channel; Home Shopping Network; TBS Superstation; The Learning Channel; WGN America.
Fee: $30.00 installation; $10.64 monthly; $5.00 converter; $20.00 additional installation.
Expanded Basic Service 1
Subscribers: N.A.
Programming (via satellite): ABC Family Channel; AMC; Animal Planet; Arts & Entertainment; Bravo; Cartoon Network; CNBC; CNN; Comedy Central; Country Music TV; C-SPAN 2; Disney Channel; E! Entertainment Television; ESPN; ESPN 2; Food Network; Fuse; FX; Headline News; HGTV; History Channel; Lifetime; Lifetime Movie Network; MSNBC; MTV; National Geographic Channel; Nickelodeon; Oxygen; QVC; ShopNBC; Spike TV; Style Network; Syfy; Travel Channel; Trinity Broadcasting Network; truTV; Turner Network TV; USA Network; Versus; VH1; WE tv; Weather Channel.
Fee: $49.45 monthly.
Digital Basic Service
Subscribers: N.A.
Programming (received off-air): WGIQ (PBS) Louisville; WJHG-TV (CW, MNT, NBC) Panama City; WSFA (NBC) Montgomery; WTVY (CBS, CW, MNT) Dothan.
Programming (via satellite): AmericanLife TV Network; BBC America; Bio; Bloomberg Television; Bravo; Current; Discovery Digital Networks; Discovery HD Theater; ESPN 2 HD; ESPN Classic Sports; ESPN HD; ESPN Now; ESPN U; ESPNews; Fox Movie Channel; Fox Reality Channel; Fox Soccer; G4; GAS; Golf Channel; Great American Country; GSN; HDNet; HDNet Movies; History Channel International; INHD; MTV Networks Digital Suite; Music Choice; Nick Jr.; NickToons TV; Outdoor Channel; Ovation; Sleuth; Speed Channel; Toon Disney; Turner Classic Movies; TV Land; Universal HD; WebMD Television.
Fee: $11.00 monthly.
Digital Pay Service 1
Pay Units: N.A.
Programming (via satellite): Cinemax (multiplexed); Encore (multiplexed); HBO (multiplexed); HBO HD; Independent Film Channel; Showtime; Showtime HD; Starz (multiplexed); Sundance Channel; The Movie Channel (multiplexed).
Fee: $10.50 monthly (each).

Pay-Per-View

iN DEMAND (delivered digitally); Fresh (delivered digitally); Shorteez (delivered digitally); Pleasure (delivered digitally); Hot Choice (delivered digitally); Ten Blue (delivered digitally); Ten Blox (delivered digitally).

Internet Service

Operational: Yes.

Fee: $32.95-$57.95 monthly.

Telephone Service

Digital: Operational

Fee: $39.95 monthly

Miles of Plant: 19.0 (coaxial); None (fiber optic). Homes passed: 939. Total homes in franchised area: 950.

Marketing Director: Nicole Hardy.

City fee: 3% of gross.

Ownership: Bright House Networks LLC (MSO).

SCOTTSBORO—Charter Communications. Now served by GUNTERSVILLE, AL [AL0033]. ICA: AL0219.

SCOTTSBORO—Scottsboro Electric Power Board, PO Box 550, Scottsboro, AL 35768-0550. Phone: 256-574-2682. Fax: 256-574-5085. E-mail: kathya@scottsboropower.com. Web Site: http://www.scottsboropower.com. ICA: AL0260.

Note: This system is an overbuild.

TV Market Ranking: 96 (SCOTTSBORO). Franchise award date: N.A. Franchise expiration date: N.A. Began: N.A.

Channel capacity: 80 (operating 2-way). Channels available but not in use: N.A.

Basic Service

Subscribers: 4,500.

Programming (received off-air): WAAY-TV (ABC) Huntsville; WAFF (NBC) Huntsville; WDEF-TV (CBS) Chattanooga; WHIQ (PBS) Huntsville; WHNT-TV (CBS) Huntsville; WRCB (NBC) Chattanooga; WTVC (ABC) Chattanooga; WZDX (FOX, MNT) Huntsville.

Programming (via satellite): C-SPAN 2; CW+; Headline News; Home Shopping Network; INSP; Radar Channel; TBS Superstation; TV Guide Network; Weather Channel; WGN America.

Fee: $14.00 monthly.

Expanded Basic Service 1

Subscribers: N.A.

Programming (via satellite): ABC Family Channel; AMC; Animal Planet; Arts & Entertainment; BET Networks; Bravo; Cartoon Network; CNBC; CNN; Comcast Sports Net Southeast; Comcast/Charter Sports Southeast (CSS); Comedy Central; Country Music TV; C-SPAN; Discovery Channel; Disney Channel; E! Entertainment Television; ESPN; ESPN 2; ESPN Classic Sports; ESPNews; Eternal Word TV Network; FitTV; Food Network; Fox News Channel; FX; G4; Golf Channel; Great American Country; HGTV; History Channel; ION Television; Lifetime; MTV; National Geographic Channel; Nickelodeon; Outdoor Channel; QVC; Speed Channel; Spike TV; Syfy; The Learning Channel; Toon Disney; Travel Channel; Trinity Broadcasting Network; Turner Classic Movies; Turner Network TV; Turner South; TV Land; USA Network; VH1.

Fee: $16.00 monthly.

Digital Basic Service

Subscribers: 500.

Programming (received off-air): WAAY-TV (ABC) Huntsville; WHDF (CW) Florence; WHIQ (PBS) Huntsville; WHNT-TV (CBS) Huntsville; WZDX (FOX, MNT) Huntsville.

Programming (via satellite): BBC America; Bio; CBS College Sports Network; Discovery Digital Networks; Discovery HD Theater; Do-It-Yourself; Fox College Sports Atlantic; Fox College Sports Central; Fox College Sports Pacific; Fox Movie Channel; GSN; Hallmark Channel; HDNet; HDNet Movies; History Channel International; Independent Film Channel; SoapNet; Style Network; The Sportsman Channel; WE tv.

Fee: $45.00 monthly; $5.00 converter.

Pay Service 1

Pay Units: N.A.

Programming (via satellite): Cinemax; Encore; HBO (multiplexed); Showtime; Starz; The Movie Channel.

Fee: $14.00 monthly (Cinemax, Showtime, TMC, or Starz/Encore), $10.00 monthly (HBO).

Digital Pay Service 1

Pay Units: N.A.

Programming (via satellite): Canales N; Cinemax (multiplexed); Encore (multiplexed); Flix; HBO (multiplexed); Showtime (multiplexed); Starz (multiplexed); Sundance Channel; The Movie Channel (multiplexed).

Fee: $6.00 monthly (Canales N), $12.00 monthly (Cinemax or Starz/Encore), $14.00 monthly (Showtime, TMC, Flix, & Sundance), $16.00 monthly (HBO).

Video-On-Demand: No

Pay-Per-View

iN DEMAND (delivered digitally), Addressable: Yes; Hot Choice (delivered digitally); Fresh (delivered digitally).

Internet Service

Operational: Yes.

Subscribers: 2,500.

Broadband Service: In-house.

Fee: $33.00-$60.00 monthly; $8.00 modem lease; $370.00 modem purchase.

Telephone Service

None

Miles of Plant: 200.0 (coaxial); None (fiber optic). Homes passed: 6,300.

Manager: Jimmy Sandlin. Chief Technician: Philip Chaney.

Ownership: Scottsboro Electric Power Board.

SELBROOK—Alabama Broadband LLC, 3447A Parkwood Rd SE, Bessemer, AL 35022. Phones: 877-840-5040; 205-426-3432. E-mail: contact@alabamabroadband.com. Web Site: http://www.alabamabroadband.net. Also serves Shady Lake Trailer Park. ICA: AL0139.

TV Market Ranking: Below 100 (SELBROOK, Shady Lake Trailer Park). Franchise award date: March 9, 1987. Franchise expiration date: N.A. Began: May 9, 1987.

Channel capacity: 32 (not 2-way capable). Channels available but not in use: 8.

Basic Service

Subscribers: 344.

Programming (received off-air): WAIQ (PBS) Montgomery; WAKA (CBS) Selma; WCOV-TV (FOX) Montgomery; WMCF-TV (TBN) Montgomery; WNCF (ABC) Montgomery; WSFA (NBC) Montgomery.

Programming (via satellite): ABC Family Channel; Arts & Entertainment; CNN; Country Music TV; Discovery Channel; Disney Channel; ESPN; ESPN 2; HGTV; Lifetime; MTV; Nickelodeon; QVC; Spike TV; Syfy; TBS Superstation; Turner Network TV; USA Network; VH1; WGN America.

Fee: $35.00 installation; $18.25 monthly.

Pay Service 1

Pay Units: 69.

Programming (via satellite): Cinemax.

Fee: $10.00 installation; $10.95 monthly.

Pay Service 2

Pay Units: 98.

Programming (via satellite): HBO.

Fee: $10.00 installation; $10.95 monthly.

Video-On-Demand: No

Internet Service

Operational: No.

Telephone Service

None

Miles of Plant: 10.0 (coaxial); None (fiber optic). Total homes in franchised area: 500.

President: Tom Early.

County fee: 3% of basic.

Ownership: Alabama Broadband LLC (MSO).

SELMA—Charter Communications, 2100 Columbiana Rd, Vestavia, AL 35216. Phone: 205-824-5400. Fax: 205-824-5490. Web Site: http://www.charter.com. Also serves Dallas County. ICA: AL0018.

TV Market Ranking: Below 100 (Dallas County, SELMA). Franchise award date: N.A. Franchise expiration date: N.A. Began: January 1, 1964.

Channel capacity: N.A. Channels available but not in use: N.A.

Basic Service

Subscribers: 10,049.

Programming (received off-air): WAIQ (PBS) Montgomery; WAKA (CBS) Selma; WBIH (IND) Selma; WBRC (FOX) Birmingham; WCOV-TV (FOX) Montgomery; WIYC (IND) Troy; WMCF-TV (TBN) Montgomery; WNCF (ABC) Montgomery; WSFA (NBC) Montgomery; allband FM.

Programming (via satellite): C-SPAN; QVC.

Fee: $29.99 installation.

Expanded Basic Service 1

Subscribers: 5,500.

Programming (via satellite): ABC Family Channel; AMC; Animal Planet; Arts & Entertainment; BET Networks; Cartoon Network; CNBC; CNN; Comcast Sports Net Southeast; Country Music TV; Discovery Channel; Disney Channel; ESPN; ESPN 2; Fox News Channel; Headline News; HGTV; Lifetime; MTV; Nickelodeon; Shop at Home; Spike TV; Syfy; TBS Superstation; The Learning Channel; Travel Channel; Turner Network TV; TV Land; USA Network; VH1; Weather Channel.

Fee: $43.00 monthly.

Digital Basic Service

Subscribers: N.A.

Programming (via satellite): BBC America; Bravo; Discovery Digital Networks; DMX Music; ESPN Classic Sports; ESPNews; Fox Sports World; Golf Channel; GSN; History Channel; Independent Film Channel; Nick Jr.; Turner Classic Movies; TV Guide Interactive Inc.; Versus; WE tv.

Fee: $16.99 monthly.

Digital Pay Service 1

Pay Units: N.A.

Programming (via satellite): Cinemax (multiplexed); Encore (multiplexed); HBO (multiplexed); Showtime (multiplexed); Starz (multiplexed); The Movie Channel.

Video-On-Demand: Yes

Pay-Per-View

iN DEMAND (delivered digitally); Playboy TV (delivered digitally).

Internet Service

Operational: Yes.

Broadband Service: Charter Pipeline.

Fee: $29.99 monthly.

Telephone Service

Digital: Operational

Miles of Plant: 196.0 (coaxial); None (fiber optic). Homes passed: 11,274. Total homes in franchised area: 11,274.

Vice President & General Manager: Don Karell. Technical Operations Director: Greg Prim. Marketing Director: David Redmond. Marketing Manager: Jeff Hatcher.

City fee: 3% of gross.

Ownership: Charter Communications Inc. (MSO).

SHELBY LAKE—Charter Communications, 2100 Columbiana Rd, Vestavia, AL 35216. Phone: 205-824-5400. Fax: 205-824-5490. Web Site: http://www.charter.com. Also serves Lay Lake & Shelby County (southern portion). ICA: AL0222.

TV Market Ranking: 40 (Lay Lake, Shelby County (southern portion), SHELBY LAKE). Franchise award date: N.A. Franchise expiration date: N.A. Began: N.A.

Channel capacity: 40 (not 2-way capable). Channels available but not in use: None.

Basic Service

Subscribers: 766.

Programming (received off-air): WABM (MNT) Birmingham; WBIQ (PBS) Birmingham; WBRC (FOX) Birmingham; WCFT-TV (ABC) Tuscaloosa; WIAT (CBS) Birmingham; WTTO (CW) Homewood; WVTM-TV (NBC) Birmingham.

Programming (via satellite): C-SPAN; Home Shopping Network; QVC; WGN America.

Fee: $29.99 installation.

Expanded Basic Service 1

Subscribers: 733.

Programming (via satellite): ABC Family Channel; AMC; Animal Planet; Arts & Entertainment; Cartoon Network; CNN; Comcast Sports Net Southeast; Country Music TV; Discovery Channel; Disney Channel; ESPN; ESPN 2; FX; Headline News; Lifetime; MTV; Nickelodeon; Spike TV; Syfy; TBS Superstation; The Learning Channel; Toon Disney; Turner Network TV; TV Land; USA Network; WE tv; Weather Channel.

Fee: $43.00 monthly.

Digital Basic Service

Subscribers: N.A.

Programming (via satellite): AmericanLife TV Network; BBC America; Bio; Bloomberg Television; Bravo; Discovery Digital Networks; DMX Music; ESPN Classic Sports; ESPNews; Fox Movie Channel; G4; GAS; Golf Channel; GSN; Halogen Network; HGTV; History Channel; History Channel International; Independent Film Channel; Lifetime Movie Network; MTV Networks Digital Suite; MuchMusic Network; Nick Jr.; Outdoor Channel; ShopNBC; Speed Channel; Style Network; Trinity Broadcasting Network; Turner Classic Movies; Versus.

Fee: $16.99 monthly.

Pay Service 1

Pay Units: 127.

Programming (via satellite): HBO.

Fee: $9.95 monthly.

Pay Service 2

Pay Units: 132.

Programming (via satellite): Showtime.

Fee: $9.95 monthly.

Digital Pay Service 1

Pay Units: N.A.

Programming (via satellite): Cinemax (multiplexed); Encore (multiplexed); HBO (multiplexed); Showtime (multiplexed); Starz (multiplexed); The Movie Channel (multiplexed).

Video-On-Demand: No

Pay-Per-View

ESPN Extra (delivered digitally); ESPN Now (delivered digitally); Hot Choice (delivered digitally); iN DEMAND (delivered digitally); Playboy TV (delivered digitally); Fresh (delivered digitally); Shorteez (delivered digitally).

Internet Service

Operational: No.

Telephone Service
None
Miles of Plant: 54.0 (coaxial); None (fiber optic). Homes passed: 1,719.
Vice President & General Manager: Don Karell. Technical Operations Director: Greg Prim. Marketing Director: David Redmond. Marketing Manager: Jeff Hatcher.
Ownership: Charter Communications Inc. (MSO).

SKYLINE—Formerly served by Almega Cable. No longer in operation. ICA: AL0223.

SOUTHSIDE—Charter Communications, 2100 Columbiana Rd, Vestavia, AL 35216. Phone: 205-824-5400. Fax: 205-824-5490. Web Site: http://www.charter.com. Also serves Hokes Bluff. ICA: AL0076.
TV Market Ranking: Below 100 (Hokes Bluff, SOUTHSIDE). Franchise award date: N.A. Franchise expiration date: N.A. Began: February 1, 1981.
Channel capacity: 52 (not 2-way capable). Channels available but not in use: None.
Basic Service
Subscribers: 3,982.
Programming (received off-air): WBRC (FOX) Birmingham; WCIQ (PBS) Mount Cheaha State Park; WIAT (CBS) Birmingham; WJSU-TV (ABC) Anniston; WTJP-TV (TBN) Gadsden; WTTO (CW) Homewood; WVTM-TV (NBC) Birmingham.
Programming (via satellite): Home Shopping Network; ION Television; TV Guide Network; WGN America.
Current originations: Public Access.
Fee: $29.99 installation.
Expanded Basic Service 1
Subscribers: 2,080.
Programming (via satellite): ABC Family Channel; AMC; Animal Planet; Arts & Entertainment; Cartoon Network; CNBC; CNN; Comcast Sports Net Southeast; Comcast/Charter Sports Southeast (CSS); Comedy Central; Country Music TV; C-SPAN; C-SPAN 2; Discovery Channel; Disney Channel; E! Entertainment Television; ESPN; ESPN 2; Fox News Channel; FX; Headline News; HGTV; History Channel; INSP; Lifetime; MTV; Nickelodeon; QVC; SoapNet; Spike TV; SportSouth; Syfy; TBS Superstation; The Learning Channel; Toon Disney; Turner Network TV; TV Land; USA Network; VH1; WE tv; Weather Channel.
Fee: $43.00 monthly.
Digital Basic Service
Subscribers: N.A.
Programming (via satellite): AmericanLife TV Network; BBC America; Bio; Bloomberg Television; Bravo; Discovery Digital Networks; ESPN Classic Sports; Fox Movie Channel; G4; GAS; Golf Channel; GSN; Halogen Network; History Channel International; Independent Film Channel; Lifetime Movie Network; MTV Networks Digital Suite; MuchMusic Network; Music Choice; Nick Jr.; Outdoor Channel; ShopNBC; Speed Channel; Style Network; Turner Classic Movies; TV Guide Interactive Inc.; Versus.
Fee: $16.99 monthly.
Digital Pay Service 1
Pay Units: 188.
Programming (via satellite): Cinemax (multiplexed).
Fee: $10.95 monthly.
Digital Pay Service 2
Pay Units: 542.
Programming (via satellite): The Movie Channel (multiplexed).
Fee: $10.95 monthly.
Digital Pay Service 3
Pay Units: 591.
Programming (via satellite): HBO (multiplexed).
Fee: $10.95 monthly.
Digital Pay Service 4
Pay Units: 787.
Programming (via satellite): Flix; Showtime (multiplexed).
Fee: $10.95 monthly.
Digital Pay Service 5
Pay Units: N.A.
Programming (via satellite): Encore (multiplexed); Starz (multiplexed).
Fee: $10.95 monthly.
Video-On-Demand: No
Pay-Per-View
Addressable homes: 355.
ESPN Extra (delivered digitally); ESPN Now (delivered digitally); iN DEMAND (delivered digitally); Playboy TV (delivered digitally); Fresh (delivered digitally); Shorteez (delivered digitally); Urban Xtra (delivered digitally).
Internet Service
Operational: Yes.
Fee: $39.99 monthly.
Telephone Service
Digital: Operational
Fee: $29.99 monthly
Miles of Plant: 157.0 (coaxial); None (fiber optic). Homes passed: 5,195. Total homes in franchised area: 8,127.
Vice President & General Manager: Don Karell. Technical Operations Manager: Greg Prim. Marketing Director: David Redmond. Marketing Manager: Jeff Hatcher.
Ownership: Charter Communications Inc. (MSO).

SPANISH COVE—Mediacom. Now served by FAIRHOPE (formerly Daphne), AL [AL0124]. ICA: AL0119.

STAPLETON—Mediacom. Now served by FAIRHOPE (formerly Daphne), AL [AL0124]. ICA: AL0235.

SULLIGENT—CommuniComm Services, 3164 Hwy 431, Ste 9, Roanoke, AL 36274-1702. Phone: 334-863-7080. Fax: 334-863-2027. Web Site: http://www.netcommander.com. Also serves Vernon. ICA: AL0084.
TV Market Ranking: Below 100 (SULLIGENT, Vernon). Franchise award date: N.A. Franchise expiration date: N.A. Began: December 1, 1964.
Channel capacity: N.A. Channels available but not in use: N.A.
Basic Service
Subscribers: 964.
Programming (received off-air): WBRC (FOX) Birmingham; WCBI-TV (CBS, CW, MNT) Columbus; WCFT-TV (ABC) Tuscaloosa; WFIQ (PBS) Florence; WIAT (CBS) Birmingham; WLOV-TV (FOX) West Point; WTTO (CW) Homewood; WTVA (NBC) Tupelo; WVTM-TV (NBC) Birmingham.
Programming (via satellite): Superstation WGN.
Fee: $25.00 installation; $12.95 monthly; $3.95 converter; $10.00 additional installation.
Expanded Basic Service 1
Subscribers: N.A.
Programming (via satellite): ABC Family Channel; American Movie Classics; Animal Planet; Arts & Entertainment; BET Networks; Bravo; Cartoon Network; CNBC; CNN; Comcast/Charter Sports Southeast (CSS); Comedy Central; Country Music TV; C-SPAN; C-SPAN 2; Discovery Channel; Disney Channel; E! Entertainment Television; ESPN; ESPN 2; ESPN Classic Sports; ESPNews; Food Network; Fox News Channel; FX; Headline News; HGTV; History Channel; Home Shopping Network; Lifetime; MSNBC; MTV; Nick Jr.; Nickelodeon; Outdoor Channel; QVC; RFD-TV; ShopNBC; Speed Channel; Spike TV; Syfy; TBS Superstation; The Learning Channel; Travel Channel; Trinity Broadcasting Network; truTV; Turner Classic Movies; Turner Network TV; TV Land; USA Network; VH1; WE tv; Weather Channel.
Digital Basic Service
Subscribers: 128.
Programming (via satellite): AmericanLife TV Network; BBC America; Bio; Blackbelt TV; Bloomberg Television; Church Channel; CMT Pure Country; Current; Discovery Health Channel; Discovery Military Channel; Discovery Planet Green; DMX Music; FitTV; Fox Movie Channel; Fox Soccer; Fuse; G4; Golf Channel; Gospel Music Channel; Great American Country; GSN; Halogen Network; Healthy Living Channel; History Channel International; ID Investigation Discovery; JCTV; Lifetime Movie Network; MTV Hits; MTV Jams; National Geographic Channel; Ovation; Science Channel; Sleuth; SoapNet; Sundance Channel; TeenNick; The Word Network; Toon Disney; Versus; VH1 Classic; VH1 Soul.
Digital Pay Service 1
Pay Units: 93.
Programming (via satellite): Cinemax (multiplexed); Encore (multiplexed); Flix; HBO (multiplexed); Showtime (multiplexed); Starz (multiplexed); The Movie Channel.
Video-On-Demand: No
Pay-Per-View
iN DEMAND (delivered digitally); Hot Choice (delivered digitally); Playboy TV (delivered digitally); Fresh (delivered digitally); Spice: Xcess (delivered digitally).
Internet Service
Operational: Yes.
Subscribers: 123.
Broadband Service: Net Commander.
Fee: $39.95 installation; $51.95 monthly.
Telephone Service
None
Miles of Plant: 64.0 (coaxial); None (fiber optic). Homes passed: 2,482.
General Manager: Brian Chase. Chief Technician: William Boyd.
City fee: $125 annually.
Ownership: James Cable LLC (MSO).

SWEET WATER—Sky Cablevision, PO Box 65, 1309 Roebuck Dr, Meridian, MS 39301. Phone: 601-485-6980. Fax: 601-483-0103. Web Site: http://skycablevision.com. ICA: AL0227.
TV Market Ranking: Outside TV Markets (SWEET WATER). Franchise award date: N.A. Franchise expiration date: N.A. Began: September 9, 1989.
Channel capacity: N.A. Channels available but not in use: N.A.
Basic Service
Subscribers: N.A.
Programming (received off-air): WGBC (NBC) Meridian; WIIQ (PBS) Demopolis; WMDN (CBS) Meridian; WTOK-TV (ABC, CW, FOX, MNT) Meridian.
Programming (via satellite): ABC Family Channel; Arts & Entertainment; CNN; Discovery Channel; Disney Channel; ESPN; TBS Superstation; Turner Network TV; USA Network; WGN America.
Fee: $34.00 monthly.
Pay Service 1
Pay Units: N.A.
Programming (via satellite): HBO.
Fee: $11.00 monthly.
Internet Service
Operational: No.
Telephone Service
None
Manager & Chief Technician: Berry Ward.
Ownership: Sky Cablevision Ltd. (MSO).

SYLACAUGA—Charter Communications. Now served by LEEDS, AL [AL0192]. ICA: AL0031.

TALLADEGA—Charter Communications. Now served by LEEDS, AL [AL0192]. ICA: AL0024.

THOMASTON—Galaxy Cablevision, PO Box 879, 118 S Jackson St, Grove Hill, AL 36451-0879. Phone: 251-275-3118. Fax: 251-275-3120. Web Site: http://www.galaxycable.com. ICA: AL0146.
TV Market Ranking: Outside TV Markets (THOMASTON). Franchise award date: September 19, 1988. Franchise expiration date: N.A. Began: November 1, 1989.
Channel capacity: 54 (not 2-way capable). Channels available but not in use: 21.
Basic Service
Subscribers: 53.
Programming (received off-air): WAKA (CBS) Selma; WCOV-TV (FOX) Montgomery; WIIQ (PBS) Demopolis; WNCF (ABC) Montgomery; WSFA (NBC) Montgomery.
Programming (via satellite): ABC Family Channel; AMC; Arts & Entertainment; Cartoon Network; CNN; Discovery Channel; Disney Channel; E! Entertainment Television; ESPN; ESPN 2; Great American Country; Hallmark Channel; Headline News; HGTV; Lifetime; Outdoor Channel; QVC; Speed Channel; SportSouth; TBS Superstation; Toon Disney; Trinity Broadcasting Network; Turner Network TV; USA Network; Weather Channel; WGN America.
Current originations: Public Access.
Fee: $25.00 installation; $39.60 monthly.
Pay Service 1
Pay Units: N.A.
Programming (via satellite): HBO.
Fee: $9.95 monthly.
Internet Service
Operational: No.
Telephone Service
None
Miles of Plant: 11.0 (coaxial); None (fiber optic). Homes passed: 260.
State Manager: Bill Flowers. Technical Manager & Engineer: Greg Berthaut. Customer Service Representative: Lisa Ray.
Ownership: Galaxy Cable Inc. (MSO).

THOMASVILLE—Mediacom, 760 Middle St, PO Box 1009, Fairhope, AL 36532. Phones: 850-934-7700 (Gulf Breeze regional office); 251-928-0374. Fax: 251-928-3804. Web Site: http://www.mediacomcable.com. Also serves Clarke County (portions) & Jackson. ICA: AL0080.
TV Market Ranking: Outside TV Markets (Clarke County (portions), Jackson, THOMASVILLE). Franchise award date: February 23, 1976. Franchise expiration date: N.A. Began: February 1, 1976.
Channel capacity: N.A. Channels available but not in use: N.A.
Basic Service
Subscribers: 2,601.
Programming (received off-air): WAKA (CBS) Selma; WALA-TV (FOX) Mobile;

WBIH (IND) Selma; WEAR-TV (ABC) Pensacola; WIIQ (PBS) Demopolis; WKRG-TV (CBS) Mobile; WMAH-TV (PBS) Biloxi; WPMI-TV (NBC) Mobile; WSFA (NBC) Montgomery; WTOK-TV (ABC, CW, FOX, MNT) Meridian; 1 FM.

Programming (via satellite): ABC Family Channel; AMC; Animal Planet; Arts & Entertainment; BET Networks; Bravo; Cartoon Network; CNBC; CNN; Comcast Sports Net Southeast; Comedy Central; Country Music TV; C-SPAN; C-SPAN 2; Discovery Channel; Disney Channel; E! Entertainment Television; ESPN; ESPN 2; Eternal Word TV Network; FitTV; Food Network; Fox News Channel; FX; Hallmark Channel; Headline News; HGTV; History Channel; Home Shopping Network; INSP; ION Television; Lifetime; MSNBC; MTV; Nickelodeon; Outdoor Channel; QVC; Speed Channel; Spike TV; SportSouth; Syfy; TBS Superstation; The Learning Channel; Travel Channel; Trinity Broadcasting Network; truTV; Turner Classic Movies; Turner Network TV; TV Land; USA Network; VH1; WE tv; Weather Channel; WGN America.

Fee: $49.95 monthly.

Digital Basic Service

Subscribers: 445.

Programming (via satellite): AmericanLife TV Network; BBC America; Bio; Bloomberg Television; Discovery Digital Networks; Fox Movie Channel; Fox Sports World; Fuse; G4; GSN; Halogen Network; History Channel International; Independent Film Channel; Lifetime Movie Network; Music Choice; Style Network; Versus.

Fee: $12.00 monthly.

Digital Pay Service 1

Pay Units: 226.

Programming (via satellite): Cinemax (multiplexed).

Fee: $10.45 monthly.

Digital Pay Service 2

Pay Units: 452.

Programming (via satellite): Encore (multiplexed); Starz (multiplexed).

Fee: $10.45 monthly.

Digital Pay Service 3

Pay Units: 420.

Programming (via satellite): Flix; Sundance Channel; The Movie Channel (multiplexed).

Fee: $10.45 monthly.

Digital Pay Service 4

Pay Units: 456.

Programming (via satellite): HBO (multiplexed).

Fee: $10.45 monthly.

Digital Pay Service 5

Pay Units: 414.

Programming (via satellite): Showtime (multiplexed).

Fee: $10.45 monthly.

Video-On-Demand: No

Pay-Per-View

Addressable homes: 445.

ESPN Now (delivered digitally), Addressable: Yes; ETC (delivered digitally); Pleasure (delivered digitally); TVN Entertainment (delivered digitally); sports (delivered digitally).

Internet Service

Operational: Yes.

Telephone Service

None

Homes passed: 4,900. Miles of plant (coax & fiber) included in Camden

Vice President: David Servies. Operations Director: Gene Wuchner. Technical Operations Manager: Mike Sneary. Sales & Marketing Manager: Joey Nagem.

City fee: 5% of gross.

Ownership: Mediacom LLC (MSO).

THORSBY—Charter Communications, 2100 Columbiana Rd, Vestavia, AL 35216. Phone: 205-824-5400. Fax: 205-824-5490. Web Site: http://www.charter.com. Also serves Jemison. ICA: AL0200.

TV Market Ranking: Below 100 (Jemison, THORSBY). Franchise award date: N.A. Franchise expiration date: N.A. Began: June 1, 1984.

Channel capacity: N.A. Channels available but not in use: N.A.

Basic Service

Subscribers: 817.

Programming (received off-air): WABM (MNT) Birmingham; WBIQ (PBS) Birmingham; WBRC (FOX) Birmingham; WCFT-TV (ABC) Tuscaloosa; WIAT (CBS) Birmingham; WPXH-TV (ION) Gadsden; WTTO (CW) Homewood; WVTM-TV (NBC) Birmingham.

Programming (via satellite): C-SPAN; Home Shopping Network; WGN America.

Current originations: Religious Access; Public Access.

Fee: $29.99 installation.

Expanded Basic Service 1

Subscribers: N.A.

Programming (via satellite): ABC Family Channel; AMC; Animal Planet; Arts & Entertainment; Bravo; Cartoon Network; CNBC; CNN; Comcast Sports Net Southeast; Comedy Central; Country Music TV; Discovery Channel; Disney Channel; E! Entertainment Television; ESPN; ESPN 2; Fox News Channel; FX; G4; Golf Channel; Headline News; HGTV; History Channel; MTV; Nickelodeon; Oxygen; Speed Channel; Spike TV; SportSouth; Syfy; TBS Superstation; The Learning Channel; Toon Disney; Travel Channel; Turner Classic Movies; Turner Network TV; TV Land; USA Network; VH1; WE tv; Weather Channel.

Fee: $43.00 monthly.

Digital Basic Service

Subscribers: N.A.

Programming (via satellite): BBC America; Bio; Bloomberg Television; Discovery Digital Networks; ESPN Classic Sports; ESPNews; Fox Movie Channel; Fox Soccer; Fuse; GAS; GSN; History Channel International; Independent Film Channel; Lifetime Movie Network; MTV Networks Digital Suite; Music Choice; Nick Jr.; Nick Too; NickToons TV; Style Network; Sundance Channel.

Fee: $16.99 monthly.

Pay Service 1

Pay Units: N.A.

Programming (via satellite): Flix (multiplexed); Showtime (multiplexed); The Movie Channel (multiplexed).

Digital Pay Service 1

Pay Units: 232.

Programming (via satellite): Cinemax (multiplexed); Encore (multiplexed); HBO (multiplexed); Starz (multiplexed).

Fee: $9.95 monthly (each).

Video-On-Demand: No

Pay-Per-View

ESPN Extra (delivered digitally); ESPN Now (delivered digitally); iN DEMAND (delivered digitally); Playboy TV (delivered digitally); Fresh (delivered digitally).

Internet Service

Operational: No.

Telephone Service

None

Miles of Plant: 53.0 (coaxial); None (fiber optic). Homes passed: 1,543.

Vice President & General Manager: Don Karell. Technical Operations Director: Greg Prim. Marketing Director: David Remond. Marketing Manager: Jeff Hatcher.

City fee: 3% of gross.

Ownership: Charter Communications Inc. (MSO).

TRAFFORD—Formerly served by Almega Cable. No longer in operation. ICA: AL0228.

TRINITY—Coosa Cable, 1701 Cogswell Ave, Pell City, AL 35125-1646. Phones: 800-824-4773; 205-884-4545. Fax: 205-884-4510. E-mail: coosacable@coosahs.net. Web Site: http://www.coosahs.net. Also serves Lawrence County (portions). ICA: AL0108.

TV Market Ranking: 96 (Lawrence County (portions), TRINITY). Franchise award date: N.A. Franchise expiration date: N.A. Began: March 1, 1987.

Channel capacity: 36 (not 2-way capable). Channels available but not in use: 10.

Basic Service

Subscribers: 507.

Programming (received off-air): WAAY-TV (ABC) Huntsville; WAFF (NBC) Huntsville; WHDF (CW) Florence; WHIQ (PBS) Huntsville; WHNT-TV (CBS) Huntsville; WZDX (FOX, MNT) Huntsville.

Programming (via satellite): ABC Family Channel; Animal Planet; Arts & Entertainment; Cartoon Network; CNN; Comcast Sports Net Southeast; Comedy Central; C-SPAN; Disney Channel; ESPN; ESPN 2; FitTV; Fox News Channel; Great American Country; Hallmark Channel; Headline News; HGTV; History Channel; Home Shopping Network; Lifetime; Nickelodeon; Spike TV; TBS Superstation; The Learning Channel; Turner Classic Movies; Turner Network TV; TV Land; USA Network; WE tv; Weather Channel; WGN America.

Fee: $40.00 installation; $30.00 monthly; $1.00 converter; $10.00 additional installation.

Pay Service 1

Pay Units: 284.

Programming (via satellite): HBO.

Fee: $12.00 monthly.

Pay Service 2

Pay Units: 136.

Programming (via satellite): Cinemax.

Fee: $9.50 monthly.

Digital Pay Service 1

Pay Units: N.A.

Programming (via satellite): Cinemax (multiplexed); HBO (multiplexed); Showtime (multiplexed); Starz (multiplexed); The Movie Channel (multiplexed).

Fee: $5.95 monthly (Starz), $12.00 monthly (HBO), $13.50 monthly (Showtime).

Video-On-Demand: No

Internet Service

Operational: Yes.

Fee: $40.00 installation; $18.50-$45.95 monthly.

Telephone Service

Digital: Operational

Fee: $46.95 monthly

Miles of Plant: 30.0 (coaxial); None (fiber optic). Additional miles planned: 1.0 (coaxial). Homes passed: 1,040. Total homes in franchised area: 1,200.

President & Technical Operations Manager: Jeff Smith. Chief Executive Officer: Arthur M. Smith. Manager: Alton D. Elliott. Chief Technician: T. Coolidge. Administrative Assistant: Wanda Scott.

Ownership: Trinity Cablevision Inc.

TROY—Charter Communications, 2100 Columbiana Rd, Vestavia, AL 35216. Phone: 205-824-5400. Fax: 205-824-5490. Web Site: http://www.charter.com. Also serves Brundidge, Dale County, Elba, Ozark & Pike County. ICA: AL0027.

TV Market Ranking: Below 100 (Brundidge, Dale County, Elba, Ozark, Pike County, TROY). Franchise award date: N.A. Franchise expiration date: N.A. Began: November 1, 1974.

Channel capacity: N.A. Channels available but not in use: N.A.

Basic Service

Subscribers: 3,186.

Programming (received off-air): WAKA (CBS) Selma; WBMM (CW) Tuskegee; WCOV-TV (FOX) Montgomery; WDIQ (PBS) Dozier; WIYC (IND) Troy; WNCF (ABC) Montgomery; WSFA (NBC) Montgomery; WTVM (ABC) Columbus; WTVY (CBS, CW, MNT) Dothan.

Programming (via satellite): ABC Family Channel; CNBC; Home Shopping Network; TBS Superstation; WGN America.

Current originations: Government Access; Educational Access; Public Access.

Fee: $29.99 installation.

Expanded Basic Service 1

Subscribers: 2,911.

Programming (via satellite): ABC Family Channel; AMC; Animal Planet; Arts & Entertainment; BET Networks; Bravo; Cartoon Network; CNN; Comcast Sports Net Southeast; Comedy Central; Country Music TV; C-SPAN; C-SPAN 2; Discovery Channel; Disney Channel; E! Entertainment Television; ESPN; ESPN 2; Food Network; Fox News Channel; FX; G4; Golf Channel; GSN; Hallmark Channel; Headline News; HGTV; History Channel; INSP; Lifetime; MSNBC; MTV; National Geographic Channel; Nickelodeon; Oxygen; SoapNet; Speed Channel; Spike TV; SportSouth; Syfy; Telemundo; The Learning Channel; Toon Disney; Travel Channel; Trinity Broadcasting Network; truTV; Turner Classic Movies; Turner Network TV; TV Land; Univision; USA Network; Versus; VH1; WE tv; Weather Channel.

Fee: $43.00 monthly.

Digital Basic Service

Subscribers: N.A.

Programming (via satellite): BBC America; Bio; Bloomberg Television; Discovery Digital Networks; Do-It-Yourself; ESPN Classic Sports; ESPNews; Fox College Sports Atlantic; Fox College Sports Central; Fox College Sports Pacific; Fox Movie Channel; Fox Sports en Espanol; Fox Sports World; Fuse; GAS; Great American Country; History Channel International; Independent Film Channel; Lifetime Movie Network; MTV Networks Digital Suite; Music Choice; NFL Network; Nick Jr.; Nick Too; NickToons TV; Sundance Channel.

Fee: $16.99 monthly.

Digital Pay Service 1

Pay Units: N.A.

Programming (via satellite): Cinemax (multiplexed); Encore (multiplexed); Flix; HBO (multiplexed); Showtime (multiplexed); Starz (multiplexed); The Movie Channel (multiplexed).

Video-On-Demand: No

Pay-Per-View

NASCAR In Car (delivered digitally); Hot Choice (delivered digitally); NHL Center Ice (delivered digitally); MLB Extra Innings (delivered digitally); Playboy TV (delivered digitally); Fresh (delivered digitally); Shorteez (delivered digitally); iN DEMAND (delivered digitally).

Internet Service
Operational: Yes.
Broadband Service: Charter Pipeline.
Fee: $29.99 monthly.
Telephone Service
Digital: Operational
Miles of Plant: 155.0 (coaxial); None (fiber optic). Homes passed: 6,946. Total homes in franchised area: 7,230.
Vice President & General Manager: Don Karell. Technical Operations Director: Greg Prim. Marketing Director: David Redmond. Marketing Manager: Jeff Hatcher.
City fee: 3% of gross.
Ownership: Charter Communications Inc. (MSO).

TROY—Troy Cablevision & Entertainment, 1006 S Brundidge St, Troy, AL 36081-3121. Phones: 800-735-9546; 334-566-3310. Fax: 334-566-3304. E-mail: support@troycable.net. Web Site: http://www.troycable.net. ICA: AL0032. **Note:** This system is an overbuild.
TV Market Ranking: Below 100 (TROY). Franchise award date: May 6, 1985. Franchise expiration date: N.A. Began: July 15, 1986.
Channel capacity: N.A. Channels available but not in use: N.A.
Basic Service
Subscribers: 2,977.
Programming (received off-air): WAKA (CBS) Selma; WBMM (CW) Tuskegee; WCIQ (PBS) Mount Cheaha State Park; WCOV-TV (FOX) Montgomery; WIYC (IND) Troy; WLTZ (CW, NBC) Columbus; WNCF (ABC) Montgomery; WSFA (NBC) Montgomery; WTVM (ABC) Columbus; WTVY (CBS, CW, MNT) Dothan.
Programming (via satellite): ABC Family Channel; AMC; Animal Planet; Arts & Entertainment; BET Networks; Bravo; CNBC; CNN; Comcast Sports Net Southeast; Comcast/Charter Sports Southeast (CSS); Comedy Central; Country Music TV; C-SPAN; C-SPAN 2; Discovery Channel; Disney Channel; E! Entertainment Television; ESPN; ESPN 2; ESPN Classic Sports; Food Network; Fox News Channel; FX; Golf Channel; GSN; Hallmark Channel; Headline News; HGTV; History Channel; Home Shopping Network; INSP; Lifetime; MSNBC; MTV; National Geographic Channel; Nickelodeon; QVC; Speed Channel; Spike TV; SportSouth; Syfy; TBS Superstation; The Learning Channel; Toon Disney; Travel Channel; Turner Classic Movies; Turner Network TV; TV Guide Network; TV Land; USA Network; VH1; Weather Channel; WGN America.
Current originations: Public Access; Educational Access.
Fee: $15.00 monthly.
Digital Basic Service
Subscribers: N.A.
Programming (via satellite): AmericanLife TV Network; BBC America; Bio; Bloomberg Television; Discovery Digital Networks; Discovery HD Theater; ESPN; ESPNews; FitTV; Fox College Sports Atlantic; Fox College Sports Central; Fox College Sports Pacific; Fox Movie Channel; Fox Soccer; Fox Sports en Espanol; Fuse; G4; GAS; Halogen Network; HDNet; HDNet Movies; History Channel International; Lifetime Movie Network; MTV Networks Digital Suite; Music Choice; Nick Jr.; Nick Too; NickToons TV; Outdoor Channel; Sleuth; SoapNet; Style Network; Toon Disney; Trinity Broadcasting Network.
Digital Pay Service 1
Pay Units: N.A.
Programming (via satellite): Cinemax (multiplexed); Encore (multiplexed); Flix; HBO (multiplexed); Showtime (multiplexed); Starz (multiplexed); Sundance Channel; The Movie Channel (multiplexed).
Fee: $7.95 monthly (Cinemax or Starz), $8.95 monthly (Encore), $10.95 monthly (Showtime & TMC), $11.95 monthly (HBO).
Video-On-Demand: No
Pay-Per-View
iN DEMAND (delivered digitally); Hot Choice (delivered digitally); Pleasure (delivered digitally); College Football (delivered digitally).
Internet Service
Operational: Yes. Began: June 1, 2000.
Subscribers: 1,550.
Broadband Service: In-house.
Fee: $49.95 installation; $41.95-$54.95 monthly.
Telephone Service
Digital: Operational
Miles of Plant: 110.0 (coaxial); None (fiber optic). Homes passed: 6,233.
Manager: William Freeman. Chief Technician: Ken Jordan.
City fee: 3% of gross.
Ownership: Troy Cablevision (MSO).

TUSCALOOSA—Comcast Cable, 1131 Whigham Place, Tuscaloosa, AL 35405-3669. Phone: 205-391-3677. Web Site: http://www.comcast.com. Also serves Abernant, Jefferson County (southern portion), Northport & Tuscaloosa County. ICA: AL0230.
TV Market Ranking: 40 (Abernant, Jefferson County (southern portion)); Below 100 (Northport, TUSCALOOSA, Tuscaloosa County). Franchise award date: N.A. Franchise expiration date: N.A. Began: July 1, 1957.
Channel capacity: 70 (operating 2-way). Channels available but not in use: N.A.
Basic Service
Subscribers: 38,000.
Programming (received off-air): WABM (MNT) Birmingham; WBIQ (PBS) Birmingham; WBRC (FOX) Birmingham; WCFT-TV (ABC) Tuscaloosa; WDBB (CW) Bessemer; WIAT (CBS) Birmingham; WVTM-TV (NBC) Birmingham.
Programming (via satellite): ABC Family Channel; AMC; Arts & Entertainment; BET Networks; Cartoon Network; CNBC; CNN; Comcast Sports Net Southeast; C-SPAN; C-SPAN 2; Deutsche Welle TV; Discovery Channel; Disney Channel; E! Entertainment Television; ESPN; ESPN 2; Eternal Word TV Network; Food Network; G4; Great American Country; GSN; Headline News; HGTV; History Channel; Home Shopping Network; INSP; Lifetime; MTV; MTV2; Music Choice; Nickelodeon; QVC; Radar Channel; Speed Channel; Spike TV; Style Network; TBS Superstation; The Learning Channel; Turner Network TV; TV Guide Network; TV Land; USA Network; VH1; Weather Channel; WGN America.
Current originations: Educational Access.
Fee: $62.99 installation; $8.85 monthly.
Expanded Basic Service 1
Subscribers: N.A.
Programming (via satellite): Animal Planet; Comedy Central; ESPN Classic Sports; Fox News Channel; Golf Channel; Syfy; Trinity Broadcasting Network.
Fee: $39.40 monthly.
Digital Basic Service
Subscribers: N.A.
Programming (via satellite): BBC America; Discovery Digital Networks; Flix; GAS; MTV Networks Digital Suite; Music Choice; Nick Jr.; Sundance Channel; Weatherscan.
Fee: $14.95 monthly.
Digital Pay Service 1
Pay Units: N.A.
Programming (via satellite): Cinemax (multiplexed); Encore; Flix; HBO (multiplexed); Showtime (multiplexed); The Movie Channel (multiplexed).
Fee: $14.95 monthly (each).
Video-On-Demand: Yes
Pay-Per-View
ESPN Extra (delivered digitally); ESPN Gameplan (delivered digitally); ESPN Now (delivered digitally); Hot Choice (delivered digitally); iN DEMAND (delivered digitally); iN DEMAND (delivered digitally); Fresh (delivered digitally); Sports PPV (delivered digitally).
Internet Service
Operational: Yes.
Broadband Service: Comcast High Speed Internet.
Fee: $42.95 monthly; $7.00 modem lease.
Telephone Service
Digital: Operational
Miles of Plant: 752.0 (coaxial); None (fiber optic).
Chief Technician: Johnny Mills.
City fee: 3% of gross.
Ownership: Comcast Cable Communications Inc. (MSO).

TUSCALOOSA COUNTY—Charter Communications. Now served by LEEDS, AL [AL0192]. ICA: AL0060.

TUSKEGEE—Charter Communications. Now served by LEEDS, AL [AL0192]. ICA: AL0041.

UNION SPRINGS—Com-Link Inc., 206 Hardaway Ave E, Union Springs, AL 36089-1609. Phones: 800-722-2805; 334-738-4400. Fax: 334-738-5555. Web Site: http://www.ustconline.net. Also serves Aberfoil & Midway. ICA: AL0088.
TV Market Ranking: Below 100 (Aberfoil, Midway, UNION SPRINGS). Franchise award date: October 1, 1980. Franchise expiration date: N.A. Began: April 1, 1981.
Channel capacity: 51 (not 2-way capable). Channels available but not in use: 9.
Basic Service
Subscribers: 1,300.
Programming (received off-air): WAIQ (PBS) Montgomery; WAKA (CBS) Selma; WCOV-TV (FOX) Montgomery; WMCF-TV (TBN) Montgomery; WNCF (ABC) Montgomery; WSFA (NBC) Montgomery; WTVM (ABC) Columbus.
Programming (via satellite): CNN; Discovery Channel; ESPN; TBS Superstation.
Current originations: Government Access; Educational Access; Public Access.
Fee: $35.00 installation; $24.70 monthly.
Expanded Basic Service 1
Subscribers: 1,069.
Programming (via satellite): ABC Family Channel; Arts & Entertainment; BET Networks; CNBC; Comcast Sports Net Southeast; ESPN 2; Headline News; History Channel; Lifetime; Nickelodeon; QVC; Spike TV; Turner Network TV; USA Network; Weather Channel; WGN America.
Fee: $16.00 monthly.
Video-On-Demand: No
Internet Service
Operational: Yes.
Broadband Service: In-house.
Fee: $42.50 installation; $34.95-$59.95 monthly.
Telephone Service
None
Miles of Plant: 30.0 (coaxial); 50.0 (fiber optic). Homes passed: 2,227.
Executive Vice President: Larry Grogan. Chief Technician: Lynn Rotton.
City fee: 3% of gross.
Ownership: Com-Link Inc. (MSO).

UNIONTOWN—Galaxy Cablevision, PO Box 879, 118 S Jackson St, Grove Hill, AL 36451-0879. Phone: 251-275-3118. Fax: 251-275-3120. Web Site: http://www.galaxycable.com. Also serves Perry County. ICA: AL0118.
TV Market Ranking: Below 100 (Perry County, UNIONTOWN). Franchise award date: N.A. Franchise expiration date: N.A. Began: N.A.
Channel capacity: 36 (not 2-way capable). Channels available but not in use: None.
Basic Service
Subscribers: 306.
Programming (received off-air): WAKA (CBS) Selma; WCFT-TV (ABC) Tuscaloosa; WCOV-TV (FOX) Montgomery; WIIQ (PBS) Demopolis; WNCF (ABC) Montgomery; WSFA (NBC) Montgomery.
Programming (via satellite): ABC Family Channel; Arts & Entertainment; BET Networks; Cartoon Network; CNN; C-SPAN; Discovery Channel; Disney Channel; ESPN; ESPN 2; Fox News Channel; FX; Great American Country; Headline News; History Channel; Outdoor Channel; QVC; Syfy; TBS Superstation; Toon Disney; Trinity Broadcasting Network; Turner Classic Movies; Turner Network TV; USA Network; Weather Channel; WGN America.
Current originations: Public Access.
Fee: $20.00 installation; $40.01 monthly.
Pay Service 1
Pay Units: 136.
Programming (via satellite): HBO.
Fee: $25.00 installation; $8.50 monthly.
Pay Service 2
Pay Units: N.A.
Programming (via satellite): Encore; Starz (multiplexed).
Internet Service
Operational: No.
Telephone Service
None
Miles of Plant: 22.0 (coaxial); None (fiber optic). Homes passed: 962. Total homes in franchised area: 962.
State Manager: Bill Flowers. Technical Manager & Engineer: Greg Berthaut. Customer Service Representative: Lisa Ray.
Ownership: Galaxy Cable Inc. (MSO).

VALLEY—Knology, 415 N Gilmer Ave, Lanett, AL 36863-2053. Phones: 706-642-2246 (Customer service); 706-645-8630. Fax: 333-644-9286. Web Site: http://www.knology.com. Also serves Lanett, AL; West Point, GA. ICA: AL0259. **Note:** This system is an overbuild.
TV Market Ranking: 94 (Lanett, VALLEY, West Point). Franchise award date: N.A. Franchise expiration date: N.A. Began: N.A.
Channel capacity: N.A. Channels available but not in use: N.A.
Basic Service
Subscribers: 3,500.
Programming (received off-air): WCAG-LP La Grange; WCIQ (PBS) Mount Cheaha State Park; WJSP-TV (PBS) Columbus; WLGA (CW) Opelika; WLTZ (CW, NBC) Columbus; WRBL (CBS) Columbus; WSB-TV (ABC) Atlanta; WSFA (NBC) Montgomery; WTVM (ABC) Columbus; WXTX (FOX) Columbus.
Programming (via satellite): ABC Family Channel; AMC; Animal Planet; Arts & Entertainment; BET Networks; Bravo; Cartoon Network; CNBC; CNN; Comcast

Sports Net Southeast; Comcast/Charter Sports Southeast (CSS); Comedy Central; Country Music TV; C-SPAN; C-SPAN 2; Discovery Channel; Disney Channel; E! Entertainment Television; ESPN; ESPN 2; ESPN Classic Sports; Food Network; Fox News Channel; FX; Golf Channel; Gospel Music Channel; Great American Country; GSN; Hallmark Channel; Headline News; HGTV; History Channel; Home Shopping Network; Lifetime; Lifetime Movie Network; MTV; Nick At Nite; Nickelodeon; Outdoor Channel; Oxygen; QVC; ShopNBC; Speed Channel; Spike TV; SportSouth; Syfy; TBS Superstation; The Learning Channel; Toon Disney; Travel Channel; Trinity Broadcasting Network; truTV; Turner Classic Movies; Turner Network TV; TV Guide Network; TV Land; USA Network; VH1; Weather Channel; WGN America.

Current originations: Public Access.

Fee: $49.95 monthly.

Digital Basic Service

Subscribers: 63,000 Includes Dothan, Huntsville, Montgomery, Panama City Beach FL, Pinellas County FL, Augusta GA, Columbus GA, Charleston SC, & Knoxville TN.

Programming (received off-air): WLTZ (CW, NBC) Columbus; WRBL (CBS) Columbus; WTVM (ABC) Columbus; WXTX (FOX) Columbus.

Programming (via satellite): BBC America; Bloomberg Television; Boomerang; Church Channel; CMT Pure Country; C-SPAN 3; Discovery Channel HD; Discovery HD Theater; Discovery Health Channel; Discovery Kids Channel; Discovery Military Channel; Discovery Planet Green; ESPN 2 HD; ESPN HD; ESPN U; FitTV; FSN HD; G4; Hallmark Movie Channel; Halogen Network; HDNet; HDNet Movies; ID Investigation Discovery; Independent Film Channel; INSP; JCTV; Jewelry Television; Lifetime Real Women; MTV Hits; MTV Jams; MTV Tres; MTV2; mtvU; Music Choice; National Geographic Channel; NFL Network; Nick Jr.; Nick Too; NickToons TV; Pentagon Channel; QVC HD; Science Channel; SoapNet; TBS in HD; TeenNick; TLC HD; Turner Network TV HD; Universal HD; Versus; Versus HD; VH1 Classic; VH1 Soul; WE tv.

Fee: $9.95 monthly.

Digital Expanded Basic Service

Subscribers: N.A.

Programming (via satellite): CBS College Sports Network; ESPNews; Fox College Sports Atlantic; Fox College Sports Central; Fox College Sports Pacific; Fox Soccer; Fuel TV; Tennis Channel; The Sportsman Channel.

Digital Pay Service 1

Pay Units: N.A.

Programming (via satellite): Cinemax (multiplexed); Cinemax HD; Cinemax On Demand; Encore (multiplexed); Flix; Flix On Demand; HBO (multiplexed); HBO HD; HBO On Demand; Showtime (multiplexed); Showtime HD; Showtime On Demand; Starz (multiplexed); Starz HDTV; Sundance Channel; The Movie Channel (multiplexed); The Movie Channel On Demand.

Fee: $56.35 monthly.

Video-On-Demand: Yes

Pay-Per-View

iN DEMAND (delivered digitally); Hot Choice (delivered digitally); ESPN Extra (delivered digitally); Spice: Xcess (delivered digitally); Playboy TV (delivered digitally); Fresh (delivered digitally); Shorteez (delivered digitally); Club Jenna (delivered digitally); ESPN Now (delivered digitally).

Internet Service

Operational: Yes.

Subscribers: 122,195.

Broadband Service: Knology.Net.

Fee: $29.95 installation; $57.95 monthly.

Telephone Service

Analog: Not Operational

Digital: Operational

Subscribers: 155,365.

Fee: $23.15 monthly

Miles of Plant: 300.0 (coaxial); None (fiber optic). Homes passed: 12,400.

General Manager: Kevin Nolan. Operations Director: Chuck Goodwin. Marketing Manager: Tammy Clark.

Ownership: Knology Inc. (MSO).

WADLEY—CommuniComm Services, 3164 Hwy 431, Ste 9, Roanoke, AL 36274-1702. Phone: 334-863-7080. Fax: 334-863-2027. Web Site: http://www.netcommander.com. ICA: AL0155.

TV Market Ranking: Outside TV Markets (WADLEY). Franchise award date: January 1, 1984. Franchise expiration date: N.A. Began: December 1, 1984.

Channel capacity: N.A. Channels available but not in use: N.A.

Basic Service

Subscribers: 199.

Programming (received off-air): WAGA-TV (FOX) Atlanta; WBRC (FOX) Birmingham; WCAG-LP La Grange; WCIQ (PBS) Mount Cheaha State Park; WGCL-TV (CBS) Atlanta; WJSU-TV (ABC) Anniston; WSB-TV (ABC) Atlanta; WSFA (NBC) Montgomery; WTTO (CW) Homewood.

Programming (via satellite): QVC; Superstation WGN; TBS Superstation.

Fee: $25.00 installation; $10.00 monthly; $15.00 additional installation.

Expanded Basic Service 1

Subscribers: N.A.

Programming (via satellite): ABC Family Channel; AMC; Animal Planet; Arts & Entertainment; BET Networks; Bravo; Cartoon Network; CNBC; CNN; Comcast/Charter Sports Southeast (CSS); Comedy Central; Country Music TV; C-SPAN; C-SPAN 2; Discovery Channel; Disney Channel; E! Entertainment Television; ESPN; ESPN 2; ESPN Classic Sports; Food Network; Fox Movie Channel; Fox News Channel; FX; Great American Country; Hallmark Channel; Headline News; HGTV; History Channel; Home Shopping Network; ION Television; Lifetime; Lifetime Movie Network; MSNBC; MTV; Nick Jr.; Nickelodeon; Outdoor Channel; ShopNBC; Spike TV; Syfy; The Learning Channel; The Sportsman Channel; Travel Channel; Trinity Broadcasting Network; truTV; Turner Classic Movies; Turner Network TV; Turner South; TV Guide Network; TV Land; USA Network; VH1; WE tv; Weather Channel.

Digital Basic Service

Subscribers: 19.

Programming (via satellite): BBC America; Bio; Bloomberg Television; Discovery Health Channel; Discovery Home Channel; Discovery Kids Channel; Discovery Military Channel; DMX Music; Fox Soccer; Fuse; Golf Channel; GSN; Halogen Network; History Channel International; ID Investigation Discovery; Independent Film Channel; National Geographic Channel; Science Channel; Sleuth; SoapNet; Speed Channel; Toon Disney; Versus.

Pay Service 1

Pay Units: N.A.

Programming (via satellite): Cinemax (multiplexed); Encore; HBO (multiplexed); MoviePlex; Starz (multiplexed).

Digital Pay Service 1

Pay Units: 68.

Programming (via satellite): Cinemax (multiplexed); Encore (multiplexed); HBO (multiplexed); Showtime (multiplexed); Starz (multiplexed).

Video-On-Demand: No

Pay-Per-View

iN DEMAND (delivered digitally); Hot Choice (delivered digitally); Playboy TV (delivered digitally); Fresh (delivered digitally).

Internet Service

Operational: Yes. Began: December 1, 2000.

Subscribers: 81.

Broadband Service: Net Commander.

Fee: $39.95 installation; $51.95 monthly.

Telephone Service

None

Miles of Plant: 8.0 (coaxial); None (fiber optic). Homes passed: 367.

General Manager: Brian Chase. Chief Technician: William Boyd.

City fee: 3% of gross.

Ownership: James Cable LLC (MSO).

WARRIOR—Time Warner Cable. Now served by CULLMAN, AL [AL0034]. ICA: AL0082.

WATERLOO—Formerly served by North Crossroads Communications Inc. No longer in operation. ICA: AL0233.

WEDOWEE—CommuniComm Services, 3164 Hwy 431, Ste 9, Roanoke, AL 36274-1702. Phone: 334-863-7080. Fax: 334-863-2027. Web Site: http://www.netcommander.com. ICA: AL0147.

TV Market Ranking: Below 100 (WEDOWEE). Franchise award date: April 20, 1983. Franchise expiration date: N.A. Began: December 1, 1983.

Channel capacity: N.A. Channels available but not in use: N.A.

Basic Service

Subscribers: 182.

Programming (received off-air): WAXC-LP (IND) Alexander City; WBRC (FOX) Birmingham; WCAG-LP La Grange; WCIQ (PBS) Mount Cheaha State Park; WGCL-TV (CBS) Atlanta; WIAT (CBS) Birmingham; WJSU-TV (ABC) Anniston; WSFA (NBC) Montgomery; WTTO (CW) Homewood; WTVM (ABC) Columbus.

Programming (via satellite): Superstation WGN; TBS Superstation.

Fee: $25.00 installation; $11.00 monthly.

Expanded Basic Service 1

Subscribers: N.A.

Programming (via satellite): ABC Family Channel; American Movie Classics; Animal Planet; Arts & Entertainment; BET Networks; Bravo; Cartoon Network; CNBC; CNN; Comcast/Charter Sports Southeast (CSS); Comedy Central; Country Music TV; C-SPAN; C-SPAN 2; Discovery Channel; Disney Channel; E! Entertainment Television; ESPN; ESPN 2; ESPN Classic Sports; Food Network; Fox Movie Channel; Fox News Channel; FX; Great American Country; Headline News; HGTV; History Channel; Home Shopping Network; ION Television; Lifetime; Lifetime Movie Network; MSNBC; MTV; Nick Jr.; Nickelodeon; Outdoor Channel; QVC; ShopNBC; Spike TV; Syfy; The Learning Channel; The Sportsman Channel; Travel Channel; Trinity Broadcasting Network; truTV; Turner Network TV; Turner South; TV Land; USA Network; VH1; WE tv; Weather Channel.

Digital Basic Service

Subscribers: 27.

Programming (via satellite): BBC America; Bloomberg Television; Discovery Health Channel; Discovery Home Channel; Discovery Kids Channel; Discovery Military Channel; DMX Music; FitTV; G4; Golf Channel; GSN; Halogen Network; ID Investigation Discovery; Independent Film Channel; Science Channel; Sleuth; SoapNet; Speed Channel; Toon Disney; Turner Classic Movies; Versus.

Digital Pay Service 1

Pay Units: 49.

Programming (via satellite): Cinemax (multiplexed); Encore (multiplexed); HBO (multiplexed); Showtime (multiplexed); Starz (multiplexed).

Video-On-Demand: No

Pay-Per-View

iN DEMAND (delivered digitally); Fresh (delivered digitally); Playboy TV (delivered digitally).

Internet Service

Operational: Yes.

Subscribers: 32.

Broadband Service: Net Commander.

Fee: $39.95 installation; $51.95 monthly.

Telephone Service

None

Miles of Plant: 11.0 (coaxial); None (fiber optic). Homes passed: 431.

General Manager: Brian Chase. Chief Technician: William Boyd.

City fee: 3% of gross.

Ownership: James Cable LLC (MSO).

WEST BLOCTON—Formerly served by Almega Cable. No longer in operation. ICA: AL0061.

WESTOVER—Charter Communications, 2100 Columbiana Rd, Vestavia, AL 35216. Phone: 205-824-5400. Fax: 205-824-5490. Web Site: http://www.charter.com. Also serves Chelsea, Harpersville, Shelby County & Vincent. ICA: AL0196.

TV Market Ranking: 40 (Chelsea, Harpersville, Shelby County, Vincent, WESTOVER). Franchise award date: January 22, 1986. Franchise expiration date: N.A. Began: N.A.

Channel capacity: N.A. Channels available but not in use: N.A.

Basic Service

Subscribers: 1,417.

Programming (received off-air): WABM (MNT) Birmingham; WBIQ (PBS) Birmingham; WBRC (FOX) Birmingham; WCFT-TV (ABC) Tuscaloosa; WIAT (CBS) Birmingham; WTTO (CW) Homewood; WVTM-TV (NBC) Birmingham.

Programming (via satellite): Comcast Sports Net Southeast; C-SPAN; TBS Superstation; WGN America.

Fee: $29.99 installation.

Expanded Basic Service 1

Subscribers: N.A.

Programming (via satellite): ABC Family Channel; AMC; Animal Planet; Arts & Entertainment; Cartoon Network; CNN; Country Music TV; Discovery Channel; Disney Channel; ESPN; ESPN 2; Headline News; MSNBC; MTV; Nickelodeon; Spike TV; Syfy; The Learning Channel; Toon Disney; Turner Network TV; USA Network; Weather Channel.

Fee: $43.00 monthly.

Digital Basic Service

Subscribers: N.A.

Programming (via satellite): AmericanLife TV Network; BBC America; Bio; Bloomberg

Television; Bravo; Discovery Digital Networks; ESPN Classic Sports; ESPNews; Fox Movie Channel; G4; GAS; Golf Channel; GSN; Halogen Network; HGTV; History Channel; History Channel International; Independent Film Channel; Lifetime Movie Network; MTV Networks Digital Suite; MuchMusic Network; Music Choice; Nick Jr.; Outdoor Channel; ShopNBC; Speed Channel; Style Network; Trinity Broadcasting Network; Turner Classic Movies; TV Guide Interactive Inc.; Versus; WE tv.
Fee: $16.99 monthly.

Digital Pay Service 1
Pay Units: 636.
Programming (via satellite): Cinemax (multiplexed); Encore (multiplexed); Flix; HBO (multiplexed); Showtime (multiplexed); Starz (multiplexed); The Movie Channel (multiplexed).
Fee: $9.95 monthly (each).

Video-On-Demand: Yes

Pay-Per-View
ESPN Extra (delivered digitally); ESPN Now (delivered digitally); iN DEMAND (delivered digitally); Playboy TV (delivered digitally); Fresh (delivered digitally).

Internet Service
Operational: Yes.
Broadband Service: Charter Pipeline.
Fee: $29.99 monthly.

Telephone Service
Digital: Operational

Miles of Plant: 79.0 (coaxial); None (fiber optic). Homes passed: 2,127.
Vice President & General Manager: Don Karell. Technical Operations Director: Greg Prim. Marketing Director: David Redmond. Marketing Manager: Jeff Hatcher.
City fee: 3% of gross.
Ownership: Charter Communications Inc. (MSO).

WETUMPKA—Bright House Networks, 3996 US Hwy 231, Wetumpka, AL 36093. Phones: 800-822-0060; 205-290-1300. Fax: 334-567-2123. Web Site: http://www.elmore.mybrighthouse.com. Also serves Coosada, Deatsville, Eclectic, Elmore County (portions), Gunter AFB, Maxwell AFB, Millbrook, Tallapoosa County (southern portion) & Tallassee. ICA: AL0016.
TV Market Ranking: Below 100 (Coosada, Deatsville, Eclectic, Elmore County (portions), Gunter AFB, Maxwell AFB, Millbrook, Tallapoosa County (southern portion), Tallassee, WETUMPKA). Franchise award date: January 1, 1977. Franchise expiration date: N.A. Began: December 1, 1977.
Channel capacity: 72 (operating 2-way). Channels available but not in use: 2.

Basic Service
Subscribers: 18,844.
Programming (received off-air): WABM (MNT) Birmingham; WBIQ (PBS) Birmingham; WBRC (FOX) Birmingham; WIAT (CBS) Birmingham; WPXH-TV (ION) Gadsden; WTJP-TV (TBN) Gadsden; WTTO (CW) Homewood; WVTM-TV (NBC) Birmingham.
Programming (via satellite): C-SPAN; C-SPAN 2; QVC; TV Guide Network; WGN America.
Fee: $35.83 installation; $1.00 converter.

Expanded Basic Service 1
Subscribers: N.A.
Programming (via satellite): ABC Family Channel; AMC; Animal Planet; Arts & Entertainment; BET Networks; Cartoon Network; CNBC; CNN; Comcast Sports Net Southeast; Comedy Central; Discovery Channel; Disney Channel; E! Entertainment Television; Encore; ESPN; ESPN 2; ESPN Classic Sports; Eternal Word TV Network; Food Network; Fox News Channel; Fuse; FX; Golf Channel; Great American Country; Hallmark Channel; Headline News; HGTV; History Channel; Home Shopping Network; Lifetime; Lifetime Movie Network; MSNBC; MTV; National Geographic Channel; Nickelodeon; Oxygen; ShopNBC; SoapNet; Spike TV; SportSouth; Style Network; Syfy; TBS Superstation; The Learning Channel; Travel Channel; truTV; Turner Classic Movies; Turner Network TV; TV Land; Univision; USA Network; Versus; VH1; WE tv; Weather Channel.
Fee: $49.45 monthly.

Digital Basic Service
Subscribers: N.A.
Programming (received off-air): WBIQ (PBS) Birmingham; WBRC (FOX) Birmingham; WIAT (CBS) Birmingham; WTVM (ABC) Columbus; WVTM-TV (NBC) Birmingham.
Programming (via satellite): American-Life TV Network; America's Store; BBC America; Bio; Black Family Channel; Boomerang; Bravo; CNN International; Cooking Channel; C-SPAN 3; Current; Discovery Digital Networks; Discovery HD Theater; Do-It-Yourself; ESPN; ESPNews; FamilyNet; FitTV; Fox Sports World; G4; GAS; GSN; HDNet; HDNet Movies; History Channel International; iN DEMAND; Lifetime Real Women; MTV2; Music Choice; NBA TV; Nick Jr.; NickToons TV; Outdoor Channel; Ovation; Speed Channel; Toon Disney; Turner Network TV; VH1 Classic.
Fee: $11.00 monthly.

Digital Expanded Basic Service
Subscribers: N.A.
Programming (via satellite): Canales N; CBS College Sports Network; Encore (multiplexed); Flix; Fox College Sports Atlantic; Fox College Sports Central; Fox College Sports Pacific; Fox Movie Channel; Fuel TV; Independent Film Channel; NBA TV; Outdoor Channel; Sundance Channel; Tennis Channel; The Sportsman Channel; WAM! America's Kidz Network.

Digital Pay Service 1
Pay Units: 6,194.
Programming (via satellite): Cinemax (multiplexed); HBO (multiplexed); Playboy TV; Showtime (multiplexed); Starz (multiplexed); The Movie Channel (multiplexed).
Fee: $10.50 monthly (each).

Video-On-Demand: No

Pay-Per-View
Movies/Events (delivered digitally); Fresh (delivered digitally); Playboy TV (delivered digitally); Hot Choice (delivered digitally); NBA TV (delivered digitally); Ten Clips (delivered digitally); Pleasure (delivered digitally); ESPN (delivered digitally); MLB Extra Innings (delivered digitally); NHL Center Ice (delivered digitally).

Internet Service
Operational: Yes.
Subscribers: 5,010.
Broadband Service: Road Runner.
Fee: $49.95 installation; $29.95 monthly.

Telephone Service
Analog: Not Operational
Digital: Operational
Fee: $39.95 monthly

Miles of Plant: 520.0 (coaxial); 70.0 (fiber optic). Homes passed: 28,874.
Manager: Bruce Burgess. Marketing Director: Dennis Burns. Chief Technician: Mike Truelove.
Ownership: Bright House Networks LLC (MSO).

WINFIELD—West Alabama TV Cable Co. Inc., PO Box 930, 213 2nd Ave NE, Fayette, AL 35555-0930. Phones: 205-487-2884; 205-932-4700 (Fayette office). Fax: 205-932-3585. E-mail: cable@watvc.com. Web Site: http://www.watvc.com. Also serves Brilliant. ICA: AL0074.
TV Market Ranking: Outside TV Markets (Brilliant, WINFIELD). Franchise award date: N.A. Franchise expiration date: N.A. Began: May 10, 1965.
Channel capacity: 60 (operating 2-way). Channels available but not in use: 4.

Basic Service
Subscribers: 2,192.
Programming (received off-air): WABM (MNT) Birmingham; WBIQ (PBS) Birmingham; WBRC (FOX) Birmingham; WCFT-TV (ABC) Tuscaloosa; WIAT (CBS) Birmingham; WTTO (CW) Homewood; WTVA (NBC) Tupelo; WVTM-TV (NBC) Birmingham.
Programming (via satellite): ABC Family Channel; AMC; Arts & Entertainment; BET Networks; Cartoon Network; CNBC; CNN; Country Music TV; C-SPAN; Discovery Channel; Disney Channel; E! Entertainment Television; ESPN; ESPN 2; Food Network; Fox News Channel; FX; Golf Channel; Gospel Music TV; Hallmark Channel; Headline News; HGTV; History Channel; Home Shopping Network; Lifetime; MTV; Nickelodeon; QVC; SportSouth; TBS Superstation; The Learning Channel; Travel Channel; Trinity Broadcasting Network; Turner Classic Movies; Turner Network TV; TV Guide Network; TV Land; USA Network; VH1; Weather Channel; WGN America.
Current originations: Leased Access.
Fee: $35.00 installation; $37.25 monthly.

Digital Basic Service
Subscribers: N.A.
Programming (via satellite): BBC America; Bio; Bloomberg Television; Discovery Health Channel; Discovery Kids Channel; Discovery Military Channel; Discovery Planet Green; DMX Music; ESPN Classic Sports; ESPNews; Fox Movie Channel; Fox Soccer; G4; History Channel International; ID Investigation Discovery; Independent Film Channel; INSP; Lifetime Movie Network; Lime; National Geographic Channel; Outdoor Channel; Science Channel; Sleuth; Speed Channel; Toon Disney; Versus; WE tv.
Fee: $14.00 monthly.

Pay Service 1
Pay Units: 237.
Programming (via satellite): HBO.
Fee: $15.00 installation; $11.95 monthly.

Pay Service 2
Pay Units: N.A.
Programming (via satellite): Cinemax.
Fee: $15.00 installation; $10.95 monthly.

Digital Pay Service 1
Pay Units: N.A.
Programming (via satellite): Cinemax (multiplexed); Encore (multiplexed); HBO (multiplexed); Showtime (multiplexed); Starz (multiplexed); The Movie Channel (multiplexed).
Fee: $10.95 monthly (Cinemax or Starz/Encore/TMC), $12.95 monthly (HBO or Showtime).

Video-On-Demand: No

Pay-Per-View
iN DEMAND (delivered digitally); Hot Choice (delivered digitally); Spice (delivered digitally); ESPN Now (delivered digitally); Sports PPV (delivered digitally).

Internet Service
Operational: Yes.
Broadband Service: In-house.
Fee: $24.95 installation.

Telephone Service
None

Miles of Plant: 150.0 (coaxial); None (fiber optic). Homes passed: 8,000. Total homes in franchised area: 10,000.
Manager: Kyle South.
City fee: $250 annually.
Ownership: West Alabama TV Cable Co. Inc. (MSO).

ALASKA

Total Systems: **30**
Total Communities Served: **55**
Franchises Not Yet Operating: **0**
Applications Pending: **0**
Communities with Applications: **0**
Number of Basic Subscribers: **199,227**
Number of Expanded Basic Subscribers: **129,467**
Number of Pay Units: **95,845**

Top 100 Markets Represented: N.A.

For a list of cable communities in this section, see the Cable Community Index located in the back of Cable Volume 2.
For explanation of terms used in cable system listings, see p. D-11.

ADAK—Adak Cablevision, 4101 Artic Blvd, Ste 205, Anchorage, AK 99503. Phones: 907-592-3735; 907-222-0844. Fax: 907-222-0845. ICA: AK0044.
TV Market Ranking: Outside TV Markets (ADAK). Franchise award date: N.A. Franchise expiration date: N.A. Began: June 1, 1983.
Channel capacity: 54 (not 2-way capable). Channels available but not in use: 29.
Basic Service
Subscribers: 60.
Programming (via satellite): ABC Family Channel; Alaska Rural Communications Service (ARCS); AMC; Arts & Entertainment; Country Music TV; Discovery Channel; Disney Channel; ESPN; Fox Sports Net; Headline News; Home Shopping Network; MTV; Netlink International; Syfy; TBS Superstation; Turner Network TV; USA Network; WGN America.
Fee: $120.00 installation; $145.00 monthly.
Pay Service 1
Pay Units: 3.
Programming (via satellite): Cinemax; HBO.
Fee: $6.99 monthly (Cinemax), $10.99 monthly (HBO).
Internet Service
Operational: Yes.
Fee: $24.95 installation; $60.00-$105.00 monthly.
Telephone Service
None
Miles of Plant: 26.0 (coaxial); None (fiber optic).
Manager & Chief Technician: John Rearick.
Ownership: Adak Cablevision.

ANCHORAGE—Formerly served by ACS Television. No longer in operation. ICA: AK0047.

ANCHORAGE—Formerly served by Sprint Corp. No longer in operation. ICA: AK0045.

ANCHORAGE—GCI, PO Box 99016, 2550 Denali St, Ste 1000, Anchorage, AK 99503-3910. Phones: 907-265-5600 (Corporate office); 800-800-4800; 907-265-5400. Fax: 907-868-8570. E-mail: rcs@gci.com. Web Site: http://www.gci.com. Also serves Chugiak, Eagle River, Elmendorf AFB, Fort Richardson, Palmer, Peters Creek & Wasilla. ICA: AK0001.
TV Market Ranking: Below 100 (ANCHORAGE, Chugiak, Eagle River, Elmendorf AFB, Fort Richardson, Palmer, Peters Creek, Wasilla). Franchise award date: N.A. Franchise expiration date: N.A. Began: October 1, 1980.
Channel capacity: 78 (operating 2-way). Channels available but not in use: N.A.
Basic Service
Subscribers: 79,269.
Programming (received off-air): KAKM (PBS) Anchorage; KCFT-LP Anchorage; KDMD (ION) Anchorage; KIMO (ABC, CW) Anchorage; KTBY (FOX) Anchorage; KTUU-TV (NBC) Anchorage; KTVA (CBS) Anchorage; KYES-TV (MNT) Anchorage; 6 FMs.
Programming (via satellite): C-SPAN; C-SPAN 2; CW+; TV Guide Network; WGN America.
Current originations: Religious Access; Government Access; Educational Access; Public Access.
Fee: $25.50 installation; $21.20 monthly; $5.99 converter; $20.00 additional installation.

Expanded Basic Service 1
Subscribers: 74,398.
Programming (via satellite): ABC Family Channel; AMC; Animal Planet; Arts & Entertainment; BET Networks; Bravo; Cartoon Network; CNBC; CNN; Comcast Sports Net Northwest; Comedy Central; Country Music TV; C-SPAN 2; Discovery Channel; Disney Channel; E! Entertainment Television; ESPN; ESPN 2; ESPN Classic Sports; Food Network; Fox News Channel; Fuse; FX; Headline News; HGTV; History Channel; Home Shopping Network; Lifetime; Lifetime Movie Network; MSNBC; MTV; National Geographic Channel; NFL Network; Nickelodeon; Outdoor Channel; Oxygen; Pentagon Channel; QVC; ShopNBC; SoapNet; Spike TV; Style Network; Syfy; TBS Superstation; The Learning Channel; Toon Disney; Travel Channel; truTV; Turner Classic Movies; Turner Network TV; TV Land; Univision; USA Network; Versus; VH1; WE tv; Weather Channel.
Fee: $35.79 monthly.

Digital Basic Service
Subscribers: 40,441.
Programming (received off-air): KAKM (PBS) Anchorage; KTUU-TV (NBC) Anchorage; KTVA (CBS) Anchorage.
Programming (via satellite): 3 Angels Broadcasting Network; AmericanLife TV Network; BBC America; Bio; Bloomberg Television; Boomerang; BYU Television; Church Channel; CNN International; Daystar TV Network; Discovery Digital Networks; Discovery HD Theater; Do-It-Yourself; ESPN HD; ESPNews; Eternal Word TV Network; FamilyNet; Fox College Sports Atlantic; Fox College Sports Central; Fox College Sports Pacific; Fox Soccer; Fuel TV; G4; GAS; Golf Channel; Gospel Music Channel; Great American Country; GSN; Halogen Network; HDNet; HDNet Movies; History Channel International; Independent Film Channel; INSP; Military History Channel; MTV Networks Digital Suite; Music Choice; NFL Network; Nick Jr.; NickToons TV; Speed Channel; Tennis Channel; The Sportsman Channel; Trinity Broadcasting Network; Turner Network TV HD; TVG Network; Universal HD; WealthTV.
Fee: $18.00 monthly.
Pay Service 1
Pay Units: N.A. Included in Digital Pay Service 1
Programming (via satellite): Cinemax (multiplexed); HBO (multiplexed); Showtime (multiplexed); The Movie Channel (multiplexed).
Fee: $10.95 monthly (Cinemax), $13.95 monthly (HBO or Showtime & TMC).
Digital Pay Service 1
Pay Units: 58,115.
Programming (via satellite): Cinemax (multiplexed); Cinemax HD; Encore (multiplexed); Filipino Channel; Flix; HBO (multiplexed); HBO HD; Korean Channel; Showtime (multiplexed); Showtime HD; Starz (multiplexed); Starz HDTV; Sundance Channel; The Movie Channel (multiplexed); The Movie Channel HD.
Fee: $10.95 monthly (Cinemax), $12.95 monthly (Starz & Encore), $13.95 monthly (HBO or Showtime), $13.99 (Filipino Channel or Korean Channel).
Video-On-Demand: No
Pay-Per-View
Addressable: Yes; ESPN (delivered digitally); iN DEMAND (delivered digitally).
Internet Service
Operational: Yes.
Subscribers: 29,639.
Broadband Service: GCI Hypernet.
Fee: $24.99 monthly.
Telephone Service
Digital: Operational
Miles of Plant: 1,367.0 (coaxial); 164.0 (fiber optic). Homes passed: 135,551.
Vice President, Content & Data: Bob Ormberg. Marketing Manager: David Fox.
City fee: None.
Ownership: General Communication Inc. (MSO).

ANGOON—Angoon Cablevision, PO Box 189, 700 Aandeine Aat, Angoon, AK 99820-0189. Phone: 907-788-3653. Fax: 907-788-3821. ICA: AK0033.
TV Market Ranking: Outside TV Markets (ANGOON). Franchise award date: N.A. Franchise expiration date: N.A. Began: January 1, 1986.
Channel capacity: 33 (not 2-way capable). Channels available but not in use: 1.
Basic Service
Subscribers: 47.
Programming (via satellite): ABC Family Channel; CNN; Discovery Channel; Disney Channel; ESPN; HBO; KCNC-TV (CBS) Denver; KUSA (NBC) Denver; Showtime; Spike TV; TBS Superstation; Turner Network TV; USA Network; WGN America.
Fee: $30.00 installation; $54.50 monthly.
Video-On-Demand: No
Internet Service
Operational: No.
Telephone Service
None
Homes passed: 135.
Manager & Chief Technician: Alan Zuboss.
Ownership: Angoon Cablevision.

BARROW—GCI, PO Box 489, 1230 Agvik St, Barrow, AK 99723. Phone: 907-852-5511. Fax: 907-852-5510. E-mail: rcs@gci.com. Web Site: http://www.gci.com. ICA: AK0013.
TV Market Ranking: Outside TV Markets (BARROW). Franchise award date: N.A. Franchise expiration date: N.A. Began: January 1, 1968.
Channel capacity: 65 (operating 2-way). Channels available but not in use: N.A.
Basic Service
Subscribers: 1,091.
Programming (received off-air): KIMO (ABC, CW) Anchorage; KTBY (FOX) Anchorage; KTOO-TV (PBS) Juneau; KTUU-TV (NBC) Anchorage; KTVA (CBS) Anchorage; KYES-TV (MNT) Anchorage.
Programming (via satellite): C-SPAN; C-SPAN 2; QVC; TV Guide Network; WGN America.
Current originations: Public Access; Educational Access.
Fee: $65.00 installation; $20.70 monthly.
Expanded Basic Service 1
Subscribers: 1,045.
Programming (via satellite): ABC Family Channel; AMC; Animal Planet; Arts & Entertainment; BET Networks; Cartoon Network; CNBC; CNN; Comedy Central; Country Music TV; Discovery Channel; Disney Channel; E! Entertainment Television; ESPN; ESPN 2; Food Network; Hallmark Channel; Headline News; HGTV; History Channel; Home Shopping Network; Lifetime; MSNBC; MTV; Nickelodeon; Outdoor Channel; Spike TV; Syfy; TBS Superstation; The Learning Channel; Toon Disney; Travel Channel; Trinity Broadcasting Network; truTV; Turner Classic Movies; Turner Network TV; TV Land; USA Network; VH1.
Fee: $66.00 monthly.
Digital Pay Service 1
Pay Units: 220.
Programming (via satellite): Cinemax (multiplexed).
Fee: $10.95 monthly.
Digital Pay Service 2
Pay Units: 407.
Programming (via satellite): HBO (multiplexed).
Fee: $13.95 monthly.
Digital Pay Service 3
Pay Units: 199.
Programming (via satellite): Encore (multiplexed); Starz (multiplexed).
Fee: $12.95 monthly.

Digital Pay Service 4
Pay Units: 329.
Programming (via satellite): Flix; Showtime (multiplexed); Sundance Channel; The Movie Channel (multiplexed).
Fee: $12.95 monthly.
Video-On-Demand: No
Pay-Per-View
iN DEMAND (delivered digitally); Adult Swim (delivered digitally).
Internet Service
Operational: Yes.
Fee: $49.99 monthly.
Telephone Service
None
Miles of Plant: 30.0 (coaxial); None (fiber optic). Homes passed: 1,540.
Manager: Dave Fawcett. Chief Technician: Robert David.
City fee: None.
Ownership: General Communication Inc.

BETHEL—GCI, PO Box 247, 210 3rd St, Bethel, AK 99559. Phones: 907-265-5600 (Anchorage office); 907-543-3226. Fax: 907-543-5127. E-mail: rcs@gci.com. Web Site: http://www.gci.com. ICA: AK0050.
TV Market Ranking: Outside TV Markets (BETHEL TWP.). Franchise award date: N.A. Franchise expiration date: N.A. Began: N.A.
Channel capacity: N.A. Channels available but not in use: N.A.
Basic Service
Subscribers: 1,189.
Programming (received off-air): KAKM (PBS) Anchorage; KIMO (ABC, CW) Anchorage; KTBY (FOX) Anchorage; KTUU-TV (NBC) Anchorage; KTVA (CBS) Anchorage; KYES-TV (MNT) Anchorage.
Programming (via satellite): C-SPAN; C-SPAN 2; QVC; TV Guide Network; WGN America.
Current originations: Educational Access; Public Access.
Fee: $35.50 installation; $19.70 monthly; $11.25 additional installation.
Expanded Basic Service 1
Subscribers: 1,059.
Programming (via satellite): ABC Family Channel; AMC; Animal Planet; Arts & Entertainment; Cartoon Network; CNBC; CNN; Comedy Central; Country Music TV; Discovery Channel; Disney Channel; ESPN; ESPN 2; Food Network; Headline News; HGTV; History Channel; Lifetime; MSNBC; MTV; Nickelodeon; Outdoor Channel; Spike TV; Syfy; TBS Superstation; The Learning Channel; Toon Disney; Travel Channel; Trinity Broadcasting Network; truTV; Turner Classic Movies; Turner Network TV; TV Land; USA Network; VH1; Weather Channel.
Fee: $66.40 monthly.
Digital Pay Service 1
Pay Units: 277.
Programming (via satellite): Cinemax (multiplexed).
Fee: $10.95 monthly.
Digital Pay Service 2
Pay Units: 501.
Programming (via satellite): HBO (multiplexed).
Fee: $13.95 monthly.
Digital Pay Service 3
Pay Units: 381.
Programming (via satellite): Flix; Showtime (multiplexed); Sundance Channel; The Movie Channel (multiplexed).
Fee: $12.95 monthly.
Digital Pay Service 4
Pay Units: 154.
Programming (via satellite): Encore (multiplexed); Starz (multiplexed).
Fee: $12.95 monthly.
Video-On-Demand: No
Pay-Per-View
iN DEMAND (delivered digitally); Adult Swim (delivered digitally).
Internet Service
Operational: Yes.
Broadband Service: GCI Hypernet.
Fee: $24.99 monthly.
Telephone Service
None
Miles of Plant: 23.0 (coaxial); None (fiber optic). Homes passed: 2,388.
Manager: Betty Ann Steciw.
Ownership: General Communication Inc. (MSO).

CORDOVA—GCI, PO Box 791, 202 Nicholoff Way, Cordova, AK 99574-0791. Phone: 907-424-7317. Fax: 907-424-5138. E-mail: rcs@gci.com. Web Site: http://www.gci.com. ICA: AK0012.
TV Market Ranking: Outside TV Markets (CORDOVA). Franchise award date: N.A. Franchise expiration date: N.A. Began: April 1, 1968.
Channel capacity: 40 (operating 2-way). Channels available but not in use: N.A.
Basic Service
Subscribers: 667.
Programming (received off-air): KIMO (ABC, CW) Anchorage; KTBY (FOX) Anchorage; KTOO-TV (PBS) Juneau; KTUU-TV (NBC) Anchorage; KTVA (CBS) Anchorage; KYES-TV (MNT) Anchorage; 8 FMs.
Programming (via satellite): C-SPAN; C-SPAN 2; Home Shopping Network; QVC; TV Guide Network; WGN America.
Current originations: Government Access; Educational Access; Public Access.
Fee: $26.50 installation; $20.70 monthly; $1.00 converter; $25.00 additional installation.
Expanded Basic Service 1
Subscribers: 569.
Programming (via satellite): ABC Family Channel; AMC; Animal Planet; Arts & Entertainment; CNBC; CNN; Comcast Sports Net Northwest; Comedy Central; Country Music TV; Discovery Channel; Disney Channel; ESPN; ESPN 2; Food Network; Fox News Channel; Headline News; HGTV; History Channel; Lifetime; MSNBC; MTV; Nickelodeon; Northwest Cable News; Outdoor Channel; Spike TV; Syfy; TBS Superstation; The Learning Channel; Toon Disney; Travel Channel; Trinity Broadcasting Network; Turner Network TV; USA Network; VH1; Weather Channel.
Fee: $36.84 installation; $69.07 monthly.
Digital Pay Service 1
Pay Units: 79.
Programming (via satellite): Cinemax (multiplexed).
Fee: $10.95 monthly.
Digital Pay Service 2
Pay Units: 153.
Programming (via satellite): HBO (multiplexed).
Fee: $13.95 monthly.
Digital Pay Service 3
Pay Units: 56.
Programming (via satellite): Flix; Showtime (multiplexed); Sundance Channel; The Movie Channel (multiplexed).
Fee: $12.95 monthly.
Digital Pay Service 4
Pay Units: 55.
Programming (via satellite): Encore (multiplexed); Starz (multiplexed).
Fee: $12.95 monthly.
Video-On-Demand: No
Pay-Per-View
iN DEMAND (delivered digitally); Adult Swim (delivered digitally).
Internet Service
Operational: Yes. Began: July 1, 2002.
Broadband Service: GCI Hypernet.
Fee: $24.99 monthly.
Telephone Service
None
Miles of Plant: 24.0 (coaxial); None (fiber optic). Homes passed: 1,193. Total homes in franchised area: 1,193.
Manager: Cindy Butler. Chief Technician: Jesse Carter.
City fee: None.
Ownership: General Communication Inc. (MSO).

CRAIG—Craig Cable TV Inc., PO Box 131, Craig, AK 99921-0131. Phone: 907-826-3470. ICA: AK0034.
TV Market Ranking: Outside TV Markets (CRAIG (VILLAGE)). Franchise award date: N.A. Franchise expiration date: N.A. Began: N.A.
Channel capacity: 40 (not 2-way capable). Channels available but not in use: 4.
Basic Service
Subscribers: 170.
Programming (received off-air): KAKM (PBS) Anchorage; KIMO (ABC, CW) Anchorage; KING-TV (NBC) Seattle; KIRO-TV (CBS, IND) Seattle; KTBY (FOX) Anchorage.
Programming (via satellite): ABC Family Channel; Alaska Rural Communications Service (ARCS); CNN; Comcast Sports Net Northwest; Country Music TV; Discovery Channel; Disney Channel; ESPN; Headline News; Lifetime; MTV; NASA TV; Nickelodeon; Showtime; Spike TV; Syfy; TBS Superstation; The Learning Channel; The Movie Channel; Turner Network TV; TV Guide Network; USA Network; VH1; WGN America.
Current originations: Public Access.
Fee: $35.00 installation; $55.00 monthly.
Video-On-Demand: No
Internet Service
Operational: No.
Telephone Service
None
Miles of Plant: 10.0 (coaxial); None (fiber optic).
Manager: Bob McNamara.
Ownership: Craig Cable TV Inc.

DILLINGHAM—Nushagak Cooperative Inc., PO Box 350, 557 Kenny Wren Rd, Dillingham, AK 99576-0350. Phones: 800-478-5296; 907-842-5251. Fax: 907-842-2799. E-mail: nushtel@nushtel.com. Web Site: http://www.nushtel.com. ICA: AK0017.
TV Market Ranking: Outside TV Markets (DILLINGHAM). Franchise award date: N.A. Franchise expiration date: N.A. Began: November 1, 1994.
Channel capacity: 45 (operating 2-way). Channels available but not in use: 10.
Basic Service
Subscribers: 502.
Programming (received off-air): KTVA (CBS) Anchorage; KUAC-TV (PBS) Fairbanks; KYES-TV (MNT) Anchorage; 2 FMs.
Programming (via satellite): Alaska Rural Communications Service (ARCS).
Current originations: Religious Access; Educational Access; Public Access.
Fee: $38.05 installation; $25.00 monthly.
Video-On-Demand: No
Internet Service
Operational: Yes.
Fee: $38.05 installation; $54.95-$144.95 monthly.
Telephone Service
None
Miles of Plant: 27.0 (coaxial); None (fiber optic). Additional miles planned: 10.0 (fiber optic). Homes passed: 635. Total homes in franchised area: 635.
President: Chris Napoli. Chief Executive Officer: Frank Corbin. Customer Service Manager: Nancy Favors.
Ownership: Nushagak Cooperative Inc.

FAIRBANKS—GCI, 505 Old Steese Hwy, No. 101, Fairbanks, AK 99701. Phones: 800-800-4800; 907-452-7191. Fax: 907-374-4673. E-mail: rcs@gci.com. Web Site: http://www.gci.com. Also serves Elelson AFB, Fairbanks County (unincorporated areas), Fort Greely, Fort Wainwright, North Pole & North Star Borough. ICA: AK0002.
TV Market Ranking: Below 100 (Elelson AFB, FAIRBANKS, Fairbanks County (unincorporated areas) (portions), Fort Wainwright, North Pole, North Star Borough); Outside TV Markets (Fairbanks County (unincorporated areas) (portions), Fort Greely). Franchise award date: N.A. Franchise expiration date: N.A. Began: September 15, 1979.
Channel capacity: 61 (operating 2-way). Channels available but not in use: N.A.
Basic Service
Subscribers: 19,878.
Programming (received off-air): K13XD (CBS) Fairbanks; KATN (ABC, CW) Fairbanks; KFXF (FOX) Fairbanks; KJNP-TV (TBN) North Pole; KTVF (NBC) Fairbanks; KUAC-TV (PBS) Fairbanks.
Programming (via satellite): C-SPAN; C-SPAN 2; CW+; TV Guide Network; WGN America.
Current originations: Government Access; Educational Access.
Fee: $25.50 installation; $20.20 monthly.
Expanded Basic Service 1
Subscribers: 19,186.
Programming (via satellite): ABC Family Channel; AMC; Animal Planet; Arts & Entertainment; BET Networks; Bravo; Cartoon Network; CNBC; CNN; Comcast Sports Net Northwest; Comedy Central; Country Music TV; Discovery Channel; Disney Channel; E! Entertainment Television; ESPN; ESPN 2; Food Network; Fox News Channel; Fuse; FX; Headline News; HGTV; History Channel; Home Shopping Network; Lifetime; Lifetime Movie Network; MSNBC; MTV; National Geographic Channel; NFL Network; Nickelodeon; Outdoor Channel; Oxygen; Pentagon Channel; QVC; ShopNBC; SoapNet; Spike TV; Syfy; TBS Superstation; The Learning Channel; Toon Disney; Travel Channel; truTV; Turner Classic Movies; Turner Network TV; TV Land; Univision; USA Network; Versus; VH1; WE tv; Weather Channel.
Fee: $9.11 installation; $57.75 monthly; $2.82 converter.
Digital Basic Service
Subscribers: 8,114.
Programming (received off-air): KUAC-TV (PBS) Fairbanks.
Programming (via satellite): 3 Angels Broadcasting Network; AmericanLife TV Network; BBC America; Bio; Bloomberg

Television; Boomerang; BYU Television; Church Channel; CNN International; Daystar TV Network; Discovery Digital Networks; Discovery HD Theater; Do-It-Yourself; ESPN HD; ESPNews; Eternal Word TV Network; FamilyNet; Fox College Sports Atlantic; Fox College Sports Central; Fox College Sports Pacific; Fox Soccer; Fuel TV; G4; GAS; Golf Channel; Gospel Music Channel; Great American Country; GSN; Halogen Network; HDNet; HDNet Movies; History Channel International; Independent Film Channel; INSP; Military History Channel; MTV Networks Digital Suite; Music Choice; NFL Network; Nick Jr.; NickToons TV; Speed Channel; Tennis Channel; The Sportsman Channel; Trinity Broadcasting Network; Turner Network TV HD; TVG Network; Universal HD; WealthTV.
Fee: $14.99 monthly.

Digital Pay Service 1
Pay Units: 2,024.
Programming (via satellite): Cinemax (multiplexed); Cinemax HD.
Fee: $10.95 monthly.

Digital Pay Service 2
Pay Units: 2,597.
Programming (via satellite): Flix; Showtime (multiplexed); Showtime HD; The Movie Channel (multiplexed); The Movie Channel HD.
Fee: $12.95 monthly.

Digital Pay Service 3
Pay Units: 8,093.
Programming (via satellite): HBO (multiplexed); HBO HD.
Fee: $13.95 monthly.

Digital Pay Service 4
Pay Units: 2,155.
Programming (via satellite): Encore (multiplexed); Starz (multiplexed); Starz HDTV.
Fee: $12.95 monthly.

Video-On-Demand: No

Pay-Per-View
Addressable homes: 11,760.
Hot Choice (delivered digitally), Addressable: Yes; ESPN (delivered digitally); iN DEMAND (delivered digitally); Fresh (delivered digitally), Addressable: Yes.

Internet Service
Operational: Yes.
Subscribers: 4,470.
Broadband Service: GCI Hypernet.
Fee: $24.99 monthly.

Telephone Service
None

Miles of Plant: 271.0 (coaxial); 62.0 (fiber optic). Homes passed: 30,928.
Interior Operations Director: Marven E Smith. Regional Technical Manager: David Schram.
Ownership: General Communication Inc. (MSO).

GALENA—Eyecom Cable, 201 E 56th Ave, Anchorage, AK 99518-1283. Phones: 907-563-2074 (Customer service); 907-563-2003. Fax: 907-565-5539. E-mail: custsvc@telalaska.com. Web Site: http://www.telalaska.com. ICA: AK0035.
TV Market Ranking: Outside TV Markets (GALENA). Franchise award date: N.A. Franchise expiration date: N.A. Began: April 1, 1984.
Channel capacity: 60 (2-way capable). Channels available but not in use: 29.

Basic Service
Subscribers: 147.
Programming (via satellite): ABC Family Channel; Animal Planet; Arts & Entertainment; Cartoon Network; CNBC; CNN; Country Music TV; Discovery Channel; Disney Channel; ESPN; ESPN 2; Headline News; History Channel; Spike TV; Syfy; TBS Superstation; The Learning Channel; Turner Classic Movies; Turner Network TV; TV Guide Network; USA Network; WGN America.
Programming (via translator): KIMO (ABC, CW) Anchorage; KTBY (FOX) Anchorage; KTUU-TV (NBC) Anchorage; KTVA (CBS) Anchorage; KUAC-TV (PBS) Fairbanks.
Current originations: Educational Access; Public Access.
Fee: $45.95 monthly.

Pay Service 1
Pay Units: 36.
Programming (via satellite): HBO.
Fee: $13.95 monthly.

Pay Service 2
Pay Units: 17.
Programming (via satellite): Cinemax.
Fee: $10.95 monthly.

Video-On-Demand: No

Internet Service
Operational: No, DSL.

Telephone Service
None

Miles of Plant: 13.0 (coaxial); None (fiber optic). Total homes in franchised area: 420.
President & Chief Executive Officer: Jack Rhyner. Chief Operations Officer: Dave Goggins. Chief Technician: Dan Christensen.
City fee: None.
Ownership: Eyecom Inc. (MSO).

GAMBELL—Formerly served by Frontier Cable Inc. No longer in operation. ICA: AK0036.

GIRDWOOD—Eyecom Cable, 201 E 56th Ave, Anchorage, AK 99518-1283. Phone: 907-563-2003 (Corporate office). Fax: 907-565-5539. E-mail: custsvc@telalaska.com. Web Site: http://www.telalaska.com. ICA: AK0018.
TV Market Ranking: Below 100 (GIRDWOOD). Franchise award date: May 1, 1986. Franchise expiration date: N.A. Began: April 1, 1987.
Channel capacity: 51 (not 2-way capable). Channels available but not in use: 11.

Basic Service
Subscribers: 562.
Programming (received off-air): KAKM (PBS) Anchorage; KIMO (ABC, CW) Anchorage; KTBY (FOX) Anchorage; KTUU-TV (NBC) Anchorage; KTVA (CBS) Anchorage; KYES-TV (MNT) Anchorage.
Programming (via satellite): ABC Family Channel; AMC; Animal Planet; Arts & Entertainment; Bravo; Cartoon Network; CNBC; CNN; Comedy Central; Country Music TV; Discovery Channel; Disney Channel; ESPN; ESPN 2; Food Network; Headline News; HGTV; History Channel; Lifetime; MSNBC; MTV; Nickelodeon; Spike TV; Syfy; TBS Superstation; The Learning Channel; Travel Channel; Turner Classic Movies; Turner Network TV; TV Land; USA Network; VH1; WGN America.
Current originations: Government Access; Educational Access; Public Access.
Fee: $35.00 installation; $41.95 monthly.

Pay Service 1
Pay Units: 37.
Programming (via satellite): Cinemax.
Fee: $10.95 monthly.

Pay Service 2
Pay Units: 91.
Programming (via satellite): HBO (multiplexed).

Fee: $13.95 monthly.

Video-On-Demand: No

Internet Service
Operational: No.

Telephone Service
None

Miles of Plant: 26.0 (coaxial); None (fiber optic). Homes passed: 1,044. Total homes in franchised area: 1,187.
President & Chief Executive Officer: Jack Rhyner. Chief Operations Officer: Dave Goggins. Chief Technician: Dan Christensen.
Ownership: Eyecom Inc. (MSO).

HAINES—Haines Cable TV, PO Box 1229, 715 Main St, Haines, AK 99827-1229. Phone: 907-766-2337. Fax: 907-766-2345. E-mail: pcampbell99827@yahoo.com. Web Site: http://www.hainescable.tvheaven.com. ICA: AK0019.
TV Market Ranking: Outside TV Markets (HAINES). Franchise award date: April 1, 1967. Franchise expiration date: N.A. Began: August 1, 1972.
Channel capacity: 35 (not 2-way capable). Channels available but not in use: 4.

Basic Service
Subscribers: 340.
Programming (via satellite): ABC Family Channel; Alaska Rural Communications Service (ARCS); CNN; Disney Channel; ESPN; FX; KCNC-TV (CBS) Denver; KING-TV (NBC) Seattle; KUSA (NBC) Denver; KWGN-TV (CW) Denver; QVC; Spike TV; Syfy; The Learning Channel; Trinity Broadcasting Network; Turner Network TV; USA Network; VH1; WGN America.
Programming (via translator): KIMO (ABC, CW) Anchorage.
Current originations: Religious Access; Government Access; Educational Access; Public Access.
Fee: $31.66 installation; $41.00 monthly.

Pay Service 1
Pay Units: 30.
Programming (via satellite): Showtime.
Fee: $15.75 installation; $12.95 monthly.

Video-On-Demand: No

Pay-Per-View
Addressable homes: 400.
iN DEMAND, Addressable: Yes.

Internet Service
Operational: No.

Telephone Service
None

Miles of Plant: 42.0 (coaxial); None (fiber optic). Additional miles planned: 15.0 (coaxial). Homes passed: 800.
Manager: Patty Campbell.
Ownership: Haines & Skagway Cable TV (MSO).

HOMER—GCI, 397 E. Pioneer Ave, Ste 3, Homer, AK 99603. Phones: 800-800-4800; 907-235-6366. Fax: 907-235-6625. E-mail: rcs@gci.com. Web Site: http://www.gci.com. Also serves Kachemak City. ICA: AK0046.
TV Market Ranking: Outside TV Markets (HOMER, Kachemak City). Franchise award date: N.A. Franchise expiration date: N.A. Began: N.A.
Channel capacity: 60 (operating 2-way). Channels available but not in use: 10.

Basic Service
Subscribers: 984.
Programming (received off-air): KAKM (PBS) Anchorage; KIMO (ABC, CW) Anchorage; KTBY (FOX) Anchorage; KTUU-TV (NBC) Anchorage; KTVA (CBS) Anchorage; KYES-TV (MNT) Anchorage.
Programming (via satellite): C-SPAN; C-SPAN 2; QVC; TV Guide Network.
Fee: $26.50 installation; $21.20 monthly.

Expanded Basic Service 1
Subscribers: 884.
Programming (via satellite): ABC Family Channel; AMC; Animal Planet; Arts & Entertainment; Bravo; Cartoon Network; CNBC; CNN; Comcast Sports Net Northwest; Comedy Central; Country Music TV; Discovery Channel; Disney Channel; ESPN; ESPN 2; Food Network; Fox News Channel; Headline News; HGTV; History Channel; Lifetime; MSNBC; MTV; Nickelodeon; Northwest Cable News; Spike TV; Syfy; TBS Superstation; The Learning Channel; Toon Disney; Travel Channel; Trinity Broadcasting Network; Turner Network TV; USA Network; Versus; VH1; Weather Channel.
Fee: $39.47 monthly.

Digital Basic Service
Subscribers: N.A.
Programming (via satellite): Music Choice.
Fee: $10.00 monthly.

Digital Pay Service 1
Pay Units: 75.
Programming (via satellite): Cinemax (multiplexed).
Fee: $10.95 monthly.

Digital Pay Service 2
Pay Units: 204.
Programming (via satellite): HBO (multiplexed).
Fee: $13.95 monthly.

Digital Pay Service 3
Pay Units: 75.
Programming (via satellite): Flix; Showtime (multiplexed); Sundance Channel; The Movie Channel (multiplexed).
Fee: $12.95 monthly.

Digital Pay Service 4
Pay Units: 54.
Programming (via satellite): Encore (multiplexed); Starz (multiplexed).
Fee: $12.95 monthly.

Video-On-Demand: No

Pay-Per-View
Adult Swim (delivered digitally); Movies (delivered digitally); special events (delivered digitally).

Internet Service
Operational: Yes. Began: September 1, 2002.
Broadband Service: GCI Hypernet.
Fee: $24.99 monthly.

Telephone Service
None

Miles of Plant: 49.0 (coaxial); None (fiber optic). Homes passed: 2,092. Total homes in franchised area: 3,400.

Manager: Bettyann Steciw. Chief Technician: Charles D. Smith.
Ownership: General Communication Inc. (MSO).

HOONAH—Formerly served by Hoonah Community TV. No longer in operation. ICA: AK0037.

HOOPER BAY—Formerly served by Frontier Cable Inc. No longer in operation. ICA: AK0023.

JUNEAU—GCI, 3161 Channel Dr, Ste 1, Juneau, AK 99801-7815. Phones: 907-265-5600 (Administrative office); 907-586-3320. Fax: 907-463-3880. E-mail: rcs@gci.com. Web Site: http://www.gci.com. Also serves Douglas. ICA: AK0003.
TV Market Ranking: Below 100 (Douglas, JUNEAU). Franchise award date: January 1, 1966. Franchise expiration date: N.A. Began: January 1, 1966.
Channel capacity: 61 (operating 2-way). Channels available but not in use: N.A.

Basic Service
Subscribers: 10,046.
Programming (received off-air): KATH-LP Juneau-Douglas; KJUD (ABC, CW) Juneau; KTBY (FOX) Anchorage; KTNL-TV (CBS, ION) Sitka; KTOO-TV (PBS) Juneau; 14 FMs.
Programming (via satellite): C-SPAN; C-SPAN 2; CW+; KYES-TV (MNT) Anchorage; Trinity Broadcasting Network; TV Guide Network; WGN America.
Current originations: Leased Access; Government Access; Educational Access; Public Access.
Fee: $25.50 installation; $19.70 monthly; $3.95 converter.

Expanded Basic Service 1
Subscribers: 8,650.
Programming (via satellite): ABC Family Channel; AMC; Animal Planet; Arts & Entertainment; Bravo; Cartoon Network; CNBC; CNN; Comcast Sports Net Northwest; Comedy Central; Country Music TV; Discovery Channel; Disney Channel; E! Entertainment Television; ESPN; ESPN 2; Food Network; Fox News Channel; Fuse; FX; Hallmark Channel; Headline News; HGTV; History Channel; Home Shopping Network; Lifetime; Lifetime Movie Network; MSNBC; MTV; National Geographic Channel; NFL Network; Nickelodeon; Northwest Cable News; Outdoor Channel; Oxygen; Pentagon Channel; QVC; ShopNBC; SoapNet; Spike TV; Syfy; TBS Superstation; The Learning Channel; Toon Disney; Travel Channel; truTV; Turner Classic Movies; Turner Network TV; TV Land; Univision; USA Network; Versus; VH1; WE tv; Weather Channel.
Fee: $24.09 monthly.

Digital Basic Service
Subscribers: 4,521.
Programming (received off-air): KTOO-TV (PBS) Juneau.
Programming (via satellite): 3 Angels Broadcasting Network; AmericanLife TV Network; BBC America; Bio; Bloomberg Television; Boomerang; BYU Television; Church Channel; CNN International; Daystar TV Network; Discovery Digital Networks; Discovery HD Theater; Do-It-Yourself; ESPN HD; ESPNews; Eternal Word TV Network; FamilyNet; Fox College Sports Atlantic; Fox College Sports Central; Fox College Sports Pacific; Fox Soccer; Fuel TV; G4; GAS; Golf Channel; Gospel Music Channel; Great American Country; GSN; Halogen Network; HDNet; HDNet Movies; History Channel International; Independent Film Channel; INSP; Military History Channel; MTV Networks Digital Suite; Music Choice; NFL Network; Nick Jr.; NickToons TV; Speed Channel; Tennis Channel; The Sportsman Channel; Turner Network TV HD; TVG Network; Universal HD; WealthTV.
Fee: $16.00 monthly.

Digital Pay Service 1
Pay Units: 631.
Programming (via satellite): Cinemax (multiplexed); Cinemax HD.
Fee: $10.95 monthly.

Digital Pay Service 2
Pay Units: 2,260.
Programming (via satellite): HBO (multiplexed); HBO HD.
Fee: $13.95 monthly.

Digital Pay Service 3
Pay Units: 737.
Programming (via satellite): Flix; Showtime (multiplexed); Showtime HD; The Movie Channel (multiplexed); The Movie Channel HD.
Fee: $12.95 monthly.

Digital Pay Service 4
Pay Units: 669.
Programming (via satellite): Encore (multiplexed); Starz (multiplexed); Starz HDTV.
Fee: $12.95 monthly.

Digital Pay Service 5
Pay Units: 218.
Programming (via satellite): Filipino Channel.
Fee: $13.99 monthly.

Video-On-Demand: No

Pay-Per-View
ESPN (delivered digitally); Movies (delivered digitally); special events (delivered digitally); Adult Swim (delivered digitally).

Internet Service
Operational: Yes. Began: December 1, 1999.
Broadband Service: GCI Hypernet.
Fee: $24.99 monthly.

Telephone Service
Digital: Operational
Miles of Plant: 153.0 (coaxial); 34.0 (fiber optic). Homes passed: 14,199.
Manager: Terry Dunlap. Plant Manager: Rob Knorr.
Ownership: General Communication Inc. (MSO).

KETCHIKAN—GCI, 2417 Tongass, Ste 104, Ketchikan, AK 99901. Phone: 907-225-2191. Fax: 907-225-4943. E-mail: rcs@gci.com. Web Site: http://www.gci.com. Also serves Saxman. ICA: AK0005.
TV Market Ranking: Below 100 (KETCHIKAN, Saxman). Franchise award date: N.A. Franchise expiration date: N.A. Began: November 11, 1953.
Channel capacity: 57 (operating 2-way). Channels available but not in use: N.A.

Basic Service
Subscribers: 3,501.
Programming (received off-air): KJUD (ABC, CW) Juneau; KTBY (FOX) Anchorage; KUBD (CBS, ION) Ketchikan; KYES-TV (MNT) Anchorage.
Programming (via satellite): C-SPAN; C-SPAN 2; CW+; KING-TV (NBC) Seattle; QVC; Trinity Broadcasting Network; TV Guide Network; WGN America.
Current originations: Government Access; Educational Access; Public Access.
Fee: $25.50 installation; $16.00 monthly; $2.74 converter.

Expanded Basic Service 1
Subscribers: 2,864.
Programming (via satellite): ABC Family Channel; AMC; Animal Planet; Arts & Entertainment; Bravo; Cartoon Network; CNBC; CNN; Comcast Sports Net Northwest; Comedy Central; Country Music TV; Discovery Channel; Disney Channel; E! Entertainment Television; ESPN; ESPN 2; Food Network; Fox News Channel; FX; Hallmark Channel; Headline News; HGTV; History Channel; Lifetime; Lifetime Movie Network; MSNBC; MTV; National Geographic Channel; NFL Network; Nickelodeon; Northwest Cable News; Outdoor Channel; SoapNet; Spike TV; Syfy; TBS Superstation; The Learning Channel; Toon Disney; Travel Channel; truTV; Turner Classic Movies; Turner Network TV; TV Land; USA Network; Versus; VH1; WE tv; Weather Channel.
Fee: $37.55 monthly.

Digital Basic Service
Subscribers: 1,146.
Programming (via satellite): 3 Angels Broadcasting Network; BBC America; Boomerang; BYU Television; Church Channel; Daystar TV Network; Discovery HD Theater; Do-It-Yourself; ESPN HD; ESPNews; Eternal Word TV Network; FamilyNet; Fox College Sports Atlantic; Fox College Sports Central; Fox College Sports Pacific; Fox Movie Channel; Fox Soccer; Fuel TV; G4; GAS; GSN; Halogen Network; HDNet; HDNet Movies; Independent Film Channel; INSP; Military History Channel; MTV Networks Digital Suite; Music Choice; NFL Network; Nick Jr.; NickToons TV; Speed Channel; The Sportsman Channel; Turner Network TV HD; TVG Network; Universal HD.
Fee: $7.00 monthly.

Digital Pay Service 1
Pay Units: 316.
Programming (via satellite): Cinemax (multiplexed); Cinemax HD.
Fee: $10.95 monthly.

Digital Pay Service 2
Pay Units: 657.
Programming (via satellite): HBO (multiplexed); HBO HD.
Fee: $13.95 monthly.

Digital Pay Service 3
Pay Units: 298.
Programming (via satellite): Flix; Showtime (multiplexed); Showtime HD; Sundance Channel; The Movie Channel (multiplexed); The Movie Channel HD.
Fee: $12.95 monthly.

Digital Pay Service 4
Pay Units: 274.
Programming (via satellite): Encore (multiplexed); Starz (multiplexed); Starz HDTV.
Fee: $12.95 monthly.

Digital Pay Service 5
Pay Units: 88.
Programming (via satellite): Filipino Channel.
Fee: $13.99 monthly.

Video-On-Demand: No

Pay-Per-View
Adult Swim (delivered digitally); Movies (delivered digitally); special events (delivered digitally).

Internet Service
Operational: Yes.
Broadband Service: GCI Hypernet.
Fee: $24.99 monthly.

Telephone Service
Analog: Not Operational
Digital: Operational
Miles of Plant: 74.0 (coaxial); 18.0 (fiber optic). Homes passed: 6,924.
Chief Technician: Russell Tramell.
Ownership: General Communication Inc. (MSO).

KING COVE—Formerly served by Mount Dutton Cable Corp. No longer in operation. ICA: AK0024.

KING SALMON—Bay Cablevision, PO Box 259, One Main St, King Salmon, AK 99613. Phones: 907-246-8235; 800-478-9100; 907-246-3300. Fax: 907-246-1115. E-mail: bbtccsr@bristolbay.com. Web Site: http://www.bristolbay.com. Also serves Naknek. ICA: AK0015.
TV Market Ranking: Outside TV Markets (KING SALMON, Naknek). Franchise award date: N.A. Franchise expiration date: N.A. Began: January 1, 1986.
Channel capacity: 45 (not 2-way capable). Channels available but not in use: 5.

Basic Service
Subscribers: 380.
Programming (received off-air): KUAC-TV (PBS) Fairbanks; 4 FMs.
Programming (via microwave): KIMO (ABC, CW) Anchorage; KTVA (CBS) Anchorage.
Programming (via satellite): ABC Family Channel; Alaska Rural Communications Service (ARCS); AMC; Animal Planet; Arts & Entertainment; CNN; Country Music TV; Discovery Channel; Disney Channel; ESPN; ESPN 2; Food Network; G4; HGTV; History Channel; Home Shopping Network; MTV; Nickelodeon; Spike TV; Syfy; TBS Superstation; The Learning Channel; Trinity Broadcasting Network; Turner Classic Movies; Turner Network TV; TV Land; USA Network; VH1; WGN America.
Current originations: Public Access.
Fee: $40.00 installation; $50.00 monthly.

Pay Service 1
Pay Units: 6.
Programming (via satellite): Cinemax.
Fee: $12.50 monthly.

Pay Service 2
Pay Units: 47.
Programming (via satellite): HBO.
Fee: $12.50 monthly.

Video-On-Demand: No

Internet Service
Operational: No, Dialup only.

Telephone Service
None
Miles of Plant: 15.0 (coaxial); None (fiber optic). Homes passed: 700. Total homes in franchised area: 750.

Manager: Todd Hoppe. Plant Supervisor: Earl Hubb. Chief Technician: Robert Hadfield.
Ownership: Bristol Bay Telephone Cooperative Inc.

KIPNUK—Formerly served by Frontier Cable Inc. No longer in operation. ICA: AK0027.

KODIAK—GCI, 2011 Mill Bay Rd, Kodiak, AK 99615-6991. Phone: 907-486-3334. Fax: 907-486-5160. Web Site: http://www.gci.com. ICA: AK0006.
TV Market Ranking: Outside TV Markets (KODIAK). Franchise award date: N.A. Franchise expiration date: N.A. Began: July 1, 1969.
Channel capacity: 54 (operating 2-way). Channels available but not in use: N.A.

Basic Service
Subscribers: 3,265.
Programming (via satellite): C-SPAN; C-SPAN 2; CW+; KTBY (FOX) Anchorage; TV Guide Network; WGN America.
Programming (via translator): KIMO (ABC, CW) Anchorage; KTUU-TV (NBC) Anchorage; KTVA (CBS) Anchorage; KYES-TV (MNT) Anchorage.
Current originations: Government Access; Educational Access; Public Access.
Fee: $35.50 installation; $21.20 monthly.

Expanded Basic Service 1
Subscribers: 2,756.
Programming (via satellite): ABC Family Channel; AMC; Animal Planet; Arts & Entertainment; BET Networks; Bravo; Cartoon Network; CNBC; CNN; Comcast Sports Net Northwest; Comedy Central; Country Music TV; Discovery Channel; Disney Channel; E! Entertainment Television; ESPN; ESPN 2; Food Network; Fox News Channel; Fuse; FX; Headline News; HGTV; History Channel; Home Shopping Network; Lifetime; Lifetime Movie Network; MSNBC; MTV; National Geographic Channel; NFL Network; Nickelodeon; Northwest Cable News; Outdoor Channel; Oxygen; Pentagon Channel; QVC; ShopNBC; SoapNet; Spike TV; Syfy; TBS Superstation; The Learning Channel; Toon Disney; Travel Channel; truTV; Turner Classic Movies; Turner Network TV; TV Land; Univision; USA Network; Versus; VH1; WE tv; Weather Channel.
Fee: $43.79 monthly.

Digital Basic Service
Subscribers: N.A.
Programming (via satellite): 3 Angels Broadcasting Network; AmericanLife TV Network; BBC America; Bio; Bloomberg Television; Boomerang; BYU Television; Church Channel; CNN International; Daystar TV Network; Discovery Digital Networks; Discovery HD Theater; Do-It-Yourself; ESPN HD; ESPNews; Eternal Word TV Network; FamilyNet; Fox College Sports Atlantic; Fox College Sports Central; Fox College Sports Pacific; Fox Soccer; Fuel TV; G4; GAS; Golf Channel; Gospel Music Channel; Great American Country; GSN; Halogen Network; HDNet; HDNet Movies; History Channel International; Independent Film Channel; INSP; Military History Channel; MTV Networks Digital Suite; Music Choice; NFL Network; Nick Jr.; NickToons TV; Speed Channel; Tennis Channel; The Sportsman Channel; Trinity Broadcasting Network; Turner Network TV HD; TVG Network; Universal HD; WealthTV.
Fee: $20.00 monthly.

Digital Pay Service 1
Pay Units: 365.
Programming (via satellite): Cinemax (multiplexed); Cinemax HD.
Fee: $10.95 monthly.

Digital Pay Service 2
Pay Units: 829.
Programming (via satellite): HBO (multiplexed); HBO HD.
Fee: $13.95 monthly.

Digital Pay Service 3
Pay Units: 250.
Programming (via satellite): Flix; Showtime (multiplexed); Showtime HD; The Movie Channel (multiplexed); The Movie Channel HD.
Fee: $12.95 monthly.

Digital Pay Service 4
Pay Units: 256.
Programming (via satellite): Encore (multiplexed); Starz (multiplexed); Starz HDTV.
Fee: $12.95 monthly.

Digital Pay Service 5
Pay Units: 439.
Programming (via satellite): Filipino Channel.
Fee: $12.95 monthly.

Video-On-Demand: No

Pay-Per-View
Adult Swim (delivered digitally); Movies (delivered digitally), Fee: $3.95; special events (delivered digitally).

Internet Service
Operational: Yes. Began: October 17, 2002.
Broadband Service: GCI Hypernet.
Fee: $24.99 monthly.

Telephone Service
Analog: Not Operational
Digital: Operational

Miles of Plant: 63.0 (coaxial); 18.0 (fiber optic). Homes passed: 5,509.
Manager: John Burnett.
Ownership: General Communication Inc. (MSO).

KOTZEBUE—GCI, PO Box 750, 606 Bison St, Kotzebue, AK 99752-0750. Phone: 907-442-2620. Fax: 907-442-3732. E-mail: rcs@gci.com. Web Site: http://www.gci.com. ICA: AK0016.
TV Market Ranking: Outside TV Markets (KOTZEBUE). Franchise award date: N.A. Franchise expiration date: N.A. Began: January 1, 1973.
Channel capacity: 63 (2-way capable). Channels available but not in use: N.A.

Basic Service
Subscribers: 791.
Programming (received off-air): KAKM (PBS) Anchorage; KYES-TV (MNT) Anchorage; 7 FMs.
Programming (via satellite): Alaska Rural Communications Service (ARCS); C-SPAN; C-SPAN 2; Home Shopping Network; KIMO (ABC, CW) Anchorage; KTBY (FOX) Anchorage; KTUU-TV (NBC) Anchorage; KTVA (CBS) Anchorage; QVC; TV Guide Network; WGN America.
Current originations: Government Access; Educational Access; Public Access.
Fee: $35.50 installation; $19.70 monthly.

Expanded Basic Service 1
Subscribers: 705.
Programming (via satellite): ABC Family Channel; AMC; Animal Planet; Arts & Entertainment; Cartoon Network; CNBC; CNN; Comedy Central; Country Music TV; Discovery Channel; Disney Channel; ESPN; ESPN 2; Food Network; Headline News; HGTV; History Channel; Lifetime; MSNBC; MTV; Nickelodeon; Outdoor Channel; Spike TV; Syfy; TBS Superstation; The Learning Channel; Toon Disney; Travel Channel; Trinity Broadcasting Network; Turner Classic Movies; Turner Network TV; TV Land; USA Network; VH1; Weather Channel.
Fee: $42.86 monthly.

Digital Basic Service
Subscribers: N.A.
Programming (via satellite): Music Choice.
Fee: $5.00 monthly.

Digital Pay Service 1
Pay Units: 196.
Programming (via satellite): Cinemax (multiplexed).
Fee: $10.95 monthly.

Digital Pay Service 2
Pay Units: 242.
Programming (via satellite): HBO (multiplexed).
Fee: $13.95 monthly.

Digital Pay Service 3
Pay Units: 219.
Programming (via satellite): Flix; Showtime (multiplexed); Sundance Channel; The Movie Channel (multiplexed).
Fee: $12.95 monthly.

Digital Pay Service 4
Pay Units: 148.
Programming (via satellite): Encore (multiplexed); Starz (multiplexed).
Fee: $12.95 monthly.

Video-On-Demand: No

Pay-Per-View
iN DEMAND (delivered digitally); Adult Swim (delivered digitally).

Internet Service
Operational: No.

Telephone Service
None

Miles of Plant: 7.0 (coaxial); None (fiber optic). Homes passed: 1,144.
Manager: Gary Samuelson. Marketing Director: Taryl Gebhardt.
Ownership: General Communication Inc. (MSO).

MOUNTAIN VILLAGE—Formerly served by Village Cable Co. No longer in operation. ICA: AK0022.

NOME—GCI, 110 Front St, Ste 103, Nome, AK 99762. Phones: 800-800-4800; 907-265-5600 (Administrative office); 907-443-2550. Fax: 907-443-5845. E-mail: rcs@gci.com. Web Site: http://www.gci.com. ICA: AK0038.
TV Market Ranking: Outside TV Markets (NOME). Franchise award date: N.A. Franchise expiration date: N.A. Began: February 1, 1971.
Channel capacity: 67 (operating 2-way). Channels available but not in use: 2.

Basic Service
Subscribers: 1,242.
Programming (received off-air): KAKM (PBS) Anchorage; KYES-TV (MNT) Anchorage; 8 FMs.
Programming (via satellite): C-SPAN; C-SPAN 2; KIMO (ABC, CW) Anchorage; KTBY (FOX) Anchorage; KTUU-TV (NBC) Anchorage; TV Guide Network; WGN America.
Current originations: Government Access; Educational Access; Public Access.
Fee: $35.50 installation; $20.70 monthly.

Expanded Basic Service 1
Subscribers: 1,129.
Programming (via satellite): ABC Family Channel; AMC; Animal Planet; Arts & Entertainment; BET Networks; Bravo; Cartoon Network; CNBC; CNN; Comedy Central; Country Music TV; Discovery Channel; Disney Channel; E! Entertainment Television; ESPN; ESPN 2; Food Network; Headline News; HGTV; History Channel; Home Shopping Network; KTVA (CBS) Anchorage; Lifetime; Lifetime Movie Network; MSNBC; MTV; Nickelodeon; Outdoor Channel; QVC; ShopNBC; SoapNet; Spike TV; Style Network; Syfy; TBS Superstation; The Learning Channel; Toon Disney; Travel Channel; truTV; Turner Classic Movies; Turner Network TV; TV Land; Univision; USA Network; VH1; WE tv; Weather Channel.
Fee: $47.29 monthly.

Digital Basic Service
Subscribers: N.A.
Programming (via satellite): 3 Angels Broadcasting Network; AmericanLife TV Network; BBC America; Bio; Bloomberg Television; Boomerang; BYU Television; Church Channel; CNN International; Daystar TV Network; Discovery HD Theater; Discovery Health Channel; Discovery Home Channel; Discovery Kids Channel; Discovery Military Channel; Discovery Times Channel; Do-It-Yourself; ESPN HD; ESPNews; FamilyNet; G4; Great American Country; GSN; Halogen Network; HDNet; HDNet Movies; History Channel International; Independent Film Channel; INSP; MTV Hits; MTV2; Music Choice; Nick Jr.; NickToons TV; Science Channel; TeenNick; The Sportsman Channel; Trinity Broadcasting Network; Turner Network TV HD; Universal HD; VH1 Classic; WealthTV; WealthTV HD.
Fee: $15.00 monthly.

Digital Pay Service 1
Pay Units: 193.
Programming (via satellite): Cinemax (multiplexed); Cinemax HD; HBO HD; Showtime HD; Starz HDTV; The Movie Channel HD.
Fee: $10.95 monthly.

Digital Pay Service 2
Pay Units: 325.
Programming (via satellite): HBO (multiplexed).
Fee: $13.95 monthly.

Digital Pay Service 3
Pay Units: 137.
Programming (via satellite): Flix; Showtime (multiplexed); The Movie Channel (multiplexed).
Fee: $12.95 monthly.

Digital Pay Service 4
Pay Units: 152.
Programming (via satellite): Encore (multiplexed); Starz (multiplexed).
Fee: $12.95 monthly.

Video-On-Demand: No

Pay-Per-View
iN DEMAND (delivered digitally); Adult Swim (delivered digitally).

Internet Service
Operational: Yes.
Broadband Service: GCI Hypernet.
Fee: $24.99 monthly.

Telephone Service
None

Miles of Plant: 21.0 (coaxial); 1.0 (fiber optic). Homes passed: 1,625.

Manager: Gary Samuelson. Chief Technician: Earl Merchant.

Ownership: General Communication Inc. (MSO).

PETERSBURG—GCI, 914 Nordic Dr, Anchorage, AK 99833. Phones: 907-265-5600 (Corporate office); 907-772-3292. Fax: 907-772-3942. E-mail: rcs@gci.com. Web Site: http://www.gci.com. ICA: AK0011.

TV Market Ranking: Outside TV Markets (PETERSBURG). Franchise award date: December 1, 1980. Franchise expiration date: N.A. Began: September 1, 1968.

Channel capacity: 40 (operating 2-way). Channels available but not in use: N.A.

Basic Service
Subscribers: 956.
Programming (received off-air): KJUD (ABC, CW) Juneau; KTOO-TV (PBS) Juneau; KYES-TV (MNT) Anchorage; 8 FMs.
Programming (via satellite): C-SPAN; C-SPAN 2; KING-TV (NBC) Seattle; KTBY (FOX) Anchorage; KTVA (CBS) Anchorage; QVC; TV Guide Network; WGN America.
Current originations: Government Access; Educational Access; Public Access.
Fee: $25.50 installation; $19.70 monthly.

Expanded Basic Service 1
Subscribers: 864.
Programming (via satellite): ABC Family Channel; AMC; Animal Planet; Arts & Entertainment; Cartoon Network; CNBC; CNN; Comcast Sports Net Northwest; Comedy Central; Country Music TV; Discovery Channel; Disney Channel; ESPN; ESPN 2; Food Network; Fox News Channel; Hallmark Channel; Headline News; HGTV; History Channel; Lifetime; MSNBC; MTV; Nickelodeon; Northwest Cable News; Outdoor Channel; Spike TV; Syfy; TBS Superstation; The Learning Channel; Toon Disney; Travel Channel; Trinity Broadcasting Network; truTV; Turner Network TV; TV Land; USA Network; Versus; VH1; Weather Channel.
Fee: $26.50 installation; $35.29 monthly.

Digital Basic Service
Subscribers: N.A.
Programming (via satellite): DMX Music.
Fee: $5.00 monthly.

Digital Pay Service 1
Pay Units: 139.
Programming (via satellite): Cinemax (multiplexed); Showtime (multiplexed).
Fee: $10.95 monthly.

Digital Pay Service 2
Pay Units: 213.
Programming (via satellite): HBO (multiplexed).
Fee: $13.95 monthly.

Digital Pay Service 3
Pay Units: 117.
Programming (via satellite): Flix; Sundance Channel; The Movie Channel (multiplexed).
Fee: $12.95 monthly.

Digital Pay Service 4
Pay Units: 80.
Programming (via satellite): Encore (multiplexed); Starz (multiplexed).
Fee: $12.95 monthly.

Video-On-Demand: No

Pay-Per-View
Adult Swim (delivered digitally); Movies (delivered digitally); special events (delivered digitally).

Internet Service
Operational: Yes. Began: July 1, 2002.
Broadband Service: GCI Hypernet.
Fee: $99.99 installation; $24.99 monthly.

Telephone Service
None

Miles of Plant: 25.0 (coaxial); None (fiber optic). Homes passed: 1,583.

Chief Technician: Perry Allen.

Ownership: General Communication Inc. (MSO).

PORT LIONS—Formerly served by Eyecom Cable. No longer in operation. ICA: AK0026.

QUINHAGAK—Formerly served by Frontier Cable Inc. No longer in operation. ICA: AK0039.

SAVOONGA—Formerly served by Frontier Cable Inc. No longer in operation. ICA: AK0040.

SEWARD—GCI, PO Box 99016, 404 Adams St, Seward, AK 99664. Phones: 800-800-4800; 907-224-8912. Fax: 907-224-7318. E-mail: rcs@gci.com. Web Site: http://www.gci.com. ICA: AK0009.

TV Market Ranking: Outside TV Markets (SEWARD). Franchise award date: December 1, 1986. Franchise expiration date: N.A. Began: June 5, 1987.

Channel capacity: N.A. Channels available but not in use: N.A.

Basic Service
Subscribers: 1,515.
Programming (received off-air): KTOO-TV (PBS) Juneau; KYES-TV (MNT) Anchorage; 12 FMs.
Programming (via satellite): Alaska Rural Communications Service (ARCS); C-SPAN; C-SPAN 2; CW+; KIMO (ABC, CW) Anchorage; KTBY (FOX) Anchorage; KTUU-TV (NBC) Anchorage; KTVA (CBS) Anchorage; TV Guide Network; WGN America.
Current originations: Public Access.
Planned originations: Educational Access.
Fee: $35.50 installation; $21.20 monthly.

Expanded Basic Service 1
Subscribers: 1,382.
Programming (via satellite): ABC Family Channel; AMC; Animal Planet; Arts & Entertainment; BET Networks; Bravo; Cartoon Network; CNBC; CNN; Comcast Sports Net Northwest; Comedy Central; Country Music TV; Discovery Channel; Disney Channel; E! Entertainment Television; ESPN; ESPN 2; Food Network; Fox News Channel; Fuse; FX; Headline News; HGTV; History Channel; Home Shopping Network; Lifetime; Lifetime Movie Network; MSNBC; MTV; National Geographic Channel; NFL Network; Nickelodeon; Outdoor Channel; Oxygen; Pentagon Channel; QVC; ShopNBC; SoapNet; Speed Channel; Spike TV; Style Network; Syfy; TBS Superstation; The Learning Channel; Toon Disney; Travel Channel; truTV; Turner Classic Movies; Turner Network TV; TV Land; Univision; USA Network; Versus; VH1; WE tv; Weather Channel.
Fee: $40.28 monthly.

Digital Basic Service
Subscribers: N.A.
Programming (via satellite): 3 Angels Broadcasting Network; AmericanLife TV Network; BBC America; Bio; Bloomberg Television; Boomerang; BYU Television; Church Channel; CNN International; Daystar TV Network; Discovery Health Channel; Discovery Home Channel; Discovery Kids Channel; Discovery Military Channel; Discovery Times Channel; Do-It-Yourself; ESPNews; Eternal Word TV Network; FamilyNet; Fox College Sports Atlantic; Fox College Sports Central; Fox College Sports Pacific; Fox Soccer; Fuel TV; G4; Golf Channel; Gospel Music Channel; Great American Country; GSN; Halogen Network; History Channel International; HorseRacing TV; Independent Film Channel; INSP; International Television (ITV); MTV Hits; MTV2; Music Choice; Nick Jr.; NickToons TV; Science Channel; TeenNick; Tennis Channel; The Sportsman Channel; Trinity Broadcasting Network; VH1 Classic; WealthTV.
Fee: $20.00 monthly.

Digital Pay Service 1
Pay Units: 111.
Programming (via satellite): Cinemax (multiplexed).
Fee: $10.95 monthly.

Digital Pay Service 2
Pay Units: 386.
Programming (via satellite): HBO (multiplexed).
Fee: $13.95 monthly.

Digital Pay Service 3
Pay Units: 115.
Programming (via satellite): Flix; Showtime (multiplexed); The Movie Channel (multiplexed).
Fee: $12.95 monthly.

Digital Pay Service 4
Pay Units: 81.
Programming (via satellite): Encore (multiplexed); Starz (multiplexed).
Fee: $12.95 monthly.

Video-On-Demand: No

Pay-Per-View
Addressable homes: 630.
Adult Swim (delivered digitally); Movies (delivered digitally), Addressable: Yes; special events (delivered digitally).

Internet Service
Operational: Yes. Began: December 1, 2001.
Broadband Service: GCI Hypernet.
Fee: $24.99 monthly.

Telephone Service
None

Miles of Plant: 43.0 (coaxial); None (fiber optic). Homes passed: 1,923.

Office Manager: Jeannette Kimes. Chief Technician: Gary Lindquist.

Ownership: General Communication Inc. (MSO).

SITKA—GCI, 208 Lake St, Ste A, Sitka, AK 99835-7582. Phone: 907-747-3535. Fax: 907-747-4929. Web Site: http://www.gci.com. Also serves Mount Edgecumbe & Sitka County. ICA: AK0007.

TV Market Ranking: Below 100 (Mount Edgecumbe, SITKA, Sitka County (portions)); Outside TV Markets (Sitka County (portions)). Franchise award date: N.A. Franchise expiration date: N.A. Began: November 15, 1959.

Channel capacity: 58 (operating 2-way). Channels available but not in use: N.A.

Basic Service
Subscribers: 2,956.
Programming (received off-air): KJUD (ABC, CW) Juneau; KSCT-LP (NBC) Sitka; KTBY (FOX) Anchorage; KTNL-TV (CBS, ION) Sitka; KTOO-TV (PBS) Juneau; KYES-TV (MNT) Anchorage.
Programming (via satellite): C-SPAN; C-SPAN 2; CW+; KING-TV (NBC) Seattle; TV Guide Network; WGN America.
Current originations: Leased Access; Public Access.
Planned originations: Educational Access.
Fee: $20.00 installation; $18.70 monthly; $1.59 converter; $12.85 additional installation.

Expanded Basic Service 1
Subscribers: 1,977.
Programming (via satellite): ABC Family Channel; AMC; Animal Planet; Arts & Entertainment; BET Networks; Bravo; Cartoon Network; CNBC; CNN; Comcast Sports Net Northwest; Comedy Central; Country Music TV; Discovery Channel; Disney Channel; E! Entertainment Television; ESPN; ESPN 2; Food Network; Fox News Channel; Fuse; FX; Headline News; HGTV; History Channel; Home Shopping Network; Lifetime; Lifetime Movie Network; MSNBC; MTV; National Geographic Channel; NFL Network; Nickelodeon; Northwest Cable News; Outdoor Channel; Oxygen; Pentagon Channel; QVC; ShopNBC; SoapNet; Spike TV; Style Network; Syfy; TBS Superstation; The Learning Channel; Toon Disney; Travel Channel; truTV; Turner Classic Movies; Turner Network TV; TV Land; Univision; USA Network; Versus; VH1; WE tv; Weather Channel.
Fee: $12.08 installation; $41.29 monthly.

Digital Basic Service
Subscribers: N.A.
Programming (via satellite): 3 Angels Broadcasting Network; AmericanLife TV Network; BBC America; Bio; Bloomberg Television; Boomerang; BYU Television; Church Channel; CNN International; Daystar TV Network; Discovery Digital Networks; Discovery HD Theater; Do-It-Yourself; ESPN HD; ESPNews; Eternal Word TV Network; FamilyNet; Fox College Sports Atlantic; Fox College Sports Central; Fox College Sports Pacific; Fox Soccer; Fuel TV; G4; GAS; Golf Channel; Gospel Music Channel; Great American Country; GSN; Halogen Network; HDNet; HDNet Movies; History Channel International; Independent Film Channel; INSP; MTV Networks Digital Suite; Music Choice; Nick Jr.; NickToons TV; Speed Channel; Tennis Channel; The Movie Channel HD; The Sportsman Channel; Trinity Broadcasting Network; Turner Network TV HD; TVG Network; Universal HD; WealthTV.
Fee: $20.00 monthly.

Digital Pay Service 1
Pay Units: 199.
Programming (via satellite): Cinemax (multiplexed); Cinemax HD; Flix.
Fee: $10.95 monthly.

Digital Pay Service 2
Pay Units: 377.
Programming (via satellite): HBO (multiplexed); HBO HD.
Fee: $13.95 monthly.
Digital Pay Service 3
Pay Units: 210.
Programming (via satellite): Showtime (multiplexed); Showtime HD; Sundance Channel; The Movie Channel (multiplexed).
Fee: $12.95 monthly.
Digital Pay Service 4
Pay Units: 67.
Programming (via satellite): Encore (multiplexed); Starz (multiplexed); Starz HDTV.
Fee: $12.95 monthly.
Digital Pay Service 5
Pay Units: 66.
Programming (via satellite): Filipino Channel.
Fee: $13.99 monthly.
Video-On-Demand: No
Pay-Per-View
Adult Swim (delivered digitally); Movies (delivered digitally), Addressable: No; special events (delivered digitally).
Internet Service
Operational: Yes.
Broadband Service: GCI Hypernet.
Fee: $24.99 monthly.
Telephone Service
None
Miles of Plant: 42.0 (coaxial); 1.0 (fiber optic). Homes passed: 4,461.
Manager & Chief Technician: Dennis Lanham. Marketing Director: Tricia Wurtz.
Ownership: General Communication Inc. (MSO).

SKAGWAY—Skagway Cable TV, PO Box 454, 715 Main St., Haines, AK 99827-0454. Phone: 907-766-2137. Fax: 907-766-2345. E-mail: pcampbell99827@yahoo.com. Web Site: http://www.hainescable.tvheaven.com. ICA: AK0020.
TV Market Ranking: Outside TV Markets (SKAGWAY). Franchise award date: April 1, 1962. Franchise expiration date: N.A. Began: January 1, 1965.
Channel capacity: 35 (operating 2-way). Channels available but not in use: 7.
Basic Service
Subscribers: 100.
Programming (via satellite): ABC Family Channel; Alaska Rural Communications Service (ARCS); CNN; Discovery Channel; Disney Channel; ESPN; KCNC-TV (CBS) Denver; KIMO (ABC, CW) Anchorage; KUSA (NBC) Denver; Spike TV; Syfy; TBS Superstation; The Learning Channel; Turner Network TV; USA Network; WGN America; WJBK (FOX) Detroit.
Fee: $41.60 installation; $47.43 monthly.
Video-On-Demand: No
Internet Service
Operational: No.
Telephone Service
None
Miles of Plant: 7.0 (coaxial); None (fiber optic). Homes passed: 277. Total homes in franchised area: 277.
Manager: Patty Campbell.
Ownership: Haines & Skagway Cable TV (MSO).

SOLDOTNA—GCI, 189 S Binkley St, Ste 101, Soldotna, AK 99669-8006. Phones: 800-800-4800; 907-262-3266. Fax: 907-262-3560. Web Site: http://www.gci.com. Also serves Kenai, Kenai Peninsula & Ridgeway. ICA: AK0051.
TV Market Ranking: Outside TV Markets (Kenai, Kenai Peninsula, Ridgeway, SOLDOTNA).
Channel capacity: N.A. Channels available but not in use: N.A.
Basic Service
Subscribers: 3,647.
Programming (received off-air): KAKM (PBS) Anchorage; KIMO (ABC, CW) Anchorage; KTBY (FOX) Anchorage; KTUU-TV (NBC) Anchorage; KTVA (CBS) Anchorage; KYES-TV (MNT) Anchorage.
Programming (via satellite): C-SPAN; C-SPAN 2; QVC; TV Guide Network; WGN America.
Fee: $35.50 installation; $21.20 monthly; $15.00 additional installation.
Expanded Basic Service 1
Subscribers: 3,476.
Programming (via satellite): ABC Family Channel; AMC; Animal Planet; Arts & Entertainment; Bravo; Cartoon Network; CNBC; CNN; Comcast Sports Net Northwest; Comedy Central; Country Music TV; Discovery Channel; Disney Channel; E! Entertainment Television; ESPN; ESPN 2; Food Network; Fox News Channel; FX; Headline News; HGTV; History Channel; Home Shopping Network; Lifetime; Lifetime Movie Network; MSNBC; MTV; Nickelodeon; Northwest Cable News; Outdoor Channel; Spike TV; Syfy; TBS Superstation; The Learning Channel; Toon Disney; Travel Channel; truTV; Turner Classic Movies; Turner Network TV; USA Network; VH1.
Fee: $33.79 monthly.
Digital Basic Service
Subscribers: 656.
Programming (via satellite): BBC America; Boomerang; Discovery Digital Networks; ESPNews; Fox College Sports Atlantic; Fox College Sports Central; Fox College Sports Pacific; Fox Soccer; G4; GSN; Independent Film Channel; Military History Channel; Music Choice; Speed Channel; The Sportsman Channel.
Fee: $18.00 monthly.
Digital Pay Service 1
Pay Units: 1,878.
Programming (via satellite): Cinemax (multiplexed); Encore (multiplexed); Flix; HBO (multiplexed); Showtime (multiplexed); Starz (multiplexed); The Movie Channel (multiplexed).
Fee: $10.95 monthly (Cinemax), $12.95 monthly (Showtime or Starz), $13.95 monthly (HBO).
Video-On-Demand: No
Pay-Per-View
Addressable homes: 656.
Adult Swim (delivered digitally); Movies (delivered digitally); special events (delivered digitally).
Internet Service
Operational: Yes.
Broadband Service: GCI Hypernet.
Fee: $54.99 monthly.
Telephone Service
None
Miles of Plant: 121.0 (coaxial); 18.0 (fiber optic). Homes passed: 6,251.
Office Manager: Denise Daley. Chief Technician: Walt Zuck.
Ownership: General Communication Inc. (MSO).

ST. MARYS—Formerly served by Frontier Cable Inc. No longer in operation. ICA: AK0030.

TANANA—Supervision Cable TV, PO Box 872100, Wasilla, AK 99687-2100. Phone: 907-373-5599. Fax: 907-373-5599. Web Site: http://www.yukontel.net. ICA: AK0031.
TV Market Ranking: Outside TV Markets (TANANA). Franchise award date: N.A. Franchise expiration date: N.A. Began: December 1, 1986.
Channel capacity: 45 (operating 2-way). Channels available but not in use: 30.
Basic Service
Subscribers: 70.
Programming (received off-air): KAKM (PBS) Anchorage; KIMO (ABC, CW) Anchorage.
Programming (via satellite): CNN; Discovery Channel; Disney Channel; ESPN; Fox News Channel; Headline News; Home Shopping Network; KCNC-TV (CBS) Denver; KUSA (NBC) Denver; MTV2; Spike TV; TBS Superstation; The Learning Channel; Turner Network TV; TV Land; USA Network; VH1; WGN America.
Current originations: Educational Access; Public Access.
Fee: $40.00 installation; $35.00 monthly.
Pay Service 1
Pay Units: 43.
Programming (via satellite): HBO; Showtime (multiplexed).
Fee: $10.00 monthly.
Video-On-Demand: No
Internet Service
Operational: Yes.
Subscribers: 35.
Broadband Service: In-house.
Fee: $30.00 installation; $45.00 monthly.
Telephone Service
None
Miles of Plant: 2.0 (coaxial); None (fiber optic). Homes passed: 104.
Manager: Chelle Sommerville. Chief Technician: Don Eller.
Ownership: Supervision Cable TV (MSO).

THORNE BAY—Formerly served by Thorne Bay Community TV Inc. No longer in operation. ICA: AK0041.

TOGIAK—Formerly served by Frontier Cable Inc. No longer in operation. ICA: AK0025.

TOKSOOK BAY—Formerly served by Frontier Cable Inc. No longer in operation. ICA: AK0029.

TUNUNAK—Formerly served by Frontier Cable Inc. No longer in operation. ICA: AK0028.

UNALAKLEET—Formerly served by Frontier Cable Inc. No longer in operation, AK. ICA: AK0021.

UNALASKA—Eyecom Cable, 201 E 56th Ave, Anchorage, AK 99518-1283. Phones: 800-478-2982; 907-563-2003. Fax: 907-565-5539. E-mail: custsvc@telalaska.com. Web Site: http://www.telalaska.com. Also serves Dutch Harbor. ICA: AK0042.
TV Market Ranking: Outside TV Markets (Dutch Harbor, UNALASKA). Franchise award date: N.A. Franchise expiration date: N.A. Began: December 1, 1984.
Channel capacity: N.A. Channels available but not in use: N.A.
Basic Service
Subscribers: 1,041.
Programming (via satellite): ABC Family Channel; Alaska Rural Communications Service (ARCS); AMC; Animal Planet; Arts & Entertainment; Bravo; Cartoon Network; CNN; Comedy Central; Cooking Channel; Country Music TV; Discovery Channel; Disney Channel; ESPN; ESPN 2; GalaVision; Headline News; History Channel; KIMO (ABC, CW) Anchorage; KTUU-TV (NBC) Anchorage; KTVA (CBS) Anchorage; KUAC-TV (PBS) Fairbanks; KYES-TV (MNT) Anchorage; Lifetime; MTV; Nickelodeon; Spike TV; Syfy; TBS Superstation; The Learning Channel; Trinity Broadcasting Network; Turner Network TV; TV Land; USA Network; VH1; WGN America.
Current originations: Educational Access; Public Access.
Fee: $35.00 installation; $42.40 monthly.
Digital Basic Service
Subscribers: N.A.
Programming (via satellite): Music Choice.
Digital Pay Service 1
Pay Units: 187.
Programming (via satellite): Cinemax.
Fee: $10.95 monthly.
Digital Pay Service 2
Pay Units: 253.
Programming (via satellite): HBO.
Fee: $13.95 monthly.
Digital Pay Service 3
Pay Units: 70.
Programming (via satellite): Playboy TV.
Fee: $7.95 monthly.
Video-On-Demand: No
Internet Service
Operational: Yes.
Broadband Service: arctic.net.
Fee: $45.00 monthly.
Telephone Service
None
Miles of Plant: 26.0 (coaxial); None (fiber optic).
President & Chief Executive Officer: Jack Rhyner. Chief Operating Officer: Dave Goggins. Chief Technician: Dan Christensen.
City fee: None.
Ownership: Eyecom Inc. (MSO).

VALDEZ—GCI, 104 Harbor Court, Valdez, AK 99686. Phones: 907-265-5600 (Administrative office); 907-835-4930. Fax: 907-835-4257. E-mail: rcs@gci.com. Web Site: http://www.gci.com. ICA: AK0010.
TV Market Ranking: Outside TV Markets (VALDEZ). Franchise award date: N.A. Franchise expiration date: N.A. Began: September 1, 1974.
Channel capacity: 36 (operating 2-way). Channels available but not in use: N.A.
Basic Service
Subscribers: 1,271.
Programming (received off-air): KAKM (PBS) Anchorage; KIMO (ABC, CW) Anchorage; KTBY (FOX) Anchorage; KTUU-TV

(NBC) Anchorage; KTVA (CBS) Anchorage; KYES-TV (MNT) Anchorage; 8 FMs.
Programming (via satellite): Alaska Rural Communications Service (ARCS); C-SPAN; C-SPAN 2; Home Shopping Network; QVC; TV Guide Network; WGN America.
Current originations: Government Access; Educational Access; Public Access.
Fee: $35.50 installation; $20.70 monthly.

Expanded Basic Service 1
Subscribers: 1,157.
Programming (via satellite): ABC Family Channel; AMC; Animal Planet; Arts & Entertainment; CNBC; CNN; Comcast Sports Net Northwest; Comedy Central; Country Music TV; Discovery Channel; Disney Channel; ESPN; ESPN 2; Food Network; Fox News Channel; Headline News; HGTV; History Channel; Lifetime; MSNBC; MTV; Nickelodeon; Northwest Cable News; Outdoor Channel; Spike TV; Syfy; TBS Superstation; The Learning Channel; Toon Disney; Travel Channel; Turner Network TV; TV Land; USA Network; Versus; VH1; Weather Channel.
Fee: $40.26 monthly.

Digital Basic Service
Subscribers: N.A.
Programming (via satellite): Music Choice.

Digital Pay Service 1
Pay Units: 455.
Programming (via satellite): HBO (multiplexed).
Fee: $13.95 monthly.

Digital Pay Service 2
Pay Units: 120.
Programming (via satellite): Cinemax (multiplexed).
Fee: $10.95 monthly.

Digital Pay Service 3
Pay Units: 74.
Programming (via satellite): Encore (multiplexed); Starz (multiplexed).
Fee: $12.95 monthly.

Digital Pay Service 4
Pay Units: 119.
Programming (via satellite): Flix; Showtime (multiplexed); Sundance Channel; The Movie Channel (multiplexed).
Fee: $12.95 monthly.

Video-On-Demand: No

Pay-Per-View
iN DEMAND (delivered digitally); Adult Swim (delivered digitally).

Internet Service
Operational: Yes. Began: January 1, 2000.
Broadband Service: GCI Hypernet.
Fee: $24.99 monthly.

Telephone Service
None

Miles of Plant: 33.0 (coaxial); 10.0 (fiber optic). Homes passed: 2,032.
Manager: Tom Zulz.
City fee: None.
Ownership: General Communication Inc. (MSO).

WASILLA—GCI, 501 N Main St, Ste 130, Wasilla, AK 99654-7023. Phones: 800-800-4800; 907-373-2288. Fax: 907-376-8888. E-mail: rcs@gci.com. Web Site: http://www.gci.com. Also serves Matanuska Valley & Palmer. ICA: AK0004.
TV Market Ranking: Below 100 (Matanuska Valley, Palmer, WASILLA). Franchise award date: N.A. Franchise expiration date: N.A. Began: October 1, 1982.
Channel capacity: 57 (operating 2-way). Channels available but not in use: N.A.

Basic Service
Subscribers: 7,874.
Programming (received off-air): KAKM (PBS) Anchorage; KCFT-LP Anchorage; KDMD (ION) Anchorage; KIMO (ABC, CW) Anchorage; KTBY (FOX) Anchorage; KTUU-TV (NBC) Anchorage; KTVA (CBS) Anchorage; KYES-TV (MNT) Anchorage.
Programming (via satellite): C-SPAN; C-SPAN 2; CW+; TV Guide Network; WGN America.
Current originations: Public Access.
Fee: $25.50 installation; $21.20 monthly.

Expanded Basic Service 1
Subscribers: 6,780.
Programming (via satellite): ABC Family Channel; AMC; Animal Planet; Arts & Entertainment; BET Networks; Bravo; Cartoon Network; CNBC; CNN; Comcast Sports Net Northwest; Comedy Central; Country Music TV; Discovery Channel; Disney Channel; E! Entertainment Television; ESPN; ESPN 2; ESPN Classic Sports; Food Network; Fox News Channel; Fuse; FX; Headline News; HGTV; History Channel; Home Shopping Network; Lifetime; Lifetime Movie Network; MSNBC; MTV; National Geographic Channel; NFL Network; Nickelodeon; Outdoor Channel; Oxygen; Pentagon Channel; QVC; ShopNBC; SoapNet; Spike TV; Syfy; TBS Superstation; The Learning Channel; Toon Disney; Travel Channel; truTV; Turner Classic Movies; Turner Network TV; TV Land; Univision; USA Network; Versus; VH1; WE tv; Weather Channel.
Fee: $35.79 monthly.

Digital Basic Service
Subscribers: N.A.
Programming (received off-air): KAKM (PBS) Anchorage; KTUU-TV (NBC) Anchorage; KTVA (CBS) Anchorage.
Programming (via satellite): 3 Angels Broadcasting Network; AmericanLife TV Network; BBC America; Bio; Bloomberg Television; Boomerang; BYU Television; Church Channel; CNN International; Daystar TV Network; Discovery Digital Networks; Discovery HD Theater; Do-It-Yourself; ESPN HD; ESPNews; Eternal Word TV Network; FamilyNet; Fox College Sports Atlantic; Fox College Sports Central; Fox College Sports Pacific; Fox Soccer; Fuel TV; G4; GAS; Golf Channel; Gospel Music Channel; Great American Country; GSN; Halogen Network; HDNet; HDNet Movies; History Channel International; Independent Film Channel; INSP; Military History Channel; MTV Networks Digital Suite; Music Choice; NFL Network; Nick Jr.; NickToons TV; Speed Channel; Tennis Channel; The Sportsman Channel; Trinity Broadcasting Network; Turner Network TV HD; TVG Network; Universal HD; WealthTV.
Fee: $18.00 monthly.

Digital Pay Service 1
Pay Units: 3,564.
Programming (via satellite): Cinemax (multiplexed); Cinemax HD; Filipino Channel; HBO (multiplexed); Korean Channel; Showtime (multiplexed); Starz (multiplexed).
Fee: $10.95 monthly (Cinemax), $12.95 monthly (Starz), $13.95 monthly (Showtime or HBO), $13.99 monthly (Korean Channel or Filipino Channel).

Video-On-Demand: No

Pay-Per-View
Hot Choice (delivered digitally), Addressable: Yes; iN DEMAND (delivered digitally); ESPN (delivered digitally).

Internet Service
Operational: Yes.
Subscribers: 534.
Broadband Service: GCI Hypernet.
Fee: $24.99 monthly.

Telephone Service
Analog: Not Operational
Digital: Operational

Miles of Plant: 371.0 (coaxial); 27.0 (fiber optic). Homes passed: 16,778.
Ownership: General Communication Inc. (MSO).

WHITTIER—Supervision Cable TV, PO Box 872100, Wasilla, AK 99687-2100. Phone: 907-373-5599. Fax: 907-373-5599. Web Site: http://www.yukontel.net. ICA: AK0032.
TV Market Ranking: Below 100 (WHITTIER). Franchise award date: N.A. Franchise expiration date: N.A. Began: March 1, 1987.
Channel capacity: 45 (operating 2-way). Channels available but not in use: 28.

Basic Service
Subscribers: 132.
Programming (received off-air): KAKM (PBS) Anchorage; KIMO (ABC, CW) Anchorage.
Programming (via satellite): CNN; Discovery Channel; Disney Channel; ESPN; Headline News; Home Shopping Network; KCNC-TV (CBS) Denver; KUSA (NBC) Denver; MTV2; Spike TV; TBS Superstation; The Learning Channel; Turner Network TV; TV Land; USA Network; VH1; WGN America.
Current originations: Educational Access.
Fee: $40.00 installation; $30.50 monthly.

Pay Service 1
Pay Units: 119.
Programming (via satellite): HBO.
Fee: $10.00 monthly.

Pay Service 2
Pay Units: 119.
Programming (via satellite): Showtime (multiplexed).
Fee: $10.00 monthly.

Video-On-Demand: No

Internet Service
Operational: Yes. Began: July 27, 2000.
Subscribers: 80.
Broadband Service: In-house.
Fee: $50.00 monthly.

Telephone Service
None

Miles of Plant: 3.0 (coaxial); None (fiber optic).
Manager: Chelle Sommerville. Chief Technician: Don Eller.
Ownership: Supervision Cable TV (MSO).

WRANGELL—GCI, PO Box 909, 325 Front St, Wrangell, AK 99929. Phone: 907-874-2392. Web Site: http://www.gci.com. ICA: AK0014.
TV Market Ranking: Outside TV Markets (WRANGELL). Franchise award date: N.A. Franchise expiration date: N.A. Began: September 1, 1968.
Channel capacity: 60 (operating 2-way). Channels available but not in use: N.A.

Basic Service
Subscribers: 656.
Programming (received off-air): KJUD (ABC, CW) Juneau; KTVA (CBS) Anchorage; KYES-TV (MNT) Anchorage.
Programming (via satellite): C-SPAN; C-SPAN 2; KING-TV (NBC) Seattle; KTBY (FOX) Anchorage; QVC; TV Guide Network; WGN America.
Current originations: Government Access; Educational Access; Public Access.
Fee: $25.50 installation; $19.70 monthly.

Expanded Basic Service 1
Subscribers: 586.
Programming (via satellite): ABC Family Channel; AMC; Animal Planet; Arts & Entertainment; Cartoon Network; CNBC; CNN; Comcast Sports Net Northwest; Comedy Central; Country Music TV; Discovery Channel; Disney Channel; ESPN; ESPN 2; Food Network; Fox News Channel; Hallmark Channel; Headline News; HGTV; History Channel; Lifetime; MSNBC; MTV; Nickelodeon; Northwest Cable News; Spike TV; Syfy; TBS Superstation; The Learning Channel; Toon Disney; Travel Channel; Trinity Broadcasting Network; truTV; Turner Network TV; TV Land; USA Network; Versus; VH1; Weather Channel.
Fee: $35.29 monthly.

Digital Basic Service
Subscribers: N.A.
Programming (via satellite): Music Choice.
Fee: $5.00 monthly.

Digital Pay Service 1
Pay Units: 72.
Programming (via satellite): Cinemax (multiplexed).
Fee: $10.95 monthly.

Digital Pay Service 2
Pay Units: 109.
Programming (via satellite): HBO (multiplexed).
Fee: $13.95 monthly.

Digital Pay Service 3
Pay Units: 84.
Programming (via satellite): Flix; Showtime (multiplexed); Sundance Channel; The Movie Channel (multiplexed).
Fee: $12.95 monthly.

Digital Pay Service 4
Pay Units: 49.
Programming (via satellite): Encore (multiplexed); Starz (multiplexed).
Fee: $12.95 monthly.

Video-On-Demand: No

Pay-Per-View
Adult Swim (delivered digitally); Movies (delivered digitally); special events (delivered digitally).

Internet Service
Operational: Yes.
Subscribers: 360.
Broadband Service: GCI Hypernet.
Fee: $49.99 monthly.

Telephone Service
None

Miles of Plant: 25.0 (coaxial); None (fiber optic). Homes passed: 1,092.
Manager: Rynda Hayes. Chief Technician: Don McConachie.
Ownership: General Communication Inc. (MSO).

ARIZONA

Total Systems: 64
Total Communities Served: 212
Franchises Not Yet Operating: 0
Applications Pending: 0
Communities with Applications: 0
Number of Basic Subscribers: 1,517,365
Number of Expanded Basic Subscribers: 149,964
Number of Pay Units: 255,759

Top 100 Markets Represented: Phoenix-Mesa (43).

For a list of cable communities in this section, see the Cable Community Index located in the back of Cable Volume 2. For explanation of terms used in cable system listings, see p. D-11.

AJO—Mediacom, 879 N Plaza Dr, Ste D101, Apache Junction, AZ 85220-4112. Phone: 480-474-2087. Fax: 480-474-2084. Web Site: http://www.mediacomcable.com. ICA: AZ0037.

TV Market Ranking: Outside TV Markets (AJO). Franchise award date: N.A. Franchise expiration date: N.A. Began: February 1, 1952.

Channel capacity: 61 (not 2-way capable). Channels available but not in use: 1.

Basic Service

Subscribers: N.A. included in Apache Junction

Programming (received off-air): KAET (PBS) Phoenix.

Programming (via microwave): KGUN-TV (ABC) Tucson; KOLD-TV (CBS) Tucson; KPAZ-TV (TBN) Phoenix; KPHO-TV (CBS) Phoenix; KPNX (NBC) Mesa; KTVK (IND) Phoenix; KUAT-TV (PBS) Tucson; KVOA (NBC) Tucson.

Programming (via satellite): ABC Family Channel; AMC; Arts & Entertainment; CNN; Country Music TV; Discovery Channel; Disney Channel; ESPN; Eternal Word TV Network; Headline News; KTLA (CW) Los Angeles; Lifetime; Nickelodeon; TBS Superstation; Telemundo; Trinity Broadcasting Network; Turner Network TV; USA Network; WGN America.

Current originations: Religious Access; Public Access.

Fee: $29.50 installation; $39.95 monthly; $2.00 converter.

Pay Service 1

Pay Units: N.A.

Programming (via satellite): Encore; HBO; Showtime; The Movie Channel.

Fee: $5.95 monthly (Encore), $12.95 monthly (HBO or Showtime & TMC).

Video-On-Demand: No

Internet Service

Operational: No.

Telephone Service

None

Homes passed: 2,000. Total homes in franchised area: 2,500. Miles of plant (coax) included in Apache Junction

General Manager: Steven Lamb.

County fee: 3% of gross.

Ownership: Mediacom LLC (MSO).

ALPINE—Formerly served by Eagle West Communications Inc. No longer in operation. ICA: AZ0083.

APACHE JUNCTION—Mediacom, 879 N Plaza Dr, Ste D101, Apache Junction, AZ 85220-4112. Phone: 480-474-2087. Fax: 480-474-2084. Web Site: http://www.mediacomcable.com. Also serves Gold Canyon, Peralta Trails, Pinal County (portions), Queen Creek, Queen Valley, Rock Shadows & Sand Banks. ICA: AZ0008.

TV Market Ranking: 43 (APACHE JUNCTION, Gold Canyon, Peralta Trails, Pinal County (portions) (portions), Queen Creek, Queen Valley, Rock Shadows, Sand Banks); Below 100 (Pinal County (portions) (portions)); Outside TV Markets (Pinal County (portions) (portions)). Franchise award date: N.A. Franchise expiration date: N.A. Began: March 1, 1985.

Channel capacity: N.A. Channels available but not in use: N.A.

Basic Service

Subscribers: 13,610 include Ajo & Nogales.

Programming (received off-air): KAET (PBS) Phoenix; KASW (CW) Phoenix; KAZT-TV (IND) Phoenix; KDTP (ETV) Holbrook; KNXV-TV (ABC) Phoenix; KPAZ-TV (TBN) Phoenix; KPHO-TV (CBS) Phoenix; KPNX (NBC) Mesa; KPPX-TV (ION) Tolleson; KSAZ-TV (FOX) Phoenix; KTVK (IND) Phoenix; KTVW-DT (UNV) Phoenix; KUTP (MNT) Phoenix.

Programming (via satellite): ABC Family Channel; AMC; Animal Planet; Arts & Entertainment; Cartoon Network; CNBC; CNN; Comedy Central; Country Music TV; C-SPAN; Discovery Channel; Disney Channel; E! Entertainment Television; ESPN; ESPN 2; Food Network; Fox News Channel; Fox Sports Net Arizona; FX; Hallmark Channel; Headline News; HGTV; History Channel; Home Shopping Network; Lifetime; MSNBC; MTV; Nickelodeon; QVC; SoapNet; Spike TV; Syfy; TBS Superstation; The Learning Channel; Travel Channel; Turner Network TV; TV Guide Network; TV Land; USA Network; VH1; Weather Channel; WGN America.

Current originations: Government Access; Educational Access.

Fee: $44.25 installation; $29.50 monthly; $20.00 additional installation.

Digital Basic Service

Subscribers: N.A.

Programming (via satellite): AmericanLife TV Network; BBC America; Bloomberg Television; Discovery Digital Networks; DMX Music; ESPN Classic Sports; Fox Movie Channel; G4; Golf Channel; GSN; Independent Film Channel; INSP; Outdoor Channel; Turner Classic Movies; Versus; WE tv; Weatherscan.

Fee: $8.00 monthly.

Pay Service 1

Pay Units: 486.

Programming (via satellite): Cinemax.

Fee: $25.00 installation; $7.95 monthly.

Pay Service 2

Pay Units: 1,144.

Programming (via satellite): HBO.

Fee: $11.95 monthly.

Pay Service 3

Pay Units: 1,077.

Programming (via satellite): Encore; Starz.

Fee: $6.95 monthly.

Digital Pay Service 1

Pay Units: N.A.

Programming (via satellite): Cinemax (multiplexed); Encore (multiplexed); HBO (multiplexed); Showtime (multiplexed); Starz (multiplexed); The Movie Channel (multiplexed).

Fee: $8.00 monthly (Starz/Encore), $9.95 (Cinemax or Showtime), $3.95 monthly (HBO).

Video-On-Demand: Yes

Pay-Per-View

Hot Choice (delivered digitally); iN DEMAND (delivered digitally); Playboy TV (delivered digitally); Fresh (delivered digitally); Sports PPV (delivered digitally).

Internet Service

Operational: Yes.

Broadband Service: Mediacom High Speed Internet.

Fee: $59.95 installation; $42.95 monthly; $3.00 modem lease; $239.95 modem purchase.

Telephone Service

Analog: Not Operational

Digital: Operational

Miles of Plant: 850.0 (coaxial); None (fiber optic). Homes passed: 30,000. Miles of plant (coax) includes Ajo & Nogales

General Manager: Steven Lamb.

City fee: 3% of gross.

Ownership: Mediacom LLC (MSO).

AVONDALE—Cox Communications. Now served by PHOENIX, AZ [AZ0001]. ICA: AZ0020.

BAGDAD—Eagle West Communications Inc, 1030 S Mesa Dr, Mesa, AZ 85210. Phones: 480-380-5855; 480-813-8371. Fax: 480-813-4596. ICA: AZ0048.

TV Market Ranking: Outside TV Markets (BAGDAD). Franchise award date: N.A. Franchise expiration date: N.A. Began: January 1, 1983.

Channel capacity: N.A. Channels available but not in use: N.A.

Basic Service

Subscribers: N.A. Included in East Mesa

Programming (received off-air): KAET (PBS) Phoenix; KASW (CW) Phoenix; KNXV-TV (ABC) Phoenix; KPHO-TV (CBS) Phoenix; KPNX (NBC) Mesa; KSAZ-TV (FOX) Phoenix; KTVK (IND) Phoenix; KTVW-DT (UNV) Phoenix; KUTP (MNT) Phoenix; 13 FMs.

Programming (via satellite): AMC; Animal Planet; Arts & Entertainment; Bravo; CNN; Country Music TV; Discovery Channel; E! Entertainment Television; ESPN; ESPN 2; Eternal Word TV Network; Fox News Channel; Fox Sports Net; FX; G4; Hallmark Channel; Headline News; HGTV; History Channel; Home Shopping Network; ION Television; Lifetime; Nickelodeon; Outdoor Channel; QVC; Spike TV; Syfy; TBS Superstation; The Learning Channel; Turner Network TV; USA Network; Weather Channel; WGN America.

Fee: $39.95 installation; $31.95 monthly.

Pay Service 1

Pay Units: 26.

Programming (via satellite): HBO.

Fee: $9.95 monthly.

Pay Service 2

Pay Units: 9.

Programming (via satellite): Cinemax.

Fee: $9.95 monthly.

Pay Service 3

Pay Units: N.A.

Programming (via satellite): The Movie Channel.

Video-On-Demand: No

Internet Service

Operational: No.

Telephone Service

None

Homes passed & miles of plant included in East Mesa

General Manager: Ernest McKay.

Ownership: Eagle West Communications (MSO).

BENSON—Cox Communications, 1440 E 15th St, Tucson, AZ 85719. Phones: 623-328-3121 (Phoenix office); 520-629-8470. Fax: 520-624-5918. Web Site: http://www.cox.com/arizona. ICA: AZ0138.

TV Market Ranking: Outside TV Markets (BENSON).

Channel capacity: N.A. Channels available but not in use: N.A.

Basic Service

Subscribers: N.A.

Programming (received off-air): KGUN-TV (ABC) Tucson; KMSB (FOX) Tucson; KOLD-TV (CBS) Tucson; KTTU (MNT) Tucson; KUAT-TV (PBS) Tucson; KVOA (NBC) Tucson; KWBA-TV (CW) Sierra Vista.

Programming (via satellite): Discovery Channel; Headline News; QVC; WGN America.

Fee: $19.95 monthly.

Expanded Basic Service 1

Subscribers: N.A.

Programming (via satellite): ABC Family Channel; AMC; Animal Planet; Arts & Entertainment; BET Networks; Cartoon Network; CNBC; CNN; Comedy Central; Country Music TV; C-SPAN; C-SPAN 2; Discovery Health Channel; Disney Channel; E! Entertainment Television; ESPN; ESPN 2; Food Network; Fox News Channel; Fox Sports Net Arizona; FX; Golf Channel; HGTV; History Channel; Home Shopping Network; INSP; Lifetime; MSNBC; MTV; Nickelodeon; Spike TV; Syfy; TBS Superstation; Telemundo; The Learning Channel; Travel Channel; truTV; Turner Network TV; TV Guide Network; TV Land; Univision; USA Network; VH1; Weather Channel.

Fee: $23.00 monthly.

Digital Basic Service
Subscribers: N.A.
Programming (via satellite): BBC America; Bio; Bloomberg Television; Bravo; Canales N; Discovery Digital Networks; Encore (multiplexed); ESPN Classic Sports; ESPNews; Fox Soccer; Fuse; G4; GSN; History Channel International; Independent Film Channel; Lifetime Movie Network; Music Choice; Outdoor Channel; Speed Channel; Sundance Channel; Toon Disney; Trinity Broadcasting Network; Turner Classic Movies; Versus; WE tv.
Fee: $23.96 monthly.

Digital Pay Service 1
Pay Units: N.A.
Programming (via satellite): Cinemax (multiplexed); Encore; HBO (multiplexed); Showtime (multiplexed); Starz (multiplexed); The Movie Channel (multiplexed).
Fee: $12.95 monthly (each).

Video-On-Demand: Planned

Internet Service
Operational: Yes.
Broadband Service: Cox High Speed Internet.

Vice President & Regional Manager: Steve Rizley. Vice President & Systems Manager: Anne Doris. Vice President, Marketing: Anthony Maldonado. Marketing Manager: Nancy Duckett. Media Relations Director: Andrea Katsones. Media Relations Manager: Monica Contreras.
Ownership: Cox Communications Inc. (MSO).

BISBEE—Cable One, 99 Bisbee Rd, Bisbee, AZ 85603-1118. Phone: 520-432-5397. Fax: 520-432-7981. Web Site: http://www.cableone.net. Also serves Cochise County & Naco. ICA: AZ0029.
TV Market Ranking: Below 100 (BISBEE, Cochise County, Naco). Franchise award date: N.A. Franchise expiration date: N.A. Began: April 1, 1952.
Channel capacity: 124 (operating 2-way). Channels available but not in use: None.

Basic Service
Subscribers: 2,600.
Programming (received off-air): KGUN-TV (ABC) Tucson; KMSB (FOX) Tucson; KOLD-TV (CBS) Tucson; KTTU (MNT) Tucson; KUAT-TV (PBS) Tucson; KVOA (NBC) Tucson.
Programming (via satellite): ABC Family Channel; Animal Planet; Arts & Entertainment; Cartoon Network; CNBC; CNN; Comedy Central; Country Music TV; C-SPAN; Discovery Channel; Disney Channel; ESPN; ESPN 2; Fox News Channel; Fox Sports Net Arizona; FX; Headline News; History Channel; Lifetime; MTV; Nickelodeon; Ovation; QVC; Spike TV; Syfy; TBS Superstation; Telemundo; The Learning Channel; Turner Classic Movies; Turner Network TV; TV Guide Network; TV Land; Univision; USA Network; VH1; Weather Channel; WGN America.
Current originations: Government Access; Leased Access.
Fee: $46.00 monthly.

Digital Basic Service
Subscribers: 300.
Programming (via satellite): Bio; Boomerang; Canales N; Discovery Digital Networks; DMX Music; ESPN Classic Sports; ESPNews; Fox Movie Channel; Fox Soccer; G4; Golf Channel; GSN; History Channel International; National Geographic Channel; Outdoor Channel; Speed Channel; Toon Disney; Trinity Broadcasting Network; Versus.
Fee: $15.00 monthly.

Digital Pay Service 1
Pay Units: N.A.
Programming (via satellite): Cinemax (multiplexed); Encore (multiplexed); Flix; HBO (multiplexed); Showtime (multiplexed); Starz (multiplexed); The Movie Channel.
Fee: $15.00 monthly (each).

Video-On-Demand: No

Pay-Per-View
Addressable homes: 300.
iN DEMAND (delivered digitally), Fee: $3.95, Addressable: Yes.

Internet Service
Operational: Yes.
Subscribers: 900.
Broadband Service: CableONE.net.
Fee: $75.00 installation; $43.00 monthly.

Telephone Service
None

Miles of Plant: 67.0 (coaxial); None (fiber optic). Homes passed: 3,949. Total homes in franchised area: 3,949.
Manager: Steve Brideau. Technical Operations Manager: Chuck Dunlap.
City fee: 2% of gross.
Ownership: Cable One Inc. (MSO).

BLACK CANYON CITY—Eagle West Communications Inc, 1030 S Mesa Dr, Mesa, AZ 85210. Phones: 800-558-5564; 480-380-5855; 480-813-8371. Fax: 480-813-4596. ICA: AZ0127.
TV Market Ranking: Outside TV Markets (BLACK CANYON CITY). Franchise award date: January 1, 1976. Franchise expiration date: N.A. Began: January 1, 1977.
Channel capacity: N.A. Channels available but not in use: N.A.

Basic Service
Subscribers: N.A. Included in East Mesa
Programming (received off-air): KAET (PBS) Phoenix; KASW (CW) Phoenix; KAZT-TV (IND) Phoenix; KNXV-TV (ABC) Phoenix; KPAZ-TV (TBN) Phoenix; KPHO-TV (CBS) Phoenix; KPNX (NBC) Mesa; KSAZ-TV (FOX) Phoenix; KTVK (IND) Phoenix; KUTP (MNT) Phoenix.
Programming (via satellite): ABC Family Channel; AMC; Arts & Entertainment; Cartoon Network; CNN; Country Music TV; Discovery Channel; E! Entertainment Television; ESPN; ESPN 2; Fox News Channel; Fox Sports Net Arizona; Hallmark Channel; Headline News; HGTV; History Channel; Home Shopping Network; ION Television; Lifetime; Nickelodeon; Outdoor Channel; QVC; Spike TV; Syfy; TBS Superstation; The Learning Channel; Turner Network TV; USA Network; Weather Channel; WGN America.
Fee: $19.95 installation; $36.95 monthly.

Video-On-Demand: No

Internet Service
Operational: No.

Telephone Service
None

Homes passed & miles of plant included in East Mesa
General Manager: Ernest McKay.
Ownership: Eagle West Communications (MSO).

BULLHEAD CITY—NPG Cable, Inc., Suite 101, 2585 Miracle Mile, Bullhead City, AZ 86442. Phones: 928-758-6641; 928-758-4844 (customer service). Fax: 928-201-2475. Web Site: http://www.npgcable.net. Also serves Fort Mohave, Mohave County (portions) & Mohave Valley. ICA: AZ0009.
TV Market Ranking: Below 100 (BULLHEAD CITY, Fort Mohave, Mohave County (portions) (portions), Mohave Valley); Outside TV Markets (Mohave County (portions) (portions)). Franchise award date: November 1, 1974. Franchise expiration date: N.A. Began: November 1, 1974.
Channel capacity: N.A. Channels available but not in use: N.A.

Basic Service
Subscribers: 11,930.
Programming (received off-air): KAET (PBS) Phoenix; KASW (CW) Phoenix; KAZT-TV (IND) Phoenix; KMOH-TV (IND) Kingman; KNXV-TV (ABC) Phoenix; KPHO-TV (CBS) Phoenix; KPNX (NBC) Mesa; KSAZ-TV (FOX) Phoenix; KTAZ (TMO) Phoenix; KTVK (IND) Phoenix; KTVW-DT (UNV) Phoenix; KUTP (MNT) Phoenix.
Programming (via satellite): ABC Family Channel; AMC; Animal Planet; Arts & Entertainment; Bravo; Cartoon Network; CNBC; CNN; Comedy Central; Country Music TV; C-SPAN; C-SPAN 2; Discovery Channel; Discovery Health Channel; Disney Channel; E! Entertainment Television; ESPN; ESPN 2; ESPN Classic Sports; Food Network; Fox News Channel; Fox Sports Net Arizona; FX; Great American Country; Headline News; HGTV; History Channel; Home Shopping Network; ION Television; KTLA Los Angeles; Lifetime; Lifetime Movie Network; MSNBC; MTV; National Geographic Channel; Nickelodeon; Product Information Network; QVC; Speed Channel; Spike TV; Syfy; TBS Superstation; The Learning Channel; Travel Channel; Trinity Broadcasting Network; truTV; Turner Classic Movies; Turner Network TV; TV Guide Network; TV Land; USA Network; VH1; Weather Channel; WGN America.
Current originations: Leased Access; Government Access; Educational Access.
Fee: $39.95 installation; $43.80 monthly.

Digital Basic Service
Subscribers: 3,276.
Programming (via satellite): BBC America; Bio; Chiller; Cooking Channel; Discovery Channel HD; Discovery Kids Channel; Discovery Military Channel; Discovery Planet Green; DMX Music; Do-It-Yourself; ESPN 2 HD; ESPN HD; ESPN U; ESPNews; Food Network HD; Fox Soccer; Fox Sports en Espanol; FSN Digital Atlantic; FSN Digital Central; FSN Digital Pacific; FSN HD; Fuel TV; FX HD; Golf Channel; GSN; Hallmark Channel; HDNet; HDNet Movies; HGTV HD; History Channel International; ID Investigation Discovery; Independent Film Channel; MTV2; Nick Jr.; NickToons TV; Oxygen; Science Channel; SoapNet; Speed Channel; Speed HD; Style Network; Syfy HD; TeenNick; Toon Disney; Turner Network TV HD; Universal HD; USA Network HD; Versus; VH1 Classic; VH1 Country; WE tv.
Fee: $11.95 monthly.

Digital Pay Service 1
Pay Units: N.A.
Programming (via satellite): Cinemax (multiplexed); Encore (multiplexed); HBO (multiplexed); Showtime (multiplexed); Starz (multiplexed); The Movie Channel (multiplexed).
Fee: $6.95 monthly (Cinemax), $9.95 monthly (Starz/Encore), $11.95 monthly (Showtime/TMC), $12.00 monthly (HBO).

Video-On-Demand: Planned

Pay-Per-View
iN DEMAND (delivered digitally); Club Jenna (delivered digitally); Fresh (delivered digitally); Spice: Xcess (delivered digitally).

Internet Service
Operational: Yes. Began: May 1, 1999.
Subscribers: 5,225.
Broadband Service: Optimum Online.
Fee: $59.95 installation; $24.95 monthly; $5.00 modem lease.

Telephone Service
Analog: Not Operational
Digital: Operational
Subscribers: 2,851.
Fee: $59.95 installation; $39.95 monthly

Miles of Plant: 426.0 (coaxial); 75.0 (fiber optic). Homes passed: 41,261. Total homes in franchised area: 41,261.
District Manager: Scott Leprich. Plant Manager: George (Chip) Acker. Marketing Director: Denise Lewis. Customer Service Manager: Lora Atchley.
City fee: 3% of gross.
Ownership: News Press & Gazette Co. (MSO).

BYLAS—San Carlos Apache Telecom, PO Box 1000, 10 Telecom Ln, Peridot, AZ 85542. Phone: 928-475-2433. Fax: 938-475-7076. Web Site: http://www.scatui.net. ICA: AZ0134.
TV Market Ranking: Franchise award date: N.A. Franchise expiration date: N.A. Began: September 1, 2004.
Channel capacity: 38 (not 2-way capable). Channels available but not in use: N.A.

Basic Service
Subscribers: 400.
Programming (received off-air): KFPH-TV (TEL) Flagstaff; KNXV-TV (ABC) Phoenix; KPHO-TV (CBS) Phoenix; KPNX (NBC) Mesa; KSAZ-TV (FOX) Phoenix; KTVK (IND) Phoenix; KTVW-DT (UNV) Phoenix.
Programming (via satellite): ABC Family Channel; AMC; Arts & Entertainment; CNN; Comedy Central; Discovery Channel; Disney Channel; ESPN; ESPN 2; Fox Sports Net Arizona; Great American Country; Hallmark Channel; Headline News; HGTV; MTV; Nickelodeon; Outdoor Channel; Spike TV; Syfy; TBS Superstation; The Learning Channel; Toon Disney; Trinity Broadcasting Network; Turner Classic Movies; USA Network; VH1; WGN America.
Fee: $15.00 installation; $24.00 monthly.

Pay Service 1
Pay Units: 200.
Programming (via satellite): HBO; Showtime; The Movie Channel.
Fee: $8.00 monthly (Showtime or TMC), $10.00 monthly (HBO).

Internet Service
Operational: No.

Telephone Service
None

Miles of Plant: 14.0 (coaxial); None (fiber optic). Homes passed: 400. Total homes in franchised area: 500.
Chief Technician: Richard Gomez. Sales & Marketing: Marion Case.
Ownership: San Carlos Apache Telecommunications Utility Inc. (MSO).

CAREFREE—Cox Communications. Now served by PHOENIX, AZ [AZ0001]. ICA: AZ0030.

CASA GRANDE—Cox Communications, 1550 W Deer Valley Rd, Phoenix, AZ 85027-2121. Phones: 623-594-1000 (Customer service); 623-328-3121. Fax: 623-328-3580. Web Site: http://www.cox.com/arizona. Also serves Pinal County. ICA: AZ0019.
TV Market Ranking: 43 (CASA GRANDE, Pinal County (portions)); Below 100 (Pinal County (portions)); Outside TV Markets (CASA GRANDE, Pinal County (portions)).

Franchise award date: N.A. Franchise expiration date: N.A. Began: April 1, 1975.
Channel capacity: 75 (operating 2-way). Channels available but not in use: None.

Basic Service

Subscribers: 3,385.

Programming (received off-air): KAET (PBS) Phoenix; KDTP (ETV) Holbrook; KNXV-TV (ABC) Phoenix; KPAZ-TV (TBN) Phoenix; KPHO-TV (CBS) Phoenix; KPNX (NBC) Mesa; KPPX-TV (ION) Tolleson; KSAZ-TV (FOX) Phoenix; KTAZ (TMO) Phoenix; KTVK (IND) Phoenix; KTVW-DT (UNV) Phoenix; KUTP (MNT) Phoenix; allband FM.

Programming (via satellite): Arizona News Channel; C-SPAN; Home Shopping Network; QVC; TBS Superstation; TV Guide Network; WGN America.

Current originations: Leased Access; Government Access; Public Access; Educational Access.

Fee: $21.95 monthly.

Expanded Basic Service 1

Subscribers: N.A.

Programming (received off-air): KPDF-CA Phoenix.

Programming (via satellite): ABC Family Channel; AMC; Animal Planet; Arts & Entertainment; BET Networks; Bravo; Cartoon Network; CNBC; CNN; Comedy Central; Country Music TV; Discovery Channel; Disney Channel; E! Entertainment Television; ESPN; ESPN 2; Food Network; Fox News Channel; Fox Sports Net Arizona; FX; GalaVision; Golf Channel; Headline News; HGTV; History Channel; Lifetime; MSNBC; MTV; Nickelodeon; Speed Channel; Spike TV; Syfy; The Learning Channel; Travel Channel; truTV; Turner Network TV; TV Land; USA Network; VH1; Weather Channel.

Fee: $26.00 monthly.

Digital Basic Service

Subscribers: N.A.

Programming (received off-air): KAET (PBS) Phoenix; KNXV-TV (ABC) Phoenix; KPNX (NBC) Mesa; KSAZ-TV (FOX) Phoenix; KTVK (IND) Phoenix; KUTP (MNT) Phoenix.

Programming (via satellite): Animal Planet HD; Arts & Entertainment HD; BYU Television; CNBC HD+; C-SPAN; C-SPAN 2; C-SPAN 3; Daystar TV Network; Discovery Channel HD; Discovery HD Theater; Discovery Health Channel; Discovery Home Channel; Discovery Kids Channel; Discovery Military Channel; ESPN 2 HD; ESPN HD; Eternal Word TV Network; Food Network HD; History Channel HD; ID Investigation Discovery; INSP; Jewelry Television; KASW (CW) Phoenix; KPHO-TV (CBS) Phoenix; Lifetime Television HD; Music Choice; National Geographic Channel; National Geographic Channel HD Network; Nick Jr.; Science Channel; Science Channel HD; ShopNBC; TBS in HD; Turner Classic Movies; Turner Network TV HD; Universal HD; USA Network HD; Versus HD.

Fee: $5.00 monthly.

Digital Expanded Basic Service

Subscribers: N.A.

Programming (via satellite): Azteca America; Bandamax; BBC America; Bio; Boomerang; Boomerang en Espanol; Canal Sur; Cine Latino; CMT Pure Country; CNN en Espanol; Cooking Channel; De Pelicula; De Pelicula Clasico; Discovery en Espanol; Discovery Familia; Do-It-Yourself; Encore (multiplexed); ESPN Classic Sports; ESPN Deportes; ESPN U; ESPNews; EWTN en Espanol; FitTV; Flix; Fox College Sports Atlantic; Fox College Sports Central; Fox College Sports Pacific; Fox Reality Channel; Fox Soccer; Fox Sports en Espanol; Fuel TV; Fuse; G4; GalaVision; Gol TV; Great American Country; GSN; Hallmark Channel; History Channel en Espanol; History Channel International; Independent Film Channel; Lifetime Movie Network; LOGO; MTV Hits; MTV Jams; MTV Tres; MTV2; mun2 television; NBA TV; NFL Network; NHL Network; NickToons TV; Oxygen; SoapNet; Sorpresa; Sundance Channel; TeenNick; Telemundo; Toon Disney; Toon Disney en Espanol; TV Chile; VeneMovies; Versus; VH1 Classic; VH1 Soul; Video Rola.

Fee: $6.00 monthly (Variety, Sports & Info, Movie or Latino.

Digital Pay Service 1

Pay Units: N.A.

Programming (via satellite): Cinemax (multiplexed); Cinemax HD; HBO (multiplexed); HBO HD; Showtime (multiplexed); Showtime HD; Starz (multiplexed); Starz HDTV; The Movie Channel (multiplexed).

Fee: $14.00 monthly (HBO, Cinemax, Showtime/TMC or Starz).

Video-On-Demand: No

Pay-Per-View

iN DEMAND (delivered digitally); iN DEMAND (delivered digitally); Hot Choice (delivered digitally); Hot Choice (delivered digitally); Ten Clips (delivered digitally); Ten Clips (delivered digitally); Club Jenna (delivered digitally); Club Jenna (delivered digitally); Playboy TV (delivered digitally); Playboy TV (delivered digitally); Ten Blox (delivered digitally); Ten Blox (delivered digitally); Fresh (delivered digitally); Fresh (delivered digitally); Spice: Xcess (delivered digitally); Spice: Xcess (delivered digitally); Sports PPV (delivered digitally); Sports PPV (delivered digitally).

Internet Service

Operational: Yes.

Broadband Service: Cox High Speed Internet.

Fee: $49.95 monthly.

Telephone Service

Digital: Operational

Fee: $5.00 installation; $20.00 monthly

Miles of Plant: 42.0 (coaxial); None (fiber optic). Additional miles planned: 35.0 (coaxial). Homes passed: 6,922.

Vice President, Network Operations: Herb Dougall. Vice President, Marketing: Anthony Maldonado. General Manager: Steve Rizley. Media Relations Director: Andrea Katsenes.

City fee: 3% of gross.

Ownership: Cox Communications Inc. (MSO).

CASA GRANDE (northern portion)—Eagle West Communications Inc, 1030 S Mesa Dr, Mesa, AZ 85210. Phones: 800-558-5564; 480-380-5855; 480-813-8371. Fax: 480-813-4596. ICA: AZ0126.

TV Market Ranking: 43 (CASA GRANDE (NORTHERN PORTION)). Franchise award date: January 1, 1988. Franchise expiration date: N.A. Began: N.A.

Channel capacity: 61 (not 2-way capable). Channels available but not in use: 9.

Basic Service

Subscribers: N.A. Included in East Mesa

Programming (received off-air): KAET (PBS) Phoenix; KASW (CW) Phoenix; KGUN-TV (ABC) Tucson; KNXV-TV (ABC) Phoenix; KOLD-TV (CBS) Tucson; KPAZ-TV (TBN) Phoenix; KPHO-TV (CBS) Phoenix; KPNX (NBC) Mesa; KSAZ-TV (FOX) Phoenix; KTVK (IND) Phoenix; KTVW-DT (UNV) Phoenix; KUTP (MNT) Phoenix; KVOA (NBC) Tucson.

Programming (via satellite): AMC; Arts & Entertainment; Cartoon Network; CNBC; CNN; Country Music TV; C-SPAN; Discovery Channel; E! Entertainment Television; ESPN; ESPN 2; Fox News Channel; Fox Sports Net; FX; Hallmark Channel; Headline News; HGTV; History Channel; ION Television; Lifetime; MTV; Nickelodeon; Outdoor Channel; QVC; Speed Channel; Spike TV; Syfy; TBS Superstation; The Learning Channel; Turner Network TV; TV Land; USA Network; Weather Channel; WGN America.

Fee: $19.95 installation; $39.00 monthly.

Video-On-Demand: No

Internet Service

Operational: No.

Telephone Service

None

Homes passed & miles of plant included in East Mesa

General Manager: Ernest McKay.

Ownership: Eagle West Communications (MSO).

CAVE CREEK—Eagle West Communications Inc, 1030 S Mesa Dr, Mesa, AZ 85210. Phone: 480-813-8371. Fax: 480-813-4596. ICA: AZ0060.

TV Market Ranking: 43 (CAVE CREEK). Franchise award date: January 25, 1990. Franchise expiration date: N.A. Began: December 1, 1990.

Channel capacity: N.A. Channels available but not in use: N.A.

Basic Service

Subscribers: N.A. Included in East Mesa

Programming (received off-air): KAET (PBS) Phoenix; KASW (CW) Phoenix; KDTP-LP Phoenix; KNXV-TV (ABC) Phoenix; KPAZ-TV (TBN) Phoenix; KPHO-TV (CBS) Phoenix; KPNX (NBC) Mesa; KSAZ-TV (FOX) Phoenix; KTVK (IND) Phoenix; KUTP (MNT) Phoenix.

Programming (via satellite): AMC; Arts & Entertainment; Cartoon Network; CNBC; CNN; Country Music TV; C-SPAN; Discovery Channel; ESPN; ESPN 2; ESPNews; Fox Sports Net Arizona; Hallmark Channel; Headline News; HGTV; History Channel; Home Shopping Network; HorseTV Channel; ION Television; Lifetime; MTV; Nickelodeon; QVC; Spike TV; TBS Superstation; Turner Network TV; USA Network; VH1; WGN America.

Fee: $31.95 monthly.

Pay Service 1

Pay Units: N.A.

Programming (via satellite): Encore; Showtime; Starz.

Video-On-Demand: No

Internet Service

Operational: No.

Telephone Service

None

Homes passed & miles of plant included in East Mesa

General Manager: Ernest McKay.

Ownership: Eagle West Communications (MSO).

CHANDLER (portions)—Qwest Choice TV. IPTV service has been discontinued.. ICA: AZ5012.

CHINLE—Formerly served by Frontier Communications. No longer in operation. ICA: AZ0038.

CLIFTON—Cable One, 1996 W Thatcher Blvd, Safford, AZ 85546-3318. Phones: 928-428-1850; 928-865-4031. Fax: 928-865-4691. E-mail: sbrideau@cableone.net. Web Site: http://www.cableone.net. Also serves Greenlee County & Morenci. ICA: AZ0034.

TV Market Ranking: Outside TV Markets (CLIFTON, Greenlee County, Morenci). Franchise award date: December 8, 1965. Franchise expiration date: N.A. Began: April 1, 1965.

Channel capacity: 48 (not 2-way capable). Channels available but not in use: None.

Basic Service

Subscribers: 460.

Programming (received off-air): KAET (PBS) Phoenix; KPHO-TV (CBS) Phoenix; KPNX (NBC) Mesa; KSAZ-TV (FOX) Phoenix; KTVK (IND) Phoenix.

Programming (via satellite): ABC Family Channel; Arts & Entertainment; Cartoon Network; CNBC; CNN; C-SPAN; Discovery Channel; Disney Channel; ESPN; ESPN 2; Fox Sports Net Arizona; Headline News; HGTV; History Channel; KUTP (MNT) Phoenix; Lifetime; MTV; Nickelodeon; QVC; Syfy; TBS Superstation; The Learning Channel; Univision; USA Network; VH1; Weather Channel; WGN America.

Fee: $48.14 installation; $46.00 monthly.

Pay Service 1

Pay Units: 72.

Programming (via satellite): HBO.

Fee: $7.00 monthly.

Pay Service 2

Pay Units: 57.

Programming (via satellite): Cinemax.

Fee: $7.00 monthly.

Pay Service 3

Pay Units: 23.

Programming (via satellite): Showtime; The Movie Channel.

Fee: $7.00 monthly.

Video-On-Demand: No

Pay-Per-View

Addressable homes: 1,176.

iN DEMAND, Addressable: Yes.

Internet Service

Operational: No.

Telephone Service

None

Miles of Plant: 36.0 (coaxial); None (fiber optic). Homes passed: 2,165. Total homes in franchised area: 2,165.

Manager: Steve Brideau. Technical Operations Manager: Chuck Dunlap.

City fee: 3% of gross.

Ownership: Cable One Inc. (MSO).

CONCHO VALLEY—Formerly served by Eagle West Communications Inc. No longer in operation. ICA: AZ0111.

COOLIGE—Cable America Corp. Now served by PHOENIX, AZ [AZ0001]. ICA: AZ0032.

CORDES LAKES—Cordes Lakes Cablevision, 20269 Conestoga Dr, Cordes Lakes, AZ 86333. Phone: 928-379-0348. ICA: AZ0065.
TV Market Ranking: Outside TV Markets (CORDES LAKES). Franchise award date: February 22, 1988. Franchise expiration date: N.A. Began: February 1, 1990.
Channel capacity: 35 (not 2-way capable). Channels available but not in use: 4.
Basic Service
Subscribers: 107.
Programming (received off-air): KAET (PBS) Phoenix; KNXV-TV (ABC) Phoenix; KPHO-TV (CBS) Phoenix; KPNX (NBC) Mesa; KSAZ-TV (FOX) Phoenix; KTVK (IND) Phoenix; KUTP (MNT) Phoenix.
Programming (via satellite): ABC Family Channel; AMC; CNN; Country Music TV; C-SPAN; Discovery Channel; ESPN; Headline News; History Channel; MSNBC; MTV; Nickelodeon; QVC; Spike TV; Syfy; TBS Superstation; Turner Network TV; TV Guide Network; USA Network; VH1; WGN America.
Fee: $31.95 monthly.
Pay Service 1
Pay Units: 5.
Programming (via satellite): Encore; Showtime; The Movie Channel.
Fee: $14.95 monthly (each).
Internet Service
Operational: No.
Telephone Service
None
Miles of Plant: 16.0 (coaxial); None (fiber optic). Homes passed: 551. Total homes in franchised area: 800.
Ownership: Cordes Lakes Cablevision (MSO).

COTTONWOOD—Cable One, 235 S 6th St, Cottonwood, AZ 86326-4241. Phone: 928-634-9677. Fax: 928-634-5394. Web Site: http://www.cableone.net. Also serves Clarkdale, Cornville, Page Springs, Yavapai County (northeastern portion) & Yavapai-Apache-Clarksdale Reservation. ICA: AZ0129.
TV Market Ranking: Below 100 (Page Springs, Yavapai County (northeastern portion) (portions)); Outside TV Markets (Clarkdale, Cornville, COTTONWOOD, Yavapai County (northeastern portion) (portions), Yavapai-Apache-Clarksdale Reservation). Franchise award date: N.A. Franchise expiration date: N.A. Began: N.A.
Channel capacity: 63 (operating 2-way). Channels available but not in use: None.
Basic Service
Subscribers: 3,673.
Programming (received off-air): KAET (PBS) Phoenix; KASW (CW) Phoenix; KCFG (IND) Flagstaff; KFPH-TV (TEL) Flagstaff; KNAZ-TV (NBC) Flagstaff; KNXV-TV (ABC) Phoenix; KPHO-TV (CBS) Phoenix; KPNX (NBC) Mesa; KSAZ-TV (FOX) Phoenix; KTAZ (TMO) Phoenix; KTVK (IND) Phoenix; KUTP (MNT) Phoenix.
Programming (via satellite): C-SPAN; C-SPAN 2; Home Shopping Network; QVC; WGN America.
Fee: $46.00 monthly.
Expanded Basic Service 1
Subscribers: N.A.
Programming (via satellite): ABC Family Channel; AMC; Animal Planet; Arts & Entertainment; Cartoon Network; CNBC; CNN; Comedy Central; Country Music TV; Discovery Channel; Disney Channel; ESPN; ESPN 2; Food Network; Fox News Channel; Fox Sports Net Arizona; FX; Headline News; HGTV; History Channel; Lifetime; MSNBC; MTV; Nickelodeon; Spike TV; Syfy; TBS Superstation; The Learning Channel; Travel Channel; Trinity Broadcasting Network; Turner Classic Movies; Turner Network TV; TV Guide Network; TV Land; USA Network; VH1; Weather Channel.
Digital Basic Service
Subscribers: 1,111.
Programming (via satellite): 3 Angels Broadcasting Network; Arts & Entertainment HD; Bio; Boomerang; Boomerang en Espanol; BYU Television; Cine Mexicano; CNN en Espanol; Discovery Channel HD; Discovery HD Theater; Discovery Health Channel; Discovery Kids Channel; Discovery Military Channel; ESPN 2 HD; ESPN Classic Sports; ESPN Deportes; ESPN HD; ESPNews; FamilyNet; Food Network HD; Fox College Sports Atlantic; Fox College Sports Central; Fox College Sports Pacific; Fox Movie Channel; Fox Soccer; Fox Sports en Espanol; Fuel TV; Golf Channel; Great American Country; GSN; Hallmark Channel; HGTV HD; History Channel HD; History Channel International; INSP; La Familia Network; Latele Novela Network; mun2 television; Music Choice; National Geographic Channel; National Geographic Channel HD Network; Outdoor Channel; Science Channel; SoapNet; Speed Channel; TBS in HD; Telemundo; TLC HD; Toon Disney; Toon Disney en Espanol; Trinity Broadcasting Network; Turner Network TV HD; TVG Network; Universal HD; WE tv.
Digital Pay Service 1
Pay Units: 620.
Programming (via satellite): HBO (multiplexed); HBO HD; HBO Latino.
Fee: $15.15 monthly.
Digital Pay Service 2
Pay Units: 595.
Programming (via satellite): Cinemax (multiplexed).
Digital Pay Service 3
Pay Units: 231.
Programming (via satellite): Flix; Showtime (multiplexed); Showtime HD; Sundance Channel; The Movie Channel (multiplexed); The Movie Channel HD.
Fee: $15.15 monthly.
Digital Pay Service 4
Pay Units: N.A.
Programming (via satellite): Encore (multiplexed); Starz (multiplexed).
Video-On-Demand: No
Pay-Per-View
Addressable homes: 1,177.
iN DEMAND (delivered digitally), Addressable: Yes; Penthouse TV (delivered digitally); Ten Clips (delivered digitally); Ten Blox (delivered digitally); Ten Blue (delivered digitally).
Internet Service
Operational: Yes.
Broadband Service: CableONE.net.
Fee: $75.00 installation; $33.00 monthly.
Telephone Service
Digital: Operational
Fee: $75.00 installation; $39.95 monthly
Homes passed: 7,948.
General Manager: Dennis Edwards. Marketing Director: J J McCormick. Office Manager: Mindy Gray.
Ownership: Cable One Inc. (MSO).

DOUGLAS—Cox Communications, 1440 E 15th St, Tucson, AZ 85719. Phones: 623-328-3121 (Phoenix office); 520-629-8470. Fax: 520-624-5918. Web Site: http://www.cox.com/arizona. Also serves Fort Huachuca & Pirtleville. ICA: AZ0023.
TV Market Ranking: Below 100 (Fort Huachuca); Outside TV Markets (DOUGLAS, Pirtleville). Franchise award date: April 1, 1976. Franchise expiration date: N.A. Began: April 1, 1976.
Channel capacity: 40 (operating 2-way). Channels available but not in use: N.A.
Basic Service
Subscribers: 4,604.
Programming (received off-air): KGUN-TV (ABC) Tucson; KOLD-TV (CBS) Tucson; KTTU (MNT) Tucson; KUAT-TV (PBS) Tucson; KVOA (NBC) Tucson; 12 FMs.
Programming (via microwave): KMSB (FOX) Tucson.
Programming (via satellite): ABC Family Channel; TBS Superstation; WGN America.
Fee: $50.21 installation; $16.08 monthly.
Expanded Basic Service 1
Subscribers: N.A.
Programming (via satellite): AMC; Arts & Entertainment; Cartoon Network; CNN; Comcast Sports Net Southwest; Disney Channel; ESPN; Fox News Channel; GalaVision; Lifetime; MTV; Nickelodeon; Spike TV; The Learning Channel; Turner Network TV; USA Network; VH1.
Fee: $17.76 monthly.
Digital Basic Service
Subscribers: 552.
Programming (via satellite): BBC America; Bravo; Discovery Digital Networks; ESPN Classic Sports; Fox Sports World; Golf Channel; GSN; HGTV; History Channel; Independent Film Channel; Syfy; Turner Classic Movies; Versus; WE tv.
Fee: $10.00 monthly.
Pay Service 1
Pay Units: 506.
Programming (via satellite): Cinemax; Encore; HBO; Showtime; Starz.
Fee: $10.95 monthly (Cinemax, HBO, Showtime, or Starz/Encore).
Digital Pay Service 1
Pay Units: N.A.
Programming (via satellite): Cinemax (multiplexed); Encore (multiplexed); HBO (multiplexed); Showtime (multiplexed); Starz (multiplexed).
Fee: $10.95 monthly (Cinemax, HBO, Showtime, or Starz/Encore).
Video-On-Demand: No
Pay-Per-View
Addressable homes: 552.
iN DEMAND (delivered digitally), Addressable: Yes; Fresh (delivered digitally).
Internet Service
Operational: Yes.
Subscribers: 322.
Broadband Service: Cox High Speed Internet.
Telephone Service
Digital: Operational
Fee: $5.00 installation; $11.75 monthly
Miles of Plant: 270.0 (coaxial); None (fiber optic). Homes passed: 9,151.
Vice President & Systems Manager: Anne Doris. Vice President & Regional Manager: Steve Rizley. Vice President, Marketing: Anthony Maldonado. Media Relations Director: Andrea Katsenes. Media Relations Manager: Monica Contreras. Marketing Manager: Nancy Duckett.
City fee: 2% of gross.
Ownership: Cox Communications Inc. (MSO).

DUDLEYVILLE—Eagle West Communications Inc, 1030 S Mesa Dr, Mesa, AZ 85210. Phone: 480-813-8371. Fax: 480-813-4596. Also serves Hayden, Indian Hills & Winkelman. ICA: AZ0075.
TV Market Ranking: Outside TV Markets (DUDLEYVILLE, Hayden, Indian Hills, Winkelman). Franchise award date: N.A. Franchise expiration date: N.A. Began: February 1, 1980.
Channel capacity: 40 (not 2-way capable). Channels available but not in use: N.A.
Basic Service
Subscribers: N.A. Included in East Mesa
Programming (received off-air): KCNC-TV (CBS) Denver; KGUN-TV (ABC) Tucson; KHRR (TMO) Tucson; KSAZ-TV (FOX) Phoenix; KTVK (IND) Phoenix; KUAT-TV (PBS) Tucson; KVOA (NBC) Tucson.
Programming (via satellite): AMC; Animal Planet; Arts & Entertainment; BET Networks; Cartoon Network; CNN; C-SPAN; Discovery Channel; ESPN; ESPN 2; Fox Sports Net Arizona; FX; GalaVision; Hallmark Channel; History Channel; Home Shopping Network; ION Television; Lifetime; Nickelodeon; Outdoor Channel; QVC; Spike TV; Syfy; TBS Superstation; Trinity Broadcasting Network; Turner Classic Movies; Turner Network TV; Univision; USA Network; VH1; WGN America.
Fee: $31.95 monthly.
Pay Service 1
Pay Units: 207.
Programming (via satellite): HBO.
Fee: $9.95 installation; $9.95 monthly.
Video-On-Demand: No
Internet Service
Operational: No.
Telephone Service
None
Homes passed & miles of plant included in East Mesa
General Manager: Ernest McKay.
Ownership: Eagle West Communications (MSO).

EAGAR—Eagle West Communications Inc, 1030 S Mesa Dr, Mesa, AZ 85210. Phones: 928-333-1444; 480-813-8371. Fax: 480-323-2234. Also serves Springerville. ICA: AZ0086.
TV Market Ranking: Outside TV Markets (EAGAR, Springerville). Franchise award date: N.A. Franchise expiration date: N.A. Began: March 1, 1979.
Channel capacity: N.A. Channels available but not in use: N.A.
Basic Service
Subscribers: N.A. Included in East Mesa
Programming (received off-air): KAET (PBS) Phoenix; KTLA (CW) Los Angeles.
Programming (via microwave): KNXV-TV (ABC) Phoenix; KPHO-TV (CBS) Phoenix; KPNX (NBC) Mesa; KSAZ-TV (FOX) Phoenix; KTVK (IND) Phoenix; KUTP (MNT) Phoenix.
Programming (via satellite): ABC Family Channel; AMC; Animal Planet; Arts & Entertainment; BYU Television; Cartoon Network; CNN; Country Music TV; Discovery Channel; ESPN; ESPN 2; Fox News Channel; Fox Sports Net Arizona; FX; Hallmark Channel; Headline News; HGTV; History Channel; Home Shopping Network; ION Television; Lifetime; Nickelodeon; Outdoor Channel; Spike TV; Syfy; The Learning Channel; Turner Classic Movies; Turner Network TV; TV Land; Univision; USA Network; VH1; Weather Channel; WGN America.
Fee: $39.95 installation; $31.95 monthly; $1.96 converter; $9.95 additional installation.
Pay Service 1
Pay Units: 58.
Programming (via satellite): HBO.
Fee: $9.95 installation; $9.95 monthly.
Pay Service 2
Pay Units: 28.
Programming (via satellite): Cinemax.

Fee: $9.95 installation; $9.95 monthly.
Video-On-Demand: No
Internet Service
Operational: No.
Telephone Service
None
Homes passed & miles of plant included in East Mesa
Chief Executive Officer: Pete Collins. General Manager: Ernest McKay.
Ownership: Eagle West Communications (MSO).

EAST MESA—Eagle West Communications Inc, 9333 E Main St, Ste 122, Mesa, AZ 85207-8872. Phone: 480-813-8371. Fax: 480-323-2234. ICA: AZ0022.
TV Market Ranking: 43 (EAST MESA). Franchise award date: January 1, 1983. Franchise expiration date: N.A. Began: December 13, 1983.
Channel capacity: 64 (not 2-way capable). Channels available but not in use: 3.
Basic Service
Subscribers: 4,000 Includes all Eagle West systems.
Programming (received off-air): KAET (PBS) Phoenix; KASW (CW) Phoenix; KNXV-TV (ABC) Phoenix; KPAZ-TV (TBN) Phoenix; KPHO-TV (CBS) Phoenix; KPNX (NBC) Mesa; KSAZ-TV (FOX) Phoenix; KTAZ (TMO) Phoenix; KTVK (IND) Phoenix; KTVW-DT (UNV) Phoenix; KUTP (MNT) Phoenix.
Programming (via satellite): AMC; AmericanLife TV Network; Animal Planet; Arts & Entertainment; BET Networks; Cartoon Network; CNBC; CNN; Comcast Sports Net Southwest; Country Music TV; C-SPAN; Current; Daystar TV Network; Discovery Channel; E! Entertainment Television; ESPN; ESPN 2; Eternal Word TV Network; Fox Movie Channel; Fox News Channel; FX; G4; Hallmark Channel; Headline News; HGTV; History Channel; Home Shopping Network; HorseTV Channel; ION Television; Lifetime; MTV; Nick Jr.; Nickelodeon; Outdoor Channel; QVC; Sleuth; Speed Channel; Spike TV; Syfy; TBS Superstation; The Learning Channel; Travel Channel; truTV; Turner Classic Movies; Turner Network TV; USA Network; VH1; Weather Channel; WGN America.
Current originations: Government Access.
Fee: $19.95 installation; $31.95 monthly; $19.95 additional installation.
Pay Service 1
Pay Units: 65.
Programming (via satellite): Showtime.
Fee: $19.95 installation; $9.00 monthly.
Pay Service 2
Pay Units: 475.
Programming (via satellite): HBO.
Fee: $15.00 installation; $9.00 monthly.
Pay Service 3
Pay Units: 200.
Programming (via satellite): The Movie Channel.
Fee: $19.95 installation; $9.00 monthly.
Video-On-Demand: No
Internet Service
Operational: No.
Telephone Service
None
Miles of Plant: 1,090.0 (coaxial); None (fiber optic). Homes passed: 45,000. Homes passed & miles of plant include all Eagle West systems
Chief Executive Officer: Pete Collins. General Manager: Ernest McKay. Marketing Manager: Don Livingston.
County fee: 5% of gross.
Ownership: Eagle West Communications (MSO).

ELOY—Eagle West Communications Inc, 1030 S Mesa Dr, Mesa, AZ 85210. Phone: 480-813-8371. Fax: 480-813-4596. Also serves Arizona City & Toltec City. ICA: AZ0043.
TV Market Ranking: Outside TV Markets (Arizona City, ELOY, Toltec City). Franchise award date: N.A. Franchise expiration date: N.A. Began: December 16, 1974.
Channel capacity: 36 (not 2-way capable). Channels available but not in use: 5.
Basic Service
Subscribers: N.A. Included in East Mesa
Programming (received off-air): KAET (PBS) Phoenix; KASW (CW) Phoenix; KAZT-TV (IND) Phoenix; KNXV-TV (ABC) Phoenix; KPHO-TV (CBS) Phoenix; KPNX (NBC) Mesa; KPPX-TV (ION) Tolleson; KSAZ-TV (FOX) Phoenix; KTVK (IND) Phoenix; KTVW-DT (UNV) Phoenix; KUAT-TV (PBS) Tucson; KUTP (MNT) Phoenix; allband FM.
Programming (via satellite): BET Networks; CNN; Country Music TV; Discovery Channel; Disney Channel; ESPN; Home Shopping Network; Lifetime; Nickelodeon; Outdoor Channel; Spike TV; TBS Superstation; Trinity Broadcasting Network; Turner Network TV; USA Network; WGN America.
Fee: $19.95 installation; $31.95 monthly.
Pay Service 1
Pay Units: 150.
Programming (via satellite): Cinemax; HBO.
Fee: $9.95 monthly (Cinemax), $12.00 monthly (HBO).
Video-On-Demand: No
Internet Service
Operational: No.
Telephone Service
None
Homes passed & miles of plant included in East Mesa
General Manager: Ernest McKay.
City fee: 3% of gross.
Ownership: Eagle West Communications (MSO).

FLAGSTAFF—Formerly served by Microwave Communication Services. No longer in operation. ICA: AZ0116.

FLAGSTAFF—NPG Cable, Inc., 1601 S Plaza Way, Flagstaff, AZ 86001-7102. Phones: 928-855-9855; 928-779-3661. Fax: 928-855-1979. Web Site: http://www.npgcable.net. Also serves Coconino County, Kachina & Mountainaire. ICA: AZ0012.
TV Market Ranking: Below 100 (Coconino County (portions), FLAGSTAFF, Kachina, Mountainaire); Outside TV Markets (Coconino County (portions)). Franchise award date: May 1, 1954. Franchise expiration date: N.A. Began: May 1, 1954.
Channel capacity: N.A. Channels available but not in use: N.A.
Basic Service
Subscribers: 13,499.
Programming (received off-air): KAET (PBS) Phoenix; KASW (CW) Phoenix; KAZT-TV (IND) Phoenix; KFPH-TV (TEL) Flagstaff; KMOH-TV (IND) Kingman; KNAZ-TV (NBC) Flagstaff; KTVW-DT (UNV) Phoenix; 10 FMs.
Programming (via microwave): KNXV-TV (ABC) Phoenix; KPHO-TV (CBS) Phoenix; KPNX (NBC) Mesa; KSAZ-TV (FOX) Phoenix; KTLA (CW) Los Angeles; KTVK (IND) Phoenix; KUTP (MNT) Phoenix.

Programming (via satellite): ABC Family Channel; AMC; Animal Planet; Arts & Entertainment; Cartoon Network; CNBC; CNN; Comedy Central; Country Music TV; C-SPAN; C-SPAN 2; Discovery Channel; Discovery Health Channel; Disney Channel; E! Entertainment Television; ESPN; ESPN 2; ESPN Classic Sports; Food Network; Fox News Channel; Fox Sports Net Arizona; FX; G4; Great American Country; Headline News; HGTV; History Channel; Home Shopping Network; ION Television; Lifetime; Lifetime Movie Network; MSNBC; MTV; National Geographic Channel; Nickelodeon; Product Information Network; QVC; Spike TV; Syfy; TBS Superstation; The Learning Channel; Travel Channel; Trinity Broadcasting Network; truTV; Turner Classic Movies; Turner Network TV; TV Guide Network; TV Land; USA Network; VH1; Weather Channel.
Current originations: Educational Access; Public Access.
Planned originations: Religious Access; Government Access.
Fee: $39.95 installation; $43.80 monthly; $2.50 converter; $9.95 additional installation.
Digital Basic Service
Subscribers: 4,318.
Programming (via satellite): BBC America; Bio; Bloomberg Television; CMT Pure Country; Cooking Channel; Discovery Digital Networks; Discovery HD Theater; DMX Music; Do-It-Yourself; ESPN 2 HD; ESPN HD; ESPN U; ESPNews; Food Network HD; Fox Movie Channel; Fox Soccer; Fox Sports en Espanol; FSN Digital Atlantic; FSN Digital Central; FSN Digital Pacific; Fuel TV; GAS; Golf Channel; GSN; HDNet; HDNet Movies; HGTV HD; History Channel International; Independent Film Channel; Lifetime Movie Network; Lime; MTV Networks Digital Suite; Nick Jr.; NickToons TV; SoapNet; Speed Channel; Style Network; Toon Disney; Versus; WE tv.
Fee: $11.95 monthly.
Digital Pay Service 1
Pay Units: N.A.
Programming (via satellite): Cinemax (multiplexed); Encore (multiplexed); HBO (multiplexed); Showtime (multiplexed); Starz (multiplexed); The Movie Channel (multiplexed).
Fee: $6.95 monthly (Cinemax), $9.95 monthly (Starz/Encore), $11.95 monthly (Showtime/TMC), $12.00 monthly (HBO).
Video-On-Demand: Planned
Pay-Per-View
iN DEMAND (delivered digitally); Fresh (delivered digitally).
Internet Service
Operational: Yes.
Subscribers: 9,667.
Broadband Service: Uneedspeed.
Fee: $59.95 installation; $24.95 monthly.
Telephone Service
Digital: Operational
Fee: $59.95 installation; $39.95 monthly
Miles of Plant: 518.0 (coaxial); None (fiber optic). Homes passed: 29,698. Total homes in franchised area: 29,698.
General Manager: Rosa Rosas. Plant Manager: Randy Meeks. Customer Service Manager: Cathy Garcia.
Ownership: News Press & Gazette Co. (MSO).

FLORENCE GARDEN MOBILE HOME PARK—Eagle West Communications Inc, 1030 S Mesa Dr, Mesa, AZ 85210. Phone: 480-813-8371. Fax: 480-813-4596. ICA: AZ0035.
TV Market Ranking: 43 (FLORENCE GARDEN MOBILE HOME PARK). Franchise award date: February 1, 1978. Franchise expiration date: N.A. Began: February 1, 1984.
Channel capacity: 41 (not 2-way capable). Channels available but not in use: N.A.
Basic Service
Subscribers: N.A. Included in East Mesa
Programming (received off-air): KAET (PBS) Phoenix; KGUN-TV (ABC) Tucson; KNXV-TV (ABC) Phoenix; KOLD-TV (CBS) Tucson; KPHO-TV (CBS) Phoenix; KPNX (NBC) Mesa; KSAZ-TV (FOX) Phoenix; KTVK (IND) Phoenix; KTVW-DT (UNV) Phoenix; KUTP (MNT) Phoenix; KVOA (NBC) Tucson.
Programming (via satellite): ABC Family Channel; AMC; Arts & Entertainment; CNBC; CNN; Country Music TV; C-SPAN; Discovery Channel; ESPN; ESPN 2; Fox News Channel; Fox Sports Net Arizona; Headline News; HGTV; History Channel; Lifetime; Nickelodeon; Spike TV; TBS Superstation; Trinity Broadcasting Network; Turner Network TV; USA Network; WGN America.
Fee: $39.95 installation; $25.88 monthly; $1.96 converter.
Pay Service 1
Pay Units: N.A.
Programming (via satellite): Cinemax; HBO.
Fee: $9.95 monthly (Cinemax), $11.95 monthly (HBO).
Video-On-Demand: No
Internet Service
Operational: No.
Telephone Service
None
Homes passed & miles of plant included in East Mesa
General Manager: Ernest McKay.
Ownership: Eagle West Communications (MSO).

FORT MOHAVE MESA—Formerly served by Americable International Arizona Inc. No longer in operation. ICA: AZ0041.

FREDONIA—Precis Communications. Now served by KANAB, UT [UT0033]. ICA: AZ0072.

GILA BEND—Cox Communications. Now served by PHOENIX, AZ [AZ0001]. ICA: AZ0055.

GILA COUNTY—San Carlos Apache Telecom, PO Box 1000, 10 Telecom Ln, Peridot, AZ 85542. Phone: 928-475-2433. Fax: 928-

475-7076. Web Site: http://www.scatui.net. ICA: AZ0135.
TV Market Ranking: Outside TV Markets (GILA COUNTY).
Channel capacity: 20 (not 2-way capable). Channels available but not in use: N.A.
Basic Service
Subscribers: 10.
Programming (received off-air): KAET (PBS) Phoenix; KPHO-TV (CBS) Phoenix; KPNX (NBC) Mesa; KSAZ-TV (FOX) Phoenix; KTVK (IND) Phoenix.
Programming (via satellite): ABC Family Channel; Discovery Channel; ESPN; ESPN 2; Fox Sports Net Arizona; Headline News; KNXV-TV (ABC) Phoenix; KUTP (MNT) Phoenix; Outdoor Channel; Spike TV; TBS Superstation; Trinity Broadcasting Network; USA Network; WGN America.
Fee: $15.00 installation; $13.76 monthly.
Pay Service 1
Pay Units: N.A.
Programming (via satellite): Encore; Starz.
Internet Service
Operational: No.
Telephone Service
None
Homes passed: 15. Total homes in franchised area: 15.
Chief Technician: Richard Gomez. Sales & Marketing: Marion Case.
Ownership: San Carlos Apache Telecommunications Utility Inc. (MSO).

GILBERT—Cox Communications. Now served by PHOENIX, AZ [AZ0001]. ICA: AZ0090.

GILBERT (portions)—Qwest Choice TV. IPTV service has been discontinued.. ICA: AZ5013.

GISELA—Indevideo Co. Inc., PO Box 422, 5901 E McKellips Rd, Ste 109, Mesa, AZ 85215. Phones: 480-656-7432; 800-234-8333. Fax: 480-656-8704. E-mail: indevideo2@juno.com. ICA: AZ0076.
TV Market Ranking: Outside TV Markets (GISELA). Franchise award date: January 1, 1982. Franchise expiration date: N.A. Began: July 1, 1982.
Channel capacity: 42 (not 2-way capable). Channels available but not in use: 5.
Basic Service
Subscribers: 90.
Programming (received off-air): KAET (PBS) Phoenix; KPHO-TV (CBS) Phoenix; KPNX (NBC) Mesa; KSAZ-TV (FOX) Phoenix; KTVK (IND) Phoenix.
Programming (via satellite): ABC Family Channel; ESPN; KCNC-TV (CBS) Denver; Turner Network TV; WGN America.
Fee: $10.00 installation; $27.50 monthly.
Video-On-Demand: No
Internet Service
Operational: No.
Telephone Service
None
Miles of Plant: 9.0 (coaxial); None (fiber optic). Homes passed: 210. Total homes in franchised area: 210.
General Manager & Chief Technician: Kevin Williams.
Ownership: Indevideo Co. Inc. (MSO).

GLENDALE (portions)—Qwest Choice TV. IPTV service has been discontinued.. ICA: AZ5014.

GLOBE-MIAMI—Cable One, PO Box 30, 727 Paxton Ave, Globe, AZ 85502-0030. Phones: 928-425-3161; 928-425-6351. Fax: 928-425-5404. E-mail: joni.maldonado@cableone.net. Web Site: http://www.cableone.net. Also serves Central Heights, Claypool, Gila County, Ice House Canyon, Six Shooter Canyon & Wheatfields. ICA: AZ0018.
TV Market Ranking: Outside TV Markets (Claypool, Gila County, GLOBE-MIAMI, Ice House Canyon, Six Shooter Canyon, Wheatfields). Franchise award date: November 12, 1972. Franchise expiration date: N.A. Began: October 1, 1953.
Channel capacity: N.A. Channels available but not in use: N.A.
Basic Service
Subscribers: 3,900.
Programming (received off-air): KAET (PBS) Phoenix.
Programming (via microwave): KGUN-TV (ABC) Tucson; KNXV-TV (ABC) Phoenix; KPHO-TV (CBS) Phoenix; KPNX (NBC) Mesa; KSAZ-TV (FOX) Phoenix; KTVK (IND) Phoenix.
Programming (via satellite): ABC Family Channel; Animal Planet; Arts & Entertainment; Cartoon Network; CNBC; CNN; Country Music TV; C-SPAN; C-SPAN 2; Discovery Channel; Disney Channel; E! Entertainment Television; ESPN; ESPN 2; Food Network; Fox News Channel; Fox Sports en Espanol; Fox Sports Net Arizona; FX; Headline News; HGTV; History Channel; Home Shopping Network; ION Television; Lifetime; MSNBC; MTV; Nickelodeon; QVC; Spike TV; Syfy; TBS Superstation; The Learning Channel; Trinity Broadcasting Network; Turner Classic Movies; Turner Network TV; TV Guide Network; TV Land; USA Network; VH1; Weather Channel; WGN America.
Current originations: Public Access.
Fee: $75.00 installation; $46.00 monthly; $30.00 additional installation.
Digital Basic Service
Subscribers: 1,168.
Programming (via satellite): Bio; Boomerang; Canales N (multiplexed); Discovery Digital Networks; DMX Music; ESPN Classic Sports; ESPNews; Fox College Sports Atlantic; Fox College Sports Central; Fox College Sports Pacific; Fox Movie Channel; Fox Soccer; Fuel TV; G4; Golf Channel; Great American Country; Hallmark Channel; History Channel International; INSP; Military History Channel; National Geographic Channel; Outdoor Channel; SoapNet; Speed Channel; Toon Disney; Trinity Broadcasting Network; truTV; TVG Network.
Fee: $10.00 ($22.00); $10.00 converter.
Digital Pay Service 1
Pay Units: 500.
Programming (via satellite): Cinemax (multiplexed); Encore (multiplexed); Flix (multiplexed); HBO (multiplexed); Showtime (multiplexed); Starz (multiplexed); Sundance Channel (multiplexed); The Movie Channel.
Fee: $7.00 monthly (each); $10.00 converter.
Video-On-Demand: No
Pay-Per-View
Addressable homes: 1,168.
Addressable: Yes.
Internet Service
Operational: Yes. Began: April 1, 2001.
Subscribers: 2,800.
Broadband Service: CableONE.net.
Fee: $75.00 installation; $43.00 monthly; $6.00 modem lease.
Telephone Service
Digital: Operational
Fee: $75.00 installation; $39.95 monthly
Miles of Plant: 141.0 (coaxial); None (fiber optic). Homes passed: 7,500. Total homes in franchised area: 7,500.
Manager: Joni Maldonado. Chief Technician: Brian Johns.
City fee: 3% of gross.
Ownership: Cable One Inc. (MSO).

GOLDEN SHORES—Rapid Cable, 1750 S Hwy 10, Price, UT 84501-4364. Phone: 435-637-6823. Fax: 435-637-9755. Also serves Topock. ICA: AZ0050.
TV Market Ranking: Below 100 (GOLDEN SHORES, Topock).
Channel capacity: 54 (not 2-way capable). Channels available but not in use: N.A.
Basic Service
Subscribers: N.A.
Programming (received off-air): KAET (PBS) Phoenix; KAZT-TV (IND) Phoenix; KLAS-TV (CBS) Las Vegas; KPHO-TV (CBS) Phoenix; KPNX (NBC) Mesa; KSAZ-TV (FOX) Phoenix; KTNV-TV (ABC) Las Vegas; KTVK (IND) Phoenix; KUTP (MNT) Phoenix.
Programming (via satellite): ABC Family Channel; AMC; Arts & Entertainment; CNN; Comedy Central; Country Music TV; C-SPAN 2; Discovery Channel; Disney Channel; ESPN; ESPN 2; Fox News Channel; FX; Headline News; History Channel; KTLA (CW) Los Angeles; Lifetime; MSNBC; MTV; Nickelodeon; QVC; Speed Channel; Spike TV; Syfy; TBS Superstation; Trinity Broadcasting Network; truTV; Turner Classic Movies; Turner Network TV; TV Guide Network; TV Land; USA Network; VH1; WGN America.
Fee: $29.95 installation; $39.81 monthly.
Pay Service 1
Pay Units: N.A.
Programming (via satellite): Encore; HBO; Showtime; The Movie Channel.
Internet Service
Operational: No.
Fee: $24.95 monthly.
Telephone Service
None
Miles of Plant: 35.0 (coaxial); None (fiber optic). Homes passed: 1,367.
Regional Manager: Shane Baggs.
Ownership: Rapid Communications LLC (MSO).

GOLDEN VALLEY—Golden Valley Cable & Communications, 4206 W Hwy 68, Golden Valley, AZ 86413. Phone: 928-565-4190. Fax: 928-565-4136. E-mail: cs@goldenvalleycable.com. Web Site: http://www.goldenvalleycable.com. ICA: AZ0051.
TV Market Ranking: Below 100 (GOLDEN VALLEY).
Channel capacity: N.A. Channels available but not in use: N.A.
Basic Service
Subscribers: 300.
Programming (received off-air): KAET (PBS) Phoenix; KASW (CW) Phoenix; KAZT-TV (IND) Phoenix; KLAS-TV (CBS) Las Vegas; KMOH-TV (IND) Kingman; KPHO-TV (CBS) Phoenix; KPNX (NBC) Mesa; KSAZ-TV (FOX) Phoenix; KTNV-TV (ABC) Las Vegas; KTVK (IND) Phoenix.
Programming (via satellite): ABC Family Channel; AMC; Animal Planet; Arts & Entertainment; AZ TV; Bio; Bloomberg Television; Cartoon Network; CNN; Comedy Central; Country Music TV; Crime & Investigation Network; C-SPAN; C-SPAN 2; Discovery Channel; ESPN; ESPN 2; Food Network; Fox Movie Channel; Fox News Channel; Fox Sports Net West; FX; Headline News; HGTV; History Channel; History Channel International; Home Shopping Network; HorseRacing TV; Lifetime; Military History Channel; MSNBC; MTV; National Geographic Channel; Nickelodeon; QVC; Speed Channel; Spike TV; Superstation WGN; Syfy; TBS Superstation; Trinity Broadcasting Network; truTV; Turner Network TV; TV Guide Network; TV Land; USA Network; VH1; Weather Channel; WGN America.
Fee: $31.95 monthly.
Expanded Basic Service 1
Subscribers: N.A.
Programming (via satellite): Hallmark Channel; Hallmark Movie Channel.
Fee: $5.95 monthly.
Pay Service 1
Pay Units: N.A.
Programming (via satellite): Encore; HBO; Showtime; The Movie Channel.
Fee: $3.00 monthly (Encore), $11.95 monthly (Showtime & TMC), $12.95 monthly (HBO), $14.95 monthly (Showtime, TMC & Encore).
Internet Service
Operational: Yes.
Fee: $29.95-$44.95 monthly.
Telephone Service
Digital: Operational
Miles of Plant: 100.0 (coaxial); None (fiber optic). Homes passed: 2,000.
Manager: Joan Huffman.; Daniel Huffman.
Ownership: Golden Valley Cable & Communications Inc.

GRAND CANYON—Indevideo Co. Inc., PO Box 422, 5901 E McKellips Rd, Ste 109, Mesa, AZ 85215. Phones: 480-656-7432; 800-234-8333. Fax: 480-656-8704. E-mail: indevideo2@juno.com. ICA: AZ0058.
TV Market Ranking: Outside TV Markets (GRAND CANYON). Franchise award date: January 1, 1983. Franchise expiration date: N.A. Began: March 1, 1984.
Channel capacity: 42 (not 2-way capable). Channels available but not in use: 4.
Basic Service
Subscribers: 320.
Programming (received off-air): KAET (PBS) Phoenix; KNXV-TV (ABC) Phoenix; KPHO-TV (CBS) Phoenix; KPNX (NBC) Mesa; KSAZ-TV (FOX) Phoenix; KTVK (IND) Phoenix; KTVW-DT (UNV) Phoenix; KUTP (MNT) Phoenix.
Programming (via satellite): ABC Family Channel; Arts & Entertainment; CNN; Country Music TV; C-SPAN; Discovery Channel; ESPN; ESPN 2; GalaVision; GSN; Headline News; History Channel; Nickelodeon; QVC; Speed Channel; Spike TV; Syfy; TBS Superstation; The Learning Channel; Turner Network TV; TV Land; Weather Channel; WGN America.
Fee: $10.00 installation; $27.50 monthly.
Pay Service 1
Pay Units: 33.
Programming (via satellite): Encore; Starz.
Fee: $10.00 monthly.
Video-On-Demand: No
Internet Service
Operational: No.
Telephone Service
None
Miles of Plant: 25.0 (coaxial); None (fiber optic). Homes passed: 450. Total homes in franchised area: 450.
General Manager & Chief Technician: Kevin Williams.
Ownership: Indevideo Co. Inc. (MSO).

GRAND MISSOURI MOBILE HOME PARK—Formerly served by Sun Valley Cable Inc. No longer in operation. ICA: AZ0122.

HEBER—Eagle West Communications Inc, 1030 S Mesa Dr, Mesa, AZ 85210. Phones: 800-558-5564; 480-380-5855; 480-813-8371. Fax: 480-813-4596. Web Site: http://www.eagletelephone.com/services.shtml. Also serves Overgaard. ICA: AZ0061.

TV Market Ranking: Outside TV Markets (HEBER, Overgaard). Franchise award date: N.A. Franchise expiration date: N.A. Began: September 1, 1974.

Channel capacity: 40 (not 2-way capable). Channels available but not in use: N.A.

Basic Service

Subscribers: N.A. Included in East Mesa

Programming (received off-air): KAET (PBS) Phoenix; KNXV-TV (ABC) Phoenix; KPNX (NBC) Mesa; KUTP (MNT) Phoenix.

Programming (via microwave): KPHO-TV (CBS) Phoenix; KPNX (NBC) Mesa; KSAZ-TV (FOX) Phoenix; KTVK (IND) Phoenix.

Programming (via satellite): AMC; Animal Planet; Arts & Entertainment; CNN; Country Music TV; Discovery Channel; ESPN; Fox Sports Net Arizona; FX; Headline News; HGTV; History Channel; ION Television; Lifetime; Nickelodeon; Outdoor Channel; QVC; Spike TV; Syfy; TBS Superstation; Telefutura; Trinity Broadcasting Network; Turner Network TV; USA Network; VH1; Weather Channel; WGN America.

Fee: $19.95 installation; $36.95 monthly.

Video-On-Demand: No

Internet Service

Operational: No.

Telephone Service

None

Homes passed & miles of plant included in East Mesa

General Manager: Ernest McKay.

Ownership: Eagle West Communications (MSO).

HOLBROOK—Cable One. Now served by SHOW LOW, AZ [AZ0014]. ICA: AZ0040.

KAYENTA—Formerly served by Frontier Communications. No longer in operation. ICA: AZ0123.

KEARNY—Eagle West Communications Inc, 9333 E Main St, Ste 122, Mesa, AZ 85207-8872. Phones: 520-363-5525; 480-813-8371. Fax: 480-813-4596. Also serves Pinal County (portions). ICA: AZ0052.

TV Market Ranking: Outside TV Markets (KEARNY, Pinal County (portions) (portions)). Franchise award date: N.A. Franchise expiration date: N.A. Began: February 1, 1980.

Channel capacity: 40 (not 2-way capable). Channels available but not in use: N.A.

Basic Service

Subscribers: N.A. Included in East Mesa

Programming (received off-air): KASW (CW) Phoenix; KNXV-TV (ABC) Phoenix; KPNX (NBC) Mesa; KSAZ-TV (FOX) Phoenix; KTVK (IND) Phoenix; KTVW-DT (UNV) Phoenix; KUTP (MNT) Phoenix; KVOA (NBC) Tucson.

Programming (via satellite): ABC Family Channel; Animal Planet; Arts & Entertainment; Cartoon Network; CNN; Country Music TV; Discovery Channel; ESPN; ESPN 2; Fox Movie Channel; Fox News Channel; Fox Sports Net; FX; GalaVision; Hallmark Channel; History Channel; Home Shopping Network; ION Television; Lifetime; Nick Jr.; Nickelodeon; Outdoor Channel; QVC; Spike TV; Syfy; Trinity Broadcasting Network; Turner Network TV; Univision; USA Network; VH1; WGN America.

Fee: $31.95 monthly.

Pay Service 1

Pay Units: 75.

Programming (via satellite): Encore Action; HBO; Starz.

Fee: $4.95 monthly (Encore), $7.95 monthly (Starz!), $9.95 monthly (HBO).

Video-On-Demand: No

Internet Service

Operational: No.

Telephone Service

None

Homes passed & miles of plant included in East Mesa

General Manager: Ernest McKay. Chief Technician: Mike French.

Ownership: Eagle West Communications (MSO).

KINGMAN—NPG Cable, Inc., 2900 Airway Blvd, Kingman, AZ 86401-3646. Phones: 928-757-8079 (Customer service); 928-758-6641. Fax: 928-757-5905. Web Site: http://www.npgcable.net. Also serves Mohave County. ICA: AZ0015.

TV Market Ranking: Below 100 (KINGMAN, Mohave County (portions)); Outside TV Markets (Mohave County (portions)). Franchise award date: N.A. Franchise expiration date: N.A. Began: June 1, 1980.

Channel capacity: N.A. Channels available but not in use: N.A.

Basic Service

Subscribers: 8,965.

Programming (received off-air): KAET (PBS) Phoenix; KASW (CW) Phoenix; KAZT-TV (IND) Phoenix; KMOH-TV (IND) Kingman; KNXV-TV (ABC) Phoenix; KPHO-TV (CBS) Phoenix; KPNX (NBC) Mesa; KSAZ-TV (FOX) Phoenix; KTVK (IND) Phoenix; KUTP (MNT) Phoenix; 7 FMs.

Programming (via satellite): ABC Family Channel; AMC; Animal Planet; Arts & Entertainment; Cartoon Network; CNBC; CNN; Comedy Central; Country Music TV; C-SPAN; Discovery Channel; Discovery Health Channel; Disney Channel; E! Entertainment Television; ESPN; ESPN 2; ESPN Classic Sports; Food Network; Fox News Channel; Fox Sports Net Arizona; FX; Great American Country; Headline News; HGTV; History Channel; Home Shopping Network; Lifetime; MSNBC; MTV; Nickelodeon; QVC; Spike TV; Syfy; TBS Superstation; The Learning Channel; Travel Channel; truTV; Turner Classic Movies; Turner Network TV; TV Guide Network; TV Land; Univision; USA Network; VH1; Weather Channel; WGN America.

Fee: $24.95 installation; $43.80 monthly; $5.00 converter.

Digital Basic Service

Subscribers: 2,662.

Programming (via satellite): BBC America; Bio; Chiller; CMT Pure Country; Cooking Channel; Discovery Channel HD; Discovery Kids Channel; Discovery Military Channel; Discovery Planet Green; DMX Music; Do-It-Yourself; ESPN 2 HD; ESPN HD; ESPNews; Food Network HD; Fox Soccer; Fox Sports en Espanol; FSN Digital Atlantic; FSN Digital Central; FSN Digital Pacific; Fuel TV; Golf Channel; GSN; Hallmark Channel; Halogen Network; HDNet; HDNet Movies; HGTV HD; History Channel International; ID Investigation Discovery; Independent Film Channel; ION Television; Lifetime Movie Network; MTV2; National Geographic Channel; Nick Jr.; NickToons TV; Oxygen; Product Information Network; Science Channel; SoapNet; Speed Channel; Style Network; Syfy HD; TeenNick; Toon Disney; Turner Network TV HD; Universal HD; USA Network HD; Versus; VH1 Classic; WE tv.

Fee: $11.95 monthly.

Digital Pay Service 1

Pay Units: N.A.

Programming (via satellite): Cinemax (multiplexed); Encore (multiplexed); HBO (multiplexed); Showtime (multiplexed); Starz (multiplexed); The Movie Channel (multiplexed).

Fee: $6.95 monthly (Cinemax), $9.95 monthly (Starz/Encore), $11.95 monthly (Showtime/TMC), $12.00 monthly (HBO).

Video-On-Demand: Planned

Pay-Per-View

Addressable homes: 3,500.

Hot Choice (delivered digitally), Addressable: Yes; iN DEMAND; iN DEMAND (delivered digitally); Spice.

Internet Service

Operational: Yes.

Subscribers: 4,678.

Broadband Service: Optimum Online.

Fee: $59.95 installation; $24.95 monthly; $5.00 modem lease.

Telephone Service

Digital: Operational

Subscribers: 2,058.

Fee: $59.95 installation; $39.95 monthly

Miles of Plant: 270.0 (coaxial); 35.0 (fiber optic). Total homes in franchised area: 15,482.

District Manager: Scott Leprich. Plant Manager: Tim Hults. Customer Service Manager: Lora Atchley.

Ownership: News Press & Gazette Co. (MSO).

LAKE HAVASU CITY—NPG Cable, Inc., 730 Acoma Blvd N, Lake Havasu City, AZ 86403-3609. Phones: 928-855-9855; 928-855-7815 (Customer service). Fax: 928-855-1979. E-mail: bakerd@npgco.com. Web Site: http://www.npgcable.net. Also serves Crystal Beach, Desert Hills, Horizan Six & Mohave County (portions). ICA: AZ0010.

TV Market Ranking: Outside TV Markets (Crystal Beach, Desert Hills, Horizan Six, LAKE HAVASU CITY, Mohave County (portions)). Franchise award date: October 16, 1973. Franchise expiration date: N.A. Began: October 16, 1973.

Channel capacity: N.A. Channels available but not in use: N.A.

Basic Service

Subscribers: 15,902.

Programming (received off-air): KAET (PBS) Phoenix; KASW (CW) Phoenix; KAZT-CA Phoenix; KMOH-TV (IND) Kingman; KNXV-TV (ABC) Phoenix; KTAZ (TMO) Phoenix; KTVW-DT (UNV) Phoenix; KUTP (MNT) Phoenix.

Programming (via microwave): KPHO-TV (CBS) Phoenix; KPNX (NBC) Mesa; KSAZ-TV (FOX) Phoenix; KTVK (IND) Phoenix.

Programming (via satellite): ABC Family Channel; AMC; Animal Planet; Arts & Entertainment; Bravo; Cartoon Network; CNBC; CNN; Comedy Central; Country Music TV; C-SPAN; Discovery Channel; Discovery Health Channel; Disney Channel; E! Entertainment Television; ESPN; ESPN 2; ESPN Classic Sports; Food Network; Fox News Channel; Fox Sports Net Arizona; FX; G4; Headline News; HGTV; History Channel; Home Shopping Network; ION Television; KLHU-CA (IND) Lake Havasu City; KTLA (CW) Los Angeles; Lifetime; Lifetime Movie Network; MSNBC; MTV; National Geographic Channel; Nickelodeon; Outdoor Channel; QVC; Speed Channel; Spike TV; Syfy; TBS Superstation; The Learning Channel; Travel Channel; Trinity Broadcasting Network; truTV; Turner Network TV; TV Guide Network; TV Land; USA Network; VH1; Weather Channel; WGN America.

Fee: $39.95 installation; $43.80 monthly.

Digital Basic Service

Subscribers: 7,664.

Programming (via satellite): Discovery Kids Channel; Music Choice; Nick Jr.; NickToons TV; Science Channel; TeenNick; Toon Disney.

Fee: $11.95 monthly.

Digital Pay Service 1

Pay Units: N.A.

Programming (via satellite): Encore (multiplexed).

Fee: $6.95 monthly (Cinemax), $9.95 monthly (Starz/Encore), $11.95 monthly (Showtime/TMC), $12.00 monthly (HBO).

Video-On-Demand: Yes

Pay-Per-View

Hot Choice (delivered digitally), Addressable: Yes; Fresh (delivered digitally); iN DEMAND; iN DEMAND (delivered digitally).

Internet Service

Operational: Yes. Began: May 1, 1998.

Subscribers: 7,391.

Broadband Service: Uneedspeed.

Fee: $59.95 installation; $24.95 monthly; $5.00 modem lease.

Telephone Service

Digital: Operational

Subscribers: 2,660.

Fee: $59.95 installation; $39.95 monthly

Miles of Plant: 493.0 (coaxial); 256.0 (fiber optic). Homes passed: 25,000. Total homes in franchised area: 25,000.

District Manager: Donna Baker. Plant Manager: Rick Hightower.

City fee: 5% of gross.

Ownership: News Press & Gazette Co. (MSO).

LEUPP—Formerly served by Indevideo Co. Inc. No longer in operation. ICA: AZ0115.

LUKE AFB—Cox Communications. Now served by PHOENIX, AZ [AZ0001]. ICA: AZ0092.

MAMMOTH—Eagle West Communications Inc, 1030 S Mesa Dr, Mesa, AZ 85210. Phone: 480-813-8371. Fax: 480-813-4596. ICA: AZ0125.

TV Market Ranking: Outside TV Markets (MAMMOTH). Franchise award date: N.A.

Franchise expiration date: N.A. Began: N.A.
Channel capacity: 40 (not 2-way capable). Channels available but not in use: N.A.

Basic Service

Subscribers: N.A. Included in East Mesa
Programming (received off-air): KGUN-TV (ABC) Tucson; KSAZ-TV (FOX) Phoenix; KUAT-TV (PBS) Tucson; KVOA (NBC) Tucson; KWGN-TV (CW) Denver.
Programming (via satellite): ABC Family Channel; AMC; Animal Planet; Arts & Entertainment; BET Networks; Cartoon Network; CNN; C-SPAN; Discovery Channel; ESPN; Fox Sports Net Arizona; G4; GalaVision; History Channel; Home Shopping Network; ION Television; KCNC-TV (CBS) Denver; Lifetime; Nickelodeon; QVC; Spike TV; Syfy; TBS Superstation; Trinity Broadcasting Network; Turner Classic Movies; Turner Network TV; TV Land; Univision; USA Network; WGN America.
Fee: $31.95 monthly.

Pay Service 1

Pay Units: N.A.
Programming (via satellite): HBO.
Fee: $9.95 monthly.

Video-On-Demand: No

Internet Service

Operational: No.

Telephone Service

None

Homes passed & miles of plant included in East Mesa
General Manager: Ernest McKay.
Ownership: Eagle West Communications (MSO).

MARICOPA—Orbitel Communications, 21116 N John Wayne Pkwy, Ste B9, Maricopa, AZ 85239. Phones: 520-568-8890; 800-247-1566; 877-274-5269. E-mail: sales@orbitelcom.com. Web Site: http://orbitelcom.com. ICA: AZ0142.
TV Market Ranking: 43 (MARICOPA). Franchise award date: N.A. Franchise expiration date: N.A. Began: January 1, 2002.
Channel capacity: N.A. Channels available but not in use: N.A.

Basic Service

Subscribers: N.A.
Programming (received off-air): KAET (PBS) Phoenix; KASW (CW) Phoenix; KAZT-TV (IND) Phoenix; KNXV-TV (ABC) Phoenix; KPAZ-TV (TBN) Phoenix; KPHO-TV (CBS) Phoenix; KPNX (NBC) Mesa; KPPX-TV (ION) Tolleson; KSAZ-TV (FOX) Phoenix; KTVK (IND) Phoenix; KTVW-DT (UNV) Phoenix; KUTP (MNT) Phoenix.
Programming (via satellite): C-SPAN; Eternal Word TV Network; Home Shopping Network; QVC; TBS Superstation; Telefutura; TV Guide Network.
Current originations: Government Access.
Fee: $19.95 monthly.

Expanded Basic Service 1

Subscribers: N.A.
Programming (via satellite): ABC Family Channel; AMC; Animal Planet; Arts & Entertainment; BET Networks; Boomerang; Bravo; Cartoon Network; CNBC; CNN; CNN en Espanol; Comedy Central; Country Music TV; C-SPAN 2; C-SPAN 3; Discovery Channel; Disney Channel; E! Entertainment Television; ESPN; ESPN 2; Food Network; Fox News Channel; Fox Sports Net Arizona; FX; GalaVision; Great American Country; Hallmark Channel; Headline News; HGTV; History Channel; Lifetime; MSNBC; MTV; NFL Network; Nickelodeon; Oxygen; SoapNet; Spike TV; The Learning Channel; Travel Channel; truTV; Turner Network TV; TV Land; USA Network; VH1; Weather Channel.
Fee: $23.95 monthly.

Digital Basic Service

Subscribers: N.A.
Programming (received off-air): KAET (PBS) Phoenix; KNXV-TV (ABC) Phoenix; KPHO-TV (CBS) Phoenix; KPNX (NBC) Mesa; KPPX-TV (ION) Tolleson; KSAZ-TV (FOX) Phoenix; KTVW-DT (UNV) Phoenix; KUTP (MNT) Phoenix.
Programming (via satellite): AmericanLife TV Network; BBC America; Bio; Discovery Channel; Discovery HD Theater; DMX Music; ESPN Classic Sports; ESPN HD; ESPNews; Fox College Sports Atlantic; Fox College Sports Central; Fox College Sports Pacific; Fox Movie Channel; Fox Soccer; Fuse; G4; GAS; Golf Channel; GSN; HDNet; HDNet Movies; History Channel International; Independent Film Channel; Lifetime Movie Network; MTV Networks Digital Suite; National Geographic Channel; Nick Jr.; NickToons TV; Outdoor Channel; Sleuth; Speed Channel; Style Network; Syfy; Toon Disney; Turner Classic Movies; Turner Network TV HD; Versus; WE tv; WGN America.
Fee: $13.00 monthly.

Digital Pay Service 1

Pay Units: N.A.
Programming (via satellite): Cinemax (multiplexed); Cinemax HD; Encore (multiplexed); HBO (multiplexed); HBO HD; Outdoor Channel 2 HD; Showtime (multiplexed); Showtime HD; Starz (multiplexed); Starz HDTV (multiplexed); The Movie Channel; The Movie Channel (multiplexed).
Fee: $9.95 monthly (Cinemax or TMC), $11.95 monthly (HBO, Showtime, or Starz/Encore).

Internet Service

Operational: Yes.
Fee: $39.95-$54.95 monthly.

Telephone Service

Digital: Operational
Fee: $24.95 monthly

Ownership: Orbitel Communications.

MARICOPA COUNTY (unincorporated)—Qwest Choice TV. IPTV service has been discontinued.. ICA: AZ5015.

MESA—Cox Communications. Now served by PHOENIX, AZ [AZ0001]. ICA: AZ0006.

MUNDS PARK—NPG Cable of Arizona. Now served by SEDONA, AZ [AZ0025]. ICA: AZ0096.

NOGALES—Mediacom, 181 N Arroyo Blvd, Nogales, AZ 85621. Phones: 800-239-8411; 480-474-2087. Fax: 480-474-2084. Web Site: http://www.mediacomcable.com. Also serves Amado, Arivaca, Rio Rico & Santa Cruz County (portions). ICA: AZ0017.
TV Market Ranking: Below 100 (Amado, Arivaca, NOGALES, Rio Rico, Santa Cruz County (portions)); Outside TV Markets (Santa Cruz County (portions)). Franchise award date: N.A. Franchise expiration date: N.A. Began: May 15, 1978.
Channel capacity: 80 (operating 2-way). Channels available but not in use: 14.

Basic Service

Subscribers: 6,272.
Programming (received off-air): KHRR (TMO) Tucson; KMSB (FOX) Tucson; KTTV (FOX) Los Angeles; KWBA-TV (CW) Sierra Vista; allband FM.
Programming (via microwave): KGUN-TV (ABC) Tucson; KOLD-TV (CBS) Tucson; KVOA (NBC) Tucson.
Programming (via satellite): ABC Family Channel; AMC; AmericanLife TV Network; Animal Planet; Arts & Entertainment; Cartoon Network; CNBC; CNN; Comedy Central; C-SPAN; Discovery Channel; Disney Channel; E! Entertainment Television; ESPN; ESPN 2; Eternal Word TV Network; Food Network; Fox News Channel; FX; GalaVision; Headline News; HGTV; History Channel; Home Shopping Network; Lifetime; MSNBC; MTV; Nickelodeon; Outdoor Channel; QVC; Speed Channel; Spike TV; Syfy; TBS Superstation; Telefutura; Televisa Networks; The Learning Channel; Toon Disney; Travel Channel; Trinity Broadcasting Network; truTV; Turner Network TV; TV Guide Network; TV Land; Univision; USA Network; VH1; W Network; Weather Channel; WGN America.
Current originations: Educational Access; Public Access.
Fee: $34.95 installation; $34.95 monthly.

Digital Basic Service

Subscribers: N.A.
Programming (via satellite): BBC America; Discovery Digital Networks; Encore (multiplexed); ESPNews; Fox Soccer; GSN; Independent Film Channel; National Geographic Channel; Nick Jr.; Turner Classic Movies; Versus; VH1 Classic.

Digital Pay Service 1

Pay Units: N.A.
Programming (via satellite): Cinemax; Flix; HBO (multiplexed); Showtime; The Movie Channel (multiplexed).
Fee: $8.00 monthly (Starz/Encore), $11.95 monthly (Cinemax or Showtime), $12.95 monthly (HBO).

Video-On-Demand: No

Pay-Per-View

iN DEMAND, Addressable: Yes.

Internet Service

Operational: Yes.
Broadband Service: Mediacom High Speed Internet.
Fee: $59.95 installation; $42.95 monthly; $3.00 modem lease.

Telephone Service

None

Homes passed: 7,495. Miles of plant (coax) included in Apache Junction
General Manager: Peter Quam. Sales & Marketing Manager: Paul Tremblay. Technical Operations Manager: Pete Purvis.
City fee: 3% of gross.
Ownership: Mediacom LLC (MSO).

ORACLE—Eagle West Communications Inc, 1030 S Mesa Dr, Mesa, AZ 85210. Phone: 480-813-8371. Fax: 480-813-4596. ICA: AZ0068.
TV Market Ranking: Below 100 (ORACLE). Franchise award date: N.A. Franchise expiration date: N.A. Began: July 1, 1985.
Channel capacity: 40 (not 2-way capable). Channels available but not in use: N.A.

Basic Service

Subscribers: N.A. Included in East Mesa
Programming (received off-air): KASW (CW) Phoenix; KGUN-TV (ABC) Tucson; KPHO-TV (CBS) Phoenix; KSAZ-TV (FOX) Phoenix; KTVK (IND) Phoenix; KUAT-TV (PBS) Tucson; KUTP (MNT) Phoenix; KVOA (NBC) Tucson.
Programming (via satellite): AMC; Animal Planet; Arts & Entertainment; BET Networks; CNN; C-SPAN; Discovery Channel; ESPN; Fox Sports Net Arizona; G4; History Channel; Home Shopping Network; ION Television; Lifetime; Nickelodeon; Outdoor Channel; QVC; Spike TV; TBS Superstation; The Learning Channel; Trinity Broadcasting Network; Turner Network TV; TV Land; Univision; USA Network; VH1; WGN America.
Fee: $31.95 monthly.

Pay Service 1

Pay Units: 136.
Programming (via satellite): HBO.
Fee: $9.95 monthly.

Video-On-Demand: No

Internet Service

Operational: No.

Telephone Service

None

Homes passed & miles of plant included in East Mesa
General Manager: Ernest McKay.
Ownership: Eagle West Communications (MSO).

PAGE—Cable One, PO Box 3049, 155 5th Ave, Page, AZ 86040. Phone: 928-645-2132. Fax: 928-645-3087. E-mail: webmaster@cableone.net. Web Site: http://www.cableone.net. Also serves Coconino County. ICA: AZ0033.
TV Market Ranking: Below 100 (Coconino County (portions)); Outside TV Markets (Coconino County (portions), PAGE). Franchise award date: N.A. Franchise expiration date: N.A. Began: April 1, 1960.
Channel capacity: 75 (operating 2-way). Channels available but not in use: N.A.

Basic Service

Subscribers: 1,415.
Programming (received off-air): KAET (PBS) Phoenix; KASW (CW) Phoenix; KNXV-TV (ABC) Phoenix; KPHO-TV (CBS) Phoenix; KPNX (NBC) Mesa; KSAZ-TV (FOX) Phoenix; KTVK (IND) Phoenix.
Programming (via satellite): ABC Family Channel; AMC; Animal Planet; Arts & Entertainment; BYU Television; Cartoon Network; CNBC; CNN; Comedy Central; Country Music TV; C-SPAN; C-SPAN 2; Discovery Channel; Disney Channel; ESPN; ESPN 2; Food Network; Fox News Channel; Fox Sports Net Arizona; FX; Hallmark Channel; Headline News; HGTV; History Channel; Home Shopping Network; Lifetime; MSNBC; MTV; Nickelodeon; QVC; Spike TV; Syfy; TBS Superstation; The Learning Channel; Trinity Broadcasting Network; Turner Classic Movies; Turner Network TV; TV Land; TVG Network; USA Network; VH1; Weather Channel.
Fee: $9.95 installation; $46.00 monthly.

Digital Basic Service

Subscribers: 300.
Programming (via satellite): Bio; Bloomberg Television; Discovery Digital Networks; DMX Music; ESPN Classic Sports; ESPNews; Fox College Sports Atlantic; Fox College Sports Central; Fox College Sports Pacific; Fox Movie Channel; Fox Soccer; G4; Golf Channel; Great American Country; GSN; History Channel International; National Geographic Channel; Outdoor Channel; Speed Channel; Toon Disney; Trinity Broadcasting Network; Turner Network TV HD; Universal HD; Versus.
Fee: $15.00 monthly.

Digital Pay Service 1

Pay Units: N.A.
Programming (via satellite): Cinemax (multiplexed); Flix; HBO (multiplexed); Showtime (multiplexed); The Movie Channel (multiplexed).
Fee: $15.00 monthly (each).

Video-On-Demand: No

Pay-Per-View
Addressable homes: 129.
Hot Network (delivered digitally), Addressable: Yes; movies (delivered digitally); Special Events (delivered digitally).
Internet Service
Operational: Yes.
Subscribers: 989.
Broadband Service: CableONE.net.
Fee: $75.00 installation; $43.00 monthly.
Telephone Service
None
Miles of Plant: 35.0 (coaxial); None (fiber optic). Additional miles planned: 2.0 (coaxial). Homes passed: 2,945. Total homes in franchised area: 2,945.
Manager: John Giattino.
City fee: 3% of gross.
Ownership: Cable One Inc. (MSO).

PARADISE VALLEY (portions)—Qwest Choice TV. IPTV service has been discontinued.. ICA: AZ5016.

PARKER—NPG Cable, Inc., 1640 California Ave, Parker, AZ 85344. Phones: 928-669-2191 (customer service); 928-855-9855. Fax: 928-855-1979. Web Site: http://www.npgcable.net. Also serves La Paz County (portions), AZ; Earp & San Bernardino County (portions), CA. ICA: AZ0016.
TV Market Ranking: Outside TV Markets (Earp, La Paz County (portions), PARKER, San Bernardino County (portions)). Franchise award date: N.A. Franchise expiration date: N.A. Began: April 1, 1970.
Channel capacity: N.A. Channels available but not in use: N.A.
Basic Service
Subscribers: 3,620.
Programming (received off-air): KAET (PBS) Phoenix; KASW (CW) Phoenix; KMOH-TV (IND) Kingman; KNXV-TV (ABC) Phoenix; KTVK (IND) Phoenix; KTVW-DT (UNV) Phoenix; KUTP (MNT) Phoenix; allband FM.
Programming (via microwave): KPHO-TV (CBS) Phoenix; KPNX (NBC) Mesa; KSAZ-TV (FOX) Phoenix; KYMA-DT (NBC) Yuma.
Programming (via satellite): ABC Family Channel; AMC; Animal Planet; Arts & Entertainment; Cartoon Network; CNBC; CNN; Comedy Central; Country Music TV; C-SPAN; Discovery Channel; Discovery Health Channel; Disney Channel; E! Entertainment Television; ESPN; ESPN 2; ESPN Classic Sports; Food Network; Fox News Channel; Fox Sports Net Arizona; FX; Great American Country; GSN; Headline News; HGTV; History Channel; Home Shopping Network; ION Television; KTLA (CW) Los Angeles; Lifetime; MSNBC; MTV; Nickelodeon; Product Information Network; QVC; Spike TV; Syfy; TBS Superstation; Telemundo; The Learning Channel; Travel Channel; Trinity Broadcasting Network; truTV; Turner Classic Movies; Turner Network TV; TV Guide Network; TV Land; USA Network; VH1; WE tv; Weather Channel; WGN America.
Current originations: Government Access; Educational Access; Leased Access; Public Access.
Fee: $24.95 installation; $38.80 monthly; $2.50 converter; $9.95 additional installation.
Digital Basic Service
Subscribers: 1,275.
Programming (via satellite): BBC America; Bio; CMT Pure Country; Cooking Channel; Discovery Digital Networks; DMX Music; Do-It-Yourself; ESPNews; Fox Soccer; Fox Sports en Espanol; FSN Digital Atlantic; FSN Digital Central; FSN Digital Pacific; Fuel TV; GAS; Golf Channel; Hallmark Channel; History Channel International; Independent Film Channel; Lime; MTV Networks Digital Suite; National Geographic Channel; Nick Jr.; NickToons TV; Outdoor Channel; SoapNet; Speed Channel; Style Network; Toon Disney; Versus.
Fee: $11.95 monthly.
Digital Pay Service 1
Pay Units: N.A.
Programming (via satellite): Cinemax (multiplexed); Encore (multiplexed); HBO (multiplexed); Showtime (multiplexed); Starz (multiplexed); The Movie Channel (multiplexed).
Fee: $6.95 monthly (Cinemax), $9.95 monthly (Starz/Encore), $11.95 monthly (Showtime/TMC), $12.00 monthly (HBO).
Video-On-Demand: No
Pay-Per-View
iN DEMAND (delivered digitally); Hot Network; Fresh (delivered digitally).
Internet Service
Operational: Yes.
Subscribers: 1,893.
Broadband Service: Optimum Online.
Fee: $59.95 installation; $24.95 monthly; $5.00 modem lease.
Telephone Service
Digital: Operational
Subscribers: 956.
Fee: $59.95 installation; $39.95 monthly
Miles of Plant: 172.0 (coaxial); 51.0 (fiber optic). Homes passed: 9,600. Total homes in franchised area: 9,600.
District Manager: Donna Baker. Plant Manager: Rick Highlander.
City fee: 5% of gross.
Ownership: News Press & Gazette Co. (MSO).

PATAGONIA—Cox Communications, 1440 E 15th St, Tucson, AZ 85719. Phones: 623-328-3121 (Phoenix office); 520-629-8470. Fax: 520-624-5918. Web Site: http://www.cox.com/arizona. Also serves Sonoita. ICA: AZ0064.
TV Market Ranking: Below 100 (PATAGONIA, Sonoita). Franchise award date: N.A. Franchise expiration date: N.A. Began: July 1, 1974.
Channel capacity: 26 (operating 2-way). Channels available but not in use: N.A.
Basic Service
Subscribers: 333.
Programming (received off-air): KGUN-TV (ABC) Tucson; KMSB (FOX) Tucson; KOLD-TV (CBS) Tucson; KTTU (MNT) Tucson; KUAT-TV (PBS) Tucson; KVOA (NBC) Tucson; allband FM.
Programming (via satellite): ABC Family Channel; AMC; Animal Planet; Cartoon Network; CNN; Comcast Sports Net Southwest; Country Music TV; Discovery Channel; Disney Channel; Encore; ESPN; Fox News Channel; History Channel; Spike TV; TBS Superstation; The Learning Channel; Turner Network TV; USA Network.
Fee: $44.95 installation; $22.70 monthly; $19.95 additional installation.
Pay Service 1
Pay Units: 37.
Programming (via satellite): HBO.
Fee: $10.95 monthly.
Video-On-Demand: No
Pay-Per-View
Addressable homes: 323.
Movies, Addressable: Yes; special events.
Internet Service
Operational: Yes.

Telephone Service
Digital: Operational
Miles of Plant: 220.0 (coaxial); None (fiber optic). Additional miles planned: 2.0 (coaxial). Homes passed: 491.
Vice President & Regional Manager: Steve Rizley. Vice President & Systems Manager: Anne Doris. Vice President, Marketing: Anthony Maldonando. Media Relations Director: Andrea Katsenes.
City fee: 3% of gross.
Ownership: Cox Communications Inc. (MSO).

PAYSON—NPG Cable, Inc., 112 W Bonita St, Payson, AZ 85541. Phone: 928-855-9855. Fax: 928-855-1979. Web Site: http://www.npgcable.net. Also serves Star Valley. ICA: AZ0024.
TV Market Ranking: Outside TV Markets (PAYSON (VILLAGE), Star Valley). Franchise award date: October 1, 1981. Franchise expiration date: N.A. Began: January 1, 1955.
Channel capacity: N.A. Channels available but not in use: N.A.
Basic Service
Subscribers: 5,127 Includes Pines.
Programming (received off-air): KAET (PBS) Phoenix; KASW (CW) Phoenix; KAZT-TV (IND) Phoenix; KMOH-TV (IND) Kingman; KNXV-TV (ABC) Phoenix; KPHO-TV (CBS) Phoenix; KPNX (NBC) Mesa; KSAZ-TV (FOX) Phoenix; KTVK (IND) Phoenix; KTVW-DT (UNV) Phoenix; KUTP (MNT) Phoenix; 12 FMs.
Programming (via satellite): ABC Family Channel; AMC; Animal Planet; Arts & Entertainment; BYU Television; Cartoon Network; CNBC; CNN; Comedy Central; Country Music TV; C-SPAN; Discovery Channel; Discovery Health Channel; Disney Channel; E! Entertainment Television; ESPN; ESPN 2; ESPN Classic Sports; ESPNews; Eternal Word TV Network; Food Network; Fox News Channel; Fox Sports Net Arizona; Great American Country; Headline News; HGTV; History Channel; Home Shopping Network; ION Television; Lifetime; MSNBC; MTV; Nickelodeon; QVC; ShopNBC; Speed Channel; Spike TV; Syfy; TBS Superstation; The Learning Channel; Travel Channel; Trinity Broadcasting Network; Turner Classic Movies; Turner Network TV; TV Guide Network; TV Land; USA Network; VH1; Weather Channel; WGN America.
Current originations: Government Access.
Fee: $39.95 installation; $43.80 monthly; $2.50 converter; $9.95 additional installation.
Digital Basic Service
Subscribers: 977.
Programming (via satellite): BBC America; Bio; CMT Pure Country; Cooking Channel; Discovery Digital Networks; DMX Music; Do-It-Yourself; Fox Soccer; Fox Sports en Espanol; FSN Digital Atlantic; FSN Digital Central; FSN Digital Pacific; Fuel TV; FX; GAS; Golf Channel; GSN; History Channel International; Independent Film Channel; Lime; MTV Networks Digital Suite; National Geographic Channel; Nick Jr.; NickToons TV; SoapNet; Style Network; Toon Disney; Versus; WE tv.
Fee: $7.95 monthly.
Digital Pay Service 1
Pay Units: N.A.
Programming (via satellite): Cinemax (multiplexed); Encore (multiplexed); HBO (multiplexed); Showtime (multiplexed); Starz; The Movie Channel (multiplexed).
Fee: $6.95 monthly (Cinemax), $9.95 monthly (Starz/Encore), $11.95 monthly (Showtime/TMC), $12.00 monthly (HBO).
Video-On-Demand: No
Pay-Per-View
iN DEMAND (delivered digitally).
Internet Service
Operational: Yes.
Subscribers: 3,121.
Broadband Service: Uneedspeed.
Fee: $59.95 installation; $24.95 monthly.
Telephone Service
Digital: Operational
Fee: $59.95 installation; $39.95 monthly
Miles of Plant: 250.0 (coaxial); None (fiber optic). Homes passed: 11,563. Total homes in franchised area: 12,000. Includes Pines
General Manager: Karen Foster. Plant Manager: Jack Buchea.
City fee: 2% of gross.
Ownership: News Press & Gazette Co. (MSO).

PEACH SPRINGS—Formerly served by Eagle West Communications Inc. No longer in operation. ICA: AZ0071.

PEORIA (portions)—Qwest Choice TV. IPTV service has been discontinued.. ICA: AZ5017.

PERRYVILLE—Formerly served by Eagle West Communications Inc. No longer in operation. ICA: AZ0078.

PHOENIX—Cox Communications, 1550 W Deer Valley Rd, Phoenix, AZ 85027-2121. Phones: 623-594-1000 (Customer service); 623-328-3121. Fax: 623-328-3580. Web Site: http://www.cox.com/arizona. Also serves Avondale, Buckeye, Carefree, Cashion, Cave Creek, Chandler, Coolidge, El Mirage, Florence, Fountain Hills, Gila Bend, Gilbert, Glendale, Goodyear, Guadalupe, Litchfield Park, Luke AFB, Maricopa County (portions), Mesa, Paradise Valley, Peoria, Queen Creek, Rio Verde, Scottsdale, Sun City, Sun City West, Sun Lakes, Surprise, Tempe, Tolleson, Wickenburg & Youngtown. ICA: AZ0001.
TV Market Ranking: 43 (Avondale, Buckeye, Carefree, Cashion, Cave Creek, Chandler, Coolidge, El Mirage, Florence, Fountain Hills, Gilbert, Glendale, Goodyear, Guadalupe, Litchfield Park, Luke AFB, Maricopa County (portions), Mesa, Paradise Valley, Peoria, PHOENIX, Queen Creek, Rio Verde, Scottsdale, Sun City, Sun City West, Sun Lakes, Surprise, Tempe, Tolleson, Tolleson, Youngtown); Below 100 (Maricopa County (portions)); Outside TV Markets (Gila Bend, Wickenburg, Maricopa County (portions)). Franchise award date:

N.A. Franchise expiration date: N.A. Began: January 1, 1960.
Channel capacity: N.A. Channels available but not in use: N.A.

Basic Service

Subscribers: 770,954.

Programming (received off-air): KAET (PBS) Phoenix; KASW (CW) Phoenix; KAZT-TV (IND) Phoenix; KNXV-TV (ABC) Phoenix; KPAZ-TV (TBN) Phoenix; KPHO-TV (CBS) Phoenix; KPNX (NBC) Mesa; KPPX-TV (ION) Tolleson; KSAZ-TV (FOX) Phoenix; KTVK (IND) Phoenix; KTVW-DT (UNV) Phoenix; KUTP (MNT) Phoenix; allband FM.

Programming (via satellite): QVC; TBS Superstation; WGN America.

Current originations: Leased Access; Government Access; Educational Access; Public Access.

Fee: $34.95 installation; $17.95 monthly; $2.65 converter; $17.28 additional installation.

Expanded Basic Service 1

Subscribers: N.A.

Programming (via satellite): ABC Family Channel; Animal Planet; Arts & Entertainment; BET Networks; Bravo; Cartoon Network; CNBC; CNN; Comedy Central; Country Music TV; C-SPAN; C-SPAN 2; Disney Channel; E! Entertainment Television; ESPN; ESPN 2; ESPN Classic Sports; Food Network; Fox Sports Net West; FX; G4; Golf Channel; Hallmark Channel; Headline News; HGTV; History Channel; Home Shopping Network; Independent Film Channel; Lifetime; MSNBC; MTV; mun2 television; Nickelodeon; Product Information Network; Speed Channel; Syfy; Telemundo; The Learning Channel; Travel Channel; Turner Classic Movies; TV Guide Network; TV Land; USA Network; Versus; VH1; Weather Channel.

Fee: $22.00 monthly.

Expanded Basic Service 2

Subscribers: N.A.

Programming (via satellite): AMC; Country Music TV; Discovery Channel; Spike TV; Turner Network TV.

Fee: $3.35 monthly.

Digital Basic Service

Subscribers: 157,344.

Programming (via satellite): BBC America; Bloomberg Television; Discovery Digital Networks; Encore Action; Flix; Fuse; GSN; Music Choice; Ovation; Sundance Channel.

Fee: $9.95 installation; $10.00 monthly; $2.82 converter.

Pay Service 1

Pay Units: 149,783.

Programming (via satellite): Cinemax (multiplexed); HBO (multiplexed); Showtime; Starz (multiplexed); The Movie Channel (multiplexed).

Fee: $7.95 monthly (Cinemax, Starz or TMC), $9.95 monthly (HBO or Showtime).

Digital Pay Service 1

Pay Units: N.A.

Programming (via satellite): Cinemax (multiplexed); HBO (multiplexed); Showtime; Starz (multiplexed); The Movie Channel (multiplexed).

Fee: $10.00 monthly (each).

Video-On-Demand: No

Pay-Per-View

Addressable homes: 157,344.

Hot Choice (delivered digitally), Addressable: Yes; iN DEMAND, Fee: $4.95; Fresh; Movies (delivered digitally); special events (delivered digitally).

Internet Service

Operational: Yes.

Subscribers: 77,343.

Broadband Service: Cox High Speed Internet.

Fee: $99.00 installation; $39.95 monthly; $15.00 modem lease; $399.00 modem purchase.

Telephone Service

Digital: Operational

Fee: $13.00 monthly

Miles of Plant: 15,000.0 (coaxial); None (fiber optic). Miles of plant (coaxial) includes both coax & fiber miles for all Cox systems in AZ

Vice President & Regional Manager: Steve Rizley. Vice President, Marketing: Anthony Maldonado. Vice President, Network Operations: Herb Dougall. Media Relations Director: Andrea Katsenes.

Ownership: Cox Communications Inc. (MSO).

PHOENIX—Formerly served by Sprint Corp. No longer in operation. ICA: AZ0120.

PHOENIX—Formerly served by TV Max. No longer in operation. ICA: AZ0136.

PHOENIX (portions)—Qwest Choice TV. IPTV service has been discontinued.. ICA: AZ5018.

PHOENIX (portions)—Qwest Choice TV. This cable system has converted to IPTV. See Phoenix (portions), AZ [AZ5018], AZ. ICA: AZ0130.

PIMA COUNTY—Comcast Cable, 8251 N Cortaro Rd, Tucson, AZ 85743-9393. Phone: 520-744-2653. Fax: 520-744-4737. E-mail: lori_green@cable.comcast.com. Web Site: http://www.comcast.com. Also serves Catalina (portions), Marana, Oro Valley, Tucson (portions), Tucson (unincorporated areas) & Tucson Estates. ICA: AZ0003.

TV Market Ranking: Below 100 (Catalina (portions), Marana, Oro Valley, PIMA COUNTY, Tucson (portions), Tucson (unincorporated areas), Tucson Estates). Franchise award date: August 1, 1979. Franchise expiration date: N.A. Began: July 1, 1982.

Channel capacity: N.A. Channels available but not in use: N.A.

Basic Service

Subscribers: 80,364.

Programming (received off-air): KGUN-TV (ABC) Tucson; KHRR (TMO) Tucson; KMSB (FOX) Tucson; KOLD-TV (CBS) Tucson; KTTU (MNT) Tucson; KUAT-TV (PBS) Tucson; KUVE-DT (UNV) Green Valley; KVOA (NBC) Tucson; KWBA-TV (CW) Sierra Vista.

Programming (via satellite): ESPN; WGN America.

Current originations: Educational Access.

Fee: $14.99 monthly.

Expanded Basic Service 1

Subscribers: 55,493.

Programming (via satellite): ABC Family Channel; AMC; Animal Planet; Arts & Entertainment; BET Networks; Bravo; Cartoon Network; CNBC; CNN; Comedy Central; Country Music TV; C-SPAN; C-SPAN 2; Discovery Channel; Disney Channel; E! Entertainment Television; ESPN 2; ESPN Classic Sports; Food Network; Fox News Channel; Fox Sports Net; FX; GalaVision; Golf Channel; Great American Country; GSN; Headline News; HGTV; History Channel; Home Shopping Network; INSP; Lifetime; MSNBC; MTV; Nickelodeon; QVC; Speed Channel; Spike TV; Style Network; Syfy; TBS Superstation; The Learning Channel; Travel Channel; Trinity Broadcasting Network; truTV; Turner Classic Movies; Turner Network TV; TV Guide Network; TV Land; USA Network; Versus; VH1; VH1 Classic; Weather Channel.

Fee: $36.00 monthly.

Digital Basic Service

Subscribers: 23,000.

Programming (via satellite): BBC America; Bravo; Cooking Channel; C-SPAN 3; Discovery Digital Networks; DMX Music; Do-It-Yourself; Encore (multiplexed); ESPNews; Flix; Fox Sports Net Mid-Atlantic; Fox Sports Net West; G4; GAS; MTV Networks Digital Suite (multiplexed); National Geographic Channel; Nick Too; NickToons TV; SoapNet; Syfy; Toon Disney; WAM! America's Kidz Network.

Fee: $11.95 monthly.

Digital Expanded Basic Service

Subscribers: N.A.

Programming (via satellite): Nick Jr.

Fee: $4.00 monthly.

Digital Pay Service 1

Pay Units: N.A.

Programming (via satellite): Cinemax; HBO; Showtime; Starz (multiplexed); The Movie Channel.

Fee: $17.95 monthly (each).

Video-On-Demand: Yes

Pay-Per-View

Addressable homes: 32,512.

Hot Network, Addressable: Yes; Spice.

Internet Service

Operational: Yes.

Broadband Service: Comcast High Speed Internet.

Fee: $42.95 monthly.

Telephone Service

Digital: Operational

Miles of Plant: 1,450.0 (coaxial); None (fiber optic). Additional miles planned: 65.0 (coaxial). Homes passed: 104,197. Total homes in franchised area: 109,647.

General Manager: Paul Pecora. Chief Technician: Scott Anderson. Marketing Manager: Hans Rhey. Community & Government Affairs Director: Kelle Maslyn.

County fee: 3% of gross.

Ownership: Comcast Cable Communications Inc. (MSO).

PINE—NPG Cable, Inc., 112 W Bonita St, Payson, AZ 85541. Phones: 928-474-4263; 928-855-9855. Fax: 928-855-1979. Web Site: http://www.npgcable.net. Also serves Strawberry. ICA: AZ0027.

TV Market Ranking: Outside TV Markets (PINE, Strawberry). Franchise award date: N.A. Franchise expiration date: N.A. Began: October 1, 1978.

Channel capacity: N.A. Channels available but not in use: N.A.

Basic Service

Subscribers: N.A. Included in Payson

Programming (received off-air): KAET (PBS) Phoenix; KASW (CW) Phoenix; KNXV-TV (ABC) Phoenix; KPHO-TV (CBS) Phoenix; KPNX (NBC) Mesa; KSAZ-TV (FOX) Phoenix; KTVK (IND) Phoenix; KTVW-DT (UNV) Phoenix; KUTP (MNT) Phoenix; allband FM.

Programming (via satellite): ABC Family Channel; AMC; Animal Planet; Arts & Entertainment; Cartoon Network; CNN; Comedy Central; C-SPAN; Discovery Channel; Discovery Health Channel; ESPN; ESPN 2; ESPN Classic Sports; Food Network; Fox News Channel; Fox Sports Net Arizona; FX; Great American Country; Headline News; HGTV; History Channel; Lifetime; MTV; Nickelodeon; QVC; ShopNBC; Spike TV; Syfy; TBS Superstation; The Learning Channel; Travel Channel; Trinity Broadcasting Network; Turner Classic Movies; Turner Network TV; TV Land; USA Network; VH1; Weather Channel; WGN America.

Fee: $39.95 installation; $35.50 monthly; $5.00 converter; $9.95 additional installation.

Pay Service 1

Pay Units: 164.

Programming (via satellite): Cinemax; HBO.

Fee: $6.95 monthly (Cinemax), $12.00 monthly (HBO).

Video-On-Demand: No

Internet Service

Operational: Yes.

Broadband Service: Uneedspeed.

Fee: $59.95 installation; $24.95 monthly.

Telephone Service

None

Homes passed: Included in Payson

General Manager: Karen Foster. Plant Manager: Jack Buchea.

City fee: None.

Ownership: News Press & Gazette Co. (MSO).

POMERENE—Midvale Telephone Exchange Inc., 2205 Keithley Creek Rd, Midvale, ID 83645-5019. Phone: 208-355-2211. Fax: 208-355-2222. ICA: AZ0133.

TV Market Ranking: Below 100 (POMERENE). Franchise award date: N.A. Franchise expiration date: N.A. Began: N.A.

Channel capacity: N.A. Channels available but not in use: N.A.

Basic Service

Subscribers: 80.

Programming (received off-air): KGUN-TV (ABC) Tucson; KMSB (FOX) Tucson; KOLD-TV (CBS) Tucson; KTTU (MNT) Tucson; KUAT-TV (PBS) Tucson; KVOA (NBC) Tucson.

Programming (via satellite): ABC Family Channel; Cartoon Network; CNN; Country Music TV; C-SPAN; Discovery Channel; Disney Channel; ESPN; Fox Sports Net Arizona; GalaVision; Hallmark Channel; Headline News; History Channel; Nickelodeon; QVC; Spike TV; TBS Superstation; The Learning Channel; Turner Classic Movies; Turner Network TV; USA Network; Versus; WGN America.

Fee: $20.00 monthly.

Pay Service 1

Pay Units: 9.

Programming (via satellite): Cinemax.

Fee: $9.00 monthly.

Pay Service 2

Pay Units: 11.

Programming (via satellite): HBO.

Fee: $9.00 monthly.

Internet Service

Operational: No.

Telephone Service

None

Miles of Plant: 5.0 (coaxial); None (fiber optic). Homes passed: 200.

Manager: John Stuart.

Ownership: Midvale Telephone Exchange Inc. (MSO).

PRESCOTT—Cable One, 3201 Tower Rd, Prescott, AZ 86305-3734. Phone: 928-445-4511. Fax: 928-443-3303. Web Site: http://www.cableone.net. Also serves Chino Valley, Dewey, Humboldt, Mayer & Prescott Valley. ICA: AZ0007.

TV Market Ranking: Outside TV Markets (Chino Valley, Dewey, Humboldt, Mayer, PRESCOTT, Prescott Valley). Franchise

award date: December 1, 1953. Franchise expiration date: N.A. Began: July 1, 1953.
Channel capacity: 64 (operating 2-way). Channels available but not in use: 10.
Basic Service
Subscribers: 31,489.
Programming (received off-air): KAET (PBS) Phoenix; KASW (CW) Phoenix; KAZT-TV (IND) Phoenix; KFPH-TV (TEL) Flagstaff; KNAZ-TV (NBC) Flagstaff; KNXV-TV (ABC) Phoenix; KPHO-TV (CBS) Phoenix; KPNX (NBC) Mesa; KSAZ-TV (FOX) Phoenix; KTVK (IND) Phoenix; KUTP (MNT) Phoenix; 17 FMs.
Programming (via satellite): ABC Family Channel; AMC; Animal Planet; Arts & Entertainment; Bravo; Cartoon Network; CNBC; CNN; Comedy Central; Country Music TV; C-SPAN; C-SPAN 2; Discovery Channel; Disney Channel; ESPN; ESPN 2; Fox News Channel; Fox Sports Net Arizona; FX; Headline News; HGTV; History Channel; Home Shopping Network; ION Television; Lifetime; MSNBC; MTV; Nickelodeon; QVC; Spike TV; Syfy; TBS Superstation; The Learning Channel; Trinity Broadcasting Network; Turner Classic Movies; Turner Network TV; TV Guide Network; TV Land; USA Network; VH1; Weather Channel; WGN America.
Current originations: Leased Access; Public Access.
Fee: $75.00 installation; $46.00 monthly; $.90 converter.
Digital Basic Service
Subscribers: 9,268.
Programming (via satellite): Bio; Boomerang; Discovery Digital Networks; ESPN Classic Sports; ESPNews; Hallmark Channel; History Channel International; National Geographic Channel; SoapNet; Speed Channel; Toon Disney; truTV.
Digital Pay Service 1
Pay Units: 4,110.
Programming (via satellite): HBO (multiplexed).
Digital Pay Service 2
Pay Units: 3,832.
Programming (via satellite): Cinemax (multiplexed).
Digital Pay Service 3
Pay Units: 1,901.
Programming (via satellite): Showtime (multiplexed); The Movie Channel (multiplexed).
Digital Pay Service 4
Pay Units: N.A.
Programming (via satellite): DMX Music; Flix (multiplexed); Sundance Channel (multiplexed).
Video-On-Demand: No
Pay-Per-View
ESPN Sports 1-6 (delivered digitally); ETC (delivered digitally); Playboy TV (delivered digitally); Pleasure (delivered digitally); Fresh (delivered digitally); Shorteez (delivered digitally).
Internet Service
Operational: Yes.
Subscribers: 4,375.
Broadband Service: CableONE.net.
Fee: $75.00 installation; $43.00 monthly.
Telephone Service
Digital: Operational
Fee: $75.00 installation; $39.95 monthly
Miles of Plant: 750.0 (coaxial); 150.0 (fiber optic). Additional miles planned: 12.0 (coaxial). Homes passed: 49,541. Total homes in franchised area: 49,541.
General Manager: Dennis Edwards. Marketing Director: J J McCormick. Customer Service Manager: Trudy Szabo.
City fee: 3% of gross.
Ownership: Cable One Inc. (MSO).

QUARTZSITE—Formerly served by Americable International Arizona Inc. No longer in operation. ICA: AZ0036.

RIO VERDE—Cox Communications. Now served by PHOENIX, AZ [AZ0001]. ICA: AZ0100.

ROBSON RANCH—Western Broadband, 9666 E Riggs Rd, Ste 108, Sun Lakes, AZ 85248. Phones: 480-895-8084; 800-998-8084. Fax: 480-895-3150. E-mail: ltaylor@wbhsi.net. Web Site: http://www.westernbroadband.net. ICA: AZ0141.
TV Market Ranking: Outside TV Markets (ROBSON RANCH).
Channel capacity: 78 (operating 2-way). Channels available but not in use: N.A.
Basic Service
Subscribers: 78.
Programming (received off-air): KAET (PBS) Phoenix; KASW (CW) Phoenix; KAZT-TV (IND) Phoenix; KDTP-LP Phoenix; KNXV-TV (ABC) Phoenix; KPAZ-TV (TBN) Phoenix; KPHO-TV (CBS) Phoenix; KPNX (NBC) Mesa; KPPX-TV (ION) Tolleson; KSAZ-TV (FOX) Phoenix; KTVK (IND) Phoenix; KTVW-DT (UNV) Phoenix; KUTP (MNT) Phoenix.
Programming (via satellite): America's Store; INSP; QVC; ShopNBC; TV Guide Network; WGN America.
Fee: $40.00 installation; $20.95 monthly.
Expanded Basic Service 1
Subscribers: N.A.
Programming (via satellite): ABC Family Channel; AMC; Animal Planet; Arts & Entertainment; Bravo; CNBC; CNN; Comedy Central; Country Music TV; C-SPAN; C-SPAN 2; Discovery Channel; Disney Channel; E! Entertainment Television; ESPN; ESPN 2; ESPN Classic Sports; Food Network; Fox News Channel; Fox Sports Net Arizona; FX; Golf Channel; GSN; Hallmark Channel; Headline News; HGTV; History Channel; Home Shopping Network; Lifetime; MSNBC; MTV; National Geographic Channel; Nickelodeon; SoapNet; Speed Channel; Spike TV; Syfy; TBS Superstation; Tennis Channel; The Learning Channel; Travel Channel; truTV; Turner Classic Movies; Turner Network TV; TV Land; USA Network; Versus; VH1; WE tv; WealthTV; Weather Channel.
Fee: $27.00 monthly.
Digital Basic Service
Subscribers: 39.
Programming (via satellite): BBC America; Bio; Bloomberg Television; Cooking Channel; Discovery Digital Networks; DMX Music; ESPNews; Fox College Sports Atlantic; Fox College Sports Central; Fox College Sports Pacific; Fox Movie Channel; G4; GAS; Great American Country; Halogen Network; History Channel International; Lifetime Movie Network; Lime; MTV Networks Digital Suite; Nick Jr.; NickToons TV; Outdoor Channel; Sleuth; Style Network; Trinity Broadcasting Network.
Fee: $11.50 monthly.
Digital Pay Service 1
Pay Units: 5.
Programming (via satellite): Cinemax (multiplexed); Encore (multiplexed); HBO (multiplexed); Showtime (multiplexed); Starz (multiplexed); The Movie Channel (multiplexed).
Fee: $13.00 monthly (HBO, Cinemax, Starz/Encore or Showtime/TMC).
Video-On-Demand: No
Pay-Per-View
iN DEMAND (delivered digitally); Hot Choice (delivered digitally).
Internet Service
Operational: Yes.
Subscribers: 57.
Broadband Service: In-house.
Fee: $99.00 installation; $41.95-$73.45 monthly.
Telephone Service
Digital: Operational
Fee: $69.95 installation; $39.95 monthly
Miles of Plant: 13.0 (coaxial); None (fiber optic). Homes passed: 388. Total homes in franchised area: 388. Coax miles includes fiber miles
President & Chief Executive Officer: Tom Basinger. Marketing & Programming Director: Bryan Johnson. Technical Operations Manager: Jerry Scullawl. Customer Service Manager: Linda Taylor.
Ownership: Western Broadband LLC (MSO).

ROOSEVELT—Formerly served by Salt River Cablevision. No longer in operation. ICA: AZ0131.

SADDLE MOUNTAIN—Formerly served by Eagle West Communications Inc. No longer in operation. ICA: AZ0109.

SADDLEBROOKE—Western Broadband, 9666 E Riggs Rd, Ste 108, Sun Lakes, AZ 85248. Phones: 480-895-8084; 800-998-8084. Fax: 480-895-3150. E-mail: ltaylor@wbhsi.net. Web Site: http://www.westernbroadband.net. ICA: AZ0140.
TV Market Ranking: Below 100 (SADDLEBROOKE).
Channel capacity: 78 (operating 2-way). Channels available but not in use: N.A.
Basic Service
Subscribers: 3,078.
Programming (received off-air): KGUN-TV (ABC) Tucson; KMSB (FOX) Tucson; KOLD-TV (CBS) Tucson; KTTU (MNT) Tucson; KUAT-TV (PBS) Tucson; KVOA (NBC) Tucson; KWBA-TV (CW) Sierra Vista.
Programming (via satellite): America's Store; C-SPAN; C-SPAN 2; QVC; ShopNBC; TBS Superstation; Telemundo; Trinity Broadcasting Network; WGN America.
Current originations: Leased Access.
Fee: $20.95 monthly.
Expanded Basic Service 1
Subscribers: N.A.
Programming (via satellite): ABC Family Channel; AMC; Animal Planet; Arts & Entertainment; Bravo; CNBC; CNN; Comedy Central; Country Music TV; Discovery Channel; Disney Channel; E! Entertainment Television; ESPN; ESPN 2; ESPN Classic Sports; Food Network; Fox News Channel; Fox Sports Net Arizona; FX; Golf Channel; GSN; Hallmark Channel; Headline News; HGTV; History Channel; Home Shopping Network; Lifetime; MSNBC; MTV; National Geographic Channel; Nickelodeon; SoapNet; Speed Channel; Spike TV; Syfy; Tennis Channel; The Learning Channel; Travel Channel; truTV; Turner Classic Movies; Turner Network TV; TV Guide Network; TV Land; USA Network; Versus; VH1; WE tv; WealthTV; Weather Channel.
Fee: $27.00 monthly.
Digital Basic Service
Subscribers: 813.
Programming (received off-air): KUSA (NBC) Denver; KWBA-TV (CW) Sierra Vista.
Programming (via satellite): BBC America; Bio; Bloomberg Television; Cooking Channel; Discovery Digital Networks; Discovery HD Theater; DMX Music; ESPNews; Fox College Sports Atlantic; Fox College Sports Central; Fox College Sports Pacific; Fox Movie Channel; G4; GAS; Great American Country; Halogen Network; HDNet; HDNet Movies; History Channel International; Lifetime Movie Network; Lime; MTV Networks Digital Suite; Nick Jr.; NickToons TV; Outdoor Channel; Sleuth; Style Network; Trinity Broadcasting Network; Universal HD.
Fee: $11.95 monthly.
Digital Pay Service 1
Pay Units: 464.
Programming (via satellite): Cinemax (multiplexed); Encore (multiplexed); HBO (multiplexed); Showtime (multiplexed); Starz (multiplexed); The Movie Channel (multiplexed).
Fee: $13.00 monthly (HBO, Cinemax, Starz/Encore or Showtime/TMC).
Video-On-Demand: No
Pay-Per-View
iN DEMAND (delivered digitally); Hot Choice (delivered digitally).
Internet Service
Operational: Yes.
Subscribers: 2,249.
Broadband Service: In-house.
Fee: $99.00 installation; $41.95-$73.45 monthly.
Telephone Service
Digital: Operational
Fee: $69.95 installation
Miles of Plant: 93.0 (coaxial); None (fiber optic). Homes passed: 4,549. Total homes in franchised area: 4,549. Coax miles includes fiber miles
President & Chief Executive Officer: Tom Basinger. Marketing & Programming Director: Bryan Johnson. Technical Operations Manager: Jerry Scullawl. Customer Service Manager: Linda Taylor.
Ownership: Western Broadband LLC (MSO).

SAFFORD—Cable One, 1996 W Thatcher Blvd, Safford, AZ 85546-3318. Phone: 928-428-1850. Fax: 928-428-0774. E-mail: sbrideau@cableone.net. Web Site: http://www.cableone.net. Also serves Graham County, Pima, Solomon, Swift Trail & Thatcher. ICA: AZ0021.
TV Market Ranking: Outside TV Markets (Graham County, Pima, SAFFORD, Solomon, Swift Trail, Thatcher). Franchise award date: N.A. Franchise expiration date: N.A. Began: April 1, 1962.
Channel capacity: 78 (operating 2-way). Channels available but not in use: None.
Basic Service
Subscribers: 4,370.
Programming (received off-air): KAET (PBS) Phoenix.
Programming (via microwave): KGUN-TV (ABC) Tucson; KNXV-TV (ABC) Phoenix; KPHO-TV (CBS) Phoenix; KPNX (NBC) Mesa; KSAZ-TV (FOX) Phoenix; KTVK (IND) Phoenix; KUTP (MNT) Phoenix.
Programming (via satellite): Animal Planet; Arts & Entertainment; BYU Television; Cartoon Network; CNBC; CNN; Comedy Central; Country Music TV; C-SPAN; C-SPAN 2; Discovery Channel; Disney Channel; ESPN; ESPN 2; Food Network; Fox News Channel; Fox Sports en Espanol; Fox Sports Net Arizona; FX; Headline News; HGTV; History Channel; Home Shopping Network; Lifetime; MSNBC; MTV; Nickelodeon; QVC; Syfy; TBS Superstation; The Learning Channel; Trinity Broadcasting Network; Turner Classic Movies; TV

Guide Network; TV Land; USA Network; VH1; Weather Channel; WGN America.
Fee: $15.47 installation; $46.00 monthly.

Digital Basic Service
Subscribers: 1,139.
Programming (via satellite): Bio; Boomerang; BYU Television; Canales N; Discovery Digital Networks; ESPN Classic Sports; ESPNews; FamilyNet; Fox College Sports Atlantic; Fox College Sports Central; Fox College Sports Pacific; Fox Movie Channel; Fox Soccer; Fuel TV; G4; Golf Channel; Great American Country; Hallmark Channel; History Channel International; INSP; Military History Channel; Music Choice; National Geographic Channel; Outdoor Channel; SoapNet; Speed Channel; Toon Disney; Trinity Broadcasting Network; truTV; TVG Network.
Fee: $9.95 monthly.

Digital Pay Service 1
Pay Units: N.A.
Programming (via satellite): Cinemax; Encore; HBO (multiplexed); Showtime; Starz; The Movie Channel.
Fee: $7.00 monthly (each).

Video-On-Demand: No

Pay-Per-View
Addressable homes: 1,805.
Addressable: Yes; Shorteez (delivered digitally); ESPN Now (delivered digitally); Pleasure (delivered digitally); ETC (delivered digitally); Playboy TV (delivered digitally); Fresh (delivered digitally).

Internet Service
Operational: Yes. Began: October 2, 2002.
Subscribers: 2,402.
Broadband Service: CableONE.net.
Fee: $75.00 installation; $43.00 monthly; $5.00 modem lease.

Telephone Service
Analog: Not Operational
Digital: Operational
Fee: $75.00 installation; $39.95 monthly

Miles of Plant: 185.0 (coaxial); None (fiber optic). Homes passed: 7,300. Total homes in franchised area: 7,300.
Manager: Stephen Brideau. Chief Technician: Chuck Dunlap.
City fee: 2% of gross.
Ownership: Cable One Inc. (MSO).

SALOME—Formerly served by San Carlos Cablevision. No longer in operation. ICA: AZ0128.

SAN CARLOS—San Carlos Apache Telecom, PO Box 1000, 10 Telecom Ln, Peridot, AZ 85542. Phone: 928-475-2433. Fax: 928-475-7076. Web Site: http://www.scatui.net. Also serves Peridot. ICA: AZ0046.
TV Market Ranking: Outside TV Markets (Peridot, SAN CARLOS). Franchise award date: N.A. Franchise expiration date: N.A. Began: April 1, 1983.
Channel capacity: 46 (not 2-way capable). Channels available but not in use: N.A.

Basic Service
Subscribers: 1,000.
Programming (received off-air): KAET (PBS) Phoenix; KFPH-TV (TEL) Flagstaff; KGUN-TV (ABC) Tucson; KNXV-TV (ABC) Phoenix; KPHO-TV (CBS) Phoenix; KPNX (NBC) Mesa; KSAZ-TV (FOX) Phoenix; KTVK (IND) Phoenix; KTVW-DT (UNV) Phoenix; KUTP (MNT) Phoenix; allband FM.
Programming (via satellite): ABC Family Channel; AMC; Arts & Entertainment; CNN; Comedy Central; C-SPAN; Discovery Channel; Disney Channel; ESPN; ESPN 2; FitTV; Fox Sports Net Arizona; Great American Country; Hallmark Channel; Headline News; HGTV; History Channel; MTV; Nickelodeon; Outdoor Channel; Spike TV; Syfy; TBS Superstation; The Learning Channel; Toon Disney; Trinity Broadcasting Network; Turner Classic Movies; Turner Network TV; TV Land; USA Network; VH1; Weather Channel.
Fee: $15.00 installation; $28.00 monthly.

Pay Service 1
Pay Units: 400.
Programming (via satellite): HBO; Showtime; The Movie Channel.
Fee: $8.00 monthly (Showtime or TMC), $10.00 monthly (HBO).

Internet Service
Operational: No.

Telephone Service
None

Miles of Plant: 34.0 (coaxial); None (fiber optic). Additional miles planned: 8.0 (coaxial). Homes passed: 1,430. Total homes in franchised area: 1,500.
Chief Technician: Richard Gomez. Sales & Marketing: Marion Case.
Ownership: San Carlos Apache Telecommunications Utility Inc. (MSO).

SAN MANUEL—Eagle West Communications Inc, 1030 S Mesa Dr, Mesa, AZ 85210. Phone: 480-813-8371. Fax: 480-813-4596. ICA: AZ0044.
TV Market Ranking: Below 100 (SAN MANUEL). Franchise award date: N.A. Franchise expiration date: N.A. Began: April 1, 1977.
Channel capacity: 40 (not 2-way capable). Channels available but not in use: N.A.

Basic Service
Subscribers: N.A. Included in East Mesa
Programming (received off-air): KGUN-TV (ABC) Tucson; KOLD-TV (CBS) Tucson; KSAZ-TV (FOX) Phoenix; KUAT-TV (PBS) Tucson; KVOA (NBC) Tucson; KWBA-TV (CW) Sierra Vista.
Programming (via satellite): AMC; Animal Planet; Arts & Entertainment; BET Networks; Cartoon Network; CNN; Comedy Central; C-SPAN; Discovery Channel; ESPN; Fox News Channel; Fox Sports Net; FX; G4; History Channel; Home Shopping Network; ION Television; Lifetime; Nickelodeon; Outdoor Channel; QVC; Syfy; TBS Superstation; The Learning Channel; Trinity Broadcasting Network; Turner Network TV; TV Land; Univision; USA Network; VH1; WGN America.
Fee: $35.00 installation; $31.95 monthly; $15.00 additional installation.

Pay Service 1
Pay Units: 43.
Programming (via satellite): Cinemax; HBO.
Fee: $9.95 monthly (each).

Video-On-Demand: No

Internet Service
Operational: No.

Telephone Service
None

Homes passed & miles of plant included in East Mesa
General Manager: Ernest McKay.
Ownership: Eagle West Communications (MSO).

SANTA RITA BEL AIRE—Cox Communications, 1440 E 15th St, Tucson, AZ 85719. Phones: 520-629-8470; 623-328-3121 (Phoenix office). Fax: 520-624-5914. Web Site: http://www.cox.com/arizona. ICA: AZ0137.
TV Market Ranking: Below 100 (SANTA RITA BEL AIRE).
Channel capacity: N.A. Channels available but not in use: N.A.

Basic Service
Subscribers: N.A.
Programming (received off-air): KGUN-TV (ABC) Tucson; KHRR (TMO) Tucson; KMSB (FOX) Tucson; KOLD-TV (CBS) Tucson; KTTU (MNT) Tucson; KUAT-TV (PBS) Tucson; KUVE-DT (UNV) Green Valley; KVOA (NBC) Tucson; KWBA-TV (CW) Sierra Vista.

Expanded Basic Service 1
Subscribers: N.A.
Programming (via satellite): CNBC; CNN; C-SPAN; C-SPAN 2; Discovery Channel; ESPN; ESPN 2; Fox News Channel; Fox Sports Net Arizona; Headline News; History Channel; Home Shopping Network; MSNBC; QVC; Speed Channel; TBS Superstation; Turner Network TV; USA Network; WGN America.

Internet Service
Operational: Yes.

Telephone Service
Digital: Operational

Vice President & Regional Manager: Steve Rizley. Vice President & Systems Manager: Anne Doris. Vice President, Marketing: Anthony Maldonado. Marketing Director: Nancy Duckett.
Ownership: Cox Communications Inc. (MSO).

SCOTTSDALE (portions)—Qwest Choice TV. IPTV service has been discontinued.. ICA: AZ5019.

SEDONA—NPG Cable, Inc., 65 Coffee Pot Dr, Ste A, Sedona, AZ 86336. Phone: 928-855-9855. Fax: 928-855-1979. Web Site: http://www.npgcable.net. Also serves Camp Verde, Cottonwood (southeastern portions), Lake Montezuma, Munds Park, Oak Creek (village), Pinewood & Verde Village. ICA: AZ0025.
TV Market Ranking: Below 100 (Munds Park, Oak Creek (village), Pinewood, SEDONA); Outside TV Markets (Camp Verde, Cottonwood (southeastern portions), Lake Montezuma, Verde Village). Franchise award date: November 1, 1959. Franchise expiration date: N.A. Began: November 1, 1959.
Channel capacity: 82 (operating 2-way). Channels available but not in use: 8.

Basic Service
Subscribers: 5,889.
Programming (received off-air): KAET (PBS) Phoenix; KASW (CW) Phoenix; KAZT-TV (IND) Phoenix; KFPH-TV (TEL) Flagstaff; KMOH-TV (IND) Kingman; KNAZ-TV (NBC) Flagstaff; KNXV-TV (ABC) Phoenix; KTVW-DT (UNV) Phoenix; KUTP (MNT) Phoenix; allband FM.
Programming (via microwave): KPHO-TV (CBS) Phoenix; KPNX (NBC) Mesa; KSAZ-TV (FOX) Phoenix; KTVK (IND) Phoenix.
Programming (via satellite): ABC Family Channel; AMC; Animal Planet; Arts & Entertainment; Cartoon Network; CNBC; CNN; Comedy Central; Country Music TV; C-SPAN; C-SPAN 2; Discovery Channel; Discovery Health Channel; E! Entertainment Television; ESPN; ESPN 2; ESPN Classic Sports; Eternal Word TV Network; Food Network; Fox News Channel; Fox Sports Net Arizona; FX; Golf Channel; Great American Country; Headline News; HGTV; History Channel; Home Shopping Network; Lifetime; MSNBC; MTV; Nickelodeon; Paxson Communications Corp.; Product Information Network; QVC; Spike TV; Syfy; TBS Superstation; The Learning Channel; Travel Channel; Trinity Broadcasting Network; truTV; Turner Classic Movies; Turner Network TV; TV Guide Network; TV Land; USA Network; VH1; Weather Channel; WGN America.
Fee: $39.95 installation; $43.80 monthly.

Digital Basic Service
Subscribers: 1,448.
Programming (via satellite): BBC America; Bio; Cooking Channel; Discovery Digital Networks; DMX Music; Do-It-Yourself; ESPNews; Fox College Sports Atlantic; Fox College Sports Central; Fox College Sports Pacific; Fox Soccer; Fox Sports en Espanol; Fuel TV; GAS; GSN; History Channel International; Independent Film Channel; Lifetime Movie Network; Lime; MTV Networks Digital Suite; National Geographic Channel; Nick Jr.; NickToons TV; Speed Channel; Versus; WE tv.
Fee: $11.95 monthly.

Digital Pay Service 1
Pay Units: N.A.
Programming (via satellite): Cinemax (multiplexed); Encore (multiplexed); HBO (multiplexed); Showtime (multiplexed); Starz (multiplexed); The Movie Channel (multiplexed).
Fee: $6.95 monthly (Cinemax), $9.95 monthly (Starz/Encore), $11.95 monthly (Showtime/TMC), $12.00 monthly (HBO).

Video-On-Demand: No

Pay-Per-View
iN DEMAND (delivered digitally).

Internet Service
Operational: Yes.
Subscribers: 2,543.
Broadband Service: Uneedspeed.
Fee: $59.95 installation; $24.95 monthly; $5.00 modem lease.

Telephone Service
Analog: Not Operational
Digital: Operational
Fee: $59.95 installation; $39.95 monthly

Miles of Plant: 360.0 (coaxial); None (fiber optic). Homes passed: 17,846. Total homes in franchised area: 20,000.
General Manager: Karen Foster. Plant Manager: John Patterson.
County fee: $50.00 annually (Coconino & Yavapai).
Ownership: News Press & Gazette Co. (MSO).

SELLS—Formerly served by Red Hawk Cable. No longer in operation. ICA: AZ0053.

SHOW LOW—Cable One, 1341 E Thornton St, Show Low, AZ 85901. Phones: 602-364-6000 (Phoenix office); 800-742-4524; 928-537-2279. Fax: 928-537-0607. E-mail: bdorsey@cableone.net. Web Site: http://www.cableone.net. Also serves Bushman Acres, Holbrook, Joseph City, Lakeside, Navajo County (portions), Pinetop, Pineview, Snowflake, Taylor, Wagon Wheel, White Mountain Lake & Winslow. ICA: AZ0014.
TV Market Ranking: Below 100 (Bushman Acres, Holbrook, Joseph City, Navajo County (portions) (portions), Pineview, Snowflake, Taylor, Wagon Wheel, Winslow); Outside TV Markets (Lakeside, Navajo County (portions) (portions), Pinetop, SHOW LOW, White Mountain Lake). Franchise award date: September 1, 1968. Franchise expiration date: N.A. Began: April 1, 1962.
Channel capacity: 62 (operating 2-way). Channels available but not in use: None.

Basic Service
Subscribers: 13,000.
Programming (received off-air): KAET (PBS) Phoenix; KNXV-TV (ABC) Phoenix; 11 FMs.
Programming (via microwave): KPHO-TV (CBS) Phoenix; KPNX (NBC) Mesa; KSAZ-TV (FOX) Phoenix; KTVK (IND) Phoenix.
Programming (via satellite): Telemundo; Univision; WGN America.
Current originations: Government Access.
Fee: $30.00 installation; $46.00 monthly; $17.95 additional installation.

Expanded Basic Service 1
Subscribers: N.A.
Programming (via satellite): ABC Family Channel; AMC; Animal Planet; Arts & Entertainment; Cartoon Network; CNBC; CNN; Country Music TV; C-SPAN; Discovery Channel; Disney Channel; ESPN; ESPN 2; Food Network; Fox News Channel; Fox Sports Net Arizona; FX; Headline News; HGTV; History Channel; Home Shopping Network; MSNBC; MTV; Nickelodeon; QVC; Spike TV; Syfy; TBS Superstation; The Learning Channel; Travel Channel; Turner Classic Movies; Turner Network TV; TV Guide Network; TV Land; USA Network; VH1; Weather Channel.
Fee: $42.50 monthly.

Digital Basic Service
Subscribers: 3,500.
Programming (via satellite): 3 Angels Broadcasting Network; Bio; Boomerang; BYU Television; Canales N; Discovery Digital Networks; ESPN Classic Sports; FamilyNet; Fox College Sports Atlantic; Fox College Sports Central; Fox College Sports Pacific; Fox Movie Channel; Fox Soccer; Fuel TV; Golf Channel; Great American Country; GSN; Hallmark Channel; History Channel International; INSP; Music Choice; National Geographic Channel; Outdoor Channel; SoapNet; Speed Channel; Toon Disney; Trinity Broadcasting Network; truTV; Turner Network TV HD; TVG Network; Universal HD; WE tv.
Fee: $8.95 monthly.

Digital Pay Service 1
Pay Units: N.A.
Programming (via satellite): Cinemax (multiplexed); HBO (multiplexed); Showtime; Showtime HD; Starz In Black; Sundance Channel; The Movie Channel (multiplexed); The Movie Channel HD.
Fee: $7.00 monthly (each).

Video-On-Demand: No

Pay-Per-View
Movies (delivered digitally); Pleasure (delivered digitally); Ten Clips (delivered digitally); Ten Blox (delivered digitally); Ten Blue (delivered digitally).

Internet Service
Operational: Yes. Began: June 1, 2002.
Subscribers: 4,500.
Broadband Service: CableONE.net.
Fee: $75.00 installation; $43.00 monthly; $5.00 modem lease.

Telephone Service
Digital: Operational
Fee: $75.00 installation; $39.95 monthly

Miles of Plant: 600.0 (coaxial); 10.0 (fiber optic). Additional miles planned: 15.0 (coaxial). Homes passed: 28,000. Total homes in franchised area: 28,000.

Manager: Brad Dorsey. Marketing Director: Glen Erickson. Chief Technician: Lyle Sumic.

City fee: 3% of gross.

Ownership: Cable One Inc. (MSO).

SIERRA VISTA—Cox Communications, 1440 E 15th St, Tucson, AZ 85719. Phones: 623-328-3121 (Phoenix office); 520-629-8470. Fax: 520-624-5918. Web Site: http://www.cox.com/arizona. Also serves Ash Canyon (unincorporated area), Carr Canyon (unincorporated area), Fort Huachuca, Hereford, Miller Canyon (unincorporated area), Ramsey Canyon (unincorporated area) & Stump Canyon (unincorporated area). ICA: AZ0005.

TV Market Ranking: Below 100 (Ash Canyon (unincorporated area), Carr Canyon (unincorporated area), Fort Huachuca, Hereford, Miller Canyon (unincorporated area), Ramsey Canyon (unincorporated area), SIERRA VISTA, Stump Canyon (unincorporated area)). Franchise award date: June 1, 1967. Franchise expiration date: N.A. Began: January 1, 1967.

Channel capacity: 75 (operating 2-way). Channels available but not in use: None.

Basic Service
Subscribers: 12,430.
Programming (received off-air): KGUN-TV (ABC) Tucson; KMSB (FOX) Tucson; KOLD-TV (CBS) Tucson; KTTU (MNT) Tucson; KUAT-TV (PBS) Tucson; KVOA (NBC) Tucson; KWBA-TV (CW) Sierra Vista; 20 FMs.
Programming (via satellite): Discovery Channel; Headline News; TBS Superstation; WGN America.
Current originations: Government Access; Educational Access.
Fee: $50.21 installation; $12.46 monthly.

Expanded Basic Service 1
Subscribers: N.A.
Programming (via satellite): ABC Family Channel; AMC; Animal Planet; Arts & Entertainment; BET Networks; Cartoon Network; CNBC; CNN; Comcast Sports Net Southwest; Comedy Central; Country Music TV; C-SPAN; Disney Channel; E! Entertainment Television; ESPN; ESPN 2; Food Network; Fox News Channel; Hallmark Channel; HGTV; History Channel; Home Shopping Network; Lifetime; MoviePlex; MTV; Nickelodeon; Spike TV; Syfy; The Learning Channel; Travel Channel; Turner Classic Movies; Turner Network TV; TV Guide Network; USA Network; VH1; Weather Channel.
Fee: $27.52 monthly.

Digital Basic Service
Subscribers: 9,100.
Programming (via satellite): BBC America; Bravo; Discovery Digital Networks; ESPN Classic Sports; Fox Sports World; Golf Channel; GSN; HGTV; Independent Film Channel; Versus; WE tv.
Fee: $12.00 monthly.

Pay Service 1
Pay Units: 1,367.
Programming (via satellite): Cinemax; Encore; HBO; Showtime; Starz; The Movie Channel.
Fee: $20.00 installation; $10.95 monthly (Cinemax, HBO, Showtime & TMC or Starz & Encore).

Digital Pay Service 1
Pay Units: N.A.
Programming (via satellite): Cinemax (multiplexed); Encore (multiplexed); HBO (multiplexed); Showtime (multiplexed); Starz (multiplexed); The Movie Channel.
Fee: $10.95 monthly (Cinemax, HBO, Showtime/TMC, or Starz/Encore).

Video-On-Demand: Planned

Pay-Per-View
Addressable homes: 9,100.
ESPN Now (delivered digitally), Addressable: Yes; iN DEMAND (delivered digitally); Fresh (delivered digitally).

Internet Service
Operational: Yes.
Subscribers: 870.
Broadband Service: Cox High Speed Internet.
Fee: $49.95 monthly.

Telephone Service
Digital: Planned

Miles of Plant: 656.0 (coaxial); None (fiber optic). Homes passed: 15,271. Total homes in franchised area: 32,697.

Vice President & Regional Manager: Steve Rizley. Vice President, Marketing: Anthony Maldonado. Vice President & Systems Manager: Anne Doris. Media Relations Manager: Andrea Katsenes.

City fee: 2% of gross.

Ownership: Cox Communications Inc. (MSO).

ST. JOHNS—Eagle West Communications Inc, 1030 S Mesa Dr, Mesa, AZ 85210. Phone: 480-813-4596. Fax: 480-813-4596. ICA: AZ0045.

TV Market Ranking: Outside TV Markets (ST. JOHNS). Franchise award date: N.A. Franchise expiration date: N.A. Began: September 1, 1977.

Channel capacity: 42 (not 2-way capable). Channels available but not in use: N.A.

Basic Service
Subscribers: N.A. Included in East Mesa
Programming (received off-air): KAET (PBS) Phoenix.
Programming (via microwave): KNXV-TV (ABC) Phoenix; KPHO-TV (CBS) Phoenix; KPNX (NBC) Mesa; KSAZ-TV (FOX) Phoenix; KTVK (IND) Phoenix; KUTP (MNT) Phoenix.
Programming (via satellite): ABC Family Channel; AMC; Arts & Entertainment; CNN; Country Music TV; Discovery Channel; Disney Channel; ESPN; ESPN 2; Fox Sports Net Arizona; History Channel; Home Shopping Network; Lifetime; Nickelodeon; Spike TV; TBS Superstation; The Learning Channel; Turner Network TV; TV Land; USA Network; Weather Channel; WGN America.
Current originations: Public Access.
Fee: $19.95 installation; $31.95 monthly.

Pay Service 1
Pay Units: 32.
Programming (via satellite): HBO.
Fee: $10.00 monthly.

Pay Service 2
Pay Units: 4.
Programming (via satellite): Cinemax.
Fee: $12.95 monthly.

Video-On-Demand: No

Internet Service
Operational: No.

Telephone Service
None

Homes passed & miles of plant included in East Mesa

General Manager: Ernest McKay.

Ownership: Eagle West Communications (MSO).

SUN LAKES—Western Broadband, 9666 E Riggs Rd, Ste 108, Sun Lakes, AZ 85248. Phones: 480-895-8084; 800-998-8084. Fax: 480-895-3150. E-mail: ltaylor@wbhsi.net. Web Site: http://www.westernbroadband.net. ICA: AZ0139.

TV Market Ranking: 43 (SUN LAKES).

Channel capacity: 78 (operating 2-way). Channels available but not in use: N.A.

Basic Service
Subscribers: 6,626.
Programming (received off-air): KAET (PBS) Phoenix; KASW (CW) Phoenix; KAZT-TV (IND) Phoenix; KDPH-LP (TMO) Phoenix; KNXV-TV (ABC) Phoenix; KPAZ-TV (TBN) Phoenix; KPHO-TV (CBS) Phoenix; KPNX (NBC) Mesa; KPPX-TV (ION) Tolleson; KSAZ-TV (FOX) Phoenix; KTVK (IND) Phoenix; KTVW-DT (UNV) Phoenix; KUTP (MNT) Phoenix.
Programming (via satellite): QVC; ShopNBC; TBS Superstation; WGN America.
Current originations: Leased Access.
Fee: $40.00 installation; $20.95 monthly.

Expanded Basic Service 1
Subscribers: N.A.
Programming (via satellite): ABC Family Channel; AMC; Animal Planet; Arts & Entertainment; Bravo; CNBC; CNN; Comedy Central; Country Music TV; C-SPAN; C-SPAN 2; Discovery Channel; Disney Channel; E! Entertainment Television; ESPN; ESPN 2; ESPN Classic Sports; Food Network; Fox News Channel; Fox Sports Net Arizona; FX; Golf Channel; GSN; Hallmark Channel; Headline News; HGTV; History Channel; Home Shopping Network; INSP; Jewelry Television; Lifetime; MSNBC; MTV; National Geographic Channel; Nickelodeon; SoapNet; Speed Channel; Spike TV; Syfy; Tennis Channel; The Learning Channel; Travel Channel; truTV; Turner Classic Movies; Turner Network TV; TV Guide Network; TV Land; USA Network; Versus; VH1; WE tv; WealthTV; Weather Channel.
Fee: $27.95 monthly.

Digital Basic Service
Subscribers: 1,568.
Programming (received off-air): KAET (PBS) Phoenix; KNXV-TV (ABC) Phoenix; KPHO-TV (CBS) Phoenix; KPNX (NBC) Mesa; KSAZ-TV (FOX) Phoenix; KWBA-TV (CW) Sierra Vista.
Programming (via satellite): BBC America; Bio; Bloomberg Television; Cooking Channel; Discovery Digital Networks; Discovery HD Theater; DMX Music; Do-It-Yourself; ESPNews; Fox College Sports Atlantic; Fox College Sports Central; Fox College Sports Pacific; Fox Movie Channel; G4; GAS; Great American Country; Halogen Network; HDNet; HDNet Movies; History Channel International; Lifetime Movie Network; Lime; MTV Networks Digital Suite; Nick Jr.; NickToons TV; Outdoor Channel; Sleuth; Style Network; Trinity Broadcasting Network; Universal HD.
Fee: $19.95 monthly.

Digital Pay Service 1
Pay Units: 796.
Programming (via satellite): Cinemax (multiplexed); Encore (multiplexed); HBO (multiplexed); Showtime (multiplexed); Starz (multiplexed); The Movie Channel (multiplexed).
Fee: $13.00 monthly (Cinemax, HBO, Starz/Encore, or Showtime/TMC).

Video-On-Demand: No

Pay-Per-View
iN DEMAND (delivered digitally); Hot Choice (delivered digitally).

Internet Service
Operational: Yes.
Subscribers: 3,750.
Fee: $99.00 installation; $41.95-$73.45 monthly.

Telephone Service
Digital: Operational
Fee: $69.95 installation

Miles of Plant: None (coaxial); 105.0 (fiber optic). Homes passed: 11,677. Total homes in franchised area: 11,677.

President & Chief Executive Officer: Tom Basinger. Marketing & Programming Director: Bryan Johnson. Technical Oper-

ations Manager: Jerry Scullawl. Customer Service Manager: Linda Taylor.
Ownership: Western Broadband LLC (MSO).

SUPERIOR—Eagle West Communications Inc, 1030 S Mesa Dr, Mesa, AZ 85210. Phone: 480-813-8371. Fax: 480-813-4596. ICA: AZ0042.
TV Market Ranking: Outside TV Markets (SUPERIOR). Franchise award date: N.A. Franchise expiration date: N.A. Began: September 15, 1981.
Channel capacity: 40 (not 2-way capable). Channels available but not in use: N.A.
Basic Service
Subscribers: N.A. Included in East Mesa
Programming (received off-air): KAET (PBS) Phoenix; KNXV-TV (ABC) Phoenix; KPHO-TV (CBS) Phoenix; KPNX (NBC) Mesa; KSAZ-TV (FOX) Phoenix; KTVK (IND) Phoenix; KTVW-DT (UNV) Phoenix; KUTP (MNT) Phoenix.
Programming (via satellite): ABC Family Channel; Animal Planet; Bloomberg Television; CNN; Comedy Central; Country Music TV; C-SPAN; Discovery Channel; E! Entertainment Television; ESPN; ESPN Classic Sports; Fox News Channel; GalaVision; Hallmark Channel; Headline News; Lifetime; MTV; Nickelodeon; Outdoor Channel; QVC; Spike TV; TBS Superstation; The Learning Channel; truTV; TV Land; USA Network; Weather Channel; WGN America.
Fee: $31.95 monthly.
Pay Service 1
Pay Units: 484.
Programming (via satellite): Cinemax; Encore; HBO; Starz.
Fee: $4.95 monthly (Starz or Encore), $13.00 monthly (HBO).
Video-On-Demand: No
Internet Service
Operational: No, DSL.
Telephone Service
None
Homes passed & miles of plant included in East Mesa
General Manager: Ernest McKay.
City fee: 2% of gross.
Ownership: Eagle West Communications (MSO).

TSAILE—Formerly served by Frontier Communications. No longer in operation. ICA: AZ0124.

TUBA CITY—Indevideo Co. Inc., PO Box 422, 5901 E McKellips Rd, Ste 109, Mesa, AZ 85215. Phones: 480-656-7432; 800-234-8333. Fax: 480-656-8704. E-mail: indevideo2@juno.com. ICA: AZ0039.
TV Market Ranking: Outside TV Markets (TUBA CITY). Franchise award date: January 1, 1972. Franchise expiration date: N.A. Began: March 1, 1972.
Channel capacity: 60 (not 2-way capable). Channels available but not in use: 43.
Basic Service
Subscribers: 1,005.
Programming (received off-air): KAET (PBS) Phoenix; KASW (CW) Phoenix; KNAZ-TV (NBC) Flagstaff; KNXV-TV (ABC) Phoenix; KPNX (NBC) Mesa; KUTP (MNT) Phoenix.
Programming (via microwave): KPHO-TV (CBS) Phoenix; KSAZ-TV (FOX) Phoenix; KTVK (IND) Phoenix.
Programming (via satellite): AMC; Arts & Entertainment; CNN; Country Music TV; C-SPAN; Discovery Channel; ESPN; ESPN 2; Fox News Channel; FX; G4; GSN; Headline News; HGTV; History Channel; National Geographic Channel; Nickelodeon; QVC; Speed Channel; Spike TV; The Learning Channel; Trinity Broadcasting Network; Turner Network TV; TV Land; VH1; WGN America.
Current originations: Educational Access.
Fee: $29.95 monthly.
Pay Service 1
Pay Units: N.A.
Programming (via satellite): Encore; HBO (multiplexed); Starz.
Fee: $10.00 monthly.
Video-On-Demand: No
Internet Service
Operational: No.
Telephone Service
None
Miles of Plant: 38.0 (coaxial); None (fiber optic). Homes passed: 1,890.
General Manager & Chief Technician: Kevin Williams.
Ownership: Indevideo Co. Inc. (MSO).

TUCSON—Cox Communications, 1440 E 15th St, Tucson, AZ 85719. Phones: 623-328-3121 (Phoenix office); 520-629-8470. Fax: 520-624-5918. Web Site: http://www.cox.com/arizona. Also serves Davis-Monthan AFB, Foothills, Green Valley, Pima County, Rita Ranch, Sahuarita, Santo Tomas & South Tucson. ICA: AZ0002.
TV Market Ranking: Below 100 (Davis-Monthan AFB, Foothills, Green Valley, Pima County (portions), Rita Ranch, Sahuarita, Santo Tomas, South Tucson, TUCSON); Outside TV Markets (Pima County (portions)). Franchise award date: December 7, 1981. Franchise expiration date: N.A. Began: September 7, 1982.
Channel capacity: N.A. Channels available but not in use: N.A.
Basic Service
Subscribers: 127,871.
Programming (received off-air): KGUN-TV (ABC) Tucson; KHRR (TMO) Tucson; KMSB (FOX) Tucson; KOLD-TV (CBS) Tucson; KTTU (MNT) Tucson; KUAT-TV (PBS) Tucson; KVOA (NBC) Tucson; KWBA-TV (CW) Sierra Vista; 30 FMs.
Programming (via satellite): C-SPAN; Hallmark Channel; Home Shopping Network; QVC; TV Guide Network; Weather Channel; WGN America.
Programming (via translator): KTVW-DT (UNV) Phoenix.
Current originations: Government Access; Educational Access; Public Access.
Planned originations: Leased Access; Religious Access.
Fee: $50.21 installation; $15.07 monthly.
Expanded Basic Service 1
Subscribers: 93,801.
Programming (via satellite): ABC Family Channel; AMC; Animal Planet; Arts & Entertainment; BET Networks; Bravo; Cartoon Network; CNBC; CNN; Comedy Central; Country Music TV; Discovery Channel; Disney Channel; E! Entertainment Television; ESPN; ESPN 2; Food Network; Fox News Channel; Fox Sports Net Arizona; FX; Golf Channel; Headline News; HGTV; History Channel; Lifetime; MSNBC; MTV; Nickelodeon; Oxygen; Speed Channel; Spike TV; TBS Superstation; The Learning Channel; Travel Channel; Turner Classic Movies; Turner Network TV; TV Land; USA Network; Versus; VH1.
Fee: $22.72 monthly.
Digital Basic Service
Subscribers: 55,691.
Programming (via satellite): Barker; BBC America; Bloomberg Television; Cartoon Network Tambien en Espanol; Discovery Digital Networks; Encore Action; ESPN Classic Sports; Fox Sports en Espanol; Fox Sports World; G4; GSN; Independent Film Channel; INSP; Lifetime Movie Network; MuchMusic Network; Music Choice; SoapNet; Sundance Channel; Syfy; Toon Disney; truTV; WE tv.
Fee: $15.45 monthly.
Pay Service 1
Pay Units: 84,615.
Programming (via satellite): Cinemax; Encore; HBO (multiplexed); Showtime; Starz; The Movie Channel.
Fee: $20.45 installation; $10.95 monthly (Cinemax, HBO, Showtime/TMC, or Starz/Encore).
Digital Pay Service 1
Pay Units: N.A.
Programming (via satellite): Cinemax (multiplexed); Encore; HBO (multiplexed); Showtime (multiplexed); Starz (multiplexed); The Movie Channel (multiplexed).
Fee: $10.95 monthly (Cinemax, HBO, Showtime/TMC, or Starz/Encore).
Video-On-Demand: No
Pay-Per-View
Addressable homes: 55,691.
ESPN Extra (delivered digitally), Addressable: Yes; ESPN Full Court (delivered digitally); ESPN Game Plan (delivered digitally); ESPN Now (delivered digitally); iN DEMAND (delivered digitally); Playboy TV (delivered digitally); Spice (delivered digitally); Spice2 (delivered digitally); The Hot Network (delivered digitally); The Hot Zone.
Internet Service
Operational: Yes.
Broadband Service: Cox High Speed Internet.
Fee: $149.95 installation; $49.95 monthly; $15.00 modem lease.
Telephone Service
None
Miles of Plant: 2,862.0 (coaxial); None (fiber optic). Homes passed: 201,619. Total homes in franchised area: 210,969.
Vice President & Systems Manager: Anne Doris. Vice President & Regional Manager: Steve Rizley. Vice President, Marketing: Anthony Maldonado. Marketing Director: Nancy Duckett. Media Relations Director: Andrea Katsenes. Media Relations Manager: Monica Contreras.
City fee: 5% of gross.
Ownership: Cox Communications Inc. (MSO).

TUCSON—Formerly served by Sprint Corp. No longer in operation. ICA: AZ0118.

TUCSON ESTATES—Comcast Cable. Now served by PIMA VALLEY, AZ [AZ0003]. ICA: AZ0105.

TUSAYAN—Indevideo Co. Inc., PO Box 422, 5901 E McKellips Rd, Ste 109, Mesa, AZ 85215. Phones: 480-656-7432; 800-234-8333. Fax: 480-656-8704. E-mail: indevideo2@juno.com. ICA: AZ0063.
TV Market Ranking: Outside TV Markets (TUSAYAN). Franchise award date: January 1, 1984. Franchise expiration date: N.A. Began: September 1, 1985.
Channel capacity: 36 (not 2-way capable). Channels available but not in use: None.
Basic Service
Subscribers: 85.
Programming (received off-air): KAET (PBS) Phoenix; KPHO-TV (CBS) Phoenix; KPNX (NBC) Mesa; KSAZ-TV (FOX) Phoenix; KTVK (IND) Phoenix.
Programming (via satellite): CNN; Discovery Channel; ESPN; TBS Superstation; WGN America.
Fee: $27.50 monthly.
Pay Service 1
Pay Units: N.A.
Programming (via satellite): The Movie Channel.
Video-On-Demand: No
Internet Service
Operational: No.
Telephone Service
None
Miles of Plant: 17.0 (coaxial); None (fiber optic). Homes passed: 250.
General Manager & Chief Technician: Kevin Williams.
Ownership: Indevideo Co. Inc. (MSO).

WELLTON—Beamspeed LLC, 2481 E Palo Verde St, Yuma, AZ 85365-3619. Phones: 928-317-6866; 928-726-0896. Fax: 928-726-3238. Web Site: http://www.beamspeed.net. ICA: AZ0062.
TV Market Ranking: Below 100 (WELLTON). Franchise award date: N.A. Franchise expiration date: N.A. Began: October 8, 1987.
Channel capacity: 35 (not 2-way capable). Channels available but not in use: None.
Basic Service
Subscribers: 145.
Programming (received off-air): KAET (PBS) Phoenix; KASW (CW) Phoenix; KECY-TV (ABC, FOX, MNT, TMO) El Centro; KNXV-TV (ABC) Phoenix; KSWT (CBS, CW) Yuma; KTVK (IND) Phoenix; KVYE (UNV) El Centro; KYMA-DT (NBC) Yuma.
Programming (via satellite): ABC Family Channel; AMC; AmericanLife TV Network; Animal Planet; Arts & Entertainment; Bravo; CNBC; CNN; Comedy Central; Country Music TV; C-SPAN; Discovery Channel; Disney Channel; E! Entertainment Television; ESPN; ESPN 2; Fox News Channel; GalaVision; Headline News; HGTV; History Channel; INSP; Lifetime; MTV; Nickelodeon; QVC; Spike TV; Syfy; TBS Superstation; The Learning Channel; Travel Channel; Turner Classic Movies; Turner Network TV; TV Land; USA Network; VH1; WE tv; WGN America.
Fee: $60.00 installation; $36.70 monthly; $2.10 converter; $31.50 additional installation.
Pay Service 1
Pay Units: 4.
Programming (via satellite): HBO.
Fee: $25.00 installation; $12.95 monthly.
Pay Service 2
Pay Units: 5.
Programming (via satellite): Cinemax.
Fee: $12.95 monthly.
Internet Service
Operational: No.
Telephone Service
None
Miles of Plant: 9.0 (coaxial); None (fiber optic). Homes passed: 525.
General Manager: Carter Hendrick. Chief Technician: Mike Straub. Marketing Director: Christi Weber.
City fee: 5% of gross.
Ownership: Beamspeed LLC (MSO).

WICKENBURG—Cox Communications. Now served by PHOENIX, AZ [AZ0001]. ICA: AZ0132.

WILLCOX—Cox Communications, 1440 E 15th St, Tucson, AZ 85719. Phones: 623-328-3121 (Phoenix office); 520-629-8470. Fax: 520-624-5918. Web Site: http://www.

cox.com/arizona. Also serves St. David & Sunsites. ICA: AZ0108.

TV Market Ranking: Below 100 (St. David); Outside TV Markets (Sunsites, WILLCOX). Franchise award date: N.A. Franchise expiration date: N.A. Began: N.A.

Channel capacity: 31 (operating 2-way). Channels available but not in use: 1.

Basic Service

Subscribers: 2,711.

Programming (received off-air): KGUN-TV (ABC) Tucson; KMSB (FOX) Tucson; KOLD-TV (CBS) Tucson; KTTU (MNT) Tucson; KUAT-TV (PBS) Tucson; KVOA (NBC) Tucson; KWBA-TV (CW) Sierra Vista.

Programming (via satellite): ABC Family Channel; Discovery Channel; Headline News; MTV; TBS Superstation; Univision; WGN America.

Fee: $50.21 installation; $13.38 monthly.

Expanded Basic Service 1

Subscribers: N.A.

Programming (via satellite): Arts & Entertainment; CNN; Country Music TV; C-SPAN; Disney Channel; ESPN; Fox Sports Net Arizona; Lifetime; MSNBC; Nickelodeon; Spike TV; Turner Network TV; USA Network.

Fee: $19.61 monthly.

Digital Basic Service

Subscribers: 325.

Programming (via satellite): BBC America; Bravo; Discovery Digital Networks; DMX Music; ESPN Classic Sports; ESPNews; Fox Soccer; Golf Channel; GSN; HGTV; History Channel; Independent Film Channel; Syfy; Turner Classic Movies; Versus; WE tv.

Fee: $10.00 monthly.

Digital Pay Service 1

Pay Units: 652.

Programming (via satellite): Cinemax (multiplexed); Encore (multiplexed); HBO (multiplexed); Showtime (multiplexed); Starz (multiplexed).

Fee: $10.95 monthly (Cinemax, HBO, Showtime, or Starz/Encore).

Video-On-Demand: Planned

Pay-Per-View

iN DEMAND (delivered digitally), Addressable: Yes; Playboy TV (delivered digitally).

Internet Service

Operational: Yes.

Telephone Service

Analog: Not Operational

Digital: Planned

Homes passed: 3,777.

Vice President & Regional Manager: Steve Rizley. Vice President & Systems Manager: Anne Doris. Vice President, Marketing: Anthony Maldonado. Marketing Manager: Nancy Duckett. Media Relations Director: Andrea Katsones. Media Relations Manager: Monica Contreras.

Ownership: Cox Communications Inc. (MSO).

WILLIAMS—Eagle West Communications Inc, 1030 S Mesa Dr, Mesa, AZ 85210. Phone: 480-813-8371. Fax: 480-813-4596. Also serves Coconino County. ICA: AZ0106.

TV Market Ranking: Below 100 (Coconino County (portions), WILLIAMS); Outside TV Markets (Coconino County (portions)). Franchise award date: December 1, 1975. Franchise expiration date: N.A. Began: December 1, 1975.

Channel capacity: 41 (not 2-way capable). Channels available but not in use: N.A.

Basic Service

Subscribers: N.A. Included in East Mesa

Programming (received off-air): KAET (PBS) Phoenix; KFPH-TV (TEL) Flagstaff; KNAZ-TV (NBC) Flagstaff; KPHO-TV (CBS) Phoenix; KPNX (NBC) Mesa; KSAZ-TV (FOX) Phoenix.

Programming (via satellite): QVC; TBS Superstation; WGN America.

Programming (via translator): KNXV-TV (ABC) Phoenix; KTVK (IND) Phoenix.

Fee: $39.95 installation; $31.95 monthly.

Expanded Basic Service 1

Subscribers: 670.

Programming (via satellite): ABC Family Channel; AMC; Arts & Entertainment; Cartoon Network; CNN; Country Music TV; Discovery Channel; ESPN; ESPN 2; History Channel; Nickelodeon; Spike TV; Syfy; The Learning Channel; Trinity Broadcasting Network; Turner Network TV; TV Land; USA Network; Weather Channel.

Fee: $7.00 monthly.

Pay Service 1

Pay Units: 54.

Programming (via satellite): HBO.

Fee: $9.95 monthly.

Video-On-Demand: No

Internet Service

Operational: No.

Telephone Service

None

Homes passed & miles of plant included in East Mesa

General Manager: Ernest McKay.

City fee: 2% of gross.

Ownership: Eagle West Communications (MSO).

WINSLOW—Cable One. Now served by SHOW LOW, AZ [AZ0014]. ICA: AZ0026.

YARNELL—Eagle West Communications Inc, 1030 S Mesa Dr, Mesa, AZ 85210. Phone: 480-813-8371. Fax: 480-813-4596. ICA: AZ0069.

TV Market Ranking: Outside TV Markets (YARNELL). Franchise award date: N.A. Franchise expiration date: N.A. Began: January 1, 1960.

Channel capacity: 41 (not 2-way capable). Channels available but not in use: N.A.

Basic Service

Subscribers: N.A. Included in East Mesa

Programming (received off-air): KAET (PBS) Phoenix; KNXV-TV (ABC) Phoenix; KPHO-TV (CBS) Phoenix; KPNX (NBC) Mesa; KSAZ-TV (FOX) Phoenix; KTVK (IND) Phoenix; KUTP (MNT) Phoenix; 1 FM.

Programming (via satellite): ABC Family Channel; AMC; Arts & Entertainment; CNN; Country Music TV; C-SPAN; Discovery Channel; ESPN; Headline News; HGTV; History Channel; Lifetime; Nickelodeon; QVC; Spike TV; Turner Network TV; USA Network; Weather Channel; WGN America.

Fee: $25.00 installation; $31.95 monthly.

Pay Service 1

Pay Units: 9.

Programming (via satellite): HBO.

Fee: $9.95 monthly.

Video-On-Demand: No

Internet Service

Operational: No.

Telephone Service

None

Homes passed & miles of plant included in East Mesa

General Manager: Ernest McKay.

Ownership: Eagle West Communications (MSO).

YUMA—Time Warner Cable, 1289 S 2nd Ave, Yuma, AZ 85364-4715. Phones: 928-782-0022 (Local office); 888-683-1000 (Customer service). Fax: 928-783-0242. Web Site: http://www.timewarnercable.com/Yuma-ElCentro. Also serves Marine Corps Air Station, San Luis, Somerton, Yuma County & Yuma Proving Ground, AZ; Winterhaven, CA. ICA: AZ0004.

TV Market Ranking: Below 100 (Marine Corps Air Station, San Luis, Somerton, Winterhaven, YUMA, Yuma County, Yuma Proving Ground). Franchise award date: N.A. Franchise expiration date: N.A. Began: August 1, 1961.

Channel capacity: N.A. Channels available but not in use: None.

Basic Service

Subscribers: 42,830 Includes El Centro.

Programming (received off-air): KAET (PBS) Phoenix; KAZT-TV (IND) Phoenix; KCOP-TV (MNT) Los Angeles; KECY-TV (ABC, FOX, MNT, TMO) El Centro; KNXV-TV (ABC) Phoenix; KSWT (CBS, CW) Yuma; KTVK (IND) Phoenix; KVYE (UNV) El Centro; KYMA-DT (NBC) Yuma; 13 FMs.

Programming (via satellite): ABC Family Channel; AMC; Animal Planet; Arts & Entertainment; BET Networks; Cartoon Network; CNBC; CNN; Country Music TV; C-SPAN; C-SPAN 2; Discovery Channel; E! Entertainment Television; ESPN; ESPN 2; Food Network; Fox Sports en Espanol; FX; GalaVision; Hallmark Channel; Headline News; HGTV; History Channel; Home Shopping Network; INSP; ION Television; Lifetime; MSNBC; MTV; Nickelodeon; QVC; ShopNBC; Syfy; Telefutura; Telemundo; The Learning Channel; Travel Channel; truTV; TV Guide Network; TV Land; USA Network; VH1; Weather Channel.

Current originations: Government Access; Public Access.

Planned originations: Educational Access.

Fee: $35.80 installation; $42.45 monthly; $.26 converter.

Expanded Basic Service 1

Subscribers: N.A.

Programming (via satellite): Bravo; Comedy Central; Disney Channel; Fox News Channel; Fox Sports Net Arizona; Oxygen; Speed Channel; Spike TV; TBS Superstation; Turner Network TV.

Fee: $10.98 monthly.

Digital Basic Service

Subscribers: 22,000 Includes El Centro.

Programming (via satellite): American-Life TV Network; BBC America; Bio; Black Family Channel; Bloomberg Television; Discovery Digital Networks; Do-It-Yourself; ESPN Classic Sports; ESPNews; FitTV; Fox Sports World; Fuse; G4; GAS; Golf Channel; Great American Country; GSN; History Channel International; INSP; MTV Networks Digital Suite; Music Choice; National Geographic Channel; Nick Jr.; Nick Too; NickToons TV; SoapNet; Style Network; Trinity Broadcasting Network; WE tv.

Fee: $6.00 monthly (each tier).

Digital Expanded Basic Service

Subscribers: N.A.

Programming (via satellite): ART America; Canales N; CCTV-4; Filipino Channel; Fox College Sports Atlantic; Fox College Sports Central; Fox College Sports Pacific; Fox Movie Channel; Independent Film Channel; Lifetime Movie Network; Outdoor Channel; RAI International; Russian Television Network; Toon Disney; Turner Classic Movies; TV Asia; TV Japan; TV5, La Television International; Versus; Zee TV USA; Zhong Tian Channel.

Digital Pay Service 1

Pay Units: N.A.

Programming (via satellite): Cinemax (multiplexed); Encore (multiplexed); Flix; HBO (multiplexed); Showtime (multiplexed); Starz (multiplexed); Sundance Channel; The Movie Channel (multiplexed).

Fee: $12.00 monthly (HBO, Cinemax, Showtime/TMC or Starz).

Video-On-Demand: Planned

Pay-Per-View

HITS PPV (delivered digitally), Addressable: Yes; Hot Choice (delivered digitally); Playboy TV (delivered digitally); Fresh (delivered digitally); Shorteez (delivered digitally); Urban American Television Network (delivered digitally).

Internet Service

Operational: Yes.

Subscribers: 22,000.

Broadband Service: Road Runner.

Fee: $44.95 monthly; $5.00 modem lease.

Telephone Service

Digital: Operational

Fee: $49.95 monthly

Miles of Plant: 1,200.0 (coaxial); None (fiber optic). Homes passed: 130,000. Homes passed & miles of plant (coax & fiber combined) includes El Centro

General Manager: Ricky Rinehart. Operations Manager: Hughie Williams. Marketing Manager: Shayne Abney. Business Manager: Jessica Haggard.

City fee: 2% of gross.

Ownership: Time Warner Cable (MSO).

ARKANSAS

Total Systems: 171
Total Communities Served: 510
Franchises Not Yet Operating: 0
Applications Pending: 0
Communities with Applications: 0
Number of Basic Subscribers: 422,438
Number of Expanded Basic Subscribers: 91,693
Number of Pay Units: 83,986

Top 100 Markets Represented: Memphis (26); Little Rock-Pine Bluff (50); Texarkana, TX-Shreveport, LA (58); Monroe, LA-El Dorado, AR (99).

**For a list of cable communities in this section, see the Cable Community Index located in the back of Cable Volume 2.
For explanation of terms used in cable system listings, see p. D-11.**

ALMYRA—Formerly served by Cebridge Connections. No longer in operation. ICA: AR0299.

ALPENA—Madison County Cable. Now served by WESTERN GROVE, AR [AR0183]. ICA: AR0197.

ALTHEIMER—Almega Cable, 4001 W Airport Frwy, Ste 530, Bedford, TX 76021. Phones: 817-685-9588; 877-725-6342. Fax: 817-685-6488. Web Site: http://almega.com. Also serves Wabbaseka. ICA: AR0130.

TV Market Ranking: 50 (ALTHEIMER, Wabbaseka). Franchise award date: N.A. Franchise expiration date: N.A. Began: N.A.

Channel capacity: 35 (not 2-way capable). Channels available but not in use: N.A.

Basic Service

Subscribers: 90.

Programming (received off-air): KARK-TV (NBC) Little Rock; KASN (CW) Pine Bluff; KATV (ABC) Little Rock; KETS (PBS) Little Rock; KLRT-TV (FOX) Little Rock; KTHV (CBS) Little Rock; KVTN-DT (IND) Pine Bluff.

Programming (via satellite): ABC Family Channel; AmericanLife TV Network; Arts & Entertainment; BET Networks; CNN; Country Music TV; Discovery Channel; Disney Channel; ESPN; Home Shopping Network; Lifetime; MTV; Nickelodeon; Spike TV; TBS Superstation; Turner Classic Movies; Turner Network TV; USA Network; Weather Channel; WGN America.

Fee: $39.95 installation; $39.99 monthly.

Pay Service 1

Pay Units: 77.

Programming (via satellite): HBO.

Fee: $10.95 monthly.

Pay Service 2

Pay Units: 78.

Programming (via satellite): Showtime.

Fee: $8.00 monthly.

Video-On-Demand: No

Internet Service

Operational: No.

Telephone Service

None

Miles of Plant: 11.0 (coaxial); None (fiber optic). Homes passed: 594.

President: Thomas Kurien.

Ownership: Almega Cable (MSO).

AMITY—Community Communications Co., 1920 Hwy 425 N, Monticello, AR 71655-4463. Phones: 800-272-2191; 870-367-7300. Fax: 870-367-9770. E-mail: generalmanager@ccc-cable.net. Web Site: http://www.ccc-cable.net. ICA: AR0158.

TV Market Ranking: Below 100 (AMITY). Franchise award date: N.A. Franchise expiration date: N.A. Began: January 1, 1979.

Channel capacity: 48 (not 2-way capable). Channels available but not in use: N.A.

Basic Service

Subscribers: 177.

Programming (received off-air): KARK-TV (NBC) Little Rock; KASN (CW) Pine Bluff; KATV (ABC) Little Rock; KETG (PBS) Arkadelphia; KLRT-TV (FOX) Little Rock; KTHV (CBS) Little Rock; KVTH-DT (IND) Hot Springs.

Programming (via satellite): ABC Family Channel; AMC; Arts & Entertainment; CNN; Country Music TV; Discovery Channel; ESPN; ESPN 2; FX; Lifetime; Nickelodeon; Outdoor Channel; QVC; Spike TV; Syfy; TBS Superstation; The Learning Channel; Trinity Broadcasting Network; Turner Network TV; TV Land; USA Network; VH1; WGN America.

Fee: $35.00 installation; $33.60 monthly.

Pay Service 1

Pay Units: N.A.

Programming (via satellite): Showtime; The Movie Channel.

Fee: $35.00 installation; $8.50 monthly (each).

Video-On-Demand: No

Internet Service

Operational: No.

Telephone Service

None

Miles of Plant: 9.0 (coaxial); None (fiber optic). Homes passed: 302.

Manager: Jackie Kennedy. Operations Manager: Larry Ivy.

Ownership: Community Communications Co. (MSO).

ARKADELPHIA—Suddenlink Communications, 2505 Pine St, Arkadelphia, AR 71923-4358. Phone: 870-246-7611. Fax: 870-246-4356. E-mail: gene.regan@suddenlink.com. Web Site: http://www.suddenlink.com. Also serves Caddo Valley. ICA: AR0216.

TV Market Ranking: Below 100 (ARKADELPHIA, Caddo Valley). Franchise award date: February 1, 1989. Franchise expiration date: N.A. Began: November 1, 1976.

Channel capacity: 59 (not 2-way capable). Channels available but not in use: None.

Basic Service

Subscribers: 3,520.

Programming (received off-air): KARK-TV (NBC) Little Rock; KARZ-TV (MNT) Little Rock; KASN (CW) Pine Bluff; KATV (ABC) Little Rock; KETG (PBS) Arkadelphia; KKAP (ETV) Little Rock; KKYK-DT (IND) Camden; KLRT-TV (FOX) Little Rock; KTHV (CBS) Little Rock; KVTH-DT (IND) Hot Springs; all-band FM.

Programming (via satellite): C-SPAN; FamilyNet; Home Shopping Network; LWS Local Weather Station; QVC; TBS Superstation; TV Guide Network; WGN America.

Fee: $30.00 installation; $19.95 monthly.

Expanded Basic Service 1

Subscribers: 3,210.

Programming (via satellite): ABC Family Channel; AMC; Animal Planet; Arts & Entertainment; BET Networks; Bravo!; Cartoon Network; CNBC; CNN; Comcast Sports Net Southwest; Comedy Central; Country Music TV; C-SPAN 2; Discovery Channel; Disney Channel; E! Entertainment Television; ESPN; ESPN 2; Eternal Word TV Network; Food Network; Fox News Channel; FX; Great American Country; Headline News; HGTV; History Channel; INSP; Lifetime; Lifetime Movie Network; MSNBC; MTV; Nickelodeon; Outdoor Channel; Speed Channel; Spike TV; Syfy; The Learning Channel; Travel Channel; Trinity Broadcasting Network; truTV; Turner Classic Movies; Turner Network TV; TV Land; USA Network; Versus; VH1; Weather Channel.

Fee: $28.05 monthly.

Digital Basic Service

Subscribers: N.A.

Programming (received off-air): KARK-TV (NBC) Little Rock; KATV (ABC) Little Rock; KLRT-TV (FOX) Little Rock; KTHV (CBS) Little Rock.

Programming (via satellite): Animal Planet HD; Arts & Entertainment HD; BBC America; Bio; Bloomberg Television; Boomerang; CBS College Sports Network; Chiller; CMT Pure Country; Cooking Channel; Cox Sports Television; Discovery Channel HD; Discovery HD Theater; Discovery Health Channel; Discovery Kids Channel; Discovery Military Channel; Discovery Planet Green; Do-It-Yourself; Encore (multiplexed); ESPN 2 HD; ESPN Classic Sports; ESPN HD; ESPN U; ESPNews; FamilyNet; Food Network HD; Fox Reality Channel; Fox Soccer; FSN HD; Fuel TV; Fuse; FX HD; G4; Golf Channel; Gospel Music Channel; GSN; Hallmark Channel; Halogen Network; HDNet; HDNet Movies; HGTV HD; History Channel HD; History Channel International; ID Investigation Discovery; Independent Film Channel; Lifetime Real Women; MTV Hits; MTV2; Music Choice; National Geographic Channel; National Geographic Channel HD Network; Nick Jr.; NickToons TV; Oxygen; Science Channel; Si TV; SoapNet; Style Network; Sundance Channel; Syfy HD; TBS in HD; TeenNick; Tennis Channel; The Sportsman Channel; TLC HD; Toon Disney; Turner Network TV HD; TV One; Universal HD; USA Network HD; VH1 Classic; VH1 Soul; WE tv; Weatherscan.

Fee: $33.00 monthly.

Digital Pay Service 1

Pay Units: N.A.

Programming (via satellite): Cinemax (multiplexed); HBO (multiplexed); HBO HD; Showtime (multiplexed); Showtime HD; Starz (multiplexed); The Movie Channel (multiplexed).

Fee: $11.99 monthly (HBO, Cinemax, Showtime/TMC or Starz).

Video-On-Demand: No

Pay-Per-View

iN DEMAND (delivered digitally); Shorteez (delivered digitally); Fresh (delivered digitally); Playboy TV (delivered digitally); Club Jenna (delivered digitally); Spice: Xcess (delivered digitally).

Internet Service

Operational: Yes.

Fee: $49.95 monthly.

Telephone Service

None

Miles of Plant: 92.0 (coaxial); None (fiber optic). Homes passed: 4,527. Total homes in franchised area: 5,610.

Manager: Robbie Lee. Chief Technician: Chris Echols. Marketing Director: Kathy Wyrick.

City fee: 3% of gross.

Ownership: Cequel Communications LLC (MSO).

ARKANSAS CITY—Community Communications Co., 1920 Hwy 425 N, Monticello, AR 71655-4463. Phones: 800-272-2191; 870-367-7300. Fax: 870-367-9770. E-mail: generalmanager@ccc-cable.net. Web Site: http://www.ccc-cable.net. ICA: AR0174.

TV Market Ranking: Below 100 (ARKANSAS CITY). Franchise award date: N.A. Franchise expiration date: N.A. Began: N.A.

Channel capacity: 48 (not 2-way capable). Channels available but not in use: N.A.

Basic Service

Subscribers: 112.

Programming (received off-air): KASN (CW) Pine Bluff; KATV (ABC) Little Rock; KLRT-TV (FOX) Little Rock; KTVE (NBC) El Dorado; WABG-TV (ABC) Greenwood; WMAO-TV (PBS) Greenwood; WXVT (CBS) Greenville.

Programming (via satellite): ABC Family Channel; AMC; Arts & Entertainment; BET Networks; CNN; Comcast Sports Net Southwest; Country Music TV; Discovery Channel; ESPN; ESPN 2; FitTV; FX; Home Shopping Network; Lifetime; Nickelodeon; Outdoor Channel; QVC; Spike TV; Syfy; TBS Superstation; Trinity Broadcasting Network; Turner Network TV; TV Land; USA Network; VH1; WGN America.

Fee: $20.00 installation; $33.60 monthly.

Pay Service 1

Pay Units: 40.

Programming (via satellite): HBO; The Movie Channel.

Fee: $10.00 monthly (each).

Video-On-Demand: No

Internet Service

Operational: No.

Telephone Service
None
Miles of Plant: 7.0 (coaxial); None (fiber optic). Homes passed: 230. Total homes in franchised area: 230.
Manager: Jackie Kennedy. Operations Manager: Larry Ivy.
Ownership: Community Communications Co. (MSO).

ASH FLAT—Crystal Broadband Networks, PO Box 180336, Chicago, IL 60618. Phone: 817-685-9588. E-mail: info@crystalbn.com. Web Site: http://crystalbn.com. ICA: AR0175.
TV Market Ranking: Outside TV Markets (ASH FLAT). Franchise award date: April 1, 1986. Franchise expiration date: N.A. Began: August 1, 1975.
Channel capacity: 36 (not 2-way capable). Channels available but not in use: N.A.
Basic Service
Subscribers: 127.
Programming (received off-air): KAIT (ABC) Jonesboro; KEMV (PBS) Mountain View; KOLR (CBS) Springfield; KTHV (CBS) Little Rock; KVTJ-DT (IND) Jonesboro; KYTV (CW, NBC) Springfield.
Programming (via satellite): ABC Family Channel; AMC; Arts & Entertainment; CNBC; CNN; Comcast Sports Net Southwest; Discovery Channel; Disney Channel; ESPN; ESPN 2; Fox News Channel; Great American Country; History Channel; Home Shopping Network; Lifetime; Nickelodeon; Spike TV; TBS Superstation; Trinity Broadcasting Network; Turner Network TV; TV Land; USA Network; Weather Channel; WGN America; WNBC (NBC) New York.
Fee: $29.95 installation; $39.95 monthly.
Pay Service 1
Pay Units: 37.
Programming (via satellite): Cinemax; HBO.
Fee: $8.99 monthly (Cinemax), $12.99 monthly (HBO).
Video-On-Demand: No
Internet Service
Operational: Yes.
Telephone Service
Digital: Operational
Miles of Plant: 12.0 (coaxial); None (fiber optic). Homes passed: 303.
Program Manager: Shawn Smith. General Manager: Nidhin Johnson.
City fee: 1% of gross.
Ownership: Crystal Broadband Networks (MSO).

ASHDOWN—NewWave Communications, 1311 Business Hwy 60 W, Dexter, MO 63841. Phone: 877-744-1212 (Customer service). E-mail: info@newwavecom.com. Web Site: http://www.newwavecom.com. Also serves Little River County (portions). ICA: AR0033.
TV Market Ranking: 58 (ASHDOWN, Little River County (portions)). Franchise award date: May 1, 1977. Franchise expiration date: N.A. Began: May 31, 1977.
Channel capacity: 136 (2-way capable). Channels available but not in use: N.A.
Basic Service
Subscribers: 570.
Programming (received off-air): KARK-TV (NBC) Little Rock; KATV (ABC) Little Rock; KETG (PBS) Arkadelphia; KJEP-CA Nashville; KMSS-TV (FOX) Shreveport; KSLA (CBS) Shreveport; KTAL-TV (NBC) Texarkana; KTBS-TV (ABC) Shreveport; KTSS-LP Hope; allband FM.
Programming (via satellite): C-SPAN; C-SPAN 2; Home Shopping Network; INSP; QVC; Trinity Broadcasting Network; WGN America.
Fee: $29.95 installation; $19.95 monthly.
Expanded Basic Service 1
Subscribers: 477.
Programming (via satellite): ABC Family Channel; AMC; Animal Planet; Arts & Entertainment; BET Networks; Bravo; Cartoon Network; CNBC; CNN; Comedy Central; Country Music TV; Discovery Channel; Disney Channel; E! Entertainment Television; ESPN; ESPN 2; ESPN Classic Sports; Food Network; Fox News Channel; FX; Golf Channel; Hallmark Channel; Headline News; HGTV; History Channel; Lifetime; MSNBC; MTV; Nickelodeon; Outdoor Channel; SoapNet; Speed Channel; Spike TV; Syfy; TBS Superstation; The Learning Channel; Travel Channel; truTV; Turner Network TV; TV Land; USA Network; VH1; Weather Channel.
Fee: $40.95 monthly.
Digital Basic Service
Subscribers: 65.
Programming (received off-air): KPXJ (CW) Minden.
Programming (via satellite): BBC America; Bio; Black Family Channel; Bloomberg Television; Discovery Digital Networks; DMX Music; ESPNews; FitTV; Fox Movie Channel; G4; GAS; Great American Country; GSN; Halogen Network; History Channel International; Independent Film Channel; Lifetime Movie Network; MTV Networks Digital Suite; Nick Jr.; NickToons TV; ShopNBC; Sleuth; Style Network; The Word Network; Toon Disney; Turner Classic Movies; Versus.
Digital Pay Service 1
Pay Units: 318.
Programming (via satellite): Cinemax (multiplexed); Encore (multiplexed); Flix; HBO (multiplexed); Showtime (multiplexed); Starz (multiplexed); The Movie Channel (multiplexed).
Pay-Per-View
Hot Choice (delivered digitally); Playboy TV (delivered digitally); Fresh (delivered digitally); Shorteez (delivered digitally); iN DEMAND (delivered digitally).
Internet Service
Operational: Yes.
Subscribers: 27.
Broadband Service: SpeedNet.
Fee: $34.95 monthly.
Telephone Service
None
Miles of Plant: 48.0 (coaxial); None (fiber optic). Homes passed: 2,296.
General Manager: Ed Gargas. Technical Operations Manager: Jerry Townsend.
Franchise fee: 4% of gross.
Ownership: NewWave Communications (MSO).

ATKINS—Suddenlink Communications, 12444 Powerscourt Dr, Saint Louis, MO 63131-3660. Phones: 800-999-6845 (Customer service); 314-965-2020. Fax: 903-561-5485. E-mail: gene.regan@suddenlink.com. Web Site: http://www.suddenlink.com. Also serves Pope County (portions). ICA: AR0079.
TV Market Ranking: Outside TV Markets (ATKINS, Pope County (portions)). Franchise award date: N.A. Franchise expiration date: N.A. Began: December 1, 1982.
Channel capacity: N.A. Channels available but not in use: N.A.
Basic Service
Subscribers: 576.
Programming (received off-air): KARK-TV (NBC) Little Rock; KARZ-TV (MNT) Little Rock; KASN (CW) Pine Bluff; KATV (ABC) Little Rock; KETS (PBS) Little Rock; KKAP (ETV) Little Rock; KKYK-DT (IND) Camden; KLRT-TV (FOX) Little Rock; KTHV (CBS) Little Rock; KVTN-DT (IND) Pine Bluff; WGN-TV (CW, IND) Chicago.
Programming (via satellite): C-SPAN; Home Shopping Network; Jewelry Television; Trinity Broadcasting Network.
Fee: $24.95 installation; $19.95 monthly.
Expanded Basic Service 1
Subscribers: N.A.
Programming (via satellite): ABC Family Channel; AMC; Animal Planet; Arts & Entertainment; BET Networks; Cartoon Network; CNBC; CNN; Comcast Sports Net Southwest; Comedy Central; Discovery Channel; Disney Channel; E! Entertainment Television; ESPN; ESPN 2; Food Network; Fox News Channel; FX; Great American Country; Hallmark Channel; Headline News; HGTV; History Channel; Lifetime; MSNBC; MTV; National Geographic Channel; Nickelodeon; Outdoor Channel; Speed Channel; Spike TV; Syfy; TBS Superstation; The Learning Channel; Travel Channel; Turner Classic Movies; Turner Network TV; TV Land; USA Network; VH1; Weather Channel.
Fee: $22.04 monthly.
Pay Service 1
Pay Units: 24.
Programming (via satellite): HBO.
Fee: $10.95 monthly.
Pay Service 2
Pay Units: 71.
Programming (via satellite): Showtime.
Fee: $10.95 monthly.
Pay Service 3
Pay Units: N.A.
Programming (via satellite): The Movie Channel.
Fee: $10.95 monthly.
Video-On-Demand: No
Internet Service
Operational: Yes. Began: May 27, 2003.
Broadband Service: Cebridge High Speed Cable Internet.
Fee: $33.00 monthly.
Telephone Service
Digital: Operational
Fee: $29.95 monthly
Miles of Plant: 37.0 (coaxial); None (fiber optic). Homes passed: 1,278.
Regional Manager: Todd Cruthird. Plant Manager: Danny Keith. Marketing Director: Beverly Gambell.
City fee: 3% of gross.
Ownership: Cequel Communications LLC (MSO).

AUGUSTA—Augusta Video Inc. Now served by SEARCY, AR [AR0017]. ICA: AR0068.

BATESVILLE—Suddenlink Communications, 2490 Harrison St, Batesville, AR 72501-7421. Phone: 870-793-7277. Fax: 870-793-6185. Web Site: http://www.suddenlink.com. Also serves Independence County (portions), Moorefield, South Side & Sulphur Rock. ICA: AR0218.
TV Market Ranking: Outside TV Markets (BATESVILLE, Independence County (portions), Moorefield, South Side, Sulphur Rock). Franchise award date: N.A. Franchise expiration date: N.A. Began: September 3, 1951.
Channel capacity: N.A. Channels available but not in use: N.A.
Basic Service
Subscribers: 5,140.
Programming (received off-air): KAIT (ABC) Jonesboro; KARK-TV (NBC) Little Rock; KARZ-TV (MNT) Little Rock; KATV (ABC) Little Rock; KKAP (ETV) Little Rock; KKYK-DT (IND) Camden; KLRT-TV (FOX) Little Rock; KTEJ (PBS) Jonesboro; KTHV (CBS) Little Rock; allband FM.
Programming (via satellite): C-SPAN; C-SPAN 2; ESPN; GalaVision; Headline News; Home Shopping Network; INSP; Jewelry Television; QVC; TBS Superstation; Trinity Broadcasting Network; Weather Channel; WGN America.
Fee: $45.00 installation; $19.95 monthly.
Expanded Basic Service 1
Subscribers: N.A.
Programming (via satellite): ABC Family Channel; AMC; Animal Planet; Arts & Entertainment; BET Networks; Bravo; Cartoon Network; CNBC; CNN; Comcast Sports Net Southwest; Comedy Central; Country Music TV; Discovery Channel; Disney Channel; E! Entertainment Television; ESPN 2; Food Network; Fox News Channel; FX; Great American Country; HGTV; History Channel; Lifetime; Lifetime Movie Network; MSNBC; MTV; Nickelodeon; Outdoor Channel; Oxygen; Speed Channel; Spike TV; Syfy; The Learning Channel; Travel Channel; truTV; Turner Network TV; TV Land; USA Network; Versus; VH1.
Fee: $13.14 monthly.
Digital Basic Service
Subscribers: N.A.
Programming (received off-air): KAIT (ABC) Jonesboro.
Programming (via satellite): Animal Planet HD; Arts & Entertainment HD; BBC America; Bio; Bloomberg Television; Boomerang; CBS College Sports Network; Chiller; CMT Pure Country; Cooking Channel; Cox Sports Television; Discovery Channel HD; Discovery en Espanol; Discovery HD Theater; Discovery Health Channel; Discovery Kids Channel; Discovery Military Channel; Discovery Planet Green; Do-It-Yourself; Encore (multiplexed); ESPN 2 HD; ESPN Classic Sports; ESPN HD; ESPN U; ESPNews; Food Network HD; Fox Reality Channel; Fox Soccer; FSN HD; Fuel TV; Fuse; FX HD; G4; Golf Channel; GSN; Hallmark Channel; Halogen Network; HDNet; HDNet Movies; HGTV HD; History Channel HD; History Channel International; ID Investigation Discovery; Independent Film Channel; Lifetime Real Women; MTV Hits; MTV2; Music Choice; National Geographic Channel; National Geographic Channel HD Network; Nick Jr.; NickToons TV; RFD-TV; Science Channel; SoapNet; Style Network; Sundance Channel; Syfy HD; TBS in HD; TeenNick; TLC HD; Toon Disney; Turner Classic Movies; Turner Network TV HD; Universal HD; USA Network HD; VH1 Classic.
Fee: $24.95 monthly.
Digital Pay Service 1
Pay Units: N.A.
Programming (via satellite): Cinemax (multiplexed); HBO (multiplexed); HBO HD; Showtime (multiplexed); Showtime HD; Starz (multiplexed); The Movie Channel (multiplexed).
Fee: $12.95 monthly (HBO, Cinemax, Showtime/TMC or Starz).
Video-On-Demand: No
Pay-Per-View
iN DEMAND (delivered digitally); Fresh (delivered digitally); Spice: Xcess (delivered digitally); Playboy TV (delivered digitally).
Internet Service
Operational: Yes.
Broadband Service: Cebridge High Speed Cable Internet.
Fee: $49.95 installation; $33.00 monthly.

Telephone Service
Digital: Operational
Fee: $33.00 monthly
Miles of Plant: 63.0 (coaxial); None (fiber optic).
Manager: Dwayne Millikin. Chief Technician: Don Province. Marketing Director: Kathy Wyrick.
City fee: $1 per subscriber annually.
Ownership: Cequel Communications LLC (MSO).

BAXTER COUNTY (unincorporated areas)—Formerly served by Almega Cable. No longer in operation. ICA: AR0119.
TV Market Ranking: Outside TV Markets (BAXTER COUNTY).

BEARDEN—Rapid Cable, 515 E Longview Dr, Arp, TX 75750. Phone: 903-859-6492. Fax: 903-859-3708. ICA: AR0107.
TV Market Ranking: Below 100 (BEARDEN). Franchise award date: N.A. Franchise expiration date: N.A. Began: N.A.
Channel capacity: 36 (not 2-way capable). Channels available but not in use: N.A.
Basic Service
Subscribers: 116.
Programming (received off-air): KARK-TV (NBC) Little Rock; KASN (CW) Pine Bluff; KATV (ABC) Little Rock; KETS (PBS) Little Rock; KLRT-TV (FOX) Little Rock; KTHV (CBS) Little Rock; KTVE (NBC) El Dorado.
Programming (via satellite): ABC Family Channel; Animal Planet; Arts & Entertainment; BET Networks; CNN; Discovery Channel; Disney Channel; ESPN; Great American Country; Headline News; HGTV; Home Shopping Network; Lifetime; National Geographic Channel; Nickelodeon; Outdoor Channel; Spike TV; TBS Superstation; The Learning Channel; Trinity Broadcasting Network; Turner Classic Movies; Turner Network TV; USA Network; Weather Channel.
Fee: $54.95 installation; $44.05 monthly.
Pay Service 1
Pay Units: 7.
Programming (via satellite): Cinemax.
Fee: $12.95 monthly.
Pay Service 2
Pay Units: 34.
Programming (via satellite): Showtime.
Fee: $12.95 monthly.
Pay Service 3
Pay Units: 45.
Programming (via satellite): HBO.
Fee: $12.95 monthly.
Video-On-Demand: No
Internet Service
Operational: No.
Telephone Service
None
Miles of Plant: 15.0 (coaxial); None (fiber optic). Homes passed: 650.
Regional Manager: Mike Taylor. Chief Technician: Larry Stafford.
Ownership: Rapid Communications LLC (MSO).

BEAVER LAKE—Cox Communications. Now served by SPRINGDALE, AR [AR0220]. ICA: AR0092.

BEEBE—Charter Communications, 19863 Interstate 30, Ste 3, Benton, AR 72015-6966. Phones: 501-315-4405; 636-207-7014 (St Louis office). Fax: 501-315-4406. Web Site: http://www.charter.com. ICA: AR0059.
TV Market Ranking: 50 (BEEBE). Franchise award date: January 1, 1984. Franchise expiration date: N.A. Began: December 1, 1984.
Channel capacity: N.A. Channels available but not in use: N.A.
Basic Service
Subscribers: 920.
Programming (received off-air): KARK-TV (NBC) Little Rock; KARZ-TV (MNT) Little Rock; KASN (CW) Pine Bluff; KATV (ABC) Little Rock; KETS (PBS) Little Rock; KLRT-TV (FOX) Little Rock; KTHV (CBS) Little Rock; KVTN-DT (IND) Pine Bluff.
Programming (via satellite): ABC Family Channel; Arts & Entertainment; CNN; Comcast Sports Net Southwest; Comedy Central; Country Music TV; C-SPAN; E! Entertainment Television; ESPN; Headline News; Home Shopping Network; Lifetime; MTV; Nickelodeon; QVC; Syfy; The Learning Channel; WGN America.
Current originations: Government Access; Educational Access; Public Access.
Fee: $29.99 installation; $3.48 converter.
Expanded Basic Service 1
Subscribers: 785.
Programming (via satellite): AMC; Animal Planet; Bravo; Cartoon Network; CNBC; Discovery Channel; Disney Channel; ESPN 2; FitTV; Food Network; Fox Movie Channel; Fox News Channel; FX; Hallmark Channel; HGTV; History Channel; MSNBC; SoapNet; Speed Channel; Spike TV; TBS Superstation; Toon Disney; Travel Channel; truTV; Turner Classic Movies; Turner Network TV; TV Guide Network; TV Land; USA Network; Versus; VH1; WE tv; Weather Channel.
Fee: $49.99 monthly.
Digital Basic Service
Subscribers: N.A.
Programming (via satellite): AmericanLife TV Network; BBC America; Bio; Bloomberg Television; Discovery Digital Networks; DMX Music; Fox Movie Channel; G4; GAS; Golf Channel; GSN; Halogen Network; HGTV; History Channel; History Channel International; Independent Film Channel; Lifetime Movie Network; MTV Networks Digital Suite; MuchMusic Network; Nick Jr.; Outdoor Channel; ShopNBC; Speed Channel; Style Network; Toon Disney; Trinity Broadcasting Network; Turner Classic Movies; Versus; WE tv.
Pay Service 1
Pay Units: 42.
Programming (via satellite): Cinemax.
Fee: $11.95 monthly.
Pay Service 2
Pay Units: 58.
Programming (via satellite): HBO (multiplexed).
Fee: $11.95 monthly.
Pay Service 3
Pay Units: 38.
Programming (via satellite): Showtime (multiplexed).
Fee: $11.95 monthly.
Pay Service 4
Pay Units: 32.
Programming (via satellite): The Movie Channel.
Fee: $11.95 monthly.
Digital Pay Service 1
Pay Units: N.A.
Programming (via satellite): Cinemax (multiplexed); Encore (multiplexed); Flix; HBO (multiplexed); Showtime (multiplexed); Starz (multiplexed); The Movie Channel (multiplexed).
Fee: $11.95 monthly (each).
Video-On-Demand: No
Pay-Per-View
Urban Xtra (delivered digitally).
Internet Service
Operational: No.
Telephone Service
None
Miles of Plant: 48.0 (coaxial); None (fiber optic). Homes passed: 2,818.
Vice President & General Manager: Steve Trippe. Operations Director: Dave Miller. Operations Manager: Dave Huntsman. Chief Technician: Jim Miller. Marketing Director: Beverly Wall. Office Manager: Missy Brown.
Franchise fee: 3% of gross.
Ownership: Charter Communications Inc. (MSO).

BENTON COUNTY—Cox Communications. Now served by SPRINGDALE, AR [AR0220]. ICA: AR0039.

BERRYVILLE—Cox Communications, 4901 S 48th St, Springdale, AR 72762. Phones: 316-262-4270 (Wichita office); 479-717-3700. Fax: 479-756-1081. Web Site: http://www.cox.com/arkansas. Also serves Beaver, Carroll County (portions), Eureka Springs, Green Forest & Holiday Island. ICA: AR0221.
TV Market Ranking: Below 100 (Beaver, BERRYVILLE, Carroll County (portions), Eureka Springs, Green Forest, Holiday Island). Franchise award date: N.A. Franchise expiration date: N.A. Began: January 1, 1963.
Channel capacity: N.A. Channels available but not in use: N.A.

Basic Service
Subscribers: N.A. Included in Wichita
Programming (received off-air): KAFT (PBS) Fayetteville; KARK-TV (NBC) Little Rock; KATV (ABC) Little Rock; KHOG-TV (ABC) Fayetteville; KOLR (CBS) Springfield; KSFX-TV (FOX) Springfield; KSPR (ABC) Springfield; KTHV (CBS) Little Rock; KYTV (CW, NBC) Springfield; allband FM.
Programming (via satellite): ABC Family Channel; Arts & Entertainment; CNN; C-SPAN; C-SPAN 2; Discovery Channel; Disney Channel; ESPN; Great American Country; ION Television; Lifetime; Nickelodeon; TBS Superstation; Trinity Broadcasting Network; Turner Network TV; TV Guide Network; Weather Channel; WGN America.
Fee: $35.00 installation; $10.00 monthly; $1.50 converter.

Expanded Basic Service 1
Subscribers: N.A.
Programming (via satellite): AMC; Animal Planet; CNBC; Comcast Sports Net Southwest; Comedy Central; ESPN 2; Fox News Channel; FX; GalaVision; Headline News; HGTV; History Channel; Home Shopping Network; MSNBC; Outdoor Channel; Oxygen; Speed Channel; Spike TV; Syfy; The Learning Channel; Trinity Broadcasting Network; Turner Classic Movies; TV Land; USA Network; Versus; VH1; WE tv.
Fee: $43.15 monthly.

Digital Basic Service
Subscribers: N.A.
Programming (via satellite): BBC America; Bloomberg Television; Discovery Digital Networks; DMX Music; Encore Action; ESPNews; Fox Sports World; Fuse; Golf Channel; GSN; Lifetime Movie Network; SoapNet; Toon Disney; truTV.
Fee: $14.00 monthly.
Pay Service 1
Pay Units: N.A.
Programming (via satellite): Encore; HBO (multiplexed); Showtime (multiplexed); Starz; The Movie Channel.
Fee: $35.00 installation; $9.00 monthly (HBO, Showtime, Starz, or Encore), $9.50 monthly (TMC).
Digital Pay Service 1
Pay Units: N.A.
Programming (via satellite): Cinemax (multiplexed); HBO (multiplexed); Showtime (multiplexed); Starz (multiplexed); The Movie Channel.
Video-On-Demand: No
Pay-Per-View
ESPN Extra (delivered digitally); ESPN Gameplan (delivered digitally); ESPN Now (delivered digitally); iN DEMAND; iN DEMAND (delivered digitally).
Internet Service
Operational: Yes.
Broadband Service: Cox High Speed Internet.
Fee: $19.99-$59.99 monthly.
Telephone Service
Digital: Operational
Fee: $15.95 monthly
Miles of Plant: 34.0 (coaxial); None (fiber optic). Additional miles planned: 1.0 (coaxial). Homes passed included in Springdale
Vice President & General Manager: Kimberly Edmunds. Vice President, Operations: Nelson Mower. Vice President, Marketing: Tony Matthews. Marketing Director: Tina Gabbard. Community Relations Manager: Kelly Zaga.
City fee: 3% of gross.
Ownership: Cox Communications Inc.

BIGGERS—Boycom Cablevision Inc., 3467 Township Line Rd, Poplar Bluff, MO 63901. Phone: 573-686-9101. Fax: 573-686-4722. Web Site: http://www.boycomonline.com. Also serves Datto, Reyno & Success. ICA: AR0109.
TV Market Ranking: Below 100 (Datto, Reyno, Success); Outside TV Markets (BIGGERS). Franchise award date: May 14, 1969. Franchise expiration date: N.A. Began: January 1, 1968.
Channel capacity: 52 (not 2-way capable). Channels available but not in use: N.A.
Basic Service
Subscribers: N.A. Included in Alton
Programming (received off-air): KAIT (ABC) Jonesboro; KFVS-TV (CBS, CW) Cape Girardeau; KTEJ (PBS) Jonesboro; KVTJ-DT (IND) Jonesboro; WMC-TV (NBC) Memphis; WNBC (NBC) New York; WSEE-TV (CBS, CW) Erie; allband FM.
Programming (via satellite): ABC Family Channel; AMC; Arts & Entertainment; CNN; Comcast Sports Net Southwest; Discovery Channel; Disney Channel; E! Entertainment Television; ESPN; ESPN 2; Fox News Channel; FX; Great American Country; History Channel; Home Shopping Network; Lifetime; MSNBC; MTV; Nickelodeon; Speed Channel; Spike TV; Syfy; TBS Superstation; The Learning Channel; Toon Disney; Trinity Broadcasting Network; Turner Network TV; TV Land; USA Network; VH1; Weather Channel; WGN America.
Fee: $29.95 installation; $39.95 monthly.
Pay Service 1
Pay Units: 176.
Programming (via satellite): Cinemax; Encore; HBO.
Fee: $2.99 monthly (Encore), $8.99 monthly (Cinemax), $12.99 monthly (HBO).

Pay Service 2
Pay Units: N.A.
Programming (via satellite): Showtime; The Movie Channel.
Video-On-Demand: No
Internet Service
Operational: No.
Telephone Service
None
Miles of Plant: 33.0 (coaxial); None (fiber optic). Homes passed: 645.
President: Steven Boyers. General Manager: Shelly Batton. Chief Technician: Phil Huett.
City fee: 2% of gross.
Ownership: Boycom Cablevision Inc. (MSO).

BISCOE—Formerly served by Cebridge Connections. No longer in operation. ICA: AR0194.

BISMARCK—Community Communications Co., 1920 Hwy 425 N, Monticello, AR 71655-4463. Phones: 800-272-2191; 870-367-7300. Fax: 870-367-9770. E-mail: generalmanager@ccc-cable.net. Web Site: http://www.ccc-cable.net. ICA: AR0135.
TV Market Ranking: Below 100 (BISMARCK). Franchise award date: N.A. Franchise expiration date: N.A. Began: August 1, 1989.
Channel capacity: 48 (not 2-way capable). Channels available but not in use: N.A.
Basic Service
Subscribers: 140.
Programming (received off-air): KARK-TV (NBC) Little Rock; KASN (CW) Pine Bluff; KATV (ABC) Little Rock; KETS (PBS) Little Rock; KLRT-TV (FOX) Little Rock; KTHV (CBS) Little Rock.
Programming (via satellite): ABC Family Channel; AMC; Arts & Entertainment; CNN; Comcast Sports Net Southwest; Country Music TV; Discovery Channel; Disney Channel; E! Entertainment Television; ESPN; ESPN 2; Fox News Channel; FX; Headline News; Lifetime; MTV; Nickelodeon; Outdoor Channel; QVC; Spike TV; Syfy; TBS Superstation; Trinity Broadcasting Network; Turner Network TV; TV Land; USA Network; VH1; Weather Channel; WGN America.
Fee: $25.00 installation; $33.60 monthly.
Pay Service 1
Pay Units: N.A.
Programming (via satellite): HBO; Showtime; The Movie Channel.
Fee: $10.00 monthly (HBO).
Video-On-Demand: No
Internet Service
Operational: No.
Telephone Service
None
Homes passed: 405.
Ownership: Community Communications Co. (MSO).

BLACK ROCK—Indco Cable TV, PO Box 3799, 2700 N Saint Louis, Batesville, AR 72503-3799. Phone: 870-793-4174. Fax: 870-793-7439. Web Site: http://www.indco.net. Also serves Imboden, Portia, Powhatan & Ravenden. ICA: AR0114.
TV Market Ranking: Below 100 (BLACK ROCK, Portia, Powhatan); Outside TV Markets (Imboden, Ravenden). Franchise award date: N.A. Franchise expiration date: N.A. Began: January 1, 1979.
Channel capacity: 20 (operating 2-way). Channels available but not in use: None.
Basic Service
Subscribers: 583.
Programming (received off-air): KAIT (ABC) Jonesboro; KATV (ABC) Little Rock; KTEJ (PBS) Jonesboro; WHBQ-TV (FOX) Memphis; WMC-TV (NBC) Memphis; WREG-TV (CBS) Memphis.
Programming (via satellite): ABC Family Channel; AMC; Cartoon Network; CNN; Comcast Sports Net Southeast; C-SPAN; Discovery Channel; Disney Channel; ESPN; ESPN 2; Fox News Channel; Fox Sports Net; Great American Country; HGTV; History Channel; Lifetime; Nickelodeon; Outdoor Channel; QVC; Spike TV; TBS Superstation; Trinity Broadcasting Network; Turner Network TV; TV Land; USA Network; VH1; Weather Channel; WGN America.
Fee: $20.00 installation; $30.95 monthly; $10.00 additional installation.
Pay Service 1
Pay Units: 9.
Programming (via satellite): Cinemax.
Fee: $8.00 monthly.
Pay Service 2
Pay Units: 8.
Programming (via satellite): HBO.
Fee: $10.00 monthly.
Pay Service 3
Pay Units: N.A.
Programming (via satellite): Showtime; The Movie Channel.
Fee: $9.00 monthly (each).
Video-On-Demand: Planned
Internet Service
Operational: Yes.
Telephone Service
Digital: Operational
Miles of Plant: 10.0 (coaxial); None (fiber optic).
Manager: J. D. Pierce. Chief Technician: Tommy Barnett. Marketing Director: Connie Barnett.
City fee: 1% of gross.
Ownership: Indco Cable TV (MSO).

BLYTHEVILLE—Ritter Communications. Now served by MARKED TREE, AR [AR0072]. ICA: AR0018.
TV Market Ranking: 26 (Mississippi County (portions)); Below 100 (Mississippi County (portions)); Outside TV Markets (Mississippi County (portions)).

BONO—Ritter Communications. Now served by MARKED TREE, AR [AR0072]. ICA: AR0105.

BOONEVILLE—Suddenlink Communications, 127 N Elmira Ave, Russellville, AR 72802-9614. Phones: 800-582-9577; 479-968-2223. Fax: 479-968-2223. Web Site: http://www.suddenlink.com. ICA: AR0053.
TV Market Ranking: Below 100 (BOONEVILLE). Franchise award date: November 1, 1963. Franchise expiration date: N.A. Began: November 1, 1963.
Channel capacity: 62 (operating 2-way). Channels available but not in use: 10.
Basic Service
Subscribers: 1,325.
Programming (received off-air): KAFT (PBS) Fayetteville; KARK-TV (NBC) Little Rock; KFSM-TV (CBS) Fort Smith; KFTA-TV (FOX) Fort Smith; KHBS (ABC) Fort Smith; KPBI-CA (FOX) Fort Smith; KTHV (CBS) Little Rock; allband FM.
Programming (via satellite): C-SPAN; QVC; TBS Superstation; Trinity Broadcasting Network; TV Guide Network; TV Land; Weather Channel; WGN America.
Current originations: Public Access.
Fee: $38.00 installation; $19.95 monthly.
Expanded Basic Service 1
Subscribers: N.A.
Programming (via satellite): ABC Family Channel; AMC; Animal Planet; Arts & Entertainment; Cartoon Network; CNBC; CNN; Comcast Sports Net Southwest; Discovery Channel; Disney Channel; E! Entertainment Television; ESPN; ESPN 2; Fox News Channel; Great American Country; Headline News; HGTV; History Channel; Lifetime; Nickelodeon; Speed Channel; Spike TV; Syfy; The Learning Channel; Trinity Broadcasting Network; Turner Network TV; USA Network; Versus; VH1.
Fee: $18.00 monthly.
Digital Basic Service
Subscribers: N.A.
Programming (via satellite): BBC America; Bio; Bloomberg Television; Discovery Health Channel; Discovery Kids Channel; Discovery Military Channel; Discovery Planet Green; DMX Music; ESPN Classic Sports; ESPNews; Fox Soccer; Fuse; G4; Golf Channel; GSN; Halogen Network; ID Investigation Discovery; Independent Film Channel; Lifetime Movie Network; Science Channel; Sundance Channel; Toon Disney.
Fee: $16.00 monthly.
Digital Pay Service 1
Pay Units: N.A.
Programming (via satellite): Cinemax (multiplexed); Encore (multiplexed); HBO (multiplexed); Showtime (multiplexed); Starz (multiplexed); The Movie Channel (multiplexed).
Fee: $12.95 monthly (HBO, Cinemax, Showtime/TMC or Starz/Encore).
Video-On-Demand: No
Pay-Per-View
iN DEMAND (delivered digitally); ESPN Gameplan (delivered digitally); ESPN Now (delivered digitally); Shorteez (delivered digitally); Fresh (delivered digitally); Playboy TV (delivered digitally); Spice: Xcess (delivered digitally).
Internet Service
Operational: Yes.
Broadband Service: Cebridge High Speed Cable Internet.
Fee: $29.95 monthly.
Telephone Service
None
Miles of Plant: 31.0 (coaxial); None (fiber optic). Homes passed: 1,792. Total homes in franchised area: 2,082.
Manager: Mike Ederington. Plant Manager: Wayne Ollis. Chief Technician: Clint Petty. Marketing Director: Kathy Wyrick.
Ownership: Cequel Communications LLC (MSO).

BOONEVILLE HUMAN DEVELOPMENT CENTER—Formerly served by Eagle Media. No longer in operation. ICA: AR0313.

BRADFORD—Indco Cable TV, PO Box 3799, 2700 N Saint Louis, Batesville, AR 72503-3799. Phone: 501-793-4174. Fax: 501-793-7439. Web Site: http://www.indco.net. ICA: AR0131.
TV Market Ranking: Outside TV Markets (BRADFORD). Franchise award date: N.A. Franchise expiration date: N.A. Began: N.A.
Channel capacity: 36 (operating 2-way). Channels available but not in use: N.A.
Basic Service
Subscribers: 307.
Programming (received off-air): KAIT (ABC) Jonesboro; KARK-TV (NBC) Little Rock; KASN (CW) Pine Bluff; KATV (ABC) Little Rock; KLRT-TV (FOX) Little Rock; KTEJ (PBS) Jonesboro; KTHV (CBS) Little Rock.
Programming (via satellite): ABC Family Channel; Arts & Entertainment; CNN; Comcast Sports Net Southwest; Country Music TV; Discovery Channel; Disney Channel; ESPN; ESPN 2; FX; Nickelodeon; Outdoor Channel; QVC; Spike TV; Syfy; TBS Superstation; Trinity Broadcasting Network; Turner Classic Movies; Turner Network TV; USA Network; Weather Channel; WGN America.
Fee: $30.95 monthly.
Pay Service 1
Pay Units: 17.
Programming (via satellite): HBO.
Fee: $10.00 monthly.
Pay Service 2
Pay Units: 4.
Programming (via satellite): Cinemax.
Fee: $8.00 monthly.
Video-On-Demand: Planned
Internet Service
Operational: Yes.
Fee: $29.95 monthly.
Telephone Service
None
Miles of Plant: 10.0 (coaxial); None (fiber optic). Homes passed: 425.
Marketing Director: Connie Barnett. Manager: J. D. Pierce. Chief Technician: Tommy Barnett.
City fee: 2% of gross.
Ownership: Indco Cable TV (MSO).

BRADLEY—Formerly served by Cebridge Connections. No longer in operation. ICA: AR0152.

BRIARCLIFF—Formerly served by Almega Cable. No longer in operation. ICA: AR0090.

BRINKLEY—East Arkansas Video Inc., PO Box 1079, 521 N Washington St, Forrest City, AR 72336-1079. Phones: 870-633-1079 (Headend); 870-633-8932. Fax: 870-633-8898. E-mail: eastarkansasvideocs@cablelynx.com. Web Site: http://www.eastarkansasvideo.com. ICA: AR0055.
TV Market Ranking: Outside TV Markets (BRINKLEY). Franchise award date: August 1, 1969. Franchise expiration date: N.A. Began: August 1, 1969.
Channel capacity: 35 (operating 2-way). Channels available but not in use: 1.
Basic Service
Subscribers: 600.
Programming (received off-air): KAIT (ABC) Jonesboro; KARK-TV (NBC) Little Rock; KATV (ABC) Little Rock; KTEJ (PBS) Jonesboro; KTHV (CBS) Little Rock; KVTN-DT (IND) Pine Bluff; WHBQ-TV (FOX) Memphis; WKNO (PBS) Memphis; WLMT (CW) Memphis; WMC-TV (NBC) Memphis; WPTY-TV (ABC) Memphis; WPXX-TV (ION, MNT) Memphis; WREG-TV (CBS) Memphis; 1 FM.
Programming (via satellite): ABC Family Channel; AMC; Animal Planet; Arts & Entertainment; BET Networks; CNBC; CNN; Comcast Sports Net Southwest; Comedy Central; Country Music TV; C-SPAN; C-SPAN 2; Discovery Channel; Disney Channel; ESPN; ESPN 2; Food Network; Fox News Channel; FX; Headline News; HGTV; History Channel; Home Shopping Network; Lifetime; MTV; Nickelodeon; ShopNBC; Sneak Prevue; Spike TV; Syfy; TBS Superstation; The Learning Channel; Toon Disney; Trinity Broadcasting Network; Turner Classic Movies; Turner Network TV; TV Guide Network; TV Land; Univision;

USA Network; VH1; Weather Channel; WGN America.
Current originations: Educational Access.
Fee: $40.00 installation; $48.90 monthly; $3.17 converter.

Digital Basic Service
Subscribers: N.A.
Programming (via satellite): AmericanLife TV Network; BBC America; Bio; CMT Pure Country; Discovery Health Channel; Discovery Kids Channel; Discovery Military Channel; Discovery Planet Green; DMX Music; ESPNews; FitTV; Fox Soccer; FSN Digital Atlantic; FSN Digital Central; FSN Digital Pacific; G4; Golf Channel; Great American Country; GSN; Halogen Network; History Channel International; ID Investigation Discovery; Lifetime Movie Network; MTV Hits; MTV Jams; MTV Tres; MTV2; National Geographic Channel; Nick Jr.; Nick Too; NickToons TV; Outdoor Channel; Science Channel; SoapNet; Speed Channel; Style Network; TeenNick; Toon Disney; VH1 Classic; VH1 Soul; WE tv.
Fee: $10.00 monthly.

Digital Expanded Basic Service
Subscribers: N.A.
Programming (received off-air): KAIT (ABC) Jonesboro; KTEJ (PBS) Jonesboro.
Programming (via satellite): CNN HD; Discovery Channel HD; ESPN HD; HDNet; HDNet Movies; Outdoor Channel 2 HD; TBS in HD; Turner Network TV HD.
Fee: $5.00 monthly.

Digital Pay Service 1
Pay Units: 166.
Programming (via satellite): Cinemax (multiplexed); Cinemax HD; Encore; HBO (multiplexed); HBO HD; Starz (multiplexed); Starz HDTV.
Fee: $12.95 monthly (HBO, Cinemax, or Starz/Encore).

Internet Service
Operational: Yes. Began: June 1, 2003.
Broadband Service: Cablelynx.
Fee: $24.95-$44.95 monthly.

Telephone Service
Digital: Operational
Fee: $45.70 monthly
Miles of Plant: 33.0 (coaxial); None (fiber optic). Additional miles planned: 2.0 (coaxial). Homes passed: 1,765.
Manager: John Harbin. Plant Manager: Billy Bechtel.
City fee: 3% of gross.
Ownership: WEHCO Video Inc. (MSO).

CABOT—Suddenlink Communications, 1421 S 2nd St, Cabot, AR 72023. Phones: 314-965-2020; 877-423-2743 (Customer service). Fax: 903-561-5485. Web Site: http://www.suddenlink.com. Also serves Austin, Faulkner County (portions), Little Rock AFB, Lonoke County (portions), Macon, Pulaski County (portions), South Bend & Ward. ICA: AR0023.
TV Market Ranking: 50 (Austin, CABOT, Faulkner County (portions), Little Rock AFB, Lonoke County (portions), Macon, Pulaski County (portions), South Bend, Ward); Outside TV Markets (Faulkner County (portions)). Franchise award date: N.A. Franchise expiration date: N.A. Began: January 1, 1983.
Channel capacity: 49 (operating 2-way). Channels available but not in use: N.A.

Basic Service
Subscribers: 8,953.
Programming (received off-air): KARK-TV (NBC) Little Rock; KARZ-TV (MNT) Little Rock; KASN (CW) Pine Bluff; KATV (ABC) Little Rock; KETS (PBS) Little Rock; KKAP (ETV) Little Rock; KKYK-DT (IND) Camden; KLRT-TV (FOX) Little Rock; KTHV (CBS) Little Rock; KTWN-LD Searcy; KVTN-DT (IND) Pine Bluff.
Programming (via satellite): C-SPAN; Hallmark Channel; QVC.
Fee: $39.95 installation; $19.95 monthly.

Expanded Basic Service 1
Subscribers: N.A.
Programming (via satellite): ABC Family Channel; AMC; Animal Planet; Arts & Entertainment; Cartoon Network; CNBC; CNN; Comcast Sports Net Southwest; Comedy Central; Discovery Channel; Disney Channel; E! Entertainment Television; ESPN; ESPN 2; Food Network; Fox News Channel; FX; Great American Country; Hallmark Channel; Headline News; HGTV; History Channel; INSP; Lifetime; MTV; National Geographic Channel; Nickelodeon; Spike TV; Syfy; TBS Superstation; The Learning Channel; Turner Classic Movies; Turner Network TV; TV Land; USA Network; VH1; Weather Channel.
Fee: $22.04 monthly.

Digital Basic Service
Subscribers: N.A.
Programming (received off-air): KARK-TV (NBC) Little Rock; KATV (ABC) Little Rock; KLRT-TV (FOX) Little Rock; KTHV (CBS) Little Rock.
Programming (via satellite): BBC America; Bio; Bloomberg Television; CMT Pure Country; Discovery HD Theater; Discovery Health Channel; Discovery Kids Channel; Discovery Military Channel; Discovery Planet Green; DMX Music; ESPN Classic Sports; ESPN HD; ESPNews; Fuse; G4; Golf Channel; GSN; HDNet; HDNet Movies; History Channel International; ID Investigation Discovery; Independent Film Channel; Lifetime Movie Network; MTV2; National Geographic Channel HD Network; Nick Jr.; NickToons TV; Outdoor Channel; Science Channel; Sleuth; Speed Channel; Style Network; Sundance Channel; TeenNick; Toon Disney; Turner Network TV HD; Versus; VH1 Classic; WE tv.
Fee: $16.00 monthly.

Pay Service 1
Pay Units: 1,394.
Programming (via satellite): Showtime.
Fee: $12.95 monthly.

Pay Service 2
Pay Units: 1,069.
Programming (via satellite): HBO.
Fee: $12.95 monthly.

Digital Pay Service 1
Pay Units: N.A.
Programming (via satellite): Cinemax (multiplexed); Encore (multiplexed); HBO (multiplexed); Showtime (multiplexed); Starz (multiplexed); The Movie Channel (multiplexed).
Fee: $12.95 monthly (HBO, Cinemax, Showtime/TMC or Starz/Encore).

Video-On-Demand: No

Pay-Per-View
iN DEMAND (delivered digitally); Playboy TV (delivered digitally); Fresh (delivered digitally); Club Jenna (delivered digitally).

Internet Service
Operational: Yes. Began: September 1, 2002.
Broadband Service: Cebridge High Speed Cable Internet.
Fee: $21.95 monthly; $9.95 modem lease.

Telephone Service
Digital: Operational
Fee: $33.00 monthly
Miles of Plant: 499.0 (coaxial); None (fiber optic). Homes passed: 14,808.
Regional Manager: Todd Cruthird. Chief Technician: Randy Oliger.
City fee: 3% of gross.
Ownership: Cequel Communications LLC (MSO).

CALDWELL—Indco Cable TV, PO Box 3799, 2700 N Saint Louis, Batesville, AR 72503-3799. Phone: 870-793-4174. Fax: 870-793-7439. Web Site: http://www.indco.net. Also serves Colt & St. Francis County. ICA: AR0222.
TV Market Ranking: 26 (St. Francis County (portions)); Outside TV Markets (CALDWELL, Colt, St. Francis County (portions)). Franchise award date: N.A. Franchise expiration date: N.A. Began: December 1, 1988.
Channel capacity: 36 (operating 2-way). Channels available but not in use: N.A.

Basic Service
Subscribers: 947.
Programming (received off-air): KAIT (ABC) Jonesboro; KATV (ABC) Little Rock; KKYK-DT (IND) Camden; KTHV (CBS) Little Rock; WHBQ-TV (FOX) Memphis; WKNO (PBS) Memphis; WLMT (CW) Memphis; WMC-TV (NBC) Memphis; WPTY-TV (ABC) Memphis; WREG-TV (CBS) Memphis.
Programming (via satellite): ABC Family Channel; Arts & Entertainment; BET Networks; CNN; Comcast Sports Net Southwest; Country Music TV; Discovery Channel; Disney Channel; ESPN; ESPN 2; Fox News Channel; FX; Headline News; HGTV; History Channel; Home Shopping Network; Lifetime; Nickelodeon; Outdoor Channel; QVC; Spike TV; Syfy; TBS Superstation; Trinity Broadcasting Network; Turner Classic Movies; Turner Network TV; USA Network; Weather Channel; WGN America.
Fee: $26.95 monthly.

Pay Service 1
Pay Units: 28.
Programming (via satellite): Cinemax.
Fee: $8.00 monthly.

Pay Service 2
Pay Units: 38.
Programming (via satellite): HBO.
Fee: $10.00 monthly.

Pay Service 3
Pay Units: 48.
Programming (via satellite): Cinemax; HBO.
Fee: $16.00 monthly.

Internet Service
Operational: Yes.

Telephone Service
Digital: Operational
Miles of Plant: 21.0 (coaxial); None (fiber optic). Homes passed: 1,050. Total homes in franchised area: 2,200.
Manager: J.D. Pierce. Chief Technician: Tom Barnett. Marketing Director: Connie Barnett.
Ownership: Indco Cable TV (MSO).

CALICO ROCK—Indco Cable TV, PO Box 3799, 2700 N Saint Louis, Batesville, AR 72503-3799. Phone: 870-793-4174. Fax: 870-793-7439. Web Site: http://www.indco.net. Also serves Pineville. ICA: AR0223.
TV Market Ranking: Outside TV Markets (CALICO ROCK, Pineville). Franchise award date: N.A. Franchise expiration date: N.A. Began: January 1, 1970.
Channel capacity: 36 (operating 2-way). Channels available but not in use: N.A.

Basic Service
Subscribers: 354.
Programming (received off-air): KAIT (ABC) Jonesboro; KARK-TV (NBC) Little Rock; KATV (ABC) Little Rock; KEMV (PBS) Mountain View; KOLR (CBS) Springfield; KTHV (CBS) Little Rock; KYTV (CW, NBC) Springfield.
Programming (via satellite): ABC Family Channel; CNN; Country Music TV; Discovery Channel; Disney Channel; ESPN; ESPN 2; Fox Sports Net; FX; Headline News; HGTV; History Channel; Lifetime; Nickelodeon; Outdoor Channel; QVC; Spike TV; Syfy; TBS Superstation; The Learning Channel; Trinity Broadcasting Network; Turner Classic Movies; Turner Network TV; USA Network; Weather Channel; WGN America.
Fee: $30.95 monthly.

Pay Service 1
Pay Units: 8.
Programming (via satellite): Cinemax.
Fee: $8.00 monthly.

Pay Service 2
Pay Units: 7.
Programming (via satellite): HBO.
Fee: $10.00 monthly.

Video-On-Demand: Planned

Internet Service
Operational: Yes.
Fee: $29.95 monthly.

Telephone Service
None
Miles of Plant: 15.0 (coaxial); None (fiber optic).
Manager: J. D. Pierce. Chief Technician: Tommy Barnett. Marketing Director: Connie Barnett.
Ownership: Indco Cable TV (MSO).

CAMDEN—Cam-Tel Co., PO Box 835, 113 Madison Ave NE, Camden, AR 71701-3514. Phones: 870-836-5969 (Headend); 870-836-8111. Fax: 870-836-2109. E-mail: camdencabletvcs@cablelynx.com. Web Site: http://www.camdencabletv.com. ICA: AR0019.
TV Market Ranking: 99 (CAMDEN). Franchise award date: N.A. Franchise expiration date: N.A. Began: March 1, 1964.
Channel capacity: 76 (operating 2-way). Channels available but not in use: 11.

Basic Service
Subscribers: 4,866.
Programming (received off-air): KARK-TV (NBC) Little Rock; KARZ-TV (MNT) Little Rock; KASN (CW) Pine Bluff; KATV (ABC) Little Rock; KETS (PBS) Little Rock; KKAP (ETV) Little Rock; KKYK-CA (IND) Little Rock; KLRT-TV (FOX) Little Rock; KTHV (CBS) Little Rock; KTVE (NBC) El Dorado; KVTN-DT (IND) Pine Bluff.
Programming (via satellite): ABC Family Channel; AMC; Animal Planet; Arts & Entertainment; BET Networks; Cartoon Network; CNBC; CNN; Comcast Sports Net Southwest; Country Music TV; C-SPAN; C-SPAN 2; Discovery Channel; Disney Channel; ESPN; ESPN 2; Food Network; Fox News Channel; FX; Hallmark Channel; Headline News; HGTV; History Channel; Home Shopping Network; Lifetime; MTV; Nickelodeon; ShopNBC; Spike TV; Syfy; TBS Superstation; The Learning Channel; Turner Classic Movies; Turner Network TV; TV Guide Network; TV Land; USA Network; VH1; Weather Channel; WGN America.
Current originations: Government Access; Public Access; Educational Access.
Fee: $40.00 installation; $52.95 monthly.

Digital Basic Service
Subscribers: N.A.
Programming (via satellite): AmericanLife TV Network; BBC America; Bio; CMT Pure Country; Discovery Health Channel; Discovery Kids Channel; Discovery Military

Channel; Discovery Planet Green; DMX Music; ESPNews; FitTV; Fox Soccer; FSN Digital Atlantic; FSN Digital Central; FSN Digital Pacific; G4; Golf Channel; Great American Country; GSN; Halogen Network; History Channel International; ID Investigation Discovery; Lifetime Movie Network; MTV Hits; MTV Jams; MTV Tres; MTV2; National Geographic Channel; Nick Jr.; Nick Too; NickToons TV; Outdoor Channel; Science Channel; SoapNet; Speed Channel; Style Network; TeenNick; Toon Disney; VH1 Classic; VH1 Soul; WE tv.
Fee: $10.00 monthly.

Digital Pay Service 1
Pay Units: 614.
Programming (via satellite): Cinemax (multiplexed).
Fee: $12.95 monthly.

Digital Pay Service 2
Pay Units: N.A.
Programming (via satellite): Encore; Starz (multiplexed).
Fee: $12.95 monthly.

Digital Pay Service 3
Pay Units: 1,284.
Programming (via satellite): HBO (multiplexed).
Fee: $12.95 monthly.

Video-On-Demand: No

Pay-Per-View
iN DEMAND (delivered digitally), Fee: $3.95, Addressable: Yes.

Internet Service
Operational: Yes. Began: August 10, 2001.
Broadband Service: Cablelynx.
Fee: $24.95-$74.95 monthly; $10.00 modem lease.

Telephone Service
Analog: Not Operational
Digital: Operational
Fee: $45.70 monthly

Miles of Plant: 189.0 (coaxial); 99.0 (fiber optic). Homes passed: 7,570.
Technical Operations & Plant Manager: Ronnie Floyd. Office Manager: Stacy Eads.
City fee: 5% of revenue.
Ownership: WEHCO Video Inc. (MSO).; Walter E Hussman Jr.

CARPENTER DAM—Community Communications Co., 1920 Highway 425 N, Monticello, AR 71655-4463. Phones: 800-272-2191; 870-367-7300. Fax: 870-367-9770. E-mail: generalmanager@ccc-cable.net. Web Site: http://www.ccc-cable.net. Also serves Diamondhead. ICA: AR0293.
TV Market Ranking: Below 100 (CARPENTER DAM, Diamondhead). Franchise award date: N.A. Franchise expiration date: N.A. Began: N.A.
Channel capacity: 48 (not 2-way capable). Channels available but not in use: N.A.

Basic Service
Subscribers: 137.
Programming (received off-air): KARK-TV (NBC) Little Rock; KASN (CW) Pine Bluff; KATV (ABC) Little Rock; KETS (PBS) Little Rock; KLRT-TV (FOX) Little Rock; KTHV (CBS) Little Rock.
Programming (via satellite): ABC Family Channel; AMC; Arts & Entertainment; Cartoon Network; CNBC; CNN; Comcast Sports Net Southwest; Country Music TV; Discovery Channel; Disney Channel; ESPN; ESPN 2; Fox News Channel; FX; Golf Channel; Headline News; Home Shopping Network; Lifetime; MTV; Nickelodeon; Outdoor Channel; QVC; Spike TV; Syfy; TBS Superstation; The Learning Channel; Trinity Broadcasting Network; Turner Classic Movies; Turner Network TV; TV Land; USA Network; Weather Channel; WGN America.
Fee: $20.00 installation; $33.60 monthly.

Pay Service 1
Pay Units: 12.
Programming (via satellite): HBO.
Fee: $12.00 monthly.

Pay Service 2
Pay Units: 10.
Programming (via satellite): Showtime; The Movie Channel.
Fee: $12.00 monthly (each).

Video-On-Demand: No

Internet Service
Operational: No.

Telephone Service
None

Miles of Plant: 14.0 (coaxial); None (fiber optic). Homes passed: 348. Total homes in franchised area: 348.
Assistant Manager: Deborah Forrest. Operations Manager: Larry Ivy.
Ownership: Community Communications Co. (MSO).

CARTHAGE—Formerly served by Almega Cable. No longer in operation. ICA: AR0185.

CARTHAGE—Formerly served by Almega Cable. No longer in operation. ICA: AR0182.

CASA—Formerly served by Eagle Media. No longer in operation. ICA: AR0308.

CAVE CITY—Indco Cable TV, PO Box 3799, 2700 N Saint Louis, Batesville, AR 72503-3799. Phones: 800-364-0831; 870-793-4174. Fax: 870-793-7439. Web Site: http://www.indco.net. Also serves Good Earth, Independence County (northern portion), Pfeiffer & Weavers Chapel. ICA: AR0224.
TV Market Ranking: Outside TV Markets (CAVE CITY, Good Earth, Independence County (northern portion), Pfeiffer, Weavers Chapel). Franchise award date: N.A. Franchise expiration date: N.A. Began: August 1, 1963.
Channel capacity: 40 (operating 2-way). Channels available but not in use: N.A.

Basic Service
Subscribers: 958.
Programming (received off-air): KAIT (ABC) Jonesboro; KARK-TV (NBC) Little Rock; KATV (ABC) Little Rock; KEMV (PBS) Mountain View; KLRT-TV (FOX) Little Rock; KTHV (CBS) Little Rock; KVTJ-DT (IND) Jonesboro.
Programming (via satellite): ABC Family Channel; AmericanLife TV Network; CNN; Comcast Sports Net Southwest; Country Music TV; Discovery Channel; Disney Channel; ESPN; ESPN 2; FX; HGTV; Lifetime; Nickelodeon; Outdoor Channel; QVC; Spike TV; Syfy; TBS Superstation; Trinity Broadcasting Network; Turner Classic Movies; Turner Network TV; USA Network; VH1; Weather Channel; WGN America.
Fee: $35.45 installation; $30.95 monthly.

Pay Service 1
Pay Units: 16.
Programming (via satellite): HBO.
Fee: $10.00 monthly.

Pay Service 2
Pay Units: 2.
Programming (via satellite): Showtime.
Fee: $9.00 monthly.

Pay Service 3
Pay Units: 1.
Programming (via satellite): The Movie Channel.
Fee: $9.00 monthly.

Pay Service 4
Pay Units: 6.
Programming (via satellite): Cinemax.
Fee: $8.00 monthly.

Video-On-Demand: Planned

Internet Service
Operational: Yes. Began: December 10, 2004.
Subscribers: 145.
Broadband Service: In-house.
Fee: $29.95 monthly.

Telephone Service
None

Miles of Plant: 60.0 (coaxial); 11.0 (fiber optic). Total homes in franchised area: 1,100.
General Manager: J.D. Pierce. Marketing Director: Connie Barnett. Chief Technician: Tom Barnett.
Ownership: Indco Cable TV (MSO).

CEDARVILLE—Cox Communications. Now served by SPRINGDALE, AR [AR0220]. ICA: AR0060.

CHARLESTON—Suddenlink Communications, 12444 Powerscourt Dr, Saint Louis, MO 63131-3660. Phones: 314-965-2020; 800-999-6845 (Customer service). Fax: 903-561-5485. Web Site: http://www.suddenlink.com. ICA: AR0225.
TV Market Ranking: Below 100 (CHARLESTON). Franchise award date: December 1, 1970. Franchise expiration date: N.A. Began: January 1, 1972.
Channel capacity: 78 (operating 2-way). Channels available but not in use: None.

Basic Service
Subscribers: 622.
Programming (received off-air): KAFT (PBS) Fayetteville; KFDF-CA Fort Smith; KFSM-TV (CBS) Fort Smith; KFTA-TV (FOX) Fort Smith; KHBS (ABC) Fort Smith; KNWA-TV (NBC) Rogers.
Programming (via satellite): C-SPAN; CW+; Home Shopping Network; INSP.
Fee: $34.95 installation; $19.95 monthly.

Expanded Basic Service 1
Subscribers: N.A.
Programming (via satellite): ABC Family Channel; AMC; Animal Planet; Arts & Entertainment; BET Networks; Cartoon Network; CNBC; CNN; Comcast Sports Net Southwest; Comedy Central; Discovery Channel; Disney Channel; E! Entertainment Television; ESPN; ESPN 2; Food Network; Fox News Channel; FX; Great American Country; Hallmark Channel; Headline News; HGTV; History Channel; Lifetime; MSNBC; MTV; National Geographic Channel; Nickelodeon; Outdoor Channel; Speed Channel; Spike TV; Syfy; TBS Superstation; The Learning Channel; Travel Channel; truTV; Turner Classic Movies; Turner Network TV; TV Land; USA Network; VH1; Weather Channel.
Fee: $22.04 monthly.

Pay Service 1
Pay Units: 76.
Programming (via satellite): HBO.
Fee: $12.95 monthly.

Pay Service 2
Pay Units: 44.
Programming (via satellite): The Movie Channel.
Fee: $12.95 monthly.

Pay Service 3
Pay Units: 50.
Programming (via satellite): Showtime.
Fee: $12.95 monthly.

Video-On-Demand: No

Internet Service
Operational: Yes. Began: November 12, 2003.
Broadband Service: Cebridge High Speed Cable Internet.
Fee: $19.95 monthly.

Telephone Service
None

Miles of Plant: 21.0 (coaxial); None (fiber optic). Homes passed: 1,050.
Regional Manager: Todd Cruthird. Plant Manager: Danny Keith. Marketing Director: Beverly Gambell.
City fee: 2% of gross.
Ownership: Cequel Communications LLC (MSO).

CHIDESTER—Formerly served by Almega Cable. No longer in operation. ICA: AR0138.

CLARENDON—Rapid Cable, 515 E Longview Dr, Arp, TX 75750. Phone: 903-859-6492. Fax: 903-859-3708. ICA: AR0084.
TV Market Ranking: Outside TV Markets (CLARENDON). Franchise award date: N.A. Franchise expiration date: N.A. Began: December 1, 1982.
Channel capacity: 54 (operating 2-way). Channels available but not in use: 9.

Basic Service
Subscribers: 306.
Programming (received off-air): KARK-TV (NBC) Little Rock; KASN (CW) Pine Bluff; KATV (ABC) Little Rock; KETS (PBS) Little Rock; KKYK-DT (IND) Camden; KLRT-TV (FOX) Little Rock; KTHV (CBS) Little Rock; 1 FM.
Programming (via satellite): Home Shopping Network; INSP.
Fee: $54.95 installation; $20.95 monthly.

Expanded Basic Service 1
Subscribers: N.A.
Programming (via satellite): ABC Family Channel; Animal Planet; Arts & Entertainment; BET Networks; Cartoon Network; CNBC; CNN; Comedy Central; C-SPAN; Discovery Channel; Disney Channel; ESPN; ESPN 2; Great American Country; Headline News; HGTV; Lifetime; MSNBC; National Geographic Channel; Nickelodeon; Outdoor Channel; Spike TV; TBS Superstation; The Learning Channel; Turner Classic Movies; Turner Network TV; USA Network; Weather Channel.
Fee: $23.10 monthly.

Digital Basic Service
Subscribers: N.A.
Programming (via satellite): BBC America; Bio; Bloomberg Television; Discovery Health Channel; Discovery Kids Channel; Discovery Military Channel; Discovery Planet Green; DMX Music; ESPN Classic Sports; ESPNews; Fox College Sports Atlantic; Fox College Sports Central; Fox College Sports Pacific; Fox Soccer; Fuse; G4; Golf Channel; GSN; History Channel; History Channel International; ID Investigation Discovery; Independent Film Channel; Science Channel; ShopNBC; Sleuth; Speed Channel; Style Network; Sundance Channel; Toon Disney; Trinity Broadcasting Network; Versus; WE tv.

Pay Service 1
Pay Units: 16.
Programming (via satellite): Cinemax.
Fee: $12.95 monthly.

Pay Service 2
Pay Units: 37.
Programming (via satellite): HBO.
Fee: $12.95 monthly.

Pay Service 3
Pay Units: 54.
Programming (via satellite): Showtime.
Fee: $12.95 monthly.
Digital Pay Service 1
Pay Units: N.A.
Programming (via satellite): Cinemax (multiplexed); Encore (multiplexed); HBO (multiplexed); Showtime (multiplexed); Starz (multiplexed); The Movie Channel.
Video-On-Demand: No
Internet Service
Operational: No.
Telephone Service
None
Miles of Plant: 11.0 (coaxial); None (fiber optic). Homes passed: 1,091. Total homes in franchised area: 1,100.
Regional Manager: Mike Taylor. Chief Technician: Larry Stafford.
City fee: 3% of gross.
Ownership: Rapid Communications LLC (MSO).

CLARKSVILLE—Suddenlink Communications, 127 N Elmira Ave, Russellville, AR 72802-9614. Phones: 800-582-9577; 479-968-2223. Fax: 479-968-1343. Web Site: http://www.suddenlink.com. ICA: AR0043.
TV Market Ranking: Outside TV Markets (CLARKSVILLE). Franchise award date: N.A. Franchise expiration date: N.A. Began: September 1, 1964.
Channel capacity: N.A. Channels available but not in use: N.A.
Basic Service
Subscribers: 2,800.
Programming (received off-air): KAFT (PBS) Fayetteville; KARK-TV (NBC) Little Rock; KATV (ABC) Little Rock; KFDF-CA Fort Smith; KFSM-TV (CBS) Fort Smith; KFTA-TV (FOX) Fort Smith; KHBS (ABC) Fort Smith; KTHV (CBS) Little Rock; KXUN-LP Fort Smith; allband FM.
Programming (via satellite): C-SPAN; Home Shopping Network; QVC; TBS Superstation; Telefutura; Weather Channel; WGN America.
Current originations: Public Access; Educational Access.
Fee: $38.00 installation; $19.95 monthly; $2.25 converter; $15.00 additional installation.
Expanded Basic Service 1
Subscribers: N.A.
Programming (via satellite): ABC Family Channel; AMC; Animal Planet; Arts & Entertainment; BET Networks; Bravo; Cartoon Network; CNBC; CNN; Comcast Sports Net Southwest; Comedy Central; Country Music TV; C-SPAN 2; Discovery Channel; Disney Channel; E! Entertainment Television; ESPN; ESPN 2; Eternal Word TV Network; Food Network; Fox News Channel; FX; GalaVision; Great American Country; Headline News; HGTV; History Channel; INSP; Jewelry Television; Lifetime; Lifetime Movie Network; MSNBC; MTV; Nickelodeon; Outdoor Channel; Speed Channel; Spike TV; Syfy; The Learning Channel; Travel Channel; Trinity Broadcasting Network; truTV; Turner Classic Movies; Turner Network TV; TV Guide Network; TV Land; USA Network; Versus; VH1.
Fee: $23.75 monthly.
Digital Basic Service
Subscribers: N.A.
Programming (received off-air): KARK-TV (NBC) Little Rock; KTHV (CBS) Little Rock.
Programming (via satellite): Animal Planet HD; Arts & Entertainment HD; Bandamax; BBC America; Bio; Bloomberg Television; Boomerang; Boomerang en Espanol; CBS College Sports Network; Chiller; Cine Latino; Cine Mexicano; CMT Pure Country; CNN en Espanol; Cooking Channel; Cox Sports Television; De Pelicula; De Pelicula Clasico; Discovery Channel HD; Discovery en Espanol; Discovery HD Theater; Discovery Health Channel; Discovery Kids Channel; Discovery Military Channel; Discovery Planet Green; Do-It-Yourself; Encore (multiplexed); ESPN 2 HD; ESPN Classic Sports; ESPN Deportes; ESPN HD; ESPN U; ESPNews; EWTN en Espanol; FamilyNet; Food Network HD; Fox Reality Channel; Fox Soccer; Fox Sports en Espanol; FSN HD; Fuel TV; Fuse; FX HD; G4; GalaVision; Golf Channel; Gospel Music Channel; GSN; Hallmark Channel; Halogen Network; HDNet; HDNet Movies; HGTV HD; History Channel en Espanol; History Channel HD; History Channel International; ID Investigation Discovery; Independent Film Channel; KATV (ABC) Little Rock; Latele Novela Network; Lifetime Real Women; MTV Hits; MTV Tres; MTV2; mtvU; mun2 television; Music Choice; National Geographic Channel; National Geographic Channel HD Network; Nick Jr.; NickToons en Espanol; NickToons TV; Oxygen; Palladia; RFD-TV; Science Channel; Si TV; SoapNet; Sorpresa; Style Network; Sundance Channel; Sur Network; Syfy HD; TBN Enlace USA; TBS in HD; TeenNick; Telehit; Telemundo; Tennis Channel; The Sportsman Channel; TLC HD; Toon Disney; Toon Disney en Espanol; Turner Network TV HD; TV Chile; TV One; Universal HD; USA Network HD; VH1 Classic; Video Rola; WE tv; Weatherscan.
Fee: $24.95 monthly.
Digital Pay Service 1
Pay Units: N.A.
Programming (via satellite): Cinemax (multiplexed); HBO (multiplexed); HBO HD; HBO Latino; Showtime (multiplexed); Showtime HD; Starz (multiplexed); The Movie Channel (multiplexed).
Fee: $12.95 monthly (HBO, Cinemax, Showtime/TMC or Starz).
Video-On-Demand: No
Pay-Per-View
iN DEMAND (delivered digitally); Fresh (delivered digitally); Playboy TV (delivered digitally); Shorteez (delivered digitally); Club Jenna (delivered digitally); Spice: Xcess (delivered digitally); Playboy en Espanol (delivered digitally).
Internet Service
Operational: Yes.
Broadband Service: Cebridge High Speed Cable Internet.
Fee: $33.00 monthly.
Telephone Service
Digital: Operational
Fee: $33.00 monthly
Miles of Plant: 53.0 (coaxial); None (fiber optic).
Manager: Mike Ederington. Chief Engineer: Wayne Ollis. Customer Service Manager: Jane Ollis.
City fee: 3% of gross.
Ownership: Cequel Communications LLC (MSO).

CLINTON—Clinton Cablevision Inc., PO Box 900, 114 Richard Rd, Clinton, AR 72031-0900. Phones: 877-383-8257; 501-745-4040. Fax: 501-745-4663. E-mail: clintoncable@clintoncable.net. Web Site: http://www.clintoncable.net. Also serves Van Buren County. ICA: AR0226.
TV Market Ranking: Outside TV Markets (CLINTON, Van Buren County). Franchise award date: N.A. Franchise expiration date: N.A. Began: November 1, 1976.
Channel capacity: 60 (operating 2-way). Channels available but not in use: N.A.
Basic Service
Subscribers: 1,074.
Programming (received off-air): KARK-TV (NBC) Little Rock; KASN (CW) Pine Bluff; KATV (ABC) Little Rock; KEMV (PBS) Mountain View; KKYK-CA (IND) Little Rock; KLRT-TV (FOX) Little Rock; KTHV (CBS) Little Rock.
Programming (via satellite): Bloomberg Television; Cartoon Network; CNN; Country Music TV; C-SPAN; Daystar TV Network; Discovery Channel; Disney Channel; ESPN; Food Network; Fox News Channel; FX; Gospel Music TV; Great American Country; Headline News; HGTV; Home Shopping Network; Lifetime; Nickelodeon; Outdoor Channel; QVC; RFD-TV; Spike TV; TBS Superstation; The Learning Channel; Trinity Broadcasting Network; Turner Classic Movies; Turner Network TV; TV Land; USA Network; Weather Channel; WGN America.
Fee: $25.00 installation; $24.75 monthly.
Digital Basic Service
Subscribers: N.A.
Programming (via satellite): BBC America; Discovery Digital Networks; DMX Music; Encore (multiplexed); ESPN 2; ESPN Classic Sports; ESPNews; FitTV; Fuse; G4; GAS; Golf Channel; GSN; Halogen Network; History Channel; Lifetime Movie Network; Nick Jr.; NickToons TV; Sleuth; Speed Channel; Syfy; Toon Disney; Versus; WE tv.
Fee: $15.95 monthly.
Digital Pay Service 1
Pay Units: N.A.
Programming (via satellite): Cinemax (multiplexed); Encore (multiplexed); HBO (multiplexed); Showtime (multiplexed); Starz (multiplexed); The Movie Channel (multiplexed).
Fee: $8.95 monthly (Cinemax or Encore/Starz), $11.95 monthly (HBO), $12.95 monthly (Showtime & TMC).
Video-On-Demand: No; No
Pay-Per-View
Movies (delivered digitally); Sports PPV (delivered digitally); Special events (delivered digitally); Adult Channels (delivered digitally).
Internet Service
Operational: Yes. Began: July 1, 2002.
Broadband Service: In-house.
Fee: $50.00 installation; $39.95 monthly.
Telephone Service
None
Miles of Plant: 18.0 (coaxial); None (fiber optic).
Manager & Chief Technician: John Hastings.
Ownership: Clinton Cable Inc.

COAL HILL—Suddenlink Communications, 12444 Powerscourt Dr, Saint Louis, MO 63131-3660. Phones: 800-999-6845 (Customer service); 314-965-2020. Fax: 903-561-5485. Web Site: http://www.suddenlink.com. Also serves Hartman & Johnson County (southwestern portion). ICA: AR0101.
TV Market Ranking: Outside TV Markets (COAL HILL, Hartman, Johnson County (southwestern portion)). Franchise award date: N.A. Franchise expiration date: N.A. Began: December 1, 1982.
Channel capacity: 36 (2-way capable). Channels available but not in use: None.
Basic Service
Subscribers: 378.
Programming (received off-air): KAFT (PBS) Fayetteville; KARK-TV (NBC) Little Rock; KATV (ABC) Little Rock; KFSM-TV (CBS) Fort Smith; KFTA-TV (FOX) Fort Smith; KHBS (ABC) Fort Smith; KTHV (CBS) Little Rock.
Programming (via satellite): Cartoon Network; CW+; Fox News Channel; Trinity Broadcasting Network.
Fee: $30.00 installation; $19.95 monthly.
Expanded Basic Service 1
Subscribers: N.A.
Programming (via satellite): ABC Family Channel; AMC; Arts & Entertainment; CNN; Discovery Channel; Disney Channel; ESPN; ESPN 2; Great American Country; Headline News; HGTV; History Channel; Home Shopping Network; Lifetime; National Geographic Channel; Nickelodeon; Outdoor Channel; Spike TV; Syfy; TBS Superstation; Turner Network TV; USA Network; Weather Channel.
Fee: $20.00 monthly.
Pay Service 1
Pay Units: 30.
Programming (via satellite): The Movie Channel.
Fee: $13.95 monthly.
Pay Service 2
Pay Units: 6.
Programming (via satellite): HBO.
Fee: $13.95 monthly.
Pay Service 3
Pay Units: 54.
Programming (via satellite): Showtime.
Fee: $13.95 monthly.
Video-On-Demand: No
Pay-Per-View
ESPN Extra (delivered digitally); ESPN Now (delivered digitally); Shorteez (delivered digitally); Fresh (delivered digitally); Playboy TV (delivered digitally); iN DEMAND (delivered digitally).
Internet Service
Operational: No.
Telephone Service
None
Miles of Plant: 31.0 (coaxial); None (fiber optic). Homes passed: 871.
Regional Manager: Todd Cruthird. Area Manager: Carl Miller. Plant Manager: Danny Keith. Marketing Director: Beverly Gambell.
Ownership: Cequel Communications LLC (MSO).

CONWAY—Conway Corp. C.T.S., PO Box 99, 1307 Prairie St, Conway, AR 72033. Phones: 501-450-6040 (Customer service); 501-450-6020; 501-450-6000. Fax: 501-450-6099. E-mail: billb@conwaycorp.net. Web Site: http://www.conwaycorp.com. ICA: AR0011.
TV Market Ranking: 50 (CONWAY). Franchise award date: May 22, 1979. Franchise expiration date: N.A. Began: June 1, 1980.
Channel capacity: 117 (operating 2-way). Channels available but not in use: 10.
Basic Service
Subscribers: 15,421.
Programming (received off-air): KARK-TV (NBC) Little Rock; KARZ-TV (MNT) Little Rock; KASN (CW) Pine Bluff; KATV (ABC) Little Rock; KETS (PBS) Little Rock; KKAP (ETV) Little Rock; KKYK-DT (IND) Camden; KLRT-TV (FOX) Little Rock; KTHV (CBS) Little Rock; KVTN-DT (IND) Pine Bluff.
Programming (via satellite): ABC Family Channel; Arts & Entertainment; CNN; Comcast Sports Net Southwest; C-SPAN; Discovery Channel; E! Entertainment Televi-

sion; ESPN; ESPN 2; Eternal Word TV Network; Fox News Channel; FX; Headline News; HGTV; Home Shopping Network; Lifetime; MSNBC; Nickelodeon; PBS Kids Channel; QVC; SoapNet; Spike TV; TBS Superstation; The Learning Channel; Toon Disney; Trinity Broadcasting Network; TV Guide Network; TV Land; USA Network; VH1; Weather Channel; WGN America.
Current originations: Leased Access; Public Access; Leased Access; Educational Access.
Fee: $38.50 installation; $25.50 monthly; $4.00 converter.

Expanded Basic Service 1
Subscribers: 12,704.
Programming (via satellite): AMC; Animal Planet; BET Networks; Bravo; Cartoon Network; CNBC; Comedy Central; Country Music TV; Disney Channel; ESPNews; FitTV; Food Network; Golf Channel; History Channel; MTV; National Geographic Channel; Outdoor Channel; Syfy; Telemundo; Travel Channel; truTV; Turner Classic Movies; Versus.
Fee: $10.50 monthly.

Digital Basic Service
Subscribers: 6,956.
Programming (via satellite): BBC America; Bio; Boomerang; Discovery Digital Networks; Do-It-Yourself; ESPN Classic Sports; Fox Movie Channel; Fox Sports World; G4; GAS; Great American Country; Hallmark Channel; History Channel International; Lifetime Movie Network; MTV Networks Digital Suite; Nick Jr.; Nick Too; Speed Channel; The Sportsman Channel; Trinity Broadcasting Network; WE tv.
Fee: $14.50 monthly; $4.00 converter.

Digital Pay Service 1
Pay Units: 1,024.
Programming (via satellite): Cinemax (multiplexed).
Fee: $5.00 installation; $9.45 monthly.

Digital Pay Service 2
Pay Units: 2,389.
Programming (via satellite): HBO (multiplexed).
Fee: $5.00 installation; $12.95 monthly.

Digital Pay Service 3
Pay Units: 1,214.
Programming (via satellite): Showtime (multiplexed).
Fee: $5.00 installation; $11.95 monthly.

Digital Pay Service 4
Pay Units: 304.
Programming (via satellite): Starz.
Fee: $8.45 monthly.

Video-On-Demand: No

Pay-Per-View
iN DEMAND, Addressable: Yes.

Internet Service
Operational: Yes.
Fee: $38.50 installation; $29.95 monthly.

Telephone Service
None

Miles of Plant: 498.0 (coaxial); 64.0 (fiber optic). Homes passed: 20,602. Total homes in franchised area: 20,602.
Chief Executive Officer: Richard Arnold. Chief Operating Officer: Tommy Shackelford. Marketing & Communications Coordinator: Crystal Kemp. Advertising & Marketing Manager: Linda Johnson.
City fee: 3% of gross.
Ownership: Conway Corp.

CONWAY (eastern portion)—Alliance Communications, PO Box 960, 290 S Broadview St, Greenbrier, AR 72058-9616. Phone: 501-679-6619. Fax: 501-679-5694. Web Site: http://www.alliancecable.net. ICA: AR0104.
TV Market Ranking: 50 (CONWAY (EASTERN PORTION)). Franchise award date: N.A. Franchise expiration date: N.A. Began: February 9, 1984.
Channel capacity: 36 (not 2-way capable). Channels available but not in use: 6.

Basic Service
Subscribers: 47.
Programming (received off-air): KARK-TV (NBC) Little Rock; KASN (CW) Pine Bluff; KATV (ABC) Little Rock; KETS (PBS) Little Rock; KLRT-TV (FOX) Little Rock; KTHV (CBS) Little Rock.
Programming (via satellite): ABC Family Channel; AmericanLife TV Network; CNN; Country Music TV; Disney Channel; ESPN; Headline News; MTV; Nickelodeon; TBS Superstation; Turner Network TV; USA Network; Weather Channel; WGN America; WPIX (CW, IND) New York.
Fee: $39.95 installation; $34.65 monthly.

Pay Service 1
Pay Units: N.A.
Programming (via satellite): HBO; Showtime.
Fee: $9.00 monthly (Showtime), $10.95 monthly (HBO).

Video-On-Demand: No

Internet Service
Operational: Yes.
Fee: $30.00 installation; $29.95 monthly.

Telephone Service
Digital: Operational
Fee: $49.95 installation; $54.95 monthly

Miles of Plant: 29.0 (coaxial); None (fiber optic). Homes passed: 710.
Vice President: Arl Cope. Operations Manager: Jeff Browers. Programming & Marketing Manager: James Fuller.
Ownership: Buford Media Group LLC (MSO).

CORNING—Allegiance Communications, 707 W Saratoga St, Shawnee, OK 74804. Phones: 405-395-1131; 405-275-6923. Web Site: http://www.allegiance.tv. ICA: AR0227.
TV Market Ranking: Below 100 (CORNING). Franchise award date: N.A. Franchise expiration date: N.A. Began: January 1, 1966.
Channel capacity: 28 (operating 2-way). Channels available but not in use: N.A.

Basic Service
Subscribers: N.A.
Programming (received off-air): KAIT (ABC) Jonesboro; KARK-TV (NBC) Little Rock; KATV (ABC) Little Rock; KBSI (FOX) Cape Girardeau; KFVS-TV (CBS, CW) Cape Girardeau; KTEJ (PBS) Jonesboro; KVTJ-DT (IND) Jonesboro; WMC-TV (NBC) Memphis; allband FM.
Programming (via satellite): CNN; C-SPAN; CW+; Home Shopping Network; QVC; Trinity Broadcasting Network; TV Guide Network; Weather Channel; WGN America.
Fee: $35.00 installation; $19.99 monthly.

Expanded Basic Service 1
Subscribers: N.A.
Programming (via satellite): ABC Family Channel; Arts & Entertainment; Cartoon Network; Comcast Sports Net Southwest; Comedy Central; Discovery Channel; Disney Channel; ESPN; ESPN 2; ESPN Classic Sports; Fox News Channel; HGTV; History Channel; INSP; Lifetime; NFL Network; Nickelodeon; Spike TV; Syfy; TBS Superstation; The Learning Channel; Travel Channel; Turner Classic Movies; Turner Network TV; TV Land; USA Network; VH1.
Fee: $32.16 monthly.

Digital Basic Service
Subscribers: N.A.
Programming (via satellite): AmericanLife TV Network; BBC America; Bio; Bloomberg Television; Bravo; Cine Latino; Cine Mexicano; CMT Pure Country; CNN en Espanol; Current; Discovery en Espanol; Discovery Health Channel; Discovery Kids Channel; Discovery Military Channel; Discovery Planet Green; DMX Music; Encore (multiplexed); ESPN 2; ESPN Classic Sports; ESPN Deportes; ESPNews; FitTV; Flix; Fox College Sports Atlantic; Fox College Sports Central; Fox College Sports Pacific; Fox Movie Channel; Fox Soccer; Fox Sports en Espanol; Fuse; G4; Golf Channel; Gospel Music Channel; Great American Country; GSN; Halogen Network; HGTV; History Channel; History Channel en Espanol; History Channel International; ID Investigation Discovery; Independent Film Channel; Lifetime Movie Network; MTV Hits; MTV Tres; MTV2; mun2 television; National Geographic Channel; Nick Jr.; NickToons TV; Outdoor Channel; Science Channel; ShopNBC; Sleuth; Speed Channel; Style Network; Sundance Channel; Syfy; TeenNick; The Word Network; Toon Disney; Trinity Broadcasting Network; Turner Classic Movies; VeneMovies; Versus; VH1 Classic; VH1 Soul; WE tv.
Fee: $10.85 monthly.

Pay Service 1
Pay Units: N.A.
Programming (via satellite): Cinemax; HBO; Showtime.

Digital Pay Service 1
Pay Units: N.A.
Programming (via satellite): Cinemax (multiplexed); HBO (multiplexed); HBO Latino; Showtime (multiplexed); Starz (multiplexed); The Movie Channel (multiplexed).

Video-On-Demand: No

Pay-Per-View
iN DEMAND (delivered digitally); Playboy TV (delivered digitally); Fresh (delivered digitally); Shorteez (delivered digitally).

Internet Service
Operational: Yes.
Fee: $24.95 installation; $39.95 monthly.

Telephone Service
None

Miles of Plant: 36.0 (coaxial); None (fiber optic).
Chief Executive Officer: Bill Haggarty. Regional Vice President: Andrew Dearth. Vice President, Marketing: Tracy Bass.
City fee: 3% of gross.
Ownership: Allegiance Communications (MSO).

CRAWFORDSVILLE—Formerly served by Ritter Communications. No longer in operation. ICA: AR0166.

CROSSETT—Cable South Media, 301 W 1st Ave, Crossett, AR 71635. Phone: 870-305-1241. Also serves North Crossett & West Crossett. ICA: AR0028.
TV Market Ranking: 99 (West Crossett); Outside TV Markets (CROSSETT, North Crossett, West Crossett). Franchise award date: N.A. Franchise expiration date: N.A. Began: November 1, 1966.
Channel capacity: 63 (not 2-way capable). Channels available but not in use: None.

Basic Service
Subscribers: 3,120.
Programming (received off-air): KAQY (ABC) Columbia; KARD (FOX) West Monroe; KATV (ABC) Little Rock; KETS (PBS) Little Rock; KLTM-TV (PBS) Monroe; KNOE-TV (CBS, CW) Monroe; KTVE (NBC) El Dorado.
Programming (via satellite): ION Television; QVC; TV Guide Network; WGN America.
Current originations: Educational Access.
Fee: $29.95 installation; $12.00 monthly; $1.37 converter.

Expanded Basic Service 1
Subscribers: 2,800.
Programming (via satellite): ABC Family Channel; AMC; Animal Planet; Arts & Entertainment; BET Networks; Bravo; Cartoon Network; CNBC; CNN; Comcast Sports Net Southwest; Comedy Central; Country Music TV; C-SPAN; Discovery Channel; Disney Channel; E! Entertainment Television; ESPN; ESPN 2; Food Network; Fox News Channel; FX; G4; Golf Channel; GSN; Hallmark Channel; Headline News; HGTV; History Channel; Home Shopping Network; INSP; Lifetime; MSNBC; MTV; National Geographic Channel; Nickelodeon; Outdoor Channel; Oxygen; Product Information Network; Shop at Home; SoapNet; Speed Channel; Spike TV; Syfy; TBS Superstation; The Learning Channel; Travel Channel; Trinity Broadcasting Network; truTV; Turner Classic Movies; Turner Network TV; TV Land; USA Network; Versus; VH1; WE tv; Weather Channel.
Fee: $29.25 monthly.

Digital Basic Service
Subscribers: N.A.
Programming (via satellite): BBC America; Bio; Bloomberg Television; Discovery Digital Networks; Do-It-Yourself; History Channel International; Independent Film Channel; MTV Networks Digital Suite; Music Choice; Nick Jr.; NickToons TV; Style Network; Sundance Channel; TV Guide Interactive Inc.

Pay Service 1
Pay Units: 252.
Programming (via satellite): The Movie Channel.
Fee: $8.00 monthly.

Digital Pay Service 1
Pay Units: N.A.
Programming (via satellite): Cinemax (multiplexed); Encore (multiplexed); Flix; HBO (multiplexed); Showtime (multiplexed); Starz (multiplexed); The Movie Channel (multiplexed).

Video-On-Demand: No

Pay-Per-View
iN DEMAND (delivered digitally); NBA TV (delivered digitally); NHL Center Ice/MLB Extra Innings (delivered digitally); Playboy TV (delivered digitally); Pleasure (delivered digitally); Fresh (delivered digitally); Shorteez (delivered digitally).

Internet Service
Operational: No.

Telephone Service
None

Miles of Plant: 81.0 (coaxial); 88.0 (fiber optic). Homes passed: 4,574.

City fee: 2% of gross.
Ownership: Cable South Media III LLC (MSO).

CURTIS—Community Communications Co., 1920 Hwy 425 N, Monticello, AR 71655-4463. Phones: 800-272-2191; 870-367-7300. Fax: 870-367-9770. E-mail: generalmanager@ccc-cable.net. Web Site: http://www.ccc-cable.net. Also serves Gum Springs. ICA: AR0147.
TV Market Ranking: Below 100 (CURTIS, Gum Springs). Franchise award date: N.A. Franchise expiration date: N.A. Began: N.A.
Channel capacity: 48 (not 2-way capable). Channels available but not in use: N.A.
Basic Service
Subscribers: 22.
Programming (received off-air): KARK-TV (NBC) Little Rock; KASN (CW) Pine Bluff; KATV (ABC) Little Rock; KETG (PBS) Arkadelphia; KLRT-TV (FOX) Little Rock; KTHV (CBS) Little Rock; KVTH-DT (IND) Hot Springs.
Programming (via satellite): ABC Family Channel; AMC; CNN; Country Music TV; Discovery Channel; Disney Channel; ESPN; Fox Sports Net; Headline News; Outdoor Channel; QVC; Syfy; TBS Superstation; USA Network; WGN America.
Fee: $15.95 monthly.
Pay Service 1
Pay Units: N.A.
Programming (via satellite): Showtime.
Fee: $10.95 monthly.
Video-On-Demand: No
Internet Service
Operational: No.
Telephone Service
None
Miles of Plant: 20.0 (coaxial); None (fiber optic). Homes passed: 350.
Ownership: Community Communications Co. (MSO).

CUSHMAN—Indco Cable TV, PO Box 3799, 2700 N Saint Louis, Batesville, AR 72503-3799. Phone: 870-793-4174. Fax: 870-793-7439. Web Site: http://www.indco.net. ICA: AR0228.
TV Market Ranking: Outside TV Markets (CUSHMAN). Franchise award date: N.A. Franchise expiration date: N.A. Began: N.A.
Channel capacity: 36 (operating 2-way). Channels available but not in use: N.A.
Basic Service
Subscribers: 107.
Programming (received off-air): KAIT (ABC) Jonesboro; KARK-TV (NBC) Little Rock; KEMV (PBS) Mountain View; KLRT-TV (FOX) Little Rock; KTHV (CBS) Little Rock.
Programming (via satellite): ABC Family Channel; CNN; Country Music TV; Discovery Channel; Disney Channel; ESPN; ESPN 2; HGTV; Lifetime; Nickelodeon; Outdoor Channel; QVC; Spike TV; Syfy; TBS Superstation; Trinity Broadcasting Network; Turner Classic Movies; Turner Network TV; USA Network; VH1; Weather Channel; WGN America.
Fee: $20.00 installation; $30.95 monthly.
Video-On-Demand: Planned
Internet Service
Operational: Yes.
Fee: $29.95 monthly.
Telephone Service
None
Manager: J. D. Pierce. Chief Technician: Tommy Barnett. Marketing Director: Connie Barnett.
Ownership: Indco Cable TV (MSO).

DAISY—Allegiance Communications, 707 W Saratoga St, Shawnee, OK 74804. Phones: 405-395-1131; 405-275-6923. Web Site: http://www.allegiance.tv. Also serves Kirby, Newhope & Salem. ICA: AR0142.
TV Market Ranking: Below 100 (Salem); Outside TV Markets (DAISY, Kirby, Newhope). Franchise award date: N.A. Franchise expiration date: N.A. Began: February 1, 1986.
Channel capacity: N.A. Channels available but not in use: N.A.
Basic Service
Subscribers: 486.
Programming (received off-air): KARK-TV (NBC) Little Rock; KASN (CW) Pine Bluff; KATV (ABC) Little Rock; KETG (PBS) Arkadelphia; KKYK-CA (IND) Little Rock; KLRT-TV (FOX) Little Rock; KTHV (CBS) Little Rock.
Programming (via satellite): ABC Family Channel; AMC; Arts & Entertainment; CNN; Country Music TV; Discovery Channel; Disney Channel; ESPN; History Channel; Nickelodeon; QVC; Spike TV; TBS Superstation; Trinity Broadcasting Network; USA Network; Weather Channel; WGN America.
Fee: $25.00 installation; $21.95 monthly.
Video-On-Demand: No
Pay-Per-View
Spice: Xcess (delivered digitally); iN DEMAND (delivered digitally); Playboy TV (delivered digitally); Fresh (delivered digitally); Club Jenna (delivered digitally).
Internet Service
Operational: No.
Telephone Service
None
Miles of Plant: 17.0 (coaxial); None (fiber optic).
Chief Executive Officer: Bill Haggarty. Regional Vice President: Andrew Dearth. Vice President, Marketing: Tracy Bass.
Ownership: Allegiance Communications (MSO).

DANVILLE—Suddenlink Communications, 12444 Powerscourt Dr, Saint Louis, MO 63131-3660. Phones: 800-999-6845 (Customer service); 314-965-2020. Fax: 903-561-5485. Web Site: http://www.suddenlink.com. Also serves Belleville, Havana & Yell County (eastern portion). ICA: AR0046.
TV Market Ranking: Below 100 (Yell County (eastern portion)); Outside TV Markets (Belleville, DANVILLE, Havana, Yell County (eastern portion)). Franchise award date: January 1, 1973. Franchise expiration date: N.A. Began: October 1, 1974.
Channel capacity: N.A. Channels available but not in use: N.A.
Basic Service
Subscribers: 1,575.
Programming (received off-air): KARK-TV (NBC) Little Rock; KARZ-TV (MNT) Little Rock; KASN (CW) Pine Bluff; KATV (ABC) Little Rock; KETS (PBS) Little Rock; KFSM-TV (CBS) Fort Smith; KKAP (ETV) Little Rock; KKYK-DT (IND) Camden; KLRT-TV (FOX) Little Rock; KTHV (CBS) Little Rock; KVTN-DT (IND) Pine Bluff; 13 FMs.
Programming (via satellite): C-SPAN; Trinity Broadcasting Network.
Fee: $30.00 installation.
Expanded Basic Service 1
Subscribers: N.A.
Programming (via satellite): ABC Family Channel; AMC; Animal Planet; Arts & Entertainment; CNBC; CNN; Discovery Channel; Disney Channel; ESPN; ESPN 2; Great American Country; Headline News; HGTV; Home Shopping Network; Lifetime; MSNBC; MTV; National Geographic Channel; Nickelodeon; Outdoor Channel; Spike TV; TBS Superstation; Turner Network TV; Univision; USA Network; Weather Channel.
Fee: $39.95 monthly.
Pay Service 1
Pay Units: 26.
Programming (via satellite): Cinemax.
Fee: $9.00 monthly.
Pay Service 2
Pay Units: 200.
Programming (via satellite): HBO.
Fee: $10.95 monthly.
Pay Service 3
Pay Units: 74.
Programming (via satellite): Showtime.
Fee: $10.95 monthly.
Video-On-Demand: No
Internet Service
Operational: No.
Telephone Service
None
Miles of Plant: 150.0 (coaxial); None (fiber optic). Homes passed: 2,400.
Regional Manager: Todd Cruthird. Plant Manager: Danny Keith. Marketing Director: Beverly Gambell.
City fee: 3% of gross.
Ownership: Cequel Communications LLC (MSO).

DE QUEEN—Allegiance Communications, 707 W Saratoga St, Shawnee, OK 74804. Phones: 405-395-1131; 405-275-6923. Web Site: http://www.allegiance.tv. Also serves Sevier County. ICA: AR0045.
TV Market Ranking: 58 (Sevier County (portions)); Outside TV Markets (DE QUEEN, Sevier County (portions)). Franchise award date: February 1, 1994. Franchise expiration date: N.A. Began: December 1, 1965.
Channel capacity: 35 (operating 2-way). Channels available but not in use: 1.
Basic Service
Subscribers: 2,356.
Programming (received off-air): KARK-TV (NBC) Little Rock; KATV (ABC) Little Rock; KETG (PBS) Arkadelphia; KMSS-TV (FOX) Shreveport; KSLA (CBS) Shreveport; KTAL-TV (NBC) Texarkana; KTBS-TV (ABC) Shreveport; KTHV (CBS) Little Rock; allband FM.
Programming (via satellite): CNN; QVC; Telemundo; Univision; Weather Channel.
Current originations: Religious Access; Government Access; Educational Access; Public Access.
Fee: $25.00 installation; $19.99 monthly.
Expanded Basic Service 1
Subscribers: 2,117.
Programming (via satellite): ABC Family Channel; AMC; Animal Planet; Arts & Entertainment; BET Networks; CMT Pure Country; CNBC; Comcast Sports Net Southwest; Discovery Channel; Disney Channel; ESPN; ESPN 2; ESPN Classic Sports; Food Network; Fox News Channel; FX; Hallmark Channel; Headline News; HGTV; History Channel; Lifetime; NFL Network; Nickelodeon; Spike TV; Syfy; TBS Superstation; The Learning Channel; truTV; Turner Classic Movies; Turner Network TV; TV Land; USA Network; VH1.
Fee: $10.56 monthly.
Digital Basic Service
Subscribers: N.A.
Programming (via satellite): 3 Angels Broadcasting Network; AmericanLife TV Network; BBC America; Bio; Black Family Channel; Bloomberg Television; Bravo; BYU Television; Church Channel; Cine Latino; Cine Mexicano; CNN en Espanol; Daystar TV Network; Discovery en Espanol; Discovery Health Channel; Discovery Kids Channel; Discovery Military Channel; Discovery Planet Green; DMX Music; Encore (multiplexed); ESPN Classic Sports; ESPNews; FamilyNet; FitTV; Flix; Fox College Sports Atlantic; Fox College Sports Central; Fox College Sports Pacific; Fox Movie Channel; Fox Soccer; Fox Sports en Espanol; Fuse; G4; GAS; Golden Eagle Broadcasting; Golf Channel; Gospel Music TV; Great American Country; GSN; Halogen Network; History Channel; History Channel en Espanol; History Channel International; ID Investigation Discovery; Independent Film Channel; JCTV; La Familia Network; Latin Television (LTV); Lifetime Movie Network; Lime; MTV Hits; MTV Tres; MTV2; National Geographic Channel; Nick Jr.; NickToons TV; Outdoor Channel; Puma TV; Science Channel; ShopNBC; Speed Channel; Style Network; Sundance Channel; Syfy; TBN Enlace USA; The Word Network; Toon Disney; Toon Disney en Espanol; Trinity Broadcasting Network; Trio; Turner Classic Movies; TV Chile; TV Colombia; TVE Internacional; Versus; VH1 Classic; VH1 Country; WE tv.
Fee: $32.16 monthly.
Pay Service 1
Pay Units: 144.
Programming (via satellite): Cinemax; Starz.
Fee: $9.95 monthly.
Pay Service 2
Pay Units: 462.
Programming (via satellite): HBO.
Fee: $10.95 monthly.
Pay Service 3
Pay Units: 387.
Programming (via satellite): Showtime.
Fee: $9.95 monthly.
Pay Service 4
Pay Units: 869.
Programming (via satellite): Encore.
Fee: $2.95 monthly.
Digital Pay Service 1
Pay Units: N.A.
Programming (via satellite): Cinemax (multiplexed); HBO (multiplexed); HBO Latino; Showtime (multiplexed); Starz (multiplexed); The Movie Channel (multiplexed).
Pay-Per-View
iN DEMAND (delivered digitally); Hot Choice (delivered digitally); Playboy TV (delivered digitally); Fresh (delivered digitally); Shorteez (delivered digitally).
Internet Service
Operational: Yes.
Fee: $24.95 installation; $39.95 monthly.
Telephone Service
Digital: Planned
Miles of Plant: 48.0 (coaxial); None (fiber optic). Homes passed: 2,499. Total homes in franchised area: 2,568.
Chief Executive Officer: Bill Haggarty. Regional Vice President: Andrew Dearth. Vice President, Marketing: Tracy Bass.
Ownership: Allegiance Communications (MSO).

DE WITT—Suddenlink Communications, 12444 Powerscourt Dr, Saint Louis, MO 63131-3660. Phones: 800-999-6845 (Customer service); 314-965-2020. Fax: 903-561-5485. Web Site: http://www.suddenlink.com. ICA: AR0064.
TV Market Ranking: Below 100 (DE WITT). Franchise award date: April 11, 1979. Fran-

chise expiration date: N.A. Began: November 15, 1980.
Channel capacity: N.A. Channels available but not in use: N.A.
Basic Service
Subscribers: 1,088.
Programming (received off-air): KARK-TV (NBC) Little Rock; KARZ-TV (MNT) Little Rock; KASN (CW) Pine Bluff; KATV (ABC) Little Rock; KETS (PBS) Little Rock; KKAP (ETV) Little Rock; KLRT-TV (FOX) Little Rock; KTHV (CBS) Little Rock; KVTN-DT (IND) Pine Bluff.
Fee: $34.95 installation; $23.00 monthly.
Expanded Basic Service 1
Subscribers: N.A.
Programming (via satellite): ABC Family Channel; AMC; Animal Planet; Arts & Entertainment; BET Networks; Cartoon Network; CNBC; CNN; Comcast Sports Net Southwest; Comedy Central; C-SPAN; Discovery Channel; Disney Channel; E! Entertainment Television; ESPN; ESPN 2; Food Network; Fox News Channel; FX; Great American Country; Hallmark Channel; Headline News; HGTV; History Channel; Jewelry Television; Lifetime; MSNBC; MTV; National Geographic Channel; Nickelodeon; Outdoor Channel; QVC; Spike TV; Syfy; TBS Superstation; The Learning Channel; Travel Channel; Turner Classic Movies; Turner Network TV; TV Land; USA Network; VH1; Weather Channel.
Fee: $31.00 monthly.
Digital Basic Service
Subscribers: N.A.
Programming (via satellite): BBC America; Bio; Bloomberg Television; Discovery Health Channel; Discovery Kids Channel; Discovery Military Channel; Discovery Planet Green; DMX Music; ESPN Classic Sports; ESPNews; Fox College Sports Atlantic; Fox College Sports Central; Fox College Sports Pacific; Fuse; G4; Golf Channel; GSN; History Channel International; ID Investigation Discovery; Independent Film Channel; Outdoor Channel; Science Channel; ShopNBC; Sleuth; Soccer Television; Speed Channel; Style Network; Sundance Channel; Toon Disney; Trinity Broadcasting Network; Versus; WE tv.
Fee: $19.00 monthly.
Pay Service 1
Pay Units: 81.
Programming (via satellite): Showtime.
Fee: $12.95 monthly.
Pay Service 2
Pay Units: 192.
Programming (via satellite): HBO.
Fee: $12.95 monthly.
Digital Pay Service 1
Pay Units: N.A.
Programming (via satellite): Cinemax (multiplexed); Encore (multiplexed); Flix; HBO (multiplexed); Showtime; Starz (multiplexed); The Movie Channel (multiplexed).
Fee: $12.95 monthly (HBO, Cinemax, Starz/Encore or Showtime/TMC).
Video-On-Demand: No
Pay-Per-View
iN DEMAND (delivered digitally); Playboy TV (delivered digitally); Club Jenna (delivered digitally); Fresh (delivered digitally); Spice: Xcess (delivered digitally).
Internet Service
Operational: Yes. Began: April 15, 2004.
Broadband Service: Cebridge High Speed Cable Internet.
Fee: $25.95 monthly.
Telephone Service
Digital: Operational
Fee: $33.00 monthly
Miles of Plant: 25.0 (coaxial); None (fiber optic). Homes passed: 1,340. Total homes in franchised area: 1,661.
Regional Manager: Todd Cruthird. Manager: Dave Walker. Chief Technician: Carl Miller. Marketing Director: Beverly Gambell.
City fee: 3% of gross.
Ownership: Cequel Communications LLC (MSO).

DELIGHT—Formerly served by Almega Cable. No longer in operation. ICA: AR0160.

DES ARC—Rapid Cable, 515 E Longview Dr, Arp, TX 75750. Phone: 903-859-6492. Fax: 903-859-3708. Also serves Prairie County (portions). ICA: AR0091.
TV Market Ranking: Outside TV Markets (DES ARC, Prairie County (portions)). Franchise award date: N.A. Franchise expiration date: N.A. Began: December 1, 1982.
Channel capacity: 60 (not 2-way capable). Channels available but not in use: N.A.
Basic Service
Subscribers: 201.
Programming (received off-air): KARK-TV (NBC) Little Rock; KASN (CW) Pine Bluff; KATV (ABC) Little Rock; KETS (PBS) Little Rock; KKYK-DT (IND) Camden; KLRT-TV (FOX) Little Rock; KTHV (CBS) Little Rock; KVTN-DT (IND) Pine Bluff.
Programming (via satellite): Home Shopping Network; National Geographic Channel.
Fee: $54.95 installation; $20.95 monthly.
Expanded Basic Service 1
Subscribers: N.A.
Programming (via satellite): ABC Family Channel; AMC; Arts & Entertainment; BET Networks; CNN; Discovery Channel; Disney Channel; ESPN; ESPN 2; Great American Country; Headline News; HGTV; History Channel; Lifetime; Nickelodeon; Outdoor Channel; Spike TV; Syfy; TBS Superstation; The Learning Channel; Trinity Broadcasting Network; Turner Network TV; USA Network; Weather Channel.
Fee: $23.10 monthly.
Digital Basic Service
Subscribers: N.A.
Programming (via satellite): AmericanLife TV Network; BBC America; Bio; Bloomberg Television; Discovery Health Channel; Discovery Kids Channel; Discovery Military Channel; Discovery Planet Green; DMX Music; ESPN 2; ESPN Classic Sports; ESPNews; Fox College Sports Atlantic; Fox College Sports Central; Fox College Sports Pacific; Fox Soccer; Fuse; G4; Golf Channel; GSN; Halogen Network; HGTV; History Channel; History Channel International; ID Investigation Discovery; Lifetime Movie Network; Outdoor Channel; Ovation; Science Channel; ShopNBC; Sleuth; Speed Channel; Style Network; Syfy; Trinity Broadcasting Network; Turner Classic Movies; Versus; WE tv.
Pay Service 1
Pay Units: 12.
Programming (via satellite): HBO.
Fee: $12.95 monthly.
Pay Service 2
Pay Units: 25.
Programming (via satellite): The Movie Channel.
Fee: $12.95 monthly.
Pay Service 3
Pay Units: 61.
Programming (via satellite): Showtime.
Fee: $12.95 monthly.
Digital Pay Service 1
Pay Units: N.A.
Programming (via satellite): Cinemax (multiplexed); Encore (multiplexed); Flix; HBO (multiplexed); Showtime (multiplexed); Starz (multiplexed); The Movie Channel (multiplexed).
Video-On-Demand: No
Pay-Per-View
iN DEMAND (delivered digitally); Playboy TV (delivered digitally); Club Jenna (delivered digitally).
Internet Service
Operational: No.
Telephone Service
None
Miles of Plant: 16.0 (coaxial); None (fiber optic). Homes passed: 910.
Regional Manager: Mike Taylor. Chief Technician: Larry Stafford.
Ownership: Rapid Communications LLC (MSO).

DIAMOND CITY—Indco Cable TV, PO Box 3799, 2700 N Saint Louis, Batesville, AR 72503-3799. Phones: 870-793-4174; 800-364-0833. Fax: 870-793-7439. Web Site: http://www.indco.net. Also serves Lead Hill. ICA: AR0124.
TV Market Ranking: Below 100 (DIAMOND CITY, Lead Hill). Franchise award date: N.A. Franchise expiration date: N.A. Began: October 1, 1984.
Channel capacity: 35 (operating 2-way). Channels available but not in use: 1.
Basic Service
Subscribers: 272.
Programming (received off-air): KEMV (PBS) Mountain View; KHOG-TV (ABC) Fayetteville; KOLR (CBS) Springfield; KOZK (PBS) Springfield; KSFX-TV (FOX) Springfield; KSPR (ABC) Springfield; KYTV (CW, NBC) Springfield.
Programming (via satellite): ABC Family Channel; AmericanLife TV Network; Arts & Entertainment; CNN; Comcast Sports Net Southwest; C-SPAN; Discovery Channel; Disney Channel; ESPN; ESPN 2; HGTV; History Channel; Lifetime; Nickelodeon; Outdoor Channel; QVC; Spike TV; TBS Superstation; Travel Channel; Trinity Broadcasting Network; Turner Classic Movies; Turner Network TV; USA Network; Weather Channel; WGN America.
Fee: $20.00 installation; $30.95 monthly; $10.00 additional installation.
Pay Service 1
Pay Units: 29.
Programming (via satellite): HBO.
Fee: $10.00 monthly.
Video-On-Demand: Planned
Internet Service
Operational: Yes.
Fee: $29.95 monthly.
Telephone Service
None
Miles of Plant: 19.0 (coaxial); None (fiber optic). Homes passed: 481.
Manager: J. D. Pierce. Chief Technician: Tommy Barnett. Marketing Director: Connie Barnett.
Ownership: Indco Cable TV (MSO).

DIERKS—Allegiance Communications, 707 W Saratoga St, Shawnee, OK 74804. Phones: 405-395-1131; 405-275-6923. Web Site: http://www.allegiance.tv. Also serves Center Point & Sevier County (portions). ICA: AR0108.
TV Market Ranking: Outside TV Markets (Center Point, DIERKS, Sevier County (portions)). Franchise award date: N.A. Franchise expiration date: N.A. Began: January 1, 1969.
Channel capacity: 30 (not 2-way capable). Channels available but not in use: 5.
Basic Service
Subscribers: 522.
Programming (received off-air): KARK-TV (NBC) Little Rock; KATV (ABC) Little Rock; KETG (PBS) Arkadelphia; KJEP-CA Nashville; KMSS-TV (FOX) Shreveport; KSHV-TV (MNT) Shreveport; KSLA (CBS) Shreveport; KTAL-TV (NBC) Texarkana; allband FM.
Programming (via satellite): ABC Family Channel; AMC; Arts & Entertainment; CNN; Country Music TV; Discovery Channel; Disney Channel; ESPN; Nickelodeon; QVC; Spike TV; Syfy; TBS Superstation; Trinity Broadcasting Network; Turner Network TV; USA Network; Weather Channel; WGN America.
Fee: $35.00 installation; $21.95 monthly; $8.50 additional installation.
Digital Basic Service
Subscribers: N.A.
Programming (via satellite): BBC America; Bio; Bloomberg Television; Bravo; Chiller; CMT Pure Country; Current; Discovery Health Channel; Discovery Kids Channel; Discovery Military Channel; Discovery Planet Green; DMX Music; Encore (multiplexed); ESPN Classic Sports; ESPNews; FitTV; Flix; Fox Movie Channel; Fox Soccer; Fuse; G4; Golf Channel; GSN; HGTV; History Channel; History Channel International; ID Investigation Discovery; Independent Film Channel; Lifetime Movie Network; MTV Hits; MTV2; National Geographic Channel; Nick Jr.; NickToons TV; Outdoor Channel; RFD-TV; Science Channel; Sleuth; SoapNet; Speed Channel; Style Network; Sundance Channel; TeenNick; Toon Disney; Turner Classic Movies; Versus; VH1 Classic; VH1 Soul; WE tv.
Fee: $30.20 monthly.
Digital Pay Service 1
Pay Units: N.A.
Programming (via satellite): Cinemax (multiplexed); HBO (multiplexed); Showtime (multiplexed); Starz (multiplexed); The Movie Channel (multiplexed).
Video-On-Demand: No
Pay-Per-View
Spice: Xcess (delivered digitally); iN DEMAND (delivered digitally); Playboy TV (delivered digitally); Fresh (delivered digitally); Club Jenna (delivered digitally).
Internet Service
Operational: No.
Telephone Service
None
Miles of Plant: 30.0 (coaxial); None (fiber optic). Additional miles planned: 2.0 (coaxial). Homes passed: 650. Total homes in franchised area: 650.
Chief Executive Officer: Bill Haggarty. Regional Vice President: Andrew Dearth. Vice President, Marketing: Tracy Bass.
City fee: 4% of basic.
Ownership: Allegiance Communications (MSO).

DOVER—Suddenlink Communications, 12444 Powerscourt Dr, Saint Louis, MO 63131-3660. Phones: 800-999-6845 (Customer service); 314-965-2020. Fax: 903-561-5485. Web Site: http://www.suddenlink.com. Also serves Pope County (unincorporated areas). ICA: AR0113.
TV Market Ranking: Outside TV Markets (DOVER, Pope County (unincorporated areas)). Franchise award date: N.A.

Franchise expiration date: N.A. Began: December 7, 1982.

Channel capacity: 60 (not 2-way capable). Channels available but not in use: 1.

Basic Service

Subscribers: 496.

Programming (received off-air): KAFT (PBS) Fayetteville; KARK-TV (NBC) Little Rock; KATV (ABC) Little Rock; KFSM-TV (CBS) Fort Smith; KLRT-TV (FOX) Little Rock; KTHV (CBS) Little Rock.

Programming (via satellite): Fox News Channel; Trinity Broadcasting Network.

Fee: $39.95 installation; $17.95 monthly.

Expanded Basic Service 1

Subscribers: N.A.

Programming (via satellite): ABC Family Channel; AMC; Animal Planet; Arts & Entertainment; CNN; Comcast Sports Net Southwest; Discovery Channel; Disney Channel; ESPN; ESPN 2; Food Network; Great American Country; Headline News; HGTV; History Channel; Lifetime; National Geographic Channel; Nickelodeon; Outdoor Channel; QVC; Spike TV; Syfy; TBS Superstation; Turner Network TV; TV Land; USA Network; VH1; Weather Channel.

Fee: $22.00 monthly.

Pay Service 1

Pay Units: 18.

Programming (via satellite): HBO.

Fee: $13.00 monthly.

Pay Service 2

Pay Units: 22.

Programming (via satellite): The Movie Channel.

Fee: $10.95 monthly.

Pay Service 3

Pay Units: 57.

Programming (via satellite): Showtime.

Fee: $10.95 monthly.

Video-On-Demand: No

Pay-Per-View

Sports PPV (delivered digitally); ESPN Extra (delivered digitally); ESPN Now (delivered digitally); Playboy TV (delivered digitally); Shorteez (delivered digitally); Fresh (delivered digitally); iN DEMAND (delivered digitally).

Internet Service

Operational: No.

Telephone Service

None

Miles of Plant: 36.0 (coaxial); None (fiber optic). Homes passed: 1,073.

Regional Manager: Todd Cruthird. Plant Manager: Danny Keith. Marketing Director: Beverly Gambell.

Ownership: Cequel Communications LLC (MSO).

DUMAS—Allegiance Communications, 707 W Saratoga St, Shawnee, OK 74804. Phones: 405-395-1131; 405-275-6923. Web Site: http://www.allegiance.tv. ICA: AR0317.

TV Market Ranking: Below 100 (DUMAS). Franchise award date: N.A. Franchise expiration date: N.A. Began: N.A.

Channel capacity: N.A. Channels available but not in use: N.A.

Basic Service

Subscribers: N.A.

Programming (received off-air): KARK-TV (NBC) Little Rock; KARZ-TV (MNT) Little Rock; KASN (CW) Pine Bluff; KATV (ABC) Little Rock; KETS (PBS) Little Rock; KKYK-CA (IND) Little Rock; KLRT-TV (FOX) Little Rock; KTHV (CBS) Little Rock; KTVE (NBC) El Dorado; WABG-TV (ABC) Greenwood; WXVT (CBS) Greenville.

Programming (via satellite): CNBC; CNN; C-SPAN; Headline News; Home Shopping Network; Trinity Broadcasting Network; Weather Channel; WGN America.

Fee: $38.00 installation; $19.99 monthly.

Expanded Basic Service 1

Subscribers: N.A.

Programming (via satellite): ABC Family Channel; Animal Planet; Arts & Entertainment; BET Networks; Cartoon Network; Comcast Sports Net Southwest; Discovery Channel; Disney Channel; ESPN; ESPN 2; ESPN Classic Sports; Fox News Channel; FX; Great American Country; Hallmark Channel; HGTV; History Channel; Lifetime; Nickelodeon; Outdoor Channel; Oxygen; Speed Channel; Spike TV; Syfy; TBS Superstation; The Learning Channel; Travel Channel; Turner Classic Movies; Turner Network TV; TV Land; USA Network; VH1.

Fee: $13.36 monthly.

Digital Basic Service

Subscribers: N.A.

Programming (via satellite): AmericanLife TV Network; BBC America; Bio; Bloomberg Television; Bravo; Cine Latino; Cine Mexicano; CMT Pure Country; CNN en Espanol; Daystar TV Network; Discovery en Espanol; Discovery HD Theater; Discovery Health Channel; Discovery Kids Channel; Discovery Military Channel; Discovery Planet Green; DMX Music; Encore (multiplexed); ESPN Classic Sports; ESPN Deportes; ESPN HD; ESPNews; FitTV; Flix; Fox College Sports Atlantic; Fox College Sports Central; Fox College Sports Pacific; Fox Movie Channel; Fox Soccer; Fox Sports en Espanol; Fuse; G4; Golf Channel; Gospel Music TV; Great American Country; GSN; Halogen Network; HDNet; HDNet Movies; History Channel; History Channel en Espanol; History Channel International; ID Investigation Discovery; Independent Film Channel; Lifetime Movie Network; MTV Hits; MTV Tres; MTV2; National Geographic Channel; Nick Jr.; NickToons TV; Outdoor Channel; Outdoor Channel 2 HD; Science Channel; ShopNBC; Sleuth; Speed Channel; Style Network; Sundance Channel; Syfy; TeenNick; The Word Network; Toon Disney; Trinity Broadcasting Network; Turner Classic Movies; Universal HD; VH1 Classic; WE tv.

Fee: $32.16 monthly.

Digital Pay Service 1

Pay Units: N.A.

Programming (via satellite): Cinemax (multiplexed); HBO (multiplexed); HBO HD; Showtime (multiplexed); Showtime HD; Starz (multiplexed); The Movie Channel (multiplexed).

Video-On-Demand: No

Pay-Per-View

iN DEMAND (delivered digitally); Hot Choice (delivered digitally); Fresh (delivered digitally); Club Jenna (delivered digitally); Playboy TV (delivered digitally).

Internet Service

Operational: Yes.

Fee: $24.95 installation; $39.95 monthly.

Telephone Service

Digital: Planned

Miles of Plant: 33.0 (coaxial); None (fiber optic). Homes passed: 2,400.

Chief Executive Officer: Bill Haggarty. Regional Vice President: Andrew Dearth. Vice President, Marketing: Tracy Bass.

Ownership: Allegiance Communications (MSO).

EARLE—Comcast Cable, 6555 Quince Rd, Ste 400, Memphis, TN 38119-8225. Phone: 901-365-1770. Fax: 901-369-4515. Web Site: http://www.comcast.com. Also serves Crittenden County & Parkin. ICA: AR0058.

TV Market Ranking: 26 (Crittenden County (portions), EARLE, Parkin); Below 100 (Crittenden County (portions)). Franchise award date: January 1, 1981. Franchise expiration date: N.A. Began: January 1, 1982.

Channel capacity: N.A. Channels available but not in use: None.

Basic Service

Subscribers: N.A. Included in Memphis

Programming (received off-air): WBUY-TV (TBN) Holly Springs; WHBQ-TV (FOX) Memphis; WKNO (PBS) Memphis; WLMT (CW) Memphis; WMC-TV (NBC) Memphis; WPTY-TV (ABC) Memphis; WREG-TV (CBS) Memphis.

Programming (via satellite): C-SPAN; QVC.

Current originations: Public Access.

Fee: $41.00 installation; $9.50 monthly; $.65 converter; $22.00 additional installation.

Expanded Basic Service 1

Subscribers: N.A.

Programming (via satellite): ABC Family Channel; AMC; Animal Planet; Arts & Entertainment; BET Networks; CNBC; CNN; Country Music TV; Discovery Channel; ESPN; ESPN 2; Eternal Word TV Network; Food Network; Fox News Channel; Fox Sports Net; FX; Golf Channel; Hallmark Channel; Headline News; HGTV; Lifetime Movie Network; MSNBC; MTV; MTV2; Nickelodeon; Oxygen; ShopNBC; Spike TV; SportSouth; Syfy; TBS Superstation; The Learning Channel; truTV; Turner Classic Movies; Turner Network TV; TV Land; USA Network; VH1; WE tv; Weather Channel; WGN America.

Fee: $42.55 monthly.

Pay Service 1

Pay Units: N.A.

Programming (via satellite): Encore; HBO (multiplexed).

Video-On-Demand: No

Internet Service

Operational: Yes.

Telephone Service

Digital: Operational

Homes passed: 1,680. Total homes in franchised area: 1,680. Miles of plant included in Memphis

Vice President & General Manager: Terry Kennedy. Technical Operations Director: Jim Davies. Marketing & Sales Director: Linda Brashear. Government Affairs Director: Otha Brando.

City fee: 3% of basic.

Ownership: Comcast Cable Communications Inc. (MSO).

EAST CAMDEN—Community Communications Co., 1920 Hwy 425 N, Monticello, AR 71655-4463. Phones: 870-367-7300; 800-272-2191. Fax: 870-367-9770. E-mail: generalmanager@ccc-cable.net. Web Site: http://www.ccc-cable.net. Also serves Ouachita County (portions). ICA: AR0127.

TV Market Ranking: 99 (EAST CAMDEN, Ouachita County (Portions)). Franchise award date: N.A. Franchise expiration date: N.A. Began: N.A.

Channel capacity: 48 (not 2-way capable). Channels available but not in use: 14.

Basic Service

Subscribers: 222.

Programming (received off-air): KARK-TV (NBC) Little Rock; KASN (CW) Pine Bluff; KATV (ABC) Little Rock; KETG (PBS) Arkadelphia; KLRT-TV (FOX) Little Rock; KTHV (CBS) Little Rock; KTVE (NBC) El Dorado.

Programming (via satellite): ABC Family Channel; AMC; Arts & Entertainment; CNBC; CNN; Comcast Sports Net Southwest; Country Music TV; Discovery Channel; E! Entertainment Television; ESPN; ESPN 2; FitTV; Fox News Channel; FX; Headline News; Lifetime; MTV; Nickelodeon; Outdoor Channel; QVC; Spike TV; Syfy; TBS Superstation; The Learning Channel; Trinity Broadcasting Network; Turner Network TV; TV Land; USA Network; VH1; Weather Channel; WGN America.

Fee: $20.00 installation; $33.60 monthly.

Pay Service 1

Pay Units: 110.

Programming (via satellite): HBO; Showtime; The Movie Channel.

Fee: $10.00 monthly (each).

Video-On-Demand: No

Internet Service

Operational: No.

Telephone Service

None

Miles of Plant: 40.0 (coaxial); None (fiber optic). Homes passed: 450. Total homes in franchised area: 450.

Chief Technician: Larry Ivy.

Ownership: Community Communications Co. (MSO).

EL DORADO—Suddenlink Communications, 1127 N Madison Ave, El Dorado, AR 71730-3805. Phone: 870-862-1306. Fax: 870-852-7080. Web Site: http://www.suddenlink.com. Also serves Lake Faircrest, Lawson, Old Union & Urbana. ICA: AR0233.

TV Market Ranking: 99 (EL DORADO, Lake Faircrest, Lawson, Old Union, Urbana). Franchise award date: N.A. Franchise expiration date: N.A. Began: September 1, 1964.

Channel capacity: 80 (operating 2-way). Channels available but not in use: N.A.

Basic Service

Subscribers: 10,202.

Programming (received off-air): KAQY (ABC) Columbia; KARD (FOX) West Monroe; KATV (ABC) Little Rock; KETG (PBS) Arkadelphia; KLMB-LP El Dorado; KNOE-TV (CBS, CW) Monroe; KTBS-TV (ABC) Shreveport; KTVE (NBC) El Dorado.

Programming (via satellite): CNN; Home Shopping Network; TV Guide Network; WGN America.

Fee: $38.00 installation; $8.62 monthly.

Expanded Basic Service 1

Subscribers: 8,968.

Programming (via satellite): ABC Family Channel; AMC; Animal Planet; Arts & Entertainment; BET Networks; Cartoon Network; Comcast Sports Net Southwest; Comedy Central; C-SPAN; Discovery Channel; Disney Channel; ESPN; ESPN 2; Food Network; Fox News Channel; FX; Golf Channel; Great American Country; Headline News; HGTV; History Channel; INSP; ION Television; Lifetime; MSNBC; MTV; Nickelodeon; Oxygen; Spike TV; Syfy; TBS Superstation; The Learning Channel; Travel Channel; Trinity Broadcasting Network; Turner Classic Movies; Turner Network TV; TV Land; USA Network; VH1; Weather Channel.

Fee: $22.33 monthly.

Digital Basic Service

Subscribers: N.A.

Programming (via satellite): BBC America; Bloomberg Television; Discovery Digital Networks; DMX Music; Encore Action; ESPNews; G4; GAS; MTV Networks Digital Suite; Nick Jr.; Outdoor Channel; SoapNet; Toon Disney.

Fee: $8.65 monthly.

Pay Service 1
Pay Units: 5,150.
Programming (via satellite): Cinemax; HBO; Showtime.
Fee: $15.00 installation; $9.00 monthly (Cinemax), $10.00 monthly (Showtime), $10.95 monthly (HBO).
Digital Pay Service 1
Pay Units: N.A.
Programming (via satellite): Cinemax (multiplexed); HBO (multiplexed); Showtime (multiplexed); Starz (multiplexed); The Movie Channel (multiplexed).
Fee: $7.95 monthly (Starz), $9.00 monthly (Cinemax), $10.95 monthly (HBO), $11.50 monthly (Showtime & TMC).
Video-On-Demand: No
Pay-Per-View
ESPN Extra (delivered digitally), Fee: $3.30, Addressable: Yes; ESPN Gameplan (delivered digitally); ESPN Now (delivered digitally); Hot Choice (delivered digitally); iN DEMAND (delivered digitally); NBA TV (delivered digitally); Fresh (delivered digitally); Sports PPV (delivered digitally).
Internet Service
Operational: Yes.
Broadband Service: Cebridge High Speed Cable Internet.
Fee: $49.95 installation; $26.95 monthly; $39.95 modem lease.
Telephone Service
None
Miles of Plant: None (coaxial); 30.0 (fiber optic).
Manager: Marilyn Warren. Chief Technician: Robbie Lee.
City fee: 3% of gross.
Ownership: Cequel Communications LLC (MSO).

EMERSON—Formerly served by Almega Cable. No longer in operation. ICA: AR0186.

EMMET—Formerly served by Almega Cable. No longer in operation. ICA: AR0304.

ENGLAND—Rapid Cable, 515 E Longview Dr, Arp, TX 75750. Phone: 903-859-6492. Fax: 903-859-3708. ICA: AR0082.
TV Market Ranking: 50 (ENGLAND). Franchise award date: November 28, 1979. Franchise expiration date: N.A. Began: November 15, 1980.
Channel capacity: 36 (2-way capable). Channels available but not in use: 6.
Basic Service
Subscribers: 184.
Programming (received off-air): KARK-TV (NBC) Little Rock; KARZ-TV (MNT) Little Rock; KASN (CW) Pine Bluff; KATV (ABC) Little Rock; KETS (PBS) Little Rock; KKYK-DT (IND) Camden; KLRT-TV (FOX) Little Rock; KTHV (CBS) Little Rock; KVTN-DT (IND) Pine Bluff; 15 FMs.
Fee: $54.95 installation; $20.95 monthly.
Expanded Basic Service 1
Subscribers: N.A.
Programming (via satellite): ABC Family Channel; BET Networks; CNN; Comcast Sports Net Southwest; Discovery Channel; Disney Channel; ESPN; ESPN 2; Fox News Channel; Great American Country; HGTV; History Channel; Lifetime; National Geographic Channel; Nickelodeon; Outdoor Channel; QVC; Spike TV; TBS Superstation; The Learning Channel; Trinity Broadcasting Network; Turner Classic Movies; Turner Network TV; TV Land; USA Network; VH1; Weather Channel.
Fee: $23.10 monthly.
Digital Basic Service
Subscribers: N.A.
Programming (via satellite): BBC America; Bio; Bloomberg Television; Discovery Health Channel; Discovery Kids Channel; Discovery Military Channel; Discovery Planet Green; ESPN Classic Sports; ESPNews; Fox College Sports Atlantic; Fox College Sports Central; Fox College Sports Pacific; Fox Soccer; Fuse; G4; Golf Channel; GSN; History Channel International; ID Investigation Discovery; Independent Film Channel; Science Channel; ShopNBC; Sleuth; Speed Channel; Style Network; Sundance Channel; Toon Disney; Versus; WE tv.
Pay Service 1
Pay Units: 69.
Programming (via satellite): Showtime.
Fee: $12.95 monthly.
Pay Service 2
Pay Units: 109.
Programming (via satellite): HBO.
Fee: $12.95 monthly.
Digital Pay Service 1
Pay Units: N.A.
Programming (via satellite): Cinemax (multiplexed); DMX Music; Encore (multiplexed); Flix; HBO (multiplexed); Showtime (multiplexed); Starz (multiplexed); The Movie Channel (multiplexed).
Video-On-Demand: No
Pay-Per-View
iN DEMAND (delivered digitally); Club Jenna (delivered digitally); Playboy TV (delivered digitally).
Internet Service
Operational: No.
Telephone Service
None
Miles of Plant: 20.0 (coaxial); None (fiber optic). Homes passed: 665. Total homes in franchised area: 1,180.
Regional Manager: Mike Taylor. Chief Technician: Larry Stafford.
City fee: 3% of gross.
Ownership: Rapid Communications LLC (MSO).

EUDORA—Community Communications Co., 1920 Hwy 425 N, Monticello, AR 71655-4463. Phones: 800-272-2191; 870-367-7300. Fax: 870-367-9770. E-mail: generalmanager@ccc-cable.net. Web Site: http://www.ccc-cable.net. ICA: AR0088.
TV Market Ranking: Below 100 (EUDORA). Franchise award date: N.A. Franchise expiration date: N.A. Began: September 1, 1978.
Channel capacity: 48 (not 2-way capable). Channels available but not in use: N.A.
Basic Service
Subscribers: 611.
Programming (received off-air): KARD (FOX) West Monroe; KARK-TV (NBC) Little Rock; KARZ-TV (MNT) Little Rock; KATV (ABC) Little Rock; KEJB (MNT)lorado; KKAP (ETV) Little Rock; KKYK-CA (IND) Little Rock; KTHV (CBS) Little Rock; KTVE (NBC) El Dorado; WABG-TV (ABC) Greenwood; WMAO-TV (PBS) Greenwood; WXVT (CBS) Greenville.
Programming (via satellite): ABC Family Channel; Arts & Entertainment; BET Networks; Bravo; CNBC; CNN; Comcast Sports Net Southwest; Country Music TV; Discovery Channel; Disney Channel; E! Entertainment Television; ESPN; ESPN 2; Eternal Word TV Network; FitTV; Fox News Channel; FX; HGTV; History Channel; Home Shopping Network; Lifetime;

MTV; National Geographic Channel; Nickelodeon; Outdoor Channel; QVC; Speed Channel; Spike TV; Syfy; TBS Superstation; Trinity Broadcasting Network; Turner Classic Movies; Turner Network TV; TV Guide Network; TV Land; USA Network; Versus; Weather Channel; WGN America.
Fee: $20.00 installation; $35.70 monthly.
Pay Service 1
Pay Units: 91.
Programming (via satellite): Cinemax; HBO; Showtime; The Movie Channel.
Fee: $10.00 monthly (each).
Internet Service
Operational: No.
Telephone Service
None
Miles of Plant: 13.0 (coaxial); None (fiber optic). Homes passed: 950. Total homes in franchised area: 1,125.
Operations Manager: Larry Ivy.
City fee: 2% of gross.
Ownership: Community Communications Co. (MSO).

EUREKA SPRINGS—Cox Communications. Now served by BERRYVILLE, AR [AR0221]. ICA: AR0080.

EVENING SHADE—Indco Cable TV, PO Box 3799, 2700 N Saint Louis, Batesville, AR 72503-3799. Phone: 870-793-4174. Fax: 870-793-7439. Web Site: http://www.indco.net. ICA: AR0234.
TV Market Ranking: Outside TV Markets (EVENING SHADE). Franchise award date: N.A. Franchise expiration date: N.A. Began: July 1, 1973.
Channel capacity: N.A. Channels available but not in use: N.A.
Basic Service
Subscribers: 96.
Programming (received off-air): KAIT (ABC) Jonesboro; KARK-TV (NBC) Little Rock; KEMV (PBS) Mountain View; KLRT-TV (FOX) Little Rock; KTHV (CBS) Little Rock; KVTJ-DT (IND) Jonesboro.
Programming (via satellite): ABC Family Channel; CNN; Country Music TV; Discovery Channel; Disney Channel; ESPN; ESPN 2; History Channel; Lifetime; Nickelodeon; Outdoor Channel; QVC; Spike TV; Syfy; TBS Superstation; Turner Classic Movies; Turner Network TV; USA Network; WDIV-TV (NBC) Detroit; WGN America; WTOL (CBS) Toledo.
Fee: $20.00 installation; $30.95 monthly; $10.00 additional installation.
Pay Service 1
Pay Units: 7.
Programming (via satellite): HBO.
Fee: $10.00 monthly.
Video-On-Demand: Planned
Internet Service
Operational: Yes.
Fee: $29.95 monthly.
Telephone Service
None
Miles of Plant: 5.0 (coaxial); None (fiber optic).
Manager: J. D. Pierce. Chief Technician: Tommy Barnett. Marketing Director: Connie Barnett.
City fee: 1% of gross.
Ownership: Indco Cable TV (MSO).

EXCELSIOR—Cox Communications. Now served by SPRINGDALE, AR [AR0220]. ICA: AR0235.

FAIRFIELD BAY—Allegiance Communications, 707 W Saratoga St, Shawnee, OK 74804. Phones: 405-395-1131; 405-275-6923. Web Site: http://www.allegiance.tv. Also serves Cleburne County (portions) & Shirley. ICA: AR0236.
TV Market Ranking: Outside TV Markets (Cleburne County (portions), FAIRFIELD BAY, Shirley). Franchise award date: N.A. Franchise expiration date: N.A. Began: N.A.
Channel capacity: 33 (operating 2-way). Channels available but not in use: N.A.
Basic Service
Subscribers: 1,200.
Programming (received off-air): KARK-TV (NBC) Little Rock; KARZ-TV (MNT) Little Rock; KASN (CW) Pine Bluff; KATV (ABC) Little Rock; KEMV (PBS) Mountain View; KLRT-TV (FOX) Little Rock; KTHV (CBS) Little Rock.
Programming (via satellite): C-SPAN; Home Shopping Network; INSP; Weather Channel.
Fee: $35.00 installation; $29.50 monthly.
Expanded Basic Service 1
Subscribers: N.A.
Programming (via satellite): ABC Family Channel; AMC; Arts & Entertainment; CNBC; CNN; Discovery Channel; Disney Channel; ESPN; Fox News Channel; Great American Country; Headline News; History Channel; Lifetime; Spike TV; TBS Superstation; The Learning Channel; truTV; Turner Network TV; TV Land; USA Network; WGN America.
Digital Basic Service
Subscribers: N.A.
Programming (via satellite): BBC America; Bio; Bloomberg Television; Bravo; Chiller; CMT Pure Country; Current; Discovery Health Channel; Discovery Kids Channel; Discovery Military Channel; Discovery Planet Green; DMX Music; Encore (multiplexed); ESPN Classic Sports; ESPNews; FitTV; Flix; Fox Business Channel; Fox College Sports Atlantic; Fox College Sports Central; Fox College Sports Pacific; Fox Movie Channel; Fox Soccer; Fuse; G4; Golf Channel; GSN; HGTV; History Channel International; ID Investigation Discovery; Independent Film Channel; Lifetime Movie Network; MTV Hits; MTV2; National Geographic Channel; Nick Jr.; NickToons TV; Outdoor Channel; RFD-TV; Science Channel; ShopNBC; Sleuth; SoapNet; Speed Channel; Style Network; Sundance Channel; Syfy; TeenNick; Toon Disney; Trinity Broadcasting Network; Turner Classic Movies; Versus; VH1 Classic; VH1 Soul; WE tv.
Fee: $22.65 monthly.

Pay Service 1
Pay Units: N.A.
Programming (via satellite): HBO.
Fee: $35.00 installation; $11.95 monthly.
Digital Pay Service 1
Pay Units: N.A.
Programming (via satellite): Cinemax (multiplexed); HBO (multiplexed); Showtime (multiplexed); Starz (multiplexed); The Movie Channel (multiplexed).
Video-On-Demand: No
Pay-Per-View
Spice: Xcess (delivered digitally); iN DEMAND (delivered digitally); Playboy TV (delivered digitally); Fresh (delivered digitally); Club Jenna (delivered digitally); Hot Choice (delivered digitally).
Internet Service
Operational: Yes.
Fee: $24.95 installation; $39.95 monthly.
Telephone Service
None
Miles of Plant: 25.0 (coaxial); None (fiber optic).
Chief Executive Officer: Bill Haggarty. Regional Vice President: Andrew Dearth. Vice President, Marketing: Tracy Bass.
Ownership: Allegiance Communications (MSO).

FAYETTEVILLE—Cox Communications. Now served by SPRINGDALE, AR [AR0220]. ICA: AR0007.

FORDYCE—Cable South Media, 301 W 1st Ave, Crossett, AR 71635. Phone: 870-305-1241. ICA: AR0056.
TV Market Ranking: 50 (FORDYCE). Franchise award date: N.A. Franchise expiration date: N.A. Began: January 1, 1977.
Channel capacity: N.A. Channels available but not in use: N.A.
Basic Service
Subscribers: 963.
Programming (received off-air): KARK-TV (NBC) Little Rock; KARZ-TV (MNT) Little Rock; KASN (CW) Pine Bluff; KATV (ABC) Little Rock; KETS (PBS) Little Rock; KLRT-TV (FOX) Little Rock; KTHV (CBS) Little Rock; KTVE (NBC) El Dorado; KVTN-DT (IND) Pine Bluff.
Programming (via satellite): C-SPAN; ESPN; Home Shopping Network; INSP; QVC; Trinity Broadcasting Network; Weather Channel; WGN America.
Fee: $29.99 installation.
Expanded Basic Service 1
Subscribers: N.A.
Programming (via satellite): ABC Family Channel; AMC; Animal Planet; Arts & Entertainment; BET Networks; Cartoon Network; CNBC; CNN; Comedy Central; Country Music TV; Discovery Channel; Disney Channel; E! Entertainment Television; ESPN 2; Food Network; Fox News Channel; FX; Hallmark Channel; Headline News; History Channel; Lifetime; MSNBC; MTV; Nickelodeon; Outdoor Channel; Oxygen; Shop at Home; Spike TV; Syfy; TBS Superstation; The Learning Channel; Travel Channel; Turner Network TV; TV Land; USA Network; VH1.
Fee: $42.99 monthly.
Digital Basic Service
Subscribers: N.A.
Programming (via satellite): AmericanLife TV Network; BBC America; Bio; Bloomberg Television; Bravo; Discovery Digital Networks; DMX Music; Fox Movie Channel; G4; GAS; Golf Channel; GSN; Halogen Network; HGTV; History Channel International; Independent Film Channel; Lifetime Movie Network; MTV Networks Digital Suite; MuchMusic Network; Nick Jr.; ShopNBC; Speed Channel; Style Network; Turner Classic Movies; Versus; WE tv.
Pay Service 1
Pay Units: 94.
Programming (via satellite): Showtime.
Fee: $9.00 monthly.
Pay Service 2
Pay Units: 40.
Programming (via satellite): The Movie Channel.
Fee: $7.00 monthly.
Pay Service 3
Pay Units: 94.
Programming (via satellite): HBO.
Fee: $11.00 monthly.
Digital Pay Service 1
Pay Units: N.A.
Programming (via satellite): Cinemax (multiplexed); Encore (multiplexed); Flix; HBO (multiplexed); Showtime (multiplexed); Starz (multiplexed); The Movie Channel (multiplexed).
Video-On-Demand: No
Pay-Per-View
Hot Choice (delivered digitally); iN DEMAND (delivered digitally); Playboy TV (delivered digitally); Fresh (delivered digitally); Shorteez (delivered digitally); Urban Xtra (delivered digitally).
Internet Service
Operational: No.
Telephone Service
None
Miles of Plant: 45.0 (coaxial); None (fiber optic). Homes passed: 2,077.
City fee: 3% of gross.
Ownership: Cable South Media III LLC (MSO).

FORREST CITY—East Arkansas Video Inc., PO Box 1079, 521 N Washington St, Forrest City, AR 72336-1079. Phones: 870-633-1079 (Headend); 870-633-8932. Fax: 870-633-8898. E-mail: eastarkansasvideocs@cablelynx.com. Web Site: http://www.eastarkansasvideo.com. Also serves Lee County (portions), Marianna & Wynne. ICA: AR0026.
TV Market Ranking: Outside TV Markets (FORREST CITY, Lee County (portions), Marianna, Wynne). Franchise award date: January 1, 1970. Franchise expiration date: N.A. Began: January 1, 1972.
Channel capacity: 35 (operating 2-way). Channels available but not in use: None.
Basic Service
Subscribers: 8,705.
Programming (received off-air): KAIT (ABC) Jonesboro; KARK-TV (NBC) Little Rock; KATV (ABC) Little Rock; KTEJ (PBS) Jonesboro; KTHV (CBS) Little Rock; KVTJ-DT (IND) Jonesboro; WHBQ-TV (FOX) Memphis; WKNO (PBS) Memphis; WLMT (CW) Memphis; WMC-TV (NBC) Memphis; WPTY-TV (ABC) Memphis; WPXX-TV (ION, MNT) Memphis; WREG-TV (CBS) Memphis; allband FM.
Programming (via satellite): ABC Family Channel; AMC; Animal Planet; Arts & Entertainment; BET Networks; CNBC; CNN; Comcast Sports Net Southwest; Comedy Central; Country Music TV; C-SPAN; C-SPAN 2; Discovery Channel; Disney Channel; ESPN; ESPN 2; Food Network; Fox News Channel; FX; Headline News; HGTV; History Channel; Home Shopping Network; Lifetime; MTV; Nickelodeon; ShopNBC; Sneak Prevue; Spike TV; Syfy; TBS Superstation; The Learning Channel; Toon Disney; Trinity Broadcasting Network; Turner Classic Movies; Turner Network TV; TV Guide Network; TV Land; Univision; USA Network; VH1; Weather Channel; WGN America.
Current originations: Educational Access.
Fee: $40.00 installation; $48.90 monthly; $3.17 converter.
Digital Basic Service
Subscribers: N.A.
Programming (via satellite): AmericanLife TV Network; BBC America; Bio; CMT Pure Country; Discovery Health Channel; Discovery Kids Channel; Discovery Military Channel; Discovery Planet Green; DMX Music; ESPNews; FitTV; Fox Soccer; FSN Digital Atlantic; FSN Digital Central; FSN Digital Pacific; G4; Golf Channel; Great American Country; GSN; Halogen Network; History Channel International; ID Investigation Discovery; Lifetime Movie Network; MTV Hits; MTV Jams; MTV Tres; MTV2; National Geographic Channel; Nick Jr.; Nick Too; NickToons TV; Outdoor Channel; Science Channel; SoapNet; Speed Channel; TeenNick; Toon Disney; VH1 Classic; VH1 Soul; WE tv.
Fee: $10.00 monthly; $4.95 converter.
Digital Expanded Basic Service
Subscribers: N.A.
Programming (received off-air): KAIT (ABC) Jonesboro; KTEJ (PBS) Jonesboro.
Programming (via satellite): CNN HD; Discovery Channel HD; ESPN HD; HDNet; HDNet Movies; Outdoor Channel 2 HD; TBS in HD; Turner Network TV HD.
Fee: $5.00 monthly.
Digital Pay Service 1
Pay Units: N.A.
Programming (via satellite): Cinemax (multiplexed); Cinemax HD; Encore (multiplexed); HBO (multiplexed); HBO HD; Starz (multiplexed); Starz HDTV.
Fee: $12.95 monthly (HBO, Cinemax or Starz & Encore).
Video-On-Demand: No
Pay-Per-View
iN DEMAND (delivered digitally), Fee: $3.99.
Internet Service
Operational: Yes. Began: April 1, 2001.
Broadband Service: Cablelynx.
Fee: $24.95-$44.95 monthly; $10.00 modem lease.
Telephone Service
Analog: Not Operational
Digital: Operational
Fee: $45.70 monthly
Miles of Plant: 176.0 (coaxial); None (fiber optic). Homes passed: 9,446.
Manager: John Harbin. Plant Manager: Billy Bechtel.
City fee: 3% of gross.
Ownership: WEHCO Video Inc. (MSO).

FORT SMITH—Cox Communications, 4901 S 48th St, Springdale, AR 72762. Phones: 316-262-4270 (Wichita office); 479-717-3700. Fax: 479-756-1081. Web Site: http://www.cox.com/arkansas. Also serves Alma, Arkola, Barling, Bloomer, Bonanza, Central City, Chester, Crawford County, Dean Springs, Dora, Dyer, Figure Five, Franklin County (western portion), Greenwood, Hackett, Hartford, Huntington, Kibler, Lavaca, Mansfield, Midland, Mountainburg, Mulberry, Rudy, Sugarloaf Lake, Van Buren & Witcherville, AR; Arkoma, Le Flore County (unincorporated areas), Muldrow, Pocola, Roland & Sequoyah County (southern portion), OK. ICA: AR0003.
TV Market Ranking: Below 100 (Alma, Arkola, Arkoma, Barling, Bloomer, Bonanza, Central City, Chester, Crawford County, Dean Springs, Dora, Dyer, Figure Five, FORT SMITH, Franklin County (western portion), Greenwood, Hackett, Hartford, Kibler, Lavaca, Le Flore County (unincorporated areas) (portions), Mansfield, Midland, Mountainburg, Mulberry, Muldrow, Pocola, Roland, Rudy, Sequoyah County (southern portion), Sugarloaf Lake, Van Buren, Witcherville); Outside TV Markets (Le Flore County (unincorporated areas) (portions)). Franchise award date: January 1, 1960. Franchise expiration date: N.A. Began: November 11, 1961.
Channel capacity: N.A. Channels available but not in use: N.A.
Basic Service
Subscribers: N.A. Included in Wichita
Programming (received off-air): KAFT (PBS) Fayetteville; KARK-TV (NBC) Little Rock; KFSM-TV (CBS) Fort Smith; KFTA-TV (FOX) Fort Smith; KHBS (ABC) Fort Smith; KOET (PBS) Eufaula; KPBI (MNT) Eureka Springs; KPBI-CA (FOX) Fort Smith; KTHV (CBS) Little Rock; KTUL (ABC) Tulsa; KWOG (IND) Springdale; 16 FMs.
Programming (via satellite): GalaVision; Home Shopping Network; INSP; TBS Superstation; Trinity Broadcasting Network; TV Guide Network; WGN America.
Current originations: Leased Access; Government Access; Educational Access; Government Access; Educational Access; Public Access.
Fee: $38.00 installation; $10.61 monthly.
Expanded Basic Service 1
Subscribers: 27,710.
Programming (via satellite): ABC Family Channel; AMC; Animal Planet; Arts & Entertainment; BET Networks; Bravo; Cartoon Network; CNBC; CNN; Comcast Sports Net Southwest; Comedy Central; Country Music TV; C-SPAN; C-SPAN 2; Discovery Channel; Disney Channel; E! Entertainment Television; ESPN; ESPN 2; Food Network; Fox News Channel; FX; Great American Country; Headline News; HGTV; History Channel; Lifetime; MSNBC; MTV; Nickelodeon; Oxygen; QVC; Speed Channel; Spike TV; The Learning Channel; Travel Channel; truTV; Turner Network TV; TV Land; Univision; USA Network; Versus; VH1; Weather Channel.
Fee: $43.15 monthly.
Digital Basic Service
Subscribers: N.A.
Programming (via satellite): BBC America; Bio; Bloomberg Television; Discovery Digital Networks; Encore Action; ESPN Classic Sports; ESPNews; Fox Sports World; G4; Golf Channel; GSN; Hallmark Channel; History Channel; Independent Film Channel; MuchMusic Network; Music Choice; SoapNet; Syfy; Toon Disney; Turner Classic Movies; WE tv.
Fee: $14.00 monthly.
Digital Pay Service 1
Pay Units: N.A.
Programming (via satellite): Cinemax (multiplexed); HBO (multiplexed); Showtime (multiplexed); Starz (multiplexed); The Movie Channel (multiplexed).
Video-On-Demand: No
Pay-Per-View
NBA TV (delivered digitally); ESPN Gameplan (delivered digitally); ESPN Now (delivered digitally); iN DEMAND (delivered digitally), Addressable: Yes; Fresh (delivered digitally).
Internet Service
Operational: Yes.
Broadband Service: Cox High Speed Internet.
Fee: $19.99-$59.99 monthly.

Telephone Service
Digital: Operational
Fee: $15.95 monthly
Miles of Plant: 699.0 (coaxial); None (fiber optic). Total homes in franchised area: 39,048. Homes passed included in Springdale
Vice President & General Manager: Kimberly Edmunds. Vice President, Operations: Nelson Mower. Vice President, Marketing: Tony Matthews. Marketing Director: Tina Gabbard. Community Relations Manager: Kelly Zaga.
City fee: 4% of gross.
Ownership: Cox Communications Inc. (MSO).

FOUKE—Rapid Cable, 515 E Longview Dr, Arp, TX 75750. Phone: 903-895-6492. Fax: 903-859-3708. Also serves Mandeville & Miller County (unincorporated areas). ICA: AR0237.
TV Market Ranking: 58 (FOUKE, Mandeville, Miller County (unincorporated areas)). Franchise award date: December 8, 1988. Franchise expiration date: N.A. Began: January 12, 1989.
Channel capacity: 54 (not 2-way capable). Channels available but not in use: 18.
Basic Service
Subscribers: 826.
Programming (received off-air): KATV (ABC) Little Rock; KETG (PBS) Arkadelphia; KLFI-LP Texarkana; KLTS-TV (PBS) Shreveport; KMSS-TV (FOX) Shreveport; KSHV-TV (MNT) Shreveport; KSLA (CBS) Shreveport; KTAL-TV (NBC) Texarkana; KTBS-TV (ABC) Shreveport.
Programming (via satellite): Home Shopping Network; TV Guide Network.
Fee: $54.95 installation; $20.95 monthly.
Expanded Basic Service 1
Subscribers: N.A.
Programming (via satellite): ABC Family Channel; AMC; Animal Planet; Arts & Entertainment; BET Networks; Cartoon Network; CNBC; CNN; Comcast Sports Net Southwest; Comedy Central; C-SPAN; Discovery Channel; Disney Channel; E! Entertainment Television; ESPN; ESPN 2; Food Network; Fox News Channel; FX; Great American Country; Headline News; HGTV; History Channel; Lifetime; MSNBC; MTV; National Geographic Channel; Nickelodeon; Outdoor Channel; Spike TV; Syfy; TBS Superstation; The Learning Channel; Trinity Broadcasting Network; Turner Classic Movies; Turner Network TV; USA Network; VH1; Weather Channel.
Fee: $23.10 monthly.
Pay Service 1
Pay Units: 185.
Programming (via satellite): Cinemax.
Fee: $12.95 monthly.
Pay Service 2
Pay Units: 228.
Programming (via satellite): HBO.
Fee: $12.95 monthly.
Pay Service 3
Pay Units: 126.
Programming (via satellite): The Movie Channel.
Fee: $12.95 monthly.
Pay Service 4
Pay Units: 226.
Programming (via satellite): Showtime.
Fee: $12.95 monthly.
Video-On-Demand: No
Internet Service
Operational: No.
Telephone Service
None
Miles of Plant: 134.0 (coaxial); None (fiber optic). Homes passed: 2,734.
Regional Manager: Mike Taylor. Chief Technician: Larry Stafford.
Ownership: Rapid Communications LLC (MSO).

FOUNTAIN HILL—Formerly served by Almega Cable. No longer in operation. ICA: AR0210.

FRIENDSHIP—Community Communications Co., 1920 Hwy 425 N, Monticello, AR 71655-4463. Phones: 870-367-7300; 800-272-2191. Fax: 870-367-9770. E-mail: generalmanager@ccc-cable.net. Web Site: http://www.ccc-cable.net. Also serves Central & Donaldson. ICA: AR0123.
TV Market Ranking: Below 100 (Central, Donaldson, FRIENDSHIP). Franchise award date: N.A. Franchise expiration date: N.A. Began: September 1, 1989.
Channel capacity: 48 (not 2-way capable). Channels available but not in use: N.A.
Basic Service
Subscribers: 56.
Programming (received off-air): KARK-TV (NBC) Little Rock; KASN (CW) Pine Bluff; KATV (ABC) Little Rock; KETG (PBS) Arkadelphia; KLRT-TV (FOX) Little Rock; KTHV (CBS) Little Rock.
Programming (via satellite): ABC Family Channel; AMC; Arts & Entertainment; CNBC; CNN; Country Music TV; Discovery Channel; Disney Channel; ESPN; ESPN 2; Headline News; Lifetime; Nickelodeon; Outdoor Channel; QVC; Speed Channel; Spike TV; Syfy; TBS Superstation; Trinity Broadcasting Network; Turner Network TV; USA Network; VH1; WGN America.
Fee: $33.60 monthly.
Pay Service 1
Pay Units: N.A.
Programming (via satellite): HBO.
Fee: $10.00 monthly.
Video-On-Demand: No
Internet Service
Operational: No.
Telephone Service
None
Homes passed: 483.
Ownership: Community Communications Co. (MSO).

FULTON—Allegiance Communications, 707 W Saratoga St, Shawnee, OK 74804. Phones: 405-275-6923; 405-395-1131. Web Site: http://www.allegiance.tv. Also serves Saratoga & Tolette. ICA: AR0282.
TV Market Ranking: 58 (FULTON, Saratoga, Tolette). Franchise award date: N.A. Franchise expiration date: N.A. Began: N.A.
Channel capacity: 23 (not 2-way capable). Channels available but not in use: N.A.
Basic Service
Subscribers: 229.
Programming (received off-air): KARK-TV (NBC) Little Rock; KETG (PBS) Arkadelphia; KJEP-CA Nashville; KMSS-TV (FOX) Shreveport; KSHV-TV (MNT) Shreveport; KSLA (CBS) Shreveport; KTAL-TV (NBC) Texarkana; KTBS-TV (ABC) Shreveport; KTHV (CBS) Little Rock; KTSS-LP Hope.
Programming (via satellite): ABC Family Channel; Arts & Entertainment; BET Networks; CNN; Discovery Channel; Disney Channel; ESPN; Nickelodeon; QVC; Spike TV; TBS Superstation; Turner Network TV; USA Network; Weather Channel; WGN America.
Fee: $35.00 installation; $19.99 monthly; $15.00 additional installation.
Pay Service 1
Pay Units: N.A.
Programming (via satellite): Cinemax; HBO; Showtime; The Movie Channel.
Fee: $11.00 monthly (each).
Video-On-Demand: No
Pay-Per-View
iN DEMAND (delivered digitally); Urban American Television Network (delivered digitally); Playboy TV (delivered digitally); Fresh (delivered digitally); Shorteez (delivered digitally).
Internet Service
Operational: No.
Telephone Service
None
Homes passed: 553.
Chief Executive Officer: Bill Haggarty. Regional Vice President: Andrew Dearth. Vice President, Marketing: Tracy Bass.
Ownership: Allegiance Communications (MSO).

GARLAND CITY—Formerly served by Cebridge Connections. No longer in operation. ICA: AR0305.

GILLETT—Community Communications Co., 1920 Hwy 425 N, Monticello, AR 71655-4463. Phones: 800-272-2191; 870-367-7300. Fax: 870-367-9770. E-mail: generalmanager@ccc-cable.net. Web Site: http://www.ccc-cable.net. ICA: AR0153.
TV Market Ranking: Below 100 (GILLETT). Franchise award date: N.A. Franchise expiration date: N.A. Began: January 1, 1984.
Channel capacity: 48 (not 2-way capable). Channels available but not in use: 9.
Basic Service
Subscribers: 182.
Programming (received off-air): KARK-TV (NBC) Little Rock; KASN (CW) Pine Bluff; KATV (ABC) Little Rock; KETS (PBS) Little Rock; KLRT-TV (FOX) Little Rock; KTHV (CBS) Little Rock; WXVT (CBS) Greenville.
Programming (via satellite): ABC Family Channel; Arts & Entertainment; BET Networks; CNN; Comcast Sports Net Southwest; Country Music TV; Discovery Channel; Disney Channel; E! Entertainment Television; ESPN; ESPN 2; FitTV; Fox News Channel; FX; Lifetime; MTV; Nickelodeon; Outdoor Channel; QVC; Spike TV; Syfy; TBS Superstation; Trinity Broadcasting Network; Turner Classic Movies; Turner Network TV; USA Network; VH1; Weather Channel; WGN America.
Fee: $35.00 installation; $33.60 monthly.
Pay Service 1
Pay Units: 27.
Programming (via satellite): HBO.
Fee: $25.00 installation; $10.00 monthly (each).
Video-On-Demand: No
Internet Service
Operational: No.
Telephone Service
None
Miles of Plant: 7.0 (coaxial); None (fiber optic). Homes passed: 340.
Chief Technician: Larry Ivy.
Ownership: Community Communications Co. (MSO).

GLENWOOD—Community Communications Co., 1920 Hwy 425 N, Monticello, AR 71655-4463. Phones: 800-272-2191; 870-367-7300. Fax: 870-367-9770. E-mail: generalmanager@ccc-cable.net. Web Site: http://www.ccc-cable.net. ICA: AR0238.
TV Market Ranking: Below 100 (GLENWOOD). Franchise award date: N.A. Franchise expiration date: N.A. Began: February 12, 1974.
Channel capacity: 48 (not 2-way capable). Channels available but not in use: N.A.
Basic Service
Subscribers: 398.
Programming (received off-air): KARK-TV (NBC) Little Rock; KARZ-TV (MNT) Little Rock; KASN (CW) Pine Bluff; KATV (ABC) Little Rock; KETG (PBS) Arkadelphia; KKAP (ETV) Little Rock; KKYK-CA (IND) Little Rock; KLRA-LP Little Rock; KLRT-TV (FOX) Little Rock; KTHV (CBS) Little Rock; KVTH-DT (IND) Hot Springs; allband FM.
Programming (via satellite): ABC Family Channel; AMC; Arts & Entertainment; CNBC; CNN; Country Music TV; Discovery Channel; ESPN; ESPN 2; FitTV; Fox News Channel; FX; Golf Channel; Headline News; Home Shopping Network; Lifetime; MTV; National Geographic Channel; Nickelodeon; Outdoor Channel; QVC; Spike TV; Syfy; TBS Superstation; The Learning Channel; Trinity Broadcasting Network; Turner Network TV; TV Land; USA Network; VH1; Weather Channel; WGN America.
Fee: $35.00 installation; $33.60 monthly.
Pay Service 1
Pay Units: N.A.
Programming (via satellite): HBO; Showtime; The Movie Channel.
Fee: $35.00 installation; $8.00 monthly (each).
Video-On-Demand: No
Internet Service
Operational: No.
Telephone Service
None
Miles of Plant: 15.0 (coaxial); None (fiber optic).
Operations Manager: Larry Ivy.
City fee: 2% of gross.
Ownership: Community Communications Co. (MSO).

GOSNELL—Ritter Communications. Now served by MARKED TREE, AR [AR0072]. ICA: AR0067.

GOULD—Community Communications Co., 1920 Hwy 425 N, Monticello, AR 71655-4463. Phones: 870-367-7300; 800-272-2191. Fax: 870-367-9770. E-mail: generalmanager@ccc-cable.net. Web Site: http://www.ccc-cable.net. ICA: AR0132.
TV Market Ranking: 50 (GOULD). Franchise award date: N.A. Franchise expiration date: N.A. Began: February 1, 1983.
Channel capacity: 48 (not 2-way capable). Channels available but not in use: N.A.
Basic Service
Subscribers: 230.
Programming (received off-air): KARK-TV (NBC) Little Rock; KASN (CW) Pine Bluff; KATV (ABC) Little Rock; KETS (PBS) Little Rock; KLRT-TV (FOX) Little Rock; KTHV (CBS) Little Rock; KTVE (NBC) El Dorado; WXVT (CBS) Greenville.
Programming (via satellite): ABC Family Channel; AMC; BET Networks; CNN; Comcast Sports Net Southwest; Country Music TV; Discovery Channel; Disney Channel; ESPN; ESPN 2; FitTV; FX; Lifetime; MTV; Nickelodeon; Outdoor Channel; QVC; Spike TV; Syfy; TBS Superstation; Trinity Broadcasting Network; Turner Network TV; TV Land; USA Network; VH1; Weather Channel; WGN America.
Fee: $19.95 installation; $33.60 monthly.

Pay Service 1
Pay Units: 10.
Programming (via satellite): HBO; The Movie Channel.
Fee: $10.00 installation.
Video-On-Demand: No
Internet Service
Operational: No.
Telephone Service
None
Miles of Plant: 7.0 (coaxial); None (fiber optic). Homes passed: 425.
Operations Manager: Larry Ivy.
Ownership: Community Communications Co. (MSO).

GRADY—Formerly served by Cebridge Connections. No longer in operation. ICA: AR0177.

GREENBRIER—Alliance Communications, PO Box 960, 290 S Broadview St, Greenbrier, AR 72058-9616. Phone: 501-679-6619. Fax: 501-679-5694. Web Site: http://www.alliancecable.net. Also serves Oppelo, Perry & Wooster. ICA: AR0077.
TV Market Ranking: 50 (GREENBRIER, Oppelo, Perry, Wooster); Outside TV Markets (Oppelo). Franchise award date: December 1, 1983. Franchise expiration date: N.A. Began: January 1, 1984.
Channel capacity: 125 (operating 2-way). Channels available but not in use: 57.
Basic Service
Subscribers: 1,502.
Programming (received off-air): KARK-TV (NBC) Little Rock; KARZ-TV (MNT) Little Rock; KASN (CW) Pine Bluff; KATV (ABC) Little Rock; KETS (PBS) Little Rock; KKAP (ETV) Little Rock; KKYK-DT (IND) Camden; KLRT-TV (FOX) Little Rock; KTHV (CBS) Little Rock; KVTN-DT (IND) Pine Bluff.
Programming (via satellite): Weather Channel; WGN America.
Fee: $15.00 installation; $38.00 monthly.
Expanded Basic Service 1
Subscribers: N.A.
Programming (via satellite): ABC Family Channel; AMC; Animal Planet; Arts & Entertainment; Cartoon Network; CNN; Comcast Sports Net Southwest; Comedy Central; Country Music TV; C-SPAN; Discovery Channel; Disney Channel; ESPN; ESPN 2; ESPN Classic Sports; Food Network; Fox News Channel; FX; Golf Channel; Great American Country; GSN; Hallmark Channel; Headline News; HGTV; History Channel; Home Shopping Network; Lifetime; MSNBC; MTV; National Geographic Channel; Nickelodeon; Outdoor Channel; Spike TV; Syfy; TBS Superstation; The Learning Channel; The Sportsman Channel; truTV; Turner Classic Movies; Turner Network TV; TV Guide Network; TV Land; USA Network; VH1.
Digital Basic Service
Subscribers: 335.
Programming (via satellite): AmericanLife TV Network; BBC America; Bio; Bloomberg Television; Bravo; Country Music TV; Current; Discovery Digital Networks; DMX Music; Encore (multiplexed); ESPN Classic Sports; ESPNews; Fox College Sports Atlantic; Fox College Sports Central; Fox College Sports Pacific; Fox Movie Channel; Fox Reality Channel; Fox Soccer; Fuse; G4; GAS; Gospel Music Channel; Halogen Network; History Channel International; Independent Film Channel; Lifetime Movie Network; MTV Networks Digital Suite; National Geographic Channel; Nick Jr.; NickToons TV; Ovation; PBS Kids Sprout; RFD-TV; ShopNBC; Sleuth; SoapNet; Speed Channel; Style Network; The Word Network; Toon Disney; Trinity Broadcasting Network; Versus; WE tv.
Fee: $46.00 monthly.
Digital Pay Service 1
Pay Units: 154.
Programming (via satellite): HBO (multiplexed).
Digital Pay Service 2
Pay Units: 66.
Programming (via satellite): Showtime (multiplexed).
Digital Pay Service 3
Pay Units: 71.
Programming (via satellite): Cinemax (multiplexed).
Digital Pay Service 4
Pay Units: 66.
Programming (via satellite): The Movie Channel (multiplexed).
Digital Pay Service 5
Pay Units: 66.
Programming (via satellite): Flix.
Digital Pay Service 6
Pay Units: 70.
Programming (via satellite): Starz (multiplexed).
Video-On-Demand: No
Pay-Per-View
iN DEMAND (delivered digitally); Playboy TV (delivered digitally); Fresh (delivered digitally); Hot Choice (delivered digitally).
Internet Service
Operational: Yes.
Subscribers: 893.
Broadband Service: In-house.
Fee: $30.00 installation; $29.95 monthly; $9.95 modem lease.
Telephone Service
Digital: Operational
Fee: $29.95 installation; $39.95 monthly
Miles of Plant: 27.0 (coaxial); None (fiber optic). Homes passed: 5,354.
Vice President: Arl Cope. Operations Manager: Jeff Browers. Programming & Marketing Manager: James Fuller.
Ownership: Buford Media Group LLC (MSO).

GREENE COUNTY (unincorporated areas)—Indco Cable TV, PO Box 3799, 2700 N Saint Louis, Batesville, AR 72503-3799. Phone: 870-793-4174. Fax: 870-793-7439. Web Site: http://www.indco.net. Also serves Craighead County (unincorporated areas). ICA: AR0319.
TV Market Ranking: Below 100 (Craighead County (unincorporated areas), GREENE COUNTY (UNINCORPORATED AREAS)). Franchise award date: N.A. Franchise expiration date: N.A. Began: N.A.
Channel capacity: N.A. Channels available but not in use: N.A.
Basic Service
Subscribers: 1,578.
Programming (received off-air): KAIT (ABC) Jonesboro; KARK-TV (NBC) Little Rock; KATV (ABC) Little Rock; KTHV (CBS) Little Rock; WHBQ-TV (FOX) Memphis; WLMT (CW) Memphis; WMC-TV (NBC) Memphis; WPTY-TV (ABC) Memphis; WREG-TV (CBS) Memphis.
Programming (via satellite): ABC Family Channel; Cartoon Network; CNBC; CNN; Country Music TV; C-SPAN; Discovery Channel; Disney Channel; ESPN; ESPN 2; FX; Headline News; HGTV; History Channel; Lifetime; Nickelodeon; Outdoor Channel; QVC; Spike TV; Syfy; TBS Superstation; The Learning Channel; Trinity Broadcasting Network; Turner Classic Movies; Turner Network TV; TV Land; USA Network; VH1; Weather Channel; WGN America.
Current originations: Educational Access.
Fee: $30.95 monthly.
Pay Service 1
Pay Units: 20.
Programming (via satellite): Cinemax.
Fee: $8.00 monthly.
Pay Service 2
Pay Units: 81.
Programming (via satellite): HBO.
Fee: $10.00 monthly.
Video-On-Demand: No
Internet Service
Operational: Yes.
Telephone Service
Digital: Operational
Manager: J. D. Pierce. Chief Technician: Tommy Barnett.
Ownership: Indco Cable TV (MSO).

GREENWOOD—Formerly served by Eagle Media. No longer in operation. ICA: AR0314.

GREERS FERRY—Formerly served by Alliance Communications. No longer in operation. ICA: AR0239.

GUION—Indco Cable TV, PO Box 3799, 2700 N Saint Louis, Batesville, AR 72503-3799. Phone: 870-793-4174. Fax: 870-793-7439. Web Site: http://www.indco.net. ICA: AR0215.
TV Market Ranking: Outside TV Markets (GUION). Franchise award date: N.A. Franchise expiration date: N.A. Began: March 1, 1955.
Channel capacity: N.A. Channels available but not in use: N.A.
Basic Service
Subscribers: 22.
Programming (received off-air): KAIT (ABC) Jonesboro; KARK-TV (NBC) Little Rock; KATV (ABC) Little Rock; KEMV (PBS) Mountain View; KTHV (CBS) Little Rock; KYTV (CW, NBC) Springfield.
Programming (via satellite): ABC Family Channel; CNN; ESPN; ESPN 2; Spike TV; TBS Superstation; Trinity Broadcasting Network; Turner Network TV; USA Network.
Fee: $24.75 monthly.
Video-On-Demand: Planned
Internet Service
Operational: Yes.
Fee: $29.95 monthly.
Telephone Service
None
Miles of Plant: 2.0 (coaxial); None (fiber optic). Homes passed: 60.
Marketing Director: Connie Barnett. Manager: J. D. Pierce. Chief Technician: Tommy Barnett.
Ownership: Indco Cable TV (MSO).

GUM SPRINGS—Indco Cable TV, PO Box 3799, 2700 N Saint Louis, Batesville, AR 72503-3799. Phone: 870-793-4174. Fax: 870-793-7439. Web Site: http://www.indco.net. ICA: AR0302.
TV Market Ranking: Below 100 (GUM SPRINGS). Franchise award date: N.A. Franchise expiration date: N.A. Began: N.A.
Channel capacity: 36 (operating 2-way). Channels available but not in use: N.A.
Basic Service
Subscribers: 277.
Programming (received off-air): KARK-TV (NBC) Little Rock; KASN (CW) Pine Bluff; KATV (ABC) Little Rock; KKYK-DT (IND) Camden; KLRT-TV (FOX) Little Rock; KTHV (CBS) Little Rock.
Programming (via satellite): ABC Family Channel; Arts & Entertainment; Cartoon Network; CNN; Comcast Sports Net Southwest; Country Music TV; C-SPAN; Discovery Channel; Disney Channel; ESPN; ESPN 2; Fox News Channel; FX; Golf Channel; HGTV; History Channel; Lifetime; MSNBC; Nickelodeon; Outdoor Channel; QVC; Spike TV; Syfy; TBS Superstation; Trinity Broadcasting Network; Turner Classic Movies; Turner Network TV; TV Land; USA Network; Weather Channel; WGN America.
Fee: $30.95 monthly.
Pay Service 1
Pay Units: 9.
Programming (via satellite): Cinemax.
Fee: $8.00 monthly.
Pay Service 2
Pay Units: 13.
Programming (via satellite): HBO.
Fee: $10.00 monthly.
Pay Service 3
Pay Units: 8.
Programming (via satellite): The Movie Channel.
Fee: $10.00 monthly.
Video-On-Demand: Planned
Internet Service
Operational: Yes.
Fee: $29.95 monthly.
Telephone Service
None
Miles of Plant: 11.0 (coaxial); None (fiber optic).
Manager: J. D. Pierce. Chief Technician: Tom Barnett. Marketing Director: Connie Barnett.
Ownership: Indco Cable TV (MSO).

GURDON—Suddenlink Communications, 2505 Pine St, Arkadelphia, AR 71923-4358. Phone: 870-246-7611. Fax: 870-246-4356. Web Site: http://www.suddenlink.com. ICA: AR0096.
TV Market Ranking: Below 100 (GURDON). Franchise award date: N.A. Franchise expiration date: N.A. Began: September 1, 1976.
Channel capacity: N.A. Channels available but not in use: N.A.
Basic Service
Subscribers: 750.
Programming (received off-air): KARK-TV (NBC) Little Rock; KARZ-TV (MNT) Little Rock; KASN (CW) Pine Bluff; KATV (ABC) Little Rock; KETG (PBS) Arkadelphia; KKAP (ETV) Little Rock; KKYK-DT (IND) Camden; KLRT-TV (FOX) Little Rock; KTHV (CBS) Little Rock; KVTH-DT (IND) Hot Springs.
Programming (via satellite): C-SPAN; FamilyNet; Home Shopping Network; QVC; TBS Superstation; TV Guide Network; WGN America.
Current originations: Religious Access; Educational Access.
Fee: $38.00 installation; $31.54 monthly.
Expanded Basic Service 1
Subscribers: N.A.
Programming (via satellite): ABC Family Channel; AMC; Animal Planet; Arts & Entertainment; BET Networks; Bravo; Cartoon Network; CNBC; CNN; Comcast Sports Net Southwest; Comedy Central; Country Music TV; C-SPAN 2; Discovery Channel; Disney Channel; E! Entertainment Television; ESPN; ESPN 2; Eternal Word TV Network; Food Network; Fox News Channel; FX; Great American Country; Headline News; HGTV; History Channel; INSP; Jewelry Television; Lifetime; Lifetime Movie Network; MSNBC; MTV; Nickelodeon; Outdoor Channel; Speed Channel; Spike TV; Syfy; The Learning Channel; Travel Channel; Trinity Broadcasting Network; truTV;

Turner Classic Movies; Turner Network TV; TV Land; USA Network; Versus; VH1; Weather Channel.

Digital Basic Service
Subscribers: N.A.
Programming (received off-air): KARK-TV (NBC) Little Rock; KATV (ABC) Little Rock; KLRT-TV (FOX) Little Rock; KTHV (CBS) Little Rock.
Programming (via satellite): Arts & Entertainment HD; BBC America; Bio; Bloomberg Television; Boomerang; CBS College Sports Network; CMT Pure Country; Cooking Channel; Cox Sports Television; Discovery HD Theater; Discovery Health Channel; Discovery Home Channel; Discovery Kids Channel; Discovery Military Channel; Discovery Times Channel; Do-It-Yourself; Encore (multiplexed); ESPN Classic Sports; ESPN HD; ESPNews; FamilyNet; Food Network HD; Fox Reality Channel; Fox Soccer; FSN HD; Fuel TV; Fuse; G4; Golf Channel; Gospel Music Channel; GSN; Hallmark Channel; Halogen Network; HDNet; HDNet Movies; HGTV HD; History Channel International; Independent Film Channel; MTV Hits; MTV Jams; MTV2; Music Choice; National Geographic Channel; National Geographic Channel HD Network; Nick Jr.; NickToons TV; Oxygen; Science Channel; Si TV; SoapNet; Style Network; Sundance Channel; TeenNick; Tennis Channel; The Sportsman Channel; Toon Disney; Turner Network TV HD; TV One; Universal HD; VH1 Classic; VH1 Soul; WE tv; Weatherscan.

Digital Pay Service 1
Pay Units: N.A.
Programming (via satellite): Cinemax (multiplexed); HBO (multiplexed); HBO HD; Showtime (multiplexed); Showtime HD; Starz (multiplexed); The Movie Channel (multiplexed).

Pay-Per-View
iN DEMAND (delivered digitally); Playboy TV (delivered digitally); Fresh (delivered digitally); Shorteez (delivered digitally); Club Jenna (delivered digitally); Spice: Xcess (delivered digitally).

Internet Service
Operational: Yes.
Fee: $35.00 monthly.

Telephone Service
Digital: Operational
Fee: $20.00 monthly

Miles of Plant: 27.0 (coaxial); None (fiber optic). Homes passed: 1,184. Total homes in franchised area: 1,308.

Chief Technician: Allen Wardlaw. Manager: Robbie Lee. Marketing Director: LaDawn Mohr.

Ownership: Cequel Communications LLC (MSO).

HAMBURG—Rapid Cable, 515 E Longview Dr, Arp, TX 75750. Phone: 903-859-6492. Fax: 903-859-3708. ICA: AR0075.

TV Market Ranking: Outside TV Markets (HAMBURG). Franchise award date: N.A. Franchise expiration date: N.A. Began: March 1, 1974.

Channel capacity: N.A. Channels available but not in use: N.A.

Basic Service
Subscribers: 502.
Programming (received off-air): KAQY (ABC) Columbia; KARD (FOX) West Monroe; KASN (CW) Pine Bluff; KATV (ABC) Little Rock; KEJB (MNT)lorado; KETS (PBS) Little Rock; KKYK-CA (IND) Little Rock; KNOE-TV (CBS, CW) Monroe; KTVE (NBC) El Dorado; allband FM.
Fee: $54.95 installation; $20.95 monthly.

Expanded Basic Service 1
Subscribers: N.A.
Programming (via satellite): ABC Family Channel; Animal Planet; Arts & Entertainment; BET Networks; Cartoon Network; CNBC; CNN; Comcast Sports Net Southwest; C-SPAN; Discovery Channel; Disney Channel; E! Entertainment Television; ESPN; ESPN 2; Food Network; Fox News Channel; FX; Great American Country; Halogen Network; Headline News; Lifetime; MTV; National Geographic Channel; Nickelodeon; Outdoor Channel; Spike TV; TBS Superstation; Turner Classic Movies; Turner Network TV; USA Network; Weather Channel.
Fee: $23.10 monthly.

Digital Basic Service
Subscribers: N.A.
Programming (via satellite): BBC America; Bio; Bloomberg Television; Discovery Health Channel; Discovery Kids Channel; Discovery Military Channel; Discovery Planet Green; DMX Music; ESPN Classic Sports; ESPNews; Fox College Sports Atlantic; Fox College Sports Central; Fox Soccer; Fuse; G4; Golf Channel; GSN; HGTV; History Channel; History Channel International; ID Investigation Discovery; Independent Film Channel; Science Channel; ShopNBC; Sleuth; Speed Channel; Style Network; Sundance Channel; Toon Disney; Trinity Broadcasting Network; Versus; WE tv.

Pay Service 1
Pay Units: 26.
Programming (via satellite): Cinemax.
Fee: $12.95 monthly.

Pay Service 2
Pay Units: 36.
Programming (via satellite): HBO.
Fee: $12.95 monthly.

Pay Service 3
Pay Units: 114.
Programming (via satellite): Showtime.
Fee: $12.95 monthly.

Digital Pay Service 1
Pay Units: N.A.
Programming (via satellite): Cinemax (multiplexed); Encore (multiplexed); Flix; HBO (multiplexed); Showtime (multiplexed); Starz (multiplexed); The Movie Channel (multiplexed).

Video-On-Demand: No

Pay-Per-View
iN DEMAND (delivered digitally); Playboy TV (delivered digitally); Club Jenna (delivered digitally).

Internet Service
Operational: No.

Telephone Service
None

Miles of Plant: 39.0 (coaxial); None (fiber optic). Homes passed: 1,280.

Regional Manager: Mike Taylor. Chief Technician: Larry Stafford.

City fee: 2% of gross.

Ownership: Rapid Communications LLC (MSO).

HAMPTON—Langco Inc., PO Box 778, Hampton, AR 71744-0778. Phone: 870-798-2201. Fax: 870-798-2289. Also serves Banks. ICA: AR0321.

TV Market Ranking: 99 (Banks, HAMPTON).

Channel capacity: N.A. Channels available but not in use: N.A.

Basic Service
Subscribers: 432.
Programming (received off-air): KARK-TV (NBC) Little Rock; KASN (CW) Pine Bluff; KATV (ABC) Little Rock; KETS (PBS) Little Rock; KKYK-CA (IND) Little Rock; KLRT-TV (FOX) Little Rock; KTHV (CBS) Little Rock; KTVE (NBC) El Dorado.
Programming (via satellite): ABC Family Channel; AMC; Arts & Entertainment; BET Networks; Boomerang; Bravo; Cartoon Network; CNBC; CNN; Comcast Sports Net Southeast; Comedy Central; Country Music TV; C-SPAN; Discovery Channel; Disney Channel; ESPN; ESPN 2; ESPN Classic Sports; ESPNews; Fox Movie Channel; Golf Channel; Hallmark Channel; Headline News; HGTV; History Channel; Home Shopping Network; Lifetime; MSNBC; MTV; National Geographic Channel; Nickelodeon; Outdoor Channel; Speed Channel; Spike TV; Syfy; TBS Superstation; The Learning Channel; Trinity Broadcasting Network; Turner Classic Movies; Turner Network TV; USA Network; Weather Channel; WGN America.
Fee: $23.95 monthly.

Digital Basic Service
Subscribers: N.A.
Programming (via satellite): BBC America; Bio; Bloomberg Television; Bravo; CMT Pure Country; Current; Discovery Health Channel; Discovery Kids Channel; Discovery Military Channel; Discovery Planet Green; Encore (multiplexed); ESPN 2; ESPN Classic Sports; ESPNews; FitTV; Fox College Sports Atlantic; Fox College Sports Central; Fox College Sports Pacific; Fox Movie Channel; Fox Soccer; Fuse; G4; Golf Channel; Gospel Music Channel; Great American Country; GSN; Halogen Network; HGTV; History Channel; History Channel International; ID Investigation Discovery; Independent Film Channel; Lifetime Movie Network; Lime; MTV Hits; MTV2; Music Choice; National Geographic Channel; Nick Jr.; NickToons TV; Outdoor Channel; Ovation; Science Channel; Sleuth; Speed Channel; Starz (multiplexed); Style Network; Sundance Channel; Syfy; TeenNick; Toon Disney; Trinity Broadcasting Network; Turner Classic Movies; Versus; VH1 Classic; VH1 Soul; WE tv.
Fee: $31.00 monthly.

Digital Pay Service 1
Pay Units: N.A.
Programming (via satellite): Cinemax (multiplexed); Flix; HBO (multiplexed); Showtime (multiplexed); Sundance Channel; The Movie Channel (multiplexed).
Fee: $12.50 monthly (HBO, Cinemax, Showtime/Flix/Sundance, or TMC).

Video-On-Demand: No

Pay-Per-View
iN DEMAND (delivered digitally); Playboy TV (delivered digitally); Spice (delivered digitally); Spice 2 (delivered digitally); Club Jenna (delivered digitally).

Internet Service
Operational: No.

Telephone Service
None

General Manager: David Wells.

Ownership: South Arkansas Telephone Co. Inc.

HARDY—Charter Communications, 312 Washington Ave, West Plains, MO 65775. Phones: 636-207-7044 (St Louis office); 573-472-0247; 417-256-2785. Web Site: http://www.charter.com. Also serves Cherokee Village, Highland & Sharp County (portions). ICA: AR0040.

TV Market Ranking: Outside TV Markets (Cherokee Village, HARDY, Highland, Sharp County (portions)). Franchise award date: June 1, 1965. Franchise expiration date: N.A. Began: June 1, 1996.

Channel capacity: N.A. Channels available but not in use: N.A.

Basic Service
Subscribers: 1,174.
Programming (received off-air): KAIT (ABC) Jonesboro; KEJC-LP Sheridan; KEMV (PBS) Mountain View; KOLR (CBS) Springfield; KPBI (MNT) Eureka Springs; KVTJ-DT (IND) Jonesboro; WSEE-TV (CBS, CW) Erie.
Programming (via satellite): C-SPAN; Eternal Word TV Network; Home Shopping Network; INSP; QVC; Trinity Broadcasting Network; WGN America; WNBC (NBC) New York.
Current originations: Educational Access; Public Access; Government Access.
Fee: $29.99 installation.

Expanded Basic Service 1
Subscribers: N.A.
Programming (via satellite): ABC Family Channel; AMC; Animal Planet; Arts & Entertainment; Bravo; Cartoon Network; CNBC; CNN; Comedy Central; Country Music TV; Discovery Channel; Disney Channel; E! Entertainment Television; ESPN; ESPN 2; Food Network; Fox News Channel; Fox Sports Net Midwest; FX; G4; Golf Channel; Headline News; HGTV; History Channel; Lifetime; MSNBC; MTV; National Geographic Channel; Nickelodeon; Outdoor Channel; Oxygen; Speed Channel; Spike TV; Style Network; Syfy; TBS Superstation; The Learning Channel; Travel Channel; Turner Classic Movies; Turner Network TV; TV Land; USA Network; VH1; Weather Channel.
Fee: $49.99 monthly.

Digital Basic Service
Subscribers: N.A.
Programming (via satellite): BBC America; Bio; Bloomberg Television; Discovery Digital Networks; Do-It-Yourself; ESPN Classic Sports; ESPNews; FitTV; Fox Movie Channel; Fox Sports World; GAS; GSN; Hallmark Channel; History Channel International; Independent Film Channel; Lifetime Movie Network; MTV Networks Digital Suite; Music Choice; Nick Jr.; Nick Too; NickToons TV; SoapNet; Sundance Channel; WE tv.

Digital Pay Service 1
Pay Units: 275.
Programming (via satellite): Cinemax (multiplexed); Encore; HBO (multiplexed); Showtime (multiplexed); Starz (multiplexed); The Movie Channel (multiplexed).
Fee: $10.95 monthly (each).

Video-On-Demand: No

Pay-Per-View
ETC (delivered digitally); The Erotic Network (delivered digitally); Pleasure (delivered digitally); iN DEMAND (delivered digitally).
Internet Service
Operational: No.
Telephone Service
None
Miles of Plant: 150.0 (coaxial); None (fiber optic). Total homes in franchised area: 3,491.
Vice President & General Manager: Steve Trippe. Operations Director: Dave Miller. Operations Manager: Dave Huntsman. Plant Manager: Kevin Goetz. Chief Technician: Randy Ward. Marketing Director: Beverly Wall.
Ownership: Charter Communications Inc. (MSO).

HARMONY GROVE—Formerly served by Almega Cable. No longer in operation. ICA: AR0297.

HARRELL—Suddenlink Communications, 12444 Powerscourt Dr, Saint Louis, MO 63131-3660. Phones: 314-965-2020; 800-999-6845 (Customer service). Fax: 903-561-5485. Web Site: http://www.suddenlink.com. ICA: AR0240.
TV Market Ranking: 99 (HARRELL). Franchise award date: N.A. Franchise expiration date: N.A. Began: August 1, 1990.
Channel capacity: 36 (not 2-way capable). Channels available but not in use: N.A.
Basic Service
Subscribers: 48.
Programming (received off-air): KARD (FOX) West Monroe; KASN (CW) Pine Bluff; KATV (ABC) Little Rock; KETG (PBS) Arkadelphia; KTHV (CBS) Little Rock; KTVE (NBC) El Dorado.
Programming (via satellite): ABC Family Channel; AMC; Arts & Entertainment; BET Networks; CNN; Discovery Channel; Disney Channel; ESPN; Great American Country; Headline News; HGTV; Lifetime; National Geographic Channel; Nickelodeon; Spike TV; Syfy; TBS Superstation; The Learning Channel; Trinity Broadcasting Network; Turner Network TV; USA Network; Weather Channel.
Fee: $39.95 installation; $39.24 monthly.
Pay Service 1
Pay Units: 12.
Programming (via satellite): The Movie Channel.
Fee: $6.95 monthly.
Pay Service 2
Pay Units: 21.
Programming (via satellite): Showtime.
Fee: $9.00 monthly.
Video-On-Demand: No
Internet Service
Operational: No.
Telephone Service
None
Miles of Plant: 5.0 (coaxial); None (fiber optic). Homes passed: 126.
Regional Manager: Todd Cruthird. Area Manager: Russell Gaston. Plant Manager: George Lewis. Marketing Director: Beverly Gambell.
Ownership: Cequel Communications LLC (MSO).

HARRISBURG—Ritter Communications. Now served by MARKED TREE, AR [AR0072]. ICA: AR0100.

HARRISON—Cox Communications, 4901 S 48th St, Springdale, AR 72762. Phones: 316-262-4270 (Wichita office); 479-717-3700. Fax: 479-756-1081. Web Site: http://www.cox.com/arkansas. Also serves Bellefonte, Bergman, Boone County & Valley Springs. ICA: AR0022.
TV Market Ranking: Below 100 (Bellefonte, Bergman, Boone County, HARRISON, Valley Springs). Franchise award date: N.A. Franchise expiration date: N.A. Began: February 1, 1954.
Channel capacity: N.A. Channels available but not in use: N.A.
Basic Service
Subscribers: N.A. Included in Wichita
Programming (received off-air): KARK-TV (NBC) Little Rock; KATV (ABC) Little Rock; KEMV (PBS) Mountain View; KOLR (CBS) Springfield; KPBI (MNT) Eureka Springs; KSFX-TV (FOX) Springfield; KSPR (ABC) Springfield; KTHV (CBS) Little Rock; KYTV (CW, NBC) Springfield.
Programming (via satellite): CNN; C-SPAN; Home Shopping Network; KWBM (MNT) Harrison [LICENSED & SILENT]; TBS Superstation; Trinity Broadcasting Network; Weather Channel; WGN America.
Fee: $38.00 installation; $17.49 monthly.
Expanded Basic Service 1
Subscribers: N.A.
Programming (via satellite): ABC Family Channel; AMC; Animal Planet; Arts & Entertainment; Bravo; Cartoon Network; CNBC; Comcast Sports Net Southwest; Comedy Central; Country Music TV; C-SPAN 2; Discovery Channel; Discovery Health Channel; Disney Channel; E! Entertainment Television; ESPN; ESPN 2; Food Network; Fox News Channel; FX; G4; Great American Country; Headline News; HGTV; History Channel; Lifetime; MSNBC; MTV; Nickelodeon; Outdoor Channel; Oxygen; QVC; Speed Channel; Spike TV; Syfy; The Learning Channel; Travel Channel; Turner Network TV; TV Guide Network; TV Land; Univision; USA Network; Versus; VH1.
Fee: $43.15 monthly.
Digital Basic Service
Subscribers: N.A.
Programming (via satellite): AmericanLife TV Network; BBC America; Bio; Bloomberg Television; Discovery Digital Networks; Encore Action; ESPN Classic Sports; ESPNews; Fox Sports World; Golf Channel; GSN; Hallmark Channel; History Channel International; Independent Film Channel; Lifetime Movie Network; MuchMusic Network; Music Choice; SoapNet; Sundance Channel; Toon Disney; Turner Classic Movies.
Fee: $14.00 monthly.
Pay Service 1
Pay Units: 775.
Programming (via satellite): Cinemax; HBO; Showtime; Starz; The Movie Channel.
Fee: $11.95 monthly (each).
Digital Pay Service 1
Pay Units: N.A.
Programming (via satellite): Cinemax (multiplexed); Flix; HBO (multiplexed); Showtime (multiplexed); Starz (multiplexed); The Movie Channel (multiplexed).
Video-On-Demand: No
Pay-Per-View
ESPN Extra (delivered digitally), Addressable: Yes; ESPN Gameplan (delivered digitally); ESPN Now (delivered digitally); Hot Choice (delivered digitally); iN DEMAND (delivered digitally); NBA TV (delivered digitally); Playboy TV (delivered digitally); Sports PPV (delivered digitally).
Internet Service
Operational: Yes.
Broadband Service: Cox High Speed Internet.
Fee: $19.99-$59.99 monthly.
Telephone Service
Digital: Operational
Fee: $15.95 monthly
Miles of Plant: 230.0 (coaxial); None (fiber optic). Homes passed included in Springdale
Vice President & General Manager: Kimberly Edmunds. Vice President, Operations: Nelson Mower. Vice President, Marketing: Tony Matthews. Marketing Director: Tina Gabbard. Community Relations Manager: Kelly Zaga.
City fee: 3% of gross.
Ownership: Cox Communications Inc. (MSO).

HATFIELD—Formerly served by Allegiance Communications. No longer in operation. ICA: AR0241.

HAZEN—Suddenlink Communications, 12444 Powerscourt Dr, Saint Louis, MO 63131-3660. Phones: 314-965-2020; 800-999-6845 (Customer service). Fax: 903-561-5485. Web Site: http://www.suddenlink.com. Also serves Carlisle, De Valls Bluff & Prairie County (unincorporated areas). ICA: AR0118.
TV Market Ranking: 50 (Carlisle); Outside TV Markets (De Valls Bluff, HAZEN, Prairie County (unincorporated areas)). Franchise award date: N.A. Franchise expiration date: N.A. Began: N.A.
Channel capacity: 36 (operating 2-way). Channels available but not in use: N.A.
Basic Service
Subscribers: 861.
Programming (received off-air): KARK-TV (NBC) Little Rock; KASN (CW) Pine Bluff; KATV (ABC) Little Rock; KETS (PBS) Little Rock; KLRT-TV (FOX) Little Rock; KVTN-DT (IND) Pine Bluff.
Programming (via satellite): Home Shopping Network; KARZ-TV (MNT) Little Rock; KTHV (CBS) Little Rock.
Fee: $17.95 installation; $19.95 monthly.
Expanded Basic Service 1
Subscribers: N.A.
Programming (via satellite): ABC Family Channel; AMC; Animal Planet; Arts & Entertainment; BET Networks; Bravo; Cartoon Network; CNBC; CNN; Comcast Sports Net Southwest; Comedy Central; C-SPAN; Discovery Channel; Disney Channel; E! Entertainment Television; ESPN; ESPN 2; Food Network; Fox News Channel; FX; Golf Channel; Great American Country; Hallmark Channel; Headline News; HGTV; History Channel; Lifetime; MSNBC; MTV; National Geographic Channel; Nickelodeon; Outdoor Channel; Spike TV; TBS Superstation; The Learning Channel; Travel Channel; Turner Network TV; TV Land; USA Network; VH1; Weather Channel.
Fee: $25.00 monthly.
Pay Service 1
Pay Units: 30.
Programming (via satellite): The Movie Channel.
Fee: $10.95 monthly.
Pay Service 2
Pay Units: 149.
Programming (via satellite): Showtime.
Fee: $9.00 monthly.
Pay Service 3
Pay Units: 83.
Programming (via satellite): HBO.
Fee: $10.95 monthly.
Video-On-Demand: No
Pay-Per-View
Sports PPV (delivered digitally); ESPN Extra (delivered digitally); ESPN Now (delivered digitally); Shorteez (delivered digitally); Fresh (delivered digitally); Playboy TV (delivered digitally); iN DEMAND (delivered digitally).
Internet Service
Operational: Yes. Began: October 10, 2003.
Broadband Service: Cebridge High Speed Cable Internet.
Fee: $49.95 installation; $26.95 monthly.
Telephone Service
None
Miles of Plant: 45.0 (coaxial); None (fiber optic). Homes passed: 1,792.
Regional Manager: Todd Cruthird. Area Manager: Carolyn Wilder. Plant Manager: Randy Oliger. Marketing Director: Beverly Gambell.
Ownership: Cequel Communications LLC (MSO).

HEBER SPRINGS—Suddenlink Communications, 903 S 7th St, Heber Springs, AR 72543-4419. Phones: 888-822-5151; 501-362-3413. Fax: 501-362-5070. Web Site: http://www.suddenlink.com. Also serves Eden Isle & Little Red River. ICA: AR0242.
TV Market Ranking: Outside TV Markets (Eden Isle, HEBER SPRINGS, Little Red River). Franchise award date: N.A. Franchise expiration date: N.A. Began: January 1, 1960.
Channel capacity: N.A. Channels available but not in use: N.A.
Basic Service
Subscribers: N.A.
Programming (received off-air): KAIT (ABC) Jonesboro; KARK-TV (NBC) Little Rock; KARZ-TV (MNT) Little Rock; KASN (CW) Pine Bluff; KATV (ABC) Little Rock; KEMV (PBS) Mountain View; KKAP (ETV) Little Rock; KKYK-DT (IND) Camden; KLRT-TV (FOX) Little Rock; KTHV (CBS) Little Rock; KVTN-DT (IND) Pine Bluff; allband FM.
Programming (via satellite): C-SPAN; Jewelry Television; QVC; TBS Superstation; WGN America.
Current originations: Leased Access.
Fee: $38.00 installation; $13.79 monthly.
Expanded Basic Service 1
Subscribers: N.A.
Programming (via satellite): ABC Family Channel; AMC; Animal Planet; Arts & Entertainment; BET Networks; Bravo; Cartoon Network; CNBC; CNN; Comcast Sports Net Southwest; Comedy Central; Country Music TV; C-SPAN 2; Discovery Channel; Disney Channel; E! Entertainment Television; ESPN; ESPN 2; Food Network; Fox News Channel; FX; GalaVision; Great American Country; Headline News; HGTV; History Channel; Home Shopping Network; Lifetime; Lifetime Movie Network; MSNBC; MTV; Nickelodeon; Outdoor Channel; Oxygen; Speed Channel; Spike TV; Syfy; The Learning Channel; Travel Channel; truTV; Turner Classic Movies; Turner Network TV; TV Land; USA Network; Versus; VH1; Weather Channel.
Fee: $22.20 monthly.
Digital Basic Service
Subscribers: N.A.
Programming (received off-air): KARK-TV (NBC) Little Rock; KATV (ABC) Little Rock; KLRT-TV (FOX) Little Rock; KTHV (CBS) Little Rock.
Programming (via satellite): Arts & Entertainment HD; BBC America; Bio; Bloomberg Television; Boomerang; CBS College Sports Network; CMT Pure Country; Cooking Channel; Discovery en

Espanol; Discovery HD Theater; Discovery Health Channel; Discovery Home Channel; Discovery Kids Channel; Discovery Military Channel; Discovery Times Channel; Do-It-Yourself; Encore (multiplexed); ESPN Classic Sports; ESPN HD; ESPNews; Food Network HD; Fox Reality Channel; Fox Soccer; FSN HD; Fuel TV; Fuse; G4; Golf Channel; GSN; Hallmark Channel; Halogen Network; HDNet; HDNet Movies; HGTV HD; History Channel International; Independent Film Channel; MTV Hits; MTV2; Music Choice; National Geographic Channel; National Geographic Channel HD Network; Nick Jr.; NickToons TV; Science Channel; SoapNet; Style Network; Sundance Channel; TeenNick; Toon Disney; Trinity Broadcasting Network; Turner Network TV HD; Universal HD; VH1 Classic.

Digital Pay Service 1
Pay Units: N.A.
Programming (via satellite): Cinemax (multiplexed); HBO (multiplexed); HBO HD; Showtime (multiplexed); Showtime HD; Starz (multiplexed); The Movie Channel (multiplexed).
Fee: $11.95 monthly (each).

Video-On-Demand: No

Pay-Per-View
iN DEMAND (delivered digitally); Spice: Xcess (delivered digitally); Playboy TV (delivered digitally); Fresh (delivered digitally).

Internet Service
Operational: Yes.
Broadband Service: Cebridge High Speed Cable Internet.
Fee: $49.95 installation; $26.95 monthly.

Telephone Service
None

Miles of Plant: 160.0 (coaxial); None (fiber optic).
Manager: Dewayne Millikin. Chief Technician: Robert Hayes.
City fee: $0.25 per subscriber annually.
Ownership: Cequel Communications LLC (MSO).

HECTOR—Suddenlink Communications, 12444 Powerscourt Dr, Saint Louis, MO 63131-3660. Phones: 314-965-2020; 800-999-6845 (Customer service). Fax: 903-561-5485. Web Site: http://www.suddenlink.com. ICA: AR0243.
TV Market Ranking: Outside TV Markets (HECTOR). Franchise award date: N.A. Franchise expiration date: N.A. Began: June 1, 1989.
Channel capacity: 36 (not 2-way capable). Channels available but not in use: N.A.

Basic Service
Subscribers: 150.
Programming (received off-air): KAFT (PBS) Fayetteville; KARK-TV (NBC) Little Rock; KATV (ABC) Little Rock; KLRT-TV (FOX) Little Rock; KTHV (CBS) Little Rock.
Programming (via satellite): C-SPAN; QVC; Trinity Broadcasting Network.
Fee: $39.95 installation; $19.95 monthly.

Expanded Basic Service 1
Subscribers: N.A.
Programming (via satellite): ABC Family Channel; AMC; CNN; Discovery Channel; Disney Channel; ESPN; Great American Country; Headline News; HGTV; Lifetime; MTV; Nickelodeon; Outdoor Channel; Spike TV; TBS Superstation; The Learning Channel; Turner Network TV; USA Network; Weather Channel.
Fee: $22.00 monthly.

Pay Service 1
Pay Units: 1.
Programming (via satellite): HBO.
Fee: $13.00 monthly.

Pay Service 2
Pay Units: 12.
Programming (via satellite): The Movie Channel.
Fee: $10.95 monthly.

Pay Service 3
Pay Units: 22.
Programming (via satellite): Showtime.
Fee: $10.95 monthly.

Video-On-Demand: No

Internet Service
Operational: No.

Telephone Service
None

Miles of Plant: 13.0 (coaxial); None (fiber optic). Homes passed: 457.
Regional Manager: Todd Cruthird. Area Manager: Carl Miller. Plant Manager: Danny Keith. Marketing Director: Beverly Gambell.
Ownership: Cequel Communications LLC (MSO).

HELENA—Suddenlink Communications, 528 Oakland Ave, Helena, AR 72342-1617. Phones: 870-338-8220; 888-822-5151; 870-338-3451. Fax: 870-338-7642. Web Site: http://www.suddenlink.com. Also serves Lexa, Phillips County, Poplar Grove & West Helena. ICA: AR0015.
TV Market Ranking: Outside TV Markets (HELENA, Lexa, Phillips County, Poplar Grove, West Helena). Franchise award date: N.A. Franchise expiration date: N.A. Began: October 20, 1968.
Channel capacity: 60 (operating 2-way). Channels available but not in use: N.A.

Basic Service
Subscribers: 6,610.
Programming (received off-air): KATV (ABC) Little Rock; KETS (PBS) Little Rock; KTHV (CBS) Little Rock; WHBQ-TV (FOX) Memphis; WKNO (PBS) Memphis; WLMT (CW) Memphis; WMC-TV (NBC) Memphis; WPTY-TV (ABC) Memphis; WPXX-TV (ION, MNT) Memphis; WREG-TV (CBS) Memphis; allband FM.
Programming (via satellite): C-SPAN; C-SPAN 2; Headline News; Home Shopping Network; Local Cable Weather; TBS Superstation; Trinity Broadcasting Network; Weather Channel; WGN America.
Fee: $38.00 installation; $14.50 monthly.

Expanded Basic Service 1
Subscribers: N.A.
Programming (via satellite): ABC Family Channel; AMC; Animal Planet; Arts & Entertainment; BET Networks; Bravo; Cartoon Network; CNBC; CNN; Comcast Sports Net Southwest; Comedy Central; Country Music TV; Discovery Channel; Disney Channel; E! Entertainment Television; ESPN; ESPN 2; Food Network; Fox News Channel; FX; Great American Country; HGTV; History Channel; Jewelry Television; Lifetime; Lifetime Movie Network; MSNBC; MTV; Nickelodeon; Outdoor Channel; Oxygen; Speed Channel; Spike TV; Syfy; The Learning Channel; Travel Channel; truTV; Turner Network TV; TV Land; USA Network; Versus; VH1.
Fee: $45.10 monthly.

Digital Basic Service
Subscribers: N.A.
Programming (received off-air): WHBQ-TV (FOX) Memphis; WPTY-TV (ABC) Memphis; WREG-TV (CBS) Memphis.
Programming (via satellite): Arts & Entertainment HD; BBC America; Bio; Bloomberg Television; Boomerang; CBS College Sports Network; CMT Pure Country; Cooking Channel; Discovery en Espanol; Discovery HD Theater; Discovery Health Channel; Discovery Home Channel; Discovery Kids Channel; Discovery Military Channel; Discovery Times Channel; Do-It-Yourself; Encore (multiplexed); ESPN Classic Sports; ESPN HD; ESPNews; Food Network HD; Fox Reality Channel; Fox Soccer; FSN HD; Fuel TV; Fuse; G4; Golf Channel; GSN; Hallmark Channel; Halogen Network; HDNet; HDNet Movies; HGTV HD; History Channel International; Independent Film Channel; MTV Hits; MTV Jams; MTV2; Music Choice; National Geographic Channel; National Geographic Channel HD Network; Nick Jr.; NickToons TV; Science Channel; SoapNet; Style Network; Sundance Channel; TeenNick; Toon Disney; Turner Classic Movies; Turner Network TV HD; Universal HD; VH1 Classic; VH1 Soul.
Fee: $11.00 monthly.

For more information call **800-771-9202** or visit **www.warren-news.com**

Pay Service 1
Pay Units: 620.
Fee: $35.00 installation; $11.95 monthly (each).

Digital Pay Service 1
Pay Units: N.A.
Programming (via satellite): Cinemax (multiplexed); HBO (multiplexed); HBO HD; Showtime (multiplexed); Showtime HD; Starz (multiplexed); The Movie Channel (multiplexed).

Video-On-Demand: Planned

Pay-Per-View
iN DEMAND (delivered digitally); Fresh (delivered digitally); Spice: Xcess (delivered digitally); Playboy TV (delivered digitally).

Internet Service
Operational: Yes.
Broadband Service: Cebridge High Speed Cable Internet.
Fee: $29.95 monthly.

Telephone Service
Digital: Operational
Fee: $44.95 monthly

Miles of Plant: 101.0 (coaxial); None (fiber optic). Additional miles planned: 5.0 (coaxial). Homes passed: 8,777.
Chief Technician: Wesley Bryan. Manager: Russ Hodges.
City fee: 3% of gross.
Ownership: Cequel Communications LLC (MSO).

HERMITAGE—Formerly served by Almega Cable. No longer in operation. ICA: AR0146.

HIGGINSON—Rapid Cable, 515 E Longview Dr, Arp, TX 75750. Phone: 903-895-6492. Fax: 903-859-3708. Also serves Garner, Griffithville, McRae, West Point & White County (portions). ICA: AR0133.
TV Market Ranking: Outside TV Markets (Garner, Griffithville, HIGGINSON, McRae, West Point, White County (portions)). Franchise award date: N.A. Franchise expiration date: N.A. Began: April 1, 1987.
Channel capacity: 36 (not 2-way capable). Channels available but not in use: N.A.

Basic Service
Subscribers: 146.
Programming (received off-air): KARK-TV (NBC) Little Rock; KASN (CW) Pine Bluff; KATV (ABC) Little Rock; KETS (PBS) Little Rock; KLRT-TV (FOX) Little Rock; KTHV (CBS) Little Rock; KVTN-DT (IND) Pine Bluff.
Programming (via satellite): Home Shopping Network; National Geographic Channel; TBS Superstation.
Fee: $54.95 installation; $20.95 monthly.

Expanded Basic Service 1
Subscribers: N.A.
Programming (via satellite): ABC Family Channel; Arts & Entertainment; Cartoon Network; CNN; Discovery Channel; Disney Channel; ESPN; Great American Country; Headline News; HGTV; Lifetime; Nickelodeon; Outdoor Channel; Spike TV; The Learning Channel; Turner Classic Movies; Turner Network TV; USA Network; Weather Channel.
Fee: $23.10 monthly.

Digital Basic Service
Subscribers: N.A.
Programming (via satellite): AmericanLife TV Network; BBC America; Bio; Bloomberg Television; Discovery Health Channel; Discovery Kids Channel; Discovery Military Channel; Discovery Planet Green; DMX Music; ESPN 2; ESPN Classic Sports; ESPNews; Fox College Sports Atlantic; Fox College Sports Central; Fox College Sports Pacific; Fox Soccer; Fuse; G4; Golf Channel; GSN; Halogen Network; HGTV; History Channel; History Channel International; ID Investigation Discovery; Lifetime Movie Network; Outdoor Channel; Ovation; Science Channel; ShopNBC; Sleuth; Speed Channel; Style Network; Syfy; Trinity Broadcasting Network; Turner Classic Movies; Versus; WE tv.

Pay Service 1
Pay Units: 34.
Programming (via satellite): The Movie Channel.
Fee: $12.95 monthly.

Pay Service 2
Pay Units: 42.
Programming (via satellite): HBO.
Fee: $12.95 monthly.

Pay Service 3
Pay Units: 45.
Programming (via satellite): Showtime.
Fee: $12.95 monthly.

Digital Pay Service 1
Pay Units: N.A.
Programming (via satellite): Cinemax (multiplexed); Encore; HBO (multiplexed); Showtime (multiplexed); Starz (multiplexed); The Movie Channel (multiplexed).

Video-On-Demand: No

Pay-Per-View
iN DEMAND (delivered digitally); Playboy TV (delivered digitally); Club Jenna (delivered digitally).

Internet Service
Operational: No.

Telephone Service
None
Miles of Plant: 40.0 (coaxial); None (fiber optic). Homes passed: 1,086.
Regional Manager: Mike Taylor. Chief Technician: Larry Stafford.
Ownership: Rapid Communications LLC (MSO).

HOLLY GROVE—Formerly served by Cebridge Connections. No longer in operation. ICA: AR0154.

HOOKER/LADD—Community Communications Co., 1920 Hwy 425 N, Monticello, AR 71655-4463. Phones: 800-272-2191; 870-367-7300. Fax: 870-367-9770. E-mail: generalmanager@ccc-cable.net. Web Site: http://www.ccc-cable.net. Also serves Ladd. ICA: AR0157.
TV Market Ranking: 50 (HOOKER, LADD). Franchise award date: N.A. Franchise expiration date: N.A. Began: May 15, 1989.
Channel capacity: 48 (not 2-way capable). Channels available but not in use: N.A.
Basic Service
Subscribers: 101.
Programming (received off-air): KARK-TV (NBC) Little Rock; KASN (CW) Pine Bluff; KATV (ABC) Little Rock; KETS (PBS) Little Rock; KLRT-TV (FOX) Little Rock; KTHV (CBS) Little Rock.
Programming (via satellite): ABC Family Channel; AMC; Arts & Entertainment; BET Networks; CNN; Country Music TV; ESPN; ESPN 2; FX; Lifetime; Nickelodeon; Outdoor Channel; QVC; Syfy; TBS Superstation; The Learning Channel; Trinity Broadcasting Network; Turner Network TV; TV Land; USA Network; VH1; WGN America.
Fee: $25.00 installation; $33.60 monthly.
Pay Service 1
Pay Units: N.A.
Programming (via satellite): HBO; Showtime.
Fee: $10.00 monthly (each).
Video-On-Demand: No
Internet Service
Operational: No.
Telephone Service
None
Homes passed: 318.
Operations Manager: Larry Ivy.
Ownership: Community Communications Co. (MSO).

HOPE—Hope Community TV, 506 S Walnut St, Hope, AR 71801-5355. Phone: 870-777-4684. Fax: 870-777-5159. E-mail: hopecabletvcs@cablelynx.com. Web Site: http://www.hopecabletv.com. Also serves Perrytown & Prescott. ICA: AR0031.
TV Market Ranking: 58 (HOPE, Perrytown); Outside TV Markets (Prescott, Perrytown). Franchise award date: N.A. Franchise expiration date: N.A. Began: December 9, 1967.
Channel capacity: 51 (operating 2-way). Channels available but not in use: None.
Basic Service
Subscribers: 8,705.
Programming (received off-air): KARK-TV (NBC) Little Rock; KATV (ABC) Little Rock; KETG (PBS) Arkadelphia; KMSS-TV (FOX) Shreveport; KSHV-TV (MNT) Shreveport; KSLA (CBS) Shreveport; KTAL-TV (NBC) Texarkana; KTBS-TV (ABC) Shreveport; KTHV (CBS) Little Rock; KTSS-LP Hope.
Programming (via satellite): ABC Family Channel; AMC; Animal Planet; Arts & Entertainment; BET Networks; Cartoon Network; CNBC; CNN; Comcast Sports Net Southwest; Country Music TV; C-SPAN; C-SPAN 2; CW+; Discovery Channel; Disney Channel; ESPN; ESPN 2; FamilyNet; Food Network; Fox News Channel; FX; GalaVision; Headline News; HGTV; History Channel; Home Shopping Network; Lifetime; MTV; Nickelodeon; ShopNBC; Sneak Prevue; Spike TV; Syfy; TBS Superstation; Telemundo; The Learning Channel; Trinity Broadcasting Network; Turner Classic Movies; Turner Network TV; TV Guide Network; TV Land; Univision; USA Network; VH1; Weather Channel.
Current originations: Government Access; Public Access.
Fee: $35.11 installation; $47.90 monthly.
Digital Basic Service
Subscribers: 232.
Programming (via satellite): AmericanLife TV Network; BBC America; Bio; CMT Pure Country; Discovery Health Channel; Discovery Kids Channel; Discovery Military Channel; Discovery Planet Green; ESPNews; FitTV; Fox Soccer; FSN Digital Atlantic; FSN Digital Central; FSN Digital Pacific; G4; Golf Channel; Great American Country; GSN; Halogen Network; History Channel International; ID Investigation Discovery; Lifetime Movie Network; MTV Hits; MTV Jams; MTV Tres; MTV2; Music Choice; National Geographic Channel; Nick Jr.; Nick Too; NickToons TV; Outdoor Channel; Science Channel; SoapNet; Speed Channel; Style Network; TeenNick; Toon Disney; VH1 Classic; VH1 Soul; WE tv.
Fee: $10.00 monthly.
Digital Expanded Basic Service
Subscribers: N.A.
Programming (via satellite): CNN HD; Discovery HD Theater; ESPN HD; HDNet; HDNet Movies; Outdoor Channel 2 HD; TBS in HD; Turner Network TV HD.
Fee: $10.00 monthly.
Pay Service 1
Pay Units: 827.
Programming (via satellite): HBO.
Fee: $12.29 installation; $12.95 monthly.
Digital Pay Service 1
Pay Units: 210.
Programming (via satellite): Cinemax (multiplexed); Cinemax HD.
Fee: $12.95 monthly.
Digital Pay Service 2
Pay Units: 49.
Programming (via satellite): HBO (multiplexed); HBO HD.
Fee: $12.95 monthly.
Digital Pay Service 3
Pay Units: N.A.
Programming (via satellite): Encore; Starz (multiplexed); Starz HDTV.
Fee: $12.95 monthly.
Video-On-Demand: No
Pay-Per-View
Addressable homes: 232.
iN DEMAND (delivered digitally), Addressable: Yes.
Internet Service
Operational: Yes. Began: May 1, 2001.
Subscribers: 58.
Broadband Service: Cablelynx.
Fee: $19.95-$74.95 monthly; $10.00 modem lease.
Telephone Service
Analog: Not Operational
Digital: Operational
Fee: $45.70 monthly
Miles of Plant: 160.0 (coaxial); 13.0 (fiber optic).
Manager: Stacy Eads. Plant Manager: Ronnie Floyd. Technician Supervisor: Dale Klare.
City fee: 3% of gross.
Ownership: WEHCO Video Inc. (MSO).; Gilmer Cable (MSO).; Kenneth W. Poindexter.

HORSESHOE BEND—Crystal Broadband Networks, PO Box 180336, Chicago, TX 60618. Phones: 877-319-0328; 630-206-0447. E-mail: info@crystalbn.com. Web Site: http://crystalbn.com. Also serves Franklin & Izard County. ICA: AR0071.
TV Market Ranking: Outside TV Markets (Franklin, HORSESHOE BEND, Izard County). Franchise award date: August 1, 1974. Franchise expiration date: N.A. Began: August 1, 1974.
Channel capacity: 52 (2-way capable). Channels available but not in use: 11.
Basic Service
Subscribers: 522.
Programming (received off-air): KAIT (ABC) Jonesboro; KEMV (PBS) Mountain View; KOLR (CBS) Springfield; KSFX-TV (FOX) Springfield; KTHV (CBS) Little Rock; KYTV (CW, NBC) Springfield; WNBC (NBC) New York; allband FM.
Programming (via satellite): C-SPAN; Home Shopping Network; Trinity Broadcasting Network; WGN America.
Fee: $29.95 installation; $19.95 monthly.
Expanded Basic Service 1
Subscribers: N.A.
Programming (via satellite): ABC Family Channel; AMC; Arts & Entertainment; Cartoon Network; CNBC; CNN; Comcast Sports Net Southwest; Discovery Channel; Disney Channel; E! Entertainment Television; ESPN; ESPN 2; Food Network; Golf Channel; Great American Country; Hallmark Channel; HGTV; History Channel; Lifetime; MTV; Nickelodeon; Spike TV; TBS Superstation; The Learning Channel; Turner Classic Movies; Turner Network TV; TV Land; USA Network; VH1; Weather Channel.
Fee: $20.00 monthly.
Pay Service 1
Pay Units: 310.
Programming (via satellite): Cinemax; Encore; HBO; Showtime; Starz; The Movie Channel.
Fee: $5.99 monthly (Encore), $8.99 monthly (Cinemax), $12.99 monthly (HBO), $13.99 monthly (Showtime & TMC).
Video-On-Demand: No
Internet Service
Operational: Yes.
Telephone Service
Digital: Operational
Miles of Plant: 59.0 (coaxial); None (fiber optic). Additional miles planned: 15.0 (coaxial). Homes passed: 1,335.
Program Manager: Shawn Smith. General Manager: Nidhin Johnson.
City fee: 2% of gross.
Ownership: Crystal Broadband Networks (MSO).

HOT SPRINGS—Resort TV Cable Co. Inc., 410 Airport Rd, Ste H, Hot Springs, AR 71913-4000. Phone: 870-836-8111. Fax: 501-624-0502. Web Site: http://www.resorttvcable.com. Also serves Garland County & Mountain Pine. ICA: AR0004.
TV Market Ranking: Below 100 (Garland County, HOT SPRINGS, Mountain Pine). Franchise award date: June 1, 1964. Franchise expiration date: N.A. Began: September 2, 1970.
Channel capacity: 62 (operating 2-way). Channels available but not in use: None.
Basic Service
Subscribers: 23,971.
Programming (received off-air): KARK-TV (NBC) Little Rock; KARZ-TV (MNT) Little Rock; KASN (CW) Pine Bluff; KATV (ABC) Little Rock; KETS (PBS) Little Rock; KKAP (ETV) Little Rock; KLRT-TV (FOX) Little Rock; KTHV (CBS) Little Rock; KVTJ-DT (IND) Jonesboro.
Programming (via satellite): ABC Family Channel; AMC; Animal Planet; Arts & Entertainment; BET Networks; Cartoon Network; CNBC; CNN; Comcast Sports Net Southwest; Comedy Central; Country Music TV; C-SPAN; C-SPAN 2; Discovery Channel; Disney Channel; ESPN; ESPN 2; ESPN Classic Sports; Food Network; Fox News Channel; FX; GalaVision; Hallmark Channel; Headline News; HGTV; History Channel; Home Shopping Network; Lifetime; MSNBC; MTV; NASA TV; Nickelodeon; ShopNBC; Sneak Prevue; Spike TV; Syfy; TBS Superstation; Telemundo; The Learning Channel; Travel Channel; Trinity Broadcasting Network; truTV; Turner Classic Movies; Turner Network TV; TV Guide Network; TV Land; Univision; USA Network; VH1; Weather Channel; WGN America.
Current originations: Government Access; Educational Access; Public Access.
Fee: $48.90 monthly; $2.19 converter.
Digital Basic Service
Subscribers: N.A.
Programming (via satellite): AmericanLife TV Network; BBC America; Bio; CMT Pure Country; Discovery Health Channel; Discovery Kids Channel; Discovery Military Channel; Discovery Planet Green; DMX Music; ESPNews; FitTV; Fox Soccer; FSN Digital Atlantic; FSN Digital Central; FSN Digital Pacific; G4; Golf Channel; Great American Country; GSN; Halogen Network; History Channel International; ID Investigation Discovery; Lifetime Movie Network; MTV Hits; MTV Jams; MTV Tres; MTV2; National Geographic Channel; Nick Jr.; Nick Too; NickToons TV; Science Channel; SoapNet; Speed Channel; Style Network; TeenNick; Toon Disney; VH1 Classic; VH1 Soul; WE tv.
Fee: $10.00 monthly.
Digital Expanded Basic Service
Subscribers: N.A.
Programming (received off-air): KARK-TV (NBC) Little Rock; KATV (ABC) Little Rock; KTEJ (PBS) Jonesboro; KTHV (CBS) Little Rock.
Programming (via satellite): CNN HD; Discovery Channel HD; ESPN HD; HDNet; HDNet Movies; Outdoor Channel 2 HD; PBS HD; TBS in HD; Turner Network TV HD.
Fee: $5.00 monthly.
Pay Service 1
Pay Units: N.A.
Programming (via satellite): HBO.
Digital Pay Service 1
Pay Units: N.A.
Programming (via satellite): Cinemax (multiplexed); Cinemax HD; Encore (multiplexed); HBO (multiplexed); HBO HD; Starz (multiplexed); Starz HDTV.
Fee: $12.95 monthly (HBO, Cinemax, or Starz/Encore).
Video-On-Demand: No
Pay-Per-View
iN DEMAND (delivered digitally), Addressable: Yes.
Internet Service
Operational: Yes. Began: April 1, 2001.
Subscribers: 301.

Broadband Service: Cablelynx.
Fee: $19.95 monthly; $10.00 modem lease.
Telephone Service
Analog: Not Operational
Digital: Operational
Fee: $45.70 monthly
Miles of Plant: 550.0 (coaxial); None (fiber optic). Homes passed: 27,765.
Manager: Harvey Oxner. Chief Technician: Charles Hill. Marketing Director: Lori Haight. Office Manager: Judy Meinecke.
Franchise fee: 3% of basic gross.
Ownership: WEHCO Video Inc. (MSO).; Gilmer Cable (MSO).

HOT SPRINGS VILLAGE—Suddenlink Communications, 4656 N Hwy 7, Ste L, Hot Springs Village, AR 71909-9482. Phone: 501-984-5010. Web Site: http://www.suddenlink.com. Also serves Garland County. ICA: AR0246.
TV Market Ranking: 50 (Garland County (portions)); Below 100 (HOT SPRINGS VILLAGE, Garland County (portions)). Franchise award date: July 27, 1972. Franchise expiration date: N.A. Began: January 1, 1973.
Channel capacity: 56 (operating 2-way). Channels available but not in use: N.A.
Basic Service
Subscribers: 4,963.
Programming (received off-air): KARK-TV (NBC) Little Rock; KARZ-TV (MNT) Little Rock; KASN (CW) Pine Bluff; KATV (ABC) Little Rock; KETS (PBS) Little Rock; KLRT-TV (FOX) Little Rock; KTHV (CBS) Little Rock; KVTN-DT (IND) Pine Bluff; allband FM.
Programming (via satellite): ABC Family Channel; Comcast Sports Net Southwest; C-SPAN; Fox News Channel; Golf Channel; HGTV; Home Shopping Network; TBS Superstation; Trinity Broadcasting Network; TV Land; WGN America.
Current originations: Government Access; Educational Access; Public Access.
Fee: $38.00 installation; $14.48 monthly.
Expanded Basic Service 1
Subscribers: 4,613.
Programming (via satellite): AMC; AmericanLife TV Network; Arts & Entertainment; CNBC; CNN; Discovery Channel; Disney Channel; ESPN; ESPN 2; Great American Country; Headline News; History Channel; Lifetime; Spike TV; Syfy; Turner Network TV; USA Network; Weather Channel.
Fee: $10.00 installation; $13.47 monthly.
Pay Service 1
Pay Units: 50.
Programming (via satellite): HBO; The Movie Channel.
Fee: $35.00 installation; $8.75 monthly (TMC), $9.75 monthly (HBO).
Video-On-Demand: No
Internet Service
Operational: Yes.
Broadband Service: Cebridge High Speed Cable Internet.
Fee: $49.95 installation; $26.95 monthly.
Telephone Service
None
Miles of Plant: 54.0 (coaxial); None (fiber optic). Additional miles planned: 9.0 (coaxial).
Manager: Mark Badgwell. Chief Technician: Chris Raburn.
City fee: None.
Ownership: Cequel Communications LLC (MSO).

HUGHES—Suddenlink Communications, 12444 Powerscourt Dr, Saint Louis, MO 63131-3660. Phones: 800-999-6845 (Customer service); 314-965-2020. Fax: 903-561-5485. Web Site: http://www.suddenlink.com. Also serves Crittenden County (portions), Horseshoe Lake, Madison & Widener. ICA: AR0112.
TV Market Ranking: 26 (Crittenden County (portions), Horseshoe Lake, HUGHES); Outside TV Markets (Madison, Widener). Franchise award date: N.A. Franchise expiration date: N.A. Began: December 1, 1982.
Channel capacity: 36 (operating 2-way). Channels available but not in use: N.A.
Basic Service
Subscribers: 869.
Programming (received off-air): KAIT (ABC) Jonesboro; KARK-TV (NBC) Little Rock; KATV (ABC) Little Rock; KVTJ-DT (IND) Jonesboro; WHBQ-TV (FOX) Memphis; WKNO (PBS) Memphis; WLMT (CW) Memphis; WMC-TV (NBC) Memphis; WPTY-TV (ABC) Memphis; WPXX-TV (ION, MNT) Memphis; WREG-TV (CBS) Memphis.
Programming (via satellite): KTHV (CBS) Little Rock; National Geographic Channel.
Fee: $17.95 installation; $19.95 monthly.
Expanded Basic Service 1
Subscribers: N.A.
Programming (via satellite): ABC Family Channel; Animal Planet; BET Networks; Cartoon Network; CNBC; CNN; C-SPAN; C-SPAN 2; Discovery Channel; Disney Channel; E! Entertainment Television; ESPN; ESPN 2; Fox News Channel; Great American Country; Headline News; HGTV; Home Shopping Network; Lifetime; MTV; Nickelodeon; Spike TV; Syfy; TBS Superstation; The Learning Channel; Travel Channel; Trinity Broadcasting Network; Turner Network TV; USA Network; Weather Channel.
Fee: $24.00 monthly.
Pay Service 1
Pay Units: 49.
Programming (via satellite): Cinemax.
Fee: $10.95 monthly.
Pay Service 2
Pay Units: 182.
Programming (via satellite): HBO.
Fee: $10.95 monthly.
Pay Service 3
Pay Units: 180.
Programming (via satellite): Showtime.
Fee: $10.95 monthly.
Video-On-Demand: No
Pay-Per-View
Sports PPV (delivered digitally); ESPN Extra (delivered digitally); ESPN Now (delivered digitally); Shorteez (delivered digitally); Fresh (delivered digitally); Playboy TV (delivered digitally); iN DEMAND (delivered digitally).
Internet Service
Operational: Yes. Began: June 3, 2004.
Broadband Service: Cebridge High Speed Cable Internet.
Fee: $49.95 installation; $26.95 monthly.
Telephone Service
None
Miles of Plant: 44.0 (coaxial); None (fiber optic). Homes passed: 1,781.
Regional Manager: Todd Cruthird. Area Manager: Al Harrison. Plant Manager: John Barnett. Marketing Director: Beverly Gambell.
Ownership: Cequel Communications LLC (MSO).

HUMNOKE—Formerly served by Cebridge Connections. No longer in operation. ICA: AR0179.

HUMPHREY—Formerly served by Cebridge Connections. No longer in operation. ICA: AR0161.

HUNTSVILLE—Madison County Cable, PO Box D, 113 Court St, Huntsville, AR 72740. Phones: 479-738-2121; 479-738-6828. Fax: 479-738-2105. Web Site: http://www.madisoncounty.net. ICA: AR0247.
TV Market Ranking: Below 100 (HUNTSVILLE). Franchise award date: N.A. Franchise expiration date: N.A. Began: October 1, 1959.
Channel capacity: 66 (operating 2-way). Channels available but not in use: N.A.
Basic Service
Subscribers: 1,000.
Programming (received off-air): KAFT (PBS) Fayetteville; KFDF-CA Fort Smith; KFSM-TV (CBS) Fort Smith; KHOG-TV (ABC) Fayetteville; KNWA-TV (NBC) Rogers; KOLR (CBS) Springfield; KPBI (MNT) Eureka Springs; KPBI-CA (FOX) Fort Smith; KSFX-TV (FOX) Springfield; KSPR (ABC) Springfield; KXUN-LP Fort Smith; KYTV (CW, NBC) Springfield.
Programming (via satellite): ABC Family Channel; Animal Planet; Arts & Entertainment; Bravo; CNBC; CNN; Comcast Sports Net Southwest; Country Music TV; C-SPAN; C-SPAN 2; CW+; Discovery Channel; Disney Channel; E! Entertainment Television; ESPN; ESPN 2; ESPN Classic Sports; FitTV; Food Network; Fox News Channel; Golf Channel; Headline News; HGTV; History Channel; Home Shopping Network; Lifetime; Lifetime Movie Network; MSNBC; MTV; MyNetworkTV Inc.; Nickelodeon; Outdoor Channel; QVC; Spike TV; Syfy; TBS Superstation; The Learning Channel; The Sportsman Channel; Toon Disney; Travel Channel; Trinity Broadcasting Network; truTV; Turner Classic Movies; Turner Network TV; TV Guide Network; TV Land; USA Network; VH1; Weather Channel; WGN America.
Fee: $21.90 installation; $28.50 monthly; $10.00 additional installation.
Digital Basic Service
Subscribers: 300.
Programming (via satellite): AmericanLife TV Network; BBC America; Bio; Bloomberg Television; Bravo; Discovery Health Channel; Discovery Home Channel; Discovery Kids Channel; Discovery Times Channel; DMX Music; Fox Movie Channel; Fuse; G4; GAS; Great American Country; GSN; Halogen Network; History Channel International; Independent Film Channel; Lifetime Movie Network; MTV Hits; MTV2; Newsworld International; Nick Jr.; NickToons TV; Ovation; Science Channel; ShopNBC; Style Network; Trio; VH1 Classic; VH1 Country; VH1 Soul; WE tv.
Fee: $37.50 monthly.
Digital Expanded Basic Service
Subscribers: N.A.
Programming (via satellite): Cine Latino; CNN en Espanol; Discovery en Espanol; Fox Sports en Espanol; HTV Musica; MTV Tres; TVE Internacional; Utilisima; VHUNO.
Fee: $5.00 monthly.
Digital Expanded Basic Service 2
Subscribers: N.A.
Programming (via satellite): ESPN Classic Sports; ESPNews; Fox Sports World; FSN Digital Atlantic; FSN Digital Central; FSN Digital Pacific; Speed Channel; Versus.
Fee: $5.00 monthly.
Pay Service 1
Pay Units: 40.
Programming (via satellite): Cinemax; HBO.
Fee: $16.00 monthly.
Digital Pay Service 1
Pay Units: N.A.
Programming (via satellite): Cinemax (multiplexed); Encore (multiplexed); Flix; HBO (multiplexed); Showtime (multiplexed); Starz (multiplexed); Sundance Channel; The Movie Channel.
Fee: $13.00 monthly (Cinemax, Starz/Encore or Showtime/Flix/Sundance/TMC), $15.00 monthly (HBO).
Video-On-Demand: No
Pay-Per-View
iN DEMAND (delivered digitally); Playboy TV (delivered digitally); Spice (delivered digitally); Spice 2 (delivered digitally); ESPN Now (delivered digitally); ESPN (delivered digitally).
Internet Service
Operational: No.
Telephone Service
None
Miles of Plant: 80.0 (coaxial); None (fiber optic).
Manager: Joe Shrum. Chief Technician: Stewart Markley.
City fee: 3% of gross.
Ownership: Madison Communications Inc. (MSO).

HUTTIG—Bayou Cable TV, PO Box 466, Marion, LA 71260-0466. Phone: 318-292-4774. Fax: 318-292-4775. Web Site: http://www.bayoucable.com. ICA: AR0315.
TV Market Ranking: 99 (HUTTIG). Franchise award date: N.A. Franchise expiration date: N.A. Began: N.A.
Channel capacity: 50 (not 2-way capable). Channels available but not in use: 6.
Basic Service
Subscribers: 257.
Programming (received off-air): KAQY (ABC) Columbia; KARD (FOX) West Monroe; KATV (ABC) Little Rock; KLTM-TV (PBS) Monroe; KNOE-TV (CBS, CW) Monroe; KTVE (NBC) El Dorado.
Programming (via satellite): AMC; Hallmark Channel; Trinity Broadcasting Network; TV Land.
Fee: $30.00 installation; $15.95 monthly.
Expanded Basic Service 1
Subscribers: N.A.
Programming (received off-air): KEJB (MNT)lorado.
Programming (via satellite): ABC Family Channel; Animal Planet; Arts & Entertainment; BET Networks; CNN; Country Music TV; Discovery Channel; ESPN; ESPN 2; Food Network; Fox News Channel; FX; History Channel; ION Television; Lifetime; MTV; National Geographic Channel; Nickelodeon; Outdoor Channel; Speed Channel; Spike TV; TBS Superstation; The Learning Channel; Turner Network TV; USA Network; VH1; Weather Channel; WGN America.
Fee: $20.00 monthly.
Pay Service 1
Pay Units: N.A.
Programming (via satellite): Cinemax; HBO.
Fee: $8.95 monthly (Cinemax), $10.95 monthly (HBO).
Video-On-Demand: No
Internet Service
Operational: No.
Telephone Service
None
Miles of Plant: 7.0 (coaxial); None (fiber optic).
Manager: Alan C. Booker. Chief Technician: Mark Andrews.
Ownership: Bayou Cable TV (MSO).

JASPER—Ritter Communications. Now served by WESTERN GROVE, AR [AR0183]. ICA: AR0178.

JONES MILL—Community Communications Co., 1920 Hwy 425 N, Monticello, AR 71655-4463. Phones: 800-272-2191; 870-367-7300. Fax: 870-367-9770. E-mail: generalmanager@ccc-cable.net. Web Site: http://www.ccc-cable.net. ICA: AR0248.

TV Market Ranking: Below 100 (JONES MILL). Franchise award date: N.A. Franchise expiration date: N.A. Began: N.A.

Channel capacity: 48 (not 2-way capable). Channels available but not in use: N.A.

Basic Service

Subscribers: 232.

Programming (received off-air): KARK-TV (NBC) Little Rock; KATV (ABC) Little Rock; KETS (PBS) Little Rock; KLRT-TV (FOX) Little Rock; KTHV (CBS) Little Rock.

Programming (via satellite): ABC Family Channel; AMC; Arts & Entertainment; CNN; Country Music TV; Discovery Channel; Disney Channel; ESPN; ESPN 2; FitTV; Fox News Channel; FX; Headline News; Lifetime; MTV; Nickelodeon; Outdoor Channel; QVC; Spike TV; Syfy; TBS Superstation; The Learning Channel; Trinity Broadcasting Network; Turner Network TV; TV Land; USA Network; VH1; Weather Channel; WGN America.

Fee: $33.60 monthly.

Pay Service 1

Pay Units: N.A.

Programming (via satellite): HBO; Showtime; The Movie Channel.

Fee: $10.00 monthly (each).

Video-On-Demand: No

Internet Service

Operational: No.

Telephone Service

None

Miles of Plant: 21.0 (coaxial); None (fiber optic).

Chief Technician: Larry Ivy.

Ownership: Community Communications Co. (MSO).

JONESBORO—Suddenlink Communications, 1520 S Caraway Rd, Jonesboro, AR 72401-5308. Phone: 870-935-3615. Fax: 870-972-8141. Web Site: http://www.suddenlink.com. Also serves Bay. ICA: AR0008.

TV Market Ranking: Below 100 (Bay, JONESBORO). Franchise award date: January 1, 1968. Franchise expiration date: N.A. Began: October 3, 1967.

Channel capacity: N.A. Channels available but not in use: N.A.

Basic Service

Subscribers: 21,433.

Programming (received off-air): KAIT (ABC) Jonesboro; KARK-TV (NBC) Little Rock; KATV (ABC) Little Rock; KTEJ (PBS) Jonesboro; KTHV (CBS) Little Rock; KVTJ-DT (IND) Jonesboro; WHBQ-TV (FOX) Memphis; WKNO (PBS) Memphis; WMC-TV (NBC) Memphis; WREG-TV (CBS) Memphis.

Programming (via satellite): CW+; INSP; ION Television; News Plus; QVC; TBS Superstation; TV Guide Network; WGN America.

Current originations: Government Access; Educational Access.

Fee: $38.00 installation; $15.13 monthly; $3.83 converter.

Expanded Basic Service 1

Subscribers: N.A.

Programming (via satellite): ABC Family Channel; AMC; Arts & Entertainment; BET Networks; Cartoon Network; CNBC; CNN; Comcast Sports Net Southwest; Comedy Central; C-SPAN; Discovery Channel; Disney Channel; ESPN; ESPN 2; Food Network; Fox News Channel; FX; Great American Country; Headline News; History Channel; Lifetime; MSNBC; MTV; Nickelodeon; Spike TV; The Learning Channel; Travel Channel; Trinity Broadcasting Network; truTV; Turner Network TV; USA Network; VH1; Weather Channel.

Fee: $27.35 monthly.

Digital Basic Service

Subscribers: N.A.

Programming (via satellite): BBC America; Discovery Digital Networks; DMX Music; Encore Action; ESPN Classic Sports; ESPNews; Fox Sports World; Golf Channel; GSN; HGTV; Syfy; Turner Classic Movies; Versus; WE tv.

Fee: $15.00 monthly.

Pay Service 1

Pay Units: 2,600.

Programming (via satellite): Cinemax; HBO; Showtime; Starz.

Fee: $19.95 installation; $11.95 monthly (each).

Digital Pay Service 1

Pay Units: N.A.

Programming (via satellite): Cinemax (multiplexed); HBO (multiplexed); Showtime (multiplexed); Starz (multiplexed); The Movie Channel (multiplexed).

Video-On-Demand: Planned

Pay-Per-View

Addressable homes: 1,095.

Hot Choice (delivered digitally), Addressable: Yes; iN DEMAND (delivered digitally); Playboy TV (delivered digitally).

Internet Service

Operational: Yes.

Broadband Service: Cebridge High Speed Cable Internet.

Fee: $29.95 monthly.

Telephone Service

Digital: Operational

Fee: $44.95 monthly

Miles of Plant: 457.0 (coaxial); None (fiber optic). Additional miles planned: 10.0 (coaxial). Homes passed: 24,000. Total homes in franchised area: 24,000.

Manager: Garry Bowman. Chief Technician: Chriss Berry. Program Director: Kevin Shirley. Customer Service Manager: Rhonda McKay.

City fee: 5% of gross.

Ownership: Cequel Communications LLC (MSO).

JUNCTION CITY—Rapid Cable, 515 E Longview Dr, Arp, TX 75750. Phone: 903-859-6492. Fax: 903-859-3708. Also serves Junction City. ICA: AR0249.

TV Market Ranking: 99 (Junction City, JUNCTION CITY). Franchise award date: N.A. Franchise expiration date: N.A. Began: N.A.

Channel capacity: 36 (not 2-way capable). Channels available but not in use: N.A.

Basic Service

Subscribers: 136.

Programming (received off-air): KAQY (ABC) Columbia; KARD (FOX) West Monroe; KATV (ABC) Little Rock; KEJB (MNT)lorado; KKYK-DT (IND) Camden; KLTM-TV (PBS) Monroe; KNOE-TV (CBS, CW) Monroe; KTVE (NBC) El Dorado.

Programming (via satellite): ABC Family Channel; Animal Planet; Arts & Entertainment; BET Networks; Cartoon Network; CNBC; CNN; Discovery Channel; Disney Channel; ESPN; FX; Great American Country; Headline News; HGTV; History Channel; Home Shopping Network; Lifetime; MTV; National Geographic Channel; Nickelodeon; Outdoor Channel; Spike TV; Syfy; TBS Superstation; The Learning Channel; Turner Classic Movies; Turner Network TV; USA Network; Weather Channel.

Fee: $54.95 installation; $44.05 monthly.

Pay Service 1

Pay Units: 32.

Programming (via satellite): HBO.

Fee: $12.95 monthly.

Pay Service 2

Pay Units: 37.

Programming (via satellite): The Movie Channel.

Fee: $12.95 monthly.

Pay Service 3

Pay Units: 61.

Programming (via satellite): Showtime.

Fee: $12.95 monthly.

Pay Service 4

Pay Units: N.A.

Programming (via satellite): Flix.

Fee: $1.95 monthly.

Video-On-Demand: No

Internet Service

Operational: No.

Telephone Service

None

Miles of Plant: 15.0 (coaxial); None (fiber optic). Homes passed: 551.

Regional Manager: Mike Taylor. Chief Technician: Larry Stafford.

Ownership: Rapid Communications LLC (MSO).

KNOBEL—Formerly served by Cebridge Connections. No longer in operation. ICA: AR0193.

KNOXVILLE—Formerly served by Quality Entertainment Corp. No longer in operation. ICA: AR0310.

LAKE CITY—Ritter Communications. Now served by MARKED TREE, AR [AR0072]. ICA: AR0251.

LAKE ERLING—Formerly served by Cebridge Connections. No longer in operation. ICA: AR0306.

LAKE VIEW—Alliance Communications, PO Box 960, 290 S Broadview St, Greenbrier, AR 72058-9616. Phone: 501-679-6619. Fax: 501-679-5694. Web Site: http://www.alliancecable.net. Also serves Elaine. ICA: AR0181.

TV Market Ranking: Outside TV Markets (Elaine, LAKE VIEW). Franchise award date: N.A. Franchise expiration date: N.A. Began: August 1, 1989.

Channel capacity: 35 (not 2-way capable). Channels available but not in use: 12.

Basic Service

Subscribers: 254.

Programming (received off-air): KASN (CW) Pine Bluff; KATV (ABC) Little Rock; WABG-TV (ABC) Greenwood; WLMT (CW) Memphis; WMAV-TV (PBS) Oxford; WMC-TV (NBC) Memphis; WREG-TV (CBS) Memphis; WXVT (CBS) Greenville.

Programming (via satellite): ABC Family Channel; Animal Planet; Arts & Entertainment; BET Networks; Cartoon Network; CNN; Country Music TV; C-SPAN; Discovery Channel; ESPN; ESPN 2; FX; Headline News (multiplexed); History Channel; Home Shopping Network; Lifetime; MTV; Nickelodeon; Outdoor Channel; Spike TV; Syfy; TBS Superstation; The Learning Channel; Trinity Broadcasting Network; truTV; Turner Classic Movies; Turner Network TV; TV Land; USA Network; VH1; Weather Channel; WGN America; WHBQ-TV (FOX) Memphis.

Fee: $10.00 installation; $33.60 monthly.

Digital Basic Service

Subscribers: 16.

Programming (via satellite): AmericanLife TV Network; BBC America; Bio; Bloomberg Television; Discovery Digital Networks; DMX Music; ESPN Classic Sports; ESPNews; Fox Movie Channel; Fox Sports World; Fuse; G4; GAS; Golf Channel; GSN; Halogen Network; HGTV; History Channel International; Independent Film Channel; MTV Networks Digital Suite; National Geographic Channel; Nick Jr.; NickToons TV; Ovation; Speed Channel; Style Network; Sundance Channel; Trio; Versus; WE tv.

Fee: $42.00 monthly.

Pay Service 1

Pay Units: N.A.

Programming (via satellite): Cinemax; HBO.

Digital Pay Service 1

Pay Units: 44.

Programming (via satellite): HBO (multiplexed).

Fee: $11.95 monthly.

Digital Pay Service 2

Pay Units: 10.

Programming (via satellite): Showtime (multiplexed).

Fee: $11.95 monthly.

Digital Pay Service 3

Pay Units: 51.

Programming (via satellite): Cinemax (multiplexed).

Fee: $11.95 monthly.

Digital Pay Service 4

Pay Units: 10.

Programming (via satellite): The Movie Channel (multiplexed).

Fee: $11.95 monthly.

Digital Pay Service 5

Pay Units: 13.

Programming (via satellite): Encore (multiplexed).

Fee: $11.95 monthly.

Digital Pay Service 6

Pay Units: 10.

Programming (via satellite): Flix.

Fee: $11.95 monthly.

Digital Pay Service 7

Pay Units: 10.

Programming (via satellite): Starz (multiplexed).

Fee: $11.95 monthly.

Video-On-Demand: No

Pay-Per-View

iN DEMAND (delivered digitally); Playboy TV (delivered digitally); Fresh (delivered digitally); Shorteez (delivered digitally).

Internet Service

Operational: No.

Telephone Service

None

Miles of Plant: 31.0 (coaxial); None (fiber optic). Homes passed: 978.

Vice President: Arl Cope. Operations Manager: Jeff Browers. Programming & Marketing Manager: James Fuller.

Ownership: Buford Media Group LLC (MSO).

LAKE VILLAGE—Allegiance Communications, 707 W Saratoga St, Shawnee, OK 74804. Phones: 405-395-1131; 405-275-6923. Web Site: http://www.allegiance.tv. ICA: AR0253.

TV Market Ranking: Below 100 (LAKE VILLAGE). Franchise award date: N.A. Franchise expiration date: N.A. Began: January 31, 1966.
Channel capacity: 39 (operating 2-way). Channels available but not in use: N.A.

Basic Service
Subscribers: 677.
Programming (received off-air): KARK-TV (NBC) Little Rock; KARZ-TV (MNT) Little Rock; KASN (CW) Pine Bluff; KATV (ABC) Little Rock; KETS (PBS) Little Rock; KKYK-CA (IND) Little Rock; KLRT-TV (FOX) Little Rock; KTHV (CBS) Little Rock; KTVE (NBC) El Dorado; WABG-TV (ABC) Greenwood; WXVT (CBS) Greenville; allband FM.
Programming (via satellite): CNBC; CNN; C-SPAN; Daystar TV Network; Headline News; Home Shopping Network; Trinity Broadcasting Network; WGN America.
Fee: $38.00 installation; $19.99 monthly.

Expanded Basic Service 1
Subscribers: 553.
Programming (via satellite): ABC Family Channel; Animal Planet; Arts & Entertainment; BET Networks; Cartoon Network; Comcast Sports Net Southwest; Discovery Channel; Disney Channel; ESPN; ESPN 2; ESPN Classic Sports; Fox News Channel; FX; Great American Country; Hallmark Channel; HGTV; History Channel; Lifetime; Nickelodeon; Outdoor Channel; Oxygen; Speed Channel; Spike TV; Syfy; TBS Superstation; The Learning Channel; Travel Channel; Turner Classic Movies; Turner Network TV; TV Land; USA Network; VH1; Weather Channel.
Fee: $32.16 monthly.

Digital Basic Service
Subscribers: 79.
Programming (via satellite): AmericanLife TV Network; BBC America; Bio; Bloomberg Television; Bravo; Cine Latino; Cine Mexicano; CMT Pure Country; CNN en Espanol; Daystar TV Network; Discovery en Espanol; Discovery HD Theater; Discovery Health Channel; Discovery Kids Channel; Discovery Military Channel; Discovery Planet Green; DMX Music; Encore (multiplexed); ESPN Classic Sports; ESPN Deportes; ESPN HD; ESPNews; FitTV; Flix; Fox College Sports Atlantic; Fox College Sports Central; Fox College Sports Pacific; Fox Movie Channel; Fox Soccer; Fox Sports en Espanol; Fuse; G4; Golf Channel; Gospel Music Channel; Great American Country; GSN; Halogen Network; HDNet; HDNet Movies; History Channel; History Channel en Espanol; History Channel International; ID Investigation Discovery; Independent Film Channel; Lifetime Movie Network; MTV Hits; MTV Tres; MTV2; National Geographic Channel; Nick Jr.; NickToons TV; Outdoor Channel; Outdoor Channel 2 HD; Science Channel; ShopNBC; Sleuth; Speed Channel; Style Network; Sundance Channel; Syfy; TeenNick; The Word Network; Toon Disney; Trinity Broadcasting Network; Turner Classic Movies; Universal HD; VH1 Classic; WE tv.
Fee: $10.85 monthly.

Digital Pay Service 1
Pay Units: N.A.
Programming (via satellite): Cinemax (multiplexed); HBO (multiplexed); HBO HD; Showtime (multiplexed); Showtime HD; Starz (multiplexed); The Movie Channel (multiplexed).
Fee: $11.95 monthly (each).

Video-On-Demand: No

Pay-Per-View
iN DEMAND (delivered digitally), Fee: $3.75; Club Jenna (delivered digitally); Fresh (delivered digitally); Playboy TV (delivered digitally); Hot Choice (delivered digitally).

Internet Service
Operational: Yes.
Fee: $24.95 installation; $39.95 monthly.

Telephone Service
None

Miles of Plant: 18.0 (coaxial); None (fiber optic). Additional miles planned: 1.0 (coaxial).
Chief Executive Officer: Bill Haggarty. Regional Vice President: Andrew Dearth. Vice President, Marketing: Tracy Bass.
City fee: 3% of gross.
Ownership: Allegiance Communications (MSO).

LAVACA—Cox Communications. Now served by FORT SMITH, AR [AR0003]. ICA: AR0254.

LEE COUNTY (southern portion)—Alliance Communications, PO Box 960, 290 S Broadview St, Greenbrier, AR 72058-9616. Phone: 501-679-6619. Fax: 501-679-5694. Web Site: http://www.alliancecable.net. Also serves Aubrey & Rondo. ICA: AR0208.
TV Market Ranking: Outside TV Markets (Aubrey, LEE COUNTY (SOUTHERN PORTION), Rondo). Franchise award date: N.A. Franchise expiration date: N.A. Began: April 24, 1990.
Channel capacity: 65 (not 2-way capable). Channels available but not in use: 10.

Basic Service
Subscribers: 224.
Programming (received off-air): KASN (CW) Pine Bluff; KATV (ABC) Little Rock; KTHV (CBS) Little Rock; WHBQ-TV (FOX) Memphis; WKNO (PBS) Memphis; WLMT (CW) Memphis; WMC-TV (NBC) Memphis; WPTY-TV (ABC) Memphis; WREG-TV (CBS) Memphis.
Programming (via satellite): ABC Family Channel; Animal Planet; Arts & Entertainment; BET Networks; Cartoon Network; CNN; Country Music TV; C-SPAN; Discovery Channel; ESPN; ESPN 2; GSN; Headline News; HGTV; History Channel; Home Shopping Network; Lifetime; MTV; Nickelodeon; Outdoor Channel; Spike TV; Syfy; TBS Superstation; The Learning Channel; Trinity Broadcasting Network; truTV; Turner Classic Movies; Turner Network TV; TV Land; USA Network; VH1; Weather Channel; WGN America.
Fee: $33.60 monthly.

Digital Basic Service
Subscribers: 17.
Programming (via satellite): AmericanLife TV Network; BBC America; Bio; Bloomberg Television; Discovery Digital Networks; DMX Music; ESPN Classic Sports; ESPNews; Fox Movie Channel; Fox Sports World; Fuse; G4; GAS; Golf Channel; Halogen Network; History Channel International; Independent Film Channel; MTV Networks Digital Suite; National Geographic Channel; Nick Jr.; NickToons TV; Ovation; Speed Channel; Style Network; Sundance Channel; Trio; Versus; WE tv.
Fee: $42.00 monthly.

Pay Service 1
Pay Units: 24.
Programming (via satellite): HBO.

Pay Service 2
Pay Units: 25.
Programming (via satellite): Cinemax.

Digital Pay Service 1
Pay Units: 40.
Programming (via satellite): HBO (multiplexed).
Fee: $11.95 monthly.

Digital Pay Service 2
Pay Units: N.A.
Programming (via satellite): Showtime (multiplexed).
Fee: $11.95 monthly.

Digital Pay Service 3
Pay Units: 12.
Programming (via satellite): Cinemax (multiplexed).
Fee: $11.95 monthly.

Digital Pay Service 4
Pay Units: 40.
Programming (via satellite): The Movie Channel (multiplexed).
Fee: $11.95 monthly.

Digital Pay Service 5
Pay Units: 12.
Programming (via satellite): Flix.
Fee: $11.95 monthly.

Digital Pay Service 6
Pay Units: 13.
Programming (via satellite): Encore (multiplexed).
Fee: $11.95 monthly.

Digital Pay Service 7
Pay Units: 13.
Programming (via satellite): Starz (multiplexed).
Fee: $11.95 monthly.

Video-On-Demand: No

Pay-Per-View
iN DEMAND (delivered digitally); Hot Choice (delivered digitally); Playboy TV (delivered digitally); Fresh (delivered digitally); Shorteez (delivered digitally).

Internet Service
Operational: No.

Telephone Service
None

Miles of Plant: 30.0 (coaxial); None (fiber optic). Homes passed: 740. Total homes in franchised area: 740.
Vice President: Arl Cope. Operations Manager: Jeff Browers. Programming & Marketing Manager: James Fuller.
Ownership: Buford Media Group LLC (MSO).

LEOLA—Formerly served by Cebridge Connections. No longer in operation. ICA: AR0184.

LESLIE—Ritter Communications, 646 Longview, Jonesboro, AR 72401. Phones: 888-336-4466; 870-336-3434. Web Site: http://www.getritter.info. ICA: AR0170.
TV Market Ranking: Outside TV Markets (LESLIE). Franchise award date: N.A. Franchise expiration date: N.A. Began: July 1, 1983.
Channel capacity: 60 (operating 2-way). Channels available but not in use: None.

Basic Service
Subscribers: 49.
Programming (received off-air): KARK-TV (NBC) Little Rock; KATV (ABC) Little Rock; KEMV (PBS) Mountain View; KLRT-TV (FOX) Little Rock; KOLR (CBS) Springfield; KTHV (CBS) Little Rock.
Programming (via satellite): Home Shopping Network; National Geographic Channel; Trinity Broadcasting Network; Weather Channel.
Fee: $39.95 installation; $17.95 monthly.

Expanded Basic Service 1
Subscribers: N.A.
Programming (via satellite): ABC Family Channel; Animal Planet; Cartoon Network; CNN; Discovery Channel; Disney Channel; ESPN; ESPN 2; Great American Country; Headline News; HGTV; Lifetime; Nickelodeon; Outdoor Channel; Spike TV; TBS Superstation; The Learning Channel; Turner Classic Movies; Turner Network TV; USA Network.
Fee: $16.00 monthly.

Pay Service 1
Pay Units: 6.
Programming (via satellite): HBO.
Fee: $11.95 monthly.

Pay Service 2
Pay Units: 5.
Programming (via satellite): Showtime.
Fee: $11.95 monthly.

Video-On-Demand: No

Internet Service
Operational: No.

Telephone Service
None

Miles of Plant: 5.0 (coaxial); None (fiber optic). Homes passed: 258.
President: Bob Mouser. Marketing Director: Jane Marie Woodruff. Headend Manager: Joe Sain.
Ownership: Ritter Communications (MSO).

LEWISVILLE—Rapid Cable, 515 E Longview Dr, Arp, TX 75750. Phone: 903-859-6492. Fax: 903-859-3708. Also serves Buckner & Stamps. ICA: AR0285.
TV Market Ranking: 58 (Buckner, LEWISVILLE, Stamps). Franchise award date: N.A. Franchise expiration date: N.A. Began: N.A.
Channel capacity: 54 (not 2-way capable). Channels available but not in use: N.A.

Basic Service
Subscribers: 496.
Programming (received off-air): KATV (ABC) Little Rock; KETG (PBS) Arkadelphia; KMSS-TV (FOX) Shreveport; KSHV-TV (MNT) Shreveport; KSLA (CBS) Shreveport; KTAL-TV (NBC) Texarkana; KTBS-TV (ABC) Shreveport; KTSS-LP Hope.
Programming (via satellite): Home Shopping Network; National Geographic Channel; Trinity Broadcasting Network.
Fee: $54.95 installation; $20.95 monthly.

Expanded Basic Service 1
Subscribers: N.A.
Programming (via satellite): ABC Family Channel; AMC; Animal Planet; Arts & Entertainment; BET Networks; Cartoon Network; CNBC; CNN; Comcast Sports Net Southwest; C-SPAN; Discovery Channel; Disney Channel; E! Entertainment Television; ESPN; ESPN 2; Food Network; Fox News Channel; FX; Great American Country; Headline News; HGTV; Lifetime; MTV; Nickelodeon; Outdoor Channel; Spike TV; TBS Superstation; Turner Classic Movies;

Turner Network TV; USA Network; VH1; Weather Channel.
Fee: $23.10 monthly.

Digital Basic Service
Subscribers: N.A.
Programming (via satellite): AmericanLife TV Network; BBC America; Bio; Bloomberg Television; Discovery Health Channel; Discovery Kids Channel; Discovery Military Channel; Discovery Planet Green; DMX Music; ESPN 2; ESPN Classic Sports; ESPNews; Fox College Sports Atlantic; Fox College Sports Central; Fox College Sports Pacific; Fox Soccer; Fuse; G4; Golf Channel; GSN; Halogen Network; HGTV; History Channel; History Channel International; ID Investigation Discovery; Lifetime Movie Network; Outdoor Channel; Ovation; Science Channel; ShopNBC; Sleuth; Speed Channel; Style Network; Syfy; Trinity Broadcasting Network; Turner Classic Movies; Versus; WE tv.

Pay Service 1
Pay Units: 98.
Programming (via satellite): HBO.
Fee: $12.95 monthly.

Pay Service 2
Pay Units: 32.
Programming (via satellite): The Movie Channel.
Fee: $12.95 monthly.

Pay Service 3
Pay Units: 167.
Programming (via satellite): Showtime.
Fee: $12.95 monthly.

Pay Service 4
Pay Units: N.A.
Programming (via satellite): Flix.
Fee: $1.95 monthly.

Digital Pay Service 1
Pay Units: N.A.
Programming (via satellite): Cinemax (multiplexed); Encore (multiplexed); Flix; HBO (multiplexed); Showtime (multiplexed); Starz (multiplexed); The Movie Channel (multiplexed).

Video-On-Demand: No

Pay-Per-View
iN DEMAND (delivered digitally); Playboy TV (delivered digitally); Club Jenna (delivered digitally).

Internet Service
Operational: No.

Telephone Service
None

Miles of Plant: 56.0 (coaxial); None (fiber optic). Homes passed: 1,983.
Regional Manager: Mike Taylor. Chief Technician: Larry Stafford.
Ownership: Rapid Communications LLC (MSO).

LITTLE ROCK—Comcast Cable, 1020 W 4th St, Little Rock, AR 72201-2010. Phone: 501-376-5700. Fax: 501-375-1042. Web Site: http://www.comcast.com. Also serves Bryant, Cammack Village, Jacksonville, North Little Rock, Pulaski County (portions) & Sherwood. ICA: AR0001.
TV Market Ranking: 50 (Bryant, Cammack Village, Jacksonville, LITTLE ROCK, North Little Rock, Pulaski County (portions), Sherwood). Franchise award date: February 1, 1980. Franchise expiration date: N.A. Began: August 19, 1980.
Channel capacity: N.A. Channels available but not in use: N.A.

Basic Service
Subscribers: 85,000.
Programming (received off-air): KARK-TV (NBC) Little Rock; KASN (CW) Pine Bluff; KATV (ABC) Little Rock; KETS (PBS) Little Rock; KKAP (ETV) Little Rock; KLRT-TV (FOX) Little Rock; KTHV (CBS) Little Rock; KVTN-DT (IND) Pine Bluff; 10 FMs.
Programming (via satellite): ABC Family Channel; AMC; Animal Planet; Arts & Entertainment; BET Networks; Black Family Channel; Bravo; Cartoon Network; CNBC; CNN; Comcast Sports Net Southwest; Comcast/Charter Sports Southeast (CSS); Comedy Central; Country Music TV; C-SPAN; C-SPAN 2; Discovery Channel; Discovery Health Channel; E! Entertainment Television; ESPN; ESPN 2; ESPN Classic Sports; Eternal Word TV Network; Food Network; Fox News Channel; FX; Golf Channel; Great American Country; GSN; Hallmark Channel; Headline News; HGTV; History Channel; Home Shopping Network; INSP; ION Television; Lifetime; MSNBC; MTV; Nickelodeon; Outdoor Channel; QVC; Speed Channel; Spike TV; Syfy; TBS Superstation; The Learning Channel; truTV; Turner Classic Movies; Turner Network TV; TV Guide Network; TV Land; Univision; USA Network; Versus; VH1; Weather Channel; WGN America.
Current originations: Leased Access; Religious Access; Government Access; Educational Access; Public Access.
Fee: $19.95 installation; $9.50 monthly.

Digital Basic Service
Subscribers: N.A.
Programming (via satellite): BBC America; Cooking Channel; C-SPAN 3; Discovery Digital Networks; Do-It-Yourself; ESPNews; Music Choice; National Geographic Channel; SoapNet; Weatherscan.
Fee: $16.90 monthly.

Pay Service 1
Pay Units: 33,067.
Programming (via satellite): HBO (multiplexed).
Fee: $25.00 installation; $13.75 monthly.

Digital Pay Service 1
Pay Units: N.A.
Programming (via satellite): Cinemax (multiplexed); Encore; HBO (multiplexed); Showtime; The Movie Channel (multiplexed).
Fee: $13.10 monthly (each).

Video-On-Demand: Yes

Pay-Per-View
iN DEMAND (delivered digitally); ShopNBC (delivered digitally).

Internet Service
Operational: Yes. Began: January 18, 2001.
Broadband Service: Comcast High Speed Internet.
Fee: $42.95 monthly; $7.00 modem lease; $199.00 modem purchase.

Telephone Service
Digital: Operational

Miles of Plant: 1,609.0 (coaxial); None (fiber optic). Homes passed: 135,123. Total homes in franchised area: 136,758.
General Manager: Gary Massaglia. Chief Technician: Jim Davies. Marketing Director: Phyllis Elliott. Customer Service Manager: Barbara Pierce.
Ownership: Comcast Cable Communications Inc. (MSO).

LITTLE ROCK—Formerly served by Charter Communications. No longer in operation. ICA: AR0296.

LOCKESBURG—Formerly served by Lockesburg Cablevision. No longer in operation. ICA: AR0122.

LOCUST BAYOU—Rapid Cable, 515 E Longview Dr, Arp, TX 75750. Phone: 903-859-6492. Fax: 903-859-3708. ICA: AR0257.
TV Market Ranking: 99 (LOCUST BAYOU). Franchise award date: N.A. Franchise expiration date: N.A. Began: August 1, 1990.
Channel capacity: 36 (not 2-way capable). Channels available but not in use: N.A.

Basic Service
Subscribers: N.A.
Programming (received off-air): KARK-TV (NBC) Little Rock; KATV (ABC) Little Rock; KETG (PBS) Arkadelphia; KTHV (CBS) Little Rock; KTVE (NBC) El Dorado.
Programming (via satellite): TBS Superstation.
Fee: $54.95 installation; $44.05 monthly.

Pay Service 1
Pay Units: 17.
Programming (via satellite): The Movie Channel.
Fee: $12.95 monthly.

Pay Service 2
Pay Units: 31.
Programming (via satellite): Showtime.
Fee: $12.95 monthly.

Video-On-Demand: No

Internet Service
Operational: No.

Telephone Service
None

Miles of Plant: 11.0 (coaxial); None (fiber optic). Homes passed: 238.
Regional Manager: Mike Taylor. Chief Technician: Larry Stafford.
Ownership: Rapid Communications LLC (MSO).

LONDON—Suddenlink Communications, 12444 Powerscourt Dr, Saint Louis, MO 63131-3660. Phones: 314-965-2020; 800-999-6845 (Customer service). Fax: 903-561-5485. Web Site: http://www.suddenlink.com. ICA: AR0258.
TV Market Ranking: Outside TV Markets (LONDON). Franchise award date: N.A. Franchise expiration date: N.A. Began: January 1, 1980.
Channel capacity: 36 (not 2-way capable). Channels available but not in use: N.A.

Basic Service
Subscribers: 190.
Programming (received off-air): KAFT (PBS) Fayetteville; KARK-TV (NBC) Little Rock; KATV (ABC) Little Rock; KHBS (ABC) Fort Smith; KLRT-TV (FOX) Little Rock; KTHV (CBS) Little Rock.
Programming (via satellite): Home Shopping Network; National Geographic Channel; Trinity Broadcasting Network.
Fee: $17.95 installation; $17.95 monthly.

Expanded Basic Service 1
Subscribers: N.A.
Programming (via satellite): ABC Family Channel; Arts & Entertainment; Cartoon Network; CNN; Discovery Channel; Disney Channel; ESPN; Great American Country; Headline News; HGTV; History Channel; Lifetime; Nickelodeon; Spike TV; TBS Superstation; The Learning Channel; Turner Classic Movies; Turner Network TV; USA Network; Weather Channel.
Fee: $20.74 monthly.

Pay Service 1
Pay Units: 3.
Programming (via satellite): HBO.
Fee: $13.00 monthly.

Pay Service 2
Pay Units: 11.
Programming (via satellite): The Movie Channel.
Fee: $10.95 monthly.

Pay Service 3
Pay Units: 31.
Programming (via satellite): Showtime.
Fee: $10.95 monthly.

Video-On-Demand: No

Pay-Per-View
iN DEMAND (delivered digitally); Playboy TV (delivered digitally); Fresh (delivered digitally); Shorteez (delivered digitally); Urban American Television Network (delivered digitally).

Internet Service
Operational: No.

Telephone Service
None

Miles of Plant: 18.0 (coaxial); None (fiber optic). Homes passed: 502.
Regional Manager: Todd Cruthird. Area Manager: Carl Miller. Plant Manager: Danny Keith. Marketing Director: Beverly Gambell.
Ownership: Cequel Communications LLC (MSO).

LONOKE—Rapid Cable, 515 E Longview Dr, Arp, TX 75750. Phone: 903-895-6492. Fax: 903-859-3708. ICA: AR0066.
TV Market Ranking: 50 (LONOKE). Franchise award date: August 10, 1981. Franchise expiration date: N.A. Began: July 1, 1981.
Channel capacity: 36 (2-way capable). Channels available but not in use: 3.

Basic Service
Subscribers: 334.
Programming (received off-air): KARK-TV (NBC) Little Rock; KARZ-TV (MNT) Little Rock; KASN (CW) Pine Bluff; KATV (ABC) Little Rock; KETS (PBS) Little Rock; KKYK-DT (IND) Camden; KLRT-TV (FOX) Little Rock; KTHV (CBS) Little Rock; KVTN-DT (IND) Pine Bluff; allband FM.
Programming (via satellite): National Geographic Channel; Spike TV; Turner Network TV.
Current originations: Public Access.
Fee: $54.95 installation; $20.95 monthly.

Expanded Basic Service 1
Subscribers: N.A.
Programming (via satellite): ABC Family Channel; BET Networks; Cartoon Network; CNN; C-SPAN; Discovery Channel; Disney Channel; ESPN; ESPN 2; Fox News Channel; FX; Great American Country; Headline News; HGTV; History Channel; Lifetime; Nickelodeon; QVC; TBS Superstation; The Learning Channel; Travel Channel; Turner Classic Movies; TV Land; USA Network; VH1; Weather Channel.
Fee: $23.10 monthly.

Pay Service 1
Pay Units: 162.
Programming (via satellite): HBO.
Fee: $12.95 monthly.

Pay Service 2
Pay Units: 96.
Programming (via satellite): Showtime.
Fee: $12.95 monthly.

Video-On-Demand: No

Internet Service
Operational: No.

Telephone Service
None

Miles of Plant: 32.0 (coaxial); None (fiber optic). Additional miles planned: 1.0 (coaxial). Homes passed: 964.
Regional Manager: Mike Taylor. Chief Technician: Larry Stafford.
City fee: 3% of gross.
Ownership: Rapid Communications LLC (MSO).

LYNN—Formerly served by Ritter Communications. No longer in operation. ICA: AR0188.

MAGAZINE—Formerly served by Almega Cable. No longer in operation. ICA: AR0134.

MAGIC SPRINGS—Community Communications Co., 1920 Hwy 425 N, Monticello, AR 71655-4463. Phones: 800-272-2191; 870-367-7300. Fax: 870-367-9770. E-mail: generalmanager@ccc-cable.net. Web Site: http://www.ccc-cable.net. ICA: AR0137.

TV Market Ranking: Below 100 (MAGIC SPRINGS). Franchise award date: N.A. Franchise expiration date: N.A. Began: October 1, 1989.

Channel capacity: 48 (not 2-way capable). Channels available but not in use: 1.

Basic Service

Subscribers: 214.

Programming (received off-air): KARK-TV (NBC) Little Rock; KASN (CW) Pine Bluff; KATV (ABC) Little Rock; KETS (PBS) Little Rock; KLRT-TV (FOX) Little Rock; KTHV (CBS) Little Rock.

Programming (via satellite): ABC Family Channel; AMC; Arts & Entertainment; CNN; Comcast Sports Net Southwest; Country Music TV; Discovery Channel; Disney Channel; E! Entertainment Television; ESPN; ESPN 2; FX; Headline News; Lifetime; MTV; Nickelodeon; Outdoor Channel; QVC; Spike TV; Syfy; TBS Superstation; Trinity Broadcasting Network; Turner Network TV; TV Land; USA Network; VH1; Weather Channel; WGN America.

Fee: $16.95 monthly.

Pay Service 1

Pay Units: N.A.

Programming (via satellite): HBO; Showtime; The Movie Channel.

Fee: $25.00 installation; $10.00 monthly (HBO).

Video-On-Demand: No

Internet Service

Operational: No.

Telephone Service

None

Miles of Plant: 22.0 (coaxial); None (fiber optic). Homes passed: 400.

Ownership: Community Communications Co. (MSO).

MAGNOLIA—Suddenlink Communications, 1911 N Jackson St, Magnolia, AR 71753-2053. Phone: 870-234-3112. Fax: 870-234-3959. Web Site: http://www.suddenlink.com. Also serves Columbia County & Waldo. ICA: AR0024.

TV Market Ranking: 99 (Columbia County (portions), MAGNOLIA); Below 100 (Waldo, Columbia County (portions)); Outside TV Markets (Columbia County (portions)). Franchise award date: N.A. Franchise expiration date: N.A. Began: June 1, 1964.

Channel capacity: 60 (not 2-way capable). Channels available but not in use: N.A.

Basic Service

Subscribers: 4,946.

Programming (received off-air): KARK-TV (NBC) Little Rock; KATV (ABC) Little Rock; KETG (PBS) Arkadelphia; KMSS-TV (FOX) Shreveport; KPXJ (CW) Minden; KSLA (CBS) Shreveport; KTAL-TV (NBC) Texarkana; KTBS-TV (ABC) Shreveport; 5 FMs.

Programming (via satellite): C-SPAN; C-SPAN 2; DMX Music; Home Shopping Network; INSP; Jewelry Television; Local Cable Weather; QVC; TBS Superstation; Trinity Broadcasting Network; Weather Channel; WGN America.

Fee: $30.00 installation; $14.64 monthly.

Expanded Basic Service 1

Subscribers: 4,056.

Programming (via satellite): ABC Family Channel; AMC; Animal Planet; Arts & Entertainment; BET Networks; Bravo; Cartoon Network; CNBC; CNN; Comcast Sports Net Southwest; Comedy Central; Country Music TV; Discovery Channel; Disney Channel; E! Entertainment Television; ESPN; ESPN 2; Food Network; Fox News Channel; FX; Great American Country; Headline News; HGTV; History Channel; Lifetime; Lifetime Movie Network; MSNBC; MTV; Nickelodeon; Speed Channel; Spike TV; Syfy; The Learning Channel; Travel Channel; truTV; Turner Network TV; TV Land; USA Network; Versus; VH1.

Fee: $15.60 monthly.

Digital Basic Service

Subscribers: 1,277.

Programming (received off-air): KMSS-TV (FOX) Shreveport; KSLA (CBS) Shreveport; KTBS-TV (ABC) Shreveport.

Programming (via satellite): Arts & Entertainment HD; BBC America; Bio; Bloomberg Television; CBS College Sports Network; CMT Pure Country; Cooking Channel; Discovery en Espanol; Discovery HD Theater; Discovery Health Channel; Discovery Home Channel; Discovery Kids Channel; Discovery Military Channel; Discovery Times Channel; Do-It-Yourself; Encore (multiplexed); ESPN Classic Sports; ESPN HD; ESPNews; Food Network HD; Fox Reality Channel; Fox Soccer; Fuel TV; Fuse; G4; Golf Channel; GSN; Hallmark Channel; Halogen Network; HDNet; HDNet Movies; HGTV HD; History Channel International; Independent Film Channel; MTV Hits; MTV Jams; MTV2; Music Choice; National Geographic Channel; National Geographic Channel HD Network; Nick Jr.; NickToons TV; Outdoor Channel; Science Channel; SoapNet; Style Network; Sundance Channel; TeenNick; Toon Disney; Turner Classic Movies; Turner Network TV HD; Universal HD; VH1 Classic; VH1 Soul.

Fee: $49.95 monthly.

Digital Pay Service 1

Pay Units: 2,527.

Programming (via satellite): Cinemax (multiplexed); HBO (multiplexed); HBO HD; Showtime (multiplexed); Showtime HD; Starz (multiplexed); The Movie Channel (multiplexed).

Fee: $27.95 monthly.

Video-On-Demand: No

Pay-Per-View

iN DEMAND (delivered digitally), Fee: $3.99; Playboy TV (delivered digitally); Fresh (delivered digitally).

Internet Service

Operational: Yes.

Fee: $29.95 monthly.

Telephone Service

None

Miles of Plant: 50.0 (coaxial); None (fiber optic). Homes passed: 5,700. Total homes in franchised area: 5,800.

Manager: Robert Banks. Marketing Director: Kathy Wyrick. Chief Technician: James Crisp. Customer Service Manager: Jennifer England.

Ownership: Cequel Communications LLC (MSO).

MALVERN—Suddenlink Communications, 528 Oakland Ave, Helena, AR 72342-1617. Phones: 888-822-5151; 501-332-6254. Fax: 501-337-7338. Web Site: http://www.suddenlink.com. Also serves Perla & Rockport. ICA: AR0259.

TV Market Ranking: 50 (Perla, Rockport); Below 100 (MALVERN). Franchise award date: N.A. Franchise expiration date: N.A. Began: January 1, 1980.

Channel capacity: N.A. Channels available but not in use: N.A.

Basic Service

Subscribers: 4,066.

Programming (received off-air): KAIT (ABC) Jonesboro; KARK-TV (NBC) Little Rock; KARZ-TV (MNT) Little Rock; KASN (CW) Pine Bluff; KATV (ABC) Little Rock; KKAP (ETV) Little Rock; KKYK-DT (IND) Camden; KLRT-TV (FOX) Little Rock; KTEJ (PBS) Jonesboro; KTHV (CBS) Little Rock; KVTJ-DT (IND) Jonesboro; WMC-TV (NBC) Memphis.

Programming (via satellite): C-SPAN 2; Headline News; Home Shopping Network; Jewelry Television; QVC; TBS Superstation; Weather Channel; WGN America.

Fee: $38.00 installation; $12.47 monthly.

Expanded Basic Service 1

Subscribers: N.A.

Programming (via satellite): ABC Family Channel; AMC; Animal Planet; Arts & Entertainment; BET Networks; Bravo; Cartoon Network; CNBC; CNN; Comcast Sports Net Southwest; Comedy Central; Country Music TV; C-SPAN; Discovery Channel; Disney Channel; E! Entertainment Television; ESPN; ESPN 2; Food Network; Fox News Channel; FX; Great American Country; HGTV; History Channel; Lifetime; Lifetime Movie Network; MSNBC; MTV; Nickelodeon; Oxygen; Speed Channel; Spike TV; Syfy; The Learning Channel; Travel Channel; truTV; Turner Classic Movies; Turner Network TV; TV Land; USA Network; Versus; VH1.

Fee: $16.13 monthly.

Digital Basic Service

Subscribers: N.A.

Programming (via satellite): BBC America; Bio; Bloomberg Television; CBS College Sports Network; CMT Pure Country; Cooking Channel; Discovery en Espanol; Discovery Health Channel; Discovery Home Channel; Discovery Kids Channel; Discovery Military Channel; Discovery Times Channel; Do-It-Yourself; Encore (multiplexed); ESPN Classic Sports; ESPNews; Fox Reality Channel; Fox Soccer; Fuel TV; Fuse; G4; Golf Channel; GSN; Hallmark Channel; History Channel International; Independent Film Channel; MTV Hits; MTV Jams; MTV2; Music Choice; National Geographic Channel; Nick Jr.; NickToons TV; Outdoor Channel; Science Channel; SoapNet; Style Network; Sundance Channel; TeenNick; Toon Disney; Trinity Broadcasting Network; VH1 Classic; VH1 Soul.

Digital Pay Service 1

Pay Units: N.A.

Programming (via satellite): Cinemax (multiplexed); HBO (multiplexed); Showtime (multiplexed); Starz (multiplexed); The Movie Channel (multiplexed).

Pay-Per-View

iN DEMAND (delivered digitally); Fresh (delivered digitally); Spice: Xcess (delivered digitally).

Internet Service

Operational: No.

Telephone Service

None

Miles of Plant: 97.0 (coaxial); None (fiber optic).

Manager: Robbie Lee. Chief Technician: Chuck Davis.

Ownership: Cequel Communications LLC (MSO).

MANILA—Ritter Communications. Now served by MARKED TREE, AR [AR0072]. ICA: AR0076.

MARKED TREE—Ritter Communications, 2815 Longview, Jonesboro, AR 72401. Phones: 888-336-4466 (Customer service); 870-336-3434 (Administrative office). Fax: 870-358-4170. Web Site: http://www.getritter.info. Also serves Bassett, Black Oak, Blytheville, Bono, Brookland, Caraway, Cash, Cherry Valley, Craighead County (northwestern portion), Dell, Dyess, Fisher, Gilmore, Gosnell, Grubbs, Harrisburg, Hickory Ridge, Joiner, Keiser, Lake City, Lake Poinsett, Leachville, Lepanto, Luxora, Manila, Mississippi County (portions), Monette, Osceola, Swifton, Trumann, Turrell, Tyronza, Weiner & Wilson, AR; Arbyrd & Cardwell, MO. ICA: AR0072.

TV Market Ranking: 26 (Bassett, Gilmore, Joiner, Turrell, Tyronza, Wilson); Below 100 (Arbyrd, Black Oak, Bono, Brookland, Caraway, Cardwell, Cash, Cherry Valley, Craighead County (northwestern portion), Dyess, Fisher, Grubbs, Harrisburg, Hickory Ridge, Keiser, Lake City, Lake Poinsett, Leachville, Lepanto, Manila, MARKED TREE, Mississippi County (portions) (portions), Monette, Swifton, Trumann, Weiner); Outside TV Markets (Blytheville, Dell, Gosnell, Luxora, Mississippi County (portions) (portions), Osceola). Franchise award date: January 1, 1981. Franchise expiration date: N.A. Began: June 28, 1982.

Channel capacity: 78 (operating 2-way). Channels available but not in use: N.A.

Basic Service

Subscribers: 16,722.

Programming (received off-air): KAIT (ABC) Jonesboro; KTEJ (PBS) Jonesboro; KVTJ-DT (IND) Jonesboro; WHBQ-TV (FOX) Memphis; WKNO (PBS) Memphis; WLMT (CW) Memphis; WMC-TV (NBC) Memphis; WPTY-TV (ABC) Memphis; WPXX-TV (ION, MNT) Memphis; WREG-TV (CBS) Memphis; 1 FM.

Programming (via microwave): KARK-TV (NBC) Little Rock; KATV (ABC) Little Rock.

Programming (via satellite): C-SPAN; C-SPAN 2; Home Shopping Network; National Geographic Channel; QVC; Travel Channel; Trinity Broadcasting Network; TV Guide Network.

Fee: $39.95 installation.

Expanded Basic Service 1

Subscribers: N.A.

Programming (via satellite): ABC Family Channel; AMC; Animal Planet; Arts & Entertainment; BET Networks; Bravo;

Cartoon Network; CNBC; CNN; Comedy Central; Country Music TV; Discovery Channel; Disney Channel; E! Entertainment Television; ESPN; ESPN 2; Food Network; Fox News Channel; FX; Great American Country; Hallmark Channel; Headline News; HGTV; Lifetime; Lifetime Movie Network; MSNBC; MTV; Nickelodeon; Outdoor Channel; Spike TV; Syfy; TBS Superstation; The Learning Channel; Turner Classic Movies; Turner Network TV; TV Land; USA Network; VH1; Weather Channel.
Fee: $45.95 monthly.

Digital Basic Service
Subscribers: 1,978.
Programming (received off-air): KAIT (ABC) Jonesboro; WHBQ-TV (FOX) Memphis; WMC-TV (NBC) Memphis; WREG-TV (CBS) Memphis.
Programming (via satellite): BBC America; CMT Pure Country; Discovery HD Theater; Discovery Health Channel; Discovery Kids Channel; Discovery Military Channel; Discovery Planet Green; DMX Music; ESPN Classic Sports; ESPN HD; ESPNews; FitTV; Fox College Sports Atlantic; Fox College Sports Central; Fox College Sports Pacific; Fox Movie Channel; Fox Soccer; Golf Channel; Gospel Music Channel; GSN; HDNet; HDNet Movies; History Channel; ID Investigation Discovery; Independent Film Channel; Lifetime Real Women; MTV Hits; MTV2; Nick Jr.; NickToons TV; PBS Kids Sprout; Science Channel; SoapNet; Speed Channel; TeenNick; Toon Disney; Universal HD; Versus; VH1 Classic; VH1 Soul; WE tv.
Fee: $15.00 monthly.

Digital Pay Service 1
Pay Units: N.A.
Programming (via satellite): Cinemax (multiplexed); Encore (multiplexed); Flix; HBO (multiplexed); HBO HD; Showtime (multiplexed); Starz (multiplexed); Starz HDTV; The Movie Channel (multiplexed).
Fee: $12.95 monthly (HBO, Cinemax, Starz/Encore or Showtime/TMC/Flix).

Video-On-Demand: No

Pay-Per-View
Playboy TV (delivered digitally); iN DEMAND (delivered digitally).

Internet Service
Operational: Yes.
Subscribers: 4,330.
Broadband Service: Cebridge High Speed Cable Internet.
Fee: $39.95 monthly.

Telephone Service
None

Miles of Plant: 648.0 (coaxial); None (fiber optic). Homes passed: 31,271.

Vice President, Operations: David Adams. General Manager: Harold Kinnell. Marketing Director: Jane Marie Woodruff. Product Development Representative: Kimberly McFarland.

City fee: 4% of basic & expanded basic; 2% of pay.

Ownership: Ritter Communications (MSO).

MARSHALL—Alliance Communications, PO Box 960, 290 S Broadview St, Greenbrier, AR 72058-9616. Phones: 501-679-6619; 903-561-4411; 800-842-8160. Fax: 501-679-5694. Web Site: http://www.alliancecable.net. ICA: AR0098.

TV Market Ranking: Outside TV Markets (MARSHALL COUNTY (PORTIONS)). Franchise award date: May 20, 1997. Franchise expiration date: N.A. Began: January 1, 1952.

Channel capacity: 65 (not 2-way capable). Channels available but not in use: 24.

Basic Service
Subscribers: 366.
Programming (received off-air): KARK-TV (NBC) Little Rock; KASN (CW) Pine Bluff; KATV (ABC) Little Rock; KETS (PBS) Little Rock; KLRT-TV (FOX) Little Rock; KTHV (CBS) Little Rock; KYTV (CW, NBC) Springfield.
Programming (via satellite): Turner Classic Movies.
Fee: $25.00 installation; $32.00 monthly.

Pay Service 1
Pay Units: 16.
Programming (via satellite): HBO.
Fee: $11.95 monthly.

Pay Service 2
Pay Units: 17.
Programming (via satellite): Showtime.
Fee: $11.95 monthly.

Pay Service 3
Pay Units: 5.
Programming (via satellite): Cinemax.
Fee: $11.95 monthly.

Pay Service 4
Pay Units: 12.
Programming (via satellite): The Movie Channel.
Fee: $11.95 monthly.

Pay Service 5
Pay Units: 5.
Programming (via satellite): Flix.
Fee: $11.95 monthly.

Pay Service 6
Pay Units: 5.
Programming (via satellite): Sundance Channel.
Fee: $11.95 monthly.

Pay Service 7
Pay Units: 9.
Programming (via satellite): Starz.
Fee: $11.95 monthly.

Pay Service 8
Pay Units: 9.
Programming (via satellite): Encore.
Fee: $11.95 monthly.

Video-On-Demand: No

Internet Service
Operational: No.

Telephone Service
None

Miles of Plant: 25.0 (coaxial); None (fiber optic). Homes passed: 936.

Vice President: Arl Cope. Operations Manager: Jeff Browers. Programming & Marketing Manager: James Fuller.

Ownership: Buford Media Group LLC (MSO).

MARVELL—Suddenlink Communications, 528 Oakland Ave, Helena, AR 72342-1617. Phone: 870-338-3451. Fax: 870-338-7642. Web Site: http://www.suddenlink.com. ICA: AR0260.

TV Market Ranking: Outside TV Markets (MARVELL). Franchise award date: N.A. Franchise expiration date: N.A. Began: N.A.

Channel capacity: 78 (operating 2-way). Channels available but not in use: N.A.

Basic Service
Subscribers: 7,020.
Programming (received off-air): KATV (ABC) Little Rock; KETS (PBS) Little Rock; KTHV (CBS) Little Rock; WHBQ-TV (FOX) Memphis; WKNO (PBS) Memphis; WLMT (CW) Memphis; WMC-TV (NBC) Memphis; WPTY-TV (ABC) Memphis; WREG-TV (CBS) Memphis.
Programming (via satellite): ABC Family Channel; AMC; Animal Planet; Arts & Entertainment; BET Networks; Bravo; Cartoon Network; CNBC; CNN; Comcast Sports Net Southwest; Comedy Central; Country Music TV; C-SPAN; Discovery Channel; Disney Channel; E! Entertainment Television; ESPN; ESPN 2; Food Network; Fox News Channel; FX; Great American Country; Headline News; HGTV; History Channel; Home Shopping Network; ION Television; Lifetime; MSNBC; MTV; Nickelodeon; Outdoor Channel; Oxygen; Speed Channel; Spike TV; Syfy; TBS Superstation; The Learning Channel; Travel Channel; Trinity Broadcasting Network; Turner Network TV; TV Land; USA Network; Versus; VH1; Weather Channel; WGN America.
Fee: $30.00 installation; $15.29 monthly.

Digital Basic Service
Subscribers: N.A.
Programming (via satellite): BBC America; Bio; Bloomberg Television; Discovery Digital Networks; Encore Action; ESPN Classic Sports; ESPNews; Fox Sports World; G4; Golf Channel; GSN; Hallmark Channel; History Channel International; Independent Film Channel; Lifetime Movie Network; MuchMusic Network; Music Choice; SoapNet; Sundance Channel; Toon Disney; truTV.

Pay Service 1
Pay Units: 6,450.
Programming (via satellite): Showtime; The Movie Channel.
Fee: $35.00 installation; $10.00 monthly (each).

Digital Pay Service 1
Pay Units: N.A.
Programming (via satellite): Cinemax (multiplexed); HBO (multiplexed); Showtime; Starz (multiplexed); The Movie Channel (multiplexed).

Video-On-Demand: No

Pay-Per-View
NBA TV (delivered digitally); ESPN Gameplan (delivered digitally); ESPN Now (delivered digitally); Fresh (delivered digitally); Hot Choice (delivered digitally); iN DEMAND (delivered digitally).

Internet Service
Operational: Yes.
Broadband Service: Cebridge High Speed Cable Internet.
Fee: $49.95 installation; $26.95 monthly.

Telephone Service
None

Miles of Plant: 210.0 (coaxial); None (fiber optic). Homes passed: 9,200.

Ownership: Cequel Communications LLC (MSO).

MAUMELLE—Charter Communications, 19863 Interstate 30, Ste 3, Benton, AR 72015-6966. Phones: 636-207-7044 (St Louis office); 501-315-4405. Fax: 501-315-4406. Web Site: http://www.charter.com. Also serves Morgan, North Little Rock & Oak Grove. ICA: AR0020.

TV Market Ranking: 50 (MAUMELLE, Morgan, North Little Rock, Oak Grove). Franchise award date: N.A. Franchise expiration date: N.A. Began: August 1, 1983.

Channel capacity: N.A. Channels available but not in use: N.A.

Basic Service
Subscribers: 3,414.
Programming (received off-air): KARK-TV (NBC) Little Rock; KARZ-TV (MNT) Little Rock; KASN (CW) Pine Bluff; KATV (ABC) Little Rock; KETS (PBS) Little Rock; KLRT-TV (FOX) Little Rock; KTHV (CBS) Little Rock; KVTN-DT (IND) Pine Bluff.
Programming (via satellite): ABC Family Channel; Arts & Entertainment; CNN; Comcast Sports Net Southwest; Comedy Central; Country Music TV; C-SPAN; E! Entertainment Television; ESPN; Headline News; Home Shopping Network; Lifetime; MTV; Nickelodeon; QVC; Sneak Prevue; VH1; WGN America.
Current originations: Government Access; Educational Access; Public Access.
Fee: $29.99 installation; $1.18 converter.

Expanded Basic Service 1
Subscribers: 3,001.
Programming (via satellite): AMC; Animal Planet; Bravo; Cartoon Network; CNBC; Discovery Channel; Disney Channel; ESPN 2; Food Network; Fox News Channel; FX; Golf Channel; HGTV; History Channel; MSNBC; Oxygen; Speed Channel; Spike TV; Syfy; TBS Superstation; The Learning Channel; Travel Channel; Turner Network TV; TV Guide Network; TV Land; USA Network; Weather Channel.
Fee: $49.99 monthly.

Digital Basic Service
Subscribers: N.A.
Programming (via satellite): AmericanLife TV Network; BBC America; Bio; Bloomberg Television; Bravo; Discovery Digital Networks; DMX Music; ESPN Classic Sports; ESPNews; Fox Movie Channel; G4; GAS; GSN; Halogen Network; History Channel International; Independent Film Channel; Lifetime Movie Network; MTV Networks Digital Suite; MuchMusic Network; Nick Jr.; Outdoor Channel; ShopNBC; Style Network; Toon Disney; Trinity Broadcasting Network; Turner Classic Movies; Versus; WE tv.

Digital Pay Service 1
Pay Units: N.A.
Programming (via satellite): Cinemax (multiplexed); Encore (multiplexed); Flix; HBO (multiplexed); Showtime (multiplexed); Starz (multiplexed); The Movie Channel (multiplexed).

Video-On-Demand: No

Pay-Per-View
Addressable homes: 812.
ESPN Extra (delivered digitally); ESPN Now (delivered digitally); Hot Choice (delivered digitally); iN DEMAND; iN DEMAND (delivered digitally); Playboy TV (delivered digitally); Fresh (delivered digitally); Shorteez (delivered digitally); Urban Xtra (delivered digitally).

Internet Service
Operational: Yes.
Broadband Service: Charter Pipeline.
Fee: $29.99 monthly.

Telephone Service
Digital: Operational

Miles of Plant: 111.0 (coaxial); None (fiber optic). Homes passed: 7,863. Total homes in franchised area: 10,000.

Vice President & General Manager: Steve Trippe. Operations Director: Dave Miller. Operations Manager: Dave Huntsman. Chief Technician: Jim Miller. Marketing Director: Beverly Wall. Office Manager: Missy Brown.

Ownership: Charter Communications Inc. (MSO).

MAYFLOWER—Reach Broadband, 515 E Longview Dr, Arp, TX 75750. Phones: 800-687-1258; 903-859-6492. Fax: 903-859-3708. Web Site: http://www.reachbroadband.net. Also serves Faulkner County (portions). ICA: AR0049.

TV Market Ranking: 50 (Faulkner County (portions), MAYFLOWER). Franchise award date: N.A. Franchise expiration date: N.A. Began: August 1, 1984.

Channel capacity: 44 (not 2-way capable). Channels available but not in use: N.A.

Basic Service
Subscribers: 337.
Programming (received off-air): KARK-TV (NBC) Little Rock; KARZ-TV (MNT) Little Rock; KASN (CW) Pine Bluff; KATV (ABC) Little Rock; KETS (PBS) Little Rock; KKAP (ETV) Little Rock; KKYK-DT (IND) Camden; KLRT-TV (FOX) Little Rock; KTHV (CBS) Little Rock; KVTN-DT (IND) Pine Bluff.
Fee: $54.95 installation; $20.95 monthly.
Expanded Basic Service 1
Subscribers: N.A.
Programming (via satellite): ABC Family Channel; Animal Planet; Arts & Entertainment; BET Networks; Cartoon Network; CNN; C-SPAN; Discovery Channel; Disney Channel; E! Entertainment Television; ESPN; ESPN 2; Fox News Channel; FX; Great American Country; Headline News; Home Shopping Network; Lifetime; MSNBC; MTV; National Geographic Channel; Nickelodeon; Outdoor Channel; Spike TV; TBS Superstation; Turner Classic Movies; Turner Network TV; USA Network; Weather Channel.
Fee: $23.10 monthly.
Digital Basic Service
Subscribers: N.A.
Programming (via satellite): AmericanLife TV Network; BBC America; Bio; Bloomberg Television; Discovery Health Channel; Discovery Kids Channel; Discovery Military Channel; Discovery Planet Green; DMX Music; ESPN 2; ESPN Classic Sports; ESPNews; Fox College Sports Atlantic; Fox College Sports Central; Fox College Sports Pacific; Fox Soccer; Fuse; G4; Golf Channel; GSN; Halogen Network; HGTV; History Channel; History Channel International; ID Investigation Discovery; Lifetime Movie Network; Outdoor Channel; Ovation; Science Channel; ShopNBC; Sleuth; Speed Channel; Style Network; Syfy; Trinity Broadcasting Network; Turner Classic Movies; Versus; WE tv.
Pay Service 1
Pay Units: 48.
Programming (via satellite): Cinemax.
Fee: $12.95 monthly.
Pay Service 2
Pay Units: 93.
Programming (via satellite): Showtime.
Fee: $12.95 monthly.
Pay Service 3
Pay Units: 54.
Programming (via satellite): HBO.
Fee: $12.95 monthly.
Digital Pay Service 1
Pay Units: N.A.
Programming (via satellite): Cinemax (multiplexed); Encore (multiplexed); Flix; HBO (multiplexed); Showtime (multiplexed); Starz (multiplexed); The Movie Channel (multiplexed).
Video-On-Demand: No
Pay-Per-View
iN DEMAND (delivered digitally); Playboy TV (delivered digitally); Club Jenna (delivered digitally).
Internet Service
Operational: No.
Telephone Service
None
Miles of Plant: 55.0 (coaxial); None (fiber optic). Homes passed: 1,892.
Regional Manager: Ronnie Stafford. Office Manager: Jan Gibson.
Ownership: RB3 LLC (MSO).

McALMONT—Charter Communications, 19863 Interstate 30, Ste 3, Benton, AR 72015-6966. Phones: 636-207-7044 (St Louis office); 501-315-4405. Fax: 501-315-4406. Web Site: http://www.charter.com. Also serves Pulaski County (eastern portion) & Sherwood. ICA: AR0034.
TV Market Ranking: 50 (MCALMONT, Pulaski County (eastern portion), Sherwood). Franchise award date: January 1, 1986. Franchise expiration date: N.A. Began: April 1, 1986.
Channel capacity: N.A. Channels available but not in use: N.A.
Basic Service
Subscribers: 2,387.
Programming (received off-air): KARK-TV (NBC) Little Rock; KARZ-TV (MNT) Little Rock; KASN (CW) Pine Bluff; KATV (ABC) Little Rock; KETS (PBS) Little Rock; KLRT-TV (FOX) Little Rock; KTHV (CBS) Little Rock; KVTN-DT (IND) Pine Bluff.
Programming (via satellite): ABC Family Channel; AMC; BET Networks; CNN; Comcast Sports Net Southwest; Comedy Central; Country Music TV; C-SPAN; E! Entertainment Television; ESPN; Headline News; Home Shopping Network; Lifetime; MTV; QVC; The Learning Channel; VH1; WGN America.
Current originations: Public Access.
Fee: $29.99 installation; $3.48 converter.
Expanded Basic Service 1
Subscribers: 525.
Programming (via satellite): Bravo; Discovery Channel; Disney Channel; ESPN 2; Nickelodeon; Spike TV; Syfy; TBS Superstation; Turner Network TV; USA Network; Weather Channel.
Fee: $49.99 monthly.
Digital Basic Service
Subscribers: N.A.
Programming (via satellite): AmericanLife TV Network; BBC America; Bio; Bloomberg Television; Discovery Digital Networks; DMX Music; Fox Movie Channel; G4; GAS; Golf Channel; GSN; Halogen Network; HGTV; History Channel; History Channel International; Independent Film Channel; Lifetime Movie Network; MTV Networks Digital Suite; MuchMusic Network; Nick Jr.; Outdoor Channel; ShopNBC; Speed Channel; Style Network; Toon Disney; Trinity Broadcasting Network; Turner Classic Movies; Versus; WE tv.
Pay Service 1
Pay Units: 68.
Programming (via satellite): Cinemax.
Fee: $11.95 monthly.
Pay Service 2
Pay Units: 67.
Programming (via satellite): HBO.
Fee: $11.95 monthly.
Pay Service 3
Pay Units: 72.
Programming (via satellite): Showtime.
Pay Service 4
Pay Units: 42.
Programming (via satellite): The Movie Channel.
Fee: $11.95 monthly.
Digital Pay Service 1
Pay Units: N.A.
Programming (via satellite): Cinemax (multiplexed); Encore (multiplexed); Flix; HBO (multiplexed); Showtime (multiplexed); Starz (multiplexed); The Movie Channel (multiplexed).
Video-On-Demand: No
Pay-Per-View
ESPN Extra (delivered digitally); ESPN Now (delivered digitally); Hot Choice (delivered digitally); iN DEMAND; iN DEMAND (delivered digitally); Playboy TV (delivered digitally); Fresh (delivered digitally); Shorteez (delivered digitally); Urban Xtra (delivered digitally).
Internet Service
Operational: No.
Telephone Service
None
Miles of Plant: 75.0 (coaxial); None (fiber optic). Homes passed: 2,387. Total homes in franchised area: 6,000.
Vice President & General Manager: Steve Trippe. Operations Director: Dave Miller. Operations Manager: Dave Huntsman. Chief Technician: Jim Miller. Marketing Director: Beverly Wall. Office Manager: Missy Brown.
Franchise fee: 3% of gross.
Ownership: Charter Communications Inc. (MSO).

MCCASKILL—Allegiance Communications, 707 W Saratoga St, Shawnee, OK 74804. Phones: 405-275-6923; 405-395-1131. Web Site: http://www.allegiance.tv. Also serves Blevins. ICA: AR0261.
TV Market Ranking: Outside TV Markets (Blevins, MCCASKILL). Franchise award date: N.A. Franchise expiration date: N.A. Began: February 1, 1990.
Channel capacity: 28 (not 2-way capable). Channels available but not in use: 4.
Basic Service
Subscribers: 164.
Programming (received off-air): KARK-TV (NBC) Little Rock; KATV (ABC) Little Rock; KETG (PBS) Arkadelphia; KMSS-TV (FOX) Shreveport; KSHV-TV (MNT) Shreveport; KSLA (CBS) Shreveport; KTAL-TV (NBC) Texarkana; KTBS-TV (ABC) Shreveport; KTHV (CBS) Little Rock; KTSS-LP Hope.
Programming (via satellite): ABC Family Channel; AMC; Arts & Entertainment; CMT Pure Country; CNN; Discovery Channel; Disney Channel; ESPN; Spike TV; Syfy; TBS Superstation; Trinity Broadcasting Network; Turner Network TV; USA Network; WGN America.
Fee: $35.00 installation; $21.95 monthly.
Pay Service 1
Pay Units: N.A.
Programming (via satellite): Cinemax; Showtime; The Movie Channel.
Fee: $11.90 monthly (Cinemax or Showtime).
Video-On-Demand: No
Pay-Per-View
Urban American Television Network (delivered digitally); iN DEMAND (delivered digitally); Playboy TV (delivered digitally); Fresh (delivered digitally); Shorteez (delivered digitally).
Internet Service
Operational: No.
Telephone Service
None
Chief Executive Officer: Bill Haggarty. Regional Vice President: Andrew Dearth. Vice President, Marketing: Tracy Bass.
Ownership: Allegiance Communications (MSO).

McCRORY—Allegiance Communications, 707 W Saratoga St, Shawnee, OK 74804. Phones: 405-275-6923; 405-395-1131. Web Site: http://www.allegiance.tv. Also serves Patterson. ICA: AR0073.
TV Market Ranking: Outside TV Markets (MCCRORY, Patterson). Franchise award date: N.A. Franchise expiration date: N.A. Began: April 1, 1974.
Channel capacity: N.A. Channels available but not in use: N.A.
Basic Service
Subscribers: 740.
Programming (received off-air): KAIT (ABC) Jonesboro; KARK-TV (NBC) Little Rock; KASN (CW) Pine Bluff; KATV (ABC) Little Rock; KLRT-TV (FOX) Little Rock; KTEJ (PBS) Jonesboro; KTHV (CBS) Little Rock; KVTJ-DT (IND) Jonesboro; WMC-TV (NBC) Memphis.
Programming (via satellite): ABC Family Channel; AMC; Arts & Entertainment; BET Networks; Cartoon Network; CNN; Comcast Sports Net Southwest; Comedy Central; C-SPAN; Discovery Channel; Disney Channel; ESPN; ESPN 2; ESPN Classic Sports; Food Network; FX; Great American Country; Hallmark Channel; HGTV; History Channel; Lifetime; NFL Network; Nickelodeon; Outdoor Channel; QVC; Spike TV; Syfy; TBS Superstation; The Learning Channel; Trinity Broadcasting Network; Turner Network TV; TV Land; USA Network; VH1; Weather Channel; WGN America.
Fee: $30.00 installation; $29.45 monthly.
Digital Basic Service
Subscribers: N.A.
Programming (via satellite): AmericanLife TV Network; BBC America; Bio; Bloomberg Television; Bravo; Cine Latino; Cine Mexicano; CMT Pure Country; CNN en Espanol; Current; Discovery en Espanol; Discovery Health Channel; Discovery Kids Channel; Discovery Military Channel; Discovery Planet Green; DMX Music; Encore (multiplexed); ESPN 2; ESPN Classic Sports; ESPN Deportes; ESPNews; FitTV; Flix; Fox College Sports Atlantic; Fox College Sports Central; Fox College Sports Pacific; Fox Movie Channel; Fox Soccer; Fox Sports en Espanol; Fuse; G4; Golf Channel; Gospel Music Channel; Great American Country; GSN; Halogen Network; HGTV; History Channel; History Channel en Espanol; History Channel International; ID Investigation Discovery; Independent Film Channel; Lifetime Movie Network; MTV Hits; MTV Tres; MTV2; mun2 television; National Geographic Channel; Nick Jr.; NickToons TV; Outdoor Channel; Science Channel; ShopNBC; Sleuth; Speed Channel; Style Network; Sundance Channel; Syfy; TeenNick; The Word Network; Toon Disney; Trinity Broadcasting Network; Turner Classic Movies; VeneMovies; Versus; VH1 Classic; VH1 Soul; WE tv.
Pay Service 1
Pay Units: N.A.
Programming (via satellite): HBO; Showtime.
Fee: $30.00 installation; $11.95 monthly (each).

Digital Pay Service 1
Pay Units: N.A.
Programming (via satellite): Cinemax (multiplexed); HBO (multiplexed); HBO Latino; Showtime (multiplexed); Starz (multiplexed); The Movie Channel (multiplexed).
Video-On-Demand: No
Pay-Per-View
iN DEMAND (delivered digitally); Playboy TV (delivered digitally); Fresh (delivered digitally); Hot Choice (delivered digitally); Spice: Xcess (delivered digitally); Club Jenna (delivered digitally).
Internet Service
Operational: Yes.
Fee: $24.95 installation; $39.95 monthly.
Telephone Service
None
Miles of Plant: 16.0 (coaxial); None (fiber optic). Homes passed: 1,320.
Chief Executive Officer: Bill Haggarty. Regional Vice President: Andrew Dearth. Vice President, Marketing: Tracy Bass.
City fee: 1% of gross.
Ownership: Allegiance Communications (MSO).

McDOUGAL—Formerly served by Almega Cable. No longer in operation. ICA: AR0201.

McGEHEE—Allegiance Communications, 707 W Saratoga St, Shawnee, OK 74804. Phones: 405-275-6923; 405-395-1131. Web Site: http://www.allegiance.tv. Also serves Dermott, Desha County & Mitchellville. ICA: AR0262.
TV Market Ranking: Below 100 (Dermott, Desha County (portions), MCGEHEE, Mitchellville); Outside TV Markets (Desha County (portions)). Franchise award date: N.A. Franchise expiration date: N.A. Began: March 1, 1964.
Channel capacity: 58 (operating 2-way). Channels available but not in use: N.A.
Basic Service
Subscribers: 3,804.
Programming (received off-air): KARK-TV (NBC) Little Rock; KARZ-TV (MNT) Little Rock; KASN (CW) Pine Bluff; KATV (ABC) Little Rock; KETS (PBS) Little Rock; KKYK-DT (IND) Camden; KLRT-TV (FOX) Little Rock; KTHV (CBS) Little Rock; KTVE (NBC) El Dorado; WABG-TV (ABC) Greenwood; WXVT (CBS) Greenville; allband FM.
Programming (via satellite): CNBC; CNN; C-SPAN; Daystar TV Network; Headline News; Home Shopping Network; Trinity Broadcasting Network; Weather Channel; WGN America.
Fee: $38.00 installation; $21.95 monthly.
Expanded Basic Service 1
Subscribers: 2,040.
Programming (via satellite): ABC Family Channel; Animal Planet; Arts & Entertainment; BET Networks; Cartoon Network; Comcast Sports Net Southwest; Discovery Channel; Disney Channel; ESPN; ESPN 2; ESPN Classic Sports; Fox News Channel; FX; Great American Country; Hallmark Channel; HGTV; History Channel; Lifetime; Nickelodeon; Outdoor Channel; Oxygen; Speed Channel; Spike TV; Syfy; TBS Superstation; The Learning Channel; Travel Channel; Turner Classic Movies; Turner Network TV; TV Land; USA Network; VH1.
Fee: $30.20 monthly.
Digital Basic Service
Subscribers: N.A.
Programming (via satellite): AmericanLife TV Network; BBC America; Bio; Bloomberg Television; Bravo; Cine Latino; Cine Mexicano; CMT Pure Country; CNN en Espanol; Daystar TV Network; Discovery en Espanol; Discovery HD Theater; Discovery Health Channel; Discovery Kids Channel; Discovery Military Channel; Discovery Planet Green; DMX Music; Encore (multiplexed); ESPN Classic Sports; ESPN Deportes; ESPN HD; ESPNews; FitTV; Flix; Fox College Sports Atlantic; Fox College Sports Central; Fox College Sports Pacific; Fox Movie Channel; Fox Soccer; Fox Sports en Espanol; Fuse; G4; Golf Channel; Gospel Music Channel; Great American Country; GSN; Halogen Network; HDNet; HDNet Movies; History Channel; History Channel en Espanol; History Channel International; ID Investigation Discovery; Independent Film Channel; Lifetime Movie Network; MTV Hits; MTV Tres; MTV2; National Geographic Channel; Nick Jr.; NickToons TV; Outdoor Channel; Outdoor Channel 2 HD; Science Channel; ShopNBC; Sleuth; Speed Channel; Style Network; Sundance Channel; Syfy; TeenNick; The Word Network; Toon Disney; Trinity Broadcasting Network; Turner Classic Movies; TV Colombia; Universal HD; Versus; VH1 Classic; WE tv.
Fee: $11.00 monthly.
Digital Pay Service 1
Pay Units: N.A.
Programming (via satellite): Cinemax (multiplexed); HBO (multiplexed); HBO HD; HBO Latino; Showtime (multiplexed); Showtime HD; Starz (multiplexed); The Movie Channel.
Video-On-Demand: No
Pay-Per-View
iN DEMAND (delivered digitally); Hot Choice (delivered digitally); Playboy TV (delivered digitally); Spice (delivered digitally); Spice 2 (delivered digitally).
Internet Service
Operational: Yes.
Fee: $24.95 installation; $39.95 monthly.
Telephone Service
None
Miles of Plant: 50.0 (coaxial); None (fiber optic).
Chief Executive Officer: Bill Haggarty. Regional Vice President: Andrew Dearth. Vice President: Tracy Bass.
City fee: 3% of gross.
Ownership: Allegiance Communications (MSO).

MELBOURNE—Indco Cable TV, PO Box 3799, 2700 N Saint Louis, Batesville, AR 72503-3799. Phone: 870-793-4174. Fax: 870-793-7439. Web Site: http://www.indco.net. ICA: AR0264.
TV Market Ranking: Outside TV Markets (MELBOURNE). Franchise award date: N.A. Franchise expiration date: N.A. Began: August 1, 1966.
Channel capacity: 35 (operating 2-way). Channels available but not in use: N.A.
Basic Service
Subscribers: 527.
Programming (received off-air): KAIT (ABC) Jonesboro; KARK-TV (NBC) Little Rock; KATV (ABC) Little Rock; KEMV (PBS) Mountain View; KOLR (CBS) Springfield; KTHV (CBS) Little Rock; KYTV (CW, NBC) Springfield.
Programming (via satellite): ABC Family Channel; CNN; Country Music TV; Discovery Channel; Disney Channel; ESPN; ESPN 2; Fox Sports Net; FX; Headline News; HGTV; Nickelodeon; Outdoor Channel; QVC; Spike TV; Syfy; TBS Superstation; Trinity Broadcasting Network; Turner Classic Movies; Turner Network TV; TV Land; USA Network; Weather Channel; WGN America; WPIX (CW, IND) New York.
Fee: $20.00 installation; $30.95 monthly; $10.00 additional installation.
Pay Service 1
Pay Units: 24.
Programming (via satellite): Cinemax.
Fee: $8.00 monthly.
Pay Service 2
Pay Units: 16.
Programming (via satellite): HBO.
Fee: $10.00 monthly.
Video-On-Demand: Planned
Internet Service
Operational: Yes.
Fee: $29.95 monthly.
Telephone Service
None
Miles of Plant: 14.0 (coaxial); None (fiber optic).
Manager: J. D. Pierce. Chief Technician: Tommy Barnett. Marketing Director: Connie Barnett.
City fee: 3% of gross.
Ownership: Indco Cable TV (MSO).

MENA—Allegiance Communications, 707 W Saratoga St, Shawnee, OK 74804. Phones: 405-275-6923; 405-395-1131. Web Site: http://www.allegiance.tv. ICA: AR0265.
TV Market Ranking: Outside TV Markets (MENA). Franchise award date: N.A. Franchise expiration date: N.A. Began: February 1, 1954.
Channel capacity: N.A. Channels available but not in use: N.A.
Basic Service
Subscribers: 2,906.
Programming (received off-air): KARK-TV (NBC) Little Rock; KARZ-TV (MNT) Little Rock; KATV (ABC) Little Rock; KETG (PBS) Arkadelphia; KFSM-TV (CBS) Fort Smith; KHBS (ABC) Fort Smith; KLRT-TV (FOX) Little Rock; KTHV (CBS) Little Rock; allband FM.
Programming (via satellite): CNN; C-SPAN; Home Shopping Network; KFDF-CA Fort Smith; QVC; Trinity Broadcasting Network; TV Guide Network; Weather Channel; WGN America.
Current originations: Educational Access.
Fee: $38.00 installation; $21.95 monthly.
Expanded Basic Service 1
Subscribers: N.A.
Programming (via satellite): ABC Family Channel; AMC; Animal Planet; Arts & Entertainment; CNBC; Comcast Sports Net Southwest; Comedy Central; Country Music TV; CW+; Discovery Channel; Disney Channel; ESPN; ESPN 2; ESPN Classic Sports; Food Network; Fox News Channel; FX; Hallmark Channel; Headline News; HGTV; History Channel; Lifetime; NFL Network; Nickelodeon; RFD-TV; Spike TV; Syfy; TBS Superstation; The Learning Channel; Travel Channel; truTV; Turner Classic Movies; Turner Network TV; TV Land; USA Network; VH1.
Fee: $17.56 monthly.
Digital Basic Service
Subscribers: N.A.
Programming (via satellite): AmericanLife TV Network; BBC America; Bio; Bloomberg Television; Bravo; Chiller; Cine Latino; Cine Mexicano; CMT Pure Country; CNN en Espanol; Current; Discovery en Espanol; Discovery Health Channel; Discovery Kids Channel; Discovery Military Channel; Discovery Planet Green; DMX Music; Encore (multiplexed); ESPN 2; ESPN Classic Sports; ESPN Deportes; ESPNews; FitTV; Flix; Fox College Sports Atlantic; Fox College Sports Central; Fox College Sports Pacific; Fox Movie Channel; Fox Soccer; Fox Sports en Espanol; Fuse; G4; Golf Channel; Gospel Music Channel; Great American Country; GSN; Halogen Network; HGTV; History Channel; History Channel en Espanol; History Channel International; ID Investigation Discovery; Independent Film Channel; Lifetime Movie Network; MTV Hits; MTV Tres; MTV2; mun2 television; National Geographic Channel; Nick Jr.; NickToons TV; Outdoor Channel; Ovation; Science Channel; ShopNBC; Sleuth; SoapNet; Speed Channel; Style Network; Sundance Channel; Syfy; TeenNick; The Word Network; Toon Disney; Trinity Broadcasting Network; Turner Classic Movies; VeneMovies; Versus; VH1 Classic; VH1 Soul; WE tv.
Pay Service 1
Pay Units: 355.
Programming (via satellite): HBO; Showtime.
Fee: $35.00 installation; $11.95 monthly (each).
Digital Pay Service 1
Pay Units: N.A.
Programming (via satellite): Cinemax (multiplexed); HBO (multiplexed); HBO Latino; Showtime (multiplexed); Starz (multiplexed); The Movie Channel (multiplexed).
Video-On-Demand: No
Pay-Per-View
iN DEMAND (delivered digitally); Playboy TV (delivered digitally); Hot Choice (delivered digitally); Spice: Xcess (delivered digitally); Club Jenna (delivered digitally); Fresh (delivered digitally).
Internet Service
Operational: Yes.
Fee: $24.95 installation; $39.95 monthly.
Telephone Service
None
Miles of Plant: 41.0 (coaxial); None (fiber optic).
Chief Executive Officer: Bill Haggarty. Regional Vice President: Andrew Dearth. Vice President, Marketing: Tracy Bass.
City fee: $100.00 per month.
Ownership: Allegiance Communications (MSO).

MIDLAND—Cox Communications. Now served by FORT SMITH, AR [AR0003]. ICA: AR0266.

MINERAL SPRINGS—Allegiance Communications, 707 W Saratoga St, Shawnee, OK 74804. Phones: 405-275-6923; 405-395-1131. Web Site: http://www.allegiance.tv. ICA: AR0148.
TV Market Ranking: 58 (MINERAL SPRINGS). Franchise award date: N.A. Franchise expiration date: N.A. Began: November 1, 1977.
Channel capacity: 30 (2-way capable). Channels available but not in use: N.A.
Basic Service
Subscribers: 265.
Programming (received off-air): KARK-TV (NBC) Little Rock; KATV (ABC) Little Rock; KETG (PBS) Arkadelphia; KJEP-CA Nashville; KMSS-TV (FOX) Shreveport; KSHV-TV (MNT) Shreveport; KSLA (CBS) Shreveport; KTAL-TV (NBC) Texarkana; KTBS-TV (ABC) Shreveport; KTSS-LP Hope.
Programming (via satellite): ABC Family Channel; AMC; Arts & Entertainment; BET Networks; CMT Pure Country; CNN; Discovery Channel; Disney Channel; ESPN; ESPN 2; HGTV; ION Television; QVC; Spike TV; TBS Superstation; Turner Network TV;

USA Network; Weather Channel; WGN America.
Fee: $35.00 installation; $21.95 monthly; $15.00 additional installation.
Pay Service 1
Pay Units: N.A.
Programming (via satellite): Cinemax; HBO; Showtime; The Movie Channel.
Fee: $11.00 monthly (each).
Video-On-Demand: No
Pay-Per-View
Urban American Television Network (delivered digitally); iN DEMAND (delivered digitally); Playboy TV (delivered digitally); Fresh (delivered digitally); Shorteez (delivered digitally).
Internet Service
Operational: No.
Telephone Service
None
Miles of Plant: 6.0 (coaxial); None (fiber optic). Homes passed: 350. Total homes in franchised area: 469.
Chief Executive Officer: Bill Haggarty. Regional Vice President: Andrew Dearth. Vice President, Marketing: Tracy Bass.
City fee: 2% of gross.
Ownership: Allegiance Communications (MSO).

MONTICELLO—Community Communications Co., 1920 Hwy 425 N, Monticello, AR 71655-4463. Phones: 800-272-2191; 870-367-7300. Fax: 870-367-9770. E-mail: generalmanager@ccc-cable.net. Web Site: http://www.ccc-cable.net. Also serves Drew County. ICA: AR0032.
TV Market Ranking: Below 100 (Drew County (portions), MONTICELLO); Outside TV Markets (Drew County (portions)). Franchise award date: N.A. Franchise expiration date: N.A. Began: May 1, 1974.
Channel capacity: 78 (operating 2-way). Channels available but not in use: None.
Basic Service
Subscribers: 3,178.
Programming (received off-air): KARK-TV (NBC) Little Rock; KARZ-TV (MNT) Little Rock; KASN (CW) Pine Bluff; KATV (ABC) Little Rock; KETS (PBS) Little Rock; KKAP (ETV) Little Rock; KKYK-DT (IND) Camden; KLRA-LP Little Rock; KLRT-TV (FOX) Little Rock; KTHV (CBS) Little Rock; KTVE (NBC) El Dorado; WABG-TV (ABC) Greenwood; WXVT (CBS) Greenville; allband FM.
Programming (via satellite): ABC Family Channel; Animal Planet; Arts & Entertainment; BET Networks; Bloomberg Television; Bravo; Cartoon Network; CNBC; CNN; Comcast Sports Net Southwest; Comedy Central; Country Music TV; Cox Sports Television; C-SPAN; C-SPAN 2; Discovery Channel; Disney Channel; E! Entertainment Television; ESPN; ESPN 2; Eternal Word TV Network; FitTV; Food Network; Fox News Channel; FX; Golf Channel; Headline News; HGTV; History Channel; Home Shopping Network; Lifetime; MSNBC; MTV; National Geographic Channel; Nickelodeon; Outdoor Channel; QVC; Speed Channel; Spike TV; Syfy; TBS Superstation; The Learning Channel; Travel Channel; Trinity Broadcasting Network; Turner Classic Movies; Turner Network TV; TV Guide Network; TV Land; USA Network; Versus; VH1; Weather Channel; WGN America.
Current originations: Public Access.
Fee: $30.00 installation; $38.70 monthly.
Digital Basic Service
Subscribers: N.A.
Programming (via satellite): BBC America; Bio; CMT Pure Country; Cooking Channel; Discovery Health Channel; Discovery Home Channel; Discovery Kids Channel; Discovery Military Channel; Discovery Times Channel; ESPNews; Fox Movie Channel; Fuse; G4; GSN; Halogen Network; History Channel International; Independent Film Channel; Lifetime Movie Network; MTV2; Music Choice; Nick Jr.; NickToons TV; Science Channel; Sleuth; SoapNet; Style Network; TeenNick; Toon Disney; VH1 Classic; WE tv.
Fee: $5.00 monthly.
Digital Pay Service 1
Pay Units: 464.
Programming (via satellite): Cinemax (multiplexed); Encore (multiplexed); HBO (multiplexed); Showtime (multiplexed); Starz (multiplexed); The Movie Channel (multiplexed).
Fee: $6.00 monthly (Starz, Encore or TMC), $12.00 monthly (HBO, Cinemax or Showtime).
Video-On-Demand: No
Pay-Per-View
Club Jenna (delivered digitally); Playboy TV (delivered digitally), Addressable: Yes; Fresh (delivered digitally); special events (delivered digitally).
Internet Service
Operational: Yes.
Broadband Service: community.internet.
Fee: $30.00 installation; $29.95 monthly.
Telephone Service
None
Miles of Plant: 110.0 (coaxial); None (fiber optic). Homes passed: 3,700.
City fee: 2% of gross.
Ownership: Community Communications Co. (MSO).

MONTROSE—Dean Hill Cable, PO Box 128, Parkdale, AR 71661. Phone: 870-473-2802. Fax: 870-737-0020. ICA: AR0322.
TV Market Ranking: Below 100 (MONTROSE).
Channel capacity: N.A. Channels available but not in use: N.A.
Basic Service
Subscribers: 49.
Programming (received off-air): KATV (ABC) Little Rock; KLTM-TV (PBS) Monroe; KNOE-TV (CBS, CW) Monroe; KTVE (NBC) El Dorado; WABG-TV (ABC) Greenwood.
Programming (via satellite): Disney Channel; ESPN; TBS Superstation; Turner Network TV; WGN America.
Fee: $35.00 installation; $30.00 monthly.
Pay Service 1
Pay Units: 5.
Programming (via satellite): HBO.
Fee: $10.00 installation; $11.55 monthly.
Internet Service
Operational: No.
Telephone Service
None
Manager: Dean Hill. Assistant Manager: Kathy Hill.
Ownership: Dean Hill Cable (MSO).

MORO—Indco Cable TV, PO Box 3799, 2700 N Saint Louis, Batesville, AR 72503-3799. Phone: 870-793-4174. Fax: 870-793-7439. Web Site: http://www.indco.net. ICA: AR0268.
TV Market Ranking: Outside TV Markets (MORO). Franchise award date: N.A. Franchise expiration date: N.A. Began: N.A.
Channel capacity: 36 (operating 2-way). Channels available but not in use: N.A.

Basic Service
Subscribers: 59.
Programming (received off-air): KARK-TV (NBC) Little Rock; KASN (CW) Pine Bluff; KATV (ABC) Little Rock; KLRT-TV (FOX) Little Rock; KTEJ (PBS) Jonesboro; KTHV (CBS) Little Rock.
Programming (via satellite): ABC Family Channel; Discovery Channel; Disney Channel; ESPN; ESPN 2; Spike TV; TBS Superstation; Trinity Broadcasting Network; Turner Network TV; USA Network; WGN America.
Fee: $30.95 monthly.
Pay Service 1
Pay Units: 2.
Programming (via satellite): The Movie Channel.
Fee: $10.00 monthly.
Video-On-Demand: Planned
Internet Service
Operational: Yes.
Fee: $29.95 monthly.
Telephone Service
None
Manager: J. D. Pierce. Chief Technician: Tommy Barnett. Marketing Director: Connie Barnett.
Ownership: Indco Cable TV (MSO).

MORRILTON—Suddenlink Communications, 127 N Elmira Ave, Russellville, AR 72802-9614. Phones: 888-822-5151; 479-354-5686. Fax: 479-969-1343. Web Site: http://www.suddenlink.com. Also serves Conway County (portions). ICA: AR0035.
TV Market Ranking: 50 (Conway County (portions), MORRILTON); Outside TV Markets (Conway County (portions), MORRILTON). Franchise award date: N.A. Franchise expiration date: N.A. Began: February 1, 1981.
Channel capacity: N.A. Channels available but not in use: N.A.
Basic Service
Subscribers: 2,194.
Programming (received off-air): KAFT (PBS) Fayetteville; KARK-TV (NBC) Little Rock; KARZ-TV (MNT) Little Rock; KASN (CW) Pine Bluff; KATV (ABC) Little Rock; KFSM-TV (CBS) Fort Smith; KKAP (ETV) Little Rock; KKYK-DT (IND) Camden; KLRA-LP Little Rock; KLRT-TV (FOX) Little Rock; KTHV (CBS) Little Rock.
Programming (via satellite): C-SPAN; Home Shopping Network; QVC; TBS Superstation; Telefutura; Weather Channel; WGN America.
Current originations: Educational Access.
Fee: $30.00 installation; $10.35 monthly.
Expanded Basic Service 1
Subscribers: 2,079.
Programming (via satellite): ABC Family Channel; AMC; Animal Planet; Arts & Entertainment; BET Networks; Bravo; Cartoon Network; CNBC; CNN; Comcast Sports Net Southwest; Comedy Central; Country Music TV; C-SPAN 2; Discovery Channel; Disney Channel; E! Entertainment Television; ESPN; ESPN 2; Eternal Word TV Network; Food Network; Fox News Channel; FX; GalaVision; Great American Country; Headline News; HGTV; History Channel; INSP; Jewelry Television; Lifetime; Lifetime Movie Network; MSNBC; MTV; Nickelodeon; Outdoor Channel; Speed Channel; Spike TV; Syfy; The Learning Channel; Travel Channel; Trinity Broadcasting Network; truTV; Turner Classic Movies; Turner Network TV; TV Guide Network; TV Land; USA Network; Versus; VH1.
Fee: $30.00 installation; $35.75 monthly.
Digital Basic Service
Subscribers: N.A.
Programming (received off-air): KARK-TV (NBC) Little Rock; KATV (ABC) Little Rock; KLRT-TV (FOX) Little Rock; KTHV (CBS) Little Rock.
Programming (via satellite): Arts & Entertainment HD; Bandamax; BBC America; Bio; Bloomberg Television; Boomerang; Boomerang en Espanol; CBS College Sports Network; Cine Latino; Cine Mexicano; CMT Pure Country; CNN en Espanol; Cooking Channel; Cox Sports Television; De Pelicula; De Pelicula Clasico; Discovery en Espanol; Discovery HD Theater; Discovery Health Channel; Discovery Home Channel; Discovery Kids Channel; Discovery Military Channel; Discovery Times Channel; Do-It-Yourself; Encore (multiplexed); ESPN Classic Sports; ESPN Deportes; ESPN HD; ESPNews; EWTN en Espanol; FamilyNet; Food Network HD; Fox Reality Channel; Fox Soccer; Fox Sports en Espanol; FSN HD; Fuel TV; Fuse; G4; GalaVision; Golf Channel; Gospel Music Channel; GSN; Hallmark Channel; Halogen Network; HDNet; HDNet Movies; HGTV HD; History Channel en Espanol; History Channel International; Independent Film Channel; Latele Novela Network; MTV Hits; MTV Tres; MTV2; mtvU; mun2 television; Music Choice; National Geographic Channel; National Geographic Channel HD Network; Nick Jr.; NickToons en Espanol; NickToons TV; Oxygen; Palladia; Ritmoson Latino; Science Channel; Si TV; SoapNet; Sorpresa; Style Network; Sundance Channel; Sur Network; TBN Enlace USA; TeenNick; Telehit; Telemundo; Tennis Channel; The Sportsman Channel; Toon Disney; Toon Disney en Espanol; Turner Network TV HD; TV Chile; TV One; Universal HD; VH1 Classic; Video Rola; WE tv; Weatherscan.
Digital Pay Service 1
Pay Units: N.A.
Programming (via satellite): Cinemax (multiplexed); HBO (multiplexed); HBO HD; HBO Latino; Showtime (multiplexed); Showtime HD; Starz (multiplexed); The Movie Channel (multiplexed).
Video-On-Demand: Yes
Pay-Per-View
iN DEMAND (delivered digitally); Playboy TV (delivered digitally); Fresh (delivered digitally); Shorteez (delivered digitally); Club Jenna (delivered digitally); Spice: Xcess (delivered digitally); Playboy en Espanol (delivered digitally).
Internet Service
Operational: Yes.
Fee: $35.00 monthly.

Telephone Service
Digital: Operational
Fee: $20.00 monthly
Miles of Plant: 79.0 (coaxial); None (fiber optic). Homes passed: 3,270.
General Manager: Mike Ederington. Marketing Director: Kathy Wyrick. Chief Technician: Clint Petty.
City fee: 3% of gross.
Ownership: Cequel Communications LLC (MSO).

MOUNT IDA—Suddenlink Communications, 12444 Powerscourt Dr, Saint Louis, MO 63131-3660. Phones: 314-965-2020; 800-999-6845 (Customer service). Fax: 903-561-5485. Web Site: http://www.suddenlink.com. Also serves Montgomery County (unincorporated areas) & Mountain Harbor Resort. ICA: AR0121.
TV Market Ranking: Below 100 (Montgomery County (unincorporated areas), MOUNT IDA, Mountain Harbor Resort). Franchise award date: N.A. Franchise expiration date: N.A. Began: May 1, 1982.
Channel capacity: 60 (operating 2-way). Channels available but not in use: N.A.
Basic Service
Subscribers: 932.
Programming (received off-air): KARK-TV (NBC) Little Rock; KARZ-TV (MNT) Little Rock; KASN (CW) Pine Bluff; KATV (ABC) Little Rock; KKYK-DT (IND) Camden; KLRT-TV (FOX) Little Rock; KTHV (CBS) Little Rock.
Programming (via satellite): Home Shopping Network; KETG (PBS) Arkadelphia; KVTN-DT (IND) Pine Bluff; Trinity Broadcasting Network; WGN America.
Fee: $17.95 installation; $19.95 monthly.
Expanded Basic Service 1
Subscribers: N.A.
Programming (via satellite): ABC Family Channel; AMC; Animal Planet; Arts & Entertainment; BET Networks; Cartoon Network; CNBC; CNN; Comcast Sports Net Southwest; Comedy Central; Discovery Channel; Disney Channel; E! Entertainment Television; ESPN; ESPN 2; Food Network; Fox News Channel; FX; Great American Country; Hallmark Channel; Headline News; HGTV; History Channel; Lifetime; MSNBC; MTV; National Geographic Channel; Nickelodeon; Outdoor Channel; Speed Channel; Spike TV; Syfy; TBS Superstation; The Learning Channel; Travel Channel; Turner Classic Movies; Turner Network TV; TV Land; USA Network; VH1; Weather Channel.
Fee: $25.00 monthly.
Pay Service 1
Pay Units: 50.
Programming (via satellite): HBO.
Fee: $13.00 monthly.
Pay Service 2
Pay Units: 34.
Programming (via satellite): The Movie Channel.
Fee: $10.95 monthly.
Pay Service 3
Pay Units: 77.
Programming (via satellite): Showtime.
Fee: $10.95 monthly.
Video-On-Demand: No
Pay-Per-View
Fresh (delivered digitally); Playboy TV (delivered digitally); iN DEMAND (delivered digitally).
Internet Service
Operational: Yes. Began: May 5, 2003.
Broadband Service: Cebridge High Speed Cable Internet.
Fee: $49.95 installation; $26.95 monthly.
Telephone Service
None
Miles of Plant: 56.0 (coaxial); None (fiber optic). Homes passed: 1,607.
Regional Manager: Todd Cruthird. Area Manager: Carolyn Wilder. Plant Manager: Donnie Burton. Marketing Director: Beverly Gambell.
Ownership: Cequel Communications LLC (MSO).

MOUNT PLEASANT—Indco Cable TV, PO Box 3799, 2700 N Saint Louis, Batesville, AR 72503-3799. Phone: 870-793-4174. Fax: 870-793-7439. Web Site: http://www.indco.net. ICA: AR0269.
TV Market Ranking: Outside TV Markets (MOUNT PLEASANT). Franchise award date: N.A. Franchise expiration date: N.A. Began: January 1, 1972.
Channel capacity: N.A. Channels available but not in use: N.A.
Basic Service
Subscribers: 79.
Programming (received off-air): KAIT (ABC) Jonesboro; KARK-TV (NBC) Little Rock; KATV (ABC) Little Rock; KEMV (PBS) Mountain View; KTHV (CBS) Little Rock.
Programming (via satellite): ABC Family Channel; CNN; Discovery Channel; Disney Channel; ESPN; ESPN 2; HGTV; Lifetime; Nickelodeon; Outdoor Channel; QVC; Spike TV; TBS Superstation; Turner Classic Movies; Turner Network TV; WGN America.
Fee: $20.00 installation; $30.95 monthly; $10.00 additional installation.
Pay Service 1
Pay Units: 4.
Programming (via satellite): HBO.
Fee: $10.00 monthly.
Video-On-Demand: Planned
Internet Service
Operational: Yes.
Fee: $29.95 monthly.
Telephone Service
None
Miles of Plant: 3.0 (coaxial); None (fiber optic).
Manager: J. D. Pierce. Marketing Director: Connie Barnett. Chief Technician: Tommy Barnett.
City fee: 1% of gross.
Ownership: Indco Cable TV (MSO).

MOUNTAIN HOME—Suddenlink Communications, PO Box 3055, 808 Club Blvd, Mountain Home, AR 72653. Phone: 870-425-3161. Fax: 870-425-3164. Web Site: http://www.suddenlink.com. Also serves Baxter County (portions), Bull Shoals, Cotter, Flippin, Gassville, Lakeview, Marion County (portions) & Midway. ICA: AR0013.
TV Market Ranking: Below 100 (Baxter County (portions) (portions), Bull Shoals, Cotter, Flippin, Gassville, Lakeview, Marion County (portions) (portions)); Outside TV Markets (Baxter County (portions) (portions), Marion County (portions) (portions), Midway, MOUNTAIN HOME). Franchise award date: N.A. Franchise expiration date: N.A. Began: March 1, 1959.
Channel capacity: N.A. Channels available but not in use: N.A.
Basic Service
Subscribers: 11,452.
Programming (received off-air): K07XL Mountain Home; KARK-TV (NBC) Little Rock; KATV (ABC) Little Rock; KEMV (PBS) Mountain View; KOLR (CBS) Springfield; KOZK (PBS) Springfield; KSFX-TV (FOX) Springfield; KSPR (ABC) Springfield; KTHV (CBS) Little Rock; KWBM (MNT) Harrison [LICENSED & SILENT]; KYTV (CW, NBC) Springfield; LWS Local Weather Station; 9 FMs.
Programming (via satellite): C-SPAN; C-SPAN 2; DMX Music; Home Shopping Network; INSP; QVC; TBS Superstation; Trinity Broadcasting Network; TV Guide Network; Weather Channel; WGN America.
Current originations: Leased Access.
Fee: $35.00 installation; $15.31 monthly.
Expanded Basic Service 1
Subscribers: 8,802.
Programming (via satellite): ABC Family Channel; AMC; Animal Planet; Arts & Entertainment; Bravo; Cartoon Network; CNBC; CNN; Comcast Sports Net Southwest; Comedy Central; Country Music TV; Discovery Channel; Disney Channel; E! Entertainment Television; ESPN; ESPN 2; Food Network; Fox News Channel; FX; Golf Channel; Great American Country; Headline News; HGTV; History Channel; Jewelry Television; Lifetime; Lifetime Movie Network; MSNBC; MTV; Nickelodeon; Outdoor Channel; Oxygen; Speed Channel; Spike TV; Syfy; The Learning Channel; Travel Channel; truTV; Turner Classic Movies; Turner Network TV; TV Land; USA Network; Versus; VH1; WE tv.
Fee: $13.64 monthly.
Digital Basic Service
Subscribers: N.A.
Programming (received off-air): KOLR (CBS) Springfield; KOZK (PBS) Springfield; KSFX-TV (FOX) Springfield; KYTV (CW, NBC) Springfield.
Programming (via satellite): Arts & Entertainment HD; BBC America; Bio; Bloomberg Television; CBS College Sports Network; CMT Pure Country; Cooking Channel; Discovery en Espanol; Discovery HD Theater; Discovery Health Channel; Discovery Home Channel; Discovery Kids Channel; Discovery Military Channel; Discovery Times Channel; Do-It-Yourself; Encore (multiplexed); ESPN Classic Sports; ESPN HD; ESPNews; Food Network HD; Fox Reality Channel; Fox Soccer; FSN HD; Fuel TV; Fuse; G4; GSN; Hallmark Channel; HDNet; HDNet Movies; HGTV HD; History Channel International; Independent Film Channel; MTV Hits; MTV2; Music Choice; National Geographic Channel; National Geographic Channel HD Network; Nick Jr.; NickToons TV; Science Channel; SoapNet; Style Network; Sundance Channel; TeenNick; Toon Disney; Turner Network TV HD; Universal HD; VH1 Classic.
Digital Pay Service 1
Pay Units: N.A.
Programming (via satellite): Cinemax (multiplexed); HBO (multiplexed); HBO HD; Showtime (multiplexed); Showtime HD; Starz (multiplexed); The Movie Channel (multiplexed).
Video-On-Demand: Planned
Pay-Per-View
iN DEMAND (delivered digitally); Playboy TV (delivered digitally); Fresh (delivered digitally); Club Jenna (delivered digitally); Spice: Xcess (delivered digitally).
Internet Service
Operational: Yes.
Subscribers: 1,250.
Broadband Service: Cebridge High Speed Cable Internet.
Fee: $29.95 monthly.
Telephone Service
None
Miles of Plant: 428.0 (coaxial); None (fiber optic). Homes passed: 14,000. Total homes in franchised area: 15,000.
Manager: Ron Vincent. Chief Technician: Eddie Thorn.
City fee: 3% of gross.
Ownership: Cequel Communications LLC (MSO).

MOUNTAIN VIEW—Indco Cable TV, PO Box 3799, 2700 N Saint Louis, Batesville, AR 72503-3799. Phone: 870-793-4174. Fax: 870-793-7439. Web Site: http://www.indco.net. ICA: AR0271.
TV Market Ranking: Outside TV Markets (MOUNTAIN VIEW). Franchise award date: N.A. Franchise expiration date: N.A. Began: November 1, 1968.
Channel capacity: 36 (not 2-way capable). Channels available but not in use: N.A.
Basic Service
Subscribers: 1,483.
Programming (received off-air): KAIT (ABC) Jonesboro; KARK-TV (NBC) Little Rock; KASN (CW) Pine Bluff; KATV (ABC) Little Rock; KLRT-TV (FOX) Little Rock; KTEJ (PBS) Jonesboro; KTHV (CBS) Little Rock; KYTV (CW, NBC) Springfield; allband FM.
Programming (via satellite): ABC Family Channel; Arts & Entertainment; CNN; Country Music TV; Discovery Channel; Disney Channel; ESPN; ESPN 2; Fox Sports Net; FX; HGTV; History Channel; Lifetime; Nickelodeon; QVC; Spike TV; Syfy; TBS Superstation; Trinity Broadcasting Network; Turner Classic Movies; Turner Network TV; TV Land; USA Network; VH1; Weather Channel; WGN America.
Fee: $20.00 installation; $26.95 monthly; $10.00 additional installation.
Pay Service 1
Pay Units: 34.
Programming (via satellite): Cinemax.
Fee: $8.00 monthly.
Pay Service 2
Pay Units: 32.
Programming (via satellite): HBO.
Fee: $10.00 monthly.
Pay Service 3
Pay Units: 29.
Programming (via satellite): Cinemax; HBO.
Fee: $16.00 monthly (HBO and Cinemax Combo).
Video-On-Demand: No
Internet Service
Operational: Yes.
Telephone Service
Digital: Operational
Miles of Plant: 35.0 (coaxial); None (fiber optic).
Manager: J. D. Pierce. Marketing Director: Connie Barnett. Chief Technician: Tommy Barnett.
City fee: $0.50 per subscriber annually.
Ownership: Indco Cable TV (MSO).

MULBERRY—Cox Communications. Now served by FORT SMITH, AR [AR0003]. ICA: AR0052.

MURFREESBORO—Allegiance Communications, 707 W Saratoga St, Shawnee, OK 74804. Phones: 405-395-1131; 405-275-6923. Web Site: http://www.allegiance.tv. Also serves Pike County (unincorporated areas). ICA: AR0095.
TV Market Ranking: Outside TV Markets (MURFREESBORO, Pike County (unincorporated areas)). Franchise award date: March 2, 1964. Franchise expiration date: N.A. Began: September 1, 1964.
Channel capacity: N.A. Channels available but not in use: N.A.

Basic Service
Subscribers: 696.
Programming (received off-air): KARK-TV (NBC) Little Rock; KATV (ABC) Little Rock; KETG (PBS) Arkadelphia; KJEP-CA Nashville; KMSS-TV (FOX) Shreveport; KSLA (CBS) Shreveport; KTAL-TV (NBC) Texarkana; KTBS-TV (ABC) Shreveport; KTHV (CBS) Little Rock; KTSS-LP Hope; KVTH-DT (IND) Hot Springs; allband FM.
Programming (via satellite): CNN; QVC; Trinity Broadcasting Network; TV Guide Network; Weather Channel; WGN America.
Fee: $25.00 installation; $21.95 monthly.
Expanded Basic Service 1
Subscribers: N.A.
Programming (via satellite): ABC Family Channel; AMC; Arts & Entertainment; Cartoon Network; CNBC; Comcast Sports Net Southwest; Comedy Central; Country Music TV; Discovery Channel; Disney Channel; ESPN; ESPN 2; Fox News Channel; Hallmark Channel; History Channel; Lifetime; MTV; NFL Network; Nickelodeon; Spike TV; Syfy; TBS Superstation; The Learning Channel; Turner Network TV; TV Land; USA Network; VH1.
Digital Basic Service
Subscribers: N.A.
Programming (via satellite): AmericanLife TV Network; BBC America; Bio; Bloomberg Television; Bravo; Cine Latino; Cine Mexicano; CMT Pure Country; CNN en Espanol; Current; Discovery en Espanol; Discovery Health Channel; Discovery Kids Channel; Discovery Military Channel; Discovery Planet Green; DMX Music; Encore (multiplexed); ESPN 2; ESPN Classic Sports; ESPN Deportes; ESPNews; FitTV; Flix; Fox College Sports Atlantic; Fox College Sports Central; Fox College Sports Pacific; Fox Movie Channel; Fox Soccer; Fox Sports en Espanol; Fuse; G4; Golf Channel; Gospel Music Channel; Great American Country; GSN; Halogen Network; HGTV; History Channel; History Channel en Espanol; History Channel International; ID Investigation Discovery; Independent Film Channel; Lifetime Movie Network; Lime; MTV Hits; MTV Tres; MTV2; mun2 television; National Geographic Channel; Nick Jr.; NickToons TV; Outdoor Channel; Science Channel; ShopNBC; Speed Channel; Style Network; Sundance Channel; Syfy; TeenNick; The Word Network; Toon Disney; Trinity Broadcasting Network; Trio; Turner Classic Movies; VeneMovies; Versus; VH1 Classic; VH1 Soul; WE tv.
Pay Service 1
Pay Units: 46.
Programming (via satellite): Starz.
Pay Service 2
Pay Units: 216.
Programming (via satellite): Encore.
Fee: $1.75 monthly.
Pay Service 3
Pay Units: 103.
Programming (via satellite): The Movie Channel.
Fee: $9.95 monthly.
Pay Service 4
Pay Units: 42.
Programming (via satellite): HBO.
Fee: $10.95 monthly.
Digital Pay Service 1
Pay Units: N.A.
Programming (via satellite): Cinemax (multiplexed); HBO (multiplexed); HBO Latino; Showtime (multiplexed); Starz (multiplexed); The Movie Channel (multiplexed).
Pay-Per-View
iN DEMAND (delivered digitally); Hot Choice (delivered digitally); Playboy TV (delivered digitally); Fresh (delivered digitally); Spice: Xcess (delivered digitally); Club Jenna (delivered digitally).
Internet Service
Operational: Yes.
Fee: $24.95 installation; $39.95 monthly.
Telephone Service
None
Miles of Plant: 20.0 (coaxial); None (fiber optic). Homes passed: 1,634. Total homes in franchised area: 1,634.
Chief Executive Officer: Bill Haggarty. Regional Vice President: Andrew Dearth. Vice President, Marketing: Tracy Bass.
City fee: 2% of gross.
Ownership: Allegiance Communications (MSO).

NASHVILLE—Suddenlink Communications, 12444 Powerscourt Dr, Saint Louis, MO 63131-3660. Phone: 314-965-2020. Web Site: http://www.suddenlink.com. Also serves Hempstead County (portions). ICA: AR0272.
TV Market Ranking: Outside TV Markets (Hempstead County (portions), NASHVILLE). Franchise award date: N.A. Franchise expiration date: N.A. Began: September 15, 1967.
Channel capacity: 26 (operating 2-way). Channels available but not in use: N.A.
Basic Service
Subscribers: 1,432.
Programming (received off-air): KARK-TV (NBC) Little Rock; KATV (ABC) Little Rock; KETG (PBS) Arkadelphia; KMSS-TV (FOX) Shreveport; KSLA (CBS) Shreveport; KTAL-TV (NBC) Texarkana; KTBS-TV (ABC) Shreveport; KTHV (CBS) Little Rock; allband FM.
Fee: $39.95 installation; $19.95 monthly.
Expanded Basic Service 1
Subscribers: N.A.
Programming (received off-air): KJEP-CA Nashville; KSJA-CA Nashville; KTSS-LP Hope.
Programming (via satellite): ABC Family Channel; AMC; Animal Planet; Arts & Entertainment; BET Networks; Cartoon Network; CNBC; CNN; Comcast Sports Net Southwest; Comedy Central; Discovery Channel; Disney Channel; E! Entertainment Television; ESPN; ESPN 2; Food Network; Fox News Channel; FX; Great American Country; Headline News; HGTV; History Channel; Home Shopping Network; Lifetime; MSNBC; MTV; National Geographic Channel; Nickelodeon; Outdoor Channel; Spike TV; Syfy; TBS Superstation; The Learning Channel; Travel Channel; Turner Classic Movies; Turner Network TV; TV Land; USA Network; Versus; VH1; Weather Channel.
Fee: $24.00 monthly.
Pay Service 1
Pay Units: 29.
Programming (via satellite): Cinemax.
Fee: $9.95 monthly.
Pay Service 2
Pay Units: 164.
Programming (via satellite): HBO.
Fee: $10.95 monthly.
Pay Service 3
Pay Units: 158.
Programming (via satellite): Showtime.
Fee: $7.00 monthly.
Video-On-Demand: No
Pay-Per-View
iN DEMAND (delivered digitally); Playboy TV (delivered digitally); Fresh (delivered digitally); Shorteez (delivered digitally); Urban American Television Network (delivered digitally).

Internet Service
Operational: Yes. Began: July 8, 2003.
Broadband Service: Cebridge High Speed Cable Internet.
Fee: $49.95 installation; $26.95 monthly.
Telephone Service
None
Miles of Plant: 53.0 (coaxial); None (fiber optic). Homes passed: 2,426.
Regional Manager: Todd Cruthird. Plant Manager: George Lewis. Marketing Director: Beverly Gambell.
City fee: 2% of gross first 300 subs.; 5% thereafter.
Ownership: Cequel Communications LLC (MSO).

NEWARK—Indco Cable TV, PO Box 3799, 2700 N Saint Louis, Batesville, AR 72503-3799. Phone: 870-793-4174. Fax: 870-793-7439. Web Site: http://www.indco.net. Also serves Magness. ICA: AR0093.
TV Market Ranking: Outside TV Markets (Magness, NEWARK). Franchise award date: N.A. Franchise expiration date: N.A. Began: October 1, 1975.
Channel capacity: 36 (not 2-way capable). Channels available but not in use: N.A.
Basic Service
Subscribers: 420.
Programming (received off-air): KAIT (ABC) Jonesboro; KARK-TV (NBC) Little Rock; KATV (ABC) Little Rock; KEMV (PBS) Mountain View; KLRT-TV (FOX) Little Rock; KTHV (CBS) Little Rock.
Programming (via satellite): ABC Family Channel; Arts & Entertainment; CNN; Comcast Sports Net Southwest; Country Music TV; Discovery Channel; Disney Channel; ESPN; ESPN 2; FX; HGTV; Lifetime; Nickelodeon; Outdoor Channel; QVC; Spike TV; Syfy; TBS Superstation; Turner Classic Movies; Turner Network TV; USA Network; Weather Channel; WGN America.
Fee: $20.00 installation; $30.95 monthly; $10.00 additional installation.
Pay Service 1
Pay Units: 9.
Programming (via satellite): Cinemax.
Fee: $8.00 monthly.
Pay Service 2
Pay Units: 3.
Programming (via satellite): HBO.
Fee: $10.00 monthly.
Pay Service 3
Pay Units: 8.
Programming (via satellite): Cinemax; HBO.
Fee: $16.00 monthly.
Internet Service
Operational: Yes.
Telephone Service
Digital: Operational
Miles of Plant: 10.0 (coaxial); None (fiber optic). Homes passed: 849.
Manager: J. D. Pierce. Chief Technician: Tommy Barnett. Marketing Director: Connie Barnett.
City fee: 1% of gross.
Ownership: Indco Cable TV (MSO).

NEWPORT—Suddenlink Communications, PO Box 608, 300 State St, Newport, AR 72112-0608. Phone: 870-523-3607. Fax: 870-523-2219. Web Site: http://www.suddenlink.com. Also serves Campbell Station, Diaz, Jackson County, Jacksonport & Tuckerman. ICA: AR0030.
TV Market Ranking: Below 100 (Campbell Station, Diaz, Jackson County (portions), NEWPORT, Tuckerman); Outside TV Markets (Jackson County (portions), Jacksonport). Franchise award date: N.A. Franchise expiration date: N.A. Began: November 2, 1964.
Channel capacity: 61 (operating 2-way). Channels available but not in use: N.A.
Basic Service
Subscribers: 4,236.
Programming (received off-air): KAIT (ABC) Jonesboro; KARK-TV (NBC) Little Rock; KARZ-TV (MNT) Little Rock; KASN (CW) Pine Bluff; KATV (ABC) Little Rock; KKAP (ETV) Little Rock; KKYK-DT (IND) Camden; KLRT-TV (FOX) Little Rock; KTEJ (PBS) Jonesboro; KTHV (CBS) Little Rock; KVTJ-DT (IND) Jonesboro; WMC-TV (NBC) Memphis; allband FM.
Programming (via satellite): C-SPAN; C-SPAN 2; Headline News; Home Shopping Network; Jewelry Television; QVC; TBS Superstation; Weather Channel; WGN America.
Fee: $30.00 installation; $19.25 monthly.
Expanded Basic Service 1
Subscribers: N.A.
Programming (via satellite): ABC Family Channel; AMC; Animal Planet; Arts & Entertainment; BET Networks; Bravo; Cartoon Network; CNBC; CNN; Comcast Sports Net Southwest; Comedy Central; Country Music TV; Discovery Channel; Disney Channel; E! Entertainment Television; ESPN; ESPN 2; Food Network; Fox News Channel; FX; Great American Country; HGTV; History Channel; Lifetime; Lifetime Movie Network; MSNBC; MTV; Nickelodeon; Oxygen; Speed Channel; Spike TV; Syfy; The Learning Channel; Travel Channel; truTV; Turner Classic Movies; Turner Network TV; TV Land; USA Network; Versus; VH1.
Digital Basic Service
Subscribers: N.A.
Programming (via satellite): BBC America; Bio; Bloomberg Television; CBS College Sports Network; CMT Pure Country; Cooking Channel; Discovery en Espanol; Discovery Health Channel; Discovery Home Channel; Discovery Kids Channel; Discovery Military Channel; Discovery Times Channel; Do-It-Yourself; Encore (multiplexed); ESPN Classic Sports; ESPNews; Fox Reality Channel; Fox Soccer; Fuel TV; Fuse; G4; Golf Channel; GSN; Hallmark Channel; History Channel International; Independent Film Channel; MTV Hits; MTV Jams; MTV2; Music Choice; National Geographic Channel; Nick Jr.; NickToons TV; Outdoor Channel; Science Channel; SoapNet; Style Network; Sundance Channel; TeenNick; Toon Disney; Trinity Broadcasting Network; VH1 Classic; VH1 Soul.
Fee: $14.34 monthly.

Digital Pay Service 1
Pay Units: N.A.
Programming (via satellite): Cinemax (multiplexed); HBO (multiplexed); Showtime (multiplexed); Starz (multiplexed); The Movie Channel (multiplexed).
Pay-Per-View
iN DEMAND (delivered digitally); Fresh (delivered digitally); Spice: Xcess (delivered digitally).
Internet Service
Operational: Yes.
Broadband Service: Cebridge High Speed Cable Internet.
Fee: $29.95 monthly.
Telephone Service
Digital: Operational
Fee: $44.95 monthly
Miles of Plant: 80.0 (coaxial); None (fiber optic). Homes passed: 4,905.
Chief Technician: Jerry Raby. Manager: Paul Eddington.
City fee: $0.50 per subscriber annually.
Ownership: Cequel Communications LLC (MSO).

NORMAN—Community Communications Co., 1920 Hwy 425 N, Monticello, AR 71655-4463. Phones: 800-272-2191; 870-367-7300. Fax: 870-367-9770. E-mail: generalmanager@ccc-cable.net. Web Site: http://www.ccc-cable.net. ICA: AR0167.
TV Market Ranking: Below 100 (NORMAN). Franchise award date: N.A. Franchise expiration date: N.A. Began: January 1, 1972.
Channel capacity: 48 (not 2-way capable). Channels available but not in use: N.A.
Basic Service
Subscribers: 64.
Programming (received off-air): KARK-TV (NBC) Little Rock; KATV (ABC) Little Rock; KETG (PBS) Arkadelphia; KFSM-TV (CBS) Fort Smith; KLRT-TV (FOX) Little Rock; KTHV (CBS) Little Rock; allband FM.
Programming (via satellite): ABC Family Channel; AMC; Arts & Entertainment; CNN; Country Music TV; Discovery Channel; ESPN; FX; Lifetime; Nickelodeon; Outdoor Channel; QVC; Spike TV; Syfy; TBS Superstation; The Learning Channel; Trinity Broadcasting Network; Turner Classic Movies; Turner Network TV; TV Land; USA Network; VH1; WGN America.
Fee: $10.00 installation; $33.60 monthly.
Pay Service 1
Pay Units: N.A.
Programming (via satellite): Showtime; The Movie Channel.
Fee: $8.00 monthly (each).
Video-On-Demand: No
Internet Service
Operational: No.
Telephone Service
None
Miles of Plant: 4.0 (coaxial); None (fiber optic). Homes passed: 260.
Manager: Larry Ivy.
City fee: 2% of gross.
Ownership: Community Communications Co. (MSO).

OAK GROVE HEIGHTS—Fusion Media, 1910 Mockingbird Ln, Paragould, AR 72450. Phones: 870-586-0216; 870-919-1454. E-mail: goodwintechnologies@gmail.com. Web Site: http://www.fusion-media.tv. Also serves Craighead County (portions) & Greene County (portions). ICA: AR0273.
TV Market Ranking: Below 100 (OAK GROVE HEIGHTS). Franchise award date: N.A. Franchise expiration date: N.A. Began: November 1, 1983.
Channel capacity: N.A. Channels available but not in use: N.A.
Basic Service
Subscribers: 175.
Programming (received off-air): KAIT (ABC) Jonesboro; KTEJ (PBS) Jonesboro; WMC-TV (NBC) Memphis; WPTY-TV (ABC) Memphis; WREG-TV (CBS) Memphis.
Programming (via satellite): Disney Channel; Headline News.
Fee: $25.00 installation; $31.45 monthly.
Pay Service 1
Pay Units: 25.
Programming (via satellite): Cinemax.
Fee: $10.00 installation; $9.95 monthly.
Pay Service 2
Pay Units: 25.
Programming (via satellite): HBO.
Fee: $10.95 monthly.
Video-On-Demand: No
Internet Service
Operational: Yes.
Fee: $29.99-$59.99 monthly.
Telephone Service
None
Miles of Plant: 15.0 (coaxial); None (fiber optic).
General Manager: Kenneth Goodwin.
Ownership: MM & G Enterprises LLC.

OIL TROUGH—Indco Cable TV, PO Box 3799, 2700 N Saint Louis, Batesville, AR 72503-3799. Phone: 870-793-4174. Fax: 870-793-7439. Web Site: http://www.indco.net. ICA: AR0274.
TV Market Ranking: Outside TV Markets (OIL TROUGH). Franchise award date: N.A. Franchise expiration date: N.A. Began: January 1, 1984.
Channel capacity: N.A. Channels available but not in use: N.A.
Basic Service
Subscribers: 51.
Programming (received off-air): KAIT (ABC) Jonesboro; KARK-TV (NBC) Little Rock; KATV (ABC) Little Rock; KEMV (PBS) Mountain View; KTHV (CBS) Little Rock.
Programming (via satellite): CNN; Discovery Channel; Disney Channel; ESPN; ESPN 2; HGTV; Lifetime; Nickelodeon; Spike TV; Syfy; TBS Superstation; Turner Classic Movies; Turner Network TV; USA Network; Weather Channel; WGN America.
Fee: $20.00 installation; $30.95 monthly; $10.00 additional installation.
Pay Service 1
Pay Units: 1.
Programming (via satellite): HBO.
Fee: $10.00 installation; $10.00 monthly.
Video-On-Demand: Planned
Internet Service
Operational: Yes.
Fee: $29.95 monthly.
Telephone Service
None
Miles of Plant: 2.0 (coaxial); None (fiber optic).
Manager: J. D. Pierce. Chief Technician: Tommy Barnett. Marketing Director: Connie Barnett.
City fee: 1% of gross.
Ownership: Indco Cable TV (MSO).

O'KEAN—Formerly served by Cebridge Connections. No longer in operation. ICA: AR0207.

OSCEOLA—Ritter Communications. Now served by MARKED TREE, AR [AR0072]. ICA: AR0029.

OXFORD—Formerly served by Almega Cable. No longer in operation. ICA: AR0205.

OZARK—Suddenlink Communications, 310 N 3rd St, Ozark, AR 72949-2810. Phones: 479-964-1076; 479-667-2738; 800-582-9577. Web Site: http://www.suddenlink.com. Also serves Altus. ICA: AR0275.
TV Market Ranking: Below 100 (OZARK); Outside TV Markets (Altus). Franchise award date: N.A. Franchise expiration date: N.A. Began: July 1, 1965.
Channel capacity: 41 (not 2-way capable). Channels available but not in use: N.A.
Basic Service
Subscribers: 1,465.
Programming (received off-air): KAFT (PBS) Fayetteville; KARK-TV (NBC) Little Rock; KFSM-TV (CBS) Fort Smith; KFTA-TV (FOX) Fort Smith; KHBS (ABC) Fort Smith; KPBI-CA (FOX) Fort Smith; KTHV (CBS) Little Rock.
Programming (via satellite): ABC Family Channel; Arts & Entertainment; CNN; Comcast Sports Net Southwest; C-SPAN; C-SPAN 2; Discovery Channel; Disney Channel; ESPN; ESPN 2; Great American Country; Headline News; HGTV; History Channel; Home Shopping Network; ION Television; Lifetime; Nickelodeon; Spike TV; TBS Superstation; The Learning Channel; Trinity Broadcasting Network; Turner Classic Movies; Turner Network TV; TV Land; USA Network; VH1; Weather Channel; WGN America.
Fee: $38.00 installation; $30.99 monthly.
Digital Basic Service
Subscribers: N.A.
Programming (via satellite): BBC America; Bio; Bloomberg Television; Discovery Digital Networks; DMX Music; Encore Action; ESPNews; Fox Sports World; G4; Golf Channel; GSN; Halogen Network; History Channel International; Lifetime Movie Network; MuchMusic Network; Outdoor Channel; Speed Channel; Sundance Channel; Toon Disney; Versus.
Pay Service 1
Pay Units: 515.
Programming (via satellite): Cinemax; HBO; Showtime.
Fee: $30.00 installation; $10.00 monthly (Showtime), $11.95 monthly (Cinemax or HBO).
Digital Pay Service 1
Pay Units: N.A.
Programming (via satellite): Cinemax (multiplexed); Encore (multiplexed); HBO (multiplexed); Showtime (multiplexed); Starz (multiplexed); The Movie Channel.
Video-On-Demand: No
Pay-Per-View
ESPN Gameplan (delivered digitally); ESPN Now (delivered digitally); Shorteez (delivered digitally); Fresh (delivered digitally); Playboy TV (delivered digitally); iN DEMAND (delivered digitally); Special events, Addressable: No.
Internet Service
Operational: No.
Telephone Service
None
Miles of Plant: 38.0 (coaxial); None (fiber optic). Homes passed: 2,721. Total homes in franchised area: 2,721.
Vice President: Mark Williams. Manager: Jeff Jech. Marketing Director: Tina Gabbard. Chief Technician: Clint Petty.
Ownership: Cequel Communications LLC (MSO).

OZARK ACRES—Formerly served by Cebridge Connections. No longer in operation. ICA: AR0155.

PALESTINE—Formerly served by Almega Cable. No longer in operation. ICA: AR0191.

PANGBURN—Indco Cable TV, PO Box 3799, 2700 N Saint Louis, Batesville, AR 72503-3799. Phone: 870-793-4174. Fax: 870-793-7439. Web Site: http://www.indco.net. Also serves Albion & Letona. ICA: AR0276.
TV Market Ranking: Outside TV Markets (Albion, Letona, PANGBURN). Franchise award date: N.A. Franchise expiration date: N.A. Began: January 1, 1984.
Channel capacity: 36 (operating 2-way). Channels available but not in use: N.A.
Basic Service
Subscribers: 572.
Programming (received off-air): KARK-TV (NBC) Little Rock; KASN (CW) Pine Bluff; KATV (ABC) Little Rock; KEMV (PBS) Mountain View; KKYK-DT (IND) Camden; KLRT-TV (FOX) Little Rock; KTHV (CBS) Little Rock.
Programming (via satellite): ABC Family Channel; Arts & Entertainment; CNN; Comcast Sports Net Southwest; Country Music TV; Discovery Channel; Disney Channel; ESPN; ESPN 2; FX; HGTV; History Channel; Lifetime; Nickelodeon; Outdoor Channel; QVC; Spike TV; Syfy; TBS Superstation; Trinity Broadcasting Network; Turner Classic Movies; Turner Network TV; USA Network; Weather Channel; WGN America.
Fee: $30.95 monthly.
Pay Service 1
Pay Units: 7.
Programming (via satellite): Cinemax.
Fee: $8.00 monthly.
Pay Service 2
Pay Units: 20.
Programming (via satellite): HBO.
Fee: $10.00 monthly.
Video-On-Demand: Planned
Internet Service
Operational: Yes.
Fee: $29.95 monthly.
Telephone Service
None
Miles of Plant: 8.0 (coaxial); None (fiber optic).
Marketing Director: Connie Barnett. Manager: J. D. Pierce. Chief Technician: Tommy Barnett.
Ownership: Indco Cable TV (MSO).

PARAGOULD—Paragould City Light & Water Commission, PO Box 9, 1901 Jones Rd, Paragould, AR 72451-0009. Phone: 870-239-7700. Fax: 870-239-7727. Web Site: http://www.clwc.com. ICA: AR0016.
TV Market Ranking: Below 100 (PARAGOULD). Franchise award date: December 1, 1989. Franchise expiration date: N.A. Began: January 31, 1991.
Channel capacity: N.A. Channels available but not in use: N.A.
Basic Service
Subscribers: 9,900.
Programming (received off-air): KAIT (ABC) Jonesboro; KARK-TV (NBC) Little Rock; KATV (ABC) Little Rock; KTEJ (PBS) Jonesboro; KVTJ-DT (IND) Jonesboro; WHBQ-TV (FOX) Memphis; WLMT (CW) Memphis; WMC-TV (NBC) Memphis; WPTY-TV (ABC) Memphis; WREG-TV (CBS) Memphis.
Programming (via satellite): C-SPAN; C-SPAN 2; HGTV; Home Shopping Network;

QVC; Trinity Broadcasting Network; TV Guide Network; Weather Channel.
Current originations: Leased Access; Religious Access; Government Access; Educational Access.
Fee: $10.67 monthly.

Expanded Basic Service 1
Subscribers: N.A.
Programming (via satellite): ABC Family Channel; AMC; AmericanLife TV Network; Animal Planet; Arts & Entertainment; Cartoon Network; CNBC; CNN; Comcast Sports Net Southwest; Comedy Central; Country Music TV; Discovery Channel; Disney Channel; E! Entertainment Television; ESPN; ESPN 2; ESPN Classic Sports; ESPNews; Food Network; Fox News Channel; FX; Hallmark Channel; Headline News; History Channel; Lifetime; MSNBC; MTV; National Geographic Channel; Nickelodeon; Outdoor Channel; Radar Channel; Spike TV; Syfy; TBS Superstation; The Learning Channel; Travel Channel; truTV; Turner Classic Movies; Turner Network TV; TV Land; USA Network; VH1; WGN America.
Fee: $20.38 monthly.

Digital Basic Service
Subscribers: N.A.
Programming (via satellite): Bio; Bloomberg Television; CMT Pure Country; Discovery Health Channel; Discovery Kids Channel; Discovery Military Channel; Discovery Planet Green; Do-It-Yourself; ESPN U; Eternal Word TV Network; FamilyNet; Fox Movie Channel; Fox Reality Channel; FSN Digital Atlantic; FSN Digital Central; FSN Digital Pacific; Fuel TV; Golf Channel; History Channel International; ID Investigation Discovery; MTV Hits; MTV2; Nick Jr.; NickToons TV; Science Channel; SoapNet; Speed Channel; Style Network; Sundance Channel; TeenNick; Toon Disney; Versus; VH1 Classic; WE tv.
Fee: $13.12 monthly.

Digital Expanded Basic Service
Subscribers: N.A.
Programming (received off-air): KAIT (ABC) Jonesboro; WHBQ-TV (FOX) Memphis; WKNO (PBS) Memphis; WMC-TV (NBC) Memphis; WREG-TV (CBS) Memphis.
Programming (via satellite): Arts & Entertainment HD; Bio HD; Discovery Channel HD; ESPN 2 HD; ESPN HD; HDNet; HDNet Movies; History Channel HD.
Fee: $7.10 monthly.

Pay Service 1
Pay Units: 1,226.
Programming (via satellite): Cinemax.
Fee: $9.77 monthly.

Pay Service 2
Pay Units: 1,268.
Programming (via satellite): Showtime; The Movie Channel.
Fee: $11.83 monthly.

Pay Service 3
Pay Units: 1,668.
Programming (via satellite): HBO (multiplexed).
Fee: $14.59 monthly.

Digital Pay Service 1
Pay Units: N.A.
Programming (via satellite): Cinemax (multiplexed); Encore (multiplexed); HBO (multiplexed); Showtime (multiplexed); Showtime; Starz (multiplexed); Starz HDTV; The Movie Channel.
Fee: $9.56 monthly (Starz/Encore), $9.77 monthly (Cinemax), $11.83 monthly (Showtime/TMC), $14.59 monthly (HBO).

Video-On-Demand: No

Pay-Per-View
Addressable homes: 508.
Hot Choice (delivered digitally), Fee: $1.95-$3.95, Addressable: Yes; iN DEMAND (delivered digitally).

Internet Service
Operational: Yes, dial-up. Began: June 1, 1998.
Broadband Service: In-house.
Fee: $22.95-$59.95 monthly.

Telephone Service
None

Miles of Plant: 180.0 (coaxial); 52.0 (fiber optic). Additional miles planned: 15.0 (fiber optic). Homes passed: 10,100.
General Manager & Chief Executive Officer: Bill Fischer. Chief Technician: Johnny Estes.
Franchise fee: 3% of gross.
Ownership: Paragould Light Water & Cable.

PARIS—Suddenlink Communications, 127 N Elmira Ave, Russellville, AR 72802-9614. Phones: 800-582-9577; 479-968-2223. Fax: 479-968-1343. Web Site: http://www.suddenlink.com. ICA: AR0054.
TV Market Ranking: Outside TV Markets (PARIS). Franchise award date: April 7, 1994. Franchise expiration date: N.A. Began: April 1, 1964.
Channel capacity: 62 (operating 2-way). Channels available but not in use: N.A.

Basic Service
Subscribers: 1,350.
Programming (received off-air): KAFT (PBS) Fayetteville; KFDF-CA Fort Smith; KFSM-TV (CBS) Fort Smith; KFTA-TV (FOX) Fort Smith; KHBS (ABC) Fort Smith; KNWA-TV (NBC) Rogers; KTHV (CBS) Little Rock.
Programming (via satellite): C-SPAN; CW+; QVC; TBS Superstation; Trinity Broadcasting Network; TV Guide Network; Weather Channel; WGN America.
Fee: $38.00 installation; $11.07 monthly; $4.15 converter.

Expanded Basic Service 1
Subscribers: 1,218.
Programming (via satellite): ABC Family Channel; AMC; Animal Planet; Arts & Entertainment; Cartoon Network; CNBC; CNN; Comcast Sports Net Southwest; Discovery Channel; Disney Channel; E! Entertainment Television; ESPN; ESPN 2; Food Network; Fox News Channel; Great American Country; Headline News; HGTV; History Channel; Lifetime; Nickelodeon; Outdoor Channel; Speed Channel; Spike TV; Syfy; The Learning Channel; Turner Network TV; TV Land; USA Network; Versus; VH1.
Fee: $25.24 monthly.

Digital Basic Service
Subscribers: N.A.
Programming (via satellite): BBC America; Bio; Bloomberg Television; Discovery Health Channel; Discovery Home Channel; Discovery Kids Channel; Discovery Military Channel; Discovery Times Channel; DMX Music; ESPN Classic Sports; ESPNews; Fox Soccer; Fuse; G4; Golf Channel; GSN; Halogen Network; History Channel International; Independent Film Channel; Lifetime Movie Network; Science Channel; Sundance Channel; Toon Disney.

Digital Pay Service 1
Pay Units: N.A.
Programming (via satellite): Cinemax (multiplexed); Encore (multiplexed); HBO (multiplexed); Showtime (multiplexed); Starz (multiplexed); The Movie Channel (multiplexed).

Video-On-Demand: No

Pay-Per-View
iN DEMAND (delivered digitally); Playboy TV (delivered digitally); Fresh (delivered digitally); Spice: Xcess (delivered digitally).

Internet Service
Operational: Yes.
Broadband Service: Cebridge High Speed Cable Internet.
Fee: $29.95 monthly.

Telephone Service
Digital: Operational
Fee: $44.95 monthly

Miles of Plant: 32.0 (coaxial); None (fiber optic). Homes passed: 1,767. Total homes in franchised area: 1,781.
System Manager: Mike Ederington. Field System Manager: Wayne Ollis. Customer Service Manager: Jane Howell. Field Services Manager: Clint Petty.
City fee: 3% of gross.
Ownership: Cequel Communications LLC (MSO).

PEARCY—Community Communications Co., 1920 Hwy 425 N, Monticello, AR 71655-4463. Phones: 800-272-2191; 870-367-7300. Fax: 870-367-9770. E-mail: generalmanager@ccc-cable.net. Web Site: http://www.ccc-cable.net. ICA: AR0089.
TV Market Ranking: Below 100 (PEARCY). Franchise award date: N.A. Franchise expiration date: N.A. Began: N.A.
Channel capacity: 48 (not 2-way capable). Channels available but not in use: N.A.

Basic Service
Subscribers: 339.
Programming (received off-air): KARK-TV (NBC) Little Rock; KATV (ABC) Little Rock; KETG (PBS) Arkadelphia; KLRT-TV (FOX) Little Rock; KTHV (CBS) Little Rock.
Programming (via satellite): ABC Family Channel; Arts & Entertainment; CNBC; CNN; Comcast Sports Net Southwest; Country Music TV; Discovery Channel; E! Entertainment Television; ESPN; ESPN 2; Fox News Channel; FX; Headline News; Lifetime; MTV; Nickelodeon; Outdoor Channel; QVC; Spike TV; Syfy; TBS Superstation; The Learning Channel; Trinity Broadcasting Network; Turner Classic Movies; Turner Network TV; TV Land; USA Network; Weather Channel; WGN America.
Fee: $30.00 installation; $23.50 monthly; $3.50 converter; $20.00 additional installation.

Pay Service 1
Pay Units: 49.
Programming (via satellite): Cinemax; HBO; Showtime; The Movie Channel.
Fee: $10.00 monthly (each).

Internet Service
Operational: No.

Telephone Service
None

Miles of Plant: 44.0 (coaxial); None (fiber optic). Homes passed: 950. Total homes in franchised area: 950.
Manager: Jackie Kennedy. Operations Manager: Larry Ivy.
Ownership: Community Communications Co. (MSO).

PERRYVILLE—Alliance Communications, PO Box 960, 290 S Broadview St, Greenbrier, AR 72058-9616. Phone: 501-679-6619. Fax: 501-679-5694. Web Site: http://www.alliancecable.net. ICA: AR0318.
TV Market Ranking: 50 (PERRYVILLE). Franchise award date: N.A. Franchise expiration date: N.A. Began: N.A.
Channel capacity: 65 (not 2-way capable). Channels available but not in use: 16.

Basic Service
Subscribers: 345.
Programming (received off-air): KARK-TV (NBC) Little Rock; KATV (ABC) Little Rock; KETS (PBS) Little Rock; KLRA-LP Little Rock; KLRT-TV (FOX) Little Rock; KTHV (CBS) Little Rock; KVTN-DT (IND) Pine Bluff.
Programming (via satellite): ABC Family Channel; Arts & Entertainment; CNN; Country Music TV; Discovery Channel; Disney Channel; ESPN; MTV; Nickelodeon; Spike TV; TBS Superstation; truTV; Turner Classic Movies; Turner Network TV; USA Network; Weather Channel; WGN America.
Fee: $32.00 monthly.

Digital Basic Service
Subscribers: 41.
Fee: $42.00 monthly.

Digital Pay Service 1
Pay Units: 1.
Programming (via satellite): HBO (multiplexed).
Fee: $11.95 monthly.

Digital Pay Service 2
Pay Units: 16.
Programming (via satellite): Showtime (multiplexed).
Fee: $11.95 monthly.

Digital Pay Service 3
Pay Units: N.A.
Programming (via satellite): Cinemax (multiplexed).
Fee: $11.95 monthly.

Digital Pay Service 4
Pay Units: 1.
Programming (via satellite): The Movie Channel (multiplexed).
Fee: $11.95 monthly.

Digital Pay Service 5
Pay Units: 1.
Programming (via satellite): Flix.
Fee: $11.95 monthly.

Digital Pay Service 6
Pay Units: 1.
Programming (via satellite): Sundance Channel.
Fee: $11.95 monthly.

Digital Pay Service 7
Pay Units: 1.
Programming (via satellite): Starz (multiplexed).
Fee: $11.95 monthly.

Digital Pay Service 8
Pay Units: 1.
Programming (via satellite): Encore (multiplexed).
Fee: $11.95 monthly.

Video-On-Demand: No

Internet Service
Operational: No.

Telephone Service
None
Miles of Plant: 57.0 (coaxial); None (fiber optic). Homes passed: 1,515. Total homes in franchised area: 1,515.
Vice President: Arl Cope. Operations Manager: Jeff Browers. Programming & Marketing Manager: James Fuller.
Ownership: Buford Media Group LLC (MSO).

PINE BLUFF—Pine Bluff Cable TV Co. Inc., PO Box 9008, 715 S Poplar St, Pine Bluff, AR 71601-4842. Phones: 870-879-4734 (Headend); 870-536-0350. Fax: 870-536-0351. E-mail: pinebluffcabletvcs@cablelynx.com. Web Site: http://www.pinebluffcabletv.com. Also serves Jefferson County (portions) & Whitehall (portions). ICA: AR0006.
TV Market Ranking: 50 (Jefferson County (portions), PINE BLUFF, Whitehall (portions)). Franchise award date: October 1, 1975. Franchise expiration date: N.A. Began: May 31, 1976.
Channel capacity: 116 (operating 2-way). Channels available but not in use: 41.
Basic Service
Subscribers: 15,500.
Programming (received off-air): KARK-TV (NBC) Little Rock; KASN (CW) Pine Bluff; KATV (ABC) Little Rock; KETS (PBS) Little Rock; KKYK-DT (IND) Camden; KLRT-TV (FOX) Little Rock; KTHV (CBS) Little Rock.
Programming (via satellite): ABC Family Channel; AMC; Animal Planet; Arts & Entertainment; BET Networks; Cartoon Network; CNBC; CNN; Comcast Sports Net Southwest; Comedy Central; Country Music TV; C-SPAN; C-SPAN 2; Discovery Channel; Disney Channel; ESPN; ESPN 2; ESPN Classic Sports; Eternal Word TV Network; Food Network; Fox News Channel; FX; Hallmark Channel; Headline News; HGTV; History Channel; Home Shopping Network; Lifetime; MSNBC; MTV; NASA TV; National Geographic Channel; Nickelodeon; ShopNBC; Sneak Prevue; Spike TV; Syfy; TBS Superstation; The Learning Channel; truTV; Turner Classic Movies; Turner Network TV; TV Guide Network; TV Land; USA Network; VH1; Weather Channel; WGN America.
Current originations: Educational Access; Government Access; Public Access.
Fee: $40.00 installation; $48.90 monthly; $3.19 converter.
Digital Basic Service
Subscribers: 1,500.
Programming (via satellite): AmericanLife TV Network; BBC America; Bio; CMT Pure Country; Discovery Health Channel; Discovery Kids Channel; Discovery Military Channel; Discovery Planet Green; DMX Music; ESPNews; FitTV; Fox Soccer; FSN Digital Atlantic; FSN Digital Central; FSN Digital Pacific; G4; Golf Channel; Great American Country; GSN; Halogen Network; History Channel International; ID Investigation Discovery; Lifetime Movie Network; MTV Hits; MTV Jams; MTV Tres; MTV2; National Geographic Channel; Nick Jr.; Nick Too; NickToons TV; Outdoor Channel; Science Channel; SoapNet; Speed Channel; Style Network; TeenNick; Toon Disney; VH1 Classic; VH1 Soul; WE tv.
Fee: $10.00 monthly.
Digital Expanded Basic Service
Subscribers: N.A.
Programming (received off-air): KARK-TV (NBC) Little Rock; KATV (ABC) Little Rock; KTHV (CBS) Little Rock.
Programming (via satellite): CNN HD; Discovery Channel HD; ESPN HD; HDNet; HDNet Movies; Outdoor Channel 2 HD; PBS HD; TBS in HD; Turner Network TV HD.
Fee: $5.00 monthly.
Digital Pay Service 1
Pay Units: N.A.
Programming (via satellite): Cinemax (multiplexed); Cinemax HD; Encore (multiplexed); HBO (multiplexed); HBO HD; Starz (multiplexed); Starz HDTV.
Fee: $12.95 monthly (HBO, Cinemax, or Starz/Encore).
Video-On-Demand: No
Pay-Per-View
Movies, Fee: $3.99, Addressable: Yes.
Internet Service
Operational: Yes.
Subscribers: 100.
Broadband Service: Cablelynx.
Fee: $24.95-$44.95 monthly; $10.00 modem lease.
Telephone Service
Digital: Operational
Fee: $45.70 monthly
Miles of Plant: 420.0 (coaxial); 400.0 (fiber optic). Additional miles planned: 17.0 (coaxial). Homes passed: 21,000. Total homes in franchised area: 25,000.
General Manager: Mark Billingsly. Technical Supervisor: Mike Spokes. Customer Service & Office Manager: Jena Jones.
Franchise fee: 3% of gross.
Ownership: WEHCO Video Inc. (MSO).

PINE BLUFF (southern portion)—Formerly served by Almega Cable. No longer in operation. ICA: AR0277.
TV Market Ranking: 50 (PINE BLUFF).

PINEBERGEN—Rapid Cable, 515 E Longview Dr, Arp, TX 75750. Phone: 903-859-6492. Fax: 903-859-3708. Also serves Jefferson County (portions) & Sulphur Springs. ICA: AR0110.
TV Market Ranking: 50 (Jefferson County (portions), PINEBERGEN, Sulphur Springs). Franchise award date: N.A. Franchise expiration date: N.A. Began: February 1, 1990.
Channel capacity: 48 (not 2-way capable). Channels available but not in use: N.A.
Basic Service
Subscribers: 364.
Programming (received off-air): KAFT (PBS) Fayetteville; KHOG-TV (ABC) Fayetteville; KNWA-TV (NBC) Rogers; KOAM-TV (CBS) Pittsburg; KODE-TV (ABC) Joplin; KSNF (NBC) Joplin; KTAJ-TV (TBN) St. Joseph; KTUL (ABC) Tulsa.
Programming (via satellite): ABC Family Channel; AMC; Animal Planet; Arts & Entertainment; Cartoon Network; CNBC; CNN; Comcast Sports Net Southwest; C-SPAN; Discovery Channel; Disney Channel; E! Entertainment Television; ESPN; ESPN 2; Food Network; Fox News Channel; GalaVision; Great American Country; Headline News; HGTV; INSP; Lifetime; National Geographic Channel; Nickelodeon; QVC; Spike TV; Syfy; TBS Superstation; The Learning Channel; Trinity Broadcasting Network; Turner Network TV; TV Land; Univision; USA Network; Weather Channel.
Fee: $54.95 installation; $44.05 monthly.
Digital Basic Service
Subscribers: N.A.
Programming (via satellite): BBC America; Bio; Bloomberg Television; Discovery Health Channel; Discovery Kids Channel; Discovery Military Channel; Discovery Planet Green; DMX Music; ESPN Classic Sports; ESPNews; Fox College Sports Atlantic; Fox College Sports Central; Fox College Sports Pacific; Fox Soccer; Fuse; G4; Golf Channel; GSN; History Channel; History Channel International; ID Investigation Discovery; Independent Film Channel; Outdoor Channel; Science Channel; ShopNBC; Sleuth; Speed Channel; Style Network; Sundance Channel; Toon Disney; Turner Classic Movies; Versus; WE tv.
Pay Service 1
Pay Units: 52.
Fee: $12.95 monthly.
Pay Service 2
Pay Units: 87.
Fee: $12.95 monthly.
Pay Service 3
Pay Units: 128.
Fee: $12.95 monthly.
Digital Pay Service 1
Pay Units: N.A.
Programming (via satellite): Cinemax (multiplexed); Encore (multiplexed); Flix; HBO (multiplexed); Showtime (multiplexed); Starz (multiplexed); The Movie Channel (multiplexed).
Video-On-Demand: No
Pay-Per-View
iN DEMAND (delivered digitally); Playboy TV (delivered digitally).
Internet Service
Operational: No.
Telephone Service
None
Miles of Plant: 87.0 (coaxial); None (fiber optic). Homes passed: 1,900.
Regional Manager: Mike Taylor. Chief Technician: Larry Stafford.
Ownership: Rapid Communications LLC (MSO).

PLAINVIEW—Indco Cable TV, PO Box 3799, 2700 N Saint Louis, Batesville, AR 72503-3799. Phone: 870-793-4174. Fax: 870-793-7439. Web Site: http://www.indco.net. ICA: AR0303.
TV Market Ranking: Outside TV Markets (PLAINVIEW). Franchise award date: N.A. Franchise expiration date: N.A. Began: N.A.
Channel capacity: 36 (operating 2-way). Channels available but not in use: N.A.
Basic Service
Subscribers: 489.
Programming (received off-air): KARK-TV (NBC) Little Rock; KASN (CW) Pine Bluff; KATV (ABC) Little Rock; KKYK-DT (IND) Camden; KLRT-TV (FOX) Little Rock; KTHV (CBS) Little Rock.
Programming (via satellite): ABC Family Channel; Arts & Entertainment; Cartoon Network; CNN; Comcast Sports Net Southwest; Country Music TV; Discovery Channel; Disney Channel; ESPN; ESPN 2; FX; HGTV; History Channel; Lifetime; Nickelodeon; Outdoor Channel; QVC; Spike TV; Syfy; TBS Superstation; Trinity Broadcasting Network; Turner Classic Movies; Turner Network TV; TV Land; USA Network; Weather Channel; WGN America.
Fee: $26.95 monthly.
Pay Service 1
Pay Units: 23.
Programming (via satellite): HBO.
Fee: $10.00 monthly.
Pay Service 2
Pay Units: 13.
Programming (via satellite): The Movie Channel.
Fee: $9.00 monthly.
Video-On-Demand: Planned
Internet Service
Operational: Yes.
Fee: $29.95 monthly.
Telephone Service
None
Manager: J.D. Pierce. Chief Technician: Tommy Barnett. Marketing Director: Connie Barnett.
Ownership: Indco Cable TV (MSO).

PLAINVIEW—Rapid Cable, 515 E Longview Dr, Arp, TX 75750. Phone: 903-859-6492. Fax: 903-859-3708. Also serves Ola & Yell County (eastern portion). ICA: AR0085.
TV Market Ranking: Below 100 (Yell County (eastern portion) (portions)); Outside TV Markets (Ola, PLAINVIEW, Yell County (eastern portion) (portions)). Franchise award date: N.A. Franchise expiration date: N.A. Began: December 1, 1982.
Channel capacity: 36 (not 2-way capable). Channels available but not in use: N.A.
Basic Service
Subscribers: 221.
Programming (received off-air): KAFT (PBS) Fayetteville; KARK-TV (NBC) Little Rock; KATV (ABC) Little Rock; KLRT-TV (FOX) Little Rock; KTHV (CBS) Little Rock.
Programming (via satellite): CNN.
Fee: $54.95 installation; $20.95 monthly.
Expanded Basic Service 1
Subscribers: N.A.
Programming (via satellite): ABC Family Channel; AMC; Animal Planet; Arts & Entertainment; CNN; Comcast Sports Net Southwest; Discovery Channel; Disney Channel; ESPN; ESPN 2; Fox News Channel; Great American Country; Headline News; HGTV; Home Shopping Network; Lifetime; National Geographic Channel; Nickelodeon; Outdoor Channel; Spike TV; TBS Superstation; The Learning Channel; Trinity Broadcasting Network; Turner Network TV; USA Network; Weather Channel.
Fee: $23.10 monthly.
Digital Basic Service
Subscribers: N.A.
Programming (via satellite): AmericanLife TV Network; BBC America; Bio; Bloomberg Television; Discovery Health Channel; Discovery Kids Channel; Discovery Military Channel; Discovery Planet Green; DMX Music; ESPN 2; ESPN Classic Sports; ESPNews; Fox College Sports Atlantic; Fox College Sports Central; Fox College Sports Pacific; Fox Soccer; Fuse; G4; Golf Channel; GSN; Halogen Network; HGTV; History Channel; History Channel International; ID Investigation Discovery; Lifetime Movie Network; Outdoor Channel; Ovation; Science Channel; ShopNBC; Sleuth; Speed Channel; Style Network; Syfy; Trinity Broadcasting Network; Turner Classic Movies; Versus; WE tv.
Pay Service 1
Pay Units: 5.
Programming (via satellite): HBO.
Fee: $12.95 monthly.
Pay Service 2
Pay Units: 12.
Programming (via satellite): The Movie Channel.
Fee: $12.95 monthly.
Pay Service 3
Pay Units: 38.
Programming (via satellite): Showtime.
Fee: $12.95 monthly.
Digital Pay Service 1
Pay Units: N.A.
Programming (via satellite): Cinemax (multiplexed); Encore (multiplexed); Flix; HBO (multiplexed); Showtime (multiplexed); Starz (multiplexed); The Movie Channel (multiplexed).
Video-On-Demand: No

Pay-Per-View
iN DEMAND (delivered digitally); Playboy TV (delivered digitally); Club Jenna (delivered digitally).
Internet Service
Operational: No.
Telephone Service
None
Miles of Plant: 29.0 (coaxial); None (fiber optic). Homes passed: 1,179.
Regional Manager: Mike Taylor. Chief Technician: Larry Stafford.
City fee: 2% of gross.
Ownership: Rapid Communications LLC (MSO).

PLEASANT PLAINS—Indco Cable TV, PO Box 3799, 2700 N Saint Louis, Batesville, AR 72503-3799. Phone: 870-793-4174. Fax: 870-793-7439. Web Site: http://www.indco.net. Also serves Independence County (unincorporated areas). ICA: AR0278.
TV Market Ranking: Outside TV Markets (Independence County (unincorporated areas), PLEASANT PLAINS). Franchise award date: N.A. Franchise expiration date: N.A. Began: November 1, 1989.
Channel capacity: 36 (operating 2-way). Channels available but not in use: N.A.
Basic Service
Subscribers: 96.
Programming (received off-air): KAIT (ABC) Jonesboro; KARK-TV (NBC) Little Rock; KASN (CW) Pine Bluff; KATV (ABC) Little Rock; KEMV (PBS) Mountain View; KLRT-TV (FOX) Little Rock; KTHV (CBS) Little Rock.
Programming (via satellite): ABC Family Channel; CNN; Country Music TV; Discovery Channel; Disney Channel; ESPN; ESPN 2; HGTV; Lifetime; Nickelodeon; Outdoor Channel; QVC; Spike TV; Syfy; TBS Superstation; Trinity Broadcasting Network; Turner Network TV; USA Network; Weather Channel; WGN America.
Fee: $30.95 monthly.
Pay Service 1
Pay Units: 2.
Programming (via satellite): Cinemax.
Fee: $8.00 monthly.
Pay Service 2
Pay Units: 2.
Programming (via satellite): Cinemax; HBO.
Fee: $16.00 monthly.
Video-On-Demand: Planned
Internet Service
Operational: Yes.
Fee: $29.95 monthly.
Telephone Service
None
Manager: J. D. Pierce. Chief Technician: Tommy Barnett. Marketing Director: Connie Barnett.
Ownership: Indco Cable TV (MSO).

PLUMERVILLE—Alliance Communications, PO Box 960, 290 S Broadview St, Greenbrier, AR 72058-9616. Phone: 501-679-6619. Fax: 501-679-5694. Web Site: http://www.alliancecable.net. Also serves Menifee. ICA: AR0149.
TV Market Ranking: 50 (Menifee, PLUMERVILLE). Franchise award date: N.A. Franchise expiration date: N.A. Began: January 1, 1990.
Channel capacity: 65 (not 2-way capable). Channels available but not in use: 10.
Basic Service
Subscribers: 288.
Programming (received off-air): KARK-TV (NBC) Little Rock; KARZ-TV (MNT) Little Rock; KASN (CW) Pine Bluff; KATV (ABC) Little Rock; KETS (PBS) Little Rock; KKYK-CA (IND) Little Rock; KLRT-TV (FOX) Little Rock; KTHV (CBS) Little Rock.
Programming (via satellite): ABC Family Channel; AMC; Animal Planet; Arts & Entertainment; BET Networks; Cartoon Network; CNN; Country Music TV; C-SPAN; Discovery Channel; Disney Channel; ESPN; ESPN 2; GSN; Hallmark Channel; HGTV; History Channel; Home Shopping Network; Lifetime; MTV; Nickelodeon; Outdoor Channel; Spike TV; Syfy; TBS Superstation; The Learning Channel; truTV; Turner Classic Movies; Turner Network TV; TV Land; USA Network; VH1; Weather Channel; WGN America.
Fee: $10.00 installation; $32.00 monthly.
Digital Basic Service
Subscribers: 23.
Programming (via satellite): AmericanLife TV Network; BBC America; Bio; Bloomberg Television; Discovery Digital Networks; DMX Music; ESPN Classic Sports; ESPNews; Fox Movie Channel; Fox Sports World; Fuse; G4; GAS; Golf Channel; Halogen Network; History Channel International; Independent Film Channel; MTV Networks Digital Suite; National Geographic Channel; Nick Jr.; NickToons TV; Ovation; Speed Channel; Style Network; Sundance Channel; Trio; Versus; WE tv.
Fee: $42.00 monthly.
Pay Service 1
Pay Units: N.A.
Programming (via satellite): Cinemax; HBO.
Digital Pay Service 1
Pay Units: 49.
Programming (via satellite): HBO (multiplexed).
Fee: $11.95 monthly.
Digital Pay Service 2
Pay Units: N.A.
Programming (via satellite): Showtime (multiplexed).
Fee: $11.95 monthly.
Digital Pay Service 3
Pay Units: 6.
Programming (via satellite): Cinemax (multiplexed).
Fee: $11.95 monthly.
Digital Pay Service 4
Pay Units: 34.
Programming (via satellite): The Movie Channel (multiplexed).
Fee: $11.95 monthly.
Digital Pay Service 5
Pay Units: 6.
Programming (via satellite): Flix.
Fee: $11.95 monthly.
Digital Pay Service 6
Pay Units: 6.
Programming (via satellite): Encore.
Fee: $11.95 monthly.
Digital Pay Service 7
Pay Units: 6.
Programming (via satellite): Starz (multiplexed).
Fee: $11.95 monthly.
Video-On-Demand: No
Pay-Per-View
iN DEMAND (delivered digitally); Hot Choice (delivered digitally); Playboy TV (delivered digitally); Fresh (delivered digitally); Shorteez (delivered digitally).
Internet Service
Operational: No.
Telephone Service
None
Miles of Plant: 25.0 (coaxial); None (fiber optic). Homes passed: 1,433.

Vice President: Arl Cope. Operations Manager: Jeff Browers. Programming & Marketing Manager: James Fuller.
Ownership: Buford Media Group LLC (MSO).

POCAHONTAS—Suddenlink Communications, PO Box 370, 2728 Thomasville Rd, Pocahontas, AR 72455. Phone: 870-892-5801. Web Site: http://www.suddenlink.com. Also serves East Pocahontas. ICA: AR0036.
TV Market Ranking: Below 100 (East Pocahontas, POCAHONTAS). Franchise award date: N.A. Franchise expiration date: N.A. Began: January 1, 1961.
Channel capacity: N.A. Channels available but not in use: N.A.
Basic Service
Subscribers: 2,834.
Programming (received off-air): KAIT (ABC) Jonesboro; KARK-TV (NBC) Little Rock; KATV (ABC) Little Rock; KTEJ (PBS) Jonesboro; KTHV (CBS) Little Rock; KVTJ-DT (IND) Jonesboro; WHBQ-TV (FOX) Memphis; WMC-TV (NBC) Memphis; WREG-TV (CBS) Memphis; allband FM.
Programming (via satellite): CNN; C-SPAN; CW+; ESPN; Home Shopping Network; ION Television; MTV; QVC; TBS Superstation; TV Guide Network; Weather Channel; WGN America.
Current originations: Leased Access.
Fee: $35.00 installation; $10.00 monthly.
Expanded Basic Service 1
Subscribers: N.A.
Programming (via satellite): ABC Family Channel; AMC; Animal Planet; Arts & Entertainment; Bravo; Cartoon Network; CNBC; Comcast Sports Net Southwest; Comedy Central; Country Music TV; Discovery Channel; Disney Channel; E! Entertainment Television; ESPN 2; Eternal Word TV Network; Food Network; Fox News Channel; FX; Great American Country; Headline News; HGTV; History Channel; INSP; Lifetime; MSNBC; Nickelodeon; Oxygen; Speed Channel; Spike TV; Syfy; The Learning Channel; Travel Channel; truTV; Turner Classic Movies; Turner Network TV; TV Land; USA Network; Versus; VH1.
Digital Basic Service
Subscribers: N.A.
Programming (via satellite): BBC America; Bio; Bloomberg Television; Discovery Digital Networks; Encore Action; ESPN Classic Sports; ESPNews; Fox Sports World; G4; Golf Channel; GSN; Hallmark Channel; History Channel International; Independent Film Channel; Lifetime Movie Network; MuchMusic Network; Music Choice; Outdoor Channel; SoapNet; Sundance Channel; Toon Disney.
Pay Service 1
Pay Units: N.A.
Programming (via satellite): Cinemax; HBO; Showtime.
Fee: $8.00 monthly (Cinemax or Showtime), $9.00 monthly (HBO).
Digital Pay Service 1
Pay Units: N.A.
Programming (via satellite): Cinemax (multiplexed); HBO (multiplexed); Showtime (multiplexed); Starz (multiplexed); The Movie Channel (multiplexed).
Pay-Per-View
Playboy TV (delivered digitally); Fresh (delivered digitally); NBA TV (delivered digitally); ESPN Gameplan (delivered digitally); ESPN Now (delivered digitally); iN DEMAND (delivered digitally); Special events, Addressable: No.
Internet Service
Operational: Yes.
Fee: $29.95 monthly.
Telephone Service
None
Miles of Plant: 53.0 (coaxial); None (fiber optic). Homes passed: 3,000.
Manager: Gary Bowman.
City fee: $0.50 per subscriber annually.
Ownership: Cequel Communications LLC (MSO).

PORTLAND—Dean Hill Cable, PO Box 128, Parkdale, AR 71661. Phone: 870-473-2802. Fax: 870-737-0020. ICA: AR0323.
TV Market Ranking: Below 100 (PORTLAND). Franchise award date: N.A. Franchise expiration date: N.A. Began: September 1, 1981.
Channel capacity: N.A. Channels available but not in use: N.A.
Basic Service
Subscribers: 64.
Programming (received off-air): KATV (ABC) Little Rock; KLTM-TV (PBS) Monroe; KNOE-TV (CBS, CW) Monroe; KTVE (NBC) El Dorado; WABG-TV (ABC) Greenwood.
Programming (via satellite): Disney Channel; ESPN; TBS Superstation; Turner Network TV; WGN America.
Fee: $35.00 installation; $30.00 monthly.
Pay Service 1
Pay Units: 5.
Programming (via satellite): HBO.
Fee: $11.55 monthly.
Pay Service 2
Pay Units: 2.
Programming (via satellite): Showtime; The Movie Channel.
Fee: $11.55 monthly.
Internet Service
Operational: No.
Telephone Service
None
Manager: Dean Hill. Assistant Manager: Kathy Hill.
Ownership: Dean Hill Cable (MSO).

PRAIRIE GROVE—Cox Communications. Now served by SPRINGDALE, AR [AR0220]. ICA: AR0279.

RATCLIFF—Formerly served by Eagle Media. No longer in operation. ICA: AR0162.

RAVENDEN SPRINGS—Formerly served by Cebridge Connections. No longer in operation. ICA: AR0211.

RECTOR—NewWave Communications, 1311 Business Hwy 60 W, Dexter, MO 63841. Phones: 888-863-9928; 873-614-4573. Fax: 573-624-4371. E-mail: info@newwavecom.com. Web Site: http://www.newwavecom.com. Also serves Clay County (portions), Greenway, Lafe, Marmaduke, Piggott, Pollard & St. Francis. ICA: AR0081.

TV Market Ranking: Below 100 (Clay County (portions), Greenway, Lafe, Marmaduke, Piggott, Pollard, RECTOR, St. Francis). Franchise award date: N.A. Franchise expiration date: N.A. Began: January 1, 1970.

Channel capacity: 52 (operating 2-way). Channels available but not in use: N.A.

Basic Service

Subscribers: 2,714.

Programming (received off-air): KAIT (ABC) Jonesboro; KBSI (FOX) Cape Girardeau; KFVS-TV (CBS, CW) Cape Girardeau; KTEJ (PBS) Jonesboro; KVTJ-DT (IND) Jonesboro; WHBQ-TV (FOX) Memphis; WMC-TV (NBC) Memphis; WPSD-TV (NBC) Paducah; WREG-TV (CBS) Memphis; allband FM.

Programming (via satellite): C-SPAN; CW+; Home Shopping Network; INSP; QVC; Trinity Broadcasting Network; WGN America.

Fee: $61.50 installation; $17.95 monthly.

Expanded Basic Service 1

Subscribers: 2,584.

Programming (via satellite): ABC Family Channel; AMC; Animal Planet; Arts & Entertainment; BET Networks; Bravo; Cartoon Network; CNBC; CNN; Comcast Sports Net Southwest; Comedy Central; Country Music TV; Discovery Channel; Disney Channel; E! Entertainment Television; ESPN; ESPN 2; ESPN Classic Sports; Food Network; Fox News Channel; FX; Golf Channel; Great American Country; GSN; Hallmark Channel; Headline News; HGTV; History Channel; Jewelry Television; Lifetime; MSNBC; MTV; National Geographic Channel; Nickelodeon; Outdoor Channel; Oxygen; SoapNet; Speed Channel; Spike TV; Syfy; TBS Superstation; The Learning Channel; Travel Channel; truTV; Turner Classic Movies; Turner Network TV; TV Land; USA Network; VH1; Weather Channel.

Fee: $21.00 monthly.

Digital Basic Service

Subscribers: N.A.

Programming (received off-air): KAIT (ABC) Jonesboro; KBSI (FOX) Cape Girardeau; KFVS-TV (CBS, CW) Cape Girardeau; WPSD-TV (NBC) Paducah.

Programming (via satellite): Arts & Entertainment HD; BBC America; Bio; Bloomberg Television; CMT Pure Country; Discovery HD Theater; Discovery Health Channel; Discovery Kids Channel; Discovery Military Channel; Discovery Planet Green; Do-It-Yourself; ESPN 2 HD; ESPN Classic Sports; ESPN HD; ESPNews; Fox Movie Channel; FSN HD; G4; Great American Country; Halogen Network; HDNet; HDNet Movies; History Channel HD; History Channel International; ID Investigation Discovery; Independent Film Channel; Lifetime Movie Network; MTV Hits; MTV2; Music Choice; Nick Jr.; NickToons TV; Palladia; RFD-TV; Science Channel; Sleuth; Style Network; TeenNick; The Sportsman Channel; Toon Disney; Turner Classic Movies; Turner Network TV HD; USA Network HD; Versus; Versus HD; VH1 Classic; VH1 Soul; Weather Channel HD.

Digital Pay Service 1

Pay Units: N.A.

Programming (via satellite): Cinemax (multiplexed); Cinemax HD; Encore (multiplexed); Flix; HBO (multiplexed); HBO HD; Showtime (multiplexed); Starz (multiplexed); Starz HDTV; The Movie Channel (multiplexed).

Video-On-Demand: No

Pay-Per-View

iN DEMAND (delivered digitally); Playboy TV (delivered digitally); Hot Choice (delivered digitally); Fresh (delivered digitally); Club Jenna (delivered digitally); Shorteez (delivered digitally).

Internet Service

Operational: Yes. Began: November 1, 2004.

Fee: $40.00 installation; $31.99 monthly.

Telephone Service

Digital: Operational

Fee: $24.99 monthly

Miles of Plant: 101.0 (coaxial); None (fiber optic). Homes passed: 4,728.

General Manager: Ed Gargas. Technical Operations Manager: Jerry Townsend.

City fee: 3% of gross.

Ownership: NewWave Communications (MSO).

REED—Community Communications Co., 1920 Hwy 425 N, Monticello, AR 71655-4463. Phones: 800-272-2191; 870-367-7300. Fax: 870-367-9770. E-mail: generalmanager@ccc-cable.net. Web Site: http://www.ccc-cable.net. Also serves Tillar. ICA: AR0169.

TV Market Ranking: Below 100 (REED, Tillar). Franchise award date: N.A. Franchise expiration date: N.A. Began: January 1, 1980.

Channel capacity: 48 (not 2-way capable). Channels available but not in use: 18.

Basic Service

Subscribers: 117.

Programming (received off-air): KASN (CW) Pine Bluff; KATV (ABC) Little Rock; KETS (PBS) Little Rock; KLRT-TV (FOX) Little Rock; KTHV (CBS) Little Rock; KTVE (NBC) El Dorado; WXVT (CBS) Greenville.

Programming (via satellite): ABC Family Channel; AMC; Arts & Entertainment; BET Networks; CNN; Country Music TV; Discovery Channel; ESPN; ESPN 2; FX; Home Shopping Network; Lifetime; Nickelodeon; Outdoor Channel; QVC; Spike TV; Syfy; TBS Superstation; The Learning Channel; Trinity Broadcasting Network; Turner Network TV; TV Land; USA Network; VH1; WGN America.

Fee: $20.00 installation; $33.60 monthly.

Pay Service 1

Pay Units: 149.

Programming (via satellite): HBO; Showtime; The Movie Channel.

Fee: $11.00 monthly.

Video-On-Demand: No

Internet Service

Operational: No.

Telephone Service

None

Miles of Plant: 30.0 (coaxial); None (fiber optic). Homes passed: 250. Total homes in franchised area: 250.

Operations Manager: Larry Ivy.

Ownership: Community Communications Co. (MSO).

RISON—Community Communications Co., 1920 Hwy 425 N, Monticello, AR 71655-4463. Phones: 800-272-2191; 870-367-7300. Fax: 870-367-9770. E-mail: generalmanager@ccc-cable.net. Web Site: http://www.ccc-cable.net. ICA: AR0150.

TV Market Ranking: 50 (RISON). Franchise award date: N.A. Franchise expiration date: N.A. Began: July 16, 1982.

Channel capacity: 48 (not 2-way capable). Channels available but not in use: N.A.

Basic Service

Subscribers: 155.

Programming (received off-air): KARK-TV (NBC) Little Rock; KASN (CW) Pine Bluff; KATV (ABC) Little Rock; KETS (PBS) Little Rock; KLRT-TV (FOX) Little Rock; KTHV (CBS) Little Rock; KTVE (NBC) El Dorado; KVTN-DT (IND) Pine Bluff.

Programming (via satellite): ABC Family Channel; AMC; Arts & Entertainment; BET Networks; CNN; Country Music TV; Discovery Channel; Disney Channel; ESPN; ESPN 2; FX; Lifetime; Nickelodeon; Outdoor Channel; QVC; Spike TV; Syfy; TBS Superstation; The Learning Channel; Trinity Broadcasting Network; Turner Network TV; TV Land; USA Network; VH1; WGN America.

Fee: $30.00 installation; $33.60 monthly; $3.50 converter; $20.00 additional installation.

Pay Service 1

Pay Units: 14.

Programming (via satellite): HBO; Showtime; The Movie Channel.

Fee: $10.00 installation; $10.00 monthly (Showtime & TMC), $11.00 monthly (HBO).

Video-On-Demand: No

Internet Service

Operational: No.

Telephone Service

None

Miles of Plant: 12.0 (coaxial); None (fiber optic). Homes passed: 350. Total homes in franchised area: 400.

Manager: Larry Ivy.

Ownership: Community Communications Co. (MSO).

ROGERS—Cox Communications. Now served by SPRINGDALE, AR [AR0220]. ICA: AR0012.

ROYAL—Community Communications Co., 1920 Hwy 425 N, Monticello, AR 71655-4463. Phone: 870-367-7300. Fax: 870-367-9770. E-mail: generalmanager@ccc-cable.net. Web Site: http://www.ccc-cable.net. ICA: AR0125.

TV Market Ranking: Below 100 (ROYAL). Franchise award date: N.A. Franchise expiration date: N.A. Began: N.A.

Channel capacity: 48 (not 2-way capable). Channels available but not in use: N.A.

Basic Service

Subscribers: 249.

Programming (received off-air): KARK-TV (NBC) Little Rock; KASN (CW) Pine Bluff; KATV (ABC) Little Rock; KETG (PBS) Arkadelphia; KLRT-TV (FOX) Little Rock; KTHV (CBS) Little Rock; KVTH-DT (IND) Hot Springs.

Programming (via satellite): ABC Family Channel; AMC; Arts & Entertainment; CNN; Comcast Sports Net Southwest; Country Music TV; Discovery Channel; Disney Channel; ESPN; ESPN 2; Fox News Channel; FX; Headline News; HGTV; Home Shopping Network; Lifetime; MTV; Nickelodeon; Outdoor Channel; QVC; Spike TV; Syfy; TBS Superstation; The Learning Channel; Trinity Broadcasting Network; Turner Network TV; TV Land; USA Network; Weather Channel; WGN America.

Fee: $33.60 monthly.

Pay Service 1

Pay Units: N.A.

Programming (via satellite): HBO; Showtime; The Movie Channel.

Video-On-Demand: No

Internet Service

Operational: No.

Telephone Service

None

Miles of Plant: 25.0 (coaxial); None (fiber optic). Homes passed: 481.

Manager: Major Blissitt.

Ownership: Community Communications Co. (MSO).

RUDY/HIGHWAY 71—Cox Communications. Now served by FORT SMITH, AR [AR0003]. ICA: AR0281.

RUSSELL—Indco Cable TV, PO Box 3799, 2700 N Saint Louis, Batesville, AR 72503-3799. Phone: 870-793-4174. Fax: 870-793-7439. Web Site: http://www.indco.net. ICA: AR0212.

TV Market Ranking: Outside TV Markets (RUSSELL). Franchise award date: N.A. Franchise expiration date: N.A. Began: June 1, 1983.

Channel capacity: 36 (operating 2-way). Channels available but not in use: N.A.

Basic Service

Subscribers: 40.

Programming (received off-air): KARK-TV (NBC) Little Rock; KASN (CW) Pine Bluff; KATV (ABC) Little Rock; KETS (PBS) Little Rock; KLRT-TV (FOX) Little Rock; KTHV (CBS) Little Rock.

Programming (via satellite): ABC Family Channel; CNN; Discovery Channel; Disney Channel; ESPN; ESPN 2; Outdoor Channel; Spike TV; Syfy; TBS Superstation; Trinity Broadcasting Network; Turner Classic Movies; Turner Network TV; USA Network; WGN America.

Fee: $30.95 monthly.

Pay Service 1

Pay Units: 6.

Programming (via satellite): HBO.

Fee: $10.00 monthly.

Video-On-Demand: Planned

Internet Service

Operational: Yes.

Fee: $29.95 monthly.

Telephone Service

None

Miles of Plant: 2.0 (coaxial); None (fiber optic). Homes passed: 90.

Manager: J. D. Pierce. Chief Technician: Tommy Barnett. Marketing Director: Connie Barnett.

Ownership: Indco Cable TV (MSO).

RUSSELLVILLE—Suddenlink Communications, 127 N Elmira Ave, Russellville, AR 72802-9614. Phones: 501-968-2223 (Customer service); 800-582-9577; 479-968-2223. Fax: 479-968-2223. Web Site: http://www.suddenlink.com. Also serves Dardanelle, Lamar, Norristown, Pope County (portions) & Pottsville. ICA: AR0014.

TV Market Ranking: Outside TV Markets (Dardanelle, Lamar, Norristown, Pope County (portions), Pottsville, RUSSELLVILLE). Franchise award date: N.A. Franchise expiration date: N.A. Began: September 1, 1964.

Channel capacity: 120 (operating 2-way). Channels available but not in use: N.A.

Basic Service

Subscribers: 14,900.

Programming (received off-air): KAFT (PBS) Fayetteville; KARK-TV (NBC) Little

Rock; KARZ-TV (MNT) Little Rock; KASN (CW) Pine Bluff; KATV (ABC) Little Rock; KFSM-TV (CBS) Fort Smith; KKAP (ETV) Little Rock; KKYK-CA (IND) Little Rock; KLRA-LP Little Rock; KLRT-TV (FOX) Little Rock; KTHV (CBS) Little Rock.

Programming (via satellite): C-SPAN; Home Shopping Network; QVC; TBS Superstation; Telefutura; Weather Channel; WGN America.

Current originations: Educational Access.

Fee: $38.00 installation; $10.35 monthly.

Expanded Basic Service 1

Subscribers: N.A.

Programming (via satellite): ABC Family Channel; AMC; Animal Planet; Arts & Entertainment; BET Networks; Bravo; Cartoon Network; CNBC; CNN; Comcast Sports Net Southwest; Comedy Central; Country Music TV; C-SPAN 2; Discovery Channel; Disney Channel; E! Entertainment Television; ESPN; ESPN 2; Eternal Word TV Network; Food Network; Fox News Channel; FX; GalaVision; Great American Country; Headline News; HGTV; History Channel; INSP; Jewelry Television; Lifetime; Lifetime Movie Network; MSNBC; MTV; Nickelodeon; Outdoor Channel; Speed Channel; Spike TV; Syfy; The Learning Channel; Travel Channel; Trinity Broadcasting Network; truTV; Turner Classic Movies; Turner Network TV; TV Guide Network; TV Land; USA Network; Versus; VH1.

Fee: $25.60 monthly.

Digital Basic Service

Subscribers: 400.

Programming (received off-air): KARK-TV (NBC) Little Rock; KATV (ABC) Little Rock; KLRT-TV (FOX) Little Rock; KTHV (CBS) Little Rock.

Programming (via satellite): Arts & Entertainment HD; Bandamax; BBC America; Bio; Bloomberg Television; Boomerang; CBS College Sports Network; Cine Latino; Cine Mexicano; CMT Pure Country; CNN en Espanol; Cooking Channel; Cox Sports Television; De Pelicula; De Pelicula Clasico; Discovery en Espanol; Discovery HD Theater; Discovery Health Channel; Discovery Home Channel; Discovery Kids Channel; Discovery Military Channel; Discovery Times Channel; Do-It-Yourself; Encore (multiplexed); ESPN Classic Sports; ESPN Deportes; ESPN HD; ESPNews; EWTN en Espanol; FamilyNet; Food Network HD; Fox Reality Channel; Fox Soccer; Fox Sports en Espanol; FSN HD; Fuel TV; Fuse; G4; GalaVision; Golf Channel; Gospel Music Channel; GSN; Hallmark Channel; Halogen Network; HDNet; HDNet Movies; HGTV HD; History Channel en Espanol; History Channel International; Independent Film Channel; Latele Novela Network; MTV Hits; MTV Tres; MTV2; mtvU; mun2 television; Music Choice; National Geographic Channel; National Geographic Channel HD Network; Nick Jr.; NickToons en Espanol; NickToons TV; Oxygen; Palladia; Ritmoson Latino; Science Channel; Si TV; SoapNet; Sorpresa; Style Network; Sundance Channel; Sur Network; TBN Enlace USA; TeenNick; Telehit; Telemundo; Tennis Channel; The Sportsman Channel; Toon Disney; Toon Disney en Espanol; Turner Network TV HD; TV Chile; TV One; Universal HD; VH1 Classic; Video Rola; WE tv; Weatherscan.

Fee: $4.99 monthly.

Digital Pay Service 1

Pay Units: N.A.

Programming (via satellite): Cinemax (multiplexed); HBO (multiplexed); HBO HD; HBO Latino; Showtime (multiplexed); Showtime HD; Starz (multiplexed); The Movie Channel (multiplexed).

Fee: $10.95 monthly (each).

Video-On-Demand: Planned

Pay-Per-View

iN DEMAND (delivered digitally); Playboy TV (delivered digitally); Shorteez (delivered digitally); Fresh (delivered digitally); Club Jenna (delivered digitally); Spice: Xcess (delivered digitally).

Internet Service

Operational: Yes.

Subscribers: 1,300.

Broadband Service: Cebridge High Speed Cable Internet.

Fee: $29.95 monthly.

Telephone Service

Digital: Operational

Fee: $44.95 monthly

Miles of Plant: 257.0 (coaxial); None (fiber optic).

Manager: Mike Ederington. Marketing Director: Kathy Wyrick. Chief Engineer: Wayne Ollis. Customer Service Manager: Jane Ollis.

City fee: 3% of gross.

Ownership: Cequel Communications LLC (MSO).

SALEM—Salem Cable Vision, PO Box 1115, Salem, AR 72576. Phone: 870-895-4993. Fax: 870-895-4905. ICA: AR0116.

TV Market Ranking: Outside TV Markets (SALEM). Franchise award date: N.A. Franchise expiration date: N.A. Began: January 1, 1965.

Channel capacity: N.A. Channels available but not in use: N.A.

Basic Service

Subscribers: 650.

Programming (received off-air): KAIT (ABC) Jonesboro; KARK-TV (NBC) Little Rock; KEMV (PBS) Mountain View; KOLR (CBS) Springfield; KSFX-TV (FOX) Springfield; KTVT (CBS) Fort Worth; KYTV (CW, NBC) Springfield.

Programming (via satellite): ABC Family Channel; AmericanLife TV Network; Arts & Entertainment; CNN; Country Music TV; C-SPAN; Discovery Channel; Disney Channel; ESPN; Headline News; Lifetime; Nickelodeon; QVC; Spike TV; TBS Superstation; The Learning Channel; Trinity Broadcasting Network; Turner Network TV; USA Network; Weather Channel; WGN America.

Current originations: Educational Access.

Fee: $25.00 installation; $32.75 monthly; $10.00 additional installation.

Pay Service 1

Pay Units: 29.

Programming (via satellite): Cinemax; HBO.

Fee: $10.00 installation; $6.00 monthly (Cinemax), $7.50 monthly (HBO).

Video-On-Demand: No

Internet Service

Operational: No.

Telephone Service

None

Miles of Plant: 330.0 (coaxial); None (fiber optic). Homes passed: 700. Total homes in franchised area: 700.

Manager: Monty McCullough. Chief Technician: Mike Innes.

City fee: 3% of gross.

Ownership: Monty McCullough.

SALINE COUNTY (unincorporated areas)—Community Communications Co., 1920 Hwy 425 N, Monticello, AR 71655-4463. Phones: 800-272-2191; 870-367-7300. Fax: 870-367-9770. E-mail: generalmanager@ccc-cable.net.

Web Site: http://www.ccc-cable.net. Also serves Glenrose. ICA: AR0083.

TV Market Ranking: 50 (Glenrose, SALINE COUNTY (UNINCORPORATED AREAS) (portions)); Below 100 (SALINE COUNTY (UNINCORPORATED AREAS) (portions)). Franchise award date: N.A. Franchise expiration date: N.A. Began: N.A.

Channel capacity: 54 (not 2-way capable). Channels available but not in use: 1.

Basic Service

Subscribers: 150.

Programming (received off-air): KARK-TV (NBC) Little Rock; KASN (CW) Pine Bluff; KATV (ABC) Little Rock; KETS (PBS) Little Rock; KLRT-TV (FOX) Little Rock; KTHV (CBS) Little Rock; KVTN-DT (IND) Pine Bluff.

Programming (via satellite): ABC Family Channel; AMC; Arts & Entertainment; CNN; Comcast Sports Net Southwest; Country Music TV; Discovery Channel; Disney Channel; ESPN; ESPN 2; Fox News Channel; FX; Headline News; Lifetime; MTV; Nickelodeon; Outdoor Channel; QVC; Spike TV; Syfy; TBS Superstation; The Learning Channel; Trinity Broadcasting Network; Turner Classic Movies; Turner Network TV; TV Guide Network; TV Land; USA Network; Weather Channel; WGN America.

Fee: $30.00 installation; $33.60 monthly; $3.50 converter; $20.00 additional installation.

Pay Service 1

Pay Units: 72.

Programming (via satellite): HBO; Showtime; The Movie Channel.

Fee: $10.00 monthly (HBO or Showtime & TMC).

Video-On-Demand: No

Internet Service

Operational: No.

Telephone Service

None

Homes passed: 1,100.

Operations Manager: Larry Ivy.

Ownership: Community Communications Co. (MSO).

SCRANTON—Formerly served by Eagle Media. No longer in operation. ICA: AR0173.

SEARCY—White County Cable TV, PO Box 340, 1927 W Beebe Capps Expy, Searcy, AR 72145-0340. Phones: 501-268-4118; 501-268-4117. Fax: 501-268-1341. E-mail: whitecountycabletvcs@cablelynx.com. Web Site: http://www.whitecountycabletv.com. Also serves Augusta, Bald Knob, Judsonia & Kensett. ICA: AR0017.

TV Market Ranking: Outside TV Markets (Augusta, Bald Knob, Judsonia, Kensett, SEARCY). Franchise award date: N.A. Franchise expiration date: N.A. Began: October 1, 1979.

Channel capacity: 78 (operating 2-way). Channels available but not in use: None.

Basic Service

Subscribers: 8,728.

Programming (received off-air): KAIT (ABC) Jonesboro; KARK-TV (NBC) Little Rock; KARZ-TV (MNT) Little Rock; KASN (CW) Pine Bluff; KATV (ABC) Little Rock; KETS (PBS) Little Rock; KKAP (ETV) Little Rock; KKYK-DT (IND) Camden; KLRT-TV (FOX) Little Rock; KTHV (CBS) Little Rock; KVTN-DT (IND) Pine Bluff; 1 FM.

Programming (via satellite): ABC Family Channel; AMC; Animal Planet; Arts & Entertainment; BET Networks; Cartoon Network; CNBC; CNN; Comcast Sports Net Southwest; Country Music TV; C-SPAN; C-SPAN 2; Discovery Channel; Disney Channel; ESPN; ESPN 2; Food Network; Fox News Channel; FX; Hallmark Channel; Headline News; HGTV; History Channel; Home Shopping Network; Lifetime; MSNBC; MTV; Nickelodeon; ShopNBC; Sneak Prevue; Spike TV; Syfy; TBS Superstation; The Learning Channel; Trinity Broadcasting Network; truTV; Turner Classic Movies; Turner Network TV; TV Guide Network; TV Land; Univision; USA Network; VH1; Weather Channel; WGN America.

Current originations: Educational Access.

Fee: $40.00 installation; $47.90 monthly.

Digital Basic Service

Subscribers: N.A.

Programming (via satellite): AmericanLife TV Network; BBC America; Bio; CMT Pure Country; Discovery Health Channel; Discovery Kids Channel; Discovery Military Channel; Discovery Planet Green; DMX Music; ESPNews; FitTV; Fox Soccer; FSN Digital Atlantic; FSN Digital Central; FSN Digital Pacific; G4; Golf Channel; Great American Country; GSN; Halogen Network; History Channel International; ID Investigation Discovery; Lifetime Movie Network; MTV Hits; MTV Jams; MTV Tres; MTV2; National Geographic Channel; Nick Jr.; Nick Too; NickToons TV; Outdoor Channel; Science Channel; SoapNet; Speed Channel; Style Network; TeenNick; Toon Disney; VH1 Classic; VH1 Soul; WE tv.

Fee: $10.00 monthly.

Digital Pay Service 1

Pay Units: N.A.

Programming (via satellite): Cinemax (multiplexed); Encore (multiplexed); HBO (multiplexed); Starz (multiplexed).

Fee: $12.95 monthly (HBO, Cinemax, or Starz/Encore).

Video-On-Demand: No

Pay-Per-View

Addressable homes: 1,644.

iN DEMAND (delivered digitally), Addressable: Yes.

Internet Service

Operational: Yes. Began: April 1, 2001.

Subscribers: 150.

Broadband Service: Cablelynx.

Fee: $24.95-$44.95 monthly; $10.00 modem lease.

Telephone Service

Digital: Operational

Fee: $45.70 monthly

Miles of Plant: 214.0 (coaxial); None (fiber optic). Homes passed: 9,722.

Area Manager: Tony Allen. Marketing & Program Director: Lori Haight. Plant Manager: Tyson Sergent. Office Manager: Christian Young.

City fee: 3% of gross.
Ownership: WEHCO Video Inc. (MSO).

SEDGWICK—Formerly served by Cebridge Connections. No longer in operation. ICA: AR0202.

SHANNON HILLS—Charter Communications, 19863 Interstate 30, Ste 3, Benton, AR 72015-6966. Phones: 636-207-7044 (St Louis office); 501-315-4405. Fax: 501-315-4406. Web Site: http://www.charter.com. Also serves Alexander, Bauxite, Benton, Haskell, Hensley, Saline County (eastern portion), Tull & Wrightsville. ICA: AR0005.

TV Market Ranking: 50 (Alexander, Bauxite, Benton, Haskell, Hensley, Saline County (eastern portion), SHANNON HILLS, Tull, Wrightsville). Franchise award date: May 1, 1980. Franchise expiration date: N.A. Began: October 15, 1980.

Channel capacity: N.A. Channels available but not in use: N.A.

Basic Service

Subscribers: 9,037.

Programming (received off-air): KARK-TV (NBC) Little Rock; KARZ-TV (MNT) Little Rock; KASN (CW) Pine Bluff; KATV (ABC) Little Rock; KETS (PBS) Little Rock; KKYK-DT (IND) Camden; KLRT-TV (FOX) Little Rock; KTHV (CBS) Little Rock; KVTN-DT (IND) Pine Bluff; allband FM.

Programming (via satellite): ABC Family Channel; Arts & Entertainment; CNN; Comcast Sports Net Southwest; Comedy Central; C-SPAN; E! Entertainment Television; ESPN; ESPN 2; Home Shopping Network; Jewelry Television; Lifetime; MTV; Nickelodeon; QVC; Syfy; The Learning Channel; VH1; Weather Channel; WGN America.

Current originations: Public Access.

Fee: $29.99 installation; $3.48 converter.

Expanded Basic Service 1

Subscribers: N.A.

Programming (via satellite): AMC; Animal Planet; Bravo; Cartoon Network; CNBC; Country Music TV; Discovery Channel; Disney Channel; Flix; Food Network; Fox Movie Channel; Fox News Channel; FX; G4; Golf Channel; Great American Country; GSN; Hallmark Channel; Headline News; HGTV; History Channel; MSNBC; National Geographic Channel; Oxygen; SoapNet; Speed Channel; Spike TV; Style Network; TBS Superstation; Toon Disney; Travel Channel; truTV; Turner Classic Movies; Turner Network TV; TV Guide Network; TV Land; USA Network; Versus; WE tv.

Fee: $49.99 monthly.

Digital Basic Service

Subscribers: 648.

Programming (via satellite): BBC America; Bio; Bloomberg Television; Discovery Digital Networks; Do-It-Yourself; FitTV; Fox College Sports Atlantic; Fox College Sports Central; Fox College Sports Pacific; Fox Soccer; Fuel TV; History Channel International; Lifetime Movie Network; Music Choice; Science Television; Sundance Channel; WE tv.

Digital Pay Service 1

Pay Units: 359.

Programming (via satellite): Cinemax (multiplexed).

Digital Pay Service 2

Pay Units: 546.

Programming (via satellite): HBO (multiplexed).

Digital Pay Service 3

Pay Units: 21.

Programming (via satellite): Encore (multiplexed); Starz (multiplexed).

Fee: $13.95 monthly.

Video-On-Demand: No

Pay-Per-View

Addressable homes: 2,443.

ETC (delivered digitally), Fee: $3.95, Addressable: Yes; Hot Choice (delivered digitally); iN DEMAND (delivered digitally), Fee: $6.95; Pleasure (delivered digitally); Sports PPV (delivered digitally).

Internet Service

Operational: Yes.

Broadband Service: Charter Pipeline.

Telephone Service

Digital: Operational

Miles of Plant: 1,600.0 (coaxial); 58.0 (fiber optic). Homes passed: 45,983. Total homes in franchised area: 78,000.

Vice President & General Manager: Steve Trippe. Operations Director: Dave Miller. Operations Manager: Dave Huntsman. Chief Technician: Jim Miller. Marketing Director: Beverly Wall. Office Manager: Missy Brown.

Ownership: Charter Communications Inc. (MSO).

SHERIDAN—Rapid Cable, 515 E Longview Dr, Arp, TX 75750. Phone: 903-859-6492. Fax: 903-859-3708. Also serves Grant County (northern portion), Poyen & Prattsville. ICA: AR0051.

TV Market Ranking: 50 (Grant County (northern portion), Poyen, Prattsville, SHERIDAN). Franchise award date: N.A. Franchise expiration date: N.A. Began: N.A.

Channel capacity: 45 (not 2-way capable). Channels available but not in use: N.A.

Basic Service

Subscribers: 874.

Programming (received off-air): KARK-TV (NBC) Little Rock; KASN (CW) Pine Bluff; KATV (ABC) Little Rock; KETS (PBS) Little Rock; KKYK-DT (IND) Camden; KLRT-TV (FOX) Little Rock; KTHV (CBS) Little Rock; KVTN-DT (IND) Pine Bluff.

Programming (via satellite): C-SPAN; Home Shopping Network; KARZ-TV (MNT) Little Rock.

Fee: $54.95 installation; $20.95 monthly.

Expanded Basic Service 1

Subscribers: N.A.

Programming (received off-air): KKAP (ETV) Little Rock.

Programming (via satellite): ABC Family Channel; Arts & Entertainment; BET Networks; Cartoon Network; CNBC; CNN; Comcast Sports Net Southwest; Discovery Channel; Disney Channel; E! Entertainment Television; ESPN; ESPN 2; Fox News Channel; FX; Great American Country; Headline News; Lifetime; MTV; National Geographic Channel; Nickelodeon; Outdoor Channel; Spike TV; TBS Superstation; The Learning Channel; Turner Classic Movies; Turner Network TV; TV Land; USA Network; Weather Channel.

Fee: $23.10 monthly.

Digital Basic Service

Subscribers: N.A.

Programming (via satellite): BBC America; Bio; Bloomberg Television; Discovery Kids Channel; Discovery Military Channel; Discovery Planet Green; DMX Music; ESPN Classic Sports; ESPNews; Fox College Sports Atlantic; Fox College Sports Central; Fox College Sports Pacific; Fox Soccer; Fuse; G4; Golf Channel; GSN; HGTV; History Channel; History Channel International; ID Investigation Discovery; Independent Film Channel; Science Channel; ShopNBC; Sleuth; Speed Channel; Style Network; Sundance Channel; Toon Disney; Trinity Broadcasting Network; Versus; WE tv.

Pay Service 1

Pay Units: 57.

Programming (via satellite): Cinemax.

Fee: $12.95 monthly.

Pay Service 2

Pay Units: 170.

Programming (via satellite): Showtime.

Fee: $12.95 monthly.

Pay Service 3

Pay Units: 129.

Programming (via satellite): HBO.

Fee: $12.95 monthly.

Digital Pay Service 1

Pay Units: N.A.

Programming (via satellite): Cinemax (multiplexed); Encore (multiplexed); Flix; HBO (multiplexed); Showtime (multiplexed); Starz (multiplexed); The Movie Channel (multiplexed).

Video-On-Demand: No

Pay-Per-View

iN DEMAND (delivered digitally); Playboy TV (delivered digitally); Club Jenna (delivered digitally).

Internet Service

Operational: No.

Telephone Service

None

Miles of Plant: 135.0 (coaxial); None (fiber optic). Homes passed: 3,218.

Regional Manager: Mike Taylor. Chief Technician: Larry Stafford.

Ownership: Rapid Communications LLC (MSO).

SIDNEY—Indco Cable TV, PO Box 3799, 2700 N Saint Louis, Batesville, AR 72503-3799. Phone: 870-793-4174. Fax: 870-793-7439. ICA: AR0320.

TV Market Ranking: Outside TV Markets (SIDNEY). Franchise award date: N.A. Franchise expiration date: N.A. Began: N.A.

Channel capacity: N.A. Channels available but not in use: N.A.

Basic Service

Subscribers: 39.

Programming (received off-air): KAIT (ABC) Jonesboro; KARK-TV (NBC) Little Rock; KTHV (CBS) Little Rock.

Programming (via satellite): ABC Family Channel; CNN; Country Music TV; Discovery Channel; ESPN; Home Shopping Network; Lifetime; Outdoor Channel; Spike TV; TBS Superstation; Trinity Broadcasting Network; Turner Network TV; TV Land; USA Network; Weather Channel; WGN America.

Current originations: Educational Access.

Fee: $20.00 installation; $30.95 monthly.

Pay Service 1

Pay Units: 2.

Programming (via satellite): HBO.

Fee: $10.00 monthly.

Video-On-Demand: Planned

Internet Service

Operational: Yes.

Telephone Service

None

Manager: J. D. Pierce. Chief Technician: Tommy Barnett. Marketing Director: Connie Barnett.

Ownership: Indco Cable TV (MSO).

SILOAM SPRINGS—Cox Communications, 4901 S 48th St, Springdale, AR 72762. Phones: 316-262-4270 (Wichita office); 479-717-3700. Fax: 479-756-1081. Web Site: http://www.cox.com/arkansas. Also serves Decatur & Gentry, AR; West Siloam Springs, OK. ICA: AR0283.

TV Market Ranking: Below 100 (Decatur, Gentry, SILOAM SPRINGS, West Siloam Springs). Franchise award date: N.A. Franchise expiration date: N.A. Began: May 1, 1953.

Channel capacity: 117 (operating 2-way). Channels available but not in use: 33.

Basic Service

Subscribers: N.A. Included in Wichita

Programming (received off-air): K45EI Bentonville & Rogers; KAFT (PBS) Fayetteville; KFSM-TV (CBS) Fort Smith; KHOG-TV (ABC) Fayetteville; KNWA-TV (NBC) Rogers; KOED-TV (PBS) Tulsa; KOTV-DT (CBS) Tulsa; KSNF (NBC) Joplin; KTUL (ABC) Tulsa; KWOG (IND) Springdale.

Programming (via satellite): TBS Superstation; WGN America.

Programming (via translator): KPBI-CA (FOX) Fort Smith.

Current originations: Public Access.

Fee: $38.00 installation; $9.26 monthly.

Expanded Basic Service 1

Subscribers: N.A.

Programming (via satellite): ABC Family Channel; Arts & Entertainment; CNBC; CNN; Comcast Sports Net Southwest; C-SPAN; C-SPAN 2; Discovery Channel; Disney Channel; ESPN; Fox News Channel; FX; G4; Great American Country; Headline News; History Channel; Home Shopping Network; INSP; ION Television; Lifetime; Nickelodeon; Oxygen; QVC; Speed Channel; Spike TV; The Learning Channel; Travel Channel; Trinity Broadcasting Network; Turner Classic Movies; Turner Network TV; TV Land; USA Network; Versus; VH1; Weather Channel.

Fee: $43.15 monthly.

Expanded Basic Service 2

Subscribers: N.A.

Programming (via satellite): AMC; Animal Planet; Cartoon Network; Comedy Central; ESPN 2; GalaVision; Golf Channel; GSN; HGTV; MoviePlex; Outdoor Channel; Syfy.

Fee: $6.95 monthly.

Digital Basic Service

Subscribers: N.A.

Programming (via satellite): BBC America; Discovery Digital Networks; Encore Action; Lifetime Movie Network; MuchMusic Network; Music Choice; Toon Disney.

Fee: $14.00 monthly.

Pay Service 1

Pay Units: N.A.

Programming (via satellite): Cinemax; HBO; Showtime.

Fee: $35.00 installation; $10.00 monthly (Cinemax or Showtime), $11.00 monthly (HBO).

Digital Pay Service 1

Pay Units: N.A.

Programming (via satellite): Cinemax (multiplexed); Flix; HBO (multiplexed); Showtime (multiplexed); Starz (multiplexed); The Movie Channel (multiplexed).

Video-On-Demand: No

Pay-Per-View

ESPN Extra (delivered digitally); ESPN Gameplan (delivered digitally); ESPN Now (delivered digitally); iN DEMAND (delivered digitally); NBA League Pass (delivered digitally).

Internet Service

Operational: Yes.

Broadband Service: Cox High Speed Internet.

Fee: $19.99-$59.99 monthly.

Telephone Service

Digital: Operational

Fee: $15.95 monthly

Miles of Plant: 150.0 (coaxial); 50.0 (fiber optic). Homes passed included in Springdale
Vice President & General Manager: Kimberly Edmunds. Vice President, Operations: Nelson Mower. Vice President, Marketing: Tony Matthews. Marketing Director: Tina Gabbard. Community Relations Manager: Kelly Zaga.
City fee: None.
Ownership: Cox Communications Inc. (MSO).

SMACKOVER—Rapid Cable, 515 E Longview Dr, Arp, TX 75750. Phone: 903-859-6492. Fax: 903-859-3708. Also serves Calion, Elliott, LouAnn, Norphlet, Ouachita County (portions) & Union County (portions). ICA: AR0069.
TV Market Ranking: 50 (Calion, Union County (portions)); 99 (Elliott, LouAnn, Norphlet, Ouachita County (portions), SMACKOVER). Franchise award date: N.A. Franchise expiration date: N.A. Began: December 1, 1980.
Channel capacity: 54 (not 2-way capable). Channels available but not in use: 5.

Basic Service
Subscribers: 848.
Programming (received off-air): KASN (CW) Pine Bluff; KATV (ABC) Little Rock; KEJB (MNT) El Dorado; KETG (PBS) Arkadelphia; KKYK-CA (IND) Little Rock; KNOE-TV (CBS, CW) Monroe; KSLA (CBS) Shreveport; KTVE (NBC) El Dorado.
Programming (via satellite): KMSS-TV (FOX) Shreveport; Weather Channel.
Fee: $54.95 installation; $20.95 monthly.

Expanded Basic Service 1
Subscribers: N.A.
Programming (via satellite): ABC Family Channel; AMC; Animal Planet; Arts & Entertainment; BET Networks; Cartoon Network; CNBC; CNN; Comcast Sports Net Southwest; Discovery Channel; Disney Channel; E! Entertainment Television; ESPN; ESPN 2; Food Network; Fox News Channel; FX; Great American Country; Headline News; HGTV; History Channel; Lifetime; MTV; National Geographic Channel; Nickelodeon; Outdoor Channel; Spike TV; TBS Superstation; The Learning Channel; Turner Classic Movies; Turner Network TV; USA Network; VH1.
Fee: $23.10 monthly.

Digital Basic Service
Subscribers: N.A.
Programming (via satellite): BBC America; Bio; Bloomberg Television; Discovery Health Channel; Discovery Kids Channel; Discovery Military Channel; Discovery Planet Green; DMX Music; ESPN Classic Sports; ESPNews; Fox College Sports Atlantic; Fox College Sports Central; Fox College Sports Pacific; Fox Soccer; Fuse; G4; Golf Channel; GSN; History Channel International; ID Investigation Discovery; Independent Film Channel; Science Channel; ShopNBC; Sleuth; Speed Channel; Style Network; Sundance Channel; Toon Disney; Trinity Broadcasting Network; Versus; WE tv.

Pay Service 1
Pay Units: 146.
Programming (via satellite): HBO.
Fee: $12.95 monthly.

Pay Service 2
Pay Units: 89.
Programming (via satellite): Cinemax.
Fee: $12.95 monthly.

Pay Service 3
Pay Units: 206.
Programming (via satellite): Showtime.
Fee: $12.95 monthly.

Digital Pay Service 1
Pay Units: N.A.
Programming (via satellite): Cinemax (multiplexed); Encore (multiplexed); Flix; HBO (multiplexed); Showtime (multiplexed); Starz (multiplexed); The Movie Channel (multiplexed).
Video-On-Demand: No

Pay-Per-View
iN DEMAND (delivered digitally); Playboy TV (delivered digitally); Club Jenna (delivered digitally).

Internet Service
Operational: No.

Telephone Service
None
Miles of Plant: 76.0 (coaxial); None (fiber optic). Homes passed: 2,474.
Regional Manager: Mike Taylor. Chief Technician: Larry Stafford.
Ownership: Rapid Communications LLC (MSO).

SONORA—Cox Communications. Now served by SPRINGDALE, AR [AR0220]. ICA: AR0117.

SPRINGDALE—Cox Communications, 1006 NW 11th St, Bentonville, AR 72712-4160. Phones: 800-822-4433; 479-273-5644. Fax: 479-273-2406. Web Site: http://www.cox.com/arkansas. Also serves Beaver Lake, Beaver Shores, Beaverama, Bella Vista, Benton County, Bentonville, Bethel Heights Twp., Blue Springs, Cave Springs, Cedarville, Centerton, Crawford County (unincorporated areas), Elkins, Elm Springs, Excelsior, Farmington, Fayetteville, Goshen, Gravette, Greenland, Harmon, Johnson, Knob Hill, Lincoln, Little Flock, Lowell, Mayfield, Monte Ne, Pea Ridge, Prairie Creek, Prairie Grove, Rivercliff, Rochell, Rogers, Sonora, Tontitown, Village Estates, Wareagle, Wareagle Cove, Washington County, Wedington, West Fork & Winslow. ICA: AR0220.
TV Market Ranking: Below 100 (Beaver Lake, Beaver Shores, Beaverama, Bella Vista, Benton County, Bentonville, Bethel Heights Twp., Blue Springs, Cave Springs, Cedarville, Centerton, Crawford County (unincorporated areas), Elkins, Elm Springs, Excelsior, Farmington, Fayetteville, Goshen, Gravette, Greenland, Harmon, Johnson, Knob Hill, Lincoln, Little Flock, Lowell, Mayfield, Monte Ne, Pea Ridge, Prairie Creek, Prairie Grove, Rivercliff, Rochell, Rogers, Sonora, SPRINGDALE, Tontitown, Village Estates, Wareagle, Wareagle Cove, Washington County, Wedington, West Fork, Winslow). Franchise award date: N.A. Franchise expiration date: N.A. Began: January 1, 1962.
Channel capacity: 77 (operating 2-way). Channels available but not in use: N.A.

Basic Service
Subscribers: N.A. Included in Wichita
Programming (received off-air): KAFT (PBS) Fayetteville; KARK-TV (NBC) Little Rock; KFSM-TV (CBS) Fort Smith; KHOG-TV (ABC) Fayetteville; KNWA-TV (NBC) Rogers; KOLR (CBS) Springfield; KSNF (NBC) Joplin; KTUL (ABC) Tulsa; KWOG (IND) Springdale; allband FM.
Programming (via satellite): C-SPAN; ESPN; Home Shopping Network; ION Television; TBS Superstation; TV Guide Network; WGN America.
Current originations: Leased Access.
Fee: $35.00 installation; $16.33 monthly.

Expanded Basic Service 1
Subscribers: N.A.
Programming (via satellite): ABC Family Channel; AMC; Animal Planet; Arts & Entertainment; CNBC; CNN; Comcast Sports Net Southwest; C-SPAN 2; Discovery Channel; Disney Channel; E! Entertainment Television; Eternal Word TV Network; Fox News Channel; FX; Great American Country; Headline News; HGTV; Lifetime; MTV; Nickelodeon; Spike TV; The Learning Channel; Travel Channel; Trinity Broadcasting Network; Turner Network TV; TV Land; USA Network; VH1; Weather Channel.
Fee: $43.15 monthly.

Digital Basic Service
Subscribers: N.A.
Programming (via satellite): BBC America; Discovery Digital Networks; DMX Music; Encore Action; ESPN Classic Sports; ESPNews; Fox Sports World; GSN; Lifetime Movie Network; MuchMusic Network; Speed Channel; Toon Disney; Versus; WE tv.
Fee: $14.00 monthly.

Digital Pay Service 1
Pay Units: N.A.
Programming (via satellite): Cinemax (multiplexed); Fresh; HBO (multiplexed); Showtime (multiplexed); The Movie Channel (multiplexed).
Fee: $11.95 monthly (each).
Video-On-Demand: No

Pay-Per-View
Addressable homes: 7,000.
iN DEMAND, Addressable: Yes.

Internet Service
Operational: Yes.
Broadband Service: Cox High Speed Internet.
Fee: $24.95 installation; $19.99-$59.99 monthly; $10.00 modem lease.

Telephone Service
None
Miles of Plant: 1,567.0 (coaxial); None (fiber optic). Homes passed: 280,649. Homes passed includes Fort Smith, Berryville, Harrison, & Siloam Springs
Vice President & General Manager: Kimberly Edmunds. Vice President, Operations: Nelson Mower. Vice President, Marketing: Tony Matthews. Marketing Director: Tina Gabbard. Community Relations Manager: Kelly Zaga.
City fee: 2% of gross.
Ownership: Cox Communications Inc.

STAR CITY—Community Communications Co., 1920 Hwy 425 N, Monticello, AR 71655-4463. Phones: 800-272-2191; 870-367-7300. Fax: 870-367-9770. E-mail: generalmanager@ccc-cable.net. Web Site: http://www.ccc-cable.net. Also serves Lincoln County & Yorktown. ICA: AR0086.
TV Market Ranking: 50 (Lincoln County (portions), STAR CITY, Yorktown); Below 100 (Lincoln County (portions)). Franchise award date: N.A. Franchise expiration date: N.A. Began: December 1, 1982.
Channel capacity: 48 (not 2-way capable). Channels available but not in use: N.A.

Basic Service
Subscribers: 447.
Programming (received off-air): KARK-TV (NBC) Little Rock; KASN (CW) Pine Bluff; KATV (ABC) Little Rock; KETS (PBS) Little Rock; KLRT-TV (FOX) Little Rock; KTHV (CBS) Little Rock; KTVE (NBC) El Dorado; KVTN-DT (IND) Pine Bluff.
Programming (via satellite): ABC Family Channel; AMC; Arts & Entertainment; BET Networks; CNBC; CNN; Comcast Sports Net Southwest; Country Music TV; Discovery Channel; Disney Channel; ESPN; ESPN 2; Fox News Channel; FX; History Channel; Home Shopping Network; MTV; Nickelodeon; Outdoor Channel; QVC; Spike TV; Syfy; TBS Superstation; The Learning Channel; Trinity Broadcasting Network; Turner Network TV; TV Guide Network; TV Land; USA Network; VH1; Weather Channel; WGN America.
Fee: $19.95 installation; $33.60 monthly.

Pay Service 1
Pay Units: 62.
Programming (via satellite): HBO; The Movie Channel.
Fee: $12.00 monthly (HBO).

Pay Service 2
Pay Units: N.A.
Programming (via satellite): Showtime.
Video-On-Demand: No

Internet Service
Operational: No.

Telephone Service
None
Miles of Plant: 19.0 (coaxial); None (fiber optic). Homes passed: 1,050.
Operations Manager: Larry Ivy.
Ownership: Community Communications Co. (MSO).

STEPHENS—Rapid Cable, 515 E Longview Dr, Arp, TX 75750. Phone: 903-859-6492. Fax: 903-859-3708. ICA: AR0106.
TV Market Ranking: 99 (STEPHENS). Franchise award date: N.A. Franchise expiration date: N.A. Began: October 1, 1981.
Channel capacity: 36 (not 2-way capable). Channels available but not in use: N.A.

Basic Service
Subscribers: 119.
Programming (received off-air): KATV (ABC) Little Rock; KETG (PBS) Arkadelphia; KKYK-CA (IND) Little Rock; KMSS-TV (FOX) Shreveport; KSLA (CBS) Shreveport; KTAL-TV (NBC) Texarkana; KTVE (NBC) El Dorado.
Programming (via satellite): Animal Planet; Arts & Entertainment; BET Networks; CNN; Discovery Channel; Disney Channel; ESPN; Great American Country; Headline News; Lifetime; MTV; National Geographic Channel; Nickelodeon; QVC; Spike TV; TBS Superstation; The Learning Channel; Trinity Broadcasting Network; Turner Classic Movies; Turner Network TV; USA Network; Weather Channel.
Fee: $54.95 installation; $44.05 monthly.

Pay Service 1
Pay Units: 22.
Programming (via satellite): The Movie Channel.
Fee: $12.95 monthly.

Pay Service 2
Pay Units: 15.
Programming (via satellite): HBO.
Fee: $12.95 monthly.

Pay Service 3
Pay Units: 51.
Programming (via satellite): Showtime.
Fee: $12.95 monthly.

Video-On-Demand: No

Internet Service
Operational: No.

Telephone Service
None

Miles of Plant: 15.0 (coaxial); None (fiber optic). Homes passed: 525.
Regional Manager: Mike Taylor. Chief Technician: Larry Stafford.
City fee: 3% of gross.
Ownership: Rapid Communications LLC (MSO).

STRONG—Bayou Cable TV, PO Box 466, Marion, LA 71260-0466. Phone: 318-292-4774. Fax: 318-292-4775. Web Site: http://www.bayoucable.com. ICA: AR0324.
Channel capacity: 50 (not 2-way capable). Channels available but not in use: 7.

Basic Service
Subscribers: 240.
Programming (received off-air): KAQY (ABC) Columbia; KARD (FOX) West Monroe; KATV (ABC) Little Rock; KLTM-TV (PBS) Monroe; KNOE-TV (CBS, CW) Monroe; KTVE (NBC) El Dorado.
Programming (via satellite): AMC; Hallmark Channel; Trinity Broadcasting Network; TV Land.
Fee: $15.95 monthly.

Expanded Basic Service 1
Subscribers: N.A.
Programming (received off-air): KEJB (MNT)lorado.
Programming (via satellite): ABC Family Channel; Animal Planet; Arts & Entertainment; BET Networks; CNN; Country Music TV; Discovery Channel; ESPN; ESPN 2; Food Network; Fox News Channel; FX; History Channel; ION Television; Lifetime; MTV; National Geographic Channel; Nickelodeon; Outdoor Channel; Speed Channel; Spike TV; TBS Superstation; The Learning Channel; Turner Network TV; USA Network; VH1; Weather Channel; WGN America.
Fee: $20.00 monthly.

Pay Service 1
Pay Units: N.A.
Programming (via satellite): Cinemax; HBO.
Fee: $8.95 monthly (Cinemax), $10.95 monthly (HBO).

Internet Service
Operational: No.

Telephone Service
None

Miles of Plant: 8.0 (coaxial); None (fiber optic).
Manager: Alan C. Booker. Chief Technician: Mark Andrews.
Ownership: Bayou Cable TV (MSO).

STUTTGART—Suddenlink Communications, 12444 Powerscourt Dr, Saint Louis, MO 63131-3660. Web Site: http://www.suddenlink.com. ICA: AR0027.
TV Market Ranking: 50 (STUTTGART). Franchise award date: March 29, 1972. Franchise expiration date: N.A. Began: October 1, 1973.
Channel capacity: 78 (operating 2-way). Channels available but not in use: N.A.

Basic Service
Subscribers: 2,756.
Programming (received off-air): KARK-TV (NBC) Little Rock; KARZ-TV (MNT) Little Rock; KASN (CW) Pine Bluff; KATV (ABC) Little Rock; KETS (PBS) Little Rock; KKAP (ETV) Little Rock; KLRT-TV (FOX) Little Rock; KTHV (CBS) Little Rock; KVTN-DT (IND) Pine Bluff; allband FM.
Programming (via satellite): WGN America.
Fee: $35.00 installation; $19.95 monthly.

Expanded Basic Service 1
Subscribers: N.A.
Programming (via satellite): ABC Family Channel; AMC; Animal Planet; Arts & Entertainment; BET Networks; Bravo; Cartoon Network; CNBC; CNN; Comcast Sports Net Southwest; Comedy Central; C-SPAN; Discovery Channel; Disney Channel; E! Entertainment Television; ESPN; ESPN 2; Food Network; Fox News Channel; FX; Golf Channel; Great American Country; Hallmark Channel; Headline News; HGTV; History Channel; Jewelry Television; Lifetime; MSNBC; MTV; National Geographic Channel; Nickelodeon; Outdoor Channel; QVC; Speed Channel; Spike TV; Syfy; TBS Superstation; The Learning Channel; Travel Channel; Turner Classic Movies; Turner Network TV; TV Guide Network; TV Land; USA Network; VH1; Weather Channel.
Fee: $24.00 monthly.

Digital Basic Service
Subscribers: N.A.
Programming (via satellite): BBC America; Bio; Bloomberg Television; CMT Pure Country; Discovery Health Channel; Discovery Home Channel; Discovery Kids Channel; Discovery Military Channel; Discovery Times Channel; DMX Music; ESPN Classic Sports; ESPNews; Fox Soccer; Fuse; G4; GSN; History Channel International; Independent Film Channel; Lifetime Movie Network; MTV Hits; MTV2; Nick Jr.; NickToons TV; Science Channel; Sleuth; Style Network; Sundance Channel; TeenNick; Toon Disney; Trinity Broadcasting Network; Versus; VH1 Classic; VH1 Soul; WE tv.
Fee: $3.99 monthly.

Pay Service 1
Pay Units: 278.
Programming (via satellite): Showtime.
Fee: $9.95 monthly.

Pay Service 2
Pay Units: 616.
Programming (via satellite): HBO.
Fee: $10.95 monthly.

Pay Service 3
Pay Units: 299.
Programming (via satellite): The Movie Channel.
Fee: $5.95 monthly.

Digital Pay Service 1
Pay Units: N.A.
Programming (via satellite): Cinemax (multiplexed); Encore (multiplexed); HBO (multiplexed); Showtime (multiplexed); Starz (multiplexed); The Movie Channel (multiplexed).

Pay-Per-View
iN DEMAND (delivered digitally), Addressable: Yes; Playboy TV (delivered digitally); Club Jenna (delivered digitally); Fresh (delivered digitally); Spice: Xcess (delivered digitally).

Internet Service
Operational: Yes. Began: June 23, 2002.
Broadband Service: Cebridge High Speed Cable Internet.
Fee: $29.95 monthly; $9.95 modem lease.

Telephone Service
Digital: Operational
Fee: $44.95 monthly

Miles of Plant: 66.0 (coaxial); None (fiber optic). Homes passed: 3,445. Total homes in franchised area: 4,489.
Manager: Dave Walker. Chief Technician: Carl Miller. Marketing Director: Beverly Gambell. Regional Manager: Todd Cruthird.
City fee: 3% of gross.
Ownership: Cequel Communications LLC (MSO).

SUBIACO—Formerly served by Eagle Media. No longer in operation. ICA: AR0187.

TAYLOR—Formerly served by Cebridge Connections. No longer in operation. ICA: AR0168.

THORNTON—Formerly served by Almega Cable. No longer in operation. ICA: AR0171.

TONTITOWN—Cox Communications. Now served by SPRINGDALE, AR [AR0220]. ICA: AR0074.

TRASKWOOD—Formerly served by Cebridge Connections. No longer in operation. ICA: AR0190.

TRUMANN—Ritter Communications. Now served by MARKED TREE, AR [AR0072]. ICA: AR0025.

TUMBLING SHOALS—Indco Cable TV, PO Box 3799, 2700 N Saint Louis, Batesville, AR 72503-3799. Phone: 870-793-4174. Fax: 870-793-7439. Web Site: http://www.indco.net. Also serves Drasco & Ida. ICA: AR0286.
TV Market Ranking: Outside TV Markets (Drasco, Ida, TUMBLING SHOALS). Franchise award date: N.A. Franchise expiration date: N.A. Began: August 1, 1990.
Channel capacity: 36 (operating 2-way). Channels available but not in use: 7.

Basic Service
Subscribers: 283.
Programming (received off-air): KAIT (ABC) Jonesboro; KARK-TV (NBC) Little Rock; KATV (ABC) Little Rock; KEMV (PBS) Mountain View; KKYK-DT (IND) Camden; KLRT-TV (FOX) Little Rock; KTHV (CBS) Little Rock.
Programming (via satellite): ABC Family Channel; CNN; Comcast Sports Net Southwest; Discovery Channel; Disney Channel; ESPN; ESPN 2; FX; HGTV; History Channel; Nickelodeon; Outdoor Channel; QVC; Spike TV; Syfy; TBS Superstation; Trinity Broadcasting Network; Turner Classic Movies; Turner Network TV; USA Network; Weather Channel; WGN America.
Fee: $20.00 installation; $30.95 monthly.

Pay Service 1
Pay Units: 6.
Programming (via satellite): Cinemax.
Fee: $8.00 monthly.

Pay Service 2
Pay Units: 8.
Programming (via satellite): HBO.
Fee: $10.00 monthly.

Video-On-Demand: Planned

Internet Service
Operational: Yes.
Fee: $29.95 monthly.

Telephone Service
None

Manager: J. D. Pierce. Chief Technician: Tommy Barnett. Marketing Director: Connie Barnett.
Ownership: Indco Cable TV (MSO).

TUPELO—Indco Cable TV, PO Box 3799, 2700 N Saint Louis, Batesville, AR 72503-3799. Phone: 870-793-4174. Fax: 870-793-7439. Web Site: http://www.indco.net/. ICA: AR0209.
TV Market Ranking: Outside TV Markets (TUPELO). Franchise award date: N.A. Franchise expiration date: N.A. Began: June 1, 1983.
Channel capacity: 36 (not 2-way capable). Channels available but not in use: N.A.

Basic Service
Subscribers: 26.
Programming (received off-air): KAIT (ABC) Jonesboro; KARK-TV (NBC) Little Rock; KATV (ABC) Little Rock; KLRT-TV (FOX) Little Rock; KTEJ (PBS) Jonesboro; KTHV (CBS) Little Rock; WMC-TV (NBC) Memphis.
Programming (via satellite): ABC Family Channel; CNN; Disney Channel; ESPN; ESPN 2; HGTV; Outdoor Channel; Spike TV; Syfy; TBS Superstation; Trinity Broadcasting Network; Turner Classic Movies; Turner Network TV; USA Network; WGN America.
Fee: $30.95 monthly.

Pay Service 1
Pay Units: 4.
Programming (via satellite): HBO.
Fee: $10.00 monthly.

Internet Service
Operational: Yes.

Telephone Service
Digital: Operational

Miles of Plant: 2.0 (coaxial); None (fiber optic). Homes passed: 100.
Manager: J. D. Pierce. Chief Technician: Tommy Barnett. Marketing Director: Connie Barnett.
Ownership: Indco Cable TV (MSO).

TURRELL—Ritter Communications. Now served by MARKED TREE, AR [AR0072]. ICA: AR0144.

VAN BUREN—Cox Communications. Now served by FORT SMITH, AR [AR0003]. ICA: AR0287.

VILONIA—Charter Communications, 19863 Interstate 30, Ste 3, Benton, AR 72015-6966. Phones: 501-315-4405; 636-207-7044 (St Louis office). Fax: 501-315-4406. Web Site: http://www.charter.com. Also serves Faulkner County (southeastern portion). ICA: AR0099.
TV Market Ranking: 50 (Faulkner County (southeastern portion), VILONIA). Franchise award date: N.A. Franchise expiration date: N.A. Began: N.A.
Channel capacity: N.A. Channels available but not in use: N.A.

Basic Service
Subscribers: 1,341.
Programming (received off-air): KARK-TV (NBC) Little Rock; KASN (CW) Pine Bluff; KATV (ABC) Little Rock; KETS (PBS) Little Rock; KLRT-TV (FOX) Little Rock; KTHV (CBS) Little Rock; KVTN-DT (IND) Pine Bluff.
Programming (via satellite): ABC Family Channel; Comcast Sports Net Southwest; Comedy Central; Country Music TV; C-SPAN; E! Entertainment Television; ESPN;

Headline News; Lifetime; MTV; Nickelodeon; QVC; The Learning Channel; USA Network; VH1; WGN America.
Current originations: Government Access; Educational Access; Public Access.
Fee: $29.99 installation; $6.95 converter.

Expanded Basic Service 1
Subscribers: 395.
Programming (via satellite): AMC; Bravo; CNN; Discovery Channel; Disney Channel; History Channel; Spike TV; Syfy; TBS Superstation; Turner Network TV; Weather Channel.
Fee: $49.99 monthly.

Digital Basic Service
Subscribers: N.A.
Programming (via satellite): AmericanLife TV Network; BBC America; Bio; Bloomberg Television; Discovery Digital Networks; DMX Music; Fox Movie Channel; G4; GAS; Golf Channel; GSN; Halogen Network; HGTV; History Channel International; Independent Film Channel; Lifetime Movie Network; MTV Networks Digital Suite; MuchMusic Network; Nick Jr.; Outdoor Channel; Speed Channel; Style Network; Toon Disney; Trinity Broadcasting Network; Turner Classic Movies; Versus; WE tv.
Fee: $25.60 monthly.

Pay Service 1
Pay Units: 25.
Programming (via satellite): Cinemax.
Fee: $11.95 monthly.

Pay Service 2
Pay Units: 37.
Programming (via satellite): HBO.
Fee: $11.95 monthly.

Pay Service 3
Pay Units: 19.
Programming (via satellite): Showtime.
Fee: $11.95 monthly.

Digital Pay Service 1
Pay Units: N.A.
Programming (via satellite): Cinemax (multiplexed); Encore (multiplexed); Flix; HBO (multiplexed); Showtime (multiplexed); Starz; The Movie Channel (multiplexed).

Video-On-Demand: No

Pay-Per-View
ESPN Extra (delivered digitally); ESPN Now (delivered digitally); Hot Choice (delivered digitally); iN DEMAND (delivered digitally); Playboy TV (delivered digitally); Fresh (delivered digitally); Shorteez (delivered digitally).

Internet Service
Operational: No.

Telephone Service
None

Miles of Plant: 62.0 (coaxial); None (fiber optic). Homes passed: 1,341.
Vice President & General Manager: Steve Trippe. Operations Director: Dave Miller. Operations Manager: Dave Huntsman. Chief Technician: Jim Miller. Marketing Director: Beverly Wall. Office Manager: Missy Brown.
Ownership: Charter Communications Inc. (MSO).

VIOLA—Salem Cable Vision, PO Box 1115, Salem, AR 72576. Phone: 870-895-4993. Fax: 870-895-4905. ICA: AR0195.
TV Market Ranking: Outside TV Markets (VIOLA). Franchise award date: December 1, 1988. Franchise expiration date: N.A. Began: April 1, 1986.
Channel capacity: 121 (2-way capable). Channels available but not in use: 13.

Basic Service
Subscribers: 150.
Programming (received off-air): KAIT (ABC) Jonesboro; KARK-TV (NBC) Little Rock; KEMV (PBS) Mountain View; KOLR (CBS) Springfield; KSFX-TV (FOX) Springfield; KTHV (CBS) Little Rock; KYTV (CW, NBC) Springfield.
Programming (via satellite): C-SPAN; Home Shopping Network; TBS Superstation; Weather Channel; WGN America.
Fee: $61.50 installation; $14.44 monthly.

Expanded Basic Service 1
Subscribers: 79.
Programming (via satellite): ABC Family Channel; AMC; CNN; Comcast Sports Net Southwest; ESPN; Great American Country; Nickelodeon; Trinity Broadcasting Network; Turner Network TV; USA Network.
Fee: $13.06 monthly.

Pay Service 1
Pay Units: 34.
Programming (via satellite): Cinemax; HBO.
Fee: $8.99 monthly (Cinemax), $12.99 monthly (HBO).

Internet Service
Operational: No.

Telephone Service
None

Miles of Plant: 7.0 (coaxial); 20.0 (fiber optic). Homes passed: 159.
Manager: Monty McCullough. Chief Technician: Mike Innes.
Ownership: Monty McCullough (MSO).

WALDRON—Suddenlink Communications, 12444 Powerscourt Dr, Saint Louis, MO 63131-3660. Phones: 800-999-6845 (Customer service); 314-965-2020. Fax: 903-561-5485. Web Site: http://www.suddenlink.com. ICA: AR0078.
TV Market Ranking: Outside TV Markets (WALDRON). Franchise award date: January 1, 1967. Franchise expiration date: N.A. Began: August 1, 1967.
Channel capacity: N.A. Channels available but not in use: N.A.

Basic Service
Subscribers: 1,242.
Programming (received off-air): KAFT (PBS) Fayetteville; KFSM-TV (CBS) Fort Smith; KFTA-TV (FOX) Fort Smith; KHBS (ABC) Fort Smith; KNWA-TV (NBC) Rogers; KTUL (ABC) Tulsa; allband FM.
Programming (via satellite): C-SPAN; National Geographic Channel; QVC; Trinity Broadcasting Network.
Fee: $35.00 installation; $18.00 monthly.

Expanded Basic Service 1
Subscribers: N.A.
Programming (via satellite): ABC Family Channel; AMC; Animal Planet; Arts & Entertainment; Cartoon Network; CNBC; CNN; Comcast Sports Net Southwest; Comedy Central; CW+; Discovery Channel; Disney Channel; E! Entertainment Television; ESPN; ESPN 2; Food Network; Fox News Channel; FX; Great American Country; Hallmark Channel; Headline News; HGTV; History Channel; Jewelry Television; Lifetime; MSNBC; MTV; Nickelodeon; Outdoor Channel; Spike TV; Syfy; TBS Superstation; The Learning Channel; Turner Classic Movies; Turner Network TV; TV Land; Univision; USA Network; VH1; Weather Channel.
Fee: $19.95 monthly.

Digital Basic Service
Subscribers: N.A.
Programming (via satellite): BBC America; Bio; Bloomberg Television; Discovery Health Channel; Discovery Home Channel; Discovery Kids Channel; Discovery Military Channel; Discovery Times Channel; DMX Music; ESPN Classic Sports; ESPNews; Fox College Sports Atlantic; Fox College Sports Central; Fox College Sports Pacific; Fox Soccer; Fuse; G4; Golf Channel; GSN; History Channel International; Independent Film Channel; Science Channel; ShopNBC; Sleuth; Speed Channel; Style Network; Sundance Channel; Versus; WE tv.

Pay Service 1
Pay Units: 160.
Programming (via satellite): HBO.
Fee: $10.95 monthly.

Pay Service 2
Pay Units: 85.
Programming (via satellite): The Movie Channel.
Fee: $5.95 monthly.

Pay Service 3
Pay Units: 82.
Programming (via satellite): Showtime.
Fee: $9.95 monthly.

Digital Pay Service 1
Pay Units: N.A.
Programming (via satellite): Cinemax (multiplexed); Encore (multiplexed); Flix; HBO (multiplexed); Showtime (multiplexed); Starz (multiplexed); The Movie Channel (multiplexed).

Video-On-Demand: No

Pay-Per-View
iN DEMAND (delivered digitally); Playboy TV (delivered digitally); Fresh (delivered digitally); Club Jenna (delivered digitally); Spice: Xcess (delivered digitally).

Internet Service
Operational: Yes. Began: March 24, 2004.
Broadband Service: Cebridge High Speed Cable Internet.
Fee: $29.95 monthly.

Telephone Service
Digital: Operational
Fee: $44.95 monthly

Miles of Plant: 23.0 (coaxial); None (fiber optic). Homes passed: 1,378.
Manager: Dave Walker. Chief Technician: Carl Miller. Marketing Director: Beverly Gambell. Regional Manager: Todd Cruthird.
City fee: 4% of gross.
Ownership: Cequel Communications LLC (MSO).

WALNUT RIDGE—Suddenlink Communications, PO Box 370, 2728 Thomasville Rd, Pocahontas, AR 72455. Phone: 870-886-2542. Fax: 870-892-5694. Web Site: http://www.suddenlink.com. Also serves College City, Hoxie & Lawrence County. ICA: AR0288.
TV Market Ranking: Below 100 (College City, Hoxie, Lawrence County, WALNUT RIDGE). Franchise award date: N.A. Franchise expiration date: N.A. Began: July 1, 1963.
Channel capacity: N.A. Channels available but not in use: N.A.

Basic Service
Subscribers: 2,581.
Programming (received off-air): KAIT (ABC) Jonesboro; KARK-TV (NBC) Little Rock; KATV (ABC) Little Rock; KTEJ (PBS) Jonesboro; KTHV (CBS) Little Rock; KVTJ-DT (IND) Jonesboro; WHBQ-TV (FOX) Memphis; WMC-TV (NBC) Memphis; WREG-TV (CBS) Memphis; 3 FMs.
Programming (via satellite): C-SPAN; CW+; ION Television; Lifetime; MTV; QVC; TBS Superstation; TV Guide Network; WGN America.
Current originations: Public Access.
Fee: $25.00 installation; $10.63 monthly; $15.00 additional installation.

Expanded Basic Service 1
Subscribers: 2,293.
Programming (via satellite): ABC Family Channel; AMC; Animal Planet; Arts & Entertainment; Bravo; Cartoon Network; CNBC; CNN; Comcast Sports Net Southwest; Comedy Central; Country Music TV; Discovery Channel; Disney Channel; E! Entertainment Television; ESPN; ESPN 2; Eternal Word TV Network; Food Network; Fox News Channel; FX; Great American Country; Headline News; HGTV; History Channel; Home Shopping Network; INSP; MSNBC; Nickelodeon; Oxygen; Speed Channel; Spike TV; Syfy; The Learning Channel; Travel Channel; truTV; Turner Classic Movies; Turner Network TV; TV Land; USA Network; Versus; VH1; Weather Channel.
Fee: $12.88 monthly.

Digital Basic Service
Subscribers: N.A.
Programming (via satellite): BBC America; Bio; Bloomberg Television; Discovery Digital Networks; Encore (multiplexed); ESPN Classic Sports; ESPNews; Fox Sports World; Fuse; G4; Golf Channel; GSN; Hallmark Channel; History Channel International; Independent Film Channel; Lifetime Movie Network; Music Choice; Outdoor Channel; SoapNet; Sundance Channel; Toon Disney.

Digital Pay Service 1
Pay Units: N.A.
Programming (via satellite): Cinemax (multiplexed); HBO (multiplexed); Showtime (multiplexed); Starz (multiplexed); The Movie Channel (multiplexed).

Video-On-Demand: No

Pay-Per-View
Playboy TV (delivered digitally); ESPN Now (delivered digitally); ESPN Gameplan (delivered digitally); NBA TV (delivered digitally); Fresh (delivered digitally); iN DEMAND (delivered digitally).

Internet Service
Operational: Yes.
Fee: $35.00 monthly.

Telephone Service
Digital: Operational
Fee: $20.00 monthly

Miles of Plant: 26.0 (coaxial); None (fiber optic). Additional miles planned: 6.0 (coaxial).
Manager: Garry Bowman.
City fee: 1% of gross.
Ownership: Cequel Communications LLC (MSO).

WARREN—Community Communications Co., 1920 Hwy 425 N, Monticello, AR 71655-4463. Phones: 800-272-2191; 870-367-7300. Fax: 870-367-9770. E-mail: generalmanager@ccc-cable.net. Web Site: http://www.ccc-cable.net. Also serves Bradley County. ICA: AR0041.
TV Market Ranking: 99 (Bradley County (portions)); Outside TV Markets (WARREN,

Bradley County (portions)). Franchise award date: N.A. Franchise expiration date: N.A. Began: December 1, 1974.

Channel capacity: 54 (not 2-way capable). Channels available but not in use: 4.

Basic Service

Subscribers: 1,740.

Programming (received off-air): KARK-TV (NBC) Little Rock; KARZ-TV (MNT) Little Rock; KASN (CW) Pine Bluff; KATV (ABC) Little Rock; KETS (PBS) Little Rock; KKYK-DT (IND) Camden; KLRT-TV (FOX) Little Rock; KTHV (CBS) Little Rock; KTVE (NBC) El Dorado; allband FM.

Programming (via satellite): ABC Family Channel; Animal Planet; Arts & Entertainment; BET Networks; CNBC; CNN; Comcast Sports Net Southwest; Comedy Central; Country Music TV; C-SPAN; Discovery Channel; Disney Channel; E! Entertainment Television; ESPN; ESPN 2; ESPNews; Fox News Channel; FX; GalaVision; Headline News; History Channel; Home Shopping Network; Lifetime; MTV; National Geographic Channel; Nickelodeon; Outdoor Channel; QVC; Speed Channel; Spike TV; Syfy; TBS Superstation; The Learning Channel; Travel Channel; Trinity Broadcasting Network; Turner Classic Movies; Turner Network TV; TV Guide Network; TV Land; USA Network; Versus; VH1; Weather Channel; WGN America.

Fee: $35.00 installation; $35.70 monthly; $20.00 additional installation.

Pay Service 1

Pay Units: 117.

Programming (via satellite): Cinemax.

Fee: $10.00 monthly.

Pay Service 2

Pay Units: 149.

Programming (via satellite): Showtime; The Movie Channel.

Fee: $10.00 monthly.

Pay Service 3

Pay Units: 165.

Programming (via satellite): HBO.

Fee: $10.00 monthly.

Video-On-Demand: No

Internet Service

Operational: No.

Telephone Service

None

Miles of Plant: 75.0 (coaxial); None (fiber optic). Homes passed: 2,750. Total homes in franchised area: 2,750.

Operations Manager: Larry Ivy.

Ownership: Community Communications Co. (MSO).

WATSON—Community Communications Co., 1920 Hwy 425 N, Monticello, AR 71655-4463. Phones: 800-272-2191; 870-367-7300. Fax: 870-367-9770. E-mail: generalmanager@ccc-cable.net. Web Site: http://www.ccc-cable.net. ICA: AR0198.

TV Market Ranking: Below 100 (WATSON). Franchise award date: N.A. Franchise expiration date: N.A. Began: July 1, 1988.

Channel capacity: 48 (not 2-way capable). Channels available but not in use: 9.

Basic Service

Subscribers: 65.

Programming (received off-air): KARZ-TV (MNT) Little Rock; KASN (CW) Pine Bluff; KATV (ABC) Little Rock; KETS (PBS) Little Rock; KKAP (ETV) Little Rock; KKYK-CA (IND) Little Rock; KPBI (MNT) Eureka Springs; KTHV (CBS) Little Rock; KTVE (NBC) El Dorado; WABG-TV (ABC) Greenwood; WXVT (CBS) Greenville.

Programming (via satellite): ABC Family Channel; AMC; Arts & Entertainment; BET Networks; CNN; Country Music TV; C-SPAN; Discovery Channel; ESPN; ESPN 2; FX; Lifetime; Nickelodeon; Outdoor Channel; QVC; Spike TV; Syfy; TBS Superstation; The Learning Channel; Trinity Broadcasting Network; Turner Network TV; TV Land; USA Network; WGN America.

Fee: $35.00 installation; $33.60 monthly.

Pay Service 1

Pay Units: 39.

Programming (via satellite): HBO.

Fee: $10.00 monthly.

Video-On-Demand: No

Internet Service

Operational: No.

Telephone Service

None

Homes passed: 143.

Operations Manager: Larry Ivy.

Ownership: Community Communications Co. (MSO).

WEST FORK—Cox Communications. Now served by SPRINGDALE, AR [AR0220]. ICA: AR0290.

WEST PULASKI—Charter Communications, 19863 Interstate 30, Ste 3, Benton, AR 72015-6966. Phones: 636-207-7044 (St Louis office); 501-315-4405. Fax: 501-315-4406. Web Site: http://www.charter.com. ICA: AR0048.

TV Market Ranking: 50 (WEST PULASKI). Franchise award date: N.A. Franchise expiration date: N.A. Began: N.A.

Channel capacity: N.A. Channels available but not in use: N.A.

Basic Service

Subscribers: 766.

Programming (received off-air): KARK-TV (NBC) Little Rock; KARZ-TV (MNT) Little Rock; KASN (CW) Pine Bluff; KATV (ABC) Little Rock; KETS (PBS) Little Rock; KLRT-TV (FOX) Little Rock; KTHV (CBS) Little Rock; KVTN-DT (IND) Pine Bluff.

Programming (via satellite): ABC Family Channel; Arts & Entertainment; CNN; Comcast Sports Net Southwest; Comedy Central; C-SPAN; Discovery Channel; E! Entertainment Television; ESPN; Headline News; Home Shopping Network; Lifetime; MTV; Nickelodeon; QVC; Syfy; The Learning Channel; VH1; WGN America.

Current originations: Government Access; Educational Access; Public Access.

Fee: $29.99 installation.

Expanded Basic Service 1

Subscribers: 684.

Programming (via satellite): AMC; Bravo; Country Music TV; Disney Channel; History Channel; Spike TV; TBS Superstation; Turner Network TV; USA Network; Weather Channel.

Fee: $49.99 monthly.

Digital Basic Service

Subscribers: N.A.

Programming (via satellite): AmericanLife TV Network; BBC America; Bio; Bloomberg Television; Discovery Digital Networks; DMX Music; ESPN 2; ESPN Classic Sports; ESPNews; Fox Movie Channel; G4; GAS; Golf Channel; GSN; Halogen Network; HGTV; History Channel International; Independent Film Channel; Lifetime Movie Network; MTV Networks Digital Suite; MuchMusic Network; Nick Jr.; Outdoor Channel; ShopNBC; Speed Channel; Style Network; Toon Disney; Trinity Broadcasting Network; Turner Classic Movies; Versus; WE tv.

Pay Service 1

Pay Units: 33.

Programming (via satellite): Cinemax.

Fee: $11.95 monthly.

Pay Service 2

Pay Units: 47.

Programming (via satellite): HBO.

Fee: $11.95 monthly.

Pay Service 3

Pay Units: 35.

Programming (via satellite): Showtime.

Fee: $11.95 monthly.

Pay Service 4

Pay Units: 28.

Programming (via satellite): The Movie Channel.

Fee: $11.95 monthly.

Digital Pay Service 1

Pay Units: N.A.

Programming (via satellite): Cinemax (multiplexed); Encore (multiplexed); Flix; HBO (multiplexed); Showtime (multiplexed); Starz (multiplexed); The Movie Channel (multiplexed).

Video-On-Demand: No

Pay-Per-View

ESPN Extra (delivered digitally); ESPN Now (delivered digitally); Hot Choice (delivered digitally); iN DEMAND; iN DEMAND (delivered digitally); Playboy TV (delivered digitally); Fresh (delivered digitally); Shorteez (delivered digitally); Urban Xtra (delivered digitally).

Internet Service

Operational: No.

Telephone Service

None

Miles of Plant: 94.0 (coaxial); None (fiber optic). Homes passed: 2,310. Total homes in franchised area: 2,500.

Vice President & General Manager: Steve Trippe. Operations Director: Dave Miller. Operations Manager: Dave Huntsman. Chief Technician: Jim Miller. Marketing Director: Beverly Wall. Office Manager: Missy Brown.

Franchise fee: 3% of gross.

Ownership: Charter Communications Inc. (MSO).

WESTERN GROVE—Ritter Communications, 2109 Fowler Ave, Jonesboro, AR 72401. Phones: 888-336-4466; 870-336-3434. Web Site: http://www.getritter.info. Also serves Alpena, Everton & Jasper. ICA: AR0183.

TV Market Ranking: Below 100 (Alpena, Everton, Jasper, WESTERN GROVE). Franchise award date: N.A. Franchise expiration date: N.A. Began: October 1, 1983.

Channel capacity: 20 (operating 2-way). Channels available but not in use: N.A.

Basic Service

Subscribers: 472.

Programming (received off-air): KARK-TV (NBC) Little Rock; KATV (ABC) Little Rock; KEMV (PBS) Mountain View; KHOG-TV (ABC) Fayetteville; KOLR (CBS) Springfield; KSFX-TV (FOX) Springfield; KSPR (ABC) Springfield; KTHV (CBS) Little Rock; KWBM (MNT) Harrison [LICENSED & SILENT]; KYTV (CW, NBC) Springfield.

Programming (via satellite): C-SPAN; CW+; Home Shopping Network; KWBM (MNT) Harrison [LICENSED & SILENT]; Trinity Broadcasting Network.

Fee: $39.95 installation; $17.95 monthly.

Expanded Basic Service 1

Subscribers: N.A.

Programming (received off-air): KTKO-LP Harrison.

Programming (via satellite): ABC Family Channel; AMC; Animal Planet; Arts & Entertainment; CNN; Comedy Central; Discovery Channel; Disney Channel; ESPN; ESPN 2; Food Network; Great American Country; Headline News; HGTV; History Channel; Lifetime; Lifetime Movie Network; National Geographic Channel; Nickelodeon; Outdoor Channel; Spike TV; TBS Superstation; The Learning Channel; Travel Channel; Turner Classic Movies; Turner Network TV; TV Land; USA Network; Weather Channel.

Fee: $33.95 monthly.

Pay Service 1

Pay Units: 12.

Programming (via satellite): HBO.

Fee: $11.95 monthly.

Pay Service 2

Pay Units: 4.

Programming (via satellite): The Movie Channel.

Fee: $11.95 monthly.

Video-On-Demand: No

Internet Service

Operational: No, DSL only.

Telephone Service

None

Miles of Plant: 97.0 (coaxial); None (fiber optic). Homes passed: 888.

President: Bob Mouser. Marketing Director: Jane Marie Woodruff. Headend Manager: Joe Sain.

Ownership: Ritter Communications (MSO).

WHEATLEY—Formerly served by Almega Cable. No longer in operation. ICA: AR0298.

WHITEHALL—Suddenlink Communications, 12444 Powerscourt Dr, Saint Louis, MO 63131-3660. Phones: 800-999-6845 (Customer service); 314-965-2020. Fax: 903-561-5485. Web Site: http://www.suddenlink.com. Also serves Grant County (portions), Hardin, Jefferson County (portions), Pine Bluff Arsenal & Redfield. ICA: AR0042.

TV Market Ranking: 50 (Grant County (portions), Hardin, Jefferson County (portions), Pine Bluff Arsenal, Redfield, WHITEHALL). Franchise award date: N.A. Franchise expiration date: N.A. Began: N.A.

Channel capacity: 36 (operating 2-way). Channels available but not in use: None.

Basic Service

Subscribers: N.A.

Programming (received off-air): KARK-TV (NBC) Little Rock; KARZ-TV (MNT) Little Rock; KASN (CW) Pine Bluff; KATV (ABC) Little Rock; KETS (PBS) Little Rock; KKYK-DT (IND) Camden; KLRT-TV (FOX) Little Rock; KTHV (CBS) Little Rock.

Programming (via satellite): KVTN-DT (IND) Pine Bluff.

Fee: $39.95 installation; $19.95 monthly.

Expanded Basic Service 1

Subscribers: N.A.

Programming (via satellite): ABC Family Channel; AMC; Animal Planet; Arts & Entertainment; BET Networks; Cartoon Network; CNBC; CNN; Comcast Sports Net Southwest; Comedy Central; Discovery Channel; Disney Channel; E! Entertainment Television; ESPN; ESPN 2; Food Network; Fox News Channel; Great American Country; Headline News; HGTV; History Channel; Home Shopping Network; Lifetime; MTV; National Geographic Channel; Nickelodeon; Outdoor Channel; Spike TV; Syfy; TBS Superstation; The Learning Channel; Turner Classic Movies; Turner Network TV; TV Land; USA Network; Weather Channel.

Fee: $24.00 monthly.

Digital Basic Service
Subscribers: N.A.
Programming (via satellite): BBC America; Bio; Bloomberg Television; Discovery Digital Networks; ESPN Classic Sports; ESPNews; Fox College Sports Atlantic; Fox College Sports Central; Fox College Sports Pacific; Fox Soccer; Fuse; G4; Golf Channel; GSN; History Channel International; Independent Film Channel; Science Television; ShopNBC; Speed Channel; Style Network; Sundance Channel; Toon Disney; Trinity Broadcasting Network; Versus; WE tv.
Digital Expanded Basic Service
Subscribers: N.A.
Programming (via satellite): DMX Music.
Pay Service 1
Pay Units: 122.
Programming (via satellite): Cinemax.
Fee: $9.00 monthly.
Pay Service 2
Pay Units: 220.
Programming (via satellite): HBO.
Fee: $10.95 monthly.
Pay Service 3
Pay Units: 192.
Programming (via satellite): Showtime.
Fee: $10.95 monthly.
Digital Pay Service 1
Pay Units: N.A.
Programming (via satellite): Cinemax (multiplexed); Encore (multiplexed); Flix (multiplexed); HBO (multiplexed); Showtime (multiplexed); Starz (multiplexed); The Movie Channel (multiplexed).
Video-On-Demand: No
Pay-Per-View
Fresh (delivered digitally); Fresh (delivered digitally); Playboy TV (delivered digitally); iN DEMAND (delivered digitally).
Internet Service
Operational: Yes. Began: November 22, 2002.
Broadband Service: Cebridge High Speed Cable Internet.
Fee: $29.95 monthly.
Telephone Service
Digital: Operational
Fee: $44.95 monthly
Miles of Plant: 127.0 (coaxial); None (fiber optic). Homes passed: 4,375.
Regional Manager: Todd Cruthird. Area Manager: Carolyn Wilder. Plant Manager: Donnie Burton.
Ownership: Cequel Communications LLC (MSO).

WILMAR—Almega Cable, 4001 W Airport Frwy, Ste 530, Bedford, TX 76021. Phone: 877-725-6342. Fax: 817-685-6488. Web Site: http://www.almegacable.com. ICA: AR0164.
TV Market Ranking: Outside TV Markets (WILMAR). Franchise award date: N.A. Franchise expiration date: N.A. Began: N.A.
Channel capacity: 36 (not 2-way capable). Channels available but not in use: 18.
Basic Service
Subscribers: N.A.
Programming (received off-air): KARK-TV (NBC) Little Rock; KASN (CW) Pine Bluff; KATV (ABC) Little Rock; KETS (PBS) Little Rock; KLRT-TV (FOX) Little Rock; KTHV (CBS) Little Rock.
Programming (via satellite): ABC Family Channel; BET Networks; CNN; Country Music TV; Discovery Channel; Disney Channel; ESPN; TBS Superstation; Turner Network TV; USA Network; WGN America.
Fee: $39.95 installation; $39.95 monthly.
Pay Service 1
Pay Units: 42.
Programming (via satellite): HBO.
Fee: $10.95 monthly.
Pay Service 2
Pay Units: 35.
Programming (via satellite): Showtime.
Fee: $10.95 monthly.
Video-On-Demand: No
Internet Service
Operational: No.
Telephone Service
None
Miles of Plant: 9.0 (coaxial); None (fiber optic). Homes passed: 274.
President: Thomas Kurien.
Ownership: Almega Cable (MSO).

WILMOT—Dean Hill Cable, PO Box 128, Parkdale, AR 71661. Phone: 870-473-2802. Fax: 870-737-0020. Also serves Parkdale. ICA: AR0129.
TV Market Ranking: Below 100 (Parkdale); Outside TV Markets (WILMOT). Franchise award date: N.A. Franchise expiration date: N.A. Began: September 1, 1981.
Channel capacity: N.A. Channels available but not in use: N.A.
Basic Service
Subscribers: 119.
Programming (received off-air): KATV (ABC) Little Rock; KLTM-TV (PBS) Monroe; KNOE-TV (CBS, CW) Monroe; KTVE (NBC) El Dorado; WABG-TV (ABC) Greenwood.
Programming (via satellite): Disney Channel; ESPN; TBS Superstation; Turner Network TV; WGN America.
Fee: $35.00 installation; $27.00 monthly.
Pay Service 1
Pay Units: 25.
Programming (via satellite): HBO.
Fee: $11.55 monthly.
Video-On-Demand: No
Internet Service
Operational: No.
Telephone Service
None
Miles of Plant: 19.0 (coaxial); None (fiber optic).
Manager: Dean Hill. Assistant Manager: Kathy Hill.
Ownership: Dean Hill Cable (MSO).

WINSLOW—Cox Communications. Now served by SPRINGDALE, AR [AR0220]. ICA: AR0291.

WITCHERVILLE—Formerly served by Eagle Media. No longer in operation. ICA: AR0311.

YELLVILLE—Indco Cable TV, PO Box 3799, 2700 N Saint Louis, Batesville, AR 72503-3799. Phone: 870-793-4174. Fax: 870-793-7439. Web Site: http://www.indco.net. Also serves Marion County & Summit. ICA: AR0292.
TV Market Ranking: Below 100 (Marion County (portions), Summit, YELLVILLE); Outside TV Markets (Marion County (portions)). Franchise award date: September 1, 1991. Franchise expiration date: N.A. Began: August 1, 1961.
Channel capacity: 35 (operating 2-way). Channels available but not in use: N.A.
Basic Service
Subscribers: 538.
Programming (received off-air): KARK-TV (NBC) Little Rock; KATV (ABC) Little Rock; KEMV (PBS) Mountain View; KOLR (CBS) Springfield; KSFX-TV (FOX) Springfield; KSPR (ABC) Springfield; KTHV (CBS) Little Rock; KWBM (MNT) Harrison [LICENSED & SILENT]; KYTV (CW, NBC) Springfield.
Programming (via satellite): ABC Family Channel; AmericanLife TV Network; Arts & Entertainment; CNBC; CNN; Country Music TV; C-SPAN; Discovery Channel; Disney Channel; ESPN; ESPN 2; FX; HGTV; History Channel; Nickelodeon; Outdoor Channel; QVC; Spike TV; Syfy; TBS Superstation; Travel Channel; Trinity Broadcasting Network; Turner Network TV; USA Network; Weather Channel; WGN America.
Fee: $20.00 installation; $30.95 monthly.
Pay Service 1
Pay Units: 9.
Programming (via satellite): Cinemax.
Fee: $8.00 monthly.
Pay Service 2
Pay Units: 15.
Programming (via satellite): HBO.
Fee: $10.00 monthly.
Video-On-Demand: Planned
Internet Service
Operational: Yes.
Fee: $29.95 monthly.
Telephone Service
None
Miles of Plant: 26.0 (coaxial); None (fiber optic).
Manager: J. D. Pierce. Chief Technician: Tommy Barnett. Marketing Director: Connie Barnett.
Ownership: Indco Cable TV (MSO).

CALIFORNIA

Total Systems: **180**
Total Communities Served: **1,172**
Franchises Not Yet Operating: **0**
Applications Pending: **0**
Communities with Applications: **0**
Number of Basic Subscribers: **8,105,648**
Number of Expanded Basic Subscribers: **1,980,713**
Number of Pay Units: **1,065,342**

Top 100 Markets Represented: Sacramento-Stockton-Modesto (25); Los Angeles-San Bernardino-Corona-Riverside-Anaheim (2); San Diego (51); Fresno-Visalia-Hanford-Clovis-Merced-Porterville (72); San Francisco-Oakland-San Jose (7).

**For a list of cable communities in this section, see the Cable Community Index located in the back of Cable Volume 2.
For explanation of terms used in cable system listings, see p. D-11.**

ADOBE WELLS MOBILE HOME PARK—Formerly served by Comcast Cable. No longer in operation. ICA: CA0305.

AGOURA HILLS—Time Warner Cable. Now served by CHATSWORTH, CA [CA0013]. ICA: CA0024.

ALAMEDA—Comcast Cable. Now served by OAKLAND, CA [CA0018]. ICA: CA0080.

ALAMEDA—Formerly served by Alameda Power & Telecom. Now served by OAKLAND, CA [CA0018]. ICA: CA0454.

ALHAMBRA—Charter Communications, 4781 Irwindale Ave, Suite 350, Irwindale, CA 91706-2175. Phone: 626-430-3300. Fax: 626-430-3420. E-mail: kari@charter.com. Web Site: http://www.charter.com. Also serves Altadena, City of Commerce, Commerce, Covina, Huntington Park, La Canada-Flintridge, Los Angeles County, Monrovia (southern portion), Montebello, Monterey Park, Norwalk, Pasadena, Rosemead, San Gabriel, South San Gabriel, Temple City, Walnut & West Covina. ICA: CA0005.

TV Market Ranking: 2 (ALHAMBRA, Altadena, City of Commerce, Commerce, Covina, Huntington Park, La Canada-Flintridge, Los Angeles County, Monrovia (southern portion), Montebello, Monterey Park, Norwalk, Pasadena, Rosemead, San Gabriel, South San Gabriel, Temple City, Walnut, West Covina). Franchise award date: N.A. Franchise expiration date: N.A. Began: August 1, 1981.

Channel capacity: N.A. Channels available but not in use: N.A.

Basic Service

Subscribers: 300,000.

Programming (received off-air): KABC-TV (ABC) Los Angeles; KAZA-TV (IND) Avalon; KCBS-TV (CBS) Los Angeles; KCET (PBS) Los Angeles; KCOP-TV (MNT) Los Angeles; KDOC-TV (IND) Anaheim; KFTR-DT (TEL) Ontario; KJLA (IND) Ventura; KLCS (PBS) Los Angeles; KLRN (PBS) San Antonio; KMEX-DT (UNV) Los Angeles; KNBC (NBC) Los Angeles; KOCE-TV (PBS) Huntington Beach; KPXN-TV (ION) San Bernardino; KRCA (IND) Riverside; KSCI (IND) Long Beach; KTBN-TV (TBN) Santa Ana; KTLA (CW) Los Angeles; KTTV (FOX) Los Angeles; KVEA (TMO) Corona; KWHY-TV (IND) Los Angeles; KXLA (IND) Rancho Palos Verdes.

Programming (via satellite): Comedy Central; C-SPAN; Product Information Network; QVC; TBS Superstation; TV Guide Network; WGN America.

Current originations: Leased Access; Government Access; Public Access.

Fee: $29.99 installation.

Expanded Basic Service 1

Subscribers: 122,867.

Programming (via satellite): ABC Family Channel; AMC; Animal Planet; Arts & Entertainment; BET Networks; Bravo; Cartoon Network; CCTV-4; CNBC; CNN; Country Music TV; C-SPAN 2; Discovery Channel; Disney Channel; E! Entertainment Television; ESPN; ESPN 2; ESPN Classic Sports; Food Network; Fox News Channel; Fox Sports en Espanol; Fox Sports Net West; Fox Sports Net West 2; FX; G4; GalaVision; Golf Channel; Headline News; HGTV; History Channel; Jade Channel; Lifetime; MSNBC; MTV; Nickelodeon; Oxygen; Speed Channel; Spike TV; Syfy; The Learning Channel; The Movie Channel; Travel Channel; truTV; Turner Classic Movies; Turner Network TV; USA Network; VH1.

Fee: $48.95 monthly.

Digital Basic Service

Subscribers: 93,500.

Programming (via satellite): BBC America; Bio; Bloomberg Television; Boomerang; Discovery Digital Networks; Do-It-Yourself; Fox College Sports Atlantic; Fox College Sports Central; Fox College Sports Pacific; GAS; Great American Country; History Channel International; Independent Film Channel; Lifetime Movie Network; MTV Networks Digital Suite; MuchMusic Network; Music Choice; Nick Jr.; Nick Too; Style Network; Sundance Channel; Toon Disney; WE tv.

Fee: $6.95 monthly.

Digital Pay Service 1

Pay Units: 13,856.

Programming (via satellite): Cinemax (multiplexed).

Fee: $10.00 monthly.

Digital Pay Service 2

Pay Units: N.A.

Programming (via satellite): Encore (multiplexed); Starz (multiplexed).

Fee: $10.00 monthly.

Digital Pay Service 3

Pay Units: 40,533.

Programming (via satellite): HBO (multiplexed).

Fee: $10.00 monthly.

Digital Pay Service 4

Pay Units: 28,903.

Programming (via satellite): Flix; Showtime (multiplexed).

Fee: $10.00 monthly.

Digital Pay Service 5

Pay Units: 11,872.

Programming (via satellite): The Movie Channel (multiplexed).

Fee: $10.00 monthly.

Video-On-Demand: Yes

Pay-Per-View

Addressable homes: 93,500.

ETC (delivered digitally), Addressable: Yes; iN DEMAND (delivered digitally); Playboy TV (delivered digitally); Pleasure (delivered digitally); Fresh; Shorteez (delivered digitally); Video On Demand (delivered digitally); sports (delivered digitally).

Internet Service

Operational: Yes.

Subscribers: 12,228.

Broadband Service: Charter Pipeline.

Fee: $29.99 monthly; $4.95 modem lease.

Telephone Service

Digital: Operational

Fee: $29.99 monthly

Miles of Plant: 2,084.0 (coaxial); None (fiber optic). Additional miles planned: 8.0 (fiber optic). Homes passed: 328,000.

Vice President & General Manager: Wendy Rasmussen. Technical Operations Manager: Tom Williams. Marketing Manager: Lily Ho.

City fee: 5% of gross.

Ownership: Charter Communications Inc. (MSO).

ALTURAS—Charter Communications, 270 Bridge St, San Luis Obispo, CA 93401. Phone: 805-544-1962. Fax: 805-541-6042. Web Site: http://www.charter.com. Also serves Modoc County (portions). ICA: CA0230.

TV Market Ranking: Outside TV Markets (ALTURAS, Modoc County (portions)). Franchise award date: N.A. Franchise expiration date: N.A. Began: January 1, 1957.

Channel capacity: 61 (not 2-way capable). Channels available but not in use: 10.

Basic Service

Subscribers: 1,342.

Programming (received off-air): KIXE-TV (PBS) Redding; KOLO-TV (ABC) Reno; KOTI (NBC) Klamath Falls; KRCR-TV (ABC) Redding; KTVL (CBS, CW) Medford; 2 FMs.

Programming (via satellite): Discovery Channel; Food Network; Hallmark Channel; Home Shopping Network; KCNC-TV (CBS) Denver; WGN America.

Current originations: Government Access; Educational Access.

Fee: $51.00 installation; $11.68 monthly; $25.50 additional installation.

Expanded Basic Service 1

Subscribers: 1,266.

Programming (via satellite): ABC Family Channel; AMC; Animal Planet; Arts & Entertainment; Cartoon Network; CNN; Comcast Sports Net Northwest; Comedy Central; Country Music TV; Disney Channel; E! Entertainment Television; ESPN; ESPN 2; FitTV; Fox News Channel; FX; Headline News; HGTV; History Channel; MoviePlex; MTV; Nickelodeon; Spike TV; Syfy; TBS Superstation; The Learning Channel; truTV; Turner Network TV; USA Network; Versus; Weather Channel.

Fee: $14.38 monthly.

Digital Basic Service

Subscribers: N.A.

Programming (via satellite): AmericanLife TV Network; BBC America; Bio; Bloomberg Television; Bravo; Discovery Digital Networks; DMX Music; ESPN Now; Fox Movie Channel; Fox Soccer; Fuse; G4; Golf Channel; GSN; Halogen Network; History Channel International; Independent Film Channel; Lifetime Movie Network; MTV Networks Digital Suite; Nick Jr.; Outdoor Channel; ShopNBC; Speed Channel; TeenNick; Toon Disney; Trinity Broadcasting Network; Turner Classic Movies; WE tv.

Pay Service 1

Pay Units: 90.

Programming (via satellite): Cinemax; Encore; HBO; Showtime; Starz.

Fee: $25.00 installation; $9.50 monthly (Cinemax).

Digital Pay Service 1

Pay Units: N.A.

Programming (via satellite): Cinemax (multiplexed); Encore (multiplexed); Flix; HBO (multiplexed); Showtime (multiplexed); Starz (multiplexed); The Movie Channel (multiplexed).

Video-On-Demand: No

Pay-Per-View

iN DEMAND (delivered digitally); Hot Choice (delivered digitally); Playboy TV (delivered digitally); Fresh (delivered digitally); Shorteez (delivered digitally); ESPN (delivered digitally).

Internet Service

Operational: No.

Telephone Service

None

Miles of Plant: 66.0 (coaxial); 6.0 (fiber optic). Homes passed: 1,691. Total homes in franchised area: 1,707.

Vice President & General Manager: Ed Merrill. Operations Manager: Donna Briggs. Marketing Director: Sarwar Assar.

City fee: 2% of gross.

Ownership: Charter Communications Inc. (MSO).

ANAHEIM—Time Warner Cable, 3430 E Miraloma Ave, Anaheim, CA 92806-2101. Phones: 310-647-3000; 714-414-1400. Fax: 714-414-1492. Web Site: http://www.timewarnercable.com/socal. Also serves Alta Loma, Anaheim Hills, Beaumont, Bloomington, Brea, Buena Park, Calimesa, Canyon Lake, Chino, Chino Hills, Colton, Corona, Corona Del Mar, Costa Mesa, Cucamonga, Cypress, Etiwanda, Fontana, Fountain Valley, Fullerton, Garden Grove, Grand Terrace, Hemet, Highland, Homeland, Huntington Beach, Idyllwild, La Habra, La Habra Heights, La Palma, Lake Elsinore, Lakeview, Loma

Linda, Los Alamitos, Lytle Creek, March AFB, Menifee, Mentone, Midway City, Montclair, Moreno Valley, Murrieta, Murrieta Hot Springs, Muscoy, Newport Beach, Nuevo, Ontario, Orange City, Orange County (unincorporated areas), Perris, Placentia, Quail Valley, Rancho California, Rancho Cucamunga, Redlands, Rialto, Riverside County (portions), Romoland, Rossmoor, San Bernardino, San Bernardino County, San Jacinto, Santa Ana, Seal Beach, Stanton, Sunset Beach, Temecula, Tustin, Upland, Villa Park, Westminster, Wildomar, Winchester, Woodcrest, Yorba Linda & Yucaipa. ICA: CA0033.

TV Market Ranking: 2 (Alta Loma, ANAHEIM, Anaheim Hills, Beaumont, Bloomington, Brea, Buena Park, Calimesa, Canyon Lake, Chino, Chino Hills, Colton, Corona, Corona Del Mar, Costa Mesa, Cucamonga, Cypress, Etiwanda, Fontana, Fullerton, Garden Grove, Grand Terrace, Hemet, Highland, Homeland, Huntington Beach, La Habra, La Habra Heights, La Palma, Lake Elsinore, Lakeview, Loma Linda, Los Alamitos, Lytle Creek, March AFB, Menifee, Mentone, Midway City, Montclair, Moreno Valley, Murrieta, Murrieta Hot Springs, Muscoy, Newport Beach, Nuevo, Ontario, Orange City, Orange County (unincorporated areas), Perris, Placentia, Quail Valley, Rancho California, Rancho Cucamunga, Redlands, Rialto, Riverside County (portions), Romoland, Rossmoor, San Bernardino, San Bernardino County, San Jacinto, Santa Ana, Seal Beach, Stanton, Sunset Beach, Temecula, Tustin, Upland, Villa Park, Westminster, Wildomar, Winchester, Woodcrest, Yorba Linda, Yucaipa); Below 100 (Fountain Valley, Idyllwild). Franchise award date: January 25, 1980. Franchise expiration date: N.A. Began: October 1, 1980.

Channel capacity: N.A. Channels available but not in use: N.A.

Basic Service

Subscribers: N.A. Included in Los Angeles

Programming (received off-air): KABC-TV (ABC) Los Angeles; KAZA-TV (IND) Avalon; KCAL-TV (IND) Los Angeles; KCBS-TV (CBS) Los Angeles; KCET (PBS) Los Angeles; KCOP-TV (MNT) Los Angeles; KDOC-TV (IND) Anaheim; KFTR-DT (TEL) Ontario; KJLA (IND) Ventura; KLCS (PBS) Los Angeles; KMEX-DT (UNV) Los Angeles; KNBC (NBC) Los Angeles; KOCE-TV (PBS) Huntington Beach; KPXN-TV (ION) San Bernardino; KRCA (IND) Riverside; KSCI (IND) Long Beach; KTBN-TV (TBN) Santa Ana; KTLA (CW) Los Angeles; KTTV (FOX) Los Angeles; KVCR-DT (PBS) San Bernardino; KVEA (TMO) Corona; KWHY-TV (IND) Los Angeles; KXLA (IND) Rancho Palos Verdes.

Programming (via satellite): Home Shopping Network; QVC; TV Guide Network.

Current originations: Leased Access; Government Access; Educational Access; Public Access.

Fee: $29.95 installation; $17.20 monthly.

Expanded Basic Service 1

Subscribers: N.A.

Programming (via satellite): ABC Family Channel; AMC; Animal Planet; Arts & Entertainment; BET Networks; Bravo; Cartoon Network; CNBC; CNN; Comedy Central; C-SPAN; C-SPAN 2; Discovery Channel; Disney Channel; E! Entertainment Television; ESPN; ESPN 2; FitTV; Food Network; Fox News Channel; Fox Sports Net West; Fox Sports Net West 2; FX; GalaVision; Headline News; HGTV; History Channel; Lifetime; MSNBC; MTV; mun2 television; National Geographic Channel; Nickelodeon; Spike TV; Style Network; Syfy; TBS Superstation; The Learning Channel; Travel Channel; truTV; Turner Classic Movies; Turner Network TV; TV Land; USA Network; VH1; Weather Channel; WGN America.

Fee: $33.80 monthly.

Digital Basic Service

Subscribers: 31,642.

Programming (via satellite): AmericanLife TV Network; BBC America; Bio; Black Family Channel; Bloomberg Television; Canales N; Colours; Country Music TV; Discovery Digital Networks; Do-It-Yourself; ESPN Classic Sports; ESPNews; Eternal Word TV Network; FamilyNet; Fox College Sports Atlantic; Fox College Sports Central; Fox College Sports Pacific; Fox Movie Channel; Fox Sports World; Fuse; G4; Gaming Entertainment Television; Golf Channel; Great American Country; GSN; Hallmark Channel; Halogen Network; History Channel International; Independent Film Channel; Lifetime Movie Network; M-2 (Movie Mania) TV Network; Outdoor Channel; Oxygen; SoapNet; Speed Channel; Sundance Channel; Tennis Channel; Versus; WE tv.

Fee: $5.00 monthly (each tier).

Digital Expanded Basic Service

Subscribers: N.A.

Programming (via satellite): GAS; MTV Networks Digital Suite; Music Choice; Nick Jr.; Nick Too; NickToons TV; Toon Disney.

Digital Pay Service 1

Pay Units: 11,000.

Programming (via satellite): ART America; CCTV-4; Cinemax (multiplexed); Encore (multiplexed); Filipino Channel; Flix; HBO (multiplexed); RAI International; Russian Television Network; Saigon Broadcasting TV Network; Showtime (multiplexed); Starz (multiplexed); The Movie Channel (multiplexed); TV Asia; TV Japan; TV5, La Television International; Zhong Tian Channel.

Fee: $11.95 monthly (Zhong Tian, CCTV, Filipino, ART or SBTN), $14.95 monthly (TV Asia, TV5, RAI, MBC or RTN), $15.00 monthly (Cinemax, HBO, Showtime/TMC or Starz).

Video-On-Demand: Yes

Pay-Per-View

Addressable homes: 31,642.

iN DEMAND (delivered digitally); Sports PPV (delivered digitally); Hot Choice (delivered digitally), Addressable: Yes; Urban Xtra (delivered digitally); Playboy TV; Spice (delivered digitally), Fee: $6.95; Shorteez (delivered digitally).

Internet Service

Operational: Yes. Began: January 1, 2002.

Broadband Service: Road Runner.

Fee: $49.95 installation; $44.95 monthly.

Telephone Service

Digital: Operational

Fee: $49.95 installation; $44.95 monthly

Miles of Plant: 12,761.0 (coaxial); None (fiber optic). Homes passed: 1,452,478. Miles of plant (coax) includes miles of plant (fiber)

President: Fred Stephany. Vice President, Technical Operations: Ike Wells. Vice President, Marketing & Sales: Bill Erickson. Vice President, Government & Public Affairs: Kristy Hennessey.

City fee: 5% of gross.

Ownership: Time Warner Cable (MSO).

ANTELOPE—SureWest Broadband. Formerly served by Sacramento, CA [CA0459]. This cable system has converted to IPTV, PO Box 969, Roseville, CA 95661. Phone: 916-772-2000. Fax: 916-786-7170. Web Site: http://www.surewest.com. ICA: CA5598.

TV Market Ranking: 25 (ANTELOPE).

Channel capacity: N.A. Channels available but not in use: N.A.

Video-On-Demand: Yes

Internet Service

Operational: Yes.

Telephone Service

Digital: Operational

Ownership: SureWest Broadband.

ARCADIA—Charter Communications, 4781 Irwindale Ave, Irwindale, CA 91706-2175. Phone: 626-430-3300. Fax: 626-430-3420. Web Site: http://www.charter.com. Also serves Monrovia & Pasadena. ICA: CA0458.

Note: This system is an overbuild.

TV Market Ranking: 2 (ARCADIA). Franchise award date: July 2, 2001. Franchise expiration date: N.A. Began: January 1, 2002.

Channel capacity: N.A. Channels available but not in use: N.A.

Basic Service

Subscribers: 3,000.

Programming (received off-air): KABC-TV (ABC) Los Angeles; KCBS-TV (CBS) Los Angeles; KCET (PBS) Los Angeles; KCOP-TV (MNT) Los Angeles; KDOC-TV (IND) Anaheim; KHSD-TV (ABC) Lead; KJLA (IND) Ventura; KLCS (PBS) Los Angeles; KMEX-DT (UNV) Los Angeles; KNBC (NBC) Los Angeles; KPXN-TV (ION) San Bernardino; KRCA (IND) Riverside; KSCI (IND) Long Beach; KTBN-TV (TBN) Santa Ana; KTLA (CW) Los Angeles; KTTV (FOX) Los Angeles; KVEA (TMO) Corona; KWHY-TV (IND) Los Angeles.

Programming (via satellite): ABC Family Channel; AMC; Animal Planet; Arts & Entertainment; BET Networks; Bravo; Cartoon Network; CNBC; CNN; Comedy Central; Country Music TV; C-SPAN; C-SPAN 2; Discovery Channel; Disney Channel; E! Entertainment Television; ESPN; ESPN 2; Food Network; Fox Movie Channel; Fox News Channel; Fox Sports Net West; Fox Sports Net West 2; FX; G4; GalaVision; Golf Channel; GSN; Headline News; HGTV; History Channel; Independent Film Channel; Lifetime; Lifetime Movie Network; MSNBC; MTV; National Geographic Channel; Nickelodeon; Oxygen; QVC; ShopNBC; Speed Channel; Spike TV; Syfy; TBS Superstation; The Learning Channel; Toon Disney; Travel Channel; Turner Network TV; TV Guide Network; TV Land; USA Network; VH1; Weather Channel; WGN America.

Fee: $45.00 installation; $42.95 monthly.

Digital Basic Service

Subscribers: 7,000.

Programming (via satellite): BBC America; Bio; Bloomberg Television; Boomerang; CCTV-4; Chinese Television Network; Discovery Digital Networks; Do-It-Yourself; ESPN Classic Sports; ESPN Extra; ESPNews; FamilyNet; Fox Sports World; GAS; Great American Country; History Channel International; Jade Channel; Lifetime Real Women; MTV Networks Digital Suite; Music Choice; NBA TV; Nick Jr.; Nick Too; Ovation; Power Link; Style Network; Sundance Channel; truTV; Turner Classic Movies; Versus.

Fee: $12.00 monthly.

Digital Pay Service 1

Pay Units: N.A.

Programming (via satellite): ART America; Canales N; Cinemax; Encore; Filipino Channel; Flix; HBO; RAI International; Showtime; Starz; The Movie Channel; TV Asia; TV Japan; TV5 USA.

Fee: $12.00 monthly (foreign language channels), $13.00 monthly (movie packages).

Video-On-Demand: Yes

Pay-Per-View

Addressable: Yes; iN DEMAND (delivered digitally); Playboy TV (delivered digitally); sports.

Internet Service

Operational: Yes. Began: December 31, 2001.

Subscribers: 6,000.

Broadband Service: Charter Pipeline.

Fee: $54.00 monthly.

Telephone Service

Analog: Not Operational

Digital: Operational

Vice President & General Manager: Wendy Rasmussen. Technical Operations Manager: Tom Williams. Marketing Manager: Lily Ho.

Ownership: Charter Communications Inc. (MSO).

ARDEN PARK—SureWest Broadband. Formerly served by Sacramento, CA [CA0459]. This cable system has converted to IPTV, PO Box 969, Roseville, CA 95661. Phone: 916-772-2000. Fax: 916-786-7170. Web Site: http://www.surewest.com. ICA: CA5599.

TV Market Ranking: 25 (ARDEN PARK).

Channel capacity: N.A. Channels available but not in use: N.A.

Video-On-Demand: Yes

Internet Service

Operational: Yes.

Telephone Service

Digital: Operational

Ownership: SureWest Broadband.

ARTESIA—Formerly served by Comcast Cable. No longer in operation. ICA: CA0187.

AUBURN—Charter Communications. Now served by PLACER COUNTY (southwestern portion), CA [CA0131]. ICA: CA0162.

AVALON/CATALINA ISLAND—Catalina Cable TV Co., PO Box 2143, 222 Metropole Ave, Avalon, CA 90704-2143. Phone: 310-510-0255. Fax: 310-510-2565. E-mail: catcable@catalinaisp.com. Web Site: http://www.catalinaisp.com. Also serves Catalina Island. ICA: CA0224.

TV Market Ranking: 2 (AVALON, CATALINA ISLAND). Franchise award date: December 19, 1986. Franchise expiration date: N.A. Began: October 1, 1986.

Channel capacity: 77 (operating 2-way). Channels available but not in use: None.

Basic Service

Subscribers: 1,300.

Programming (received off-air): KABC-TV (ABC) Los Angeles; KCBS-TV (CBS) Los Angeles; KCET (PBS) Los Angeles; KCOP-TV (MNT) Los Angeles; KDOC-TV (IND) Anaheim; KNBC (NBC) Los Angeles; KOCE-TV (PBS) Huntington Beach; KTLA (CW) Los Angeles; KTTV (FOX) Los Angeles.

Programming (via satellite): ABC Family Channel; AMC; Arts & Entertainment; Cartoon Network; CNBC; CNN; Comedy Central; C-SPAN; Discovery Channel; ESPN; ESPN 2; Food Network; Fox Sports Net; GalaVision; Headline News; Home Shopping Network; Lifetime; MTV; Nick Jr.; Nickelodeon; QVC; Spike TV; TBS Superstation; The Learning Channel; Travel Channel; Turner Network TV; USA Network; VH1; WGN America.

Current originations: Religious Access; Government Access; Educational Access; Public Access.
Fee: $29.95 installation; $41.50 monthly.
Digital Basic Service
Subscribers: 305.
Fee: $12.95 monthly.
Digital Pay Service 1
Pay Units: 46.
Programming (via satellite): Encore; Starz; Sundance Channel.
Video-On-Demand: Planned
Internet Service
Operational: Yes. Began: August 31, 1999.
Subscribers: 400.
Broadband Service: ISP Channel.
Fee: $99.00 installation; $39.95 monthly.
Telephone Service
None
Miles of Plant: 13.0 (coaxial); None (fiber optic). Homes passed: 1,650. Total homes in franchised area: 1,707.
Manager: Ralph Morrow.
City fee: 5% of gross.
Ownership: Catalina Cable TV Co.

AVENAL—Bright House Networks, 3701 Sillect Ave, Bakersfield, CA 93308-6330. Phones: 800-734-4615; 661-634-2200. Fax: 661-634-2245. E-mail: bakersfield.customercare@mybrighthouse.com. Web Site: http://www.bakersfield.mybrighthouse.com. ICA: CA0221.
TV Market Ranking: 72 (AVENAL). Franchise award date: April 1, 1968. Franchise expiration date: N.A. Began: April 1, 1968.
Channel capacity: 78 (operating 2-way). Channels available but not in use: N.A.
Basic Service
Subscribers: N.A.
Programming (received off-air): KAIL (MNT) Fresno; KFAZ-CA Visalia; KFRE-TV (CW) Sanger; KFSN-TV (ABC) Fresno; KFTV-DT (UNV) Hanford; KGPE (CBS) Fresno; KMPH-TV (FOX) Visalia; KNSO (TMO) Merced; KNXT (ETV) Visalia; KSEE (NBC) Fresno; KTFF-DT (TEL) Porterville; KVPT (PBS) Fresno.
Programming (via satellite): California Channel; QVC; ShopNBC; TV Guide Network; WGN America.
Fee: $44.95 installation; $12.95 monthly; $5.95 additional installation.
Expanded Basic Service 1
Subscribers: N.A.
Programming (via satellite): ABC Family Channel; AMC; Animal Planet; Arts & Entertainment; Cartoon Network; CNBC; CNN; CNN en Espanol; Comedy Central; C-SPAN; C-SPAN 2; Discovery Channel; Disney Channel; E! Entertainment Television; ESPN; ESPN 2; ESPN Classic Sports; Food Network; Fox News Channel; Fox Sports en Espanol; Fox Sports Net West; FX; GalaVision; Great American Country; Hallmark Channel; Headline News; HGTV; History Channel; Lifetime; Lifetime Movie Network; MSNBC; MTV; mun2 television; National Geographic Channel; Nickelodeon; Speed Channel; Spike TV; Syfy; TBS Superstation; The Learning Channel; Travel Channel; truTV; Turner Classic Movies; Turner Network TV; TV Land; USA Network; Versus; VH1; WE tv; Weather Channel.
Fee: $33.00 monthly.
Digital Basic Service
Subscribers: N.A.
Programming (via satellite): Bloomberg Television; Discovery Digital Networks; DMX Music; Encore; ESPNews; Fox College Sports Atlantic; Fox College Sports Central; Fox College Sports Pacific; Fox Movie Channel; Fox Soccer; G4; GAS; Golf Channel; GSN; Independent Film Channel; MTV Networks Digital Suite; Nick Jr.; Toon Disney; Trio; Versus.
Fee: $12.00 monthly.
Digital Pay Service 1
Pay Units: 66.
Programming (via satellite): Cinemax (multiplexed).
Fee: $13.95 monthly.
Digital Pay Service 2
Pay Units: 120.
Programming (via satellite): HBO (multiplexed).
Fee: $13.95 monthly.
Digital Pay Service 3
Pay Units: 48.
Programming (via satellite): Showtime (multiplexed).
Fee: $13.95 monthly.
Digital Pay Service 4
Pay Units: 19.
Programming (via satellite): The Movie Channel (multiplexed).
Fee: $13.95 monthly.
Digital Pay Service 5
Pay Units: 37.
Programming (via satellite): Starz (multiplexed).
Fee: $13.95 monthly.
Pay-Per-View
Addressable homes: 371.
iN DEMAND (delivered digitally); Fresh (delivered digitally); Hot Choice (delivered digitally); Playboy TV (delivered digitally); ESPN Now (delivered digitally); Sports PPV (delivered digitally).
Internet Service
Operational: No.
Telephone Service
None
Miles of Plant: 18.0 (coaxial); 2.0 (fiber optic). Homes passed: 2,242.
Manager: Joe Schoenstein. Marketing Director: Danielle Armstrong. Chief Technician: Chris Gravis. Advertising Manager: Don Stone. Customer Service Manager: Becky Mitchell.
City fee: 5% of gross.
Ownership: Bright House Networks LLC (MSO).

AZUSA—Charter Communications, 4781 Irwindale Ave, Irwindale, CA 91706-2175. Phone: 626-430-3300. Fax: 626-430-3420. Web Site: http://www.charter.com. Also serves Citrus, Duarte & Irwindale. ICA: CA0429.
TV Market Ranking: 2 (AZUSA, Citrus, Duarte, Irwindale). Franchise award date: N.A. Franchise expiration date: N.A. Began: N.A.
Channel capacity: N.A. Channels available but not in use: N.A.
Basic Service
Subscribers: 12,500.
Programming (received off-air): KABC-TV (ABC) Los Angeles; KAZA-TV (IND) Avalon; KCBS-TV (CBS) Los Angeles; KCET (PBS) Los Angeles; KCOP-TV (MNT) Los Angeles; KDOC-TV (IND) Anaheim; KFTR-DT (TEL) Ontario; KJLA (IND) Ventura; KMEX-DT (UNV) Los Angeles; KNBC (NBC) Los Angeles; KOCE-TV (PBS) Huntington Beach; KPXN-TV (ION) San Bernardino; KRCA (IND) Riverside; KSCI (IND) Long Beach; KTBN-TV (TBN) Santa Ana; KTLA (CW) Los Angeles; KTTV (FOX) Los Angeles; KVEA (TMO) Corona; KWHY-TV (IND) Los Angeles.
Programming (via satellite): Arts & Entertainment; C-SPAN; C-SPAN 2; History Channel; QVC; TBS Superstation; TV Guide Network; WGN America.
Current originations: Public Access.
Expanded Basic Service 1
Subscribers: N.A.
Programming (via satellite): ABC Family Channel; AMC; Animal Planet; BET Networks; Bravo; Cartoon Network; CNBC; CNN; Comedy Central; Country Music TV; Discovery Channel; Disney Channel; E! Entertainment Television; ESPN; ESPN 2; ESPN Classic Sports; Food Network; Fox News Channel; Fox Sports en Espanol; Fox Sports Net West; Fox Sports Net West 2; G4; GalaVision; Golf Channel; Headline News; HGTV; Jade Channel; Lifetime; MSNBC; MTV; Nickelodeon; Oxygen; Speed Channel; Spike TV; Syfy; The Learning Channel; Travel Channel; truTV; Turner Classic Movies; Turner Network TV; TV Land; USA Network; VH1.
Fee: $48.95 monthly.
Digital Basic Service
Subscribers: 4,330.
Programming (via satellite): BBC America; Bio; Bloomberg Television; Boomerang; CCTV-4; Discovery Digital Networks; Do-It-Yourself; Fox College Sports Atlantic; Fox College Sports Central; Fox College Sports Pacific; GAS; Great American Country; History Channel International; Independent Film Channel; Lifetime Movie Network; MTV Networks Digital Suite; MuchMusic Network; Music Choice; Nick Jr.; Nick Too; Style Network; Sundance Channel; Toon Disney; WE tv.
Digital Pay Service 1
Pay Units: 5,930.
Programming (via satellite): Cinemax (multiplexed); Encore (multiplexed); Flix; HBO (multiplexed); Showtime (multiplexed); Starz (multiplexed); The Movie Channel (multiplexed).
Video-On-Demand: Yes
Pay-Per-View
Addressable homes: 4,330.
ETC (delivered digitally), Addressable: Yes; iN DEMAND (delivered digitally); Playboy TV (delivered digitally); Pleasure (delivered digitally); Shorteez (delivered digitally); sports (delivered digitally).
Internet Service
Operational: Yes.
Subscribers: 729.
Broadband Service: Charter Pipeline.
Fee: $29.99 monthly.
Telephone Service
Analog: Not Operational
Digital: Operational
Fee: $29.99 monthly
Miles of Plant: 261.0 (coaxial); None (fiber optic). Homes passed: 15,700.
Vice President & General Manager: Wendy Rasmussen. Technical Operations Manager: Tom Williams. Marketing Manager: Lily Ho.
Ownership: Charter Communications Inc. (MSO).

BAKERSFIELD—Bright House Networks, 3701 Sillect Ave, Bakersfield, CA 93308-6330. Phones: 661-323-4892 (Customer service); 800-734-4615; 661-634-2200. Fax: 661-634-2245. E-mail: bakersfield.customercare@mybrighthouse.com. Web Site: http://www.bakersfield.mybrighthouse.com. Also serves Buttonwillow, Delano, Kern County, McFarland, Shafter & Wasco. ICA: CA0025.
TV Market Ranking: 72 (Delano, Kern County (portions), McFarland); Below 100 (BAKERSFIELD, Buttonwillow, Shafter, Wasco, Kern County (portions)); Outside TV Markets (Kern County (portions)). Franchise award date: September 17, 1966. Franchise expiration date: N.A. Began: September 17, 1966.
Channel capacity: 78 (operating 2-way). Channels available but not in use: None.
Basic Service
Subscribers: 110,000.
Programming (received off-air): KABC-TV (ABC) Los Angeles; KABE-LP Bakersfield; KBAK-TV (CBS) Bakersfield; KBFX-CA (FOX) Bakersfield; KCAL-TV (IND) Los Angeles; KCET (PBS) Los Angeles; KCOP-TV (MNT) Los Angeles; KERO-TV (ABC) Bakersfield; KETV (ABC) Omaha; KGET-TV (CW, NBC) Bakersfield; KTLA (CW) Los Angeles; KUVI-DT (MNT) Bakersfield; KVPT (PBS) Fresno.
Programming (via satellite): California Channel; QVC; ShopNBC; TV Guide Network.
Current originations: Government Access; Educational Access.
Fee: $44.95 installation; $12.95 monthly.
Expanded Basic Service 1
Subscribers: 71,329.
Programming (received off-air): Versus.
Programming (via satellite): ABC Family Channel; AMC; Animal Planet; Arts & Entertainment; Azteca America; BET Networks; Bravo; Cartoon Network; CNBC; CNN; Comedy Central; C-SPAN; C-SPAN 2; Discovery Channel; Disney Channel; E! Entertainment Television; ESPN; ESPN 2; ESPN Classic Sports; Food Network; Fox News Channel; Fox Sports Net West; Fox Sports Net West 2; Fuse; FX; GalaVision; Golf Channel; Great American Country; Hallmark Channel; Headline News; HGTV; History Channel; Lifetime; Lifetime Movie Network; MSNBC; MTV; National Geographic Channel; Nickelodeon; Spike TV; Style Network; Syfy; TBS Superstation; Telefutura; Telemundo; The Learning Channel; Travel Channel; Trinity Broadcasting Network; truTV; Turner Classic Movies; Turner Network TV; TV Land; USA Network; VH1; WE tv; Weather Channel.
Fee: $33.00 monthly.
Digital Basic Service
Subscribers: N.A.
Programming (received off-air): KBAK-TV (CBS) Bakersfield; KERO-TV (ABC) Bakersfield; KGET-TV (CW, NBC) Bakersfield.
Programming (via satellite): AmericanLife TV Network; Arts & Entertainment HD; BBC America; BBC America On Demand; Beauty and Fashion Channel; Bio; Bloomberg Television; Boomerang; Canales N; CBS College Sports Network; CNBC; CNN International; Cooking Channel; Country Music TV; C-SPAN 2; C-SPAN 3; Current; Discovery Digital Networks; Discovery HD Theater; Do-It-Yourself; Encore (multiplexed); ESPN HD; ESPNews; Eternal Word TV Network; Exercise TV; Fox College Sports Atlantic; Fox College Sports Central; Fox College Sports Pacific; Fox Movie Channel; Fox Reality Channel; Fox Soccer; Fuel TV; G4; GAS; GSN; HDNet; HDNet Movies; Healthy Living Channel; History Channel International; Independent Film Channel; INHD; Jewelry Television; Lifetime Real Women; Men's Channel; MoviePlex; MTV Networks Digital Suite; Music Choice; National Geographic Channel On Demand; NBA TV; Nick Jr.; NickToons TV; Outdoor Channel; Ovation; Si TV; Sleuth; Speed Channel; Speed On Demand; Tennis Channel; The Word Network; Toon Disney; Turner Network TV HD; Universal HD.
Fee: $12.00 monthly.

Digital Pay Service 1
Pay Units: N.A.
Programming (via satellite): Cinemax (multiplexed); Filipino Channel; HBO (multiplexed); HBO HD; Showtime (multiplexed); Showtime HD; Starz (multiplexed); The Movie Channel (multiplexed); Zee TV USA.
Fee: $13.95 monthly (HBO, Cinemax, Starz, Showtime, TMC or Filipino), $16.95 monthly (Zee TV).
Video-On-Demand: Yes
Pay-Per-View
Addressable homes: 33,333.
iN DEMAND, Fee: $3.95, Addressable: Yes; Playboy TV, Fee: $6.95; Fresh, Fee: $6.95; Shorteez.
Internet Service
Operational: Yes. Began: April 15, 2000.
Subscribers: 7,000.
Broadband Service: Road Runner.
Fee: $29.95 monthly.
Telephone Service
Analog: Not Operational
Digital: Operational
Fee: $33.95 monthly
Miles of Plant: 463.0 (coaxial); 30.0 (fiber optic). Homes passed: 184,478. Total homes in franchised area: 235,000.
Manager: Joe Schoenstein. Marketing & Program Director: Danielle Armstrong. Advertising Director: Don Stone. Chief Technician: Chris Gravis. Customer Service Manager: Becky Mitchell.
City fee: 5% of gross.
Ownership: Bright House Networks LLC (MSO).

BAKERSFIELD—Suddenlink Communications. Now served by BAKERSFIELD, CA [CA0025]. ICA: CA0073.

BANNING—Time Warner Cable, 41725 Cook St, Palm Desert, CA 92211-5100. Phones: 858-695-3110 (San Diego administrative office); 760-340-1312. Fax: 760-340-9764. Web Site: http://www.timewarnercable.com/desertcities. Also serves Beaumont, Cherry Valley (portions) & Riverside County. ICA: CA0176.
TV Market Ranking: 2 (BANNING, Beaumont, Cherry Valley (portions), Riverside County). Franchise award date: November 25, 1952. Franchise expiration date: N.A. Began: February 1, 1953.
Channel capacity: N.A. Channels available but not in use: N.A.
Basic Service
Subscribers: N.A. Included in San Diego
Programming (received off-air): KABC-TV (ABC) Los Angeles; KAZA-TV (IND) Avalon; KCBS-TV (CBS) Los Angeles; KCET (PBS) Los Angeles; KCOP-TV (MNT) Los Angeles; KESQ-TV (ABC, CW) Palm Springs; KFTR-DT (TEL) Ontario; KJLA (IND) Ventura; KMEX-DT (UNV) Los Angeles; KMIR-TV (NBC) Palm Springs; KNBC (NBC) Los Angeles; KPXN-TV (ION) San Bernardino; KRCA (IND) Riverside; KTLA (CW) Los Angeles; KTTV (FOX) Los Angeles; KVCR-DT (PBS) San Bernardino; KXLA (IND) Rancho Palos Verdes; 14 FMs.
Programming (via satellite): C-SPAN; C-SPAN 2; Home Shopping Network; QVC; Weather Channel; WGN America.
Fee: $43.09 installation; $10.99 monthly.
Expanded Basic Service 1
Subscribers: 2,428.
Programming (via satellite): ABC Family Channel; AMC; AmericanLife TV Network; Animal Planet; Arts & Entertainment; BET Networks; Bravo; Cartoon Network; CNBC; CNN; Comedy Central; Discovery Channel; Disney Channel; E! Entertainment Television; ESPN; ESPN 2; ESPN Classic Sports; Eternal Word TV Network; Food Network; Fox News Channel; Fox Sports Net; FX; Hallmark Channel; Headline News; HGTV; History Channel; Lifetime; MSNBC; MTV; National Geographic Channel; Nickelodeon; SoapNet; Spike TV; TBS Superstation; The Learning Channel; Travel Channel; Trinity Broadcasting Network; truTV; Turner Classic Movies; Turner Network TV; TV Guide Network; TV Land; USA Network; VH1; WE tv; Weather Channel.
Fee: $30.00 monthly.
Digital Basic Service
Subscribers: N.A.
Programming (via satellite): ABC Family Channel; AMC; America's Store; Animal Planet; Arts & Entertainment; BBC America; BET Networks; Bio; Bloomberg Television; Bravo; Cartoon Network; CNBC; CNN; CNN International; Comedy Central; Cooking Channel; C-SPAN; C-SPAN 2; C-SPAN 3; Discovery Digital Networks; Disney Channel; Do-It-Yourself; E! Entertainment Television; Encore (multiplexed); ESPN; ESPN 2; ESPN Classic Sports; ESPNews; FitTV; Flix; Food Network; Fox News Channel; Fox Soccer; Fox Sports Net West; Fox Sports Net West 2; Fuse; FX; G4; Golf Channel; GSN; Hallmark Channel; Halogen Network; Headline News; HGTV; History Channel; History Channel International; Independent Film Channel; INSP; Lifetime; Lifetime Movie Network; Lifetime Real Women; MoviePlex; MSNBC; MTV; MTV2; National Geographic Channel; Nick Jr.; Nickelodeon; Ovation; Oxygen; SoapNet; Speed Channel; Spike TV; Style Network; Sundance Channel; Syfy; TBS Superstation; The Learning Channel; Toon Disney; Travel Channel; truTV; Turner Classic Movies; Turner Network TV; TV Land; USA Network; Versus; VH1; VH1 Classic; WE tv; Weather Channel.
Digital Pay Service 1
Pay Units: 324.
Programming (via satellite): Cinemax (multiplexed).
Fee: $12.00 monthly.
Digital Pay Service 2
Pay Units: 48.
Programming (via satellite): Starz (multiplexed).
Fee: $12.00 monthly.
Digital Pay Service 3
Pay Units: 903.
Programming (via satellite): HBO (multiplexed).
Fee: $12.00 monthly.
Digital Pay Service 4
Pay Units: 339.
Programming (via satellite): Showtime (multiplexed); The Movie Channel (multiplexed).
Fee: $12.00 monthly.
Video-On-Demand: Yes
Pay-Per-View
Playboy TV (delivered digitally); Fresh (delivered digitally); Shorteez (delivered digitally).
Internet Service
Operational: Yes.
Broadband Service: Road Runner.
Fee: $50.00 installation; $44.95 monthly.
Telephone Service
Digital: Operational
Fee: $39.95 monthly
Homes passed included in San Diego. Miles of plant (coax & fiber) included in Palm Desert
President: Bob Barlow. Vice President & General Manager: Tad Yo. Technical Operations Director: Dessi Ochoa. Engineering Director: Mike Sagona. Marketing Director: Jimmy Kelly. Government & Community Affairs Director: Kathi Jacobs. Vice President, Customer Service: Armando Rancano.
City fee: 4% of gross.
Ownership: Time Warner Cable (MSO).

BARSTOW—Time Warner Cable, 10450 Pacific Center Court, San Diego, CA 92121-2222. Phones: 858-695-3110; 858-635-8297. Fax: 858-566-6248. Web Site: http://www.timewarnercable.com/Barstow. Also serves Daggett, San Bernardino County & Yermo. ICA: CA0151.
TV Market Ranking: Below 100 (BARSTOW, Daggett, San Bernardino County, Yermo). Franchise award date: January 1, 1952. Franchise expiration date: N.A. Began: November 1, 1952.
Channel capacity: 77 (operating 2-way). Channels available but not in use: 12.
Basic Service
Subscribers: N.A. Included in San Diego
Programming (received off-air): KABC-TV (ABC) Los Angeles; KCAL-TV (IND) Los Angeles; KHIZ (IND) Barstow; KJLA (IND) Ventura; 15 FMs.
Programming (via microwave): KCBS-TV (CBS) Los Angeles; KCET (PBS) Los Angeles; KCOP-TV (MNT) Los Angeles; KNBC (NBC) Los Angeles; KTLA (CW) Los Angeles; KTTV (FOX) Los Angeles.
Programming (via satellite): ABC Family Channel; Arts & Entertainment; BET Networks; CNBC; CNN; C-SPAN; C-SPAN 2; Discovery Channel; E! Entertainment Television; ESPN; Fox Sports Net; Headline News; Home Shopping Network; ION Television; Lifetime; MTV; Nickelodeon; QVC; Spike TV; TBS Superstation; Trinity Broadcasting Network; Turner Network TV; USA Network; VH1.
Current originations: Government Access; Educational Access; Public Access.
Fee: $25.00 installation; $10.99 monthly; $11.00 additional installation.
Expanded Basic Service 1
Subscribers: N.A.
Programming (via satellite): AMC; Animal Planet; Bravo; California Channel; Cartoon Network; Comedy Central; Disney Channel; ESPN 2; ESPN Classic Sports; Food Network; Fox News Channel; FX; GalaVision; Golf Channel; GSN; HGTV; History Channel; INSP; MSNBC; Outdoor Channel; ShopNBC; Speed Channel; Syfy; The Learning Channel; Travel Channel; Turner Classic Movies; TV Guide Network; TV Land; Univision; Weather Channel.
Fee: $30.00 monthly.
Digital Basic Service
Subscribers: N.A.
Programming (via satellite): BBC America; Bloomberg Television; Canales N; Country Music TV; C-SPAN 3; Discovery Digital Networks; Do-It-Yourself; ESPNews; FitTV; Fox Movie Channel; Fox Sports World; Great American Country; Independent Film Channel; Lifetime Movie Network; MTV2; Music Choice; National Geographic Channel; Nick Jr.; Toon Disney; truTV.
Fee: $20.00 installation; $13.05 monthly.
Digital Pay Service 1
Pay Units: N.A.
Programming (via satellite): Cinemax (multiplexed); HBO (multiplexed); Showtime (multiplexed); The Movie Channel (multiplexed).
Fee: $12.00 monthly (each).
Video-On-Demand: Yes
Pay-Per-View
Playboy TV (delivered digitally); iN DEMAND (delivered digitally); Shorteez (delivered digitally); Pleasure (delivered digitally).
Internet Service
Operational: Yes.
Broadband Service: Road Runner.
Fee: $99.95 installation; $44.95 monthly.
Telephone Service
Digital: Operational
Fee: $39.95 monthly
Miles of Plant: 190.0 (coaxial); 11.0 (fiber optic). Total homes in franchised area: 15,000. Homes passed included in San Diego
President: Bob Barlow. Vice President, Engineering: Ron Johnson. Vice President, Technical Services: Bob Jones. Vice President, Public Affairs: Marc Farrar. Vice President, Customer Care: Vinit Ahooja.
Ownership: Time Warner Cable (MSO).; Advance/Newhouse Partnership (MSO).

BEAR VALLEY—New Day Broadband, PO Box 535, 9155 Deschutes Rd, #D, Palo Cedro, CA 96073-8714. Phone: 530-547-2226. Fax: 530-547-4948. ICA: CA0307.
TV Market Ranking: Outside TV Markets (BEAR VALLEY). Franchise award date: N.A. Franchise expiration date: N.A. Began: October 1, 1970.
Channel capacity: 36 (not 2-way capable). Channels available but not in use: 10.
Basic Service
Subscribers: 165.
Programming (received off-air): KCRA-TV (NBC) Sacramento; KOVR (CBS) Stockton; KTVU (FOX) Oakland; KVIE (PBS) Sacramento; KXTV (ABC) Sacramento.
Fee: $29.95 installation; $28.03 monthly.
Pay Service 1
Pay Units: 4.
Programming (via satellite): HBO.
Fee: $11.00 monthly.
Pay Service 2
Pay Units: 1.
Programming (via satellite): Cinemax.
Fee: $11.00 monthly.
Internet Service
Operational: No.
Telephone Service
None
Miles of Plant: 5.0 (coaxial); None (fiber optic). Homes passed: 294.
Chief Executive Officer: Neal Sehnog.
City fee: None.
Ownership: New Day Broadband (MSO).

BELL—Formerly served by Comcast Cable. No longer in operation. ICA: CA0139.

BENICIA—Comcast Cable. Now served by NAPA/SONOMA, CA [CA0038]. ICA: CA0166.

BIG BEAR LAKE—Charter Communications, 7337 Central Ave, Riverside, CA 92504. Phone: 951-343-5100. Fax: 951-354-5942. Web Site: http://www.charter.com. Also serves Big Bear City & San Bernardino County (portions). ICA: CA0309.
TV Market Ranking: 2 (Big Bear City, BIG BEAR LAKE, San Bernardino County (portions)). Franchise award date: N.A. Franchise expiration date: N.A. Began: January 1, 1952.
Channel capacity: N.A. Channels available but not in use: N.A.
Basic Service
Subscribers: 13,000.
Programming (received off-air): KABC-TV (ABC) Los Angeles; KCAL-TV (IND) Los An-

geles; KCBS-TV (CBS) Los Angeles; KCET (PBS) Los Angeles; KCOP-TV (MNT) Los Angeles; KHIZ (IND) Barstow; KJLA (IND) Ventura; KNBC (NBC) Los Angeles; KTLA (CW) Los Angeles; KTTV (FOX) Los Angeles; KXLA (IND) Rancho Palos Verdes; 15 FMs.
Programming (via satellite): C-SPAN; FX; Home Shopping Network; QVC; TBS Superstation; TV Guide Network.
Current originations: Educational Access.
Fee: $30.00 installation.

Expanded Basic Service 1
Subscribers: 10,124.
Programming (received off-air): KBEH (IND) Oxnard; KVEA (TMO) Corona; KVMD (IND) Twentynine Palms.
Programming (via satellite): ABC Family Channel; AMC; Animal Planet; Arts & Entertainment; BET Networks; Bravo; Cartoon Network; CNBC; CNN; Comedy Central; Country Music TV; Discovery Channel; Disney Channel; E! Entertainment Television; ESPN; ESPN 2; ESPN Classic Sports; Eternal Word TV Network; Food Network; Fox News Channel; Fox Sports en Espanol; Fox Sports Net North; G4; GalaVision; Golf Channel; Great American Country; GSN; Hallmark Channel; Headline News; HGTV; History Channel; ION Television; Lifetime; MSNBC; MTV; MTV2; National Geographic Channel; Nickelodeon; Oxygen; ShopNBC; SoapNet; Speed Channel; Spike TV; Syfy; The Learning Channel; Travel Channel; Trinity Broadcasting Network; truTV; Turner Classic Movies; Turner Network TV; TV Land; Univision; USA Network; Versus; VH1; WE tv; Weather Channel.
Fee: $45.45 monthly.

Digital Basic Service
Subscribers: N.A.
Programming (received off-air): KABC-TV (ABC) Los Angeles; KCBS-TV (CBS) Los Angeles; KCET (PBS) Los Angeles; KNBC (NBC) Los Angeles; KTLA (CW) Los Angeles.
Programming (via satellite): 3 Angels Broadcasting Network; BBC America; Bio; Black Family Channel; Bloomberg Television; Boomerang; BYU Television; Canales N; Discovery Digital Networks; Discovery HD Theater; Do-It-Yourself; ESPN; ESPNews; Eternal Word TV Network; FitTV; Fox College Sports Atlantic; Fox College Sports Central; Fox College Sports Pacific; Fox Soccer; Fuel TV; Fuse; GAS; Gol TV; Gospel Music Channel; Halogen Network; HDNet; HDNet Movies; History Channel International; Independent Film Channel; INSP; KTTV (FOX) Los Angeles; Lifetime Movie Network; Lifetime Real Women; MTV Networks Digital Suite; Music Choice; NFL Network; Nick Jr.; NickToons TV; Sundance Channel; Toon Disney; Turner Network TV HD; TV One; TVG Network; WealthTV.

Digital Pay Service 1
Pay Units: N.A.
Programming (via satellite): Cinemax (multiplexed); Encore (multiplexed); Flix; HBO; HBO (multiplexed); LOGO; Showtime; Showtime (multiplexed); Starz (multiplexed); The Movie Channel (multiplexed).

Video-On-Demand: Yes

Pay-Per-View
iN DEMAND (delivered digitally); Spice Hot (delivered digitally); Playboy TV (delivered digitally); TEN Clips (delivered digitally).

Internet Service
Operational: Yes.
Broadband Service: Charter Pipeline.
Fee: $29.99 monthly.

Telephone Service
Digital: Operational
Fee: $29.99 monthly

Miles of Plant: 194.0 (coaxial); None (fiber optic). Homes passed: 21,162.
Vice President & General Manager: Fred Lutz. Technical Operations Manager: George Noel. Marketing Director: Chris Bailey.
Ownership: Charter Communications Inc. (MSO).

BISHOP—Suddenlink Communications, 201 E Line St, Bishop, CA 93515. Phone: 760-873-4123. Fax: 760-873-5145. Web Site: http://www.suddenlink.com. Also serves Big Pine, Independence, Inyo County & Round Valley. ICA: CA0310.
TV Market Ranking: Outside TV Markets (Big Pine, BISHOP, Independence, Inyo County, Round Valley). Franchise award date: May 13, 1967. Franchise expiration date: N.A. Began: February 28, 1966.
Channel capacity: 61 (operating 2-way). Channels available but not in use: 4.

Basic Service
Subscribers: 4,008.
Programming (received off-air): KABC-TV (ABC) Los Angeles; KCBS-TV (CBS) Los Angeles; KLVX-TV (PBS) Las Vegas; KNBC (NBC) Los Angeles; KOLO-TV (ABC) Reno; KTLA (CW) Los Angeles; KTTV (FOX) Los Angeles; 17 FMs.
Programming (via satellite): QVC; TBS Superstation; TV Guide Network; Weather Channel.
Current originations: Leased Access; Educational Access; Public Access.
Fee: $49.95 installation; $18.31 monthly; $29.95 additional installation.

Expanded Basic Service 1
Subscribers: 3,567.
Programming (via satellite): Arts & Entertainment; CNBC; CNN; Discovery Channel; Disney Channel; E! Entertainment Television; ESPN; ESPN 2; Fox News Channel; Fox Sports Net; FX; Headline News; History Channel; Home Shopping Network; MSNBC; Nickelodeon; Spike TV; Style Network; Syfy; The Learning Channel; Toon Disney; Trinity Broadcasting Network; Turner Network TV; USA Network.
Fee: $15.54 monthly.

Digital Basic Service
Subscribers: N.A.
Programming (via satellite): BBC America; Bravo; Canales N; Discovery Digital Networks; DMX Music; Encore; ESPN Classic Sports; ESPNews; Fox Sports World; Golf Channel; GSN; HGTV; Independent Film Channel; Speed Channel; Turner Classic Movies; Versus; VH1 Classic; VH1 Country.
Fee: $3.95 monthly.

Digital Pay Service 1
Pay Units: 492.
Programming (via satellite): Cinemax (multiplexed).
Fee: $10.95 monthly.

Digital Pay Service 2
Pay Units: 690.
Programming (via satellite): HBO (multiplexed).
Fee: $13.95 monthly.

Digital Pay Service 3
Pay Units: 636.
Programming (via satellite): Showtime (multiplexed).
Fee: $10.95 monthly.

Digital Pay Service 4
Pay Units: 570.
Programming (via satellite): The Movie Channel (multiplexed).
Fee: $10.95 monthly.

Video-On-Demand: No

Pay-Per-View
Hot Choice (delivered digitally); iN DEMAND (delivered digitally); Fresh (delivered digitally).

Internet Service
Operational: Yes. Began: August 7, 2002.
Subscribers: 24.
Broadband Service: Cebridge High Speed Cable Internet.
Fee: $99.99 installation; $24.95 monthly.

Telephone Service
None

Miles of Plant: 108.0 (coaxial); None (fiber optic).
Manager: Dawn McWithey. Chief Technician: David Gibbs. Marketing Director: Jason Oelkers.
Ownership: Cequel Communications LLC (MSO).

BLYTHE—NPG Cable, Inc., 129 S 2nd St, Blythe, CA 92225-2623. Phones: 928-855-9855; 760-922-2133 (Customer service). Fax: 760-922-5885. Web Site: http://www.npgcable.net. Also serves Ehrenberg, AZ; East Blythe & Riverside County (eastern portion), CA. ICA: CA0183.
TV Market Ranking: 2 (East Blythe); Outside TV Markets (BLYTHE, Ehrenberg, Riverside County (eastern portion), East Blythe). Franchise award date: N.A. Franchise expiration date: N.A. Began: July 12, 1957.
Channel capacity: 117 (operating 2-way). Channels available but not in use: N.A.

Basic Service
Subscribers: 3,511.
Programming (received off-air): KABC-TV (ABC) Los Angeles; KAET (PBS) Phoenix; KASW (CW) Phoenix; KCAL-TV (IND) Los Angeles; KECY-TV (ABC, FOX, MNT, TMO) El Centro; KMOH-TV (IND) Kingman; KSWT (CBS, CW) Yuma; KTVW-DT (UNV) Phoenix; KUTP (MNT) Phoenix; KYMA-DT (NBC) Yuma; 10 FMs.
Programming (via microwave): KPHO-TV (CBS) Phoenix; KPNX (NBC) Mesa; KSAZ-TV (FOX) Phoenix; KTLA (CW) Los Angeles; KTTV (FOX) Los Angeles.
Programming (via satellite): ABC Family Channel; AMC; Animal Planet; Arts & Entertainment; BET Networks; Cartoon Network; CNBC; CNN; Comedy Central; Country Music TV; C-SPAN; Discovery Channel; Discovery Health Channel; Disney Channel; E! Entertainment Television; ESPN; ESPN 2; ESPN Classic Sports; Eternal Word TV Network; Food Network; Fox News Channel; Fox Sports Net West; FX; GalaVision; Great American Country; Headline News; HGTV; History Channel; Home Shopping Network; ION Television; Lifetime; MSNBC; MTV; Nickelodeon; Product Information Network; QVC; Spike TV; Syfy; TBS Superstation; Telefutura; Telemundo; The Learning Channel; Travel Channel; Trinity Broadcasting Network; truTV; Turner Classic Movies; Turner Network TV; TV Guide Network; TV Land; USA Network; VH1; Weather Channel.
Current originations: Public Access.
Fee: $39.95 installation; $43.80 monthly; $2.50 converter; $9.95 additional installation.

Digital Basic Service
Subscribers: 838.
Programming (via satellite): BBC America; Bio; Canales N; CMT Pure Country; Cooking Channel; Discovery HD Theater; DMX Music; Do-It-Yourself; ESPNews; Fox Soccer; FSN Digital Atlantic; FSN Digital Central; FSN Digital Pacific; Fuel TV; GAS; Golf Channel; GSN; Hallmark Channel; History Channel International; Independent Film Channel; Lime; MTV Networks Digital Suite; National Geographic Channel; Nick Jr.; NickToons TV; Outdoor Channel; SoapNet; Speed Channel; Style Network; Toon Disney; Versus; WE tv.
Fee: $11.95 monthly.

Digital Pay Service 1
Pay Units: N.A.
Programming (via satellite): Cinemax (multiplexed); Encore (multiplexed); HBO (multiplexed); Showtime (multiplexed); Starz (multiplexed); The Movie Channel (multiplexed).
Fee: $6.95 monthly (Cinemax), $9.95 monthly (Starz/Encore), $11.95 monthly (Showtime/TMC), $12.00 monthly (HBO).

Video-On-Demand: No

Pay-Per-View
iN DEMAND (delivered digitally); Fresh (delivered digitally).

Internet Service
Operational: Yes.
Subscribers: 856.
Fee: $59.95 installation; $24.95 monthly; $5.00 modem lease.

Telephone Service
Analog: Not Operational
Digital: Operational
Subscribers: 125.
Fee: $59.95 installation; $39.95 monthly

Miles of Plant: 81.0 (coaxial); 18.0 (fiber optic). Additional miles planned: 3.0 (coaxial). Homes passed: 5,213. Total homes in franchised area: 5,872.
District Manager: Donna Baker. Plant Manager: Rick Hightower.
City fee: 5% of gross.
Ownership: News Press & Gazette Co. (MSO).

BOMBAY BEACH—Cable USA, PO Box 336, 2455 Stirrup Rd, Borrego Springs, CA 92004-0336. Phones: 308-236-1512 (Kearney, NE corporate office); 800-300-6989; 760-767-5607. Fax: 760-767-3609. Web Site: http://www.cableusa.com. ICA: CA0275.
TV Market Ranking: Below 100 (BOMBAY BEACH). Franchise award date: N.A. Franchise expiration date: N.A. Began: N.A.
Channel capacity: N.A. Channels available but not in use: N.A.

Basic Service
Subscribers: 117.
Programming (received off-air): KECY-TV (ABC, FOX, MNT, TMO) El Centro; KESQ-TV (ABC, CW) Palm Springs; KRMA-TV (PBS) Denver; KSWT (CBS, CW) Yuma; KYMA-DT (NBC) Yuma.
Programming (via satellite): Cartoon Network; Comedy Central; C-SPAN; C-SPAN 2; E! Entertainment Television; Headline News; Home Shopping Network; TBS Superstation; The Learning Channel; Trinity Broadcasting Network; TV Land; VH1; WGN America.
Fee: $24.95 installation; $21.99 monthly; $21.50 additional installation.

Expanded Basic Service 1
Subscribers: N.A.
Programming (via satellite): ABC Family Channel; AMC; Animal Planet; Arts & Entertainment; CNN; Discovery Channel; ESPN; ESPN 2; History Channel; Lifetime; Nickelodeon; Spike TV; Syfy; Turner Classic Movies; Turner Network TV; USA Network.
Fee: $36.51 monthly.

Pay Service 1
Pay Units: 47.
Programming (via satellite): Cinemax; HBO.
Fee: $13.00 monthly (Cinemax), $13.50 monthly (HBO).

Internet Service
Operational: No.
Telephone Service
None
Miles of Plant: 10.0 (coaxial); None (fiber optic). Homes passed: 250.
Manager & Chief Technician: Joe Gustafson.
Franchise fee: 3% of gross.
Ownership: USA Companies (MSO).

BORON—Charter Communications, 7337 Central Ave, Riverside, CA 92504. Phone: 951-343-5100. Fax: 951-354-5942. Web Site: http://www.charter.com. ICA: CA0242.
TV Market Ranking: Below 100 (BORON). Franchise award date: N.A. Franchise expiration date: N.A. Began: December 30, 1969.
Channel capacity: N.A. Channels available but not in use: N.A.
Basic Service
Subscribers: 1,330.
Programming (received off-air): KABC-TV (ABC) Los Angeles; KBAK-TV (CBS) Bakersfield; KCBS-TV (CBS) Los Angeles; KCOP-TV (MNT) Los Angeles; KERO-TV (ABC) Bakersfield; KHIZ (IND) Barstow; KNBC (NBC) Los Angeles; KTLA (CW) Los Angeles; KTTV (FOX) Los Angeles; allband FM.
Programming (via satellite): ABC Family Channel; C-SPAN; ESPN; Home Shopping Network; MTV; Nickelodeon; QVC.
Fee: $15.00 installation; $15.90 monthly.
Expanded Basic Service 1
Subscribers: 683.
Programming (via satellite): AMC; Lifetime.
Fee: $1.79 monthly.
Expanded Basic Service 2
Subscribers: 652.
Programming (via satellite): CNN; Discovery Channel; Disney Channel; Food Network; TBS Superstation; Turner Network TV.
Fee: $5.65 monthly.
Pay Service 1
Pay Units: 41.
Programming (via satellite): HBO.
Fee: $11.95 monthly.
Pay Service 2
Pay Units: 14.
Programming (via satellite): The Movie Channel.
Fee: $10.95 monthly.
Pay Service 3
Pay Units: 34.
Programming (via satellite): Showtime.
Fee: $10.95 monthly.
Video-On-Demand: No
Internet Service
Operational: No.
Telephone Service
None
Miles of Plant: 132.0 (coaxial); 32.0 (fiber optic). Total homes in franchised area: 5,870.
Vice President & General Manager: Fred Lutz. Technical Operations Manager: George Noel. Marketing Director: Chris Bailey.
Ownership: Charter Communications Inc. (MSO).

BORREGO SPRINGS—Cable USA, PO Box 336, 2455 Stirrup Rd, Borrego Springs, CA 92004-0336. Phones: 305-236-1512 (Corporate office); 800-300-6989; 760-767-5607. Fax: 760-767-3609. Web Site: http://www.cableusa.com. ICA: CA0236.
TV Market Ranking: Outside TV Markets (BORREGO SPRINGS). Franchise award date: June 1, 1963. Franchise expiration date: N.A. Began: June 1, 1963.
Channel capacity: N.A. Channels available but not in use: N.A.
Basic Service
Subscribers: 878.
Programming (received off-air): KCOP-TV (MNT) Los Angeles; KSWT (CBS, CW) Yuma; KYMA-DT (NBC) Yuma; various Mexican stations; allband FM.
Programming (via microwave): KFMB-TV (CBS) San Diego; KGTV (ABC) San Diego; KNSD (NBC) San Diego; KPBS (PBS) San Diego; KSWB-TV (FOX) San Diego; KTLA (CW) Los Angeles; KUSI-TV (IND) San Diego.
Programming (via satellite): Eternal Word TV Network; GalaVision; Headline News; QVC; Telefutura; Telemundo; Trinity Broadcasting Network; TV Guide Network; Univision; Weather Channel.
Current originations: Government Access; Educational Access; Public Access.
Fee: $50.00 installation; $26.70 monthly; $32.00 additional installation.
Expanded Basic Service 1
Subscribers: N.A.
Programming (via satellite): ABC Family Channel; AMC; Animal Planet; Arts & Entertainment; Cartoon Network; CNBC; CNN; Comedy Central; C-SPAN; C-SPAN 2; Discovery Channel; E! Entertainment Television; ESPN; ESPN 2; ESPN Classic Sports; Food Network; Fox News Channel; Fox Sports Net; FX; Golf Channel; Great American Country; Hallmark Channel; HGTV; History Channel; ION Television; Lifetime; MSNBC; MTV; National Geographic Channel; Nickelodeon; Spike TV; Syfy; TBS Superstation; The Learning Channel; Travel Channel; truTV; Turner Classic Movies; Turner Network TV; TV Land; USA Network; VH1; WGN America.
Digital Basic Service
Subscribers: N.A.
Programming (via satellite): Alterna'TV; AZ TV; BBC America; Bio; Bloomberg Television; Canales N; CMT Pure Country; Current; Daystar TV Network; Discovery Channel HD; Discovery Health Channel; Discovery Home Channel; Discovery Kids Channel; Discovery Military Channel; Discovery Times Channel; DMX Music; Encore (multiplexed); ESPN HD; ESPNews; FitTV; Fox College Sports Atlantic; Fox College Sports Central; Fox College Sports Pacific; Fox Movie Channel; Fox Soccer; G4; GSN; Halogen Network; History Channel International; MTV Hits; MTV2; Nick Jr.; Outdoor Channel; Ovation; Science Channel; ShopNBC; Sleuth; Speed Channel; Starz (multiplexed); Style Network; Syfy; TBS in HD; TeenNick; Turner Network TV HD; Versus; VH1 Classic; VH1 Soul; WE tv.
Digital Pay Service 1
Pay Units: N.A.
Programming (via satellite): Cinemax (multiplexed); Flix; HBO (multiplexed); Lifetime Movie Network; Showtime (multiplexed); The Movie Channel (multiplexed).
Video-On-Demand: No
Pay-Per-View
iN DEMAND (delivered digitally); Playboy TV (delivered digitally); Hot Choice (delivered digitally); Fresh (delivered digitally); Spice: Xcess (delivered digitally); Club Jenna (delivered digitally).
Internet Service
Operational: Yes.
Broadband Service: In-house.
Telephone Service
Digital: Operational
Miles of Plant: 100.0 (coaxial); None (fiber optic). Additional miles planned: 50.0 (coaxial). Total homes in franchised area: 2,500.
Manager & Chief Technician: Joe Gustafson.
County fee: 5% of basic gross.
Ownership: USA Companies (MSO).

BOX CANYON—Charter Communications, 3806 Cross Creek Rd, Malibu, CA 90265-4971. Phones: 626-430-3300 (Irwindale office); 310-456-9010. Fax: 310-579-7010. Web Site: http://www.charter.com. Also serves Los Angeles County (portions) & Ventura County (portions). ICA: CA0433.
TV Market Ranking: 2 (BOX CANYON, Los Angeles County (portions), Ventura County (portions)); Below 100 (Los Angeles County (portions), Ventura County (portions)); Outside TV Markets (Los Angeles County (portions), Ventura County (portions)). Franchise award date: N.A. Franchise expiration date: N.A. Began: N.A.
Channel capacity: 59 (not 2-way capable). Channels available but not in use: None.
Basic Service
Subscribers: 396.
Programming (received off-air): KABC-TV (ABC) Los Angeles; KCAL-TV (IND) Los Angeles; KCBS-TV (CBS) Los Angeles; KCET (PBS) Los Angeles; KCOP-TV (MNT) Los Angeles; KDOC-TV (IND) Anaheim; KFTR-DT (TEL) Ontario; KLCS (PBS) Los Angeles; KMEX-DT (UNV) Los Angeles; KNBC (NBC) Los Angeles; KTBN-TV (TBN) Santa Ana; KTLA (CW) Los Angeles; KVEA (TMO) Corona; KVMD (IND) Twentynine Palms; KWHY-TV (IND) Los Angeles.
Programming (via satellite): ABC Family Channel; Arts & Entertainment; CNBC; Comedy Central; Country Music TV; C-SPAN; C-SPAN 2; E! Entertainment Television; Food Network; Headline News; Home Shopping Network; Lifetime; MTV; Nickelodeon; Spike TV; Syfy; The Learning Channel; USA Network; VH1; WGN America.
Current originations: Government Access; Educational Access; Public Access.
Fee: $15.85 monthly.
Expanded Basic Service 1
Subscribers: 332.
Programming (via satellite): AMC; Animal Planet; Cartoon Network; CNN; Discovery Channel; Disney Channel; ESPN; ESPN 2; Fox Sports Net West; Fox Sports Net West 2; FX; GSN; Hallmark Channel; MSNBC; National Geographic Channel; TBS Superstation; truTV; Turner Network TV.
Fee: $6.93 monthly.
Pay Service 1
Pay Units: 37.
Programming (via satellite): Cinemax.
Fee: $15.65 monthly.
Pay Service 2
Pay Units: 92.
Programming (via satellite): HBO.
Fee: $15.65 monthly.
Pay Service 3
Pay Units: 31.
Programming (via satellite): Showtime.
Fee: $15.65 monthly.
Video-On-Demand: Yes
Internet Service
Operational: No.
Telephone Service
None
Miles of Plant: 10.0 (coaxial); None (fiber optic). Homes passed: 609.
Vice President & General Manager: Wendy Rasmussen. Technical Operations Director: Peter Arredondo. Marketing Manager: Lily Ho.
Ownership: Charter Communications Inc. (MSO).

BREA—Formerly served by Adelphia Communications. Now served by ANAHEIM, CA [CA0033]. ICA: CA0084.

BRIDGEPORT—Satview Broadband, 3550 Barron Way, Ste 13A, Reno, NV 89511. Phones: 800-225-0605; 775-338-6626. Fax: 775-333-0225. E-mail: taroil@yahoo.com. Web Site: http://www.iwantone.tv. ICA: CA0292.
TV Market Ranking: Outside TV Markets (BRIDGEPORT). Franchise award date: April 29, 1988. Franchise expiration date: N.A. Began: August 1, 1990.
Channel capacity: 36 (not 2-way capable). Channels available but not in use: 11.
Basic Service
Subscribers: 77.
Programming (received off-air): KOLO-TV (ABC) Reno; KTVN (CBS) Reno.
Programming (via satellite): Arts & Entertainment; CNN; Discovery Channel; Disney Channel; ESPN; ESPN 2; Headline News; KCNC-TV (CBS) Denver; KRMA-TV (PBS) Denver; KTLA (CW) Los Angeles; KUSA (NBC) Denver; Nickelodeon; Spike TV; TBS Superstation; Trinity Broadcasting Network; Turner Classic Movies; Turner Network TV; USA Network.
Fee: $49.95 installation; $33.49 monthly.
Pay Service 1
Pay Units: 25.
Programming (via satellite): HBO.
Fee: $13.95 monthly.
Pay Service 2
Pay Units: N.A.
Programming (via satellite): Showtime.
Fee: $8.95 monthly.
Internet Service
Operational: No.
Telephone Service
None
Miles of Plant: 10.0 (coaxial); None (fiber optic). Homes passed: 300.
Chief Executive Officer: Tariq Ahmad.
Ownership: Satview Broadband Ltd. (MSO).

BURLINGAME—Comcast Cable. Now served by SAN FRANCISCO, CA [CA0003]. ICA: CA0149.

BURNEY—Windjammer Cable, 4400 PGA Blvd, Ste 902, Palm Beach Gardens, FL 33410. Phones: 877-450-5558; 561-775-1208. Fax: 561-775-7811. Web Site: http://www.windjammercable.com. Also serves Johnson Park. ICA: CA0217.
TV Market Ranking: Outside TV Markets (BURNEY, Johnson Park). Franchise award date: N.A. Franchise expiration date: N.A. Began: October 1, 1971.
Channel capacity: N.A. Channels available but not in use: N.A.
Basic Service
Subscribers: 1,480.
Programming (received off-air): KCVU (FOX) Paradise; KIXE-TV (PBS) Redding; KNVN (NBC) Chico; KRCR-TV (ABC) Redding; KRVU-LD (MNT) Redding.
Programming (via satellite): California Channel; C-SPAN; C-SPAN 2; Hallmark Channel; Home Shopping Network; KCNC-TV (CBS) Denver; KHSL-TV (CBS, CW) Chico; KUSA (NBC) Denver; QVC; ShopNBC; TBS Superstation; TV Guide Network; WGN America.
Current originations: Public Access.
Fee: $35.80 installation; $27.91 monthly.
Expanded Basic Service 1
Subscribers: 1,152.
Programming (via satellite): ABC Family Channel; AMC; Animal Planet; Arts & Enter-

tainment; Bravo; Cartoon Network; CNBC; CNN; Comcast Sports Net Bay Area; Comedy Central; Country Music TV; Discovery Channel; Disney Channel; E! Entertainment Television; ESPN; ESPN 2; Food Network; Fox News Channel; FX; Headline News; HGTV; History Channel; Lifetime; MSNBC; MTV; Nickelodeon; Spike TV; Syfy; The Learning Channel; Travel Channel; truTV; Turner Network TV; Univision; USA Network; VH1; Weather Channel.
Fee: $33.93 monthly.

Digital Basic Service
Subscribers: N.A.
Programming (via satellite): AmericanLife TV Network; BBC America; Black Family Channel; Bloomberg Television; Discovery Digital Networks; FitTV; Fox Movie Channel; Fox Sports World; Fuse; G4; GAS; Great American Country; GSN; Halogen Network; Lifetime Movie Network; MTV; MTV Hits; MTV2; National Geographic Channel; Nick Jr.; Nick Too; NickToons TV; SoapNet; Speed Channel; Style Network; The Word Network; Trinity Broadcasting Network; Turner Classic Movies; VH1; VH1 Classic; VH1 Country; VH1 Soul; WE tv.
Fee: $61.99 monthly.

Digital Expanded Basic Service
Subscribers: N.A.
Programming (via satellite): Bio; Canales N; DMX Music; Do-It-Yourself; ESPN Classic Sports; ESPNews; Fox Sports Net; Golf Channel; History Channel International; Independent Film Channel; Outdoor Channel; Sundance Channel; Toon Disney; Versus.

Digital Pay Service 1
Pay Units: N.A.
Programming (via satellite): ART America; CCTV-4; Cinemax (multiplexed); Encore; Filipino Channel; Flix (multiplexed); HBO (multiplexed); RAI International; Russian Television Network; Showtime (multiplexed); The Movie Channel (multiplexed); TV Asia; TV Japan; TV5, La Television International; Zee TV USA; Zhong Tian Channel.
Fee: $12.00 monthly (Cinemax, HBO, Showtime/TMC or Starz), $15.00 monthly (CCTV, Filipino, ART, TV Asia, TV5, RAI, CTN or RTN).

Video-On-Demand: No

Pay-Per-View
Sports PPV (delivered digitally); Urban American Television Network (delivered digitally); Hot Choice (delivered digitally); Playboy TV (delivered digitally); Fresh (delivered digitally).

Internet Service
Operational: Yes.
Broadband Service: In-house.
Fee: $20.99-$49.99 installation; $44.95 monthly.

Telephone Service
Digital: Operational
Fee: $49.95 monthly

Miles of Plant: 42.0 (coaxial); None (fiber optic). Homes passed: 2,000. Total homes in franchised area: 2,000.
General Manager: Timothy Evard. Operations Director: Belinda Graham. Engineering Director: Mike Earehart. Finance & Accounting Director: Cindy Johnson.
City fee: 5% of gross.
Ownership: Windjammer Communications LLC (MSO).

CABAZON—Formerly served by TV Max. No longer in operation. ICA: CA0263.

CALABASAS—Time Warner Cable. Now served by CHATSWORTH, CA [CA0013]. ICA: CA0227.

CALIFORNIA CITY—Charter Communications, 7337 Central Ave, Riverside, CA 92504. Phone: 951-343-5100. Fax: 951-354-5942. Web Site: http://www.charter.com. ICA: CA0399.
TV Market Ranking: Outside TV Markets (CALIFORNIA CITY). Franchise award date: N.A. Franchise expiration date: N.A. Began: N.A.
Channel capacity: N.A. Channels available but not in use: N.A.

Basic Service
Subscribers: 2,024.
Programming (received off-air): KABC-TV (ABC) Los Angeles; KBAK-TV (CBS) Bakersfield; KCAL-TV (IND) Los Angeles; KCBS-TV (CBS) Los Angeles; KCET (PBS) Los Angeles; KCOP-TV (MNT) Los Angeles; KERO-TV (ABC) Bakersfield; KHIZ (IND) Barstow; KNBC (NBC) Los Angeles; KTLA (CW) Los Angeles; KTTV (FOX) Los Angeles.
Programming (via satellite): AMC; Arts & Entertainment; CNN; Comedy Central; C-SPAN; Discovery Channel; Disney Channel; Food Network; Headline News; History Channel; Home Shopping Network; MTV; Nickelodeon; Oxygen; QVC; TBS Superstation; The Learning Channel; Trinity Broadcasting Network; Turner Network TV; USA Network; VH1; Weather Channel; WGN America.
Current originations: Government Access.
Fee: $14.64 monthly.

Expanded Basic Service 1
Subscribers: 1,946.
Programming (received off-air): KVMD (IND) Twentynine Palms.
Programming (via satellite): ABC Family Channel; Country Music TV; ESPN; Lifetime; Spike TV; Syfy.
Fee: $6.00 monthly.

Digital Basic Service
Subscribers: N.A.
Programming (via satellite): BBC America; Bio; Discovery Digital Networks; Do-It-Yourself; Fox College Sports Atlantic; Fox College Sports Central; Fox College Sports Pacific; Fuse; GAS; History Channel International; Independent Film Channel; Music Choice; Nick Jr.; Nickelodeon; Science Television; Sundance Channel; WE tv.

Digital Pay Service 1
Pay Units: N.A.
Programming (via satellite): Cinemax (multiplexed); Encore (multiplexed); HBO (multiplexed); Starz (multiplexed).

Video-On-Demand: No

Pay-Per-View
Fresh (delivered digitally); Shorteez (delivered digitally).

Internet Service
Operational: Yes.
Broadband Service: Charter Pipeline.
Fee: $29.99 monthly.

Telephone Service
None

Miles of Plant: 90.0 (coaxial); None (fiber optic). Homes passed: 2,858.
Vice President & General Manager: Fred Lutz. Technical Operations Director: George Noel. Marketing Director: Chris Bailey. Government Relations Director: Sandra Magana.
Ownership: Charter Communications Inc. (MSO).

CALIFORNIA HOT SPRINGS—Charter Communications, 270 Bridge St, San Luis Obispo, CA 93401. Phone: 805-544-1962. Fax: 805-541-6042. Web Site: http://www.charter.com. ICA: CA0402.
TV Market Ranking: 72 (CALIFORNIA HOT SPRINGS). Franchise award date: N.A. Franchise expiration date: N.A. Began: N.A.
Channel capacity: 32 (not 2-way capable). Channels available but not in use: 18.

Basic Service
Subscribers: 157.
Programming (received off-air): KBAK-TV (CBS) Bakersfield; KERO-TV (ABC) Bakersfield; KMPH-TV (FOX) Visalia; KSEE (NBC) Fresno; KVPT (PBS) Fresno.
Programming (via satellite): Arts & Entertainment; CNN; Discovery Channel; ESPN; QVC; Syfy.
Fee: $19.91 monthly.

Pay Service 1
Pay Units: 13.
Programming (via satellite): Showtime.
Fee: $11.45 monthly.

Video-On-Demand: No

Internet Service
Operational: No.

Telephone Service
None

Miles of Plant: 19.0 (coaxial); None (fiber optic). Homes passed: 487.
Vice President & General Manager: Ed Merrill. Technical Operations Director: Ken Arellano. Marketing Director: Sarwar Assar.
Ownership: Charter Communications Inc. (MSO).

CALIPATRIA—Cable USA, PO Box 336, 2455 Stirrup Rd, Borrego Springs, CA 92004-0336. Phones: 308-236-1512 (Kearney, NE corporate office); 800-300-6989; 760-767-5607. Fax: 760-767-3609. Web Site: http://www.cableusa.com. Also serves Niland. ICA: CA0256.
TV Market Ranking: Below 100 (CALIPATRIA, Niland). Franchise award date: N.A. Franchise expiration date: N.A. Began: January 21, 1982.
Channel capacity: 61 (not 2-way capable). Channels available but not in use: N.A.

Basic Service
Subscribers: 408.
Programming (received off-air): KCET (PBS) Los Angeles; KECY-TV (ABC, FOX, MNT, TMO) El Centro; KESQ-TV (ABC, CW) Palm Springs; KSWT (CBS, CW) Yuma; KTLA (CW) Los Angeles; KVYE (UNV) El Centro; KYMA-DT (NBC) Yuma; various Mexican stations.
Programming (via satellite): ABC Family Channel; CNN en Espanol; GalaVision; QVC; Telefutura; Telemundo.
Fee: $24.95 installation; $21.99 monthly; $21.50 additional installation.

Expanded Basic Service 1
Subscribers: N.A.
Programming (via satellite): AMC; Animal Planet; Arts & Entertainment; Cartoon Network; CNBC; CNN; Comedy Central; C-SPAN; C-SPAN 2; Discovery Channel; E! Entertainment Television; ESPN; ESPN 2; Eternal Word TV Network; Fox News Channel; Great American Country; Headline News; HGTV; History Channel; Home Shopping Network; INSP; Lifetime; MSNBC; MTV; Nickelodeon; Spike TV; Syfy; TBS Superstation; The Learning Channel; Trinity Broadcasting Network; truTV; Turner Classic Movies; Turner Network TV; TV Land; WGN America.
Fee: $36.51 monthly.

Pay Service 1
Pay Units: 173.
Programming (via satellite): Cinemax; HBO (multiplexed).
Fee: $13.00 monthly (Cinemax), $13.95 monthly (HBO).

Internet Service
Operational: No.

Telephone Service
None

Miles of Plant: 29.0 (coaxial); 6.0 (fiber optic). Homes passed: 939.
Manager & Chief Technician: Joe Gustafson.
City fee: 4% of gross.
Ownership: USA Companies (MSO).

CAMARILLO—No longer in operation. Also serves CAMARILLO. ICA: CA0311.

CAMARILLO—Time Warner Cable. Now served by CHATSWORTH, CA [CA0013]. ICA: CA0138.

CANYON COUNTRY—Comcast Cable. Now served by CHATSWORTH, CA [CA0013]. ICA: CA0313.

CAPE COD MOBILE HOME PARK—Formerly served by Comcast Cable. No longer in operation. ICA: CA0314.

CARLSBAD—Time Warner Cable, 10450 Pacific Center Court, San Diego, CA 92121-2222. Phones: 858-635-8297; 760-438-7741 (Carlsbad office). Fax: 858-566-6248. Web Site: http://www.timewarnercable.com/sandiego. Also serves Del Mar, Encinitas (portions), Fallbrook, San Diego County (unincorporated areas), San Marcos (portions), Solana Beach & Vista. ICA: CA0048.
TV Market Ranking: 51 (CARLSBAD, Del Mar, Encinitas (portions), San Diego County (unincorporated areas), San Marcos (portions), Solana Beach, Vista); Outside TV Markets (Fallbrook). Franchise award date: November 18, 1977. Franchise expiration date: N.A. Began: November 18, 1977.
Channel capacity: N.A. Channels available but not in use: N.A.

Basic Service
Subscribers: N.A. Included in San Diego
Programming (received off-air): KDTF-CA (UNV) San Diego; KFMB-TV (CBS) San Diego; KGTV (ABC) San Diego; KNSD (NBC) San Diego; KPBS (PBS) San Diego; KSWB-TV (FOX) San Diego; KUSI-TV (IND) San Diego; various Mexican stations; 18 FMs.
Programming (via satellite): Azteca America; California Channel; C-SPAN; C-SPAN 2; Home Shopping Network; Jewelry Television; ShopNBC; TBS Superstation; WGN America.
Current originations: Leased Access.
Fee: $30.00 installation; $16.95 monthly.

Expanded Basic Service 1
Subscribers: 56,134.
Programming (via satellite): ABC Family Channel; AMC; Animal Planet; Arts & Entertainment; BET Networks; Bravo; Cartoon Network; CNBC; CNN; Comedy Central; Country Music TV; Discovery Channel; Disney Channel; E! Entertainment Television; ESPN; ESPN 2; Food Network; Fox News Channel; Fox Sports Net West; FX; Golf Channel; Hallmark Channel; Headline News; HGTV; History Channel; ION Television; Lifetime; Lifetime Movie Network; MSNBC; MTV; Nickelodeon; QVC; Spike TV; Syfy; Telefutura; Telemundo; The Learning Channel; Travel Channel; truTV; Turner Classic Movies; Turner Network TV; TV Guide Network; TV Land; USA Network; Versus; VH1; Weather Channel.
Fee: $14.12 installation; $30.00 monthly.

Digital Basic Service
Subscribers: 14,211.
Programming (received off-air): KFMB-TV (CBS) San Diego; KGTV (ABC) San Diego; KNSD (NBC) San Diego; KPBS (PBS) San Diego; KSWB-TV (FOX) San Diego.
Programming (via satellite): 10 News Channel; AmericanLife TV Network; Arts & Entertainment HD; BBC America; Bio; Bloomberg Television; Boomerang; Boomerang en Espanol; Canal Sur; CBS College Sports Network; CCTV-9 (CCTV International); Cine Latino; CNN en Espanol; CNN International; Cooking Channel; C-SPAN 3; Current; Discovery en Espanol; Discovery HD Theater; Discovery Health Channel; Discovery Home Channel; Discovery Kids Channel; Discovery Military Channel; Disney Channel; Do-It-Yourself; Encore (multiplexed); ESPN 2 HD; ESPN Classic Sports; ESPN Deportes; ESPN HD; ESPN U; ESPNews; Eternal Word TV Network; EWTN en Espanol; FitTV; Flix; Fox Business Channel; Fox College Sports Atlantic; Fox College Sports Central; Fox College Sports Pacific; Fox Movie Channel; Fox Reality Channel; Fox Soccer; Fox Sports en Espanol; FSN HD; Fuel TV; Fuse; G4; Gospel Music Channel; Great American Country; GSN; Halogen Network; HDNet; HDNet Movies; History Channel en Espanol; History Channel HD; History Channel International; ID Investigation Discovery; Independent Film Channel; INSP; La Familia Network; Lifetime Movie Network HD; Lifetime Real Women; LOGO; MTV Tres; MTV2; mun2 television; Music Choice; National Geographic Channel; National Geographic Channel HD Network; NBA TV; NBA TV HD; Nick Jr.; NickToons TV; Outdoor Channel; Ovation; Oxygen; Palladia; Puma TV; Science Channel; Sleuth; SoapNet; Sorpresa; Speed Channel; Style Network; Sundance Channel; TBS in HD; TeenNick; Tennis Channel; The Word Network; Toon Disney; Toon Disney en Espanol; Trinity Broadcasting Network; Turner Network TV HD; TVG Network; Universal HD; Versus HD; VH1 Classic; Video Rola; V-me TV; WE tv.
Digital Pay Service 1
Pay Units: N.A.
Programming (via satellite): Cinemax (multiplexed); Filipino Channel; HBO (multiplexed); Playboy TV; Saigon Broadcasting TV Network; Showtime (multiplexed); Starz (multiplexed); The Movie Channel (multiplexed).
Fee: $12.00 monthly (each).
Video-On-Demand: Yes
Pay-Per-View
iN DEMAND (delivered digitally); Playboy TV (delivered digitally); Club Jenna (delivered digitally); Ten Blox (delivered digitally); NHL Center Ice (delivered digitally); MLB Extra Innings (delivered digitally); ESPN Full Court (delivered digitally); ESPN Gameplan (delivered digitally); NBA League Pass (delivered digitally); MLS Direct Kick (delivered digitally); Ten Clips (delivered digitally).
Internet Service
Operational: Yes. Began: December 8, 1997.
Subscribers: 500.
Broadband Service: Road Runner.
Fee: $44.95 monthly; $254.00 modem purchase.
Telephone Service
Digital: Operational
Miles of Plant: 824.0 (coaxial); 173.0 (fiber optic). Additional miles planned: 30.0 (coaxial). Homes passed: 76,892.
President: Bob Barlow. Vice President, Technical Services: Ron Johnson. Vice President, Engineering: Bob Jones. Vice President, Public Affairs: Marc Farrar. Vice President, Customer Care: Vinit Ahooja.
City fee: 5% of basic.
Ownership: Time Warner Cable (MSO).

CARMICHAEL—SureWest Broadband. Formerly served by Sacramento, CA [CA0459]. This cable system has converted to IPTV, PO Box 969, Roseville, CA 95661. Phone: 916-772-2000. Fax: 916-786-7170. Web Site: http://www.surewest.com. ICA: CA5600.
TV Market Ranking: 25 (CARMICHAEL).
Channel capacity: N.A. Channels available but not in use: N.A.
Video-On-Demand: Yes
Internet Service
Operational: Yes.
Telephone Service
Digital: Operational
Ownership: SureWest Broadband.

CARSON—Astound Broadband, 215 Mason Cir, Concord, CA 94520-1203. Phone: 800-427-8686. Web Site: http://www.astound.net. Also serves Gardena. ICA: CA0456. **Note:** This system is an overbuild.
TV Market Ranking: 2 (CARSON, Gardena). Franchise award date: N.A. Franchise expiration date: N.A. Began: N.A.
Channel capacity: N.A. Channels available but not in use: N.A.
Basic Service
Subscribers: 374.
Programming (received off-air): KABC-TV (ABC) Los Angeles; KAZA-TV (IND) Avalon; KCAL-TV (IND) Los Angeles; KCBS-TV (CBS) Los Angeles; KCET (PBS) Los Angeles; KCOP-TV (MNT) Los Angeles; KDOC-TV (IND) Anaheim; KFTR-DT (TEL) Ontario; KJLA (IND) Ventura; KLCS (PBS) Los Angeles; KMEX-DT (UNV) Los Angeles; KNBC (NBC) Los Angeles; KOCE-TV (PBS) Huntington Beach; KPXN-TV (ION) San Bernardino; KRCA (IND) Riverside; KSCI (IND) Long Beach; KTBN-TV (TBN) Santa Ana; KTLA (CW) Los Angeles; KTTV (FOX) Los Angeles; KVEA (TMO) Corona; KWHY-TV (IND) Los Angeles; KXLA (IND) Rancho Palos Verdes.
Programming (via satellite): California Channel; C-SPAN; C-SPAN 2; QVC; WGN America.
Expanded Basic Service 1
Subscribers: N.A.
Programming (via satellite): ABC Family Channel; AMC; Animal Planet; Arts & Entertainment; BET Networks; Bravo; Cartoon Network; CNBC; CNN; Comedy Central; Country Music TV; Discovery Channel; Disney Channel; E! Entertainment Television; ESPN; ESPN 2; ESPN Classic Sports; ESPNews; Eternal Word TV Network; Food Network; Fox Movie Channel; Fox News Channel; Fox Sports Net West; Fox Sports Net West 2; FX; GalaVision; Golf Channel; Headline News; HGTV; History Channel; Home Shopping Network; Home Shopping Network 2; Lifetime; MTV; mun2 television; National Geographic Channel; Nickelodeon; Oxygen; Speed Channel; Spike TV; Syfy; TBS Superstation; The Learning Channel; Travel Channel; truTV; Turner Classic Movies; Turner Network TV; TV Land; USA Network; VH1; WE tv; Weather Channel.
Digital Basic Service
Subscribers: N.A.
Programming (via satellite): BBC America; Black Family Channel; Bloomberg Television; Boomerang; Discovery Digital Networks; Fox Soccer; Fuel TV; G4; GAS; Independent Film Channel; Lifetime Movie Network; MTV Networks Digital Suite; Nick Jr.; Nick Too; NickToons TV; Sundance Channel; Tennis Channel; The Word Network; TVG Network.
Digital Pay Service 1
Pay Units: N.A.
Programming (via satellite): ART America; CCTV-4; Cinemax (multiplexed); Encore (multiplexed); Filipino Channel; Flix; HBO (multiplexed); MBC America; Power Link; RAI International; Russian Television Network; Saigon Broadcasting TV Network; Showtime (multiplexed); Starz (multiplexed); The Movie Channel (multiplexed); TV Asia; TV Japan; TV5, La Television International; Zee TV USA.
Video-On-Demand: No
Pay-Per-View
iN DEMAND (delivered digitally), Addressable: Yes; Ten Clips (delivered digitally); Ten Blue (delivered digitally); Ten Blox (delivered digitally).
Internet Service
Operational: Yes.
Telephone Service
Digital: Operational
Fee: $49.95 installation; $20.00 monthly
Homes passed: 9,737.
Ownership: WaveDivision Holdings LLC (MSO).

CARSON—Comcast Cable. Now served by LOS ANGELES, CA [CA0009]. ICA: CA0112.

CASA DE AMIGOS MOBILE HOME PARK—Formerly served by Comcast Cable. No longer in operation. ICA: CA0316.

CEDARVILLE—Formerly served by Almega Cable. No longer in operation. ICA: CA0282.

CENTRAL ORANGE COUNTY—Time Warner Cable. Now served by ANAHEIM, CA [CA0033]. ICA: CA0042.

CERRITOS—Charter Communications, 4781 Irwindale Ave, Irwindale, CA 91706-2175. Phone: 626-430-3300. Fax: 626-430-3420. Web Site: http://www.charter.com. ICA: CA0137.
TV Market Ranking: 2 (CERRITOS). Franchise award date: February 19, 1987. Franchise expiration date: N.A. Began: September 26, 1988.
Channel capacity: 82 (operating 2-way). Channels available but not in use: None.
Basic Service
Subscribers: 14,200 Includes Ventura.
Programming (received off-air): KABC-TV (ABC) Los Angeles; KAZA-TV (IND) Avalon; KCAL-TV (IND) Los Angeles; KCBS-TV (CBS) Los Angeles; KCET (PBS) Los Angeles; KCOP-TV (MNT) Los Angeles; KDOC-TV (IND) Anaheim; KFTR-DT (TEL) Ontario; KJLA (IND) Ventura; KLCS (PBS) Los Angeles; KMEX-DT (UNV) Los Angeles; KNBC (NBC) Los Angeles; KOCE-TV (PBS) Huntington Beach; KPXN-TV (ION) San Bernardino; KRCA (IND) Riverside; KSCI (IND) Long Beach; KTBN-TV (TBN) Santa Ana; KTLA (CW) Los Angeles; KTTV (FOX) Los Angeles; KVEA (TMO) Corona; KVMD (IND) Twentynine Palms; KWHY-TV (IND) Los Angeles; KXLA (IND) Rancho Palos Verdes.
Programming (via satellite): California Channel; C-SPAN; QVC.
Current originations: Leased Access; Educational Access.
Fee: $60.00 installation; $22.95 monthly; $25.00 additional installation.
Expanded Basic Service 1
Subscribers: 6,422.
Programming (via satellite): ABC Family Channel; AMC; Animal Planet; Arts & Entertainment; BET Networks; Bravo; Cartoon Network; CNBC; CNN; Comedy Central; Discovery Channel; Disney Channel; E! Entertainment Television; ESPN; ESPN 2; Food Network; Fox News Channel; Fox Sports Net; Fox Sports Net West 2; FX; G4; Golf Channel; GSN; Hallmark Channel; Headline News; HGTV; History Channel; Lifetime; MTV; Nickelodeon; ShopNBC; Spike TV; Syfy; TBS Superstation; The Learning Channel; Travel Channel; truTV; Turner Classic Movies; Turner Network TV; TV Land; USA Network; VH1; Weather Channel.
Fee: $21.00 monthly; $25.00 additional installation.
Digital Basic Service
Subscribers: N.A.
Programming (received off-air): KABC-TV (ABC) Los Angeles; KCBS-TV (CBS) Los Angeles; KCET (PBS) Los Angeles; KNBC (NBC) Los Angeles; KTLA (CW) Los Angeles; KTTV (FOX) Los Angeles.
Programming (via satellite): AmericanLife TV Network; Discovery Digital Networks; Discovery HD Theater; DMX Music; E! Entertainment Television; ESPNews; Fox College Sports Atlantic; Fox College Sports Central; Fox College Sports Pacific; GAS; GSN; Halogen Network; HDNet; Lifetime Real Women; National Geographic Channel; NFL Network; Nick Jr.; NickToons TV; Outdoor Channel; Speed Channel; Toon Disney; truTV; Turner Network TV HD; WE tv.
Fee: $9.00 monthly.
Digital Expanded Basic Service
Subscribers: N.A.
Programming (via satellite): Canales N; CCTV-4; Chinese Television Network; Filipino Channel; MBC America; New Tang Dynasty TV; TV Asia; Zee TV USA.
Fee: $7.00 monthly.
Digital Pay Service 1
Pay Units: N.A.
Programming (via satellite): Cinemax (multiplexed); Encore (multiplexed); Flix; HBO (multiplexed); Showtime (multiplexed); Starz (multiplexed); The Movie Channel (multiplexed).
Fee: $12.00 monthly (Showtime, Cinemax, or Starz/Encore), $14.00 monthly (HBO).
Video-On-Demand: Yes
Pay-Per-View
Movies (delivered digitally); Special events (delivered digitally); ESPN (delivered digitally).
Internet Service
Operational: Yes.
Broadband Service: Charter Pipeline.
Fee: $39.95 monthly.
Telephone Service
Digital: Operational
Miles of Plant: 175.0 (coaxial); None (fiber optic). Homes passed: 15,976. Total homes in franchised area: 15,976.
Vice President & General Manager: Wendy Rasumssen. Technical Operations Manager: Tom Williams.
City fee: 2% of gross.
Ownership: Charter Communications Inc. (MSO).

CHALFANT VALLEY—Formerly served by Satview Broadband. No longer in operation. ICA: CA0319.

CHATSWORTH—Time Warner Cable, 9260 Topanga Canyon Blvd, Chatsworth, CA 91311-5726. Phones: 818-407-4400;

818-700-6500 (Customer service). Fax: 818-998-0858. Web Site: http://www.timewarnercable.com/socal. Also serves Acton, Agoura Hills, Aqua Dulce, Beverly Hills, Calabasas, Calabasas Park, Camarillo, Canoga Park, Canyon Country, Castaic, CBC Naval Base, Edwards AFB, El Rio, Elizabeth Lake, Encino, Fillmore, Granada Hills, Green Valley, Kagel Canyon, Lancaster, Leona Valley, Littlerock, Los Angeles County (portions), Mission Hills (portions), Moorpark, Newbury Park, Newhall, North Hills, Northridge, Oak Park, Ojai, Oxnard, Palmdale, Pearblossom, Port Hueneme, Quartz Hill, Reseda, Santa Clarita, Santa Monica, Santa Paula, Saugus, Sherman Oaks, Sherman Oaks (portions), Simi Valley, Stevenson Ranch, Studio City, Sunland, Sylmar, Tarzana, Thousand Oaks, Tujunga, Valencia, Van Nuys, Ventura, Ventura County (portions), West Hills, West Hollywood, West San Fernando Valley, Westlake Village, Winnetka & Woodland Hills. ICA: CA0013.

TV Market Ranking: 2 (Agoura Hills, Aqua Dulce, Beverly Hills, Calabasas, Calabasas Park, Canoga Park, Canyon Country, Castaic, CHATSWORTH, Encino, Granada Hills, Kagel Canyon, Los Angeles County (portions) (portions), Mission Hills (portions), Moorpark, Newbury Park, Newhall, North Hills, Northridge, Oak Park, Reseda, San Fernando, Santa Clarita, Santa Monica, Saugus, Sherman Oaks, Sherman Oaks (portions), Simi Valley, Stevenson Ranch, Studio City, Sunland, Sylmar, Tarzana, Thousand Oaks, Tujunga, Valencia, Van Nuys, Ventura County (portions) (portions), West Hills, West Hollywood, West San Fernando Valley, Westlake Village, Winnetka, Woodland Hills); Below 100 (Camarillo, CBC Naval Base, El Rio, Fillmore, Ojai, Oxnard, Port Hueneme, Santa Paula, Ventura, Ventura County (portions) (portions)); Outside TV Markets (Acton, Edwards AFB, Elizabeth Lake, Green Valley, Lancaster, Leona Valley, Littlerock, Palmdale, Pearblossom, Quartz Hill, Los Angeles County (portions) (portions)). Franchise award date: June 8, 1980. Franchise expiration date: N.A. Began: June 6, 1981.

Channel capacity: N.A. Channels available but not in use: N.A.

Basic Service

Subscribers: N.A. Included in Los Angeles

Programming (received off-air): KABC-TV (ABC) Los Angeles; KCAL-TV (IND) Los Angeles; KCBS-TV (CBS) Los Angeles; KCET (PBS) Los Angeles; KCOP-TV (MNT) Los Angeles; KDOC-TV (IND) Anaheim; KFTR-DT (TEL) Ontario; KJLA (IND) Ventura; KLCS (PBS) Los Angeles; KMEX-DT (UNV) Los Angeles; KNBC (NBC) Los Angeles; KOCE-TV (PBS) Huntington Beach; KPXN-TV (ION) San Bernardino; KRCA (IND) Riverside; KSCI (IND) Long Beach; KTBN-TV (TBN) Santa Ana; KTLA (CW) Los Angeles; KTTV (FOX) Los Angeles; KVEA (TMO) Corona; KWHY-TV (IND) Los Angeles; KXLA (IND) Rancho Palos Verdes; 17 FMs.

Programming (via satellite): C-SPAN; TV Guide Network.

Current originations: Leased Access; Religious Access; Government Access; Educational Access; Public Access.

Fee: $29.95 installation; $14.61 monthly; $3.00 converter.

Expanded Basic Service 1

Subscribers: N.A.

Programming (via satellite): ABC Family Channel; AMC; Arts & Entertainment; BET Networks; Bravo; Cartoon Network; CNBC; CNN; Comedy Central; Discovery Channel; Disney Channel; E! Entertainment Television; ESPN; ESPN 2; Food Network; Fox News Channel; Fox Sports Net West; FX; GalaVision; Golf Channel; Headline News; HGTV; History Channel; Home Shopping Network; MSNBC; MTV; Nickelodeon; Oxygen; QVC; ShopNBC; Spike TV; Syfy; TBS Superstation; The Learning Channel; truTV; Turner Network TV; TV Land; USA Network; VH1; Weather Channel.

Fee: $35.29 monthly.

Digital Basic Service

Subscribers: 79,186.

Programming (received off-air): KABC-TV (ABC) Los Angeles; KCAL-TV (IND) Los Angeles; KCBS-TV (CBS) Los Angeles; KCET (PBS) Los Angeles; KNBC (NBC) Los Angeles; KOCE-TV (PBS) Huntington Beach; KTLA (CW) Los Angeles; KTTV (FOX) Los Angeles.

Programming (via satellite): American-Life TV Network; America's Store; Animal Planet; BBC America; Bio; Bloomberg Television; Boomerang; Boomerang en Espanol; California Channel; Cartoon Network Tambien en Espanol; CB Television Michoacan; CCTV-9 (CCTV International); Cine Latino; CNN en Espanol; Cooking Channel; Country Music TV; C-SPAN 2; C-SPAN 3; Current; Discovery en Espanol; Discovery HD Theater; Discovery Health Channel; Discovery Home Channel; Discovery Kids Channel; Discovery Military Channel; Discovery Times Channel; Do-It-Yourself; Encore (multiplexed); ESPN 2 HD; ESPN Classic Sports; ESPN Deportes; ESPN HD; ESPN U; ESPNews; Eternal Word TV Network; EWTN en Espanol; FitTV; Flix; Fox Business Channel; Fox College Sports Atlantic; Fox College Sports Central; Fox College Sports Pacific; Fox Movie Channel; Fox Reality Channel; Fox Soccer; Fox Sports en Espanol; Fuse; G4; GalaVision; Gospel Music Channel; Great American Country; GSN; Hallmark Channel; HDNet; HDNet Movies; History Channel International; HTV Musica; ImaginAsian TV; Independent Film Channel; Infinito; INSP; Korean Channel; La Familia Network; Lifetime Movie Network; Lifetime Real Women; LOGO; MTV Hits; MTV Jams; MTV2; mun2 television; Music Choice; National Geographic Channel; Nick Jr.; NickToons TV; Once Mexico; Outdoor Channel; Ovation; Palladia; Playboy en Espanol; Science Channel; Si TV; Sleuth; SoapNet; Sorpresa; Speed Channel; Starz HDTV; Style Network; Sundance Channel; Sur Network; TBS in HD; TeenNick; The Word Network; Toon Disney; Toon Disney en Espanol; Travel Channel; Turner Classic Movies; Turner Network TV HD; TV One; TVE Internacional; Universal HD; Utilisima; Versus; VH1 Classic; VH1 Soul; Video Rola; WE tv.

Fee: $5.00 monthly (each tier).

Digital Pay Service 1

Pay Units: 51,166.

Programming (via satellite): ART America; Cinemax (multiplexed); Cinemax HD; Filipino Channel; HBO (multiplexed); HBO HD; MBC America; RAI International; Russian Television Network; Saigon Broadcasting TV Network; Showtime (multiplexed); Showtime HD; Starz (multiplexed); The Movie Channel (multiplexed); TV Asia; TV Japan; TV5, La Television International; Zhong Tian Channel.

Fee: $11.95 monthly (Zhong Tian, CCTV, Filipino, ART or SBTN), $14.95 monthly (TV Asia, TV5, RAI, MBC or RTN), $15.00 monthly (Cinemax, HBO, Showtime/TMC, Starz or Playboy), $24.95 monthly (TV Japan).

Video-On-Demand: Yes

Pay-Per-View

Addressable homes: 79,186.

Hot Choice (delivered digitally), Addressable: Yes; Playboy TV (delivered digitally); Pleasure (delivered digitally); Fresh (delivered digitally); Shorteez (delivered digitally); sports (delivered digitally).

Internet Service

Operational: Yes.

Subscribers: 28,020.

Broadband Service: Road Runner.

Fee: $49.95 installation; $44.95 monthly.

Telephone Service

Digital: Operational

Fee: $44.95 monthly

Miles of Plant: 1,542.0 (coaxial); None (fiber optic). Homes passed: 194,196.

President: Deborah Picciolo. Vice President, Technical Operations: Mike Snider. Vice President, Engineering: Jose Leon. Vice President, Marketing & Sales: Bill Erickson. Vice President, Public & Community Affairs: Patricia Fregoso-Cox. Public Relations Manager: Katie Himes.

City fee: 5% of gross.

Ownership: Time Warner Cable (MSO).

CHICO—Comcast Cable, 311 B St, Yuba City, CA 95991-5054. Phone: 530-790-3322. Web Site: http://www.comcast.com. Also serves Biggs, Butte County, Colusa, Corning, Durham, Gridley, Hamilton City, Orland, Oroville, Paradise & Willows. ICA: CA0066.

TV Market Ranking: Below 100 (Biggs, Butte County, CHICO, Corning, Durham, Gridley, Hamilton City, Orland, Oroville, Paradise, Willows); Outside TV Markets (Colusa). Franchise award date: July 12, 1964. Franchise expiration date: N.A. Began: January 1, 1969.

Channel capacity: N.A. Channels available but not in use: N.A.

Basic Service

Subscribers: 55,483.

Programming (received off-air): KCRA-TV (NBC) Sacramento; KCVU (FOX) Paradise; KHSL-TV (CBS, CW) Chico; KIXE-TV (PBS) Redding; KNVN (NBC) Chico; KOVR (CBS) Stockton; KRCR-TV (ABC) Redding; KRVU-LD (MNT) Redding; KTFK-DT (TEL) Stockton; KTXL (FOX) Sacramento; KVIE (PBS) Sacramento; KXTV (ABC) Sacramento; 27 FMs.

Programming (via satellite): California Channel; C-SPAN; C-SPAN 2; Discovery Channel; Home Shopping Network; QVC; TV Guide Network; Univision.

Current originations: Government Access; Educational Access; Public Access.

Fee: $43.99 installation; $14.97 monthly.

Expanded Basic Service 1

Subscribers: N.A.

Programming (via satellite): ABC Family Channel; AMC; Animal Planet; Arts & Entertainment; Cartoon Network; CNBC; CNN; Comcast Sports Net Bay Area; Comcast SportsNet West; Comedy Central; Country Music TV; Disney Channel; E! Entertainment Television; ESPN; ESPN 2; Food Network; Fox News Channel; FX; Golf Channel; Hallmark Channel; Headline News; HGTV; History Channel; Lifetime; MSNBC; MTV; Nickelodeon; Spike TV; Style Network; TBS Superstation; The Learning Channel; Travel Channel; truTV; Turner Network TV; USA Network; Versus; VH1; Weather Channel.

Fee: $33.78 monthly.

Digital Basic Service

Subscribers: N.A.

Programming (via satellite): AmericanLife TV Network; Arabic Channel; BBC America; Bio; Black Family Channel; Bloomberg Television; Bravo; BYU Television; Canales N; CBS College Sports Network; CCTV-4; Discovery Digital Networks; Discovery HD Theater; DMX Music; ESPN; ESPN Classic Sports; ESPNews; Filipino Channel; FitTV; Fox College Sports Atlantic; Fox College Sports Central; Fox College Sports Pacific; Fox Movie Channel; Fox Sports World; Fuse; G4; GAS; Great American Country; GSN; Halogen Network; HDNet; History Channel International; Independent Film Channel; International Television (ITV); Lifetime Movie Network; Lime; MTV Networks Digital Suite; National Geographic Channel; NBA TV; NFL Network; Nick Jr.; Nick Too; NickToons TV; Outdoor Channel; Ovation; RAI International; Russian Television Network; Saigon Broadcasting TV Network; ShopNBC; Speed Channel; Sundance Channel; Syfy; The Word Network; Toon Disney; Trinity Broadcasting Network; Turner Classic Movies; TV Asia; TV Japan; TV Land; TV5, La Television International; TVG Network; WAM! America's Kidz Network; WE tv; Zee TV USA; Zhong Tian Channel.

Fee: $11.95 monthly.

Digital Pay Service 1

Pay Units: 6,100.

Programming (via satellite): Cinemax (multiplexed); Encore (multiplexed); HBO (multiplexed); Showtime (multiplexed); Starz (multiplexed); The Movie Channel (multiplexed).

Fee: $17.99 monthly (Cinemax, Starz or TMC), $18.99 monthly (HBO or Showtime).

Video-On-Demand: Yes

Pay-Per-View

iN DEMAND (delivered digitally); Fresh (delivered digitally); Shorteez (delivered digitally); Playboy TV (delivered digitally).

Internet Service

Operational: Yes.

Broadband Service: Comcast High Speed Internet.

Fee: $42.95 monthly.

Telephone Service

Digital: Operational

Miles of Plant: 911.0 (coaxial); 10.0 (fiber optic). Homes passed: 81,400. Total homes in franchised area: 81,400.

General Manager: DeeDee Brady. Technical Operations Director: Tom Baer.

City fee: 5% of gross.

Ownership: Comcast Cable Communications Inc. (MSO).

CHINO—Now served by ANAHEIM, CA [CA0033]. ICA: CA0320.

CHOWCHILLA—Comcast Cable, 2441 N Grove Industrial Dr, Fresno, CA 93727-1535. Phone: 559-253-4050. Fax: 559-253-4090. Web Site: http://www.comcast.com. Also serves Madera County (southwestern portion). ICA: CA0218.

TV Market Ranking: 72 (CHOWCHILLA, Madera County (southwestern portion)). Franchise award date: N.A. Franchise expiration date: N.A. Began: July 1, 1982.

Channel capacity: 36 (operating 2-way). Channels available but not in use: 6.

Basic Service

Subscribers: 1,375.

Programming (received off-air): KAIL (MNT) Fresno; KFSN-TV (ABC) Fresno;

KFTV-DT (UNV) Hanford; KGMC (IND) Clovis; KGPE (CBS) Fresno; KMPH-TV (FOX) Visalia; KSEE (NBC) Fresno; KVPT (PBS) Fresno.
Programming (via satellite): ABC Family Channel; AMC; Arts & Entertainment; Cartoon Network; CNN; C-SPAN; Discovery Channel; Disney Channel; ESPN; ESPN 2; FX; GalaVision; Headline News; Home Shopping Network; Spike TV; TBS Superstation; The Learning Channel; Travel Channel; Trinity Broadcasting Network; Turner Network TV; USA Network; WGN America.
Fee: $43.99 installation; $38.87 monthly.

Pay Service 1
Pay Units: 176.
Programming (via satellite): Cinemax; HBO.
Fee: $15.00 installation; $10.97 monthly (Cinemax), $12.87 monthly (HBO).

Video-On-Demand: No

Pay-Per-View
Addressable homes: 1,375.
WWF Wrestlemania, Addressable: Yes.

Internet Service
Operational: Yes.

Telephone Service
Digital: Operational
Miles of Plant: 23.0 (coaxial); None (fiber optic). Homes passed: 2,000. Total homes in franchised area: 2,000.
General Manager: Len Falter. Marketing Director: Stewart Butler. Communications Director: Erica Smith.
City fee: 5% of gross.
Ownership: Comcast Cable Communications Inc. (MSO).

CHULA VISTA—NexHorizon Communications, 581 C St, Chula Vista, CA 91910-1406. Phone: 619-476-0177. Fax: 619-422-4060. Web Site: http://www.nexhorizon.us. Also serves National City. ICA: CA0113. **Note:** This system is an overbuild.
TV Market Ranking: 51 (CHULA VISTA, National City). Franchise award date: September 15, 1987. Franchise expiration date: N.A. Began: February 8, 1988.
Channel capacity: 68 (operating 2-way). Channels available but not in use: None.

Basic Service
Subscribers: 3,400.
Programming (received off-air): KFMB-TV (CBS) San Diego; KGTV (ABC) San Diego; KNSD (NBC) San Diego; KPBS (PBS) San Diego; KSWB-TV (FOX) San Diego; KUSI-TV (IND) San Diego.
Programming (via microwave): KTLA (CW) Los Angeles.
Programming (via satellite): ABC Family Channel; AMC; America's Store; Animal Planet; Arts & Entertainment; BET Networks; Bravo; Cartoon Network; CNBC; CNN; Comedy Central; C-SPAN; C-SPAN 2; Discovery Channel; Disney Channel; E! Entertainment Television; ESPN; ESPN 2; Food Network; Fox News Channel; Fox Sports Net West; Hallmark Channel; Headline News; HGTV; History Channel; Home Shopping Network; Lifetime; MTV; National Geographic Channel; Nickelodeon; QVC; SoapNet; Syfy; TBS Superstation; The Learning Channel; Travel Channel; Trinity Broadcasting Network; truTV; Turner Classic Movies; Turner Network TV; TV Land; USA Network; VH1; Weather Channel; WGN America.
Current originations: Government Access.
Fee: $35.00 installation; $38.90 monthly.

Pay Service 1
Pay Units: N.A.
Programming (via satellite): Cinemax (multiplexed); Filipino Channel; HBO (multiplexed); Showtime (multiplexed); The Movie Channel (multiplexed).
Fee: $10.95 monthly (Showtime or TMC), $11.95 monthly (Cinemax), $12.95 monthly (Filipino Channel), $13.95 monthly (HBO).

Video-On-Demand: No

Pay-Per-View
Addressable homes: 1,525.
iN DEMAND, Addressable: Yes; Playboy TV, Fee: $10.95.

Internet Service
Operational: Yes.
Subscribers: 148.
Broadband Service: In-house.
Fee: $39.95 monthly.

Telephone Service
Analog: Not Operational
Digital: Operational
Fee: $34.95 monthly
Miles of Plant: 98.0 (coaxial); None (fiber optic). Homes passed: 17,000. Total homes in franchised area: 45,000.
Manager: Monica Villasenor. Chief Technician: Randy Watson.
Franchise fee: 3% of gross.
Ownership: NexHorizon Communications Inc. (MSO).

CITRUS HEIGHTS—SureWest Broadband. Formerly served by Sacramento, CA [CA0459]. This cable system has converted to IPTV, PO Box 969, Roseville, CA 95661. Phone: 916-772-2000. Fax: 916-786-7170. Web Site: http://www.surewest.com. ICA: CA5601.
TV Market Ranking: 25 (CITRUS HEIGHTS).
Channel capacity: N.A. Channels available but not in use: N.A.

Video-On-Demand: Yes

Internet Service
Operational: Yes.

Telephone Service
Digital: Operational
Ownership: SureWest Broadband.

CLAREMONT—Comcast Cable. Now served by LOS ANGELES, CA [CA0009]. ICA: CA0150.

CLEARLAKE OAKS—Mediacom, 13221 E Hwy 20, Clearlake Oaks, CA 95423-9329. Phones: 707-998-1187; 800-239-8411 (Customer service). Fax: 707-998-9317. Web Site: http://www.mediacomcable.com. Also serves Clearlake, Clearlake Park, Cobb, Finley, Glenhaven, Hidden Valley Lake, Kelseyville, Konocti Bay, Lake County, Lakeport, Lower Lake, Lucerne, Nice & Upper Lake. ICA: CA0104.
TV Market Ranking: Below 100 (Hidden Valley Lake, Lake County (portions), Lower Lake); Outside TV Markets (Clearlake, CLEARLAKE OAKS, Clearlake Park, Cobb, Finley, Glenhaven, Kelseyville, Konocti Bay, Lake County (portions), Lakeport, Lucerne, Nice, Upper Lake). Franchise award date: October 1, 1962. Franchise expiration date: N.A. Began: October 1, 1962.
Channel capacity: N.A. Channels available but not in use: N.A.

Basic Service
Subscribers: 13,700.
Programming (received off-air): KBCW (CW) San Francisco; KCRA-TV (NBC) Sacramento; KFTY (IND) Santa Rosa; KGO-TV (ABC) San Francisco; KICU-TV (IND) San Jose; KNTV (NBC) San Jose; KOVR (CBS) Stockton; KPIX-TV (CBS) San Francisco; KQED (PBS) San Francisco; KRON-TV (MNT) San Francisco; KTNC-TV (IND) Concord; KTVU (FOX) Oakland; KTXL (FOX) Sacramento; 22 FMs.
Programming (via satellite): ABC Family Channel; C-SPAN; FitTV; QVC; TV Guide Network; Weather Channel.
Current originations: Leased Access.
Fee: $29.50 installation; $20.95 monthly; $2.00 converter.

Expanded Basic Service 1
Subscribers: N.A.
Programming (via satellite): AMC; Animal Planet; Arts & Entertainment; Bravo; Cartoon Network; CNBC; CNN; Comcast Sports Net Bay Area; Comedy Central; Country Music TV; Discovery Channel; Disney Channel; E! Entertainment Television; ESPN; ESPN 2; Food Network; Fox News Channel; Fox Sports Net; FX; Headline News; HGTV; History Channel; Home Shopping Network; Lifetime; MSNBC; MTV; Nickelodeon; ShopNBC; SoapNet; Speed Channel; Spike TV; Syfy; TBS Superstation; Telemundo; The Learning Channel; Travel Channel; Trinity Broadcasting Network; truTV; Turner Network TV; TV Land; Univision; USA Network; VH1; WE tv.
Fee: $25.95 monthly.

Digital Basic Service
Subscribers: N.A.
Programming (via satellite): BBC America; Discovery Digital Networks; ESPN; ESPN 2; ESPNews; Fox Soccer; G4; Golf Channel; GSN; Independent Film Channel; Music Choice; National Geographic Channel; Nick Jr.; Turner Classic Movies; Turner Network TV; Versus; VH1 Classic.
Fee: $8.00 monthly.

Digital Pay Service 1
Pay Units: N.A.
Programming (via satellite): Cinemax (multiplexed); Encore (multiplexed); Flix; HBO (multiplexed); Showtime (multiplexed); Starz (multiplexed); Sundance Channel; The Movie Channel (multiplexed).
Fee: $13.95 monthly (HBO), $9.95 monthly (Showtime or Cinemax), $8.00 monthly (Starz/Encore).

Video-On-Demand: No

Pay-Per-View
Movies (delivered digitally).

Internet Service
Operational: Yes.
Subscribers: 7,500.
Broadband Service: Mediacom High Speed Internet.
Fee: $59.95 installation; $42.95 monthly; $3.00 modem lease; $239.95 modem purchase.

Telephone Service
Digital: Operational
Miles of Plant: 795.0 (coaxial); 180.0 (fiber optic). Homes passed: 29,988. Total homes in franchised area: 29,988.
Senior Manager, Operations: Shawn Swatosh. Chief Technician: Mike Caruthers.
City fee: 3% of gross.
Ownership: Mediacom LLC (MSO).

COALINGA—Comcast Cable, 2441 N Grove Industrial Dr, Fresno, CA 93727-1535. Phone: 559-253-4050. Fax: 559-253-4090. Web Site: http://www.comcast.com. ICA: CA0208.
TV Market Ranking: Outside TV Markets (COALINGA). Franchise award date: August 15, 1977. Franchise expiration date: N.A. Began: January 1, 1979.
Channel capacity: 60 (operating 2-way). Channels available but not in use: N.A.

Basic Service
Subscribers: 2,300.
Programming (received off-air): KAIL (MNT) Fresno; KFRE-TV (CW) Sanger; KFSN-TV (ABC) Fresno; KFTV-DT (UNV) Hanford; KGMC (IND) Clovis; KGPE (CBS) Fresno; KMPH-TV (FOX) Visalia; KNSO (TMO) Merced; KNXT (ETV) Visalia; KSEE (NBC) Fresno; KTFF-DT (TEL) Porterville; KVPT (PBS) Fresno.
Programming (via satellite): ABC Family Channel; AMC; AmericanLife TV Network; Animal Planet; Arts & Entertainment; CNN; Comcast Sports Net Bay Area; Comedy Central; C-SPAN; Discovery Channel; Disney Channel; E! Entertainment Television; ESPN; ESPN 2; Fox News Channel; FX; GalaVision; Great American Country; Headline News; HGTV; History Channel; Home Shopping Network; ION Television; Lifetime; MTV; Nickelodeon; Spike TV; Syfy; TBS Superstation; The Learning Channel; Trinity Broadcasting Network; Turner Classic Movies; Turner Network TV; TV Guide Network; TV Land; USA Network; VH1; Weather Channel; WGN America.
Current originations: Public Access.
Fee: $43.99 installation; $34.95 monthly; $1.00 converter.

Digital Basic Service
Subscribers: N.A.
Programming (via satellite): AmericanLife TV Network; BBC America; Bio; Black Family Channel; Bloomberg Television; Bravo; Canales N; Current; Discovery Digital Networks; DMX Music; ESPN 2; ESPN Classic Sports; ESPNews; Fox College Sports Atlantic; Fox College Sports Central; Fox College Sports Pacific; Fox Movie Channel; Fox Soccer; Fuse; G4; GAS; Golf Channel; Great American Country; GSN; Halogen Network; HGTV; History Channel; History Channel International; Independent Film Channel; Lifetime Movie Network; Lime; MTV Networks Digital Suite; National Geographic Channel; Nick Jr.; NickToons TV; Outdoor Channel; Ovation; ShopNBC; Speed Channel; Style Network; Sundance Channel; Syfy; The Word Network; Toon Disney; Trinity Broadcasting Network; Trio; Turner Classic Movies; TV Land; TVG Network; Versus; WE tv.

Digital Pay Service 1
Pay Units: N.A.
Programming (via satellite): Cinemax (multiplexed); Encore (multiplexed); Flix; HBO (multiplexed); Showtime (multiplexed); Starz (multiplexed); The Movie Channel (multiplexed).

Video-On-Demand: No

Pay-Per-View
iN DEMAND (delivered digitally); Fresh (delivered digitally); Shorteez (delivered digitally); Playboy TV (delivered digitally); Hot Choice (delivered digitally).

Internet Service
Operational: Yes.

Telephone Service
Digital: Operational

Miles of Plant: 26.0 (coaxial); None (fiber optic). Additional miles planned: 2.0 (coaxial). Homes passed: 3,800. Total homes in franchised area: 3,800.

General Manager: Len Falter. Marketing Director: Stewart Butler.

City fee: 3% of gross.

Ownership: Comcast Cable Communications Inc. (MSO).

COARSEGOLD—Northland Cable Television, 40108 Hwy 49, Ste A, Oakhurst, CA 93644-8826. Phones: 800-736-1414; 559-683-7388. Fax: 559-642-2432. E-mail: oakhurst@northlandcabletv.com. Web Site: http://www.northlandcabletv.com. Also serves Yosemite Lake Park. ICA: CA0259.

TV Market Ranking: 72 (COARSEGOLD, Yosemite Lake Park); Outside TV Markets (Yosemite Lake Park). Franchise award date: April 11, 1990. Franchise expiration date: N.A. Began: July 1, 1990.

Channel capacity: 36 (operating 2-way). Channels available but not in use: 6.

Basic Service
Subscribers: 500.
Programming (received off-air): KAIL (MNT) Fresno; KFRE-TV (CW) Sanger; KFSN-TV (ABC) Fresno; KFTV-DT (UNV) Hanford; KGPE (CBS) Fresno; KMPH-TV (FOX) Visalia; KNSO (TMO) Merced; KNXT (ETV) Visalia; KSEE (NBC) Fresno; KVPT (PBS) Fresno.
Programming (via satellite): Arts & Entertainment; CNN; C-SPAN; Discovery Channel; ESPN; Fox News Channel; Hallmark Channel; Headline News; National Geographic Channel; QVC; TBS Superstation; The Learning Channel; Turner Network TV; TV Guide Network; USA Network; Weather Channel; WGN America.
Fee: $55.00 installation; $34.99 monthly.

Expanded Basic Service 1
Subscribers: N.A.
Programming (via satellite): Cartoon Network; CNBC; Comcast Sports Net Bay Area; Country Music TV; E! Entertainment Television; ESPN 2; Food Network; Fox Movie Channel; HGTV; History Channel; Lifetime; Nickelodeon; Spike TV; Turner Classic Movies.
Fee: $39.99 monthly.

Digital Basic Service
Subscribers: 200.
Programming (via satellite): BBC America; Bloomberg Television; Discovery Digital Networks; DMX Music; Golf Channel; Great American Country; GSN; INSP; Outdoor Channel; Speed Channel; Syfy; Trinity Broadcasting Network.
Fee: $12.00 monthly.

Digital Expanded Basic Service
Subscribers: N.A.
Programming (via satellite): AmericanLife TV Network; Bravo; FitTV; G4; Independent Film Channel; WE tv.

Pay Service 1
Pay Units: 101.
Programming (via satellite): HBO.
Fee: $15.00 installation; $13.50 monthly.

Digital Pay Service 1
Pay Units: N.A.
Programming (via satellite): Cinemax (multiplexed); Encore (multiplexed); Flix; HBO (multiplexed); Showtime (multiplexed); Starz (multiplexed); Sundance Channel; The Movie Channel (multiplexed).

Pay-Per-View
Hot Choice (delivered digitally); Playboy TV (delivered digitally); Fresh (delivered digitally).

Internet Service
Operational: Yes.
Broadband Service: Northland Express.
Fee: $42.99 monthly.

Telephone Service
None

Homes passed: 1,032. Total homes in franchised area: 2,500.

Manager: Ken Musgrove. Chief Technician: Roger Conroy. Office Manager: Karen Bradley.

County fee: 5% of gross.

Ownership: Northland Communications Corp. (MSO).

COLEVILLE—Satview Broadband, 3550 Barron Way, Ste 13A, Reno, NV 89511. Phones: 775-333-6626; 800-225-0605. Fax: 775-333-0225. E-mail: taroil@yahoo.com. Web Site: http://www.iwantone.tv. ICA: CA0432.

TV Market Ranking: Outside TV Markets (COLEVILLE). Franchise award date: N.A. Franchise expiration date: N.A. Began: N.A.

Channel capacity: 50 (not 2-way capable). Channels available but not in use: N.A.

Basic Service
Subscribers: 700.
Programming (received off-air): KAME-TV (MNT) Reno; KOLO-TV (ABC) Reno; KRNV-DT (ABC) Reno; KTVN (CBS) Reno; 8 FMs.
Programming (via satellite): ABC Family Channel; AMC; AmericanLife TV Network; Discovery Channel; ESPN; KRXI-TV (FOX) Reno; KTLA (CW) Los Angeles; MSNBC; Nickelodeon; QVC; TBS Superstation; Turner Network TV; USA Network; WGN America.
Current originations: Religious Access.
Fee: $40.00 installation; $26.50 monthly.

Pay Service 1
Pay Units: 255.
Programming (via satellite): HBO.
Fee: $12.00 monthly.

Pay Service 2
Pay Units: 241.
Programming (via satellite): The Movie Channel.
Fee: $9.00 monthly.

Internet Service
Operational: No.

Telephone Service
None

Miles of Plant: 65.0 (coaxial); None (fiber optic). Additional miles planned: 5.0 (coaxial). Total homes in franchised area: 1,600. Total homes in franchised area includes Topaz Lake, NV

Chief Executive Officer: Tariq Ahmad.

Ownership: Satview Broadband Ltd. (MSO).

COLTON—Now served by ANAHEIM, CA [CA0033]. ICA: CA0134.

COMPTON—Time Warner Cable. Now served by LOS ANGELES, CA [CA0009]. ICA: CA0041.

CONCORD—Astound Broadband, 215 Mason Cir, Concord, CA 94520-1203. Phones: 800-427-8686; 925-459-1000. Fax: 425-576-8221. Web Site: http://www.wavebroadband.com. Also serves Contra Costa County (unincorporated areas) & Walnut Creek. ICA: CA0457. **Note:** This system is an overbuild.

TV Market Ranking: 7 (CONCORD (VILLAGE), Conta Costa County (unincorporated areas), Walnut Creek). Franchise award date: N.A. Franchise expiration date: N.A. Began: N.A.

Channel capacity: N.A. Channels available but not in use: N.A.

Basic Service
Subscribers: 14,000.
Programming (received off-air): KBCW (CW) San Francisco; KCNS (IND) San Francisco; KCRA-TV (NBC) Sacramento; KCSM-TV (PBS) San Mateo; KDTV-TV (UNV) San Francisco; KFSF-DT (TEL) Vallejo; KGO-TV (ABC) San Francisco; KICU-TV (IND) San Jose; KKPX-TV (ION) San Jose; KMTP-TV (ETV) San Francisco; KNTV (NBC) San Jose; KOFY-TV (IND) San Francisco; KPIX-TV (CBS) San Francisco; KQED (PBS) San Francisco; KRON-TV (MNT) San Francisco; KSTS (TMO) San Jose; KTEH (PBS) San Jose; KTLN-TV (IND) Novato; KTNC-TV (IND) Concord; KTSF (IND) San Francisco; KTVU (FOX) Oakland.
Programming (via satellite): California Channel; QVC; TBS Superstation; Trinity Broadcasting Network; Weather Channel; WGN America.
Current originations: Government Access; Public Access.
Fee: $19.95 installation; $21.95 monthly.

Expanded Basic Service 1
Subscribers: N.A.
Programming (via satellite): ABC Family Channel; AMC; AmericanLife TV Network; Animal Planet; Arts & Entertainment; BET Networks; Bravo; Cartoon Network; CNBC; CNN; Comcast Sports Net Bay Area; Comedy Central; Country Music TV; C-SPAN; C-SPAN 2; Discovery Channel; Discovery Health Channel; Disney Channel; E! Entertainment Television; ESPN; ESPN 2; ESPN Classic Sports; ESPNews; Food Network; Fox News Channel; FX; G4; GalaVision; Golf Channel; GSN; Hallmark Channel; Headline News; HGTV; History Channel; Lifetime; MSNBC; MTV; mun2 television; Nickelodeon; SoapNet; Speed Channel; Spike TV; Syfy; The Learning Channel; Toon Disney; Travel Channel; truTV; Turner Network TV; TV Land; USA Network; VH1.
Fee: $28.00 monthly.

Digital Basic Service
Subscribers: N.A.
Programming (received off-air): KBCW (CW) San Francisco; KGO-TV (ABC) San Francisco; KNTV (NBC) San Jose; KOFY-TV (IND) San Francisco; KPIX-TV (CBS) San Francisco; KQED (PBS) San Francisco; KTVU (FOX) Oakland.
Programming (via satellite): Arts & Entertainment HD; BBC America; Bio; Bloomberg Television; Boomerang; Classic Arts Showcase; Cooking Channel; Current; Discovery Digital Networks; Discovery HD Theater; Do-It-Yourself; Encore Wam; ESPN 2 HD; ESPN HD; ESPN U; Food Network HD; Fox College Sports Atlantic; Fox College Sports Central; Fox College Sports Pacific; Fox Movie Channel; Fuel TV; Fuse; GAS; Great American Country; Hallmark Channel; Halogen Network; HDNet; HDNet Movies; HGTV HD; History Channel International; Independent Film Channel; Lifetime Movie Network; Lifetime Real Women; MTV Networks Digital Suite; Music Choice; National Geographic Channel; National Geographic Channel HD Network; NFL Network; Nick Jr.; NickToons TV; Outdoor Channel; Ovation; Oxygen; PBS Kids Channel; Sleuth; Soccer Television; Style Network; Turner Classic Movies; Turner Network TV HD; Universal HD; Versus; WE tv.
Fee: $31.00 monthly.

Digital Pay Service 1
Pay Units: N.A.
Programming (via satellite): Canales N; CCTV-4; Cinemax (multiplexed); Cinemax HD; Cinemax On Demand; Encore (multiplexed); Filipino Channel; Flix; HBO (multiplexed); HBO HD; HBO On Demand; here! On Demand; here! TV; Russian Television Network; Showtime (multiplexed); Showtime HD; Showtime On Demand; Starz (multiplexed); Starz HDTV; Starz On Demand; The Movie Channel (multiplexed); The Movie Channel HD; The Movie Channel On Demand; Zee TV USA; Zhong Tian Channel.
Fee: $8.95 monthly (Starz or Flix, Sundance & TMC), $9.95 monthly (Cinemax, HBO or Showtime), $11.95 monthly (Canales n, CTN or Filipino).

Video-On-Demand: Yes

Pay-Per-View
iN DEMAND (delivered digitally).

Internet Service
Operational: Yes.
Subscribers: 20,000.
Broadband Service: BroadbandNOW!.
Fee: $19.95 installation; $19.95-$74.95 monthly.

Telephone Service
Digital: Operational
Subscribers: 11,000.
Fee: $19.95 installation; $24.95-$49.95 monthly

Marketing Manager: Bob Green.

Ownership: WaveDivision Holdings LLC (MSO).

CONCORD—Comcast Cable, 2500 Bates Ave, Concord, CA 94520-1208. Phones: 925-973-7000 (San Ramon regional office); 925-349-3300. Web Site: http://www.comcast.com. Also serves Alameda County, Antioch, Bay Point, Bethel Island, Brentwood, Byron, Castro Valley, Clayton, Clyde, Contra Costa County, Danville, Discovery Bay, Dublin, Knightsen, Lafayette, Livermore, Martinez, Moraga, Oakley, Orinda, Pacheco, Pittsburg, Pleasant Hill, Pleasanton, Rossmoor, San Ramon, Sunol & Walnut Creek. ICA: CA0101.

TV Market Ranking: 7 (Alameda County, Antioch, Bay Point, Bethel Island, Brentwood, Byron, Castro Valley, Clayton, Clyde, CONCORD (VILLAGE), Contra Costa County, Danville, Discovery Bay, Dublin, Knightsen, Lafayette, Livermore, Martinez, Moraga, Oakley, Orinda, Pacheco, Pittsburg, Pleasant Hill, Pleasanton, Rossmoor, San Ramon, Sunol, Walnut Creek); Below 100 (Danville). Franchise award date: March 1, 1967. Franchise expiration date: N.A. Began: March 1, 1967.

Channel capacity: N.A. Channels available but not in use: N.A.

Basic Service
Subscribers: N.A. Included in San Francisco
Programming (received off-air): KBCW (CW) San Francisco; KCNS (IND) San Francisco; KCRA-TV (NBC) Sacramento; KDTV-TV (UNV) San Francisco; KFSF-DT (TEL) Vallejo; KGO-TV (ABC) San Francisco; KICU-TV (IND) San Jose; KKPX-TV (ION) San Jose; KNTV (NBC) San Jose; KOFY-TV (IND) San Francisco; KPIX-TV (CBS) San Francisco; KQED (PBS) San

Francisco; KRON-TV (MNT) San Francisco; KSTS (TMO) San Jose; KTEH (PBS) San Jose; KTLN-TV (IND) Novato; KTNC-TV (IND) Concord; KTSF (IND) San Francisco; KTVU (FOX) Oakland; allband FM.

Programming (via satellite): Discovery Channel; Home Shopping Network 2; QVC; TBS Superstation; TV Guide Network.

Current originations: Government Access; Educational Access; Public Access.

Fee: $43.99 installation; $16.77 monthly.

Expanded Basic Service 1

Subscribers: 200,000.

Programming (via satellite): ABC Family Channel; AMC; Animal Planet; Arts & Entertainment; BET Networks; Cartoon Network; CNBC; CNN; Comcast Sports Net Bay Area; Comedy Central; C-SPAN; C-SPAN 2; Disney Channel; E! Entertainment Television; ESPN; ESPN 2; Food Network; Fox News Channel; FX; Golf Channel; Hallmark Channel; Headline News; History Channel; Lifetime; MSNBC; MTV; Nickelodeon; Spike TV; The Learning Channel; Travel Channel; Turner Network TV; TV Land; USA Network; Versus; VH1; Weather Channel.

Fee: $33.22 monthly.

Digital Basic Service

Subscribers: 14,677.

Programming (via satellite): American-Life TV Network; BBC America; Bio; Bloomberg Television; Bravo; Canales N; Discovery Digital Networks; DragonTV; Encore Action; ESPN Classic Sports; ESPNews; Eternal Word TV Network; FitTV; Fox College Sports Atlantic; Fox College Sports Central; Fox College Sports Pacific; Fox Movie Channel; Fox Sports World; Fuse; G4; GAS; Great American Country; GSN; Halogen Network; HGTV; History Channel International; Independent Film Channel; International Television (ITV); Lifetime Movie Network; Lime; MTV Networks Digital Suite; Music Choice; National Geographic Channel; Nick Jr.; NickToons TV; Outdoor Channel; Ovation; ShopNBC; Speed Channel; Style Network; Sundance Channel; Syfy; The Word Network; Toon Disney; Trinity Broadcasting Network; Turner Classic Movies; WE tv; Weatherscan.

Fee: $11.46 monthly.

Digital Pay Service 1

Pay Units: 13,000.

Programming (via satellite): CCTV-4; Cinemax (multiplexed); Filipino Channel; Flix; HBO (multiplexed); RAI Internacional; Russian Television Network; Saigon Broadcasting TV Network; Showtime (multiplexed); Starz (multiplexed); The Movie Channel (multiplexed); TV Asia; TV Japan; TV5, La Television International; Zee TV USA; Zhong Tian Channel.

Fee: $17.00 monthly (each).

Video-On-Demand: Yes

Pay-Per-View

Addressable homes: 14,677.

iN DEMAND (delivered digitally), Addressable: Yes; Hot Choice (delivered digitally); Barker (delivered digitally); Urban Xtra (delivered digitally); Fresh (delivered digitally); Shorteez (delivered digitally); Playboy TV (delivered digitally); ESPN Now (delivered digitally); Sports PPV (delivered digitally).

Internet Service

Operational: Yes.

Broadband Service: Comcast High Speed Internet.

Fee: $42.95 monthly.

Telephone Service

Digital: Operational

Fee: $44.95 monthly

Miles of Plant: 3,276.0 (coaxial); 173.0 (fiber optic). Homes passed: 389,014.

Area Vice President: Marty Robinson. Vice President, Communications: Andrew Johnson. Technical Operations Director: Joe Raposa. Marketing Director: David Jew.

City fee: 5% of gross.

Ownership: Comcast Cable Communications Inc. (MSO).

CONCORD—Comcast Cable. Now served by CONCORD (formerly Walnut Creek), CA [CA0101]. ICA: CA0057.

COPPER COVE COPPEROPOLIS—Formerly served by Mountain View Cable. No longer in operation. ICA: CA0323.

CORONA—Time Warner Cable. Now served by ANAHEIM, CA [CA0033]. ICA: CA0087.

CORONADO—Time Warner Cable. Now served by SAN DIEGO, CA [CA0007]. ICA: CA0163.

COSTA MESA—Time Warner Cable. Now served by ANAHEIM, CA [CA0033]. ICA: CA0069.

COVINA—Comcast Cable. Now served by LOS ANGELES, CA [CA0009]. ICA: CA0110.

CRESCENT CITY—Charter Communications, 1286 Northcrest Dr, Crescent City, CA 95531-2321. Phones: 360-828-6600 (Vancouver office); 707-464-5722. Fax: 707-464-4849. Web Site: http://www.charter.com. Also serves Del Norte County & Gasquet, CA; North Smith River, OR. ICA: CA0155.

TV Market Ranking: Outside TV Markets (CRESCENT CITY, Del Norte County, Gasquet, North Smith River). Franchise award date: N.A. Franchise expiration date: N.A. Began: January 1, 1958.

Channel capacity: N.A. Channels available but not in use: N.A.

Basic Service

Subscribers: 6,192.

Programming (received off-air): KAEF-TV (ABC) Arcata; KBLN (IND) Grants Pass; KBSC-LP (IND) Brookings; KBVU (FOX) Eureka; KEET (PBS) Eureka; KIEM-TV (NBC) Eureka; KOBI (NBC) Medford; KVIQ (CBS, CW) Eureka; 4 FMs.

Programming (via satellite): C-SPAN; C-SPAN 2; Eternal Word TV Network; Home Shopping Network; INSP; QVC; ShopNBC; Telemundo; Trinity Broadcasting Network; TV Guide Network; Univision; Weather Channel; WGN America.

Current originations: Public Access; Leased Access.

Fee: $29.95 installation.

Expanded Basic Service 1

Subscribers: N.A.

Programming (via satellite): ABC Family Channel; AMC; Animal Planet; Arts & Entertainment; Bravo!; Cartoon Network; CNBC; CNN; Comcast Sports Net Bay Area; Comedy Central; Country Music TV; Discovery Channel; Disney Channel; Do-It-Yourself; E! Entertainment Television; ESPN; ESPN 2; Food Network; Fox News Channel; FX; G4; Golf Channel; Great American Country; GSN; Hallmark Channel; Headline News; HGTV; History Channel; Lifetime; MSNBC; MTV; MTV2; National Geographic Channel; Nickelodeon; Northwest Cable News; Oxygen; Speed Channel; Spike TV; Syfy; TBS Superstation; The Learning Channel; Toon Disney; Travel Channel; truTV; Turner Classic Movies; Turner Network TV; TV Land; USA Network; Versus; VH1; WE tv.

Fee: $42.95 monthly.

Digital Basic Service

Subscribers: N.A.

Programming (via satellite): BBC America; Bio; Boomerang; CNN en Espanol; CNN International; Discovery Digital Networks; DMX Music; ESPN Classic Sports; ESPNews; Fox College Sports Atlantic; Fox College Sports Central; Fox College Sports Pacific; Fox Movie Channel; Fox Soccer; Fox Sports en Espanol; Fuel TV; GAS; History Channel International; Independent Film Channel; Lifetime Movie Network; MTV Networks Digital Suite; NFL Network; Nick Jr.; NickToons TV; SoapNet; Sundance Channel.

Digital Pay Service 1

Pay Units: N.A.

Programming (via satellite): Cinemax; Encore; Flix; HBO (multiplexed); Showtime (multiplexed); Starz (multiplexed); The Movie Channel (multiplexed).

Video-On-Demand: No

Pay-Per-View

iN DEMAND (delivered digitally); Hot Choice (delivered digitally); Playboy TV (delivered digitally); Fresh (delivered digitally); Shorteez (delivered digitally); NASCAR In Car.

Internet Service

Operational: Yes.

Broadband Service: Charter Pipeline.

Fee: $29.95 monthly.

Telephone Service

Digital: Operational

Miles of Plant: 240.0 (coaxial); None (fiber optic). Homes passed: 7,611.

Vice President: Frank Antonovich. General Manager: Linda Kimberly. Plant Manager: Earl Desomber. Chief Technician: Dennis Putman. Marketing Director: Diane Long. Office Manager: Sandra Milunich.

City fee: 5% of gross.

Ownership: Charter Communications Inc. (MSO).

CRESCENT MILLS—Wave Broadband, 401 Kirkland Parkplace, Ste 500, Kirkland, WA 98033. Phone: 425-576-8200. Fax: 425-576-8221. Web Site: http://wavebroadband.com. Also serves Greenville. ICA: CA0447.

TV Market Ranking: Outside TV Markets (CRESCENT MILLS, Greenville). Franchise award date: N.A. Franchise expiration date: N.A. Began: N.A.

Channel capacity: N.A. Channels available but not in use: N.A.

Basic Service

Subscribers: N.A. Included in West Sacramento

Programming (received off-air): KCRA-TV (NBC) Sacramento; KHSL-TV (CBS, CW) Chico; KOVR (CBS) Stockton; KTVU (FOX) Oakland; KVIE (PBS) Sacramento; KXTV (ABC) Sacramento.

Programming (via satellite): ABC Family Channel; Animal Planet; Arts & Entertainment; Cartoon Network; CNBC; CNN; Comcast Sports Net Bay Area; Country Music TV; C-SPAN; Discovery Channel; Disney Channel; ESPN; ESPN 2; Headline News; History Channel; Lifetime; MTV; Nickelodeon; QVC; Spike TV; Syfy; TBS Superstation; The Learning Channel; Turner Classic Movies; Turner Network TV; USA Network; Weather Channel; WGN America.

Fee: free installation; $40.95 monthly; $.98 converter.

Digital Basic Service

Subscribers: N.A.

Programming (via satellite): AmericanLife TV Network; BBC America; Bio; Bloomberg Television; Bravo!; Discovery Digital Networks; FitTV; Fox Movie Channel; Fox Soccer; Fuse; G4; GAS; Golf Channel; GSN; HGTV; Independent Film Channel; INSP; Lifetime Movie Network; MTV Networks Digital Suite; Music Choice; Nick Jr.; Outdoor Channel; Science Television; ShopNBC; Speed Channel; Toon Disney; Trinity Broadcasting Network; Versus; WE tv.

Pay Service 1

Pay Units: N.A.

Programming (via satellite): HBO; Showtime.

Fee: $12.45 monthly (Showtime), $13.95 monthly (HBO).

Digital Pay Service 1

Pay Units: N.A.

Programming (via satellite): Cinemax (multiplexed); Encore (multiplexed); Flix (multiplexed); HBO (multiplexed); Showtime (multiplexed); Starz; The Movie Channel.

Video-On-Demand: No

Pay-Per-View

Hot Choice (delivered digitally); Playboy TV (delivered digitally); Fresh (delivered digitally); Shorteez (delivered digitally).

Internet Service

Operational: No.

Telephone Service

None

General Manager: Tim Peters. Marketing Director: Adam Lazara.

Ownership: WaveDivision Holdings LLC (MSO).

CROWLEY LAKE—Satview Broadband, 3550 Barron Way, Ste 13A, Reno, NV 89511. Phones: 800-225-0605; 775-338-6626. Fax: 775-333-0225. Web Site: http://www.iwantone.tv. ICA: CA0289.

TV Market Ranking: Outside TV Markets (CROWLEY LAKE). Franchise award date: N.A. Franchise expiration date: N.A. Began: January 1, 1984.

Channel capacity: 36 (not 2-way capable). Channels available but not in use: 12.

Basic Service

Subscribers: 57.

Programming (received off-air): KABC-TV (ABC) Los Angeles; KCAL-TV (IND) Los Angeles; KCBS-TV (CBS) Los Angeles; KJLA (IND) Ventura; KLVX-TV (PBS) Las Vegas; KNBC (NBC) Los Angeles; KTTV (FOX) Los Angeles.

Programming (via satellite): Animal Planet; Arts & Entertainment; Bravo; Cartoon Network; CNBC; CNN; Comedy Central; Discovery Channel; Discovery Health Channel; Disney Channel; E! Entertainment Tele-

vision; ESPN; ESPN 2; Food Network; Fox News Channel; Fox Sports Net; FX; Golf Channel; Great American Country; Headline News; History Channel; Home Shopping Network; ION Television; Lifetime; MSNBC; MTV; Nickelodeon; QVC; ShopNBC; SoapNet; Spike TV; Style Network; Syfy; TBS Superstation; The Learning Channel; Toon Disney; Travel Channel; Trinity Broadcasting Network; Turner Network TV; TV Guide Network; Univision; USA Network; VH1; Weather Channel.
Programming (via translator): KOLO-TV (ABC) Reno; KTLA (CW) Los Angeles.
Current originations: Public Access.
Fee: $49.95 installation; $27.90 monthly.
Pay Service 1
Pay Units: 38.
Fee: $15.00 installation; $13.95 monthly.
Pay Service 2
Pay Units: 27.
Fee: $15.00 installation; $10.95 monthly.
Pay-Per-View
Hot Choice (delivered digitally); Fresh (delivered digitally); Viewer's Choice (delivered digitally).
Internet Service
Operational: No.
Telephone Service
None
Miles of Plant: 4.0 (coaxial); None (fiber optic). Homes passed: 300.
Chief Executive Officer: Tariq Ahmad.
Ownership: Satview Broadband Ltd. (MSO).

CUPERTINO—Matrix Cablevision Inc. Now served by SAN JOSE, CA [CA0004]. ICA: CA0466.

CYPRESS—Time Warner Cable. Now served by ANAHEIM, CA [CA0033]. ICA: CA0117.

DAVIS—Comcast Cable. Now served by SACRAMENTO, CA [CA0002]. ICA: CA0122.

DEL PASO HEIGHTS (portions)—SureWest Broadband. Formerly served by Sacramento, CA [CA0459]. This cable system has converted to IPTV, PO Box 969, Roseville, CA 95661. Phone: 916-772-2000. Fax: 916-786-7170. Web Site: http://www.surewest.com. ICA: CA5602.
TV Market Ranking: 25 (DEL PASO HEIGHTS (PORTIONS)).
Channel capacity: N.A. Channels available but not in use: N.A.
Video-On-Demand: Yes
Internet Service
Operational: Yes.
Telephone Service
Digital: Operational
Ownership: SureWest Broadband.

DESERT CENTER—Formerly served by American Pacific Co. No longer in operation. ICA: CA0327.

DESERT HOT SPRINGS—Time Warner Cable. Now served by PALM DESERT, CA [CA0036]. ICA: CA0156.

DIAMOND BAR—Time Warner Cable. Now served by LOS ANGELES, CA [CA0009]. ICA: CA0082.

DORRIS—Almega Cable, 4001 W Airport Frwy, Ste 530, Bedford, TX 76021. Phones: 877-725-6342; 817-685-9588. Fax: 817-685-6488. Web Site: http://almegacable.com. ICA: CA0274.
TV Market Ranking: Below 100 (DORRIS). Franchise award date: N.A. Franchise expiration date: N.A. Began: June 3, 1981.
Channel capacity: 40 (2-way capable). Channels available but not in use: 8.
Basic Service
Subscribers: 63.
Programming (received off-air): KDKF (ABC) Klamath Falls; KMVU-DT (FOX) Medford; KOTI (NBC) Klamath Falls; KRCR-TV (ABC) Redding; KSYS (PBS) Medford; KTVL (CBS, CW) Medford.
Programming (via satellite): ABC Family Channel; Arts & Entertainment; Bravo; CNBC; CNN; Comedy Central; Discovery Channel; Disney Channel; ESPN; HGTV; MSNBC; National Geographic Channel; Spike TV; Syfy; TBS Superstation; Turner Classic Movies; Turner Network TV; Univision; USA Network; WGN America.
Current originations: Educational Access; Public Access.
Fee: $29.95 installation; $31.95 monthly.
Pay Service 1
Pay Units: 9.
Programming (via satellite): HBO.
Fee: $15.00 installation; $10.95 monthly.
Video-On-Demand: No
Internet Service
Operational: No.
Telephone Service
None
Miles of Plant: 7.0 (coaxial); None (fiber optic). Homes passed: 430.
President: Thomas Kurien.
Franchise fee: 5% of basic.
Ownership: Almega Cable (MSO).

DOWNEY—Formerly served by Comcast Cable. No longer in operation. ICA: CA0022.

DOWNIEVILLE—Downieville TV Corp. No longer in operation. ICA: CA0287.

EAGLE ROCK—Time Warner Cable. Now served by LOS ANGELES, CA [CA0009]. ICA: CA0472.

EARLIMART—Charter Communications. Now served by PORTERVILLE, CA [CA0152]. ICA: CA0328.

EAST LOS ANGELES—Time Warner Cable. Now served by LOS ANGELES, CA [CA0009]. ICA: CA0063.

EAST SAN FERNANDO VALLEY—Time Warner Cable. Now served by LOS ANGELES, CA [CA0009]. ICA: CA0012.

EL CENTRO—Time Warner Cable, 1289 S 2nd Ave, Yuma, AZ 85364-4715. Phone: 928-329-9723. Fax: 928-783-0242. Web Site: http://www.timewarnercable.com/Yuma-ElCentro. Also serves Brawley, Calexico, El Centro NAF, Heber, Holtville, Imperial & Westmorland. ICA: CA0088.
TV Market Ranking: Below 100 (Brawley, Calexico, EL CENTRO, El Centro NAF, Heber, Holtville, Imperial, Westmorland). Franchise award date: March 1, 1960. Franchise expiration date: N.A. Began: March 1, 1960.
Channel capacity: N.A. Channels available but not in use: N.A.
Basic Service
Subscribers: N.A. Included in Yuma, AZ
Programming (received off-air): KABC-TV (ABC) Los Angeles; KECY-TV (ABC, FOX, MNT, TMO) El Centro; KSWT (CBS, CW) Yuma; KVYE (UNV) El Centro; KYMA-DT (NBC) Yuma; 5 FMs.
Programming (via microwave): KCOP-TV (MNT) Los Angeles; KPBS (PBS) San Diego.
Programming (via satellite): ABC Family Channel; AMC; Animal Planet; Arts & Entertainment; BET Networks; Bravo!; California Channel; Cartoon Network; CNBC; CNN; Comedy Central; Country Music TV; C-SPAN; C-SPAN 2; Discovery Channel; E! Entertainment Television; ESPN; ESPN 2; Eternal Word TV Network; Food Network; Fox News Channel; Fox Sports en Espanol; Fox Sports Net West; Fox Sports Net West 2; FX; GalaVision; Hallmark Channel; Headline News; HGTV; History Channel; Home Shopping Network; ION Television; Lifetime; MSNBC; MTV; Nickelodeon; Oxygen; QVC; ShopNBC; Syfy; TBS Superstation; Telemundo; The Learning Channel; Travel Channel; truTV; Turner Network TV; TV Land; USA Network; VH1; Weather Channel.
Current originations: Educational Access.
Planned originations: Public Access.
Fee: $35.80 installation; $42.71 monthly; $2.01 converter.
Expanded Basic Service 1
Subscribers: 13,900.
Programming (via satellite): Disney Channel; Fox Sports Net West 2; Spike TV.
Fee: $7.00 monthly.
Digital Basic Service
Subscribers: N.A. Included in Yuma, AZ
Programming (via satellite): American-Life TV Network; BBC America; Bloomberg Television; Canales N; Discovery Digital Networks; Do-It-Yourself; ESPN Classic Sports; ESPNews; Fuse; G4; GAS; Golf Channel; GSN; Halogen Network; Independent Film Channel; MTV Networks Digital Suite; Music Choice; National Geographic Channel; Nick Jr.; Nick Too; Outdoor Channel; SoapNet; Speed Channel; Style Network; Sundance Channel; Toon Disney; Trinity Broadcasting Network; Turner Classic Movies; Versus; WE tv.
Fee: $6.00 monthly (Variety, Choice, Movies, Sports or Espanol).
Digital Pay Service 1
Pay Units: N.A.
Programming (via satellite): ART America; CCTV-4; Cinemax (multiplexed); Encore (multiplexed); Filipino Channel; Flix; HBO (multiplexed); RAI International; Russian Television Network; Showtime (multiplexed); Starz (multiplexed); The Movie Channel (multiplexed); TV Asia; TV Japan; TV5, La Television International.
Fee: $12.00 monthly (HBO, Cinemax, Showitme, TMC, Starz or Encore), $15.00 monthly (TV Japan, RTN, CCTV, TV Asia, TV-5, Filipino Channel, RAI or ART).
Video-On-Demand: Planned
Pay-Per-View
Special events, Addressable: Yes; Playboy TV (delivered digitally); Fresh (delivered digitally); Hot Choice (delivered digitally).
Internet Service
Operational: Yes.
Broadband Service: Road Runner.
Fee: $44.95 monthly; $5.00 modem lease.
Telephone Service
Digital: Operational
Fee: $49.95 monthly
Homes passed & miles of plant included in Yuma, AZ
General Manager: Ricky Rinehart. Operations Manager: Hughie Williams. Marketing Manager: Shayne Abney. Business Manager: Jessica Haggard.
Franchise fee: 3% of gross.
Ownership: Time Warner Cable (MSO).

EL MONTE—Now served by LOS ANGELES, CA [CA0009]. ICA: CA0047.

ELK GROVE—SureWest Broadband. Formerly served by Sacramento, CA [CA0459]. This cable system has converted to IPTV, PO Box 969, Roseville, CA 95661. Phone: 916-772-2000. Fax: 916-786-7170. Web Site: http://www.surewest.com. ICA: CA5603.
TV Market Ranking: 25 (ELK GROVE).
Channel capacity: N.A. Channels available but not in use: N.A.
Video-On-Demand: Yes
Internet Service
Operational: Yes.
Telephone Service
Digital: Operational
Ownership: SureWest Broadband.

ETNA—Formerly served by Siskiyou Cablevision Inc. No longer in operation. ICA: CA0233.

EUREKA—Suddenlink Communications, 911 W Wabash Ave, Eureka, CA 95501-2131. Phones: 877-443-3127; 707-268-5380. Fax: 707-444-9017. Web Site: http://www.suddenlink.com. Also serves Arcata, Blue Lake, Ferndale, Fieldbrook, Fortuna, Humboldt County, Rio Dell, Scotia & Trinidad. ICA: CA0065.
TV Market Ranking: Below 100 (Arcata, Blue Lake, EUREKA, Ferndale, Fieldbrook, Fortuna, Humboldt County, Rio Dell, Scotia, Trinidad). Franchise award date: October 1, 1967. Franchise expiration date: N.A. Began: May 1, 1968.
Channel capacity: 79 (operating 2-way). Channels available but not in use: 6.
Basic Service
Subscribers: 30,912.
Programming (received off-air): KAEF-TV (ABC) Arcata; KBVU (FOX) Eureka; KEET (PBS)ureka; KIEM-TV (NBC) Eureka; KPIX-TV (CBS) San Francisco; KVIQ (CBS, CW) Eureka.
Programming (via microwave): KPIX-TV (CBS) San Francisco; KRON-TV (MNT) San Francisco.
Programming (via satellite): C-SPAN; TBS Superstation.
Current originations: Educational Access; Public Access.
Fee: $30.00 installation; $6.79 monthly.
Expanded Basic Service 1
Subscribers: 30,260.
Programming (via satellite): ABC Family Channel; AMC; Animal Planet; Arts & Entertainment; Bravo; Cartoon Network; CNBC; CNN; Comcast Sports Net Bay Area; Comedy Central; C-SPAN 2; Discovery Channel; Discovery Health Channel; Disney Channel; E! Entertainment Television; ESPN; ESPN 2; Food Network; Fox News Channel; FX; Golf Channel; Headline News; HGTV; History Channel; Home Shopping Network; Independent Film Channel; ION Television; Lifetime; MSNBC; MTV; Nickelodeon; Product Information Network; QVC; Sneak Prevue; Speed Channel; Spike TV; Syfy; The Learning Channel; Travel Channel; Trinity Broadcasting Network; truTV; Turner Classic Movies; Turner Network TV; TV Guide Network; TV Land; USA Network; Versus; VH1; Weather Channel.
Fee: $30.00 installation; $8.33 monthly.
Digital Basic Service
Subscribers: N.A.
Programming (via satellite): BBC America; Bloomberg Television; Discovery Digital Networks; ESPN Now; ESPNews; Fox Sports World; G4; Golf Channel; GSN; Inde-

pendent Film Channel; Lifetime Movie Network; MuchMusic Network; Music Choice; NBA TV; Outdoor Channel; SoapNet; Sundance Channel; Toon Disney.

Pay Service 1

Pay Units: 13,000.

Programming (via satellite): Cinemax (multiplexed); HBO (multiplexed); Showtime (multiplexed); The Movie Channel.

Fee: $10.75 monthly (each).

Digital Pay Service 1

Pay Units: N.A.

Programming (via satellite): Cinemax (multiplexed); Encore; HBO (multiplexed); Showtime (multiplexed); Starz (multiplexed); The Movie Channel.

Video-On-Demand: Yes

Pay-Per-View

Addressable homes: 12,760.

Hot Choice (delivered digitally), Addressable: Yes; iN DEMAND; iN DEMAND (delivered digitally); Playboy TV (delivered digitally); Fresh (delivered digitally); Shorteez (delivered digitally).

Internet Service

Operational: Yes.

Broadband Service: Cebridge High Speed Cable Internet.

Fee: $99.99 installation; $24.95 monthly.

Telephone Service

Digital: Operational

Fee: $39.95 monthly

Miles of Plant: 601.0 (coaxial); 100.0 (fiber optic). Homes passed: 41,090. Total homes in franchised area: 51,984.

Manager: Dorothy Lovfald. Marketing Director: Wendy Purnell. Chief Technician: Carl Moon.

Franchise fee: 5% of gross.

Ownership: Cequel Communications LLC (MSO).

FAIR OAKS (portions)—SureWest Broadband. Formerly served by Sacramento, CA [CA0459]. This cable system has converted to IPTV, PO Box 969, Roseville, CA 95661. Phone: 916-772-2000. Fax: 916-786-7170. Web Site: http://www.surewest.com. ICA: CA5604.

TV Market Ranking: 25 (FAIR OAKS (PORTIONS)).

Channel capacity: N.A. Channels available but not in use: N.A.

Video-On-Demand: Yes

Internet Service

Operational: Yes.

Telephone Service

Digital: Operational

Ownership: SureWest Broadband.

FAIRFIELD—Comcast Cable. Now served by NAPA/SONOMA, CA [CA0038]. ICA: CA0078.

FALL RIVER MILLS—Almega Cable, 4001 W Airport Frwy, Ste 530, Bedford, TX 76021. Phones: 877-725-6342; 817-685-9588. Fax: 817-685-6488. Web Site: http://almegacable.com. Also serves McArthur & Pittville. ICA: CA0329.

TV Market Ranking: Outside TV Markets (FALL RIVER MILLS, McArthur, Pittville). Franchise award date: N.A. Franchise expiration date: N.A. Began: February 19, 1982.

Channel capacity: 19 (not 2-way capable). Channels available but not in use: 4.

Basic Service

Subscribers: 264.

Programming (received off-air): KHSL-TV (CBS, CW) Chico; KIXE-TV (PBS) Redding; KOTI (NBC) Klamath Falls; KRCR-TV (ABC) Redding.

Programming (via satellite): ABC Family Channel; Arts & Entertainment; Bravo; Cartoon Network; CNBC; CNN; Discovery Channel; Disney Channel; ESPN; Fox News Channel; HGTV; MSNBC; Spike TV; Syfy; TBS Superstation; Turner Classic Movies; Turner Network TV; USA Network; WGN America.

Fee: $43.50 installation; $19.95 monthly; $21.50 additional installation.

Pay Service 1

Pay Units: 42.

Programming (via satellite): HBO.

Fee: $10.00 installation; $11.00 monthly.

Video-On-Demand: No

Internet Service

Operational: No.

Telephone Service

None

Miles of Plant: 12.0 (coaxial); None (fiber optic). Homes passed: 720.

President: Thomas Kurien. Regional Service Manager: Tom Wilert.

County fee: 5% of gross.

Ownership: Almega Cable (MSO).

FISH CAMP—Formerly served by Northland Cable Television. No longer in operation. ICA: CA0330.

FOREST FALLS—Charter Communications, 7337 Central Ave, Riverside, CA 92504. Phone: 951-343-5100. Fax: 951-354-5942. E-mail: jehrle@chartercom.com. Web Site: http://www.charter.com. Also serves Angelus Oaks, Mill Creek Park & Yucaipa. ICA: CA0211.

TV Market Ranking: 2 (Angelus Oaks, FOREST FALLS, Mill Creek Park, Yucaipa). Franchise award date: N.A. Franchise expiration date: N.A. Began: October 1, 1986.

Channel capacity: 36 (not 2-way capable). Channels available but not in use: N.A.

Basic Service

Subscribers: 273.

Programming (received off-air): KABC-TV (ABC) Los Angeles; KCBS-TV (CBS) Los Angeles; KCET (PBS) Los Angeles; KCOP-TV (MNT) Los Angeles; KDOC-TV (IND) Anaheim; KFTR-DT (TEL) Ontario; KHIZ (IND) Barstow; KMEX-DT (UNV) Los Angeles; KNBC (NBC) Los Angeles; KPXN-TV (ION) San Bernardino; KRCA (IND) Riverside; KSCI (IND) Long Beach; KTBN-TV (TBN) Santa Ana; KTLA (CW) Los Angeles; KTTV (FOX) Los Angeles; KVCR-DT (PBS) San Bernardino; KVEA (TMO) Corona.

Programming (via satellite): ABC Family Channel; AMC; Arts & Entertainment; BET Networks; Cartoon Network; CNBC; CNN; Comedy Central; Country Music TV; C-SPAN; Discovery Channel; Disney Channel; E! Entertainment Television; ESPN; ESPN 2; Eternal Word TV Network; Food Network; Fox News Channel; Fox Sports Net West; FX; Headline News; History Channel; Lifetime; MSNBC; MTV; Nickelodeon; Oxygen; QVC; Spike TV; Syfy; TBS Superstation; The Learning Channel; Turner Classic Movies; Turner Network TV; TV Guide Network; USA Network; VH1; Weather Channel; WGN America.

Fee: $11.95 monthly.

Pay Service 1

Pay Units: N.A.

Programming (via satellite): Cinemax; HBO (multiplexed); Showtime; The Movie Channel.

Video-On-Demand: No

Pay-Per-View

iN DEMAND.

Internet Service

Operational: No.

Telephone Service

None

Miles of Plant: 35.0 (coaxial); None (fiber optic). Additional miles planned: 30.0 (coaxial). Homes passed: 850. Total homes in franchised area: 5,800.

Vice President & General Manager: Fred Lutz. Marketing Director: Chris Bailey. Technical Operations Manager: George Noel.

Ownership: Charter Communications Inc. (MSO).

FORESTHILL—Suddenlink Communications, 12444 Powerscourt Dr, Saint Louis, MO 63131-3660. Phones: 314-965-2020; 530-268-3771. Web Site: http://www.suddenlink.com. Also serves Todd Valley. ICA: CA0238.

TV Market Ranking: Outside TV Markets (FORESTHILL, Todd Valley). Franchise award date: April 1, 1987. Franchise expiration date: N.A. Began: September 1, 1989.

Channel capacity: 62 (operating 2-way). Channels available but not in use: 19.

Basic Service

Subscribers: N.A.

Programming (received off-air): KCRA-TV (NBC) Sacramento; KMAX-TV (CW) Sacramento; KOVR (CBS) Stockton; KQCA (MNT) Stockton; KTFK-DT (TEL) Stockton; KTXL (FOX) Sacramento; KUVS-DT (UNV) Modesto; KVIE (PBS) Sacramento; KXTV (ABC) Sacramento.

Programming (via satellite): ABC Family Channel; AmericanLife TV Network; Animal Planet; Arts & Entertainment; CNBC; CNN; Comedy Central; C-SPAN; C-SPAN 2; Discovery Channel; Disney Channel; E! Entertainment Television; ESPN; ESPN 2; Eternal Word TV Network; Food Network; Fox News Channel; Great American Country; Headline News; HGTV; History Channel; Home Shopping Network; Lifetime; MTV; Nickelodeon; QVC; Spike TV; Style Network; Syfy; TBS Superstation; The Learning Channel; Trinity Broadcasting Network; Turner Classic Movies; Turner Network TV; TV Land; USA Network; VH1; Weather Channel; WGN America.

Fee: $19.95 monthly.

Digital Basic Service

Subscribers: N.A.

Programming (via satellite): BBC America; Bio; Bravo; Discovery Digital Networks; DMX Music; Encore Action; ESPN Classic Sports; ESPNews; Fox Sports World; Fuse; GAS; Golf Channel; GSN; History Channel International; Independent Film Channel; Lifetime Movie Network; MTV2; National Geographic Channel; Nick Jr.; Speed Channel; Starz; Toon Disney; Versus; VH1 Classic; VH1 Country; WE tv.

Fee: $3.95 monthly.

Pay Service 1

Pay Units: N.A.

Programming (via satellite): Cinemax; HBO; Showtime; The Movie Channel.

Digital Pay Service 1

Pay Units: N.A.

Programming (via satellite): Cinemax (multiplexed); HBO (multiplexed); Showtime (multiplexed); The Movie Channel (multiplexed).

Video-On-Demand: No

Internet Service

Operational: Yes. Began: January 1, 1998.

Broadband Service: Cebridge High Speed Cable Internet.

Fee: $99.99 installation; $24.95 monthly.

Telephone Service

None

Miles of Plant: 35.0 (coaxial); None (fiber optic). Homes passed: 1,500. Total homes in franchised area: 5,000.

Manager: Doug Landaker. Chief Technician: Tim Lenz. Marketing Director: Jason Oelkers.

Ownership: Cequel Communications LLC (MSO).

FORT IRWIN—Formerly served by Total TV of Fort Irwin Inc. No longer in operation. ICA: CA0405.

FORT ORD—Suddenlink Communications, 142 4th Ave, Marina, CA 93933. Phones: 314-965-2020; 800-446-6745; 530-587-6100. Web Site: http://www.suddenlink.com. Also serves Presidio of Monterey. ICA: CA0153.

TV Market Ranking: Below 100 (FORT ORD, Presidio of Monterey). Franchise award date: November 19, 1980. Franchise expiration date: N.A. Began: May 5, 1981.

Channel capacity: 77 (operating 2-way). Channels available but not in use: 20.

Basic Service

Subscribers: 1,918.

Programming (received off-air): KCBA (FOX) Salinas; KICU-TV (IND) San Jose; KION-TV (CBS, CW) Monterey; KNTV (NBC) San Jose; KSBW (NBC) Salinas; KSMS-TV (UNV) Monterey.

Programming (via microwave): KQED (PBS) San Francisco; KTEH (PBS) San Jose.

Programming (via satellite): TBS Superstation; WGN America.

Current originations: Government Access.

Fee: $35.00 installation; $18.50 monthly; $15.00 additional installation.

Expanded Basic Service 1

Subscribers: 1,701.

Programming (via satellite): ABC Family Channel; Arts & Entertainment; BET Networks; CNN; Comcast Sports Net Bay Area; Comedy Central; Discovery Channel; Disney Channel; E! Entertainment Television; ESPN; Headline News; Home Shopping Network; Lifetime; MTV; Nickelodeon; Spike TV; Turner Network TV; USA Network; VH1.

Fee: $5.00 monthly.

Pay Service 1

Pay Units: 7.

Programming (via satellite): Flix.

Pay Service 2

Pay Units: 213.

Programming (via satellite): HBO.

Fee: $9.95 monthly.

Pay Service 3

Pay Units: 192.

Programming (via satellite): The Movie Channel.

Fee: $9.95 monthly.

Pay Service 4

Pay Units: 74.

Programming (via satellite): Playboy TV.

Fee: $8.95 monthly.

Pay Service 5

Pay Units: 217.

Programming (via satellite): Showtime.

Fee: $9.95 monthly.

Video-On-Demand: No

Pay-Per-View

iN DEMAND, Fee: $4.95.

Internet Service

Operational: No.

Telephone Service
None
Miles of Plant: 50.0 (coaxial); None (fiber optic). Homes passed: 5,000. Total homes in franchised area: 12,333.
Marketing Director: Jason Oelkers.
Ownership: Cequel Communications LLC (MSO).

FOSTER CITY—Comcast Cable. Now served by SAN FRANCISCO, CA [CA0003]. ICA: CA0136.

FRANCISCAN MOBILE HOME PARK—Comcast Cable, 2055 Folsom St, San Francisco, CA 94110-1330. Phone: 415-863-8500. Fax: 415-863-1659. Web Site: http://www.comcast.com. ICA: CA0331.
TV Market Ranking: 7 (FRANCISCAN MOBILE HOME). Franchise award date: N.A. Franchise expiration date: N.A. Began: August 1, 1988.
Channel capacity: N.A. Channels available but not in use: N.A.
Basic Service
Subscribers: N.A.
Programming (received off-air): KBCW (CW) San Francisco; KGO-TV (ABC) San Francisco; KICU-TV (IND) San Jose; KNTV (NBC) San Jose; KOFY-TV (IND) San Francisco; KPIX-TV (CBS) San Francisco; KQED (PBS) San Francisco; KRON-TV (MNT) San Francisco; KTVU (FOX) Oakland.
Programming (via satellite): TBS Superstation; WGN America.
Internet Service
Operational: Yes.
Telephone Service
Digital: Operational
Area Vice President: Doug Schultz. Technical Operations Director: Adam Goyer. Marketing Director: Jeff Farr.
Ownership: Comcast Cable Communications Inc. (MSO).

FRAZIER PARK—CalNeva Broadband, PO Box 2169, 3341 Los Padres Dr, Frazier Park, CA 93225. Phones: 800-330-2028; 866-668-0169 (Technical support). Also serves Pine Mountain Club. ICA: CA0225.
TV Market Ranking: Outside TV Markets (FRAZIER PARK, Pine Mountain Club). Franchise award date: September 4, 1974. Franchise expiration date: N.A. Began: January 1, 1981.
Channel capacity: 65 (operating 2-way). Channels available but not in use: 9.
Basic Service
Subscribers: 2,737.
Programming (received off-air): KABC-TV (ABC) Los Angeles; KBAK-TV (CBS) Bakersfield; KCAL-TV (IND) Los Angeles; KCBS-TV (CBS) Los Angeles; KCET (PBS) Los Angeles; KCOP-TV (MNT) Los Angeles; KERO-TV (ABC) Bakersfield; KGET-TV (CW, NBC) Bakersfield; KMPH-TV (FOX) Visalia; KNBC (NBC) Los Angeles; KTFF-DT (TEL) Porterville; KTLA (CW) Los Angeles; KTTV (FOX) Los Angeles; KUVI-DT (MNT) Bakersfield; allband FM.
Programming (via satellite): Animal Planet; Arts & Entertainment; Cartoon Network; CNN; Comedy Central; Country Music TV; C-SPAN; C-SPAN 2; Discovery Channel; E! Entertainment Television; ESPN; ESPN 2; ESPN Classic Sports; Food Network; Fox News Channel; Fox Sports Net; FX; Hallmark Channel; Halogen Network; HGTV; History Channel; Home Shopping Network; Lifetime; MTV; National Geographic Channel; Nickelodeon; QVC; SoapNet; Spike TV; Syfy; TBS Superstation; The Learning Channel; Travel Channel; Trinity Broadcasting Network; truTV; Turner Classic Movies; Turner Network TV; TV Guide Network; TV Land; VH1; Weather Channel; WGN America.
Current originations: Educational Access.
Fee: $29.95 installation; $39.81 monthly.
Digital Basic Service
Subscribers: N.A.
Programming (via satellite): BBC America; Bio; Bloomberg Television; Bravo; CMT Pure Country; Current; Discovery Health Channel; Discovery Kids Channel; Discovery Military Channel; Discovery Planet Green; DMX Music; ESPNews; Fox Movie Channel; Fox Soccer; G4; Golf Channel; GSN; History Channel International; ID Investigation Discovery; Independent Film Channel; Lifetime Movie Network; MTV Jams; MTV2; Nick Jr.; NickToons TV; Outdoor Channel; Ovation; Science Channel; Speed Channel; Style Network; Sundance Channel; TeenNick; VH1 Classic; VH1 Soul.
Fee: $12.95 monthly.
Digital Pay Service 1
Pay Units: N.A.
Programming (via satellite): Cinemax (multiplexed); Encore (multiplexed); HBO (multiplexed); Showtime (multiplexed); Starz (multiplexed); The Movie Channel (multiplexed).
Fee: $12.50 monthly (HBO, Showtime/TMC, Starz/Encore or Cinemax).
Video-On-Demand: No
Pay-Per-View
iN DEMAND (delivered digitally).
Internet Service
Operational: Yes.
Broadband Service: Rapid High Speed Internet.
Fee: $29.25 installation; $24.95 monthly.
Telephone Service
None
Miles of Plant: 105.0 (coaxial); None (fiber optic).
Manager: Tom Gelardi.
City fee: 3% of gross.
Ownership: CalNeva Broadband LLC (MSO).

FREMONT—Comcast Cable. Now served by OAKLAND, CA [CA0018]. ICA: CA0046.

FRESNO—Comcast Cable, 2441 N Grove Industrial Dr, Fresno, CA 93727-1535. Phone: 559-253-4050. Fax: 559-253-4090. Web Site: http://www.comcast.com. Also serves Armona, Clovis, Corcoran, Dinuba, Dos Palos, Firebaugh, Fowler, Fresno County, Grangeville, Hanford, Hardwick, Kerman, Kings County, Kingsburg, Laton, Lemoore, Lemoore Naval Air Station, Madera, Madera County (southern portion), Mendota, Parlier, Reedley, San Joaquin (portions), Sanger, Selma, Tulare, Tulare County & Visalia. ICA: CA0011.
TV Market Ranking: 72 (Armona, Clovis, Corcoran, Dinuba, Dos Palos, Firebaugh, Fowler, FRESNO, Fresno County (portions), Grangeville, Hanford, Hardwick, Kerman, Kings County, Kingsburg, Laton, Lemoore, Lemoore Naval Air Station, Madera, Madera County (southern portion), Mendota, Parlier, Reedley, San Joaquin (portions), Sanger, Selma, Tulare, Tulare County, Visalia); Outside TV Markets (Fresno County (portions)). Franchise award date: N.A. Franchise expiration date: N.A. Began: May 9, 1977.
Channel capacity: N.A. Channels available but not in use: N.A.
Basic Service
Subscribers: 168,500.
Programming (received off-air): KAIL (MNT) Fresno; KFRE-TV (CW) Sanger; KFSN-TV (ABC) Fresno; KFTV-DT (UNV) Hanford; KGMC (IND) Clovis; KGPE (CBS) Fresno; KMPH-TV (FOX) Visalia; KNSO (TMO) Merced; KNXT (ETV) Visalia; KSEE (NBC) Fresno; KVPT (PBS) Fresno; 17 FMs.
Programming (via satellite): California Channel; C-SPAN; C-SPAN 2; Home Shopping Network; ION Television; TV Guide Network.
Current originations: Government Access; Educational Access; Public Access.
Fee: $43.99 installation; $13.50 monthly; $.24 converter.
Expanded Basic Service 1
Subscribers: N.A.
Programming (via satellite): ABC Family Channel; AMC; Animal Planet; Arts & Entertainment; BET Networks; Bravo; Cartoon Network; CNBC; CNN; Comcast Sports Net Bay Area; Comedy Central; Discovery Channel; Disney Channel; E! Entertainment Television; ESPN; ESPN 2; ESPN Classic Sports; Food Network; Fox News Channel; Fox Sports en Espanol; FX; GalaVision; Golf Channel; Great American Country; Headline News; HGTV; History Channel; Lifetime; MSNBC; MTV; mun2 television; Nickelodeon; Oxygen; Speed Channel; Spike TV; Syfy; TBS Superstation; The Learning Channel; Travel Channel; Trinity Broadcasting Network; truTV; Turner Network TV; TV Land; USA Network; Versus; VH1; WE tv; Weather Channel; WGN America.
Fee: $32.30 monthly.
Digital Basic Service
Subscribers: 56,875.
Programming (via satellite): AmericanLife TV Network; ART America; BBC America; Bio; Black Family Channel; Bloomberg Television; Canales N; Discovery Digital Networks; DMX Music; ESPNews; Filipino Channel; Fox College Sports Atlantic; Fox College Sports Central; Fox College Sports Pacific; Fox Movie Channel; Fox Sports World; Fuse; G4; GAS; Halogen Network; History Channel International; Independent Film Channel; Lifetime Movie Network; Lime; National Geographic Channel; Nick Jr.; NickToons TV; Outdoor Channel; Ovation; RAI USA; Russian Television Network; ShopNBC; Star India Gold; Star India News; Star India Plus; Star One; Style Network; Sundance Channel; Toon Disney; Turner Classic Movies; TV Asia; TV Japan; TV5 USA; Vijay.
Fee: $14.95 monthly.
Digital Pay Service 1
Pay Units: 102,025.
Programming (via satellite): Cinemax (multiplexed); Encore (multiplexed); Flix; HBO (multiplexed); Showtime (multiplexed); Starz (multiplexed); The Movie Channel (multiplexed).
Fee: $13.00 monthly (each).
Video-On-Demand: Yes
Pay-Per-View
Addressable homes: 56,875.
Addressable: Yes; iN DEMAND; ESPN Now (delivered digitally); Hot Choice (delivered digitally); iN DEMAND (delivered digitally); Playboy TV (delivered digitally); Fresh (delivered digitally); Shorteez (delivered digitally); sports (delivered digitally).
Internet Service
Operational: Yes.
Subscribers: 31,500.
Broadband Service: Comcast High Speed Internet.
Fee: $42.95 monthly; $3.00 modem lease.
Telephone Service
Analog: Not Operational
Digital: Planned
Miles of Plant: 3,540.0 (coaxial); 160.0 (fiber optic). Additional miles planned: 40.0 (coaxial). Homes passed: 405,000.
General Manager: Len Falter. Marketing Director: Stewart Butler. Communications Director: Erica Smith.
City fee: 5% of gross.
Ownership: Comcast Cable Communications Inc. (MSO).

FRESNO—Formerly served by Sprint Corp. No longer in operation. ICA: CA0407.

GARBERVILLE—Wave Broadband, PO Box 3520, 4120 Citrus Ave, Rocklin, CA 95677. Phone: 866-928-3123. Web Site: http://www.wavebroadband.com. Also serves Benbow & Redway. ICA: CA0244.
TV Market Ranking: Outside TV Markets (Benbow, GARBERVILLE, Redway). Franchise award date: N.A. Franchise expiration date: N.A. Began: June 1, 1975.
Channel capacity: 80 (operating 2-way). Channels available but not in use: N.A.
Basic Service
Subscribers: 850.
Programming (received off-air): KEET (PBS)ureka; KIEM-TV (NBC) Eureka; KRCR-TV (ABC) Redding; KVIQ (CBS, CW) Eureka; allband FM.
Programming (via microwave): KRON-TV (MNT) San Francisco; KTVU (FOX) Oakland.
Programming (via satellite): ABC Family Channel; Arts & Entertainment; CNN; Comcast Sports Net Bay Area; Discovery Channel; Disney Channel; ESPN; Headline News; Lifetime; MTV; Nickelodeon; QVC; Spike TV; TBS Superstation; Turner Classic Movies; Turner Network TV; USA Network; WGN America.
Current originations: Government Access.
Fee: free installation; $40.95 monthly; $2.00 converter.
Pay Service 1
Pay Units: 160.
Programming (via satellite): Cinemax; HBO.
Fee: $10.95 monthly (Starz/Encore), $11.95 monthly (HBO, Cinemax or Showtime/TMC/Sundance).
Video-On-Demand: No
Internet Service
Operational: Yes.
Broadband Service: Wave Broadband.
Fee: $59.95 monthly.
Telephone Service
Digital: Operational
Fee: $49.95 monthly
Miles of Plant: 17.0 (coaxial); None (fiber optic). Homes passed: 1,329.
Technology Manager: Seth Johannson. Sales Director: Tom Carroll.
County fee: 3% of gross.
Ownership: WaveDivision Holdings LLC (MSO).

GEORGIAN MANOR MOBILE HOME PARK—Formerly served by Comcast Cable. No longer in operation. ICA: CA0333.

GILROY—Charter Communications, 8120 Camino Arroyo, Gilroy, CA 95020. Phones: 805-544-1962 (San Luis Obispo office); 408-847-2020. Fax: 408-847-2993. Web Site: http://www.charter.com. Also serves Aromas, Carmel Highlands, Castroville, Hollister, Las Lomas, Morgan Hill, Moss Landing,

Oakhills, Prunedale, San Benito County (portions), San Juan Bautista (portions) & San Martin. ICA: CA0425.

TV Market Ranking: 7 (Aromas, GILROY, Hollister, Las Lomas, Morgan Hill, San Benito County (portions), San Martin); Below 100 (Carmel Highlands, Moss Landing, Oakhills, Prunedale, San Juan Bautista (portions), San Benito County (portions)); Outside TV Markets (Castroville, San Benito County (portions)). Franchise award date: N.A. Franchise expiration date: N.A. Began: N.A.

Channel capacity: N.A. Channels available but not in use: N.A.

Basic Service

Subscribers: 6,041.

Programming (received off-air): KCBA (FOX) Salinas; KCNS (IND) San Francisco; KDTV-TV (UNV) San Francisco; KFSF-DT (TEL) Vallejo; KION-TV (CBS, CW) Monterey; KKPX-TV (ION) San Jose; KNTV (NBC) San Jose; KOFY-TV (IND) San Francisco; KSBW (NBC) Salinas; KSTS (TMO) San Jose; KTEH (PBS) San Jose; KTNC-TV (IND) Concord.

Programming (via microwave): KBCW (CW) San Francisco; KGO-TV (ABC) San Francisco; KICU-TV (IND) San Jose; KPIX-TV (CBS) San Francisco; KQED (PBS) San Francisco; KRON-TV (MNT) San Francisco; KTVU (FOX) Oakland.

Programming (via satellite): California Channel; C-SPAN; GalaVision; Home Shopping Network; QVC; ShopNBC; TBS Superstation; Weather Channel.

Current originations: Government Access; Educational Access; Public Access.

Fee: $29.99 installation.

Expanded Basic Service 1

Subscribers: 5,508.

Programming (via satellite): AMC; Animal Planet; Arts & Entertainment; BET Networks; Bravo; Cartoon Network; CNBC; CNN; Comcast Sports Net Bay Area; Comedy Central; Country Music TV; Discovery Channel; Disney Channel; E! Entertainment Television; ESPN; ESPN 2; FitTV; Food Network; Fox News Channel; Fox Sports en Espanol; FX; G4; Golf Channel; GSN; Hallmark Channel; Headline News; HGTV; History Channel; Lifetime; MSNBC; MTV; National Geographic Channel; Nickelodeon; Oxygen; SoapNet; Speed Channel; Spike TV; Syfy; The Learning Channel; Toon Disney; Travel Channel; truTV; Turner Classic Movies; Turner Network TV; TV Land; USA Network; Versus; VH1; WE tv.

Fee: $38.99 monthly.

Digital Basic Service

Subscribers: N.A.

Programming (via satellite): BBC America; Bio; Discovery Digital Networks; Do-It-Yourself; ESPN Classic Sports; ESPNews; Fox College Sports Atlantic; Fox College Sports Central; Fox College Sports Pacific; Fox Soccer; Fuel TV; Fuse; GAS; History Channel International; Independent Film Channel; Lifetime Movie Network; MTV Networks Digital Suite; Music Choice; NFL Network; Nick Jr.; Nick Too; Outdoor Channel; Science Television; TVG Network.

Digital Pay Service 1

Pay Units: N.A.

Programming (via satellite): Cinemax (multiplexed); HBO (multiplexed); Starz (multiplexed).

Video-On-Demand: Yes

Pay-Per-View

Hot Choice (delivered digitally); Playboy TV (delivered digitally); Fresh (delivered digitally); Shorteez (delivered digitally).

Internet Service

Operational: Yes.

Broadband Service: Charter Pipeline.

Fee: $29.99 monthly.

Telephone Service

Digital: Operational

Miles of Plant: 188.0 (coaxial); None (fiber optic). Homes passed: 11,409.

Vice President & General Manager: Ed Merrill. Marketing Director: Sarwar Assar.

Ownership: Charter Communications Inc. (MSO).

GLENDALE—Charter Communications, 4781 Irwindale Ave, Irwindale, CA 91706-2175. Phone: 626-430-3300. Fax: 626-430-3420. Web Site: http://www.charter.com. Also serves Burbank, La Canada, La Crescenta & Montrose. ICA: CA0021.

TV Market Ranking: 2 (Burbank, GLENDALE, La Canada, La Crescenta, Montrose). Franchise award date: January 1, 1962. Franchise expiration date: N.A. Began: January 1, 1962.

Channel capacity: 78 (operating 2-way). Channels available but not in use: None.

Basic Service

Subscribers: 81,782.

Programming (received off-air): KABC-TV (ABC) Los Angeles; KCBS-TV (CBS) Los Angeles; KCET (PBS) Los Angeles; KCOP-TV (MNT) Los Angeles; KDOC-TV (IND) Anaheim; KFTR-DT (TEL) Ontario; KJLA (IND) Ventura; KLCS (PBS) Los Angeles; KMEX-DT (UNV) Los Angeles; KNBC (NBC) Los Angeles; KPXN-TV (ION) San Bernardino; KRCA (IND) Riverside; KSCI (IND) Long Beach; KTBN-TV (TBN) Santa Ana; KTLA (CW) Los Angeles; KTTV (FOX) Los Angeles; KVEA (TMO) Corona; KWHY-TV (IND) Los Angeles.

Programming (via satellite): G4; QVC; TBS Superstation; USA Network.

Current originations: Leased Access; Government Access; Educational Access; Public Access.

Fee: $29.99 installation.

Expanded Basic Service 1

Subscribers: N.A.

Programming (via satellite): ABC Family Channel; AMC; Animal Planet; Arts & Entertainment; BET Networks; Bravo; Cartoon Network; CNBC; CNN; Comedy Central; C-SPAN; C-SPAN 2; Discovery Channel; Disney Channel; E! Entertainment Television; ESPN; ESPN 2; ESPN Classic Sports; Food Network; Fox News Channel; Fox Sports Net West; Fox Sports Net West 2; Fox Sports World; FX; GalaVision; Golf Channel; GSN; Headline News; HGTV; History Channel; Home Shopping Network; Lifetime; MSNBC; MTV; Nickelodeon; Oxygen; Spike TV; Syfy; The Learning Channel; Toon Disney; Travel Channel; truTV; Turner Classic Movies; Turner Network TV; TV Guide Network; TV Land; VH1; Weather Channel.

Fee: $48.95 monthly.

Digital Basic Service

Subscribers: N.A.

Programming (via satellite): BBC America; Bio; Bloomberg Television; Discovery Digital Networks; GAS; History Channel International; Independent Film Channel; Lifetime Movie Network; Music Choice; Nick Jr.; Style Network; WE tv.

Fee: $8.95 monthly.

Digital Pay Service 1

Pay Units: 11,826.

Programming (via satellite): Cinemax (multiplexed).

Fee: $10.95 monthly.

Digital Pay Service 2

Pay Units: 1,361.

Programming (via satellite): HBO (multiplexed).

Fee: $12.95 monthly.

Digital Pay Service 3

Pay Units: 295.

Programming (via satellite): Flix; Showtime (multiplexed); Sundance Channel.

Fee: $12.95 monthly.

Digital Pay Service 4

Pay Units: 5,084.

Programming (via satellite): Encore (multiplexed); Starz (multiplexed); The Movie Channel (multiplexed).

Fee: $10.90 monthly (TMC), $10.95 monthly (Starz & Encore).

Video-On-Demand: Yes

Pay-Per-View

Addressable homes: 32,000.

Addressable: Yes; iN DEMAND (delivered digitally); Fresh (delivered digitally); Shorteez (delivered digitally).

Internet Service

Operational: Yes.

Subscribers: 106,225.

Broadband Service: Charter Pipeline.

Fee: $29.99 monthly; $4.95 modem lease.

Telephone Service

Analog: Not Operational

Digital: Operational

Miles of Plant: 603.0 (coaxial); None (fiber optic). Homes passed: 170,000. Homes passed includes Whittier

Vice President & General Manager: Wendy Rasmusson. Technical Operations Manager: Tom Williams. Marketing Manager: Lily Ho.

City fee: 5% of gross.

Ownership: Charter Communications Inc. (MSO).

GLENDORA—Time Warner Cable. Now served by LOS ANGELES, CA [CA0009]. ICA: CA0035.

GLENWOOD—Formerly served by Comcast Cable. No longer in operation. ICA: CA0335.

GRASS VALLEY—Comcast Cable, 311 B St, Yuba City, CA 95991-5054. Phones: 530-790-3322; 800-266-2278. Fax: 530-671-3822. Web Site: http://www.comcast.com. Also serves Lake Wildwood, Nevada City, Nevada County & Penn Valley. ICA: CA0164.

TV Market Ranking: Below 100 (Lake Wildwood, Penn Valley); Outside TV Markets (GRASS VALLEY, Nevada City, Nevada County). Franchise award date: N.A. Franchise expiration date: N.A. Began: February 1, 1964.

Channel capacity: 41 (operating 2-way). Channels available but not in use: N.A.

Basic Service

Subscribers: 10,677.

Programming (received off-air): KCRA-TV (NBC) Sacramento; KMAX-TV (CW) Sacramento; KOVR (CBS) Stockton; KQCA (MNT) Stockton; KSPX-TV (ION) Sacramento; KTFK-DT (TEL) Stockton; KTXL (FOX) Sacramento; KUVS-DT (UNV) Modesto; KVIE (PBS) Sacramento; KXTV (ABC) Sacramento; 11 FMs.

Programming (via satellite): C-SPAN; C-SPAN 2; Hallmark Channel; QVC; TBS Superstation; TV Guide Network.

Current originations: Public Access; Educational Access.

Fee: $43.99 installation; $15.50 monthly.

Expanded Basic Service 1

Subscribers: 8,334.

Programming (via satellite): ABC Family Channel; AMC; Animal Planet; Arts & Entertainment; BET Networks; Cartoon Network; CNBC; CNN; Comcast Sports Net Bay Area; Comedy Central; Country Music TV; Discovery Channel; Disney Channel; E! Entertainment Television; ESPN; ESPN 2; Food Network; Fox News Channel; FX; GalaVision; Golf Channel; GSN; Hallmark Channel; Headline News; HGTV; Lifetime; MSNBC; MTV; Nick Jr.; Nickelodeon; Spike TV; Syfy; TBS Superstation; The Learning Channel; Travel Channel; truTV; Turner Classic Movies; Turner Network TV; TV Land; USA Network; VH1; Weather Channel.

Fee: $48.75 monthly.

Digital Basic Service

Subscribers: N.A.

Programming (via satellite): BBC America; Bio; Bloomberg Television; Bravo; Discovery Digital Networks; DMX Music; ESPN 2; ESPN Classic Sports; ESPNews; FitTV; Fox Movie Channel; Fox Sports World; Fuse; G4; GAS; Golf Channel; GSN; Halogen Network; HGTV; History Channel; History Channel International; Independent Film Channel; International Television (ITV); Lifetime Movie Network; Lime; MTV Networks Digital Suite; National Geographic Channel; NickToons TV; Outdoor Channel; Ovation; Speed Channel; Style Network; Sundance Channel; Syfy; Toon Disney; Trinity Broadcasting Network; Turner Classic Movies; TV Land; WE tv.

Fee: $49.75 monthly.

Digital Pay Service 1

Pay Units: 1,133.

Programming (via satellite): Cinemax (multiplexed); Encore (multiplexed); HBO; Showtime (multiplexed); Starz (multiplexed); The Movie Channel (multiplexed).

Fee: $20.00 installation; $17.99 monthly (Cinemax, Starz or TMC), $18.99 monthly (HBO or Showtime).

Video-On-Demand: No

Pay-Per-View

iN DEMAND (delivered digitally); Fresh (delivered digitally); Shorteez (delivered digitally); Playboy TV (delivered digitally).

Internet Service

Operational: Yes.

Fee: $42.95 monthly.

Telephone Service

Digital: Operational

Fee: $39.95 monthly

Miles of Plant: 229.0 (coaxial); None (fiber optic). Homes passed: 14,358. Total homes in franchised area: 14,467.

General Manager: DeeDee Brady. Marketing Director: Tom Baer.

City fee: 3% of gross.
Ownership: Comcast Cable Communications Inc. (MSO).

GREENFIELD—Charter Communications, 8120 Camino Arroyo, Gilroy, CA 95020. Phones: 408-847-2020; 805-544-1962 (San Luis Obispo office). Fax: 408-847-2993. Web Site: http://www.charter.com. Also serves Monterey County (portions). ICA: CA0337.
TV Market Ranking: Below 100 (GREENFIELD, Monterey County (portions)). Franchise award date: N.A. Franchise expiration date: N.A. Began: January 1, 1974.
Channel capacity: 35 (not 2-way capable). Channels available but not in use: None.
Basic Service
Subscribers: 1,444.
Programming (received off-air): KCBA (FOX) Salinas; KION-TV (CBS, CW) Monterey; KKPX-TV (ION) San Jose; KQED (PBS) San Francisco; KSBW (NBC) Salinas; KSMS-TV (UNV) Monterey.
Programming (via microwave): KTVU (FOX) Oakland.
Programming (via satellite): ABC Family Channel; AMC; Arts & Entertainment; Bravo; Comcast Sports Net Bay Area; Country Music TV; ESPN; Home Shopping Network; KGO-TV (ABC) San Francisco; Lifetime; MTV; Nickelodeon; QVC; Spike TV; Syfy; The Learning Channel; USA Network; Weather Channel.
Current originations: Government Access; Educational Access; Public Access.
Fee: $29.99 installation.
Expanded Basic Service 1
Subscribers: 1,401.
Programming (via satellite): CNN; Discovery Channel; Disney Channel; GalaVision; Headline News; TBS Superstation; Turner Network TV; WGN America.
Fee: $28.99 monthly.
Digital Basic Service
Subscribers: N.A.
Programming (via satellite): AmericanLife TV Network; BBC America; Bio; Bloomberg Television; Discovery Digital Networks; DMX Music; ESPN 2; ESPN Classic Sports; ESPNews; FitTV; Fox Movie Channel; Fuse; G4; GAS; Golf Channel; GSN; HGTV; History Channel; History Channel International; Independent Film Channel; INSP; Lifetime Movie Network; MTV Networks Digital Suite; Nick Jr.; Outdoor Channel; Science Television; ShopNBC; Speed Channel; Toon Disney; Trinity Broadcasting Network; Turner Classic Movies; Versus; WE tv.
Pay Service 1
Pay Units: 160.
Programming (via satellite): Showtime; The Movie Channel.
Fee: $15.00 installation; $10.95 monthly.
Digital Pay Service 1
Pay Units: N.A.
Programming (via satellite): Cinemax (multiplexed); Encore (multiplexed); HBO (multiplexed); Showtime (multiplexed); Starz; The Movie Channel.
Video-On-Demand: No
Pay-Per-View
iN DEMAND (delivered digitally); ESPN Now (delivered digitally); ESPN Sports PPV (delivered digitally); Hot Choice (delivered digitally); Playboy TV (delivered digitally); Fresh (delivered digitally); Shorteez (delivered digitally).
Internet Service
Operational: Yes.
Broadband Service: Charter Pipeline.
Telephone Service
Digital: Operational
Miles of Plant: 41.0 (coaxial); None (fiber optic). Homes passed: 2,735.
Vice President & General Manager: Ed Merrill. Chief Technician: Mark Beech. Marketing Director: Sarwar Assar.
Ownership: Charter Communications Inc. (MSO).

GROVELAND—SNC Cable, PO Box 281, Sonora, CA 95373. Phone: 209-586-7622. Web Site: http://www.snccable.com. Also serves Big Oak Flat. ICA: CA0209.
TV Market Ranking: Outside TV Markets (Big Oak Flat, GROVELAND). Franchise award date: N.A. Franchise expiration date: N.A. Began: October 1, 1978.
Channel capacity: N.A. Channels available but not in use: N.A.
Basic Service
Subscribers: 409.
Programming (received off-air): KCRA-TV (NBC) Sacramento; KMAX-TV (CW) Sacramento; KOVR (CBS) Stockton; KQCA (MNT) Stockton; KTXL (FOX) Sacramento; KUVS-DT (UNV) Modesto; KVIE (PBS) Sacramento; KXTV (ABC) Sacramento.
Programming (via satellite): ABC Family Channel; AMC; Animal Planet; Arts & Entertainment; CNN; Comedy Central; C-SPAN; Discovery Channel; Disney Channel; ESPN; Fox News Channel; FX; Headline News; Home Shopping Network; Lifetime; Nickelodeon; Shop at Home; Spike TV; TBS Superstation; Turner Network TV; USA Network; VH1; WGN America.
Fee: $50.00 installation; $27.95 monthly.
Pay Service 1
Pay Units: N.A.
Programming (via satellite): HBO.
Fee: $13.95 monthly.
Internet Service
Operational: Yes.
Fee: $39.95 monthly.
Telephone Service
None
Miles of Plant: 65.0 (coaxial); None (fiber optic). Homes passed: 4,000.
Manager: Tim Holden.
Ownership: Sierra Nevada Communications (MSO).

GUADALUPE—Charter Communications. Now served by SAN LUIS OBISPO, CA [CA0045]. ICA: CA0400.

HACIENDA HEIGHTS—Time Warner Cable. Now served by LOS ANGELES, CA [CA0009]. ICA: CA0027.

HACIENDA HEIGHTS—Time Warner Cable. Now served by LOS ANGELES, CA [CA0009]. ICA: CA0338.

HALF MOON BAY—Comcast Cable. Now served by SAN FRANCISCO, CA [CA0003]. ICA: CA0179.

HAPPY CAMP—Formerly served by Almega Cable. No longer in operation. ICA: CA0260.

HAYFORK—New Day Broadband, PO Box 535, 9155 Deschutes Rd, #D, Palo Cedro, CA 96073-8714. Phone: 530-547-2226. Fax: 530-547-4849. ICA: CA0279.
TV Market Ranking: Outside TV Markets (HAYFORK). Franchise award date: January 1, 1984. Franchise expiration date: N.A. Began: April 1, 1985.
Channel capacity: 36 (not 2-way capable). Channels available but not in use: None.
Basic Service
Subscribers: 150.
Programming (received off-air): KHSL-TV (CBS, CW) Chico; KIXE-TV (PBS) Redding; KRCR-TV (ABC) Redding.
Programming (via satellite): ABC Family Channel; CNN; Disney Channel; ESPN; Nickelodeon; TBS Superstation; USA Network; WGN America.
Current originations: Public Access.
Fee: $15.00 installation; $36.75 monthly.
Pay Service 1
Pay Units: 25.
Programming (via satellite): HBO.
Fee: $20.00 installation; $11.50 monthly.
Internet Service
Operational: No.
Telephone Service
None
Miles of Plant: 15.0 (coaxial); None (fiber optic). Additional miles planned: 2.0 (coaxial). Homes passed: 501.
Chief Executive Officer: Neal Sehnog.
City fee: 3% of gross.
Ownership: New Day Broadband.

HAYWARD—Comcast Cable. Now served by OAKLAND, CA [CA0018]. ICA: CA0026.

HEMET—Time Warner Cable. Now served by ANAHEIM, CA [CA0033]. ICA: CA0044.

HERLONG—Formerly served by Almega Cable. No longer in operation. ICA: CA0340.

HERMOSA BEACH—Time Warner Cable. Now served by LOS ANGELES, CA [CA0009]. ICA: CA0094.

HESPERIA—Charter Communications, 7337 Central Ave, Riverside, CA 92504. Phone: 951-343-5100. Fax: 951-354-5942. Web Site: http://www.charter.com. Also serves Adelanto, Apple Valley, Big Bear, Crestline, Lake Arrowhead, San Bernardino County (portions), Silver Lakes, Spring Valley Lake & Victorville. ICA: CA0158.
TV Market Ranking: 2 (Adelanto, Apple Valley, Big Bear, Crestline, HESPERIA, Lake Arrowhead, San Bernardino County (portions) (portions), Silver Lakes, Spring Valley Lake, Victorville); Below 100 (San Bernardino County (portions) (portions)); Outside TV Markets (San Bernardino County (portions) (portions)). Franchise award date: May 1, 1981. Franchise expiration date: N.A. Began: N.A.
Channel capacity: N.A. Channels available but not in use: N.A.
Basic Service
Subscribers: 56,938.
Programming (received off-air): KABC-TV (ABC) Los Angeles; KHIZ (IND) Barstow; KJLA (IND) Ventura; KVEA (TMO) Corona; KXLA (IND) Rancho Palos Verdes; 28 FMs.
Programming (via microwave): KCAL-TV (IND) Los Angeles; KCBS-TV (CBS) Los Angeles; KCET (PBS) Los Angeles; KCOP-TV (MNT) Los Angeles; KNBC (NBC) Los Angeles; KTLA (CW) Los Angeles; KTTV (FOX) Los Angeles.
Programming (via satellite): C-SPAN; FX; Home Shopping Network; QVC; TBS Superstation; TV Guide Network.
Current originations: Government Access; Educational Access.
Fee: $29.99 installation; $21.50 monthly; $6.95 converter; $9.99 additional installation.
Expanded Basic Service 1
Subscribers: 46,321.
Programming (via satellite): ABC Family Channel; AMC; Animal Planet; Arts & Entertainment; BET Networks; Bravo; Cartoon Network; CNBC; CNN; Comedy Central; Country Music TV; Discovery Channel; Disney Channel; E! Entertainment Television; ESPN; ESPN 2; ESPN Classic Sports; Eternal Word TV Network; Food Network; Fox News Channel; Fox Sports en Espanol; Fox Sports Net West 2; Fox Sports World; G4; GalaVision; Golf Channel; Great American Country; GSN; Hallmark Channel; Headline News; HGTV; History Channel; ION Television; Lifetime; MSNBC; MTV; MTV2; National Geographic Channel; Nickelodeon; Oxygen; ShopNBC; SoapNet; Speed Channel; Spike TV; Syfy; The Learning Channel; Travel Channel; Trinity Broadcasting Network; truTV; Turner Classic Movies; Turner Network TV; TV Land; Univision; USA Network; Versus; VH1; WE tv; Weather Channel.
Fee: $29.99 installation; $28.15 monthly; $9.99 additional installation.
Digital Basic Service
Subscribers: N.A.
Programming (via satellite): BBC America; Bio; Black Family Channel; Bloomberg Television; Boomerang; BYU Television; CNN en Espanol; Discovery Digital Networks; Discovery HD Theater; Do-It-Yourself; ESPN; ESPNews; Eternal Word TV Network; Fox College Sports Atlantic; Fox College Sports Central; Fox College Sports Pacific; Fox Soccer; Fuel TV; Fuse; GAS; HDNet; HDNet Movies; History Channel International; Independent Film Channel; International Television (ITV); Lifetime Movie Network; Lifetime Real Women; MTV Networks Digital Suite; Music Choice; NFL Network; Nick Jr.; NickToons TV; Style Network; Sundance Channel; Toon Disney; TV One; TVG Network; WealthTV.
Digital Pay Service 1
Pay Units: N.A.
Programming (via satellite): Cinemax (multiplexed); Filipino Channel; HBO (multiplexed); Showtime; Starz (multiplexed).
Video-On-Demand: Yes
Pay-Per-View
@Max (delivered digitally); Playboy TV (delivered digitally); Fresh (delivered digitally).
Internet Service
Operational: Yes.
Subscribers: 20,897.
Broadband Service: Charter Pipeline.
Fee: $29.99 monthly; $2.96 modem lease.
Telephone Service
Digital: Operational
Miles of Plant: 520.0 (coaxial); None (fiber optic). Homes passed: 146,000. Total homes in franchised area: 165,000.
Vice President & General Manager: Fred Lutz. Technical Operations Manager: George Noel. Marketing Director: Chris Bailey.
Franchise fee: 5% of gross.
Ownership: Charter Communications Inc. (MSO).

HURON—Comcast Cable, 2441 N Grove Industrial Dr, Fresno, CA 93727-1535. Phones: 800-266-2278; 559-455-4305. Fax: 559-253-4090. Web Site: http://www.comcast.com. ICA: CA0273.
TV Market Ranking: 72 (HURON). Franchise award date: N.A. Franchise expiration date: N.A. Began: January 1, 1983.
Channel capacity: 36 (2-way capable). Channels available but not in use: 10.
Basic Service
Subscribers: 350.
Programming (received off-air): KAIL (MNT) Fresno; KFRE-TV (CW) Sanger; KFSN-TV (ABC) Fresno; KFTV-DT (UNV) Hanford; KGPE (CBS) Fresno; KJEO-LD

Fresno; KMPH-TV (FOX) Visalia; KSEE (NBC) Fresno; KVPT (PBS) Fresno.
Programming (via satellite): ABC Family Channel; AMC; AmericanLife TV Network; Animal Planet; Arts & Entertainment; CNN; Comedy Central; C-SPAN; Discovery Channel; Disney Channel; E! Entertainment Television; ESPN; ESPN 2; Fox Sports Net; FX; GalaVision; Headline News; HGTV; History Channel; Home Shopping Network; Lifetime; MTV; MTV Latin America; Nickelodeon; Spike TV; Syfy; TBS Superstation; Telemundo; The Learning Channel; Turner Classic Movies; Turner Network TV; TV Guide Network; TV Land; USA Network; VH1; Weather Channel; WGN America.
Fee: $43.99 installation; $35.95 monthly.

Digital Basic Service
Subscribers: N.A.
Programming (via satellite): BBC America; Black Family Channel; Bloomberg Television; Bravo; Discovery Health Channel; Discovery Home Channel; Discovery Kids Channel; Discovery Times Channel; ESPN 2; ESPN Classic Sports; ESPNews; FitTV; Fox College Sports Atlantic; Fox College Sports Central; Fox College Sports Pacific; Fuse; G4; Golf Channel; Great American Country; GSN; HGTV; History Channel; MTV Hits; MTV2; National Geographic Channel; NickToons TV; Outdoor Channel; Science Channel; ShopNBC; Speed Channel; Style Network; Syfy; Trinity Broadcasting Network; TV Land; Versus; VH1 Classic; VH1 Country; VH1 Soul.
Fee: $52.50 monthly.

Pay Service 1
Pay Units: 154.
Programming (via satellite): HBO (multiplexed).
Fee: $20.00 installation; $12.17 monthly.

Pay Service 2
Pay Units: N.A.
Programming (via satellite): Encore; Starz.
Fee: $11.43 monthly.

Internet Service
Operational: Yes.

Telephone Service
Digital: Operational

Miles of Plant: 10.0 (coaxial); None (fiber optic). Additional miles planned: 2.0 (coaxial). Homes passed: 800. Total homes in franchised area: 800.
General Manager: Len Falter. Marketing Director: Stewart Butler.
City fee: 3% of gross.
Ownership: Comcast Cable Communications Inc. (MSO).

IONE—Volcano Vision, PO Box 1070, 20000 Hwy 88, Pine Grove, CA 95665. Phone: 209-274-2660. Fax: 209-296-2230. E-mail: rayc@volcanotel.com. Web Site: http://www.volcanocommunications.com. Also serves Buena Vista. ICA: CA0265.
TV Market Ranking: 25 (Buena Vista, IONE). Franchise award date: December 10, 1976. Franchise expiration date: N.A. Began: May 1, 1977.
Channel capacity: 135 (operating 2-way). Channels available but not in use: 65.

Digital Basic Service
Subscribers: 635.
Programming (received off-air): KCRA-TV (NBC) Sacramento; KMAX-TV (CW) Sacramento; KOVR (CBS) Stockton; KQCA (MNT) Stockton; KSPX-TV (ION) Sacramento; KTXL (FOX) Sacramento; KUVS-DT (UNV) Modesto; KVIE (PBS) Sacramento; KXTV (ABC) Sacramento.
Programming (via satellite): AMC; AmericanLife TV Network; Arts & Entertainment; Arts & Entertainment HD; BBC America; BBC World News; BET Networks; Bloomberg Television; Boomerang; Bravo; Bravo HD; Chiller; CNBC; CNBC HD+; CNN; Colours; Comcast Sports Net Bay Area; Comcast SportsNet West; Comedy Central; Cooking Channel; Country Music TV; Discovery Channel; Discovery HD Theater; Discovery Military Channel; DMX Music; E! Entertainment Television; ESPN; ESPN 2; ESPN 2 HD; ESPN Classic Sports; ESPN HD; ESPNews; FitTV; Food Network; Food Network HD; Fox Movie Channel; Fox News Channel; Fox Sports Net West 2; Fuel TV; FX; Gospel Music Channel; GSN; HDNet; HDNet Movies; Headline News; HGTV; HGTV HD; History Channel; History Channel HD; HorseRacing TV; Lifetime; Lifetime Movie Network; Lifetime Movie Network HD; Mojo Mix; MSNBC; MTV; National Geographic Channel; National Geographic Channel HD Network; Outdoor Channel; Outdoor Channel 2 HD; Ovation; Oxygen; ReelzChannel; Smile of a Child; SoapNet; Soundtrack Channel; Speed Channel; Spike TV; Syfy; Syfy HD; TBS in HD; TBS Superstation; Toon Disney; Travel Channel; truTV; Turner Classic Movies; Turner Network TV; Turner Network TV HD; TV Land; Universal HD; USA Network; USA Network HD; Versus; VH1; WE tv; WealthTV; WealthTV HD; World Harvest Television.
Current originations: Leased Access; Government Access; Educational Access.
Fee: $35.00 installation; $18.99 monthly; $2.00 converter.

Digital Expanded Basic Service
Subscribers: N.A.
Programming (via satellite): Bio; CBS College Sports Network; Country Music TV; Current; Discovery Health Channel; Do-It-Yourself; ESPN U; Fox Business Channel; Fox College Sports Atlantic; Fox College Sports Central; Fox College Sports Pacific; G4; GAS; Hallmark Movie Channel; History Channel International; Lifetime Real Women; MTV Hits; MTV Jams; MTV2; Nick Jr.; NickToons TV; RFD-TV; Sleuth; Style Network; VH1 Classic; VH1 Soul; VHUNO.
Fee: $16.00 monthly.

Digital Expanded Basic Service 2
Subscribers: N.A.
Programming (via satellite): CMT Pure Country; Crime & Investigation Network; C-SPAN 3; Fox Soccer; Fuse; Golf Channel; Great American Country; Independent Film Channel; Military History Channel; Tennis Channel.
Fee: $6.00 monthly.

Digital Pay Service 1
Pay Units: N.A.
Programming (via satellite): Cinemax (multiplexed); Encore (multiplexed); Flix; HBO (multiplexed); Showtime (multiplexed); Showtime HD; Starz (multiplexed); Starz HDTV; Sundance Channel; The Movie Channel (multiplexed); The Movie Channel HD.
Fee: $8.95 monthly (Starz or Encore), $12.95 monthly (Cinemax), $14.95 monthly (HBO).

Video-On-Demand: No

Pay-Per-View
iN DEMAND (delivered digitally); Hot Choice (delivered digitally); Playboy TV (delivered digitally); Fresh (delivered digitally); Shorteez (delivered digitally).

Internet Service
Operational: Yes, Both DSL & dial-up. Began: October 17, 2002.
Subscribers: 400.
Broadband Service: Volcano.
Fee: $29.95-$59.95 monthly.

Telephone Service
None

Miles of Plant: 35.0 (coaxial); None (fiber optic). Homes passed: 1,450.
Manager: Ray Crabtree. Chief Technician: Ramel Chand. Marketing Director: Duke Milunovich.
City fee: 5% of gross.
Ownership: Volcano Communications Co. (MSO).

JACK RANCH/POSEY—Charter Communications, 270 Bridge St, San Luis Obispo, CA 93401. Phone: 805-544-1962. Fax: 805-541-6042. Web Site: http://www.charter.com. Also serves Posey. ICA: CA0403.
TV Market Ranking: 72 (JACK RANCH, POSEY). Franchise award date: N.A. Franchise expiration date: N.A. Began: N.A.
Channel capacity: 32 (not 2-way capable). Channels available but not in use: 18.

Basic Service
Subscribers: 110.
Programming (received off-air): KBAK-TV (CBS) Bakersfield; KFSN-TV (ABC) Fresno; KGPE (CBS) Fresno; KMPH-TV (FOX) Visalia; KSEE (NBC) Fresno; KVPT (PBS) Fresno.
Programming (via satellite): CNN; Discovery Channel; ESPN; Headline News; QVC; Syfy.
Fee: $19.72 monthly.

Pay Service 1
Pay Units: 4.
Programming (via satellite): The Movie Channel.
Fee: $11.45 monthly.

Video-On-Demand: No

Internet Service
Operational: No.

Telephone Service
None

Miles of Plant: 12.0 (coaxial); None (fiber optic). Homes passed: 318.
Vice President & General Manager: Ed Merrill. Technical Operations Director: Ken Arellano. Marketing Director: Sarwar Assar.
Ownership: Charter Communications Inc. (MSO).

JULIAN—Cable USA, PO Box 336, 2455 Stirrup Rd, Borrego Springs, CA 92004-0336. Phones: 308-236-1512 (Kearney, NE corporate office); 760-767-5607; 800-300-6989. Fax: 760-767-3609. Web Site: http://www.cableusa.com. ICA: CA0254.
TV Market Ranking: Outside TV Markets (JULIAN). Franchise award date: N.A. Franchise expiration date: N.A. Began: December 1, 1982.
Channel capacity: N.A. Channels available but not in use: N.A.

Basic Service
Subscribers: 687.
Programming (received off-air): KCAL-TV (IND) Los Angeles; KCOP-TV (MNT) Los Angeles; KFMB-TV (CBS) San Diego; KGTV (ABC) San Diego; KNSD (NBC) San Diego; KPBS (PBS) San Diego; KSWB-TV (FOX) San Diego; KTLA (CW) Los Angeles; KUSI-TV (IND) San Diego; 15 FMs.
Programming (via satellite): C-SPAN; Eternal Word TV Network; Headline News; HGTV; International Television (ITV); QVC; TBS Superstation; Trinity Broadcasting Network; Weather Channel.
Fee: $24.95 installation; $24.99 monthly.

Expanded Basic Service 1
Subscribers: 583.
Programming (via satellite): ABC Family Channel; AMC; Arts & Entertainment; CNN; Discovery Channel; ESPN; ESPN 2; History Channel; Lifetime; MTV; Nickelodeon; Outdoor Channel; Spike TV; Turner Network TV; TV Land; USA Network; VH1.
Fee: $39.99 monthly.

Digital Basic Service
Subscribers: N.A.
Programming (via satellite): Bio; Bloomberg Television; Discovery Digital Networks; DMX Music; Encore (multiplexed); ESPN 2; ESPN Classic Sports; ESPNews; FitTV; Flix; Fox Movie Channel; Fox Sports World; Fuse; G4; Golf Channel; Great American Country; GSN; HGTV; History Channel; History Channel International; Independent Film Channel; Lifetime; National Geographic Channel; Outdoor Channel; Speed Channel; Starz (multiplexed); Style Network; Turner Classic Movies; Versus; WE tv.
Fee: $14.00 monthly.

Digital Pay Service 1
Pay Units: N.A.
Programming (via satellite): Cinemax (multiplexed); Flix; HBO (multiplexed); Showtime (multiplexed); Starz; The Movie Channel (multiplexed).
Fee: $12.00 monthly (Cinemax), $14.00 monthly (Starz or Showtime), $15.00 monthly (HBO).

Video-On-Demand: No

Pay-Per-View
iN DEMAND (delivered digitally); Playboy TV (delivered digitally).

Internet Service
Operational: Yes.
Broadband Service: In-house.
Fee: $35.95 monthly.

Telephone Service
Digital: Operational
Fee: $39.95 monthly

Miles of Plant: 24.0 (coaxial); None (fiber optic). Homes passed: 1,087. Total homes in franchised area: 1,087.
Manager & Chief Technician: Joe Gustafson.
City fee: 5% of basic.
Ownership: USA Companies (MSO).

JUNE LAKE—NPG Cable Inc., 123 Commerce Dr, Ste B6, Mammoth Lakes, CA 93546. Phones: 760-934-8553; 760-934-9640. Fax: 760-934-9640. Web Site: http://www.npgcable.com. ICA: CA0475.
TV Market Ranking: Outside TV Markets (June Lake).
Channel capacity: N.A. Channels available but not in use: N.A.

Basic Service
Subscribers: N.A. Included in Mammoth Lakes
Programming (received off-air): KAME-TV (MNT) Reno; KNPB (PBS) Reno; KOLO-TV (ABC) Reno; KREN-TV (CW, UNV) Reno; KRNV-DT (ABC) Reno; KRXI-TV (FOX) Reno; KSRW-LP Mammoth Lakes, etc.; KTVN (CBS) Reno.
Programming (via satellite): ABC Family Channel; American Movie Classics; Animal Planet; Arts & Entertainment; Cartoon Network; CNBC; CNN; Comedy Central; Country Music TV; Discovery Channel; Discovery Health Channel; Disney Channel; ESPN; ESPN 2; ESPN Classic Sports; Fox News Channel; Fox Sports Net West; GalaVision; Great American Country; Headline News; History Channel; Home Shopping Network; ION Television; Lifetime; Lifetime Movie Network; MSNBC; MTV; Nickelodeon; QVC; Spike TV; Syfy; TBS Superstation; The Learning Channel; Turner Classic Movies; Turner Network TV; TV Guide Network; Univision; USA Network; Versus; VH1; Weather Channel.

Current originations: Government Access.
Fee: $39.95 installation; $43.80 monthly; $9.95 additional installation.
Pay Service 1
Pay Units: N.A.
Programming (via satellite): HBO; Showtime; The Movie Channel.
Fee: $9.00 monthly (HBO), $11.95 monthly (Showtime/TMC).
Video-On-Demand: No
Internet Service
Operational: Yes.
Fee: $59.95 installation; $49.95 monthly.
Telephone Service
None
Homes passed, total homes in area, and miles of plant included in Mammoth Lakes
General Manager: Maggie Thompson. Plant Manager: Joe Warta. Customer Service Manager: Janine Arvisu.
Ownership: News Press & Gazette Co. (MSO).

KERNVILLE—Mediacom, 27192 Sun City Blvd, Ste A, Sun City, CA 92586. Phone: 951-679-3977. Fax: 951-679-9087. Web Site: http://www.mediacomcable.com. Also serves Bodfish, Kern River Valley, Lake Isabella, Mountain Mesa, Onyx, Weldon & Wofford Heights. ICA: CA0168.
TV Market Ranking: Below 100 (Bodfish, Kern River Valley, Lake Isabella, Weldon); Outside TV Markets (KERNVILLE, Mountain Mesa, Onyx, Wofford Heights). Franchise award date: N.A. Franchise expiration date: N.A. Began: N.A.
Channel capacity: N.A. Channels available but not in use: N.A.
Basic Service
Subscribers: 6,698.
Programming (received off-air): KBAK-TV (CBS) Bakersfield; KBFX-CA (FOX) Bakersfield; KCAL-TV (IND) Los Angeles; KERO-TV (ABC) Bakersfield; KGET-TV (CW, NBC) Bakersfield; KTVU (FOX) Oakland; KUVI-DT (MNT) Bakersfield.
Programming (via satellite): Disney Channel; Eternal Word TV Network; FX; Home Shopping Network; QVC; TV Guide Network.
Fee: $29.50 installation; $19.80 monthly.
Expanded Basic Service 1
Subscribers: 6,423.
Programming (via satellite): ABC Family Channel; AmericanLife TV Network; Animal Planet; Arts & Entertainment; Bravo; Cartoon Network; CNBC; CNN; Comedy Central; Country Music TV; C-SPAN; C-SPAN 2; Discovery Channel; E! Entertainment Television; ESPN; ESPN 2; Food Network; Fox News Channel; Fox Sports Net; Golf Channel; Headline News; HGTV; History Channel; ION Television; Lifetime; MSNBC; MTV; Nickelodeon; Speed Channel; Spike TV; Syfy; TBS Superstation; The Learning Channel; Travel Channel; Trinity Broadcasting Network; truTV; Turner Classic Movies; Turner Network TV; TV Land; USA Network; Versus; VH1; WE tv; Weather Channel.
Fee: $26.15 monthly.
Digital Basic Service
Subscribers: N.A.
Programming (via satellite): BBC America; Discovery Digital Networks; DMX Music; ESPNews; Fox Soccer; GSN; Independent Film Channel; National Geographic Channel; Nick Jr.; VH1 Classic.
Fee: $8.00 monthly.
Digital Pay Service 1
Pay Units: N.A.
Programming (via satellite): Cinemax (multiplexed); Encore (multiplexed); HBO (multiplexed); Showtime (multiplexed); Starz (multiplexed); The Movie Channel (multiplexed).
Fee: $8.00 monthly (Starz/Encore), $9.95 monthly (Cinemax or Showtime), $13.95 monthly (HBO).
Video-On-Demand: No
Pay-Per-View
Movies (delivered digitally), Fee: $3.99.
Internet Service
Operational: Yes.
Broadband Service: Mediacom High Speed Internet.
Fee: $40.95 monthly.
Telephone Service
None
Miles of Plant: 144.0 (coaxial); None (fiber optic). Homes passed: 8,250. Total homes in franchised area: 8,500.
General Manager: Allen Boblitz. Engineering Director: Jon Tatilano.
Franchise fee: 5% of gross.
Ownership: Mediacom LLC (MSO).

KING CITY—Charter Communications, 8120 Camino Arroyo, Gilroy, CA 95020. Phones: 408-847-2020; 805-544-1962 (San Luis Obispo administrative office). Fax: 408-847-2993. Web Site: http://www.charter.com. Also serves Monterey County (portions). ICA: CA0345.
TV Market Ranking: Outside TV Markets (KING CITY, Monterey County (portions)). Franchise award date: N.A. Franchise expiration date: N.A. Began: December 10, 1974.
Channel capacity: N.A. Channels available but not in use: N.A.
Basic Service
Subscribers: 2,481.
Programming (received off-air): KCBA (FOX) Salinas; KION-TV (CBS, CW) Monterey; KKPX-TV (ION) San Jose; KQED (PBS) San Francisco; KSBW (NBC) Salinas; KSMS-TV (UNV) Monterey.
Programming (via microwave): KTVU (FOX) Oakland.
Programming (via satellite): ABC Family Channel; AMC; Bravo; Comcast Sports Net Bay Area; Country Music TV; Discovery Channel; ESPN; GalaVision; Home Shopping Network; KGO-TV (ABC) San Francisco; Lifetime; MTV; Nickelodeon; QVC; Spike TV; Syfy; USA Network.
Current originations: Government Access; Educational Access; Public Access.
Fee: $29.99 installation.
Expanded Basic Service 1
Subscribers: 2,117.
Programming (via satellite): Arts & Entertainment; CNN; Disney Channel; Headline News; The Learning Channel; Turner Network TV; Weather Channel; WGN America.
Fee: $38.99 monthly.
Digital Basic Service
Subscribers: N.A.
Programming (via satellite): AmericanLife TV Network; BBC America; Bio; Bloomberg Television; Discovery Digital Networks; DMX Music; ESPN 2; ESPN Classic Sports; ESPNews; FitTV; Fox Movie Channel; Fuse; G4; GAS; Golf Channel; GSN; HGTV; History Channel; History Channel International; Independent Film Channel; INSP; Lifetime Movie Network; MTV Networks Digital Suite; Nick Jr.; Outdoor Channel; Science Television; ShopNBC; Speed Channel; Toon Disney; Trinity Broadcasting Network; Turner Classic Movies; Versus; WE tv.
Pay Service 1
Pay Units: 415.
Programming (via satellite): Showtime; The Movie Channel.
Fee: $15.00 installation; $10.95 monthly.
Digital Pay Service 1
Pay Units: N.A.
Programming (via satellite): Cinemax (multiplexed); Encore (multiplexed); HBO (multiplexed); Showtime (multiplexed); Starz (multiplexed); The Movie Channel (multiplexed).
Video-On-Demand: No
Pay-Per-View
iN DEMAND (delivered digitally); ESPN Now (delivered digitally); ESPN (delivered digitally); Hot Choice (delivered digitally); Playboy TV (delivered digitally); Fresh (delivered digitally); Shorteez (delivered digitally).
Internet Service
Operational: No.
Telephone Service
None
Miles of Plant: 63.0 (coaxial); None (fiber optic). Homes passed: 3,550.
Vice President & General Manager: Ed Merrill. Chief Technician: Mark Beech. Marketing Director: Sarwar Assar.
Ownership: Charter Communications Inc. (MSO).

KLAMATH—Almega Cable, 4001 W Airport Frwy, Ste 530, Bedford, TX 76021. Phones: 877-725-6342; 817-685-9588. Fax: 817-685-6488. Web Site: http://almegacable.com. Also serves Del Norte County, Hunters Valley, Klamath Glen, Requa & Terwer Valley. ICA: CA0228.
TV Market Ranking: Outside TV Markets (Del Norte County, Hunters Valley, KLAMATH, Klamath Glen, Requa, Terwer Valley). Franchise award date: N.A. Franchise expiration date: N.A. Began: January 1, 1956.
Channel capacity: N.A. Channels available but not in use: N.A.
Basic Service
Subscribers: 261.
Programming (received off-air): KAEF-TV (ABC) Arcata; KEET (PBS)ureka; KIEM-TV (NBC) Eureka; KOBI (NBC) Medford; KVIQ (CBS, CW) Eureka; allband FM.
Programming (via satellite): ABC Family Channel; Arts & Entertainment; Bravo; CNBC; CNN; Country Music TV; Discovery Channel; Disney Channel; ESPN; HGTV; INSP; MSNBC; QVC; Spike TV; Syfy; TBS Superstation; The Learning Channel; Turner Classic Movies; Turner Network TV; USA Network; WGN America.
Fee: $43.50 installation; $21.00 monthly; $21.50 additional installation.
Pay Service 1
Pay Units: 77.
Programming (via satellite): HBO.
Fee: $15.00 installation; $10.95 monthly.
Video-On-Demand: No
Internet Service
Operational: No.
Telephone Service
None
Miles of Plant: 22.0 (coaxial); None (fiber optic). Homes passed: 765.
President: Thomas Kurien.
City fee: 5% of basic.
Ownership: Almega Cable (MSO).

KNIGHTSEN—Comcast Cable. Now served by CONCORD, CA [CA0101]. ICA: CA0145.

KYBURZ—Comcast Cable. Now served by PLACERVILLE, CA [CA0108]. ICA: CA0422.

LAKE ALMANOR—CalNeva Broadband, PO Box 1470, 322 Ash St, Westwood, CA 96137. Phones: 530-256-2028; 866-330-2028. Also serves Chester, Clear Creek, Dyre Mountain, East Shore, Hamilton Branch, West Shore & Westwood. ICA: CA0200.
TV Market Ranking: Outside TV Markets (Chester, Clear Creek, Dyre Mountain, East Shore, Hamilton Branch, LAKE ALMANOR, West Shore, Westwood). Franchise award date: January 1, 1962. Franchise expiration date: N.A. Began: January 1, 1962.
Channel capacity: 65 (not 2-way capable). Channels available but not in use: 7.
Basic Service
Subscribers: 2,514.
Programming (received off-air): KHSL-TV (CBS, CW) Chico; KIXE-TV (PBS) Redding; KOVR (CBS) Stockton; KRCR-TV (ABC) Redding; KRXI-TV (FOX) Reno; allband FM.
Programming (via microwave): KCRA-TV (NBC) Sacramento; KMAX-TV (CW) Sacramento.
Programming (via satellite): 3 Angels Broadcasting Network; ABC Family Channel; AMC; Animal Planet; Arts & Entertainment; Cartoon Network; CNBC; CNN; College Sports Television; Comedy Central; Country Music TV; C-SPAN; Discovery Channel; E! Entertainment Television; ESPN; ESPN 2; ESPN Classic Sports; Food Network; Fox News Channel; FX; Golf Channel; Great American Country; Hallmark Channel; Headline News; HGTV; History Channel; Home Shopping Network; Lifetime; MSNBC; MTV; National Geographic Channel; Nickelodeon; Outdoor Channel; Product Information Network; Spike TV; Syfy; TBS Superstation; The Learning Channel; truTV; Turner Classic Movies; Turner Network TV; TV Guide Network; TV Land; USA Network; VH1; WE tv; Weather Channel; WGN America.
Current originations: Educational Access.
Fee: $29.95 installation; $39.00 monthly; $1.00 converter; $19.00 additional installation.
Digital Basic Service
Subscribers: N.A.
Programming (via satellite): BBC America; Bio; Bloomberg Television; Bravo; CMT Pure Country; Current; Discovery Health Channel; Discovery Kids Channel; Discovery Military Channel; Discovery Planet Green; DMX Music; ESPNews; Fox Movie Channel; Fox Soccer; G4; GSN; Halogen Network; History Channel International; ID Investigation Discovery; Independent Film Channel; Lifetime Movie Network; MTV Jams; MTV2; Nick Jr.; NickToons TV; Ovation; Science Channel; Speed Channel; Style Network; Sundance Channel; TeenNick; The Movie Channel (multiplexed); Toon Disney; VH1 Soul.
Fee: $12.95 monthly.
Pay Service 1
Pay Units: N.A.
Programming (via satellite): HBO.
Digital Pay Service 1
Pay Units: N.A.
Programming (via satellite): Cinemax (multiplexed); Encore (multiplexed); HBO (multiplexed); Showtime (multiplexed); Starz (multiplexed).
Fee: $8.35 monthly (Starz), $13.00 monthly (HBO or Cinemax).
Pay-Per-View
Fresh (delivered digitally); Playboy TV (delivered digitally).
Internet Service
Operational: Yes.
Fee: $29.95 installation; $24.95 monthly.
Telephone Service
None
Miles of Plant: 97.0 (coaxial); None (fiber optic). Homes passed: 4,070. Total homes in franchised area: 5,342.

Manager: Tom Gelardi.
City fee: 2% of gross.
Ownership: CalNeva Broadband LLC (MSO).

LAKE ARROWHEAD—Charter Communications, 7337 Central Ave, Riverside, CA 92504. Phone: 951-343-5100. Fax: 951-354-5942. Web Site: http://www.charter.com. Also serves Blue Jay, Cedarpines Park, Crestline, Green Valley Lake, Rimforest, Running Springs & Twin Peaks. ICA: CA0127.

TV Market Ranking: 2 (Blue Jay, Cedarpines Park, Crestline, Green Valley Lake, LAKE ARROWHEAD, Rimforest, Running Springs, Twin Peaks). Franchise award date: March 26, 1962. Franchise expiration date: N.A. Began: January 1, 1963.

Channel capacity: N.A. Channels available but not in use: N.A.

Basic Service

Subscribers: 17,000.

Programming (received off-air): KABC-TV (ABC) Los Angeles; KAZA-TV (IND) Avalon; KCAL-TV (IND) Los Angeles; KCBS-TV (CBS) Los Angeles; KCET (PBS) Los Angeles; KCOP-TV (MNT) Los Angeles; KDOC-TV (IND) Anaheim; KFTR-DT (TEL) Ontario; KHIZ (IND) Barstow; KJLA (IND) Ventura; KLCS (PBS) Los Angeles; KMEX-DT (UNV) Los Angeles; KNBC (NBC) Los Angeles; KPXN-TV (ION) San Bernardino; KRCA (IND) Riverside; KSCI (IND) Long Beach; KTBN-TV (TBN) Santa Ana; KTLA (CW) Los Angeles; KTTV (FOX) Los Angeles; KVCR-DT (PBS) San Bernardino; KVEA (TMO) Corona; KVMD (IND) Twentynine Palms; KWHY-TV (IND) Los Angeles; KXLA (IND) Rancho Palos Verdes.

Programming (via satellite): C-SPAN; ESPN; Eternal Word TV Network; Home Shopping Network; QVC; TBS Superstation; WGN America.

Fee: $29.99 installation.

Expanded Basic Service 1

Subscribers: 10,715.

Programming (via satellite): ABC Family Channel; AMC; Animal Planet; Arts & Entertainment; BET Networks; Bravo!; Cartoon Network; CNBC; CNN; Comedy Central; Country Music TV; Discovery Channel; Disney Channel; E! Entertainment Television; ESPN 2; Food Network; Fox News Channel; Fox Sports Net West; Fox Sports Net West 2; FX; G4; GalaVision; GSN; Hallmark Channel; Headline News; HGTV; History Channel; INSP; Lifetime; MSNBC; MTV; National Geographic Channel; Nickelodeon; Oxygen; SoapNet; Speed Channel; Spike TV; Syfy; The Learning Channel; Travel Channel; truTV; Turner Classic Movies; Turner Network TV; TV Land; USA Network; Versus; VH1; WE tv; Weather Channel.

Fee: $45.45 monthly.

Digital Basic Service

Subscribers: N.A.

Programming (received off-air): KABC-TV (ABC) Los Angeles; KNBC (NBC) Los Angeles; KTTV (FOX) Los Angeles.

Programming (via satellite): BBC America; Bio; Black Family Channel; Bloomberg Television; Boomerang; BYU Television; Canales N; Discovery Digital Networks; Discovery HD Theater; Do-It-Yourself; ESPN Classic Sports; ESPNews; Eternal Word TV Network; Fox College Sports Atlantic; Fox College Sports Central; Fox College Sports Pacific; Fox Soccer; Fuel TV; Fuse; GAS; Golf Channel; Great American Country; HDNet; HDNet Movies; History Channel International; Independent Film Channel; International Television (ITV); Lifetime Movie Network; Lifetime Real Women; MTV Networks Digital Suite; Music Choice; NFL Network; Nick Jr.; NickToons TV; Science Television; Sundance Channel; Toon Disney; TV One; TVG Network; WealthTV.

Digital Pay Service 1

Pay Units: N.A.

Programming (via satellite): Cinemax (multiplexed); Filipino Channel; HBO; Starz (multiplexed).

Video-On-Demand: Yes

Pay-Per-View

Special events.

Internet Service

Operational: Yes. Began: February 1, 2001.

Broadband Service: Charter Pipeline.

Fee: $29.99 monthly.

Telephone Service

Digital: Operational

Fee: $29.99 monthly

Miles of Plant: 272.0 (coaxial); None (fiber optic). Homes passed: 24,042.

Vice President & General Manager: Fred Lutz. Technical Operations Manager: George Noel. Marketing Director: Chris Bailey.

Ownership: Charter Communications Inc. (MSO).

LAKE ELSINORE—Comcast Cable. Now served by ANAHEIM, CA [CA0033]. ICA: CA0079.

LAKE HUGHES—Lake Hughes Cable TV Service, 1399 Arundell Ave, Ventura, CA 93003-5025. Phones: 800-227-7747; 805-642-0241. Fax: 805-650-1869. E-mail: cappsinc@pacbell.net. Web Site: http://www.cappsinc.net. ICA: CA0286.

TV Market Ranking: Outside TV Markets (LAKE HUGHES). Franchise award date: N.A. Franchise expiration date: N.A. Began: September 1, 1954.

Channel capacity: 42 (2-way capable). Channels available but not in use: 7.

Basic Service

Subscribers: 62.

Programming (received off-air): KABC-TV (ABC) Los Angeles; KCAL-TV (IND) Los Angeles; KCBS-TV (CBS) Los Angeles; KCET (PBS) Los Angeles; KCOP-TV (MNT) Los Angeles; KHIZ (IND) Barstow; KNBC (NBC) Los Angeles; KTLA (CW) Los Angeles; KTTV (FOX) Los Angeles; allband FM.

Programming (via satellite): Arts & Entertainment; CNBC; CNN; Comedy Central; C-SPAN; Discovery Channel; Disney Channel; ESPN; ESPN 2; Fox News Channel; Headline News; History Channel; Nickelodeon; QVC; Syfy; The Learning Channel; Trinity Broadcasting Network; truTV; Turner Classic Movies; Turner Network TV; Weather Channel.

Current originations: Government Access; Educational Access; Public Access.

Fee: $31.50 installation; $26.00 monthly; $15.75 additional installation.

Pay Service 1

Pay Units: 12.

Programming (via satellite): Cinemax.

Fee: $4.67 monthly.

Pay Service 2

Pay Units: 11.

Programming (via satellite): HBO.

Fee: $11.95 monthly.

Pay Service 3

Pay Units: 6.

Programming (via satellite): Showtime.

Fee: $10.00 monthly.

Pay Service 4

Pay Units: 6.

Programming (via satellite): The Movie Channel.

Fee: $7.25 monthly.

Internet Service

Operational: No.

Telephone Service

None

Miles of Plant: 8.0 (coaxial); None (fiber optic). Homes passed: 253. Total homes in franchised area: 253.

Manager: Capp Loughboro. Program Director: Gilbert Yniguez. Chief Technician: Charles Zych.

County fee: 5% of gross.

Ownership: Capp's TV Electronics Inc.

LAKE OF THE PINES—Suddenlink Communications, 10101 Streeter Rd, Ste 1, Auburn, CA 95602. Phones: 314-965-2020; 530-268-3731. Web Site: http://www.suddenlink.com. Also serves Alta Sierra, Alta Sierra Estates, Christian Valley & Meadow Vista. ICA: CA0202.

TV Market Ranking: 25 (Christian Valley); Outside TV Markets (Alta Sierra, Alta Sierra Estates, LAKE OF THE PINES, Meadow Vista). Franchise award date: July 1, 1984. Franchise expiration date: N.A. Began: June 2, 1987.

Channel capacity: 62 (operating 2-way). Channels available but not in use: 7.

Basic Service

Subscribers: 5,418.

Programming (received off-air): KCRA-TV (NBC) Sacramento; KMAX-TV (CW) Sacramento; KOVR (CBS) Stockton; KQCA (MNT) Stockton; KSPX-TV (ION) Sacramento; KTFK-DT (TEL) Stockton; KTXL (FOX) Sacramento; KVIE (PBS) Sacramento; KXTV (ABC) Sacramento; WGN-TV (CW, IND) Chicago.

Programming (via satellite): Weather Channel.

Current originations: Government Access; Public Access.

Fee: $45.00 installation; $19.95 monthly.

Expanded Basic Service 1

Subscribers: 3,039.

Programming (via satellite): ABC Family Channel; AMC; Animal Planet; Arts & Entertainment; Cartoon Network; CNBC; CNN; Comcast Sports Net Bay Area; Comedy Central; C-SPAN; C-SPAN 2; Discovery Channel; Disney Channel; E! Entertainment Television; ESPN; ESPN 2; Eternal Word TV Network; Food Network; Fox News Channel; FX; Golf Channel; Great American Country; Hallmark Channel; Headline News; HGTV; History Channel; Home Shopping Network; Lifetime; MTV; Nickelodeon; QVC; Spike TV; TBS Superstation; The Learning Channel; Travel Channel; Trinity Broadcasting Network; Turner Network TV; TV Land; USA Network; VH1.

Fee: $19.04 monthly.

Digital Basic Service

Subscribers: N.A.

Programming (via satellite): BBC America; Bio; Bloomberg Television; Bravo!; Discovery Digital Networks; DMX Music; ESPN Classic Sports; ESPNews; Fox Movie Channel; Fox Soccer; Fuse; G4; GSN; History Channel International; Independent Film Channel; Lifetime Movie Network; Military History Channel; National Geographic Channel; Outdoor Channel; Science Television; Speed Channel; Toon Disney; Turner Classic Movies; Versus; WE tv.

Fee: $3.95 monthly.

Pay Service 1

Pay Units: 147.

Programming (via satellite): Cinemax.

Fee: $9.95 monthly.

Pay Service 2

Pay Units: 265.

Programming (via satellite): HBO.

Fee: $10.95 monthly.

Pay Service 3

Pay Units: 186.

Programming (via satellite): Showtime.

Fee: $9.95 monthly.

Pay Service 4

Pay Units: 149.

Programming (via satellite): The Movie Channel.

Fee: $9.95 monthly.

Pay Service 5

Pay Units: 69.

Programming (via satellite): Starz.

Fee: $4.99 monthly.

Pay Service 6

Pay Units: 70.

Programming (via satellite): Encore.

Fee: $1.35 monthly.

Digital Pay Service 1

Pay Units: N.A.

Programming (via satellite): Cinemax; Encore (multiplexed); HBO (multiplexed); Showtime (multiplexed); Starz (multiplexed); The Movie Channel (multiplexed).

Video-On-Demand: No

Pay-Per-View

iN DEMAND (delivered digitally); Playboy TV (delivered digitally); Fresh (delivered digitally).

Internet Service

Operational: Yes.

Broadband Service: Cebridge High Speed Cable Internet.

Fee: $99.99 installation; $24.95 monthly.

Telephone Service

None

Miles of Plant: 305.0 (coaxial); None (fiber optic). 450/550 MHz

Manager: Doug Landaker. Chief Technician: Tim Lenz. Marketing Director: Jason Oelkers.

Franchise fee: 5% of gross.

Ownership: Cequel Communications LLC (MSO).

LAKE WILDWOOD—Comcast Cable. Now served by GRASS VALLEY, CA [CA0164]. ICA: CA0207.

LAKEWOOD—Formerly served by Time Warner Cable. No longer in operation. ICA: CA0092.

LE GRAND—Comcast Cable, 2441 N Grove Industrial Dr, Fresno, CA 93727-1535. Phone: 559-253-4050. Fax: 559-253-4090.

Web Site: http://www.comcast.com. ICA: CA0349.
TV Market Ranking: 25 (LE GRAND); Outside TV Markets (LE GRAND). Franchise award date: N.A. Franchise expiration date: N.A. Began: January 1, 1987.
Channel capacity: 33 (not 2-way capable). Channels available but not in use: N.A.
Basic Service
Subscribers: 200.
Programming (received off-air): KAIL (MNT) Fresno; KFSN-TV (ABC) Fresno; KFTV-DT (UNV) Hanford; KGPE (CBS) Fresno; KMPH-TV (FOX) Visalia; KSEE (NBC) Fresno; KVPT (PBS) Fresno.
Programming (via satellite): ABC Family Channel; AMC; Arts & Entertainment; Cartoon Network; CNN; C-SPAN; Discovery Channel; ESPN; ESPN 2; FX; GalaVision; Headline News; Home Shopping Network; Spike TV; TBS Superstation; The Learning Channel; Trinity Broadcasting Network; Turner Network TV; USA Network; WGN America.
Fee: $43.99 installation; $33.04 monthly.
Pay Service 1
Pay Units: N.A.
Programming (via satellite): Cinemax; HBO.
Fee: $10.97 monthly (Cinemax), $12.87 monthly (HBO).
Internet Service
Operational: Yes.
Telephone Service
None
General Manager: Len Falter. Marketing Director: Stewart Butler. Communications Director: Erica Smith.
Ownership: Comcast Cable Communications Inc.

LEE VINING—Formerly served by Satview Broadband. No longer in operation. ICA: CA0350.

LEWISTON—New Day Broadband, PO Box 535, 9155 Deschutes Rd, #D, Palo Cedro, CA 96073-8714. Phone: 530-547-2226. Fax: 530-547-4948. ICA: CA0351.
TV Market Ranking: Below 100 (LEWISTON). Franchise award date: N.A. Franchise expiration date: N.A. Began: October 1, 1990.
Channel capacity: 36 (not 2-way capable). Channels available but not in use: 4.
Basic Service
Subscribers: 150.
Programming (received off-air): KHSL-TV (CBS, CW) Chico; KIXE-TV (PBS) Redding; KRCR-TV (ABC) Redding.
Programming (via satellite): ABC Family Channel; CNN; Discovery Channel; Disney Channel; ESPN; KCNC-TV (CBS) Denver; TBS Superstation; WGN America.
Fee: $15.00 installation; $36.75 monthly.
Pay Service 1
Pay Units: 13.
Programming (via satellite): HBO.
Fee: $11.50 monthly.
Internet Service
Operational: No.
Telephone Service
None
Miles of Plant: 16.0 (coaxial); None (fiber optic). Homes passed: 375.
Chief Executive Officer: Neal Sehnog.
Ownership: New Day Broadband (MSO).

LINCOLN—SureWest Broadband. Formerly served by Sacramento, CA [CA0459]. This cable system has converted to IPTV, PO Box 969, Roseville, CA 95661. Phone: 916-772-2000. Fax: 916-786-7170. Web Site: http://www.surewest.com. ICA: CA5605.
TV Market Ranking: 25 (LINCOLN).
Channel capacity: N.A. Channels available but not in use: N.A.
Video-On-Demand: Yes
Internet Service
Operational: Yes.
Telephone Service
Digital: Operational
Ownership: SureWest Broadband.

LODI—Comcast Cable, 6505 Tam O Shanter Dr, Stockton, CA 95210-3349. Phone: 209-473-4955. Fax: 209-473-8177. Web Site: http://www.comcast.com. Also serves Acampo, Lockeford, Victor & Woodbridge. ICA: CA0100.
TV Market Ranking: 25 (Acampo, Lockeford, LODI, Victor, Woodbridge). Franchise award date: August 5, 1968. Franchise expiration date: N.A. Began: August 5, 1968.
Channel capacity: N.A. Channels available but not in use: N.A.
Basic Service
Subscribers: 10,850.
Programming (received off-air): KCRA-TV (NBC) Sacramento; KCSO-LP Sacramento; KGO-TV (ABC) San Francisco; KICU-TV (IND) San Jose; KMAX-TV (CW) Sacramento; KOFY-TV (IND) San Francisco; KOVR (CBS) Stockton; KQCA (MNT) Stockton; KRON-TV (MNT) San Francisco; KSPX-TV (ION) Sacramento; KTFK-DT (TEL) Stockton; KTNC-TV (IND) Concord; KTVU (FOX) Oakland; KTXL (FOX) Sacramento; KUVS-DT (UNV) Modesto; KVIE (PBS) Sacramento; KXTV (ABC) Sacramento.
Programming (via satellite): CNBC; CNN; C-SPAN; C-SPAN 2; Fox News Channel; Headline News; MSNBC; TV Guide Network; Weather Channel.
Current originations: Religious Access; Government Access; Educational Access; Public Access.
Fee: $43.99 installation; $15.00 monthly.
Expanded Basic Service 1
Subscribers: N.A.
Programming (via satellite): ABC Family Channel; AMC; Animal Planet; Arts & Entertainment; BET Networks; Bravo; Cartoon Network; Comcast Sports Net Bay Area; Comedy Central; Discovery Channel; Disney Channel; E! Entertainment Television; ESPN; ESPN 2; ESPN Classic Sports; Food Network; FX; GalaVision; Golf Channel; Great American Country; GSN; Hallmark Channel; HGTV; History Channel; Home Shopping Network; International Television (ITV); Lifetime; MTV; mun2 television; Nickelodeon; Oxygen; QVC; ShopNBC; Spike TV; Syfy; TBS Superstation; The Learning Channel; Travel Channel; truTV; Turner Network TV; TV Land; USA Network; Versus; VH1; WE tv.
Fee: $34.95 monthly.
Digital Basic Service
Subscribers: 3,255.
Programming (via satellite): AmericanLife TV Network; ART America; BBC America; Bio; Black Family Channel; Bloomberg Television; Canales N; CCTV-4; Discovery Digital Networks; Encore; ESPNews; Filipino Channel; FitTV; Fox College Sports Atlantic; Fox College Sports Central; Fox College Sports Pacific; Fox Movie Channel; Fox Sports World; Fuse; G4; GAS; Halogen Network; History Channel International; Independent Film Channel; International Television (ITV); Lifetime Movie Network; Lime; MTV Networks Digital Suite; Music Choice; National Geographic Channel; Nick Jr.; NickToons TV; Outdoor Channel; Ovation; Power Link; RAI International; Russian Television Network; Saigon Broadcasting TV Network; Speed Channel; Style Network; Sundance Channel; The Word Network; Toon Disney; Trinity Broadcasting Network; Turner Classic Movies; TV Asia; TV Japan; TV5, La Television International; Zee TV USA.
Fee: $11.95 monthly.
Digital Pay Service 1
Pay Units: N.A.
Programming (via satellite): Cinemax (multiplexed); HBO (multiplexed); Showtime (multiplexed); Starz (multiplexed); The Movie Channel (multiplexed).
Fee: $17.99 monthly (Cinemax, Starz or TMC), $18.99 monthly (HBO or Showtime).
Video-On-Demand: Yes
Pay-Per-View
iN DEMAND (delivered digitally); Urban Xtra (delivered digitally); Fresh (delivered digitally); Shorteez (delivered digitally); Playboy TV (delivered digitally); Hot Choice (delivered digitally); ESPN Now (delivered digitally); Sports PPV (delivered digitally).
Internet Service
Operational: Yes.
Broadband Service: Comcast High Speed Internet.
Fee: $42.95 monthly.
Telephone Service
Digital: Operational
Miles of Plant: 256.0 (coaxial); None (fiber optic). Homes passed: 15,581.
Technical Operations Director: Fred Walkover. Marketing Manager: Terry Dowling.
Franchise fee: 3% of gross.
Ownership: Comcast Cable Communications Inc. (MSO).

LONE PINE—Lone Pine TV Inc., PO Box 867, 223 Jackson St, Lone Pine, CA 93545-0867. Phones: 888-876-5461; 760-876-5461. Fax: 760-876-9101. E-mail: BjBranson@lonepinetv.com. Web Site: http://www.lonepine.lonepinetv.com. Also serves Alabama Hills. ICA: CA0353.
TV Market Ranking: Outside TV Markets (Alabama Hills, LONE PINE). Franchise award date: January 1, 1956. Franchise expiration date: N.A. Began: January 1, 1956.
Channel capacity: 80 (2-way capable). Channels available but not in use: N.A.
Basic Service
Subscribers: 500.
Programming (received off-air): KABC-TV (ABC) Los Angeles; KCAL-TV (IND) Los Angeles; KCET (PBS) Los Angeles; KCOP-TV (MNT) Los Angeles; KTTV (FOX) Los Angeles; allband FM.
Programming (via satellite): ABC Family Channel; AMC; Animal Planet; Arts & Entertainment; Cartoon Network; CNBC; CNN; Comedy Central; Country Music TV; Discovery Channel; Disney Channel; ESPN; ESPN 2; ESPN Classic Sports; Eternal Word TV Network; Food Network; Fox News Channel; Fox Sports Net Prime Ticket; Fox Sports Net West; FX; GalaVision; Great American Country; Hallmark Channel; Headline News; HGTV; History Channel; Home Shopping Network; Lifetime; MSNBC; MTV; National Geographic Channel; Nickelodeon; QVC; SoapNet; Spike TV; Syfy; TBS Superstation; Telefutura; Telemundo; The Learning Channel; Toon Disney; Travel Channel; Trinity Broadcasting Network; truTV; Turner Network TV; TV Land; Univision; USA Network; VH1; Weather Channel.
Programming (via translator): KCBS-TV (CBS) Los Angeles; KNBC (NBC) Los Angeles; KTLA (CW) Los Angeles.
Fee: $25.00 installation; $37.00 monthly.
Digital Basic Service
Subscribers: N.A.
Programming (via satellite): AmericanLife TV Network; BBC America; Bio; Bloomberg Television; Church Channel; Cooking Channel; Current; Discovery Health Channel; Discovery Military Channel; Discovery Planet Green; FitTV; Gospel Music Channel; Halogen Network; History Channel International; ID Investigation Discovery; JCTV; RFD-TV; Science Channel; ShopNBC; Sleuth; The Word Network.
Fee: $5.00 monthly.
Digital Expanded Basic Service
Subscribers: N.A.
Programming (via satellite): Bravo; Fox Movie Channel; Independent Film Channel; Lifetime Movie Network; Sundance Channel; Trio; Turner Classic Movies; WE tv.
Fee: $5.00 monthly.
Digital Expanded Basic Service 2
Subscribers: N.A.
Programming (via satellite): Discovery Kids Channel; G4; GSN; Nick Jr.; NickToons TV; PBS Kids Sprout; TeenNick.
Fee: $5.00 monthly.
Digital Expanded Basic Service 3
Subscribers: N.A.
Programming (via satellite): Fuse; MTV Hits; MTV Jams; MTV2; VH1 Classic; VH1 Country; VH1 Soul.
Fee: $5.00 monthly.
Digital Expanded Basic Service 4
Subscribers: N.A.
Programming (via satellite): ESPN 2; ESPN Classic Sports; ESPNews; Fox College Sports Atlantic; Fox College Sports Central; Fox College Sports Pacific; Fox Soccer; Golf Channel; Outdoor Channel; Speed Channel; Versus.
Fee: $5.00 monthly.
Digital Expanded Basic Service 5
Subscribers: N.A.
Programming (via satellite): Cine Latino; Cine Mexicano; CNN en Espanol; Discovery en Espanol; ESPN Deportes; Fox Sports en Espanol; HBO Latino; History Channel en Espanol; MTV Tres; mun2 television; VeneMovies.
Fee: $5.00 monthly.
Pay Service 1
Pay Units: 135.
Programming (via satellite): Showtime; The Movie Channel.
Fee: $15.00 installation; $8.00 monthly (each).
Pay Service 2
Pay Units: N.A.
Programming (via satellite): HBO.
Fee: $15.00 installation; $12.00 monthly.
Digital Pay Service 1
Pay Units: N.A.
Programming (via satellite): Cinemax (multiplexed); Encore (multiplexed); Flix; HBO (multiplexed); Showtime (multiplexed); Starz (multiplexed); The Movie Channel (multiplexed).
Fee: $11.99 monthly (HBO, Cinemax, Starz/Encore or Showtime/Flix/TMC).
Internet Service
Operational: Yes.
Subscribers: 300.
Broadband Service: In-house.
Fee: $41.99-$61.99 monthly.
Telephone Service
Digital: Operational
Subscribers: 10.
Fee: $30.00-$40.00 monthly

Miles of Plant: 8.0 (coaxial); None (fiber optic). Homes passed: 902. Total homes in franchised area: 902.
Manager, Marketing & Program Director: Bruce Branson. Chief Technician: Steve Stukas.
City fee: 2% of gross.
Ownership: Lone Pine TV Inc. (MSO).

LONG BARN—SNC Cable, PO Box 281, Sonora, CA 95373. Phone: 209-586-7622. Web Site: http://www.snccable.com. ICA: CA0354.
TV Market Ranking: Outside TV Markets (LONG BARN). Franchise award date: N.A. Franchise expiration date: N.A. Began: January 1, 1984.
Channel capacity: N.A. Channels available but not in use: N.A.
Basic Service
Subscribers: 139.
Programming (received off-air): KCRA-TV (NBC) Sacramento; KMAX-TV (CW) Sacramento; KOVR (CBS) Stockton; KQCA (MNT) Stockton; KTFK-DT (TEL) Stockton; KTNC-TV (IND) Concord; KTXL (FOX) Sacramento; KVIE (PBS) Sacramento; KXTV (ABC) Sacramento; allband FM.
Programming (via satellite): Arts & Entertainment; CNBC; CNN; Discovery Channel; ESPN; Fox News Channel; History Channel; TBS Superstation; Trinity Broadcasting Network; Turner Network TV.
Fee: $50.00 installation; $27.95 monthly.
Pay Service 1
Pay Units: 4.
Programming (via satellite): HBO.
Fee: $13.95 monthly.
Video-On-Demand: No
Internet Service
Operational: No.
Telephone Service
None
Miles of Plant: 10.0 (coaxial); None (fiber optic). Homes passed: 200.
General Manager: Tim Holden.
Ownership: Sierra Nevada Communications (MSO).

LONG BEACH—Charter Communications, 4781 Irwindale Ave, Irwindale, CA 91706-2175. Phone: 626-430-3300. Fax: 626-430-3420. Web Site: http://www.charter.com. Also serves Signal Hill. ICA: CA0014.
TV Market Ranking: 2 (LONG BEACH, Signal Hill). Franchise award date: N.A. Franchise expiration date: N.A. Began: June 1, 1965.
Channel capacity: 124 (operating 2-way). Channels available but not in use: N.A.
Basic Service
Subscribers: 110,000.
Programming (received off-air): KABC-TV (ABC) Los Angeles; KAZA-TV (IND) Avalon; KCAL-TV (IND) Los Angeles; KCBS-TV (CBS) Los Angeles; KCET (PBS) Los Angeles; KCOP-TV (MNT) Los Angeles; KDOC-TV (IND) Anaheim; KFTR-DT (TEL) Ontario; KJLA (IND) Ventura; KLCS (PBS) Los Angeles; KMEX-DT (UNV) Los Angeles; KNBC (NBC) Los Angeles; KOCE-TV (PBS) Huntington Beach; KPXN-TV (ION) San Bernardino; KRCA (IND) Riverside; KSCI (IND) Long Beach; KTBN-TV (TBN) Santa Ana; KTLA (CW) Los Angeles; KTTV (FOX) Los Angeles; KVEA (TMO) Corona; KVMD (IND) Twentynine Palms; KWHY-TV (IND) Los Angeles; KXLA (IND) Rancho Palos Verdes; 4 FMs.
Programming (via satellite): America's Store; C-SPAN; C-SPAN 2; E! Entertainment Television; Home Shopping Network; Jewelry Television; ShopNBC; WGN America.
Fee: $29.99 installation.
Expanded Basic Service 1
Subscribers: N.A.
Programming (via satellite): ABC Family Channel; AMC; Animal Planet; Arts & Entertainment; BET Networks; Bravo; Cartoon Network; CNBC; CNN; Comedy Central; Country Music TV; Discovery Channel; Disney Channel; ESPN; ESPN 2; ESPN Classic Sports; Eternal Word TV Network; FitTV; Food Network; Fox Movie Channel; Fox News Channel; Fox Sports en Espanol; Fox Sports Net West; Fox Sports Net West 2; FX; G4; GalaVision; Golf Channel; GSN; Hallmark Channel; Headline News; HGTV; History Channel; Lifetime; MSNBC; MTV; MTV2; Nickelodeon; Oxygen; Product Information Network; QVC; Speed Channel; Spike TV; TBS Superstation; The Learning Channel; Travel Channel; truTV; Turner Classic Movies; Turner Network TV; TV Guide Network; TV Land; USA Network; Versus; VH1; WE tv; Weather Channel.
Fee: $48.95 monthly.
Digital Basic Service
Subscribers: 68,200.
Programming (via satellite): BBC America; Bio; Bloomberg Television; Boomerang; CNN en Espanol; Discovery Digital Networks; Do-It-Yourself; Encore Action; Fox College Sports Atlantic; Fox College Sports Central; Fox College Sports Pacific; Fuse; GAS; Great American Country; History Channel International; HTV Musica; Independent Film Channel; Lifetime Movie Network; MTV Networks Digital Suite; mun2 television; Music Choice; National Geographic Channel; Nick Jr.; NickToons TV; Style Network; Sundance Channel; Syfy; Telemundo; Toon Disney.
Fee: $10.00 monthly.
Digital Pay Service 1
Pay Units: 9,646.
Programming (via satellite): Canales N; Cinemax (multiplexed); Flix; HBO (multiplexed); Showtime (multiplexed); Starz (multiplexed); The Movie Channel (multiplexed).
Fee: $10.00 monthly (Cinemax, Showtime or TMC), $11.00 monthly (HBO).
Video-On-Demand: Yes
Pay-Per-View
Addressable homes: 68,200.
Playboy TV (delivered digitally), Fee: $4.95, Addressable: Yes; Shorteez (delivered digitally); Sports PPV (delivered digitally); iN DEMAND (delivered digitally); ETC (delivered digitally); Pleasure (delivered digitally).
Internet Service
Operational: Yes.
Broadband Service: Charter Pipeline.
Fee: $29.99 monthly.
Telephone Service
Digital: Operational
Fee: $29.99 monthly
Miles of Plant: 750.0 (coaxial); None (fiber optic). Additional miles planned: 10.0 (coaxial). Homes passed: 185,738.
Vice President & General Manager: Wendy Rasmusson. Technical Operations Manager: Tom Williams. Marketing Manager: Lily Ho.
City fee: 5% of gross.
Ownership: Charter Communications Inc. (MSO).

LONG BEACH NAVAL BASE—Formerly served by Americable International. No longer in operation. ICA: CA0355.

LOS ALAMOS—Charter Communications, 270 Bridge St, San Luis Obispo, CA 93401. Phone: 805-544-1962. Fax: 818-541-6042. Web Site: http://www.charter.com. ICA: CA0280.
TV Market Ranking: Below 100 (LOS ALAMOS). Franchise award date: February 1, 1984. Franchise expiration date: N.A. Began: October 31, 1984.
Channel capacity: 53 (operating 2-way). Channels available but not in use: 32.
Basic Service
Subscribers: 320.
Programming (received off-air): KCOY-TV (CBS) Santa Maria; KEYT-TV (ABC, MNT) Santa Barbara; KJLA (IND) Ventura; KSBY (CW, NBC) San Luis Obispo.
Programming (via satellite): ABC Family Channel; Bravo; ESPN; MTV; QVC; The Learning Channel.
Current originations: Government Access.
Fee: $45.00 installation; $21.80 monthly.
Expanded Basic Service 1
Subscribers: 232.
Programming (via satellite): Country Music TV; Lifetime; USA Network.
Fee: $2.79 monthly.
Expanded Basic Service 2
Subscribers: 205.
Programming (via satellite): CNN; Discovery Channel; Disney Channel; Headline News; TBS Superstation.
Fee: $6.25 monthly.
Pay Service 1
Pay Units: 53.
Programming (via satellite): Cinemax.
Fee: $11.95 monthly.
Pay Service 2
Pay Units: 68.
Programming (via satellite): HBO.
Fee: $11.95 monthly.
Pay Service 3
Pay Units: N.A.
Programming (via satellite): GalaVision.
Fee: $3.95 monthly.
Video-On-Demand: No
Internet Service
Operational: Yes.
Telephone Service
Digital: Operational
Miles of Plant: 6.0 (coaxial); None (fiber optic). Homes passed: 500.
Vice President & General Manager: Ed Merrill. Chief Technician: Dan Joseph. Marketing Manager: Sarwar Assar.
Franchise fee: 5% of gross.
Ownership: Charter Communications Inc. (MSO).

LOS ALTOS HILLS—Comcast Cable. Now served by SAN FRANCISCO, CA [CA0003]. ICA: CA0213.

LOS ANGELES—Comcast Cable. Now served by CHATSWORTH, CA [CA0013]. ICA: CA0062.

LOS ANGELES—Time Warner Cable, 550 N Continental Blvd, Ste 250, El Segundo, CA 90245-5050. Phone: 310-647-3000. Fax: 310-647-3036. Web Site: http://www.timewarnercable.com/socal. Also serves Arcadia, Athens, Baldwin Hills, Baldwin Park, Boyle Heights, Bradbury, Brentwood, Carson, Charter Oak, City of Industry, Claremont, Compton, Covina, Culver City, Diamond Bar, Eagle Rock, East Compton, East Los Angeles, East San Fernando Valley, El Monte, El Segundo, Florence, Gardena, Glendora, Hacienda Heights, Harbor City, Hawaiian Gardens, Hawthorne, Hermosa Beach, Hollywood, Inglewood, La Puente, La Verne, Ladera Heights, Lawndale, Lennox, Lomita, Los Angeles County (portions), Manhattan Beach, Marina Del Ray, Mission Hills, Monrovia, Pacific Palisades, Pacoima, Palms, Pico Rivera, Playa Del Ray, Playa Vista, Pomona, Rancho Park, Redondo Beach, Rowland Heights, San Dimas, San Fernando, San Marino, San Pedro, Sepulveda, Sierra Madre, South Gate, South Pasadena, South Whittier, Sun Valley, Torrance, Venice, Walnut Park, West Los Angeles, Westchester, Willowbrook, Wilmington, Wilshire & Windsor Hills. ICA: CA0009.
TV Market Ranking: 2 (Arcadia, Athens, Baldwin Hills, Baldwin Park, Boyle Heights, Bradbury, Brentwood, Carson, Charter Oak, City of Industry, Claremont, Compton, Covina, Culver City, Diamond Bar, Eagle Rock, East Compton, East Los Angeles, East San Fernando Valley, El Monte, El Segundo, Florence, Gardena, Glendora, Hacienda Heights, Harbor City, Hawaiian Gardens, Hawthorne, Hermosa Beach, Hollywood, Inglewood, La Puente, La Verne, Ladera Heights, Lawndale, Lennox, Lomita, LOS ANGELES, Los Angeles County (portions), Manhattan Beach, Marina Del Ray, Mission Hills, Monrovia, Pacific Palisades, Pacoima, Palms, Pico Rivera, Playa Del Ray, Playa Vista, Pomona, Rancho Park, Redondo Beach, Rowland Heights, San Dimas, San Fernando, San Marino, San Pasadena, San Pedro, Sepulveda, Sierra Madre, South Gate, South Whittier, Sun Valley, Torrance, Venice, Walnut Park, West Los Angeles, Westchester, Willowbrook, Wilmington, Wilshire, Windsor Hills). Franchise award date: N.A. Franchise expiration date: N.A. Began: November 1, 1980.
Channel capacity: 78 (operating 2-way). Channels available but not in use: N.A.
Basic Service
Subscribers: 1,900,000 Includes Anaheim & Chatsworth.
Programming (received off-air): KABC-TV (ABC) Los Angeles; KAZA-TV (IND) Avalon; KCAL-TV (IND) Los Angeles; KCBS-TV (CBS) Los Angeles; KCET (PBS) Los Angeles; KCOP-TV (MNT) Los Angeles; KDOC-TV (IND) Anaheim; KFTR-DT (TEL) Ontario; KJLA (IND) Ventura; KLCS (PBS) Los Angeles; KMEX-DT (UNV) Los Angeles; KNBC (NBC) Los Angeles; KOCE-TV (PBS) Huntington Beach; KPXN-TV (ION) San Bernardino; KRCA (IND) Riverside; KSCI (IND) Long Beach; KTBN-TV (TBN) Santa Ana; KTLA (CW) Los Angeles; KTTV (FOX) Los Angeles; KVEA (TMO) Corona; KWHY-TV (IND) Los Angeles; KXLA (IND) Rancho Palos Verdes; LATV Networks.
Programming (via satellite): California Channel; CNBC; C-SPAN; C-SPAN 2; Fox News Channel; Home Shopping Network; MSNBC; QVC; TV Guide Network; WGN America.
Current originations: Public Access; Leased Access; Government Access; Educational Access; Public Access.
Fee: $28.99 installation; $9.24 monthly.
Expanded Basic Service 1
Subscribers: N.A.
Programming (via satellite): ABC Family Channel; AMC; Animal Planet; Arts & Entertainment; BET Networks; Bravo; Cartoon Network; CNN; Comedy Central; Country Music TV; Discovery Channel; Disney Channel; E! Entertainment Television; ESPN; ESPN 2; ESPN Classic Sports; Food Network; Fox Sports en Espanol; Fox Sports Net West; Fox Sports Net West 2; FX; GalaVision; Golf Channel; Headline News; HGTV; History Channel;

Lifetime; MTV; Nickelodeon; Oxygen; Spike TV; Syfy; TBS Superstation; The Learning Channel; Travel Channel; truTV; Turner Network TV; TV Land; USA Network; VH1; Weather Channel.
Fee: $41.21 monthly.
Digital Basic Service
Subscribers: N.A.
Programming (via satellite): BBC America; Discovery Digital Networks; Discovery Kids Channel; ESPNews; G4; GSN; Independent Film Channel; Lime; Music Choice; National Geographic Channel; Nick Jr.; Style Network; The Word Network; Turner Classic Movies; Versus; WE tv; Weatherscan.
Fee: $5.00 monthly (each tier).
Digital Expanded Basic Service
Subscribers: N.A.
Programming (via satellite): Bio; Encore (multiplexed); GAS; Halogen Network; History Channel International; MTV Networks Digital Suite; NickToons TV; Outdoor Channel; Sundance Channel; Toon Disney.
Fee: $5.00 monthly.
Digital Pay Service 1
Pay Units: 10,060.
Programming (via satellite): ART America; Cinemax (multiplexed); Filipino Channel; Flix; HBO (multiplexed); MBC America; RAI International; Russian Television Network; Saigon Broadcasting TV Network; Showtime (multiplexed); Starz (multiplexed); The Movie Channel (multiplexed); TV Asia; TV Japan; TV5, La Television International; Zhong Tian Channel.
Fee: $11.95 monthly (Zhong Tian, CCTV, Filipino, ART or SBTN), $14.95 monthly (TV Asia, TV5, RAI, MBC or RTN), $15.00 monthly (Cinemax, HBO, Showtime/TMC, Starz or Playboy), $24.95 monthly (TV Japan).
Video-On-Demand: Yes
Pay-Per-View
iN DEMAND (delivered digitally), Addressable: Yes.
Internet Service
Operational: Yes.
Broadband Service: Road Runner.
Fee: $49.95 installation; $44.95 monthly.
Telephone Service
Digital: Operational
Fee: $49.95 installation; $44.95 monthly
Miles of Plant: 9,569.0 (coaxial); 2,722.0 (fiber optic). Homes passed: 4,100,000.
President: Jeffrey Hirsch. Vice President, Technical Operations: Mitchel Christopher. Vice President, Engineering: Jose Leon. Vice President, Marketing & Sales: Bill Erickson. Vice President, Public Relations: Patti Rockenwagner. Vice President, External Affairs: Deane Leavenworth. Corporate Communications Manager: Toni Mathews.
City fee: 5% of gross.
Ownership: Time Warner Cable (MSO).

LOS ANGELES (south central portion)—Comcast Cable. Now served by LOS ANGELES, CA [CA0009]. ICA: CA0008.

LOS ANGELES (western portion)—Comcast Cable. Now served by LOS ANGELES, CA [CA0009]. ICA: CA0019.

LOS GATOS—Comcast Cable. Now served by SAN JOSE, CA [CA0004]. ICA: CA0144.

LOS GATOS (unincorporated areas)—Matrix Cablevision Inc. Now served by SAN JOSE, CA [CA0004]. ICA: CA0306.

LUSHMEADOWS—Northland Cable Television, 40108 Hwy 49, Ste A, Oakhurst, CA 93644-8826. Phones: 800-736-1414; 559-683-7388. Fax: 559-642-2432. E-mail: oakhurst@northlandcabletv.com. Web Site: http://www.northlandcabletv.com. Also serves Mariposa County (portions). ICA: CA0357.
TV Market Ranking: 72 (Mariposa County (portions)); Outside TV Markets (LUSHMEADOWS). Franchise award date: N.A. Franchise expiration date: N.A. Began: N.A.
Channel capacity: 24 (not 2-way capable). Channels available but not in use: N.A.
Basic Service
Subscribers: 206.
Programming (received off-air): KAIL (MNT) Fresno; KFRE-TV (CW) Sanger; KFSN-TV (ABC) Fresno; KGPE (CBS) Fresno; KMPH-TV (FOX) Visalia; KNSO (TMO) Merced; KSEE (NBC) Fresno; KVPT (PBS) Fresno.
Programming (via satellite): AMC; Arts & Entertainment; CNN; Country Music TV; C-SPAN; Discovery Channel; ESPN; Hallmark Channel; QVC; Spike TV; TBS Superstation; The Learning Channel; Turner Classic Movies; Turner Network TV; WGN America.
Fee: $32.99 monthly.
Pay Service 1
Pay Units: 143.
Programming (via satellite): HBO.
Fee: $10.50 monthly.
Internet Service
Operational: No.
Telephone Service
None
Miles of Plant: 27.0 (coaxial); None (fiber optic). Homes passed: 419. Total homes in franchised area: 419.
Manager: Ken Musgrove. Chief Technician: Roger Conroy. Office Manager: Karen Bradley.
Ownership: Northland Communications Corp. (MSO).

MALIBU—Charter Communications, 3806 Cross Creek Rd, Malibu, CA 90265-4971. Phones: 626-430-3300 (Irwindale office); 310-456-9010. Fax: 310-579-7010. Web Site: http://www.charter.com. Also serves Agoura (portions), Agoura Hills, Calabasas, Calabasas (unincorporated areas), Hidden Hills, Los Angeles (unincorporated areas), Los Angeles County (portions), Lost Hills, Topanga & Ventura County (portions). ICA: CA0129.
TV Market Ranking: 2 (Agoura (portions), Agoura Hills, Calabasas, Calabasas (unincorporated areas), Hidden Hills, Los Angeles (unincorporated areas), Los Angeles County (portions), Lost Hills, MALIBU, Topanga, Ventura County (portions)). Franchise award date: N.A. Franchise expiration date: N.A. Began: January 1, 1958.
Channel capacity: 95 (operating 2-way). Channels available but not in use: 7.
Basic Service
Subscribers: 15,000.
Programming (received off-air): KABC-TV (ABC) Los Angeles; KBEH (IND) Oxnard; KCBS-TV (CBS) Los Angeles; KCET (PBS) Los Angeles; KCOP-TV (MNT) Los Angeles; KFTR-DT (TEL) Ontario; KJLA (IND) Ventura; KLCS (PBS) Los Angeles; KMEX-DT (UNV) Los Angeles; KNBC (NBC) Los Angeles; KPXN-TV (ION) San Bernardino; KRCA (IND) Riverside; KSCI (IND) Long Beach; KTBN-TV (TBN) Santa Ana; KTLA (CW) Los Angeles; KTTV (FOX) Los Angeles; KVEA (TMO) Corona; KWHY-TV (IND) Los Angeles; allband FM.
Programming (via satellite): ABC Family Channel; Arts & Entertainment; California Channel; CNBC; C-SPAN; E! Entertainment Television; Fox News Channel; Hallmark Channel; Lifetime; MTV; Nickelodeon; Oxygen; QVC; Syfy; TBS Superstation; The Learning Channel; Travel Channel; Turner Network TV; TV Guide Network; USA Network; VH1; Weather Channel; WGN America.
Current originations: Government Access; Educational Access; Public Access.
Fee: $29.99 installation.
Expanded Basic Service 1
Subscribers: 14,068.
Programming (via satellite): AMC; Animal Planet; Bravo; Cartoon Network; CNN; Comedy Central; Country Music TV; Discovery Channel; Disney Channel; ESPN; ESPN 2; Food Network; Fox Movie Channel; Fox Sports Net West; Fox Sports Net West 2; FX; G4; Golf Channel; GSN; Headline News; HGTV; History Channel; MSNBC; SoapNet; Speed Channel; Spike TV; truTV; Turner Classic Movies; Turner Network TV; TV Land; Versus.
Fee: $48.95 monthly.
Digital Basic Service
Subscribers: 7,331.
Programming (via satellite): BBC America; Bio; Bloomberg Television; Boomerang; Discovery Digital Networks; Do-It-Yourself; GAS; History Channel International; Independent Film Channel; Lifetime Movie Network; MTV Networks Digital Suite; MuchMusic Network; Music Choice; Nick Jr.; Nick Too; Style Network; Sundance Channel; Toon Disney; WE tv.
Fee: $10.00 monthly.
Digital Pay Service 1
Pay Units: N.A.
Programming (via satellite): Cinemax (multiplexed); Flix; HBO (multiplexed); Showtime (multiplexed); The Movie Channel (multiplexed).
Fee: $10.00 monthly (each).
Video-On-Demand: Yes
Pay-Per-View
Hot Choice (delivered digitally); iN DEMAND; iN DEMAND (delivered digitally); Playboy TV; Playboy TV (delivered digitally); Fresh (delivered digitally); Shorteez (delivered digitally); sports (delivered digitally).
Internet Service
Operational: Yes.
Broadband Service: Charter Pipeline.
Fee: $29.99 monthly.
Telephone Service
Digital: Operational
Fee: $29.99 monthly
Miles of Plant: 582.0 (coaxial); None (fiber optic). Homes passed: 22,600.
Vice President & General Manager: Wendy Rasmusson. Technical Operations Director: Peter Arredondo. Marketing Manager: Lily Ho.
Franchise fee: 5% of gross.
Ownership: Charter Communications Inc. (MSO).

MAMMOTH LAKES—NPG Cable, Inc., 123 Commerce Dr, Ste B6, Mammoth Lakes, CA 93546. Phones: 760-934-9640; 760-934-8553. Fax: 760-934-6512. Web Site: http://www.npgcable.net. ICA: CA0358.
TV Market Ranking: Outside TV Markets (MAMMOTH LAKES). Franchise award date: January 1, 1970. Franchise expiration date: N.A. Began: September 1, 1970.
Channel capacity: N.A. Channels available but not in use: N.A.
Basic Service
Subscribers: 6,237 Includes June Lake.
Programming (received off-air): KAME-TV (MNT) Reno; KBEH (IND) Oxnard; KNPB (PBS) Reno; KOLO-TV (ABC) Reno; KRENTV (CW, UNV) Reno; KRNV-DT (ABC) Reno; KRXI-TV (FOX) Reno; KSRW-LP Mammoth Lakes, etc.; KTVN (CBS) Reno; allband FM.
Programming (via satellite): ABC Family Channel; AMC; Animal Planet; Arts & Entertainment; Cartoon Network; CNBC; CNN; Comedy Central; Country Music TV; C-SPAN; Discovery Channel; Discovery Health Channel; Disney Channel; ESPN; ESPN 2; ESPN Classic Sports; Food Network; Fox News Channel; Fox Sports Net West; FX; GalaVision; Great American Country; Headline News; HGTV; History Channel; Home Shopping Network; INSP; ION Television; KTLA (CW) Los Angeles; Lifetime; Lifetime Movie Network; MSNBC; MTV; National Geographic Channel; Nickelodeon; QVC; Spike TV; Syfy; TBS Superstation; The Learning Channel; Travel Channel; Turner Classic Movies; Turner Network TV; TV Guide Network; TV Land; Univision; USA Network; Versus; VH1; Weather Channel.
Current originations: Leased Access; Public Access.
Fee: $39.95 installation; $43.80 monthly; $2.50 converter; $9.95 additional installation.
Digital Basic Service
Subscribers: 1,156.
Programming (via satellite): BBC America; Bio; Cooking Channel; Discovery Digital Networks; Discovery HD Theater; DMX Music; Do-It-Yourself; ESPN 2 HD; ESPN HD; ESPN U; ESPNews; Food Network HD; Fox Soccer; Fox Sports en Espanol; FSN Digital Atlantic; FSN Digital Central; FSN Digital Pacific; Fuel TV; GAS; Golf Channel; GSN; HDNet; HDNet Movies; HGTV HD; History Channel International; Independent Film Channel; MTV Networks Digital Suite; Nick Jr.; NickToons TV; SoapNet; Speed Channel; Toon Disney; Turner Network TV HD; Universal HD; WE tv.
Fee: $11.95 monthly.
Digital Pay Service 1
Pay Units: N.A.
Programming (via satellite): Cinemax (multiplexed); Encore (multiplexed); HBO (multiplexed); Showtime (multiplexed); Starz (multiplexed); The Movie Channel (multiplexed).
Fee: $6.95 monthly (Cinemax), $9.95 monthly (Starz/Encore), $11.95 monthly (Showtime/TMC), $12.00 monthly (HBO).
Video-On-Demand: No
Pay-Per-View
iN DEMAND (delivered digitally); Fresh (delivered digitally).
Internet Service
Operational: Yes.
Subscribers: 2,196.
Broadband Service: Optimum Online.
Fee: $59.95 installation; $24.95 monthly; $5.00 modem lease.
Telephone Service
Analog: Not Operational
Digital: Planned
Miles of Plant: 105.0 (coaxial); 19.0 (fiber optic). Homes passed: 9,000. Total homes in franchised area: 9,000. Homes passed, total homes in area, and miles of plant (coax) include June Lake
General Manager: Maggie Thompson. Plant Manager: Joe Warta. Customer Service Manager: Janine Arrisu.
City fee: 3% of gross.
Ownership: News Press & Gazette Co. (MSO).

MANTECA—Comcast Cable. Now served by STOCKTON, CA [CA0028]. ICA: CA0126.

MARIPOSA—Northland Cable Television, 40108 Hwy 49, Ste A, Oakhurst, CA 93644-8826. Phones: 800-736-1414; 559-683-7388. Fax: 559-642-2432. E-mail: oakhurst@northlandcabletv.com. Web Site: http://www.northlandcabletv.com. ICA: CA0359.

TV Market Ranking: 72 (MARIPOSA). Franchise award date: January 1, 1981. Franchise expiration date: N.A. Began: N.A.

Channel capacity: 43 (not 2-way capable). Channels available but not in use: 7.

Basic Service

Subscribers: 400.

Programming (received off-air): KAIL (MNT) Fresno; KFRE-TV (CW) Sanger; KFSN-TV (ABC) Fresno; KFTV-DT (UNV) Hanford; KGMC (IND) Clovis; KGPE (CBS) Fresno; KMPH-TV (FOX) Visalia; KNSO (TMO) Merced; KSEE (NBC) Fresno; KTVU (FOX) Oakland; KVPT (PBS) Fresno; allband FM.

Programming (via satellite): Animal Planet; Arts & Entertainment; Cartoon Network; CNBC; CNN; C-SPAN; Discovery Channel; ESPN; Fox News Channel; Headline News; History Channel; Lifetime; QVC; TBS Superstation; The Learning Channel; Turner Network TV; USA Network; WGN America.

Fee: $55.00 installation; $31.99 monthly.

Expanded Basic Service 1

Subscribers: N.A.

Programming (via satellite): AMC; Comcast Sports Net Bay Area; Country Music TV; E! Entertainment Television; ESPN 2; Food Network; Hallmark Channel; HGTV; Nickelodeon; Spike TV; Syfy; Turner Classic Movies.

Fee: $39.99 monthly.

Digital Basic Service

Subscribers: 25.

Programming (via satellite): BBC America; Bloomberg Television; Discovery Digital Networks; DMX Music; Fox Movie Channel; Golf Channel; Great American Country; GSN; Halogen Network; Speed Channel; Trinity Broadcasting Network.

Fee: $12.00 monthly.

Digital Expanded Basic Service

Subscribers: N.A.

Programming (via satellite): AmericanLife TV Network; FitTV; G4; Outdoor Channel; WE tv.

Pay Service 1

Pay Units: 146.

Programming (via satellite): HBO.

Fee: $13.50 monthly.

Digital Pay Service 1

Pay Units: N.A.

Programming (via satellite): Cinemax (multiplexed); Encore; Flix; HBO (multiplexed); Showtime (multiplexed); The Movie Channel (multiplexed).

Fee: $10.00 monthly (each).

Pay-Per-View

Fresh (delivered digitally); Playboy TV (delivered digitally); Hot Choice (delivered digitally); Sports PPV (delivered digitally).

Internet Service

Operational: Yes.

Fee: $44.99 monthly.

Telephone Service

None

Miles of Plant: 14.0 (coaxial); None (fiber optic). Homes passed: 956. Total homes in franchised area: 956.

Manager: Ken Musgrove. Chief Technician: Roger Conroy. Office Manager: Karen Bradley.

Ownership: Northland Communications Corp. (MSO).

MARSH CREEK MOTOR HOME PARK—Formerly served by Comcast Cable. No longer in operation. ICA: CA0291.

MCCLELLAN PARK—SureWest Broadband. Formerly served by Sacramento, CA [CA0459]. This cable system has converted to IPTV, PO Box 969, Roseville, CA 95661. Phone: 916-772-2000. Fax: 916-786-7170. Web Site: http://www.surewest.com. ICA: CA5606.

TV Market Ranking: 25 (MCCLELLAN PARK).

Channel capacity: N.A. Channels available but not in use: N.A.

Video-On-Demand: Yes

Internet Service

Operational: Yes.

Telephone Service

Digital: Operational

Ownership: SureWest Broadband.

MEADOW VISTA—Formerly served by Cebridge Connections. Now served by LAKE OF THE PINES, CA [CA0202]. ICA: CA0196.

MECCA—Cable USA, PO Box 336, 2455 Stirrup Rd, Borrego Springs, CA 92004-0336. Phones: 308-236-1512 (Kearney, NE corporate office); 760-767-5607; 800-300-6989. Fax: 760-767-3609. Web Site: http://www.cableusa.com. ICA: CA0281.

TV Market Ranking: Below 100 (MECCA). Franchise award date: N.A. Franchise expiration date: N.A. Began: January 1, 1983.

Channel capacity: N.A. Channels available but not in use: N.A.

Basic Service

Subscribers: N.A.

Programming (received off-air): KDFX-CA Indio/Palm Springs; KESQ-TV (ABC, CW) Palm Springs; KFMB-TV (CBS) San Diego; KMIR-TV (NBC) Palm Springs; KPBS (PBS) San Diego.

Programming (via satellite): QVC; TBS Superstation; Trinity Broadcasting Network; Weather Channel; WGN America.

Fee: $24.95 installation; $14.95 monthly.

Expanded Basic Service 1

Subscribers: N.A.

Programming (via satellite): ABC Family Channel; Animal Planet; Arts & Entertainment; Cartoon Network; CNBC; CNN; CNN en Espanol; Country Music TV; C-SPAN; C-SPAN 2; Discovery Channel; Discovery en Espanol; E! Entertainment Television; ESPN; ESPN 2; ESPN Classic Sports; Eternal Word TV Network; Food Network; Fox News Channel; Fox Sports en Espanol; G4; Hallmark Channel; Headline News; History Channel; Home Shopping Network; MTV Tres; Nickelodeon; ShopNBC; Spike TV; Syfy; The Learning Channel; Turner Classic Movies; Turner Network TV; USA Network; VeneMovies; WE tv.

Fee: $24.95 installation; $35.45 monthly.

Expanded Basic Service 2

Subscribers: N.A.

Programming (via satellite): Canal 52MX; Cine Latino; Cine Mexicano; GalaVision; History Channel en Espanol; Telefutura; Telemundo; Toon Disney en Espanol; Univision.

Fee: $9.95 monthly.

Pay Service 1

Pay Units: N.A.

Programming (via satellite): Showtime.

Fee: $7.75 monthly.

Internet Service

Operational: No.

Telephone Service

None

Miles of Plant: 5.0 (coaxial); None (fiber optic). Homes passed: 350.

Manager & Chief Technician: Joe Gustafson.

Ownership: USA Companies (MSO).

MENLO PARK—Matrix Cablevision Inc. Now served by SAN JOSE, CA [CA0004]. ICA: CA0361.

MERCED—Comcast Cable, 2441 N Grove Industrial Dr, Fresno, CA 93727-1535. Phone: 559-253-4050. Fax: 559-253-4090. Web Site: http://www.comcast.com. Also serves Atwater, Castle AFB & Winton. ICA: CA0072.

TV Market Ranking: 25 (MERCED); 25,72 (Atwater, Castle AFB, Winton). Franchise award date: January 1, 1965. Franchise expiration date: N.A. Began: January 1, 1967.

Channel capacity: N.A. Channels available but not in use: N.A.

Basic Service

Subscribers: 24,000.

Programming (received off-air): KAIL (MNT) Fresno; KFRE-TV (CW) Sanger; KFSN-TV (ABC) Fresno; KFTV-DT (UNV) Hanford; KGPE (CBS) Fresno; KMAX-TV (CW) Sacramento; KMPH-TV (FOX) Visalia; KNSO (TMO) Merced; KQED (PBS) San Francisco; KSEE (NBC) Fresno; KTVU (FOX) Oakland; 22 FMs.

Programming (via satellite): ABC Family Channel; AMC; Animal Planet; Arts & Entertainment; BET Networks; Cartoon Network; CNBC; CNN; Comcast Sports Net Bay Area; C-SPAN; Discovery Channel; Disney Channel; ESPN; Fox News Channel; FX; GalaVision; Headline News; Lifetime; MTV; Nickelodeon; QVC; Spike TV; TBS Superstation; Turner Network TV; TV Guide Network; USA Network.

Current originations: Public Access.

Fee: $43.99 installation; $16.00 monthly.

Digital Basic Service

Subscribers: 6,198.

Programming (via satellite): BBC America; Bio; Black Family Channel; Bloomberg Television; Bravo; Canales N; Discovery Digital Networks; DMX Music; ESPN 2; ESPN Classic Sports; ESPNews; Fox College Sports Atlantic; Fox College Sports Central; Fox College Sports Pacific; Fox Movie Channel; Fox Sports World; Fuse; G4; GAS; Golf Channel; Great American Country; GSN; Halogen Network; HGTV; History Channel; History Channel International; Independent Film Channel; Lifetime Movie Network; Lime; MTV Networks Digital Suite; National Geographic Channel; Nick Jr.; NickToons TV; Outdoor Channel; Ovation; ShopNBC; Speed Channel; Style Network; Sundance Channel; Syfy; The Word Network; Toon Disney; Trinity Broadcasting Network; Turner Classic Movies; TV Land; Versus; WE tv.

Fee: $11.95 monthly.

Digital Pay Service 1

Pay Units: 3,984.

Programming (via satellite): Cinemax (multiplexed); Encore (multiplexed); Flix; HBO (multiplexed); Showtime (multiplexed); Starz (multiplexed); The Movie Channel (multiplexed).

Fee: $20.00 installation; $17.99 monthly each (Cinemax, Starz & TMC), $18.99 monthly (HBO & Showtime).

Video-On-Demand: Yes

Pay-Per-View

iN DEMAND (delivered digitally), Addressable: Yes; Fresh (delivered digitally); Shorteez (delivered digitally); Playboy TV (delivered digitally).

Internet Service

Operational: Yes.

Subscribers: 3,646.

Broadband Service: Comcast High Speed Internet.

Fee: $42.95 installation; $3.00 modem lease.

Telephone Service

Digital: Operational

Miles of Plant: 401.0 (coaxial); 16.0 (fiber optic). Additional miles planned: 15.0 (coaxial). Homes passed: 38,000. Total homes in franchised area: 38,350.

General Manager: Len Falter. Marketing Director: Stewart Butler. Communications Director: Erica Smith.

Franchise fee: 5% of gross.

Ownership: Comcast Cable Communications Inc. (MSO).

MERCED—Formerly served by Sprint Corp. No longer in operation. ICA: CA0436.

MEYERS—Charter Communications, 9335 Prototype Dr, Reno, NV 89521. Phone: 775-850-1200. Fax: 775-850-1279. Web Site: http://www.charter.com. Also serves El Dorado County (portions) & Tahoe Paradise. ICA: CA0194.

TV Market Ranking: Outside TV Markets (El Dorado County (portions), MEYERS, Tahoe Paradise). Franchise award date: N.A. Franchise expiration date: N.A. Began: August 25, 1978.

Channel capacity: 42 (not 2-way capable). Channels available but not in use: None.

Basic Service

Subscribers: N.A. Included in Reno NV

Programming (received off-air): K38FW Stateline; KAME-TV (MNT) Reno; KCRA-TV (NBC) Sacramento; KGO-TV (ABC) San Francisco; KNPB (PBS) Reno; KOLO-TV (ABC) Reno; KREN-TV (CW, UNV) Reno; KRNV-DT (ABC) Reno; KRXI-TV (FOX) Reno; KTVN (CBS) Reno; allband FM.

Programming (via satellite): C-SPAN; QVC; TBS Superstation; WGN America.

Current originations: Leased Access.

Fee: $35.95 installation; $16.32 monthly; $2.01 converter; $24.95 additional installation.

Expanded Basic Service 1

Subscribers: 3,718.

Programming (via satellite): ABC Family Channel; AMC; Arts & Entertainment; CNBC; CNN; Comcast Sports Net Bay Area; Comedy Central; Discovery Channel; Disney Channel; E! Entertainment Television; ESPN; ESPN 2; Headline News; HGTV; History Channel; Lifetime; MTV; Nickelodeon; Spike TV; Syfy; The Learning

Channel; Turner Network TV; USA Network; VH1; Weather Channel.
Fee: $19.95 installation; $23.91 monthly.

Digital Basic Service
Subscribers: N.A.
Programming (via satellite): BBC America; Bio; Black Family Channel; Bravo; Discovery Digital Networks; DMX Music; ESPN Classic Sports; ESPNews; Fox College Sports Atlantic; Fox College Sports Central; Fox College Sports Pacific; Fox Movie Channel; Fox Soccer; Fuse; G4; GAS; Golf Channel; Great American Country; GSN; Halogen Network; Independent Film Channel; International Television (ITV); Lifetime Movie Network; MTV Networks Digital Suite; National Geographic Channel; Nick Jr.; Outdoor Channel; Speed Channel; Style Network; Sundance Channel; The Word Network; Toon Disney; Trinity Broadcasting Network; Turner Classic Movies; TV Guide Interactive Inc.; Versus; WE tv.

Digital Pay Service 1
Pay Units: N.A.
Programming (via satellite): Cinemax (multiplexed); Encore (multiplexed); HBO (multiplexed); Showtime (multiplexed); Starz (multiplexed); The Movie Channel (multiplexed).

Video-On-Demand: No

Pay-Per-View
iN DEMAND (delivered digitally); Fresh (delivered digitally); Shorteez (delivered digitally); Playboy TV (delivered digitally).

Internet Service
Operational: Yes.
Fee: $39.95 monthly.

Telephone Service
Digital: Operational
Fee: $29.99 monthly

Miles of Plant: 113.0 (coaxial); None (fiber optic).
Vice President & General Manager: Manny Martinez. Technical Operations Manager: Carol Eure.
City fee: 5% of gross.
Ownership: Charter Communications Inc. (MSO).

MIDPINES—Formerly served by Timber TV. No longer in operation. ICA: CA0299.

MILPITAS—Comcast Cable. Now served by SAN JOSE, CA [CA0004]. ICA: CA0142.

MISSION BAY MOBILE HOME PARK—Formerly served by Comcast Cable. No longer in operation. ICA: CA0362.

MODESTO & OAKDALE—Comcast Cable, 6505 Tam O Shanter Dr, Stockton, CA 95210-3349. Phone: 209-473-4955. Fax: 209-473-8177. Web Site: http://www.comcast.com. Also serves Stanislaus County. ICA: CA0040.
TV Market Ranking: 25 (MODESTO & OAKDALE); 25,72 (Stanislaus County). Franchise award date: January 1, 1969. Franchise expiration date: N.A. Began: June 2, 1970.
Channel capacity: N.A. Channels available but not in use: N.A.

Basic Service
Subscribers: 46,081.
Programming (received off-air): KBSV (ETV) Ceres; KCRA-TV (NBC) Sacramento; KMAX-TV (CW) Sacramento; KOVR (CBS) Stockton; KQCA (MNT) Stockton; KQED (PBS) San Francisco; KSPX-TV (ION) Sacramento; KTFK-DT (TEL) Stockton; KTNC-TV (IND) Concord; KTXL (FOX) Sacramento; KUVS-DT (UNV) Modesto; KVIE (PBS) Sacramento; KXTV (ABC) Sacramento; 14 FMs.
Programming (via satellite): CNBC; CNN; C-SPAN; C-SPAN 2; Fox News Channel; Headline News; MSNBC; Telemundo; TV Guide Network; Weather Channel.
Current originations: Educational Access; Public Access.
Fee: $43.99 installation; $14.00 monthly; $.69 converter.

Expanded Basic Service 1
Subscribers: 45,000.
Programming (via satellite): ABC Family Channel; AMC; Animal Planet; Arts & Entertainment; BET Networks; Bravo; California Channel; Cartoon Network; Comcast Sports Net Bay Area; Comedy Central; Country Music TV; Discovery Channel; Disney Channel; E! Entertainment Television; ESPN; ESPN 2; ESPN Classic Sports; Eternal Word TV Network; Food Network; Fox Sports en Espanol; FX; GalaVision; Golf Channel; GSN; Hallmark Channel; HGTV; History Channel; Home Shopping Network; INSP; Lifetime; MTV; Nickelodeon; QVC; ShopNBC; Spike TV; Style Network; Syfy; TBS Superstation; The Learning Channel; Travel Channel; truTV; Turner Network TV; TV Land; USA Network; Versus; VH1.
Fee: $38.55 monthly.

Digital Basic Service
Subscribers: 13,824.
Programming (via satellite): AmericanLife TV Network; BBC America; Bio; Black Family Channel; Bloomberg Television; Canales N; Discovery Digital Networks; DMX Music; Encore Action; ESPNews; FitTV; Fox College Sports Atlantic; Fox College Sports Central; Fox College Sports Pacific; Fox Movie Channel; Fox Sports World; Fuse; G4; GAS; Great American Country; Halogen Network; History Channel International; Independent Film Channel; International Television (ITV); Lifetime Movie Network; Lime; MTV Networks Digital Suite; National Geographic Channel; Nick Jr.; NickToons TV; Outdoor Channel; Ovation; Speed Channel; Sundance Channel; The Word Network; Toon Disney; Trinity Broadcasting Network; Turner Classic Movies; WE tv.
Fee: $11.95 monthly.

Digital Pay Service 1
Pay Units: 23,690.
Programming (via satellite): Cinemax (multiplexed); Flix; HBO (multiplexed); Showtime (multiplexed); Starz (multiplexed); The Movie Channel (multiplexed).
Fee: $17.99 monthly (Cinemax, Starz or TMC), $18.99 monthly (HBO or Showtime).

Video-On-Demand: Yes

Pay-Per-View
Addressable homes: 23,000.
iN DEMAND (delivered digitally), Addressable: No; Urban Xtra (delivered digitally); Fresh (delivered digitally); Shorteez (delivered digitally); Playboy TV (delivered digitally); Sports PPV (delivered digitally).

Internet Service
Operational: Yes.
Broadband Service: Comcast High Speed Internet.
Fee: $42.95 monthly.

Telephone Service
Digital: Operational

Miles of Plant: 734.0 (coaxial); 15.0 (fiber optic). Homes passed: 96,636. Total homes in franchised area: 96,636.
Technical Operations Director: Fred Walkover. Marketing Manager: Terry Dowling.
City fee: 3% of gross.
Ownership: Comcast Cable Communications Inc. (MSO).

MOFFETT FIELD NAVAL AIRSTATION—Formerly served by Americable International-Moffett Inc. No longer in operation. ICA: CA0226.

MOJAVE—Charter Communications, 7337 Central Ave, Riverside, CA 92504. Phone: 951-343-5100. Fax: 951-354-5942. Web Site: http://www.charter.com. Also serves Rosamond. ICA: CA0206.
TV Market Ranking: Outside TV Markets (MOJAVE, Rosamond). Franchise award date: N.A. Franchise expiration date: N.A. Began: May 28, 1984.
Channel capacity: N.A. Channels available but not in use: N.A.

Basic Service
Subscribers: 1,685.
Programming (received off-air): KABC-TV (ABC) Los Angeles; KBAK-TV (CBS) Bakersfield; KCAL-TV (IND) Los Angeles; KCBS-TV (CBS) Los Angeles; KCET (PBS) Los Angeles; KCOP-TV (MNT) Los Angeles; KERO-TV (ABC) Bakersfield; KHIZ (IND) Barstow; KNBC (NBC) Los Angeles; KTBN-TV (TBN) Santa Ana; KTLA (CW) Los Angeles; KTTV (FOX) Los Angeles; KVMD (IND) Twentynine Palms.
Programming (via satellite): California Channel; C-SPAN; GalaVision; Home Shopping Network; QVC; Weather Channel; WGN America.
Current originations: Government Access; Educational Access; Public Access.
Fee: $30.00 installation.

Expanded Basic Service 1
Subscribers: 1,683.
Programming (via satellite): ABC Family Channel; AMC; Arts & Entertainment; BET Networks; Bravo; Cartoon Network; CNBC; CNN; Comedy Central; Country Music TV; Discovery Channel; Disney Channel; E! Entertainment Television; ESPN; ESPN 2; Food Network; Fox News Channel; Fox Sports Net West; Fox Sports Net West 2; Headline News; HGTV; History Channel; Lifetime; MTV; MTV2; Nickelodeon; Outdoor Channel; Oxygen; Spike TV; Syfy; TBS Superstation; The Learning Channel; Turner Network TV; TV Guide Network; TV One; Univision; USA Network; VH1.
Fee: $45.45 monthly.

Digital Basic Service
Subscribers: N.A.
Programming (via satellite): Bandamax; BBC America; Bio; Bloomberg Television; Canales N; CMT Pure Country; C-SPAN 3; Discovery Digital Networks; Do-It-Yourself; ESPN Classic Sports; ESPNews; FitTV; Fox College Sports Atlantic; Fox College Sports Central; Fox College Sports Pacific; Fuse; G4; GAS; Gol TV; GSN; Hallmark Channel; History Channel International; Independent Film Channel; Lifetime Movie Network; Lifetime Real Women; Military History Channel; MTV Networks Digital Suite; National Geographic Channel; Nick Jr.; Nick Too; Pentagon Channel; SoapNet; Sundance Channel; Toon Disney; TV Land; Versus; WE tv.

Digital Pay Service 1
Pay Units: N.A.
Programming (via satellite): Cinemax (multiplexed); Encore (multiplexed); Flix; Fox Movie Channel; HBO (multiplexed); Showtime (multiplexed); Starz (multiplexed); The Movie Channel (multiplexed).

Video-On-Demand: No

Pay-Per-View
iN DEMAND (delivered digitally); Playboy TV (delivered digitally); Fresh (delivered digitally); Club Jenna (delivered digitally); Fresh! (delivered digitally).

Internet Service
Operational: Yes.
Fee: $39.99 monthly.

Telephone Service
None

Miles of Plant: 85.0 (coaxial); 10.0 (fiber optic). Homes passed: 5,432. Total homes in franchised area: 6,908.
Vice President & General Manager: Fred Lutz. Technical Operations Manager: George Noel. Marketing Director: Chris Bailey.
Franchise fee: 5% of gross.
Ownership: Charter Communications Inc. (MSO).

MONTEREY—Comcast Cable, 1900 S 10th St, San Jose, CA 95112-4110. Phones: 408-918-3200; 925-973-7000 (San Ramon regional office). Fax: 408-294-7280. Web Site: http://www.comcast.com. Also serves Carmel Valley, Carmel-by-the-Sea, Del Monte Forest, Del Rey Oaks, Marina, Monterey County (portions), Pacific Grove, Salinas, Sand City & Seaside. ICA: CA0030.
TV Market Ranking: Below 100 (Carmel Valley, Carmel-by-the-Sea, Del Monte Forest, Del Rey Oaks, Marina, MONTEREY, Monterey County (portions), Pacific Grove, Salinas, Sand City, Seaside). Franchise award date: January 1, 1952. Franchise expiration date: N.A. Began: March 5, 1952.
Channel capacity: 82 (operating 2-way). Channels available but not in use: 9.

Basic Service
Subscribers: 63,578.
Programming (received off-air): KCBA (FOX) Salinas; KION-TV (CBS, CW) Monterey; KKPX-TV (ION) San Jose; KSBW (NBC) Salinas; KSMS-TV (UNV) Monterey.
Programming (via microwave): KICU-TV (IND) San Jose; KQED (PBS) San Francisco; KTEH (PBS) San Jose; KTVU (FOX) Oakland.
Programming (via satellite): California Channel; C-SPAN; C-SPAN 2; Discovery Channel; Home Shopping Network 2; QVC; ShopNBC; Telemundo; TV Guide Network.
Current originations: Leased Access; Public Access.
Fee: $16.21 monthly.

Expanded Basic Service 1
Subscribers: N.A.
Programming (via microwave): KGO-TV (ABC) San Francisco.
Programming (via satellite): ABC Family Channel; AMC; Animal Planet; Arts & Entertainment; BET Networks; Bravo; Cartoon Network; CNBC; CNN; Comedy Cen-

tral; Country Music TV; Disney Channel; E! Entertainment Television; ESPN; ESPN 2; Food Network; Fox News Channel; Fox Sports Net; FX; GalaVision; Golf Channel; Hallmark Channel; Headline News; HGTV; History Channel; Lifetime; MSNBC; MTV; Nickelodeon; Oxygen; Spike TV; TBS Superstation; The Learning Channel; truTV; Turner Network TV; TV Land; USA Network; Versus; VH1; Weather Channel.
Fee: $39.19 monthly.

Digital Basic Service
Subscribers: N.A.
Programming (via satellite): AmericanLife TV Network; BBC America; Bio; Black Family Channel; Bloomberg Television; Canales N; Discovery Digital Networks; Encore Action; ESPN Classic Sports; ESPNews; FitTV; Fox College Sports Atlantic; Fox College Sports Central; Fox College Sports Pacific; Fox Movie Channel; Fox Sports World; Fuse; G4; GAS; Great American Country; GSN; Halogen Network; History Channel International; Independent Film Channel; International Television (ITV); Lifetime Movie Network; Lime; MTV Networks Digital Suite; Music Choice; National Geographic Channel; Nick Jr.; NickToons TV; Outdoor Channel; Ovation; Speed Channel; Style Network; Sundance Channel; Syfy; The Word Network; Toon Disney; Trinity Broadcasting Network; Turner Classic Movies; WE tv.
Fee: $11.95 monthly.

Digital Pay Service 1
Pay Units: N.A.
Programming (via satellite): CCTV-4; Cinemax (multiplexed); Filipino Channel; Flix; HBO (multiplexed); RAI International; Russian Television Network; Saigon Broadcasting TV Network; Showtime (multiplexed); Starz (multiplexed); The Movie Channel (multiplexed); TV Asia; TV Japan; TV5, La Television International; Zee TV USA; Zhong Tian Channel.
Fee: $17.00 monthly (each).

Video-On-Demand: Yes

Pay-Per-View
iN DEMAND (delivered digitally); Hot Choice (delivered digitally); Urban Xtra (delivered digitally); Fresh (delivered digitally); Playboy TV (delivered digitally); ESPN Now (delivered digitally); Comcast/Charter Sports Southeast (CSS) (delivered digitally); Sports PPV (delivered digitally).

Internet Service
Operational: Yes.
Broadband Service: Comcast High Speed Internet.
Fee: $42.95 monthly.

Telephone Service
Digital: Operational
Fee: $44.95 monthly

Miles of Plant: 850.0 (coaxial); None (fiber optic). Homes passed: 96,205. Total homes in franchised area: 122,566.
Area Vice President: Navarra Williams. Technical Operations Director: David Walton. Network Manager: Curt Christenson. Sales & Marketing Director: Eden Godsoe. Vice President, Communications: Andrew Johnson.
City fee: 5% of gross.
Ownership: Comcast Cable Communications Inc. (MSO).

MONTEREY—Formerly served by Sprint Corp. No longer in operation. ICA: CA0437.

MORGAN HILL—Charter Communications. Now served by GILROY, CA [CA0425]. ICA: CA0334.

MOUNT SHASTA—Northland Cable Television, PO Box 8, 219 E Alma St, Mount Shasta, CA 96067-0008. Phone: 530-926-6128. Fax: 530-926-6546. E-mail: mtshasta@northlandcabletv.com. Web Site: http://www.northlandcabletv.com. Also serves Cragview, Dunsmuir, McCloud, Siskiyou County & Weed. ICA: CA0171.
TV Market Ranking: Below 100 (Siskiyou County (portions)); Outside TV Markets (Cragview, Dunsmuir, McCloud, MOUNT SHASTA, Siskiyou County (portions), Weed). Franchise award date: N.A. Franchise expiration date: N.A. Began: December 26, 1972.
Channel capacity: N.A. Channels available but not in use: N.A.

Basic Service
Subscribers: 4,500.
Programming (received off-air): KBLN (IND) Grants Pass; KDRV (ABC) Medford; KHSL-TV (CBS, CW) Chico; KIXE-TV (PBS) Redding; KNVN (NBC) Chico; KOBI (NBC) Medford; KRCR-TV (ABC) Redding; KRVU-LD (MNT) Redding; KTVL (CBS, CW) Medford.
Programming (via satellite): Animal Planet; Arts & Entertainment; Cartoon Network; CNBC; CNN; Comcast Sports Net Bay Area; Comedy Central; Cooking Channel; C-SPAN; CW+; Discovery Channel; ESPN; ESPN 2; Food Network; Fox Movie Channel; Fox News Channel; FX; Golf Channel; Great American Country; Hallmark Channel; Headline News; HGTV; History Channel; Lifetime; MTV; NFL Network; Nickelodeon; Outdoor Channel; QVC; Spike TV; Syfy; TBS Superstation; Telemundo; The Learning Channel; Turner Classic Movies; Turner Network TV; TV Land; USA Network; Versus; VH1; Weather Channel; WGN America.
Current originations: Government Access; Educational Access; Public Access.

Digital Basic Service
Subscribers: 500.
Programming (via satellite): BBC America; Bloomberg Television; Bravo; Discovery Health Channel; Discovery Kids Channel; Discovery Military Channel; Discovery Planet Green; DMX Music; ESPNews; Eternal Word TV Network; FitTV; Fox Soccer; G4; ID Investigation Discovery; Independent Film Channel; INSP; Lifetime Movie Network; National Geographic Channel; Science Channel; Speed Channel; Trinity Broadcasting Network; WE tv.
Fee: $49.99 monthly.

Pay Service 1
Pay Units: 670.
Programming (via satellite): HBO.
Fee: $10.00 installation; $11.45 monthly.

Digital Pay Service 1
Pay Units: N.A.
Programming (via satellite): Cinemax (multiplexed); Encore (multiplexed); Flix; HBO (multiplexed); Showtime (multiplexed); Starz (multiplexed); The Movie Channel (multiplexed).
Fee: $14.75 monthly (HBO, Cinemax, Starz/Encore or Showtime/TMC/Flix).

Video-On-Demand: No

Pay-Per-View
iN DEMAND (delivered digitally); Playboy TV (delivered digitally); Fresh (delivered digitally); Club Jenna (delivered digitally).

Internet Service
Operational: Yes.
Broadband Service: Northland Express.
Fee: $42.99 monthly.

Telephone Service
Analog: Not Operational
Digital: Planned

Miles of Plant: 135.0 (coaxial); None (fiber optic). Homes passed: 8,500. Total homes in franchised area: 8,610.
District Manager: Vince Reinig.
City fee: 2% of gross.
Ownership: Northland Communications Corp. (MSO).

MOUNTAIN MEADOWS—Formerly served by Entertainment Express. No longer in operation. ICA: CA0240.

MOUNTAIN VIEW—Comcast Cable. Now served by SAN JOSE, CA [CA0004]. ICA: CA0090.

NAPA—Comcast Cable. Now served by NAPA/SONOMA, CA [CA0038]. ICA: CA0091.

NAPA/SONOMA—Comcast Cable, 1111 Andersen Dr, San Rafael, CA 94901-5336. Phones: 925-973-7000 (San Ramon regional office); 415-459-5333. Web Site: http://www.comcast.com. Also serves American Canyon, Belvedere, Benica, Black Point, Calistoga, Camp Meeker, Cazadero, Cloverdale, Corte Madera, Cotati, Fairfax, Fairfield, Forest Knolls, Forestville, Fulton, Geyserville, Green Brae, Guerneville, Healdsburg, Kentfield, Kenwood, Lagunitas, Larkspur, Marin City, Marin County (southeastern portion), Mill Valley, Napa, Napa County, Novato, Oakmont, Penngrove, Petaluma, Rio Nido, Rio Vista, Rohnert Park, Ross, San Anselmo, San Geronimo, San Quentin, San Rafael, Santa Rosa, Santa Venetia, Sausalito, Sebastopol, Solano County, Sonoma County, St. Helena, Strawberry, Suisin City, Tamalpais, Tamelac, Tiburon, Travis AFB, Vacaville, Vallejo, Windsor, Woodacre & Yountville. ICA: CA0038.
TV Market Ranking: 25 (Vacaville); 7 (American Canyon, Belvedere, Benica, Black Point, Corte Madera, Fairfax, Fairfield, Forest Knolls, Green Brae, Kentfield, Lagunitas, Larkspur, Marin City, Marin County (southeastern portion), Mill Valley, Napa County (portions), Novato, Rio Vista, Ross, San Anselmo, San Geronimo, San Quentin, San Rafael, Santa Venetia, Sausalito, Sonoma County (portions), Strawberry, Suisin City, Tamalpais, Temelac, Tiburon, Travis AFB, Vallejo, Woodacre); 7,25 (Solano County); Below 100 (Calistoga, Camp Meeker, Cazadero, Cloverdale, Cotati, Forestville, Fulton, Geyserville, Guerneville, Healdsburg, Kenwood, NAPA, Oakmont, Penngrove, Rio Nida, Rohnert Park, Santa Rosa, Sebastopol, SONOMA, St. Helena, Windsor, Yountville, Napa County (portions), Sonoma County (portions)); Outside TV Markets (Petaluma). Franchise award date: N.A. Franchise expiration date: N.A. Began: N.A.
Channel capacity: 75 (operating 2-way). Channels available but not in use: None.

Basic Service
Subscribers: N.A. Included in San Francisco
Programming (received off-air): KBCW (CW) San Francisco; KCNS (IND) San Francisco; KDTV-TV (UNV) San Francisco; KFSF-DT (TEL) Vallejo; KFTY (IND) Santa Rosa; KGO-TV (ABC) San Francisco; KICU-TV (IND) San Jose; KKPX-TV (ION) San Jose; KMTP-TV (ETV) San Francisco; KNTV (NBC) San Jose; KOFY-TV (IND) San Francisco; KPIX-TV (CBS) San Francisco; KQED (PBS) San Francisco; KRCB (PBS) Cotati; KRON-TV (MNT) San Francisco; KSTS (TMO) San Jose; KTEH (PBS) San Jose; KTLN-TV (IND) Novato; KTNC-TV (IND) Concord; KTSF (IND) San Francisco; KTVU (FOX) Oakland; 20 FMs.
Programming (via satellite): America's Store; C-SPAN; C-SPAN 2; Discovery Channel; Home Shopping Network 2; QVC; ShopNBC; TV Guide Network.
Fee: $43.99 installation; $17.65 monthly.

Expanded Basic Service 1
Subscribers: 76,250.
Programming (via satellite): ABC Family Channel; AMC; Animal Planet; Arts & Entertainment; BET Networks; Bravo; Cartoon Network; CNBC; CNN; Comcast Sports Net Bay Area; Comedy Central; Country Music TV; Disney Channel; E! Entertainment Television; ESPN; ESPN 2; Food Network; Fox News Channel; FX; GalaVision; Golf Channel; Hallmark Channel; Headline News; HGTV; History Channel; Lifetime; MSNBC; MTV; Nickelodeon; Oxygen; Spike TV; TBS Superstation; The Learning Channel; Travel Channel; truTV; Turner Network TV; TV Land; USA Network; Versus; VH1; Weather Channel.
Fee: $34.85 monthly.

Digital Basic Service
Subscribers: N.A.
Programming (via satellite): AmericanLife TV Network; BBC America; Bio; Black Family Channel; Bloomberg Television; Canales N; CCTV-4; Discovery Digital Networks; DragonTV; ESPN Classic Sports; ESPNews; Eternal Word TV Network; Filipino Channel; FitTV; Fox College Sports Atlantic; Fox College Sports Central; Fox College Sports Pacific; Fox Movie Channel; Fox Sports World; Fuse; G4; GAS; Great American Country; GSN; Halogen Network; History Channel International; Independent Film Channel; International Television (ITV); Lifetime Movie Network; Lime; MTV Networks Digital Suite; Music Choice; National Geographic Channel; Nick Jr.; NickToons TV; Outdoor Channel; Ovation; RAI International; Russian Television Network; Speed Channel; Style Network; Sundance Channel; Syfy; The Word Network; Toon Disney; Trinity Broadcasting Network; Turner Classic Movies; TV5, La Television International; WE tv; Weatherscan; Zhong Tian Channel.
Fee: $11.95 monthly.

Digital Pay Service 1
Pay Units: 4,100.
Programming (via satellite): Cinemax (multiplexed); Encore (multiplexed); Flix; HBO (multiplexed); Showtime (multiplexed); Starz (multiplexed); The Movie Channel (multiplexed).
Fee: $17.00 monthly (each).

Video-On-Demand: Yes

Pay-Per-View
iN DEMAND (delivered digitally); Barker (delivered digitally); Urban Xtra (delivered digitally); Fresh (delivered digitally); Shorteez (delivered digitally); Playboy TV (delivered digitally); ESPN Now (delivered digitally); Sports PPV (delivered digitally).

Internet Service
Operational: Yes.
Broadband Service: Comcast High Speed Internet.
Fee: $42.95 monthly.

Telephone Service
Digital: Operational
Fee: $44.95 monthly

Miles of Plant: 4,081.0 (coaxial); None (fiber optic). Homes passed: 404,247.
Area Vice President: Paul Gibson. Vice President, Communications: Andrew Johnson. Technical Operations Director: John

Portelli. Sales & Marketing Director: Susan Blum.
Ownership: Comcast Cable Communications Inc. (MSO).

NEEDLES—CalNeva Broadband, 1032 E Broadway St, Needles, CA 92363. Phone: 760-326-2030. Also serves Mohave Valley. ICA: CA0222.
TV Market Ranking: Below 100 (Mohave Valley, NEEDLES). Franchise award date: N.A. Franchise expiration date: N.A. Began: December 1, 1982.
Channel capacity: 54 (operating 2-way). Channels available but not in use: 19.
Basic Service
Subscribers: 768.
Programming (received off-air): KAET (PBS) Phoenix; KAZT-TV (IND) Phoenix; KNXV-TV (ABC) Phoenix; KSNV-DT (NBC) Las Vegas; KUTP (MNT) Phoenix; KVVU-TV (FOX) Henderson.
Programming (via satellite): Animal Planet; Arts & Entertainment; Cartoon Network; CNN; Country Music TV; C-SPAN; C-SPAN 2; Discovery Channel; Disney Channel; ESPN; ESPN 2; Great American Country; Headline News; History Channel; Home Shopping Network; KTLA (CW) Los Angeles; Lifetime; Lifetime Movie Network; MTV; Nickelodeon; Spike TV; Syfy; TBS Superstation; The Learning Channel; Trinity Broadcasting Network; Turner Classic Movies; Turner Network TV; TV Guide Network; TV Land; Univision; USA Network; VH1; Weather Channel; WGN America.
Programming (via translator): KPHO-TV (CBS) Phoenix; KPNX (NBC) Mesa; KSAZ-TV (FOX) Phoenix; KTVK (IND) Phoenix.
Fee: $29.95 installation; $39.81 monthly; $19.00 additional installation.
Pay Service 1
Pay Units: 309.
Programming (via satellite): Cinemax; HBO; Showtime.
Fee: $10.45 monthly (each).
Video-On-Demand: No
Internet Service
Operational: Yes.
Broadband Service: Rapid High Speed Internet.
Fee: $29.95 installation; $24.95 monthly.
Telephone Service
None
Miles of Plant: 32.0 (coaxial); None (fiber optic). Additional miles planned: 5.0 (coaxial). Homes passed: 1,900. Total homes in franchised area: 3,100.
Manager: Tom Gelardi.
City fee: 3% of gross.
Ownership: CalNeva Broadband LLC (MSO).

NEW CUYAMA—Formerly served by Wave Broadband. No longer in operation. ICA: CA0290.

NEWARK—Comcast Cable. Now served by OAKLAND, CA [CA0018]. ICA: CA0154.

NEWMAN—Comcast Cable, 2441 N Grove Industrial Dr, Fresno, CA 93727-1535. Phones: 559-253-4050; 800-266-2278. Fax: 559-253-4090. Web Site: http://www.comcast.com. Also serves Crow's Landing, Gustine, Los Banos, Patterson & Stanislaus County (portions). ICA: CA0178.
TV Market Ranking: 25 (Crow's Landing, Gustine, Los Banos, NEWMAN, Patterson, Stanislaus County (portions)). Franchise award date: N.A. Franchise expiration date: N.A. Began: N.A.
Channel capacity: N.A. Channels available but not in use: N.A.
Basic Service
Subscribers: 5,000.
Programming (received off-air): KAIL (MNT) Fresno; KFRE-TV (CW) Sanger; KFSN-TV (ABC) Fresno; KFTV-DT (UNV) Hanford; KMAX-TV (CW) Sacramento; KMPH-TV (FOX) Visalia; KNSO (TMO) Merced; KQED (PBS) San Francisco; KSEE (NBC) Fresno; KTXL (FOX) Sacramento.
Programming (via satellite): ABC Family Channel; Arts & Entertainment; CNN; C-SPAN; Discovery Channel; Headline News; Lifetime; MTV; Nickelodeon; QVC; TBS Superstation; Turner Network TV.
Fee: $43.99 installation; $16.00 monthly.
Expanded Basic Service 1
Subscribers: 4,221.
Programming (via satellite): AMC; Animal Planet; Arts & Entertainment; Bravo; Cartoon Network; CMT Pure Country; Comcast Sports Net Bay Area; Comedy Central; Disney Channel; E! Entertainment Television; ESPN; ESPN 2; Food Network; Fox News Channel; FX; GalaVision; Golf Channel; GSN; Hallmark Channel; HGTV; Home Shopping Network; ShopNBC; Spike TV; Syfy; TBS Superstation; The Learning Channel; Turner Network TV; TV Land; USA Network; Versus.
Fee: $51.50 monthly.
Digital Basic Service
Subscribers: 1,625.
Programming (via satellite): American-Life TV Network; BBC America; Bio; Black Family Channel; Bloomberg Television; Bravo; Canales N; Discovery Digital Networks; DMX Music; ESPN 2; ESPN Classic Sports; ESPN Now; ESPNews; Fox College Sports Atlantic; Fox College Sports Central; Fox College Sports Pacific; Fox Movie Channel; Fox Sports World; Fuse; G4; GAS; Golf Channel; Great American Country; GSN; Halogen Network; HGTV; History Channel; History Channel International; Independent Film Channel; Lifetime Movie Network; MTV Networks Digital Suite; National Geographic Channel; Nick Jr.; NickToons TV; Outdoor Channel; Ovation; PBS Kids Sprout; ShopNBC; Speed Channel; Style Network; Sundance Channel; Syfy; The Word Network; Toon Disney; Trinity Broadcasting Network; Turner Classic Movies; TV Land; TV One; Versus; WE tv.
Fee: $11.95 monthly.
Digital Pay Service 1
Pay Units: 2,915.
Programming (via satellite): Cinemax (multiplexed); Encore (multiplexed); Flix; HBO (multiplexed); Showtime (multiplexed); Starz (multiplexed); The Movie Channel (multiplexed).
Fee: $17.99 monthly (Cinemax, Starz, or TMC), $18.99 monthly (HBO or Showtime).
Video-On-Demand: Yes
Pay-Per-View
Addressable homes: 1,625.
iN DEMAND (delivered digitally), Addressable: Yes; Urban Xtra (delivered digitally); Fresh (delivered digitally); Shorteez (delivered digitally); Playboy TV (delivered digitally); Hot Choice (delivered digitally); Sports PPV (delivered digitally).
Internet Service
Operational: Yes.
Subscribers: 900.
Broadband Service: Comcast High Speed Internet.
Fee: $42.95 monthly; $3.00 modem lease.
Telephone Service
Digital: Planned
Fee: $39.95 monthly
Miles of Plant: 83.0 (coaxial); None (fiber optic). Homes passed: 7,000. Total homes in franchised area: 7,000.
General Manager: Len Falter. Marketing Director: Stewart Butler. Communications Director: Erica Smith.
Ownership: Comcast Cable Communications Inc. (MSO).

NEWPORT BEACH—Formerly served by Adelphia Communications. Now served by ANAHEIM, CA [CA0033]. ICA: CA0115.

NORTH EDWARDS—Charter Communications, 7337 Central Ave, Riverside, CA 92504. Phone: 951-343-5100. Fax: 951-354-5942. Web Site: http://www.charter.com. ICA: CA0404.
TV Market Ranking: Outside TV Markets (NORTH EDWARDS). Franchise award date: N.A. Franchise expiration date: N.A. Began: N.A.
Channel capacity: N.A. Channels available but not in use: N.A.
Basic Service
Subscribers: 212.
Programming (received off-air): KABC-TV (ABC) Los Angeles; KBAK-TV (CBS) Bakersfield; KCAL-TV (IND) Los Angeles; KCBS-TV (CBS) Los Angeles; KCET (PBS) Los Angeles; KCOP-TV (MNT) Los Angeles; KERO-TV (ABC) Bakersfield; KHIZ (IND) Barstow; KNBC (NBC) Los Angeles; KTBN-TV (TBN) Santa Ana; KTLA (CW) Los Angeles; KTTV (FOX) Los Angeles; KVMD (IND) Twentynine Palms.
Programming (via satellite): California Channel; Comedy Central; C-SPAN; GalaVision; Home Shopping Network; QVC; TV Guide Network; Weather Channel; WGN America.
Current originations: Government Access.
Fee: $29.99 installation.
Expanded Basic Service 1
Subscribers: 207.
Programming (via satellite): ABC Family Channel; AMC; Arts & Entertainment; BET Networks; Bravo; Cartoon Network; CNBC; CNN; Country Music TV; Discovery Channel; Disney Channel; E! Entertainment Television; ESPN; ESPN 2; Food Network; Fox News Channel; Fox Sports Net West; Fox Sports Net West 2; Headline News; HGTV; History Channel; Lifetime; MTV; MTV2; Nickelodeon; Outdoor Channel; Oxygen; Spike TV; Syfy; TBS Superstation; The Learning Channel; Turner Network TV; TV One; Univision; USA Network; VH1.
Fee: $45.45 monthly.
Digital Basic Service
Subscribers: N.A.
Programming (via satellite): Bandamax; BBC America; Bio; Bloomberg Television; Canales N; CMT Pure Country; C-SPAN 3; Discovery Digital Networks; Do-It-Yourself; ESPN Classic Sports; ESPNews; FitTV; Fox College Sports Atlantic; Fox College Sports Central; Fox College Sports Pacific; Fuse; G4; GAS; Gol TV; GSN; Hallmark Channel; History Channel International; Independent Film Channel; Lifetime Movie Network; Lifetime Real Women; Military History Channel; MTV Networks Digital Suite; National Geographic Channel; Nick Jr.; Nick Too; Pentagon Channel; SoapNet; Sundance Channel; Toon Disney; TV Land; Versus; WE tv.
Digital Pay Service 1
Pay Units: N.A.
Programming (via satellite): Cinemax (multiplexed); Encore (multiplexed); Flix; Fox Movie Channel; HBO (multiplexed); Showtime (multiplexed); Starz (multiplexed); The Movie Channel (multiplexed).
Video-On-Demand: No
Pay-Per-View
iN DEMAND (delivered digitally); Playboy TV (delivered digitally); Fresh (delivered digitally); Club Jenna (delivered digitally); Fresh! (delivered digitally).
Internet Service
Operational: Yes.
Fee: $39.99 monthly.
Telephone Service
None
Miles of Plant: 7.0 (coaxial); None (fiber optic). Homes passed: 235.
Vice President & General Manager: Fred Lutz. Technical Operations Manager: George Noel. Marketing Director: Chris Bailey.
Ownership: Charter Communications Inc. (MSO).

NORTH FORK—Ponderosa Cablevision, PO Box 21, 47671 Rd 200, O'Neals, CA 93645. Phones: 800-682-1878; 559-868-6000. E-mail: customercare@goponderosa.com. Web Site: http://www.goponderosa.com. ICA: CA0469.
TV Market Ranking: 72 (NORTH FORK).
Channel capacity: N.A. Channels available but not in use: N.A.
Basic Service
Subscribers: 403.
Programming (received off-air): KAIL (MNT) Fresno; KFRE-TV (CW) Sanger; KFSN-TV (ABC) Fresno; KFTV-DT (UNV) Hanford; KJEO-LD Fresno; KMPH-TV (FOX) Visalia; KSEE (NBC) Fresno; KTFF-DT (TEL) Porterville; KVPT (PBS) Fresno.
Programming (via satellite): ABC Family Channel; AMC; Animal Planet; Arts & Entertainment; CNBC; CNN; Comedy Central; Country Music TV; C-SPAN; Discovery Channel; Disney Channel; ESPN; ESPN 2; ESPN Classic Sports; Food Network; Fox News Channel; Hallmark Channel; Headline News; HGTV; History Channel; MSNBC; MTV; Nickelodeon; Outdoor Channel; QVC; Spike TV; Syfy; TBS Superstation; The Learning Channel; Travel Channel; Trinity Broadcasting Network; Turner Classic Movies; Turner Network TV; TV Land; USA Network; VH1.
Fee: $30.00 installation; $30.95 monthly.
Pay Service 1
Pay Units: 66.
Programming (via satellite): HBO.
Fee: $10.00 installation; $10.95 monthly.
Pay Service 2
Pay Units: 23.
Programming (via satellite): Showtime.
Fee: $10.00 installation; $9.95 monthly.
Pay Service 3
Pay Units: 20.
Programming (via satellite): Cinemax.
Fee: $10.00 installation; $9.95 monthly.
Internet Service
Operational: No, DSL & dialup.
Telephone Service
None
Homes passed: 800.
General Manager: Matt Boos. Technical Supervisor: Doug Wickham. Marketing Manager: Cheryl Frank.
Ownership: Ponderosa Cablevision.

NORTHSTAR—Charter Communications, 9335 Prototype Dr, Reno, NV 89521. Phone: 775-850-1200. Fax: 775-850-1279. Web

Site: http://www.charter.com. Also serves Agate Bay, Brockway, Carnelian Bay, Cedar Flat, Kings Beach, Placer County (eastern portion), Tahoe City & Tahoe Vista, CA; Incline Village & Washoe County (southern portion), NV. ICA: CA0246.

TV Market Ranking: Below 100 (Agate Bay, Brockway, Carnelian Bay, Cedar Flat, Incline Village, Kings Beach, NORTHSTAR, Placer County (portions), Tahoe City, Tahoe Vista, Washoe County (portions)); Outside TV Markets (Placer County (portions), Washoe County (portions)). Franchise award date: N.A. Franchise expiration date: N.A. Began: January 1, 1963.

Channel capacity: 29 (not 2-way capable). Channels available but not in use: None.

Basic Service

Subscribers: N.A. Included in Reno NV

Programming (received off-air): KNPB (PBS) Reno; KOLO-TV (ABC) Reno; KREN-TV (CW, UNV) Reno; KRNS-CA (IND) Reno; KRNV-DT (ABC) Reno; KRXI-TV (FOX) Reno; 10 FMs.

Programming (via microwave): KCRA-TV (NBC) Sacramento; KGO-TV (ABC) San Francisco; KTVN (CBS) Reno.

Programming (via satellite): C-SPAN; Discovery Channel; FX; QVC; TV Guide Network; Weather Channel.

Fee: $60.00 installation; $15.20 monthly.

Expanded Basic Service 1

Subscribers: 1,063.

Programming (via satellite): ABC Family Channel; AMC; Animal Planet; Arts & Entertainment; Cartoon Network; CNBC; CNN; Comcast Sports Net Bay Area; Disney Channel; E! Entertainment Television; ESPN; Fox News Channel; Headline News; Home Shopping Network; Lifetime; MTV; Nickelodeon; Spike TV; Turner Network TV; USA Network.

Fee: $22.89 monthly.

Digital Basic Service

Subscribers: N.A.

Programming (via satellite): BBC America; Bravo; CMT Pure Country; Discovery Digital Networks; DMX Music; ESPN 2; ESPN Classic Sports; ESPNews; Fox Soccer; Golf Channel; GSN; HGTV; History Channel; Independent Film Channel; National Geographic Channel; Nick Jr.; Speed Channel; Syfy; Turner Classic Movies; TV Land; Versus; VH1 Classic; WE tv.

Fee: $11.00 monthly.

Digital Pay Service 1

Pay Units: N.A.

Programming (via satellite): Cinemax (multiplexed); Encore (multiplexed); HBO (multiplexed); Showtime (multiplexed); Starz (multiplexed); The Movie Channel (multiplexed).

Video-On-Demand: No

Pay-Per-View

movies & events (delivered digitally); Playboy TV (delivered digitally); Hot Choice (delivered digitally).

Internet Service

Operational: No.

Telephone Service

None

Miles of Plant: 17.0 (coaxial); None (fiber optic). Homes passed: 1,122. Total homes in franchised area: 1,122.

Vice President & General Manager: Manny Martinez. Technical Operations Manager: Carol Eure.

City fee: 3% of gross (California only).

Ownership: Charter Communications Inc. (MSO).

NOVATO—Comcast Cable. Now served by NAPA/SONOMA, CA [CA0038]. ICA: CA0118.

NOVATO—Horizon Cable TV Inc., 520 Mesa Rd, Point Reyes Station, CA 94956. Phones: 888-663-9610; 415-663-9610. Fax: 415-663-9608. E-mail: info@horizoncable.com. Web Site: http://www.horizoncable.com. ICA: CA0239.

TV Market Ranking: 7 (NOVATO). Franchise award date: N.A. Franchise expiration date: N.A. Began: January 1, 1968.

Channel capacity: 81 (operating 2-way). Channels available but not in use: N.A.

Basic Service

Subscribers: 357.

Programming (received off-air): KBCW (CW) San Francisco; KCNS (IND) San Francisco; KDTV-TV (UNV) San Francisco; KFTY (IND) Santa Rosa; KGO-TV (ABC) San Francisco; KICU-TV (IND) San Jose; KKPX-TV (ION) San Jose; KNTV (NBC) San Jose; KOFY-TV (IND) San Francisco; KPIX-TV (CBS) San Francisco; KQED (PBS) San Francisco; KRCB (PBS) Cotati; KRON-TV (MNT) San Francisco; KSTS (TMO) San Jose; KTEH (PBS) San Jose; KTLN-TV (IND) Novato; KTNC-TV (IND) Concord; KTSF (IND) San Francisco; KTVU (FOX) Oakland.

Programming (via satellite): ABC Family Channel; AMC; Animal Planet; Arts & Entertainment; Bloomberg Television; Bravo; California Channel; CNBC; CNN; Comcast Sports Net Bay Area; Comedy Central; C-SPAN; C-SPAN 2; Discovery Channel; Disney Channel; E! Entertainment Television; ESPN; ESPN 2; Food Network; Fox News Channel; FX; G4; Hallmark Channel; Headline News; HGTV; History Channel; Lifetime; MSNBC; MTV; Nickelodeon; QVC; Spike TV; Syfy; TBS Superstation; The Learning Channel; Toon Disney; Travel Channel; truTV; Turner Network TV; USA Network; VH1; Weather Channel.

Current originations: Government Access; Educational Access; Public Access.

Fee: $39.95 installation; $38.45 monthly; $49.95 additional installation.

Digital Basic Service

Subscribers: 79.

Programming (via satellite): American-Life TV Network; BBC America; Bio; Black Family Channel; Discovery Digital Networks; DMX Music; ESPN Classic Sports; Fox Sports World; GAS; GSN; Halogen Network; History Channel International; MTV2; National Geographic Channel; Nick Jr.; ShopNBC; Trinity Broadcasting Network; Turner Classic Movies; Versus; VH1 Classic.

Fee: $12.95 monthly; $9.95 converter.

Digital Expanded Basic Service

Subscribers: N.A.

Programming (via satellite): ESPNews; FitTV; Fox College Sports Atlantic; Fox College Sports Central; Fox College Sports Pacific; Fox Movie Channel; Golf Channel; Great American Country; Independent Film Channel; Lifetime Movie Network; Lime; MTV Networks Digital Suite; Outdoor Channel; Ovation; Speed Channel; Style Network; Sundance Channel; WE tv.

Fee: $5.00 monthly.

Pay Service 1

Pay Units: N.A.

Programming (via satellite): Encore; HBO (multiplexed); Showtime; Starz; Sundance Channel; The Movie Channel.

Fee: $10.00 installation; $8.95 monthly (Cinemax), $10.95 monthly (Showtime, Sundance & TMC), $12.95 monthly (HBO).

Digital Pay Service 1

Pay Units: N.A.

Programming (via satellite): Cinemax (multiplexed); Encore (multiplexed); Flix; HBO (multiplexed); Showtime (multiplexed); Starz (multiplexed); Sundance Channel; The Movie Channel (multiplexed).

Fee: $9.95 monthly (Encore & Starz), $10.95 monthly (Cinemax), $12.95 monthly (HBO or Showtime & TMC).

Video-On-Demand: No

Pay-Per-View

ESPN Extra (delivered digitally); ESPN Now (delivered digitally); Hot Choice (delivered digitally); Playboy TV (delivered digitally); Fresh (delivered digitally); Shorteez (delivered digitally); Sports PPV (delivered digitally); movies (delivered digitally).

Internet Service

Operational: Yes.

Subscribers: 182.

Broadband Service: ISP Alliance.

Fee: $89.95 installation; $35.95 monthly; $5.00 modem lease; $119.00 modem purchase.

Telephone Service

None

Miles of Plant: 15.0 (coaxial); None (fiber optic). Homes passed: 798.

Manager & Program Director: Susan Daniel. Chief Engineer: Kevin Daniel. Marketing Director & Customer Service Manager: Andrea Clark.

Ownership: Horizon Cable TV Inc. (MSO).

OAKHURST—Northland Cable Television, 40108 Hwy 49, Ste A, Oakhurst, CA 93644-8826. Phones: 800-736-1414; 559-683-7388. Fax: 559-642-2432. E-mail: oakhurst@northlandcabletv.com. Web Site: http://www.northlandcabletv.com. Also serves Ahwahnee, Bass Lake & Cedar Valley. ICA: CA0364.

TV Market Ranking: 72 (Ahwahnee, Bass Lake, Cedar Valley, OAKHURST). Franchise award date: N.A. Franchise expiration date: N.A. Began: March 1, 1963.

Channel capacity: 52 (not 2-way capable). Channels available but not in use: 2.

Basic Service

Subscribers: 2,185.

Programming (received off-air): KAIL (MNT) Fresno; KFRE-TV (CW) Sanger; KFSN-TV (ABC) Fresno; KFTV-DT (UNV) Hanford; KGPE (CBS) Fresno; KNSO (TMO) Merced; KSEE (NBC) Fresno; KVPT (PBS) Fresno; 13 FMs.

Programming (via microwave): KMPH-TV (FOX) Visalia.

Programming (via satellite): Arts & Entertainment; CNBC; CNN; C-SPAN; Discovery Channel; ESPN; Fox News Channel; Hallmark Channel; Headline News; QVC; TBS Superstation; The Learning Channel; Travel Channel; Trinity Broadcasting Network; Turner Network TV; TV Guide Network; USA Network; Weather Channel.

Current originations: Leased Access; Public Access.

Fee: $75.00 installation; $35.00 monthly.

Expanded Basic Service 1

Subscribers: N.A.

Programming (via satellite): Animal Planet; Bravo; Cartoon Network; Comcast Sports Net Bay Area; Comedy Central; E! Entertainment Television; ESPN 2; Food Network; Fox Movie Channel; Golf Channel; Great American Country; HGTV; History Channel; Lifetime; NFL Network; Nickelodeon; Spike TV; Syfy; Turner Classic Movies; TV Land.

Fee: $43.29 monthly.

Digital Basic Service

Subscribers: N.A.

Programming (via satellite): BBC America; Bloomberg Television; Discovery Health Channel; Discovery Kids Channel; Discovery Military Channel; Discovery Planet Green; DMX Music; ESPNews; FitTV; Fox Soccer; ID Investigation Discovery; Independent Film Channel; Lifetime Movie Network; Science Channel; Speed Channel; WE tv.

Fee: $40.69 monthly.

Pay Service 1

Pay Units: 458.

Programming (via satellite): HBO.

Fee: $15.00 installation; $11.95 monthly.

Digital Pay Service 1

Pay Units: N.A.

Programming (via satellite): Cinemax (multiplexed); Encore (multiplexed); Flix; HBO (multiplexed); Showtime (multiplexed); Starz (multiplexed); Sundance Channel; The Movie Channel (multiplexed).

Fee: $14.75 monthly (HBO, Cinemax, Starz/Encore or Showtime/TMC/Flix.

Video-On-Demand: No

Pay-Per-View

iN DEMAND (delivered digitally); Playboy TV (delivered digitally); Fresh (delivered digitally).

Internet Service

Operational: Yes.

Fee: $44.99 monthly.

Telephone Service

None

Miles of Plant: 106.0 (coaxial); None (fiber optic). Homes passed: 4,387. Total homes in franchised area: 4,387.

Manager: Ken Musgrove. Office Manager: Karen Bradley. Chief Technician: Roger Conroy.

Ownership: Northland Communications Corp. (MSO).

OAKLAND—Comcast Cable, 2900 Technology Ct, Richmond, CA 94806-1952. Phones: 925-973-7000 (San Ramon regional office); 510-243-3000. Web Site: http://www.comcast.com. Also serves Alameda, Alameda County (unincorporated areas), Albany, Berkeley, Contra Costa County (portions), Crockett, El Cerrito, El Sobrante, Emeryville, Fremont, Hayward, Hercules, Kensington, Newark, Piedmont, Pinole, Porta Costa, Richmond, Rodeo, San Leandro, San Lorenzo, San Pablo, Treasure Island Naval Station & Union City. ICA: CA0018.

TV Market Ranking: 7 (Alameda, Alameda County (unincorporated areas), Albany, Berkeley, Contra Costa County (portions), Crockett, El Cerrito, El Sobrante, Emeryville, Fremont, Hayward, Hercules, Kensington, Newark, OAKLAND, Piedmont, Pinole, Porta Costa, Richmond, Rodeo, San Leandro, San Lorenzo, San Pablo, Treasure Island Naval Station, Union City). Franchise award date: January 1, 1969. Franchise expiration date: N.A. Began: January 1, 1970.

Channel capacity: 70 (operating 2-way). Channels available but not in use: None.

Basic Service

Subscribers: N.A. Included in San Francisco

Programming (received off-air): KBCW (CW) San Francisco; KCNS (IND) San Francisco; KCSM-TV (PBS) San Mateo; KFSF-DT (TEL) Vallejo; KGO-TV (ABC) San Francisco; KICU-TV (IND) San Jose; KKPX-TV (ION) San Jose; KNTV (NBC) San Jose; KOFY-TV (IND) San Francisco; KPIX-TV (CBS) San Francisco; KQED (PBS) San Francisco; KRON-TV (MNT) San Francisco; KSTS (TMO) San Jose; KTEH (PBS) San Jose; KTLN-TV (IND) Novato; KTNC-TV (IND) Concord; KTSF (IND) San Francisco; KTVU (FOX) Oakland.

Programming (via satellite): C-SPAN; C-SPAN 2; Discovery Channel; QVC; TBS Superstation; TV Guide Network; Weather Channel.

Current originations: Leased Access; Religious Access; Government Access; Educational Access; Public Access.

Fee: $43.99 installation; $13.90 monthly; $1.60 converter.

Expanded Basic Service 1

Subscribers: N.A.

Programming (via satellite): ABC Family Channel; AMC; Animal Planet; Arts & Entertainment; BET Networks; Bravo; Cartoon Network; CNBC; CNN; Comcast Sports Net Bay Area; Comedy Central; Disney Channel; ESPN; Food Network; Fox News Channel; Headline News; History Channel; Lifetime; MTV; Nickelodeon; Syfy; The Learning Channel; truTV; Turner Network TV; USA Network; VH1.

Fee: $35.35 monthly.

Digital Basic Service

Subscribers: 195,076.

Programming (via satellite): BBC America; Canadian Learning Television; Discovery Digital Networks; Encore Action; ESPN 2; ESPN Classic Sports; ESPNews; Fox Sports World; G4; Golf Channel; GSN; HGTV; Independent Film Channel; MTV Hits; Music Choice; Nick Jr.; Ovation; Star India Gold; Star India News; Star India Plus; Star One; Sundance Channel; Turner Classic Movies; TV Land; VH1 Soul; Vijay; WE tv.

Fee: $15.20 monthly.

Digital Pay Service 1

Pay Units: N.A.

Programming (via satellite): Cinemax (multiplexed); HBO (multiplexed); Showtime (multiplexed); Starz (multiplexed); The Movie Channel (multiplexed).

Fee: $17.00 monthly (each).

Video-On-Demand: Yes

Pay-Per-View

Addressable homes: 53,103.

iN DEMAND (delivered digitally), Addressable: Yes; Shorteez (delivered digitally); Playboy TV (delivered digitally).

Internet Service

Operational: Yes.

Subscribers: 69,860.

Broadband Service: Comcast High Speed Internet.

Fee: $42.95 monthly.

Telephone Service

Digital: Operational

Subscribers: 18,238.

Fee: $44.95 monthly

Miles of Plant: 800.0 (coaxial); 52.0 (fiber optic). Homes passed: 575,927.

Area Vice President: Hank Fore. Vice President, Communications: Andrew Johnson. Technical Operations Director: Kevin Perry. Marketing Director: Bill Rivas.

City fee: 5% of gross.

Ownership: Comcast Cable Communications Inc. (MSO).

OCOTILLO—Cable USA, PO Box 336, 2455 Stirrup Rd, Borrego Springs, CA 92004-0336. Phones: 308-236-1512 (Kearney, NE corporate office); 800-300-6989; 760-767-5607. Fax: 760-767-3609. Web Site: http://www.cableusa.com. ICA: CA0297.

TV Market Ranking: Below 100 (OCOTILLO). Franchise award date: May 31, 1988. Franchise expiration date: N.A. Began: February 1, 1988.

Channel capacity: N.A. Channels available but not in use: N.A.

Basic Service

Subscribers: 42.

Programming (received off-air): KECY-TV (ABC, FOX, MNT, TMO) El Centro; KPBS (PBS) San Diego.

Programming (via satellite): AMC; Arts & Entertainment; CNN; Discovery Channel; ESPN; KSWT (CBS, CW) Yuma; KYMA-DT (NBC) Yuma; Lifetime; Spike TV; TBS Superstation; USA Network.

Fee: $24.95 installation; $26.00 monthly.

Pay Service 1

Pay Units: N.A.

Programming (via satellite): The Movie Channel.

Video-On-Demand: No

Internet Service

Operational: No.

Telephone Service

None

Miles of Plant: 10.0 (coaxial); None (fiber optic). Homes passed: 100. Total homes in franchised area: 150.

Manager & Chief Technician: Joe Gustafson.

County fee: 3% of basic.

Ownership: USA Companies (MSO).

OJAI—Formerly served by Adelphia Communications. Now served by CHATSWORTH, CA [CA0013]. ICA: CA0440.

OLINDA—Formerly served by Almega Cable. No longer in operation. ICA: CA0455.

ONTARIO—Time Warner Cable. Now served by ANAHEIM, CA [CA0033]. ICA: CA0010.

ORANGE COUNTY—Cox Communications, 29947 Avenida De Las Banderas, Rancho Santa Margarita, CA 92688-2113. Phones: 949-240-1212 (Customer service); 949-546-2000 (Administrative office). Fax: 949-546-3514. Web Site: http://www.cox.com/oc. Also serves Aliso Viejo, Dana Point, Irvine, Ladera Ranch, Laguna Beach, Laguna Hills, Laguna Niguel, Lake Forest, Los Angeles County (portions), Mission Viejo, Newport Beach, Palos Verdes Estates, Palos Verdes Peninsula, Rancho Santa Margarita, Ranchos Palos Verdes, Rolling Hills, Rolling Hills Estates, San Clemente, San Juan Capistrano, San Pedro & Tustin. ICA: CA0015.

TV Market Ranking: 2 (Aliso Viejo, Dana Point, Irvine, Ladera Ranch, Laguna Beach, Laguna Hills, Laguna Niguel, Lake Forest, Los Angeles County (portions) (portions), Mission Viejo, Newport Beach, ORANGE COUNTY, Palos Verdes Estates, Palos Verdes Peninsula, Rancho Santa Margarita, Ranchos Palos Verdes, Rolling Hills, Rolling Hills Estates, San Clemente, San Juan Capistrano, San Pedro, Tustin (portions)); Below 100 (Los Angeles County (portions) (portions)); Outside TV Markets (Los Angeles County (portions) (portions)). Franchise award date: N.A. Franchise expiration date: N.A. Began: N.A.

Channel capacity: 110 (operating 2-way). Channels available but not in use: 41.

Basic Service

Subscribers: 280,000.

Programming (received off-air): KABC-TV (ABC) Los Angeles; KCBS-TV (CBS) Los Angeles; KCET (PBS) Los Angeles; KCOP-TV (MNT) Los Angeles; KDOC-TV (IND) Anaheim; KFTR-DT (TEL) Ontario; KLCS (PBS) Los Angeles; KMEX-DT (UNV) Los Angeles; KNBC (NBC) Los Angeles; KOCE-TV (PBS) Huntington Beach; KPXN-TV (ION) San Bernardino; KRCA (IND) Riverside; KSCI (IND) Long Beach; KTBN-TV (TBN) Santa Ana; KTLA (CW) Los Angeles; KTTV (FOX) Los Angeles; KVEA (TMO) Corona; KWHY-TV (IND) Los Angeles; KXLA (IND) Rancho Palos Verdes.

Programming (via satellite): California Channel; C-SPAN; C-SPAN 2; Home Shopping Network; QVC; TBS Superstation; TV Guide Network; WGN America.

Current originations: Leased Access; Government Access; Educational Access; Public Access.

Fee: $52.50 installation; $16.20 monthly; $7.10 converter.

Expanded Basic Service 1

Subscribers: 209,954.

Programming (via satellite): ABC Family Channel; AMC; Animal Planet; Arts & Entertainment; BET Networks; Bravo; Cartoon Network; CNBC; CNN; Comedy Central; Discovery Channel; Disney Channel; E! Entertainment Television; Encore Action; ESPN; ESPN 2; ESPN Classic Sports; Flix; Food Network; Fox News Channel; Fox Sports Net; Fox Sports Net West; FX; GalaVision; Hallmark Channel; Headline News; HGTV; History Channel; Independent Film Channel; Lifetime; MSNBC; MTV; Nickelodeon; Speed Channel; Spike TV; Sundance Channel; Syfy; The Learning Channel; Travel Channel; Turner Classic Movies; Turner Network TV; TV Land; USA Network; Versus; VH1; Weather Channel.

Fee: $44.99 monthly.

Digital Basic Service

Subscribers: 137,940.

Programming (via satellite): BBC America; Bio; Bloomberg Television; Discovery Digital Networks; DMX Music; Flix; Fox Sports World; G4; Golf Channel; GSN; History Channel International; Independent Film Channel; Lifetime Movie Network; MuchMusic Network; Ovation; Sundance Channel; Toon Disney; Weatherscan.

Fee: $13.50 monthly.

Pay Service 1

Pay Units: 16,799.

Programming (via satellite): Cinemax.

Fee: $20.00 installation; $9.95 monthly.

Pay Service 2

Pay Units: 38,837.

Programming (via satellite): HBO.

Fee: $20.00 installation; $9.95 monthly.

Pay Service 3

Pay Units: 28,360.

Programming (via satellite): Showtime.

Fee: $20.00 installation; $9.95 monthly.

Digital Pay Service 1

Pay Units: N.A.

Programming (via satellite): Cinemax (multiplexed); Encore (multiplexed); HBO (multiplexed); Showtime (multiplexed); Starz (multiplexed); The Movie Channel (multiplexed).

Fee: $9.95 monthly (each).

Video-On-Demand: Yes

Pay-Per-View

Addressable homes: 137,940.

Hot Choice, Fee: $4.95, Addressable: Yes; iN DEMAND (delivered digitally); Playboy TV (delivered digitally); Fresh (delivered digitally); Shorteez (delivered digitally).

Internet Service

Operational: Yes.

Subscribers: 106,722.

Broadband Service: Cox High Speed Internet.

Fee: $99.95 installation; $44.95 monthly; $15.00 modem lease; $79.00 modem purchase.

Telephone Service

Digital: Operational

Subscribers: 94,100.

Fee: $10.69 monthly

Miles of Plant: 2,790.0 (coaxial); 289.0 (fiber optic). Homes passed: 400,000. Total homes in franchised area: 318,698.

Vice President & General Manager: Duffy Leone. Vice President, Network Operations: Rick Guerrero. Marketing Director: Colleen Lagner. Communications Manager: Ayn Craciun.

City fee: 5% of gross.

Ownership: Cox Communications Inc. (MSO).

ORANGE COUNTY (western portion)—Time Warner Cable. Now served by ANAHEIM, CA [CA0033]. ICA: CA0071.

ORICK—Formerly served by Almega Cable. No longer in operation. ICA: CA0366.

OROVILLE—Comcast Cable. Now served by CHICO, CA [CA0066]. ICA: CA0077.

OXNARD—Time Warner Cable. Now served by CHATSWORTH, CA [CA0013]. ICA: CA0052.

PACIFICA—Comcast Cable. Now served by SAN FRANCISCO, CA [CA0003]. ICA: CA0116.

PALM DESERT—Time Warner Cable, 41725 Cook St, Palm Desert, CA 92211-5100. Phones: 858-695-3110 (San Diego office); 760-340-1312. Fax: 760-340-9764. Web Site: http://www.timewarnercable.com/desertcities. Also serves Bermuda Dunes, Cathedral City, Coachella, Desert Hot Springs, Indian Wells, Indio, La Quinta, Palm Springs, Palm Springs Oasis, Rancho Mirage, Riverside County (portions), Shadow Ridge Creek, Thousand Palms, Tri-Palm Estates & Western Village. ICA: CA0036.

TV Market Ranking: Below 100 (Bermuda Dunes, Cathedral City, Coachella, Desert Hot Springs, Indian Wells, Indio, La Quinta, PALM DESERT, Palm Springs, Palm Springs Oasis, Rancho Mirage, Riverside County (portions), Shadow Ridge Creek, Thousand Palms, Tri-Palm Estates, Western Village). Franchise award date: N.A. Franchise expiration date: N.A. Began: January 1, 1959.

Channel capacity: 206 (operating 2-way). Channels available but not in use: 27.

Basic Service

Subscribers: N.A. Included in San Diego

Programming (received off-air): KABC-TV (ABC) Los Angeles; KCWQ-LP Palm Springs; KDFX-CA Indio/Palm Springs; KESQ-TV (ABC, CW) Palm Springs; KEVC-CA Indio; KMIR-TV (NBC) Palm Springs; KPSP-LP (CBS) Cathedral City; KUNA-LP (TMO) Indio; KVCR-DT (PBS) San Bernardino; KVER-CA Indio; KYAV-LP Palm Springs; 11 FMs.

Programming (via microwave): KCAL-TV (IND) Los Angeles; KCET (PBS) Los Angeles; KNBC (NBC) Los Angeles.

Programming (via satellite): C-SPAN; C-SPAN 2; Eternal Word TV Network; ION Television; MyNetworkTV Inc.; QVC; ShopNBC; Trinity Broadcasting Network; TV Guide Network; WGN America.

Current originations: Leased Access; Religious Access.

Planned originations: Government Access; Educational Access; Public Access.

Fee: $36.00 installation; $10.99 monthly; $5.00 converter.

Expanded Basic Service 1

Subscribers: N.A.

Programming (via satellite): ABC Family Channel; AMC; Animal Planet; Arts & Entertainment; BET Networks; Bravo; Cartoon Network; CNBC; CNN; Comedy Central; Discovery Channel; Disney Channel; E! Entertainment Television; ESPN; ESPN 2; Food Network; Fox News Channel; Fox Sports en Espanol; Fox Sports Net West; FX; Golf Channel; Hallmark Channel; Headline News; HGTV; History Channel; Home Shopping Network; Lifetime; Lifetime Movie Network; MSNBC; MTV; Nickelodeon; Spike TV; Syfy; TBS Superstation; The Learning Channel; Travel Channel; truTV; Turner Classic Movies; Turner Network TV; TV Land; USA Network; Versus; VH1; WE tv; Weather Channel.

Digital Basic Service

Subscribers: N.A.

Programming (via satellite): Arts & Entertainment HD; BBC America; BBC America On Demand; Bio; Bloomberg Television; Boomerang; Boomerang en Espanol; California Channel; Canal Sur; CBS College Sports Network; Cine Latino; CNN en Espanol; CNN International; Cooking Channel; Country Music TV; C-SPAN 3; Current; Discovery en Espanol; Discovery HD Theater; Discovery Health Channel; Discovery Home Channel; Discovery Kids Channel; Discovery Military Channel; Do-It-Yourself; Encore (multiplexed); ESPN 2 HD; ESPN Classic Sports; ESPN Deportes; ESPN HD; ESPN U; ESPNews; EWTN en Espanol; Exercise TV; FitTV; Flix; Fox Business Channel; Fox College Sports Atlantic; Fox College Sports Central; Fox College Sports Pacific; Fox HD; Fox Movie Channel; Fox Reality Channel; Fox Soccer; Fox Sports en Espanol; Fuel TV; Fuse; GSN; Halogen Network; HDNet; History Channel HD; History Channel International; Howard TV; ID Investigation Discovery; Independent Film Channel; INSP; La Familia Network; Lifetime Real Women; LOGO; MTV Tres; MTV2; mun2 television; Music Choice; National Geographic Channel; National Geographic Channel HD Network; National Geographic Channel On Demand; NBA TV; Nick Jr.; NickToons TV; Ovation; Oxygen; Oxygen On Demand; Puma TV; Science Channel; Sleuth; SoapNet; Sorpresa; Style Network; Sundance Channel; TBS in HD; TeenNick; Tennis Channel; Toon Disney; Toon Disney en Espanol; Turner Network TV HD; TV Guide SPOT; Universal HD; Versus HD; VH1 Classic; Video Rola.

Fee: $29.60 monthly.

Digital Pay Service 1

Pay Units: 2,351.

Programming (via satellite): Cinemax (multiplexed); Cinemax On Demand; HBO HD; HDNet Movies; Showtime HD.

Fee: $12.00 monthly.

Digital Pay Service 2

Pay Units: 1,180.

Programming (via satellite): Starz (multiplexed).

Fee: $12.00 monthly.

Digital Pay Service 3

Pay Units: 4,387.

Programming (via satellite): HBO (multiplexed); HBO On Demand.

Fee: $12.00 monthly.

Digital Pay Service 4

Pay Units: 2,129.

Programming (via satellite): Showtime (multiplexed); Showtime On Demand; The Movie Channel (multiplexed); The Movie Channel On Demand.

Fee: $12.00 monthly.

Video-On-Demand: Yes

Pay-Per-View

Addressable homes: 9,781.

iN DEMAND, Addressable: Yes; Playboy TV (delivered digitally); Fresh (delivered digitally); Shorteez (delivered digitally); ESPN (delivered digitally).

Internet Service

Operational: Yes.

Broadband Service: Road Runner, EarthLink, AOL.

Fee: $50.00 installation; $44.95 monthly.

Telephone Service

Digital: Operational

Fee: $39.95 monthly

Miles of Plant: 2,610.0 (coaxial); 73.0 (fiber optic). Total homes in franchised area: 199,575. Homes passed included in San Diego. Miles of plant (coax & fiber) includes Banning

President: Bob Barlow. Vice President & General Manager: Tad Yo. Vice President, Customer Care: Vinit Ahooja. Technical Operations Director: Dessi Ocho. Marketing Director: Jimmy Kelly. Engineering Director: Mike Sagona. Public Affairs Director: Kathi Jacobs.

City fee: 5% of gross.

Ownership: Time Warner Cable (MSO).

PALMDALE—Time Warner Cable. Now served by CHATSWORTH, CA [CA0013]. ICA: CA0031.

PALO ALTO—Comcast Cable. Now served by SAN JOSE, CA [CA0004]. ICA: CA0055.

PALO CEDRO—New Day Broadband, PO Box 535, 9155 Deschutes Rd, #D, Palo Cedro, CA 96073-8714. Phone: 530-547-2226. Fax: 530-547-4948. Also serves Anderson, Bear Mountain, Bella Vista, Cottonwood, Jones Valley, Millville, Mountain Gate & Shasta County (portions). ICA: CA0172.

TV Market Ranking: Below 100 (Anderson, Bear Mountain, Bella Vista, Cottonwood, Jones Valley, Millville, Mountain Gate, PALO CEDRO, Shasta County (portions)). Franchise award date: April 6, 1982. Franchise expiration date: N.A. Began: October 15, 1982.

Channel capacity: 59 (not 2-way capable). Channels available but not in use: 10.

Basic Service

Subscribers: 2,982.

Programming (received off-air): KCVU (FOX) Paradise; KIXE-TV (PBS) Redding; KNVN (NBC) Chico; KRCR-TV (ABC) Redding.

Programming (via satellite): ABC Family Channel; Arts & Entertainment; CNN; Country Music TV; C-SPAN; Discovery Channel; Disney Channel; ESPN; Headline News; Lifetime; MTV; Nickelodeon; QVC; Spike TV; TBS Superstation; Turner Network TV; USA Network; Weather Channel; WGN America.

Fee: $15.00 installation; $36.75 monthly.

Pay Service 1

Pay Units: 93.

Programming (via satellite): Cinemax.

Fee: $11.50 monthly.

Pay Service 2

Pay Units: 303.

Programming (via satellite): HBO.

Fee: $11.50 monthly.

Pay Service 3

Pay Units: 147.

Programming (via satellite): Showtime; The Movie Channel.

Fee: $10.45 monthly.

Pay Service 4

Pay Units: 47.

Programming (via satellite): Encore.

Fee: $7.30 monthly.

Video-On-Demand: No

Internet Service

Operational: No.

Telephone Service

None

Miles of Plant: 325.0 (coaxial); 18.0 (fiber optic).

Chief Executive Officer: Neal Sehnog.

City fee: 5% of gross.

Ownership: New Day Broadband (MSO).

PALOS VERDES PENINSULA—Cox Communications. Now served by ORANGE COUNTY, CA [CA0015]. ICA: CA0060.

PERRIS—Time Warner Cable. Now served by ANAHEIM, CA [CA0033]. ICA: CA0159.

PETALUMA—Comcast Cable. Now served by NAPA/SONOMA, CA [CA0038]. ICA: CA0068.

PETALUMA COAST GUARD STATION—MWR Cable, 599 Tomales Rd, Petaluma, CA 94952-5000. Phone: 707-765-7343 (Office Phone). Fax: 707-765-7329. E-mail: lawrence.a.streeter@uscg.mil. ICA: CA0368.

TV Market Ranking: 7 (PETALUMA COAST GUARD STATION). Franchise award date: N.A. Franchise expiration date: N.A. Began: December 22, 1988.

Channel capacity: 95 (operating 2-way). Channels available but not in use: None.

Basic Service

Subscribers: 220.

Programming (received off-air): KBCW (CW) San Francisco; KGO-TV (ABC) San Francisco; KICU-TV (IND) San Jose; KOFY-TV (IND) San Francisco; KPIX-TV (CBS) San Francisco; KQED (PBS) San Francisco; KRON-TV (MNT) San Francisco; KTVU (FOX) Oakland.

Programming (via satellite): ABC Family Channel; AMC; Animal Planet; Arts & Entertainment; BET Networks; Cartoon Network; CNN; Comedy Central; Country Music TV; Discovery Channel; Disney Channel; E! Entertainment Television; ESPN; ESPN 2; ESPN Classic Sports; ESPNews; Food Network; Fox Movie Channel; Fox News Channel; Fox Sports Net West; GSN; HBO (multiplexed); HGTV; History Channel; Lifetime; MTV; Nickelodeon; Speed Channel; Spike TV; Syfy; TBS Superstation; The Learning Channel; Toon Disney; Travel Channel; Turner Network TV; Univision; USA Network; VH1; Weather Channel.

Current originations: Government Access.

Fee: $20.00 installation; $25.00 monthly.

Internet Service

Operational: Yes. Began: October 1, 2004.

Subscribers: 140.

Broadband Service: In-house.

Fee: $20.00 installation; $25.00 monthly; $50.00 modem purchase.

Telephone Service

None

Homes passed: 500.

Manager: Larry Streeter.

Ownership: MWR Cable.

PHELAN—Charter Communications, 7337 Central Ave, Riverside, CA 92504. Phone: 951-343-5100. Fax: 951-354-5942. Web Site: http://www.charter.com. Also serves Wrightwood. ICA: CA0398.

TV Market Ranking: 2 (PHELAN, Wrightwood). Franchise award date: N.A. Franchise expiration date: N.A. Began: N.A.

Channel capacity: 36 (not 2-way capable). Channels available but not in use: None.

Basic Service

Subscribers: 807.

Programming (received off-air): KABC-TV (ABC) Los Angeles; KCBS-TV (CBS) Los Angeles; KCET (PBS) Los Angeles; KCOP-TV (MNT) Los Angeles; KHIZ (IND) Barstow; KNBC (NBC) Los Angeles; KTLA (CW) Los Angeles; KTTV (FOX) Los Angeles; KWHY-TV (IND) Los Angeles.

Programming (via satellite): AMC; Arts & Entertainment; CNN; Comedy Central; ESPN; Home Shopping Network; MTV; Nickelodeon; QVC; Spike TV; TBS Superstation; Turner Network TV; USA Network; VH1.

Fee: $26.95 monthly.

Expanded Basic Service 1

Subscribers: 783.

Programming (via satellite): ABC Family Channel; Discovery Channel; Disney Channel; Food Network; Headline News; The Learning Channel.

Fee: $7.68 monthly.

Pay Service 1

Pay Units: 102.

Programming (via satellite): Cinemax.

Fee: $10.95 monthly.

Pay Service 2

Pay Units: 235.

Programming (via satellite): HBO.

Fee: $11.95 monthly.

Pay Service 3
Pay Units: 173.
Programming (via satellite): Showtime.
Fee: $10.95 monthly.

Pay Service 4
Pay Units: 115.
Programming (via satellite): The Movie Channel.
Fee: $10.95 monthly.

Pay Service 5
Pay Units: N.A.
Programming (via satellite): Encore; Fox Sports Net.

Video-On-Demand: No

Pay-Per-View
Special events.

Internet Service
Operational: No.

Telephone Service
None

Miles of Plant: 102.0 (coaxial); 17.0 (fiber optic). Homes passed: 3,815. Total homes in franchised area: 4,581.

Vice President & General Manager: Fred Lutz. Technical Operations Manager: George Noel. Marketing Director: Chris Bailey.

Ownership: Charter Communications Inc. (MSO).

PINE GROVE—Volcano Vision, PO Box 1070, 20000 Hwy 88, Pine Grove, CA 95665. Phones: 209-296-2288 (Information); 209-274-2660. Fax: 209-296-2230. E-mail: info@volcanotel.com. Web Site: http://www.volcanocommunications.com. Also serves Amador County, Buck Horn, Kirkwood, Pioneer, Volcano & West Point. ICA: CA0197.

TV Market Ranking: 25 (Amador County (portions)); Outside TV Markets (Buck Horn, Kirkwood, PINE GROVE, Pioneer, Volcano, West Point, Amador County (portions)). Franchise award date: May 2, 1983. Franchise expiration date: N.A. Began: May 2, 1983.

Channel capacity: 78 (operating 2-way). Channels available but not in use: 65.

Digital Basic Service
Subscribers: N.A.
Programming (received off-air): KCRA-TV (NBC) Sacramento; KMAX-TV (CW) Sacramento; KOVR (CBS) Stockton; KQCA (MNT) Stockton; KSPX-TV (ION) Sacramento; KTXL (FOX) Sacramento; KUVS-DT (UNV) Modesto; KVIE (PBS) Sacramento; KXTV (ABC) Sacramento.
Programming (via satellite): AMC; AmericanLife TV Network; Arts & Entertainment; Arts & Entertainment HD; BBC America; BBC World News; BET Networks; Bloomberg Television; Boomerang; Bravo; Bravo HD; Chiller; CNBC; CNBC HD+; CNN; Colours; Comcast Sports Net Bay Area; Comcast SportsNet West; Comedy Central; Cooking Channel; Country Music TV; Discovery Channel; Discovery HD Theater; Discovery Military Channel; DMX Music; E! Entertainment Television; ESPN; ESPN 2; ESPN 2 HD; ESPN Classic Sports; ESPN HD; ESPNews; FitTV; Food Network; Food Network HD; Fox Movie Channel; Fox News Channel; Fox Sports Net West 2; Fuel TV; FX; Gospel Music Channel; GSN; HDNet; HDNet Movies; Headline News; HGTV; HGTV HD; History Channel; History Channel HD; HorseRacing TV; Lifetime; Lifetime Movie Network; Lifetime Movie Network HD; Mojo Mix; MSNBC; MTV; National Geographic Channel; National Geographic Channel HD Network; Outdoor Channel; Outdoor Channel 2 HD; Ovation; Oxygen; ReelzChannel; Smile of a Child; SoapNet; Soundtrack Channel; Speed Channel; Spike TV; Syfy; Syfy HD; TBS in HD; TBS Superstation; Toon Disney; Travel Channel; truTV; Turner Classic Movies; Turner Network TV; Turner Network TV HD; TV Land; Universal HD; USA Network; USA Network HD; Versus; VH1; WE tv; WealthTV; WealthTV HD; World Harvest Television.
Current originations: Public Access.
Fee: $29.99 monthly.

Digital Expanded Basic Service
Subscribers: N.A.
Programming (via satellite): Bio; CBS College Sports Network; Current; Do-It-Yourself; ESPN U; Fox Business Channel; Fox College Sports Atlantic; Fox College Sports Central; Fox College Sports Pacific; G4; GAS; Hallmark Movie Channel; History Channel International; Lifetime Real Women; MTV Hits; MTV Jams; MTV2; Nick Jr.; NickToons TV; RFD-TV; Sleuth; Style Network; VH1 Classic; VH1 Soul; VHUNO.
Fee: $16.00 monthly.

Digital Expanded Basic Service 2
Subscribers: N.A.
Programming (via satellite): CMT Pure Country; Crime & Investigation Network; Fox Soccer; Fuse; Golf Channel; Great American Country; Independent Film Channel; Military History Channel; Tennis Channel.
Fee: $6.00 monthly.

Digital Pay Service 1
Pay Units: N.A.
Programming (via satellite): Cinemax (multiplexed); Encore (multiplexed); Flix; HBO (multiplexed); Showtime (multiplexed); Showtime HD; Starz (multiplexed); Starz HDTV; Sundance Channel; The Movie Channel; The Movie Channel HD.
Fee: $8.95 monthly (Starz or Encore), $12.95 monthly (Cinemax), $14.95 monthly (HBO).

Video-On-Demand: No

Pay-Per-View
Addressable homes: 3,850.
iN DEMAND (delivered digitally), Fee: $3.99, Addressable: Yes; Hot Choice (delivered digitally); Playboy TV (delivered digitally); Fresh (delivered digitally); Shorteez (delivered digitally).

Internet Service
Operational: Yes, DSL & dialup.
Subscribers: 175.
Broadband Service: Volcano.
Fee: $29.95-$59.95 monthly.

Telephone Service
None

Miles of Plant: 260.0 (coaxial); None (fiber optic). Homes passed: 7,000.

Manager & Chief Technician: Duke Milunovich. Marketing Director: Ramel Chand.

County fee: 5% of gross.

Ownership: Volcano Communications Co. (MSO).

PINECREST—SNC Cable, PO Box 281, Sonora, CA 95373. Phone: 209-586-7622. Web Site: http://www.snccable.com. Also serves Cold Springs & Strawberry. ICA: CA0251.

TV Market Ranking: Outside TV Markets (Cold Springs, PINECREST, Strawberry). Franchise award date: N.A. Franchise expiration date: N.A. Began: August 1, 1961.

Channel capacity: 30 (not 2-way capable). Channels available but not in use: N.A.

Digital Basic Service
Subscribers: 175.
Programming (received off-air): KCRA-TV (NBC) Sacramento; KMAX-TV (CW) Sacramento; KOVR (CBS) Stockton; KQCA (MNT) Stockton; KTFK-DT (TEL) Stockton; KTNC-TV (IND) Concord; KTXL (FOX) Sacramento; KVIE (PBS) Sacramento; KXTV (ABC) Sacramento; allband FM.
Programming (via satellite): Arts & Entertainment; CNBC; CNN; Discovery Channel; ESPN; Fox News Channel; History Channel; TBS Superstation; Trinity Broadcasting Network; Turner Network TV.
Fee: $50.00 installation; $27.95 monthly.

Digital Pay Service 1
Pay Units: 4.
Programming (via satellite): HBO.
Fee: $13.95 monthly.

Video-On-Demand: No

Internet Service
Operational: No.

Telephone Service
None

Miles of Plant: 18.0 (coaxial); None (fiber optic). Additional miles planned: 2.0 (coaxial). Homes passed: 1,000. Total homes in franchised area: 1,050.

General Manager: Tim Holden.

County fee: 2% of gross.

Ownership: Sierra Nevada Communications (MSO).

PINOLE—Comcast Cable. Now served by OAKLAND, CA [CA0018]. ICA: CA0032.

PITTSBURG—Comcast Cable. Now served by CONCORD, CA [CA0101]. ICA: CA0056.

PLACER COUNTY (southwestern portion)—Wave Broadband, PO Box 3520, 4120 Citrus Ave, Rocklin, CA 95677. Phone: 866-928-3123. Web Site: http://www.wavebroadband.com. Also serves Auburn, Christian Valley (unincorporated areas), Colfax, Granite Bay, Lincoln, Loomis, Nevada County (western portion), Newcastle, Penryn, Placer County (western portion) & Rocklin. ICA: CA0131.

TV Market Ranking: 25 (Auburn, Christian Valley (unincorporated areas), Granite Bay, Lincoln, Loomis, Nevada County (western portion), Newcastle, Penryn, PLACER COUNTY, Placer County (western portion), Rocklin); Below 100 (Placer County (western portion) (portions)); Outside TV Markets (Colfax, Nevada County (western portion), Placer County (western portion) (portions)). Franchise award date: May 1, 1980. Franchise expiration date: N.A. Began: January 1, 1981.

Channel capacity: 97 (operating 2-way). Channels available but not in use: None.

Basic Service
Subscribers: N.A.
Programming (received off-air): KCRA-TV (NBC) Sacramento; KMAX-TV (CW) Sacramento; KOVR (CBS) Stockton; KQCA (MNT) Stockton; KSPX-TV (ION) Sacramento; KTFK-DT (TEL) Stockton; KTXL (FOX) Sacramento; KUVS-DT (UNV) Modesto; KVIE (PBS) Sacramento; KXTV (ABC) Sacramento.
Programming (via satellite): California Channel; C-SPAN; C-SPAN 2; Home Shopping Network; Jewelry Television; QVC; WGN America.
Current originations: Educational Access; Leased Access; Government Access; Public Access.
Fee: $29.95 installation; $22.95 monthly.

Expanded Basic Service 1
Subscribers: N.A.
Programming (via satellite): ABC Family Channel; AMC; Animal Planet; Arts & Entertainment; Bravo; Cartoon Network; CBS College Sports Network; CNBC; CNN; Comcast Sports Net Bay Area; Comcast SportsNet West; Comedy Central; Country Music TV; Discovery Channel; Disney Channel; Disney XD; E! Entertainment Television; ESPN; ESPN 2; ESPN Classic Sports; Food Network; Fox Movie Channel; Fox News Channel; FX; Golf Channel; Hallmark Channel; Headline News; HGTV; History Channel; INSP; Lifetime; MSNBC; MTV; National Geographic Channel; Nickelodeon; Oxygen; Spike TV; Syfy; TBS Superstation; The Learning Channel; Travel Channel; truTV; Turner Classic Movies; Turner Network TV; TV Land; USA Network; VH1; Weather Channel.
Fee: $25.55 monthly.

Digital Basic Service
Subscribers: N.A.
Programming (via satellite): BBC America; Bio; BYU Television; CMT Pure Country; C-SPAN 2; Current; Discovery Health Channel; Discovery Kids Channel; Discovery Military Channel; Discovery Planet Green; Disney XD; Eternal Word TV Network; FitTV; Fox Business Channel; History Channel International; ID Investigation Discovery; MTV Hits; MTV2; Music Choice; Nick Jr.; NickToons TV; PBS Kids Sprout; Science Channel; Sleuth; SoapNet; TeenNick; Trinity Broadcasting Network; VH1 Classic; VH1 Soul.
Fee: $18.45 monthly.

Digital Expanded Basic Service
Subscribers: N.A.
Programming (via satellite): ABC News Now; AmericanLife TV Network; Bloomberg Television; Boomerang; Bravo; Cooking Channel; Do-It-Yourself; Fox Movie Channel; Fuse; G4; Gospel Music Channel; Great American Country; GSN; Halogen Network; HGTV; History Channel; Independent Film Channel; Lifetime Movie Network; Lifetime Real Women; mun2 television; Ovation; Style Network; Syfy; truTV; Turner Classic Movies; WE tv; WealthTV.

Digital Expanded Basic Service 2
Subscribers: N.A.
Programming (via satellite): CBS College Sports Network; ESPN 2; ESPN Classic Sports; ESPN U; ESPNews; Fox Soccer; FSN Digital Atlantic; FSN Digital Central; FSN Digital Pacific; Fuel TV; Gol TV; Golf Channel; NBA TV; NFL Network; Outdoor Channel; Speed Channel; Tennis Channel; Versus.

Digital Expanded Basic Service 3
Subscribers: N.A.
Programming (via satellite): Azteca America; Bandamax; Canal 52MX; Cine Latino; Cine Mexicano; CNN en Espanol; De Pelicula; De Pelicula Clasico; Discovery en Espanol; Discovery Familia; Disney XD en Espanol; ESPN Deportes; Gol TV; History Channel en Espanol; MTV Tres; Once Mexico; Sorpresa; Telemundo; VeneMovies; V-me TV.

Digital Expanded Basic Service 4
Subscribers: N.A.
Programming (received off-air): KCRA-TV (NBC) Sacramento; KMAX-TV (CW) Sacramento; KOVR (CBS) Stockton; KQCA (MNT) Stockton; KTXL (FOX) Sacramento; KVIE (PBS) Sacramento; KXTV (ABC) Sacramento.
Programming (via satellite): Animal Planet HD; Arts & Entertainment HD; Discovery Channel HD; Discovery HD Theater; Disney Channel HD; ESPN 2 HD; ESPN HD; Food Network HD; Hallmark Channel HD; HDNet; HDNet Movies; HGTV HD; History Channel HD; MGM HD; National Geographic Channel HD Network; NFL Network HD; Science

Channel HD; TBS in HD; TLC HD; Travel Channel HD; Turner Network TV HD; Universal HD; WealthTV HD.

Digital Pay Service 1

Pay Units: N.A.

Programming (via satellite): Cinemax (multiplexed); Encore (multiplexed); Filipino Channel; Flix; HBO (multiplexed); HBO HD; MoviePlex; Showtime (multiplexed); Showtime HD; Starz (multiplexed); The Movie Channel (multiplexed).

Fee: $12.00 monthly (Showtime/TMC/Flix), $15.00 monthly (HBO, Cinemax or Starz/ Encore).

Video-On-Demand: Yes

Pay-Per-View

Playboy TV (delivered digitally); Fresh (delivered digitally); iN DEMAND (delivered digitally); NBA League Pass (delivered digitally).

Internet Service

Operational: Yes.

Broadband Service: Wave Broadband.

Fee: $24.95-$74.95 monthly; $5.00 modem lease.

Telephone Service

Digital: Operational

Fee: $29.95-$49.95 monthly

Miles of Plant: 257.0 (coaxial); None (fiber optic). Additional miles planned: 40.0 (coaxial). Homes passed: 20,045.

Manager: Seth Johanson. Sales Director: Tom Carroll.

City fee: 3% of gross. County fee: 5% of gross.

Ownership: WaveDivision Holdings LLC (MSO).

PLACERVILLE—Comcast Cable, 4350 Pell Dr, Sacramento, CA 95838-2531. Phone: 916-927-2225. Fax: 916-927-0805. Web Site: http://www.comcast.com. Also serves Auburn Lake Trails, Cameron Park, Camino, Cool, Diamond Springs, El Dorado County (portions), El Dorado Hills, Georgetown, Kyburz, Mount Ralston, Pollock Pines, Rescue, Shingle Springs, Strawberry & Twin Bridges. ICA: CA0108.

TV Market Ranking: 25 (Cameron Park, El Dorado County (portions), El Dorado Hills, Rescue, Shingle Springs); Outside TV Markets (Auburn Lake Trails, Camino, Cool, Diamond Springs, Georgetown, Kyburz, Mount Ralston, PLACERVILLE, Pollock Pines, Strawberry, Twin Bridges, El Dorado County (portions)). Franchise award date: March 3, 1982. Franchise expiration date: N.A. Began: April 1, 1967.

Channel capacity: N.A. Channels available but not in use: N.A.

Basic Service

Subscribers: 17,626.

Programming (received off-air): KCRA-TV (NBC) Sacramento; KCSO-LP Sacramento; KMAX-TV (CW) Sacramento; KOVR (CBS) Stockton; KQCA (MNT) Stockton; KSPX-TV (ION) Sacramento; KTFK-DT (TEL) Stockton; KTXL (FOX) Sacramento; KUVS-DT (UNV) Modesto; KVIE (PBS) Sacramento; KXTV (ABC) Sacramento.

Programming (via satellite): C-SPAN; C-SPAN 2; Home Shopping Network; QVC; TV Guide Network.

Current originations: Leased Access; Government Access; Educational Access; Public Access.

Fee: $43.99 installation; $9.24 monthly; $1.23 converter.

Expanded Basic Service 1

Subscribers: 17,250.

Programming (via satellite): ABC Family Channel; AMC; Animal Planet; Arts & Entertainment; Bravo; Cartoon Network; CNBC; CNN; Comcast Sports Net Bay Area; Comedy Central; Country Music TV; Discovery Channel; Disney Channel; E! Entertainment Television; ESPN; Food Network; Fox News Channel; FX; Golf Channel; GSN; Hallmark Channel; Headline News; HGTV; History Channel; Lifetime; MSNBC; MTV; Nickelodeon; Oxygen; Spike TV; Style Network; Syfy; TBS Superstation; The Learning Channel; Travel Channel; truTV; Turner Network TV; TV Land; USA Network; Versus; VH1; Weather Channel.

Fee: $41.91 monthly.

Digital Basic Service

Subscribers: N.A.

Programming (via satellite): AmericanLife TV Network; ART America; BBC America; Bio; Black Family Channel; Bloomberg Television; Canales N; CCTV-4; Discovery Digital Networks; DMX Music; ESPN 2; ESPN Classic Sports; ESPNews; Filipino Channel; FitTV; Fox College Sports Atlantic; Fox College Sports Central; Fox College Sports Pacific; Fox Movie Channel; Fox Sports World; Fuse; G4; GAS; Great American Country; Halogen Network; History Channel International; Independent Film Channel; International Television (ITV); Lifetime Movie Network; Lime; MTV Networks Digital Suite; National Geographic Channel; Nick Jr.; NickToons TV; Outdoor Channel; Ovation; RAI International; Russian Television Network; Saigon Broadcasting TV Network; ShopNBC; Speed Channel; Sundance Channel; The Word Network; Toon Disney; Trinity Broadcasting Network; Turner Classic Movies; TV Asia; TV Japan; TV5, La Television International; WE tv; Zee TV USA; Zhong Tian Channel.

Fee: $11.95 monthly.

Digital Pay Service 1

Pay Units: 996.

Programming (via satellite): Cinemax (multiplexed); HBO (multiplexed); Showtime; Starz (multiplexed); The Movie Channel (multiplexed).

Fee: $17.99 monthly (Cinemax, TMC or Starz), $18.99 monthly (HBO or Showtime).

Video-On-Demand: Yes

Pay-Per-View

iN DEMAND; ESPN Now (delivered digitally); Sports PPV (delivered digitally); iN DEMAND (delivered digitally); Urban Xtra (delivered digitally); Fresh (delivered digitally); Shorteez (delivered digitally); Playboy TV (delivered digitally); Hot Choice (delivered digitally).

Internet Service

Operational: Yes.

Broadband Service: Comcast High Speed Internet.

Fee: $42.95 monthly.

Telephone Service

Digital: Operational

Miles of Plant: 545.0 (coaxial); None (fiber optic). Homes passed: 26,654. Total homes in franchised area: 43,117.

Area Vice President: Dan McCarty. Technical Operations Director: Joe Trassare. Marketing Manager: Christi Rossi.

Franchise fee: 5% of gross.

Ownership: Comcast Cable Communications Inc. (MSO).

PLANADA—Comcast Cable, 2441 N Grove Industrial Dr, Fresno, CA 93727-1535. Phones: 559-253-4050; 800-266-2278. Fax: 559-253-4090. Web Site: http://www.comcast.com. ICA: CA0268.

TV Market Ranking: 72 (PLANADA). Franchise award date: N.A. Franchise expiration date: N.A. Began: January 1, 1984.

Channel capacity: 36 (not 2-way capable). Channels available but not in use: 16.

Basic Service

Subscribers: 220.

Programming (received off-air): KAIL (MNT) Fresno; KFRE-TV (CW) Sanger; KFSN-TV (ABC) Fresno; KFTV-DT (UNV) Hanford; KGPE (CBS) Fresno; KMPH-TV (FOX) Visalia; KNSO (TMO) Merced; KSEE (NBC) Fresno; KVPT (PBS) Fresno.

Programming (via satellite): ABC Family Channel; AMC; Arts & Entertainment; Cartoon Network; CNN; Comcast Sports Net Bay Area; Comedy Central; Discovery Channel; Disney Channel; ESPN; GalaVision; Great American Country; Headline News; Home Shopping Network; Lifetime; MTV; Nickelodeon; QVC; Spike TV; Syfy; TBS Superstation; The Learning Channel; Turner Network TV; USA Network; VH1.

Fee: $43.99 installation; $35.95 monthly.

Pay Service 1

Pay Units: 58.

Programming (via satellite): HBO.

Fee: $12.87 monthly.

Pay Service 2

Pay Units: 40.

Programming (via satellite): Showtime.

Fee: $11.50 monthly.

Internet Service

Operational: Yes.

Telephone Service

Digital: Operational

Miles of Plant: 10.0 (coaxial); None (fiber optic). Homes passed: 650. Total homes in franchised area: 750.

General Manager: Len Falter. Marketing Director: Stewart Butler. Communications Director: Erica Smith.

County fee: 3% of gross.

Ownership: Comcast Cable Communications Inc. (MSO).

PLANTATION-BY-THE-SEA—Formerly served by Cox Communications. No longer in operation. ICA: CA0293.

PLEASANT HILL—Comcast Cable. Now served by CONCORD, CA [CA0101]. ICA: CA0029.

PLEASANTON—Comcast Cable. Now served by CONCORD, CA [CA0101]. ICA: CA0037.

POINT MUGU NAVAL AIR STATION—Communication Services, 4564 Telephone Rd, Ste 805, Ventura, CA 93003-5661. Phone: 805-658-1579. Fax: 805-658-0929. Web Site: http://www.commservcable.com. ICA: CA0252.

TV Market Ranking: Below 100 (POINT MUGU NAVAL AIR STATION). Franchise award date: N.A. Franchise expiration date: N.A. Began: September 1, 1992.

Channel capacity: 40 (operating 2-way). Channels available but not in use: 4.

Basic Service

Subscribers: 652.

Programming (received off-air): KABC-TV (ABC) Los Angeles; KBEH (IND) Oxnard; KCAL-TV (IND) Los Angeles; KCBS-TV (CBS) Los Angeles; KCET (PBS) Los Angeles; KCOP-TV (MNT) Los Angeles; KJLA (IND) Ventura; KMEX-DT (UNV) Los Angeles; KNBC (NBC) Los Angeles; KTLA (CW) Los Angeles; KTTV (FOX) Los Angeles.

Programming (via satellite): ABC Family Channel; Animal Planet; Arts & Entertainment; BET Networks; Cartoon Network; CNBC; CNN; Comedy Central; Country Music TV; C-SPAN; Discovery Channel; Disney Channel; E! Entertainment Television; ESPN; ESPN 2; Food Network; Fox News Channel; Fox Sports Net West; Fox Sports Net West 2; Great American Country; Headline News; HGTV; History Channel; INSP; Lifetime; MTV; National Geographic Channel; Nickelodeon; QVC; SoapNet; Syfy; TBS Superstation; The Learning Channel; Travel Channel; Turner Classic Movies; Turner Network TV; TV Guide Network; TV Land; USA Network; VH1; Weather Channel; WGN America.

Fee: $25.00 installation; $34.85 monthly.

Digital Basic Service

Subscribers: N.A.

Programming (received off-air): KABC-TV (ABC) Los Angeles; KCBS-TV (CBS) Los Angeles; KCET (PBS) Los Angeles; KNBC (NBC) Los Angeles; KTLA (CW) Los Angeles; KTTV (FOX) Los Angeles.

Programming (via satellite): BBC America; Bloomberg Television; Discovery Digital Networks; DMX Music; ESPN U; ESPNews; Fox College Sports Atlantic; Fox College Sports Central; Fox College Sports Pacific; Fox Movie Channel; G4; Halogen Network; Lime; Outdoor Channel; Toon Disney.

Fee: $10.95 monthly.

Pay Service 1

Pay Units: N.A.

Programming (via satellite): HBO.

Fee: $10.95 monthly.

Digital Pay Service 1

Pay Units: N.A.

Programming (via satellite): Cinemax (multiplexed); HBO (multiplexed).

Fee: $10.06 monthly (Cinemax), $11.12 monthly (HBO).

Video-On-Demand: Yes

Pay-Per-View

iN DEMAND (delivered digitally); Fresh (delivered digitally); Playboy TV (delivered digitally).

Internet Service

Operational: Yes. Began: July 1, 2000.

Broadband Service: Cable Rocket.

Fee: $99.00 installation; $42.50 monthly; $10.00 modem lease.

Telephone Service

None

Miles of Plant: 13.0 (coaxial); None (fiber optic). Homes passed: 1,000.

Manager: Phil Shockley. Chief Technician: Wayne Shockley.

Ownership: Coaxial Properties Inc.

POINT REYES STATION—Horizon Cable TV Inc., 520 Mesa Rd, Point Reyes Station, CA 94956. Phones: 888-663-9610; 415-663-9610. Fax: 415-663-9608. E-mail: info@horizoncable.com. Web Site: http://www.horizoncable.com. Also serves Dillon Beach, Inverness, Olema & Stinson Beach. ICA: CA0453.

TV Market Ranking: 7 (Dillon Beach, Inverness, Olema, POINT REYES STATION, Stinson Beach). Franchise award date: N.A. Franchise expiration date: N.A. Began: N.A.

Channel capacity: 89 (operating 2-way). Channels available but not in use: N.A.

Basic Service

Subscribers: 736.

Programming (received off-air): KBCW (CW) San Francisco; KFTY (IND) Santa Rosa; KGO-TV (ABC) San Francisco; KNTV (NBC) San Jose; KOFY-TV (IND) San Francisco; KPIX-TV (CBS) San Francisco; KQED (PBS) San Francisco; KRCB (PBS) Cotati; KRON-TV (MNT) San Francisco; KTLN-TV (IND) Novato; KTSF (IND) San Francisco; KTVU (FOX) Oakland.

Programming (via satellite): AMC; Animal Planet; Arts & Entertainment; Bravo; CNBC; CNN; Comedy Central; C-SPAN; C-SPAN 2; Discovery Channel; Disney Channel; Encore; ESPN; ESPN 2; Fox Sports Net; Headline News; HGTV; History Channel; Lifetime; MSNBC; MTV; Nickelodeon; QVC; Spike TV; Syfy; TBS Superstation; The Learning Channel; Travel Channel; Turner Classic Movies; Turner Network TV; TV Land; Univision; USA Network; VH1; Weather Channel.

Fee: $39.95 installation; $36.95 monthly.

Pay Service 1

Pay Units: N.A.

Programming (via satellite): Cinemax (multiplexed); HBO (multiplexed); Showtime; Sundance Channel; The Movie Channel.

Fee: $8.95 monthly (Cinemax), $10.95 monthly (Showtime, TMC or Sundance), $12.95 monthly (HBO).

Video-On-Demand: No

Internet Service

Operational: Yes.

Subscribers: 462.

Broadband Service: ISP Alliance.

Fee: $89.95 installation; $35.95 monthly; $10.00 modem lease; $199.00 modem purchase.

Telephone Service

None

Homes passed: 1,994.

Manager: Susan Daniel. Marketing Director & Customer Service Manager: Andrea Clark. Chief Engineer: Kevin Daniel.

Ownership: Horizon Cable TV Inc. (MSO).

POMONA—Comcast Cable. Now served by LOS ANGELES, CA [CA0009]. ICA: CA0076.

PORTERVILLE—Charter Communications, 270 Bridge St, San Luis Obispo, CA 93401. Phone: 805-544-1962. Fax: 805-541-6042. Web Site: http://www.charter.com. Also serves Camp Nelson, Cutler, Ducor, Earlimart, Exeter, Farmersville, Ivanhoe, Lindsay, Oak Ranch, Orange Cove, Orosi, Pixley, Plainview, Poplar, Springville, Strathmore, Terra Bella, Three Rivers, Tipton, Tulare County (northeastern portion), Woodlake & Woodville. ICA: CA0152.

TV Market Ranking: 72 (Camp Nelson, Cutler, Ducor, Earlimart, Exeter, Farmersville, Ivanhoe, Lindsay, Oak Ranch, Orange Cove, Orosi, Pixley, Plainview, Poplar, PORTERVILLE, Springville, Strathmore, Terra Bella, Three Rivers, Tipton, Tulare County (northeastern portion), Woodlake, Woodville). Franchise award date: October 6, 1965. Franchise expiration date: N.A. Began: January 1, 1968.

Channel capacity: 39 (not 2-way capable). Channels available but not in use: None.

Basic Service

Subscribers: 15,865.

Programming (received off-air): KAIL (MNT) Fresno; KBAK-TV (CBS) Bakersfield; KERO-TV (ABC) Bakersfield; KFRE-TV (CW) Sanger; KFSN-TV (ABC) Fresno; KFTV-DT (UNV) Hanford; KGET-TV (CW, NBC) Bakersfield; KGMC (IND) Clovis; KJEO-LD Fresno; KMPH-TV (FOX) Visalia; KNXT (ETV) Visalia; KSEE (NBC) Fresno; KVPT (PBS) Fresno; allband FM.

Programming (via satellite): C-SPAN; E! Entertainment Television; GalaVision; ION Television; MTV; QVC; Speed Channel; TBS Superstation; Telemundo; Weather Channel.

Fee: $29.99 installation; $17.60 monthly.

Expanded Basic Service 1

Subscribers: N.A.

Programming (via satellite): Arts & Entertainment; CNBC; CNN; Country Music TV; Discovery Channel; Disney Channel; ESPN; ESPN 2; Headline News; Lifetime; Nickelodeon; Spike TV; Turner Network TV; USA Network.

Fee: $8.00 installation; $38.99 monthly.

Digital Basic Service

Subscribers: N.A.

Programming (via satellite): BBC America; Bio; Discovery Digital Networks; ESPNews; Fuse; GAS; Golf Channel; GSN; History Channel International; Independent Film Channel; Lifetime Movie Network; MTV2; Music Choice; Nick Jr.; Science Television; Syfy; Toon Disney; Turner Classic Movies; Versus; Vida Vision; WE tv.

Pay Service 1

Pay Units: 1,070.

Programming (via satellite): Showtime (multiplexed); The Movie Channel (multiplexed).

Fee: $10.45 monthly.

Digital Pay Service 1

Pay Units: N.A.

Programming (via satellite): Cinemax (multiplexed); HBO (multiplexed).

Video-On-Demand: No

Pay-Per-View

Playboy TV (delivered digitally).

Internet Service

Operational: Yes.

Broadband Service: Charter Pipeline.

Fee: $29.99 monthly.

Telephone Service

Digital: Operational

Miles of Plant: 656.0 (coaxial); None (fiber optic). Homes passed: 40,860.

Vice President & General Manager: Ed Merrill. Technical Operations Director: Ken Arellano. Marketing Director: Sarwar Assar.

City fee: 5% of gross.

Ownership: Charter Communications Inc. (MSO).

PORTOLA—Wave Broadband, 401 Kirkland Parkplace, Ste 500, Kirkland, WA 98033. Phone: 425-576-8200. Fax: 425-576-8221. Web Site: http://wavebroadband.com. Also serves Delleker, Graeagle, Loyalton, Plumas County, Quincy & Sierra County (portions). ICA: CA0185.

TV Market Ranking: Below 100 (Loyalton); Outside TV Markets (Delleker, Graeagle, Plumas County, PORTOLA, Quincy, Sierra County (portions)). Franchise award date: N.A. Franchise expiration date: N.A. Began: January 1, 1963.

Channel capacity: N.A. Channels available but not in use: N.A.

Basic Service

Subscribers: N.A. Included in West Sacramento

Programming (received off-air): KAME-TV (MNT) Reno; KCRA-TV (NBC) Sacramento; KOVR (CBS) Stockton; KQCA (MNT) Stockton; KRNV-DT (ABC) Reno; KTVU (FOX) Oakland; KVIE (PBS) Sacramento; KXTV (ABC) Sacramento; allband FM.

Programming (via satellite): ABC Family Channel; Animal Planet; Arts & Entertainment; California Channel; Cartoon Network; CNBC; CNN; Comcast SportsNet West; Comedy Central; Country Music TV; C-SPAN; Discovery Channel; Disney Channel; ESPN; ESPN 2; Food Network; Fox News Channel; FX; G4; GalaVision; Golf Channel; Headline News; HGTV; History Channel; Home Shopping Network; Lifetime; MTV; Nickelodeon; Oxygen; Speed Channel; Spike TV; Syfy; TBS Superstation; The Learning Channel; Travel Channel; Turner Classic Movies; Turner Network TV; TV Guide Network; TV Land; USA Network; Versus; VH1; WE tv; Weather Channel; WGN America.

Current originations: Public Access.

Fee: $40.00 installation; $42.95 monthly; $.98 converter.

Pay Service 1

Pay Units: 627.

Programming (via satellite): HBO; Showtime.

Fee: $12.95 monthly (Showtime), $13.95 monthly (HBO).

Video-On-Demand: No

Internet Service

Operational: No.

Telephone Service

None

Miles of Plant: 129.0 (coaxial); None (fiber optic). Homes passed: 5,551.

General Manager: Tim Peters. Marketing Director: Adam Lazara.

City fee: 5% of gross.

Ownership: WaveDivision Holdings LLC (MSO).

PORTOLA VALLEY—Comcast Cable. Now served by SAN FRANCISCO, CA [CA0003]. ICA: CA0356.

QUINCY—Quincy Community TV Assn. Inc., PO Box 834, 81 Bradley St, Quincy, CA 95971-0834. Phone: 530-283-2330. ICA: CA0214.

TV Market Ranking: Outside TV Markets (QUINCY). Franchise award date: November 1, 1956. Franchise expiration date: N.A. Began: January 1, 1957.

Channel capacity: 62 (not 2-way capable). Channels available but not in use: N.A.

Basic Service

Subscribers: 1,008.

Programming (received off-air): KCRA-TV (NBC) Sacramento; KHSL-TV (CBS, CW) Chico; KICU-TV (IND) San Jose; KMAX-TV (CW) Sacramento; KOVR (CBS) Stockton; KQCA (MNT) Stockton; KTFK-DT (TEL) Stockton; KTVU (FOX) Oakland; KTXL (FOX) Sacramento; KVIE (PBS) Sacramento; KXTV (ABC) Sacramento; 12 FMs.

Programming (via satellite): ABC Family Channel; AMC; Animal Planet; Arts & Entertainment; California Channel; CNBC; CNN; Comcast Sports Net Bay Area; Country Music TV; C-SPAN; Discovery Channel; ESPN; Golf Channel; HGTV; History Channel; Lifetime; MTV; NASA TV; Nickelodeon; Spike TV; Syfy; TBS Superstation; The Learning Channel; Turner Network TV; USA Network; VH1; Weather Channel.

Current originations: Educational Access.

Fee: $45.00 installation; $38.00 monthly.

Pay Service 1

Pay Units: 128.

Programming (via satellite): HBO.

Fee: $45.00 installation; $38.00 monthly.

Pay Service 2

Pay Units: 27.

Programming (via satellite): Showtime; The Movie Channel.

Fee: $12.00 monthly.

Pay Service 3

Pay Units: 46.

Programming (via satellite): Cinemax.

Fee: $7.00 monthly.

Internet Service

Operational: No.

Telephone Service

None

Miles of Plant: 43.0 (coaxial); None (fiber optic). Additional miles planned: 1.0 (coaxial). Homes passed: 2,025. Total homes in franchised area: 2,200.

Manager: Todd Crabtree. Chief Technician: Michael Stockton.

City fee: 2% of gross.

Ownership: Quincy Community TV Assn. Inc.

QUINCY (portions)—Charter Communications. Now served by PORTOLA, CA [CA0185]. ICA: CA0278.

RAINBOW—Venture Communications, 26667 Madison Suite A, Murrieta, CA 92562. Phone: 800-203-6469. E-mail: tketterer@ranchopacific.biz. Also serves Oak Crest Moble Home Park. ICA: CA0296.

TV Market Ranking: Below 100 (Oak Crest Moble Home Park); Outside TV Markets (RAINBOW). Franchise award date: January 1, 1989. Franchise expiration date: N.A. Began: N.A.

Channel capacity: 80 (not 2-way capable). Channels available but not in use: 47.

Basic Service

Subscribers: 664.

Programming (received off-air): KFMB-TV (CBS) San Diego; KGTV (ABC) San Diego; KNSD (NBC) San Diego; KPBS (PBS) San Diego; KSWB-TV (FOX) San Diego; KTLA (CW) Los Angeles; KUSI-TV (IND) San Diego.

Programming (via satellite): ABC Family Channel; Arts & Entertainment; CNBC; CNN; Comedy Central; C-SPAN; Discovery Channel; Disney Channel; ESPN; ESPN 2; Food Network; Hallmark Channel; Headline News; HGTV; History Channel; Lifetime; MSNBC; Spike TV; Syfy; TBS Superstation; The Learning Channel; truTV; Turner Classic Movies; Turner Network TV; USA Network; various Mexican stations; Weather Channel; WGN America.

Fee: $45.00 installation; $24.95 monthly.

Pay Service 1

Pay Units: 40.

Programming (via satellite): Cinemax; HBO.

Fee: $8.95 monthly (Cinemax), $11.95 monthly (HBO).

Video-On-Demand: No

Internet Service

Operational: No.

Telephone Service

None

Miles of Plant: 10.0 (coaxial); None (fiber optic).

Manager: Tim Ketterer. Business Manager: Jason Martin. Chief Technician: Vince Showalter.
Ownership: DAK Communications Inc.

RANCHO CORDOVA—Comcast Cable. Now served by SACRAMENTO, CA [CA0002]. ICA: CA0215.

RANCHO CORDOVA (portions)—SureWest Broadband. Formerly served by Sacramento, CA [CA0459]. This cable system has converted to IPTV, PO Box 969, Roseville, CA 95661. Phone: 916-772-2000. Fax: 916-786-7170. Web Site: http://www.surewest.com. ICA: CA5607.
TV Market Ranking: 25 (RANCHO CORDOVA (PORTIONS)).
Channel capacity: N.A. Channels available but not in use: N.A.
Video-On-Demand: Yes
Internet Service
Operational: Yes.
Telephone Service
Digital: Operational
Ownership: SureWest Broadband.

RANCHO YOLO MOBILE HOME PARK—Formerly served by Wave Broadband. No longer in operation. ICA: CA0448.

RASNOW—No longer in operation. ICA: CA0439.

RED BLUFF—Charter Communications, 270 Bridge St, San Luis Obispo, CA 93401. Phone: 805-544-1962. Fax: 805-541-6042. Web Site: http://www.charter.com. ICA: CA0464.
TV Market Ranking: Below 100 (RED BLUFF).
Channel capacity: N.A. Channels available but not in use: N.A.
Basic Service
Subscribers: N.A.
Programming (received off-air): KCVU (FOX) Paradise; KHSL-TV (CBS, CW) Chico; KIXE-TV (PBS) Redding; KNVN (NBC) Chico; KRCR-TV (ABC) Redding; KRVU-LD (MNT) Redding.
Programming (via satellite): California Channel; Country Music TV; C-SPAN; Discovery Channel; Hallmark Channel; Home Shopping Network; QVC; TBS Superstation; The Learning Channel; truTV; Univision; Weather Channel.
Expanded Basic Service 1
Subscribers: N.A.
Programming (via satellite): ABC Family Channel; AMC; Arts & Entertainment; Cartoon Network; CNBC; CNN; Comcast Sports Net Bay Area; Comedy Central; Disney Channel; E! Entertainment Television; ESPN; ESPN 2; Headline News; Lifetime; MTV; Nickelodeon; Spike TV; Syfy; Turner Network TV; USA Network; VH1.
Digital Basic Service
Subscribers: N.A.
Programming (via satellite): BBC America; Bio; Bravo; Discovery Digital Networks; DMX Music; ESPN Classic Sports; ESPNews; Fox Soccer; Fuse; GAS; Golf Channel; GSN; HGTV; History Channel; History Channel International; Independent Film Channel; Lifetime Movie Network; MTV Networks Digital Suite; National Geographic Channel; Nick Jr.; Speed Channel; Style Network; Toon Disney; Turner Classic Movies; TV Guide Interactive Inc.; Versus; WE tv.
Digital Pay Service 1
Pay Units: N.A.
Programming (via satellite): Cinemax (multiplexed); Encore (multiplexed); HBO (multiplexed); Showtime (multiplexed); Starz (multiplexed); The Movie Channel.
Video-On-Demand: No
Pay-Per-View
iN DEMAND (delivered digitally); Playboy TV (delivered digitally).
Internet Service
Operational: Yes.
Broadband Service: Charter Pipeline.
Telephone Service
Digital: Operational
Vice President & General Manager: Ed Merrill. Operations Director: Donna Briggs. Marketing Director: Sarwar Assar.
Ownership: Charter Communications Inc. (MSO).

REDDING—Charter Communications, 270 Bridge St, San Luis Obispo, CA 93401. Phone: 805-544-1962. Fax: 805-541-6042. Web Site: http://www.charter.com. Also serves Anderson, Cottonwood, Finer Living, Shasta County & Tehama County. ICA: CA0058.
TV Market Ranking: Below 100 (Anderson, Cottonwood, Finer Living, REDDING, Shasta County, Tehama County). Franchise award date: N.A. Franchise expiration date: N.A. Began: May 1, 1967.
Channel capacity: N.A. Channels available but not in use: N.A.
Basic Service
Subscribers: 34,019.
Programming (received off-air): KCVU (FOX) Paradise; KGEC-LP (IND) Redding; KHSL-TV (CBS, CW) Chico; KIXE-TV (PBS) Redding; KNVN (NBC) Chico; KRCR-TV (ABC) Redding; KRVU-LD (MNT) Redding; 19 FMs.
Programming (via satellite): 3 Angels Broadcasting Network; California Channel; C-SPAN; C-SPAN 2; Eternal Word TV Network; Home Shopping Network; INSP; ION Television; Product Information Network; QVC; TBS Superstation; Telemundo; Trinity Broadcasting Network; TV Guide Network; Univision; Weather Channel.
Current originations: Leased Access; Government Access; Educational Access; Public Access.
Fee: $29.99 installation.
Expanded Basic Service 1
Subscribers: 31,000.
Programming (via satellite): ABC Family Channel; AMC; Animal Planet; Arts & Entertainment; BET Networks; Bravo; Cartoon Network; CNBC; CNN; Comcast Sports Net Bay Area; Comedy Central; Country Music TV; Discovery Channel; Disney Channel; E! Entertainment Television; ESPN; ESPN 2; ESPN Classic Sports; Food Network; Fox News Channel; Fox Sports World; FX; G4; Golf Channel; GSN; Hallmark Channel; Headline News; HGTV; History Channel; Lifetime; MSNBC; MTV; National Geographic Channel; Nickelodeon; Oxygen; SoapNet; Speed Channel; Spike TV; Syfy; The Learning Channel; Toon Disney; Travel Channel; truTV; Turner Network TV; TV Land; USA Network; Versus; VH1; WE tv.
Fee: $48.95 monthly.
Digital Basic Service
Subscribers: N.A.
Programming (via satellite): BBC America; Bio; Bloomberg Television; Boomerang; CNN en Espanol; Discovery Digital Networks; Do-It-Yourself; ESPNews; Fox College Sports Atlantic; Fox College Sports Central; Fox College Sports Pacific; Fox Sports en Espanol; Fuel TV; Fuse; GAS; Great American Country; History Channel International; Independent Film Channel; Lifetime Movie Network; MTV Networks Digital Suite; Music Choice; NFL Network; Nick Jr.; NickToons TV; Outdoor Channel; Style Network; Sundance Channel; Turner Classic Movies; TV Guide Interactive Inc.; TVG Network.
Fee: $10.00 monthly.
Digital Pay Service 1
Pay Units: N.A.
Programming (via satellite): Cinemax (multiplexed); Encore (multiplexed); Flix; HBO (multiplexed); Showtime (multiplexed); Starz (multiplexed); The Movie Channel (multiplexed).
Fee: $19.95 installation; $10.95 monthly (each).
Video-On-Demand: Yes
Pay-Per-View
Addressable homes: 13,200.
iN DEMAND (delivered digitally), Addressable: Yes; Playboy TV (delivered digitally); Fresh (delivered digitally); Shorteez (delivered digitally); NASCAR In Car (delivered digitally).
Internet Service
Operational: Yes.
Broadband Service: Charter Pipeline.
Fee: $29.99 monthly.
Telephone Service
Digital: Operational
Miles of Plant: 600.0 (coaxial); 3.0 (fiber optic). Homes passed: 55,800. Total homes in franchised area: 58,000.
Vice President & General Manager: Ed Merrill. Operations Manager: Donna Briggs. Marketing Director: Sarwar Assar.
City fee: 5% of gross.
Ownership: Charter Communications Inc. (MSO).

REDDING—Formerly served by Sprint Corp. No longer in operation. ICA: CA0408.

REDLANDS—Time Warner Cable. Now served by ANAHEIM, CA [CA0033], CA. ICA: CA0039.

REDONDO BEACH—Time Warner Cable. Now served by LOS ANGELES, CA [CA0009]. ICA: CA0097.

RIDGECREST—Mediacom, 27192 Sun City Blvd, Ste A, Sun City, CA 92586. Phone: 951-679-3977. Fax: 951-679-9087. Web Site: http://www.mediacomcable.com. Also serves Argus, China Lake Naval Weapons Center, Indian Wells Valley, Inyokern, Kern County (unincorporated areas), Searles Valley & Trona. ICA: CA0128.
TV Market Ranking: Below 100 (Kern County (unincorporated areas) (portions)); Outside TV Markets (Argus, China Lake Naval Weapons Center, Indian Wells Valley, Inyokern, Kern County (unincorporated areas) (portions), RIDGECREST, Searles Valley, Trona). Franchise award date: N.A. Franchise expiration date: N.A. Began: N.A.
Channel capacity: 62 (operating 2-way). Channels available but not in use: None.
Basic Service
Subscribers: 11,000.
Programming (received off-air): CCTV-4; KABC-TV (ABC) Los Angeles; KCAL-TV (IND) Los Angeles; KCBS-TV (CBS) Los Angeles; KCET (PBS) Los Angeles; KNBC (NBC) Los Angeles; KTLA (CW) Los Angeles; KTTV (FOX) Los Angeles; 16 FMs.
Programming (via satellite): C-SPAN; C-SPAN 2; Food Network; MSNBC; TBS Superstation; TV Guide Network; WGN America.
Current originations: Leased Access; Government Access; Public Access.
Fee: $44.25 installation; $20.70 monthly.
Expanded Basic Service 1
Subscribers: 9,500.
Programming (via satellite): ABC Family Channel; AMC; Animal Planet; Arts & Entertainment; BET Networks; Bravo; Cartoon Network; CNBC; CNN; Comedy Central; Country Music TV; Discovery Channel; Disney Channel; E! Entertainment Television; ESPN; ESPN 2; Eternal Word TV Network; Fox News Channel; Fox Sports Net; FX; Headline News; History Channel; Home Shopping Network; Lifetime; MTV; Nickelodeon; QVC; Spike TV; Syfy; The Learning Channel; Trinity Broadcasting Network; truTV; Turner Network TV; TV Land; Univision; USA Network; VH1; Weather Channel.
Fee: $25.25 monthly.
Digital Basic Service
Subscribers: N.A.
Programming (via satellite): BBC America; Bio; Bloomberg Television; Discovery Digital Networks; DMX Music; ESPNews; FitTV; Fox Movie Channel; Fox Soccer; Fuse; Golf Channel; GSN; Halogen Network; HGTV; History Channel International; Independent Film Channel; Lifetime Movie Network; Lime; National Geographic Channel; Nick Jr.; NickToons TV; Outdoor Channel; Speed Channel; Style Network; Turner Classic Movies; TV Land; Versus.
Fee: $8.00 monthly.
Digital Pay Service 1
Pay Units: N.A.
Programming (via satellite): Cinemax (multiplexed); Encore (multiplexed); HBO (multiplexed); Showtime (multiplexed); Starz (multiplexed); The Movie Channel (multiplexed).
Fee: $8.00 monthly (Starz/Encore), $9.95 monthly (Cinemax or Showtime), $13.95 monthly (HBO).
Video-On-Demand: No
Pay-Per-View
Movies (delivered digitally).
Internet Service
Operational: Yes.
Broadband Service: Mediacom High Speed Internet.
Fee: $40.95 monthly; $3.00 modem lease; $239.95 modem purchase.
Telephone Service
Analog: Not Operational
Digital: Operational
Miles of Plant: 280.0 (coaxial); None (fiber optic). Homes passed: 17,500. Total homes in franchised area: 18,000.
General Manager: Allen Bublitz. Engineering Director: Jon Tatilano.
City fee: 5% of gross.
Ownership: Mediacom LLC (MSO).

RIO VISTA—Comcast Cable. Now served by NAPA/SONOMA, CA [CA0038]. ICA: CA0232.

RIO VISTA—Wave Broadband, 401 Kirkland Parkplace, Ste 500, Kirkland, WA 98033. Phones: 866-928-3123; 425-576-8200. Fax: 425-576-8221. Web Site: http://wavebroadband.com. ICA: CA0449.
TV Market Ranking: 7,25 (RIO VISTA). Franchise award date: N.A. Franchise expiration date: N.A. Began: N.A.
Channel capacity: N.A. Channels available but not in use: N.A.

Basic Service
Subscribers: N.A. Included in West Sacramento
Programming (received off-air): KCRA-TV (NBC) Sacramento; KMAX-TV (CW) Sacramento; KOVR (CBS) Stockton; KQCA (MNT) Stockton; KTNC-TV (IND) Concord; KTXL (FOX) Sacramento; KUVS-DT (UNV) Modesto; KVIE (PBS) Sacramento; KXTV (ABC) Sacramento.
Programming (via satellite): ABC Family Channel; AMC; Arts & Entertainment; BET Networks; California Channel; Cartoon Network; CNBC; CNN; Comcast Sports Net Bay Area; Comedy Central; Country Music TV; C-SPAN; C-SPAN 2; Discovery Channel; Disney Channel; E! Entertainment Television; ESPN; ESPN 2; Food Network; Golf Channel; Headline News; HGTV; History Channel; Lifetime; MTV; Nickelodeon; QVC; Spike TV; Syfy; TBS Superstation; The Learning Channel; Turner Classic Movies; Turner Network TV; TV Guide Network; TV Land; USA Network; VH1; Weather Channel; WGN America.
Fee: $49.95 installation; $47.95 monthly; $21.00 additional installation.

Pay Service 1
Pay Units: N.A.
Programming (via satellite): Cinemax (multiplexed); Encore; HBO (multiplexed); Showtime (multiplexed); The Movie Channel.
Fee: $29.00 monthly.

Video-On-Demand: No

Internet Service
Operational: No.

Telephone Service
None

General Manager: Tim Peters. Marketing Director: Adam Lazara.
Ownership: WaveDivision Holdings LLC (MSO).

RIVERDALE—Comcast Cable, 2441 N Grove Industrial Dr, Fresno, CA 93727-1535. Phones: 800-266-2278; 559-253-4050. Fax: 559-253-4090. Web Site: http://www.comcast.com. ICA: CA0270.
TV Market Ranking: 72 (EAST RIVERDALE). Franchise award date: N.A. Franchise expiration date: N.A. Began: June 15, 1984.
Channel capacity: 36 (2-way capable). Channels available but not in use: 14.

Basic Service
Subscribers: N.A.
Programming (received off-air): KAIL (MNT) Fresno; KFRE-TV (CW) Sanger; KFSN-TV (ABC) Fresno; KFTV-DT (UNV) Hanford; KGPE (CBS) Fresno; KMPH-TV (FOX) Visalia; KNSO (TMO) Merced; KSEE (NBC) Fresno; KVPT (PBS) Fresno.
Programming (via satellite): Home Shopping Network; QVC; Trinity Broadcasting Network; TV Guide Network; WGN America.
Fee: $13.50 monthly.

Expanded Basic Service 1
Subscribers: 169.
Programming (via satellite): ABC Family Channel; AMC; Animal Planet; Arts & Entertainment; BET Networks; Bravo; Cartoon Network; CNBC; CNN; Comcast Sports Net Bay Area; Comcast SportsNet West; Comedy Central; Country Music TV; C-SPAN; Discovery Channel; Disney Channel; E! Entertainment Television; ESPN; ESPN 2; Food Network; Fox News Channel; Fox Sports en Espanol; FX; GalaVision; Golf Channel; GSN; Hallmark Channel; Headline News; HGTV; History Television; Lifetime; MSNBC; MTV; Nickelodeon; Oxygen; Speed Channel; Spike TV; Syfy; TBS Superstation; The Learning Channel; Travel Channel; truTV; Turner Classic Movies; Turner Network TV; TV Land; USA Network; Versus; VH1; Weather Channel.
Fee: $51.50 monthly.

Digital Basic Service
Subscribers: N.A.
Programming (via satellite): BBC America; Black Family Channel; Bloomberg Television; Discovery HD Theater; Discovery Health Channel; Discovery Kids Channel; ESPN 2 HD; ESPN Classic Sports; ESPN HD; ESPNews; Flix; Fox Reality Channel; Fuse; G4; Great American Country; Independent Film Channel; MoviePlex; MTV2; National Geographic Channel; Nick Jr.; Science Channel; Si TV; SoapNet; Style Network; The Word Network; Turner Classic Movies; Turner Network TV HD; TV One; Universal HD; Versus HD; VH1 Classic; VH1 Soul; WE tv; Weatherscan.
Fee: $52.50 monthly.

Pay Service 1
Pay Units: 37.
Programming (via satellite): Showtime; The Movie Channel.
Fee: $15.00 installation; $9.95 monthly (TMC), $11.50 monthly (Showtime).

Digital Pay Service 1
Pay Units: N.A.
Programming (via satellite): Cinemax (multiplexed); HBO (multiplexed); Showtime (multiplexed); Starz (multiplexed); The Movie Channel (multiplexed).

Internet Service
Operational: Yes.
Fee: $42.95 monthly.

Telephone Service
None

Miles of Plant: 9.0 (coaxial); None (fiber optic). Homes passed: 600.
General Manager: Len Falter. Marketing Director: Rafael Vasquez. Communications Director: Bryan Byrd.
County fee: 3% of gross.
Ownership: Comcast Cable Communications Inc. (MSO).

RIVERSIDE—Charter Communications, 7337 Central Ave, Riverside, CA 92504. Phone: 951-343-5100. Fax: 951-354-5942. Web Site: http://www.charter.com. Also serves Jurupa Hills, Mira Loma, Norco, Rubidoux & Sunnyslope. ICA: CA0023.
TV Market Ranking: 2 (Jurupa Hills, Mira Loma, Norco, RIVERSIDE, Rubidoux, Sunnyslope). Franchise award date: N.A. Franchise expiration date: N.A. Began: September 30, 1980.
Channel capacity: N.A. Channels available but not in use: N.A.

Basic Service
Subscribers: 58,650.
Programming (received off-air): KABC-TV (ABC) Los Angeles; KAZA-TV (IND) Avalon; KCAL-TV (IND) Los Angeles; KCBS-TV (CBS) Los Angeles; KCET (PBS) Los Angeles; KCOP-TV (MNT) Los Angeles; KDOC-TV (IND) Anaheim; KFTR-DT (TEL) Ontario; KHIZ (IND) Barstow; KLCS (PBS) Los Angeles; KMEX-DT (UNV) Los Angeles; KNBC (NBC) Los Angeles; KPXN-TV (ION) San Bernardino; KRCA (IND) Riverside; KSCI (IND) Long Beach; KTBN-TV (TBN) Santa Ana; KTLA (CW) Los Angeles; KTTV (FOX) Los Angeles; KVCR-DT (PBS) San Bernardino; KVEA (TMO) Corona; KVMD (IND) Twentynine Palms; KWHY-TV (IND) Los Angeles; KXLA (IND) Rancho Palos Verdes.
Programming (via satellite): C-SPAN; Home Shopping Network; QVC; TBS Superstation; WGN America.
Current originations: Leased Access; Government Access; Educational Access; Public Access.
Fee: $29.95 installation; $20.95 monthly.

Expanded Basic Service 1
Subscribers: 44,520.
Programming (via satellite): ABC Family Channel; AMC; Animal Planet; Arts & Entertainment; BET Networks; Bravo; Cartoon Network; CNBC; CNN; Comedy Central; Country Music TV; Discovery Channel; Disney Channel; E! Entertainment Television; ESPN; ESPN 2; Food Network; Fox News Channel; Fox Sports Net West; Fox Sports Net West 2; FX; G4; GalaVision; GSN; Hallmark Channel; Headline News; HGTV; History Channel; INSP; Lifetime; MSNBC; MTV; National Geographic Channel; Nickelodeon; Oxygen; SoapNet; Speed Channel; Spike TV; Syfy; The Learning Channel; Travel Channel; truTV; Turner Classic Movies; Turner Network TV; TV Land; USA Network; Versus; VH1; WE tv; Weather Channel.
Fee: $33.20 monthly.

Digital Basic Service
Subscribers: N.A.
Programming (via satellite): BBC America; Bio; Black Family Channel; Bloomberg Television; Boomerang; BYU Television; CNN en Espanol; Discovery Digital Networks; DMX Music; Do-It-Yourself; ESPN Classic Sports; ESPN Deportes; ESPNews; Eternal Word TV Network; Fox College Sports Atlantic; Fox College Sports Central; Fox College Sports Pacific; Fox Soccer; Fox Sports en Espanol; Fuel TV; Fuse; GAS; Golf Channel; Great American Country; History Channel International; Independent Film Channel; International Television (ITV); Lifetime Movie Network; Lifetime Real Women; MTV Networks Digital Suite; NFL Network; Nick Jr.; NickToons TV; Science Television; Sundance Channel; Toon Disney; TV One; TVG Network; WealthTV.

Digital Pay Service 1
Pay Units: N.A.
Programming (via satellite): Cinemax (multiplexed); Encore (multiplexed); Filipino Channel; Flix; HBO (multiplexed); Showtime (multiplexed); Starz (multiplexed); The Movie Channel (multiplexed).

Video-On-Demand: Yes

Pay-Per-View
iN DEMAND (delivered digitally); Playboy TV (delivered digitally); The Erotic Network (delivered digitally); Spice Hot (delivered digitally); ETC (Erotic TV Clips) (delivered digitally); NHL Center Ice/MLB Extra Innings (delivered digitally).

Internet Service
Operational: Yes.
Fee: $29.99 monthly.

Telephone Service
Digital: Operational
Fee: $29.99 monthly

Miles of Plant: 1,158.0 (coaxial); 25.0 (fiber optic). Homes passed: 108,000. Total homes in franchised area: 118,000.
Vice President & General Manager: Fred Lutz. Technical Operations Manager: George Noel. Marketing Director: Chris Bailey.
City fee: 5% of gross.
Ownership: Charter Communications Inc. (MSO).

RIVERSIDE—Formerly served by Cross Country Wireless Cable. No longer in operation. ICA: CA0409.

ROHNERT PARK—Comcast Cable. Now served by NAPA/SONOMA, CA [CA0038]. ICA: CA0050.

ROSEVILLE—Comcast Cable. Now served by SACRAMENTO, CA [CA0002]. ICA: CA0124.

ROSEVILLE—SureWest Broadband. Formerly served by Sacramento, CA [CA0459]. This cable system has converted to IPTV, PO Box 969, Roseville, CA 95661. Phone: 916-772-2000. Fax: 916-786-7170. Web Site: http://www.surewest.com. ICA: CA5608.
TV Market Ranking: 25 (ROSEVILLE).
Channel capacity: N.A. Channels available but not in use: N.A.

Video-On-Demand: Yes

Internet Service
Operational: Yes.

Telephone Service
Digital: Operational

Ownership: SureWest Broadband.

SACRAMENTO—Comcast Cable, 4350 Pell Dr, Sacramento, CA 95838-2531. Phone: 916-927-2225. Fax: 916-927-0805. Web Site: http://www.comcast.com. Also serves Citrus Heights, Davis, El Macero, Elk Grove, Folsom, Galt, Greater Willowbank, Isleton, McClellan Park, Meadowview, Oak Park, Placer County (western portion), Rancho Cordova, Roseville, Sacramento County & Yolo County. ICA: CA0002.
TV Market Ranking: 25 (Citrus Heights, Davis, El Macero, Elk Grove, Folsom, Galt, Greater Willowbank, Isleton, McClellan Park, Meadowview, Oak Park, Placer County (western portion), Rancho Cordova, Roseville, SACRAMENTO, Sacramento County, Yolo County (portions)); Below 100 (Yolo County (portions)); Outside TV Markets (Yolo County (portions)). Franchise award date: December 1, 1983. Franchise expiration date: N.A. Began: August 25, 1985.
Channel capacity: N.A. Channels available but not in use: N.A.

Basic Service
Subscribers: 252,060.
Programming (received off-air): KCRA-TV (NBC) Sacramento; KCSO-LP Sacramento; KMAX-TV (CW) Sacramento; KOVR (CBS) Stockton; KQCA (MNT) Stockton; KSPX-TV (ION) Sacramento; KTFK-DT (TEL) Stockton; KTNC-TV (IND) Concord; KTXL (FOX) Sacramento; KUVS-DT (UNV) Modesto; KVIE (PBS) Sacramento; KXTV (ABC) Sacramento; 28 FMs.
Programming (via satellite): California Channel; C-SPAN; C-SPAN 2; GalaVision;

Home Shopping Network; QVC; TV Guide Network.
Current originations: Leased Access; Religious Access; Government Access; Educational Access; Public Access.
Fee: $43.99 installation; $12.11 monthly.

Expanded Basic Service 1
Subscribers: N.A.
Programming (via satellite): ABC Family Channel; AMC; Animal Planet; Arts & Entertainment; BET Networks; Bravo; Cartoon Network; CNBC; CNN; Comcast Sports Net Bay Area; Comedy Central; Country Music TV; Discovery Channel; E! Entertainment Television; ESPN; ESPN 2; Food Network; Fox News Channel; FX; Golf Channel; GSN; Headline News; HGTV; History Channel; Lifetime; MSNBC; MTV; Nickelodeon; Speed Channel; Spike TV; Style Network; Syfy; TBS Superstation; The Learning Channel; truTV; Turner Classic Movies; Turner Network TV; TV Land; USA Network; Versus; VH1; Weather Channel.
Fee: $39.05 monthly.

Digital Basic Service
Subscribers: N.A.
Programming (via satellite): AmericanLife TV Network; BBC America; Black Family Channel; Bloomberg Television; Discovery Digital Networks; ESPN Classic Sports; ESPNews; Fox College Sports Atlantic; Fox College Sports Central; Fox College Sports Pacific; Fox Movie Channel; Fox Sports World; G4; GAS; Great American Country; Halogen Network; History Channel International; Independent Film Channel; KRCA (IND) Riverside; KXTV (ABC) Sacramento; Lifetime Movie Network; Lime; MTV Networks Digital Suite; MuchMusic Network; National Geographic Channel; Nick Jr.; NickToons TV; Outdoor Channel; Ovation; ShopNBC; Star India Gold; Star India News; Star India Plus; Star One; Sundance Channel; The Word Network; Toon Disney; Trinity Broadcasting Network; Vijay; WE tv.
Fee: $11.95 monthly.

Digital Pay Service 1
Pay Units: N.A.
Programming (via satellite): Canales N; Cinemax (multiplexed); Encore (multiplexed); Flix; HBO (multiplexed); Music Choice; Showtime (multiplexed); Starz (multiplexed); The Movie Channel (multiplexed).
Fee: $17.99 monthly (Cinemax, TMC, or Starz), $18.99 monthly (HBO or Showtime).

Video-On-Demand: Yes

Pay-Per-View
Addressable homes: 250,000.
iN DEMAND (delivered digitally), Addressable: Yes; Hot Choice (delivered digitally); Playboy TV (delivered digitally); Fresh (delivered digitally); Shorteez (delivered digitally); ESPN Extra (delivered digitally); ESPN Now (delivered digitally); Sports PPV (delivered digitally); iN DEMAND.

Internet Service
Operational: Yes.
Broadband Service: Comcast High Speed Internet.
Fee: $42.95 monthly; $7.00 modem lease; $149.00 modem purchase.

Telephone Service
Digital: Operational
Miles of Plant: 4,059.0 (coaxial); 500.0 (fiber optic). Homes passed: 513,000.
Area Vice President: Dan McCarty. Technical Operations Director: Joe Trassare. Marketing Manager: Christi Rossi. Communications Director: Erica Smith.
City fee: 5% of gross.
Ownership: Comcast Cable Communications Inc. (MSO).

SACRAMENTO—Formerly [CA0459]. This cable system has converted to IPTV, PO Box 969, Roseville, CA 95661. Phone: 916-772-2000. Fax: 916-786-7170. Web Site: http://www.surewest.com. ICA: CA5597.
TV Market Ranking: 25 (SACRAMENTO).
Channel capacity: N.A. Channels available but not in use: N.A.

Basic Service
Subscribers: 21,000 (Includes Antelope, Arden Park, Carmichael, Citrus Heights, Del Paso Heights, Elk Grove, Fair Oaks, Lincoln, McClellan Park, Rancho Cordova, Roseville, Sacramento, S. Natomas).

Video-On-Demand: Yes

Internet Service
Operational: Yes.
Subscribers: 21,000.

Telephone Service
Digital: Operational
Subscribers: 19,800.
Miles of Plant: None (coaxial); 573.0 (fiber optic). Homes passed: 192,867. (Sub counts & fiber miles includes Antelope, Arden Park, Carmichael, Citrus Heights, Del Paso Heights, Elk Grove, Fair Oaks, Lincoln, McClellan Park, Rancho Cordova, Roseville, Sacramento, S. Natomas)
Ownership: SureWest Broadband.

SACRAMENTO—Formerly served by Wireless Broadcasting Services. No longer in operation. ICA: CA0410.

SACRAMENTO—SureWest Broadband. This cable system has converted to IPTV. See Sacramento, CA [CA5597]. ICA: CA0459.

SALTON CITY—Cable USA, PO Box 336, 2455 Stirrup Rd, Borrego Springs, CA 92004-0336. Phone: 760-767-5607. Fax: 760-767-3609. Web Site: http://www.cableusa.com. ICA: CA0473.
TV Market Ranking: Below 100 (SALTON CITY).
Channel capacity: N.A. Channels available but not in use: N.A.

Basic Service
Subscribers: N.A.
Programming (received off-air): KDFX-CA Indio/Palm Springs; KESQ-TV (ABC, CW) Palm Springs; KFMB-TV (CBS) San Diego; KMIR-TV (NBC) Palm Springs; KPBS (PBS) San Diego.
Programming (via satellite): Canal 52MX; Cine Latino; Cine Mexicano; CNN en Espanol; Discovery en Espanol; History Channel en Espanol; MTV Tres; QVC; TBS Superstation; Toon Disney en Espanol; Trinity Broadcasting Network; VeneMovies; Weather Channel; WGN America.

Expanded Basic Service 1
Subscribers: N.A.
Programming (via satellite): ABC Family Channel; Animal Planet; Arts & Entertainment; Cartoon Network; CNBC; CNN; Country Music TV; C-SPAN; C-SPAN 2; Discovery Channel; E! Entertainment Television; ESPN; ESPN 2; ESPN Classic Sports; Eternal Word TV Network; Food Network; Fox News Channel; Fox Sports en Espanol; G4; GalaVision; Hallmark Channel; Headline News; History Channel; Home Shopping Network; MTV; Nickelodeon; ShopNBC; Spike TV; Syfy; Telefutura; The Learning Channel; Turner Classic Movies; Turner Network TV; Univision; USA Network; VH1; WE tv.

Digital Basic Service
Subscribers: N.A.
Programming (via satellite): AmericanLife TV Network; BBC America; Bio; Bloomberg Television; CMT Pure Country; Current; Daystar TV Network; Discovery Health Channel; Discovery Kids Channel; Discovery Military Channel; Discovery Planet Green; DMX Music; ESPN 2; ESPN Classic Sports; ESPNews; FitTV; Fox College Sports Atlantic; Fox College Sports Central; Fox College Sports Pacific; Fox Movie Channel; Fox Soccer; G4; Golf Channel; Gospel Music Channel; GSN; Halogen Network; History Channel International; ID Investigation Discovery; MTV Hits; MTV2; National Geographic Channel; Nick Jr.; Outdoor Channel; Ovation; Science Channel; ShopNBC; Speed Channel; Style Network; Syfy; TeenNick; Trinity Broadcasting Network; Versus; VH1 Classic; VH1 Soul; WE tv.

Digital Expanded Basic Service
Subscribers: N.A.
Programming (via satellite): Cine Latino; Cine Mexicano; CNN en Espanol; Discovery en Espanol; Fox Sports en Espanol; History Channel en Espanol; MTV Tres; Toon Disney en Espanol; Utilisima.

Digital Pay Service 1
Pay Units: N.A.
Programming (via satellite): Cinemax (multiplexed); Encore (multiplexed); Flix; Fox Movie Channel; HBO (multiplexed); HBO Latino; Lifetime Movie Network; Showtime (multiplexed); Starz (multiplexed); Sundance Channel; The Movie Channel (multiplexed).

Video-On-Demand: No

Pay-Per-View
iN DEMAND (delivered digitally); Hot Choice (delivered digitally); Playboy TV (delivered digitally); Shorteez (delivered digitally); Fresh (delivered digitally); Club Jenna (delivered digitally).

Internet Service
Operational: Yes.

Telephone Service
None
Manager & Chief Technician: Joe Gustafson.
Ownership: USA Companies (MSO).

SALTON SEA BEACH—Cable USA, PO Box 336, 2455 Stirrup Rd, Borrego Springs, CA 92004-0336. Phones: 308-236-1512 (Kearney, NE corporate office); 800-300-6989; 760-767-5607. Fax: 760-767-3609. Web Site: http://www.cableusa.com. Also serves Desert Shores. ICA: CA0255.
TV Market Ranking: Below 100 (Desert Shores); Outside TV Markets (SALTON SEA BEACH). Franchise award date: April 5, 1984. Franchise expiration date: N.A. Began: June 1, 1984.
Channel capacity: N.A. Channels available but not in use: N.A.

Basic Service
Subscribers: 386.
Programming (received off-air): KECY-TV (ABC, FOX, MNT, TMO) El Centro; KESQ-TV (ABC, CW) Palm Springs; KMIR-TV (NBC) Palm Springs; KRMA-TV (PBS) Denver; KSWT (CBS, CW) Yuma; KTLA (CW) Los Angeles.
Programming (via satellite): ABC Family Channel; Cartoon Network; C-SPAN 2; Great American Country; Headline News; Home Shopping Network; TBS Superstation; The Learning Channel; Trinity Broadcasting Network; TV Land; Weather Channel; WGN America.
Current originations: Public Access.
Fee: $24.95 installation; $21.99 monthly; $3.00 converter.

Expanded Basic Service 1
Subscribers: N.A.
Programming (via satellite): AMC; Animal Planet; Arts & Entertainment; Comedy Central; Court TV; Discovery Channel; E! Entertainment Television; ESPN; ESPN 2; History Channel; Lifetime; MTV; Nickelodeon; Spike TV; Syfy; Turner Classic Movies; Turner Network TV; USA Network; VH1.

Pay Service 1
Pay Units: N.A.
Programming (via satellite): HBO; The Movie Channel.
Fee: $13.00 monthly (The Movie Channel), $14.50 monthly (HBO).

Internet Service
Operational: No.

Telephone Service
None
Miles of Plant: 12.0 (coaxial); None (fiber optic). Homes passed: 900. Total homes in franchised area: 2,000.
Manager & Chief Technician: Joe Gustafson.
County fee: 3% of basic.
Ownership: USA Companies (MSO).

SAN ANDREAS—Comcast Cable, 6505 Tam O Shanter Dr, Stockton, CA 95210-3349. Phones: 209-473-4555; 800-266-2278. Fax: 209-473-8177. Web Site: http://www.comcast.com. Also serves Amador County (portions), Angels Camp, Arnold, Avery, Big Trees, Calaveras County, Douglas Flat, Hathaway Pines, Mokelumne Hill, Murphys, Rancho Calaveras, Vallecito & Valley Springs. ICA: CA0133.
TV Market Ranking: 25 (Amador County (portions), Calaveras County (portions), SAN ANDREAS); Outside TV Markets (Angels Camp, Arnold, Avery, Big Trees, Douglas Flat, Hathaway Pines, Mokelumne Hill, Murphys, Rancho Calaveras, Vallecito, Valley Springs, Amador County (portions), Calaveras County (portions), SAN ANDREAS). Franchise award date: N.A. Franchise expiration date: N.A. Began: January 1, 1965.
Channel capacity: 60 (operating 2-way). Channels available but not in use: None.

Basic Service
Subscribers: 9,376.
Programming (received off-air): KCRA-TV (NBC) Sacramento; KCSO-LP Sacramento; KMAX-TV (CW) Sacramento; KOVR (CBS) Stockton; KQCA (MNT) Stockton; KSPX-TV (ION) Sacramento; KTFK-DT (TEL) Stockton; KTXL (FOX) Sacramento; KUVS-DT (UNV) Modesto; KVIE (PBS) Sacramento; KXTV (ABC) Sacramento; allband FM.
Programming (via satellite): CNBC; CNN; C-SPAN; C-SPAN 2; Fox News Channel;

Headline News; Home Shopping Network; MSNBC; QVC; TV Guide Network; Weather Channel.
Current originations: Leased Access; Government Access; Educational Access; Public Access.
Fee: $43.99 installation; $12.00 monthly; $2.50 converter.

Expanded Basic Service 1
Subscribers: N.A.
Programming (via satellite): ABC Family Channel; AMC; Animal Planet; Arts & Entertainment; BET Networks; Cartoon Network; Comcast Sports Net Bay Area; Comedy Central; Discovery Channel; Disney Channel; E! Entertainment Television; ESPN; ESPN 2; ESPN Classic Sports; Food Network; FX; Great American Country; GSN; HGTV; History Channel; Lifetime; MTV; Nickelodeon; Oxygen; ShopNBC; Spike TV; TBS Superstation; The Learning Channel; Travel Channel; truTV; Turner Network TV; TV Land; USA Network; Versus; VH1; WE tv.
Fee: $49.95 monthly.

Digital Basic Service
Subscribers: 2,812.
Programming (via satellite): AmericanLife TV Network; BBC America; Bio; Black Family Channel; Bloomberg Television; Bravo; Canales N; Discovery Digital Networks; DMX Music; Encore Action; ESPNews; FitTV; Fox College Sports Atlantic; Fox College Sports Central; Fox College Sports Pacific; Fox Movie Channel; Fox Sports World; Fuse; G4; GAS; Golf Channel; GSN; Halogen Network; History Channel International; Independent Film Channel; International Television (ITV); Lifetime Movie Network; Lime; MTV Networks Digital Suite; National Geographic Channel; Nick Jr.; NickToons TV; Outdoor Channel; Ovation; Speed Channel; Style Network; Sundance Channel; Syfy; The Word Network; Toon Disney; Trinity Broadcasting Network; Turner Classic Movies.
Fee: $50.95 monthly.

Digital Pay Service 1
Pay Units: 203.
Programming (via satellite): Cinemax (multiplexed); Flix; HBO (multiplexed); Showtime (multiplexed); Starz (multiplexed); The Movie Channel (multiplexed).
Fee: $10.00 installation; $17.99 monthly (Cinemax, Starz or TMC), $18.99 monthly (HBO or Showtime).

Video-On-Demand: No

Pay-Per-View
Addressable homes: 2,812.
iN DEMAND (delivered digitally), Addressable: Yes; Urban Xtra (delivered digitally); Fresh (delivered digitally); Shorteez (delivered digitally); Playboy TV (delivered digitally); Hot Choice (delivered digitally); ESPN Now (delivered digitally); Sports PPV (delivered digitally).

Internet Service
Operational: Yes.
Broadband Service: Comcast High Speed Internet.
Fee: $42.95 monthly.

Telephone Service
Digital: Operational
Miles of Plant: 362.0 (coaxial); 5.0 (fiber optic). Homes passed: 18,901. Total homes in franchised area: 25,731.
Technical Operations Director: Fred Walkover. Marketing Manager: Terry Dowling.
County fee: 5% of gross.
Ownership: Comcast Cable Communications Inc. (MSO).

SAN BERNARDINO—Charter Communications, 7337 Central Ave, Riverside, CA 92504. Phone: 951-343-5100. Web Site: http://www.charter.com. Also serves Devore, Rancho Cucamonga & San Bernardino County (portions). ICA: CA0120.
TV Market Ranking: 2 (Devore, Rancho Cucamonga, SAN BERNARDINO, San Bernardino County (portions)). Franchise award date: November 21, 1961. Franchise expiration date: N.A. Began: June 1, 1952.
Channel capacity: N.A. Channels available but not in use: N.A.

Basic Service
Subscribers: 38,729.
Programming (received off-air): KABC-TV (ABC) Los Angeles; KAZA-TV (IND) Avalon; KDOC-TV (IND) Anaheim; KFTR-DT (TEL) Ontario; KHIZ (IND) Barstow; KJLA (IND) Ventura; KPXN-TV (ION) San Bernardino; KRCA (IND) Riverside; KSCI (IND) Long Beach; KTBN-TV (TBN) Santa Ana; KVCR-DT (PBS) San Bernardino; KVEA (TMO) Corona; KVMD (IND) Twentynine Palms; KXLA (IND) Rancho Palos Verdes; WGN-TV (CW, IND) Chicago; 25 FMs.
Programming (via microwave): KCAL-TV (IND) Los Angeles; KCBS-TV (CBS) Los Angeles; KCET (PBS) Los Angeles; KCOP-TV (MNT) Los Angeles; KLCS (PBS) Los Angeles; KMEX-DT (UNV) Los Angeles; KNBC (NBC) Los Angeles; KTLA (CW) Los Angeles; KTTV (FOX) Los Angeles; KWHY-TV (IND) Los Angeles.
Programming (via satellite): C-SPAN; Eternal Word TV Network; Home Shopping Network; QVC; TBS Superstation.
Current originations: Government Access; Educational Access; Public Access.
Fee: $29.99 installation; $4.00 converter.

Expanded Basic Service 1
Subscribers: N.A.
Programming (via satellite): ABC Family Channel; AMC; Animal Planet; Arts & Entertainment; BET Networks; Bravo!; Cartoon Network; CNBC; CNN; Comedy Central; Country Music TV; Discovery Channel; Disney Channel; E! Entertainment Television; ESPN; ESPN 2; Food Network; Fox News Channel; Fox Sports Net; Fox Sports Net West 2; FX; G4; GalaVision; GSN; Hallmark Channel; Headline News; HGTV; History Channel; INSP; Lifetime; MSNBC; MTV; National Geographic Channel; Nickelodeon; Oxygen; SoapNet; Speed Channel; Spike TV; Syfy; The Learning Channel; Travel Channel; truTV; Turner Classic Movies; Turner Network TV; TV Land; USA Network; Versus; VH1; WE tv; Weather Channel.
Fee: $45.45 monthly.

Digital Basic Service
Subscribers: N.A.
Programming (via satellite): BBC America; Bio; Black Family Channel; Bloomberg Television; Boomerang; BYU Television; CNN en Espanol; Discovery Digital Networks; DMX Music; Do-It-Yourself; ESPN Classic Sports; ESPN Deportes; ESPNews; Eternal Word TV Network; Fox College Sports Atlantic; Fox College Sports Central; Fox College Sports Pacific; Fox Soccer; Fuel TV; Fuse; GAS; Golf Channel; Great American Country; History Channel International; Independent Film Channel; Lifetime Movie Network; Lifetime Real Women; MTV Networks Digital Suite; NFL Network; Nick Jr.; Nick Too; Science Television; Sundance Channel; Toon Disney; TV One; TVG Network; WealthTV.

Digital Pay Service 1
Pay Units: N.A.
Programming (via satellite): Cinemax (multiplexed); Filipino Channel; HBO (multiplexed); Starz (multiplexed).

Video-On-Demand: Yes

Pay-Per-View
iN DEMAND (delivered digitally), Fee: $3.95; NHL Center Ice/MLB Extra Innings (delivered digitally); Spice Hot (delivered digitally), Fee: $7.95; Playboy TV (delivered digitally); The Erotic Network (delivered digitally); ETC (Erotic TV Clips) (delivered digitally).

Internet Service
Operational: Yes.
Broadband Service: Charter Pipeline.
Fee: $29.99 monthly.

Telephone Service
Digital: Operational
Fee: $29.99 monthly
Miles of Plant: 522.0 (coaxial); 33.0 (fiber optic). Additional miles planned: 10.0 (coaxial); 3.0 (fiber optic). Homes passed: 55,486. Total homes in franchised area: 55,486.
Vice President & General Manager: Fred Lutz. Technical Operations Manager: George Noel. Marketing Director: Chris Bailey.
City fee: 5% of gross.
Ownership: Charter Communications Inc. (MSO).

SAN BERNARDINO—Now served by ANAHEIM, CA [CA0033]. ICA: CA0370.

SAN BERNARDINO—Now served by ANAHEIM, CA [CA0033]. ICA: CA0103.

SAN BRUNO—City of San Bruno Municipal Cable TV, 398 El Camino Real, San Bruno, CA 94066-4946. Phones: 866-668-0165 (Internet & Phone technical support); 650-616-3100. Fax: 650-871-5526. E-mail: info@sanbrunocable.com. Web Site: http://www.sanbrunocable.com. ICA: CA0140.
TV Market Ranking: 7 (SAN BRUNO). Franchise award date: January 1, 1971. Franchise expiration date: N.A. Began: October 1, 1971.
Channel capacity: 78 (operating 2-way). Channels available but not in use: 6.

Basic Service
Subscribers: 9,000.
Programming (received off-air): KBCW (CW) San Francisco; KCNS (IND) San Francisco; KCSM-TV (PBS) San Mateo; KDTV-TV (UNV) San Francisco; KFSF-DT (TEL) Vallejo; KGO-TV (ABC) San Francisco; KICU-TV (IND) San Jose; KKPX-TV (ION) San Jose; KMTP-TV (ETV) San Francisco; KNTV (NBC) San Jose; KOFY-TV (IND) San Francisco; KPIX-TV (CBS) San Francisco; KQED (PBS) San Francisco; KRON-TV (MNT) San Francisco; KSTS (TMO) San Jose; KTEH (PBS) San Jose; KTLN-TV (IND) Novato; KTNC-TV (IND) Concord; KTSF (IND) San Francisco; KTVU (FOX) Oakland.
Programming (via satellite): California Channel; Home Shopping Network; QVC.
Current originations: Government Access; Educational Access.
Fee: $18.75 monthly.

Expanded Basic Service 1
Subscribers: N.A.
Programming (via satellite): ABC Family Channel; AMC; Animal Planet; Arts & Entertainment; BET Networks; Bravo; Cartoon Network; CBS College Sports Network; CNBC; CNN; Comcast SportsNet West; Comedy Central; Country Music TV; C-SPAN; Discovery Channel; Disney Channel; E! Entertainment Television; ESPN; ESPN 2; ESPN Classic Sports; ESPN U; Food Network; Fox News Channel; FX; Hallmark Channel; Headline News; HGTV; History Channel; Lifetime; MSNBC; MTV; MTV2; National Geographic Channel; Nickelodeon; Oxygen; PBS Kids Sprout; SoapNet; Spike TV; Syfy; TBS Superstation; The Learning Channel; Toon Disney; Travel Channel; truTV; Turner Classic Movies; Turner Network TV; TV Guide Network; TV Land; USA Network; VH1; Weather Channel.
Fee: $30.06 monthly.

Digital Basic Service
Subscribers: 2,100.
Programming (via satellite): American-Life TV Network; BBC America; Bio; Bloomberg Television; Boomerang; BYU Television; CMT Pure Country; CNN International; Cooking Channel; C-SPAN 2; Current; Discovery Health Channel; Discovery Kids Channel; Discovery Military Channel; Discovery Planet Green; DMX Music; Do-It-Yourself; ESPN Deportes; ESPNews; Eternal Word TV Network; Fox Business Channel; Fox Movie Channel; Fox Soccer; Fuse; G4; Gol TV; Golf Channel; GSN; Hallmark Movie Channel; Halogen Network; History Channel International; HorseRacing TV; ID Investigation Discovery; Independent Film Channel; Lifetime Movie Network; Lifetime Real Women; LOGO; MTV Hits; MTV Jams; Nick Jr.; NickToons TV; Outdoor Channel; Ovation; Science Channel; Sleuth; Speed Channel; Style Network; Sundance Channel; TeenNick; Tennis Channel; Trinity Broadcasting Network; TVG Network; Versus; VH1 Classic; VH1 Soul; WE tv.
Fee: $35.23 monthly.

Digital Expanded Basic Service
Subscribers: N.A.
Programming (received off-air): KBCW (CW) San Francisco; KGO-TV (ABC) San Francisco; KNTV (NBC) San Jose; KOFY-TV (IND) San Francisco; KPIX-TV (CBS) San Francisco; KRON-TV (MNT) San Francisco; KTEH (PBS) San Jose; KTVU (FOX) Oakland.
Programming (via satellite): Animal Planet HD; Arts & Entertainment HD; Azteca America; Bio HD; CNN HD; Discovery Channel HD; Discovery HD Theater; Discovery Planet Green; ESPN 2 HD; ESPN HD; Food Network HD; Fox Business Channel HD; Fox News HD; FX HD; Hallmark Movie Channel HD; HDNet; HDNet Movies; HGTV HD; History Channel HD; KQED (PBS) San Francisco; National Geographic Channel HD Network; Outdoor Channel 2 HD; QVC HD; Science Channel HD; Speed HD; TBS in HD; TLC HD; Turner Network TV HD; Universal HD; Versus HD; Weather Channel HD.
Fee: $7.30 monthly (HD Broadcast & Basic or HD Plus).

Digital Expanded Basic Service 2
Subscribers: N.A.
Programming (via satellite): AYM Sports; Bandamax; Canal 24 Horas; Canal Sur; CB Television Michoacan; Cine Latino; Cine Mexicano; CNN en Espanol; De Pelicula; De Pelicula Clasico; Discovery en Espanol; Discovery Familia; Docu TVE; Ecuavisia Internacional; EWTN en Espanol; Fox Sports en Espanol; Gol TV; History Channel en Espanol; HITN; HTV Musica; Infinito; La Familia Network; Latele Novela Network; Latino America TV; MTV Tres; mun2 television; Once Mexico; Ritmoson Latino; Sorpresa; Sur Mex; TBN Enlace USA; Telefe In-

ternational; Teleformula; Telehit; Telemicro Internacional; TV Chile; TV Colombia; TVE Internacional; Utilisima; VeneMovies; Video Rola.
Fee: $15.70 monthly.

Pay Service 1
Pay Units: N.A.
Programming (via satellite): Cinemax; Encore; HBO; Showtime; Starz; The Movie Channel.
Fee: $8.35 monthly (Starz/Encore), $10.95 monthly (HBO, Cinemax, Showtime or TMC).

Digital Pay Service 1
Pay Units: N.A.
Programming (via satellite): ART America; CCTV-4; Cinemax (multiplexed); Cinemax HD; Encore (multiplexed); Filipino Channel; GMA Pinoy TV; HBO (multiplexed); HBO HD; Korean Channel; RAI Internazional; Russian Television Network; Saigon Broadcasting TV Network; Showtime (multiplexed); Showtime HD; Smithsonian Channel HD; Starz (multiplexed); Starz Comedy HD; Starz Edge HD; Starz HDTV; Starz Kids & Family HD; The Movie Channel (multiplexed); The Movie Channel HD; TV Asia; TV Japan; TV5 USA; Zee TV USA; Zhong Tian Channel.
Fee: $3.54 monthly (Encore), $10.45 monthly (Rai or TV5), $12.55 monthly (Zhong Tian & CCTV), $13.60 monthly (HBO, Showtime, TMC, Cinemax, Starz, ART or Korean), $15.70 monthly (SBTN, Russian, or TV Asia & Zee TV), $20.95 monthly (Filipino), $26.20 monthly (TV Jap.

Video-On-Demand: Yes

Pay-Per-View
iN DEMAND (delivered digitally), Addressable: Yes; Playboy TV (delivered digitally); Sports PPV (delivered digitally); Fresh (delivered digitally); Hot Choice (delivered digitally); Spice: Xcess (delivered digitally).

Internet Service
Operational: Yes. Began: September 1, 1999.
Subscribers: 4,500.
Broadband Service: sanbrunocable.com.
Fee: $99.00 installation; $32.95 monthly; $75.00 modem purchase.

Telephone Service
Analog: Not Operational
Digital: Operational
Fee: $26.80 monthly

Miles of Plant: 75.0 (coaxial); 25.0 (fiber optic). Homes passed: 15,600.
Director: Tenzin Gyaltsen. Chief Engineer: Al Johnson. Business Manager: Stephen Firpo. Program Manager: Miriam Schalit.
City fee: 5% of gross.
Ownership: San Bruno Municipal Cable TV.

SAN DIEGO—Cox Communications, 5159 Federal Blvd, San Diego, CA 92105-5428. Phone: 619-263-9251. Fax: 619-266-5540. Web Site: http://www.cox.com/sandiego. Also serves Bonsall, Camp Pendleton, Cardiff-by-the-Sea, Chula Vista, Crest, El Cajon, Encinitas, Escondido, Imperial Beach, Jamul, La Mesa, Lemon Grove, Leucadia, National City, Oceanside, Pine Valley, Poway, Ramona, Rancho San Diego, Rancho Santa Fe, San Diego (unincorporated areas), San Diego County, San Marcos, Santee, Solana Beach, Spring Valley & Vista. ICA: CA0001.
TV Market Ranking: 51 (Bonsall, Camp Pendleton, Cardiff-by-the-Sea, Chula Vista, Crest, El Cajon, Encinitas, Escondido, Imperial Beach, Jamul, La Mesa, Lemon Grove, Leucadia, National City, Oceanside, Poway, Ramona, Rancho San Diego, Rancho Santa Fe, SAN DIEGO, San Diego (unincorporated areas), San Marcos, Santee, Solana Beach, Spring Valley, Vista); Outside TV Markets (Pine Valley). Franchise award date: January 1, 1962. Franchise expiration date: N.A. Began: January 1, 1964.
Channel capacity: N.A. Channels available but not in use: N.A.

Basic Service
Subscribers: 537,000.
Programming (received off-air): KFMB-TV (CBS) San Diego; KGTV (ABC) San Diego; KNSD (NBC) San Diego; KPBS (PBS) San Diego; KSWB-TV (FOX) San Diego; KTLA (CW) Los Angeles; KUSI-TV (IND) San Diego; allband FM.
Programming (via microwave): 10 News Channel; KCOP-TV (MNT) Los Angeles; KFMB-TV (CBS) San Diego; KGTV (ABC) San Diego; KNSD (NBC) San Diego; KPBS (PBS) San Diego.
Programming (via satellite): California Channel; C-SPAN; C-SPAN 2; Eternal Word TV Network; QVC; TBS Superstation; Weather Channel; WGN America.
Current originations: Leased Access; Government Access; Educational Access; Public Access.
Fee: $60.00 installation; $12.00 monthly.

Expanded Basic Service 1
Subscribers: 453,525.
Programming (via satellite): ABC Family Channel; AMC; Animal Planet; Arts & Entertainment; BET Networks; Bravo; Cartoon Network; CNBC; CNN; Comedy Central; Country Music TV; Discovery Channel; Disney Channel; E! Entertainment Television; ESPN; ESPN 2; ESPN Classic Sports; Eternal Word TV Network; Food Network; Fox News Channel; Fox Sports en Espanol; Fox Sports Net; FX; Golf Channel; Headline News; HGTV; History Channel; Home Shopping Network; ION Television; Lifetime; MSNBC; MTV; Nickelodeon; ShopNBC; Speed Channel; Spike TV; Syfy; The Learning Channel; Travel Channel; truTV; Turner Classic Movies; Turner Network TV; TV Guide Network; TV Land; USA Network; Versus; VH1.
Fee: $27.95 monthly.

Digital Basic Service
Subscribers: N.A.
Programming (via satellite): BBC America; Bloomberg Television; Discovery Digital Networks; Encore Action; Eternal Word TV Network; Flix; Fox Sports World; G4; GSN; Hallmark Channel; Halogen Network; Independent Film Channel; Lifetime Movie Network; MuchMusic Network; Music Choice; NBA TV; Oxygen; SoapNet; Sundance Channel; Toon Disney; Trinity Broadcasting Network; Weatherscan.
Fee: $7.00 monthly.

Pay Service 1
Pay Units: 55,588.
Programming (via satellite): Cinemax.
Fee: $12.50 monthly.

Pay Service 2
Pay Units: 95,558.
Programming (via satellite): HBO.
Fee: $12.50 monthly.

Pay Service 3
Pay Units: 48,032.
Programming (via satellite): Showtime.
Fee: $12.50 monthly.

Digital Pay Service 1
Pay Units: N.A.
Programming (via satellite): Cinemax (multiplexed); Filipino Channel; HBO (multiplexed); Saigon Broadcasting TV Network; Showtime (multiplexed); Starz (multiplexed); The Movie Channel (multiplexed); TV Japan.
Fee: $9.00 (Cinemax, HBO, Showtime, Starz!, TMC); $10.00 monthly (Filipino Channel); $15.00 monthly (Saigon Brodcasting TV Network); $25.00 monthly (TV Japan).

Video-On-Demand: Yes

Pay-Per-View
Addressable homes: 223,694.
ESPN Extra (delivered digitally), Addressable: Yes; ESPN Gameplan (delivered digitally); iN DEMAND; iN DEMAND (delivered digitally); sports (delivered digitally).

Internet Service
Operational: Yes. Began: May 1, 1997.
Broadband Service: Cox High Speed Internet.
Fee: $49.95 installation; $29.95 monthly; $10.00 modem lease; $399.00 modem purchase.

Telephone Service
Digital: Operational
Fee: $9.99 monthly

Miles of Plant: 5,454.0 (coaxial); 213.0 (fiber optic). Homes passed: 750,000. Total homes in franchised area: 750,000.
Vice President & Regional Manager: William K. Geppert. Vice President, Marketing: Colette Jelineo. Chief Technician: Steve Gautereaux. Media & Public Relations Manager: Ceanne Guerra.
City fee: 3% of gross.
Ownership: Cox Communications Inc. (MSO).

SAN DIEGO—Time Warner Cable, 10450 Pacific Center Court, San Diego, CA 92121-2222. Phones: 865-635-8297; 858-695-3110. Fax: 858-566-6248. Web Site: http://www.timewarnercable.com/sandiego. Also serves Coronado, Del Mar, La Jolla, Pacific Beach, Poway, Rancho Bernardo & San Diego County. ICA: CA0007.
TV Market Ranking: 51 (Coronado, Del Mar, La Jolla, Pacific Beach, Poway, Rancho Bernardo, SAN DIEGO); 51,2 (San Diego County (portions)); Below 100 (San Diego County (portions)); Outside TV Markets (San Diego County (portions)). Franchise award date: January 1, 1964. Franchise expiration date: N.A. Began: January 1, 1964.
Channel capacity: N.A. Channels available but not in use: N.A.

Basic Service
Subscribers: 425,000 Includes Banning, Barstow, Carlsbad, Palm Desert, & Yucca Valley.
Programming (received off-air): KDTF-CA (UNV) San Diego; KFMB-TV (CBS) San Diego; KGTV (ABC) San Diego; KNSD (NBC) San Diego; KPBS (PBS) San Diego; KSWB-TV (FOX) San Diego; KUSI-TV (IND) San Diego; allband FM.
Programming (via satellite): Azteca America; C-SPAN; C-SPAN 2; Home Shopping Network; Jewelry Television; NASA TV; TBS Superstation; TV Guide Network; various Mexican stations; WGN America.
Current originations: Leased Access; Government Access; Educational Access; Public Access.
Fee: $36.00 installation; $12.49 monthly; $2.19 converter.

Expanded Basic Service 1
Subscribers: 177,700.
Programming (via satellite): ABC Family Channel; AMC; Animal Planet; Arts & Entertainment; BET Networks; Bravo; Cartoon Network; CNBC; CNN; Comedy Central; Country Music TV; Discovery Channel; Disney Channel; E! Entertainment Television; ESPN; ESPN 2; Food Network; Fox News Channel; Fox Sports Net West; FX; Golf Channel; Hallmark Channel; Headline News; HGTV; History Channel; ION Television; Lifetime; Lifetime Movie Network; MSNBC; MTV; Nickelodeon; QVC; Spike TV; Syfy; Telefutura; Telemundo; The Learning Channel; Travel Channel; truTV; Turner Classic Movies; Turner Network TV; TV Land; USA Network; Versus; VH1; WE tv; Weather Channel.
Fee: $36.46 monthly.

Digital Basic Service
Subscribers: 60,000.
Programming (received off-air): KFMB-TV (CBS) San Diego; KGTV (ABC) San Diego; KNSD (NBC) San Diego; KPBS (PBS) San Diego; KSWB-TV (FOX) San Diego.
Programming (via microwave): 10 News Channel.
Programming (via satellite): AmericanLife TV Network; Arts & Entertainment HD; BBC America; BBC America On Demand; Bio; Bloomberg Television; Boomerang; Boomerang en Espanol; Canal Sur; CBS College Sports Network; CCTV-9 (CCTV International); Cine Latino; CNN en Espanol; CNN International; Cooking Channel; C-SPAN 3; Current; Discovery en Espanol; Discovery HD Theater; Discovery Health Channel; Discovery Home Channel; Discovery Kids Channel; Discovery Military Channel; Discovery Times Channel; Disney Channel; Do-It-Yourself; Encore (multiplexed); ESPN 2 HD; ESPN Classic Sports; ESPN Deportes; ESPN HD; ESPN U; ESPNews; Eternal Word TV Network; EWTN en Espanol; Exercise TV; FitTV; Fox Business Channel; Fox College Sports Atlantic; Fox College Sports Central; Fox College Sports Pacific; Fox Movie Channel; Fox Reality Channel; Fox Soccer; Fox Sports en Espanol; FSN HD; Fuel TV; Fuse; G4; Gospel Music Channel; Great American Country; GSN; Halogen Network; HDNet; HDNet Movies; History Channel Internazional; HorseRacing TV; Independent Film Channel; INSP; La Familia Network; Lifetime Real Women; LOGO; MTV Tres; MTV2; mun2 television; Music Choice; National Geographic Channel; National Geographic Channel HD Network; National Geographic Channel On Demand; NBA TV; Nick Jr.; NickToons TV; Ovation; Oxygen; Oxygen On Demand; Palladia; Puma TV; Science Channel; Sleuth; SoapNet; Speed Channel; Style Network; Sundance Channel; TBS in HD; TeenNick; Tennis Channel; The Word Network; Toon Disney; Toon Disney en Espanol; Trinity Broadcasting Network; Turner Network TV HD; TV Guide SPOT; Universal HD; Versus HD; VH1 Classic; VHUNO; Video Rola.
Fee: $5.00 monthly (each pack).

Digital Pay Service 1
Pay Units: 19,400.
Programming (via satellite): Cinemax (multiplexed); Cinemax HD.
Fee: $12.00 monthly.

Digital Pay Service 2
Pay Units: 55,000.
Programming (via satellite): HBO (multiplexed); HBO HD.
Fee: $12.00 monthly.

Digital Pay Service 3
Pay Units: 21,900.
Programming (via satellite): Showtime (multiplexed); Showtime HD.
Fee: $12.00 monthly.

Digital Pay Service 4
Pay Units: 13,000.
Programming (via satellite): Starz; Starz HDTV.
Fee: $12.00 monthly.

Digital Pay Service 5
Pay Units: 2,500.
Programming (via satellite): Filipino Channel; Playgirl TV; Saigon Broadcasting TV Network.
Fee: $11.00 monthly.
Video-On-Demand: Yes
Pay-Per-View
iN DEMAND (delivered digitally); NHL Center Ice (delivered digitally); Ten Blox (delivered digitally); MLB Extra Innings (delivered digitally); ESPN Gameplan (delivered digitally); NBA League Pass (delivered digitally); Howard TV (delivered digitally); Ten Clips (delivered digitally); Playboy TV (delivered digitally); Club Jenna (delivered digitally).
Internet Service
Operational: Yes. Began: January 1, 1997.
Subscribers: 120,000.
Broadband Service: Road Runner.
Fee: $50.00 installation; $44.95 monthly.
Telephone Service
Digital: Operational
Fee: $39.95 monthly
Miles of Plant: 1,916.0 (coaxial); 468.0 (fiber optic). Homes passed: 460,000. Homes passed includes Banning, Barstow & Palm Desert
President: Bob Barlow. Vice President, Technical Services: Ron Johnson. Vice President, Engineering: Bob Jones. Vice President, Public Affairs: Marc Farrar. Vice President, Customer Care: Vinit Ahooja.
Ownership: Time Warner Cable (MSO).

SAN DIEGO NAVAL BASE—NWS Communications, 79 Mainline Dr, Westfield, MA 01085-3313. Phone: 800-562-7081. Fax: 413-562-5415. E-mail: info@nwscorp.net. Web Site: http://www.nwscorp.net. ICA: CA0372.
TV Market Ranking: 51 (SAN DIEGO NAVAL BASE). Franchise award date: October 1, 1986. Franchise expiration date: N.A. Began: June 1, 1987.
Channel capacity: 63 (2-way capable). Channels available but not in use: None.
Basic Service
Subscribers: 5,516.
Programming (received off-air): KFMB-TV (CBS) San Diego; KGTV (ABC) San Diego; KNSD (NBC) San Diego; KPBS (PBS) San Diego; KSWB-TV (FOX) San Diego; KTLA (CW) Los Angeles; KUSI-TV (IND) San Diego.
Programming (via satellite): ABC Family Channel; AMC; Animal Planet; Arts & Entertainment; BET Networks; Cartoon Network; CNBC; CNN; Comedy Central; Country Music TV; C-SPAN; C-SPAN 2; Discovery Channel; Disney Channel; E! Entertainment Television; ESPN; ESPN 2; Eternal Word TV Network; Fox Movie Channel; FX; Headline News; History Channel; Lifetime; MTV; Nickelodeon; QVC; Spike TV; Syfy; TBS Superstation; The Learning Channel; Trinity Broadcasting Network; Turner Classic Movies; Turner Network TV; TV Guide Network; TV Land; USA Network; VH1; Weather Channel; WGN America.
Fee: $34.95 monthly.
Pay Service 1
Pay Units: 941.
Programming (via satellite): Cinemax; Encore; HBO; Showtime; The Movie Channel.
Fee: $2.95 monthly (Encore), $11.95 monthly (Showtime), $12.95 monthly (Cinemax, HBO or TMC).
Video-On-Demand: No
Internet Service
Operational: No.
Telephone Service
None
Miles of Plant: 50.0 (coaxial); None (fiber optic). Additional miles planned: 25.0 (coaxial). Homes passed: 14,811.
Manager: James Smith.
Ownership: NWS Communications.

SAN FRANCISCO—Comcast Cable, 2055 Folsom St, San Francisco, CA 94110-1330. Phones: 925-973-7000 (San Ramon regional office); 415-863-8500. Fax: 415-863-1659. Web Site: http://www.comcast.com. Also serves Belmont, Brisbane, Burlingame, Colma, Daly City, El Granada, Foster City, Half Moon Bay, Hillsborough, La Honda, Los Altos Hills, Los Trancos Woods, Millbrae, Miramar, Montara, Moss Beach, Pacifica, Pescadero, Portola Valley, Redwood City, San Carlos, San Mateo, San Mateo County, South San Francisco & Woodside. ICA: CA0003.
TV Market Ranking: 7 (Belmont, Brisbane, Burlingame, Colma, Daly City, El Granada, Foster City, Half Moon Bay, Hillsborough, La Honda, Los Altos Hills, Los Trancos Woods, Millbrae, Miramar, Montara, Moss Beach, Pacifica, Pescadero, Portola Valley, Redwood City, San Carlos, SAN FRANCISCO, San Mateo, San Mateo County, South San Francisco, Woodside). Franchise award date: N.A. Franchise expiration date: N.A. Began: January 1, 1953.
Channel capacity: 75 (operating 2-way). Channels available but not in use: None.
Basic Service
Subscribers: 1,700,000 Includes Concord, Napa/Sonoma, Oakland, & San Jose.
Programming (received off-air): KBCW (CW) San Francisco; KCNS (IND) San Francisco; KCSM-TV (PBS) San Mateo; KDTV-TV (UNV) San Francisco; KFSF-DT (TEL) Vallejo; KGO-TV (ABC) San Francisco; KICU-TV (IND) San Jose; KKPX-TV (ION) San Jose; KNTV (NBC) San Jose; KOFY-TV (IND) San Francisco; KPIX-TV (CBS) San Francisco; KQED (PBS) San Francisco; KRCB (PBS) Cotati; KRON-TV (MNT) San Francisco; KSTS (TMO) San Jose; KTEH (PBS) San Jose; KTLN-TV (IND) Novato; KTNC-TV (IND) Concord; KTSF (IND) San Francisco; KTVU (FOX) Oakland; 24 FMs.
Programming (via satellite): California Channel; C-SPAN; C-SPAN 2; Discovery Channel; Home Shopping Network; TV Guide Network.
Current originations: Leased Access; Educational Access; Public Access.
Fee: $43.99 installation; $17.99 monthly.
Expanded Basic Service 1
Subscribers: N.A.
Programming (via satellite): ABC Family Channel; AMC; Animal Planet; Arts & Entertainment; BET Networks; Bravo; Cartoon Network; CNBC; CNN; Comcast Sports Net Bay Area; Comedy Central; Disney Channel; E! Entertainment Television; ESPN; ESPN 2; Food Network; Fox News Channel; FX; Golf Channel; Hallmark Channel; Headline News; HGTV; History Channel; International Television (ITV); Jade Channel; Lifetime; MSNBC; MTV; Nickelodeon; QVC; Spike TV; Syfy; TBS Superstation; The Learning Channel; Travel Channel; truTV; Turner Network TV; TV Land; USA Network; Versus; VH1; Weather Channel.
Fee: $52.50 monthly.
Digital Basic Service
Subscribers: N.A.
Programming (received off-air): KGO-TV (ABC) San Francisco; KNTV (NBC) San Jose; KPIX-TV (CBS) San Francisco; KQED (PBS) San Francisco.
Programming (via satellite): AmericanLife TV Network; BBC America; Bio; Black Family Channel; Bloomberg Television; Canales N; CCTV-4; CNN en Espanol; Discovery Health Channel; Discovery Home Channel; Discovery Kids Channel; Discovery Military Channel; Discovery Times Channel; ESPN Classic Sports; ESPN Now; ESPNews; Eternal Word TV Network; Filipino Channel; FitTV; Fox Movie Channel; Fox Sports en Espanol; Fox Sports Net Mid-Atlantic; Fox Sports World; Fuse; G4; GAS; Gol TV; Great American Country; GSN; History Channel International; Independent Film Channel; INSP; Lifetime Movie Network; Lime; MTV Networks Digital Suite; MTV2; Music Choice; National Geographic Channel; Nick Jr.; NickToons TV; Outdoor Channel; Ovation; RAI International; Russian Television Network; Saigon Broadcasting TV Network; Science Television; ShopNBC; Sorpresa; Speed Channel; Star India Gold; Star India News; Star India Plus; Star One; Sundance Channel; The Word Network; Toon Disney; Trinity Broadcasting Network; Turner Classic Movies; TV Asia; TV Japan; TVE Internacional; Video Rola; Vijay; WAM! America's Kidz Network; WE tv; Weatherscan; Zee TV USA; Zhong Tian Channel.
Fee: $53.50 monthly.
Digital Pay Service 1
Pay Units: N.A.
Programming (via satellite): Cinemax (multiplexed); Flix; HBO (multiplexed); Showtime (multiplexed); The Movie Channel (multiplexed).
Fee: $17.00 monthly (each).
Video-On-Demand: Yes
Pay-Per-View
Addressable: Yes; iN DEMAND, Fee: $4.95; Playboy TV (delivered digitally); Fresh (delivered digitally); UrbanXtra (delivered digitally).
Internet Service
Operational: Yes.
Broadband Service: Comcast High Speed Internet.
Fee: $42.95 monthly.
Telephone Service
Digital: Operational
Fee: $44.95 monthly
Miles of Plant: 2,110.0 (coaxial); 80.0 (fiber optic). Homes passed: 481,931.
Area Vice President: Doug Schulz. Vice President, Communications: Andrew Johnson. Technical Operations Director: Adam Goyer. Marketing Director: Jeff Farr.
City fee: 5% of gross.
Ownership: Comcast Cable Communications Inc. (MSO).

SAN FRANCISCO—Formerly served by TV Max. No longer in operation. ICA: CA0411.

SAN FRANCISCO (southern portion)—Astound Broadband, 2841 S El Camino Real, San Mateo, CA 94403. Phone: 800-427-8686. Fax: 425-576-8221. Web Site: http://www.astound.net. Also serves Burlingame, Daly City, Redwood City, San Mateo & South San Francisco. ICA: CA0452. **Note:** This system is an overbuild.
TV Market Ranking: 7 (Burlingame, Daly City, Redwood City, SAN FRANCISCO, San Mateo, South San Francisco). Franchise award date: N.A. Franchise expiration date: N.A. Began: July 28, 1999.
Channel capacity: N.A. Channels available but not in use: N.A.
Basic Service
Subscribers: 20,000.
Programming (received off-air): KBCW (CW) San Francisco; KCNS (IND) San Francisco; KDTV-TV (UNV) San Francisco; KGO-TV (ABC) San Francisco; KICU-TV (IND) San Jose; KKPX-TV (ION) San Jose; KMTP-TV (ETV) San Francisco; KNTV (NBC) San Jose; KOFY-TV (IND) San Francisco; KPIX-TV (CBS) San Francisco; KQED (PBS) San Francisco; KRON-TV (MNT) San Francisco; KSTS (TMO) San Jose; KTEH (PBS) San Jose; KTLN-TV (IND) Novato; KTNC-TV (IND) Concord; KTSF (IND) San Francisco; KTVU (FOX) Oakland; Telefutura.
Programming (via satellite): California Channel; C-SPAN; C-SPAN 2; TV Guide Network.
Current originations: Government Access.
Planned originations: Public Access.
Fee: $46.50 monthly.
Expanded Basic Service 1
Subscribers: N.A.
Programming (via satellite): ABC Family Channel; AMC; Animal Planet; Arts & Entertainment; BET Networks; Bloomberg Television; Bravo; Cartoon Network; CNBC; CNN; Comcast Sports Net Bay Area; Comedy Central; Country Music TV; Discovery Channel; Disney Channel; E! Entertainment Television; ESPN; ESPN 2; ESPN Classic Sports; ESPNews; Eternal Word TV Network; Food Network; Fox Movie Channel; Fox News Channel; Fox Sports Net; FX; G4; GalaVision; Golf Channel; Headline News; HGTV; History Channel; Home Shopping Network; Independent Film Channel; Lifetime; MTV; MTV2; National Geographic Channel; Nickelodeon; Oxygen; QVC; Speed Channel; Spike TV; Syfy; TBS Superstation; The Learning Channel; Toon Disney; Travel Channel; truTV; Turner Classic Movies; Turner Network TV; TV Land; USA Network; VH1; WE tv; Weather Channel.
Fee: $3.45 monthly.
Digital Basic Service
Subscribers: N.A.
Programming (received off-air): KGO-TV (ABC) San Francisco; KNTV (NBC) San Jose; KPIX-TV (CBS) San Francisco; KQED (PBS) San Francisco; KTVU (FOX) Oakland.
Programming (via satellite): BBC America; Bio; Boomerang; Comcast Sports Net Bay Area; Discovery Digital Networks; Discovery HD Theater; ESPN; Fox Soccer; Fuel TV; Gaming Entertainment Television; GAS; HDNet; HDNet Movies; History Channel International; Lifetime Movie Network; MTV Networks Digital Suite; Music Choice; Nick Jr.; Nick Too; NickToons TV; PBS Kids Sprout; SoapNet; Style Network; Sundance Channel; Tennis Channel.
Fee: $17.00 monthly.
Digital Pay Service 1
Pay Units: N.A.
Programming (via satellite): ART America; CCTV-4; Cinemax (multiplexed); Encore (multiplexed); Filipino Channel; Flix; HBO (multiplexed); RAI International; Russian Television Network; Showtime (multiplexed); Starz (multiplexed); Starz HDTV; The Movie Channel (multiplexed); TV Asia; TV Japan; TV5, La Television International; Zee TV USA; Zhong Tian Channel.
Video-On-Demand: Yes
Pay-Per-View
iN DEMAND (delivered digitally), Addressable: Yes; Ten Clips (delivered digitally); Ten Blue (delivered digitally); Ten Blox (delivered digitally).

Internet Service
Operational: Yes.
Broadband Service: In-house.
Fee: $19.95-$74.95 monthly.

Telephone Service
Digital: Operational
Fee: $24.95-$49.95 monthly
Homes passed: 92,000. Total homes in franchised area: 92,000.
Ownership: WaveDivision Holdings LLC (MSO).

SAN JOSE—Comcast Cable, 1900 S 10th St, San Jose, CA 95112-4110. Phones: 925-973-7000 (San Ramon regional office); 408-918-3200. Fax: 408-294-7280. Web Site: http://www.comcast.com. Also serves Atherton, Campbell, Cape Cod Village, Cupertino, East Palo Alto, Ladera, Los Altos, Los Gatos, Menlo Park, Milpitas, Monte Sereno, Mountain View, Palo Alto, San Mateo County (portions), Santa Clara, Santa Clara County, Saratoga, Stanford & Sunnyvale. ICA: CA0004.
TV Market Ranking: 7 (Atherton, Campbell, Cape Cod Village, Cupertino, East Palo Alto, Ladera, Los Altos, Los Gatos, Menlo Park, Milpitas, Monte Sereno, Mountain View, Palo Alto, SAN JOSE, San Mateo County (portions), Santa Clara, Santa Clara County, Saratoga, Stanford, Sunnyvale). Franchise award date: December 1, 1967. Franchise expiration date: N.A. Began: March 1, 1968.
Channel capacity: N.A. Channels available but not in use: N.A.

Basic Service
Subscribers: N.A. Included in San Francisco
Programming (received off-air): KBCW (CW) San Francisco; KCNS (IND) San Francisco; KDTV-TV (UNV) San Francisco; KFSF-DT (TEL) Vallejo; KGO-TV (ABC) San Francisco; KICU-TV (IND) San Jose; KKPX-TV (ION) San Jose; KMTP-TV (ETV) San Francisco; KNTV (NBC) San Jose; KOFY-TV (IND) San Francisco; KPIX-TV (CBS) San Francisco; KQED (PBS) San Francisco; KRON-TV (MNT) San Francisco; KSBW (NBC) Salinas; KSTS (TMO) San Jose; KTEH (PBS) San Jose; KTLN-TV (IND) Novato; KTNC-TV (IND) Concord; KTSF (IND) San Francisco; KTVU (FOX) Oakland; 30 FMs.
Programming (via satellite): California Channel; C-SPAN; C-SPAN 2; Discovery Channel; Home Shopping Network 2; QVC; TV Guide Network.
Current originations: Government Access; Educational Access; Public Access.
Fee: $43.99 installation; $14.07 monthly; $4.85 converter; $40.00 additional installation.

Expanded Basic Service 1
Subscribers: 158,409.
Programming (via satellite): ABC Family Channel; AMC; Animal Planet; Arts & Entertainment; BET Networks; Bravo; Cartoon Network; CNBC; CNN; Comedy Central; Country Music TV; Disney Channel; E! Entertainment Television; ESPN; ESPN 2; Food Network; Fox News Channel; Fox Sports Net; FX; GalaVision; Golf Channel; Hallmark Channel; Headline News; HGTV; History Channel; Lifetime; MSNBC; MTV; mun2 television; Nickelodeon; Spike TV; Syfy; TBS Superstation; The Learning Channel; Travel Channel; truTV; Turner Network TV; TV Land; USA Network; Versus; VH1; Weather Channel.
Fee: $38.33 monthly.

Digital Basic Service
Subscribers: 76,691.
Programming (via satellite): AmericanLife TV Network; BBC America; Bio; Black Family Channel; Bloomberg Television; Discovery Digital Networks; DragonTV; Encore Action; ESPN Classic Sports; ESPNews; Eternal Word TV Network; FitTV; Fox College Sports Atlantic; Fox College Sports Central; Fox College Sports Pacific; Fox Movie Channel; Fox Sports World; Fuse; G4; GAS; Great American Country; GSN; Halogen Network; History Channel International; Independent Film Channel; Lifetime Movie Network; Lime; MTV Networks Digital Suite; Music Choice; National Geographic Channel; Nick Jr.; NickToons TV; Outdoor Channel; Ovation; ShopNBC; Speed Channel; Star India Gold; Star India News; Star India Plus; Star One; Style Network; Sundance Channel; The Word Network; Toon Disney; Trinity Broadcasting Network; Turner Classic Movies; Vijay; WE tv; Weatherscan.
Fee: $11.95 monthly.

Digital Pay Service 1
Pay Units: 9,994.
Programming (via satellite): Cinemax (multiplexed).
Fee: $24.95 installation; $17.00 monthly.

Digital Pay Service 2
Pay Units: 11,533.
Programming (via satellite): Starz (multiplexed).
Fee: $17.00 monthly.

Digital Pay Service 3
Pay Units: 45,692.
Programming (via satellite): Canales N.
Fee: $17.00 monthly.

Digital Pay Service 4
Pay Units: 33,168.
Programming (via satellite): HBO (multiplexed).
Fee: $17.00 monthly.

Digital Pay Service 5
Pay Units: 3,493.
Programming (via satellite): RAI International; Russian Television Network; TV5, La Television International.

Digital Pay Service 6
Pay Units: 15,193.
Programming (via satellite): Showtime (multiplexed).
Fee: $17.00 monthly.

Digital Pay Service 7
Pay Units: 10,242.
Programming (via satellite): CCTV-4; Filipino Channel; Saigon Broadcasting TV Network; TV Asia; TV Japan; Zee TV USA; Zhong Tian Channel.

Digital Pay Service 8
Pay Units: 6,069.
Programming (via satellite): Flix; The Movie Channel (multiplexed).
Fee: $17.00 monthly.
Video-On-Demand: Yes

Pay-Per-View
Addressable homes: 76,646.
iN DEMAND (delivered digitally), Fee: $4.95-$7.95, Addressable: Yes; Hot Choice (delivered digitally); Urban Xtra (delivered digitally); Fresh (delivered digitally); Playboy TV (delivered digitally); ESPN Now (delivered digitally); Sports PPV (delivered digitally).

Internet Service
Operational: Yes.
Broadband Service: Comcast High Speed Internet.
Fee: $42.95 monthly.

Telephone Service
Digital: Operational
Miles of Plant: 2,413.0 (coaxial); None (fiber optic). Homes passed: 290,264. Total homes in franchised area: 296,459.
Area Vice President: Navarra Williams. Vice President, Communications: Andrew Johnson. Technical Operations Director: Dave Walton. Network Manager: Curt Christenson. Sales & Marketing Director: Eden Godsoe.
City fee: 5% of gross.
Ownership: Comcast Cable Communications Inc. (MSO).

SAN JOSE—Formerly served by Pacific Bell Video Services. No longer in operation. ICA: CA0441.

SAN JOSE—Formerly served by TV Max. No longer in operation. ICA: CA0412.

SAN JOSE—Matrix Cablevision Inc. Now served by SAN JOSE, CA [CA0004]. ICA: CA0467.

SAN LUIS OBISPO—Charter Communications, 270 Bridge St, San Luis Obispo, CA 93401. Phone: 805-544-1962. Fax: 805-541-6042. Web Site: http://www.charter.com. Also serves Arroyo Grande, Atascadero, Avila Beach, Cambria, Cayucos, Country Club Estates, Grover Beach, Guadalupe, Heritage Ranch, Los Osos, Morro Bay, Nipomo, Oceano, Paso Robles, Pismo/Shell Beach, San Luis Obispo County (portions), San Miguel, Santa Margarita & Templeton. ICA: CA0045.
TV Market Ranking: Below 100 (Arroyo Grande, Atascadero, Avila Beach, Cambria, Cayucos, Country Club Estates, Grover Beach, Guadalupe, Heritage Ranch, Los Osos, Morro Bay, Nipomo, Oceano, Paso Robles, Pismo/Shell Beach, SAN LUIS OBISPO, San Luis Obispo County (portions), San Miguel, Santa Margarita, Templeton). Franchise award date: August 2, 1967. Franchise expiration date: N.A. Began: August 2, 1968.
Channel capacity: N.A. Channels available but not in use: N.A.

Basic Service
Subscribers: 64,849.
Programming (received off-air): KBEH (IND) Oxnard; KCBS-TV (CBS) Los Angeles; KCET (PBS) Los Angeles; KCOP-TV (MNT) Los Angeles; KCOY-TV (CBS) Santa Maria; KEYT-TV (ABC, MNT) Santa Barbara; KKFX-CA San Luis Obispo; KPMR (UNV) Santa Barbara; KSBY (CW, NBC) San Luis Obispo; KTAS (TMO) San Luis Obispo; KTLA (CW) Los Angeles; 25 FMs.
Programming (via satellite): California Channel; C-SPAN; C-SPAN 2; Eternal Word TV Network; Home Shopping Network; INSP; ION Television; QVC; Speed Channel; Syfy; Trinity Broadcasting Network; TV Guide Network; Weather Channel.
Current originations: Leased Access; Government Access; Educational Access; Public Access.
Fee: $29.99 installation.

Expanded Basic Service 1
Subscribers: 54,210.
Programming (via satellite): ABC Family Channel; AMC; Animal Planet; Arts & Entertainment; Bravo; Cartoon Network; CNBC; CNN; Comedy Central; Country Music TV; Discovery Channel; Disney Channel; E! Entertainment Television; ESPN; ESPN 2; Food Network; Fox News Channel; Fox Sports Net West; Fox Sports Net West 2; G4; GalaVision; Golf Channel; Hallmark Channel; Headline News; HGTV; History Channel; Lifetime; MSNBC; MTV; National Geographic Channel; Nickelodeon; Oxygen; SoapNet; Speed Channel; Spike TV; Syfy; TBS Superstation; The Learning Channel; Travel Channel; truTV; Turner Classic Movies; Turner Network TV; TV Land; USA Network; Versus; VH1; Weather Channel.
Fee: $38.99 monthly.

Digital Basic Service
Subscribers: N.A.
Programming (via satellite): BBC America; Bio; Bloomberg Television; Boomerang; Discovery Digital Networks; Do-It-Yourself; Fox College Sports Atlantic; Fox College Sports Central; Fox College Sports Pacific; GAS; Great American Country; History Channel International; Independent Film Channel; Lifetime Movie Network; MTV Networks Digital Suite; MuchMusic Network; Music Choice; Nick Jr.; NickToons TV; Style Network; Sundance Channel; Toon Disney; WE tv.
Fee: $15.00 monthly.

Pay Service 1
Pay Units: 3,006.
Programming (via satellite): Cinemax.
Fee: $11.90 monthly.

Pay Service 2
Pay Units: 1,895.
Programming (via satellite): The Movie Channel.
Fee: $11.90 monthly.

Pay Service 3
Pay Units: 10,092.
Programming (via satellite): HBO.
Fee: $11.90 monthly.

Pay Service 4
Pay Units: 3,603.
Programming (via satellite): Showtime.
Fee: $11.90 monthly.

Digital Pay Service 1
Pay Units: N.A.
Programming (via satellite): Cinemax (multiplexed); Encore (multiplexed); Flix; HBO (multiplexed); Showtime (multiplexed); Starz (multiplexed); The Movie Channel (multiplexed).
Fee: $10.00 monthly (Cinemax, HBO, TMC, Flix/Showtime, or Starz/Encore).
Video-On-Demand: Yes

Pay-Per-View
Addressable homes: 16,000.
iN DEMAND; iN DEMAND (delivered digitally); Playboy TV (delivered digitally); Fresh (delivered digitally); Shorteez (delivered digitally).

Internet Service
Operational: Yes. Began: March 1, 2000.
Broadband Service: Charter Pipeline.
Fee: $29.99 monthly; $4.95 modem lease.
Telephone Service
Digital: Operational
Fee: $29.99 monthly
Miles of Plant: 1,658.0 (coaxial); 199.0 (fiber optic). Homes passed: 80,490. Total homes in franchised area: 105,411.
Vice President & General Manager: Ed Merrill. Chief Technician: Dan Joseph. Marketing Director: Sarwar Assar.
City fee: 4% of gross.
Ownership: Charter Communications Inc. (MSO).

SAN LUIS OBISPO—Formerly served by TVCN. No longer in operation. ICA: CA0413.

SAN MATEO—Comcast Cable. Now served by SAN FRANCISCO, CA [CA0003]. ICA: CA0081.

SAN PABLO—Comcast Cable. Now served by OAKLAND, CA [CA0018]. ICA: CA0123.

SAN SIMEON ACRES—San Simeon Community Cable Inc., PO Box 84, San Simeon, CA 93452-0084. Phone: 805-927-5555. ICA: CA0295.
TV Market Ranking: Below 100 (SAN SIMEON ACRES). Franchise award date: N.A. Franchise expiration date: N.A. Began: August 1, 1982.
Channel capacity: 36 (operating 2-way). Channels available but not in use: N.A.
Basic Service
Subscribers: 500.
Programming (received off-air): KCOY-TV (CBS) Santa Maria; KSBY (CW, NBC) San Luis Obispo; KTLA (CW) Los Angeles.
Programming (via satellite): Arts & Entertainment; CNBC; CNN; C-SPAN; Discovery Channel; ESPN; History Channel; KRMA-TV (PBS) Denver; KUSA (NBC) Denver; Lifetime; Nickelodeon; Spike TV; TBS Superstation; The Learning Channel; Turner Classic Movies; Turner Network TV; USA Network; Weather Channel; WGN America.
Current originations: Government Access; Educational Access; Public Access.
Fee: $22.50 monthly.
Pay Service 1
Pay Units: N.A.
Programming (via satellite): Cinemax; HBO.
Fee: $10.00 monthly (each).
Internet Service
Operational: Yes.
Subscribers: 50.
Broadband Service: Paralynx.
Fee: $49.00 monthly.
Telephone Service
None
Miles of Plant: 4.0 (coaxial); None (fiber optic). Homes passed: 1,200.
Ownership: San Simeon Community Cable Inc.

SANTA ANA—Formerly served by Adelphia Communications. Now served by ANAHEIM, CA [CA0033]. ICA: CA0376.

SANTA BARBARA—Cox Communications, 3303 State St, Santa Barbara, CA 93301. Phones: 805-683-7751; 805-683-6651 (Customer service). Fax: 805-964-6069. Web Site: http://www.cox.com/santabarbara. Also serves Carpinteria, Goleta, Isla Vista, Montecito, Santa Barbara County (portions) & Ventura County (portions). ICA: CA0034.
TV Market Ranking: Below 100 (Carpinteria, Goleta, Isla Vista, Montecito, SANTA BARBARA, Santa Barbara County (portions), Ventura County (portions)). Franchise award date: October 1, 1961. Franchise expiration date: N.A. Began: May 1, 1962.
Channel capacity: N.A. Channels available but not in use: N.A.

Basic Service
Subscribers: 66,000.
Programming (received off-air): KBEH (IND) Oxnard; KCET (PBS) Los Angeles; KCOP-TV (MNT) Los Angeles; KCOY-TV (CBS) Santa Maria; KEYT-TV (ABC, MNT) Santa Barbara; KNBC (NBC) Los Angeles; KSBY (CW, NBC) San Luis Obispo; KTAS (TMO) San Luis Obispo; 24 FMs.
Programming (via satellite): CNN; C-SPAN; C-SPAN 2; FX; Home Shopping Network; Lifetime; MSNBC; mun2 television; Product Information Network; TBS Superstation; Trinity Broadcasting Network; truTV; Turner Network TV; TV Guide Network; USA Network; VH1; Weather Channel.
Current originations: Leased Access; Government Access; Educational Access; Public Access.
Fee: $49.95 installation; $16.70 monthly; $35.00 additional installation.

Expanded Basic Service 1
Subscribers: N.A.
Programming (via satellite): ABC Family Channel; AMC; Animal Planet; Arts & Entertainment; Bravo; Canales N; Cartoon Network; CNBC; Comedy Central; Discovery Channel; Disney Channel; E! Entertainment Television; ESPN; ESPN 2; Food Network; Fox News Channel; Fox Sports en Espanol; Fox Sports Net West; Fox Sports Net West 2; GalaVision; Golf Channel; Hallmark Channel; HBO; Headline News; HGTV; History Channel; Independent Film Channel; MTV; Nickelodeon; QVC; Speed Channel; Spike TV; Syfy; The Learning Channel; Travel Channel; Turner Classic Movies; TV Land; Versus.
Fee: $11.95 monthly.

Digital Basic Service
Subscribers: N.A.
Programming (via satellite): BBC America; Bloomberg Television; Discovery Digital Networks; Fox College Sports Atlantic; Fox Sports World; G4; GSN; Independent Film Channel; Lifetime Movie Network; MuchMusic Network; Music Choice; NBA TV; Oxygen; SoapNet; Sundance Channel; Toon Disney.

Pay Service 1
Pay Units: 30,000.
Programming (via satellite): Cinemax; HBO; Showtime.
Fee: $5.00 installation; $13.95 monthly (each).

Digital Pay Service 1
Pay Units: N.A.
Programming (via satellite): Cinemax (multiplexed); Encore; HBO (multiplexed); Showtime (multiplexed); Starz (multiplexed); The Movie Channel.
Video-On-Demand: No

Pay-Per-View
ESPN Extra (delivered digitally), Addressable: Yes; ESPN Gameplan (delivered digitally); ESPN Now (delivered digitally); iN DEMAND; Sports PPV (delivered digitally); movies (delivered digitally).

Internet Service
Operational: Yes. Began: December 1, 1999.
Broadband Service: Cox High Speed Internet.
Fee: $149.95 installation; $39.95 monthly; $15.00 modem lease; $199.00 modem purchase.
Telephone Service
Digital: Operational
Fee: $15.25 monthly
Miles of Plant: 902.0 (coaxial); 231.0 (fiber optic). Homes passed: 93,317. Total homes in franchised area: 93,317.
Vice President & General Manager: Julie McGovern. Marketing Director: Scott James. Government & Public Affairs Director: David Edelman. Chief Technician: Rodney Baker.
County fee: 5% of gross.
Ownership: Cox Communications Inc. (MSO).

SANTA CLARA—Comcast Cable. Now served by SAN JOSE, CA [CA0004]. ICA: CA0075.

SANTA CLARITA—Time Warner Cable. Now served by CHATSWORTH, CA [CA0013]. ICA: CA0083.

SANTA CRUZ—Comcast Cable, 1900 S 10th St, San Jose, CA 95112-4110. Phones: 925-973-7000 (San Ramon regional office); 408-918-3200. Fax: 408-294-7280. Web Site: http://www.comcast.com. Also serves Aptos, Ben Lomond, Bonny Doon, Boulder Creek, Brookdale, Davenport, Felton, La Selva Beach, Lompico, Mount Hermon, Rio Del Mar, Santa Cruz County (unincorporated areas), Scotts Valley & Soquel. ICA: CA0043.
TV Market Ranking: 7 (Aptos, Ben Lomond, Bonny Doon, Boulder Creek, Brookdale, Davenport, Felton, La Selva Beach, Lompico, Mount Hermon, Rio Del Mar, SANTA CRUZ, Santa Cruz County (unincorporated areas), Scotts Valley, Soquel). Franchise award date: June 1, 1989. Franchise expiration date: N.A. Began: September 1, 1954.
Channel capacity: N.A. Channels available but not in use: N.A.
Basic Service
Subscribers: 48,560.
Programming (received off-air): KCBA (FOX) Salinas; KDJT-CA (TEL) Salinas/Monterey, etc.; KGO-TV (ABC) San Francisco; KICU-TV (IND) San Jose; KION-TV (CBS, CW) Monterey; KKPX-TV (ION) San Jose; KMCE-LP Monterey; KMUV-LP Monterey; KPIX-TV (CBS) San Francisco; KQED (PBS) San Francisco; KRON-TV (MNT) San Francisco; KSBW (NBC) Salinas; KSMS-TV (UNV) Monterey; KTEH (PBS) San Jose; KTSF (IND) San Francisco; KTVU (FOX) Oakland; allband FM.
Programming (via satellite): C-SPAN; C-SPAN 2; CW+; Discovery Channel; Hallmark Channel; Jewelry Television; QVC; TV Guide Network.
Current originations: Public Access; Leased Access; Government Access; Educational Access; Public Access.
Fee: $12.62 monthly; $4.25 converter.
Expanded Basic Service 1
Subscribers: N.A.
Programming (via satellite): ABC Family Channel; AMC; Animal Planet; Arts & Entertainment; BET Networks; Bravo; California Channel; Cartoon Network; CNBC; CNN; Comedy Central; Country Music TV; Disney Channel; E! Entertainment Television; ESPN; ESPN 2; Food Network; Fox News Channel; FX; GalaVision; Headline News; History Channel; MSNBC; MTV; MTV2; Nickelodeon; Spike TV; Syfy; TBS Superstation; The Learning Channel; Travel Channel; truTV; Turner Network TV; USA Network; VH1; Weather Channel.
Fee: $39.78 monthly.
Digital Basic Service
Subscribers: 32,509.
Programming (received off-air): KCBA (FOX) Salinas; KGO-TV (ABC) San Francisco; KION-TV (CBS, CW) Monterey; KQED (PBS) San Francisco; KSBW (NBC) Salinas.
Programming (via satellite): BBC America; Bio; CB Television Michoacan; Cine Latino; CMT Pure Country; CNN en Espanol; Comcast SportsNet West; Cooking Channel; Discovery en Espanol; Discovery Health Channel; Discovery Kids Channel; Discovery Military Channel; Discovery Planet Green; DMX Music; Do-It-Yourself; Encore (multiplexed); ESPN 2 HD; ESPN Classic Sports; ESPN Deportes; ESPN HD; ESPNews; Fox Soccer; Fox Sports en Espanol; G4; Gol TV; Golf Channel; Golf Channel HD; GSN; HDNet; HGTV; History Channel en Espanol; History Channel International; ID Investigation Discovery; Independent Film Channel; Infinito; Lifetime Movie Network; MoviePlex; MTV Hits; mun2 television; National Geographic Channel; National Geographic Channel HD Network; NBA TV; NFL Network; Nick Jr.; NickToons TV; PBS Kids Sprout; Playboy en Espanol; Science Channel; SoapNet; Speed Channel; Style Network; Sundance Channel; Sur Network; TeenNick; Toon Disney; Toon Disney en Espanol; Trinity Broadcasting Network; Turner Classic Movies; Turner Network TV HD; TV Land; VeneMovies; Versus; Versus HD; VH1 Classic; VH1 Soul; V-me TV; WE tv.
Fee: $11.95 monthly.
Digital Pay Service 1
Pay Units: N.A.
Programming (via satellite): Cinemax (multiplexed); HBO (multiplexed); HBO HD; Showtime (multiplexed); Starz (multiplexed); The Movie Channel (multiplexed).
Fee: $13.00 monthly (each).
Video-On-Demand: Yes
Pay-Per-View
Playboy TV (delivered digitally); Club Jenna (delivered digitally); iN DEMAND (delivered digitally).
Internet Service
Operational: Yes.
Telephone Service
Digital: Operational
Fee: $44.95 monthly
Miles of Plant: 836.0 (coaxial); 51.0 (fiber optic). Homes passed: 64,912. Total homes in franchised area: 86,517.
Area Vice President: Navarra Williams. Technical Operations Director: David Walton. Network Manager: Curt Christenson. Sales & Marketing Director: Eden Godsoe. Vice President, Communications: Andrew Johnson.
City fee: 7% of gross.
Ownership: Comcast Cable Communications Inc. (MSO).

SANTA MARIA—Comcast Cable, 2323 Thompson Way, Santa Maria, CA 93455. Phone: 805-349-7185. Fax: 805-349-7649. Web Site: http://www.comcast.com. Also serves Ballard, Buellton, Lompoc, Los Olivos, Mission Hills, Orcutt, Santa Barbara County, Santa Ynez, Solvang & Vandenburg Village. ICA: CA0352.
TV Market Ranking: Below 100 (Ballard, Buellton, Lompoc, Los Olivos, Mission

Hills, Orcutt, Santa Barbara County, SANTA MARIA, Santa Ynez, Solvang, Vandenburg Village). Franchise award date: January 1, 2003. Franchise expiration date: N.A. Began: February 1, 1964.

Channel capacity: N.A. Channels available but not in use: N.A.

Basic Service

Subscribers: 39,001.

Programming (received off-air): KCOY-TV (CBS) Santa Maria; KEYT-TV (ABC, MNT) Santa Barbara; KKFX-CA San Luis Obispo; KPMR (UNV) Santa Barbara; KPXN-TV (ION) San Bernardino; KSBY (CW, NBC) San Luis Obispo; KTAS (TMO) San Luis Obispo; 14 FMs.

Programming (via microwave): KCET (PBS) Los Angeles; KCOP-TV (MNT) Los Angeles; KNBC (NBC) Los Angeles; KTLA (CW) Los Angeles.

Programming (via satellite): ABC Family Channel; AMC; Animal Planet; Arts & Entertainment; BET Networks; Cartoon Network; CNBC; CNN; Comedy Central; Country Music TV; C-SPAN; Discovery Channel; Disney Channel; E! Entertainment Television; ESPN; ESPN 2; Eternal Word TV Network; Food Network; Fox News Channel; Fox Sports Net West; FX; GalaVision; Golf Channel; Headline News; HGTV; History Channel; Lifetime; MTV; Nickelodeon; QVC; Speed Channel; Spike TV; Syfy; The Learning Channel; Trinity Broadcasting Network; truTV; Turner Network TV; TV Guide Network; TV Land; USA Network; Versus; VH1; Weather Channel.

Current originations: Government Access.

Fee: $49.95 installation; $41.24 monthly; $1.95 converter; $24.95 additional installation.

Digital Basic Service

Subscribers: 10,000.

Programming (via satellite): BBC America; Discovery Digital Networks; DMX Music; GSN; Turner Classic Movies.

Fee: $12.95 monthly.

Digital Pay Service 1

Pay Units: 3,500.

Programming (via satellite): Cinemax (multiplexed).

Fee: $9.00 monthly.

Digital Pay Service 2

Pay Units: 6,700.

Programming (via satellite): HBO (multiplexed).

Fee: $12.00 monthly.

Digital Pay Service 3

Pay Units: 2,000.

Programming (via satellite): Showtime (multiplexed).

Fee: $9.00 monthly.

Digital Pay Service 4

Pay Units: 3,450.

Programming (via satellite): Encore (multiplexed); Starz (multiplexed).

Fee: $9.00 monthly.

Digital Pay Service 5

Pay Units: N.A.

Programming (via satellite): Canales N.

Fee: $7.00 monthly.

Video-On-Demand: Yes

Pay-Per-View

Addressable homes: 10,000.

iN DEMAND (delivered digitally); Playboy TV (delivered digitally); Fresh (delivered digitally).

Internet Service

Operational: Yes.

Broadband Service: Comcast High Speed Internet.

Fee: $42.95 monthly.

Telephone Service

Digital: Operational

Miles of Plant: 650.0 (coaxial); 80.0 (fiber optic). Total homes in franchised area: 62,000.

General Manager: Christina Villanueva. Technical Operations Director: Bob Guzman. Marketing Manager: Kathryn Scott.

Ownership: Comcast Cable Communications Inc. (MSO).

SANTA MONICA—Time Warner Cable. Now served by CHATSWORTH, CA [CA0013]. ICA: CA0460.

SANTA ROSA—Comcast Cable. Now served by NAPA/SONOMA, CA [CA0038]. ICA: CA0049.

SARATOGA—Comcast Cable. Now served by SAN JOSE, CA [CA0004]. ICA: CA0165.

SEAL BEACH—Formerly served by Adelphia Communications. Now served by ANAHEIM, CA [CA0033]. ICA: CA0147.

SHAVER LAKE—Suddenlink Communications, 12444 Powerscourt Dr, Saint Louis, MO 63131-3660. Phones: 314-965-2020; 760-873-4123. Web Site: http://www.suddenlink.com. ICA: CA0247.

TV Market Ranking: 72 (SHAVER LAKE). Franchise award date: August 23, 1983. Franchise expiration date: N.A. Began: N.A.

Channel capacity: 42 (not 2-way capable). Channels available but not in use: None.

Basic Service

Subscribers: 962.

Programming (received off-air): KFRE-TV (CW) Sanger; KFSN-TV (ABC) Fresno; KJEO-LD Fresno; KMPH-TV (FOX) Visalia; KMSG-LP (IND) Fresno; KNXT (ETV) Visalia; KPXN-TV (ION) San Bernardino; KSEE (NBC) Fresno; KVPT (PBS) Fresno.

Programming (via satellite): ABC Family Channel; AMC; Animal Planet; Arts & Entertainment; CNBC; CNN; Comcast Sports Net Bay Area; C-SPAN; Discovery Channel; Disney Channel; ESPN; ESPN 2; Fox News Channel; History Channel; Lifetime; Nickelodeon; Spike TV; TBS Superstation; The Learning Channel; Toon Disney; Turner Network TV; USA Network; Weather Channel; WGN America.

Fee: $49.95 installation; $37.99 monthly.

Pay Service 1

Pay Units: 83.

Programming (via satellite): Encore.

Fee: $10.95 monthly.

Pay Service 2

Pay Units: 70.

Programming (via satellite): HBO.

Fee: $10.00 monthly.

Pay Service 3

Pay Units: 100.

Programming (via satellite): Showtime.

Fee: $10.95 monthly.

Pay Service 4

Pay Units: 111.

Programming (via satellite): The Movie Channel.

Fee: $10.95 monthly.

Video-On-Demand: No

Internet Service

Operational: No.

Telephone Service

Digital: Operational

Miles of Plant: 26.0 (coaxial); None (fiber optic). Additional miles planned: 12.0 (coaxial). Homes passed: 1,076.

Marketing Director: Jason Oelkers.

Ownership: Cequel Communications LLC (MSO).

SHERMAN OAKS—Time Warner Cable. Now served by CHATSWORTH, CA [CA0013]. ICA: CA0471.

SIERRA DAWN ESTATES—Sierra Dawn Cablevision, 950 S Lyon Ave, Hemet, CA 92543-6872. Phone: 951-925-6502. Fax: 951-925-6503. ICA: CA0379.

TV Market Ranking: 2 (SIERRA DAWN ESTATES). Franchise award date: N.A. Franchise expiration date: N.A. Began: N.A.

Channel capacity: 45 (not 2-way capable). Channels available but not in use: N.A.

Basic Service

Subscribers: 1,474.

Programming (received off-air): KABC-TV (ABC) Los Angeles; KCBS-TV (CBS) Los Angeles; KCET (PBS) Los Angeles; KCOP-TV (MNT) Los Angeles; KNBC (NBC) Los Angeles; KTLA (CW) Los Angeles; KTTV (FOX) Los Angeles.

Programming (via satellite): AMC; Arts & Entertainment; CNBC; CNN; C-SPAN; Discovery Channel; ESPN; Food Network; Fox News Channel; HGTV; History Channel; ION Television; KTBN-TV (TBN) Santa Ana; KVCR-DT (PBS) San Bernardino; Lifetime; MSNBC; Spike TV; TBS Superstation; Turner Network TV; USA Network; WE tv; Weather Channel; WGN America.

Video-On-Demand: No

Telephone Service

None

Manager: Dan Goodrich. Chief Technician: Steve Hulstrom.

Ownership: Sierra Dawn Estates Homeowners Assn.

SIERRA MADRE—Now served by LOS ANGELES, CA [CA0009]. ICA: CA0093.

SIMI VALLEY—Time Warner Cable. Now served by CHATSWORTH, CA [CA0013]. ICA: CA0380.

SOLEDAD—Charter Communications, 8120 Camino Arroyo, Gilroy, CA 95020. Phones: 408-847-2020; 805-544-1962 (San Luis Obispo administrative office). Fax: 408-847-2993. Web Site: http://www.charter.com. Also serves Chualar, Gonzales & Monterey County (portions). ICA: CA0382.

TV Market Ranking: Below 100 (Chualar, Gonzales, Monterey County (portions), SOLEDAD). Franchise award date: N.A. Franchise expiration date: N.A. Began: March 1, 1972.

Channel capacity: N.A. Channels available but not in use: N.A.

Basic Service

Subscribers: 2,850.

Programming (received off-air): KCBA (FOX) Salinas; KGO-TV (ABC) San Francisco; KICU-TV (IND) San Jose; KION-TV (CBS, CW) Monterey; KKPX-TV (ION) San Jose; KSBW (NBC) Salinas; KSMS-TV (UNV) Monterey; KTVU (FOX) Oakland; allband FM.

Programming (via satellite): Arts & Entertainment; Comcast Sports Net Bay Area; Home Shopping Network; MTV; QVC; TBS Superstation; USA Network.

Programming (via translator): KQED (PBS) San Francisco.

Current originations: Government Access; Educational Access; Public Access.

Fee: $25.00 installation; $12.37 monthly; $20.00 additional installation.

Expanded Basic Service 1

Subscribers: 2,588.

Programming (via satellite): ABC Family Channel; AMC; Cartoon Network; CNN; Country Music TV; Discovery Channel; Disney Channel; ESPN; GalaVision; Headline News; Lifetime; Nickelodeon; Spike TV.

Fee: $8.58 monthly.

Digital Basic Service

Subscribers: N.A.

Programming (via satellite): AmericanLife TV Network; BBC America; Bio; Bloomberg Television; Bravo!; Discovery Digital Networks; DMX Music; ESPN 2; ESPN Classic Sports; ESPNews; FitTV; Fox Movie Channel; Fuse; G4; GAS; Golf Channel; GSN; HGTV; History Channel; History Channel International; Independent Film Channel; INSP; Lifetime Movie Network; MTV Networks Digital Suite; Nick Jr.; Outdoor Channel; Science Television; ShopNBC; Speed Channel; Syfy; Toon Disney; Trinity Broadcasting Network; Turner Classic Movies; Versus; WE tv.

Pay Service 1

Pay Units: 99.

Programming (via satellite): Cinemax; HBO; Showtime; The Movie Channel.

Fee: $25.00 installation; $10.95 monthly.

Digital Pay Service 1

Pay Units: N.A.

Programming (via satellite): Cinemax (multiplexed); Encore (multiplexed); HBO (multiplexed); Showtime (multiplexed); Starz (multiplexed); The Movie Channel (multiplexed).

Video-On-Demand: No

Pay-Per-View

iN DEMAND (delivered digitally); ESPN Now (delivered digitally); ESPN Sports PPV (delivered digitally); Hot Choice (delivered digitally); Playboy TV (delivered digitally); Fresh (delivered digitally); Shorteez (delivered digitally).

Internet Service

Operational: No.

Telephone Service

None

Miles of Plant: 36.0 (coaxial); None (fiber optic). Homes passed: 4,629.

Vice President & General Manager: Ed Merrill. Chief Technician: Mark Beech. Marketing Director: Sarwar Assar.

Franchise fee: 5% of gross.

Ownership: Charter Communications Inc. (MSO).

SONORA—Comcast Cable. Now served by TWAIN HARTE, CA [CA0148]. ICA: CA0130.

SOUTH GATE—Time Warner Cable. Now served by LOS ANGELES, CA [CA0009]. ICA: CA0468.

SOUTH LAKE TAHOE—Charter Communications, 9335 Prototype Dr, Reno, NV 89521. Phone: 775-850-1200. Fax: 775-850-1279. Web Site: http://www.charter.com. Also serves Douglas County, Glenbrook & Stateline. ICA: CA0132.

TV Market Ranking: Below 100 (Douglas County (portions), Glenbrook); Outside TV Markets (Douglas County (portions), SOUTH LAKE TAHOE, Stateline). Franchise award date: N.A. Franchise expiration date: N.A. Began: January 1, 1962.

Channel capacity: 66 (operating 2-way). Channels available but not in use: N.A.

Basic Service

Subscribers: 13,066.

Programming (received off-air): K38FW Stateline; KAME-TV (MNT) Reno; KNPB (PBS) Reno; KNVV-LP Reno; KRXI-TV (FOX) Reno; 14 FMs.

Programming (via microwave): KCRA-TV (NBC) Sacramento; KGO-TV (ABC) San Francisco; KOLO-TV (ABC) Reno; KPIX-TV (CBS) San Francisco; KREN-TV (CW, UNV) Reno; KRNV-DT (ABC) Reno; KTVN (CBS) Reno.

Programming (via satellite): C-SPAN; C-SPAN 2; ION Television; KRNS-CA (IND) Reno; QVC; TBS Superstation; TV Guide Network.

Current originations: Educational Access; Public Access.

Fee: $29.99 installation; $16.66 monthly.

Expanded Basic Service 1

Subscribers: 12,488.

Programming (via satellite): ABC Family Channel; AMC; Animal Planet; Arts & Entertainment; Cartoon Network; CNBC; CNN; Comcast Sports Net Bay Area; Comedy Central; Discovery Channel; Disney Channel; E! Entertainment Television; ESPN; FitTV; Food Network; Fox News Channel; Fox Sports en Espanol; FX; GalaVision; Hallmark Channel; Headline News; HGTV; Home Shopping Network; Lifetime; MSNBC; MTV; Nickelodeon; Oxygen; Spike TV; Style Network; The Learning Channel; Travel Channel; truTV; Turner Network TV; TV Land; USA Network; VH1; Weather Channel.

Fee: $32.58 monthly.

Digital Basic Service

Subscribers: N.A.

Programming (via satellite): BBC America; Bio; Black Family Channel; Bloomberg Television; Bravo; Canales N; Discovery Digital Networks; DMX Music; ESPN Classic Sports; ESPNews; Fox College Sports Atlantic; Fox College Sports Central; Fox College Sports Pacific; Fox Movie Channel; Fox Soccer; Fuse; G4; GAS; Golf Channel; Great American Country; GSN; Halogen Network; History Channel; History Channel International; Independent Film Channel; International Television (ITV); Lifetime Movie Network; MTV Networks Digital Suite; National Geographic Channel; Nick Jr.; Outdoor Channel; Speed Channel; Sundance Channel; Syfy; The Word Network; Toon Disney; Trinity Broadcasting Network; Turner Classic Movies; TV Guide Interactive Inc.; Versus; WE tv.

Fee: $10.95 monthly.

Digital Pay Service 1

Pay Units: N.A.

Programming (via satellite): Cinemax (multiplexed); Encore (multiplexed); HBO (multiplexed); Showtime (multiplexed); Starz (multiplexed); The Movie Channel (multiplexed).

Video-On-Demand: Yes

Pay-Per-View

iN DEMAND (delivered digitally); NASCAR In Car (delivered digitally); Fresh (delivered digitally); Shorteez (delivered digitally); Playboy TV (delivered digitally).

Internet Service

Operational: Yes.

Broadband Service: Charter Pipeline.

Fee: $29.99 monthly; $10.00 modem lease; $199.00 modem purchase.

Telephone Service

Digital: Operational

Miles of Plant: 159.0 (coaxial); None (fiber optic). Homes passed: 16,459. Total homes in franchised area: 16,744.

Vice President & General Manager: Manny Martinez. Technical Operations Manager: Carol Eure.

City fee: 5% of gross.

Ownership: Charter Communications Inc. (MSO).

SOUTH NATOMAS—SureWest Broadband. Formerly served by Sacramento, CA [CA0459]. This cable system has converted to IPTV, PO Box 969, Roseville, CA 95661. Phone: 916-772-2000. Fax: 916-786-7170. Web Site: http://www.surewest.com. ICA: CA5609.

TV Market Ranking: 25 (SOUTH NATOMAS).

Channel capacity: N.A. Channels available but not in use: N.A.

Video-On-Demand: Yes

Internet Service

Operational: Yes.

Telephone Service

Digital: Operational

Ownership: SureWest Broadband.

SOUTH PASADENA—Time Warner Cable. Now served by LOS ANGELES, CA [CA0009]. ICA: CA0161.

SOUTH SAN FRANCISCO—Comcast Cable. Now served by SAN FRANCISCO, CA [CA0003]. ICA: CA0106.

SPANISH RANCH MOBILE HOME PARK—Formerly served by Comcast Cable. No longer in operation. ICA: CA0383.

STEVENSON RANCH—Time Warner Cable. Now served by CHATSWORTH, CA [CA0013]. ICA: CA0465.

STOCKTON—Comcast Cable, 6505 Tam O Shanter Dr, Stockton, CA 95210-3349. Phone: 209-473-4955. Fax: 209-473-8177. Web Site: http://www.comcast.com. Also serves French Camp, Lathrop, Linden, Manteca & San Joaquin County. ICA: CA0028.

TV Market Ranking: 25 (French Camp, Lathrop, Linden, Manteca, San Joaquin County, STOCKTON). Franchise award date: April 1, 1972. Franchise expiration date: N.A. Began: January 1, 1973.

Channel capacity: N.A. Channels available but not in use: N.A.

Basic Service

Subscribers: 72,928.

Programming (received off-air): KCRA-TV (NBC) Sacramento; KCSO-LP Sacramento; KICU-TV (IND) San Jose; KMAX-TV (CW) Sacramento; KOVR (CBS) Stockton; KQCA (MNT) Stockton; KRON-TV (MNT) San Francisco; KSPX-TV (ION) Sacramento; KTFK-DT (TEL) Stockton; KTNC-TV (IND) Concord; KTXL (FOX) Sacramento; KUVS-DT (UNV) Modesto; KVIE (PBS) Sacramento; KXTV (ABC) Sacramento; allband FM.

Programming (via microwave): KGO-TV (ABC) San Francisco; KOFY-TV (IND) San Francisco; KQED (PBS) San Francisco.

Programming (via satellite): California Channel; CNBC; CNN; C-SPAN; C-SPAN 2; Eternal Word TV Network; Fox News Channel; Headline News; MSNBC; QVC; TV Guide Network; Weather Channel.

Current originations: Government Access; Educational Access; Public Access.

Fee: $43.99 installation; $14.00 monthly.

Expanded Basic Service 1

Subscribers: N.A.

Programming (via satellite): ABC Family Channel; AMC; Animal Planet; Arts & Entertainment; BET Networks; Bravo; Cartoon Network; Comcast Sports Net Bay Area; Comedy Central; Discovery Channel; Disney Channel; E! Entertainment Television; ESPN; ESPN 2; ESPN Classic Sports; Food Network; FX; GalaVision; Golf Channel; Great American Country; GSN; Hallmark Channel; HGTV; History Channel; Home Shopping Network; Lifetime; MTV; mun2 television; Nickelodeon; Oxygen; ShopNBC; Spike TV; Syfy; TBS Superstation; The Learning Channel; Travel Channel; truTV; Turner Network TV; TV Land; USA Network; Versus; VH1; WE tv.

Fee: $35.95 monthly.

Digital Basic Service

Subscribers: 21,878.

Programming (via satellite): AmericanLife TV Network; BBC America; Bio; Black Family Channel; Bloomberg Television; Canales N; Discovery Digital Networks; Encore Action; ESPNews; FitTV; Fox College Sports Atlantic; Fox College Sports Central; Fox College Sports Pacific; Fox Movie Channel; Fox Sports World; Fuse; G4; GAS; Halogen Network; History Channel International; Independent Film Channel; Lifetime Movie Network; Lime; MTV Networks Digital Suite; Music Choice; National Geographic Channel; Nick Jr.; NickToons TV; Outdoor Channel; Ovation; Speed Channel; Star India Gold; Star India News; Star India Plus; Star One; Style Network; Sundance Channel; The Word Network; Toon Disney; Trinity Broadcasting Network; Turner Classic Movies; Vijay.

Fee: $11.95 monthly.

Digital Pay Service 1

Pay Units: 55,127.

Programming (via satellite): ART America; CCTV-4; Cinemax (multiplexed); Filipino Channel; Flix; HBO (multiplexed); RAI International; Russian Television Network; Saigon Broadcasting TV Network; Showtime (multiplexed); Starz (multiplexed); The Movie Channel (multiplexed); TV Asia; TV Japan; TV5, La Television International; Zee TV USA; Zhong Tian Channel.

Fee: $10.00 installation; $17.99 monthly (Cinemax, Starz or TMC), $18.99 monthly (HBO or Showtime).

Video-On-Demand: Yes

Pay-Per-View

Addressable homes: 21,878.

iN DEMAND, Addressable: Yes; ESPN Now (delivered digitally); Sports PPV (delivered digitally); iN DEMAND (delivered digitally); Urban Xtra (delivered digitally); Fresh (delivered digitally); Shorteez (delivered digitally); Playboy TV (delivered digitally); Hot Choice (delivered digitally).

Internet Service

Operational: Yes. Began: August 17, 1999.

Broadband Service: Comcast High Speed Internet.

Fee: $42.95 monthly.

Telephone Service

Digital: Operational

Miles of Plant: 975.0 (coaxial); 116.0 (fiber optic). Homes passed: 139,444.

Technical Operations Director: Fred Walkover. Marketing Manager: Terry Dowling.

City fee: 5% of gross.

Ownership: Comcast Cable Communications Inc. (MSO).

STRAWBERRY—Comcast Cable. Now served by PLACERVILLE, CA [CA0108]. ICA: CA0421.

STUDIO CITY—Formerly served by Adelphia Communications. Now served by CHATSWORTH, CA [CA0013]. ICA: CA0461.

SUN CITY—Mediacom, 27192 Sun City Blvd, Ste A, Sun City, CA 92586. Phone: 951-679-3977. Fax: 951-679-9087. Web Site: http://www.mediacomcable.com. ICA: CA0385.

TV Market Ranking: 2 (SUN CITY). Franchise award date: April 10, 1964. Franchise expiration date: N.A. Began: April 10, 1964.

Channel capacity: N.A. Channels available but not in use: N.A.

Basic Service

Subscribers: 10,463.

Programming (received off-air): KABC-TV (ABC) Los Angeles; KCAL-TV (IND) Los Angeles; KCBS-TV (CBS) Los Angeles; KCET (PBS) Los Angeles; KCOP-TV (MNT) Los Angeles; KDOC-TV (IND) Anaheim; KHSC-LP (HSN) Fresno; KJLA (IND) Ventura; KLCS (PBS) Los Angeles; KMEX-DT (UNV) Los Angeles; KNBC (NBC) Los Angeles; KPXN-TV (ION) San Bernardino; KRCA (IND) Riverside; KSCI (IND) Long Beach; KTBN-TV (TBN) Santa Ana; KTLA (CW) Los Angeles; KTTV (FOX) Los Angeles; KVCR-DT (PBS) San Bernardino; KVEA (TMO) Corona; KWHY-TV (IND) Los Angeles.

Programming (via satellite): California Channel; C-SPAN; C-SPAN 2; FX; QVC; TBS Superstation; truTV; TV Guide Network; WGN America.

Current originations: Public Access.

Fee: $29.50 installation; $21.00 monthly; $2.18 converter.

Expanded Basic Service 1

Subscribers: N.A.

Programming (via satellite): ABC Family Channel; AMC; AmericanLife TV Network; Animal Planet; Arts & Entertainment; BET Networks; CNBC; CNN; Comedy Central; Discovery Channel; Disney Channel; ESPN; ESPN 2; Food Network; Fox News Channel; Fox Sports Net West; Fox Sports Net West 2; Golf Channel; Headline News; HGTV; History Channel; INSP; Lifetime; MSNBC; MTV; Nickelodeon; Spike TV; Syfy; The Learning Channel; Toon Disney; Travel Channel; Turner Classic Movies; Turner Network TV; TV Land; USA Network; VH1; WE tv; Weather Channel.

Fee: $24.95 monthly.

Digital Basic Service

Subscribers: N.A.

Programming (via satellite): BBC America; Discovery Digital Networks; ESPNews; Music Choice; National Geographic Channel; Nick Jr.; Speed Channel.

Fee: $8.00 monthly.

Digital Pay Service 1
Pay Units: N.A.
Programming (via satellite): Cinemax (multiplexed); Encore (multiplexed); Flix (multiplexed); HBO (multiplexed); Showtime (multiplexed); Starz (multiplexed); Sundance Channel (multiplexed); The Movie Channel (multiplexed).
Fee: $8.00 monthly (Starz/Encore), $9.95 monthly (Showtime or Cinemax), $13.95 monthly (HBO).
Video-On-Demand: No
Pay-Per-View
Addressable homes: 1,202.
iN DEMAND, Fee: $3.95, Addressable: Yes.
Internet Service
Operational: Yes.
Broadband Service: Mediacom High Speed Internet.
Fee: $59.95 installation; $40.95 monthly; $3.00 modem lease; $239.95 modem purchase.
Telephone Service
Analog: Not Operational
Digital: Operational
Miles of Plant: 145.0 (coaxial); None (fiber optic). Homes passed: 10,501. Total homes in franchised area: 13,232.
General Manager: Allen Bublitz. Regional Engineering Director: Jon Tatilano.
County fee: 5% of gross.
Ownership: Mediacom LLC (MSO).

SUNNYVALE—Comcast Cable. Now served by SAN JOSE, CA [CA0004]. ICA: CA0067.

SUSANVILLE—Windjammer Cable, 4400 PGA Blvd, Ste 902, Palm Beach Gardens, FL 33410. Phones: 561-775-1208; 877-450-5558. Fax: 561-775-7811. Web Site: http://www.windjammercable.com. Also serves Janesville, Johnstonville, Lassen County & Leavitt Lake. ICA: CA0191.
TV Market Ranking: Outside TV Markets (Janesville, Johnstonville, Lassen County, Leavitt Lake, SUSANVILLE). Franchise award date: January 1, 1965. Franchise expiration date: N.A. Began: January 1, 1955.
Channel capacity: 78 (operating 2-way). Channels available but not in use: 19.
Basic Service
Subscribers: 8,800.
Programming (received off-air): KAME-TV (MNT) Reno; KCRA-TV (NBC) Sacramento; KHSL-TV (CBS, CW) Chico; allband FM.
Programming (via microwave): KNPB (PBS) Reno; KOLO-TV (ABC) Reno; KRNV-DT (ABC) Reno; KRXI-TV (FOX) Reno; KTVN (CBS) Reno.
Programming (via satellite): California Channel; C-SPAN; C-SPAN 2; CW+; Daystar TV Network; Home Shopping Network; Product Information Network; QVC; TBS Superstation; TV Guide Network; WGN America.
Fee: $35.80 installation; $27.91 monthly.
Expanded Basic Service 1
Subscribers: N.A.
Programming (via satellite): ABC Family Channel; AMC; Animal Planet; Arts & Entertainment; Bravo; Cartoon Network; CNBC; CNN; Comcast Sports Net Bay Area; Comedy Central; Country Music TV; Discovery Channel; Disney Channel; E! Entertainment Television; ESPN; ESPN 2; Food Network; Fox News Channel; FX; Hallmark Channel; Headline News; HGTV; History Channel; Lifetime; MSNBC; MTV; Nickelodeon; Spike TV; Syfy; The Learning Channel; Travel Channel; truTV; Turner Network TV; TV Land; USA Network; VH1; Weather Channel.
Fee: $33.93 monthly.
Digital Basic Service
Subscribers: N.A.
Programming (received off-air): KOLO-TV (ABC) Reno; KRNV-DT (ABC) Reno; KTVN (CBS) Reno.
Programming (via satellite): AmericanLife TV Network; BBC America; Bio; Bloomberg Television; Boomerang; Canal 52MX; CBS College Sports Network; Cine Latino; CMT Pure Country; CNN en Espanol; Cooking Channel; C-SPAN 3; Discovery en Espanol; Discovery HD Theater; Discovery Health Channel; Discovery Home Channel; Discovery Kids Channel; Discovery Military Channel; Discovery Times Channel; Do-It-Yourself; Encore (multiplexed); ESPN 2 HD; ESPN Classic Sports; ESPN HD; ESPN U; ESPNews; Eternal Word TV Network; FitTV; Flix; Fox Business Channel; Fox College Sports Atlantic; Fox College Sports Central; Fox College Sports Pacific; Fox Movie Channel; Fox Reality Channel; Fox Soccer; Fox Sports en Espanol; Fuel TV; Fuse; G4; GAS; Golf Channel; Gospel Music Channel; Great American Country; GSN; Halogen Network; HDNet Movies; History Channel en Espanol; History Channel International; Independent Film Channel; Lifetime Movie Network; LOGO; MTV Hits; MTV Jams; MTV Tres; MTV2; Music Choice; National Geographic Channel; NBA TV; Nick Jr.; Nick Too; NickToons TV; Outdoor Channel; Science Channel; SoapNet; Speed Channel; Style Network; Sundance Channel; The Sportsman Channel; The Word Network; Toon Disney; Trinity Broadcasting Network; Turner Classic Movies; Turner Network TV HD; Universal HD; Versus; VH1 Classic; VH1 Soul; WE tv.
Fee: $61.99 monthly.
Digital Pay Service 1
Pay Units: N.A.
Programming (via satellite): ART America; CCTV-4; Cinemax (multiplexed); Cinemax HD; Filipino Channel; HBO (multiplexed); HBO HD; RAI International; Russian Television Network; Showtime (multiplexed); Showtime HD; Starz (multiplexed); Starz HDTV; The Movie Channel (multiplexed); TV Asia; TV5, La Television International; Zhong Tian Channel.
Fee: $12.00 monthly (Cinemax, HBO, Showtime/TMC or Starz), $15.00 monthly (Zhong Tian, CCTV, TV Asia, TV5, RAI, Filipino, TV Russia or ART).
Video-On-Demand: No
Pay-Per-View
Playboy TV (delivered digitally); Fresh (delivered digitally); Hot Choice (delivered digitally); Special events (delivered digitally); iN DEMAND (delivered digitally).
Internet Service
Operational: Yes.
Broadband Service: In-house.
Fee: $20.99-$49.99 monthly.
Telephone Service
Digital: Operational
Fee: $49.95 monthly
Miles of Plant: 93.0 (coaxial); None (fiber optic).
General Manager: Timothy Evard. Operations Director: Belinda Graham. Engineering Director: Mike Earehart. Finance & Accounting Director: Cindy Johnson.
City fee: 3% of gross.
Ownership: Windjammer Communications LLC (MSO).

TASSAJARA VALLEY—Formerly served by Comcast Cable. No longer in operation. ICA: CA0387.

TEHACHAPI—Bright House Networks, 117 S Mill St, Tehachapi, CA 93561. Phones: 800-734-4615 (Customer service); 661-323-4892; 661-634-2200. Fax: 661-634-2245. E-mail: bakersfield.customercare@mybrighthouse.com. Web Site: http://www.bakersfield.mybrighthouse.com. Also serves Arvin, Ford City, Kern County, Lamont, Maricopa, South Taft, Taft & Taft Heights. ICA: CA0170.
TV Market Ranking: 72 (Kern County (portions)); Below 100 (Arvin, Ford City, Lamont, Maricopa, South Taft, Taft, Taft Heights, TEHACHAPI, Kern County (portions)); Outside TV Markets (Kern County (portions)). Franchise award date: January 1, 1964. Franchise expiration date: N.A. Began: April 1, 1964.
Channel capacity: 122 (operating 2-way). Channels available but not in use: None.
Basic Service
Subscribers: 9,942.
Programming (received off-air): KABC-TV (ABC) Los Angeles; KABE-LP Bakersfield; KBAK-TV (CBS) Bakersfield; KERO-TV (ABC) Bakersfield; KGET-TV (CW, NBC) Bakersfield; KUVI-DT (MNT) Bakersfield; KVPT (PBS) Fresno.
Programming (via microwave): KCAL-TV (IND) Los Angeles; KCET (PBS) Los Angeles; KCOP-TV (MNT) Los Angeles; KNBC (NBC) Los Angeles; KTLA (CW) Los Angeles.
Programming (via satellite): California Channel; QVC; ShopNBC; TV Guide Network.
Current originations: Public Access; Government Access.
Fee: $44.95 installation; $12.45 monthly.
Expanded Basic Service 1
Subscribers: 7,349.
Programming (via satellite): ABC Family Channel; AMC; Animal Planet; Arts & Entertainment; Azteca America; BET Networks; Bravo; Cartoon Network; CNBC; CNN; Comedy Central; C-SPAN; Discovery Channel; Disney Channel; E! Entertainment Television; ESPN; ESPN 2; ESPN Classic Sports; Fox News Channel; Fox Sports Net West; FX; GalaVision; Golf Channel; Great American Country; Hallmark Channel; Headline News; HGTV; Lifetime; Lifetime Movie Network; MSNBC; MTV; Nickelodeon; Spike TV; Style Network; Syfy; TBS Superstation; Telefutura; Telemundo; The Learning Channel; Travel Channel; Trinity Broadcasting Network; truTV; Turner Classic Movies; Turner Network TV; TV Land; USA Network; VH1; WE tv; Weather Channel.
Fee: $33.00 monthly.
Digital Basic Service
Subscribers: N.A.
Programming (received off-air): KBAK-TV (CBS) Bakersfield; KERO-TV (ABC) Bakersfield; KGET-TV (CW, NBC) Bakersfield.
Programming (via satellite): AmericanLife TV Network; America's Store; Arts & Entertainment HD; BBC America; Beauty and Fashion Channel; Bio; Black Family Channel; Bloomberg Television; Boomerang; Canales N; CNN International; Cooking Channel; Country Music TV; C-SPAN 2; C-SPAN 3; Current; Discovery Digital Networks; Discovery HD Theater; Disney Channel; Do-It-Yourself; Encore (multiplexed); ESPN HD; ESPNews; Eternal Word TV Network; Exercise TV; Filipino Channel; Fox College Sports Atlantic; Fox College Sports Central; Fox College Sports Pacific; Fox Movie Channel; Fox Soccer; G4; GAS; GSN; HDNet; HDNet Movies; Healthy Living Channel; History Channel International; Independent Film Channel; INHD; International Television (ITV); Jewelry Television; Lifetime Real Women; Men's Channel; MoviePlex; Music Choice; National Geographic Channel On Demand; Nick Jr.; NickToons TV; Ovation; Oxygen; Shop at Home; Si TV; Sleuth; SoapNet; Speed Channel; Speed On Demand; Spike TV; Tennis Channel; The Word Network; Toon Disney; Turner Network TV HD; Universal HD; Zee TV USA.
Fee: $12.00 monthly.
Digital Pay Service 1
Pay Units: N.A.
Programming (via satellite): Cinemax (multiplexed); Cinemax On Demand; HBO (multiplexed); HBO HD; HBO On Demand; Showtime (multiplexed); Showtime HD; Showtime On Demand; Starz (multiplexed); The Movie Channel (multiplexed); The Movie Channel On Demand.
Fee: $13.00 monthly (HBO, Starz, Cinemax, Showtime, TMC or Filipino) $16.95 monthly (Zee TV).
Video-On-Demand: Yes
Pay-Per-View
Addressable homes: 1,584.
iN DEMAND, Addressable: Yes; iN DEMAND (delivered digitally), Fee: $6.95; ESPN Gameplan (delivered digitally); MLB Extra Innings (delivered digitally); NASCAR In Car (delivered digitally); MLS Direct Kick (delivered digitally); Fresh (delivered digitally), Fee: $6.95; Playboy TV (delivered digitally); Hot Choice (delivered digitally); Shorteez (delivered digitally); Movies (delivered digitally); NBA League Pass (delivered digitally); ESPN Full Court (delivered digitally); NHL Center Ice (delivered digitally).
Internet Service
Operational: Yes.
Broadband Service: Road Runner.
Fee: $29.95 monthly.
Telephone Service
Analog: Not Operational
Digital: Operational
Fee: $33.95 monthly
Miles of Plant: 151.0 (coaxial); 22.0 (fiber optic). Homes passed: 13,187. Total homes in franchised area: 13,187.
Manager: Joe Schoenstein. Marketing & Programming Director: Danielle Armstrong. Advertising Director: Don Stone. Chief Technician: Chris Gravis. Customer Service Manager: Becky Mitchell.

County fee: 5% of gross.
Ownership: Bright House Networks LLC (MSO).

TEHAMA—New Day Broadband, PO Box 535, 9155 Deschutes Rd, #D, Palo Cedro, CA 96073-8714. Phone: 530-547-2226. Fax: 530-547-4948. Also serves Gerber & Los Molinos. ICA: CA0241.
TV Market Ranking: Below 100 (Gerber, Los Molinos, TEHAMA). Franchise award date: N.A. Franchise expiration date: N.A. Began: February 1, 1984.
Channel capacity: 37 (not 2-way capable). Channels available but not in use: 3.
Basic Service
Subscribers: 600.
Programming (received off-air): KCVU (FOX) Paradise; KHSL-TV (CBS, CW) Chico; KIXE-TV (PBS) Redding; KNVN (NBC) Chico; KRCR-TV (ABC) Redding.
Programming (via satellite): ABC Family Channel; CNN; Disney Channel; ESPN; MTV; Nickelodeon; TBS Superstation; USA Network; WGN America.
Fee: $15.00 installation; $36.75 monthly.
Pay Service 1
Pay Units: N.A.
Programming (via satellite): HBO.
Fee: $11.50 monthly.
Internet Service
Operational: No.
Telephone Service
None
Miles of Plant: 26.0 (coaxial); None (fiber optic). Homes passed: 1,800.
Chief Executive Officer: Neal Sehnog. Chief Technician: Tony Kelly.
Ownership: New Day Broadband (MSO).

THE SEA RANCH—Central Valley Cable, 38951 S Hwy 1, Gualala, CA 95445-8596. Phone: 707-884-4111. Fax: 707-884-4116. E-mail: cvccable@mcn.org. Also serves Gualala. ICA: CA0389.
TV Market Ranking: Below 100 (Manchester); Outside TV Markets (Gualala, Point Arena, THE SEA RANCH). Franchise award date: N.A. Franchise expiration date: N.A. Began: August 13, 1966.
Channel capacity: 60 (operating 2-way). Channels available but not in use: None.
Basic Service
Subscribers: 1,185.
Programming (received off-air): KBCW (CW) San Francisco; KGO-TV (ABC) San Francisco; KICU-TV (IND) San Jose; KNTV (NBC) San Jose; KOFY-TV (IND) San Francisco; KPIX-TV (CBS) San Francisco; KQED (PBS) San Francisco; KRCB (PBS) Cotati; KRON-TV (MNT) San Francisco; KTVU (FOX) Oakland; 21 FMs.
Programming (via satellite): AMC; Arts & Entertainment; BBC America; Bravo; Cartoon Network; CNBC; CNN; Comedy Central; C-SPAN; C-SPAN 2; Discovery Channel; E! Entertainment Television; ESPN; ESPN 2; ESPNews; Fox Movie Channel; Fox News Channel; Fox Sports Net; FX; Golf Channel; Great American Country; Headline News; HGTV; History Channel; Lifetime; MTV; National Geographic Channel; Nickelodeon; QVC; Syfy; TBS Superstation; Telemundo; The Learning Channel; Turner Classic Movies; Turner Network TV; Univision; USA Network; VH1; Weather Channel; WGN America.
Current originations: Public Access.
Fee: $65.00 installation; $44.50 monthly; $1.00 converter.
Pay Service 1
Pay Units: 20.
Programming (via satellite): Cinemax (multiplexed).
Fee: $12.10 monthly.
Pay Service 2
Pay Units: 60.
Programming (via satellite): HBO (multiplexed).
Fee: $13.15 monthly.
Video-On-Demand: No
Internet Service
Operational: Yes.
Broadband Service: Mendocino Community Network (MCN).
Fee: $65.00 installation; $39.99 monthly.
Telephone Service
None
Miles of Plant: 110.0 (coaxial); None (fiber optic). Total homes in franchised area: 3,350.
Plant Manager: David Ramsey.
County fee: 5% of gross (Mendocino); 5% of gross (Sonoma).
Ownership: Central Valley Cable TV LLC.

THERMAL—Cable USA, PO Box 336, 2455 Stirrup Rd, Borrego Springs, CA 92004-0336. Phones: 800-300-6989; 308-236-1512 (Corporate office); 760-767-5607. Fax: 760-767-3609. Web Site: http://www.cableusa.com. ICA: CA0474.
TV Market Ranking: Below 100 (THERMAL).
Channel capacity: N.A. Channels available but not in use: N.A.
Basic Service
Subscribers: N.A.
Programming (received off-air): KDFX-CA Indio/Palm Springs; KESQ-TV (ABC, CW) Palm Springs; KMIR-TV (NBC) Palm Springs.
Programming (via satellite): ABC Family Channel; Arts & Entertainment; GalaVision; Home Shopping Network; TBS Superstation; Telefutura; Telemundo; Univision; WGN America.
Internet Service
Operational: No.
Manager & Chief Technician: Joe Gustafson.
Ownership: USA Companies (MSO).

THOUSAND OAKS—Charter Communications, 3806 Cross Creek Rd, Malibu, CA 90265-4971. Phones: 626-430-3300 (Irwindale office); 310-456-9010. Fax: 310-579-7010. Web Site: http://www.charter.com. ICA: CA0188.
TV Market Ranking: 2 (THOUSAND OAKS). Franchise award date: September 1, 1967. Franchise expiration date: N.A. Began: September 1, 1967.
Channel capacity: 60 (2-way capable). Channels available but not in use: N.A.
Basic Service
Subscribers: 3,748.
Programming (received off-air): KABC-TV (ABC) Los Angeles; KADY-LP Sherman; KAZA-TV (IND) Avalon; KCAL-TV (IND) Los Angeles; KCBS-TV (CBS) Los Angeles; KCET (PBS) Los Angeles; KCOP-TV (MNT) Los Angeles; KEYT-TV (ABC, MNT) Santa Barbara; KFTR-DT (TEL) Ontario; KJLA (IND) Ventura; KMEX-DT (UNV) Los Angeles; KNBC (NBC) Los Angeles; KPXN-TV (ION) San Bernardino; KRCA (IND) Riverside; KSCI (IND) Long Beach; KTBN-TV (TBN) Santa Ana; KTLA (CW) Los Angeles; KTTV (FOX) Los Angeles; KVEA (TMO) Corona; KVMD (IND) Twentynine Palms; KWHY-TV (IND) Los Angeles; KXLA (IND) Rancho Palos Verdes.
Programming (via satellite): ABC Family Channel; AMC; Arts & Entertainment; Bravo; CNBC; CNN; Comedy Central; C-SPAN; E! Entertainment Television; ESPN; Food Network; FX; Headline News; Home Shopping Network; Lifetime; MTV; Nickelodeon; Oxygen; QVC; Spike TV; USA Network; VH1.
Current originations: Government Access; Educational Access; Public Access.
Fee: $65.00 installation; $22.45 monthly; $.98 converter.
Expanded Basic Service 1
Subscribers: N.A.
Programming (via satellite): Animal Planet; Discovery Channel; Disney Channel; ESPN 2; Fox Movie Channel; Fox News Channel; Fox Sports Net West; Fox Sports Net West 2; GSN; History Channel; MSNBC; Syfy; TBS Superstation; The Learning Channel; Turner Classic Movies; Turner Network TV; WE tv; Weather Channel; WGN America.
Pay Service 1
Pay Units: 713.
Programming (via satellite): HBO.
Fee: $5.00 monthly.
Pay Service 2
Pay Units: 204.
Programming (via satellite): Showtime.
Fee: $5.00 monthly.
Video-On-Demand: No
Pay-Per-View
iN DEMAND (delivered digitally); NASCAR In Car (delivered digitally); Playboy TV (delivered digitally); Fresh (delivered digitally); Shorteez (delivered digitally).
Internet Service
Operational: Yes.
Telephone Service
Digital: Operational
Miles of Plant: 65.0 (coaxial); None (fiber optic). Homes passed: 4,709.
Vice President & General Manager: Wendy Rasmussen. Technical Operations Director: Peter Arredondo. Marketing Manager: Lily Ho.
Franchise fee: 3% of gross.
Ownership: Charter Communications Inc. (MSO).

THOUSAND OAKS—Time Warner Cable. Now served by CHATSWORTH, CA [CA0013]. ICA: CA0446.

TORRANCE—Time Warner Cable. Now served by LOS ANGELES, CA [CA0009]. ICA: CA0020.

TRACY—Comcast Cable, 6505 Tam O Shanter Dr, Stockton, CA 95210-3349. Phones: 209-473-4955; 800-266-2278. Fax: 209-473-8177. E-mail: farrell_moseley@cable.comcast.com. Web Site: http://www.comcast.com. Also serves San Joaquin County. ICA: CA0143.
TV Market Ranking: 7,25 (San Joaquin County, TRACY). Franchise award date: N.A. Franchise expiration date: N.A. Began: January 1, 1966.
Channel capacity: N.A. Channels available but not in use: N.A.
Basic Service
Subscribers: 12,021.
Programming (received off-air): KCRA-TV (NBC) Sacramento; KCSO-LP Sacramento; KGO-TV (ABC) San Francisco; KICU-TV (IND) San Jose; KMAX-TV (CW) Sacramento; KOVR (CBS) Stockton; KPIX-TV (CBS) San Francisco; KQCA (MNT) Stockton; KQED (PBS) San Francisco; KSPX-TV (ION) Sacramento; KTFK-DT (TEL) Stockton; KTNC-TV (IND) Concord; KTVU (FOX) Oakland; KTXL (FOX) Sacramento; KUVS-DT (UNV) Modesto; KVIE (PBS) Sacramento; KXTV (ABC) Sacramento; 20 FMs.
Programming (via satellite): CNBC; CNN; C-SPAN; C-SPAN 2; Fox News Channel; Headline News; MSNBC; TV Guide Network; Weather Channel.
Current originations: Government Access; Educational Access; Public Access.
Fee: $43.99 installation; $11.80 monthly; $1.13 converter.
Expanded Basic Service 1
Subscribers: N.A.
Programming (via satellite): ABC Family Channel; AMC; Animal Planet; Arts & Entertainment; BET Networks; Bravo; Cartoon Network; Comcast Sports Net Bay Area; Comedy Central; Country Music TV; Discovery Channel; Disney Channel; E! Entertainment Television; ESPN; ESPN 2; Eternal Word TV Network; Food Network; FX; GalaVision; Golf Channel; GSN; HGTV; History Channel; Home Shopping Network 2; Lifetime; MTV; mun2 television; Nickelodeon; QVC; ShopNBC; Spike TV; Style Network; Syfy; TBS Superstation; The Learning Channel; Turner Network TV; TV Land; USA Network; Versus; VH1.
Fee: $52.55 monthly.
Digital Basic Service
Subscribers: 3,606.
Programming (via satellite): AmericanLife TV Network; BBC America; Bio; Black Family Channel; Bloomberg Television; Canales N; Discovery Digital Networks; Encore Action; ESPN Classic Sports; ESPNews; FitTV; Fox College Sports Atlantic; Fox College Sports Central; Fox College Sports Pacific; Fox Movie Channel; Fox Sports World; Fuse; G4; GAS; Great American Country; Halogen Network; History Channel International; Independent Film Channel; Lifetime Movie Network; Lime; MTV Networks Digital Suite; Music Choice; National Geographic Channel; Nick Jr.; NickToons TV; Outdoor Channel; Ovation; Speed Channel; Sundance Channel; The Word Network; Toon Disney; Trinity Broadcasting Network; Turner Classic Movies; WE tv.
Fee: $11.95 monthly.
Digital Pay Service 1
Pay Units: 1,424.
Programming (via satellite): ART America; CCTV-4; Cinemax (multiplexed); Filipino Channel; Flix; HBO (multiplexed); Power Link; RAI International; Russian Television Network; Saigon Broadcasting TV Network; Showtime (multiplexed); Starz (multiplexed); The Movie Channel (multiplexed); TV Asia; TV Japan; TV5, La Television International; Zee TV USA.

Fee: $17.99 monthly (Cinemax, Starz or TMC), $18.99 monthly (HBO or Showtime).

Video-On-Demand: Yes

Pay-Per-View

Addressable homes: 3,606.

iN DEMAND (delivered digitally), Fee: $4.95, Addressable: Yes; Playboy TV (delivered digitally); Fresh (delivered digitally); Urban Xtra (delivered digitally); Shorteez (delivered digitally); Hot Choice (delivered digitally); ESPN Now (delivered digitally); Sports PPV (delivered digitally).

Internet Service

Operational: Yes.

Broadband Service: Comcast High Speed Internet.

Fee: $42.95 monthly.

Telephone Service

Digital: Operational

Fee: $39.95 monthly

Miles of Plant: 144.0 (coaxial); 225.0 (fiber optic). Total homes in franchised area: 17,772.

Technical Operations Director: Fred Walkover. Marketing Manager: Terry Dowling.

City fee: 5% of gross.

Ownership: Comcast Cable Communications Inc. (MSO).

TRAVIS AFB—Comcast Cable. Now served by NAPA/SONOMA, CA [CA0038]. ICA: CA0192.

TRINITY CENTER—Formerly served by Almega Cable. No longer in operation. ICA: CA0391.

TRUCKEE—Suddenlink Communications, 10607 West River St, Truckee, CA 96161. Phones: 314-965-2020; 530-587-6100. Fax: 530-587-1468. Web Site: http://www.suddenlink.com. Also serves Alpine Meadows, Donner Lake, Donner Summit, Glenshire, Lake Tahoe, Meeks Bay-Tahoma Area, Serene Lakes, Sierra Meadows, Soda Springs, Squaw Valley, Sugar Bowl, Tahoe City (southeastern portion), Tahoe Donner, Ward Valley & West Lake Tahoe. ICA: CA0181.

TV Market Ranking: 25 (Sierra Meadows); Below 100 (Alpine Meadows, Donner Lake, Donner Summit, Glenshire, Lake Tahoe, Meeks Bay-Tahoma Area, Soda Springs, Squaw Valley, Sugar Bowl, Tahoe City (southeastern portion), Tahoe Donner, TRUCKEE); Outside TV Markets (Serene Lakes, Ward Valley, West Lake Tahoe). Franchise award date: February 3, 1964. Franchise expiration date: N.A. Began: September 1, 1964.

Channel capacity: 58 (operating 2-way). Channels available but not in use: 9.

Basic Service

Subscribers: 11,642.

Programming (received off-air): KCRA-TV (NBC) Sacramento; KGO-TV (ABC) San Francisco; KOLO-TV (ABC) Reno; KOVR (CBS) Stockton; KPIX-TV (CBS) San Francisco; KQED (PBS) San Francisco; KREN-TV (CW, UNV) Reno; KTVU (FOX) Oakland; KTXL (FOX) Sacramento; allband FM.

Programming (via satellite): ABC Family Channel; Arts & Entertainment; CNBC; CNN; Comcast Sports Net Bay Area; Comedy Central; C-SPAN; Discovery Channel; Disney Channel; ESPN; ESPN 2; Fox News Channel; Great American Country; Headline News; Lifetime; MTV; Nickelodeon; QVC; Spike TV; The Learning Channel; Toon Disney; Turner Network TV; USA Network; Versus; VH1; Weather Channel.

Current originations: Government Access; Educational Access.

Fee: $49.95 installation; $18.04 monthly.

Digital Basic Service

Subscribers: N.A.

Programming (via satellite): BBC America; Box; Bravo; Canales N; Discovery Digital Networks; DMX Music; Encore; ESPN Classic Sports; ESPNews; Fox Sports World; Golf Channel; GSN; HGTV; Independent Film Channel; Speed Channel; Syfy; Turner Classic Movies.

Fee: $3.95 monthly.

Pay Service 1

Pay Units: N.A.

Programming (via satellite): Encore; HBO; Showtime; Starz; The Movie Channel; Univision.

Digital Pay Service 1

Pay Units: N.A.

Programming (via satellite): Cinemax (multiplexed); HBO (multiplexed); Showtime (multiplexed); The Movie Channel (multiplexed).

Video-On-Demand: No

Pay-Per-View

Movies (delivered digitally); Special events (delivered digitally).

Internet Service

Operational: Yes. Began: June 1, 2001.

Subscribers: 350.

Broadband Service: Cebridge High Speed Cable Internet.

Fee: $99.99 installation; $24.95 monthly; $10.00 modem lease; $240.00 modem purchase.

Telephone Service

None

Miles of Plant: 350.0 (coaxial); None (fiber optic). Homes passed: 18,543.

Manager: Dawn McWithey. Marketing Director: Jason Oelkers. Chief Technician: Dave Woods.

Ownership: Cequel Communications LLC (MSO).

TUJUNGA—Time Warner Cable. Now served by CHATSWORTH, CA [CA0013]. ICA: CA0470.

TULELAKE—Almega Cable, 4001 W Airport Frwy, Ste 530, Bedford, TX 76021. Phones: 877-725-6342; 817-685-9588. Fax: 817-685-6488. Web Site: http://almegacable.com. ICA: CA0392.

TV Market Ranking: Below 100 (TULELAKE). Franchise award date: N.A. Franchise expiration date: N.A. Began: N.A.

Channel capacity: 45 (not 2-way capable). Channels available but not in use: 24.

Basic Service

Subscribers: 161.

Programming (received off-air): KDKF (ABC) Klamath Falls; KIXE-TV (PBS) Redding; KMVU-DT (FOX) Medford; KOTI (NBC) Klamath Falls; KTVL (CBS, CW) Medford.

Programming (via satellite): ABC Family Channel; Arts & Entertainment; Bravo; CNBC; CNN; Discovery Channel; Disney Channel; ESPN; HGTV; INSP; MSNBC; Syfy; TBS Superstation; Turner Classic Movies; Turner Network TV; Univision; USA Network; WGN America.

Current originations: Educational Access.

Fee: $29.95 installation; $28.45 monthly.

Pay Service 1

Pay Units: 30.

Programming (via satellite): HBO.

Fee: $10.95 monthly.

Video-On-Demand: No

Internet Service

Operational: Yes.

Fee: $39.95 installation; $39.95 monthly.

Telephone Service

None

Miles of Plant: 15.0 (coaxial); None (fiber optic). Homes passed: 472.

President: Thomas Kurien.

Franchise fee: 3% of gross less installations.

Ownership: Almega Cable (MSO).

TURLOCK—Charter Communications, 270 Bridge St, San Luis Obispo, CA 93401. Phone: 805-544-1962. Fax: 805-541-6042. Web Site: http://www.charter.com. Also serves Ceres, Del Rio, Delhi, Denair, Empire, Escalon, Hickman, Hilmar, Hughson, Keyes, Livingston, Ripon, Riverbank, Salida, San Joaquin County (portions), Stanislaus County (portions) & Waterford. ICA: CA0095.

TV Market Ranking: 25 (Ceres, Del Rio, Delhi, Denair, Escalon, Hilmar, Keyes, Ripon, Salida, San Joaquin County (portions)); 25,72 (Empire, Hickman, Hughson, Livingston, Riverbank, Stanislaus County (portions), TURLOCK, Waterford). Franchise award date: N.A. Franchise expiration date: N.A. Began: June 13, 1973.

Channel capacity: N.A. Channels available but not in use: N.A.

Basic Service

Subscribers: 44,297.

Programming (received off-air): KBSV (ETV) Ceres; KCRA-TV (NBC) Sacramento; KFSN-TV (ABC) Fresno; KMAX-TV (CW) Sacramento; KOVR (CBS) Stockton; KQCA (MNT) Stockton; KSPX-TV (ION) Sacramento; KTFK-DT (TEL) Stockton; KTXL (FOX) Sacramento; KUVS-DT (UNV) Modesto; KVIE (PBS) Sacramento; KXTV (ABC) Sacramento; allband FM.

Programming (via satellite): ABC Family Channel; AMC; Animal Planet; Arts & Entertainment; BET Networks; Bravo; Cartoon Network; CNBC; CNN; Comcast Sports Net Bay Area; Comedy Central; Country Music TV; C-SPAN; C-SPAN 2; Discovery Channel; Disney Channel; E! Entertainment Television; ESPN; ESPN 2; ESPN Classic Sports; Eternal Word TV Network; Food Network; Fox News Channel; Fox Sports en Espanol; FX; GalaVision; Golf Channel; GSN; Hallmark Channel; Headline News; HGTV; History Channel; Home Shopping Network; Lifetime; MSNBC; MTV; National Geographic Channel; Nickelodeon; Oxygen; QVC; SoapNet; Speed Channel; Spike TV; Syfy; TBS Superstation; Telemundo; The Learning Channel; Travel Channel; Trinity Broadcasting Network; truTV; Turner Classic Movies; Turner Network TV; TV Guide Network; TV Land; USA Network; Versus; VH1; Weather Channel.

Current originations: Leased Access; Religious Access; Government Access; Educational Access; Public Access.

Fee: $29.99 installation; $38.99 monthly.

Digital Basic Service

Subscribers: 14,000.

Programming (via satellite): BBC America; Bio; Bloomberg Television; Boomerang; Discovery Digital Networks; Do-It-Yourself; GAS; History Channel International; Lifetime Movie Network; Music Choice; Nick Jr.; Style Network; Sundance Channel; Toon Disney; WE tv.

Digital Pay Service 1

Pay Units: N.A.

Programming (via satellite): Cinemax (multiplexed); Encore (multiplexed); Flix; HBO (multiplexed); Showtime (multiplexed); Starz (multiplexed); The Movie Channel (multiplexed).

Video-On-Demand: Yes

Pay-Per-View

Addressable homes: 16,971.

Hot Choice (delivered digitally), Addressable: Yes; iN DEMAND; Fresh; Fresh (delivered digitally); Shorteez (delivered digitally); Sports PPV (delivered digitally); movies (delivered digitally).

Internet Service

Operational: Yes. Began: December 1, 1999.

Subscribers: 2,500.

Broadband Service: Charter Pipeline.

Fee: $29.99 monthly; $199.00 modem purchase.

Telephone Service

Digital: Operational

Miles of Plant: 461.0 (coaxial); 29.0 (fiber optic). Homes passed: 66,000.

Vice President & General Manager: Ed Merrill. Technical Operations Director: Ken Arellano. Marketing Director: Sarwar Assar. Office Manager: Joanne Yee.

City fee: 5% of gross.

Ownership: Charter Communications Inc. (MSO).

TUSTIN—Comcast Cable. Now served by ANAHEIM, CA [CA0033]. ICA: CA0121.

TWAIN HARTE—Comcast Cable, 6505 Tam O Shanter Dr, Stockton, CA 95210-3349. Phone: 209-473-4955. Fax: 209-473-8177. Web Site: http://www.comcast.com. Also serves Columbia, Jamestown, Mi-Wuk Village, Mono Vista, Phoenix Lake-Cedar Ridge, Sierra Village, Sonora, Soulsbyville, Standard (portions of Tuolmne County), Sugar Pine & Tuolumne City (portions of Tuolumne County). ICA: CA0148.

TV Market Ranking: Outside TV Markets (Columbia, Jamestown, Mi-Wuk Village, Mono Vista, Phoenix Lake-Cedar Ridge, Sierra Village, Sonora, Soulsbyville, Standard, Sugar Pine, Tuolumne City, TWAIN HARTE (portions)). Franchise award date: N.A. Franchise expiration date: N.A. Began: June 1, 1967.

Channel capacity: 39 (operating 2-way). Channels available but not in use: 5.

Basic Service

Subscribers: 18,744.

Programming (received off-air): KCRA-TV (NBC) Sacramento; KMAX-TV (CW) Sacramento; KOVR (CBS) Stockton; KQCA (MNT) Stockton; KSPX-TV (ION) Sacramento; KTFK-DT (TEL) Stockton; KTVU (FOX) Oakland; KTXL (FOX) Sacramento; KUVS-DT (UNV) Modesto; KVIE (PBS) Sacramento; 11 FMs.

Programming (via satellite): C-SPAN; QVC; TBS Superstation; TV Guide Network; Weather Channel.

Current originations: Public Access.

Planned originations: Educational Access.

Fee: $43.99 installation; $15.00 monthly; $.60 converter.

Expanded Basic Service 1

Subscribers: 18,000.

Programming (via satellite): ABC Family Channel; AMC; Arts & Entertainment; CNBC; CNN; Comcast Sports Net Bay Area; Country Music TV; Discovery Channel; Disney Channel; ESPN; Fox News Channel; FX; Lifetime; MTV; Nickelodeon; Spike TV; Turner Network TV; USA Network; Weather Channel.

Fee: $41.95 monthly.

Digital Basic Service
Subscribers: 5,623.
Programming (via satellite): BBC America; Bio; Bloomberg Television; Bravo; Discovery Digital Networks; Discovery Kids Channel; DMX Music; Encore Action; ESPN 2; ESPN Classic Sports; ESPNews; FitTV; Fox Movie Channel; Fox Sports World; Fuse; G4; GAS; Golf Channel; GSN; Halogen Network; HGTV; History Channel; History Channel International; Independent Film Channel; International Television (ITV); Lifetime Movie Network; Lime; MTV Networks Digital Suite; National Geographic Channel; Nick Jr.; NickToons TV; Outdoor Channel; Ovation; Speed Channel; Style Network; Sundance Channel; Syfy; Toon Disney; Trinity Broadcasting Network; Turner Classic Movies; TV Land; Versus; VH1 Classic; WE tv.
Fee: $53.55 monthly.
Digital Pay Service 1
Pay Units: 8,446.
Programming (via satellite): Cinemax (multiplexed); HBO (multiplexed); Showtime (multiplexed); Starz (multiplexed); The Movie Channel (multiplexed).
Fee: $10.00 installation; $17.99 monthly (Cinemax, Starz or TMC), $18.99 monthly (HBO or Showtime).
Video-On-Demand: No
Pay-Per-View
Addressable homes: 5,623.
iN DEMAND (delivered digitally), Addressable: Yes; Fresh (delivered digitally); Shorteez (delivered digitally); Playboy TV (delivered digitally).
Internet Service
Operational: Yes.
Broadband Service: Comcast High Speed Internet.
Fee: $42.95 monthly.
Telephone Service
None
Miles of Plant: 622.0 (coaxial); None (fiber optic). Homes passed: 40,666. Total homes in franchised area: 40,666.
Technical Operations Director: Fred Walkover. Marketing Manager: Terry Dowling.
City fee: 3% of basic.
Ownership: Comcast Cable Communications Inc. (MSO).

UKIAH—Comcast Cable, 1060 N State St, Ukiah, CA 95482-3414. Phones: 415-459-5333 (San Rafael office); 707-462-8646. Fax: 707-462-6973. Web Site: http://www.comcast.com. Also serves Albion, Brooktrails, Calpella, Caspar, Fort Bragg, Littleriver, Mendocino, Mendocino County, Redwood Valley, Talmage & Willits. ICA: CA0111.
TV Market Ranking: Below 100 (Albion, Caspar, Fort Bragg, Littleriver, Mendocino, Mendocino County (portions), Redwood Valley, Willits); Outside TV Markets (Brooktrails, Calpella, Mendocino County (portions), Talmage, UKIAH). Franchise award date: January 1, 1952. Franchise expiration date: N.A. Began: December 1, 1952.
Channel capacity: N.A. Channels available but not in use: N.A.
Basic Service
Subscribers: 12,755.
Programming (received off-air): KFTY (IND) Santa Rosa; KGO-TV (ABC) San Francisco; KNTV (NBC) San Jose; KPIX-TV (CBS) San Francisco; KQED (PBS) San Francisco; KTVU (FOX) Oakland; 13 FMs.
Programming (via satellite): ABC Family Channel; AMC; Animal Planet; Arts & Entertainment; Bravo; Cartoon Network; CNBC; CNN; Comcast Sports Net Bay Area; Comedy Central; Country Music TV; C-SPAN; C-SPAN 2; Discovery Channel; Disney Channel; E! Entertainment Television; ESPN; ESPN 2; Eternal Word TV Network; Food Network; Fox News Channel; FX; Headline News; HGTV; History Channel; Home Shopping Network; Lifetime; MSNBC; MTV; Nickelodeon; QVC; Spike TV; Syfy; TBS Superstation; Telemundo; The Learning Channel; Travel Channel; truTV; Turner Network TV; TV Guide Network; TV Land; Univision; USA Network; VH1; Weather Channel; WGN America.
Current originations: Government Access; Public Access; Leased Access; Educational Access.
Fee: $43.99 installation; $17.65 monthly.
Digital Basic Service
Subscribers: 4,500.
Programming (via satellite): AmericanLife TV Network; BBC America; Bio; Black Family Channel; Bloomberg Television; Canales N; Discovery Digital Networks; DMX Music; Do-It-Yourself; ESPN Classic Sports; ESPNews; FitTV; Flix; Fox College Sports Atlantic; Fox College Sports Central; Fox College Sports Pacific; Fox Movie Channel; Fox Sports World; Fuse; G4; GAS; Golf Channel; Great American Country; GSN; Halogen Network; History Channel International; Independent Film Channel; Lifetime Movie Network; MTV Networks Digital Suite; Music Choice; National Geographic Channel; Nick Jr.; Nick Too; NickToons TV; Outdoor Channel; Ovation; SoapNet; Speed Channel; Style Network; Sundance Channel; The Word Network; Toon Disney; Trinity Broadcasting Network; Turner Classic Movies; Versus; WE tv.
Fee: $11.95 monthly.
Digital Pay Service 1
Pay Units: 109.
Programming (via satellite): Cinemax (multiplexed).
Fee: $17.00 monthly.
Digital Pay Service 2
Pay Units: 450.
Programming (via satellite): HBO (multiplexed).
Fee: $17.00 monthly.
Digital Pay Service 3
Pay Units: 140.
Programming (via satellite): Showtime (multiplexed).
Fee: $17.00 monthly.
Digital Pay Service 4
Pay Units: N.A.
Programming (via satellite): ART America; CCTV-4; Encore (multiplexed); Filipino Channel; RAI International; Starz (multiplexed); The Movie Channel (multiplexed); TV Asia; TV Japan; TV5, La Television International; Zee TV USA; Zhong Tian Channel.
Fee: $17.00 monthly (each).
Video-On-Demand: No
Pay-Per-View
Addressable homes: 4,500.
iN DEMAND (delivered digitally), Addressable: Yes; Playboy TV (delivered digitally); Fresh (delivered digitally); Shorteez (delivered digitally); Hot Choice (delivered digitally); Urban Xtra (delivered digitally); Sports PPV (delivered digitally).
Internet Service
Operational: Yes. Began: December 31, 2001.
Broadband Service: Comcast High Speed Internet.
Fee: $42.95 monthly.
Telephone Service
None
Miles of Plant: 408.0 (coaxial); 40.0 (fiber optic). Homes passed: 23,500. Total homes in franchised area: 40,000.
Area Vice President: Paul Gibson. Technical Operations Director: John Portelli. Chief Technician: Robert Reid. Sales & Marketing Director: Susan Blum.
Ownership: Comcast Cable Communications Inc. (MSO).

UNION CITY—Comcast Cable. Now served by OAKLAND, CA [CA0018]. ICA: CA0135.

VACAVILLE—Comcast Cable. Now served by NAPA/SONOMA, CA [CA0038]. ICA: CA0098.

VALLEJO—Comcast Cable. Now served by NAPA/SONOMA, CA [CA0038]. ICA: CA0061.

VALLEY CENTER—Mediacom, 27192 Sun City Blvd, Ste A, Sun City, CA 92586. Phone: 951-679-3977. Fax: 951-679-9087. Web Site: http://www.mediacomcable.com. Also serves Pauma Valley & Rincon. ICA: CA0223.
TV Market Ranking: 51 (VALLEY CENTER); Outside TV Markets (Pauma Valley, Rincon). Franchise award date: N.A. Franchise expiration date: N.A. Began: September 1, 1966.
Channel capacity: 60 (2-way capable). Channels available but not in use: 15.
Basic Service
Subscribers: 2,030.
Programming (received off-air): KFMB-TV (CBS) San Diego; KGTV (ABC) San Diego; KNSD (NBC) San Diego; KPBS (PBS) San Diego; KSWB-TV (FOX) San Diego; KTLA (CW) Los Angeles; KUSI-TV (IND) San Diego; allband FM.
Programming (via satellite): ABC Family Channel; AMC; AmericanLife TV Network; Animal Planet; Arts & Entertainment; CNBC; CNN; Comedy Central; C-SPAN; C-SPAN 2; Discovery Channel; Disney Channel; E! Entertainment Television; ESPN; ESPN 2; Eternal Word TV Network; Food Network; Fox News Channel; Fox Sports Net West; Golf Channel; Headline News; HGTV; History Channel; Home Shopping Network; Lifetime; MSNBC; MTV; Nickelodeon; Outdoor Channel; QVC; Spike TV; Telemundo; The Learning Channel; Toon Disney; Travel Channel; Trinity Broadcasting Network; Turner Network TV; TV Land; Univision; USA Network; VH1; Weather Channel; WGN America.
Current originations: Educational Access.
Fee: $41.25 installation; $45.95 monthly; $20.00 additional installation.
Digital Basic Service
Subscribers: N.A.
Programming (via satellite): BBC America; Bio; Discovery Digital Networks; DMX Music; ESPNews; Fox Soccer; Fuse; GAS; GSN; History Channel International; Independent Film Channel; Lifetime Movie Network; National Geographic Channel; Nick Jr.; Speed Channel; Style Network; Turner Classic Movies; Versus; VH1 Classic.
Fee: $8.00 monthly.
Digital Pay Service 1
Pay Units: N.A.
Programming (via satellite): Cinemax (multiplexed); Encore (multiplexed); Flix; HBO (multiplexed); Showtime (multiplexed); Starz (multiplexed); The Movie Channel (multiplexed).
Fee: $8.00 monthly (Starz/Encore), $9.95 monthly (Cinemax or Showtime/TMC), $13.95 monthly (HBO).
Video-On-Demand: No
Pay-Per-View
iN DEMAND (delivered digitally); Adult PPV (delivered digitally).
Internet Service
Operational: Yes.
Broadband Service: Mediacom High Speed Internet.
Fee: $59.95 installation; $40.95 monthly.
Telephone Service
None
Miles of Plant: 150.0 (coaxial); None (fiber optic). Additional miles planned: 10.0 (coaxial). Homes passed: 2,100. Total homes in franchised area: 2,700.
General Manager: Allen Bublitz. Engineering Director: Jon Tatilano.
City fee: 3% of basic.
Ownership: Mediacom LLC.

VAN NUYS—Formerly served by Adelphia Communications. Now served by CHATSWORTH, CA [CA0013]. ICA: CA0462.

VANDENBERG AFB—Vandenberg Broadband, 2312 104th Ave SE, Bellevue, WA 98004. Phones: 805-734-5578 (Local office); 425-451-1470. Fax: 425-451-1471. E-mail: corporateoffice@ruralwest.com. Web Site: http://www.vafb.net. ICA: CA0393.
TV Market Ranking: Below 100 (VANDENBERG AFB). Franchise award date: February 1, 1986. Franchise expiration date: N.A. Began: May 10, 1986.
Channel capacity: 78 (operating 2-way). Channels available but not in use: N.A.
Basic Service
Subscribers: 1,400.
Programming (received off-air): KCOY-TV (CBS) Santa Maria; KEYT-TV (ABC, MNT) Santa Barbara; KRMA-TV (PBS) Denver; KSBY (CW, NBC) San Luis Obispo; KTLA (CW) Los Angeles; KTVD (MNT) Denver.
Programming (via satellite): ABC Family Channel; AMC; Animal Planet; Arts & Entertainment; BET Networks; Boomerang; Cartoon Network; CNBC; CNN; Comedy Central; Country Music TV; C-SPAN; C-SPAN 2; Discovery Channel; Disney Channel; E! Entertainment Television; ESPN; ESPN 2; ESPN Classic Sports; Eternal Word TV Network; Food Network; Fox News Channel; Fox Sports Net; FX; Hallmark Channel; Headline News; HGTV; History Channel; Lifetime; MSNBC; MTV; NASA TV; Nickelodeon; Oxygen; QVC; Speed Channel; Spike TV; Syfy; TBS Superstation; The Learning Channel; Travel Channel; Trinity Broadcasting Network; Turner Network TV; TV Land; Univision; USA Network; VH1; WE tv; Weather Channel; WGN America; WPIX (CW, IND) New York.
Current originations: Public Access; Public Access.
Fee: $37.95 monthly.
Digital Basic Service
Subscribers: 262.
Programming (via satellite): BBC America; Bio; Bloomberg Television; Bravo; Current; Discovery Health Channel; Discovery Kids Channel; Discovery Military Channel; Discovery Planet Green; DMX Music; ESPN 2; ESPN Classic Sports; FitTV; Fox College Sports Atlantic; Fox College Sports Central; Fox College Sports Pacific; Fox Movie Channel; Fox Soccer; Fuse; G4; Golf Channel; Great American Country; GSN; Halogen

Network; HGTV; History Channel; History Channel International; ID Investigation Discovery; Independent Film Channel; International Television (ITV); Lifetime Movie Network; Lime; MTV Hits; MTV2; National Geographic Channel; Nick Jr.; NickToons TV; Outdoor Channel; Ovation; Science Channel; Speed Channel; Style Network; Sundance Channel; TeenNick; Toon Disney; Trio; Turner Classic Movies; VH1 Classic; VH1 Country; VH1 Soul.
Fee: $51.95 monthly.

Digital Pay Service 1
Pay Units: 300.
Programming (via satellite): Cinemax (multiplexed); HBO (multiplexed); Showtime (multiplexed); The Movie Channel (multiplexed).
Fee: $10.95 monthly.

Digital Pay Service 2
Pay Units: N.A.
Programming (via satellite): Encore (multiplexed); Flix; Starz (multiplexed).

Video-On-Demand: No

Pay-Per-View
iN DEMAND.

Internet Service
Operational: Yes.
Subscribers: 475.
Broadband Service: In-house.
Fee: $34.99 monthly.

Telephone Service
Analog: Not Operational
Digital: Planned

Miles of Plant: 25.0 (coaxial); 12.0 (fiber optic). Homes passed: 3,000.
Manager: Dave Bowland. Chief Technician: Sean Esman.
Ownership: RuralWest - Western Rural Broadband Inc. (MSO).

VENTURA—Charter Communications, 3806 Cross Creek Rd, Malibu, CA 90265-4971. Phones: 310-456-9010; 626-430-3300 (Irwindale office). Fax: 310-579-7010. Web Site: http://www.charter.com. Also serves Casitas Springs, La Conchita & Ventura County (Rincon area). ICA: CA0146.
TV Market Ranking: Below 100 (Casitas Springs, La Conchita, VENTURA, Ventura County (Rincon area)). Franchise award date: December 31, 1999. Franchise expiration date: N.A. Began: January 1, 1951.
Channel capacity: 74 (operating 2-way). Channels available but not in use: None.

Basic Service
Subscribers: N.A. Included in Cerritos
Programming (received off-air): KABC-TV (ABC) Los Angeles; KBEH (IND) Oxnard; KCAL-TV (IND) Los Angeles; KCBS-TV (CBS) Los Angeles; KCET (PBS) Los Angeles; KCOP-TV (MNT) Los Angeles; KEYT-TV (ABC, MNT) Santa Barbara; KFTR-DT (TEL) Ontario; KJLA (IND) Ventura; KMEX-DT (UNV) Los Angeles; KNBC (NBC) Los Angeles; KTLA (CW) Los Angeles; KTTV (FOX) Los Angeles; KVEA (TMO) Corona; allband FM.
Programming (via satellite): California Channel; Fox Sports Net West; Home Shopping Network; Jewelry Television; KAZA-TV (IND) Avalon; KRCA (IND) Riverside; QVC; Trinity Broadcasting Network.
Current originations: Public Access; Leased Access.
Fee: $52.50 installation; $22.95 monthly; $2.10 converter; $20.00 additional installation.

Expanded Basic Service 1
Subscribers: N.A.
Programming (via satellite): ABC Family Channel; AMC; Animal Planet; Arts & Entertainment; BET Networks; Bravo; Cartoon Network; CNBC; CNN; Comedy Central; Country Music TV; C-SPAN; C-SPAN 2; Discovery Channel; Discovery Health Channel; Disney Channel; E! Entertainment Television; ESPN; ESPN 2; ESPN Classic Sports; ESPNews; Eternal Word TV Network; FitTV; Food Network; Fox Movie Channel; Fox News Channel; Fox Sports en Espanol; Fox Sports Net West 2; FX; GalaVision; Golf Channel; Great American Country; Hallmark Channel; Headline News; HGTV; History Channel; ION Television; Lifetime; MSNBC; MTV; Nickelodeon; Oxygen; ShopNBC; SoapNet; Spike TV; Syfy; TBS Superstation; The Learning Channel; Toon Disney; Travel Channel; truTV; Turner Classic Movies; Turner Network TV; TV Guide Network; TV Land; USA Network; VH1; Weather Channel.
Fee: $23.55 monthly.

Digital Basic Service
Subscribers: 1,800.
Programming (received off-air): KABC-TV (ABC) Los Angeles; KCBS-TV (CBS) Los Angeles; KCET (PBS) Los Angeles; KCOP-TV (MNT) Los Angeles; KNBC (NBC) Los Angeles; KTLA (CW) Los Angeles; KTTV (FOX) Los Angeles.
Programming (via satellite): Arts & Entertainment HD; BBC America; Bio; CMT Pure Country; Discovery Digital Networks; Discovery HD Theater; ESPN 2 HD; ESPN HD; Food Network HD; Fox Reality Channel; GAS; HDNet; HDNet Movies; HGTV HD; History Channel International; INSP; MTV Networks Digital Suite; Music Choice; National Geographic Channel HD Network; Nick Jr.; NickToons TV; PBS Kids Sprout; Turner Network TV HD; Universal HD.
Fee: $13.00 monthly.

Digital Expanded Basic Service
Subscribers: N.A.
Programming (via satellite): American-Life TV Network; Bloomberg Television; Boomerang; Canales N; Discovery Health Channel; Do-It-Yourself; ESPN U; Fox College Sports Atlantic; Fox College Sports Central; Fox College Sports Pacific; Fox Movie Channel; Fox Soccer; Fuel TV; Fuse; G4; Gol TV; GSN; Hallmark Channel; Halogen Network; Independent Film Channel; Lifetime Movie Network; National Geographic Channel; NFL Network; Outdoor Channel; Sleuth; Speed Channel; Style Network; Syfy; Tennis Channel; Toon Disney; TV Land; Versus; WE tv.
Fee: $5.00 monthly (variety or sports), $7.00 monthly (Canales).

Digital Pay Service 1
Pay Units: 1,800.
Programming (via satellite): Cinemax (multiplexed); Cinemax HD; Encore (multiplexed); Flix; HBO (multiplexed); HBO HD; Showtime (multiplexed); Showtime HD; Starz (multiplexed); Starz HDTV; The Movie Channel (multiplexed); The Movie Channel HD.
Fee: $12.00 monthly (Showtime/TMC/Flix) $15.00 monthly (Cinemax, HBO or Starz/Encore).

Video-On-Demand: Planned

Pay-Per-View
Addressable homes: 6,000.
Playboy TV (delivered digitally), Addressable: Yes; Fresh (delivered digitally); Movies (delivered digitally); special events.

Internet Service
Operational: Yes. Began: April 1, 1998.
Subscribers: 220.
Broadband Service: Charter Pipeline.
Fee: $49.95 installation; $39.95 monthly; $3.00 modem lease.

Telephone Service
Digital: Operational

Miles of Plant: 126.0 (coaxial); 36.0 (fiber optic). Homes passed: 16,000. Total homes in franchised area: 16,000.
Vice President & General Manager: Wendy Rasmussen. Technical Operations Manager: Peter Arrendondo. Marketing Manager: Lily Ho.
City fee: 5% of gross.
Ownership: Charter Communications Inc. (MSO).

VENTURA—Time Warner Cable. Now served by CHATSWORTH, CA [CA0013]. ICA: CA0099.

VICTORVILLE—Charter Communications. Now served by HESPERIA, CA [CA0158]. ICA: CA0064.

VISALIA—Formerly served by Sprint Corp. No longer in operation. ICA: CA0420.

WATSONVILLE—Charter Communications, 270 Bridge St, San Luis Obispo, CA 93401. Phones: 805-544-1962; 831-724-7337. Fax: 805-541-6042. Web Site: http://www.charter.com. Also serves Capitola, Corralitos, Freedom, Pajaro Dunes & Santa Cruz County (portions). ICA: CA0107.
TV Market Ranking: 7 (Capitola, Corralitos, Freedom, Pajaro Dunes, Santa Cruz County (portions), WATSONVILLE). Franchise award date: January 1, 1964. Franchise expiration date: N.A. Began: January 1, 1964.
Channel capacity: N.A. Channels available but not in use: N.A.

Basic Service
Subscribers: 13,183.
Programming (received off-air): KCBA (FOX) Salinas; KDJT-CA (TEL) Salinas/Monterey, etc.; KION-TV (CBS, CW) Monterey; KMCE-LP Monterey; KNTV (NBC) San Jose; KPPX-TV (ION) Tolleson; KSBW (NBC) Salinas; KSMS-TV (UNV) Monterey; KTEH (PBS) San Jose; 24 FMs.
Programming (via microwave): KBCW (CW) San Francisco; KGO-TV (ABC) San Francisco; KICU-TV (IND) San Jose; KQED (PBS) San Francisco; KTSF (IND) San Francisco; KTVU (FOX) Oakland.
Programming (via satellite): ABC Family Channel; AMC; Animal Planet; Arts & Entertainment; Bravo; California Channel; Cartoon Network; CNBC; CNN; Comcast Sports Net Bay Area; Comedy Central; C-SPAN; C-SPAN 2; Discovery Channel; Disney Channel; E! Entertainment Television; ESPN; ESPN 2; Eternal Word TV Network; Food Network; Fox News Channel; Fox Sports en Espanol; FX; G4; GalaVision; Hallmark Channel; Headline News; HGTV; History Channel; Home Shopping Network; International Television (ITV); Lifetime; MSNBC; MTV; mun2 television; National Geographic Channel; Nickelodeon; Oxygen; Portuguese Channel; QVC; SoapNet; Speed Channel; Spike TV; Syfy; TBS Superstation; The Learning Channel; Toon Disney; Travel Channel; truTV; Turner Classic Movies; Turner Network TV; TV Guide Network; TV Land; USA Network; Versus; VH1; WE tv; Weather Channel.
Current originations: Government Access; Educational Access; Public Access; Religious Access.
Fee: $29.99 installation; $38.99 monthly.

Digital Basic Service
Subscribers: N.A.
Programming (via satellite): BBC America; Bio; Discovery Digital Networks; DMX Music; Do-It-Yourself; ESPN Classic Sports; ESPNews; Fox College Sports Atlantic; Fox College Sports Central; Fox College Sports Pacific; Fox Movie Channel; Fuel TV; Fuse; GAS; History Channel International; Independent Film Channel; Lifetime Movie Network; MTV Networks Digital Suite; NFL Network; Nick Jr.; Nick Too; Outdoor Channel; TV Guide Interactive Inc.; TVG Network.

Digital Pay Service 1
Pay Units: 950.
Programming (via satellite): Cinemax (multiplexed); Encore (multiplexed); Flix; HBO (multiplexed); Showtime (multiplexed); Starz (multiplexed); The Movie Channel (multiplexed).

Video-On-Demand: Yes

Pay-Per-View
iN DEMAND (delivered digitally); NASCAR In Car (delivered digitally); NHL Center Ice (delivered digitally); MLB Extra Innings (delivered digitally); Hot Choice (delivered digitally); Playboy TV (delivered digitally); Fresh (delivered digitally); Shorteez (delivered digitally).

Internet Service
Operational: Yes.
Broadband Service: Charter Pipeline.
Fee: $29.99 monthly.

Telephone Service
Digital: Operational

Miles of Plant: 200.0 (coaxial); None (fiber optic). Homes passed: 22,934. Total homes in franchised area: 28,782.
Vice President & General Manager: Ed Merrill. Technical Operations Director: Ken Arellano. Chief Technician: Mark Beech. Marketing Director: Sarwar Assar.
City fee: 4% of gross.
Ownership: Charter Communications Inc. (MSO).

WEAVERVILLE—New Day Broadband, PO Box 535, 9155 Deschutes Rd, #D, Palo Cedro, CA 96073-8714. Phone: 530-547-2226. Fax: 530-547-4948. ICA: CA0249.
TV Market Ranking: Below 100 (WEAVERVILLE). Franchise award date: January 1, 1978. Franchise expiration date: N.A. Began: October 15, 1979.
Channel capacity: 37 (operating 2-way). Channels available but not in use: 2.

Basic Service
Subscribers: 850.
Programming (received off-air): KCVU (FOX) Paradise; KHSL-TV (CBS, CW) Chico; KIXE-TV (PBS) Redding; KRCR-TV (ABC) Redding.
Programming (via satellite): ABC Family Channel; CNN; Disney Channel; ESPN; Nickelodeon; TBS Superstation; WGN America.
Fee: $15.00 installation; $36.75 monthly.

Pay Service 1
Pay Units: 125.
Programming (via satellite): HBO.
Fee: $11.50 monthly.

Pay Service 2
Pay Units: 22.
Programming (via satellite): Showtime.
Fee: $11.50 monthly.

Internet Service
Operational: No.

Telephone Service
None
Miles of Plant: 23.0 (coaxial); None (fiber optic). Homes passed: 1,680. Total homes in franchised area: 1,680.
Chief Executive Officer: Neal Sehnog.
City fee: 5% of gross.
Ownership: New Day Broadband (MSO).

WEST HOLLYWOOD—Time Warner Cable. Now served by CHATSWORTH, CA [CA0013]. ICA: CA0463.

WEST LOS ANGELES—Time Warner Cable. Now served by LOS ANGELES, CA [CA0009]. ICA: CA0006.

WEST SACRAMENTO—Wave Broadband, 401 Kirkland Parkplace, Ste 500, Kirkland, WA 98033. Phones: 866-928-3123; 425-576-8200. Fax: 425-576-8221. Web Site: http://wavebroadband.com. Also serves Dixon, Winters & Woodland. ICA: CA0086.
TV Market Ranking: 25 (Dixon, WEST SACRAMENTO, Winters, Woodland). Franchise award date: N.A. Franchise expiration date: N.A. Began: September 14, 1973.
Channel capacity: N.A. Channels available but not in use: N.A.

Basic Service
Subscribers: 19,000 Includes Crescent Mills, Portola, & Rio Vista.
Programming (received off-air): KCRA-TV (NBC) Sacramento; KCSO-LP Sacramento; KMAX-TV (CW) Sacramento; KOVR (CBS) Stockton; KQCA (MNT) Stockton; KQED (PBS) San Francisco; KSPX-TV (ION) Sacramento; KTFK-DT (TEL) Stockton; KTNC-TV (IND) Concord; KTVU (FOX) Oakland; KTXL (FOX) Sacramento; KUVS-DT (UNV) Modesto; KVIE (PBS) Sacramento; KXTV (ABC) Sacramento; 30 FMs.
Programming (via satellite): California Channel; C-SPAN; C-SPAN 2; Home Shopping Network; Jewelry Television; Product Information Network; QVC; Trinity Broadcasting Network; TV Guide Network.
Current originations: Leased Access; Government Access; Educational Access; Public Access.
Fee: $29.99 installation.

Expanded Basic Service 1
Subscribers: 17,000.
Programming (via satellite): ABC Family Channel; AMC; Animal Planet; Arts & Entertainment; BET Networks; Bravo!; Cartoon Network; CNBC; CNN; Comcast SportsNet West; Comedy Central; Country Music TV; Discovery Channel; Disney Channel; Disney XD; E! Entertainment Television; ESPN; ESPN 2; Food Network; Fox News Channel; Fox Sports en Espanol; FX; G4; GalaVision; Golf Channel; GSN; Hallmark Channel; Headline News; HGTV; History Channel; INSP; Lifetime; MSNBC; MTV; National Geographic Channel; Nickelodeon; Oxygen; SoapNet; Speed Channel; Spike TV; Style Network; Syfy; TBS Superstation; The Learning Channel; Travel Channel; truTV; Turner Classic Movies; Turner Network TV; TV Land; USA Network; Versus; VH1; Weather Channel.
Fee: $38.99 monthly.

Digital Basic Service
Subscribers: N.A.
Programming (via satellite): BBC America; Bio; BYU Television; CMT Pure Country; Current; Discovery Health Channel; Discovery Kids Channel; Discovery Military Channel; Discovery Planet Green; Eternal Word TV Network; FitTV; Fox Business Channel; History Channel International; ID Investigation Discovery; MTV Hits; MTV Jams; MTV Networks Digital Suite; MTV Tres; MTV2; mtvU; Music Choice; Nick Jr.; NickToons TV; PBS Kids Sprout; Science Channel; Sleuth; SoapNet; TeenNick; VH1 Classic; VH1 Soul.

Digital Expanded Basic Service
Subscribers: N.A.
Programming (via satellite): American-Life TV Network; Bloomberg Television; Boomerang; Cooking Channel; Do-It-Yourself; Fox Movie Channel; Fuse; G4; Gospel Music Channel; Great American Country; Halogen Network; Independent Film Channel; Lifetime Movie Network; Lifetime Real Women; mun2 television; Ovation; WE tv; WealthTV.

Digital Expanded Basic Service 2
Subscribers: N.A.
Programming (via satellite): 22 Mexico; Azteca America; Bandamax; Canal 52MX; Cine Latino; Cine Mexicano; CNN en Espanol; De Pelicula; De Pelicula Clasico; Discovery en Espanol; Discovery Familia; Disney XD en Espanol; ESPN Deportes; Gol TV; History Channel en Espanol; HITN; Infinito; La Familia Network; MTV Tres; Once Mexico; Sorpresa; TV Chile; Utilisima; VeneMovies; Video Rola.

Digital Expanded Basic Service 3
Subscribers: N.A.
Programming (via satellite): Filipino Channel.

Digital Expanded Basic Service 4
Subscribers: N.A.
Programming (via satellite): CBS College Sports Network; ESPN Classic Sports; ESPN U; ESPNews; Fox Soccer; FSN Digital Atlantic; FSN Digital Central; FSN Digital Pacific; Fuel TV; Gol TV; NFL Network; Outdoor Channel; Tennis Channel; TVG Network.

Digital Expanded Basic Service 5
Subscribers: N.A.
Programming (via satellite): Animal Planet HD; Arts & Entertainment HD; Discovery Channel HD; Discovery HD Theater; Disney Channel HD; ESPN 2 HD; ESPN HD; Food Network HD; Hallmark Movie Channel HD; HDNet; HDNet Movies; HGTV HD; History Channel HD; MGM HD; National Geographic Channel HD Network; NFL Network HD; Science Channel HD; TBS in HD; TLC HD; Travel Channel HD; Turner Network TV HD; Universal HD; WealthTV HD.

Digital Pay Service 1
Pay Units: N.A.
Programming (via satellite): Cinemax (multiplexed); Cinemax HD; Encore (multiplexed); Flix; HBO (multiplexed); HBO HD; MoviePlex; Showtime (multiplexed); Showtime HD; Starz (multiplexed); Starz HDTV; The Movie Channel (multiplexed); The Movie Channel HD.

Video-On-Demand: Yes

Pay-Per-View
Addressable homes: 9,200.
iN DEMAND, Fee: $2.96-$4.46, Addressable: Yes; Playboy TV (delivered digitally); Fresh (delivered digitally); Club Jenna (delivered digitally); Movies (delivered digitally); Special events (delivered digitally).

Internet Service
Operational: Yes.
Broadband Service: Wave Broadband.
Fee: $24.95-$74.95 monthly.

Telephone Service
Digital: Operational
Fee: $29.95-$49.95 monthly
Miles of Plant: 284.0 (coaxial); 6.0 (fiber optic). Homes passed: 34,130.
General Manager: Tim Peters. Marketing Director: Adam Lazara.
City fee: 5% of gross.
Ownership: WaveDivision Holdings LLC (MSO).

WHITTIER—Charter Communications, 4781 Irwindale Ave, Irwindale, CA 91706-2175. Phone: 626-430-3300. Fax: 626-430-3420. Web Site: http://www.charter.com. ICA: CA0096.
TV Market Ranking: 2 (WHITTIER). Franchise award date: January 1, 1976. Franchise expiration date: N.A. Began: January 1, 1982.
Channel capacity: 76 (operating 2-way). Channels available but not in use: N.A.

Basic Service
Subscribers: 13,341.
Programming (received off-air): KABC-TV (ABC) Los Angeles; KCBS-TV (CBS) Los Angeles; KCET (PBS) Los Angeles; KCOP-TV (MNT) Los Angeles; KDOC-TV (IND) Anaheim; KFTR-DT (TEL) Ontario; KJLA (IND) Ventura; KLCS (PBS) Los Angeles; KMEX-DT (UNV) Los Angeles; KNBC (NBC) Los Angeles; KOCE-TV (PBS) Huntington Beach; KPXN-TV (ION) San Bernardino; KRCA (IND) Riverside; KSCI (IND) Long Beach; KTBN-TV (TBN) Santa Ana; KTLA (CW) Los Angeles; KTTV (FOX) Los Angeles; KVEA (TMO) Corona; KWHY-TV (IND) Los Angeles.
Programming (via satellite): C-SPAN; C-SPAN 2; Home Shopping Network; QVC; TBS Superstation; TV Guide Network.
Current originations: Leased Access; Government Access.
Fee: $29.99 installation.

Expanded Basic Service 1
Subscribers: N.A.
Programming (via satellite): ABC Family Channel; AMC; Animal Planet; Arts & Entertainment; BET Networks; Bravo; Cartoon Network; CNBC; CNN; Comedy Central; Discovery Channel; Disney Channel; E! Entertainment Television; ESPN; ESPN 2; ESPN Classic Sports; Food Network; Fox News Channel; Fox Sports Net West; Fox Sports Net West 2; Fox Sports World; FX; G4; GalaVision; Golf Channel; GSN; Headline News; HGTV; History Channel; Lifetime; MSNBC; MTV; Nickelodeon; Speed Channel; Spike TV; Syfy; The Learning Channel; Toon Disney; Travel Channel; truTV; Turner Classic Movies; Turner Network TV; TV Land; USA Network; Versus; VH1; Weather Channel.
Fee: $48.95 monthly.

Digital Basic Service
Subscribers: N.A.
Programming (via satellite): BBC America; Bio; Bloomberg Television; Discovery Digital Networks; GAS; History Channel International; Lifetime Movie Network; Music Choice; Nick Jr.; Style Network; WE tv.
Fee: $8.95 monthly.

Digital Pay Service 1
Pay Units: 1,424.
Programming (via satellite): Cinemax (multiplexed); Encore (multiplexed); Flix; HBO (multiplexed); Showtime (multiplexed); Starz (multiplexed); Sundance Channel; The Movie Channel (multiplexed).
Fee: $10.90 monthly (TMC), $10.95 monthly (Cinemax or Starz & Encore), $12.95 monthly (Flix, Showtime & Sundance or HBO).

Video-On-Demand: Yes

Pay-Per-View
Addressable: Yes; iN DEMAND; Fresh (delivered digitally); Shorteez (delivered digitally).

Internet Service
Operational: Yes.
Broadband Service: Charter Pipeline.
Fee: $29.99 monthly; $4.95 modem lease.

Telephone Service
Digital: Operational
Fee: $29.99 monthly
Miles of Plant: 246.0 (coaxial); 4.0 (fiber optic). Total homes in franchised area: 30,772. Homes passed included in Glendale
Vice President & General Manager: Wendy Rasmusson. Technical Operations Manager: Tom Williams. Marketing Manager: Lily Ho.
City fee: 3% of gross.
Ownership: Charter Communications Inc. (MSO).

WILLIAMS—Comcast Cable, 311 B St, Yuba City, CA 95991-5054. Phones: 800-266-2278; 530-790-3322. Fax: 530-671-3822. E-mail: deedee_brady@cable.comcast.com. Web Site: http://www.comcast.com. Also serves Arbuckle & Maxwell. ICA: CA0229.
TV Market Ranking: Outside TV Markets (Arbuckle, Maxwell, WILLIAMS). Franchise award date: August 1, 1981. Franchise expiration date: N.A. Began: N.A.
Channel capacity: 42 (not 2-way capable). Channels available but not in use: 3.

Basic Service
Subscribers: 1,559.
Programming (received off-air): KCRA-TV (NBC) Sacramento; KHSL-TV (CBS, CW) Chico; KMAX-TV (CW) Sacramento; KNVN (NBC) Chico; KOVR (CBS) Stockton; KQCA (MNT) Stockton; KRCR-TV (ABC) Redding; KSPX-TV (ION) Sacramento; KTXL (FOX) Sacramento; KVIE (PBS) Sacramento; KXTV (ABC) Sacramento.
Programming (via satellite): ABC Family Channel; AMC; Animal Planet; Arts & Entertainment; CNN; Comcast Sports Net Bay Area; C-SPAN; Discovery Channel; Disney Channel; E! Entertainment Television; ESPN; ESPN 2; Fox News Channel; Fox Sports en Espanol; FX; GalaVision; Great American Country; Headline News; HGTV; History Channel; Home Shopping Network; Lifetime; MTV; Nickelodeon; SoapNet; Spike TV; TBS Superstation; Telemundo; The Learning Channel; Turner Classic Movies; Turner Network TV; TV Guide Network; USA Network; VH1; Weather Channel.
Fee: $44.99 installation; $33.38 monthly; $2.00 converter.

Pay Service 1
Pay Units: 125.
Programming (via satellite): Cinemax (multiplexed).
Fee: $17.99 monthly.

Pay Service 2
Pay Units: 230.
Programming (via satellite): HBO (multiplexed).
Fee: $17.99 monthly.

Pay Service 3
Pay Units: 70.
Programming (via satellite): Showtime.
Fee: $17.99 monthly.

Pay-Per-View
iN DEMAND (delivered digitally).

Internet Service
Operational: Yes.

Telephone Service
Digital: Operational
Miles of Plant: 34.0 (coaxial); None (fiber optic). Homes passed: 2,200. Total homes in franchised area: 2,200.
General Manager: DeeDee Brady. Marketing Director: Tom Baer.

Franchise fee: 5% of gross.
Ownership: Comcast Cable Communications Inc. (MSO).

WILLOW CREEK—Almega Cable, 4001 W Airport Frwy, Ste 530, Bedford, TX 76021. Phones: 877-725-6342; 817-685-9588. Fax: 817-685-6488. Web Site: http://almegacable.com. ICA: CA0264.
TV Market Ranking: Below 100 (WILLOW CREEK). Franchise award date: N.A. Franchise expiration date: N.A. Began: January 26, 1981.
Channel capacity: 45 (not 2-way capable). Channels available but not in use: 15.
Basic Service
Subscribers: 354.
Programming (received off-air): KIEM-TV (NBC) Eureka; KRCR-TV (ABC) Redding; KVIQ (CBS, CW) Eureka.
Programming (via satellite): ABC Family Channel; Arts & Entertainment; Bravo; Cartoon Network; CNBC; CNN; Discovery Channel; Disney Channel; ESPN; ESPN 2; Fox News Channel; HGTV; History Channel; INSP; MSNBC; National Geographic Channel; Spike TV; Syfy; TBS Superstation; Turner Classic Movies; Turner Network TV; USA Network; WE tv; WGN America.
Fee: $29.95 installation; $27.45 monthly.
Pay Service 1
Pay Units: 79.
Programming (via satellite): HBO.
Fee: $10.00 installation; $10.95 monthly.
Video-On-Demand: No
Internet Service
Operational: Yes.
Fee: $39.95 installation; $19.95 monthly.
Telephone Service
None
Miles of Plant: 32.0 (coaxial); None (fiber optic). Homes passed: 712.
President: Thomas Kurien.
City fee: 3% of basic.
Ownership: Almega Cable (MSO).

WILLOW RANCH MOBILE HOME PARK—Formerly served by Comcast Cable. No longer in operation. ICA: CA0394.

WILMINGTON—Time Warner Cable. Now served by LOS ANGELES, CA [CA0009]. ICA: CA0054.

YORBA LINDA—Now served by ANAHEIM, CA [CA0033]. ICA: CA0397.

YOUNTVILLE—Comcast Cable. Now served by NAPA/SONOMA, CA [CA0038]. ICA: CA0261.

YREKA—Northland Cable Television, PO Box 840, 315 W Miner St, Yreka, CA 96097-0840. Phone: 530-842-4228. Fax: 530-842-2516. E-mail: yreka@northlandcabletv.com. Web Site: http://www.northlandcabletv.com. Also serves Grenada, Montague & Siskiyou County. ICA: CA0189.
TV Market Ranking: Outside TV Markets (Grenada, Montague, Siskiyou County, YREKA). Franchise award date: N.A. Franchise expiration date: N.A. Began: August 1, 1954.
Channel capacity: 53 (not 2-way capable). Channels available but not in use: None.
Basic Service
Subscribers: 3,500.
Programming (received off-air): KBLN (IND) Grants Pass; KDRV (ABC) Medford; KIXE-TV (PBS) Redding; KMVU-DT (FOX) Medford; KRCR-TV (ABC) Redding; KRVU-LD (MNT) Redding; KTVL (CBS, CW) Medford; allband FM.
Programming (via microwave): KOBI (NBC) Medford.
Programming (via satellite): Animal Planet; Arts & Entertainment; Cartoon Network; CNBC; CNN; Comcast Sports Net Bay Area; Comedy Central; C-SPAN; CW+; Discovery Channel; E! Entertainment Television; ESPN; ESPN 2; Food Network; Fox Movie Channel; Fox News Channel; FX; Great American Country; Hallmark Channel; Headline News; HGTV; History Channel; Lifetime; National Geographic Channel; NFL Network; Nickelodeon; Outdoor Channel; QVC; Spike TV; Syfy; TBS Superstation; The Learning Channel; Travel Channel; Trinity Broadcasting Network; Turner Classic Movies; Turner Network TV; TV Land; Univision; USA Network; VH1; Weather Channel; WGN America.
Current originations: Government Access; Educational Access; Public Access.
Fee: $50.00 installation; $48.99 monthly.
Digital Basic Service
Subscribers: N.A.
Programming (via satellite): BBC America; Bloomberg Television; Bravo; Discovery Health Channel; Discovery Home Channel; Discovery Kids Channel; Discovery Military Channel; Discovery Times Channel; DMX Music; ESPNews; FitTV; Fox Soccer; G4; Golf Channel; Independent Film Channel; Lifetime Movie Network; Science Channel; Speed Channel; Versus; WE tv.
Fee: $6.00 monthly.
Pay Service 1
Pay Units: 683.
Programming (via satellite): Encore.
Fee: $2.95 monthly.
Pay Service 2
Pay Units: 230.
Programming (via satellite): HBO.
Fee: $13.50 monthly.
Digital Pay Service 1
Pay Units: N.A.
Programming (via satellite): Cinemax (multiplexed); Encore (multiplexed); Flix; HBO (multiplexed); Showtime (multiplexed); Starz (multiplexed); The Movie Channel (multiplexed).
Fee: $14.00 monthly (HBO, Cinemax, Starz/Encore or Showtime/TMC/Flix).
Video-On-Demand: No
Internet Service
Operational: Yes.
Fee: $42.99 monthly.
Telephone Service
None
Miles of Plant: 98.0 (coaxial); 4.0 (fiber optic). Homes passed: 4,381.
Manager: Coralene Arkfeld.
City fee: 2% of gross.
Ownership: Northland Communications Corp. (MSO).

YUBA CITY—Comcast Cable, 311 B St, Yuba City, CA 95991-5054. Phone: 530-790-3322. Fax: 530-671-3822. Web Site: http://www.comcast.com. Also serves Beale AFB, Linda, Live Oak, Marysville, Olivehurst, Sutter County (portions), Wheatland & Yuba County (portions). ICA: CA0070.
TV Market Ranking: 25 (Sutter County (portions) (portions), Wheatland); Below 100 (Live Oak, Yuba County (portions) (portions)); Outside TV Markets (Beale AFB, Linda, Marysville, Olivehurst, YUBA CITY, Yuba County (portions) (portions), Sutter County (portions) (portions)). Franchise award date: December 15, 1968. Franchise expiration date: N.A. Began: December 15, 1968.
Channel capacity: N.A. Channels available but not in use: N.A.

Basic Service
Subscribers: 29,477.
Programming (received off-air): KCRA-TV (NBC) Sacramento; KGO-TV (ABC) San Francisco; KHSL-TV (CBS, CW) Chico; KICU-TV (IND) San Jose; KMAX-TV (CW) Sacramento; KNVN (NBC) Chico; KOVR (CBS) Stockton; KQCA (MNT) Stockton; KSPX-TV (ION) Sacramento; KTFK-DT (TEL) Stockton; KTVU (FOX) Oakland; KTXL (FOX) Sacramento; KUVS-DT (UNV) Modesto; KVIE (PBS) Sacramento; KXTV (ABC) Sacramento; 18 FMs.
Programming (via satellite): California Channel; C-SPAN; C-SPAN 2; Home Shopping Network 2; INSP; QVC; ShopNBC; Telemundo; TV Guide Network; WGN America.
Current originations: Government Access; Educational Access; Public Access.
Fee: $43.99 installation; $11.89 monthly.

Expanded Basic Service 1
Subscribers: N.A.
Programming (via satellite): ABC Family Channel; AMC; Animal Planet; Arts & Entertainment; BET Networks; Cartoon Network; CNBC; CNN; Comcast Sports Net Bay Area; Comedy Central; Discovery Channel; Disney Channel; E! Entertainment Television; ESPN; ESPN 2; ESPN Classic Sports; Food Network; Fox News Channel; FX; GalaVision; Golf Channel; Great American Country; GSN; Hallmark Channel; Headline News; HGTV; History Channel; Lifetime; MSNBC; MTV; Nickelodeon; Spike TV; Style Network; Syfy; TBS Superstation; The Learning Channel; truTV; Turner Classic Movies; Turner Network TV; TV Land; USA Network; Versus; VH1; WE tv; Weather Channel.
Fee: $36.86 monthly.

Digital Basic Service
Subscribers: N.A.
Programming (via satellite): AmericanLife TV Network; ART America; BBC America; Bio; Black Family Channel; Bloomberg Television; Bravo; Canales N; CCTV-4; Discovery Digital Networks; DMX Music; ESPNews; Filipino Channel; FitTV; Fox College Sports Atlantic; Fox College Sports Central; Fox College Sports Pacific; Fox Movie Channel; Fox Sports World; Fuse; G4; GAS; Halogen Network; History Channel International; Independent Film Channel; Lifetime Movie Network; Lime; MTV Networks Digital Suite; National Geographic Channel; Nick Jr.; NickToons TV; Outdoor Channel; Ovation; Power Link; RAI International; Russian Television Network; Saigon Broadcasting TV Network; Speed Channel; Sundance Channel; The Word Network; Toon Disney; Trinity Broadcasting Network; Turner Classic Movies; TV Asia; TV Japan; TV5, La Television International; Zee TV USA.
Fee: $11.95 monthly.
Digital Pay Service 1
Pay Units: N.A.
Programming (via satellite): Cinemax (multiplexed); HBO (multiplexed); Showtime; Starz (multiplexed); The Movie Channel (multiplexed).
Fee: $17.99 monthly (Starz, Cinemax or TMC), $18.99 monthly (HBO or Showtime).
Video-On-Demand: Yes
Pay-Per-View
Addressable homes: 11,283.
iN DEMAND (delivered digitally); Urban Xtra (delivered digitally); Fresh (delivered digitally); Shorteez (delivered digitally); Playboy TV (delivered digitally); Hot Choice (delivered digitally); iN DEMAND; ESPN Now (delivered digitally), Addressable: Yes; Sports PPV (delivered digitally).
Internet Service
Operational: Yes.
Broadband Service: Comcast High Speed Internet.
Fee: $42.95 monthly.
Telephone Service
Digital: Operational
Miles of Plant: 463.0 (coaxial); 36.0 (fiber optic). Homes passed: 44,125. Total homes in franchised area: 64,467.
General Manager: DeeDee Brady. Marketing Director: Tom Baer. Communications Director: Erica Smith.
City fee: 5% of gross.
Ownership: Comcast Cable Communications Inc. (MSO).

YUBA CITY—Formerly served by Sprint Corp. No longer in operation. ICA: CA0443.

YUCCA VALLEY—Time Warner Cable, 41725 Cook St, Palm Desert, CA 92211-5100. Phones: 858-635-8297 (San Diego office); 760-340-1312. Fax: 760-340-9764. Web Site: http://www.timewarnercable.com/desertcities. Also serves Joshua Tree, Morongo Valley, Twentynine Palms & Twentynine Palms Marine Corps Base. ICA: CA0119.
TV Market Ranking: Below 100 (Joshua Tree, Morongo Valley, Twentynine Palms, Twentynine Palms Marine Corps Base, YUCCA VALLEY). Franchise award date: N.A. Franchise expiration date: N.A. Began: January 1, 1957.
Channel capacity: N.A. Channels available but not in use: N.A.
Basic Service
Subscribers: N.A. Included in San Diego
Programming (received off-air): KABC-TV (ABC) Los Angeles; KESQ-TV (ABC, CW) Palm Springs; KJLA (IND) Ventura; KPXN-TV (ION) San Bernardino; KVEA (TMO) Corona; KXLA (IND) Rancho Palos Verdes; KYAV-LP Palm Springs; 20 FMs.
Programming (via microwave): KCAL-TV (IND) Los Angeles; KCET (PBS) Los Angeles; KMEX-DT (UNV) Los Angeles; KNBC (NBC) Los Angeles; KPSP-LP (CBS) Cathedral City; KTLA (CW) Los Angeles; KTTV (FOX) Los Angeles.
Programming (via satellite): BYU Television; C-SPAN; C-SPAN 2; Eternal Word TV Network; GalaVision; MyNetworkTV Inc.; QVC;

ShopNBC; Trinity Broadcasting Network; TV Guide Network; WGN America.
Current originations: Government Access; Educational Access; Public Access.
Fee: $31.11 installation; $10.99 monthly; $1.40 converter.

Expanded Basic Service 1
Subscribers: 10,417.
Programming (via satellite): ABC Family Channel; AMC; Animal Planet; Arts & Entertainment; BET Networks; Bravo; Cartoon Network; CNBC; CNN; Comedy Central; Discovery Channel; Disney Channel; E! Entertainment Television; ESPN; ESPN 2; Food Network; Fox News Channel; Fox Sports Net West; FX; Hallmark Channel; Headline News; HGTV; History Channel; Home Shopping Network; Lifetime; MSNBC; MTV; Nickelodeon; Spike TV; Syfy; TBS Superstation; The Learning Channel; Travel Channel; truTV; Turner Network TV; TV Land; USA Network; VH1; Weather Channel.
Fee: $30.00 monthly.

Digital Basic Service
Subscribers: N.A.
Programming (received off-air): KABC-TV (ABC) Los Angeles; KCBS-TV (CBS) Los Angeles; KNBC (NBC) Los Angeles; KTTV (FOX) Los Angeles; KVMD (IND) Twentynine Palms.
Programming (via satellite): BBC America; Bio; Bloomberg Television; Boomerang; California Channel; Canales N; CBS College Sports Network; Cooking Channel; Country Music TV; Current; Discovery HD Theater; Discovery Health Channel; Discovery Home Channel; Discovery Kids Channel; Discovery Military Channel; Discovery Times Channel; Do-It-Yourself; Do-It-Yourself On Demand; ESPN Classic Sports; ESPN HD; ESPN U; ESPNews; Exercise TV; FitTV; Food Network On Demand; Fox Business Channel; Fox College Sports Atlantic; Fox College Sports Central; Fox College Sports Pacific; Fox Movie Channel; Fox Reality Channel; Fox Soccer; Fuel TV; Fuse; G4; GAS; Golf Channel; Great American Country; GSN; Halogen Network; HDNet; HDNet Movies; HGTV On Demand; History Channel International; Howard TV; Independent Film Channel; INSP; Lifetime Movie Network; Lifetime Real Women; LOGO; MTV Tres; MTV2; Music Choice; National Geographic Channel; National Geographic Channel On Demand; NBA TV; Nick Jr.; NickToons TV; Outdoor Channel; Ovation; Oxygen; Science Channel; Sleuth; SoapNet; Speed Channel; Style Network; Tennis Channel; Toon Disney; Turner Classic Movies; Turner Network TV HD; Universal HD; Versus; VH1 Classic; WE tv.

Digital Pay Service 1
Pay Units: N.A.
Programming (via satellite): Cinemax (multiplexed); Cinemax HD; Cinemax On Demand; Encore (multiplexed); Filipino Channel; Flix; HBO (multiplexed); HBO HD; HBO On Demand; Showtime (multiplexed); Showtime HD; Showtime On Demand; Starz (multiplexed); Starz HDTV; Sundance Channel; The Movie Channel (multiplexed); The Movie Channel On Demand; TV Japan.
Fee: $12.00 monthly (each).

Video-On-Demand: Yes

Pay-Per-View
iN DEMAND (delivered digitally); Playboy TV (delivered digitally); NHL Center Ice (delivered digitally); ESPN Full Court (delivered digitally); MLB Extra Innings (delivered digitally); ESPN Gameplan (delivered digitally); NBA League Pass (delivered digitally); MLS Direct Kick (delivered digitally).

Internet Service
Operational: Yes.
Broadband Service: Road Runner.
Fee: $44.95 installation; $5.00 modem lease.

Telephone Service
Digital: Operational
Fee: $39.95 monthly

Miles of Plant: 405.0 (coaxial); None (fiber optic). Homes passed: 29,152.
President: Bob Barlow Walsh. Vice President & General Manager: Tad Yo. Engineering Director: Mike Sagona. Technical Operations Director: Dessi Ochoa. Marketing Director: Jimmy Kelly. Vice President, Customer Service: Armando Rancando. Public Affairs Director: Kathi Jacobs.
City fee: 5% of gross.
Ownership: Time Warner Cable (MSO).

COLORADO

Total Systems: **109**
Total Communities Served: **339**
Franchises Not Yet Operating: **0**
Applications Pending: **0**

Communities with Applications: **0**
Number of Basic Subscribers: **1,385,455**
Number of Expanded Basic Subscribers: **64,360**
Number of Pay Units: **15,810**

Top 100 Markets Represented: Denver-Castle Rock (32).

**For a list of cable communities in this section, see the Cable Community Index located in the back of Cable Volume 2.
For explanation of terms used in cable system listings, see p. D-11.**

AKRON—CommuniComm Services. Now served by OTIS, CO [CO0128]. ICA: CO0086.

ALAMOSA—Bresnan Communications, 312 State Ave, Alamosa, CO 81101-2638. Phones: 877-273-7626 (Customer service); 719-275-8356; 719-589-3775. Fax: 719-589-5002. Web Site: http://www.bresnan.com. Also serves Alamosa County, Alamosa East, Monte Vista & Rio Grande County (portions). ICA: CO0035.

TV Market Ranking: Outside TV Markets (ALAMOSA, Alamosa County, Alamosa East, Monte Vista, Rio Grande County (portions)). Franchise award date: N.A. Franchise expiration date: N.A. Began: March 1, 1955.

Channel capacity: N.A. Channels available but not in use: N.A.

Basic Service

Subscribers: 2,823.

Programming (received off-air): KCNC-TV (CBS) Denver; KDVR (FOX) Denver; KMGH-TV (ABC) Denver; KRDO-TV (ABC) Colorado Springs; KRMA-TV (PBS) Denver; KTSC (PBS) Pueblo; KTVD (MNT) Denver; KUSA (NBC) Denver; KWGN-TV (CW) Denver.

Programming (via satellite): BYU Television; C-SPAN; C-SPAN 2; FX; Home Shopping Network; ION Television; Lifetime; QVC; TV Guide Network.

Fee: $60.00 installation; $9.37 monthly; $60.00 additional installation.

Expanded Basic Service 1

Subscribers: 2,558.

Programming (via satellite): ABC Family Channel; Altitude Sports & Entertainment; AMC; Animal Planet; Arts & Entertainment; Cartoon Network; CNBC; CNN; Comedy Central; Country Music TV; Discovery Channel; Disney Channel; E! Entertainment Television; ESPN; ESPN 2; Eternal Word TV Network; Food Network; Fox News Channel; Fox Sports Net Rocky Mountain; Hallmark Channel; Headline News; HGTV; History Channel; INSP; MSNBC; MTV; Nickelodeon; Oxygen; Spike TV; Syfy; TBS Superstation; Telefutura; The Learning Channel; Travel Channel; truTV; Turner Classic Movies; Turner Network TV; TV Land; Univision; USA Network; VH1; Weather Channel.

Fee: $41.62 monthly.

Digital Basic Service

Subscribers: N.A.

Programming (via satellite): AmericanLife TV Network; Animal Planet HD; Arts & Entertainment HD; Bandamax; BBC America; Bio; Bloomberg Television; Bravo; CBS College Sports Network; Cine Latino; Cine Mexicano; CMT Pure Country; CNN en Espanol; Cooking Channel; De Pelicula; De Pelicula Clasico; Discovery Channel HD; Discovery en Espanol; Discovery HD Theater; Discovery Health Channel; Discovery Kids Channel; Discovery Military Channel; Discovery Planet Green; DMX Music; Do-It-Yourself; ESPN Classic Sports; ESPN Deportes; ESPN HD; ESPNews; FitTV; Food Network HD; Fox College Sports Atlantic; Fox College Sports Central; Fox College Sports Pacific; Fox Movie Channel; Fox Reality Channel; Fox Soccer; Fox Sports en Espanol; Fuse; G4; Gol TV; Golf Channel; Gospel Music Channel; GSN; Halogen Network; HGTV HD; History Channel en Espanol; History Channel HD; History Channel International; ID Investigation Discovery; Independent Film Channel; ION Television; Lifetime Movie Network; Mountain West TV; MTV Hits; MTV Jams; MTV Tres; MTV2; mun2 television; National Geographic Channel; National Geographic Channel HD Network; NFL Network; Nick Jr.; Nick Too; NickToons TV; Outdoor Channel; PBS Kids Sprout; RFD-TV; Science Channel; SoapNet; Speed Channel; Style Network; Syfy HD; TeenNick; Telefutura; Telehit; The Sportsman Channel; Toon Disney; Trinity Broadcasting Network; Universal HD; Univision; USA Network HD; VeneMovies; Versus; VH1 Classic; VH1 Soul.

Fee: $6.00 monthly.

Digital Pay Service 1

Pay Units: N.A.

Programming (via satellite): Cinemax (multiplexed); Encore (multiplexed); Flix; HBO (multiplexed); HBO HD; Showtime (multiplexed); Starz (multiplexed); Starz HDTV; The Movie Channel (multiplexed).

Video-On-Demand: No

Pay-Per-View

iN DEMAND (delivered digitally), Addressable: Yes.

Internet Service

Operational: Yes.

Broadband Service: Bresnan OnLine.

Fee: $39.95 monthly.

Telephone Service

Digital: Operational

Fee: $49.99 monthly

Miles of Plant: 80.0 (coaxial); 31.0 (fiber optic). Homes passed: 7,512.

General Manager: Jerry Parker. Technical Operations Manager: Doyle Rouna.

City fee: 2% of gross.

Ownership: Bresnan Communications Inc. (MSO). Sale pends to Cablevision Systems Corp.

ANTONITO—Bresnan Communications, 402 Main St, Canon City, CO 81212. Phone: 877-273-7626. Web Site: http://www.bresnan.com. ICA: CO0120.

TV Market Ranking: Outside TV Markets (ANTONITO). Franchise award date: N.A. Franchise expiration date: N.A. Began: October 1, 1986.

Channel capacity: 37 (not 2-way capable). Channels available but not in use: N.A.

Basic Service

Subscribers: 116.

Programming (received off-air): KCNC-TV (CBS) Denver; KMGH-TV (ABC) Denver; KRMA-TV (PBS) Denver; KUSA (NBC) Denver; KWGN-TV (CW) Denver.

Programming (via satellite): ABC Family Channel; CNN; Country Music TV; Discovery Channel; Disney Channel; ESPN; GalaVision; TBS Superstation; Turner Network TV; USA Network; WGN America.

Fee: $20.00 installation; $14.58 monthly; $15.00 additional installation.

Pay Service 1

Pay Units: 9.

Programming (via satellite): HBO; The Movie Channel.

Fee: $10.00 installation; $11.00 monthly (each).

Video-On-Demand: No

Internet Service

Operational: Yes.

Fee: $39.95 monthly.

Telephone Service

Digital: Operational

Fee: $49.99 monthly

Miles of Plant: 7.0 (coaxial); None (fiber optic). Homes passed: 455.

General Manager: Jerry Parker. Technical Operations Manager: Doyle Ruena.

City fee: 3% of gross and basic.

Ownership: Bresnan Communications Inc. (MSO). Sale pends to Cablevision Systems Corp.

ARRIBA—Formerly served by Rebeltec Communications. No longer in operation. ICA: CO0156.

ASPEN—Comcast Cable, 1605 Grand Ave, Ste I, Glenwood Springs, CO 81601. Phone: 970-928-7784. Fax: 970-945-0270. Web Site: http://www.comcast.com. Also serves Basalt, Carbondale, Eagle County, El Jebel, Garfield County, Glenwood Springs, Pitkin County & Snowmass Village. ICA: CO0017.

TV Market Ranking: Below 100 (Basalt, Carbondale, Eagle County, El Jebel, Garfield County, Glenwood Springs, Pitkin County (portions), Snowmass Village); Outside TV Markets (ASPEN, Pitkin County (portions)). Franchise award date: January 1, 1962. Franchise expiration date: N.A. Began: April 1, 1963.

Channel capacity: 55 (operating 2-way). Channels available but not in use: None.

Basic Service

Subscribers: 58,858 Includes Avon, Granby, Kremmling, Parachute, Rifle, Silverthorne, & Steamboat Springs.

Programming (received off-air): KCNC-TV (CBS) Denver; KCXP-LP Eagle,tc.; KDVR (FOX) Denver; KMGH-TV (ABC) Denver; KREX-TV (CBS, MNT) Grand Junction; KRMA-TV (PBS) Denver; KSZG-LD Aspen; KTVD (MNT) Denver; KUSA (NBC) Denver; KWGN-TV (CW) Denver; 21 FMs.

Programming (via satellite): Azteca America; CET - Comcast Entertainment TV; C-SPAN; Discovery Channel; ION Television; QVC; TBS Superstation.

Current originations: Leased Access; Government Access; Educational Access; Public Access.

Fee: $44.99 installation; $14.99 monthly; $3.00 converter.

Expanded Basic Service 1

Subscribers: N.A.

Programming (via satellite): ABC Family Channel; Altitude Sports & Entertainment; AMC; Animal Planet; Arts & Entertainment; Bravo; Cartoon Network; CNBC; CNN; Comedy Central; Disney Channel; E! Entertainment Television; ESPN; ESPN 2; Food Network; Fox News Channel; Fox Sports Net Rocky Mountain; FX; G4; Golf Channel; Hallmark Channel; Headline News; HGTV; History Channel; Lifetime; MSNBC; MTV; Nickelodeon; Oxygen; Spike TV; Syfy; The Learning Channel; Travel Channel; Turner Classic Movies; Turner Network TV; TV Land; Univision; USA Network; Versus; VH1; Weather Channel.

Fee: $35.00 monthly.

Digital Basic Service

Subscribers: 20,215 Includes Avon, Granby, Kremmling, Parachute, Rifle, Silverthorne, & Steamboat Springs.

Programming (received off-air): KCNC-TV (CBS) Denver; KDVR (FOX) Denver; KMGH-TV (ABC) Denver; KRMA-TV (PBS) Denver; KTVD (MNT) Denver; KUSA (NBC) Denver; KWGN-TV (CW) Denver.

Programming (via satellite): BBC America; Bio; Bloomberg Television; Canal 52MX; Canales N; CBS College Sports Network; Country Music TV; Current; Discovery Digital Networks; Discovery HD Theater; DMX Music; Encore (multiplexed); ESPN 2 HD; ESPN Classic Sports; ESPN HD; ESPNews; Flix; Fox College Sports Atlantic; Fox College Sports Central; Fox College Sports Pacific; Fox Movie Channel; Fox Reality Channel; Fox Soccer; Fuse; GAS; GSN; Halogen Network; History Channel International; Independent Film Channel; INHD; Lifetime Movie Network; LOGO; MoviePlex; MTV Networks Digital Suite; National Geographic Channel; NBA TV; NFL Network; Nick Jr.; Nick Too; NickToons TV; Outdoor Channel; Palladia; PBS Kids Sprout; Si TV; SoapNet; Speed Channel; Style Network; Sundance Channel; the mtn; Toon Disney; Trinity Broadcasting Network; Turner Network TV HD; TV One; Versus HD; WE tv.

Fee: $9.95 monthly.

Digital Pay Service 1

Pay Units: N.A.

Programming (via satellite): Cinemax (multiplexed); Cinemax HD; HBO (multiplexed); HBO HD; Showtime (multiplexed); Show-

time HD; Starz (multiplexed); Starz HDTV; The Movie Channel (multiplexed).
Fee: $15.99 monthly (each).
Video-On-Demand: No
Pay-Per-View
ESPN (delivered digitally); NBA League Pass (delivered digitally); iN DEMAND (delivered digitally); Playboy TV (delivered digitally); Fresh (delivered digitally); NHL Center Ice; MLB Extra Innings (delivered digitally).
Internet Service
Operational: Yes.
Subscribers: 25,045.
Broadband Service: Comcast High Speed Internet.
Fee: $42.95 monthly.
Telephone Service
None
Miles of Plant: 1,130.0 (coaxial); None (fiber optic). Homes passed: 106,170. Homes passed includes Avon, Granby, Kremmling, Parachute, Rifle, Silverthorne, & Steamboat Springs; miles of plant (coax) includes Rifle & Avon
Vice President: Mike Trueblood. General Manager: Ben Miller. Technical Operations Manager: James Comiskey. Customer Service Manager: Anita Robinson.
City fee: 5% of gross.
Ownership: Comcast Cable Communications Inc. (MSO).

AVON—Comcast Cable, 281 Metcalf Rd, Ste 110, Avon, CO 81620-0439. Phone: 970-949-1224. Fax: 970-970-9138. Web Site: http://www.comcast.com. Also serves Beaver Creek, East Vail, Edwards, Minturn & Vail. ICA: CO0020.
TV Market Ranking: Outside TV Markets (AVON-BY-THE-SEA, Beaver Creek, East Vail, Edwards, Minturn, Vail). Franchise award date: N.A. Franchise expiration date: N.A. Began: February 1, 1969.
Channel capacity: N.A. Channels available but not in use: N.A.
Basic Service
Subscribers: N.A. Included in Aspen
Programming (received off-air): KCNC-TV (CBS) Denver; KDVR (FOX) Denver; KMGH-TV (ABC) Denver; KRMA-TV (PBS) Denver; KTVD (MNT) Denver; KUSA (NBC) Denver; KWGN-TV (CW) Denver.
Programming (via satellite): C-SPAN 2; Discovery Channel; Hallmark Channel; TBS Superstation.
Current originations: Government Access; Leased Access; Public Access.
Fee: $44.99 installation; $14.29 monthly.
Expanded Basic Service 1
Subscribers: 9,087.
Programming (via satellite): ABC Family Channel; AMC; Animal Planet; Arts & Entertainment; Cartoon Network; CNBC; CNN; Comedy Central; C-SPAN; Disney Channel; E! Entertainment Television; ESPN; ESPN 2; Fox News Channel; Fox Sports Net Rocky Mountain; FX; GalaVision; Headline News; History Channel; Lifetime; MSNBC; MTV; Nickelodeon; Oxygen; QVC; Spike TV; Telemundo; The Learning Channel; Travel Channel; truTV; Turner Network TV; TV Land; Univision; USA Network; VH1; Weather Channel; WGN America.
Fee: $35.70 monthly.
Digital Basic Service
Subscribers: N.A. Included in Aspen
Programming (via satellite): BBC America; Black Family Channel; Bravo; Discovery Digital Networks; DMX Music; Encore (multiplexed); ESPN Classic Sports; ESPN Now; ESPNews; Fox College Sports Atlantic; Fox College Sports Central; Fox College Sports Pacific; Fox Movie Channel; Fox Sports World; Fuse; G4; Golf Channel; Great American Country; GSN; HGTV; Independent Film Channel; Lifetime Movie Network; National Geographic Channel; Nick Jr.; Outdoor Channel; ShopNBC; Speed Channel; Style Network; Sundance Channel; Syfy; The Word Network; Trinity Broadcasting Network; Turner Classic Movies; Versus; WE tv.
Fee: $9.95 monthly.
Digital Pay Service 1
Pay Units: N.A.
Programming (via satellite): Cinemax (multiplexed); Flix; HBO (multiplexed); Showtime (multiplexed); Starz (multiplexed); The Movie Channel (multiplexed).
Fee: $15.99 monthly (each).
Video-On-Demand: No
Pay-Per-View
Sports PPV (delivered digitally); iN DEMAND (delivered digitally); Urban Xtra (delivered digitally); Fresh (delivered digitally); Shorteez (delivered digitally); Playboy TV (delivered digitally); Hot Choice (delivered digitally).
Internet Service
Operational: Yes.
Broadband Service: Comcast High Speed Internet.
Fee: $42.95 monthly.
Telephone Service
None
Homes passed & miles of plant included in Aspen
Vice President: Mike Trueblood. General Manager: Ben Miller. Technical Operations Manager: James Comiskey. Customer Service Manager: Anita Robinson.
Ownership: Comcast Cable Communications Inc. (MSO).

BAILEY—Formerly served by US Cable of Coastal Texas LP. No longer in operation. ICA: CO0059.

BAYFIELD—Rocky Mountain Cable, 40 County Rd 600, Unit F, Pagosa Springs, CO 81147-9473. Phones: 800-222-1332; 970-731-2211. Fax: 970-731-5510. Web Site: http://www.rockymtncable.com. ICA: CO0105.
TV Market Ranking: Below 100 (BAYFIELD). Franchise award date: July 5, 1983. Franchise expiration date: N.A. Began: March 1, 1984.
Channel capacity: 52 (not 2-way capable). Channels available but not in use: None.
Basic Service
Subscribers: 420.
Programming (received off-air): KDVR (FOX) Denver; KREZ-TV (CBS) Durango; KWGN-TV (CW) Denver.
Programming (via satellite): CNBC; CNN; Discovery Channel; Disney Channel; Do-It-Yourself; Food Network; Headline News; HGTV; History Channel; KMGH-TV (ABC) Denver; KRMA-TV (PBS) Denver; KUSA (NBC) Denver; Nickelodeon; QVC; TBS Superstation; The Learning Channel; truTV; USA Network; Weather Channel.
Fee: $20.00 installation; $27.24 monthly.
Expanded Basic Service 1
Subscribers: 338.
Programming (via satellite): ABC Family Channel; Arts & Entertainment; Bravo; Cartoon Network; Comedy Central; Country Music TV; ESPN; ESPN 2; Fox News Channel; Fox Sports Net Rocky Mountain; FX; Great American Country; GSN; Hallmark Channel; MSNBC; MTV; Outdoor Channel; Speed Channel; Spike TV; Turner Classic Movies; Turner Network TV; TV Land; Univision; Versus; WE tv.
Fee: $14.75 monthly.
Pay Service 1
Pay Units: 44.
Programming (via satellite): HBO (multiplexed).
Fee: $13.49 monthly.
Video-On-Demand: No
Internet Service
Operational: No.
Telephone Service
None
Miles of Plant: 16.0 (coaxial); None (fiber optic). Homes passed: 780.
President: Wayne Vestal. Chief Technician: Mark Dardnell.
City fee: 3% of gross minus signal rental costs.
Ownership: ICE Cable Holdings LLC (MSO).

BENNETT—Comcast Cable. Now served by DENVER (suburbs), CO [CO0001]. ICA: CO0157.

BEULAH—Beulah Land Communications Inc., 8611 Central Ave, Beulah, CO 81023-9740. Phone: 719-485-2400. Fax: 719-485-3500. Web Site: http://www.fone.net. ICA: CO0158.
TV Market Ranking: Below 100 (BEULAH). Franchise award date: March 1, 1992. Franchise expiration date: N.A. Began: September 1, 1992.
Channel capacity: 41 (not 2-way capable). Channels available but not in use: N.A.
Basic Service
Subscribers: 264.
Programming (received off-air): KKTV (CBS, MNT) Colorado Springs; KOAA-TV (NBC) Pueblo; KRDO-TV (ABC) Colorado Springs; KTSC (PBS) Pueblo; KWGN-TV (CW) Denver; KXRM-TV (FOX) Colorado Springs.
Programming (via satellite): ABC Family Channel; Animal Planet; Arts & Entertainment; CNN; Country Music TV; Discovery Channel; Disney Channel; ESPN; ESPN 2; Food Network; Fox News Channel; Fox Sports Net Rocky Mountain; Hallmark Channel; Headline News; HGTV; History Channel; Lifetime; NASA TV; National Geographic Channel; Nickelodeon; Spike TV; Syfy; TBS Superstation; The Learning Channel; Travel Channel; Turner Classic Movies; Turner Network TV; TV Land; USA Network; Versus; Weather Channel.
Current originations: Educational Access.
Fee: $125.00 installation; $21.26 monthly.
Pay Service 1
Pay Units: 5.
Programming (via satellite): The Movie Channel.
Fee: $7.50 monthly.
Pay Service 2
Pay Units: 33.
Programming (via satellite): HBO.
Fee: $10.00 monthly.
Video-On-Demand: No
Internet Service
Operational: No, DSL only.
Telephone Service
None
Miles of Plant: 15.0 (coaxial); None (fiber optic). Homes passed: 350. Total homes in franchised area: 350.
Manager & Chief Technician: Richard Sellers.
Ownership: Beulah Land Communications Inc.

BLACK HAWK—Rocky Mountain Cable, 40 County Rd 600, Unit F, Pagosa Springs, CO 81147-9473. Phones: 800-222-1332; 970-731-2211. Fax: 970-731-5510. Web Site: http://www.rockymtncable.com. Also serves Central City. ICA: CO0097.
TV Market Ranking: 32 (BLACK HAWK, Central City). Franchise award date: May 8, 1984. Franchise expiration date: N.A. Began: November 20, 1985.
Channel capacity: 59 (not 2-way capable). Channels available but not in use: 1.
Basic Service
Subscribers: 318.
Programming (via satellite): Discovery Channel; Fox News Channel; KCNC-TV (CBS) Denver; KDVR (FOX) Denver; KMGH-TV (ABC) Denver; KRMA-TV (PBS) Denver; KUSA (NBC) Denver; KWGN-TV (CW) Denver; Nickelodeon; QVC; TBS Superstation; The Learning Channel; Travel Channel; TV Guide Network; TV Land; USA Network; WGN America.
Fee: $20.00 installation; $27.24 monthly.
Expanded Basic Service 1
Subscribers: 284.
Programming (via satellite): ABC Family Channel; Animal Planet; Arts & Entertainment; Bravo; Cartoon Network; CNBC; CNN; Comedy Central; Country Music TV; Disney Channel; Do-It-Yourself; ESPN; ESPN 2; Food Network; Fox Sports Net Rocky Mountain; Headline News; History Channel; MSNBC; MTV; Outdoor Channel; Speed Channel; Spike TV; Syfy; Trinity Broadcasting Network; truTV; Turner Classic Movies; Turner Network TV; Univision; Versus; WE tv; Weather Channel.
Fee: $14.75 monthly.
Pay Service 1
Pay Units: 33.
Programming (via satellite): HBO (multiplexed).
Fee: $12.49 monthly.
Pay Service 2
Pay Units: 67.
Programming (via satellite): Cinemax (multiplexed).
Fee: $13.49 monthly.
Video-On-Demand: No
Pay-Per-View
Spice, Fee: $7.95, Addressable: Yes; Spice2, Fee: $7.95.
Internet Service
Operational: Yes.
Fee: $35.00 installation; $39.95 monthly.
Telephone Service
None
Miles of Plant: 41.0 (coaxial); None (fiber optic). Homes passed: 814.
President: Wayne Vestal. Chief Technician: Bobby Smith.
City fee: 3% of gross.
Ownership: ICE Cable Holdings LLC (MSO).

BLANCA—Jade Communications-Direct TV, PO Box 1138, 129 Santa Fe Rd, Alamosa, CO 81101-1138. Phones: 719-589-2964; 719-379-3839; 719-589-5140. Fax: 719-206-8133. E-mail: jade@gojade.org. Web Site: http://www.gojade.org. Also serves Fort Garland. ICA: CO0198.
TV Market Ranking: Outside TV Markets (BLANCA, Fort Garland). Franchise award date: October 1, 1991. Franchise expiration date: N.A. Began: October 1, 1991.
Channel capacity: 32 (not 2-way capable). Channels available but not in use: 10.
Basic Service
Subscribers: 120.
Programming (received off-air): KASA-TV (FOX) Santa Fe; KKTV (CBS, MNT) Colorado Springs; KOAT-TV (ABC) Albuquerque; KOB (NBC) Albuquerque; KRDO-TV (ABC) Colorado Springs; KRQE (CBS) Albuquerque; KTSC (PBS) Pueblo.

Programming (via satellite): ABC Family Channel; CNN; Discovery Channel; Disney Channel; ESPN; KCNC-TV (CBS) Denver; KMGH-TV (ABC) Denver; KRMA-TV (PBS) Denver; KUSA (NBC) Denver; KWGN-TV (CW) Denver; QVC; Spike TV; TBS Superstation; Turner Network TV.

Fee: $35.00 installation; $18.55 monthly.

Pay Service 1

Pay Units: 70.

Programming (via satellite): HBO.

Fee: $10.99 monthly.

Internet Service

Operational: No.

Telephone Service

None

Miles of Plant: 15.0 (coaxial); None (fiber optic). Homes passed: 300. Total homes in franchised area: 300.

Manager: Alan Wehe.

Ownership: Jade Communications LLC.

BOULDER—Comcast Cable. Now served by Denver (suburbs), CO [CO0001]. ICA: CO0007.

BOULDER (portions)—Qwest Choice TV. IPTV service has been discontinued.. ICA: CO5002.

BRECKENRIDGE—Comcast Cable. Now served by SILVERTHORNE (formerly Dillon), CO [CO0015]. ICA: CO0022.

BRIGHTON—Comcast Cable. Now served by DENVER (suburbs), CO [CO0001]. ICA: CO0024.

BROOMFIELD—Comcast Cable. Now served by Denver (suburbs), CO [CO0001]. ICA: CO0014.

BUENA VISTA—Bresnan Communications, 402 Main St, Canon City, CO 81212. Phone: 877-273-7626. Web Site: http://www.bresnan.com. Also serves Chaffee County & Johnson Village. ICA: CO0047.

TV Market Ranking: Outside TV Markets (BUENA VISTA, Chaffee County, Johnson Village). Franchise award date: N.A. Franchise expiration date: N.A. Began: October 1, 1973.

Channel capacity: N.A. Channels available but not in use: N.A.

Basic Service

Subscribers: 720.

Programming (received off-air): KCNC-TV (CBS) Denver; KDVR (FOX) Denver; KMGH-TV (ABC) Denver; KRDO-TV (ABC) Colorado Springs; KRMA-TV (PBS) Denver; KTSC (PBS) Pueblo; KTVD (MNT) Denver; KUSA (NBC) Denver; KWGN-TV (CW) Denver; allband FM.

Programming (via satellite): C-SPAN; C-SPAN 2; Home Shopping Network; ION Television; Lifetime.

Current originations: Public Access.

Fee: $40.00 installation; $19.95 monthly; $2.00 converter.

Expanded Basic Service 1

Subscribers: N.A.

Programming (via satellite): ABC Family Channel; Altitude Sports & Entertainment; AMC; Animal Planet; Arts & Entertainment; Cartoon Network; CNBC; CNN; Comedy Central; Country Music TV; Discovery Channel; Disney Channel; E! Entertainment Television; ESPN; ESPN 2; Eternal Word TV Network; Food Network; Fox News Channel; Fox Sports Net Rocky Mountain; FX; Hallmark Channel; Headline News; HGTV; History Channel; Independent Film Channel; MSNBC; MTV; Nickelodeon; Oxygen; QVC; Spike TV; Syfy; TBS Superstation; The Learning Channel; The Sportsman Channel; Travel Channel; truTV; Turner Classic Movies; Turner Network TV; TV Guide Network; TV Land; USA Network; VH1; Weather Channel.

Fee: $35.00 monthly.

Digital Basic Service

Subscribers: N.A.

Programming (via satellite): AmericanLife TV Network; Animal Planet HD; Arts & Entertainment HD; BBC America; Bio; Bloomberg Television; Bravo; CBS College Sports Network; Cine Latino; Cine Mexicano; CMT Pure Country; CNN en Espanol; Discovery Channel HD; Discovery en Espanol; Discovery HD Theater; Discovery Health Channel; Discovery Military Channel; Discovery Planet Green; DMX Music; ESPN Classic Sports; ESPN Deportes; ESPN HD; ESPNews; FitTV; Food Network HD; Fox College Sports Atlantic; Fox College Sports Central; Fox College Sports Pacific; Fox Movie Channel; Fox Reality Channel; Fox Soccer; Fox Sports en Espanol; G4; Golf Channel; Gospel Music Channel; GSN; Halogen Network; HGTV HD; History Channel en Espanol; History Channel HD; History Channel International; ID Investigation Discovery; Independent Film Channel; ION Television; Lifetime Movie Network; Mountain West TV; MTV Hits; MTV Jams; MTV Tres; MTV2; mun2 television; National Geographic Channel; National Geographic Channel HD Network; NFL Network; Nick Jr.; Nick Too; NickToons TV; Outdoor Channel; PBS Kids Sprout; RFD-TV; Science Channel; SoapNet; Speed Channel; Style Network; Syfy HD; TeenNick; Toon Disney; Trinity Broadcasting Network; Universal HD; USA Network HD; VeneMovies; Versus; VH1 Classic; VH1 Soul.

Fee: $56.99 monthly.

Digital Pay Service 1

Pay Units: N.A.

Programming (via satellite): Cinemax (multiplexed); Encore (multiplexed); Flix; HBO (multiplexed); HBO HD; Showtime (multiplexed); Starz (multiplexed); Starz HDTV; The Movie Channel (multiplexed).

Video-On-Demand: No

Internet Service

Operational: Yes.

Broadband Service: Bresnan OnLine.

Fee: $35.00 installation; $55.95 monthly.

Telephone Service

Digital: Operational

Fee: $49.99 monthly

Miles of Plant: 52.0 (coaxial); 9.0 (fiber optic). Homes passed: 2,314.

General Manager: Jerry Parker. Technical Operations Manager: Doyle Ruona.

City fee: 3% of gross.

Ownership: Bresnan Communications Inc. (MSO). Sale pends to Cablevision Systems Corp.

BURLINGTON—Baja Broadband, 403 14th St, Burlington, CO 80807-1609. Phones: 970-565-4031 (Cortez office); 719-346-8101. Fax: 719-346-8119. Web Site: http://www.bajabroadband.com. ICA: CO0057.

TV Market Ranking: Below 100 (BURLINGTON). Franchise award date: September 1, 1963. Franchise expiration date: N.A. Began: September 1, 1963.

Channel capacity: 62 (not 2-way capable). Channels available but not in use: None.

Basic Service

Subscribers: 1,053.

Programming (received off-air): KBSL-DT (CBS) Goodland; KDVR (FOX) Denver; KLBY (ABC) Colby; KTVD (MNT) Denver.

Programming (via microwave): KCNC-TV (CBS) Denver; KMGH-TV (ABC) Denver; KRMA-TV (PBS) Denver; KUSA (NBC) Denver; KWGN-TV (CW) Denver.

Programming (via satellite): ABC Family Channel; AMC; Animal Planet; Arts & Entertainment; Bravo; Cartoon Network; CNBC; CNN; Comedy Central; Country Music TV; C-SPAN; Discovery Channel; Disney Channel; E! Entertainment Television; ESPN; ESPN 2; Food Network; Fox News Channel; Fox Sports Net Rocky Mountain; FX; Hallmark Channel; Headline News; HGTV; History Channel; Home Shopping Network; Lifetime; MSNBC; MTV; National Geographic Channel; Nickelodeon; Product Information Network; QVC; Speed Channel; Spike TV; Syfy; TBS Superstation; The Learning Channel; the mtn; Travel Channel; truTV; Turner Classic Movies; Turner Network TV; TV Land; Univision; USA Network; VH1; Weather Channel; WGN America.

Current originations: Public Access; Educational Access.

Fee: $49.95 installation; $25.45 monthly.

Digital Basic Service

Subscribers: 459.

Programming (via satellite): BBC America; Bio; Bloomberg Television; CMT Pure Country; Discovery Health Channel; Discovery Kids Channel; Discovery Military Channel; Discovery Planet Green; Disney XD; ESPNews; FitTV; Fox Movie Channel; Fox Soccer; Fuse; G4; Golf Channel; GSN; Halogen Network; History Channel International; ID Investigation Discovery; Independent Film Channel; Lifetime Movie Network; MTV2; Music Choice; Nick Jr.; NickToons TV; Outdoor Channel; Science Channel; Style Network; TeenNick; Trinity Broadcasting Network; Versus; VH1 Classic; WE tv.

Digital Pay Service 1

Pay Units: N.A.

Programming (via satellite): Cinemax (multiplexed); Encore (multiplexed); HBO (multiplexed); Showtime (multiplexed); Starz; The Movie Channel (multiplexed).

Fee: $9.95 monthly (each).

Video-On-Demand: No

Pay-Per-View

iN DEMAND (delivered digitally); Club Jenna (delivered digitally); Playboy TV (delivered digitally); Fresh (delivered digitally).

Internet Service

Operational: No.

Telephone Service

None

Miles of Plant: 29.0 (coaxial); None (fiber optic). Homes passed: 1,769.

Area Vice President & General Manager: Tom Jaskiewicz. Technical Operations Director: Matt Warford.

City fee: 3% of gross.

Ownership: Baja Broadband (MSO).

CALHAN—FairPoint Communications, PO Box 218, Simla, CO 80835. Phone: 719-541-2261. Fax: 719-541-2129. ICA: CO0140.

TV Market Ranking: Below 100 (CALHAN). Franchise award date: April 1, 1985. Franchise expiration date: N.A. Began: September 10, 1985.

Channel capacity: 35 (not 2-way capable). Channels available but not in use: 7.

Basic Service

Subscribers: 95.

Programming (received off-air): KKTV (CBS, MNT) Colorado Springs; KOAA-TV (NBC) Pueblo; KRDO-TV (ABC) Colorado Springs; KTSC (PBS) Pueblo; KXRM-TV (FOX) Colorado Springs.

Programming (via satellite): ABC Family Channel; America's Store; Arts & Entertainment; CNN; Discovery Channel; Disney Channel; ESPN; ESPN 2; Great American Country; Headline News; History Channel; KWGN-TV (CW) Denver; Lifetime; Spike TV; Syfy; TBS Superstation; The Learning Channel; Turner Classic Movies; Turner Network TV; USA Network; Weather Channel; WGN America.

Fee: $20.95 monthly; $.75 converter.

Pay Service 1

Pay Units: 21.

Programming (via satellite): Cinemax.

Fee: $10.00 monthly.

Pay Service 2

Pay Units: 27.

Programming (via satellite): HBO.

Fee: $11.50 monthly.

Internet Service

Operational: No.

Broadband Service: DSL service only.

Telephone Service

None

Miles of Plant: 5.0 (coaxial); None (fiber optic). Homes passed: 300. Total homes in franchised area: 310.

Lead Technician: Dennis McKnight.

City fee: 3% of basic gross.

Ownership: FairPoint Communications Inc. (MSO).

CANON CITY—Bresnan Communications, 402 Main St, Canon City, CO 81212. Phone: 877-273-7626. Web Site: http://www.bresnan.com. Also serves Brookside, Coal Creek, Florence, Fremont County, Lincoln Park, Penrose, Rockvale & Williamsburg. ICA: CO0016.

TV Market Ranking: Below 100 (Brookside, Coal Creek, Florence, Fremont County (portions), Lincoln Park, Penrose, Rockvale, Williamsburg); Outside TV Markets (CANON CITY, Fremont County (portions)). Franchise award date: July 1, 1978. Franchise expiration date: N.A. Began: October 1, 1978.

Channel capacity: N.A. Channels available but not in use: N.A.

Basic Service

Subscribers: 7,336.

Programming (received off-air): KKTV (CBS, MNT) Colorado Springs; KOAA-TV (NBC) Pueblo; KRDO-TV (ABC) Colorado Springs; KTSC (PBS) Pueblo; KWGN-TV (CW) Denver; KXRM-TV (FOX) Colorado Springs.

Programming (via satellite): C-SPAN; C-SPAN 2; CW+; Home Shopping Network; MyNetworkTV Inc.; QVC; TBS Superstation; Trinity Broadcasting Network; TV Guide Network; V-me TV.

Fee: $44.95 installation; $19.95 monthly.

Expanded Basic Service 1

Subscribers: 6,994.

Programming (via satellite): ABC Family Channel; Altitude Sports & Entertainment; AMC; Animal Planet; Arts & Entertainment; BYU Television; Cartoon Network; CNBC; CNN; Comedy Central; Country Music TV; Discovery Channel; Disney Channel; E! Entertainment Television; ESPN; ESPN 2; Eternal Word TV Network; Food Network; Fox News Channel; Fox Sports Net Rocky Mountain; FX; Hallmark Channel; Headline

News; HGTV; History Channel; ION Television; Lifetime; MSNBC; MTV; Nickelodeon; Oxygen; Spike TV; Syfy; Telefutura; The Learning Channel; Travel Channel; truTV; Turner Classic Movies; Turner Network TV; TV Land; Univision; USA Network; VH1; Weather Channel.
Fee: $35.00 monthly.

Digital Basic Service
Subscribers: 3,000.
Programming (received off-air): KKTV (CBS, MNT) Colorado Springs; KOAA-TV (NBC) Pueblo; KRDO-TV (ABC) Colorado Springs; KTSC (PBS) Pueblo; KXRM-TV (FOX) Colorado Springs.
Programming (via satellite): ABC Family HD; AmericanLife TV Network; Animal Planet HD; Arts & Entertainment HD; BBC America; Bio; Bloomberg Television; Bravo; Bravo HD; CBS College Sports Network; CMT Pure Country; CNBC HD+; CNN HD; Cooking Channel; Discovery Channel HD; Discovery HD Theater; Discovery Health Channel; Discovery Kids Channel; Discovery Planet Green; Disney Channel HD; DMX Music; Do-It-Yourself; ESPN 2 HD; ESPN Classic Sports; ESPN HD; ESPNews; FitTV; Food Network HD; Fox College Sports Atlantic; Fox College Sports Central; Fox College Sports Pacific; Fox Movie Channel; Fox Reality Channel; Fox Soccer; FSN HD; Fuse; G4; Golf Channel; Gospel Music Channel; GSN; Halogen Network; HDNet; HDNet Movies; HGTV HD; History Channel HD; History Channel International; ID Investigation Discovery; Independent Film Channel; ION Life; ION Television; Jewelry Television; Lifetime Movie Network; Lifetime Movie Network HD; Mountain West TV; MTV Hits; MTV Jams; MTV Tres; MTV2; National Geographic Channel; National Geographic Channel HD Network; NFL Network; NFL Network HD; Nick Jr.; Nick Too; NickToons TV; Outdoor Channel; Outdoor Channel 2 HD; Palladia; PBS Kids Sprout; Qubo; RFD-TV; Science Channel; Science Channel HD; SoapNet; Speed Channel; Speed HD; Style Network; Syfy HD; TBS in HD; TeenNick; The Sportsman Channel; TLC HD; Toon Disney; Trinity Broadcasting Network; Turner Network TV HD; Universal HD; USA Network HD; Versus; Versus HD; VH1 Classic; VH1 Soul; Weather Channel HD.
Fee: $2.04 monthly.

Digital Pay Service 1
Pay Units: 4,000.
Programming (via satellite): Cinemax (multiplexed); Cinemax HD; Encore (multiplexed); Flix; HBO (multiplexed); HBO HD; Showtime (multiplexed); Showtime HD; Starz (multiplexed); Starz HDTV; The Movie Channel (multiplexed); The Movie Channel HD.

Video-On-Demand: Yes

Pay-Per-View
Hot Choice (delivered digitally), Addressable: No; Fresh (delivered digitally).

Internet Service
Operational: Yes.
Broadband Service: Bresnan OnLine.
Fee: $35.00 installation; $60.95 monthly.

Telephone Service
Digital: Operational
Fee: $49.95 monthly

Miles of Plant: 286.0 (coaxial); 104.0 (fiber optic). Total homes in franchised area: 15,705.
General Manager: Jerry Parker. Technical Operations Manager: Doyle Ruona.
City fee: 3% of gross.
Ownership: Bresnan Communications Inc. (MSO). Sale pends to Cablevision Systems Corp.

CANTERBURY PARK—Formerly served by Island Cable. No longer in operation. ICA: CO0160.

CASTLE ROCK—Comcast Cable. Now served by DENVER (suburbs), CO [CO0001]. ICA: CO0200.

CENTER—Formerly served by Center Municipal Cable System. No longer in operation. ICA: CO0102.

CHAPPELL—Charter Communications. Now served by JULESBURG, CO [CO0084]. ICA: NE0084.

CHEYENNE WELLS—Champion Broadband, 380 Perry St, Ste 230, Castle Rock, CO 80104. Phones: 303-688-7766; 866-801-1122. E-mail: mhaverkate@championbroadband.com. Web Site: http://www.championbroadband.com. ICA: CO0104.
TV Market Ranking: Outside TV Markets (CHEYENNE WELLS). Franchise award date: N.A. Franchise expiration date: N.A. Began: April 4, 1984.
Channel capacity: 41 (operating 2-way). Channels available but not in use: 5.

Basic Service
Subscribers: 86.
Programming (received off-air): KBSL-DT (CBS) Goodland; KCNC-TV (CBS) Denver; KKTV (CBS, MNT) Colorado Springs; KMGH-TV (ABC) Denver; KOAA-TV (NBC) Pueblo; KRDO-TV (ABC) Colorado Springs; KTSC (PBS) Pueblo; KUSA (NBC) Denver; KWGN-TV (CW) Denver.
Programming (via satellite): ABC Family Channel; AMC; Arts & Entertainment; Cartoon Network; CNN; Discovery Channel; Disney Channel; ESPN; ESPN 2; Fox News Channel; Fox Sports Net Rocky Mountain; Fuse; FX; Headline News; INSP; MSNBC; Outdoor Channel; QVC; TBS Superstation; Turner Network TV; USA Network; WGN America.
Current originations: Public Access.
Fee: $35.00 installation; $36.45 monthly.

Pay Service 1
Pay Units: 89.
Programming (via satellite): HBO.
Fee: $10.00 installation; $10.95 monthly.

Video-On-Demand: No

Internet Service
Operational: Yes.
Fee: $45.00 installation; $45.00 monthly.

Telephone Service
None

Miles of Plant: 8.0 (coaxial); None (fiber optic). Homes passed: 542.
General Manager: Mark Haverkate.
City fee: 3% of basic.
Ownership: Champion Broadband (MSO).

COLLBRAN—KiRock Communications, 14761 Deer Run Rd, Delta, CO 81416. Phone: 970-874-9934. Fax: 970-240-8122. ICA: CO0147.
TV Market Ranking: Below 100 (COLLBRAN). Franchise award date: N.A. Franchise expiration date: N.A. Began: June 1, 1990.
Channel capacity: 42 (not 2-way capable). Channels available but not in use: N.A.

Basic Service
Subscribers: 74.
Programming (received off-air): KCNC-TV (CBS) Denver; KMGH-TV (ABC) Denver; KRMA-TV (PBS) Denver; KUSA (NBC) Denver; KWGN-TV (CW) Denver.
Programming (via satellite): ABC Family Channel; CNN; Discovery Channel; ESPN; Spike TV; TBS Superstation; Turner Network TV; USA Network.
Fee: $25.50 monthly.

Pay Service 1
Pay Units: 18.
Programming (via satellite): Cinemax; HBO; Showtime.
Fee: $11.95 monthly (each).

Miles of Plant: 6.0 (coaxial); None (fiber optic). Homes passed: 165.
Manager & Chief Technician: Ki R. Nelson.
City fee: 5% of gross.
Ownership: Kirock Cable.

COLORADO CITY—Bresnan Communications, 402 Main St, Canon City, CO 81212. Phones: 877-273-7626; 719-384-8434. Fax: 719-275-6068. Web Site: http://www.bresnan.com. Also serves Pueblo County & Rye. ICA: CO0094.
TV Market Ranking: Below 100 (COLORADO CITY, Pueblo County, Rye). Franchise award date: June 1, 1983. Franchise expiration date: N.A. Began: April 8, 1985.
Channel capacity: N.A. Channels available but not in use: N.A.

Basic Service
Subscribers: 385.
Programming (received off-air): ION Television; KCNC-TV (CBS) Denver; KKTV (CBS, MNT) Colorado Springs; KMGH-TV (ABC) Denver; KOAA-TV (NBC) Pueblo; KRDO-TV (ABC) Colorado Springs; KTSC (PBS) Pueblo; KWGN-TV (CW) Denver; KXRM-TV (FOX) Colorado Springs.
Programming (via satellite): ABC Family Channel; Altitude Sports & Entertainment; AMC; Animal Planet; Arts & Entertainment; BYU Television; Cartoon Network; CNBC; CNN; Comedy Central; Country Music TV; C-SPAN; C-SPAN 2; CW+; Discovery Channel; Disney Channel; E! Entertainment Television; ESPN; ESPN 2; Eternal Word TV Network; Food Network; Fox News Channel; Fox Sports Net Rocky Mountain; FX; Hallmark Channel; Headline News; HGTV; History Channel; Home Shopping Network; KUSA (NBC) Denver; Lifetime; MSNBC; MTV; MyNetworkTV Inc.; Nickelodeon; Oxygen; QVC; Spike TV; Syfy; TBS Superstation; Telefutura; The Learning Channel; The Sportsman Channel; Travel Channel; truTV; Turner Classic Movies; Turner Network TV; TV Guide Network; Univision; USA Network; VH1; Weather Channel.
Fee: $60.00 installation; $54.95 monthly; $2.00 converter.

Digital Basic Service
Subscribers: N.A.
Programming (received off-air): KKTV (CBS, MNT) Colorado Springs; KOAA-TV (NBC) Pueblo; KRDO-TV (ABC) Colorado Springs; KXRM-TV (FOX) Colorado Springs.
Programming (via satellite): ABC Family HD; AmericanLife TV Network; Animal Planet HD; Arts & Entertainment HD; Bandamax; BBC America; Bio; Bloomberg Television; Bravo; CBS College Sports Network; Cine Latino; Cine Mexicano; CMT Pure Country; CNN en Espanol; De Pelicula; De Pelicula Clasico; Discovery Channel HD; Discovery en Espanol; Discovery HD Theater; Discovery Health Channel; Discovery Kids Channel; Discovery Planet Green; Disney Channel HD; DMX Music; ESPN Classic Sports; ESPN Deportes; ESPN HD; ESPNews; FitTV; Food Network HD; Fox College Sports Atlantic; Fox College Sports Central; Fox College Sports Pacific; Fox Movie Channel; Fox Reality Channel; Fox Soccer; Fox Sports en Espanol; Fuse; G4; Gol TV; Golf Channel; Gospel Music Channel; GSN; Halogen Network; HGTV HD; History Channel en Espanol; History Channel HD; History Channel International; ID Investigation Discovery; Independent Film Channel; ION Television; Lifetime Movie Network; Mountain West TV; MTV Hits; MTV Jams; MTV Tres; MTV2; mun2 television; National Geographic Channel; National Geographic Channel HD Network; NFL Network; Nick Jr.; NickToons TV; Outdoor Channel; PBS Kids Sprout; RFD-TV; Science Channel; Science Channel HD; SoapNet; Speed Channel; Style Network; Syfy HD; TeenNick; Telefutura; Telehit; Toon Disney; Trinity Broadcasting Network; TV Land; Universal HD; Univision; USA Network HD; VeneMovies; Versus; VH1 Classic; VH1 Soul.

Digital Pay Service 1
Pay Units: N.A.
Programming (via satellite): Cinemax (multiplexed); Encore (multiplexed); Flix; HBO (multiplexed); Showtime (multiplexed); Starz (multiplexed); Starz HDTV; The Movie Channel (multiplexed).

Video-On-Demand: No

Internet Service
Operational: Yes.
Broadband Service: Bresnan OnLine.
Fee: $35.00 installation; $55.95 monthly.

Telephone Service
Digital: Operational
Fee: $49.99 monthly

Miles of Plant: 52.0 (coaxial); 13.0 (fiber optic). Homes passed: 1,196.
General Manager: Jerry Parker. Chief Technician: Matt Harris.
Franchise fee: 3% of gross.
Ownership: Bresnan Communications Inc. (MSO). Sale pends to Cablevision Systems Corp.

COLORADO SPRINGS—Comcast Cable, 213 N Union Blvd, Colorado Springs, CO 80909. Phone: 719-457-4501. Fax: 719-457-4503. Web Site: http://www.comcast.com. Also serves Black Forest, Cascade, Chipita Park, Cimarron Hills, El Paso County, Fountain, Green Mountain Falls, Manitou Springs, Monument, Palmer Lake, Rockrimmon & Woodmoor. ICA: CO0003.
TV Market Ranking: 32 (Black Forest, Cascade, Chipita Park, El Paso County (portions), Green Mountain Falls, Manitou Springs, Monument, Palmer Lake, Rockrimmon, Woodmoor); Below 100 (Cimarron Hills, COLORADO SPRINGS, Fountain, El Paso County (portions)). Franchise award date: N.A. Franchise expiration date: N.A. Began: June 23, 1969.
Channel capacity: 135 (operating 2-way). Channels available but not in use: 57.

Basic Service
Subscribers: 98,881 Includes Trinidad.
Programming (received off-air): KBDI-TV (PBS) Broomfield; KCNC-TV (CBS) Denver; KGHB-CA Pueblo, etc.; KKTV (CBS, MNT) Colorado Springs; KOAA-TV (NBC) Pueblo; KRDO-TV (ABC) Colorado Springs; KTSC (PBS) Pueblo; KUSA (NBC) Denver; KWGN-TV (CW) Denver; KXRM-TV (FOX) Colorado Springs; KXTU-LP (CW) Colorado Springs; 24 FMs.

Programming (via satellite): KRMZ (PBS) Steamboat Springs; QVC.

Current originations: Leased Access; Government Access; Educational Access; Public Access.

Fee: $23.99 installation; $18.54 monthly.

Expanded Basic Service 1

Subscribers: N.A.

Programming (received off-air): KWHS-LP (IND) Colorado Springs.

Programming (via satellite): ABC Family Channel; AMC; Animal Planet; Arts & Entertainment; BET Networks; Bravo; Cartoon Network; CNBC; CNN; Comedy Central; Country Music TV; C-SPAN; C-SPAN 2; Discovery Channel; Disney Channel; E! Entertainment Television; ESPN; ESPN 2; Eternal Word TV Network; Food Network; Fox News Channel; Fox Sports en Espanol; Fox Sports Net Rocky Mountain; FX; Golf Channel; Hallmark Channel; Headline News; HGTV; History Channel; Home Shopping Network; INSP; ION Television; Lifetime; MSNBC; MTV; Nickelodeon; Oxygen; ShopNBC; Speed Channel; Spike TV; Syfy; TBS Superstation; The Learning Channel; Travel Channel; Turner Classic Movies; Turner Network TV; TV Guide Network; TV Land; USA Network; Versus; VH1; WE tv; Weather Channel; WGN America.

Fee: $27.94 monthly.

Digital Basic Service

Subscribers: 52,512 Includes Trinidad.

Programming (via satellite): American-Life TV Network; BBC America; Bio; Black Family Channel; Bloomberg Television; Chinese Television Network; Discovery Digital Networks; Do-It-Yourself; ESPN Classic Sports; ESPNews; FamilyNet; FitTV; Fox Movie Channel; Fox Sports World; Fuse; G4; GAS; Great American Country; GSN; Halogen Network; History Channel International; Independent Film Channel; M-2 (Movie Mania) TV Network; MTV Networks Digital Suite; Music Choice; National Geographic Channel; Nick Jr.; Nick Too; NickToons TV; Outdoor Channel; SoapNet; Style Network; Toon Disney; Trinity Broadcasting Network.

Fee: $11.95 monthly.

Digital Expanded Basic Service

Subscribers: N.A.

Programming (via satellite): Canales N; Fox College Sports Atlantic; Fox College Sports Central; Fox College Sports Pacific; Sundance Channel.

Fee: $4.95 monthly.

Digital Pay Service 1

Pay Units: N.A.

Programming (via satellite): ART America; Canales N; CCTV-4; Cinemax (multiplexed); Encore (multiplexed); Filipino Channel; Flix; HBO (multiplexed); International Television (ITV); RAI International; Russian Television Network; Showtime (multiplexed); Starz (multiplexed); The Movie Channel (multiplexed); TV Asia; TV Japan; TV5 USA; Zee TV USA.

Fee: $18.99 monthly (each).

Video-On-Demand: Planned

Pay-Per-View

Addressable homes: 52,007.

Shorteez (delivered digitally); Fresh (delivered digitally); Urban American Television Network (delivered digitally); Playboy TV (delivered digitally); Hot Choice (delivered digitally); HITS PPV (delivered digitally), Addressable: Yes.

Internet Service

Operational: Yes.

Subscribers: 64,458.

Broadband Service: Comcast High Speed Internet.

Fee: $42.95 monthly; $6.95 modem lease; $264.99 modem purchase.

Telephone Service

None

Miles of Plant: 2,267.0 (coaxial); 80.0 (fiber optic). Homes passed: 248,330. Homes passed includes Trinidad

Vice President & General Manager: Jim Commers. Technical Operations Director: Jim Garcia. Vice President, Marketing: Zach Street. Public Relations Manager: Sandra Mann.

City fee: 5% of gross.

Ownership: Comcast Cable Communications Inc. (MSO).

COLORADO SPRINGS—Formerly served by Sprint Corp. No longer in operation. ICA: CO0192.

CONIFER—US Cable, 266 Basher Dr, #4, Berthoud, CO 80513. Phones: 800-480-7020; 970-587-2243. Fax: 970-587-4208. Web Site: http://www.uscable.com. Also serves Clear Creek County (eastern portion), Evergreen (portions), Jefferson County (southern portion), Marshdale Park & Park County (northwestern portion). ICA: CO0163.

TV Market Ranking: 32 (Clear Creek County (eastern portion) (portions), CONIFER, Evergreen (portions), Jefferson County (southern portion), Marshdale Park, Park County (northwestern portion) (portions)); Outside TV Markets (Clear Creek County (eastern portion) (portions), Park County (northwestern portion) (portions)). Franchise award date: N.A. Franchise expiration date: N.A. Began: October 1, 1988.

Channel capacity: 54 (not 2-way capable). Channels available but not in use: N.A.

Basic Service

Subscribers: N.A. Included in Johnstown

Programming (via satellite): ABC Family Channel; AMC; Animal Planet; Arts & Entertainment; Bravo; Cartoon Network; CNBC; CNN; Comedy Central; Country Music TV; C-SPAN; C-SPAN 2; Discovery Channel; Disney Channel; ESPN; ESPN 2; ESPNews; Food Network; Fox Sports Net Rocky Mountain; Headline News; HGTV; History Channel; Home Shopping Network; KBDI-TV (PBS) Broomfield; KCNC-TV (CBS) Denver; KDVR (FOX) Denver; KMGH-TV (ABC) Denver; KPXC-TV (ION) Denver; KRMA-TV (PBS) Denver; KTVD (MNT) Denver; KUSA (NBC) Denver; KWGN-TV (CW) Denver; Lifetime; MTV; Nickelodeon; ShopNBC; Spike TV; Syfy; TBS Superstation; The Learning Channel; Travel Channel; truTV; Turner Classic Movies; Turner Network TV; TV Land; USA Network; VH1; Weather Channel; WGN America.

Fee: $75.00 installation; $24.95 monthly.

Pay Service 1

Pay Units: 800.

Programming (via satellite): HBO.

Fee: $8.95 monthly.

Pay Service 2

Pay Units: N.A.

Programming (via satellite): Cinemax; Showtime.

Video-On-Demand: No

Internet Service

Operational: No.

Telephone Service

None

General Manager: Dave Kavanagh. Chief Technician: Josh Patchett. Office Manager: Debbie Hernandez. Marketing Manager: Jennifer Lideman. Construction Manager: Rich Fromstad.

Ownership: US Cable Corp. (MSO).; Comcast Cable Communications Inc. (MSO).

COPPER MOUNTAIN—Copper Mountain Consolidated Metropolitan District, PO Box 3002, 0154 Wheeler Pl, Copper Mountain, CO 80443-3002. Phone: 970-968-2537. Fax: 970-968-2932. ICA: CO0083.

TV Market Ranking: Outside TV Markets (COPPER MOUNTAIN). Franchise award date: January 1, 1976. Franchise expiration date: N.A. Began: December 31, 1976.

Channel capacity: 61 (operating 2-way). Channels available but not in use: 18.

Basic Service

Subscribers: 1,440.

Programming (via satellite): ABC Family Channel; Altitude Sports & Entertainment; AMC; Animal Planet; Arts & Entertainment; Bravo; CNBC; CNN; Comedy Central; Country Music TV; C-SPAN; C-SPAN 2; Discovery Channel; Disney Channel; ESPN; ESPN 2; Food Network; Fox News Channel; Golf Channel; Headline News; HGTV; History Channel; Independent Film Channel; KCNC-TV (CBS) Denver; KDVR (FOX) Denver; KMGH-TV (ABC) Denver; KRMA-TV (PBS) Denver; KTVD (MNT) Denver; KUSA (NBC) Denver; KWGN-TV (CW) Denver; Lifetime; MSNBC; MTV; National Geographic Channel; Nickelodeon; Speed Channel; Spike TV; TBS Superstation; The Learning Channel; Toon Disney; Turner Classic Movies; Turner Network TV; TV Guide Network; TV Land; USA Network; Versus; VH1; Weather Channel; WGN America.

Fee: $30.00 installation; $40.00 monthly.

Digital Basic Service

Subscribers: N.A.

Programming (via satellite): Bio; Bravo; DMX Music; Encore (multiplexed); ESPN Classic Sports; Flix; Fuse; GAS; HGTV; History Channel; History Channel International; Lifetime Movie Network; MTV2; Style Network; Trio.

Fee: $16.00 monthly.

Pay Service 1

Pay Units: 26.

Programming (via satellite): HBO.

Digital Pay Service 1

Pay Units: N.A.

Programming (via satellite): Cinemax (multiplexed); HBO (multiplexed); Showtime (multiplexed); Starz (multiplexed); The Movie Channel (multiplexed).

Fee: $7.00 monthly (Starz), $8.00 monthly (Cinemax), $10.00 monthly (HBO), $12.50 monthly (Showtime & TMC).

Pay-Per-View

Addressable homes: 625.

Hot Choice, Fee: $5.95-$6.95, Addressable: Yes; iN DEMAND; movies; special events.

Internet Service

Operational: Yes.

Fee: $25.00 installation; $24.00 monthly.

Telephone Service

None

Miles of Plant: 6.0 (coaxial); None (fiber optic).

Manager: David Erickson. Chief Technician: David Arnesen.

Ownership: Copper Mountain Consolidated Metropolitan District.

CORTEZ—Baja Broadband, 107 S Washington St, Cortez, CO 81321-3739. Phone: 970-565-4031. Fax: 970-565-7404. Web Site: http://www.bajabroadband.com. ICA: CO0044.

TV Market Ranking: Outside TV Markets (CORTEZ). Franchise award date: N.A. Franchise expiration date: N.A. Began: September 1, 1981.

Channel capacity: N.A. Channels available but not in use: N.A.

Basic Service

Subscribers: 2,025.

Programming (via satellite): C-SPAN; Home Shopping Network; INSP; QVC; WGN America.

Programming (via translator): KASA-TV (FOX) Santa Fe; KJCT (ABC, TMO) Grand Junction; KLUZ-TV (UNV) Albuquerque; KOAT-TV (ABC) Albuquerque; KOBF (NBC) Farmington; KREZ-TV (CBS) Durango; KRMJ (PBS) Grand Junction; KRPV-DT (IND) Roswell; KTEL-LP Albuquerque; KTVD (MNT) Denver; KUSA (NBC) Denver; KWGN-TV (CW) Denver.

Current originations: Government Access; Educational Access; Public Access.

Fee: $49.95 installation; $23.00 monthly.

Expanded Basic Service 1

Subscribers: 1,634.

Programming (via satellite): ABC Family Channel; AMC; Animal Planet; Arts & Entertainment; Bravo; Cartoon Network; CNBC; CNN; Comedy Central; Country Music TV; C-SPAN 2; Discovery Channel; Disney Channel; E! Entertainment Television; ESPN; ESPN 2; Food Network; Fox News Channel; Fox Sports Net Rocky Mountain; FX; G4; GalaVision; Golf Channel; Great American Country; GSN; Hallmark Channel; Headline News; HGTV; History Channel; Lifetime; Lifetime Movie Network; MSNBC; MTV; National Geographic Channel; Nickelodeon; Outdoor Channel; SoapNet; Speed Channel; Spike TV; Syfy; TBS Superstation; The Learning Channel; Travel Channel; Trinity Broadcasting Network; truTV; Turner Network TV; TV Land; USA Network; VH1; WE tv; Weather Channel.

Fee: $25.30 monthly.

Digital Basic Service

Subscribers: N.A.

Programming (via satellite): BBC America; Bio; Bloomberg Television; CMT Pure Country; Discovery Health Channel; Discovery Kids Channel; Discovery Military Channel; Discovery Planet Green; Disney XD; FitTV; Fox Business Channel; Fox Movie Channel; Fox Reality Channel; Fuse; History Channel International; ID Investigation Discovery; Independent Film Channel; Lifetime Real Women; MTV Hits; MTV2; Music Choice; Nick Jr.; Science Channel; Style Network; TeenNick; the mtn; Turner Classic Movies; VH1 Classic; VH1 Soul.

Fee: $8.95 monthly.

Digital Expanded Basic Service

Subscribers: N.A.

Programming (via satellite): ESPN Classic Sports; Fox Soccer; Versus.

Digital Expanded Basic Service 2

Subscribers: N.A.

Programming (via satellite): Arts & Entertainment HD; ESPN HD; Food Network HD; FSN HD; FX HD; HGTV HD; History Channel HD; National Geographic Channel HD Network; Speed HD; TBS in HD; Turner Network TV HD.

Digital Expanded Basic Service 3

Subscribers: N.A.

Programming (via satellite): HDNet; HDNet Movies; Universal HD.

Digital Pay Service 1
Pay Units: 691.
Programming (via satellite): Cinemax (multiplexed); Cinemax HD; Encore (multiplexed); Flix; HBO (multiplexed); HBO HD; Showtime (multiplexed); Showtime HD; Starz (multiplexed); Starz HDTV; The Movie Channel (multiplexed); The Movie Channel HD.
Fee: $9.00 monthly (each).
Video-On-Demand: No
Pay-Per-View
iN DEMAND (delivered digitally); Ten Blox (delivered digitally); Ten Xtsy (delivered digitally); Sports PPV (delivered digitally); Hot Choice (delivered digitally); Ten Blue (delivered digitally); Playboy TV (delivered digitally); Fresh (delivered digitally); Spice: Xcess (delivered digitally); Ten On Demand (delivered digitally); Ten Clips (delivered digitally).
Internet Service
Operational: Yes. Began: May 1, 2002.
Subscribers: 300.
Broadband Service: In-house.
Fee: $49.99 installation; $52.99 monthly; $4.96 modem lease; $69.95 modem purchase.
Telephone Service
None
Miles of Plant: 48.0 (coaxial); None (fiber optic). Homes passed: 2,770. Total homes in franchised area: 2,900.
Area Vice President & General Manager: Tom Jaskiewicz. Technical Operations Director: Matt Warford.
City fee: 3% of gross.
Ownership: Baja Broadband (MSO).

CRAIG—Bresnan Communications, 580 Russell St, Craig, CO 81625. Phones: 877-273-7626; 970-824-3298. Fax: 970-824-5529. Web Site: http://www.bresnan.com. Also serves Hayden & Moffat County. ICA: CO0039.
TV Market Ranking: Below 100 (Hayden, Moffat County (portions)); Outside TV Markets (CRAIG (VILLAGE), Moffat County (portions)). Franchise award date: N.A. Franchise expiration date: N.A. Began: June 1, 1980.
Channel capacity: N.A. Channels available but not in use: N.A.
Basic Service
Subscribers: 3,105.
Programming (received off-air): KCNC-TV (CBS) Denver; KDVR (FOX) Denver; KMGH-TV (ABC) Denver; KPXC-TV (ION) Denver; KRMA-TV (PBS) Denver; KTVD (MNT) Denver; KUSA (NBC) Denver; KWGN-TV (CW) Denver; 6 FMs.
Programming (via satellite): America One Television; C-SPAN; C-SPAN 2; Discovery Channel; Home Shopping Network; Lifetime; QVC; TBS Superstation.
Fee: $19.95 monthly; $1.50 converter.
Expanded Basic Service 1
Subscribers: 2,600.
Programming (via satellite): ABC Family Channel; Altitude Sports & Entertainment; AMC; Animal Planet; Arts & Entertainment; Cartoon Network; CNBC; CNN; Comedy Central; Country Music TV; Disney Channel; E! Entertainment Television; ESPN; ESPN 2; Eternal Word TV Network; Food Network; Fox News Channel; Fox Sports Net Rocky Mountain; FX; GalaVision; Great American Country; Hallmark Channel; Headline News; HGTV; History Channel; MSNBC; MTV; Nickelodeon; Oxygen; Spike TV; Syfy; Telefutura; The Learning Channel; Travel Channel; truTV; Turner Classic Movies; Turner Network TV; TV Guide Network; TV Land; Univision; USA Network; VH1; Weather Channel.
Fee: $35.00 monthly.
Digital Basic Service
Subscribers: N.A.
Programming (via satellite): AmericanLife TV Network; Animal Planet HD; Arts & Entertainment HD; Bandamax; BBC America; Bio; Bloomberg Television; Bravo; CBS College Sports Network; Cine Latino; Cine Mexicano; CMT Pure Country; CNN en Espanol; CNN HD; Cooking Channel; De Pelicula; De Pelicula Clasico; Discovery en Espanol; Discovery HD Theater; Discovery Health Channel; Discovery Kids Channel; Discovery Military Channel; Discovery Planet Green; DMX Music; Do-It-Yourself; ESPN 2 HD; ESPN Classic Sports; ESPN Deportes; ESPN HD; ESPNews; FitTV; Food Network HD; Fox College Sports Atlantic; Fox College Sports Central; Fox College Sports Pacific; Fox Movie Channel; Fox Reality Channel; Fox Soccer; Fox Sports en Espanol; Fuse; G4; GalaVision; Gol TV; Golf Channel; Gospel Music Channel; GSN; Halogen Network; HDNet; HDNet Movies; HGTV HD; History Channel en Espanol; History Channel HD; History Channel International; ID Investigation Discovery; Independent Film Channel; Jewelry Television; Lifetime Movie Network; Lifetime Movie Network HD; Mountain West TV; MTV Hits; MTV Jams; MTV Tres; MTV2; mun2 television; National Geographic Channel; National Geographic Channel HD Network; NFL Network; NFL Network HD; Nick Jr.; Nick Too; NickToons TV; Outdoor Channel; PBS Kids Sprout; RFD-TV; Science Channel; Science Channel HD; SoapNet; Speed Channel; Style Network; Syfy HD; TBS in HD; TeenNick; Telefutura; Telehit; The Sportsman Channel; TLC HD; Toon Disney; Trinity Broadcasting Network; Turner Network TV HD; Universal HD; Univision; USA Network HD; VeneMovies; Versus; Versus HD; VH1 Classic; VH1 Soul; Weather Channel HD.
Pay Service 1
Pay Units: 453.
Programming (via satellite): HBO.
Fee: $24.95 installation; $13.59 monthly.
Digital Pay Service 1
Pay Units: N.A.
Programming (via satellite): Cinemax (multiplexed); Cinemax HD; Encore (multiplexed); Flix; HBO (multiplexed); HBO HD; Showtime (multiplexed); Showtime HD; Starz (multiplexed); Starz HDTV; The Movie Channel (multiplexed); The Movie Channel HD.
Video-On-Demand: No
Pay-Per-View
ESPN (delivered digitally); iN DEMAND (delivered digitally).
Internet Service
Operational: Yes.
Broadband Service: Bresnan OnLine.
Fee: $35.00 installation; $55.95 monthly.
Telephone Service
Digital: Operational
Fee: $49.99 monthly
Miles of Plant: 58.0 (coaxial); None (fiber optic). Homes passed: 5,000. Total homes in franchised area: 5,000.
Regional General Manager: Tommy Cotton.
Ownership: Bresnan Communications Inc. (MSO). Sale pends to Cablevision Systems Corp.

CREEDE—Rocky Mountain Cable, 40 County Rd 600, Unit F, Pagosa Springs, CO 81147-9473. Phones: 800-222-1332; 970-731-2211. Fax: 970-731-5510. Web Site: http://www.rockymtncable.com. ICA: CO0126.
TV Market Ranking: Outside TV Markets (CREEDE). Franchise award date: June 28, 1983. Franchise expiration date: N.A. Began: December 1, 1983.
Channel capacity: 35 (not 2-way capable). Channels available but not in use: 1.
Basic Service
Subscribers: 40.
Programming (via satellite): Arts & Entertainment; Bravo; CNN; Comedy Central; Country Music TV; C-SPAN; Discovery Channel; Disney Channel; ESPN; ESPN 2; Fox News Channel; Hallmark Channel; Headline News; History Channel; KCNC-TV (CBS) Denver; KDVR (FOX) Denver; KMGH-TV (ABC) Denver; KRMA-TV (PBS) Denver; KUSA (NBC) Denver; KWGN-TV (CW) Denver; MSNBC; Nickelodeon; QVC; Spike TV; Syfy; TBS Superstation; The Learning Channel; TV Land; USA Network; Versus; WE tv; WGN America.
Current originations: Public Access.
Fee: $20.00 installation; $36.99 monthly.
Pay Service 1
Pay Units: N.A.
Programming (via satellite): HBO.
Fee: $13.49 monthly.
Video-On-Demand: No
Internet Service
Operational: No.
Telephone Service
None
Miles of Plant: 5.0 (coaxial); None (fiber optic). Homes passed: 329.
President: Wayne Vestal. Chief Technician: Bobby Smith.
City fee: 5% of gross minus signal rental cost.
Ownership: ICE Cable Holdings LLC (MSO).

CRIPPLE CREEK—US Cable, 266 Basher Dr, #4, Berthoud, CO 80513. Phone: 970-587-2243. Fax: 970-587-4208. Web Site: http://www.uscable.com. ICA: CO0165.
TV Market Ranking: Below 100 (CRIPPLE CREEK). Franchise award date: N.A. Franchise expiration date: N.A. Began: N.A.
Channel capacity: 42 (not 2-way capable). Channels available but not in use: N.A.
Basic Service
Subscribers: N.A. Included in Johnstown
Programming (received off-air): KCNC-TV (CBS) Denver; KDVR (FOX) Denver; KRDO-TV (ABC) Colorado Springs; KUSA (NBC) Denver; KWGN-TV (CW) Denver.
Programming (via satellite): ABC Family Channel; Animal Planet; Arts & Entertainment; CNN; Comedy Central; Country Music TV; Discovery Channel; Disney Channel; ESPN; ESPN 2; Fox Sports Net Rocky Mountain; FX; Headline News; History Channel; Nickelodeon; Outdoor Channel; QVC; ShopNBC; Speed Channel; Spike TV; Syfy; TBS Superstation; The Learning Channel; Turner Classic Movies; Turner Network TV; TV Land; USA Network; VH1; Weather Channel; WGN America.
Fee: $15.00 installation; $14.95 monthly; $2.00 converter.
Pay Service 1
Pay Units: 57.
Programming (via satellite): Cinemax.
Fee: $9.50 monthly.
Pay Service 2
Pay Units: N.A.
Programming (via satellite): HBO.
Internet Service
Operational: Yes.
Fee: $27.95 monthly.
Telephone Service
None
Miles of Plant: 8.0 (coaxial); None (fiber optic).
General Manager: Dave Kavanagh. Chief Technician: Josh Patchett. Office Manager: Debbie Hernandez. Marketing Manager: Jennifer Lideman. Construction Manager: Rich Fromstad.
Ownership: US Cable Corp. (MSO).; Comcast Cable Communications Inc. (MSO).

CUCHARA VALLEY—Formerly served by Westcom II LLC. No longer in operation. ICA: CO0130.

DEER TRAIL—Champion Broadband, 380 Perry St, Ste 230, Castle Rock, CO 80104. Phones: 303-688-7766; 866-801-1122. E-mail: mhaverkate@championbroadband.com. Web Site: http://www.championbroadband.com. ICA: CO0139.
TV Market Ranking: Outside TV Markets (DEER TRAIL). Franchise award date: N.A. Franchise expiration date: N.A. Began: December 1, 1986.
Channel capacity: 41 (operating 2-way). Channels available but not in use: 8.
Basic Service
Subscribers: 37.
Programming (received off-air): KCNC-TV (CBS) Denver; KDVR (FOX) Denver; KMGH-TV (ABC) Denver; KRMA-TV (PBS) Denver; KRMT (ETV) Denver; KTVD (MNT) Denver; KUSA (NBC) Denver; KWGN-TV (CW) Denver.
Programming (via satellite): ABC Family Channel; AMC; Arts & Entertainment; Cartoon Network; CNN; Discovery Channel; Disney Channel; ESPN; ESPN 2; Great American Country; HGTV; ION Television; Lifetime; Outdoor Channel; QVC; TBS Superstation; Travel Channel; Turner Network TV; USA Network; Weather Channel; WGN America.
Fee: $35.00 installation; $37.45 monthly.
Pay Service 1
Pay Units: 27.
Programming (via satellite): HBO.
Fee: $10.00 installation; $10.95 monthly.
Video-On-Demand: No
Internet Service
Operational: Yes.
Fee: $45.00 installation; $45.00 monthly.
Telephone Service
None
Miles of Plant: 5.0 (coaxial); None (fiber optic). Homes passed: 217.
General Manager: Mark Haverkate.
City fee: 3% of gross.
Ownership: Champion Broadband (MSO).

DEL NORTE—Bresnan Communications, 402 Main St, Canon City, CO 81212. Phones: 970-263-2300; 877-273-7626. Web Site: http://www.bresnan.com. Also serves Rio Grande County. ICA: CO0089.
TV Market Ranking: Outside TV Markets (DEL NORTE, Rio Grande County). Franchise award date: N.A. Franchise expiration date: N.A. Began: February 1, 1983.
Channel capacity: 38 (not 2-way capable). Channels available but not in use: N.A.
Basic Service
Subscribers: 188.
Programming (received off-air): KCNC-TV (CBS) Denver; KDVR (FOX) Denver; KMGH-TV (ABC) Denver; KRMA-TV (PBS) Denver; KTVD (MNT) Denver; KUSA (NBC) Denver; KWGN-TV (CW) Denver.

Programming (via satellite): Altitude Sports & Entertainment; C-SPAN; Discovery Channel; TBS Superstation.
Fee: $39.99 installation; $20.99 monthly.

Expanded Basic Service 1
Subscribers: N.A.
Programming (via satellite): ABC Family Channel; AMC; Animal Planet; Cartoon Network; CNN; Disney Channel; ESPN; ESPN 2; Fox News Channel; Fox Sports Net Rocky Mountain; FX; INSP; Lifetime; MTV; Nickelodeon; Spike TV; The Learning Channel; truTV; Turner Network TV; Univision; USA Network; Weather Channel.
Fee: $28.00 monthly.

Pay Service 1
Pay Units: 30.
Programming (via satellite): Encore; HBO; Showtime.
Fee: $8.95 monthly (HBO).

Video-On-Demand: No

Internet Service
Operational: No.

Telephone Service
None

Miles of Plant: 13.0 (coaxial); None (fiber optic). Homes passed: 882.
General Manager: Jerry Parker. Technical Operations Manager: Doyle Ruona.
Ownership: Bresnan Communications Inc. (MSO). Sale pends to Cablevision Systems Corp.

DELTA—Bresnan Communications, 2502 Foresight Cir, Grand Junction, CO 81505. Phones: 970-874-4629 (Customer service); 970-263-2300. E-mail: shogue@bresnan.com. Web Site: http://www.bresnan.com. Also serves Delta County. ICA: CO0042.
TV Market Ranking: Below 100 (DELTA, Delta County). Franchise award date: N.A. Franchise expiration date: N.A. Began: December 1, 1965.
Channel capacity: N.A. Channels available but not in use: N.A.

Basic Service
Subscribers: 2,300.
Programming (received off-air): KCNC-TV (CBS) Denver; KDVR (FOX) Denver; KJCT (ABC, TMO) Grand Junction; KKCO (CW, NBC) Grand Junction; KREY-TV (CBS) Montrose; KRMA-TV (PBS) Denver; KTSC (PBS) Pueblo; KTVD (MNT) Denver; KWGN-TV (CW) Denver.
Programming (via satellite): C-SPAN; C-SPAN 2; Discovery Channel; Home Shopping Network; Lifetime; QVC; Spike TV; TBS Superstation; Telemundo.
Current originations: Government Access; Educational Access.
Fee: $43.59 installation; $19.99 monthly.

Expanded Basic Service 1
Subscribers: 2,000.
Programming (via satellite): ABC Family Channel; Altitude Sports & Entertainment; AMC; Animal Planet; Arts & Entertainment; Bravo; Cartoon Network; CNBC; CNN; Comedy Central; Country Music TV; Disney Channel; E! Entertainment Television; ESPN; ESPN 2; Eternal Word TV Network; Food Network; Fox News Channel; Fox Sports Net Rocky Mountain; FX; Hallmark Channel; Headline News; HGTV; History Channel; ION Television; MSNBC; MTV; Nickelodeon; Oxygen; Syfy; Telefutura; The Learning Channel; Travel Channel; truTV; Turner Classic Movies; Turner Network TV; TV Guide Network; TV Land; Univision; USA Network; VH1; Weather Channel.
Fee: $34.96 monthly.

Digital Basic Service
Subscribers: 300.
Programming (received off-air): KJCT (ABC, TMO) Grand Junction; KKCO (CW, NBC) Grand Junction; KREX-TV (CBS, MNT) Grand Junction.
Programming (via satellite): ABC Family HD; AmericanLife TV Network; Animal Planet HD; Arts & Entertainment HD; Bandamax; BBC America; Bio; Bloomberg Television; Bravo HD; BYU Television; CBS College Sports Network; Cine Latino; Cine Mexicano; CMT Pure Country; CNBC HD+; CNN en Espanol; CNN HD; Cooking Channel; De Pelicula; De Pelicula Clasico; Discovery Channel HD; Discovery en Espanol; Discovery HD Theater; Discovery Health Channel; Discovery Kids Channel; Discovery Military Channel; Discovery Planet Green; Disney Channel HD; DMX Music; Do-It-Yourself; ESPN 2 HD; ESPN Classic Sports; ESPN Deportes; ESPN HD; ESPNews; FitTV; Food Network HD; Fox College Sports Atlantic; Fox College Sports Central; Fox College Sports Pacific; Fox Movie Channel; Fox Reality Channel; Fox Soccer; Fox Sports en Espanol; FSN HD; Fuse; G4; Gol TV; Golf Channel; Gospel Music Channel; GSN; Halogen Network; HDNet; HDNet Movies; HGTV HD; History Channel en Espanol; History Channel HD; History Channel International; ID Investigation Discovery; Independent Film Channel; ION Life; ION Television; Jewelry Television; Lifetime Movie Network; Lifetime Movie Network HD; Mountain West TV; MTV Hits; MTV Jams; MTV Tres; MTV2; mun2 television; National Geographic Channel; National Geographic Channel HD Network; NFL Network; NFL Network HD; NHL Network; Nick Jr.; Nick Too; NickToons TV; Outdoor Channel; Outdoor Channel 2 HD; Palladia; PBS Kids Sprout; Qubo; RFD-TV; Science Channel; Science Channel HD; SoapNet; Speed Channel; Speed HD; Style Network; Syfy HD; TBS in HD; TeenNick; Telefutura; Telehit; The Sportsman Channel; TLC HD; Toon Disney; Trinity Broadcasting Network; Turner Network TV HD; Universal HD; Univision; USA Network HD; VeneMovies; Versus; Versus HD; VH1 Classic; VH1 Soul; Weather Channel HD.

Pay Service 1
Pay Units: 472.
Programming (via satellite): HBO.
Fee: $14.19 monthly.

Digital Pay Service 1
Pay Units: N.A.
Programming (via satellite): Cinemax (multiplexed); Cinemax HD; Cinemax On Demand; Encore (multiplexed); Flix; HBO (multiplexed); HBO HD; HBO On Demand; Showtime (multiplexed); Showtime HD; Showtime On Demand; Starz (multiplexed); Starz HDTV; Starz On Demand; The Movie Channel (multiplexed); The Movie Channel HD.
Fee: $15.15 monthly (HBO, Cinemax, Starz/Encore or Showtime/TMC/Flix).

Video-On-Demand: Yes

Pay-Per-View
iN DEMAND (delivered digitally); ESPN (delivered digitally); NBA League Pass (delivered digitally); MLS Direct Kick (delivered digitally); MLB Extra Innings (delivered digitally); NHL Center Ice (delivered digitally).

Internet Service
Operational: Yes.
Broadband Service: Bresnan OnLine.
Fee: $20.00 installation; $55.95 monthly.

Telephone Service
Digital: Operational
Fee: $49.99 monthly

Miles of Plant: 72.0 (coaxial); None (fiber optic). Homes passed: 4,000.
Regional Vice President: Sean Hogue. Chief Technician: Rich Lett.
City fee: 3% of gross.
Ownership: Bresnan Communications Inc. (MSO). Sale pends to Cablevision Systems Corp.

DENVER—Comcast Cable, 8000 E Iliff Ave, Denver, CO 80231. Phones: 303-603-2000; 800-266-2278. Fax: 303-603-2600. Web Site: http://www.comcast.com. Also serves Glendale. ICA: CO0002.
TV Market Ranking: 32 (DENVER, Glendale). Franchise award date: N.A. Franchise expiration date: N.A. Began: June 20, 1983.
Channel capacity: N.A. Channels available but not in use: N.A.

Basic Service
Subscribers: 536,870 Includes Denver (suburbs).
Programming (received off-air): KBDI-TV (PBS) Broomfield; KCEC (UNV) Denver; KCNC-TV (CBS) Denver; KDEN-TV (TMO) Longmont; KDVR (FOX) Denver; KMGH-TV (ABC) Denver; KPXC-TV (ION) Denver; KRMA-TV (PBS) Denver; KRMT (ETV) Denver; KRMZ (PBS) Steamboat Springs; KTFD-DT (UNV) Boulder; KTVD (MNT) Denver; KUSA (NBC) Denver; KWGN-TV (CW) Denver; KWHD (IND) Castle Rock.
Programming (via satellite): Bravo; Comcast SportsNet West; C-SPAN; C-SPAN 2; Discovery Channel; Hallmark Channel; Home Shopping Network; QVC; TBS Superstation; TV Guide Network; WGN America.
Current originations: Leased Access; Religious Access; Government Access; Educational Access; Public Access.
Fee: $44.99 installation; $14.49 monthly; $20.00 additional installation.

Expanded Basic Service 1
Subscribers: N.A.
Programming (via satellite): ABC Family Channel; AMC; Animal Planet; Arts & Entertainment; BET Networks; Cartoon Network; CNBC; CNN; Comedy Central; Country Music TV; Disney Channel; E! Entertainment Television; ESPN; ESPN 2; Food Network; Fox News Channel; Fox Sports Net Rocky Mountain; FX; GalaVision; Headline News; HGTV; History Channel; Lifetime; MoviePlex; MSNBC; MTV; Nickelodeon; Oxygen; Spike TV; Syfy; The Learning Channel; Toon Disney; Travel Channel; truTV; Turner Classic Movies; Turner Network TV; TV Land; USA Network; Versus; VH1; Weather Channel.
Fee: $48.99 monthly.

Digital Basic Service
Subscribers: 316,957 Includes Denver (suburbs).
Programming (via satellite): BBC America; Black Family Channel; Discovery Digital Networks; DMX Music; ESPN Classic Sports; ESPN Now; ESPNews; Fox Sports World; G4; Golf Channel; Great American Country; GSN; Independent Film Channel; Lifetime Movie Network; Music Choice; National Geographic Channel; Nick Jr.; ShopNBC; Style Network; The Word Network; Trinity Broadcasting Network; WE tv; Weatherscan.
Fee: $12.95 installation; $6.65 monthly; $3.25 converter.

Digital Expanded Basic Service
Subscribers: N.A.
Programming (via satellite): AmericanLife TV Network; Bio; Bloomberg Television; Encore; Fox College Sports Atlantic; Fox College Sports Central; Fox College Sports Pacific; Fox Movie Channel; Fuse; GAS; Halogen Network; History Channel International; Lime; MTV Networks Digital Suite; NickToons TV; Northwest Cable News; Outdoor Channel; Ovation; Sundance Channel.
Fee: $63.95 monthly.

Digital Pay Service 1
Pay Units: N.A.
Programming (via satellite): Cinemax (multiplexed); Flix; HBO (multiplexed); Showtime (multiplexed); Starz (multiplexed); The Movie Channel (multiplexed).
Fee: $18.99 monthly (each).

Video-On-Demand: Yes

Pay-Per-View
Addressable homes: 65,000.
iN DEMAND, Addressable: Yes; Fresh (delivered digitally); Sports PPV (delivered digitally); Barker (delivered digitally); Urban Xtra (delivered digitally); Shorteez (delivered digitally); Playboy TV (delivered digitally); Hot Choice (delivered digitally); iN DEMAND (delivered digitally).

Internet Service
Operational: Yes.
Subscribers: 325,585.
Broadband Service: Comcast High Speed Internet.
Fee: $42.95 monthly; $10.00 modem lease.

Telephone Service
Digital: Operational
Fee: $44.95 monthly

Miles of Plant: 9,755.0 (coaxial); None (fiber optic). Homes passed: 1,140,200. Homes passed includes Denver (suburbs)
Senior Vice President: Scott Binder. Vice President, Marketing & Sales: William Mosher. General Manager: Rich Jennings. Technical Operations Director: Dale Kirk. Network Operations Director: David Krook. Marketing Manager: Carolyn O'Hearn. Public Relations Director: Cindy Parsons.
City fee: 5% of gross; 2% of gross to local access.
Ownership: Comcast Cable Communications Inc. (MSO).

DENVER—Formerly served by Sprint Corp. No longer in operation. ICA: CO0195.

DENVER (suburbs)—Comcast Cable, 8000 E Iliff Ave, Denver, CO 80231. Phone: 303-603-2000. Fax: 303-603-2600. Web Site: http://www.comcast.com. Also serves Adams County, Arapahoe County, Arvada, Aurora, Bennett, Boulder, Boulder County (portions), Bow Mar, Brighton, Broomfield, Byers, Castle Rock, Cherry Hills Village, Clear Creek County, Columbine Valley, Commerce City, Deer Trail, Douglas County, Downieville, Dumont, Edgewater, Elbert County, Elizabeth, Empire, Englewood, Evergreen, Federal Heights, Foxfield, Franktown, Georgetown, Golden, Greenwood Village, Highlands Ranch, Idaho Springs, Idledale, Indian Hills, Jefferson County, Kiowa, Kittredge, Lakewood, Larkspur, Lawson, Littleton, Lochbuie, Lone Tree, Louviers, Morrison, Niwot, Northglenn, Parker, Sedalia, Sheridan, Silver Plume, Strasburg, Thornton, Welby, Westminster & Wheat Ridge. ICA: CO0001.
TV Market Ranking: 32 (Adams County, Arapahoe County, Arvada, Aurora, Bennett, Boulder, Boulder County (portions), Bow Mar, Brighton, Broomfield, Byers, Castle Rock, Cherry Hills Village, Clear Creek County (portions), Columbine Valley, Commerce City, Deer Trail, DENVER (SUBURBS), Douglas County, Edgewater, Elbert County, Elizabeth, Englewood, Evergreen, Federal Heights, Foxfield, Franktown, Golden, Greenwood Village,

Highlands Ranch, Highlands Ranch, Idaho Springs, Idledale, Indian Hills, Jefferson County, Kiowa, Kittredge, Lakewood, Larkspur, Littleton, Littleton, Lochbuie, Lone Tree, Louviers, Morrison, Niwot, Northglenn, Parker, Sedalia, Sheridan, Strasburg, Thornton, Welby, Westminster, Wheat Ridge); Below 100 (Downieville, Dumont, Empire, Georgetown, Lawson, Silver Plume); Outside TV Markets (Clear Creek County (portions)).

Channel capacity: N.A. Channels available but not in use: N.A.

Basic Service

Subscribers: N.A. Included in Denver

Programming (received off-air): KBDI-TV (PBS) Broomfield; KCEC (UNV) Denver; KCNC-TV (CBS) Denver; KDEN-TV (TMO) Longmont; KDVR (FOX) Denver; KMGH-TV (ABC) Denver; KRMA-TV (PBS) Denver; KRMT (ETV) Denver; KTFD-DT (UNV) Boulder; KTVD (MNT) Denver; KUSA (NBC) Denver; KWGN-TV (CW) Denver; KWHD (IND) Castle Rock.

Programming (via satellite): Azteca America; Bravo; CET - Comcast Entertainment TV; C-SPAN; Discovery Channel; FitTV; Hallmark Channel; Home Shopping Network; ION Television; QVC; TBS Superstation; WGN America.

Current originations: Leased Access; Government Access; Public Access.

Fee: $23.99 installation; $14.49 monthly.

Expanded Basic Service 1

Subscribers: N.A.

Programming (via satellite): ABC Family Channel; Altitude Sports & Entertainment; AMC; Animal Planet; Arts & Entertainment; BET Networks; Cartoon Network; CNBC; CNN; Comedy Central; Disney Channel; E! Entertainment Television; ESPN; ESPN 2; Food Network; Fox News Channel; Fox Sports Net Rocky Mountain; FX; GalaVision; Golf Channel; Headline News; HGTV; History Channel; Lifetime; MSNBC; MTV; Nickelodeon; Oxygen; Speed Channel; Spike TV; Syfy; The Learning Channel; Toon Disney; Travel Channel; truTV; Turner Classic Movies; Turner Network TV; TV Land; USA Network; Versus; VH1; Weather Channel.

Fee: $34.50 monthly.

Digital Basic Service

Subscribers: N.A. Included in Denver

Programming (received off-air): KCNC-TV (CBS) Denver; KDVR (FOX) Denver; KMGH-TV (ABC) Denver; KRMA-TV (PBS) Denver; KTVD (MNT) Denver; KUSA (NBC) Denver; KWGN-TV (CW) Denver.

Programming (via satellite): AmericanLife TV Network; BBC America; Bio; Black Family Channel; Bloomberg Television; Bravo; BYU Television; Canales N; CBS College Sports Network; Cooking Channel; Country Music TV; Current; Discovery Digital Networks; Discovery HD Theater; Do-It-Yourself; Encore (multiplexed); ESPN 2 HD; ESPN Classic Sports; ESPN HD; ESPNews; Eternal Word TV Network; Flix; Fox College Sports Atlantic; Fox College Sports Central; Fox College Sports Pacific; Fox Movie Channel; Fox Reality Channel; Fox Soccer; Fuse; G4; GAS; Great American Country; GSN; Halogen Network; History Channel International; Independent Film Channel; INHD; Lifetime Movie Network; Lime; LOGO; MoviePlex; MTV Networks Digital Suite; National Geographic Channel; NBA TV; NFL Network; Nick Jr.; Nick Too; NickToons TV; Outdoor Channel; Palladia; PBS Kids Sprout; ShopNBC; SoapNet; Style Network; Sundance Channel; the mtn; The Word Network; Trinity Broadcasting Network; Turner Network TV HD; TV One; Universal HD; Versus HD; WE tv; Weatherscan.

Fee: $14.95 monthly.

Digital Pay Service 1

Pay Units: N.A.

Programming (via satellite): Cinemax (multiplexed); Cinemax HD; Flix; HBO (multiplexed); HBO HD; Showtime (multiplexed); Showtime HD; Starz (multiplexed); Starz HDTV; The Movie Channel (multiplexed).

Fee: $18.99 monthly (each).

Pay-Per-View

iN DEMAND (delivered digitally); Sports PPV (delivered digitally); NBA League Pass (delivered digitally); NHL Center Ice (delivered digitally); MLB Extra Innings (delivered digitally); Playboy TV (delivered digitally); Hot Choice (delivered digitally).

Internet Service

Operational: Yes.

Broadband Service: Comcast High Speed Internet.

Fee: $42.95 monthly.

Telephone Service

Digital: Operational

Fee: $44.95 monthly

Homes passed included in Denver

Senior Vice President: Scott Binder. Vice President, Sales & Marketing: William Mosher. General Manager (northern portion): Rich Jennings. General Manager (southern portion): Dan Buchanan. Technical Operations Director: Dale Kirk. Network Operations Director: David Krook. Marketing Manager: Carolyn O'Hearn. Public Relations Director: Cindy Parsons.

Ownership: Comcast Cable Communications Inc. (MSO).

DOLORES—Bresnan Communications, 2502 Foresight Cir, Grand Junction, CO 81505. Phones: 877-273-7626; 970-263-2300. E-mail: shogue@bresnan.com. Web Site: http://www.bresnan.com. Also serves Mancos. ICA: CO0106.

TV Market Ranking: Below 100 (Mancos); Outside TV Markets (DOLORES). Franchise award date: N.A. Franchise expiration date: N.A. Began: January 1, 1983.

Channel capacity: N.A. Channels available but not in use: N.A.

Basic Service

Subscribers: 185.

Programming (received off-air): KASA-TV (FOX) Santa Fe; KLUZ-TV (UNV) Albuquerque; KOAT-TV (ABC) Albuquerque; KOBF (NBC) Farmington; KREZ-TV (CBS) Durango; KRMJ (PBS) Grand Junction; KRPV-DT (IND) Roswell.

Programming (via satellite): C-SPAN; C-SPAN 2; CW+; Discovery Channel; Fox News Channel; Home Shopping Network; KCNC-TV (CBS) Denver; KRMA-TV (PBS) Denver; KUSA (NBC) Denver; QVC; TBS Superstation.

Current originations: Government Access.

Fee: $20.00 installation; $19.99 monthly; $15.00 additional installation.

Expanded Basic Service 1

Subscribers: N.A.

Programming (via satellite): ABC Family Channel; Altitude Sports & Entertainment; AMC; Animal Planet; Arts & Entertainment; Cartoon Network; CNBC; CNN; Comedy Central; Country Music TV; Disney Channel; E! Entertainment Television; ESPN; ESPN 2; Food Network; Fox Sports Net Rocky Mountain; FX; Hallmark Channel; Headline News; HGTV; History Channel; INSP; ION Television; Lifetime; MSNBC; MTV; Nickelodeon; Oxygen; Spike TV; Syfy; The Learning Channel; Travel Channel; truTV; Turner Classic Movies; Turner Network TV; TV Guide Network; TV Land; USA Network; VH1; Weather Channel.

Fee: $34.96 monthly.

Digital Basic Service

Subscribers: N.A.

Programming (via satellite): AmericanLife TV Network; Animal Planet HD; Arts & Entertainment HD; Bandamax; BBC America; Bio; Bloomberg Television; Bravo; BYU Television; CBS College Sports Network; Cine Latino; Cine Mexicano; CMT Pure Country; CNN en Espanol; Cooking Channel; De Pelicula; De Pelicula Clasico; Discovery Channel HD; Discovery en Espanol; Discovery HD Theater; Discovery Health Channel; Discovery Kids Channel; Discovery Military Channel; Discovery Planet Green; DMX Music; Do-It-Yourself; ESPN 2 HD; ESPN Classic Sports; ESPN Deportes; ESPN HD; ESPNews; FitTV; Food Network HD; Fox College Sports Atlantic; Fox College Sports Central; Fox College Sports Pacific; Fox Movie Channel; Fox Reality Channel; Fox Soccer; Fox Sports en Espanol; FSN HD; Fuse; G4; Gol TV; Golf Channel; Gospel Music Channel; Great American Country; GSN; Halogen Network; HDNet; HDNet Movies; HGTV HD; History Channel en Espanol; History Channel HD; History Channel International; ID Investigation Discovery; Independent Film Channel; ION Life; ION Television; Jewelry Television; Lifetime Movie Network; Lifetime Movie Network HD; Mountain West TV; MTV Hits; MTV Jams; MTV Tres; MTV2; mun2 television; National Geographic Channel; National Geographic Channel HD Network; NFL Network; NFL Network HD; NHL Network; Nick Jr.; Nick Too; NickToons TV; Outdoor Channel; PBS Kids Sprout; Qubo; RFD-TV; Science Channel; Science Channel HD; SoapNet; Speed Channel; Style Network; Syfy HD; TBS in HD; TeenNick; Telehit; The Sportsman Channel; TLC HD; Toon Disney; Trinity Broadcasting Network; Turner Network TV HD; Universal HD; USA Network HD; VeneMovies; Versus; Versus HD; VH1 Classic; VH1 Soul.

Digital Pay Service 1

Pay Units: N.A.

Programming (via satellite): Cinemax (multiplexed); Cinemax On Demand; Encore (multiplexed); Flix; HBO (multiplexed); HBO HD; HBO On Demand; Showtime (multiplexed); Showtime HD; Showtime On Demand; Starz (multiplexed); Starz HDTV; Starz On Demand; The Movie Channel (multiplexed); The Movie Channel HD.

Video-On-Demand: No

Pay-Per-View

iN DEMAND (delivered digitally); ESPN (delivered digitally); NBA League Pass (delivered digitally); MLS Direct Kick (delivered digitally); MLB Extra Innings (delivered digitally); NHL Center Ice (delivered digitally).

Internet Service

Operational: Yes.

Fee: $35.00 installation; $55.00 monthly.

Telephone Service

Digital: Operational

Fee: $49.95 monthly

Miles of Plant: 19.0 (coaxial); None (fiber optic). Homes passed: 1,006.

Regional Vice President: Sean Hogue. Technical Operations Manager: Gary Young. Public Relations Specialist: Sean Howard.

City fee: 3% of basic gross.

Ownership: Bresnan Communications Inc. (MSO). Sale pends to Cablevision Systems Corp.

DOVE CREEK—Bresnan Communications, 2502 Foresight Cir, Grand Junction, CO 81505. Phones: 877-273-7626; 970-247-2681. E-mail: shogue@bresnan.com. Web Site: http://www.bresnan.com. ICA: CO0118.

TV Market Ranking: Outside TV Markets (DOVE CREEK). Franchise award date: June 20, 1988. Franchise expiration date: N.A. Began: September 1, 1989.

Channel capacity: N.A. Channels available but not in use: N.A.

Basic Service

Subscribers: 165.

Programming (received off-air): KCNC-TV (CBS) Denver; KDVR (FOX) Denver; KMGH-TV (ABC) Denver; KRMA-TV (PBS) Denver; KUSA (NBC) Denver; KWGN-TV (CW) Denver.

Programming (via satellite): ABC Family Channel; C-SPAN; Discovery Channel; Lifetime; QVC; TBS Superstation.

Current originations: Government Access.

Fee: $20.00 installation; $20.99 monthly; $15.00 additional installation.

Expanded Basic Service 1

Subscribers: N.A.

Programming (via satellite): Altitude Sports & Entertainment; Animal Planet; Arts & Entertainment; Cartoon Network; CNN; Comedy Central; Country Music TV; Disney Channel; ESPN; Food Network; Fox News Channel; Fox Sports Net Rocky Mountain; Headline News; HGTV; History Channel; Nickelodeon; Spike TV; The Learning Channel; Turner Network TV; USA Network; VH1; Weather Channel.

Fee: $24.00 monthly.

Pay Service 1

Pay Units: 12.

Programming (via satellite): HBO; Starz; The Movie Channel.

Fee: $11.65 monthly (TMC), $12.62 monthly (HBO).

Video-On-Demand: No

Internet Service

Operational: No.

Telephone Service

None

Miles of Plant: 9.0 (coaxial); None (fiber optic). Homes passed: 400.

Regional Vice President: Sean Hogue. Technical Operations Manager: Gary Young.

City fee: 3% of gross.

Ownership: Bresnan Communications Inc. (MSO). Sale pends to Cablevision Systems Corp.

DURANGO—Bresnan Communications, 2502 Foresight Cir, Grand Junction, CO 81505. Phone: 970-263-2300. E-mail: shogue@bresnan.com. Web Site: http://www.bresnan.com. Also serves Hermosa & La Plata County. ICA: CO0023.

TV Market Ranking: Below 100 (DURANGO, Hermosa, La Plata County). Franchise award date: N.A. Franchise expiration date: N.A. Began: December 1, 1954.

Channel capacity: N.A. Channels available but not in use: N.A.

Basic Service

Subscribers: 5,430.

Programming (received off-air): KASA-TV (FOX) Santa Fe; KOBF (NBC) Farmington; KREZ-TV (CBS) Durango; KRMJ (PBS) Grand Junction; KRPV-DT (IND) Roswell; 1 FM.

Programming (via microwave): KLUZ-TV (UNV) Albuquerque; KOAT-TV (ABC) Albuquerque.

Programming (via satellite): C-SPAN; C-SPAN 2; Discovery Channel; Home

Shopping Network; KCNC-TV (CBS) Denver; KRMA-TV (PBS) Denver; KUSA (NBC) Denver; KWGN-TV (CW) Denver; QVC; TBS Superstation; Telemundo.
Current originations: Government Access; Public Access.
Fee: $39.99 installation.

Expanded Basic Service 1
Subscribers: N.A.
Programming (via satellite): ABC Family Channel; AMC; Animal Planet; Arts & Entertainment; Cartoon Network; CNBC; CNN; Comedy Central; Country Music TV; Disney Channel; E! Entertainment Television; ESPN; ESPN 2; Food Network; Fox News Channel; Fox Sports Net Rocky Mountain; FX; Hallmark Channel; Headline News; HGTV; History Channel; INSP; ION Television; Lifetime; MSNBC; MTV; Nickelodeon; Oxygen; Spike TV; Syfy; The Learning Channel; Travel Channel; truTV; Turner Classic Movies; Turner Network TV; TV Guide Network; TV Land; USA Network; VH1; Weather Channel.
Fee: $56.99 monthly.

Digital Basic Service
Subscribers: N.A.
Programming (via satellite): AmericanLife TV Network; Animal Planet HD; Arts & Entertainment HD; Bandamax; BBC America; Bio; Bloomberg Television; Bravo; BYU Television; CBS College Sports Network; Cine Latino; Cine Mexicano; CMT Pure Country; CNN en Espanol; Cooking Channel; De Pelicula; De Pelicula Clasico; Discovery Channel HD; Discovery en Espanol; Discovery HD Theater; Discovery Health Channel; Discovery Kids Channel; Discovery Military Channel; Discovery Planet Green; DMX Music; Do-It-Yourself; ESPN 2 HD; ESPN Classic Sports; ESPN Deportes; ESPN HD; ESPNews; FitTV; Food Network HD; Fox College Sports Atlantic; Fox College Sports Central; Fox College Sports Pacific; Fox Movie Channel; Fox Reality Channel; Fox Soccer; Fox Sports en Espanol; FSN HD; Fuse; G4; Gol TV; Golf Channel; Gospel Music Channel; Great American Country; GSN; Halogen Network; HDNet; HDNet Movies; HGTV HD; History Channel en Espanol; History Channel HD; History Channel International; ID Investigation Discovery; Independent Film Channel; ION Life; ION Television; Jewelry Television; Lifetime Movie Network; Lifetime Movie Network HD; Mountain West TV; MTV Hits; MTV Jams; MTV Tres; MTV2; mun2 television; National Geographic Channel; National Geographic Channel HD Network; NFL Network; NFL Network HD; NHL Network; Nick Jr.; Nick Too; NickToons TV; Outdoor Channel; PBS Kids Sprout; Qubo; RFD-TV; Science Channel; Science Channel HD; SoapNet; Speed Channel; Style Network; Syfy HD; TBS in HD; TeenNick; Telehit; The Sportsman Channel; TLC HD; Toon Disney; Trinity Broadcasting Network; Turner Network TV HD; Universal HD; USA Network HD; VeneMovies; Versus; Versus HD; VH1 Classic; VH1 Soul.

Digital Pay Service 1
Pay Units: N.A.
Programming (via satellite): Cinemax (multiplexed); Cinemax On Demand; Encore (multiplexed); Flix; HBO (multiplexed); HBO HD; HBO On Demand; Showtime (multiplexed); Showtime HD; Showtime On Demand; Starz (multiplexed); Starz HDTV; Starz On Demand; The Movie Channel (multiplexed); The Movie Channel HD.
Video-On-Demand: Yes

Pay-Per-View
iN DEMAND (delivered digitally); ESPN (delivered digitally); NBA League Pass (delivered digitally); MLS Direct Kick (delivered digitally); MLB Extra Innings (delivered digitally); NHL Center Ice (delivered digitally).

Internet Service
Operational: Yes.
Broadband Service: Bresnan OnLine.
Fee: $39.95 monthly; $3.00 modem lease.

Telephone Service
Digital: Operational
Fee: $49.99 monthly
Miles of Plant: 57.0 (coaxial); None (fiber optic). Homes passed: 11,110.
Regional Vice President: Sean Hogue. Technical Operations Manager: Gary Young.
City fee: 2% of basic gross.
Ownership: Bresnan Communications Inc. (MSO). Sale pends to Cablevision Systems Corp.

DURANGO WEST—Bresnan Communications, 2502 Foresight Cir, Grand Junction, CO 81505. Phone: 970-263-2300. E-mail: shogue@bresnan.com. Web Site: http://www.bresnan.com. Also serves Pinetop-Durango West. ICA: CO0125.
TV Market Ranking: Below 100 (DURANGO WEST, Pinetop-Durango West). Franchise award date: N.A. Franchise expiration date: N.A. Began: January 1, 1983.
Channel capacity: 36 (not 2-way capable). Channels available but not in use: N.A.

Basic Service
Subscribers: 150.
Programming (received off-air): KASA-TV (FOX) Santa Fe; KOBF (NBC) Farmington; KREZ-TV (CBS) Durango.
Programming (via satellite): ABC Family Channel; Altitude Sports & Entertainment; Animal Planet; Arts & Entertainment; Cartoon Network; CNN; Comedy Central; C-SPAN; Discovery Channel; Disney Channel; ESPN; Food Network; Fox News Channel; Fox Sports Net Rocky Mountain; FX; Headline News; HGTV; History Channel; KCNC-TV (CBS) Denver; KMGH-TV (ABC) Denver; KRMA-TV (PBS) Denver; KUSA (NBC) Denver; KWGN-TV (CW) Denver; Lifetime; Nickelodeon; QVC; Spike TV; TBS Superstation; The Learning Channel; Turner Network TV; USA Network; VH1; Weather Channel.
Fee: $35.00 installation; $22.99 monthly; $15.00 additional installation.

Pay Service 1
Pay Units: 77.
Programming (via satellite): Cinemax; HBO; Starz.
Fee: $10.00 installation; $12.00 monthly (each).
Video-On-Demand: No

Internet Service
Operational: Yes.
Fee: $39.95 monthly.

Telephone Service
Digital: Operational
Fee: $49.99 monthly
Miles of Plant: 7.0 (coaxial); None (fiber optic). Homes passed: 586.
Regional Vice President: Sean Hogue. Technical Operations Manager: Gary Young.
City fee: 3% of gross.
Ownership: Bresnan Communications Inc. (MSO). Sale pends to Cablevision Systems Corp.

EADS—Champion Broadband, 380 Perry St, Ste 230, Castle Rock, CO 80104. Phones: 303-688-7766; 866-801-1122. Web Site: http://www.championbroadband.com. ICA: CO0114.
TV Market Ranking: Outside TV Markets (EADS). Franchise award date: N.A. Franchise expiration date: N.A. Began: October 8, 1982.
Channel capacity: 41 (operating 2-way). Channels available but not in use: 9.

Basic Service
Subscribers: 200.
Programming (received off-air): KCNC-TV (CBS) Denver; KKTV (CBS, MNT) Colorado Springs; KMGH-TV (ABC) Denver; KOAA-TV (NBC) Pueblo; KRDO-TV (ABC) Colorado Springs; KTSC (PBS) Pueblo; KUSA (NBC) Denver; KWGN-TV (CW) Denver; KXRM-TV (FOX) Colorado Springs.
Programming (via satellite): ABC Family Channel; Arts & Entertainment; Cartoon Network; CNN; Discovery Channel; Disney Channel; ESPN; Fox Sports Net Rocky Mountain; Great American Country; Headline News; INSP; Lifetime; Outdoor Channel; QVC; Syfy; TBS Superstation; Turner Network TV; USA Network; Weather Channel; WGN America.
Current originations: Public Access.
Fee: $30.00 installation; $20.45 monthly.

Pay Service 1
Pay Units: 54.
Programming (via satellite): HBO; Showtime; The Movie Channel.
Fee: $9.95 monthly (Showtime or TMC), $10.95 monthly (HBO).
Video-On-Demand: No

Internet Service
Operational: Yes.
Fee: $45.00 installation; $45.00 monthly.

Telephone Service
None
Miles of Plant: 7.0 (coaxial); None (fiber optic). Homes passed: 410.
General Manager: Mark Haverkate.
City fee: 1% of gross.
Ownership: Champion Broadband (MSO).

EAGLE—CenturyTel, 100 CenturyTel Dr, Monroe, LA 71203. Phones: 318-388-9000 (Corporate office); 970-328-6618. Fax: 970-328-1578. Web Site: http://www.centurytel.com. Also serves Gypsum. ICA: CO0096.
TV Market Ranking: Below 100 (EAGLE, Gypsum). Franchise award date: October 26, 1982. Franchise expiration date: N.A. Began: May 1, 1983.
Channel capacity: 35 (operating 2-way). Channels available but not in use: 7.

Basic Service
Subscribers: 1,929.
Programming (via satellite): ABC Family Channel; CNN; Country Music TV; ESPN; KCNC-TV (CBS) Denver; KDVR (FOX) Denver; KMGH-TV (ABC) Denver; KRMA-TV (PBS) Denver; KTVD (MNT) Denver; KUSA (NBC) Denver; KWGN-TV (CW) Denver; Lifetime; TBS Superstation.
Fee: $35.00 installation; $28.95 monthly.

Expanded Basic Service 1
Subscribers: 725.
Programming (via satellite): Animal Planet; Arts & Entertainment; CNBC; Discovery Channel; Discovery Health Channel; ESPN 2; Fox Sports Net Rocky Mountain; Great American Country; Headline News; Nickelodeon; QVC; Spike TV; Syfy; The Learning Channel; Travel Channel; truTV; Turner Network TV; USA Network; VH1; Weather Channel; WGN America.
Fee: $28.94 monthly.

Digital Basic Service
Subscribers: N.A.
Programming (via satellite): BBC America; Bio; Bloomberg Television; Discovery Digital Networks; DMX Music; ESPN Classic Sports; ESPNews; Fox Sports World; G4; GAS; Golf Channel; GSN; Halogen Network; History Channel; History Channel International; Lifetime Movie Network; Nick Jr.; NickToons TV; Speed Channel; Style Network; Toon Disney; Versus; WE tv.
Fee: $11.95 monthly.

Pay Service 1
Pay Units: 106.
Programming (via satellite): HBO.
Fee: $14.95 monthly.

Pay Service 2
Pay Units: N.A.
Programming (via satellite): Starz.
Fee: $10.95 monthly.

Pay Service 3
Pay Units: 12.
Programming (via satellite): Showtime.
Fee: $12.95 monthly.

Pay Service 4
Pay Units: 49.
Programming (via satellite): Cinemax.
Fee: $14.95 monthly.

Digital Pay Service 1
Pay Units: N.A.
Programming (via satellite): Cinemax (multiplexed); Encore (multiplexed); HBO (multiplexed); Showtime (multiplexed); Starz (multiplexed); The Movie Channel (multiplexed).
Fee: $10.95 monthly (Encore & Starz), $12.95 monthly (Showtime & TMC), $14.95 monthly (HBO or Cinemax).
Video-On-Demand: No

Pay-Per-View
iN DEMAND (delivered digitally), Fee: $3.95-$7.95.

Internet Service
Operational: Yes.
Broadband Service: In-house.
Fee: $35.00 installation; $29.95 monthly.

Telephone Service
Analog: Operational
Miles of Plant: 25.0 (coaxial); None (fiber optic).
Manager: Rob Jones. Chief Technician: Brian Fischer.
City fee: 5% of gross.
Ownership: CenturyLink (MSO).

EATON—US Cable, 266 Basher Dr, #4, Berthoud, CO 80513. Phones: 970-587-2243; 800-480-7020. Fax: 970-587-4208. E-mail: dkavanagh@uscable.com. Web Site: http://www.uscable.com. Also serves Ault, Laporte, Larimer County (portions), Nunn, Pierce, Poudre Valley Mobile Home Park & Wellington. ICA: CO0055.
TV Market Ranking: Below 100 (Ault, EATON, Laporte, Larimer County (portions), Nunn, Pierce, Poudre Valley Mobile Home Park, Wellington). Franchise award date: N.A. Franchise expiration date: N.A. Began: October 14, 1981.
Channel capacity: N.A. Channels available but not in use: N.A.

Basic Service
Subscribers: N.A. Included in Johnstown
Programming (received off-air): KBDI-TV (PBS) Broomfield; KCEC (UNV) Denver; KCNC-TV (CBS) Denver; KDEN-TV (TMO) Longmont; KDVR (FOX) Denver; KGWN-TV (CBS, CW) Cheyenne; KMGH-TV (ABC) Denver; KPXC-TV (ION) Denver; KRMA-TV (PBS) Denver; KTFD-DT (UNV) Boulder; KTVD (MNT) Denver; KUSA (NBC) Denver; KWGN-TV (CW) Denver.
Programming (via satellite): ABC Family Channel; Altitude Sports & Entertainment; AMC; Animal Planet; Arts & Entertainment; Cartoon Network; CNBC; CNN; Comedy Central; Country Music TV; C-SPAN;

Discovery Channel; Disney Channel; E! Entertainment Television; ESPN; ESPN 2; Food Network; Fox News Channel; Fox Sports Net Rocky Mountain; FX; GalaVision; Hallmark Channel; Headline News; HGTV; History Channel; Home Shopping Network; Lifetime; MTV; mun2 television; National Geographic Channel; Nickelodeon; Oxygen; QVC; ShopNBC; Speed Channel; Spike TV; Syfy; TBS Superstation; The Learning Channel; Travel Channel; truTV; Turner Network TV; TV Guide Network; TV Land; USA Network; Versus; VH1; Weather Channel; WGN America.

Current originations: Government Access; Leased Access; Public Access.

Fee: $20.00 installation; $43.95 monthly.

Digital Basic Service

Subscribers: N.A.

Programming (via satellite): Animal Planet HD; Arts & Entertainment HD; BBC America; Bloomberg Television; Bravo; Daystar TV Network; Discovery Channel HD; Discovery HD Theater; Discovery Health Channel; Discovery Kids Channel; DMX Music; Encore; ESPN 2; ESPN Classic Sports; ESPN HD; ESPNews; Food Network HD; Fox Soccer; Fuse; G4; Golf Channel; Gospel Music Channel; Great American Country; GSN; HDNet; HDNet Movies; HGTV; HGTV HD; History Channel; History Channel HD; Independent Film Channel; Lifetime Movie Network; MTV2; National Geographic Channel HD Network; Nick Jr.; Science Channel; ShopNBC; Sleuth; Style Network; Syfy HD; TeenNick; Toon Disney; Trinity Broadcasting Network; Turner Classic Movies; Universal HD; USA Network HD; Versus; VH1 Classic; WE tv; WealthTV HD.

Fee: $16.95 monthly.

Digital Expanded Basic Service

Subscribers: N.A.

Programming (via satellite): Bio; CMT Pure Country; Discovery Military Channel; Encore (multiplexed); FitTV; Fox Movie Channel; Halogen Network; History Channel International; ID Investigation Discovery; Ovation.

Fee: $2.95 monthly.

Digital Expanded Basic Service 2

Subscribers: N.A.

Programming (via satellite): Fox College Sports Atlantic; Fox College Sports Central; Fox College Sports Pacific; Fox Soccer; NFL Network; Outdoor Channel; Speed Channel.

Fee: $2.00 monthly.

Digital Pay Service 1

Pay Units: N.A.

Programming (via satellite): Cinemax (multiplexed); HBO (multiplexed); Showtime; Starz; The Movie Channel (multiplexed).

Fee: $11.95 monthly.

Video-On-Demand: No

Pay-Per-View

iN DEMAND (delivered digitally); Playboy TV (delivered digitally).

Internet Service

Operational: Yes.

Fee: $27.95 monthly.

Telephone Service

None

Miles of Plant: 25.0 (coaxial); None (fiber optic). Homes passed: 1,658.

General Manager: Dave Kavanaugh. Chief Technician: Josh Patchett. Marketing Manager: Jennifer Lideman. Office Manager: Debbie Hernandez. Construction Manager: Rich Fromstad.

City fee: 3% of gross.

Ownership: Comcast Cable Communications Inc. (MSO).; US Cable Corp. (MSO).

EL PASO COUNTY (eastern portions)—Falcon PTC. Formerly Falcon, CO [CO0213]. This cable system has converted to IPTV, 707 Hathaway Dr, Colorado Springs, CO 80915. Phone: 719-573-5343. Fax: 719-886-7925. E-mail: sales@falconbroadband.net. Web Site: http://www.falconbroadband.net. ICA: CO5007.

Channel capacity: N.A. Channels available but not in use: N.A.

Internet Service

Operational: Yes.

Ownership: Falcon Broadband.

EMPIRE—Comcast Cable. Now served by DENVER (suburbs), CO [CO0001]. ICA: CO0080.

ESTES PARK—Baja Broadband, 14120 Ballanytyne Corp. Pl, Ste 500, Charlotte, NC 28277. Phones: 970-565-4031 (Cortez office); 980-235-7600 (Corporate office). E-mail: info@bajabroadband.com. Web Site: http://www.bajabroadband.com. Also serves Larimer County. ICA: CO0038.

TV Market Ranking: Below 100 (ESTES PARK, Larimer County). Franchise award date: N.A. Franchise expiration date: N.A. Began: June 1, 1953.

Channel capacity: 78 (operating 2-way). Channels available but not in use: None.

Basic Service

Subscribers: 3,688.

Programming (received off-air): KCNC-TV (CBS) Denver; KDVR (FOX) Denver; KMGH-TV (ABC) Denver; KRMA-TV (PBS) Denver; KTVD (MNT) Denver; KUSA (NBC) Denver; KWGN-TV (CW) Denver; 18 FMs.

Programming (via satellite): C-SPAN; C-SPAN 2; Home Shopping Network; QVC; Univision; Weather Channel; WGN America.

Current originations: Leased Access.

Fee: $49.95 installation; $48.30 monthly.

Expanded Basic Service 1

Subscribers: N.A.

Programming (via satellite): ABC Family Channel; Altitude Sports & Entertainment; AMC; Animal Planet; Arts & Entertainment; Bravo; Cartoon Network; CNBC; CNN; Comedy Central; Country Music TV; Discovery Channel; Disney Channel; Disney XD; E! Entertainment Television; ESPN; ESPN 2; FitTV; Food Network; Fox News Channel; Fox Sports Net Rocky Mountain; FX; G4; Golf Channel; GSN; Hallmark Channel; Headline News; HGTV; History Channel; Lifetime; MSNBC; MTV; National Geographic Channel; Nickelodeon; SoapNet; Speed Channel; Spike TV; Syfy; TBS Superstation; The Learning Channel; Travel Channel; truTV; Turner Classic Movies; Turner Network TV; TV Land; USA Network; Versus; VH1.

Digital Basic Service

Subscribers: 947.

Programming (via satellite): BBC America; Bloomberg Television; CMT Pure Country; Discovery en Espanol; Discovery Health Channel; Discovery Kids Channel; Discovery Military Channel; Discovery Planet Green; ESPN Classic Sports; ID Investigation Discovery; MTV Hits; MTV Jams; MTV Tres; MTV2; Music Choice; Nick Jr.; Nick Too; NickToons TV; Science Channel; Style Network; TeenNick; VH1 Classic; VH1 Soul; WE tv.

Fee: $8.95 monthly.

Digital Expanded Basic Service

Subscribers: N.A.

Programming (via satellite): LOGO.

Digital Expanded Basic Service 2

Subscribers: N.A.

Programming (via satellite): ESPN HD; Golf Channel HD; Turner Network TV HD; Versus HD.

Digital Expanded Basic Service 3

Subscribers: N.A.

Programming (via satellite): HDNet; HDNet Movies; Universal HD.

Digital Pay Service 1

Pay Units: N.A.

Programming (via satellite): Cinemax (multiplexed); Encore (multiplexed); Flix; HBO (multiplexed); Showtime (multiplexed); Showtime HD; Starz (multiplexed); Starz HDTV; The Movie Channel (multiplexed); The Movie Channel HD.

Video-On-Demand: No

Pay-Per-View

iN DEMAND (delivered digitally); Hot Choice (delivered digitally).

Internet Service

Operational: Yes. Began: September 1, 2000.

Subscribers: 847.

Broadband Service: In-house.

Fee: $49.99 installation; $52.99 monthly; $4.95 modem lease; $69.95 modem purchase.

Telephone Service

None

Miles of Plant: 162.0 (coaxial); None (fiber optic). Homes passed: 5,447.

Chief Executive Officer: William A. Schuler. Area Vice President & General Manager: Tom Jaskiewicz. Chief Operating Officer: Phillip Klein. Technical Operations Director: Matt Warford.

City fee: 3% of gross.

Ownership: Baja Broadband (MSO).

FAIRPLAY—Formerly served by Cebridge Connections. No longer in operation. ICA: CO0124.

FALCON—Falcon PTC. This cable system has converted to IPTV. See El Paso County (eastern portions), CO [CO5007]. ICA: CO0213.

FLAGLER—Champion Broadband, 380 Perry St, Ste 230, Castle Rock, CO 80104. Phones: 303-688-7766; 866-801-1122. Web Site: http://www.championbroadband.com. ICA: CO0133.

TV Market Ranking: Outside TV Markets (FLAGLER). Franchise award date: October 15, 1982. Franchise expiration date: N.A. Began: November 15, 1982.

Channel capacity: 36 (operating 2-way). Channels available but not in use: N.A.

Basic Service

Subscribers: 36.

Programming (received off-air): KCNC-TV (CBS) Denver; KDVR (FOX) Denver; KMGH-TV (ABC) Denver; KUSA (NBC) Denver; KWGN-TV (CW) Denver.

Programming (via satellite): ABC Family Channel; Arts & Entertainment; CNBC; CNN; Discovery Channel; Disney Channel; ESPN; ESPN 2; Fox Sports Net Rocky Mountain; Great American Country; Headline News; Lifetime; Outdoor Channel; QVC; TBS Superstation; The Learning Channel; Toon Disney; Turner Classic Movies; Turner Network TV; USA Network; Weather Channel; WGN America.

Fee: $30.00 installation; $37.45 monthly.

Pay Service 1

Pay Units: 27.

Programming (via satellite): HBO; The Movie Channel.

Fee: $9.95 monthly (TMC),$10.95 monthly (HBO).

Video-On-Demand: No

Internet Service

Operational: Yes.

Fee: $45.00 installation; $45.00 monthly.

Telephone Service

None

Miles of Plant: 6.0 (coaxial); None (fiber optic). Homes passed: 259.

General Manager: Mark Haverkate.

Ownership: Champion Broadband (MSO).

FLEMING—PC Telcom, 120 N Sunflower Dr, Holyoke, CO 80734. Phones: 866-854-2111; 970-854-2201. Fax: 970-854-2668. E-mail: customerservice@pctelcom.coop. Web Site: http://my.pctelcom.coop. ICA: CO0167.

TV Market Ranking: Below 100 (FLEMING). Franchise award date: August 29, 1988. Franchise expiration date: N.A. Began: August 1, 1989.

Channel capacity: 36 (not 2-way capable). Channels available but not in use: N.A.

Basic Service

Subscribers: N.A. Included in Holyoke

Programming (received off-air): KCDO-TV (IND) Sterling; KCNC-TV (CBS) Denver; KDVR (FOX) Denver; KMGH-TV (ABC) Denver; KPNE-TV (PBS) North Platte; KUSA (NBC) Denver; KWGN-TV (CW) Denver.

Programming (via satellite): ABC Family Channel; AMC; Arts & Entertainment; CNN; Discovery Channel; E! Entertainment Television; ESPN; ESPN 2; Fox Sports Net Rocky Mountain; Great American Country; Headline News; HGTV; History Channel; Lifetime; Nickelodeon; Spike TV; TBS Superstation; The Learning Channel; Turner Network TV; TV Land; USA Network; Weather Channel; WGN America.

Fee: $33.99 monthly.

Pay Service 1

Pay Units: N.A.

Programming (via satellite): HBO.

Fee: $12.45 monthly.

Video-On-Demand: No

Internet Service

Operational: No.

Telephone Service

None

Miles of Plant: 5.0 (coaxial); None (fiber optic). Total homes in franchised area: 110.

General Manager: Vincent Kropp. Operations Director: Pete Markle. Chief Technician: J.C. Peckham. Marketing & Public Relations Manager: Sharon Crist.

Ownership: PC Telcorp (MSO).

FORT CARSON—Baja Broadband, PO Box 13261, 1519 McDonald St, Bldg 1519, Fort Carson, CO 80913-0261. Phone: 719-576-7404. Fax: 719-579-8231. Web Site: http://www.bajabroadband.com. ICA: CO0026.

TV Market Ranking: Below 100 (FORT CARSON). Franchise award date: May 4, 1989. Franchise expiration date: N.A. Began: November 15, 1979.

Channel capacity: 135 (operating 2-way). Channels available but not in use: 60.

Basic Service

Subscribers: 2,019.

Programming (received off-air): KKTV (CBS, MNT) Colorado Springs; KMAS-LP Denver; KOAA-TV (NBC) Pueblo; KRDO-TV (ABC) Colorado Springs; KTSC (PBS) Pueblo; KWGN-TV (CW) Denver; KXRM-TV (FOX) Colorado Springs; KXTU-LP (CW) Colorado Springs.

Programming (via satellite): C-SPAN; Home Shopping Network; INSP; Product Infor-

mation Network; QVC; Trinity Broadcasting Network; WGN America.
Current originations: Government Access; Educational Access.
Fee: $49.95 installation; $18.99 monthly.

Expanded Basic Service 1
Subscribers: 2,000.
Programming (via satellite): ABC Family Channel; AMC; Animal Planet; Arts & Entertainment; BET Networks; Bravo; Cartoon Network; CNBC; CNN; Comedy Central; Country Music TV; Discovery Channel; Disney Channel; E! Entertainment Television; ESPN; ESPN 2; Food Network; Fox News Channel; Fox Sports Net Rocky Mountain; FX; G4; Golf Channel; Great American Country; GSN; Hallmark Channel; Headline News; HGTV; History Channel; Lifetime; Lifetime Movie Network; MSNBC; MTV; National Geographic Channel; Nickelodeon; SoapNet; Speed Channel; Spike TV; Style Network; Syfy; TBS Superstation; The Learning Channel; Travel Channel; truTV; Turner Classic Movies; Turner Network TV; TV Land; Univision; USA Network; VH1; WE tv; Weather Channel.
Fee: $30.00 monthly.

Digital Basic Service
Subscribers: N.A.
Programming (via satellite): BBC America; Bio; Bloomberg Television; CMT Pure Country; Discovery en Espanol; Discovery Health Channel; Discovery Kids Channel; Discovery Military Channel; Discovery Planet Green; Disney XD; Do-It-Yourself; ESPN Classic Sports; FitTV; Fox Business Channel; Fox College Sports Atlantic; Fox College Sports Central; Fox College Sports Pacific; Fox Movie Channel; Fox Reality Channel; Fox Soccer; Fuel TV; History Channel International; ID Investigation Discovery; Independent Film Channel; Lifetime Real Women; MTV Hits; MTV Jams; MTV Tres; MTV2; Music Choice; Nick Jr.; Nick Too; NickToons TV; Science Channel; Sundance Channel; TeenNick; the mtn; VH1 Classic; VH1 Soul.
Fee: $8.95 monthly.

Digital Expanded Basic Service
Subscribers: N.A.
Programming (received off-air): KKTV (CBS, MNT) Colorado Springs; KRDO-TV (ABC) Colorado Springs; KTSC (PBS) Pueblo; KWGN-TV (CW) Denver; KXRM-TV (FOX) Colorado Springs.
Programming (via satellite): Arts & Entertainment HD; ESPN HD; Food Network HD; FX HD; HGTV HD; History Channel HD; National Geographic Channel HD Network; Speed HD; TBS in HD; Turner Network TV HD.

Digital Expanded Basic Service 2
Subscribers: N.A.
Programming (via satellite): HDNet; HDNet Movies; Universal HD.

Digital Pay Service 1
Pay Units: N.A.
Programming (via satellite): Cinemax (multiplexed); Cinemax HD; Encore; Flix; HBO (multiplexed); HBO HD; Showtime (multiplexed); Showtime HD; Starz (multiplexed); Starz HDTV; The Movie Channel (multiplexed); The Movie Channel HD.

Video-On-Demand: No

Pay-Per-View
iN DEMAND (delivered digitally); Ten On Demand (delivered digitally); Hot Choice (delivered digitally); Ten Clips (delivered digitally).

Internet Service
Operational: Yes. Began: November 1, 2002.
Broadband Service: In-house.
Fee: $9.99 installation; $55.99 monthly; $4.96 modem lease; $69.95 modem purchase.

Telephone Service
None

Miles of Plant: 32.0 (coaxial); None (fiber optic). Homes passed: 5,097. Total homes in franchised area: 5,097.
Area Vice President & General Manager: Tom Jaskiewicz. Technical Operations Director: Matt Warford.
City fee: 4% of basic.
Ownership: Baja Broadband (MSO).

FORT COLLINS—Comcast Cable, 1201 University Ave, Fort Collins, CO 80521. Phones: 303-776-2108 (Longmont office); 970-419-3113. Fax: 970-493-4958. Web Site: http://www.comcast.com. Also serves Larimer County (portions). ICA: CO0008.
TV Market Ranking: Below 100 (FORT COLLINS, Larimer County (portions)). Franchise award date: November 1, 1978. Franchise expiration date: N.A. Began: October 15, 1979.
Channel capacity: 78 (operating 2-way). Channels available but not in use: None.

Basic Service
Subscribers: N.A. Included in Longmont
Programming (received off-air): KBDI-TV (PBS) Broomfield; KCEC (UNV) Denver; KCNC-TV (CBS) Denver; KDVR (FOX) Denver; KMGH-TV (ABC) Denver; KPXC-TV (ION) Denver; KRMA-TV (PBS) Denver; KRMZ (PBS) Steamboat Springs; KTVD (MNT) Denver; KUSA (NBC) Denver; KWGN-TV (CW) Denver; 19 FMs.
Programming (via satellite): C-SPAN; C-SPAN 2; TV Guide Network; WGN America.
Current originations: Leased Access; Government Access; Educational Access; Public Access.
Fee: $23.99 installation; $14.99 monthly.

Expanded Basic Service 1
Subscribers: N.A.
Programming (received off-air): KDEN-TV (TMO) Longmont.
Programming (via satellite): ABC Family Channel; Altitude Sports & Entertainment; AMC; Animal Planet; Arts & Entertainment; BET Networks; Cartoon Network; CNBC; CNN; Comedy Central; Country Music TV; Discovery Channel; Disney Channel; E! Entertainment Television; ESPN; ESPN 2; Food Network; Fox News Channel; Fox Sports Net Rocky Mountain; FX; Golf Channel; Hallmark Channel; Headline News; HGTV; History Channel; Home Shopping Network; Lifetime; MoviePlex; MSNBC; MTV; Nickelodeon; Oxygen; Spike TV; TBS Superstation; The Learning Channel; Travel Channel; truTV; Turner Network TV; TV Land; USA Network; Versus; VH1; Weather Channel.
Fee: $33.50 monthly.

Digital Basic Service
Subscribers: N.A. Included in Longmont
Programming (received off-air): KCNC-TV (CBS) Denver; KDVR (FOX) Denver; KMGH-TV (ABC) Denver; KRMA-TV (PBS) Denver; KTVD (MNT) Denver; KUSA (NBC) Denver; KWGN-TV (CW) Denver.
Programming (via satellite): BBC America; Bio; Black Family Channel; Bloomberg Television; Bravo; BYU Television; Canal 52MX; Canales N; CBS College Sports Network; CET - Comcast Entertainment TV; Cooking Channel; Country Music TV; Current; Discovery Digital Networks; Discovery HD Theater; Do-It-Yourself; Encore (multiplexed); ESPN 2 HD; ESPN Classic Sports; ESPN HD; ESPNews; Eternal Word TV Network; Flix; Fox College Sports Atlantic; Fox College Sports Central; Fox College Sports Pacific; Fox Movie Channel; Fox Reality Channel; Fox Soccer; Fuse; G4; GAS; Great American Country; GSN; Halogen Network; History Channel International; Independent Film Channel; INHD; Lifetime Movie Network; Lime; LOGO; MTV Networks Digital Suite; Music Choice; National Geographic Channel; NBA TV; NFL Network; Nick Jr.; NickToons TV; Outdoor Channel; Palladia; PBS Kids Sprout; ShopNBC; Si TV; SoapNet; Speed Channel; Style Network; Sundance Channel; Syfy; the mtn; The Word Network; Toon Disney; Trinity Broadcasting Network; Turner Classic Movies; Turner Network TV HD; Universal HD; Versus HD; WE tv.
Fee: $11.95 monthly.

For more information call **800-771-9202** or visit **www.warren-news.com**

Digital Pay Service 1
Pay Units: N.A.
Programming (via satellite): Cinemax (multiplexed); Cinemax HD; Flix; HBO (multiplexed); HBO HD; Showtime (multiplexed); Showtime HD; Starz (multiplexed); Starz HDTV; The Movie Channel (multiplexed).
Fee: $15.99 monthly (each).

Video-On-Demand: No

Pay-Per-View
Addressable homes: 9,859.
iN DEMAND (delivered digitally), Addressable: Yes; ESPN Gameplan (delivered digitally); NBA League Pass (delivered digitally); NHL Center Ice (delivered digitally); MLB Extra Innings (delivered digitally); Playboy TV (delivered digitally).

Internet Service
Operational: Yes.
Broadband Service: Comcast High Speed Internet.
Fee: $42.95 monthly; $10.00 modem lease.

Telephone Service
None

Miles of Plant: 615.0 (coaxial); 62.0 (fiber optic). Homes passed included in Longmont
Vice President & General Manager: Mike Trueblood. Technical Operations Manager: Stan Reifschneider.
City fee: 3% of gross.
Ownership: Comcast Cable Communications Inc. (MSO).

FORT COLLINS—Formerly served by Sprint Corp. No longer in operation. ICA: CO0197.

FORT LUPTON—Comcast Cable. Now served by LONGMONT, CO [CO0011]. ICA: CO0056.

FORT MORGAN—Bresnan Communications, 506 W 17th St, Cheyenne, WY 82001. Phone: 877-273-7626. Web Site: http://www.bresnan.com. Also serves Brush, Log Lane Village & Morgan County. ICA: CO0029.
TV Market Ranking: Below 100 (Brush, Morgan County (portions)); Outside TV Markets (FORT MORGAN, Log Lane Village, Morgan County (portions)). Franchise award date: N.A. Franchise expiration date: N.A. Began: September 1, 1970.
Channel capacity: N.A. Channels available but not in use: N.A.

Basic Service
Subscribers: 3,500.
Programming (received off-air): KCNC-TV (CBS) Denver; KDVR (FOX) Denver; KMGH-TV (ABC) Denver; KRMA-TV (PBS) Denver; KTVD (MNT) Denver; KUSA (NBC) Denver; KWGN-TV (CW) Denver.
Programming (via satellite): C-SPAN; C-SPAN 2; Discovery Channel; Home Shopping Network; Lifetime; QVC; TBS Superstation; Univision.
Current originations: Educational Access.
Fee: $44.95 installation; $13.08 monthly.

Expanded Basic Service 1
Subscribers: 3,250.
Programming (via satellite): ABC Family Channel; Altitude Sports & Entertainment; AMC; Animal Planet; Arts & Entertainment; Cartoon Network; CNBC; CNN; Comedy Central; Country Music TV; C-SPAN; Disney Channel; E! Entertainment Television; ESPN; ESPN 2; Eternal Word TV Network; Food Network; Fox News Channel; Fox Sports Net Rocky Mountain; FX; GalaVision; Hallmark Channel; Headline News; HGTV; History Channel; ION Television; MSNBC; MTV; Nickelodeon; Spike TV; Syfy; Telefutura; Telemundo; The Learning Channel; Travel Channel; truTV; Turner Classic Movies; Turner Network TV; TV Guide Network; TV Land; USA Network; VH1; Weather Channel.
Fee: $44.90 monthly.

Digital Basic Service
Subscribers: N.A.
Programming (via satellite): ABC Family HD; AmericanLife TV Network; Animal Planet HD; Arts & Entertainment HD; Azteca America; Bandamax; BBC America; Bio; Bloomberg Television; Bravo; CB Television Michoacan; CBS College Sports Network; Cine Latino; Cine Mexicano; CMT Pure Country; CNBC HD+; CNN en Espanol; CNN HD; Cooking Channel; De Pelicula; De Pelicula Clasico; Discovery Channel HD; Discovery en Espanol; Discovery HD Theater; Discovery Health Channel; Discovery Kids Channel; Discovery Military Channel; Discovery Planet Green; Disney Channel HD; DMX Music; Do-It-Yourself; ESPN 2 HD; ESPN Classic Sports; ESPN Deportes; ESPN HD; ESPNews; EWTN en Espanol; FitTV; Food Network HD; Fox College Sports Atlantic; Fox College Sports Central; Fox College Sports Pacific; Fox Movie Channel; Fox Reality Channel; Fox Soccer; Fox Sports en Espanol; FSN HD; Fuse; G4; GalaVision; Gol TV; Golf Channel; Gospel Music Channel; GSN; Halogen Network; HDNet; HDNet Movies; HGTV HD; History Channel en Espanol; History Channel HD; History Channel International; ID Investigation Discovery; Independent Film Channel; ION Television; Lifetime Movie Network; Lifetime Movie Network HD; Mountain West TV; MTV Hits; MTV Jams; MTV Tres; MTV2; mun2 television; National Geo-

graphic Channel; National Geographic Channel HD Network; NFL Network; NFL Network HD; Nick Jr.; Nick Too; NickToons TV; Once Mexico; Outdoor Channel; PBS Kids Sprout; RFD-TV; Science Channel; Science Channel HD; SoapNet; Speed Channel; Style Network; Syfy HD; TBS in HD; TeenNick; Telefutura; Telehit; The Sportsman Channel; TLC HD; Toon Disney; Trinity Broadcasting Network; Turner Network TV HD; Universal HD; Univision; USA Network HD; VeneMovies; Versus; Versus HD; VH1 Classic; VH1 Soul; Weather Channel HD.

Pay Service 1
Pay Units: 198.
Programming (via satellite): Encore; HBO; Starz.
Fee: $1.75 monthly (Encore), $13.56 monthly (HBO).

Digital Pay Service 1
Pay Units: N.A.
Programming (via satellite): Cinemax (multiplexed); Cinemax HD; Encore (multiplexed); HBO (multiplexed); HBO HD; Showtime (multiplexed); Showtime HD; Starz (multiplexed); Starz HDTV; The Movie Channel (multiplexed); The Movie Channel HD.

Video-On-Demand: No

Pay-Per-View
Sports PPV (delivered digitally); ESPN Now (delivered digitally); iN DEMAND (delivered digitally).

Internet Service
Operational: Yes.
Broadband Service: Bresnan OnLine.
Fee: $39.95 monthly.

Telephone Service
Digital: Operational
Fee: $49.99 monthly

Miles of Plant: 100.0 (coaxial); 21.0 (fiber optic). Homes passed: 7,782.
Regional Vice President: Clint Rodeman. General Manager: Wes Frost. Technical Operations Manager: Mitch Winter.
City fee: 5% of gross.
Ownership: Bresnan Communications Inc. (MSO). Sale pends to Cablevision Systems Corp.

FOWLER—Bresnan Communications. Now served by LA JUNTA, CO [CO0040]. ICA: CO0091.

FREDERICK—Comcast Cable. Now served by LONGMONT, CO [CO0011]. ICA: CO0050.

GENESEE—Formerly served by Comcast Cable. No longer in operation. ICA: CO0169.

GILCREST—US Cable, 266 Basher Dr, #4, Berthoud, CO 80513. Phones: 800-480-7020; 970-587-2243. Fax: 970-587-4208. Web Site: http://www.uscable.com. Also serves Platteville. ICA: CO0170.
TV Market Ranking: 32 (Platteville); Below 100 (GILCREST). Franchise award date: N.A. Franchise expiration date: N.A. Began: N.A.
Channel capacity: 49 (not 2-way capable). Channels available but not in use: N.A.

Basic Service
Subscribers: N.A. Included in Johnstown
Programming (received off-air): KBDI-TV (PBS) Broomfield; KCEC (UNV) Denver; KCNC-TV (CBS) Denver; KDEN-TV (TMO) Longmont; KDVR (FOX) Denver; KMGH-TV (ABC) Denver; KPXC-TV (ION) Denver; KRMA-TV (PBS) Denver; KRMT (ETV) Denver; KTVD (MNT) Denver; KUSA (NBC) Denver; KWGN-TV (CW) Denver.
Programming (via satellite): ABC Family Channel; AMC; Animal Planet; Arts & Entertainment; Cartoon Network; CNN; Country Music TV; Discovery Channel; Disney Channel; ESPN; ESPN 2; Fox Sports Net Rocky Mountain; GalaVision; HGTV; History Channel; Lifetime; MTV; Nickelodeon; QVC; Spike TV; Syfy; TBS Superstation; The Learning Channel; Travel Channel; Turner Classic Movies; Turner Network TV; USA Network; Weather Channel; WGN America.
Current originations: Leased Access.
Fee: $49.95 installation; $30.00 monthly.

Digital Basic Service
Subscribers: N.A.
Programming (via satellite): BBC America; Bio; Bloomberg Television; Discovery Health Channel; Discovery Home Channel; Discovery Kids Channel; Discovery Times Channel; FitTV; Fuse; G4; GSN; HGTV; History Channel; History Channel International; INSP; Lime; Military History Channel; MTV2; Nick Jr.; Science Television; Sleuth; Style Network; Syfy; Toon Disney; Trinity Broadcasting Network.
Fee: $17.90 monthly.

Digital Expanded Basic Service
Subscribers: N.A.
Programming (via satellite): Bravo; Encore; Encore Action; Encore Drama; Encore Love; Encore Mystery; Encore Wam; Encore Westerns; Fox Movie Channel; Independent Film Channel; Lifetime Movie Network; Turner Classic Movies; WE tv.

Digital Expanded Basic Service 2
Subscribers: N.A.
Programming (via satellite): ESPN 2; ESPN Classic Sports; ESPNews; Fox Soccer; GAS; Golf Channel; Outdoor Channel; Speed Channel; Versus.

Pay Service 1
Pay Units: N.A.
Programming (via satellite): Cinemax; HBO.
Fee: $20.00 installation; $9.95 monthly (each).

Digital Pay Service 1
Pay Units: N.A.
Programming (via satellite): Cinemax (multiplexed); HBO (multiplexed); Showtime (multiplexed); Starz (multiplexed); The Movie Channel.

Video-On-Demand: No

Internet Service
Operational: Yes.

Telephone Service
None

General Manager: Dave Kavanagh. Chief Technician: Josh Patchett. Office Manager: Debbie Hernandez. Marketing Manager: Jennifer Lideman. Construction Manager: Rich Fromstad.
City fee: 3% of gross.
Ownership: US Cable Corp. (MSO).; Comcast Cable Communications Inc. (MSO).

GILPIN COUNTY—Champion Broadband, 380 Perry St, Ste 230, Castle Rock, CO 80104. Phones: 303-688-7766; 866-801-1122. Web Site: http://www.championbroadband.com. Also serves Boulder County (portions), Coal Creek Canyon & Jefferson County. ICA: CO0060.
TV Market Ranking: 32 (Boulder County (portions), COAL CREEK CANYON (portions), Gilpin County (portions), Jefferson County); Below 100 (Boulder County (portions), COAL CREEK CANYON (portions), Gilpin County (portions)). Franchise award date: January 1, 1988. Franchise expiration date: N.A. Began: March 1, 1989.
Channel capacity: 41 (operating 2-way). Channels available but not in use: None.

Basic Service
Subscribers: 179.
Programming (received off-air): KCNC-TV (CBS) Denver; KDVR (FOX) Denver; KMGH-TV (ABC) Denver; KRMA-TV (PBS) Denver; KTVD (MNT) Denver; KUSA (NBC) Denver; KWGN-TV (CW) Denver; KWHD (IND) Castle Rock.
Programming (via satellite): ABC Family Channel; AMC; Arts & Entertainment; Cartoon Network; CNBC; CNN; C-SPAN; Discovery Channel; Disney Channel; ESPN; ESPN 2; Fox News Channel; Fox Sports Net Rocky Mountain; Fuse; FX; Great American Country; Headline News; HGTV; History Channel; INSP; Lifetime; MSNBC; Outdoor Channel; Syfy; TBS Superstation; The Learning Channel; Travel Channel; Turner Network TV; USA Network; Weather Channel; WGN America.
Fee: $45.00 installation; $35.45 monthly.

Pay Service 1
Pay Units: N.A.
Programming (via satellite): Encore; HBO.
Fee: $9.95 monthly (HBO).

Video-On-Demand: No

Internet Service
Operational: No.

Telephone Service
None

Miles of Plant: 62.0 (coaxial); None (fiber optic). Homes passed: 1,500. Total homes in franchised area: 2,000.
General Manager: Mark Haverkate.
Ownership: Champion Broadband (MSO).

GLENWOOD SPRINGS—Comcast Cable. Now served by ASPEN, CO [CO0017]. ICA: CO0025.

GRANADA—Champion Broadband, 380 Perry St, Ste 230, Castle Rock, CO 80104. Phones: 303-688-7766; 866-801-1122. Web Site: http://www.championbroadband.com. ICA: CO0144.
TV Market Ranking: Outside TV Markets (GRANADA). Franchise award date: N.A. Franchise expiration date: N.A. Began: N.A.
Channel capacity: 36 (operating 2-way). Channels available but not in use: 8.

Basic Service
Subscribers: 62.
Programming (received off-air): KCNC-TV (CBS) Denver; KDVR (FOX) Denver; KMGH-TV (ABC) Denver; KRDO-TV (ABC) Colorado Springs; KTSC (PBS) Pueblo; KUSA (NBC) Denver; KWGN-TV (CW) Denver.
Programming (via satellite): ABC Family Channel; AMC; Arts & Entertainment; CNBC; CNN; Discovery Channel; Disney Channel; E! Entertainment Television; ESPN; ESPN 2; Great American Country; Lifetime; Outdoor Channel; QVC; TBS Superstation; The Learning Channel; Turner Network TV; USA Network; Weather Channel.
Fee: $30.00 installation; $36.45 monthly.

Pay Service 1
Pay Units: 49.
Programming (via satellite): HBO.
Fee: $10.95 monthly.

Video-On-Demand: No

Internet Service
Operational: Yes.
Fee: $45.00 installation; $45.00 monthly.

Telephone Service
None

Miles of Plant: 5.0 (coaxial); None (fiber optic). Homes passed: 232.
General Manager: Mark Haverkate.
Ownership: Champion Broadband (MSO).

GRANBY—Comcast Cable, 249 Warren Ave, Ste 250, Silverthorne, CO 80498. Phone: 970-262-2601. Fax: 970-468-2672. Web Site: http://www.comcast.com. Also serves Fraser, Grand County, Grand Lake, Hot Sulphur Springs, Silver Creek & Winter Park. ICA: CO0021.
TV Market Ranking: Below 100 (Fraser, Grand County (portions), Grand Lake, Silver Creek, Winter Park); Outside TV Markets (GRANBY, Grand County (portions), Hot Sulphur Springs). Franchise award date: N.A. Franchise expiration date: N.A. Began: N.A.
Channel capacity: N.A. Channels available but not in use: N.A.

Basic Service
Subscribers: N.A. Included in Aspen
Programming (via satellite): ABC Family Channel; Animal Planet; Arts & Entertainment; CNN; Discovery Channel; Disney Channel; ESPN; ESPN 2; Fox News Channel; Fox Sports Net Rocky Mountain; FX; Great American Country; KCNC-TV (CBS) Denver; KDVR (FOX) Denver; KMGH-TV (ABC) Denver; KPXC-TV (ION) Denver; KRMA-TV (PBS) Denver; KTVD (MNT) Denver; KUSA (NBC) Denver; KWGN-TV (CW) Denver; MoviePlex; MSNBC; MTV; Nickelodeon; Spike TV; TBS Superstation; Turner Network TV; USA Network; Weather Channel.
Current originations: Public Access.
Fee: $44.99 installation; $49.99 monthly.

Digital Basic Service
Subscribers: N.A. Included in Aspen
Programming (via satellite): BBC America; Bravo; Discovery Kids Channel; DMX Music; Encore; ESPN Classic Sports; ESPNews; Fox Sports World; Golf Channel; HGTV; Independent Film Channel; Nick Jr.; Science Channel; Syfy; Turner Classic Movies; TV Land; Versus; WE tv.
Fee: $9.95 monthly.

Pay Service 1
Pay Units: 140.
Programming (via satellite): Encore; HBO; Starz.

Digital Pay Service 1
Pay Units: N.A.
Programming (via satellite): Cinemax (multiplexed); HBO (multiplexed); Showtime (multiplexed); Starz (multiplexed); The Movie Channel (multiplexed).
Fee: $15.99 monthly (each).

Video-On-Demand: No

Pay-Per-View
iN DEMAND (delivered digitally), Fee: $3.99-$6.95, Addressable: Yes; Playboy TV (delivered digitally).

Internet Service
Operational: Yes.
Broadband Service: Comcast High Speed Internet.
Fee: $42.95 monthly.

Telephone Service
None

Miles of Plant: 203.0 (coaxial); None (fiber optic). Homes passed included in Aspen
Vice President: Mike Trueblood. General Manager: Ben Miller. Technical Operations Manager: David Farran. Customer Service Manager: Sherry Higgins.
Ownership: Comcast Cable Communications Inc. (MSO).

GRAND JUNCTION—Bresnan Communications, 2502 Foresight Cir, Grand Junction, CO 81505. Phones: 877-273-7626; 970-263-2300. Fax: 970-245-6803. E-mail: shogue@bresnan.com. Web Site: http://www.bresnan.com. Also serves Fruita,

Fruitvale, Mesa County & Palisade. ICA: CO0006.

TV Market Ranking: Below 100 (Fruita, Fruitvale, GRAND JUNCTION, Mesa County, Palisade). Franchise award date: March 1, 1966. Franchise expiration date: N.A. Began: October 1, 1966.

Channel capacity: N.A. Channels available but not in use: N.A.

Basic Service

Subscribers: 27,900.

Programming (received off-air): KFQX (FOX) Grand Junction; KJCT (ABC, TMO) Grand Junction; KKCO (CW, NBC) Grand Junction; KREX-TV (CBS, MNT) Grand Junction; KRMJ (PBS) Grand Junction; 14 FMs.

Programming (via satellite): C-SPAN; Discovery Channel; Home Shopping Network; Lifetime; MSNBC; MyNetworkTV Inc.; QVC; TBS Superstation; Telemundo; Trinity Broadcasting Network.

Current originations: Government Access.

Fee: $38.00 installation; $.72 converter.

Expanded Basic Service 1

Subscribers: N.A.

Programming (via satellite): ABC Family Channel; Altitude Sports & Entertainment; AMC; Animal Planet; Arts & Entertainment; Bravo; BYU Television; Cartoon Network; CNBC; CNN; Comedy Central; Country Music TV; C-SPAN 2; Disney Channel; E! Entertainment Television; ESPN; ESPN 2; Eternal Word TV Network; Food Network; Fox News Channel; Fox Sports Net Rocky Mountain; FX; Hallmark Channel; Headline News; HGTV; History Channel; INSP; ION Television; MTV; Nickelodeon; Oxygen; Spike TV; Syfy; Telefutura; The Learning Channel; Travel Channel; truTV; Turner Classic Movies; Turner Network TV; TV Guide Network; TV Land; Univision; USA Network; VH1; Weather Channel.

Fee: $56.99 monthly.

Digital Basic Service

Subscribers: N.A.

Programming (received off-air): KFQX (FOX) Grand Junction; KJCT (ABC, TMO) Grand Junction; KKCO (CW, NBC) Grand Junction; KREX-TV (CBS, MNT) Grand Junction.

Programming (via satellite): ABC Family HD; AmericanLife TV Network; Animal Planet HD; Arts & Entertainment HD; Bandamax; BBC America; Bio; Bloomberg Television; BlueHighways TV; Bravo HD; CBS College Sports Network; Cine Latino; Cine Mexicano; CMT Pure Country; CNBC HD+; CNN en Espanol; CNN HD; Cooking Channel; C-SPAN 3; De Pelicula; De Pelicula Clasico; Discovery Channel HD; Discovery en Espanol; Discovery HD Theater; Discovery Health Channel; Discovery Kids Channel; Discovery Military Channel; Discovery Planet Green; Disney Channel HD; DMX Music; Do-It-Yourself; ESPN 2 HD; ESPN Classic Sports; ESPN Deportes; ESPN HD; ESPNews; FitTV; Food Network HD; Fox College Sports Atlantic; Fox College Sports Central; Fox College Sports Pacific; Fox Movie Channel; Fox Reality Channel; Fox Soccer; Fox Sports en Espanol; FSN HD; Fuse; G4; Gol TV; Golf Channel; Gospel Music Channel; Great American Country; GSN; Halogen Network; HDNet; HDNet Movies; HGTV HD; History Channel en Espanol; History Channel HD; History Channel International; ID Investigation Discovery; Independent Film Channel; ION Television; Jewelry Television; Lifetime Movie Network; Lifetime Movie Network HD; Mountain West TV; MTV Hits; MTV Jams; MTV Tres; MTV2; mun2 television; National Geographic Channel; National Geographic Channel HD Network; NFL Network; NFL Network HD; NHL Network; Nick Jr.; Nick Too; NickToons TV; Outdoor Channel; Outdoor Channel 2 HD; Palladia; PBS Kids Sprout; RFD-TV; Science Channel; Science Channel HD; SoapNet; Speed Channel; Speed HD; Style Network; Syfy HD; TBS in HD; TeenNick; Telefutura; Telehit; The Sportsman Channel; TLC HD; Toon Disney; Trinity Broadcasting Network; Turner Network TV HD; Universal HD; Univision; USA Network HD; VenеMovies; Versus; Versus HD; VH1 Classic; VH1 Soul; Weather Channel HD.

Digital Pay Service 1

Pay Units: N.A.

Programming (via satellite): Cinemax (multiplexed); Cinemax HD; Cinemax On Demand; Encore (multiplexed); Flix; HBO (multiplexed); HBO HD; HBO On Demand; Showtime (multiplexed); Showtime HD; Showtime On Demand; Starz (multiplexed); Starz HDTV; Starz On Demand; The Movie Channel (multiplexed); The Movie Channel HD.

Video-On-Demand: Yes

Pay-Per-View

iN DEMAND (delivered digitally); ESPN (delivered digitally); NBA League Pass (delivered digitally); MLS Direct Kick (delivered digitally); MLB Extra Innings (delivered digitally); NHL Center Ice (delivered digitally).

Internet Service

Operational: Yes.

Broadband Service: Bresnan OnLine.

Fee: $39.95 monthly.

Telephone Service

Digital: Operational

Fee: $49.99 monthly

Miles of Plant: 606.0 (coaxial); 38.0 (fiber optic). Additional miles planned: 12.0 (coaxial). Homes passed: 54,900.

Regional Vice President: Sean Hogue. Technical Operations Manager: Gary Young.

City fee: 2% of gross.

Ownership: Bresnan Communications Inc. (MSO). Sale pends to Cablevision Systems Corp.

GREELEY—Comcast Cable, 3737 W 10th St, Greeley, CO 80634-1818. Phones: 303-776-2108 (Longmont office); 970-356-1079. Fax: 970-353-4363. Web Site: http://www.comcast.com. Also serves Evans, Garden City, La Salle, Weld County & Windsor. ICA: CO0009.

TV Market Ranking: Below 100 (Evans, Garden City, GREELEY, La Salle, Weld County (portions), Windsor); Outside TV Markets (Weld County (portions)). Franchise award date: N.A. Franchise expiration date: N.A. Began: November 1, 1980.

Channel capacity: 63 (operating 2-way). Channels available but not in use: N.A.

Basic Service

Subscribers: N.A. Included in Longmont

Programming (received off-air): KBDI-TV (PBS) Broomfield; KCEC (UNV) Denver; KCNC-TV (CBS) Denver; KDEN-TV (TMO) Longmont; KDVR (FOX) Denver; KMGH-TV (ABC) Denver; KPXC-TV (ION) Denver; KRMA-TV (PBS) Denver; KTVD (MNT) Denver; KUSA (NBC) Denver; KWGN-TV (CW) Denver.

Programming (via satellite): Azteca America; C-SPAN; MyNetworkTV Inc.; QVC; TV Guide Network; WGN America.

Current originations: Government Access; Leased Access; Educational Access; Public Access.

Fee: $44.99 installation; $14.99 monthly.

Expanded Basic Service 1

Subscribers: 18,729.

Programming (via satellite): ABC Family Channel; Altitude Sports & Entertainment; AMC; Animal Planet; Arts & Entertainment; BET Networks; Cartoon Network; CNBC; CNN; Comedy Central; Country Music TV; Discovery Channel; Disney Channel; E! Entertainment Television; ESPN; ESPN 2; Food Network; Fox News Channel; Fox Sports Net Rocky Mountain; FX; GalaVision; Golf Channel; Great American Country; Hallmark Channel; Headline News; HGTV; History Channel; Lifetime; MoviePlex; MSNBC; MTV; MTV2; Nickelodeon; Oxygen; Spike TV; TBS Superstation; The Learning Channel; Travel Channel; truTV; Turner Network TV; TV Land; USA Network; Versus; VH1; Weather Channel.

Fee: $33.50 monthly.

Digital Basic Service

Subscribers: N.A. Included in Longmont

Programming (received off-air): KCNC-TV (CBS) Denver; KDVR (FOX) Denver; KMGH-TV (ABC) Denver; KRMA-TV (PBS) Denver; KTVD (MNT) Denver; KUSA (NBC) Denver; KWGN-TV (CW) Denver.

Programming (via satellite): AmericanLife TV Network; BBC America; Bio; Black Family Channel; Bloomberg Television; Bravo; BYU Television; Canal 52MX; Canales N; CBS College Sports Network; CET - Comcast Entertainment TV; Cooking Channel; Country Music TV; Current; Discovery Digital Networks; Discovery HD Theater; DMX Music; Do-It-Yourself; Encore (multiplexed); ESPN 2 HD; ESPN Classic Sports; ESPN HD; ESPNews; Eternal Word TV Network; Flix; Fox College Sports Atlantic; Fox College Sports Central; Fox College Sports Pacific; Fox Movie Channel; Fox Reality Channel; Fox Soccer; Fuse; G4; GAS; GSN; Halogen Network; History Channel International; Independent Film Channel; INHD; Lifetime Movie Network; Lime; LOGO; MTV Networks Digital Suite; National Geographic Channel; NBA TV; NFL Network; Nick Jr.; NickToons TV; Outdoor Channel; Palladia; PBS Kids Sprout; ShopNBC; Si TV; SoapNet; Speed Channel; Style Network; Sundance Channel; Syfy; the mtn; The Word Network; Toon Disney; Turner Classic Movies; Turner Network TV HD; TV One; Universal HD; Versus HD; WE tv; Weatherscan.

Fee: $9.15 monthly.

Digital Pay Service 1

Pay Units: N.A.

Programming (via satellite): Cinemax (multiplexed); Cinemax HD; Flix; HBO (multiplexed); HBO HD; Showtime (multiplexed); Showtime HD; Starz (multiplexed); Starz HDTV; The Movie Channel (multiplexed).

Fee: $15.95 monthly (each).

Video-On-Demand: No

Pay-Per-View

iN DEMAND (delivered digitally); Hot Choice (delivered digitally); Playboy TV (delivered digitally); Sports PPV (delivered digitally); NBA League Pass (delivered digitally); MLB Extra Innings (delivered digitally); NHL Center Ice (delivered digitally).

Internet Service

Operational: Yes.

Broadband Service: Comcast High Speed Internet.

Fee: $42.95 monthly.

Telephone Service

Digital: Operational

Miles of Plant: 550.0 (coaxial); 90.0 (fiber optic). Homes passed included in Longmont

Vice President & General Manager: Mike Trueblood. Technical Operations Director: Stan Reifschneider. Administrative Assistant: Diane Romero.

City fee: 8% of gross.

Ownership: Comcast Cable Communications Inc. (MSO).

GUNNISON—Time Warner Cable, 412 W Tomichi Ave, Gunnison, CO 81230-2711. Phone: 970-641-6412. Fax: 970-641-6159. Web Site: http://www.timewarnercable.com. Also serves Crested Butte, Gunnison County, Mount Crested Butte, Riverbend & Skyland. ICA: CO0036.

TV Market Ranking: Outside TV Markets (Crested Butte, GUNNISON, Gunnison County, Mount Crested Butte, Riverbend, Skyland). Franchise award date: N.A. Franchise expiration date: N.A. Began: March 1, 1984.

Channel capacity: N.A. Channels available but not in use: N.A.

Basic Service

Subscribers: N.A.

Programming (received off-air): KCNC-TV (CBS) Denver; KDVR (FOX) Denver; KMGH-TV (ABC) Denver; KRMA-TV (PBS) Denver; KTVD (MNT) Denver; KUSA (NBC) Denver; KWGN-TV (CW) Denver; 8 FMs.

Programming (via satellite): C-SPAN; C-SPAN 2; ESPNews; GalaVision; QVC; ShopNBC; TV Guide Network; TV Land; WGN America.

Current originations: Leased Access; Educational Access.

Fee: $39.95 installation; $24.46 monthly; $35.00 additional installation.

Expanded Basic Service 1

Subscribers: N.A.

Programming (via satellite): ABC Family Channel; AMC; Animal Planet; Arts & Entertainment; Cartoon Network; CNBC; CNN; Comedy Central; Country Music TV; Discovery Channel; Disney Channel; E! Entertainment Television; ESPN; ESPN 2; Food Network; Fox News Channel; Fox Sports Net Rocky Mountain; FX; Hallmark Channel; Headline News; HGTV; History Channel; Home Shopping Network; ION Television; Lifetime; MSNBC; MTV; Nickelodeon; Oxygen; Speed Channel; Spike TV; Syfy; TBS Superstation; The Learning Channel; Travel Channel; truTV; Turner Network TV; USA Network; Versus; VH1; Weather Channel.

Fee: $29.75 monthly.

Digital Basic Service

Subscribers: N.A.

Programming (via satellite): AmericanLife TV Network; BBC America; Bloomberg Television; Discovery Digital Networks; ESPN Classic Sports; ESPNews; FitTV; Fox Movie

Channel; Fox Sports World; G4; Golf Channel; GSN; INSP; Music Choice; National Geographic Channel; Nick Jr.; NickToons TV; Outdoor Channel; Trinity Broadcasting Network; Turner Classic Movies; Versus; VH1 Classic; VH1 Country; WE tv.
Fee: $10.99 monthly.

Digital Pay Service 1
Pay Units: N.A.
Programming (via satellite): Cinemax (multiplexed); Encore (multiplexed); HBO (multiplexed); Showtime (multiplexed); Starz (multiplexed); The Movie Channel (multiplexed).
Fee: $15.95 monthly (each).

Video-On-Demand: No

Pay-Per-View
Fresh (delivered digitally); Urban American Television Network (delivered digitally); Hot Choice (delivered digitally); Playboy TV (delivered digitally); HITS PPV (delivered digitally).

Internet Service
Operational: Yes.
Broadband Service: Road Runner.
Fee: $69.95 installation; $44.95 monthly.

Telephone Service
Digital: Operational
Fee: $44.95 monthly

Miles of Plant: 80.0 (coaxial); None (fiber optic). Homes passed: 4,000.
Manager: Ernie Young. Chief Technician: Dan Ward.
City fee: 3% of gross.
Ownership: Time Warner Cable (MSO).

HAYDEN—Bresnan Communications. Now served by CRAIG, CO [CO0039]. ICA: CO0098.

HERMOSA—Hermosa Cablevision Inc. Now served by DURANGO, CO [CO0023]. ICA: CO0087.

HIGHLANDS RANCH—Comcast Cable. Now served by DENVER (suburbs), CO [CO0001]. ICA: CO0180.

HIGHLANDS RANCH—Qwest Choice TV. IPTV service has been discontinued.. ICA: CO5003.

HIGHLANDS RANCH—Qwest Choice TV. This cable system has converted to IPTV. See Highlands Ranch, CO [CO5003], CO. ICA: CO0208.

HOLIDAY VILLAGE—Formerly served by Island Cable. No longer in operation. ICA: CO0209.

HOLLY—Champion Broadband, 380 Perry St, Ste 230, Castle Rock, CO 80104. Phones: 866-801-1122; 303-688-7766. Web Site: http://www.championbroadband.com. ICA: CO0101.

TV Market Ranking: Outside TV Markets (HOLLY). Franchise award date: January 20, 1983. Franchise expiration date: N.A. Began: January 23, 1983.
Channel capacity: 41 (operating 2-way). Channels available but not in use: 7.

Basic Service
Subscribers: 93.
Programming (received off-air): KCNC-TV (CBS) Denver; KDVR (FOX) Denver; KKTV (CBS, MNT) Colorado Springs; KMGH-TV (ABC) Denver; KOAA-TV (NBC) Pueblo; KRDO-TV (ABC) Colorado Springs; KTSC (PBS) Pueblo; KUSA (NBC) Denver; KWGN-TV (CW) Denver.
Programming (via satellite): ABC Family Channel; Arts & Entertainment; Cartoon Network; CNN; Discovery Channel; Disney Channel; ESPN; ESPN 2; Fox News Channel; Fox Sports Net Rocky Mountain; FX; Great American Country; INSP; Outdoor Channel; QVC; TBS Superstation; Turner Network TV; USA Network; Weather Channel; WGN America.
Current originations: Public Access.
Fee: $35.00 installation; $37.45 monthly.

Pay Service 1
Pay Units: 48.
Programming (via satellite): HBO; The Movie Channel.
Fee: $9.95 monthly (TMC), $10.95 monthly (HBO).

Video-On-Demand: No

Internet Service
Operational: Yes.
Fee: $45.00 installation; $45.00 monthly.

Telephone Service
None

Miles of Plant: 7.0 (coaxial); None (fiber optic). Homes passed: 550.
General Manager: Mark Haverkate.
City fee: 3% of gross.
Ownership: Champion Broadband (MSO).

HOLYOKE—PC Telcom, 120 N Sunflower Dr, Holyoke, CO 80734. Phones: 866-854-2111; 970-854-2201. Fax: 970-854-2668. E-mail: customerservice@pctelcom.coop. Web Site: http://my.pctelcom.coop. Also serves Haxtun. ICA: CO0065.

TV Market Ranking: Below 100 (Haxtun); Outside TV Markets (HOLYOKE). Franchise award date: N.A. Franchise expiration date: N.A. Began: March 1, 1972.
Channel capacity: 50 (not 2-way capable). Channels available but not in use: None.

Basic Service
Subscribers: 1,002 Includes Fleming & Sedgwick.
Programming (received off-air): KCDO-TV (IND) Sterling; KPNE-TV (PBS) North Platte; allband FM.
Programming (via microwave): KCNC-TV (CBS) Denver; KDVR (FOX) Denver; KMGH-TV (ABC) Denver; KUSA (NBC) Denver; KWGN-TV (CW) Denver.
Programming (via satellite): ABC Family Channel; AMC; Animal Planet; Arts & Entertainment; CNBC; CNN; C-SPAN; Discovery Channel; Disney Channel; E! Entertainment Television; ESPN; ESPN 2; Fox News Channel; Fox Sports Net Rocky Mountain; Great American Country; Headline News; HGTV; History Channel; Home Shopping Network; Lifetime; MTV; Nickelodeon; SoapNet; Spike TV; Syfy; TBS Superstation; Turner Network TV; TV Land; Univision; USA Network; VH1; Weather Channel; WGN America.
Current originations: Public Access.
Fee: $34.95 monthly.

Pay Service 1
Pay Units: N.A.
Programming (via satellite): Cinemax; HBO.
Fee: $11.10 monthly (Cinemax), $13.35 monthly (HBO).

Video-On-Demand: No

Internet Service
Operational: Yes.

Telephone Service
None

Miles of Plant: 22.0 (coaxial); None (fiber optic). Additional miles planned: 5.0 (coaxial). Homes passed: 1,300.
General Manager: Vincent Kropp. Operations Director: Pete Markle. Chief Technician: J.C. Peckham. Marketing & Public Relations Manager: Sharon Crist. Customer Service Manager: Patty Freel.
City fee: None.
Ownership: PC Telcorp (MSO).

HOTCHKISS—Rocky Mountain Cable, 40 County Rd 600, Unit F, Pagosa Springs, CO 81147-9473. Phones: 800-222-1332; 970-731-2211. Fax: 970-731-5510. Web Site: http://www.rockymtncable.com. Also serves Austin, Cedaredge, Crawford, Eckert, Lazear, Orchard City, Paonia (unincorporated portions) & Rogers Mesa. ICA: CO0172.

TV Market Ranking: Below 100 (Austin, Cedaredge, Crawford, Eckert, HOTCHKISS, Lazear, Orchard City, Paonia (unincorporated portions), Rogers Mesa). Franchise award date: N.A. Franchise expiration date: N.A. Began: December 15, 1982.
Channel capacity: 49 (2-way capable). Channels available but not in use: None.

Basic Service
Subscribers: 1,509.
Programming (received off-air): KREY-TV (CBS) Montrose.
Programming (via satellite): Comedy Central; C-SPAN; Fox News Channel; Hallmark Channel; History Channel; KCNC-TV (CBS) Denver; KDVR (FOX) Denver; KMGH-TV (ABC) Denver; KRMA-TV (PBS) Denver; KUSA (NBC) Denver; KWGN-TV (CW) Denver; QVC; TBS Superstation; The Learning Channel; Travel Channel; TV Land; USA Network; WE tv; Weather Channel.
Current originations: Public Access.
Fee: $20.00 installation; $27.24 monthly; $5.00 converter.

Expanded Basic Service 1
Subscribers: 1,313.
Programming (via satellite): ABC Family Channel; Altitude Sports & Entertainment; AMC; Arts & Entertainment; CNN; Country Music TV; Discovery Channel; Disney Channel; ESPN; ESPN 2; Fox Sports Net Rocky Mountain; FX; G4; Headline News; HGTV; Home Shopping Network; Lifetime; Nickelodeon; Spike TV; Syfy; Turner Network TV; Versus.
Fee: $14.75 monthly.

Digital Basic Service
Subscribers: 432.
Programming (via satellite): BBC America; Bio; Bloomberg Television; Bravo; Discovery Digital Networks; ESPN Classic Sports; ESPNews; Fox Movie Channel; Fox Soccer; Fuse; GAS; Golf Channel; Gospel Music Channel; GSN; Halogen Network; History Channel International; Independent Film Channel; Lifetime Movie Network; MTV Networks Digital Suite; National Geographic Channel; Nick Jr.; NickToons TV; Outdoor Channel; Speed Channel; Trinity Broadcasting Network; Trio; Turner Classic Movies.
Fee: $8.00 monthly.

Pay Service 1
Pay Units: 91.
Programming (via satellite): HBO.
Fee: $13.49 monthly.

Digital Pay Service 1
Pay Units: N.A.
Programming (via satellite): Cinemax (multiplexed); Encore (multiplexed); Flix; HBO (multiplexed); Showtime (multiplexed); Starz (multiplexed); The Movie Channel (multiplexed).
Fee: $12.49 monthly (Starz/Encore or Cinemax), $13.49 monthly (HBO or Showtime/TMC/Flix).

Video-On-Demand: No

Internet Service
Operational: No.

Telephone Service
None

Miles of Plant: 225.0 (coaxial); 45.0 (fiber optic).
President: Wayne Vestal. Chief Engineer: Bobby Smith.
City fee: 3% of gross.
Ownership: ICE Cable Holdings LLC (MSO).

HUDSON—Formerly served by US Cable of Coastal Texas LP. No longer in operation. ICA: CO0173.

HUGO—Champion Broadband, 380 Perry St, Ste 230, Castle Rock, CO 80104. Phones: 303-688-7766; 866-801-1122. Web Site: http://www.championbroadband.com. ICA: CO0174.

TV Market Ranking: Outside TV Markets (HUGO). Franchise award date: January 1, 1983. Franchise expiration date: N.A. Began: January 1, 1983.
Channel capacity: 36 (operating 2-way). Channels available but not in use: 1.

Basic Service
Subscribers: 82.
Programming (received off-air): KCNC-TV (CBS) Denver; KDVR (FOX) Denver; KKTV (CBS, MNT) Colorado Springs; KMGH-TV (ABC) Denver; KRDO-TV (ABC) Colorado Springs; KRMA-TV (PBS) Denver; KUSA (NBC) Denver; KWGN-TV (CW) Denver.
Programming (via satellite): ABC Family Channel; Arts & Entertainment; CNBC; CNN; Discovery Channel; Disney Channel; ESPN; ESPN 2; Fox News Channel; Fox Sports Net Rocky Mountain; Fuse; FX; Great American Country; INSP; Lifetime; MSNBC; Outdoor Channel; TBS Superstation; The Learning Channel; Toon Disney; Turner Classic Movies; Turner Network TV; USA Network; Weather Channel; WGN America.
Fee: $35.00 installation; $36.45 monthly.

Pay Service 1
Pay Units: 77.
Programming (via satellite): HBO; The Movie Channel.
Fee: $10.00 installation; $9.95 monthly (TMC),$10.95 monthly (HBO).

Video-On-Demand: Yes

Internet Service
Operational: Yes.
Fee: $45.00 installation; $45.00 monthly.

Telephone Service
None

Miles of Plant: 7.0 (coaxial); None (fiber optic). Homes passed: 467.
General Manager: Mark Haverkate.
City fee: 3% of gross.
Ownership: Champion Broadband (MSO).

IDAHO SPRINGS—Comcast Cable. Now served by DENVER (suburbs), CO [CO0001]. ICA: CO0082.

IGNACIO—Rural Route Video, PO Box 640, Ignacio, CO 81137-0640. Phone: 970-563-9593. Fax: 970-563-9381. Web Site: http://www.westernet.net. Also serves Southern Ute Indian Reservation. ICA: CO0076.

TV Market Ranking: Below 100 (IGNACIO, Southern Ute Indian Reservation). Franchise award date: February 1, 1987. Franchise expiration date: N.A. Began: December 1, 1986.
Channel capacity: 36 (operating 2-way). Channels available but not in use: 5.

Basic Service
Subscribers: 254.
Programming (received off-air): KLUZ-TV (UNV) Albuquerque; KOAT-TV (ABC) Albu-

querque; KOBF (NBC) Farmington; KREZ-TV (CBS) Durango.
Programming (via satellite): ABC Family Channel; Animal Planet; Cartoon Network; CNBC; Country Music TV; C-SPAN; C-SPAN 2; ESPN 2; Food Network; FX; G4; HGTV; History Channel; Home Shopping Network; KRMJ (PBS) Grand Junction; Syfy; Telefutura; The Learning Channel; Travel Channel; Trinity Broadcasting Network; Turner Classic Movies; TV Land; WE tv.
Fee: $60.00 installation; $34.75 monthly; $3.00 converter.
Pay Service 1
Pay Units: 164.
Programming (via satellite): Cinemax; HBO.
Fee: $10.50 monthly (Cinemax), $11.50 monthly (HBO).
Video-On-Demand: No
Internet Service
Operational: Yes. Began: December 31, 1999.
Subscribers: 30.
Broadband Service: In-house.
Fee: $150.00 installation; $45.00 monthly.
Telephone Service
None
Miles of Plant: 14.0 (coaxial); None (fiber optic). Additional miles planned: 1.0 (coaxial). Homes passed: 1,000. Total homes in franchised area: 1,200.
Manager: Christopher L. May.
City fee: 5% of gross.
Ownership: Rural Route Video (MSO).

JOHNSTOWN—US Cable, 266 Basher Dr, #4, Berthoud, CO 80513. Phones: 970-587-2243; 800-480-7020. Fax: 970-587-4208. Web Site: http://www.uscable.com. Also serves Milliken & Weld County (portions). ICA: CO0073.
TV Market Ranking: 32 (Weld County (portions)); Below 100 (JOHNSTOWN, Milliken, Weld County (portions)); Outside TV Markets (Weld County (portions)). Franchise award date: N.A. Franchise expiration date: N.A. Began: July 1, 1982.
Channel capacity: 86 (operating 2-way). Channels available but not in use: N.A.
Basic Service
Subscribers: 7,000 Includes Conifer, Cripple Creek, Eaton, Gilcrest, Kersey, Table Mountain, & Woodland Park.
Programming (received off-air): KBDI-TV (PBS) Broomfield; KCEC (UNV) Denver; KCNC-TV (CBS) Denver; KDEN-TV (TMO) Longmont; KDVR (FOX) Denver; KGWN-TV (CBS, CW) Cheyenne; KMGH-TV (ABC) Denver; KPXC-TV (ION) Denver; KRMA-TV (PBS) Denver; KTFD-DT (UNV) Boulder; KTVD (MNT) Denver; KUSA (NBC) Denver; KWGN-TV (CW) Denver.
Programming (via satellite): ABC Family Channel; Altitude Sports & Entertainment; AMC; Animal Planet; Arts & Entertainment; BYU Television; Cartoon Network; CNN; Comedy Central; Country Music TV; C-SPAN; Discovery Channel; Disney Channel; E! Entertainment Television; ESPN; ESPN 2; Food Network; Fox News Channel; Fox Sports Net Rocky Mountain; FX; GalaVision; Hallmark Channel; Headline News; HGTV; History Channel; Home Shopping Network; Lifetime; MTV; mun2 television; National Geographic Channel; Nickelodeon; Oxygen; QVC; ShopNBC; Speed Channel; Spike TV; Syfy; TBS Superstation; The Learning Channel; Travel Channel; truTV; Turner Network TV; TV Guide Network; TV Land; USA Network; Versus; VH1; Weather Channel; WGN America.
Current originations: Leased Access.
Fee: $49.95 installation; $43.95 monthly.
Digital Basic Service
Subscribers: N.A.
Programming (via satellite): Animal Planet HD; Arts & Entertainment HD; BBC America; Bloomberg Television; Bravo; Current; Daystar TV Network; Discovery Channel HD; Discovery HD Theater; Discovery Health Channel; Discovery Kids Channel; DMX Music; ESPN Classic Sports; ESPN HD; ESPNews; Food Network HD; Fox Soccer; Fuse; G4; Golf Channel; Gospel Music Channel; Great American Country; GSN; HDNet; HGTV HD; History Channel HD; Independent Film Channel; Lifetime Movie Network; MTV2; National Geographic Channel HD Network; Nick Jr.; Science Channel; Sleuth; Style Network; Syfy; Syfy HD; TeenNick; The Word Network; Toon Disney; Trinity Broadcasting Network; Turner Classic Movies; Universal HD; USA Network HD; VH1 Classic; WE tv; WealthTV HD.
Fee: $16.95 monthly.
Digital Expanded Basic Service
Subscribers: N.A.
Programming (via satellite): Fox College Sports Atlantic; Fox College Sports Central; Fox College Sports Pacific; NFL Network; Outdoor Channel.
Fee: $2.00 monthly.
Digital Expanded Basic Service 2
Subscribers: N.A.
Programming (via satellite): Bio; CMT Pure Country; Discovery Home Channel; Discovery Times Channel; Encore (multiplexed); FitTV; Fox Movie Channel; Halogen Network; History Channel International; Ovation.
Fee: $2.95 monthly.
Digital Pay Service 1
Pay Units: N.A.
Programming (via satellite): Cinemax (multiplexed); Cinemax HD; HBO (multiplexed); HBO HD; Showtime (multiplexed); Showtime HD; The Movie Channel (multiplexed).
Fee: $11.95 monthly (HBO, Cinemax, Showtime or TMC).
Video-On-Demand: No
Pay-Per-View
iN DEMAND (delivered digitally); Playboy TV (delivered digitally); Fresh (delivered digitally); Spice: Xcess (delivered digitally); Club Jenna (delivered digitally).
Internet Service
Operational: Yes.
Subscribers: 5,500.
Broadband Service: Warp Drive Online.
Fee: $27.95 monthly.
Telephone Service
None
Miles of Plant: 13.0 (coaxial); None (fiber optic). Homes passed: 1,073.
General Manager: Dave Kavanagh. Chief Technician: Josh Patchett. Office Manager: Debbie Hernandez. Marketing Manager: Jennifer Lideman. Construction Manager: Rich Fromstad.
Ownership: US Cable Corp. (MSO).; Comcast Cable Communications Inc. (MSO).

JULESBURG—PC Telcom, 120 N Sunflower Dr, Holyoke, CO 80734. Phones: 866-854-2111; 970-854-2201. Fax: 970-854-2668. E-mail: customerservice@pctelcom.coop. Web Site: http://my.pctelcom.coop. Also serves Ovid, CO; Chappell, NE. ICA: CO0084.
TV Market Ranking: Outside TV Markets (Chappell, JULESBURG, Ovid). Franchise award date: May 1, 1957. Franchise expiration date: N.A. Began: December 1, 1975.
Channel capacity: 50 (not 2-way capable). Channels available but not in use: 1.
Basic Service
Subscribers: 895.
Programming (received off-air): KCDO-TV (IND) Sterling; KCNC-TV (CBS) Denver; KDVR (FOX) Denver; KMGH-TV (ABC) Denver; KNOP-TV (NBC) North Platte; KPNE-TV (PBS) North Platte; KRMA-TV (PBS) Denver; KUSA (NBC) Denver; KWGN-TV (CW) Denver; KWNB-TV (ABC) Hayes Center.
Programming (via satellite): ABC Family Channel; Animal Planet; Arts & Entertainment; CNBC; CNN; C-SPAN; Discovery Channel; Disney Channel; E! Entertainment Television; ESPN; ESPN 2; Fox News Channel; Fox Sports Net Rocky Mountain; Great American Country; HGTV; History Channel; Home Shopping Network; Lifetime; MTV; Nickelodeon; SoapNet; Spike TV; Syfy; TBS Superstation; The Learning Channel; Trinity Broadcasting Network; Turner Classic Movies; Turner Network TV; Univision; USA Network; VH1; Weather Channel; WGN America.
Fee: $34.95 monthly.
Pay Service 1
Pay Units: N.A.
Programming (via satellite): Cinemax; HBO; Showtime.
Fee: $9.15 monthly (Cinemax or Showtime), $10.40 monthly (HBO).
Video-On-Demand: No
Pay-Per-View
ESPN Extra (delivered digitally); ESPN Now (delivered digitally); iN DEMAND (delivered digitally); Playboy TV (delivered digitally); Fresh (delivered digitally); Shorteez (delivered digitally).
Internet Service
Operational: No.
Telephone Service
None
Miles of Plant: 25.0 (coaxial); None (fiber optic). Homes passed: 1,324.
General Manager: Vincent Kropp. Operations Director: Pete Markle. Chief Technician: J.C. Peckam. Marketing & Public Relations Manager: Sharon Crist.
Ownership: PC Telcorp (MSO).

KERSEY—US Cable. No longer in operation. ICA: CO0116.

KIT CARSON—Rebeltec Communications, PO Box 10, Kit Carson, CO 80825. Phone: 719-767-8902. Fax: 719-767-8906. E-mail: cable@rebeltec.net. Web Site: http://www.rebeltec.net. ICA: CO0152.
TV Market Ranking: Outside TV Markets (KIT CARSON). Franchise award date: January 1, 1991. Franchise expiration date: N.A. Began: June 1, 1991.
Channel capacity: 36 (not 2-way capable). Channels available but not in use: 19.
Basic Service
Subscribers: 65.
Programming (via microwave): KKTV (CBS, MNT) Colorado Springs; KOAA-TV (NBC) Pueblo; KRDO-TV (ABC) Colorado Springs.
Programming (via satellite): ABC Family Channel; Altitude Sports & Entertainment; Arts & Entertainment; CNN; Country Music TV; Discovery Channel; Disney Channel; ESPN; ESPN 2; Fox News Channel; Fox Sports Net Rocky Mountain; Hallmark Channel; HGTV; History Channel; ION Television; KCNC-TV (CBS) Denver; KDVR (FOX) Denver; KMGH-TV (ABC) Denver; KRMA-TV (PBS) Denver; KTVD (MNT) Denver; KUSA (NBC) Denver; KWGN-TV (CW) Denver; RFD-TV; Shop at Home; TBS Superstation; Trinity Broadcasting Network; Turner Classic Movies; Turner Network TV; USA Network; Versus; Weather Channel; WGN America.
Current originations: Public Access.
Fee: $30.00 installation; $30.00 monthly; $3.00 converter.
Pay Service 1
Pay Units: 5.
Programming (via satellite): Cinemax; HBO.
Fee: $15.00 monthly.
Internet Service
Operational: Yes, DSL.
Fee: $75.00 installation; $25.00 monthly.
Telephone Service
None
Miles of Plant: 3.0 (coaxial); None (fiber optic). Homes passed: 130. Total homes in franchised area: 130.
Manager & Chief Technician: B.J. Mayhan. Marketing Director: Angela Mayhan.
Ownership: Rebeltec Communications LLC (MSO).

KREMMLING—Comcast Cable, 249 Warren Ave, Ste 250, Silverthorne, CO 80498. Phone: 970-262-2601. Fax: 970-468-2672. Web Site: http://www.comcast.com. Also serves Grand County (unincorporated areas). ICA: CO0093.
TV Market Ranking: Below 100 (Grand County (unincorporated areas) (portions)); Outside TV Markets (Grand County (unincorporated areas) (portions), KREMMLING). Franchise award date: N.A. Franchise expiration date: N.A. Began: February 1, 1970.
Channel capacity: N.A. Channels available but not in use: N.A.
Basic Service
Subscribers: N.A. Included in Aspen
Programming (via satellite): ABC Family Channel; Animal Planet; Arts & Entertainment; CNN; Disney Channel; E! Entertainment Television; ESPN; Fox News Channel; Fox Sports Net Rocky Mountain; FX; Great American Country; KCNC-TV (CBS) Denver; KDVR (FOX) Denver; KMGH-TV (ABC) Denver; KRMA-TV (PBS) Denver; KTVD (MNT) Denver; KUSA (NBC) Denver; KWGN-TV (CW) Denver; MSNBC; MTV; Nickelodeon; Spike TV; TBS Superstation; Turner Network TV; USA Network.
Current originations: Public Access.
Fee: $44.99 installation; $49.99 monthly.
Digital Basic Service
Subscribers: N.A. Included in Aspen
Programming (via satellite): BBC America; Bravo; Discovery Digital Networks; DMX Music; ESPN Classic Sports; ESPNews; Fox Soccer; Golf Channel; GSN; HGTV; His-

tory Channel; Independent Film Channel; Nick Jr.; Syfy; Turner Classic Movies; TV Land; Versus; WE tv.
Fee: $9.95 monthly.

Pay Service 1
Pay Units: 20.
Programming (via satellite): Cinemax; Encore; HBO; Starz.
Fee: $25.00 installation; $9.95 monthly (Cinemax or HBO), $10.45 monthly (Starz & Encore).

Digital Pay Service 1
Pay Units: N.A.
Programming (via satellite): Encore (multiplexed); HBO (multiplexed); Showtime; Starz; The Movie Channel.
Fee: $15.99 monthly (each).

Video-On-Demand: No

Pay-Per-View
iN DEMAND (delivered digitally); Playboy TV (delivered digitally).

Internet Service
Operational: Yes.
Broadband Service: Comcast High Speed Internet.
Fee: $42.95 monthly.

Telephone Service
None

Miles of Plant: 11.0 (coaxial); None (fiber optic). Homes passed included in Aspen
Vice President: Mike Trueblood. General Manager: Ben Miller. Technical Operations Manager: David Farran. Customer Service Manager: Sherry Higgins.
City fee: 5% of gross.
Ownership: Comcast Cable Communications Inc. (MSO).

LA JUNTA—Bresnan Communications, 2218 San Juan Ave, La Junta, CO 81050. Phone: 877-273-7626. Web Site: http://www.bresnan.com. Also serves Fowler, Manzanola, Otero County (unincorporated areas), Rocky Ford & Swink. ICA: CO0040.
TV Market Ranking: Below 100 (Fowler, Otero County (unincorporated areas) (portions)); Outside TV Markets (LA JUNTA, Manzanola, Otero County (unincorporated areas) (portions), Rocky Ford, Swink). Franchise award date: April 1, 1981. Franchise expiration date: N.A. Began: June 1, 1977.
Channel capacity: 33 (operating 2-way). Channels available but not in use: N.A.

Basic Service
Subscribers: 3,259.
Programming (received off-air): KKTV (CBS, MNT) Colorado Springs; KOAA-TV (NBC) Pueblo; KRDO-TV (ABC) Colorado Springs; KTSC (PBS) Pueblo; KXRM-TV (FOX) Colorado Springs.
Programming (via satellite): CNBC; C-SPAN; C-SPAN 2; Home Shopping Network; ION Television; KWGN-TV (CW) Denver; Lifetime; QVC; TV Guide Network; Univision.
Fee: $60.00 installation; $29.73 monthly; $3.95 converter.

Expanded Basic Service 1
Subscribers: N.A.
Programming (via satellite): ABC Family Channel; Altitude Sports & Entertainment; AMC; Animal Planet; Arts & Entertainment; Cartoon Network; CNN; Comedy Central; Country Music TV; Discovery Channel; Disney Channel; E! Entertainment Television; ESPN; ESPN 2; Eternal Word TV Network; Food Network; Fox News Channel; Fox Sports Net Rocky Mountain; FX; GalaVision; Hallmark Channel; Headline News; HGTV; History Channel; MSNBC; MTV; Nickelodeon; Oxygen; Spike TV; Syfy; TBS Superstation; Telefutura; The Learning Channel; Travel Channel; truTV; Turner Classic Movies; Turner Network TV; TV Land; USA Network; VH1; Weather Channel.
Fee: $28.56 monthly.

Digital Basic Service
Subscribers: N.A.
Programming (received off-air): KKTV (CBS, MNT) Colorado Springs; KRDO-TV (ABC) Colorado Springs; KTSC (PBS) Pueblo; KXRM-TV (FOX) Colorado Springs.
Programming (via satellite): ABC Family HD; AmericanLife TV Network; Animal Planet HD; Arts & Entertainment HD; Bandamax; BBC America; Bio; Bloomberg Television; Bravo; CBS College Sports Network; Cine Latino; Cine Mexicano; CMT Pure Country; CNN en Espanol; Cooking Channel; De Pelicula; De Pelicula Clasico; Discovery Channel HD; Discovery en Espanol; Discovery HD Theater; Discovery Health Channel; Discovery Military Channel; Discovery Planet Green; Disney Channel HD; DMX Music; Do-It-Yourself; ESPN Classic Sports; ESPN Deportes; ESPN HD; ESPNews; FitTV; Food Network HD; Fox College Sports Atlantic; Fox College Sports Central; Fox College Sports Pacific; Fox Movie Channel; Fox Reality Channel; Fox Soccer; Fox Sports en Espanol; Fuse; G4; GalaVision; Gol TV; Golf Channel; Gospel Music Channel; GSN; Halogen Network; HGTV HD; History Channel en Espanol; History Channel International; ID Investigation Discovery; Independent Film Channel; ION Television; KOAA-TV (NBC) Pueblo; Lifetime Movie Network; Mountain West TV; MTV Hits; MTV Jams; MTV Tres; MTV2; mun2 television; National Geographic Channel; National Geographic Channel HD Network; NFL Network; Nick Jr.; Nick Too; NickToons TV; Outdoor Channel; PBS Kids Sprout; RFD-TV; Science Channel; Science Channel HD; SoapNet; Speed Channel; Style Network; Syfy HD; TeenNick; Telefutura; Telehit; The Sportsman Channel; Toon Disney; Trinity Broadcasting Network; Universal HD; Univision; USA Network HD; VeneMovies; Versus; VH1 Classic; VH1 Soul.

Digital Pay Service 1
Pay Units: 493.
Programming (via satellite): Cinemax (multiplexed); Encore (multiplexed); Flix; HBO (multiplexed); HBO HD; Showtime (multiplexed); Starz (multiplexed); Starz HDTV; The Movie Channel (multiplexed).

Video-On-Demand: No

Pay-Per-View
iN DEMAND (delivered digitally).

Internet Service
Operational: Yes.
Fee: $39.95 monthly.

Telephone Service
Digital: Operational
Fee: $49.99 monthly

Miles of Plant: 94.0 (coaxial); 20.0 (fiber optic). Homes passed: 5,092.
General Manager: Jerry Parker. Chief Technician: Matt Harris.
City fee: 5% of gross.
Ownership: Bresnan Communications Inc. (MSO). Sale pends to Cablevision Systems Corp.

LA VETA—Formerly served by Westcom II LLC. No longer in operation. ICA: CO0199.

LAKE CITY—Rocky Mountain Cable, 40 County Rd 600, Unit F, Pagosa Springs, CO 81147-9473. Phones: 800-222-1332; 970-731-2211. Fax: 970-731-5510. Web Site: http://www.rockymtncable.com. ICA: CO0127.
TV Market Ranking: Outside TV Markets (LAKE CITY). Franchise award date: January 1, 1982. Franchise expiration date: N.A. Began: January 1, 1986.
Channel capacity: 42 (not 2-way capable). Channels available but not in use: 1.

Basic Service
Subscribers: 131.
Programming (via satellite): ABC Family Channel; AMC; Animal Planet; Arts & Entertainment; Bravo; CNBC; CNN; Comedy Central; Country Music TV; Discovery Channel; Disney Channel; ESPN; ESPN 2; Fox News Channel; G4; Hallmark Channel; History Channel; KCNC-TV (CBS) Denver; KDVR (FOX) Denver; KMGH-TV (ABC) Denver; KRMA-TV (PBS) Denver; KUSA (NBC) Denver; KWGN-TV (CW) Denver; MSNBC; Nickelodeon; Outdoor Channel; QVC; Spike TV; Syfy; TBS Superstation; The Learning Channel; Travel Channel; Turner Network TV; TV Land; USA Network; VH1; WE tv; Weather Channel; WGN America.
Fee: $20.00 installation; $37.24 monthly.

Pay Service 1
Pay Units: 11.
Programming (via satellite): HBO.
Fee: $15.00 installation; $13.49 monthly.

Video-On-Demand: No

Internet Service
Operational: No.

Telephone Service
None

Miles of Plant: 11.0 (coaxial); None (fiber optic). Homes passed: 300.
President: Wayne Vestal. Chief Technician: Bobby Smith.
City fee: 3% of gross.
Ownership: ICE Cable Holdings LLC.

LAKEWOOD—Comcast Cable, 8000 E Iliff Ave, Denver, CO 80231. Phone: 303-603-2000. Fax: 303-6-3-2600. Web Site: http://www.comcast.com. Also serves Aurora & Denver (portions). ICA: CO0207. **Note:** This system is an overbuild.
TV Market Ranking: 32 (Aurora, Denver (portions), LAKEWOOD). Franchise award date: September 13, 2001. Franchise expiration date: N.A. Began: April 1, 2001.
Channel capacity: 80 (operating 2-way). Channels available but not in use: None.

Basic Service
Subscribers: 1,674.
Programming (received off-air): KBDI-TV (PBS) Broomfield; KCEC (UNV) Denver; KCNC-TV (CBS) Denver; KDEN-TV (TMO) Longmont; KDVR (FOX) Denver; KMGH-TV (ABC) Denver; KPXC-TV (ION) Denver; KRMA-TV (PBS) Denver; KRMT (ETV) Denver; KRMZ (PBS) Steamboat Springs; KTVD (MNT) Denver; KTVJ-LP Santa Rosa; KUSA (NBC) Denver; KWGN-TV (CW) Denver; KWHD (IND) Castle Rock.
Programming (via satellite): ABC Family Channel; Altitude Sports & Entertainment; AMC; Animal Planet; Arts & Entertainment; BET Networks; Bravo; Cartoon Network; CNBC; CNN; Comedy Central; Country Music TV; C-SPAN; C-SPAN 2; Discovery Channel; Discovery Health Channel; Disney Channel; E! Entertainment Television; ESPN; ESPN 2; ESPN Classic Sports; ESPNews; Eternal Word TV Network; Food Network; Fox News Channel; Fox Sports Net Rocky Mountain; FX; GalaVision; Golf Channel; GSN; Hallmark Channel; Headline News; HGTV; History Channel; Home Shopping Network; Lifetime; MSNBC; MTV; National Geographic Channel; Nickelodeon; QVC; ShopNBC; Speed Channel; Spike TV; Syfy; TBS Superstation; The Learning Channel; Toon Disney; Travel Channel; Trinity Broadcasting Network; truTV; Turner Classic Movies; Turner Network TV; TV Land; USA Network; Versus; VH1; Weather Channel; WGN America.
Fee: $49.95 installation; $37.95 monthly; $19.95 additional installation.

Digital Basic Service
Subscribers: 1,000.
Programming (received off-air): KCNC-TV (CBS) Denver; KDVR (FOX) Denver; KMGH-TV (ABC) Denver; KRMA-TV (PBS) Denver; KUSA (NBC) Denver.
Programming (via satellite): BBC America; Bio; Discovery Digital Networks; Discovery HD Theater; Encore (multiplexed); ESPN HD; Fox College Sports Atlantic; Fox College Sports Central; Fox College Sports Pacific; Fox Soccer; G4; GAS; History Channel International; Independent Film Channel; MTV Networks Digital Suite; Music Choice; Nick Jr.; NickToons TV; Ovation; Style Network; The Sportsman Channel; Turner Network TV HD.
Fee: $12.95 monthly.

Digital Pay Service 1
Pay Units: N.A.
Programming (via satellite): ART America; Canales N; CCTV-4; Chinese Television Network; Cinemax (multiplexed); Filipino Channel; Flix; HBO (multiplexed); HBO HD; RAI International; Russian Television Network; Showtime (multiplexed); Starz (multiplexed); The Movie Channel (multiplexed); TV Asia; TV Japan; TV5, La Television International.
Fee: $5.00 monthly (Canales), $10.95 monthly (Cinemax), $11.95 monthly (Starz/Encore), $12.95 monthly (HBO), $13.95 monthly (Flix, Showtime & TMC), $14.95 monthly (ART, CCTV-4, Filipino, RAI, RTN or TV 5), $24.95 monthly (TV Asia), $29.95 monthly (TV Japan).

Video-On-Demand: No

Pay-Per-View
ETC (delivered digitally), Addressable: Yes; iN DEMAND (delivered digitally), Fee: $3.95; sports (delivered digitally).

Internet Service
Operational: Yes. Began: April 1, 2001.
Subscribers: 1,500.
Broadband Service: Champion Broadband.
Fee: $69.95 installation; $44.95 monthly.

Telephone Service
Digital: Operational

Miles of Plant: 120.0 (coaxial); None (fiber optic). Homes passed: 12,500.
Senior Vice President: Scott Binder. General Manager: Rich Jenning.
Ownership: Comcast Cable Communications Inc. (MSO).

LAMAR—Bresnan Communications, 2218 San Juan Ave, La Junta, CO 81050. Phones: 719-384-8434 (La Junta office); 719-275-8356. Fax: 719-275-6068. Web Site: http://www.bresnan.com. Also serves Prowers County (unincorporated areas). ICA: CO0034.
TV Market Ranking: Outside TV Markets (LAMAR, Prowers County (unincorporated areas)). Franchise award date: N.A. Franchise expiration date: N.A. Began: January 10, 1964.
Channel capacity: N.A. Channels available but not in use: N.A.

Basic Service
Subscribers: 1,875.
Programming (received off-air): KKTV (CBS, MNT) Colorado Springs; KOAA-TV

(NBC) Pueblo; KRDO-TV (ABC) Colorado Springs; KTSC (PBS) Pueblo; 1 FM.

Programming (via satellite): CNBC; C-SPAN; C-SPAN 2; Home Shopping Network; KCNC-TV (CBS) Denver; KDVR (FOX) Denver; KKTV (CBS, MNT) Colorado Springs; KMGH-TV (ABC) Denver; KPXC-TV (ION) Denver; KTVD (MNT) Denver; KUSA (NBC) Denver; KWGN-TV (CW) Denver; Lifetime; MyNetworkTV Inc.; QVC; TV Guide Network; Univision.

Programming (via translator): KTSC (PBS) Pueblo.

Fee: $60.00 installation; $20.99 monthly; $3.95 converter.

Expanded Basic Service 1

Subscribers: N.A.

Programming (via satellite): ABC Family Channel; Altitude Sports & Entertainment; AMC; Animal Planet; Arts & Entertainment; Cartoon Network; CNN; Comedy Central; Country Music TV; Discovery Channel; Disney Channel; E! Entertainment Television; ESPN; ESPN 2; Eternal Word TV Network; Food Network; Fox News Channel; Fox Sports Net Rocky Mountain; FX; Hallmark Channel; Headline News; HGTV; History Channel; MSNBC; MTV; Nickelodeon; Oxygen; Spike TV; Syfy; TBS Superstation; Telefutura; The Learning Channel; Travel Channel; truTV; Turner Classic Movies; Turner Network TV; TV Land; USA Network; VH1; Weather Channel.

Digital Basic Service

Subscribers: N.A.

Programming (received off-air): KKTV (CBS, MNT) Colorado Springs; KOAA-TV (NBC) Pueblo; KRDO-TV (ABC) Colorado Springs; KTSC (PBS) Pueblo.

Programming (via satellite): ABC Family HD; AmericanLife TV Network; Animal Planet HD; Arts & Entertainment HD; Bandamax; BBC America; Bio; Bloomberg Television; Bravo; CBS College Sports Network; Cine Latino; Cine Mexicano; CMT Pure Country; CNN en Espanol; Cooking Channel; De Pelicula; De Pelicula Clasico; Discovery Channel HD; Discovery en Espanol; Discovery HD Theater; Discovery Health Channel; Discovery Kids Channel; Discovery Military Channel; Discovery Planet Green; Disney Channel HD; DMX Music; Do-It-Yourself; ESPN Classic Sports; ESPN Deportes; ESPN HD; ESPNews; FitTV; Food Network HD; Fox College Sports Atlantic; Fox College Sports Central; Fox College Sports Pacific; Fox Movie Channel; Fox Reality Channel; Fox Soccer; Fox Sports en Espanol; Fuse; G4; Gol TV; Golf Channel; Gospel Music Channel; GSN; Halogen Network; HGTV HD; History Channel en Espanol; History Channel International; ID Investigation Discovery; Independent Film Channel; ION Television; Lifetime Movie Network; Mountain West TV; MTV Hits; MTV Jams; MTV Tres; MTV2; mun2 television; National Geographic Channel; National Geographic Channel HD Network; NFL Network; Nick Jr.; Nick Too; NickToons TV; Outdoor Channel; PBS Kids Sprout; RFD-TV; Science Channel; Science Channel HD; SoapNet; Speed Channel; Style Network; Syfy HD; TeenNick; Telefutura; Telehit; The Sportsman Channel; Toon Disney; Trinity Broadcasting Network; Universal HD; Univision; USA Network HD; VeneMovies; Versus; VH1 Classic; VH1 Soul.

Digital Pay Service 1

Pay Units: N.A.

Programming (via satellite): Cinemax (multiplexed); Encore (multiplexed); Flix; HBO (multiplexed); HBO HD; Showtime (multiplexed); Starz (multiplexed); Starz HDTV; The Movie Channel (multiplexed).

Video-On-Demand: No

Internet Service

Operational: Yes.

Fee: $39.95 monthly.

Telephone Service

Digital: Operational

Fee: $49.99 monthly

Miles of Plant: 44.0 (coaxial); 8.0 (fiber optic). Homes passed: 5,092.

General Manager: Jerry Parker. Chief Technician: Matt Harris.

City fee: 5% of gross.

Ownership: Bresnan Communications Inc. (MSO). Sale pends to Cablevision Systems Corp.

LAPORTE—US Cable of Coastal Texas LP. Now served by EATON, CO [CO0055]. ICA: CO0177.

LARIMER COUNTY—Champion Broadband, 380 Perry St, Ste 230, Castle Rock, CO 80104. Phones: 303-688-7766; 866-801-1122. Web Site: http://www.championbroadband.com. ICA: CO0211.

TV Market Ranking: Below 100 (LARIMER COUNTY). Franchise award date: November 2, 1988. Franchise expiration date: N.A. Began: N.A.

Channel capacity: 41 (not 2-way capable). Channels available but not in use: None.

Basic Service

Subscribers: 264.

Programming (received off-air): KBDI-TV (PBS) Broomfield; KCNC-TV (CBS) Denver; KDVR (FOX) Denver; KMGH-TV (ABC) Denver; KPXC-TV (ION) Denver; KRMA-TV (PBS) Denver; KTVD (MNT) Denver; KUSA (NBC) Denver; KWGN-TV (CW) Denver.

Programming (via satellite): ABC Family Channel; AMC; Arts & Entertainment; Cartoon Network; CNBC; CNN; C-SPAN; Discovery Channel; Disney Channel; ESPN; ESPN 2; Fox News Channel; Fox Sports Net Rocky Mountain; Fuse; FX; Great American Country; Headline News; HGTV; History Channel; Lifetime; MSNBC; Outdoor Channel; QVC; Syfy; TBS Superstation; The Learning Channel; Travel Channel; Turner Network TV; USA Network; Weather Channel; WGN America.

Fee: $49.95 installation; $37.95 monthly.

Digital Basic Service

Subscribers: 1.

Fee: $12.95 monthly.

Pay Service 1

Pay Units: N.A.

Programming (via satellite): HBO; The Movie Channel.

Fee: $10.95 monthly (Cinemax), $11.95 monthly (Starz), $12.95 monthly (HBO), $13.95 monthly (Showtime/TMC).

Internet Service

Operational: Yes.

Fee: $45.00 installation; $45.00 monthly.

Telephone Service

None

Miles of Plant: 61.0 (coaxial); None (fiber optic). Homes passed: 1,150.

General Manager: Mark Haverkate.

Ownership: Champion Broadband.

LAS ANIMAS—Baja Broadband, 344 W 6th St, Las Animas, CO 81054-1750. Phones: 970-565-4031 (Cortez office); 719-456-0243. Fax: 970-565-7407. Web Site: http://www.bajabroadband.com. ICA: CO0066.

TV Market Ranking: Outside TV Markets (LAS ANIMAS). Franchise award date: N.A. Franchise expiration date: N.A. Began: July 1, 1981.

Channel capacity: 62 (not 2-way capable). Channels available but not in use: 2.

Basic Service

Subscribers: 951.

Programming (received off-air): KKTV (CBS, MNT) Colorado Springs; KOAA-TV (NBC) Pueblo; KRDO-TV (ABC) Colorado Springs; KTSC (PBS) Pueblo; KTVD (MNT) Denver; KWGN-TV (CW) Denver; KXRM-TV (FOX) Colorado Springs.

Programming (via satellite): ABC Family Channel; AMC; Animal Planet; Arts & Entertainment; Bravo; Cartoon Network; CNBC; CNN; Comedy Central; Country Music TV; C-SPAN; Discovery Channel; Disney Channel; E! Entertainment Television; ESPN; ESPN 2; Eternal Word TV Network; Food Network; Fox News Channel; Fox Sports Net Rocky Mountain; FX; G4; Headline News; HGTV; History Channel; Home Shopping Network; Lifetime; MSNBC; MTV; National Geographic Channel; Nickelodeon; Product Information Network; QVC; Speed Channel; Spike TV; Syfy; TBS Superstation; The Learning Channel; Travel Channel; Trinity Broadcasting Network; truTV; Turner Classic Movies; Turner Network TV; TV Land; Univision; USA Network; VH1; Weather Channel; WGN America.

Current originations: Public Access.

Fee: $49.95 installation; $40.99 monthly.

Digital Basic Service

Subscribers: N.A.

Programming (via satellite): BBC America; Bio; Bloomberg Television; CMT Pure Country; Discovery Health Channel; Discovery Kids Channel; Discovery Military Channel; Discovery Planet Green; Disney XD; ESPNews; FitTV; Fox Movie Channel; Fox Soccer; Fuse; G4; Golf Channel; GSN; Halogen Network; History Channel International; ID Investigation Discovery; Independent Film Channel; Lifetime Movie Network; MTV2; Music Choice; Nick Jr.; Outdoor Channel; Science Channel; Style Network; TeenNick; Versus; VH1 Classic.

Digital Pay Service 1

Pay Units: N.A.

Programming (via satellite): Cinemax (multiplexed); Encore (multiplexed); HBO (multiplexed); Showtime (multiplexed); Starz; The Movie Channel (multiplexed).

Video-On-Demand: No

Pay-Per-View

Club Jenna (delivered digitally); iN DEMAND (delivered digitally); Playboy TV (delivered digitally); Fresh (delivered digitally).

Internet Service

Operational: No.

Telephone Service

None

Miles of Plant: 23.0 (coaxial); None (fiber optic). Homes passed: 1,125.

Area Vice President & General Manager: Tom Jaskiewicz. Technical Operations Director: Matt Warford.

Ownership: Baja Broadband (MSO).

LEADVILLE—Bresnan Communications, 402 Main St, Canon City, CO 81212. Phone: 719-275-8356. Fax: 719-275-6068. Web Site: http://www.bresnan.com. Also serves Lake County & Leadville North. ICA: CO0045.

TV Market Ranking: Outside TV Markets (Lake County, LEADVILLE, Leadville North). Franchise award date: N.A. Franchise expiration date: N.A. Began: March 1, 1954.

Channel capacity: N.A. Channels available but not in use: N.A.

Basic Service

Subscribers: 1,055.

Programming (via satellite): C-SPAN; C-SPAN 2; Home Shopping Network; ION Television; KCNC-TV (CBS) Denver; KDVR (FOX) Denver; KMGH-TV (ABC) Denver; KRMA-TV (PBS) Denver; KTVD (MNT) Denver; KUSA (NBC) Denver; KWGN-TV (CW) Denver; Lifetime; QVC; Weather Channel.

Fee: $60.00 installation; $11.00 monthly; $60.00 additional installation.

Expanded Basic Service 1

Subscribers: 836.

Programming (via satellite): ABC Family Channel; Altitude Sports & Entertainment; AMC; Animal Planet; Arts & Entertainment; Cartoon Network; CNBC; CNN; Comedy Central; Country Music TV; Discovery Channel; Disney Channel; E! Entertainment Television; ESPN; ESPN 2; Eternal Word TV Network; Food Network; Fox News Channel; Fox Sports Net Rocky Mountain; FX; Hallmark Channel; Headline News; HGTV; History Channel; MSNBC; MTV; Nickelodeon; Oxygen; Spike TV; Syfy; TBS Superstation; Telemundo; The Learning Channel; The Sportsman Channel; Travel Channel; truTV; Turner Classic Movies; Turner Network TV; TV Guide Network; TV Land; USA Network; VH1.

Fee: $12.60 monthly.

Digital Basic Service

Subscribers: N.A.

Programming (via satellite): AmericanLife TV Network; Animal Planet HD; Arts & Entertainment HD; Bandamax; BBC America; Bio; Bloomberg Television; Bravo; CBS College Sports Network; Cine Latino; Cine Mexicano; CMT Pure Country; CNN en Espanol; De Pelicula; De Pelicula Clasico; Discovery Channel HD; Discovery en Espanol; Discovery HD Theater; Discovery Health Channel; Discovery Kids Channel; Discovery Military Channel; DMX Music; ESPN Classic Sports; ESPN Deportes; ESPN HD; ESPNews; FitTV; Food Network HD; Fox College Sports Atlantic; Fox College Sports Central; Fox College Sports Pacific; Fox Movie Channel; Fox Reality Channel; Fox Soccer; Fox Sports en Espanol; Fuse; G4; Gol TV; Golf Channel; Gospel Music Channel; GSN; Halogen Network; HGTV HD; History Channel en Espanol; History Channel HD; History Channel International; ID Investigation Discovery; Independent Film Channel; ION Television; Lifetime Movie Network; Mountain West TV; MTV Hits; MTV Jams; MTV Tres; MTV2; mun2 television; National Geographic Channel; National Geographic Channel HD Network; NFL Network; Nick Jr.; Nick Too; NickToons TV; Outdoor Channel; PBS Kids Sprout; RFD-TV; Science Channel; SoapNet; Speed Channel; Style Network; Syfy HD; TeenNick; Telehit; Toon Disney; Trinity Broadcasting Network; Universal HD; USA Network HD; VeneMovies; Versus; VH1 Classic; VH1 Soul.

Digital Pay Service 1

Pay Units: N.A.

Programming (via satellite): Cinemax (multiplexed); Encore (multiplexed); Flix; HBO (multiplexed); HBO HD; Showtime (multiplexed); Starz (multiplexed); Starz HDTV; The Movie Channel (multiplexed).

Video-On-Demand: No

Pay-Per-View

iN DEMAND (delivered digitally).

Internet Service
Operational: Yes.
Broadband Service: Bresnan OnLine.
Fee: $39.95 monthly.
Telephone Service
Analog: Not Operational
Digital: Operational
Miles of Plant: 47.0 (coaxial); 19.0 (fiber optic). Homes passed: 3,826.
General Manager: Jerry Parker. Technical Operations Manager: Doyle Ruona.
City fee: 5% of gross.
Ownership: Bresnan Communications Inc. (MSO). Sale pends to Cablevision Systems Corp.

LIMON—Champion Broadband, 380 Perry St, Ste 230, Castle Rock, CO 80104. Phones: 303-688-7766; 866-801-1122. Web Site: http://www.championbroadband.com. ICA: CO0069.
TV Market Ranking: Outside TV Markets (LIMON). Franchise award date: N.A. Franchise expiration date: N.A. Began: January 1, 1963.
Channel capacity: 41 (operating 2-way). Channels available but not in use: None.
Basic Service
Subscribers: 384.
Programming (received off-air): KCEC (UNV) Denver; KCNC-TV (CBS) Denver; KDVR (FOX) Denver; KKTV (CBS, MNT) Colorado Springs; KMGH-TV (ABC) Denver; KRDO-TV (ABC) Colorado Springs; KRMA-TV (PBS) Denver; KUSA (NBC) Denver; KWGN-TV (CW) Denver; allband FM.
Programming (via satellite): ABC Family Channel; AMC; Arts & Entertainment; Cartoon Network; Comedy Central; C-SPAN; Discovery Channel; Disney Channel; ESPN; ESPN 2; Fox News Channel; Fox Sports Net Rocky Mountain; FX; Great American Country; Headline News; HGTV; History Channel; INSP; Lifetime; Outdoor Channel; QVC; TBS Superstation; The Learning Channel; Toon Disney; Turner Classic Movies; Turner Network TV; USA Network; Weather Channel; WGN America.
Current originations: Public Access.
Fee: $45.00 installation; $34.95 monthly.
Digital Basic Service
Subscribers: N.A.
Programming (via satellite): AmericanLife TV Network; BBC America; Bio; Bloomberg Television; Discovery Digital Networks; DMX Music; ESPN Classic Sports; ESPNews; FitTV; Fox College Sports Atlantic; Fox College Sports Central; Fox College Sports Pacific; Fox Sports World; Fuse; G4; Golf Channel; Halogen Network; History Channel; History Channel International; Lime; National Geographic Channel; Speed Channel; Style Network; WE tv.
Fee: $13.95 monthly.
Digital Expanded Basic Service
Subscribers: N.A.
Programming (via satellite): DMX Music; Encore; Fox Movie Channel; Lifetime Movie Network.
Fee: $13.95 monthly.
Pay Service 1
Pay Units: 63.
Programming (via satellite): Cinemax; HBO.
Fee: $15.00 installation; $10.95 monthly (HBO).
Digital Pay Service 1
Pay Units: N.A.
Programming (via satellite): Cinemax (multiplexed); Flix; HBO (multiplexed); Showtime (multiplexed); The Movie Channel (multiplexed).
Fee: $16.55 monthly.
Video-On-Demand: No
Pay-Per-View
ESPN Now (delivered digitally), Fee: $3.99, Addressable: Yes; Hot Choice (delivered digitally); Movies (delivered digitally); Playboy TV (delivered digitally); Fresh (delivered digitally); Shorteez (delivered digitally); sports (delivered digitally); Urban Xtra (delivered digitally).
Internet Service
Operational: Yes.
Broadband Service: Champion Broadband.
Fee: $45.00 installation; $24.95 monthly.
Telephone Service
None
Miles of Plant: 20.0 (coaxial); None (fiber optic). Homes passed: 1,112.
General Manager: Mark Haverkate.
City fee: 3% of gross.
Ownership: Champion Broadband (MSO).

LONGMONT—Comcast Cable, 434 Kimbark St, Longmont, CO 80501-5526. Phone: 303-776-2108. Fax: 303-678-5308. Web Site: http://www.comcast.com. Also serves Berthoud, Campion, Dacono, Erie, Evanston, Firestone, Fort Lupton, Frederick, Hygiene, Lafayette, Larimer County, Louisville, Loveland & Superior. ICA: CO0011.
TV Market Ranking: 32 (Dacono, Erie, Evanston, Firestone, Fort Lupton, Frederick, Hygiene, Lafayette, LONGMONT, Louisville, Superior); Below 100 (Berthoud, Campion, Larimer County, Loveland). Franchise award date: May 1, 1982. Franchise expiration date: N.A. Began: March 15, 1983.
Channel capacity: 77 (operating 2-way). Channels available but not in use: 8.
Basic Service
Subscribers: 97,944 Includes Fort Collins & Greeley.
Programming (received off-air): KBDI-TV (PBS) Broomfield; KCEC (UNV) Denver; KCNC-TV (CBS) Denver; KDEN-TV (TMO) Longmont; KDVR (FOX) Denver; KMGH-TV (ABC) Denver; KPXC-TV (ION) Denver; KRMA-TV (PBS) Denver; KRMT (ETV) Denver; KTVD (MNT) Denver; KUSA (NBC) Denver; KWGN-TV (CW) Denver; KWHD (IND) Castle Rock; 1 FM.
Programming (via satellite): C-SPAN; Hallmark Channel; Home Shopping Network; QVC; Telefutura; WGN America.
Current originations: Government Access; Educational Access.
Fee: $44.99 installation; $12.79 monthly.
Expanded Basic Service 1
Subscribers: N.A.
Programming (via satellite): ABC Family Channel; Altitude Sports & Entertainment; AMC; Animal Planet; Arts & Entertainment; Cartoon Network; CNBC; CNN; Comedy Central; Country Music TV; Discovery Channel; Disney Channel; E! Entertainment Television; ESPN; ESPN 2; Food Network; Fox News Channel; Fox Sports Net Rocky Mountain; FX; Golf Channel; Headline News; HGTV; History Channel; Lifetime; MSNBC; MTV; Nickelodeon; Speed Channel; Spike TV; Style Network; Syfy; TBS Superstation; The Learning Channel; Travel Channel; truTV; Turner Network TV; TV Land; USA Network; Versus; VH1; Weather Channel.
Fee: $35.70 monthly.
Digital Basic Service
Subscribers: 48,434 Includes Fort Collins & Greeley.
Programming (received off-air): KCNC-TV (CBS) Denver; KDVR (FOX) Denver; KMGH-TV (ABC) Denver; KUSA (NBC) Denver.
Programming (via satellite): BBC America; Bio; Black Family Channel; Bloomberg Television; Bravo; Canal 52MX; Canales N; CBS College Sports Network; CET - Comcast Entertainment TV; Country Music TV; Current; Discovery Digital Networks; Encore (multiplexed); ESPN Classic Sports; ESPN HD; ESPNews; Flix; Fox College Sports Atlantic; Fox College Sports Central; Fox College Sports Pacific; Fox Movie Channel; Fox Reality Channel; Fox Soccer; Fuse; G4; GAS; Great American Country; GSN; Halogen Network; History Channel International; Independent Film Channel; INHD; Lifetime Movie Network; Lime; LOGO; MoviePlex; MTV Networks Digital Suite; Music Choice; National Geographic Channel; NFL Network; Nick Jr.; NickToons TV; Outdoor Channel; PBS Kids Sprout; ShopNBC; SoapNet; Sundance Channel; the mtn; The Word Network; Toon Disney; Trinity Broadcasting Network; Turner Classic Movies; TV Guide Network; Versus HD; WE tv; Weatherscan.
Fee: $8.45 monthly.
Digital Pay Service 1
Pay Units: 151.
Programming (via satellite): Cinemax (multiplexed); Flix; HBO (multiplexed); Showtime (multiplexed); Starz (multiplexed); The Movie Channel (multiplexed).
Fee: $15.99 monthly (each).
Video-On-Demand: No
Pay-Per-View
iN DEMAND (delivered digitally); ESPN (delivered digitally); Starz (delivered digitally); Playboy TV (delivered digitally).
Internet Service
Operational: Yes.
Subscribers: 59,135.
Broadband Service: Comcast High Speed Internet.
Fee: $42.95 monthly.
Telephone Service
Digital: Operational
Miles of Plant: 1,050.0 (coaxial); None (fiber optic). Homes passed: 225,750. Homes passed includes Fort Collins & Greeley
Vice President & General Manager: Mike Trueblood. Technical Operations Director: Stan Reifschneider. Marketing Director: Kier Kristenson.
City fee: 5% of gross.
Ownership: Comcast Cable Communications Inc. (MSO).

LOVELAND (Columbine Mobile Home Park)—Formerly served by US Cable of Coastal Texas LP. No longer in operation. ICA: CO0178.

LYONS—Champion Broadband, 380 Perry St, Ste 230, Castle Rock, CO 80104. Phones: 303-688-7766; 866-801-1122. Web Site: http://www.championbroadband.com. ICA: CO0110.
TV Market Ranking: Below 100 (LYONS). Franchise award date: N.A. Franchise expiration date: N.A. Began: February 1, 1985.
Channel capacity: 61 (operating 2-way). Channels available but not in use: 21.
Basic Service
Subscribers: 202.
Programming (received off-air): KCNC-TV (CBS) Denver; KDVR (FOX) Denver; KMGH-TV (ABC) Denver; KRMA-TV (PBS) Denver; KRMT (ETV) Denver; KTVD (MNT) Denver; KUSA (NBC) Denver; KWGN-TV (CW) Denver.
Programming (via satellite): ABC Family Channel; Arts & Entertainment; Bravo; Cartoon Network; CNBC; CNN; Discovery Channel; Disney Channel; ESPN; ESPN 2; Fox News Channel; Fox Sports Net Rocky Mountain; Fuse; FX; Great American Country; Headline News; HGTV; Lifetime; MSNBC; Outdoor Channel; QVC; TBS Superstation; The Learning Channel; Turner Classic Movies; Turner Network TV; Univision; USA Network; Weather Channel; WGN America.
Fee: $30.00 installation; $33.50 monthly.
Pay Service 1
Pay Units: 52.
Programming (via satellite): HBO; Showtime.
Fee: $10.95 monthly (HBO).
Video-On-Demand: No
Internet Service
Operational: Yes.
Broadband Service: Champion Broadband.
Fee: $45.00 installation; $45.00 monthly.
Telephone Service
None
Miles of Plant: 20.0 (coaxial); None (fiber optic). Homes passed: 850.
General Manager: Mark Haverkate.
Ownership: Champion Broadband (MSO).

MANASSA—Bresnan Communications, 402 Main St, Canon City, CO 81212. Phone: 877-273-7626. Web Site: http://www.bresnan.com. Also serves La Jara, Romeo & Sanford. ICA: CO0068.
TV Market Ranking: Outside TV Markets (La Jara, MANASSA, Romeo, Sanford). Franchise award date: N.A. Franchise expiration date: N.A. Began: August 1, 1986.
Channel capacity: N.A. Channels available but not in use: N.A.
Basic Service
Subscribers: 294.
Programming (via satellite): ABC Family Channel; Altitude Sports & Entertainment; Animal Planet; Cartoon Network; CNN; Country Music TV; Discovery Channel; Disney Channel; ESPN; ESPN 2; GalaVision; Hallmark Channel; KCNC-TV (CBS) Denver; KDVR (FOX) Denver; KMGH-TV (ABC) Denver; KRMA-TV (PBS) Denver; KTVD (MNT) Denver; KUSA (NBC) Denver; KWGN-TV (CW) Denver; Nickelodeon; Oxygen; Spike TV; TBS Superstation; Telefutura; The Learning Channel; Turner Network TV; Univision; USA Network.
Fee: $39.99 installation; $56.99 monthly; $15.00 additional installation.
Digital Basic Service
Subscribers: N.A.
Programming (via satellite): Bandamax; BBC America; Bravo; CBS College Sports Network; Cine Latino; Cine Mexicano; CMT Pure Country; CNN en Espanol; De Pelicula; De Pelicula Clasico; Discovery en Espanol; Discovery Health Channel; Discovery Kids Channel; Discovery Military Channel; Discovery Planet Green; DMX Music; ESPN Classic Sports; ESPN Deportes; ESPNews; Fox Soccer; Fox Sports en Espanol; GalaVision; Gol TV; Golf Channel; GSN; HGTV; History Channel; History Channel en Espanol; ID Investigation Discovery; Independent Film Channel; Mountain West TV; MTV Tres; mun2 television; National Geographic Channel; Nick Jr.; Science Channel; SoapNet; Speed Channel; Syfy; Telefutura; Telehit; Turner Classic Movies; TV Land; Univision; VeneMovies; Versus; VH1 Classic.
Digital Pay Service 1
Pay Units: N.A.
Programming (via satellite): Cinemax (multiplexed); Encore (multiplexed); HBO (multiplexed); Showtime (multiplexed);

Starz (multiplexed); The Movie Channel (multiplexed).
Video-On-Demand: No
Pay-Per-View
iN DEMAND (delivered digitally).
Internet Service
Operational: Yes.
Fee: $39.95 monthly.
Telephone Service
Digital: Operational
Fee: $49.99 monthly
Miles of Plant: 50.0 (coaxial); 10.0 (fiber optic). Homes passed: 1,227.
General Manager: Jerry Parker. Technical Operations Manager: Doyle Ruona.
Ownership: Bresnan Communications Inc. (MSO). Sale pends to Cablevision Systems Corp.

MANCOS—Bresnan Communications. Now served by DOLORES, CO [CO0106]. ICA: CO0111.

MANZANOLA—Bresnan Communications. Now served by LA JUNTA, CO [CO0040]. ICA: CO0149.

MEAD—K2 Communications, PO Box 232, Mead, CO 80542-0232. Phones: 866-525-2253; 303-828-0369; 970-535-6323. Fax: 303-265-9001. E-mail: info@k2cable.com. Web Site: http://www.k2cable.com. ICA: CO0196.
TV Market Ranking: 32 (MEAD). Franchise award date: July 1, 1993. Franchise expiration date: N.A. Began: March 1, 1994.
Channel capacity: 36 (operating 2-way). Channels available but not in use: N.A.
Basic Service
Subscribers: 325.
Programming (received off-air): KBDI-TV (PBS) Broomfield; KCNC-TV (CBS) Denver; KDVR (FOX) Denver; KMGH-TV (ABC) Denver; KPXC-TV (ION) Denver; KRMA-TV (PBS) Denver; KTFD-DT (UNV) Boulder; KTVD (MNT) Denver; KUSA (NBC) Denver; KWGN-TV (CW) Denver.
Fee: $35.00 installation.
Expanded Basic Service 1
Subscribers: 160.
Programming (received off-air): KDEN-TV (TMO) Longmont.
Programming (via satellite): ABC Family Channel; Altitude Sports & Entertainment; AMC; Animal Planet; Arts & Entertainment; Bravo; Cartoon Network; CNBC; CNN; Comedy Central; C-SPAN; Discovery Channel; Disney Channel; Do-It-Yourself; Encore; ESPN; ESPN 2; ESPN Classic Sports; Food Network; Fox Sports Net; FX; Golf Channel; Great American Country; Hallmark Channel; Headline News; HGTV; History Channel; Home Shopping Network; Independent Film Channel; INSP; Lifetime; MoviePlex; MSNBC; National Geographic Channel; Nickelodeon; Oxygen; Speed Channel; Spike TV; Syfy; TBS Superstation; The Learning Channel; Travel Channel; truTV; Turner Classic Movies; Turner Network TV; TV Land; USA Network; Versus; VH1; Weather Channel; WGN America.
Fee: $37.95 monthly.
Pay Service 1
Pay Units: 31.
Programming (via satellite): HBO.
Fee: $14.95 monthly.
Pay Service 2
Pay Units: 34.
Programming (via satellite): Flix; Showtime; Sundance Channel; The Movie Channel.
Fee: $14.95 monthly.
Video-On-Demand: No
Internet Service
Operational: Yes.
Subscribers: 200.
Broadband Service: In-house.
Fee: $49.99 installation; $38.95 monthly.
Telephone Service
Digital: Operational
Fee: $29.99 monthly
Miles of Plant: 14.0 (coaxial); None (fiber optic). Total homes in franchised area: 1,000.
Manager & Chief Technician: Gary Shields.
Ownership: K2 Communications.

MEEKER—Bresnan Communications, 580 Russell St, Craig, CO 81625. Phones: 970-824-3298; 970-824-3296 (Customer service). Fax: 970-824-5528. Web Site: http://www.bresnan.com. Also serves Rio Blanco County. ICA: CO0078.
TV Market Ranking: Below 100 (Rio Blanco County (portions)); Outside TV Markets (MEEKER, Rio Blanco County (portions)). Franchise award date: N.A. Franchise expiration date: N.A. Began: June 1, 1982.
Channel capacity: N.A. Channels available but not in use: N.A.
Basic Service
Subscribers: 189.
Programming (via satellite): ABC Family Channel; Altitude Sports & Entertainment; AMC; Animal Planet; Cartoon Network; CNBC; CNN; Discovery Channel; Disney Channel; E! Entertainment Television; ESPN; Fox News Channel; Fox Sports Net Rocky Mountain; FX; Great American Country; Headline News; KCNC-TV (CBS) Denver; KDVR (FOX) Denver; KMGH-TV (ABC) Denver; KRMA-TV (PBS) Denver; KTVD (MNT) Denver; KUSA (NBC) Denver; KWGN-TV (CW) Denver; Lifetime; MSNBC; MTV; Nickelodeon; QVC; Spike TV; TBS Superstation; The Learning Channel; truTV; Turner Network TV; USA Network; Weather Channel.
Fee: $39.99 installation; $42.50 monthly; $1.50 converter; $18.75 additional installation.
Pay Service 1
Pay Units: 82.
Programming (via satellite): Cinemax; Encore; HBO; Showtime; Starz.
Fee: $1.75 monthly (Encore), $13.20 monthly (Cinemax), $14.19 monthly (HBO or Showtime).
Video-On-Demand: No
Pay-Per-View
Movies; special events.
Internet Service
Operational: Yes.
Fee: $36.95 monthly.
Telephone Service
Digital: Operational
Fee: $46.95 monthly
Miles of Plant: 16.0 (coaxial); None (fiber optic). Homes passed: 975. Total homes in franchised area: 1,150.
General Manager: Tommy Cotton.
Ownership: Bresnan Communications Inc. (MSO). Sale pends to Cablevision Systems Corp.

MERINO—Kentec Communications, 915 W Main St, Sterling, CO 80751. Phone: 970-522-8107. Fax: 970-521-9457. Web Site: http://www.kci.net. ICA: CO0191.
TV Market Ranking: Below 100 (MERINO). Franchise award date: May 4, 1992. Franchise expiration date: N.A. Began: September 1, 1992.
Channel capacity: 63 (not 2-way capable). Channels available but not in use: N.A.

Basic Service
Subscribers: 53.
Programming (via satellite): ABC Family Channel; Altitude Sports & Entertainment; AMC; Animal Planet; Arts & Entertainment; CNN; Comedy Central; Discovery Channel; Discovery Health Channel; Disney Channel; ESPN; ESPN 2; Fox News Channel; Fox Sports Net Rocky Mountain; Headline News; HGTV; History Channel; Home Shopping Network; KCNC-TV (CBS) Denver; KDVR (FOX) Denver; KMGH-TV (ABC) Denver; KRMA-TV (PBS) Denver; KTVD (MNT) Denver; KUSA (NBC) Denver; KWGN-TV (CW) Denver; National Geographic Channel; Nickelodeon; Paxson Communications Corp.; ShopNBC; Speed Channel; Syfy; TBS Superstation; The Learning Channel; Travel Channel; Trinity Broadcasting Network; Turner Classic Movies; Turner Network TV; USA Network; WE tv; Weather Channel; WGN America.
Fee: $30.00 installation; $25.00 monthly.
Pay Service 1
Pay Units: 5.
Programming (via satellite): HBO.
Fee: $10.00 monthly.
Internet Service
Operational: No.
Telephone Service
None
Miles of Plant: 3.0 (coaxial); None (fiber optic). Homes passed: 100. Total homes in franchised area: 100.
Manager & Chief Technician: Kent Sager. Marketing Director: Tiffany Stewart.
Ownership: Kentec Communications Inc. (MSO).

MONTE VISTA—Bresnan Communications. Now served by ALAMOSA, CO [CO0035]. ICA: CO0048.

MONTROSE—Bresnan Communications, 2502 Foresight Cir, Grand Junction, CO 81505. Phone: 970-263-2300. E-mail: shogue@bresnan.com. Web Site: http://www.bresnan.com. Also serves Montrose County. ICA: CO0028.
TV Market Ranking: Below 100 (MONTROSE, Montrose County (portions)); Outside TV Markets (Montrose County (portions)). Franchise award date: N.A. Franchise expiration date: N.A. Began: January 1, 1966.
Channel capacity: N.A. Channels available but not in use: N.A.
Basic Service
Subscribers: 4,955.
Programming (received off-air): KFQX (FOX) Grand Junction; KJCT (ABC, TMO) Grand Junction; KKCO (CW, NBC) Grand Junction; KREY-TV (CBS) Montrose; KRMA-TV (PBS) Denver.
Programming (via satellite): C-SPAN; C-SPAN 2; CW+; Discovery Channel; HGTV; History Channel; Home Shopping Network; Lifetime; MyNetworkTV Inc.; Spike TV; TBS Superstation; Telemundo; Weather Channel.
Current originations: Government Access.
Fee: $43.50 installation; $10.97 monthly.
Expanded Basic Service 1
Subscribers: 3,500.
Programming (via satellite): ABC Family Channel; AMC; Animal Planet; Arts & Entertainment; Cartoon Network; CNBC; CNN; Comedy Central; Country Music TV; Disney Channel; E! Entertainment Television; ESPN; ESPN 2; Eternal Word TV Network; Food Network; Fox News Channel; Fox Sports Net Rocky Mountain; FX; Hallmark Channel; Headline News; ION Television; MSNBC; MTV; Nickelodeon; Oxygen; QVC; Syfy; Telefutura; The Learning Channel; Travel Channel; truTV; Turner Classic Movies; Turner Network TV; TV Guide Network; TV Land; Univision; USA Network; VH1.
Fee: $26.99 monthly.
Digital Basic Service
Subscribers: N.A.
Programming (received off-air): KFQX (FOX) Grand Junction; KJCT (ABC, TMO) Grand Junction; KKCO (CW, NBC) Grand Junction; KREX-TV (CBS, MNT) Grand Junction.
Programming (via satellite): ABC Family HD; Altitude Sports & Entertainment; AmericanLife TV Network; Animal Planet HD; Arts & Entertainment HD; Bandamax; BBC America; Bio; Bloomberg Television; Bravo; Bravo HD; BYU Television; CBS College Sports Network; Cine Latino; Cine Mexicano; CMT Pure Country; CNBC HD+; CNN en Espanol; CNN HD; Cooking Channel; De Pelicula; De Pelicula Clasico; Discovery Channel HD; Discovery en Espanol; Discovery HD Theater; Discovery Health Channel; Discovery Kids Channel; Discovery Military Channel; Discovery Planet Green; Disney Channel HD; DMX Music; Do-It-Yourself; ESPN 2 HD; ESPN Classic Sports; ESPN Deportes; ESPN HD; ESPNews; FitTV; Food Network HD; Fox College Sports Atlantic; Fox College Sports Central; Fox College Sports Pacific; Fox Movie Channel; Fox Reality Channel; Fox Soccer; Fox Sports en Espanol; FSN HD; Fuse; G4; Gol TV; Golf Channel; Gospel Music Channel; GSN; Halogen Network; HDNet; HDNet Movies; HGTV HD; History Channel en Espanol; History Channel HD; History Channel International; ID Investigation Discovery; Independent Film Channel; ION Life; ION Television; Jewish Television (JTV); Lifetime Movie Network; Lifetime Movie Network HD; Mountain West TV; MTV Hits; MTV Jams; MTV Tres; MTV2; mun2 television; National Geographic Channel; National Geographic Channel HD Network; NFL Network; NFL Network HD; NHL Network; Nick Jr.; Nick Too; NickToons TV; Outdoor Channel; Outdoor Channel 2 HD; Palladia; PBS Kids Sprout; Qubo; RFD-TV; Science Channel; Science Channel HD; SoapNet; Speed Channel; Speed HD; Style Network; Syfy HD; TBS in HD; TeenNick; Telefutura; Telehit; The Sportsman Channel; TLC HD; Toon Disney; Trinity Broadcasting Network; Turner Network TV HD; Universal HD; Univision; USA Network HD; VeneMovies; Versus; Versus HD; VH1 Classic; VH1 Soul; Weather Channel HD.

Pay Service 1
Pay Units: 341.
Programming (via satellite): Cinemax.
Fee: $20.00 installation; $13.20 monthly.
Pay Service 2
Pay Units: 1,232.
Programming (via satellite): HBO.
Fee: $14.19 monthly.
Digital Pay Service 1
Pay Units: N.A.
Programming (via satellite): Cinemax (multiplexed); Cinemax HD; Cinemax On Demand; Encore (multiplexed); Flix; HBO (multiplexed); HBO HD; HBO On Demand; Showtime; Showtime HD; Showtime On Demand; Starz (multiplexed); Starz HDTV; Starz On Demand; The Movie Channel (multiplexed); The Movie Channel HD.
Video-On-Demand: Yes
Pay-Per-View
Movies (delivered digitally); special events (delivered digitally); ESPN (delivered digitally); NBA League Pass (delivered digitally); MLS Direct Kick (delivered digitally); MLB Extra Innings (delivered digitally); NHL Center Ice (delivered digitally).
Internet Service
Operational: Yes.
Broadband Service: Bresnan OnLine.
Fee: $55.95 monthly.
Telephone Service
Digital: Operational
Fee: $39.99 monthly
Miles of Plant: 116.0 (coaxial); None (fiber optic). Homes passed: 9,100.
Regional Vice President: Sean Hogue. Technical Operations Manager: Gary Young.
City fee: 3% of gross.
Ownership: Bresnan Communications Inc. (MSO). Sale pends to Cablevision Systems Corp.

MONUMENT—Formerly served by Adelphia Communications. Now served by COLORADO SPRINGS, CO [CO0003]. ICA: CO0032.

NEDERLAND—Rocky Mountain Cable, 40 County Rd 600, Unit F, Pagosa Springs, CO 81147-9473. Phones: 800-222-1332; 970-731-2211. Fax: 970-731-5510. Web Site: http://www.rockymtncable.com. ICA: CO0100.
TV Market Ranking: Below 100 (NEDERLAND). Franchise award date: January 15, 1983. Franchise expiration date: N.A. Began: December 30, 1983.
Channel capacity: 44 (not 2-way capable). Channels available but not in use: None.
Basic Service
Subscribers: 137.
Programming (via satellite): Animal Planet; Cartoon Network; Discovery Channel; ESPN; History Channel; KCNC-TV (CBS) Denver; KDVR (FOX) Denver; KMGH-TV (ABC) Denver; KRMA-TV (PBS) Denver; KUSA (NBC) Denver; KWGN-TV (CW) Denver; MSNBC; Nickelodeon; Outdoor Channel; QVC; TBS Superstation; The Learning Channel; Travel Channel; TV Land; USA Network; WE tv.
Fee: $20.00 installation; $27.24 monthly.
Expanded Basic Service 1
Subscribers: 110.
Programming (via satellite): ABC Family Channel; Arts & Entertainment; CNBC; CNN; Comedy Central; Country Music TV; Disney Channel; ESPN 2; Fox Sports Net Rocky Mountain; Headline News; MTV; Spike TV; Syfy; Turner Classic Movies; Turner Network TV; Versus; Weather Channel.
Fee: $14.75 monthly.
Pay Service 1
Pay Units: 25.
Programming (via satellite): HBO (multiplexed).
Fee: $13.49 monthly.
Video-On-Demand: No
Internet Service
Operational: No.
Telephone Service
None
Miles of Plant: 14.0 (coaxial); None (fiber optic). Homes passed: 541.
President: Wayne Vestal. Chief Technician: Bobby Smith.
City fee: 3% of gross.
Ownership: ICE Cable Holdings LLC (MSO).

NEW CASTLE—Comcast Cable. Now served by RIFLE, CO [CO0043]. ICA: CO0092.

NORWOOD—B & C Cable, PO Box 548, Norwood, CO 81423-0548. Phone: 970-327-0122. E-mail: bccable@rtebb.net. ICA: CO0137.
TV Market Ranking: Below 100 (NORWOOD). Franchise award date: N.A. Franchise expiration date: N.A. Began: August 1, 1991.
Channel capacity: 42 (not 2-way capable). Channels available but not in use: 16.
Basic Service
Subscribers: 62.
Programming (received off-air): KJCT (ABC, TMO) Grand Junction; KKCO (CW, NBC) Grand Junction; KREY-TV (CBS) Montrose; KRMA-TV (PBS) Denver; KWGN-TV (CW) Denver.
Programming (via satellite): ABC Family Channel; AMC; Arts & Entertainment; CNN; Discovery Channel; ESPN; Spike TV; TBS Superstation; Turner Network TV; USA Network.
Current originations: Public Access.
Fee: $15.00 installation; $23.00 monthly.
Pay Service 1
Pay Units: 5.
Programming (via satellite): Cinemax.
Fee: $8.00 monthly.
Pay Service 2
Pay Units: 11.
Programming (via satellite): HBO.
Fee: $8.00 monthly.
Pay Service 3
Pay Units: 7.
Programming (via satellite): Showtime.
Fee: $8.00 monthly.
Internet Service
Operational: No.
Telephone Service
None
Miles of Plant: 5.0 (coaxial); None (fiber optic). Homes passed: 245. Total homes in franchised area: 245.
Manager & Chief Technician: Craig Greager.
City fee: 5% of basic.
Ownership: B & C Cable.

NUCLA—Bresnan Communications, 2502 Foresight Cir, Grand Junction, CO 81505. Phone: 970-263-2300. E-mail: shogue@bresnan.com. Web Site: http://www.bresnan.com. Also serves Naturita. ICA: CO0090.
TV Market Ranking: Outside TV Markets (Naturita, NUCLA). Franchise award date: N.A. Franchise expiration date: N.A. Began: N.A.
Channel capacity: 36 (not 2-way capable). Channels available but not in use: 14.
Basic Service
Subscribers: 150.
Programming (received off-air): KREY-TV (CBS) Montrose.
Programming (via satellite): ABC Family Channel; Altitude Sports & Entertainment; Animal Planet; CNN; Country Music TV; Discovery Channel; Disney Channel; ESPN; KCNC-TV (CBS) Denver; KDVR (FOX) Denver; KMGH-TV (ABC) Denver; KRMA-TV (PBS) Denver; KUSA (NBC) Denver; KWGN-TV (CW) Denver; Spike TV; TBS Superstation; Turner Network TV; USA Network.
Fee: $43.50 installation; $20.99 monthly.
Pay Service 1
Pay Units: 74.
Programming (via satellite): HBO.
Fee: $10.00 installation; $12.95 monthly.
Pay Service 2
Pay Units: 91.
Programming (via satellite): The Movie Channel.
Fee: $10.00 installation; $12.95 monthly.
Video-On-Demand: No
Internet Service
Operational: Yes.
Fee: $39.95 monthly.
Telephone Service
Digital: Operational
Fee: $49.99 monthly
Miles of Plant: 14.0 (coaxial); None (fiber optic). Homes passed: 760. Total homes in franchised area: 790.
Regional Vice President: Sean Hogue. Technical Operations Manager: Gary Young.
Ownership: Bresnan Communications Inc. (MSO). Sale pends to Cablevision Systems Corp.

OAK CREEK—Formerly served by Westcom II LLC. No longer in operation. ICA: CO0119.

OLATHE—Rocky Mountain Cable, 40 County Rd 600, Unit F, Pagosa Springs, CO 81147-9473. Phones: 800-222-1332; 970-731-2211. Fax: 970-731-5510. Web Site: http://www.rockymtncable.com. ICA: CO0112.
TV Market Ranking: Below 100 (OLATHE). Franchise award date: January 1, 1981. Franchise expiration date: N.A. Began: N.A.
Channel capacity: 48 (not 2-way capable). Channels available but not in use: 1.
Basic Service
Subscribers: 244.
Programming (received off-air): KJCT (ABC, TMO) Grand Junction; KREY-TV (CBS) Montrose; KRMA-TV (PBS) Denver; KWGN-TV (CW) Denver.
Programming (via satellite): ABC Family Channel; AMC; Animal Planet; Arts & Entertainment; Bravo; Cartoon Network; CNBC; CNN; Comedy Central; Country Music TV; C-SPAN; Discovery Channel; Disney Channel; ESPN; ESPN 2; Eternal Word TV Network; GalaVision; Hallmark Channel; Headline News; History Channel; MSNBC; Nickelodeon; Outdoor Channel; QVC; Spike TV; Syfy; TBS Superstation; Telefutura; The Learning Channel; Trinity Broadcasting Network; Turner Classic Movies; Turner Network TV; TV Land; Univision; USA Network; Versus; WE tv; Weather Channel; WGN America.
Fee: $20.00 installation; $34.99 monthly.
Pay Service 1
Pay Units: 32.
Programming (via satellite): HBO.
Fee: $13.49 monthly (HBO).
Video-On-Demand: No
Internet Service
Operational: No.
Telephone Service
None
Miles of Plant: 9.0 (coaxial); None (fiber optic). Homes passed: 450. Total homes in franchised area: 450.
President: Wayne Vestal. Chief Technician: Bobby Smith.
Ownership: ICE Cable Holdings LLC (MSO).

ORDWAY—Champion Broadband, 380 Perry St, Ste 230, Castle Rock, CO 80104. Phones: 303-688-7766; 866-801-1122. Web Site: http://www.championbroadband.com. ICA: CO0099.
TV Market Ranking: Outside TV Markets (ORDWAY). Franchise award date: December 1, 1983. Franchise expiration date: N.A. Began: February 1, 1982.
Channel capacity: 41 (not 2-way capable). Channels available but not in use: 6.
Basic Service
Subscribers: 138.
Programming (received off-air): KKTV (CBS, MNT) Colorado Springs; KOAA-TV (NBC) Pueblo; KRDO-TV (ABC) Colorado Springs; KTSC (PBS) Pueblo; KWGN-TV (CW) Denver; KXRM-TV (FOX) Colorado Springs.
Programming (via satellite): ABC Family Channel; AMC; Arts & Entertainment; Cartoon Network; CNN; Discovery Channel; Disney Channel; ESPN; ESPN 2; Fox News Channel; Fox Sports Net Rocky Mountain; Fuse; FX; Great American Country; Headline News; INSP; Lifetime; Outdoor Channel; QVC; TBS Superstation; The Learning Channel; Turner Network TV; Univision; USA Network; Weather Channel; WGN America.
Fee: $25.00 installation; $36.45 monthly.
Pay Service 1
Pay Units: 37.
Programming (via satellite): HBO; The Movie Channel.
Fee: $9.95 monthly (TMC),$10.95 monthly (HBO).
Video-On-Demand: No
Internet Service
Operational: No.
Telephone Service
None
Miles of Plant: 7.0 (coaxial); None (fiber optic). Homes passed: 768.
General Manager: Mark Haverkate.
Ownership: Champion Broadband (MSO).

OTIS—CommuniComm Services, 234 Wind River Dr, Douglas, WY 82633-2338. Phone: 307-358-3861. Fax: 307-358-3849. Web Site: http://www.netcommander.com. Also serves Akron & Yuma. ICA: CO0128.
TV Market Ranking: Below 100 (Akron); Outside TV Markets (OTIS (RURAL), Yuma). Franchise award date: January 1, 1969. Franchise expiration date: N.A. Began: December 1, 1969.
Channel capacity: N.A. Channels available but not in use: N.A.
Basic Service
Subscribers: 608.
Programming (received off-air): KTVS-LD Albuquerque.
Programming (via microwave): KCNC-TV (CBS) Denver; KDVR (FOX) Denver; KMGH-TV (ABC) Denver; KRMA-TV (PBS) Denver; KUSA (NBC) Denver; KWGN-TV (CW) Denver.
Programming (via satellite): Home Shopping Network; QVC; Univision; WGN America.
Fee: $39.95 installation; $29.95 monthly.
Expanded Basic Service 1
Subscribers: 39.
Programming (via satellite): 3 Angels Broadcasting Network; ABC Family Channel; AMC; Animal Planet; Arts & Entertainment; Bravo; Cartoon Network;

CNBC; CNN; Comedy Central; Country Music TV; C-SPAN; C-SPAN 2; Discovery Channel; Discovery Health Channel; E! Entertainment Television; ESPN; ESPN 2; ESPN Classic Sports; ESPNews; Food Network; Fox News Channel; Fox Sports Net Rocky Mountain; FX; Great American Country; Hallmark Channel; Headline News; HGTV; History Channel; MSNBC; MTV; Nick Jr.; Nickelodeon; Outdoor Channel; Spike TV; Syfy; TBS Superstation; The Learning Channel; Travel Channel; Turner Classic Movies; Turner Network TV; TV Land; USA Network; VH1; WE tv; Weather Channel.
Fee: $19.04 monthly.

Digital Basic Service
Subscribers: 8.
Programming (via satellite): BBC America; Bio; Blackbelt TV; Bloomberg Television; Bravo; Discovery Digital Networks; ESPN 2; ESPN Classic Sports; ESPNews; Fox College Sports Atlantic; Fox College Sports Central; Fox College Sports Pacific; Fox Movie Channel; Fox Sports World; Fuse; G4; GAS; Golf Channel; Great American Country; GSN; Halogen Network; HGTV; History Channel; History Channel International; Independent Film Channel; International Television (ITV); Lifetime Movie Network; MBC America; MTV Networks Digital Suite; Music Choice; National Geographic Channel; Nick Jr.; NickToons TV; Outdoor Channel; Ovation; ShopNBC; Speed Channel; Style Network; Sundance Channel; Syfy; The Word Network; Trinity Broadcasting Network; Trio; Turner Classic Movies; TV Land; Versus; WE tv.
Fee: $11.95 monthly.

Digital Pay Service 1
Pay Units: 5.
Programming (via satellite): HBO (multiplexed).
Fee: $15.00 installation; $13.95 monthly.

Digital Pay Service 2
Pay Units: 5.
Programming (via satellite): Cinemax (multiplexed).
Fee: $11.95 monthly.

Digital Pay Service 3
Pay Units: 4.
Programming (via satellite): Encore (multiplexed); Starz (multiplexed).
Fee: $13.95 monthly.

Digital Pay Service 4
Pay Units: 2.
Programming (via satellite): Flix; Showtime (multiplexed); The Movie Channel (multiplexed).
Fee: $13.95 monthly (Showtime/Flix or TMC).

Video-On-Demand: No

Pay-Per-View
Hot Choice, Fee: $3.95-$50.00; Playboy TV, Fee: $3.95-$50.00; Fresh, Fee: $3.95-$50.00; Shorteez, Fee: $3.95-$50.00.

Internet Service
Operational: Yes.
Subscribers: 6.
Broadband Service: Net Commander.
Fee: $39.95 installation; $21.95 monthly.

Telephone Service
None

Miles of Plant: 38.0 (coaxial); None (fiber optic). Homes passed: 2,550.
General Manager: Merritt Engleberetsen. Chief Technician: Eric Garland. Marketing Director: Darby Edelman.
Franchise fee: None.
Ownership: James Cable LLC (MSO).

PAGOSA SPRINGS—Rocky Mountain Cable, 40 County Rd 600, Unit F, Pagosa Springs, CO 81147-9473. Phones: 800-222-1332; 970-731-2211. Fax: 970-731-5510. Web Site: http://www.rockymtncable.com. Also serves Archuleta County. ICA: CO0053.
TV Market Ranking: Outside TV Markets (Archuleta County, PAGOSA SPRINGS). Franchise award date: February 7, 1984. Franchise expiration date: N.A. Began: August 15, 1984.
Channel capacity: 67 (not 2-way capable). Channels available but not in use: 7.

Basic Service
Subscribers: 1,592.
Programming (received off-air): KRPV-DT (IND) Roswell.
Programming (via microwave): KOAT-TV (ABC) Albuquerque; KOBF (NBC) Farmington.
Programming (via satellite): CNN; Discovery Channel; Fox News Channel; Hallmark Channel; Headline News; KCNC-TV (CBS) Denver; KMGH-TV (ABC) Denver; KRMA-TV (PBS) Denver; KUSA (NBC) Denver; KWGN-TV (CW) Denver; Lifetime; QVC; The Learning Channel; Travel Channel; TV Guide Network; Weather Channel.
Fee: $20.00 installation; $27.24 monthly.

Expanded Basic Service 1
Subscribers: 1,352.
Programming (via microwave): KLUZ-TV (UNV) Albuquerque.
Programming (via satellite): ABC Family Channel; AMC; Animal Planet; Arts & Entertainment; Bravo; CNBC; Comedy Central; Country Music TV; C-SPAN; Disney Channel; Do-It-Yourself; ESPN; ESPN 2; Food Network; Fox Sports Net Rocky Mountain; FX; Great American Country; GSN; HGTV; History Channel; Home Shopping Network; MSNBC; MTV; Nickelodeon; Outdoor Channel; SoapNet; Speed Channel; Spike TV; TBS Superstation; truTV; Turner Network TV; TV Land; USA Network; Versus; VH1; WE tv.
Fee: $14.75 monthly.

Digital Basic Service
Subscribers: N.A.
Programming (via satellite): BBC America; Bio; Bloomberg Television; Bravo; Discovery Digital Networks; ESPN 2; ESPN Classic Sports; ESPNews; FitTV; Fox Movie Channel; Fox Sports World; Fuse; G4; GAS; Golf Channel; Gospel Music TV; GSN; Halogen Network; HGTV; History Channel; History Channel International; Independent Film Channel; Lifetime Movie Network; MTV Networks Digital Suite; Nick Jr.; NickToons TV; Outdoor Channel; Speed Channel; Trinity Broadcasting Network; Trio; Turner Classic Movies; TV Land; Versus; WE tv.
Fee: $3.00 monthly.

Pay Service 1
Pay Units: N.A.
Programming (via satellite): HBO.
Fee: $13.49 monthly.

Digital Pay Service 1
Pay Units: N.A.
Programming (via satellite): Cinemax (multiplexed); Encore (multiplexed); Flix; HBO (multiplexed); Showtime (multiplexed); Starz (multiplexed); The Movie Channel (multiplexed).
Fee: $12.49 monthly (Starz/Encore or Cinemax), $13.49 monthly (HBO or Showtime).

Video-On-Demand: No

Pay-Per-View
Playboy TV, Fee: $3.95-$7.95; Spice; Spice2.

Internet Service
Operational: Yes.
Fee: $35.00 installation; $39.95 monthly.

Telephone Service
None

Miles of Plant: 65.0 (coaxial); None (fiber optic). Homes passed: 2,093.
President: Wayne Vestal. Chief Technician: Mark Darnell.
City fee: 3% of gross.
Ownership: ICE Cable Holdings LLC (MSO).

PAONIA—Bresnan Communications, 2502 Foresight Cir, Grand Junction, CO 81505. Phone: 970-263-2300. E-mail: shogue@bresnan.com. Web Site: http://www.bresnan.com. Also serves Delta County. ICA: CO0079.
TV Market Ranking: Below 100 (Delta County (portions), PAONIA); Outside TV Markets (Delta County (portions)). Franchise award date: N.A. Franchise expiration date: N.A. Began: June 1, 1982.
Channel capacity: 35 (operating 2-way). Channels available but not in use: 2.

Basic Service
Subscribers: 230.
Programming (received off-air): KKCO (CW, NBC) Grand Junction; KREY-TV (CBS) Montrose; KTVD (MNT) Denver.
Programming (via satellite): ABC Family Channel; Altitude Sports & Entertainment; AMC; Animal Planet; CNN; C-SPAN; Discovery Channel; Disney Channel; ESPN; Fox News Channel; Fox Sports Net Rocky Mountain; FX; Headline News; KCNC-TV (CBS) Denver; KDVR (FOX) Denver; KMGH-TV (ABC) Denver; KRMA-TV (PBS) Denver; KUSA (NBC) Denver; KWGN-TV (CW) Denver; MTV; Nickelodeon; Spike TV; TBS Superstation; truTV; Turner Network TV; USA Network; Weather Channel.
Planned originations: Public Access.
Fee: $43.50 installation; $23.99 monthly.

Digital Basic Service
Subscribers: N.A.
Programming (via satellite): BBC America; Bravo; CBS College Sports Network; CMT Pure Country; Discovery Health Channel; Discovery Kids Channel; Discovery Military Channel; Discovery Planet Green; DMX Music; ESPN 2; ESPN Classic Sports; ESPNews; Fox Soccer; Golf Channel; GSN; HGTV; History Channel; ID Investigation Discovery; Independent Film Channel; Mountain West TV; National Geographic Channel; Nick Jr.; Science Channel; SoapNet; Speed Channel; Syfy; Turner Classic Movies; TV Land; Versus; VH1 Classic.

Digital Pay Service 1
Pay Units: N.A.
Programming (via satellite): Encore (multiplexed); HBO (multiplexed); Showtime Too; Starz Edge; The Movie Channel.

Video-On-Demand: No

Internet Service
Operational: Yes.
Fee: $39.95 monthly.

Telephone Service
Digital: Operational
Fee: $49.99 monthly

Miles of Plant: 26.0 (coaxial); None (fiber optic). Homes passed: 990.
Regional Vice President: Sean Hogue. Technical Operations Manager: Gary Young.
City fee: 3% of gross.
Ownership: Bresnan Communications Inc. (MSO). Sale pends to Cablevision Systems Corp.

PARACHUTE—Comcast Cable, 1605 Grand Ave, Ste I, Glenwood Springs, CO 81601. Phone: 970-928-7784. Fax: 970-945-0270. Web Site: http://www.comcast.com. Also serves Battlement Mesa. ICA: CO0072.
TV Market Ranking: Outside TV Markets (Battlement Mesa, PARACHUTE). Franchise award date: July 9, 1981. Franchise expiration date: N.A. Began: November 1, 1981.
Channel capacity: 66 (operating 2-way). Channels available but not in use: None.

Basic Service
Subscribers: N.A. Included in Aspen
Programming (received off-air): KCEC (UNV) Denver; KCNC-TV (CBS) Denver; KDVR (FOX) Denver; KJCT (ABC, TMO) Grand Junction; KMGH-TV (ABC) Denver; KPXC-TV (ION) Denver; KRMA-TV (PBS) Denver; KTVD (MNT) Denver; KUSA (NBC) Denver; KWGN-TV (CW) Denver.
Programming (via satellite): ABC Family Channel; Altitude Sports & Entertainment; C-SPAN; ESPN; ESPN 2; Fox Sports Net Rocky Mountain; TV Guide Network.
Current originations: Religious Access; Educational Access.
Fee: $44.99 installation; $14.99 monthly.

Expanded Basic Service 1
Subscribers: N.A.
Programming (via satellite): AMC; Animal Planet; Arts & Entertainment; Bio; Bravo; CNBC; CNN; Comedy Central; Country Music TV; Discovery Channel; Disney Channel; Food Network; Fox News Channel; Great American Country; Headline News; HGTV; History Channel; History Channel International; Home Shopping Network; Lifetime; MSNBC; MTV; National Geographic Channel; Nickelodeon; Outdoor Channel; QVC; ShopNBC; SoapNet; Spike TV; Syfy; TBS Superstation; The Learning Channel; Toon Disney; Travel Channel; Trinity Broadcasting Network; Turner Classic Movies; Turner Network TV; TV Land; USA Network; VH1; Weather Channel; WGN America.
Fee: $35.00 monthly.

Digital Basic Service
Subscribers: N.A. Included in Aspen
Programming (via satellite): BBC America; Bloomberg Television; Discovery Health Channel; Discovery Kids Channel; ESPN Classic Sports; ESPNews; FitTV; Fox Movie Channel; Fox Soccer; G4; Golf Channel; GSN; Halogen Network; Independent Film Channel; LOGO; MoviePlex; Music Choice; Nick Jr.; NickToons TV; PBS Kids Sprout; Science Television; Versus; WE tv.
Fee: $9.95 monthly.

Pay Service 1
Pay Units: 83.
Programming (via satellite): Cinemax.
Fee: $9.95 monthly.

Pay Service 2
Pay Units: 316.
Programming (via satellite): HBO (multiplexed).
Fee: $9.95 monthly.
Pay Service 3
Pay Units: 109.
Programming (via satellite): Showtime.
Fee: $9.95 monthly.
Digital Pay Service 1
Pay Units: N.A.
Programming (via satellite): Encore (multiplexed); Showtime; Starz; The Movie Channel.
Fee: $15.99 monthly (each).
Video-On-Demand: No
Pay-Per-View
Playboy TV; Fresh.
Internet Service
Operational: Yes.
Broadband Service: Comcast High Speed Internet.
Fee: $42.95 monthly.
Telephone Service
None
Miles of Plant: 30.0 (coaxial); None (fiber optic). Homes passed included in Aspen
Vice President: Mike Trueblood. General Manager: Ben Miller. Technical Operations Manager: James Comiskey. Customer Service Manager: Anita Robinson.
City fee: 5% of gross.
Ownership: Comcast Cable Communications Inc. (MSO).

PENROSE (unincorporated areas)—Bresnan Communications. Now served by CANON CITY, CO [CO0016]. ICA: CO0075.

PETERSON AFB—Peterson Broadband, 802 Mitchell Rd, Colorado Springs, CO 80914. Phones: 719-597-0873; 719-597-0164; 425-451-1470 (Corporate office). Fax: 425-451-1471. Web Site: http://www.pafb.net. ICA: CO0081.
TV Market Ranking: Below 100 (PETERSON AFB). Franchise award date: N.A. Franchise expiration date: N.A. Began: January 1, 1983.
Channel capacity: 74 (operating 2-way). Channels available but not in use: N.A.
Basic Service
Subscribers: 750.
Programming (received off-air): KKTV (CBS, MNT) Colorado Springs; KOAA-TV (NBC) Pueblo; KRDO-TV (ABC) Colorado Springs; KTSC (PBS) Pueblo; KXRM-TV (FOX) Colorado Springs; KXTU-LP (CW) Colorado Springs.
Programming (via satellite): ABC Family Channel; AMC; Animal Planet; Arts & Entertainment; BBC America; BET Networks; Bio; Cartoon Network; CNBC; CNN; Comedy Central; Country Music TV; C-SPAN; C-SPAN 2; Discovery Channel; Discovery Kids Channel; Discovery Military Channel; Disney Channel; E! Entertainment Television; ESPN; ESPN 2; ESPN Classic Sports; Food Network; Fox Movie Channel; Fox News Channel; FX; G4; Golf Channel; Hallmark Channel; Headline News; HGTV; History Channel; History Channel International; KWGN-TV (CW) Denver; Lifetime; Lifetime Movie Network; MSNBC; MTV; NASA TV; National Geographic Channel; Nickelodeon; Outdoor Channel; Oxygen; Pentagon Channel; QVC; Speed Channel; Spike TV; Syfy; TBS Superstation; The Learning Channel; Travel Channel; Trinity Broadcasting Network; Turner Classic Movies; Turner Network TV; TV Land; Univision; USA Network; Versus; VH1; WE tv; Weather Channel; WGN America.
Fee: $40.00 installation; $37.95 monthly.
Digital Basic Service
Subscribers: 107.
Programming (via satellite): Bravo; CMT Pure Country; Discovery Planet Green; DMX Music; ESPN Classic Sports; Fuse; HGTV; History Channel International; ID Investigation Discovery; Lifetime Movie Network; MTV2; National Geographic Channel; Speed Channel; Style Network; TeenNick; Toon Disney; Trio; VH1 Classic.
Fee: $43.90 monthly.
Digital Pay Service 1
Pay Units: 150.
Programming (via satellite): Cinemax (multiplexed); Encore (multiplexed); Flix; HBO (multiplexed); Showtime (multiplexed); Starz (multiplexed); The Movie Channel (multiplexed).
Fee: $10.95 monthly (each).
Video-On-Demand: No
Internet Service
Operational: Yes.
Subscribers: 300.
Broadband Service: In-house.
Fee: $26.95 installation; $34.95 monthly.
Telephone Service
None
Miles of Plant: 4.0 (coaxial); 4.0 (fiber optic). Homes passed: 1,549.
Manager: Kevin Abriam. Office Manager: Kim Abriam.
Ownership: RuralWest - Western Rural Broadband Inc. (MSO).

PUEBLO—Comcast Cable, 807 N Greenwood St, Pueblo, CO 81003-2925. Phone: 719-546-3216. Fax: 719-546-1597. Web Site: http://www.comcast.com. Also serves Blende, Pueblo County, Pueblo West & St. Charles Mesa. ICA: CO0005.
TV Market Ranking: Below 100 (Blende, PUEBLO, Pueblo County, Pueblo West, St. Charles Mesa). Franchise award date: N.A. Franchise expiration date: N.A. Began: June 1, 1970.
Channel capacity: 67 (operating 2-way). Channels available but not in use: None.
Basic Service
Subscribers: 27,447.
Programming (received off-air): KKTV (CBS, MNT) Colorado Springs; KOAA-TV (NBC) Pueblo; KRDO-TV (ABC) Colorado Springs; KTSC (PBS) Pueblo; KXRM-TV (FOX) Colorado Springs; KXTU-LP (CW) Colorado Springs.
Programming (via satellite): ABC Family Channel; Animal Planet; CNN; C-SPAN; C-SPAN 2; Discovery Channel; Eternal Word TV Network; Fox News Channel; Great American Country; Hallmark Channel; Headline News; HGTV; Home Shopping Network; KCNC-TV (CBS) Denver; KMGH-TV (ABC) Denver; KUSA (NBC) Denver; KWGN-TV (CW) Denver; Lifetime; Nickelodeon; QVC; TBS Superstation; Travel Channel; TV Land; Univision; VH1; Weather Channel.
Current originations: Government Access; Educational Access; Public Access.
Fee: $60.00 installation; $23.99 monthly; $3.00 converter.
Expanded Basic Service 1
Subscribers: N.A.
Programming (via satellite): Altitude Sports & Entertainment; AMC; Arts & Entertainment; BET Networks; Cartoon Network; CNBC; Comedy Central; Country Music TV; Disney Channel; E! Entertainment Television; ESPN; ESPN 2; Food Network; Fox Sports Net Rocky Mountain; FX; Golf Channel; History Channel; ION Television; MSNBC; MTV; Oxygen; Syfy; The Learning Channel; truTV; Turner Network TV; TV Guide Network; USA Network; Versus.
Fee: $12.10 monthly.
Digital Basic Service
Subscribers: 12,284.
Programming (received off-air): KKTV (CBS, MNT) Colorado Springs; KOAA-TV (NBC) Pueblo; KRDO-TV (ABC) Colorado Springs; KXRM-TV (FOX) Colorado Springs.
Programming (via satellite): American-Life TV Network; BBC America; Bio; Black Family Channel; Bloomberg Television; Bravo; Canal 52MX; Canales N; CBS College Sports Network; Country Music TV; Discovery Digital Networks; Discovery HD Theater; Encore (multiplexed); ESPN 2 HD; ESPN Classic Sports; ESPN HD; ESPNews; Flix; Fox College Sports Atlantic; Fox College Sports Central; Fox College Sports Pacific; Fox Movie Channel; Fox Reality Channel; Fox Soccer; Fuse; G4; GAS; GSN; Halogen Network; History Channel International; Independent Film Channel; INHD; Lifetime Movie Network; LOGO; MoviePlex; MTV Networks Digital Suite; Music Choice; MyNetworkTV Inc.; National Geographic Channel; NBA TV; NFL Network; Nick Jr.; NickToons TV; Outdoor Channel; Palladia; PBS Kids Sprout; ShopNBC; Si TV; SoapNet; Speed Channel; Sundance Channel; the mtn; The Word Network; Toon Disney; Trinity Broadcasting Network; Turner Classic Movies; Turner Network TV HD; TV One; Versus HD; WE tv.
Fee: $23.95 monthly.
Pay Service 1
Pay Units: 2,742.
Programming (via satellite): Encore (multiplexed); HBO.
Fee: $20.00 installation; $10.95 monthly (Showtime or Starz & Encore), $12.75 monthly (Cinemax or HBO).
Digital Pay Service 1
Pay Units: N.A.
Programming (via satellite): Cinemax (multiplexed); Cinemax HD; Flix; HBO (multiplexed); HBO HD; Showtime (multiplexed); Showtime HD; Starz (multiplexed); Starz HDTV; The Movie Channel (multiplexed).
Video-On-Demand: Planned
Pay-Per-View
Sports PPV (delivered digitally); iN DEMAND (delivered digitally); Fresh (delivered digitally); NBA League Pass (delivered digitally); Playboy TV (delivered digitally); Hot Choice (delivered digitally); NHL Center Ice (delivered digitally); MLB Extra Innings (delivered digitally).
Internet Service
Operational: Yes.
Subscribers: 9,779.
Broadband Service: Comcast High Speed Internet.
Fee: $42.95 monthly.
Telephone Service
None
Miles of Plant: 707.0 (coaxial); None (fiber optic). Homes passed: 64,497.
Vice President: Jim Commers. General Manager: Kyle Ford. Technical Operations Director: Jim Garcia. Vice President, Marketing: Zach Street. Public Relations Manager: Sandra Mann.
City fee: 3% of gross.
Ownership: Comcast Cable Communications Inc. (MSO).

PUEBLO WEST—Comcast Cable. Now served by PUEBLO, CO [CO0005]. ICA: CO0077.

RANGELY—Bresnan Communications, 580 Russell St, Craig, CO 81625. Phone: 970-824-3298. Fax: 970-824-5529. Web Site: http://www.bresnan.com. Also serves Rio Blanco County. ICA: CO0085.
TV Market Ranking: Outside TV Markets (RANGELY, Rio Blanco County). Franchise award date: N.A. Franchise expiration date: N.A. Began: August 1, 1982.
Channel capacity: N.A. Channels available but not in use: N.A.
Basic Service
Subscribers: 169.
Programming (via satellite): ABC Family Channel; Altitude Sports & Entertainment; AMC; Animal Planet; Cartoon Network; CNBC; CNN; C-SPAN; Discovery Channel; Disney Channel; E! Entertainment Television; ESPN; Fox News Channel; Fox Sports Net Rocky Mountain; FX; Great American Country; Hallmark Channel; Headline News; KCNC-TV (CBS) Denver; KDVR (FOX) Denver; KMGH-TV (ABC) Denver; KRMA-TV (PBS) Denver; KTVD (MNT) Denver; KUSA (NBC) Denver; KWGN-TV (CW) Denver; Lifetime; MoviePlex; MSNBC; MTV; Nickelodeon; QVC; Spike TV; TBS Superstation; The Learning Channel; truTV; Turner Network TV; USA Network; Weather Channel.
Fee: $37.50 installation; $24.78 monthly; $1.50 converter; $17.55 additional installation.
Pay Service 1
Pay Units: 123.
Programming (via satellite): Cinemax; Encore; HBO; Showtime; Starz.
Fee: $9.95 monthly (each).
Video-On-Demand: No
Internet Service
Operational: Yes.
Fee: $39.95 monthly.
Telephone Service
Digital: Operational
Fee: $49.99 monthly
Miles of Plant: 15.0 (coaxial); None (fiber optic). Homes passed: 867. Total homes in franchised area: 1,042.
General Manager: Tommy Cotton.
City fee: 5% of gross.
Ownership: Bresnan Communications Inc. (MSO). Sale pends to Cablevision Systems Corp.

RIFLE—Comcast Cable, 1605 Grand Ave, Ste I, Glenwood Springs, CO 81601. Phone: 970-928-7784. Fax: 970-945-0270. E-mail: mike_trueblood@cable.comcast.com. Web Site: http://www.comcast.com. Also serves Apple Tree Mobile Home Park, Garfield County, Mountain Shadow Subdivision, New Castle & Silt. ICA: CO0043.
TV Market Ranking: Below 100 (Apple Tree Mobile Home Park, Garfield County (portions), Mountain Shadow Subdivision, New Castle, RIFLE, Silt); Outside TV Markets (Garfield County (portions)). Franchise award date: July 1, 1978. Franchise expiration date: N.A. Began: July 31, 1963.
Channel capacity: N.A. Channels available but not in use: N.A.
Basic Service
Subscribers: N.A. Included in Aspen
Programming (received off-air): KJCT (ABC, TMO) Grand Junction; KREG-TV (CBS) Glenwood Springs; 19 FMs.
Programming (via satellite): Arts & Entertainment; Discovery Channel; KCNC-TV

(CBS) Denver; KDVR (FOX) Denver; KMGH-TV (ABC) Denver; KPXC-TV (ION) Denver; KRMA-TV (PBS) Denver; KTVD (MNT) Denver; KUSA (NBC) Denver; KWGN-TV (CW) Denver; QVC; TBS Superstation.
Current originations: Government Access; Educational Access; Public Access.
Fee: $44.99 installation; $14.99 monthly.

Expanded Basic Service 1
Subscribers: 1,812.
Programming (via satellite): ABC Family Channel; Animal Planet; Cartoon Network; CNBC; CNN; Comedy Central; Country Music TV; C-SPAN; Disney Channel; ESPN; ESPN 2; Fox News Channel; Fox Sports Net Rocky Mountain; FX; Lifetime; MoviePlex; MSNBC; MTV; Nickelodeon; Oxygen; Spike TV; Turner Network TV; Univision; USA Network; Weather Channel.
Fee: $35.00 monthly.

Digital Basic Service
Subscribers: N.A. Included in Aspen
Programming (via satellite): BBC America; Bravo; Discovery Digital Networks; DMX Music; Encore; ESPN Classic Sports; ESPNews; Fox Sports World; Golf Channel; GSN; History Channel; Independent Film Channel; Nick Jr.; Syfy; Turner Classic Movies; TV Land; Versus; WE tv.
Fee: $9.95 monthly.

Pay Service 1
Pay Units: 241.
Programming (via satellite): Encore; HBO.
Fee: $10.00 installation; $1.75 monthly (Encore), $10.95 monthly (HBO).

Digital Pay Service 1
Pay Units: N.A.
Programming (via satellite): Cinemax (multiplexed); HBO (multiplexed); Showtime (multiplexed); Starz (multiplexed); The Movie Channel (multiplexed).
Fee: $15.99 monthly (each).

Video-On-Demand: No

Pay-Per-View
iN DEMAND (delivered digitally); Playboy TV (delivered digitally).

Internet Service
Operational: Yes.
Broadband Service: Comcast High Speed Internet.
Fee: $42.95 monthly.

Telephone Service
None

Homes passed & miles of plant included in Aspen
Vice President: Mike Trueblood. General Manager: Amy Lynch. Technical Operations Manager: James Comiskey. Customer Service Supervisor: Anita Robinson.
City fee: 5% of gross.
Ownership: Comcast Cable Communications Inc. (MSO).

ROCKY FORD—Bresnan Communications. Now served by LA JUNTA, CO [CO0040]. ICA: CO0051.

SAGUACHE—Rocky Mountain Cable, 40 County Rd 600, Unit F, Pagosa Springs, CO 81147-9473. Phones: 800-222-1332; 970-731-2211. Fax: 970-731-5510. Web Site: http://www.rockymtncable.com. ICA: CO0138.
TV Market Ranking: Outside TV Markets (SAGUACHE). Franchise award date: N.A. Franchise expiration date: N.A. Began: July 8, 1992.
Channel capacity: 53 (not 2-way capable). Channels available but not in use: 4.

Basic Service
Subscribers: 88.
Programming (via satellite): ABC Family Channel; AMC; Arts & Entertainment; Bravo; Cartoon Network; CNN; Comedy Central; Country Music TV; C-SPAN; Discovery Channel; Disney Channel; ESPN; ESPN 2; Fox Sports Net Rocky Mountain; G4; History Channel; KCNC-TV (CBS) Denver; KDVR (FOX) Denver; KMGH-TV (ABC) Denver; KRMA-TV (PBS) Denver; KUSA (NBC) Denver; KWGN-TV (CW) Denver; MSNBC; Nickelodeon; QVC; Spike TV; Syfy; TBS Superstation; The Learning Channel; Travel Channel; Trinity Broadcasting Network; Turner Classic Movies; Turner Network TV; TV Guide Network; TV Land; Univision; USA Network; VH1; WE tv; Weather Channel; WGN America.
Programming (via translator): KKTV (CBS, MNT) Colorado Springs; KOB (NBC) Albuquerque.
Fee: $20.00 installation; $36.99 monthly.

Pay Service 1
Pay Units: 3.
Programming (via satellite): Cinemax.
Fee: $12.49 monthly.

Pay Service 2
Pay Units: 5.
Programming (via satellite): HBO.
Fee: $13.49 monthly.

Video-On-Demand: No

Internet Service
Operational: No.

Telephone Service
None

Miles of Plant: 5.0 (coaxial); None (fiber optic). Homes passed: 250. Total homes in franchised area: 250.
President: Wayne Vestal. Chief Technician: Bobby Smith.
Ownership: ICE Cable Holdings LLC.

SALIDA—Bresnan Communications, 402 Main St, Canon City, CO 81212. Phone: 877-273-7626. Web Site: http://www.bresnan.com. Also serves Chaffee County & Poncha Springs. ICA: CO0037.
TV Market Ranking: Outside TV Markets (Chaffee County, Poncha Springs, SALIDA). Franchise award date: N.A. Franchise expiration date: N.A. Began: August 1, 1954.
Channel capacity: N.A. Channels available but not in use: N.A.

Basic Service
Subscribers: 1,545.
Programming (via satellite): C-SPAN 2; Discovery Channel; Home Shopping Network; KCNC-TV (CBS) Denver; KDVR (FOX) Denver; KMGH-TV (ABC) Denver; KPXC-TV (ION) Denver; KRDO-TV (ABC) Colorado Springs; KRMA-TV (PBS) Denver; KTSC (PBS) Pueblo; KTVD (MNT) Denver; KUSA (NBC) Denver; KWGN-TV (CW) Denver; Lifetime; QVC; TV Guide Network.
Current originations: Leased Access.
Fee: $60.00 installation; $9.33 monthly; $60.00 additional installation.

Expanded Basic Service 1
Subscribers: 1,436.
Programming (via satellite): ABC Family Channel; Altitude Sports & Entertainment; AMC; Animal Planet; Arts & Entertainment; Cartoon Network; CNBC; CNN; Comedy Central; Country Music TV; C-SPAN; Disney Channel; E! Entertainment Television; ESPN; ESPN 2; Eternal Word TV Network; Food Network; Fox News Channel; Fox Sports Net Rocky Mountain; FX; Hallmark Channel; Headline News; HGTV; History Channel; MSNBC; MTV; Nickelodeon; Oxygen; Spike TV; Syfy; TBS Superstation; The Learning Channel; Travel Channel; truTV; Turner Classic Movies; Turner Network TV; TV Land; USA Network; VH1; Weather Channel.
Fee: $12.21 monthly.

Digital Basic Service
Subscribers: 850.
Programming (via satellite): American-Life TV Network; Animal Planet HD; Arts & Entertainment HD; BBC America; Bio; Bloomberg Television; Bravo; CBS College Sports Network; Cine Latino; Cine Mexicano; CMT Pure Country; CNN en Espanol; Cooking Channel; Discovery Channel HD; Discovery en Espanol; Discovery HD Theater; Discovery Health Channel; Discovery Kids Channel; Discovery Military Channel; Discovery Planet Green; DMX Music; Do-It-Yourself; ESPN Classic Sports; ESPN Deportes; ESPN HD; ESPNews; FitTV; Food Network HD; Fox College Sports Atlantic; Fox College Sports Central; Fox College Sports Pacific; Fox Movie Channel; Fox Reality Channel; Fox Soccer; Fox Sports en Espanol; Fuse; G4; Golf Channel; Gospel Music Channel; GSN; Halogen Network; HGTV HD; History Channel en Espanol; History Channel HD; History Channel International; ID Investigation Discovery; Independent Film Channel; ION Television; Lifetime Movie Network; Mountain West TV; MTV Jams; MTV Tres; MTV2; mun2 television; National Geographic Channel; National Geographic Channel HD Network; NFL Network; Nick Jr.; Nick Too; NickToons TV; Outdoor Channel; PBS Kids Sprout; RFD-TV; Science Channel; SoapNet; Speed Channel; Style Network; Syfy HD; TeenNick; The Sportsman Channel; Toon Disney; Trinity Broadcasting Network; Universal HD; USA Network HD; VeneMovies; Versus; VH1 Classic; VH1 Soul.

Digital Pay Service 1
Pay Units: N.A.
Programming (via satellite): Cinemax (multiplexed); Encore (multiplexed); Flix; HBO; HBO HD; Showtime (multiplexed); Starz (multiplexed); Starz HDTV; The Movie Channel (multiplexed).

Video-On-Demand: No

Internet Service
Operational: Yes.
Broadband Service: Bresnan OnLine.
Fee: $39.95 monthly.

Telephone Service
Digital: Operational
Fee: $49.99 monthly

Miles of Plant: 50.0 (coaxial); 10.0 (fiber optic). Homes passed: 4,303.
General Manager: Jerry Parker. Technical Operations Manager: Doyle Ruena.
City fee: 5% of gross.
Ownership: Bresnan Communications Inc. (MSO). Sale pends to Cablevision Systems Corp.

SAN LUIS—Bresnan Communications, 402 Main St, Canon City, CO 81212. Phone: 877-273-7626. Web Site: http://www.bresnan.com. Also serves Chama & San Pablo. ICA: CO0107.
TV Market Ranking: Outside TV Markets (Chama, SAN LUIS, San Pablo). Franchise award date: July 10, 1985. Franchise expiration date: N.A. Began: January 1, 1986.
Channel capacity: N.A. Channels available but not in use: N.A.

Basic Service
Subscribers: 166.
Programming (via satellite): ABC Family Channel; Altitude Sports & Entertainment; Animal Planet; BYU Television; Cartoon Network; CNN; Country Music TV; Discovery Channel; Disney Channel; ESPN; GalaVision; Hallmark Channel; KCNC-TV (CBS) Denver; KDVR (FOX) Denver; KMGH-TV (ABC) Denver; KRMA-TV (PBS) Denver; KTVD (MNT) Denver; KUSA (NBC) Denver; KWGN-TV (CW) Denver; Nickelodeon; Oxygen; Spike TV; TBS Superstation; Telefutura; The Learning Channel; Turner Network TV; Univision; USA Network.
Fee: $20.00 installation; $14.99 monthly; $15.00 additional installation.

Digital Basic Service
Subscribers: N.A.
Programming (via satellite): Bandamax; BBC America; Bravo; CBS College Sports Network; Cine Latino; Cine Mexicano; CMT Pure Country; CNN en Espanol; De Pelicula; De Pelicula Clasico; Discovery en Espanol; Discovery Health Channel; Discovery Kids Channel; Discovery Military Channel; Discovery Planet Green; DMX Music; ESPN Classic Sports; ESPN Deportes; ESPNews; Fox Soccer; Fox Sports en Espanol; GalaVision; Gol TV; Golf Channel; GSN; HGTV; History Channel; History Channel en Espanol; ID Investigation Discovery; Independent Film Channel; Mountain West TV; MTV Tres; mun2 television; National Geographic Channel; Nick Jr.; Science Channel; SoapNet; Speed Channel; Syfy; Telefutura; Telehit; Turner Classic Movies; TV Land; Univision; VeneMovies; Versus; VH1 Classic.

Digital Pay Service 1
Pay Units: N.A.
Programming (via satellite): Cinemax (multiplexed); Encore (multiplexed); HBO (multiplexed); Showtime (multiplexed); Starz (multiplexed); The Movie Channel (multiplexed).

Video-On-Demand: No

Internet Service
Operational: Yes.
Fee: $39.95 monthly.

Telephone Service
Digital: Operational
Fee: $49.99 monthly

Miles of Plant: 16.0 (coaxial); None (fiber optic). Homes passed: 600.
Regional Manager: Joe Stackhouse.
Ownership: Bresnan Communications Inc. (MSO). Sale pends to Cablevision Systems Corp.

SEDGWICK—PC Telcom, 120 N Sunflower Dr, Holyoke, CO 80734. Phone: 970-854-2201. Fax: 970-854-2668. E-mail: customerservice@pctelcom.coop. Web Site: http://my.pctelcom.coop. ICA: CO0214.

TV Market Ranking: Outside TV Markets (SEDGWICK).
Channel capacity: N.A. Channels available but not in use: N.A.
Basic Service
Subscribers: N.A. Included in Holyoke
Programming (received off-air): KCNC-TV (CBS) Denver; KDVR (FOX) Denver; KMGH-TV (ABC) Denver; KPNE-TV (PBS) North Platte; KTVS-LD Albuquerque; KUSA (NBC) Denver; KWGN-TV (CW) Denver.
Programming (via satellite): ABC Family Channel; Altitude Sports & Entertainment; AMC; Animal Planet; Arts & Entertainment; CNBC; CNN; Country Music TV; C-SPAN; Discovery Channel; Disney Channel; E! Entertainment Television; ESPN; ESPN 2; Fox News Channel; Fox Sports Net Rocky Mountain; Great American Country; Hallmark Channel; Headline News; HGTV; History Channel; Home Shopping Network; Lifetime; MTV; Nickelodeon; Spike TV; Syfy; TBS Superstation; The Learning Channel; Trinity Broadcasting Network; Turner Network TV; TV Land; USA Network; VH1; Weather Channel; WGN America.
Fee: $34.95 monthly.
Pay Service 1
Pay Units: N.A.
Programming (via satellite): Cinemax.
Fee: $10.85 monthly.
Internet Service
Operational: No.
Telephone Service
None
General Manager: Vincent Kropp. Operations Director: Pete Markle. Chief Technician: J.C. Peckham. Marketing & Public Relations Manager: Sharon Crist.
Ownership: PC Telcorp.

SEIBERT—Formerly served by B & C Cablevision Inc. No longer in operation. ICA: CO0181.

SILT—Comcast Cable. Now served by RIFLE, CO [CO0043]. ICA: CO0108.

SILVERTHORNE—Comcast Cable, 249 Warren Ave, Ste 250, Silverthorne, CO 80498. Phone: 970-260-2601. Fax: 970-468-2672. Web Site: http://www.comcast.com. Also serves Blue River, Breckenridge, Dillon, Frisco, Keystone & Summit County. ICA: CO0015.
TV Market Ranking: Outside TV Markets (Blue River, Breckenridge, Dillon, Frisco, Keystone, SILVERTHORNE, Summit County). Franchise award date: N.A. Franchise expiration date: N.A. Began: June 1, 1971.
Channel capacity: N.A. Channels available but not in use: N.A.
Basic Service
Subscribers: N.A. Included in Aspen
Programming (received off-air): KCNC-TV (CBS) Denver; KDVR (FOX) Denver; KMGH-TV (ABC) Denver; KRMA-TV (PBS) Denver; KTVD (MNT) Denver; KUSA (NBC) Denver; KWGN-TV (CW) Denver; 5 FMs.
Programming (via satellite): Discovery Channel; TBS Superstation.
Current originations: Leased Access; Government Access; Public Access.
Fee: $44.99 installation; $14.99 monthly.
Expanded Basic Service 1
Subscribers: N.A.
Programming (via satellite): ABC Family Channel; AMC; Animal Planet; Arts & Entertainment; CNBC; CNN; C-SPAN; Disney Channel; ESPN; ESPN 2; Fox News Channel; Fox Sports Net Rocky Mountain; FX; Home Shopping Network; Lifetime; MSNBC; MTV; Nickelodeon; Spike TV; Turner Network TV; USA Network; Weather Channel.
Fee: $35.00 monthly.
Digital Basic Service
Subscribers: N.A. Included in Aspen
Programming (via satellite): BBC America; Bravo; Discovery Digital Networks; DMX Music; Encore; ESPN Classic Sports; ESPNews; Fox Sports World; Golf Channel; GSN; HGTV; History Channel; Independent Film Channel; Nick Jr.; Syfy; Turner Classic Movies; TV Land; Versus; WE tv.
Fee: $9.95 monthly.
Digital Pay Service 1
Pay Units: 378.
Programming (via satellite): Cinemax (multiplexed); HBO (multiplexed); Showtime (multiplexed); Starz (multiplexed); The Movie Channel (multiplexed).
Fee: $15.99 monthly (each).
Video-On-Demand: No
Pay-Per-View
Addressable homes: 3,085.
Playboy TV (delivered digitally), Fee: $5.95-$7.95, Addressable: Yes; Fresh (delivered digitally); iN DEMAND (delivered digitally).
Internet Service
Operational: Yes.
Broadband Service: Comcast High Speed Internet.
Fee: $42.95 monthly.
Telephone Service
Digital: Operational
Miles of Plant: 330.0 (coaxial); None (fiber optic). Homes passed included in Aspen
Vice President: Mike Trueblood. General Manager: Ben Miller. Technical Operations Manager: David Farran. Customer Service Manager: Sherry Higgins.
City fee: 3% of gross.
Ownership: Comcast Cable Communications Inc. (MSO).

SILVERTON—Rocky Mountain Cable, 40 County Rd 600, Unit F, Pagosa Springs, CO 81147-9473. Phones: 800-222-1332; 970-731-2211. Fax: 970-731-5510. Web Site: http://www.rockymtncable.com. ICA: CO0103.
TV Market Ranking: Outside TV Markets (SILVERTON). Franchise award date: September 21, 1982. Franchise expiration date: N.A. Began: January 27, 1983.
Channel capacity: 35 (not 2-way capable). Channels available but not in use: 2.
Basic Service
Subscribers: 100.
Programming (via satellite): Arts & Entertainment; Bravo; CNN; Comedy Central; Country Music TV; C-SPAN; Discovery Channel; Disney Channel; ESPN; ESPN 2; Fox News Channel; Hallmark Channel; Headline News; KCNC-TV (CBS) Denver; KDVR (FOX) Denver; KMGH-TV (ABC) Denver; KRMA-TV (PBS) Denver; KUSA (NBC) Denver; KWGN-TV (CW) Denver; MSNBC; Nickelodeon; Outdoor Channel; QVC; Syfy; TBS Superstation; The Learning Channel; TV Land; USA Network; WE tv; Weather Channel; WGN America.
Fee: $20.00 installation; $36.95 monthly.
Pay Service 1
Pay Units: 9.
Programming (via satellite): Cinemax.
Fee: $12.49 monthly.
Pay Service 2
Pay Units: 26.
Programming (via satellite): HBO.
Fee: $13.49 monthly.
Video-On-Demand: No
Internet Service
Operational: No.
Telephone Service
None
Miles of Plant: 8.0 (coaxial); None (fiber optic). Additional miles planned: 3.0 (fiber optic). Homes passed: 420.
President: Wayne Vestal. Chief Technician: Bobby Smith.
City fee: 1% of basic gross.
Ownership: ICE Cable Holdings LLC (MSO).

SIMLA—FairPoint Communications, PO Box 218, Simla, CO 80835. Phone: 719-541-2261. Fax: 719-541-2129. ICA: CO0142.
TV Market Ranking: Outside TV Markets (SIMLA). Franchise award date: N.A. Franchise expiration date: N.A. Began: February 1, 1985.
Channel capacity: 35 (not 2-way capable). Channels available but not in use: 5.
Basic Service
Subscribers: 95.
Programming (received off-air): KKTV (CBS, MNT) Colorado Springs; KOAA-TV (NBC) Pueblo; KRDO-TV (ABC) Colorado Springs; KXRM-TV (FOX) Colorado Springs.
Programming (via satellite): ABC Family Channel; America's Store; Arts & Entertainment; CNN; Discovery Channel; Disney Channel; ESPN; ESPN 2; Great American Country; Headline News; History Channel; KRMA-TV (PBS) Denver; KWGN-TV (CW) Denver; Lifetime; Spike TV; Syfy; TBS Superstation; The Learning Channel; Turner Classic Movies; Turner Network TV; USA Network; Weather Channel; WGN America.
Fee: $35.00 installation; $20.95 monthly; $.75 converter.
Pay Service 1
Pay Units: 9.
Programming (via satellite): Cinemax.
Fee: $10.00 monthly.
Pay Service 2
Pay Units: 15.
Programming (via satellite): HBO.
Fee: $11.50 monthly.
Video-On-Demand: No
Internet Service
Operational: No.
Broadband Service: DSL service only.
Telephone Service
None
Miles of Plant: 4.0 (coaxial); None (fiber optic). Homes passed: 220. Total homes in franchised area: 225.
Lead Technician: Dennis McKnight.
Ownership: FairPoint Communications Inc. (MSO).

SOUTH FORK—Rocky Mountain Cable, 40 County Rd 600, Unit F, Pagosa Springs, CO 81147-9473. Phones: 800-222-1332; 970-731-2211. Fax: 970-731-5510. Web Site: http://www.rockymtncable.com. Also serves Torres. ICA: CO0131.
TV Market Ranking: Outside TV Markets (SOUTH FORK, Torres). Franchise award date: April 19, 1989. Franchise expiration date: N.A. Began: August 26, 1989.
Channel capacity: 36 (not 2-way capable). Channels available but not in use: 1.
Basic Service
Subscribers: 100.
Programming (via satellite): ABC Family Channel; AMC; Arts & Entertainment; Bravo; CNN; Comedy Central; Country Music TV; C-SPAN; Discovery Channel; ESPN; ESPN 2; Fox News Channel; G4; Hallmark Channel; Headline News; History Channel; KCNC-TV (CBS) Denver; KDVR (FOX) Denver; KMGH-TV (ABC) Denver; KRMA-TV (PBS) Denver; KUSA (NBC) Denver; KWGN-TV (CW) Denver; MSNBC; QVC; Spike TV; Syfy; TBS Superstation; The Learning Channel; Travel Channel; TV Land; USA Network; WE tv; Weather Channel; WGN America.
Fee: $20.00 installation; $36.99 monthly.
Pay Service 1
Pay Units: 11.
Programming (via satellite): HBO.
Fee: $13.49 monthly.
Video-On-Demand: No
Internet Service
Operational: No.
Telephone Service
None
Miles of Plant: 26.0 (coaxial); None (fiber optic). Homes passed: 531.
President: Wayne Vestal. Chief Technician: Bobby Smith.
Ownership: ICE Cable Holdings LLC (MSO).

SPRINGFIELD—Baja Broadband, 900 Main St, Springfield, CO 81073. Phones: 970-565-4031 (Cortez office); 719-523-6382. Fax: 970-565-7407. Web Site: http://www.bajabroadband.com. ICA: CO0088.
TV Market Ranking: Outside TV Markets (SPRINGFIELD). Franchise award date: N.A. Franchise expiration date: N.A. Began: October 1, 1961.
Channel capacity: 62 (not 2-way capable). Channels available but not in use: None.
Basic Service
Subscribers: 577.
Programming (received off-air): KDVR (FOX) Denver; KKTV (CBS, MNT) Colorado Springs; KOAA-TV (NBC) Pueblo; KPXC-TV (ION) Denver; KRDO-TV (ABC) Colorado Springs; KTSC (PBS) Pueblo; KWGN-TV (CW) Denver; 2 FMs.
Programming (via satellite): ABC Family Channel; AMC; Animal Planet; Arts & Entertainment; Bravo; Cartoon Network; CNBC; CNN; Comedy Central; Country Music TV; C-SPAN; Discovery Channel; Disney Channel; E! Entertainment Television; ESPN; ESPN 2; Food Network; Fox News Channel; Fox Sports Net Rocky Mountain; FX; Hallmark Channel; Headline News; HGTV; History Channel; Home Shopping Network; Lifetime; MSNBC; MTV; National Geographic Channel; Nickelodeon; Product Information Network; QVC; Spike TV; Syfy; TBS Superstation; The Learning Channel; the mtn; Travel Channel; truTV; Turner Network TV; TV Land; Univision; USA Network; VH1; Weather Channel; WGN America.
Current originations: Public Access.
Fee: $49.95 installation; $23.50 monthly.
Digital Basic Service
Subscribers: N.A.
Programming (via satellite): BBC America; Bio; Bloomberg Television; CMT Pure Country; Discovery Health Channel; Discovery Kids Channel; Discovery Military Channel; Discovery Planet Green; Disney XD; ESPNews; FitTV; Fox Movie Channel; Fox Soccer; Fuse; G4; Golf Channel; GSN; Halogen Network; History Channel International; ID Investigation Discovery; Independent Film Channel; MTV Networks Digital Suite; MTV2; Music Choice; Nick Jr.; NickToons TV; Outdoor Channel; Science Channel; Speed Channel; Style Network; TeenNick; Trinity Broadcasting Network; Versus; VH1 Classic; WE tv.
Digital Pay Service 1
Pay Units: N.A.
Programming (via satellite): Cinemax (multiplexed); Encore (multiplexed); HBO (multiplexed); Showtime (multiplexed); Starz; The Movie Channel (multiplexed).
Video-On-Demand: No

Pay-Per-View
iN DEMAND (delivered digitally); Club Jenna (delivered digitally); Playboy TV (delivered digitally); Fresh (delivered digitally).
Internet Service
Operational: No.
Telephone Service
None
Miles of Plant: 17.0 (coaxial); None (fiber optic). Homes passed: 716.
Area Vice President & General Manager: Tom Jaskiewicz. Technical Operations Director: Matt Warford.
Ownership: Baja Broadband (MSO).

STAGECOACH—Formerly served by Westcom II LLC. No longer in operation. ICA: CO0205.

STEAMBOAT SPRINGS—Comcast Cable, 625 S Lincoln Ave, Ste 205, Steamboat Springs, CO 80487-8902. Phone: 970-870-6225. Fax: 970-870-0877. Web Site: http://www.comcast.com. Also serves Routt County. ICA: CO0027.
TV Market Ranking: Below 100 (Routt County, STEAMBOAT SPRINGS). Franchise award date: N.A. Franchise expiration date: N.A. Began: January 1, 1982.
Channel capacity: N.A. Channels available but not in use: N.A.
Basic Service
Subscribers: N.A. Included in Aspen
Programming (received off-air): KCNC-TV (CBS) Denver; KDVR (FOX) Denver; KMGH-TV (ABC) Denver; KPXC-TV (ION) Denver; KRMA-TV (PBS) Denver; KTVD (MNT) Denver; KUSA (NBC) Denver; KWGN-TV (CW) Denver; Telemundo; 3 FMs.
Programming (via satellite): C-SPAN; C-SPAN 2; Discovery Channel; Home Shopping Network; QVC; TBS Superstation.
Current originations: Leased Access; Government Access; Educational Access; Public Access.
Fee: $44.99 installation; $14.29 monthly.
Expanded Basic Service 1
Subscribers: 2,403.
Programming (via satellite): ABC Family Channel; Altitude Sports & Entertainment; AMC; Animal Planet; Arts & Entertainment; Cartoon Network; CNBC; CNN; Comedy Central; Disney Channel; E! Entertainment Television; ESPN; ESPN 2; Fox News Channel; Fox Sports Net Rocky Mountain; FX; G4; Golf Channel; Hallmark Channel; Headline News; HGTV; History Channel; Lifetime; MoviePlex; MSNBC; MTV; Nickelodeon; Spike TV; The Learning Channel; Travel Channel; truTV; Turner Classic Movies; Turner Network TV; TV Land; USA Network; Versus; VH1; Weather Channel.
Fee: $35.70 monthly.
Digital Basic Service
Subscribers: N.A. Included in Aspen
Programming (via satellite): AmericanLife TV Network; BBC America; Bio; Black Family Channel; Bloomberg Television; Bravo; Canal 52MX; Canales N; CBS College Sports Network; Country Music TV; Current; Discovery Digital Networks; Discovery HD Theater; DMX Music; Encore (multiplexed); ESPN 2 HD; ESPN Classic Sports; ESPN HD; ESPNews; Flix; Fox College Sports Atlantic; Fox College Sports Central; Fox College Sports Pacific; Fox Movie Channel; Fox Reality Channel; Fox Soccer; Fuse; GAS; Great American Country; GSN; Halogen Network; History Channel International; Independent Film Channel; INHD; Lifetime Movie Network; Lime; LOGO; MTV Networks Digital Suite; National Geographic Channel; NBA TV; NFL Network; Nick Jr.; Nick Too; NickToons TV; Outdoor Channel; Palladia; PBS Kids Sprout; ShopNBC; SoapNet; Speed Channel; Style Network; Sundance Channel; Syfy; the mtn; The Word Network; Toon Disney; Trinity Broadcasting Network; Turner Network TV HD; TV One; Versus HD; WE tv.
Fee: $9.45 monthly.
Digital Pay Service 1
Pay Units: N.A.
Programming (via satellite): Cinemax (multiplexed); Cinemax HD; HBO (multiplexed); HBO HD; Showtime (multiplexed); Showtime HD; Starz (multiplexed); Starz HDTV; The Movie Channel (multiplexed).
Fee: $15.99 monthly (each).
Video-On-Demand: No
Pay-Per-View
iN DEMAND (delivered digitally); Hot Choice (delivered digitally); Ten Clips (delivered digitally); NBA League Pass (delivered digitally); NHL Center Ice (delivered digitally); MLB Extra Innings (delivered digitally).
Internet Service
Operational: Yes.
Broadband Service: Comcast High Speed Internet.
Fee: $42.95 monthly.
Telephone Service
Digital: Operational
Miles of Plant: 126.0 (coaxial); None (fiber optic). Homes passed included in Aspen
Vice President: Mike Trueblood. General Manager: Ben Miller. Technical Operations Manager: David Farran. Customer Service Manager: Sherry Higgins.
City fee: 3% of gross.
Ownership: Comcast Cable Communications Inc. (MSO).

STERLING—Bresnan Communications, 506 W 17th St, Cheyenne, WY 82001. Phone: 877-273-7626. Web Site: http://www.bresnan.com. Also serves Logan County. ICA: CO0019.
TV Market Ranking: Below 100 (Logan County, STERLING). Franchise award date: January 1, 1951. Franchise expiration date: N.A. Began: September 1, 1952.
Channel capacity: N.A. Channels available but not in use: N.A.
Basic Service
Subscribers: 3,600.
Programming (via satellite): C-SPAN; Discovery Channel; Home Shopping Network; ION Television; KCNC-TV (CBS) Denver; KDVR (FOX) Denver; KMGH-TV (ABC) Denver; KRMA-TV (PBS) Denver; KTVD (MNT) Denver; KUSA (NBC) Denver; KWGN-TV (CW) Denver; Lifetime; QVC; Univision.
Current originations: Public Access.
Fee: $60.00 installation; $9.19 monthly; $60.00 additional installation.
Expanded Basic Service 1
Subscribers: N.A.
Programming (via satellite): ABC Family Channel; Altitude Sports & Entertainment; AMC; Animal Planet; Arts & Entertainment; Cartoon Network; CNBC; CNN; Comedy Central; Country Music TV; C-SPAN 2; Disney Channel; E! Entertainment Television; ESPN; ESPN 2; Eternal Word TV Network; Food Network; Fox News Channel; Fox Sports Net Rocky Mountain; FX; Great American Country; Hallmark Channel; Headline News; HGTV; History Channel; INSP; MSNBC; MTV; Nickelodeon; Oxygen; Spike TV; Syfy; Telefutura; The Learning Channel; Travel Channel; truTV; Turner Classic Movies; Turner Network TV; TV Guide Network; TV Land; USA Network; VH1; Weather Channel.
Fee: $47.80 monthly.
Digital Basic Service
Subscribers: N.A.
Programming (via satellite): ABC Family HD; AmericanLife TV Network; Animal Planet HD; Arts & Entertainment HD; Bandamax; BBC America; Bio; Bloomberg Television; Bravo; CBS College Sports Network; Cine Latino; CMT Pure Country; CNBC HD+; CNN en Espanol; CNN HD; Cooking Channel; Current; De Pelicula; De Pelicula Clasico; Discovery Channel HD; Discovery en Espanol; Discovery HD Theater; Discovery Health Channel; Discovery Kids Channel; Discovery Military Channel; Discovery Planet Green; Disney Channel HD; DMX Music; Do-It-Yourself; ESPN 2 HD; ESPN Classic Sports; ESPN Deportes; ESPN HD; ESPNews; FitTV; Food Network HD; Fox College Sports Atlantic; Fox College Sports Central; Fox College Sports Pacific; Fox Movie Channel; Fox Reality Channel; Fox Soccer; Fox Sports en Espanol; FSN HD; Fuse; G4; Gol TV; Golf Channel; Gospel Music Channel; GSN; Halogen Network; HDNet; HDNet Movies; HGTV HD; History Channel en Espanol; History Channel HD; History Channel International; HorseRacing TV; ID Investigation Discovery; Independent Film Channel; ION Television; Lifetime Movie Network; Lifetime Movie Network HD; Mountain West TV; MTV Hits; MTV Jams; MTV Tres; MTV2; mun2 television; National Geographic Channel; National Geographic Channel HD Network; NFL Network; NFL Network HD; Nick Jr.; Nick Too; NickToons TV; Outdoor Channel; PBS Kids Sprout; RFD-TV; Science Channel; Science Channel HD; Speed Channel; Style Network; Syfy HD; TBS in HD; TeenNick; Telefutura; Telehit; The Sportsman Channel; TLC HD; Toon Disney; Trinity Broadcasting Network; Turner Network TV HD; Universal HD; Univision; USA Network HD; VeneMovies; Versus; Versus HD; VH1 Classic; VH1 Soul; Weather Channel HD.
Pay Service 1
Pay Units: 333.
Programming (via satellite): Encore; HBO; Starz.
Fee: $20.00 installation; $11.95 monthly (HBO or Showtime).
Digital Pay Service 1
Pay Units: N.A.
Programming (via satellite): Cinemax (multiplexed); Cinemax HD; Encore (multiplexed); HBO (multiplexed); HBO HD; Showtime (multiplexed); Showtime HD; Starz (multiplexed); Starz HDTV; The Movie Channel (multiplexed); The Movie Channel HD.
Video-On-Demand: No
Pay-Per-View
Sports PPV (delivered digitally); ESPN Now (delivered digitally); iN DEMAND (delivered digitally).
Internet Service
Operational: Yes.
Broadband Service: Bresnan OnLine.
Fee: $39.95 monthly.
Telephone Service
Digital: Operational
Fee: $49.99 monthly
Miles of Plant: 97.0 (coaxial); None (fiber optic). Homes passed: 6,900.
Regional Vice President: Clint Rodeman. General Manager: Wes Frost. Technical Operations Manager: Mitch Winter.
City fee: 4% of gross.
Ownership: Bresnan Communications Inc. (MSO). Sale pends to Cablevision Systems Corp.

STRATTON—Champion Broadband, 380 Perry St, Ste 230, Castle Rock, CO 80104. Phones: 303-688-7766; 866-801-1122. Web Site: http://www.championbroadband.com. ICA: CO0184.
TV Market Ranking: Outside TV Markets (STRATTON). Franchise award date: N.A. Franchise expiration date: N.A. Began: August 15, 1983.
Channel capacity: 41 (operating 2-way). Channels available but not in use: 11.
Basic Service
Subscribers: 33.
Programming (received off-air): KCNC-TV (CBS) Denver; KDVR (FOX) Denver; KMGH-TV (ABC) Denver; KUSA (NBC) Denver; KWGN-TV (CW) Denver.
Programming (via satellite): ABC Family Channel; AMC; Arts & Entertainment; CNN; Discovery Channel; Disney Channel; ESPN; ESPN 2; Fox News Channel; Fox Sports Net Rocky Mountain; FX; INSP; MSNBC; Outdoor Channel; QVC; TBS Superstation; The Learning Channel; Toon Disney; Turner Network TV; USA Network; WGN America.
Current originations: Public Access.
Fee: $35.00 installation; $36.45 monthly; $15.00 additional installation.
Pay Service 1
Pay Units: 39.
Programming (via satellite): HBO; The Movie Channel.
Fee: $9.95 monthly (TMC),$10.95 monthly (HBO).
Video-On-Demand: No
Internet Service
Operational: Yes.
Fee: $45.00 installation; $45.00 monthly.
Telephone Service
None
Miles of Plant: 6.0 (coaxial); None (fiber optic). Homes passed: 330.
General Manager: Mark Haverkate.
City fee: 3% of gross.
Ownership: Champion Broadband (MSO).

SUGAR CITY—Formerly served by CableDirect. No longer in operation. ICA: CO0206.

SUNNYSIDE—Rural Route Video, PO Box 640, Ignacio, CO 81137-0640. Phone: 970-563-9593. Web Site: http://www.westernet.net. ICA: CO0154.
TV Market Ranking: Below 100 (SUNNYSIDE). Franchise award date: N.A. Franchise expiration date: N.A. Began: November 1, 1988.
Channel capacity: 36 (not 2-way capable). Channels available but not in use: N.A.
Basic Service
Subscribers: 19.
Programming (received off-air): KREZ-TV (CBS) Durango; KRMA-TV (PBS) Denver; KUSA (NBC) Denver; KWGN-TV (CW) Denver.
Programming (via satellite): ABC Family Channel; ESPN; TBS Superstation; USA Network.
Fee: $40.00 installation; $37.75 monthly.
Pay Service 1
Pay Units: 6.
Programming (via satellite): HBO.
Fee: $10.95 monthly.
Video-On-Demand: No
Internet Service
Operational: No.

Telephone Service
None
Miles of Plant: 2.0 (coaxial); None (fiber optic). Homes passed: 75.
Manager: Christopher L. May.
Ownership: Rural Route Video (MSO).

SUNSET CREEK—Formerly served by Island Cable. No longer in operation. ICA: CO0210.

TABLE MOUNTAIN—US Cable, 266 Basher Dr, #4, Berthoud, CO 80513. Phones: 800-480-7020; 970-587-2243. Fax: 970-587-4208. E-mail: dkavanagh@uscable.com. Web Site: http://www.uscable.com. ICA: CO0185.
TV Market Ranking: 32 (TABLE MOUNTAIN). Franchise award date: N.A. Franchise expiration date: N.A. Began: N.A.
Channel capacity: 74 (operating 2-way). Channels available but not in use: N.A.
Basic Service
Subscribers: N.A. Included in Johnstown
Programming (received off-air): KBDI-TV (PBS) Broomfield; KCEC (UNV) Denver; KCNC-TV (CBS) Denver; KDVR (FOX) Denver; KMGH-TV (ABC) Denver; KPXC-TV (ION) Denver; KRMA-TV (PBS) Denver; KRMT (ETV) Denver; KTVD (MNT) Denver; KUSA (NBC) Denver; KWGN-TV (CW) Denver; KWHD (IND) Castle Rock.
Programming (via satellite): ABC Family Channel; Altitude Sports & Entertainment; AMC; Animal Planet; Arts & Entertainment; Bravo; Cartoon Network; CNBC; CNN; Comedy Central; Country Music TV; C-SPAN; C-SPAN 2; Discovery Channel; Disney Channel; E! Entertainment Television; ESPN; ESPN 2; Food Network; Fox News Channel; Fox Sports Net Rocky Mountain; FX; Hallmark Channel; Headline News; HGTV; History Channel; Home Shopping Network; Lifetime; MSNBC; MTV; National Geographic Channel; Nickelodeon; ShopNBC; Speed Channel; Spike TV; Syfy; TBS Superstation; The Learning Channel; Travel Channel; truTV; Turner Network TV; TV Guide Network; TV Land; USA Network; VH1; Weather Channel; WGN America.
Current originations: Government Access.
Fee: $50.00 installation; $18.45 monthly.
Digital Basic Service
Subscribers: N.A.
Programming (via satellite): AZ TV; BBC America; Bloomberg Television; Current; Daystar TV Network; Discovery Health Channel; Discovery Kids Channel; DMX Music; ESPN Classic Sports; ESPNews; Fox Soccer; Fuse; G4; GAS; Golf Channel; Great American Country; GSN; Independent Film Channel; Lifetime Movie Network; MTV2; Nick Jr.; Ovation; Science Channel; Sleuth; Style Network; The Word Network; Toon Disney; Trinity Broadcasting Network; Turner Classic Movies; Versus; VH1 Classic; WE tv.
Fee: $16.95 monthly.
Digital Expanded Basic Service
Subscribers: N.A.
Programming (via satellite): Fox College Sports Atlantic; Fox College Sports Central; Fox College Sports Pacific; NFL Network; Outdoor Channel.
Fee: $2.00 monthly.
Digital Expanded Basic Service 2
Subscribers: N.A.
Programming (via satellite): Bio; Discovery Home Channel; Discovery Military Channel; Discovery Times Channel; Encore (multiplexed); FitTV; Fox Movie Channel; Halogen Network; History Channel International.
Fee: $2.95 monthly.
Pay Service 1
Pay Units: N.A.
Programming (via satellite): Cinemax; HBO; Showtime.
Digital Pay Service 1
Pay Units: N.A.
Programming (via satellite): Cinemax (multiplexed); HBO (multiplexed); Showtime (multiplexed); Starz; The Movie Channel (multiplexed).
Fee: $6.95 monthly (Starz), $11.95 monthly (Cinemax, HBO, Showtime, or TMC).
Video-On-Demand: No
Pay-Per-View
iN DEMAND (delivered digitally); Playboy TV (delivered digitally); Fresh (delivered digitally); Spice: Xcess (delivered digitally); Club Jenna (delivered digitally).
Internet Service
Operational: Yes.
Broadband Service: Warp Drive Online.
Fee: $27.95 monthly.
Telephone Service
None
General Manager: Dave Kavanagh. Chief Technician: Josh Patchett. Office Manager: Debbie Hernandez. Marketing Manager: Jennifer Lideman. Construction Manager: Rich Fromstad.
Ownership: Comcast Cable Communications Inc. (MSO).; US Cable Corp. (MSO).

TELLURIDE—Time Warner Cable, 412 W Tomichi Ave, Gunnison, CO 81230-2711. Phone: 970-641-6412. Fax: 970-641-6159. Web Site: http://www.timewarnercable.com. ICA: CO0061.
TV Market Ranking: Outside TV Markets (TELLURIDE). Franchise award date: January 1, 1980. Franchise expiration date: N.A. Began: January 30, 1981.
Channel capacity: N.A. Channels available but not in use: N.A.
Basic Service
Subscribers: 980.
Programming (received off-air): KCNC-TV (CBS) Denver; KMGH-TV (ABC) Denver; KRMA-TV (PBS) Denver; KUSA (NBC) Denver; KWGN-TV (CW) Denver.
Programming (via satellite): Arts & Entertainment; CNN; C-SPAN; C-SPAN 2; Discovery Health Channel; Disney Channel; Hallmark Channel; MSNBC; QVC; Spike TV; TBS Superstation; The Word Network; WGN America.
Current originations: Leased Access; Government Access; Educational Access; Public Access.
Fee: $39.95 installation; $24.46 monthly; $2.00 converter; $20.00 additional installation.
Expanded Basic Service 1
Subscribers: 900.
Programming (via satellite): ABC Family Channel; Altitude Sports & Entertainment; AMC; Animal Planet; Bravo; Cartoon Network; CNBC; Comedy Central; Country Music TV; Discovery Channel; E! Entertainment Television; ESPN; ESPN 2; Food Network; Fox News Channel; Fox Sports Net Rocky Mountain; FX; GalaVision; Great American Country; Headline News; History Channel; Lifetime; MTV; Nickelodeon; Oxygen; Speed Channel; Syfy; The Learning Channel; Travel Channel; truTV; Turner Classic Movies; Turner Network TV; TV Land; USA Network; Versus; VH1; Weather Channel.
Fee: $29.75 monthly.
Digital Basic Service
Subscribers: N.A.
Programming (via satellite): American-Life TV Network; BBC America; Bio; Bloomberg Television; Discovery Health Channel; Discovery Home Channel; Discovery Kids Channel; Discovery Military Channel; Discovery Times Channel; ESPN Classic Sports; ESPNews; Eternal Word TV Network; FitTV; Fox Business Channel; Fox Movie Channel; Fox Soccer; FSN Digital Atlantic; FSN Digital Central; FSN Digital Pacific; Fuse; G4; Golf Channel; Gospel Music Channel; Great American Country; GSN; Halogen Network; HGTV; History Channel International; Independent Film Channel; Lifetime Movie Network; MTV2; Music Choice; National Geographic Channel; Nick Jr.; NickToons TV; Outdoor Channel; Science Channel; Style Network; Toon Disney; Trinity Broadcasting Network; Versus; VH1 Classic; VH1 Country; WE tv.
Fee: $10.99 monthly.
Digital Pay Service 1
Pay Units: N.A.
Programming (via satellite): Cinemax (multiplexed); Encore (multiplexed); HBO (multiplexed); Showtime (multiplexed); Starz; The Movie Channel.
Fee: $15.95 monthly (each package).
Video-On-Demand: Planned
Pay-Per-View
Urban Xtra (delivered digitally); Hot Choice (delivered digitally); Fresh (delivered digitally); Playboy TV (delivered digitally); Sports PPV (delivered digitally).
Internet Service
Operational: Yes.
Broadband Service: Road Runner.
Fee: $69.95 installation; $44.95 monthly.
Telephone Service
Digital: Operational
Fee: $44.95 monthly
Miles of Plant: 14.0 (coaxial); None (fiber optic). Homes passed: 1,500. Total homes in franchised area: 1,500.
General Manager: Mike Miller. Chief Technician: Dan Ward.
City fee: 3% of basic gross.
Ownership: Time Warner Cable (MSO).

TOWAOC—Ute Mountain Cable TV, PO Box 68, 100 Mike Wash Rd, Towaoc, CO 81334-0068. Phone: 970-564-5490. Fax: 970-564-5489. ICA: CO0121.
TV Market Ranking: Outside TV Markets (TOWAOC). Franchise award date: N.A. Franchise expiration date: N.A. Began: January 1, 1985.
Channel capacity: 41 (not 2-way capable). Channels available but not in use: None.
Basic Service
Subscribers: 330.
Programming (via satellite): America's Store; Arts & Entertainment; CNN; C-SPAN; C-SPAN 2; Discovery Channel; Disney Channel; ESPN; Fox Movie Channel; Fox Sports Net Rocky Mountain; FX; G4; Headline News; History Channel; MTV; Nickelodeon; Outdoor Channel; Spike TV; Syfy; TBS Superstation; Trinity Broadcasting Network; Turner Classic Movies; Turner Network TV; USA Network; WGN America.
Programming (via translator): KCNC-TV (CBS) Denver; KMGH-TV (ABC) Denver; KOAT-TV (ABC) Albuquerque; KRMA-TV (PBS) Denver; KUSA (NBC) Denver; KWGN-TV (CW) Denver.
Fee: $25.00 installation; $15.00 monthly.
Pay Service 1
Pay Units: N.A.
Programming (via satellite): Cinemax; HBO; Showtime; The Movie Channel.
Fee: $10.00 monthly (each).
Internet Service
Operational: Yes.
Broadband Service: In-house.
Telephone Service
Digital: Planned
Miles of Plant: 25.0 (coaxial); None (fiber optic). Homes passed: 425. Total homes in franchised area: 425.
General Manager: Michael Elkriver. Chief Technician: Aldo Hammond. Office Manager: Yvonne House.
Ownership: Ute Mountain Indian Tribe.

TRINIDAD—Comcast Cable, 213 N Union Blvd, Colorado Springs, CO 80909. Phones: 719-457-4501; 800-266-2278. Fax: 719-457-4503. Web Site: http://www.comcast.com. Also serves Jansen & Las Animas County (portions). ICA: CO0031.
TV Market Ranking: Outside TV Markets (Jansen, Las Animas County (portions), TRINIDAD). Franchise award date: N.A. Franchise expiration date: N.A. Began: March 1, 1953.
Channel capacity: N.A. Channels available but not in use: N.A.
Basic Service
Subscribers: N.A. Included in Colorado Springs
Programming (received off-air): KKTV (CBS, MNT) Colorado Springs; KOAA-TV (NBC) Pueblo; KRDO-TV (ABC) Colorado Springs; KTSC (PBS) Pueblo; KWGN-TV (CW) Denver; KXRM-TV (FOX) Colorado Springs; KXTU-LP (CW) Colorado Springs; 15 FMs.
Programming (via satellite): ABC Family Channel; AMC; Animal Planet; Arts & Entertainment; CNBC; CNN; Country Music TV; C-SPAN; Discovery Channel; Disney Channel; ESPN; ESPN 2; Eternal Word TV Network; Food Network; Fox News Channel; FX; GalaVision; Hallmark Channel; Headline News; HGTV; History Channel; Home Shopping Network; Lifetime; MTV; Nickelodeon; Oxygen; QVC; Syfy; The Learning Channel; Trinity Broadcasting Network; truTV; TV Land; USA Network; VH1; Weather Channel; WGN America.
Current originations: Government Access; Educational Access; Public Access.
Fee: $35.00 installation; $35.17 monthly; $1.00 converter.
Expanded Basic Service 1
Subscribers: N.A.
Programming (via satellite): Comedy Central; Fox Sports Net Rocky Mountain; MSNBC; Spike TV; TBS Superstation; Travel Channel; Turner Network TV.
Fee: $48.20 monthly.
Digital Basic Service
Subscribers: N.A. Included in Colorado Springs
Programming (via satellite): BBC America; Bloomberg Television; Bravo; Discovery Digital Networks; ESPN Classic Sports; ESPNews; FitTV; Fox Sports World; G4; Golf Channel; GSN; INSP; Music Choice; Nick Jr.; NickToons TV; Outdoor Channel; Versus; WE tv.
Fee: $62.15 monthly.
Digital Pay Service 1
Pay Units: N.A.
Programming (via satellite): Cinemax (multiplexed); Encore (multiplexed); HBO (multiplexed); Showtime (multiplexed); Starz (multiplexed); The Movie Channel (multiplexed).

Fee: $14.95 monthly.
Video-On-Demand: Planned
Pay-Per-View
Fresh (delivered digitally); Playboy TV (delivered digitally); HITS PPV (delivered digitally).
Internet Service
Operational: Yes.
Broadband Service: Comcast High Speed Internet.
Fee: $42.95 monthly.
Telephone Service
None
Miles of Plant: 69.0 (coaxial); 69.0 (fiber optic). Homes passed included in Colorado Springs
Vice President & General Manager: Jim Commers. Senior Vice President, Colorado Region: Scott Binder. Vice President, Marketing: Zach Street. Technical Operations Director: Jim Garcia. Public Relations Manager: Sandra Mann.
Ownership: Comcast Cable Communications Inc. (MSO).

VALDEZ—Formerly served by Wozniak TV. No longer in operation. ICA: CO0135.

VICTOR—Bresnan Communications, 402 Main St, Canon City, CO 81212. Phone: 877-273-7626. Web Site: http://www.bresnan.com. ICA: CO0123.
TV Market Ranking: Below 100 (VICTOR). Franchise award date: October 1, 1986. Franchise expiration date: N.A. Began: March 1, 1987.
Channel capacity: N.A. Channels available but not in use: N.A.
Basic Service
Subscribers: 39.
Programming (received off-air): KKTV (CBS, MNT) Colorado Springs; KOAA-TV (NBC) Pueblo; KRDO-TV (ABC) Colorado Springs; KTSC (PBS) Pueblo; KTVD (MNT) Denver.
Programming (via satellite): CNBC; C-SPAN; C-SPAN 2; Disney Channel; Home Shopping Network; ION Television; KCNC-TV (CBS) Denver; KDVR (FOX) Denver; KMGH-TV (ABC) Denver; KUSA (NBC) Denver; KWGN-TV (CW) Denver; Lifetime; MyNetworkTV Inc.; QVC; TV Guide Network; Univision; V-me TV.
Fee: $25.00 installation; $20.00 monthly; $15.00 additional installation.
Expanded Basic Service 1
Subscribers: N.A.
Programming (via satellite): ABC Family Channel; Altitude Sports & Entertainment; AMC; Animal Planet; Arts & Entertainment; Cartoon Network; CNN; Comedy Central; Country Music TV; Discovery Channel; E! Entertainment Television; ESPN; ESPN 2; Eternal Word TV Network; Food Network; Fox News Channel; Fox Sports Net Rocky Mountain; FX; Hallmark Channel; Headline News; HGTV; History Channel; MSNBC; MTV; Nickelodeon; Oxygen; Spike TV; Syfy; TBS Superstation; Telefutura; The Learning Channel; Travel Channel; truTV; Turner Classic Movies; Turner Network TV; TV Land; USA Network; VH1; Weather Channel.
Digital Basic Service
Subscribers: N.A.
Programming (received off-air): KKTV (CBS, MNT) Colorado Springs; KOAA-TV (NBC) Pueblo; KRDO-TV (ABC) Colorado Springs; KTSC (PBS) Pueblo.
Programming (via satellite): ABC Family HD; AmericanLife TV Network; Animal Planet HD; Arts & Entertainment HD; Bandamax; BBC America; Bio; Bloomberg Television; Bravo; CBS College Sports Network; Cine Latino; Cine Mexicano; CMT Pure Country; CNN en Espanol; Cooking Channel; De Pelicula; De Pelicula Clasico; Discovery Channel HD; Discovery en Espanol; Discovery HD Theater; Discovery Health Channel; Discovery Kids Channel; Discovery Military Channel; Discovery Planet Green; Disney Channel HD; DMX Music; Do-It-Yourself; ESPN Classic Sports; ESPN Deportes; ESPN HD; ESPNews; FitTV; Food Network HD; Fox College Sports Atlantic; Fox College Sports Central; Fox College Sports Pacific; Fox Movie Channel; Fox Reality Channel; Fox Soccer; Fox Sports en Espanol; Fuse; G4; Gol TV; Golf Channel; Gospel Music Channel; GSN; Halogen Network; HGTV HD; History Channel en Espanol; History Channel International; ID Investigation Discovery; Independent Film Channel; ION Television; Lifetime Movie Network; Mountain West TV; MTV Hits; MTV Jams; MTV Tres; MTV2; mun2 television; National Geographic Channel; National Geographic Channel HD Network; NFL Network; Nick Jr.; Nick Too; NickToons TV; Outdoor Channel; PBS Kids Sprout; RFD-TV; Science Channel; Science Channel HD; SoapNet; Speed Channel; Style Network; Syfy HD; TeenNick; Telefutura; Telehit; The Sportsman Channel; Toon Disney; Trinity Broadcasting Network; Universal HD; Univision; USA Network HD; VeneMovies; Versus; VH1 Classic; VH1 Soul.
Digital Pay Service 1
Pay Units: N.A.
Programming (via satellite): Cinemax (multiplexed); Encore (multiplexed); Flix; HBO (multiplexed); HBO HD; Showtime (multiplexed); Starz (multiplexed); Starz HDTV; The Movie Channel (multiplexed).
Video-On-Demand: No
Internet Service
Operational: Yes.
Fee: $39.95 monthly.
Telephone Service
Digital: Operational
Fee: $49.99 monthly
Miles of Plant: 4.0 (coaxial); None (fiber optic). Homes passed: 347. Total homes in franchised area: 400.
General Manager: Jerry Parker. Technical Operations Manager: Doyle Ruona.
County fee: 3% of gross.
Ownership: Bresnan Communications Inc. (MSO). Sale pends to Cablevision Systems Corp.

WALDEN—Bresnan Communications, 580 Russell St, Craig, CO 81625. Phones: 307-635-7760; 970-824-3296. Fax: 307-637-5973. Web Site: http://www.bresnan.com. ICA: CO0115.
TV Market Ranking: Below 100 (WALDEN). Franchise award date: N.A. Franchise expiration date: N.A. Began: July 1, 1982.
Channel capacity: 39 (not 2-way capable). Channels available but not in use: None.
Basic Service
Subscribers: 150.
Programming (via satellite): ABC Family Channel; Animal Planet; Arts & Entertainment; Cartoon Network; CNBC; CNN; Discovery Channel; Disney Channel; E! Entertainment Television; ESPN; ESPN 2; Fox Sports Net Rocky Mountain; FX; Great American Country; Headline News; History Channel; Independent Film Channel; KCNC-TV (CBS) Denver; KMGH-TV (ABC) Denver; KRMA-TV (PBS) Denver; KUSA (NBC) Denver; KWGN-TV (CW) Denver; Lifetime; MoviePlex; MSNBC; Nickelodeon; Spike TV; The Learning Channel; Travel Channel; Turner Network TV; USA Network; Weather Channel.
Fee: $49.95 installation; $34.95 monthly; $60.00 additional installation.
Pay Service 1
Pay Units: 36.
Programming (via satellite): Encore; HBO.
Fee: $12.87 monthly (Encore), $15.15 monthly (HBO).
Video-On-Demand: No
Internet Service
Operational: Yes.
Fee: $39.95 monthly.
Telephone Service
Digital: Operational
Fee: $49.99 monthly
Miles of Plant: 6.0 (coaxial); None (fiber optic). Homes passed: 500.
Regional Vice President: Clint Rodeman. General Manager: Wes Frost. Technical Operations Manager: Mitch Winter.
City fee: 3% of gross.
Ownership: Bresnan Communications Inc. (MSO). Sale pends to Cablevision Systems Corp.

WALSENBURG—Bresnan Communications, 402 Main St, Canon City, CO 81212. Phones: 970-824-3296; 877-273-7626. Web Site: http://www.bresnan.com. Also serves Huerfano County (portions). ICA: CO0058.
TV Market Ranking: Outside TV Markets (Huerfano County (portions), WALSENBURG). Franchise award date: July 5, 1977. Franchise expiration date: N.A. Began: October 1, 1969.
Channel capacity: N.A. Channels available but not in use: N.A.
Basic Service
Subscribers: 800.
Programming (received off-air): KKTV (CBS, MNT) Colorado Springs; KOAA-TV (NBC) Pueblo; KRDO-TV (ABC) Colorado Springs; KTSC (PBS) Pueblo; KXRM-TV (FOX) Colorado Springs; 2 FMs.
Programming (via satellite): BYU Television; C-SPAN; CW+; FX; ION Television; KCNC-TV (CBS) Denver; KMGH-TV (ABC) Denver; KUSA (NBC) Denver; KWGN-TV (CW) Denver; Lifetime; MyNetworkTV Inc.; TBS Superstation; Turner Network TV.
Fee: $60.00 installation; $20.00 monthly; $3.95 converter; $15.00 additional installation.
Expanded Basic Service 1
Subscribers: 300.
Programming (via satellite): ABC Family Channel; Altitude Sports & Entertainment; AMC; Animal Planet; Arts & Entertainment; Cartoon Network; CNBC; CNN; Comedy Central; Country Music TV; C-SPAN 2; Discovery Channel; Disney Channel; E! Entertainment Television; ESPN; ESPN 2; Eternal Word TV Network; Food Network; Fox News Channel; Fox Sports Net Rocky Mountain; Hallmark Channel; Headline News; HGTV; History Channel; Home Shopping Network; MSNBC; MTV; Nickelodeon; Oxygen; QVC; Spike TV; Syfy; Telefutura; The Learning Channel; The Sportsman Channel; Travel Channel; truTV; Turner Classic Movies; TV Guide Network; Univision; USA Network; VH1; Weather Channel.
Fee: $28.99 monthly.
Digital Basic Service
Subscribers: N.A.
Programming (received off-air): KKTV (CBS, MNT) Colorado Springs; KOAA-TV (NBC) Pueblo; KRDO-TV (ABC) Colorado Springs; KTSC (PBS) Pueblo; KXRM-TV (FOX) Colorado Springs.
Programming (via satellite): ABC Family HD; AmericanLife TV Network; Animal Planet HD; Arts & Entertainment HD; Bandamax; BBC America; Bio; Bloomberg Television; Bravo; CBS College Sports Network; Cine Latino; Cine Mexicano; CMT Pure Country; CNN en Espanol; De Pelicula; De Pelicula Clasico; Discovery Channel HD; Discovery en Espanol; Discovery HD Theater; Discovery Health Channel; Discovery Kids Channel; Discovery Military Channel; Discovery Planet Green; Disney Channel HD; DMX Music; ESPN Classic Sports; ESPN Deportes; ESPN HD; ESPNews; FitTV; Food Network HD; Fox College Sports Atlantic; Fox College Sports Central; Fox College Sports Pacific; Fox Movie Channel; Fox Reality Channel; Fox Soccer; Fox Sports en Espanol; Fuse; G4; Gol TV; Golf Channel; Gospel Music Channel; GSN; Halogen Network; HGTV HD; History Channel en Espanol; History Channel HD; History Channel International; ID Investigation Discovery; Independent Film Channel; ION Television; Lifetime Movie Network; Mountain West TV; MTV Hits; MTV Jams; MTV Tres; MTV2; mun2 television; National Geographic Channel; National Geographic Channel HD Network; NFL Network; Nick Jr.; Nick Too; NickToons TV; Outdoor Channel; PBS Kids Sprout; RFD-TV; Science Channel; SoapNet; Speed Channel; Style Network; Syfy HD; TeenNick; Telefutura; Telehit; Toon Disney; Trinity Broadcasting Network; TV Land; Universal HD; Univision; USA Network HD; VeneMovies; Versus; VH1 Classic; VH1 Soul.
Digital Pay Service 1
Pay Units: N.A.
Programming (via satellite): Cinemax (multiplexed); Encore (multiplexed); Flix; HBO (multiplexed); HBO HD; Showtime (multiplexed); Starz (multiplexed); Starz HDTV; The Movie Channel (multiplexed).
Video-On-Demand: No
Internet Service
Operational: Yes.
Broadband Service: Bresnan OnLine.
Fee: $39.95 monthly.
Telephone Service
Digital: Operational
Fee: $49.99 monthly
Miles of Plant: 23.0 (coaxial); 6.0 (fiber optic). Homes passed: 2,307.
General Manager: Jerry Parker. Chief Technician: Matt Harris.
City fee: 2% of gross.
Ownership: Bresnan Communications Inc. (MSO). Sale pends to Cablevision Systems Corp.

WALSH—Champion Broadband, 380 Perry St, Ste 230, Castle Rock, CO 80104. Phones: 303-688-7766; 866-801-1122. Web Site: http://www.championbroadband.com. ICA: CO0113.

TV Market Ranking: Outside TV Markets (WALSH). Franchise award date: February 7, 1983. Franchise expiration date: N.A. Began: February 7, 1983.

Channel capacity: 41 (operating 2-way). Channels available but not in use: 9.

Basic Service

Subscribers: 80.

Programming (received off-air): KCNC-TV (CBS) Denver; KKTV (CBS, MNT) Colorado Springs; KMGH-TV (ABC) Denver; KOAA-TV (NBC) Pueblo; KRDO-TV (ABC) Colorado Springs; KTSC (PBS) Pueblo; KUSA (NBC) Denver; KWGN-TV (CW) Denver.

Programming (via satellite): ABC Family Channel; AMC; Arts & Entertainment; Cartoon Network; CNN; Discovery Channel; Disney Channel; ESPN; ESPN 2; Fox News Channel; Fox Sports Net Rocky Mountain; FX; Headline News; INSP; Outdoor Channel; QVC; TBS Superstation; Turner Network TV; USA Network; WGN America.

Current originations: Public Access.

Fee: $35.00 installation; $36.45 monthly.

Pay Service 1

Pay Units: 34.

Programming (via satellite): HBO; The Movie Channel.

Fee: $9.95 monthly (TMC), $10.95 monthly (HBO).

Video-On-Demand: No

Internet Service

Operational: Yes.

Fee: $45.00 installation; $45.00 monthly.

Telephone Service

None

Miles of Plant: 7.0 (coaxial); None (fiber optic). Homes passed: 350.

General Manager: Mark Haverkate.

Ownership: Champion Broadband (MSO).

WELD COUNTY—Champion Broadband, 380 Perry St, Ste 230, Castle Rock, CO 80104. Phones: 303-688-7766; 866-801-1122. Web Site: http://www.championbroadband.com. Also serves River Valley Village Mobile Home Park. ICA: CO0212.

TV Market Ranking: Below 100 (River Valley Village Mobile Home Park, WELD COUNTY).

Channel capacity: 36 (not 2-way capable). Channels available but not in use: None.

Basic Service

Subscribers: 72.

Programming (received off-air): KBDI-TV (PBS) Broomfield; KCNC-TV (CBS) Denver; KDVR (FOX) Denver; KMGH-TV (ABC) Denver; KRMA-TV (PBS) Denver; KTVD (MNT) Denver; KUSA (NBC) Denver; KWGN-TV (CW) Denver.

Programming (via satellite): ABC Family Channel; AMC; Arts & Entertainment; CNN; Discovery Channel; Disney Channel; ESPN; ESPN 2; Fox News Channel; Fox Sports Net Rocky Mountain; Fuse; Great American Country; Headline News; Lifetime; Outdoor Channel; QVC; Speed Channel; Syfy; TBS Superstation; The Learning Channel; Toon Disney; Travel Channel; Turner Network TV; USA Network; Weather Channel; WGN America.

Fee: $33.45 monthly.

Pay Service 1

Pay Units: N.A.

Programming (via satellite): HBO; The Movie Channel.

Internet Service

Operational: Yes.

Fee: $45.00 installation; $45.00 monthly.

Telephone Service

None

Miles of Plant: 2.0 (coaxial); None (fiber optic). Homes passed: 350.

General Manager: Mark Haverkate.

Ownership: Champion Broadband (MSO).

WESTCLIFFE—NexHorizon Communications. No longer in operation. ICA: CO0190.

WIGGINS—Formerly served by Northern Colorado Communications Inc. No longer in operation. ICA: CO0145.

WILEY—NexHorizon Communications. No longer in operation. ICA: CO0150.

WINTER PARK—Comcast Cable. Now served by GRANBY, CO [CO0021]. ICA: CO0188.

WOODLAND PARK—US Cable, 266 Basher Dr, #4, Berthoud, CO 80513. Phones: 800-480-7020; 970-587-2243. Fax: 970-587-4208. Web Site: http://www.uscable.com. ICA: CO0189.

TV Market Ranking: 32 (WOODLAND PARK). Franchise award date: January 1, 1981. Franchise expiration date: N.A. Began: June 1, 1982.

Channel capacity: 66 (not 2-way capable). Channels available but not in use: None.

Basic Service

Subscribers: N.A. Included in Johnstown

Programming (received off-air): KKTV (CBS, MNT) Colorado Springs; KOAA-TV (NBC) Pueblo; KRDO-TV (ABC) Colorado Springs; KTSC (PBS) Pueblo; KUSA (NBC) Denver; KWGN-TV (CW) Denver; KXRM-TV (FOX) Colorado Springs.

Programming (via satellite): ABC Family Channel; Altitude Sports & Entertainment; AMC; Animal Planet; Arts & Entertainment; Bravo; Cartoon Network; CNBC; CNN; Comedy Central; Country Music TV; C-SPAN; C-SPAN 2; Discovery Channel; Disney Channel; E! Entertainment Television; ESPN; ESPN 2; Eternal Word TV Network; Food Network; Fox News Channel; Fox Sports Net Rocky Mountain; FX; Hallmark Channel; Headline News; History Channel; Home Shopping Network; Lifetime; MTV; National Geographic Channel; Nickelodeon; QVC; ShopNBC; Speed Channel; Spike TV; Syfy; TBS Superstation; The Learning Channel; Travel Channel; truTV; Turner Classic Movies; Turner Network TV; TV Guide Network; TV Land; USA Network; VH1; Weather Channel; WGN America.

Current originations: Public Access; Government Access.

Fee: $49.95 installation; $43.95 monthly; $1.15 converter.

Digital Basic Service

Subscribers: N.A.

Programming (via satellite): Animal Planet HD; Arts & Entertainment HD; AZ TV; BBC America; Bloomberg Television; Current; Daystar TV Network; Discovery Channel HD; Discovery HD Theater; Discovery Health Channel; Discovery Kids Channel; DMX Music; ESPN Classic Sports; ESPN HD; ESPNews; Food Network HD; Fox Soccer; Fuse; G4; GAS; Golf Channel; Great American Country; GSN; HDNet; HDNet Movies; HGTV; HGTV HD; History Channel HD; Independent Film Channel; Lifetime Movie Network; MBC America; MTV2; National Geographic Channel HD Network; Nick Jr.; Ovation; Science Channel; Sleuth; Style Network; Syfy HD; The Word Network; Toon Disney; Trinity Broadcasting Network; Universal HD; USA Network HD; Versus; VH1 Classic; WE tv; WealthTV HD.

Fee: $16.95 monthly.

Digital Expanded Basic Service

Subscribers: N.A.

Programming (via satellite): Fox College Sports Atlantic; Fox College Sports Central; Fox College Sports Pacific; NFL Network; Outdoor Channel.

Fee: $2.95 monthly.

Digital Expanded Basic Service 2

Subscribers: N.A.

Programming (via satellite): Bio; Discovery Home Channel; Discovery Military Channel; Discovery Times Channel; Encore (multiplexed); FitTV; Fox Movie Channel; Halogen Network; History Channel International; VH1 Country.

Fee: $2.00 monthly.

Digital Pay Service 1

Pay Units: N.A.

Programming (via satellite): Cinemax (multiplexed); HBO (multiplexed); Showtime (multiplexed); The Movie Channel (multiplexed).

Fee: $11.95 monthly (each).

Digital Pay Service 2

Pay Units: N.A.

Programming (via satellite): Starz (multiplexed).

Fee: $6.95 monthly.

Video-On-Demand: No

Pay-Per-View

iN DEMAND (delivered digitally); Playboy TV (delivered digitally); Fresh (delivered digitally); Spice: Xcess (delivered digitally); Club Jenna (delivered digitally).

Internet Service

Operational: Yes. Began: September 1, 2003.

Broadband Service: Warp Drive Online.

Fee: $27.95 monthly.

Telephone Service

None

Miles of Plant: 81.0 (coaxial); None (fiber optic).

General Manager: Dave Kavanagh. Chief Technician: Josh Patchett. Office Manager: Debbie Hernandez. Marketing Manager: Jennifer Lideman. Construction Manager: Rich Fromstad.

Ownership: Comcast Cable Communications Inc. (MSO).; US Cable Corp. (MSO).

WRAY—Eagle Communications, PO Box 817, 2703 Hall St, Ste 13, Hays, KS 67601. Phone: 785-625-4000. Fax: 785-625-8030. E-mail: comments@eaglecom.net. Web Site: http://www.eaglecom.net. ICA: CO0071.

TV Market Ranking: Outside TV Markets (WRAY). Franchise award date: July 1, 1980. Franchise expiration date: N.A. Began: December 1, 1980.

Channel capacity: 36 (operating 2-way). Channels available but not in use: 1.

Basic Service

Subscribers: 196.

Programming (received off-air): KBSL-DT (CBS) Goodland; KCNC-TV (CBS) Denver; KDVR (FOX) Denver; KMGH-TV (ABC) Denver; KRMA-TV (PBS) Denver; KUSA (NBC) Denver; KWGN-TV (CW) Denver.

Programming (via satellite): C-SPAN; QVC; Weather Channel.

Fee: $35.00 installation; $19.95 monthly.

Expanded Basic Service 1

Subscribers: N.A.

Programming (via satellite): ABC Family Channel; Animal Planet; Arts & Entertainment; CNN; Country Music TV; Discovery Channel; Disney Channel; E! Entertainment Television; ESPN; ESPN 2; Fox News Channel; Fox Sports Net Rocky Mountain; Great American Country; Headline News; History Channel; Lifetime; MTV; National Geographic Channel; Nickelodeon; Spike TV; TBS Superstation; The Learning Channel; Turner Network TV; TV Land; USA Network; VH1.

Fee: $24.50 monthly.

Digital Basic Service

Subscribers: N.A.

Programming (via satellite): BBC America; Bio; Bloomberg Television; CMT Pure Country; Cooking Channel; Current; Discovery Health Channel; Discovery Kids Channel; Discovery Military Channel; Discovery Planet Green; DMX Music; ESPN Classic Sports; ESPNews; FitTV; Fox Movie Channel; Fox Soccer; Fuse; G4; Golf Channel; GSN; Halogen Network; History Channel International; ID Investigation Discovery; Independent Film Channel; Lifetime Movie Network; MTV Hits; MTV2; Nick Jr.; NickToons TV; Outdoor Channel; PBS Kids Sprout; RFD-TV; Science Channel; Sleuth; SoapNet; Speed Channel; Style Network; Sundance Channel; TeenNick; Toon Disney; Trinity Broadcasting Network; Turner Classic Movies; Versus; VH1 Classic; VH1 Soul; WE tv.

Fee: $3.95 monthly (variety, sports or entertainment package), $5.95 monthly (basic).

Pay Service 1

Pay Units: 81.

Programming (via satellite): HBO.

Fee: $11.95 monthly.

Pay Service 2

Pay Units: 78.

Programming (via satellite): Showtime.

Fee: $11.95 monthly.

Pay Service 3

Pay Units: 89.

Programming (via satellite): The Movie Channel.

Fee: $11.95 monthly.

Digital Pay Service 1

Pay Units: N.A.

Programming (via satellite): Cinemax (multiplexed); Encore (multiplexed); HBO (multiplexed); Showtime (multiplexed); Starz (multiplexed); The Movie Channel (multiplexed).

Fee: $11.95 monthly (HBO, Cinemax, Showtime/TMC/Flix or Starz/Encore.

Video-On-Demand: No

Pay-Per-View

Spice: Xcess (delivered digitally); Club Jenna (delivered digitally); iN DEMAND (delivered digitally); Playboy TV (delivered digitally); Fresh (delivered digitally).

Internet Service

Operational: Yes.

Fee: $22.95 monthly.

Telephone Service

None

Miles of Plant: 12.0 (coaxial); None (fiber optic). Homes passed: 1,104.

President & Chief Executive Officer: Gary Shorman. General Manager: Rex Skiles. Chief Technician: Les Libal.

City fee: 3% of gross.

Ownership: Eagle Communications Inc. (KS) (MSO).

YUMA—CommuniComm Services. Now served by OTIS, CO [CO0128]. ICA: CO0063.

CONNECTICUT

Total Systems: **24**
Total Communities Served: **204**
Franchises Not Yet Operating: **0**
Applications Pending: **0**
Communities with Applications: **0**
Number of Basic Subscribers: **1,159,226**
Number of Expanded Basic Subscribers: **288,253**
Number of Pay Units: **78,812**

Top 100 Markets Represented: Hartford-New Haven-New Britain-Waterbury-New London (19); New York, NY-Linden-Paterson-Newark, NJ (1); Providence, RI-New Bedford, MA (33); Boston-Cambridge-Worcester-Lawrence (6).

**For a list of cable communities in this section, see the Cable Community Index located in the back of Cable Volume 2.
For explanation of terms used in cable system listings, see p. D-11.**

ASHFORD—Charter Communications, 9 Commerce Rd, Newtown, CT 6470. Phones: 508-853-1515 (Worcester office); 203-304-4001 (Newtown office). Fax: 203-304-8713. Web Site: http://www.charter.com. Also serves Brooklyn, Canterbury, Chaplin, Columbia, Coventry, Eastford, Hampton, Lebanon, Mansfield, Pomfret, Scotland, Thompson, Willimantic, Willington, Windham & Woodstock. ICA: CT0012.

TV Market Ranking: 19 (Columbia, Coventry, Lebanon, Mansfield, Willimantic, Windham); 19,33 (Scotland); 33 (Brooklyn, Pomfret); 6,19 (ASHFORD, Canterbury, Chaplin, Eastford, Hampton, Willington); 6,33 (Thompson, Woodstock). Franchise award date: August 3, 1983. Franchise expiration date: N.A. Began: December 1, 1984.

Channel capacity: N.A. Channels available but not in use: N.A.

Basic Service

Subscribers: 31,401.

Programming (received off-air): WBZ-TV (CBS) Boston; WCCT-TV (CW) Waterbury; WCTX (MNT) New Haven; WCVB-TV (ABC) Boston; WEDH (PBS) Hartford; WFSB (CBS) Hartford; WGBH-TV (PBS) Boston; WHPX-TV (ION) New London; WSAH (IND) Bridgeport; WSBE-TV (PBS) Providence; WTIC-TV (FOX) Hartford; WTNH (ABC) New Haven; WUVN (UNV) Hartford; WVIT (NBC) New Britain; 26 FMs.

Programming (via satellite): C-SPAN; C-SPAN 2; Eternal Word TV Network; Home Shopping Network; QVC; TV Guide Network.

Current originations: Government Access; Educational Access; Public Access.

Fee: $29.99 installation.

Expanded Basic Service 1

Subscribers: 11,680.

Programming (via satellite): ABC Family Channel; AMC; Animal Planet; Arts & Entertainment; BET Networks; Bravo; Cartoon Network; CNBC; CNN; Comcast Sports Net New England; Comedy Central; Discovery Channel; Disney Channel; E! Entertainment Television; ESPN; ESPN 2; Food Network; Fox News Channel; GalaVision; Golf Channel; Hallmark Channel; Headline News; HGTV; History Channel; INSP; Lifetime; MSNBC; MTV; National Geographic Channel; New England Sports Network; Nickelodeon; Oxygen; SoapNet; Speed Channel; Spike TV; Syfy; TBS Superstation; The Learning Channel; Travel Channel; truTV; Turner Classic Movies; Turner Network TV; TV Land; USA Network; Versus; VH1; Weather Channel.

Fee: $55.00 monthly.

Digital Basic Service

Subscribers: 28,000.

Programming (via satellite): BBC America; Bio; Bloomberg Television; Discovery Digital Networks; Do-It-Yourself; ESPNews; G4; GAS; Great American Country; History Channel International; Independent Film Channel; Lifetime Movie Network; MTV Networks Digital Suite; MuchMusic Network; Music Choice; Nick Jr.; Nick Too; NickToons TV; Style Network; Sundance Channel; Toon Disney; WE tv.

Fee: $8.43 monthly.

Pay Service 1

Pay Units: 1,981.

Programming (via satellite): Cinemax; HBO; Showtime; The Movie Channel.

Fee: $10.00 installation; $10.00 monthly (Cinemax or TMC), $12.00 monthly (HBO or Showtime).

Digital Pay Service 1

Pay Units: N.A.

Programming (via satellite): Cinemax (multiplexed); Encore (multiplexed); Flix; HBO (multiplexed); Showtime (multiplexed); Starz (multiplexed); The Movie Channel (multiplexed).

Fee: $13.95 monthly (Cinemax, HBO or Flix, Showtime & TMC or Starz & Encore).

Video-On-Demand: Yes

Pay-Per-View

Addressable homes: 16,518.

ETC (delivered digitally), Addressable: Yes; Hot Choice (delivered digitally); iN DEMAND; Playboy TV (delivered digitally); Pleasure (delivered digitally); Fresh (delivered digitally); sports (delivered digitally).

Internet Service

Operational: Yes.

Broadband Service: Charter Pipeline.

Fee: $29.99 monthly; $5.00 modem lease; $120.00 modem purchase.

Telephone Service

Digital: Operational

Fee: $29.99 monthly

Miles of Plant: 1,518.0 (coaxial); None (fiber optic). Homes passed: 51,560. Total homes in franchised area: 61,360.

Vice President & General Manager: Greg Garabedian. Technical Operations Director: George Duffy. Marketing Director: Dennis Jerome.

State fee: 5% of gross.

Ownership: Charter Communications Inc. (MSO).

BOLTON—Comcast of Connecticut. Now served by VERNON, CT [CT0034]. ICA: CT0036.

BRANFORD—Comcast Cable, 44 N Branford Rd, Branford, CT 6405. Phones: 800-266-2278; 860-505-6248. Fax: 860-505-3597. Web Site: http://www.comcast.com. Also serves East Haven, Guilford, Madison, North Branford, North Haven, Northford & Wallingford. ICA: CT0006.

TV Market Ranking: 19 (BRANFORD, East Haven, Guilford, Madison, North Branford, North Haven, Northford, Wallingford). Franchise award date: March 1, 1967. Franchise expiration date: N.A. Began: February 1, 1975.

Channel capacity: N.A. Channels available but not in use: N.A.

Basic Service

Subscribers: 61,075.

Programming (received off-air): WABC-TV (ABC) New York; WCBS-TV (CBS) New York; WCCT-TV (CW) Waterbury; WCTX (MNT) New Haven; WEDH (PBS) Hartford; WFSB (CBS) Hartford; WHPX-TV (ION) New London; WNBC (NBC) New York; WNET (PBS) Newark; WNYW (FOX) New York; WPIX (CW, IND) New York; WRDM-CA (TMO) Hartford; WTIC-TV (FOX) Hartford; WTNH (ABC) New Haven; WUVN (UNV) Hartford; WVIT (NBC) New Britain; WWOR-TV (MNT) Secaucus; 22 FMs.

Programming (via microwave): WSAH (IND) Bridgeport.

Programming (via satellite): ABC Family Channel; AMC; Arts & Entertainment; BET Networks; Cartoon Network; CNBC; CNN; Comcast Sports Net New England; Country Music TV; C-SPAN; C-SPAN 2; Discovery Channel; E! Entertainment Television; ESPN; ESPN 2; Eternal Word TV Network; FX; Headline News; Home Shopping Network; Lifetime; MSG; MSNBC; MTV; New England Cable News; Nickelodeon; QVC; Spike TV; TBS Superstation; The Comcast Network; The Learning Channel; truTV; Turner Network TV; USA Network; VH1; Weather Channel.

Current originations: Government Access; Educational Access; Public Access.

Fee: $45.50 installation; $13.32 monthly; $1.25 converter; $28.55 additional installation.

Expanded Basic Service 1

Subscribers: N.A.

Programming (via satellite): Animal Planet; Comedy Central; Disney Channel; Food Network; Fox News Channel; HGTV; History Channel; New England Sports Network; Oxygen; ShopNBC; Syfy; Travel Channel; TV Guide Network; Yankees Entertainment & Sports.

Fee: $51.61 monthly.

Digital Basic Service

Subscribers: N.A.

Programming (via satellite): BBC America; Bio; Black Family Channel; Bloomberg Television; Bravo; Discovery Digital Networks; DMX Music; ESPN Classic Sports; ESPNews; FitTV; Fox College Sports Atlantic (multiplexed); Fox Movie Channel; Fox Sports World; Fuse; G4; GAS; Golf Channel; Great American Country; GSN; Halogen Network; History Channel International; Independent Film Channel; International Television (ITV); Lifetime Movie Network; Lime; MTV Networks Digital Suite; MTV2; Music Choice; National Geographic Channel; National Jewish TV (NJT); Nick Jr.; NickToons TV; Outdoor Channel; Science Television; ShopNBC; Speed Channel; Style Network; Sundance Channel; The Word Network; Toon Disney; Trinity Broadcasting Network; Turner Classic Movies; Versus; WAM! America's Kidz Network; WE tv.

Fee: $45.23 monthly.

Pay Service 1

Pay Units: 2,725.

Programming (via satellite): HBO.

Fee: $19.95 monthly.

Digital Pay Service 1

Pay Units: N.A.

Programming (via satellite): Cinemax (multiplexed); Encore (multiplexed); HBO (multiplexed); Showtime (multiplexed); The Movie Channel (multiplexed).

Fee: $19.95 monthly.

Video-On-Demand: Yes

Pay-Per-View

Spice (delivered digitally); Playboy TV (delivered digitally); iN DEMAND (delivered digitally).

Internet Service

Operational: Yes.

Broadband Service: Comcast High Speed Internet.

Fee: $42.95 monthly.

Telephone Service

Digital: Operational

Fee: $39.95 monthly

Miles of Plant: 1,307.0 (coaxial); None (fiber optic). Homes passed: 83,420.

Vice President & General Manager: Michael Parker. Technical Operations Director: Bob Burns. Marketing Director: Carolyne Hannan. Marketing Manager: Judi Cyr. Marketing Coordinator: Marcia McElroy.

State fee: 5% of gross.

Ownership: Comcast Cable Communications Inc. (MSO).

BRIDGEPORT—Cablevision Systems Corp., 28 Cross St, Norwalk, CT 6851. Phones: 516-803-2300; 203-750-5600. Fax: 203-354-0921. Web Site: http://www.cablevision.com. Also serves Fairfield County, Milford, Orange, Stratford & Woodbridge. ICA: CT0003.

TV Market Ranking: 19 (BRIDGEPORT, Fairfield County, Milford, Orange, Stratford, Woodbridge). Franchise award date: N.A. Franchise expiration date: N.A. Began: June 15, 1977.

Channel capacity: 110 (operating 2-way). Channels available but not in use: N.A.

Basic Service

Subscribers: 98,100.

Programming (received off-air): WABC-TV (ABC) New York; WCCT-TV (CW) Waterbury; WEDW (PBS) Bridgeport; WFSB (CBS) Hartford; WFUT-DT (TEL) Newark; WLIW (PBS) Garden City; WLNY-TV (IND) Riverhead; WNBC (NBC) New York; WNET (PBS) Newark; WNJU (TMO) Linden; WPIX (CW, IND) New York; WPXN-TV (ION) New York; WRNN-TV (IND) Kingston; WSAH (IND) Bridgeport; WTIC-TV (FOX) Hartford; WTNH (ABC) New Haven; WVIT (NBC) New Britain; WWOR-TV (MNT) Secaucus; WXTV-DT (UNV) Paterson; 29 FMs.

Programming (via microwave): News 12 Connecticut; WCBS-TV (CBS) New York; WNYW (FOX) New York.

Current originations: Leased Access; Religious Access; Government Access; Educational Access; Public Access.

Fee: $49.95 installation; $15.70 monthly; $21.95 additional installation.

Expanded Basic Service 1

Subscribers: N.A.

Programming (via satellite): ABC Family Channel; AMC; Animal Planet; Arts & Entertainment; BET Networks; Bravo; Cartoon Network; CNBC; CNN; Comedy Central; C-SPAN; C-SPAN 2; CT-N; Discovery Channel; Disney Channel; E! Entertainment Television; ESPN; ESPN 2; Food Network; Fox News Channel; Fuse; FX; GalaVision; GSN; Headline News; HGTV; History Channel; Home Shopping Network; Lifetime; MSNBC; MTV; MTV2; News 12 Traffic & Weather; Nickelodeon; QVC; ShopNBC; SoapNet; Speed Channel; Spike TV; SportsNet New York; Syfy; TBS Superstation; The Learning Channel; Travel Channel; truTV; Turner Classic Movies; Turner Network TV; TV Land; USA Network; VH1; WE tv; Weather Channel; Yankees Entertainment & Sports.

Fee: $31.25 monthly.

Digital Basic Service

Subscribers: N.A.

Programming (received off-air): WABC-TV (ABC) New York; WCBS-TV (CBS) New York; WNBC (NBC) New York; WNYW (FOX) New York; WPIX (CW, IND) New York; WWOR-TV (MNT) Secaucus.

Programming (via satellite): Azteca America; BBC World News; Bio; Bloomberg Television; Canal Sur; Caracol; Cartoon Network Tambien en Espanol; CBS College Sports Network; Cine Latino; CNN en Espanol; CNN HD; Country Music TV; C-SPAN 3; Discovery en Espanol; Discovery HD Theater; Discovery Kids Channel; Discovery Military Channel; Discovery Planet Green; Docu TVE; Ecuavisia Internacional; ESPN 2 HD; ESPN Classic Sports; ESPN Deportes; ESPN HD; ESPNews; EuroNews; EWTN en Espanol; Food Network HD; Fox College Sports Atlantic; Fox College Sports Central; Fox College Sports Pacific; Fox Movie Channel; Fox Soccer; Fox Sports en Espanol; Fuel TV; G4; Gol TV; Golf Channel; Great American Country; Hallmark Channel; here! On Demand; HGTV HD; History Channel en Espanol; History Channel International; Howard TV; HTV Musica; ID Investigation Discovery; Infinito; Jewelry Television; La Familia Network; Latele Novela Network; LOGO; Maria+Vision; Momentum TV; MoviePlex; MSG; MSG Plus; MTV Hits; MTV Tres; mun2 television; Music Choice; National Geographic Channel; National Geographic Channel HD Network; NBA TV; New England Cable News; NHL Network; Nick Jr.; NickToons TV; Outdoor Channel; Oxygen; Science Channel; ShopNBC; Sorpresa; Sundance Channel; Supercanal Caribe; TBS in HD; TeenNick; Telefe International; Telemicro Internacional; Toon Disney; Toon Disney en Espanol; Turner Network TV HD; TV Chile; TV Colombia; TVE Internacional; TVG Network; Universal HD; Utilisima; VeneMovies; Versus; Versus HD; VH1 Classic; VH1 Soul; V-me TV; WAPA America; YES HD.

Fee: $10.95 monthly.

Pay Service 1

Pay Units: N.A.

Programming (via satellite): Cinemax; Flix; HBO (multiplexed); Independent Film Channel; Showtime (multiplexed); Starz; The Movie Channel.

Fee: $40.00 installation; $9.95 monthly (each).

Digital Pay Service 1

Pay Units: N.A.

Programming (via satellite): CCTV-4; Channel One; Cinemax (multiplexed); Cinemax HD; Cinemax On Demand; Encore (multiplexed); Filipino Channel; GMA Pinoy TV; HBO (multiplexed); HBO HD; HBO On Demand; Korean Channel; MBC America; MKTV; Portuguese Channel; RAI USA; Russian Television Network; Showtime (multiplexed); Showtime HD; Showtime On Demand; Sino TV; Starz (multiplexed); Starz HDTV; Starz On Demand; The Jewish Channel; The Movie Channel (multiplexed); The Movie Channel HD; TV Asia; TV Japan; TV Polonia; TV5 USA; Zee TV USA.

Fee: $9.95 monthly (Cinemax, Showtime/TMC, Starz/Encore or Playboy), $11.95 monthly (HBO).

Video-On-Demand: Yes

Pay-Per-View

Anime Network (delivered digitally); Independent Film Channel (delivered digitally); Disney Channel (delivered digitally); MSG Plus (delivered digitally); MSG (delivered digitally); MoviePlex (delivered digitally); iN DEMAND (delivered digitally); Playboy TV (delivered digitally).

Internet Service

Operational: Yes.

Broadband Service: Optimum Online.

Fee: $46.95 installation; $34.95 monthly; $299.00 modem purchase.

Telephone Service

Digital: Operational

Fee: $34.95 monthly

Miles of Plant: 1,313.0 (coaxial); None (fiber optic). Homes passed: 134,627.

Vice President, Field Operations: Mark Fitchett. Area Director, Government Affairs: Michael Chowaniec. Director, Government Affairs: Jennifer Young.

State fee: 5% of gross.

Ownership: Cablevision Systems Corp. (MSO).

CLINTON—Comcast Cable, 21 E Main St, Clinton, CT 6413. Phones: 800-266-2278; 860-505-6248. Fax: 860-505-3597. Web Site: http://www.comcast.com. Also serves Centerbrook, Chester, Deep River, Durham, Essex, Haddam, Higganum, Ivoryton, Killingworth, Old Saybrook & Westbrook. ICA: CT0017.

TV Market Ranking: 19 (Centerbrook, Chester, CLINTON, Deep River, Durham, Essex, Haddam, Higganum, Ivoryton, Killingworth, Old Saybrook, Westbrook). Franchise award date: N.A. Franchise expiration date: N.A. Began: March 1, 1977.

Channel capacity: N.A. Channels available but not in use: N.A.

Basic Service

Subscribers: 23,463.

Programming (received off-air): WCCT-TV (CW) Waterbury; WCTX (MNT) New Haven; WFSB (CBS) Hartford; WHPX-TV (ION) New London; WNET (PBS) Newark; WTIC-TV (FOX) Hartford; WTNH (ABC) New Haven; WUVN (UNV) Hartford; WVIT (NBC) New Britain; WWOR-TV (MNT) Secaucus; 28 FMs.

Programming (via satellite): ABC Family Channel; Arts & Entertainment; Bravo; Cartoon Network; CNBC; CNN; Comedy Central; Country Music TV; C-SPAN; C-SPAN 2; Discovery Channel; Discovery Health Channel; Disney Channel; E! Entertainment Television; ESPN; ESPN 2; Eternal Word TV Network; Fox News Channel; FX; Golf Channel; GSN; HGTV; Home Shopping Network 2; Lifetime; MSNBC; MTV; New England Sports Network; Nickelodeon; QVC; Speed Channel; Style Network; Syfy; TBS Superstation; The Comcast Network; The Learning Channel; truTV; TV Guide Network; USA Network; Versus; VH1; Weather Channel; WSAH (IND) Bridgeport; Yankees Entertainment & Sports.

Current originations: Educational Access; Public Access.

Fee: $45.50 installation; $12.01 monthly; $1.25 converter.

Expanded Basic Service 1

Subscribers: 8,855.

Programming (via satellite): AMC; Animal Planet; Comcast Sports Net New England; ESPN Classic Sports; Food Network; Spike TV; Turner Classic Movies; Turner Network TV; TV Land.

Fee: $25.00 installation; $51.50 monthly.

Digital Basic Service

Subscribers: N.A.

Programming (via satellite): BBC America; Catholic Television Network; C-SPAN 3; Discovery Digital Networks; DMX Music; ESPNews; Flix (multiplexed); G4; GAS; MTV Networks Digital Suite; National Geographic Channel; Nick Jr.; Nick Too; Science Television; ShopNBC; SoapNet; Sundance Channel (multiplexed); Toon Disney; WAM! America's Kidz Network; Weatherscan.

Fee: $45.23 monthly.

Pay Service 1

Pay Units: 1,488.

Programming (via satellite): HBO (multiplexed).

Fee: $19.95 monthly.

Digital Pay Service 1

Pay Units: N.A.

Programming (via satellite): Cinemax (multiplexed); Encore (multiplexed); Showtime (multiplexed); The Movie Channel (multiplexed).

Fee: $11.20 monthly (each).

Video-On-Demand: Yes

Pay-Per-View

Addressable homes: 8,000.

Hot Choice (delivered digitally), Addressable: Yes; Playboy TV (delivered digitally); Fresh (delivered digitally); Pleasure (delivered digitally).

Internet Service

Operational: Yes.

Broadband Service: Comcast High Speed Internet.

Fee: $42.95 monthly.

Telephone Service

Digital: Operational

Fee: $39.95 monthly

Miles of Plant: 921.0 (coaxial); None (fiber optic). Homes passed: 62,518.

Vice President & General Manager: Michael Parker. Technical Operations Director: Bob Burns. Marketing Director: Carolyne Hannan. Marketing Manager: Judi Cyr. Marketing Coordinator: Marcia McElroy.

State fee: 5% of gross.

Ownership: Comcast Cable Communications Inc. (MSO).

DANBURY—Comcast Cable, 5 Shelter Rock Rd, Danbury, CT 6810. Phone: 860-505-6248. Fax: 860-505-3597. Web Site: http://www.comcast.com. Also serves Bethel & Ridgefield. ICA: CT0024.

TV Market Ranking: 19 (Bethel, DANBURY, Ridgefield). Franchise award date: N.A. Franchise expiration date: N.A. Began: February 29, 1972.

Channel capacity: N.A. Channels available but not in use: N.A.

Basic Service

Subscribers: 34,142.

Programming (received off-air): WABC-TV (ABC) New York; WCBS-TV (CBS) New York; WCCT-TV (CW) Waterbury; WFSB (CBS) Hartford; WFUT-DT (TEL) Newark; WNBC (NBC) New York; WNET (PBS) Newark; WNJU (TMO) Linden; WNYE-TV (PBS) New York; WNYW (FOX) New York; WPIX (CW, IND) New York; WPXN-TV (ION) New York; WRNN-TV (IND) Kingston; WSAH (IND) Bridgeport; WTBY-TV (TBN) Poughkeepsie; WTIC-TV (FOX) Hartford; WTNH (ABC) New Haven; WVIT (NBC) New Britain; WWOR-TV (MNT) Secaucus; WXTV-DT (UNV) Paterson; allband FM.

Programming (via satellite): AMC; Animal Planet; Arts & Entertainment; Bravo; Cartoon Network; CNBC; CNN; Comedy Central; Country Music TV; C-SPAN; C-SPAN 2; Discovery Channel; Discovery Health Channel; Disney Channel; E! Entertainment Television; ESPN; ESPN 2; ESPN Classic Sports; Eternal Word TV Network; Food Network; Fox News Channel; FX; GSN; Headline News; HGTV; History Channel; Home Shopping Network 2; Lifetime; MSG; MSNBC; MTV; Nickelodeon; QVC; Speed Channel; Style Network; Syfy; The Comcast Network; The Learning Channel; truTV; Turner Classic Movies; TV Guide Network; TV Land; USA Network; Versus; VH1; Weather Channel; Yankees Entertainment & Sports.

Current originations: Educational Access; Public Access.

Fee: $45.50 installation; $17.53 monthly.

Expanded Basic Service 1

Subscribers: 34,000.

Programming (via satellite): Comcast Sports Net New England; Spike TV; TBS Superstation; Turner Network TV.

Fee: $52.52 monthly.

Digital Basic Service

Subscribers: N.A.

Programming (via satellite): BBC America; Catholic Television Network; C-SPAN 3; Discovery Digital Networks; Disney Channel; ESPNews; G4; GAS; MTV Networks Digital Suite; Music Choice; National Geographic Channel; Nick Jr.; Nick Too; SoapNet; Toon Disney; WAM! America's Kidz Network; Weatherscan.

Fee: $45.23 monthly.

Pay Service 1

Pay Units: N.A.

Programming (via satellite): Cinemax; Encore; Golf Channel; HBO (multiplexed); Showtime; Starz.

Fee: $19.95 monthly (HBO, Cinemax, Showtime & Starz!), $4.00 monthly (Encore).

Digital Pay Service 1

Pay Units: N.A.

Programming (via satellite): Canales N; Cinemax (multiplexed); Encore; Flix (multiplexed); HBO (multiplexed); Showtime (multiplexed); Sundance Channel (multiplexed); The Movie Channel (multiplexed); Zee TV USA; Zhong Tian Channel.

Fee: $19.95 monthly.

Video-On-Demand: Yes

Pay-Per-View
iN DEMAND (delivered digitally); Playboy TV (delivered digitally); Fresh (delivered digitally); Shorteez (delivered digitally); Pleasure (delivered digitally); iN DEMAND.

Internet Service
Operational: Yes.
Broadband Service: Comcast High Speed Internet.
Fee: $42.95 monthly; $7.00 modem lease; $199.00 modem purchase.

Telephone Service
Digital: Operational
Fee: $39.95 monthly
Miles of Plant: 780.0 (coaxial); None (fiber optic). Homes passed: 49,550.
Vice President: Michael Parker. General Manager: Andrew McCarthy. Technical Operations Director: Bob Burns. Marketing Director: Carolyne Hannan. Marketing Manager: Judi Cyr. Marketing Coordinator: Marcia McElroy. Government & Community Relations Manager: Sharon Corieanne.
State fee: 5% of gross.
Ownership: Comcast Cable Communications Inc. (MSO).

ENFIELD—Cox Communications, 5 Niblick Rd, Enfield, CT 6082. Phones: 800-955-9515; 401-821-1919 (Customer service); 401-383-1919 (Administrative office). Fax: 860-741-6249. Web Site: http://www.cox.com. Also serves East Granby, East Windsor, Granby, Hartland, Somers, Stafford, Suffield, Union & Windsor Locks. ICA: CT0011.
TV Market Ranking: 19 (East Granby, East Windsor, ENFIELD, Granby, Hartland, Somers, Suffield, Windsor Locks); 19,6 (Stafford, Union). Franchise award date: December 23, 1982. Franchise expiration date: N.A. Began: April 1, 1984.
Channel capacity: N.A. Channels available but not in use: N.A.

Basic Service
Subscribers: 37,689.
Programming (received off-air): WCCT-TV (CW) Waterbury; WDMR-LP (TMO) Springfield; WEDH (PBS) Hartford; WFSB (CBS) Hartford; WGBY-TV (PBS) Springfield; WGGB-TV (ABC) Springfield; WHPX-TV (ION) New London; WTIC-TV (FOX) Hartford; WTNH (ABC) New Haven; WUVN (UNV) Hartford; WVIT (NBC) New Britain; allband FM.
Programming (via satellite): Cox Sports Television; C-SPAN; C-SPAN 2; CT-N; MyNetworkTV Inc.; QVC; TBS Superstation; TV Guide Network.
Current originations: Leased Access; Government Access; Educational Access; Public Access.
Fee: $29.99 installation; $29.14 monthly.

Expanded Basic Service 1
Subscribers: N.A.
Programming (via satellite): ABC Family Channel; AMC; Animal Planet; Arts & Entertainment; BET Networks; Bravo; Cartoon Network; CNBC; CNN; Comcast SportsNet Mid-Atlantic; Comedy Central; Discovery Channel; Discovery Health Channel; Disney Channel; E! Entertainment Television; ESPN; ESPN 2; Eternal Word TV Network; Food Network; Fox News Channel; FX; Headline News; HGTV; History Channel; Home Shopping Network; Lifetime; MSNBC; MTV; New England Sports Network; Nickelodeon; ShopNBC; Spike TV; Syfy; The Learning Channel; Travel Channel; truTV; Turner Network TV; TV Land; USA Network; VH1; Weather Channel.
Fee: $42.05 installation; $32.59 monthly.

Digital Basic Service
Subscribers: N.A.
Programming (received off-air): WCCT-TV (CW) Waterbury; WEDH (PBS) Hartford; WFSB (CBS) Hartford; WGGB-TV (ABC) Springfield; WTIC-TV (FOX) Hartford; WTNH (ABC) New Haven; WVIT (NBC) New Britain.
Programming (via satellite): AMC HD; Animal Planet HD; Arts & Entertainment HD; Bio; Bio HD; Bloomberg Television; Boomerang; Bravo HD; Cartoon Network HD; CBS College Sports Network; CMT HD; CNBC HD+; CNN HD; CNN International; Comcast SportsNet Mid-Atlantic; Comedy Central; Discovery Channel HD; Discovery HD Theater; Discovery Kids Channel; Discovery Planet Green; Discovery Planet Green HD; E! Entertainment Television HD; ESPN 2 HD; ESPN Classic Sports; ESPN HD; ESPN U; ESPNews; FitTV; Food Network HD; Fox Business Channel; Fox Business Channel HD; Fox News HD; Fox Soccer; Fuel TV; FX HD; G4; Gol TV; Golf Channel; Golf Channel HD; Hallmark Movie Channel HD; HGTV HD; History Channel HD; History Channel International; ID Investigation Discovery; Lifetime Movie Network HD; Lifetime Television HD; Military History Channel; MLB Network; MTV Networks HD; Music Choice; MyNetworkTV Inc.; National Geographic Channel; National Geographic Channel HD Network; NBA TV; NBA TV HD; New England Sports Network; NFL Network; NFL Network HD; NHL Network; NHL Network HD; Nick HD; Nick Jr.; Palladia; Science Channel HD; Science Television; Speed Channel; Speed HD; Spike TV HD; Syfy HD; TBS in HD; TLC HD; Travel Channel HD; Trinity Broadcasting Network; Turner Network TV HD; Universal HD; USA Network HD; Versus; Versus HD; VH1 HD; Weatherscan.
Fee: $55.74 monthly.

Digital Expanded Basic Service
Subscribers: N.A.
Programming (via satellite): BBC America; Boomerang; Chiller; CMT Pure Country; Cooking Channel; Country Music TV; Disney XD; Fuse; Great American Country; GSN; Hallmark Channel; Halogen Network; Independent Film Channel; INSP; Lifetime Movie Network; LOGO; MTV Hits; MTV Jams; MTV Tres; mtvU; mun2 television; NickToons TV; Oxygen; PBS Kids Sprout; SoapNet; Sundance Channel; TeenNick; Turner Classic Movies; TV One; VH1 Classic.
Fee: $68.74 monthly.

Digital Expanded Basic Service 2
Subscribers: N.A.
Programming (via satellite): Canal Sur; Cine Latino; CNN en Espanol; De Pelicula; De Pelicula Clasico; Discovery en Espanol; Disney XD en Espanol; ESPN Deportes; Fox Sports en Espanol; GalaVision; History Channel en Espanol; NickToons en Espanol; RAI International; Ritmoson Latino; Sorpresa; TV Chile; TV Colombia; TV5 USA; WAPA America.
Fee: $9.95 monthly (RAI Italia), $11.95 monthly (TV5), $44.95 (various Spanish channels).

Digital Pay Service 1
Pay Units: N.A.
Programming (via satellite): Cinemax (multiplexed); Cinemax HD; Encore (multiplexed); Flix; HBO (multiplexed); HBO HD; Showtime (multiplexed); Showtime HD; Starz (multiplexed); Starz HDTV; The Movie Channel (multiplexed).

Fee: $13.00 monthly (Cinemax, HBO, Starz/Encore or Flix/Showtime/TMC).
Video-On-Demand: Yes

Pay-Per-View
iN DEMAND (delivered digitally), Addressable: Yes; NHL Center Ice (delivered digitally); Playboy TV (delivered digitally); Shorteez (delivered digitally); Club Jenna (delivered digitally); ESPN Gameplan (delivered digitally); ESPN Full Court (delivered digitally); NBA League Pass (delivered digitally); MLS Direct Kick (delivered digitally); MLB Extra Innings (delivered digitally); Spice: Xcess (delivered digitally).

Internet Service
Operational: Yes. Began: May 1, 2000.
Broadband Service: Cox High Speed Internet.
Fee: $79.95 installation; $39.95 monthly; $15.00 modem lease; $299.00 modem purchase.

Telephone Service
Digital: Operational
Fee: $29.95 installation; $22.00 monthly
Miles of Plant: 956.0 (coaxial); None (fiber optic). Homes passed: 52,988.
Senior Vice President & General Manager: Paul Cronin. Vice President, Network Services: Allan Gardiner. Vice President, Marketing: Doreen Studley. Vice President, Government & Public Affairs: John L Wolfe. Residential Product Management Director: Jonathan Leepson. Public Relations Director: Amy Quinn.
State fee: 5% of gross.
Ownership: Cox Communications Inc. (MSO).

GROTON—Comcast Cable, 401 Gold Star Hwy, Groton, CT 6340. Phones: 800-266-2278; 860-505-6248. Fax: 860-505-3597. Web Site: http://www.comcast.com. Also serves Gales Ferry, Ledyard, Mystic, New London Submarine Base, North Stonington, Old Mystic, Pawcatuck, Stonington & Voluntown. ICA: CT0013.
TV Market Ranking: 19 (Gales Ferry, GROTON, Ledyard, Mystic, New London Submarine Base, North Stonington, Old Mystic, Pawcatuck, Stonington, Voluntown). Franchise award date: N.A. Franchise expiration date: N.A. Began: January 1, 1975.
Channel capacity: N.A. Channels available but not in use: N.A.

Basic Service
Subscribers: 22,991.
Programming (received off-air): WCCT-TV (CW) Waterbury; WCTX (MNT) New Haven; WFSB (CBS) Hartford; WGBH-TV (PBS) Boston; WJAR (NBC) Providence; WLNE-TV (ABC) New Bedford; WTIC-TV (FOX) Hartford; WTNH (ABC) New Haven; WUVN (UNV) Hartford; WVIT (NBC) New Britain; 14 FMs.
Programming (via satellite): C-SPAN; Eternal Word TV Network; Home Shopping Network; ION Television; New England Cable News; QVC; TBS Superstation.
Current originations: Leased Access; Religious Access; Government Access; Educational Access; Public Access.
Fee: $45.50 installation; $11.60 monthly.

Expanded Basic Service 1
Subscribers: N.A.
Programming (via satellite): ABC Family Channel; AMC; Animal Planet; Arts & Entertainment; BET Networks; Bravo; Cartoon Network; CNBC; CNN; Comedy Central; Country Music TV; Discovery Channel; Disney Channel; E! Entertainment Television; ESPN; ESPN 2; Food Network; Fox News Channel; FX; Golf Channel; Hallmark Channel; Headline News; HGTV; History Channel; Lifetime; MSNBC; MTV; New England Sports Network; Nickelodeon; Speed Channel; Spike TV; Style Network; Syfy; The Comcast Network; The Learning Channel; Travel Channel; truTV; Turner Network TV; TV Land; USA Network; Versus; VH1; Weather Channel; Yankees Entertainment & Sports.
Fee: $48.51 monthly.

Digital Basic Service
Subscribers: N.A.
Programming (received off-air): WCCT-TV (CW) Waterbury; WFSB (CBS) Hartford; WTIC-TV (FOX) Hartford; WTNH (ABC) New Haven; WVIT (NBC) New Britain.
Programming (via satellite): ABC Family HD; Animal Planet HD; Arts & Entertainment HD; BBC America; Big Ten Network; Bio; Bloomberg Television; CBS College Sports Network; Cine Latino; Cine Mexicano; CMT Pure Country; CNBC HD+; CNN en Espanol; CNN HD; Cooking Channel; Country Music TV; C-SPAN 2; C-SPAN 3; Current; Daystar TV Network; Discovery Channel HD; Discovery en Espanol; Discovery Health Channel; Discovery Kids Channel; Discovery Military Channel; Discovery Planet Green; Disney Channel HD; Do-It-Yourself; Encore (multiplexed); ESPN 2 HD; ESPN Classic Sports; ESPN Deportes; ESPN HD; ESPNews; Flix; Food Network HD; Fox Business Channel; Fox Business Channel HD; Fox College Sports Atlantic; Fox College Sports Central; Fox College Sports Pacific; Fox News HD; Fox Reality Channel; Fox Soccer; Fox Sports en Espanol; Fuse; FX HD; G4; Gol TV; Great American Country; GSN; Hallmark Channel; Hallmark Movie Channel; Hallmark Movie Channel HD; HDNet; HGTV HD; History Channel en Espanol; History Channel HD; History Channel International; ID Investigation Discovery; Independent Film Channel; Lifetime Movie Network; LOGO; MLB Network; MoviePlex; MTV Hits; MTV Tres; MTV2; mun2 television; National Geographic Channel; National Geographic Channel HD Network; NBA TV; New England Cable News; NFL Network; NHL Network; Nick Jr.; Nick Too; NickToons TV; Oxygen; PBS Kids Sprout; QVC HD; RAI International; Retro Television Network; Science Channel; Science Channel HD; ShopNBC; SoapNet; Speed Channel; Sundance Channel; Syfy HD; TBS in HD; TeenNick; Tennis Channel; TLC HD; Toon Disney; Travel Channel HD; Trinity Broadcasting Network; truTV; Turner Network TV HD; TV One; TV5 USA; TVG Network; Universal HD; USA Network HD; VeneMovies;

Versus HD; VH1 Classic; VH1 Soul; WAPA America; WE tv; YES HD; Zee Gold.
Fee: $6.20 monthly.

Digital Pay Service 1
Pay Units: N.A.
Programming (via satellite): Cinemax (multiplexed); Cinemax HD; HBO (multiplexed); HBO HD; Showtime (multiplexed); Showtime HD; Starz (multiplexed); Starz HDTV; The Movie Channel; The Movie Channel (multiplexed); The Movie Channel HD.
Fee: $19.95 monthly.

Video-On-Demand: Yes

Pay-Per-View
iN DEMAND (delivered digitally); Playboy TV (delivered digitally); Fresh (delivered digitally); Shorteez (delivered digitally); Penthouse TV (delivered digitally).

Internet Service
Operational: Yes.
Broadband Service: Comcast High Speed Internet.
Fee: $42.95 monthly.

Telephone Service
Digital: Operational
Fee: $44.95 monthly

Miles of Plant: 812.0 (coaxial); None (fiber optic). Homes passed: 40,263.

Vice President & General Manager: Michael Parker. Technical Operations Director: Bob Burns. Marketing Director: Carolyne Hannan. Marketing Manager: Judi Cyr. Marketing Coordinator: Marcia McElroy.

State fee: 3% of gross.

Ownership: Comcast Cable Communications Inc. (MSO).

HARTFORD—Comcast Cable, 222 New Park Dr, Berlin, CT 06037-3741. Phones: 800-266-2278; 860-505-6248. Fax: 860-505-3597. Web Site: http://www.comcast.com. Also serves Bloomfield, East Hartford, Simsbury, West Hartford & Windsor. ICA: CT0001.

TV Market Ranking: 19 (Bloomfield, East Hartford, HARTFORD, Simsbury, West Hartford, Windsor). Franchise award date: January 1, 1974. Franchise expiration date: N.A. Began: January 1, 1975.

Channel capacity: 78 (operating 2-way). Channels available but not in use: None.

Basic Service
Subscribers: 91,800.
Programming (received off-air): WCCT-TV (CW) Waterbury; WCTX (MNT) New Haven; WEDH (PBS) Hartford; WFSB (CBS) Hartford; WGBY-TV (PBS) Springfield; WHCT-LP Hartford & New Haven; WHPX-TV (ION) New London; WRDM-CA (TMO) Hartford; WTIC-TV (FOX) Hartford; WTNH (ABC) New Haven; WVIT (NBC) New Britain.
Programming (via satellite): Discovery Channel; Product Information Network; Shop at Home; TBS Superstation.
Current originations: Leased Access; Government Access; Educational Access; Public Access.
Fee: $45.50 installation; $11.90 monthly; $1.25 converter; $25.00 additional installation.

Expanded Basic Service 1
Subscribers: 79,846.
Programming (via satellite): ABC Family Channel; AMC; Animal Planet; Arts & Entertainment; BET Networks; Cartoon Network; CNBC; CNN; Comcast Sports Net New England; Comedy Central; C-SPAN; C-SPAN 2; Disney Channel; E! Entertainment Television; ESPN; ESPN 2; Eternal Word TV Network; Food Network; Fox News Channel; FX; Headline News; HGTV; History Channel; Home Shopping Network; Lifetime; MSG; MSNBC; MTV; National Jewish TV (NJT); New England Cable News; New England Sports Network; Nickelodeon; Oxygen; QVC; ShopNBC; Spike TV; Syfy; The Learning Channel; truTV; Turner Network TV; TV Guide Network; TV Land; USA Network; VH1; Weather Channel.
Fee: $37.90 monthly.

Digital Basic Service
Subscribers: N.A.
Programming (via satellite): BBC America; Bravo; Discovery Digital Networks; DMX Music; Encore; ESPN Classic Sports; ESPNews; Fox Sports World; G4; Golf Channel; GSN; Independent Film Channel; National Geographic Channel; NBA TV; Nick Jr.; Style Network; Turner Classic Movies; Versus; WE tv.
Fee: $6.20 monthly.

Digital Expanded Basic Service
Subscribers: N.A.
Programming (via satellite): Bio; Black Family Channel; Bloomberg Television; Canales N; Fox College Sports Atlantic; Fox College Sports Central; Fox College Sports Pacific; Fox Movie Channel; GAS; Great American Country; Halogen Network; History Channel International; Independent Film Channel; Lifetime Movie Network; MTV Networks Digital Suite; MuchMusic Network; Outdoor Channel; Ovation; Speed Channel; Sundance Channel; The Word Network; Toon Disney; Trinity Broadcasting Network; Turner Classic Movies; WE tv.

Pay Service 1
Pay Units: 4,988.
Programming (via satellite): Cinemax; Encore; HBO; Showtime; Starz; The Movie Channel.
Fee: $20.00 installation; $19.95 monthly (each).

Digital Pay Service 1
Pay Units: N.A.
Programming (via satellite): Cinemax (multiplexed); HBO (multiplexed); Showtime (multiplexed); Starz; The Movie Channel (multiplexed).
Fee: $19.95 monthly.

Video-On-Demand: Yes

Pay-Per-View
iN DEMAND; iN DEMAND (delivered digitally); Playboy TV (delivered digitally); Fresh (delivered digitally); Shorteez (delivered digitally); sports (delivered digitally).

Internet Service
Operational: Yes.
Broadband Service: Comcast High Speed Internet.
Fee: $42.95 monthly.

Telephone Service
Digital: Operational
Fee: $30.00 installation; $44.95 monthly

Miles of Plant: 1,147.0 (coaxial); None (fiber optic). Homes passed: 147,994.

Regional Vice President: Douglas Guthrie. Marketing Coordinator: Marcia McElroy. Vice President & General Manager: Pamela Mackenzie. Technical Operations Director: Jim Jones. Marketing Director: Carolyne Hannan. Marketing Manager: Judy Cyr.

State fee: 5% of gross.

Ownership: Comcast Cable Communications Inc. (MSO).

LAKEVILLE—Comcast Cable, 10 Gandolfo Dr, Canaan, CT 6018. Phones: 800-266-2278; 860-505-6248. Fax: 860-505-3597. Web Site: http://www.comcast.com. Also serves Canaan, Falls Village, Norfolk, North Canaan, Salisbury, Sharon & West Cornwall. ICA: CT0023.

TV Market Ranking: 19 (Falls Village, Norfolk, Sharon, West Cornwall); Below 100 (Canaan, LAKEVILLE, North Canaan, Salisbury). Franchise award date: N.A. Franchise expiration date: N.A. Began: July 1, 1979.

Channel capacity: N.A. Channels available but not in use: N.A.

Basic Service
Subscribers: 1,232.
Programming (received off-air): WCCT-TV (CW) Waterbury; WCTX (MNT) New Haven; WEDH (PBS) Hartford; WFSB (CBS) Hartford; WTIC-TV (FOX) Hartford; WTNH (ABC) New Haven; WUVN (UNV) Hartford; WVIT (NBC) New Britain; 1 FM.
Programming (via satellite): Arts & Entertainment; Cartoon Network; CNBC; CNN; C-SPAN; Discovery Channel; FX; MTV; New England Sports Network; Nickelodeon; QVC; The Learning Channel; Turner Network TV; Weather Channel.
Fee: $45.50 installation; $13.44 monthly.

Expanded Basic Service 1
Subscribers: 997.
Programming (via satellite): AMC; Animal Planet; Comedy Central; Disney Channel; ESPN; ESPN 2; Food Network; Fox News Channel; Lifetime; MSG; Spike TV; TBS Superstation; TV Guide Network; USA Network; Yankees Entertainment & Sports.
Fee: $52.50 monthly.

Digital Basic Service
Subscribers: N.A.
Programming (via satellite): BBC America; Bio; Black Family Channel; Bloomberg Television; Bravo; Discovery Digital Networks; DMX Music; ESPN Classic Sports; ESPNews; FitTV; Fox College Sports Atlantic (multiplexed); Fox Movie Channel; Fox Sports World; Fuse; G4; GAS; Great American Country; GSN; Halogen Network; History Channel International; Independent Film Channel; International Television (ITV); Lifetime Movie Network; Lime; MTV Networks Digital Suite; MTV2; Music Choice; National Geographic Channel; Nick Jr.; NickToons TV; Outdoor Channel; Science Television; Speed Channel; Style Network; Sundance Channel; The Word Network; Toon Disney; Trinity Broadcasting Network; Turner Classic Movies; WAM! America's Kidz Network; WE tv.
Fee: $45.23 monthly.

Pay Service 1
Pay Units: 502.
Programming (via satellite): Cinemax; Encore; HBO; Starz.
Fee: $19.95 monthly (HBO).

Digital Pay Service 1
Pay Units: N.A.
Programming (via satellite): Cinemax (multiplexed); Encore (multiplexed); HBO (multiplexed); Showtime (multiplexed); The Movie Channel (multiplexed).
Fee: $19.95 monthly.

Video-On-Demand: Yes

Pay-Per-View
iN DEMAND (delivered digitally); Fresh (delivered digitally); Playboy TV (delivered digitally).

Internet Service
Operational: Yes.
Broadband Service: Comcast High Speed Internet.
Fee: $42.95 monthly.

Telephone Service
Digital: Operational
Fee: $44.95 monthly

Miles of Plant: 290.0 (coaxial); None (fiber optic). Homes passed: 7,625.

Vice President & General Manager: Pamela Mackenzie. Marketing Director: Carolyne Hannan. Marketing Manager: Judi Cyr. Marketing Coordinator: Marcia McElroy. Technical Operations Director: Jim Jones.

State fee: 5% of gross.

Ownership: Comcast Cable Communications Inc. (MSO).

LITCHFIELD—Cablevision Systems Corp., 28 Cross St, Norwalk, CT 6851. Phones: 516-803-2300 (Corporate office); 203-750-5600. Fax: 203-354-0921. Web Site: http://www.cablevision.com. Also serves Bantam, Bethlehem, Burrville, Cornwall, Goshen, Milton, Morris, Northfield, Oakville, Thomaston, Torrington, Warren & Watertown. ICA: CT0015.

TV Market Ranking: 19 (Bantam, Bethlehem, Burrville, Cornwall, Goshen, LITCHFIELD, Milton, Morris, Northfield, Oakville, Thomaston, Torrington, Warren, Watertown). Franchise award date: January 1, 1968. Franchise expiration date: N.A. Began: December 1, 1974.

Channel capacity: N.A. Channels available but not in use: N.A.

Basic Service
Subscribers: 27,173.
Programming (received off-air): WCCT-TV (CW) Waterbury; WCTX (MNT) New Haven; WEDH (PBS) Hartford; WFSB (CBS) Hartford; WHPX-TV (ION) New London; WNBC (NBC) New York; WRDM-CA (TMO) Hartford; WTIC-TV (FOX) Hartford; WTNH (ABC) New Haven; WVIT (NBC) New Britain; allband FM.
Programming (via satellite): CT-N; Home Shopping Network; QVC; ShopNBC; WGN America.
Current originations: Leased Access; Religious Access; Government Access; Educational Access; Public Access.
Fee: $49.95 installation; $12.42 monthly; $21.95 additional installation.

Expanded Basic Service 1
Subscribers: N.A.
Programming (received off-air): WUVN (UNV) Hartford.
Programming (via satellite): ABC Family Channel; AMC; Animal Planet; Arts & Entertainment; BET Networks; Bravo; Cartoon Network; CNBC; CNN; Comedy Central; C-SPAN; C-SPAN 2; Discovery Channel; Disney Channel; E! Entertainment Television; ESPN; ESPN 2; Food Network; Fox News Channel; Fuse; FX; GSN; Headline News; HGTV; History Channel; Lifetime; MSG; MSNBC; MTV; MTV2; New England Sports Network; Nickelodeon; SoapNet; Speed Channel; Spike TV; SportsNet New York; Syfy; TBS Superstation; The Learning Channel; Travel Channel; truTV; Turner Classic Movies; Turner Network TV; TV Land; USA Network; VH1; WE tv; Weather Channel; Yesterday USA.
Fee: $34.53 monthly.

Digital Basic Service
Subscribers: N.A.
Programming (received off-air): WCCT-TV (CW) Waterbury; WCTX (MNT) New Haven; WFSB (CBS) Hartford; WTIC-TV (FOX) Hartford; WTNH (ABC) New Haven; WVIT (NBC) New Britain.
Programming (via satellite): Animal Planet HD; Azteca America; BBC World News; Bio; Bloomberg Television; Bravo HD; Canal Sur; Caracol; Cartoon Network Tambien en Espanol; CBS College Sports Network; CCTV-4; Channel One; Chiller; Cine Latino; CNBC HD+; CNN en Espanol; CNN HD; Country Music TV; C-SPAN 3; Discovery Channel HD; Discovery en Espanol; Discovery HD Theater; Discovery Kids Channel; Discovery Military Channel; Discovery Planet

Green; Docu TVE; Ecuavisia Internacional; ESPN 2 HD; ESPN Classic Sports; ESPN Deportes; ESPN HD; ESPNews; EuroNews; EWTN en Espanol; Filipino Channel; Food Network HD; Fox College Sports Atlantic; Fox College Sports Central; Fox College Sports Pacific; Fox Movie Channel; Fox News HD; Fox Soccer; Fox Sports en Espanol; Fuel TV; FX HD; G4; GMA Pinoy TV; Gol TV; Golf Channel; Great American Country; Hallmark Channel; Hallmark Movie Channel; Hallmark Movie Channel HD; here! On Demand; HGTV HD; History Channel en Espanol; History Channel International; Howard TV; HTV Musica; ID Investigation Discovery; IFC Films On Demand; Infinito; Jewelry Television; Korean Channel; La Familia Network; Latele Novela Network; LOGO; Maria+Vision; MBC America; MKTV; Momentum TV; MTV Hits; MTV Tres; mun2 television; Music Choice; National Geographic Channel; National Geographic Channel HD Network; NBA TV; NHL Network; Nick HD; Nick Jr.; NickToons TV; Outdoor Channel; Oxygen; RAI USA; Russian Television Network; Science Channel; Science Channel HD; Sleuth; Society of Portuguese Television; Sorpresa; Speed HD; Spike TV HD; Sundance Channel; Supercanal Caribe; Syfy HD; TBS in HD; TeenNick; Telefe International; Telemicro Internacional; TLC HD; Toon Disney; Toon Disney en Espanol; Travel Channel HD; Turner Network TV HD; TV Asia; TV Chile; TV Colombia; TV Japan; TV Polonia; TV5 USA; TVE Internacional; TVG Network; Universal HD; USA Network HD; Utilisima; VeneMovies; Versus; Versus HD; VH1 Classic; VH1 Soul; WAPA America; Weather Channel HD; YES HD; Zee TV USA.
Fee: $10.95 monthly.

Pay Service 1
Pay Units: N.A.
Programming (via satellite): Cinemax; Flix; HBO (multiplexed); Independent Film Channel; Showtime (multiplexed); The Movie Channel.

Digital Pay Service 1
Pay Units: N.A.
Programming (via satellite): Cinemax; Cinemax HD; Cinemax On Demand; Encore (multiplexed); HBO (multiplexed); HBO HD; HBO On Demand; Playboy TV; Showtime (multiplexed); Showtime HD; Showtime On Demand; Starz (multiplexed); Starz HDTV; Starz On Demand; The Movie Channel (multiplexed); The Movie Channel HD.
Fee: $9.95 monthly (Cinemax, Showtime/TMC, Playboy or Starz/Encore), $11.95 monthly (HBO).

Video-On-Demand: Yes

Pay-Per-View
Playboy TV; Independent Film Channel (delivered digitally); Anime Network (delivered digitally); Disney Channel (delivered digitally); iN DEMAND (delivered digitally); NBA TV (delivered digitally); Playboy TV (delivered digitally).

Internet Service
Operational: Yes.
Broadband Service: Optimum Online.
Fee: $46.95 installation; $34.95 monthly; $299.00 modem purchase.

Telephone Service
Digital: Operational
Fee: $46.95 installation; $34.95 monthly
Miles of Plant: 906.0 (coaxial); None (fiber optic). Homes passed: 38,826.
Vice President, Fleld Operations: Mark Fitchett. Government Affairs Area Director: Michael Chowaniec. Government Affairs Director: Jennifer Young.
Ownership: Cablevision Systems Corp. (MSO).

MANCHESTER—Cox Communications, 170 Utopia Rd, Machester, CT 6040. Phones: 800-955-9515; 860-436-4269; 401-383-1919 (Customer service & administrative office). Fax: 860-512-5115. E-mail: newengland.services@cox.com. Web Site: http://www.cox.com. Also serves East Glastonbury, Glastonbury, Newington, Rocky Hill, South Glastonbury, South Windsor & Wethersfield. ICA: CT0005.
TV Market Ranking: 19 (East Glastonbury, Glastonbury, MANCHESTER, Newington, Rocky Hill, South Glastonbury, South Windsor, Wethersfield). Franchise award date: October 13, 1973. Franchise expiration date: N.A. Began: March 1, 1975.
Channel capacity: N.A. Channels available but not in use: N.A.

Basic Service
Subscribers: 66,227.
Programming (received off-air): WCCT-TV (CW) Waterbury; WEDH (PBS) Hartford; WFSB (CBS) Hartford; WGBY-TV (PBS) Springfield; WHPX-TV (ION) New London; WRDM-CA (TMO) Hartford; WSAH (IND) Bridgeport; WTIC-TV (FOX) Hartford; WTNH (ABC) New Haven; WUVN (UNV) Hartford; WVIT (NBC) New Britain.
Programming (via satellite): Cox Sports Television; C-SPAN; C-SPAN 2; CT-N; Home Shopping Network; MyNetworkTV Inc.; QVC; TBS Superstation; TV Guide Network.
Current originations: Government Access; Leased Access; Educational Access; Public Access.
Fee: $29.99 installation; $29.14 monthly; $2.84 converter; $21.23 additional installation.

Expanded Basic Service 1
Subscribers: N.A.
Programming (via satellite): ABC Family Channel; AMC; Animal Planet; Arts & Entertainment; BET Networks; Bravo; Cartoon Network; CNBC; CNN; Comcast SportsNet Mid-Atlantic; Comedy Central; Discovery Channel; Discovery Health Channel; Disney Channel; E! Entertainment Television; ESPN; ESPN 2; Eternal Word TV Network; Food Network; Fox News Channel; FX; Headline News; HGTV; History Channel; Lifetime; MSNBC; MTV; New England Sports Network; Nickelodeon; ShopNBC; Spike TV; Syfy; The Learning Channel; Travel Channel; truTV; Turner Network TV; TV Land; USA Network; VH1; Weather Channel; Yankees Entertainment & Sports.
Fee: $21.35 monthly.

Digital Basic Service
Subscribers: N.A.
Programming (received off-air): WCCT-TV (CW) Waterbury; WEDH (PBS) Hartford; WFSB (CBS) Hartford; WTIC-TV (FOX) Hartford; WTNH (ABC) New Haven; WVIT (NBC) New Britain.
Programming (via satellite): AMC HD; Animal Planet HD; Arts & Entertainment HD; Bio; Bio HD; Bloomberg Television; Bravo HD; Cartoon Network HD; CBS College Sports Network; CMT HD; CNBC HD+; CNN HD; CNN International; Comcast SportsNet Mid-Atlantic; Comedy Central; Discovery Channel HD; Discovery HD Theater; Discovery Kids Channel; Discovery Planet Green; Discovery Planet Green HD; E! Entertainment Television HD; ESPN 2 HD; ESPN Classic Sports; ESPN HD; ESPN U; ESPNews; FitTV; Food Network HD; Fox Business Channel; Fox Business Channel HD; Fox News HD; Fox Soccer; Fuel TV; FX HD; G4; Gol TV; Golf Channel; Golf Channel HD; Hallmark Movie Channel HD; HGTV HD; History Channel HD; History Channel International; ID Investigation Discovery; Lifetime Movie Network HD; Lifetime Television HD; Military History Channel; MLB Network; MTV Networks HD; MyNetworkTV Inc.; National Geographic Channel; National Geographic Channel HD Network; NBA TV; NBA TV HD; New England Sports Network; NFL Network; NFL Network HD; NHL Network; NHL Network HD; Nick HD; Nick Jr.; Palladia; Science Channel; Science Channel HD; Speed Channel; Speed HD; Spike TV HD; Syfy HD; TBS in HD; TLC HD; Travel Channel HD; Turner Network TV HD; Universal HD; USA Network HD; Versus; Versus HD; VH1 HD; Weatherscan; YES HD.
Fee: $55.74 monthly.

Digital Expanded Basic Service
Subscribers: N.A.
Programming (via satellite): BBC America; Boomerang; Chiller; CMT Pure Country; Cooking Channel; Country Music TV; Disney XD; Do-It-Yourself; Fuse; Great American Country; GSN; Hallmark Channel; Halogen Network; Independent Film Channel; INSP; Lifetime Movie Network; LOGO; MTV Hits; MTV Jams; MTV Tres; MTV2; mtvU; mun2 television; NickToons TV; Oxygen; PBS Kids Sprout; SoapNet; Sundance Channel; TeenNick; Trinity Broadcasting Network; Turner Classic Movies; TV One; VH1 Classic; WE tv.
Fee: $68.74 monthly.

Digital Expanded Basic Service 2
Subscribers: N.A.
Programming (via satellite): Canal Sur; Cine Latino; CNN en Espanol; De Pelicula; De Pelicula Clasico; Discovery en Espanol; Disney XD en Espanol; ESPN Deportes; Fox Sports en Espanol; GalaVision; History Channel en Espanol; NickToons en Espanol; RAI International; Ritmoson Latino; Sorpresa; TV Chile; TV Colombia; TV5 USA; WAPA America.
Fee: $9.95 monthly (RAI Italia), $11.95 monthly (TV5), $44.39 monthly (various Spanish channels).

Digital Pay Service 1
Pay Units: N.A.
Programming (via satellite): Cinemax (multiplexed); Cinemax HD; Encore (multiplexed); Flix; HBO (multiplexed); HBO HD; Showtime (multiplexed); Showtime HD; Starz (multiplexed); Starz HDTV; The Movie Channel (multiplexed).
Fee: $13.00 monthly (Cinemax, HBO, Starz/Encore or Flix/Showtime/TMC).

Video-On-Demand: Yes

Pay-Per-View
Addressable homes: 26,330.
iN DEMAND, Addressable: Yes; iN DEMAND (delivered digitally); Club Jenna (delivered digitally); Playboy TV (delivered digitally); Shorteez (delivered digitally); NHL Center Ice (delivered digitally); ESPN Gameplan (delivered digitally); ESPN Full Court (delivered digitally); NBA League Pass (delivered digitally); MLS Direct Kick (delivered digitally); MLB Extra Innings (delivered digitally); Spice: Xcess (delivered digitally).

Internet Service
Operational: Yes. Began: January 1, 1997.
Broadband Service: Cox High Speed Internet.
Fee: $99.95 installation; $39.95 monthly; $15.00 modem lease; $299.00 modem purchase.

Telephone Service
None
Miles of Plant: 1,039.0 (coaxial); None (fiber optic). Homes passed: 88,176.
Senior Vice President & General Manager: Paul Cronin. Vice President, Network Services: Allan Gardiner. Vice President, Government & Public Affairs: John L Wolfe. Vice President, Marketing: Doreen Studley. Public Relations Director: Amy Quinn. Residential Product Management Director: Jonathan Leepson.
State fee: 5% of gross.
Ownership: Cox Communications Inc. (MSO).

MERIDEN—Cox Communications, 683 E Main St, Meriden, CT 6450. Phones: 800-955-9515; 401-383-1919; 203-439-4269 (Customer service). Fax: 203-514-6037. Web Site: http://www.cox.com. Also serves Cheshire & Southington. ICA: CT0010.
TV Market Ranking: 19 (Cheshire, MERIDEN, Southington). Franchise award date: January 1, 1974. Franchise expiration date: N.A. Began: July 1, 1974.
Channel capacity: 79 (operating 2-way). Channels available but not in use: 20.

Basic Service
Subscribers: 39,734.
Programming (received off-air): WCCT-TV (CW) Waterbury; WEDH (PBS) Hartford; WFSB (CBS) Hartford; WGBY-TV (PBS) Springfield; WHPX-TV (ION) New London; WRDM-CA (TMO) Hartford; WSAH (IND) Bridgeport; WTIC-TV (FOX) Hartford; WTNH (ABC) New Haven; WUVN (UNV) Hartford; WVIT (NBC) New Britain.
Programming (via microwave): WPIX (CW, IND) New York.
Programming (via satellite): Cox Sports Television; C-SPAN; C-SPAN 2; CT-N; Home Shopping Network; MyNetworkTV Inc.; TBS Superstation; TV Guide Network.
Current originations: Leased Access; Educational Access; Public Access.
Planned originations: Government Access.
Fee: $29.99 installation; $29.14 monthly; $1.25 converter; $21.23 additional installation.

Expanded Basic Service 1
Subscribers: 39,050.
Programming (via satellite): ABC Family Channel; AMC; Animal Planet; Arts & Entertainment; BET Networks; Bravo!; Cartoon Network; CNBC; CNN; Comcast SportsNet Mid-Atlantic; Comedy Central; Discovery Channel; Discovery Health Channel; Disney Channel; E! Entertainment Television; ESPN; ESPN 2; Eternal Word TV Network; Food Network; Fox News Channel; FX; Headline News; HGTV; History

Channel; Home Shopping Network; Lifetime; MSNBC; MTV; New England Sports Network; Nickelodeon; QVC; Spike TV; Syfy; The Learning Channel; Travel Channel; truTV; Turner Network TV; TV Land; USA Network; VH1; Weather Channel; Yankees Entertainment & Sports.
Fee: $26.08 installation; $21.35 monthly.

Digital Basic Service
Subscribers: N.A.
Programming (received off-air): WCCT-TV (CW) Waterbury; WEDH (PBS) Hartford; WFSB (CBS) Hartford; WTIC-TV (FOX) Hartford; WTNH (ABC) New Haven; WVIT (NBC) New Britain.
Programming (via satellite): AMC HD; Animal Planet HD; Arts & Entertainment HD; Bio; Bio HD; Bloomberg Television; Bravo HD; Cartoon Network HD; CBS College Sports Network; CMT HD; CNBC HD+; CNN HD; CNN International; Comcast SportsNet Mid-Atlantic; Comedy Central; Discovery Channel HD; Discovery HD Theater; Discovery Kids Channel; Discovery Planet Green; Discovery Planet Green HD; E! Entertainment Television HD; ESPN 2 HD; ESPN Classic Sports; ESPN HD; ESPN U; ESPNews; FitTV; Food Network HD; Fox Business Channel; Fox Business Channel HD; Fox News HD; Fox Soccer; Fuel TV; FX HD; G4; Gol TV; Golf Channel; Golf Channel HD; Hallmark Movie Channel HD; HGTV HD; History Channel HD; History Channel International; ID Investigation Discovery; Lifetime Movie Network HD; Lifetime Television HD; Military History Channel; MLB Network; MTV Networks HD; Music Choice; MyNetworkTV Inc.; National Geographic Channel; National Geographic Channel HD Network; NBA TV; NBA TV HD; New England Sports Network; NFL Network; NFL Network HD; NHL Network; NHL Network HD; Nick HD; Nick Jr.; Palladia; Science Channel; Science Channel HD; Speed Channel; Speed HD; Spike TV HD; Syfy HD; TBS in HD; TLC HD; Travel Channel HD; Turner Network TV HD; Universal HD; USA Network HD; Versus; Versus HD; VH1 HD; Weatherscan; YES HD.
Fee: $55.74 monthly.

Digital Expanded Basic Service
Subscribers: N.A.
Programming (via satellite): BBC America; Boomerang; Chiller; CMT Pure Country; Cooking Channel; Country Music TV; Disney XD; Do-It-Yourself; Fuse; Great American Country; GSN; Hallmark Channel; Halogen Network; Independent Film Channel; INSP; Lifetime Movie Network; LOGO; MTV Hits; MTV Jams; MTV Tres; MTV2; mtvU; mun2 television; NickToons TV; Oxygen; PBS Kids Sprout; SoapNet; Sundance Channel; TeenNick; Trinity Broadcasting Network; Turner Classic Movies; TV One; VH1 Classic; WE tv.
Fee: $68.74 monthly.

Digital Expanded Basic Service 2
Subscribers: N.A.
Programming (via satellite): Canal Sur; Cine Latino; CNN en Espanol; De Pelicula; De Pelicula Clasico; Discovery en Espanol; Disney XD en Espanol; ESPN Deportes; Fox Sports en Espanol; GalaVision; History Channel en Espanol; NickToons en Espanol; RAI International; Ritmoson Latino; Sorpresa; TV Chile; TV Colombia; TV5 USA; WAPA America.
Fee: $9.95 monthly (RAI Italia), $11.95 monthly (TV5), $44.39 monthly (various Spanish channels).

Digital Pay Service 1
Pay Units: N.A.
Programming (via satellite): Cinemax (multiplexed); Cinemax HD; Encore (multiplexed); Flix; HBO (multiplexed); HBO HD; Showtime (multiplexed); Showtime HD; Starz (multiplexed); Starz HDTV; The Movie Channel (multiplexed).
Fee: $13.00 monthly (HBO, Cinemax, Showtime/Flix/TMC or Starz/Encore).
Video-On-Demand: Yes
Pay-Per-View
iN DEMAND (delivered digitally); Fresh (delivered digitally); Playboy TV (delivered digitally); Shorteez (delivered digitally); NHL Center Ice (delivered digitally); ESPN Full Court (delivered digitally); ESPN Gameplan (delivered digitally); NBA League Pass (delivered digitally); MLS Direct Kick (delivered digitally); MLB Extra Innings (delivered digitally); Spice: Xcess (delivered digitally).
Internet Service
Operational: Yes. Began: September 30, 1997.
Broadband Service: Cox High Speed Internet.
Fee: $39.95 monthly; $15.00 modem lease; $299.00 modem purchase.
Telephone Service
Digital: Operational
Fee: $15.99 installation; $11.95 monthly
Miles of Plant: 680.0 (coaxial); None (fiber optic). Homes passed: 56,908.
Senior Vice President & General Manager: Paul Cronin. Vice President, Network Services: Allan Gardner. Vice President, Government & Public Affairs: John Wolfe. Vice President, Marketing: Doreen Studley. Public Relations Director: Amy Quinn. Residential Product Management Director: Jonathan Leepson.
State fee: 5% of gross.
Ownership: Cox Communications Inc. (MSO).

MIDDLETOWN—Comcast Cable, 19 Tuttle Pl, Middletown, CT 6457. Phones: 800-266-2278; 860-505-6248. Fax: 860-505-3597. Web Site: http://www.comcast.com. Also serves Cromwell, East Hampton, Middlefield, Portland & Rockfall. ICA: CT0019.
TV Market Ranking: 19 (Cromwell, East Hampton, Middlefield, MIDDLETOWN TWP., Portland). Franchise award date: N.A. Franchise expiration date: N.A. Began: September 1, 1977.
Channel capacity: N.A. Channels available but not in use: N.A.
Basic Service
Subscribers: 24,558.
Programming (received off-air): WCCT-TV (CW) Waterbury; WCTX (MNT) New Haven; WFSB (CBS) Hartford; WGBY-TV (PBS) Springfield; WHPX-TV (ION) New London; WRDM-CA (TMO) Hartford; WTIC-TV (FOX) Hartford; WTNH (ABC) New Haven; WUVN (UNV) Hartford; WVIT (NBC) New Britain; WWLP (NBC) Springfield; WWOR-TV (MNT) Secaucus; 1 FM.
Programming (via microwave): WNYW (FOX) New York.
Programming (via satellite): ABC Family Channel; Arts & Entertainment; BET Networks; Bravo; Cartoon Network; CNBC; CNN; Comedy Central; Country Music TV; C-SPAN; C-SPAN 2; Discovery Channel; Discovery Health Channel; ESPN; ESPN 2; FX; Golf Channel; Headline News; HGTV; History Channel; Home Shopping Network; Lifetime; MSNBC; MTV; New England Sports Network; Nickelodeon; QVC; Style Network; Syfy; TBS Superstation; The Comcast Network; The Learning Channel; Travel Channel; truTV; TV Guide Network; USA Network; VH1; Weather Channel; Yankees Entertainment & Sports.
Current originations: Educational Access; Public Access.
Fee: $45.50 installation; $12.88 monthly; $1.25 converter; $26.32 additional installation.
Expanded Basic Service 1
Subscribers: N.A.
Programming (via satellite): AMC; Animal Planet; Comcast Sports Net New England; ESPN Classic Sports; Food Network; GSN; Spike TV; Turner Network TV; TV Land.
Fee: $51.52 monthly.
Digital Basic Service
Subscribers: N.A.
Programming (via satellite): BBC America; Catholic Television Network; C-SPAN 3; Discovery Digital Networks; Disney Channel; DMX Music; ESPNews; Flix; G4; GAS; MTV Networks Digital Suite; National Geographic Channel; Nick Jr.; Nick Too; Science Television; ShopNBC; SoapNet; Sundance Channel; Toon Disney; WAM! America's Kidz Network; Weatherscan.
Fee: $48.23 monthly.
Pay Service 1
Pay Units: N.A.
Programming (via satellite): HBO (multiplexed).
Fee: $19.95 monthly.
Digital Pay Service 1
Pay Units: N.A.
Programming (via satellite): Cinemax (multiplexed); Encore (multiplexed); HBO (multiplexed); Showtime (multiplexed); The Movie Channel (multiplexed).
Fee: $19.95 monthly (each).
Video-On-Demand: Yes
Pay-Per-View
iN DEMAND (delivered digitally), Addressable: Yes; Playboy TV (delivered digitally); Spice (delivered digitally); Hot Choice (delivered digitally); Pleasure (delivered digitally).
Internet Service
Operational: Yes.
Broadband Service: Comcast High Speed Internet.
Fee: $42.95 monthly.
Telephone Service
Digital: Operational
Fee: $39.95 monthly
Miles of Plant: 596.0 (coaxial); None (fiber optic). Homes passed: 40,527.
Vice President & General Manager: Michael Parker. Technical Operations Director: Bob Burns. Marketing Director: Carolyn Hannan. Marketing Manager: Judi Cyr. Marketing Coordinator: Marcia McElroy.
State fee: 5% of gross.
Ownership: Comcast Cable Communications Inc. (MSO).

NEW HAVEN—Comcast Cable, 630 Chapel Street, New Haven, CT 6510. Phones: 866-200-6670; 877-870-4310 (Customer service); 203-785-8195. Fax: 203-865-0429. Web Site: http://www.comcast.com. ICA: CT0004.
TV Market Ranking: 19 (NEW HAVEN (PORTIONS)).
Channel capacity: N.A. Channels available but not in use: N.A.
Basic Service
Subscribers: 62,227.
Programming (received off-air): WABC-TV (ABC) New York; WCBS-TV (CBS) New York; WCCT-TV (CW) Waterbury; WCTX (MNT) New Haven; WEDH (PBS) Hartford; WFSB (CBS) Hartford; WHPX-TV (ION) New London; WNBC (NBC) New York; WNET (PBS) Newark; WNYW (FOX) New York; WPIX (CW, IND) New York; WRDM-CA (TMO) Hartford; WSAH (IND) Bridgeport; WTNH (ABC) New Haven; WUTH-CA Hartford; WUVN (UNV) Hartford; WVIT (NBC) New Britain.
Programming (via satellite): ABC Family Channel; AMC; Animal Planet; Arts & Entertainment; BET Networks; Bravo; Cartoon Network; CNBC; CNN; Comedy Central; C-SPAN; Discovery Channel; Disney Channel; E! Entertainment Television; ESPN; ESPN 2; Eternal Word TV Network; Food Network; Fox News Channel; FX; Golf Channel; Headline News; HGTV; History Channel; Home Shopping Network; Lifetime; MSG; MSNBC; MTV; New England Cable News; New England Sports Network; Nickelodeon; QVC; Speed Channel; Spike TV; SportsNet New York; Syfy; TBS Superstation; The Comcast Network; The Learning Channel; Travel Channel; Turner Classic Movies; Turner Network TV; TV Land; USA Network; Versus; VH1; Weather Channel; Yankees Entertainment & Sports.
Current originations: Public Access; Government Access.
Fee: $48.95 installation; $12.68 monthly.
Digital Basic Service
Subscribers: N.A.
Programming (received off-air): WCCT-TV (CW) Waterbury; WFSB (CBS) Hartford; WTIC-TV (FOX) Hartford; WTNH (ABC) New Haven; WVIT (NBC) New Britain.
Programming (via satellite): ABC Family HD; Animal Planet HD; Arts & Entertainment HD; BBC America; Big Ten Network; Bio; Bloomberg Television; CBS College Sports Network; Cine Latino; Cine Mexicano; CMT Pure Country; CNBC HD+; CNN en Espanol; CNN HD; Cooking Channel; Country Music TV; C-SPAN 2; C-SPAN 3; Current; Daystar TV Network; Discovery Channel HD; Discovery en Espanol; Discovery Health Channel; Discovery Kids Channel; Discovery Military Channel; Discovery Planet Green; Disney Channel HD; Do-It-Yourself; Encore (multiplexed); ESPN 2 HD; ESPN Classic Sports; ESPN Deportes; ESPN HD; ESPNews; Flix; Food Network HD; Fox Business Channel; Fox Business Channel HD; Fox College Sports Atlantic; Fox College Sports Central; Fox College Sports Pacific; Fox News HD; Fox Reality Channel; Fox Soccer; Fox Sports en Espanol; Fuse; FX HD; G4; Gol TV; Great American Country; GSN; Hallmark Channel; Hallmark Movie Channel; Hallmark Movie Channel HD; HDNet; HGTV HD; History Channel en Espanol; History Channel HD; History Channel International; ID Investigation Discovery; Independent Film Channel; Lifetime Movie Network; LOGO; MLB Network; MoviePlex; MTV Hits; MTV Tres; MTV2; mun2 television; National Geographic Channel; National Geographic Channel HD Network; NBA TV; New England Cable News; NFL Network; NHL Network; Nick Jr.; Nick Too; NickToons TV; Oxygen; PBS HD; PBS Kids Sprout; QVC HD; RAI USA; Retro Television Network; Science Channel; Science Channel HD; ShopNBC; SoapNet; Speed Channel; Style Network; Sundance Channel; Syfy HD; TBS in HD; TeenNick; Tennis Channel; TLC HD; Toon Disney; Travel Channel HD; Trinity Broadcasting Network; truTV; Turner Network TV HD; TV Guide Interactive Inc.; TV One; TV5 USA; TVG Network; Universal HD; USA Network HD; VeneMovies; Versus HD; VH1 Classic; VH1 Soul; WAPA America; WE tv; YES HD; Zee TV USA.

Digital Pay Service 1
Pay Units: N.A.
Programming (via satellite): Cinemax (multiplexed); Cinemax HD; HBO (multiplexed); HBO HD; Showtime (multiplexed); Showtime HD; Starz (multiplexed); Starz HDTV; The Movie Channel (multiplexed); The Movie Channel HD.
Pay-Per-View
iN DEMAND (delivered digitally); Playboy TV (delivered digitally); Fresh (delivered digitally); Shorteez (delivered digitally); Penthouse TV (delivered digitally).
Internet Service
Operational: Yes.
Broadband Service: Comcast High Speed Internet.
Fee: $42.95 monthly.
Telephone Service
Digital: Operational
Fee: $39.95 monthly
Miles of Plant: 732.0 (coaxial); None (fiber optic). Homes passed: 115,689.
General Manager: Michael Parker. Chief Technician: Bob Burns. Marketing Manager: Marcia McElroy.
Ownership: Comcast Cable Communications Inc. (MSO).

NEW LONDON—MetroCast Communications of Connecticut, PO Box 6008, 61 Myrock Ave, Waterford, CT 6385. Phone: 860-442-8525. Fax: 860-443-6031. Web Site: http://www.metrocastcommunications.com. Also serves Central Village, Danielson, Dayville, East Lyme, Griswold, Killingly, Montville, Moosup, Niantic, Oakdale, Oneco, Plainfield, Putnam, Quaker Hill, Rogers, Sterling, Waterford & Wauregan. ICA: CT0008.
TV Market Ranking: 19 (East Lyme, Griswold, Montville, NEW LONDON, Niantic, Oakdale, Plainfield, Quaker Hill, Waterford); 19,33 (Central Village, Killingly, Moosup, Oneco, Sterling, Wauregan); 19,6 (Danielson); 6,33 (Dayville, Putnam, Rogers). Franchise award date: N.A. Franchise expiration date: N.A. Began: May 1, 1973.
Channel capacity: 78 (operating 2-way). Channels available but not in use: N.A.
Basic Service
Subscribers: 36,334.
Programming (received off-air): WCCT-TV (CW) Waterbury; WCTX (MNT) New Haven; WEDN (PBS) Norwich; WFSB (CBS) Hartford; WGBH-TV (PBS) Boston; WHPX-TV (ION) New London; WJAR (NBC) Providence; WLNE-TV (ABC) New Bedford; WPRI-TV (CBS) Providence; WTIC-TV (FOX) Hartford; WTNH (ABC) New Haven; WUVN (UNV) Hartford; WVIT (NBC) New Britain; 28 FMs.
Programming (via satellite): Country Music TV; C-SPAN; C-SPAN 2; CT-N; Home Shopping Network; QVC; TBS Superstation; TV Guide Network; WGN America.
Current originations: Government Access; Educational Access; Public Access.
Fee: $25.90 installation; $9.95 monthly.
Expanded Basic Service 1
Subscribers: 34,595.
Programming (via satellite): ABC Family Channel; Animal Planet; Arts & Entertainment; BET Networks; Bravo; Cartoon Network; CNBC; CNN; Comcast Sports Net New England; Comedy Central; Discovery Channel; Disney Channel; ESPN; ESPN 2; ESPN Classic Sports; Eternal Word TV Network; Food Network; Fox News Channel; FX; HGTV; History Channel; Lifetime; MSNBC; MTV; New England Sports Network; Nickelodeon; Spike TV; Syfy; The Learning Channel; Travel Channel; Turner Network TV; TV Land; USA Network; VH1; Weather Channel; Yankees Entertainment & Sports.
Fee: $32.15 monthly.
Digital Basic Service
Subscribers: 7,314.
Programming (received off-air): WEDN (PBS) Norwich; WFSB (CBS) Hartford; WTIC-TV (FOX) Hartford; WVIT (NBC) New Britain.
Programming (via satellite): BBC America; Boomerang; Cooking Channel; Country Music TV; Discovery Digital Networks; Discovery HD Theater; ESPN U; ESPNews; G4; GAS; Hallmark Channel; HDNet; HDNet Movies; Lifetime Movie Network; LOGO; MTV Networks Digital Suite; Music Choice; Nick Jr.; Nick Too; NickToons TV; PBS Kids Sprout; Toon Disney; Turner Network TV HD; Weatherscan.
Fee: $8.95 monthly.
Digital Expanded Basic Service
Subscribers: N.A.
Programming (via satellite): Bio; Bloomberg Television; Fox College Sports Atlantic; Fox College Sports Central; Fox College Sports Pacific; Fox Movie Channel; Fox Soccer; Golf Channel; History Channel International; Independent Film Channel; NFL Network; Speed Channel; Style Network; Turner Classic Movies; Versus.
Fee: $8.95 monthly.
Digital Pay Service 1
Pay Units: N.A.
Programming (via satellite): Cinemax (multiplexed); Flix; HBO (multiplexed); Showtime (multiplexed); Sundance Channel; The Movie Channel (multiplexed).
Fee: $9.95 monthly (Showtime or Cinemax), $10.95 monthly (HBO).
Video-On-Demand: Planned
Pay-Per-View
iN DEMAND; Fresh; iN DEMAND (delivered digitally); Pleasure (delivered digitally).
Internet Service
Operational: Yes. Began: September 1, 2000.
Subscribers: 10,223.
Broadband Service: In-house.
Fee: $75.00 installation; $39.95 monthly; $2.50 modem lease; $99.00 modem purchase.
Telephone Service
None
Miles of Plant: 1,149.0 (coaxial); None (fiber optic). Homes passed: 56,810.
General Manager: John Dee. Operations Director: Hugh O'Brien. Technical Operations Manager: John Ort. Marketing Manager: Katherine Diaz.
State fee: 5% of gross.
Ownership: Harron Communications LP (MSO).

NEWTOWN—Charter Communications, 9 Commerce Rd, Newtown, CT 6470. Phones: 508-853-1515 (Worcester office); 203-304-4001. Fax: 203-304-8713. Web Site: http://www.charter.com. Also serves Bethlehem, Bridgewater, Brookfield, Kent, Monroe, New Fairfield, New Milford, Roxbury, Sherman, Southbury, Trumbull, Washington & Woodbury. ICA: CT0014.
TV Market Ranking: 19 (Bethlehem, Bridgewater, Brookfield, Kent, Monroe, New Fairfield, New Milford, NEWTOWN, Roxbury, Sherman, Southbury, Trumbull, Washington, Woodbury). Franchise award date: N.A. Franchise expiration date: N.A. Began: July 1, 1978.
Channel capacity: N.A. Channels available but not in use: N.A.
Basic Service
Subscribers: 70,568.
Programming (received off-air): WABC-TV (ABC) New York; WCBS-TV (CBS) New York; WCCT-TV (CW) Waterbury; WCTX (MNT) New Haven; WEDW (PBS) Bridgeport; WFSB (CBS) Hartford; WNBC (NBC) New York; WNET (PBS) Newark; WNYW (FOX) New York; WPIX (CW, IND) New York; WPXN-TV (ION) New York; WRNN-TV (IND) Kingston; WSAH (IND) Bridgeport; WTIC-TV (FOX) Hartford; WTNH (ABC) New Haven; WVIT (NBC) New Britain; WWOR-TV (MNT) Secaucus; WXTV-DT (UNV) Paterson; allband FM.
Programming (via satellite): C-SPAN; Home Shopping Network; QVC; TV Guide Network.
Current originations: Leased Access; Government Access; Educational Access.
Expanded Basic Service 1
Subscribers: 57,312.
Programming (via satellite): ABC Family Channel; AMC; Animal Planet; Arts & Entertainment; Bravo; Cartoon Network; CNBC; CNN; Comedy Central; C-SPAN 2; Discovery Channel; Disney Channel; E! Entertainment Television; ESPN; ESPN 2; ESPN Classic Sports; Eternal Word TV Network; Food Network; Fox News Channel; G4; Golf Channel; Hallmark Channel; Headline News; HGTV; History Channel; INSP; Lifetime; MSG; MSG Plus; MSNBC; MTV; National Geographic Channel; Nickelodeon; Oxygen; ShopNBC; Speed Channel; Spike TV; Syfy; TBS Superstation; The Learning Channel; Travel Channel; Trinity Broadcasting Network; truTV; Turner Classic Movies; Turner Network TV; TV Land; USA Network; Versus; VH1; Weather Channel; Yankees Entertainment & Sports.
Fee: $55.00 monthly.
Digital Basic Service
Subscribers: 58,000.
Programming (via satellite): BBC America; Bio; Bloomberg Television; Discovery Digital Networks; Do-It-Yourself; ESPNews; GAS; Great American Country; History Channel International; Independent Film Channel; Lifetime Movie Network; MTV Networks Digital Suite; MuchMusic Network; Music Choice; Nick Jr.; Nick Too; NickToons TV; SoapNet; Style Network; Sundance Channel; Toon Disney; WE tv.
Fee: $8.43 monthly.
Digital Pay Service 1
Pay Units: 6,351.
Programming (via satellite): Cinemax (multiplexed).
Fee: $13.95 monthly.
Digital Pay Service 2
Pay Units: 11,611.
Programming (via satellite): HBO (multiplexed).
Fee: $13.95 monthly.
Digital Pay Service 3
Pay Units: 6,671.
Programming (via satellite): Flix; Showtime (multiplexed); The Movie Channel (multiplexed).
Fee: $13.95 monthly.
Digital Pay Service 4
Pay Units: N.A.
Programming (via satellite): Encore (multiplexed); Starz (multiplexed).
Fee: $13.95 monthly.
Video-On-Demand: Yes
Pay-Per-View
Addressable homes: 58,000.
ETC (delivered digitally); iN DEMAND (delivered digitally); Playboy TV (delivered digitally); Pleasure (delivered digitally); Fresh (delivered digitally).
Internet Service
Operational: Yes. Began: May 1, 1998.
Broadband Service: Charter Pipeline.
Fee: $29.99 monthly; $5.00 modem lease; $79.00 modem purchase.
Telephone Service
Digital: Operational
Fee: $29.99 monthly
Miles of Plant: 2,803.0 (coaxial); None (fiber optic). Homes passed: 101,046.
Vice President & General Manager: Greg Garabedian. Technical Operations Director: George Duffy. Marketing Director: Dennis Jerome.
Ownership: Charter Communications Inc. (MSO).

NORWALK—Cablevision Systems Corp., 28 Cross St, Norwalk, CT 6851. Phones: 203-750-5600; 516-803-2300 (Corporate office). Fax: 203-354-0921. Web Site: http://www.cablevision.com. Also serves Darien, Easton, Greenwich, New Canaan, Redding, Stamford, Weston, Westport & Wilton. ICA: CT0002.
TV Market Ranking: 1 (Greenwich, Stamford); 19 (Darien, Easton, New Canaan, NORWALK, Redding, Weston, Westport, Wilton). Franchise award date: July 1, 1981. Franchise expiration date: N.A. Began: August 16, 1982.
Channel capacity: 110 (operating 2-way). Channels available but not in use: N.A.
Basic Service
Subscribers: 123,084.
Programming (received off-air): WABC-TV (ABC) New York; WCCT-TV (CW) Waterbury; WEDW (PBS) Bridgeport; WFSB (CBS) Hartford; WFUT-DT (TEL) Newark; WLIW (PBS) Garden City; WLNY-TV (IND) Riverhead; WNET (PBS) Newark; WNJU (TMO) Linden; WPIX (CW, IND) New York; WPXN-TV (ION) New York; WRNN-TV (IND) Kingston; WSAH (IND) Bridgeport; WTIC-TV (FOX) Hartford; WTNH (ABC) New Haven; WVIT (NBC) New Britain; WWOR-TV (MNT) Secaucus; WXTV-DT (UNV) Paterson; 12 FMs.
Programming (via microwave): News 12 Connecticut; WCBS-TV (CBS) New York; WNBC (NBC) New York; WNYW (FOX) New York.
Current originations: Leased Access; Religious Access; Government Access; Educational Access; Public Access.
Fee: $49.95 installation; $16.72 monthly; $3.50 converter; $21.95 additional installation.
Expanded Basic Service 1
Subscribers: N.A.
Programming (via satellite): ABC Family Channel; AMC; Animal Planet; Arts & Entertainment; BET Networks; Bravo; Cartoon Network; CNBC; CNN; Comedy Central; C-SPAN; C-SPAN 2; CT-N; Discovery Channel; Disney Channel; E! Entertainment Television; ESPN; ESPN 2; Food Network; Fox News Channel; Fuse; FX; GSN; Headline News; HGTV; History Channel; Home Shopping Network; Lifetime; MSG; MSG Plus; MSNBC; MTV; MTV2; News 12 Traffic & Weather; Nickelodeon; QVC; ShopNBC; SoapNet; Speed Channel; Spike TV; SportsNet New York; Syfy; TBS Superstation; The Learning Channel; Travel Channel; truTV; Turner Classic Movies; Turner Network TV; TV Land; USA Network; VH1; WE tv; Weather Channel; Yankees Entertainment & Sports.
Fee: $33.23 monthly.
Digital Basic Service
Subscribers: N.A.
Programming (received off-air): WABC-TV (ABC) New York; WCBS-TV (CBS) New

York; WNBC (NBC) New York; WNYW (FOX) New York; WPIX (CW, IND) New York; WWOR-TV (MNT) Secaucus.
Programming (via satellite): Azteca America; BBC World News; Bio; Bloomberg Television; Canal Sur; Caracol; Cartoon Network Tambien en Espanol; CBS College Sports Network; Cine Latino; CNN en Espanol; CNN HD; Country Music TV; C-SPAN 3; Discovery en Espanol; Discovery HD Theater; Discovery Kids Channel; Discovery Military Channel; Discovery Planet Green; Docu TVE; Ecuavisia Internacional; ESPN 2 HD; ESPN Classic Sports; ESPN Deportes; ESPN HD; ESPNews; EuroNews; EWTN en Espanol; Food Network HD; Fox College Sports Atlantic; Fox College Sports Central; Fox College Sports Pacific; Fox Movie Channel; Fox Soccer; Fox Sports en Espanol; Fuel TV; G4; Gol TV; Golf Channel; Great American Country; Hallmark Channel; here! On Demand; HGTV HD; History Channel en Espanol; History Channel International; Howard TV; HTV Musica; ID Investigation Discovery; Infinito; Jewelry Television; La Familia Network; Latele Novela Network; LOGO; Maria+Vision; Momentum TV; MoviePlex; MTV Hits; MTV Tres; mun2 television; Music Choice; National Geographic Channel; National Geographic Channel HD Network; NBA TV; New England Cable News; NHL Network; Nick Jr.; NickToons TV; Outdoor Channel; Oxygen; Science Channel; ShopNBC; Sorpresa; Sundance Channel; Supercanal Caribe; TBS in HD; TeenNick; Telefe Internacional; Telemicro Internacional; The Jewish Channel; Toon Disney; Toon Disney en Espanol; Turner Network TV HD; TV Chile; TV Colombia; TVE Internacional; TVG Network; Universal HD; Utilisima; VeneMovies; Versus; Versus HD; VH1 Classic; VH1 Soul; WAPA America; YES HD.
Fee: $10.95 monthly.

Pay Service 1
Pay Units: 33,500.
Programming (via satellite): Cinemax; Club Jenna; Flix; HBO (multiplexed); Independent Film Channel; Showtime (multiplexed); The Movie Channel (multiplexed).
Fee: $40.00 installation.

Digital Pay Service 1
Pay Units: N.A.
Programming (via satellite): CCTV-4; Channel One; Cinemax (multiplexed); Cinemax HD; Cinemax On Demand; Encore (multiplexed); Filipino Channel; GMA Pinoy TV; HBO (multiplexed); HBO HD; HBO On Demand; Korean Channel; MBC America; MKTV; Portuguese Channel; RAI USA; Russian Television Network; Showtime (multiplexed); Showtime HD; Showtime On Demand; Sino TV; Starz (multiplexed); Starz HDTV; Starz On Demand; The Movie Channel (multiplexed); The Movie Channel HD; TV Asia; TV Japan; TV Polonia; TV5 USA; Zee TV USA.
Fee: $9.95 monthly (Cinemax, Showtime/TMC, Starz/Encore or Playboy), $11.95 monthly (HBO).

Video-On-Demand: Yes

Pay-Per-View
Independent Film Channel (delivered digitally); Anime Network (delivered digitally); iN DEMAND (delivered digitally); Disney Channel (delivered digitally); Playboy TV (delivered digitally).

Internet Service
Operational: Yes. Began: January 1, 1997.
Broadband Service: Optimum Online.
Fee: $46.95 installation; $34.95 monthly; $299.00 modem purchase.

Telephone Service
Digital: Operational
Fee: $46.95 installation; $34.95 monthly
Miles of Plant: 2,524.0 (coaxial); None (fiber optic). Homes passed: 149,903.
Government Affairs Area Director: Michael Chowaniec. Vice President, Field Operations: Mark Fitchett. Government Affairs Director: Jennifer Young.
State fee: 5% of gross.
Ownership: Cablevision Systems Corp. (MSO).

NORWICH—Comcast Cable, 1 Hilltop Rd, Norwich, CT 6360. Phones: 888-683-1000; 860-505-6248. Fax: 860-505-3597. Web Site: http://www.comcast.com. Also serves Bozrah, Colchester, Franklin, Lisbon, Preston & Sprague. ICA: CT0018.
TV Market Ranking: 19 (Bozrah, Colchester, Franklin, NORWICH, Sprague); 33,19 (Lisbon, Preston). Franchise award date: N.A. Franchise expiration date: N.A. Began: December 28, 1975.
Channel capacity: N.A. Channels available but not in use: None.

Basic Service
Subscribers: 17,871.
Programming (received off-air): WCCT-TV (CW) Waterbury; WCTX (MNT) New Haven; WCVB-TV (ABC) Boston; WEDN (PBS) Norwich; WFSB (CBS) Hartford; WGBH-TV (PBS) Boston; WHPX-TV (ION) New London; WJAR (NBC) Providence; WPRI-TV (CBS) Providence; WTIC-TV (FOX) Hartford; WTNH (ABC) New Haven; WUVN (UNV) Hartford; WVIT (NBC) New Britain; 18 FMs.
Programming (via satellite): C-SPAN; C-SPAN 2; Home Shopping Network; TV Guide Network.
Current originations: Government Access; Educational Access; Public Access.
Fee: $10.45 installation; $9.50 monthly; $.90 converter.

Expanded Basic Service 1
Subscribers: 10,791.
Programming (via satellite): ABC Family Channel; AMC; Animal Planet; Arts & Entertainment; BET Networks; Bravo; Cartoon Network; CNBC; CNN; Comcast Sports Net New England; Comedy Central; Country Music TV; Discovery Channel; Disney Channel; E! Entertainment Television; ESPN; ESPN 2; Eternal Word TV Network; Food Network; Fox News Channel; FX; Hallmark Channel; Headline News; HGTV; History Channel; Lifetime; MSNBC; MTV; New England Cable News; New England Sports Network; Nickelodeon; Oxygen; QVC; ShopNBC; Spike TV; Syfy; TBS Superstation; The Learning Channel; Travel Channel; truTV; Turner Classic Movies; Turner Network TV; TV Land; USA Network; VH1; Weather Channel; Yankees Entertainment & Sports.
Fee: $10.00 installation; $40.45 monthly.

Digital Basic Service
Subscribers: N.A.
Programming (via satellite): AmericanLife TV Network; BBC America; Black Family Channel; Bloomberg Television; Discovery Digital Networks; DMX Music; FitTV; Fox Movie Channel; Fox Sports World; Fuse; G4; GAS; Golf Channel; Great American Country; GSN; Halogen Network; Lifetime Movie Network; MTV Networks Digital Suite; National Geographic Channel; Nick Jr.; Nick Too; NickToons TV; SoapNet; Speed Channel; Style Network; The Sportsman Channel; The Word Network; Toon Disney; Trinity Broadcasting Network; WE tv.

Digital Expanded Basic Service
Subscribers: N.A.
Programming (via satellite): Bio; CBS College Sports Network; CCTV-4; Do-It-Yourself; ESPN Classic Sports; ESPNews; Fox College Sports Central; Fox College Sports Pacific; History Channel International; Independent Film Channel; International Television (ITV); Outdoor Channel; Sundance Channel; Tennis Channel; Versus.

Digital Pay Service 1
Pay Units: 7,222.
Programming (via satellite): Cinemax (multiplexed); Encore (multiplexed); HBO (multiplexed); Showtime (multiplexed); Starz (multiplexed); The Movie Channel (multiplexed).

Video-On-Demand: Planned

Pay-Per-View
Sports PPV (delivered digitally); Fresh (delivered digitally); Hot Choice (delivered digitally); Playboy TV (delivered digitally); HITS PPV (delivered digitally), Addressable: Yes.

Internet Service
Operational: Yes.
Broadband Service: Comcast High Speed Internet.
Fee: $42.95 monthly.

Telephone Service
Digital: Operational
Miles of Plant: 580.0 (coaxial); None (fiber optic). Homes passed: 30,223.
Vice President & General Manager: Michael Parker. Technical Operations Director: Bob Burns. Marketing Director: Carolyn Hannan. Marketing Manager: Jodi Cyr. Marketing Coordinator: Marcia McElroy.
State fee: 3% of gross.
Ownership: Comcast Cable Communications Inc. (MSO).

OLD LYME—Comcast Cable, 1 Hilltop Rd, Norwich, CT 6360. Phones: 888-683-1000; 860-505-6248. Fax: 860-505-3597. Web Site: http://www.comcast.com. Also serves East Haddam, Haddam Neck, Lyme & Salem. ICA: CT0025.
TV Market Ranking: 19 (East Haddam, Haddam Neck, Lyme, OLD LYME, Salem). Franchise award date: N.A. Franchise expiration date: N.A. Began: July 1, 1980.
Channel capacity: N.A. Channels available but not in use: None.

Basic Service
Subscribers: 7,721.
Programming (received off-air): WCCT-TV (CW) Waterbury; WCTX (MNT) New Haven; WCVB-TV (ABC) Boston; WEDN (PBS) Norwich; WFSB (CBS) Hartford; WGBH-TV (PBS) Boston; WHPX-TV (ION) New London; WJAR (NBC) Providence; WPRI-TV (CBS) Providence; WTIC-TV (FOX) Hartford; WTNH (ABC) New Haven; WUVN (UNV) Hartford; WVIT (NBC) New Britain; 28 FMs.
Programming (via satellite): C-SPAN; C-SPAN 2; Home Shopping Network; QVC; TV Guide Network.
Current originations: Government Access; Educational Access; Public Access.
Fee: $10.45 installation; $9.50 monthly.

Expanded Basic Service 1
Subscribers: 3,487.
Programming (via satellite): ABC Family Channel; AMC; Animal Planet; Arts & Entertainment; Bravo; Cartoon Network; CNBC; CNN; Comcast Sports Net New England; Comedy Central; Country Music TV; Discovery Channel; Disney Channel; E! Entertainment Television; ESPN; ESPN 2; Eternal Word TV Network; Food Network; Fox News Channel; FX; Hallmark Channel; Headline News; HGTV; History Channel; Lifetime; MSNBC; MTV; New England Cable News; New England Sports Network; Nickelodeon; Oxygen; Spike TV; Syfy; TBS Superstation; The Learning Channel; Travel Channel; truTV; Turner Network TV; TV Land; USA Network; VH1; Weather Channel; Yankees Entertainment & Sports.
Fee: $49.95 monthly.

Digital Basic Service
Subscribers: N.A.
Programming (via satellite): American-Life TV Network; BBC America; Bloomberg Television; Discovery Digital Networks; FitTV; Fox Movie Channel; Fox Sports World; Fuse; G4; GAS; Golf Channel; Great American Country; GSN; Halogen Network; Lifetime Movie Network; MTV Networks Digital Suite; Music Choice; National Geographic Channel; Nick Jr.; Nick Too; NickToons TV; SoapNet; Speed Channel; Style Network; The Sportsman Channel; The Word Network; Toon Disney; Trinity Broadcasting Network; WE tv.
Fee: $45.23 monthly.

Digital Expanded Basic Service
Subscribers: N.A.
Programming (via satellite): Bio; CCTV-4; Do-It-Yourself; ESPN Classic Sports; ESPNews; Fox College Sports Atlantic; Fox College Sports Central; Fox College Sports Pacific; History Channel International; Independent Film Channel; International Television (ITV); Outdoor Channel; Sundance Channel; Tennis Channel; Turner Classic Movies; Versus.
Fee: $68.69 monthly.

Digital Pay Service 1
Pay Units: N.A.
Programming (via satellite): Cinemax (multiplexed); Encore (multiplexed); Flix; HBO (multiplexed); Showtime; Starz (multiplexed); The Movie Channel.

Video-On-Demand: Planned

Pay-Per-View
Sports PPV (delivered digitally); Fresh (delivered digitally); Hot Choice (delivered digitally); Playboy TV (delivered digitally); HITS PPV (delivered digitally), Addressable: Yes.

Internet Service
Operational: Yes.
Broadband Service: Comcast High Speed Internet.
Fee: $42.95 monthly.

Telephone Service
Digital: Operational
Miles of Plant: 437.0 (coaxial); None (fiber optic). Homes passed: 12,480.
Vice President & General Manager: Michael Parker. Technical Operations Director: Bob Burns. Marketing Director: Carolyn Hannan. Marketing Manager: Judi Cyr. Marketing Coordinator: Marcia McElroy.
State fee: 5% of gross.
Ownership: Comcast Cable Communications Inc. (MSO).

PLAINVILLE—Comcast Cable, 222 New Park Dr, Berlin, CT 06037-3741. Phones: 800-266-2278; 860-505-6248. Fax: 860-505-3597. Web Site: http://www.comcast.com. Also serves Avon, Berlin, Bristol, Burlington, Canton, Farmington & New Britain. ICA: CT0037.
TV Market Ranking: 19 (Avon, Berlin, Bristol, Burlington, Canton, Farmington, New Britain, PLAINVILLE (VILLAGE)).
Channel capacity: N.A. Channels available but not in use: N.A.

Basic Service

Subscribers: 70,218.

Programming (received off-air): WCCT-TV (CW) Waterbury; WCTX (MNT) New Haven; WFSB (CBS) Hartford; WGBY-TV (PBS) Springfield; WHPX-TV (ION) New London; WRDM-CA (TMO) Hartford; WTIC-TV (FOX) Hartford; WTNH (ABC) New Haven; WUVN (UNV) Hartford; WVIT (NBC) New Britain.

Programming (via satellite): C-SPAN; C-SPAN 2; Eternal Word TV Network; National Jewish TV (NJT); New England Cable News; Shop at Home; TBS Superstation; The Comcast Network.

Current originations: Government Access; Educational Access; Public Access.

Fee: $12.20 monthly.

Expanded Basic Service 1

Subscribers: N.A.

Programming (via satellite): ABC Family Channel; AMC; Animal Planet; Arts & Entertainment; BET Networks; Cartoon Network; CNBC; CNN; Comcast Sports Net New England; Comedy Central; Discovery Channel; Disney Channel; E! Entertainment Television; ESPN; ESPN 2; Food Network; Fox News Channel; FX; Golf Channel; Headline News; HGTV; History Channel; Home Shopping Network; Lifetime; MSNBC; MTV; New England Sports Network; Nickelodeon; QVC; ShopNBC; Spike TV; Syfy; The Learning Channel; truTV; Turner Network TV; TV Guide Network; TV Land; USA Network; VH1; Weather Channel.

Fee: $37.90 monthly.

Expanded Basic Service 2

Subscribers: N.A.

Programming (via satellite): Fuse; Turner Classic Movies; Versus.

Digital Basic Service

Subscribers: N.A.

Programming (received off-air): WFSB (CBS) Hartford; WTIC-TV (FOX) Hartford; WTNH (ABC) New Haven; WVIT (NBC) New Britain.

Programming (via satellite): Bio; Bloomberg Television; Canales N; Discovery Digital Networks; ESPN; ESPN Classic Sports; ESPNews; FitTV; Fox Movie Channel; Fox Soccer; G4; GAS; GSN; Halogen Network; History Channel International; Independent Film Channel; INHD (multiplexed); Lifetime Movie Network; MTV Networks Digital Suite; National Geographic Channel; NFL Network; Nick Jr.; Nick Too; NickToons TV; Outdoor Channel; Speed Channel; Style Network; Sundance Channel; Toon Disney; Trinity Broadcasting Network; TVG Network; WE tv.

Fee: $38.79 monthly.

Pay Service 1

Pay Units: N.A.

Programming (via satellite): HBO; The Movie Channel.

Fee: $19.95 monthly.

Digital Pay Service 1

Pay Units: N.A.

Programming (via satellite): Cinemax (multiplexed); Encore (multiplexed); HBO (multiplexed); Showtime (multiplexed); Starz (multiplexed); The Movie Channel (multiplexed).

Fee: $19.95 monthly (each).

Video-On-Demand: Yes

Pay-Per-View

iN DEMAND; iN DEMAND (delivered digitally); Playboy TV (delivered digitally); Fresh (delivered digitally); Shorteez (delivered digitally).

Internet Service

Operational: Yes.

Broadband Service: Comcast High Speed Internet.

Fee: $42.95 monthly; $3.00 modem lease.

Telephone Service

Digital: Operational

Fee: $44.95 monthly

Miles of Plant: 1,249.0 (coaxial); None (fiber optic). Total homes in franchised area: 111,358.

Vice President & General Manager: Pamela Mackenzie. Technical Operations Director: Jim Jones. Marketing Director: Carolyne Hannan. Marketing Coordinator: Marcia McElroy. Marketing Manager: Judy Cyr.

Ownership: Comcast Cable Communications Inc. (MSO).

SEYMOUR—Comcast Cable, 80 Great Hill Rd, Seymour, CT 06483-2299. Phones: 888-683-1000; 860-505-6248. Fax: 203-505-3597. Web Site: http://www.comcast.com. Also serves Ansonia, Beacon Falls, Bethany, Derby, Huntington, Naugatuck, Oxford & Shelton. ICA: CT0009.

TV Market Ranking: 19 (Ansonia, Beacon Falls, Bethany, Derby, Huntington, Naugatuck, Oxford, SEYMOUR, Shelton). Franchise award date: January 1, 1963. Franchise expiration date: N.A. Began: March 28, 1972.

Channel capacity: 78 (operating 2-way). Channels available but not in use: None.

Basic Service

Subscribers: 34,885.

Programming (received off-air): WABC-TV (ABC) New York; WCBS-TV (CBS) New York; WCCT-TV (CW) Waterbury; WCTX (MNT) New Haven; WEDW (PBS) Bridgeport; WFSB (CBS) Hartford; WHPX-TV (ION) New London; WNBC (NBC) New York; WNET (PBS) Newark; WNYW (FOX) New York; WPIX (CW, IND) New York; WRDM-CA (TMO) Hartford; WSAH (IND) Bridgeport; WTIC-TV (FOX) Hartford; WTNH (ABC) New Haven; WUVN (UNV) Hartford; WVIT (NBC) New Britain; WWOR-TV (MNT) Secaucus.

Programming (via satellite): C-SPAN; C-SPAN 2; Eternal Word TV Network; Home Shopping Network; QVC; TBS Superstation; Trinity Broadcasting Network; TV Guide Network.

Current originations: Leased Access; Religious Access; Educational Access; Public Access.

Fee: $58.00 installation; $25.00 monthly; $4.03 converter.

Expanded Basic Service 1

Subscribers: N.A.

Programming (via satellite): ABC Family Channel; AMC; Animal Planet; Arts & Entertainment; BET Networks; Bravo; Cartoon Network; CNBC; CNN; Comedy Central; Country Music TV; Discovery Channel; Disney Channel; E! Entertainment Television; ESPN; ESPN 2; Food Network; Fox News Channel; FX; Hallmark Channel; Headline News; HGTV; History Channel; Lifetime; MSG; MSNBC; MTV; Nickelodeon; Spike TV; Syfy; The Learning Channel; Travel Channel; truTV; Turner Classic Movies; Turner Network TV; TV Land; USA Network; VH1; Weather Channel; Yankees Entertainment & Sports.

Fee: $53.35 monthly.

Digital Basic Service

Subscribers: 9,000.

Programming (via satellite): AmericanLife TV Network; BBC America; Black Family Channel; Bloomberg Television; Discovery Digital Networks; FitTV; Fox Movie Channel; Fox Sports World; Fuse; G4; GAS; Golf Channel; Great American Country; GSN; Halogen Network; Lifetime Movie Network; Lime; Music Choice; National Geographic Channel; Nick Jr.; Nick Too; NickToons TV; Oxygen; SoapNet; Speed Channel; Style Network; The Sportsman Channel; The Word Network; Toon Disney; Trinity Broadcasting Network; TVG Network; WE tv.

Fee: $45.23 monthly.

Digital Expanded Basic Service

Subscribers: N.A.

Programming (via satellite): Bio; Canales N; CBS College Sports Network; Do-It-Yourself; ESPN Classic Sports; ESPNews; Fox College Sports Atlantic; Fox College Sports Central; Fox College Sports Pacific; Fuel TV; History Channel International; Independent Film Channel; Outdoor Channel; Sundance Channel; Tennis Channel; Versus.

Pay Service 1

Pay Units: N.A.

Programming (via satellite): Cinemax; Encore; Showtime (multiplexed); Starz; The Movie Channel.

Fee: $8.00 monthly (Starz), $10.00 monthly (Cinemax, Showtime or TMC), $11.00 monthly (HBO).

Digital Pay Service 1

Pay Units: N.A.

Programming (via satellite): ART America; CCTV-4; Cinemax (multiplexed); Encore (multiplexed); Flix; HBO (multiplexed); RAI International; Showtime (multiplexed); Starz (multiplexed); The Movie Channel (multiplexed); TV5 USA.

Fee: $4.95 monthly (Encore), $6.00 monthly (Music Choice), $8.00 monthly (Starz), $10.00 monthly (ART, CCTV-4, CTN, Filipino, RAI, TV Asia or TV5), $12.95 monthly (Cinemax, HBO or Flix, Showtime & TMC), $25.00 monthly (TV Japan).

Video-On-Demand: Planned

Pay-Per-View

Playboy TV (delivered digitally); Shorteez (delivered digitally); iN DEMAND (delivered digitally); Fresh; Sports PPV (delivered digitally).

Internet Service

Operational: Yes. Began: June 1, 2002.

Subscribers: 500.

Broadband Service: Comcast High Speed Internet.

Fee: $42.95 monthly; $10.00 modem lease.

Telephone Service

Digital: Operational

Fee: $39.95 monthly

Miles of Plant: 899.0 (coaxial); None (fiber optic). Homes passed: 62,271.

Vice President & General Manager: Michael Parker. Technical Operations Director: Bob Burns. Marketing Director: Carolyn Hannan. Marketing Manager: Judi Cyr. Marketing Coordinator: Marcia McElroy.

State fee: 5% of gross.

Ownership: Comcast Cable Communications Inc. (MSO).

VERNON—Comcast Cable, 222 New Park Dr, Berlin, CT 06037-3741. Phones: 800-266-2278; 860-505-6248. Fax: 860-505-3597. Web Site: http://www.comcast.com. Also serves Andover, Bolton, Ellington, Hebron, Marlborough & Tolland. ICA: CT0034.

TV Market Ranking: 19 (Andover, Bolton, Ellington, Hebron, Marlborough, Tolland, VERNON). Franchise award date: N.A. Franchise expiration date: N.A. Began: N.A.

Channel capacity: N.A. Channels available but not in use: N.A.

Basic Service

Subscribers: 26,005.

Programming (received off-air): WCCT-TV (CW) Waterbury; WCTX (MNT) New Haven; WEDH (PBS) Hartford; WFSB (CBS) Hartford; WGBY-TV (PBS) Springfield; WHPX-TV (ION) New London; WRDM-CA (TMO) Hartford; WTIC-TV (FOX) Hartford; WTNH (ABC) New Haven; WUVN (UNV) Hartford; WVIT (NBC) New Britain; WWLP (NBC) Springfield.

Programming (via satellite): Comedy Central; C-SPAN; C-SPAN 2; Discovery Channel; Fox News Channel; New England Cable News; New England Sports Network; QVC; TBS Superstation; The Comcast Network; The Learning Channel; TV Guide Network; Univision; VH1.

Current originations: Government Access; Educational Access.

Fee: $45.50 installation; $12.10 monthly.

Expanded Basic Service 1

Subscribers: N.A.

Programming (via satellite): ABC Family Channel; AMC; Animal Planet; Arts & Entertainment; BET Networks; Bio; Bloomberg Television; Cartoon Network; CNBC; CNN; Comcast Sports Net New England; Country Music TV; Disney Channel; E! Entertainment Television; ESPN; ESPN 2; Eternal Word TV Network; FitTV; Food Network; Fox Movie Channel; Fox Sports Net Mid-Atlantic; Fox Sports Net Midwest; Fox Sports Net West; Fox Sports World; FX; Golf Channel; Great American Country; GSN; Hallmark Channel; Halogen Network; Headline News; HGTV; History Channel; Home Shopping Network; Lifetime; Lifetime Movie Network; MSNBC; MTV; NBA TV; Nickelodeon; Outdoor Channel; Speed Channel; Spike TV; Sundance Channel; Syfy; Travel Channel; Trinity Broadcasting Network; truTV; Turner Classic Movies; Turner Network TV; USA Network; Versus; Yankees Entertainment & Sports.

Fee: $51.57 monthly.

Digital Basic Service

Subscribers: N.A.

Programming (via satellite): BBC America; Black Family Channel; Bravo; Discovery Digital Networks; Fuse; G4; GAS; HGTV; History Channel International; Independent Film Channel; International Television (ITV); MTV Networks Digital Suite; MTV2; Music Choice; National Geographic Channel; Nick Jr.; NickToons TV; Style Network; The Word Network; Toon Disney; TV Land; WE tv.

Fee: $45.23 monthly.

Digital Pay Service 1

Pay Units: N.A.

Programming (via satellite): Canales N; Cinemax (multiplexed); Encore; HBO (multiplexed); Showtime (multiplexed).

Fee: $19.95 monthly (each).

Video-On-Demand: Yes

Pay-Per-View

Fresh (delivered digitally); iN DEMAND (delivered digitally); Playboy TV (delivered digitally); Shorteez (delivered digitally).

Internet Service

Operational: Yes.

Broadband Service: Comcast High Speed Internet.

Fee: $42.95 monthly.

Telephone Service

Digital: Operational

Fee: $44.95 monthly

Homes passed: 36,585.

Area Vice President & General Manager: Pamela Mackenzie. Technical Operations Director: Jim Jones. Marketing Director: Carolyne Hannan. Marketing Manager: Judi Cyr. Marketing Coordinator: Marcia McElroy.

Ownership: Comcast Cable Communications Inc. (MSO).

WATERBURY—Comcast Cable, 80 Great Hill Rd, Seymour, CT 06483-2299. Phones: 888-683-1000; 860-505-6248. Fax: 860-505-3597. Web Site: http://www.comcast.com. Also serves Middlebury, Plymouth, Prospect, Terryville & Wolcott. ICA: CT0007.

TV Market Ranking: 19 (Middlebury, Plymouth, Prospect, Terryville, WATERBURY (VILLAGE), Wolcott). Franchise award date: March 1, 1975. Franchise expiration date: N.A. Began: March 14, 1975.

Channel capacity: N.A. Channels available but not in use: N.A.

Basic Service

Subscribers: 39,938.

Programming (received off-air): WABC-TV (ABC) New York; WCCT-TV (CW) Waterbury; WCTX (MNT) New Haven; WEDH (PBS) Hartford; WFSB (CBS) Hartford; WHPX-TV (ION) New London; WNBC (NBC) New York; WNYW (FOX) New York; WPIX (CW, IND) New York; WRDM-CA (TMO) Hartford; WSAH (IND) Bridgeport; WTIC-TV (FOX) Hartford; WTNH (ABC) New Haven; WUVN (UNV) Hartford; WVIT (NBC) New Britain; WWOR-TV (MNT) Secaucus.

Programming (via satellite): C-SPAN; C-SPAN 2; Eternal Word TV Network; Home Shopping Network; QVC; TBS Superstation; TV Guide Network.

Current originations: Government Access; Educational Access; Public Access.

Fee: $25.00 installation; $16.35 monthly; $2.75 converter.

Expanded Basic Service 1

Subscribers: N.A.

Programming (via satellite): ABC Family Channel; AMC; Animal Planet; Arts & Entertainment; BET Networks; Bravo; Cartoon Network; CNBC; CNN; Comedy Central; Country Music TV; Discovery Channel; Disney Channel; E! Entertainment Television; ESPN; ESPN 2; Food Network; Fox News Channel; FX; Hallmark Channel; Headline News; HGTV; History Channel; Lifetime; MSG; MSNBC; MTV; Nickelodeon; Spike TV; Syfy; The Learning Channel; Travel Channel; Trinity Broadcasting Network; truTV; Turner Classic Movies; Turner Network TV; TV Land; USA Network; VH1; Weather Channel; Yankees Entertainment & Sports.

Fee: $49.95 monthly.

Digital Basic Service

Subscribers: N.A.

Programming (received off-air): WCCT-TV (CW) Waterbury; WEDH (PBS) Hartford; WFSB (CBS) Hartford; WNYW (FOX) New York; WTNH (ABC) New Haven; WVIT (NBC) New Britain.

Programming (via satellite): BBC America; Bio; Black Family Channel; Bloomberg Television; Canales N; CBS College Sports Network; Cooking Channel; Country Music TV; Current; Discovery Digital Networks; Discovery HD Theater; Do-It-Yourself; Encore (multiplexed); ESPN 2 HD; ESPN Classic Sports; ESPN Deportes; ESPN HD; Flix; Fox College Sports Atlantic; Fox College Sports Central; Fox College Sports Pacific; Fox Movie Channel; Fox Reality Channel; Fox Soccer; G4; GAS; Golf Channel; Great American Country; GSN; Halogen Network; History Channel International; Independent Film Channel; INHD; Lifetime Movie Network; LOGO; MTV Networks Digital Suite; Music Choice; National Geographic Channel; NFL Network; Nick Jr.; Nick Too; Outdoor Channel; Oxygen; SoapNet; Speed Channel; Style Network; Sundance Channel; Tennis Channel; The Sportsman Channel; The Word Network; Toon Disney; Trinity Broadcasting Network; Turner Network TV HD; TVG Network; Versus; WE tv.

Fee: $45.23 monthly.

Digital Pay Service 1

Pay Units: N.A.

Programming (via satellite): ART America; CCTV-4; Cinemax (multiplexed); Cinemax HD; Flix; HBO (multiplexed); HBO HD; RAI International; Showtime (multiplexed); Showtime HD; Starz (multiplexed); Starz HDTV; The Movie Channel (multiplexed); TV5 USA.

Fee: $4.95 monthly (Encore), $8.00 monthly (Starz), $10.00 monthly (ART, CCTV-4, CTN, Filipino, RAI, TV Asia or TV5), $12.95 monthly (Cinemax, HBO or Flix, Showtime & TMC), $25.00 monthly (TV Japan).

Video-On-Demand: Planned

Pay-Per-View

Addressable homes: 12,000.

iN DEMAND (delivered digitally), Fee: $3.99, Addressable: Yes; Fresh, Fee: $3.99; ESPN (delivered digitally), Fee: $3.99; NBA League Pass (delivered digitally); NHL Center Ice (delivered digitally); MLB Extra Innings (delivered digitally); Playboy TV (delivered digitally).

Internet Service

Operational: Yes. Began: June 1, 2002.

Subscribers: 500.

Broadband Service: Comcast High Speed Internet.

Fee: $42.95 monthly; $10.00 modem lease.

Telephone Service

Digital: Operational

Fee: $39.95 monthly

Miles of Plant: 691.0 (coaxial); None (fiber optic). Homes passed: 72,726.

Vice President & General Manager: Michael Parker. Technical Operations Director: Bob Burns. Marketing Director: Carolyn Hannan. Marketing Manager: Judi Cyr. Marketing Coordinator: Marcia McElroy.

State fee: 5% of gross.

Ownership: Comcast Cable Communications Inc. (MSO).

WINSTED—Charter Communications, 9 Commerce Rd, Newtown, CT 6470. Phones: 800-827-8288; 203-304-4001. Fax: 203-304-8713. Web Site: http://www.charter.com. Also serves Barkhamsted, Colebrook, Goshen, Harwinton, New Hartford, West Hartland & Winchester. ICA: CT0021.

TV Market Ranking: 19 (Barkhamsted, Colebrook, Goshen, Harwinton, New Hartford, West Hartland, Winchester, WINSTED). Franchise award date: January 1, 1975. Franchise expiration date: N.A. Began: March 18, 1975.

Channel capacity: 78 (operating 2-way). Channels available but not in use: None.

Basic Service

Subscribers: 8,476.

Programming (received off-air): WCCT-TV (CW) Waterbury; WCTX (MNT) New Haven; WEDH (PBS) Hartford; WFSB (CBS) Hartford; WGBY-TV (PBS) Springfield; WHPX-TV (ION) New London; WTIC-TV (FOX) Hartford; WTNH (ABC) New Haven; WUVN (UNV) Hartford; WVIT (NBC) New Britain; allband FM.

Programming (via satellite): C-SPAN; C-SPAN 2; Eternal Word TV Network; Home Shopping Network; QVC; Shop at Home; Trinity Broadcasting Network; TV Guide Network.

Current originations: Government Access; Educational Access; Public Access.

Expanded Basic Service 1

Subscribers: 7,640.

Programming (via satellite): ABC Family Channel; AMC; Animal Planet; Arts & Entertainment; Bravo; Cartoon Network; CNBC; CNN; Comcast Sports Net New England; Comedy Central; Discovery Channel; Disney Channel; E! Entertainment Television; ESPN; Food Network; Fox News Channel; FX; G4; Golf Channel; Hallmark Channel; Headline News; HGTV; History Channel; INSP; Lifetime; MSG; MSNBC; MTV; National Geographic Channel; New England Sports Network; Nickelodeon; Oxygen; ShopNBC; Speed Channel; Spike TV; Syfy; TBS Superstation; The Learning Channel; Travel Channel; truTV; Turner Classic Movies; Turner Network TV; TV Land; USA Network; Versus; VH1; Weather Channel; Yankees Entertainment & Sports.

Fee: $55.00 monthly.

Digital Basic Service

Subscribers: N.A.

Programming (via satellite): BBC America; Bio; Bloomberg Television; Discovery Digital Networks; Do-It-Yourself; GAS; Great American Country; History Channel International; Independent Film Channel; Lifetime Movie Network; MTV Networks Digital Suite; MuchMusic Network; Music Choice; Nick Jr.; Nick Too; NickToons TV; SoapNet; Style Network; Sundance Channel; Toon Disney; WE tv.

Fee: $5.71 monthly.

Digital Pay Service 1

Pay Units: 326.

Programming (via satellite): Cinemax (multiplexed).

Fee: $13.95 monthly.

Digital Pay Service 2

Pay Units: 549.

Programming (via satellite): HBO (multiplexed).

Fee: $13.95 monthly.

Digital Pay Service 3

Pay Units: 470.

Programming (via satellite): Flix; Showtime (multiplexed); The Movie Channel (multiplexed).

Fee: $13.95 monthly.

Digital Pay Service 4

Pay Units: 428.

Programming (via satellite): Encore (multiplexed); Starz (multiplexed).

Fee: $13.95 monthly.

Video-On-Demand: Yes

Pay-Per-View

ETC (delivered digitally); iN DEMAND (delivered digitally); Playboy TV (delivered digitally); Pleasure (delivered digitally); Fresh (delivered digitally); sports (delivered digitally).

Internet Service

Operational: Yes. Began: November 1, 2001.

Broadband Service: Charter Pipeline.

Fee: $29.99 monthly; $5.00 modem lease; $79.00 modem purchase.

Telephone Service

Digital: Operational

Fee: $29.99 monthly

Miles of Plant: 455.0 (coaxial); None (fiber optic). Homes passed: 11,352. Total homes in franchised area: 12,385.

Vice President & General Manager: Greg Garabedian. Technical Operations Director: George Duffy. Marketing Director: Dennis Jerome.

Ownership: Charter Communications Inc. (MSO).

DELAWARE

Total Systems: 5
Total Communities Served: 80
Franchises Not Yet Operating: 0
Applications Pending: 0
Communities with Applications: 0
Number of Basic Subscribers: 118,752
Number of Expanded Basic Subscribers: 156,027
Number of Pay Units: 12,363

Top 100 Markets Represented: Baltimore (14); Philadelphia, PA-Burlington, NJ (4).

For a list of cable communities in this section, see the Cable Community Index located in the back of Cable Volume 2.
For explanation of terms used in cable system listings, see p. D-11.

DAGSBORO—Mediacom, 601 Clayton St, Dagsboro, DE 19939-1738. Phones: 302-732-9332; 302-732-6600 (Customer service). Fax: 302-732-6697. E-mail: ptremblay@mediacomcc.com. Web Site: http://www.mediacomcable.com. Also serves Bethany Beach, Clarksville, Frankford, Millsboro, Millville, Ocean View, Roxana, Selbyville, South Bethany & Sussex County, DE; Bishopville, Ocean Pines, Pittsville, Whaleysville & Willards, MD. ICA: DE0001.

TV Market Ranking: Below 100 (Bethany Beach, Bishopville, Clarksville, DAGSBORO, Frankford, Millsboro, Millville, Ocean Pines, Ocean View, Pittsville, Roxana, Selbyville, South Bethany, Sussex County (portions), Whaleysville, Willards); Outside TV Markets (Sussex County (portions)). Franchise award date: March 12, 1975. Franchise expiration date: N.A. Began: October 1, 1968.

Channel capacity: N.A. Channels available but not in use: N.A.

Basic Service

Subscribers: 36,838.

Programming (received off-air): WBOC-TV (CBS, FOX) Salisbury; WCPB (PBS) Salisbury; WDPB (PBS) Seaford; WEWE-LP (IND) Sussex County; WMDT (ABC, CW) Salisbury.

Programming (via microwave): WBAL-TV (NBC) Baltimore; WJZ-TV (CBS) Baltimore; WTTG (FOX) Washington; WTXF-TV (FOX) Philadelphia.

Programming (via satellite): ABC Family Channel; AMC; Animal Planet; Arts & Entertainment; BET Networks; Bravo; Cartoon Network; CNBC; CNN; Comcast SportsNet Mid-Atlantic; Comedy Central; Country Music TV; C-SPAN; C-SPAN 2; Discovery Channel; Disney Channel; E! Entertainment Television; ESPN; ESPN 2; Eternal Word TV Network; Food Network; Fox News Channel; FX; Golf Channel; Headline News; HGTV; History Channel; Home Shopping Network; Lifetime; MSNBC; MTV; Nickelodeon; Outdoor Channel; QVC; ShopNBC; Spike TV; Syfy; TBS Superstation; The Learning Channel; Travel Channel; truTV; Turner Network TV; TV Guide Network; TV Land; USA Network; VH1; WE tv; Weather Channel.

Current originations: Government Access; Public Access.

Fee: $29.50 installation; $27.95 monthly; $3.00 converter; $20.00 additional installation.

Digital Basic Service

Subscribers: N.A.

Programming (received off-air): WBOC-TV (CBS, FOX) Salisbury.

Programming (via satellite): BBC America; Bio; Bloomberg Television; Bravo; Discovery Digital Networks; Discovery HD Theater; DMX Music; ESPN; ESPNews; Fox Movie Channel; Fox Soccer; Fuse; G4; GAS; GSN; Halogen Network; HDNet; HDNet Movies; History Channel International; Independent Film Channel; Lifetime Movie Network; Lime; Mid-Atlantic Sports Network; MTV2; National Geographic Channel; Nick Jr.; NickToons TV; Speed Channel; Style Network; Turner Classic Movies; Versus; VH1 Classic; Weatherscan.

Fee: $8.00 monthly.

Digital Pay Service 1

Pay Units: N.A.

Programming (via satellite): Cinemax (multiplexed); Encore (multiplexed); HBO (multiplexed); HBO HD; Showtime (multiplexed); Showtime HD; Starz (multiplexed); Starz HDTV; The Movie Channel (multiplexed).

Fee: $8.00 monthly (Starz), $9.95 monthly (Showtime or Cinemax), $13.95 monthly (HBO).

Video-On-Demand: Planned

Pay-Per-View

ESPN (delivered digitally); Mediacom PPV (delivered digitally).

Internet Service

Operational: Yes.

Subscribers: 6,956.

Broadband Service: Mediacom High Speed Internet.

Fee: $59.95 installation; $42.95 monthly; $3.00 modem lease; $239.00 modem purchase.

Telephone Service

Analog: Not Operational

Digital: Planned

Miles of Plant: 1,100.0 (coaxial); None (fiber optic). Total homes in franchised area: 51,219. Miles of plant (coax) includes fiber miles

Regional Vice President: David Kane. Marketing Director: Martin Wills. Customer Service Manager: Dulce Olexo. Area Technical Operations Manager: Gary McEachern. Chief Technician: Tim Baker.

Ownership: Mediacom LLC (MSO).

DOVER—Comcast Cable, 5729 W Denneys Rd, Dover, DE 19904-1365. Phone: 302-674-2494. Fax: 302-674-2538. Web Site: http://www.comcast.com. Also serves Bowers Beach, Camden, Cheswold, Clayton, Dover AFB, Farmington, Felton, Frederica, Harrington, Hartly, Houston, Kent County, Kenton, Leipsic, Little Creek, Magnolia, Marydel, New Castle County (southern portion), Smyrna, Viola, Woodside & Wyoming. ICA: DE0004.

TV Market Ranking: Below 100 (Bowers Beach, Clayton, DOVER, Farmington, Frederica, Kent County (portions), Leipsic, Little Creek, New Castle County (portions), Smyrna); Outside TV Markets (Camden, Cheswold, Dover AFB, Felton, Harrington, Hartly, Houston, Kent County (portions), Kenton, Magnolia, Marydel, Viola, Woodside, Wyoming). Franchise award date: January 1, 1962. Franchise expiration date: N.A. Began: January 1, 1963.

Channel capacity: N.A. Channels available but not in use: N.A.

Basic Service

Subscribers: 34,424.

Programming (received off-air): KYW-TV (CBS) Philadelphia; WBOC-TV (CBS, FOX) Salisbury; WCAU (NBC) Philadelphia; WHYY-TV (PBS) Wilmington; WMDT (ABC, CW) Salisbury; WPHL-TV (MNT) Philadelphia; WPPX-TV (ION) Wilmington; WPSG (CW) Philadelphia; WPVI-TV (ABC) Philadelphia; WTXF-TV (FOX) Philadelphia; WUVP-DT (UNV) Vineland; allband FM.

Programming (via satellite): Disney Channel; Eternal Word TV Network; QVC; TBS Superstation; Trinity Broadcasting Network; TV Guide Network.

Fee: $44.95 installation; $18.75 monthly; $3.33 converter.

Expanded Basic Service 1

Subscribers: N.A.

Programming (received off-air): WGTW-TV (IND) Burlington.

Programming (via satellite): ABC Family Channel; AMC; Animal Planet; Arts & Entertainment; BET Networks; Bravo; Cartoon Network; CNBC; CNN; Comcast SportsNet Philly; Comedy Central; Country Music TV; C-SPAN; C-SPAN 2; Discovery Channel; Discovery Health Channel; E! Entertainment Television; ESPN; ESPN 2; Food Network; Fox News Channel; FX; GAS; Golf Channel; Great American Country; Hallmark Channel; Headline News; HGTV; History Channel; Home Shopping Network; Lifetime; MSNBC; MTV; Nickelodeon; SoapNet; Speed Channel; Spike TV; Style Network; Syfy; The Learning Channel; truTV; Turner Classic Movies; Turner Network TV; TV Land; TV One; Univision; USA Network; Versus; VH1; Weather Channel.

Fee: $32.90 monthly.

Digital Basic Service

Subscribers: N.A.

Programming (via satellite): BBC America; Canales N; C-SPAN 3; Discovery Digital Networks; Disney Channel; DMX Music; Encore (multiplexed); ESPNews; G4; GAS; Mid-Atlantic Sports Network; National Geographic Channel; Nick Jr.; Nick Too; Science Television; Telemundo; Toon Disney; WAM! America's Kidz Network; Weatherscan.

Fee: $14.30 monthly.

Pay Service 1

Pay Units: N.A.

Programming (via satellite): Cinemax; HBO; Showtime; The Movie Channel.

Fee: $18.00 monthly.

Digital Pay Service 1

Pay Units: N.A.

Programming (via satellite): Cinemax (multiplexed); HBO (multiplexed); Showtime (multiplexed); Starz (multiplexed); The Movie Channel (multiplexed).

Fee: $11.00 monthly (each).

Video-On-Demand: Yes

Pay-Per-View

Fresh (delivered digitally); Pleasure (delivered digitally); Shorteez (delivered digitally); ESPN Now (delivered digitally); ESPN PPV (delivered digitally); NBA (delivered digitally); NHL/MLB (delivered digitally); Playboy TV (delivered digitally); iN DEMAND (delivered digitally).

Internet Service

Operational: Yes. Began: December 1, 2000.

Subscribers: 2,000.

Broadband Service: Comcast High Speed Internet.

Fee: $42.95 monthly; $449.00 modem purchase.

Telephone Service

Digital: Operational

Fee: $44.95 monthly

Miles of Plant: 252.0 (coaxial); None (fiber optic). Total homes in franchised area: 50,219. Miles of plant (coax) includes Rehoboth Beach, Cambridge MD, Cecilton MD, Elkton MD, Ocean City MD, & Salisbury MD

Vice President & General Manager: Henry Pearl. Area Engineering Manager: Cliff Jones. Marketing Director: David Tashjian. Marketing Coordinator: Kelly Kaiser. Business Operations Director: Cara Dever. Government & Public Affairs Director: Tom Worley.

City fee: 3% of gross.

Ownership: Comcast Cable Communications Inc. (MSO).

MIDDLETOWN—Atlantic Broadband, 600 N Broad St, Middletown, DE 19709-1032. Phones: 800-441-7068 (Customer service); 800-559-1746; 302-378-0780; 302-378-7050. Fax: 302-378-1478. E-mail: info@atlanticbb.com. Web Site: http://www.atlanticbb.com. Also serves Delaware City, New Castle County, Odessa, St. Georges & Townsend, DE; Cecil County (portions), Chesapeake City, Elkton (portions), Kent County (portions), Perry Point, Perryville & Port Deposit, MD. ICA: DE0005.

TV Market Ranking: 14 (Perry Point, Perryville, Port Deposit); Below 100 (Cecil County (portions), Chesapeake City, Delaware City, Elkton (portions), Kent County (portions), MIDDLETOWN TWP., New Castle County, Odessa, St. Georges, Townsend). Franchise award date: N.A. Franchise expiration date: N.A. Began: September 17, 1980.

Channel capacity: N.A. Channels available but not in use: N.A.

Basic Service

Subscribers: 7,500.

Programming (received off-air): KYW-TV (CBS) Philadelphia; WBAL-TV (NBC) Baltimore; WCAU (NBC) Philadelphia; WGTW-TV (IND) Burlington; WHYY-TV

(PBS) Wilmington; WJZ-TV (CBS) Baltimore; WMAR-TV (ABC) Baltimore; WNUV (CW) Baltimore; WPHL-TV (MNT) Philadelphia; WPPX-TV (ION) Wilmington; WPSG (CW) Philadelphia; WPVI-TV (ABC) Philadelphia; WTXF-TV (FOX) Philadelphia.
Programming (via satellite): C-SPAN; C-SPAN 2; Home Shopping Network; Mid-Atlantic Sports Network; QVC.
Current originations: Public Access.
Fee: $25.00 installation; $12.89 monthly.

Expanded Basic Service 1
Subscribers: 6,012.
Programming (via satellite): ABC Family Channel; AMC; Animal Planet; Arts & Entertainment; BET Networks; Bravo; Cartoon Network; CNBC; CNN; Comcast SportsNet Philly; Comedy Central; Country Music TV; Discovery Channel; Discovery Health Channel; Disney Channel; E! Entertainment Television; ESPN; ESPN 2; Food Network; Fox News Channel; FX; Headline News; HGTV; History Channel; Lifetime; Lifetime Movie Network; Mid-Atlantic Sports Network; MSNBC; MTV; National Geographic Channel; Nickelodeon; NickToons TV; Speed Channel; Spike TV; Syfy; TBS Superstation; The Learning Channel; Travel Channel; Turner Network TV; TV Land; USA Network; Versus; VH1; Weather Channel.
Fee: $39.52 monthly.

Digital Basic Service
Subscribers: 4,400.
Programming (received off-air): KYW-TV (CBS) Philadelphia; WBAL-TV (NBC) Baltimore; WCAU (NBC) Philadelphia; WHYY-TV (PBS) Wilmington; WJZ-TV (CBS) Baltimore; WMAR-TV (ABC) Baltimore; WPHL-TV (MNT) Philadelphia; WPPX-TV (ION) Wilmington; WPSG (CW) Philadelphia; WPVI-TV (ABC) Philadelphia; WTXF-TV (FOX) Philadelphia.
Programming (via satellite): Animal Planet HD; Arts & Entertainment HD; BBC America; Bio; Bloomberg Television; CCTV-4; Cooking Channel; Discovery Channel HD; Discovery HD Theater; Discovery Kids Channel; Discovery Military Channel; Discovery Planet Green; DMX Music; Do-It-Yourself; Encore (multiplexed); ESPN 2 HD; ESPN Classic Sports; ESPN HD; ESPNews; Eternal Word TV Network; Fuel TV; G4; Golf Channel; Great American Country; GSN; Hallmark Channel; History Channel International; ID Investigation Discovery; Independent Film Channel; Jewelry Television; Lifetime Real Women; LOGO; Mid-Atlantic Sports Network; MTV Hits; MTV Jams; MTV Tres; MTV2; NFL Network; Nick Jr.; Nick Too; Oxygen; Science Channel; SoapNet; Starz (multiplexed); Starz HDTV; TBS in HD; TeenNick; The Sportsman Channel; Toon Disney; Trinity Broadcasting Network; Turner Classic Movies; Turner Network TV HD; TVG Network; VH1 Classic; VH1 Country; VH1 Soul; WE tv; Weatherscan.
Fee: $18.95 monthly.

Digital Pay Service 1
Pay Units: 2,300.
Programming (via satellite): Cinemax (multiplexed); Cinemax HD; Flix; HBO (multiplexed); HBO HD; Showtime (multiplexed); The Movie Channel (multiplexed).
Fee: $16.95 monthly (HBO, Cinemax, or Showtime/TMC/Flix).

Video-On-Demand: Yes

Pay-Per-View
Hot Choice (delivered digitally), Fee: $8.99-$9.99; iN DEMAND (delivered digitally), Fee: $3.99.

Internet Service
Operational: Yes. Began: January 1, 2004.
Broadband Service: Atlantic Broadband High-Speed Internet.
Fee: $25.00 installation; $22.95-$56.95 monthly.

Telephone Service
Digital: Operational
Fee: $49.95 monthly

Miles of Plant: 453.0 (coaxial); None (fiber optic). Additional miles planned: 107.0 (coaxial). Homes passed: 19,000.
Vice President & General Manager: Joseph DiJulio. Plant Manager: Lenny Gilbert. Personnel Manager: Susan Gresh. Marketing Director: Sam McGill. Construction Manager: Rick Hudkins.
City fee: 3% of gross.
Ownership: Atlantic Broadband (MSO).

REHOBOTH BEACH—Comcast Cable, 5729 W Denneys Rd, Dover, DE 19904-1365. Phone: 302-674-2494. Fax: 302-674-2538. Web Site: http://www.comcast.com. Also serves Bethel, Blades, Bridgeville, Dewey Beach, Ellendale, Georgetown, Greenwood, Henlopen Acres, Kent County (unincorporated areas), Laurel, Lewes, Lincoln, Milford, Milton, Seaford, Slaughter Beach & Sussex County (portions). ICA: DE0003.
TV Market Ranking: Below 100 (Bethel, Blades, Bridgeville, Dewey Beach, Ellendale, Georgetown, Greenwood, Henlopen Acres, Kent County (unincorporated areas) (portions), Laurel, Lewes, Lincoln, Milford, Milton, REHOBOTH BEACH, Seaford, Slaughter Beach, Sussex County (portions)); Outside TV Markets (Kent County (unincorporated areas) (portions)). Franchise award date: N.A. Franchise expiration date: N.A. Began: February 14, 1966.
Channel capacity: N.A. Channels available but not in use: N.A.

Basic Service
Subscribers: 35,590.
Programming (received off-air): WBOC-TV (CBS, FOX) Salisbury; WDPB (PBS) Seaford; WMDT (ABC, CW) Salisbury; WMPT (PBS) Annapolis; 9 FMs.
Programming (via microwave): WBAL-TV (NBC) Baltimore; WCAU (NBC) Philadelphia; WJZ-TV (CBS) Baltimore; WTTG (FOX) Washington; WTXF-TV (FOX) Philadelphia.
Programming (via satellite): Eternal Word TV Network; Golf Channel; ION Television; TBS Superstation; The Comcast Network.
Current originations: Public Access.
Fee: $44.95 installation; $19.45 monthly.

Expanded Basic Service 1
Subscribers: 13,301.
Programming (via satellite): ABC Family Channel; AMC; America's Store; Animal Planet; Arts & Entertainment; BET Networks; Cartoon Network; CNBC; CNN; Comcast SportsNet Mid-Atlantic; Comedy Central; Country Music TV; C-SPAN; C-SPAN 2; Discovery Channel; Discovery Health Channel; Disney Channel; E! Entertainment Television; ESPN; ESPN 2; Food Network; Fox News Channel; FX; Great American Country; GSN; Hallmark Channel; Headline News; HGTV; History Channel; Home Shopping Network 2; Lifetime; MSNBC; MTV; Nickelodeon; QVC; ShopNBC; SoapNet; Speed Channel; Spike TV; Style Network; Syfy; The Learning Channel; Trinity Broadcasting Network; truTV; Turner Classic Movies; Turner Network TV; TV Guide Network; TV Land; TV One; Univision; USA Network; Versus; VH1; Weather Channel.
Fee: $54.95 monthly.

Digital Basic Service
Subscribers: N.A.
Programming (via satellite): BBC America; Canales N; C-SPAN 3; Discovery Digital Networks; Disney Channel; DMX Music; Encore (multiplexed); ESPNews; G4; GAS; Mid-Atlantic Sports Network; MTV Networks Digital Suite; National Geographic Channel; Nick Jr.; Nick Too; SoapNet; Toon Disney; WAM! America's Kidz Network; Weatherscan.
Fee: $10.95 monthly.

Pay Service 1
Pay Units: 10,063.
Programming (via satellite): Cinemax; HBO (multiplexed); Showtime; The Movie Channel.
Fee: $18.00 monthly (each).

Digital Pay Service 1
Pay Units: N.A.
Programming (via satellite): Cinemax (multiplexed); HBO (multiplexed); Showtime (multiplexed); Starz (multiplexed); The Movie Channel (multiplexed).
Fee: $11.00 monthly (each).

Video-On-Demand: Yes

Pay-Per-View
iN DEMAND (delivered digitally); Pleasure (delivered digitally); Playboy TV (delivered digitally); Fresh (delivered digitally); Shorteez (delivered digitally).

Internet Service
Operational: Yes.
Broadband Service: Comcast High Speed Internet.
Fee: $42.95 monthly.

Telephone Service
Digital: Operational
Fee: $44.95 monthly

Miles of Plant: 531.0 (coaxial); None (fiber optic). Total homes in franchised area: 51,920. Miles of plant (coax) included in Dover
Vice President & General Manager: Henry Pearl. Area Engineering Manager: Cliff Jones. Marketing Director: David Tashjian. Government & Public Affairs Director: Tom Worley. Business Operations Director: Cara Dever.
Ownership: Comcast Cable Communications Inc. (MSO).

WILMINGTON—Comcast Cable, 3220 Tillman Dr, Bensalem, PA 19010. Phone: 215-642-6400. Fax: 215-638-6510. Web Site: http://www.comcast.com. Also serves Arden, Ardencroft, Ardentown, Bellefonte, Elsmere, New Castle, New Castle County, Newark & Newport. ICA: DE0006.
TV Market Ranking: 4 (Arden, Ardencroft, Ardentown, Bellefonte, Elsmere, New Castle, New Castle County (portions), Newport, WILMINGTON); Below 100 (Newark, New Castle County (portions)). Franchise award date: December 1, 1969. Franchise expiration date: N.A. Began: December 1, 1969.
Channel capacity: N.A. Channels available but not in use: N.A.

Basic Service
Subscribers: N.A. Included in Bensalem Twp., PA
Programming (received off-air): KYW-TV (CBS) Philadelphia; WCAU (NBC) Philadelphia; WFMZ-TV (IND) Allentown; WGTW-TV (IND) Burlington; WHYY-TV (PBS) Wilmington; WMCN-TV (IND) Atlantic City; WNJS (PBS) Camden; WPHL-TV (MNT) Philadelphia; WPPX-TV (ION) Wilmington; WPSG (CW) Philadelphia; WPVI-TV (ABC) Philadelphia; WTVE (IND) Reading; WTXF-TV (FOX) Philadelphia; WUVP-DT (UNV) Vineland; WWSI (TMO) Atlantic City; WYBE (ETV) Philadelphia; allband FM.
Programming (via satellite): Headline News; TBS Superstation; The Comcast Network.
Current originations: Leased Access; Government Access.
Fee: $9.95 monthly.

Expanded Basic Service 1
Subscribers: 136,714.
Programming (via satellite): ABC Family Channel; AMC; Animal Planet; Arts & Entertainment; BET Networks; Bravo; Cartoon Network; CNBC; CNN; Comcast SportsNet Mid-Atlantic; Comedy Central; Country Music TV; C-SPAN; C-SPAN 2; Discovery Channel; Discovery Health Channel; Disney Channel; E! Entertainment Television; ESPN; ESPN 2; Eternal Word TV Network; Food Network; Fox News Channel; FX; Golf Channel; GSN; HGTV; History Channel; Home Shopping Network; INSP; Lifetime; MSNBC; MTV; MTV2; Nickelodeon; QVC; Speed Channel; Spike TV; Syfy; The Learning Channel; truTV; Turner Classic Movies; Turner Network TV; TV Guide Network; TV Land; USA Network; Versus; VH1; Weather Channel.
Fee: $42.25 monthly.

Digital Basic Service
Subscribers: N.A.
Programming (via satellite): BBC America; Bio; Cooking Channel; C-SPAN 3; Discovery Digital Networks; DMX Music; Do-It-Yourself; ESPNews; G4; GAS; History Channel International; Independent Film Channel; Mid-Atlantic Sports Network; MTV Networks Digital Suite; National Geographic Channel; Nick Jr.; Nick Too; Science Television; ShopNBC; SoapNet; Toon Disney; WAM! America's Kidz Network; Weatherscan.
Fee: $24.90 monthly.

Digital Pay Service 1
Pay Units: N.A.
Programming (via satellite): Cinemax (multiplexed); Encore (multiplexed); Flix (multiplexed); HBO (multiplexed); Showtime (multiplexed); Sundance Channel (multiplexed); The Movie Channel (multiplexed).

Video-On-Demand: Yes

Pay-Per-View
Addressable homes: 64,544.
Playboy TV (delivered digitally), Fee: $5.95, Addressable: Yes; Spice (delivered digitally), Fee: $5.95; iN DEMAND (delivered digitally); Pleasure (delivered digitally); ESPN Now (delivered digitally); NBA (delivered digitally); NHL/MLB (delivered digitally).

Internet Service
Operational: Yes. Began: August 9, 1999.
Broadband Service: Comcast High Speed Internet.
Fee: $59.95 installation; $42.95 monthly; $7.00 modem lease; $199.00 modem purchase.

Telephone Service
Digital: Operational
Fee: $44.95 monthly

Miles of Plant: 2,318.0 (coaxial); 200.0 (fiber optic). Additional miles planned: 30.0 (coaxial); 70.0 (fiber optic). Homes passed: 194,101. Total homes in franchised area: 208,977.
Senior Regional Vice President: Amy Smith. Vice President, Technical Operations: Rich Massi. Vice President, Marketing: Chip Goodman.
City fee: 5% of gross.
Ownership: Comcast Cable Communications Inc. (MSO).

DISTRICT OF COLUMBIA

Total Systems: 20
Total Communities Served: 22
Franchises Not Yet Operating: 0
Applications Pending: 0
Communities with Applications: 0
Number of Basic Subscribers: 176,000
Number of Expanded Basic Subscribers: 0
Number of Pay Units: 0

Top 100 Markets Represented: Washington, DC (9).

For a list of cable communities in this section, see the Cable Community Index located in the back of Cable Volume 2. For explanation of terms used in cable system listings, see p. D-11.

ADAMS MORGAN—RCN Corp. Formerly [DC0006]. This cable system has converted to IPTV, 196 Van Buren St, Herndon, VA 20170. Phone: 703-434-8200. Web Site: http://www.rcn.com. ICA: DC5001.
TV Market Ranking: 9 (ADAMS MORGAN). Franchise award date: N.A. Franchise expiration date: N.A. Began: N.A.
Channel capacity: N.A. Channels available but not in use: N.A.
Digital Basic Service
Subscribers: N.A.
Fee: $65.50 monthly; 3.95-$17.95 converter.
Digital Expanded Basic Service
Subscribers: N.A.
Fee: $82.45 monthly.
A la Carte 1
Subscribers: N.A.
Fee: $2.95 -$24.95 monthly (International); $8.99 monthly (HD); $14.95 monthly (Sentana Sports); $19.95 monthly (International Soccer); $49 per season (MLS Direct Kick); $79 per season (NHL Center Ice); $139 per season (MLB Extra Innings).
Pay Service 1
Pay Units: N.A.
Fee: $8.95 monthly (Cinemax); $11.95 monthly (Starz); $16.95 monthly (Showtime & TMC); $19.95 (HBO).
Video-On-Demand: Yes
Internet Service
Operational: Yes.
Broadband Service: RCN.
Fee: $53.00 monthly.
Telephone Service
Digital: Operational
Fee: $50.00 monthly
Chairman: Steven J. Simmons. Chief Executive Officer: Jim Holanda.
Ownership: RCN Corp. (MSO).

ANACOSTIA—RCN Corp. Formerly [DC0006]. This cable system has converted to IPTV, 196 Van Buren St, Herndon, VA 20170. Phone: 703-434-8200. Web Site: http://www.rcn.com. ICA: DC5002.
TV Market Ranking: 9 (ANACOSTIA).
Channel capacity: N.A. Channels available but not in use: N.A.
Digital Basic Service
Subscribers: N.A.
Fee: $65.50 monthly; 3.95-$17.95 converter.
Digital Expanded Basic Service
Subscribers: N.A.
Fee: $82.45 monthly.
A la Carte 1
Subscribers: N.A.
Fee: $2.95 -$24.95 monthly (International); $8.99 monthly (HD); $14.95 monthly (Sentana Sports); $19.95 monthly (International Soccer); $49 per season (MLS Direct Kick); $79 per season (NHL Center Ice); $139 per season (MLB Extra Innings).
Pay Service 1
Pay Units: N.A.
Fee: $8.95 monthly (Cinemax); $11.95 monthly (Starz); $16.95 monthly (Showtime & TMC); $19.95 (HBO).
Internet Service
Operational: Yes.
Fee: $53.00 monthly.
Telephone Service
Digital: Operational
Fee: $50.00 monthly
Chairman: Steven J. Simmons. Chief Executive Officer: Jim Holanda.
Ownership: RCN Corp.

BENNING ROAD—RCN Corp. Formerly [DC0006]. This cable system has converted to IPTV, 196 Van Buren St, Herndon, VA 20170. Phone: 703-434-8200. Web Site: http://www.rcn.com. ICA: DC5003.
TV Market Ranking: 9 (BENNING ROAD).
Channel capacity: N.A. Channels available but not in use: N.A.
Digital Basic Service
Subscribers: N.A.
Fee: $65.50 monthly; 3.95-$17.95 converter.
Digital Expanded Basic Service
Subscribers: N.A.
Fee: $82.45 monthly.
A la Carte 1
Subscribers: N.A.
Fee: $2.95 -$24.95 monthly (International); $8.99 monthly (HD); $14.95 monthly (Sentana Sports); $19.95 monthly (International Soccer); $49 per season (MLS Direct Kick); $79 per season (NHL Center Ice); $139 per season (MLB Extra Innings).
Pay Service 1
Pay Units: N.A.
Fee: $8.95 monthly (Cinemax); $11.95 monthly (Starz); $16.95 monthly (Showtime & TMC); $19.95 (HBO).
Internet Service
Operational: Yes.
Fee: $53.00 monthly.
Telephone Service
Digital: Operational
Fee: $50.00 monthly
Chairman: Steven J. Simmons. Chief Executive Officer: Jim Holanda.
Ownership: RCN Corp.

BOLLING AFB—Mid-Atlantic Communications. Now served by WASHINGTON, DC [DC0001]. ICA: DC0002.

BROOKLAND—RCN Corp. Formerly [DC0006]. This cable system has converted to IPTV, 196 Van Buren St, Herndon, VA 20170. Phone: 703-434-8200. Web Site: http://www.rcn.com. ICA: DC5004.
TV Market Ranking: 9 (BROOKLAND).
Channel capacity: N.A. Channels available but not in use: N.A.
Digital Basic Service
Subscribers: N.A.
Fee: $65.50 monthly; 3.95-$17.95 converter.
Digital Expanded Basic Service
Subscribers: N.A.
Fee: $82.45 monthly.
A la Carte 1
Subscribers: N.A.
Fee: $2.95 -$24.95 monthly (International); $8.99 monthly (HD); $14.95 monthly (Sentana Sports); $19.95 monthly (International Soccer); $49 per season (MLS Direct Kick); $79 per season (NHL Center Ice); $139 per season (MLB Extra Innings).
Pay Service 1
Pay Units: N.A.
Fee: $8.95 monthly (Cinemax); $11.95 monthly (Starz); $16.95 monthly (Showtime & TMC); $19.95 (HBO).
Internet Service
Operational: Yes.
Fee: $53.00 monthly.
Telephone Service
Digital: Operational
Fee: $50.00 monthly
Chairman: Steven J. Simmons. Chief Executive Officer: Jim Holanda.
Ownership: RCN Corp.

CAPITOL HILL—RCN Corp. Formerly [DC0006]. This cable system has converted to IPTV, 196 Van Buren St, Herndon, VA 20170. Phone: 703-434-8200. Web Site: http://www.rcn.com. ICA: DC5005.
TV Market Ranking: 9 (CAPITOL HILL).
Channel capacity: N.A. Channels available but not in use: N.A.
Digital Basic Service
Subscribers: N.A.
Fee: $65.50 monthly; 3.95-$17.95 converter.
Digital Expanded Basic Service
Subscribers: N.A.
Fee: $82.45 monthly.
A la Carte 1
Subscribers: N.A.
Fee: $2.95 -$24.95 monthly (International); $8.99 monthly (HD); $14.95 monthly (Sentana Sports); $19.95 monthly (International Soccer); $49 per season (MLS Direct Kick); $79 per season (NHL Center Ice); $139 per season (MLB Extra Innings).
Pay Service 1
Pay Units: N.A.
Fee: $8.95 monthly (Cinemax); $11.95 monthly (Starz); $16.95 monthly (Showtime & TMC); $19.95 (HBO).
Internet Service
Operational: Yes.
Fee: $53.00 monthly.
Telephone Service
Digital: Operational
Fee: $50.00 monthly
Chairman: Steven J. Simmons. Chief Executive Officer: Jim Holanda.
Ownership: RCN Corp.

CHINATOWN—RCN Corp. Formerly [DC0006]. This cable system has converted to IPTV, 196 Van Buren St, Herndon, VA 20170. Phone: 703-434-8200. Web Site: http://www.rcn.com. ICA: DC5006.
TV Market Ranking: 9 (CHINATOWN).
Channel capacity: N.A. Channels available but not in use: N.A.
Digital Basic Service
Subscribers: N.A.
Fee: $65.50 monthly; 3.95-$17.95 converter.
Digital Expanded Basic Service
Subscribers: N.A.
Fee: $82.45 monthly.
A la Carte 1
Subscribers: N.A.
Fee: $2.95 -$24.95 monthly (International); $8.99 monthly (HD); $14.95 monthly (Sentana Sports); $19.95 monthly (International Soccer); $49 per season (MLS Direct Kick); $79 per season (NHL Center Ice); $139 per season (MLB Extra Innings).
Pay Service 1
Pay Units: N.A.
Fee: $8.95 monthly (Cinemax); $11.95 monthly (Starz); $16.95 monthly (Showtime & TMC); $19.95 (HBO).
Internet Service
Operational: Yes.
Fee: $53.00 monthly.
Telephone Service
Digital: Operational
Fee: $50.00 monthly
Chairman: Steven J. Simmons. Chief Executive Officer: Jim Holanda.
Ownership: RCN Corp.

CLEVELAND PARK—RCN Corp. Formerly [DC0006]. This cable system has converted to IPTV, 196 Van Buren St, Herndon, VA 20170. Phone: 703-434-8200. Web Site: http://www.rcn.com. ICA: DC5007.
TV Market Ranking: 9 (CLEVELAND PARK).
Channel capacity: N.A. Channels available but not in use: N.A.
Digital Basic Service
Subscribers: N.A.
Fee: $65.50 monthly; 3.95-$17.95 converter.
Digital Expanded Basic Service
Subscribers: N.A.
Fee: $82.45 monthly.
A la Carte 1
Subscribers: N.A.
Fee: $2.95 -$24.95 monthly (International); $8.99 monthly (HD); $14.95 monthly (Sentana Sports); $19.95 monthly (Inter-

national Soccer); $49 per season (MLS Direct Kick); $79 per season (NHL Center Ice); $139 per season (MLB Extra Innings).

Pay Service 1
Pay Units: N.A.
Fee: $8.95 monthly (Cinemax); $11.95 monthly (Starz); $16.95 monthly (Showtime & TMC); $19.95 (HBO).

Internet Service
Operational: Yes.
Fee: $53.00 monthly.

Telephone Service
Digital: Operational
Fee: $50.00 monthly

Chairman: Steven J. Simmons. Chief Executive Officer: Jim Holanda.
Ownership: RCN Corp.

COLUMBIA HEIGHTS—RCN Corp. Formerly [DC0006]. This cable system has converted to IPTV, 196 Van Buren St, Herndon, VA 20170. Phone: 703-434-8200. Web Site: http://www.rcn.com. ICA: DC5008.
TV Market Ranking: 9 (COLUMBIA HEIGHTS).
Channel capacity: N.A. Channels available but not in use: N.A.

Digital Basic Service
Subscribers: N.A.
Fee: $65.50 monthly; 3.95-$17.95 converter.

Digital Expanded Basic Service
Subscribers: N.A.
Fee: $82.45 monthly.

A la Carte 1
Subscribers: N.A.
Fee: $2.95 -$24.95 monthly (International); $8.99 monthly (HD); $14.95 monthly (Sentana Sports); $19.95 monthly (International Soccer); $49 per season (MLS Direct Kick); $79 per season (NHL Center Ice); $139 per season (MLB Extra Innings).

Pay Service 1
Pay Units: N.A.
Fee: $8.95 monthly (Cinemax); $11.95 monthly (Starz); $16.95 monthly (Showtime & TMC); $19.95 (HBO).

Internet Service
Operational: Yes.
Fee: $53.00 monthly.

Telephone Service
Digital: Operational
Fee: $50.00 monthly

Chairman: Steven J. Simmons. Chief Executive Officer: Jim Holanda.
Ownership: RCN Corp.

CONGRESS HEIGHTS—RCN Corp. Formerly [DC0006]. This cable system has converted to IPTV, 196 Van Buren St, Herndon, VA 20170. Phone: 703-434-8200. Web Site: http://www.rcn.com. ICA: DC5009.
TV Market Ranking: 9 (CONGRESS HEIGHTS).
Channel capacity: N.A. Channels available but not in use: N.A.

Digital Basic Service
Subscribers: N.A.
Fee: $65.50 monthly; 3.95-$17.95 converter.

Digital Expanded Basic Service
Subscribers: N.A.
Fee: $82.45 monthly.

A la Carte 1
Subscribers: N.A.
Fee: $2.95 -$24.95 monthly (International); $8.99 monthly (HD); $14.95 monthly (Sentana Sports); $19.95 monthly (International Soccer); $49 per season (MLS Direct Kick); $79 per season (NHL Center Ice); $139 per season (MLB Extra Innings).

Pay Service 1
Pay Units: N.A.
Fee: $8.95 monthly (Cinemax); $11.95 monthly (Starz); $16.95 monthly (Showtime & TMC); $19.95 (HBO).

Internet Service
Operational: Yes.
Fee: $53.00 monthly.

Telephone Service
Digital: Operational
Fee: $50.00 monthly

Chairman: Steven J. Simmons. Chief Executive Officer: Jim Holanda.
Ownership: RCN Corp.

DUPONT CIRCLE—RCN Corp. Formerly [DC0006]. This cable system has converted to IPTV, 196 Van Buren St, Herndon, VA 20170. Phone: 703-434-8200. Web Site: http://www.rcn.com. ICA: DC5010.
TV Market Ranking: 9 (DUPONT CIRCLE).
Channel capacity: N.A. Channels available but not in use: N.A.

Digital Basic Service
Subscribers: N.A.
Fee: $65.50 monthly; 3.95-$17.95 converter.

Digital Expanded Basic Service
Subscribers: N.A.
Fee: $82.45 monthly.

A la Carte 1
Subscribers: N.A.
Fee: $2.95 -$24.95 monthly (International); $8.99 monthly (HD); $14.95 monthly (Sentana Sports); $19.95 monthly (International Soccer); $49 per season (MLS Direct Kick); $79 per season (NHL Center Ice); $139 per season (MLB Extra Innings).

Pay Service 1
Pay Units: N.A.
Fee: $8.95 monthly (Cinemax); $11.95 monthly (Starz); $16.95 monthly (Showtime & TMC); $19.95 (HBO).

Internet Service
Operational: Yes.
Fee: $53.00 monthly.

Telephone Service
Digital: Operational
Fee: $50.00 monthly

Chairman: Steven J. Simmons. Chief Executive Officer: Jim Holanda.
Ownership: RCN Corp.

FORT TOTTEN—RCN Corp. Formerly [DC0006]. This cable system has converted to IPTV, 196 Van Buren St, Herndon, VA 20170. Phone: 703-434-8200. Web Site: http://www.rcn.com. ICA: DC5011.
TV Market Ranking: 9 (FORT TOTTEN).
Channel capacity: N.A. Channels available but not in use: N.A.

Digital Basic Service
Subscribers: N.A.
Fee: $65.50 monthly; 3.95-$17.95 converter.

Digital Expanded Basic Service
Subscribers: N.A.
Fee: $82.45 monthly.

A la Carte 1
Subscribers: N.A.
Fee: $2.95 -$24.95 monthly (International); $8.99 monthly (HD); $14.95 monthly (Sentana Sports); $19.95 monthly (International Soccer); $49 per season (MLS Direct Kick); $79 per season (NHL Center Ice); $139 per season (MLB Extra Innings).

Pay Service 1
Pay Units: N.A.
Fee: $8.95 monthly (Cinemax); $11.95 monthly (Starz); $16.95 monthly (Showtime & TMC); $19.95 (HBO).

Pay Service 1
Pay Units: N.A.
Fee: $8.95 monthly (Cinemax); $11.95 monthly (Starz); $16.95 monthly (Showtime & TMC); $19.95 (HBO).

Internet Service
Operational: Yes.
Fee: $53.00 monthly.

Telephone Service
Digital: Operational
Fee: $50.00 monthly

Chairman: Steven J. Simmons. Chief Executive Officer: Jim Holanda.
Ownership: RCN Corp.

Internet Service
Operational: Yes.
Fee: $53.00 monthly.

Telephone Service
Digital: Operational
Fee: $50.00 monthly

Chairman: Steven J. Simmons. Chief Executive Officer: Jim Holanda.
Ownership: RCN Corp.

FRIENDSHIP HEIGHTS—RCN Corp. Formerly [DC0006]. This cable system has converted to IPTV, 196 Van Buren St, Herndon, VA 20170. Phone: 703-434-8200. Web Site: http://www.rcn.com. ICA: DC5012.
TV Market Ranking: 9 (FRIENDSHIP HEIGHTS).
Channel capacity: N.A. Channels available but not in use: N.A.

Digital Basic Service
Subscribers: N.A.
Fee: $65.50 monthly; 3.95-$17.95 converter.

Digital Expanded Basic Service
Subscribers: N.A.
Fee: $82.45 monthly.

A la Carte 1
Subscribers: N.A.
Fee: $2.95 -$24.95 monthly (International); $8.99 monthly (HD); $14.95 monthly (Sentana Sports); $19.95 monthly (International Soccer); $49 per season (MLS Direct Kick); $79 per season (NHL Center Ice); $139 per season (MLB Extra Innings).

Pay Service 1
Pay Units: N.A.
Fee: $8.95 monthly (Cinemax); $11.95 monthly (Starz); $16.95 monthly (Showtime & TMC); $19.95 (HBO).

Internet Service
Operational: Yes.
Fee: $53.00 monthly.

Telephone Service
Digital: Operational
Fee: $50.00 monthly

Chairman: Steven J. Simmons. Chief Executive Officer: Jim Holanda.
Ownership: RCN Corp.

GLOVER PARK—RCN Corp. Formerly [DC0006]. This cable system has converted to IPTV, 196 Van Buren St, Herndon, VA 20170. Phone: 703-434-8200. Web Site: http://www.rcn.com. ICA: DC5013.
TV Market Ranking: 9 (GLOVER PARK).
Channel capacity: N.A. Channels available but not in use: N.A.

Digital Basic Service
Subscribers: N.A.
Fee: $65.503 monthly; 3.95-$17.95 converter.

Digital Expanded Basic Service
Subscribers: N.A.
Fee: $82.45 monthly.

A la Carte 1
Subscribers: N.A.
Fee: $2.95 -$24.95 monthly (International); $8.99 monthly (HD); $14.95 monthly (Sentana Sports); $19.95 monthly (International Soccer); $49 per season (MLS Direct Kick); $79 per season (NHL Center Ice); $139 per season (MLB Extra Innings).

Pay Service 1
Pay Units: N.A.
Fee: $8.95 monthly (Cinemax); $11.95 monthly (Starz); $16.95 monthly (Showtime & TMC); $19.95 (HBO).

Internet Service
Operational: Yes.
Fee: $53.00 monthly.

Telephone Service
Digital: Operational
Fee: $50.00 monthly

Chairman: Steven J. Simmons. Chief Executive Officer: Jim Holanda.
Ownership: RCN Corp.

MOUNT PLEASANT—RCN Corp. Formerly [DC0006]. This cable system has converted to IPTV, 196 Van Buren St, Herndon, VA 20170. Phone: 703-434-8200. Web Site: http://www.rcn.com. ICA: DC5014.
TV Market Ranking: 9 (MOUNT PLEASANT).
Channel capacity: N.A. Channels available but not in use: N.A.

Digital Basic Service
Subscribers: N.A.
Fee: $65.50 monthly; 3.95-$17.95 converter.

Digital Expanded Basic Service
Subscribers: N.A.
Fee: $82.45 monthly.

A la Carte 1
Subscribers: N.A.
Fee: $2.95 -$24.95 monthly (International); $8.99 monthly (HD); $14.95 monthly (Sentana Sports); $19.95 monthly (International Soccer); $49 per season (MLS Direct Kick); $79 per season (NHL Center Ice); $139 per season (MLB Extra Innings).

Pay Service 1
Pay Units: N.A.
Fee: $8.95 monthly (Cinemax); $11.95 monthly (Starz); $16.95 monthly (Showtime & TMC); $19.95 (HBO).

Internet Service
Operational: Yes.
Fee: $53.00 monthly.

Telephone Service
Digital: Operational
Fee: $50.00 monthly

Chairman: Steven J. Simmons. Chief Executive Officer: Jim Holanda.
Ownership: RCN Corp.

MOUNT VERNON SQUARE—RCN Corp. Formerly [DC0006]. This cable system has converted to IPTV, 196 Van Buren St, Herndon, VA 20170. Phone: 703-434-8200. Web Site: http://www.rcn.com. ICA: DC5015.
TV Market Ranking: 9 (MOUNT VERNON SQUARE).
Channel capacity: N.A. Channels available but not in use: N.A.

Digital Basic Service
Subscribers: N.A.
Fee: $65.50 monthly; 3.95-$17.95 converter.

Digital Expanded Basic Service
Subscribers: N.A.
Fee: $82.45 monthly.

A la Carte 1
Subscribers: N.A.
Fee: $2.95 -$24.95 monthly (International); $8.99 monthly (HD); $14.95 monthly (Sentana Sports); $19.95 monthly (International Soccer); $49 per season (MLS Direct Kick); $79 per season (NHL Center Ice); $139 per season (MLB Extra Innings).

Pay Service 1
Pay Units: N.A.
Fee: $8.95 monthly (Cinemax); $11.95 monthly (Starz); $16.95 monthly (Showtime & TMC); $19.95 (HBO).

Internet Service
Operational: Yes.
Fee: $53.00 monthly.

Telephone Service
Digital: Operational
Fee: $50.00 monthly

Chairman: Steven J. Simmons. Chief Executive Officer: Jim Holanda.
Ownership: RCN Corp.

PETWORTH—RCN Corp. Formerly [DC0006]. This cable system has converted to IPTV, 196 Van Buren St, Herndon, VA 20170. Phone: 703-434-8200. Web Site: http://www.rcn.com. ICA: DC5016.
TV Market Ranking: 9 (PETWORTH).
Channel capacity: N.A. Channels available but not in use: N.A.
Digital Basic Service
Subscribers: N.A.
Fee: $65.50 monthly; 3.95-$17.95 converter.
Digital Expanded Basic Service
Subscribers: N.A.
Fee: $82.45 monthly.
A la Carte 1
Subscribers: N.A.
Fee: $2.95 -$24.95 monthly (International); $8.99 monthly (HD); $14.95 monthly (Sentana Sports); $19.95 monthly (International Soccer); $49 per season (MLS Direct Kick); $79 per season (NHL Center Ice); $139 per season (MLB Extra Innings).
Pay Service 1
Pay Units: N.A.
Fee: $8.95 monthly (Cinemax); $11.95 monthly (Starz); $16.95 monthly (Showtime & TMC); $19.95 (HBO).
Internet Service
Operational: Yes.
Fee: $53.00 monthly.
Telephone Service
Digital: Operational
Fee: $50.00 monthly
Chairman: Steven J. Simmons. Chief Executive Officer: Jim Holanda.
Ownership: RCN Corp.

SHAW—RCN Corp. Formerly [DC0006]. This cable system has converted to IPTV, 196 Van Buren St, Herndon, VA 20170. Phone: 703-434-8200. Web Site: http://www.rcn.com. ICA: DC5017.
TV Market Ranking: 9 (SHAW).
Channel capacity: N.A. Channels available but not in use: N.A.
Digital Basic Service
Subscribers: N.A.
Fee: $65.50 monthly; 3.95-$17.95 converter.
Digital Expanded Basic Service
Subscribers: N.A.
Fee: $82.45 monthly.
A la Carte 1
Subscribers: N.A.
Fee: $2.95 -$24.95 monthly (International); $8.99 monthly (HD); $14.95 monthly (Sentana Sports); $19.95 monthly (International Soccer); $49 per season (MLS Direct Kick); $79 per season (NHL Center Ice); $139 per season (MLB Extra Innings).
Pay Service 1
Pay Units: N.A.
Fee: $8.95 monthly (Cinemax); $11.95 monthly (Starz); $16.95 monthly (Showtime & TMC); $19.95 (HBO).
Internet Service
Operational: Yes.
Fee: $53.00 monthly.
Telephone Service
Digital: Operational
Fee: $50.00 monthly
Chairman: Steven J. Simmons. Chief Executive Officer: Jim Holanda.
Ownership: RCN Corp.

TENLEYTOWN—RCN Corp. Formerly [DC0006]. This cable system has converted to IPTV, 196 Van Buren St, Herndon, VA 20170. Phone: 703-434-8200. Web Site: http://www.rcn.com. ICA: DC5018.
TV Market Ranking: 9 (TENLEYTOWN).
Channel capacity: N.A. Channels available but not in use: N.A.
Digital Basic Service
Subscribers: N.A.
Fee: $65.50 monthly; 3.95-$17.95 converter.
Digital Expanded Basic Service
Subscribers: N.A.
Fee: $82.45 monthly.
A la Carte 1
Subscribers: N.A.
Fee: $2.95 -$24.95 monthly (International); $8.99 monthly (HD); $14.95 monthly (Sentana Sports); $19.95 monthly (International Soccer); $49 per season (MLS Direct Kick); $79 per season (NHL Center Ice); $139 per season (MLB Extra Innings).
Pay Service 1
Pay Units: N.A.
Fee: $8.95 monthly (Cinemax); $11.95 monthly (Starz); $16.95 monthly (Showtime & TMC); $19.95 (HBO).
Internet Service
Operational: Yes.
Fee: $53.00 monthly.
Telephone Service
Digital: Operational
Fee: $50.00 monthly
Chairman: Steven J. Simmons. Chief Executive Officer: Jim Holanda.
Ownership: RCN Corp.

U.S. SOLDIERS' & AIRMEN'S HOME—Chesapeake Cable Partners. Now served by WASHINGTON, DC [DC0001]. ICA: DC0003.

VAN NESS—RCN Corp. Formerly [DC0006]. This cable system has converted to IPTV, 196 Van Buren St, Herndon, VA 20170. Phone: 703-434-8200. Web Site: http://www.rcn.com. ICA: DC5019.
TV Market Ranking: 9 (VAN NESS).
Channel capacity: N.A. Channels available but not in use: N.A.
Digital Basic Service
Subscribers: N.A.
Fee: $65.50 monthly; 3.95-$17.95 converter.
Digital Expanded Basic Service
Subscribers: N.A.
Fee: $82.45 monthly.
A la Carte 1
Subscribers: N.A.
Fee: $2.95 -$24.95 monthly (International); $8.99 monthly (HD); $14.95 monthly (Sentana Sports); $19.95 monthly (International Soccer); $49 per season (MLS Direct Kick); $79 per season (NHL Center Ice); $139 per season (MLB Extra Innings).
Pay Service 1
Pay Units: N.A.
Fee: $8.95 monthly (Cinemax); $11.95 monthly (Starz); $16.95 monthly (Showtime & TMC); $19.95 (HBO).
Internet Service
Operational: Yes.
Fee: $53.00 monthly.
Telephone Service
Digital: Operational
Fee: $50.00 monthly
Chairman: Steven J. Simmons. Chief Executive Officer: Jim Holanda.
Ownership: RCN Corp.

WASHINGTON—Comcast Cable, 900 Michigan Ave NE, Washington, DC 20017-1833. Phone: 202-832-2001. Fax: 202-635-5120. Web Site: http://www.comcast.com. Also serves Bolling AFB & U.S. Soldiers' & Airmen's Home. ICA: DC0001.
TV Market Ranking: 9 (Bolling AFB, U.S. Soldiers' & Airmen's Home, WASHINGTON). Franchise award date: March 14, 1985. Franchise expiration date: N.A. Began: September 1, 1968.
Channel capacity: N.A. Channels available but not in use: N.A.
Basic Service
Subscribers: 110,000.
Programming (received off-air): WDCA (MNT) Washington; WDCW (CW) Washington; WETA-TV (PBS) Washington; WFDC-DT (UNV) Arlington; WHUT-TV (PBS) Washington; WJLA-TV (ABC) Washington; WMPT (PBS) Annapolis; WPXW-TV (ION) Manassas; WRC-TV (NBC) Washington; WTTG (FOX) Washington; WUSA (CBS) Washington; WZDC-CA (TMO) Washington.
Programming (via microwave): NewsChannel 8.
Programming (via satellite): ABC Family Channel; AMC; Animal Planet; Arts & Entertainment; BET Networks; Cartoon Network; CNBC; CNN; Comcast SportsNet Mid-Atlantic; Comedy Central; Country Music TV; C-SPAN; C-SPAN 2; Discovery Channel; Discovery Health Channel; Disney Channel; E! Entertainment Television; ESPN; ESPN 2; Food Network; Fox News Channel; FX; G4; Golf Channel; GSN; Hallmark Channel; Headline News; HGTV; History Channel; Home Shopping Network; Lifetime; MHz Networks; MSNBC; MTV; Nickelodeon; Oxygen; QVC; Spike TV; Style Network; Syfy; TBS Superstation; Telefutura; The Learning Channel; Travel Channel; truTV; Turner Classic Movies; Turner Network TV; TV Guide Network; TV Land; TV One; USA Network; Versus; VH1; Weather Channel; WGN America.
Current originations: Leased Access; Educational Access; Public Access.
Fee: $41.95 installation; $13.45 monthly; $12.95 additional installation.
Digital Basic Service
Subscribers: 66,000.
Programming (received off-air): WDCW (CW) Washington; WETA-TV (PBS) Washington; WJLA-TV (ABC) Washington; WRC-TV (NBC) Washington; WTTG (FOX) Washington; WUSA (CBS) Washington.
Programming (via satellite): BBC America; Bio; Black Family Channel; Bloomberg Television; Canales N; CBS College Sports Network; Comcast SportsNet Mid-Atlantic; Cooking Channel; Country Music TV; C-SPAN 3; Discovery Digital Networks; Discovery HD Theater; Do-It-Yourself; Encore Wam; ESPN; ESPN Classic Sports; ESPNews; Eternal Word TV Network; Flix; Fox College Sports Atlantic; Fox College Sports Central; Fox College Sports Pacific; Fox Soccer; GAS; Gol TV; Great American Country; History Channel International; Independent Film Channel; INHD; INHD2; INSP; Lifetime Movie Network; LOGO; Mid-Atlantic Sports Network; MoviePlex; MTV Networks Digital Suite; National Geographic Channel; NBA TV; NFL Network; Nick Jr.; Nick Too; NickToons TV; PBS Kids Sprout; RAI International; SoapNet; Speed Channel; Sundance Channel (multiplexed); Tennis Channel; The Word Network; Toon Disney; Trinity Broadcasting Network; TV Asia; TV5, La Television International; Universal HD; WE tv; Weatherscan; Zee TV USA.
Fee: $14.90 monthly.
Pay Service 1
Pay Units: N.A.
Programming (via satellite): HBO; Showtime.
Fee: $14.95 monthly (Showtime), $16.95 monthly (HBO).
Digital Pay Service 1
Pay Units: N.A.
Programming (via satellite): Cinemax (multiplexed); Cinemax HD; DMX Music; Encore (multiplexed); HBO (multiplexed); HBO HD; Showtime (multiplexed); Showtime HD; Starz (multiplexed); Starz HDTV; The Movie Channel (multiplexed).
Fee: $21.95 installation; $11.95 monthly (Starz), $14.25 monthly (Showtime, Cinemax, or TMC), $16.95 monthly (HBO).
Video-On-Demand: Yes
Pay-Per-View
iN DEMAND (delivered digitally); Fresh (delivered digitally); Hot Choice (delivered digitally); Playboy TV (delivered digitally); Shorteez (delivered digitally); Pleasure (delivered digitally); Sports PPV (delivered digitally).
Internet Service
Operational: Yes. Began: January 1, 2001.
Broadband Service: Comcast High Speed Internet.
Fee: $42.95 monthly.
Telephone Service
Digital: Operational
Fee: $44.95 monthly
Miles of Plant: 1,105.0 (coaxial); 120.0 (fiber optic). Homes passed: 325,000.
Vice President & General Manager: Tony Hollinger. Technical Director: Kelwin Mebane. Marketing Director: Maxine Gill. Government & Public Affairs Director: Kathy Etemad-Hollinger.
City fee: 5% of gross.
Ownership: Comcast Cable Communications Inc. (MSO).

WASHINGTON—RCN Corp. This cable system has converted to IPTV and has been broken into 19 communities. See [DC5001] through [DC5019], DC. ICA: DC0006.

WASHINGTON (northwestern portion)—RCN Corp. Now served by WASHINGTON (formerly WASHINGTON southeastern portion), DC [DC0006]. ICA: DC0005.

FLORIDA

Total Systems: 150
Total Communities Served: 837
Franchises Not Yet Operating: 0
Applications Pending: 0
Communities with Applications: 0
Number of Basic Subscribers: 6,654,664
Number of Expanded Basic Subscribers: 787,708
Number of Pay Units: 539,754

Top 100 Markets Represented: Miami (21); Tampa-St. Petersburg-Clearwater-Lakeland (28); Orlando-Daytona Beach-Melbourne-Cocoa-Clermont (55); Mobile, AL-Pensacola, FL (59); Jacksonville (68).

For a list of cable communities in this section, see the Cable Community Index located in the back of Cable Volume 2.
For explanation of terms used in cable system listings, see p. D-11.

ADVENT CHRISTIAN VILLAGE—Advent Christian Village Cable TV, PO Box 4329, Dowling Park, FL 32060. Phone: 386-658-5155. Fax: 386-658-5151. ICA: FL0315.

TV Market Ranking: Below 100 (ADVENT CHRISTIAN VILLAGE). Franchise award date: N.A. Franchise expiration date: N.A. Began: March 1, 1985.

Channel capacity: 27 (not 2-way capable). Channels available but not in use: N.A.

Basic Service

Subscribers: 400.

Programming (received off-air): WCJB-TV (ABC, CW) Gainesville; WCTV (CBS, MNT) Thomasville; WTWC-TV (NBC) Tallahassee; WTXL-TV (ABC) Tallahassee; WUFT (PBS) Gainesville.

Programming (via satellite): ABC Family Channel; Discovery Channel; ESPN; TBS Superstation; USA Network; WGN America.

Fee: $26.00 monthly.

Video-On-Demand: No

Internet Service

Operational: No.

Telephone Service

None

Miles of Plant: 10.0 (coaxial); None (fiber optic).

Manager: Tim Goyette.

Ownership: Advent Christian Village Inc.

ALACHUA—CommuniComm Services, 17774 NW US Highway 441, High Springs, FL 32643-8749. Phone: 386-454-2299. Fax: 386-454-3705. Web Site: http://www.communicomm.com. Also serves Alachua County. ICA: FL0209.

TV Market Ranking: Below 100 (ALACHUA, Alachua County). Franchise award date: N.A. Franchise expiration date: N.A. Began: December 1, 1968.

Channel capacity: N.A. Channels available but not in use: N.A.

Basic Service

Subscribers: N.A. Included in High Springs

Programming (received off-air): WACX (IND) Leesburg; WCJB-TV (ABC, CW) Gainesville; WCWJ (CW) Jacksonville; WJXT (IND) Jacksonville; WMYG-LP Lake City; WOGX (FOX) Ocala; WTLV (NBC) Jacksonville; WUFT (PBS) Gainesville; allband FM.

Programming (via satellite): QVC; Trinity Broadcasting Network; TV Guide Network.

Fee: $50.00 installation; $16.00 monthly; $3.52 converter; $30.00 additional installation.

Expanded Basic Service 1

Subscribers: N.A.

Programming (via satellite): ABC Family Channel; AMC; Animal Planet; Arts & Entertainment; BET Networks; Cartoon Network; CNBC; CNN; Comedy Central; Country Music TV; C-SPAN; Discovery Channel; Disney Channel; Do-It-Yourself; ESPN; ESPN 2; ESPN Classic Sports; ESPNews; Food Network; Fox News Channel; FX; Hallmark Channel; Headline News; HGTV; History Channel; ION Television; Lifetime; MTV; Nick Jr.; Nickelodeon; Outdoor Channel; ShopNBC; Speed Channel; Spike TV; SunSports TV; Syfy; TBS Superstation; The Learning Channel; Travel Channel; truTV; Turner Network TV; TV Land; Univision; USA Network; VH1; Weather Channel.

Digital Basic Service

Subscribers: N.A.

Programming (via satellite): BBC America; Bloomberg Television; Bravo; CMT Pure Country; Discovery Digital Networks; DMX Music; FitTV; Fox Movie Channel; Fox Soccer; G4; Golf Channel; GSN; Halogen Network; Independent Film Channel; Military History Channel; National Geographic Channel; NickToons TV; SoapNet; Turner Classic Movies; Versus; VH1 Classic; WE tv.

Pay Service 1

Pay Units: N.A. Included in High Springs

Programming (via satellite): Cinemax; Encore; HBO; Starz.

Fee: $9.95 monthly (Cinemax), $11.95 monthly (HBO).

Digital Pay Service 1

Pay Units: N.A.

Programming (via satellite): Cinemax (multiplexed); Encore (multiplexed); HBO (multiplexed); Starz (multiplexed).

Video-On-Demand: No

Pay-Per-View

iN DEMAND (delivered digitally); Club Jenna (delivered digitally); Playboy TV (delivered digitally); Fresh (delivered digitally).

Internet Service

Operational: Yes. Began: February 1, 2002.

Broadband Service: Net Commander.

Fee: $39.95 installation; $51.95 monthly.

Telephone Service

None

Homes passed and miles of plant included in High Springs

General Manager: Darrell Laird. Chief Technician: Michael Smith. Customer Service Manager: Cindy Ross.

City fee: 3% of gross.

Ownership: James Cable LLC (MSO).

ALLIGATOR POINT—Mediacom. Now served by WEWAHITCHKA, FL [FL0159]. ICA: FL0191.

ALVA—Time Warner Cable. Now served by NAPLES, FL [FL0029]. ICA: FL0324.

APALACHICOLA—Mediacom. Now served by WEWAHITCHKA, FL [FL0159]. ICA: FL0103.

ARCADIA—Comcast Cable, 5205 Fruitville Rd, Sarasota, FL 34232. Phone: 941-371-4444. Fax: 941-371-5097. Web Site: http://www.comcast.com. Also serves Fort Ogden. ICA: FL0101.

TV Market Ranking: Below 100 (Fort Ogden); Outside TV Markets (ARCADIA). Franchise award date: N.A. Franchise expiration date: N.A. Began: January 1, 1965.

Channel capacity: 60 (operating 2-way). Channels available but not in use: N.A.

Basic Service

Subscribers: 2,503.

Programming (received off-air): WBBH-TV (NBC) Fort Myers; WFLA-TV (NBC) Tampa; WFTT-DT (TEL) Tampa; WFTX-TV (FOX) Cape Coral; WGCU (PBS) Fort Myers; WINK-TV (CBS) Fort Myers; WMOR-TV (IND) Lakeland; WRXY-TV (IND) Tice; WTOG (CW) St. Petersburg; WTVT (FOX) Tampa; WVEA-TV (UNV) Venice; WWSB (ABC) Sarasota; WXCW (CW) Naples; WXPX-TV (ION) Bradenton; WZVN-TV (ABC) Naples; allband FM.

Programming (via satellite): ABC Family Channel; AMC; Animal Planet; Arts & Entertainment; BET Networks; Cartoon Network; CNN; Comcast/Charter Sports Southeast (CSS); Comedy Central; Country Music TV; C-SPAN; Discovery Channel; Discovery Health Channel; Disney Channel; E! Entertainment Television; ESPN; ESPN 2; Fox News Channel; FX; Golf Channel; GSN; Headline News; HGTV; History Channel; Home Shopping Network; Lifetime; MTV; Nickelodeon; QVC; Speed Channel; Spike TV; SunSports TV; TBS Superstation; The Learning Channel; truTV; Turner Network TV; TV Land; USA Network; Versus; VH1; Weather Channel; WGN America.

Fee: $63.35 installation; $40.30 monthly.

Pay Service 1

Pay Units: N.A.

Programming (via satellite): Cinemax; HBO; Showtime; The Movie Channel.

Fee: $25.00 installation; $10.00 monthly (Cinemax or Showtime), $10.95 monthly (HBO).

Video-On-Demand: No

Internet Service

Operational: Yes.

Telephone Service

Digital: Operational

Miles of Plant: 78.0 (coaxial); None (fiber optic). Homes passed: 4,500. Total homes in franchised area: 6,902.

Regional Vice President: Rod Dagenais. Vice President & General Manager: Steve Dvoskin. Technical Operations Director: Danny Maxwell. Technical Operations Manager: Andrew Behn. Marketing Director: Vince Maffeo.

City fee: 3% of gross.

Ownership: Comcast Cable Communications Inc. (MSO).

ARCHER—Comcast Cable, 20775 W Pennsylvania Ave, Dunnellon, FL 34431. Phones: 352-787-9601 (Leesburg office); 352-489-0939. Fax: 352-365-6279. Web Site: http://www.comcast.com. ICA: FL0189.

TV Market Ranking: Below 100 (ARCHER). Franchise award date: N.A. Franchise expiration date: N.A. Began: January 1, 1984.

Channel capacity: N.A. Channels available but not in use: N.A.

Basic Service

Subscribers: N.A. Included in Inverness

Programming (received off-air): WCJB-TV (ABC, CW) Gainesville; WESH (NBC) Daytona Beach; WJXT (IND) Jacksonville; WOGX (FOX) Ocala; WUFT (PBS) Gainesville.

Programming (via satellite): ABC Family Channel; CNN; Discovery Channel; ESPN; Headline News; TBS Superstation; Turner Network TV; USA Network; WGN America.

Fee: $15.86 installation; $18.30 monthly.

Pay Service 1

Pay Units: 77.

Programming (via satellite): Cinemax; HBO.

Fee: $10.00 installation; $11.60 monthly (each).

Video-On-Demand: No

Internet Service

Operational: Yes.

Telephone Service

Digital: Operational

Miles of Plant: 20.0 (coaxial); None (fiber optic). Homes passed: 660.

General Manager: Mike Davenport. Marketing Manager: Melanie Melvin.

Ownership: Comcast Cable Communications Inc. (MSO).

ASTOR—Florida Cable, PO Box 498, 23748 State Rd 40, Astor, FL 32102-0498. Phones: 800-779-2788; 352-759-2788. Fax: 352-759-3577. Web Site: http://www.floridacable.com. Also serves Altoona, Astatula, Eustis, Lake County (unincorporated areas), Pierson, Sorrento, Volusia & Volusia County (unincorporated areas). ICA: FL0171.

TV Market Ranking: 55 (Altoona, Astatula, ASTOR, Eustis, Lake County (unincorporated areas), Pierson, Sorrento, Volusia, Volusia County (unincorporated areas)). Franchise award date: N.A. Franchise expiration date: N.A. Began: September 15, 1984.

Channel capacity: 77 (operating 2-way). Channels available but not in use: N.A.

Basic Service

Subscribers: 10,000.

Programming (received off-air): WDSC-TV (PBS) New Smyrna Beach; WESH (NBC) Daytona Beach; WFTV (ABC) Orlando; WKCF (CW) Clermont; WKMG-TV (CBS) Orlando; WMFE-TV (PBS) Orlando; WOFL (FOX) Orlando; WRBW (MNT) Orlando; WRDQ (IND) Orlando.

Programming (via satellite): ABC Family Channel; AMC; Animal Planet; Arts & Entertainment; Cartoon Network; CNBC; CNN; Country Music TV; C-SPAN; Discovery Channel; E! Entertainment Television; ESPN; ESPN 2; Food Network; Fox News Channel; FX; GalaVision; Headline News; HGTV; History Channel; Home Shopping Network; Lifetime; MTV; Nickelodeon; PBS Kids Channel; Speed Channel; Spike TV; SunSports TV; Syfy; TBS Superstation; The Learning Channel; Travel Channel; Turner Classic Movies; Turner Network TV; TV Guide Network; TV Land; TVE Internacional; Univision; USA Network; VH1; Weather Channel; WGN America.
Fee: $25.00 installation; $11.95 monthly.

Digital Basic Service
Subscribers: N.A.
Programming (via satellite): American-Life TV Network; BBC America; Bio; Black Family Channel; Bloomberg Television; Bravo; Canales N; Discovery Digital Networks; DMX Music; ESPN Classic Sports; ESPNews; FitTV; Fox Movie Channel; Fox Soccer; Fuse; G4; GAS; Golf Channel; Great American Country; GSN; Halogen Network; History Channel International; Independent Film Channel; Lifetime Movie Network; MTV Networks Digital Suite; National Geographic Channel; Nick Jr.; Outdoor Channel; Ovation; ShopNBC; Style Network; Sundance Channel; The Word Network; Trinity Broadcasting Network; Versus; WE tv.

Digital Pay Service 1
Pay Units: 85.
Programming (via satellite): Cinemax (multiplexed); Encore (multiplexed); HBO (multiplexed); Showtime (multiplexed); Starz (multiplexed); The Movie Channel (multiplexed).
Fee: $9.95 installation; $10.50 monthly (each).

Video-On-Demand: No

Pay-Per-View
iN DEMAND (delivered digitally); Hot Choice (delivered digitally); Playboy TV (delivered digitally); Fresh (delivered digitally); Shorteez (delivered digitally).

Internet Service
Operational: Yes. Began: January 1, 2000.
Broadband Service: USA2net.net.
Fee: $49.95 installation; $24.95 monthly.

Telephone Service
None

Miles of Plant: 22.0 (coaxial); None (fiber optic). Additional miles planned: 7.0 (coaxial).
General Manager: Jim Pierce. Office Manager: Aleta Dawson. Plant Manager: Larry English.
County fee: 3% of gross.
Ownership: Florida Cable Inc.

ATLANTA (metro area)—Comcast Cable, 2925 Courtyards Dr, Norcross, GA 30071. Phones: 770-559-2424; 770-559-2727. Fax: 770-559-2479. Web Site: http://www.comcast.com. Also serves Avondale Estates, Berkeley Lake, Chamblee, Clarkston, College Park, Decatur, DeKalb County, Doraville, Druid Hills, Dunwoody, East Point, Fairburn, Fulton County (southern portion), Grayson, Hapeville, Lilburn, Lithonia, Norcross, Palmetto, Pine Lake, Snellville, Stone Mountain & Union City. ICA: GA0001.
TV Market Ranking: 18 (ATLANTA (METRO AREA), Avondale Estates, Berkeley Lake, Chamblee, Clarkston, College Park, Decatur, DeKalb County, Doraville, Druid Hills, Dunwoody, East Point, Fairburn, Fulton County (southern portion), Grayson, Hapeville, Lilburn, Lithonia, Norcross, Palmetto, Pine Lake, Snellville, Stone Mountain, Union City). Franchise award date: N.A. Franchise expiration date: N.A. Began: May 1, 1968.
Channel capacity: N.A. Channels available but not in use: N.A.

Basic Service
Subscribers: 522,000 Includes Atlanta (perimeter north) & Atlanta (perimeter south).
Programming (received off-air): WAGA-TV (FOX) Atlanta; WATC-DT (ETV) Atlanta; WATL (MNT) Atlanta; WGCL-TV (CBS) Atlanta; WGTV (PBS) Athens; WHSG-TV (TBN) Monroe; WPBA (PBS) Atlanta; WPCH-TV (IND) Atlanta; WPXA-TV (ION) Rome; WSB-TV (ABC) Atlanta; WUPA (CW) Atlanta; WUVG-DT (UNV) Athens; WXIA-TV (NBC) Atlanta.
Programming (via microwave): Atlanta Interfaith Broadcasters.
Programming (via satellite): Home Shopping Network; QVC; TV Guide Network.
Current originations: Leased Access; Government Access; Educational Access; Public Access.
Fee: $25.00 installation; $16.95 monthly.

Expanded Basic Service 1
Subscribers: N.A.
Programming (via satellite): ABC Family Channel; AMC; Animal Planet; Arts & Entertainment; BET Networks; Bravo; Cartoon Network; CNBC; CNN; Comcast Sports Net Southeast; Comcast/Charter Sports Southeast (CSS); Comedy Central; Country Music TV; C-SPAN; C-SPAN 2; Discovery Channel; Disney Channel; E! Entertainment Television; ESPN; ESPN 2; Food Network; Fox News Channel; FX; Golf Channel; Headline News; HGTV; History Channel; Lifetime; MTV; Nickelodeon; Oxygen; Speed Channel; Spike TV; SportSouth; Syfy; Telemundo; The Learning Channel; Travel Channel; truTV; Turner Classic Movies; Turner Network TV; TV Land; USA Network; VH1; WE tv; Weather Channel.
Fee: $33.04 monthly.

Digital Basic Service
Subscribers: 194,091.
Programming (via satellite): C-SPAN 3; Discovery Digital Networks; ESPN Classic Sports; ESPNews; GAS; GSN; Lime; Music Choice; NASA TV; Nick Jr.; ShopNBC; Style Network; Toon Disney; Weatherscan.
Fee: $11.95 monthly.

Digital Expanded Basic Service
Subscribers: N.A.
Programming (via satellite): AmericanLife TV Network; BBC America; Bio; Black Family Channel; Bloomberg Television; Daystar TV Network; Encore Action; Eternal Word TV Network; FamilyNet; Fox College Sports Atlantic; Fox College Sports Central; Fox College Sports Pacific; Fox Movie Channel; Fox Sports World; G4; Great American Country; Halogen Network; History Channel International; Independent Film Channel; Lifetime Movie Network; MSNBC; MTV Networks Digital Suite; National Geographic Channel; NickToons TV; Outdoor Channel; Ovation; Sundance Channel; The Word Network; Versus.
Fee: $4.00 monthly.

Digital Pay Service 1
Pay Units: 15,625.
Programming (via satellite): Canales N; Cinemax (multiplexed); Flix; HBO (multiplexed); Korean Channel; Showtime (multiplexed); Starz (multiplexed); The Movie Channel (multiplexed); TV Japan.
Fee: $10.00 installation; $5.99 monthly (Canales N), $14.99 monthly (HBO, Cinemax, Showtime, Starz, or Flix/TMC), $14.99 monthly (Korean), $29.95 monthly (TV Japan).

Video-On-Demand: Yes

Pay-Per-View
Addressable homes: 194,091.
sports (delivered digitally); Shorteez (delivered digitally); Fresh (delivered digitally); Playboy TV (delivered digitally); iN DEMAND (delivered digitally); ESPN Now (delivered digitally), Addressable: Yes; Hot Choice (delivered digitally).

Internet Service
Operational: Yes.
Subscribers: 48,491.
Broadband Service: Comcast High Speed Internet.
Fee: $49.95 installation; $42.95 monthly; $3.00 modem lease; $139.00 modem purchase.

Telephone Service
Digital: Operational
Fee: $44.95 monthly

Miles of Plant: 20,000.0 (coaxial); None (fiber optic). Miles of plant (coax & fiber combined) includes Atlanta (perimeter north) & Atlanta (perimeter south)
Regional Vice President: Gene Shatlock. Regional Vice President, Operations: Michael Hewitt. General Manager: Trevor Yant. Technical Operations Director: Phil Dente. Marketing Director: Lillian Harding. Communications Manager: Cindy Kicklighter.
City fee: 5% of gross.
Ownership: Comcast Cable Communications Inc. (MSO).

AUBURNDALE—Bright House Networks, 1004 US Hwy 92 W, Auburndale, FL 33823. Phones: 727-856-3278 (Customer service); 863-965-7733. Fax: 863-288-2204. E-mail: tampabay.customercare@mybrighthouse.com. Web Site: http://tampabay.brighthouse.com. Also serves Davenport, Deer Creek Golf RV Park, Dundee, Eagle Lake, Haines City, Lake Alfred, Lake Hamilton, Lake Wales (portions), Lakeland, Mulberry, Polk City, Polk County, Three World RV Park, Winter Haven & Winter Haven Oaks Mobile Home Park. ICA: FL0036.
TV Market Ranking: 28 (AUBURNDALE, Deer Creek Golf RV Resort, Dundee, Eagle Lake, Lake Alfred, Lake Hamilton, Lake Wales (portions), Lakeland, Mulberry, Polk City, Three World RV Park, Winter Haven, Winter Haven Oaks Mobile Home Park); 28,55 (Polk County (portions)); 55 (Davenport, Haines City); Outside TV Markets (Polk County (portions)). Franchise award date: January 1, 1966. Franchise expiration date: N.A. Began: January 1, 1968.
Channel capacity: N.A. Channels available but not in use: None.

Basic Service
Subscribers: 104,140.
Programming (received off-air): WCLF (IND) Clearwater; WEDU (PBS) Tampa; WFLA-TV (NBC) Tampa; WFTS-TV (ABC) Tampa; WFTT-DT (TEL) Tampa; WTOG (CW) St. Petersburg; WTSP (CBS) St. Petersburg; WTTA (MNT) St. Petersburg; WUSF-TV (PBS) Tampa; WVEA-TV (UNV) Venice; WXPX-TV (ION) Bradenton.
Programming (via satellite): Bay News 9; Home Shopping Network; QVC; ShopNBC; TV Guide Network; WFTV (ABC) Orlando; WGN America.
Current originations: Government Access.
Fee: $42.95 installation; $16.00 monthly.

Expanded Basic Service 1
Subscribers: N.A.
Programming (via satellite): ABC Family Channel; AMC; Animal Planet; Arts & Entertainment; BET Networks; Bravo; Cartoon Network; CNBC; CNN; Comedy Central; Country Music TV; C-SPAN; C-SPAN 2; Discovery Channel; Disney Channel; E! Entertainment Television; ESPN; ESPN 2; ESPN Classic Sports; Flix; Food Network; Fox News Channel; Fox Sports Net Florida; FX; Golf Channel; Hallmark Channel; Headline News; HGTV; History Channel; Jewelry Television; Lifetime; Lifetime Movie Network; MoviePlex; MSNBC; MTV; National Geographic Channel; Nickelodeon; Oxygen; Shop at Home; Spike TV; SunSports TV; Syfy; TBS Superstation; The Learning Channel; Travel Channel; truTV; Turner Network TV; TV Land; USA Network; Versus; VH1; WE tv; Weather Channel.
Fee: $28.95 monthly.

Digital Basic Service
Subscribers: 45,054.
Programming (received off-air): WFTS-TV (ABC) Tampa; WTVT (FOX) Tampa.
Programming (via satellite): AmericanLife TV Network; America's Store; Bay News 9; BBC America; Bloomberg Television; Cooking Channel; C-SPAN 3; Discovery Digital Networks; Do-It-Yourself; ESPNews; FitTV; Fox Sports World; Fuse; G4; GAS; Great American Country; GSN; Lifetime Real Women; MTV2; Nick Jr.; Outdoor Channel; Ovation; Science Television; SoapNet; Speed Channel; Style Network; Sundance Channel; Toon Disney; Trinity Broadcasting Network; VH1 Classic.
Fee: $11.95 monthly.

Digital Expanded Basic Service
Subscribers: N.A.
Programming (via satellite): Encore Action; Fox Movie Channel; Independent Film Channel.
Fee: $6.00 monthly.

Digital Pay Service 1
Pay Units: N.A.
Programming (via satellite): Cinemax (multiplexed).

Video-On-Demand: Yes

Pay-Per-View
Addressable homes: 45,054.
iN DEMAND (delivered digitally); Playboy TV (delivered digitally), Fee: $3.95, Addressable: Yes; Pleasure (delivered digitally); Fresh (delivered digitally), Fee: $3.95; Shorteez (delivered digitally).

Internet Service
Operational: Yes.
Subscribers: 30,201.
Broadband Service: Road Runner.
Fee: $39.95 installation; $29.95 monthly.

Telephone Service
Digital: Operational
Fee: $39.95 monthly

Miles of Plant: 3,064.0 (coaxial); None (fiber optic). Homes passed: 167,140.
Division President: Kevin Hyman. Vice President & General Manager: Dave Ross. Vice President, Engineering: Gene White. Engineering Director: Scott Twyman. Marketing Director: Robb Bennett. Marketing Coordinator: Mike Schaal.
City fee: 5% of gross.
Ownership: Bright House Networks LLC (MSO).

BAKER—Mediacom. Now served by MILTON, FL [FL0380]. ICA: FL0182.
TV Market Ranking: Franchise award date: N.A. Franchise expiration date: N.A. Began: N.A.

BANYON SPRINGS—No longer in operation. ICA: FL0212.

BARTOW—Comcast Cable, 5205 Fruitville Rd, Sarasota, FL 34232. Phone: 941-371-4444. Fax: 941-371-5097. Web Site: http://www.comcast.com. Also serves Fort Meade & Homeland. ICA: FL0050.

TV Market Ranking: 28 (BARTOW, Fort Meade, Homeland). Franchise award date: N.A. Franchise expiration date: N.A. Began: January 1, 1969.

Channel capacity: N.A. Channels available but not in use: N.A.

Basic Service

Subscribers: 6,154.

Programming (received off-air): WCLF (IND) Clearwater; WEDU (PBS) Tampa; WFLA-TV (NBC) Tampa; WFTS-TV (ABC) Tampa; WFTT-DT (TEL) Tampa; WFTV (ABC) Orlando; WKMG-TV (CBS) Orlando; WMOR-TV (IND) Lakeland; WTOG (CW) St. Petersburg; WTSP (CBS) St. Petersburg; WTTA (MNT) St. Petersburg; WTVT (FOX) Tampa; WUSF-TV (PBS) Tampa; WVEA-TV (UNV) Venice; WXPX-TV (ION) Bradenton; 14 FMs.

Programming (via satellite): QVC; Style Network; TV Guide Network.

Current originations: Educational Access; Government Access.

Fee: $63.35 installation; $13.75 monthly.

Expanded Basic Service 1

Subscribers: N.A.

Programming (via satellite): ABC Family Channel; AMC; Animal Planet; Arts & Entertainment; BET Networks; Cartoon Network; CNBC; CNN; Comcast/Charter Sports Southeast (CSS); Comedy Central; Country Music TV; C-SPAN; C-SPAN 2; Discovery Channel; Discovery Health Channel; E! Entertainment Television; ESPN; ESPN 2; Food Network; Fox News Channel; FX; Golf Channel; GSN; Hallmark Channel; Headline News; HGTV; History Channel; Home Shopping Network; Lifetime; MTV; Nickelodeon; Speed Channel; Spike TV; SunSports TV; Syfy; TBS Superstation; The Learning Channel; Turner Network TV; TV Land; USA Network; Versus; VH1; Weather Channel.

Fee: $47.50 monthly.

Digital Basic Service

Subscribers: 1,539.

Programming (received off-air): WFLA-TV (NBC) Tampa.

Programming (via satellite): BBC America; CMT Pure Country; Discovery Digital Networks; Disney Channel; Encore; ESPNews; Flix; GAS; MTV Networks Digital Suite; Music Choice; Nick Jr.; Nick Too; SoapNet; Sundance Channel; Toon Disney; WE tv; Weatherscan.

Fee: $14.95 monthly.

Pay Service 1

Pay Units: 9,666.

Programming (via satellite): HBO; Showtime.

Fee: $25.00 installation; $10.00 monthly (each).

Digital Pay Service 1

Pay Units: N.A.

Programming (via satellite): Cinemax (multiplexed); HBO (multiplexed); Showtime (multiplexed); Starz (multiplexed); The Movie Channel (multiplexed).

Fee: $13.50 monthly (each).

Video-On-Demand: No

Pay-Per-View

Addressable homes: 1,539.

iN DEMAND (delivered digitally), Addressable: Yes; Hot Choice (delivered digitally); Playboy TV (delivered digitally).

Internet Service

Operational: Yes.

Broadband Service: Comcast High Speed Internet.

Fee: $42.95 monthly.

Telephone Service

None

Regional Vice President: Rod Dagenais. Vice President & General Manager: Steve Dvoskin. Technical Operations Director: Danny Maxwell. Technical Operations Manager: Andrew Behn. Marketing Director: Vince Maffeo.

City fee: 3% of gross.

Ownership: Comcast Cable Communications Inc. (MSO).

BAY INDIES MOBILE HOME PARK—Formerly served by Mobile Home Properties Inc. No longer in operation. ICA: FL0213.

BELLE GLADE—Comcast Cable, 450 E Palm Beach Rd, South Bay, FL 33493. Phones: 561-996-3087; 561-996-8455. Fax: 561-996-3091. Web Site: http://www.comcast.com. Also serves Canal Point, Clewiston, Hendry County (northeastern portion), Pahokee, Palm Beach County (portions) & South Bay. ICA: FL0073.

TV Market Ranking: Below 100 (BELLE GLADE, Canal Point, Pahokee, Palm Beach County (portions)); Outside TV Markets (Clewiston, Hendry County (northeastern portion), Palm Beach County (portions), South Bay). Franchise award date: September 23, 1968. Franchise expiration date: N.A. Began: April 1, 1972.

Channel capacity: N.A. Channels available but not in use: N.A.

Basic Service

Subscribers: 8,057.

Programming (received off-air): WFGC (IND) Palm Beach; WFLX (FOX) West Palm Beach; WHDT-LP Miami; WLTV-DT (UNV) Miami; WPBF (ABC) Tequesta; WPBT (PBS) Miami; WPEC (CBS) West Palm Beach; WPLG (ABC) Miami; WPTV-TV (NBC) West Palm Beach; WPXP-TV (ION) Lake Worth; WTCE-TV (ETV) Fort Pierce; WTVX (CW) Fort Pierce; WXEL-TV (PBS) West Palm Beach.

Programming (via satellite): Home Shopping Network; QVC; TV Guide Network; WGN America.

Current originations: Government Access; Educational Access.

Fee: $50.00 installation; $14.65 monthly; $1.55 converter; $10.00 additional installation.

Expanded Basic Service 1

Subscribers: N.A.

Programming (received off-air): WSCV (TMO) Fort Lauderdale.

Programming (via satellite): ABC Family Channel; AMC; Animal Planet; Arts & Entertainment; BET Networks; Bravo; Cartoon Network; CNBC; CNN; Comedy Central; Country Music TV; C-SPAN; C-SPAN 2; Discovery Channel; Disney Channel; E! Entertainment Television; ESPN; ESPN 2; Eternal Word TV Network; Food Network; Fox News Channel; Fox Sports Net Florida; FX; Golf Channel; Hallmark Channel; Headline News; HGTV; History Channel; Lifetime; MSNBC; MTV; Nickelodeon; Oxygen; Product Information Network; ShopNBC; Spike TV; Style Network; SunSports TV; Syfy; TBS Superstation; The Learning Channel; Travel Channel; truTV; Turner Network TV; TV Land; Univision; USA Network; VH1; Weather Channel.

Fee: $47.99 monthly.

Digital Basic Service

Subscribers: N.A.

Programming (via satellite): AmericanLife TV Network; BBC America; Bio; Black Family Channel; Bloomberg Television; Discovery Digital Networks; Do-It-Yourself; ESPN Classic Sports; ESPNews; FamilyNet; FitTV; Fox Sports World; Fuse; G4; GSN; Halogen Network; History Channel International; Lifetime Movie Network; M-2 (Movie Mania) TV Network; Music Choice; Outdoor Channel; SoapNet; Speed Channel; Toon Disney; Trinity Broadcasting Network; Versus; WE tv.

Fee: $53.49 monthly.

Digital Expanded Basic Service

Subscribers: N.A.

Programming (via satellite): Fox College Sports Atlantic; Fox College Sports Central; Fox College Sports Pacific; Fox Movie Channel; GAS; Independent Film Channel; MTV Networks Digital Suite; National Geographic Channel; Nick Jr.; Nick Too; NickToons TV; Sundance Channel; Turner Classic Movies.

Fee: $5.00 monthly.

Digital Pay Service 1

Pay Units: N.A.

Programming (via satellite): Cinemax (multiplexed); Encore (multiplexed); Flix; HBO (multiplexed); Showtime (multiplexed); Starz (multiplexed); The Movie Channel (multiplexed).

Video-On-Demand: No

Pay-Per-View

Hot Choice (delivered digitally); Playboy TV (delivered digitally); Fresh (delivered digitally); Shorteez (delivered digitally); Movies (delivered digitally); special events (delivered digitally); sports (delivered digitally).

Internet Service

Operational: Yes. Began: December 31, 2001.

Broadband Service: Comcast High Speed Internet.

Fee: $42.95 monthly; $5.00 modem lease.

Telephone Service

Digital: Operational

Miles of Plant: 218.0 (coaxial); None (fiber optic). Homes passed: 20,000.

Area Vice President: Gary Waterfield. General Manager: Geoff Shook. Technical Operations Manager: John Barnard. Marketing Director: Christopher Derario. Marketing Manager: Diane Bissoon. Marketing Coordinator: Janet Epstien. Government & Community Affairs Director: Marta Casas-Celayas.

City fee: 5% of gross.

Ownership: Comcast Cable Communications Inc. (MSO).

BEVERLY BEACH—Formerly served by TV Max. No longer in operation. ICA: FL0186.

BIG CYPRESS SEMINOLE INDIAN RESERVATION—Comcast Cable, 141 NW 16th St, Pompano Beach, FL 33060. Phone: 954-252-1937. Fax: 954-532-7256. Web Site: http://www.comcast.com. ICA: FL0376.

TV Market Ranking: Outside TV Markets (BIG CYPRESS SEMINOLE INDIAN RESERVATION).

Channel capacity: 19 (not 2-way capable). Channels available but not in use: N.A.

Basic Service

Subscribers: N.A. Included in Miami

Video-On-Demand: No

Internet Service

Operational: No.

Telephone Service

None

Vice President & General Manager: Rick Seamon. Technical Operations Director: Ross Pappas.

Ownership: Comcast Cable Communications Inc. (MSO).

BLOUNTSTOWN—Bright House Networks, 94 Walton Rd, DeFuniak Springs, FL 32433. Phones: 800-288-1664; 727-791-7730. Fax: 850-892-1318. Web Site: http://panhandle.brighthouse.com. Also serves Bristol, Calhoun County (portions) & Liberty County. ICA: FL0133.

TV Market Ranking: Below 100 (BLOUNTSTOWN, Bristol, Calhoun County (portions), Liberty County). Franchise award date: N.A. Franchise expiration date: N.A. Began: January 1, 1971.

Channel capacity: N.A. Channels available but not in use: N.A.

Basic Service

Subscribers: 1,394.

Programming (received off-air): WCTV (CBS, MNT) Thomasville; WFSU-TV (PBS) Tallahassee; WJHG-TV (CW, MNT, NBC) Panama City; WMBB (ABC) Panama City; WPGX (FOX) Panama City; WTVY (CBS, CW, MNT) Dothan.

Programming (via satellite): ABC Family Channel; AMC; Animal Planet; Arts & Entertainment; BET Networks; Bravo; Cartoon Network; CNBC; CNN; Country Music TV; C-SPAN; Discovery Channel; Disney Channel; E! Entertainment Television; ESPN; ESPN 2; Food Network; Fox News Channel; FX; Headline News; HGTV; History Channel; Home Shopping Network; Lifetime; Lifetime Movie Network; MSNBC; MTV; National Geographic Channel; Nickelodeon; Oxygen; QVC; ShopNBC; Spike TV; Style Network; SunSports TV; Syfy; TBS Superstation; The Learning Channel; Travel Channel; Trinity Broadcasting Network; Turner Network TV; USA Network; VH1; WE tv; Weather Channel.

Fee: $53.75 installation; $44.35 monthly; $17.90 additional installation.

Digital Basic Service

Subscribers: N.A.

Programming (via satellite): AmericanLife TV Network; BBC America; Bloomberg Television; Discovery Digital Networks; DMX Music; ESPN Classic Sports; ESPN Now; ESPNews; Fox Sports World; G4; GAS; Golf Channel; GSN; MTV2; Nick Jr.; Outdoor Channel; Ovation; Speed Channel; Toon Disney; Turner Classic Movies; Versus; VH1 Classic.

Fee: $12.45 monthly.

Digital Pay Service 1

Pay Units: N.A.

Programming (via satellite): Cinemax (multiplexed); Encore (multiplexed); HBO (multiplexed); Independent Film Channel; Showtime (multiplexed); Sundance Channel; The Movie Channel (multiplexed); WAM! America's Kidz Network.

Fee: $10.50 monthly (each).

Video-On-Demand: No

Pay-Per-View

Fresh (delivered digitally); Shorteez (delivered digitally); Hot Choice (delivered digitally); iN DEMAND (delivered digitally); Sports PPV (delivered digitally).

Internet Service

Operational: Yes.

Broadband Service: Road Runner.

Fee: $49.95 installation; $29.95 monthly.

Telephone Service

Analog: Not Operational

Digital: Operational

Fee: $39.95 monthly
Miles of Plant: 72.0 (coaxial); None (fiber optic). Homes passed: 2,330. Total homes in franchised area: 2,496.
Marketing Director: Nicole Hardy. Technical Operations Manager: Lynn Miller. Chief Technician: Edward Harrison. Business Manager: Elaine West.
Ownership: Bright House Networks LLC (MSO).

BOCA RATON—Now served by DELRAY BEACH, FL [FL0091]. ICA: FL0035.

BOCA RATON—Now served by DELRAY BEACH, FL [FL0091]. ICA: FL0051.

BONIFAY—Mediacom. Now served by WEWAHITCHKA, FL [FL0159]. ICA: FL0152.

BOWLING GREEN—Comcast Cable, 3010 Herring Ave, Sebring, FL 33870. Phones: 941-371-6700; 800-266-2278. Web Site: http://www.comcast.com. ICA: FL0167.
TV Market Ranking: 28 (BOWLING GREEN). Franchise award date: September 9, 1986. Franchise expiration date: N.A. Began: N.A.
Channel capacity: 25 (not 2-way capable). Channels available but not in use: N.A.

Basic Service
Subscribers: 300.
Programming (received off-air): WEDU (PBS) Tampa; WFLA-TV (NBC) Tampa; WFTS-TV (ABC) Tampa; WKMG-TV (CBS) Orlando; WMOR-TV (IND) Lakeland; WTOG (CW) St. Petersburg; WTVT (FOX) Tampa; WUSF-TV (PBS) Tampa; WVEA-TV (UNV) Venice.
Programming (via satellite): ABC Family Channel; C-SPAN; Eternal Word TV Network; Hallmark Channel; History Channel; QVC; TBS Superstation; TV Guide Network; WGN America.
Fee: $34.95 installation; $27.95 monthly.

Expanded Basic Service 1
Subscribers: N.A.
Programming (via satellite): AMC; Animal Planet; Arts & Entertainment; CNBC; CNN; Comedy Central; Discovery Channel; Disney Channel; ESPN; ESPN 2; Fox Sports Net Florida; Headline News; Lifetime; MSNBC; MTV; Nickelodeon; Shop at Home; Spike TV; SunSports TV; Turner Classic Movies; Turner Network TV; USA Network; VH1; Weather Channel.

Pay Service 1
Pay Units: N.A.
Programming (via satellite): HBO (multiplexed); Showtime; The Movie Channel.

Pay-Per-View
iN DEMAND.

Internet Service
Operational: Yes.

Telephone Service
None
Miles of Plant: 15.0 (coaxial); None (fiber optic). Homes passed: 1,095.
General Manager: Geoff Shook.
City fee: 3% of gross.
Ownership: Comcast Cable Communications Inc. (MSO).

BRADENTON—Bright House Networks, 5413 E State Rd 64, Bradenton, FL 34208. Phones: 941-748-1822; 941-345-1019 (Broadband technical support); 941-746-3816 (Administrative office). Fax: 941-345-1321. E-mail: tampabay.mancustsrv@mybrighthouse.com. Web Site: http://tampabay.brighthouse.com. Also serves Anna Maria, Bradenton Beach, Ellenton, Holmes Beach, Manatee County, Palmetto, Parrish & Terra Ceia. ICA: FL0019.
TV Market Ranking: 28 (Anna Maria, BRADENTON, Bradenton Beach, Ellenton, Holmes Beach, Manatee County (portions), Palmetto, Parrish, Terra Ceia); Below 100 (Manatee County (portions)). Franchise award date: N.A. Franchise expiration date: N.A. Began: December 1, 1969.
Channel capacity: N.A. Channels available but not in use: N.A.

Basic Service
Subscribers: 97,782.
Programming (received off-air): WCLF (IND) Clearwater; WEDU (PBS) Tampa; WFLA-TV (NBC) Tampa; WMOR-TV (IND) Lakeland; WTOG (CW) St. Petersburg; WTSP (CBS) St. Petersburg; WTTA (MNT) St. Petersburg; WTVT (FOX) Tampa; WUSF-TV (PBS) Tampa; WVEA-TV (UNV) Venice; WWSB (ABC) Sarasota; WXPX-TV (ION) Bradenton.
Programming (via satellite): Bay News 9; C-SPAN; History Channel; Home Shopping Network; Promoter; QVC; Shop at Home; ShopNBC; TBS Superstation; TV Guide Network; WFTT-DT (TEL) Tampa; WGN America.
Fee: $26.62 installation; $16.95 monthly.

Expanded Basic Service 1
Subscribers: 82,000.
Programming (via satellite): ABC Family Channel; AMC; Animal Planet; Arts & Entertainment; BET Networks; Bravo; Cartoon Network; Catch 47; CNBC; CNN; Comedy Central; Country Music TV; C-SPAN 2; Discovery Channel; Discovery Health Channel; Disney Channel; E! Entertainment Television; ESPN; ESPN 2; ESPN Classic Sports; Food Network; Fox News Channel; Fox Sports Net; FX; Golf Channel; Hallmark Channel; Headline News; HGTV; Lifetime; Lifetime Movie Network; MoviePlex; MSNBC; MTV; National Geographic Channel; Nickelodeon; Oxygen; Spike TV; SunSports TV; Syfy; Telemundo; The Learning Channel; Travel Channel; truTV; Turner Classic Movies; Turner Network TV; TV Land; USA Network; Versus; VH1; WE tv; Weather Channel.
Fee: $46.45 monthly.

Digital Basic Service
Subscribers: 22,000.
Programming (received off-air): WEDU (PBS) Tampa; WFTS-TV (ABC) Tampa; WTVT (FOX) Tampa.
Programming (via satellite): AmericanLife TV Network; America's Store; Bay News 9 Espanol; BBC America; BBC America On Demand; Bio; Black Family Channel; Bloomberg Television; Cooking Channel; C-SPAN 3; Current; Discovery Digital Networks; Discovery HD Theater; Disney Channel; Do-It-Yourself; Do-It-Yourself On Demand; ESPN; ESPNews; Eternal Word TV Network; Fine Living On Demand; FitTV; Flix; Florida Channel; Food Network On Demand; Fox College Sports Atlantic; Fox College Sports Central; Fox College Sports Pacific; Fox Soccer; Fuel TV; Fuse; G4; GAS; Great American Country; Great American Country On Demand; GSN; HDNet; HDNet Movies; HGTV On Demand; History Channel International; INHD; INHD2; Lifetime Real Women; Military History Channel; MTV2; Music Choice; National Geographic Channel On Demand; NBA TV; Nick Jr.; NickToons TV; Outdoor Channel; Ovation; Science Television; Sleuth; SoapNet; Speed Channel; Speed On Demand; Style Network; Sundance Channel; Tampa Bay On Demand; Tennis Channel; Toon Disney; Trinity Broadcasting Network; Turner Network TV HD; TV One; Universal HD; various Mexican stations; VH1 Classic.
Fee: $11.95 monthly.

Digital Pay Service 1
Pay Units: N.A.
Programming (via satellite): Cinemax (multiplexed); HBO; HBO (multiplexed); Showtime (multiplexed); Showtime HD; Starz (multiplexed); The Movie Channel (multiplexed).
Fee: $7.95 monthly; $6.95 converter.

Digital Pay Service 2
Pay Units: N.A.
Programming (via satellite): Fox Movie Channel; The New Encore.

Video-On-Demand: No

Pay-Per-View
Addressable homes: 22,000.
iN DEMAND; Movies (delivered digitally); Shorteez (delivered digitally); Playboy TV (delivered digitally); Pleasure (delivered digitally).

Internet Service
Operational: Yes.
Subscribers: 26,100.
Broadband Service: Road Runner.
Fee: $29.95 monthly.

Telephone Service
Digital: Operational
Fee: $49.95 monthly
Miles of Plant: 1,570.0 (coaxial); 415.0 (fiber optic). Additional miles planned: 40.0 (coaxial); 10.0 (fiber optic). Homes passed: 145,000. Total homes in franchised area: 145,000.
Division President: Kevin Hyman. Vice President, Engineering: Gene White. General Manager: Rosemary Carlson. Senior Technical Director: Rick Hoffmeister. Marketing Director: Gretchen Adams. Customer Service Director: Dorothy Stephens.
County fee: 3% of gross. City fee: 4% of gross.
Ownership: Bright House Networks LLC (MSO).

BRADENTON—Florida Cable, PO Box 498, 23748 State Rd 40, Astor, FL 32102-0498. Phone: 352-759-2788. Fax: 352-759-3577. Web Site: http://www.floridacable.com. ICA: FL0348.
TV Market Ranking: Below 100 (BRADENTON). Franchise award date: N.A. Franchise expiration date: N.A. Began: N.A.
Channel capacity: 65 (not 2-way capable). Channels available but not in use: 11.

Basic Service
Subscribers: 235.
Programming (received off-air): WCJB-TV (ABC, CW) Gainesville; WEDU (PBS) Tampa; WFLA-TV (NBC) Tampa; WFTS-TV (ABC) Tampa; WMOR-TV (IND) Lakeland; WOGX (FOX) Ocala; WTOG (CW) St. Petersburg; WTSP (CBS) St. Petersburg; WTTA (MNT) St. Petersburg; WTVT (FOX) Tampa; WUFT (PBS) Gainesville; WVEA-TV (UNV) Venice.
Programming (via satellite): ABC Family Channel; Animal Planet; Arts & Entertainment; CNN; Comedy Central; Country Music TV; C-SPAN; C-SPAN 2; Discovery Channel; Disney Channel; E! Entertainment Television; ESPN; ESPN 2; Eternal Word TV Network; FX; Hallmark Channel; Headline News; HGTV; History Channel; Home Shopping Network; Lifetime; MTV; Nickelodeon; Spike TV; Syfy; TBS Superstation; The Learning Channel; Travel Channel; Trinity Broadcasting Network; truTV; Turner Classic Movies; Turner Network TV; TV Land; USA Network; VH1; Weather Channel; WGN America.
Fee: $29.95 installation; $29.95 monthly.

Pay Service 1
Pay Units: 25.
Programming (via satellite): Cinemax.
Fee: $10.95 monthly.

Pay Service 2
Pay Units: 14.
Programming (via satellite): Showtime.
Fee: $10.95 monthly.

Pay Service 3
Pay Units: 46.
Programming (via satellite): HBO.
Fee: $10.95 monthly.

Video-On-Demand: No

Internet Service
Operational: No.

Telephone Service
None
Miles of Plant: 45.0 (coaxial); None (fiber optic). Homes passed: 990.
General Manager: Jim Pierce. Plant Manager: Larry English. Office Manager: Alita Dawson.
Ownership: Florida Cable Inc. (MSO).

BRADENTON—Formerly served by Sprint Corp. No longer in operation. ICA: FL0301.

BRADENTON (unincorporated areas)—Universal Cablevision Inc., 4440 26th St W, Bradenton, FL 34207. Phone: 941-756-5460. Fax: 941-756-5460. E-mail: cabletv.providers@verizon.net. ICA: FL0215.
TV Market Ranking: 28 (BRADENTON). Franchise award date: N.A. Franchise expiration date: N.A. Began: September 1, 1990.
Channel capacity: 62 (not 2-way capable). Channels available but not in use: 17.

Basic Service
Subscribers: 852.
Programming (received off-air): various Mexican stations; WCLF (IND) Clearwater; WEDU (PBS) Tampa; WFLA-TV (NBC) Tampa; WFTS-TV (ABC) Tampa; WFTT-DT (TEL) Tampa; WTOG (CW) St. Petersburg; WTSP (CBS) St. Petersburg; WTTA (MNT) St. Petersburg; WTVT (FOX) Tampa; WUSF-TV (PBS) Tampa; WWSB (ABC) Sarasota; WXPX-TV (ION) Bradenton.
Programming (via satellite): QVC; TBS Superstation; WGN America.
Current originations: Public Access.
Fee: $35.00 installation; $16.20 monthly; $2.50 converter.

Expanded Basic Service 1
Subscribers: 650.
Programming (received off-air): WMOR-TV (IND) Lakeland.
Programming (via satellite): ABC Family Channel; AMC; Animal Planet; Arts & Entertainment; CNBC; CNN; Comedy Central; Country Music TV; C-SPAN; Discovery Channel; E! Entertainment Television; ESPN; ESPN 2; Flix; Food Network; Hallmark Channel; Headline News; HGTV; History Channel; Home Shopping Network; Lifetime; MTV; Nickelodeon; Spike TV; Syfy; The Learning Channel; Travel Channel; Turner Network TV; TV Land; USA Network; VH1; Weather Channel.
Fee: $25.00 monthly.

Pay Service 1
Pay Units: 35.
Programming (via satellite): HBO.
Fee: $10.00 installation; $9.16 monthly.

Pay Service 2
Pay Units: 19.
Programming (via satellite): Showtime.
Fee: $7.59 monthly.

Pay Service 3
Pay Units: 18.
Programming (via satellite): Cinemax.
Fee: $7.58 monthly.
Video-On-Demand: No
Internet Service
Operational: No.
Telephone Service
None
Miles of Plant: 6.0 (coaxial); None (fiber optic). Additional miles planned: 10.0 (coaxial).
Manager & Chief Technician: David Manny. Office Coordinator: Jo Hunley.
City fee: 5% of gross.
Ownership: Universal Cablevision Inc.

BRANDON (northern portion)—Comcast Cable, 8130 County Rd 44, Leg A, Leesburg, FL 34788. Phones: 888-255-5789 (Jacksonville); 352-787-9601 (Leesburg office). Fax: 352-365-6279. Web Site: http://www.comcast.com. Also serves Plant City (unincorporated areas). ICA: FL0085.
TV Market Ranking: 28 (BRANDON, Plant City (unincorporated areas)). Franchise award date: June 1, 1988. Franchise expiration date: N.A. Began: September 16, 1988.
Channel capacity: N.A. Channels available but not in use: N.A.
Basic Service
Subscribers: 3,937.
Programming (received off-air): WCLF (IND) Clearwater; WEDU (PBS) Tampa; WFLA-TV (NBC) Tampa; WFTS-TV (ABC) Tampa; WMOR-TV (IND) Lakeland; WTOG (CW) St. Petersburg; WTSP (CBS) St. Petersburg; WTVT (FOX) Tampa; WUSF-TV (PBS) Tampa; WXPX-TV (ION) Bradenton.
Programming (via satellite): Home Shopping Network; WGN America.
Fee: $16.11 monthly.
Expanded Basic Service 1
Subscribers: N.A.
Programming (via satellite): ABC Family Channel; AMC; Animal Planet; Arts & Entertainment; BET Networks; Cartoon Network; CNBC; CNN; Comedy Central; Country Music TV; C-SPAN; C-SPAN 2; Discovery Channel; Disney Channel; E! Entertainment Television; ESPN; ESPN 2; Food Network; Fox News Channel; Fox Sports Net Florida; FX; Hallmark Channel; Headline News; HGTV; History Channel; Lifetime; MSNBC; MTV; Nickelodeon; Spike TV; Style Network; SunSports TV; Syfy; TBS Superstation; The Learning Channel; Travel Channel; truTV; Turner Classic Movies; Turner Network TV; TV Guide Network; TV Land; USA Network; VH1; Weather Channel.
Fee: $43.95 monthly.
Digital Basic Service
Subscribers: N.A.
Programming (via satellite): AmericanLife TV Network; BBC America; Bio; Bloomberg Television; Discovery Digital Networks; Do-It-Yourself; ESPN Classic Sports; FitTV; Fox Movie Channel; Fox Sports Net; Fuse; G4; Golf Channel; GSN; Halogen Network; History Channel International; National Geographic Channel; Nick Jr.; NickToons TV; Outdoor Channel; SoapNet; Speed Channel; Toon Disney; Trinity Broadcasting Network; Versus; VH1 Classic; VH1 Country; WE tv.
Fee: $19.95 monthly.
Digital Expanded Basic Service
Subscribers: N.A.
Programming (via satellite): DMX Music.
Digital Pay Service 1
Pay Units: N.A.
Programming (via satellite): Cinemax (multiplexed); Encore (multiplexed); HBO (multiplexed); Showtime (multiplexed); The Movie Channel (multiplexed).
Video-On-Demand: Planned
Pay-Per-View
HITS PPV 1-6 (delivered digitally); Playboy (delivered digitally); Hot Network (delivered digitally); Spice (delivered digitally).
Internet Service
Operational: Yes. Began: January 1, 2005.
Broadband Service: Comcast High Speed Internet.
Fee: $42.95 monthly.
Telephone Service
None
Miles of Plant: 223.0 (coaxial); None (fiber optic). Homes passed: 12,426. Total homes in franchised area: 12,426.
Vice President & General Manager: Mike Davenport. Chief Engineer: Sean Curley. Marketing Manager: Melanie Melvin.
Ownership: Comcast Cable Communications Inc. (MSO).

BRANFORD—CommuniComm Services, 17774 NW US Highway 441, High Springs, FL 32643-8749. Phone: 386-454-2299. Fax: 386-454-3705. Web Site: http://www.communicomm.com. Also serves Suwannee County. ICA: FL0197.
TV Market Ranking: Below 100 (BRANFORD, Suwannee County). Franchise award date: N.A. Franchise expiration date: N.A. Began: August 1, 1969.
Channel capacity: N.A. Channels available but not in use: N.A.
Basic Service
Subscribers: N.A. Included in High Springs
Programming (received off-air): WACX (IND) Leesburg; WCJB-TV (ABC, CW) Gainesville; WCWJ (CW) Jacksonville; WJXT (IND) Jacksonville; WOGX (FOX) Ocala; WTLV (NBC) Jacksonville; WUFT (PBS) Gainesville.
Programming (via satellite): QVC; Trinity Broadcasting Network; TV Guide Network.
Fee: $50.00 installation; $31.00 monthly; $3.52 converter.
Expanded Basic Service 1
Subscribers: N.A.
Programming (via satellite): ABC Family Channel; AMC; Animal Planet; Arts & Entertainment; BET Networks; Cartoon Network; CNBC; CNN; Comedy Central; Country Music TV; C-SPAN; Discovery Channel; Disney Channel; Do-It-Yourself; ESPN; ESPN 2; ESPN Classic Sports; ESPNews; Food Network; Fox News Channel; FX; Hallmark Channel; Headline News; HGTV; History Channel; ION Television; Lifetime; MTV; Nick Jr.; Nickelodeon; Outdoor Channel; ShopNBC; Speed Channel; Spike TV; SunSports TV; Syfy; TBS Superstation; The Learning Channel; Travel Channel; truTV; Turner Network TV; TV Land; Univision; USA Network; VH1; Weather Channel.
Digital Basic Service
Subscribers: N.A.
Programming (via satellite): BBC America; Bloomberg Television; Bravo; CMT Pure Country; Discovery Health Channel; Discovery Kids Channel; Discovery Military Channel; Discovery Planet Green; DMX Music; FitTV; Fox Movie Channel; Fox Soccer; G4; Golf Channel; GSN; Halogen Network; ID Investigation Discovery; Independent Film Channel; National Geographic Channel; NickToons TV; Science Channel; SoapNet; Turner Classic Movies; Versus; VH1 Classic; WE tv.
Pay Service 1
Pay Units: N.A. Included in High Springs
Programming (via satellite): Cinemax; Encore; HBO; Starz.
Fee: $30.00 installation; $9.95 monthly (Cinemax), $11.95 monthly (HBO).
Digital Pay Service 1
Pay Units: N.A.
Programming (via satellite): Cinemax (multiplexed); Encore (multiplexed); HBO (multiplexed); Starz (multiplexed).
Video-On-Demand: No
Pay-Per-View
iN DEMAND (delivered digitally); Club Jenna (delivered digitally); Fresh (delivered digitally); Playboy TV (delivered digitally).
Internet Service
Operational: Yes.
Broadband Service: Net Commander.
Fee: $39.95 installation; $51.95 monthly.
Telephone Service
None
Total homes in franchised area: 424. Homes passed and miles of plant included in High Springs
General Manager: Darrell Laird. Chief Technician: Michael Smith. Customer Service Manager: Cindy Ross.
City fee: 3% of gross.
Ownership: James Cable LLC (MSO).

BRATT—Formerly served by CableSouth Inc. No longer in operation. ICA: FL0184.

BRIGHTON SEMINOLE RESERVE—Comcast Cable, 141 NW 16th St, Pompano Beach, FL 33060. Phone: 954-252-1937. Fax: 954-532-7256. Web Site: http://www.comcast.com. ICA: FL0314.
TV Market Ranking: Outside TV Markets (BRIGHTON SEMINOLE RESERVE). Franchise award date: N.A. Franchise expiration date: N.A. Began: November 1, 1991.
Channel capacity: 19 (not 2-way capable). Channels available but not in use: None.
Basic Service
Subscribers: N.A. Included in Miami
Programming (received off-air): WBBH-TV (NBC) Fort Myers; WFTX-TV (FOX) Cape Coral; WGCU (PBS) Fort Myers; WINK-TV (CBS) Fort Myers; WZVN-TV (ABC) Naples.
Programming (via satellite): ABC Family Channel; Arts & Entertainment; CNN; Discovery Channel; Disney Channel; ESPN; Spike TV; TBS Superstation.
Fee: $14.95 monthly.
Pay Service 1
Pay Units: N.A.
Programming (via satellite): HBO; Showtime.
Fee: $10.00 monthly (each).
Video-On-Demand: No
Internet Service
Operational: No.
Telephone Service
None
Miles of Plant: 3.0 (coaxial); None (fiber optic). Homes passed: 150.
Vice President & General Manager: Rick Seamon. Technical Operations Director: Ross Pappas.
Ownership: Comcast Cable Communications Inc. (MSO).

BRONSON—Florida Cable, PO Box 498, 23748 State Rd 40, Astor, FL 32102-0498. Phones: 800-779-2788; 352-759-2788. Fax: 352-759-3777. E-mail: support@floridacable.com. Web Site: http://www.floridacable.com. Also serves Levy County. ICA: FL0169.
TV Market Ranking: Below 100 (BRONSON, Levy County). Franchise award date: June 9, 1985. Franchise expiration date: N.A. Began: July 1, 1988.
Channel capacity: 36 (not 2-way capable). Channels available but not in use: None.
Basic Service
Subscribers: 364.
Programming (received off-air): WCJB-TV (ABC, CW) Gainesville; WGFL (CBS, MNT) High Springs; WOGX (FOX) Ocala; WUFT (PBS) Gainesville.
Programming (via satellite): ABC Family Channel; Arts & Entertainment; Cartoon Network; CNN; Comedy Central; Discovery Channel; Disney Channel; E! Entertainment Television; ESPN; ESPN 2; Food Network; Fox News Channel; Fuse; FX; Great American Country; Headline News; Home Shopping Network; Lifetime; Speed Channel; Syfy; TBS Superstation; The Learning Channel; Toon Disney; Turner Classic Movies; Turner Network TV; USA Network; Weather Channel; WGN America; WNBC (NBC) New York.
Programming (via translator): WACX (IND) Leesburg.
Fee: $39.45 monthly.
Pay Service 1
Pay Units: 90.
Programming (via satellite): Cinemax; HBO; Showtime; The Movie Channel.
Fee: $10.95 monthly (each).
Internet Service
Operational: No, Both DSL & dial-up.
Telephone Service
None
Miles of Plant: 49.0 (coaxial); None (fiber optic). Homes passed: 977.
General Manager: Jim Pierce. Plant Manager: Larry English. Office Manager: Alita Dawson.
Ownership: Florida Cable Inc. (MSO).

BROOKER—New River Cablevision Inc., PO Box 128, 11401 SW State Rd 231, Brooker, FL 32622. Phone: 352-485-1362. Fax: 352-485-1352. E-mail: tamralindsey@alltel.net. Also serves Worthington Springs. ICA: FL0196.
TV Market Ranking: Below 100 (BROOKER, Worthington Springs). Franchise award date: January 1, 1989. Franchise expiration date: N.A. Began: N.A.
Channel capacity: 54 (2-way capable). Channels available but not in use: 16.
Basic Service
Subscribers: 234.
Programming (received off-air): WCJB-TV (ABC, CW) Gainesville; WGFL (CBS, MNT) High Springs; WJXT (IND) Jacksonville; WOGX (FOX) Ocala; WTEV-TV (CBS) Jacksonville; WTLV (NBC) Jacksonville; WUFT (PBS) Gainesville.
Programming (via satellite): ABC Family Channel; AMC; Arts & Entertainment; CNN; Country Music TV; Discovery Channel; Disney Channel; ESPN; ESPN 2; Headline News; History Channel; INSP; Lifetime; Nickelodeon; Spike TV; Syfy; TBS Superstation; The Learning Channel; Trinity Broadcasting Network; Turner Network TV; TV Land; USA Network; VH1; Weather Channel.
Fee: $24.95 installation; $21.69 monthly.
Pay Service 1
Pay Units: 67.
Programming (via satellite): HBO.
Fee: $9.95 monthly.
Pay Service 2
Pay Units: 42.
Programming (via satellite): Showtime.

Fee: $9.95 monthly.
Video-On-Demand: No
Internet Service
Operational: No.
Telephone Service
None
Miles of Plant: 25.0 (coaxial); None (fiber optic). Homes passed: 574. Total homes in franchised area: 900.
Manager & Chief Technician: Mike McCoy.
Ownership: New River Cablevision Inc.

BROWARD COUNTY—Comcast Cable, 141 NW 16th St, Pompano Beach, FL 33060. Phone: 954-252-1937. Fax: 954-532-7256. Web Site: http://www.comcast.com. Also serves Bonaventure, Coconut Creek, Cooper City, Dania, Davie, Deerfield Beach, Fort Lauderdale, Hallandale, Hillsboro Beach, Hollywood, Hollywood Seminole Reserve, Lauderdale Lakes, Lauderdale-by-the-Sea, Lauderhill, Lazy Lake, Lighthouse Point, Margate, Miramar, North Lauderdale, Oakland Park, Parkland, Pembroke Park, Pembroke Pines, Plantation, Pompano Beach, Sea Ranch Lakes, Sunrise, Tamarac, Wilton Manors & Wynmoor Village. ICA: FL0016.
TV Market Ranking: 21 (Bonaventure, BROWARD COUNTY (portions), Coconut Creek, Cooper City, Dania, Davie, Fort Lauderdale, Hallandale, Hollywood, Lauderdale Lakes, Lauderdale-by-the-Sea, Lauderhill, Lazy Lake, Margate, Miramar, North Lauderdale, Oakland Park, Parkland, Pembroke Park, Pembroke Pines, Plantation, Pompano Beach, Sea Ranch Lakes, Sunrise, Tamarac, Wilton Manors, Wynmoor Village); Below 100 (Deerfield Beach, Hillsboro Beach, Lighthouse Point, BROWARD COUNTY (portions)); Outside TV Markets (Hollywood Seminole Reserve, BROWARD COUNTY (portions)). Franchise award date: October 1, 1983. Franchise expiration date: N.A. Began: May 1, 1975.
Channel capacity: N.A. Channels available but not in use: N.A.
Basic Service
Subscribers: N.A. Included in Miami
Programming (received off-air): WAMI-DT (TEL) Hollywood; WBFS-TV (MNT) Miami; WFOR-TV (CBS) Miami; WHFT-TV (TBN) Miami; WLRN-TV (PBS) Miami; WLTV-DT (UNV) Miami; WPBT (PBS) Miami; WPLG (ABC) Miami; WPXM-TV (ION) Miami; WSBS-TV (IND) Key West; WSCV (TMO) Fort Lauderdale; WSFL-TV (CW) Miami; WSVN (FOX) Miami; WTVJ (NBC) Miami; WXEL-TV (PBS) West Palm Beach; 25 FMs.
Programming (via satellite): C-SPAN; C-SPAN 2; QVC; TV Guide Network; WGN America.
Current originations: Leased Access; Religious Access; Government Access; Educational Access; Public Access.
Fee: $45.00 installation; $13.00 monthly; $15.00 additional installation.
Expanded Basic Service 1
Subscribers: N.A.
Programming (via satellite): ABC Family Channel; AMC; Animal Planet; Arts & Entertainment; BET Networks; Bravo; Cartoon Network; CNBC; CNN; Comcast/Charter Sports Southeast (CSS); Comedy Central; Discovery Channel; Disney Channel; E! Entertainment Television; ESPN; ESPN 2; Food Network; Fox News Channel; Fox Sports Net Florida; FX; Golf Channel; Great American Country; GSN; Hallmark Channel; Headline News; HGTV; History Channel; Home Shopping Network; Lifetime; MSNBC; MTV; Nickelodeon; Speed Channel; Spike TV; Style Network; Syfy; TBS Superstation; The Learning Channel; Travel Channel; truTV; Turner Network TV; TV Land; USA Network; Versus; VH1; Weather Channel.
Fee: $39.95 monthly.
Digital Basic Service
Subscribers: N.A.
Programming (received off-air): WTVJ (NBC) Miami.
Programming (via satellite): BBC America; Bio; Bloomberg Television; Canales N; Cooking Channel; Discovery Digital Networks; Discovery HD Theater; Do-It-Yourself; Encore; ESPN; ESPNews; Eternal Word TV Network; FitTV; Flix; Fox Movie Channel; Fox Soccer; G4; GAS; History Channel International; International Television (ITV); Lifetime Movie Network; Lime; MTV Networks Digital Suite; Music Choice; National Geographic Channel; NFL Network; NickToons TV; Ovation; Sundance Channel; The Word Network; Toon Disney; Turner Classic Movies; WAM! America's Kidz Network; WE tv; WFOR-TV (CBS) Miami; WPBT (PBS) Miami; WPLG (ABC) Miami; WSVN (FOX) Miami.
Fee: $11.95 monthly.
Digital Expanded Basic Service
Subscribers: N.A.
Programming (via satellite): Black Family Channel; ESPN Classic Sports; Fox College Sports Atlantic; Fox College Sports Central; Fox College Sports Pacific; Halogen Network; Jewelry Television; Nick Jr.; Outdoor Channel; ShopNBC.
Fee: $5.00 monthly.
Pay Service 1
Pay Units: 25,367.
Programming (via satellite): HBO.
Fee: $15.99 monthly.
Digital Pay Service 1
Pay Units: 4,008.
Programming (via satellite): Cinemax (multiplexed); HBO (multiplexed); Showtime (multiplexed); Starz (multiplexed); The Movie Channel (multiplexed).
Video-On-Demand: Yes
Pay-Per-View
Addressable homes: 74,479.
Addressable: Yes; iN DEMAND (delivered digitally); Playboy TV (delivered digitally); Fresh (delivered digitally); Shorteez (delivered digitally); Sports PPV (delivered digitally).
Internet Service
Operational: Yes.
Broadband Service: Comcast High Speed Internet.
Fee: $42.95 monthly; $10.00 modem lease.
Telephone Service
Digital: Operational
Miles of Plant: 5,000.0 (coaxial); None (fiber optic). Homes passed: 715,000.
Vice President & General Manager: Rick Seamon. Vice President, Regional Marketing: David Lucoff. Technical Operations Director: Ross Pappas. Government & Community Relations Manager: Cindy Stoddart. Public Relations Director: Spero Canton.
City fee: 3% of gross.
Ownership: Comcast Cable Communications Inc. (MSO).

CALLAHAN—Comcast Cable. Now served by HILLIARD, FL [FL0157]. ICA: FL0128.

CAMPBELLTON—Campbellton Cable TV, PO Box 80, Siloam, NC 27047-0080. Phone: 850-263-1442. Fax: 850-263-1442. ICA: FL0323.
TV Market Ranking: Outside TV Markets (CAMPBELLTON). Franchise award date: November 11, 1991. Franchise expiration date: N.A. Began: February 1, 1993.
Channel capacity: 60 (not 2-way capable). Channels available but not in use: 44.
Basic Service
Subscribers: 40.
Programming (received off-air): WDHN (ABC) Dothan; WFSU-TV (PBS) Tallahassee; WJHG-TV (CW, MNT, NBC) Panama City; WPGX (FOX) Panama City; WTVY (CBS, CW, MNT) Dothan.
Programming (via satellite): ABC Family Channel; BET Networks; CNN; ESPN; TBS Superstation; Trinity Broadcasting Network; Turner Network TV; USA Network; WGN America.
Fee: $25.00 installation; $13.50 monthly.
Pay Service 1
Pay Units: 24.
Programming (via satellite): HBO.
Fee: $11.00 monthly.
Internet Service
Operational: No.
Miles of Plant: 5.0 (coaxial); None (fiber optic). Homes passed: 139. Total homes in franchised area: 180.
General Manager: Dale Norman.
Ownership: Norman & Associates Inc. (MSO).

CANTONMENT—Bright House Networks, 151 London Pkwy, Birmingham, AL 35211-4541. Phones: 850-968-6959; 800-866-2061; 205-290-1300. Fax: 850-968-2550. Web Site: http://panhandle.brighthouse.com. Also serves Cottage Hills, Escambia County & Molina. ICA: FL0090.
TV Market Ranking: 59 (CANTONMENT, Cottage Hills, Escambia County (portions), Molina); Outside TV Markets (Escambia County (portions)). Franchise award date: February 1, 1987. Franchise expiration date: N.A. Began: May 1, 1987.
Channel capacity: N.A. Channels available but not in use: N.A.
Basic Service
Subscribers: 6,276.
Programming (received off-air): WALA-TV (FOX) Mobile; WEAR-TV (ABC) Pensacola; WHBR (IND) Pensacola; WJTC (IND) Pensacola; WKRG-TV (CBS) Mobile; WMPV-TV (TBN) Mobile; WPAN (IND) Fort Walton Beach; WPMI-TV (NBC) Mobile; WSRE (PBS) Pensacola.
Programming (via satellite): ABC Family Channel; AMC; Animal Planet; Arts & Entertainment; BET Networks; Cartoon Network; CNBC; CNN; Comedy Central; Country Music TV; C-SPAN; C-SPAN 2; Discovery Channel; Disney Channel; E! Entertainment Television; ESPN; ESPN 2; Eternal Word TV Network; Food Network; Fox News Channel; FX; Hallmark Channel; Headline News; HGTV; History Channel; Home Shopping Network; Lifetime; MSNBC; MTV; National Geographic Channel; Nickelodeon; Oxygen; QVC; Spike TV; SunSports TV; Syfy; TBS Superstation; The Learning Channel; Travel Channel; truTV; Turner Network TV; USA Network; VH1; WE tv; Weather Channel.
Fee: $53.75 installation; $42.00 monthly; $17.90 additional installation.
Digital Basic Service
Subscribers: 1,920.
Programming (via satellite): AmericanLife TV Network; BBC America; Bloomberg Television; Discovery Digital Networks; DMX Music; ESPN Classic Sports; ESPN Now; ESPNews; Fox Sports World; G4; GAS; Golf Channel; GSN; MTV2; Nick Jr.; Outdoor Channel; Ovation; Speed Channel; Toon Disney; Turner Classic Movies; Versus; VH1 Classic.
Fee: $13.00 monthly.
Digital Pay Service 1
Pay Units: N.A.
Programming (via satellite): Cinemax (multiplexed); Encore (multiplexed); Fox Movie Channel; HBO (multiplexed); Independent Film Channel; Showtime (multiplexed); Starz (multiplexed); Sundance Channel; The Movie Channel (multiplexed).
Fee: $10.50 monthly (each).
Video-On-Demand: Yes
Pay-Per-View
Hot Choice (delivered digitally); iN DEMAND (delivered digitally); Fresh (delivered digitally); Shorteez (delivered digitally); Sports PPV (delivered digitally).
Internet Service
Operational: Yes.
Broadband Service: Road Runner.
Fee: $29.95 monthly.
Telephone Service
Digital: Operational
Fee: $39.95 monthly
Miles of Plant: 410.0 (coaxial); None (fiber optic). Additional miles planned: 30.0 (coaxial). Homes passed: 10,720. Total homes in franchised area: 10,720.
Marketing Director: Nicole Hardy. Chief Technician: Ed Harrison.
Ownership: Bright House Networks LLC (MSO).

CAPE CORAL—Time Warner Cable. Now served by NAPLES, FL [FL0029]. ICA: FL0039.

CAPE SAN BLAS—Mediacom. Now served by WEWAHITCHKA, FL [FL0159]. ICA: FL0206.

CEDAR KEY—Bright House Networks, 2600 McCormick Dr, Ste 255, Clearwater, FL 33759-1070. Phone: 727-791-7730. Fax: 727-791-8201. Web Site: http://tampabay.brighthouse.com. ICA: FL0190.
TV Market Ranking: Outside TV Markets (CEDAR KEY). Franchise award date: September 1, 1977. Franchise expiration date: N.A. Began: September 1, 1977.
Channel capacity: N.A. Channels available but not in use: N.A.
Basic Service
Subscribers: 600.
Programming (received off-air): WCLF (IND) Clearwater; WEDU (PBS) Tampa; WFLA-TV (NBC) Tampa; WFTS-TV (ABC) Tampa; WFTT-DT (TEL) Tampa; WMOR-TV (IND) Lakeland; WTOG (CW) St. Petersburg; WTSP (CBS) St. Petersburg; WTTA (MNT) St. Petersburg; WTVT (FOX) Tampa; WUSF-TV (PBS) Tampa; WVEA-TV (UNV) Venice; WXPX-TV (ION) Bradenton.
Programming (via satellite): Bay News 9; Home Shopping Network; QVC; ShopNBC; TV Guide Network; WGN America.
Fee: $34.95 installation; $18.50 monthly.
Expanded Basic Service 1
Subscribers: N.A.
Programming (via satellite): ABC Family Channel; AMC; Animal Planet; Arts & Entertainment; BET Networks; Bravo; Cartoon Network; Catch 47; CNBC; CNN; Comedy Central; Country Music TV; C-SPAN; C-SPAN 2; Discovery Channel; Discovery Health Channel; Disney Channel; ESPN; ESPN 2; ESPN Classic Sports; Eternal Word TV Network; Food Network; Fox News Channel; Fox Sports Net; FX; GalaVision; Golf Channel; Hallmark Channel; Headline News; HGTV; History

Channel; Lifetime; Lifetime Movie Network; MoviePlex; MSNBC; MTV; National Geographic Channel; Nickelodeon; Oxygen; ReacTV; Spike TV; SunSports TV; Syfy; TBS Superstation; The Learning Channel; Travel Channel; truTV; Turner Classic Movies; Turner Network TV; TV Land; USA Network; Versus; VH1; WE tv; Weather Channel.

Digital Basic Service

Subscribers: N.A.

Programming (received off-air): WEDU (PBS) Tampa; WFLA-TV (NBC) Tampa; WFTS-TV (ABC) Tampa; WMOR-TV (IND) Lakeland; WTOG (CW) St. Petersburg; WTSP (CBS) St. Petersburg; WTVT (FOX) Tampa; WUSF-TV (PBS) Tampa.

Programming (via satellite): AmericanLife TV Network; Arts & Entertainment HD; Bay News 9; BBC America; BBC America On Demand; Bio; Black Family Channel; Bloomberg Television; Canales N; Cooking Channel; C-SPAN 3; Current; Discovery Digital Networks; Discovery HD Theater; Disney Channel; Do-It-Yourself; Encore; ESPN HD; ESPNews; Eternal Word TV Network; Flix; Fox College Sports Atlantic; Fox College Sports Central; Fox College Sports Pacific; Fox Movie Channel; Fox Reality Channel; Fox Soccer; Fuel TV; Fuse; G4; GAS; Great American Country; Great American Country On Demand; GSN; HDNet; HDNet Movies; History Channel International; Howard TV; Independent Film Channel; INHD; Jewelry Television; Lifetime Real Women; LOGO; MTV Networks Digital Suite; Music Choice; National Geographic Channel On Demand; NBA TV; Nick Jr.; NickToons TV; Outdoor Channel; Ovation; Palladia; Sleuth; SoapNet; Speed Channel; Speed On Demand; Style Network; Sundance Channel; Tennis Channel; Toon Disney; Trinity Broadcasting Network; Turner Network TV HD; TV Guide SPOT; TV One; Universal HD.

Digital Pay Service 1

Pay Units: N.A.

Programming (via satellite): Cinemax (multiplexed); Cinemax On Demand; HBO (multiplexed); HBO HD; HBO On Demand; Showtime (multiplexed); Showtime HD; Showtime On Demand; Starz (multiplexed); The Movie Channel (multiplexed); The Movie Channel On Demand.

Pay-Per-View

iN DEMAND (delivered digitally); ESPN Gameplan (delivered digitally); Pleasure (delivered digitally); Playboy TV (delivered digitally); ESPN Full Court (delivered digitally); NBA League Pass (delivered digitally); NHL Center Ice (delivered digitally); MLS Direct Kick (delivered digitally).

Internet Service

Operational: No.

Telephone Service

None

Miles of Plant: 21.0 (coaxial); 1.0 (fiber optic). Homes passed: 963.

Division President: Kevin Hyman. Vice President, Engineering: Gene White. Chief Technician: Roger Carroll.

Ownership: Bright House Networks LLC (MSO).

CELEBRATION—Comcast Cable, 8130 County Rd 44, Leg A, Leesburg, FL 34788. Phone: 352-787-9601. Fax: 352-365-6279. Web Site: http://www.comcast.com. ICA: FL0334.

TV Market Ranking: 55 (CELEBRATION). Franchise award date: May 6, 1996. Franchise expiration date: N.A. Began: N.A.

Channel capacity: N.A. Channels available but not in use: N.A.

Basic Service

Subscribers: 72,940 Includes Debary, Leesburg, & Silver Springs Shores.

Programming (received off-air): WDSC-TV (PBS) New Smyrna Beach; WESH (NBC) Daytona Beach; WFTV (ABC) Orlando; WHLV-TV (IND) Cocoa; WKCF (CW) Clermont; WKMG-TV (CBS) Orlando; WMFE-TV (PBS) Orlando; WOFL (FOX) Orlando; WOPX-TV (ION) Melbourne; WOTF-DT (TEL) Melbourne; WRBW (MNT) Orlando; WRDQ (IND) Orlando; WTGL (ETV) Leesburg; WVEN-TV (UNV) Daytona Beach.

Programming (via satellite): C-SPAN 2; TV Guide Network; WGN America.

Current originations: Government Access.

Fee: $36.95 installation; $16.45 monthly.

Expanded Basic Service 1

Subscribers: N.A.

Programming (via satellite): ABC Family Channel; AMC; Animal Planet; Arts & Entertainment; BET Networks; Bravo; Cartoon Network; CNBC; CNN; Comcast/Charter Sports Southeast (CSS); Comedy Central; Country Music TV; C-SPAN; Discovery Channel; Discovery Health Channel; E! Entertainment Television; ESPN; ESPN 2; Eternal Word TV Network; Food Network; Fox News Channel; FX; Golf Channel; GSN; Hallmark Channel; Headline News; HGTV; History Channel; Home Shopping Network; Lifetime; MSNBC; MTV; Nickelodeon; QVC; Speed Channel; Spike TV; Style Network; SunSports TV; Syfy; TBS Superstation; The Learning Channel; Travel Channel; truTV; Turner Classic Movies; Turner Network TV; TV Land; USA Network; Versus; VH1; Weather Channel.

Fee: $45.05 monthly.

Digital Basic Service

Subscribers: N.A.

Programming (via satellite): BBC America; C-SPAN 3; Discovery Digital Networks; ESPNews; GAS; MTV Networks Digital Suite; National Geographic Channel; Nick Jr.; Nick Too; NickToons TV; SoapNet; Toon Disney; WAM! America's Kidz Network.

Fee: $14.95 monthly.

Pay Service 1

Pay Units: N.A.

Programming (via satellite): Cinemax (multiplexed); HBO (multiplexed); Showtime (multiplexed).

Fee: $10.00 monthly (each).

Digital Pay Service 1

Pay Units: N.A.

Programming (via satellite): Cinemax (multiplexed); Encore (multiplexed); Flix; HBO (multiplexed); Showtime (multiplexed); Starz (multiplexed); Sundance Channel (multiplexed); The Movie Channel (multiplexed).

Fee: $13.25 monthly (each).

Video-On-Demand: Planned

Pay-Per-View

Addressable homes: 156.

iN DEMAND (delivered digitally), Addressable: Yes; Hot Choice (delivered digitally); Playboy TV (delivered digitally); Fresh (delivered digitally); Shorteez (delivered digitally); Pleasure (delivered digitally).

Internet Service

Operational: Yes.

Subscribers: 18,031.

Broadband Service: Comcast High Speed Internet.

Fee: $42.95 monthly.

Telephone Service

Analog: Not Operational

Digital: Operational

Homes passed: 124,812. Homes passed includes Debary, Leesburg, & Silver Springs Shores

Vice President & General Manager: Mike Davenport. Chief Engineer: Sean Curley. Marketing Manager: Melanie Melvin.

Ownership: Comcast Cable Communications Inc. (MSO).

CENTURY—Bright House Networks, 240 Hwy 97 S, Cantonment, FL 32533. Phones: 850-968-6959; 800-866-2061. Fax: 850-892-1318. Web Site: http://panhandle.brighthouse.com. Also serves Flomaton, AL; Jay & Santa Rosa County (northern portion), FL. ICA: FL0217.

TV Market Ranking: 59 (Santa Rosa County (northern portion) (portions)); Outside TV Markets (CENTURY, Flomaton, Jay, Santa Rosa County (northern portion) (portions)). Franchise award date: N.A. Franchise expiration date: N.A. Began: March 1, 1983.

Channel capacity: 36 (operating 2-way). Channels available but not in use: None.

Basic Service

Subscribers: N.A.

Programming (received off-air): WALA-TV (FOX) Mobile; WEAR-TV (ABC) Pensacola; WHBR (IND) Pensacola; WJTC (IND) Pensacola; WKRG-TV (CBS) Mobile; WMPV-TV (TBN) Mobile; WPAN (IND) Fort Walton Beach; WPMI-TV (NBC) Mobile; WSRE (PBS) Pensacola.

Programming (via satellite): ABC Family Channel; AMC; Animal Planet; Arts & Entertainment; BET Networks; Cartoon Network; CNBC; CNN; Comedy Central; Country Music TV; C-SPAN; C-SPAN 2; Discovery Channel; Disney Channel; E! Entertainment Television; ESPN; ESPN 2; Eternal Word TV Network; Food Network; Fox News Channel; Fuse; FX; Hallmark Channel; Headline News; HGTV; History Channel; Home Shopping Network; Lifetime; Lifetime Movie Network; MSNBC; MTV; National Geographic Channel; Nickelodeon; NickToons TV; Oxygen; QVC; ShopNBC; Spike TV; Style Network; Syfy; TBS Superstation; The Learning Channel; Travel Channel; truTV; Turner Network TV; USA Network; Versus; VH1; WE tv; Weather Channel; WGN America.

Fee: $17.55 monthly.

Digital Basic Service

Subscribers: N.A.

Programming (via satellite): BBC America; Bio; Bloomberg Television; Bravo; Discovery Digital Networks; DMX Music; ESPN Classic Sports; ESPNews; Fox Movie Channel; Fox Sports World; G4; GAS; Golf Channel; GSN; History Channel International; MTV Networks Digital Suite; Nick Jr.; Outdoor Channel; Ovation; Speed Channel; Toon Disney; Turner Classic Movies; TV Land; VH1 Classic.

Digital Pay Service 1

Pay Units: N.A.

Programming (via satellite): Cinemax (multiplexed); Encore (multiplexed); HBO (multiplexed); Independent Film Channel; Showtime (multiplexed); Starz (multiplexed); Sundance Channel; The Movie Channel (multiplexed).

Video-On-Demand: No

Pay-Per-View

Hot Choice (delivered digitally); iN DEMAND (delivered digitally); Fresh (delivered digitally); Shorteez (delivered digitally); Sports PPV (delivered digitally).

Internet Service

Operational: Yes.

Broadband Service: RoadRunner.

Fee: $29.95 monthly.

Telephone Service

Digital: Operational

Fee: $39.95 monthly

Miles of Plant: 89.0 (coaxial); None (fiber optic). Total homes in franchised area: 2,000.

Marketing Director: Nicole Hardy. Chief Technician: Scott Horn.

Ownership: Bright House Networks LLC (MSO).

CHASEWOOD—Now served by PALM BEACH GARDENS, FL [FL0030]. ICA: FL0219.

CHATTAHOOCHEE—Bright House Networks, 94 Walton Rd, DeFuniak Springs, FL 32433. Phones: 800-288-1664; 727-791-7730. Fax: 850-892-1315. Web Site: http://panhandle.brighthouse.com. Also serves Gadsden County (portions). ICA: FL0151.

TV Market Ranking: Below 100 (CHATTAHOOCHEE, Gadsden County (portions)). Franchise award date: N.A. Franchise expiration date: N.A. Began: February 1, 1971.

Channel capacity: N.A. Channels available but not in use: N.A.

Basic Service

Subscribers: 802.

Programming (received off-air): WCTV (CBS, MNT) Thomasville; WFSU-TV (PBS) Tallahassee; WJHG-TV (CW, MNT, NBC) Panama City; WMBB (ABC) Panama City; WTLH (CW, FOX) Bainbridge; WTVY (CBS, CW, MNT) Dothan; WTWC-TV (NBC) Tallahassee; WTXL-TV (ABC) Tallahassee.

Programming (via satellite): ABC Family Channel; AMC; Animal Planet; Arts & Entertainment; BET Networks; Bravo; Cartoon Network; CNBC; CNN; Country Music TV; C-SPAN; Discovery Channel; Disney Channel; E! Entertainment Television; ESPN; ESPN 2; Food Network; Fox News Channel; FX; Hallmark Channel; Headline News; HGTV; History Channel; Home Shopping Network; Lifetime; Lifetime Movie Network; MSNBC; MTV; National Geographic Channel; Nickelodeon; Oxygen; QVC; ShopNBC; Spike TV; SunSports TV; Syfy; TBS Superstation; The Learning Channel; Travel Channel; Trinity Broadcasting Network; Turner Network TV; USA Network; VH1; WE tv; Weather Channel; WGN America.

Fee: $53.75 installation; $44.35 monthly; $17.90 additional installation.

Digital Basic Service

Subscribers: N.A.

Programming (via satellite): AmericanLife TV Network; BBC America; Bloomberg Television; Discovery Digital Networks; DMX Music; ESPN Classic Sports; ESPN Now; ESPNews; FitTV; Fox Sports World; G4; GAS; Golf Channel; GSN; MTV2; Nick Jr.; Outdoor Channel; Ovation; Speed Channel; Toon Disney; Turner Classic Movies; Versus; VH1 Classic.

Fee: $12.45 monthly.

Digital Pay Service 1

Pay Units: N.A.

Programming (via satellite): Cinemax (multiplexed); Encore (multiplexed); Fox Movie Channel; HBO (multiplexed); Independent Film Channel; Showtime (multiplexed); Sundance Channel; The Movie Channel (multiplexed).

Fee: $10.50 monthly (each).

Video-On-Demand: No

Pay-Per-View
Hot Choice (delivered digitally); Fresh (delivered digitally); iN DEMAND (delivered digitally); Shorteez (delivered digitally).

Internet Service
Operational: Yes.
Broadband Service: Road Runner.
Fee: $49.95 installation; $29.95 monthly.

Telephone Service
Digital: Operational
Fee: $39.95 monthly

Miles of Plant: 26.0 (coaxial); None (fiber optic). Homes passed: 1,432. Total homes in franchised area: 1,499.

Marketing Director: Nicole Hardy. Technical Operations Manager: Lynn Miller. Chief Technician: Edward Harrison. Business Manager: Elaine West.

Ownership: Bright House Networks LLC (MSO).

CHIEFLAND—CommuniComm Services, 17774 NW US Highway 441, High Springs, FL 32643-8749. Phone: 386-454-2299. Fax: 386-454-3705. Web Site: http://www.communicomm.com. ICA: FL0140.

TV Market Ranking: Below 100 (CHIEFLAND). Franchise award date: N.A. Franchise expiration date: N.A. Began: June 1, 1969.

Channel capacity: N.A. Channels available but not in use: N.A.

Basic Service
Subscribers: N.A. Included in High Springs
Programming (received off-air): WACX (IND) Leesburg; WCJB-TV (ABC, CW) Gainesville; WCWJ (CW) Jacksonville; WJXT (IND) Jacksonville; WOGX (FOX) Ocala; WTLV (NBC) Jacksonville; WUFT (PBS) Gainesville.
Programming (via satellite): QVC; Trinity Broadcasting Network; TV Guide Network.
Fee: $50.00 installation; $31.00 monthly; $30.00 additional installation.

Expanded Basic Service 1
Subscribers: N.A.
Programming (via satellite): ABC Family Channel; AMC; Animal Planet; Arts & Entertainment; BET Networks; Cartoon Network; CNBC; CNN; Comedy Central; Country Music TV; C-SPAN; Discovery Channel; Disney Channel; Do-It-Yourself; ESPN; ESPN 2; ESPN Classic Sports; ESPNews; Food Network; Fox News Channel; FX; Hallmark Channel; Headline News; HGTV; History Channel; ION Television; Lifetime; MTV; Nick Jr.; Nickelodeon; Outdoor Channel; ShopNBC; Speed Channel; Spike TV; SunSports TV; Syfy; TBS Superstation; The Learning Channel; Travel Channel; truTV; Turner Network TV; TV Land; Univision; USA Network; VH1; Weather Channel.

Digital Basic Service
Subscribers: N.A.
Programming (via satellite): BBC America; Bloomberg Television; Bravo; CMT Pure Country; Discovery Digital Networks; DMX Music; FitTV; Fox Movie Channel; Fox Soccer; G4; Golf Channel; GSN; Halogen Network; Independent Film Channel; Military History Channel; National Geographic Channel; NickToons TV; SoapNet; Turner Classic Movies; Versus; VH1 Classic; WE tv.

Pay Service 1
Pay Units: N.A. Included in High Springs
Programming (via satellite): Cinemax; Encore; HBO (multiplexed); Starz.
Fee: $30.00 installation; $9.95 monthly (Cinemax), $11.95 monthly (HBO).

Digital Pay Service 1
Pay Units: N.A.
Programming (via satellite): Cinemax (multiplexed); Encore (multiplexed); HBO (multiplexed); Starz (multiplexed).

Video-On-Demand: No

Pay-Per-View
iN DEMAND (delivered digitally); Playboy TV (delivered digitally); Fresh (delivered digitally); Club Jenna (delivered digitally).

Internet Service
Operational: Yes.
Broadband Service: Net Commander.

Telephone Service
None

Total homes in franchised area: 2,000. Homes passed and miles of plant included in High Springs

General Manager: Darrell Laird. Chief Technician: Michael Smith. Customer Service Manager: Cindy Ross.

City fee: 3% of gross.

Ownership: James Cable LLC (MSO).

CHIPLEY—Bright House Networks, 94 Walton Rd, DeFuniak Springs, FL 32433. Phones: 800-288-1664; 205-290-1300. Fax: 850-892-1318. Web Site: http://panhandle.brighthouse.com. Also serves Graceville, Jackson County & Washington County. ICA: FL0126.

TV Market Ranking: Below 100 (CHIPLEY, Graceville, Jackson County, Washington County). Franchise award date: N.A. Franchise expiration date: N.A. Began: August 1, 1970.

Channel capacity: N.A. Channels available but not in use: N.A.

Basic Service
Subscribers: 1,797.
Programming (received off-air): The Learning Channel; WCTV (CBS, MNT) Thomasville; WFSU-TV (PBS) Tallahassee; WJHG-TV (CW, MNT, NBC) Panama City; WMBB (ABC) Panama City; WPGX (FOX) Panama City; WTVY (CBS, CW, MNT) Dothan.
Programming (via satellite): ABC Family Channel; AMC; Animal Planet; Arts & Entertainment; BET Networks; Bravo; Cartoon Network; CNBC; CNN; Country Music TV; C-SPAN; Discovery Channel; Disney Channel; E! Entertainment Television; ESPN; ESPN 2; Food Network; FX; Hallmark Channel; Headline News; HGTV; History Channel; Home Shopping Network; Lifetime; Lifetime Movie Network; MSNBC; MTV; National Geographic Channel; Nickelodeon; Oxygen; QVC; ShopNBC; Spike TV; Style Network; SunSports TV; Syfy; TBS Superstation; Travel Channel; Trinity Broadcasting Network; Turner Network TV; USA Network; VH1; WE tv; Weather Channel.
Current originations: Government Access; Educational Access; Public Access.
Fee: $53.75 installation; $44.35 monthly; $17.90 additional installation.

Digital Basic Service
Subscribers: N.A.
Programming (via satellite): Bloomberg Television; Discovery Digital Networks; ESPN Now; ESPNews; Fox Sports World; G4; GAS; Golf Channel; GSN; MTV2; Nick Jr.; Outdoor Channel; Ovation; Speed Channel; Toon Disney; Turner Classic Movies; Versus; VH1 Classic.
Fee: $12.45 monthly.

Digital Pay Service 1
Pay Units: N.A.
Programming (via satellite): BBC America; Encore (multiplexed); HBO (multiplexed); Showtime (multiplexed); The Movie Channel (multiplexed).
Fee: $10.50 monthly (each).

Video-On-Demand: No

Pay-Per-View
Special events.

Internet Service
Operational: Yes.
Fee: $49.95 installation; $29.95 monthly.

Telephone Service
Digital: Operational
Fee: $39.95 monthly

Miles of Plant: 91.0 (coaxial); None (fiber optic). Homes passed: 2,839. Total homes in franchised area: 3,155.

Marketing Director: Nicole Hardy. Technical Operations Manager: Lynn Miller. Chief Technician: Edward Harrison.

Ownership: Bright House Networks LLC (MSO).

CHRISTMAS—Florida Cable, PO Box 498, 23748 State Rd 40, Astor, FL 32102-0498. Phones: 352-759-2788; 800-779-2788. Fax: 352-759-3577. Web Site: http://www.floridacable.com. ICA: FL0342.

TV Market Ranking: 55 (CHRISTMAS). Franchise award date: N.A. Franchise expiration date: N.A. Began: N.A.

Channel capacity: 40 (not 2-way capable). Channels available but not in use: N.A.

Basic Service
Subscribers: N.A.
Programming (received off-air): WACX (IND) Leesburg; WESH (NBC) Daytona Beach; WFTV (ABC) Orlando; WKCF (CW) Clermont; WKMG-TV (CBS) Orlando; WMFE-TV (PBS) Orlando; WOFL (FOX) Orlando; WRBW (MNT) Orlando; WRDQ (IND) Orlando.
Programming (via satellite): ABC Family Channel; Animal Planet; Arts & Entertainment; CNN; Country Music TV; Discovery Channel; ESPN; ESPN 2; Headline News; Home Shopping Network; Lifetime; MTV; Nickelodeon; QVC; Spike TV; TBS Superstation; The Learning Channel; Turner Network TV; USA Network; VH1; Weather Channel; WGN America.
Fee: $40.00 installation; $22.95 monthly.

Pay Service 1
Pay Units: 41.
Programming (via satellite): Showtime; The Movie Channel.
Fee: $10.95 monthly.

Internet Service
Operational: No.

Telephone Service
None

General Manager: Jim Pierce. Office Manager: Aleta Dawson. Plant Manager: Larry English.

Ownership: Florida Cable Inc. (MSO).

CITRA—Florida Cable, PO Box 498, 23748 State Rd 40, Astor, FL 32102-0498. Phones: 352-759-2788; 800-779-2788. Fax: 352-759-3797. E-mail: support@floridacable.com. Web Site: http://www.floridacable.com. Also serves Anthony, Hideaway Mobile Home Park, Marion County (northern portion) & Sparr. ICA: FL0153.

TV Market Ranking: Below 100 (Anthony, CITRA, Hideaway Mobile Home Park, Marion County (northern portion), Sparr). Franchise award date: N.A. Franchise expiration date: N.A. Began: July 1, 1988.

Channel capacity: 36 (not 2-way capable). Channels available but not in use: None.

Basic Service
Subscribers: 758.
Programming (received off-air): WACX (IND) Leesburg; WCJB-TV (ABC, CW) Gainesville; WESH (NBC) Daytona Beach; WFTV (ABC) Orlando; WGFL (CBS, MNT) High Springs; WKMG-TV (CBS) Orlando; WOGX (FOX) Ocala; WUFT (PBS) Gainesville.
Programming (via satellite): ABC Family Channel; Animal Planet; Arts & Entertainment; CNN; Comedy Central; Discovery Channel; Disney Channel; ESPN; Food Network; Fox News Channel; Fuse; FX; Great American Country; Headline News; History Channel; Lifetime; QVC; Speed Channel; Syfy; TBS Superstation; Travel Channel; Turner Classic Movies; Turner Network TV; USA Network; Weather Channel; WGN America.
Fee: $39.45 monthly.

Pay Service 1
Pay Units: 107.
Programming (via satellite): Cinemax; HBO; Showtime.

Video-On-Demand: No

Internet Service
Operational: No.

Telephone Service
None

Miles of Plant: 99.0 (coaxial); None (fiber optic). Homes passed: 2,100.

General Manager: Jim Pierce. Plant Manager: Larry English. Office Manager: Alita Dawson.

Ownership: Florida Cable Inc. (MSO).

CLAY COUNTY—Florida Cable, PO Box 498, 23748 State Rd 40, Astor, FL 32102-0498. Phones: 352-759-2788; 800-779-2788. Fax: 352-759-3797. E-mail: support@floridacable.com. Web Site: http://www.floridacable.com. Also serves Clay Hill & Middleburg. ICA: FL0125.

TV Market Ranking: 68 (CLAY COUNTY, Clay Hill, MIDDLEBURG); Below 100 (CLAY COUNTY). Franchise award date: May 26, 1987. Franchise expiration date: N.A. Began: July 26, 1988.

Channel capacity: 41 (not 2-way capable). Channels available but not in use: None.

Basic Service
Subscribers: 390.
Programming (received off-air): WAWS (FOX, MNT) Jacksonville; WCWJ (CW) Jacksonville; WJCT (PBS) Jacksonville; WJEB-TV (ETV) Jacksonville; WJXT (IND) Jacksonville; WJXX (ABC) Orange Park; WTEV-TV (CBS) Jacksonville; WTLV (NBC) Jacksonville; WUFT (PBS) Gainesville.
Programming (via satellite): ABC Family Channel; AMC; Arts & Entertainment; Cartoon Network; CNBC; CNN; Comedy Central; Discovery Channel; Disney Channel; ESPN; Food Network; Fox News Channel; Fuse; FX; Great American Country; Headline News; History Channel; Home Shopping Network; Lifetime; QVC; Speed Channel; SunSports TV; TBS Superstation; Travel Channel; Turner Network TV; USA Network; Weather Channel; WGN America.
Current originations: Public Access.
Fee: $30.00 installation; $36.45 monthly.

Pay Service 1
Pay Units: 228.
Programming (via satellite): Cinemax; HBO; Showtime; The Movie Channel.
Fee: $9.95 monthly (each).

Video-On-Demand: No

Internet Service
Operational: Yes.
Fee: $24.95-$49.95 monthly.

Telephone Service
Digital: Planned

Miles of Plant: 86.0 (coaxial); None (fiber optic). Homes passed: 1,909.

General Manager: Jim Pierce. Plant Manager: Larry English. Office Manager: Alita Dawson.
Ownership: Florida Cable Inc. (MSO).

CLEWISTON—Now served by BELLE GLADE, FL [FL0073]. ICA: FL0105.

CORAL SPRINGS—Advanced Cable Communications, 12409 NW 35th St, Coral Springs, FL 33065-2413. Phone: 954-753-0100. Fax: 954-345-0783. E-mail: info@advancedcable.net. Web Site: http://www.advancedcable.net. Also serves Broward County (portions). ICA: FL0045.
TV Market Ranking: 21 (Broward County (portions), CORAL SPRINGS). Franchise award date: June 12, 1980. Franchise expiration date: N.A. Began: September 1, 1975.
Channel capacity: 77 (operating 2-way). Channels available but not in use: None.

Basic Service
Subscribers: 28,329.
Programming (received off-air): WAMI-DT (TEL) Hollywood; WBFS-TV (MNT) Miami; WFOR-TV (CBS) Miami; WGEN-TV (IND) Key West; WHFT-TV (TBN) Miami; WLRN-TV (PBS) Miami; WLTV-DT (UNV) Miami; WPBT (PBS) Miami; WPLG (ABC) Miami; WPXM-TV (ION) Miami; WSBS-TV (IND) Key West; WSCV (TMO) Fort Lauderdale; WSFL-TV (CW) Miami; WSVN (FOX) Miami; WTVJ (NBC) Miami; WXEL-TV (PBS) West Palm Beach.
Programming (via satellite): C-SPAN; Home Shopping Network; QVC; TV Guide Network; Weather Channel; WGN America.
Current originations: Government Access.
Fee: $43.00 installation; $18.00 monthly; $2.32 converter; $19.10 additional installation.

Expanded Basic Service 1
Subscribers: N.A.
Programming (via satellite): ABC Family Channel; AMC; Animal Planet; Arts & Entertainment; BET Networks; Bravo; Cartoon Network; CNBC; CNN; Comedy Central; Country Music TV; Discovery Channel; Discovery Health Channel; Disney Channel; E! Entertainment Television; ESPN; ESPN 2; ESPN U; Eternal Word TV Network; Food Network; Fox News Channel; Fox Sports Net Florida; FX; G4; Golf Channel; Hallmark Channel; Headline News; HGTV; History Channel; Lifetime; MSNBC; MTV; MTV2; National Geographic Channel; Nickelodeon; Speed Channel; Spike TV; Style Network; SunSports TV; Syfy; TBS Superstation; The Learning Channel; Travel Channel; truTV; Turner Classic Movies; Turner Network TV; TV Land; USA Network; Versus; VH1; WE tv.
Fee: $30.75 monthly.

Digital Basic Service
Subscribers: N.A.
Programming (received off-air): WBFS-TV (MNT) Miami; WFOR-TV (CBS) Miami; WPBT (PBS) Miami; WPLG (ABC) Miami; WSVN (FOX) Miami; WTVJ (NBC) Miami.
Programming (via satellite): Arts & Entertainment HD; BBC America; Bio; Bloomberg Television; CMT Pure Country; College Sports Television; Cooking Channel; C-SPAN 3; Discovery HD Theater; Discovery Kids Channel; Discovery Military Channel; Discovery Planet Green; DMX Music; ESPN 2 HD; ESPN HD; ESPNews; Fox College Sports Atlantic; Fox College Sports Central; Fox College Sports Pacific; Fox Movie Channel; Fox Reality Channel; Fox Soccer; Fox Sports en Espanol; FSN HD; Fuel TV; Fuse; G4; Gol TV; GSN; HDNet; HDNet Movies; History Channel HD; History Channel International; ID Investigation Discovery; LATV Networks; Lifetime Movie Network; MTV Hits; mun2 television; National Geographic Channel HD Network; NFL Network; NFL Network HD; Nick Jr.; NickToons TV; PBS Kids Sprout; Science Channel; ShopNBC; Sleuth; SoapNet; TBS in HD; TeenNick; Toon Disney; Turner Network TV HD; Universal HD; VH1 Classic; VH1 Soul.
Fee: $21.90 monthly; $2.32 converter.

Digital Expanded Basic Service
Subscribers: N.A.
Programming (via satellite): Canal 24 Horas; Canal 52MX; Canal Sur; Cine Latino; Cine Mexicano; CNN en Espanol; Discovery en Espanol; Docu TVE; ESPN Deportes; Fox Sports en Espanol; Gol TV; History Channel en Espanol; Latele Novela Network; MTV Tres; mun2 television; Telefe International; Toon Disney en Espanol; TV Chile; TV Colombia; TVE Internacional; VeneMovies.
Fee: $10.95 monthly.

Digital Pay Service 1
Pay Units: N.A.
Programming (via satellite): Cinemax (multiplexed); Cinemax HD; Encore (multiplexed); Flix; HBO (multiplexed); HBO HD; Showtime (multiplexed); Showtime HD; Starz (multiplexed); Starz HDTV; Sundance Channel; The Movie Channel (multiplexed).
Fee: $10.00 monthly (Cinemax), $16.95 monthly (Starz/Encore or Showtime/TMC/Flix/Sundance), $18.95 monthly (HBO), $26.95 monthly (Cinemax & HBO).

Video-On-Demand: Planned

Pay-Per-View
Addressable homes: 12,889.
iN DEMAND, Fee: $3.95, Addressable: Yes; iN DEMAND (delivered digitally); Playboy TV (delivered digitally), Fee: $7.99; Fresh (delivered digitally), Fee: $7.99; special events; special events (delivered digitally); sports.

Internet Service
Operational: Yes. Began: August 1, 1998.
Subscribers: 1,572.
Broadband Service: In-house.
Fee: $99.00 installation; $42.95 monthly; $10.00 modem lease.

Telephone Service
Analog: Not Operational
Digital: Operational

Miles of Plant: 430.0 (coaxial); 84.0 (fiber optic). Additional miles planned: 28.0 (coaxial). Homes passed: 45,222. Total homes in franchised area: 45,222.
Vice President, Engineering: Rick Scheller. Manager: Jim Pagano. Marketing Director: Michelle Fitzpatrick. Program Director & Production Manager: Mike Milo. Customer Service Manager: Michelle Martinie.
City fee: 5% of monthly gross.
Ownership: Schurz Communications Inc. (MSO).

CRAWFORDVILLE—Comcast Cable. Now served by TALLAHASSEE, FL [FL0283]. ICA: FL0116.

CRESCENT CITY—Comcast Cable, 6805 Southpoint Pkwy, Jacksonville, FL 32216. Phone: 904-374-8000. Fax: 904-374-7622. Web Site: http://www.comcast.com. Also serves Pomona Park & Putnam County. ICA: FL0131.
TV Market Ranking: 55 (CRESCENT CITY, Putnam County (portions)); Below 100 (Putnam County (portions)); Outside TV Markets (Pomona Park, Putnam County (portions)). Franchise award date: August 1, 1981. Franchise expiration date: N.A. Began: June 1, 1982.
Channel capacity: 40 (2-way capable). Channels available but not in use: 1.

Basic Service
Subscribers: N.A. Included with Jacksonville
Programming (received off-air): WAWS (FOX, MNT) Jacksonville; WCWJ (CW) Jacksonville; WESH (NBC) Daytona Beach; WJEB-TV (ETV) Jacksonville; WJGV-CD (IND) Palatka; WJXT (IND) Jacksonville; WJXX (ABC) Orange Park; WTEV-TV (CBS) Jacksonville; WTLV (NBC) Jacksonville; WUFT (PBS) Gainesville; 12 FMs.
Programming (via satellite): C-SPAN; History Channel; INSP; TBS Superstation; Weather Channel; WKMG-TV (CBS) Orlando.
Current originations: Educational Access.
Fee: $43.99 installation; $24.83 monthly; $1.65 converter.

Expanded Basic Service 1
Subscribers: 1,233.
Programming (via satellite): ABC Family Channel; AMC; Arts & Entertainment; BET Networks; CNN; Discovery Channel; Disney Channel; E! Entertainment Television; ESPN; ESPN 2; Food Network; Fox News Channel; FX; Headline News; Lifetime; MTV; Nickelodeon; QVC; Spike TV; The Learning Channel; Turner Network TV; USA Network.
Fee: $36.05 monthly.

Digital Basic Service
Subscribers: 272.
Programming (via satellite): AmericanLife TV Network; BBC America; Bio; Bloomberg Television; Bravo; CMT Pure Country; Current; Discovery Health Channel; Discovery Kids Channel; Discovery Military Channel; Discovery Planet Green; ESPN 2; ESPN Classic Sports; ESPNews; Fox Movie Channel; Fox Soccer; G4; Golf Channel; GSN; Halogen Network; HGTV; History Channel; History Channel International; ID Investigation Discovery; Independent Film Channel; Lifetime Movie Network; MTV2; Nick Jr.; Outdoor Channel; Ovation; Science Channel; Speed Channel; Style Network; Sundance Channel; Syfy; TeenNick; Toon Disney; Trinity Broadcasting Network; Turner Classic Movies; TV Land; Versus; VH1 Classic; VH1 Soul.
Fee: $13.94 monthly.

Pay Service 1
Pay Units: 722.
Programming (via satellite): Cinemax; HBO.
Fee: $15.95 monthly (each).

Digital Pay Service 1
Pay Units: N.A.
Programming (via satellite): HBO (multiplexed).
Fee: $15.95 monthly.

Video-On-Demand: No

Pay-Per-View
Addressable homes: 272.
iN DEMAND (delivered digitally), Addressable: Yes.

Internet Service
Operational: Yes.

Telephone Service
Digital: Operational

Miles of Plant: 119.0 (coaxial); None (fiber optic). Homes passed: 3,876.
Vice President & General Manager: Doug McMillan. Engineering Director: Mike Humphrey. Vice President, Marketing: Vic Scarborough. Government Affairs Director: Bill Ferry.
Ownership: Comcast Cable Communications Inc. (MSO).

CRESTVIEW—Cox Communications. Now served by FORT WALTON BEACH, FL [FL0023]. ICA: FL0074.

CROSS CITY—CommuniComm Services, 17774 NW US Highway 441, High Springs, FL 32643-8749. Phone: 386-454-2299. Fax: 386-454-3705. Web Site: http://www.netcommander.com. Also serves Dixie County. ICA: FL0158.
TV Market Ranking: Below 100 (CROSS CITY, Dixie County (portions)); Outside TV Markets (Dixie County (portions)). Franchise award date: N.A. Franchise expiration date: N.A. Began: December 1, 1968.
Channel capacity: N.A. Channels available but not in use: N.A.

Basic Service
Subscribers: N.A. Included in High Springs
Programming (received off-air): WCJB-TV (ABC, CW) Gainesville; WCWJ (CW) Jacksonville; WGFL (CBS, MNT) High Springs; WJXT (IND) Jacksonville; WOGX (FOX) Ocala; WTLV (NBC) Jacksonville; WUFT (PBS) Gainesville.
Programming (via satellite): QVC; Trinity Broadcasting Network; TV Guide Network.
Fee: $50.00 installation; $31.00 monthly.

Expanded Basic Service 1
Subscribers: N.A.
Programming (via satellite): ABC Family Channel; AMC; Animal Planet; Arts & Entertainment; BET Networks; Cartoon Network; CNBC; CNN; Comedy Central; Country Music TV; C-SPAN; Discovery Channel; Disney Channel; Do-It-Yourself; ESPN; ESPN 2; ESPN Classic Sports; ESPNews; Food Network; Fox News Channel; FX; Hallmark Channel; Headline News; HGTV; History Channel; ION Television; Lifetime; MTV; Nick Jr.; Nickelodeon; Outdoor Channel; ShopNBC; Speed Channel; Spike TV; SunSports TV; Syfy; TBS Superstation; The Learning Channel; Travel Channel; truTV; Turner Network TV; TV Land; Univision; USA Network; VH1; Weather Channel.

Digital Basic Service
Subscribers: N.A.
Programming (via satellite): BBC America; Bloomberg Television; Bravo; CMT Pure Country; Discovery Health Channel; Discovery Kids Channel; Discovery Military Channel; Discovery Planet Green; DMX Music; Fox Movie Channel; Fox Soccer; G4; Golf Channel; GSN; Halogen Network; ID Investigation Discovery; Independent Film Channel; Military History Channel; National Geographic Channel; NickToons TV; Science Channel; SoapNet; Turner Classic Movies; Versus; VH1 Classic; WE tv.

Pay Service 1
Pay Units: N.A. Included in High Springs
Programming (via satellite): Cinemax; Encore; HBO; Starz.
Fee: $30.00 installation; $9.95 monthly (Cinemax), $11.95 monthly (HBO).

Digital Pay Service 1
Pay Units: N.A.
Programming (via satellite): Cinemax (multiplexed); Encore (multiplexed); HBO (multiplexed); Starz (multiplexed).

Video-On-Demand: No

Pay-Per-View
iN DEMAND (delivered digitally); Playboy TV (delivered digitally); Club Jenna (delivered digitally); Fresh (delivered digitally).

Internet Service
Operational: Yes.
Broadband Service: Net Commander.
Fee: $39.95 installation; $51.95 monthly.
Telephone Service
None
Homes passed and miles of plant included in High Springs
General Manager: Darrell Laird. Chief Technician: Michael Smith. Customer Service Manager: Cindy Ross.
Franchise fee: 3% of gross.
Ownership: James Cable LLC (MSO).

DAVIE—Comcast Cable. Now served by BROWARD COUNTY, FL [FL0016]. ICA: FL0022.

DE FUNIAK SPRINGS—Bright House Networks, 94 Walton Rd, DeFuniak Springs, FL 32433. Phones: 850-892-3155; 205-290-1300. Fax: 850-892-1318. Web Site: http://panhandle.brighthouse.com. Also serves Hartford & Slocomb, AL; Walton County (portions), FL. ICA: FL0111.
TV Market Ranking: Below 100 (Hartford, Slocomb, Walton County (portions) (portions)); Outside TV Markets (DE FUNIAK SPRINGS, Walton County (portions) (portions)). Franchise award date: N.A. Franchise expiration date: N.A. Began: November 1, 1969.
Channel capacity: N.A. Channels available but not in use: N.A.
Basic Service
Subscribers: 5,863.
Programming (received off-air): WFSU-TV (PBS) Tallahassee; WJHG-TV (CW, MNT, NBC) Panama City; WMBB (ABC) Panama City; WPGX (FOX) Panama City; WTVY (CBS, CW, MNT) Dothan; WWEO-CA De Funiak Springs.
Programming (via satellite): ABC Family Channel; AMC; Animal Planet; Arts & Entertainment; BET Networks; Bravo; Cartoon Network; CNBC; CNN; Country Music TV; C-SPAN; Discovery Channel; Disney Channel; E! Entertainment Television; ESPN; ESPN 2; Food Network; Fox News Channel; FX; Hallmark Channel; Headline News; HGTV; History Channel; Home Shopping Network; Lifetime; Lifetime Movie Network; MSNBC; MTV; National Geographic Channel; Nickelodeon; Oxygen; QVC; ShopNBC; Spike TV; Style Network; SunSports TV; Syfy; TBS Superstation; The Learning Channel; Travel Channel; Trinity Broadcasting Network; Turner Network TV; USA Network; VH1; WE tv; Weather Channel.
Current originations: Government Access; Educational Access; Public Access.
Fee: $53.76 installation; $44.35 monthly; $17.90 additional installation.
Digital Basic Service
Subscribers: N.A.
Programming (via satellite): AmericanLife TV Network; Discovery Digital Networks; G4; GAS; GSN; MTV2; MuchMoreMusic; Nick Jr.; Ovation; Toon Disney; Turner Classic Movies; VH1 Classic.
Fee: $12.45 monthly.
Digital Pay Service 1
Pay Units: N.A.
Programming (via satellite): Cinemax (multiplexed); Encore; Fox Movie Channel; HBO (multiplexed); Showtime (multiplexed); Sundance Channel; The Movie Channel (multiplexed).
Fee: $10.50 monthly (each).
Video-On-Demand: No
Internet Service
Operational: Yes.
Broadband Service: Road Runner.
Fee: $49.95 monthly.
Telephone Service
Digital: Operational
Fee: $39.95 monthly
Miles of Plant: 167.0 (coaxial); None (fiber optic).
Marketing Director: Nicole Hardy. Technical Operations Manager: Lynn Miller. Chief Technician: Edward Harrison. Business Manager: Elaine West.
City fee: 6% of gross.
Ownership: Bright House Networks LLC (MSO).

DE LAND—Bright House Networks, 1655 State Rd 472, DeLand, FL 32724. Phones: 386-775-7300 (Customer service); 407-215-5524. Fax: 386-775-0769. E-mail: john.doctor@mybrighthouse.com. Web Site: http://cfl.mybrighthouse.com. Also serves Beverly Beach, Bunnell, Daytona Beach, Daytona Beach Shores, De Bary (portions), De Leon Springs, Deltona, District Five, District Four, Edgewater, Flagler Beach, Flagler County, Holly Hill, Lake Helen, New Smyrna Beach, Oak Hill, Orange City, Ormond Beach, Ormond by the Sea, Osteen, Palm Coast, Ponce Inlet, Port Orange, Rima Ridge, South Daytona, Spruce Creek & Volusia County. ICA: FL0033.
TV Market Ranking: 55 (Bunnell, Daytona Beach, Daytona Beach Shores, De Bary (portions), DE LAND, De Leon Springs, Deltona, District Five, District Four, Edgewater, Flagler Beach, Flagler County, Holly Hill, Lake Helen, New Smyrna Beach, Oak Hill, Orange City, Ormond Beach, Ormond by the Sea, Osteen, Palm Coast, Ponce Inlet, Port Orange, Rima Ridge, South Daytona, Spruce Creek, Volusia County); 85 (Beverly Beach). Franchise award date: N.A. Franchise expiration date: N.A. Began: January 4, 1971.
Channel capacity: 300 (operating 2-way). Channels available but not in use: N.A.
Basic Service
Subscribers: 183,026.
Programming (received off-air): WACX (IND) Leesburg; WDSC-TV (PBS) New Smyrna Beach; WESH (NBC) Daytona Beach; WFTV (ABC) Orlando; WHLV-TV (IND) Cocoa; WKCF (CW) Clermont; WKMG-TV (CBS) Orlando; WMFE-TV (PBS) Orlando; WOFL (FOX) Orlando; WOPX-TV (ION) Melbourne; WOTF-DT (TEL) Melbourne; WRBW (MNT) Orlando; WRDQ (IND) Orlando; 12 FMs.
Programming (via satellite): Central Florida News 13; TBS Superstation; Turner Network TV; WGN America.
Current originations: Educational Access.
Fee: $50.00 installation; $11.22 monthly; $1.55 converter; $20.00 additional installation.
Expanded Basic Service 1
Subscribers: N.A.
Programming (via satellite): AMC; Animal Planet; Arts & Entertainment; BET Networks; Bravo; Cartoon Network; CNBC; CNN; Comedy Central; Country Music TV; C-SPAN; C-SPAN 2; Discovery Channel; Disney Channel; E! Entertainment Television; ESPN; ESPN 2; Eternal Word TV Network; Food Network; Fox News Channel; FX; GalaVision; Golf Channel; Hallmark Channel; Headline News; HGTV; History Channel; Home Shopping Network; Lifetime; Lifetime Movie Network; MSNBC; MTV; Nickelodeon; Oxygen; Product Information Network; QVC; ShopNBC; SoapNet; Speed Channel; SunSports TV; Syfy; Telemundo; The Learning Channel; Travel Channel; truTV; Turner Classic Movies; TV Land; USA Network; VH1; WE tv; Weather Channel.
Fee: $39.57 monthly.
Digital Basic Service
Subscribers: N.A.
Programming (via satellite): ABC Family Channel; America's Store; BBC America; Bloomberg Television; C-SPAN 2; C-SPAN 3; Discovery Digital Networks; DMX Music; Do-It-Yourself; ESPN Classic Sports; ESPN Now; ESPNews; Eternal Word TV Network; FitTV; Fox Sports World; Fuse; G4; GAS; Lifetime Real Women; MTV2; NASA TV; National Geographic Channel; Nick Jr.; Outdoor Channel; Ovation; PBS Kids Channel; Science Television; Style Network; Toon Disney; Versus; VH1 Classic.
Fee: $7.70 monthly.
Digital Expanded Basic Service
Subscribers: N.A.
Programming (via satellite): Canales N.
Digital Pay Service 1
Pay Units: N.A.
Programming (via satellite): Cinemax (multiplexed); Encore (multiplexed); Flix; HBO (multiplexed); Independent Film Channel; MoviePlex; Showtime (multiplexed); Starz; Sundance Channel; The Movie Channel (multiplexed).
Fee: $10.95 monthly (each).
Video-On-Demand: Yes
Pay-Per-View
Addressable homes: 25,823.
ESPN Now (delivered digitally); Sports PPV (delivered digitally); Hot Choice (delivered digitally); Playboy TV (delivered digitally); Pleasure (delivered digitally); Shorteez (delivered digitally); iN DEMAND (delivered digitally), Addressable: Yes; Fresh (delivered digitally).
Internet Service
Operational: Yes.
Broadband Service: Road Runner.
Fee: $24.95 installation; $44.95 monthly.
Telephone Service
Digital: Operational
Fee: $24.95 installation; $49.95 monthly
Miles of Plant: 2,691.0 (coaxial); 247.0 (fiber optic). Total homes in franchised area: 225,000.
Division President: J. Christian Fenger. General Manager: John Doctor. Customer Service Manager: Valerie Gabaree.
City fee: 5% of basic gross.
Ownership: Bright House Networks LLC (MSO).

DEBARY—Comcast Cable, 8130 County Rd 44, Leg A, Leesburg, FL 34788. Phone: 352-787-9601. Fax: 352-365-6279. Web Site: http://www.comcast.com. Also serves Volusia County (portions). ICA: FL0124.
TV Market Ranking: 55 (DE BARY, Volusia County (portions)). Franchise award date: January 1, 1981. Franchise expiration date: N.A. Began: July 27, 1981.
Channel capacity: N.A. Channels available but not in use: N.A.
Basic Service
Subscribers: N.A. Included in Celebration
Programming (received off-air): WBCC (PBS) Cocoa; WESH (NBC) Daytona Beach; WFTV (ABC) Orlando; WHLV-TV (IND) Cocoa; WKCF (CW) Clermont; WKMG-TV (CBS) Orlando; WMFE-TV (PBS) Orlando; WOFL (FOX) Orlando; WOPX-TV (ION) Melbourne; WOTF-DT (TEL) Melbourne; WRBW (MNT) Orlando; WRDQ (IND) Orlando; WVEN-TV (UNV) Daytona Beach.
Programming (via satellite): C-SPAN 2; TV Guide Network.
Current originations: Leased Access.
Fee: $36.95 installation; $10.78 monthly.
Expanded Basic Service 1
Subscribers: N.A. Included in Celebration
Programming (via satellite): ABC Family Channel; AMC; Animal Planet; Arts & Entertainment; BET Networks; Bravo; Cartoon Network; CNBC; CNN; Comcast/Charter Sports Southeast (CSS); Comedy Central; C-SPAN; Discovery Channel; Discovery Health Channel; Disney Channel; E! Entertainment Television; ESPN; ESPN 2; Food Network; Fox News Channel; FX; Golf Channel; Great American Country; GSN; Hallmark Channel; Headline News; HGTV; History Channel; Home Shopping Network; Lifetime; MSNBC; MTV; Nickelodeon; Product Information Network; QVC; Speed Channel; Spike TV; Style Network; SunSports TV; Syfy; TBS Superstation; The Learning Channel; Travel Channel; truTV; Turner Classic Movies; Turner Network TV; TV Land; USA Network; Versus; VH1; Weather Channel; WGN America.
Fee: $37.17 monthly.
Digital Basic Service
Subscribers: N.A. Included in Celebration
Programming (received off-air): WESH (NBC) Daytona Beach; WFTV (ABC) Orlando; WKMG-TV (CBS) Orlando; WMFE-TV (PBS) Orlando; WOFL (FOX) Orlando; WRDQ (IND) Orlando.
Programming (via satellite): BBC America; C-SPAN 3; Discovery Digital Networks; Discovery HD Theater; Disney Channel; Encore (multiplexed); ESPN 2; ESPNews; Flix (multiplexed); Florida Channel; Fox Sports Net; G4; GAS; INHD (multiplexed); MTV Networks Digital Suite; Music Choice; National Geographic Channel; Nick Jr.; Nick Too; NickToons TV; SoapNet; Sundance Channel (multiplexed); The Movie Channel; Toon Disney; WAM! America's Kidz Network; Weatherscan.
Fee: $14.95 monthly.
Pay Service 1
Pay Units: 164.
Programming (via satellite): Cinemax (multiplexed); HBO (multiplexed); Showtime (multiplexed).
Fee: $13.95 monthly each (Cinemax & Showtime), $14.95 monthly (HBO).
Digital Pay Service 1
Pay Units: N.A.
Programming (via satellite): Cinemax (multiplexed); HBO (multiplexed); HBO HD; Showtime (multiplexed); Showtime HD; Starz (multiplexed); The Movie Channel.
Fee: $13.50 monthly (each).
Video-On-Demand: Planned
Pay-Per-View
ShopNBC (delivered digitally); iN DEMAND (delivered digitally); Playboy TV (delivered digitally); Fresh (delivered digitally); Shorteez (delivered digitally); Pleasure (delivered digitally); NASCAR In Car (delivered digitally); MAX HD (delivered digitally); Hot Choice (delivered digitally); Starz HDTV (delivered digitally).
Internet Service
Operational: Yes.
Broadband Service: Comcast High Speed Internet.
Fee: $42.95 monthly.
Telephone Service
Analog: Not Operational
Digital: Operational
Homes passed included in Celebration
Regional Vice President: Rod Dagenais. Marketing Manager: Melanie Melvin. General

Manager: Mike Davenport. Chief Engineer: Sean Curley.
Ownership: Comcast Cable Communications Inc. (MSO).

DELRAY BEACH—Comcast Cable, 1595 SW 4th Ave, Delray Beach, FL 33444-8133. Phone: 561-272-2522. Fax: 561-272-8776. Web Site: http://www.comcast.com. Also serves Boca Raton, Boynton Beach, Golf Village, Gulf Stream, Highland Beach, Ocean Ridge, Palm Beach County (portions) & West Delray Beach. ICA: FL0091.
TV Market Ranking: Below 100 (Boca Raton, Boynton Beach, DELRAY BEACH, Golf Village, Gulf Stream, Highland Beach, Ocean Ridge, Palm Beach County (portions), West Delray Beach); Outside TV Markets (Palm Beach County (portions)). Franchise award date: July 1, 1974. Franchise expiration date: N.A. Began: December 1, 1976.
Channel capacity: N.A. Channels available but not in use: N.A.

Basic Service
Subscribers: 116,337.
Programming (received off-air): WFGC (IND) Palm Beach; WFLX (FOX) West Palm Beach; WLRN-TV (PBS) Miami; WLTV-DT (UNV) Miami; WPBF (ABC) Tequesta; WPBT (PBS) Miami; WPEC (CBS) West Palm Beach; WPTV-TV (NBC) West Palm Beach; WPXP-TV (ION) Lake Worth; WSFL-TV (CW) Miami; WSVN (FOX) Miami; WTVX (CW) Fort Pierce; WXEL-TV (PBS) West Palm Beach.
Programming (via satellite): Home Shopping Network; MSNBC; Product Information Network; QVC; TBS Superstation; TV Guide Network; USA Network; WGN America.
Current originations: Government Access.
Fee: $21.93 installation; $14.65 monthly.

Expanded Basic Service 1
Subscribers: N.A.
Programming (via satellite): ABC Family Channel; AMC; Animal Planet; Arts & Entertainment; BET Networks; Bravo; CNBC; CNN; Comedy Central; C-SPAN; C-SPAN 2; Discovery Channel; Discovery Health Channel; Disney Channel; E! Entertainment Television; ESPN; ESPN 2; Eternal Word TV Network; FitTV; Food Network; Fox News Channel; Fox Sports Net Florida; FX; Golf Channel; Hallmark Channel; Headline News; HGTV; History Channel; Lifetime; MTV; Nickelodeon; Oxygen; Spike TV; Style Network; SunSports TV; Syfy; The Learning Channel; Travel Channel; Turner Network TV; TV Land; VH1; Weather Channel.
Fee: $47.99 monthly.

Digital Basic Service
Subscribers: 14,400.
Programming (via satellite): American-Life TV Network; BBC America; Bio; Black Family Channel; Bloomberg Television; Discovery Digital Networks; Do-It-Yourself; ESPN Classic Sports; ESPNews; FitTV; Fox Sports World; Fuse; G4; Great American Country; GSN; Halogen Network; History Channel International; Outdoor Channel; SoapNet; Speed Channel; Toon Disney; Trinity Broadcasting Network; Versus; WE tv.
Fee: $53.49 monthly.

Digital Expanded Basic Service
Subscribers: N.A.
Programming (via satellite): DMX Music; Fox Movie Channel; GAS; Independent Music Network; MTV Networks Digital Suite; National Geographic Channel; Nick Jr.; Sundance Channel; Turner Classic Movies.

Pay Service 1
Pay Units: 56,251.
Programming (via satellite): Cinemax; HBO; Showtime; The Movie Channel.
Fee: $15.00 installation; $10.50 monthly.

Digital Pay Service 1
Pay Units: N.A.
Programming (via satellite): Cinemax (multiplexed); Encore (multiplexed); Flix; HBO (multiplexed); Showtime (multiplexed); Starz (multiplexed); The Movie Channel (multiplexed).

Video-On-Demand: Yes

Pay-Per-View
Addressable homes: 14,400.
Playboy TV (delivered digitally), Addressable: Yes.

Internet Service
Operational: Yes.
Broadband Service: Comcast High Speed Internet.
Fee: $42.95 monthly.

Telephone Service
Digital: Operational
Fee: $39.95 monthly
Miles of Plant: 1,591.0 (coaxial); None (fiber optic). Homes passed: 144,122.
Area Vice President: Gary Waterfield. General Manager: Mike Ligouri. Technical Operations Manager: George Benjamin. Marketing Manager: Diane Bissoon. Marketing Coordinator: Janet Epstein. Government & Community Affairs Director: Marta Casas-Celayas.
County fee: 5% of gross.
Ownership: Comcast Cable Communications Inc. (MSO).

DOWLING PARK—KLiP Interactive, 455 Gees Mill Business Court, Conyers, GA 30013. Phones: 800-388-6577; 678-727-7100. Fax: 678-727-7002. E-mail: jsheehan@klipia.com. Web Site: http://www.klipia.com. ICA: FL0347.
TV Market Ranking: Outside TV Markets (DOWLING PARK). Franchise award date: N.A. Franchise expiration date: N.A. Began: N.A.
Channel capacity: 56 (not 2-way capable). Channels available but not in use: 20.

Basic Service
Subscribers: 56.
Programming (received off-air): WCJB-TV (ABC, CW) Gainesville; WCTV (CBS, MNT) Thomasville; WTLF (CW, FOX) Tallahassee; WTLH (CW, FOX) Bainbridge; WTWC-TV (NBC) Tallahassee; WTXL-TV (ABC) Tallahassee; WUFT (PBS) Gainesville.
Programming (via satellite): ABC Family Channel; Animal Planet; Arts & Entertainment; Cartoon Network; CNN; Country Music TV; C-SPAN; C-SPAN 2; Discovery Channel; ESPN; ESPN 2; Headline News; HGTV; History Channel; Lifetime; MTV; Nickelodeon; QVC; Spike TV; TBS Superstation; The Learning Channel; Travel Channel; Trinity Broadcasting Network; Turner Classic Movies; Turner Network TV; USA Network; Weather Channel; WGN America.
Fee: $29.95 installation; $31.13 monthly.

Pay Service 1
Pay Units: 1.
Programming (via satellite): Cinemax.
Fee: $10.95 monthly.

Pay Service 2
Pay Units: 2.
Programming (via satellite): HBO.
Fee: $10.95 monthly.

Video-On-Demand: No

Internet Service
Operational: No.

Telephone Service
None
Miles of Plant: 17.0 (coaxial); None (fiber optic). Homes passed: 321.
Chief Executive Officer: Joseph A. Sheehan. General Manager East: Mark Miller. General Manager West: Vance Johnson.
Ownership: KLiP Interactive LLC (MSO).

DUNNELLON—Now served by INVERNESS, FL [FL0319]. ICA: FL0227.

EAST MILTON—Mediacom. Now served by GULF BREEZE, FL [FL0070]. ICA: FL0170.
TV Market Ranking: Franchise award date: N.A. Franchise expiration date: N.A. Began: N.A.

EASTPOINT—Mediacom. Now served by WEWAHITCHKA, FL [FL0159]. ICA: FL0180.

ENGLEWOOD—Comcast Cable, 5205 Fruitville Rd, Sarasota, FL 34232. Phone: 941-371-4444. Fax: 941-371-5097. Web Site: http://www.comcast.com. Also serves Boca Grande, Rotonda & Sarasota County (portions). ICA: FL0229.
TV Market Ranking: 28 (Sarasota County (portions) (portions)); Below 100 (Boca Grande, ENGLEWOOD, Rotonda, Sarasota County (portions) (portions)). Franchise award date: N.A. Franchise expiration date: N.A. Began: October 1, 1969.
Channel capacity: N.A. Channels available but not in use: N.A.

Basic Service
Subscribers: 13,605.
Programming (received off-air): WCLF (IND) Clearwater; WEDU (PBS) Tampa; WFLA-TV (NBC) Tampa; WFTT-DT (TEL) Tampa; WFTX-TV (FOX) Cape Coral; WINK-TV (CBS) Fort Myers; WMOR-TV (IND) Lakeland; WTOG (CW) St. Petersburg; WTSP (CBS) St. Petersburg; WTTA (MNT) St. Petersburg; WTVT (FOX) Tampa; WVEA-TV (UNV) Venice; WWSB (ABC) Sarasota; WXPX-TV (ION) Bradenton; allband FM.
Programming (via satellite): ABC Family Channel; AMC; Animal Planet; Arts & Entertainment; BET Networks; Bravo; Cartoon Network; CNBC; CNN; Comcast/Charter Sports Southeast (CSS); Comedy Central; Country Music TV; C-SPAN; C-SPAN 2; Discovery Channel; Discovery Health Channel; Disney Channel; E! Entertainment Television; ESPN; ESPN 2; Food Network; Fox News Channel; Golf Channel; GSN; Hallmark Channel; Headline News; HGTV; History Channel; Home Shopping Network; Lifetime; MSNBC; MTV; Nickelodeon; QVC; Sneak Prevue; Speed Channel; Spike TV; Style Network; SunSports TV; Syfy; TBS Superstation; The Learning Channel; truTV; Turner Classic Movies; Turner Network TV; TV Guide Network; TV Land; USA Network; Versus; VH1; WE tv; Weather Channel; WGN America.
Current originations: Educational Access; Government Access.
Fee: $63.35 installation; $11.55 monthly.

Digital Basic Service
Subscribers: 3,401.
Programming (via satellite): BBC America; C-SPAN 3; Discovery Digital Networks; Encore Action; ESPNews; Flix; G4; GAS; MTV Networks Digital Suite; Music Choice; National Geographic Channel; Nick Jr.; Nick Too; ShopNBC; SoapNet; Sundance Channel; Toon Disney; Weatherscan.
Fee: $14.95 monthly.

Digital Pay Service 1
Pay Units: N.A.
Programming (via satellite): Cinemax (multiplexed); HBO (multiplexed); Showtime (multiplexed); Starz (multiplexed); The Movie Channel (multiplexed).
Fee: $13.50 monthly (each).

Video-On-Demand: Yes

Pay-Per-View
Addressable homes: 3,401.
iN DEMAND (delivered digitally), Addressable: Yes; Hot Choice (delivered digitally); Playboy TV (delivered digitally); Fresh (delivered digitally); Shorteez (delivered digitally); Pleasure (delivered digitally); NBA TV (delivered digitally).

Internet Service
Operational: Yes.
Subscribers: 1,497.
Broadband Service: Comcast High Speed Internet.
Fee: $42.95 monthly.

Telephone Service
Digital: Operational
Regional Vice President: Rod Dagenais. Vice President & General Manager: Steve Dvoskin. Technical Operations Director: Danny Maxwell. Technical Operations Manager: Andrew Behn. Marketing Director: Vince Maffeo.
Ownership: Comcast Cable Communications Inc. (MSO).

EVERGLADES CITY—Comcast Cable. Now served by NAPLES (formerly BONITA SPRINGS), FL [FL0029]. ICA: FL0150.

FANNING SPRINGS—Florida Cable, PO Box 498, 23748 State Rd 40, Astor, FL 32102-0498. Phone: 352-759-2788. Fax: 352-759-3577. Web Site: http://www.floridacable.com. Also serves Old Town. ICA: FL0378.
TV Market Ranking: Below 100 (FANNING SPRINGS, Old Town).
Channel capacity: N.A. Channels available but not in use: N.A.

Basic Service
Subscribers: N.A.
Programming (received off-air): WCJB-TV (ABC, CW) Gainesville; WESH (NBC) Daytona Beach; WGFL (CBS, MNT) High Springs; WOGX (FOX) Ocala; WUFT (PBS) Gainesville.
Programming (via satellite): ABC Family Channel; Arts & Entertainment; Cartoon Network; CNN; Country Music TV; C-SPAN; C-SPAN 2; Discovery Channel; ESPN; ESPN 2; Headline News; HGTV; History Channel; Home Shopping Network; Lifetime; MTV; Nickelodeon; QVC; Spike TV; Syfy; TBS Superstation; The Learning Channel; Trinity Broadcasting Network; Turner Classic Movies; Turner Network TV; USA Network; VH1; Weather Channel; WGN America.

Pay Service 1
Pay Units: N.A.
Programming (via satellite): HBO (multiplexed).

Internet Service
Operational: No.

Telephone Service
None
General Manager: Jim Pierce. Plant Manager: Larry English. Office Manager: Alita Dawson.
Ownership: Florida Cable Inc. (MSO).

FERNANDINA BEACH—Comcast Cable. Now served by JACKSONVILLE, FL [FL0002]. ICA: FL0088.

FLORAHOME—Florida Cable, PO Box 498, 23748 State Rd 40, Astor, FL 32102-0498. Phone: 352-759-2788. Fax: 352-759-3577. Web Site: http://www.floridacable.com. Also serves Grandin & Keystone Heights. ICA: FL0221.

TV Market Ranking: Below 100 (FLORAHOME, Grandin, Keystone Heights). Franchise award date: August 29, 1990. Franchise expiration date: N.A. Began: December 1, 1990.

Channel capacity: N.A. Channels available but not in use: N.A.

Basic Service

Subscribers: 150.

Programming (received off-air): WAWS (FOX, MNT) Jacksonville; WCJB-TV (ABC, CW) Gainesville; WCWJ (CW) Jacksonville; WJCT (PBS) Jacksonville; WJXT (IND) Jacksonville; WJXX (ABC) Orange Park; WOGX (FOX) Ocala; WTEV-TV (CBS) Jacksonville; WTLV (NBC) Jacksonville; WUFT (PBS) Gainesville.

Programming (via satellite): ABC Family Channel; AMC; Animal Planet; Arts & Entertainment; Cartoon Network; CNBC; CNN; Comedy Central; Cooking Channel; Country Music TV; C-SPAN; Discovery Channel; Discovery Health Channel; Disney Channel; Do-It-Yourself; ESPN; ESPN 2; ESPNews; Food Network; Fox News Channel; FX; GSN; Hallmark Channel; Headline News; HGTV; History Channel; Lifetime; MoviePlex; MTV; Nickelodeon; Outdoor Channel; QVC; SoapNet; Speed Channel; Spike TV; Syfy; TBS Superstation; The Learning Channel; Travel Channel; Trinity Broadcasting Network; truTV; Turner Classic Movies; Turner Network TV; TV Land; USA Network; VH1; WE tv; Weather Channel; WGN America.

Fee: $45.00 installation; $33.42 monthly.

Pay Service 1

Pay Units: 30.

Programming (via satellite): Cinemax; HBO; The Movie Channel.

Fee: $8.95 monthly (TMC), $10.95 monthly (Cinemax or HBO).

Video-On-Demand: No

Internet Service

Operational: No.

Telephone Service

None

General Manager: Jim Pierce. Plant Manager: Larry English. Office Manager: Alita Dawson.

Ownership: Florida Cable Inc. (MSO).

FLORIDA HIGHLANDS—Formerly served by KLiP Interactive. No longer in operation. ICA: FL0231.

FOREST GLEN—Now served by WEST PALM BEACH, FL [FL0008]. ICA: FL0232.

FORT LAUDERDALE—Comcast Cable. Now served by BROWARD COUNTY, FL [FL0016]. ICA: FL0014.

FORT MYERS—Comcast Cable. Now served by NAPLES (formerly BONITA SPRINGS), FL [FL0029]. ICA: FL0025.

FORT PIERCE—Comcast Cable. Now served by VERO BEACH, FL [FL0040]. ICA: FL0043.

FORT PIERCE—Formerly served by Wireless Broadcasting of Fort Pierce. No longer in operation. ICA: FL0303.

FORT WALTON BEACH—Cox Communications, 2205 La Vista Ave, Pensacola, FL 32504. Phone: 850-862-4142. Fax: 850-479-3912. Web Site: http://www.cox.com/gulfcoast. Also serves Cinco Bayou, Crestview, Destin, Eglin Air Force Base, Freeport, Hurlburt Field, Mary Esther, Niceville, Okaloosa County (portions), Okaloosa Island, Shalimar, Topsil & Walton County (portions). ICA: FL0023.

TV Market Ranking: 59 (Cinco Bayou, FORT WALTON BEACH, Hurlburt Field, Mary Esther, Okaloosa County (portions), Okaloosa Island); Below 100 (Crestview, Destin, Eglin Air Force Base, Niceville, Shalimar, Topsil, Walton County (portions), Okaloosa County (portions)). Franchise award date: April 18, 1985. Franchise expiration date: N.A. Began: June 12, 1963.

Channel capacity: N.A. Channels available but not in use: N.A.

Basic Service

Subscribers: N.A. Included in Pensacola

Programming (received off-air): WALA-TV (FOX) Mobile; WEAR-TV (ABC) Pensacola; WFGX (MNT) Fort Walton Beach; WHBR (IND) Pensacola; WJHG-TV (CW, MNT, NBC) Panama City; WJTC (IND) Pensacola; WKRG-TV (CBS) Mobile; WMBB (ABC) Panama City; WMPV-TV (TBN) Mobile; WPAN (IND) Fort Walton Beach; WPMI-TV (NBC) Mobile; WSRE (PBS) Pensacola; WTVY (CBS, CW, MNT) Dothan; 14 FMs.

Programming (via satellite): C-SPAN; C-SPAN 2; Home Shopping Network; QVC; TBS Superstation; WGN America.

Current originations: Leased Access; Public Access.

Fee: $56.50 installation; $11.54 monthly.

Expanded Basic Service 1

Subscribers: 30,649.

Programming (via satellite): ABC Family Channel; AMC; Animal Planet; Arts & Entertainment; BET Networks; Bravo; Cartoon Network; CNBC; CNN; Comedy Central; Discovery Channel; Disney Channel; E! Entertainment Television; ESPN; Eternal Word TV Network; Fox News Channel; Fox Sports Net Florida; Headline News; HGTV; INSP; Lifetime; MSNBC; MTV; Nickelodeon; Product Information Network; Sneak Prevue; Speed Channel; Spike TV; SunSports TV; Syfy; The Learning Channel; Turner Network TV; TV Guide Network; USA Network; Versus; VH1; Weather Channel.

Fee: $35.00 installation; $31.69 monthly.

Expanded Basic Service 2

Subscribers: N.A.

Programming (via satellite): ESPN 2; Golf Channel; History Channel; Turner Classic Movies.

Fee: $6.45 monthly.

Digital Basic Service

Subscribers: 12,118.

Programming (via satellite): BBC America; Bloomberg Television; Discovery Digital Networks; G4; Golf Channel; GSN; Independent Film Channel; Lifetime Movie Network; MuchMusic Network; Music Choice; Sundance Channel; Toon Disney.

Fee: $12.99 monthly.

Pay Service 1

Pay Units: 40,150.

Programming (via satellite): Cinemax (multiplexed); HBO (multiplexed); Showtime; The Movie Channel.

Fee: $11.00 monthly (each).

Digital Pay Service 1

Pay Units: N.A.

Programming (via satellite): Cinemax (multiplexed); Encore; HBO (multiplexed); Showtime (multiplexed); Starz; The Movie Channel (multiplexed).

Fee: $27.00 monthly.

Video-On-Demand: Planned

Pay-Per-View

Addressable homes: 11,981.

ESPN Extra, Addressable: Yes; ESPN Now; iN DEMAND; iN DEMAND (delivered digitally); Playboy TV; Playboy TV (delivered digitally); Fresh; Fresh (delivered digitally).

Internet Service

Operational: Yes.

Subscribers: 8,906.

Broadband Service: Cox High Speed Internet.

Fee: $99.00 installation; $19.95-$59.95 monthly; $10.00 modem lease; $99.00 modem purchase.

Telephone Service

Digital: Operational

Fee: $10.99-$44.79 monthly

Miles of plant & homes passed included in Pensacola

Vice President & General Manager: Keith Gregory. Vice President, Network Operations: Mark O'Ceallaigh. Vice President, Marketing: Dale Tapley. Marketing Director: Bob Hartnet. Public Affairs Director: Shela Nichols.

Ownership: Cox Communications Inc. (MSO).

FREEPORT—Cox Communications. Now served by FORT WALTON BEACH, FL [FL0023]. ICA: FL0357.

FRUITLAND PARK—Florida Cable, PO Box 498, 23748 State Rd 40, Astor, FL 32102-0498. Phones: 352-759-3577; 800-388-6577; 352-759-2788. E-mail: support@floridacable.com. Web Site: http://www.floridacable.com. ICA: FL0350.

TV Market Ranking: Below 100 (FRUITLAND PARK). Franchise award date: N.A. Franchise expiration date: N.A. Began: N.A.

Channel capacity: 56 (not 2-way capable). Channels available but not in use: 10.

Basic Service

Subscribers: 220.

Programming (received off-air): WCJB-TV (ABC, CW) Gainesville; WCLF (IND) Clearwater; WEDU (PBS) Tampa; WFLA-TV (NBC) Tampa; WFTS-TV (ABC) Tampa; WMOR-TV (IND) Lakeland; WOGX (FOX) Ocala; WTOG (CW) St. Petersburg; WTSP (CBS) St. Petersburg; WTTA (MNT) St. Petersburg; WTVT (FOX) Tampa; WUFT (PBS) Gainesville; WVEA-TV (UNV) Venice.

Programming (via satellite): ABC Family Channel; Animal Planet; Arts & Entertainment; Cartoon Network; CNN; Country Music TV; C-SPAN; Discovery Channel; Disney Channel; E! Entertainment Television; ESPN; ESPN 2; Headline News; HGTV; History Channel; Home Shopping Network; Nickelodeon; Spike TV; Syfy; TBS Superstation; The Learning Channel; truTV; Turner Classic Movies; Turner Network TV; TV Land; USA Network; VH1; Weather Channel; WGN America.

Fee: $29.95 installation; $29.95 monthly.

Pay Service 1

Pay Units: 39.

Programming (via satellite): Cinemax.

Pay Service 2

Pay Units: 56.

Programming (via satellite): HBO.

Video-On-Demand: No

Internet Service

Operational: No.

Telephone Service

None

Miles of Plant: 45.0 (coaxial); None (fiber optic). Homes passed: 847.

General Manager: Jim Pierce. Plant Manager: Larry English. Office Manager: Alita Dawson.

Ownership: Florida Cable Inc. (MSO).

GADSDEN COUNTY (portions)—Mediacom. Now served by HAVANA, FL [FL0144]. ICA: FL0360.

GAINESVILLE—Cox Communications, 6020 NW 43rd St, Gainesville, FL 32653-3338. Phone: 352-377-1741. Fax: 352-378-2790. Web Site: http://www.cox.com/gainesvilleocala. Also serves Alachua, Alachua County (portions), Marion County (portions), Newberry & Ocala. ICA: FL0027.

TV Market Ranking: Below 100 (Alachua, Alachua County (portions), GAINESVILLE, Marion County (portions), Newberry, Ocala). Franchise award date: January 1, 1963. Franchise expiration date: N.A. Began: May 1, 1965.

Channel capacity: 70 (operating 2-way). Channels available but not in use: N.A.

Basic Service

Subscribers: 107,000.

Programming (received off-air): WCJB-TV (ABC, CW) Gainesville; WGFL (CBS, MNT) High Springs; WKCF (CW) Clermont; WLUF-LP Gainesville; WNBW-DT (NBC) Gainesville; WOGX (FOX) Ocala; WOPX-TV (ION) Melbourne; WUFT (PBS) Gainesville.

Programming (via microwave): WESH (NBC) Daytona Beach; WJXT (IND) Jacksonville.

Programming (via satellite): C-SPAN; C-SPAN 2; Home Shopping Network; MyNetworkTV Inc.; QVC; ShopNBC; TBS Superstation; TV Guide Network; WGN America.

Current originations: Leased Access; Government Access; Educational Access.

Fee: $21.36 installation; $11.10 monthly; $.81 converter.

Expanded Basic Service 1

Subscribers: N.A.

Programming (via satellite): ABC Family Channel; AMC; Animal Planet; Arts & Entertainment; BET Networks; Bravo; Cartoon Network; CNBC; CNN; Comedy Central; Country Music TV; Discovery Channel; Discovery Health Channel; Disney Channel; E! Entertainment Television; ESPN; ESPN 2; Food Network; Fox News Channel; Fox Sports Net Florida; FX; Golf Channel; Headline News; HGTV; History Channel; Lifetime; MSNBC; MTV; MTV2; Nickelodeon; Speed Channel; Spike TV; SunSports TV; Syfy; The Learning Channel; Travel Channel; Turner Classic Movies; Turner Network TV; TV Land; Univision; USA Network; Versus; VH1; Weather Channel.

Fee: $34.89 monthly.

Digital Basic Service

Subscribers: N.A.

Programming (via satellite): Discovery Kids Channel; Discovery Military Channel; Discovery Planet Green; History Channel International; ID Investigation Discovery; MLB Network; Music Choice; National Geographic Channel; Nick Jr.; Science Channel; Weatherscan.

Fee: $4.50 monthly.

Digital Expanded Basic Service

Subscribers: N.A.

Programming (via satellite): Encore (multiplexed); Independent Film Channel; Lifetime Movie Network; LOGO; Sundance Channel.

Fee: $5.00 monthly.

Digital Expanded Basic Service 2

Subscribers: N.A.

Programming (via satellite): BBC America; Boomerang; BYU Television; Chiller; CMT

Pure Country; Cooking Channel; Disney XD; Encore Wam; Eternal Word TV Network; Fox Reality Channel; Fuse; GSN; Hallmark Channel; MTV Hits; MTV Jams; MTV Tres; mtvU; NickToons TV; Oxygen; PBS Kids Sprout; SoapNet; Style Network; TeenNick; truTV; TV One; VH1 Classic; VH1 Soul; WE tv.
Fee: $5.00 monthly.

Digital Expanded Basic Service 3
Subscribers: N.A.
Programming (via satellite): Bio; Bloomberg Television; Cox Sports Television; Do-It-Yourself; ESPN Classic Sports; ESPN U; ESPNews; FitTV; Fox Business Channel; Fox Soccer; Fuel TV; G4; History Channel International; HorseRacing TV; NBA TV; NFL Network; NHL Network; Tennis Channel; TVG Network.
Fee: $5.00 monthly.

Digital Expanded Basic Service 4
Subscribers: N.A.
Programming (via satellite): Boomerang en Espanol; Canal Sur; CNN en Espanol; De Pelicula; Discovery en Espanol; Discovery Familia; Disney XD en Espanol; ESPN Deportes; Fox Sports en Espanol; GalaVision; History Channel en Espanol; MTV Tres; Ritmoson Latino; Telehit; Telemundo; TV Colombia; Univision.
Fee: $5.00 monthly.

Digital Expanded Basic Service 5
Subscribers: N.A.
Programming (received off-air): WCJB-TV (ABC, CW) Gainesville; WESH (NBC) Daytona Beach; WGFL (CBS, MNT) High Springs; WNBW-DT (NBC) Gainesville; WOGX (FOX) Ocala; WUFT (PBS) Gainesville.
Programming (via satellite): AMC HD; Animal Planet HD; Arts & Entertainment HD; Bravo HD; CNBC HD+; CNN HD; Discovery Channel HD; Discovery HD Theater; Discovery Planet Green HD; ESPN 2 HD; ESPN HD; Food Network HD; Golf Channel HD; Hallmark Movie Channel HD; History Channel HD; Lifetime Movie Network HD; Lifetime Television HD; National Geographic Channel HD Network; NFL Network HD; Palladia; Science Channel HD; Syfy HD; TBS in HD; TLC HD; Turner Network TV HD; Universal HD; USA Network HD; Versus HD.

Digital Pay Service 1
Pay Units: N.A.
Programming (via satellite): Cinemax (multiplexed); Cinemax HD; Encore; HBO (multiplexed); HBO HD; Showtime (multiplexed); Showtime HD; Starz (multiplexed); Starz HDTV; The Movie Channel (multiplexed).
Fee: $11.99 monthly (HBO, Cinemax, Showtime/TMC or Starz/Encore).

Video-On-Demand: Yes

Pay-Per-View
Addressable homes: 22,097.
Hot Choice (delivered digitally), Addressable: Yes; Spice: Xcess (delivered digitally); Club Jenna (delivered digitally); iN DEMAND; iN DEMAND (delivered digitally); Playboy TV (delivered digitally); Fresh; Shorteez (delivered digitally).

Internet Service
Operational: Yes.
Broadband Service: Cox High Speed Internet.
Fee: $29.95 installation; $19.99-$44.99 monthly; $10.00 modem lease; $299.95 modem purchase.

Telephone Service
Digital: Operational
Fee: $30.00 installation; $9.97-$39.95 monthly

Miles of Plant: 2,100.0 (coaxial); None (fiber optic). Homes passed: 164,754. Total homes in franchised area: 164,754. Miles of plant (coax) includes miles of plant (fiber)

Vice President & General Manager: Mike Giampietro. Vice President, Human Resources: Kia Painter. Network Operations Director: Brad Spatz. Sales & Marketing Director: David Saldarriago. Business Operations Director: Steve Chapman. Public Affairs Specialist: Devon Chestnut.

Franchise fee: 5% of gross.

Ownership: Cox Communications Inc. (MSO).

GOLDEN GATE—Time Warner Cable. Now served by NAPLES, FL [FL0029]. ICA: FL0062.

GOLF VILLAGE—Now served by DELRAY BEACH, FL [FL0091]. ICA: FL0193.

GREENACRES CITY—Now served by WEST PALM BEACH, FL [FL0008]. ICA: FL0053.

GREENSBORO—Mediacom. Now served by HAVANA, FL [FL0144]. ICA: FL0204.

GREENVILLE—KLiP Interactive, 455 Gees Mill Business Court, Conyers, GA 30013. Phone: 678-727-7100. Fax: 678-727-7002. E-mail: jsheehan@klipia.com. Web Site: http://www.klipia.com. ICA: FL0235.

TV Market Ranking: Below 100 (GREENVILLE). Franchise award date: N.A. Franchise expiration date: N.A. Began: N.A.

Channel capacity: 45 (not 2-way capable). Channels available but not in use: 13.

Basic Service
Subscribers: 84.
Programming (received off-air): WCTV (CBS, MNT) Thomasville; WFSU-TV (PBS) Tallahassee; WTLH (CW, FOX) Bainbridge; WTWC-TV (NBC) Tallahassee; WTXL-TV (ABC) Tallahassee.
Programming (via satellite): ABC Family Channel; Animal Planet; Arts & Entertainment; BET Networks; CNN; Country Music TV; Discovery Channel; Disney Channel; ESPN; ESPN 2; Fox News Channel; FX; Headline News; Lifetime; Nickelodeon; QVC; Spike TV; TBS Superstation; The Learning Channel; Travel Channel; Trinity Broadcasting Network; Turner Network TV; USA Network; Weather Channel; WGN America.
Fee: $29.95 installation; $33.47 monthly.

Pay Service 1
Pay Units: 12.
Programming (via satellite): Cinemax; HBO.
Fee: $25.00 installation; $10.95 monthly (each).

Video-On-Demand: No

Internet Service
Operational: No.

Telephone Service
None

Miles of Plant: 20.0 (coaxial); None (fiber optic). Homes passed: 436.

Chief Executive Officer: Joseph A. Sheehan. General Manager East: Mark Miller. General Manager West: Vance Johnson.

Ownership: KLiP Interactive LLC (MSO).

GRETNA—Mediacom. Now served by HAVANA, FL [FL0144]. ICA: FL0202.

GULF BREEZE—Mediacom, 1613 Nantahala Beach Rd, Gulf Breeze, FL 32563-8944. Phones: 850-934-2520 (Southern division office); 850-934-7700. Fax: 850-934-2508. Web Site: http://www.mediacomcable.com. Also serves Atmore, Brewton & East Brewton, AL; Baker, East Milton, Escambia County (portions), Holley (portions), Milton, Navarre Beach, Pensacola Beach, Pensacola Naval Air Station, Santa Rosa County (portions) & Whiting Field Naval Air Station, FL. ICA: FL0070.

TV Market Ranking: 59 (East Milton, Escambia County (portions), GULF BREEZE, Holley (portions), Milton, Navarre Beach, Pensacola Beach, Pensacola Naval Air Station, Santa Rosa County (portions), Whiting Field Naval Air Station); Below 100 (Baker); Outside TV Markets (Atmore, Brewton, East Brewton). Franchise award date: March 21, 1977. Franchise expiration date: N.A. Began: December 29, 1978.

Channel capacity: N.A. Channels available but not in use: N.A.

Basic Service
Subscribers: 27,702.
Programming (received off-air): WALA-TV (FOX) Mobile; WEAR-TV (ABC) Pensacola; WFGX (MNT) Fort Walton Beach; WFNA (CW) Gulf Shores; WHBR (IND) Pensacola; WJTC (IND) Pensacola; WKRG-TV (CBS) Mobile; WMPV-TV (TBN) Mobile; WPAN (IND) Fort Walton Beach; WPMI-TV (NBC) Mobile; WSRE (PBS) Pensacola.
Programming (via satellite): ABC Family Channel; AMC; Animal Planet; Arts & Entertainment; BET Networks; Bravo; Cartoon Network; CNBC; CNN; Comedy Central; Country Music TV; C-SPAN; C-SPAN 2; Discovery Channel; Disney Channel; E! Entertainment Television; ESPN; ESPN 2; Eternal Word TV Network; FitTV; Food Network; Fox News Channel; FX; Golf Channel; Hallmark Channel; Headline News; HGTV; History Channel; Home Shopping Network; ION Television; Lifetime; MSNBC; MTV; Nickelodeon; Outdoor Channel; Oxygen; QVC; Speed Channel; Spike TV; SunSports TV; Syfy; TBS Superstation; The Learning Channel; Travel Channel; truTV; Turner Network TV; TV Guide Network; TV Land; USA Network; VH1; WE tv; Weather Channel; WGN America.
Fee: $24.95 installation; $44.95 monthly; $2.95 converter; $15.00 additional installation.

Digital Basic Service
Subscribers: 6,820.
Programming (via satellite): BBC America; Bio; Discovery Digital Networks; Fox Movie Channel; Fox Sports World; Fuse; G4; GSN; Halogen Network; History Channel International; Independent Film Channel; Lifetime Movie Network; Music Choice; Style Network; Turner Classic Movies.
Fee: $12.00 monthly.

Digital Pay Service 1
Pay Units: 4,035.
Programming (via satellite): Cinemax (multiplexed); Encore (multiplexed); Flix; HBO (multiplexed); Showtime (multiplexed); Starz (multiplexed); Sundance Channel; The Movie Channel (multiplexed).

Video-On-Demand: Yes

Pay-Per-View
Addressable homes: 6,820.
ESPN Now (delivered digitally), Addressable: Yes; ETC (delivered digitally); Pleasure (delivered digitally); TVN Entertainment (delivered digitally); sports (delivered digitally).

Internet Service
Operational: Yes.
Subscribers: 4,908.
Broadband Service: Mediacom High Speed Internet.
Fee: $42.95 monthly.

Telephone Service
Digital: Operational

Miles of Plant: 940.0 (coaxial); None (fiber optic). Homes passed: 38,446.

Vice President: David Servies. Regional Technical Operations Director: Eddie Arnold. Engineering Director: Powell Bedgood. Technical Operations Manager: Shayne Routhe. Sales & Marketing Manager: Joey Nagem. Government Relations Director: Barbara Bonowicz.

City fee: 5% of gross.

Ownership: Mediacom LLC (MSO).

HAMPTON—Florida Cable, PO Box 498, 23748 State Rd 40, Astor, FL 32102-0498. Phones: 352-759-2788; 800-779-2788. Fax: 352-759-3577. E-mail: support@floridacable.com. Web Site: http://www.floridacable.com. Also serves Hampton 2 & Starke. ICA: FL0237.

TV Market Ranking: Below 100 (HAMPTON, Hampton 2, Starke). Franchise award date: August 8, 1989. Franchise expiration date: N.A. Began: N.A.

Channel capacity: 36 (not 2-way capable). Channels available but not in use: None.

Basic Service
Subscribers: 245.
Programming (received off-air): WAWS (FOX, MNT) Jacksonville; WCWJ (CW) Jacksonville; WJCT (PBS) Jacksonville; WJEB-TV (ETV) Jacksonville; WJXT (IND) Jacksonville; WJXX (ABC) Orange Park; WTEV-TV (CBS) Jacksonville; WTLV (NBC) Jacksonville; WUFT (PBS) Gainesville.
Programming (via satellite): ABC Family Channel; Animal Planet; Arts & Entertainment; Cartoon Network; CNN; Comedy Central; Discovery Channel; Disney Channel; E! Entertainment Television; ESPN; Food Network; Fox News Channel; Fuse; FX; Great American Country; Headline News; Home Shopping Network; Lifetime; Speed Channel; Syfy; TBS Superstation; Toon Disney; Turner Network TV; USA Network; Weather Channel; WGN America.
Fee: $30.00 installation; $39.45 monthly.

Pay Service 1
Pay Units: 88.
Programming (via satellite): Cinemax; HBO; Showtime; The Movie Channel.
Fee: $9.95 monthly (each).

Internet Service
Operational: No.

Telephone Service
None

Miles of Plant: 19.0 (coaxial); None (fiber optic). Homes passed: 1,492.

General Manager: Jim Pierce. Plant Manager: Larry English. Office Manager: Alita Dawson.

Ownership: Florida Cable Inc. (MSO).

HASTINGS—Comcast Cable, 6805 Southpoint Pkwy, Jacksonville, FL 32216. Phone: 904-374-8000. Fax: 904-374-7622. Web Site: http://www.comcast.com. Also serves St. Johns County. ICA: FL0187.

TV Market Ranking: 68 (St. Johns County (portions)); Outside TV Markets (HASTINGS, St. Johns County (portions)). Franchise award date: N.A. Franchise expiration date: N.A. Began: December 1, 1982.

Channel capacity: 40 (not 2-way capable). Channels available but not in use: 12.

Basic Service
Subscribers: N.A. Included with Jacksonville
Programming (received off-air): WAWS (FOX, MNT) Jacksonville; WCWJ (CW) Jacksonville; WJCT (PBS) Jacksonville;

WJEB-TV (ETV) Jacksonville; WJXT (IND) Jacksonville; WJXX (ABC) Orange Park; WTEV-TV (CBS) Jacksonville; WTLV (NBC) Jacksonville; WUFT (PBS) Gainesville.
Programming (via satellite): C-SPAN; TBS Superstation; TV Guide Network; Weather Channel.
Current originations: Educational Access; Leased Access.
Fee: $43.99 installation; $20.17 monthly; $1.65 converter.

Expanded Basic Service 1
Subscribers: 216.
Programming (via satellite): ABC Family Channel; AMC; Animal Planet; Arts & Entertainment; BET Networks; Bravo; Cartoon Network; CNBC; CNN; Comcast/Charter Sports Southeast (CSS); Comedy Central; Country Music TV; C-SPAN 2; Discovery Channel; Disney Channel; E! Entertainment Television; ESPN; ESPN 2; ESPN Classic Sports; Eternal Word TV Network; Food Network; Fox News Channel; Fox Sports Net; Fuse; FX; Golf Channel; Great American Country; Hallmark Channel; Headline News; HGTV; History Channel; Home Shopping Network; Lifetime; MTV; MTV2; Nickelodeon; QVC; Speed Channel; Spike TV; SunSports TV; Syfy; The Learning Channel; truTV; Turner Network TV; TV Land; Univision; USA Network; Versus; VH1; WE tv; Weatherscan; WGN America.
Fee: $27.00 monthly.

Digital Basic Service
Subscribers: N.A.
Programming (received off-air): WAWS (FOX, MNT) Jacksonville; WJCT (PBS) Jacksonville; WJXX (ABC) Orange Park; WTLV (NBC) Jacksonville.
Programming (via satellite): BBC America; Bio; Black Family Channel; Bloomberg Television; Bravo; Canales N; Cooking Channel; Discovery Digital Networks; Discovery HD Theater; DMX Music; Do-It-Yourself; ESPN; ESPNews; FamilyNet; Fox College Sports Atlantic; Fox College Sports Central; Fox College Sports Pacific; Fox Sports World; G4; GAS; GSN; Halogen Network; History Channel International; Independent Film Channel; INHD; International Television (ITV); Jewelry Television; Lifetime Movie Network; Lime; MSNBC; MTV Networks Digital Suite; Music Choice; National Geographic Channel; NBA TV; NFL Network; Nick Jr.; Nick Too; NickToons TV; Outdoor Channel; Ovation; ShopNBC; Sundance Channel; The Word Network; Toon Disney; Trinity Broadcasting Network; Turner Classic Movies; Turner Network TV; TV One; WTEV-TV (CBS) Jacksonville.
Fee: $22.99 monthly.

Pay Service 1
Pay Units: 167.
Programming (via satellite): Cinemax; HBO.
Fee: $15.95 monthly (each).

Digital Pay Service 1
Pay Units: N.A.
Programming (via satellite): Cinemax (multiplexed); Cinemax HD; Encore (multiplexed); Flix; HBO (multiplexed); HBO HD; Showtime (multiplexed); Showtime HD; Starz (multiplexed); Starz HDTV; The Movie Channel (multiplexed).
Fee: $15.95 monthly (each).

Video-On-Demand: No

Pay-Per-View
iN DEMAND (delivered digitally); ESPN (delivered digitally); NASCAR In Car (delivered digitally); NBA League Pass (delivered digitally); NHL Center Ice (delivered digitally); MLB Extra Innings (delivered digitally); Fresh (delivered digitally); Shorteez (delivered digitally); Playboy TV (delivered digitally).

Internet Service
Operational: Yes.

Telephone Service
Digital: Operational

Miles of Plant: 12.0 (coaxial); None (fiber optic). Homes passed: 709.
Vice President & General Manager: Doug McMillan. Engineering Director: Mike Humphrey. Vice President, Marketing: Vic Scarborough. Government Affairs Director: Bill Ferry.
City fee: 4% of gross.
Ownership: Comcast Cable Communications Inc. (MSO).

HAVANA—Mediacom, 275 Norman Dr, Valdosta, GA 31601. Phone: 229-244-3852. Fax: 229-244-0724. Web Site: http://www.mediacomcable.com. Also serves Gadsden County (portions), Greensboro & Gretna. ICA: FL0144.
TV Market Ranking: Below 100 (Gadsden County (portions), Greensboro, Gretna, HAVANA). Franchise award date: October 3, 1977. Franchise expiration date: N.A. Began: December 1, 1977.
Channel capacity: N.A. Channels available but not in use: N.A.

Basic Service
Subscribers: 2,508.
Programming (received off-air): WCTV (CBS, MNT) Thomasville; WFSU-TV (PBS) Tallahassee; WJHG-TV (CW, MNT, NBC) Panama City; WMBB (ABC) Panama City; WTLH (CW, FOX) Bainbridge; WTWC-TV (NBC) Tallahassee; WTXL-TV (ABC) Tallahassee.
Programming (via satellite): ABC Family Channel; AMC; AmericanLife TV Network; Animal Planet; Arts & Entertainment; BET Networks; Bravo; Cartoon Network; CNBC; CNN; Comedy Central; Country Music TV; C-SPAN; C-SPAN 2; Discovery Channel; Disney Channel; E! Entertainment Television; ESPN; ESPN 2; Eternal Word TV Network; Food Network; Fox News Channel; FX; Golf Channel; Hallmark Channel; Headline News; HGTV; History Channel; Home Shopping Network; INSP; ION Television; Jewelry Television; Lifetime; MSNBC; MTV; MTV2; Nickelodeon; Outdoor Channel; QVC; ShopNBC; SoapNet; Speed Channel; Spike TV; SunSports TV; Syfy; TBS Superstation; The Learning Channel; Toon Disney; Travel Channel; Trinity Broadcasting Network; truTV; Turner Network TV; TV Guide Network; TV Land; Univision; USA Network; VH1; WE tv; Weather Channel; WGN America.
Current originations: Government Access.
Fee: $29.50 installation; $44.95 monthly; $3.35 converter.

Digital Basic Service
Subscribers: N.A.
Programming (received off-air): WCTV (CBS, MNT) Thomasville; WFSU-TV (PBS) Tallahassee; WTLH (CW, FOX) Bainbridge; WTXL-TV (ABC) Tallahassee.
Programming (via satellite): ABC News Now; BBC America; Bio; Bloomberg Television; CCTV-9 (CCTV International); CMT Pure Country; Discovery Health Channel; Discovery Home Channel; Discovery Kids Channel; Discovery Military Channel; DMX Music; ESPN 2 HD; ESPN HD; ESPNews; Fox Movie Channel; Fox Soccer; Fuse; G4; Golf Channel; Great American Country; GSN; Halogen Network; HDNet; HDNet Movies; History Channel International; ID Investigation Discovery; Independent Film Channel; ION Life; Lifetime Movie Network; MTV Hits; National Geographic Channel; Nick Jr.; NickToons TV; Ovation; Qubo; ReelzChannel; RFD-TV; Science Television; Sleuth; Style Network; TeenNick; The Word Network; Turner Classic Movies; Universal HD; Versus; VH1 Classic; VH1 Soul.
Fee: $7.00 monthly; $5.00 converter.

Digital Pay Service 1
Pay Units: 255.
Programming (via satellite): Cinemax (multiplexed); Encore (multiplexed); HBO (multiplexed); HBO HD; Showtime (multiplexed); Showtime HD; Starz (multiplexed); Starz HDTV; The Movie Channel (multiplexed); The Movie Channel HD.
Fee: $9.95 monthly (Cinemax, Showtime or Starz), $11.95 monthly (HBO).

Video-On-Demand: Yes

Pay-Per-View
Addressable homes: 708.
iN DEMAND (delivered digitally); Sports PPV (delivered digitally).

Internet Service
Operational: Yes.
Broadband Service: Mediacom High Speed Internet.
Fee: $49.95 installation; $45.95 monthly.

Telephone Service
Analog: Not Operational
Digital: Operational

Homes passed: 4,537. Miles of plant (coax & fiber) included in Thomasville, GA
Regional Vice President: Sue Misiunas. Regional Technical Operations Manager: Gary McDougall. Regional Marketing Director: Melanie Hannasch. Marketing Manager: Daryl Channey.
Ownership: Mediacom LLC (MSO).

HAWTHORNE—CommuniComm Services, 17774 NW US Highway 441, High Springs, FL 32643-8749. Phone: 386-454-2299. Fax: 386-454-3705. Web Site: http://www.communicomm.com. ICA: FL0183.
TV Market Ranking: Below 100 (HAWTHORNE). Franchise award date: January 1, 1974. Franchise expiration date: N.A. Began: N.A.
Channel capacity: N.A. Channels available but not in use: N.A.

Basic Service
Subscribers: N.A. Included in High Springs
Programming (received off-air): WCJB-TV (ABC, CW) Gainesville; WJCT (PBS) Jacksonville; WKMG-TV (CBS) Orlando; WOGX (FOX) Ocala; WTLV (NBC) Jacksonville; WUFT (PBS) Gainesville.
Programming (via satellite): HGTV; Nick Jr.; QVC; TBS Superstation; WGN America.
Fee: $50.00 installation; $31.00 monthly.

Expanded Basic Service 1
Subscribers: N.A.
Programming (via satellite): ABC Family Channel; AMC; Arts & Entertainment; BET Networks; CNBC; CNN; Comedy Central; Country Music TV; Discovery Channel; ESPN; ESPN 2; Fox News Channel; FX; Headline News; Nickelodeon; Spike TV; SunSports TV; Trinity Broadcasting Network; Turner Network TV; USA Network; Weather Channel.

Digital Basic Service
Subscribers: N.A.
Programming (via satellite): Alterna'TV; BBC America; Bio; Blackbelt TV; Bloomberg Television; Bravo; Discovery Health Channel; Discovery Kids Channel; Discovery Military Channel; Discovery Planet Green; DMX Music; FitTV; Fox Soccer; Fuse; G4; Golf Channel; GSN; Halogen Network; History Channel; ID Investigation Discovery; Independent Film Channel; Lifetime Movie Network; Outdoor Channel; Science Channel; Speed Channel; Syfy; Turner Classic Movies; TVG Network; Versus; WE tv.

Pay Service 1
Pay Units: N.A. Included in High Springs
Programming (via satellite): Cinemax; Encore; HBO (multiplexed); Starz.
Fee: $30.00 installation; $9.95 monthly (Cinemax), $11.95 monthly (HBO).

Digital Pay Service 1
Pay Units: N.A.
Programming (via satellite): Cinemax (multiplexed); Encore (multiplexed); HBO (multiplexed); Starz (multiplexed).

Video-On-Demand: No

Pay-Per-View
iN DEMAND (delivered digitally); Hot Choice (delivered digitally); Playboy TV (delivered digitally); Fresh (delivered digitally).

Internet Service
Operational: No.
Fee: $51.95 monthly.

Telephone Service
None

Total homes in franchised area: 600. Homes passed and miles of plant included in High Springs
General Manager: Darrell Laird. Chief Technician: Michael Smith. Customer Service Manager: Cindy Ross.
Ownership: James Cable LLC (MSO).

HERNANDO COUNTY—Bright House Networks, 1004 US Hwy 92 W, Auburndale, FL 33823. Phones: 352-796-3006 (Customer service); 863-965-7733. Fax: 863-228-2204. Web Site: http://tampabay.brighthouse.com. Also serves Brooksville (portions), Brooksville (unincorporated areas), Cloverleaf Mobile Home Park, Spring Hill & Weeki Wachee. ICA: FL0238.
TV Market Ranking: 28 (HERNANDO COUNTY (portions)); Below 100 (Cloverleaf Mobile Home Park, HERNANDO COUNTY (portions)); Outside TV Markets (Brooksville (portions), Brooksville (unincorporated areas), Spring Hill, Weeki Wachee, HERNANDO COUNTY (portions)). Franchise award date: N.A. Franchise expiration date: N.A. Began: October 1, 1982.
Channel capacity: N.A. Channels available but not in use: None.

Basic Service
Subscribers: 119,566.
Programming (received off-air): WCLF (IND) Clearwater; WEDU (PBS) Tampa; WFLA-TV (NBC) Tampa; WFTS-TV (ABC) Tampa; WFTT-DT (TEL) Tampa; WMOR-TV (IND) Lakeland; WTOG (CW) St. Petersburg; WTSP (CBS) St. Petersburg; WTTA (MNT) St. Petersburg; WUSF-TV (PBS)

Tampa; WVEA-TV (UNV) Venice; WXPX-TV (ION) Bradenton.
Programming (via satellite): Bay News 9; Home Shopping Network; QVC; ShopNBC; TV Guide Network; WGN America.
Current originations: Educational Access.
Fee: $42.95 installation; $16.00 monthly.

Expanded Basic Service 1
Subscribers: N.A.
Programming (via satellite): ABC Family Channel; AMC; Animal Planet; Arts & Entertainment; BET Networks; Bravo; Cartoon Network; Catch 47; CNBC; CNN; Comedy Central; Country Music TV; C-SPAN; C-SPAN 2; Discovery Channel; Discovery Health Channel; Disney Channel; ESPN; ESPN 2; ESPN Classic Sports; Eternal Word TV Network; Food Network; Fox News Channel; Fox Sports Net Florida; FX; Golf Channel; Hallmark Channel; Headline News; HGTV; History Channel; Lifetime; Lifetime Movie Network; MoviePlex; MSNBC; MTV; National Geographic Channel; Nickelodeon; Oxygen; Spike TV; SunSports TV; Syfy; TBS Superstation; The Learning Channel; Travel Channel; truTV; Turner Classic Movies; Turner Network TV; TV Land; USA Network; Versus; VH1; WE tv; Weather Channel.
Fee: $28.95 monthly.

Digital Basic Service
Subscribers: 10,315.
Programming (received off-air): WEDU (PBS) Tampa; WFLA-TV (NBC) Tampa; WFTS-TV (ABC) Tampa; WMOR-TV (IND) Lakeland; WTSP (CBS) St. Petersburg; WTVT (FOX) Tampa.
Programming (via satellite): American-Life TV Network; America's Store; Auction TV; Bay News 9; BBC America; Bio; Black Family Channel; Bloomberg Television; Canales N; Cooking Channel; C-SPAN 3; Current; Discovery Digital Networks; Discovery HD Theater; Disney Channel; Do-It-Yourself; ESPN; ESPNews; Eternal Word TV Network; FitTV; Flix; Fox College Sports Atlantic; Fox College Sports Central; Fox College Sports Pacific; Fox Soccer; Fuel TV; G4; GAS; Great American Country; GSN; HDNet; HDNet Movies; History Channel International; INHD; Lifetime Real Women; MTV2; Music Choice; NBA TV; Nick Jr.; NickToons TV; Outdoor Channel; Ovation; Sleuth; SoapNet; Speed Channel; Style Network; Sundance Channel; Tennis Channel; Toon Disney; Trinity Broadcasting Network; Turner Network TV; TV One; Universal HD; VH1 Classic.
Fee: $11.95 monthly.

Digital Pay Service 1
Pay Units: N.A.
Programming (via satellite): Cinemax (multiplexed); HBO (multiplexed); HBO HD; Showtime (multiplexed); Showtime HD; Starz (multiplexed); The Movie Channel (multiplexed).
Fee: $25.00 installation; $12.55 monthly (each).

Video-On-Demand: Yes

Pay-Per-View
Addressable homes: 10,315.
iN DEMAND (delivered digitally), Addressable: Yes; Playboy TV (delivered digitally); Pleasure (delivered digitally); Fresh (delivered digitally); Shorteez (delivered digitally).

Internet Service
Operational: Yes.
Subscribers: 10,864.
Broadband Service: Road Runner.
Fee: $39.95 installation; $29.95 monthly.

Telephone Service
Digital: Operational
Fee: $39.95 monthly
Miles of Plant: 1,138.0 (coaxial); None (fiber optic).
Division President: Kevin Hyman. Vice President & General Manager: Dave Ross. Vice President, Engineering: Gene White. Engineering Director: Scott Twyman. Marketing Director: Robb Bennett.
County fee: 5% of gross.
Ownership: Bright House Networks LLC (MSO).

HERNANDO COUNTY—Florida Cable, PO Box 498, 23748 State Rd 40, Astor, FL 32102-0498. Phones: 800-779-2788; 352-759-2788. Fax: 352-759-3797. E-mail: support@floridacable.com. Web Site: http://www.floridacable.com. Also serves Brooksville, Bushnell, Nobleton, Sumter County & Webster. ICA: FL0148.
TV Market Ranking: 55 (Brooksville, Bushnell, HERNANDO COUNTY, Nobleton, Sumter County, Webster). Franchise award date: May 18, 1989. Franchise expiration date: N.A. Began: N.A.
Channel capacity: 37 (not 2-way capable). Channels available but not in use: None.

Basic Service
Subscribers: 336.
Programming (received off-air): WACX (IND) Leesburg; WEDU (PBS) Tampa; WFLA-TV (NBC) Tampa; WFTS-TV (ABC) Tampa; WFTT-DT (TEL) Tampa; WKCF (CW) Clermont; WMOR-TV (IND) Lakeland; WTOG (CW) St. Petersburg; WTSP (CBS) St. Petersburg; WTVT (FOX) Tampa.
Programming (via satellite): ABC Family Channel; Animal Planet; Arts & Entertainment; Cartoon Network; CNN; Comedy Central; Discovery Channel; Disney Channel; ESPN; Food Network; Fox News Channel; Fuse; FX; Great American Country; Headline News; Lifetime; QVC; Showtime; Speed Channel; SunSports TV; TBS Superstation; Turner Network TV; USA Network; Weather Channel; WGN America.
Fee: $30.00 installation; $39.45 monthly.

Pay Service 1
Pay Units: 108.
Programming (via satellite): Cinemax; HBO; Showtime.
Fee: $9.95 monthly (each).

Video-On-Demand: No

Internet Service
Operational: No.

Telephone Service
None
Miles of Plant: 63.0 (coaxial); None (fiber optic). Homes passed: 1,414.
General Manager: Jim Pierce. Plant Manager: Larry English. Office Manager: Alita Dawson.
Ownership: Florida Cable Inc. (MSO).

HIALEAH—Comcast Cable. Now served by MIAMI, FL [FL0006]. ICA: FL0010.

HIDDEN ACRES—Formerly served by Comcast Cable. No longer in operation. ICA: FL0240.

HIGH SPRINGS—CommuniComm Services, 17774 NW US Highway 441, High Springs, FL 32643-8749. Phones: 356-454-3588; 386-454-2299. Fax: 386-454-3705. Web Site: http://www.netcommander.com. ICA: FL0160.
TV Market Ranking: Below 100 (HIGH SPRINGS). Franchise award date: N.A. Franchise expiration date: N.A. Began: September 1, 1968.
Channel capacity: N.A. Channels available but not in use: N.A.

Basic Service
Subscribers: 3,979 (includes Alachua, Branford, Chiefland, Cross City, Hawthorne, Micanopy, Orange Lake & Steinhatchee).
Programming (received off-air): WCJB-TV (ABC, CW) Gainesville; WCWJ (CW) Jacksonville; WJXT (IND) Jacksonville; WMYG-LP Lake City; WOGX (FOX) Ocala; WTLV (NBC) Jacksonville; WUFT (PBS) Gainesville; allband FM.
Programming (via satellite): QVC; Trinity Broadcasting Network; TV Guide Network.
Fee: $50.00 installation; $15.00 monthly; $3.52 converter.

Expanded Basic Service 1
Subscribers: N.A.
Programming (via satellite): ABC Family Channel; American Movie Classics; Animal Planet; Arts & Entertainment; BET Networks; Cartoon Network; CNBC; CNN; Comedy Central; Country Music TV; C-SPAN; Discovery Channel; Disney Channel; Do-It-Yourself; ESPN; ESPN 2; ESPN Classic Sports; ESPNews; Food Network; Fox News Channel; FX; Hallmark Channel; Headline News; HGTV; History Channel; ION Television; Lifetime; MTV; Nick Jr.; Nickelodeon; Outdoor Channel; ShopNBC; Speed Channel; Spike TV; SunSports TV; Syfy; TBS Superstation; The Learning Channel; Travel Channel; truTV; Turner Network TV; TV Land; Univision; USA Network; VH1; Weather Channel.

Digital Basic Service
Subscribers: N.A.
Programming (via satellite): BBC America; Bloomberg Television; CMT Pure Country; Discovery Health Channel; Discovery Kids Channel; Discovery Military Channel; Discovery Planet Green; DMX Music; FitTV; Fox Movie Channel; Fox Soccer; G4; Golf Channel; GSN; Halogen Network; ID Investigation Discovery; Independent Film Channel; National Geographic Channel; NickToons TV; Science Channel; SoapNet; Turner Classic Movies; Versus; VH1 Classic; WE tv.

Pay Service 1
Pay Units: 1,237 (includes Alachua, Branford, Chiefland, Cross City, Hawthorne, Micanopy, Orange Lake & Steinhatchee).
Programming (via satellite): Cinemax; Encore; HBO (multiplexed); Starz.
Fee: $15.00 installation; $9.95 monthly.

Digital Pay Service 1
Pay Units: N.A.
Programming (via satellite): Bravo; Cinemax (multiplexed); Encore (multiplexed); HBO (multiplexed); Starz (multiplexed).

Video-On-Demand: No

Pay-Per-View
iN DEMAND (delivered digitally); Club Jenna (delivered digitally); Playboy TV (delivered digitally); Fresh (delivered digitally).

Internet Service
Operational: Yes. Began: February 1, 2002.
Broadband Service: Net Commander.
Fee: $39.95 installation; $51.95 monthly.

Telephone Service
None
Miles of Plant: 398.0 (coaxial); None (fiber optic). Homes passed: 13,015. Homes passed includes Alachua, Branford, Chiefland, Cross City, Hawthorne, Micanopy, Orange Lake & Steinhatchee
General Manager: Darrell Laird. Chief Technician: Michael Smith. Customer Service Manager: Cindy Ross.
City fee: 3% of gross.
Ownership: James Cable LLC (MSO).

HIGHLAND BEACH—Now served by DELRAY BEACH, FL [FL0091]. ICA: FL0117.

HILLIARD—Comcast Cable, 6805 Southpoint Pkwy, Jacksonville, FL 32216. Phone: 904-374-8000. Fax: 904-374-7622. Web Site: http://www.comcast.com. Also serves Callahan & Nassau County (portions). ICA: FL0157.
TV Market Ranking: 68 (Callahan, HILLIARD, Nassau County (portions)). Franchise award date: October 1, 1980. Franchise expiration date: N.A. Began: April 10, 1981.
Channel capacity: N.A. Channels available but not in use: N.A.

Basic Service
Subscribers: N.A. Included with Jacksonville
Programming (received off-air): WAWS (FOX, MNT) Jacksonville; WCWJ (CW) Jacksonville; WJCT (PBS) Jacksonville; WJXT (IND) Jacksonville; WJXX (ABC) Orange Park; WTEV-TV (CBS) Jacksonville; WTLV (NBC) Jacksonville; WUFT (PBS) Gainesville; 1 FM.
Programming (via satellite): BET Networks; Bravo; C-SPAN; E! Entertainment Television; HGTV; ION Television; TBS Superstation; The Learning Channel; TV Guide Network; Weather Channel.
Current originations: Leased Access; Educational Access.
Fee: $43.99 installation; $1.65 converter.

Expanded Basic Service 1
Subscribers: 576.
Programming (via satellite): ABC Family Channel; AMC; Animal Planet; Arts & Entertainment; BET Networks; CNBC; CNN; Comcast/Charter Sports Southeast (CSS); Comedy Central; Discovery Channel; Disney Channel; ESPN; ESPN 2; Eternal Word TV Network; Food Network; Fox News Channel; Fox Sports Net; Fuse; FX; Golf Channel; Hallmark Channel; Headline News; History Channel; MTV; MTV2; Nickelodeon; Speed Channel; Spike TV; SunSports TV; Syfy; truTV; Turner Network TV; TV Land; Univision; USA Network; Versus; VH1; WGN America.
Fee: $36.05 monthly.

Digital Basic Service
Subscribers: N.A.
Programming (received off-air): WAWS (FOX, MNT) Jacksonville; WCWJ (CW) Jacksonville; WJCT (PBS) Jacksonville; WJXX (ABC) Orange Park; WTEV-TV (CBS) Jacksonville; WTLV (NBC) Jacksonville.
Programming (via satellite): BBC America; Bio; Bloomberg Television; Bravo; Cartoon Network; Cine Latino; Cine Mexicano; CMT Pure Country; CNN en Espanol; Cooking Channel; Country Music TV; C-SPAN 2; C-SPAN 3; Current; Daystar TV Network; Discovery en Espanol; Discovery Health Channel; Discovery Kids Channel; Discovery Military Channel; Do-It-Yourself; Encore (multiplexed); ESPN 2 HD; ESPN Classic Sports; ESPN Deportes; ESPN HD; ESPNews; FamilyNet; FitTV; Flix; Fox College Sports Atlantic; Fox College Sports Central; Fox College Sports Pacific; Fox Reality Channel; Fox Soccer; Fox Sports en Espanol; FSN HD; G4; Gol TV; Gospel Music Channel; Great American Country; GSN; HDNet; History Channel en Espanol; History Channel International; ID Investigation Discovery; Independent Film Channel; INSP; Jewelry Television; Latele Novela Network; Lifetime Movie Network; LOGO;

MoviePlex; MSNBC; mun2 television; National Geographic Channel; National Geographic Channel HD Network; NBA TV; NFL Network; Nick Jr.; Nickelodeon; NickToons TV; Outdoor Channel; Oxygen; PBS Kids Sprout; Retro Television Network; Science Channel; ShopNBC; Si TV; SoapNet; Sorpresa; Speed Channel; Style Network; Sundance Channel; SunSports TV; Sur Network; TeenNick; The Sportsman Channel; The Word Network; Toon Disney; Travel Channel; Trinity Broadcasting Network; Turner Classic Movies; Turner Network TV HD; TV Colombia; TV One; TVN Entertainment; Universal HD; VeneMovies; Versus HD; VH1 Classic; VH1 Soul.
Fee: $11.95 monthly.

Pay Service 1
Pay Units: 531.
Programming (via satellite): HBO.
Fee: $9.95 monthly (each).

Digital Pay Service 1
Pay Units: N.A.
Programming (via satellite): Cinemax (multiplexed); Cinemax HD; HBO (multiplexed); HBO HD; Showtime (multiplexed); Showtime HD; Starz (multiplexed); Starz HDTV; The Movie Channel (multiplexed).
Fee: $15.95 monthly (each).

Video-On-Demand: No

Pay-Per-View
iN DEMAND (delivered digitally); Playboy TV (delivered digitally); Fresh (delivered digitally); Shorteez (delivered digitally); Club Jenna (delivered digitally).

Internet Service
Operational: Yes.

Telephone Service
Digital: Operational

Miles of Plant: 41.0 (coaxial); None (fiber optic). Homes passed: 1,950.

Vice President & General Manager: Doug McMillan. Engineering Director: Mike Humphrey. Vice President, Marketing: Vic Scarborough. Government Affairs Director: Bill Ferry.

Ownership: Comcast Cable Communications Inc. (MSO).

HILLSBOROUGH COUNTY—Bright House Networks, 525 Grand Regency Blvd, Brandon, FL 33510. Phones: 813-436-2128 (Customer service); 813-684-6100. Fax: 813-436-2128. Web Site: http://tampabay.brighthouse.com. Also serves Apollo Beach, Balm, Bloomingdale, Brandon (southern portion), Gibsonton, MacDill, MacDill AFB, Pasco County (southern portion), Plant City, Riverview, Ruskin, Sun City Center, Tampa, Temple Terrace, Valrico (southern portion) & Wimauma. ICA: FL0003.

TV Market Ranking: 28 (Apollo Beach, Balm, Bloomingdale, Brandon (southern portion), Gibsonton, HILLSBOROUGH COUNTY, MacDill, MacDill AFB, Pasco County (southern portion), Plant City, Riverview, Ruskin, Sun City Center, Tampa, Temple Terrace, Valrico (southern portion), Wimauma). Franchise award date: April 1, 1970. Franchise expiration date: N.A. Began: February 10, 1971.

Channel capacity: N.A. Channels available but not in use: N.A.

Basic Service
Subscribers: 273,944.
Programming (received off-air): Bay News 9; WCLF (IND) Clearwater; WEDU (PBS) Tampa; WFLA-TV (NBC) Tampa; WFTS-TV (ABC) Tampa; WFTT-DT (TEL) Tampa; WMOR-TV (IND) Lakeland; WRMD-CA (TMO) Tampa; WTOG (CW) St. Petersburg; WTSP (CBS) St. Petersburg; WTTA (MNT) St. Petersburg; WTVT (FOX) Tampa; WUSF-TV (PBS) Tampa; WVEA-LP Tampa; WXPX-TV (ION) Bradenton; 3 FMs.
Programming (via satellite): BET Networks; C-SPAN; Home Shopping Network; ShopNBC; TBS Superstation; TV Guide Network; WGN America.
Current originations: Leased Access; Government Access; Educational Access; Public Access.
Fee: $32.00 installation; $8.87 monthly.

Expanded Basic Service 1
Subscribers: N.A.
Programming (via satellite): ABC Family Channel; AMC; Animal Planet; Arts & Entertainment; Bravo; Cartoon Network; CNBC; CNN; Comedy Central; Country Music TV; C-SPAN 2; Discovery Channel; Disney Channel; E! Entertainment Television; ESPN; ESPN 2; ESPN Classic Sports; Eternal Word TV Network; Food Network; Fox News Channel; Fox Sports Net; FX; Golf Channel; Hallmark Channel; Headline News; HGTV; History Channel; Lifetime; Lifetime Movie Network; MoviePlex; MSNBC; MTV; National Geographic Channel; Nickelodeon; Oxygen; QVC; Spike TV; SunSports TV; Syfy; The Learning Channel; Travel Channel; truTV; Turner Classic Movies; Turner Network TV; TV Land; USA Network; Versus; VH1; WE tv; Weather Channel.
Fee: $31.95 monthly.

Digital Basic Service
Subscribers: 108,000.
Programming (received off-air): WEDU (PBS) Tampa; WFLA-TV (NBC) Tampa; WFTS-TV (ABC) Tampa; WMOR-TV (IND) Lakeland; WTSP (CBS) St. Petersburg; WTVT (FOX) Tampa; WUSF-TV (PBS) Tampa.
Programming (via satellite): AmericanLife TV Network; America's Store; Bay News 9; Bay News 9 Espanol; BBC America; Bio; Black Family Channel; Bloomberg Television; Canales N; Catch 47; Cooking Channel; C-SPAN 3; Current; Discovery Digital Networks; Discovery HD Theater; Disney Channel; Do-It-Yourself; Do-It-Yourself On Demand; ESPN; ESPNews; Eternal Word TV Network; Fine Living On Demand; Flix; Food Network On Demand; Fox Soccer; Fuse; G4; GAS; Great American Country; Great American Country On Demand; GSN; HDNet; HDNet Movies; HGTV On Demand; History Channel International; Independent Film Channel; INHD; INHD2; Lifetime Real Women; MTV2; Music Choice; Nick Jr.; NickToons TV; Ovation; SoapNet; Speed Channel; Sundance Channel; Tampa Bay On Demand; Toon Disney; Trinity Broadcasting Network; Trio; Turner Network TV HD; TV One; Universal HD; VH1 Classic.
Fee: $14.90 monthly.

Digital Expanded Basic Service
Subscribers: N.A.
Programming (via satellite): Encore; Fox College Sports Atlantic; Fox College Sports Central; Fox College Sports Pacific; Fox Movie Channel; Fuel TV; NBA TV; Outdoor Channel; Tennis Channel.

Digital Pay Service 1
Pay Units: N.A.
Programming (via satellite): Cinemax (multiplexed); HBO (multiplexed); HBO HD; HBO On Demand; Showtime (multiplexed); Showtime HD; Showtime On Demand; Starz (multiplexed); The Movie Channel (multiplexed); The Movie Channel On Demand.

Fee: $10.50 installation; $9.95 monthly (each).

Video-On-Demand: Yes

Pay-Per-View
Addressable homes: 108,000.
Hot Choice (delivered digitally), Addressable: Yes; iN DEMAND (delivered digitally); Playboy TV (delivered digitally); Pleasure (delivered digitally); Fresh (delivered digitally); Shorteez (delivered digitally).

Internet Service
Operational: Yes.
Subscribers: 66,049.
Broadband Service: AOL for Broadband, EarthLink, Internet Junction, Road Runner.
Fee: $44.95 monthly.

Telephone Service
Digital: Operational
Fee: $49.95 monthly

Miles of Plant: 5,000.0 (coaxial); 1,000.0 (fiber optic). Homes passed: 425,000. Total homes in franchised area: 450,000.

Division President: Kevin Hyman. Vice President, Engineering: Gene White. General Manager: Harry F. Sheraw. Engineering Director: Mike Vanderkodde. Marketing Director: Robb Bennett.

County fee: 5% of gross.

Ownership: Bright House Networks LLC (MSO).

HOLOPAW—Florida Cable, PO Box 498, 23748 State Rd 40, Astor, FL 32102-0498. Phone: 352-759-2788. Fax: 352-759-3577. Web Site: http://www.floridacable.com. ICA: FL0242.

TV Market Ranking: 55 (HOLOPAW). Franchise award date: N.A. Franchise expiration date: N.A. Began: September 1, 1990.

Channel capacity: N.A. Channels available but not in use: N.A.

Basic Service
Subscribers: N.A.
Programming (received off-air): WESH (NBC) Daytona Beach; WFTV (ABC) Orlando; WKCF (CW) Clermont; WKMG-TV (CBS) Orlando; WMFE-TV (PBS) Orlando; WOFL (FOX) Orlando; WOPX-TV (ION) Melbourne; WOTF-DT (TEL) Melbourne; WRBW (MNT) Orlando; WTGL (ETV) Leesburg.
Programming (via satellite): ABC Family Channel; AMC; Animal Planet; Arts & Entertainment; Cartoon Network; CNBC; CNN; Comedy Central; Country Music TV; C-SPAN; C-SPAN 2; Discovery Channel; Discovery Health Channel; ESPN; Food Network; Fox News Channel; GSN; Headline News; HGTV; History Channel; Lifetime; MoviePlex; MTV; Nickelodeon; Outdoor Channel; QVC; SoapNet; Spike TV; TBS Superstation; The Learning Channel; Travel Channel; Trinity Broadcasting Network; truTV; Turner Classic Movies; Turner Network TV; TV Land; Univision; USA Network; WE tv; Weather Channel; WGN America.
Fee: $40.00 installation; $33.42 monthly.

Pay Service 1
Pay Units: N.A.
Programming (via satellite): Cinemax; HBO.
Fee: $10.95 monthly (each).

Internet Service
Operational: No.

Telephone Service
None

General Manager: Jim Pierce. Plant Manager: Larry English. Office Manager: Aleta Dawson.

Ownership: Florida Cable Inc. (MSO).

HOMOSASSA—Bright House Networks, 1004 US Hwy 92 W, Auburndale, FL 33823. Phones: 863-965-7733 (Regional office); 727-746-0755. Fax: 863-288-2204. Web Site: http://tampabay.brighthouse.com. Also serves Beverly Hills, Citrus County, Citrus Springs, Crystal River, Hernando, Homosassa Springs, Inverness & Lecanto. ICA: FL0046.

TV Market Ranking: Below 100 (Beverly Hills, Citrus County (portions), Citrus Springs, Crystal River, Hernando, Inverness, Lecanto); Outside TV Markets (Citrus County (portions), HOMOSASSA, Homosassa Springs). Franchise award date: N.A. Franchise expiration date: N.A. Began: December 17, 1985.

Channel capacity: N.A. Channels available but not in use: N.A.

Basic Service
Subscribers: 33,938.
Programming (received off-air): WCLF (IND) Clearwater; WEDU (PBS) Tampa; WFLA-TV (NBC) Tampa; WFTS-TV (ABC) Tampa; WFTT-DT (TEL) Tampa; WFTV (ABC) Orlando; WMOR-TV (IND) Lakeland; WTOG (CW) St. Petersburg; WTSP (CBS) St. Petersburg; WTTA (MNT) St. Petersburg; WTVT (FOX) Tampa; WUFT (PBS) Gainesville; WVEA-TV (UNV) Venice; WXPX-TV (ION) Bradenton; allband FM.
Programming (via satellite): Home Shopping Network; QVC; ShopNBC; TV Guide Network; WFTV (ABC) Orlando; WGN America.
Current originations: Educational Access.
Fee: $42.95 installation; $16.00 monthly.

Expanded Basic Service 1
Subscribers: N.A.
Programming (via satellite): ABC Family Channel; AMC; Animal Planet; Arts & Entertainment; BET Networks; Bravo; Cartoon Network; CNBC; CNN; Comedy Central; Country Music TV; C-SPAN; C-SPAN 2; Discovery Channel; Disney Channel; ESPN 2; ESPN Classic Sports; Eternal Word TV Network; Flix; Food Network; Fox News Channel; Fox Sports Net Florida; FX; Golf Channel; Hallmark Channel; Headline News; HGTV; History Channel; Jewelry Television; Lifetime; Lifetime Movie Network; MoviePlex; MSNBC; MTV; National Geographic Channel; Nickelodeon; Oxygen; Product Information Network; Shop at Home; Spike TV; SunSports TV; Syfy; TBS Superstation; The Learning Channel; Travel Channel; truTV; Turner Classic Movies; Turner Network TV; TV Land; USA Network; Versus; VH1; WE tv; Weather Channel.
Fee: $28.95 monthly.

Digital Basic Service
Subscribers: 14,683.
Programming (received off-air): WFTS-TV (ABC) Tampa; WTVT (FOX) Tampa.
Programming (via satellite): AmericanLife TV Network; America's Store; Bay News 9; BBC America; Bloomberg Television; Cooking Channel; C-SPAN 3; Discovery Digital Networks; Do-It-Yourself; ESPNews; FitTV; Flix; Fox Sports World; Fuse; G4; GAS; Great American Country; GSN; MTV2; Music Choice; Nick Jr.; Outdoor Channel; Ovation; SoapNet; Speed Channel; Style Network; Sundance Channel; Toon Disney; Trinity Broadcasting Network; VH1 Classic.
Digital Expanded Basic Service
Subscribers: N.A.
Programming (via satellite): Encore Action; Fox Movie Channel; Independent Film Channel.
Digital Pay Service 1
Pay Units: N.A.
Programming (via satellite): Cinemax (multiplexed); HBO (multiplexed); Showtime (multiplexed); Starz (multiplexed); The Movie Channel (multiplexed).
Video-On-Demand: Yes
Pay-Per-View
Addressable homes: 14,683.
Playboy TV (delivered digitally); Pleasure (delivered digitally); Fresh (delivered digitally); Shorteez (delivered digitally); iN DEMAND (delivered digitally), Addressable: Yes.
Internet Service
Operational: Yes.
Subscribers: 9,842.
Broadband Service: Road Runner.
Fee: $39.95 installation; $29.95 monthly.
Telephone Service
Digital: Operational
Fee: $39.95 monthly
Miles of Plant: 1,309.0 (coaxial); None (fiber optic). Homes passed: 54,469. Total homes in franchised area: 54,469.
Division President: Kevin Hyman. Vice President & General Manager: Dave Ross. Vice President, Engineering: Gene White. Engineering Director: Scott Twyman. Marketing Director: Robb Bennett.
County fee: 5% of gross.
Ownership: Bright House Networks LLC (MSO).

HOSFORD—Southeast Cable TV Inc., PO Box 584, 107 S Main St, Boston, GA 31626-0584. Phone: 229-498-4191. Fax: 229-498-1026. ICA: FL0312.
TV Market Ranking: Below 100 (HOSFORD). Franchise award date: N.A. Franchise expiration date: N.A. Began: December 1, 1991.
Channel capacity: 40 (not 2-way capable). Channels available but not in use: 16.
Basic Service
Subscribers: 168.
Programming (received off-air): WCTV (CBS, MNT) Thomasville; WFSU-TV (PBS) Tallahassee; WJHG-TV (CW, MNT, NBC) Panama City; WMBB (ABC) Panama City; WPGX (FOX) Panama City; WTWC-TV (NBC) Tallahassee; WTXL-TV (ABC) Tallahassee.
Programming (via satellite): ABC Family Channel; Arts & Entertainment; CNN; Country Music TV; Discovery Channel; ESPN; Headline News; Nickelodeon; QVC; Spike TV; TBS Superstation; Turner Network TV; USA Network; WGN America.
Fee: $15.00 installation; $17.95 monthly.
Pay Service 1
Pay Units: 52.
Programming (via satellite): HBO.
Fee: $10.00 monthly.
Pay Service 2
Pay Units: 26.
Programming (via satellite): Encore.
Fee: $5.00 monthly.
Video-On-Demand: No
Internet Service
Operational: No.
Telephone Service
None
Miles of Plant: 13.0 (coaxial); None (fiber optic). Homes passed: 300.
Manager: Bob Heide.
Ownership: Southeast Cable TV Inc. (MSO).

IMMOKALEE—Time Warner Cable. Now served by NAPLES, FL [FL0029]. ICA: FL0099.

IMMOKALEE SEMINOLE INDIAN RESERVATION—Comcast Cable, 141 NW 16th St, Pompano Beach, FL 33060. Phone: 954-252-1937. Fax: 954-532-7256. Web Site: http://www.comcast.com. ICA: FL0375.
TV Market Ranking: Outside TV Markets (IMMOKALEE SEMINOLE INDIAN RESERVATION).
Channel capacity: 19 (not 2-way capable). Channels available but not in use: N.A.
Basic Service
Subscribers: N.A. Included in Miami
Video-On-Demand: No
Internet Service
Operational: No.
Telephone Service
None
Vice President & General Manager: Rick Seamon. Technical Operations Director: Ross Pappas.
Ownership: Comcast Cable Communications Inc. (MSO).

INDIAN SPRINGS—Now served by DELRAY BEACH, FL [FL0091]. ICA: FL0243.

INDIANTOWN—Now served by STUART, FL [FL0024]. ICA: FL0244.

INVERNESS—Comcast Cable, 2020 Highway 44 W, Inverness, FL 34453. Phones: 352-787-9601 (Leesburg office); 352-637-0123. Fax: 352-365-6279. Web Site: http://www.comcast.com. Also serves Beverly Hills, Citrus County (northern portion), Dunnellon, Hernando (portions), Inglis, Marion County (southwestern portion) & Yankeetown. ICA: FL0319. **Note:** This system is an overbuild.
TV Market Ranking: Below 100 (Beverly Hills, Citrus County (northern portion), Dunnellon, Hernando (portions), Inglis, INVERNESS, Marion County (southwestern portion)); Outside TV Markets (Yankeetown). Franchise award date: July 7, 1987. Franchise expiration date: N.A. Began: October 1, 1987.
Channel capacity: N.A. Channels available but not in use: N.A.
Basic Service
Subscribers: 10,906 Includes Archer, Trenton & Williston, FL.
Programming (received off-air): WACX (IND) Leesburg; WCJB-TV (ABC, CW) Gainesville; WCLF (IND) Clearwater; WEDU (PBS) Tampa; WESH (NBC) Daytona Beach; WFLA-TV (NBC) Tampa; WFTS-TV (ABC) Tampa; WFTV (ABC) Orlando; WGFL (CBS, MNT) High Springs; WMOR-TV (IND) Lakeland; WOGX (FOX) Ocala; WTOG (CW) St. Petersburg; WTSP (CBS) St. Petersburg; WTVT (FOX) Tampa; WUFT (PBS) Gainesville; WVEA-TV (UNV) Venice; WYKE-CD Inglis/Yankeetown.
Programming (via satellite): C-SPAN; Home Shopping Network; QVC; Travel Channel; TV Guide Network; WGN America.
Fee: $19.95 monthly.
Expanded Basic Service 1
Subscribers: N.A.
Programming (via satellite): ABC Family Channel; AMC; Animal Planet; Arts & Entertainment; BET Networks; Cartoon Network; CNBC; CNN; Comcast/Charter Sports Southeast (CSS); Comedy Central; Country Music TV; Discovery Channel; Disney Channel; E! Entertainment Television; ESPN; ESPN 2; Eternal Word TV Network; Food Network; Fox News Channel; Fox Sports Net Florida; FX; Hallmark Channel; Headline News; HGTV; History Channel; Lifetime; MSNBC; MTV; Nickelodeon; Spike TV; SunSports TV; Syfy; TBS Superstation; The Learning Channel; truTV; Turner Network TV; TV Land; USA Network; VH1; Weather Channel.
Digital Basic Service
Subscribers: N.A.
Programming (via satellite): BBC America; Bloomberg Television; Bravo; CMT Pure Country; Discovery Health Channel; Discovery Home Channel; Discovery Kids Channel; Discovery Military Channel; Encore (multiplexed); ESPNews; FitTV; Fox Movie Channel; G4; GSN; ID Investigation Discovery; Independent Film Channel; Music Choice; National Geographic Channel; Nick Jr.; NickToons TV; Science Channel; Trinity Broadcasting Network; Turner Classic Movies; VH1 Classic; WE tv.
Fee: $8.50 monthly.
Digital Pay Service 1
Pay Units: N.A.
Programming (via satellite): Cinemax (multiplexed); HBO (multiplexed); Showtime (multiplexed); Starz (multiplexed); The Movie Channel (multiplexed).
Fee: $9.95 monthly (each).
Video-On-Demand: No
Pay-Per-View
iN DEMAND (delivered digitally); Playboy TV (delivered digitally); Club Jenna (delivered digitally); Fresh (delivered digitally).
Internet Service
Operational: Yes.
Broadband Service: Comcast High Speed Internet.
Telephone Service
None
Miles of Plant: 480.0 (coaxial); None (fiber optic). Homes passed: 24,129.
Vice President & General Manager: Mike Davenport. Marketing Manager: Melanie Melvin. Chief Technician: Hal Priest.
Ownership: Comcast Cable Communications Inc. (MSO).

JACKSONVILLE—Comcast Cable, 6805 Southpoint Pkwy, Jacksonville, FL 32216. Phone: 904-374-8000. Fax: 904-374-7622. E-mail: Doug_Mcmillan2@cable.comcast.com. Web Site: http://www.comcast.com. Also serves Amelia Island, Atlantic Beach, Baldwin, Bradford County (portions), Cecil Field Naval Air Station, Clay County (portions), Fernandina Beach, Green Cove Springs, Jacksonville Beach, Jacksonville Naval Air Station, Mayport Naval Air Station, Nassau County, Neptune Beach, Orange Park, Ponte Vedra Beach, St. Johns County (northern portion) & Starke. ICA: FL0002.
TV Market Ranking: 68 (Amelia Island, Atlantic Beach, Baldwin, Bradford County (portions), Cecil Field Naval Air Station, Clay County (portions), Fernandina Beach, Green Cove Springs, JACKSONVILLE, Jacksonville Beach, Jacksonville Naval Air Station, Mayport Naval Air Station, Nassau County, Neptune Beach, Orange Park, Ponte Vedra Beach, St. Johns County (northern portion)); Below 100 (Starke, Bradford County (portions), Clay County (portions)). Franchise award date: N.A. Franchise expiration date: N.A. Began: June 15, 1979.
Channel capacity: N.A. Channels available but not in use: N.A.
Basic Service
Subscribers: 226,439 Includes Folkston GA & Nahunta GA.
Programming (received off-air): WAWS (FOX, MNT) Jacksonville; WCWJ (CW) Jacksonville; WJCT (PBS) Jacksonville; WJEB-TV (ETV) Jacksonville; WJXT (IND) Jacksonville; WJXX (ABC) Orange Park; WTEV-TV (CBS) Jacksonville; WTLV (NBC) Jacksonville; WUFT (PBS) Gainesville.
Programming (via satellite): C-SPAN; C-SPAN 2; Lifetime; QVC; TBS Superstation; Turner Network TV; Weather Channel.
Current originations: Leased Access; Government Access; Educational Access; Public Access.
Fee: $49.95 installation; $6.95 monthly; $3.00 converter.
Expanded Basic Service 1
Subscribers: 216,717.
Programming (via satellite): ABC Family Channel; AMC; Animal Planet; Arts & Entertainment; BET Networks; Bravo; Cartoon Network; CNBC; CNN; Comedy Central; Country Music TV; Discovery Channel; Disney Channel; E! Entertainment Television; ESPN; ESPN 2; ESPN Classic Sports; Eternal Word TV Network; Food Network; Fox News Channel; Fox Sports Net Florida; Fuse; FX; Golf Channel; Great American Country; Hallmark Channel; Headline News; HGTV; Home Shopping Network; ION Television; MTV; Nickelodeon; Speed Channel; Spike TV; SunSports TV; Syfy; The Learning Channel; truTV; TV Guide Network; TV Land; Univision; USA Network; Versus; VH1.
Fee: $49.99 monthly.
Digital Basic Service
Subscribers: 47,553.
Programming (via satellite): BBC America; Bio; Black Family Channel; Bloomberg Television; Canal D; Comcast/Charter Sports Southeast (CSS); Discovery Digital Networks; DMX Music; Encore (multiplexed); ESPNews; Fox College Sports Atlantic; Fox College Sports Central; Fox College Sports

Pacific; Fox Movie Channel; Fox Sports World; G4; GAS; GSN; Halogen Network; History Channel; History Channel International; Independent Film Channel; Lifetime Movie Network; Lime; MoviePlex; MSNBC; MTV Networks Digital Suite; National Geographic Channel; Nick Jr.; NickToons TV; Outdoor Channel; Ovation; ShopNBC; Style Network; The Word Network; Toon Disney; Turner Classic Movies.
Fee: $11.95 monthly.

Pay Service 1
Pay Units: 167,596.
Programming (via satellite): Encore; HBO (multiplexed); The Movie Channel.
Fee: $15.95 monthly.

Digital Pay Service 1
Pay Units: N.A.
Programming (via satellite): Cinemax (multiplexed); Flix; HBO (multiplexed); Showtime (multiplexed); Starz (multiplexed); The Movie Channel (multiplexed).
Fee: $15.95 monthly (each).

Video-On-Demand: Yes

Pay-Per-View
Addressable homes: 47,553.
NBA TV (delivered digitally), Addressable: Yes; iN DEMAND (delivered digitally); Fresh (delivered digitally); Shorteez (delivered digitally); Playboy TV (delivered digitally); Sports PPV (delivered digitally).

Internet Service
Operational: Yes.
Subscribers: 16,983.
Broadband Service: Comcast High Speed Internet.
Fee: $39.95 installation; $42.95 monthly; $10.00 modem lease.

Telephone Service
Digital: Operational
Fee: $44.95 monthly

Miles of Plant: 4,056.0 (coaxial); 282.0 (fiber optic). Homes passed: 441,715. Total homes in franchised area: 441,715.

Vice President & General Manager: Doug McMillan. Vice President, Marketing: Vic Scarborough. Engineering Director: Mke Humprey. Government Affairs Director: Bill Ferry.

City fee: 3% of gross.

Ownership: Comcast Cable Communications Inc. (MSO).

JASPER—Comcast Cable, PO Box 812, 203 Hatley St W, Jasper, FL 32052-0812. Phones: 850-574-4016 (Tallahassee office); 386-792-1820 (Jasper office). Fax: 386-792-2415. Web Site: http://www.comcast.com. ICA: FL0168.

TV Market Ranking: Below 100 (JASPER). Franchise award date: N.A. Franchise expiration date: N.A. Began: January 1, 1969.

Channel capacity: N.A. Channels available but not in use: N.A.

Basic Service
Subscribers: N.A. Included in Tallahassee
Programming (received off-air): WALB (NBC) Albany; WCJB-TV (ABC, CW) Gainesville; WCTV (CBS, MNT) Thomasville; WJCT (PBS) Jacksonville; WJXT (IND) Jacksonville; WTLH (CW, FOX) Bainbridge.
Programming (via satellite): QVC; TBS Superstation; Weather Channel; WGN America.
Fee: $39.88 installation; $11.95 monthly.

Expanded Basic Service 1
Subscribers: N.A.
Programming (via satellite): ABC Family Channel; AMC; Arts & Entertainment; BET Networks; Cartoon Network; CNBC; CNN; Comcast/Charter Sports Southeast (CSS); Comedy Central; Country Music TV; C-SPAN; Discovery Channel; Discovery Health Channel; Disney Channel; E! Entertainment Television; ESPN; ESPN 2; Food Network; Fox News Channel; FX; Golf Channel; Great American Country; GSN; Hallmark Channel; Headline News; HGTV; History Channel; Home Shopping Network; Lifetime; MTV; Nickelodeon; Speed Channel; Spike TV; Style Network; SunSports TV; The Learning Channel; Travel Channel; Trinity Broadcasting Network; truTV; Turner Network TV; TV Land; TV One; USA Network; Versus; VH1.
Fee: $36.55 monthly.

Pay Service 1
Pay Units: 82.
Programming (via satellite): Cinemax; HBO.
Fee: $11.95 monthly (Cinemax), $13.94 monthly (HBO).

Video-On-Demand: No

Internet Service
Operational: Yes.

Telephone Service
Digital: Operational

Miles of plant (coax) & homes passed included in Tallahassee

General Manager: K. C. McWilliams. Technical Operations Director: Terry Pullen. Area Technical Manager: Andy Musgrove. Chief Technician: Dwayne Hicks. Marketing Director: Claire Evans.

City fee: 3% of gross.

Ownership: Comcast Cable Communications Inc. (MSO).

JENNINGS—Comcast Cable, 2288 SW Main Blvd, Lake City, FL 32025-0029. Phone: 386-752-6161. Fax: 386-752-6613. Web Site: http://www.comcast.com. ICA: FL0203.

TV Market Ranking: Below 100 (JENNINGS). Franchise award date: February 1, 1985. Franchise expiration date: N.A. Began: February 1, 1985.

Channel capacity: N.A. Channels available but not in use: N.A.

Basic Service
Subscribers: 71.
Programming (received off-air): WALB (NBC) Albany; WCTV (CBS, MNT) Thomasville; WFXU (IND) Live Oak; WTLH (CW, FOX) Bainbridge; WTXL-TV (ABC) Tallahassee; WXGA-TV (PBS) Waycross.
Programming (via satellite): ABC Family Channel; BET Networks; CNN; C-SPAN; Discovery Channel; Disney Channel; E! Entertainment Television; ESPN; ESPN 2; Spike TV; TBS Superstation; Travel Channel; Turner Network TV; TV Land; USA Network; Weather Channel.
Fee: $44.79 installation; $13.34 monthly.

Pay Service 1
Pay Units: 24.
Programming (via satellite): Showtime; The Movie Channel.
Fee: $12.00 monthly (each).

Video-On-Demand: No

Internet Service
Operational: Yes.

Telephone Service
Digital: Operational

Miles of Plant: 8.0 (coaxial); None (fiber optic). Homes passed: 242. Total homes in franchised area: 242.

Vice President: Doug McMillan. General Manager: Mark Russell. Manager: Bob Garner. Chief Technician: Jonathan Norton.

City fee: 4% of gross.

Ownership: Comcast Cable Communications Inc. (MSO).

KEATON BEACH—Southeast Cable TV Inc., PO Box 584, 107 S Main St, Boston, GA 31626-0584. Phone: 229-498-4191. Fax: 229-498-1026. Also serves Dekle Beach. ICA: FL0225.

TV Market Ranking: Outside TV Markets (Dekle Beach, KEATON BEACH). Franchise award date: N.A. Franchise expiration date: N.A. Began: July 1, 1992.

Channel capacity: 40 (not 2-way capable). Channels available but not in use: 16.

Basic Service
Subscribers: 185.
Programming (received off-air): WCJB-TV (ABC, CW) Gainesville; WCTV (CBS, MNT) Thomasville; WFSU-TV (PBS) Tallahassee; WTLH (CW, FOX) Bainbridge; WTWC-TV (NBC) Tallahassee; WTXL-TV (ABC) Tallahassee.
Programming (via satellite): ABC Family Channel; Arts & Entertainment; CNN; Country Music TV; Discovery Channel; ESPN; Headline News; Nickelodeon; QVC; TBS Superstation; Turner Network TV; USA Network; Weather Channel; WGN America.
Fee: $15.00 installation; $17.95 monthly.

Pay Service 1
Pay Units: 16.
Programming (via satellite): Encore.
Fee: $4.00 monthly.

Pay Service 2
Pay Units: 25.
Programming (via satellite): HBO.
Fee: $10.00 monthly.

Video-On-Demand: No

Internet Service
Operational: No.

Telephone Service
None

Miles of Plant: 14.0 (coaxial); None (fiber optic). Homes passed: 250.

Manager: Bob Heide.

Ownership: Southeast Cable TV Inc. (MSO).

KENANSVILLE—Florida Cable, PO Box 498, 23748 State Rd 40, Astor, FL 32102-0498. Phone: 352-759-2788. Fax: 352-759-3577. Web Site: http://www.floridacable.com. ICA: FL0246.

TV Market Ranking: 55 (KENANSVILLE). Franchise award date: N.A. Franchise expiration date: N.A. Began: June 1, 1990.

Channel capacity: N.A. Channels available but not in use: N.A.

Basic Service
Subscribers: 72.
Programming (received off-air): WESH (NBC) Daytona Beach; WFTV (ABC) Orlando; WKCF (CW) Clermont; WKMG-TV (CBS) Orlando; WMFE-TV (PBS) Orlando; WOFL (FOX) Orlando; WOTF-DT (TEL) Melbourne; WRBW (MNT) Orlando; WRDQ (IND) Orlando; WTGL (ETV) Leesburg.
Programming (via satellite): ABC Family Channel; AMC; AmericanLife TV Network; Animal Planet; Arts & Entertainment; Cartoon Network; CNBC; CNN; Comedy Central; Country Music TV; C-SPAN; Discovery Channel; Discovery Health Channel; ESPN; Food Network; Fox News Channel; GSN; Headline News; HGTV; History Channel; Lifetime; MoviePlex; MTV; Nickelodeon; Outdoor Channel; QVC; SoapNet; Spike TV; TBS Superstation; The Learning Channel; Travel Channel; Trinity Broadcasting Network; truTV; Turner Classic Movies; Turner Network TV; TV Land; USA Network; WE tv; Weather Channel; WGN America.
Fee: $45.00 installation; $33.42 monthly.

Pay Service 1
Pay Units: N.A.
Programming (via satellite): Cinemax; HBO.
Fee: $10.95 monthly (each).

Internet Service
Operational: No.

Telephone Service
None

Miles of Plant: 11.0 (coaxial); None (fiber optic). Total homes in franchised area: 300.

General Manager: Jim Pierce. Plant Manager: Larry English. Office Manager: Alita Dawson.

Ownership: Florida Cable Inc. (MSO).

KENDALL—Comcast Cable. Now served by MIAMI, FL [FL0006]. ICA: FL0021.

KEY COLONY BEACH—Comcast Cable. Now served by KEY WEST, FL [FL0055]. ICA: FL0081.

KEY LARGO—Comcast Cable. Now served by KEY WEST, FL [FL0055]. ICA: FL0068.

KEY WEST—Comcast Cable, 1010 Kennedy Dr, Ste 200, Key West, FL 33040. Phones: 954-534-7419 (Miramar regional office); 305-292-8376 (Customer service). Fax: 305-296-9620. E-mail: bill_underwood@cable.comcast.com. Web Site: http://www.comcast.com. Also serves Big Coppitt Key, Big Pine Key, Duck Key, Grassy Key, Islamorada, Key Colony Beach, Key Largo, Little Torch Key, Marathon, Marathon Shores, Monroe County (portions), Ocean Reef Club, Ramrod Key, Stock Island, Sugarloaf Key, Summerland Key, Tavernier & Upper Matecumbe Key. ICA: FL0055.

TV Market Ranking: Below 100 (Big Coppitt Key, Big Pine Key, KEY WEST, Little Torch Key, Monroe County (portions), Ramrod Key, Stock Island, Sugarloaf Key, Summerland Key); Outside TV Markets (Duck Key, Grassy Key, Islamorada, Key Colony Beach, Key Largo, Marathon, Marathon Shores, Monroe County (portions), Ocean Reef Club, Tavernier, Upper Matecumbe Key). Franchise award date: N.A. Franchise expiration date: N.A. Began: June 1, 1955.

Channel capacity: N.A. Channels available but not in use: N.A.

Basic Service
Subscribers: N.A. Included in Miami
Programming (received off-air): WAMI-DT (TEL) Hollywood; WBFS-TV (MNT) Miami; WDLP-CA Pompano Beach; WFOR-TV (CBS) Miami; WGEN-TV (IND) Key West; WHFT-TV (TBN) Miami; WLTV-DT (UNV) Miami; WPBT (PBS) Miami; WPLG (ABC) Miami; WPXM-TV (ION) Miami; WSCV (TMO) Fort Lauderdale; WSFL-TV (CW) Miami; WSVN (FOX) Miami; WTVJ (NBC) Miami; allband FM.

Programming (via satellite): C-SPAN; Home Shopping Network; QVC; TV Guide Network; WGN-TV (CW, IND) Chicago.
Current originations: Government Access; Educational Access.
Fee: $45.00 installation; $13.10 monthly.

Expanded Basic Service 1
Subscribers: 30,000.
Programming (via satellite): ABC Family Channel; AMC; Animal Planet; Arts & Entertainment; BET Networks; Bravo; CNBC; CNN; Comedy Central; Country Music TV; Discovery Channel; Disney Channel; E! Entertainment Television; ESPN; ESPN 2; Food Network; Fox News Channel; Fox Sports en Espanol; Fox Sports Net Florida; FX; Golf Channel; GSN; Hallmark Channel; Headline News; HGTV; History Channel; Lifetime; MSNBC; MTV; mun2 television; Nickelodeon; Spike TV; Style Network; SunSports TV; Syfy; TBS Superstation; The Learning Channel; truTV; Turner Network TV; TV Land; USA Network; Versus; VH1; Weather Channel.
Fee: $52.95 monthly.

Digital Basic Service
Subscribers: 14,400.
Programming (via satellite): BBC America; Discovery Digital Networks; ESPN Classic Sports; ESPNews; Fox Sports World; Independent Film Channel; Music Choice; National Geographic Channel; Nick Jr.; Speed Channel; Turner Classic Movies; VH1 Classic; VH1 Country; WE tv.
Fee: $11.95 monthly.

Digital Pay Service 1
Pay Units: N.A.
Programming (via satellite): Cinemax (multiplexed); Encore (multiplexed); HBO; Showtime; Starz (multiplexed); The Movie Channel (multiplexed).

Video-On-Demand: Yes

Pay-Per-View
iN DEMAND (delivered digitally), Addressable: Yes; Playboy TV (delivered digitally), Addressable: Yes.

Internet Service
Operational: Yes.
Subscribers: 6,500.
Broadband Service: Comcast High Speed Internet.
Fee: $42.95 monthly; $3.00 modem lease.

Telephone Service
Digital: Planned

Miles of Plant: 700.0 (coaxial); None (fiber optic). Homes passed: 60,000.
Area Vice President: Tom Autry. Regional Vice President, Marketing: David Lucoff. General Manager: Bill Underwood. Technical Operations Director: Kurt Decker. Marketing Supervisor: Mary Lou Bochenick. Public Relations Director: Spero Canton.
Ownership: Comcast Cable Communications Inc. (MSO).

LA BELLE—Time Warner Cable. Now served by NAPLES, FL [FL0029]. ICA: FL0106.

LAKE BUTLER—Comcast Cable, 6805 Southpoint Pkwy, Jacksonville, FL 32216. Phone: 904-374-8000. Fax: 904-374-7622. Web Site: http://www.comcast.com. Also serves Union County. ICA: FL0155.
TV Market Ranking: 68 (Union County (portions)); Below 100 (LAKE BUTLER, Union County (portions)). Franchise award date: September 1, 1981. Franchise expiration date: N.A. Began: December 1, 1982.
Channel capacity: 40 (operating 2-way). Channels available but not in use: None.

Basic Service
Subscribers: N.A. Included in Jacksonville
Programming (received off-air): WAWS (FOX, MNT) Jacksonville; WCJB-TV (ABC, CW) Gainesville; WCWJ (CW) Jacksonville; WJCT (PBS) Jacksonville; WJEB-TV (ETV) Jacksonville; WJXT (IND) Jacksonville; WJXX (ABC) Orange Park; WOGX (FOX) Ocala; WTEV-TV (CBS) Jacksonville; WTLV (NBC) Jacksonville; WUFT (PBS) Gainesville.
Programming (via satellite): ABC Family Channel; BET Networks; C-SPAN; C-SPAN 2; INSP; Lifetime; TBS Superstation.
Current originations: Educational Access.
Fee: $43.99 installation; $10.09 monthly; $1.65 converter.

Expanded Basic Service 1
Subscribers: 519.
Programming (via satellite): AMC; Arts & Entertainment; CNN; Discovery Channel; Disney Channel; ESPN; ESPN 2; Food Network; Fox News Channel; FX; Great American Country; Hallmark Channel; Headline News; Home Shopping Network; MTV; Nickelodeon; QVC; Spike TV; The Learning Channel; Turner Network TV; TV Guide Network; TV Land; USA Network; Weather Channel.
Fee: $32.05 monthly.

Digital Basic Service
Subscribers: N.A.
Programming (via satellite): AmericanLife TV Network; BBC America; Bio; Bloomberg Television; Bravo; Discovery Digital Networks; ESPN Classic Sports; ESPNews; Fox Movie Channel; Fox Sports World; G4; GAS; Golf Channel; GSN; HGTV; History Channel; History Channel International; Independent Film Channel; International Television (ITV); Lifetime Movie Network; MTV Networks Digital Suite; Nick Jr.; Outdoor Channel; Ovation; Speed Channel; Sundance Channel; Syfy; Toon Disney; Trinity Broadcasting Network; Turner Classic Movies; TV Land; Versus.
Fee: $17.94 monthly.

Pay Service 1
Pay Units: 116.
Programming (via satellite): Cinemax; HBO.
Fee: $15.95 monthly (each).

Digital Pay Service 1
Pay Units: N.A.
Programming (via satellite): HBO (multiplexed).
Fee: $15.95 monthly.

Video-On-Demand: No

Pay-Per-View
iN DEMAND (delivered digitally).

Internet Service
Operational: Yes.

Telephone Service
Digital: Operational

Miles of Plant: 51.0 (coaxial); None (fiber optic). Homes passed: 1,907.
Vice President & General Manager: Doug McMillan. Engineering Director: Mike Humphrey. Vice President, Marketing: Vic Scarborough. Government Affairs Director: Bill Ferry.
Ownership: Comcast Cable Communications Inc. (MSO).

LAKE CITY—Comcast Cable, 2288 SW Main Blvd, Lake City, FL 32025-0029. Phone: 386-752-6161. Fax: 386-752-6613. Web Site: http://www.comcast.com. Also serves Columbia County, Live Oak & Suwannee County (portions). ICA: FL0079.
TV Market Ranking: Below 100 (Columbia County (portions), Live Oak, Suwannee County (portions)); Outside TV Markets (Columbia County (portions), LAKE CITY). Franchise award date: January 1, 1966. Franchise expiration date: N.A. Began: January 1, 1967.
Channel capacity: N.A. Channels available but not in use: N.A.

Basic Service
Subscribers: 9,582.
Programming (received off-air): WAWS (FOX, MNT) Jacksonville; WCJB-TV (ABC, CW) Gainesville; WCWJ (CW) Jacksonville; WJXT (IND) Jacksonville; WTEV-TV (CBS) Jacksonville; WTLV (NBC) Jacksonville; WUFT (PBS) Gainesville.
Programming (via satellite): ABC Family Channel; AMC; Animal Planet; Arts & Entertainment; BET Networks; Bravo; Cartoon Network; CNBC; CNN; Comedy Central; Country Music TV; C-SPAN; C-SPAN 2; Discovery Channel; Disney Channel; E! Entertainment Television; ESPN; Food Network; Fox Sports Net; GSN; Headline News; HGTV; History Channel; Lifetime; Lifetime Movie Network; MSNBC; MTV; Nickelodeon; Oxygen; QVC; Spike TV; SunSports TV; Syfy; TBS Superstation; The Learning Channel; Travel Channel; Trinity Broadcasting Network; Turner Network TV; TV Land; USA Network; VH1; WE tv; Weather Channel; WGN America.
Current originations: Public Access.
Fee: $44.79 installation; $15.56 monthly; $17.92 additional installation.

Expanded Basic Service 1
Subscribers: N.A.
Programming (via satellite): Discovery Health Channel; ESPN 2; FX; Hallmark Channel; Home Shopping Network; INSP; ION Television; ShopNBC; Spike TV; truTV; TV Guide Network.
Fee: $30.40 monthly.

Digital Basic Service
Subscribers: N.A.
Programming (via satellite): AmericanLife TV Network; BBC America; Bio; Bloomberg Television; Cooking Channel; Discovery Digital Networks; Do-It-Yourself; ESPN Classic Sports; ESPNews; FitTV; Fox College Sports Atlantic; Fox College Sports Central; Fox College Sports Pacific; Fox Sports World; Fuel TV; Fuse; G4; GAS; Golf Channel; Great American Country; Halogen Network; History Channel International; MTV Hits; MTV2; National Geographic Channel; Nick Jr.; NickToons TV; Outdoor Channel; Ovation; Science Television; Speed Channel; Tennis Channel; Toon Disney; Turner Classic Movies; Versus; VH1 Classic.
Fee: $12.03 monthly.

Digital Expanded Basic Service
Subscribers: N.A.
Programming (via satellite): Fox Movie Channel; Independent Film Channel; Sundance Channel; WAM! America's Kidz Network.
Fee: $6.00 monthly.

Digital Pay Service 1
Pay Units: N.A.
Programming (via satellite): Cinemax (multiplexed); Encore (multiplexed); HBO (multiplexed); Showtime (multiplexed); The Movie Channel (multiplexed).
Fee: $12.00 monthly (each).

Video-On-Demand: No

Pay-Per-View
Playboy TV (delivered digitally); Pleasure (delivered digitally); iN DEMAND (delivered digitally); ESPN Extra (delivered digitally); Fresh (delivered digitally); Shorteez (delivered digitally); Hot Choice (delivered digitally).

Internet Service
Operational: Yes. Began: October 1, 2002.
Broadband Service: Comcast High Speed Internet.
Fee: $99.95 installation; $42.95 monthly.

Telephone Service
Digital: Operational

Miles of Plant: 259.0 (coaxial); None (fiber optic). Homes passed: 10,255. Total homes in franchised area: 15,733.
Vice President: Doug McMillan. Manager: Bob Garner. General Manager: Mark Russell. Chief Technician: Jonathan Norton.
City fee: 5% of gross.
Ownership: Comcast Cable Communications Inc. (MSO).

LAKE MARY JANE—Florida Cable, PO Box 498, 23748 State Rd 40, Astor, FL 32102-0498. Phones: 352-759-2788; 800-779-2788. Fax: 352-759-2788. Web Site: http://www.floridacable.com. ICA: FL0344.
TV Market Ranking: 55 (LAKE MARY JANE). Franchise award date: N.A. Franchise expiration date: N.A. Began: N.A.
Channel capacity: 40 (not 2-way capable). Channels available but not in use: N.A.

Basic Service
Subscribers: N.A.
Programming (received off-air): WESH (NBC) Daytona Beach; WFTV (ABC) Orlando; WHLV-TV (IND) Cocoa; WKCF (CW) Clermont; WKMG-TV (CBS) Orlando; WMFE-TV (PBS) Orlando; WOFL (FOX) Orlando; WRBW (MNT) Orlando; WRDQ (IND) Orlando.
Programming (via satellite): ABC Family Channel; Animal Planet; Arts & Entertainment; CNN; Country Music TV; Discovery Channel; ESPN; ESPN 2; Headline News; Home Shopping Network; Lifetime Movie Network; MTV; Nickelodeon; QVC; Spike TV; TBS Superstation; The Learning Channel; Turner Network TV; USA Network; Weather Channel; WGN America.
Fee: $40.00 installation; $22.95 monthly.

Pay Service 1
Pay Units: 50.
Programming (via satellite): Showtime; The Movie Channel.
Fee: $10.95 monthly.

Internet Service
Operational: No.

Telephone Service
None

General Manager: Jim Pierce. Plant Manager: Larry English. Office Manager: Aleta Dawson.
Ownership: Florida Cable Inc. (MSO).

LAKE PLACID—Comcast Cablevision of West Florida Inc. Now served by SEBRING, FL [FL0063]. ICA: FL0250.

LAKE WALES—Comcast Cable, 5205 Fruitville Rd, Sarasota, FL 34232. Phone: 941-371-4444. Fax: 941-371-5097. Web Site: http://www.comcast.com. Also serves Frostproof & Polk County (portions). ICA: FL0251.
TV Market Ranking: 28 (Frostproof, LAKE WALES); 28,55 (Polk County (portions)). Franchise award date: N.A. Franchise expiration date: N.A. Began: October 1, 1967.
Channel capacity: N.A. Channels available but not in use: N.A.

Basic Service
Subscribers: 6,683.
Programming (received off-air): WBBH-TV (NBC) Fort Myers; WCLF (IND) Clearwater; WEDU (PBS) Tampa; WFLA-TV (NBC) Tampa; WFTS-TV (ABC) Tampa; WFTT-DT

(TEL) Tampa; WFTV (ABC) Orlando; WINK-TV (CBS) Fort Myers; WMOR-TV (IND) Lakeland; WTOG (CW) St. Petersburg; WTTA (MNT) St. Petersburg; WTVT (FOX) Tampa; WVEA-TV (UNV) Venice; WXPX-TV (ION) Bradenton.
Programming (via satellite): ABC Family Channel; AMC; Animal Planet; Arts & Entertainment; BET Networks; Cartoon Network; CNBC; CNN; Comcast/Charter Sports Southeast (CSS); C-SPAN; Discovery Channel; Discovery Health Channel; E! Entertainment Television; ESPN; ESPN 2; Eternal Word TV Network; Food Network; Fox News Channel; FX; Golf Channel; Great American Country; GSN; Headline News; HGTV; History Channel; Home Shopping Network; INSP; Lifetime; MSNBC; MTV; Nickelodeon; QVC; Speed Channel; Spike TV; Style Network; SunSports TV; Syfy; TBS Superstation; The Learning Channel; truTV; Turner Network TV; TV Guide Network; TV Land; USA Network; Versus; VH1; Weather Channel; WGN America.
Current originations: Government Access; Educational Access; Public Access.
Fee: $49.95 installation; $43.35 monthly.
Digital Basic Service
Subscribers: 1,671.
Programming (via satellite): BBC America; Canales N; Discovery Digital Networks; Disney Channel; Encore; ESPNews; Flix (multiplexed); GAS; MTV Networks Digital Suite; Music Choice; Nick Jr.; Nick Too; SoapNet; Sundance Channel (multiplexed); Toon Disney; WAM! America's Kidz Network; WE tv; Weatherscan.
Fee: $14.95 monthly.
Pay Service 1
Pay Units: N.A.
Programming (via satellite): Cinemax; HBO (multiplexed); Showtime.
Fee: $24.95 installation; $10.00 monthly (each).
Digital Pay Service 1
Pay Units: N.A.
Programming (via satellite): Cinemax (multiplexed); HBO (multiplexed); Showtime (multiplexed); Starz (multiplexed); The Movie Channel (multiplexed).
Fee: $10.00 monthly (each).
Video-On-Demand: No
Pay-Per-View
iN DEMAND (delivered digitally); Hot Choice (delivered digitally); Playboy TV (delivered digitally); Fresh (delivered digitally); Shorteez (delivered digitally); Pleasure (delivered digitally).
Internet Service
Operational: Yes.
Broadband Service: Comcast High Speed Internet.
Fee: $42.95 monthly.
Telephone Service
Digital: Operational
Regional Vice President: Rod Dagenais. Vice President & General Manager: Steve Dvoskin. Technical Operations Director: Danny Maxwell. Technical Operations Manager: Andrew Behn. Marketing Director: Vince Maffeo.
City fee: 3% of gross.
Ownership: Comcast Cable Communications Inc. (MSO).

LAWTEY—Florida Cable, PO Box 498, 23748 State Rd 40, Astor, FL 32102-0498. Phones: 352-759-2788; 800-779-2788. Fax: 352-759-3797. E-mail: support@floridacable.com. Web Site: http://www.floridacable.com. Also serves Bradford County, Clay County, Kingsley Lake, Raiford & Union County. ICA: FL0137.
TV Market Ranking: 68 (Bradford County, Clay County, Kingsley Lake, LAWTEY, Union County); Below 100 (Raiford, Bradford County, Clay County, Union County). Franchise award date: December 7, 2002. Franchise expiration date: N.A. Began: N.A.
Channel capacity: 41 (not 2-way capable). Channels available but not in use: 1.
Basic Service
Subscribers: 419.
Programming (received off-air): WAWS (FOX, MNT) Jacksonville; WCWJ (CW) Jacksonville; WJCT (PBS) Jacksonville; WJEB-TV (ETV) Jacksonville; WJXT (IND) Jacksonville; WJXX (ABC) Orange Park; WTEV-TV (CBS) Jacksonville; WTLV (NBC) Jacksonville; WUFT (PBS) Gainesville.
Programming (via satellite): ABC Family Channel; AMC; Arts & Entertainment; BET Networks; Cartoon Network; CNBC; CNN; Comedy Central; Discovery Channel; Disney Channel; ESPN; Food Network; Fox News Channel; Fuse; FX; Great American Country; Headline News; Home Shopping Network; Lifetime; QVC; Speed Channel; SunSports TV; TBS Superstation; Turner Network TV; USA Network; Weather Channel; WGN America.
Fee: $30.00 installation; $39.45 monthly.
Pay Service 1
Pay Units: 189.
Programming (via satellite): Cinemax; HBO; Showtime; The Movie Channel.
Fee: $9.95 monthly (each).
Video-On-Demand: No
Internet Service
Operational: No.
Telephone Service
None
Miles of Plant: 108.0 (coaxial); None (fiber optic). Homes passed: 1,954.
Manager: Jim Pierce. Plant Manager: Larry English. Office Manager: Alita Dawson.
Ownership: Florida Cable Inc. (MSO).

LEE—KLiP Interactive, 455 Gees Mill Business Court, Conyers, GA 30013. Phones: 800-388-6577; 678-727-7100. Fax: 678-727-7002. E-mail: jsheehan@klipia.com. Web Site: http://www.klipia.com. Also serves Madison County (portions). ICA: FL0349.
TV Market Ranking: Below 100 (LEE, Madison County (portions)); Outside TV Markets (Madison County (portions)). Franchise award date: N.A. Franchise expiration date: N.A. Began: N.A.
Channel capacity: 45 (not 2-way capable). Channels available but not in use: 15.
Basic Service
Subscribers: 41.
Programming (received off-air): WABW-TV (PBS) Pelham; WCTV (CBS, MNT) Thomasville; WTLF (CW, FOX) Tallahassee; WTLH (CW, FOX) Bainbridge; WTWC-TV (NBC) Tallahassee; WTXL-TV (ABC) Tallahassee.
Programming (via satellite): ABC Family Channel; AMC; Animal Planet; Arts & Entertainment; CNN; Country Music TV; Discovery Channel; Disney Channel; ESPN; ESPN 2; Lifetime; MTV; Nickelodeon; QVC; Spike TV; Syfy; TBS Superstation; The Learning Channel; Travel Channel; Trinity Broadcasting Network; Turner Classic Movies; Turner Network TV; USA Network; WGN America.
Fee: $29.95 installation; $32.55 monthly.
Pay Service 1
Pay Units: 5.
Programming (via satellite): HBO.
Fee: $10.95 monthly.
Video-On-Demand: No
Internet Service
Operational: No.
Telephone Service
None
Miles of Plant: 23.0 (coaxial); None (fiber optic). Homes passed: 273.
Chief Executive Officer: Joseph A. Sheehan. General Manager East: Mark Miller. General Manager West: Vance Johnson.
Ownership: KLiP Interactive LLC (MSO).

LEESBURG—Comcast Cable, 8130 County Rd 44, Leg A, Leesburg, FL 34788. Phone: 352-787-9601. Fax: 352-365-6279. Web Site: http://www.comcast.com. Also serves Eustis, Fruitland Park, Grand Island, Howey-in-the-Hills, Lady Lake, Mont Verde, Mount Dora, Mount Plymouth, Sorrento, Tavares, The Villages & Umatilla. ICA: FL0034.
TV Market Ranking: 55 (De Bary, Eustis, Fruitland Park, Grand Island, Howey-in-the-Hills, Lady Lake, LEESBURG, Mont Verde, Mount Dora, Mount Plymouth, Sorrento, Tavares, The Villages, Umatilla). Franchise award date: N.A. Franchise expiration date: N.A. Began: December 1, 1968.
Channel capacity: N.A. Channels available but not in use: N.A.
Basic Service
Subscribers: N.A. Included in Celebration
Programming (received off-air): WESH (NBC) Daytona Beach; WFTV (ABC) Orlando; WHLV-TV (IND) Cocoa; WKCF (CW) Clermont; WKMG-TV (CBS) Orlando; WMFE-TV (PBS) Orlando; WOPX-TV (ION) Melbourne; WOTF-DT (TEL) Melbourne; WRBW (MNT) Orlando; WRDQ (IND) Orlando; WVEN-TV (UNV) Daytona Beach.
Programming (via satellite): C-SPAN 2; TV Guide Network; WGN America.
Current originations: Leased Access.
Fee: $36.95 installation; $11.00 monthly.
Expanded Basic Service 1
Subscribers: N.A. Included in Celebration
Programming (via satellite): ABC Family Channel; AMC; Animal Planet; Arts & Entertainment; BET Networks; Bravo; Cartoon Network; CNBC; CNN; Comcast/Charter Sports Southeast (CSS); Comedy Central; Country Music TV; C-SPAN; Discovery Channel; Discovery Health Channel; Disney Channel; E! Entertainment Television; ESPN; ESPN 2; Eternal Word TV Network; Food Network; Fox News Channel; FX; Golf Channel; GSN; Headline News; HGTV; History Channel; Home Shopping Network 2; Jewelry Television; Lifetime; MSNBC; MTV; Nickelodeon; QVC; Shop at Home; Speed Channel; Spike TV; Style Network; SunSports TV; Syfy; TBS Superstation; The Learning Channel; Turner Network TV; TV Guide Network; TV Land; USA Network; Versus; VH1; Weather Channel.
Fee: $49.99 monthly.
Digital Basic Service
Subscribers: N.A. Included in Celebration
Programming (via satellite): BBC America; C-SPAN 3; Discovery Digital Networks; Encore Action; ESPNews; Flix; GAS; MTV Networks Digital Suite; Music Choice; Nick Jr.; Nick Too; SoapNet; Sundance Channel; Toon Disney; Weatherscan.
Fee: $14.95 monthly.
Digital Pay Service 1
Pay Units: N.A. Included in Celebration
Programming (via satellite): Cinemax (multiplexed); HBO (multiplexed); Showtime (multiplexed); Starz (multiplexed); The Movie Channel (multiplexed).
Fee: $13.50 monthly (each).
Video-On-Demand: Planned
Pay-Per-View
Addressable homes: 14,059.
iN DEMAND, Fee: $3.95, Addressable: Yes; iN DEMAND (delivered digitally); Playboy TV (delivered digitally); Fresh (delivered digitally); Shorteez (delivered digitally); Pleasure (delivered digitally); ESPN Now (delivered digitally); ESPN Extra (delivered digitally); NBA TV (delivered digitally).
Internet Service
Operational: Yes.
Broadband Service: Comcast High Speed Internet.
Fee: $42.95 monthly; $7.00 modem lease; $199.00 modem purchase.
Telephone Service
Digital: Operational
Homes passed included in Celebration
Regional Vice President: Rod Dagenais. Vice President & General Manager: Mike Davenport. Technical Operations Manager: Jeff Martin.; Jose Galarza. Chief Engineer: Sean Curley. Marketing Manager: Melanie Melvin. Business Operations Director: Leisa Sellers.
City fee: 3% of gross.
Ownership: Comcast Cable Communications Inc. (MSO).

LEESBURG LAKESHORE MOBILE HOME PARK—Leesburg Lakeshore Mobile Home Park Inc. No longer in operation. ICA: FL0205.

LEHIGH ACRES—Comcast Cablevision of West Florida Inc. Now served by NAPLES (formerly BONITA SPRINGS, FL [FL0029]. ICA: FL0095.

LITTLE TORCH KEY—Comcast Cable. Now served by KEY WEST, FL [FL0055]. ICA: FL0089.

LIVE OAK—Comcast Cable. Now served by LAKE CITY, FL [FL0079]. ICA: FL0100.

LIVE OAK—Florida Cable, PO Box 498, 23748 State Rd 40, Astor, FL 32102-0498. Phones: 352-759-2788; 800-779-2788. Fax: 352-759-3797. E-mail: support@floridacable.com. Web Site: http://www.floridacable.com. Also serves Condo 7. ICA: FL0361.
TV Market Ranking: Below 100 (Condo 7, LIVE OAK). Franchise award date: May 31, 1991. Franchise expiration date: N.A. Began: N.A.
Channel capacity: 36 (not 2-way capable). Channels available but not in use: None.
Basic Service
Subscribers: 295.
Programming (received off-air): WACX-LP Tallahassee; WESH (NBC) Daytona Beach; WFTV (ABC) Orlando; WKCF (CW) Clermont; WKMG-TV (CBS) Orlando; WMFE-TV (PBS) Orlando; WOFL (FOX) Orlando; WOGX (FOX) Ocala; WRBW (MNT) Orlando; WRDQ (IND) Orlando.
Programming (via satellite): ABC Family Channel; AMC; Animal Planet; Arts & Entertainment; BBC America; BET Networks; CNBC; CNN; Comedy Central; Country Music TV; C-SPAN; C-SPAN 2; Discovery Channel; Discovery Health Channel; E! Entertainment Television; ESPN; ESPN 2; ESPN Classic Sports; ESPNews; FitTV; Food Network; Fox News Channel; FX; G4; GalaVision; Golf Channel; Hallmark Channel; Headline News; HGTV; History Channel; Home Shopping Network; Lifetime; Lifetime Movie Network; MSNBC; MTV; Nickelodeon; QVC; ShopNBC; Speed Channel; Spike TV; Syfy; TBS Supersta-

tion; The Learning Channel; Travel Channel; truTV; Turner Classic Movies; Turner Network TV; TV Land; Univision; USA Network; Versus; VH1; WE tv; Weather Channel; WGN America.
Fee: $32.00 monthly.
Internet Service
Operational: No.
Telephone Service
None
Miles of Plant: 2.0 (coaxial); None (fiber optic). Homes passed: 295.
General Manager: Jim Pierce. Plant Manager: Larry English. Office Manager: Alita Dawson.
Ownership: Florida Cable Inc. (MSO).

LIVE OAK—KLiP Interactive, 455 Gees Mill Business Court, Conyers, GA 30013. Phones: 800-388-6577; 706-215-1385. Fax: 706-343-1041. E-mail: jsheehan@klipia.com. Web Site: http://www.klipia.com. Also serves Wellborn. ICA: FL0352.
TV Market Ranking: Below 100 (LIVE OAK, Wellborn). Franchise award date: N.A. Franchise expiration date: N.A. Began: N.A.
Channel capacity: N.A. Channels available but not in use: N.A.
Basic Service
Subscribers: 178.
Programming (received off-air): WCJB-TV (ABC, CW) Gainesville; WCTV (CBS, MNT) Thomasville; WJXT (IND) Jacksonville; WOGX (FOX) Ocala; WTLV (NBC) Jacksonville; WTXL-TV (ABC) Tallahassee; WUFT (PBS) Gainesville.
Programming (via satellite): ABC Family Channel; Animal Planet; BET Networks; CNN; Country Music TV; C-SPAN; Discovery Channel; ESPN; Fox News Channel; History Channel; MTV; Nickelodeon; QVC; Spike TV; Syfy; TBS Superstation; Turner Classic Movies; Turner Network TV; USA Network; Weather Channel; WGN America.
Fee: $20.50 installation; $35.45 monthly.
Pay Service 1
Pay Units: 6.
Programming (via satellite): Cinemax.
Fee: $10.95 monthly.
Pay Service 2
Pay Units: 8.
Programming (via satellite): HBO.
Fee: $10.95 monthly.
Video-On-Demand: No
Internet Service
Operational: No.
Telephone Service
None
Miles of Plant: 60.0 (coaxial); None (fiber optic). Homes passed: 956.
President: Joe Sheehan.
Ownership: KLiP Interactive LLC (MSO).

MACCLENNY—Comcast Cable, 6805 Southpoint Pkwy, Jacksonville, FL 32216. Phone: 904-374-8000. Fax: 904-374-7622. Web Site: http://www.comcast.com. Also serves Baker County & Glen St. Mary. ICA: FL0107.
TV Market Ranking: 68 (Baker County (portions), Glen St. Mary, MACCLENNY); Below 100 (Baker County (portions)); Outside TV Markets (Baker County (portions)). Franchise award date: December 1, 1979. Franchise expiration date: N.A. Began: N.A.
Channel capacity: N.A. Channels available but not in use: N.A.
Basic Service
Subscribers: N.A. Included with Jacksonville
Programming (received off-air): WAWS (FOX, MNT) Jacksonville; WCWJ (CW) Jacksonville; WJCT (PBS) Jacksonville; WJEB-TV (ETV) Jacksonville; WJXT (IND) Jacksonville; WJXX (ABC) Orange Park; WTEV-TV (CBS) Jacksonville; WTLV (NBC) Jacksonville; WUFT (PBS) Gainesville.
Programming (via satellite): C-SPAN; Home Shopping Network; ION Television; QVC; TV Guide Network; Weatherscan; WGN America.
Current originations: Government Access; Educational Access.
Fee: $49.95 installation; $9.61 monthly; $1.65 converter.
Expanded Basic Service 1
Subscribers: 2,282.
Programming (via satellite): ABC Family Channel; AMC; Animal Planet; Arts & Entertainment; BET Networks; Bravo; Cartoon Network; CNBC; CNN; Comcast/Charter Sports Southeast (CSS); Comedy Central; Country Music TV; Discovery Channel; Disney Channel; E! Entertainment Television; ESPN; ESPN 2; Eternal Word TV Network; Food Network; Fox News Channel; Fox Sports Net; Fuse; FX; Golf Channel; Great American Country; Hallmark Channel; Headline News; HGTV; History Channel; Lifetime; MTV; MTV2; Nickelodeon; Speed Channel; Spike TV; SunSports TV; Syfy; TBS Superstation; The Learning Channel; truTV; Turner Network TV; TV Land; Univision; USA Network; Versus; VH1; WE tv; Weather Channel.
Fee: $32.04 monthly.
Digital Basic Service
Subscribers: 503.
Programming (received off-air): WAWS (FOX, MNT) Jacksonville; WCWJ (CW) Jacksonville; WJCT (PBS) Jacksonville; WJXX (ABC) Orange Park; WTEV-TV (CBS) Jacksonville; WTLV (NBC) Jacksonville.
Programming (via satellite): BBC America; Bio; Black Family Channel; Bloomberg Television; Bravo; Canales N; Cooking Channel; Country Music TV; C-SPAN 2; C-SPAN 3; Current; Discovery Digital Networks; Discovery HD Theater; Do-It-Yourself; Encore (multiplexed); ESPN 2 HD; ESPN Classic Sports; ESPN HD; ESPNews; FamilyNet; Fox College Sports Atlantic; Fox College Sports Central; Fox College Sports Pacific; Fox Soccer; G4; GAS; GSN; Halogen Network; History Channel International; Independent Film Channel; INHD; Jewelry Television; Lifetime Movie Network; LOGO; MoviePlex; MSNBC; MTV Networks Digital Suite; Music Choice; National Geographic Channel; NBA TV; NFL Network; Nick Jr.; Nick Too; NickToons TV; Outdoor Channel; Oxygen; Palladia; PBS Kids Sprout; ShopNBC; Style Network; Sundance Channel; Tennis Channel; The Sportsman Channel; The Word Network; Toon Disney; Travel Channel; Trinity Broadcasting Network; Turner Classic Movies; Turner Network TV HD; TV One; Versus HD.
Fee: $9.95 monthly.
Digital Pay Service 1
Pay Units: N.A.
Programming (via satellite): Cinemax (multiplexed); Cinemax HD; Flix; HBO (multiplexed); HBO HD; Showtime (multiplexed); Showtime HD; Starz (multiplexed); Starz HDTV; The Movie Channel (multiplexed).
Fee: $15.95 monthly (each).
Video-On-Demand: No
Pay-Per-View
Addressable homes: 503.
Movies & Events (delivered digitally), Addressable: Yes; Playboy TV (delivered digitally); ESPN (delivered digitally); NBA League Pass (delivered digitally); NHL Center Ice (delivered digitally); MLB Extra Innings (delivered digitally).
Internet Service
Operational: Yes.
Subscribers: 3,930.
Broadband Service: Comcast High Speed Internet.
Fee: $42.95 monthly.
Telephone Service
Digital: Operational
Miles of Plant: 169.0 (coaxial); None (fiber optic). Homes passed: 6,446.
Vice President & General Manager: Doug McMillan. Engineering Director: Mike Humphrey. Vice President, Marketing: Vic Scarborough. Government Affairs Director: Bill Ferry.
Ownership: Comcast Cable Communications Inc. (MSO).

MACON—Cox Communications, 6601 Hawkinsville Rd, Macon, GA 31216-6837. Phone: 478-784-8000. Fax: 478-784-5100. Web Site: http://www.cox.com/middlega. Also serves Bibb County, Byron, Centerville, Houston County, Jones County (portions), Monroe County (portions), Payne City, Peach County (portions), Perry, Robins AFB & Warner Robins. ICA: GA0003.
TV Market Ranking: Below 100 (Bibb County, Byron, Centerville, Houston County, Jones County (portions), MACON, Monroe County (portions), Payne City, Peach County (portions), Perry, Robins AFB, Warner Robins). Franchise award date: December 14, 1964. Franchise expiration date: N.A. Began: December 31, 1964.
Channel capacity: N.A. Channels available but not in use: N.A.
Basic Service
Subscribers: 70,000.
Programming (received off-air): WGNM (IND) Macon; WGXA (FOX, MNT) Macon; WMAZ-TV (CBS) Macon; WMGT-TV (MNT, NBC) Macon; WMUM-TV (PBS) Cochran; WPGA-TV (ABC) Perry; WSB-TV (ABC) Atlanta.
Programming (via satellite): C-SPAN; CW+; Home Shopping Network; INSP; TBS Superstation; WGN America.
Current originations: Government Access; Educational Access; Public Access.
Fee: $56.50 installation; $13.00 monthly; $1.00 converter.
Expanded Basic Service 1
Subscribers: N.A.
Programming (via satellite): ABC Family Channel; AMC; Animal Planet; Arts & Entertainment; BET Networks; Bravo; Cartoon Network; CNBC; CNN; Comcast Sports Net Southeast; Comedy Central; Country Music TV; C-SPAN 2; Discovery Channel; Discovery Health Channel; Disney Channel; E! Entertainment Television; ESPN; ESPN 2; Eternal Word TV Network; Food Network; Fox News Channel; FX; Golf Channel; Hallmark Channel; Headline News; HGTV; History Channel; ION Television; Lifetime; MSNBC; MTV; Nickelodeon; QVC; Speed Channel; Spike TV; SportSouth; Syfy; The Learning Channel; Travel Channel; Trinity Broadcasting Network; truTV; Turner Network TV; TV Guide Network; TV Land; Univision; USA Network; Versus; VH1; Weather Channel.
Fee: $35.99 monthly.
Digital Basic Service
Subscribers: N.A.
Programming (via satellite): AmericanLife TV Network; BYU Television; Daystar TV Network; Discovery Kids Channel; Discovery Military Channel; Discovery Planet Green; Eternal Word TV Network; FamilyNet; Gospel Music Channel; GSN; Halogen Network; ID Investigation Discovery; Jewelry Television; Music Choice; National Geographic Channel; Nick Jr.; Science Channel; ShopNBC; Trinity Broadcasting Network; Weatherscan.
Fee: $7.51 monthly.
Digital Expanded Basic Service
Subscribers: N.A.
Programming (via satellite): Encore (multiplexed); Flix; Hallmark Movie Channel; Independent Film Channel; Lifetime Movie Network; MoviePlex; Sundance Channel; Turner Classic Movies.
Fee: $10.51 monthly.
Digital Expanded Basic Service 2
Subscribers: N.A.
Programming (via satellite): Bio; Bloomberg Television; CNN International; Cooking Channel; Cox Sports Television; Do-It-Yourself; ESPN Classic Sports; ESPN U; ESPNews; FitTV; Fox Soccer; Fuel TV; G4; History Channel International; NBA TV; NFL Network; NHL Network; Outdoor Channel; Tennis Channel; The Sportsman Channel.
Fee: $10.51 monthly.
Digital Expanded Basic Service 3
Subscribers: N.A.
Programming (via satellite): Africa Channel; BBC America; Boomerang; CMT Pure Country; Disney XD; Encore Wam; Fuse; Great American Country; GSN; MTV Hits; MTV Jams; MTV Tres; MTV2; NickToons TV; Oxygen; PBS Kids Sprout; SoapNet; Style Network; TeenNick; TV One; VH1 Classic; VH1 Soul; WE tv.
Fee: $10.51 monthly.
Digital Expanded Basic Service 4
Subscribers: N.A.
Programming (via satellite): CNN en Espanol; Discovery en Espanol; Discovery Familia; ESPN Deportes; Fox Sports en Espanol; GalaVision; Gol TV; MTV Tres; Sorpresa; Telefutura; Telemundo; VeneMovies.
Fee: $30.71 monthly.
Digital Pay Service 1
Pay Units: N.A.
Programming (via satellite): Cinemax (multiplexed); Cinemax HD; Encore; HBO (multiplexed); HBO HD; Showtime (multiplexed); Showtime HD; Starz (multiplexed); Starz HDTV; The Movie Channel (multiplexed).
Fee: $11.00 monthly (HBO, Cinemax, Showtime/TMC or Starz/Encore).
Video-On-Demand: Yes
Pay-Per-View
Addressable homes: 31,179.
ESPN Extra (delivered digitally), Fee: $2.95-$3.95, Addressable: Yes; Spice: Xcess (delivered digitally); MLB Extra Innings (delivered digitally); NHL Center Ice (delivered digitally); Club Jenna (delivered digitally);

NBA League Pass (delivered digitally); iN DEMAND; iN DEMAND (delivered digitally); MLS Direct Kick (delivered digitally); Playboy TV (delivered digitally); Ten Blox (delivered digitally); Ten Clips (delivered digitally).

Internet Service

Operational: Yes.

Broadband Service: Cox High Speed Internet.

Fee: $79.99 installation; $29.99-$56.99 monthly; $15.00 modem lease.

Telephone Service

Digital: Operational

Fee: $15.70-$54.95 monthly

Miles of Plant: 1,623.0 (coaxial); 176.0 (fiber optic). Additional miles planned: 35.0 (coaxial); 159.0 (fiber optic). Homes passed: 106,568. Total homes in franchised area: 135,630.

Vice President & General Manager: J. Michael Dyer. Vice President, Operations: Karen Whitaker. Marketing Director: Mark Watkins. Community & Government Relations Director: Lynn Murphey.

City fee: 5% of gross.

Ownership: Cox Communications Inc. (MSO).

MADISON—Comcast Cable, 3760 Hartsfield Rd, Tallahassee, FL 32303-1121. Phones: 850-574-4016 (Tallahassee office); 912-487-2224 (Local office). Fax: 850-574-4030. Web Site: http://www.comcast.com. Also serves Madison County. ICA: FL0138.

TV Market Ranking: Below 100 (MADISON, Madison County (portions)); Outside TV Markets (Madison County (portions)). Franchise award date: N.A. Franchise expiration date: N.A. Began: November 1, 1970.

Channel capacity: 66 (not 2-way capable). Channels available but not in use: None.

Basic Service

Subscribers: N.A. Included in Tallahassee

Programming (received off-air): WABW-TV (PBS) Pelham; WCTV (CBS, MNT) Thomasville; WFSU-TV (PBS) Tallahassee; WTLH (CW, FOX) Bainbridge; WTWC-TV (NBC) Tallahassee; WTXL-TV (ABC) Tallahassee.

Programming (via satellite): ABC Family Channel; AmericanLife TV Network; Animal Planet; Arts & Entertainment; BET Networks; CNBC; CNN; Comcast/Charter Sports Southeast (CSS); Comedy Central; Country Music TV; C-SPAN; C-SPAN 2; Discovery Channel; Discovery Health Channel; Disney Channel; E! Entertainment Television; ESPN; ESPN 2; Eternal Word TV Network; Food Network; Fox News Channel; FX; Golf Channel; Great American Country; GSN; Hallmark Channel; Headline News; HGTV; History Channel; Home Shopping Network; ION Television; Lifetime; MBC America; MSNBC; MTV; MTV2; Nickelodeon; QVC; Speed Channel; Spike TV; Style Network; SunSports TV; Syfy; TBS Superstation; The Learning Channel; Trinity Broadcasting Network; truTV; Turner Network TV; TV Guide Network; TV Land; TV One; USA Network; Versus; VH1; Weather Channel; WGN America.

Fee: $39.88 installation; $11.95 monthly.

Digital Basic Service

Subscribers: N.A.

Programming (via satellite): Music Choice; Nick Jr.; Nick Too.

Pay Service 1

Pay Units: N.A.

Programming (via satellite): Cinemax; HBO; Showtime.

Fee: $11.95 monthly each (Showtime & TMC), $13.95 monthly (HBO).

Digital Pay Service 1

Pay Units: 367.

Programming (via satellite): Cinemax (multiplexed); Flix; HBO (multiplexed); Showtime (multiplexed); The Movie Channel (multiplexed).

Video-On-Demand: No

Pay-Per-View

Addressable homes: 367.

iN DEMAND (delivered digitally); Hot Choice (delivered digitally); Playboy TV (delivered digitally); Fresh (delivered digitally); Shorteez (delivered digitally).

Internet Service

Operational: Yes.

Telephone Service

Digital: Operational

Miles of plant (coax) & homes passed included in Tallahassee

General Manager: K. C. McWilliams. Area Technical Manager: Andy Musgrove. Technical Operations Director: Terry Pullen. Marketing Director: Claire Evans. System Coordinator: Carla Musgrove.

City fee: 3% of gross.

Ownership: Comcast Cable Communications Inc. (MSO).

MARCO ISLAND—Marco Island Cable Inc., PO Box 368, 926 Windward Dr, Marco Island, FL 34145-2528. Phone: 239-642-4545 (Customer service). Fax: 239-394-4895. E-mail: marcocable@marcocable.com. Web Site: http://marcocable.net. ICA: FL0359.

TV Market Ranking: Below 100 (MARCO ISLAND). Franchise award date: N.A. Franchise expiration date: N.A. Began: N.A.

Channel capacity: 263 (operating 2-way). Channels available but not in use: N.A.

Basic Service

Subscribers: N.A.

Programming (received off-air): WBBH-TV (NBC) Fort Myers; WEVU-CA Fort Myers; WFTX-TV (FOX) Cape Coral; WGCU (PBS) Fort Myers; WINK-TV (CBS) Fort Myers; WRXY-TV (IND) Tice; WXCW (CW) Naples; WZVN-TV (ABC) Naples; 15 FMs.

Programming (via satellite): ABC Family Channel; AMC; AmericanLife TV Network; Animal Planet; Arts & Entertainment; Bravo; CNBC; CNN; Comedy Central; Country Music TV; C-SPAN; C-SPAN 2; Deutsche Welle TV; Discovery Channel; Disney Channel; E! Entertainment Television; ESPN; ESPN 2; Eternal Word TV Network; Food Network; Fox News Channel; Golf Channel; Headline News; HGTV; History Channel; Home Shopping Network; Lifetime; MSNBC; MTV; Nickelodeon; QVC; Sneak Prevue; Spike TV; Syfy; TBS Superstation; The Learning Channel; Toon Disney; Travel Channel; truTV; Turner Classic Movies; Turner Network TV; TV Guide Network; TV Land; USA Network; VH1; Weather Channel; WGN America.

Current originations: Government Access.

Fee: $51.95 monthly.

Digital Basic Service

Subscribers: N.A.

Programming (received off-air): WBBH-TV (NBC) Fort Myers; WFTX-TV (FOX) Cape Coral; WGCU (PBS) Fort Myers; WZVN-TV (ABC) Naples.

Programming (via satellite): BBC America; Cinemax; Cooking Channel; Deutsche Welle TV; Discovery Digital Networks; Encore Action; ESPN; G4; GAS; HBO; iN DEMAND; MTV Networks Digital Suite; Music Choice; NFL Network; Nick Jr.; Nick Too; NickToons TV; Tennis Channel.

Fee: $25.00 installation; $19.95 monthly.

Digital Pay Service 1

Pay Units: N.A.

Programming (via satellite): Cinemax (multiplexed); Deutsche Welle TV; Flix; HBO (multiplexed); Playboy TV; Showtime (multiplexed); Starz (multiplexed); The Movie Channel (multiplexed).

Fee: $9.95 monthly (Deutsche Welle), $10.00 monthly (Showtime/TMC/Flix or Starz), $10.95 monthly (Cinemax), $15.95 monthly (HBO), $29.95 monthly (Playboy).

Video-On-Demand: No

Pay-Per-View

Playboy TV (delivered digitally), Addressable: Yes; iN DEMAND (delivered digitally); MLB Extra Innings (delivered digitally); Hot Choice (delivered digitally); Pleasure (delivered digitally); Fresh (delivered digitally); Shorteez (delivered digitally); ESPN Now (delivered digitally); NHL Center Ice (delivered digitally).

Internet Service

Operational: Yes.

Broadband Service: Marco Island Cable.

Fee: $50.00 installation; $29.95 monthly; $5.00 modem lease; $99.00 modem purchase.

Telephone Service

None

Homes passed: 12,000.

President: William Gaston.

Ownership: Marco Island Cable.

MARGATE—Comcast Cable. Now served by BROWARD COUNTY, FL [FL0016]. ICA: FL0041.

MARIANNA—Comcast Cable, 1316 Harrison Ave, Panama City, FL 32401. Phone: 850-769-2929. Fax: 850-769-2988. Web Site: http://www.comcast.com. Also serves Alford, Altha, Bascom, Cottondale, Cypress, Greenwood, Jackson County (portions) & Malone. ICA: FL0134.

TV Market Ranking: Below 100 (Alford, Altha, Bascom, Cottondale, Cypress, Greenwood, Jackson County (portions), Malone, MARIANNA). Franchise award date: N.A. Franchise expiration date: N.A. Began: March 4, 1980.

Channel capacity: 55 (operating 2-way). Channels available but not in use: N.A.

Basic Service

Subscribers: 3,841.

Programming (received off-air): WBIF (IND) Marianna [LICENSED & SILENT]; WCTV (CBS, MNT) Thomasville; WFSU-TV (PBS) Tallahassee; WJHG-TV (CW, MNT, NBC) Panama City; WMBB (ABC) Panama City; WPGX (FOX) Panama City; WTVY (CBS, CW, MNT) Dothan.

Programming (via satellite): Catholic Television Network; Country Music TV; C-SPAN; QVC.

Fee: $43.30 installation; $8.20 monthly.

Expanded Basic Service 1

Subscribers: N.A.

Programming (via satellite): ABC Family Channel; AMC; Animal Planet; Arts & Entertainment; BET Networks; Cartoon Network; CNBC; CNN; Comcast/Charter Sports Southeast (CSS); Discovery Channel; Disney Channel; E! Entertainment Television; ESPN; ESPN 2; Food Network; Fox News Channel; FX; Golf Channel; Great American Country; GSN; Headline News; HGTV; History Channel; Home Shopping Network; Lifetime; MTV; Nickelodeon; Speed Channel; Spike TV; Style Network; SunSports TV; Syfy; TBS Superstation; The Learning Channel; Trinity Broadcasting Network; Turner Network TV; TV Land; USA Network; VH1; Weather Channel.

Fee: $30.75 monthly.

Digital Basic Service

Subscribers: 960.

Programming (via satellite): BBC America; CMT Pure Country; Discovery Digital Networks; Encore (multiplexed); Flix; GAS; MTV Networks Digital Suite; Music Choice; Nick Jr.; Nick Too; Sundance Channel.

Fee: $14.95 monthly.

Pay Service 1

Pay Units: 395.

Programming (via satellite): Cinemax; HBO; Showtime.

Fee: $19.95 installation; $11.95 monthly (each).

Digital Pay Service 1

Pay Units: N.A.

Programming (via satellite): Cinemax (multiplexed); HBO (multiplexed); Showtime (multiplexed); The Movie Channel (multiplexed).

Fee: $3.95 monthly (each).

Video-On-Demand: No

Pay-Per-View

Addressable homes: 960.

Hot Choice (delivered digitally); iN DEMAND (delivered digitally); Playboy TV (delivered digitally); Fresh (delivered digitally).

Internet Service

Operational: Yes.

Subscribers: 423.

Broadband Service: Comcast High Speed Internet.

Fee: $42.95 monthly.

Telephone Service

Analog: Not Operational

Digital: Operational

Miles of Plant: 130.0 (coaxial); None (fiber optic).

General Manager: Fritz Hoehne. Technical Operations Manager: Tim Denton. Marketing Manager: Kevin Canel.

City fee: 3% of gross.

Ownership: Comcast Cable Communications Inc. (MSO).

MARION COUNTY (southeastern portion)—Cablevision of Marion County, 8296 SW 103rd St Rd, Ste 3, Ocala, FL 34481. Phone: 352-854-0408. Fax: 352-854-0086. Web Site: http://www.lightningspeed.net. ICA: FL0368.

TV Market Ranking: Below 100 (MARION COUNTY (SOUTHEASTERN PORTION)).

Channel capacity: N.A. Channels available but not in use: N.A.

Basic Service

Subscribers: 1,998.

Programming (received off-air): WACX (IND) Leesburg; WCJB-TV (ABC, CW) Gainesville; WESH (NBC) Daytona Beach; WFTV (ABC) Orlando; WKCF (CW) Clermont; WKMG-TV (CBS) Orlando; WOFL (FOX) Orlando; WOGX (FOX) Ocala; WRBW (MNT) Orlando; WUFT (PBS) Gainesville.

Programming (via satellite): ABC Family Channel; AMC; Animal Planet; Arts & Entertainment; Bravo; Cartoon Network; CNBC; CNN; C-SPAN; C-SPAN 2; Discovery Channel; ESPN; ESPN 2; Food Network; Fox Movie Channel; Fox News Channel; FX; Golf Channel; Great American Country; Headline News; HGTV; History Channel; Home Shopping Network; Lifetime; MSNBC; QVC; Speed Channel; SunSports TV; Syfy; TBS Superstation; The Learning Channel; Travel Channel; truTV; Turner Classic Movies; Turner Network TV; TV Guide Network; TV Land; Univision; USA Network; Weather Channel; WGN America.

Current originations: Public Access.
Fee: $50.00 installation; $39.45 monthly.
Digital Basic Service
Subscribers: N.A.
Programming (via satellite): AmericanLife TV Network; BBC America; Bio; Bloomberg Television; Discovery Digital Networks; DMX Music; ESPN Classic Sports; ESP-News; FitTV; Fox College Sports Atlantic; Fox Movie Channel; Fox Sports Net; Fuse; G4; GSN; History Channel International; INSP; Lifetime Movie Network; National Geographic Channel; Outdoor Channel; Sleuth; Speed Channel; Style Network; Toon Disney; WE tv.
Fee: $13.95 monthly.
Pay Service 1
Pay Units: N.A.
Programming (via satellite): Cinemax; HBO (multiplexed); Showtime; The Movie Channel.
Fee: $10.25 monthly (Showtime or TMC), $10.95 monthly (Cinemax), $14.95 monthly (HBO).
Digital Pay Service 1
Pay Units: N.A.
Programming (via satellite): Cinemax (multiplexed); Encore (multiplexed); Flix; HBO (multiplexed); Showtime (multiplexed); Starz (multiplexed); The Movie Channel (multiplexed).
Fee: $14.95 monthly (Starz/Encore), $23.95 monthly (HBO Superpak or Movieplex).
Video-On-Demand: No
Pay-Per-View
iN DEMAND (delivered digitally); Playboy TV (delivered digitally); Fresh (delivered digitally); Shorteez (delivered digitally); Hot Choice (delivered digitally).
Internet Service
Operational: Yes.
Fee: $50.00 installation; $34.95 monthly.
Telephone Service
Digital: Operational
Fee: $40.00 installation; $49.99 monthly
Miles of Plant: 40.0 (coaxial); 7.0 (fiber optic). Homes passed: 3,505.
President: Jess King. Vice President, Plant Services: Richard Black. Vice President, Customer Care: Kerri King. Office Manager: Louise Brush.
Ownership: Cablevision of Marion County LLC (MSO).

MARION COUNTY (southern portion)—Florida Cable, PO Box 498, 23748 State Rd 40, Astor, FL 32102-0498. Phones: 352-759-2788; 800-779-2788. Fax: 352-759-3577. E-mail: support@floridacable.com. Web Site: http://www.floridacable.com. Also serves Eustis, Lake Yale Estates, Palm Shores Mobile Home Park, Sandpiper Mobile Home Park & Umatilla. ICA: FL0364.
TV Market Ranking: 55 (Eustis, Lake Yale Estates, MARION COUNTY (SOUTHERN PORTION), Palm Shores Mobile Home Park, Sandpiper Mobile Home Park, Umatilla).
Channel capacity: 36 (not 2-way capable). Channels available but not in use: None.
Basic Service
Subscribers: 257.
Programming (received off-air): WACX (IND) Leesburg; WESH (NBC) Daytona Beach; WFTV (ABC) Orlando; WKCF (CW) Clermont; WKMG-TV (CBS) Orlando; WMFE-TV (PBS) Orlando; WOFL (FOX) Orlando; WOGX (FOX) Ocala; WRBW (MNT) Orlando.
Programming (via satellite): ABC Family Channel; Animal Planet; Arts & Entertainment; Cartoon Network; CNBC; CNN; Comedy Central; C-SPAN; Discovery Channel; Disney Channel; ESPN; Food Network; Fuse; Great American Country; Headline News; Lifetime; QVC; Speed Channel; Syfy; TBS Superstation; Turner Network TV; USA Network; Weather Channel; WGN America.
Fee: $26.45 monthly.
Pay Service 1
Pay Units: N.A.
Programming (via satellite): Cinemax; HBO; Showtime.
Internet Service
Operational: No.
Telephone Service
None
Miles of Plant: 41.0 (coaxial); None (fiber optic). Homes passed: 1,180.
General Manager: Jim Pierce. Plant Manager: Larry English. Office Manager: Alita Dawson.
Ownership: Florida Cable Inc. (MSO).

MAYO—Comcast Cable, 2288 SW Main Blvd, Lake City, FL 32025-0029. Phone: 386-752-6161. Fax: 386-752-6613. Web Site: http://www.comcast.com. ICA: FL0192.
TV Market Ranking: Outside TV Markets (MAYO). Franchise award date: August 3, 1982. Franchise expiration date: N.A. Began: August 3, 1982.
Channel capacity: 36 (not 2-way capable). Channels available but not in use: 1.
Basic Service
Subscribers: 160.
Programming (received off-air): WCJB-TV (ABC, CW) Gainesville; WCTV (CBS, MNT) Thomasville; WOGX (FOX) Ocala; WTWC-TV (NBC) Tallahassee; WTXL-TV (ABC) Tallahassee; WUFT (PBS) Gainesville.
Programming (via satellite): ABC Family Channel; AMC; Animal Planet; Arts & Entertainment; BET Networks; CNN; Comedy Central; Country Music TV; Discovery Channel; Disney Channel; E! Entertainment Television; ESPN; ESPN 2; History Channel; Home Shopping Network; Lifetime; Nickelodeon; ShopNBC; Spike TV; SunSports TV; TBS Superstation; Travel Channel; Trinity Broadcasting Network; Turner Network TV; TV Land; USA Network; Weather Channel.
Fee: $44.79 installation; $14.37 monthly.
Pay Service 1
Pay Units: 66.
Programming (via satellite): HBO; Showtime.
Fee: $12.00 monthly (each).
Video-On-Demand: Yes
Internet Service
Operational: Yes.
Telephone Service
Digital: Operational
Miles of Plant: 9.0 (coaxial); None (fiber optic). Additional miles planned: 1.0 (coaxial). Homes passed: 715.
Vice President: Doug McMillan. General Manager: Mark Russell. Manager: Bob Garner. Chief Technician: Jonathan Norton.
City fee: 3% of gross.
Ownership: Comcast Cable Communications Inc. (MSO).

MELBOURNE—Bright House Networks, 720 Magnolia Way, Melbourne, FL 32935. Phones: 321-254-3300 (Customer service); 321-254-3326. Fax: 321-254-1307. E-mail: paul.hanson@mybrighthouse.com. Web Site: http://cfl.mybrighthouse.com. Also serves Barefoot Bay, Brevard County, Cape Canaveral, Charleston Place, Cocoa, Cocoa Beach, Greenwood Manor, Greenwood Village, Indian Harbor Beach, Indiatlantic, Malabar, Melbourne Beach, Melbourne Village, Merritt Island, Palm Bay, Palm Shores, Patrick AFB, Rockledge, Satellite Beach, Snug Harbor Village, Titusville, Viera & West Melbourne. ICA: FL0015.
TV Market Ranking: 55 (Barefoot Bay, Brevard County, Cape Canaveral, Charleston Place, Cocoa, Cocoa Beach, Greenwood Manor, Greenwood Village, Indian Harbor Beach, Indiatlantic, Malabar, MELBOURNE, Melbourne Beach, Melbourne Village, Merritt Island, Palm Bay, Palm Shores, Patrick AFB, Rockledge, Satellite Beach, Snug Harbor Village, Titusville, Viera, West Melbourne). Franchise award date: N.A. Franchise expiration date: N.A. Began: October 1, 1964.
Channel capacity: N.A. Channels available but not in use: N.A.
Basic Service
Subscribers: 177,694.
Programming (received off-air): WBCC (PBS) Cocoa; WESH (NBC) Daytona Beach; WFTV (ABC) Orlando; WHLV-TV (IND) Cocoa; WKCF (CW) Clermont; WKMG-TV (CBS) Orlando; WMFE-TV (PBS) Orlando; WOFL (FOX) Orlando; WOPX-TV (ION) Melbourne; WOTF-DT (TEL) Melbourne; WRBW (MNT) Orlando; WRDQ (IND) Orlando; WVEN-TV (UNV) Daytona Beach; 18 FMs.
Programming (via microwave): Central Florida News 13.
Programming (via satellite): AMC; Animal Planet; Arts & Entertainment; BET Networks; Bravo; Cartoon Network; CNBC; CNN; Comedy Central; Country Music TV; C-SPAN; C-SPAN 2; Discovery Channel; Discovery Health Channel; Disney Channel; E! Entertainment Television; ESPN; ESPN 2; Food Network; Fox News Channel; FX; GalaVision; Golf Channel; Hallmark Channel; Headline News; HGTV; History Channel; Home Shopping Network; Lifetime; Lifetime Movie Network; Lifetime Real Women; MSNBC; MTV; NASA TV; Nickelodeon; Oxygen; QVC; ShopNBC; SoapNet; Speed Channel; Spike TV; Style Network; SunSports TV; Syfy; TBS Superstation; Telemundo; The Learning Channel; Travel Channel; truTV; Turner Classic Movies; Turner Network TV; TV Land; USA Network; VH1; WE tv; Weather Channel; WGN America.
Current originations: Government Access; Leased Access.
Fee: $36.83 installation; $50.79 monthly; $.97 converter; $27.96 additional installation.
Digital Basic Service
Subscribers: N.A.
Programming (received off-air): Local Cable Weather; WDSC-TV (PBS) New Smyrna Beach; WESH (NBC) Daytona Beach; WFTV (ABC) Orlando; WKCF (CW) Clermont; WKMG-TV (CBS) Orlando; WMFE-TV (PBS) Orlando; WOFL (FOX) Orlando; WRBW (MNT) Orlando.
Programming (via satellite): ABC Family Channel; America's Store; BBC America; Black Family Channel; Bloomberg Television; CBS College Sports Network; Cooking Channel; C-SPAN 3; Current; Discovery Digital Networks; Discovery HD Theater; Discovery Kids Channel; DMX Music; Do-It-Yourself; ESPN; ESPN Classic Sports; ESP-News; Eternal Word TV Network; FitTV; Fox Movie Channel; Fox Soccer; Fuel TV; Fuse; G4; GAS; Great American Country; HDNet; HDNet Movies; INHD; MTV2; National Geographic Channel; NBA TV; Nick Jr.; Nick-Toons TV; Outdoor Channel; Ovation; Tennis Channel; Toon Disney; Trio; Turner Network TV HD; Versus; VH1 Classic; Weatherscan.
Fee: $7.70 monthly.
Digital Expanded Basic Service
Subscribers: N.A.
Programming (via satellite): Canales N.
Digital Pay Service 1
Pay Units: N.A.
Programming (via satellite): Cinemax (multiplexed); Encore (multiplexed); Flix; HBO (multiplexed); HBO HD; Independent Film Channel; MoviePlex; Showtime (multiplexed); Showtime HD; Starz (multiplexed); Sundance Channel; The Movie Channel (multiplexed).
Fee: $10.95 monthly (each).
Video-On-Demand: Yes
Pay-Per-View
iN DEMAND (delivered digitally); Pleasure (delivered digitally); Playboy TV (delivered digitally); Fresh (delivered digitally); Shorteez (delivered digitally); Sports PPV (delivered digitally).
Internet Service
Operational: Yes.
Broadband Service: Road Runner.
Fee: $29.95 monthly.
Telephone Service
Digital: Operational
Fee: $28.95 monthly
Miles of Plant: 1,502.0 (coaxial); 77.0 (fiber optic).
President: Kevin Hyman. Division President: J. Christian Fenger. General Manager: Paul Hanson. Engineering Director: Robert Sell. Marketing Director: Duggan Kowalski. Customer Service Manager: Debbie Kelly.
City fee: 3% of gross.
Ownership: Bright House Networks LLC (MSO).

MELBOURNE—Formerly served by Wireless Broadcasting of Melbourne. No longer in operation. ICA: FL0305.

MEXICO BEACH—Mediacom. Now served by WEWAHITCHKA, FL [FL0159]. ICA: FL0141.

MIAMI—Comcast Cable, 18601 NW 2nd Ave, Miami, FL 33169-4507. Phones: 954-534-7419 (Miramar regional office); 305-232-8132 (Customer service). Fax: 305-770-5440. Web Site: http://www.comcast.com. Also serves Aventura, Biscayne Park, Coral Gables, Cutler Ridge, Dade County, Doral, El Portal, Florida City, Goulds, Hialeah, Hialeah Gardens, Homestead, Kendall, Leisure City, Medley, Miami Shores, Miami Springs, Naranja, North Miami, North Miami Beach, Opa-Locka, Perrine, Pinecrest, South Miami Heights, Sweetwater, Virginia Gardens & West Miami. ICA: FL0006.
TV Market Ranking: 21 (Aventura, Biscayne Park, Coral Gables, Cutler Ridge, Dade County (portions), Doral, El Portal, Florida City, Goulds, Hialeah, Hialeah Gardens, Homestead, Kendall, Leisure City, Medley, MIAMI, Miami Shores, Miami Springs, Naranja, North Miami, North Miami Beach, Opa-Locka, Perrine, Pinecrest, South Miami Heights, Sweetwater, Virginia Gardens, West Miami); Outside TV Markets (Dade County (portions)). Franchise award date: N.A. Franchise expiration date: N.A. Began: August 1, 1984.
Channel capacity: N.A. Channels available but not in use: N.A.
Basic Service
Subscribers: 740,000 Includes Big Cypress Seminole Indian Reservation,

Brighton Seminole Reserve, Broward County, Immokalee Seminole Indian Reservation, & Key West.
Programming (received off-air): WAMI-DT (TEL) Hollywood; WBFS-TV (MNT) Miami; WFOR-TV (CBS) Miami; WGEN-TV (IND) Key West; WHFT-TV (TBN) Miami; WLRN-TV (PBS) Miami; WLTV-DT (UNV) Miami; WPBT (PBS) Miami; WPLG (ABC) Miami; WPXM-TV (ION) Miami; WSCV (TMO) Fort Lauderdale; WSFL-TV (CW) Miami; WSVN (FOX) Miami; WTVJ (NBC) Miami.
Programming (via satellite): Discovery Channel; QVC; Sneak Prevue; TBS Superstation; Telemiami.
Current originations: Leased Access; Religious Access; Government Access; Educational Access.
Fee: $45.00 installation; $15.50 monthly.

Expanded Basic Service 1
Subscribers: 56,000.
Programming (via satellite): ABC Family Channel; AMC; Animal Planet; Arts & Entertainment; BET Networks; CNBC; CNN; C-SPAN; Disney Channel; E! Entertainment Television; ESPN; Fox News Channel; Fox Sports Net Florida; FX; GalaVision; Headline News; Home Shopping Network; Lifetime; MSNBC; MTV; MTV2; mun2 television; Nickelodeon; Spike TV; SunSports TV; The Learning Channel; Turner Network TV; USA Network; Weather Channel.
Fee: $52.50 monthly.

Digital Basic Service
Subscribers: 15,329.
Programming (via satellite): BBC America; Bravo; Canales N; Discovery Digital Networks; DMX Music; ESPN 2; ESPN Classic Sports; ESPNews; Fox Sports World; Golf Channel; GSN; HGTV; History Channel; Independent Film Channel; National Geographic Channel; Nick Jr.; Speed Channel; Syfy; Turner Classic Movies; TV Land; Versus; VH1 Classic; VH1 Country; WE tv.
Fee: $11.95 monthly.

Digital Pay Service 1
Pay Units: N.A.
Programming (via satellite): Cinemax (multiplexed); HBO (multiplexed); Showtime; Starz (multiplexed); The Movie Channel (multiplexed).

Video-On-Demand: Yes

Pay-Per-View
Addressable homes: 15,329.
Addressable: Yes; iN DEMAND (delivered digitally); Playboy TV (delivered digitally).

Internet Service
Operational: Yes.
Subscribers: 5,110.
Broadband Service: Comcast High Speed Internet.
Fee: $42.95 monthly; $10.00 modem lease.

Telephone Service
Digital: Planned

Miles of Plant: 4,200.0 (coaxial); None (fiber optic). Homes passed: 600,000.
Vice President & General Manager: Tom Autry. Vice President, Regional Marketing: David Lucoff. Technical Operations Director: Kurt Decker. Engineering Director: Julio Segoria. Marketing Director: Nedelka Tejada-Phillips. Government & Community Affairs Manager: Jeannie Hernandez. Public Relations Director: Spero Canton.
City fee: 4% of gross. County fee: 1% of gross.
Ownership: Comcast Cable Communications Inc. (MSO).

MIAMI—Comcast Cable. Now served by MIAMI, FL [FL0006]. ICA: FL0011.

MIAMI (portions)—Bright House Networks, 2251 Lucien Way, Maitland, FL 32751-7005. Phones: 888-534-1230; 407-215-5524. Fax: 786-845-5533. Web Site: http://cfl.mybrighthouse.com. ICA: FL0355.
TV Market Ranking: 21 (MIAMI (PORTIONS)). Franchise award date: N.A. Franchise expiration date: N.A. Began: N.A.
Channel capacity: N.A. Channels available but not in use: N.A.

Basic Service
Subscribers: N.A.
Programming (received off-air): WAMI-DT (TEL) Hollywood; WBFS-TV (MNT) Miami; WFOR-TV (CBS) Miami; WHFT-TV (TBN) Miami; WJAN-CA Miami; WLRN-TV (PBS) Miami; WLTV-DT (UNV) Miami; WPBT (PBS) Miami; WPLG (ABC) Miami; WPXM-TV (ION) Miami; WSCV (TMO) Fort Lauderdale; WSFL-TV (CW) Miami; WSVN (FOX) Miami; WTVJ (NBC) Miami.
Programming (via satellite): ABC Family Channel; Arts & Entertainment; BET Networks; Bravo; CNBC; CNN; Country Music TV; C-SPAN; C-SPAN 2; Discovery Channel; E! Entertainment Television; ESPN; ESPN 2; Food Network; FX; GalaVision; Headline News; HGTV; History Channel; Home Shopping Network; Lifetime; MTV; Nickelodeon; QVC; SoapNet; Spike TV; Sur Network; TBS Superstation; The Learning Channel; truTV; Turner Network TV; TV Guide Network; USA Network; VH1; Weather Channel; WGN America.
Current originations: Public Access.

Expanded Basic Service 1
Subscribers: N.A.
Programming (via satellite): AMC; Cartoon Network; Comedy Central; Disney Channel; Fox Sports en Espanol; Fox Sports Net; Golf Channel; mun2 television; SunSports TV; Syfy; Turner Classic Movies.

Pay Service 1
Pay Units: N.A.
Programming (via satellite): Cinemax; Encore; HBO; Playboy TV; Showtime; Starz; The Movie Channel.

Internet Service
Operational: Yes.
Broadband Service: AOL for Broadband, EarthLink, Internet Junction, Road Runner.

Telephone Service
None

Manager: Bruce Baron.
Ownership: Bright House Networks LLC (MSO).

MIAMI BEACH—Atlantic Broadband, 1681 Kennedy Cswy, North Bay Village, FL 33141. Phones: 888-752-4222; 305-861-1564; 305-861-8069. Fax: 305-861-9047. E-mail: info@atlanticbb.com. Web Site: http://www.atlanticbb.com. Also serves Aventura, Bal Harbour, Bay Harbor Islands, Dade County (portions), Golden Beach, North Bay Village, Pinecrest (portions), South Miami, Sunny Isles & Surfside. ICA: FL0020.
TV Market Ranking: 21 (Aventura, Bal Harbour, Bay Harbor Islands, Dade County (portions), Golden Beach, MIAMI BEACH, North Bay Village, Pinecrest (portions), South Miami, Sunny Isles, Surfside). Franchise award date: July 1, 1978. Franchise expiration date: N.A. Began: March 1, 1980.
Channel capacity: 82 (operating 2-way). Channels available but not in use: N.A.

Basic Service
Subscribers: 51,000.
Programming (received off-air): WAMI-DT (TEL) Hollywood; WBFS-TV (MNT) Miami; WFOR-TV (CBS) Miami; WGEN-TV (IND) Key West; WHFT-TV (TBN) Miami; WJAN-CA Miami; WLRN-TV (PBS) Miami; WLTV-DT (UNV) Miami; WPBT (PBS) Miami; WPLG (ABC) Miami; WPXM-TV (ION) Miami; WSBS-TV (IND) Key West; WSCV (TMO) Fort Lauderdale; WSFL-TV (CW) Miami; WSVN (FOX) Miami; WTVJ (NBC) Miami.
Programming (via satellite): BeachTV; CaribeVision Television Networks; C-SPAN; C-SPAN 2; Home Shopping Network; Plum TV; QVC; Telemiami; TV Guide; Weather Channel.
Current originations: Public Access; Leased Access; Government Access; Educational Access.
Fee: $25.00 installation; $18.68 monthly; $3.05 converter; $26.25 additional installation.

Expanded Basic Service 1
Subscribers: N.A.
Programming (via satellite): ABC Family Channel; AMC; Animal Planet; Arts & Entertainment; BET Networks; Bravo; Cartoon Network; CNBC; CNN; Comedy Central; Country Music TV; Discovery Channel; Disney Channel; E! Entertainment Television; ESPN; ESPN 2; Fashion Network; Food Network; Fox News Channel; Fox Sports Net Florida; FX; GalaVision; Golf Channel; GSN; Hallmark Channel; Headline News; HGTV; History Channel; Lifetime; MSNBC; MTV; MTV2; National Geographic Channel; Nickelodeon; Oxygen; Speed Channel; Spike TV; SunSports TV; Syfy; TBS Superstation; The Learning Channel; Travel Channel; truTV; Turner Network TV; TV Land; USA Network; Versus; VH1.
Fee: $39.47 monthly.

Digital Basic Service
Subscribers: 21,000.
Programming (received off-air): WAMI-DT (TEL) Hollywood; WBFS-TV (MNT) Miami; WFOR-TV (CBS) Miami; WGEN-TV (IND) Key West; WHFT-TV (TBN) Miami; WLRN-TV (PBS) Miami; WLTV-DT (UNV) Miami; WPBT (PBS) Miami; WPLG (ABC) Miami; WPXM-TV (ION) Miami; WSBS-TV (IND) Key West; WSCV (TMO) Fort Lauderdale; WSFL-TV (CW) Miami; WSVN (FOX) Miami; WTVJ (NBC) Miami.
Programming (via satellite): Animal Planet HD; Arts & Entertainment HD; BBC America; Bio; Bloomberg Television; CCTV-4; Chiller; Cooking Channel; Discovery Channel HD; Discovery HD Theater; Discovery Health Channel; Discovery Kids Channel; Discovery Military Channel; Discovery Planet Green; Disney Channel HD; Do-It-Yourself; Encore; ESPN 2 HD; ESPN Classic Sports; ESPN HD; ESPN U; ESPNews; Eternal Word TV Network; Fox Sports Net Florida; Fuel TV; Fuse; G4; Gol TV; Great American Country; HDNet; HDNet Movies; History Channel International; ID Investigation Discovery; Independent Film Channel; INSP; Jewelry Television; LATV Networks; Lifetime Movie Network; Lifetime Real Women; LOGO; MTV Hits; MTV Jams; mun2 television; Music Choice; NFL Network; NFL Network HD; Nick Jr.; Nick Too; NickToons TV; Science Channel; SoapNet; Soundtrack Channel; Starz; Style Network; SunSports TV; Syfy HD; TBS in HD; TeenNick; Tennis Channel; Toon Disney; Turner Classic Movies; Turner Network TV HD; USA Network HD; VH1 Classic; VH1 Country; VH1 Soul; WE tv; Weatherscan.
Fee: $20.95 monthly.

Digital Pay Service 1
Pay Units: 1,290.
Programming (via satellite): Canal Sur; Caracol; Cine Latino; Cinemax (multiplexed); Cinemax HD; CNN en Espanol; De Pelicula; De Pelicula Clasico; Discovery en Espanol; Discovery Familia; Docu TVE; ESPN Deportes; EWTN en Espanol; Flix; Fox Sports en Espanol; HBO (multiplexed); HBO HD; History Channel en Espanol; HTV Musica; Infinito; Latele Novela Network; MTV Tres; Ole TV; Portuguese Channel; Ritmoson Latino; Russian Television Network; Showtime (multiplexed); Showtime HD; Starz HDTV; Sundance Channel; TBN Enlace USA; Telefe International; Telehit; The Movie Channel (multiplexed); TV Chile; TVE Internacional; Utilisima.
Fee: $2.99 monthly (Sundance), $8.95 monthly (HERE!), $17.95 monthly (HBO, Cinemax, Showtime/Flix/TMC, Mundo Latino, Portugese or Russian).

Video-On-Demand: Yes

Pay-Per-View
iN DEMAND (delivered digitally), Fee: $3.99; Playboy TV (delivered digitally), Fee: $10.99-$12.99; Hot Choice (delivered digitally), Fee: $10.99-$12.99.

Internet Service
Operational: Yes. Began: January 1, 1998.
Subscribers: 6,300.
Broadband Service: Atlantic Broadband High-Speed Internet.
Fee: $24.95-$67.45 monthly; $5.00 modem lease.

Telephone Service
Digital: Operational
Fee: $49.95 monthly

Miles of Plant: 862.0 (coaxial); None (fiber optic). Homes passed: 101,000. Total homes in franchised area: 109,000.
Vice President & General Manager: Jim Waldo. Chief Technician: David Conkle. Marketing Administrator: Ira Levy.
County fee: 5% of gross.
Ownership: Atlantic Broadband (MSO).

MICANOPY—CommuniComm Services, 17774 NW US Highway 441, High Springs, FL 32643-8749. Phones: 800-881-9740; 386-454-2299. Fax: 386-454-3705. Web Site: http://www.communicomm.com. ICA: FL0201.
TV Market Ranking: Below 100 (MICANOPY). Franchise award date: N.A. Franchise expiration date: N.A. Began: March 1, 1968.
Channel capacity: N.A. Channels available but not in use: N.A.

Basic Service
Subscribers: N.A. Included in High Springs
Programming (received off-air): WCJB-TV (ABC, CW) Gainesville; WESH (NBC) Daytona Beach; WGFL (CBS, MNT) High Springs; WKMG-TV (CBS) Orlando; WOGX (FOX) Ocala; WSST-TV (IND) Cordele; WUFT (PBS) Gainesville; allband FM.
Programming (via satellite): Home Shopping Network; QVC; Trinity Broadcasting Network; TV Guide Network.
Fee: $39.99 installation; $35.45 monthly.

Expanded Basic Service 1
Subscribers: N.A.
Programming (via satellite): ABC Family Channel; AMC; Animal Planet; Arts & Entertainment; BET Networks; Bravo; Cartoon Network; CNBC; CNN; Comedy Central; Country Music TV; C-SPAN; C-SPAN 2; CW+; Discovery Channel; Disney Channel; Do-It-Yourself; E! Entertainment Television; ESPN; ESPN 2; ESPN Classic Sports; ESPNews; Food Network; Fox News Channel; FX; Hallmark Channel; Headline News; HGTV; History Channel;

ION Television; Lifetime; MSNBC; MTV; Nick Jr.; Nickelodeon; Outdoor Channel; Speed Channel; Spike TV; SunSports TV; Syfy; TBS Superstation; The Learning Channel; Travel Channel; truTV; Turner Classic Movies; Turner Network TV; TV Land; USA Network; VH1; WE tv; Weather Channel; WGN America.

Digital Basic Service

Subscribers: N.A.

Programming (via satellite): Alterna'TV; BBC America; Bio; Blackbelt TV; Bloomberg Television; Church Channel; CMT Pure Country; College Sports Television; Current; Daystar TV Network; Discovery Health Channel; Discovery Home Channel; Discovery Kids Channel; Discovery Military Channel; DMX Music; FitTV; Fox Movie Channel; Fox Soccer; Fuse; G4; Golf Channel; Gospel Music TV; Great American Country; GSN; Halogen Network; ID Investigation Discovery; Independent Film Channel; JCTV; Lifetime Movie Network; MTV Hits; MTV Jams; MTV2; National Geographic Channel; NickToons TV; Ovation; Science Channel; ShopNBC; Sleuth; SoapNet; Style Network; Sundance Channel; TeenNick; The Word Network; Versus; VH1 Classic; VH1 Soul.

Fee: $13.95 monthly.

Digital Pay Service 1

Pay Units: N.A.

Programming (via satellite): Cinemax (multiplexed); Encore; Flix; HBO (multiplexed); Showtime (multiplexed); Starz (multiplexed); The Movie Channel (multiplexed).

Fee: $10.95 monthly (Showtime/TMC or Starz/Encore), $11.95 monthly (Cinemax) $13.95 monthly (HBO).

Video-On-Demand: No

Pay-Per-View

iN DEMAND (delivered digitally); Hot Choice (delivered digitally); Playboy TV (delivered digitally); Fresh (delivered digitally); Spice: Xcess (delivered digitally).

Internet Service

Operational: Yes.

Broadband Service: Net Commander.

Fee: $39.95 installation; $51.95 monthly.

Telephone Service

None

Homes passed and miles of plant included in High Springs

General Manager: Darrell Laird. Chief Technician: Michael Smith. Customer Service Manager: Cindy Ross.

City fee: 3% of gross.

Ownership: James Cable LLC (MSO).

MIDWAY—Comcast Cablevision of Tallahassee Inc. Now served by TALLAHASSEE, FL [FL0283]. ICA: FL0194.

MILTON—Mediacom. Now served by GULF BREEZE, FL [FL0070]. ICA: FL0380.

MIMS—Comcast Cable, 8130 County Rd 44, Leg A, Leesburg, FL 34788. Phone: 352-787-9601. Fax: 352-365-6279. Web Site: http://www.comcast.com. Also serves Brevard County (northern portion). ICA: FL0130.

TV Market Ranking: 55 (Brevard County (northern portion), MIMS). Franchise award date: January 1, 1982. Franchise expiration date: N.A. Began: N.A.

Channel capacity: 51 (not 2-way capable). Channels available but not in use: None.

Basic Service

Subscribers: 1,320.

Programming (received off-air): WACX (IND) Leesburg; WBCC (PBS) Cocoa; WESH (NBC) Daytona Beach; WFTV (ABC) Orlando; WHLV-TV (IND) Cocoa; WKCF (CW) Clermont; WKMG-TV (CBS) Orlando; WMFE-TV (PBS) Orlando; WOFL (FOX) Orlando; WOTF-DT (TEL) Melbourne; WRBW (MNT) Orlando.

Programming (via satellite): Home Shopping Network; ION Television; TBS Superstation.

Current originations: Government Access.

Fee: $19.95 installation; $9.95 monthly.

Expanded Basic Service 1

Subscribers: N.A.

Programming (via satellite): ABC Family Channel; AMC; Animal Planet; Arts & Entertainment; BET Networks; CNBC; CNN; Comedy Central; Country Music TV; Discovery Channel; Disney Channel; E! Entertainment Television; ESPN; ESPN 2; Fox News Channel; FX; Headline News; HGTV; History Channel; Lifetime; MSNBC; NASA TV; Nickelodeon; SoapNet; Spike TV; SunSports TV; Syfy; Turner Network TV; TV Land; USA Network; VH1; WE tv; Weather Channel; WGN America.

Fee: $19.95 monthly.

Pay Service 1

Pay Units: 151.

Programming (via satellite): Cinemax; HBO; Showtime.

Fee: $10.95 monthly (each).

Video-On-Demand: No

Internet Service

Operational: Yes.

Telephone Service

Digital: Operational

Miles of Plant: 26.0 (coaxial); None (fiber optic). Additional miles planned: 10.0 (coaxial). Homes passed: 3,360.

Vice President & General Manager: Mike Davenport. Chief Engineer: Sean Curley. Technical Operations Manager: Jose Galarzo.; Jeff Martin. Marketing Manager: Melanie Melvin.

Franchise fee: 3% of gross.

Ownership: Comcast Cable Communications Inc. (MSO).

MONTICELLO—Comcast Cable, 3760 Hartsfield Rd, Tallahassee, FL 32303-1121. Phone: 850-574-4016. Fax: 850-574-4030. E-mail: claire_evans@cable.comcast.com. Web Site: http://www.comcast.com. Also serves Jefferson County, Killearn Lakes & Leon County (portions). ICA: FL0165.

TV Market Ranking: Below 100 (Jefferson County, Killearn Lakes, Leon County (portions), MONTICELLO). Franchise award date: April 1, 1980. Franchise expiration date: N.A. Began: April 1, 1980.

Channel capacity: N.A. Channels available but not in use: N.A.

Basic Service

Subscribers: N.A. Included in Tallahassee

Programming (received off-air): WABW-TV (PBS) Pelham; WCTV (CBS, MNT) Thomasville; WFSU-TV (PBS) Tallahassee; WTLH (CW, FOX) Bainbridge; WTWC-TV (NBC) Tallahassee; WTXL-TV (ABC) Tallahassee.

Programming (via satellite): C-SPAN; CW+; QVC; TV Guide Network; WGN America.

Current originations: Educational Access.

Fee: $39.88 installation; $13.95 monthly.

Expanded Basic Service 1

Subscribers: N.A.

Programming (via satellite): ABC Family Channel; AMC; Animal Planet; Arts & Entertainment; BET Networks; Cartoon Network; CNN; Comcast/Charter Sports Southeast (CSS); Comedy Central; Country Music TV; Discovery Channel; Discovery Health Channel; Disney Channel; E! Entertainment Television; ESPN; ESPN 2; Food Network; Fox News Channel; Golf Channel; Great American Country; GSN; Hallmark Channel; Headline News; HGTV; History Channel; Home Shopping Network; ION Television; Lifetime; MSNBC; MTV; Nickelodeon; Speed Channel; Spike TV; Style Network; SunSports TV; TBS Superstation; The Learning Channel; Travel Channel; Trinity Broadcasting Network; truTV; Turner Network TV; TV Land; TV One; USA Network; Versus; Weather Channel.

Fee: $13.49 monthly.

Pay Service 1

Pay Units: 27.

Programming (via satellite): HBO; Showtime; The Movie Channel.

Fee: $10.00 monthly (each).

Internet Service

Operational: Yes.

Telephone Service

None

Miles of plant (coax) & homes passed included in Tallahassee

General Manager: K. C. McWilliams. Technical Operations Director: Terry Pullen. Technical Operations Manager: Dave Morawski. Marketing Director: Claire Evans.

City fee: 3% of gross.

Ownership: Comcast Cable Communications Inc. (MSO).

MOORE HAVEN—Comcast Cable, 450 E Palm Beach Rd, South Bay, FL 33493. Phones: 561-996-8455; 561-996-3087. Fax: 561-996-3091. Web Site: http://www.comcast.com. Also serves Glades County. ICA: FL0146.

TV Market Ranking: Below 100 (Glades County (portions)); Outside TV Markets (Glades County (portions), MOORE HAVEN). Franchise award date: June 1, 1983. Franchise expiration date: N.A. Began: January 1, 1983.

Channel capacity: N.A. Channels available but not in use: N.A.

Basic Service

Subscribers: 383.

Programming (received off-air): WBBH-TV (NBC) Fort Myers; WFLX (FOX) West Palm Beach; WGCU (PBS) Fort Myers; WINK-TV (CBS) Fort Myers; WPBF (ABC) Tequesta; WTVX (CW) Fort Pierce.

Programming (via satellite): ABC Family Channel; AMC; Animal Planet; Arts & Entertainment; BET Networks; CNN; Comedy Central; Country Music TV; Discovery Channel; Disney Channel; ESPN; ESPN 2; Food Network; FX; Headline News; HGTV; History Channel; Home Shopping Network; MTV; Nickelodeon; QVC; Spike TV; SunSports TV; TBS Superstation; Travel Channel; truTV; Turner Network TV; TV Land; Univision; USA Network; VH1; Weather Channel; WGN America.

Fee: $43.85 monthly.

Pay Service 1

Pay Units: 153.

Programming (via satellite): Cinemax.

Fee: $8.90 monthly.

Pay Service 2

Pay Units: 225.

Programming (via satellite): HBO.

Fee: $8.90 monthly.

Pay Service 3

Pay Units: 32.

Programming (via satellite): Showtime.

Fee: $8.90 monthly.

Video-On-Demand: No

Internet Service

Operational: Yes.

Telephone Service

Digital: Operational

Miles of Plant: 24.0 (coaxial); None (fiber optic). Homes passed: 1,203. Total homes in franchised area: 1,203.

Area Vice President: Gary Waterfield. General Manager: Geof Shook. Technical Operations Manager: John Barnard. Marketing Director: Christopher Derario. Marketing Manager: Diane Bissoon. Marketing Coordinator: Janet Epstien. Government & Community Affairs Director: Marta Casas-Celayas.

City fee: 3% of gross.

Ownership: Comcast Cable Communications Inc. (MSO).

NAPLES—Comcast Cable, 301 Tower Rd, Naples, FL 34113. Phone: 239-793-9600. Fax: 239-793-1317. Web Site: http://www.comcast.com. Also serves Alva, Boca Grande Island, Bokeelia, Bonita Beach, Bonita Springs, Cape Coral, Captiva Island, Collier County, Estero, Everglades City, Fort Myers, Fort Myers Beach, Glades County (southern portion), Golden Gate, Hendry County (portions), Immokalee, La Belle, Lee County (unincorporated areas), Lehigh Acres, Marco Island, Matlacha, North Fort Myers, Pineland, Punta Gorda, San Carlos Island, Sanibel Island, St. James City & Vanderbilt Beach. ICA: FL0029.

TV Market Ranking: Below 100 (Alva, Boca Grande Island, Bokeelia, Bonita Beach, Bonita Springs, Cape Coral, Captiva Island, Collier County (portions), Estero, Everglades City, Fort Myers, Fort Myers Beach, Glades County (southern portion) (portions), Golden Gate, Hendry County (portions) (portions), Immokalee, La Belle, Lee County (unincorporated areas), Lehigh Acres, Marco Island, Matlacha, NAPLES, North Fort Myers, Pineland, Punta Gorda, San Carlos Island, Sanibel Island, St. James City, Vanderbilt Beach); Outside TV Markets (Glades County (southern portion) (portions), Hendry County (portions) (portions)). Franchise award date: January 1, 1967. Franchise expiration date: N.A. Began: March 1, 1968.

Channel capacity: N.A. Channels available but not in use: N.A.

Basic Service

Subscribers: 350,000.

Programming (received off-air): WBBH-TV (NBC) Fort Myers; WFTX-TV (FOX) Cape Coral; WGCU (PBS) Fort Myers; WINK-TV (CBS) Fort Myers; WRXY-TV (IND) Tice; WWDT-CA Naples; WXCW (CW) Naples; WZVN-TV (ABC) Naples.

Programming (via satellite): BET Networks; Comedy Central; Country Music TV; C-SPAN; C-SPAN 2; Eternal Word TV Network; Home Shopping Network; ION Television; MSNBC; QVC; Radar Channel; Spike TV; The Learning Channel; TV Guide Network; Univision; VH1; WGN America.

Current originations: Educational Access; Leased Access; Government Access.

Fee: $63.35 installation; $16.00 monthly.

Expanded Basic Service 1

Subscribers: N.A.

Programming (via satellite): ABC Family Channel; AMC; Animal Planet; Arts & Entertainment; Cartoon Network; CNBC; CNN; Comcast/Charter Sports Southeast (CSS); Discovery Channel; Discovery Health Channel; Disney Channel; E! Entertainment Television; ESPN; ESPN 2; ESPN Classic Sports; Food Network; Fox News Channel; Fox Sports Net Florida; FX; Golf Channel; GSN; Hallmark Channel; Headline News; HGTV; History Channel; Lifetime;

MTV; Nickelodeon; Oxygen; Speed Channel; Style Network; Syfy; TBS Superstation; Toon Disney; Travel Channel; truTV; Turner Classic Movies; Turner Network TV; TV Land; USA Network; Versus; Weather Channel.
Fee: $51.95 monthly.

Digital Basic Service
Subscribers: 12,351.
Programming (received off-air): WBBH-TV (NBC) Fort Myers; WGCU (PBS) Fort Myers; WZVN-TV (ABC) Naples.
Programming (via satellite): BBC America; Bio; Canales N; CMT Pure Country; Cooking Channel; C-SPAN 3; Discovery Digital Networks; Do-It-Yourself; Encore (multiplexed); ESPN HD; ESPNews; Flix; Fox College Sports Atlantic; Fox College Sports Central; Fox College Sports Pacific; Fox Soccer; G4; GAS; Gol TV; History Channel International; INHD; Lifetime Movie Network; LOGO; MoviePlex; MTV Networks Digital Suite; Music Choice; National Geographic Channel; NBA TV; NFL Network; Nick Jr.; Nick Too; NickToons TV; PBS HD; PBS Kids Sprout; ShopNBC; SoapNet; Sundance Channel; Tennis Channel; Toon Disney; Turner Network TV HD; WE tv; Weatherscan.
Fee: $14.95 monthly.

Pay Service 1
Pay Units: 3,554.
Programming (via satellite): HBO.
Fee: $10.95 monthly.

Digital Pay Service 1
Pay Units: 2,042.
Programming (via satellite): Cinemax (multiplexed); Cinemax HD; HBO (multiplexed); HBO HD; Showtime (multiplexed); Showtime HD; Starz (multiplexed); Starz HDTV; The Movie Channel (multiplexed).
Fee: $14.00 monthly (each).

Video-On-Demand: Yes

Pay-Per-View
Addressable homes: 12,351.
iN DEMAND (delivered digitally), Fee: $3.95, Addressable: Yes; Playboy TV (delivered digitally); Fresh (delivered digitally); Shorteez (delivered digitally); Pleasure (delivered digitally); Sports PPV (delivered digitally).

Internet Service
Operational: Yes.
Subscribers: 9,705.
Broadband Service: Comcast High Speed Internet.
Fee: $42.95 monthly.

Telephone Service
Digital: Operational
Fee: $44.95 monthly

750/860 MHz

Vice President & General Manager: Larry Schweber. Technical Operations Director, Construction: Joe Crone. Marketing Director: Brad Gear. Public Relations Manager: Sandra Wilson. Technical Operations Director, Engineering: Mary Beth Bower.

County fee: 5% of gross (Collier); 2% of gross (Lee).

Ownership: Comcast Cable Communications Inc. (MSO).

NAPLES—Comcast Cable. Now served by BONITA SPRINGS, FL [FL0029]. ICA: FL0028.

NEWBERRY—Cox Communications. Now served by GAINESVILLE, FL [FL0027]. ICA: FL0257.

NORTH DADE COUNTY—Comcast Cable. Now served by MIAMI, FL [FL0006]. ICA: FL0007.

NORTH OLD TOWN—Florida Cable, PO Box 498, 23748 State Rd 40, Astor, FL 32102-0498. Phone: 352-759-2788. Fax: 352-759-3577. Web Site: http://www.floridacable.com. Also serves Gilchrist County (portions). ICA: FL0379.

TV Market Ranking: Below 100 (Gilchrist County (portions), NORTH OLD TOWN).

Channel capacity: N.A. Channels available but not in use: N.A.

Basic Service
Subscribers: N.A.
Programming (received off-air): WCJB-TV (ABC, CW) Gainesville; WESH (NBC) Daytona Beach; WGFL (CBS, MNT) High Springs; WOGX (FOX) Ocala; WUFT (PBS) Gainesville.
Programming (via satellite): ABC Family Channel; America's Store; Arts & Entertainment; Cartoon Network; CNN; Country Music TV; C-SPAN; Discovery Channel; ESPN; ESPN 2; G4; Headline News; HGTV; History Channel; Lifetime; Outdoor Channel; Spike TV; Syfy; TBS Superstation; Trinity Broadcasting Network; Turner Network TV; USA Network; Weather Channel; WGN America.

Pay Service 1
Pay Units: N.A.
Programming (via satellite): HBO.

Internet Service
Operational: No.

Telephone Service
None

General Manager: Jim Pierce. Plant Manager: Larry English. Office Manager: Alita Dawson.

Ownership: Florida Cable Inc. (MSO).

OCALA—Cox Cable Greater Ocala. Now served by GAINESVILLE, FL [FL0027]. ICA: FL0038.

OKEECHOBEE—Comcast Cable, 107 NW 7th Ave, Okeechobee, FL 34972-4111. Phone: 863-763-9391. Fax: 863-467-7776. Web Site: http://www.comcast.com. Also serves Buckhead Ridge, Glades County & Lakeport. ICA: FL0064.

TV Market Ranking: Below 100 (Glades County (portions), OKEECHOBEE); Outside TV Markets (Buckhead Ridge, Glades County (portions), Lakeport). Franchise award date: May 1, 1972. Franchise expiration date: N.A. Began: January 1, 1977.

Channel capacity: N.A. Channels available but not in use: N.A.

Basic Service
Subscribers: 6,100.
Programming (received off-air): WFGC (IND) Palm Beach; WFLX (FOX) West Palm Beach; WGN-TV (CW, IND) Chicago; WPBF (ABC) Tequesta; WPEC (CBS) West Palm Beach; WPTV-TV (NBC) West Palm Beach; WPXP-TV (ION) Lake Worth; WTCE-TV (ETV) Fort Pierce; WTVX (CW) Fort Pierce; WWHB-CA Stuart; WXEL-TV (PBS) West Palm Beach; allband FM.
Programming (via satellite): Home Shopping Network; NASA TV; QVC; TV Guide Network.
Current originations: Government Access; Educational Access; Public Access.
Fee: $50.00 installation; $14.65 monthly; $10.00 additional installation.

Expanded Basic Service 1
Subscribers: N.A.
Programming (via satellite): ABC Family Channel; AMC; Animal Planet; Arts & Entertainment; BET Networks; Bravo; Cartoon Network; CNBC; CNN; Comedy Central; Country Music TV; C-SPAN; C-SPAN 2; Discovery Channel; Disney Channel; E! Entertainment Television; ESPN; ESPN 2; Eternal Word TV Network; Food Network; Fox News Channel; Fox Sports Net Florida; FX; Golf Channel; Hallmark Channel; Headline News; HGTV; History Channel; Lifetime; MSNBC; MTV; Nickelodeon; Oxygen; Product Information Network; ShopNBC; Spike TV; Style Network; SunSports TV; Syfy; TBS Superstation; Telemundo; The Learning Channel; Travel Channel; truTV; Turner Network TV; TV Land; Univision; USA Network; VH1; Weather Channel.
Fee: $47.99 monthly.

Digital Basic Service
Subscribers: N.A.
Programming (via satellite): American-Life TV Network; BBC America; Bio; Black Family Channel; Bloomberg Television; Discovery Digital Networks; Do-It-Yourself; ESPN Classic Sports; ESPNews; FitTV; Fox Sports World; Fuse; G4; Great American Country; GSN; Halogen Network; History Channel International; Lifetime Movie Network; Outdoor Channel; SoapNet; Speed Channel; Toon Disney; Trinity Broadcasting Network; Versus; WE tv.
Fee: $20.15 monthly.

Digital Expanded Basic Service
Subscribers: N.A.
Programming (via satellite): Fox College Sports Atlantic; Fox College Sports Central; Fox College Sports Pacific; Fox Movie Channel; GAS; Independent Film Channel; MTV Networks Digital Suite; Music Choice; National Geographic Channel; Nick Jr.; Nick Too; NickToons TV; Sundance Channel; Turner Classic Movies.

Pay Service 1
Pay Units: N.A.
Programming (via satellite): Cinemax; HBO; Showtime; The Movie Channel.

Digital Pay Service 1
Pay Units: N.A.
Programming (via satellite): Cinemax (multiplexed); Encore (multiplexed); Flix; HBO (multiplexed); Showtime (multiplexed); Starz (multiplexed); The Movie Channel (multiplexed).

Video-On-Demand: No

Pay-Per-View
Hot Choice (delivered digitally); Fresh (delivered digitally); Shorteez (delivered digitally); Movies (delivered digitally), Addressable: Yes; special events (delivered digitally); sports (delivered digitally); Playboy TV (delivered digitally).

Internet Service
Operational: Yes.
Broadband Service: Comcast High Speed Internet.
Fee: $42.95 monthly.

Telephone Service
Digital: Operational

Miles of Plant: 279.0 (coaxial); None (fiber optic). Homes passed: 19,009.

Area Vice President: Gary Waterfield. General Manager: Geoff Shook. Chief Technician: Ernie Pinto. Marketing Director: Christopher Derario. Marketing Manager: Diane Bissoon. Marketing Coordinator: Janet Epstein. Government & Community Affairs Director: Marta Casas-Celayas.

Franchise fee: 3% of gross.

Ownership: Comcast Cable Communications Inc. (MSO).

ORANGE COUNTY (unincorporated areas)—Comcast Cable, 8130 County Rd 44, Leg A, Leesburg, FL 34788. Phone: 352-787-9601. Fax: 352-365-6279. Web Site: http://www.comcast.com. Also serves Sand Lake Point. ICA: FL0037.

TV Market Ranking: 28 (Sand Lake Point); 28,55 (ORANGE COUNTY (UNINCORPORATED AREAS)). Franchise award date: June 23, 1986. Franchise expiration date: N.A. Began: June 1, 1986.

Channel capacity: N.A. Channels available but not in use: N.A.

Basic Service
Subscribers: 24,784.
Programming (received off-air): WACX (IND) Leesburg; WESH (NBC) Daytona Beach; WFTV (ABC) Orlando; WHLV-TV (IND) Cocoa; WKCF (CW) Clermont; WKMG-TV (CBS) Orlando; WMFE-TV (PBS) Orlando; WOFL (FOX) Orlando; WOPX-TV (ION) Melbourne; WRBW (MNT) Orlando; WRDQ (IND) Orlando.
Programming (via satellite): QVC; ShopNBC; Telemundo; WGN America.
Current originations: Leased Access; Government Access; Educational Access.
Fee: $19.95 monthly.

Expanded Basic Service 1
Subscribers: N.A.
Programming (via satellite): ABC Family Channel; AMC; Animal Planet; Arts & Entertainment; BET Networks; Bravo; Cartoon Network; CNBC; CNN; Comedy Central; Country Music TV; C-SPAN; C-SPAN 2; Discovery Channel; Disney Channel; E! Entertainment Television; ESPN; ESPN 2; Eternal Word TV Network; Food Network; Fox News Channel; Fox Sports Net Florida; FX; GalaVision; Golf Channel; Hallmark Channel; Headline News; HGTV; History Channel; Home Shopping Network; Lifetime; MSNBC; MTV; NASA TV; Nickelodeon; Oxygen; Product Information Network; Speed Channel; Spike TV; Style Network; SunSports TV; Syfy; TBS Superstation; The Learning Channel; Travel Channel; Trinity Broadcasting Network; truTV; Turner Network TV; TV Land; USA Network; VH1; Weather Channel.

Digital Basic Service
Subscribers: N.A.
Programming (via satellite): AmericanLife TV Network; ART America; BBC America; Bio; Black Family Channel; Bloomberg Television; Canales N; CCTV-4; Discovery Digital Networks; Do-It-Yourself; ESPN Classic Sports; ESPNews; FamilyNet; Filipino Channel; FitTV; Fox College Sports Atlantic; Fox College Sports Central; Fox College Sports Pacific; Fox Movie Channel; Fox Sports World; Fuse; G4; GAS; Great American Country; GSN; Halogen Network; History Channel International; Independent Film Channel; Lifetime Movie Network; M-2 (Movie Mania) TV Network; MTV Networks Digital Suite; Music Choice; National Geographic Channel; Nick Jr.; Nick Too; NickToons TV; Outdoor Channel; RAI International; Russian Television Network; SoapNet; Sundance Channel; Toon Disney; Turner Classic Movies; TV Asia; TV Japan; TV5, La Television International; Versus; Zee TV USA; Zhong Tian Channel.

Pay Service 1
Pay Units: N.A.
Programming (via satellite): Cinemax; HBO; Showtime; The Movie Channel.

Digital Pay Service 1
Pay Units: N.A.
Programming (via satellite): Cinemax (multiplexed); Encore (multiplexed); Flix; HBO (multiplexed); Showtime (multiplexed); Starz (multiplexed); The Movie Channel (multiplexed).

Video-On-Demand: Planned

Pay-Per-View

Hot Choice (delivered digitally); iN DEMAND (delivered digitally), Addressable: Yes; Playboy TV (delivered digitally); Fresh (delivered digitally); Shorteez (delivered digitally); Sports PPV (delivered digitally); Urban Xtra (delivered digitally).

Internet Service

Operational: Yes.

Broadband Service: Comcast High Speed Internet.

Fee: $42.95 monthly; $5.00 modem lease.

Telephone Service

Digital: Operational

Miles of Plant: 564.0 (coaxial); None (fiber optic). Homes passed: 78,935.

Vice President & General Manager: Mike Davenport. Marketing Manager: Melanie Melvin. Chief Engineer: Sean Curley.

Ownership: Comcast Cable Communications Inc. (MSO).

ORANGE LAKE—CommuniComm Services, 17774 NW US Highway 441, High Springs, FL 32643-8749. Phone: 386-454-2299. Fax: 386-454-3705. Web Site: http://www.netcommander.com. Also serves McIntosh & Reddick. ICA: FL0260.

TV Market Ranking: Below 100 (McIntosh, ORANGE LAKE, Reddick). Franchise award date: N.A. Franchise expiration date: N.A. Began: June 1, 1984.

Channel capacity: N.A. Channels available but not in use: N.A.

Basic Service

Subscribers: N.A. Included in High Springs

Programming (received off-air): WCJB-TV (ABC, CW) Gainesville; WESH (NBC) Daytona Beach; WKMG-TV (CBS) Orlando; WOGX (FOX) Ocala; WUFT (PBS) Gainesville.

Programming (via satellite): Home Shopping Network; QVC; Trinity Broadcasting Network; TV Guide Network.

Fee: $50.00 installation; $31.00 monthly; $30.00 additional installation.

Expanded Basic Service 1

Subscribers: N.A.

Programming (via satellite): ABC Family Channel; AMC; Animal Planet; Arts & Entertainment; BET Networks; Bravo; Cartoon Network; CNBC; CNN; Comedy Central; Country Music TV; C-SPAN; C-SPAN 2; CW+; Discovery Channel; Disney Channel; Do-It-Yourself; E! Entertainment Television; ESPN; ESPN 2; ESPN Classic Sports; ESPNews; Food Network; Fox News Channel; FX; Hallmark Channel; Headline News; HGTV; History Channel; ION Television; Lifetime; MSNBC; MTV; Nick Jr.; Nickelodeon; Outdoor Channel; Speed Channel; Spike TV; SunSports TV; Syfy; TBS Superstation; The Learning Channel; Travel Channel; truTV; Turner Classic Movies; Turner Network TV; TV Land; USA Network; VH1; WE tv; Weather Channel; WGN America.

Digital Basic Service

Subscribers: N.A.

Programming (via satellite): Alterna'TV; BBC America; Bio; Blackbelt TV; Bloomberg Television; Church Channel; CMT Pure Country; College Sports Television; Current; Daystar TV Network; Discovery Health Channel; Discovery Kids Channel; Discovery Military Channel; Discovery Planet Green; DMX Music; FitTV; Fox Movie Channel; Fox Soccer; Fuse; G4; Golf Channel; Gospel Music Channel; Great American Country; GSN; Halogen Network; ID Investigation Discovery; Independent Film Channel; JCTV; Lifetime Movie Network; MTV Networks Digital Suite; National Geographic Channel; NickToons TV; Ovation; Science Channel; ShopNBC; Sleuth; SoapNet; Style Network; Sundance Channel; TeenNick; The Word Network; Versus.

Pay Service 1

Pay Units: N.A. Included in High Springs

Programming (via satellite): Cinemax; HBO.

Fee: $30.00 installation; $9.95 monthly (Cinemax), $11.95 monthly (HBO).

Digital Pay Service 1

Pay Units: N.A.

Programming (via satellite): Cinemax (multiplexed); Encore (multiplexed); Flix; HBO (multiplexed); Showtime (multiplexed); Starz (multiplexed); The Movie Channel (multiplexed).

Video-On-Demand: No

Pay-Per-View

iN DEMAND (delivered digitally); Hot Choice (delivered digitally); Playboy TV (delivered digitally); Fresh (delivered digitally); Spice: Xcess (delivered digitally).

Internet Service

Operational: Yes.

Broadband Service: Net Commander.

Fee: $39.95 installation; $51.95 monthly.

Telephone Service

None

Homes passed and miles of plant included in High Springs

General Manager: Darrell Laird. Chief Technician: Michael Smith. Customer Service Manager: Cindy Ross.

Ownership: James Cable LLC (MSO).

ORANGE PARK—Comcast Cable. Now served by JACKSONVILLE, FL [FL0002]. ICA: FL0047.

ORANGE SPRINGS—Florida Cable, PO Box 498, 23748 State Rd 40, Astor, FL 32102-0498. Phone: 352-759-2788. Fax: 352-759-3577. Web Site: http://www.floridacable.com. Also serves Johnson & Marion County (portions). ICA: FL0261.

TV Market Ranking: Below 100 (Johnson, Marion County (portions), ORANGE SPRINGS). Franchise award date: N.A. Franchise expiration date: N.A. Began: May 1, 1990.

Channel capacity: 62 (not 2-way capable). Channels available but not in use: None.

Basic Service

Subscribers: 369.

Programming (received off-air): WAWS (FOX, MNT) Jacksonville; WCJB-TV (ABC, CW) Gainesville; WESH (NBC) Daytona Beach; WFTV (ABC) Orlando; WGFL (CBS, MNT) High Springs; WJXT (IND) Jacksonville; WKCF (CW) Clermont; WKMG-TV (CBS) Orlando; WOFL (FOX) Orlando; WOGX (FOX) Ocala; WUFT (PBS) Gainesville.

Programming (via satellite): ABC Family Channel; AMC; Animal Planet; Arts & Entertainment; Cartoon Network; CNBC; CNN; Comedy Central; Cooking Channel; Country Music TV; C-SPAN; Discovery Channel; Discovery Health Channel; Disney Channel; Do-It-Yourself; ESPN; ESPN 2; ESPNews; Food Network; Fox News Channel; FX; GSN; Hallmark Channel; Headline News; HGTV; History Channel; Lifetime; MoviePlex; MTV; Nickelodeon; Outdoor Channel; QVC; SoapNet; Speed Channel; Spike TV; Syfy; TBS Superstation; The Learning Channel; Travel Channel; Trinity Broadcasting Network; truTV; Turner Classic Movies; Turner Network TV; TV Land; USA Network; WE tv; Weather Channel; WGN America.

Fee: $40.00 installation; $33.42 monthly.

Pay Service 1

Pay Units: N.A.

Programming (via satellite): Cinemax; HBO; The Movie Channel.

Fee: $10.95 monthly (each).

Internet Service

Operational: Yes.

Fee: $49.95 installation; $24.95 monthly.

Telephone Service

None

General Manager: Jim Pierce. Plant Manager: Larry English. Office Manager: Aleta Dawson.

Ownership: Florida Cable Inc. (MSO).

ORLANDO—Bright House Networks, 2251 Lucien Way, Maitland, FL 32751-7005. Phone: 407-291-2500. E-mail: michel.champagne@mybrighthouse.com. Web Site: http://cfl.mybrighthouse.com. Also serves Altamonte Springs, Apopka, Belle Isle, Caribbean Isle, Casselberry, Clermont, Eatonville, Edgewood, Geneva, Groveland, Hunters Creek, Kissimmee, Lake County (southern portion), Lake Mary, Longwood, Maitland, Mascotte, Minneola, Monterey Lakes, Oakland, Ocoee, Orange County, Osceola County, Oviedo, Park South, Polo's of Kissimmee, Sanford, Seminole County, St. Cloud, Taft, Windermere, Winter Garden, Winter Park & Winter Springs. ICA: FL0001.

TV Market Ranking: 28,55 (Orange County (portions)); 55 (Altamonte Springs, Apopka, Belle Isle, Caribbean Isle, Casselberry, Clermont, Eatonville, Edgewood, Geneva, Hunters Creek, Kissimmee, Lake Mary, Longwood, Maitland, Mascotte, Minneola, Monterey Lakes, Oakland, Ocoee, ORLANDO, Osceola County, Oviedo, Park South, Polo's of Kissimmee, Sanford, Seminole County, St. Cloud, Taft, Windermere, Winter Garden, Winter Park, Winter Springs); 55,28 (Groveland, Lake County (southern portion)); Outside TV Markets (Osceola County). Franchise award date: N.A. Franchise expiration date: N.A. Began: January 7, 1985.

Channel capacity: 60 (operating 2-way). Channels available but not in use: N.A.

Basic Service

Subscribers: 425,000.

Programming (received off-air): Central Florida News 13; WACX (IND) Leesburg; WBCC (PBS) Cocoa; WDSC-TV (PBS) New Smyrna Beach; WESH (NBC) Daytona Beach; WFTV (ABC) Orlando; WHLV-TV (IND) Cocoa; WKCF (CW) Clermont; WKMG-TV (CBS) Orlando; WMFE-TV (PBS) Orlando; WOFL (FOX) Orlando; WOPX-TV (ION) Melbourne; WOTF-DT (TEL) Melbourne; WRBW (MNT) Orlando; WRDQ (IND) Orlando; WTGL (ETV) Leesburg.

Programming (via satellite): AMC; Animal Planet; Arts & Entertainment; BET Networks; Bravo; Cartoon Network; CNBC; CNN; Comedy Central; Country Music TV; C-SPAN; C-SPAN 2; Discovery Channel; Disney Channel; E! Entertainment Television; ESPN; ESPN 2; Food Network; Fox News Channel; FX; GalaVision; Golf Channel; Hallmark Channel; Headline News; HGTV; History Channel; Home Shopping Network; Lifetime; Lifetime Movie Network; MSNBC; MTV; Nickelodeon; Oxygen; QVC; ShopNBC; SoapNet; Speed Channel; Spike TV; SunSports TV; Syfy; TBS Superstation; Telemundo; The Learning Channel; Travel Channel; truTV; Turner Classic Movies; Turner Network TV; TV Land; USA Network; VH1; WE tv; Weather Channel; WGN America.

Current originations: Government Access; Educational Access; Public Access.

Fee: $49.95 installation; $50.79 monthly.

Digital Basic Service

Subscribers: N.A.

Programming (via satellite): ABC Family Channel; America's Store; BBC America; Bloomberg Television; C-SPAN 2; C-SPAN 3; Discovery Digital Networks; DMX Music; Do-It-Yourself; ESPN Classic Sports; ESPN Now; ESPNews; Eternal Word TV Network; Fox Sports World; Fuse; G4; GAS; Lifetime Real Women; MTV Networks Digital Suite; NASA TV; National Geographic Channel; Nick Jr.; Outdoor Channel; Ovation; PBS Kids Channel; Style Network; Toon Disney; Versus; Weatherscan.

Fee: $7.70 monthly.

Digital Expanded Basic Service

Subscribers: N.A.

Programming (via satellite): Canales N.

Digital Pay Service 1

Pay Units: N.A.

Programming (via satellite): Cinemax (multiplexed); Encore; Flix; HBO (multiplexed); Independent Film Channel; MoviePlex; Showtime (multiplexed); Starz (multiplexed); Sundance Channel; The Movie Channel (multiplexed).

Fee: $10.95 monthly (each).

Video-On-Demand: Yes

Pay-Per-View

Addressable homes: 61,594.

Sports PPV (delivered digitally); ESPN Now (delivered digitally); Playboy TV (delivered digitally); Fresh (delivered digitally); Shorteez (delivered digitally); Playboy TV (delivered digitally); iN DEMAND (delivered digitally); Pleasure (delivered digitally); Fresh; Playboy TV; Pleasure; Hot Choice (delivered digitally), Addressable: Yes; iN DEMAND.

Internet Service

Operational: Yes.

Broadband Service: Road Runner.

Fee: $29.95 monthly.

Telephone Service

Digital: Operational

Fee: $32.95 monthly

Miles of Plant: 3,760.0 (coaxial); None (fiber optic).

Division President: J. Christian Fenger. Vice President & General Manager: Michel Champagne. Senior Operations Director: Mark Clark. Engineering Director: Fred Celi. Marketing Director: Sue Ruwe. Program Director: Jeff Pashley. General Manager: Richard Leibe. Senior Customer Service Director: Susan Bonsor.

Ownership: Bright House Networks LLC (MSO).

ORLANDO—Bright House Networks, 1004 US Hwy 92 W, Auburndale, FL 33823. Phone: 866-976-3279. Fax: 407-343-4021. E-mail: jeffpashley@hotmail.com. Web Site: http://www.mybrighthouse.com. Also serves Kissimmee, Osceola County, Poinciana & Polk County. ICA: FL0113.

TV Market Ranking: 28 (ORLANDO); 28,55 (Kissimmee, Osceola County, POINCIANA, Polk County). Franchise award date: May 1, 1971. Franchise expiration date: N.A. Began: March 1, 1974.

Channel capacity: 80 (operating 2-way). Channels available but not in use: 5.

Basic Service

Subscribers: 4,000.

Programming (received off-air): WACX (IND) Leesburg; WBCC (PBS) Cocoa; WDSC-TV (PBS) New Smyrna Beach; WESH (NBC) Daytona Beach; WFTV (ABC) Orlando; WHLV-TV (IND) Cocoa; WKCF

(CW) Clermont; WKMG-TV (CBS) Orlando; WMFE-TV (PBS) Orlando; WOFL (FOX) Orlando; WOPX-TV (ION) Melbourne; WOTF-DT (TEL) Melbourne; WRBW (MNT) Orlando; WRDQ (IND) Orlando; WTGL (ETV) Leesburg; WVEN-TV (UNV) Daytona Beach.

Programming (via satellite): Central Florida News 13; TBS Superstation; Turner Network TV; WGN America.

Current originations: Government Access.

Fee: $30.00 installation; $11.22 monthly; $15.00 additional installation.

Expanded Basic Service 1

Subscribers: N.A.

Programming (via satellite): AMC; Animal Planet; Arts & Entertainment; BET Networks; Bravo; Cartoon Network; CNBC; CNN; Comedy Central; Country Music TV; C-SPAN; Discovery Channel; Discovery Health Channel; Disney Channel; E! Entertainment Television; ESPN; ESPN 2; Food Network; Fox News Channel; FX; GalaVision; Golf Channel; Hallmark Channel; Headline News; HGTV; History Channel; Home Shopping Network; Lifetime; Lifetime Movie Network; MSNBC; MTV; Nickelodeon; Oxygen; QVC; ShopNBC; SoapNet; Speed Channel; Spike TV; Style Network; SunSports TV; Syfy; Telemundo; The Learning Channel; Travel Channel; truTV; Turner Classic Movies; TV Land; USA Network; VH1; WE tv; Weather Channel.

Fee: $39.57 monthly.

Digital Basic Service

Subscribers: N.A.

Programming (received off-air): WDSC-TV (PBS) New Smyrna Beach; WESH (NBC) Daytona Beach; WFTV (ABC) Orlando; WKCF (CW) Clermont; WKMG-TV (CBS) Orlando; WMFE-TV (PBS) Orlando; WOFL (FOX) Orlando; WRBW (MNT) Orlando.

Programming (via satellite): ABC Family Channel; America's Store; BBC America; Black Family Channel; Bloomberg Television; Canales N; Cooking Channel; C-SPAN 2; C-SPAN 3; Current; Discovery Digital Networks; Discovery HD Theater; DMX Music; Do-It-Yourself; ESPN; ESPN Classic Sports; ESPNews; Eternal Word TV Network; Fox Movie Channel; Fox Soccer; Fuse; G4; GAS; Great American Country; HDNet; HDNet Movies; INHD (multiplexed); Lifetime Real Women; MTV2; NASA TV; National Geographic Channel; Nick Jr.; NickToons TV; Outdoor Channel; Ovation; Toon Disney; Turner Network TV HD; Universal HD; Versus; VH1 Classic.

Fee: $7.70 monthly.

Digital Pay Service 1

Pay Units: N.A.

Programming (via satellite): CBS College Sports Network; Cinemax (multiplexed); Encore (multiplexed); Flix; Fuel TV; HBO; HBO HD (multiplexed); Independent Film Channel; MLB Extra Innings; MoviePlex; NASCAR In Car; NBA TV; NHL Center Ice; Showtime; Showtime HD (multiplexed); Starz (multiplexed); Sundance Channel; Tennis Channel; The Movie Channel (multiplexed).

Fee: $10.95 monthly (each).

Video-On-Demand: No

Internet Service

Operational: Yes. Began: December 1, 2002.

Broadband Service: Road Runner.

Fee: $32.95 monthly; $4.00 modem lease.

Telephone Service

Digital: Operational

Fee: $44.95 monthly

Miles of Plant: 150.0 (coaxial); None (fiber optic). Additional miles planned: 6.0 (coaxial). Homes passed: 8,700. Total homes in franchised area: 11,000.

Manager: Richard Leibe. Customer Service Manager: Jean McLean. Chief Technician: Tim Blytenburg. Program Director: Jeff Pashley.

County fee: 5% of gross.

Ownership: Bright House Networks LLC.

ORTONA—Comcast Cable, 450 E Palm Beach Rd, South Bay, FL 33493. Phone: 561-996-3087. Fax: 561-996-3091. Web Site: http://www.comcast.com. ICA: FL0262.

TV Market Ranking: Below 100 (ORTONA). Franchise award date: N.A. Franchise expiration date: N.A. Began: N.A.

Channel capacity: N.A. Channels available but not in use: N.A.

Basic Service

Subscribers: N.A.

Programming (received off-air): WBBH-TV (NBC) Fort Myers; WFTX-TV (FOX) Cape Coral; WGCU (PBS) Fort Myers; WINK-TV (CBS) Fort Myers; WRXY-TV (IND) Tice; WXCW (CW) Naples; WZVN-TV (ABC) Naples.

Programming (via satellite): Home Shopping Network; QVC; WGN America.

Fee: $50.00 installation; $14.95 monthly.

Expanded Basic Service 1

Subscribers: N.A.

Programming (via satellite): ABC Family Channel; AMC; Animal Planet; Arts & Entertainment; CNN; Comedy Central; Country Music TV; C-SPAN; C-SPAN 2; Discovery Channel; Disney Channel; ESPN; ESPN 2; Great American Country; Headline News; Lifetime; MSNBC; ShopNBC; Spike TV; TBS Superstation; The Learning Channel; truTV; USA Network.

Fee: $28.90 monthly.

Pay Service 1

Pay Units: N.A.

Programming (via satellite): Cinemax; HBO.

Fee: $8.90 monthly (each).

Video-On-Demand: No

Internet Service

Operational: No.

Telephone Service

None

Miles of Plant: 6.0 (coaxial); None (fiber optic). Homes passed: 200.

Area Vice President: Gary Waterfield. General Manager: Geoff Shook. Technical Operations Manager: John Barnard. Marketing Director: Christopher Derario. Marketing Manager: Diane Bissoon. Marketing Coordinator: Janet Epstein. Government & Community Affairs Director: Marta Casas-Celayas.

Ownership: Comcast Cable Communications Inc. (MSO).

OSCEOLA COUNTY (eastern portion)—Comcast Cable, 8130 County Rd 44, Leg A, Leesburg, FL 34788. Phone: 352-787-9601. Fax: 352-365-6279. Web Site: http://www.comcast.com. ICA: FL0094.

TV Market Ranking: 28,55 (OSCEOLA COUNTY (EASTERN PORTION)). Franchise award date: October 20, 1986. Franchise expiration date: N.A. Began: N.A.

Channel capacity: N.A. Channels available but not in use: N.A.

Basic Service

Subscribers: 4,584.

Programming (received off-air): WBSF (CW) Bay City; WESH (NBC) Daytona Beach; WFTV (ABC) Orlando; WHLV-TV (IND) Cocoa; WKCF (CW) Clermont; WKMG-TV (CBS) Orlando; WMFE-TV (PBS) Orlando; WOFL (FOX) Orlando; WOPX-TV (ION) Melbourne; WRBW (MNT) Orlando; WRDQ (IND) Orlando; WTGL (ETV) Leesburg.

Programming (via satellite): QVC; TV Guide Network; Univision; WGN America.

Current originations: Government Access; Educational Access; Public Access.

Fee: $19.95 monthly.

Expanded Basic Service 1

Subscribers: N.A.

Programming (received off-air): WKME-CA Kissimmee.

Programming (via satellite): ABC Family Channel; AMC; Animal Planet; Arts & Entertainment; BET Networks; Bio; Bravo; Cartoon Network; CNBC; CNN; Comedy Central; Country Music TV; C-SPAN; C-SPAN 2; Discovery Channel; Disney Channel; E! Entertainment Television; ESPN; ESPN 2; Eternal Word TV Network; Food Network; Fox News Channel; Fox Sports Net Florida; FX; GalaVision; Golf Channel; Hallmark Channel; Headline News; HGTV; History Channel; History Channel International; Home Shopping Network; Lifetime; MSNBC; MTV; NASA TV; Nickelodeon; Oxygen; Product Information Network; ShopNBC; Speed Channel; Spike TV; Style Network; SunSports TV; Syfy; TBS Superstation; The Learning Channel; Travel Channel; Trinity Broadcasting Network; truTV; Turner Network TV; TV Land; USA Network; VH1; Weather Channel.

Digital Basic Service

Subscribers: N.A.

Programming (received off-air): WESH (NBC) Daytona Beach; WKMG-TV (CBS) Orlando; WMFE-TV (PBS) Orlando; WOFL (FOX) Orlando.

Programming (via satellite): AmericanLife TV Network; BBC America; Black Family Channel; Bloomberg Television; Canales N; Colours; Discovery Digital Networks; DMX Music; Do-It-Yourself; ESPN; ESPN Classic Sports; ESPN U; ESPNews; FamilyNet; Fox Movie Channel; Fox Soccer; Fuel TV; Fuse; G4; GAS; Great American Country; GSN; Halogen Network; HDNet; HDNet Movies; INHD; Lifetime Movie Network; LOGO; M-2 (Movie Mania) TV Network; MTV Networks Digital Suite; National Geographic Channel; Nick Jr.; Nick Too; NickToons TV; SoapNet; Toon Disney; Turner Classic Movies; TVG Network; WE tv.

Digital Expanded Basic Service

Subscribers: N.A.

Programming (via satellite): Fox College Sports Atlantic; Fox College Sports Central; Fox College Sports Pacific; Fox Reality Channel; Independent Film Channel; Outdoor Channel; Sundance Channel; Versus.

Digital Pay Service 1

Pay Units: N.A.

Programming (via satellite): ART America; CCTV-4; Cinemax (multiplexed); Encore (multiplexed); Filipino Channel; Flix (multiplexed); HBO (multiplexed); HBO HD; RAI International; Russian Television Network; Showtime (multiplexed); Showtime HD; Starz (multiplexed); Starz HDTV; The Movie Channel (multiplexed); TV Asia; TV Japan; TV5, La Television International; TVN Entertainment; Zhong Tian Channel.

Video-On-Demand: Planned

Pay-Per-View

Playboy TV (delivered digitally); Fresh (delivered digitally); Shorteez (delivered digitally); Hot Choice (delivered digitally); Urban American Television Network (delivered digitally).

Internet Service

Operational: Yes.

Broadband Service: Comcast High Speed Internet.

Fee: $42.95 monthly.

Telephone Service

Digital: Operational

Miles of Plant: 83.0 (coaxial); None (fiber optic). Homes passed: 8,414.

Vice President & General Manager: Mike Davenport. Chief Engineer: Sean Curley. Marketing Manager: Melanie Melvin.

Ownership: Comcast Cable Communications Inc. (MSO).

OSCEOLA COUNTY (western portion)—Comcast Cable, 8130 County Rd 44, Leg A, Leesburg, FL 34788. Phone: 352-787-9601 (Leesburg office). Fax: 352-365-6279. Web Site: http://www.comcast.com. Also serves Davenport (portions), Kissimmee (portions) & Polk County (northern portion). ICA: FL0139.

TV Market Ranking: 28,55 (OSCEOLA COUNTY (WESTERN PORTION) (portions), Polk County (northern portion) (portions)); 55 (Davenport (portions), Kissimmee (portions)). Franchise award date: September 24, 1987. Franchise expiration date: N.A. Began: September 24, 1987.

Channel capacity: N.A. Channels available but not in use: N.A.

Basic Service

Subscribers: 4,264.

Programming (received off-air): WACX (IND) Leesburg; WESH (NBC) Daytona Beach; WFTV (ABC) Orlando; WHLV-TV (IND) Cocoa; WKCF (CW) Clermont; WKME-CA Kissimmee; WKMG-TV (CBS) Orlando; WMFE-TV (PBS) Orlando; WOFL (FOX) Orlando; WOPX-TV (ION) Melbourne; WRBW (MNT) Orlando; WRDQ (IND) Orlando; WTGL (ETV) Leesburg; WVEN-TV (UNV) Daytona Beach.

Programming (via satellite): QVC; ShopNBC; WGN America.

Current originations: Government Access; Educational Access; Leased Access.

Fee: $20.57 monthly.

Expanded Basic Service 1

Subscribers: N.A.

Programming (via satellite): ABC Family Channel; AMC; Animal Planet; Arts & Entertainment; BET Networks; Bravo; Cartoon Network; CNBC; CNN; Comedy Central; Country Music TV; C-SPAN; C-SPAN 2; Discovery Channel; Disney Channel; E! Entertainment Television; ESPN; ESPN 2; Eternal Word TV Network; Food Network; Fox News Channel; Fox Sports Net Florida; FX; GalaVision; Golf Channel; Headline News; HGTV; History Channel; Home Shopping Network; Lifetime; MSNBC; MTV; NASA TV; Nickelodeon; Oxygen; Product Information Network; Speed Channel; Spike TV; SunSports TV; Syfy; TBS Superstation; The Learning Channel; Travel Channel; Trinity Broadcasting Network; truTV; Turner Network TV; TV Guide Network; TV Land; USA Network; VH1; Weather Channel.

Digital Basic Service

Subscribers: N.A.

Programming (via satellite): AmericanLife TV Network; America's Store; BBC America; Bio; Black Family Channel; Bloomberg Television; Canales N; Colours; Discovery Digital Networks; Do-It-Yourself; ESPN Classic Sports; ESPNews; FamilyNet; Fox College Sports Atlantic; Fox College Sports Central; Fox College Sports Pacific; Fox Movie Channel; Fox Sports World; Fuse; G4; Gaming Entertainment Television; GAS; Great American Country; GSN; Halogen

Network; History Channel International; Independent Film Channel; International Television (ITV); Lifetime Movie Network; M-2 (Movie Mania) TV Network; MTV Networks Digital Suite; Music Choice; National Geographic Channel; Nick Jr.; Nick Too; NickToons TV; Outdoor Channel; SoapNet; Sundance Channel; Toon Disney; Turner Classic Movies; Versus; WE tv.

Pay Service 1

Pay Units: 258.

Programming (via satellite): Cinemax.

Fee: $10.00 monthly.

Pay Service 2

Pay Units: 626.

Programming (via satellite): HBO.

Fee: $10.00 monthly.

Pay Service 3

Pay Units: 88.

Programming (via satellite): Showtime; The Movie Channel.

Fee: $10.00 monthly.

Digital Pay Service 1

Pay Units: N.A.

Programming (via satellite): ART America; CCTV-4; Cinemax (multiplexed); Encore (multiplexed); Filipino Channel; Flix; HBO (multiplexed); RAI International; Russian Television Network; Showtime (multiplexed); Starz; The Movie Channel (multiplexed); TV Asia; TV Japan; TV5, La Television International; Zhong Tian Channel.

Video-On-Demand: Planned

Pay-Per-View

HITS (Headend In The Sky) (delivered digitally); Playboy TV (delivered digitally); Fresh (delivered digitally); Shorteez (delivered digitally); Hot Choice (delivered digitally); ESPN (delivered digitally); NBA League Pass (delivered digitally); NHL Center Ice (delivered digitally); MLB Extra Innings (delivered digitally).

Internet Service

Operational: Yes.

Broadband Service: Comcast High Speed Internet.

Fee: $42.95 monthly.

Telephone Service

Digital: Operational

Miles of Plant: 222.0 (coaxial); None (fiber optic). Additional miles planned: 30.0 (coaxial). Homes passed: 7,668.

Vice President & General Manager: Mike Davenport. Chief Engineer: Sean Curley. Marketing Manager: Melanie Melvin.

Ownership: Comcast Cable Communications Inc. (MSO).

OZELLO—Formerly served by KLiP Interactive. No longer in operation. ICA: FL0263.

PAISLEY—Florida Cable, PO Box 498, 23748 State Rd 40, Astor, FL 32102-0498. Phones: 800-779-2788; 352-759-2788. Fax: 352-759-3577. E-mail: support@floridacable.com. Web Site: http://www.floridacable.com. Also serves Lake County (eastern portion). ICA: FL0248.

TV Market Ranking: 55 (Lake County (eastern portion), PAISLEY). Franchise award date: May 3, 1988. Franchise expiration date: N.A. Began: N.A.

Channel capacity: 41 (not 2-way capable). Channels available but not in use: 3.

Basic Service

Subscribers: 285.

Programming (received off-air): WACX (IND) Leesburg; WESH (NBC) Daytona Beach; WFTV (ABC) Orlando; WKCF (CW) Clermont; WKMG-TV (CBS) Orlando; WMFE-TV (PBS) Orlando; WOFL (FOX) Orlando; WRBW (MNT) Orlando.

Programming (via satellite): ABC Family Channel; AMC; Animal Planet; Arts & Entertainment; Cartoon Network; CNBC; CNN; Comedy Central; Country Music TV; C-SPAN; Discovery Channel; E! Entertainment Television; ESPN; ESPN 2; Eternal Word TV Network; Food Network; Fox News Channel; FX; Headline News; HGTV; History Channel; Home Shopping Network; Lifetime; MSNBC; MTV; Nickelodeon; Speed Channel; Spike TV; SunSports TV; Syfy; TBS Superstation; The Learning Channel; Travel Channel; Trinity Broadcasting Network; Turner Classic Movies; Turner Network TV; TV Land; USA Network; VH1; Weather Channel; WGN America.

Fee: $30.00 installation; $38.45 monthly.

Pay Service 1

Pay Units: 96.

Programming (via satellite): HBO; Showtime; The Movie Channel.

Fee: $10.95 monthly (each).

Video-On-Demand: No

Internet Service

Operational: No.

Telephone Service

None

Miles of Plant: 67.0 (coaxial); None (fiber optic). Homes passed: 1,629.

General Manager: Jim Pierce. Plant Manager: Larry English. Office Manager: Aleta Dawson.

Ownership: Florida Cable Inc. (MSO).

PALATKA—Comcast Cable, 200 N 3rd St, Palatka, FL 32177. Phone: 386-328-4205. Fax: 386-325-4602. Web Site: http://www.comcast.com. Also serves Bradford County, Clay County, East Palatka, Hollister, Interlachen, Keystone Heights, Lake Geneva, Melrose, San Mateo & Satsuma. ICA: FL0076.

TV Market Ranking: 68 (Bradford County (portions), Clay County (portions)); Below 100 (Hollister, Interlachen, Keystone Heights, Lake Geneva, Bradford County (portions), Clay County (portions)); Outside TV Markets (East Palatka, PALATKA, San Mateo, Satsuma). Franchise award date: N.A. Franchise expiration date: N.A. Began: February 1, 1968.

Channel capacity: N.A. Channels available but not in use: N.A.

Basic Service

Subscribers: 10,320.

Programming (received off-air): WAWS (FOX, MNT) Jacksonville; WCJB-TV (ABC, CW) Gainesville; WCWJ (CW) Jacksonville; WESH (NBC) Daytona Beach; WJCT (PBS) Jacksonville; WJEB-TV (ETV) Jacksonville; WJGV-CD (IND) Palatka; WJXT (IND) Jacksonville; WJXX (ABC) Orange Park; WTEV-TV (CBS) Jacksonville; WTLV (NBC) Jacksonville; WUFT (PBS) Gainesville; allband FM.

Current originations: Educational Access; Public Access.

Fee: $49.95 installation; $14.06 monthly.

Expanded Basic Service 1

Subscribers: N.A.

Programming (via satellite): ABC Family Channel; AMC; Animal Planet; Arts & Entertainment; BET Networks; Bravo; Cartoon Network; CNBC; CNN; Comcast/Charter Sports Southeast (CSS); Comedy Central; Country Music TV; C-SPAN; Discovery Channel; Discovery Health Channel; Disney Channel; E! Entertainment Television; ESPN; ESPN 2; ESPN Classic Sports; FitTV; Food Network; Fox News Channel; Fox Sports Net Florida; FX; Golf Channel; Hallmark Channel; Headline News; HGTV; History Channel; Home Shopping Network; INSP; ION Television; Lifetime; MoviePlex; MSNBC; MTV; National Geographic Channel; Nickelodeon; Oxygen; QVC; ShopNBC; Speed Channel; Spike TV; SunSports TV; Syfy; TBS Superstation; The Learning Channel; Travel Channel; truTV; Turner Classic Movies; Turner Network TV; TV Guide Network; TV Land; Univision; USA Network; WE tv; Weather Channel.

Fee: $33.00 monthly.

Digital Basic Service

Subscribers: N.A.

Programming (via satellite): AmericanLife TV Network; BBC America; Bloomberg Television; Discovery Digital Networks; ESPN Classic Sports; ESPN Now; ESPNews; Fox Sports World; Fuse; G4; GAS; GSN; Lifetime; MTV2; Music Choice; Nick Jr.; Outdoor Channel; Ovation; Style Network; Toon Disney; Versus; VH1 Classic.

Fee: $5.15 monthly.

Digital Expanded Basic Service

Subscribers: N.A.

Programming (via satellite): Encore Action; Fox Movie Channel; Independent Film Channel; Sundance Channel.

Fee: $8.00 monthly.

Digital Pay Service 1

Pay Units: N.A.

Programming (via satellite): Cinemax (multiplexed); HBO (multiplexed); Showtime (multiplexed); Starz (multiplexed); The Movie Channel.

Fee: $12.00 monthly (each).

Video-On-Demand: Yes

Pay-Per-View

Addressable homes: 3,200.

Hot Choice (delivered digitally); iN DEMAND (delivered digitally); Fresh (delivered digitally); Shorteez (delivered digitally); Movies; special events (delivered digitally), Addressable: Yes.

Internet Service

Operational: Yes. Began: September 1, 2002.

Broadband Service: Comcast High Speed Internet.

Fee: $99.95 installation; $44.95 monthly.

Telephone Service

None

Miles of Plant: 375.0 (coaxial); 100.0 (fiber optic). Additional miles planned: 1.0 (coaxial). Homes passed: 24,410.

Vice President & General Manager: Doug McMillan. Chief Technician: Dean Dabney. Vice President, Marketing: Vic Scarborough. Customer Service Manager: Wendy Thurston. Business Manager: Rosalie Shelor.

City fee: 5% of gross.

Ownership: Comcast Cable Communications Inc. (MSO).

PALM BAY—Comcast Cable, 940 12th St, Vero Beach, FL 32960-3715. Phone: 772-567-3473. Fax: 772-778-9635. Web Site: http://www.comcast.com. ICA: FL0377.

TV Market Ranking: 55 (PALM BAY).

Channel capacity: N.A. Channels available but not in use: N.A.

Basic Service

Subscribers: N.A.

Programming (received off-air): WBCC (PBS) Cocoa; WESH (NBC) Daytona Beach; WFTV (ABC) Orlando; WHLV-TV (IND) Cocoa; WKCF (CW) Clermont; WKMG-TV (CBS) Orlando; WMFE-TV (PBS) Orlando; WOFL (FOX) Orlando; WOPX-TV (ION) Melbourne; WOTF-DT (TEL) Melbourne; WRBW (MNT) Orlando.

Programming (via satellite): ABC Family Channel; AMC; Arts & Entertainment; BET Networks; Bravo; CNBC; CNN; Country Music TV; C-SPAN; C-SPAN 2; Discovery Channel; Disney Channel; ESPN; Headline News; Lifetime; MTV; Nickelodeon; QVC; Spike TV; TBS Superstation; The Learning Channel; Turner Network TV; Univision; USA Network; VH1; Weather Channel.

Pay Service 1

Pay Units: N.A.

Programming (via satellite): Cinemax; HBO; Showtime; The Movie Channel.

Video-On-Demand: No

Internet Service

Operational: Yes.

Telephone Service

Digital: Operational

Area Vice President: Gary Waterford. General Manager: Geoff Shook. Marketing Director: Leigh Ann Dunleavy. Marketing Coordinator: Joey Sergliano. Chief Technician: Michael L. Brooks. Government & Community Director: Marta Casas-Celayas.

Ownership: Comcast Cable Communications Inc. (MSO).

PALM BEACH COUNTY—Now served by WEST PALM BEACH, FL [FL0008]. ICA: FL0057.

PALM BEACH COUNTY (southeastern portion)—Now served by WEST PALM BEACH, FL [FL0008]. ICA: FL0264.

PALM BEACH GARDENS—Comcast Cable, 1401 Northpoint Pkwy, West Palm Beach, FL 33407-1965. Phone: 561-227-4240. Fax: 561-478-5866. Web Site: http://www.comcast.com. Also serves Juno Beach, Jupiter, Jupiter Inlet Colony, Jupiter Island, Lake Park, Loxahatchee, Martin County (southern portion), Palm Beach City, Palm Beach Shores, Royal Palm Beach & Tequesta. ICA: FL0030.

TV Market Ranking: Below 100 (Juno Beach, Jupiter, Jupiter Inlet Colony, Jupiter Island, Lake Park, Loxahatchee, Martin County (southern portion), Palm Beach City, PALM BEACH GARDENS, Palm Beach Shores, Royal Palm Beach, Tequesta). Franchise award date: N.A. Franchise expiration date: N.A. Began: September 1, 1967.

Channel capacity: N.A. Channels available but not in use: N.A.

Basic Service

Subscribers: 101,785.

Programming (received off-air): WFGC (IND) Palm Beach; WFLX (FOX) West Palm Beach; WHDT-LP Miami; WPBF (ABC) Tequesta; WPBT (PBS) Miami; WPEC (CBS) West Palm Beach; WPTV-TV (NBC) West Palm Beach; WPXP-TV (ION) Lake Worth; WSCV (TMO) Fort Lauderdale; WTCE-TV (ETV) Fort Pierce; WTCN-CA (MNT) Palm Beach; WTVX (CW) Fort Pierce; WXEL-TV (PBS) West Palm Beach; 20 FMs.

Programming (via satellite): Home Shopping Network; QVC; TV Guide Network; WGN America.

Current originations: Government Access; Public Access.

Fee: $49.95 installation; $14.65 monthly.

Expanded Basic Service 1

Subscribers: N.A.

Programming (received off-air): WPLG (ABC) Miami.

Programming (via satellite): ABC Family Channel; AMC; Animal Planet; Arts & Entertainment; BET Networks; Bravo; Cartoon Network; CNBC; CNN; Comcast/Charter Sports Southeast (CSS); Comedy Central; Country Music TV; C-SPAN; C-SPAN

2; Discovery Channel; Disney Channel; E! Entertainment Television; ESPN; ESPN 2; Eternal Word TV Network; Food Network; Fox News Channel; Fox Sports Net Florida; FX; Golf Channel; Hallmark Channel; Headline News; HGTV; History Channel; Lifetime; MSNBC; MTV; Nickelodeon; Oxygen; Product Information Network; ShopNBC; Spike TV; Style Network; SunSports TV; Syfy; TBS Superstation; The Learning Channel; Travel Channel; truTV; Turner Network TV; TV Land; Univision; USA Network; VH1; Weather Channel.
Fee: $47.99 monthly.

Digital Basic Service
Subscribers: 60,000.
Programming (received off-air): WFLX (FOX) West Palm Beach; WPBF (ABC) Tequesta; WPEC (CBS) West Palm Beach; WPTV-TV (NBC) West Palm Beach; WXEL-TV (PBS) West Palm Beach.
Programming (via satellite): BBC America; Bio; Black Family Channel; Bloomberg Television; Canales N; CBS College Sports Network; Cooking Channel; Country Music TV; C-SPAN 3; Discovery Digital Networks; Discovery HD Theater; Do-It-Yourself; ESPN Classic Sports; ESPNews; FamilyNet; FitTV; Flix; Fox Movie Channel; Fox Reality Channel; Fox Soccer; FSN Digital Atlantic; FSN Digital Central; FSN Digital Pacific; Fuel TV; Fuse; G4; GAS; Gol TV; Great American Country; GSN; Halogen Network; History Channel International; Independent Film Channel; Lifetime Movie Network; LOGO; MTV Networks Digital Suite; Music Choice; National Geographic Channel; NBA TV; NFL Network; Nick Jr.; Nick Too; NickToons TV; Outdoor Channel; PBS Kids Sprout; Si TV; SoapNet; Speed Channel; Sundance Channel; Tennis Channel; Toon Disney; Trinity Broadcasting Network; Turner Classic Movies; TV One; Versus; WE tv; Weatherscan.
Fee: $53.49 monthly.

Pay Service 1
Pay Units: 31,787.
Programming (via satellite): Cinemax; HBO (multiplexed); Showtime; The Movie Channel.
Fee: $10.95 monthly (Cinemax, Showtime or TMC), $11.95 monthly (HBO).

Digital Pay Service 1
Pay Units: N.A.
Programming (via satellite): Cinemax (multiplexed); Cinemax On Demand; Encore (multiplexed); HBO (multiplexed); HBO HD; HBO On Demand; Showtime (multiplexed); Showtime HD; Showtime On Demand; Starz (multiplexed); Starz HDTV; Starz On Demand; The Movie Channel (multiplexed); The Movie Channel On Demand.

Video-On-Demand: Yes

Pay-Per-View
Addressable homes: 60,000.
Playboy TV (delivered digitally), Fee: $3.95-$4.95, Addressable: Yes; Fresh (delivered digitally); Hot Choice (delivered digitally); Movies (delivered digitally); Special events (delivered digitally); NBA League Pass (delivered digitally).

Internet Service
Operational: Yes.
Broadband Service: Comcast High Speed Internet.
Fee: $42.95 monthly.

Telephone Service
Digital: Operational

Miles of Plant: 1,226.0 (coaxial); None (fiber optic). Homes passed: 141,610.

Area Vice President: Gary Waterfield. General Manager: Beth Fulcher. Chief Technician: Dan Sprunger. Marketing Director: Christopher Derano. Marketing Manager: Diane Bisson. Marketing Coordinator: Janet Epstein. Government & Community Affairs Director: Marta Casas-Celayas.

City fee: 6% of gross.

Ownership: Comcast Cable Communications Inc.

PALM CAY—Cablevision of Marion County, 8296 SW 103rd St Rd, Ste 3, Ocala, FL 34481. Phone: 352-854-0408. Fax: 352-854-0086. E-mail: com@lightningspeed.net. Web Site: http://www.lightningspeed.net. Also serves Fairfield & Marion County (southwestern portion). ICA: FL0311.

TV Market Ranking: Below 100 (Fairfield, Marion County (southwestern portion), PALM CAY). Franchise award date: June 1, 1988. Franchise expiration date: N.A. Began: June 1, 1993.

Channel capacity: 64 (operating 2-way). Channels available but not in use: None.

Basic Service
Subscribers: 790.
Programming (received off-air): WCJB-TV (ABC, CW) Gainesville; WESH (NBC) Daytona Beach; WFOR-TV (CBS) Miami; WKCF (CW) Clermont; WKMG-TV (CBS) Orlando; WOGX (FOX) Ocala; WRBW (MNT) Orlando; WUFT (PBS) Gainesville.
Programming (via satellite): ABC Family Channel; AMC; Animal Planet; Arts & Entertainment; CNBC; CNN; Comedy Central; Country Music TV; C-SPAN; C-SPAN 2; Discovery Channel; Disney Channel; E! Entertainment Television; ESPN; ESPN 2; Eternal Word TV Network; Food Network; Fox Movie Channel; Fox News Channel; Fox Sports Net; FX; Golf Channel; Great American Country; Hallmark Channel; Headline News; HGTV; History Channel; Home Shopping Network; Lifetime; MSNBC; MTV; Nickelodeon; Oxygen; Paxson Communications Corp.; QVC; Radar Channel; Shop at Home; SoapNet; Spike TV; Style Network; SunSports TV; Syfy; TBS Superstation; The Learning Channel; Toon Disney; Travel Channel; truTV; Turner Classic Movies; Turner Network TV; TV Guide Network; TV Land; Univision; USA Network; VH1; Weather Channel; WGN America.
Current originations: Educational Access.
Fee: $50.00 installation; $39.45 monthly.

Digital Basic Service
Subscribers: N.A.
Programming (received off-air): WCJB-TV (ABC, CW) Gainesville.
Programming (via satellite): BBC America; Bio; Bloomberg Television; Bravo; Canales N; Discovery Digital Networks; DMX Music; ESPN 2; ESPN Classic Sports; ESPNews; FitTV; Fox College Sports Atlantic; Fox College Sports Central; Fox College Sports Pacific; Fox Movie Channel; Fox Soccer; GAS; Golf Channel; Halogen Network; HGTV; History Channel; History Channel International; Independent Film Channel; Lime; MTV Networks Digital Suite; National Geographic Channel; Nick Jr.; NickToons TV; Outdoor Channel; Speed Channel; Syfy; Trinity Broadcasting Network; Turner Classic Movies; WE tv.
Fee: $13.95 monthly.

Pay Service 1
Pay Units: 42.
Programming (via satellite): Cinemax; HBO; Showtime; The Movie Channel.
Fee: $45.00 installation; $10.25 monthly (Showtime or TMC), $10.95 monthly (Cinemax), $14.95 monthly (HBO).

Digital Pay Service 1
Pay Units: N.A.
Programming (via satellite): Cinemax (multiplexed); Encore (multiplexed); Flix; HBO (multiplexed); Showtime (multiplexed); Starz (multiplexed); Sundance Channel; The Movie Channel (multiplexed).
Fee: $13.00 monthly (Starz/Encore), $13.95 monthly (Showtime/TMC), $23.95 monthly (HBO & Cinemax).

Video-On-Demand: No

Pay-Per-View
Movies (delivered digitally); Special events (delivered digitally); NASCAR In Car (delivered digitally); Playboy TV (delivered digitally); Fresh (delivered digitally); Shorteez (delivered digitally).

Internet Service
Operational: Yes.
Broadband Service: In-house.
Fee: $34.95 monthly.

Telephone Service
Analog: Not Operational
Digital: Operational
Fee: $40.00 installation; $49.99 monthly

Miles of Plant: 21.0 (coaxial); None (fiber optic). Homes passed: 1,500.

President: Jess R. King. Vice President, Customer Care: Kerri King. Vice President, Plant Services: Richard Black. Network Administrator: Samson Massingill. Office Manager: Louise Brush.

Ownership: Cablevision of Marion County LLC (MSO).

PALM CHASE—Now served by STUART, FL [FL0024]. ICA: FL0265.

PALM COAST—Bright House Networks. Now served by DE LAND, FL [FL0033]. ICA: FL0097.

PALM SPRINGS—Now served by WEST PALM BEACH, FL [FL0008]. ICA: FL0266.

PANAMA CITY—Comcast Cable, 1316 Harrison Ave, Panama City, FL 32401. Phone: 850-769-2929. Fax: 850-769-2988. Web Site: http://www.comcast.com. Also serves Bay County, Callaway, Cedar Grove, Lynn Haven, Panama City Beach, Parker, Springfield & Youngstown. ICA: FL0267.

TV Market Ranking: Below 100 (Bay County, Callaway, Cedar Grove, Lynn Haven, PANAMA CITY, Panama City Beach, Parker, Springfield, Youngstown). Franchise award date: April 1, 1963. Franchise expiration date: N.A. Began: April 1, 1963.

Channel capacity: N.A. Channels available but not in use: N.A.

Basic Service
Subscribers: 39,417.
Programming (received off-air): WFSG (PBS) Panama City; WJHG-TV (CW, MNT, NBC) Panama City; WMBB (ABC) Panama City; WPCT (IND) Panama City Beach; WPGX (FOX) Panama City; WTVY (CBS, CW, MNT) Dothan.
Programming (via satellite): Country Music TV; Discovery Health Channel; Eternal Word TV Network; Home Shopping Network; ION Television; QVC; TV Guide Network; WGN America.
Current originations: Educational Access.
Fee: $44.95 installation; $11.80 monthly; $.82 converter; $24.74 additional installation.

Expanded Basic Service 1
Subscribers: N.A.
Programming (via satellite): ABC Family Channel; AMC; Animal Planet; Arts & Entertainment; BET Networks; Bravo; Cartoon Network; CNBC; CNN; Comcast/Charter Sports Southeast (CSS); Comedy Central; C-SPAN; C-SPAN 2; Discovery Channel; Disney Channel; E! Entertainment Television; ESPN; ESPN 2; ESPN Classic Sports; Food Network; Fox News Channel; Fox Sports Net Florida; FX; Golf Channel; Great American Country; GSN; Headline News; HGTV; History Channel; INSP; Lifetime; MSNBC; MTV; Nickelodeon; Speed Channel; Spike TV; Style Network; SunSports TV; Syfy; TBS Superstation; The Learning Channel; Travel Channel; Trinity Broadcasting Network; truTV; Turner Classic Movies; Turner Network TV; TV Land; USA Network; Versus; VH1; Weather Channel; Weatherscan.
Fee: $31.95 monthly.

Digital Basic Service
Subscribers: 7,783.
Programming (via satellite): BBC America; C-SPAN 3; Discovery Digital Networks; Encore; ESPNews; Flix; G4; GAS; MTV Networks Digital Suite; Music Choice; National Geographic Channel; Nick Jr.; Nick Too; SoapNet; Sundance Channel; Toon Disney.
Fee: $14.95 monthly.

Pay Service 1
Pay Units: 4,650.
Programming (via satellite): Cinemax.
Fee: $12.95 monthly.

Pay Service 2
Pay Units: 8,873.
Programming (via satellite): HBO (multiplexed).
Fee: $13.95 monthly.

Pay Service 3
Pay Units: 2,294.
Programming (via satellite): Showtime.
Fee: $12.95 monthly.

Pay Service 4
Pay Units: 2,116.
Programming (via satellite): The Movie Channel.
Fee: $12.95 monthly.

Digital Pay Service 1
Pay Units: N.A.
Programming (via satellite): Cinemax (multiplexed); HBO (multiplexed); Showtime (multiplexed); Starz (multiplexed); The Movie Channel (multiplexed).
Fee: $11.05 monthly (each).

Video-On-Demand: Yes

Pay-Per-View
Addressable homes: 9,010.
iN DEMAND (delivered digitally), Addressable: Yes; iN DEMAND; Hot Choice (delivered digitally); Playboy TV (delivered digitally); Fresh (delivered digitally); Shorteez (delivered digitally); Pleasure (delivered digitally); ESPN Now (delivered digitally); ESPN Extra (delivered digitally); NBA TV (delivered digitally).

Internet Service
Operational: Yes.
Subscribers: 3,425.
Broadband Service: Comcast High Speed Internet.
Fee: $42.95 monthly; $7.00 modem lease; $199.00 modem purchase.

Telephone Service
Analog: Not Operational
Digital: Operational

Miles of Plant: 1,600.0 (coaxial); None (fiber optic). Homes passed: 57,965. Miles of plant (coax & fiber combined) includes Marianna

Regional Vice President: Rod Dagenais. General Manager: Fritz Hoehne. Technical Operations Manager: Tim Denton. Engineering

Manager: Sonny Spencer. Marketing Manager: Kevin Canel.
Ownership: Comcast Cable Communications Inc. (MSO).

PANAMA CITY BEACH—Comcast Cable. Now served by PANAMA CITY, FL [FL0267]. ICA: FL0075.

PANAMA CITY BEACH—Knology, 235 W. 15th St, Panama City, FL 32401. Phones: 706-645-8553 (Corporate office); 850-215-1000. Fax: 850-215-5800. Web Site: http://www.knology.com. ICA: FL0336. **Note:** This system is an overbuild.
TV Market Ranking: Below 100 (PANAMA CITY BEACH). Franchise award date: N.A. Franchise expiration date: N.A. Began: N.A.
Channel capacity: 110 (operating 2-way). Channels available but not in use: 30.

Basic Service
Subscribers: 9,708.
Programming (received off-air): WBIF (IND) Marianna [LICENSED & SILENT]; WFSG (PBS) Panama City; WJHG-TV (CW, MNT, NBC) Panama City; WMBB (ABC) Panama City; WPCT (IND) Panama City Beach; WPGX (FOX) Panama City; WTVY (CBS, CW, MNT) Dothan.
Programming (via satellite): ABC Family Channel; AMC; Animal Planet; Arts & Entertainment; BET Networks; Bravo; Cartoon Network; CNBC; CNN; Comedy Central; Country Music TV; C-SPAN; C-SPAN 2; CW+; Discovery Channel; Disney Channel; E! Entertainment Television; ESPN; ESPN 2; Eternal Word TV Network; Food Network; Fox News Channel; Fox Sports Net Florida; FX; G4; Golf Channel; Hallmark Channel; Headline News; HGTV; History Channel; Home Shopping Network; INSP; Lifetime; Lifetime Movie Network; MoviePlex; MSNBC; MTV; MyNetworkTV Inc.; NASA TV; Nick At Nite; Nickelodeon; Outdoor Channel; Oxygen; QVC; ShopNBC; Speed Channel; Spike TV; SunSports TV; Syfy; TBS Superstation; The Learning Channel; Toon Disney; Travel Channel; Trinity Broadcasting Network; truTV; Turner Classic Movies; Turner Network TV; TV Guide Network; TV Land; Univision; USA Network; Versus; VH1; WE tv; Weather Channel; Weatherscan; WGN America.
Current originations: Leased Access; Religious Access; Government Access; Educational Access; Public Access.
Fee: $46.25 monthly.

Digital Basic Service
Subscribers: N.A. Included in Valley, AL
Programming (received off-air): WFSG (PBS) Panama City; WJHG-TV (CW, MNT, NBC) Panama City; WMBB (ABC) Panama City; WPGX (FOX) Panama City; WTVY (CBS, CW, MNT) Dothan.
Programming (via satellite): BBC America; Bloomberg Television; Boomerang; CBS College Sports Network; Church Channel; CMT Pure Country; C-SPAN 3; Discovery HD Theater; Discovery Health Channel; Discovery Kids Channel; Discovery Military Channel; Discovery Planet Green; ESPN 2 HD; ESPN HD; ESPN U; ESPNews; FamilyNet; FitTV; Florida Channel; Fox College Sports Atlantic; Fox College Sports Central; Fox College Sports Pacific; Fox Soccer; Fuel TV; GSN; HDNet; HDNet Movies; ID Investigation Discovery; Independent Film Channel; JCTV; Jewelry Television; Lifetime Real Women; MTV Hits; MTV Jams; MTV Tres; MTV2; mtvU; Music Choice; National Geographic Channel; NFL Network; Nick Jr.; Nick Too; NickToons TV; Ovation; Pentagon Channel; Research Channel; Science Channel; SoapNet; Starz HDTV; TeenNick; Tennis Channel; The Sportsman Channel; Turner Network TV HD; Universal HD; VH1 Classic; VH1 Soul.

Pay Service 1
Pay Units: N.A.
Programming (via satellite): HBO (multiplexed); Showtime (multiplexed).
Fee: $7.95 monthly (Showtime), $9.95 monthly (HBO).

Digital Pay Service 1
Pay Units: N.A.
Programming (via satellite): Cinemax (multiplexed); Encore (multiplexed); Flix; HBO (multiplexed); HBO HD; Showtime (multiplexed); Starz (multiplexed); Sundance Channel; The Movie Channel (multiplexed).
Fee: $3.00 monthly (Encore), $4.50 monthly (Starz), $7.95 monthly (Showtime or Sundance & TMC), $8.95 monthly (Cinemax), $9.95 monthly (HBO).

Video-On-Demand: Yes

Pay-Per-View
Urban Xtra (delivered digitally); ESPN Now (delivered digitally); ESPN Extra (delivered digitally); Spice: Xcess (delivered digitally); Club Jenna (delivered digitally); iN DEMAND (delivered digitally); Playboy TV (delivered digitally); Fresh (delivered digitally); Shorteez (delivered digitally).

Internet Service
Operational: Yes.
Broadband Service: Knology.Net.
Fee: $29.95 installation; $59.95 monthly.

Telephone Service
Analog: Not Operational
Digital: Operational
Fee: $18.60 monthly
Miles of Plant: 150.0 (coaxial); 720.0 (fiber optic). Homes passed: 61,700.
General Manager: Al McCambry. Technical Operations Manager: Steve Thomas. Sales & Marketing Manager: Michelle Gilbert.
Ownership: Knology Inc. (MSO).

PASCO COUNTY (central & eastern portions)—Bright House Networks, 30432 State Rd 54, Wesley Chapel, FL 33543. Phones: 813-862-0500; 813-862-0522. Fax: 863-288-2204. Web Site: http://tampabay.brighthouse.com. Also serves Dade City, Land O' Lakes, Lutz, San Antonio, St. Leo, Wesley Chapel & Zephyrhills. ICA: FL0042.
TV Market Ranking: 28 (Dade City, Land O' Lakes, Lutz, San Antonio, St. Leo, Wesley Chapel, Zephyrhills); 28,55 (PASCO COUNTY (CENTRAL & EASTERN PORTIONS) (portions)). Franchise award date: June 2, 1981. Franchise expiration date: N.A. Began: November 1, 1982.
Channel capacity: 60 (operating 2-way). Channels available but not in use: 2.

Basic Service
Subscribers: 45,000.
Programming (received off-air): WCLF (IND) Clearwater; WEDU (PBS) Tampa; WFLA-TV (NBC) Tampa; WFTS-TV (ABC) Tampa; WFTT-DT (TEL) Tampa; WMOR-TV (IND) Lakeland; WTOG (CW) St. Petersburg; WTSP (CBS) St. Petersburg; WTTA (MNT) St. Petersburg; WTVT (FOX) Tampa; WUSF-TV (PBS) Tampa; WVEA-TV (UNV) Venice; WXPX-TV (ION) Bradenton; 10 FMs.
Programming (via satellite): Bay News 9; Florida Channel; Home Shopping Network; Jewelry Television; QVC; ShopNBC; TBS Superstation; TV Guide Network; WGN America.
Current originations: Leased Access; Religious Access; Government Access; Educational Access; Public Access.
Fee: $48.95 installation; $29.25 monthly; $1.75 converter.

Expanded Basic Service 1
Subscribers: N.A.
Programming (via satellite): ABC Family Channel; AMC; Animal Planet; Arts & Entertainment; BET Networks; Bravo; Cartoon Network; Catch 47; CNBC; CNN; Comedy Central; Country Music TV; C-SPAN; C-SPAN 2; Discovery Channel; Discovery Health Channel; Disney Channel; E! Entertainment Television; ESPN; ESPN 2; ESPN Classic Sports; Eternal Word TV Network; Food Network; Fox News Channel; Fox Sports Net Florida; FX; Golf Channel; Hallmark Channel; Headline News; HGTV; History Channel; Lifetime; Lifetime Movie Network; MoviePlex; MSNBC; MTV; National Geographic Channel; Nickelodeon; Oxygen; Spike TV; SunSports TV; Syfy; Telemundo; The Learning Channel; Travel Channel; truTV; Turner Classic Movies; Turner Network TV; TV Land; USA Network; Versus; VH1; WE tv; Weather Channel.

Digital Basic Service
Subscribers: N.A.
Programming (received off-air): WFLA-TV (NBC) Tampa; WFTS-TV (ABC) Tampa; WMOR-TV (IND) Lakeland; WTSP (CBS) St. Petersburg; WTVT (FOX) Tampa; WUSF-TV (PBS) Tampa.
Programming (via satellite): AmericanLife TV Network; America's Store; Bay News 9; BBC America; Bio; Black Family Channel; Bloomberg Television; Cooking Channel; C-SPAN 3; Current; Discovery Digital Networks; Discovery HD Theater; Disney Channel; Do-It-Yourself; Encore (multiplexed); ESPN Gameplan (multiplexed); ESPNews; Eternal Word TV Network; Flix; Fox College Sports Atlantic; Fox College Sports Central; Fox College Sports Pacific; Fox Movie Channel; Fox Soccer; Fuel TV; Fuse; G4; GAS; Great American Country; HDNet; HDNet Movies; History Channel International; Independent Film Channel; INHD; INHD2; Lifetime Real Women; MLB Extra Innings (multiplexed); MLS Direct Kick (multiplexed); MTV2; Music Choice; NASCAR In Car (multiplexed); NBA League Pass (multiplexed); NBA TV; NHL Center Ice (multiplexed); Nick Jr.; NickToons TV; Outdoor Channel; Ovation; Sleuth; SoapNet; Speed Channel; Style Network; Tennis Channel; Toon Disney; Trinity Broadcasting Network; Turner Network TV HD; TV One; Universal HD; VH1 Classic; WEDU (PBS) Tampa.

Digital Pay Service 1
Pay Units: N.A.
Programming (via satellite): Cinemax (multiplexed); HBO (multiplexed); Showtime (multiplexed); Showtime HD; Starz (multiplexed); The Movie Channel (multiplexed).

Video-On-Demand: Yes

Pay-Per-View
Movies (delivered digitally); Special events (delivered digitally); Pleasure (delivered digitally); Playboy TV (delivered digitally).

Internet Service
Operational: Yes.
Subscribers: 13,050.
Broadband Service: Road Runner.
Fee: $29.95 monthly.

Telephone Service
Analog: Not Operational
Digital: Operational
Fee: $39.95 monthly
Miles of Plant: 648.0 (coaxial); 32.0 (fiber optic). Additional miles planned: 17.0 (coaxial). Homes passed: 72,223. Total homes in franchised area: 72,223.
Division President: Kevin Hyman. Vice President & General Manager: Dave Ross. Vice President, Engineering: Gene White. Engineering Director: Scott Twyman. Marketing Director: Robb Bennett.
County fee: 3% of gross. City fee: 5% of gross.
Ownership: Bright House Networks LLC (MSO).

PASCO COUNTY (western portion)—Bright House Networks, 1004 US Hwy 92 W, Auburndale, FL 33823. Phones: 727-856-3278 (Customer service); 863-965-7733. Fax: 863-288-2204. Web Site: http://tampabay.brighthouse.com. Also serves Elfers, Holiday, Hudson, New Port Richey & Port Richey. ICA: FL0009.
TV Market Ranking: 28 (Elfers, Holiday, Hudson, New Port Richey, Pasco County (western portion), PORT RICHEY). Franchise award date: N.A. Franchise expiration date: N.A. Began: February 1, 1971.
Channel capacity: N.A. Channels available but not in use: N.A.

Basic Service
Subscribers: 119,595.
Programming (received off-air): WCLF (IND) Clearwater; WEDU (PBS) Tampa; WFLA-TV (NBC) Tampa; WFTS-TV (ABC) Tampa; WFTT-DT (TEL) Tampa; WMOR-TV (IND) Lakeland; WTOG (CW) St. Petersburg; WTSP (CBS) St. Petersburg; WTTA (MNT) St. Petersburg; WUSF-TV (PBS) Tampa; WVEA-TV (UNV) Venice; WXPX-TV (ION) Bradenton; allband FM.
Programming (via satellite): Bay News 9; Florida Channel; Home Shopping Network; QVC; ShopNBC; TV Guide Network; WGN America.
Current originations: Government Access; Educational Access.
Fee: $42.95 installation; $16.00 monthly.

Expanded Basic Service 1
Subscribers: N.A.
Programming (via satellite): ABC Family Channel; AMC; Animal Planet; Arts & Entertainment; BET Networks; Bravo; Cartoon Network; Catch 47; CNBC; CNN; Comedy Central; Country Music TV; C-SPAN; C-SPAN 2; Discovery Channel; Discovery Health Channel; Disney Channel; E! Entertainment Television; ESPN; ESPN 2; ESPN Classic Sports; Eternal Word TV Network; Food Network; Fox News Channel; Fox Sports Net Florida; FX; Golf Channel; Hallmark Channel; Headline News; HGTV; History Channel; Lifetime; Lifetime Movie Network; MoviePlex; MSNBC; MTV; National Geographic Channel; Nickelodeon; Oxygen; Spike TV; SunSports TV; Syfy; TBS Superstation; Telemundo; The Learning Channel; Travel Channel; truTV; Turner Classic Movies; Turner Network TV; TV Land; USA Network; Versus; VH1; WE tv; Weather Channel.
Fee: $28.95 monthly.

Digital Basic Service
Subscribers: 20,688.
Programming (received off-air): WEDU (PBS) Tampa; WFLA-TV (NBC) Tampa; WFTS-TV (ABC) Tampa; WMOR-TV (IND) Lakeland; WTSP (CBS) St. Petersburg; WTVT (FOX) Tampa; WUSF-TV (PBS) Tampa.
Programming (via satellite): AmericanLife TV Network; America's Store; Bay News 9; Bay News 9 Espanol; BBC America; Bio; Black Family Channel; Bloomberg Television; Cooking Channel; C-SPAN 3; Current; Discovery Digital Networks; Discovery HD Theater; Disney Channel; Do-It-

Yourself; Do-It-Yourself On Demand; ESPN; ESPNews; Eternal Word TV Network; Fine Living On Demand; Flix (multiplexed); Food Network On Demand; Fox Soccer; Fuse; G4; GAS; Great American Country; Great American Country On Demand; GSN; HD-Net; HDNet Movies; HGTV On Demand; History Channel International; Independent Film Channel; INHD; INHD2; Lifetime Real Women; MTV2; Music Choice; Nick Jr.; NickToons TV; Ovation; Sleuth; SoapNet; Speed Channel; Style Network; Sundance Channel; Tampa Bay On Demand; Toon Disney; Trinity Broadcasting Network; Turner Network TV HD; TV One; Universal HD; VH1 Classic.
Fee: $11.95 monthly.

Digital Expanded Basic Service
Subscribers: N.A.
Programming (via satellite): Canales N; Encore (multiplexed); Fox College Sports Atlantic; Fox College Sports Central; Fox College Sports Pacific; Fox Movie Channel; Fuel TV; NBA TV; Outdoor Channel; Tennis Channel.

Digital Pay Service 1
Pay Units: N.A.
Programming (via satellite): Cinemax (multiplexed); HBO (multiplexed); HBO HD; Showtime (multiplexed); Showtime HD; Starz (multiplexed); The Movie Channel (multiplexed).

Video-On-Demand: Yes

Pay-Per-View
Addressable homes: 20,688.
iN DEMAND (delivered digitally), Addressable: Yes; Sports PPV (delivered digitally); Playboy TV (delivered digitally); ESPN Gameplan (delivered digitally); Pleasure (delivered digitally); NBA League Pass (delivered digitally); NHL Center Ice (delivered digitally); MLB Extra Innings (delivered digitally); NASCAR In Car (delivered digitally); MLS Direct Kick (delivered digitally).

Internet Service
Operational: Yes.
Subscribers: 23,008.
Broadband Service: Road Runner.
Fee: $39.95 installation; $29.95 monthly.

Telephone Service
Digital: Operational
Fee: $39.95 monthly

Miles of Plant: 1,652.0 (coaxial); 1.0 (fiber optic). Homes passed: 127,336. Total homes in franchised area: 194,610.

Division President: Kevin Hyman. Vice President & General Manager: Dave Ross. Vice President, Engineering: Gene White. Marketing Director: Robb Bennett.

County fee: 6% of gross.

Ownership: Bright House Networks LLC.

PEDRO—Cablevision of Marion County, 8296 SW 103rd St Rd, Ste 3, Ocala, FL 34481. Phone: 352-854-0408. Fax: 352-854-0086. Web Site: http://www.lightningspeed.net. Also serves Summerfield. ICA: FL0362.

TV Market Ranking: Below 100 (PEDRO, Summerfield).

Channel capacity: 41 (operating 2-way). Channels available but not in use: 3.

Basic Service
Subscribers: 300.
Programming (received off-air): WCJB-TV (ABC, CW) Gainesville; WESH (NBC) Daytona Beach; WKCF (CW) Clermont; WKMG-TV (CBS) Orlando; WOGX (FOX) Ocala; WUFT (PBS) Gainesville.
Programming (via satellite): ABC Family Channel; AMC; Animal Planet; Arts & Entertainment; Cartoon Network; CNN; Discovery Channel; Disney Channel; ESPN; Food Network; Fox News Channel; Fuse; FX; Great American Country; Headline News; Lifetime; QVC; Speed Channel; SunSports TV; Syfy; TBS Superstation; Toon Disney; Travel Channel; Turner Network TV; USA Network; Weather Channel; WGN America.
Fee: $50.00 installation; $40.95 monthly.

Pay Service 1
Pay Units: N.A.
Programming (via satellite): Cinemax; HBO; Showtime; The Movie Channel.
Fee: $9.95 monthly (Showtime & TMC), $10.95 monthly (Cinemax), $14.95 monthly (HBO).

Video-On-Demand: No

Internet Service
Operational: Yes.
Fee: $50.00 installation; $34.95 monthly.

Telephone Service
Digital: Operational
Fee: $40.00 installation; $49.99 monthly

Miles of Plant: 74.0 (coaxial); None (fiber optic). Homes passed: 1,382.

President: Jess R. King. Vice President, Plant Services: Richard Black. Vice President, Customer Care: Kerri King. Office Manager: Louise Brush.

Ownership: Cablevision of Marion County LLC (MSO).

PEMBROKE PINES—Comcast Cable. Now served by BROWARD COUNTY, FL [FL0016]. ICA: FL0372.

PENNEY FARMS—Florida Cable, PO Box 498, 23748 State Rd 40, Astor, FL 32102-0498. Phones: 352-759-2788; 800-779-2788. Fax: 352-759-3797. E-mail: support@floridacable.com. Web Site: http://www.floridacable.com. ICA: FL0363.

TV Market Ranking: 68 (PENNEY FARMS).

Channel capacity: 41 (not 2-way capable). Channels available but not in use: None.

Basic Service
Subscribers: 337.
Programming (received off-air): WAWS (FOX, MNT) Jacksonville; WCWJ (CW) Jacksonville; WJCT (PBS) Jacksonville; WJEB-TV (ETV) Jacksonville; WJXT (IND) Jacksonville; WJXX (ABC) Orange Park; WTEV-TV (CBS) Jacksonville; WTLV (NBC) Jacksonville; WUFT (PBS) Gainesville.
Programming (via satellite): ABC Family Channel; AMC; Arts & Entertainment; Cartoon Network; CNBC; CNN; Comedy Central; Discovery Channel; Disney Channel; ESPN; Food Network; Fox News Channel; Fuse; FX; Great American Country; Headline News; Home Shopping Network; Lifetime; QVC; Speed Channel; Syfy; TBS Superstation; Travel Channel; Turner Classic Movies; Turner Network TV; USA Network; Weather Channel; WGN America.
Fee: $32.45 monthly.

Pay Service 1
Pay Units: N.A.
Programming (via satellite): Cinemax; HBO; Showtime; The Movie Channel.

Internet Service
Operational: No.

Telephone Service
None

Miles of Plant: 40.0 (coaxial); None (fiber optic). Homes passed: 1,359.

General Manager: Jim Pierce. Plant Manager: Larry English. Office Manager: Alita Dawson.

Ownership: Florida Cable Inc. (MSO).

PENSACOLA—Cox Communications, 2205 La Vista Ave, Pensacola, FL 32504. Phones: 850-862-4142; 850-477-2695. Fax: 850-479-3912. Web Site: http://www.cox.com/gulfcoast. Also serves Escambia County & University of West Florida. ICA: FL0018.

TV Market Ranking: 59 (Escambia County, PENSACOLA, University of West Florida); Outside TV Markets (Escambia County). Franchise award date: January 26, 1967. Franchise expiration date: N.A. Began: January 1, 1969.

Channel capacity: N.A. Channels available but not in use: N.A.

Basic Service
Subscribers: 176,000 Includes Fort Walton Beach.
Programming (received off-air): WALA-TV (FOX) Mobile; WEAR-TV (ABC) Pensacola; WFGX (MNT) Fort Walton Beach; WFNA (CW) Gulf Shores; WHBR (IND) Pensacola; WJTC (IND) Pensacola; WKRG-TV (CBS) Mobile; WMPV-TV (TBN) Mobile; WPAN (IND) Fort Walton Beach; WPMI-TV (NBC) Mobile; WSRE (PBS) Pensacola.
Programming (via satellite): C-SPAN; C-SPAN 2; Home Shopping Network; QVC; Sneak Prevue; TBS Superstation; TV Guide Network; WGN America.
Current originations: Leased Access; Educational Access; Public Access.
Planned originations: Government Access.
Fee: $56.50 installation; $11.54 monthly; $1.25 converter.

Expanded Basic Service 1
Subscribers: N.A.
Programming (via satellite): ABC Family Channel; AMC; Animal Planet; Arts & Entertainment; BET Networks; Bravo; Cartoon Network; CNBC; CNN; Comedy Central; Country Music TV; Discovery Channel; Disney Channel; E! Entertainment Television; ESPN; ESPN 2; Food Network; Fox News Channel; Fox Sports Net Florida; FX; Golf Channel; Headline News; HGTV; History Channel; Lifetime; MSNBC; MTV; Nickelodeon; Oxygen; ShopNBC; Speed Channel; Spike TV; SunSports TV; Syfy; The Learning Channel; Travel Channel; Turner Classic Movies; Turner Network TV; TV Land; USA Network; Versus; VH1; Weather Channel.
Fee: $31.69 monthly.

Digital Basic Service
Subscribers: 13,944.
Programming (received off-air): WJTC (IND) Pensacola; WPMI-TV (NBC) Mobile; WSRE (PBS) Pensacola.
Programming (via satellite): BBC America; Bloomberg Television; Discovery Digital Networks; Discovery HD Theater; ESPN; ESPNews; Eternal Word TV Network; Fox Sports World; G4; GalaVision; Golf Channel; Great American Country; GSN; Halogen Network; Independent Film Channel; INHD (multiplexed); Lifetime Movie Network; MuchMusic Network; Music Choice; NBA TV; SoapNet; Sundance Channel; Toon Disney; Turner Network TV; Universal HD.
Fee: $12.99 monthly.

Pay Service 1
Pay Units: 46,200.
Programming (via satellite): Cinemax (multiplexed); HBO (multiplexed); Showtime (multiplexed); The Movie Channel.
Fee: $11.00 monthly (each).

Digital Pay Service 1
Pay Units: N.A.
Programming (via satellite): Cinemax (multiplexed); Encore; HBO (multiplexed); HBO HD; Showtime (multiplexed); Showtime HD; Starz (multiplexed).
Fee: $11.00 monthly (each).

Video-On-Demand: Planned

Pay-Per-View
ESPN Extra (delivered digitally); Hot Choice; iN DEMAND; iN DEMAND (delivered digitally); Fresh; Shorteez; sports (delivered digitally).

Internet Service
Operational: Yes.
Subscribers: 10,248.
Broadband Service: Cox High Speed Internet.
Fee: $149.00 installation; $19.95-$59.95 monthly; $15.00 modem lease; $175.00 modem purchase.

Telephone Service
Digital: Operational
Fee: $10.99-$44.79 monthly

Miles of Plant: 2,877.0 (coaxial); None (fiber optic). Homes passed: 236,627. Miles of plant & homes passed include Fort Walton Beach

Vice President & General Manager: Keith Gregory. Vice President, Network Operations: Mark O'Ceallaigh. Vice President, Marketing: Dale Tapley. Marketing Manager: Bob Hartnett. Government & Public Affairs Director: Sheila Nichols.

Franchise fee: 5% of gross.

Ownership: Cox Communications Inc. (MSO).

PERRY—Comcast Cable, 217 E Green St, Perry, FL 32347-2737. Phones: 850-574-4016 (Tallahassee office); 850-584-2295. Fax: 850-584-6499. Web Site: http://www.comcast.com. Also serves Taylor County. ICA: FL0269.

TV Market Ranking: Below 100 (Taylor County (portions)); Outside TV Markets (PERRY, Taylor County (portions)). Franchise award date: N.A. Franchise expiration date: N.A. Began: July 1, 1963.

Channel capacity: N.A. Channels available but not in use: N.A.

Basic Service
Subscribers: N.A. Included in Tallahassee
Programming (received off-air): WCTV (CBS, MNT) Thomasville; WFSU-TV (PBS) Tallahassee; WTLH (CW, FOX) Bainbridge; WTWC-TV (NBC) Tallahassee; WTXL-TV (ABC) Tallahassee.
Programming (via satellite): C-SPAN; C-SPAN 2; CW+; Home Shopping Network; QVC; Weather Channel; WGN America.
Current originations: Educational Access.
Fee: $39.88 installation; $9.25 monthly.

Expanded Basic Service 1
Subscribers: N.A.
Programming (via satellite): ABC Family Channel; AMC; Animal Planet; Arts & Entertainment; BET Networks; Cartoon Network; CNBC; CNN; Comcast/Charter Sports Southeast (CSS); Country Music TV; Discovery Channel; Discovery Health Channel; Disney Channel; E! Entertainment Television; ESPN; ESPN 2; Food Network; Fox News Channel; FX; Great American Country; GSN; Hallmark Channel; Headline News; HGTV; History Channel; Lifetime; MTV; Nickelodeon; Speed Channel; Spike TV; Style Network; SunSports TV; Syfy; TBS Superstation; The Learning Channel; Travel Channel; truTV; Turner Network TV; TV Land; USA Network; Versus; VH1.
Fee: $39.95 monthly.

Digital Basic Service
Subscribers: N.A.
Programming (received off-air): WCTV (CBS, MNT) Thomasville.
Programming (via satellite): 3 Angels Broadcasting Network; BBC America; C-SPAN 3; Discovery Digital Networks; Encore (multiplexed); ESPNews; Flix; GAS; Halogen Network; INSP; Lifetime Movie Network; MTV Networks Digital Suite; Mu-

sic Choice; Nick Jr.; Nick Too; PBS Kids Sprout; SoapNet; Sundance Channel; Toon Disney; Trinity Broadcasting Network; TV One.
Fee: $6.90 monthly.

Pay Service 1
Pay Units: N.A.
Programming (via satellite): HBO.
Fee: $24.95 installation; $13.95 monthly.

Digital Pay Service 1
Pay Units: N.A.
Programming (via satellite): Cinemax (multiplexed); HBO (multiplexed); Showtime (multiplexed); Starz (multiplexed); The Movie Channel (multiplexed).
Fee: $13.00 monthly (each).

Video-On-Demand: No

Pay-Per-View
Movies (delivered digitally); Hot Choice (delivered digitally); Playboy TV (delivered digitally); Fresh (delivered digitally); Shorteez (delivered digitally).

Internet Service
Operational: Yes. Began: November 4, 2004.
Broadband Service: Comcast High Speed Internet.
Fee: $42.95 monthly.

Telephone Service
Digital: Operational

Miles of plant (coax) & homes passed included in Tallahassee

General Manager: K. C. McWilliams. Chief Technician: Chris Osborne. Technical Operations Director: Terry Pullen. Area Technical Manager: Andy Musgrove. Marketing Director: Claire Evans.

City fee: 5% of gross. County fee: 3% of gross.

Ownership: Comcast Cable Communications Inc. (MSO).

PINELLAS COUNTY—Bright House Networks, 700 Carillon Pkwy, St Petersburg, FL 33716. Phones: 727-329-5020 (Customer service); 727-329-2000. Fax: 727-329-2869. Web Site: http://tampabay.brighthouse.com. Also serves Bay Pines, Belleair, Belleair Beach, Belleair Bluffs, Belleair Shores, Clearwater, Dunedin, East Lake Woodlands, Gulfport, Indian Rocks Beach, Indian Shores, Isla del Sol, Kenneth City, Largo, Madeira Beach, North Redington Beach, Oldsmar, Palm Harbor, Pinellas County (unincorporated areas), Pinellas Park, Redington Beach, Redington Shores, Safety Harbor, Seminole, South Pasadena, South St. Petersburg, St. Petersburg, St. Petersburg Beach, Tarpon Springs, Tierra Verde, Treasure Island & Venice (portions). ICA: FL0005.

TV Market Ranking: 28 (Bay Pines, Belleair, Belleair, Belleair Bluffs, Belleair Shores, Clearwater, Dunedin, East Lake Woodlands, Gulfport, Indian Rocks Beach, Indian Shores, Isla del Sol, Isla del Sol, Kenneth City, Largo, Madeira Beach, North Redington Beach, Oldsmar, Palm Harbor, PINELLAS COUNTY, Pinellas County (unincorporated areas), Pinellas Park, Redington Beach, Redington Shores, Safety Harbor, Seminole, South Pasadena, South St. Petersburg, St. Petersburg, St. Petersburg Beach, Tarpon Springs, Tierra Verde, Tierra Verde, Treasure Island, Venice (portions)). Franchise award date: January 1, 1972. Franchise expiration date: N.A. Began: January 1, 1972.

Channel capacity: 141 (operating 2-way). Channels available but not in use: None.

Basic Service
Subscribers: 354,739.
Programming (received off-air): WCLF (IND) Clearwater; WEDU (PBS) Tampa; WFLA-TV (NBC) Tampa; WFTS-TV (ABC) Tampa; WFTT-DT (TEL) Tampa; WTOG (CW) St. Petersburg; WTSP (CBS) St. Petersburg; WTTA (MNT) St. Petersburg; WTVT (FOX) Tampa; WUSF-TV (PBS) Tampa; WVEA-TV (UNV) Venice; WXPX-TV (ION) Bradenton; 3 FMs.
Programming (via satellite): Bay News 9; C-SPAN; C-SPAN 2; Home Shopping Network; TV Guide Network; WGN America.
Current originations: Leased Access; Government Access; Educational Access.
Fee: $17.00 installation; $8.50 monthly.

Expanded Basic Service 1
Subscribers: 277,000.
Programming (received off-air): WMOR-TV (IND) Lakeland.
Programming (via satellite): ABC Family Channel; AMC; Animal Planet; Arts & Entertainment; BET Networks; Bravo; Cartoon Network; Catch 47; CNBC; CNN; Comedy Central; Country Music TV; C-SPAN 2; Discovery Channel; Discovery Health Channel; Disney Channel; E! Entertainment Television; ESPN; ESPN 2; ESPN Classic Sports; Eternal Word TV Network; Food Network; Fox News Channel; Fox Sports Net; FX; Golf Channel; Hallmark Channel; Headline News; HGTV; History Channel; Lifetime; Lifetime Movie Network; MoviePlex; MSNBC; MTV; National Geographic Channel; Nickelodeon; Oxygen; QVC; Shop at Home; ShopNBC; Spike TV; SunSports TV; Syfy; TBS Superstation; Telemundo; The Learning Channel; Travel Channel; truTV; Turner Classic Movies; Turner Network TV; TV Land; USA Network; Versus; VH1; WE tv; Weather Channel.
Fee: $17.00 installation; $36.45 monthly.

Digital Basic Service
Subscribers: 150,000.
Programming (received off-air): WUSF-TV (PBS) Tampa.
Programming (via satellite): American-Life TV Network; America's Store; Bay News 9; Bay News 9 Espanol; BBC America; BBC America On Demand; Bio; Black Family Channel; Bloomberg Television; Cooking Channel; C-SPAN 3; Current; Discovery Digital Networks; Discovery HD Theater; Disney Channel; Do-It-Yourself; Do-It-Yourself On Demand; ESPN; ESPNews; Eternal Word TV Network; Fine Living On Demand; Flix; Florida Channel; Food Network On Demand; Fox College Sports Atlantic; Fox College Sports Central; Fox College Sports Pacific; Fox Soccer; Fuel TV; Fuse; G4; GAS; Great American Country; Great American Country On Demand; GSN; HDNet; HDNet Movies; HGTV On Demand; History Channel International; Independent Film Channel; INHD; INHD2; Lifetime Real Women; MTV2; Music Choice; National Geographic Channel On Demand; NBA TV; Nick Jr.; NickToons TV; Outdoor Channel; Ovation; Science Television; Sleuth; SoapNet; Speed Channel; Speed On Demand; Style Network; Sundance Channel; Tampa Bay On Demand; Tennis Channel; Toon Disney; Trinity Broadcasting Network; Turner Network TV HD; TV One; Universal HD; various Mexican stations; VH1 Classic; WEDU (PBS) Tampa; WFLA-TV (NBC) Tampa; WMOR-TV (IND) Lakeland.
Fee: $11.95 monthly.

Digital Pay Service 1
Pay Units: 14,000.
Programming (via satellite): Cinemax (multiplexed).
Fee: $14.95 installation; $10.95 monthly.

Digital Pay Service 2
Pay Units: 25,300.
Programming (via satellite): HBO; HBO (multiplexed).
Fee: $14.95 installation; $10.95 monthly.

Digital Pay Service 3
Pay Units: 8,500.
Programming (via satellite): Showtime; Showtime (multiplexed).
Fee: $14.95 installation; $10.95 monthly.

Digital Pay Service 4
Pay Units: 3,100.
Programming (via satellite): The Movie Channel (multiplexed).
Fee: $14.95 installation; $10.95 monthly.

Digital Pay Service 5
Pay Units: N.A.
Programming (via satellite): Starz (multiplexed); The New Encore.
Fee: $10.95 monthly.

Video-On-Demand: Yes

Pay-Per-View
Addressable homes: 150,000.
iN DEMAND (delivered digitally), Addressable: Yes; Playboy TV (delivered digitally); Pleasure (delivered digitally).

Internet Service
Operational: Yes.
Subscribers: 88,701.
Broadband Service: Road Runner.
Fee: $44.95 monthly.

Telephone Service
Digital: Operational
Fee: $49.95 monthly

Miles of Plant: 429.0 (coaxial); 3,765.0 (fiber optic). Homes passed: 510,103. Total homes in franchised area: 510,103.

Division President: Kevin Hyman. Vice President, Engineering: Gene White. Manager: Mike Robertson. Marketing Director: Mike Betts. Chief Technician: Steve Eichler. Customer Service Manager: Ellen Adams.

City fee: 5% of gross (St. Petersburg).

Ownership: Bright House Networks LLC (MSO).

PINELLAS COUNTY—Knology, 3001 Gandy Blvd, Pinellas Park, FL 33782-6200. Phones: 727-239-1000 (customer service); 706-645-8553 (Corporate office). Fax: 727-576-4800. Web Site: http://www.knology.com. Also serves Clearwater, Dunedin, Largo, Oldsmar, Safety Harbor, Seminole, St. Petersburg & Tarpon Springs. ICA: FL0339. **Note:** This system is an overbuild.

TV Market Ranking: 28 (Clearwater, Dunedin, Largo, Oldsmar, PINELLAS COUNTY, Safety Harbor, Seminole, St. Petersburg, Tarpon Springs). Franchise award date: N.A. Franchise expiration date: N.A. Began: N.A.

Channel capacity: N.A. Channels available but not in use: N.A.

Basic Service
Subscribers: 77,186.
Programming (received off-air): WCLF (IND) Clearwater; WEDU (PBS) Tampa; WFLA-TV (NBC) Tampa; WFTS-TV (ABC) Tampa; WFTT-DT (TEL) Tampa; WMOR-TV (IND) Lakeland; WTOG (CW) St. Petersburg; WTSP (CBS) St. Petersburg; WTTA (MNT) St. Petersburg; WTVT (FOX) Tampa; WUSF-TV (PBS) Tampa; WVEA-TV (UNV) Venice.
Programming (via satellite): ABC Family Channel; AMC; Animal Planet; Arts & Entertainment; BET Networks; Bio; Bravo; Cartoon Network; CNBC; CNN; Comedy Central; Country Music TV; C-SPAN; Discovery Channel; Discovery Health Channel; Disney Channel; E! Entertainment Television; ESPN; ESPN 2; ESPN Classic Sports; FitTV; Food Network; Fox News Channel; Fox Sports Net Florida; FX; G4; GalaVision; Golf Channel; GSN; Hallmark Channel; Headline News; HGTV; History Channel; Home Shopping Network; ION Television; Lifetime; Lifetime Movie Network; Local Cable Weather; MTV; National Geographic Channel; Nickelodeon; Outdoor Channel; Oxygen; QVC; ShopNBC; Speed Channel; Spike TV; SunSports TV; Syfy; TBS Superstation; The Learning Channel; Travel Channel; truTV; Turner Classic Movies; Turner Network TV; TV Land; USA Network; Versus; VH1; Weather Channel; WGN America.
Current originations: Leased Access; Religious Access; Government Access; Educational Access; Public Access.
Fee: $45.95 monthly.

Digital Basic Service
Subscribers: N.A. Included in Valley AL
Programming (received off-air): WEDU (PBS) Tampa; WFLA-TV (NBC) Tampa; WFTS-TV (ABC) Tampa; WTSP (CBS) St. Petersburg; WTVT (FOX) Tampa.
Programming (via satellite): American-Life TV Network; Animal Planet HD; BBC America; Boomerang; CBS College Sports Network; CMT Pure Country; C-SPAN 2; C-SPAN 3; Current; Discovery Channel HD; Discovery HD Theater; Discovery Kids Channel; Discovery Military Channel; Discovery Planet Green; Do-It-Yourself; ESPN 2 HD; ESPN HD; ESPN U; ESPNews; Eternal Word TV Network; Florida Channel; Fox College Sports Atlantic; Fox College Sports Central; Fox College Sports Pacific; Fox Soccer; FSN HD; Fuel TV; Fuse; Hallmark Movie Channel; HDNet; HDNet Movies; History Channel International; ID Investigation Discovery; Independent Film Channel; INSP; Jewelry Television; Lifetime Real Women; MSNBC; MTV Hits; MTV Jams; MTV Tres; MTV2; mtvU; Music Choice; National Geographic Channel HD Network; NFL Network; NFL Network HD; Nick Jr.; Nick Too; NickToons TV; PBS World; Pentagon Channel; QVC HD; Science Channel; Shop at Home; SoapNet; TBS in HD; TeenNick; Telemundo; Tennis Channel; The Sportsman Channel; TLC HD; Trinity Broadcasting Network; Turner Network TV HD; Universal HD; Versus HD; VH1 Classic; VH1 Soul; V-me TV; WE tv; Weatherscan.

Digital Pay Service 1
Pay Units: N.A.
Programming (via satellite): Cinemax (multiplexed); Cinemax HD; Encore (multiplexed); Flix; HBO (multiplexed); HBO HD; Playboy TV; Showtime (multiplexed); Showtime HD; Starz (multiplexed); Starz HDTV; The Movie Channel (multiplexed).

Video-On-Demand: No

Pay-Per-View
iN DEMAND (delivered digitally); ESPN (delivered digitally); Hot Choice (delivered digitally); Spice: Xcess (delivered digitally); Playboy TV (delivered digitally); Club Jenna (delivered digitally); Penthouse TV (delivered digitally); Ten Clips (delivered digitally).

Internet Service
Operational: Yes.
Broadband Service: Knology.Net.
Fee: $29.95 installation; $54.95 monthly.

Telephone Service
Digital: Operational
Fee: $18.91 monthly

Miles of Plant: 2,100.0 (coaxial); None (fiber optic). Homes passed: 274,000. Miles of plant include both coax & fiber

General Manager: Chuck Blaine. Technical Operations Manager: Tim Kimbler. Marketing Director: Richard Lightle.
Ownership: Knology Inc. (MSO).

POLK COUNTY—Formerly served by People's Wireless Cable. No longer in operation. ICA: FL0307.

PORT CHARLOTTE—Comcast Cable, 5205 Fruitville Rd, Sarasota, FL 34232. Phones: 941-371-4444; 941-371-6700 (Customer service). Fax: 941-371-5097. Web Site: http://www.comcast.com. Also serves Charlotte County (unincorporated areas) & Punta Gorda. ICA: FL0044.
TV Market Ranking: Below 100 (Charlotte County (unincorporated areas), PORT CHARLOTTE, Punta Gorda). Franchise award date: September 1, 1964. Franchise expiration date: N.A. Began: January 1, 1965.
Channel capacity: N.A. Channels available but not in use: N.A.
Basic Service
Subscribers: 28,356.
Programming (received off-air): WBBH-TV (NBC) Fort Myers; WFTX-TV (FOX) Cape Coral; WGCU (PBS) Fort Myers; WINK-TV (CBS) Fort Myers; WRXY-TV (IND) Tice; WUVF-CA (UNV) Naples; WWSB (ABC) Sarasota; WXCW (CW) Naples; WZVN-TV (ABC) Naples; allband FM.
Programming (via satellite): C-SPAN; Eternal Word TV Network; Hallmark Channel; ION Television; MyNetworkTV Inc.; QVC; WGN America.
Current originations: Leased Access; Government Access.
Fee: $63.35 installation; $12.55 monthly.
Expanded Basic Service 1
Subscribers: N.A.
Programming (via satellite): ABC Family Channel; AMC; Animal Planet; Arts & Entertainment; BET Networks; Bravo; Cartoon Network; CNBC; CNN; Comcast/Charter Sports Southeast (CSS); Comedy Central; Country Music TV; Discovery Channel; Discovery Health Channel; E! Entertainment Television; ESPN; ESPN 2; Food Network; Fox News Channel; Fox Sports Net; FX; Golf Channel; Headline News; HGTV; History Channel; Home Shopping Network; Jewelry Television; Lifetime; MSNBC; MTV; Nickelodeon; Speed Channel; Spike TV; Style Network; SunSports TV; Syfy; TBS Superstation; The Learning Channel; Travel Channel; truTV; Turner Classic Movies; Turner Network TV; TV Guide Network; TV Land; USA Network; Versus; VH1; Weather Channel.
Fee: $38.40 monthly.
Digital Basic Service
Subscribers: 7,089.
Programming (received off-air): WBBH-TV (NBC) Fort Myers; WFTX-TV (FOX) Cape Coral; WGCU (PBS) Fort Myers; WINK-TV (CBS) Fort Myers; WZVN-TV (ABC) Naples.
Programming (via satellite): Arts & Entertainment HD; BBC America; Bio; CMT Pure Country; Cooking Channel; C-SPAN 2; C-SPAN 3; Current; Discovery Digital Networks; Discovery HD Theater; Disney Channel; Do-It-Yourself; Encore (multiplexed); ESPN 2 HD; ESPN HD; ESPNews; Eternal Word TV Network; Flix; Fox College Sports Atlantic; Fox College Sports Central; Fox College Sports Pacific; Fox Reality Channel; Fox Soccer; G4; GAS; Gol TV; Great American Country; GSN; History Channel International; INHD; Lifetime Movie Network; LOGO; MoviePlex; MTV Networks Digital Suite; Music Choice; National Geographic Channel; National Geographic Channel HD Network; NBA TV; Nick Jr.; Nick Too; NickToons TV; Outdoor Channel; Palladia; PBS Kids Sprout; Playboy TV; ShopNBC; Showcase Television; SoapNet; Sundance Channel; Tennis Channel; The Sportsman Channel; Toon Disney; Turner Network TV HD; TV One; TVG Network; Universal HD; Versus HD; WE tv; Weatherscan.
Fee: $14.95 monthly.
Pay Service 1
Pay Units: 9,600.
Programming (via satellite): HBO.
Fee: $12.95 monthly.
Digital Pay Service 1
Pay Units: N.A.
Programming (via satellite): Cinemax (multiplexed); Cinemax HD; HBO (multiplexed); HBO HD; Showtime (multiplexed); Showtime HD; Starz (multiplexed); Starz HDTV; The Movie Channel (multiplexed).
Fee: $13.50 monthly (each).
Video-On-Demand: Yes
Pay-Per-View
Addressable homes: 7,089.
iN DEMAND (delivered digitally), Addressable: Yes; Hot Choice (delivered digitally); Playboy TV (delivered digitally); SunSports TV (delivered digitally); Sports PPV (delivered digitally); NBA League Pass (delivered digitally).
Internet Service
Operational: Yes.
Subscribers: 3,119.
Broadband Service: Comcast High Speed Internet.
Fee: $42.95 monthly; $7.00 modem lease; $199.00 modem purchase.
Telephone Service
Digital: Operational
Fee: $29.95 installation; $44.95 monthly
Miles of Plant: 762.0 (coaxial); None (fiber optic). Homes passed: 34,297. Total homes in franchised area: 40,192.
Regional Vice President: Rod Dagenais. Vice President & General Manager: Steve Dvoskin. Technical Operations Director: Danny Maxwell. Technical Operations Manager: Andrew Behn. Marketing Director: Vince Maffeo.
City fee: 3% of gross.
Ownership: Comcast Cable Communications Inc. (MSO).

PORT ST. JOE—Mediacom. Now served by WEWAHITCHKA, FL [FL0159]. ICA: FL0142.

PUTNAM COUNTY—Formerly served by Florida Cable. No longer in operation. ICA: FL0272.

PUTNAM COUNTY (eastern portion)—Florida Cable, PO Box 498, 23748 State Rd 40, Astor, FL 32102-0498. Phones: 352-759-2788; 800-779-2788. Fax: 352-759-2788. E-mail: support@floridacable.com. Web Site: http://www.floridacable.com. Also serves Bostwick & Palatka. ICA: FL0271.
TV Market Ranking: Below 100 (Bostwick, PUTNAM COUNTY (EASTERN PORTION) (portions)); Outside TV Markets (Palatka, PUTNAM COUNTY (EASTERN PORTION) (portions)). Franchise award date: N.A. Franchise expiration date: N.A. Began: N.A.
Channel capacity: 41 (not 2-way capable). Channels available but not in use: 2.
Basic Service
Subscribers: 192.
Programming (received off-air): WAWS (FOX, MNT) Jacksonville; WCWJ (CW) Jacksonville; WJCT (PBS) Jacksonville; WJGV-CD (IND) Palatka; WJXT (IND) Jacksonville; WJXX (ABC) Orange Park; WTEV-TV (CBS) Jacksonville; WTLV (NBC) Jacksonville; WUFT (PBS) Gainesville.
Programming (via satellite): ABC Family Channel; Animal Planet; Arts & Entertainment; Cartoon Network; CNN; Comedy Central; C-SPAN; Discovery Channel; Disney Channel; ESPN; Food Network; Fox News Channel; Fuse; FX; Great American Country; Headline News; Home Shopping Network; Lifetime; Speed Channel; Syfy; TBS Superstation; Travel Channel; Turner Network TV; USA Network; Weather Channel; WGN America.
Fee: $39.45 monthly.
Pay Service 1
Pay Units: 103.
Programming (via satellite): Cinemax; HBO; Showtime; The Movie Channel.
Fee: $9.95 monthly (each).
Internet Service
Operational: No.
Telephone Service
None
Miles of Plant: 45.0 (coaxial); None (fiber optic). Homes passed: 916.
General Manager: Jim Pierce. Plant Manager: Larry English. Office Manager: Alita Dawson.
Ownership: Florida Cable Inc. (MSO).

PUTNAM COUNTY (western portion)—Florida Cable, PO Box 498, 23748 State Rd 40, Astor, FL 32102-0498. Phone: 352-759-2788. Fax: 352-759-3577. Web Site: http://www.floridacable.com. Also serves Hawthorne. ICA: FL0371.
TV Market Ranking: Below 100 (Hawthorne, PUTNAM COUNTY (WESTERN PORTION)).
Channel capacity: N.A. Channels available but not in use: N.A.
Basic Service
Subscribers: 521.
Programming (received off-air): WAWS (FOX, MNT) Jacksonville; WCJB-TV (ABC, CW) Gainesville; WCWJ (CW) Jacksonville; WESH (NBC) Daytona Beach; WJXT (IND) Jacksonville; WJXX (ABC) Orange Park; WKMG-TV (CBS) Orlando; WOGX (FOX) Ocala; WTEV-TV (CBS) Jacksonville; WTLV (NBC) Jacksonville; WUFT (PBS) Gainesville.
Programming (via satellite): ABC Family Channel; Animal Planet; Arts & Entertainment; BET Networks; Cartoon Network; CNN; Comedy Central; Discovery Channel; Disney Channel; ESPN; Fox News Channel; Fuse; FX; Great American Country; Headline News; Lifetime; QVC; Speed Channel; Syfy; TBS Superstation; Turner Classic Movies; Turner Network TV; USA Network; Weather Channel; WGN America.
Pay Service 1
Pay Units: N.A.
Programming (via satellite): Cinemax; HBO; Showtime.
Internet Service
Operational: No.
Telephone Service
None
Miles of Plant: 7.0 (coaxial); None (fiber optic). Homes passed: 1,083.
General Manager: Jim Pierce. Plant Manager: Larry English. Office Manager: Alita Dawson.
Ownership: Florida Cable Inc. (MSO).

QUINCY—Comcast Cable. Now served by TALLAHASSEE, FL [FL0283]. ICA: FL0273.

RIVER RANCH—SAT STAR Communications, 5155 Rio Vista Ave, Tampa, FL 33634. Phone: 800-445-1139. Fax: 813-249-2809. ICA: FL0161.
TV Market Ranking: 28 (RIVER RANCH). Franchise award date: December 1, 1989. Franchise expiration date: N.A. Began: June 1, 1990.
Channel capacity: 63 (not 2-way capable). Channels available but not in use: 26.
Basic Service
Subscribers: 450.
Programming (received off-air): WEDU (PBS) Tampa; WFLA-TV (NBC) Tampa; WFTS-TV (ABC) Tampa; WFTV (ABC) Orlando; WKMG-TV (CBS) Orlando; WMOR-TV (IND) Lakeland; WOPX-TV (ION) Melbourne; WTOG (CW) St. Petersburg; WTVT (FOX) Tampa.
Programming (via satellite): ABC Family Channel; AMC; Arts & Entertainment; CNBC; CNN; Country Music TV; C-SPAN; Discovery Channel; Disney Channel; ESPN; Headline News; Lifetime; QVC; Spike TV; Syfy; TBS Superstation; Travel Channel; Turner Network TV; USA Network; Weather Channel; WGN America.
Fee: $40.00 installation; $28.47 monthly.
Pay Service 1
Pay Units: N.A.
Programming (via satellite): Encore; HBO; Showtime; The Movie Channel.
Fee: $6.95 monthly (Encore), $10.95 monthly (Showtime or TMC), $12.95 monthly (HBO).
Internet Service
Operational: No.
Telephone Service
None
Miles of Plant: 1.0 (coaxial); None (fiber optic).
Vice President, Operations: George Gioe.
Ownership: SAT STAR Communications.

SAMSULA—Formerly served by Consolidated Cablevision. No longer in operation. ICA: FL0287.

SANDESTIN BEACH RESORT—Mediacom. Now served by WEWAHITCHKA, FL [FL0159]. ICA: FL0276.

SAND-N-SEA—Now served by STUART, FL [FL0024]. ICA: FL0275.

SARALAKE ESTATES MOBILE HOME PARK—Nalman Electronics, 4440 26th St W, Bradenton, FL 34207. Phone: 941-758-5533. Fax: 941-756-5460. ICA: FL0277.
TV Market Ranking: 28 (SARALAKE ESTATES). Franchise award date: N.A. Franchise expiration date: N.A. Began: January 1, 1971.
Channel capacity: 35 (not 2-way capable). Channels available but not in use: N.A.
Basic Service
Subscribers: N.A.
Programming (received off-air): WEDU (PBS) Tampa; WFLA-TV (NBC) Tampa; WFTS-TV (ABC) Tampa; WINK-TV (CBS) Fort Myers; WMYT-TV (MNT) Rock Hill; WTOG (CW) St. Petersburg; WTSP (CBS) St. Petersburg; WTTA (MNT) St. Petersburg; WTVT (FOX) Tampa; WUSF-TV (PBS) Tampa; WWSB (ABC) Sarasota; WXPX-TV (ION) Bradenton.
Programming (via satellite): ABC Family Channel; Arts & Entertainment; CNN; Discovery Channel; ESPN; Headline News; Lifetime; Spike TV; TBS Superstation; Turner Network TV; USA Network; WGN America.

Current originations: Religious Access.
Fee: $3.00 monthly.
Internet Service
Operational: No.
Miles of Plant: 1.0 (coaxial); None (fiber optic).
Manager: Sharon Douglas.
Ownership: Nalman Electronics.

SARASOTA—Comcast Cable, 5205 Fruitville Rd, Sarasota, FL 34232. Phone: 941-371-4444. Fax: 941-371-5097. Web Site: http://www.comcast.com. Also serves Longboat Key, Manatee County (portions) & Sarasota County. ICA: FL0017.
TV Market Ranking: 28 (Longboat Key, Manatee County (portions) (portions), SARASOTA, Sarasota County (portions)); Below 100 (Manatee County (portions) (portions), Sarasota County (portions)). Franchise award date: August 1, 1962. Franchise expiration date: N.A. Began: January 1, 1962.
Channel capacity: N.A. Channels available but not in use: N.A.
Basic Service
Subscribers: 56,484.
Programming (received off-air): WCLF (IND) Clearwater; WEDU (PBS) Tampa; WFLA-TV (NBC) Tampa; WFTS-TV (ABC) Tampa; WMOR-TV (IND) Lakeland; WTOG (CW) St. Petersburg; WTSP (CBS) St. Petersburg; WTTA (MNT) St. Petersburg; WTVT (FOX) Tampa; WUSF-TV (PBS) Tampa; WVEA-TV (UNV) Venice; WWSB (ABC) Sarasota; WXPX-TV (ION) Bradenton; 16 FMs.
Programming (via satellite): C-SPAN; Fox Sports Net; FX; Jewelry Television; QVC; TV Guide Network; WGN America.
Current originations: Government Access; Educational Access; Public Access.
Fee: $63.35 installation; $12.55 monthly.
Expanded Basic Service 1
Subscribers: N.A.
Programming (via satellite): ABC Family Channel; AMC; Animal Planet; Arts & Entertainment; BET Networks; Bravo; Cartoon Network; CNBC; CNN; Comcast/Charter Sports Southeast (CSS); Comedy Central; Country Music TV; C-SPAN 2; Discovery Channel; Discovery Health Channel; E! Entertainment Television; ESPN; ESPN 2; Food Network; Fox News Channel; Golf Channel; GSN; Headline News; HGTV; History Channel; Home Shopping Network; Lifetime; MSNBC; MTV; Nickelodeon; Speed Channel; Spike TV; Style Network; SunSports TV; Syfy; TBS Superstation; The Learning Channel; truTV; Turner Classic Movies; Turner Network TV; TV Land; USA Network; Versus; VH1; WE tv; Weather Channel.
Fee: $34.95 monthly.
Digital Basic Service
Subscribers: 14,121.
Programming (received off-air): WEDU (PBS) Tampa; WFLA-TV (NBC) Tampa; WTOG (CW) St. Petersburg; WTSP (CBS) St. Petersburg; WTTA (MNT) St. Petersburg; WTVT (FOX) Tampa; WWSB (ABC) Sarasota.
Programming (via satellite): ABC Family HD; Animal Planet HD; Arts & Entertainment HD; BBC America; Big Ten Network; Bio; Cartoon Network; CMT Pure Country; CNN HD; Cooking Channel; C-SPAN 2; C-SPAN 3; Current; Discovery Channel HD; Discovery Kids Channel; Discovery Military Channel; Discovery Planet Green; Disney Channel; Disney Channel HD; Do-It-Yourself; Encore (multiplexed); ESPN 2 HD; ESPN HD; ESPNews; Eternal Word TV Network; Flix; Food Network HD; Fox Business Channel; Fox College Sports Atlantic; Fox College Sports Central; Fox College Sports Pacific; Fox News HD; Fox Reality Channel; Fuse; FX HD; G4; Gol TV; Golf Channel HD; Great American Country; GSN; Hallmark Movie Channel; HDNet; HGTV HD; History Channel; History Channel HD; History Channel International; ID Investigation Discovery; Independent Film Channel; Jewelry Television; Lifetime Movie Network; LOGO; MLB Network; MoviePlex; MTV Hits; MTV Tres; MTV2; Music Choice; National Geographic Channel; National Geographic Channel HD Network; NBA TV; NFL Network; NHL Network; Nick Jr.; Nick Too; NickToons TV; Outdoor Channel; Oxygen; PBS Kids Sprout; Retro Television Network; Science Channel; Science Channel HD; ShopNBC; SoapNet; Speed HD; Sundance Channel; SunSports TV; Syfy HD; TBS in HD; TeenNick; Tennis Channel; The Sportsman Channel; TLC HD; Toon Disney; Turner Network TV HD; TV One; TVG Network; Universal HD; USA Network HD; Versus HD; VH1 Classic; VH1 Soul; WE tv.
Fee: $14.95 monthly.
Digital Pay Service 1
Pay Units: N.A.
Programming (via satellite): Cinemax (multiplexed); Cinemax HD; HBO (multiplexed); HBO HD; Showtime (multiplexed); Showtime HD; Starz (multiplexed); Starz HDTV; The Movie Channel (multiplexed).
Fee: $13.50 monthly (each).
Video-On-Demand: Yes
Pay-Per-View
Addressable homes: 14,121.
iN DEMAND (delivered digitally), Addressable: Yes; Penthouse TV (delivered digitally); Playboy TV (delivered digitally); Fresh (delivered digitally); Shorteez (delivered digitally); Pleasure (delivered digitally).
Internet Service
Operational: Yes.
Subscribers: 6,213.
Broadband Service: Comcast High Speed Internet.
Fee: $42.95 monthly; $7.00 modem lease; $199.00 modem purchase.
Telephone Service
Digital: Operational
Fee: $29.95 installation; $44.95 monthly
Miles of Plant: 1,252.0 (coaxial); None (fiber optic). Homes passed: 105,771. Total homes in franchised area: 131,731.
Regional Vice President: Rod Dagenais. Vice President & General Manager: Steve Dvoskin. Technical Operations Director: Danny Maxwell. Technical Operations Manager: Andrew Behn. Marketing Director: Vince Maffeo.
City fee: 4% of gross (Longboat Key & Sarasota).
Ownership: Comcast Cable Communications Inc. (MSO).

SEBASTIAN—Comcast Cable. Now served by VERO BEACH, FL [FL0040]. ICA: FL0077.

SEBRING—Comcast Cable, 5205 Fruitville Rd, Sarasota, FL 34232. Phone: 941-371-4444. Fax: 941-371-5097. Web Site: http://www.comcast.com. Also serves Avon Park, Avon Park AFB, Highlands County (portions) & Lake Placid. ICA: FL0063.
TV Market Ranking: Outside TV Markets (Avon Park, Avon Park AFB, Highlands County (portions), Lake Placid, SEBRING). Franchise award date: January 1, 1963. Franchise expiration date: N.A. Began: January 1, 1963.
Channel capacity: N.A. Channels available but not in use: N.A.
Basic Service
Subscribers: 12,518.
Programming (received off-air): WCLF (IND) Clearwater; WEDU (PBS) Tampa; WFLA-TV (NBC) Tampa; WFTS-TV (ABC) Tampa; WFTT-DT (TEL) Tampa; WFTV (ABC) Orlando; WINK-TV (CBS) Fort Myers; WMOR-TV (IND) Lakeland; WTOG (CW) St. Petersburg; WTTA (MNT) St. Petersburg; WTVT (FOX) Tampa; WVEA-TV (UNV) Venice; allband FM.
Programming (via satellite): Comcast/Charter Sports Southeast (CSS); C-SPAN; Eternal Word TV Network; INSP; ION Television; QVC; Speed Channel; SunSports TV; Syfy; TBS Superstation; TV Guide Network; Versus; Weather Channel; WGN America.
Fee: $63.35 installation; $13.75 monthly.
Expanded Basic Service 1
Subscribers: N.A.
Programming (via satellite): ABC Family Channel; AMC; Animal Planet; Arts & Entertainment; BET Networks; Bravo; Cartoon Network; CNBC; CNN; Discovery Channel; Discovery Health Channel; E! Entertainment Television; ESPN; ESPN 2; Food Network; Fox News Channel; Golf Channel; Great American Country; GSN; Headline News; HGTV; History Channel; Home Shopping Network; Lifetime; MSNBC; MTV; Nickelodeon; Spike TV; Style Network; The Learning Channel; truTV; Turner Network TV; TV Land; USA Network; VH1.
Fee: $47.50 monthly.
Digital Basic Service
Subscribers: 3,130.
Programming (received off-air): WEDU (PBS) Tampa; WTSP (CBS) St. Petersburg.
Programming (via satellite): BBC America; Cine Latino; CMT Pure Country; CNN en Espanol; Discovery Kids Channel; Discovery Military Channel; Discovery Planet Green; Disney Channel; Do-It-Yourself; Encore (multiplexed); ESPNews; Flix; Fox Business Channel; Fox Sports en Espanol; HDNet; ID Investigation Discovery; MoviePlex; MTV Tres; MTV2; Music Choice; National Geographic Channel; Nick Jr.; Nick Too; PBS Kids Sprout; Science Channel; SoapNet; Sundance Channel; TeenNick; Toon Disney; Toon Disney en Espanol; TVE Internacional; Utilisima; VH1 Classic; VH1 Soul; WE tv; WFTS-TV (ABC) Tampa.
Fee: $14.95 monthly.
Digital Pay Service 1
Pay Units: N.A.
Programming (via satellite): Cinemax (multiplexed); HBO (multiplexed); Showtime (multiplexed); Starz (multiplexed); The Movie Channel (multiplexed).
Fee: $13.50 monthly (each).
Video-On-Demand: No
Pay-Per-View
Addressable homes: 3,130.
Hot Choice, Addressable: Yes; iN DEMAND; Playboy TV; iN DEMAND (delivered digitally); Playboy TV (delivered digitally); Pleasure (delivered digitally); Fresh (delivered digitally); Shorteez (delivered digitally).
Internet Service
Operational: Yes.
Subscribers: 1,377.
Broadband Service: Comcast High Speed Internet.
Fee: $42.95 monthly.
Telephone Service
Digital: Operational
Miles of Plant: 327.0 (coaxial); None (fiber optic). Additional miles planned: 10.0 (coaxial). Homes passed: 15,268. Total homes in franchised area: 15,846.
Regional Vice President: Rod Dagenais. Vice President & General Manager: Steve Dvoskin. Technical Operations Director: Danny Maxwell. Technical Operations Manager: Andrew Behn. Marketing Director: Vince Maffeo.
City fee: 3% of gross.
Ownership: Comcast Cable Communications Inc. (MSO).

SHARPES FERRY—Florida Cable, PO Box 498, 23748 State Rd 40, Astor, FL 32102-0498. Phones: 352-759-2788; 800-779-2788. Fax: 352-759-3797. E-mail: support@floridacable.com. Web Site: http://www.floridacable.com. ICA: FL0365.
TV Market Ranking: Below 100 (SHARPES FERRY).
Channel capacity: 36 (not 2-way capable). Channels available but not in use: None.
Basic Service
Subscribers: 262.
Programming (received off-air): WACX (IND) Leesburg; WCJB-TV (ABC, CW) Gainesville; WESH (NBC) Daytona Beach; WFTV (ABC) Orlando; WKCF (CW) Clermont; WKMG-TV (CBS) Orlando; WOFL (FOX) Orlando; WOGX (FOX) Ocala; WRBW (MNT) Orlando; WUFT (PBS) Gainesville.
Programming (via satellite): ABC Family Channel; AmericanLife TV Network; Arts & Entertainment; Cartoon Network; CNN; Comedy Central; Discovery Channel; Disney Channel; ESPN; Food Network; Fox News Channel; FX; Great American Country; Headline News; Home Shopping Network; Lifetime; Speed Channel; Spike TV; Syfy; TBS Superstation; Turner Classic Movies; USA Network; Weather Channel; WGN America.
Fee: $39.45 monthly.
Pay Service 1
Pay Units: N.A.
Programming (via satellite): Cinemax; HBO; Showtime.
Internet Service
Operational: No.
Telephone Service
None
Miles of Plant: 20.0 (coaxial); None (fiber optic). Homes passed: 550.
General Manager: Jim Pierce. Plant Manager: Larry English. Office Manager: Alita Dawson.
Ownership: Florida Cable Inc. (MSO).

SILVER SPRINGS SHORES—Comcast Cable, 8130 County Rd 44, Leg A, Leesburg, FL 34788. Phone: 352-787-9601. Fax: 352-365-6279. Web Site: http://www.comcast.com. Also serves Rolling Greens. ICA: FL0112.
TV Market Ranking: Below 100 (Rolling Greens, SILVER SPRINGS SHORES). Franchise award date: N.A. Franchise expiration date: N.A. Began: May 1, 1975.
Channel capacity: N.A. Channels available but not in use: N.A.
Basic Service
Subscribers: N.A. Included in Celebration
Programming (received off-air): WACX (IND) Leesburg; WESH (NBC) Daytona Beach; WFTV (ABC) Orlando; WHLV-TV (IND) Cocoa; WKCF (CW) Clermont; WKMG-TV (CBS) Orlando; WMFE-TV (PBS)

Orlando; WOFL (FOX) Orlando; WOPX-TV (ION) Melbourne; WRBW (MNT) Orlando; WRDQ (IND) Orlando; WVEN-TV (UNV) Daytona Beach.
Programming (via satellite): C-SPAN 2; TV Guide Network; WGN America.
Fee: $36.95 installation; $12.00 monthly.

Expanded Basic Service 1
Subscribers: N.A. Included in Celebration
Programming (via satellite): ABC Family Channel; AMC; Animal Planet; Arts & Entertainment; BET Networks; Bravo; Cartoon Network; CNBC; CNN; Comcast/Charter Sports Southeast (CSS); Comedy Central; Country Music TV; C-SPAN; Discovery Channel; Discovery Health Channel; Disney Channel; E! Entertainment Television; ESPN; ESPN 2; Eternal Word TV Network; Food Network; Fox News Channel; FX; Golf Channel; GSN; Headline News; HGTV; History Channel; Home Shopping Network 2; Jewelry Television; Lifetime; MSNBC; MTV; Nickelodeon; QVC; Shop at Home; Speed Channel; Spike TV; Style Network; SunSports TV; Syfy; TBS Superstation; The Learning Channel; Turner Network TV; TV Land; USA Network; Versus; VH1; Weather Channel.
Fee: $42.95 monthly.

Digital Basic Service
Subscribers: N.A. Included in Celebration
Programming (via satellite): BBC America; C-SPAN 3; Discovery Digital Networks; Encore Action; ESPNews; Flix; GAS; MTV Networks Digital Suite; Music Choice; Nick Jr.; Nick Too; SoapNet; Sundance Channel; Toon Disney; Weatherscan.
Fee: $14.95 monthly.

Pay Service 1
Pay Units: 540.
Programming (via satellite): Cinemax.
Fee: $1.99 installation; $9.00 monthly.

Pay Service 2
Pay Units: 826.
Programming (via satellite): HBO.
Fee: $1.99 installation; $12.00 monthly.

Pay Service 3
Pay Units: 431.
Programming (via satellite): Showtime.
Fee: $1.99 installation; $9.00 monthly.

Digital Pay Service 1
Pay Units: N.A. Included in Celebration
Programming (via satellite): Cinemax (multiplexed); HBO (multiplexed); Showtime (multiplexed); Starz (multiplexed); The Movie Channel (multiplexed).
Fee: $7.95 monthly (each).

Video-On-Demand: Planned

Pay-Per-View
Addressable homes: 1,614.
iN DEMAND, Addressable: Yes; iN DEMAND (delivered digitally); Playboy TV (delivered digitally); Fresh (delivered digitally); Shorteez (delivered digitally); Pleasure (delivered digitally); ESPN Now (delivered digitally); ESPN Extra (delivered digitally); NBA TV (delivered digitally).

Internet Service
Operational: Yes.
Broadband Service: Comcast High Speed Internet.
Fee: $42.95 monthly.

Telephone Service
Digital: Operational

Homes passed included in Celebration

Vice President & General Manager: Mike Davenport. Marketing Manager: Melanie Melvin. Chief Engineer: Sean Curley.

Ownership: Comcast Cable Communications Inc. (MSO).

SMITH LAKE SHORES MOBILE HOME PARK—Florida Cable, PO Box 498, 23748 State Rd 40, Astor, FL 32102-0498. Phones: 352-759-2788; 800-779-2788. Fax: 352-759-3797. E-mail: support@floridacable.com. Web Site: http://www.floridacable.com. ICA: FL0366.

TV Market Ranking: Below 100 (SMITH LAKE SHORES MOBILE HOME PARK).

Channel capacity: 36 (not 2-way capable). Channels available but not in use: 10.

Basic Service
Subscribers: 58.
Programming (received off-air): WACX (IND) Leesburg; WCJB-TV (ABC, CW) Gainesville; WESH (NBC) Daytona Beach; WKCF (CW) Clermont; WKMG-TV (CBS) Orlando; WOFL (FOX) Orlando; WOGX (FOX) Ocala; WRBW (MNT) Orlando; WUFT (PBS) Gainesville.
Programming (via satellite): ABC Family Channel; AMC; Arts & Entertainment; CNN; Discovery Channel; ESPN; Headline News; History Channel; Lifetime; QVC; Speed Channel; Syfy; TBS Superstation; USA Network; Weather Channel; WGN America.
Fee: $23.45 monthly.

Pay Service 1
Pay Units: N.A.
Programming (via satellite): HBO.

Internet Service
Operational: No.

Telephone Service
None

Miles of Plant: 3.0 (coaxial); None (fiber optic). Homes passed: 101.

General Manager: Jim Pierce. Plant Manager: Larry English. Office Manager: Alita Dawson.

Ownership: Florida Cable Inc. (MSO).

SOUTH BROWARD COUNTY—Comcast Cable. No longer in operation. ICA: FL0374.

SOUTHPORT—Mediacom. Now served by WEWAHITCHKA, FL [FL0159]. ICA: FL0119.

SPRING LAKE—Comcast Cable, 5205 Fruitville Rd, Sarasota, FL 34232. Phone: 941-371-4444. Fax: 941-371-5097. Web Site: http://www.comcast.com. Also serves Lorida. ICA: FL0280.

TV Market Ranking: Outside TV Markets (Lorida, SPRING LAKE). Franchise award date: N.A. Franchise expiration date: N.A. Began: January 1, 1984.

Channel capacity: N.A. Channels available but not in use: N.A.

Basic Service
Subscribers: 702.
Programming (received off-air): WBBH-TV (NBC) Fort Myers; WCLF (IND) Clearwater; WEDU (PBS) Tampa; WFLA-TV (NBC) Tampa; WFTS-TV (ABC) Tampa; WFTT-DT (TEL) Tampa; WINK-TV (CBS) Fort Myers; WMOR-TV (IND) Lakeland; WTOG (CW) St. Petersburg; WTTA (MNT) St. Petersburg; WTVT (FOX) Tampa; WVEA-TV (UNV) Venice; WWSB (ABC) Sarasota.
Programming (via satellite): ABC Family Channel; AMC; Arts & Entertainment; BET Networks; Cartoon Network; CNBC; CNN; Comcast/Charter Sports Southeast (CSS); C-SPAN; Discovery Channel; Discovery Health Channel; E! Entertainment Television; ESPN; Eternal Word TV Network; Food Network; Fox News Channel; Golf Channel; Great American Country; GSN; Headline News; HGTV; History Channel; Home Shopping Network; INSP; ION Television; Lifetime; MSNBC; MTV; Nickelodeon; QVC; Spike TV; Style Network; SunSports TV; Syfy; TBS Superstation; The Learning Channel; truTV; Turner Network TV; TV Guide Network; TV Land; USA Network; Versus; VH1; Weather Channel; WGN America.
Fee: $63.35 installation; $22.45 monthly.

Pay Service 1
Pay Units: N.A.
Programming (via satellite): Cinemax; HBO; Showtime.
Fee: $9.95 monthly (each).

Video-On-Demand: No

Pay-Per-View
Addressable homes: 175.
iN DEMAND, Addressable: Yes; Playboy TV; Hot Choice; iN DEMAND (delivered digitally); Hot Choice (delivered digitally); Playboy TV (delivered digitally); Fresh (delivered digitally); Shorteez (delivered digitally); Pleasure (delivered digitally); NBA TV (delivered digitally).

Internet Service
Operational: No.

Telephone Service
None

Miles of Plant: 84.0 (coaxial); None (fiber optic). Additional miles planned: 55.0 (coaxial). Homes passed: 1,488.

Regional Vice President: Rod Dagenais. Vice President & General Manager: Steve Dvoskin. Technical Operations Director: Danny Maxwell. Technical Operations Manager: Andrew Behn. Marketing Director: Vince Maffeo.

Ownership: Comcast Cable Communications Inc. (MSO).

SPRINGFIELD—Springfield Cablevision, 3529 E 3rd St, Springfield, FL 32401. Phone: 850-872-7570. Fax: 850-747-5663. Also serves Cedar Grove & Hiland Park. ICA: FL0122. **Note:** This system is an overbuild.

TV Market Ranking: Below 100 (Cedar Grove, Hiland Park, SPRINGFIELD). Franchise award date: October 14, 1989. Franchise expiration date: N.A. Began: N.A.

Channel capacity: 62 (not 2-way capable). Channels available but not in use: 4.

Basic Service
Subscribers: 2,500.
Programming (received off-air): WFSG (PBS) Panama City; WJHG-TV (CW, MNT, NBC) Panama City; WMBB (ABC) Panama City; WPGX (FOX) Panama City; WTVY (CBS, CW, MNT) Dothan.
Programming (via satellite): KTLA (CW) Los Angeles; TBS Superstation; truTV; TV Guide Network; USA Network; WGN America.
Fee: $15.00 installation; $7.95 monthly; $1.95 converter; $30.00 additional installation.

Expanded Basic Service 1
Subscribers: 2,450.
Programming (via satellite): ABC Family Channel; AMC; Arts & Entertainment; BET Networks; Cartoon Network; CNBC; CNN; Country Music TV; C-SPAN; C-SPAN 2; Discovery Channel; Disney Channel; E! Entertainment Television; ESPN; Fox Sports Net Florida; Headline News; History Channel; Home Shopping Network; INSP; Lifetime; MTV; Nickelodeon; QVC; ShopNBC; Spike TV; SunSports TV; Syfy; The Learning Channel; Travel Channel; Trinity Broadcasting Network; Turner Classic Movies; Turner Network TV; VH1; Weather Channel; WPIX (CW, IND) New York.
Fee: $15.00 installation; $17.50 monthly.

Pay Service 1
Pay Units: N.A.
Programming (via satellite): Cinemax; Encore; HBO; Showtime; Starz; The Movie Channel.
Fee: $10.00 installation; $10.28 monthly (Starz & Encore), $10.34 monthly (Showtime or TMC), $10.79 monthly (Cinemax), $12.40 monthly (HBO).

Video-On-Demand: No

Pay-Per-View
Addressable homes: 1,194.
Hot Choice, Fee: $3.95, Addressable: Yes; iN DEMAND, Fee: $3.95.

Internet Service
Operational: No.

Telephone Service
None

Miles of Plant: 55.0 (coaxial); None (fiber optic). Additional miles planned: 7.0 (coaxial). Homes passed: 3,000. Total homes in franchised area: 3,000.

General Manager: Annette Williams. Chief Technician: Lewis Johnson. Technician: Chris Griffin.

Ownership: Springfield Cablevision.

SPRUCE CREEK NORTH—Galaxy Cablevision. Now served by PALM CAY, FL [FL0311]. ICA: FL0367.

ST. AUGUSTINE—Comcast Cable, 200 N 3rd St, Palatka, FL 32177. Phone: 386-328-4205. Fax: 386-325-4602. Web Site: http://www.comcast.com. Also serves Crescent Beach, St. Augustine Beach & St. Johns County (unincorporated areas). ICA: FL0059.

TV Market Ranking: 68 (St. Johns County (unincorporated areas) (portions)); Outside TV Markets (Crescent Beach, ST. AUGUSTINE, St. Augustine Beach, St. Johns County (unincorporated areas) (portions)). Franchise award date: January 1, 1965. Franchise expiration date: N.A. Began: June 1, 1969.

Channel capacity: N.A. Channels available but not in use: N.A.

Basic Service
Subscribers: 18,006.
Programming (received off-air): WAWS (FOX, MNT) Jacksonville; WCWJ (CW) Jacksonville; WJCT (PBS) Jacksonville; WJEB-TV (ETV) Jacksonville; WJXT (IND) Jacksonville; WJXX (ABC) Orange Park; WTEV-TV (CBS) Jacksonville; WTLV (NBC) Jacksonville; WUFT (PBS) Gainesville; allband FM.
Programming (via satellite): C-SPAN; WGN America.
Current originations: Government Access; Educational Access.
Fee: $49.95 installation; $15.83 monthly.

Expanded Basic Service 1
Subscribers: N.A.
Programming (via satellite): ABC Family Channel; AMC; Animal Planet; Arts & Entertainment; BET Networks; Bravo; Cartoon Network; CNBC; CNN; Comcast/Charter Sports Southeast (CSS); Comedy Central; Country Music TV; Discovery Channel; Discovery Health Channel; Disney Channel; E! Entertainment Television; ESPN; ESPN 2; ESPN Classic Sports; ESPNews; Eternal Word TV Network; FitTV; Food Network; Fox News Channel; Fox Sports Net Florida; FX; Golf Channel; GSN; Hallmark Channel; Headline News; HGTV; History Channel; Home Shopping Network; INSP; ION Television; Lifetime; MoviePlex; MSNBC; MTV; National Geographic Channel; Nickelodeon; Oxygen; QVC; ShopNBC; Speed Channel; Spike TV; SunSports TV; Syfy; TBS Superstation; The Learning Channel; Travel Channel; truTV; Turner Classic Movies; Turner Network TV; TV Guide Network; TV Land; Univision; USA Network; VH1; WE tv; Weather Channel.
Fee: $31.97 monthly.

Digital Basic Service
Subscribers: N.A.
Programming (via satellite): AmericanLife TV Network; BBC America; Bio; Bloomberg Television; Cooking Channel; Discovery Digital Networks; Do-It-Yourself; Encore (multiplexed); Fox Sports World; Fuel TV; Fuse; G4; GAS; GSN; History Channel International; INSP; Lifetime Movie Network; MTV Hits; MTV2; Music Choice; NBA TV; Nick Jr.; NickToons TV; Outdoor Channel; Ovation; Style Network; Tennis Channel; Toon Disney; Versus; VH1 Classic.
Fee: $5.15 monthly.
Digital Expanded Basic Service
Subscribers: N.A.
Programming (via satellite): Fox College Sports Atlantic; Fox College Sports Central; Fox College Sports Pacific; Fox Movie Channel; Independent Film Channel; Sundance Channel; WAM! America's Kidz Network.
Fee: $8.00 monthly.
Digital Pay Service 1
Pay Units: 1,603.
Programming (via satellite): Cinemax (multiplexed); HBO (multiplexed); Showtime (multiplexed); The Movie Channel (multiplexed).
Fee: $12.00 monthly (each).
Video-On-Demand: Yes
Pay-Per-View
iN DEMAND (delivered digitally); Playboy TV (delivered digitally); Fresh (delivered digitally); Shorteez (delivered digitally); Hot Choice (delivered digitally).
Internet Service
Operational: Yes. Began: September 1, 2002.
Broadband Service: Comcast High Speed Internet.
Fee: $99.95 installation; $44.95 monthly.
Telephone Service
None
Miles of Plant: 450.0 (coaxial); None (fiber optic).
Vice President & General Manager: Doug McMillan. Chief Technician: Dean Dabney. Vice President, Marketing: Vic Scarborough. Customer Service Manager: Wendy Thurston. Business Manager: Rosalie Shelor.
City fee: 5% of gross.
Ownership: Comcast Cable Communications Inc. (MSO).

STEINHATCHEE—CommuniComm Services, 17774 NW US Highway 441, High Springs, FL 32643-8749. Phone: 386-454-2299. Fax: 386-454-3705. Web Site: http://www.netcommander.com. ICA: FL0179.
TV Market Ranking: Outside TV Markets (STEINHATCHEE). Franchise award date: N.A. Franchise expiration date: N.A. Began: June 1, 1983.
Channel capacity: N.A. Channels available but not in use: N.A.
Basic Service
Subscribers: N.A. Included in High Springs
Programming (received off-air): WCJB-TV (ABC, CW) Gainesville; WCTV (CBS, MNT) Thomasville; WOGX (FOX) Ocala; WTWC-TV (NBC) Tallahassee; WUFT (PBS) Gainesville.
Programming (via satellite): Home Shopping Network; QVC; Trinity Broadcasting Network; TV Guide Network.
Fee: $50.00 installation; $31.00 monthly.
Expanded Basic Service 1
Subscribers: N.A.
Programming (via satellite): ABC Family Channel; AMC; Animal Planet; Arts & Entertainment; Bravo; Cartoon Network; CNBC; CNN; Comedy Central; Country Music TV; C-SPAN; C-SPAN 2; CW+; Discovery Channel; Disney Channel; Do-It-Yourself; E! Entertainment Television; ESPN; ESPN 2; ESPN Classic Sports; ESPNews; Food Network; Fox News Channel; FX; Hallmark Channel; Headline News; HGTV; History Channel; ION Television; Lifetime; MSNBC; MTV; Nick Jr.; Nickelodeon; Outdoor Channel; Speed Channel; Spike TV; SunSports TV; Syfy; TBS Superstation; The Learning Channel; Travel Channel; truTV; Turner Classic Movies; Turner Network TV; TV Land; USA Network; VH1; WE tv; Weather Channel; WGN America.
Digital Basic Service
Subscribers: N.A.
Programming (via satellite): AmericanLife TV Network; BBC America; Bio; Blackbelt TV; Bloomberg Television; Church Channel; CMT Pure Country; College Sports Television; Current; Daystar TV Network; Discovery Health Channel; Discovery Home Channel; Discovery Kids Channel; Discovery Military Channel; DMX Music; FitTV; Fox Movie Channel; Fox Soccer; Fuse; G4; Golf Channel; Gospel Music Channel; Great American Country; GSN; Halogen Network; History Channel International; ID Investigation Discovery; Independent Film Channel; JCTV; Lifetime Movie Network; MTV Networks Digital Suite; National Geographic Channel; NickToons TV; Ovation; Science Channel; ShopNBC; Sleuth; SoapNet; Style Network; Sundance Channel; TeenNick; The Word Network; Versus.
Pay Service 1
Pay Units: N.A. Included in High Springs
Programming (via satellite): Cinemax; HBO.
Fee: $30.00 installation; $9.95 monthly (Cinemax), $11.95 monthly (HBO).
Digital Pay Service 1
Pay Units: N.A.
Programming (via satellite): Cinemax (multiplexed); Encore (multiplexed); Flix; HBO (multiplexed); Showtime (multiplexed); Starz (multiplexed); The Movie Channel (multiplexed).
Video-On-Demand: No
Pay-Per-View
iN DEMAND (delivered digitally); Hot Choice (delivered digitally); Playboy TV (delivered digitally); Fresh; Spice: Xcess (delivered digitally); Club Jenna (delivered digitally).
Internet Service
Operational: Yes.
Broadband Service: Net Commander.
Fee: $39.95 installation; $51.95 monthly.
Telephone Service
None
Homes passed and miles of plant included in High Springs
General Manager: Darrell Laird. Chief Technician: Michael Smith. Customer Service Manager: Cindy Ross.
County fee: 3% of gross.
Ownership: James Cable LLC (MSO).

STUART—Comcast Cable, 1495 North Britt Rd, Stuart, FL 34994. Phones: 561-227-4240 (West Palm Beach office); 772-692-9010 (Local office). Fax: 772-692-1585. Web Site: http://www.comcast.com. Also serves Fort Pierce (portions), Hobe Sound, Hutchinson, Hutchinson Island South, Indiantown, Jensen Beach, Martin County, Ocean Breeze Park, Palm City, Port Salerno, Port St. Lucie, Ridgeway, Sewall's Point & St. Lucie County. ICA: FL0024.
TV Market Ranking: Below 100 (Fort Pierce (portions), Hobe Sound, Hutchinson, Hutchinson Island South, Indiantown, Jensen Beach, Martin County, Ocean Breeze Park, Palm City, Port Salerno, Port St. Lucie, Ridgeway, Sewall's Point, St. Lucie County, STUART). Franchise award date: N.A. Franchise expiration date: N.A. Began: October 1, 1967.
Channel capacity: N.A. Channels available but not in use: N.A.
Basic Service
Subscribers: 90,000.
Programming (received off-air): WFGC (IND) Palm Beach; WFLX (FOX) West Palm Beach; WHDT-LP Miami; WPBF (ABC) Tequesta; WPBT (PBS) Miami; WPEC (CBS) West Palm Beach; WPTV-TV (NBC) West Palm Beach; WPXP-TV (ION) Lake Worth; WTCE-TV (ETV) Fort Pierce; WTVX (CW) Fort Pierce; WXEL-TV (PBS) West Palm Beach; 20 FMs.
Programming (via satellite): WGN America.
Fee: $32.00 installation; $14.65 monthly.
Expanded Basic Service 1
Subscribers: 87,163.
Programming (via satellite): ABC Family Channel; AMC; Animal Planet; Arts & Entertainment; BET Networks; Bravo; Cartoon Network; CNBC; CNN; Comedy Central; Country Music TV; C-SPAN; C-SPAN 2; Discovery Channel; E! Entertainment Television; ESPN; ESPN 2; Eternal Word TV Network; Food Network; Fox News Channel; Fox Sports Net Florida; FX; Golf Channel; Hallmark Channel; Headline News; HGTV; History Channel; Home Shopping Network; Lifetime; MSNBC; MTV; Nickelodeon; Oxygen; QVC; ShopNBC; Spike TV; Style Network; SunSports TV; Syfy; TBS Superstation; Telemundo; The Learning Channel; Travel Channel; truTV; Turner Network TV; TV Guide Network; TV Land; USA Network; VH1; Weather Channel.
Fee: $47.99 monthly.
Digital Basic Service
Subscribers: 30,665.
Programming (via satellite): AmericanLife TV Network; BBC America; Bio; Black Family Channel; Bloomberg Television; Discovery Digital Networks; Do-It-Yourself; ESPN Classic Sports; ESPNews; FitTV; Fox Sports World; G4; Great American Country; GSN; History Channel International; INSP; MuchMusic Network; Music Choice; Outdoor Channel; Product Information Network; SoapNet; Speed Channel; Toon Disney; Trinity Broadcasting Network; Versus; WE tv.
Fee: $53.44 monthly.
Digital Expanded Basic Service
Subscribers: N.A.
Programming (via satellite): Disney Channel; Fox College Sports Atlantic; Fox College Sports Central; Fox College Sports Pacific; Fox Movie Channel; GAS; Independent Film Channel; MTV Networks Digital Suite; National Geographic Channel; Nick Jr.; Nick Too; NickToons TV; Sundance Channel; Turner Classic Movies.
Fee: $5.00 monthly.
Pay Service 1
Pay Units: 26,668.
Programming (via satellite): Cinemax; HBO (multiplexed); Showtime; The Movie Channel.
Fee: $2.00 installation; $11.95 monthly (Cinemax, Showtime or TMC), $12.95 monthly (HBO).
Digital Pay Service 1
Pay Units: N.A.
Programming (via satellite): Cinemax (multiplexed); Encore (multiplexed); Flix; HBO (multiplexed); Showtime (multiplexed); Starz (multiplexed); The Movie Channel.
Video-On-Demand: Yes
Pay-Per-View
Addressable homes: 30,665.
iN DEMAND, Fee: $4.95, Addressable: Yes; Hot Choice (delivered digitally); Playboy TV (delivered digitally); Fresh (delivered digitally); Shorteez (delivered digitally).
Internet Service
Operational: Yes. Began: February 1, 1997.
Subscribers: 571.
Broadband Service: Comcast High Speed Internet.
Fee: $42.95 monthly.
Telephone Service
Digital: Operational
Fee: $39.95 monthly
Miles of Plant: None (coaxial); 24,000.0 (fiber optic). Homes passed: 113,309.
Area Vice President: Gary Waterfield. General Manager: Geoff Waterfield. Technical Operations Manager: Terry Murphy. Marketing Director: Christopher Derario. Marketing Coordinator: Janet Epstein. Marketing Manager: Leigh Ann Dunleavy. Government & Community Affairs Director: Marta Casas-Celayas.
City fee: 3% of gross. County fee: 6% of gross.
Ownership: Comcast Cable Communications Inc. (MSO).

SUMTER COUNTY—Galaxy Cablevision. Now served by HERNANDO COUNTY, FL [FL0148]. ICA: FL0369.

SUNNY HILLS—Formerly served by Community Cable. No longer in operation. ICA: FL0200.

SUWANNEE CAMPGROUND—Formerly served by KLiP Interactive. No longer in operation. ICA: FL0351.

SWEETWATER GOLF & TENNIS CLUB EAST—Formerly served by Sweetwater Golf & Tennis Club East Inc. No longer in operation. ICA: FL0318.

SWEETWATER OAKS—Formerly served by Galaxy Cablevision. No longer in operation. ICA: FL0370.

TALLAHASSEE—Comcast Cable, 3760 Hartsfield Rd, Tallahassee, FL 32303-1121. Phone: 850-574-4016. Fax: 850-574-4030. Web Site: http://www.comcast.com. Also serves Crawfordville, Gadsden County, Leon County, Midway, Quincy, Shell Point & Sopchoppy. ICA: FL0283.
TV Market Ranking: Below 100 (Crawfordville, Gadsden County, Leon County, Midway, Quincy, Shell Point, Sopchoppy, TALLAHASSEE). Franchise award date: N.A. Franchise expiration date: N.A. Began: January 1, 1962.
Channel capacity: 82 (operating 2-way). Channels available but not in use: N.A.
Basic Service
Subscribers: 90,000 Includes Homerville GA, Quitman GA, Jasper, Madison, Monticello, & Perry.
Programming (received off-air): WABW-TV (PBS) Pelham; WBXT-CA Tallahassee; WCTV (CBS, MNT) Thomasville; WFSU-TV (PBS) Tallahassee; WTBC-LP Tallahassee; WTLF (CW, FOX) Tallahassee; WTLH (CW, FOX) Bainbridge; WTWC-TV (NBC) Tallahassee; WTXL-TV (ABC) Tallahassee; 12 FMs.
Programming (via satellite): ABC Family Channel; AMC; Animal Planet; Arts

& Entertainment; BET Networks; Bravo; Cartoon Network; CNBC; CNN; Comcast/Charter Sports Southeast (CSS); Comedy Central; Country Music TV; C-SPAN; C-SPAN 2; Discovery Channel; Discovery Health Channel; E! Entertainment Television; ESPN; ESPN 2; ESPN Classic Sports; Food Network; Fox News Channel; FX; Golf Channel; Great American Country; GSN; Headline News; HGTV; History Channel; Home Shopping Network 2; ION Television; Lifetime; MSNBC; MTV; Nickelodeon; QVC; Speed Channel; Spike TV; Style Network; SunSports TV; Syfy; TBS Superstation; The Learning Channel; truTV; Turner Classic Movies; Turner Network TV; TV Guide Network; TV Land; Univision; USA Network; Versus; VH1; Weather Channel; Weatherscan; WGN America.

Current originations: Leased Access; Educational Access; Public Access.

Fee: $39.88 installation; $9.52 monthly.

Digital Basic Service

Subscribers: 14,973.

Programming (via satellite): BBC America; Black Family Channel; C-SPAN 3; Discovery Digital Networks; Disney Channel; Encore Action; ESPNews; Eternal Word TV Network; Flix; G4; GAS; INSP; MTV Networks Digital Suite; Music Choice; National Geographic Channel; Nick Jr.; Nick Too; SoapNet; Sundance Channel; The Word Network; Toon Disney; Trinity Broadcasting Network.

Fee: $14.95 monthly.

Pay Service 1

Pay Units: N.A.

Programming (via satellite): HBO; Showtime.

Fee: $9.95 monthly (Showtime), $13.95 monthly (HBO).

Digital Pay Service 1

Pay Units: N.A.

Programming (via satellite): Cinemax (multiplexed); HBO (multiplexed); Showtime (multiplexed); Starz (multiplexed); The Movie Channel (multiplexed).

Video-On-Demand: Yes

Pay-Per-View

Addressable homes: 14,973.

iN DEMAND; iN DEMAND (delivered digitally); Playboy TV (delivered digitally); Fresh (delivered digitally); Shorteez (delivered digitally); Pleasure (delivered digitally).

Internet Service

Operational: Yes.

Subscribers: 6,588.

Broadband Service: Comcast High Speed Internet.

Fee: $149.00 installation; $42.95 monthly; $7.00 modem lease; $199.00 modem purchase.

Telephone Service

Digital: Operational

Miles of Plant: 1,250.0 (coaxial); None (fiber optic). Homes passed: 150,000. Miles of plant (coax) & homes passed include Homerville GA, Quitman GA, Jasper, Madison, Monticello, & Perry

Regional Vice President: Rod Dagenais. General Manager: K. C. McWilliams. Engineering Manager: Mike Gainey. Marketing Director: Claire Evans.

City fee: 5% of gross.

Ownership: Comcast Cable Communications Inc. (MSO).

TAMPA—Formerly served by V TV Video Television. No longer in operation. ICA: FL0309.

TEQUESTA—Now served by PALM BEACH GARDENS, FL [FL0030]. ICA: FL0284.

TRENTON—Comcast Cable, 20775 W Pennsylvania Ave, Dunnellon, FL 34431. Phones: 352-787-9601 (Leesburg office); 354-489-0939. Fax: 352-365-6279. Web Site: http://www.comcast.com. ICA: FL0188.

TV Market Ranking: Below 100 (TRENTON). Franchise award date: N.A. Franchise expiration date: N.A. Began: March 1, 1983.

Channel capacity: N.A. Channels available but not in use: N.A.

Basic Service

Subscribers: N.A. Included with Inverness, FL

Programming (received off-air): WCJB-TV (ABC, CW) Gainesville; WGFL (CBS, MNT) High Springs; WOGX (FOX) Ocala; WUFT (PBS) Gainesville.

Programming (via satellite): ABC Family Channel; AMC; BET Networks; CNBC; CNN; Country Music TV; C-SPAN; Discovery Channel; Disney Channel; E! Entertainment Television; ESPN; ESPN 2; Food Network; Fox Sports Net; FX; HGTV; History Channel; Home Shopping Network; Lifetime; Nickelodeon; QVC; Spike TV; Syfy; TBS Superstation; The Learning Channel; Trinity Broadcasting Network; Turner Classic Movies; Turner Network TV; USA Network; Weather Channel; WGN America; WNBC (NBC) New York.

Fee: $15.86 installation; $19.64 monthly.

Pay Service 1

Pay Units: 38.

Programming (via satellite): Cinemax; HBO.

Fee: $10.00 installation; $11.50 monthly (each).

Video-On-Demand: No

Internet Service

Operational: Yes.

Telephone Service

Digital: Operational

Miles of Plant: 20.0 (coaxial); None (fiber optic). Homes passed: 660.

General Manager: Mike Davenport. Marketing Manager: Melanie Melvin.

City fee: 3% of gross.

Ownership: Comcast Cable Communications Inc. (MSO).

TYNDALL AFB—Mediacom. Now served by WEWAHITCHKA, FL [FL0159]. ICA: FL0143.

VALPARAISO—Valparaiso Communications System, 465 Valparaiso Pkwy, Valparaiso, FL 32580-1274. Phones: 850-729-5404; 850-729-5402. Fax: 850-678-4553. E-mail: bbennett@valp.org. Web Site: http://www.valp.net. ICA: FL0145.

TV Market Ranking: Below 100 (VALPARAISO). Franchise award date: N.A. Franchise expiration date: N.A. Began: June 12, 1976.

Channel capacity: 66 (operating 2-way). Channels available but not in use: 6.

Basic Service

Subscribers: 1,700.

Programming (received off-air): WALA-TV (FOX) Mobile; WEAR-TV (ABC) Pensacola; WFGX (MNT) Fort Walton Beach; WFNA (CW) Gulf Shores; WJHG-TV (CW, MNT, NBC) Panama City; WJTC (IND) Pensacola; WKRG-TV (CBS) Mobile; WPAN (IND) Fort Walton Beach; WPMI-TV (NBC) Mobile; WSRE (PBS) Pensacola; WTVY (CBS, CW, MNT) Dothan; allband FM.

Programming (via satellite): ABC Family Channel; AMC; Animal Planet; Arts & Entertainment; BET Networks; Bravo; Cartoon Network; CNBC; CNN; Comedy Central; Country Music TV; C-SPAN; C-SPAN 2; Discovery Channel; Disney Channel; Do-It-Yourself; ESPN; ESPN 2; Eternal Word TV Network; Food Network; Fox News Channel; FX; Headline News; HGTV; History Channel; INSP; Lifetime; MSNBC; MTV; National Geographic Channel; Nickelodeon; QVC; Spike TV; Syfy; TBS Superstation; The Learning Channel; Toon Disney; Travel Channel; Trinity Broadcasting Network; Turner Classic Movies; Turner Network TV; TV Guide Network; TV Land; USA Network; VH1; Weather Channel; WFBD (IND) Destin; WGN America.

Current originations: Public Access.

Fee: free installation; $33.03 monthly.

Digital Basic Service

Subscribers: 180.

Programming (via satellite): AmericanLife TV Network; BBC America; Bio; Blackbelt TV; Bloomberg Television; Chiller; Church Channel; CMT Pure Country; Cooking Channel; Current; Discovery Health Channel; Discovery Kids Channel; Discovery Military Channel; Discovery Planet Green; DMX Music; Encore (multiplexed); ESPNews; FitTV; Fox Business Channel; Fox Movie Channel; Fox Reality Channel; Fox Soccer; Fuse; G4; Golf Channel; GSN; Halogen Network; History Channel International; ID Investigation Discovery; Independent Film Channel; JCTV; Lifetime Movie Network; Lime; LOGO; MTV Hits; MTV Jams; MTV2; Nick Jr.; NickToons TV; Outdoor Channel; Ovation; PBS Kids Sprout; RFD-TV; Science Channel; Sleuth; SoapNet; Speed Channel; Style Network; TeenNick; TV One; TVG Network; Versus; VH1 Classic; VH1 Soul; WE tv.

Fee: $3.05 monthly.

Digital Pay Service 1

Pay Units: N.A.

Programming (via satellite): Cinemax (multiplexed); Flix; HBO (multiplexed); Showtime (multiplexed); Starz (multiplexed); Sundance Channel; The Movie Channel (multiplexed).

Fee: $7.50 monthly (Cinemax), $10.50 monthly (Starz), $12.50 motnthly (HBO or Showtime/TMC/Sundance).

Video-On-Demand: No

Pay-Per-View

Playboy TV (delivered digitally); Fresh (delivered digitally); iN DEMAND (delivered digitally); Hot Choice (delivered digitally); Club Jenna (delivered digitally); Spice: Xcess (delivered digitally).

Internet Service

Operational: Yes. Began: July 1, 2000.

Subscribers: 1,000.

Broadband Service: Valparaiso Communications Systems.

Fee: $29.95-$44.95 installation; $10.00 modem lease; $99.95 modem purchase.

Telephone Service

None

Miles of Plant: 28.0 (coaxial); None (fiber optic). Homes passed: 1,850.

Manager: Burt B. Bennett. Chief Technician: Jerry Richter.

Ownership: Valparaiso Communication Systems.

VENICE—Comcast Cable, 5205 Fruitville Rd, Sarasota, FL 34232. Phone: 941-371-4444. Fax: 941-371-5097. Web Site: http://www.comcast.com. Also serves Laurel, Nokomis & Sarasota County. ICA: FL0032.

TV Market Ranking: 28 (Sarasota County (portions)); Below 100 (Laurel, Nokomis, VENICE, Sarasota County (portions)). Franchise award date: N.A. Franchise expiration date: N.A. Began: June 1, 1965.

Channel capacity: N.A. Channels available but not in use: N.A.

Basic Service

Subscribers: 45,151.

Programming (received off-air): WCLF (IND) Clearwater; WEDU (PBS) Tampa; WFLA-TV (NBC) Tampa; WFTT-DT (TEL) Tampa; WFTX-TV (FOX) Cape Coral; WINK-TV (CBS) Fort Myers; WMOR-TV (IND) Lakeland; WTOG (CW) St. Petersburg; WTSP (CBS) St. Petersburg; WTTA (MNT) St. Petersburg; WTVT (FOX) Tampa; WVEA-TV (UNV) Venice; WWSB (ABC) Sarasota; WXPX-TV (ION) Bradenton; 14 FMs.

Programming (via satellite): C-SPAN; Hallmark Channel; Headline News; QVC; WGN America.

Current originations: Educational Access; Government Access.

Fee: $63.35 installation; $12.55 monthly.

Expanded Basic Service 1

Subscribers: N.A.

Programming (via satellite): ABC Family Channel; AMC; Animal Planet; Arts & Entertainment; BET Networks; Bravo; Cartoon Network; CNBC; CNN; Comcast/Charter Sports Southeast (CSS); Comedy Central; Country Music TV; Discovery Channel; Discovery Health Channel; E! Entertainment Television; ESPN; ESPN 2; Food Network; Fox News Channel; Fox Sports Net; FX; Golf Channel; HGTV; History Channel; Home Shopping Network; Jewelry Television; Lifetime; MSNBC; MTV; Nickelodeon; Speed Channel; Spike TV; Style Network; SunSports TV; Syfy; TBS Superstation; The Learning Channel; Travel Channel; truTV; Turner Classic Movies; Turner Network TV; TV Guide Network; TV Land; USA Network; Versus; VH1; Weather Channel.

Fee: $36.60 monthly.

Digital Basic Service

Subscribers: 11,288.

Programming (received off-air): WBBH-TV (NBC) Fort Myers; WFTX-TV (FOX) Cape Coral; WGCU (PBS) Fort Myers; WINK-TV (CBS) Fort Myers; WZVN-TV (ABC) Naples.

Programming (via satellite): Arts & Entertainment HD; BBC America; Bio; Cinemax HD; CMT Pure Country; Cooking Channel; C-SPAN 2; C-SPAN 3; Current; Discovery Digital Networks; Discovery HD Theater; Disney Channel; Do-It-Yourself; Encore (multiplexed); ESPN 2 HD; ESPN HD; ESPNews; Eternal Word TV Network; Flix; Florida Channel; Fox College Sports Atlantic; Fox College Sports Central; Fox College Sports Pacific; Fox Reality Channel; Fox Soccer; G4; GAS; Gol TV; Great American Country; GSN; History Channel International; INHD; Lifetime Movie Network; LOGO; MoviePlex; MTV Networks Digital Suite; Music Choice; National Geographic Channel; National Geographic Channel HD Network; NBA TV; Nick Jr.; Nick Too; NickToons TV; Outdoor Channel; Palladia; PBS Kids Sprout; Playboy TV; ShopNBC; SoapNet; Sundance Channel; Tennis Channel; The Sportsman Channel; Toon Disney; Turner Network TV HD; TV One; TVG Network; Universal HD; Versus HD; WE tv; Weatherscan.

Fee: $14.95 monthly.

Pay Service 1

Pay Units: 12,714.

Programming (via satellite): HBO (multiplexed).

Fee: $10.00 monthly.

Digital Pay Service 1

Pay Units: N.A.

Programming (via satellite): Cinemax (multiplexed); HBO (multiplexed); HBO HD; Showtime (multiplexed); Showtime HD;

Starz (multiplexed); Starz HDTV; The Movie Channel (multiplexed).
Fee: $13.50 monthly (each).
Video-On-Demand: Yes
Pay-Per-View
Addressable homes: 11,288.
iN DEMAND, Addressable: Yes; Hot Choice (delivered digitally); Playboy TV (delivered digitally); SunSports TV (delivered digitally); Sports PPV (delivered digitally); NBA League Pass (delivered digitally).
Internet Service
Operational: Yes.
Subscribers: 4,967.
Broadband Service: Comcast High Speed Internet.
Fee: $42.95 monthly; $7.00 modem lease; $199.00 modem purchase.
Telephone Service
Digital: Operational
Fee: $44.95 monthly
Miles of Plant: 667.0 (coaxial); None (fiber optic). Homes passed: 50,571.
Regional Vice President: Rod Dagenais. Vice President & General Manager: Steve Dvoskin. Technical Operations Director: Danny Maxwell. Technical Operations Manager: Andrew Behn. Marketing Director: Vince Maffeo.
City fee: 3% of gross.
Ownership: Comcast Cable Communications Inc. (MSO).

VERO BEACH—Comcast Cable, 940 12th St, Vero Beach, FL 32960-3715. Phone: 772-567-3473. Fax: 772-778-9635. Web Site: http://www.comcast.com. Also serves Fellsmere, Fort Pierce, Indian River County, Indian River Shores, Orchid, Roseland, Sebastian, St. Lucie County, St. Lucie Village, Wabasso & Winter Beach. ICA: FL0040.
TV Market Ranking: 55 (Fellsmere, Indian River County, Indian River Shores, Orchid, Roseland, Sebastian, Wabasso, Winter Beach); Below 100 (Fort Pierce, St. Lucie County, St. Lucie Village, VERO BEACH). Franchise award date: N.A. Franchise expiration date: N.A. Began: January 1, 1959.
Channel capacity: N.A. Channels available but not in use: N.A.
Basic Service
Subscribers: 75,000.
Programming (received off-air): WFLX (FOX) West Palm Beach; WOTF-DT (TEL) Melbourne; WPBF (ABC) Tequesta; WPBT (PBS) Miami; WPEC (CBS) West Palm Beach; WPTV-TV (NBC) West Palm Beach; WTCE-TV (ETV) Fort Pierce; WTCN-CA (MNT) Palm Beach; WTVX (CW) Fort Pierce; WWCI-CA Vero Beach; WXEL-TV (PBS) West Palm Beach; 21 FMs.
Programming (via satellite): C-SPAN; C-SPAN 2; Eternal Word TV Network; Fox Sports Net Florida; Hallmark Channel; QVC; SunSports TV; TBS Superstation; truTV; TV Guide Network; Weather Channel.
Current originations: Educational Access; Government Access.
Fee: $45.00 installation; $14.95 monthly.
Expanded Basic Service 1
Subscribers: N.A.
Programming (via satellite): ABC Family Channel; AMC; Animal Planet; Arts & Entertainment; BET Networks; Cartoon Network; CNBC; CNN; Comedy Central; Country Music TV; Discovery Channel; Disney Channel; E! Entertainment Television; ESPN; ESPN 2; Food Network; Fox News Channel; FX; Headline News; History Channel; Lifetime; MTV; Nickelodeon; Oxygen; Spike TV; The Learning Channel; Travel Channel; Turner Network TV; USA Network; VH1.
Fee: $50.95 monthly.
Digital Basic Service
Subscribers: N.A.
Programming (received off-air): WFLX (FOX) West Palm Beach; WPBF (ABC) Tequesta; WPTV-TV (NBC) West Palm Beach; WTVX (CW) Fort Pierce; WXEL-TV (PBS) West Palm Beach.
Programming (via satellite): Arts & Entertainment HD; BBC America; Big Ten Network; Bio; Bloomberg Television; Bravo; Cine Latino; Cine Mexicano; CMT Pure Country; CNN en Espanol; Cooking Channel; Country Music TV; C-SPAN 3; Current; Discovery Channel HD; Discovery en Espanol; Discovery Kids Channel; Discovery Military Channel; Discovery Planet Green; DMX Music; Do-It-Yourself; Encore (multiplexed); ESPN 2 HD; ESPN Classic Sports; ESPN Deportes; ESPN HD; ESPNews; Eternal Word TV Network; EWTN en Espanol; Flix; Food Network HD; Fox Business Channel; Fox College Sports Atlantic; Fox College Sports Central; Fox College Sports Pacific; Fox Reality Channel; Fox Soccer; Fox Sports en Espanol; FSN HD; Fuel TV; Fuse; G4; Gol TV; GSN; HDNet; HGTV; HGTV HD; History Channel en Espanol; History Channel HD; History Channel International; ID Investigation Discovery; Independent Film Channel; Jewelry Television; LOGO; MLB Network; MoviePlex; MTV Hits; MTV Tres; MTV2; mun2 television; National Geographic Channel; National Geographic Channel HD Network; NBA TV; NFL Network; NHL Network; Nick Jr.; Nick Too; NickToons TV; Oxygen; PBS Kids Sprout; Retro Television Network; Science Channel; Science Channel HD; ShopNBC; SoapNet; Sorpresa; Style Network; SunSports TV; Sur Network; Syfy; TBS in HD; TeenNick; Tennis Channel; Toon Disney; Toon Disney en Espanol; Turner Network TV HD; TV Colombia; TV Land; TV One; TVE Internacional; TVG Network; TVN Entertainment; Universal HD; USA Network HD; VeneMovies; Versus HD; VH1 Classic; VH1 Soul; WE tv.
Fee: $9.95 monthly.
Pay Service 1
Pay Units: 1,723.
Fee: $10.00 installation; $9.00 monthly (each).
Digital Pay Service 1
Pay Units: N.A.
Programming (via satellite): Cinemax (multiplexed); Cinemax HD; HBO (multiplexed); HBO HD; Showtime (multiplexed); Showtime HD; Starz (multiplexed); Starz HDTV; The Movie Channel (multiplexed).
Fee: $8.04 monthly.
Video-On-Demand: Yes
Pay-Per-View
Fresh (delivered digitally); iN DEMAND (delivered digitally); Playboy TV (delivered digitally); Shorteez (delivered digitally); Club Jenna (delivered digitally); Penthouse TV (delivered digitally).
Internet Service
Operational: Yes. Began: December 1, 2001.
Subscribers: 2,885.
Broadband Service: Comcast High Speed Internet.
Fee: $42.95 monthly.
Telephone Service
Digital: Operational
Fee: $39.95 monthly
Miles of Plant: 1,500.0 (coaxial); None (fiber optic). Homes passed: 120,000.
Area Vice President: Gary Waterford. General Manager: Geoff Shock. Chief Technician: Michael Brooks. Marketing Director: Christopher Derario. Marketing Manager: Leigh Ann Dunleavy. Marketing Coordinator: Joey Cirgliano. Government & Community Affairs Director: Marta Casas-Celayas.
County fee: 5% of gross.
Ownership: Comcast Cable Communications Inc. (MSO).

WALDO—Comcast Cable, 6805 Southpoint Pkwy, Jacksonville, FL 32216. Phones: 800-266-2278; 904-374-8000. Fax: 904-374-7622. Web Site: http://www.comcast.com. ICA: FL0185.
TV Market Ranking: Below 100 (WALDO). Franchise award date: October 1, 1982. Franchise expiration date: N.A. Began: December 1, 1983.
Channel capacity: 40 (operating 2-way). Channels available but not in use: 8.
Basic Service
Subscribers: N.A. Included in Jacksonville
Programming (received off-air): WAWS (FOX, MNT) Jacksonville; WCJB-TV (ABC, CW) Gainesville; WGFL (CBS, MNT) High Springs; WJXT (IND) Jacksonville; WOGX (FOX) Ocala; WTLV (NBC) Jacksonville; WUFT (PBS) Gainesville.
Programming (via satellite): C-SPAN; QVC; TBS Superstation; Weather Channel.
Fee: $49.95 installation; $14.61 monthly; $1.65 converter.
Expanded Basic Service 1
Subscribers: 253.
Programming (via satellite): ABC Family Channel; AMC; Arts & Entertainment; BET Networks; CNN; Discovery Channel; Disney Channel; ESPN; Food Network; Fox News Channel; FX; Great American Country; Headline News; INSP; Lifetime; MTV; Nickelodeon; Spike TV; SunSports TV; The Learning Channel; Turner Network TV; USA Network.
Fee: $29.71 monthly.
Digital Basic Service
Subscribers: N.A.
Programming (via satellite): AmericanLife TV Network; BBC America; Bio; Bloomberg Television; Bravo; Discovery Digital Networks; ESPN 2; ESPN Classic Sports; ESPNews; Fox Movie Channel; Fox Sports World; G4; GAS; Golf Channel; GSN; Halogen Network; HGTV; History Channel; History Channel International; Independent Film Channel; International Television (ITV); Lifetime Movie Network; MTV Networks Digital Suite; Nick Jr.; Outdoor Channel; Ovation; Speed Channel; Sundance Channel; Syfy; Toon Disney; Trinity Broadcasting Network; Turner Classic Movies; TV Land; Versus.
Pay Service 1
Pay Units: 75.
Programming (via satellite): Cinemax; HBO.
Fee: $15.95 monthly (each).
Digital Pay Service 1
Pay Units: N.A.
Programming (via satellite): HBO (multiplexed).
Fee: $15.95 monthly.
Video-On-Demand: No
Pay-Per-View
iN DEMAND (delivered digitally).
Internet Service
Operational: Yes.
Telephone Service
Digital: Operational
Miles of Plant: 12.0 (coaxial); None (fiber optic). Homes passed: 607.
Vice President, Marketing: Vic Scarborough. Engineering Director: Mike Humphrey. Government Affairs Director: Bill Ferry. Vice President & General Manager: Doug McMillan.
Ownership: Comcast Cable Communications Inc. (MSO).

WAUCHULA—Comcast Cable, 5205 Fruitville Rd, Sarasota, FL 34232. Phones: 941-625-6000; 941-371-6700 (Customer service); 941-371-4444. Fax: 941-371-5097. Web Site: http://www.comcast.com. Also serves Hardee County (portions) & Zolfo Springs. ICA: FL0288.
TV Market Ranking: 28 (Hardee County (portions)); Below 100 (Hardee County (portions)); Outside TV Markets (WAUCHULA, Zolfo Springs, Hardee County (portions)). Franchise award date: N.A. Franchise expiration date: N.A. Began: June 1, 1970.
Channel capacity: N.A. Channels available but not in use: N.A.
Basic Service
Subscribers: 3,116.
Programming (received off-air): WCLF (IND) Clearwater; WEDU (PBS) Tampa; WFLA-TV (NBC) Tampa; WFTS-TV (ABC) Tampa; WFTT-DT (TEL) Tampa; WFTV (ABC) Orlando; WKMG-TV (CBS) Orlando; WMOR-TV (IND) Lakeland; WTOG (CW) St. Petersburg; WTSP (CBS) St. Petersburg; WTTA (MNT) St. Petersburg; WTVT (FOX) Tampa; WUSF-TV (PBS) Tampa; WVEA-TV (UNV) Venice; WXPX-TV (ION) Bradenton.
Programming (via satellite): ABC Family Channel; AMC; Animal Planet; Arts & Entertainment; BET Networks; Cartoon Network; CNBC; CNN; Comcast/Charter Sports Southeast (CSS); Comedy Central; Country Music TV; C-SPAN; C-SPAN 2; Discovery Channel; Discovery Health Channel; E! Entertainment Television; ESPN; ESPN 2; Food Network; Fox News Channel; FX; Golf Channel; GSN; Hallmark Channel; Headline News; HGTV; History Channel; Home Shopping Network; Lifetime; MTV; Nickelodeon; QVC; Speed Channel; Spike TV; Style Network; SunSports TV; Syfy; TBS Superstation; The Learning Channel; Turner Network TV; TV Guide Network; TV Land; USA Network; Versus; VH1; Weather Channel; WGN America.
Current originations: Government Access; Educational Access; Public Access.
Fee: $54.47 installation; $21.20 monthly.
Digital Basic Service
Subscribers: N.A.
Programming (via satellite): BBC America; Discovery Digital Networks; Disney Channel; ESPNews; Flix; MTV Networks Digital Suite; Music Choice; Nick Jr.; Nick Too; SoapNet; Sundance Channel; TeenNick; Toon Disney; WAM! America's Kidz Network; WE tv.
Pay Service 1
Pay Units: N.A.
Programming (via satellite): Cinemax; HBO; Showtime.
Fee: $24.95 installation; $9.50 monthly (each).
Digital Pay Service 1
Pay Units: N.A.
Programming (via satellite): Cinemax (multiplexed); Encore (multiplexed); HBO (multiplexed); Showtime (multiplexed); Starz (multiplexed); The Movie Channel (multiplexed).
Video-On-Demand: No

Pay-Per-View
Addressable homes: 779.
iN DEMAND; Hot Choice (delivered digitally); Playboy TV (delivered digitally); Pleasure (delivered digitally); Fresh (delivered digitally); Shorteez (delivered digitally).
Internet Service
Operational: Yes.
Telephone Service
Analog: Not Operational
Digital: Operational
Miles of Plant: 87.0 (coaxial); None (fiber optic).
Regional Vice President: Rod Dagenais. Vice President & General Manager: Steve Dvoskin. Technical Operations Director: Danny Maxwell. Technical Operations Manager: Andrew Behn. Marketing Director: Vince Maffeo.
City fee: 5% of gross.
Ownership: Comcast Cable Communications Inc. (MSO).

WELAKA—Comcast Cable, 6805 Southpoint Pkwy, Jacksonville, FL 32216. Phones: 800-266-2278; 904-374-8000. Fax: 904-374-7622. Web Site: http://www.comcast.com. Also serves Georgetown & Palatka. ICA: FL0326.
TV Market Ranking: Below 100 (Georgetown, WELAKA); Outside TV Markets (Palatka). Franchise award date: N.A. Franchise expiration date: N.A. Began: N.A.
Channel capacity: 40 (not 2-way capable). Channels available but not in use: 2.
Basic Service
Subscribers: N.A. Included in Jacksonville
Programming (received off-air): WAWS (FOX, MNT) Jacksonville; WCWJ (CW) Jacksonville; WESH (NBC) Daytona Beach; WJGV-CD (IND) Palatka; WJXT (IND) Jacksonville; WJXX (ABC) Orange Park; WKMG-TV (CBS) Orlando; WTEV-TV (CBS) Jacksonville; WTLV (NBC) Jacksonville; WUFT (PBS) Gainesville.
Programming (via satellite): BET Networks; C-SPAN; INSP; QVC; TBS Superstation; Weather Channel.
Current originations: Educational Access.
Fee: $49.95 installation; $15.29 monthly; $1.65 converter.
Expanded Basic Service 1
Subscribers: N.A. Included in Jacksonville
Programming (via satellite): ABC Family Channel; AMC; Arts & Entertainment; CNN; Discovery Channel; Disney Channel; E! Entertainment Television; ESPN; ESPN 2; Food Network; Fox News Channel; FX; Headline News; History Channel; Lifetime; MTV; Nickelodeon; Spike TV; The Learning Channel; Turner Network TV; USA Network.
Fee: $32.05 monthly.
Digital Basic Service
Subscribers: N.A.
Programming (via satellite): AmericanLife TV Network; BBC America; Bio; Bloomberg Television; Bravo; Discovery Digital Networks; ESPN 2; ESPN Classic Sports; ESPNews; Fox Movie Channel; Fox Sports World; G4; GAS; Golf Channel; GSN; Halogen Network; HGTV; History Channel; History Channel International; Independent Film Channel; International Television (ITV); Lifetime Movie Network; MTV Networks Digital Suite; Nick Jr.; Outdoor Channel; Ovation; Speed Channel; Sundance Channel; Syfy; Toon Disney; Trinity Broadcasting Network; Turner Classic Movies; TV Land; Versus.
Pay Service 1
Pay Units: N.A.
Programming (via satellite): Cinemax; HBO.
Fee: $15.95 monthly (each).
Digital Pay Service 1
Pay Units: N.A.
Programming (via satellite): HBO (multiplexed).
Fee: $15.95 monthly.
Video-On-Demand: No
Pay-Per-View
iN DEMAND (delivered digitally).
Internet Service
Operational: Yes.
Telephone Service
Digital: Operational
Miles of Plant: 115.0 (coaxial); None (fiber optic). Homes passed: 4,266.
Vice President & General Manager: Doug McMillan. Engineering Director: Mike Humphrey. Vice President, Marketing: Vic Scarborough. Marketing Manager: Kevin Grant. Government Affairs Director: Bill Ferry.
Ownership: Comcast Cable Communications Inc. (MSO).

WELLINGTON—Bright House Networks, 1655 State Rd 472, DeLand, FL 32724. Phone: 888-534-1230. Fax: 786-845-5533. E-mail: john.doctor@mybrighthouse.com. Web Site: http://cfl.mybrighthouse.com. ICA: FL0356.
TV Market Ranking: Below 100 (WELLINGTON). Franchise award date: N.A. Franchise expiration date: N.A. Began: N.A.
Channel capacity: N.A. Channels available but not in use: N.A.
Basic Service
Subscribers: 1,363.
Programming (received off-air): WBFS-TV (MNT) Miami; WFGC (IND) Palm Beach; WFLX (FOX) West Palm Beach; WLTV-DT (UNV) Miami; WPBT (PBS) Miami; WPEC (CBS) West Palm Beach; WPTV-TV (NBC) West Palm Beach; WSFL-TV (CW) Miami; WTVX (CW) Fort Pierce; WXEL-TV (PBS) West Palm Beach.
Programming (via satellite): ABC Family Channel; AMC; Animal Planet; Arts & Entertainment; BET Networks; CNBC; CNN; Country Music TV; C-SPAN; C-SPAN 2; Discovery Channel; ESPN; Food Network; FX; Headline News; HGTV; Home Shopping Network; ION Television; Lifetime; MTV; Nickelodeon; QVC; TBS Superstation; The Learning Channel; Turner Network TV; TV Guide Network; VH1; Weather Channel.
Current originations: Government Access; Public Access.
Expanded Basic Service 1
Subscribers: N.A.
Programming (via satellite): American-Life TV Network; Bravo!; Cartoon Network; Comedy Central; Disney Channel; E! Entertainment Television; ESPN 2; Fox Sports Net; Golf Channel; History Channel; Spike TV; SunSports TV; Syfy; Turner Classic Movies; USA Network; WGN America.
Pay Service 1
Pay Units: N.A.
Programming (via satellite): Cinemax; HBO; Playboy TV; Showtime; The Movie Channel.
Internet Service
Operational: Yes.
Broadband Service: Road Runner.
Fee: $44.95 monthly.
Telephone Service
Digital: Operational
Fee: $44.95 monthly
Division President: J. Christian Fenger. General Manager: John Doctor.
Ownership: Bright House Networks LLC (MSO).

WEST PALM BEACH—Comcast Cable, 1401 Northpoint Pkwy, West Palm Beach, FL 33407-1965. Phones: 561-478-5866; 561-227-4240. Fax: 561-640-3996. Web Site: http://www.comcast.com. Also serves Atlantis, Boynton Beach, Cloud Lake, Glen Ridge, Greenacres City, Haverhill, Hypoluxo, Lake Clarke Shores, Lake Worth, Lantana, Manalapan, Mangonia Park, Martin County, Palm Beach, Palm Beach County, Palm Springs, Riviera Beach, Singer Island, South Palm Beach & Wellington. ICA: FL0008.
TV Market Ranking: Below 100 (Atlantis, Boynton Beach, Cloud Lake, Glen Ridge, Greenacres City, Haverhill, Hypoluxo, Lake Clarke Shores, Lake Worth, Lantana, Manalapan, Mangonia Park, Martin County, Palm Beach, Palm Springs, Riviera Beach, Singer Island, South Palm Beach, Wellington, WEST PALM BEACH). Franchise award date: N.A. Franchise expiration date: N.A. Began: December 15, 1968.
Channel capacity: N.A. Channels available but not in use: N.A.
Basic Service
Subscribers: 419,584.
Programming (received off-air): WFGC (IND) Palm Beach; WFLX (FOX) West Palm Beach; WHDT-LP Miami; WLTV-DT (UNV) Miami; WPBF (ABC) Tequesta; WPBT (PBS) Miami; WPEC (CBS) West Palm Beach; WPLG (ABC) Miami; WPTV-TV (NBC) West Palm Beach; WPXP-TV (ION) Lake Worth; WSCV (TMO) Fort Lauderdale; WTCE-TV (ETV) Fort Pierce; WTVX (CW) Fort Pierce; WXEL-TV (PBS) West Palm Beach; 12 FMs.
Programming (via satellite): AMC; Discovery Channel; History Channel; Home Shopping Network; TBS Superstation; Turner Network TV; WGN America.
Current originations: Leased Access; Government Access.
Fee: $54.60 installation; $13.00 monthly.
Expanded Basic Service 1
Subscribers: N.A.
Programming (via satellite): ABC Family Channel; Animal Planet; Arts & Entertainment; BET Networks; Bravo; Cartoon Network; CNBC; CNN; Comedy Central; C-SPAN; C-SPAN 2; Disney Channel; E! Entertainment Television; ESPN; ESPN 2; Eternal Word TV Network; Food Network; Fox News Channel; Fox Sports Net Florida; FX; Golf Channel; Hallmark Channel; Headline News; HGTV; Lifetime; MSNBC; MTV; Nickelodeon; QVC; Spike TV; Style Network; SunSports TV; Syfy; The Learning Channel; Travel Channel; truTV; TV Guide Network; TV Land; USA Network; VH1; Weather Channel.
Fee: $18.30 monthly.
Digital Basic Service
Subscribers: 40,000.
Programming (received off-air): WFLX (FOX) West Palm Beach; WPBF (ABC) Tequesta; WPEC (CBS) West Palm Beach; WPTV-TV (NBC) West Palm Beach; WTVX (CW) Fort Pierce; WXEL-TV (PBS) West Palm Beach.
Programming (via satellite): Animal Planet HD; Arts & Entertainment HD; BBC America; Bloomberg Television; CBS College Sports Network; Cine Latino; Cine Mexicano; CMT Pure Country; CNN en Espanol; Cooking Channel; Country Music TV; C-SPAN 2; C-SPAN 3; Current; Discovery Channel HD; Discovery en Espanol; Discovery Health Channel; Discovery Kids Channel; Discovery Military Channel; Discovery Planet Green; Do-It-Yourself; Encore (multiplexed); ESPN 2 HD; ESPN Classic Sports; ESPN Deportes; ESPN HD; ESPNews; FamilyNet; FitTV; Flix; Food Network HD; Fox Business Channel; Fox College Sports Atlantic; Fox College Sports Central; Fox College Sports Pacific; Fox Movie Channel; Fox Reality Channel; Fox Soccer; Fox Sports en Espanol; FSN HD; Fuel TV; Fuse; G4; Gol TV; Golf Channel HD; Gospel Music Channel; Great American Country; GSN; Halogen Network; HDNet; HGTV HD; History Channel HD; History Channel International; ID Investigation Discovery; Independent Film Channel; Jewelry Television; La Familia Network; Lifetime Movie Network; LOGO; MLB Network; MoviePlex; MTV Hits; MTV Tres; MTV2; mun2 television; Music Choice; National Geographic Channel; National Geographic Channel HD Network; NBA TV; NFL Network; NHL Network; Nick Jr.; Nick Too; Outdoor Channel; Oxygen; PBS Kids Sprout; Retirement Living; Retro Television Network; Science Channel; Si TV; Speed Channel; Sundance Channel; Syfy HD; TeenNick; Tennis Channel; Toon Disney; Toon Disney en Espanol; Trinity Broadcasting Network; Turner Classic Movies; Turner Network TV HD; TV Colombia; TV One; TVG Network; TVN Entertainment; Universal HD; USA Network HD; VeneMovies; Versus; Versus HD; VH1 Classic; VH1 Soul; WE tv.
Digital Pay Service 1
Pay Units: N.A.
Programming (via satellite): Cinemax (multiplexed); HBO (multiplexed); HBO HD; Showtime (multiplexed); Showtime HD; Starz (multiplexed); Starz HDTV; The Movie Channel (multiplexed).
Video-On-Demand: Yes
Pay-Per-View
iN DEMAND; Club Jenna (delivered digitally); Penthouse TV (delivered digitally); Playboy TV (delivered digitally); Fresh; Shorteez (delivered digitally).
Internet Service
Operational: Yes.
Broadband Service: Comcast High Speed Internet.
Fee: $42.95 monthly.
Telephone Service
Digital: Operational
Miles of Plant: 1,433.0 (coaxial); 118.0 (fiber optic).
Area Vice President: Gary Waterfield. Manager: Beth Fulcher. Technical Operations Director: Barry Rhodes. Technical Operations Manager: Van Gordon. Chief Technician: Skip Buck. Marketing Director: Christopher Derario. Marketing Manager: Dianne Bissoon. Marketing Coordinator: Janet Epstien.; Gary Goldman. Community & Government Affairs Director: Marta CasasCelayas.
City fee: 5% of gross.
Ownership: Comcast Cable Communications Inc. (MSO).

WESTON—Advanced Cable Communications, 1274 Weston Rd, Weston, FL 33326-1916. Phone: 954-753-0100. Fax: 954-345-0783. E-mail: info@advancedcable.net. Web Site: http://www.advancedcable.com. ICA: FL0321.
TV Market Ranking: 21 (WESTON (VILLAGE)). Franchise award date: September 1, 1983. Franchise expiration date: N.A. Began: April 1, 1986.
Channel capacity: 78 (operating 2-way). Channels available but not in use: N.A.
Basic Service
Subscribers: 16,202.
Programming (received off-air): WAMI-DT (TEL) Hollywood; WBFS-TV (MNT) Miami; WFOR-TV (CBS) Miami; WHFT-TV (TBN)

Miami; WLRN-TV (PBS) Miami; WLTV-DT (UNV) Miami; WPBT (PBS) Miami; WPXM-TV (ION) Miami; WSBS-TV (IND) Key West; WSCV (TMO) Fort Lauderdale; WSFL-TV (CW) Miami; WSVN (FOX) Miami; WTVJ (NBC) Miami; WXEL-TV (PBS) West Palm Beach.

Programming (via satellite): ABC Family Channel; AMC; Animal Planet; Arts & Entertainment; BET Networks; Bravo; Cartoon Network; CNBC; CNN; Comedy Central; Country Music TV; C-SPAN; Discovery Channel; Discovery Health Channel; Disney Channel; E! Entertainment Television; ESPN; ESPN 2; Eternal Word TV Network; Food Network; Fox Movie Channel; Fox News Channel; Fox Sports Net Florida; FX; G4; Golf Channel; Hallmark Channel; Headline News; HGTV; History Channel; Home Shopping Network; Lifetime; MSNBC; MTV; MTV2; National Geographic Channel; Nickelodeon; QVC; Speed Channel; Spike TV; Style Network; SunSports TV; Syfy; TBS Superstation; The Learning Channel; Travel Channel; truTV; Turner Classic Movies; Turner Network TV; TV Guide Network; TV Land; USA Network; Versus; VH1; WE tv; Weather Channel; WGN America; WPLG (ABC) Miami.

Current originations: Leased Access; Government Access; Educational Access; Public Access.

Fee: $43.00 installation; $40.05 monthly; $2.32 converter; $19.10 additional installation.

Digital Basic Service

Subscribers: N.A.

Programming (received off-air): WBFS-TV (MNT) Miami; WFOR-TV (CBS) Miami; WPBT (PBS) Miami; WPLG (ABC) Miami; WSVN (FOX) Miami; WTVJ (NBC) Miami.

Programming (via satellite): Arts & Entertainment HD; BBC America; Bio; Bloomberg Television; CMT Pure Country; College Sports Television; Cooking Channel; C-SPAN 3; Discovery HD Theater; Discovery Kids Channel; Discovery Military Channel; Discovery Planet Green; DMX Music; ESPN 2 HD; ESPN Classic Sports; ESPN HD; ESPN U; ESPNews; Fox College Sports Atlantic; Fox College Sports Central; Fox College Sports Pacific; Fox Reality Channel; Fox Soccer; Fox Sports en Espanol; FSN HD; Fuel TV; Fuse; Gol TV; GSN; HDNet; HDNet Movies; History Channel HD; History Channel International; ID Investigation Discovery; LATV Networks; Lifetime Movie Network; MTV Hits; mun2 television; National Geographic Channel HD Network; NFL Network; NFL Network HD; Nick Jr.; NickToons TV; PBS Kids Sprout; Science Channel; ShopNBC; Sleuth; SoapNet; TBS in HD; TeenNick; Toon Disney; Turner Network TV HD; Universal HD; VH1 Classic; VH1 Soul.

Fee: $21.90 monthly.

Digital Expanded Basic Service

Subscribers: N.A.

Programming (via satellite): Canal 24 Horas; Canal 52MX; Canal Sur; Cine Latino; Cine Mexicano; CNN en Espanol; Discovery en Espanol; Docu TVE; ESPN Deportes; Fox Sports en Espanol; Gol TV; History Channel en Espanol; Latele Novela Network; MTV Tres; mun2 television; Telefe International; Toon Disney en Espanol; TV Chile; TV Colombia; TVE Internacional; VeneMovies.

Fee: $10.95 monthly.

Digital Pay Service 1

Pay Units: 1,489.

Programming (via satellite): Cinemax (multiplexed); Cinemax HD; Encore (multiplexed); Flix; HBO (multiplexed); HBO HD; Showtime (multiplexed); Showtime HD; Starz (multiplexed); Starz HDTV; Sundance Channel; The Movie Channel (multiplexed).

Fee: $10.00 monthly (Cinemax), $16.95 monthly (Showtime/TMC/Flix/Sundance or Starz/Encore), $18.95 monthly (HBO).

Video-On-Demand: Yes

Pay-Per-View

Addressable homes: 3,300.

iN DEMAND, Addressable: Yes; Playboy TV (delivered digitally), Fee: $7.99; Fresh (delivered digitally), Fee: $7.99; special events (delivered digitally); sports (delivered digitally).

Internet Service

Operational: Yes.

Broadband Service: In-house.

Fee: $47.95 monthly; $10.00 modem lease.

Telephone Service

Analog: Not Operational

Digital: Operational

Miles of Plant: 100.0 (coaxial); 1.0 (fiber optic). Additional miles planned: 80.0 (coaxial); 150.0 (fiber optic). Homes passed: 17,000.

Manager: Jim Pagano. Marketing & Program Director: Michelle Fitzpatrick. Vice President, Engineering: Rick Scheller.

Ownership: Schurz Communications Inc. (MSO).

WESTVILLE—Formerly served by Community Cable. No longer in operation. ICA: FL0289.

WEWAHITCHKA—Mediacom, 1613 Nantahala Beach Rd, Gulf Breeze, FL 32563-8944. Phone: 850-934-7700. Fax: 850-934-2506. Web Site: http://www.mediacomcable.com. Also serves Alligator Point, Apalachicola, Bay County (portions), Bonifay, Cape San Blas, Carrabelle, Eastpoint, Franklin County (portions), Gulf County (portions), Holmes County (portions), Lanark Village, Mexico Beach, Okaloosa County (portions), Panama City (portions), Port St. Joe, Sandestin Beach Resort, Santa Rosa Beach, Southport, St. Georges Island, Tyndall AFB, Vernon & Walton County (portions). ICA: FL0159.

TV Market Ranking: Below 100 (Bay County (portions), Bonifay, Cape San Blas, Dune Allen Beach, Gulf County (portions) (portions), Holmes County (portions), Mexico Beach, Okaloosa County (portions), Panama City (portions), Port St. Joe, Sandestin Beach Resort, Santa Rosa Beach, Seagrove Beach, Southport, Tyndall AFB, Vernon, Walton County (portions), WEWAHITCHKA); Outside TV Markets (Alligator Point, Apalachicola, Carrabelle, Eastpoint, Franklin County (portions), Gulf County (portions), Lanark Village, St. Georges Island). Franchise award date: August 24, 1982. Franchise expiration date: N.A. Began: June 1, 1983.

Channel capacity: N.A. Channels available but not in use: N.A.

Basic Service

Subscribers: 13,687.

Programming (received off-air): WFSU-TV (PBS) Tallahassee; WJHG-TV (CW, MNT, NBC) Panama City; WMBB (ABC) Panama City; WPGX (FOX) Panama City; WTVY (CBS, CW, MNT) Dothan.

Programming (via satellite): ABC Family Channel; AMC; Animal Planet; Arts & Entertainment; BET Networks; Bravo; Cartoon Network; CNBC; CNN; Comedy Central; Country Music TV; C-SPAN; C-SPAN 2; Discovery Channel; Disney Channel; E! Entertainment Television; ESPN; ESPN 2; Eternal Word TV Network; FitTV; Food Network; Fox News Channel; Fox Sports Net Florida; FX; GalaVision; Golf Channel; Hallmark Channel; Headline News; HGTV; History Channel; Home Shopping Network; INSP; ION Television; Lifetime; MSNBC; MTV; Nickelodeon; Outdoor Channel; Oxygen; QVC; Speed Channel; Spike TV; SunSports TV; Syfy; TBS Superstation; The Learning Channel; Toon Disney; Travel Channel; Trinity Broadcasting Network; truTV; Turner Network TV; TV Guide Network; TV Land; Univision; USA Network; VH1; WE tv; Weather Channel; WGN America.

Fee: $29.50 installation; $44.95 monthly; $3.35 converter; $20.00 additional installation.

Digital Basic Service

Subscribers: N.A.

Programming (via satellite): AmericanLife TV Network; BBC America; Bio; Bloomberg Television; Discovery Digital Networks; DMX Music; Fox Sports World; G4; GSN; Halogen Network; History Channel International; Independent Film Channel; Lifetime Movie Network; MuchMusic Network; Science Television; Style Network; Turner Classic Movies.

Fee: $7.00 monthly.

Digital Pay Service 1

Pay Units: N.A.

Programming (via satellite): Cinemax (multiplexed); Encore (multiplexed); HBO (multiplexed); Showtime (multiplexed); Starz (multiplexed).

Fee: $9.95 monthly (Cinemax, Showtime or Starz & Encore), $11.95 monthly (HBO).

Video-On-Demand: No

Internet Service

Operational: Yes.

Broadband Service: Mediacom High Speed Internet.

Fee: $49.95 installation; $40.95 monthly.

Telephone Service

Digital: Operational

Vice President: David Servies. Engineering Director: Powell Bedgood. Regional Technical Operations Director: Eddie Arnold. Government Relations Director: Barbara Bonowicz. Sales & Marketing Manager: Joey Nagem. Technical Operations Manager: Shayne Routhe.

City fee: 3% of gross.

Ownership: Mediacom LLC (MSO).

WHITE SPRINGS—Southeast Cable TV Inc. No longer in operation. ICA: FL0290.

WILDWOOD—Bright House Networks, 730 S Main St, Wildwood, FL 34785. Phone: 352-330-2897. E-mail: john.doctor@mybrighthouse.com. Web Site: http://cfl.mybrighthouse.com. Also serves Belleview, Clermont (portions), Eureka, Fort McCoy, Lake County (northern portions), Lynne, Marion County (portions), Marion Oaks, Moss Bluff, Pennbrook, Rainbow Park, Salt Springs, Silver Springs, Southgate, Sumter County (portions) & Webster. ICA: FL0291.

TV Market Ranking: 55 (Clemont (portions), Lake County (northern portions), Pennbrook, Sumter County (portions), Webster, WILDWOOD); Below 100 (Belleview, Eureka, Fort McCoy, Lynne, Marion County (portions), Marion Oaks, Moss Bluff, Rainbow Park, Salt Springs, Silver Springs, Southgate). Franchise award date: April 1, 1984. Franchise expiration date: N.A. Began: April 9, 1984.

Channel capacity: N.A. Channels available but not in use: N.A.

Basic Service

Subscribers: 41,335.

Programming (received off-air): Central Florida News 13; WACX (IND) Leesburg; WCJB-TV (ABC, CW) Gainesville; WESH (NBC) Daytona Beach; WFTV (ABC) Orlando; WHLV-TV (IND) Cocoa; WKCF (CW) Clermont; WKMG-TV (CBS) Orlando; WOFL (FOX) Orlando; WOPX-TV (ION) Melbourne; WRBW (MNT) Orlando; WRDQ (IND) Orlando; WVEN-TV (UNV) Daytona Beach.

Programming (via satellite): TBS Superstation; Turner Network TV; WGN America.

Current originations: Government Access; Leased Access.

Fee: $39.57 installation; $11.22 monthly.

Expanded Basic Service 1

Subscribers: N.A.

Programming (via satellite): AMC; Animal Planet; Arts & Entertainment; BET Networks; Bravo; Cartoon Network; CNBC; CNN; Comedy Central; Country Music TV; C-SPAN; Discovery Channel; Disney Channel; E! Entertainment Television; ESPN; ESPN 2; Food Network; Fox News Channel; FX; GalaVision; Golf Channel; Hallmark Channel; Headline News; HGTV; History Channel; Home Shopping Network; Lifetime; Lifetime Movie Network; MSNBC; MTV; Nickelodeon; Oxygen; QVC; SoapNet; Speed Channel; SunSports TV; Syfy; Telemundo; The Learning Channel; Travel Channel; truTV; Turner Classic Movies; TV Land; USA Network; VH1; WE tv; Weather Channel.

Fee: $39.57 monthly.

Digital Basic Service

Subscribers: N.A.

Programming (via satellite): ABC Family Channel; America's Store; BBC America; Bloomberg Television; C-SPAN 2; C-SPAN 3; Discovery Digital Networks; DMX Music; Do-It-Yourself; ESPN Classic Sports; ESPNews; Eternal Word TV Network; FitTV; Fox Sports World; Fuse; G4; GAS; Lifetime Real Women; MTV2; NASA TV; National Geographic Channel; Nick Jr.; Outdoor Channel; Ovation; PBS Kids Channel; Science Television; Style Network; Toon Disney; Versus; VH1 Classic.

Fee: $7.70 monthly.

Digital Expanded Basic Service

Subscribers: N.A.

Programming (via satellite): Canales N.

Pay Service 1

Pay Units: 85.

Programming (via satellite): MoviePlex.

Fee: $1.99 monthly.

Digital Pay Service 1

Pay Units: N.A.

Programming (via satellite): Cinemax (multiplexed); Encore; Flix; Fox Movie Channel; HBO (multiplexed); Showtime (multiplexed); Sundance Channel; The Movie Channel (multiplexed).

Fee: $10.95 monthly (each).

Video-On-Demand: Yes

Pay-Per-View

Shorteez (delivered digitally); Fresh (delivered digitally); Playboy TV (delivered digitally); Pleasure (delivered digitally); iN DEMAND (delivered digitally); ESPN Now (delivered digitally); Sports PPV (delivered digitally).

Internet Service

Operational: Yes.

Broadband Service: Road Runner.

Fee: $29.95 monthly.

Telephone Service
Analog: Not Operational
Digital: Operational
Fee: $28.95 monthly
Homes passed: 75,000. Total homes in franchised area: 75,000.
Division President: J. Christian Fenger. General Manager: John Doctor. Marketing Director: David Saldarrigo. Chief Technician: Wayne Zimmerman. Customer Service Manager: Valarie Gabaree.
City fee: 3% of basic.
Ownership: Bright House Networks LLC (MSO).

WILLISTON—Comcast Cable, 20775 W Pennsylvania Ave, Dunnellon, FL 34431. Phones: 352-787-9601 (Leesburg office); 352-489-0939. Fax: 352-365-6279. Web Site: http://www.comcast.com. Also serves Levy County. ICA: FL0166.
TV Market Ranking: Below 100 (Levy County (portions), WILLISTON); Outside TV Markets (Levy County (portions)). Franchise award date: N.A. Franchise expiration date: N.A. Began: April 1, 1967.
Channel capacity: N.A. Channels available but not in use: N.A.
Basic Service
Subscribers: N.A. Included with Inverness, FL
Programming (received off-air): WCJB-TV (ABC, CW) Gainesville; WGFL (CBS, MNT) High Springs; WKMG-TV (CBS) Orlando; WOGX (FOX) Ocala; WUFT (PBS) Gainesville; WVEA-TV (UNV) Venice.
Programming (via satellite): CNBC; CNN; Discovery Channel; Disney Channel; Fox News Channel; History Channel; Home Shopping Network; QVC; The Learning Channel; Travel Channel; Trinity Broadcasting Network; USA Network; Weather Channel; WGN America; WNBC (NBC) New York.
Current originations: Public Access.
Fee: $15.86 installation; $20.16 monthly.
Expanded Basic Service 1
Subscribers: N.A.
Programming (via satellite): ABC Family Channel; AMC; Animal Planet; Arts & Entertainment; BET Networks; Cartoon Network; Comedy Central; Country Music TV; C-SPAN; E! Entertainment Television; ESPN; ESPN 2; Food Network; Fox Sports Net Florida; FX; HGTV; Lifetime; Nickelodeon; Spike TV; SunSports TV; Syfy; TBS Superstation; truTV; Turner Network TV; TV Land; VH1.
Fee: $43.95 monthly.
Digital Basic Service
Subscribers: N.A.
Programming (via satellite): BBC America; Bloomberg Television; Discovery Digital Networks; DMX Music; ESPN Classic Sports; ESPNews; FitTV; Fox Movie Channel; Fox Soccer; G4; GSN; Halogen Network; National Geographic Channel; Nick Jr.; NickToons TV; Speed Channel; Trinity Broadcasting Network; Turner Classic Movies; VH1 Classic; VH1 Country; WE tv.
Digital Expanded Basic Service
Subscribers: N.A.
Programming (via satellite): Golf Channel; Independent Film Channel; Outdoor Channel; Versus.
Digital Pay Service 1
Pay Units: N.A.
Programming (via satellite): Cinemax (multiplexed); Encore; HBO (multiplexed); Showtime (multiplexed); Starz (multiplexed); The Movie Channel (multiplexed).
Video-On-Demand: No
Pay-Per-View
HITS (Headend In The Sky) (delivered digitally); Playboy TV (delivered digitally); Fresh (delivered digitally).
Internet Service
Operational: Yes.
Telephone Service
Digital: Operational
Miles of Plant: 38.0 (coaxial); None (fiber optic). Homes passed: 1,277.
General Manager: Mike Davenport. Marketing Manager: Melanie Melvin.
City fee: 3% of gross.
Ownership: Comcast Cable Communications Inc. (MSO).

WOODFIELD—Now served by DELRAY BEACH, FL [FL0091]. ICA: FL0295.

WYNMOOR VILLAGE—Comcast Cable. Now served by BROWARD COUNTY, FL [FL0016]. ICA: FL0373.

YANKEETOWN—Now served by INVERNESS, FL [FL0319]. ICA: FL0177.

YULEE—Comcast Cable, 6805 Southpoint Pkwy, Jacksonville, FL 32216. Phone: 904-374-8000. Fax: 904-374-7622. Web Site: http://www.comcast.com. Also serves Nassau County (portions). ICA: FL0129.
TV Market Ranking: 68 (Nassau County (portions), YULEE). Franchise award date: January 1, 1985. Franchise expiration date: N.A. Began: April 18, 1986.
Channel capacity: N.A. Channels available but not in use: N.A.
Basic Service
Subscribers: N.A.
Programming (received off-air): WAWS (FOX, MNT) Jacksonville; WCWJ (CW) Jacksonville; WJCT (PBS) Jacksonville; WJEB-TV (ETV) Jacksonville; WJXT (IND) Jacksonville; WJXX (ABC) Orange Park; WPXC-TV (ION) Brunswick; WTEV-TV (CBS) Jacksonville; WTLV (NBC) Jacksonville; allband FM.
Programming (via satellite): ABC Family Channel; AMC; Animal Planet; Arts & Entertainment; BET Networks; Bloomberg Television; Cartoon Network; CNBC; Comedy Central; Country Music TV; C-SPAN; C-SPAN 2; Discovery Channel; E! Entertainment Television; ESPN; ESPN 2; ESPN Classic Sports; FitTV; Food Network; FX; G4; GalaVision; Headline News; HGTV; Home Shopping Network; Lifetime; MSNBC; MTV; Nickelodeon; Product Information Network; QVC; Spike TV; Syfy; The Learning Channel; Travel Channel; Turner Network TV; TV Guide Network; TV Land; USA Network; VH1; Weather Channel; WGN America.
Fee: $49.99 monthly; $49.95 converter; $15.00 additional installation.
Expanded Basic Service 1
Subscribers: N.A.
Programming (via satellite): CNN; Disney Channel; Fox News Channel; Golf Channel; Hallmark Channel; History Channel; Oxygen; ShopNBC; TBS Superstation; truTV.
Fee: $6.97 monthly.
Digital Basic Service
Subscribers: N.A.
Programming (via satellite): AmericanLife TV Network; BBC America; Black Family Channel; Bravo; Discovery Digital Networks; ESPNews; Eternal Word TV Network; Fox Movie Channel; Great American Country; GSN; Independent Film Channel; MuchMusic Network; Music Choice; SoapNet; Speed Channel; Toon Disney; Trinity Broadcasting Network; WE tv.
Fee: $14.95 monthly.
Digital Expanded Basic Service
Subscribers: N.A.
Programming (via satellite): Bio; Do-It-Yourself; Fox Sports World; GAS; History Channel International; INSP; MTV Networks Digital Suite; National Geographic Channel; Nick Jr.; Nick Too; NickToons TV; Outdoor Channel; Style Network; Sundance Channel; Turner Classic Movies; Versus.
Digital Pay Service 1
Pay Units: N.A.
Programming (via satellite): Cinemax (multiplexed); Encore (multiplexed); Flix; HBO (multiplexed); Showtime (multiplexed); Starz (multiplexed); The Movie Channel (multiplexed).
Fee: $15.95 monthly (each).
Video-On-Demand: No
Pay-Per-View
Fresh (delivered digitally); Playboy TV (delivered digitally).
Internet Service
Operational: Yes.
Broadband Service: Comcast High Speed Internet.
Fee: $42.95 monthly; $3.00 modem lease.
Telephone Service
Digital: Operational
Miles of Plant: 152.0 (coaxial); None (fiber optic). Homes passed: 4,000. Total homes in franchised area: 4,000.
Vice President & General Manager: Doug McMillan. Engineering Director: Mike Humphrey. Vice President, Marketing: Vic Scarborough. Government Affairs Director: Bill Ferry.
County fee: 4% of gross.
Ownership: Comcast Cable Communications Inc. (MSO).

ZELLWOOD—Florida Cable, PO Box 498, 23748 State Rd 40, Astor, FL 32102-0498. Phones: 352-759-2788; 800-779-2788. Fax: 352-759-3577. Web Site: http://www.floridacable.com. ICA: FL0346.
TV Market Ranking: 55 (ZELLWOOD). Franchise award date: N.A. Franchise expiration date: N.A. Began: N.A.
Channel capacity: 52 (not 2-way capable). Channels available but not in use: N.A.
Basic Service
Subscribers: 138.
Programming (received off-air): WESH (NBC) Daytona Beach; WFTV (ABC) Orlando; WHLV-TV (IND) Cocoa; WKCF (CW) Clermont; WKMG-TV (CBS) Orlando; WMFE-TV (PBS) Orlando; WOFL (FOX) Orlando; WRBW (MNT) Orlando; WRDQ (IND) Orlando; WTGL (ETV) Leesburg.
Programming (via satellite): ABC Family Channel; AMC; AmericanLife TV Network; Animal Planet; Arts & Entertainment; CNBC; CNN; Country Music TV; C-SPAN; Discovery Channel; ESPN; ESPN 2; Fox News Channel; FX; History Channel; Home Shopping Network; Lifetime; MTV; Nickelodeon; Spike TV; SunSports TV; TBS Superstation; The Learning Channel; Travel Channel; Trinity Broadcasting Network; Turner Network TV; USA Network; VH1; Weather Channel; WGN America.
Fee: $22.95 monthly.
Pay Service 1
Pay Units: N.A.
Programming (via satellite): Cinemax; HBO.
Internet Service
Operational: No.
Telephone Service
None
Miles of Plant: 14.0 (coaxial); None (fiber optic). Total homes in franchised area: 425.
Ownership: Florida Cable Inc. (MSO).

GEORGIA

Total Systems: **216**
Total Communities Served: **841**
Franchises Not Yet Operating: **0**
Applications Pending: **0**
Communities with Applications: **0**
Number of Basic Subscribers: **1,415,962**
Number of Expanded Basic Subscribers: **871,839**
Number of Pay Units: **272,063**

Top 100 Markets Represented: Atlanta-Rome (18); Greenville-Spartanburg-Anderson, SC-Asheville, NC (46); Jacksonville, FL (68); Chattanooga, TN (78); Columbus (94).

For a list of cable communities in this section, see the Cable Community Index located in the back of Cable Volume 2.
For explanation of terms used in cable system listings, see p. D-11.

ABBEVILLE—KLiP Interactive, 455 Gees Mill Business Court, Conyers, GA 30013. Phone: 678-727-7100. Fax: 678-727-7002. E-mail: jsheehan@klipia.com. Web Site: http://www.klipia.com. ICA: GA0146.

TV Market Ranking: Below 100 (ABBEVILLE). Franchise award date: N.A. Franchise expiration date: N.A. Began: March 1, 1983.

Channel capacity: 65 (not 2-way capable). Channels available but not in use: 30.

Basic Service

Subscribers: 130.

Programming (received off-air): WALB (NBC) Albany; WFXL (FOX) Albany; WGXA (FOX, MNT) Macon; WMAZ-TV (CBS) Macon; WMGT-TV (MNT, NBC) Macon; WMUM-TV (PBS) Cochran; WPGA-TV (ABC) Perry; WSST-TV (IND) Cordele.

Programming (via satellite): ABC Family Channel; Arts & Entertainment; BET Networks; CNN; Comcast Sports Net Southeast; Country Music TV; Discovery Channel; Disney Channel; ESPN; ESPN 2; Fox News Channel; History Channel; Home Shopping Network; Lifetime; MTV; Nickelodeon; QVC; Spike TV; TBS Superstation; The Learning Channel; Trinity Broadcasting Network; Turner Network TV; TV Land; USA Network; VH1; Weather Channel; WGN America.

Fee: $29.95 installation; $38.45 monthly.

Pay Service 1

Pay Units: 20.

Programming (via satellite): HBO.

Fee: $10.95 monthly.

Pay Service 2

Pay Units: 10.

Programming (via satellite): Cinemax.

Fee: $10.95 monthly.

Internet Service

Operational: No.

Telephone Service

None

Miles of Plant: 10.0 (coaxial); None (fiber optic). Homes passed: 360.

Chief Executive Officer: Joseph A. Sheehan. General Manager East: Mark Miller. General Manager West: Vance Johnson.

Ownership: KLiP Interactive LLC (MSO).

ACWORTH—KLiP Interactive, 455 Gees Mill Business Court, Conyers, GA 30013. Phone: 678-801-4020. Fax: 678-727-7002. E-mail: jsheehan@klipia.com. Web Site: http://www.klipia.com. ICA: GA0292. **Note:** This system is an overbuild.

TV Market Ranking: 18 (ACWORTH). Franchise award date: June 1, 2000. Franchise expiration date: N.A. Began: January 29, 2001.

Channel capacity: 83 (operating 2-way). Channels available but not in use: N.A.

Basic Service

Subscribers: 1,962.

Programming (received off-air): WAGA-TV (FOX) Atlanta; WATC-DT (ETV) Atlanta; WATL (MNT) Atlanta; WGCL-TV (CBS) Atlanta; WGTV (PBS) Athens; WHSG-TV (TBN) Monroe; WPBA (PBS) Atlanta; WPXA-TV (ION) Rome; WSB-TV (ABC) Atlanta; WUPA (CW) Atlanta; WUVG-DT (UNV) Athens; WXIA-TV (NBC) Atlanta.

Programming (via satellite): Home Shopping Network; TBS Superstation; TV Guide Network; Weather Channel; WGN America.

Current originations: Educational Access; Government Access.

Fee: $13.75 monthly.

Expanded Basic Service 1

Subscribers: 1,631.

Programming (via satellite): ABC Family Channel; AMC; Animal Planet; Arts & Entertainment; BET Networks; Bravo; Cartoon Network; CNBC; CNN; Comcast Sports Net Southeast; Comedy Central; Country Music TV; C-SPAN; C-SPAN 2; Discovery Channel; Disney Channel; E! Entertainment Television; ESPN; ESPN 2; ESPN Classic Sports; Eternal Word TV Network; FitTV; Food Network; Fox News Channel; FX; GalaVision; Golf Channel; Great American Country; GSN; Headline News; HGTV; History Channel; INSP; Lifetime; MSNBC; MTV; National Geographic Channel; Nickelodeon; Outdoor Channel; QVC; Speed Channel; Spike TV; SportSouth; Style Network; Syfy; The Learning Channel; Travel Channel; truTV; Turner Classic Movies; Turner Network TV; TV Land; USA Network; Versus; VH1; WE tv.

Fee: $27.00 monthly.

Digital Basic Service

Subscribers: 1,981.

Programming (via satellite): BBC America; Bio; Bloomberg Television; Boomerang; CNN; CNN International; Discovery Digital Networks; Do-It-Yourself; Encore; Fox Movie Channel; Fuse; G4; Hallmark Channel; History Channel International; Independent Film Channel; Lifetime Movie Network; Military History Channel; Music Choice; Toon Disney.

Fee: $11.50 monthly.

Pay Service 1

Pay Units: 248.

Programming (via satellite): HBO.

Fee: $12.95 monthly.

Digital Pay Service 1

Pay Units: N.A.

Programming (via satellite): Cinemax (multiplexed); Flix; HBO (multiplexed); Showtime (multiplexed); Starz (multiplexed); Sundance Channel; The Movie Channel (multiplexed).

Fee: $5.95 monthly (Flix, IFC & Sundance), $8.95 monthly (Starz & Encore), $9.95 monthly (Cinemax or TMC), $12.95 monthly (HBO), $14.75 monthly (Showtime).

Video-On-Demand: No

Pay-Per-View

iN DEMAND (delivered digitally), Fee: $3.95, Addressable: Yes; Hot Choice (delivered digitally); Hustler TV (delivered digitally).

Internet Service

Operational: No.

Telephone Service

None

Miles of Plant: None (coaxial); 120.0 (fiber optic). Homes passed: 5,250.

Chief Executive Officer: Joseph A. Sheehan. General Manager East: Mark Miller. General Manager West: Vance Johnson.

Ownership: KLiP Interactive LLC (MSO).

ADRIAN—Comcast Cable, 141 Park of Commerce Dr, Savannah, GA 31405. Phone: 912-356-3113. Web Site: http://www.comcast.com. Also serves Emanuel County & Johnson County. ICA: GA0136.

TV Market Ranking: Outside TV Markets (ADRIAN, Emanuel County (portions), Johnson County). Franchise award date: April 5, 1982. Franchise expiration date: N.A. Began: November 2, 1982.

Channel capacity: N.A. Channels available but not in use: N.A.

Basic Service

Subscribers: N.A. Included in Savannah

Programming (received off-air): WAGT (CW, NBC) Augusta; WGXA (FOX, MNT) Macon; WJBF (ABC) Augusta; WMAZ-TV (CBS) Macon; WMGT-TV (MNT, NBC) Macon; WMUM-TV (PBS) Cochran; WPGA-TV (ABC) Perry; WRDW-TV (CBS, MNT) Augusta.

Programming (via satellite): HGTV; ION Television; QVC; Speed Channel; Spike TV; SportSouth; Style Network; Syfy; TBS Superstation; Turner Network TV; TV Land; USA Network; VH1; Weather Channel.

Fee: $47.99 installation; $11.00 monthly; $20.00 additional installation.

Expanded Basic Service 1

Subscribers: N.A.

Programming (via satellite): ABC Family Channel; AMC; Animal Planet; Arts & Entertainment; BET Networks; Cartoon Network; CNN; Comcast/Charter Sports Southeast (CSS); Comedy Central; Country Music TV; Discovery Channel; Discovery Health Channel; E! Entertainment Television; ESPN; ESPN 2; Food Network; Fox News Channel; Fox Sports Net; FX; Golf Channel; GSN; Hallmark Channel; Headline News; History Channel; Home Shopping Network; INSP; Lifetime; Nickelodeon; The Learning Channel; Versus.

Fee: $35.99 monthly.

Pay Service 1

Pay Units: 46.

Programming (via satellite): HBO; Showtime.

Fee: $15.00 installation; $7.00 monthly.

Video-On-Demand: No

Internet Service

Operational: Yes.

Telephone Service

Digital: Operational

Homes passed & miles of plant (coax & fiber) included in Savannah

General Manager: MIchael Daves. Technical Operations Director: Joel Godsen. Marketing Director: Jerry Avery. Marketing Manager: Ken Torres.

City fee: 2% of gross.

Ownership: Comcast Cable Communications Inc. (MSO).

ALBANY—Mediacom, 509 Flint Ave, Albany, GA 31701. Phones: 229-244-3852 (Valdosta regional office); 229-888-0242. Fax: 229-436-4819. Web Site: http://www.mediacomcable.com. Also serves Bridgeboro, Dawson, Dougherty County (portions), Lee County (portions), Leesburg, Pine Glen, Poulan, Putney, Radium Springs, Sylvester, Terrell County (southern portion), U.S. Marine Logistics Base (Government Reserve) & Worth County (eastern portion). ICA: GA0011.

TV Market Ranking: Below 100 (ALBANY, Bridgeboro, Dawson, Dougherty County (portions), Lee County (portions), Leesburg, Pine Glen, Poulan, Putney, Radium Springs, Sylvester, Terrell County (southern portion), U.S. Marine Logistics Base (Government Reserve), Worth County (eastern portion)). Franchise award date: May 1, 1966. Franchise expiration date: N.A. Began: October 1, 1965.

Channel capacity: 71 (operating 2-way). Channels available but not in use: None.

Basic Service

Subscribers: 39,421.

Programming (received off-air): WABW-TV (PBS) Pelham; WALB (NBC) Albany; WCTV (CBS, MNT) Thomasville; WFXL (FOX) Albany; WRBL (CBS) Columbus; WSST-TV (IND) Cordele; WSWG (CBS, MNT) Valdosta; WTVM (ABC) Columbus.

Programming (via microwave): WSB-TV (ABC) Atlanta.

Programming (via satellite): CNBC; C-SPAN; C-SPAN 2; CW+; Eternal Word TV Network; Hallmark Channel; Home Shopping Network; QVC; Trinity Broadcasting Network.

Current originations: Leased Access; Religious Access; Government Access; Educational Access; Public Access.

Fee: $19.95 installation; $10.18 monthly; $1.90 converter.

Expanded Basic Service 1
Subscribers: 35,714.
Programming (via satellite): ABC Family Channel; AMC; Animal Planet; Arts & Entertainment; BET Networks; Black Family Channel; Bravo; Cartoon Network; CNN; Comcast Sports Net Southeast; Comedy Central; Country Music TV; Discovery Channel; Disney Channel; ESPN; ESPN 2; Food Network; Fox News Channel; FX; Headline News; HGTV; History Channel; INSP; ION Television; Lifetime; MSNBC; MTV; Nickelodeon; Spike TV; Syfy; TBS Superstation; The Learning Channel; truTV; Turner Network TV; TV Guide Network; TV Land; USA Network; VH1; WE tv; Weather Channel.
Fee: $21.66 monthly.

Digital Basic Service
Subscribers: 11,500.
Programming (via satellite): BBC America; Bio; Discovery Digital Networks; DMX Music; Fox Sports World; Fuse; G4; GAS; Golf Channel; GSN; History Channel International; Independent Film Channel; Lifetime Movie Network; Lime; MTV Networks Digital Suite; National Geographic Channel; Nick Jr.; Ovation; Speed Channel; Style Network; Toon Disney; Turner Classic Movies; Versus.

Digital Pay Service 1
Pay Units: 1,737.
Programming (via satellite): Cinemax (multiplexed); Encore (multiplexed); HBO (multiplexed); Showtime (multiplexed); Starz (multiplexed); Sundance Channel; The Movie Channel (multiplexed).
Fee: $10.30 monthly (Cinemax, HBO, Showtime, Sundance/TMC, or Starz/Encore).

Video-On-Demand: Yes

Pay-Per-View
Addressable homes: 11,500.
ESPN Now (delivered digitally), Addressable: Yes; ETC (delivered digitally); TVN Entertainment (delivered digitally); sports (delivered digitally).

Internet Service
Operational: Yes.
Broadband Service: Mediacom High Speed Internet.
Fee: $70.00 installation; $42.95 monthly; $3.00 modem lease.

Telephone Service
Analog: Not Operational
Digital: Operational

Miles of Plant: 2,090.0 (coaxial); None (fiber optic). Homes passed: 48,615. Total homes in franchised area: 105,781.
Regional Vice President: Sue Misiunas. General Manager: Gary Crosby. Regional Technical Operations Manager: Gary McDougall. Technical Operations Manager: David Jones. Regional Marketing Director: Melanie Hannasch. Marketing Manager: Daryl Channey.
City fee: 5% of gross.
Ownership: Mediacom LLC (MSO).

ALLENTOWN—KLiP Interactive, 455 Gees Mill Business Court, Conyers, GA 30013. Phone: 678-727-7100. Fax: 678-727-7002. E-mail: jsheehan@klipia.com. Web Site: http://www.klipia.com. Also serves Danville, Laurens County (portions) & Twiggs County (eastern portion). ICA: GA0186.
TV Market Ranking: Below 100 (ALLENTOWN, Danville, Laurens County (portions), Twiggs County (eastern portion)). Franchise award date: N.A. Franchise expiration date: N.A. Began: January 1, 1988.
Channel capacity: 45 (not 2-way capable). Channels available but not in use: 8.

Basic Service
Subscribers: 133.
Programming (received off-air): WGNM (IND) Macon; WGXA (FOX, MNT) Macon; WMAZ-TV (CBS) Macon; WMGT-TV (MNT, NBC) Macon; WPCH-TV (IND) Atlanta; WPGA-TV (ABC) Perry.
Programming (via satellite): ABC Family Channel; Arts & Entertainment; BET Networks; Bravo!; CNBC; CNN; Comcast Sports Net Southeast; Country Music TV; C-SPAN; Discovery Channel; Disney Channel; ESPN; ESPN 2; Fox News Channel; FX; Headline News; History Channel; Lifetime; MTV; Nickelodeon; QVC; Speed Channel; Spike TV; Syfy; The Learning Channel; Trinity Broadcasting Network; Turner Network TV; TV Land; USA Network; Weather Channel; WGN America.
Fee: $29.95 installation; $39.95 monthly.

Pay Service 1
Pay Units: 25.
Programming (via satellite): HBO.
Fee: $10.95 monthly.

Pay Service 2
Pay Units: 14.
Programming (via satellite): Showtime.
Fee: $10.95 monthly.

Internet Service
Operational: No.

Telephone Service
None

Miles of Plant: 34.0 (coaxial); None (fiber optic). Homes passed: 544.
Chief Executive Officer: Joseph A. Sheehan. General Manager East: Mark Miller. General Manager West: Vance Johnson.
Ownership: KLiP Interactive LLC (MSO).

ALMA—Alma Telephone Co., PO Box 2027, 407 W 11th St, Alma, GA 31510-2027. Phone: 912-632-8603. Fax: 912-632-4519. E-mail: info@atc.cc. Web Site: http://www.accessatc.net. ICA: GA0098.
TV Market Ranking: Below 100 (ALMA). Franchise award date: January 1, 1979. Franchise expiration date: N.A. Began: December 31, 1965.
Channel capacity: 65 (not 2-way capable). Channels available but not in use: None.

Basic Service
Subscribers: 1,800.
Programming (received off-air): WAWS (FOX, MNT) Jacksonville; WCWJ (CW) Jacksonville; WGSA (CW) Baxley; WJCL (ABC) Savannah; WJXT (IND) Jacksonville; WJXX (ABC) Orange Park; WPXC-TV (ION) Brunswick; WSAV-TV (MNT, NBC) Savannah; WTEV-TV (CBS) Jacksonville; WTGS (FOX) Hardeeville; WTLV (NBC) Jacksonville; WTOC-TV (CBS) Savannah; WXGA-TV (PBS) Waycross; allband FM.
Programming (via satellite): ABC Family Channel; AMC; Animal Planet; Arts & Entertainment; BET Networks; Cartoon Network; CNBC; CNN; Comcast Sports Net Southeast; Comcast/Charter Sports Southeast (CSS); Comedy Central; Country Music TV; C-SPAN; C-SPAN 2; Discovery Channel; Disney Channel; E! Entertainment Television; ESPN; ESPN 2; ESPN Classic Sports; FitTV; Food Network; Fox News Channel; FX; Golf Channel; Hallmark Channel; Headline News; HGTV; History Channel; Home Shopping Network; INSP; Lifetime; Local Cable Weather; MTV; National Geographic Channel; Nickelodeon; Outdoor Channel; QVC; Speed Channel; Spike TV; SportSouth; Syfy; TBS Superstation; The Learning Channel; Travel Channel; Trinity Broadcasting Network; truTV; Turner Network TV; TV Guide Network; TV Land; USA Network; VH1; Weather Channel.
Current originations: Public Access.
Fee: $35.00 installation; $46.95 monthly; $3.00 converter.

Digital Basic Service
Subscribers: 450.
Programming (via satellite): BBC America; Bio; Bloomberg Television; Boomerang; Current; Discovery Military Channel; DMX Music; ESPN 2; ESPN Classic Sports; ESPN U; ESPNews; FitTV; Flix; Fox Movie Channel; Fox Soccer; FSN Digital Atlantic; FSN Digital Central; FSN Digital Pacific; Fuse; G4; Golf Channel; Gospel Music Channel; Great American Country; GSN; Hallmark Movie Channel; Halogen Network; HGTV; History Channel; History Channel International; ID Investigation Discovery; Lifetime Movie Network; Lime; MTV Hits; MTV2; National Geographic Channel; Nick Jr.; NickToons TV; Outdoor Channel; RFD-TV; Science Channel; Sleuth; SoapNet; Speed Channel; Style Network; Sundance Channel; TeenNick; Toon Disney; Trinity Broadcasting Network; Turner Classic Movies; Versus; VH1 Classic; WE tv.
Fee: $16.95 monthly.

Digital Expanded Basic Service
Subscribers: N.A.
Programming (received off-air): WAWS (FOX, MNT) Jacksonville; WCWJ (CW) Jacksonville; WJCT (PBS) Jacksonville; WJXT (IND) Jacksonville; WJXX (ABC) Orange Park; WSAV-TV (MNT, NBC) Savannah; WTEV-TV (CBS) Jacksonville; WTGS (FOX) Hardeeville; WTLV (NBC) Jacksonville; WTOC-TV (CBS) Savannah.
Programming (via satellite): Animal Planet HD; Arts & Entertainment HD; Bravo HD; CNBC HD+; CNN HD; Discovery Channel HD; ESPN 2 HD; ESPN HD; Golf Channel HD; History Channel HD; National Geographic Channel HD Network; Outdoor Channel 2 HD; Science Channel HD; Syfy HD; TBS in HD; TLC HD; Turner Network TV HD; USA Network HD; Versus HD; Weather Channel HD.

Digital Expanded Basic Service 2
Subscribers: N.A.
Programming (via satellite): Discovery HD Theater; HDNet; HDNet Movies; Universal HD.

Digital Pay Service 1
Pay Units: 141.
Programming (via satellite): HBO (multiplexed); HBO HD.
Fee: $12.95 monthly.

Digital Pay Service 2
Pay Units: 71.
Programming (via satellite): Showtime (multiplexed); Showtime HD; The Movie Channel (multiplexed).
Fee: $12.95 monthly.

Digital Pay Service 3
Pay Units: 34.
Programming (via satellite): Cinemax (multiplexed); Cinemax HD.
Fee: $8.00 monthly.

Digital Pay Service 4
Pay Units: 85.
Programming (via satellite): Encore (multiplexed); Starz (multiplexed); Starz HDTV.
Fee: $12.95 monthly.

Video-On-Demand: No

Pay-Per-View
iN DEMAND (delivered digitally); Playboy TV (delivered digitally); Fresh (delivered digitally); Spice: Xcess (delivered digitally); Club Jenna (delivered digitally).

Internet Service
Operational: No.
Broadband Service: DSL service only.

Telephone Service
None

Miles of Plant: 80.0 (coaxial); 10.0 (fiber optic). Homes passed: 2,600.
Manager & Marketing Director: Kevin Brooks. Chief Technician: Tony McKinnon.
City fee: 3% of gross.
Ownership: ATC.

AMERICUS—Mediacom, 509 Flint Ave, Albany, GA 31701. Phones: 229-244-3852 (Valdosta regional office); 229-888-0242. Fax: 229-436-4819. Web Site: http://www.mediacomcable.com. Also serves Ellaville, Randolph County (portions), Schley County (portions), Shellman & Sumter County (portions). ICA: GA0039.
TV Market Ranking: Below 100 (AMERICUS, Randolph County (portions), Schley County (portions), Shellman, Sumter County (portions)); Outside TV Markets (Ellaville, Randolph County (portions), Schley County (portions), Sumter County (portions)). Franchise award date: N.A. Franchise expiration date: N.A. Began: January 1, 1969.
Channel capacity: N.A. Channels available but not in use: N.A.

Basic Service
Subscribers: 6,852.
Programming (received off-air): WACS-TV (PBS) Dawson; WALB (NBC) Albany; WLTZ (CW, NBC) Columbus; WMAZ-TV (CBS) Macon; WRBL (CBS) Columbus; WSB-TV (ABC) Atlanta; WSST-TV (IND) Cordele; WTVM (ABC) Columbus; WXTX (FOX) Columbus; allband FM.
Programming (via satellite): Hallmark Channel; Home Shopping Network; Lifetime; Weather Channel.
Current originations: Government Access; Leased Access; Public Access.
Fee: $27.67 installation; $24.60 monthly; $1.77 converter.

Expanded Basic Service 1
Subscribers: 6,596.
Programming (via satellite): ABC Family Channel; AMC; Animal Planet; Arts & Entertainment; BET Networks; Cartoon Network; CNBC; CNN; Comcast Sports Net Southeast; Country Music TV; C-SPAN; Discovery Channel; Disney Channel; ESPN; ESPN 2; Fox News Channel; FX; Headline News; HGTV; ION Television; MoviePlex; MSNBC; MTV; Nickelodeon; QVC; Spike TV; SportSouth; Syfy; TBS Superstation; The Learning Channel; Travel Channel; Trinity Broadcasting Network; truTV; Turner Network TV; TV Guide Network; USA Network; VH1.
Fee: $17.45 monthly.

Digital Basic Service
Subscribers: N.A.
Programming (via satellite): BBC America; Bravo; Discovery Digital Networks; DMX Music; ESPN Classic Sports; ESPNews; Fox Sports World; Golf Channel; GSN; History Channel; Independent Film Channel; National Geographic Channel; Nick Jr.; Speed Channel; Turner Classic Movies; TV Land; Versus; VH1 Classic; VH1 Country; WE tv.

Digital Pay Service 1
Pay Units: N.A.
Programming (via satellite): Cinemax (multiplexed); Encore (multiplexed); HBO

(multiplexed); Showtime (multiplexed); Starz (multiplexed); The Movie Channel (multiplexed).

Video-On-Demand: Yes

Pay-Per-View

Addressable: Yes; Playboy TV (delivered digitally).

Internet Service

Operational: Yes.

Broadband Service: Mediacom High Speed Internet.

Fee: $42.95 monthly; $3.00 modem lease.

Telephone Service

Analog: Not Operational

Digital: Operational

Miles of Plant: 189.0 (coaxial); None (fiber optic). Homes passed: 9,617.

Regional Vice President: Sue Misiunas. General Manager: Gary Crosby. Technical Operations Manager: David Jones. Regional Marketing Director: Melanie Hannasch. Regional Technical Operations Manager: Gary McDougall. Marketing Manager: Daryl Channey.

City fee: 5% of gross.

Ownership: Mediacom LLC (MSO).

ARABI—Citizens Cable TV, PO Box 465, Leslie, GA 31764. Phones: 229-268-2288; 866-341-3050; 229-853-1600. Web Site: http://www.citizenscatv.com. ICA: GA0168.

TV Market Ranking: Below 100 (ARABI). Franchise award date: N.A. Franchise expiration date: N.A. Began: April 1, 1984.

Channel capacity: 65 (not 2-way capable). Channels available but not in use: 34.

Basic Service

Subscribers: 79.

Programming (received off-air): WALB (NBC) Albany; WFXL (FOX) Albany; WPGA-TV (ABC) Perry; WRBL (CBS) Columbus; WSST-TV (IND) Cordele.

Programming (via satellite): ABC Family Channel; Animal Planet; Arts & Entertainment; BET Networks; CNN; Country Music TV; Discovery Channel; ESPN; ESPN 2; Home Shopping Network; Lifetime; Nickelodeon; QVC; Spike TV; TBS Superstation; The Learning Channel; Travel Channel; Trinity Broadcasting Network; Turner Network TV; TV Land; USA Network; VH1; Weather Channel; WGN America.

Fee: $29.95 installation; $31.45 monthly.

Pay Service 1

Pay Units: 11.

Programming (via satellite): HBO.

Fee: $10.95 monthly.

Internet Service

Operational: No.

Telephone Service

None

Miles of Plant: 7.0 (coaxial); None (fiber optic). Homes passed: 90.

Chief Executive Officer: Joseph A. Sheehan. General Manager East: Mark Miller. General Manager West: Vance Johnson.

Ownership: Citizens Cable TV (MSO).

ARNOLDSVILLE—KLiP Interactive, 455 Gees Mill Business Court, Conyers, GA 30013. Phone: 678-727-7100. Fax: 678-727-7002. E-mail: jsheehan@klipia.com. Web Site: http://www.klipia.com. Also serves Clarke County (portions), Oglethorpe County (unincorporated areas) & Winterville. ICA: GA0125.

TV Market Ranking: Below 100 (ARNOLDSVILLE, Clarke County (portions), Oglethorpe County, Winterville). Franchise award date: April 18, 1989. Franchise expiration date: N.A. Began: September 1, 1989.

Channel capacity: 37 (not 2-way capable). Channels available but not in use: None.

Basic Service

Subscribers: 101.

Programming (received off-air): WAGA-TV (FOX) Atlanta; WATL (MNT) Atlanta; WGCL-TV (CBS) Atlanta; WGTV (PBS) Athens; WNEG-TV (CBS) Toccoa; WPCH-TV (IND) Atlanta; WSB-TV (ABC) Atlanta; WUVG-DT (UNV) Athens; WXIA-TV (NBC) Atlanta.

Programming (via satellite): ABC Family Channel; AMC; Animal Planet; Arts & Entertainment; Cartoon Network; CNBC; CNN; Comcast Sports Net Southeast; Country Music TV; C-SPAN; Discovery Channel; Disney Channel; ESPN; ESPN 2; Fuse; Headline News; INSP; Lifetime; QVC; Speed Channel; SportSouth; Syfy; The Learning Channel; Trinity Broadcasting Network; Turner Network TV; USA Network; Weather Channel; WGN America.

Fee: $30.00 installation; $40.95 monthly; $3.50 converter.

Pay Service 1

Pay Units: 5.

Programming (via satellite): HBO.

Fee: $14.95 monthly.

Pay Service 2

Pay Units: 5.

Programming (via satellite): Cinemax.

Fee: $10.95 monthly.

Pay Service 3

Pay Units: 8.

Programming (via satellite): Showtime.

Fee: $9.95 monthly.

Internet Service

Operational: No.

Telephone Service

None

Miles of Plant: 37.0 (coaxial); None (fiber optic). Homes passed: 678. Total homes in franchised area: 678.

Chief Executive Officer: Joseph A. Sheehan. General Manager East: Mark Miller. General Manager West: Vance Johnson.

Ownership: KLiP Interactive LLC (MSO).

ATHENS—Charter Communications, 1925 Breckenridge Plaza, Ste 100, Duluth, GA 30096-4918. Phone: 770-806-7060. Fax: 706-806-7099. Web Site: http://www.charter.com. Also serves Bogart, Clarke County (portions), Colbert, Comer, Danielsville, Hull, Madison County, Oconee County, Watkinsville & Winterville. ICA: GA0014.

TV Market Ranking: Below 100 (ATHENS, Bogart, Clarke County (portions), Colbert, Comer, Danielsville, Hull, Madison County, Oconee County, Watkinsville, Winterville). Franchise award date: N.A. Franchise expiration date: N.A. Began: January 1, 1964.

Channel capacity: N.A. Channels available but not in use: N.A.

Basic Service

Subscribers: 34,643.

Programming (received off-air): WAGA-TV (FOX) Atlanta; WATC-DT (ETV) Atlanta; WATL (MNT) Atlanta; WGCL-TV (CBS) Atlanta; WGTV (PBS) Athens; WHSG-TV (TBN) Monroe; WNEG-TV (CBS) Toccoa; WPCH-TV (IND) Atlanta; WPXA-TV (ION) Rome; WSB-TV (ABC) Atlanta; WUPA (CW) Atlanta; WUVG-DT (UNV) Athens; WXIA-TV (NBC) Atlanta; allband FM.

Programming (via satellite): BET Networks; Comcast/Charter Sports Southeast (CSS); C-SPAN; C-SPAN 2; Home Shopping Network; INSP; QVC; TV Guide Network; WGN America.

Current originations: Government Access; Educational Access.

Fee: $29.99 installation.

Expanded Basic Service 1

Subscribers: N.A.

Programming (via satellite): ABC Family Channel; AMC; Animal Planet; Arts & Entertainment; Bravo; Cartoon Network; CNBC; CNN; Comcast Sports Net Southeast; Comedy Central; Country Music TV; Discovery Channel; Disney Channel; E! Entertainment Television; ESPN; ESPN 2; Food Network; Fox News Channel; FX; G4; GalaVision; Golf Channel; GSN; Hallmark Channel; Headline News; HGTV; History Channel; Lifetime; MSNBC; MTV; National Geographic Channel; Nickelodeon; Outdoor Channel; Oxygen; Product Information Network; Shop at Home; ShopNBC; SoapNet; Speed Channel; Spike TV; SportSouth; Syfy; Telemundo; The Learning Channel; Toon Disney; Travel Channel; truTV; Turner Classic Movies; Turner Network TV; TV Land; USA Network; Versus; VH1; WE tv; Weather Channel.

Fee: $48.99 monthly.

Digital Basic Service

Subscribers: N.A.

Programming (via satellite): BBC America; Bio; Bloomberg Television; Boomerang; Canales N; Discovery Digital Networks; Do-It-Yourself; ESPN Classic Sports; ESPNews; Fox College Sports Atlantic; Fox College Sports Central; Fox College Sports Pacific; Fox Sports World; Fuse; GAS; Great American Country; History Channel International; Independent Film Channel; Lifetime Movie Network; MTV Networks Digital Suite; Music Choice; Nick Jr.; Nick Too; NickToons TV; Style Network; Sundance Channel; TV Guide Interactive Inc.

Fee: $14.00 monthly.

Digital Pay Service 1

Pay Units: 13,054.

Programming (via satellite): Cinemax (multiplexed); Encore (multiplexed); Flix; HBO (multiplexed); Showtime (multiplexed); Starz (multiplexed); The Movie Channel (multiplexed).

Video-On-Demand: Yes

Pay-Per-View

Addressable: Yes; iN DEMAND (delivered digitally); Playboy TV (delivered digitally); Fresh (delivered digitally); Shorteez (delivered digitally); sports (delivered digitally).

Internet Service

Operational: Yes.

Broadband Service: Charter Pipeline.

Fee: $29.99 monthly.

Telephone Service

Digital: Operational

Fee: $29.99 monthly

Miles of Plant: 637.0 (coaxial); 110.0 (fiber optic). Homes passed: 46,988. Total homes in franchised area: 50,000.

Vice President & General Manager: Matt Favre. Operations Director: Jeff Osbourne. Sales & Marketing Director: Antoinette Carpenter.

City fee: 3% of gross.

Ownership: Charter Communications Inc. (MSO).

ATLANTA (northern portion)—Comcast Cable, 150 Hembry Park Dr, Roswell, GA 30076. Phones: 770-559-2424 (Norcross office); 770-888-6527. Fax: 770-559-2479. Web Site: http://www.comcast.com. Also serves Acworth, Alpharetta, Austell, Cherokee County (southern portion), Cobb County, Dallas, Douglas County, Douglasville, Fulton County (northern portion), Hiram, Kennesaw, Lithia Springs, Mableton, Marietta, Paulding County, Powder Springs, Roswell, Sandy Spring, Villa Rica, Vinings, Winston & Woodstock. ICA: GA0007.

TV Market Ranking: 18 (Acworth, Alpharetta, ATLANTA (NORTHERN PORTION), Austell, Cherokee County (southern portion), Cobb County, Dallas, Douglas County, Douglasville, Fulton County (northern portion), Hiram, Kennesaw, Lithia Springs, Mableton, Marietta, Paulding County, Powder Springs, Roswell, Sandy Spring, Villa Rica, Vinings, Winston, Woodstock). Franchise award date: February 25, 1975. Franchise expiration date: N.A. Began: January 1, 1978.

Channel capacity: N.A. Channels available but not in use: N.A.

Basic Service

Subscribers: 300,000 Includes Tallapoosa.

Programming (received off-air): WAGA-TV (FOX) Atlanta; WATC-DT (ETV) Atlanta; WATL (MNT) Atlanta; WGCL-TV (CBS) Atlanta; WGTV (PBS) Athens; WHSG-TV (TBN) Monroe; WPBA (PBS) Atlanta; WPCH-TV (IND) Atlanta; WPXA-TV (ION) Rome; WSB-TV (ABC) Atlanta; WUPA (CW) Atlanta; WUVG-DT (UNV) Athens; WXIA-TV (NBC) Atlanta; 1 FM.

Programming (via microwave): Atlanta Interfaith Broadcasters.

Programming (via satellite): Home Shopping Network; QVC; TV Guide Network.

Current originations: Leased Access.

Fee: $25.00 installation; $16.95 monthly; $19.99 additional installation.

Expanded Basic Service 1

Subscribers: 210,760.

Programming (via satellite): ABC Family Channel; AMC; Animal Planet; Arts & Entertainment; BET Networks; Bravesvision; Bravo; Cartoon Network; CNBC; CNN; Comcast Sports Net Southeast; Comcast/Charter Sports Southeast (CSS); Comedy Central; Country Music TV; C-SPAN; C-SPAN 2; Discovery Channel; E! Entertainment Television; ESPN; ESPN 2; Falconsvision; Food Network; Fox News Channel; FX; Golf Channel; Headline News; HGTV; History Channel; Lifetime; MTV; Nickelodeon; Oxygen; Speed Channel; Spike TV; SportSouth; Syfy; Telemundo; The Learning Channel; Travel Channel; truTV; Turner Classic Movies; Turner Network TV; TV Land; USA Network; VH1; WE tv; Weather Channel.

Fee: $26.61 monthly.

Digital Basic Service

Subscribers: 96,100.

Programming (via satellite): C-SPAN 3; Discovery Digital Networks; ESPN Classic Sports; ESPNews; GAS; GSN; Lime; Music Choice; NASA TV; Nick Jr.; ShopNBC; Style Network; Toon Disney; Weatherscan.

Fee: $14.19 monthly.

Digital Expanded Basic Service

Subscribers: N.A.

Programming (via satellite): AmericanLife TV Network; BBC America; Bio; Black Family Channel; Bloomberg Television; Daystar TV Network; Encore Action; Eternal Word TV Network; FamilyNet; Fox College Sports Atlantic; Fox College Sports Central; Fox College Sports Pacific; Fox Movie Channel; Fox Sports World; G4; Great American Country; Halogen Network; History Channel International; Independent Film Channel; Lifetime Movie Network; MSNBC; MTV Networks Digital Suite; National Geographic Channel; NickToons TV; Outdoor Channel; Ovation; Sundance Channel; Versus.

Fee: $4.00 monthly.

Digital Pay Service 1
Pay Units: 10,428.
Programming (via satellite): Canales N; Cinemax (multiplexed); Flix; HBO (multiplexed); Korean Channel; Showtime (multiplexed); Starz (multiplexed); The Movie Channel (multiplexed); TV Japan.
Fee: $14.99 monthly (Cinemax, HBO, Showtime, Starz, or Flix/TMC), $15.99 monthly (Korean), $30.99 monthly (TV Japan).
Video-On-Demand: Yes
Pay-Per-View
Addressable homes: 96,100.
ESPN Now (delivered digitally), Fee: $4.95, Addressable: Yes; Hot Choice (delivered digitally); iN DEMAND (delivered digitally); Playboy TV (delivered digitally); Fresh (delivered digitally); Shorteez (delivered digitally); sports (delivered digitally).
Internet Service
Operational: Yes.
Broadband Service: Comcast High Speed Internet.
Fee: $49.95 installation; $42.95 monthly; $3.00 modem lease; $139.00 modem purchase.
Telephone Service
Analog: Not Operational
Digital: Operational
Fee: $44.95 monthly
Miles of Plant: 9,744.0 (coaxial); None (fiber optic). Homes passed: 550,000. Homes passed & miles of plant (coax & fiber combined) include Tallapoosa
Vice President & General Manager: Ed Dunbar. Regional Vice President: Gene Shatlock. Regional Vice President, Operations: Michael Hewitt. Technical Operations Director: Robert Harris. Marketing Director: Taylor Nipper. Communications Manager: Cindy Kicklighter.
City fee: 5% of gross.
Ownership: Comcast Cable Communications Inc. (MSO).

ATLANTA (perimeter north)—Comcast Cable, 2925 Courtyards Dr, Norcross, GA 30071. Phones: 770-559-2424 (regional office); 770-888-6527. Fax: 770-887-0079. Web Site: http://www.comcast.com. Also serves Adairsville, Arcade, Auburn, Banks County (western portion), Barrow County, Bartow County, Bethlehem, Braselton, Calhoun, Canton, Carl, Cartersville, Cherokee County (northern portion), Clarke County, Clermont, Cumming, Emerson, Euharlee, Floyd County (portions), Forsyth County (western portion), Gillsville, Gordon County (portions), Gwinnett County (eastern portion), Hall County, Holly Springs, Hoschton, Jackson County (northwestern portion), Kingston, Lake Arrowhead, Lula, Maysville, Oconee County, Pendergrass, Polk County (northeastern portion), Rome, Statham, Talmo, Taylorsville, Waleska, Walton County, White & Winder. ICA: GA0033.
TV Market Ranking: 18 (Adairsville, ATLANTA (PARAMETER NORTH), Bartow County, Calhoun, Canton, Cartersville, Cherokee County (northern portion) (portions), Cumming, Emerson, Euharlee, Floyd County (portions), Forsyth County (western portion), Gordon County (portions), Gwinnett County (eastern portion) (portions), Holly Springs, Kingston, Lake Arrowhead, Polk County (northeastern portion), Rome, Taylorsville, Walton County (portions), White); Below 100 (Arcade, Auburn, Banks County (western portion), Barrow County, Bethlehem, Braselton, Carl, Clarke County, Clermont, Gillsville, Hall County (portions) (portions), Hoschton, Jackson County (northwest portion), Lula, Maysville, Oconee County, Pendergrass, Statham, Talmo, Winder, Cherokee County (northern portion) (portions), Gwinnett County (eastern portion) (portions), Walton County (portions)); Outside TV Markets (Hall County (portions) (portions), Waleska, Cherokee County (northern portion) (portions)). Franchise award date: November 1, 1973. Franchise expiration date: N.A. Began: January 6, 1976.
Channel capacity: N.A. Channels available but not in use: N.A.

Basic Service
Subscribers: N.A. Included in Atlanta (metro area)
Programming (received off-air): WAGA-TV (FOX) Atlanta; WATC-DT (ETV) Atlanta; WATL (MNT) Atlanta; WGCL-TV (CBS) Atlanta; WGTV (PBS) Athens; WPBA (PBS) Atlanta; WPXA-TV (ION) Rome; WSB-TV (ABC) Atlanta; WUPA (CW) Atlanta; WUVG-DT (UNV) Athens; WXIA-TV (NBC) Atlanta; allband FM.
Programming (via satellite): Home Shopping Network; QVC; TBS Superstation; TV Guide Network; WDTA-LP Fayetteville; WGN America.
Current originations: Leased Access; Religious Access; Public Access.
Fee: $25.00 installation; $19.26 monthly.

Expanded Basic Service 1
Subscribers: 25,749.
Programming (via satellite): ABC Family Channel; AMC; Animal Planet; Arts & Entertainment; Bravo; Cartoon Network; CNBC; CNN; Comcast Sports Net Southeast; Comedy Central; Country Music TV; C-SPAN; Discovery Channel; Disney Channel; E! Entertainment Television; ESPN; ESPN 2; Food Network; Fox News Channel; FX; G4; Golf Channel; GSN; Headline News; HGTV; History Channel; INSP; Lifetime; MSNBC; MTV; Nickelodeon; Speed Channel; Spike TV; SportSouth; Syfy; The Learning Channel; Travel Channel; truTV; Turner Classic Movies; Turner Network TV; TV Land; USA Network; VH1; Weather Channel.
Fee: $30.73 monthly.

Digital Basic Service
Subscribers: 15,300.
Programming (via satellite): AmericanLife TV Network; BBC America; Bio; Bloomberg Television; Canales N; Discovery Digital Networks; Do-It-Yourself; ESPN Classic Sports; ESPNews; Fox Movie Channel; Fox Sports World; Fuse; History Channel International; Lifetime Movie Network; Music Choice; National Geographic Channel; NickToons TV; Outdoor Channel; Style Network; Toon Disney; Versus; VH1 Country; WE tv.
Fee: $11.95 monthly.

Digital Pay Service 1
Pay Units: 1,185.
Programming (via satellite): Cinemax (multiplexed).
Fee: $14.99 monthly.

Digital Pay Service 2
Pay Units: 1,537.
Programming (via satellite): Encore (multiplexed).
Fee: $14.99 monthly.

Digital Pay Service 3
Pay Units: 4,635.
Programming (via satellite): HBO (multiplexed).
Fee: $14.99 monthly.

Digital Pay Service 4
Pay Units: 1,172.
Programming (via satellite): Flix; Showtime (multiplexed); The Movie Channel (multiplexed).
Fee: $14.99 monthly.
Digital Pay Service 5
Pay Units: 732.
Programming (via satellite): Starz (multiplexed).
Fee: $14.99 monthly.
Video-On-Demand: Planned
Pay-Per-View
Addressable homes: 15,300.
iN DEMAND (delivered digitally), Addressable: Yes; Sports PPV (delivered digitally).
Internet Service
Operational: Yes.
Broadband Service: Comcast High Speed Internet.
Fee: $42.95 monthly.
Telephone Service
Digital: Operational
Homes passed: 48,970. Total homes in franchised area: 62,000. Miles of plant (coax & fiber combined) included in Atlanta (metro)
Regional Vice President: Gene Shatlock. Regional Vice President, Operations: Michael Hewitt. General Manager: McKnight Brown. Technical Operations Manager: Jim Sherman. Marketing Manager: Tomeka Williams. Communications Manager: Cindy Kicklighter.
City fee: 3% of gross.
Ownership: Comcast Cable Communications Inc. (MSO).

ATLANTA (perimeter south)—Comcast Cable, 2925 Courtyards Dr, Norcross, GA 30071. Phones: 770-559-2424; 770-559-6807. Fax: 770-559-2479. E-mail: kenny_faust@cable.comcast.com. Web Site: http://www.comcast.com. Also serves Between, Brooks, Carroll County (unincorporated areas), Clayton County, Conley, Conyers, Coweta County, Ellenwood, Fayette County, Fayetteville, Forest Park, Fort Gillem, Good Hope, Grantville, Griffin, Hampton, Hogansville, Jersey, Jonesboro, Lake City, Loganville, Lovejoy, Mansfield, Monticello, Morrow, Newborn, Newton County, Orchard Hill, Peachtree City, Riverdale, Rockdale County, Senoia, Social Circle, Spalding County, Sunny Side, Tyrone, Walnut Grove, Walton County (western portion) & Woolsey. ICA: GA0017.
TV Market Ranking: 18 (ATLANTA (PERIMETER SOUTH), Brooks, Carroll County (unincorporated areas), Clayton County, Conley, Conyers, Coweta County, Ellenwood, Fayette County, Fayetteville, Forest Park, Fort Gillem, Grantville (Coweta County), Hampton, Hogansville, Jonesboro, Lake City, Loganville, Lovejoy, Mansfield, Morrow, Newborn, Newton County, Peachtree City, Riverdale, Rockdale County, Senoia, Spalding County (portions), Sunny Side, Tyrone, Walnut Grove, Walton County (western portion), Woolsey); Below 100 (Between, Good Hope, Jersey, Monticello, Social Circle); Outside TV Markets (Griffin, Orchard Hill, Spalding County (portions)). Franchise award date: August 21, 1978. Franchise expiration date: N.A. Began: October 28, 1967.
Channel capacity: N.A. Channels available but not in use: N.A.
Basic Service
Subscribers: N.A. Included in Atlanta (metro area)
Programming (received off-air): WAGA-TV (FOX) Atlanta; WATC-DT (ETV) Atlanta; WATL (MNT) Atlanta; WGCL-TV (CBS) Atlanta; WGTV (PBS) Athens; WHSG-TV (TBN) Monroe; WPBA (PBS) Atlanta; WPCH-TV (IND) Atlanta; WPXA-TV (ION) Rome; WRCB (NBC) Chattanooga; WSB-TV (ABC) Atlanta; WUPA (CW) Atlanta; WUVG-DT (UNV) Athens; WXIA-TV (NBC) Atlanta; allband FM.
Programming (via microwave): Atlanta Interfaith Broadcasters.
Programming (via satellite): Home Shopping Network; QVC; TV Guide Network.
Current originations: Religious Access; Public Access.
Fee: $25.00 installation; $16.95 monthly.
Expanded Basic Service 1
Subscribers: 109,532.
Programming (via satellite): ABC Family Channel; AMC; Animal Planet; Arts & Entertainment; BET Networks; Bravesvision; Bravo; Cartoon Network; CNBC; CNN; Comcast Sports Net Southeast; Comcast/Charter Sports Southeast (CSS); Comedy Central; Country Music TV; C-SPAN; C-SPAN 2; Discovery Channel; Disney Channel; E! Entertainment Television; ESPN; ESPN 2; Falconsvision; Food Network; Fox News Channel; FX; Golf Channel; Headline News; HGTV; History Channel; Lifetime; MTV; Nickelodeon; Oxygen; Speed Channel; Spike TV; SportSouth; Syfy; Telemundo; The Learning Channel; Travel Channel; truTV; Turner Classic Movies; Turner Network TV; TV Land; USA Network; VH1; WE tv; Weather Channel.
Fee: $35.00 installation; $33.04 monthly.
Digital Basic Service
Subscribers: 18,651.
Programming (via satellite): C-SPAN 3; Discovery Digital Networks; ESPN Classic Sports; ESPNews; GAS; GSN; Lime; Music Choice; NASA TV; Nick Jr.; ShopNBC; Style Network; Toon Disney; Weatherscan.
Fee: $11.95 monthly.
Digital Expanded Basic Service
Subscribers: N.A.
Programming (via satellite): AmericanLife TV Network; BBC America; Bio; Black Family Channel; Bloomberg Television; Daystar TV Network; Encore Action; Eternal Word TV Network; FamilyNet; Fox College Sports Atlantic; Fox College Sports Central; Fox College Sports Pacific; Fox Movie Channel; Fox Sports World; G4; Great American Country; Halogen Network; History Channel International; Independent Film Channel; Lifetime Movie Network; MSNBC; MTV Networks Digital Suite; National Geographic Channel; NickToons TV; Outdoor Channel; Ovation; Sundance Channel; Versus.
Fee: $4.00 monthly.

Digital Pay Service 1
Pay Units: 24,622.
Programming (via satellite): Canales N; Cinemax (multiplexed); Flix; HBO (multiplexed); Korean Channel; Showtime (multiplexed); Starz (multiplexed); The Movie Channel (multiplexed); TV Japan.
Fee: $5.99 monthly (Canales n), $14.99 monthly (HBO, Cinemax, Showtime, Starz, or Flix/TMC), $14.99 monthly (Korean), $29.95 monthly (TV Japan).
Video-On-Demand: Yes
Pay-Per-View
Addressable homes: 18,651.
ESPN Now (delivered digitally), Addressable: Yes; Hot Choice (delivered digitally); iN DEMAND (delivered digitally); Playboy TV (delivered digitally); Fresh (delivered digitally); Shorteez (delivered digitally); sports (delivered digitally).
Internet Service
Operational: Yes. Began: April 1, 2001.
Subscribers: 852.
Broadband Service: Comcast High Speed Internet.
Fee: $49.95 installation; $42.95 monthly; $3.00 modem lease; $139.00 modem purchase.
Telephone Service
Digital: Operational
Fee: $44.95 monthly
Homes passed: 116,982. Miles of plant (coax & fiber combined) included in Atlanta (metro area)
Regional Vice President: Gene Shatlock. Regional Vice President, Operations: Michael Hewitt. General Manager: Kenny Faust. Technical Operations Manager: Deborah Collins. Marketing Manager: Maleka Burnett. Communications Manager: Cindy Kicklighter.
City fee: 5% of gross.
Ownership: Comcast Cable Communications Inc. (MSO).

ATTAPULGUS—KLiP Interactive, 455 Gees Mill Business Court, Conyers, GA 30013. Phone: 678-727-7100. Fax: 678-727-7002. E-mail: jsheehan@klipia.com. Web Site: http://www.klipia.com. ICA: GA0173.
TV Market Ranking: Below 100 (ATTAPULGUS). Franchise award date: N.A. Franchise expiration date: N.A. Began: September 1, 1988.
Channel capacity: 65 (not 2-way capable). Channels available but not in use: 32.
Basic Service
Subscribers: 61.
Programming (received off-air): WALB (NBC) Albany; WCTV (CBS, MNT) Thomasville; WFSU-TV (PBS) Tallahassee; WPCH-TV (IND) Atlanta; WTLH (CW, FOX) Bainbridge; WTVY (CBS, CW, MNT) Dothan; WTWC-TV (NBC) Tallahassee; WTXL-TV (ABC) Tallahassee.
Programming (via satellite): ABC Family Channel; Animal Planet; Arts & Entertainment; BET Networks; CNBC; CNN; Comcast Sports Net Southeast; Country Music TV; Discovery Channel; Disney Channel; ESPN; ESPN 2; Headline News; Lifetime; QVC; Spike TV; The Learning Channel; Travel Channel; Trinity Broadcasting Network; Turner Network TV; TV Land; USA Network; Weather Channel; WGN America.
Fee: $30.45 installation; $35.95 monthly.
Pay Service 1
Pay Units: 10.
Programming (via satellite): HBO.
Fee: $25.00 installation; $9.95 monthly.
Internet Service
Operational: No.
Telephone Service
None
Miles of Plant: 8.0 (coaxial); None (fiber optic). Homes passed: 300.
Chief Executive Officer: Joseph A. Sheehan. General Manager East: Mark Miller. General Manager West: Vance Johnson.
Ownership: KLiP Interactive LLC (MSO).

AUGUSTA—Comcast Cable, 105 River Shoals Pkwy, Augusta, GA 30909. Phone: 706-738-0091. Fax: 706-739-1871. E-mail: jerry_fortier@cable.comcast.com. Web Site: http://www.comcast.com. Also serves Blythe, Burke County, Columbia County, Dearing, Evans, Grovetown (portions), Hephzibah, Martinez, Richmond County, South Augusta, Thomson & Waynesboro, GA; Aiken County (portions), North Augusta & Trenton, SC. ICA: GA0004.
TV Market Ranking: Below 100 (Aiken County (portions), AUGUSTA (VILLAGE), Blythe, Burke County, Columbia County, Dearing, Evans, Grovetown (portions), Hephzibah, Martinez, North Augusta, Richmond County, South Augusta, Thomson, Trenton, Waynesboro). Franchise award date: March 1, 1970. Franchise expiration date: N.A. Began: March 1, 1970.
Channel capacity: N.A. Channels available but not in use: N.A.
Basic Service
Subscribers: 97,000.
Programming (received off-air): WAGT (CW, NBC) Augusta; WBPI-CD Augusta; WCES-TV (PBS) Wrens; WEBA-TV (PBS) Allendale; WFXG (FOX) Augusta; WIS (NBC) Columbia; WJBF (ABC) Augusta; WRDW-TV (CBS, MNT) Augusta; 24 FMs.
Programming (via satellite): Comcast/Charter Sports Southeast (CSS); Eternal Word TV Network; Home Shopping Network; ION Television; MyNetworkTV Inc.; QVC; TBS Superstation; USA Network; WGN America.
Fee: $50.00 installation; $14.95 monthly.
Expanded Basic Service 1
Subscribers: 81,019.
Programming (via satellite): ABC Family Channel; AMC; Animal Planet; Arts & Entertainment; BET Networks; Cartoon Network; CNBC; CNN; Comcast Sports Net Southeast; Comedy Central; C-SPAN; C-SPAN 2; Discovery Channel; Discovery Health Channel; Disney Channel; E! Entertainment Television; ESPN; ESPN 2; Food Network; Fox News Channel; FX; Golf Channel; Great American Country; Hallmark Channel; Headline News; HGTV; History Channel; Lifetime; MTV; Nickelodeon; Speed Channel; Spike TV; Syfy; The Learning Channel; Travel Channel; truTV; Turner Classic Movies; Turner Network TV; Turner South; TV Land; Univision; Versus; VH1; Weather Channel.
Fee: $30.04 monthly.
Digital Basic Service
Subscribers: N.A.
Programming (received off-air): WAGT (CW, NBC) Augusta.
Programming (via satellite): BBC America; Bio; Black Family Channel; CBS College Sports Network; Cooking Channel; Country Music TV; C-SPAN 3; Discovery Digital Networks; Discovery HD Theater; DMX Music; Do-It-Yourself; Encore (multiplexed); ESPN 2 HD; ESPN HD; ESPNews; FearNet; Flix; Fox College Sports Atlantic; Fox College Sports Central; Fox College Sports Pacific; Fox Reality Channel; Fox Soccer; G4; GAS; Gol TV; Gospel Music TV; GSN; Halogen Network; History Channel International; INHD; Lifetime Movie Network; MoviePlex; MSNBC; MTV Networks Digital Suite; National Geographic Channel; NBA TV; NFL Network; Nick Jr.; Nick Too; Outdoor Channel; Oxygen; Palladia; PBS Kids Sprout; SoapNet; Style Network; Sundance Channel; Tennis Channel; The Sportsman Channel; The Word Network; Toon Disney; Trinity Broadcasting Network; Turner Network TV HD; TV Asia; TV One; WE tv; Weatherscan; Zee TV USA.
Fee: $14.95 monthly.
Pay Service 1
Pay Units: 12,095.
Programming (via satellite): HBO.
Fee: $9.50 monthly.
Digital Pay Service 1
Pay Units: N.A.
Programming (via satellite): Cinemax (multiplexed); Cinemax HD; HBO (multiplexed); HBO HD; Showtime (multiplexed); Showtime HD; Starz (multiplexed); Starz HDTV; The Movie Channel (multiplexed).
Fee: $12.05 monthly (each).
Video-On-Demand: Yes
Pay-Per-View
iN DEMAND (delivered digitally); Hot Choice (delivered digitally); Playboy TV (delivered digitally); Sports PPV (delivered digitally).
Internet Service
Operational: Yes.
Broadband Service: Comcast High Speed Internet.
Fee: $42.95 monthly.
Telephone Service
Digital: Operational
Miles of Plant: 2,825.0 (coaxial); 246.0 (fiber optic). Homes passed: 123,068.
Engineering Director: Harry Hess. Technical Operations Director: Butch Jernigan. Marketing Director: Joey Fortier.
City fee: 3% of gross.
Ownership: Comcast Cable Communications Inc. (MSO).

AUGUSTA—Knology, 3714 Wheeler Rd, Augusta, GA 30909. Phones: 706-645-8553 (Corporate office); 706-364-1000 (Customer service). Fax: 706-364-1011. Web Site: http://www.knology.com. Also serves Evans, Forest Hills, Grovetown & Martinez. ICA: GA0288.
Note: This system is an overbuild.
TV Market Ranking: Below 100 (AUGUSTA (VILLAGE), Evans, Forest Hills, Grovetown, Martinez). Franchise award date: N.A. Franchise expiration date: N.A. Began: N.A.
Channel capacity: N.A. Channels available but not in use: N.A.
Basic Service
Subscribers: 5,418.
Programming (received off-air): WAGT (CW, NBC) Augusta; WBEK-CA (IND) Augusta; WBPI-CD Augusta; WCES-TV (PBS) Wrens; WEBA-TV (PBS) Allendale; WFXG (FOX) Augusta; WJBF (ABC) Augusta; WRDW-TV (CBS, MNT) Augusta.
Programming (via satellite): ABC Family Channel; AMC; Animal Planet; Arts & Entertainment; BET Networks; Bravo; Cartoon Network; CNBC; CNN; Comcast Sports Net Southeast; Comedy Central; Country Music TV; C-SPAN; C-SPAN 2; CW+; Discovery Channel; Discovery Health Channel; Disney Channel; E! Entertainment Television; ESPN; ESPN 2; ESPN Classic Sports; Food Network; Fox News Channel; FX; G4; Golf Channel; Great American Country; Hallmark Channel; Headline News; HGTV; History Channel; Home Shopping Network; Lifetime; Lifetime Movie Network; MSNBC; MTV; MTV2; MyNetworkTV Inc.; Nick At Nite; Nickelodeon; Outdoor Channel; Oxygen; QVC; ShopNBC; Speed Channel; Spike TV; SportSouth; Syfy; TBS Superstation; The Learning Channel; Toon Disney; Travel Channel; Trinity Broadcasting Network; truTV; Turner Classic Movies; Turner Network TV; TV Guide Network; TV Land; Univision; USA Network; VH1; Weather Channel; WGN America.
Current originations: Public Access.
Fee: $49.95 monthly.
Digital Basic Service
Subscribers: N.A. Included in Valley, AL
Programming (received off-air): WAGT (CW, NBC) Augusta; WFXG (FOX) Augusta; WJBF (ABC) Augusta; WRDW-TV (CBS, MNT) Augusta.
Programming (via satellite): Animal Planet HD; BBC America; Bloomberg Television; Boomerang; CBS College Sports Network; Church Channel; CMT Pure Country; Cooking Channel; C-SPAN 3; Discovery Channel HD; Discovery HD Theater; Discovery Kids Channel; Discovery Military Channel; Discovery Planet Green; Do-It-Yourself; ESPN 2 HD; ESPN HD; ESPN U; ESPNews; Eternal Word TV Network; FitTV; Fox College Sports Atlantic; Fox College Sports Central; Fox College Sports Pacific; Fox Soccer; Fuel TV; Gospel Music Channel; GSN; Hallmark Movie Channel; HDNet; HDNet Movies; ID Investigation Discovery; Independent Film Channel; INSP; JCTV; Jewelry Television; Lifetime Real Women; MTV Hits; MTV Jams; MTV Tres; mtvU; Music Choice; National Geographic Channel; National Geographic Channel HD Network; NFL Network; Nick Jr.; Nick Too; NickToons TV; Outdoor Channel On Demand; Pentagon Channel; QVC HD; Science Channel; Science Channel HD; SoapNet; Starz HDTV; TBS in HD; TeenNick; Tennis Channel; The Sportsman Channel; The Word Network; TLC HD; Turner Network TV HD; Universal HD; Versus; Versus HD; VH1 Classic; VH1 Soul; WE tv.
Pay Service 1
Pay Units: N.A.
Programming (via satellite): HBO; Showtime.
Fee: $8.95 monthly (Showtime), $9.95 monthly (HBO).
Digital Pay Service 1
Pay Units: N.A.
Programming (via satellite): Cinemax (multiplexed); Cinemax HD; Cinemax On Demand; Encore (multiplexed); Flix; Flix On Demand; HBO (multiplexed); HBO HD; HBO On Demand; Showtime (multiplexed); Showtime HD; Showtime On Demand; Starz (multiplexed); Sundance Channel; The Movie Channel (multiplexed); The Movie Channel On Demand.
Video-On-Demand: Yes
Pay-Per-View
iN DEMAND (delivered digitally); Hot Choice (delivered digitally); ESPN Extra (delivered digitally); Playboy TV (delivered digitally); Fresh (delivered digitally); Shorteez (delivered digitally); Spice: Xcess (delivered digitally); Club Jenna (delivered digitally); ESPN Now (delivered digitally).
Internet Service
Operational: Yes.
Broadband Service: Knology.Net.
Fee: $29.95 installation; $61.95 monthly; $7.00 modem lease; $199.00 modem purchase.
Telephone Service
Analog: Not Operational
Digital: Operational
Fee: $23.80 monthly
Homes passed: 55,300.

General Manager: Mike Adams. Technical Operations Manager: James Phillips. Marketing Manager: Roger Gibson.
Ownership: Knology Inc. (MSO).

AVALON—Galaxy Cablevision. Now served by HARTWELL (unincorporated areas), GA [GA0293]. ICA: GA0126.

AVERA—Formerly served by National Cable Inc. No longer in operation. ICA: GA0174.

BACONTON—Blakely Cable TV Inc., 65 Liberty St, Blakely, GA 39823-2257. Phone: 229-723-3555. Fax: 229-723-2000. ICA: GA0294.
TV Market Ranking: Below 100 (BACONTON). Franchise award date: N.A. Franchise expiration date: N.A. Began: N.A.
Channel capacity: 37 (not 2-way capable). Channels available but not in use: None.
Basic Service
Subscribers: 99.
Programming (received off-air): WABW-TV (PBS) Pelham; WALB (NBC) Albany; WCTV (CBS, MNT) Thomasville; WFXL (FOX) Albany; WTVM (ABC) Columbus.
Programming (via satellite): ABC Family Channel; Arts & Entertainment; BET Networks; CNN; Country Music TV; ESPN; Spike TV; TBS Superstation; Turner Network TV; USA Network; WGN America.
Fee: $25.00 installation; $25.95 monthly.
Pay Service 1
Pay Units: 17.
Programming (via satellite): HBO.
Fee: $10.00 monthly.
Video-On-Demand: No
Internet Service
Operational: No.
Telephone Service
None
Manager: William C. De Loach, Jr. Office Manager: Anne Harroll.
Ownership: Blakely Cable TV Inc. (MSO).

BAINBRIDGE—Mediacom, 275 Norman Dr, Valdosta, GA 31601. Phone: 229-244-3852. Fax: 229-244-0724. Web Site: http://www.mediacomcable.com. Also serves Decatur County (portions), Donalsonville & Seminole County (portions). ICA: GA0060.
TV Market Ranking: Below 100 (BAINBRIDGE, Decatur County (portions), Donalsonville, Seminole County (portions)). Franchise award date: N.A. Franchise expiration date: N.A. Began: July 20, 1968.
Channel capacity: N.A. Channels available but not in use: None.
Basic Service
Subscribers: 5,777.
Programming (received off-air): WABW-TV (PBS) Pelham; WALB (NBC) Albany; WBXT-CA Tallahassee; WCTV (CBS, MNT) Thomasville; WFSU-TV (PBS) Tallahassee; WMBB (ABC) Panama City; WSB-TV (ABC) Atlanta; WSWG (CBS, MNT) Valdosta; WTLH (CW, FOX) Bainbridge; WTVY (CBS, CW, MNT) Dothan; WTWC-TV (NBC) Tallahassee; WTXL-TV (ABC) Tallahassee; allband FM.
Programming (via satellite): ABC Family Channel; Arts & Entertainment; BET Networks; CNBC; CNN; Comedy Central; C-SPAN; Discovery Channel; Headline News; Home Shopping Network; Lifetime; Nickelodeon; TBS Superstation; Turner Network TV; VH1; Weather Channel.
Current originations: Government Access; Educational Access; Public Access.
Expanded Basic Service 1
Subscribers: 4,280.
Programming (via satellite): AMC; Animal Planet; Bravo; Cartoon Network; Comcast Sports Net Southeast; Country Music TV; C-SPAN 2; Disney Channel; E! Entertainment Television; ESPN; ESPN 2; Eternal Word TV Network; FitTV; Food Network; Fox News Channel; FX; Gaming Entertainment Television; Golf Channel; Hallmark Channel; HGTV; History Channel; INSP; ION Television; MSNBC; MTV; Outdoor Channel; QVC; Speed Channel; Spike TV; SportSouth; Syfy; The Learning Channel; Travel Channel; Trinity Broadcasting Network; truTV; TV Guide Network; TV Land; USA Network; WE tv.
Fee: $11.13 monthly.
Digital Basic Service
Subscribers: N.A.
Programming (via satellite): BBC America; Discovery Digital Networks; Fox Sports World; G4; GSN; Independent Film Channel; International Television (ITV); Lime; MTV Networks Digital Suite; Music Choice; National Geographic Channel; Nick Jr.; Ovation; Turner Classic Movies; Versus.
Digital Pay Service 1
Pay Units: 221.
Programming (via satellite): Cinemax (multiplexed); Sundance Channel; The Movie Channel (multiplexed).
Fee: $10.00 installation; $10.75 monthly.
Digital Pay Service 2
Pay Units: 1,935.
Programming (via satellite): Encore (multiplexed).
Fee: $1.75 monthly.
Digital Pay Service 3
Pay Units: 1,382.
Programming (via satellite): HBO (multiplexed).
Fee: $13.15 monthly.
Digital Pay Service 4
Pay Units: 526.
Programming (via satellite): Showtime (multiplexed).
Fee: $11.75 monthly.
Digital Pay Service 5
Pay Units: 874.
Programming (via satellite): Starz (multiplexed).
Fee: $4.75 monthly.
Video-On-Demand: Yes
Pay-Per-View
ETC (delivered digitally); ESPN Now (delivered digitally); Sports PPV (delivered digitally).
Internet Service
Operational: Yes.
Broadband Service: Mediacom High Speed Internet.
Fee: $59.95 installation; $42.95 monthly; $3.00 modem lease.
Telephone Service
Analog: Not Operational
Digital: Operational
Homes passed: 8,111. Miles of plant (coax & fiber) included in Thomasville
Regional Vice President: Sue Misiunas. Regional Technical Operations Manager: Gary McDougall. Regional Marketing Director: Melanie Hannasch. Marketing Manager: Daryl Channey.
City fee: 6% of gross.
Ownership: Mediacom LLC (MSO).

BALDWIN COUNTY (eastern portion)—KLiP Interactive, 455 Gees Mill Business Court, Conyers, GA 30013. Phone: 706-215-1385. Fax: 678-727-7002. E-mail: jsheehan@klipia.com. Web Site: http://www.klipia.com. Also serves Milledgeville (portions). ICA: GA0175.

TV Market Ranking: Below 100 (BALDWIN COUNTY (portions), Milledgeville (portions)); Outside TV Markets (BALDWIN COUNTY (portions)). Franchise award date: N.A. Franchise expiration date: N.A. Began: September 1, 1982.
Channel capacity: 65 (not 2-way capable). Channels available but not in use: 31.
Basic Service
Subscribers: 89.
Programming (received off-air): CW+; WGNM (IND) Macon; WGXA (FOX, MNT) Macon; WMAZ-TV (CBS) Macon; WMGT-TV (MNT, NBC) Macon; WPCH-TV (IND) Atlanta; WPGA-TV (ABC) Perry.
Programming (via satellite): ABC Family Channel; Animal Planet; Arts & Entertainment; BET Networks; CNBC; CNN; Comcast Sports Net Southeast; Country Music TV; Discovery Channel; Disney Channel; ESPN; ESPN 2; Fox News Channel; History Television; Home Shopping Network; Lifetime; Nickelodeon; QVC; Spike TV; SportSouth; The Learning Channel; Travel Channel; Trinity Broadcasting Network; Turner Network TV; TV Land; USA Network; Weather Channel; WGN America.
Fee: $29.95 installation; $39.95 monthly.
Pay Service 1
Pay Units: 13.
Programming (via satellite): Cinemax.
Fee: $10.95 monthly.
Pay Service 2
Pay Units: 20.
Programming (via satellite): HBO.
Fee: $10.95 monthly.
Internet Service
Operational: No.
Telephone Service
None
Miles of Plant: 20.0 (coaxial); None (fiber optic). Homes passed: 570.
Chief Executive Officer: Joseph Sheehan. General Manager East: Mark Miller. General Manager West: Vance Johnson.
Ownership: KLiP Interactive LLC (MSO).

BALDWIN COUNTY (northern portion)—KLiP Interactive, 455 Gees Mill Business Court, Conyers, GA 30013. Phone: 706-215-1385. Fax: 678-727-7002. E-mail: jsheehan@klipia.com. Web Site: http://www.klipia.com. Also serves Putnam County. ICA: GA0129.
TV Market Ranking: Below 100 (BALDWIN COUNTY (NORTHERN PORTION), Putnam County). Franchise award date: N.A. Franchise expiration date: N.A. Began: N.A.
Channel capacity: 45 (not 2-way capable). Channels available but not in use: 3.
Basic Service
Subscribers: 421.
Programming (received off-air): CW+; WGXA (FOX, MNT) Macon; WMAZ-TV (CBS) Macon; WMGT-TV (MNT, NBC) Macon; WPCH-TV (IND) Atlanta; WPGA-TV (ABC) Perry.
Programming (via satellite): ABC Family Channel; AMC; Animal Planet; Arts & Entertainment; BET Networks; Cartoon Network; CNBC; CNN; Comcast Sports Net Southeast; Country Music TV; Discovery Channel; Disney Channel; ESPN; ESPN 2; Fox News Channel; FX; GSN; Home Shopping Network; Lifetime; National Geographic Channel; Nickelodeon; Outdoor Channel; QVC; Speed Channel; Spike TV; SportSouth; The Learning Channel; Trinity Broadcasting Network; truTV; Turner Network TV; TV Land; USA Network; Weather Channel; WGN America.
Fee: $29.95 installation; $39.95 monthly.
Pay Service 1
Pay Units: 26.
Programming (via satellite): Cinemax.
Fee: $10.95 monthly.
Pay Service 2
Pay Units: 49.
Programming (via satellite): HBO.
Fee: $10.95 monthly.
Internet Service
Operational: No.
Telephone Service
None
Miles of Plant: 40.0 (coaxial); None (fiber optic). Homes passed: 1,500.
Chief Executive Officer: Joseph A. Sheehan. General Manager East: Mark Miller. General Manager West: Vance Johnson.
Ownership: KLiP Interactive LLC (MSO).

BAXLEY—ATC Cable, 371 West Parker St, Baxley, GA 31515. Phones: 877-552-5946 (Sales); 912-705-5000. Fax: 912-705-2059. E-mail: info@atc.cc. Web Site: http://www.accessatc.net. ICA: GA0082.
TV Market Ranking: Below 100 (BAXLEY). Franchise award date: N.A. Franchise expiration date: N.A. Began: April 1, 1966.
Channel capacity: 12 (operating 2-way). Channels available but not in use: None.
Basic Service
Subscribers: 1,900.
Programming (received off-air): WAWS (FOX, MNT) Jacksonville; WCWJ (CW) Jacksonville; WGSA (CW) Baxley; WJCL (ABC) Savannah; WJXT (IND) Jacksonville; WJXX (ABC) Orange Park; WPXC-TV (ION) Brunswick; WSAV-TV (MNT, NBC) Savannah; WTEV-TV (CBS) Jacksonville; WTGS (FOX) Hardeeville; WTLV (NBC) Jacksonville; WTOC-TV (CBS) Savannah; WXGA-TV (PBS) Waycross; allband FM.
Programming (via satellite): ABC Family Channel; AMC; Animal Planet; Arts & Entertainment; BET Networks; Cartoon Network; CNBC; CNN; Comcast Sports Net Southeast; Comcast/Charter Sports Southeast (CSS); Comedy Central; Country Music TV; C-SPAN; C-SPAN 2; Discovery Channel; Disney Channel; E! Entertainment Television; ESPN; ESPN 2; ESPN Classic Sports; FitTV; Food Network; Fox News Channel; FX; Golf Channel; Hallmark Channel; Headline News; HGTV; History Channel; Home Shopping Network; INSP; Lifetime; Local Cable Weather; MTV; National Geographic Channel; Nickelodeon; Outdoor Channel; QVC; Speed Channel; Spike TV; SportSouth; Syfy; TBS Superstation; The Learning Channel; Travel Channel; Trinity Broadcasting Network; truTV; Turner Network TV;

TV Guide Network; TV Land; USA Network; VH1; Weather Channel.
Current originations: Public Access.
Fee: $35.00 installation; $46.95 monthly.

Digital Basic Service
Subscribers: 34.
Programming (via satellite): BBC America; Bio; Bloomberg Television; Boomerang; Current; Discovery Military Channel; Disney XD; DMX Music; ESPN 2; ESPN Classic Sports; ESPN U; ESPNews; FitTV; Flix; Fox Movie Channel; Fox Soccer; FSN Digital Atlantic; FSN Digital Central; FSN Digital Pacific; Fuse; G4; Golf Channel; Gospel Music Channel; Great American Country; GSN; Hallmark Movie Channel; Halogen Network; HGTV; History Channel; History Channel International; ID Investigation Discovery; Lifetime Movie Network; Lime; MTV Hits; MTV2; National Geographic Channel; Nick Jr.; NickToons TV; Outdoor Channel; RFD-TV; Science Channel; Sleuth; SoapNet; Speed Channel; Style Network; Sundance Channel; TeenNick; Trinity Broadcasting Network; Turner Classic Movies; Versus; VH1 Classic; WE tv.
Fee: $16.95 monthly.

Digital Expanded Basic Service
Subscribers: N.A.
Programming (received off-air): WAWS (FOX, MNT) Jacksonville; WCWJ (CW) Jacksonville; WJCT (PBS) Jacksonville; WJXT (IND) Jacksonville; WJXX (ABC) Orange Park; WSAV-TV (MNT, NBC) Savannah; WTEV-TV (CBS) Jacksonville; WTGS (FOX) Hardeeville; WTLV (NBC) Jacksonville; WTOC-TV (CBS) Savannah.
Programming (via satellite): Animal Planet HD; Arts & Entertainment HD; Bravo HD; CNBC HD+; CNN HD; Discovery Channel HD; ESPN 2 HD; ESPN HD; Golf Channel HD; History Channel HD; National Geographic Channel HD Network; Outdoor Channel 2 HD; Science Channel HD; Syfy HD; TBS in HD; TLC HD; Turner Network TV HD; USA Network HD; Versus HD; Weather Channel HD.

Digital Expanded Basic Service 2
Subscribers: N.A.
Programming (via satellite): Discovery HD Theater; HDNet; HDNet Movies; Universal HD.

Digital Pay Service 1
Pay Units: N.A.
Programming (via satellite): Cinemax (multiplexed); Cinemax HD; Encore (multiplexed); HBO (multiplexed); HBO HD; Showtime (multiplexed); Showtime HD; Starz (multiplexed); Starz HDTV; The Movie Channel (multiplexed).
Fee: $8.00 monthly (Cinemax), $12.95 monthly (HBO, Showtime/TMC, or Starz/Encore).

Video-On-Demand: No

Pay-Per-View
iN DEMAND (delivered digitally); Playboy TV (delivered digitally); Fresh (delivered digitally); Spice: Xcess (delivered digitally); Club Jenna (delivered digitally).

Internet Service
Operational: Yes, DSL.
Broadband Service: atcnet.
Fee: $49.95-$64.95 monthly.

Telephone Service
None

Miles of Plant: 48.0 (coaxial); None (fiber optic). Additional miles planned: 5.0 (coaxial). Homes passed: 2,300.
Manager: Nathan Lingenfelter. Customer Service: Brooke Brown.
City fee: 3% of gross.
Ownership: ATC (MSO).

BENT TREE COMMUNITY—Ellijay Telephone Cooperative. Now served by ELLIJAY, GA [GA0044]. ICA: GA0138.

BERLIN—Mega Cable LLC, 333 Langford St, Berlin, GA 31722. Phone: 229-798-5335. Also serves Barney, Brooks County (portions), Colquitt County (portions), Ellenton & Morven. ICA: GA0122.
TV Market Ranking: Below 100 (Barney, BERLIN, Brooks County (portions), Colquitt County (portions), Ellenton, Morven). Franchise award date: February 16, 1988. Franchise expiration date: N.A. Began: October 10, 1988.
Channel capacity: 65 (not 2-way capable). Channels available but not in use: 32.

Basic Service
Subscribers: 182.
Programming (received off-air): WABW-TV (PBS) Pelham; WALB (NBC) Albany; WCTV (CBS, MNT) Thomasville; WFXL (FOX) Albany; WTXL-TV (ABC) Tallahassee.
Programming (via satellite): ABC Family Channel; AMC; Arts & Entertainment; BET Networks; CNN; Country Music TV; C-SPAN; Discovery Channel; Disney Channel; ESPN; Fox Sports Net; Headline News; Lifetime; Nickelodeon; QVC; Spike TV; Syfy; TBS Superstation; The Learning Channel; Travel Channel; Trinity Broadcasting Network; Turner Network TV; TV Land; USA Network; VH1; Weather Channel; WGN America.
Fee: $25.00 installation; $17.50 monthly.

Pay Service 1
Pay Units: 72.
Programming (via satellite): Encore.

Internet Service
Operational: No.

Telephone Service
None

Miles of Plant: 79.0 (coaxial); None (fiber optic).
President: Joe Sheehan.
City fee: 2% of net.
Ownership: Mega Cable LLC (MSO).

BIG CANOE—Windstream, 2000 Communications Blvd, Baldwin, GA 30511. Phones: 800-345-3874; 877-807-9463. Fax: 706-896-5170. Web Site: http://www.windstreamcable.com. Also serves Pickens County (portions). ICA: GA0095.
TV Market Ranking: Outside TV Markets (BIG CANOE, Pickens County (portions)). Franchise award date: N.A. Franchise expiration date: N.A. Began: April 6, 1976.
Channel capacity: 50 (not 2-way capable). Channels available but not in use: 4.

Basic Service
Subscribers: 1,362.
Programming (received off-air): WAGA-TV (FOX) Atlanta; WATL (MNT) Atlanta; WGCL-TV (CBS) Atlanta; WGTV (PBS) Athens; WHSG-TV (TBN) Monroe; WPCH-TV (IND) Atlanta; WPXA-TV (ION) Rome; WSB-TV (ABC) Atlanta; WUPA (CW) Atlanta; WUVG-DT (UNV) Athens; WXIA-TV (NBC) Atlanta.
Programming (via satellite): ABC Family Channel; AMC; Arts & Entertainment; Bloomberg Television; Bravo; CNBC; CNN; Comcast Sports Net Southeast; Comedy Central; C-SPAN; Discovery Channel; ESPN; ESPN 2; Food Network; Fox News Channel; Golf Channel; Headline News; HGTV; History Channel; Lifetime; Nickelodeon; QVC; Spike TV; SportSouth; Travel Channel; Turner Classic Movies; Turner Network TV; TV Guide Network; USA Network; Weather Channel; WGN America.
Fee: $42.25 monthly.

Digital Basic Service
Subscribers: 191.
Programming (via satellite): BBC America; Bio; Discovery Digital Networks; DMX Music; ESPN Classic Sports; ESPNews; Fox Sports World; Fuse; GAS; GSN; History Channel International; Independent Film Channel; Lifetime Movie Network; MTV; Nick Jr.; Sleuth; Style Network; Versus; WE tv.
Fee: $8.95 monthly.

Digital Pay Service 1
Pay Units: N.A.
Programming (via satellite): Cinemax (multiplexed); Encore (multiplexed); HBO (multiplexed); Showtime (multiplexed); Starz (multiplexed); The Movie Channel (multiplexed).
Fee: $10.95 monthly (Starz & Encore), $12.99 monthly (Showtime & TMC), $24.95 monthly (HBO & Cinemax).

Video-On-Demand: No

Pay-Per-View
iN DEMAND (delivered digitally).

Internet Service
Operational: No, Both DSL & dial-up.

Telephone Service
None

Miles of Plant: 45.0 (coaxial); None (fiber optic). Homes passed: 1,800.
President & Chief Executive Officer: Jeff Gardner. Executive Vice President & Chief Financial Officer: Brent Whittington. Executive Vice President, Network Operations: Grant Raney. Executive Vice President & Chief Marketing Officer: Ric Crane. Senior Vice President, Network Services: Frank Schueneman. Senior Vice President, Information Technology: Cindy Nash. Senior Vice President, Consumer Sales: Gregg Richey. Senior Vice President, Customer Services: Joe Marano.
City fee: None.
Ownership: Windstream Communications Inc. (MSO).

BISHOP—KLiP Interactive, 455 Gees Mill Business Court, Conyers, GA 30013. Phone: 678-727-7100. Fax: 678-727-7002. E-mail: jsheehan@klipia.com. Web Site: http://www.klipia.com. Also serves Good Hope, High Shoals, Oconee County (portions), Walton County (portions) & Watkinsville. ICA: GA0144.
TV Market Ranking: Below 100 (BISHOP, Good Hope, High Shoals, Oconee County (portions), Walton County (portions), Watkinsville). Franchise award date: N.A. Franchise expiration date: N.A. Began: N.A.
Channel capacity: 37 (not 2-way capable). Channels available but not in use: None.

Basic Service
Subscribers: 48.
Programming (received off-air): WAGA-TV (FOX) Atlanta; WATL (MNT) Atlanta; WGCL-TV (CBS) Atlanta; WGTV (PBS) Athens; WHSG-TV (TBN) Monroe; WPCH-TV (IND) Atlanta; WSB-TV (ABC) Atlanta; WUVG-DT (UNV) Athens; WXIA-TV (NBC) Atlanta.
Programming (via satellite): ABC Family Channel; AMC; Animal Planet; Arts & Entertainment; Cartoon Network; CNBC; CNN; C-SPAN; Discovery Channel; Disney Channel; ESPN; ESPN 2; Fuse; Great American Country; Headline News; HGTV; History Channel; Home Shopping Network; INSP; Lifetime; Speed Channel; SportSouth; Syfy; The Learning Channel; Turner Network TV; USA Network; Weather Channel; WGN America.
Fee: $30.00 installation; $37.95 monthly; $3.50 converter.

Pay Service 1
Pay Units: 3.
Programming (via satellite): Cinemax.
Fee: $10.95 monthly.

Pay Service 2
Pay Units: 3.
Programming (via satellite): HBO.
Fee: $14.95 monthly.

Internet Service
Operational: No.

Telephone Service
None

Miles of Plant: 17.0 (coaxial); None (fiber optic). Homes passed: 582.
Chief Executive Officer: Joseph A. Sheehan. General Manager East: Mark Miller. General Manager West: Vance Johnson.
Ownership: KLiP Interactive LLC (MSO).

BLACKSHEAR—ATC Cable, 3349 Hwy 84 W, Ste 104, Blackshear, GA 31516. Phones: 912-449-5443; 877-552-5946. Fax: 912-449-2602. E-mail: info@atc.cc. Web Site: http://www.accessatc.net. ICA: GA0100.
TV Market Ranking: Below 100 (BLACKSHEAR). Franchise award date: N.A. Franchise expiration date: N.A. Began: December 1, 1968.
Channel capacity: 80 (operating 2-way). Channels available but not in use: N.A.

Basic Service
Subscribers: 2,043.
Programming (received off-air): WAWS (FOX, MNT) Jacksonville; WCWJ (CW) Jacksonville; WGSA (CW) Baxley; WJCL (ABC) Savannah; WJXT (IND) Jacksonville; WJXX (ABC) Orange Park; WPXC-TV (ION) Brunswick; WSAV-TV (MNT, NBC) Savannah; WTEV-TV (CBS) Jacksonville; WTGS (FOX) Hardeeville; WTLV (NBC) Jacksonville; WTOC-TV (CBS) Savannah; WXGA-TV (PBS) Waycross; allband FM.
Programming (via satellite): ABC Family Channel; AMC; Animal Planet; Arts & Entertainment; BET Networks; Cartoon Network; CNBC; CNN; Comcast Sports Net Southeast; Comcast/Charter Sports Southeast (CSS); Comedy Central; Country Music TV; C-SPAN; C-SPAN 2; Discovery Channel; Disney Channel; E! Entertainment Television; ESPN; ESPN 2; ESPN Classic Sports; FitTV; Food Network; Fox News Channel; FX; Golf Channel; Hallmark Channel; Headline News; HGTV; History Channel; Home Shopping Network; INSP; Lifetime; Local Cable Weather; MTV; National Geographic Channel; Nickelodeon; Outdoor Channel; QVC; Speed Channel; Spike TV; SportSouth; Syfy; TBS Superstation; The Learning Channel; Travel Channel; Trinity Broadcasting Network; truTV; Turner Network TV; TV Guide Network; TV Land; USA Network; VH1; Weather Channel.
Current originations: Public Access.
Fee: $35.00 installation; $46.95 monthly.

Digital Basic Service
Subscribers: 300.
Programming (via satellite): AmericanLife TV Network; BBC America; Bio; Bloomberg Television; Boomerang; Current; Discovery Military Channel; Disney XD; DMX Music; ESPN 2; ESPN Classic Sports; ESPN U; ESPNews; FitTV; Flix; Fox Movie Channel; Fox Soccer; FSN Digital Atlantic; FSN Digital Central; FSN Digital Pacific; Fuse; G4; Golf Channel; Gospel Music Channel; Great American Country; GSN; Hallmark Movie Channel; Halogen Network; HGTV; History Channel; History Channel International; ID Investigation Discovery; Lifetime Movie Network; Lime; Local Cable Weather; MTV Hits; MTV2; Newsworld International; Nick Jr.; NickToons TV; Outdoor Channel;

RFD-TV; Science Channel; Sleuth; SoapNet; Speed Channel; Style Network; Sundance Channel; TeenNick; Trinity Broadcasting Network; Turner Classic Movies; Versus; VH1 Classic; WE tv.
Fee: $16.95 monthly.

Digital Expanded Basic Service
Subscribers: N.A.
Programming (received off-air): WAWS (FOX, MNT) Jacksonville; WCWJ (CW) Jacksonville; WJCT (PBS) Jacksonville; WJXT (IND) Jacksonville; WJXX (ABC) Orange Park; WSAV-TV (MNT, NBC) Savannah; WTEV-TV (CBS) Jacksonville; WTGS (FOX) Hardeeville; WTLV (NBC) Jacksonville; WTOC-TV (CBS) Savannah.
Programming (via satellite): Animal Planet HD; Arts & Entertainment HD; Bravo HD; CNBC HD+; CNN HD; Discovery Channel HD; ESPN 2 HD; ESPN HD; Golf Channel HD; History Channel HD; National Geographic Channel HD Network; Outdoor Channel 2 HD; Science Channel HD; Syfy HD; TBS in HD; TLC HD; Turner Network TV HD; USA Network HD; Versus HD; Weather Channel HD.

Digital Expanded Basic Service 2
Subscribers: N.A.
Programming (via satellite): Discovery HD Theater; HDNet; HDNet Movies; Universal HD.

Digital Pay Service 1
Pay Units: 78.
Programming (via satellite): Showtime (multiplexed); Showtime HD.
Fee: $12.95 monthly.

Digital Pay Service 2
Pay Units: 72.
Programming (via satellite): HBO (multiplexed); HBO HD.
Fee: $12.95 monthly.

Digital Pay Service 3
Pay Units: 12.
Programming (via satellite): Starz (multiplexed); Starz HDTV.
Fee: $12.95 monthly.

Digital Pay Service 4
Pay Units: N.A.
Programming (via satellite): Cinemax (multiplexed); Cinemax HD; Encore (multiplexed); The Movie Channel (multiplexed).
Fee: $8.00 monthly.

Video-On-Demand: No

Pay-Per-View
iN DEMAND (delivered digitally); Playboy TV (delivered digitally); Fresh (delivered digitally); Spice: Xcess (delivered digitally); Club Jenna (delivered digitally).

Internet Service
Operational: Yes, Both DSL & dial-up.
Broadband Service: atcnet.
Fee: $49.95-$64.95 monthly.

Telephone Service
Digital: Operational
Miles of Plant: 35.0 (coaxial); None (fiber optic). Homes passed: 2,500.
Manager: Nathan Lingenfelter. Customer Service: Jennifer Barnette.
Ownership: ATC (MSO).

BLAIRSVILLE—Windstream, 2000 Communications Blvd, Baldwin, GA 30511. Phones: 800-345-3874; 877-807-9463. Fax: 706-745-6230. Web Site: http://www.windstreamcable.com. Also serves Union County. ICA: GA0113.
TV Market Ranking: Below 100 (Union County (portions)); Outside TV Markets (BLAIRSVILLE, Union County (portions)). Franchise award date: N.A. Franchise expiration date: N.A. Began: January 1, 1982.
Channel capacity: 75 (not 2-way capable). Channels available but not in use: 12.

Basic Service
Subscribers: 3,458.
Programming (received off-air): WAGA-TV (FOX) Atlanta; WATL (MNT) Atlanta; WGCL-TV (CBS) Atlanta; WGTV (PBS) Athens; WHSG-TV (TBN) Monroe; WNEG-TV (CBS) Toccoa; WPXA-TV (ION) Rome; WRCB (NBC) Chattanooga; WSB-TV (ABC) Atlanta; WUPA (CW) Atlanta; WUVG-DT (UNV) Athens; WXIA-TV (NBC) Atlanta.
Programming (via satellite): Boomerang; C-SPAN; Home Shopping Network; TBS Superstation; WGN America.
Fee: $12.58 monthly.

Expanded Basic Service 1
Subscribers: 3,134.
Programming (via satellite): ABC Family Channel; AMC; Animal Planet; Arts & Entertainment; Bravo; Cartoon Network; CNBC; CNN; Comcast Sports Net Southeast; Comedy Central; Country Music TV; Discovery Channel; ESPN; ESPN 2; ESPN Classic Sports; Food Network; Fox News Channel; FX; Golf Channel; Headline News; HGTV; History Channel; Lifetime; MSNBC; MTV; Nickelodeon; Outdoor Channel; QVC; Speed Channel; Spike TV; SportSouth; The Learning Channel; Travel Channel; Turner Classic Movies; Turner Network TV; TV Guide Network; TV Land; USA Network; VH1; Weather Channel.
Fee: $32.67 monthly.

Digital Basic Service
Subscribers: 293.
Programming (via satellite): BBC America; Bio; CBS College Sports Network; Cooking Channel; Discovery Digital Networks; DMX Music; Do-It-Yourself; ESPNews; Eternal Word TV Network; FamilyNet; Fox College Sports Atlantic; Fox College Sports Central; Fox College Sports Pacific; Fox Movie Channel; Fox Sports World; Fuel TV; Fuse; GAS; Gospel Music TV; GSN; Hallmark Channel; Halogen Network; History Channel International; Independent Film Channel; Lifetime Movie Network; MTV2; National Geographic Channel; Nick Jr.; NickToons TV; Praise Television; Science Television; Sleuth; Style Network; The Sportsman Channel; Versus; VH1 Classic; VH1 Country; WE tv.
Fee: $12.92 monthly.

Digital Pay Service 1
Pay Units: N.A.
Programming (via satellite): Cinemax (multiplexed); Encore (multiplexed); HBO (multiplexed); Showtime (multiplexed); Starz (multiplexed); The Movie Channel (multiplexed).
Fee: $10.95 monthly (Starz & Encore), $12.99 monthly (Showtime & TMC), $24.95 monthly (HBO & Cinemax).

Video-On-Demand: No

Pay-Per-View
iN DEMAND (delivered digitally).

Internet Service
Operational: No, Both DSL & dial-up.

Telephone Service
None
Miles of Plant: 35.0 (coaxial); None (fiber optic). Additional miles planned: 5.0 (coaxial).
President & Chief Executive Officer: Jeff Gardner. Executive Vice President & Chief Financial Officer: Brent Whittington. Executive Vice President, Network Operations: Grant Raney. Executive Vice President & Chief Marketing Officer: Ric Crane. Senior Vice President, Network Services: Frank Schueneman. Senior Vice President, Information Technology: Cindy Nash. Senior Vice President, Consumer Sales: Gregg Richey. Senior Vice President, Customer Services: Joe Marano.
Ownership: Windstream Communications Inc. (MSO).

BLAKELY—Blakely Cable TV Inc., 65 Liberty St, Blakely, GA 39823-2257. Phone: 229-723-3555. Fax: 229-723-2000. Also serves Columbia. ICA: GA0085.
TV Market Ranking: Below 100 (BLAKELY, Columbia). Franchise award date: N.A. Franchise expiration date: N.A. Began: December 1, 1979.
Channel capacity: 58 (not 2-way capable). Channels available but not in use: 1.

Basic Service
Subscribers: 1,518.
Programming (received off-air): WACS-TV (PBS) Dawson; WALB (NBC) Albany; WCTV (CBS, MNT) Thomasville; WDHN (ABC) Dothan; WTVM (ABC) Columbus; WTVY (CBS, CW, MNT) Dothan; WXTX (FOX) Columbus.
Programming (via satellite): ABC Family Channel; Animal Planet; Arts & Entertainment; BET Networks; Cartoon Network; CNBC; CNN; Comedy Central; Country Music TV; C-SPAN; C-SPAN 2; Discovery Channel; Disney Channel; E! Entertainment Television; ESPN; ESPN 2; Food Network; Fox News Channel; FX; Golf Channel; Hallmark Channel; Headline News; HGTV; History Channel; Home Shopping Network; Lifetime; MTV; National Geographic Channel; Nickelodeon; Speed Channel; Spike TV; SportSouth; Syfy; TBS Superstation; The Learning Channel; Travel Channel; Trinity Broadcasting Network; truTV; Turner Classic Movies; Turner Network TV; Turner South; TV Land; USA Network; Versus; VH1; Weather Channel; WGN America.
Fee: $25.00 installation; $32.95 monthly.

Pay Service 1
Pay Units: 52.
Programming (via satellite): Cinemax.
Fee: $8.95 monthly.

Pay Service 2
Pay Units: 159.
Programming (via satellite): HBO.
Fee: $10.00 monthly.

Video-On-Demand: No

Internet Service
Operational: No.

Telephone Service
None
Miles of Plant: 35.0 (coaxial); None (fiber optic). Additional miles planned: 10.0 (coaxial). Homes passed: 2,200. Total homes in franchised area: 2,500.
Manager: William C. De Loach Jr. Office Manager: Anne Harroll.
City fee: 3% of gross.
Ownership: Blakely Cable TV Inc. (MSO).

BLUE RIDGE—Ellijay Telephone Co., PO Box 0, 224 Dalton St, Ellijay, GA 30540-3119. Phones: 706-946-2271; 706-276-2271. Fax: 706-276-9888. E-mail: cabletv@ellijay.com. Web Site: http://www.etcnow.com. Also serves McCaysville, Mineral Bluff & Morganton, GA; Copperhill, Ducktown & Turtletown, TN. ICA: GA0075.
TV Market Ranking: Below 100 (Copperhill, Ducktown, McCaysville, Turtletown); Outside TV Markets (BLUE RIDGE, Mineral Bluff, Morganton). Franchise award date: May 6, 1969. Franchise expiration date: N.A. Began: N.A.
Channel capacity: N.A. Channels available but not in use: N.A.

Basic Service
Subscribers: 2,319.
Programming (received off-air): WDEF-TV (CBS) Chattanooga; WDSI-TV (FOX, MNT) Chattanooga; WNGH-TV (PBS) Chatsworth; WRCB (NBC) Chattanooga; WSB-TV (ABC) Atlanta; WTVC (ABC) Chattanooga; 6 FMs.
Programming (via satellite): ABC Family Channel; Animal Planet; Arts & Entertainment; Cartoon Network; CNBC; CNN; Comcast/Charter Sports Southeast (CSS); Country Music TV; C-SPAN; Discovery Channel; E! Entertainment Television; ESPN; ESPN 2; Fox News Channel; Fox Sports Net; FX; Golf Channel; Hallmark Channel; Headline News; HGTV; History Channel; INSP; Lifetime; MTV; Nickelodeon; QVC; Spike TV; SportSouth; TBS Superstation; The Learning Channel; Turner Network TV; TV Land; USA Network; Versus; Weather Channel; WGN America.
Fee: $20.00 installation; $44.95 monthly; $2.00 additional installation.

Digital Basic Service
Subscribers: N.A.
Programming (via satellite): BBC America; C-SPAN 3; Discovery Digital Networks; Disney Channel; DMX Music; Encore (multiplexed); ESPNews; Flix; GAS; MTV Networks Digital Suite; NFL Network; Nick Jr.; Nick Too; NickToons TV; Science Television; SoapNet; Sundance Channel; Toon Disney.
Fee: $15.95 monthly.

Digital Pay Service 1
Pay Units: N.A.
Programming (via satellite): Cinemax (multiplexed); HBO (multiplexed); Showtime (multiplexed); Starz (multiplexed); The Movie Channel (multiplexed).
Fee: $4.95 monthly (Encore), $6.95 monthly (Cinemax), $11.95 monthly (Starz/Encore), $12.95 monthly (HBO or Showtime/TMC).

Pay-Per-View
iN DEMAND (delivered digitally); Hot Choice (delivered digitally); Playboy TV (delivered digitally); Fresh (delivered digitally); Shorteez (delivered digitally); Pleasure (delivered digitally).

Internet Service
Operational: Yes.
Broadband Service: In-house.
Fee: $49.95 monthly; $99.95 modem purchase.

Telephone Service
None
Note: Homes passed & miles of plant (coax) included in Ellijay
President: Dwight Roeland. Operations Director: Daryl Harper. Engineering Director: Frank Rigdon.

County fee: 1% of gross. City fee: 3% of gross.
Ownership: Ellijay Telephone Co.

BOLINGBROKE—Reynolds Cable TV Inc., PO Box 782, 528 S Main St, Swainsboro, GA 30401. Phone: 478-237-2853. Fax: 47-237-8730. E-mail: reynoldscable@reynoldscable.net. Web Site: http://www.reynoldscable.net. ICA: GA0123.
TV Market Ranking: Below 100 (BOLINGBROKE). Franchise award date: N.A. Franchise expiration date: N.A. Began: August 1, 1989.
Channel capacity: 60 (operating 2-way). Channels available but not in use: 17.

Basic Service
Subscribers: 675.
Programming (received off-air): WGNM (IND) Macon; WGXA (FOX, MNT) Macon; WMAZ-TV (CBS) Macon; WMGT-TV (MNT, NBC) Macon; WMUM-TV (PBS) Cochran; WPGA-TV (ABC) Perry; WSB-TV (ABC) Atlanta.
Programming (via satellite): ABC Family Channel; AMC; Animal Planet; Arts & Entertainment; Cartoon Network; CNBC; CNN; Comcast Sports Net Southeast; Comcast/Charter Sports Southeast (CSS); Comedy Central; Country Music TV; C-SPAN; CW+; Discovery Channel; Disney Channel; E! Entertainment Television; ESPN; ESPN 2; Food Network; Fox News Channel; FX; Golf Channel; Hallmark Channel; Headline News; HGTV; History Channel; Home Shopping Network; Lifetime; MTV; NFL Network; Nickelodeon; Outdoor Channel; QVC; Radar Channel; Spike TV; SportSouth; Syfy; TBS Superstation; The Learning Channel; Travel Channel; Trinity Broadcasting Network; truTV; Turner Network TV; TV Land; USA Network; VH1; Weather Channel.
Fee: $49.99 monthly.

Digital Basic Service
Subscribers: N.A.
Programming (received off-air): WGXA (FOX, MNT) Macon; WMAZ-TV (CBS) Macon; WMGT-TV (MNT, NBC) Macon.
Programming (via satellite): AmericanLife TV Network; BBC America; Bio; Bloomberg Television; Bravo; Chiller; Church Channel; CMT Pure Country; Cooking Channel; Current; Daystar TV Network; Discovery Health Channel; Discovery Kids Channel; Discovery Military Channel; Discovery Planet Green; DMX Music; ESPN 2; ESPN Classic Sports; ESPNews; FitTV; Fox College Sports Atlantic; Fox College Sports Central; Fox College Sports Pacific; Fox Movie Channel; Fox Reality Channel; Fox Soccer; Fuse; G4; Golf Channel; Gospel Music Channel; Great American Country; GSN; Halogen Network; HGTV; History Channel; History Channel International; ID Investigation Discovery; Independent Film Channel; JCTV; Lifetime Movie Network; MTV Hits; MTV2; Nick Jr.; NickToons TV; Outdoor Channel; Ovation; PBS Kids Sprout; RFD-TV; Science Channel; ShopNBC; Sleuth; SoapNet; Speed Channel; Starz IndiePlex; Starz RetroPlex; Style Network; Syfy; TeenNick; The Word Network; Toon Disney; Trinity Broadcasting Network; Turner Classic Movies; TV Land; TVG Network; Versus; VH1 Classic; VH1 Soul; WE tv.
Fee: $11.00 monthly.

Digital Expanded Basic Service
Subscribers: N.A.
Programming (via satellite): Arts & Entertainment HD; Discovery Channel HD; ESPN 2 HD; ESPN HD; HDNet; HDNet Movies; HGTV HD; NFL Network HD; Outdoor Channel 2 HD.
Fee: $9.99 monthly.

Digital Pay Service 1
Pay Units: N.A.
Programming (via satellite): Cinemax (multiplexed); Encore (multiplexed); HBO (multiplexed); Playboy TV; Showtime (multiplexed); Starz (multiplexed); The Movie Channel (multiplexed).
Fee: $1.99 monthly (HBO, Cinemax, Showtime/TMC or Starz/Encore), 17.99 monthly (Playboy).

Video-On-Demand: No

Internet Service
Operational: Yes. Began: April 1, 2002.
Subscribers: 300.
Broadband Service: Comcast High Speed Internet.
Fee: $21.99 monthly.

Telephone Service
Digital: Operational
Subscribers: 2.
Fee: $99.00 installation; $34.99 monthly
Miles of Plant: 55.0 (coaxial); None (fiber optic). Homes passed: 1,350.
Manager: Terry Reynolds.
Ownership: Reynolds Cable TV Inc. (MSO).

BOSTON—Southeast Cable TV Inc., PO Box 584, 107 S Main St, Boston, GA 31626-0584. Phone: 229-498-4191. Fax: 229-498-1026. ICA: GA0176.
TV Market Ranking: Below 100 (BOSTON). Franchise award date: N.A. Franchise expiration date: N.A. Began: N.A.
Channel capacity: 40 (not 2-way capable). Channels available but not in use: N.A.

Basic Service
Subscribers: 370.
Programming (received off-air): WABW-TV (PBS) Pelham; WALB (NBC) Albany; WCTV (CBS, MNT) Thomasville; WFSU-TV (PBS) Tallahassee; WTLH (CW, FOX) Bainbridge; WTWC-TV (NBC) Tallahassee; WTXL-TV (ABC) Tallahassee.
Programming (via satellite): ABC Family Channel; AMC; Arts & Entertainment; BET Networks; CNBC; CNN; Comedy Central; Country Music TV; C-SPAN; Discovery Channel; ESPN; ESPN 2; Fox News Channel; Fox Sports Net; Headline News; HGTV; History Channel; Lifetime; MTV; Nickelodeon; Outdoor Channel; QVC; Spike TV; SportSouth; TBS Superstation; The Learning Channel; Trinity Broadcasting Network; Turner Network TV; TV Land; USA Network; VH1; Weather Channel; WGN America.
Fee: $15.00 installation; $17.95 monthly.

Pay Service 1
Pay Units: 124.
Programming (via satellite): Cinemax; HBO.
Fee: $10.00 monthly.

Internet Service
Operational: No.

Telephone Service
None
Miles of Plant: 15.0 (coaxial); None (fiber optic). Homes passed: 550.
Manager & Chief Technician: Bob Heide.
Ownership: Southeast Cable TV Inc. (MSO).

BOWMAN—Comcast Cablevision of the South. Now served by ELBERTON, GA [GA0192]. ICA: GA0147.

BRONWOOD—Citizens Cable TV, PO Box 465, Leslie, GA 31764. Phones: 229-268-2288; 229-853-1600; 866-341-3050. Web Site: http://www.citizenscatv.com. ICA: GA0158.
TV Market Ranking: Below 100 (BRONWOOD). Franchise award date: N.A. Franchise expiration date: N.A. Began: September 1, 1988.
Channel capacity: 33 (not 2-way capable). Channels available but not in use: 27.

Basic Service
Subscribers: 150.
Programming (received off-air): WACS-TV (PBS) Dawson; WALB (NBC) Albany; WFXL (FOX) Albany; WRBL (CBS) Columbus; WSST-TV (IND) Cordele; WTVM (ABC) Columbus.
Programming (via satellite): ABC Family Channel; Arts & Entertainment; BET Networks; Boomerang; Cartoon Network; CNN; Comcast Sports Net Southeast; Comcast/Charter Sports Southeast (CSS); Country Music TV; Discovery Channel; ESPN; ESPN 2; Food Network; Fox News Channel; FX; HGTV; Home Shopping Network; Lifetime; Nickelodeon; Speed Channel; Spike TV; TBS Superstation; The Learning Channel; Turner Network TV; TV Land; USA Network; Weather Channel; WGN America.
Fee: $45.00 installation; $34.95 monthly.

Pay Service 1
Pay Units: 30.
Programming (via satellite): HBO.
Fee: $13.50 monthly.

Pay Service 2
Pay Units: 30.
Programming (via satellite): Cinemax.
Fee: $13.50 monthly.

Video-On-Demand: No

Internet Service
Operational: No.

Telephone Service
None
Miles of Plant: 9.0 (coaxial); None (fiber optic). Additional miles planned: 1.0 (coaxial). Homes passed: 230. Total homes in franchised area: 240.
Manager & Chief Engineer: Milton Foster.
Ownership: Citizens Cable TV (MSO).

BROWNS CROSSING—Formerly served by National Cable Inc. No longer in operation. ICA: GA0276.

BRUNSWICK—Comcast Cable, 1967 Glynn Ave, Brunswick, GA 31520. Phone: 912-264-5956. Fax: 912-264-4618. Web Site: http://www.comcast.com. Also serves Glynn County. ICA: GA0019.
TV Market Ranking: Below 100 (BRUNSWICK, Glynn County). Franchise award date: N.A. Franchise expiration date: N.A. Began: December 28, 1965.
Channel capacity: N.A. Channels available but not in use: None.

Basic Service
Subscribers: 22,432.
Programming (received off-air): WAWS (FOX, MNT) Jacksonville; WCWJ (CW) Jacksonville; WJCT (PBS) Jacksonville; WJXT (IND) Jacksonville; WJXX (ABC) Orange Park; WPXC-TV (ION) Brunswick; WSAV-TV (MNT, NBC) Savannah; WTEV-TV (CBS) Jacksonville; WTLV (NBC) Jacksonville; WTOC-TV (CBS) Savannah; WXGA-TV (PBS) Waycross; 10 FMs.
Programming (via satellite): ABC Family Channel; AMC; Animal Planet; Arts & Entertainment; BET Networks; Bravo; Cartoon Network; CNBC; Comcast Sports Net Southeast; Comedy Central; Country Music TV; C-SPAN; C-SPAN 2; Discovery Channel; E! Entertainment Television; ESPN; Eternal Word TV Network; Fox News Channel; FX; Hallmark Channel; HGTV; History Channel; Home Shopping Network; Lifetime; MTV; Nickelodeon; Product Information Network; QVC; Speed Channel; Spike TV; Syfy; The Learning Channel; Travel Channel; TV Guide Network; USA Network; VH1; Weather Channel; WGN America; WJEB-TV (ETV) Jacksonville; WTGS (FOX) Hardeeville.
Current originations: Religious Access; Public Access.
Fee: $39.95 installation; $27.50 monthly.

Expanded Basic Service 1
Subscribers: 11,500.
Programming (via satellite): CNN; Disney Channel; ESPN 2; Food Network; Golf Channel; Headline News; MSNBC; Oxygen; ShopNBC; TBS Superstation; truTV; Turner Network TV; TV Land.
Fee: $50.99 monthly.

Digital Basic Service
Subscribers: N.A.
Programming (via satellite): AmericanLife TV Network; BBC America; Black Family Channel; Bloomberg Television; Discovery Digital Networks; FitTV; G4; Great American Country; GSN; INSP; MuchMusic Network; Outdoor Channel; Trinity Broadcasting Network; Turner Classic Movies; WE tv.
Fee: $51.99 monthly.

Digital Expanded Basic Service
Subscribers: N.A.
Programming (via satellite): Bio; DMX Music; Do-It-Yourself; ESPN Classic Sports; ESPNews; GAS; History Channel International; Independent Film Channel; MTV Networks Digital Suite; National Geographic Channel; Nick Jr.; Nick Too; NickToons TV; SoapNet; Style Network; Sundance Channel; Toon Disney; Versus.

Digital Pay Service 1
Pay Units: N.A.
Programming (via satellite): Canales N; Cinemax (multiplexed); Encore (multiplexed); Flix; HBO (multiplexed); Showtime (multiplexed); Starz (multiplexed); The Movie Channel (multiplexed).
Fee: $14.95 monthly (each).

Video-On-Demand: Planned

Pay-Per-View
Urban American Television Network (delivered digitally); Hot Choice (delivered digitally); Fresh (delivered digitally); Playboy TV (delivered digitally); Movies (delivered digitally).

Internet Service
Operational: Yes.
Broadband Service: Comcast High Speed Internet.
Fee: $42.95 monthly.

Telephone Service
Digital: Operational
Fee: $39.95 monthly
Miles of Plant: 712.0 (coaxial); None (fiber optic). Total homes in franchised area: 42,000.
Vice President: Doug McMillan. General Manager: Mark Russell. Technical Operations Manager: William Baines. Marketing Manager: Jerald Mitchell. Office Manager: Kathleen Bartchlett.
City fee: 5% of gross.
Ownership: Comcast Cable Communications Inc. (MSO).

BUENA VISTA—Flint Cable TV, PO Box 669, 105 W Marion, Reynolds, GA 31076-0669. Phone: 888-593-7782. Fax: 478-847-2010. Web Site: http://www.flintcatv.com. Also serves Marion County. ICA: GA0130.
TV Market Ranking: 94 (BUENA VISTA, Marion County (portions)). Franchise award

date: N.A. Franchise expiration date: N.A. Began: August 1, 1983.
Channel capacity: 40 (not 2-way capable). Channels available but not in use: 5.

Basic Service
Subscribers: 288.
Programming (received off-air): WGNM (IND) Macon; WGXA (FOX, MNT) Macon; WLGA (CW) Opelika; WLTZ (CW, NBC) Columbus; WMAZ-TV (CBS) Macon; WMGT-TV (MNT, NBC) Macon; WMUM-TV (PBS) Cochran; WPGA-TV (ABC) Perry; WRBL (CBS) Columbus; WTVM (ABC) Columbus; WXTX (FOX) Columbus.
Programming (via satellite): INSP; QVC; TBS Superstation; Weather Channel.
Fee: $35.00 installation; $19.99 monthly.

Expanded Basic Service 1
Subscribers: N.A.
Programming (via satellite): ABC Family Channel; Animal Planet; Arts & Entertainment; BET Networks; Bloomberg Television; Boomerang; Bravesvision; Bravo; Cartoon Network; CNBC; CNN; Comcast Sports Net Southeast; Comedy Central; Country Music TV; C-SPAN; C-SPAN 2; C-SPAN 3; CW+; Discovery Channel; Disney Channel; E! Entertainment Television; ESPN; ESPN 2; ESPN Classic Sports; ESPN U; Food Network; Fox Business Channel; Fox News Channel; FX; Gospel Music Channel; GSN; Hallmark Channel; Headline News; HGTV; History Channel; Lifetime; MSNBC; MTV; National Geographic Channel; Nickelodeon; RFD-TV; Speed Channel; Spike TV; SportSouth; Syfy; The Learning Channel; The Sportsman Channel; Travel Channel; Trinity Broadcasting Network; truTV; Turner Classic Movies; Turner Network TV; TV Land; Univision; USA Network; VH1; WE tv; WGN America.
Fee: $23.00 monthly.

Digital Basic Service
Subscribers: N.A.
Programming (via satellite): ABC Family HD; AmericanLife TV Network; Animal Planet HD; BBC America; Chiller; Cooking Channel; Discovery Channel HD; Discovery HD Theater; Discovery Health Channel; Discovery Kids Channel; Discovery Military Channel; Discovery Planet Green; Disney Channel HD; DMX Music; FitTV; Fox News HD; Fox Soccer; Halogen Network; ID Investigation Discovery; Independent Film Channel; Lifetime Movie Network; Nick Jr.; Science Channel; Science Channel HD; SoapNet; Syfy HD; TLC HD; Travel Channel HD; USA Network HD.
Fee: $5.00 monthly.

Digital Expanded Basic Service
Subscribers: N.A.
Programming (via satellite): Arts & Entertainment HD; Food Network HD; FX HD; HGTV HD; History Channel HD; National Geographic Channel HD Network; Speed HD; Universal HD.
Fee: $6.99 monthly.

Digital Expanded Basic Service 2
Subscribers: N.A.
Programming (via satellite): Encore (multiplexed).
Fee: $6.99 monthly.

Digital Expanded Basic Service 3
Subscribers: N.A.
Programming (via satellite): Bio; ESPNews; Fox College Sports Atlantic; Fox College Sports Central; Fox College Sports Pacific; Golf Channel; History Channel International; Outdoor Channel; Outdoor Channel 2 HD; Versus.
Fee: $6.99 monthly.

Digital Expanded Basic Service 4
Subscribers: N.A.
Programming (via satellite): BET J; CMT Pure Country; Current; Disney XD; Flix; Fox Movie Channel; Fuse; G4; Gospel Music Channel; Great American Country; MTV Hits; MTV2; NickToons TV; Sleuth; Style Network; Sundance Channel; TeenNick; VH1 Classic; VH1 Soul.
Fee: $6.99 monthly.

Digital Expanded Basic Service 5
Subscribers: N.A.
Programming (via satellite): Cine Latino; Cine Mexicano; CNN en Espanol; Discovery en Espanol; ESPN Deportes; Fox Sports en Espanol; History Channel en Espanol; MTV Tres; mun2 television; VeneMovies.
Fee: $6.99 monthly.

Digital Pay Service 1
Pay Units: N.A.
Programming (via satellite): Cinemax (multiplexed); HBO (multiplexed); Showtime (multiplexed); Starz (multiplexed); Starz HDTV; The Movie Channel (multiplexed).
Fee: $12.99 monthly (HBO, Cinemax, Showtime/TMC or Starz).

Video-On-Demand: No

Internet Service
Operational: Yes.
Fee: $49.95 installation; $24.95-$59.95 monthly.

Telephone Service
Digital: Operational
Fee: $49.95 installation

Miles of Plant: 12.0 (coaxial); None (fiber optic). Homes passed: 703.
Manager: Jim Bond. Marketing Director: Laurie Long.
Ownership: Flint Cable Television Inc. (MSO).

BURKE COUNTY (portions)—Pineland Telephone Coop Inc. Formerly served by Midville, GA [GA0152]. This cable system has converted to IPTV, 30 S Roundtree St, Metter, GA 30439. Phones: 800-247-1266; 912-685-2121. Fax: 912-685-3539. E-mail: pineland@pineland.net. Web Site: http://www.pineland.net. ICA: GA5256.
Channel capacity: N.A. Channels available but not in use: N.A.

Internet Service
Operational: Yes.

General Manager: Richard P. Price.
Ownership: Pineland Telephone Cooperative Inc.

BUTLER—Flint Cable TV, PO Box 669, 105 W Marion, Reynolds, GA 31076-0669. Phone: 478-847-3101. Fax: 478-847-2010. Web Site: http://www.flintcatv.com. ICA: GA0128.
TV Market Ranking: Below 100 (BUTLER). Franchise award date: N.A. Franchise expiration date: N.A. Began: April 1, 1983.
Channel capacity: 40 (not 2-way capable). Channels available but not in use: 3.

Basic Service
Subscribers: 530.
Programming (received off-air): WGNM (IND) Macon; WGXA (FOX, MNT) Macon; WLGA (CW) Opelika; WLTZ (CW, NBC) Columbus; WMAZ-TV (CBS) Macon; WMGT-TV (MNT, NBC) Macon; WMUM-TV (PBS) Cochran; WPCH-TV (IND) Atlanta; WPGA-TV (ABC) Perry; WRBL (CBS) Columbus; WTVM (ABC) Columbus; WXTX (FOX) Columbus.
Programming (via satellite): CNBC; C-SPAN; C-SPAN 2; C-SPAN 3; INSP; QVC; RFD-TV; Weather Channel.
Fee: $35.00 installation; $19.99 monthly.

Expanded Basic Service 1
Subscribers: N.A.
Programming (via satellite): ABC Family Channel; Animal Planet; Arts & Entertainment; BET Networks; Bloomberg Television; Boomerang; Bravo; Cartoon Network; CNN; Comcast Sports Net Southeast; Comedy Central; Country Music TV; Discovery Channel; Disney Channel; E! Entertainment Television; ESPN; ESPN 2; ESPN Classic Sports; Food Network; Fox News Channel; FX; Gospel Music Channel; GSN; Hallmark Channel; Headline News; HGTV; History Channel; Lifetime; MSNBC; MTV; National Geographic Channel; Nickelodeon; Speed Channel; Spike TV; SportSouth; Syfy; The Learning Channel; The Sportsman Channel; Travel Channel; Trinity Broadcasting Network; truTV; Turner Classic Movies; Turner Network TV; TV Land; USA Network; VH1; WE tv; WGN America; WPIX (CW, IND) New York.
Fee: $20.00 monthly.

Digital Basic Service
Subscribers: N.A.
Programming (via satellite): BBC America; Bio; Canales N; Chiller; CMT Pure Country; Current; Discovery Digital Networks; DMX Music; Encore (multiplexed); ESPNews; Flix; Fox College Sports Atlantic; Fox College Sports Central; Fox College Sports Pacific; Fox Movie Channel; Fox Soccer; Fuse; G4; GAS; Golf Channel; Gospel Music Channel; Great American Country; Halogen Network; History Channel International; Independent Film Channel; MTV Networks Digital Suite; Nick Jr.; NickToons TV; Outdoor Channel; Ovation; Sleuth; SoapNet; Style Network; Sundance Channel; Toon Disney; Versus.

Pay Service 1
Pay Units: N.A.
Programming (via satellite): Cinemax; Encore; HBO.
Fee: $20.00 installation; $2.99 monthly (Encore), 11.99 monthly (Cinemax or HBO).

Digital Pay Service 1
Pay Units: N.A.
Programming (via satellite): Cinemax (multiplexed); HBO (multiplexed); Showtime (multiplexed); Starz (multiplexed); The Movie Channel (multiplexed).
Fee: $11.99 monthly (each).

Video-On-Demand: No

Internet Service
Operational: No.

Telephone Service
None

Miles of Plant: 16.0 (coaxial); None (fiber optic). Homes passed: 1,095.
Manager: James L. Bond. Marketing Director: Laurie Long.
Ownership: Flint Cable Television Inc. (MSO).

CAIRO—CNS, 100 2nd St, Cairo, GA 31728. Phones: 229-227-7001; 229-377-3653. E-mail: marketing@cns-internet.com. Web Site: http://www.cns-internet.com. ICA: GA0306. **Note:** This system is an overbuild.
TV Market Ranking: Below 100 (CAIRO). Franchise award date: N.A. Franchise expiration date: N.A. Began: June 27, 2001.
Channel capacity: 75 (operating 2-way). Channels available but not in use: None.

Basic Service
Subscribers: 1,960.
Programming (received off-air): WABW-TV (PBS) Pelham; WALB (NBC) Albany; WBXT-CA Tallahassee; WCTV (CBS, MNT) Thomasville; WFSU-TV (PBS) Tallahassee; WSB-TV (ABC) Atlanta; WTLF (CW, FOX) Tallahassee; WTLH (CW, FOX) Bainbridge; WTWC-TV (NBC) Tallahassee; WTXL-TV (ABC) Tallahassee; WXIA-TV (NBC) Atlanta.
Programming (via satellite): Bloomberg Television; C-SPAN; C-SPAN 2; Discovery Channel; Disney Channel; FamilyNet; FitTV; Fox News Channel; G4; Gospel Music TV; Hallmark Channel; Headline News; Home Shopping Network; ION Television; QVC; SportSouth; TBS Superstation; Toon Disney; Travel Channel; Trinity Broadcasting Network; Weather Channel.
Fee: $10.50 monthly.

Expanded Basic Service 1
Subscribers: 1,758.
Programming (via satellite): ABC Family Channel; AMC; Animal Planet; Arts & Entertainment; BET Networks; Bravo; Cartoon Network; CNBC; CNN; Comcast Sports Net Southeast; Comedy Central; E! Entertainment Television; ESPN; ESPN 2; ESPN Classic Sports; Food Network; FX; Golf Channel; Great American Country; GSN; HGTV; History Channel; Lifetime; MSNBC; MTV; Nickelodeon; Outdoor Channel; Speed Channel; Spike TV; Syfy; The Learning Channel; truTV; Turner Classic Movies; Turner Network TV; TV Land; Univision; USA Network; VH1; WE tv; WGN America.
Fee: $29.95 monthly.

Digital Basic Service
Subscribers: 564.
Programming (via satellite): BBC America; Bio; Boomerang; CNN en Espanol; CNN International; Discovery Digital Networks; Do-It-Yourself; Fox Movie Channel; Fox Sports en Espanol; Fox Sports World; Fuse; GAS; History Channel International; Independent Film Channel; Lifetime Movie Network; MTV Networks Digital Suite; Music Choice; National Geographic Channel; Nick Jr.; Nick Too; Style Network.
Fee: $39.95 monthly.

Pay Service 1
Pay Units: N.A.
Programming (via satellite): Cinemax; Encore; HBO; Showtime; Starz.
Fee: $8.95 monthly.

Digital Pay Service 1
Pay Units: N.A.
Programming (via satellite): Cinemax (multiplexed); Encore (multiplexed); Flix; HBO (multiplexed); Showtime (multiplexed); Starz (multiplexed); Sundance Channel.
Fee: $10.00 monthly (each).

Pay-Per-View
iN DEMAND.

Internet Service
Operational: Yes.
Subscribers: 769.

Broadband Service: SyrupCity.net.
Fee: $28.95 monthly.

Telephone Service
None

Miles of Plant: 100.0 (coaxial); None (fiber optic).

Marketing Coordinator: Sherri Nix. Broadband Engineer: Chris White.

Ownership: Community Network Services (MSO).

CAMILLA—CNS, PO Box 328, 30 E Broad St, Camilla, GA 31730. Phones: 229-227-7001; 229-336-7856. E-mail: marketing@cns-internet.com. Web Site: http://www.cns-internet.com. ICA: GA0307. **Note:** This system is an overbuild.

TV Market Ranking: Below 100 (CAMILLA).

Channel capacity: 75 (operating 2-way). Channels available but not in use: None.

Basic Service
Subscribers: 1,569.
Programming (received off-air): WABW-TV (PBS) Pelham; WALB (NBC) Albany; WCTV (CBS, MNT) Thomasville; WFSU-TV (PBS) Tallahassee; WFXL (FOX) Albany; WSB-TV (ABC) Atlanta; WSWG (CBS, MNT) Valdosta; WTXL-TV (ABC) Tallahassee.
Programming (via satellite): Bloomberg Television; C-SPAN; C-SPAN 2; CW+; Discovery Channel; Disney Channel; FamilyNet; FitTV; Fox News Channel; G4; Gospel Music TV; Hallmark Channel; Headline News; Home Shopping Network; ION Television; QVC; SportSouth; TBS Superstation; Toon Disney; Travel Channel; Trinity Broadcasting Network; Weather Channel.
Fee: $11.50 monthly.

Expanded Basic Service 1
Subscribers: 1,384.
Programming (via satellite): ABC Family Channel; AMC; Animal Planet; Arts & Entertainment; BET Networks; Bravo; Cartoon Network; CNBC; CNN; Comcast Sports Net Southeast; Comedy Central; E! Entertainment Television; ESPN; ESPN 2; Food Network; FX; Golf Channel; Great American Country; GSN; HGTV; History Channel; Lifetime; MSNBC; MTV; Nickelodeon; Outdoor Channel; Speed Channel; Spike TV; Syfy; The Learning Channel; truTV; Turner Classic Movies; Turner Network TV; TV Land; Univision; USA Network; VH1; WE tv; WGN America.
Fee: $32.95 monthly.

Digital Basic Service
Subscribers: 539.
Programming (via satellite): BBC America; Bio; Boomerang; CNN en Espanol; CNN International; Discovery Digital Networks; Do-It-Yourself; Fox Movie Channel; Fox Sports en Espanol; Fox Sports World; Fuse; GAS; History Channel International; Independent Film Channel; Lifetime Movie Network; MTV Networks Digital Suite; Music Choice; National Geographic Channel; Nick Jr.; Nick Too; Style Network.
Fee: $39.95 monthly.

Pay Service 1
Pay Units: N.A.
Programming (via satellite): Cinemax; Encore; HBO; Showtime; Starz.
Fee: $8.95 monthly (HBO).

Digital Pay Service 1
Pay Units: N.A.
Programming (via satellite): Cinemax (multiplexed); Encore (multiplexed); Flix; HBO (multiplexed); Showtime (multiplexed); Starz (multiplexed); Sundance Channel; The Movie Channel (multiplexed).
Fee: $10.00 monthly (each).

Pay-Per-View
iN DEMAND.

Internet Service
Operational: Yes.
Subscribers: 527.
Broadband Service: SyrupCity.net.
Fee: $28.95 monthly.

Telephone Service
None

Miles of Plant: 80.0 (coaxial); None (fiber optic).

Marketing Coordinator: Sherri Nix. Broadband Engineer: Chris White.

Ownership: Community Network Services (MSO).

CAMILLA—Mediacom, 509 Flint Ave, Albany, GA 31701. Phones: 229-244-3852 (Valdosta regional office); 229-888-0242. Fax: 229-436-4819. Web Site: http://www.mediacomcable.com. Also serves Meigs, Mitchell County (portions), Pelham & Thomas County (portions). ICA: GA0065.

TV Market Ranking: Below 100 (CAMILLA, Meigs, Mitchell County (portions), Pelham, Thomas County (portions)). Franchise award date: N.A. Franchise expiration date: N.A. Began: December 1, 1973.

Channel capacity: N.A. Channels available but not in use: N.A.

Basic Service
Subscribers: 2,800.
Programming (received off-air): WABW-TV (PBS) Pelham; WALB (NBC) Albany; WCTV (CBS, MNT) Thomasville; WFXL (FOX) Albany; WSBK-TV (IND) Boston; WSB-TV (ABC) Atlanta; WSWG (CBS, MNT) Valdosta; WTVM (ABC) Columbus; allband FM.
Programming (via satellite): ABC Family Channel; Arts & Entertainment; BET Networks; CNBC; CNN; Comedy Central; C-SPAN; Discovery Channel; Hallmark Channel; Headline News; Home Shopping Network; Lifetime; Nickelodeon; TBS Superstation; Turner Network TV; VH1; Weather Channel.
Current originations: Leased Access; Public Access.
Fee: $35.00 installation; $9.15 monthly.

Expanded Basic Service 1
Subscribers: 2,676.
Programming (via satellite): AMC; Animal Planet; Black Family Channel; Bravo; Cartoon Network; Comcast Sports Net Southeast; Country Music TV; C-SPAN 2; Disney Channel; E! Entertainment Television; ESPN; ESPN 2; Eternal Word TV Network; Food Network; Fox News Channel; Fox Sports World; FX; Gaming Entertainment Television; HGTV; History Channel; INSP; ION Television; Lifetime Movie Network; MSNBC; MTV; Outdoor Channel; QVC; Speed Channel; Spike TV; SportSouth; Syfy; The Learning Channel; Travel Channel; Trinity Broadcasting Network; truTV; TV Guide Network; TV Land; Univision; USA Network; WE tv.
Fee: $10.67 monthly.

Digital Basic Service
Subscribers: N.A.
Programming (via satellite): BBC America; Bio; Bloomberg Television; Canales N; Discovery Digital Networks; Fox Movie Channel; Fuse; G4; GAS; GSN; Halogen Network; History Channel International; Independent Film Channel; International Television (ITV); Lime; MTV Networks Digital Suite; Music Choice; National Geographic Channel; Nick Jr.; Ovation; Speed Channel; Style Network; Toon Disney; Turner Classic Movies; Versus.

Digital Pay Service 1
Pay Units: N.A.
Programming (via satellite): Cinemax (multiplexed); Encore (multiplexed); Flix; HBO (multiplexed); Showtime (multiplexed); Starz (multiplexed); Sundance Channel; The Movie Channel (multiplexed).
Fee: $10.75 monthly (Showtime or TMC), $12.70 monthly (HBO, Cinemax, Flix, Starz, Sundance or Encore).

Video-On-Demand: Yes

Pay-Per-View
TVN Entertainment (delivered digitally); Pleasure (delivered digitally); ETC (delivered digitally); ESPN Now (delivered digitally); Sports PPV (delivered digitally).

Internet Service
Operational: Yes. Began: December 31, 2002.
Broadband Service: Mediacom High Speed Internet.
Fee: $42.95 monthly; $3.00 modem lease.

Telephone Service
Digital: Operational

Homes passed: 5,041. Miles of plant (coax & fiber) included in Thomasville

Vice President: Sue Misiunas. General Manager: Gary Crosby. Marketing Director: Melanie Hannasch. Marketing Manager: Daryl Channey. Regional Technical Operations Manager: Gary McDougall.

City fee: 3% of gross.

Ownership: Mediacom LLC (MSO).

CARNESVILLE—Carnesville Cable, 1591 S Fairview Rd, Lavonia, GA 30553. Phone: 706-356-1714. Fax: 706-356-1737. E-mail: sales2u@gumlog.net. Web Site: http://www.gumlog.net. Also serves Franklin County (portions). ICA: GA0290.

TV Market Ranking: 46 (CARNESVILLE, Franklin County (portions)). Franchise award date: N.A. Franchise expiration date: N.A. Began: N.A.

Channel capacity: 52 (operating 2-way). Channels available but not in use: N.A.

Basic Service
Subscribers: 271.
Programming (received off-air): WAGA-TV (FOX) Atlanta; WGGS-TV (IND) Greenville; WGTV (PBS) Athens; WHNS (FOX) Greenville; WLOS (ABC) Asheville; WNEG-TV (CBS) Toccoa; WNTV (PBS) Greenville; WSB-TV (ABC) Atlanta; WXIA-TV (NBC) Atlanta; WYCW (CW) Asheville; WYFF (NBC) Greenville.
Programming (via satellite): ABC Family Channel; Arts & Entertainment; Cartoon Network; CNBC; CNN; Comcast Sports Net Southeast; Comedy Central; Country Music TV; C-SPAN; C-SPAN 2; Discovery Channel; Disney Channel; E! Entertainment Television; ESPN; ESPN 2; Fox News Channel; Headline News; HGTV; Lifetime; MTV; Nickelodeon; Outdoor Channel; QVC; Spike TV; SportSouth; Syfy; TBS Superstation; The Learning Channel; Trinity Broadcasting Network; Turner Classic Movies; Turner Network TV; TV Land; USA Network; Weather Channel; WGN America.
Fee: $54.95 installation; $41.75 monthly.

Digital Basic Service
Subscribers: 113.
Programming (via satellite): BBC America; Bloomberg Television; Bravo; Discovery Digital Networks; DMX Music; ESPN Classic Sports; ESPNews; FitTV; Fox Sports World; G4; Golf Channel; GSN; History Channel; Independent Film Channel; Nick Jr.; NickToons TV; Outdoor Channel; Speed Channel; Versus; VH1 Classic; VH1 Country; WE tv.
Fee: $9.95 monthly.

Pay Service 1
Pay Units: N.A.
Programming (via satellite): Cinemax; HBO; Showtime.
Fee: $10.95 monthly (Cinemax), $11.95 monthly (Showtime), $12.95 monthly (HBO).

Digital Pay Service 1
Pay Units: N.A.
Programming (via satellite): Cinemax (multiplexed); Encore (multiplexed); HBO (multiplexed); Showtime (multiplexed); Starz (multiplexed); The Movie Channel (multiplexed).
Fee: $10.05 monthly (each).

Pay-Per-View
iN DEMAND (delivered digitally); Playboy TV (delivered digitally); Hot Choice (delivered digitally); Fresh (delivered digitally).

Internet Service
Operational: Yes.
Subscribers: 125.
Broadband Service: Depot Street Comm.
Fee: $39.95-$69.95 monthly.

Telephone Service
Digital: Operational

Miles of Plant: 15.0 (coaxial); None (fiber optic). Homes passed: 500.

Manager: John Williamson.

Ownership: Carnesville Gumlog Cable (MSO).

CARROLLTON—Charter Communications, 1925 Breckenridge Plaza, Ste 100, Duluth, GA 30096-4918. Phones: 770-832-7225; 770-304-5833. Fax: 770-806-7099. Web Site: http://www.charter.com. Also serves Carroll County (portions) & Heard County (unincorporated areas). ICA: GA0054.

TV Market Ranking: Outside TV Markets (Carroll County (portions), CARROLLTON, Heard County (unincorporated areas)). Franchise award date: N.A. Franchise expiration date: N.A. Began: July 1, 1971.

Channel capacity: N.A. Channels available but not in use: N.A.

Basic Service
Subscribers: N.A.
Programming (received off-air): WAGA-TV (FOX) Atlanta; WATL (MNT) Atlanta; WCAG-LP La Grange; WDTA-LP Fayetteville; WGCL-TV (CBS) Atlanta; WGTV (PBS) Athens; WPCH-TV (IND) Atlanta; WPXA-TV (ION) Rome; WSB-TV (ABC) Atlanta; WUPA (CW) Atlanta; WUVG-DT (UNV) Athens; WXIA-TV (NBC) Atlanta; 9 FMs.
Programming (via satellite): C-SPAN; Home Shopping Network; INSP; Product Information Network; QVC; Trinity Broadcasting Network; TV Guide Network; WGN America.
Current originations: Leased Access; Educational Access.
Fee: $29.95 installation.

Expanded Basic Service 1
Subscribers: 3,607.
Programming (via satellite): ABC Family Channel; AMC; Animal Planet; Arts & Entertainment; BET Networks; Bravo; Cartoon Network; CNBC; CNN; Comcast Sports Net Southeast; Comcast/Charter Sports Southeast (CSS); Comedy Central; Country Music TV; Discovery Channel; Disney Channel; E! Entertainment Television; ESPN; ESPN 2; ESPN Classic Sports; Eternal Word TV Network; FitTV; Food Network; Fox News Channel; FX; G4; GalaVision; Golf Channel; GSN; Hallmark Channel; Headline News; HGTV; History Channel; Lifetime; MSNBC; MTV; National Geographic Channel; Nickelodeon; Outdoor Channel; Shop at Home; ShopNBC; SoapNet; Speed Channel; Spike TV; Sport-

South; Syfy; Telemundo; The Learning Channel; Toon Disney; Travel Channel; truTV; Turner Classic Movies; Turner Network TV; TV Land; USA Network; Versus; VH1; WE tv; Weather Channel.
Fee: $48.99 monthly.

Digital Basic Service
Subscribers: N.A.
Programming (via satellite): BBC America; Bio; Bloomberg Television; Boomerang; Canales N; Discovery Digital Networks; Do-It-Yourself; ESPNews; Fox College Sports Atlantic; Fox College Sports Central; Fox College Sports Pacific; Fox Sports World; GAS; Great American Country; History Channel International; Independent Film Channel; Lifetime Movie Network; MTV Networks Digital Suite; MuchMusic Network; Music Choice; Nick Jr.; Nick Too; NickToons TV; Style Network; Sundance Channel.
Fee: $14.00 monthly.

Digital Pay Service 1
Pay Units: 141.
Programming (via satellite): Cinemax (multiplexed); Encore (multiplexed); Flix; HBO (multiplexed); Showtime (multiplexed); Starz (multiplexed); The Movie Channel (multiplexed).

Video-On-Demand: Yes

Pay-Per-View
iN DEMAND (delivered digitally); NBA League Pass/WNBA (delivered digitally); NHL Center Ice/MLB Extra Innings (delivered digitally); Playboy TV (delivered digitally); Fresh (delivered digitally); Shorteez (delivered digitally).

Internet Service
Operational: Yes.
Broadband Service: Charter Pipeline.
Fee: $29.99 monthly; $9.95 modem lease.

Telephone Service
Digital: Operational
Fee: $29.99 monthly

Miles of Plant: 110.0 (coaxial); None (fiber optic). Homes passed: 6,733. Total homes in franchised area: 7,066.
Vice President & General Manager: Matt Favre. Operations Manager: David Spriggs. Sales & Marketing Director: Antoinette Carpenter.
City fee: 4% of gross.
Ownership: Charter Communications Inc. (MSO).

CARTERSVILLE—Now served by ATLANTA (perimeter north), GA [GA0033]. ICA: GA0026.

CEDARTOWN—Charter Communications, 1925 Breckenridge Plaza, Ste 100, Duluth, GA 30096-4918. Phones: 770-806-7060 (Duluth office); 770-748-5443 (Cedartown office). Fax: 770-806-7099. Web Site: http://www.charter.com. Also serves Cave Spring, Floyd & Polk County. ICA: GA0178.
TV Market Ranking: 18 (Cave Spring, CEDARTOWN, Floyd, Polk County). Franchise award date: July 31, 1966. Franchise expiration date: N.A. Began: December 29, 1968.
Channel capacity: N.A. Channels available but not in use: N.A.

Basic Service
Subscribers: 7,321.
Programming (received off-air): WAGA-TV (FOX) Atlanta; WATL (MNT) Atlanta; WDTA-LP Fayetteville; WGCL-TV (CBS) Atlanta; WGTV (PBS) Athens; WPCH-TV (IND) Atlanta; WPXA-TV (ION) Rome; WSB-TV (ABC) Atlanta; WUPA (CW) Atlanta; WUVG-DT (UNV) Athens; WXIA-TV (NBC) Atlanta; allband FM.
Programming (via satellite): C-SPAN; Home Shopping Network; INSP; QVC; Trinity Broadcasting Network; TV Guide Network; WGN America.
Current originations: Leased Access.
Fee: $29.95 installation.

Expanded Basic Service 1
Subscribers: 6,944.
Programming (via satellite): ABC Family Channel; AMC; Animal Planet; Arts & Entertainment; BET Networks; Bravo; Cartoon Network; CNBC; CNN; Comcast Sports Net Southeast; Comcast/Charter Sports Southeast (CSS); Comedy Central; Country Music TV; Discovery Channel; Disney Channel; E! Entertainment Television; ESPN; ESPN 2; ESPN Classic Sports; Eternal Word TV Network; Food Network; Fox News Channel; FX; G4; GalaVision; Golf Channel; GSN; Hallmark Channel; Headline News; HGTV; History Channel; Lifetime; MSNBC; MTV; MTV2; National Outdoor Geographic Channel; Nickelodeon; Outdoor Channel; Oxygen; SoapNet; Speed Channel; Spike TV; SportSouth; Syfy; Telefutura; Telemundo; The Learning Channel; Toon Disney; Travel Channel; truTV; Turner Classic Movies; Turner Network TV; TV Land; USA Network; Versus; VH1; WE tv; Weather Channel.
Fee: $48.99 monthly.

Digital Basic Service
Subscribers: N.A.
Programming (received off-air): WAGA-TV (FOX) Atlanta; WGCL-TV (CBS) Atlanta; WPCH-TV (IND) Atlanta; WSB-TV (ABC) Atlanta; WXIA-TV (NBC) Atlanta.
Programming (via satellite): BBC America; Bio; Bloomberg Television; Boomerang; Canales N; CNN International; Discovery Digital Networks; Do-It-Yourself; ESPN HD; ESPNews; Fox College Sports Atlantic; Fox College Sports Central; Fox College Sports Pacific; Fox Soccer; Fuel TV; Fuse; GAS; Gospel Music Channel; Great American Country; HDNet; HDNet Movies; History Channel International; Independent Film Channel; Lifetime Movie Network; MTV Networks Digital Suite; Music Choice; Nick Jr.; Nick Too; NickToons TV; Style Network; Sundance Channel; Tennis Channel; TV Guide Interactive Inc.
Fee: $14.00 monthly.

Digital Pay Service 1
Pay Units: N.A.
Programming (via satellite): Cinemax (multiplexed); Cinemax HD; Encore (multiplexed); Flix; HBO (multiplexed); HBO HD; LOGO; Showtime (multiplexed); Showtime HD; Starz (multiplexed); The Movie Channel (multiplexed).

Video-On-Demand: Yes

Pay-Per-View
iN DEMAND (delivered digitally); ESPN (delivered digitally); NHL Center Ice (delivered digitally); MLB Extra Innings (delivered digitally); Spice Platinum (delivered digitally); Playboy TV (delivered digitally); Spice Live (delivered digitally); Spice Hot (delivered digitally).

Internet Service
Operational: Yes. Began: January 1, 2002.
Broadband Service: Charter Pipeline.
Fee: $29.99 monthly.

Telephone Service
Digital: Operational
Fee: $29.99 monthly

Miles of Plant: 284.0 (coaxial); None (fiber optic). Homes passed: 7,874.
Vice President & General Manager: Matt Favre. Operations Manager: David Spriggs. Sales & Marketing Director: Antoinette Carpenter.

Franchise fee: 5% of gross.
Ownership: Charter Communications Inc. (MSO).

CHATSWORTH—Charter Communications, 1103 S Hamilton St, Dalton, GA 30720-7860. Phones: 706-428-2290; 865-984-1400 (Maryville, TN office). Fax: 706-260-2520. Web Site: http://www.charter.com. Also serves Eton & Murray County (central portion). ICA: GA0051.
TV Market Ranking: 78 (CHATSWORTH, Eton); 78,18 (Murray County (portions)); Below 100 (Murray County (portions)). Franchise award date: September 12, 1977. Franchise expiration date: N.A. Began: N.A.
Channel capacity: N.A. Channels available but not in use: N.A.

Basic Service
Subscribers: 6,200.
Programming (received off-air): MyNetworkTV Inc.; WATL (MNT) Atlanta; WDEF-TV (CBS) Chattanooga; WDNN-CA (IND) Dalton; WDSI-TV (FOX, MNT) Chattanooga; WELF-TV (TBN) Dalton; WFLI-TV (CW) Cleveland; WNGH-TV (PBS) Chatsworth; WPXA-TV (ION) Rome; WRCB (NBC) Chattanooga; WSB-TV (ABC) Atlanta; WTVC (ABC) Chattanooga.
Programming (via satellite): C-SPAN; C-SPAN 2; Daystar TV Network; Eternal Word TV Network; Home Shopping Network; QVC; TV Guide Network; Weather Channel; WGN America.
Current originations: Government Access.
Fee: $29.95 installation.

Expanded Basic Service 1
Subscribers: N.A.
Programming (via satellite): ABC Family Channel; AMC; Animal Planet; Arts & Entertainment; BET Networks; Bravo; Cartoon Network; CNBC; CNN; Comcast Sports Net Southeast; Comcast/Charter Sports Southeast (CSS); Comedy Central; Country Music TV; Discovery Channel; Disney Channel; E! Entertainment Television; ESPN; ESPN 2; Food Network; Fox News Channel; FX; G4; GalaVision; Golf Channel; GSN; Hallmark Channel; Headline News; HGTV; History Channel; Lifetime; MSNBC; MTV; National Geographic Channel; Nickelodeon; Oxygen; SoapNet; Speed Channel; Spike TV; SportSouth; Style Network; Syfy; TBS Superstation; Telemundo; The Learning Channel; Toon Disney; Travel Channel; truTV; Turner Classic Movies; Turner Network TV; TV Land; Univision; USA Network; Versus; VH1; WE tv; Weather Channel.
Fee: $50.99 monthly.

Digital Basic Service
Subscribers: N.A.
Programming (via satellite): AmericanLife TV Network; BBC America; Bio; Bloomberg Television; Canales N; CBS College Sports Network; CMT Pure Country; CNN International; Cooking Channel; Discovery Digital Networks; Discovery HD Theater; Do-It-Yourself; ESPN 2 HD; ESPN Classic Sports; ESPN HD; ESPN U; ESPNews; Fox College Sports Atlantic; Fox College Sports Central; Fox College Sports Pacific; Fox Movie Channel; Fox Soccer; Fuel TV; Fuse; GAS; Gospel Music Channel; Great American Country; Halogen Network; HDNet; HDNet Movies; History Channel International; Independent Film Channel; INSP; Jewelry Television; Lifetime Movie Network; Lifetime Real Women; MTV Networks Digital Suite; Music Choice; Nick Jr.; Nick Too; NickToons TV; Palladia; Sundance Channel; Tennis Channel; The Sportsman Channel; Turner Network TV HD; TV Guide Interactive Inc.; Universal HD.

Digital Pay Service 1
Pay Units: N.A.
Programming (via satellite): Cinemax (multiplexed); Encore (multiplexed); Flix; HBO (multiplexed); HBO HD; Showtime (multiplexed); Showtime HD; Starz (multiplexed); Starz HDTV; The Movie Channel (multiplexed).

Video-On-Demand: Yes

Pay-Per-View
Hot Choice (delivered digitally); iN DEMAND (delivered digitally).

Internet Service
Operational: Yes. Began: December 1, 2002.
Broadband Service: Charter Pipeline.
Fee: $29.99 monthly.

Telephone Service
Digital: Operational

Miles of Plant: 280.0 (coaxial); None (fiber optic). Homes passed: 9,333.
Operations Manager: Mike Burns. Technical Operations Director: Grant Evans. Marketing Director: Pat Hollenbeck.
City fee: 3% of gross.
Ownership: Charter Communications Inc. (MSO).

CHAUNCEY—KLiP Interactive, 455 Gees Mill Business Court, Conyers, GA 30013. Phone: 678-727-7100. Fax: 678-727-7002. E-mail: jsheehan@klipia.com. Web Site: http://www.klipia.com. ICA: GA0179.
TV Market Ranking: Outside TV Markets (CHAUNCEY). Franchise award date: N.A. Franchise expiration date: N.A. Began: N.A.
Channel capacity: 65 (not 2-way capable). Channels available but not in use: 37.

Basic Service
Subscribers: 19.
Programming (received off-air): WFXL (FOX) Albany; WGXA (FOX, MNT) Macon; WMAZ-TV (CBS) Macon; WMGT-TV (MNT, NBC) Macon; WPCH-TV (IND) Atlanta.
Programming (via satellite): ABC Family Channel; Animal Planet; Arts & Entertainment; BET Networks; CNN; Country Music TV; C-SPAN; Discovery Channel; Disney Channel; ESPN; ESPN 2; Headline News; Nickelodeon; QVC; Spike TV; The Learning Channel; Travel Channel; Trinity Broadcasting Network; Turner Network TV; USA Network; Weather Channel; WGN America.
Fee: $29.95 installation; $30.45 monthly.

Pay Service 1
Pay Units: 2.
Programming (via satellite): HBO.
Fee: $10.95 monthly.

Internet Service
Operational: No.
Telephone Service
None
Miles of Plant: 4.0 (coaxial); None (fiber optic). Homes passed: 160.
Chief Executive Officer: Joseph A. Sheehan. General Manager East: Mark Miller. General Manager West: Vance Johnson.
Ownership: KLiP Interactive LLC (MSO).

CLAXTON—Comcast Cable, 141 Park of Commerce Dr, Savannah, GA 31405. Phone: 912-356-3113. Web Site: http://www.comcast.com. Also serves Bellville, Evans County (portions) & Hagan. ICA: GA0180.
TV Market Ranking: Below 100 (Bellville, Evans County (portions)); Outside TV Markets (CLAXTON, Evans County (portions), Hagan). Franchise award date: March 4, 1968. Franchise expiration date: N.A. Began: January 12, 1970.
Channel capacity: N.A. Channels available but not in use: 5.
Basic Service
Subscribers: N.A. Included in Savannah
Programming (received off-air): WGSA (CW) Baxley; WJBF (ABC) Augusta; WJCL (ABC) Savannah; WSAV-TV (MNT, NBC) Savannah; WTGS (FOX) Hardeeville; WTOC-TV (CBS) Savannah; WVAN-TV (PBS) Savannah; 1 FM.
Programming (via satellite): QVC; WGN America.
Fee: $47.99 installation; $9.00 monthly; $20.00 additional installation.
Expanded Basic Service 1
Subscribers: N.A.
Programming (via satellite): ABC Family Channel; AMC; Animal Planet; Arts & Entertainment; BET Networks; Cartoon Network; CNBC; CNN; Comcast/Charter Sports Southeast (CSS); Comedy Central; C-SPAN; C-SPAN 2; Discovery Channel; Disney Channel; E! Entertainment Television; ESPN; ESPN 2; Food Network; Fox News Channel; Fox Sports Net; FX; Golf Channel; Great American Country; GSN; Hallmark Channel; Headline News; HGTV; History Channel; Home Shopping Network; INSP; ION Television; Lifetime; MSNBC; MTV; MTV2; Nickelodeon; Speed Channel; Spike TV; SportSouth; Syfy; TBS Superstation; The Learning Channel; truTV; Turner Classic Movies; Turner Network TV; TV Guide Network; TV Land; TV One; USA Network; Versus; VH1; Weather Channel.
Fee: $34.99 monthly.
Digital Basic Service
Subscribers: N.A.
Programming (via satellite): BBC America; Discovery Digital Networks; GAS; MTV Networks Digital Suite; Music Choice; Nick Jr.; Nick Too.
Fee: $11.95 monthly.
Pay Service 1
Pay Units: 119.
Programming (via satellite): Cinemax; HBO; Showtime.
Fee: $15.00 installation; $9.95 monthly (Cinemax), $10.95 monthly (HBO).
Digital Pay Service 1
Pay Units: N.A.
Programming (via satellite): Flix; HBO (multiplexed); Showtime (multiplexed); The Movie Channel (multiplexed).
Video-On-Demand: No
Internet Service
Operational: Yes.
Telephone Service
Digital: Operational
Homes passed & miles of plant (coax & fiber) included in Savannah
General Manager: Michael Dares. Technical Operations Director: Joel Godson. Marketing Director: Jerry Avery. Marketing Manager: Ken Torres.
City fee: 3% of gross.
Ownership: Comcast Cable Communications Inc. (MSO).

CLAYTON—Northland Cable Television, PO Box N, 130 Shepard St, Mountain City, GA 30562. Phone: 706-746-2717. Fax: 706-746-2756. Web Site: http://www.northlandcabletv.com. Also serves Dillard, Lake Rabun, Mountain City, Sky Valley & Tiger. ICA: GA0096.
TV Market Ranking: Below 100 (CLAYTON (VILLAGE), Dillard, Lake Rabun, Mountain City, Sky Valley, Tiger). Franchise award date: N.A. Franchise expiration date: N.A. Began: March 1, 1969.
Channel capacity: 50 (operating 2-way). Channels available but not in use: None.
Basic Service
Subscribers: 2,200.
Programming (received off-air): WAGA-TV (FOX) Atlanta; WATL (MNT) Atlanta; WGCL-TV (CBS) Atlanta; WGTV (PBS) Athens; WHNS (FOX) Greenville; WNEG-TV (CBS) Toccoa; WSB-TV (ABC) Atlanta; WUVG-DT (UNV) Athens; WYFF (NBC) Greenville; all-band FM.
Programming (via satellite): Animal Planet; Arts & Entertainment; Cartoon Network; CNBC; CNN; Comcast Sports Net Southeast; Comedy Central; C-SPAN; Discovery Channel; E! Entertainment Television; ESPN; ESPN 2; Food Network; Fox Movie Channel; Fox News Channel; Great American Country; Hallmark Channel; Headline News; HGTV; History Channel; Lifetime; National Geographic Channel; Nickelodeon; QVC; RFD-TV; SoapNet; Speed Channel; Spike TV; Syfy; TBS Superstation; The Learning Channel; Trinity Broadcasting Network; Turner Classic Movies; Turner Network TV; Turner South; TV Land; USA Network; Weather Channel.
Fee: $50.00 installation; $49.99 monthly.
Digital Basic Service
Subscribers: 130.
Programming (via satellite): Discovery Health Channel; Discovery Home Channel; Discovery Kids Channel; Discovery Military Channel; Discovery Times Channel; DMX Music; ESPNews; Fox Soccer; Golf Channel; Outdoor Channel; Science Channel; Versus; WE tv.
Fee: $8.00 monthly.
Pay Service 1
Pay Units: N.A.
Programming (via satellite): Cinemax; Encore; HBO; Starz.
Fee: $11.50 monthly (Cinemax), $13.50 monthly (HBO).
Digital Pay Service 1
Pay Units: N.A.
Programming (via satellite): Cinemax (multiplexed); Encore (multiplexed); Flix; HBO (multiplexed); Showtime (multiplexed); Starz (multiplexed); The Movie Channel (multiplexed).
Fee: $14.75 monthly (each).
Pay-Per-View
iN DEMAND (delivered digitally), Addressable: No.
Internet Service
Operational: Yes.
Subscribers: 215.
Fee: $42.99 monthly.
Telephone Service
None
Miles of Plant: 120.0 (coaxial); None (fiber optic). Homes passed: 4,020.
Regional Manager: Jack Corley. Business & Marketing Manager: Derrick Addison. Marketing Director: Becky Stovall. Office Manager: Robbin McClure.
City fee: 3% of gross.
Ownership: Northland Communications Corp. (MSO).

CLERMONT—Now served by ATLANTA (perimeter north), GA [GA0033]. ICA: GA0101.

CLEVELAND—Windstream, 2000 Communications Blvd, Baldwin, GA 30511. Phones: 800-345-3874; 877-807-9463. Fax: 706-896-5170. Web Site: http://www.windstreamcable.com. ICA: GA0181.
TV Market Ranking: Below 100 (CLEVELAND). Franchise award date: N.A. Franchise expiration date: N.A. Began: July 1, 1981.
Channel capacity: 62 (not 2-way capable). Channels available but not in use: 7.
Basic Service
Subscribers: 2,506.
Programming (received off-air): WAGA-TV (FOX) Atlanta; WATL (MNT) Atlanta; WGCL-TV (CBS) Atlanta; WGTV (PBS) Athens; WHSG-TV (TBN) Monroe; WNEG-TV (CBS) Toccoa; WPCH-TV (IND) Atlanta; WPXA-TV (ION) Rome; WSB-TV (ABC) Atlanta; WUPA (CW) Atlanta; WUVG-DT (UNV) Athens; WXIA-TV (NBC) Atlanta.
Programming (via satellite): Boomerang; C-SPAN; QVC; TV Guide Network; WGN America.
Fee: $14.51 monthly.
Expanded Basic Service 1
Subscribers: 2,088.
Programming (via satellite): ABC Family Channel; AMC; Animal Planet; Arts & Entertainment; Bravo; Cartoon Network; CNBC; CNN; Comcast Sports Net Southeast; Comedy Central; Country Music TV; Discovery Channel; ESPN; ESPN 2; ESPN Classic Sports; Food Network; Fox News Channel; FX; Headline News; HGTV; History Channel; Lifetime; MTV; National Geographic Channel; Nickelodeon; Speed Channel; Spike TV; SportSouth; The Learning Channel; Turner Network TV; TV Land; USA Network; VH1; Weather Channel.
Fee: $30.74 monthly.
Digital Basic Service
Subscribers: 281.
Programming (via satellite): BBC America; Bio; Canales N; CBS College Sports Network; Cooking Channel; Discovery Digital Networks; DMX Music; Do-It-Yourself; ESPNews; Eternal Word TV Network; FamilyNet; Fox College Sports Atlantic; Fox College Sports Central; Fox College Sports Pacific; Fox Movie Channel; Fox Sports World; Fuel TV; Fuse; GAS; Golf Channel; Gospel Music TV; GSN; Hallmark Channel; Halogen Network; History Channel International; Independent Film Channel; Lifetime Movie Network; MTV2; Nick Jr.; NickToons TV; Outdoor Channel; Praise Television; Science Television; Sleuth; Style Network; The Sportsman Channel; Toon Disney; Turner Classic Movies; Versus; VH1 Classic; VH1 Country; WE tv.
Fee: $10.99 monthly.
Digital Pay Service 1
Pay Units: N.A.
Programming (via satellite): Cinemax (multiplexed); Encore (multiplexed); HBO (multiplexed); Showtime (multiplexed); Starz (multiplexed); The Movie Channel (multiplexed).
Fee: $10.95 monthly (Starz & Encore), $12.99 monthly (Showtime & TMC), $24.95 monthly (HBO & Cinemax).
Video-On-Demand: No
Pay-Per-View
iN DEMAND (delivered digitally).
Internet Service
Operational: No, Both DSL & dial-up.
Telephone Service
None
Miles of Plant: 16.0 (coaxial); None (fiber optic).
President & Chief Executive Officer: Jeff Gardner. Executive Vice President & Chief Financial Officer: Brent Whittington. Executive Vice President, Network Operations: Grant Raney. Executive Vice President & Chief Marketing Officer: Ric Crane. Senior Vice President, Network Services: Frank Schueneman. Senior Vice President, Information Technology: Cindy Nash. Senior Vice President, Consumer Sales: Gregg Richey. Senior Vice President, Customer Services: Joe Marano.
Ownership: Windstream Communications Inc. (MSO).

CLIMAX—KLiP Interactive, 455 Gees Mill Business Court, Conyers, GA 30013. Phone: 678-727-7100. Fax: 678-727-7002. E-mail: jsheehan@klipia.com. Web Site: http://www.klipia.com. ICA: GA0159.
TV Market Ranking: Below 100 (CLIMAX). Franchise award date: N.A. Franchise expiration date: N.A. Began: N.A.
Channel capacity: 65 (not 2-way capable). Channels available but not in use: 31.
Basic Service
Subscribers: 26.
Programming (received off-air): WABW-TV (PBS) Pelham; WALB (NBC) Albany; WCTV (CBS, MNT) Thomasville; WFSU-TV (PBS) Tallahassee; WFXL (FOX) Albany; WPCH-TV (IND) Atlanta; WTLH (CW, FOX) Bainbridge; WTWC-TV (NBC) Tallahassee; WTXL-TV (ABC) Tallahassee.
Programming (via satellite): ABC Family Channel; Arts & Entertainment; BET Networks; CNBC; CNN; Comedy Central; Country Music TV; C-SPAN; Discovery Channel; Disney Channel; E! Entertainment Television; ESPN; ESPN 2; Headline News; History Channel; QVC; Spike TV; The Learning Channel; Trinity Broadcasting Network; Turner Network TV; TV Land; USA Network; Weather Channel; WGN America.
Fee: $29.95 installation; $31.45 monthly.
Pay Service 1
Pay Units: 4.
Programming (via satellite): HBO.
Fee: $10.95 monthly.
Internet Service
Operational: No.
Telephone Service
None
Miles of Plant: 12.0 (coaxial); None (fiber optic). Homes passed: 165.
Chief Executive Officer: Joseph A. Sheehan. General Manager East: Mark Miller. General Manager West: Vance Johnson.
Ownership: KLiP Interactive LLC (MSO).

COLLINS—Worth Cable, PO Box 2059, Hwy 280 W, Reidsville, GA 30453. Phone: 912-557-6133. Fax: 912-557-6545. Web Site: http://www.kennedynetworkservices.com. Also serves Tattnall County (portions). ICA: GA0156.
TV Market Ranking: Below 100 (COLLINS, Tattnall County (portions)); Outside TV Markets (Tattnall County (portions)). Franchise

award date: N.A. Franchise expiration date: N.A. Began: August 1, 1983.
Channel capacity: 45 (not 2-way capable). Channels available but not in use: 14.

Basic Service
Subscribers: 125.
Programming (received off-air): WGSA (CW) Baxley; WJCL (ABC) Savannah; WSAV-TV (MNT, NBC) Savannah; WTGS (FOX) Hardeeville; WTOC-TV (CBS) Savannah; WVAN-TV (PBS) Savannah.
Programming (via satellite): ABC Family Channel; Animal Planet; Arts & Entertainment; BET Networks; CNN; Comcast Sports Net Southeast; Comedy Central; Country Music TV; Discovery Channel; ESPN; Fox News Channel; Home Shopping Network; TBS Superstation; The Learning Channel; Turner Network TV; TV Land; USA Network; Weather Channel; WGN America.
Fee: $29.95 installation; $30.45 monthly.

Pay Service 1
Pay Units: 17.
Programming (via satellite): Cinemax.
Fee: $10.95 monthly.

Pay Service 2
Pay Units: 24.
Programming (via satellite): HBO.
Fee: $10.95 monthly.

Video-On-Demand: No

Internet Service
Operational: No.

Telephone Service
None

Miles of Plant: 10.0 (coaxial); None (fiber optic). Homes passed: 185.
Manager: Gina Sheridan. Chief Technician: Nick Burns.
Ownership: J. Roger Kennedy Jr. (MSO).

COLONELS ISLAND—Comcast Cable, 141 Park of Commerce Dr, Savannah, GA 31405. Phone: 912-354-2813. Fax: 912-353-6063. Web Site: http://www.comcast.com. ICA: GA0165.
TV Market Ranking: Below 100 (COLONELS ISLAND). Franchise award date: N.A. Franchise expiration date: N.A. Began: January 11, 1990.
Channel capacity: N.A. Channels available but not in use: N.A.

Basic Service
Subscribers: N.A. Included in Savannah
Programming (received off-air): WJCL (ABC) Savannah; WSAV-TV (MNT, NBC) Savannah; WTGS (FOX) Hardeeville; WTOC-TV (CBS) Savannah; WVAN-TV (PBS) Savannah.
Programming (via satellite): CNN; TBS Superstation; Turner Network TV; USA Network; Weather Channel; WGN America.
Fee: $47.99 installation; $11.00 monthly.

Expanded Basic Service 1
Subscribers: 38.
Programming (via satellite): AMC; Cartoon Network; CNBC; Comcast Sports Net Southeast; Discovery Channel; Disney Channel; ESPN; ESPN 2; Lifetime; Nickelodeon; Spike TV; Syfy; truTV.

Pay Service 1
Pay Units: 12.
Programming (via satellite): Cinemax; HBO; Showtime.

Video-On-Demand: No

Internet Service
Operational: No.

Telephone Service
None

Homes passed & miles of plant (coax & fiber) included in Savannah
General Manager: Michael Daves. Technical Operations Manager: Joel Godsen. Marketing Director: Jerry Avery. Marketing Manager: Ken Torres.
Ownership: Comcast Cable Communications Inc. (MSO).

COLQUITT—KLiP Interactive, 455 Gees Mill Business Court, Conyers, GA 30013. Phone: 678-727-7100. Fax: 678-727-7002. E-mail: jsheehan@klipia.com. Web Site: http://www.klipia.com. Also serves Damascus, Early County (portions) & Miller County (portions). ICA: GA0114.
TV Market Ranking: Below 100 (COLQUITT, Damascus, Early County (portions), Miller County (portions)). Franchise award date: N.A. Franchise expiration date: N.A. Began: N.A.
Channel capacity: 45 (not 2-way capable). Channels available but not in use: 5.

Basic Service
Subscribers: 361.
Programming (received off-air): WABW-TV (PBS) Pelham; WALB (NBC) Albany; WCTV (CBS, MNT) Thomasville; WDHN (ABC) Dothan; WPCH-TV (IND) Atlanta; WTLH (CW, FOX) Bainbridge; WTWC-TV (NBC) Tallahassee; WTXL-TV (ABC) Tallahassee.
Programming (via satellite): ABC Family Channel; Animal Planet; Arts & Entertainment; BET Networks; CNBC; CNN; Comcast Sports Net Southeast; Comedy Central; Country Music TV; C-SPAN; Discovery Channel; Disney Channel; E! Entertainment Television; ESPN; ESPN 2; FX; Headline News; Lifetime; MTV; National Geographic Channel; Nickelodeon; QVC; Speed Channel; Spike TV; The Learning Channel; Trinity Broadcasting Network; Turner Network TV; TV Land; USA Network; Weather Channel; WGN America.
Fee: $29.95 installation; $39.22 monthly.

Pay Service 1
Pay Units: 21.
Programming (via satellite): Cinemax.
Fee: $25.00 installation; $10.95 monthly.

Pay Service 2
Pay Units: 44.
Programming (via satellite): HBO.
Fee: $10.95 monthly.

Internet Service
Operational: No.

Telephone Service
None

Miles of Plant: 42.0 (coaxial); None (fiber optic). Homes passed: 911.
Chief Executive Officer: Joseph A. Sheehan. General Manager East: Mark Miller. General Manager West: Vance Johnson.
Ownership: KLiP Interactive LLC (MSO).

COLUMBUS—Charter Communications, 1349 Warren Williams Rd, Columbus, GA 31901. Phones: 706-576-6808; 770-806-7060 (Administrative office). Fax: 706-324-4031. Web Site: http://www.charter.com. Also serves Bibb City & Harris County (unincorporated areas). ICA: GA0018.
TV Market Ranking: 94 (Bibb City, COLUMBUS, Harris County (unincorporated areas)). Franchise award date: N.A. Franchise expiration date: N.A. Began: July 1, 1970.
Channel capacity: N.A. Channels available but not in use: N.A.

Basic Service
Subscribers: 11,962.
Programming (received off-air): WJSP-TV (PBS) Columbus; WLTZ (CW, NBC) Columbus; WRBL (CBS) Columbus; WTVM (ABC) Columbus; WXTX (FOX) Columbus; WYBU-CD (IND) Columbus; 3 FMs.

Programming (via satellite): CNN; Comcast/Charter Sports Southeast (CSS); C-SPAN; Home Shopping Network; INSP; ION Television; Product Information Network; QVC; TBS Superstation; Trinity Broadcasting Network; TV Guide Network; Weather Channel; WGN America.
Current originations: Government Access; Educational Access.
Fee: $29.99 installation.

Expanded Basic Service 1
Subscribers: N.A.
Programming (via satellite): ABC Family Channel; AMC; Animal Planet; Arts & Entertainment; BET Networks; Bravo; Cartoon Network; CNBC; Comcast Sports Net Southeast; Comedy Central; Country Music TV; Discovery Channel; Disney Channel; E! Entertainment Television; ESPN; ESPN 2; ESPN Classic Sports; Food Network; Fox News Channel; FX; G4; Golf Channel; GSN; Hallmark Channel; Headline News; HGTV; History Channel; Lifetime; MSNBC; MTV; Nickelodeon; Oxygen; SoapNet; Speed Channel; Spike TV; SportSouth; Syfy; Telemundo; The Learning Channel; Travel Channel; truTV; Turner Classic Movies; Turner Network TV; TV Land; USA Network; Versus; VH1; WE tv.
Fee: $48.99 monthly.

Digital Basic Service
Subscribers: N.A.
Programming (via satellite): BBC America; Discovery Digital Networks; ESPNews; Fox Sports World; GAS; Independent Film Channel; MTV Networks Digital Suite; Music Choice; Nick Jr.; Nick Too; NickToons TV; Ovation; Sundance Channel; TV Guide Interactive Inc.
Fee: $14.00 monthly.

Digital Pay Service 1
Pay Units: N.A.
Programming (via satellite): Cinemax (multiplexed); Encore (multiplexed); HBO (multiplexed); Showtime (multiplexed); Starz (multiplexed); The Movie Channel (multiplexed).
Fee: $12.20 monthly (Cinemax, HBO, Showtime or TMC).

Video-On-Demand: Yes

Pay-Per-View
iN DEMAND (delivered digitally); Playboy TV (delivered digitally).

Internet Service
Operational: Yes.
Broadband Service: Charter Pipeline.
Fee: $29.99 monthly.

Telephone Service
Digital: Operational
Fee: $29.99 monthly

Miles of Plant: 312.0 (coaxial); None (fiber optic). Homes passed: 27,259. Total homes in franchised area: 27,425.
Vice President & General Manager: Matt Favre. Operations Manager: David Spriggs. Technical Operations Manager: Brenda Ivey. Sales & Marketing Director: Antoinette Carpenter.
City fee: 3% of gross.
Ownership: Charter Communications Inc. (MSO).

COLUMBUS—Knology, 6050 Knology Way, Columbus, GA 31909. Phones: 706-645-8553 (Corporate office); 706-221-1000 (Customer service). Fax: 706-221-1050. Web Site: http://www.knology.com. ICA: GA0029. **Note:** This system is an overbuild.
TV Market Ranking: 94 (COLUMBUS, Midland). Franchise award date: June 1, 1988. Franchise expiration date: N.A. Began: October 7, 1988.
Channel capacity: N.A. Channels available but not in use: N.A.

Basic Service
Subscribers: 10,451.
Programming (received off-air): WJSP-TV (PBS) Columbus; WLGA (CW) Opelika; WLTZ (CW, NBC) Columbus; WRBL (CBS) Columbus; WTVM (ABC) Columbus; WXTX (FOX) Columbus; WYBU-CD (IND) Columbus.
Programming (via satellite): ABC Family Channel; AMC; Animal Planet; Arts & Entertainment; BET Networks; Bravo; Cartoon Network; CNBC; CNN; Comcast Sports Net Southeast; Comedy Central; Country Music TV; C-SPAN; C-SPAN 2; Discovery Channel; Discovery Health Channel; Disney Channel; E! Entertainment Television; ESPN; ESPN 2; ESPN Classic Sports; Food Network; Fox News Channel; FX; Great American Country; Hallmark Channel; Headline News; HGTV; History Channel; Home Shopping Network; Lifetime; Lifetime Movie Network; MSNBC; MTV; National Geographic Channel; Nickelodeon; Outdoor Channel; Oxygen; QVC; ShopNBC; Speed Channel; Spike TV; SportSouth; Syfy; TBS Superstation; The Learning Channel; Toon Disney; Travel Channel; Trinity Broadcasting Network; truTV; Turner Classic Movies; Turner Network TV; TV Guide Network; TV Land; Univision; USA Network; VH1; Weather Channel; WGN America.
Current originations: Government Access.
Fee: $49.95 monthly.

Digital Basic Service
Subscribers: N.A. Included in Valley AL
Programming (via satellite): BBC America; Bloomberg Television; Boomerang; CBS College Sports Network; Church Channel; CMT Pure Country; C-SPAN 3; Discovery Channel HD; Discovery HD Theater; Discovery Kids Channel; Discovery Military Channel; Discovery Planet Green; Do-It-Yourself; ESPN 2 HD; ESPN HD; ESPN U; ESPNews; Eternal Word TV Network; Fox College Sports Atlantic; Fox College Sports Central; Fox College Sports Pacific; Fox Soccer; FSN HD; Fuel TV; G4; Golf Channel; Gospel Music Channel; GSN; Hallmark Movie Channel; HDNet; HDNet Movies; ID Investigation Discovery; Independent Film Channel; INSP; JCTV; Jewelry Television; Lifetime Real Women; MTV Hits; MTV Jams; MTV Tres; MTV2; mtvU; Music Choice; National Geographic Channel HD Network; NFL Network; Nick Jr.; Nick Too; NickToons TV; Pentagon Channel; QVC HD; Science Channel; SoapNet; TBS in HD; TeenNick; Tennis Channel; The Sports-

man Channel; TLC HD; Turner Network TV HD; Universal HD; Versus; Versus HD; VH1 Classic; VH1 Soul; WE tv.

Pay Service 1

Pay Units: 1,205.

Programming (via satellite): HBO.

Fee: $13.95 monthly.

Pay Service 2

Pay Units: N.A.

Programming (via satellite): Showtime.

Digital Pay Service 1

Pay Units: N.A.

Programming (via satellite): Cinemax (multiplexed); Cinemax HD; Cinemax On Demand; Encore (multiplexed); Flix; Flix On Demand; HBO (multiplexed); HBO HD; HBO On Demand; Showtime (multiplexed); Showtime HD; Showtime On Demand; Starz (multiplexed); Starz HDTV; Sundance Channel; The Movie Channel (multiplexed); The Movie Channel On Demand.

Fee: $32.35 monthly.

Video-On-Demand: Yes

Pay-Per-View

ESPN (delivered digitally); iN DEMAND (delivered digitally); Playboy TV (delivered digitally); Fresh (delivered digitally); Shorteez (delivered digitally); Spice: Xcess (delivered digitally); Hot Choice (delivered digitally); Club Jenna (delivered digitally).

Internet Service

Operational: Yes.

Broadband Service: Knology.Net.

Fee: $29.95 installation; $61.95 monthly.

Telephone Service

Analog: Not Operational

Digital: Operational

Fee: $23.25 monthly

Miles of Plant: 221.0 (coaxial); 35.0 (fiber optic). Additional miles planned: 800.0 (coaxial); 30.0 (fiber optic). Homes passed: 71,500.

General Manager: Royce Ard. Operations Director: Richard Deenard. Sales & Marketing Manager: George Avant.

Ownership: Knology Inc. (MSO).

COLUMBUS—Mediacom, 6700 Macon Rd, Columbus, GA 31907-5735. Phones: 229-244-3852 (Valdosta regional office); 229-888-0242 (Albany administrative office); 706-568-8292. Fax: 706-568-8270. Web Site: http://www.mediacomcable.com. Also serves Cataula, Ellerslie, Fortson & Harris County (southern portion). ICA: GA0012.

TV Market Ranking: 94 (Cataula, COLUMBUS, Ellerslie, Fortson, Harris County (southern portion)). Franchise award date: N.A. Franchise expiration date: N.A. Began: December 1, 1970.

Channel capacity: N.A. Channels available but not in use: N.A.

Basic Service

Subscribers: 21,969.

Programming (received off-air): WJSP-TV (PBS) Columbus; WLGA (CW) Opelika; WLTZ (CW, NBC) Columbus; WRBL (CBS) Columbus; WTVM (ABC) Columbus; WXTX (FOX) Columbus; WYBU-CD (IND) Columbus; 1 FM.

Programming (via satellite): ABC Family Channel; BET Networks; Bravo; CNBC; Comedy Central; Country Music TV; C-SPAN; C-SPAN 2; E! Entertainment Television; Hallmark Channel; Home Shopping Network; QVC; Shop at Home; TBS Superstation; The Learning Channel; Travel Channel; Trinity Broadcasting Network; truTV; TV Guide Network; VH1; Weather Channel; WGN America.

Current originations: Government Access.

Fee: $44.25 installation; $12.24 monthly.

Expanded Basic Service 1

Subscribers: 20,211.

Programming (via satellite): AMC; Animal Planet; Arts & Entertainment; Black Family Channel; Cartoon Network; CNN; Comcast Sports Net Southeast; Discovery Channel; Disney Channel; ESPN; ESPN 2; Food Network; Fox News Channel; FX; GalaVision; Headline News; HGTV; History Channel; ION Television; Lifetime; MSNBC; MTV; Nickelodeon; SoapNet; Spike TV; SportSouth; Syfy; Turner Network TV; TV Land; USA Network; WE tv.

Fee: $15.00 installation; $7.53 monthly.

Digital Basic Service

Subscribers: 27,600.

Programming (via satellite): AmericanLife TV Network; BBC America; Bio; Bloomberg Television; Canales N; Discovery Digital Networks; ESPN Classic Sports; ESPNews; Fox Movie Channel; Fox Sports World; Fuse; G4; GAS; Golf Channel; GSN; Halogen Network; History Channel International; Independent Film Channel; Lifetime Movie Network; MTV Networks Digital Suite; Music Choice; National Geographic Channel; Nick Jr.; Outdoor Channel; Ovation; Speed Channel; Style Network; Toon Disney; Turner Classic Movies; Versus.

Digital Pay Service 1

Pay Units: 40,275.

Programming (via satellite): Cinemax (multiplexed); Encore (multiplexed); HBO (multiplexed); Showtime (multiplexed); Starz (multiplexed); Sundance Channel; The Movie Channel (multiplexed).

Fee: $10.00 monthly (Cinemax, HBO, Showtime, Starz/Encore, or Sundance/TMC).

Video-On-Demand: Yes

Pay-Per-View

Addressable homes: 27,600.

Addressable: Yes; Sports PPV (delivered digitally); ETC (delivered digitally); Pleasure (delivered digitally).

Internet Service

Operational: Yes.

Broadband Service: Mediacom High Speed Internet.

Fee: $49.00 installation; $40.95 monthly; $10.00 modem lease; $249.00 modem purchase.

Telephone Service

Analog: Not Operational

Digital: Operational

Miles of Plant: 900.0 (coaxial); None (fiber optic). Homes passed: 42,000. Total homes in franchised area: 70,000. Miles of plant (coax) includes miles of plant (fiber)

Regional Vice President: Sue Misiunas. General Manager: Gary Crosby. Regional Marketing Director: Melanie Hannasch. Regional Technical Operations Manager: Gary McDougall. Chief Technician: Darrin Best. Marketing Manager: Daryl Channey.

City fee: 3% of gross.

Ownership: Mediacom LLC (MSO).

COMER—Charter Communications. Now served by ATHENS, GA [GA0014]. ICA: GA0086.

COMMERCE—Windstream, 2000 Communications Blvd, Baldwin, GA 30511. Phones: 800-345-3874; 877-807-9463. Fax: 706-896-5170. Web Site: http://www.windstreamcable.com. Also serves Banks County (portions), Homer, Jackson County (portions) & Nicholson. ICA: GA0099.

TV Market Ranking: Below 100 (Banks County (portions), COMMERCE, Homer, Jackson County (portions), Nicholson). Franchise award date: December 18, 1982. Franchise expiration date: N.A. Began: September 1, 1981.

Channel capacity: 62 (not 2-way capable). Channels available but not in use: 2.

Basic Service

Subscribers: 2,428.

Programming (received off-air): WAGA-TV (FOX) Atlanta; WATL (MNT) Atlanta; WGCL-TV (CBS) Atlanta; WGTV (PBS) Athens; WHSG-TV (TBN) Monroe; WNEG-TV (CBS) Toccoa; WPBA (PBS) Atlanta; WPCH-TV (IND) Atlanta; WPXA-TV (ION) Rome; WSB-TV (ABC) Atlanta; WUPA (CW) Atlanta; WUVG-DT (UNV) Athens; WXIA-TV (NBC) Atlanta; WYFF (NBC) Greenville.

Programming (via satellite): C-SPAN; TV Guide Network.

Fee: $16.55 monthly; $1.00 converter.

Expanded Basic Service 1

Subscribers: 2,237.

Programming (via satellite): ABC Family Channel; AMC; Arts & Entertainment; BET Networks; Boomerang; Bravo; Cartoon Network; CNBC; CNN; Comcast Sports Net Southeast; Comedy Central; Country Music TV; Discovery Channel; ESPN; ESPN 2; ESPN Classic Sports; Food Network; Fox News Channel; Fuse; FX; Golf Channel; Headline News; HGTV; History Channel; Lifetime; MSNBC; MTV; National Geographic Channel; Nickelodeon; QVC; Speed Channel; Spike TV; SportSouth; The Learning Channel; Turner Classic Movies; Turner Network TV; TV Land; USA Network; VH1; Weather Channel; WGN America.

Fee: $28.70 monthly.

Digital Basic Service

Subscribers: 112.

Programming (via satellite): BBC America; Bio; Canales N; CBS College Sports Network; Cooking Channel; Discovery Digital Networks; DMX Music; ESPNews; Eternal Word TV Network; FamilyNet; Fox College Sports Atlantic; Fox College Sports Central; Fox College Sports Pacific; Fox Movie Channel; Fox Sports World; Fuel TV; GAS; Gospel Music TV; GSN; Hallmark Channel; Halogen Network; History Channel International; Independent Film Channel; Lifetime Movie Network; MTV2; Nick Jr.; NickToons TV; Outdoor Channel; Praise Television; Science Television; Sleuth; Style Network; The Sportsman Channel; Versus; VH1 Classic; VH1 Country; WE tv.

Fee: $8.95 monthly.

Digital Pay Service 1

Pay Units: N.A.

Programming (via satellite): Cinemax (multiplexed); Encore (multiplexed); HBO (multiplexed); Showtime (multiplexed); Starz (multiplexed); The Movie Channel (multiplexed).

Fee: $10.95 monthly (Starz & Encore), $12.99 monthly (Showtime & TMC), $24.95 monthly (HBO & Cinemax).

Video-On-Demand: No

Pay-Per-View

iN DEMAND (delivered digitally).

Internet Service

Operational: No, Both DSL & dial-up.

Telephone Service

None

Miles of Plant: 87.0 (coaxial); None (fiber optic). Homes passed: 3,575.

President & Chief Executive Officer: Jeff Gardner. Executive Vice President & Chief Financial Officer: Brent Whittington. Executive Vice President, Network Operations: Grant Raney. Executive Vice President & Chief Marketing Officer: Ric Crane. Senior Vice President, Network Services: Frank Schueneman. Senior Vice President, Information Technology: Cindy Nash. Senior Vice President, Consumer Sales: Gregg Richey. Senior Vice President, Customer Services: Joe Marano.

Ownership: Windstream Communications Inc. (MSO).

CONCORD—Georgia Broadband, 118 W Main St, Manchester, GA 31816. Phone: 706-846-4568. Web Site: http://www.georgia-broadband.com. ICA: GA0319.

TV Market Ranking: Outside TV Markets (CONCORD (VILLAGE)).

Channel capacity: N.A. Channels available but not in use: N.A.

Basic Service

Subscribers: N.A.

Programming (received off-air): WAGA-TV (FOX) Atlanta; WGCL-TV (CBS) Atlanta; WGTV (PBS) Athens; WPBA (PBS) Atlanta; WSB-TV (ABC) Atlanta; WUPA (CW) Atlanta; WUVG-DT (UNV) Athens; WXIA-TV (NBC) Atlanta.

Programming (via satellite): TBS Superstation; WGN America.

Current originations: Leased Access.

Fee: $29.95 installation; $11.95 monthly.

Expanded Basic Service 1

Subscribers: N.A.

Programming (via satellite): ABC Family Channel; AMC; Animal Planet; Arts & Entertainment; BET Networks; Cartoon Network; CNN; Comcast Sports Net Southeast; Comcast/Charter Sports Southeast (CSS); Comedy Central; Country Music TV; C-SPAN; Discovery Channel; Disney Channel; E! Entertainment Television; ESPN; ESPN 2; Fox News Channel; FX; G4; Headline News; HGTV; History Channel; Home Shopping Network; INSP; MTV; Nickelodeon; Oxygen; Spike TV; Syfy; The Learning Channel; Travel Channel; Turner Network TV; Turner South; TV Land; USA Network; VH1; Weather Channel.

Fee: $11.95 monthly.

Digital Basic Service

Subscribers: N.A.

Programming (via satellite): BBC America; Bio; Bloomberg Television; CMT Pure Country; Discovery en Espanol; Discovery Health Channel; Discovery Kids Channel; Discovery Military Channel; Discovery Planet Green; DMX Music; Do-It-Yourself; Fuse; GSN; History Channel International; ID Investigation Discovery; MTV Hits; MTV Jams; MTV Tres; Nick Jr.; Nick Too; NickToons TV; Science Channel; Style Network; Sundance Channel; TeenNick; VH1 Classic; VH1 Soul.

Fee: $11.95 monthly.

Digital Pay Service 1

Pay Units: N.A.

Programming (via satellite): Cinemax (multiplexed); Encore (multiplexed); HBO (multiplexed); Showtime (multiplexed); Starz (multiplexed); The Movie Channel (multiplexed).

Video-On-Demand: Yes

Pay-Per-View

iN DEMAND (delivered digitally).

Internet Service

Operational: Yes.

Fee: $19.95 installation; $24.95 monthly.

Telephone Service

Digital: Operational

Fee: $29.95 monthly

Chief Executive Officer: Michelle Oneil. General Manager: Jerry Oneil.

Ownership: Georgia Broadband LLC (MSO).

COOLIDGE—Southeast Cable TV Inc., PO Box 584, 107 S Main St, Boston, GA 31626-0584. Phone: 229-498-4191. Fax: 229-498-1026. ICA: GA0182.

TV Market Ranking: Below 100 (COOLIDGE). Franchise award date: N.A. Franchise expiration date: N.A. Began: January 1, 1989.

Channel capacity: 40 (not 2-way capable). Channels available but not in use: 20.

Basic Service

Subscribers: 103.

Programming (received off-air): WABW-TV (PBS) Pelham; WALB (NBC) Albany; WCTV (CBS, MNT) Thomasville; WTLH (CW, FOX) Bainbridge; WTWC-TV (NBC) Tallahassee; WTXL-TV (ABC) Tallahassee.

Programming (via satellite): ABC Family Channel; AMC; Arts & Entertainment; BET Networks; CNBC; CNN; Comedy Central; Country Music TV; C-SPAN; Discovery Channel; ESPN; ESPN 2; Fox Sports Net; Headline News; HGTV; History Channel; Lifetime; MTV; Nickelodeon; QVC; Spike TV; SportSouth; TBS Superstation; The Learning Channel; Trinity Broadcasting Network; Turner Network TV; TV Land; VH1; Weather Channel; WGN America.

Fee: $15.00 installation; $13.50 monthly.

Pay Service 1

Pay Units: 33.

Programming (via satellite): Cinemax.

Fee: $10.00 monthly.

Pay Service 2

Pay Units: 41.

Programming (via satellite): HBO.

Fee: $10.00 monthly.

Internet Service

Operational: No.

Telephone Service

None

Miles of Plant: 6.0 (coaxial); None (fiber optic). Homes passed: 210.

Manager & Chief Technician: Bob Heide.

Ownership: Southeast Cable TV Inc. (MSO).

CORDELE—Mediacom. Now served by FITZGERALD, GA [GA0052]. ICA: GA0047.

CORNELIA—Windstream, 2000 Communications Blvd, Baldwin, GA 30511. Phones: 800-345-3874; 877-807-9463. Fax: 706-896-5170. Web Site: http://www.windstreamcable.com. Also serves Alto, Baldwin, Clarkesville, Demorest, Habersham County & Mount Airy. ICA: GA0183.

TV Market Ranking: Below 100 (Alto, Baldwin, Clarkesville, CORNELIA, Demorest, Habersham County, Mount Airy). Franchise award date: N.A. Franchise expiration date: N.A. Began: March 31, 1967.

Channel capacity: 62 (not 2-way capable). Channels available but not in use: 2.

Basic Service

Subscribers: 6,667.

Programming (received off-air): WAGA-TV (FOX) Atlanta; WATL (MNT) Atlanta; WGCL-TV (CBS) Atlanta; WGTV (PBS) Athens; WHSG-TV (TBN) Monroe; WNEG-TV (CBS) Toccoa; WPCH-TV (IND) Atlanta; WPXA-TV (ION) Rome; WSB-TV (ABC) Atlanta; WUPA (CW) Atlanta; WUVG-DT (UNV) Athens; WXIA-TV (NBC) Atlanta; WYFF (NBC) Greenville.

Programming (via satellite): C-SPAN; Shop at Home; WGN America.

Fee: $16.55 monthly.

Expanded Basic Service 1

Subscribers: 6,015.

Programming (via satellite): ABC Family Channel; AMC; Animal Planet; Arts & Entertainment; Boomerang; Bravo; Cartoon Network; CNBC; CNN; Comcast Sports Net Southeast; Comedy Central; Country Music TV; Discovery Channel; ESPN; ESPN 2; ESPN Classic Sports; Food Network; Fox News Channel; FX; Headline News; HGTV; History Channel; Home Shopping Network; Lifetime; MSNBC; MTV; National Geographic Channel; Nickelodeon; Outdoor Channel; QVC; Speed Channel; Spike TV; SportSouth; The Learning Channel; Turner Network TV; TV Guide Network; TV Land; USA Network; VH1; Weather Channel.

Fee: $28.70 monthly.

Digital Basic Service

Subscribers: 636.

Programming (via satellite): BBC America; Bio; Canales N; CBS College Sports Network; Cooking Channel; Discovery Digital Networks; DMX Music; Do-It-Yourself; ESPNews; Eternal Word TV Network; FamilyNet; Fox College Sports Atlantic; Fox College Sports Central; Fox College Sports Pacific; Fox Movie Channel; Fox Sports World; Fuel TV; Fuse; GAS; Golf Channel; Gospel Music TV; GSN; Hallmark Channel; Halogen Network; History Channel International; Independent Film Channel; Lifetime Movie Network; MTV2; Nick Jr.; NickToons TV; Science Television; Sleuth; Style Network; The Sportsman Channel; Versus; VH1 Classic; VH1 Country; WE tv.

Fee: $8.95 monthly.

Digital Pay Service 1

Pay Units: N.A.

Programming (via satellite): Cinemax (multiplexed); Encore (multiplexed); HBO (multiplexed); Showtime (multiplexed); Starz (multiplexed); The Movie Channel (multiplexed).

Fee: $10.95 monthly (Starz & Encore) $12.99 monthly (Showtime & TMC), $24.95 monthly (HBO & Cinemax).

Video-On-Demand: No

Pay-Per-View

iN DEMAND (delivered digitally).

Internet Service

Operational: No, Both DSL & dial-up.

Telephone Service

None

Miles of Plant: 250.0 (coaxial); None (fiber optic).

President & Chief Executive Officer: Jeff Gardner. Executive Vice President & Chief Financial Officer: Brent Whittington. Executive Vice President, Network Operations: Grant Raney. Executive Vice President & Chief Marketing Officer: Ric Crane. Senior Vice President, Network Services: Frank Schueneman. Senior Vice President, Information Technology: Cindy Nash. Senior Vice President, Consumer Sales: Gregg Richey. Senior Vice President, Customer Services: Joe Marano.

Ownership: Windstream Communications Inc. (MSO).

COVINGTON—Charter Communications, 1167 Pace St, Covington, GA 30014. Phones: 770-385-2133; 770-385-2044. Fax: 770-385-2045. E-mail: mfavre@chartercom.com. Web Site: http://www.charter.com. Also serves Newton County, Oxford & Porterdale. ICA: GA0040.

TV Market Ranking: 18 (COVINGTON, Newton County (portions), Oxford, Porterdale); Below 100 (Newton County (portions)). Franchise award date: January 1, 1979. Franchise expiration date: N.A. Began: October 24, 1980.

Channel capacity: 79 (operating 2-way). Channels available but not in use: 4.

Basic Service

Subscribers: 11,093.

Programming (received off-air): LWS Local Weather Station; WAGA-TV (FOX) Atlanta; WATL (MNT) Atlanta; WGCL-TV (CBS) Atlanta; WGTV (PBS) Athens; WPBA (PBS) Atlanta; WPCH-TV (IND) Atlanta; WPXA-TV (ION) Rome; WSB-TV (ABC) Atlanta; WUPA (CW) Atlanta; WUVG-DT (UNV) Athens; WXIA-TV (NBC) Atlanta.

Programming (via satellite): C-SPAN; Trinity Broadcasting Network; TV Guide Network; WGN America.

Current originations: Leased Access.

Fee: $29.99 installation; $15.95 monthly.

Expanded Basic Service 1

Subscribers: 9,970.

Programming (via satellite): ABC Family Channel; AMC; AmericanLife TV Network; Animal Planet; Arts & Entertainment; BET Networks; Bravo; Cartoon Network; CNBC; CNN; Comedy Central; Country Music TV; C-SPAN 2; Discovery Channel; Discovery Health Channel; Disney Channel; Do-It-Yourself; E! Entertainment Television; ESPN; ESPN 2; ESPN Classic Sports; Food Network; Fox Movie Channel; Fox News Channel; Fox Sports Net; FX; G4; GalaVision; Golf Channel; Gospel Music Channel; Great American Country; GSN; Hallmark Channel; Headline News; HGTV; History Channel; Home Shopping Network; Lifetime; MSNBC; MTV; National Geographic Channel; Nickelodeon; Outdoor Channel; Oxygen; QVC; SoapNet; Speed Channel; Spike TV; SportSouth; Style Network; Syfy; Telefutura; The Learning Channel; truTV; Turner Classic Movies; Turner Network TV; TV Land; USA Network; VH1; WE tv; Weather Channel.

Fee: $30.04 monthly.

Digital Basic Service

Subscribers: 706.

Programming (received off-air): WAGA-TV (FOX) Atlanta; WGCL-TV (CBS) Atlanta; WSB-TV (ABC) Atlanta; WXIA-TV (NBC) Atlanta.

Programming (via satellite): BBC America; Bio; Black Family Channel; Bloomberg Television; Church Channel; Current; Daystar TV Network; Discovery Digital Networks; Discovery HD Theater; DMX Music; ESPNews; Fox College Sports Atlantic; Fox College Sports Central; Fox College Sports Pacific; Fox Soccer; Fuse; GAS; Gospel Music Channel; Halogen Network; History Channel International; Independent Film Channel; JCTV; Lifetime Movie Network; Lime; MTV Networks Digital Suite; Nick Jr.; NickToons TV; Ovation; PBS HD; ShopNBC; Sleuth; The Word Network; TV One; TVG Network; Versus.

Fee: $5.00 monthly.

Digital Pay Service 1

Pay Units: 305.

Programming (via satellite): Cinemax (multiplexed); HBO (multiplexed).

Fee: $11.00 monthly (each).

Digital Pay Service 2

Pay Units: 146.

Programming (via satellite): Flix; Showtime (multiplexed); The Movie Channel (multiplexed).

Fee: $11.00 monthly.

Digital Pay Service 3

Pay Units: 137.

Programming (via satellite): Encore (multiplexed); Starz (multiplexed).

Fee: $11.00 monthly.

Video-On-Demand: No

Internet Service

Operational: Yes.

Subscribers: 2,500.

Broadband Service: Charter Pipeline.

Fee: $29.50 monthly.

Telephone Service

None

Miles of Plant: 600.0 (coaxial); 200.0 (fiber optic). Total homes in franchised area: 17,379.

Vice President & General Manager: Matt Favre.

City fee: 5% of gross for Oxford; 3% for all other communities.

Ownership: Charter Communications Inc.

CRAWFORD—CommuniComm Services, PO Box 3668, 104 E Marion St, Eatonton, GA 31024. Phones: 800-554-3235; 706-485-2288. Fax: 706-485-0118. Web Site: http://www.netcommander.com. ICA: GA0273.

TV Market Ranking: Below 100 (CRAWFORD). Franchise award date: N.A. Franchise expiration date: N.A. Began: N.A.

Channel capacity: N.A. Channels available but not in use: N.A.

Basic Service

Subscribers: N.A. Included in Eatonton

Programming (received off-air): WAGA-TV (FOX) Atlanta; WATL (MNT) Atlanta; WGCL-TV (CBS) Atlanta; WGTV (PBS) Athens; WPCH-TV (IND) Atlanta; WSB-TV (ABC) Atlanta; WTBS-LP (IND) Atlanta; WUVG-DT (UNV) Athens; WXIA-TV (NBC) Atlanta.

Programming (via satellite): WGN America; WHSG-TV (TBN) Monroe.

Fee: $39.95 installation.

Expanded Basic Service 1

Subscribers: N.A.

Programming (via satellite): ABC Family Channel; AMC; Arts & Entertainment; BET Networks; Cinemax; CNBC; CNN; Country Music TV; Discovery Channel; ESPN; ESPN 2; Headline News; HGTV; History Channel; Home Shopping Network; Lifetime; MTV; Nick Jr.; Nickelodeon; Spike TV; SportSouth; Syfy; The Learning Channel; Turner Network TV; USA Network; VH1; Weather Channel.

Fee: $36.99 monthly.

Digital Basic Service

Subscribers: N.A. Included in Eatonton

Programming (via satellite): AmericanLife TV Network; BBC America; Bio; Blackbelt TV; Bloomberg Television; Bravo; CMT Pure Country; Discovery Health Channel; Discovery Home Channel; Discovery Kids Channel; Discovery Military Channel; Discovery Times Channel; DMX Music; ESPN Classic Sports; ESPNews; FitTV; Fox

Movie Channel; Fox Soccer; Fuse; G4; Golf Channel; GSN; Halogen Network; History Channel International; Independent Film Channel; Lifetime Movie Network; MTV2; National Geographic Channel; NickToons TV; Outdoor Channel; Science Channel; Sleuth; Speed Channel; Style Network; TeenNick; Turner Classic Movies; Versus; VH1 Classic; WE tv.
Fee: $11.95 monthly.

Pay Service 1
Pay Units: N.A.
Programming (via satellite): HBO.
Fee: $13.95 monthly.

Digital Pay Service 1
Pay Units: N.A.
Programming (via satellite): Cinemax (multiplexed); Encore (multiplexed); HBO (multiplexed); Showtime (multiplexed); Starz (multiplexed); The Movie Channel (multiplexed).
Fee: $11.95 monthly (Cinemax), $13.95 monthly (HBO, Showtime/TMC or Starz/ Encore).

Video-On-Demand: No

Pay-Per-View
Club Jenna (delivered digitally); Playboy TV (delivered digitally); Fresh (delivered digitally); Hot Choice; iN DEMAND (delivered digitally).

Internet Service
Operational: No.

Telephone Service
None

Homes passed and total homes in franchised are included in Eatonton
General Manager: Brian Chase. Chief Technician: Scott Richardson. Customer Care Manager: Diane Simmons.
Franchise fee: 5% of gross.
Ownership: James Cable LLC (MSO).

CRAWFORD COUNTY (Eastern portion)—Piedmont Cable Corp., PO Box 2059, 228 West Brazell St, Reidsville, GA 30453. Phone: 478-825-3578. Fax: 912-557-6545. Also serves Byron, Fort Valley & Lizella. ICA: GA0120.
TV Market Ranking: Below 100 (Byron, CRAWFORD COUNTY, Fort Valley, Lizella). Franchise award date: October 1, 1989. Franchise expiration date: N.A. Began: August 1, 1990.
Channel capacity: 54 (not 2-way capable). Channels available but not in use: 11.

Basic Service
Subscribers: 545.
Programming (received off-air): WGNM (IND) Macon; WGXA (FOX, MNT) Macon; WLTZ (CW, NBC) Columbus; WMAZ-TV (CBS) Macon; WMGT-TV (MNT, NBC) Macon; WMUM-TV (PBS) Cochran; WPGA-TV (ABC) Perry; WRBL (CBS) Columbus; WTVM (ABC) Columbus.
Programming (via satellite): ABC Family Channel; AMC; Arts & Entertainment; Cartoon Network; CNN; Comcast Sports Net Southeast; Comedy Central; Country Music TV; C-SPAN; Discovery Channel; ESPN; Hallmark Channel; Headline News; History Channel; Home Shopping Network; Lifetime; Nickelodeon; Spike TV; Syfy; TBS Superstation; The Learning Channel; Travel Channel; Trinity Broadcasting Network; Turner Network TV; TV Land; USA Network; VH1; Weather Channel; WGN America.
Current originations: Educational Access.
Fee: $25.00 installation; $34.75 monthly; $3.50 converter; $20.00 additional installation.

Pay Service 1
Pay Units: 86.
Programming (via satellite): HBO.
Fee: $9.95 monthly.

Pay Service 2
Pay Units: 52.
Programming (via satellite): Showtime.
Fee: $9.95 monthly.

Internet Service
Operational: No.

Miles of Plant: 60.0 (coaxial); None (fiber optic). Additional miles planned: 10.0 (coaxial). Homes passed: 850. Total homes in franchised area: 1,800.
Manager & Marketing Director: Gina Sheridan. Chief Engineer & Program Director: Nick Bruns.
County fee: 3% of basic.
Ownership: Piedmont Cable Corp.

CRAWFORD COUNTY (portions)—Flint Cable TV, PO Box 669, 105 W Marion St, Reynolds, GA 31074. Phone: 478-847-3101. Web Site: http://www.flintcatv.com. Also serves PIEDMONT. ICA: GA0324.
TV Market Ranking: Below 100 (CRAWFORD COUNTY (PORTIONS)); Outside TV Markets (PIEDMONT).
Channel capacity: N.A. Channels available but not in use: N.A.

Basic Service
Subscribers: N.A.
Programming (received off-air): WGNM (IND) Macon; WGXA (FOX, MNT) Macon; WMAZ-TV (CBS) Macon; WMGT-TV (MNT, NBC) Macon; WMUM-TV (PBS) Cochran; WPGA-TV (ABC) Perry; WRBL (CBS) Columbus; WTVM (ABC) Columbus.
Programming (via satellite): C-SPAN; Home Shopping Network; TBS Superstation; Weather Channel.

Expanded Basic Service 1
Subscribers: N.A.
Programming (via satellite): ABC Family Channel; AMC; Animal Planet; Arts & Entertainment; BET Networks; Cartoon Network; CNN; Comcast Sports Net Southeast; Comedy Central; Country Music TV; Discovery Channel; Disney Channel; E! Entertainment Television; ESPN; ESPN 2; Food Network; Fox News Channel; FX; Hallmark Channel; Hallmark Movie Channel; Headline News; HGTV; History Channel; Lifetime; MTV; National Geographic Channel; Nickelodeon; Speed Channel; Spike TV; SportSouth; Syfy; The Learning Channel; Travel Channel; truTV; Turner Network TV; TV Land; USA Network; VH1.

Digital Basic Service
Subscribers: N.A.
Programming (via satellite): AmericanLife TV Network; BBC America; Bio; Bloomberg Television; Bravo; Chiller; CMT Pure Country; Cooking Channel; Current; Discovery Health Channel; Discovery Kids Channel; Discovery Military Channel; Discovery Planet Green; Disney XD; DMX Music; Encore (multiplexed); ESPN Classic Sports; ESPNews; FitTV; Flix; Fox College Sports Atlantic; Fox College Sports Central; Fox College Sports Pacific; Fox Movie Channel; Fox Soccer; Fuse; G4; Golf Channel; Gospel Music Channel; Great American Country; GSN; History Channel International; ID Investigation Discovery; i-Lifetv; Independent Film Channel; Lifetime Movie Network; MTV Hits; MTV2; Nick At Nite; Nick Jr.; NickToons TV; Outdoor Channel; RFD-TV; Science Channel; Sleuth; SoapNet; Style Network; Sundance Channel; Trinity Broadcasting Network; Turner Classic Movies; Versus; VH1 Classic; VH1 Soul; WE tv.
Fee: $54.99 monthly.

Digital Pay Service 1
Pay Units: N.A.
Programming (via satellite): Cinemax (multiplexed); HBO (multiplexed); Showtime (multiplexed); Starz (multiplexed); The Movie Channel (multiplexed).
Fee: $12.99 monthly (HBO, Cinemax, Starz or Showtime/TMC).

Internet Service
Operational: No.

Telephone Service
None

Manager: James Bond. Marketing Manager: Shania Long.
Ownership: Flint Cable Television Inc. (MSO).

CRAWFORDVILLE—Formerly served by CommuniComm Services. No longer in operation. ICA: GA0148.

CUMMING—Now served by CANTON, GA [GA0033]. ICA: GA0027.

CUSSETA—Formerly served by Almega Cable. No longer in operation. ICA: GA0127.

CUTHBERT—Mediacom, 509 Flint Ave, Albany, GA 31701. Phones: 229-244-3852 (Valdosta office); 229-888-0242. Fax: 229-436-4819. Web Site: http://www.mediacomcable.com. Also serves Arlington, Edison, Fort Gaines, Lumpkin & Richland. ICA: GA0184.
TV Market Ranking: 94 (Lumpkin, Richland); Below 100 (Arlington, Edison, Fort Gaines); Outside TV Markets (CUTHBERT). Franchise award date: September 4, 1979. Franchise expiration date: N.A. Began: October 1, 1980.
Channel capacity: N.A. Channels available but not in use: N.A.

Basic Service
Subscribers: 1,070.
Programming (received off-air): WACS-TV (PBS) Dawson; WALB (NBC) Albany; WLTZ (CW, NBC) Columbus; WRBL (CBS) Columbus; WSB-TV (ABC) Atlanta; WSST-TV (IND) Cordele; WTVM (ABC) Columbus; WXTX (FOX) Columbus.
Programming (via satellite): Home Shopping Network; INSP; QVC; TV Guide Network; Weather Channel.
Current originations: Religious Access; Government Access; Educational Access.
Fee: $47.78 installation; $12.75 monthly; $2.50 converter.

Expanded Basic Service 1
Subscribers: N.A.
Programming (via satellite): ABC Family Channel; Animal Planet; Arts & Entertainment; BET Networks; Cartoon Network; CNBC; CNN; Comcast Sports Net Southeast; Comedy Central; Country Music TV; C-SPAN; C-SPAN 2; CW+; Discovery Channel; Disney Channel; ESPN; ESPN 2; Eternal Word TV Network; Fox News Channel; Headline News; History Channel; ION Television; Lifetime; MSNBC; MTV; Nickelodeon; Spike TV; SportSouth; TBS Superstation; The Learning Channel; Turner Network TV; TV Land; USA Network; VH1; Weatherscan; WGN America.
Fee: $30.00 installation; $3.95 monthly.

Digital Basic Service
Subscribers: N.A.
Programming (via satellite): 3 Angels Broadcasting Network; BBC America; Bio; Bloomberg Television; CMT Pure Country; Discovery Digital Networks; Discovery Military Channel; ESPNews; Fox Movie Channel; Fox Soccer; G4; Golf Channel; GSN; Halogen Network; History Channel International; ID Investigation Discovery; Independent Film Channel; ION Life; Lifetime Movie Network; MTV Hits; MTV2; National Geographic Channel; Nick Jr.; NickToons TV; Outdoor Channel; Ovation; Qubo; ReelzChannel; Science Channel; Sleuth; Speed Channel; Style Network; TeenNick; Toon Disney; Turner Classic Movies; TV One; Versus; VH1 Soul.

Digital Pay Service 1
Pay Units: N.A.
Programming (via satellite): Cinemax (multiplexed); Encore (multiplexed); HBO (multiplexed); Showtime (multiplexed); Starz (multiplexed); The Movie Channel (multiplexed).

Video-On-Demand: No

Internet Service
Operational: Yes.
Broadband Service: Mediacom High Speed Internet.
Fee: $42.95 monthly; $3.00 modem lease.

Telephone Service
Analog: Not Operational
Digital: Operational

Homes passed: 4,453.
Regional Vice President: Sue Misiunas. Marketing Manager: Daryl Channey. General Manager: Gary Crosby. Regional Marketing Director: Melanie Hannasch. Regional Technical Operations Manager: Gary McDougall. Technical Operations Manager: David Jones.
City fee: 3% of gross.
Ownership: Mediacom LLC (MSO).

DAHLONEGA—Windstream, 2000 Communications Blvd, Baldwin, GA 30511. Phones: 800-345-3874; 877-807-9463. Fax: 706-864-2213. Web Site: http://www.windstreamcable.com. Also serves Lumpkin County (portions). ICA: GA0185.
TV Market Ranking: Below 100 (Lumpkin County (portions)); Outside TV Markets (DAHLONEGA, Lumpkin County (portions)). Franchise award date: N.A. Franchise expiration date: N.A. Began: March 1, 1982.
Channel capacity: 62 (not 2-way capable). Channels available but not in use: 5.

Basic Service
Subscribers: 2,564.
Programming (received off-air): WAGA-TV (FOX) Atlanta; WATL (MNT) Atlanta; WGCL-TV (CBS) Atlanta; WGTV (PBS) Athens; WHSG-TV (TBN) Monroe; WNEG-TV (CBS) Toccoa; WPCH-TV (IND) Atlanta; WPXA-TV (ION) Rome; WSB-TV (ABC) Atlanta; WUPA (CW) Atlanta; WUVG-DT (UNV) Athens; WXIA-TV (NBC) Atlanta.
Programming (via satellite): Boomerang; C-SPAN; QVC; TV Guide Network; WGN America.
Fee: $14.51 monthly.

Expanded Basic Service 1
Subscribers: 2,225.
Programming (via satellite): ABC Family Channel; AMC; Animal Planet; Arts & Entertainment; Bravo; Cartoon Network; CNBC; CNN; Comcast Sports Net Southeast; Comedy Central; Country Music TV; Discovery Channel; ESPN; ESPN 2; ESPN Classic Sports; Food Network; Fox News Channel; FX; Headline News; HGTV; History Channel; Lifetime; MSNBC; MTV; National Geographic Channel; Nickelodeon; Speed Channel; Spike TV; SportSouth; The Learn-

ing Channel; Turner Network TV; TV Land; USA Network; VH1; Weather Channel.
Fee: $30.74 monthly.

Digital Basic Service
Subscribers: 369.
Programming (via satellite): BBC America; Bio; Canales N; CBS College Sports Network; Cooking Channel; Discovery Digital Networks; DMX Music; Do-It-Yourself; ESPNews; Fox College Sports Atlantic; Fox College Sports Central; Fox College Sports Pacific; Fox Movie Channel; Fox Sports World; Fuel TV; Fuse; GAS; Golf Channel; GSN; Hallmark Channel; History Channel International; Independent Film Channel; Lifetime Movie Network; MTV2; Nick Jr.; NickToons TV; Outdoor Channel; Science Television; Sleuth; Style Network; The Sportsman Channel; Toon Disney; Versus; VH1 Classic; VH1 Country; WE tv.
Fee: $10.99 monthly.

Pay Service 1
Pay Units: 385.
Programming (via satellite): Cinemax; HBO; Showtime.
Fee: $14.95 monthly.

Digital Pay Service 1
Pay Units: N.A.
Programming (via satellite): Cinemax (multiplexed); Encore (multiplexed); HBO (multiplexed); Showtime (multiplexed); Starz (multiplexed); The Movie Channel (multiplexed).
Fee: $10.95 monthly (Starz/Encore), $12.99 monthly (Showtime/TMC), $24.95 monthly (HBO/Cinemax).

Video-On-Demand: No

Pay-Per-View
iN DEMAND (delivered digitally).

Internet Service
Operational: No, Both DSL & dial-up.

Telephone Service
None

President & Chief Executive Officer: Jeff Gardner. Executive Vice President & Chief Financial Officer: Brent Whittington. Executive Vice President, Network Operations: Grant Raney. Executive Vice President & Chief Marketing Officer: Ric Crane. Senior Vice President, Network Services: Frank Schueneman. Senior Vice President, Consumer Sales: Gregg Richey. Senior Vice President, Information Technology: Cindy Nash. Senior Vice President, Customer Services: Joe Marano.
Ownership: Windstream Communications Inc. (MSO).

DALTON—Charter Communications, 1103 S Hamilton St, Dalton, GA 30720-7860. Phones: 706-428-2290; 865-984-1400 (Maryville office). Fax: 706-260-2520. Web Site: http://www.charter.com. Also serves Cohutta, Tunnel Hill, Varnell & Whitfield County. ICA: GA0025.
TV Market Ranking: 18,78 (Whitfield County (portions)); 78 (Cohutta, DALTON, Tunnel Hill, Varnell). Franchise award date: N.A. Franchise expiration date: N.A. Began: September 24, 1965.
Channel capacity: N.A. Channels available but not in use: N.A.

Basic Service
Subscribers: 19,600.
Programming (received off-air): WDEF-TV (CBS) Chattanooga; WDNN-CA (IND) Dalton; WDSI-TV (FOX, MNT) Chattanooga; WELF-TV (TBN) Dalton; WFLI-TV (CW) Cleveland; WNGH-TV (PBS) Chatsworth; WPCH-TV (IND) Atlanta; WPXA-TV (ION) Rome; WRCB (NBC) Chattanooga; WSB-TV (ABC) Atlanta; WTCI (PBS) Chattanooga; WTVC (ABC) Chattanooga; WXIA-TV (NBC) Atlanta; WYHB-CA (IND) Chattanooga; 15 FMs.
Programming (via satellite): C-SPAN; Home Shopping Network; QVC; WGN America.
Current originations: Public Access.
Fee: $29.99 installation.

Expanded Basic Service 1
Subscribers: 18,803.
Programming (via satellite): ABC Family Channel; AMC; Animal Planet; Arts & Entertainment; BET Networks; Bravo; Cartoon Network; CNBC; CNN; Comcast Sports Net Southeast; Comcast/Charter Sports Southeast (CSS); Comedy Central; Country Music TV; C-SPAN 2; Discovery Channel; Disney Channel; E! Entertainment Television; ESPN; ESPN 2; Eternal Word TV Network; Fox News Channel; FX; G4; GalaVision; Golf Channel; GSN; Hallmark Channel; Headline News; HGTV; History Channel; INSP; Lifetime; MSNBC; MTV; National Geographic Channel; Nickelodeon; Oxygen; Speed Channel; SportSouth; Syfy; Telemundo; The Learning Channel; Travel Channel; TV Guide Network; TV Land; USA Network; Versus; VH1; Weather Channel.
Fee: $50.99 monthly.

Digital Basic Service
Subscribers: N.A.
Programming (via satellite): BBC America; Bio; Canales N; Discovery Digital Networks; Do-It-Yourself; Fox College Sports Atlantic; Fox College Sports Central; Fox College Sports Pacific; Fox Sports World; Great American Country; History Channel International; Independent Film Channel; Music Choice; Nick Jr.; Sundance Channel; TV Guide Interactive Inc.

Digital Pay Service 1
Pay Units: 7,000.
Programming (via satellite): Cinemax (multiplexed); Encore (multiplexed); Flix (multiplexed); HBO (multiplexed); Showtime (multiplexed); Starz (multiplexed); The Movie Channel (multiplexed).
Fee: $11.98 monthly (each).

Video-On-Demand: Yes

Pay-Per-View
Hot Choice (delivered digitally); iN DEMAND (delivered digitally); Playboy TV (delivered digitally); Playboy TV en Espanol (delivered digitally); Fresh (delivered digitally); Shorteez (delivered digitally).

Internet Service
Operational: Yes. Began: November 1, 2001.
Broadband Service: Charter Pipeline.
Fee: $29.99 monthly.

Telephone Service
None

Miles of Plant: 631.0 (coaxial); None (fiber optic). Homes passed: 26,173.
Operations Manager: Mike Burns. Technical Operations Director: Grant Evans. Marketing Director: Pat Hollenbeck.
Ownership: Charter Communications Inc. (MSO).

DARIEN—Comcast Cable, 141 Park of Commerce Dr, Savannah, GA 31405. Phone: 912-356-3113. Web Site: http://www.comcast.com. Also serves McIntosh County. ICA: GA0117.
TV Market Ranking: Below 100 (DARIEN, McIntosh County). Franchise award date: N.A. Franchise expiration date: N.A. Began: November 1, 1982.
Channel capacity: N.A. Channels available but not in use: N.A.

Basic Service
Subscribers: N.A. Included in Savannah
Programming (received off-air): WJCL (ABC) Savannah; WPXC-TV (ION) Brunswick; WSAV-TV (MNT, NBC) Savannah; WTGS (FOX) Hardeeville; WTLV (NBC) Jacksonville; WTOC-TV (CBS) Savannah; WVAN-TV (PBS) Savannah.
Programming (via satellite): ABC Family Channel; BET Networks; C-SPAN; Lifetime; Trinity Broadcasting Network.
Current originations: Public Access; Government Access.
Fee: $47.99 installation; $11.75 monthly.

Expanded Basic Service 1
Subscribers: 595.
Programming (via satellite): AMC; Animal Planet; Arts & Entertainment; Cartoon Network; CNBC; CNN; Comcast/Charter Sports Southeast (CSS); Comedy Central; Country Music TV; C-SPAN 2; Discovery Channel; Discovery Health Channel; Disney Channel; E! Entertainment Television; ESPN; ESPNews; Food Network; Fox News Channel; Fox Sports Net; FX; Golf Channel; Great American Country; Hallmark Channel; Headline News; HGTV; History Channel; Home Shopping Network; MTV; Nickelodeon; Outdoor Channel; ShopNBC; Speed Channel; Spike TV; SportSouth; Syfy; TBS Superstation; The Learning Channel; Travel Channel; truTV; Turner Classic Movies; Turner Network TV; TV Guide Network; TV Land; TV One; USA Network; Versus; VH1; Weather Channel; WGN America.
Fee: $33.49 monthly.

Digital Basic Service
Subscribers: N.A.
Programming (via satellite): BBC America; Bio; Black Family Channel; Bloomberg Television; Cooking Channel; Discovery Digital Networks; DMX Music; Do-It-Yourself; Encore (multiplexed); ESPN Classic Sports; ESPNews; Flix (multiplexed); Fox Sports World; G4; GAS; GSN; History Channel International; MTV Networks Digital Suite; National Geographic Channel; NFL Network; Nick Jr.; Nick Too; NickToons TV; Style Network; Sundance Channel; The Word Network; Toon Disney; WE tv.

Pay Service 1
Pay Units: 98.
Programming (via satellite): HBO.
Fee: $18.88 installation; $13.95 monthly.

Digital Pay Service 1
Pay Units: N.A.
Programming (via satellite): Cinemax (multiplexed); HBO (multiplexed); Showtime (multiplexed); The Movie Channel (multiplexed).

Video-On-Demand: No

Pay-Per-View
iN DEMAND (delivered digitally); Hot Choice (delivered digitally); Playboy TV (delivered digitally); Fresh (delivered digitally); Pleasure (delivered digitally).

Internet Service
Operational: Yes.
Fee: $42.95 monthly.

Telephone Service
Digital: Operational

Homes passed & miles of plant (coax & fiber) included in Savannah
General Manager: Michael Daves. Technical Operations Director: Joel Godsen. Marketing Director: Jerry Avery. Marketing Manager: Ken Torres.
City fee: 3% of gross. County fee: 3% of gross.
Ownership: Comcast Cable Communications Inc.

DARIEN—Darien Communications, PO Box 575, 1011 North Way, Darien, GA 31305. Phone: 912-437-4111. Fax: 912-437-7006. E-mail: dtcadmin@darientel.net. Web Site: http://www.darientelephone.com. Also serves McIntosh County. ICA: GA0270.
TV Market Ranking: Below 100 (DARIEN, McIntosh County). Franchise award date: N.A. Franchise expiration date: N.A. Began: January 3, 1992.
Channel capacity: N.A. Channels available but not in use: N.A.

Basic Service
Subscribers: 2,700.
Programming (received off-air): WJCL (ABC) Savannah; WPXC-TV (ION) Brunswick; WSAV-TV (MNT, NBC) Savannah; WTGS (FOX) Hardeeville; WTLV (NBC) Jacksonville; WTOC-TV (CBS) Savannah; WVAN-TV (PBS) Savannah.
Programming (via satellite): C-SPAN; C-SPAN 2; Eternal Word TV Network; QVC; TBS Superstation; Trinity Broadcasting Network; TV Guide Network; WGN America.
Fee: $25.00 installation; $12.00 monthly.

Expanded Basic Service 1
Subscribers: 2,581.
Programming (via satellite): ABC Family Channel; Animal Planet; Arts & Entertainment; BET Networks; Bio; Bravo; Cartoon Network; CNBC; CNN; Comcast Sports Net Southeast; Comedy Central; Country Music TV; Discovery Channel; Disney Channel; E! Entertainment Television; ESPN; ESPN 2; ESPN Classic Sports; ESPNews; FamilyNet; Food Network; Fox News Channel; FX; Golf Channel; GSN; Hallmark Channel; Headline News; HGTV; History Channel; History Channel International; Home Shopping Network; Lifetime; MSNBC; MTV; National Geographic Channel; Nickelodeon; Outdoor Channel; Oxygen; Speed Channel; Spike TV; SportSouth; Syfy; The Learning Channel; Travel Channel; truTV; Turner Network TV; TV Land; Univision; USA Network; VH1; Weather Channel.
Fee: $20.50 monthly.

Digital Basic Service
Subscribers: 605.
Programming (via satellite): BBC America; Bloomberg Television; Discovery Digital Networks; Encore; Fox Movie Channel; GAS; Great American Country; Independent Film Channel; Lifetime Movie Network; MTV Networks Digital Suite; Music Choice; Nick Jr.; NickToons TV; Sundance Channel; Turner Classic Movies.
Fee: $13.95 monthly.

Digital Pay Service 1
Pay Units: N.A.
Programming (via satellite): Cinemax (multiplexed); HBO (multiplexed); Showtime (multiplexed); Starz (multiplexed); The Movie Channel (multiplexed).
Fee: $10.95 monthly (HBO, Cinemax, Starz or Showtime/TMC).
Video-On-Demand: No
Pay-Per-View
iN DEMAND (delivered digitally); Playboy TV (delivered digitally); Fresh (delivered digitally).
Internet Service
Operational: Yes.
Fee: $100.00 installation; $42.95-$62.95 monthly; $3.95 modem lease.
Telephone Service
Digital: Operational
Fee: $18.17 monthly
Miles of Plant: 35.0 (coaxial); None (fiber optic). Homes passed: 7,000. Total homes in franchised area: 7,000.
President: Mary Lou Forsyth. Chief Operating Officer: Johnny Zoucks. Central Office Manager: Chuck Durant. Technical Operations Manager: Neil Elder. Chief Engineer: Robert Brigman. Marketing Manager: Julia Dodd. Customer Service Manager: Bess Wolfes.
Ownership: Darien Communications.

DAVISBORO—Formerly served by Walker Cablevision. No longer in operation. ICA: GA0166.

DAWSONVILLE—Windstream, 2000 Communications Blvd, Baldwin, GA 30511. Phones: 800-345-3874; 706-216-2222. Fax: 706-896-5170. Web Site: http://www.windstreamcable.com. Also serves Dawson County (portions). ICA: GA0187.
TV Market Ranking: Outside TV Markets (Dawson County (portions), DAWSONVILLE). Franchise award date: N.A. Franchise expiration date: N.A. Began: May 1, 1985.
Channel capacity: 71 (not 2-way capable). Channels available but not in use: 10.
Basic Service
Subscribers: 2,757.
Programming (received off-air): WAGA-TV (FOX) Atlanta; WATL (MNT) Atlanta; WGCL-TV (CBS) Atlanta; WGTV (PBS) Athens; WHSG-TV (TBN) Monroe; WPBA (PBS) Atlanta; WPCH-TV (IND) Atlanta; WPXA-TV (ION) Rome; WSB-TV (ABC) Atlanta; WUPA (CW) Atlanta; WUVG-DT (UNV) Athens; WXIA-TV (NBC) Atlanta.
Programming (via satellite): Boomerang; C-SPAN; Food Network; G4; QVC; TV Guide Network; WGN America.
Fee: $14.51 monthly.
Expanded Basic Service 1
Subscribers: 2,458.
Programming (via satellite): ABC Family Channel; AMC; Animal Planet; Arts & Entertainment; Bravo; Cartoon Network; CNBC; CNN; Comcast Sports Net Southeast; Comedy Central; Country Music TV; Discovery Channel; ESPN; ESPN 2; ESPN Classic Sports; Fox News Channel; FX; Golf Channel; Headline News; HGTV; History Channel; Lifetime; MSNBC; MTV; Nickelodeon; Outdoor Channel; Speed Channel; Spike TV; SportSouth; The Learning Channel; Turner Classic Movies; Turner Network TV; TV Land; USA Network; VH1; WE tv; Weather Channel.
Fee: $30.74 monthly.
Digital Basic Service
Subscribers: 411.
Programming (via satellite): BBC America; Bio; Bravo; Canales N; CBS College Sports Network; Cooking Channel; Discovery Digital Networks; DMX Music; Do-It-Yourself; Encore Action; ESPNews; Eternal Word TV Network; FamilyNet; Fox College Sports Atlantic; Fox College Sports Central; Fox College Sports Pacific; Fox Movie Channel; Fox Sports World; Fuel TV; Fuse; GAS; Gospel Music TV; GSN; Hallmark Channel; Halogen Network; History Channel International; Independent Film Channel; Lifetime Movie Network; MTV2; National Geographic Channel; Nick Jr.; NickToons TV; Praise Television; Science Television; Sleuth; Style Network; The Sportsman Channel; Versus; VH1 Classic; VH1 Country.
Fee: $10.99 monthly.
Digital Pay Service 1
Pay Units: N.A.
Programming (via satellite): Cinemax (multiplexed); HBO (multiplexed); Showtime (multiplexed); Starz; The Movie Channel (multiplexed).
Fee: $10.95 monthly (Starz & Encore), $12.99 monthly (Showtime & TMC), $24.95 monthly (HBO & Cinemax).
Video-On-Demand: No
Pay-Per-View
iN DEMAND (delivered digitally).
Internet Service
Operational: No, Both DSL & dial-up.
Telephone Service
None
President & Chief Executive Officer: Jeff Gardner. Executive Vice President & Chief Financial Officer: Brent Whittington. Executive Vice President, Network Operations: Grant Randy. Executive Vice President & Chief Marketing Officer: Ric Crane. Senior Vice President, Network Services: Frank Schueneman. Senior Vice President, Information Technology: Cindy Nash. Senior Vice President, Consumer Sales: Gregg Richey. Senior Vice President, Customer Services: Joe Marano.
Ownership: Windstream Communications Inc. (MSO).

DOERUN—Doerun Cable TV, PO Box 37, 223 W Broad Ave, Doerun, GA 31744. Phone: 229-782-5444. Fax: 229-782-5224. ICA: GA0286.
TV Market Ranking: Below 100 (DOERUN). Franchise award date: N.A. Franchise expiration date: N.A. Began: N.A.
Channel capacity: 48 (not 2-way capable). Channels available but not in use: None.
Basic Service
Subscribers: 278.
Programming (received off-air): WALB (NBC) Albany; WCTV (CBS, MNT) Thomasville; WFXL (FOX) Albany; WSWG (CBS, MNT) Valdosta; WTXL-TV (ABC) Tallahassee.
Programming (via satellite): ABC Family Channel; AMC; Animal Planet; Arts & Entertainment; BET Networks; Cartoon Network; CNN; Comcast Sports Net Southeast; Country Music TV; C-SPAN; C-SPAN 2; Discovery Channel; Disney Channel; Do-It-Yourself; ESPN; ESPN 2; Food Network; Fox News Channel; G4; Hallmark Channel; Headline News; HGTV; History Channel; Home Shopping Network; Lifetime; National Geographic Channel; Nickelodeon; Outdoor Channel; QVC; Spike TV; TBS Superstation; The Learning Channel; Trinity Broadcasting Network; Turner Network TV; TV Land; USA Network; WE tv; Weather Channel; WGN America.
Fee: $25.00 installation; $29.99 monthly.
Pay Service 1
Pay Units: 45.
Programming (via satellite): The Movie Channel.
Fee: $9.00 monthly.
Pay Service 2
Pay Units: 79.
Programming (via satellite): Encore.
Fee: $3.50 monthly.
Pay Service 3
Pay Units: 54.
Programming (via satellite): HBO.
Fee: $16.00 monthly.
Internet Service
Operational: No.
Telephone Service
None
Miles of Plant: 10.0 (coaxial); None (fiber optic). Homes passed: 370. Total homes in franchised area: 370.
Manager & Chief Technician: Herchel Finch. Office Manager: Patrice Bryant.
Ownership: City of Doerun.

DONALSONVILLE—Mediacom. Now served by BAINBRIDGE, GA [GA0060]. ICA: GA0110.

DOUGLAS—Charter Communications, 1925 Breckenridge Plaza, Ste 100, Duluth, GA 30096-4918. Phone: 770-806-7060. Fax: 770-806-7099. Web Site: http://www.charter.com. Also serves Ambrose, Broxton, Coffee County (unincorporated areas), Nicholls & West Green. ICA: GA0037.
TV Market Ranking: Below 100 (Broxton, Coffee County (unincorporated areas) (portions), DOUGLAS, Nicholls, West Green); Outside TV Markets (Ambrose, Coffee County (unincorporated areas) (portions)). Franchise award date: N.A. Franchise expiration date: N.A. Began: December 1, 1963.
Channel capacity: 75 (not 2-way capable). Channels available but not in use: N.A.
Basic Service
Subscribers: 6,767.
Programming (received off-air): WALB (NBC) Albany; WFXL (FOX) Albany; WTOC-TV (CBS) Savannah; WXGA-TV (PBS) Waycross; 6 FMs.
Programming (via microwave): WAGA-TV (FOX) Atlanta; WSB-TV (ABC) Atlanta; WXIA-TV (NBC) Atlanta.
Programming (via satellite): Home Shopping Network; INSP; QVC; WGN America.
Current originations: Leased Access.
Fee: $29.99 installation.
Expanded Basic Service 1
Subscribers: N.A.
Programming (via satellite): ABC Family Channel; AMC; Animal Planet; Arts & Entertainment; BET Networks; Bravo; Cartoon Network; CNBC; CNN; Comcast Sports Net Southeast; Comcast/Charter Sports Southeast (CSS); Comedy Central; Country Music TV; C-SPAN; C-SPAN 2; CW+; Discovery Channel; Disney Channel; E! Entertainment Television; ESPN; ESPN 2; Eternal Word TV Network; Food Network; Fox News Channel; FX; G4; GalaVision; Golf Channel; GSN; Hallmark Channel; Headline News; HGTV; History Channel; ION Television; Lifetime; MSNBC; MTV; National Geographic Channel; Nickelodeon; Oxygen; Product Information Network; Shop at Home; ShopNBC; SoapNet; Speed Channel; Spike TV; SportSouth; Syfy; TBS Superstation; Telemundo; The Learning Channel; Toon Disney; Travel Channel; Trinity Broadcasting Network; truTV; Turner Classic Movies; Turner Network TV; TV Guide Network; TV Land; USA Network; Versus; VH1; WE tv; Weather Channel.
Fee: $48.99 monthly.
Digital Basic Service
Subscribers: N.A.
Programming (via satellite): BBC America; Bio; Bloomberg Television; Boomerang; Canales N; Discovery Digital Networks; Do-It-Yourself; ESPN Classic Sports; ESPNews; Fox Sports World; GAS; History Channel International; Independent Film Channel; Lifetime Movie Network; MTV Networks Digital Suite; Music Choice; Nick Jr.; Nick Too; NickToons TV; Style Network; Sundance Channel; TV Guide Interactive Inc.
Fee: $14.00 monthly.
Digital Pay Service 1
Pay Units: 930.
Programming (via satellite): Cinemax (multiplexed); Encore (multiplexed); Flix; HBO (multiplexed); Showtime (multiplexed); Starz (multiplexed); The Movie Channel (multiplexed).
Fee: $10.95 monthly (each).
Video-On-Demand: Yes
Pay-Per-View
Addressable: Yes; iN DEMAND (delivered digitally); Playboy TV (delivered digitally); Fresh (delivered digitally); Shorteez (delivered digitally); sports (delivered digitally).
Internet Service
Operational: Yes.
Broadband Service: Charter Pipeline.
Fee: $29.99 monthly.
Telephone Service
Digital: Operational
Miles of Plant: 115.0 (coaxial); None (fiber optic). Homes passed: 10,000.
Vice President & General Manager: Matt Favre. Operations Manager: David Spriggs. Technical Supervisor: Hank Crews. Sales & Marketing Director: Antoinette Carptenter.
City fee: 3% of gross.
Ownership: Charter Communications Inc. (MSO).

DRY BRANCH—KLiP Interactive, 455 Gees Mill Business Court, Conyers, GA 30013. Phone: 678-727-7100. Fax: 678-727-7002. E-mail: jsheehan@klipia.com. Web Site: http://www.klipia.com. Also serves Twiggs County (northern portion). ICA: GA0189.
TV Market Ranking: Below 100 (DRY BRANCH, Twiggs County (northern portion)). Franchise award date: N.A. Franchise expiration date: N.A. Began: August 1, 1990.
Channel capacity: 45 (not 2-way capable). Channels available but not in use: 12.
Basic Service
Subscribers: 146.
Programming (received off-air): WGNM (IND) Macon; WGXA (FOX, MNT) Macon; WMAZ-TV (CBS) Macon; WMGT-TV (MNT, NBC) Macon; WPCH-TV (IND) Atlanta; WPGA-TV (ABC) Perry.
Programming (via satellite): ABC Family Channel; Arts & Entertainment; BET Networks; Bravo; CNBC; CNN; Comcast Sports Net Southeast; Country Music TV; C-SPAN; Discovery Channel; Disney Channel; ESPN; ESPN 2; Fox News Channel; FX; Headline News; Lifetime; Nickelodeon; QVC; Spike TV; Syfy; The Learning Channel; Trinity Broadcasting Network; Turner Network TV; USA Network; Weather Channel; WGN America.
Fee: $44.95 installation; $39.05 monthly.

Digital Basic Service
Subscribers: N.A.
Programming (via satellite): AmericanLife TV Network; BBC America; Bio; Bloomberg Television; Current; Discovery Digital Networks; DMX Music; ESPN Classic Sports; ESPNews; FitTV; Fox Movie Channel; Fox Soccer; Fuse; G4; Golf Channel; GSN; HGTV; History Channel; History Channel International; Independent Film Channel; INSP; Lifetime Movie Network; Military History Channel; Outdoor Channel; Ovation; Sleuth; Speed Channel; Sundance Channel; Turner Classic Movies; Versus; WE tv.

Pay Service 1
Pay Units: 14.
Programming (via satellite): HBO.
Fee: $10.95 monthly.

Pay Service 2
Pay Units: 11.
Programming (via satellite): Showtime.
Fee: $10.95 monthly.

Digital Pay Service 1
Pay Units: N.A.
Programming (via satellite): Cinemax (multiplexed); Encore (multiplexed); Flix; HBO (multiplexed); Showtime (multiplexed); Starz (multiplexed); The Movie Channel (multiplexed).
Fee: $10.95 monthly (HBO or Showtime).

Pay-Per-View
iN DEMAND (delivered digitally); Hot Choice (delivered digitally); Playboy TV (delivered digitally); Fresh (delivered digitally); Shorteez (delivered digitally).

Internet Service
Operational: No.

Telephone Service
None

Miles of Plant: 49.0 (coaxial); None (fiber optic). Homes passed: 1,168.
Chief Executive Officer: Joseph A. Sheehan. General Manager East: Mark Miller. General Manager West: Vance Johnson.
Ownership: KLiP Interactive LLC (MSO).

DUBLIN—Charter Communications, 1925 Breckenridge Plaza, Ste 100, Duluth, GA 30096-4918. Phones: 770-806-7060; 478-272-1162. Fax: 770-806-7099. Web Site: http://www.charter.com. Also serves East Dublin & Laurens County. ICA: GA0043.
TV Market Ranking: Below 100 (Laurens County (portions)); Outside TV Markets (DUBLIN, East Dublin, Laurens County (portions)). Franchise award date: July 8, 1965. Franchise expiration date: N.A. Began: July 8, 1965.
Channel capacity: 78 (not 2-way capable). Channels available but not in use: 5.

Basic Service
Subscribers: 8,874.
Programming (received off-air): WGNM (IND) Macon; WGXA (FOX, MNT) Macon; WMAZ-TV (CBS) Macon; WMGT-TV (MNT, NBC) Macon; WMUM-TV (PBS) Cochran; WPGA-TV (ABC) Perry.
Programming (via microwave): WSB-TV (ABC) Atlanta; WXIA-TV (NBC) Atlanta.
Programming (via satellite): Comcast/Charter Sports Southeast (CSS); C-SPAN; CW+; Home Shopping Network; INSP; ION Television; Product Information Network; QVC; Trinity Broadcasting Network; TV Guide Network; WGN America.
Current originations: Public Access; Government Access.
Fee: $29.99 installation; $9.10 monthly; $1.12 converter.

Expanded Basic Service 1
Subscribers: 7,218.
Programming (via satellite): ABC Family Channel; AMC; Animal Planet; Arts & Entertainment; BET Networks; Bravo; Cartoon Network; CNBC; CNN; Comcast Sports Net Southeast; Comedy Central; Country Music TV; Discovery Channel; Disney Channel; E! Entertainment Television; ESPN; ESPN 2; ESPN Classic Sports; ESPNews; Food Network; Fox News Channel; FX; G4; Golf Channel; Hallmark Channel; Headline News; HGTV; History Channel; Lifetime; MTV; National Geographic Channel; Nickelodeon; Oxygen; SoapNet; Speed Channel; Spike TV; SportSouth; Syfy; TBS Superstation; Telemundo; The Learning Channel; Travel Channel; truTV; Turner Classic Movies; Turner Network TV; TV Land; USA Network; Versus; VH1; WE tv; Weather Channel.
Fee: $48.99 monthly.

Digital Basic Service
Subscribers: N.A.
Programming (via satellite): BBC America; Bio; Boomerang; Canales N; Discovery Digital Networks; Do-It-Yourself; GAS; History Channel International; Independent Film Channel; Lifetime Movie Network; MTV Networks Digital Suite; Music Choice; Nick Jr.; Nick Too; NickToons TV; Sundance Channel; TV Guide Interactive Inc.

Digital Pay Service 1
Pay Units: 559.
Programming (via satellite): Cinemax (multiplexed); Encore (multiplexed); Flix; HBO (multiplexed); Showtime (multiplexed); Starz (multiplexed); The Movie Channel (multiplexed).
Fee: $40.00 installation; $12.20 monthly (Showtime), $12.70 monthly (Cinemax or HBO).

Video-On-Demand: Yes

Pay-Per-View
iN DEMAND (delivered digitally); Playboy TV (delivered digitally); Fresh (delivered digitally); Shorteez (delivered digitally).

Internet Service
Operational: Yes.
Broadband Service: Charter Pipeline.
Fee: $29.99 monthly.

Telephone Service
Digital: Operational
Fee: $29.99 monthly

Miles of Plant: 244.0 (coaxial); 32.0 (fiber optic). Homes passed: 10,400. Total homes in franchised area: 11,394.
Vice President & General Manager: Matt Favre. Operations Manager: David Spriggs. Technical Operations Manager: Tim Hardeman. Sales & Marketing Director: Antoinette Carpenter.
City fee: 5% of gross (Dublin & East Dublin).
Ownership: Charter Communications Inc. (MSO).

DUDLEY—KLiP Interactive, 455 Gees Mill Business Court, Conyers, GA 30013. Phone: 678-727-7100. Fax: 678-727-7002. E-mail: jsheehan@klipia.com. Web Site: http://www.klipia.com. Also serves Laurens County (portions). ICA: GA0298.
TV Market Ranking: Outside TV Markets (DUDLEY, Laurens County (portions)). Franchise award date: N.A. Franchise expiration date: N.A. Began: N.A.
Channel capacity: 45 (not 2-way capable). Channels available but not in use: 10.

Basic Service
Subscribers: 212.
Programming (received off-air): WGNM (IND) Macon; WGXA (FOX, MNT) Macon; WMAZ-TV (CBS) Macon; WMGT-TV (MNT, NBC) Macon; WPCH-TV (IND) Atlanta; WPGA-TV (ABC) Perry.
Programming (via satellite): ABC Family Channel; Arts & Entertainment; BET Networks; Bravo; CNBC; CNN; Comcast Sports Net Southeast; Country Music TV; C-SPAN; Discovery Channel; Disney Channel; ESPN; ESPN 2; Fox News Channel; FX; Headline News; History Channel; Lifetime; MTV; Nickelodeon; QVC; Spike TV; SportSouth; Syfy; Trinity Broadcasting Network; Turner Network TV; USA Network; Weather Channel; WGN America.
Fee: $44.95 installation; $33.95 monthly (county), $39.86 monthly (city).

Digital Basic Service
Subscribers: N.A.
Programming (via satellite): AmericanLife TV Network; BBC America; Bio; Bloomberg Television; Current; Discovery Digital Networks; DMX Music; ESPN Classic Sports; ESPNews; FitTV; Fox Movie Channel; Fox Soccer; Fuse; G4; Golf Channel; GSN; HGTV; History Channel International; Independent Film Channel; INSP; Lifetime Movie Network; Military History Channel; Outdoor Channel; Ovation; Sleuth; Speed Channel; Sundance Channel; Turner Classic Movies; Versus; WE tv.

Pay Service 1
Pay Units: 28.
Programming (via satellite): HBO.
Fee: $10.95 monthly.

Pay Service 2
Pay Units: 9.
Programming (via satellite): Showtime.
Fee: $10.95 monthly.

Pay Service 3
Pay Units: 2.
Programming (via satellite): The Movie Channel.
Fee: $10.95 monthly.

Digital Pay Service 1
Pay Units: N.A.
Programming (via satellite): Cinemax (multiplexed); Encore (multiplexed); Flix; HBO (multiplexed); Showtime (multiplexed); Starz (multiplexed); The Movie Channel (multiplexed).
Fee: $10.95 monthly (HBO, Showtime or TMC).

Pay-Per-View
iN DEMAND (delivered digitally); Hot Choice (delivered digitally); Playboy TV (delivered digitally); Fresh (delivered digitally); Shorteez (delivered digitally).

Internet Service
Operational: No.

Telephone Service
None

Miles of Plant: 41.0 (coaxial); None (fiber optic). Homes passed: 532.
Chief Executive Officer: Joseph A. Sheehan. General Manager East: Mark Miller. General Manager West: Vance Johnson.
Ownership: KLiP Interactive LLC (MSO).

DULUTH—Charter Communications, 1925 Breckenridge Plaza, Ste 100, Duluth, GA 30096-4918. Phone: 770-806-7060. Fax: 770-806-7099. Web Site: http://www.charter.com. Also serves Buford, Dacula, Gwinnett County (portions), Lawrenceville, Rest Haven, Sugar Hill & Suwanee. ICA: GA0009.
TV Market Ranking: 18 (Buford, Dacula, DULUTH, Gwinnett County (portions), Lawrenceville, Sugar Hill, Suwanee); Below 100 (Rest Haven). Franchise award date: October 15, 1979. Franchise expiration date: N.A. Began: October 15, 1979.
Channel capacity: N.A. Channels available but not in use: N.A.

Basic Service
Subscribers: 39,790.
Programming (received off-air): WAGA-TV (FOX) Atlanta; WATC-DT (ETV) Atlanta; WATL (MNT) Atlanta; WDTA-LP Fayetteville; WGCL-TV (CBS) Atlanta; WGN-TV (CW, IND) Chicago; WGTV (PBS) Athens; WHSG-TV (TBN) Monroe; WPBA (PBS) Atlanta; WPCH-TV (IND) Atlanta; WPXA-TV (ION) Rome; WSB-TV (ABC) Atlanta; WUPA (CW) Atlanta; WUVG-DT (UNV) Athens; WXIA-TV (NBC) Atlanta.
Programming (via satellite): Home Shopping Network; INSP; Product Information Network; QVC; TV Guide Network.
Current originations: Leased Access; Government Access; Educational Access.
Fee: $29.99 installation.

Expanded Basic Service 1
Subscribers: 35,940.
Programming (via satellite): ABC Family Channel; AMC; Animal Planet; Arts & Entertainment; BET Networks; Bravo; Cartoon Network; CNBC; CNN; Comcast Sports Net Southeast; Comcast/Charter Sports Southeast (CSS); Comedy Central; Country Music TV; C-SPAN; C-SPAN 2; Discovery Channel; Disney Channel; E! Entertainment Television; ESPN; ESPN 2; ESPN Classic Sports; Eternal Word TV Network; FitTV; Food Network; Fox News Channel; FX; G4; GalaVision; Golf Channel; GSN; Hallmark Channel; Headline News; HGTV; History Channel; Lifetime; MSNBC; MTV; National Geographic Channel; Nickelodeon; Oxygen; Shop at Home; SoapNet; Speed Channel; Spike TV; SportSouth; Telemundo; The Learning Channel; Toon Disney; Travel Channel; truTV; Turner Classic Movies; Turner Network TV; TV Land; USA Network; Versus; VH1; WE tv; Weather Channel.
Fee: $48.99 monthly.

Digital Basic Service
Subscribers: N.A.
Programming (via satellite): BBC America; Bio; Bloomberg Television; Boomerang; Canales N; Discovery Digital Networks; Do-It-Yourself; ESPNews; Fox College Sports Atlantic; Fox College Sports Central; Fox College Sports Pacific; Fox Sports World; Fuse; GAS; Great American Country; History Channel International; Independent Film Channel; Lifetime Movie Network; MTV Networks Digital Suite; Music Choice; Nick Jr.; Nick Too; NickToons TV; Style Network; Sundance Channel; TV Guide Interactive Inc.; Weatherscan.
Fee: $14.00 monthly.

Digital Pay Service 1
Pay Units: 8,100.
Programming (via satellite): HBO (multiplexed).
Fee: $10.95 monthly.
Digital Pay Service 2
Pay Units: 4,950.
Programming (via satellite): Showtime (multiplexed).
Fee: $10.95 monthly.
Digital Pay Service 3
Pay Units: 1,090.
Programming (via satellite): Encore (multiplexed).
Fee: $5.95 monthly.
Digital Pay Service 4
Pay Units: 2,210.
Programming (via satellite): Cinemax (multiplexed).
Fee: $10.95 monthly.
Digital Pay Service 5
Pay Units: 1,220.
Programming (via satellite): The Movie Channel (multiplexed).
Fee: $10.95 monthly.
Digital Pay Service 6
Pay Units: N.A.
Programming (via satellite): Flix; Starz (multiplexed).
Video-On-Demand: Yes
Pay-Per-View
Addressable homes: 5,307.
Fee: $3.95, Addressable: Yes; iN DEMAND (delivered digitally); NBA League Pass/WNBA (delivered digitally); NHL Center Ice/MLB Extra Innings (delivered digitally); Playboy TV (delivered digitally); Fresh (delivered digitally), Fee: $5.95; Shorteez (delivered digitally).
Internet Service
Operational: Yes.
Broadband Service: Charter Pipeline.
Fee: $29.99 monthly; $5.00 modem lease; $99.00 modem purchase.
Telephone Service
Digital: Operational
Fee: $29.99 monthly
Miles of Plant: 1,254.0 (coaxial); 25.0 (fiber optic). Additional miles planned: 100.0 (coaxial). Homes passed: 51,115. Total homes in franchised area: 51,115.
Vice President & General Manager: Matt Favre. Operations Director: Jeff Osborne. Marketing Director: Antoinette Carpenter. Marketing Manager: Christopher Bolton.
Ownership: Charter Communications Inc. (MSO).

EAST DUBLIN—Charter Communications. Now served by DUBLIN, GA [GA0043]. ICA: GA0299.

EASTMAN—Mediacom, 509 Flint Ave, Albany, GA 31701. Phones: 229-888-0242; 229-244-3852 (Valdosta regional office). Fax: 229-436-4819. Web Site: http://www.mediacomcable.com. Also serves Dodge County (portions), Helena, McRae & Telfair County (portions). ICA: GA0076.
TV Market Ranking: Below 100 (Dodge County (portions), Helena, McRae, Telfair County (portions)); Outside TV Markets (Dodge County (portions), EASTMAN, Telfair County (portions)). Franchise award date: June 1, 1966. Franchise expiration date: N.A. Began: May 1, 1966.
Channel capacity: N.A. Channels available but not in use: N.A.
Basic Service
Subscribers: 4,218.
Programming (received off-air): WALB (NBC) Albany; WGXA (FOX, MNT) Macon; WMAZ-TV (CBS) Macon; WPGA-TV (ABC) Perry; WSST-TV (IND) Cordele; 1 FM.
Programming (via microwave): WSB-TV (ABC) Atlanta.
Programming (via satellite): ABC Family Channel; Arts & Entertainment; BET Networks; CNBC; CNN; Comedy Central; C-SPAN; Discovery Channel; Hallmark Channel; Headline News; MTV; Nickelodeon; QVC; TBS Superstation; Turner Network TV; VH1; Weather Channel.
Fee: $35.00 installation; $9.23 monthly.
Expanded Basic Service 1
Subscribers: 2,372.
Programming (via satellite): AMC; Animal Planet; Black Family Channel; Bravo; Cartoon Network; Comcast Sports Net Southeast; Country Music TV; C-SPAN 2; CW+; Disney Channel; E! Entertainment Television; ESPN; Eternal Word TV Network; FitTV; Food Network; Fox News Channel; FX; GalaVision; HGTV; History Channel; Home Shopping Network; ION Television; Lifetime; MSNBC; Oxygen; Spike TV; SportSouth; The Learning Channel; Travel Channel; Trinity Broadcasting Network; truTV; TV Guide Network; TV Land; Univision; USA Network; WE tv.
Fee: $22.43 monthly.
Digital Basic Service
Subscribers: N.A.
Programming (via satellite): BBC America; Bio; Bloomberg Television; Canales N; Discovery Digital Networks; Fox Movie Channel; Fox Sports World; Fuse; G4; GAS; Golf Channel; GSN; Halogen Network; History Channel International; Independent Film Channel; Lifetime Movie Network; Lime; MTV Networks Digital Suite; Music Choice; National Geographic Channel; Nick Jr.; Outdoor Channel; Ovation; Speed Channel; Style Network; Toon Disney; Turner Classic Movies; Versus.
Digital Pay Service 1
Pay Units: 69.
Programming (via satellite): Cinemax (multiplexed); Encore (multiplexed); Flix; HBO (multiplexed); Showtime (multiplexed); Starz (multiplexed); Sundance Channel; The Movie Channel (multiplexed).
Fee: $25.00 installation; $11.95 monthly (each).
Video-On-Demand: Yes
Pay-Per-View
TVN Entertainment (delivered digitally); Pleasure (delivered digitally); ETC (delivered digitally); ESPN Now (delivered digitally); Sports PPV (delivered digitally).
Internet Service
Operational: Yes. Began: April 1, 2003.
Broadband Service: Mediacom High Speed Internet.
Fee: $42.95 monthly; $3.00 modem lease.
Telephone Service
Digital: Operational
Homes passed: 5,592. Total homes in franchised area: 10,693. Miles of plant included in Fitzgerald
Regional Vice President: Sue Misiunas. General Manager: Gary Crosby. Regional Marketing Director: Melanie Hannasch. Regional Technical Operations Manager: Gary McDougall. Marketing Manager: Daryl Channey.
City fee: 5% of gross.
Ownership: Mediacom LLC (MSO).

EATONTON—CommuniComm Services, PO Box 3668, 104 E Marion St, Eatonton, GA 31024. Phones: 800-554-3235; 706-485-2288. Fax: 706-485-0118. Web Site: http://www.communicomm.com. Also serves Madison, Morgan County (portions) & Putnam County (portions). ICA: GA0191.
TV Market Ranking: Below 100 (Madison, Morgan County (portions), Putnam County (portions)); Outside TV Markets (EATONTON, Putnam County (portions)). Franchise award date: January 1, 1979. Franchise expiration date: N.A. Began: September 1, 1979.
Channel capacity: N.A. Channels available but not in use: N.A.

Basic Service
Subscribers: 5,943 Includes Crawford, Gray, & Greensboro.
Programming (received off-air): WAGA-TV (FOX) Atlanta; WATL (MNT) Atlanta; WGCL-TV (CBS) Atlanta; WGTV (PBS) Athens; WMAZ-TV (CBS) Macon; WPCH-TV (IND) Atlanta; WPGA-TV (ABC) Perry; WSB-TV (ABC) Atlanta; WUPA (CW) Atlanta; WUVG-DT (UNV) Athens; WXIA-TV (NBC) Atlanta; allband FM.
Programming (via satellite): TV Guide Network.
Fee: $49.95 installation; $29.99 monthly.

Expanded Basic Service 1
Subscribers: N.A.
Programming (via satellite): ABC Family Channel; AMC; Animal Planet; Arts & Entertainment; BET Networks; Bravo; Cartoon Network; CNBC; CNN; Comcast/Charter Sports Southeast (CSS); Comedy Central; Country Music TV; C-SPAN; C-SPAN 2; Discovery Channel; Disney Channel; E! Entertainment Television; ESPN; ESPN 2; ESPNews; Food Network; Fox Movie Channel; Fox News Channel; FX; G4; Hallmark Channel; Headline News; HGTV; History Channel; Home Shopping Network; ION Television; Lifetime; MSNBC; MTV; Nick Jr.; Nickelodeon; QVC; ShopNBC; Spike TV; SportSouth; Syfy; TBS Superstation; The Learning Channel; Travel Channel; Trinity Broadcasting Network; truTV; Turner Network TV; TV Land; USA Network; VH1; WE tv; Weather Channel.
Fee: $49.99 monthly.

Digital Basic Service
Subscribers: 1,086 Includes Crawford, Gray, & Greensboro.
Programming (received off-air): WAGA-TV (FOX) Atlanta; WGCL-TV (CBS) Atlanta; WSB-TV (ABC) Atlanta; WXIA-TV (NBC) Atlanta.
Programming (via satellite): Arts & Entertainment HD; BBC America; Bio; Bloomberg Television; Bravo; Cine Latino; CMT Pure Country; CNN en Espanol; Discovery en Espanol; Discovery HD Theater; Discovery Health Channel; Discovery Home Channel; Discovery Kids Channel; Discovery Military Channel; DMX Music; ESPN 2; ESPN 2 HD; ESPN Classic Sports; ESPN HD; FitTV; Fox Soccer; Fox Sports en Espanol; Fuse; G4; Golf Channel; GSN; Halogen Network; History Channel en Espanol; History Channel International; ID Investigation Discovery; Independent Film Channel; Lifetime Movie Network; MTV Hits; MTV Tres; MTV2; National Geographic Channel; NickToons TV; Outdoor Channel; Science Channel; Sleuth; SoapNet; Speed Channel; Style Network; TeenNick; Toon Disney; Toon Disney en Espanol; Turner Classic Movies; Turner Network TV HD; TVE Internacional; Universal HD; Versus; VH1 Classic; VH1 Soul; WE tv.
Fee: $20.00 installation; $11.95 monthly.

Pay Service 1
Pay Units: 1,329.
Programming (via satellite): Cinemax (multiplexed); Encore; HBO (multiplexed); Starz (multiplexed).
Fee: $11.95 monthly (Cinemax), $13.95 monthly (HBO or Starz).
Digital Pay Service 1
Pay Units: N.A.
Programming (via satellite): Cinemax (multiplexed); Encore (multiplexed); Flix; HBO (multiplexed); Showtime (multiplexed); Starz (multiplexed); Starz HDTV; The Movie Channel (multiplexed).
Fee: $11.95 monthly (Cinemax), $13.95 monthly (HBO, Showtime or Starz/Encore).
Video-On-Demand: No
Pay-Per-View
iN DEMAND (delivered digitally); Playboy TV (delivered digitally); Fresh (delivered digitally); Club Jenna (delivered digitally).
Internet Service
Operational: Yes. Began: December 31, 2001.
Subscribers: 1,705.
Broadband Service: Net Commander.
Fee: $41.95 monthly.
Telephone Service
None
Miles of Plant: 355.0 (coaxial); 110.0 (fiber optic). Homes passed: 11,215. Total homes in franchised area: 12,715. Homes passed & total homes in franchised area include Crawford, Gray, & Greensboro
General Manager: Brian Chase. Chief Technician: Scott Richardson. Customer Care Manager: Diane Simmons.
City fee: 3% of gross.
Ownership: James Cable LLC (MSO).

ELBERTON—Comcast Cable, 105 River Shoals Pkwy, Augusta, GA 30909. Phones: 706-738-0091 (Administrative); 706-733-7712 (Customer service). Fax: 706-739-1871. Web Site: http://www.comcast.com. Also serves Bowman, Elbert County, Hart County (portions) & Hartwell. ICA: GA0192.
TV Market Ranking: 46 (Bowman, Elbert County (portions), ELBERTON, Hart County (portions), Hartwell); Below 100 (Elbert County (portions)). Franchise award date: N.A. Franchise expiration date: N.A. Began: September 1, 1966.
Channel capacity: N.A. Channels available but not in use: N.A.
Basic Service
Subscribers: 5,407.
Programming (received off-air): WAGA-TV (FOX) Atlanta; WGGS-TV (IND) Greenville; WGTV (PBS) Athens; WHNS (FOX) Greenville; WLOS (ABC) Asheville; WMYA-TV (MNT) Anderson; WNEG-TV (CBS) Toccoa; WNTV (PBS) Greenville; WSB-TV (ABC) Atlanta; WXIA-TV (NBC) Atlanta; WYCW (CW) Asheville; WYFF (NBC) Greenville.
Programming (via satellite): Home Shopping Network; ION Television; QVC; WGN America.
Fee: $50.00 installation; $10.25 monthly.
Expanded Basic Service 1
Subscribers: 2,325.
Programming (via satellite): ABC Family Channel; AMC; Animal Planet; Arts & Entertainment; BET Networks; Cartoon Network; CNBC; CNN; Comcast Sports Net Southeast; Comcast/Charter Sports Southeast (CSS); Comedy Central; Country Music TV; C-SPAN; C-SPAN 2; Discovery Channel; Disney Channel; E! Entertainment Television; ESPN; ESPN 2; Food Network;

Fox News Channel; FX; Golf Channel; GSN; Headline News; HGTV; History Channel; MSNBC; MTV; Nickelodeon; Speed Channel; Spike TV; SportSouth; Style Network; Syfy; TBS Superstation; The Learning Channel; Travel Channel; Trinity Broadcasting Network; truTV; Turner Classic Movies; Turner Network TV; TV Guide Network; TV Land; USA Network; Versus; VH1; Weather Channel.
Fee: $42.95 monthly.

Digital Basic Service
Subscribers: 1,132.
Programming (received off-air): WHNS (FOX) Greenville; WOLO-TV (ABC) Columbia; WSPA-TV (CBS) Spartanburg; WYFF (NBC) Greenville.
Programming (via satellite): BBC America; CMT Pure Country; Discovery Kids Channel; Discovery Military Channel; Discovery Planet Green; DMX Music; Encore (multiplexed); ESPN HD; Flix; ID Investigation Discovery; MTV Tres; MTV2; Nick Jr.; NickToons TV; Science Channel; Sundance Channel; TeenNick; VH1 Classic; VH1 Soul.
Fee: $14.95 monthly.

Pay Service 1
Pay Units: 273.
Programming (via satellite): HBO.
Fee: $9.95 monthly.

Digital Pay Service 1
Pay Units: N.A.
Programming (via satellite): Cinemax (multiplexed); HBO (multiplexed); Showtime (multiplexed); The Movie Channel (multiplexed).
Fee: $7.05 monthly (each).

Video-On-Demand: Planned

Pay-Per-View
iN DEMAND (delivered digitally); Hot Choice (delivered digitally); Playboy TV (delivered digitally); Fresh (delivered digitally); Shorteez (delivered digitally); Pleasure (delivered digitally).

Internet Service
Operational: Yes.
Broadband Service: Comcast High Speed Internet.
Fee: $42.95 monthly.

Telephone Service
Digital: Operational

Miles of Plant: 324.0 (coaxial); None (fiber optic).
Technical Operations Director: Butch Jernigan. Engineering Director: Harry Hess. Chief Technician: Jeff Bartlett. Marketing Director: Joey Fortier.
City fee: 3% of gross.
Ownership: Comcast Cable Communications Inc. (MSO).

ELBERTON—ElbertonNet Broadband TV, 234 N McIntosh St, Elberton, GA 30635-1552. Phone: 706-213-3278. E-mail: customerservice@cityofelberton.net. Web Site: http://www.elberton.net. ICA: GA0304. **Note:** This system is an overbuild.
TV Market Ranking: 46 (ELBERTON).
Channel capacity: 96 (operating 2-way). Channels available but not in use: N.A.

Basic Service
Subscribers: 2,100.
Programming (received off-air): WAGA-TV (FOX) Atlanta; WGGS-TV (IND) Greenville; WGTV (PBS) Athens; WHNS (FOX) Greenville; WLOS (ABC) Asheville; WMYA-TV (MNT) Anderson; WNEG-TV (CBS) Toccoa; WRDW-TV (CBS, MNT) Augusta; WSPA-TV (CBS) Spartanburg; WXIA-TV (NBC) Atlanta; WYCW (CW) Asheville; WYFF (NBC) Greenville.
Programming (via satellite): C-SPAN; C-SPAN 2; Home Shopping Network; QVC; TBS Superstation; Trinity Broadcasting Network; TV Guide Network; Univision; Weather Channel; Weatherscan; WGN America.
Fee: $12.95 monthly.

Expanded Basic Service 1
Subscribers: 1,814.
Programming (via satellite): ABC Family Channel; AMC; Animal Planet; Arts & Entertainment; BET Networks; Boomerang; Bravo; Cartoon Network; CNBC; CNN; Comcast Sports Net Southeast; Comedy Central; Country Music TV; Discovery Channel; Disney Channel; E! Entertainment Television; ESPN; ESPN 2; ESPN Classic Sports; ESPNews; Food Network; Fox News Channel; FX; G4; Golf Channel; GSN; Hallmark Channel; Headline News; HGTV; History Channel; Lifetime; Lifetime Movie Network; MSNBC; MTV; National Geographic Channel; Nickelodeon; Outdoor Channel; Ovation; Oxygen; SoapNet; Speed Channel; Spike TV; SportSouth; Syfy; Telefutura; Telemundo; The Learning Channel; Toon Disney; Travel Channel; truTV; Turner Classic Movies; Turner Network TV; TV Land; USA Network; VH1; WE tv.
Fee: $34.95 monthly.

Digital Basic Service
Subscribers: 400.
Programming (received off-air): WAGA-TV (FOX) Atlanta; WLOS (ABC) Asheville; WMYA-TV (MNT) Anderson; WSPA-TV (CBS) Spartanburg; WXIA-TV (NBC) Atlanta; WYCW (CW) Asheville.
Programming (via satellite): AmericanLife TV Network; Arts & Entertainment HD; BBC America; Bio; Bloomberg Television; CMT Pure Country; Discovery Health Channel; Discovery Home Channel; Discovery Kids Channel; Discovery Military Channel; DMX Music; FitTV; Food Network HD; Fox College Sports Atlantic; Fox College Sports Central; Fox College Sports Pacific; Fox Movie Channel; Fox Reality Channel; Fox Soccer; Fuse; Gospel Music Channel; Great American Country; Hallmark Movie Channel; Halogen Network; HGTV HD; History Channel International; ID Investigation Discovery; Independent Film Channel; LOGO; MTV Hits; MTV2; National Geographic Channel HD Network; Nick Jr.; NickToons TV; PBS Kids Sprout; RFD-TV; Science Channel; Science Channel HD; Sleuth; Style Network; TeenNick; Universal HD; Versus; VH1 Classic; VH1 Soul.
Fee: $46.95 monthly.

Digital Expanded Basic Service
Subscribers: N.A.
Programming (via satellite): Canal 52MX; Cine Latino; Cine Mexicano; CNN en Espanol; Discovery en Espanol; ESPN Deportes; Fox Sports en Espanol; History Channel en Espanol; MTV Tres; VeneMovies.
Fee: $4.00 monthly.

Pay Service 1
Pay Units: N.A.
Programming (via satellite): Cinemax (multiplexed); HBO (multiplexed); Showtime (multiplexed); Starz.
Fee: $9.00 monthly (Cinemax or Starz/Encore), $12.00 monthly (HBO or Showtime/TMC/Flix).

Digital Pay Service 1
Pay Units: N.A.
Programming (via satellite): Cinemax; Encore; Flix; HBO (multiplexed); Playboy TV; Showtime (multiplexed); Starz (multiplexed); Starz HDTV; Sundance Channel; The Movie Channel (multiplexed).
Fee: $10.00 monthly (Cinemax), $11.00 monthly (Starz & Encore), $12.00 monthly (HBO or Showtime/TMC/Sundance/Flix).

Pay-Per-View
iN DEMAND (delivered digitally).

Internet Service
Operational: Yes.
Subscribers: 1,130.
Broadband Service: In-house.
Fee: $37.95-$71.95 monthly; $10.00 modem lease.

Telephone Service
Digital: Operational
Subscribers: 165.
Fee: $44.95 monthly

Miles of Plant: 30.0 (coaxial); None (fiber optic).
Marketing Director: Amy Bond.
Ownership: Elberton Utilities.

ELLIJAY—Ellijay Telephone Co., PO Box 0, 224 Dalton St, Ellijay, GA 30540-3119. Phones: 800-660-6826; 706-276-2271. Fax: 706-276-9888. E-mail: cabletv@ellijay.com. Web Site: http://www.etcnow.com. Also serves Ball Ground, Bent Tree, Blue Ridge, Cherokee County (portions), East Ellijay, Fannin County (portions), Gilmer County, Jasper, McKaysville, Mineral Bluff, Morganton, Nelson & Pickens County (portions), GA; Copperhill, Ducktown & Turtletown, TN. ICA: GA0044.
TV Market Ranking: Below 100 (Copperhill, Ducktown, East Ellijay, ELLIJAY, Gilmer County (portions), McKaysville, Turtletown); Outside TV Markets (Ball Ground, Bent Tree, Blue Ridge, Cherokee County (portions), Fannin County (portions), Gilmer County (portions), Jasper, Mineral Bluff, Morganton, Nelson, Pickens County (portions)). Franchise award date: N.A. Franchise expiration date: N.A. Began: May 1, 1968.
Channel capacity: N.A. Channels available but not in use: N.A.

Basic Service
Subscribers: 17,500.
Programming (received off-air): WAGA-TV (FOX) Atlanta; WATC-DT (ETV) Atlanta; WATL (MNT) Atlanta; WDEF-TV (CBS) Chattanooga; WDSI-TV (FOX, MNT) Chattanooga; WGCL-TV (CBS) Atlanta; WGTV (PBS) Athens; WPXA-TV (ION) Rome; WRCB (NBC) Chattanooga; WSB-TV (ABC) Atlanta; WTVC (ABC) Chattanooga; WUPA (CW) Atlanta; WUVG-DT (UNV) Athens; WXIA-TV (NBC) Atlanta.
Programming (via satellite): ABC Family Channel; Animal Planet; Arts & Entertainment; Cartoon Network; CNBC; CNN; Comcast Sports Net Southeast; Comedy Central; Country Music TV; C-SPAN; C-SPAN 2; Discovery Channel; Disney Channel; ESPN; ESPN 2; FamilyNet; Food Network; Fox News Channel; FX; Gospel Music Channel; Hallmark Channel; Headline News; HGTV; History Channel; Home Shopping Network; Lifetime; MTV; Nickelodeon; Outdoor Channel; QVC; Spike TV; SportSouth; Syfy; TBS Superstation; The Learning Channel; Toon Disney; Travel Channel; Trinity Broadcasting Network; Turner Classic Movies; Turner Network TV; TV Guide Network; TV Land; USA Network; VH1; Weather Channel.
Fee: $44.95 monthly.

Digital Basic Service
Subscribers: 4,500.
Programming (received off-air): WAGA-TV (FOX) Atlanta; WATL (MNT) Atlanta; WDEF-TV (CBS) Chattanooga; WDSI-TV (FOX, MNT) Chattanooga; WGCL-TV (CBS) Atlanta; WPCH-TV (IND) Atlanta; WRCB (NBC) Chattanooga; WSB-TV (ABC) Atlanta; WXIA-TV (NBC) Atlanta.
Programming (via satellite): AmericanLife TV Network; BBC America; Bio; Bloomberg Television; Discovery Digital Networks; Discovery HD Theater; DMX Music; Encore; ESPN Classic Sports; ESPNews; Fox Movie Channel; Fox Soccer; Fuel TV; G4; GAS; Golf Channel; GSN; Hallmark Movie Channel; HDNet; HDNet Movies; History Channel International; Independent Film Channel; Lifetime Movie Network; Lime; MTV Networks Digital Suite; Nick Jr.; NickToons TV; Speed Channel; Turner Network TV HD; Versus; WE tv.
Fee: $15.15 monthly.

Digital Pay Service 1
Pay Units: N.A.
Programming (via satellite): Cinemax; Flix; HBO (multiplexed); Showtime (multiplexed); Starz; The Movie Channel (multiplexed).
Fee: $4.95 monthly (Encore), $6.95 monthly (Cinemax), $11.95 monthly (Starz/Encore), $12.95 monthly (HBO or Showtime/TMC/Flix).

Video-On-Demand: No

Internet Service
Operational: Yes.
Subscribers: 2,000.
Fee: $49.95 monthly.

Telephone Service
None

Miles of Plant: 1,100.0 (coaxial); None (fiber optic). Homes passed: 20,000. Homes passed & miles of plant (coax) include Blue Ridge
President: Dwight Roeland. Operations Director: Daryl Harper. Engineering Director: Frank Rigdon.
Ownership: Ellijay Telephone Co. (MSO).

ENIGMA—Mediacom. Now served by PEARSON, GA [GA0063]. ICA: GA0119.

EULONIA—Comcast Cable, 141 Park of Commerce Dr, Savannah, GA 31405. Phone: 912-356-3113. Web Site: http://www.comcast.com. Also serves Belvedere Island, Crescent, Meridian, Sapelo Gardens, Shellman Bluff & Townsend. ICA: GA0091.
TV Market Ranking: Below 100 (Belvedere Island, Crescent, EULONIA, Meridian, Sapelo Gardens, Shellman Bluff, Townsend). Franchise award date: N.A. Franchise expiration date: N.A. Began: N.A.
Channel capacity: N.A. Channels available but not in use: N.A.

Basic Service
Subscribers: 866.
Programming (received off-air): WJCL (ABC) Savannah; WPXC-TV (ION) Brunswick; WSAV-TV (MNT, NBC) Savannah; WTGS (FOX) Hardeeville; WTLV (NBC) Jacksonville; WTOC-TV (CBS) Savannah; WVAN-TV (PBS) Savannah.
Programming (via satellite): ABC Family Channel; BET Networks; C-SPAN; Lifetime; TBS Superstation; Trinity Broadcasting Network; WGN America.
Current originations: Government Access; Public Access.
Fee: $11.00 monthly.
Expanded Basic Service 1
Subscribers: 655.
Programming (via satellite): AMC; Animal Planet; Arts & Entertainment; Cartoon Network; CNBC; CNN; Comcast Sports Net Southeast; Comcast/Charter Sports Southeast (CSS); Comedy Central; Country Music TV; C-SPAN 2; CW+; Discovery Channel; Discovery Health Channel; Disney Channel; E! Entertainment Television; ESPN; ESPN 2; Food Network; Fox News Channel; FX; Golf Channel; Great American Country; Hallmark Channel; Headline News; HGTV; History Channel; Home Shopping Network; MTV; Nickelodeon; Outdoor Channel; ShopNBC; Speed Channel; Spike TV; SportSouth; Syfy; The Learning Channel; Travel Channel; truTV; Turner Classic Movies; Turner Network TV; TV Guide Network; TV Land; TV One; USA Network; Versus; VH1; Weather Channel.
Fee: $28.32 monthly.
Digital Basic Service
Subscribers: N.A.
Programming (via satellite): BBC America; Bio; Black Family Channel; Bloomberg Television; Cooking Channel; Discovery Digital Networks; DMX Music; Do-It-Yourself; Encore (multiplexed); ESPN Classic Sports; ESPNews; Flix (multiplexed); Fox Sports World; G4; GAS; GSN; History Channel International; MTV Networks Digital Suite; National Geographic Channel; NFL Network; Nick Jr.; Nick Too; NickToons TV; Sundance Channel; The Word Network; Toon Disney; WE tv.
Fee: $38.27 monthly.
Pay Service 1
Pay Units: 132.
Programming (via satellite): HBO.
Digital Pay Service 1
Pay Units: N.A.
Programming (via satellite): Cinemax (multiplexed); HBO (multiplexed); Showtime (multiplexed); Starz (multiplexed); The Movie Channel (multiplexed).
Video-On-Demand: No
Pay-Per-View
iN DEMAND (delivered digitally); Hot Choice (delivered digitally); Playboy TV (delivered digitally).
Internet Service
Operational: Yes.
Fee: $42.95 monthly.
Telephone Service
Digital: Operational
Miles of Plant: 76.0 (coaxial); None (fiber optic). Homes passed: 2,291.
General Manager: Michael Daves. Marketing Director: Jerry Avery. Marketing Manager: Ken Torres. Chief Technician: Joel Godsen.
Ownership: Comcast Cable Communications Inc. (MSO).

FAIRBURN—Comcast Cable, 305 Bucknell Ct SW, Atlanta, GA 30336-2406. Phones: 770-559-2000; 404-266-2278. Fax: 770-559-7621. Web Site: http://www.comcast.com. ICA: GA0305. **Note:** This system is an overbuild.
TV Market Ranking: 18 (FAIRBURN).
Channel capacity: 78 (operating 2-way). Channels available but not in use: None.
Basic Service
Subscribers: N.A.
Programming (received off-air): WAGA-TV (FOX) Atlanta; WATL (MNT) Atlanta; WGCL-TV (CBS) Atlanta; WGTV (PBS) Athens; WPBA (PBS) Atlanta; WPCH-TV (IND) Atlanta; WSB-TV (ABC) Atlanta; WUPA (CW) Atlanta; WUVG-DT (UNV) Athens; WXIA-TV (NBC) Atlanta.
Programming (via satellite): Bravo; Disney Channel; ESPNews; INSP; ION Television; QVC; Telefutura; Trinity Broadcasting Network; TV Guide Network; TV Land; Weather Channel; WGN America.
Current originations: Public Access.
Fee: $16.95 monthly.
Expanded Basic Service 1
Subscribers: N.A.
Programming (via satellite): ABC Family Channel; AMC; Animal Planet; Arts & Entertainment; BET Networks; Cartoon Network; CNBC; CNN; Comcast Sports Net Southeast; Comedy Central; Country Music TV; C-SPAN; Discovery Channel; Discovery Health Channel; E! Entertainment Television; Encore; ESPN; ESPN 2; Eternal Word TV Network; Food Network; Fox Movie Channel; Fox News Channel; FX; G4; Golf Channel; Gospel Music TV; Great American Country; Hallmark Channel; Headline News; HGTV; History Channel; Home Shopping Network; Lifetime; MSNBC; MTV; Nickelodeon; Outdoor Channel; Speed Channel; Spike TV; SportSouth; Syfy; The Learning Channel; Toon Disney; Travel Channel; truTV; Turner Classic Movies; Turner Network TV; USA Network; Versus; VH1; WE tv.
Fee: $49.99 monthly.
Pay Service 1
Pay Units: N.A.
Programming (via satellite): Cinemax (multiplexed); HBO (multiplexed); Showtime (multiplexed); The Movie Channel (multiplexed).
Fee: $8.50 monthly (each).
Pay-Per-View
iN DEMAND.
Internet Service
Operational: Yes. Began: November 1, 1998.
Broadband Service: Comcast High Speed Internet.
Fee: $75.00 installation; $42.95 monthly.
Telephone Service
Digital: Operational
Fee: $39.95 monthly
General Manager: K C McWilliams.
Ownership: Comcast Cable Communications Inc.

FITZGERALD—Mediacom, 509 Flint Ave, Albany, GA 31701. Phones: 229-244-3852 (Valdosta regional office); 229-888-0242. Fax: 229-436-4819. Web Site: http://www.mediacomcable.com. Also serves Ben Hill County (portions), Cordele, Crisp County (portions), Dooly County (portions), Irwin County (portions), Ocilla & Vienna. ICA: GA0052.
TV Market Ranking: Below 100 (Ben Hill County (portions), Cordele, Crisp County (portions), Dooly County (portions), Irwin County (portions), Vienna); Outside TV Markets (Ben Hill County (portions), FITZGERALD, Irwin County (portions), Ocilla). Franchise award date: N.A. Franchise expiration date: N.A. Began: November 1, 1962.
Channel capacity: N.A. Channels available but not in use: None.
Basic Service
Subscribers: 10,305.
Programming (received off-air): WALB (NBC) Albany; WFXL (FOX) Albany; WMAZ-TV (CBS) Macon; WPGA-TV (ABC) Perry; WSST-TV (IND) Cordele; WXGA-TV (PBS) Waycross; 1 FM.
Programming (via microwave): WSB-TV (ABC) Atlanta.
Programming (via satellite): ABC Family Channel; Arts & Entertainment; BET Networks; CNBC; CNN; C-SPAN; Discovery Channel; Hallmark Channel; Headline News; Lifetime; MTV; Nickelodeon; QVC; TBS Superstation; Turner Network TV; Weather Channel.
Fee: $35.00 installation; $9.96 monthly; $.11 converter.
Expanded Basic Service 1
Subscribers: 4,805.
Programming (via satellite): AMC; Animal Planet; Black Family Channel; Bravo; Cartoon Network; Comcast Sports Net Southeast; Comedy Central; Country Music TV; C-SPAN 2; CW+; Disney Channel; E! Entertainment Television; ESPN; ESPN 2; Eternal Word TV Network; FitTV; Food Network; Fox News Channel; FX; GalaVision; Golf Channel; HGTV; History Channel; Home Shopping Network; ION Television; MSNBC; Oxygen; Spike TV; SportSouth; Syfy; The Learning Channel; Travel Channel; Trinity Broadcasting Network; truTV; TV Guide Network; TV Land; Univision; USA Network; VH1; WE tv.
Fee: $2.15 monthly.
Digital Basic Service
Subscribers: N.A.
Programming (via satellite): BBC America; Bio; Bloomberg Television; Canales N; Discovery Digital Networks; Fox Movie Channel; Fox Sports World; Fuse; G4; Gaming Entertainment Television; GAS; GSN; Halogen Network; History Channel International; Independent Film Channel; Lifetime Movie Network; Lime; MTV Networks Digital Suite; Music Choice; National Geographic Channel; Nick Jr.; Outdoor Channel; Ovation; Speed Channel; Style Network; Toon Disney; Turner Classic Movies; Versus.
Digital Pay Service 1
Pay Units: N.A.
Programming (via satellite): Cinemax (multiplexed); Encore (multiplexed); Flix; HBO (multiplexed); Showtime (multiplexed); Starz (multiplexed); Sundance Channel; The Movie Channel (multiplexed).
Video-On-Demand: Yes
Pay-Per-View
TVN Entertainment (delivered digitally); Pleasure (delivered digitally); ETC (delivered digitally); ESPN Now (delivered digitally); Sports PPV (delivered digitally).
Internet Service
Operational: Yes. Began: November 1, 2001.
Broadband Service: Mediacom High Speed Internet.
Fee: $50.00 installation; $42.95 monthly; $3.00 modem lease.
Telephone Service
Analog: Not Operational
Digital: Operational
Miles of Plant: 743.0 (coaxial); 120.0 (fiber optic). Homes passed: 14,360. Miles of plant (coax & fiber) includes Eastman, Hazlehurst, Moultrie, & Pearson
Regional Vice President: Sue Misiunas. General Manager: Gary Crosby. Regional Marketing Director: Melanie Hannasch. Regional Technical Operations Manager: Gary McDougall. Marketing Manager: Daryl Channey.
City fee: 3% of gross.
Ownership: Mediacom LLC (MSO).

FLINT RIVER—KLiP Interactive, 455 Gees Mill Business Court, Conyers, GA 30013. Phone: 678-727-7100. Fax: 678-727-7002. E-mail: jsheehan@klipia.com. Web Site: http://www.klipia.com. ICA: GA0280.
TV Market Ranking: Below 100 (FLINT RIVER). Franchise award date: N.A. Franchise expiration date: N.A. Began: N.A.
Channel capacity: 65 (not 2-way capable). Channels available but not in use: 33.
Basic Service
Subscribers: 16.
Programming (received off-air): WABW-TV (PBS) Pelham; WALB (NBC) Albany; WCTV (CBS, MNT) Thomasville; WFSU-TV (PBS) Tallahassee; WPCH-TV (IND) Atlanta; WTLH (CW, FOX) Bainbridge; WTXL-TV (ABC) Tallahassee.
Programming (via satellite): ABC Family Channel; Animal Planet; Arts & Entertainment; BET Networks; Bravo; CNN; Country Music TV; Discovery Channel; Disney Channel; ESPN; ESPN 2; Headline News; Lifetime; Nickelodeon; QVC; Spike TV; The Learning Channel; Travel Channel; Trinity Broadcasting Network; Turner Network TV; TV Land; USA Network; Weather Channel; WGN America.
Fee: $29.95 installation; $33.02 monthly.
Pay Service 1
Pay Units: 3.
Programming (via satellite): HBO.
Fee: $10.95 monthly.
Internet Service
Operational: No.
Telephone Service
None
Miles of Plant: 6.0 (coaxial); None (fiber optic). Homes passed: 150.
Chief Executive Officer: Joseph A. Sheehan. General Manager East: Mark Miller. General Manager West: Vance Johnson.
Ownership: KLiP Interactive LLC (MSO).

FOLKSTON—Comcast Cable, 6805 Southpoint Pkwy, Jacksonville, FL 32216. Phone: 904-374-8000. Fax: 904-374-7622. Web Site: http://www.comcast.com. Also serves Charlton County & Homeland. ICA: GA0093.
TV Market Ranking: Below 100 (Charlton County (portions)); Outside TV Markets (Charlton County (portions), FOLKSTON, Homeland). Franchise award date: June 1, 1980. Franchise expiration date: N.A. Began: December 19, 1980.
Channel capacity: 40 (2-way capable). Channels available but not in use: 2.
Basic Service
Subscribers: N.A. Included in Jacksonville, FL
Programming (received off-air): WAWS (FOX, MNT) Jacksonville; WCWJ (CW) Jacksonville; WJCT (PBS) Jacksonville; WJEB-TV (ETV) Jacksonville; WJXT (IND) Jacksonville; WJXX (ABC) Orange Park; WPXC-TV (ION) Brunswick; WTEV-TV (CBS) Jacksonville; WTLV (NBC) Jacksonville; WUFT (PBS) Gainesville; 4 FMs.
Programming (via satellite): C-SPAN; Home Shopping Network; QVC; TV Guide Network; Weatherscan; WGN America.

Current originations: Educational Access; Government Access; Public Access.
Fee: $43.99 installation.

Expanded Basic Service 1
Subscribers: 967.
Programming (via satellite): ABC Family Channel; AMC; Animal Planet; Arts & Entertainment; BET Networks; Bravo; Cartoon Network; CNBC; CNN; Comcast/Charter Sports Southeast (CSS); Comedy Central; Country Music TV; Discovery Channel; Disney Channel; E! Entertainment Television; ESPN; ESPN 2; Eternal Word TV Network; Fox News Channel; Fox Sports Net Florida; Fuse; Golf Channel; Great American Country; Hallmark Channel; Headline News; HGTV; History Channel; Lifetime; MTV; MTV2; Nickelodeon; Speed Channel; Spike TV; SunSports TV; Syfy; TBS Superstation; The Learning Channel; truTV; Turner Network TV; TV Land; Univision; USA Network; Versus; VH1; WE tv; Weather Channel.
Fee: $36.05 monthly.

Digital Basic Service
Subscribers: 215.
Programming (received off-air): WAWS (FOX, MNT) Jacksonville; WCWJ (CW) Jacksonville; WJCT (PBS) Jacksonville; WJXX (ABC) Orange Park; WTEV-TV (CBS) Jacksonville; WTLV (NBC) Jacksonville.
Programming (via satellite): BBC America; Bio; Black Family Channel; Bloomberg Television; Bravo; Canales N; Cooking Channel; Country Music TV; C-SPAN 2; C-SPAN 3; Current; Daystar TV Network; Discovery Digital Networks; Discovery HD Theater; Do-It-Yourself; Encore (multiplexed); ESPN 2 HD; ESPN Classic Sports; ESPN HD; ESPNews; FamilyNet; Fox College Sports Atlantic; Fox College Sports Central; Fox College Sports Pacific; Fox Reality Channel; Fox Soccer; G4; GAS; Gol TV; GSN; Halogen Network; History Channel International; Independent Film Channel; INHD; Jewelry Television; Lifetime Movie Network; LOGO; MoviePlex; MSNBC; MTV Networks Digital Suite; Music Choice; MyNetworkTV Inc.; National Geographic Channel; NBA TV; NFL Network; Nick Jr.; Nick Too; NickToons TV; Outdoor Channel; Oxygen; Palladia; PBS Kids Sprout; ShopNBC; Style Network; Sundance Channel; Tennis Channel; The Sportsman Channel; The Word Network; Toon Disney; Travel Channel; Trinity Broadcasting Network; Turner Classic Movies; Turner Network TV HD; TV One; Versus HD.
Fee: $10.00 monthly.

Pay Service 1
Pay Units: 744.
Programming (via satellite): HBO.
Fee: $10.00 installation; $15.95 monthly.

Digital Pay Service 1
Pay Units: N.A.
Programming (via satellite): Cinemax (multiplexed); Cinemax HD; Flix; HBO (multiplexed); HBO HD; Showtime (multiplexed); Showtime HD; Starz (multiplexed); Starz HDTV; The Movie Channel (multiplexed).
Fee: $15.95 monthly (each).
Video-On-Demand: No

Pay-Per-View
Movies & Events (delivered digitally); Playboy TV (delivered digitally); ESPN (delivered digitally); NBA League Pass (delivered digitally); NHL Center Ice (delivered digitally).

Internet Service
Operational: Yes.

Telephone Service
Digital: Operational
Miles of Plant: 49.0 (coaxial); None (fiber optic). Homes passed: 2,202.
Vice President & General Manager: Doug McMillan. Engineering Director: Mike Humphrey. Vice President, Marketing: Vic Scarborough. Government Affairs Director: Bill Ferry.
Ownership: Comcast Cable Communications Inc. (MSO).

FORSYTH—Forsyth Cable, 26 N Jackson St, Forsyth, GA 31029-2103. Phone: 478-992-5096. Fax: 478-993-1002. E-mail: khartley@forsythcable.com. Web Site: http://www.forsythcable.com. ICA: GA0080.
TV Market Ranking: Below 100 (FORSYTH). Franchise award date: N.A. Franchise expiration date: N.A. Began: February 20, 1979.
Channel capacity: 89 (operating 2-way). Channels available but not in use: 7.

Basic Service
Subscribers: 2,400.
Programming (received off-air): WAGA-TV (FOX) Atlanta; WATL (MNT) Atlanta; WGCL-TV (CBS) Atlanta; WGNM (IND) Macon; WGTV (PBS) Athens; WGXA (FOX, MNT) Macon; WMGT-TV (MNT, NBC) Macon; WPGA-TV (ABC) Perry; WSB-TV (ABC) Atlanta; WXIA-TV (NBC) Atlanta; 1 FM.
Programming (via satellite): Disney Channel; Headline News; ION Television; truTV; TV Guide Network; WGN America.
Current originations: Religious Access; Government Access; Public Access.
Fee: $49.95 installation; $9.95 monthly; $32.95 additional installation.

Expanded Basic Service 1
Subscribers: 1,584.
Programming (via satellite): ABC Family Channel; AMC; Animal Planet; Arts & Entertainment; BET Networks; Bloomberg Television; Cartoon Network; CNBC; CNN; Comcast Sports Net Southeast; Comedy Central; Country Music TV; C-SPAN; C-SPAN 2; Discovery Channel; ESPN; ESPN 2; ESPNews; FitTV; Food Network; Fox News Channel; FX; Golf Channel; HGTV; History Channel; Home Shopping Network; INSP; Lifetime; MSNBC; MTV; Nickelodeon; Outdoor Channel; QVC; Spike TV; SportSouth; Syfy; TBS Superstation; The Learning Channel; Toon Disney; Travel Channel; Trinity Broadcasting Network; Turner Classic Movies; Turner Network TV; TV Land; USA Network; VH1; WE tv; Weather Channel.
Fee: $39.90 monthly.

Pay Service 1
Pay Units: 720.
Programming (via satellite): Cinemax (multiplexed); Encore (multiplexed); HBO (multiplexed); Showtime (multiplexed); Starz.
Fee: $10.84 monthly (Starz & Encore), $10.94 monthly (Showtime), $12.04 monthly (Cinemax), $14.25 monthly (HBO).
Video-On-Demand: No

Pay-Per-View
iN DEMAND.

Internet Service
Operational: Yes. Began: January 1, 2000.
Subscribers: 150.
Broadband Service: Metropolitan Electrical Association of Georgia.
Fee: $99.00 installation; $24.95-$49.95 monthly.

Telephone Service
None
Miles of Plant: 40.0 (coaxial); 80.0 (fiber optic). Homes passed: 2,600. Total homes in franchised area: 3,000.
Manager: Alvin Randall. Chief Technician: Mark Beaubien.
Ownership: Forsyth Cable.

FORT BENNING—Windjammer Cable, 4400 PGA Blvd, Ste 902, Palm Beach Gardens, FL 33410. Phones: 561-775-1208; 877-450-5558. Fax: 561-775-7811. Web Site: http://www.windjammercable.com. ICA: GA0071.
TV Market Ranking: 94 (FORT BENNING). Franchise award date: N.A. Franchise expiration date: N.A. Began: November 1, 1974.
Channel capacity: N.A. Channels available but not in use: N.A.

Basic Service
Subscribers: N.A.
Programming (received off-air): KHGI-CA North Platte; WJSP-TV (PBS) Columbus; WLTZ (CW, NBC) Columbus; WRBL (CBS) Columbus; WTVM (ABC) Columbus; WXTX (FOX) Columbus; WYBU-CD (IND) Columbus.
Programming (via satellite): WGN America.
Current originations: Government Access.
Fee: $49.95 installation; $17.44 monthly.

Expanded Basic Service 1
Subscribers: N.A.
Programming (via satellite): ABC Family Channel; AMC; Animal Planet; Arts & Entertainment; BET Networks; Bravo!; Cartoon Network; CNN; Comcast Sports Net Southeast; Comedy Central; Country Music TV; C-SPAN; C-SPAN 2; Discovery Channel; Discovery Health Channel; Disney Channel; ESPN; ESPN 2; ESPN Classic Sports; Eternal Word TV Network; FitTV; Food Network; Fox News Channel; FX; Golf Channel; Hallmark Channel; Headline News; HGTV; History Channel; Home Shopping Network; ION Television; Lifetime; Lifetime Movie Network; MSNBC; MTV; National Geographic Channel; Nickelodeon; Oxygen; QVC; Spike TV; SportSouth; Syfy; TBS Superstation; The Learning Channel; Travel Channel; Trinity Broadcasting Network; truTV; Turner Network TV; TV Guide Network; TV Land; Univision; USA Network; VH1; WE tv; Weather Channel.
Fee: $34.87 monthly.

Digital Basic Service
Subscribers: N.A.
Programming (via satellite): AmericanLife TV Network; BBC America; Bio; Bloomberg Television; Current; Discovery HD Theater; Discovery Home Channel; Discovery Kids Channel; Discovery Times Channel; DMX Music; ESPN; ESPNews; Fox Soccer; Fuse; G4; GAS; GSN; HBO; HDNet; HDNet Movies; History Channel International; INHD; MTV Hits; MTV2; Nick Jr.; NickToons TV; Outdoor Channel; Ovation; Science Television; Showtime; Sleuth; Speed Channel; Toon Disney; Turner Classic Movies; Turner Network TV HD; Versus; VH1 Classic.
Fee: $51.77 monthly.

Digital Pay Service 1
Pay Units: 573.
Programming (via satellite): Encore; HBO; Independent Film Channel; Showtime; Starz; The Movie Channel.
Fee: $12.00 monthly (each).
Video-On-Demand: Yes

Pay-Per-View
iN DEMAND (delivered digitally); Ten Blox (delivered digitally); Fresh (delivered digitally); Shorteez (delivered digitally); Playboy TV (delivered digitally); Pleasure (delivered digitally); Hot Choice (delivered digitally); Ten Blue (delivered digitally); Ten Clips (delivered digitally).

Internet Service
Operational: Yes.
Broadband Service: In-house.
Fee: $99.00 installation; $20.99-$49.99 monthly.

Telephone Service
Digital: Operational
Fee: $74.95 installation; $44.95 monthly
Miles of Plant: 80.0 (coaxial); None (fiber optic).
General Manager: Timothy Evard. Operations Director: Belinda Graham. Engineering Director: Mike Earehart. Finance & Accounting Director: Cindy Johnson.
Franchise fee: None.
Ownership: Windjammer Communications LLC (MSO).

FORT GORDON—Charter Communications, 536 E Robinson, Grovetown, GA 30813. Phones: 770-806-7060 (Duluth office); 706-855-5680. Web Site: http://www.charter.com. Also serves Columbia County (portions), Grovetown & Harlem. ICA: GA0198.
TV Market Ranking: Below 100 (Columbia County (portions), FORT GORDON, Grovetown, Harlem). Franchise award date: September 1, 1979. Franchise expiration date: N.A. Began: April 15, 1990.
Channel capacity: N.A. Channels available but not in use: N.A.

Basic Service
Subscribers: N.A.
Programming (received off-air): WAGT (CW, NBC) Augusta; WBEK-CA (IND) Augusta; WBPI-CD Augusta; WCES-TV (PBS) Wrens; WFXG (FOX) Augusta; WJBF (ABC) Augusta; WRDW-TV (CBS, MNT) Augusta.
Programming (via satellite): C-SPAN; CW+; Home Shopping Network; ION Television; MyNetworkTV Inc.; QVC; ShopNBC; TBS Superstation; TV Guide Network; Univision; WGN America.
Current originations: Government Access.
Fee: $29.99 installation.

Expanded Basic Service 1
Subscribers: N.A.
Programming (via satellite): ABC Family Channel; AMC; Animal Planet; Arts & Entertainment; BET Networks; Bravo!; Cartoon Network; CNBC; CNN; Comcast Sports Net Southeast; Comcast/Charter Sports Southeast (CSS); Comedy Central; Country Music TV; Discovery Channel; Disney Channel; E! Entertainment Television; ESPN; ESPN 2; ESPN Classic Sports; Food Network;

Fox News Channel; FX; Golf Channel; GSN; Hallmark Channel; Headline News; HGTV; History Channel; Lifetime; MSNBC; MTV; MTV2; National Geographic Channel; Nickelodeon; Oxygen; SoapNet; Speed Channel; Spike TV; SportSouth; Style Network; Syfy; Telefutura; Telemundo; The Learning Channel; Travel Channel; truTV; Turner Classic Movies; Turner Network TV; TV Land; USA Network; VH1; Weather Channel.
Fee: $19.00 monthly.

Digital Basic Service
Subscribers: N.A.
Programming (received off-air): WAGA-TV (FOX) Atlanta; WGCL-TV (CBS) Atlanta; WSB-TV (ABC) Atlanta; WXIA-TV (NBC) Atlanta.
Programming (via satellite): Arts & Entertainment HD; BBC America; Bio; Bloomberg Television; Boomerang; Cine Latino; CMT Pure Country; CNN en Espanol; CNN International; Discovery en Espanol; Discovery HD Theater; Discovery Health Channel; Discovery Home Channel; Discovery Kids Channel; Discovery Military Channel; Do-It-Yourself; ESPN 2 HD; ESPN Deportes; ESPN HD; ESPNews; Eternal Word TV Network; FitTV; Fox College Sports Atlantic; Fox College Sports Central; Fox College Sports Pacific; Fox Soccer; Fox Sports en Espanol; Fuel TV; G4; HDNet; HDNet Movies; History Channel HD; History Channel International; ID Investigation Discovery; Independent Film Channel; INSP; La Familia Network; Lifetime Movie Network; MTV Hits; MTV Jams; MTV Tres; Music Choice; Nick Jr.; Nick Too; NickToons TV; Palladia; Science Channel; Sundance Channel; TBS in HD; TeenNick; Toon Disney; Turner Network TV HD; TVN Entertainment; Universal HD; Versus; Versus HD; VH1; VH1 Classic; VH1 Soul; WE tv.
Fee: $19.00 monthly.

Digital Pay Service 1
Pay Units: N.A.
Programming (via satellite): Cinemax (multiplexed); Cinemax HD; Encore (multiplexed); Flix; HBO (multiplexed); HBO HD; Showtime (multiplexed); Showtime HD; Starz (multiplexed); Starz HDTV; The Movie Channel (multiplexed); The Movie Channel HD.
Fee: $9.50 monthly (each).

Video-On-Demand: No

Pay-Per-View
iN DEMAND (delivered digitally), Addressable: Yes; NBA League Pass/WNBA (delivered digitally); NHL Center Ice/MLB Extra Innings (delivered digitally); Playboy TV (delivered digitally); Fresh (delivered digitally); Shorteez (delivered digitally).

Internet Service
Operational: Yes.
Broadband Service: Charter Pipeline.
Fee: $29.99 monthly.

Telephone Service
Digital: Operational
Fee: $29.99 monthly

Vice President & General Manager: Matt Favre. Operations Manager: Jeff Osborne. Technical Supervisor: Marcus Webb. Sales & Marketing Director: Antoinette Carpenter.
Ownership: Charter Communications Inc. (MSO).

FORT VALLEY—ComSouth, PO Box 508, 602 College St, Fort Valley, GA 31030-0508. Phones: 478-987-0172; 478-825-3626. Fax: 478-825-1639. Web Site: http://www.comsouth.net. Also serves Peach County. ICA: GA0077.
TV Market Ranking: Below 100 (FORT VALLEY, Peach County). Franchise award date: May 1, 1969. Franchise expiration date: N.A. Began: May 1, 1970.
Channel capacity: N.A. Channels available but not in use: N.A.

Basic Service
Subscribers: 2,000.
Programming (received off-air): WAGA-TV (FOX) Atlanta; WGNM (IND) Macon; WGXA (FOX, MNT) Macon; WMAZ-TV (CBS) Macon; WMGT-TV (MNT, NBC) Macon; WMUM-TV (PBS) Cochran; WPGA-TV (ABC) Perry; WRBL (CBS) Columbus; WSB-TV (ABC) Atlanta; WTBS-LP (IND) Atlanta; WTVM (ABC) Columbus.
Programming (via satellite): C-SPAN; CW+; Discovery Channel; Disney Channel; QVC; Radar Channel; Weather Channel.
Current originations: Government Access; Educational Access; Public Access.
Fee: $25.00 installation; $14.00 monthly; $10.00 additional installation.

Pay Service 1
Pay Units: N.A.
Programming (via satellite): Cinemax; HBO; Showtime; The Movie Channel.
Fee: $10.00 monthly (each).

Video-On-Demand: No

Internet Service
Operational: Yes, Both DSL & dial-up.
Subscribers: 325.
Fee: $14.95 monthly.

Telephone Service
Analog: Not Operational
Digital: Operational
Fee: $31.05 monthly

Miles of Plant: 58.0 (coaxial); 6.0 (fiber optic). Additional miles planned: 2.0 (coaxial). Homes passed: 3,300. Total homes in franchised area: 3,300.
Manager: Robert Barnes. Chief Technician: Larry Smiddle. Customer Service Manager: Debra Wells.
City fee: 5% of gross.
Ownership: ComSouth Corp. (MSO).

FUNSTON—Wainwright Cable Inc., PO Box 614, 352 N Railroad St, Norman Park, GA 31771. Phone: 229-769-3785. Fax: 229-769-5656. ICA: GA0269.
TV Market Ranking: Below 100 (FUNSTON). Franchise award date: October 1, 1990. Franchise expiration date: N.A. Began: March 1, 1991.
Channel capacity: 36 (not 2-way capable). Channels available but not in use: 1.

Basic Service
Subscribers: N.A. Included in Norman Park
Programming (received off-air): WABW-TV (PBS) Pelham; WALB (NBC) Albany; WCTV (CBS, MNT) Thomasville; WFXL (FOX) Albany.
Programming (via satellite): ABC Family Channel; Arts & Entertainment; Cartoon Network; CNN; Country Music TV; Discovery Channel; ESPN; Lifetime; Spike TV; Syfy; TBS Superstation; The Learning Channel; Travel Channel; Trinity Broadcasting Network; Turner Classic Movies; Turner Network TV; USA Network; Weather Channel; WGN America.
Fee: $25.00 installation; $20.00 monthly.

Pay Service 1
Pay Units: 20.
Programming (via satellite): HBO.
Fee: $10.00 monthly.

Video-On-Demand: No

Internet Service
Operational: No.

Telephone Service
None

Miles of Plant: 10.0 (coaxial); None (fiber optic). Homes passed: 180.
Manager & Chief Technician: Chris Wainwright.
Ownership: Wainwright Cable Inc. (MSO).

GAINESVILLE—Charter Communications, 1102 Thompson Bridge Rd, Gainesville, GA 30501-1706. Phones: 770-806-7060 (Duluth office); 770-532-4504. Fax: 770-531-4212. Web Site: http://www.charter.com. Also serves Buford, Chestnut Mountain, Flowery Branch, Gwinnett County (portions), Hall County, Murrayville & Oakwood. ICA: GA0016.
TV Market Ranking: 18 (Buford, Gwinnett County (portions)); Below 100 (Chestnut Mountain, Flowery Branch, GAINESVILLE, Hall County (portions), Murrayville, Oakwood, Gwinnett County (portions)); Outside TV Markets (Hall County (portions)). Franchise award date: December 1, 1967. Franchise expiration date: N.A. Began: December 6, 1967.
Channel capacity: N.A. Channels available but not in use: N.A.

Basic Service
Subscribers: 27,247.
Programming (received off-air): WAGA-TV (FOX) Atlanta; WATL (MNT) Atlanta; WGCL-TV (CBS) Atlanta; WGTV (PBS) Athens; WHSG-TV (TBN) Monroe; WNEG-TV (CBS) Toccoa; WPCH-TV (IND) Atlanta; WSB-TV (ABC) Atlanta; WUPA (CW) Atlanta; WUVG-DT (UNV) Athens; WXIA-TV (NBC) Atlanta.
Programming (via satellite): BET Networks; C-SPAN 2; Home Shopping Network; ION Television; QVC; TV Guide Network; Weather Channel.
Current originations: Leased Access; Government Access.
Fee: $29.99 installation.

Expanded Basic Service 1
Subscribers: 27,012.
Programming (via satellite): ABC Family Channel; AMC; Animal Planet; Arts & Entertainment; Bravo; Cartoon Network; CNBC; CNN; Comcast Sports Net Southeast; Comcast/Charter Sports Southeast (CSS); Comedy Central; Country Music TV; C-SPAN; Discovery Channel; Disney Channel; E! Entertainment Television; ESPN; ESPN 2; ESPN Deportes; Eternal Word TV Network; Food Network; Fox News Channel; FX; G4; GalaVision; Golf Channel; GSN; Hallmark Channel; Headline News; HGTV; History Channel; Lifetime; MSNBC; MTV; National Geographic Channel; Nickelodeon; Oxygen; Product Information Network; Shop at Home; ShopNBC; SoapNet; Speed Channel; Spike TV; SportSouth; Syfy; Telemundo; The Learning Channel; Toon Disney; Travel Channel; truTV; Turner Classic Movies; Turner Network TV; TV Land; USA Network; Versus; VH1; WE tv.
Fee: $48.99 monthly.

Digital Basic Service
Subscribers: 8,780.
Programming (via satellite): BBC America; Bio; Bloomberg Television; Boomerang; Canales N; Discovery Digital Networks; Do-It-Yourself; ESPN Classic Sports; ESPNews; Fox College Sports Atlantic; Fox College Sports Central; Fox College Sports Pacific; Fox Sports World; Fuse; GAS; Great American Country; History Channel International; Independent Film Channel; Lifetime Movie Network; MTV Networks Digital Suite; Music Choice; Nick Jr.; Nick Too; NickToons TV; Outdoor Channel; Style Network; Sundance Channel; TV Guide Interactive Inc.
Fee: $14.00 monthly.

Digital Pay Service 1
Pay Units: 3,946.
Programming (via satellite): Starz (multiplexed).
Fee: $12.95 monthly.

Digital Pay Service 2
Pay Units: 7,175.
Programming (via satellite): Cinemax (multiplexed).
Fee: $12.95 monthly.

Digital Pay Service 3
Pay Units: 3,946.
Programming (via satellite): Encore (multiplexed).
Fee: $12.95 monthly.

Digital Pay Service 4
Pay Units: 4,599.
Programming (via satellite): Flix.
Fee: $12.95 monthly.

Digital Pay Service 5
Pay Units: 8,596.
Programming (via satellite): HBO (multiplexed).
Fee: $12.95 monthly.

Digital Pay Service 6
Pay Units: 6,239.
Programming (via satellite): The Movie Channel (multiplexed).
Fee: $12.95 monthly.

Digital Pay Service 7
Pay Units: 4,599.
Programming (via satellite): Showtime (multiplexed).
Fee: $12.95 monthly.

Video-On-Demand: Yes

Pay-Per-View
Addressable homes: 8,745.
Fee: $3.95, Addressable: Yes, Fee: $6.95; iN DEMAND (delivered digitally); Playboy TV (delivered digitally); Fresh (delivered digitally); Shorteez (delivered digitally); sports (delivered digitally).

Internet Service
Operational: Yes. Began: October 1, 1998.
Subscribers: 3,986.
Broadband Service: Charter Pipeline.
Fee: $29.99 monthly; $5.00 modem lease; $199.95 modem purchase.

Telephone Service
Digital: Operational
Fee: $29.99 monthly

Miles of Plant: 967.0 (coaxial); 200.0 (fiber optic). Homes passed: 44,897. Total homes in franchised area: 51,542.
Vice President & General Manager: Matt Favre. Operations Manager: Jeff Osborne. Chief Technician: Justin Sears. Sales & Marketing Director: Antoinette Carpenter. Advertising Manager: Sherry Kelly. Office Manager: Joyce Galloway.
City fee: 5% of gross.
Ownership: Charter Communications Inc. (MSO).

GIBSON—KLiP Interactive, 455 Gees Mill Business Court, Conyers, GA 30013. Phone: 706-215-1385. Fax: 678-727-7002. E-mail: jsheehan@klipia.com. Web Site: http://www.klipia.com. Also serves Glascock County. ICA: GA0195.
TV Market Ranking: Below 100 (Glascock County (portions)); Outside TV Markets (GIBSON, Glascock County (portions)). Franchise award date: N.A. Franchise expiration date: N.A. Began: N.A.
Channel capacity: 45 (not 2-way capable). Channels available but not in use: 12.

Basic Service
Subscribers: 105.
Programming (received off-air): WAGT (CW, NBC) Augusta; WCES-TV (PBS) Wrens; WFXG (FOX) Augusta; WJBF

(ABC) Augusta; WPCH-TV (IND) Atlanta; WRDW-TV (CBS, MNT) Augusta.

Programming (via satellite): ABC Family Channel; Animal Planet; Arts & Entertainment; BET Networks; Bravo; CNBC; CNN; Comcast Sports Net Southeast; Country Music TV; CW+; Discovery Channel; Disney Channel; ESPN; ESPN 2; Fox News Channel; History Channel; Home Shopping Network; Lifetime; Nickelodeon; Spike TV; The Learning Channel; Travel Channel; Trinity Broadcasting Network; Turner Network TV; TV Land; USA Network; Weather Channel; WGN America.

Fee: $29.95 installation; $37.23 monthly.

Pay Service 1

Pay Units: 16.

Programming (via satellite): HBO.

Fee: $10.95 monthly.

Internet Service

Operational: No.

Telephone Service

None

Miles of Plant: 22.0 (coaxial); None (fiber optic). Homes passed: 355.

Chief Executive Officer: Joseph A. Sheehan. General Manager East: Mark Miller. General Manager West: Vance Johnson.

Ownership: KLiP Interactive LLC (MSO).

GLENNVILLE—Comcast Cable, 141 Park of Commerce Dr, Savannah, GA 31405. Phone: 912-356-3113. Web Site: http://www.comcast.com. ICA: GA0115.

TV Market Ranking: Below 100 (GLENNVILLE). Franchise award date: October 21, 1970. Franchise expiration date: N.A. Began: December 1, 1971.

Channel capacity: N.A. Channels available but not in use: N.A.

Basic Service

Subscribers: N.A. Included in Savannah

Programming (received off-air): WGSA (CW) Baxley; WJCL (ABC) Savannah; WSAV-TV (MNT, NBC) Savannah; WTGS (FOX) Hardeeville; WTOC-TV (CBS) Savannah; WVAN-TV (PBS) Savannah.

Programming (via satellite): Comcast/Charter Sports Southeast (CSS); ION Television; QVC; TBS Superstation; WGN America.

Fee: $41.99 installation; $11.00 monthly; $20.00 additional installation.

Expanded Basic Service 1

Subscribers: N.A.

Programming (via satellite): ABC Family Channel; AMC; Animal Planet; Arts & Entertainment; BET Networks; Cartoon Network; CNBC; CNN; Country Music TV; C-SPAN; Discovery Channel; Discovery Health Channel; Disney Channel; E! Entertainment Television; ESPN; ESPN 2; Food Network; Fox News Channel; Fox Sports Net; FX; Golf Channel; GSN; Hallmark Channel; Headline News; HGTV; Home Shopping Network; Lifetime; MTV; Nickelodeon; Speed Channel; Spike TV; SportSouth; Style Network; Syfy; The Learning Channel; Trinity Broadcasting Network; truTV; Turner Classic Movies; Turner Network TV; TV Land; USA Network; Versus; VH1; Weather Channel.

Fee: $30.99 monthly.

Digital Basic Service

Subscribers: N.A.

Programming (via satellite): BBC America; CMT Pure Country; Discovery Military Channel; Discovery Planet Green; DMX Music; Encore (multiplexed); ID Investigation Discovery; MTV Tres; MTV2; Nick Jr.; Nick Too; Science Channel; TeenNick; VH1 Classic; VH1 Soul.

Fee: $4.95 monthly.

Pay Service 1

Pay Units: N.A.

Programming (via satellite): HBO; Showtime.

Digital Pay Service 1

Pay Units: N.A.

Programming (via satellite): Cinemax (multiplexed); HBO (multiplexed); Showtime (multiplexed); Starz (multiplexed); The Movie Channel (multiplexed).

Fee: $3.50 monthly (TMC), $7.95 monthly (Starz), $11.95 monthly (HBO, Showtime or Cinemax).

Video-On-Demand: No

Pay-Per-View

iN DEMAND (delivered digitally); Hot Choice (delivered digitally).

Internet Service

Operational: Yes.

Telephone Service

Digital: Operational

Homes passed & miles of plant (coax & fiber) included in Savannah

General Manager: Michael Daves. Technical Operations Director: Joel Godsen. Marketing Director: Jerry Avery. Marketing Manager: Ken Torres.

City fee: 3% of gross.

Ownership: Comcast Cable Communications Inc. (MSO).

GORDON—KLiP Interactive, 455 Gees Mill Business Court, Conyers, GA 30013. Phones: 800-388-6577; 678-727-7100. Fax: 678-727-7002. E-mail: jsheehan@klipia.com. Web Site: http://www.klipia.com. Also serves Coopers, Ivey & Wilkinson County. ICA: GA0090.

TV Market Ranking: Below 100 (Coopers, GORDON, Ivey, Wilkinson County). Franchise award date: N.A. Franchise expiration date: N.A. Began: December 1, 1982.

Channel capacity: 65 (not 2-way capable). Channels available but not in use: 22.

Basic Service

Subscribers: 224.

Programming (received off-air): CW+; WGNM (IND) Macon; WGXA (FOX, MNT) Macon; WMAZ-TV (CBS) Macon; WMGT-TV (MNT, NBC) Macon; WPCH-TV (IND) Atlanta; WPGA-TV (ABC) Perry.

Programming (via satellite): ABC Family Channel; AMC; Animal Planet; Arts & Entertainment; BET Networks; Cartoon Network; CNN; Comcast Sports Net Southeast; Comedy Central; Country Music TV; Discovery Channel; Disney Channel; ESPN; ESPN 2; Fox News Channel; FX; GSN; Hallmark Channel; Home Shopping Network; Lifetime; MTV; National Geographic Channel; Nickelodeon; Spike TV; SportSouth; The Learning Channel; Trinity Broadcasting Network; truTV; Turner Network TV; TV Land; USA Network; Versus; WE tv; Weather Channel.

Fee: $44.95 installation; $39.95 monthly; $.45 converter.

Pay Service 1

Pay Units: 34.

Programming (via satellite): HBO.

Fee: $10.95 monthly.

Pay Service 2

Pay Units: 21.

Programming (via satellite): Showtime.

Fee: $10.95 monthly.

Internet Service

Operational: No.

Telephone Service

None

Miles of Plant: 55.0 (coaxial); None (fiber optic). Homes passed: 1,704.

Chief Executive Officer: Joseph A. Sheehan. General Manager East: Mark Miller. General Manager West: Vance Johnson.

City fee: 3% of gross.

Ownership: KLiP Interactive LLC (MSO).

GRAY—CommuniComm Services, PO Box 3668, 104 E Marion St, Eatonton, GA 31024. Phones: 800-554-3235; 706-485-2288. Fax: 706-485-0118. Web Site: http://www.netcommander.com. ICA: GA0196.

TV Market Ranking: Below 100 (GRAY). Franchise award date: N.A. Franchise expiration date: N.A. Began: February 1, 1981.

Channel capacity: N.A. Channels available but not in use: N.A.

Basic Service

Subscribers: N.A. Included in Eatonton

Programming (received off-air): WAGA-TV (FOX) Atlanta; WGNM (IND) Macon; WGTV (PBS) Athens; WGXA (FOX, MNT) Macon; WMAZ-TV (CBS) Macon; WMGT-TV (MNT, NBC) Macon; WPCH-TV (IND) Atlanta; WSB-TV (ABC) Atlanta; WXIA-TV (NBC) Atlanta.

Programming (via satellite): CW+; TV Guide Network; WPGA-TV (ABC) Perry.

Fee: $39.95 installation; $8.65 monthly.

Expanded Basic Service 1

Subscribers: N.A.

Programming (via satellite): ABC Family Channel; AMC; Animal Planet; Arts & Entertainment; BET Networks; Bravo; Cartoon Network; CNBC; CNN; Comcast/Charter Sports Southeast (CSS); Comedy Central; Country Music TV; C-SPAN; C-SPAN 2; Discovery Channel; Disney Channel; E! Entertainment Television; ESPN; ESPN 2; ESPNews; Food Network; Fox Movie Channel; Fox News Channel; FX; G4; Hallmark Channel; Headline News; HGTV; History Channel; Home Shopping Network; ION Television; Lifetime; MSNBC; MTV; Nick Jr.; Nickelodeon; QVC; ShopNBC; Spike TV; SportSouth; Syfy; TBS Superstation; The Learning Channel; Travel Channel; Trinity Broadcasting Network; truTV; Turner Network TV; TV Land; USA Network; VH1; WE tv; Weather Channel.

Fee: $49.99 monthly.

Digital Basic Service

Subscribers: N.A. Included in Eatonton

Programming (received off-air): WGXA (FOX, MNT) Macon; WMAZ-TV (CBS) Macon; WMGT-TV (MNT, NBC) Macon; WPGA-TV (ABC) Perry.

Programming (via satellite): Arts & Entertainment HD; BBC America; Bio; Bloomberg Television; Bravo; Cine Latino; CMT Pure Country; CNN en Espanol; Discovery en Espanol; Discovery HD Theater; Discovery Health Channel; Discovery Home Channel; Discovery Kids Channel; Discovery Military Channel; DMX Music; ESPN 2; ESPN 2 HD; ESPN Classic Sports; ESPN HD; FitTV; Fox Soccer; Fox Sports en Espanol; Fuse; Golf Channel; GSN; Halogen Network; History Channel International; ID Investigation Discovery; Independent Film Channel; Lifetime Movie Network; MTV Hits; MTV Tres; MTV2; National Geographic Channel; NickToons TV; Outdoor Channel; Sleuth; SoapNet; Speed Channel; Style Network; TeenNick; Toon Disney; Toon Disney en Espanol; Turner Classic Movies; Turner Network TV HD; TVE Internacional; Universal HD; Versus; VH1 Classic; VH1 Soul; WE tv.

Fee: $11.95 monthly.

Pay Service 1

Pay Units: 256.

Programming (via satellite): Cinemax (multiplexed); Encore; HBO (multiplexed); Starz (multiplexed).

Fee: $11.95 monthly (Cinemax), $13.95 monthly (HBO or Starz/Encore).

Digital Pay Service 1

Pay Units: N.A.

Programming (via satellite): Cinemax (multiplexed); Encore (multiplexed); Flix; HBO (multiplexed); Showtime (multiplexed); Starz (multiplexed); Starz HDTV; The Movie Channel (multiplexed).

Fee: $11.95 monthly (Cinemax), $13.95 monthly (HBO, Showtime/TMC/Flix or Starz/Encore).

Video-On-Demand: No

Pay-Per-View

iN DEMAND (delivered digitally); Playboy TV (delivered digitally); Fresh (delivered digitally); Club Jenna (delivered digitally).

Internet Service

Operational: Yes.

Broadband Service: Net Commander.

Fee: $39.95 installation; $51.95 monthly.

Telephone Service

None

Homes passed & total homes in franchised area included in Eatonton

General Manager: Brian Chase. Chief Technician: Scott Richardson. Customer Care Manager: Diane Simmons.

Ownership: James Cable LLC (MSO).

GREENE COUNTY (unincorporated areas)—Plantation Cablevision Inc., PO Box 4494, 865 Harmony Rd, Eatonton, GA 31024-4494. Phones: 877-830-5454; 706-485-7740. Fax: 706-485-2590. Web Site: http://www.plantationcable.net. Also serves Lake Oconee & Putnam County (unincorporated areas). ICA: GA0197.

TV Market Ranking: Below 100 (GREENE COUNTY (UNINCORPORATED AREAS) (portions), Lake Oconee, Putnam County (unincorporated areas) (portions)); Outside TV Markets (GREENE COUNTY (UNINCORPORATED AREAS) (portions), Putnam County (unincorporated areas) (portions)). Franchise award date: N.A. Franchise expiration date: N.A. Began: N.A.

Channel capacity: N.A. Channels available but not in use: N.A.

Basic Service

Subscribers: 1,800.

Programming (received off-air): WAGA-TV (FOX) Atlanta; WATL (MNT) Atlanta; WGCL-TV (CBS) Atlanta; WGTV (PBS) Athens; WGXA (FOX, MNT) Macon; WMAZ-TV (CBS) Macon; WMGT-TV (MNT, NBC) Macon; WPBA (PBS) Atlanta; WPCH-TV (IND) Atlanta; WSB-TV (ABC) Atlanta; WUPA (CW) Atlanta; WUVG-DT (UNV) Athens; WXIA-TV (NBC) Atlanta.

Programming (via satellite): AMC; Animal Planet; Arts & Entertainment; CNBC; CNN; Comedy Central; Country Music TV; C-SPAN; C-SPAN 2; Discovery Channel; Disney Channel; Do-It-Yourself; E! Entertainment Television; ESPN; ESPN 2; Food Network; Fox News Channel; Fox Sports Net; FX; Golf Channel; Headline News; HGTV; History Channel; ION Television; Lifetime; MSNBC; MTV; National Geographic Channel; Nickelodeon; Outdoor Channel; QVC; Spike TV; SportSouth; The Learning Channel; Travel Channel; truTV; Turner Network TV; TV Guide Network; TV Land; USA Network; VH1; Weather Channel; WHSG-TV (TBN) Monroe; WPGA-TV (ABC) Perry.
Fee: $50.00 installation; $39.95 monthly.

Digital Basic Service
Subscribers: N.A.
Programming (via satellite): BBC America; Discovery Health Channel; Discovery Home Channel; Discovery Kids Channel; Discovery Times Channel; ESPN Now; National Geographic Channel; Nick Jr.; NickToons TV; Outdoor Channel; Science Channel; Syfy; Toon Disney; Turner Classic Movies.
Fee: $15.95 monthly.

Pay Service 1
Pay Units: 630.
Programming (via satellite): HBO.
Fee: $12.95 monthly.

Digital Pay Service 1
Pay Units: N.A.
Programming (via satellite): Cinemax; Encore; HBO; Showtime; Starz; The Movie Channel.
Fee: $5.95 monthly (Encore), $10.95 monthly (Cinemax, Starz/Encore, or Showtime/TMC), $12.95 monthly (HBO).

Video-On-Demand: No

Pay-Per-View
Movies, Fee: $3.95, Addressable: Yes; special events.

Internet Service
Operational: Yes. Began: December 31, 1998.
Broadband Service: Plantation Cable.net.
Fee: $39.95 monthly; $9.95 modem lease.

Telephone Service
Analog: Not Operational
Digital: Operational

Miles of Plant: 150.0 (coaxial); None (fiber optic). Homes passed: 5,000.
Manager: Joel Hall. Chief Engineer: John H. Hall.
Ownership: Plantation Cablevision Inc.

GREENSBORO—CommuniComm Services, PO Box 3668, 104 E Marion St, Eatonton, GA 31024. Phones: 800-554-3235; 706-485-2298. Fax: 706-485-0118. Web Site: http://www.communicomm.com. Also serves Rutledge, Union Point & Woodville. ICA: GA0323.
TV Market Ranking: Below 100 (GREENSBORO, Rutledge, Union Point, Woodville).
Channel capacity: N.A. Channels available but not in use: N.A.

Basic Service
Subscribers: N.A. Included in Eatonton
Programming (received off-air): WAGA-TV (FOX) Atlanta; WATL (MNT) Atlanta; WGCL-TV (CBS) Atlanta; WGTV (PBS) Athens; WMAZ-TV (CBS) Macon; WPCH-TV (IND) Atlanta; WPGA-TV (ABC) Perry; WSB-TV (ABC) Atlanta; WUPA (CW) Atlanta; WUVG-DT (UNV) Athens; WXIA-TV (NBC) Atlanta.
Programming (via satellite): TV Guide Network.

Expanded Basic Service 1
Subscribers: N.A.
Programming (via satellite): ABC Family Channel; AMC; Animal Planet; Arts & Entertainment; BET Networks; Bravo; Cartoon Network; CNBC; CNN; Comcast/Charter Sports Southeast (CSS); Comedy Central; Country Music TV; C-SPAN; Discovery Channel; Disney Channel; E! Entertainment Television; ESPN; ESPN 2; Food Network; Fox News Channel; FX; G4; Hallmark Channel; Headline News; HGTV; History Channel; Home Shopping Network; ION Television; Lifetime; MSNBC; MTV; National Geographic Channel; Nick Jr.; Nickelodeon; QVC; Spike TV; SportSouth; Syfy; TBS Superstation; The Learning Channel; Travel Channel; Trinity Broadcasting Network; truTV; Turner Network TV; TV Land; USA Network; VH1; WE tv; Weather Channel.

Digital Basic Service
Subscribers: N.A. Included in Eatonton
Programming (via satellite): BBC America; Bio; Bloomberg Television; Bravo; Cine Latino; CMT Pure Country; CNN en Espanol; Discovery en Espanol; Discovery Health Channel; Discovery Kids Channel; Discovery Military Channel; Discovery Planet Green; DMX Music; ESPN 2; ESPN Classic Sports; ESPNews; FitTV; Fox Soccer; Fuse; G4; Golf Channel; GSN; Halogen Network; History Channel en Espanol; History Channel International; ID Investigation Discovery; Independent Film Channel; Lifetime Movie Network; MTV Hits; MTV Tres; MTV2; National Geographic Channel; NickToons TV; Outdoor Channel; Science Channel; Sleuth; Speed Channel; Style Network; TeenNick; Toon Disney en Espanol; Turner Classic Movies; TVE Internacional; Versus; VH1 Classic; VH1 Soul; WE tv.

Digital Expanded Basic Service
Subscribers: N.A.
Programming (via satellite): Encore (multiplexed); Fox Movie Channel.

Digital Pay Service 1
Pay Units: N.A.
Programming (via satellite): Cinemax (multiplexed); Flix; HBO (multiplexed); Showtime (multiplexed); Starz (multiplexed); The Movie Channel (multiplexed).

Video-On-Demand: No

Pay-Per-View
iN DEMAND (delivered digitally); Playboy TV (delivered digitally); Fresh (delivered digitally); Club Jenna (delivered digitally); Hot Choice (delivered digitally); Spice: Xcess (delivered digitally).

Internet Service
Operational: Yes.
Broadband Service: Net Commander.

Telephone Service
None

Homes passed & total homes in area included in Eatonton
General Manager: Brian Chase. Chief Technician: Scott Richardson. Customer Care Manager: Diane Simmons.
Ownership: James Cable LLC (MSO).

GREENVILLE—Charter Communications. Now served by STOCKBRIDGE, GA [GA0083]. ICA: GA0132.

GREENVILLE—Formerly served by Almega Cable. No longer in operation. ICA: GA0317.

GREENVILLE—Georgia Broadband, 118 W Main St, Manchester, GA 31816. Phone: 706-846-4568. Web Site: http://www.georgia-broadband.com. ICA: GA0321. **Note:** This system is an overbuild.
TV Market Ranking: Outside TV Markets (GREENVILLE).
Channel capacity: N.A. Channels available but not in use: N.A.

Basic Service
Subscribers: N.A.
Programming (received off-air): WAGA-TV (FOX) Atlanta; WATL (MNT) Atlanta; WGCL-TV (CBS) Atlanta; WPBA (PBS) Atlanta; WSB-TV (ABC) Atlanta; WUPA (CW) Atlanta; WXIA-TV (NBC) Atlanta.
Programming (via satellite): TBS Superstation; WGN America.
Fee: $15.95 monthly.

Expanded Basic Service 1
Subscribers: N.A.
Programming (via satellite): ABC Family Channel; AMC; Animal Planet; Arts & Entertainment; BET Networks; Cartoon Network; CNBC; CNN; Comcast Sports Net Southeast; Comcast/Charter Sports Southeast (CSS); Comedy Central; Country Music TV; C-SPAN; Discovery Channel; Disney Channel; E! Entertainment Television; ESPN; ESPN 2; Fox News Channel; FX; G4; Headline News; HGTV; History Channel; Home Shopping Network; INSP; MTV; Nickelodeon; Oxygen; Spike TV; Syfy; The Learning Channel; Travel Channel; Turner Network TV; TV Land; USA Network; VH1; Weather Channel.
Fee: $24.00 monthly.

Digital Basic Service
Subscribers: N.A.
Programming (via satellite): BBC America; Bloomberg Television; CMT Pure Country; Discovery en Espanol; Discovery Health Channel; Discovery Kids Channel; Discovery Military Channel; Discovery Planet Green; DMX Music; Do-It-Yourself; Fuse; GSN; History Channel International; ID Investigation Discovery; MTV Hits; MTV Jams; MTV Tres; MTV2; Nick Jr.; Nick Too; NickToons TV; Science Channel; Style Network; Sundance Channel; TeenNick; VH1 Classic; VH1 Soul.
Fee: $12.95 monthly.

Digital Pay Service 1
Pay Units: N.A.
Programming (via satellite): Cinemax (multiplexed); Encore (multiplexed); HBO (multiplexed); Showtime (multiplexed); Starz (multiplexed); The Movie Channel (multiplexed).

Video-On-Demand: Yes

Pay-Per-View
iN DEMAND (delivered digitally).

Internet Service
Operational: Yes.
Fee: $19.95 installation; $24.95 monthly.

Telephone Service
Digital: Operational
Fee: $29.95 monthly

Chief Executive Officer: Michelle Oneil. General Manager: Jerry Oneil.
Ownership: Georgia Broadband LLC (MSO).

GRIFFIN—Comcast Cable. Now served by ATLANTA (perimeter south), GA [GA0017]. ICA: GA0028.

GUYTON—Comcast Cable, 141 Park of Commerce Dr, Savannah, GA 31405. Phones: 912-354-2813 (Administrative office); 912-368-5800 (Customer service). Fax: 912-353-6063. Web Site: http://www.comcast.com. Also serves Effingham County (portions), Rincon & Springfield. ICA: GA0199.
TV Market Ranking: Below 100 (Effingham County (portions), GUYTON, Rincon, Springfield). Franchise award date: N.A. Franchise expiration date: N.A. Began: January 1, 1986.
Channel capacity: N.A. Channels available but not in use: N.A.

Basic Service
Subscribers: N.A. Included in Savannah
Programming (received off-air): WGSA (CW) Baxley; WJCL (ABC) Savannah; WSAV-TV (MNT, NBC) Savannah; WTGS (FOX) Hardeeville; WTOC-TV (CBS) Savannah; WVAN-TV (PBS) Savannah.
Programming (via satellite): ABC Family Channel; AMC; Animal Planet; Arts & Entertainment; BET Networks; Bravo; Cartoon Network; CNBC; CNN; Comcast Sports Net Southeast; Comcast/Charter Sports Southeast (CSS); Comedy Central; Country Music TV; C-SPAN; C-SPAN 2; Discovery Channel; Discovery Health Channel; Disney Channel; E! Entertainment Television; ESPN; ESPN 2; Eternal Word TV Network; Food Network; Fox News Channel; FX; Golf Channel; Great American Country; GSN; Hallmark Channel; Headline News; HGTV; History Channel; Home Shopping Network; INSP; ION Television; Lifetime; MSNBC; MTV; Nickelodeon; Product Information Network; QVC; Speed Channel; Spike TV; SportSouth; Syfy; TBS Superstation; The Learning Channel; Travel Channel; Trinity Broadcasting Network; truTV; Turner Network TV; TV Guide Network; TV Land; TV One; Univision; USA Network; Versus; VH1; WE tv; Weather Channel; WGN America.
Current originations: Educational Access; Government Access.
Fee: $29.98 installation; $49.99 monthly.

Digital Basic Service
Subscribers: N.A.
Programming (received off-air): WSAV-TV (MNT, NBC) Savannah; WTGS (FOX) Hardeeville; WTOC-TV (CBS) Savannah.
Programming (via satellite): BBC America; Bio; Black Family Channel; Cooking Channel; C-SPAN 3; Discovery Digital Networks; Discovery HD Theater; DMX Music; Do-It-Yourself; Encore; ESPN; ESPNews; Flix; Fresh; G4; GAS; History Channel International; INHD; Jewelry Television; Lifetime Movie Network; Local Cable Weather; LOGO; MoviePlex; MTV Networks Digital Suite; National Geographic Channel; NFL Network; Nick Jr.; Nick Too; NickToons TV; Outdoor Channel; PBS Kids Sprout; Playboy TV; Pleasure; Shorteez; SoapNet; Sundance Channel; The Word Network; Toon Disney; Turner Classic Movies; Turner Network TV HD; Weatherscan.
Fee: $11.95 monthly.

Digital Pay Service 1
Pay Units: 315.
Programming (via satellite): Cinemax (multiplexed); Cinemax HD; HBO (multiplexed); HBO HD; Showtime (multiplexed); Showtime HD; Starz (multiplexed); Starz HDTV; The Movie Channel (multiplexed).
Fee: $5.50 monthly (TMC), $10.00 monthly (Starz), $14.95 monthly (HBO, Cinemax or Showtime).

Video-On-Demand: Yes

Pay-Per-View
ESPN (delivered digitally).

Internet Service
Operational: Yes.
Broadband Service: Comcast High Speed Internet.
Fee: $42.95 monthly.

Telephone Service
Digital: Operational

Homes passed & miles of plant (coax & fiber) included in Savannah

General Manager: Michael Daves. Technical Operations Director: Joel Godsen. Marketing Director: Jerry Avery. Marketing Manager: Ken Torres.
Ownership: Comcast Cable Communications Inc.

HADDOCK—KLiP Interactive, 455 Gees Mill Business Court, Conyers, GA 30013. Phone: 678-727-7100. Fax: 678-727-7002. E-mail: jsheehan@klipia.com. Web Site: http://www.klipia.com. Also serves Jones County (portions). ICA: GA0160.
TV Market Ranking: Below 100 (HADDOCK, Jones County (portions)). Franchise award date: N.A. Franchise expiration date: N.A. Began: March 1, 1985.
Channel capacity: 45 (not 2-way capable). Channels available but not in use: 13.
Basic Service
Subscribers: 56.
Programming (received off-air): CW+; WGCL-TV (CBS) Atlanta; WGNM (IND) Macon; WGXA (FOX, MNT) Macon; WMAZ-TV (CBS) Macon; WMGT-TV (MNT, NBC) Macon; WPCH-TV (IND) Atlanta; WPGA-TV (ABC) Perry; WSB-TV (ABC) Atlanta; WXIA-TV (NBC) Atlanta.
Programming (via satellite): ABC Family Channel; Animal Planet; Arts & Entertainment; BET Networks; CNN; Comcast Sports Net Southeast; Country Music TV; Discovery Channel; ESPN; ESPN 2; Fox News Channel; Home Shopping Network; Lifetime; MTV; Nickelodeon; Spike TV; The Learning Channel; Travel Channel; TV Land; USA Network; Weather Channel; WGN America.
Fee: $29.95 installation; $33.01 monthly.
Pay Service 1
Pay Units: 13.
Programming (via satellite): Cinemax; HBO.
Fee: $10.95 monthly (each).
Internet Service
Operational: No.
Telephone Service
None
Miles of Plant: 20.0 (coaxial); None (fiber optic). Homes passed: 190.
Chief Executive Officer: Joseph A. Sheehan. General Manager East: Mark Miller. General Manager West: Vance Johnson.
Ownership: KLiP Interactive LLC (MSO).

HARRISON—Formerly served by Walker Cablevision. No longer in operation. ICA: GA0169.

HARTWELL—Comcast Cablevision of the South. Now served by ELBERTON, GA [GA0192]. ICA: GA0200.

HARTWELL (unincorporated areas)—Hart Communications, PO Box 388, 196 N Forest Ave, Hartwell, GA 30643. Phones: 800-276-3925; 706-376-4701. Fax: 706-376-2009. Web Site: http://www.hartcabletv.com. Also serves Avalon, Franklin County (northern portion), Martin & Stephens County (southern portion). ICA: GA0293.
TV Market Ranking: 46 (Avalon, HARTWELL (UNINCORPORATED AREAS), Martin, Stephens County (southern portion) (portions)); Below 100 (Franklin County (northern portion), Stephens County (southern portion) (portions)). Franchise award date: N.A. Franchise expiration date: N.A. Began: N.A.
Channel capacity: N.A. Channels available but not in use: N.A.
Basic Service
Subscribers: 804.
Programming (received off-air): WAGA-TV (FOX) Atlanta; WGGS-TV (IND) Greenville; WGTV (PBS) Athens; WHNS (FOX) Greenville; WLOS (ABC) Asheville; WMYA-TV (MNT) Anderson; WNEG-TV (CBS) Toccoa; WNTV (PBS) Greenville; WSB-TV (ABC) Atlanta; WSPA-TV (CBS) Spartanburg; WXIA-TV (NBC) Atlanta; WYCW (CW) Asheville; WYFF (NBC) Greenville.
Programming (via satellite): ABC Family Channel; AMC; Animal Planet; Arts & Entertainment; BET Networks; Cartoon Network; CNBC; CNN; Comcast Sports Net Southeast; Country Music TV; C-SPAN; C-SPAN 2; Discovery Channel; Disney Channel; E! Entertainment Television; ESPN; ESPN 2; Food Network; Fox News Channel; FX; Golf Channel; GSN; HGTV; History Channel; Lifetime; MTV; Nickelodeon; Outdoor Channel; QVC; Speed Channel; Spike TV; Syfy; TBS Superstation; The Learning Channel; Travel Channel; Turner Classic Movies; Turner Network TV; Turner South; TV Land; USA Network; VH1; Weather Channel; WGN America.
Current originations: Public Access.
Fee: $30.00 installation; $29.95 monthly; $2.50 converter; $10.00 additional installation.
Digital Basic Service
Subscribers: N.A.
Programming (via satellite): BBC America; Bio; Bloomberg Television; Bravo; Discovery Digital Networks; Encore (multiplexed); ESPN Classic Sports; ESPNews; Fox Movie Channel; Fox Soccer; G4; GAS; Halogen Network; History Channel International; Independent Film Channel; Lifetime Movie Network; Lime; MTV Networks Digital Suite; Nick Jr.; NickToons TV; Sleuth; Starz (multiplexed); Style Network; Toon Disney; Trinity Broadcasting Network; Versus.
Fee: $20.00 monthly.
Pay Service 1
Pay Units: N.A.
Programming (via satellite): HBO; Showtime.
Fee: $12.95 monthly (each).
Digital Pay Service 1
Pay Units: N.A.
Programming (via satellite): Cinemax (multiplexed); Flix; HBO (multiplexed); Showtime (multiplexed); The Movie Channel (multiplexed).
Fee: $13.00 monthly (Showtime, TMC & Flix), $15.00 monthly (HBO & Cinemax).
Internet Service
Operational: Yes, DSL.
Fee: $49.95 monthly.
Telephone Service
None
President: Michael C. McInerney. Vice President, Network Operations: J.R. Anderson. Customer Service Manager: Debbie Anderson.
Ownership: Hart Cable.

HAWKINSVILLE—CommuniComm Services. Now served by PERRY, GA [GA0229]. ICA: GA0062.

HAYNEVILLE—ComSouth Telesys Inc. Now served by PERRY, GA [GA0229]. ICA: GA0281.

HAZLEHURST—Mediacom, 509 Flint Ave, Albany, GA 31701. Phones: 229-244-3852 (Valdosta Regional office); 229-888-0242. Fax: 229-436-4819. Web Site: http://www.mediacomcable.com. Also serves Jeff Davis County (portions) & Lumber City. ICA: GA0073.
TV Market Ranking: Below 100 (HAZLEHURST, Jeff Davis County (portions), Lumber City). Franchise award date: N.A. Franchise expiration date: N.A. Began: January 1, 1965.
Channel capacity: N.A. Channels available but not in use: N.A.
Basic Service
Subscribers: 2,670.
Programming (received off-air): WALB (NBC) Albany; WGSA (CW) Baxley; WJCL (ABC) Savannah; WSAV-TV (MNT, NBC) Savannah; WTGS (FOX) Hardeeville; WTOC-TV (CBS) Savannah; WXGA-TV (PBS) Waycross.
Programming (via microwave): WSB-TV (ABC) Atlanta; WXIA-TV (NBC) Atlanta.
Programming (via satellite): ABC Family Channel; Arts & Entertainment; BET Networks; CNBC; CNN; C-SPAN; Discovery Channel; Disney Channel; Headline News; MTV; Nickelodeon; QVC; TBS Superstation; Turner Network TV; Weather Channel.
Fee: $35.00 installation; $21.27 monthly; $.11 converter; $10.00 additional installation.
Digital Basic Service
Subscribers: N.A.
Programming (via satellite): BBC America; Bio; Bloomberg Television; Canales N; Discovery Digital Networks; Food Network; Fox Movie Channel; Fox Sports World; Fuse; G4; GAS; Golf Channel; GSN; Halogen Network; HGTV; History Channel International; Independent Film Channel; Lifetime Movie Network; Lime; MTV Networks Digital Suite; Music Choice; National Geographic Channel; Nick Jr.; Outdoor Channel; Ovation; Speed Channel; Style Network; Toon Disney; Travel Channel; Turner Classic Movies; Versus.
Digital Pay Service 1
Pay Units: 188.
Programming (via satellite): Cinemax (multiplexed); Encore (multiplexed); Flix; HBO (multiplexed); Showtime (multiplexed); Starz (multiplexed); Sundance Channel; The Movie Channel (multiplexed).
Fee: $20.00 installation; $11.95 monthly (Cinemax or HBO), $12.50 monthly (Showtime).
Video-On-Demand: Yes
Pay-Per-View
TVN Entertainment (delivered digitally); ETC (delivered digitally); Pleasure; ESPN Now (delivered digitally); Sports PPV (delivered digitally).
Internet Service
Operational: Yes. Began: March 14, 2003.
Broadband Service: Mediacom High Speed Internet.
Fee: $42.95 monthly; $3.00 modem lease.
Telephone Service
Digital: Operational
Miles of Plant: 88.0 (coaxial); None (fiber optic). Homes passed: 3,584. Total homes in franchised area: 5,563. Miles of plant (coax & fiber) included in Fitzgerald
Regional Vice President: Sue Misiunas. General Manager: Gary Crosby. Regional Technical Operations Manager: Gary McDougall. Regional Marketing Director: Melanie Hannasch. Marketing Manager: Daryl Channey.
City fee: 3% of gross.
Ownership: Mediacom LLC (MSO).

HELEN—Windstream, 2000 Communications Blvd, Baldwin, GA 30511. Phones: 800-345-3874; 877-807-9463. Fax: 706-896-5170. Web Site: http://www.windstreamcable.com. Also serves White County (portions). ICA: GA0201.
TV Market Ranking: Below 100 (HELEN, White County (portions)). Franchise award date: N.A. Franchise expiration date: N.A. Began: December 1, 1980.
Channel capacity: 62 (not 2-way capable). Channels available but not in use: 7.
Basic Service
Subscribers: 1,197.
Programming (received off-air): WAGA-TV (FOX) Atlanta; WATL (MNT) Atlanta; WGCL-TV (CBS) Atlanta; WGTV (PBS) Athens; WHSG-TV (TBN) Monroe; WNEG-TV (CBS) Toccoa; WPCH-TV (IND) Atlanta; WPXA-TV (ION) Rome; WSB-TV (ABC) Atlanta; WUPA (CW) Atlanta; WUVG-DT (UNV) Athens; WXIA-TV (NBC) Atlanta.
Programming (via satellite): Boomerang; C-SPAN; QVC; TV Guide Network; TV Land; VH1; WGN America.
Current originations: Government Access.
Fee: $14.51 monthly.
Expanded Basic Service 1
Subscribers: 1,020.
Programming (via satellite): ABC Family Channel; AMC; Animal Planet; Arts & Entertainment; Bravo; CNBC; CNN; Comcast Sports Net Southeast; Comedy Central; Country Music TV; Discovery Channel; ESPN; ESPN 2; ESPN Classic Sports; Food Network; Fox News Channel; FX; Headline News; HGTV; History Channel; Lifetime; MTV; National Geographic Channel; Nickelodeon; Speed Channel; Spike TV; SportSouth; The Learning Channel; Turner Network TV; USA Network; Weather Channel.
Fee: $30.74 monthly.
Digital Basic Service
Subscribers: 81.
Programming (via satellite): BBC America; Bio; CBS College Sports Network; Cooking Channel; Discovery Digital Networks; DMX Music; Do-It-Yourself; ESPNews; Eternal Word TV Network; FamilyNet; Fox College Sports Atlantic; Fox College Sports Central; Fox College Sports Pacific; Fox Movie Channel; Fox Sports World; Fuel TV; Fuse; GAS; Golf Channel; Gospel Music TV; GSN; Hallmark Channel; Halogen Network; History Channel International; Independent Film Channel; Lifetime Movie Network; MTV2; Nick Jr.; NickToons TV; Outdoor Channel; Praise Television; Science Television; Sleuth; Style Network; The Sportsman Channel; Toon Disney; Turner Classic Movies; Versus; VH1 Classic; VH1 Country; WE tv.
Fee: $10.99 monthly.

Digital Pay Service 1
Pay Units: N.A.
Programming (via satellite): Cinemax (multiplexed); Encore (multiplexed); HBO (multiplexed); Showtime (multiplexed); Starz (multiplexed); The Movie Channel (multiplexed).
Fee: $10.95 monthly (Starz & Encore) $12.99 monthly (Showtime & TMC), $24.95 monthly (HBO & Cinemax).
Video-On-Demand: No
Pay-Per-View
iN DEMAND (delivered digitally).
Internet Service
Operational: No, Both DSL & dial-up.
Telephone Service
None
Miles of Plant: 20.0 (coaxial); None (fiber optic).
President & Chief Executive Officer: Jeff Gardner. Executive Vice President & Chief Financial Officer: Brent Whittington. Executive Vice President, Network Operations: Grant Raney. Executive Vice President & Chief Marketing Officer: Ric Crane. Senior Vice President, Network Services: Frank Schueneman. Senior Vice President, Information Technology: Cindy Nash. Senior Vice President, Consumer Sales: Gregg Richey. Senior Vice President, Customer Services: Joe Marano.
Ownership: Windstream Communications Inc. (MSO).

HIAWASSEE—Windstream, 2000 Communications Blvd, Baldwin, GA 30511. Phones: 800-345-3874; 877-807-9463. Fax: 706-896-5170. Web Site: http://www.windstreamcable.com. Also serves Towns County & Young Harris, GA; Clay County & Hayesville, NC. ICA: GA0202.
TV Market Ranking: Below 100 (Towns County (portions)); Outside TV Markets (Clay County, Hayesville, HIAWASSEE, Towns County (portions), Young Harris). Franchise award date: N.A. Franchise expiration date: N.A. Began: October 30, 1981.
Channel capacity: 75 (not 2-way capable). Channels available but not in use: 12.
Basic Service
Subscribers: 6,852.
Programming (received off-air): WAGA-TV (FOX) Atlanta; WATL (MNT) Atlanta; WGCL-TV (CBS) Atlanta; WGTV (PBS) Athens; WHSG-TV (TBN) Monroe; WNEG-TV (CBS) Toccoa; WPXA-TV (ION) Rome; WRCB (NBC) Chattanooga; WSB-TV (ABC) Atlanta; WUPA (CW) Atlanta; WUVG-DT (UNV) Athens; WXIA-TV (NBC) Atlanta.
Programming (via satellite): C-SPAN; Home Shopping Network; TBS Superstation; WGN America.
Fee: $12.58 monthly.
Expanded Basic Service 1
Subscribers: 6,317.
Programming (via satellite): ABC Family Channel; AMC; Animal Planet; Arts & Entertainment; Boomerang; Bravo; Cartoon Network; CNBC; CNN; Comcast Sports Net Southeast; Comedy Central; Country Music TV; Discovery Channel; ESPN; ESPN 2; ESPN Classic Sports; Food Network; Fox News Channel; FX; Golf Channel; Headline News; HGTV; History Channel; Lifetime; MSNBC; MTV; Nickelodeon; Outdoor Channel; QVC; Speed Channel; Spike TV; SportSouth; The Learning Channel; Travel Channel; Turner Classic Movies; Turner Network TV; TV Guide Network; TV Land; USA Network; VH1; Weather Channel.
Fee: $32.67 monthly.
Digital Basic Service
Subscribers: 481.
Programming (via satellite): BBC America; Bio; CBS College Sports Network; Cooking Channel; Discovery Digital Networks; DMX Music; Do-It-Yourself; ESPNews; Eternal Word TV Network; FamilyNet; Fox College Sports Atlantic; Fox College Sports Central; Fox College Sports Pacific; Fox Movie Channel; Fox Sports World; Fuel TV; Fuse; GAS; Gospel Music TV; GSN; Hallmark Channel; Halogen Network; History Channel International; Independent Film Channel; Lifetime Movie Network; MTV2; National Geographic Channel; Nick Jr.; NickToons TV; Praise Television; Science Television; Sleuth; Style Network; The Sportsman Channel; Versus; VH1 Classic; VH1 Country; WE tv.
Fee: $12.92 monthly.
Digital Pay Service 1
Pay Units: N.A.
Programming (via satellite): Cinemax (multiplexed); Encore (multiplexed); HBO (multiplexed); Showtime (multiplexed); Starz (multiplexed); The Movie Channel (multiplexed).
Fee: $10.95 monthly (Starz & Encore), $12.99 monthly (Showtime & TMC), $24.95 monthly (HBO & Cinemax).
Video-On-Demand: No
Pay-Per-View
iN DEMAND (delivered digitally).
Internet Service
Operational: No, Both DSL & dial-up.
Telephone Service
None
Miles of Plant: 210.0 (coaxial); None (fiber optic).
President & Chief Executive Officer: Jeff Gardner. Executive Vice President & Chief Financial Officer: Brent Whittington. Executive Vice President, Network Operations: Grant Raney. Executive Vice President & Chief Marketing Officer: Ric Crane. Senior Vice President, Network Services: Frank Schueneman. Senior Vice President, Information Technology: Cindy Nash. Senior Vice President, Consumer Sales: Gregg Richey. Senior Vice President, Customer Services: Joe Marano.
Ownership: Windstream Communications Inc. (MSO).

HINESVILLE—Comcast Cable, 141 Park of Commerce Dr, Savannah, GA 31405. Phone: 912-356-3113. Web Site: http://www.comcast.com. Also serves Allenhurst, Bryan County (eastern portion), Fleming, Flemington, Fort Stewart, Gardi, Gumbranch, Jesup, Lake George, Liberty County (portions), Long County (eastern portion), Ludowici, Odum, Riceboro, Richmond Hill, Screven, Walthourville, Wayne County (unincorporated areas) & Woodland Lakes Resort. ICA: GA0024.
TV Market Ranking: Below 100 (Allenhurst, Bryan County (eastern portion), Fleming, Flemington, Fort Stewart, Gardi, Gumbranch, HINESVILLE, Jesup, Lake George, Liberty County (portions), Long County (eastern portion) (portions), Odum, Riceboro, Richmond Hill, Screven, Walthourville, Wayne County (unincorporated areas), Woodland Lakes Resort); Outside TV Markets (Liberty County (portions), Long County (eastern portion) (portions), Ludowici). Franchise award date: N.A. Franchise expiration date: N.A. Began: March 18, 1972.
Channel capacity: 120 (operating 2-way). Channels available but not in use: 44.
Basic Service
Subscribers: N.A. Included in Savannah
Programming (received off-air): WGSA (CW) Baxley; WJCL (ABC) Savannah; WSAV-TV (MNT, NBC) Savannah; WTGS (FOX) Hardeeville; WTOC-TV (CBS) Savannah; WVAN-TV (PBS) Savannah.
Programming (via satellite): C-SPAN; C-SPAN 2; E! Entertainment Television; Home Shopping Network; QVC; TBS Superstation; TV Guide Network; Weather Channel.
Current originations: Government Access.
Fee: $47.99 installation; $14.95 monthly.
Expanded Basic Service 1
Subscribers: 15,549.
Programming (via satellite): ABC Family Channel; AMC; Animal Planet; Arts & Entertainment; BET Networks; Bravo; Cartoon Network; CNBC; CNN; Comcast Sports Net Southeast; Comcast/Charter Sports Southeast (CSS); Comedy Central; Country Music TV; Discovery Channel; Discovery Health Channel; Disney Channel; ESPN; ESPN 2; Eternal Word TV Network; Food Network; Fox News Channel; FX; Golf Channel; Great American Country; GSN; Hallmark Channel; Headline News; HGTV; History Channel; INSP; ION Television; Lifetime; MTV; Nickelodeon; Product Information Network; Speed Channel; Spike TV; SportSouth; Syfy; The Learning Channel; Travel Channel; truTV; Turner Network TV; TV Land; Univision; USA Network; Versus; VH1; WE tv.
Fee: $35.04 monthly.
Digital Basic Service
Subscribers: N.A.
Programming (via satellite): BBC America; Black Family Channel; Canales N; Cooking Channel; C-SPAN 3; Discovery Digital Networks; Do-It-Yourself; ESPNews; Flix; G4; GAS; MTV Networks Digital Suite; Music Choice; National Geographic Channel; Nick Jr.; Nick Too; Outdoor Channel; SoapNet; Sundance Channel; The Word Network; Toon Disney; WAM! America's Kidz Network; Weatherscan.
Fee: $11.95 monthly.
Digital Pay Service 1
Pay Units: 1,248.
Programming (via satellite): Cinemax (multiplexed).
Fee: $15.54 monthly.
Digital Pay Service 2
Pay Units: 558.
Programming (via satellite): Starz (multiplexed).
Fee: $15.54 monthly.
Digital Pay Service 3
Pay Units: 5,044.
Programming (via satellite): HBO (multiplexed).
Fee: $15.54 monthly.
Digital Pay Service 4
Pay Units: 1,360.
Programming (via satellite): Showtime (multiplexed).
Fee: $15.54 monthly.
Digital Pay Service 5
Pay Units: 2,791.
Programming (via satellite): Encore (multiplexed).
Fee: $15.54 monthly.
Digital Pay Service 6
Pay Units: 676.
Programming (via satellite): The Movie Channel (multiplexed).
Fee: $15.54 monthly.
Video-On-Demand: Yes
Pay-Per-View
Addressable homes: 3,498.
Fresh (delivered digitally), Addressable: Yes; iN DEMAND (delivered digitally); Playboy TV (delivered digitally); Shorteez (delivered digitally); Pleasure (delivered digitally); ESPN (delivered digitally).
Internet Service
Operational: Yes.
Broadband Service: Comcast High Speed Internet.
Fee: $42.95 monthly.
Telephone Service
Digital: Operational
Homes passed & miles of plant (coax & fiber) included in Savannah
General Manager: Michael Daves. Technical Operations Director: Joel Godson. Marketing Director: Jerry Avery. Marketing Manager: Ken Torres.
Ownership: Comcast Cable Communications Inc. (MSO).

HOBOKEN—Worth Cable, PO Box 2056, 3 Commissioner Dr, Darien, GA 31305-2056. Phones: 912-437-3422; 866-206-0656. Fax: 912-437-2065. Also serves Brantley County (unincorporated areas). ICA: GA0203.
TV Market Ranking: Below 100 (Brantley County (unincorporated areas) (portions)); Outside TV Markets (Brantley County (unincorporated areas) (portions), HOBOKEN). Franchise award date: N.A. Franchise expiration date: N.A. Began: N.A.
Channel capacity: 45 (not 2-way capable). Channels available but not in use: 13.
Basic Service
Subscribers: 107.
Programming (received off-air): WAWS (FOX, MNT) Jacksonville; WCWJ (CW) Jacksonville; WJCL (ABC) Savannah; WJXT (IND) Jacksonville; WPXC-TV (ION) Brunswick; WTLV (NBC) Jacksonville; WTOC-TV (CBS) Savannah; WXGA-TV (PBS) Waycross.
Programming (via satellite): ABC Family Channel; AMC; Animal Planet; Arts & Entertainment; BET Networks; CNN; Comcast Sports Net Southeast; Country Music TV; Disney Channel; ESPN; Fox News Channel; Home Shopping Network; Nickelodeon; Spike TV; TBS Superstation; The Learning Channel; Travel Channel; Trinity Broadcasting Network; Turner Network TV; TV Land; USA Network; Weather Channel; WGN America.
Fee: $29.95 installation; $30.45 monthly.
Pay Service 1
Pay Units: 48.
Programming (via satellite): HBO.
Fee: $10.95 monthly.
Video-On-Demand: No
Internet Service
Operational: No.
Telephone Service
None
Miles of Plant: 12.0 (coaxial); None (fiber optic). Homes passed: 300.
Manager: Dennis B. Wortham.
Ownership: Worth Cable Services (MSO).

HOMERVILLE—Comcast Cable, 471 South Church St, Ste C, Homerville, GA 31634. Phones: 850-574-4016 (Tallahassee office); 912-487-2224. Fax: 850-574-4030. E-mail: claire_evans@cable.comcast.com. Web Site: http://www.comcast.com. Also serves Argyle (portions) & Clinch County (portions). ICA: GA0204.
TV Market Ranking: Below 100 (Clinch County (portions) (portions), HOMERVILLE); Outside TV Markets (Argyle (portions), Clinch County (portions) (portions)). Franchise award date: August 1, 1968. Franchise ex-

piration date: N.A. Began: November 1, 1968.

Channel capacity: 67 (operating 2-way). Channels available but not in use: None.

Basic Service

Subscribers: N.A. Included in Tallahassee, FL

Programming (received off-air): WALB (NBC) Albany; WBXT-CA Tallahassee; WCTV (CBS, MNT) Thomasville; WFXL (FOX) Albany; WJXT (IND) Jacksonville; WTLV (NBC) Jacksonville; WTXL-TV (ABC) Tallahassee; WXGA-TV (PBS) Waycross.

Programming (via satellite): Disney Channel; ESPN; Great American Country; QVC; WGN America.

Fee: $39.88 installation; $7.25 monthly.

Expanded Basic Service 1

Subscribers: 1,201.

Programming (via satellite): ABC Family Channel; AMC; Animal Planet; Arts & Entertainment; BET Networks; Cartoon Network; CNBC; CNN; Comcast Sports Net Southeast; Comcast/Charter Sports Southeast (CSS); Comedy Central; Country Music TV; C-SPAN; C-SPAN 2; Discovery Channel; Discovery Health Channel; E! Entertainment Television; ESPN 2; Food Network; Fox News Channel; FX; Golf Channel; GSN; Hallmark Channel; Headline News; HGTV; History Channel; Home Shopping Network; INSP; ION Television; Lifetime; MTV; Nickelodeon; Speed Channel; Spike TV; SportSouth; Style Network; Syfy; TBS Superstation; The Learning Channel; Travel Channel; Trinity Broadcasting Network; truTV; Turner Classic Movies; Turner Network TV; TV Guide Network; TV Land; TV One; USA Network; Versus; VH1; Weather Channel.

Fee: $37.60 monthly.

Digital Basic Service

Subscribers: N.A.

Programming (via satellite): CMT Pure Country; Discovery Kids Channel; Discovery Military Channel; Discovery Planet Green; Encore (multiplexed); Flix; Gospel Music Channel; ID Investigation Discovery; Lifetime Movie Network; MoviePlex; MTV Tres; MTV2; Music Choice; Nick Jr.; Nick Too; PBS Kids Sprout; Retro Television Network; Science Channel; TeenNick; VH1 Classic; VH1 Soul.

Fee: $12.15 monthly.

Pay Service 1

Pay Units: 276.

Programming (via satellite): HBO; Showtime.

Fee: $15.00 installation; $9.95 monthly (Showtime), $11.95 monthly (HBO).

Digital Pay Service 1

Pay Units: 344.

Programming (via satellite): Cinemax (multiplexed); HBO (multiplexed); Showtime (multiplexed); Starz (multiplexed); The Movie Channel (multiplexed).

Fee: $9.95 monthly (each).

Video-On-Demand: No

Pay-Per-View

Addressable homes: 344.

iN DEMAND (delivered digitally); Hot Choice (delivered digitally); Playboy TV (delivered digitally); Fresh (delivered digitally); Shorteez (delivered digitally).

Internet Service

Operational: Yes.

Telephone Service

Digital: Operational

Miles of plant (coax) & homes passed included in Tallahassee, FL

General Manager: K. C. McWilliams. Technical Operations Director: Terry Pullen. Area Technical Manager: Andy Musgrove. Marketing Director: Claire Evans. System Coordinator: Carla Musgrove.

City fee: 3% of gross.

Ownership: Comcast Cable Communications Inc. (MSO).

IRON CITY—KLiP Interactive, 455 Gees Mill Business Court, Conyers, GA 30013. Phone: 678-727-7100. Fax: 678-727-7002. E-mail: jsheehan@klipia.com. Web Site: http://www.klipia.com. Also serves Brinson, Decatur County (portions), Early County (portions) & Seminole County (portions). ICA: GA0137.

TV Market Ranking: Below 100 (Brinson, Decatur County (portions), Early County (portions), IRON CITY, Seminole County (portions)). Franchise award date: N.A. Franchise expiration date: N.A. Began: September 1, 1990.

Channel capacity: 65 (not 2-way capable). Channels available but not in use: 31.

Basic Service

Subscribers: 74.

Programming (received off-air): WABW-TV (PBS) Pelham; WALB (NBC) Albany; WCTV (CBS, MNT) Thomasville; WDHN (ABC) Dothan; WPCH-TV (IND) Atlanta; WTLH (CW, FOX) Bainbridge; WTVY (CBS, CW, MNT) Dothan; WTWC-TV (NBC) Tallahassee; WTXL-TV (ABC) Tallahassee.

Programming (via satellite): ABC Family Channel; Arts & Entertainment; BET Networks; CNN; Comcast Sports Net Southeast; Comedy Central; Country Music TV; C-SPAN; Discovery Channel; Disney Channel; E! Entertainment Television; ESPN; ESPN 2; Fox News Channel; FX; Headline News; QVC; Spike TV; The Learning Channel; Trinity Broadcasting Network; Turner Network TV; USA Network; Weather Channel; WGN America.

Fee: $29.95 installation; $34.13 monthly.

Pay Service 1

Pay Units: 14.

Programming (via satellite): HBO.

Fee: $25.00 installation; $10.95 monthly.

Internet Service

Operational: No.

Telephone Service

None

Miles of Plant: 25.0 (coaxial); None (fiber optic). Homes passed: 435.

Chief Executive Officer: Joseph A. Sheehan. General Manager East: Mark Miller. General Manager West: Vance Johnson.

Ownership: KLiP Interactive LLC (MSO).

IRWINTON—KLiP Interactive, 455 Gees Mill Business Court, Conyers, GA 30013. Phone: 678-727-7100. Fax: 678-727-7002. E-mail: jsheehan@klipia.com. Web Site: http://www.klipia.com. Also serves McIntyre & Wilkinson County (portions). ICA: GA0300.

TV Market Ranking: Below 100 (IRWINTON, McIntyre, Wilkinson County (portions)). Franchise award date: N.A. Franchise expiration date: N.A. Began: N.A.

Channel capacity: 45 (not 2-way capable). Channels available but not in use: 12.

Basic Service

Subscribers: 31.

Programming (received off-air): CW+; WGNM (IND) Macon; WGXA (FOX, MNT) Macon; WMAZ-TV (CBS) Macon; WMGT-TV (MNT, NBC) Macon; WPCH-TV (IND) Atlanta; WPGA-TV (ABC) Perry.

Programming (via satellite): ABC Family Channel; AMC; Animal Planet; BET Networks; Bravo; CNN; Comcast Sports Net Southeast; Comedy Central; Country Music TV; Discovery Channel; Disney Channel; ESPN; ESPN 2; Fox News Channel; FX; GSN; Home Shopping Network; MTV; Nickelodeon; Spike TV; The Learning Channel; Trinity Broadcasting Network; Turner Network TV; TV Land; USA Network; Weather Channel.

Fee: $29.95 installation; $38.55 monthly.

Pay Service 1

Pay Units: 4.

Programming (via satellite): HBO.

Fee: $10.95 monthly.

Pay Service 2

Pay Units: 2.

Programming (via satellite): Showtime.

Fee: $10.95 monthly.

Internet Service

Operational: No.

Telephone Service

None

Miles of Plant: 45.0 (coaxial); None (fiber optic). Homes passed: 600.

Chief Executive Officer: Joseph A. Sheehan. General Manager East: Mark Miller. General Manager West: Vance Johnson.

Ownership: KLiP Interactive LLC (MSO).

JACKSON COUNTY—Now served by ATLANTA (perimeter north), GA [GA0033]. ICA: GA0112.

JEFFERSON—Windstream, 2000 Communications Blvd, Baldwin, GA 30511. Phones: 800-345-3874; 706-335-6640. Fax: 706-896-5170. Web Site: http://www.windstreamcable.com. Also serves Arcade, Banks County (portions) & Jackson County (southern portion). ICA: GA0206.

TV Market Ranking: Below 100 (Arcade, Banks County (portions), Jackson County (southern portion), JEFFERSON). Franchise award date: February 16, 1983. Franchise expiration date: N.A. Began: August 1, 1981.

Channel capacity: 62 (not 2-way capable). Channels available but not in use: 2.

Basic Service

Subscribers: 901.

Programming (received off-air): WAGA-TV (FOX) Atlanta; WATL (MNT) Atlanta; WGCL-TV (CBS) Atlanta; WGTV (PBS) Athens; WHSG-TV (TBN) Monroe; WNEG-TV (CBS) Toccoa; WPBA (PBS) Atlanta; WPCH-TV (IND) Atlanta; WPXA-TV (ION) Rome; WSB-TV (ABC) Atlanta; WUPA (CW) Atlanta; WUVG-DT (UNV) Athens; WXIA-TV (NBC) Atlanta; WYFF (NBC) Greenville.

Programming (via satellite): C-SPAN; TV Guide Network; WGN America.

Fee: $16.55 monthly.

Expanded Basic Service 1

Subscribers: 737.

Programming (via satellite): ABC Family Channel; AMC; Arts & Entertainment; BET Networks; Boomerang; Bravo; Cartoon Network; CNBC; CNN; Comcast Sports Net Southeast; Comedy Central; Country Music TV; Discovery Channel; ESPN; ESPN 2; Fox News Channel; G4; Golf Channel; Headline News; HGTV; History Channel; Lifetime; MSNBC; MTV; National Geographic Channel; Nickelodeon; QVC; Speed Channel; Spike TV; SportSouth; The Learning Channel; Turner Classic Movies; Turner Network TV; TV Land; USA Network; VH1; Weather Channel.

Fee: $28.70 monthly.

Digital Basic Service

Subscribers: N.A.

Programming (via satellite): BBC America; Bio; Canales N; CBS College Sports Network; Cooking Channel; Discovery Digital Networks; DMX Music; Do-It-Yourself; ESPN Classic Sports; ESPNews; Eternal Word TV Network; FamilyNet; Fox College Sports Atlantic; Fox College Sports Central; Fox College Sports Pacific; Fox Movie Channel; Fox Sports World; Fuel TV; Fuse; GAS; Gospel Music TV; GSN; Hallmark Channel; Halogen Network; History Channel International; Independent Film Channel; Lifetime Movie Network; MTV2; Nick Jr.; NickToons TV; Outdoor Channel; Praise Television; Science Television; Sleuth; Style Network; The Sportsman Channel; VH1 Classic; VH1 Country; WE tv.

Fee: $8.95 monthly.

Digital Pay Service 1

Pay Units: N.A.

Programming (via satellite): Cinemax (multiplexed); Encore (multiplexed); HBO (multiplexed); Showtime (multiplexed); Starz (multiplexed); The Movie Channel (multiplexed).

Fee: $10.95 monthly (Starz/Encore), $12.99 monthly (Cinemax or Showtime/TMC), $14.95 monthly (HBO).

Video-On-Demand: No

Pay-Per-View

iN DEMAND (delivered digitally).

Internet Service

Operational: No, Both DSL & dial-up.

Telephone Service

None

Miles of Plant: 84.0 (coaxial); None (fiber optic). Homes passed: 4,396.

President & Chief Executive Officer: Jeff Gardner. Executive Vice President & Chief Financial Officer: Brent Whittington. Executive Vice President, Network Operations: Grant Raney. Executive Vice President & Chief Marketing Officer: Ric Crane. Senior Vice President, Network Services: Frank Schueneman. Senior Vice President, Consumer Sales: Gregg Richey. Senior Vice President, Information Technology: Cindy Nash. Senior Vice President, Customer Services: Joe Marano.

Ownership: Windstream Communications Inc. (MSO).

JEFFERSONVILLE—KLiP Interactive, 455 Gees Mill Business Court, Conyers, GA 30013. Phone: 678-727-7100. Fax: 678-727-7002. E-mail: jsheehan@klipia.com. Web Site: http://www.klipia.com. Also serves Twiggs County (portions). ICA: GA0207.

TV Market Ranking: Below 100 (JEFFERSONVILLE, Twiggs County (portions)). Franchise award date: N.A. Franchise expiration date: N.A. Began: November 1, 1983.

Channel capacity: 45 (not 2-way capable). Channels available but not in use: 14.

Basic Service
Subscribers: 120.
Programming (received off-air): WGNM (IND) Macon; WGXA (FOX, MNT) Macon; WMAZ-TV (CBS) Macon; WMGT-TV (MNT, NBC) Macon; WPCH-TV (IND) Atlanta; WPGA-TV (ABC) Perry.
Programming (via satellite): ABC Family Channel; Animal Planet; Arts & Entertainment; BET Networks; CNN; Comcast Sports Net Southeast; Comedy Central; Country Music TV; Discovery Channel; Disney Channel; ESPN; ESPN 2; Fox News Channel; Home Shopping Network; Lifetime; MTV; Nickelodeon; Spike TV; The Learning Channel; Travel Channel; Trinity Broadcasting Network; Turner Network TV; TV Land; USA Network; Weather Channel.
Fee: $29.95 installation; $35.41 monthly.
Pay Service 1
Pay Units: 32.
Programming (via satellite): HBO.
Fee: $10.95 monthly.
Pay Service 2
Pay Units: 14.
Programming (via satellite): Showtime.
Fee: $10.95 monthly.
Internet Service
Operational: No.
Telephone Service
None
Miles of Plant: 24.0 (coaxial); None (fiber optic). Homes passed: 360.
Chief Executive Officer: Joseph A. Sheehan. General Manager East: Mark Miller. General Manager West: Vance Johnson.
Ownership: KLiP Interactive LLC (MSO).

JEKYLL ISLAND—Comcast Cable, 6805 Southpoint Pkwy, Jacksonville, FL 32216. Phone: 904-374-8000. Fax: 904-374-7622. Web Site: http://www.comcast.com. ICA: GA0121.
TV Market Ranking: Below 100 (JEKYLL ISLAND). Franchise award date: N.A. Franchise expiration date: N.A. Began: May 1, 1970.
Channel capacity: 62 (not 2-way capable). Channels available but not in use: 10.
Basic Service
Subscribers: 884.
Programming (received off-air): WAWS (FOX, MNT) Jacksonville; WCWJ (CW) Jacksonville; WJCL (ABC) Savannah; WJCT (PBS) Jacksonville; WJEB-TV (ETV) Jacksonville; WJXT (IND) Jacksonville; WPXC-TV (ION) Brunswick; WTEV-TV (CBS) Jacksonville; WTLV (NBC) Jacksonville; WTOC-TV (CBS) Savannah; WXGA-TV (PBS) Waycross.
Programming (via satellite): C-SPAN; Home Shopping Network; Lifetime.
Fee: $49.95 installation; $13.78 monthly.
Expanded Basic Service 1
Subscribers: 874.
Programming (via satellite): ABC Family Channel; AMC; Animal Planet; Arts & Entertainment; CNBC; CNN; Comcast Sports Net Southeast; C-SPAN 2; Discovery Channel; Disney Channel; ESPN; Food Network; Fox News Channel; Golf Channel; HGTV; History Channel; MSNBC; Nickelodeon; ShopNBC; Spike TV; SportSouth; TBS Superstation; The Learning Channel; Travel Channel; Turner Classic Movies; Turner Network TV; USA Network; VH1; WE tv; Weather Channel; WGN America.
Fee: $36.00 monthly.
Digital Basic Service
Subscribers: 21.
Programming (via satellite): BBC America; Bio; Bloomberg Television; Bravo!; Discovery Digital Networks; Discovery Kids Channel; DMX Music; FitTV; Fox Movie Channel; Fuse; G4; GAS; GSN; Halogen Network; History Channel International; Independent Film Channel; Lifetime Movie Network; Lime; MTV Networks Digital Suite; National Geographic Channel; Nick Jr.; Style Network; Syfy; Toon Disney; Trinity Broadcasting Network; Trio; WE tv.
Fee: $11.95 monthly.
Digital Expanded Basic Service
Subscribers: N.A.
Programming (via satellite): ESPN 2; ESPN Classic Sports; ESPNews; Fox Soccer; Outdoor Channel; Speed Channel; Versus.
Fee: $3.00 monthly.
Pay Service 1
Pay Units: 22.
Programming (via satellite): Cinemax (multiplexed).
Fee: $18.88 installation; $12.95 monthly.
Pay Service 2
Pay Units: 57.
Programming (via satellite): HBO.
Fee: $18.88 installation; $13.95 monthly.
Digital Pay Service 1
Pay Units: 12.
Programming (via satellite): Cinemax; Encore; HBO; Showtime; Starz; The Movie Channel.
Fee: $2.00 installation; $15.95 monthly.
Video-On-Demand: No
Pay-Per-View
Movies (delivered digitally); special events (delivered digitally).
Internet Service
Operational: Yes.
Telephone Service
None
Miles of Plant: 25.0 (coaxial); None (fiber optic). Homes passed: 1,067.
Vice President & General Manager: Doug McMillan. Vice President, Marketing: Vic Scarborough. Engineering Director: Mike Humphrey. Government Affairs Director: Bill Ferry.
Ownership: Comcast Cable Communications Inc. (MSO).

JESUP—Comcast Cable. Now served by HINESVILLE, GA [GA0024]. ICA: GA0036.

KITE—Formerly served by Walker Cablevision. No longer in operation. ICA: GA0170.

LA FAYETTE—Comcast Cable, 2030 Polymer Dr, Chattanooga, TN 37421. Phone: 423-855-3900. Fax: 423-892-5893. Web Site: http://www.comcast.com. Also serves Linwood, Rock Spring & Walker. ICA: GA0074.
TV Market Ranking: 18,78 (LA FAYETTE, Linwood); 78 (Rock Spring, Walker). Franchise award date: August 10, 1974. Franchise expiration date: N.A. Began: September 1, 1974.
Channel capacity: N.A. Channels available but not in use: N.A.
Basic Service
Subscribers: N.A. Included in Chattanooga, TN
Programming (received off-air): WAGA-TV (FOX) Atlanta; WDEF-TV (CBS) Chattanooga; WDNN-CA (IND) Dalton; WDSI-TV (FOX, MNT) Chattanooga; WELF-TV (TBN) Dalton; WFLI-TV (CW) Cleveland; WNGH-TV (PBS) Chatsworth; WRCB (NBC) Chattanooga; WTCI (PBS) Chattanooga; WTVC (ABC) Chattanooga; 13 FMs.
Programming (via satellite): ABC Family Channel; AMC; Animal Planet; Arts & Entertainment; BET Networks; Bravo; Cartoon Network; CNBC; CNN; Comcast SportsNet Mid-Atlantic; Comedy Central; Country Music TV; C-SPAN; C-SPAN 2; Discovery Channel; Discovery Health Channel; E! Entertainment Television; ESPN; ESPN 2; Food Network; Fox News Channel; Fox Sports Net; FX; Golf Channel; GSN; Hallmark Channel; Headline News; HGTV; History Channel; INSP; Lifetime; MSNBC; MTV; Nickelodeon; QVC; Speed Channel; Spike TV; Style Network; Syfy; TBS Superstation; The Learning Channel; Turner Classic Movies; Turner Network TV; TV Guide Network; TV Land; USA Network; Versus; VH1; Weather Channel; WGN America.
Fee: $39.75 installation; $49.99 monthly; $20.00 additional installation.
Digital Basic Service
Subscribers: N.A.
Programming (received off-air): WRCB (NBC) Chattanooga.
Programming (via satellite): BBC America; Canales N; C-SPAN 3; Discovery Digital Networks; Disney Channel; ESPNews; G4; GAS; MTV Latin America; MTV Networks Digital Suite; MTV2; Music Choice; National Geographic Channel; Nick Jr.; Nick Too; Science Television; SoapNet; Toon Disney; WAM! America's Kidz Network; Weatherscan.
Fee: $14.95 monthly.
Digital Pay Service 1
Pay Units: N.A.
Programming (via satellite): Cinemax (multiplexed); Encore; Flix; HBO (multiplexed); Showtime (multiplexed); Sundance Channel; The Movie Channel (multiplexed).
Video-On-Demand: Yes
Pay-Per-View
Hot Choice (delivered digitally); iN DEMAND (delivered digitally); Pleasure (delivered digitally); Shorteez (delivered digitally); Sports PPV (delivered digitally).
Internet Service
Operational: Yes. Began: March 1, 2002.
Broadband Service: Comcast High Speed Internet.
Fee: $42.95 monthly.
Telephone Service
Digital: Operational
Homes passed & miles of plant included in Chattanooga, TN
Vice President & General Manager: Valerie Gillespie. Technical Operations Director: Tom Bailey. Marketing Director: Mike Kehrer.
City fee: 4% of gross.
Ownership: Comcast Cable Communications Inc. (MSO).

LAGRANGE—Charter Communications, 1925 Breckenridge Plaza, Ste 100, Duluth, GA 30096-4918. Phones: 770-253-2668 (Newnan office); 770-806-7060 (Duluth office). Fax: 770-806-7099. Web Site: http://www.charter.com. Also serves Centralhatches, Corinth, Franklin, Manchester, Talbotton, Troup County & Woodland. ICA: GA0208.
TV Market Ranking: 94 (Manchester, Talbotton, Troup County (portions), Woodland); Outside TV Markets (Centralhatches, Corinth, Franklin, LAGRANGE, Troup County (portions)). Franchise award date: January 1, 1965. Franchise expiration date: N.A. Began: September 1, 1966.
Channel capacity: N.A. Channels available but not in use: N.A.
Basic Service
Subscribers: N.A.
Programming (received off-air): WAGA-TV (FOX) Atlanta; WATL (MNT) Atlanta; WGCL-TV (CBS) Atlanta; WJSP-TV (PBS) Columbus; WLTZ (CW, NBC) Columbus; WPCH-TV (IND) Atlanta; WPXA-TV (ION) Rome; WRBL (CBS) Columbus; WSB-TV (ABC) Atlanta; WTVM (ABC) Columbus; WUPA (CW) Atlanta; WUVG-DT (UNV) Athens; WXIA-TV (NBC) Atlanta; WXTX (FOX) Columbus; allband FM.
Programming (via satellite): C-SPAN; Trinity Broadcasting Network; WGN America.
Current originations: Government Access; Public Access.
Fee: $29.99 installation.
Expanded Basic Service 1
Subscribers: 5,000.
Programming (via satellite): ABC Family Channel; AMC; Animal Planet; Arts & Entertainment; BET Networks; Bravo; Cartoon Network; CNBC; CNN; Comcast Sports Net Southeast; Comedy Central; Country Music TV; Discovery Channel; Disney Channel; E! Entertainment Television; ESPN; ESPN 2; Eternal Word TV Network; Food Network; Fox News Channel; FX; G4; GalaVision; Golf Channel; GSN; Hallmark Channel; Headline News; HGTV; History Channel; Home Shopping Network; INSP; Lifetime; MSNBC; MTV; National Geographic Channel; Nickelodeon; Oxygen; Product Information Network; QVC; Shop at Home; SoapNet; Speed Channel; Spike TV; SportSouth; Syfy; Telemundo; The Learning Channel; Travel Channel; truTV; Turner Classic Movies; Turner Network TV; TV Guide Network; TV Land; USA Network; Versus; VH1; WE tv; Weather Channel.
Fee: $48.99 monthly.
Digital Basic Service
Subscribers: N.A.
Programming (via satellite): BBC America; Bio; Bloomberg Television; Boomerang; Canales N; CNN International; Discovery Digital Networks; Do-It-Yourself; ESPN Classic Sports; ESPNews; Fox Sports World; Great American Country; History Channel International; Independent Film Channel; Lifetime Movie Network; MTV Networks Digital Suite; MuchMusic Network; Music Choice; Nick Jr.; NickToons TV; Style Network; Sundance Channel; Toon Disney.
Fee: $14.00 monthly.
Digital Pay Service 1
Pay Units: N.A.
Programming (via satellite): Cinemax (multiplexed); Encore (multiplexed); Flix; HBO (multiplexed); Showtime (multiplexed); Starz (multiplexed); The Movie Channel (multiplexed).
Video-On-Demand: Yes
Pay-Per-View
iN DEMAND (delivered digitally); Playboy TV (delivered digitally); Fresh (delivered digitally); Shorteez (delivered digitally); Sports PPV (delivered digitally).
Internet Service
Operational: Yes.
Broadband Service: Charter Pipeline.
Fee: $29.99 monthly; $5.00 modem lease.
Telephone Service
Digital: Operational
Fee: $29.99 monthly
Miles of Plant: 322.0 (coaxial); None (fiber optic).
Vice President & General Manager: Matt Favre. Operations Manager: David Spriggs. Technical Operations Manager: Brenda Ivey. Sales & Marketing Manager: Antoinette Carpenter.
City fee: 3% of gross.
Ownership: Charter Communications Inc. (MSO).

LAKE BLACKSHEAR—Citizens Cable TV, 134 N Bailey Ave, Leslie, GA 31764. Phones: 229-874-4145; 229-853-1600. Fax: 229-874-2211. Web Site: http://www.citizenscatv.com. Also serves Cobb, De Soto, Leslie, Lilly, Plains & Sumter County (portions). ICA: GA0150.

TV Market Ranking: Below 100 (Cobb, De Soto, LAKE BLACKSHEAR, Leslie, Lilly, Plains, Sumter County (portions)). Franchise award date: N.A. Franchise expiration date: N.A. Began: January 1, 1990.

Channel capacity: 65 (operating 2-way). Channels available but not in use: 34.

Basic Service

Subscribers: 1,055.

Programming (received off-air): WACS-TV (PBS) Dawson; WALB (NBC) Albany; WFXL (FOX) Albany; WLGA (CW) Opelika; WLTZ (CW, NBC) Columbus; WMAZ-TV (CBS) Macon; WPIX (CW, IND) New York; WRBL (CBS) Columbus; WSB-TV (ABC) Atlanta; WSST-TV (IND) Cordele; WTVM (ABC) Columbus; WXTX (FOX) Columbus.

Programming (via satellite): ABC Family Channel; Animal Planet; Arts & Entertainment; BET Networks; Bloomberg Television; Cartoon Network; CNN; Comcast Sports Net Southeast; Comedy Central; Country Music TV; Discovery Channel; ESPN; ESPN 2; Food Network; Fox News Channel; Hallmark Channel; History Channel; ION Television; Lifetime; Nickelodeon; Speed Channel; Spike TV; TBS Superstation; The Learning Channel; Travel Channel; Trinity Broadcasting Network; Turner Classic Movies; Turner Network TV; Turner South; TV Land; USA Network; VH1; Weather Channel.

Fee: $19.95 installation; $28.95 monthly; $12.95 additional installation.

Digital Basic Service

Subscribers: 12.

Programming (via satellite): AmericanLife TV Network; BBC America; Bio; Black Family Channel; Bloomberg Television; Bravo; Current; Discovery Digital Networks; DMX Music; ESPN 2; ESPN Classic Sports; ESPNews; Fox College Sports Atlantic; Fox College Sports Central; Fox College Sports Pacific; Fox Movie Channel; Fox Soccer; Fuse; G4; GAS; Golf Channel; Great American Country; GSN; Halogen Network; HGTV; History Channel; History Channel International; Independent Film Channel; Lifetime Movie Network; Lime; National Geographic Channel; Nick Jr.; NickToons TV; Outdoor Channel; Ovation; PBS Kids Sprout; Sleuth; Speed Channel; Style Network; Toon Disney; Trinity Broadcasting Network; Versus; WE tv.

Pay Service 1

Pay Units: 61.

Programming (via satellite): HBO.

Fee: $10.95 monthly.

Pay Service 2

Pay Units: 33.

Programming (via satellite): Cinemax.

Fee: $10.95 monthly.

Pay Service 3

Pay Units: 47.

Programming (via satellite): Encore; Starz.

Fee: $9.00 monthly.

Digital Pay Service 1

Pay Units: N.A.

Programming (via satellite): Cinemax (multiplexed); Encore (multiplexed); HBO (multiplexed); Showtime (multiplexed); Starz (multiplexed); The Movie Channel.

Internet Service

Operational: Yes.

Subscribers: 23.

Fee: $35.00 installation; $39.95 monthly.

Telephone Service

None

Miles of Plant: 36.0 (coaxial); None (fiber optic). Homes passed: 1,200.

Administrative Assistant: Gloria Taylor. Chief Technician: Alan Braddy.

Ownership: Citizens Cable TV (MSO).

LAKE PARK—Charter Communications, 1925 Breckenridge Plaza, Ste 100, Duluth, GA 30096-4918. Phones: 770-806-7060 (Administrative office); 229-559-6104 (Valdosta office). Fax: 770-806-7099. Web Site: http://www.charter.com. Also serves Clyattville, Dasher, Lanier County, Lowndes County, Moody Air Force Base, Statenville & Valdosta (portions). ICA: GA0214.

TV Market Ranking: Below 100 (Clyattville, Clyattville, Dasher, Dasher, Lake Park, LAKE PARK, Lanier County, Lowndes County, Moody Air Force Base, Statenville, Statesville, Valdosta (portions)). Franchise award date: June 1, 1981. Franchise expiration date: N.A. Began: March 1, 1982.

Channel capacity: N.A. Channels available but not in use: N.A.

Basic Service

Subscribers: 6,548.

Programming (received off-air): WALB (NBC) Albany; WCTV (CBS, MNT) Thomasville; WSWG (CBS, MNT) Valdosta; WTLH (CW, FOX) Bainbridge; WTWC-TV (NBC) Tallahassee; WTXL-TV (ABC) Tallahassee; WXGA-TV (PBS) Waycross.

Programming (via satellite): C-SPAN; QVC; Trinity Broadcasting Network; WGN America.

Current originations: Public Access.

Fee: $29.99 installation.

Expanded Basic Service 1

Subscribers: 5,362.

Programming (via satellite): ABC Family Channel; AMC; Animal Planet; Arts & Entertainment; BET Networks; Bravo; Cartoon Network; CNBC; CNN; Comcast Sports Net Southeast; Comcast/Charter Sports Southeast (CSS); Country Music TV; Discovery Channel; Disney Channel; ESPN; ESPN 2; Food Network; FX; Headline News; HGTV; History Channel; Home Shopping Network; Lifetime; MTV; Nickelodeon; Product Information Network; SoapNet; Speed Channel; Spike TV; Syfy; TBS Superstation; The Learning Channel; Travel Channel; Turner Network TV; TV Land; USA Network; VH1; Weather Channel.

Fee: $48.99 monthly.

Digital Basic Service

Subscribers: N.A.

Programming (via satellite): BBC America; Discovery Digital Networks; Do-It-Yourself; G4; GAS; Independent Film Channel; MTV Networks Digital Suite; Music Choice; Nick Jr.; Nick Too; NickToons TV; Sundance Channel.

Digital Pay Service 1

Pay Units: 307.

Programming (via satellite): Cinemax (multiplexed).

Fee: $10.95 monthly.

Digital Pay Service 2

Pay Units: 1,269.

Programming (via satellite): HBO (multiplexed).

Fee: $11.95 monthly.

Digital Pay Service 3

Pay Units: 582.

Programming (via satellite): Flix; Showtime (multiplexed).

Fee: $10.95 monthly.

Digital Pay Service 4

Pay Units: 455.

Programming (via satellite): The Movie Channel (multiplexed).

Fee: $10.95 monthly.

Video-On-Demand: No

Pay-Per-View

Hot Choice (delivered digitally), Addressable: Yes; iN DEMAND (delivered digitally).

Internet Service

Operational: No.

Telephone Service

None

Miles of Plant: 361.0 (coaxial); None (fiber optic). Homes passed: 7,500.

Vice President & General Manager: Matt Favre. Operations Manager: David Spriggs. Technical Supervisor: Hank Crews. Sales & Marketing Director: Antoinette Carpenter.

Franchise fee: 3% of gross.

Ownership: Charter Communications Inc. (MSO).

LAKELAND—Mediacom. Now served by PEARSON, GA [GA0063]. ICA: GA0108.

LEARY—Blakely Cable TV Inc., 65 Liberty St, Blakely, GA 39823-2257. Phone: 229-723-3555. Fax: 229-723-2000. ICA: GA0295.

TV Market Ranking: Below 100 (LEARY). Franchise award date: N.A. Franchise expiration date: N.A. Began: N.A.

Channel capacity: 37 (not 2-way capable). Channels available but not in use: None.

Basic Service

Subscribers: 99.

Programming (received off-air): WABW-TV (PBS) Pelham; WALB (NBC) Albany; WCTV (CBS, MNT) Thomasville; WFXL (FOX) Albany; WTVM (ABC) Columbus.

Programming (via satellite): ABC Family Channel; BET Networks; CNN; ESPN; Spike TV; TBS Superstation; Turner Network TV; USA Network; WGN America.

Fee: $25.00 installation; $25.95 monthly.

Pay Service 1

Pay Units: 30.

Programming (via satellite): HBO.

Fee: $10.00 monthly.

Video-On-Demand: No

Internet Service

Operational: No.

Telephone Service

None

Manager: William C. De Loach, Jr. Office Manager: Anne Harroll.

Ownership: Blakely Cable TV Inc. (MSO).

LESLIE—Citizens Cable TV. Now served by LAKE BLACKSHEAR, GA [GA0150]. ICA: GA0210.

LINCOLNTON—Comcast Cable, 105 River Shoals Pkwy, Augusta, GA 30909. Phone: 706-738-0091. Fax: 706-739-1871. Web Site: http://www.comcast.com. ICA: GA0311.

TV Market Ranking: Outside TV Markets (LINCOLNTON).

Channel capacity: N.A. Channels available but not in use: N.A.

Basic Service

Subscribers: 420.

Programming (received off-air): WAGT (CW, NBC) Augusta; WCES-TV (PBS) Wrens; WFXG (FOX) Augusta; WJBF (ABC) Augusta; WRDW-TV (CBS, MNT) Augusta.

Programming (via satellite): QVC; TBS Superstation; TV Guide Network; WGN America.

Fee: $39.95 installation; $14.84 monthly.

Expanded Basic Service 1

Subscribers: N.A.

Programming (via satellite): ABC Family Channel; Animal Planet; Arts & Entertainment; BET Networks; CNBC; CNN; Comcast/Charter Sports Southeast (CSS); Comedy Central; Country Music TV; C-SPAN; C-SPAN 2; Discovery Channel; Discovery Health Channel; Disney Channel; E! Entertainment Television; ESPN; ESPN 2; Fox News Channel; Fox Sports Net; FX; Golf Channel; Headline News; HGTV; History Channel; Lifetime; MTV; Nickelodeon; Spike TV; SportSouth; Syfy; The Learning Channel; Turner Classic Movies; Turner Network TV; TV Land; USA Network; Weather Channel.

Fee: $38.00 monthly.

Video-On-Demand: No

Internet Service

Operational: No.

Broadband Service: DSL service only.

Telephone Service

None

Miles of Plant: 21.0 (coaxial); None (fiber optic).

Technical Operations Director: Butch Jernigan. Engineering Director: Harry Hess. Chief Technician: Jeff Bartlett. Area Marketing Director: Joey Fortier.

Ownership: Comcast Cable Communications Inc. (MSO).

LINCOLNTON—KLiP Interactive, 455 Gees Mill Business Court, Conyers, GA 30013. Phone: 678-727-7100. Fax: 678-727-7002. E-mail: jsheehan@klipia.com. Web Site: http://www.klipia.com. Also serves Lincoln County (portions). ICA: GA0211.

TV Market Ranking: Below 100 (Lincoln County (portions)); Outside TV Markets (Lincoln County (portions), LINCOLNTON). Franchise award date: July 5, 1983. Franchise expiration date: N.A. Began: May 1, 1984.

Channel capacity: 37 (not 2-way capable). Channels available but not in use: 1.

Basic Service

Subscribers: 116.

Programming (received off-air): WAGT (CW, NBC) Augusta; WCES-TV (PBS) Wrens; WFXG (FOX) Augusta; WJBF (ABC) Augusta; WPCH-TV (IND) Atlanta; WRDW-TV (CBS, MNT) Augusta.

Programming (via satellite): ABC Family Channel; AMC; Animal Planet; Arts & Entertainment; BET Networks; Cartoon Network; CNN; CW+; Discovery Channel; Disney Channel; ESPN; ESPN 2; Fox News Channel; FX; Headline News; HGTV; History Channel; INSP; Lifetime; QVC; Speed Channel; SportSouth; The Learning Channel;

Turner Network TV; USA Network; Weather Channel; WGN America.
Fee: $20.00 installation; $38.95 monthly; $20.00 additional installation.

Pay Service 1
Pay Units: 9.
Programming (via satellite): HBO.
Fee: $20.00 installation; $14.95 monthly.

Pay Service 2
Pay Units: 14.
Programming (via satellite): Showtime.
Fee: $13.95 monthly.

Pay Service 3
Pay Units: 12.
Programming (via satellite): The Movie Channel.
Fee: $13.95 monthly.

Internet Service
Operational: No.

Telephone Service
None
Miles of Plant: 37.0 (coaxial); None (fiber optic). Homes passed: 703.
Chief Executive Officer: Joseph A. Sheehan. General Manager East: Mark Miller. General Manager West: Vance Johnson.
City fee: 3% of gross.
Ownership: KLiP Interactive LLC (MSO).

LIZELLA—Flint Cable TV, PO Box 669, 105 W Marion St, Reynolds, GA 31076. Phone: 478-847-3101. Web Site: http://www.flintcatv.com. ICA: GA0325.
TV Market Ranking: Below 100 (LIZELLA).
Channel capacity: N.A. Channels available but not in use: N.A.

Basic Service
Subscribers: N.A.
Programming (received off-air): WGNM (IND) Macon; WGXA (FOX, MNT) Macon; WLGA (CW) Opelika; WLTZ (CW, NBC) Columbus; WMAZ-TV (CBS) Macon; WMGT-TV (MNT, NBC) Macon; WMUM-TV (PBS) Cochran; WPGA-TV (ABC) Perry; WRBL (CBS) Columbus; WTVM (ABC) Columbus; WXTX (FOX) Columbus.
Programming (via satellite): INSP; QVC; TBS Superstation; Weather Channel.
Fee: $55.00 installation; $19.99 monthly.

Expanded Basic Service 1
Subscribers: N.A.
Programming (via satellite): ABC Family Channel; Animal Planet; Arts & Entertainment; BET Networks; Bloomberg Television; Boomerang; Bravo; Cartoon Network; CNBC; CNN; Comcast Sports Net Southeast; Comedy Central; Country Music TV; C-SPAN; C-SPAN 2; C-SPAN 3; Discovery Channel; Disney Channel; E! Entertainment Television; ESPN; ESPN 2; ESPN Classic Sports; Food Network; Fox Business Channel; Fox News Channel; FX; Gospel Music Channel; GSN; Hallmark Channel; Headline News; HGTV; History Channel; Lifetime; MSNBC; MTV; National Geographic Channel; Nickelodeon; RFD-TV; RTV21; Speed Channel; Spike TV; SportSouth; Syfy; The Learning Channel; The Sportsman Channel; Travel Channel; Trinity Broadcasting Network; truTV; Turner Classic Movies; Turner Network TV; TV Land; Univision; USA Network; VH1; WE tv; WGN America.
Fee: $23.00 monthly.

Digital Basic Service
Subscribers: N.A.
Programming (via satellite): ABC Family HD; AmericanLife TV Network; Animal Planet HD; BBC America; Chiller; Cooking Channel; Discovery Channel HD; Discovery HD Theater; Discovery Health Channel; Discovery Kids Channel; Discovery Military Channel; Discovery Planet Green; Disney Channel HD; DMX Music; FitTV; Fox News HD; Fox Soccer; Halogen Network; ID Investigation Discovery; Independent Film Channel; Lifetime Movie Network; Nick Jr.; Science Channel; Science Channel HD; SoapNet; Syfy HD; TLC HD; Travel Channel HD; USA Network HD.
Fee: $49.95 installation; $47.99 monthly.

Digital Expanded Basic Service
Subscribers: N.A.
Programming (via satellite): Arts & Entertainment HD; Food Network HD; FX HD; HGTV HD; History Channel HD; National Geographic Channel HD Network; Speed HD; Universal HD.
Fee: $6.99 monthly.

Digital Expanded Basic Service 2
Subscribers: N.A.
Programming (via satellite): Encore (multiplexed).
Fee: $6.99 monthly.

Digital Expanded Basic Service 3
Subscribers: N.A.
Programming (via satellite): Bio; ESPNews; Fox College Sports Atlantic; Fox College Sports Central; Fox College Sports Pacific; Golf Channel; History Channel International; Outdoor Channel; Outdoor Channel 2 HD; Versus.
Fee: $6.99 monthly.

Digital Expanded Basic Service 4
Subscribers: N.A.
Programming (via satellite): CMT Pure Country; Current; Disney XD; Flix; Fox Movie Channel; Fuse; G4; Gospel Music Channel; Great American Country; MTV Hits; MTV2; NickToons TV; Sleuth; Style Network; Sundance Channel; VH1 Classic; VH1 Soul.
Fee: $6.99 monthly.

Digital Expanded Basic Service 5
Subscribers: N.A.
Programming (via satellite): Cine Latino; Cine Mexicano; CNN en Espanol; Discovery en Espanol; ESPN Deportes; Fox Sports en Espanol; History Channel en Espanol; MTV Tres; mun2 television; VeneMovies.
Fee: $6.99 monthly.

Digital Pay Service 1
Pay Units: N.A.
Programming (via satellite): Cinemax (multiplexed); HBO (multiplexed); Showtime; Starz (multiplexed); Starz HDTV; The Movie Channel (multiplexed).
Fee: $12.99 monthly (HBO, Cinemax, Showtime/TMC or Starz).

Internet Service
Operational: No.

Telephone Service
None
Manager: James Bond. Marketing Manager: Shania Long.
Ownership: Flint Cable Television Inc. (MSO).

LOUISVILLE—Comcast Cable, 105 River Shoals Pkwy, Augusta, GA 30909. Phones: 706-738-0091 (Administrative); 706-733-7712 (Customer service). Fax: 706-739-1871. Web Site: http://www.comcast.com. Also serves Bartow, Jefferson County, Moxley, Wadley & Wren's Quarters. ICA: GA0213.
TV Market Ranking: Below 100 (Jefferson County (portions), Wren's Quarters); Outside TV Markets (Bartow, Jefferson County (portions), LOUISVILLE, Moxley, Wadley). Franchise award date: December 31, 1980. Franchise expiration date: N.A. Began: July 17, 1981.
Channel capacity: N.A. Channels available but not in use: N.A.

Basic Service
Subscribers: 2,025.
Programming (received off-air): WAGT (CW, NBC) Augusta; WCES-TV (PBS) Wrens; WFXG (FOX) Augusta; WJBF (ABC) Augusta; WRDW-TV (CBS, MNT) Augusta.
Programming (via satellite): C-SPAN; ION Television; Lifetime; QVC; TBS Superstation; Trinity Broadcasting Network; Weather Channel; WGN America.
Fee: $50.00 installation; $12.00 monthly.

Expanded Basic Service 1
Subscribers: N.A.
Programming (via satellite): ABC Family Channel; AMC; Arts & Entertainment; BET Networks; Cartoon Network; CNBC; CNN; Comcast Sports Net Southeast; Comcast/Charter Sports Southeast (CSS); Comedy Central; Country Music TV; C-SPAN 2; Discovery Channel; Disney Channel; E! Entertainment Television; ESPN; ESPN 2; Food Network; Fox News Channel; FX; Golf Channel; GSN; Headline News; HGTV; History Channel; MTV; Nickelodeon; Speed Channel; Spike TV; SportSouth; Style Network; Syfy; The Learning Channel; Turner Classic Movies; Turner Network TV; TV Land; USA Network; Versus.
Fee: $25.00 installation; $43.50 monthly.

Digital Basic Service
Subscribers: N.A.
Programming (via satellite): BBC America; Discovery Digital Networks; DMX Music; Flix; GAS; MTV Networks Digital Suite; Nick Jr.; Nick Too.
Fee: $42.50 monthly.

Pay Service 1
Pay Units: 1,001.
Programming (via satellite): HBO.
Fee: $20.00 installation; $10.00 monthly.

Digital Pay Service 1
Pay Units: N.A.
Programming (via satellite): Cinemax (multiplexed); HBO (multiplexed); Showtime (multiplexed); Starz (multiplexed); The Movie Channel (multiplexed).
Fee: $8.00 monthly.

Video-On-Demand: No

Pay-Per-View
Hot Choice (delivered digitally); iN DEMAND (delivered digitally).

Internet Service
Operational: No.
Broadband Service: DSL service only.

Telephone Service
None
Miles of Plant: 72.0 (coaxial); None (fiber optic).
Technical Operations Director: Butch Jernigan. Engineering Director: Harry Hess. Area Marketing Director: Joey Fortier.
City fee: 3% of gross.
Ownership: Comcast Cable Communications Inc. (MSO).

LULA—Now served by ATLANTA (perimeter north), GA [GA0033]. ICA: GA0141.

LUTHERSVILLE—Luthersville Cablevision, 6301 Broad Branch Rd, Chevy Chase, MD 20815-3343. E-mail: luthersvillecable@mail.com. Also serves Meriwether County. ICA: GA0131.
TV Market Ranking: Outside TV Markets (LUTHERSVILLE, Meriwether County). Franchise award date: N.A. Franchise expiration date: N.A. Began: N.A.
Channel capacity: 40 (not 2-way capable). Channels available but not in use: 4.

Basic Service
Subscribers: 825.
Programming (received off-air): WAGA-TV (FOX) Atlanta; WGCL-TV (CBS) Atlanta; WJSP-TV (PBS) Columbus; WLTZ (CW, NBC) Columbus; WPCH-TV (IND) Atlanta; WRBL (CBS) Columbus; WSB-TV (ABC) Atlanta; WTVM (ABC) Columbus; WUPA (CW) Atlanta; WXIA-TV (NBC) Atlanta.
Programming (via satellite): ABC Family Channel; AMC; Arts & Entertainment; Cartoon Network; CNN; Country Music TV; C-SPAN; Discovery Channel; Disney Channel; E! Entertainment Television; Encore; ESPN; Hallmark Channel; Headline News; Lifetime; MTV; Nickelodeon; QVC; Spike TV; The Learning Channel; Turner Network TV; USA Network; VH1; Weather Channel.
Fee: $39.95 installation; $23.95 monthly.

Pay Service 1
Pay Units: 213.
Programming (via satellite): Cinemax; HBO; Showtime.
Fee: $25.00 installation; $10.95 monthly (Cinemax or Showtime), $11.95 monthly (HBO).

Internet Service
Operational: No.
Miles of Plant: 41.0 (coaxial); None (fiber optic). Homes passed: 845.
Manager: Sarah Chet. Chief Technician: Morgan Madigan.
Ownership: South Shore Cable TV Inc. (MSO).

MANCHESTER—Charter Communications, 1925 Breckenridge Plaza, Ste 100, Duluth, GA 30096-4918. Phones: 706-647-1575 (Thomaston office); 770-806-7060 (Administrative office). Fax: 770-806-7099. Web Site: http://www.charter.com. Also serves Chalybeate Springs, Meriwether County, Shiloh, Talbotton, Warm Springs & Woodland. ICA: GA0097.
TV Market Ranking: 94 (Chalybeate Springs, MANCHESTER, Meriwether County (portions), Shiloh, Talbotton, Warm Springs, Woodland); Outside TV Markets (Meriwether County (portions)). Franchise award date: January 1, 1970. Franchise expiration date: N.A. Began: June 1, 1976.
Channel capacity: N.A. Channels available but not in use: N.A.

Basic Service
Subscribers: N.A.
Programming (received off-air): WAGA-TV (FOX) Atlanta; WATL (MNT) Atlanta; WGCL-TV (CBS) Atlanta; WJSP-TV (PBS) Columbus; WLTZ (CW, NBC) Columbus; WPCH-TV (IND) Atlanta; WRBL (CBS) Columbus; WSB-TV (ABC) Atlanta; WTVM (ABC) Columbus; WUPA (CW) Atlanta; WXIA-TV (NBC) Atlanta.
Programming (via satellite): Trinity Broadcasting Network; WGN America.
Current originations: Leased Access.
Fee: $29.99 installation.

Expanded Basic Service 1
Subscribers: N.A.
Programming (via satellite): ABC Family Channel; AMC; Animal Planet; Arts & Entertainment; BET Networks; Cartoon Network; CNBC; CNN; Comcast Sports Net Southeast; Comedy Central; Country Music TV; Discovery Channel; Disney Channel; E! Entertainment Television; ESPN; ESPN 2; Fox News Channel; G4; Headline News; HGTV; History Channel; Home Shopping Network; INSP; Lifetime; MTV; Nickelodeon; Oxygen; Product Information Network; QVC; Speed Channel; Spike TV; SportSouth; Syfy; The Learning Channel; Travel Channel; Turner Classic Movies; Turner Network TV; TV Guide Network; TV Land; USA Network; VH1; Weather Channel.
Fee: $48.99 monthly.

Digital Basic Service
Subscribers: N.A.
Programming (via satellite): BBC America; Boomerang; Canales N; Discovery Digital Networks; GAS; MTV Networks Digital Suite; Music Choice; Nick Jr.; Nick Too; NickToons TV.
Fee: $14.00 monthly.
Digital Pay Service 1
Pay Units: N.A.
Programming (via satellite): Cinemax (multiplexed); Flix; HBO (multiplexed); Showtime (multiplexed); The Movie Channel (multiplexed).
Video-On-Demand: No
Pay-Per-View
Addressable: Yes; iN DEMAND (delivered digitally); Playboy TV (delivered digitally); Fresh (delivered digitally); Shorteez (delivered digitally).
Internet Service
Operational: Yes.
Fee: $39.99 monthly.
Telephone Service
Digital: Operational
Fee: $29.99 monthly
Miles of Plant: 120.0 (coaxial); None (fiber optic). Total homes in franchised area: 2,000.
Vice President & General Manager: Matt Favre. Operations Manager: David Spriggs. Technical Operations Manager: Tim Hardeman. Sales & Marketing Director: Antoinette Carpenter.
City fee: 3% of gross.
Ownership: Charter Communications Inc. (MSO).

McRAE—Mediacom. Now served by EASTMAN, GA [GA0076]. ICA: GA0084.

METRO ATLANTA—BellSouth Entertainment, 660 Hembree Pkwy, Ste 120, Roswell, GA 30076-4974. Phone: 469-624-5800. Fax: 770-360-4877. E-mail: jay.abbazia@bellsouth.com. Web Site: http://www.att.com. Also serves Chamblee (portions), Cherokee County (portions), Cobb County (portions), DeKalb County (portions), Duluth (portions), Gwinnett County (portions), Lawrenceville (portions) & Woodstock (portions). ICA: GA0271. **Note:** This system is an overbuild.
TV Market Ranking: 18 (ATLANTA, Chamblee (portions), Cherokee County (portions), Cobb County (portions), Dekalb County (portions), Duluth (portions), Gwinnett County (portions), Lawrenceville (portions), Woodstock (portions)). Franchise award date: N.A. Franchise expiration date: N.A. Began: N.A.
Channel capacity: N.A. Channels available but not in use: None.
Basic Service
Subscribers: N.A.
Programming (received off-air): WAGA-TV (FOX) Atlanta; WATL (MNT) Atlanta; WGCL-TV (CBS) Atlanta; WGTV (PBS) Athens; WHSG-TV (TBN) Monroe; WPBA (PBS) Atlanta; WPCH-TV (IND) Atlanta; WPXA-TV (ION) Rome; WSB-TV (ABC) Atlanta; WUPA (CW) Atlanta; WUVG-DT (UNV) Athens; WXIA-TV (NBC) Atlanta.
Programming (via satellite): C-SPAN; C-SPAN 2; QVC; TV Guide Network; WGN America.
Fee: $12.99 monthly.
Expanded Basic Service 1
Subscribers: N.A.
Programming (via satellite): ABC Family Channel; AMC; Animal Planet; Arts & Entertainment; BET Networks; Bravo; Cartoon Network; CNBC; CNN; Comcast Sports Net Southeast; Comedy Central; Country Music TV; Discovery Channel; Discovery Health Channel; Disney Channel; E! Entertainment Television; ESPN; ESPN 2; ESPN Classic Sports; ESPNews; Food Network; Fox News Channel; FX; Golf Channel; Headline News; HGTV; History Channel; Lifetime; MTV; Nickelodeon; Speed Channel; Spike TV; SportSouth; Syfy; The Learning Channel; Travel Channel; truTV; Turner Classic Movies; Turner Network TV; TV Land; USA Network; VH1; Weather Channel.
Fee: $32.00 monthly.
Digital Basic Service
Subscribers: N.A.
Programming (via satellite): Eternal Word TV Network; Fox Sports en Espanol; Independent Film Channel; Lifetime Movie Network; MSNBC; Versus; WE tv.
Fee: $44.99 installation; $2.00 monthly; $5.00 additional installation.
Digital Pay Service 1
Pay Units: N.A.
Programming (via satellite): Cinemax (multiplexed); Encore (multiplexed); HBO (multiplexed); Showtime (multiplexed); Starz; Sundance Channel; The Movie Channel (multiplexed).
Video-On-Demand: No
Pay-Per-View
iN DEMAND (delivered digitally), Addressable: Yes; Playboy TV (delivered digitally); Fresh (delivered digitally).
Internet Service
Operational: No.
Telephone Service
None
Manager: Daryl Johnson. Marketing Director: Jay M. Abbazia.
Ownership: BellSouth Entertainment Inc.

METTER—Comcast Cable, 141 Park of Commerce Dr, Savannah, GA 31405. Phone: 912-356-3113. Web Site: http://www.comcast.com. ICA: GA0218.
TV Market Ranking: Outside TV Markets (METTER). Franchise award date: June 18, 1968. Franchise expiration date: N.A. Began: December 12, 1969.
Channel capacity: N.A. Channels available but not in use: N.A.
Basic Service
Subscribers: N.A. Included in Savannah
Programming (received off-air): WJBF (ABC) Augusta; WJCL (ABC) Savannah; WSAV-TV (MNT, NBC) Savannah; WTGS (FOX) Hardeeville; WTOC-TV (CBS) Savannah; WVAN-TV (PBS) Savannah; 1 FM.
Programming (via satellite): CW+; Trinity Broadcasting Network; WGN America.
Fee: $47.99 installation; $11.50 monthly.
Expanded Basic Service 1
Subscribers: N.A.
Programming (via satellite): ABC Family Channel; AMC; Animal Planet; Arts & Entertainment; BET Networks; Bravo; Cartoon Network; CNBC; CNN; Comcast/Charter Sports Southeast (CSS); Comedy Central; Country Music TV; C-SPAN; C-SPAN 2; Discovery Channel; Discovery Health Channel; Disney Channel; E! Entertainment Television; ESPN; ESPN 2; Food Network; Fox News Channel; Fox Sports Net; FX; Golf Channel; Great American Country; GSN; Headline News; HGTV; History Channel; Home Shopping Network; INSP; ION Television; Lifetime; MTV; Nickelodeon; QVC; Speed Channel; Spike TV; SportSouth; Style Network; Syfy; TBS Superstation; The Learning Channel; truTV; Turner Classic Movies; Turner Network TV; TV Guide Network; TV Land; USA Network; Versus; VH1; Weather Channel.
Fee: $32.49 monthly.
Digital Basic Service
Subscribers: N.A.
Programming (via satellite): BBC America; Country Music TV; Discovery Digital Networks; Flix; GAS; MTV Networks Digital Suite; Music Choice; Nick Jr.; Nick Too.
Fee: $6.95 monthly.
Pay Service 1
Pay Units: N.A.
Programming (via satellite): Cinemax; HBO; Showtime; The Movie Channel.
Fee: $10.95 monthly (each).
Digital Pay Service 1
Pay Units: N.A.
Programming (via satellite): Cinemax (multiplexed); HBO (multiplexed); Showtime (multiplexed); The Movie Channel (multiplexed).
Fee: $8.68 monthly (each).
Video-On-Demand: No
Pay-Per-View
iN DEMAND (delivered digitally); Hot Choice (delivered digitally).
Internet Service
Operational: Yes.
Telephone Service
Digital: Operational
Homes passed & miles of plant (coax & fiber) included in Savannah
General Manager: Michael Daves. Technical Operations Director: Joel Godsen. Marketing Director: Jerry Avery. Marketing Manager: Ken Torres.
City fee: 3% of gross.
Ownership: Comcast Cable Communications Inc. (MSO).

MIDVILLE—Pineland Telephone Coop Inc. This cable system has converted to IPTV. See Midville, GA [GA5009]. ICA: GA0152.

MIDVILLE—Pineland Telephone Coop. Inc. Formerly [GA0152]. This cable system has converted to IPTV, 30 S Roundtree St, Metter, GA 30439. Phones: 800-247-1266; 912-685-2121. Fax: 912-685-3539. E-mail: pineland@pineland.net. Web Site: http://www.pineland.net. ICA: GA5009.
Channel capacity: N.A. Channels available but not in use: N.A.
Internet Service
Operational: Yes.
General Manager: Richard P. Price.
Ownership: Pineland Telephone Cooperative Inc.

MILAN—KLiP Interactive, 455 Gees Mill Business Court, Conyers, GA 30013. Phone: 678-727-7100. Fax: 678-727-7002. E-mail: jsheehan@klipia.com. Web Site: http://www.klipia.com. Also serves Dodge County (portions) & Telfair County (portions). ICA: GA0219.
TV Market Ranking: Below 100 (Dodge County (portions), Telfair County (portions)); Outside TV Markets (MILAN). Franchise award date: N.A. Franchise expiration date: N.A. Began: January 1, 1982.
Channel capacity: 65 (not 2-way capable). Channels available but not in use: 34.
Basic Service
Subscribers: 91.
Programming (received off-air): WALB (NBC) Albany; WFXL (FOX) Albany; WMAZ-TV (CBS) Macon; WMGT-TV (MNT, NBC) Macon; WPCH-TV (IND) Atlanta; WPGA-TV (ABC) Perry.
Programming (via satellite): ABC Family Channel; Animal Planet; BET Networks; CNN; Comcast Sports Net Southeast; Discovery Channel; Disney Channel; ESPN; ESPN 2; Fox News Channel; Home Shopping Network; Lifetime; MTV; Nickelodeon; Spike TV; The Learning Channel; Travel Channel; Turner Network TV; TV Land; USA Network; VH1; Weather Channel; WGN America.
Fee: $29.95 installation; $37.03 monthly.
Pay Service 1
Pay Units: 3.
Programming (via satellite): Cinemax.
Fee: $10.95 monthly.
Pay Service 2
Pay Units: 8.
Programming (via satellite): HBO.
Fee: $10.95 monthly.
Internet Service
Operational: No.
Telephone Service
None
Miles of Plant: 12.0 (coaxial); None (fiber optic). Homes passed: 400.
Chief Executive Officer: Joseph A. Sheehan. General Manager East: Mark Miller. General Manager West: Vance Johnson.
Ownership: KLiP Interactive LLC (MSO).

MILLEDGEVILLE—Charter Communications, 1925 Breckenridge Plaza, Ste 100, Duluth, GA 30096-4918. Phones: 478-451-3056; 770-806-7060 (Duluth office). Fax: 478-452-1942. Web Site: http://www.charter.com. Also serves Baldwin County, Hardwick & Midway-Hardwick. ICA: GA0046.
TV Market Ranking: Below 100 (Baldwin County, Hardwick, Midway-Hardwick, MILLEDGEVILLE). Franchise award date: January 1, 1964. Franchise expiration date: N.A. Began: September 20, 1965.
Channel capacity: N.A. Channels available but not in use: N.A.
Basic Service
Subscribers: 9,743.
Programming (received off-air): WAGA-TV (FOX) Atlanta; WGXA (FOX, MNT) Macon; WMAZ-TV (CBS) Macon; WMGT-TV (MNT, NBC) Macon; WMUM-TV (PBS) Cochran; WPGA-TV (ABC) Perry; WSB-TV (ABC) Atlanta; WXIA-TV (NBC) Atlanta; allband FM.
Programming (via satellite): BET Networks; C-SPAN; C-SPAN 2; CW+; Food Network; Home Shopping Network; INSP; ION Television; QVC; Trinity Broadcasting Network; truTV; TV Guide Network.
Current originations: Government Access; Public Access.
Fee: $35.00 installation; $2.00 converter.

Expanded Basic Service 1
Subscribers: 7,337.
Programming (via satellite): ABC Family Channel; AMC; Animal Planet; Arts & Entertainment; Bravo; Cartoon Network; CNBC; CNN; Comcast Sports Net Southeast; Comcast/Charter Sports Southeast (CSS); Comedy Central; Country Music TV; Discovery Channel; Disney Channel; E! Entertainment Television; ESPN; ESPN 2; Fox News Channel; FX; G4; Golf Channel; Hallmark Channel; Headline News; HGTV; History Channel; Lifetime; MSNBC; MTV; National Geographic Channel; Nickelodeon; Oxygen; Product Information Network; SoapNet; Speed Channel; Spike TV; SportSouth; Syfy; TBS Superstation; The Learning Channel; Toon Disney; Travel Channel; Turner Classic Movies; Turner Network TV; TV Land; USA Network; Versus; VH1; Weather Channel.
Fee: $48.99 monthly.

Digital Basic Service
Subscribers: N.A.
Programming (via satellite): BBC America; Bio; Bloomberg Television; Boomerang; Discovery Digital Networks; Do-It-Yourself; ESPN Classic Sports; ESPNews; GAS; History Channel International; Independent Film Channel; Lifetime Movie Network; MTV Networks Digital Suite; Music Choice; Nick Jr.; Nick Too; NickToons TV; Style Network; Sundance Channel; TV Guide Interactive Inc.; WE tv.

Digital Pay Service 1
Pay Units: 695.
Programming (via satellite): Cinemax (multiplexed); Encore (multiplexed); HBO (multiplexed); Showtime (multiplexed); Starz (multiplexed); The Movie Channel (multiplexed).
Fee: $25.00 installation; $12.78 monthly (Cinemax, HBO or Showtime).

Video-On-Demand: Yes

Pay-Per-View
iN DEMAND (delivered digitally); Playboy TV (delivered digitally); Fresh (delivered digitally); Shorteez (delivered digitally).

Internet Service
Operational: Yes. Began: December 1, 2001.
Broadband Service: Charter Pipeline.
Fee: $29.99 monthly.

Telephone Service
Digital: Operational
Fee: $29.99 monthly

Miles of Plant: 178.0 (coaxial); None (fiber optic). Total homes in franchised area: 15,812.

Vice President & General Manager: Matt Favre. Operations Director: Jeff Osborne. Technical Supervisor: Marcus Webb. Sales & Marketing Director: Antoinette Carpenter.

City fee: 3% of gross.

Ownership: Charter Communications Inc. (MSO).

MILLEN—Comcast Cable, 105 River Shoals Pkwy, Augusta, GA 30909. Phones: 706-738-0091 (Administrative); 706-733-7712 (Customer service). Fax: 706-739-1871. Web Site: http://www.comcast.com. Also serves Jenkins County (portions). ICA: GA0220.

TV Market Ranking: Outside TV Markets (Jenkins County (portions), MILLEN). Franchise award date: March 9, 1976. Franchise expiration date: N.A. Began: March 1, 1977.

Channel capacity: N.A. Channels available but not in use: N.A.

Basic Service
Subscribers: N.A.
Programming (received off-air): WAGT (CW, NBC) Augusta; WBEK-CA (IND) Augusta; WCES-TV (PBS) Wrens; WFXG (FOX) Augusta; WJBF (ABC) Augusta; WRDW-TV (CBS, MNT) Augusta; WTLH (CW, FOX) Bainbridge.
Programming (via satellite): Comcast/Charter Sports Southeast (CSS); Eternal Word TV Network; Home Shopping Network; ION Television; MyNetworkTV Inc.; QVC; TBS Superstation; USA Network; WGN America.
Fee: $49.95 installation; $17.50 monthly.

Expanded Basic Service 1
Subscribers: N.A.
Programming (via satellite): ABC Family Channel; AMC; Animal Planet; Arts & Entertainment; BET Networks; Cartoon Network; CNBC; CNN; Comcast Sports Net Southeast; Comedy Central; C-SPAN; Discovery Channel; Discovery Health Channel; Disney Channel; E! Entertainment Television; ESPN; ESPN 2; Food Network; Fox News Channel; FX; Golf Channel; Great American Country; Headline News; HGTV; History Channel; Lifetime; MTV; Nickelodeon; Speed Channel; Spike TV; Syfy; The Learning Channel; Travel Channel; truTV; Turner Classic Movies; Turner Network TV; Turner South; TV Land; Univision; Versus; VH1; Weather Channel.
Fee: $42.95 monthly.

Digital Basic Service
Subscribers: N.A.
Programming (received off-air): WAGT (CW, NBC) Augusta; WFXG (FOX) Augusta; WJBF (ABC) Augusta; WRDW-TV (CBS, MNT) Augusta.
Programming (via satellite): BBC America; Bio; Black Family Channel; CBS College Sports Network; Cooking Channel; Country Music TV; C-SPAN 3; Discovery Digital Networks; Discovery HD Theater; Do-It-Yourself; Encore (multiplexed); ESPN 2 HD; ESPN HD; ESPNews; FearNet; Flix; Fox College Sports Atlantic; Fox College Sports Central; Fox College Sports Pacific; Fox Reality Channel; Fox Soccer; G4; GAS; Gol TV; Gospel Music Channel; GSN; History Channel International; INHD; INSP; Lifetime Movie Network; LOGO; MoviePlex; MSNBC; MTV Networks Digital Suite; Music Choice; National Geographic Channel; NBA TV; NFL Network; Nick Jr.; Nick Too; Outdoor Channel; Oxygen; Palladia; PBS Kids Sprout; SoapNet; Style Network; Sundance Channel; Tennis Channel; The Sportsman Channel; The Word Network; Toon Disney; Trinity Broadcasting Network; Turner Network TV HD; TV Guide Network; TV One; WE tv; Weatherscan.
Fee: $14.95 monthly.

Pay Service 1
Pay Units: 121.
Programming (via satellite): HBO.
Fee: $15.00 installation; $10.95 monthly.

Digital Pay Service 1
Pay Units: N.A.
Programming (via satellite): Cinemax (multiplexed); Cinemax HD; HBO (multiplexed); HBO HD; Showtime (multiplexed); Showtime HD; Starz (multiplexed); Starz HDTV; The Movie Channel (multiplexed); TV Asia; Zee TV USA.

Video-On-Demand: No

Pay-Per-View
iN DEMAND (delivered digitally); Hot Choice (delivered digitally); Playboy TV (delivered digitally); Sports PPV (delivered digitally).

Internet Service
Operational: Yes.
Broadband Service: Comcast High Speed Internet.
Fee: $42.95 monthly.

Telephone Service
None

Miles of Plant: 41.0 (coaxial); None (fiber optic).

Engineering Director: Harry Hess. Technical Operations Director: Butch Jernigan. Area Marketing Director: Joey Fortier.

City fee: 3% of gross.

Ownership: Comcast Cable Communications Inc. (MSO).

MONROE—Monroe Utilities Network, PO Box 725, 215 N Broad St, Monroe, GA 30655-0725. Phone: 770-267-3429. Fax: 770-267-3698. Also serves Good Hope (portions) & Social Circle (portions). ICA: GA0068.

TV Market Ranking: Below 100 (Good Hope (portions), MONROE, Social Circle (portions)). Franchise award date: N.A. Franchise expiration date: N.A. Began: February 15, 1972.

Channel capacity: 68 (operating 2-way). Channels available but not in use: None.

Basic Service
Subscribers: 5,658.
Programming (received off-air): WAGA-TV (FOX) Atlanta; WATL (MNT) Atlanta; WGCL-TV (CBS) Atlanta; WGTV (PBS) Athens; WHSG-TV (TBN) Monroe; WPCH-TV (IND) Atlanta; WSB-TV (ABC) Atlanta; WUPA (CW) Atlanta; WUVG-DT (UNV) Athens; WXIA-TV (NBC) Atlanta; allband FM.
Programming (via satellite): ABC Family Channel; AMC; Animal Planet; Arts & Entertainment; BET Networks; Cartoon Network; CNBC; CNN; Comcast Sports Net Southeast; Comedy Central; Country Music TV; C-SPAN; Discovery Channel; Disney Channel; E! Entertainment Television; ESPN; ESPN 2; Food Network; Fox News Channel; Golf Channel; Headline News; HGTV; History Channel; Home Shopping Network; INSP; Lifetime; MTV; Nickelodeon; Outdoor Channel; QVC; Speed Channel; Spike TV; SportSouth; Syfy; Telemundo; The Learning Channel; Travel Channel; truTV; Turner Classic Movies; Turner Network TV; TV Guide Network; TV Land; USA Network; VH1; WE tv; Weather Channel; WGN America.
Fee: $15.00 installation; $13.50 monthly.

Pay Service 1
Pay Units: 568.
Programming (via satellite): Cinemax.
Fee: $10.00 installation; $9.95 monthly.

Pay Service 2
Pay Units: 1,866.
Programming (via satellite): HBO.
Fee: $10.00 installation; $9.95 monthly.

Pay Service 3
Pay Units: 112.
Programming (via satellite): Playboy TV.
Fee: $10.00 installation; $10.95 monthly.

Pay Service 4
Pay Units: 593.
Programming (via satellite): Showtime.
Fee: $10.00 installation; $9.95 monthly.

Video-On-Demand: No

Pay-Per-View
iN DEMAND, Addressable: No.

Internet Service
Operational: Yes.
Subscribers: 300.
Broadband Service: In-house.
Fee: $25.00 installation; $39.95 monthly.

Telephone Service
None

Miles of Plant: 150.0 (coaxial); 30.0 (fiber optic). Homes passed: 6,000. Total homes in franchised area: 6,000.

Cable TV Division Chief: Brian Thompson.

City fee: 5% of gross.

Ownership: City of Monroe, Water, Light & Gas Commission.

MONTEZUMA—Comcast Cable, 141 Park of Commerce Dr, Savannah, GA 31405. Phone: 912-356-3113. Web Site: http://www.comcast.com. Also serves Macon County (portions) & Oglethorpe. ICA: GA0081.

TV Market Ranking: Below 100 (Macon County (portions), MONTEZUMA, Oglethorpe). Franchise award date: June 14, 1976. Franchise expiration date: N.A. Began: October 1, 1977.

Channel capacity: N.A. Channels available but not in use: N.A.

Basic Service
Subscribers: N.A. Included in Savannah
Programming (received off-air): WACS-TV (PBS) Dawson; WALB (NBC) Albany; WGNM (IND) Macon; WLTZ (CW, NBC) Columbus; WMAZ-TV (CBS) Macon; WPGA-TV (ABC) Perry; WTVM (ABC) Columbus; WXTX (FOX) Columbus; 7 FMs.
Programming (via satellite): QVC; TV Guide Network; WGN America.
Fee: $47.99 installation; $11.00 monthly.

Expanded Basic Service 1
Subscribers: N.A.
Programming (via satellite): ABC Family Channel; AMC; Animal Planet; Arts & Entertainment; BET Networks; Cartoon Network; CNBC; CNN; Comcast/Charter Sports Southeast (CSS); Comedy Central; Country Music TV; CW+; Discovery Channel; Discovery Health Channel; Disney Channel; E! Entertainment Television; ESPN; ESPN 2; Food Network; Fox News Channel; Fox Sports Net; Golf Channel; GSN; Headline News; HGTV; History Television; Home Shopping Network; INSP; ION Television; Lifetime; MTV; Nickelodeon; Speed Channel; Spike TV; SportSouth; Style Network; Syfy; TBS Superstation; The Learning Channel; truTV; Turner Network TV; TV Land; USA Network; Versus; Weather Channel.
Fee: $26.99 monthly.

Digital Basic Service
Subscribers: N.A.
Programming (via satellite): BBC America; Country Music TV; Discovery Digital Networks; Flix; GAS; MTV Networks Digital Suite; Music Choice; Nick Jr.; Nick Too.
Fee: $6.95 monthly.

Pay Service 1
Pay Units: 137.
Programming (via satellite): Cinemax; HBO; Showtime.
Fee: $20.00 installation; $7.95 monthly (Showtime), $10.95 monthly (HBO).

Digital Pay Service 1
Pay Units: N.A.
Programming (via satellite): Cinemax (multiplexed); HBO (multiplexed); Showtime (multiplexed); The Movie Channel (multiplexed).
Fee: $10.05 monthly (each).

Video-On-Demand: No

Internet Service
Operational: Yes.

Telephone Service
Digital: Operational

Homes passed & miles of plant (coax & fiber) included in Savannah

General Manager: Michael Daves. Technical Operations Director: Joel Godsen. Market-

ing Director: Jerry Avery. Marketing Manager: Ken Torres.
City fee: 3% of gross.
Ownership: Comcast Cable Communications Inc. (MSO).

MORGAN—Blakely Cable TV Inc., 65 Liberty St, Blakely, GA 39823-2257. Phone: 229-723-3555. Fax: 229-723-2000. ICA: GA0314.
TV Market Ranking: Below 100 (MORGAN).
Channel capacity: 37 (not 2-way capable). Channels available but not in use: 13.
Basic Service
Subscribers: 40.
Programming (received off-air): WABW-TV (PBS) Pelham; WALB (NBC) Albany; WCTV (CBS, MNT) Thomasville; WFXL (FOX) Albany; WTVM (ABC) Columbus.
Programming (via satellite): ABC Family Channel; BET Networks; CNN; ESPN; Turner Network TV; USA Network; WGN America.
Fee: $25.95 monthly.
Pay Service 1
Pay Units: 6.
Programming (via satellite): HBO.
Fee: $10.00 monthly.
Internet Service
Operational: No.
Telephone Service
None
Manager: William C. De Loach, Jr. Office Manager: Anne Harroll.
Ownership: Blakely Cable TV Inc. (MSO).

MOULTRIE—CNS, PO Box 3368, 21 Ast Avenue NE, Moultrie, GA 31776. Phone: 229-985-5400. E-mail: marketing@cns-internet.com. Web Site: http://www.cns-internet.com. ICA: GA0308. **Note:** This system is an overbuild.
TV Market Ranking: Below 100 (MOULTRIE). Franchise award date: N.A. Franchise expiration date: N.A. Began: December 12, 2001.
Channel capacity: 75 (operating 2-way). Channels available but not in use: None.
Basic Service
Subscribers: 3,559.
Programming (received off-air): WABW-TV (PBS) Pelham; WALB (NBC) Albany; WCTV (CBS, MNT) Thomasville; WFSU-TV (PBS) Tallahassee; WFXL (FOX) Albany; WSB-TV (ABC) Atlanta; WSWG (CBS, MNT) Valdosta; WTXL-TV (ABC) Tallahassee.
Programming (via satellite): Bloomberg Television; C-SPAN; C-SPAN 2; CW+; Discovery Channel; Disney Channel; FamilyNet; FitTV; Fox News Channel; G4; Gospel Music TV; Hallmark Channel; Headline News; Home Shopping Network; ION Television; QVC; SportSouth; TBS Superstation; Toon Disney; Travel Channel; Trinity Broadcasting Network; Weather Channel.
Fee: $10.50 monthly.
Expanded Basic Service 1
Subscribers: 3,204.
Programming (via satellite): ABC Family Channel; AMC; Animal Planet; Arts & Entertainment; BET Networks; Bravo; Cartoon Network; CNBC; CNN; Comcast Sports Net Southeast; Comedy Central; E! Entertainment Television; ESPN; ESPN 2; Food Network; FX; Golf Channel; Great American Country; GSN; HGTV; History Channel; Lifetime; MSNBC; MTV; Nickelodeon; Outdoor Channel; Speed Channel; Spike TV; Syfy; The Learning Channel; truTV; Turner Classic Movies; Turner Network TV; TV Land; Univision; USA Network; VH1; WE tv; WGN America.
Fee: $34.95 monthly.
Digital Basic Service
Subscribers: 1,248.
Programming (via satellite): BBC America; Bio; Boomerang; CNN en Espanol; CNN International; Discovery Digital Networks; Do-It-Yourself; Fox Movie Channel; Fox Sports en Espanol; Fox Sports World; Fuse; GAS; History Channel International; Independent Film Channel; Lifetime Movie Network; MTV Networks Digital Suite; Music Choice; National Geographic Channel; Nick Jr.; Nick Too; Style Network.
Fee: $39.95 monthly.
Pay Service 1
Pay Units: N.A.
Programming (via satellite): Cinemax; Encore; HBO; Showtime; Starz.
Fee: $8.95 monthly.
Digital Pay Service 1
Pay Units: N.A.
Programming (via satellite): Cinemax (multiplexed); Encore (multiplexed); Flix; HBO (multiplexed); Showtime (multiplexed); Starz (multiplexed); Sundance Channel; The Movie Channel (multiplexed).
Fee: $10.00 monthly (each).
Pay-Per-View
iN DEMAND.
Internet Service
Operational: Yes.
Subscribers: 1,286.
Broadband Service: SyrupCity.net.
Fee: $28.95 monthly.
Telephone Service
None
Miles of Plant: 220.0 (coaxial); None (fiber optic).
Marketing Coordinator: Sherri Nix. Broadband Engineer: Chris White.
Ownership: Community Network Services (MSO).

MOULTRIE—Mediacom, 275 Norman Dr, Valdosta, GA 31601. Phone: 229-244-3852. Fax: 229-244-0724. Web Site: http://www.mediacomcable.com. Also serves Colquitt County (portions). ICA: GA0041.
TV Market Ranking: Below 100 (Colquitt County (portions), MOULTRIE). Franchise award date: February 18, 1986. Franchise expiration date: N.A. Began: November 1, 1967.
Channel capacity: 71 (operating 2-way). Channels available but not in use: None.
Basic Service
Subscribers: 5,500.
Programming (received off-air): WABW-TV (PBS) Pelham; WALB (NBC) Albany; WCTV (CBS, MNT) Thomasville; WFXL (FOX) Albany; WSB-TV (ABC) Atlanta; WSST-TV (IND) Cordele; WSWG (CBS, MNT) Valdosta; allband FM.
Programming (via satellite): Arts & Entertainment; Comedy Central; C-SPAN; Hallmark Channel; Home Shopping Network; VH1; Weather Channel.
Current originations: Leased Access; Government Access; Public Access.
Fee: $27.67 installation; $10.43 monthly; $2.72 converter; $9.22 additional installation.
Expanded Basic Service 1
Subscribers: 4,976.
Programming (via satellite): ABC Family Channel; AMC; Animal Planet; BET Networks; Bravo; Cartoon Network; CNBC; CNN; Comcast Sports Net Southeast; Country Music TV; C-SPAN 2; Discovery Channel; Disney Channel; E! Entertainment Television; ESPN; ESPN 2; Eternal Word TV Network; FitTV; Food Network; Fox News Channel; FX; GalaVision; Golf Channel; Headline News; HGTV; History Channel; ION Television; Lifetime; MSNBC; MTV; Nickelodeon; Oxygen; QVC; Spike TV; SportSouth; Syfy; TBS Superstation; The Learning Channel; Travel Channel; Trinity Broadcasting Network; truTV; Turner Network TV; TV Guide Network; TV Land; Univision; USA Network; WE tv; WSBK-TV (IND) Boston.
Fee: $25.95 monthly.
Digital Basic Service
Subscribers: N.A.
Programming (via satellite): BBC America; Bio; Bloomberg Television; Canales N; Discovery Digital Networks; Fox Movie Channel; Fox Sports World; Fuse; G4; GAS; GSN; Halogen Network; History Channel International; Independent Film Channel; Lifetime Movie Network; Lime; MTV Networks Digital Suite; Music Choice; National Geographic Channel; Nick Jr.; Outdoor Channel; Ovation; Speed Channel; Style Network; Toon Disney; Turner Classic Movies; Versus.
Pay Service 1
Pay Units: 170.
Programming (via satellite): Encore; HBO; Showtime; Starz.
Fee: $10.00 installation; $1.75 monthly (Encore), $4.75 monthly (Starz), $12.75 monthly (Showtime), $13.90 monthly (HBO).
Digital Pay Service 1
Pay Units: N.A.
Programming (via satellite): Cinemax (multiplexed); Encore (multiplexed); Flix; HBO (multiplexed); Showtime (multiplexed); Starz (multiplexed); Sundance Channel; The Movie Channel (multiplexed).
Video-On-Demand: Yes
Pay-Per-View
TVN Entertainment (delivered digitally); Pleasure (delivered digitally); ETC (delivered digitally); ESPN Now (delivered digitally); Sports PPV (delivered digitally).
Internet Service
Operational: Yes.
Broadband Service: Mediacom High Speed Internet.
Fee: $40.95 monthly.
Telephone Service
Digital: Operational
Miles of Plant: 188.0 (coaxial); None (fiber optic). Homes passed: 9,241.
Vice President: Don Zagorski. Manager: Sally Bloom. Technical Operations Manager: Donald Swanson. Chief Technician: Wendell Pitts.
City fee: 5% of gross.
Ownership: Mediacom LLC (MSO).

MOUNT VERNON—Comcast Cable, 141 Park of Commerce Dr, Savannah, GA 31405. Phone: 912-356-3113. Web Site: http://www.comcast.com. Also serves Ailey, Alamo, Glenwood, Montgomery County (portions) & Wheeler County (portions). ICA: GA0106.
TV Market Ranking: Below 100 (Ailey, Glenwood, Montgomery County (portions), MOUNT VERNON, Wheeler County (portions)); Outside TV Markets (Alamo, Montgomery County (portions), Wheeler County (portions)). Franchise award date: March 6, 1978. Franchise expiration date: N.A. Began: March 7, 1978.
Channel capacity: N.A. Channels available but not in use: N.A.
Basic Service
Subscribers: N.A. Included in Savannah
Programming (received off-air): WGSA-CA (CW) Savannah; WJCL (ABC) Savannah; WSAV-TV (MNT, NBC) Savannah; WTGS (FOX) Hardeeville; WTOC-TV (CBS) Savannah; WVAN-TV (PBS) Savannah.
Programming (via satellite): Comcast/Charter Sports Southeast (CSS); ION Television; QVC; TBS Superstation; WGN America.
Fee: $47.99 installation; $11.50 monthly; $20.00 additional installation.
Expanded Basic Service 1
Subscribers: N.A.
Programming (via satellite): ABC Family Channel; AMC; Animal Planet; Arts & Entertainment; BET Networks; Cartoon Network; CNBC; CNN; Country Music TV; C-SPAN; Discovery Channel; Discovery Health Channel; Disney Channel; E! Entertainment Television; ESPN; ESPN 2; Food Network; Fox News Channel; Fox Sports Net; FX; Golf Channel; GSN; Hallmark Channel; Headline News; HGTV; Home Shopping Network; Lifetime; MTV; Nickelodeon; Speed Channel; Spike TV; SportSouth; Style Network; Syfy; The Learning Channel; Trinity Broadcasting Network; truTV; Turner Classic Movies; Turner Network TV; TV Land; USA Network; Versus; VH1; Weather Channel.
Fee: $32.49 monthly.
Digital Basic Service
Subscribers: N.A.
Programming (via satellite): BBC America; Country Music TV; Discovery Digital Networks; Encore; GAS; MTV Networks Digital Suite; Music Choice; Nick Jr.; Nick Too.
Fee: $4.95 monthly.
Pay Service 1
Pay Units: 608.
Programming (via satellite): HBO; Showtime.
Fee: $20.00 installation; $10.00 monthly (each).
Digital Pay Service 1
Pay Units: N.A.
Programming (via satellite): Cinemax (multiplexed); HBO (multiplexed); Showtime (multiplexed); Starz (multiplexed); The Movie Channel (multiplexed).
Video-On-Demand: No
Internet Service
Operational: Yes.
Telephone Service
Digital: Operational
Homes passed & miles of plant (coax & fiber) included in Savannah
General Manager: Michael Daves. Technical Operations Director: Joel Godson. Marketing Director: Jerry Avery. Marketing Manager: Ken Torres.
City fee: 2% of gross.
Ownership: Comcast Cable Communications Inc. (MSO).

NAHUNTA—Comcast Cable, 6805 Southpoint Pkwy, Jacksonville, FL 32216. Phones: 800-266-2278; 904-374-8000. Fax: 904-374-7622. Web Site: http://www.comcast.com. ICA: GA0134.

TV Market Ranking: Below 100 (NAHUNTA). Franchise award date: April 1, 1981. Franchise expiration date: N.A. Began: January 1, 1982.

Channel capacity: 40 (2-way capable). Channels available but not in use: 7.

Basic Service

Subscribers: N.A. Included with Jacksonville, FL

Programming (received off-air): WAWS (FOX, MNT) Jacksonville; WCWJ (CW) Jacksonville; WJCL (ABC) Savannah; WJXT (IND) Jacksonville; WPXC-TV (ION) Brunswick; WSAV-TV (MNT, NBC) Savannah; WTEV-TV (CBS) Jacksonville; WTLV (NBC) Jacksonville; WXGA-TV (PBS) Waycross.

Programming (via satellite): C-SPAN; TBS Superstation.

Fee: $43.99 installation; $29.73 monthly; $1.65 converter.

Expanded Basic Service 1

Subscribers: 226.

Programming (via satellite): ABC Family Channel; Arts & Entertainment; BET Networks; CNN; Comcast Sports Net Southeast; Discovery Channel; Disney Channel; ESPN; Food Network; Fox News Channel; FX; Great American Country; Headline News; INSP; Lifetime; Nickelodeon; QVC; Spike TV; The Learning Channel; Turner Network TV; USA Network; Weather Channel.

Fee: $28.59 monthly.

Digital Basic Service

Subscribers: N.A.

Programming (via satellite): AmericanLife TV Network; BBC America; Bio; Bloomberg Television; Bravo; Discovery Digital Networks; ESPN 2; ESPN Classic Sports; ESPNews; Fox Movie Channel; Fox Sports World; G4; GAS; Golf Channel; GSN; Halogen Network; HGTV; History Channel; History Channel International; Independent Film Channel; International Television (ITV); Lifetime Movie Network; MTV Networks Digital Suite; Nick Jr.; Outdoor Channel; Ovation; Speed Channel; Sundance Channel; Syfy; Toon Disney; Trinity Broadcasting Network; Turner Classic Movies; TV Land; Versus.

Fee: $21.14 monthly.

Pay Service 1

Pay Units: 183.

Programming (via satellite): Cinemax; HBO.

Fee: $15.95 monthly (each).

Digital Pay Service 1

Pay Units: N.A.

Programming (via satellite): HBO (multiplexed).

Fee: $15.95 monthly.

Video-On-Demand: No

Pay-Per-View

iN DEMAND (delivered digitally).

Internet Service

Operational: Yes.

Telephone Service

Digital: Operational

Miles of Plant: 13.0 (coaxial); None (fiber optic). Homes passed: 553.

Vice President & General Manager: Doug McMillan. Vice President, Marketing: Vic Scarborough. Engineering Director: Mike Humphrey. Government Affairs Director: Bill Ferry.

Ownership: Comcast Cable Communications Inc. (MSO).

NEWNAN—Charter Communications, 1925 Breckenridge Plaza, Ste 100, Duluth, GA 30096-4918. Phones: 770-806-7060 (Duluth office); 770-253-2668. Fax: 770-806-7099. Web Site: http://www.charter.com. Also serves Coweta County, Lone Oak, Luthersville, Moreland, Sharpsburg & Turin. ICA: GA0042.

TV Market Ranking: 18 (Coweta County (portions), NEWNAN, Sharpsburg, Turin); Outside TV Markets (Lone Oak, Luthersville, Moreland, Coweta County (portions)). Franchise award date: January 1, 1971. Franchise expiration date: N.A. Began: March 25, 1972.

Channel capacity: N.A. Channels available but not in use: N.A.

Basic Service

Subscribers: 12,265.

Programming (received off-air): WAGA-TV (FOX) Atlanta; WATL (MNT) Atlanta; WCAG-LP La Grange; WDTA-LP Fayetteville; WGCL-TV (CBS) Atlanta; WGTV (PBS) Athens; WPCH-TV (IND) Atlanta; WPXA-TV (ION) Rome; WSB-TV (ABC) Atlanta; WUPA (CW) Atlanta; WXIA-TV (NBC) Atlanta.

Programming (via satellite): C-SPAN; C-SPAN 2; Home Shopping Network; INSP; Product Information Network; QVC; Trinity Broadcasting Network; Turner Network TV; TV Guide Network; WGN America.

Fee: $29.99 installation.

Expanded Basic Service 1

Subscribers: N.A.

Programming (via satellite): ABC Family Channel; AMC; Animal Planet; Arts & Entertainment; BET Networks; Bravo; Cartoon Network; CNBC; CNN; Comcast Sports Net Southeast; Comcast/Charter Sports Southeast (CSS); Comedy Central; Country Music TV; Discovery Channel; Disney Channel; E! Entertainment Television; ESPN; ESPN 2; ESPN Classic Sports; Eternal Word TV Network; FitTV; Food Network; Fox News Channel; FX; G4; GalaVision; Golf Channel; GSN; Hallmark Channel; Headline News; HGTV; History Channel; Lifetime; MSNBC; MTV; National Geographic Channel; Nickelodeon; Outdoor Channel; Shop at Home; ShopNBC; SoapNet; Speed Channel; Spike TV; SportSouth; Syfy; Telemundo; The Learning Channel; Toon Disney; Travel Channel; truTV; Turner Classic Movies; TV Land; USA Network; Versus; VH1; WE tv; Weather Channel.

Fee: $48.99 monthly.

Digital Basic Service

Subscribers: N.A.

Programming (via satellite): BBC America; Bio; Bloomberg Television; Boomerang; Canales N; Discovery Digital Networks; Do-It-Yourself; ESPNews; Fox College Sports Atlantic; Fox College Sports Central; Fox College Sports Pacific; Fox Sports World; Fuse; GAS; Great American Country; History Channel International; Independent Film Channel; Lifetime Movie Network; MTV Networks Digital Suite; Music Choice; Nick Jr.; Nick Too; NickToons TV; Style Network; Sundance Channel.

Fee: $14.00 monthly.

Digital Pay Service 1

Pay Units: N.A.

Programming (via satellite): Cinemax (multiplexed); Encore (multiplexed); Flix; HBO (multiplexed); Showtime (multiplexed); Starz (multiplexed); The Movie Channel (multiplexed).

Fee: $9.95 monthly (Cinemax, HBO, Showtime or TMC).

Video-On-Demand: Yes

Pay-Per-View

iN DEMAND (delivered digitally); NBA League Pass/WNBA (delivered digitally); NHL Center Ice/MLB Extra Innings (delivered digitally); Playboy TV (delivered digitally); Fresh (delivered digitally); Shorteez (delivered digitally).

Internet Service

Operational: Yes.

Broadband Service: Charter Pipeline.

Fee: $29.99 monthly; $199.00 modem purchase.

Telephone Service

Digital: Operational

Fee: $29.99 monthly

Miles of Plant: 129.0 (coaxial); None (fiber optic). Additional miles planned: 10.0 (coaxial).

Vice President & General Manager: Matt Favre. Operations Manager: David Spriggs. Technical Operations Manager: Brenda Ivey. Sales & Marketing Director: Antoinette Carpenter.

City fee: 2% of gross (first 700 subscribers).

Ownership: Charter Communications Inc. (MSO).

NEWNAN—NuLink, 70B Sewell Rd, Newnan, GA 30263. Phone: 770-683-5516. ICA: GA0310. **Note:** This system is an overbuild.

TV Market Ranking: 18 (NEWNAN).

Channel capacity: 81 (2-way capable). Channels available but not in use: N.A.

Basic Service

Subscribers: 17,500.

Programming (received off-air): WAGA-TV (FOX) Atlanta; WATL (MNT) Atlanta; WGCL-TV (CBS) Atlanta; WGTV (PBS) Athens; WPBA (PBS) Atlanta; WPCH-TV (IND) Atlanta; WSB-TV (ABC) Atlanta; WUPA (CW) Atlanta; WUVG-DT (UNV) Athens; WXIA-TV (NBC) Atlanta.

Programming (via satellite): Disney Channel; ION Television; Trinity Broadcasting Network; TV Guide Network; Weather Channel.

Current originations: Educational Access; Public Access.

Fee: $10.75 monthly.

Expanded Basic Service 1

Subscribers: N.A.

Programming (via satellite): ABC Family Channel; AMC; Animal Planet; Arts & Entertainment; BET Networks; Bravo; Cartoon Network; CNBC; CNN; Comcast Sports Net Southeast; Comedy Central; Country Music TV; C-SPAN; Daystar TV Network; Discovery Channel; Discovery Health Channel; E! Entertainment Television; ESPN; ESPN 2; Eternal Word TV Network; Food Network; Fox Movie Channel; Fox News Channel; FX; G4; Golf Channel; Gospel Music TV; Great American Country; Hallmark Channel; Headline News; HGTV; History Channel; Home Shopping Network; Lifetime; MSNBC; MTV; Nickelodeon; Outdoor Channel; Speed Channel; Spike TV; SportSouth; Syfy; The Learning Channel; Toon Disney; Travel Channel; truTV; Turner Classic Movies; Turner Network TV; TV Land; USA Network; VH1; Weather Channel; WGN America.

Fee: $36.60 monthly.

Digital Basic Service

Subscribers: N.A.

Programming (via satellite): AmericanLife TV Network; BBC America; Bio; Bloomberg Television; Boomerang; CNN en Espanol; C-SPAN 2; Discovery Digital Networks; Do-It-Yourself; ESPNews; Fox Sports en Espanol; Fox Sports World; Fuse; GAS; GSN; Halogen Network; History Channel International; Independent Film Channel; MTV Networks Digital Suite; Music Choice; National Geographic Channel; Nick Jr.; NickToons TV; Oxygen; QVC; Style Network; Versus; WAM! America's Kidz Network.

Fee: $54.74 monthly.

Pay Service 1

Pay Units: N.A.

Programming (via satellite): Cinemax; Encore; HBO; Showtime.

Fee: $12.85 monthly (each).

Digital Pay Service 1

Pay Units: N.A.

Programming (via satellite): Cinemax (multiplexed); Encore (multiplexed); Flix; HBO (multiplexed); Showtime (multiplexed); Starz (multiplexed); Sundance Channel; The Movie Channel (multiplexed).

Fee: $13.60 monthly (each).

Pay-Per-View

iN DEMAND; iN DEMAND (delivered digitally); Playboy TV (delivered digitally); Pleasure (delivered digitally); Fresh (delivered digitally); sports (delivered digitally).

Internet Service

Operational: Yes.

Subscribers: 10,000.

Broadband Service: In-house.

Fee: $44.20 monthly.

Telephone Service

None

Miles of Plant: 450.0 (coaxial); None (fiber optic). Homes passed: 36,000.

Chief Executive Officer: John Brooks. Chief Technician: Ron Lee. Marketing Coordinator: Paul Lisborg.

Ownership: H C Cable Holdings LLC.

NEWTON—Formerly served by Blakely Cable TV Inc. No longer in operation. ICA: GA0313.

NEWTON COUNTY (southern portion)—KLiP Interactive, 455 Gees Mill Business Court, Conyers, GA 30013. Phone: 678-727-7100. Fax: 678-727-7002. E-mail: jsheehan@klipia.com. Web Site: http://www.klipia.com. Also serves Butts County (portions) & Jasper County (portions). ICA: GA0301.

TV Market Ranking: Below 100 (Butts County (portions), Jasper County (portions), NEWTON COUNTY (SOUTHERN PORTION)). Franchise award date: N.A. Franchise expiration date: N.A. Began: N.A.

Channel capacity: 65 (not 2-way capable). Channels available but not in use: 19.

Basic Service

Subscribers: 445.

Programming (received off-air): WAGA-TV (FOX) Atlanta; WATL (MNT) Atlanta; WGCL-TV (CBS) Atlanta; WGTV (PBS) Athens; WHSG-TV (TBN) Monroe; WPBA (PBS) Atlanta; WPCH-TV (IND) Atlanta; WSB-TV (ABC) Atlanta; WUPA (CW) Atlanta; WXIA-TV (NBC) Atlanta.

Programming (via satellite): ABC Family Channel; AMC; Animal Planet; Arts & Entertainment; Cartoon Network; CNBC; CNN; Comcast Sports Net Southeast; Comedy Central; Country Music TV; C-SPAN; Discovery Channel; Disney Channel; E! Entertainment Television; ESPN; ESPN 2; Fox News Channel; FX; Hallmark Channel; Headline News; History Channel; Lifetime; MTV; National Geographic Channel; Nickelodeon; QVC; Spike TV; SportSouth; Syfy; The Learning Channel; truTV; Turner Network TV; TV Land; USA Network; Weather Channel; WGN America.

Fee: $29.95 installation; $39.95 monthly.

Pay Service 1
Pay Units: 47.
Programming (via satellite): HBO.
Fee: $10.95 monthly.
Pay Service 2
Pay Units: 24.
Programming (via satellite): Showtime.
Fee: $10.95 monthly.
Pay Service 3
Pay Units: 19.
Programming (via satellite): The Movie Channel.
Fee: $10.95 monthly.
Internet Service
Operational: No.
Telephone Service
None
Miles of Plant: 10.0 (coaxial); None (fiber optic). Homes passed: 2,113.
Chief Executive Officer: Joseph A. Sheehan. General Manager East: Mark Miller. General Manager West: Vance Johnson.
Ownership: KLiP Interactive LLC (MSO).

NORMAN PARK—Wainwright Cable Inc., PO Box 614, 352 N Railroad St, Norman Park, GA 31771. Phone: 229-769-3785. Fax: 229-769-5656. Also serves Bear Creek & Indian Lake. ICA: GA0140.
TV Market Ranking: Below 100 (Bear Creek, Indian Lake, NORMAN PARK). Franchise award date: September 1, 1988. Franchise expiration date: N.A. Began: March 19, 1989.
Channel capacity: 36 (not 2-way capable). Channels available but not in use: N.A.
Basic Service
Subscribers: 300 Includes Funston.
Programming (received off-air): WABW-TV (PBS) Pelham; WALB (NBC) Albany; WCTV (CBS, MNT) Thomasville; WFXL (FOX) Albany; WSWG (CBS, MNT) Valdosta; WTXL-TV (ABC) Tallahassee.
Programming (via satellite): ABC Family Channel; Arts & Entertainment; BET Networks; Cartoon Network; CNN; Comcast Sports Net Southeast; Country Music TV; Discovery Channel; ESPN; Lifetime; Spike TV; Syfy; TBS Superstation; The Learning Channel; Travel Channel; Trinity Broadcasting Network; Turner Classic Movies; Turner Network TV; USA Network; Weather Channel; WGN America.
Fee: $25.00 installation; $20.00 monthly.
Pay Service 1
Pay Units: 62.
Programming (via satellite): HBO.
Fee: $10.00 monthly.
Video-On-Demand: No
Internet Service
Operational: No.
Telephone Service
None
Miles of Plant: 15.0 (coaxial); None (fiber optic). Homes passed: 580. Total homes in franchised area: 580.
Manager & Chief Technician: Chris Wainwright.
County fee: 5% of net. City fee: 2% of net.
Ownership: Wainwright Cable Inc. (MSO).

OAK PARK—Pineland Telephone Coop. Inc. Formerly [GA0224]. This cable system has converted to IPTV, 30 S Roundtree St, Metter, GA 30439. Phones: 800-247-1266; 912-685-2121. Fax: 912-685-3539. E-mail: pineland@pineland.net. Web Site: http://www.pineland.net. ICA: GA5010.
Channel capacity: N.A. Channels available but not in use: N.A.
Internet Service
Operational: Yes.
General Manager: Richard P. Price.
Ownership: Pineland Telephone Cooperative Inc.

OAK PARK—Pineland Telephone Coop. Inc. This cable system has converted to IPTV. See Oak Park, GA [GA5010]. ICA: GA0224.

OCHLOCKNEE—Southeast Cable TV Inc., PO Box 584, 107 S Main St, Boston, GA 31626-0584. Phone: 229-498-4191. Fax: 229-498-1026. ICA: GA0225.
TV Market Ranking: Below 100 (OCHLOCKNEE). Franchise award date: N.A. Franchise expiration date: N.A. Began: May 1, 1989.
Channel capacity: 40 (not 2-way capable). Channels available but not in use: 24.
Basic Service
Subscribers: 188.
Programming (received off-air): WABW-TV (PBS) Pelham; WALB (NBC) Albany; WCTV (CBS, MNT) Thomasville; WFSU-TV (PBS) Tallahassee; WTLH (CW, FOX) Bainbridge; WTWC-TV (NBC) Tallahassee; WTXL-TV (ABC) Tallahassee.
Programming (via satellite): ABC Family Channel; Arts & Entertainment; BET Networks; CNN; Country Music TV; Discovery Channel; ESPN; Headline News; Nickelodeon; QVC; Spike TV; TBS Superstation; Turner Network TV; USA Network; WGN America.
Fee: $15.00 installation; $17.95 monthly.
Pay Service 1
Pay Units: 74.
Programming (via satellite): HBO.
Fee: $10.00 monthly.
Internet Service
Operational: No.
Telephone Service
None
Miles of Plant: 14.0 (coaxial); None (fiber optic). Homes passed: 390.
Manager & Chief Technician: Bob Heide.
Ownership: Southeast Cable TV Inc. (MSO).

OCONEE—Formerly served by National Cable Inc. No longer in operation. ICA: GA0226.

PATTERSON—ATC Cable, 3349 Hwy 84 W, Ste 104, Blackshear, GA 31516. Phones: 877-552-5946 (Sales); 912-449-5443. Fax: 912-449-2602. E-mail: info@atc.cc. Web Site: http://www.accessatc.net. Also serves Offerman. ICA: GA0272.
TV Market Ranking: Below 100 (Offerman, PATTERSON). Franchise award date: N.A. Franchise expiration date: N.A. Began: N.A.
Channel capacity: 80 (not 2-way capable). Channels available but not in use: N.A.
Basic Service
Subscribers: 350.
Programming (received off-air): WAWS (FOX, MNT) Jacksonville; WCWJ (CW) Jacksonville; WGSA (CW) Baxley; WJCL (ABC) Savannah; WJXT (IND) Jacksonville; WJXX (ABC) Orange Park; WPXC-TV (ION) Brunswick; WSAV-TV (MNT, NBC) Savannah; WTEV-TV (CBS) Jacksonville; WTGS (FOX) Hardeeville; WTLV (NBC) Jacksonville; WTOC-TV (CBS) Savannah; WXGA-TV (PBS) Waycross.
Programming (via satellite): ABC Family Channel; AMC; Animal Planet; Arts & Entertainment; BET Networks; Cartoon Network; CNBC; CNN; Comcast Sports Net Southeast; Comcast/Charter Sports Southeast (CSS); Comedy Central; Country Music TV; C-SPAN; C-SPAN 2; Discovery Channel; Disney Channel; E! Entertainment Television; ESPN; ESPN 2; ESPN Classic Sports; FitTV; Food Network; Fox News Channel; FX; Golf Channel; Hallmark Channel; Headline News; HGTV; History Channel; Home Shopping Network; INSP; Lifetime; Local Cable Weather; MTV; National Geographic Channel; Nickelodeon; Outdoor Channel; QVC; Speed Channel; Spike TV; SportSouth; Syfy; TBS Superstation; The Learning Channel; Travel Channel; Trinity Broadcasting Network; truTV; Turner Network TV; TV Guide Network; TV Land; USA Network; VH1; Weather Channel.
Current originations: Public Access.
Fee: $35.00 installation; $46.95 monthly.
Digital Basic Service
Subscribers: N.A.
Programming (via satellite): BBC America; Bio; Bloomberg Television; Boomerang; Current; Discovery Military Channel; Disney XD; DMX Music; ESPN 2; ESPN Classic Sports; ESPN U; ESPNews; FitTV; Flix; Fox Movie Channel; Fox Soccer; FSN Digital Atlantic; FSN Digital Central; FSN Digital Pacific; Fuse; G4; Golf Channel; Gospel Music Channel; Great American Country; GSN; Hallmark Movie Channel; Halogen Network; HGTV; History Channel; History Channel International; ID Investigation Discovery; Lifetime Movie Network; Lime; MTV Hits; MTV2; National Geographic Channel; Nick Jr.; NickToons TV; Outdoor Channel; RFD-TV; Science Channel; Sleuth; Soap-Net; Speed Channel; Style Network; Sundance Channel; TeenNick; Trinity Broadcasting Network; Turner Classic Movies; Versus; VH1 Classic; WE tv.
Fee: $16.95 monthly.
Digital Expanded Basic Service
Subscribers: N.A.
Programming (received off-air): WAWS (FOX, MNT) Jacksonville; WCWJ (CW) Jacksonville; WJCT (PBS) Jacksonville; WJXT (IND) Jacksonville; WJXX (ABC) Orange Park; WSAV-TV (MNT, NBC) Savannah; WTEV-TV (CBS) Jacksonville; WTGS (FOX) Hardeeville; WTLV (NBC) Jacksonville; WTOC-TV (CBS) Savannah.
Programming (via satellite): Animal Planet HD; Arts & Entertainment HD; Bravo HD; CNBC HD+; CNN HD; Discovery Channel HD; ESPN 2 HD; ESPN HD; Golf Channel HD; History Channel HD; National Geographic Channel HD Network; Outdoor Channel 2 HD; Science Channel HD; Syfy HD; TBS in HD; TLC HD; Turner Network TV HD; USA Network HD; Versus HD; Weather Channel HD.
Digital Expanded Basic Service 2
Subscribers: N.A.
Programming (via satellite): Discovery HD Theater; HDNet; HDNet Movies; Universal HD.
Digital Pay Service 1
Pay Units: N.A.
Programming (via satellite): Cinemax (multiplexed); Cinemax HD; Encore (multiplexed); HBO (multiplexed); HBO HD; Showtime (multiplexed); Showtime HD; Starz (multiplexed); Starz HDTV; The Movie Channel (multiplexed).

Pay-Per-View
iN DEMAND (delivered digitally); Playboy TV (delivered digitally); Fresh (delivered digitally); Spice: Xcess (delivered digitally); Club Jenna (delivered digitally).
Internet Service
Operational: No.
Broadband Service: DSL service only.
Telephone Service
None
Miles of Plant: 20.0 (coaxial); None (fiber optic). Homes passed: 600.
Manager: Nathan Lingenfelter. Customer Service: Jennifer Barnette.
Ownership: ATC (MSO).

PAVO—Southeast Cable TV Inc., PO Box 584, 107 S Main St, Boston, GA 31626-0584. Phone: 229-498-4191. Fax: 229-498-1026. Also serves Barwick. ICA: GA0227.
TV Market Ranking: Below 100 (Barwick, PAVO). Franchise award date: N.A. Franchise expiration date: N.A. Began: March 1, 1983.
Channel capacity: 40 (not 2-way capable). Channels available but not in use: 25.
Basic Service
Subscribers: 224.
Programming (received off-air): WABW-TV (PBS) Pelham; WALB (NBC) Albany; WCTV (CBS, MNT) Thomasville; WTLH (CW, FOX) Bainbridge; WTWC-TV (NBC) Tallahassee; WTXL-TV (ABC) Tallahassee.
Programming (via satellite): ABC Family Channel; Arts & Entertainment; BET Networks; CNN; Country Music TV; Discovery Channel; ESPN; Headline News; Nickelodeon; QVC; Spike TV; TBS Superstation; Turner Network TV; USA Network; WGN America.
Fee: $15.00 installation; $17.95 monthly.
Pay Service 1
Pay Units: 87.
Programming (via satellite): HBO.
Fee: $10.00 monthly.
Pay Service 2
Pay Units: 40.
Programming (via satellite): The Movie Channel.
Fee: $9.00 monthly.
Pay Service 3
Pay Units: N.A.
Programming (via satellite): The Movie Channel.
Fee: $8.00 monthly.
Internet Service
Operational: No.
Telephone Service
None
Miles of Plant: 16.0 (coaxial); None (fiber optic). Homes passed: 475.
Manager & Chief Technician: Bob Heide.
Ownership: Southeast Cable TV Inc. (MSO).

PEARSON—Mediacom, 509 Flint Ave, Albany, GA 31701. Phones: 229-888-0242; 229-244-3852 (Regional office). Fax: 229-436-4819. Web Site: http://www.mediacomcable.com. Also serves Adel, Alapaha, Berrien County (portions), Cook County (portions), Enigma, Lakeland, Lenox,

Nashville, Ray City, Sparks & Willacoochee. ICA: GA0063.

TV Market Ranking: Below 100 (Adel, Berrien County (portions) (portions), Cook County (portions), Enigma, Lakeland, Lenox, Nashville, Ray City, Sparks); Outside TV Markets (Alapaha, Berrien County (portions) (portions), PEARSON, Willacoochee). Franchise award date: N.A. Franchise expiration date: N.A. Began: April 1, 1968.

Channel capacity: N.A. Channels available but not in use: N.A.

Basic Service

Subscribers: 7,432.

Programming (received off-air): WALB (NBC) Albany; WCTV (CBS, MNT) Thomasville; WFXL (FOX) Albany; WSB-TV (ABC) Atlanta; WSWG (CBS, MNT) Valdosta; WTXL-TV (ABC) Tallahassee; WXGA-TV (PBS) Waycross; 9 FMs.

Programming (via satellite): C-SPAN; C-SPAN 2; Eternal Word TV Network; Hallmark Channel; Home Shopping Network; ION Television; QVC; Trinity Broadcasting Network; WSBK-TV (IND) Boston.

Current originations: Leased Access; Public Access.

Fee: $27.67 installation; $10.30 monthly; $2.72 converter.

Expanded Basic Service 1

Subscribers: 4,516.

Programming (via satellite): ABC Family Channel; AMC; Animal Planet; Arts & Entertainment; BET Networks; Cartoon Network; CNBC; CNN; Comcast Sports Net Southeast; Comedy Central; Country Music TV; Discovery Channel; Disney Channel; ESPN; ESPN 2; FitTV; Food Network; Fox News Channel; FX; GalaVision; Golf Channel; Headline News; HGTV; History Channel; Lifetime; MSNBC; MTV; Nickelodeon; Oxygen; Spike TV; Syfy; TBS Superstation; The Learning Channel; Travel Channel; truTV; Turner Network TV; TV Guide Network; TV Land; Univision; USA Network; VH1; WE tv; Weather Channel.

Fee: $28.84 monthly.

Digital Basic Service

Subscribers: N.A.

Programming (via satellite): AmericanLife TV Network; BBC America; Bio; Bloomberg Television; Canales N; Discovery Digital Networks; DMX Music; Fox Movie Channel; Fox Sports World; Fuse; G4; GAS; Golf Channel; GSN; Halogen Network; History Channel International; Independent Film Channel; Lifetime Movie Network; Lime; MTV Networks Digital Suite; National Geographic Channel; Nick Jr.; Outdoor Channel; Ovation; Speed Channel; Style Network; Toon Disney; Turner Classic Movies; Versus.

Digital Pay Service 1

Pay Units: 81.

Programming (via satellite): Cinemax (multiplexed); Encore (multiplexed); Flix; HBO (multiplexed); Showtime (multiplexed); Starz (multiplexed); Sundance Channel; The Movie Channel (multiplexed).

Fee: $10.30 monthly (Cinemax, HBO, Showtime/Sundance/TMC, or Starz/Encore).

Video-On-Demand: Yes

Pay-Per-View

ESPN Now (delivered digitally); ETC (delivered digitally); TVN Entertainment (delivered digitally); sports (delivered digitally).

Internet Service

Operational: Yes.

Broadband Service: Mediacom High Speed Internet.

Fee: $70.00 installation; $40.95 monthly.

Telephone Service

Digital: Operational

Homes passed: 9,318. Miles of plant included in Fitzgerald

Regional Vice President: Sue Misiunas. General Manager: Gary Crosby. Regional Technical Operations Manager: Gary McDougall. Regional Marketing Director: Melanie Hannasch. Marketing Manager: Daryl Channey.

City fee: 5% of gross (Nashville & Sparks).

Ownership: Mediacom LLC (MSO).

PEMBROKE—Comcast Cable, 141 Park of Commerce Dr, Savannah, GA 31405. Phone: 912-356-3113. Web Site: http://www.comcast.com. Also serves Bryan County (northern portion) & Ellabelle. ICA: GA0228.

TV Market Ranking: Below 100 (Bryan County (northern portion) (portions), Ellabelle, PEMBROKE); Outside TV Markets (Bryan County (northern portion) (portions)). Franchise award date: May 10, 1983. Franchise expiration date: N.A. Began: March 6, 1984.

Channel capacity: N.A. Channels available but not in use: N.A.

Basic Service

Subscribers: N.A. Included in Savannah

Programming (received off-air): WGSA (CW) Baxley; WJCL (ABC) Savannah; WSAV-TV (MNT, NBC) Savannah; WTGS (FOX) Hardeeville; WTOC-TV (CBS) Savannah; WVAN-TV (PBS) Savannah; 2 FMs.

Programming (via satellite): ABC Family Channel; AMC; Animal Planet; Arts & Entertainment; BET Networks; CNBC; CNN; Comcast Sports Net Southeast; Country Music TV; C-SPAN; Discovery Channel; Disney Channel; ESPN; Headline News; History Channel; Home Shopping Network; Lifetime; Nickelodeon; ShopNBC; Speed Channel; Spike TV; Syfy; TBS Superstation; The Learning Channel; Travel Channel; Trinity Broadcasting Network; truTV; Turner Classic Movies; Turner Network TV; USA Network; VH1; Weather Channel; WGN America.

Fee: $47.99 installation; $33.20 monthly; $1.00 converter.

Digital Expanded Basic Service

Subscribers: N.A.

Programming (via satellite): Bravo; Encore Action; Fox Movie Channel; Independent Film Channel; Lifetime Movie Network; WE tv.

Fee: $4.95 monthly.

Digital Expanded Basic Service 2

Subscribers: N.A.

Programming (via satellite): ESPN 2; ESPN Classic Sports; ESPNews; Fox Sports World; GAS; Golf Channel; Outdoor Channel; Versus.

Fee: $5.95 monthly.

Pay Service 1

Pay Units: 167.

Programming (via satellite): Cinemax; HBO; Showtime.

Fee: $20.00 installation; $7.95 monthly (Cinemax), $8.95 monthly (Showtime), $9.95 monthly (HBO).

Digital Pay Service 1

Pay Units: N.A.

Programming (via satellite): Cinemax (multiplexed); HBO (multiplexed); Showtime (multiplexed); Starz (multiplexed); The Movie Channel (multiplexed).

Fee: $5.95 monthly (Starz), $9.95 monthly (Cinemax or TMC), $12.95 monthly (Showtime), $13.95 monthly (HBO).

Video-On-Demand: Yes

Pay-Per-View

Addressable homes: 80.

iN DEMAND (delivered digitally); Playboy TV (delivered digitally); Fresh (delivered digitally).

Internet Service

Operational: Yes.

Broadband Service: Comcast High Speed Internet.

Fee: $42.95 monthly.

Telephone Service

None

Homes passed & miles of plant (coax & fiber) included in Savannah

General Manager: Michael Daves. Technical Operations Director: Joel Godsen. Marketing Director: Jerry Avery. Marketing Manager: Ken Torres.

City fee: 3% of gross.

Ownership: Comcast Cable Communications Inc.

PERRY—ComSouth Telesys Inc., PO Box 910, 1357-D Sam Nunn Blvd, Perry, GA 31069. Phone: 478-987-0172. Fax: 478-987-9932. E-mail: cable@comsouth.net. Web Site: http://www.comsouth.net. Also serves Bleckley County (portions), Cochran, Fort Valley, Hawkinsville, Hayneville, Kathleen, Marshallville, Pulaski County (portions), Unadilla & Warner Robins. ICA: GA0229.

TV Market Ranking: Below 100 (Bleckley County (portions), Cochran, Fort Valley, Hawkinsville, Hayneville, Kathleen, Marshallville, PERRY, Pulaski County (portions), Unadilla, Warner Robins). Franchise award date: N.A. Franchise expiration date: N.A. Began: January 1, 1968.

Channel capacity: N.A. Channels available but not in use: N.A.

Basic Service

Subscribers: 11,014.

Programming (received off-air): WGNM (IND) Macon; WGXA (FOX, MNT) Macon; WMAZ-TV (CBS) Macon; WMGT-TV (MNT, NBC) Macon; WMUM-TV (PBS) Cochran; WPGA-TV (ABC) Perry; WSB-TV (ABC) Atlanta.

Programming (via satellite): TBS Superstation; TV Guide Network; WGN America.

Current originations: Educational Access.

Fee: $29.95 installation; $12.95 monthly; $3.25 converter.

Expanded Basic Service 1

Subscribers: 5,420.

Programming (via satellite): ABC Family Channel; AMC; AmericanLife TV Network; Animal Planet; Arts & Entertainment; BET Networks; Cartoon Network; CNBC; CNN; Comcast Sports Net Southeast; Comedy Central; Country Music TV; C-SPAN; Discovery Channel; Disney Channel; E! Entertainment Television; ESPN; ESPN 2; ESPN Classic Sports; Fox News Channel; FX; Golf Channel; Hallmark Channel; Headline News; HGTV; History Channel; Home Shopping Network; Lifetime; MTV; National Geographic Channel; Nickelodeon; QVC; Speed Channel; Spike TV; Syfy; The Learning Channel; Travel Channel; truTV; Turner Classic Movies; Turner Network TV; TV Land; USA Network; Versus; VH1; Weather Channel.

Fee: $27.00 monthly.

Digital Basic Service

Subscribers: 600.

Programming (via satellite): Arts & Entertainment; BBC America; Bloomberg Television; Bravo; Discovery Digital Networks; Fox Movie Channel; Fox Sports World; G4; GSN; Halogen Network; History Channel International; Independent Film Channel; Lifetime Movie Network; MuchMusic Network; Outdoor Channel; Ovation; SportSouth; Style Network; WE tv.

Fee: $8.95 installation; $12.95 monthly.

Digital Pay Service 1

Pay Units: N.A.

Programming (via satellite): Cinemax; Encore; HBO (multiplexed); Showtime (multiplexed); Starz; Sundance Channel; The Movie Channel.

Fee: $11.00 monthly (HBO, Cinemax, Showtime/TMC/Flix or Starz/Encore).

Video-On-Demand: No

Pay-Per-View

Addressable homes: 2,850.

iN DEMAND (delivered digitally), Addressable: Yes; Playboy TV (delivered digitally); Fresh (delivered digitally); Shorteez (delivered digitally).

Internet Service

Operational: Yes.

Fee: $19.95 installation; $29.95 monthly.

Telephone Service

Analog: Operational

Fee: $49.95 installation; $19.95 monthly

Digital: Operational

Miles of Plant: 525.0 (coaxial); 75.0 (fiber optic). Additional miles planned: 10.0 (coaxial). Homes passed: 15,552.

General Manager: Rob Brooks. Plant Manager: Ray Trice. Office Manager: Lynn Trice.

City fee: 5% of gross.

Ownership: ComSouth Corp. (MSO).

PINE MOUNTAIN—Charter Communications, 1925 Breckenridge Plaza, Ste 100, Duluth, GA 30096-4918. Phones: 770-253-2668 (Newnan); 770-806-7060. Fax: 770-806-7099. Web Site: http://www.charter.com. Also serves Hamilton, Harris County & Troup County. ICA: GA0230.

TV Market Ranking: 94 (Hamilton, Harris County, PINE MOUNTAIN, Troup County (portions)); Below 100 (Troup County (portions)); Outside TV Markets (Troup County (portions)). Franchise award date: N.A. Franchise expiration date: N.A. Began: August 15, 1982.

Channel capacity: 35 (not 2-way capable). Channels available but not in use: N.A.

Basic Service

Subscribers: 1,400.

Programming (received off-air): WJSP-TV (PBS) Columbus; WLTZ (CW, NBC) Columbus; WRBL (CBS) Columbus; WTVM (ABC) Columbus; WXTX (FOX) Columbus.

Programming (via satellite): C-SPAN; C-SPAN 2; WGN America.

Fee: $29.99 installation.

Expanded Basic Service 1

Subscribers: N.A.

Programming (via satellite): ABC Family Channel; AMC; Animal Planet; Arts & Entertainment; BET Networks; Bravo; Cartoon Network; CNBC; CNN; Comcast Sports Net Southeast; Country Music TV; Discovery Channel; Disney Channel; E! Entertainment Television; ESPN; ESPN 2; Food Network; Fox News Channel; Hallmark Channel; Headline News; HGTV; History Channel; Home Shopping Network; Lifetime; MSNBC; MTV; Nickelodeon; Speed Channel; Spike TV; SportSouth; Syfy; TBS Superstation; The Learning Channel; Toon Disney; Travel Channel; Trinity Broadcasting Network; truTV; Turner Network TV; TV Land; USA Network; VH1; Weather Channel.

Fee: $48.99 monthly.

Digital Basic Service

Subscribers: N.A.

Programming (via satellite): BBC America; Discovery Digital Networks; ESPNews; Fox

Sports World; GAS; GSN; Independent Film Channel; MTV Networks Digital Suite; Music Choice; Nick Jr.; Nick Too; NickToons TV; Ovation; Sundance Channel.

Digital Pay Service 1

Pay Units: 462.

Programming (via satellite): Cinemax; Encore (multiplexed); HBO (multiplexed); Showtime (multiplexed); Starz (multiplexed); The Movie Channel (multiplexed).

Fee: $10.00 installation; $10.95 monthly (HBO or Showtime).

Video-On-Demand: No

Pay-Per-View

iN DEMAND (delivered digitally); Playboy TV (delivered digitally).

Internet Service

Operational: No.

Telephone Service

None

Miles of Plant: 11.0 (coaxial); None (fiber optic).

Vice President & General Manager: Matt Favre. Operations Manager: David Spriggs. Technical Operations Manager: Brenda Ivey. Marketing Director: Antoinette Carpenter.

Ownership: Charter Communications Inc. (MSO).

PINEHURST—ComSouth Inc., PO Box 910, 1357-D Sam Nunn Blvd, Perry, GA 31069. Phone: 478-987-0172. Fax: 478-987-9932. Web Site: http://www.comsouth.net. ICA: GA0231.

TV Market Ranking: Below 100 (PINEHURST). Franchise award date: N.A. Franchise expiration date: N.A. Began: April 1, 1986.

Channel capacity: 35 (not 2-way capable). Channels available but not in use: 8.

Basic Service

Subscribers: 50.

Programming (received off-air): WALB (NBC) Albany; WGNM (IND) Macon; WGXA (FOX, MNT) Macon; WMAZ-TV (CBS) Macon; WMGT-TV (MNT, NBC) Macon; WMUM-TV (PBS) Cochran; WRBL (CBS) Columbus; WSST-TV (IND) Cordele; WTVM (ABC) Columbus.

Programming (via satellite): ABC Family Channel; AMC; Animal Planet; Arts & Entertainment; BET Networks; Bravo; Cartoon Network; CNBC; CNN; Comedy Central; Country Music TV; C-SPAN; C-SPAN 2; Discovery Channel; E! Entertainment Television; ESPN; Food Network; Fox News Channel; FX; Hallmark Channel; Headline News; HGTV; History Channel; Home Shopping Network; ION Television; Lifetime; MSNBC; MTV; Nick Jr.; Nickelodeon; QVC; Spike TV; SportSouth; Syfy; The Learning Channel; Travel Channel; truTV; Turner Classic Movies; Turner Network TV; TV Land; USA Network; VH1; Weather Channel; WGN America; WPCH-TV (IND) Atlanta; WPGA-TV (ABC) Perry.

Fee: $49.95 installation; $29.99 monthly.

Video-On-Demand: No

Internet Service

Operational: Yes.

Fee: $49.95 installation; $29.95 monthly.

Telephone Service

None

Miles of Plant: 5.0 (coaxial); None (fiber optic).

General Manager: Rob Brooks. Plant Manager: Ray Trice. Office Manager: Lynn Trice.

Ownership: ComSouth Corp. (MSO).

PINEVIEW—KLiP Interactive, 455 Gees Mill Business Court, Conyers, GA 30013. Phone: 678-727-7100. Fax: 678-727-7002. E-mail: jsheehan@klipia.com. Web Site: http://www.klipia.com. Also serves Pulaski County (southern portion) & Wilcox County (northern portion). ICA: GA0154.

TV Market Ranking: Below 100 (PINEVIEW, Pulaski County (southern portion), Wilcox County (northern portion)). Franchise award date: N.A. Franchise expiration date: N.A. Began: August 1, 1989.

Channel capacity: 65 (not 2-way capable). Channels available but not in use: 31.

Basic Service

Subscribers: 63.

Programming (received off-air): WGXA (FOX, MNT) Macon; WMAZ-TV (CBS) Macon; WMGT-TV (MNT, NBC) Macon; WPCH-TV (IND) Atlanta; WPGA-TV (ABC) Perry; WSST-TV (IND) Cordele.

Programming (via satellite): ABC Family Channel; Animal Planet; Arts & Entertainment; BET Networks; CNBC; CNN; Comcast Sports Net Southeast; Comedy Central; Discovery Channel; Disney Channel; E! Entertainment Television; ESPN; ESPN 2; Fox News Channel; Hallmark Channel; Headline News; Lifetime; QVC; Spike TV; The Learning Channel; Travel Channel; Trinity Broadcasting Network; Turner Network TV; USA Network; Weather Channel; WGN America.

Fee: $29.95 installation; $34.83 monthly.

Pay Service 1

Pay Units: 5.

Programming (via satellite): Cinemax.

Fee: $10.95 monthly.

Pay Service 2

Pay Units: 9.

Programming (via satellite): HBO.

Fee: $10.95 monthly.

Internet Service

Operational: No.

Telephone Service

None

Miles of Plant: 10.0 (coaxial); None (fiber optic). Homes passed: 214.

Chief Executive Officer: Joseph A. Sheehan. General Manager East: Mark Miller. General Manager West: Vance Johnson.

Ownership: KLiP Interactive LLC (MSO).

PITTS—KLiP Interactive, 455 Gees Mill Business Court, Conyers, GA 30013. Phone: 678-727-7100. Fax: 678-727-7002. E-mail: jsheehan@klipia.com. Web Site: http://www.klipia.com. Also serves Seville & Wilcox County (northern portion). ICA: GA0151.

TV Market Ranking: Below 100 (PITTS, Seville, Wilcox County (northern portion)). Franchise award date: N.A. Franchise expiration date: N.A. Began: N.A.

Channel capacity: 65 (not 2-way capable). Channels available but not in use: 33.

Basic Service

Subscribers: 62.

Programming (received off-air): WALB (NBC) Albany; WGXA (FOX, MNT) Macon; WMAZ-TV (CBS) Macon; WPCH-TV (IND) Atlanta; WPGA-TV (ABC) Perry; WSST-TV (IND) Cordele.

Programming (via satellite): ABC Family Channel; AMC; Animal Planet; BET Networks; CNBC; CNN; Comcast Sports Net Southeast; Comedy Central; Discovery Channel; Disney Channel; ESPN; ESPN 2; Fox News Channel; FX; Headline News; Lifetime; QVC; Spike TV; The Learning Channel; Trinity Broadcasting Network; Turner Network TV; USA Network; Weather Channel; WGN America.

Fee: $29.95 installation; $34.73 monthly.

Pay Service 1

Pay Units: 5.

Programming (via satellite): HBO.

Fee: $10.95 monthly.

Pay Service 2

Pay Units: 7.

Programming (via satellite): Cinemax.

Fee: $10.95 monthly.

Internet Service

Operational: No.

Telephone Service

None

Miles of Plant: 12.0 (coaxial); None (fiber optic). Homes passed: 282.

Chief Executive Officer: Joseph A. Sheehan. General Manager East: Mark Miller. General Manager West: Vance Johnson.

Ownership: KLiP Interactive LLC (MSO).

PLAINS—Citizens Cable TV. Now served by LAKE BLACKSHEAR, GA [GA0150]. ICA: GA0232.

POOLER—Hargray, PO Box 5986, Hilton Head, SC 29938. Phone: 843-686-5000. Fax: 843-842-8559. Web Site: http://www.hargray.com. ICA: GA0315. **Note:** This system is an overbuild.

TV Market Ranking: Below 100 (POOLER).

Channel capacity: N.A. Channels available but not in use: N.A.

Basic Service

Subscribers: N.A.

Programming (received off-air): WCIV (ABC) Charleston; WGSA (CW) Baxley; WJCL (ABC) Savannah; WJWJ-TV (PBS) Beaufort; WSAV-TV (MNT, NBC) Savannah; WTGS (FOX) Hardeeville; WTOC-TV (CBS) Savannah; WVAN-TV (PBS) Savannah.

Programming (via satellite): ABC Family Channel; AMC; Animal Planet; Arts & Entertainment; BET Networks; Bio; Bravo; Cartoon Network; CNBC; CNN; Comcast Sports Net Southeast; Comedy Central; Country Music TV; C-SPAN; Discovery Channel; Disney Channel; E! Entertainment Television; ESPN; ESPN 2; ESPN Classic Sports; FitTV; Food Network; Fox News Channel; FX; Golf Channel; Headline News; HGTV; History Channel; Home Shopping Network; Lifetime; MSNBC; MTV; National Geographic Channel; NFL Network; Nickelodeon; Oxygen; QVC; Speed Channel; Spike TV; SportSouth; Syfy; TBS Superstation; The Learning Channel; Toon Disney; Travel Channel; truTV; Turner Classic Movies; Turner Network TV; TV Guide Network; TV Land; Univision; USA Network; Versus; VH1; WE tv; Weather Channel; WGN America.

Current originations: Public Access.

Digital Basic Service

Subscribers: N.A.

Programming (received off-air): WSAV-TV (MNT, NBC) Savannah; WTOC-TV (CBS) Savannah.

Programming (via satellite): BBC America; Boomerang; Canales N; Discovery Channel HD; Discovery Digital Networks; Do-It-Yourself; ESPN HD; ESPNews; Eternal Word TV Network; Fox College Sports Atlantic; Fox College Sports Central; Fox College Sports Pacific; Fox Movie Channel; Fox Soccer; Fuel TV; G4; GAS; Great American Country; GSN; Hallmark Channel; HDNet; HDNet Movies; History Channel International; Independent Film Channel; ION Television; Lifetime Movie Network; MTV Networks Digital Suite; Music Choice; MyNetworkTV Inc.; Nick Jr.; NickToons TV; Outdoor Channel; SoapNet; Style Network; Tennis Channel; The Sportsman Channel; Trinity Broadcasting Network; Universal HD.

Digital Pay Service 1

Pay Units: N.A.

Programming (via satellite): Cinemax (multiplexed); Cinemax HD; Encore (multiplexed); Flix; HBO (multiplexed); HBO HD; Showtime (multiplexed); Starz (multiplexed); Sundance Channel; The Movie Channel (multiplexed).

Video-On-Demand: Yes

Pay-Per-View

Special events (delivered digitally).

Internet Service

Operational: Yes.

Fee: $35.00 monthly.

Telephone Service

Digital: Operational

Operations Manager: Mark Reinhardt. Marketing Director: Karen Ehrhardt. Media Relations Manager: Tray Hunter.

Ownership: Hargray Communications Group Inc. (MSO).

PORT WENTWORTH (portions)—Comcast Cable. Now served by SAVANNAH, GA [GA0005]. ICA: GA0233.

PORTAL—KLiP Interactive, 455 Gees Mill Business Court, Conyers, GA 30013. Phone: 678-727-7100. Fax: 678-727-7002. E-mail: jsheehan@klipia.com. Web Site: http://www.klipia.com. Also serves Bulloch County. ICA: GA0153.

TV Market Ranking: Outside TV Markets (Bulloch County, PORTAL). Franchise award date: N.A. Franchise expiration date: N.A. Began: October 1, 1984.

Channel capacity: 45 (not 2-way capable). Channels available but not in use: 14.

Basic Service

Subscribers: 27.

Programming (received off-air): WJBF (ABC) Augusta; WJCL (ABC) Savannah; WPCH-TV (IND) Atlanta; WRDW-TV (CBS, MNT) Augusta; WSAV-TV (MNT, NBC) Savannah; WTGS (FOX) Hardeeville; WTOC-TV (CBS) Savannah; WVAN-TV (PBS) Savannah.

Programming (via satellite): ABC Family Channel; Animal Planet; Arts & Entertainment; BET Networks; CNBC; CNN; Comedy Central; Country Music TV; Discovery Channel; E! Entertainment Television; ESPN; ESPN 2; History Channel; Home Shopping Network; Lifetime; Nickelodeon; Spike TV; The Learning Channel; Travel Channel; Trinity Broadcasting Network; Turner Network TV; TV Land; Weather Channel.

Fee: $29.95 installation; $30.45 monthly.

Pay Service 1
Pay Units: 8.
Programming (via satellite): HBO.
Fee: $10.95 monthly.
Internet Service
Operational: No.
Telephone Service
None
Miles of Plant: 7.0 (coaxial); None (fiber optic). Homes passed: 200.
President: Joseph A. Sheehan. General Manager East: Mark Miller. General Manager West: Vance Johnson.
Ownership: KLiP Interactive LLC (MSO).

PRESTON—Citizens Cable TV, PO Box 465, Leslie, GA 31764. Phones: 229-268-2288; 866-341-3050; 229-853-1600. Fax: 229-995-6224. Web Site: http://www.citizenscatv.com. ICA: GA0162.
TV Market Ranking: 94 (PRESTON). Franchise award date: N.A. Franchise expiration date: N.A. Began: January 1, 1989.
Channel capacity: 34 (not 2-way capable). Channels available but not in use: 2.
Basic Service
Subscribers: 130.
Programming (received off-air): WACS-TV (PBS) Dawson; WALB (NBC) Albany; WLGA (CW) Opelika; WLTZ (CW, NBC) Columbus; WRBL (CBS) Columbus; WTVM (ABC) Columbus; WXTX (FOX) Columbus.
Programming (via satellite): ABC Family Channel; Arts & Entertainment; BET Networks; CNBC; CNN; Comcast Sports Net Southeast; Comcast/Charter Sports Southeast (CSS); Country Music TV; Discovery Channel; ESPN; ESPN 2; Fox News Channel; FX; HGTV; History Channel; Home Shopping Network; Lifetime; Nickelodeon; Speed Channel; Spike TV; TBS Superstation; The Learning Channel; Turner Network TV; TV Land; USA Network; Weather Channel; WGN America.
Fee: $19.95 installation; $34.95 monthly.
Pay Service 1
Pay Units: 30.
Programming (via satellite): HBO.
Fee: $13.50 monthly.
Pay Service 2
Pay Units: 30.
Programming (via satellite): Cinemax.
Fee: $13.50 monthly.
Video-On-Demand: No
Internet Service
Operational: No.
Telephone Service
None
Miles of Plant: 8.0 (coaxial); None (fiber optic). Additional miles planned: 3.0 (coaxial). Homes passed: 175. Total homes in franchised area: 235.
General Manager: Milton Foster.
Ownership: Citizens Cable TV (MSO).

QUITMAN—Comcast Cable, 471 South Church St, Ste C, Homerville, GA 31634. Phones: 850-574-4016 (Tallahassee office); 912-487-2224. Fax: 850-574-4030. Web Site: http://www.comcast.com. Also serves Brooks County (portions). ICA: GA0234.
TV Market Ranking: Below 100 (Brooks County (portions), QUITMAN). Franchise award date: March 3, 1970. Franchise expiration date: N.A. Began: November 1, 1970.
Channel capacity: 69 (operating 2-way). Channels available but not in use: None.
Basic Service
Subscribers: N.A. Included in Tallahassee, FL
Programming (received off-air): WABW-TV (PBS) Pelham; WALB (NBC) Albany; WCTV (CBS, MNT) Thomasville; WFXL (FOX) Albany; WTLH (CW, FOX) Bainbridge; WTWC-TV (NBC) Tallahassee; WTXL-TV (ABC) Tallahassee; 20 FMs.
Programming (via satellite): QVC.
Fee: $27.92 installation; $15.16 monthly.
Expanded Basic Service 1
Subscribers: N.A.
Programming (via satellite): ABC Family Channel; AMC; Animal Planet; Arts & Entertainment; BET Networks; Cartoon Network; CNN; Comcast/Charter Sports Southeast (CSS); Comedy Central; Country Music TV; C-SPAN; C-SPAN 2; CW+; Discovery Channel; Discovery Health Channel; Disney Channel; E! Entertainment Television; ESPN; ESPN 2; Eternal Word TV Network; Food Network; Fox News Channel; Fox Sports Net; FX; Golf Channel; Great American Country; GSN; Hallmark Channel; Headline News; HGTV; History Channel; Home Shopping Network; ION Television; Lifetime; MTV; Nickelodeon; Speed Channel; Spike TV; Style Network; Syfy; TBS Superstation; The Learning Channel; Travel Channel; Trinity Broadcasting Network; truTV; Turner Classic Movies; Turner Network TV; Turner South; TV Land; TV One; USA Network; Versus; VH1; Weather Channel; WGN America.
Fee: $23.11 monthly.
Digital Basic Service
Subscribers: N.A.
Programming (via satellite): Country Music TV; Encore (multiplexed); Flix; GAS; Lifetime Movie Network; MoviePlex; MTV Networks Digital Suite; Music Choice; Nick Jr.; Nick Too; PBS Kids Sprout; WAM! America's Kidz Network.
Pay Service 1
Pay Units: N.A.
Programming (via satellite): Cinemax; HBO; Showtime; The Movie Channel.
Fee: $20.00 installation; $9.95 monthly (each).
Digital Pay Service 1
Pay Units: 265.
Programming (via satellite): Cinemax (multiplexed); HBO (multiplexed); Showtime (multiplexed); Starz; The Movie Channel (multiplexed).
Fee: $9.95 monthly (each).
Video-On-Demand: No
Pay-Per-View
Addressable homes: 265.
iN DEMAND (delivered digitally); Hot Choice (delivered digitally); Playboy TV (delivered digitally); Fresh (delivered digitally); Shorteez (delivered digitally).
Internet Service
Operational: Yes.
Telephone Service
None
Miles of plant (coax) & homes passed included in Tallahassee, FL
General Manager: K. C. McWilliams. Technical Operations Director: Terry Pullen. Area Technical Manager: Andy Musgrove. Marketing Director: Claire Evans. System Coordinator: Carla Musgrove.
City fee: 3% of gross.
Ownership: Comcast Cable Communications Inc. (MSO).

RANGER—Formerly served by 3D Cable Inc. No longer in operation. ICA: GA0171.

RAYLE—Formerly served by KLiP Interactive. No longer in operation. ICA: GA0303.

RAYSVILLE—Formerly served by KLiP Interactive. No longer in operation. ICA: GA0302.

REBECCA—KLiP Interactive, 455 Gees Mill Business Court, Conyers, GA 30013. Phone: 678-727-7100. Fax: 678-727-7002. E-mail: jsheehan@klipia.com. Web Site: http://www.klipia.com. ICA: GA0235.
TV Market Ranking: Below 100 (REBECCA). Franchise award date: N.A. Franchise expiration date: N.A. Began: N.A.
Channel capacity: 65 (not 2-way capable). Channels available but not in use: 35.
Basic Service
Subscribers: 31.
Programming (received off-air): WALB (NBC) Albany; WFXL (FOX) Albany; WMAZ-TV (CBS) Macon; WPCH-TV (IND) Atlanta; WPGA-TV (ABC) Perry; WSST-TV (IND) Cordele.
Programming (via satellite): ABC Family Channel; AMC; Animal Planet; BET Networks; CNBC; CNN; Comedy Central; Discovery Channel; E! Entertainment Television; ESPN; ESPN 2; Headline News; Lifetime; Nickelodeon; QVC; Spike TV; The Learning Channel; Trinity Broadcasting Network; Turner Network TV; USA Network; Weather Channel; WGN America.
Fee: $29.95 installation; $31.45 monthly.
Pay Service 1
Pay Units: 6.
Programming (via satellite): Cinemax.
Fee: $10.95 monthly.
Pay Service 2
Pay Units: 3.
Programming (via satellite): HBO.
Fee: $10.95 monthly.
Internet Service
Operational: No.
Telephone Service
None
Miles of Plant: 8.0 (coaxial); None (fiber optic). Homes passed: 113.
Chief Executive Officer: Joseph A. Sheehan. General Manager East: Mark Miller. General Manager West: Vance Johnson.
Ownership: KLiP Interactive LLC (MSO).

RECOVERY—KLiP Interactive, 455 Gees Mill Business Court, Conyers, GA 30013. Phone: 678-727-7100. Fax: 678-727-7002. E-mail: jsheehan@klipia.com. Web Site: http://www.klipia.com. ICA: GA0296.
TV Market Ranking: Below 100 (RECOVERY). Franchise award date: N.A. Franchise expiration date: N.A. Began: N.A.
Channel capacity: 65 (not 2-way capable). Channels available but not in use: 35.
Basic Service
Subscribers: 27.
Programming (received off-air): WABW-TV (PBS) Pelham; WCTV (CBS, MNT) Thomasville; WJHG-TV (CW, MNT, NBC) Panama City; WMBB (ABC) Panama City; WPCH-TV (IND) Atlanta; WTLH (CW, FOX) Bainbridge; WTVY (CBS, CW, MNT) Dothan.
Programming (via satellite): ABC Family Channel; Animal Planet; Arts & Entertainment; Bravo; CNBC; CNN; Country Music TV; Discovery Channel; Disney Channel; ESPN; ESPN 2; Headline News; History Channel; Lifetime; Nickelodeon; QVC; Spike TV; The Learning Channel; Travel Channel; Trinity Broadcasting Network; Turner Network TV; USA Network; Weather Channel.
Fee: $29.95 installation; $31.95 monthly.
Pay Service 1
Pay Units: 1.
Programming (via satellite): HBO.
Fee: $10.95 monthly.
Internet Service
Operational: No.
Telephone Service
None
Miles of Plant: 8.0 (coaxial); None (fiber optic). Homes passed: 143.
Chief Executive Officer: Joeseph A. Sheehan. General Manager East: Mark Miller. General Manager West: Vance Johnson.
Ownership: KLiP Interactive LLC (MSO).

REIDSVILLE—Kennedy Cablevision Inc., PO Box 2059, Hwy 280 W, Reidsville, GA 30453. Phone: 912-557-6133. Fax: 912-557-6545. E-mail: kencable@alltel.net. Web Site: http://www.kennedynetworkservices.com. Also serves Cobbtown & Georgia State Prison. ICA: GA0103.
TV Market Ranking: Below 100 (Georgia State Prison, REIDSVILLE); Outside TV Markets (Cobbtown). Franchise award date: N.A. Franchise expiration date: N.A. Began: February 1, 1974.
Channel capacity: 64 (operating 2-way). Channels available but not in use: None.
Basic Service
Subscribers: 1,377.
Programming (received off-air): WJCL (ABC) Savannah; WSAV-TV (MNT, NBC) Savannah; WTGS (FOX) Hardeeville; WTOC-TV (CBS) Savannah; WVAN-TV (PBS) Savannah; allband FM.
Programming (via satellite): ABC Family Channel; AMC; Animal Planet; Arts & Entertainment; BET Networks; Cartoon Network; CNBC; CNN; Comcast Sports Net Southeast; Country Music TV; C-SPAN; Discovery Channel; Disney Channel; E! Entertainment Television; ESPN; Fox Movie Channel; Fox News Channel; FX; GSN; Hallmark Channel; Headline News; HGTV; History Channel; Home Shopping Network; Lifetime; Nickelodeon; Speed Channel; Spike TV; SportSouth; Syfy; TBS Superstation; The Learning Channel; Travel Channel; Trinity Broadcasting Network; truTV; Turner Classic Movies; Turner Network TV; TV Guide Network; TV Land; USA Network; Versus; VH1; Weather Channel; WGN America.
Current originations: Religious Access.
Fee: $40.00 installation; $38.95 monthly; $3.00 converter; $30.00 additional installation.
Pay Service 1
Pay Units: 212.
Programming (via satellite): HBO.
Fee: $10.00 installation; $10.95 monthly.
Pay Service 2
Pay Units: 150.
Programming (via satellite): Showtime.
Fee: $10.00 installation; $10.95 monthly.
Pay Service 3
Pay Units: 102.
Programming (via satellite): Cinemax.
Fee: $10.00 installation; $9.95 monthly.
Pay Service 4
Pay Units: 67.
Programming (via satellite): The Movie Channel.
Fee: $10.00 installation; $9.95 monthly.
Pay Service 5
Pay Units: N.A.
Programming (via satellite): DMX Music.
Video-On-Demand: No
Internet Service
Operational: Yes.
Subscribers: 298.
Fee: $45.00 installation; $29.95 monthly.
Telephone Service
None
Miles of Plant: 67.0 (coaxial); None (fiber optic). Homes passed: 2,278.
Manager: Gina Sheridan. Chief Technician: Nick Burns.

City fee: 3% of gross.
Ownership: J. Roger Kennedy Jr. (MSO).

RENTZ—KLiP Interactive, 455 Gees Mill Business Court, Conyers, GA 30013. Phone: 678-727-7100. Fax: 678-727-7002. E-mail: jsheehan@klipia.com. Web Site: http://www.klipia.com. Also serves Caldwell, Chester, Dexter & Laurens County (eastern portion). ICA: GA0209.
TV Market Ranking: Below 100 (Chester, Laurens County (eastern portion) (portions)); Outside TV Markets (Caldwell, Dexter, Laurens County (eastern portion) (portions), Laurens County (eastern portion), RENTZ). Franchise award date: N.A. Franchise expiration date: N.A. Began: January 1, 1988.
Channel capacity: 45 (not 2-way capable). Channels available but not in use: 7.

Basic Service
Subscribers: 301.
Programming (received off-air): WGXA (FOX, MNT) Macon; WMAZ-TV (CBS) Macon; WMGT-TV (MNT, NBC) Macon; WPCH-TV (IND) Atlanta; WPGA-TV (ABC) Perry.
Programming (via satellite): ABC Family Channel; Arts & Entertainment; BET Networks; CNBC; CNN; Comcast Sports Net Southeast; Country Music TV; C-SPAN; Discovery Channel; Disney Channel; E! Entertainment Television; ESPN; ESPN 2; FX; Headline News; History Channel; Lifetime; MTV; Nickelodeon; QVC; Spike TV; SportSouth; Syfy; Trinity Broadcasting Network; truTV; Turner Network TV; USA Network; Weather Channel; WGN America.
Fee: $44.95 installation; $39.95 monthly.

Digital Basic Service
Subscribers: N.A.
Programming (via satellite): AmericanLife TV Network; BBC America; Bio; Bloomberg Television; Bravo; Current; Discovery Digital Networks; DMX Music; ESPN Classic Sports; ESPNews; FitTV; Fox Movie Channel; Fox Soccer; Fuse; G4; Golf Channel; GSN; HGTV; History Channel International; Independent Film Channel; INSP; Lifetime Movie Network; Military History Channel; Outdoor Channel; Ovation; Sleuth; Speed Channel; Style Network; Sundance Channel; Turner Classic Movies; Versus; WE tv.

Pay Service 1
Pay Units: 39.
Programming (via satellite): HBO.
Fee: $10.95 monthly.

Pay Service 2
Pay Units: 32.
Programming (via satellite): Showtime.
Fee: $10.95 monthly.

Pay Service 3
Pay Units: 9.
Programming (via satellite): The Movie Channel.
Fee: $10.95 monthly.

Digital Pay Service 1
Pay Units: N.A.
Programming (via satellite): Cinemax (multiplexed); Encore (multiplexed); Flix; HBO (multiplexed); Showtime (multiplexed); Starz (multiplexed); The Movie Channel (multiplexed).
Fee: $10.95 monthly (HBO, Showtime or TMC).

Pay-Per-View
iN DEMAND (delivered digitally), Addressable: Yes; Playboy TV (delivered digitally); Fresh (delivered digitally); Shorteez (delivered digitally); Sports PPV (delivered digitally); Hot Choice (delivered digitally).

Internet Service
Operational: No.

Telephone Service
None
Miles of Plant: 48.0 (coaxial); None (fiber optic). Homes passed: 1,527.
Chief Executive Officer: Joseph A. Sheehan. General Manager East: Mark Miller. General Manager West: Vance Johnson.
Ownership: KLiP Interactive LLC (MSO).

REYNOLDS—Flint Cable TV, PO Box 669, 105 W Marion, Reynolds, GA 31076-0669. Phone: 478-847-3101. Fax: 478-847-2010. Web Site: http://www.flintcatv.com. ICA: GA0236.
TV Market Ranking: Below 100 (REYNOLDS). Franchise award date: October 21, 1981. Franchise expiration date: N.A. Began: N.A.
Channel capacity: 40 (not 2-way capable). Channels available but not in use: 5.

Basic Service
Subscribers: 420.
Programming (received off-air): WGNM (IND) Macon; WGXA (FOX, MNT) Macon; WLGA (CW) Opelika; WLTZ (CW, NBC) Columbus; WMAZ-TV (CBS) Macon; WMGT-TV (MNT, NBC) Macon; WMUM-TV (PBS) Cochran; WPGA-TV (ABC) Perry; WRBL (CBS) Columbus; WTVM (ABC) Columbus; WXTX (FOX) Columbus.
Programming (via satellite): INSP; QVC; TBS Superstation; Weather Channel.
Fee: $35.00 installation; $19.99 monthly.

Expanded Basic Service 1
Subscribers: N.A.
Programming (via satellite): ABC Family Channel; Animal Planet; Arts & Entertainment; BET Networks; Bloomberg Television; Boomerang; Bravo; Cartoon Network; CNBC; CNN; Comcast Sports Net Southeast; Comedy Central; Country Music TV; C-SPAN; C-SPAN 2; C-SPAN 3; Discovery Channel; Disney Channel; E! Entertainment Television; ESPN; ESPN 2; ESPN Classic Sports; Food Network; Fox News Channel; FX; Gospel Music Channel; GSN; Hallmark Channel; Headline News; HGTV; History Channel; Lifetime; MSNBC; MTV; National Geographic Channel; Nickelodeon; RFD-TV; Speed Channel; Spike TV; SportSouth; Syfy; The Learning Channel; The Sportsman Channel; Travel Channel; Trinity Broadcasting Network; truTV; Turner Classic Movies; Turner Network TV; TV Land; USA Network; VH1; WE tv; WGN America; WPIX (CW, IND) New York.
Fee: $20.00 monthly.

Digital Basic Service
Subscribers: N.A.
Programming (via satellite): BBC America; Chiller; Discovery Health Channel; Discovery Home Channel; Discovery Kids Channel; Discovery Military Channel; Discovery Times Channel; DMX Music; Fox Soccer; Halogen Network; Independent Film Channel; International Television (ITV); Nick Jr.; Science Channel; SoapNet.
Fee: $3.00 monthly.

Digital Expanded Basic Service
Subscribers: N.A.
Programming (via satellite): Bio; Canal 52MX; Cine Latino; Cine Mexicano; CMT Pure Country; CNN en Espanol; Current; Discovery en Espanol; Encore (multiplexed); ESPN Deportes; ESPNews; Flix; Fox College Sports Atlantic; Fox College Sports Central; Fox College Sports Pacific; Fox Movie Channel; Fox Sports en Espanol; Fuse; G4; GAS; Golf Channel; Gospel Music Channel; Great American Country; History Channel en Espanol; History Channel International; MTV Hits; MTV Tres; MTV2; NickToons TV; Outdoor Channel; Ovation; Sleuth; Style Network; Sundance Channel; Toon Disney; Versus; VH1 Classic; VH1 Soul.
Fee: $6.99 monthly (encore movies tier, sports & exploration tier, entertainment tier or Latino tier)).

Pay Service 1
Pay Units: N.A.
Programming (via satellite): Cinemax; Encore; HBO.
Fee: $2.99 monthly (Encore), $11.99 monthly (HBO or Cinemax).

Digital Pay Service 1
Pay Units: N.A.
Programming (via satellite): Cinemax (multiplexed); HBO (multiplexed); Showtime (multiplexed); Starz (multiplexed); The Movie Channel (multiplexed).
Fee: $11.99 monthly (HBO, Cinemax, Showtime/TMC or Starz).

Video-On-Demand: No

Internet Service
Operational: No.

Telephone Service
None
Homes passed: 509. Total homes in franchised area: 509.
Manager: Jim Bond. Marketing Manager: Laurie Long. Engineer: Mark Geiger.
Ownership: Flint Cable Television Inc. (MSO).

RHINE—KLiP Interactive, 455 Gees Mill Business Court, Conyers, GA 30013. Phone: 678-727-7100. Fax: 678-727-7002. E-mail: jsheehan@klipia.com. Web Site: http://www.klipia.com. ICA: GA0164.
TV Market Ranking: Outside TV Markets (RHINE). Franchise award date: N.A. Franchise expiration date: N.A. Began: N.A.
Channel capacity: 45 (not 2-way capable). Channels available but not in use: 17.

Basic Service
Subscribers: 54.
Programming (received off-air): WALB (NBC) Albany; WFXL (FOX) Albany; WMAZ-TV (CBS) Macon; WPCH-TV (IND) Atlanta; WPGA-TV (ABC) Perry.
Programming (via satellite): ABC Family Channel; Animal Planet; Arts & Entertainment; BET Networks; Bravo; CNN; Discovery Channel; ESPN; ESPN 2; History Channel; Lifetime; Nickelodeon; QVC; Speed Channel; Spike TV; The Learning Channel; Travel Channel; Turner Network TV; TV Land; USA Network; Weather Channel; WGN America.
Fee: $29.95 installation; $31.00 monthly.

Pay Service 1
Pay Units: 9.
Programming (via satellite): HBO.
Fee: $10.95 monthly.

Internet Service
Operational: No.

Telephone Service
None
Miles of Plant: 7.0 (coaxial); None (fiber optic). Homes passed: 160.
Chief Executive Officer: Joseph A Sheehan. General Manager West: Vance Miller. General Manager East: Mark Miller.
Ownership: KLiP Interactive LLC (MSO).

RINGGOLD—Charter Communications, 1103 S Hamilton St, Dalton, GA 30720-7860. Phones: 706-428-2290; 865-984-1400 (Maryville, TN office). Fax: 706-260-2520. Web Site: http://www.charter.com. Also serves Catoosa County. ICA: GA0238.
TV Market Ranking: 78 (Catoosa County, RINGGOLD). Franchise award date: January 16, 1984. Franchise expiration date: N.A. Began: N.A.
Channel capacity: N.A. Channels available but not in use: N.A.

Basic Service
Subscribers: 6,059.
Programming (received off-air): WDEF-TV (CBS) Chattanooga; WDSI-TV (FOX, MNT) Chattanooga; WELF-TV (TBN) Dalton; WFLI-TV (CW) Cleveland; WNGH-TV (PBS) Chatsworth; WRCB (NBC) Chattanooga; WTCI (PBS) Chattanooga; WTVC (ABC) Chattanooga.
Programming (via satellite): C-SPAN; C-SPAN 2; INSP; QVC; TBS Superstation; Weather Channel; WGN America.
Current originations: Public Access.
Fee: $29.99 installation.

Expanded Basic Service 1
Subscribers: 5,673.
Programming (via satellite): ABC Family Channel; AMC; Animal Planet; Arts & Entertainment; BET Networks; Bravo; Cartoon Network; CNBC; CNN; Comcast Sports Net Southeast; Comcast/Charter Sports Southeast (CSS); Comedy Central; Country Music TV; Discovery Channel; Disney Channel; E! Entertainment Television; ESPN; ESPN 2; Eternal Word TV Network; Food Network; Fox News Channel; FX; G4; GalaVision; Golf Channel; GSN; Hallmark Channel; Headline News; HGTV; History Channel; Home Shopping Network; Lifetime; MTV; National Geographic Channel; Nickelodeon; SoapNet; Speed Channel; SportSouth; Syfy; The Learning Channel; Travel Channel; Turner Classic Movies; Turner Network TV; TV Land; Univision; USA Network; Versus; VH1; WE tv.
Fee: $50.99 monthly.

Digital Basic Service
Subscribers: N.A.
Programming (via satellite): BBC America; Bio; Discovery Digital Networks; Do-It-Yourself; Fox College Sports Atlantic; Fox College Sports Central; Fox College Sports Pacific; Fox Sports en Espanol; Fox Sports World; Great American Country; History Channel International; Independent Film Channel; Music Choice; Nick Jr.; Sundance Channel; TV Guide Interactive Inc.

Digital Pay Service 1
Pay Units: 831.
Programming (via satellite): Cinemax (multiplexed).
Fee: $25.00 installation; $10.95 monthly.

Digital Pay Service 2
Pay Units: 1,242.
Programming (via satellite): HBO (multiplexed).
Fee: $11.95 monthly.

Digital Pay Service 3
Pay Units: 1.
Programming (via satellite): Showtime (multiplexed).

Digital Pay Service 4
Pay Units: N.A.
Programming (via satellite): Encore (multiplexed); Flix; Starz (multiplexed); The Movie Channel (multiplexed).

Video-On-Demand: No

Pay-Per-View
Hot Choice (delivered digitally), Addressable: Yes; iN DEMAND (delivered digitally); Playboy TV (delivered digitally); Fresh (delivered digitally); Shorteez (delivered digitally).

Internet Service
Operational: Yes. Began: September 1, 2001.
Broadband Service: Charter Pipeline.
Fee: $29.99 monthly.

Telephone Service
Digital: Operational
Miles of Plant: 170.0 (coaxial); None (fiber optic). Homes passed: 7,207. Total homes in franchised area: 13,368.
Operations Manager: Mike Burns. Technical Operations Director: Grant Evans. Marketing Director: Pat Hollenbeck.
Ownership: Charter Communications Inc. (MSO).

ROBERTA—Flint Cable TV, PO Box 669, 105 W Marion, Reynolds, GA 31076-0669. Phone: 478-847-3101. Fax: 478-847-1200. Web Site: http://www.flintcatv.com. ICA: GA0240.
TV Market Ranking: Below 100 (ROBERTA). Franchise award date: July 7, 1981. Franchise expiration date: N.A. Began: N.A.
Channel capacity: 40 (not 2-way capable). Channels available but not in use: 8.

Basic Service
Subscribers: 397.
Programming (received off-air): WGNM (IND) Macon; WGXA (FOX, MNT) Macon; WLTZ (CW, NBC) Columbus; WMAZ-TV (CBS) Macon; WMGT-TV (MNT, NBC) Macon; WMUM-TV (PBS) Cochran; WPGA-TV (ABC) Perry; WRBL (CBS) Columbus; WTVM (ABC) Columbus; WXTX (FOX) Columbus.
Programming (via satellite): INSP; QVC; TBS Superstation; Weather Channel; WLGA (CW) Opelika.
Fee: $35.00 installation; $19.99 monthly.

Expanded Basic Service 1
Subscribers: N.A.
Programming (via satellite): ABC Family Channel; Animal Planet; Arts & Entertainment; BET Networks; Bloomberg Television; Boomerang; Bravo; Cartoon Network; CNBC; CNN; Comcast Sports Net Southeast; Comedy Central; Country Music TV; C-SPAN; C-SPAN 2; C-SPAN 3; Discovery Channel; Disney Channel; E! Entertainment Television; ESPN; ESPN 2; ESPN Classic Sports; Food Network; Fox News Channel; FX; Gospel Music Channel; GSN; Hallmark Channel; Headline News; HGTV; History Channel; Lifetime; MSNBC; MTV; National Geographic Channel; Nickelodeon; RFD-TV; Speed Channel; Spike TV; SportSouth; Syfy; The Learning Channel; The Sportsman Channel; Travel Channel; Trinity Broadcasting Network; truTV; Turner Classic Movies; Turner Network TV; TV Land; USA Network; VH1; WE tv; WGN America; WPIX (CW, IND) New York.
Fee: $20.00 monthly.

Digital Basic Service
Subscribers: N.A.
Programming (via satellite): BBC America; Chiller; Discovery Digital Networks; Discovery Health Channel; Discovery Home Channel; Discovery Kids Channel; Discovery Military Channel; Discovery Times Channel; DMX Music; Fox Soccer; Independent Film Channel; International Television (ITV); Nick Jr.; Science Channel; SoapNet.
Fee: $3.00 monthly.

Digital Expanded Basic Service
Subscribers: N.A.
Programming (via satellite): Bio; Canal 52MX; Cine Latino; Cine Mexicano; CMT Pure Country; CNN en Espanol; Current; Discovery en Espanol; Encore (multiplexed); ESPN Deportes; ESPNews; Flix; Fox College Sports Atlantic; Fox College Sports Central; Fox College Sports Pacific; Fox Movie Channel; Fox Sports en Espanol; Fuse; G4; GAS; Golf Channel; Gospel Music Channel; Great American Country; History Channel en Espanol; History Channel International; MTV Hits; MTV Tres; MTV2; NickToons TV; Outdoor Channel; Ovation; Sleuth; Style Network; Sundance Channel; Toon Disney; Versus; VH1 Classic; VH1 Soul.

Pay Service 1
Pay Units: N.A.
Programming (via satellite): Cinemax; Encore; HBO.
Fee: $2.99 monthly (Encore), $11.99 monthly (HBO or Cinemax).

Digital Pay Service 1
Pay Units: N.A.
Programming (via satellite): Cinemax (multiplexed); HBO (multiplexed); Showtime (multiplexed); Starz (multiplexed); The Movie Channel.
Fee: $11.99 monthly (HBO, Cinemax, Starz or Showtime/TMC).

Video-On-Demand: No

Internet Service
Operational: No.

Telephone Service
None
Homes passed: 617. Total homes in franchised area: 617.
Manager: Jim Bond. Marketing Manager: Laurie Long.
Ownership: Flint Cable Television Inc. (MSO).

ROCHELLE—KLiP Interactive, 455 Gees Mill Business Court, Conyers, GA 30013. Phone: 678-727-7100. Fax: 678-727-7002. E-mail: jsheehan@klipia.com. Web Site: http://www.klipia.com. ICA: GA0241.
TV Market Ranking: Below 100 (ROCHELLE). Franchise award date: N.A. Franchise expiration date: N.A. Began: August 1, 1982.
Channel capacity: 65 (not 2-way capable). Channels available but not in use: 31.

Basic Service
Subscribers: 193.
Programming (received off-air): WALB (NBC) Albany; WFXL (FOX) Albany; WGXA (FOX, MNT) Macon; WMAZ-TV (CBS) Macon; WMGT-TV (MNT, NBC) Macon; WPCH-TV (IND) Atlanta; WPGA-TV (ABC) Perry; WSST-TV (IND) Cordele.
Programming (via satellite): ABC Family Channel; Animal Planet; Arts & Entertainment; BET Networks; CNN; Comcast Sports Net Southeast; Country Music TV; Discovery Channel; Disney Channel; ESPN; ESPN 2; Fox News Channel; Hallmark Channel; Home Shopping Network; Lifetime; MTV; Nickelodeon; Spike TV; The Learning Channel; Turner Network TV; TV Land; USA Network; VH1; Weather Channel; WGN America.
Fee: $29.95 installation; $38.21 monthly.

Pay Service 1
Pay Units: 21.
Programming (via satellite): Cinemax.
Fee: $10.95 monthly.

Pay Service 2
Pay Units: 36.
Programming (via satellite): HBO.
Fee: $10.95 monthly.

Internet Service
Operational: No.

Telephone Service
None
Miles of Plant: 15.0 (coaxial); None (fiber optic). Homes passed: 500.
Chief Executive Officer: Joseph A. Sheehan. General Manager East: Mark Miller. General Manager West: Vance Johnson.
Ownership: KLiP Interactive LLC (MSO).

ROCKMART—Charter Communications, 1925 Breckenridge Plaza, Ste 100, Duluth, GA 30096-4918. Phones: 770-748-5443 (Cedartown office); 770-806-7060 (Administrative office). Fax: 770-806-7099. Web Site: http://www.charter.com. Also serves Aragon & Polk County (eastern portion). ICA: GA0242.
TV Market Ranking: 18 (Aragon, Polk County (eastern portion), ROCKMART). Franchise award date: February 1, 1973. Franchise expiration date: N.A. Began: March 1, 1974.
Channel capacity: N.A. Channels available but not in use: N.A.

Basic Service
Subscribers: 2,477.
Programming (received off-air): WAGA-TV (FOX) Atlanta; WATC-DT (ETV) Atlanta; WATL (MNT) Atlanta; WGCL-TV (CBS) Atlanta; WGTV (PBS) Athens; WHSG-TV (TBN) Monroe; WPBA (PBS) Atlanta; WPCH-TV (IND) Atlanta; WPXA-TV (ION) Rome; WSB-TV (ABC) Atlanta; WUPA (CW) Atlanta; WUVG-DT (UNV) Athens; WXIA-TV (NBC) Atlanta; allband FM.
Programming (via satellite): C-SPAN; ESPN; INSP; TV Guide Network; WGN America.
Current originations: Government Access; Leased Access.
Fee: $29.95 installation.

Expanded Basic Service 1
Subscribers: 2,332.
Programming (via satellite): ABC Family Channel; AMC; Animal Planet; Arts & Entertainment; BET Networks; Bravo; Cartoon Network; CNBC; CNN; Comcast Sports Net Southeast; Comcast/Charter Sports Southeast (CSS); Comedy Central; Country Music TV; C-SPAN 2; Discovery Channel; Disney Channel; E! Entertainment Television; ESPN 2; Eternal Word TV Network; Food Network; Fox News Channel; FX; Golf Channel; Great American Country; GSN; Hallmark Channel; Headline News; HGTV; History Channel; Home Shopping Network; Lifetime; MSNBC; MTV; MTV2; Nickelodeon; QVC; Speed Channel; Spike TV; SportSouth; Style Network; Syfy; The Learning Channel; Travel Channel; truTV; Turner Classic Movies; Turner Network TV; TV Land; TV One; USA Network; Versus; VH1; Weather Channel.
Fee: $48.99 monthly.

Digital Basic Service
Subscribers: N.A.
Programming (via satellite): BBC America; Bio; Canales N; Cooking Channel; C-SPAN 3; Discovery Digital Networks; Discovery HD Theater; DMX Music; Do-It-Yourself; Encore; ESPN; ESPNews; Falconsvision; Flix (multiplexed); Fox College Sports Atlantic; Fox College Sports Central; Fox College Sports Pacific; Fox Soccer; G4; GAS; Gol TV; Great American Country; History Channel International; Jewelry Television; Lifetime Movie Network; LOGO; MTV Networks Digital Suite; National Geographic Channel; NBA TV; NFL Network; Nick Jr.; Nick Too; NickToons TV; PBS Kids Sprout; SoapNet; Sundance Channel (multiplexed); The Learning Channel; Toon Disney; Turner Network TV HD; TV Guide Interactive Inc.; WAM! America's Kidz Network; Weatherscan.
Fee: $14.00 monthly.

Digital Pay Service 1
Pay Units: N.A.
Programming (via satellite): Cinemax (multiplexed); HBO (multiplexed); Showtime (multiplexed); Starz (multiplexed); The Movie Channel (multiplexed).

Video-On-Demand: Yes

Pay-Per-View
iN DEMAND; Hot Choice (delivered digitally); Playboy TV (delivered digitally); Fresh (delivered digitally); Shorteez (delivered digitally).

Internet Service
Operational: Yes.
Broadband Service: Charter Pipeline.
Fee: $29.99 monthly.

Telephone Service
Digital: Operational
Fee: $29.99 monthly
Miles of Plant: 72.0 (coaxial); None (fiber optic). Homes passed: 3,019. Total homes in franchised area: 5,162.
Vice President & General Manager: Matt Favre. Operations Manager: David Spriggs. Technical Operations Manager: Darrell Currier. Sales & Marketing Director: Antoinette Carpenter.
Ownership: Charter Communications Inc. (MSO).

ROSSVILLE—Comcast Cable, 2030 Polymer Dr, Chattanooga, TN 37421. Phone: 423-855-3900. Fax: 423-892-5893. Web Site: http://www.comcast.com. Also serves Catoosa County (portions), Chattanooga Valley, Chickamauga, Fairview, Fort Oglethorpe, Lakeview & Walker County (portions). ICA: GA0022.
TV Market Ranking: 18 (ROSSVILLE (portions)); 18,78 (Walker County (portions) (portions)); 78 (Catoosa County (portions), Chattanooga Valley, Chickamauga, Fairview, Fort Oglethorpe, Lakeview). Franchise award date: N.A. Franchise expiration date: N.A. Began: N.A.
Channel capacity: N.A. Channels available but not in use: N.A.

Basic Service
Subscribers: N.A. Included in Chattanooga
Programming (received off-air): WDEF-TV (CBS) Chattanooga; WDSI-TV (FOX, MNT) Chattanooga; WELF-TV (TBN) Dalton; WFLI-TV (CW) Cleveland; WNGH-TV (PBS) Chatsworth; WRCB (NBC) Chattanooga; WTCI (PBS) Chattanooga; WTVC (ABC) Chattanooga.
Programming (via satellite): ION Television; Nickelodeon; QVC; TBS Superstation; Turner Network TV; WGN America.
Current originations: Educational Access; Leased Access.
Fee: $53.99 installation; $10.20 monthly.

Expanded Basic Service 1
Subscribers: 13,340.
Programming (received off-air): WDNN-CA (IND) Dalton.

Programming (via satellite): ABC Family Channel; AMC; Animal Planet; Arts & Entertainment; BET Networks; Bravesvision; Bravo; Cartoon Network; CNBC; CNN; Comcast/Charter Sports Southeast (CSS); Comedy Central; Country Music TV; C-SPAN; C-SPAN 2; Discovery Channel; Discovery Health Channel; E! Entertainment Television; ESPN; ESPN 2; Food Network; Fox News Channel; Fox Sports Net; FX; Golf Channel; GSN; Hallmark Channel; Headline News; HGTV; Lifetime; MSNBC; MTV; Speed Channel; Spike TV; SportSouth; Style Network; The Learning Channel; Turner Classic Movies; TV Guide Network; TV Land; USA Network; Versus; VH1; Weather Channel.
Fee: $39.79 monthly.

Digital Basic Service
Subscribers: 3,000.
Programming (via satellite): BBC America; Canales N; C-SPAN 3; Discovery Digital Networks; Disney Channel; DMX Music; Encore Action; ESPNews; Flix; G4; GAS; History Channel; INSP; MTV Networks Digital Suite; Nick Jr.; Nick Too; SoapNet; Sundance Channel; Syfy; Toon Disney; WAM! America's Kidz Network; Weatherscan.
Fee: $14.95 monthly.

Digital Pay Service 1
Pay Units: N.A.
Programming (via satellite): Cinemax (multiplexed); HBO (multiplexed); Showtime (multiplexed); Starz (multiplexed).
Fee: $12.00 monthly (each).

Video-On-Demand: Yes

Pay-Per-View
Addressable homes: 3,000.
iN DEMAND (delivered digitally), Addressable: Yes; Sports PPV (delivered digitally); Playboy TV (delivered digitally); Fresh (delivered digitally); Shorteez (delivered digitally); Hot Choice (delivered digitally); Pleasure (delivered digitally); ESPN Gameplan (delivered digitally); ESPN Full Court (delivered digitally).

Internet Service
Operational: Yes.
Broadband Service: Comcast High Speed Internet.
Fee: $42.95 monthly.

Telephone Service
Analog: Not Operational
Digital: Operational
Homes passed & miles of plant included in Chattanooga
Vice President & General Manager: Valerie Gillespie. Technical Operations Director: Tom Bailey. Marketing Director: Mike Kehrer.
City fee: 3% of gross.
Ownership: Comcast Cable Communications Inc. (MSO).

ROSWELL—Charter Communications, 1925 Breckenridge Plaza, Ste 100, Duluth, GA 30096-4918. Phone: 770-806-7060. Fax: 770-806-7099. Web Site: http://www.charter.com. Also serves Mountain Park. ICA: GA0274.
TV Market Ranking: 18 (Mountain Park, ROSWELL). Franchise award date: October 15, 1979. Franchise expiration date: N.A. Began: October 15, 1979.
Channel capacity: N.A. Channels available but not in use: N.A.

Basic Service
Subscribers: 16,379.
Programming (received off-air): WAGA-TV (FOX) Atlanta; WATC-DT (ETV) Atlanta; WATL (MNT) Atlanta; WDTA-LP Fayetteville; WGCL-TV (CBS) Atlanta; WGTV (PBS) Athens; WHSG-TV (TBN) Monroe; WPBA (PBS) Atlanta; WPCH-TV (IND) Atlanta; WPXA-TV (ION) Rome; WSB-TV (ABC) Atlanta; WUPA (CW) Atlanta; WUVG-DT (UNV) Athens; WXIA-TV (NBC) Atlanta.
Programming (via satellite): Home Shopping Network; INSP; Product Information Network; QVC; TV Guide Network; WGN America.
Current originations: Religious Access; Government Access; Educational Access; Public Access.
Fee: $29.99 installation.

Expanded Basic Service 1
Subscribers: 13,775.
Programming (via satellite): ABC Family Channel; AMC; Animal Planet; Arts & Entertainment; BET Networks; Bravo; Cartoon Network; CNBC; CNN; Comcast Sports Net Southeast; Comcast/Charter Sports Southeast (CSS); Comedy Central; Country Music TV; C-SPAN; C-SPAN 2; Discovery Channel; Disney Channel; E! Entertainment Television; ESPN; ESPN 2; ESPN Classic Sports; Eternal Word TV Network; FitTV; Food Network; Fox News Channel; FX; G4; GalaVision; Golf Channel; GSN; Hallmark Channel; Headline News; HGTV; History Channel; Lifetime; MSNBC; MTV; National Geographic Channel; Nickelodeon; Oxygen; Shop at Home; SoapNet; Speed Channel; Spike TV; SportSouth; Syfy; Telemundo; The Learning Channel; Toon Disney; Travel Channel; truTV; Turner Classic Movies; TV Land; USA Network; Versus; VH1; WE tv; Weather Channel.
Fee: $48.99 monthly.

Digital Basic Service
Subscribers: N.A.
Programming (via satellite): BBC America; Bio; Bloomberg Television; Boomerang; Canales N; Discovery Digital Networks; Do-It-Yourself; ESPNews; Fox College Sports Atlantic; Fox College Sports Central; Fox College Sports Pacific; Fox Sports World; Fuse; GAS; Great American Country; History Channel International; Independent Film Channel; Lifetime Movie Network; MTV Networks Digital Suite; Music Choice; Nick Jr.; Nick Too; NickToons TV; Style Network; Sundance Channel; TV Guide Interactive Inc.; Weatherscan.
Fee: $14.00 monthly.

Digital Pay Service 1
Pay Units: 3,475.
Programming (via satellite): HBO (multiplexed).
Fee: $10.95 monthly.

Digital Pay Service 2
Pay Units: 2,120.
Programming (via satellite): Showtime (multiplexed).
Fee: $10.95 monthly.

Digital Pay Service 3
Pay Units: 2,860.
Programming (via satellite): Encore (multiplexed); Flix.
Fee: $7.95 monthly.

Digital Pay Service 4
Pay Units: 950.
Programming (via satellite): Cinemax (multiplexed).
Fee: $10.95 monthly.

Digital Pay Service 5
Pay Units: 523.
Programming (via satellite): The Movie Channel (multiplexed).
Fee: $10.95 monthly.

Digital Pay Service 6
Pay Units: 465.
Programming (via satellite): Starz (multiplexed).
Fee: $5.95 monthly.

Video-On-Demand: Yes

Pay-Per-View
Addressable homes: 1,620.
iN DEMAND (delivered digitally), Fee: $5.95; Fresh (delivered digitally), Fee: $3.95; NBA League Pass/WNBA (delivered digitally); NHL Center Ice/MLB Extra Innings (delivered digitally); Playboy TV (delivered digitally); Shorteez (delivered digitally).

Internet Service
Operational: Yes.
Broadband Service: Charter Pipeline.
Fee: $29.99 monthly; $199.95 modem purchase.

Telephone Service
Digital: Operational
Fee: $29.99 monthly
Miles of Plant: 330.0 (coaxial); 100.0 (fiber optic). Homes passed: 19,000.
Vice President & General Manager: Matt Favre. Operations Director: Jeff Osborne. Sales & Marketing Director: Antoinette Carpenter.
Ownership: Charter Communications Inc. (MSO).

ROYSTON—Northland Cable Television, PO Box 1667, 203 Doyle St E, Toccoa, GA 30577. Phones: 706-886-2727; 706-245-9336. Fax: 706-886-0144. E-mail: betty.chastain@northlandcabletv.com. Web Site: http://www.northlandcabletv.com. Also serves Bowersville, Franklin County, Franklin Springs, Hart County (portions) & Lavonia. ICA: GA0078.
TV Market Ranking: 46 (Bowersville, Franklin County (portions), Franklin Springs, Hart County (portions), Lavonia, ROYSTON); Below 100 (Franklin County (portions)). Franchise award date: N.A. Franchise expiration date: N.A. Began: October 30, 1981.
Channel capacity: 44 (not 2-way capable). Channels available but not in use: None.

Basic Service
Subscribers: 1,700.
Programming (received off-air): WAGA-TV (FOX) Atlanta; WGGS-TV (IND) Greenville; WGTV (PBS) Athens; WHNS (FOX) Greenville; WLOS (ABC) Asheville; WMYA-TV (MNT) Anderson; WNEG-TV (CBS) Toccoa; WSB-TV (ABC) Atlanta; WXIA-TV (NBC) Atlanta; WYCW (CW) Asheville; WYFF (NBC) Greenville.
Programming (via satellite): ABC Family Channel; Arts & Entertainment; BET Networks; Cartoon Network; CNN; Comcast Sports Net Southeast; C-SPAN; Discovery Channel; ESPN; ESPN 2; FX; Great American Country; Hallmark Channel; Headline News; HGTV; INSP; Lifetime; Nickelodeon; QVC; SoapNet; SportSouth; TBS Superstation; The Learning Channel; Turner Classic Movies; Turner Network TV; TV Guide Network; USA Network; Weather Channel.
Fee: $40.00 installation; $38.99 monthly.

Pay Service 1
Pay Units: 50.
Programming (via satellite): Cinemax; Encore Action; HBO; Showtime.

Video-On-Demand: No

Internet Service
Operational: Yes.
Fee: $39.99 monthly.

Telephone Service
Analog: Not Operational
Digital: Operational
Fee: $23.99 monthly
Miles of Plant: 90.0 (coaxial); None (fiber optic). Homes passed: 2,800.
Marketing Director: Debbie Blackwell. Marketing Manager: Becky Stovall. Chief Technician: Jerry Shirley. Office Manager: Becky Chastain.
City fee: 3% of gross.
Ownership: Northland Communications Corp. (MSO).

SANDERSVILLE—Northland Cable Television, 125 E Church St, Ste F, Sandersville, GA 31082-2429. Phone: 478-552-2905. Fax: 478-552-0532. Web Site: http://www.northlandcabletv.com. Also serves Tennille & Washington County (portions). ICA: GA0069.
TV Market Ranking: Outside TV Markets (SANDERSVILLE, Tennille, Washington County (portions)). Franchise award date: N.A. Franchise expiration date: N.A. Began: September 1, 1966.
Channel capacity: 52 (operating 2-way). Channels available but not in use: None.

Basic Service
Subscribers: 3,218.
Programming (received off-air): WAGA-TV (FOX) Atlanta; WCES-TV (PBS) Wrens; WGNM (IND) Macon; WGXA (FOX, MNT) Macon; WJBF (ABC) Augusta; WMAZ-TV (CBS) Macon; WMGT-TV (MNT, NBC) Macon.
Programming (via satellite): CW+; Hallmark Channel; Trinity Broadcasting Network; Weather Channel.
Fee: $52.25 installation.

Expanded Basic Service 1
Subscribers: 1,600.
Programming (via satellite): ABC Family Channel; Animal Planet; Arts & Entertainment; BET Networks; Cartoon Network; CNBC; CNN; Comcast Sports Net Southeast; C-SPAN; Discovery Channel; ESPN; ESPN 2; Food Network; Fox Movie Channel; Fox News Channel; FX; Golf Channel; Great American Country; Headline News; HGTV; History Channel; Lifetime; MTV; Nickelodeon; Outdoor Channel; QVC; Spike TV; Syfy; TBS Superstation; The Learning Channel; Travel Channel; truTV; Turner Classic Movies; Turner Network TV; Turner South; TV Land; USA Network.
Fee: $49.99 monthly.

Digital Basic Service
Subscribers: N.A.
Programming (via satellite): BBC America; Bloomberg Television; Bravo; Discovery Health Channel; Discovery Home Channel; Discovery Kids Channel; Discovery Military Channel; Discovery Times Channel; DMX Music; ESPNews; FitTV; Fox Soccer; Independent Film Channel; Lifetime Movie Network; National Geographic Channel; Science Channel; Speed Channel; WE tv.
Fee: $5.00 monthly.

Pay Service 1
Pay Units: N.A.
Programming (via satellite): HBO; Showtime.
Fee: $10.00 installation; $13.95 monthly (Showtime), $14.60 monthly (HBO).
Digital Pay Service 1
Pay Units: N.A.
Programming (via satellite): Cinemax (multiplexed); Encore (multiplexed); Flix; HBO (multiplexed); Showtime (multiplexed); Starz (multiplexed); The Movie Channel (multiplexed).
Fee: $14.75 monthly (HBO, Cinemax, Showtime/TMC/Flix or Starz/Encore).
Video-On-Demand: No
Internet Service
Operational: Yes.
Fee: $42.99 monthly.
Telephone Service
None
Miles of Plant: 78.0 (coaxial); None (fiber optic). Homes passed: 4,445. Total homes in franchised area: 7,645.
Manager: Penny Grice. Chief Technician: Bruce Lindsey.
City fee: 3% of gross.
Ownership: Northland Communications Corp. (MSO).

SANFORD—KLiP Interactive, 455 Gees Mill Business Court, Conyers, GA 30013. Phone: 678-801-4020. Fax: 678-727-7002. E-mail: jsheehan@klipia.com. Web Site: http://www.klipia.com. Also serves Athens, Clarke County (northwestern portion), Colbert, Commerce, Danielsville, Hull, Ila, Jackson County (unincorporated areas) & Madison County (unincorporated areas). ICA: GA0105.
TV Market Ranking: 46 (Madison County (unincorporated areas) (portions), SANFORD (portions)); Below 100 (Athens, Clarke County (northwestern portion), Colbert, Commerce, Danielsville, Hull, Ila, Jackson County (unincorporated areas), Madison County (unincorporated areas) (portions), SANFORD (portions)). Franchise award date: N.A. Franchise expiration date: N.A. Began: October 1, 1989.
Channel capacity: 37 (not 2-way capable). Channels available but not in use: None.
Basic Service
Subscribers: 175.
Programming (received off-air): WAGA-TV (FOX) Atlanta; WGCL-TV (CBS) Atlanta; WGTV (PBS) Athens; WHSG-TV (TBN) Monroe; WLOS (ABC) Asheville; WNEG-TV (CBS) Toccoa; WPCH-TV (IND) Atlanta; WSB-TV (ABC) Atlanta; WUVG-DT (UNV) Athens; WXIA-TV (NBC) Atlanta; WYFF (NBC) Greenville.
Programming (via satellite): ABC Family Channel; AMC; Animal Planet; Arts & Entertainment; Cartoon Network; CNBC; CNN; Comcast Sports Net Southeast; Discovery Channel; Disney Channel; ESPN; ESPN 2; Fuse; Great American Country; Headline News; HGTV; Lifetime; Speed Channel; SportSouth; The Learning Channel; Turner Network TV; TV Land; USA Network; Weather Channel; WGN America.
Fee: $30.00 installation; $39.95 monthly; $3.50 converter.
Pay Service 1
Pay Units: 8.
Programming (via satellite): Cinemax.
Fee: $10.95 monthly.
Pay Service 2
Pay Units: 7.
Programming (via satellite): HBO.
Fee: $14.95 monthly.
Pay Service 3
Pay Units: 6.
Programming (via satellite): Showtime.
Fee: $9.95 monthly.
Internet Service
Operational: No.
Telephone Service
None
Miles of Plant: 83.0 (coaxial); None (fiber optic). Homes passed: 2,245. Total homes in franchised area: 2,245.
Chief Executive Officer: Joseph A. Sheehan. General Manager East: Mark Miller. General Manager West: Vance Johnson.
Ownership: KLiP Interactive LLC (MSO).

SARDIS—KLiP Interactive, 455 Gees Mill Business Court, Conyers, GA 30013. Phone: 678-727-7100. Fax: 678-727-7002. E-mail: jsheehan@klipia.com. Web Site: http://www.klipia.com. Also serves Burke County (portions). ICA: GA0243.
TV Market Ranking: Below 100 (Burke County (portions) (portions)); Outside TV Markets (Burke County (portions) (portions), SARDIS). Franchise award date: N.A. Franchise expiration date: N.A. Began: January 1, 1985.
Channel capacity: 45 (not 2-way capable). Channels available but not in use: 13.
Basic Service
Subscribers: 61.
Programming (received off-air): WAGT (CW, NBC) Augusta; WCES-TV (PBS) Wrens; WFXG (FOX) Augusta; WJBF (ABC) Augusta; WPCH-TV (IND) Atlanta; WRDW-TV (CBS, MNT) Augusta.
Programming (via satellite): ABC Family Channel; Animal Planet; Arts & Entertainment; BET Networks; CNN; Comcast Sports Net Southeast; Comedy Central; Country Music TV; Discovery Channel; Disney Channel; ESPN; ESPN 2; Fox News Channel; History Channel; Home Shopping Network; Lifetime; Nickelodeon; Spike TV; The Learning Channel; Travel Channel; Trinity Broadcasting Network; Turner Network TV; TV Land; USA Network; Weather Channel; WGN America.
Fee: $29.95 installation; $36.63 monthly.
Pay Service 1
Pay Units: 11.
Programming (via satellite): HBO.
Fee: $10.95 monthly.
Internet Service
Operational: No.
Telephone Service
None
Miles of Plant: 10.0 (coaxial); None (fiber optic). Homes passed: 270.
Chief Executive Officer: Joseph A. Sheehan. General Manager East: Mark Miller. General Manager West: Vance Johnson.
Ownership: KLiP Interactive LLC (MSO).

SASSER—Citizens Cable TV, PO Box 465, Leslie, GA 31764. Phones: 229-268-2288; 229-853-1600; 866-341-3050. Web Site: http://www.citizenscatv.com. ICA: GA0167.
TV Market Ranking: Below 100 (SASSER). Franchise award date: N.A. Franchise expiration date: N.A. Began: June 1, 1988.
Channel capacity: 33 (not 2-way capable). Channels available but not in use: 27.
Basic Service
Subscribers: 130.
Programming (received off-air): WACS-TV (PBS) Dawson; WALB (NBC) Albany; WCTV (CBS, MNT) Thomasville; WFXL (FOX) Albany; WRBL (CBS) Columbus; WSST-TV (IND) Cordele; WTVM (ABC) Columbus.
Programming (via satellite): ABC Family Channel; AMC; Arts & Entertainment; BET Networks; Cartoon Network; CNN; Comcast Sports Net Southeast; Comcast/Charter Sports Southeast (CSS); Country Music TV; Discovery Channel; ESPN; ESPN 2; Food Network; Fox News Channel; FX; History Channel; Home Shopping Network; Lifetime; Nickelodeon; Speed Channel; Spike TV; Syfy; TBS Superstation; The Learning Channel; Turner Network TV; USA Network; Weather Channel; WGN America.
Fee: $45.00 installation; $34.95 monthly.
Pay Service 1
Pay Units: 30.
Programming (via satellite): HBO.
Fee: $13.50 monthly.
Pay Service 2
Pay Units: 30.
Programming (via satellite): Cinemax.
Fee: $13.50 monthly.
Video-On-Demand: No
Internet Service
Operational: No.
Telephone Service
None
Miles of Plant: 7.0 (coaxial); None (fiber optic). Additional miles planned: 1.0 (coaxial). Homes passed: 159. Total homes in franchised area: 180.
Manager & Chief Technician: Milton Foster.
Ownership: Citizens Cable TV (MSO).

SAVANNAH—Comcast Cable, 141 Park of Commerce Dr, Savannah, GA 31405. Phones: 912-354-7531 (Customer service); 912-356-3113. Fax: 912-353-6063. Web Site: http://www.comcast.com. Also serves Blitchton, Bloomingdale, Bryan County (eastern portion), Chatham County (portions), Effingham County, Garden City, Gumbranch, Hunter Army Airfield, Isle of Hope-Dutch Island, Liberty County (southern portion), Midway, Pooler, Port Wentworth, Rincon, Skidaway Island, Southbridge, Springfield, Thunderbolt, Vernonburg, Whitemarsh Island & Wilmington Island. ICA: GA0005.
TV Market Ranking: Below 100 (Blitchton, Bloomingdale, Bryan County (eastern portion), Chatham County (portions), Effingham County, Garden City, Gumbranch, Hunter Army Airfield, Isle of Hope-Dutch Island, Liberty County (southern portion), Midway, Pooler, Port Wentworth, Rincon, SAVANNAH, Skidaway Island, Southbridge, Springfield, Thunderbolt, Vernonburg, Whitemarsh Island, Wilmington Island). Franchise award date: N.A. Franchise expiration date: N.A. Began: January 1, 1965.
Channel capacity: N.A. Channels available but not in use: N.A.
Basic Service
Subscribers: 109,859 Includes Adrian, Claxton, Colonels Island, Darien, Glennville, Guyton, Hinesville, Metter, Montezuma, Mount Vernon, Pembroke, Soperton, Twin City, Tybee Island, & Wrightsville.
Programming (received off-air): WGSA (CW) Baxley; WJCL (ABC) Savannah; WSAV-TV (MNT, NBC) Savannah; WTGS (FOX) Hardeeville; WTOC-TV (CBS) Savannah; WVAN-TV (PBS) Savannah; 15 FMs.
Programming (via satellite): INSP; ION Television; QVC; TV Guide Network; WGN America.
Current originations: Government Access; Public Access.
Planned originations: Educational Access.
Fee: $47.99 installation; $9.00 monthly; $3.25 converter.
Expanded Basic Service 1
Subscribers: 60,080.
Programming (via satellite): ABC Family Channel; AMC; Animal Planet; Arts & Entertainment; BET Networks; Bravo; Cartoon Network; CNBC; CNN; Comcast Sports Net Southeast; Comcast/Charter Sports Southeast (CSS); Comedy Central; Country Music TV; C-SPAN; C-SPAN 2; Discovery Channel; Discovery Health Channel; Disney Channel; E! Entertainment Television; ESPN; ESPN 2; Eternal Word TV Network; Food Network; Fox News Channel; FX; Golf Channel; Great American Country; GSN; Hallmark Channel; Headline News; HGTV; History Channel; Home Shopping Network; Lifetime; MSNBC; MTV; Nickelodeon; Speed Channel; Spike TV; SportSouth; Style Network; Syfy; TBS Superstation; The Learning Channel; Travel Channel; Trinity Broadcasting Network; Turner Network TV; TV Land; TV One; Univision; USA Network; Versus; VH1; WE tv; Weather Channel.
Fee: $51.99 monthly.
Digital Basic Service
Subscribers: N.A.
Programming (received off-air): WSAV-TV (MNT, NBC) Savannah; WTGS (FOX) Hardeeville; WTOC-TV (CBS) Savannah.
Programming (via satellite): BBC America; Bio; Black Family Channel; Canales N; Cooking Channel; Country Music TV; C-SPAN 3; Current; Discovery Digital Networks; Discovery HD Theater; Do-It-Yourself; Encore (multiplexed); ESPN 2 HD; ESPN HD; ESPNews; Flix; Fox College Sports Atlantic; Fox College Sports Central; Fox College Sports Pacific; Fox Reality Channel; Fox Soccer; G4; GAS; Gol TV; Gospel Music Channel; History Channel International; INHD; Jewelry Television; Lifetime Movie Network; LOGO; MoviePlex; MTV Networks Digital Suite; Music Choice; National Geographic Channel; NBA TV; NFL Network; Nick Jr.; Nick Too; NickToons TV; Outdoor Channel; Palladia; PBS Kids Sprout; SoapNet; Sundance Channel; Tennis Channel; The Sportsman Channel; The Word Network; Toon Disney; truTV; Turner Classic Movies; Turner Network TV HD; Versus HD; Weatherscan.
Fee: $45.49 monthly.
Digital Pay Service 1
Pay Units: 7,699.
Programming (via satellite): Cinemax (multiplexed); Cinemax HD; HBO (multiplexed); HBO HD; Showtime (multiplexed); Showtime HD; Starz (multiplexed); Starz HDTV; The Movie Channel (multiplexed).
Fee: $51.98 monthly.
Video-On-Demand: Yes
Pay-Per-View
Addressable homes: 17,285.
Hot Choice (delivered digitally), Addressable: Yes; iN DEMAND (delivered digitally); ESPN Gameplan (delivered digitally); Playboy TV (delivered digitally); NBA League Pass (delivered digitally); MLB Extra Innings (delivered digitally).
Internet Service
Operational: Yes. Began: July 28, 2000.
Subscribers: 940.
Broadband Service: Comcast High Speed Internet.
Fee: $42.95 monthly; $7.00 modem lease.
Telephone Service
Digital: Operational
Miles of Plant: 3,738.0 (coaxial); 598.0 (fiber optic). Homes passed: 237,000. Homes passed & miles of plant (coax & fiber) include Adrian, Claxton, Colonels Island, Darien, Glennville, Guyton, Hinesville,

Metter, Montezuma, Mount Vernon, Pembroke, Soperton, Twin City, Tybee Island, & Wrightsville
General Manager: Michael Daves. Marketing Director: Jerry Avery. Marketing Manager: Ken Torres. Technical Operations Director: Joel Godsen.
City fee: 5% of gross.
Ownership: Comcast Cable Communications Inc. (MSO).

SEMINOLE COUNTY—KLiP Interactive, 455 Gees Mill Business Court, Conyers, GA 30013. Phone: 678-727-7100. Fax: 678-727-7002. E-mail: jsheehan@klipia.com. Web Site: http://www.klipia.com. Also serves Grand Ridge & Sneads, FL; Lake Seminole, GA. ICA: GA0244.
TV Market Ranking: Below 100 (Grand Ridge, Lake Seminole, SEMINOLE COUNTY, Sneads). Franchise award date: N.A. Franchise expiration date: N.A. Began: N.A.
Channel capacity: 65 (not 2-way capable). Channels available but not in use: 23.
Basic Service
Subscribers: 225.
Programming (received off-air): WABW-TV (PBS) Pelham; WALB (NBC) Albany; WCTV (CBS, MNT) Thomasville; WFSU-TV (PBS) Tallahassee; WJHG-TV (CW, MNT, NBC) Panama City; WTLH (CW, FOX) Bainbridge; WTVY (CBS, CW, MNT) Dothan; WTWC-TV (NBC) Tallahassee; WTXL-TV (ABC) Tallahassee.
Programming (via satellite): ABC Family Channel; AMC; Arts & Entertainment; CNBC; CNN; Comcast Sports Net Southeast; Comedy Central; Country Music TV; C-SPAN; Discovery Channel; Disney Channel; ESPN; ESPN 2; Fox News Channel; FX; Headline News; History Channel; MTV; Nickelodeon; QVC; Speed Channel; Spike TV; TBS Superstation; The Learning Channel; Trinity Broadcasting Network; Turner Classic Movies; Turner Network TV; USA Network; Weather Channel; WGN America.
Fee: $29.95 installation; $39.95 monthly.
Pay Service 1
Pay Units: 8.
Programming (via satellite): Cinemax.
Fee: $10.95 monthly.
Pay Service 2
Pay Units: 16.
Programming (via satellite): HBO.
Fee: $10.95 monthly.
Pay Service 3
Pay Units: 5.
Programming (via satellite): Showtime.
Fee: $10.95 monthly.
Pay Service 4
Pay Units: 1.
Programming (via satellite): The Movie Channel.
Fee: $10.95 monthly.
Internet Service
Operational: No.
Telephone Service
None
Miles of Plant: 60.0 (coaxial); None (fiber optic). Homes passed: 941.
Chief Executive Officer: Joseph A. Sheehan. General Manager East: Mark Miller. General Manager West: Vance Johnson.
Ownership: KLiP Interactive LLC (MSO).

SKIDAWAY ISLAND—US Cable of Coastal Texas LP. Now served by SAVANNAH, GA [GA0005]. ICA: GA0107.

SMITHVILLE—Citizens Cable TV, 134 N Bailey Ave, Leslie, GA 31764. Phones: 229-874-4145; 229-853-1600. Fax: 229-874-2211. Web Site: http://www.citizenscatv.com. Also serves Lee County. ICA: GA0246.
TV Market Ranking: Below 100 (Lee County, SMITHVILLE). Franchise award date: N.A. Franchise expiration date: N.A. Began: N.A.
Channel capacity: 45 (operating 2-way). Channels available but not in use: 13.
Basic Service
Subscribers: 130.
Programming (received off-air): WACS-TV (PBS) Dawson; WALB (NBC) Albany; WFXL (FOX) Albany; WRBL (CBS) Columbus; WSST-TV (IND) Cordele; WTVM (ABC) Columbus.
Programming (via satellite): ABC Family Channel; Animal Planet; Arts & Entertainment; BET Networks; Bloomberg Television; Cartoon Network; CNN; Comcast Sports Net Southeast; Comedy Central; Country Music TV; Discovery Channel; ESPN; ESPN 2; Food Network; Fox News Channel; History Channel; Lifetime; Nickelodeon; Spike TV; TBS Superstation; The Learning Channel; Travel Channel; Trinity Broadcasting Network; Turner Classic Movies; Turner Network TV; Turner South; TV Land; USA Network; Weather Channel; WGN America; WPIX (CW, IND) New York.
Fee: $19.95 installation; $32.95 monthly; $12.95 additional installation.
Pay Service 1
Pay Units: 41.
Programming (via satellite): HBO.
Fee: $10.95 monthly.
Pay Service 2
Pay Units: 9.
Programming (via satellite): Cinemax.
Fee: $10.95 monthly.
Pay Service 3
Pay Units: 11.
Programming (via satellite): Encore; Starz.
Fee: $9.00 monthly.
Internet Service
Operational: Yes.
Fee: $35.00 installation; $39.95 monthly.
Telephone Service
None
Miles of Plant: 11.0 (coaxial); None (fiber optic). Homes passed: 220.
Ownership: Citizens Cable TV (MSO).

SMYRNA—Charter Communications, 1925 Breckenridge Plaza, Ste 100, Duluth, GA 30096-4918. Phone: 770-806-7060. Fax: 770-806-7099. Web Site: http://www.charter.com. Also serves Cobb County, Fulton County (portions) & Mableton (portions). ICA: GA0013.
TV Market Ranking: 18 (Cobb County, Fulton County (portions), Mableton (portions), SMYRNA). Franchise award date: N.A. Franchise expiration date: N.A. Began: September 1, 1967.
Channel capacity: N.A. Channels available but not in use: N.A.
Basic Service
Subscribers: 30,939.
Programming (received off-air): WAGA-TV (FOX) Atlanta; WATC-DT (ETV) Atlanta; WATL (MNT) Atlanta; WDTA-LP Fayetteville; WGCL-TV (CBS) Atlanta; WGTV (PBS) Athens; WHSG-TV (TBN) Monroe; WPBA (PBS) Atlanta; WPCH-TV (IND) Atlanta; WPXA-TV (ION) Rome; WSB-TV (ABC) Atlanta; WUPA (CW) Atlanta; WUVG-DT (UNV) Athens; WXIA-TV (NBC) Atlanta.
Programming (via satellite): Home Shopping Network; INSP; Product Information Network; QVC; TV Guide Network; WGN America.

Current originations: Leased Access; Government Access.
Fee: $29.99 installation.
Expanded Basic Service 1
Subscribers: N.A.
Programming (via satellite): ABC Family Channel; AMC; Animal Planet; Arts & Entertainment; BET Networks; Bravo; Cartoon Network; CNBC; CNN; Comcast Sports Net Southeast; Comcast/Charter Sports Southeast (CSS); Comedy Central; Country Music TV; C-SPAN; C-SPAN 2; Discovery Channel; Disney Channel; E! Entertainment Television; ESPN; ESPN 2; Eternal Word TV Network; Food Network; Fox News Channel; FX; G4; GalaVision; Golf Channel; GSN; Hallmark Channel; Headline News; HGTV; History Channel; Lifetime; MSNBC; MTV; National Geographic Channel; Nickelodeon; QVC; Shop at Home; SoapNet; Speed Channel; Spike TV; SportSouth; Syfy; Telemundo; The Learning Channel; Toon Disney; Travel Channel; truTV; Turner Classic Movies; Turner Network TV; TV Land; USA Network; Versus; VH1; WE tv; Weather Channel.
Fee: $48.99 monthly.
Digital Basic Service
Subscribers: N.A.
Programming (via satellite): BBC America; Bio; Bloomberg Television; Boomerang; Canales N; Discovery Digital Networks; Do-It-Yourself; Fox College Sports Atlantic; Fox College Sports Central; Fox College Sports Pacific; Fox Sports World; Fuse; GAS; Great American Country; History Channel International; Independent Film Channel; Lifetime Movie Network; MTV Networks Digital Suite; Music Choice; Nick Jr.; Nick Too; NickToons TV; Style Network; Sundance Channel; TV Guide Interactive Inc.
Fee: $14.00 monthly.
Digital Pay Service 1
Pay Units: 16,500.
Programming (via satellite): Cinemax (multiplexed); Encore (multiplexed); Flix; HBO (multiplexed); Showtime (multiplexed); Starz (multiplexed); The Movie Channel (multiplexed).
Fee: $20.00 installation; $6.25 monthly (Encore), $8.00 monthly (Showtime), $8.95 monthly (Flix), $9.00 monthly (TMC), $10.00 monthly (HBO), $10.45 monthly (Cinemax).
Video-On-Demand: Yes
Pay-Per-View
Addressable homes: 5,200.
Addressable: Yes; iN DEMAND (delivered digitally); Playboy TV (delivered digitally); Fresh (delivered digitally); NBA League Pass/WNBA (delivered digitally); NHL Center Ice/MLB Extra Innings (delivered digitally); Shorteez (delivered digitally).
Internet Service
Operational: Yes. Began: November 1, 1998.
Broadband Service: Charter Pipeline.
Fee: $29.99 monthly.
Telephone Service
Digital: Operational
Fee: $29.99 monthly
Miles of Plant: 420.0 (coaxial); 16.0 (fiber optic). Homes passed: 44,000.
Vice President & General Manager: Matt Favre. Operations Director: Jeff Osborne. Sales & Marketing Director: Antoinette Carpenter.
City fee: 3% of gross.
Ownership: Charter Communications Inc. (MSO).

SOPERTON—Comcast Cable, 141 Park of Commerce Dr, Savannah, GA 31405. Phone: 912-354-2813. Fax: 912-353-6063. Web Site: http://www.comcast.com. ICA: GA0247.
TV Market Ranking: Outside TV Markets (SOPERTON). Franchise award date: April 15, 1975. Franchise expiration date: N.A. Began: April 1, 1975.
Channel capacity: N.A. Channels available but not in use: N.A.
Basic Service
Subscribers: N.A. Included in Savannah
Programming (received off-air): WJBF (ABC) Augusta; WMAZ-TV (CBS) Macon; WMGT-TV (MNT, NBC) Macon; WMUM-TV (PBS) Cochran; WTOC-TV (CBS) Savannah.
Programming (via satellite): MTV; QVC; TBS Superstation; Weather Channel; WGN America.
Fee: $47.99 installation; $9.95 monthly.
Expanded Basic Service 1
Subscribers: N.A.
Programming (via satellite): ABC Family Channel; BET Networks; CNN; Disney Channel; ESPN; Headline News; Nickelodeon; Spike TV; Turner Network TV; USA Network; VH1.
Fee: $25.00 installation; $19.95 monthly; $20.00 additional installation.
Pay Service 1
Pay Units: 76.
Programming (via satellite): Cinemax; HBO.
Fee: $15.00 installation; $10.00 monthly (Cinemax), $10.95 monthly (HBO).
Video-On-Demand: No
Internet Service
Operational: Yes.
Telephone Service
Digital: Operational
Homes passed & miles of plant (coax & fiber) included in Savannah
General Manager: Michael Daves. Technical Operations Director: Joel Godsen. Marketing Director: Jerry Avery. Marketing Manager: Ken Torres.
City fee: 3% of gross.
Ownership: Comcast Cable Communications Inc. (MSO).

SOUTHBRIDGE—Comcast Cable. Now served by SAVANNAH, GA [GA0005]. ICA: GA0248.

SPARTA—KLiP Interactive, 455 Gees Mill Business Court, Conyers, GA 30013. Phone: 678-727-7100. Fax: 678-727-7002. E-mail: jsheehan@klipia.com. Web Site: http://www.klipia.com. Also serves Hancock County. ICA: GA0116.
TV Market Ranking: Outside TV Markets (Hancock County, SPARTA). Franchise award

date: N.A. Franchise expiration date: N.A. Began: N.A.

Channel capacity: 45 (not 2-way capable). Channels available but not in use: 7.

Basic Service

Subscribers: 440.

Programming (received off-air): WGTV (PBS) Athens; WGXA (FOX, MNT) Macon; WMAZ-TV (CBS) Macon; WMGT-TV (MNT, NBC) Macon; WPCH-TV (IND) Atlanta; WPGA-TV (ABC) Perry; WXIA-TV (NBC) Atlanta.

Programming (via satellite): ABC Family Channel; Animal Planet; Arts & Entertainment; BET Networks; CNN; Comcast Sports Net Southeast; Comedy Central; Discovery Channel; Disney Channel; E! Entertainment Television; ESPN; ESPN 2; Fox News Channel; FX; GSN; Home Shopping Network; Lifetime; National Geographic Channel; Nickelodeon; Speed Channel; Spike TV; The Learning Channel; Trinity Broadcasting Network; truTV; Turner Network TV; TV Land; USA Network; Weather Channel.

Fee: $44.95 installation; $39.95 monthly.

Digital Basic Service

Subscribers: N.A.

Programming (via satellite): AmericanLife TV Network; BBC America; Bio; Bloomberg Television; Bravo; Current; Discovery Digital Networks; DMX Music; ESPN Classic Sports; ESPNews; FitTV; Fox Movie Channel; Fox Soccer; Fuse; G4; Golf Channel; HGTV; History Channel International; Independent Film Channel; INSP; Lifetime Movie Network; Military History Channel; Outdoor Channel; Ovation; Sleuth; Sundance Channel; Turner Classic Movies; Versus; WE tv.

Pay Service 1

Pay Units: 51.

Programming (via satellite): HBO.

Fee: $10.95 monthly.

Pay Service 2

Pay Units: 72.

Programming (via satellite): Showtime.

Fee: $10.95 monthly.

Digital Pay Service 1

Pay Units: N.A.

Programming (via satellite): Cinemax (multiplexed); Encore (multiplexed); Flix; HBO (multiplexed); Showtime (multiplexed); Starz (multiplexed); The Movie Channel (multiplexed).

Fee: $10.95 monthly (HBO or Showtime).

Pay-Per-View

iN DEMAND (delivered digitally); Hot Choice (delivered digitally); Playboy TV (delivered digitally); Fresh (delivered digitally); Shorteez (delivered digitally).

Internet Service

Operational: No.

Telephone Service

None

Miles of Plant: 25.0 (coaxial); None (fiber optic). Homes passed: 1,180.

Chief Executive Officer: Joseph A. Sheehan. General Manager East: Mark Miller. General Manager West: Vance Johnson.

Ownership: KLiP Interactive LLC (MSO).

ST. MARYS—Comcast Cable, 1967 Glynn Ave, Brunswick, GA 31520. Phones: 912-264-9803; 912-264-5956. Fax: 912-264-4618. Web Site: http://www.comcast.com. Also serves Camden County & Kings Bay. ICA: GA0055.

TV Market Ranking: 68 (Camden County (portions), Kings Bay, ST. MARYS); Below 100 (Camden County (portions)). Franchise award date: December 1, 1977. Franchise expiration date: N.A. Began: July 1, 1980.

Channel capacity: 62 (not 2-way capable). Channels available but not in use: None.

Basic Service

Subscribers: 4,086.

Programming (received off-air): WAWS (FOX, MNT) Jacksonville; WCWJ (CW) Jacksonville; WJCT (PBS) Jacksonville; WJEB-TV (ETV) Jacksonville; WJXT (IND) Jacksonville; WJXX (ABC) Orange Park; WPXC-TV (ION) Brunswick; WTEV-TV (CBS) Jacksonville; WTLV (NBC) Jacksonville; WXGA-TV (PBS) Waycross.

Programming (via satellite): Country Music TV; C-SPAN; Discovery Channel; TV Guide Network.

Current originations: Leased Access.

Fee: $49.95 installation; $8.89 monthly.

Expanded Basic Service 1

Subscribers: 3,576.

Programming (via satellite): ABC Family Channel; AMC; Arts & Entertainment; BET Networks; Bravo; Cartoon Network; CNBC; CNN; Comcast Sports Net Southeast; Comedy Central; Disney Channel; E! Entertainment Television; ESPN; ESPN 2; Eternal Word TV Network; Fox News Channel; FX; Headline News; HGTV; History Channel; Home Shopping Network; Lifetime; MTV; Nickelodeon; Outdoor Channel; QVC; Spike TV; TBS Superstation; The Learning Channel; Travel Channel; Turner Classic Movies; Turner Network TV; Turner South; TV Land; Univision; USA Network; VH1; WE tv; Weather Channel; WGN America.

Fee: $49.99 monthly.

Digital Basic Service

Subscribers: 376.

Programming (via satellite): BBC America; Bio; Bloomberg Television; CMT Pure Country; Discovery Digital Networks; DMX Music; Encore (multiplexed); ESPN Classic Sports; ESPNews; Fox Movie Channel; Fox Soccer; Fuse; G4; GAS; Golf Channel; GSN; Halogen Network; History Channel International; IFC in Theaters; Lifetime Movie Network; Lime; MTV Networks Digital Suite; National Geographic Channel; Nick Jr.; NickToons TV; Speed Channel; Style Network; Syfy; Toon Disney; Trinity Broadcasting Network; Versus.

Fee: $11.95 monthly.

Pay Service 1

Pay Units: 574.

Programming (via satellite): HBO.

Fee: $15.95 monthly.

Pay Service 2

Pay Units: 170.

Programming (via satellite): Cinemax.

Fee: $18.88 installation; $15.95 monthly.

Pay Service 3

Pay Units: 121.

Programming (via satellite): Showtime.

Fee: $15.95 monthly.

Digital Pay Service 1

Pay Units: 179.

Programming (via satellite): HBO (multiplexed).

Fee: $2.00 installation; $15.95 monthly.

Digital Pay Service 2

Pay Units: 47.

Programming (via satellite): Cinemax (multiplexed).

Fee: $2.00 installation; $15.95 monthly.

Digital Pay Service 3

Pay Units: 72.

Programming (via satellite): Showtime (multiplexed).

Fee: $2.00 installation; $15.95 monthly.

Digital Pay Service 4

Pay Units: 16.

Programming (via satellite): The Movie Channel (multiplexed).

Fee: $2.00 installation; $15.95 monthly.

Digital Pay Service 5

Pay Units: 58.

Programming (via satellite): Starz (multiplexed).

Fee: $2.00 installation; $15.95 monthly.

Video-On-Demand: No

Pay-Per-View

iN DEMAND (delivered digitally).

Internet Service

Operational: Yes.

Telephone Service

Digital: Operational

Miles of Plant: 168.0 (coaxial); None (fiber optic). Homes passed: 9,168. Total homes in franchised area: 12,200.

Vice President: Doug McMillan. General Manager: Mark Russell. Technical Operations Manager: William Baines. Marketing Manager: Jerald Mitchell. Office Manager: Kathleen Bartchlett.

City fee: 3% of gross.

Ownership: Comcast Cable Communications Inc. (MSO).

STAPLETON—KLiP Interactive, 455 Gees Mill Business Court, Conyers, GA 30013. Phone: 678-727-7100. Fax: 678-727-7002. E-mail: jsheehan@klipia.com. Web Site: http://www.klipia.com. ICA: GA0249.

TV Market Ranking: Below 100 (STAPLETON). Franchise award date: N.A. Franchise expiration date: N.A. Began: N.A.

Channel capacity: 45 (not 2-way capable). Channels available but not in use: 5.

Basic Service

Subscribers: 35.

Programming (received off-air): WAGT (CW, NBC) Augusta; WCES-TV (PBS) Wrens; WFXG (FOX) Augusta; WJBF (ABC) Augusta; WRDW-TV (CBS, MNT) Augusta.

Programming (via satellite): ABC Family Channel; Arts & Entertainment; BET Networks; CNN; Comedy Central; C-SPAN 2; Disney Channel; E! Entertainment Television; ESPN; History Channel; Spike TV; TBS Superstation; The Learning Channel; Turner Network TV; TV Land; USA Network; Weather Channel; WGN America.

Fee: $29.95 installation; $29.45 monthly.

Pay Service 1

Pay Units: 8.

Programming (via satellite): HBO.

Fee: $10.95 monthly.

Internet Service

Operational: No.

Telephone Service

None

Miles of Plant: 32.0 (coaxial); None (fiber optic). Homes passed: 140.

Chief Executive Officer: Joseph A. Sheehan. General Manager East: Mark Miller. General Manager West: Vance Johnson. Marketing & Communications Director: Lizbeth A. Dison.

Ownership: KLiP Interactive LLC (MSO).

STATESBORO—Northland Cable Television, PO Box 407, 32 E Vine St, Statesboro, GA 30458-4843. Phone: 912-489-8715. Fax: 912-489-5479. Web Site: http://www.northlandcabletv.com. Also serves Brooklet & Bulloch County. ICA: GA0038.

TV Market Ranking: Below 100 (Bulloch County (portions)); Outside TV Markets (Brooklet, Bulloch County (portions), STATESBORO). Franchise award date: January 1, 1970. Franchise expiration date: N.A. Began: December 1, 1970.

Channel capacity: 60 (operating 2-way). Channels available but not in use: None.

Basic Service

Subscribers: 8,346.

Programming (received off-air): WGSA (CW) Baxley; WJCL (ABC) Savannah; WSAV-TV (MNT, NBC) Savannah; WTGS (FOX) Hardeeville; WTOC-TV (CBS) Savannah; WVAN-TV (PBS) Savannah.

Programming (via satellite): Animal Planet; Arts & Entertainment; BET Networks; Bravo; Cartoon Network; CNBC; CNN; Comcast Sports Net Southeast; Comcast/Charter Sports Southeast (CSS); Comedy Central; C-SPAN; Discovery Channel; E! Entertainment Television; ESPN; ESPN 2; Food Network; Fox Movie Channel; Fox News Channel; FX; Golf Channel; Great American Country; Hallmark Channel; Headline News; HGTV; History Channel; Lifetime; MTV; National Geographic Channel; NFL Network; Nickelodeon; QVC; Spike TV; Syfy; TBS Superstation; The Learning Channel; Travel Channel; Trinity Broadcasting Network; Turner Classic Movies; Turner Network TV; Turner South; USA Network; Weather Channel.

Current originations: Government Access; Educational Access.

Fee: $50.00 installation; $43.29 monthly.

Digital Basic Service

Subscribers: N.A.

Programming (received off-air): WJCL (ABC) Savannah; WSAV-TV (MNT, NBC) Savannah; WTGS (FOX) Hardeeville; WTOC-TV (CBS) Savannah.

Programming (via satellite): BBC America; Bloomberg Television; Discovery HD Theater; Discovery Home Channel; Discovery Kids Channel; Discovery Military Channel; Discovery Times Channel; DMX Music; ESPN 2 HD; ESPN HD; ESPNews; FitTV; Food Network HD; Fox Soccer; G4; HDNet; HDNet Movies; Independent Film Channel; Outdoor Channel; Science Television; Speed Channel; Turner Network TV HD; Universal HD; Versus; Versus HD; WE tv.

Fee: $51.99 monthly.

Pay Service 1

Pay Units: 2,267.

Programming (via satellite): Cinemax; HBO.

Fee: $11.50 monthly (Cinemax), $13.50 monthly (HBO).

Digital Pay Service 1

Pay Units: N.A.

Programming (via satellite): Cinemax (multiplexed); Encore; Flix; HBO (multiplexed); Showtime (multiplexed); Starz (multiplexed); The Movie Channel.

Fee: $14.75 monthly (HBO, Cinemax, Starz/Encore or Showtime/TMC/Flix).

Video-On-Demand: Planned

Pay-Per-View

iN DEMAND (delivered digitally); Playboy TV (delivered digitally); Fresh (delivered digitally); Hot Choice (delivered digitally).

Internet Service

Operational: Yes.

Fee: $42.99 monthly.

Telephone Service

Digital: Operational

Fee: $29.99 monthly

Miles of Plant: 255.0 (coaxial); None (fiber optic). Homes passed: 11,180.

Regional Manager: Richard W. Hutchison. Marketing Director: Steve Hudgins. Chief Technician: Daniel Cullimore. Customer Service Manager: Danielle Nixon.

City fee: 5% of gross.
Ownership: Northland Communications Corp. (MSO).

STATHAM—Now served by ATLANTA (perimeter north), GA [GA0033]. ICA: GA0250.

STILLMORE—Pineland Telephone Coop Inc. This cable system has converted to IPTV. See Stillmore, GA [GA5011]. ICA: GA0161.

STILLMORE—Pineland Telephone Coop. Inc. Formerly [GA0161]. This cable system has converted to IPTV, 30 S Roundtree St, Metter, GA 30439. Phones: 800-247-1266; 912-685-2121. Fax: 912-685-3539. E-mail: pineland@pineland.net. Web Site: http://www.pineland.net. ICA: GA5011.
Channel capacity: N.A. Channels available but not in use: N.A.
Internet Service
Operational: Yes.
General Manager: Richard P. Price.
Ownership: Pineland Telephone Cooperative Inc.

STOCKBRIDGE—Charter Communications, 1920 Brannan Rd, McDonough, GA 30253. Phones: 770-389-8907; 770-806-7060 (Duluth office). Fax: 770-389-0166. Web Site: http://www.charter.com. Also serves Aldora, Barnesville, Butts County (portions), Clayton County (portions), Concord, Flovilla, Hampton, Henry County, Highfalls, Indian Springs, Jackson, Jenkinsburg, Lamar County, Locust Grove, McDonough, Meansville, Milner, Molena, Monroe County (northern portion), Rockdale County (unincorporated areas) & Williamson. ICA: GA0083.
TV Market Ranking: 18 (Butts County (portions), Clayton County (portions), Hampton, Henry County, Locust Grove, McDonough, Rockdale County (unincorporated areas), STOCKBRIDGE); Below 100 (Aldora, Barnesville, Flovilla, Highfalls, Indian Springs, Lamar County (portions), Monroe County (northern portion), Butts County (portions)); Outside TV Markets (Concord, Jackson, Jenkinsburg, Lamar County (portions), Meansville, Milner, Molena, Williamson, Butts County (portions)). Franchise award date: September 5, 1989. Franchise expiration date: N.A. Began: April 26, 1990.
Channel capacity: N.A. Channels available but not in use: N.A.
Basic Service
Subscribers: 26,271.
Programming (received off-air): WAGA-TV (FOX) Atlanta; WATC-DT (ETV) Atlanta; WATL (MNT) Atlanta; WDTA-LP Fayetteville; WGCL-TV (CBS) Atlanta; WGTV (PBS) Athens; WHSG-TV (TBN) Monroe; WPBA (PBS) Atlanta; WPXA-TV (ION) Rome; WSB-TV (ABC) Atlanta; WUPA (CW) Atlanta; WUVG-DT (UNV) Athens; WXIA-TV (NBC) Atlanta.
Programming (via satellite): Home Shopping Network; QVC; Shop at Home; TBS Superstation; WGN America.
Current originations: Leased Access.
Fee: $29.99 installation; $19.95 monthly; $2.00 converter.
Expanded Basic Service 1
Subscribers: N.A.
Programming (via satellite): ABC Family Channel; AMC; Animal Planet; Arts & Entertainment; BET Networks; Bravo; Cartoon Network; CNBC; CNN; Comcast Sports Net Southeast; Comcast/Charter Sports Southeast (CSS); Comedy Central; Country Music TV; C-SPAN; C-SPAN 2; Discovery Channel; Disney Channel; E! Entertainment Television; ESPN; ESPN 2; Food Network; Fox News Channel; FX; G4; GalaVision; Golf Channel; GSN; Hallmark Channel; Headline News; HGTV; History Channel; INSP; Lifetime; MSNBC; MTV; National Geographic Channel; Nickelodeon; Oxygen; Product Information Network; SoapNet; Speed Channel; Spike TV; SportSouth; Syfy; Telemundo; The Learning Channel; Toon Disney; Travel Channel; truTV; Turner Network TV; TV Guide Network; TV Land; USA Network; Versus; VH1; WE tv; Weather Channel.
Fee: $48.99 monthly.
Digital Basic Service
Subscribers: N.A.
Programming (via satellite): BBC America; Bio; Bloomberg Television; Boomerang; Canales N; Discovery Digital Networks; Fox College Sports Atlantic; Fox College Sports Central; Fox College Sports Pacific; Fox Sports World; GAS; Great American Country; History Channel International; Independent Film Channel; MTV Networks Digital Suite; MuchMusic Network; Music Choice; Nick Jr.; Nick Too; NickToons TV; Style Network; Sundance Channel; Turner Classic Movies; TV Guide Interactive Inc.
Digital Pay Service 1
Pay Units: N.A.
Programming (via satellite): Cinemax (multiplexed); Encore (multiplexed); Flix; HBO (multiplexed); Showtime (multiplexed); Starz (multiplexed); The Movie Channel (multiplexed).
Fee: $7.95 monthly (Cinemax), $9.95 monthly (HBO or Showtime).
Video-On-Demand: Yes
Pay-Per-View
iN DEMAND (delivered digitally); Playboy TV (delivered digitally); NBA League Pass/WNBA (delivered digitally); NHL Center Ice/MLB Extra Innings (delivered digitally); Fresh (delivered digitally); Shorteez (delivered digitally).
Internet Service
Operational: Yes.
Broadband Service: Charter Pipeline.
Fee: $29.99 monthly.
Telephone Service
Analog: Not Operational
Digital: Operational
Miles of Plant: 1,200.0 (coaxial); 17.0 (fiber optic). Homes passed: 37,872.
Vice President & General Manager: Matt Favre. Operations Manager: David Spriggs. Technical Operations Manager: Bob Ballew. Sales & Marketing Director: Antoinette Carpenter.
County fee: 5% of gross.
Ownership: Charter Communications Inc. (MSO).

SUMMERVILLE—Charter Communications, 1103 S Hamilton St, Dalton, GA 30720-7860. Phones: 706-428-2290; 865-984-1400 (Maryville, TN office). Fax: 706-260-2520. Web Site: http://www.charter.com. Also serves Lyerly, Menlo & Trion. ICA: GA0251.
TV Market Ranking: 18 (Lyerly, Menlo, SUMMERVILLE); 18,78 (Trion). Franchise award date: N.A. Franchise expiration date: N.A. Began: January 1, 1972.
Channel capacity: N.A. Channels available but not in use: N.A.
Basic Service
Subscribers: 5,000.
Programming (received off-air): WAGA-TV (FOX) Atlanta; WATL (MNT) Atlanta; WDEF-TV (CBS) Chattanooga; WDSI-TV (FOX, MNT) Chattanooga; WELF-TV (TBN) Dalton; WGCL-TV (CBS) Atlanta; WNGH-TV (PBS) Chatsworth; WPCH-TV (IND) Atlanta; WPXA-TV (ION) Rome; WRCB (NBC) Chattanooga; WTVC (ABC) Chattanooga; WUPA (CW) Atlanta; WXIA-TV (NBC) Atlanta; 14 FMs.
Programming (via satellite): Comcast/Charter Sports Southeast (CSS); C-SPAN; Home Shopping Network; QVC.
Fee: $29.99 installation.
Expanded Basic Service 1
Subscribers: N.A.
Programming (via satellite): ABC Family Channel; AMC; Animal Planet; Arts & Entertainment; BET Networks; Cartoon Network; CNBC; CNN; Comcast Sports Net Southeast; Comedy Central; Country Music TV; Discovery Channel; Disney Channel; E! Entertainment Television; ESPN; ESPN 2; FitTV; Fox News Channel; FX; G4; Golf Channel; Headline News; HGTV; History Channel; Lifetime; MSNBC; MTV; Nickelodeon; Oxygen; Product Information Network; Shop at Home; SoapNet; Speed Channel; Spike TV; SportSouth; Syfy; The Learning Channel; Toon Disney; Travel Channel; Turner Network TV; TV Land; USA Network; Versus; VH1; WE tv; Weather Channel.
Fee: $50.99 monthly.
Digital Basic Service
Subscribers: N.A.
Programming (via satellite): AmericanLife TV Network; BBC America; Bio; Bloomberg Television; Bravo; Discovery Digital Networks; DMX Music; Fox Movie Channel; GAS; Golf Channel; GSN; Halogen Network; History Channel International; Independent Film Channel; Lifetime Movie Network; MTV Networks Digital Suite; MuchMusic Network; Nick Jr.; Outdoor Channel; ShopNBC; Style Network; Turner Classic Movies.
Digital Pay Service 1
Pay Units: N.A.
Programming (via satellite): Cinemax (multiplexed); Encore (multiplexed); HBO (multiplexed); Showtime (multiplexed); Starz (multiplexed); The Movie Channel (multiplexed).
Video-On-Demand: No
Pay-Per-View
ESPN Now (delivered digitally), Addressable: Yes; Hot Choice (delivered digitally); iN DEMAND (delivered digitally); Playboy TV (delivered digitally); Fresh (delivered digitally); Shorteez (delivered digitally); ESPN Extra (delivered digitally).
Internet Service
Operational: Yes.
Broadband Service: Charter Pipeline.
Fee: $29.99 monthly.
Telephone Service
Digital: Operational
Miles of Plant: 60.0 (coaxial); None (fiber optic). Additional miles planned: 10.0 (coaxial).
Operations Manager: Mike Burns. Technical Operations Director: Grant Evans. Marketing Director: Pat Hollenbeck.
City fee: 3% of gross.
Ownership: Charter Communications Inc. (MSO).

SURRENCY—Worth Cable, PO Box 2056, 3 Commissioner Dr, Darien, GA 31305-2056. Phone: 912-437-3422. Fax: 912-437-2065. Also serves Appling County (unincorporated areas). ICA: GA0252.
TV Market Ranking: Below 100 (Appling County (unincorporated areas), SURRENCY). Franchise award date: N.A. Franchise expiration date: N.A. Began: N.A.
Channel capacity: 45 (not 2-way capable). Channels available but not in use: 17.
Basic Service
Subscribers: 50.
Programming (received off-air): WGSA (CW) Baxley; WJCL (ABC) Savannah; WPXC-TV (ION) Brunswick; WSAV-TV (MNT, NBC) Savannah; WTGS (FOX) Hardeeville; WTOC-TV (CBS) Savannah; WXGA-TV (PBS) Waycross.
Programming (via satellite): ABC Family Channel; Animal Planet; Arts & Entertainment; BET Networks; CNN; Discovery Channel; Disney Channel; ESPN; History Channel; Lifetime; Nickelodeon; Spike TV; TBS Superstation; The Learning Channel; Travel Channel; Turner Network TV; TV Land; USA Network; Weather Channel; WGN America.
Fee: $29.95 installation; $29.45 monthly.
Pay Service 1
Pay Units: 5.
Programming (via satellite): HBO.
Fee: $10.95 monthly.
Video-On-Demand: No
Internet Service
Operational: No.
Telephone Service
None
Miles of Plant: 4.0 (coaxial); None (fiber optic). Homes passed: 67.
General Manager: Dennis Wortham.
Ownership: Worth Cable Services (MSO).

SWAINSBORO—Northland Cable Television, 123 Roger Shaw St, Ste 417, Swainsboro, GA 30401-3130. Phone: 478-237-6434. Fax: 478-237-9569. Web Site: http://www.northlandcabletv.com. Also serves Emanuel County. ICA: GA0072.
TV Market Ranking: Outside TV Markets (Emanuel County, SWAINSBORO). Franchise award date: N.A. Franchise expiration date: N.A. Began: April 15, 1965.
Channel capacity: 60 (not 2-way capable). Channels available but not in use: None.
Basic Service
Subscribers: 3,394.
Programming (received off-air): WAGT (CW, NBC) Augusta; WFXG (FOX) Augusta; WJBF (ABC) Augusta; WJCL (ABC) Savannah; WRDW-TV (CBS, MNT) Augusta; WSAV-TV (MNT, NBC) Savannah; WTOC-TV (CBS) Savannah; WVAN-TV (PBS) Savannah; allband FM.
Programming (via satellite): C-SPAN; QVC.
Fee: $2.00 converter.

Expanded Basic Service 1
Subscribers: 3,022.
Programming (via satellite): Arts & Entertainment; BET Networks; Cartoon Network; CNBC; CNN; Comcast Sports Net Southeast; Country Music TV; Discovery Channel; E! Entertainment Television; ESPN; ESPN 2; Food Network; Fox Movie Channel; Fox News Channel; FX; Golf Channel; Great American Country; Hallmark Channel; Headline News; HGTV; History Channel; Lifetime; MTV; Nickelodeon; Outdoor Channel; Spike TV; Syfy; TBS Superstation; The Learning Channel; Travel Channel; Trinity Broadcasting Network; Turner Classic Movies; Turner Network TV; Turner South; TV Land; USA Network; Weather Channel.

Digital Basic Service
Subscribers: 450.
Programming (received off-air): WAGT (CW, NBC) Augusta; WRDW-TV (CBS, MNT) Augusta.
Programming (via satellite): BBC America; Bravo; Discovery Health Channel; Discovery Kids Channel; Discovery Military Channel; Discovery Times Channel; DMX Music; ESPNews; Fox Soccer; G4; Independent Film Channel; National Geographic Channel; Science Channel; Speed Channel; WE tv.
Fee: $49.99 monthly.

Pay Service 1
Pay Units: 266.
Programming (via satellite): HBO.
Fee: $11.95 monthly (HBO).

Digital Pay Service 1
Pay Units: N.A.
Programming (via satellite): Cinemax (multiplexed); Encore (multiplexed); Flix; HBO (multiplexed); Showtime (multiplexed); Starz (multiplexed); The Movie Channel (multiplexed).
Fee: $14.75 monthly (HBO, Cinemax, Starz/Encore or Showtime/TMC/Flix).

Video-On-Demand: No

Pay-Per-View
iN DEMAND (delivered digitally); Hot Choice (delivered digitally); Playboy TV (delivered digitally); Fresh (delivered digitally).

Internet Service
Operational: Yes.
Subscribers: 450.
Fee: $42.99 monthly.

Telephone Service
None

Miles of Plant: 99.0 (coaxial); None (fiber optic). Homes passed: 3,620. Total homes in franchised area: 7,416.

Regional Manager: Richard Hutchinson. Chief Technician: Arthur Jones. Office Manager: Becky Williams.

City fee: 3% of gross.

Ownership: Northland Communications Corp. (MSO).

SYLVANIA—Comcast Cable, 105 River Shoals Pkwy, Augusta, GA 30909. Phone: 706-733-7712. Fax: 706-739-1871. E-mail: joey_fortier@cable.comcast.com. Web Site: http://www.comcast.com. Also serves Screven County (portions). ICA: GA0253.

TV Market Ranking: Outside TV Markets (Screven County (portions), SYLVANIA). Franchise award date: September 6, 1974. Franchise expiration date: N.A. Began: July 1, 1976.

Channel capacity: N.A. Channels available but not in use: N.A.

Basic Service
Subscribers: N.A.
Programming (received off-air): WAGT (CW, NBC) Augusta; WJBF (ABC) Augusta; WJCL (ABC) Savannah; WRDW-TV (CBS, MNT) Augusta; WSAV-TV (MNT, NBC) Savannah; WTGS (FOX) Hardeeville; WTOC-TV (CBS) Savannah; WVAN-TV (PBS) Savannah; 8 FMs.
Programming (via satellite): QVC; Trinity Broadcasting Network.
Fee: $39.95 installation; $7.28 monthly.

Expanded Basic Service 1
Subscribers: N.A.
Programming (via satellite): ABC Family Channel; AMC; Animal Planet; Arts & Entertainment; BET Networks; Cartoon Network; CNBC; CNN; Comcast Sports Net Southeast; Comcast/Charter Sports Southeast (CSS); Comedy Central; Country Music TV; C-SPAN; Discovery Channel; Discovery Health Channel; Disney Channel; E! Entertainment Television; ESPN; ESPN 2; Food Network; Fox News Channel; FX; Golf Channel; GSN; Headline News; HGTV; History Channel; INSP; ION Television; Lifetime; MTV; Nickelodeon; Spike TV; SportSouth; Style Network; Syfy; TBS Superstation; The Learning Channel; truTV; Turner Network TV; TV Land; USA Network; Versus; VH1; Weather Channel; WGN America.
Fee: $39.28 monthly.

Digital Basic Service
Subscribers: N.A.
Programming (via satellite): BBC America; Discovery Digital Networks; DMX Music; Encore (multiplexed); Flix; GAS; MTV Networks Digital Suite; Nick Jr.; Nick Too.
Fee: $55.33 monthly.

Pay Service 1
Pay Units: 101.
Programming (via satellite): Cinemax; HBO; Showtime.
Fee: $15.00 installation; $7.95 monthly (Showtime), $10.95 monthly (Cinemax or HBO).

Digital Pay Service 1
Pay Units: N.A.
Programming (via satellite): Cinemax (multiplexed); HBO (multiplexed); Showtime (multiplexed); Starz (multiplexed); The Movie Channel (multiplexed).

Video-On-Demand: No

Pay-Per-View
iN DEMAND (delivered digitally); Hot Choice (delivered digitally); Playboy TV (delivered digitally); Fresh (delivered digitally); Shorteez (delivered digitally); Pleasure (delivered digitally).

Internet Service
Operational: No.
Broadband Service: DSL service only.

Telephone Service
None

Miles of Plant: 78.0 (coaxial); None (fiber optic).

Engineering Director: Harry Hess. Marketing Director: Joey Fortier. Technical Operations Director: Butch Jernigan.

City fee: 3% of gross.

Ownership: Comcast Cable Communications Inc. (MSO).

TALLAPOOSA—Comcast Cable, 150 Hembry Park Dr, Roswell, GA 30076. Phones: 404-266-2278; 770-559-2424 (Norcross office). Fax: 770-559-2479. Web Site: http://www.comcast.com. Also serves Bremen, Buchanan, Mount Zion & Whitesburg. ICA: GA0104.

TV Market Ranking: 18 (Buchanan, Whitesburg); Below 100 (Mount Zion, TALLAPOOSA); Outside TV Markets (Bremen). Franchise award date: February 24, 1977. Franchise expiration date: N.A. Began: September 1, 1977.

Channel capacity: N.A. Channels available but not in use: N.A.

Basic Service
Subscribers: N.A. Included in Atlanta (northern portion)
Programming (received off-air): WAGA-TV (FOX) Atlanta; WATC-DT (ETV) Atlanta; WATL (MNT) Atlanta; WGCL-TV (CBS) Atlanta; WGTV (PBS) Athens; WHSG-TV (TBN) Monroe; WPBA (PBS) Atlanta; WPCH-TV (IND) Atlanta; WPXA-TV (ION) Rome; WSB-TV (ABC) Atlanta; WUPA (CW) Atlanta; WUVG-DT (UNV) Athens; WXIA-TV (NBC) Atlanta; 14 FMs.
Programming (via satellite): WGN America.
Fee: $25.00 installation; $16.95 monthly; $2.10 converter.

Expanded Basic Service 1
Subscribers: 1,350.
Programming (via satellite): ABC Family Channel; AMC; Animal Planet; Arts & Entertainment; BET Networks; Bravo; Cartoon Network; CNBC; CNN; Comcast/Charter Sports Southeast (CSS); Comedy Central; Country Music TV; C-SPAN; Discovery Channel; Disney Channel; E! Entertainment Television; ESPN; ESPN 2; Food Network; Fox News Channel; Fox Sports Net; FX; Golf Channel; Great American Country; GSN; Hallmark Channel; Headline News; HGTV; History Channel; Home Shopping Network; INSP; Lifetime; MSNBC; MTV; Nickelodeon; Oxygen; QVC; Spike TV; SportSouth; Style Network; Syfy; Telemundo; The Learning Channel; Travel Channel; truTV; Turner Classic Movies; Turner Network TV; TV Guide Network; TV Land; TV One; USA Network; Versus; VH1; Weather Channel.
Fee: $49.95 monthly.

Digital Basic Service
Subscribers: N.A.
Programming (received off-air): WAGA-TV (FOX) Atlanta; WATL (MNT) Atlanta; WGCL-TV (CBS) Atlanta; WPCH-TV (IND) Atlanta; WSB-TV (ABC) Atlanta; WUPA (CW) Atlanta; WUVG-DT (UNV) Athens; WUVM-LP Atlanta; WXIA-TV (NBC) Atlanta.
Programming (via satellite): Africa Channel; Arts & Entertainment HD; Atlanta Interfaith Broadcasters; BBC America; BET Networks; Bio; Black Family Channel; Bloomberg Television; Boomerang; Canales N; CMT Pure Country; CNN International; Cooking Channel; C-SPAN 2; C-SPAN 3; Current; Daystar TV Network; Discovery Digital Networks; Discovery HD Theater; Discovery Health Channel; Do-It-Yourself; Encore (multiplexed); ESPN 2 HD; ESPN Classic Sports; ESPN HD; ESPNews; FamilyNet; FearNet; Flix; Fox College Sports Atlantic; Fox College Sports Central; Fox College Sports Pacific; Fox Movie Channel; Fox Reality Channel; Fuse; G4; GAS; Gol TV; Gospel Music TV; Halogen Network; History Channel International; Independent Film Channel; INHD; Jewelry Television; Lifetime Movie Network; LOGO; MoviePlex; MTV Networks Digital Suite; Music Choice; NASA TV; National Geographic Channel; National Geographic Channel HD Network; NBA TV; NFL Network; Nick Jr.; Nick Too; NickToons TV; Outdoor Channel; Palladia; PBS Kids Sprout; ShopNBC; SoapNet; Sundance Channel; Tennis Channel; The Word Network; Toon Disney; Turner Network TV HD; Universal HD; Versus HD; WE tv; Weatherscan.

Digital Pay Service 1
Pay Units: N.A.
Programming (via satellite): Cinemax (multiplexed); Cinemax HD; HBO (multiplexed); HBO HD; Playboy TV; Showtime (multiplexed); Showtime HD; Starz (multiplexed); Starz HDTV; The Movie Channel (multiplexed); TV Japan.

Video-On-Demand: No

Pay-Per-View
Addressable homes: 412.
iN DEMAND, Fee: $4.95, Addressable: Yes.

Internet Service
Operational: Yes.

Telephone Service
Digital: Operational

Homes passed & miles of plant (coax & fiber combined) included in Atlanta (northern portion)

Vice President & General Manager: Ed Dunbar. Regional Vice President, Operations: Michael Hewitt. Regional Vice President: Gene Shatlock. Technical Operations Director: Robert Harris. Marketing Director: Taylor Nipper. Communications Manager: Cindy Kicklighter.

City fee: 5% of gross.

Ownership: Comcast Cable Communications Inc. (MSO).

THOMASTON—Charter Communications, 1925 Breckenridge Plaza, Ste 100, Duluth, GA 30096-4918. Phones: 770-806-7060 (Administrative office); 706-647-1575. Fax: 770-806-7099. Web Site: http://www.charter.com. Also serves Upson County (unincorporated areas). ICA: GA0061.

TV Market Ranking: Outside TV Markets (THOMASTON, Upson County (unincorporated areas)). Franchise award date: January 1, 1969. Franchise expiration date: N.A. Began: August 1, 1972.

Channel capacity: N.A. Channels available but not in use: N.A.

Basic Service
Subscribers: 5,849.
Programming (received off-air): WAGA-TV (FOX) Atlanta; WATL (MNT) Atlanta; WGCL-TV (CBS) Atlanta; WJSP-TV (PBS) Columbus; WMAZ-TV (CBS) Macon; WPCH-TV (IND) Atlanta; WSB-TV (ABC) Atlanta; WTVM (ABC) Columbus; WUPA (CW) Atlanta; WXIA-TV (NBC) Atlanta.
Programming (via satellite): WGN America.
Current originations: Leased Access.
Fee: $29.99 installation.

Expanded Basic Service 1
Subscribers: N.A.
Programming (via satellite): ABC Family Channel; AMC; Animal Planet; Arts & Entertainment; BET Networks; Bravo!; Cartoon Network; CNBC; CNN; Comcast Sports Net Southeast; Comcast/Charter Sports Southeast (CSS); Comedy Central; Country Music TV; C-SPAN; C-SPAN 2; Discovery Channel; Disney Channel; E! Entertainment Television; ESPN; ESPN 2; ESPN Classic Sports; Food Network; Fox News Channel; FX; G4; GalaVision; Golf Channel; Hallmark Channel; Headline News; HGTV; History Channel; Home Shopping Network; INSP; ION Television; Lifetime; MSNBC; MTV; National Geographic Channel; Nickelodeon; Oxygen; Product Information Network; QVC; SoapNet; Speed Channel; Spike TV; SportSouth; Syfy; Telemundo; The Learning Channel; Toon Disney; Travel Channel; Trinity Broadcasting Network; truTV; Turner Classic Movies; Turner Network TV; TV Guide Network; TV Land; Univision; USA Network; Versus; VH1; WE tv; Weather Channel.
Fee: $48.99 monthly.

Digital Basic Service
Subscribers: N.A.
Programming (via satellite): BBC America; Bio; Bloomberg Television; Boomerang; Canales N; Discovery Digital Networks; Do-It-Yourself; Fox College Sports Atlantic; Fox College Sports Central; Fox College Sports Pacific; Fox Sports World; Fuse; GAS; History Channel International; Independent Film Channel; Lifetime Movie Network; MTV Networks Digital Suite; Music Choice; Nick Jr.; Nick Too; NickToons TV; Style Network; Sundance Channel.
Fee: $14.00 monthly.

Digital Pay Service 1
Pay Units: N.A.
Programming (via satellite): Cinemax (multiplexed); Encore; Flix; HBO (multiplexed); Showtime (multiplexed); Starz (multiplexed); The Movie Channel (multiplexed).
Fee: $9.95 monthly (each).

Video-On-Demand: Yes

Pay-Per-View
iN DEMAND (delivered digitally); NBA League Pass/WNBA (delivered digitally); NHL Center Ice/MLB Extra Innings (delivered digitally); Playboy TV (delivered digitally); Fresh (delivered digitally); Shorteez (delivered digitally).

Internet Service
Operational: Yes.
Broadband Service: Charter Pipeline.
Fee: $29.99 monthly; $200.00 modem purchase.

Telephone Service
Digital: Operational
Fee: $29.99 monthly

Miles of Plant: 290.0 (coaxial); None (fiber optic). Total homes in franchised area: 6,000.
Vice President & General Manager: Matt Favre. Operations Manager: David Spriggs. Technical Operations Manager: Tim Hardeman. Sales & Marketing Director: Antoinette Carpenter.
City fee: 4% of gross.
Ownership: Charter Communications Inc. (MSO).

THOMASVILLE—CNS, PO Box 1397, 111 Victoria Pl, Thomasville, GA 31799. Phone: 229-227-7001. E-mail: marketing@cns-internet.com. Web Site: http://www.cns-internet.com. ICA: GA0309. **Note:** This system is an overbuild.
TV Market Ranking: Below 100 (THOMASVILLE). Franchise award date: N.A. Franchise expiration date: N.A. Began: May 14, 2001.
Channel capacity: 75 (operating 2-way). Channels available but not in use: None.

Basic Service
Subscribers: 7,536.
Programming (received off-air): WABW-TV (PBS) Pelham; WALB (NBC) Albany; WBXT-CA Tallahassee; WCTV (CBS, MNT) Thomasville; WFSU-TV (PBS) Tallahassee; WSB-TV (ABC) Atlanta; WTLF (CW, FOX) Tallahassee; WTLH (CW, FOX) Bainbridge; WTWC-TV (NBC) Tallahassee; WTXL-TV (ABC) Tallahassee; WXIA-TV (NBC) Atlanta.
Programming (via satellite): Bloomberg Television; C-SPAN; C-SPAN 2; Discovery Channel; Disney Channel; FamilyNet; FitTV; Fox News Channel; G4; Gospel Music TV; Hallmark Channel; Headline News; Home Shopping Network; ION Television; QVC; SportSouth; TBS Superstation; Toon Disney; Travel Channel; Trinity Broadcasting Network; Weather Channel.
Fee: $10.50 monthly.

Expanded Basic Service 1
Subscribers: 6,939.
Programming (via satellite): ABC Family Channel; AMC; Animal Planet; Arts & Entertainment; BET Networks; Bravo; Cartoon Network; CNBC; CNN; Comcast Sports Net Southeast; Comedy Central; E! Entertainment Television; ESPN; ESPN 2; ESPN Classic Sports; Food Network; FX; Golf Channel; Great American Country; GSN; HGTV; History Channel; Lifetime; MSNBC; MTV; Nickelodeon; Outdoor Channel; Speed Channel; Spike TV; Syfy; The Learning Channel; truTV; Turner Classic Movies; Turner Network TV; TV Land; USA Network; VH1; WE tv; WGN America.
Fee: $34.95 monthly.

Digital Basic Service
Subscribers: 2,551.
Programming (via satellite): BBC America; Bio; Boomerang; CNN en Espanol; CNN International; Discovery Digital Networks; Do-It-Yourself; Fox Movie Channel; Fox Sports en Espanol; Fox Sports World; Fuse; GAS; History Channel International; Independent Film Channel; Lifetime Movie Network; MTV Networks Digital Suite; Music Choice; National Geographic Channel; Nick Jr.; Nick Too; Style Network.
Fee: $59.95 monthly.

Pay Service 1
Pay Units: N.A.
Programming (via satellite): Cinemax (multiplexed); Encore (multiplexed); Flix; HBO (multiplexed); Showtime; Starz (multiplexed); Sundance Channel; The Movie Channel.
Fee: $8.95 monthly (HBO).

Digital Pay Service 1
Pay Units: N.A.
Programming (via satellite): Cinemax (multiplexed); Encore (multiplexed); Flix; HBO (multiplexed); Showtime (multiplexed); Starz (multiplexed); Sundance Channel; The Movie Channel (multiplexed).
Fee: $10.00 monthly (each).

Pay-Per-View
iN DEMAND.

Internet Service
Operational: Yes.
Subscribers: 4,095.
Broadband Service: SyrupCity.net.
Fee: $28.95 monthly.

Telephone Service
None

Miles of Plant: 280.0 (coaxial); None (fiber optic).
Marketing Coordinator: Sherri Nix. Broadband Engineer: Chris White.
Ownership: Community Network Services (MSO).

THOMASVILLE—Mediacom, 275 Norman Dr, Valdosta, GA 31601. Phone: 229-244-3852. Fax: 229-244-0724. Web Site: http://www.mediacomcable.com. Also serves Cairo, Grady County & Thomas County. ICA: GA0035.
TV Market Ranking: Below 100 (Cairo, Grady County, Thomas County, THOMASVILLE). Franchise award date: N.A. Franchise expiration date: N.A. Began: March 1, 1969.
Channel capacity: N.A. Channels available but not in use: None.

Basic Service
Subscribers: 10,596.
Programming (received off-air): WABW-TV (PBS) Pelham; WALB (NBC) Albany; WBXT-CA Tallahassee; WCTV (CBS, MNT) Thomasville; WFSU-TV (PBS) Tallahassee; WSWG (CBS, MNT) Valdosta; WTLH (CW, FOX) Bainbridge; WTWC-TV (NBC) Tallahassee; WTXL-TV (ABC) Tallahassee; 15 FMs.
Programming (via microwave): WSB-TV (ABC) Atlanta.
Current originations: Government Access.
Fee: $10.00 monthly; $2.00 converter.

For more information call **800-771-9202** or visit **www.warren-news.com**

Expanded Basic Service 1
Subscribers: N.A.
Programming (via satellite): ABC Family Channel; AMC; Animal Planet; Arts & Entertainment; BET Networks; Bravo; Cartoon Network; CNBC; CNN; Comcast Sports Net Southeast; Comedy Central; Country Music TV; C-SPAN; C-SPAN 2; Discovery Channel; Disney Channel; E! Entertainment Television; ESPN; Eternal Word TV Network; Food Network; Fox News Channel; FX; Gaming Entertainment Television; Hallmark Channel; Headline News; HGTV; History Channel; INSP; ION Television; Lifetime; MSNBC; MTV; Nickelodeon; Outdoor Channel; QVC; Speed Channel; Spike TV; SportSouth; Syfy; TBS Superstation; The Learning Channel; Travel Channel; Trinity Broadcasting Network; truTV; Turner Network TV; TV Guide Network; TV Land; Univision; USA Network; VH1; WE tv; Weather Channel.
Fee: $60.00 installation; $9.43 monthly.

Digital Basic Service
Subscribers: N.A.
Programming (via satellite): BBC America; Discovery Digital Networks; DMX Music; Fox Sports World; G4; Golf Channel; GSN; Independent Film Channel; Lime; MTV Networks Digital Suite; National Geographic Channel; Nick Jr.; Ovation; Turner Classic Movies; Versus.

Digital Pay Service 1
Pay Units: N.A.
Programming (via satellite): Cinemax (multiplexed); Encore (multiplexed); HBO (multiplexed); Showtime (multiplexed); Starz (multiplexed); Sundance Channel; The Movie Channel.

Video-On-Demand: Yes

Pay-Per-View
TVN Entertainment (delivered digitally); ETC (delivered digitally); ESPN Now (delivered digitally); Sports PPV (delivered digitally).

Internet Service
Operational: Yes.
Broadband Service: Mediacom High Speed Internet.
Fee: $40.95 monthly.

Telephone Service
Digital: Operational

Miles of Plant: 502.0 (coaxial); 62.0 (fiber optic). Homes passed: 10,804. Total homes in franchised area: 19,783. Miles of plant (coax & fiber) includes Havana FL, Bainbridge, & Camilla
Regional Vice President: Sue Misiunas. Regional Technical Operations Manager: Gary McDougall. Regional Marketing Director: Melanie Hannasch. Marketing Manager: Daryl Channey.
City fee: 6% of gross.
Ownership: Mediacom LLC (MSO).

TIFTON—Mediacom, 275 Norman Dr, Valdosta, GA 31601. Phone: 229-244-3852. Fax: 229-244-0724. Web Site: http://www.mediacomcable.com. Also serves Ashburn, Omega, Sycamore, Turner County (southern portion) & Ty Ty. ICA: GA0032.
TV Market Ranking: Below 100 (Ashburn, Sycamore, Turner County (southern portion), Ty Ty); Outside TV Markets (Omega, TIFTON). Franchise award date: N.A. Franchise expiration date: N.A. Began: February 1, 1969.
Channel capacity: 73 (operating 2-way). Channels available but not in use: None.

Basic Service
Subscribers: 8,300.
Programming (received off-air): WALB (NBC) Albany; WCTV (CBS, MNT) Thomasville; WFXL (FOX) Albany; WGCL-TV (CBS) Atlanta; WSB-TV (ABC) Atlanta; WSST-TV (IND) Cordele; WSWG (CBS, MNT) Valdosta; WTWC-TV (NBC) Tallahassee; WTXL-TV (ABC) Tallahassee; allband FM.
Programming (via satellite): C-SPAN; C-SPAN 2; Home Shopping Network; QVC.
Current originations: Leased Access; Government Access; Educational Access; Public Access.

Expanded Basic Service 1
Subscribers: 8,187.
Programming (via satellite): ABC Family Channel; AMC; Animal Planet; Arts & Entertainment; BET Networks; Bio; Bravo; Cartoon Network; CNBC; CNN; Comcast Sports Net Southeast; Comedy Central; Country Music TV; Discovery Channel; Discovery Health Channel; Disney Channel; Do-It-Yourself; E! Entertainment Television; ESPN; ESPN 2; ESPN Classic Sports; FitTV; Food Network; Fox News Channel; FX; GalaVision; Golf Channel; Great American Country; Hallmark Channel; Headline News; HGTV; History Channel; Lifetime; Lifetime Movie Network; MSNBC; MTV; National Geographic Channel; Nickelodeon; Outdoor Channel; Oxygen; Paxson Communications Corp.; SoapNet; Speed Channel; Spike TV; SportSouth; Syfy; TBS Superstation; The Learning Channel; Toon Disney; Travel Channel; Trinity Broadcasting Network; truTV; Turner Network TV; TV Guide Network; TV Land; Univision; USA Network; Versus; VH1; WE tv; Weather Channel; WGN America; WPIX (CW, IND) New York.
Fee: $27.73 monthly.

Digital Basic Service
Subscribers: N.A.
Programming (via satellite): 3 Angels Broadcasting Network; AmericanLife TV Network; BBC America; Bloomberg Television; Boomerang; BYU Television; Church Channel; CNN International; Daystar TV Network; Discovery Digital Networks; Discovery HD Theater; ESPNews; Eternal Word TV Network; Fox College Sports Atlantic; Fox College Sports Central; Fox College Sports Pacific; Fox Movie Channel; Fox Soccer; Fuse; G4; GAS; Golden Eagle Broadcasting; Gospel Music TV; GSN; Halogen Network; HDNet; HDNet Movies;

History Channel International; Independent Film Channel; INSP; JCTV; Lifetime Real Women; MTV Networks Digital Suite; Nick Jr.; NickToons TV; Outdoor Channel 2 HD; Ovation; Style Network; Tennis Channel; The Sportsman Channel; Turner Classic Movies; Universal HD.

Pay Service 1
Pay Units: 555.
Programming (via satellite): Cinemax.
Fee: $10.00 installation; $11.75 monthly.

Pay Service 2
Pay Units: 3,150.
Programming (via satellite): Encore (multiplexed).
Fee: $1.75 monthly.

Pay Service 3
Pay Units: 2,016.
Programming (via satellite): HBO (multiplexed).
Fee: $13.15 monthly.

Pay Service 4
Pay Units: 796.
Programming (via satellite): Showtime.
Fee: $11.75 monthly.

Pay Service 5
Pay Units: 1,106.
Programming (via satellite): Starz.
Fee: $4.75 monthly.

Digital Pay Service 1
Pay Units: N.A.
Programming (via satellite): Cinemax (multiplexed); Encore (multiplexed); Flix; HBO (multiplexed); HBO HD; Showtime (multiplexed); Starz (multiplexed); Starz HDTV; Sundance Channel; The Movie Channel (multiplexed).
Fee: $10.30 monthly (Cinemax, HBO, Showtime, Sundance/TMC, or Starz/Encore).

Video-On-Demand: Yes

Pay-Per-View
ESPN Now (delivered digitally), Addressable: Yes; ETC (delivered digitally); TVN Entertainment (delivered digitally); sports (delivered digitally).

Internet Service
Operational: Yes.
Broadband Service: Mediacom High Speed Internet.
Fee: $70.00 installation; $40.95 monthly.

Telephone Service
Digital: Operational
Fee: $39.99 monthly

Miles of Plant: 297.0 (coaxial); None (fiber optic). Homes passed: 13,794. Total homes in franchised area: 17,334.
Vice President: Don Zagorski. Manager: Sally A. Bloom. Technical Operations Manager: Donald Swanson. Chief Technician: Wendell Pitts.
City fee: 9% of gross. County fee: 8.2% of gross.
Ownership: Mediacom LLC (MSO).

TIGNALL—Formerly served by Almega Cable. No longer in operation. ICA: GA0254.

TOCCOA—Northland Cable Television, PO Box 1667, 203 Doyle St E, Toccoa, GA 30577. Phone: 706-886-2727. Fax: 706-886-0144. Web Site: http://www.northlandcabletv.com. Also serves Eastanollee (portions), Stephens County & Toccoa Falls. ICA: GA0050.
TV Market Ranking: Below 100 (Eastanollee (portions), Stephens County, TOCCOA, Toccoa Falls). Franchise award date: N.A. Franchise expiration date: N.A. Began: January 1, 1965.
Channel capacity: 237 (not 2-way capable). Channels available but not in use: None.

Basic Service
Subscribers: 5,506.
Programming (received off-air): WAGA-TV (FOX) Atlanta; WGGS-TV (IND) Greenville; WGTV (PBS) Athens; WHNS (FOX) Greenville; WLOS (ABC) Asheville; WMYA-TV (MNT) Anderson; WNEG-TV (CBS) Toccoa; WSB-TV (ABC) Atlanta; WXIA-TV (NBC) Atlanta; WYCW (CW) Asheville; WYFF (NBC) Greenville; 3 FMs.
Programming (via satellite): Arts & Entertainment; BET Networks; Cartoon Network; C-SPAN; Discovery Channel; ESPN; ESPN 2; Fox Movie Channel; Fox News Channel; HGTV; History Channel; Nickelodeon; QVC; The Learning Channel; Trinity Broadcasting Network; TV Guide Network; Weather Channel.
Fee: $40.00 installation.

Expanded Basic Service 1
Subscribers: 4,296.
Programming (via satellite): ABC Family Channel; AMC; Animal Planet; CNBC; CNN; Comcast Sports Net Southeast; Comedy Central; Country Music TV; E! Entertainment Television; Food Network; FX; Great American Country; Hallmark Channel; Headline News; Lifetime; MTV; SoapNet; Speed Channel; Spike TV; SportSouth; Syfy; TBS Superstation; Turner Classic Movies; Turner Network TV; TV Land; USA Network.
Fee: $40.00 installation.

Digital Basic Service
Subscribers: N.A.
Programming (via satellite): BBC America; Discovery Digital Networks; DMX Music; Golf Channel; GSN; INSP; Outdoor Channel.
Fee: $51.99 monthly.

Pay Service 1
Pay Units: 193.
Programming (via satellite): HBO; Showtime; The Movie Channel.
Fee: $12.20 monthly (HBO, Showtime, or TMC).

Digital Pay Service 1
Pay Units: N.A.
Programming (via satellite): Cinemax (multiplexed); Encore; Flix; HBO (multiplexed); Showtime (multiplexed); Starz (multiplexed); The Movie Channel (multiplexed).
Fee: $14.75 monthly (HBO, Cinemax, Showtime/TMC/Flix or Starz/Encore).

Video-On-Demand: No

Pay-Per-View
Fresh (delivered digitally); Playboy TV (delivered digitally).

Internet Service
Operational: Yes.
Fee: $42.99 monthly.

Telephone Service
Analog: Not Operational
Digital: Operational
Fee: $29.99 monthly

Miles of Plant: 196.0 (coaxial); None (fiber optic). Homes passed: 7,403. Total homes in franchised area: 7,497.
Regional Manager: Jack Corley. Office Manager: Betty Chastain. Marketing Manager: Becky Stovall. Technical Manager: Jerry Shirley.
City fee: 3% of gross.
Ownership: Northland Communications Corp. (MSO).

TOOMSBORO—KLiP Interactive, 455 Gees Mill Business Court, Conyers, GA 30013. Phone: 678-727-7100. Fax: 678-727-7002. E-mail: jsheehan@klipia.com. Web Site: http://www.klipia.com. ICA: GA0157.
TV Market Ranking: Below 100 (TOOMSBORO). Franchise award date: N.A. Franchise expiration date: N.A. Began: N.A.
Channel capacity: 45 (not 2-way capable). Channels available but not in use: 14.

Basic Service
Subscribers: 14.
Programming (received off-air): WMAZ-TV (CBS) Macon; WMGT-TV (MNT, NBC) Macon; WPCH-TV (IND) Atlanta; WPGA-TV (ABC) Perry.
Programming (via satellite): ABC Family Channel; Animal Planet; Arts & Entertainment; BET Networks; CNN; Comcast Sports Net Southeast; Discovery Channel; Disney Channel; ESPN; ESPN 2; Fox News Channel; Home Shopping Network; Lifetime; Nickelodeon; Speed Channel; Spike TV; The Learning Channel; Travel Channel; Trinity Broadcasting Network; Turner Network TV; TV Land; USA Network; Weather Channel; WGN America.
Fee: $29.95 installation; $36.50 monthly.

Pay Service 1
Pay Units: 2.
Programming (via satellite): HBO.
Fee: $10.95 monthly.

Internet Service
Operational: No.

Telephone Service
None

Miles of Plant: 5.0 (coaxial); None (fiber optic). Homes passed: 220.
Chief Executive Officer: Joseph A. Sheehan. General Manager East: Mark Miller. General Manager West: Vance Johnson.
Ownership: KLiP Interactive LLC (MSO).

TRENTON—Charter Communications, 1103 S Hamilton St, Dalton, GA 30720-7860. Phones: 865-984-1400 (Maryville, TN office); 706-428-2290. Fax: 706-260-2520. Web Site: http://www.charter.com. Also serves Hinkles, Rising Fawn & Wildwood. ICA: GA0255.
TV Market Ranking: 78 (Hinkles, Rising Fawn, TRENTON, Wildwood). Franchise award date: N.A. Franchise expiration date: N.A. Began: September 1, 1979.
Channel capacity: N.A. Channels available but not in use: N.A.

Basic Service
Subscribers: 2,250.
Programming (received off-air): WDEF-TV (CBS) Chattanooga; WDSI-TV (FOX, MNT) Chattanooga; WELF-TV (TBN) Dalton; WFLI-TV (CW) Cleveland; WNGH-TV (PBS) Chatsworth; WRCB (NBC) Chattanooga; WTCI (PBS) Chattanooga; WTVC (ABC) Chattanooga.
Programming (via satellite): C-SPAN; C-SPAN 2; INSP; QVC; TBS Superstation; Weather Channel; WGN America.
Current originations: Public Access.
Fee: $29.99 installation.

Expanded Basic Service 1
Subscribers: N.A.
Programming (via satellite): ABC Family Channel; AMC; Animal Planet; Arts & Entertainment; BET Networks; Bravo; Cartoon Network; CNBC; CNN; Comcast Sports Net Southeast; Comcast/Charter Sports Southeast (CSS); Comedy Central; Country Music TV; Discovery Channel; Disney Channel; E! Entertainment Television; ESPN; ESPN 2; Eternal Word TV Network; Food Network; Fox News Channel; FX; GalaVision; Golf Channel; GSN; Hallmark Channel; Headline News; HGTV; History Channel; Home Shopping Network; Lifetime; MTV; National Geographic Channel; Nickelodeon; SoapNet; Speed Channel; Spike TV; SportSouth; Syfy; The Learning Channel; Travel Channel; Turner Classic Movies; Turner Network TV; TV Land; Univision; USA Network; Versus; VH1; WE tv.
Fee: $50.99 monthly.

Digital Basic Service
Subscribers: N.A.
Programming (via satellite): BBC America; Bio; Discovery Digital Networks; Do-It-Yourself; Fox College Sports Atlantic; Fox College Sports Central; Fox College Sports Pacific; Fox Sports en Espanol; Fox Sports World; G4; Great American Country; History Channel International; Independent Film Channel; Music Choice; Nick Jr.; Sundance Channel; TV Guide Interactive Inc.

Digital Pay Service 1
Pay Units: N.A.
Programming (via satellite): Cinemax (multiplexed); Encore; Flix; HBO (multiplexed); Showtime (multiplexed); Starz (multiplexed); The Movie Channel (multiplexed).

Video-On-Demand: No

Pay-Per-View
Hot Choice (delivered digitally); iN DEMAND (delivered digitally); Playboy TV (delivered digitally), Addressable: Yes; Fresh (delivered digitally); Shorteez (delivered digitally).

Internet Service
Operational: Yes.
Broadband Service: Charter Pipeline.
Fee: $29.99 monthly.

Telephone Service
Digital: Operational

Miles of Plant: 25.0 (coaxial); None (fiber optic).
Operations Manager: Mike Burns. Technical Operations Director: Grant Evans. Marketing Director: Pat Hollenbeck.
Ownership: Charter Communications Inc. (MSO).

TWIN CITY—Comcast Cable, 141 Park of Commerce Dr, Savannah, GA 31405. Phone: 912-356-3113. Web Site: http://www.comcast.com. ICA: GA0256.
TV Market Ranking: Outside TV Markets (TWIN CITY). Franchise award date: July 7, 1981. Franchise expiration date: N.A. Began: August 1, 1982.
Channel capacity: N.A. Channels available but not in use: N.A.

Basic Service
Subscribers: N.A. Included in Savannah
Programming (received off-air): WAGT (CW, NBC) Augusta; WCES-TV (PBS) Wrens; WFXG (FOX) Augusta; WJBF (ABC) Augusta; WJCL (ABC) Savannah; WRDW-TV (CBS, MNT) Augusta; WSAV-TV (MNT, NBC) Savannah; WTOC-TV (CBS) Savannah.
Programming (via satellite): QVC; USA Network.
Fee: $47.99 installation; $20.00 additional installation.

Expanded Basic Service 1
Subscribers: N.A.
Programming (via satellite): ABC Family Channel; AMC; Animal Planet; Arts & Entertainment; BET Networks; Bravo; Cartoon Network; CNBC; CNN; Comcast/Charter Sports Southeast (CSS); Comedy Central; Country Music TV; C-SPAN; C-SPAN 2; Discovery Channel; Discovery Health Channel; Disney Channel; E! Entertainment Television; ESPN; ESPN 2; Food Network; Fox News Channel; Fox Sports Net; FX; Golf Channel; Great American Country; GSN; Hallmark Channel; Headline News; HGTV; History Channel; Home

Shopping Network; INSP; ION Television; Lifetime; MTV; Nickelodeon; Speed Channel; Spike TV; SportSouth; Style Network; Syfy; TBS Superstation; The Learning Channel; Trinity Broadcasting Network; truTV; Turner Classic Movies; Turner Network TV; TV Land; Versus; VH1; Weather Channel; WGN America.
Fee: $25.00 installation; $17.50 monthly.

Pay Service 1
Pay Units: 131.
Programming (via satellite): HBO; Showtime; The Movie Channel.
Fee: $10.00 monthly.

Video-On-Demand: No

Internet Service
Operational: No.

Telephone Service
None

Homes passed & miles of plant (coax & fiber) included in Savannah

General Manager: Michael Daves. Technical Operations Director: Joel Godsen. Marketing Director: Jerry Avery. Marketing Manager: Ken Torres.

City fee: 3% of gross.

Ownership: Comcast Cable Communications Inc. (MSO).

TYBEE ISLAND—Comcast Cable, 141 Park of Commerce Dr, Savannah, GA 31405. Phone: 912-356-3113. Web Site: http://www.comcast.com. Also serves Chatham County. ICA: GA0087.

TV Market Ranking: Below 100 (Chatham County, TYBEE ISLAND). Franchise award date: N.A. Franchise expiration date: N.A. Began: July 1, 1982.

Channel capacity: N.A. Channels available but not in use: N.A.

Basic Service
Subscribers: N.A. Included in Savannah
Programming (received off-air): WGSA (CW) Baxley; WJCL (ABC) Savannah; WJWJ-TV (PBS) Beaufort; WSAV-TV (MNT, NBC) Savannah; WTGS (FOX) Hardeeville; WTOC-TV (CBS) Savannah; WVAN-TV (PBS) Savannah.
Programming (via satellite): ABC Family Channel; INSP; ION Television; QVC; TV Guide Network; WGN America.
Current originations: Government Access; Educational Access; Public Access.
Fee: $47.99 installation; $9.00 monthly.

Expanded Basic Service 1
Subscribers: 1,744.
Programming (via satellite): AMC; Animal Planet; Arts & Entertainment; BET Networks; Bravo; Cartoon Network; CNBC; CNN; Comcast/Charter Sports Southeast (CSS); Comedy Central; Country Music TV; C-SPAN; C-SPAN 2; Discovery Channel; Discovery Health Channel; Disney Channel; E! Entertainment Television; ESPN; ESPN 2; Eternal Word TV Network; Food Network; Fox News Channel; Fox Sports Net; FX; Golf Channel; Great American Country; GSN; Hallmark Channel; Headline News; HGTV; History Channel; Home Shopping Network; Lifetime; MSNBC; MTV; Nickelodeon; Product Information Network; Speed Channel; Spike TV; SportSouth; Style Network; Syfy; TBS Superstation; The Learning Channel; Travel Channel; Trinity Broadcasting Network; truTV; Turner Network TV; TV Land; TV One; Univision; USA Network; Versus; VH1; WE tv; Weather Channel.
Fee: $40.99 monthly.

Digital Basic Service
Subscribers: N.A.
Programming (via satellite): BBC America; Bio; Black Family Channel; Canales N; Cooking Channel; C-SPAN 3; Discovery Digital Networks; Discovery HD Theater; DMX Music; Do-It-Yourself; Encore (multiplexed); Encore; ESPN; ESPNews; Flix (multiplexed); G4; GAS; History Channel International; INHD (multiplexed); Jewelry Television; Lifetime Movie Network; LOGO; MoviePlex; MTV Networks Digital Suite; National Geographic Channel; NFL Network; Nick Jr.; Nick Too; NickToons TV; Outdoor Channel; PBS Kids Sprout; SoapNet; Sundance Channel; The Word Network; Toon Disney; Turner Classic Movies; Turner Network TV HD; Weatherscan.
Fee: $11.95 monthly.

Digital Pay Service 1
Pay Units: N.A.
Programming (via satellite): Cinemax (multiplexed); Cinemax HD; HBO (multiplexed); HBO HD; Showtime (multiplexed); Showtime HD; Starz (multiplexed); Starz HDTV; The Movie Channel (multiplexed).
Fee: $15.54 monthly (each).

Video-On-Demand: Yes

Pay-Per-View
iN DEMAND (delivered digitally); Hot Choice (delivered digitally); Playboy TV (delivered digitally); Fresh (delivered digitally); Shorteez (delivered digitally); Pleasure (delivered digitally); ESPN (delivered digitally).

Internet Service
Operational: Yes.
Broadband Service: Comcast High Speed Internet.

Telephone Service
Digital: Operational

Homes passed & miles of plant (coax & fiber) included in Savannah

General Manager: Michael Daves. Technical Operations Director: Joel Godson. Marketing Director: Jerry Avery. Marketing Manager: Ken Torres.

City fee: 3% of gross.

Ownership: Comcast Cable Communications Inc.

UNADILLA—CommuniComm Services. Now served by PERRY, GA [GA0229]. ICA: GA0275.

UVALDA—Worth Cable, PO Box 2056, 3 Commissioner Dr, Darien, GA 31305-2056. Phones: 912-437-3422; 866-206-0656. Fax: 912-437-2065. Also serves Montgomery County (portions) & Toombs County (portions). ICA: GA0135.

TV Market Ranking: Below 100 (Montgomery County (portions), Toombs County (portions), UVALDA). Franchise award date: N.A. Franchise expiration date: N.A. Began: N.A.

Channel capacity: 45 (not 2-way capable). Channels available but not in use: 13.

Basic Service
Subscribers: 195.
Programming (received off-air): WFXL (FOX) Albany; WGSA (CW) Baxley; WJCL (ABC) Savannah; WSAV-TV (MNT, NBC) Savannah; WTOC-TV (CBS) Savannah; WVAN-TV (PBS) Savannah.
Programming (via satellite): ABC Family Channel; Animal Planet; Arts & Entertainment; BET Networks; CNN; Comcast Sports Net Southeast; Discovery Channel; Disney Channel; ESPN; Fox News Channel; History Channel; Home Shopping Network; Lifetime; Nickelodeon; Spike TV; TBS Superstation; The Learning Channel; Travel Channel; Turner Network TV; TV Land; USA Network; Weather Channel; WGN America.
Fee: $29.95 installation; $32.50 monthly.

Pay Service 1
Pay Units: 50.
Programming (via satellite): HBO.
Fee: $10.95 monthly.

Video-On-Demand: No

Internet Service
Operational: No.

Telephone Service
None

Miles of Plant: 15.0 (coaxial); None (fiber optic). Homes passed: 370.

General Manager: Dennis Wortham.

Ownership: Worth Cable Services (MSO).

VALDOSTA—Mediacom, 275 Norman Dr, Valdosta, GA 31601. Phone: 229-244-3852. Fax: 229-244-0724. Web Site: http://www.mediacomcable.com. Also serves Brooks County (eastern portion), Cecil, Hahira, Lowndes County & Remerton. ICA: GA0020.

TV Market Ranking: Below 100 (Brooks County (eastern portion), Cecil, Hahira, Lowndes County, Remerton, VALDOSTA). Franchise award date: N.A. Franchise expiration date: N.A. Began: July 1, 1965.

Channel capacity: N.A. Channels available but not in use: N.A.

Basic Service
Subscribers: 21,000.
Programming (received off-air): WALB (NBC) Albany; WBXT-CA Tallahassee; WCTV (CBS, MNT) Thomasville; WFXU (IND) Live Oak; WSWG (CBS, MNT) Valdosta; WTLH (CW, FOX) Bainbridge; WTWC-TV (NBC) Tallahassee; WTXL-TV (ABC) Tallahassee; WXGA-TV (PBS) Waycross; 19 FMs.
Programming (via microwave): WPCH-TV (IND) Atlanta; WSB-TV (ABC) Atlanta.
Programming (via satellite): ABC Family Channel; Arts & Entertainment; BET Networks; CNBC; CNN; Comedy Central; C-SPAN; Discovery Channel; Hallmark Channel; Headline News; Lifetime; MTV; Nickelodeon; QVC; Turner Network TV; VH1; Weather Channel.
Current originations: Government Access; Educational Access; Public Access.

Expanded Basic Service 1
Subscribers: 17,637.
Programming (via satellite): AMC; Animal Planet; Black Family Channel; Bravo; Cartoon Network; Comcast Sports Net Southeast; Country Music TV; C-SPAN 2; E! Entertainment Television; ESPN; ESPN 2; Eternal Word TV Network; FitTV; Food Network; Fox News Channel; FX; GalaVision; Golf Channel; HGTV; History Channel; Home Shopping Network; ION Television; MSNBC; Oxygen; Spike TV; SportSouth; Syfy; The Learning Channel; Travel Channel; Trinity Broadcasting Network; truTV; TV Guide Network; TV Land; USA Network; WE tv.

Digital Basic Service
Subscribers: N.A.
Programming (via satellite): BBC America; Bio; Bloomberg Television; Canales N; Discovery Digital Networks; Fox Movie Channel; Fox Sports World; Fuse; G4; Gaming Entertainment Television; GAS; GSN; Halogen Network; History Channel International; Independent Film Channel; Lifetime Movie Network; Lime; MTV Networks Digital Suite; Music Choice; National Geographic Channel; Nick Jr.; Outdoor Channel; Ovation; Speed Channel; Style Network; Toon Disney; Turner Classic Movies; Versus.

Digital Pay Service 1
Pay Units: N.A.
Programming (via satellite): Cinemax (multiplexed); Encore (multiplexed); Flix; HBO (multiplexed); Showtime (multiplexed); Starz (multiplexed); Sundance Channel; The Movie Channel (multiplexed).

Video-On-Demand: Yes

Pay-Per-View
TVN Entertainment (delivered digitally); Pleasure (delivered digitally); ETC (delivered digitally); ESPN Now (delivered digitally); Sports PPV (delivered digitally).

Internet Service
Operational: Yes.
Broadband Service: Mediacom High Speed Internet.
Fee: $59.95 installation; $42.95 monthly; $3.00 modem lease.

Telephone Service
Analog: Not Operational
Digital: Operational

Miles of Plant: 380.0 (coaxial); 63.0 (fiber optic). Homes passed: 25,636. Total homes in franchised area: 40,200.

Regional Vice President: Sue Misiunas. Regional Technical Operations Manager: Gary McDougall. Regional Marketing Director: Melanie Hannasch. Marketing Manager: Daryl Channey. Government Affairs Director: Sally Bloom.

Ownership: Mediacom LLC (MSO).

VIDALIA—Northland Cable Television, PO Box 547, 320 Commerce Way, Vidalia, GA 30475-0547. Phone: 912-537-3200. Fax: 912-537-7395. Web Site: http://www.northlandcabletv.com. Also serves Higgston, Lyons, Montgomery County, Santa Claus & Toombs County. ICA: GA0049.

TV Market Ranking: Below 100 (Higgston, Lyons, Montgomery County (portions), Santa Claus, Toombs County (portions), VIDALIA); Outside TV Markets (Montgomery County (portions), Toombs County (portions)). Franchise award date: N.A. Franchise expiration date: N.A. Began: June 1, 1963.

Channel capacity: 50 (not 2-way capable). Channels available but not in use: 7.

Basic Service
Subscribers: 5,729.
Programming (received off-air): WGSA (CW) Baxley; WJCL (ABC) Savannah; WMAZ-TV (CBS) Macon; WSAV-TV (MNT, NBC) Savannah; WTOC-TV (CBS) Savannah; WVAN-TV (PBS) Savannah; 6 FMs.
Programming (via microwave): WXIA-TV (NBC) Atlanta.
Programming (via satellite): Animal Planet; BET Networks; CNBC; CNN; C-SPAN; Discovery Channel; ESPN; FX; Great American Country; Hallmark Channel; INSP; Nickelodeon; QVC; SportSouth; TBS Superstation; The Learning Channel; Travel Chan-

nel; TV Guide Network; TV Land; Univision; Weather Channel; WTGS (FOX) Hardeeville.
Fee: $29.99 installation; $30.99 monthly; $3.00 converter.

Expanded Basic Service 1
Subscribers: N.A.
Programming (via satellite): AMC; Arts & Entertainment; Cartoon Network; Comcast Sports Net Southeast; E! Entertainment Television; ESPN 2; Food Network; FX; Golf Channel; Headline News; HGTV; History Channel; Lifetime; MTV; Speed Channel; Spike TV; Syfy; Turner Classic Movies; Turner Network TV; USA Network.
Fee: $42.29 monthly.

Digital Basic Service
Subscribers: N.A.
Programming (via satellite): BBC America; Bloomberg Television; Discovery Digital Networks; DMX Music; G4; GSN; INSP; Outdoor Channel; Trinity Broadcasting Network.
Fee: $51.99 monthly.

Digital Expanded Basic Service
Subscribers: N.A.
Programming (via satellite): Bravo; FitTV; Independent Film Channel; Versus; WE tv.

Pay Service 1
Pay Units: 765.
Programming (via satellite): HBO; Showtime.
Fee: $11.95 monthly (each).

Digital Pay Service 1
Pay Units: N.A.
Programming (via satellite): Cinemax (multiplexed); Encore; Flix; HBO (multiplexed); Showtime (multiplexed); The Movie Channel (multiplexed).

Video-On-Demand: No

Pay-Per-View
Playboy TV (delivered digitally); Fresh (delivered digitally).

Internet Service
Operational: Yes.
Fee: $42.99 monthly.

Telephone Service
Analog: Not Operational
Digital: Operational
Fee: $29.99 monthly

Miles of Plant: 168.0 (coaxial); None (fiber optic). Homes passed: 7,192. Total homes in franchised area: 12,329.
Manager: Diana Joyner. Chief Technician: Mike Dawkins.
City fee: 3% of gross.
Ownership: Northland Communications Corp. (MSO).

VILLA RICA—Charter Communications, 1925 Breckenridge Plaza, Ste 100, Duluth, GA 30096-4918. Phone: 770-806-7060. Fax: 770-806-7099. Web Site: http://www.charter.com. Also serves Bowdon, Bremen, Buchanan, Carroll County (portions), Haralson County & Temple. ICA: GA0258.
TV Market Ranking: 18 (Buchanan, Carroll County (portions), VILLA RICA); Below 100 (Bowdon, Haralson County, Carroll County (portions)); Outside TV Markets (Bremen, Temple, Carroll County (portions)). Franchise award date: January 1, 1980. Franchise expiration date: N.A. Began: September 1, 1981.
Channel capacity: N.A. Channels available but not in use: N.A.

Basic Service
Subscribers: 6,242.
Programming (received off-air): WAGA-TV (FOX) Atlanta; WATL (MNT) Atlanta; WCAG-LP La Grange; WDTA-LP Fayetteville; WGCL-TV (CBS) Atlanta; WGTV (PBS) Athens; WPCH-TV (IND) Atlanta; WPXA-TV (ION) Rome; WSB-TV (ABC) Atlanta; WUPA (CW) Atlanta; WUVG-DT (UNV) Athens; WXIA-TV (NBC) Atlanta.
Programming (via satellite): C-SPAN; Home Shopping Network; INSP; QVC; Trinity Broadcasting Network; TV Guide Network; WGN America.
Current originations: Educational Access; Leased Access.
Fee: $29.99 installation.

Expanded Basic Service 1
Subscribers: 5,979.
Programming (via satellite): ABC Family Channel; AMC; Animal Planet; Arts & Entertainment; BET Networks; Bravo; Cartoon Network; CNBC; CNN; Comcast Sports Net Southeast; Comcast/Charter Sports Southeast (CSS); Comedy Central; Country Music TV; Discovery Channel; Disney Channel; E! Entertainment Television; ESPN; ESPN 2; ESPN Classic Sports; Eternal Word TV Network; FitTV; Food Network; Fox News Channel; FX; G4; GalaVision; Golf Channel; GSN; Hallmark Channel; Headline News; HGTV; History Channel; Lifetime; MSNBC; MTV; National Geographic Channel; Nickelodeon; Outdoor Channel; Product Information Network; Shop at Home; ShopNBC; SoapNet; Speed Channel; Spike TV; SportSouth; Syfy; Telemundo; The Learning Channel; Toon Disney; Travel Channel; truTV; Turner Classic Movies; Turner Network TV; TV Land; USA Network; Versus; VH1; WE tv; Weather Channel.
Fee: $48.99 monthly.

Digital Basic Service
Subscribers: N.A.
Programming (via satellite): BBC America; Bio; Bloomberg Television; Boomerang; Canales N; Discovery Digital Networks; Do-It-Yourself; ESPNews; Fox College Sports Atlantic; Fox College Sports Central; Fox College Sports Pacific; Fox Sports World; Fuse; GAS; Great American Country; History Channel International; Independent Film Channel; Lifetime Movie Network; MTV Networks Digital Suite; Music Choice; Nick Jr.; Nick Too; NickToons TV; Style Network; Sundance Channel.
Fee: $14.00 monthly.

Digital Pay Service 1
Pay Units: 235.
Programming (via satellite): Cinemax (multiplexed).
Fee: $15.00 installation; $10.95 monthly.

Digital Pay Service 2
Pay Units: 300.
Programming (via satellite): HBO (multiplexed).
Fee: $15.00 installation; $11.95 monthly.

Digital Pay Service 3
Pay Units: 171.
Programming (via satellite): The Movie Channel (multiplexed).
Fee: $15.00 installation; $10.95 monthly.

Digital Pay Service 4
Pay Units: 158.
Programming (via satellite): Flix; Showtime (multiplexed).
Fee: $15.00 installation; $10.95 monthly.

Digital Pay Service 5
Pay Units: N.A.
Programming (via satellite): Encore; Starz.

Video-On-Demand: Yes

Pay-Per-View
iN DEMAND (delivered digitally); NBA League Pass/WNBA (delivered digitally); NHL Center Ice/MLB Extra Innings (delivered digitally); Playboy TV (delivered digitally); Fresh (delivered digitally); Shorteez (delivered digitally).

Internet Service
Operational: Yes. Began: January 1, 2002.
Broadband Service: Charter Pipeline.
Fee: $29.99 monthly.

Telephone Service
Digital: Operational

Miles of Plant: 354.0 (coaxial); None (fiber optic). Homes passed: 9,091.
Vice President & General Manager: Sherita Ceaser. Operations Manager: John Anglin. Technical Operations Manager: Ken Minton. Marketing Director: Mark Watkins. Office Manager: Cindy Giley.
Franchise fee: 4% of gross.
Ownership: Charter Communications Inc. (MSO).

WARRENTON—Comcast Cable, 105 River Shoals Pkwy, Augusta, GA 30909. Phones: 706-283-6036; 706-733-7712. Fax: 706-739-1871. Web Site: http://www.comcast.com. Also serves Camak & Warren County (portions). ICA: GA0124.
TV Market Ranking: Below 100 (Warren County (portions) (portions)); Outside TV Markets (Camak, Warren County (portions) (portions), WARRENTON). Franchise award date: July 1, 1980. Franchise expiration date: N.A. Began: December 1, 1981.
Channel capacity: N.A. Channels available but not in use: N.A.

Basic Service
Subscribers: 668.
Programming (received off-air): WAGT (CW, NBC) Augusta; WCES-TV (PBS) Wrens; WFXG (FOX) Augusta; WJBF (ABC) Augusta; WRDW-TV (CBS, MNT) Augusta.
Programming (via satellite): BET Networks; C-SPAN; CW+; Fox News Channel; Lifetime; MSNBC; QVC; Trinity Broadcasting Network; truTV; Weather Channel; WGN America.
Fee: $25.00 installation; $11.50 monthly.

Expanded Basic Service 1
Subscribers: N.A.
Programming (via satellite): ABC Family Channel; AmericanLife TV Network; CNN; Comcast Sports Net Southeast; Comcast/Charter Sports Southeast (CSS); Comedy Central; C-SPAN 2; Disney Channel; E! Entertainment Television; ESPN; ESPN 2; Eternal Word TV Network; Golf Channel; Great American Country; Headline News; HGTV; Home Shopping Network; INSP; ION Television; MTV; Nickelodeon; Speed Channel; Style Network; Syfy; The Learning Channel; Turner Classic Movies; TV Guide Network; USA Network; Versus; VH1.
Fee: $40.75 monthly.

Expanded Basic Service 2
Subscribers: N.A.
Programming (via satellite): AMC; Animal Planet; Arts & Entertainment; CNBC; Discovery Channel; Discovery Health Channel; Food Network; GSN; History Channel; Spike TV; TBS Superstation; Turner Network TV; Turner South; TV Land.
Fee: $5.98 monthly.

Pay Service 1
Pay Units: 170.
Programming (via satellite): HBO; Showtime.
Fee: $15.00 installation; $7.95 (Showtime), $11.95 monthly (HBO).

Internet Service
Operational: Yes.

Telephone Service
None

Miles of Plant: 28.0 (coaxial); None (fiber optic). Homes passed: 700.
Technical Operations Director: Butch Jernigan. Engineering Director: Harry Hess. Area Marketing Director: Joey Fortier.
City fee: 3% of basic gross.
Ownership: Comcast Cable Communications Inc. (MSO).

WARWICK—Citizens Cable TV, 134 N Bailey Ave, Leslie, GA 31764. Phones: 229-853-1600; 866-341-3050. Fax: 229-874-2211. Web Site: http://www.citizenscatv.com. Also serves Crisp County (southern portion), Lake Blackshear & Worth County. ICA: GA0259.
TV Market Ranking: Below 100 (Crisp County (southern portion), Lake Blackshear, WARWICK, Worth County). Franchise award date: N.A. Franchise expiration date: N.A. Began: N.A.
Channel capacity: 65 (operating 2-way). Channels available but not in use: 17.

Basic Service
Subscribers: 655.
Programming (received off-air): WACS-TV (PBS) Dawson; WALB (NBC) Albany; WFXL (FOX) Albany; WRBL (CBS) Columbus; WSST-TV (IND) Cordele; WTVM (ABC) Columbus.
Programming (via satellite): ABC Family Channel; AMC; Animal Planet; Arts & Entertainment; BET Networks; Bloomberg Television; Cartoon Network; CNN; Comcast Sports Net Southeast; Comedy Central; Country Music TV; Discovery Channel; Disney Channel; E! Entertainment Television; ESPN; ESPN 2; Food Network; Fox News Channel; FX; Hallmark Channel; HGTV; History Channel; Lifetime; MTV; National Geographic Channel; Nickelodeon; QVC; Speed Channel; Spike TV; Syfy; TBS Superstation; The Learning Channel; Travel Channel; Trinity Broadcasting Network; truTV; Turner Classic Movies; Turner Network TV; Turner South; TV Land; USA Network; VH1; Weather Channel.
Fee: $19.95 installation; $32.95 monthly; $12.95 additional installation.

Digital Basic Service
Subscribers: 14.
Programming (via satellite): AmericanLife TV Network; BBC America; Bio; Black Family Channel; Bloomberg Television; Bravo; Current; Discovery Digital Networks; DMX Music; ESPN 2; ESPN Classic Sports; ESPNews; Fox College Sports Atlantic; Fox College Sports Central; Fox College Sports Pacific; Fox Movie Channel; Fox Soccer; Fuse; G4; GAS; Golf Channel; Great American Country; GSN; Halogen Network; HGTV; History Channel; History Channel International; Independent Film Channel; Lifetime Movie Network; Lime; National Geographic Channel; Nick Jr.; NickToons TV; Outdoor Channel; Ovation; PBS Kids Sprout; Sleuth; Speed Channel; Style Network; Toon Disney; Trinity Broadcasting Network; Versus; WE tv.

Pay Service 1
Pay Units: 78.
Programming (via satellite): HBO.
Fee: $10.95 monthly.

Pay Service 2
Pay Units: 61.
Programming (via satellite): Showtime.
Fee: $10.95 monthly.

Digital Pay Service 1
Pay Units: N.A.
Programming (via satellite): Cinemax (multiplexed); Encore (multiplexed); HBO (multiplexed); Showtime (multiplexed); Starz (multiplexed); The Movie Channel.

Internet Service
Operational: Yes.
Subscribers: 39.
Fee: $35.00 installation; $39.95 monthly.
Telephone Service
None
Miles of Plant: 56.0 (coaxial); None (fiber optic). Homes passed: 951.
Engineer: Bill Gregory.
Ownership: Citizens Cable TV (MSO).

WASHINGTON—Comcast Cable, 105 River Shoals Pkwy, Augusta, GA 30909. Phones: 706-738-0091 (administrative office); 706-733-7712. Fax: 706-739-1871. Web Site: http://www.comcast.com. Also serves Wilkes County (portions). ICA: GA0260.
TV Market Ranking: Below 100 (Wilkes County (portions)); Outside TV Markets (BARRY FARMS, Wilkes County (portions)). Franchise award date: N.A. Franchise expiration date: N.A. Began: December 1, 1978.
Channel capacity: N.A. Channels available but not in use: N.A.
Basic Service
Subscribers: 1,600.
Programming (received off-air): WAGA-TV (FOX) Atlanta; WAGT (CW, NBC) Augusta; WCES-TV (PBS) Wrens; WFXG (FOX) Augusta; WGGS-TV (IND) Greenville; WGTV (PBS) Athens; WJBF (ABC) Augusta; WPCH-TV (IND) Atlanta; WRDW-TV (CBS, MNT) Augusta; WSB-TV (ABC) Atlanta; WXIA-TV (NBC) Atlanta; 1 FM.
Programming (via satellite): C-SPAN; C-SPAN 2; Home Shopping Network; ION Television; Nickelodeon; QVC; Trinity Broadcasting Network; WGN America.
Fee: $50.00 installation; $13.32 monthly.
Expanded Basic Service 1
Subscribers: N.A.
Programming (via satellite): ABC Family Channel; Animal Planet; Arts & Entertainment; BET Networks; Cartoon Network; CNBC; CNN; Comcast Sports Net Southeast; Comcast/Charter Sports Southeast (CSS); Comedy Central; Country Music TV; Discovery Channel; Disney Channel; E! Entertainment Television; ESPN; ESPN 2; Food Network; Fox News Channel; FX; Golf Channel; GSN; Headline News; HGTV; History Channel; Lifetime; MSNBC; MTV; Speed Channel; Spike TV; Style Network; Syfy; The Learning Channel; Travel Channel; Turner Classic Movies; Turner Network TV; Turner South; TV Land; USA Network; Versus; Weather Channel.
Fee: $42.50 monthly.
Digital Basic Service
Subscribers: 361.
Programming (via satellite): Music Choice.
Fee: $8.31 monthly.
Digital Pay Service 1
Pay Units: N.A.
Programming (via satellite): Cinemax (multiplexed); Flix; HBO (multiplexed); Showtime (multiplexed); The Movie Channel (multiplexed).
Video-On-Demand: No
Pay-Per-View
Hot Choice (delivered digitally); iN DEMAND (delivered digitally); Playboy TV (delivered digitally); Pleasure (delivered digitally); Fresh (delivered digitally); Shorteez (delivered digitally).
Internet Service
Operational: No.
Broadband Service: DSL service only.
Telephone Service
None
Miles of Plant: 50.0 (coaxial); None (fiber optic).
Engineering Director: Harry Hess. Technical Operations Director: Butch Jernigan. Area Marketing Director: Joey Fortier.
City fee: 3% of gross.
Ownership: Comcast Cable Communications Inc. (MSO).

WAVERLY HALL—Charter Communications, 1349 Warren Williams Rd, Columbus, GA 31901. Phones: 770-806-7060 (Administrative office); 706-576-6806. Fax: 706-324-4031. Web Site: http://www.charter.com. ICA: GA0261.
TV Market Ranking: 94 (WAVERLY HALL). Franchise award date: N.A. Franchise expiration date: N.A. Began: N.A.
Channel capacity: N.A. Channels available but not in use: N.A.
Basic Service
Subscribers: 327.
Programming (received off-air): WJSP-TV (PBS) Columbus; WLGA (CW) Opelika; WLTZ (CW, NBC) Columbus; WRBL (CBS) Columbus; WTVM (ABC) Columbus; WXTX (FOX) Columbus; WYBU-CD (IND) Columbus.
Programming (via satellite): CNN; Comcast/Charter Sports Southeast (CSS); C-SPAN; Home Shopping Network; INSP; ION Television; QVC; TBS Superstation; Trinity Broadcasting Network; TV Guide Network; Weather Channel; WGN America.
Fee: $29.99 installation.
Expanded Basic Service 1
Subscribers: N.A.
Programming (via satellite): ABC Family Channel; AMC; Animal Planet; Arts & Entertainment; BET Networks; Bravo; Cartoon Network; CNBC; Comcast Sports Net Southeast; Comedy Central; Country Music TV; Discovery Channel; Disney Channel; E! Entertainment Television; ESPN; ESPN 2; ESPN Classic Sports; Food Network; Fox News Channel; FX; G4; Golf Channel; GSN; Hallmark Channel; Headline News; HGTV; History Channel; Lifetime; MSNBC; MTV; Nickelodeon; Oxygen; Product Information Network; SoapNet; Speed Channel; Spike TV; SportSouth; Syfy; Telemundo; The Learning Channel; Travel Channel; truTV; Turner Classic Movies; Turner Network TV; TV Land; Univision; USA Network; Versus; VH1; WE tv.
Fee: $48.99 monthly.
Digital Basic Service
Subscribers: N.A.
Programming (via satellite): BBC America; Discovery Digital Networks; ESPNews; Fox Soccer; GAS; Independent Film Channel; International Television (ITV); MTV Networks Digital Suite; Music Choice; Nick Jr.; Nick Too; NickToons TV; Ovation; Sundance Channel; The Word Network; TV Guide Interactive Inc.
Digital Pay Service 1
Pay Units: N.A.
Programming (via satellite): Cinemax (multiplexed); Encore (multiplexed); HBO (multiplexed); Playboy TV; Showtime (multiplexed); Starz (multiplexed); The Movie Channel (multiplexed).
Video-On-Demand: No
Internet Service
Operational: Yes.
Fee: $29.99 monthly.
Telephone Service
None
Miles of Plant: 10.0 (coaxial); None (fiber optic).
Vice President & General Manager: Matt Favre. Operations Manager: David Spriggs. Technical Operations Manager: Brenda Ivey. Sales & Marketing Director: Antoinette Carpenter.
Ownership: Charter Communications Inc. (MSO).

WAYCROSS—Media Stream, 126 Havanna Ave, Waycross, GA 31501-1075. Phone: 912-283-2332. Fax: 912-285-9836. E-mail: admin@mediastreamga.com. Web Site: http://www.mediastreamga.com. Also serves Brantley County (western portion) & Ware County (eastern portion). ICA: GA0031.
TV Market Ranking: Below 100 (Brantley County (western portion) (portions), Ware County (eastern portion) (portions)); Outside TV Markets (Brantley County (western portion) (portions), Ware County (eastern portion) (portions), WAYCROSS). Franchise award date: January 1, 1962. Franchise expiration date: N.A. Began: May 1, 1964.
Channel capacity: 73 (operating 2-way). Channels available but not in use: None.
Basic Service
Subscribers: 12,000.
Programming (received off-air): WALB (NBC) Albany; WAWS (FOX, MNT) Jacksonville; WCWJ (CW) Jacksonville; WJCL (ABC) Savannah; WJXT (IND) Jacksonville; WJXX (ABC) Orange Park; WPXC-TV (ION) Brunswick; WTEV-TV (CBS) Jacksonville; WTGS (FOX) Hardeeville; WTLV (NBC) Jacksonville; WTOC-TV (CBS) Savannah; WXGA-TV (PBS) Waycross; allband FM.
Programming (via satellite): ABC Family Channel; AMC; Animal Planet; Arts & Entertainment; BET Networks; Boomerang; Bravo; Cartoon Network; CNBC; CNN; Comcast Sports Net Southeast; Comedy Central; Cooking Channel; Country Music TV; C-SPAN; Discovery Channel; Disney Channel; Do-It-Yourself; E! Entertainment Television; ESPN; ESPN 2; ESPN Classic Sports; Eternal Word TV Network; FamilyNet; FitTV; Food Network; Fox News Channel; FX; G4; Golf Channel; Gospel Music TV; Hallmark Channel; Headline News; HGTV; History Channel; Home Shopping Network; INSP; Lifetime; LWS Local Weather Station; MSNBC; MTV; National Geographic Channel; Nickelodeon; QVC; SoapNet; Speed Channel; Spike TV; Syfy; TBS Superstation; The Learning Channel; Travel Channel; Trinity Broadcasting Network; truTV; Turner Classic Movies; Turner Network TV; Turner South; TV Guide Network; TV Land; USA Network; Versus; VH1; Weather Channel; WGN America.
Current originations: Religious Access; Government Access; Educational Access.
Fee: free installation; $43.95 monthly; $4.95 converter; $15.00 additional installation.
Digital Basic Service
Subscribers: 31.
Programming (via satellite): BBC America; Black Family Channel; Bloomberg Television; CMT Pure Country; Discovery en Espanol; Discovery Health Channel; Discovery Kids Channel; Discovery Military Channel; Discovery Planet Green; ESPN U; ESPNews; Fox College Sports Atlantic; Fox College Sports Central; Fox College Sports Pacific; Great American Country; GSN; Hallmark Movie Channel; ID Investigation Discovery; Lifetime Movie Network; MTV Hits; MTV2; Music Choice; Newsworld International; NFL Network; Nick Jr.; Outdoor Channel; Ovation; Science Channel; Sleuth; Style Network; TeenNick; Toon Disney; TVG Network; VH1 Classic; VH1 Soul; WE tv.
Fee: $10.00 monthly.
Digital Expanded Basic Service
Subscribers: N.A.
Programming (received off-air): WAWS (FOX, MNT) Jacksonville; WCWJ (CW) Jacksonville; WJXX (ABC) Orange Park; WTEV-TV (CBS) Jacksonville; WTLV (NBC) Jacksonville.
Programming (via satellite): ESPN 2 HD; ESPN HD; Outdoor Channel 2 HD; Universal HD; WealthTV HD.
Fee: $13.95 monthly.
Digital Pay Service 1
Pay Units: 662.
Programming (via satellite): Cinemax (multiplexed); Cinemax HD; HBO (multiplexed); HBO HD.
Fee: $8.95 monthly (Cinemax), $13.95 monthly (HBO).
Digital Pay Service 2
Pay Units: 291.
Programming (via satellite): Flix; Showtime (multiplexed); Showtime HD; Sundance Channel; The Movie Channel (multiplexed); The Movie Channel HD.
Fee: $11.95 monthly.
Digital Pay Service 3
Pay Units: 486.
Programming (via satellite): Encore (multiplexed); Starz (multiplexed); Starz HDTV.
Fee: $11.95 monthly.
Video-On-Demand: No
Pay-Per-View
Addressable homes: 1,558.
iN DEMAND (delivered digitally), Fee: $3.95, Addressable: Yes; Playboy TV (delivered digitally), Addressable: Yes.
Internet Service
Operational: Yes.
Subscribers: 3,300.
Broadband Service: In-house.
Fee: $34.95 monthly.
Telephone Service
None
Miles of Plant: 350.0 (coaxial); 70.0 (fiber optic).
Executive Vice President: Mike Jury. Chief Technician: Mike Kellish.
City fee: 5% of gross.
Ownership: Mediastream.

WAYNESBORO—Comcast Cablevision of the South. Now served by AUGUSTA, GA [GA0004]. ICA: GA0262.

WAYNESVILLE—Comcast Cable, 141 Park of Commerce Dr, Savannah, GA 31405. Phone: 912-356-3113. Web Site: http://www.comcast.com. ICA: GA0143.
TV Market Ranking: Below 100 (WAYNESVILLE). Franchise award date: N.A. Franchise expiration date: N.A. Began: January 1, 1990.
Channel capacity: N.A. Channels available but not in use: N.A.
Basic Service
Subscribers: 275.
Programming (received off-air): WJCL (ABC) Savannah; WPXC-TV (ION) Brunswick; WSAV-TV (MNT, NBC) Savannah; WTGS (FOX) Hardeeville; WTOC-TV (CBS) Savannah; WXGA-TV (PBS) Waycross.
Programming (via satellite): QVC; Spike TV; TBS Superstation; Trinity Broadcasting Network; Weather Channel; WGN America.
Fee: $49.95 installation.
Expanded Basic Service 1
Subscribers: 239.
Programming (via satellite): AMC; Animal Planet; BET Networks; Cartoon Network; CNBC; CNN; Comcast/Charter Sports Southeast (CSS); Comedy Central; Discovery Channel; Discovery Health Channel; Disney Channel; E! Entertainment Televi-

sion; ESPN; ESPN 2; Food Network; Fox News Channel; Fox Soccer; FX; Golf Channel; Great American Country; Headline News; HGTV; Lifetime; MTV; Nickelodeon; Speed Channel; SportSouth; Style Network; Syfy; The Learning Channel; truTV; Turner Network TV; TV Land; USA Network; Versus; VH1.
Fee: $49.99 monthly.

Pay Service 1
Pay Units: 21.
Programming (via satellite): Cinemax.
Fee: $15.95 monthly.

Pay Service 2
Pay Units: 39.
Programming (via satellite): HBO.
Fee: $15.95 monthly.

Pay Service 3
Pay Units: 18.
Programming (via satellite): Showtime.
Fee: $15.95 monthly.

Video-On-Demand: No

Internet Service
Operational: Yes.

Telephone Service
Analog: Planned

Miles of Plant: 45.0 (coaxial); None (fiber optic). Homes passed: 896.

Vice President & General Manager: Doug McMillan. Vice President, Marketing: Vic Scarborough. Engineering Director: Mike Humphrey. Government Affairs Director: Bill Ferry.

Ownership: Comcast Cable Communications Inc. (MSO).

WEST POINT—Charter Communications, 401 S 6th St, Lanett, AL 36863-2673. Phone: 770-806-7060 (Duluth office). Fax: 334-644-2131. Web Site: http://www.charter.com. Also serves Chambers County, Fairfax, Lanett, River View, Shawmut & Valley, AL; Troup County, GA. ICA: GA0034.

TV Market Ranking: 94 (Chambers County (portions), Fairfax, Lanett, River View, Shawmut, Troup County (portions), Valley, WEST POINT); Below 100 (Chambers County (portions)); Outside TV Markets (Troup County (portions)). Franchise award date: September 1, 1958. Franchise expiration date: N.A. Began: September 1, 1958.

Channel capacity: N.A. Channels available but not in use: N.A.

Basic Service
Subscribers: 12,654.
Programming (received off-air): WCAG-LP La Grange; WCIQ (PBS) Mount Cheaha State Park; WJSP-TV (PBS) Columbus; WLTZ (CW, NBC) Columbus; WRBL (CBS) Columbus; WSFA (NBC) Montgomery; WTVM (ABC) Columbus; WXTX (FOX) Columbus; 22 FMs.
Programming (via satellite): Product Information Network; WGN America.
Current originations: Religious Access; Educational Access.
Fee: $29.99 installation.

Expanded Basic Service 1
Subscribers: N.A.
Programming (via satellite): ABC Family Channel; AMC; Animal Planet; Arts & Entertainment; BET Networks; Bravo; Cartoon Network; CNBC; CNN; Comcast Sports Net Southeast; Comcast/Charter Sports Southeast (CSS); Comedy Central; Country Music TV; C-SPAN; C-SPAN 2; Discovery Channel; Disney Channel; E! Entertainment Television; ESPN; ESPN 2; ESPN Classic Sports; FitTV; Food Network; Fox News Channel; FX; G4; Golf Channel; GSN; Hallmark Channel; Headline News; HGTV; History Channel; Home Shopping Network; INSP; ION Television; Lifetime; MSNBC; MTV; National Geographic Channel; Nickelodeon; Outdoor Channel; Oxygen; QVC; ShopNBC; SoapNet; Speed Channel; Spike TV; SportSouth; Syfy; TBS Superstation; Telemundo; The Learning Channel; Toon Disney; Travel Channel; Trinity Broadcasting Network; truTV; Turner Classic Movies; Turner Network TV; TV Guide Network; TV Land; USA Network; Versus; VH1; WE tv; Weather Channel.
Fee: $48.99 monthly.

Digital Basic Service
Subscribers: N.A.
Programming (via satellite): BBC America; Discovery Digital Networks; GAS; MTV Networks Digital Suite; Music Choice; Nick Jr.; Nick Too; Nickelodeon; NickToons TV; Sundance Channel; TV Guide Interactive Inc.
Fee: $14.00 monthly.

Digital Pay Service 1
Pay Units: 2,886.
Programming (via satellite): Cinemax (multiplexed); Encore (multiplexed); Flix; HBO (multiplexed); Showtime (multiplexed); Starz (multiplexed); The Movie Channel (multiplexed).
Fee: $10.00 installation; $8.95 monthly (Cinemax), $10.95 monthly (HBO or Showtime).

Video-On-Demand: Yes

Pay-Per-View
NBA League Pass/WNBA (delivered digitally); iN DEMAND (delivered digitally); Playboy TV (delivered digitally); Fresh (delivered digitally); Shorteez (delivered digitally).

Internet Service
Operational: Yes.
Broadband Service: Charter Pipeline.
Fee: $29.99 monthly.

Telephone Service
Digital: Operational

Miles of Plant: 182.0 (coaxial); None (fiber optic). Additional miles planned: 2.0 (coaxial).

Vice President & General Manager: Matt Favre. Operations Manager: David Spriggs. Technical Supervisor: Trey Crosby. Sales & Marketing Director: Antoinette Carpenter. Office Manager: Deborah Gilbert.

City fee: 3% of gross.

Ownership: Charter Communications Inc. (MSO).

WHIGHAM—KLiP Interactive, 455 Gees Mill Business Court, Conyers, GA 30013. Phone: 678-727-7100. Fax: 678-727-7002. E-mail: jsheehan@klipia.com. Web Site: http://www.klipia.com. ICA: GA0263.

TV Market Ranking: Below 100 (WHIGHAM). Franchise award date: N.A. Franchise expiration date: N.A. Began: September 1, 1988.

Channel capacity: 65 (not 2-way capable). Channels available but not in use: 18.

Basic Service
Subscribers: 92.
Programming (received off-air): WABW-TV (PBS) Pelham; WALB (NBC) Albany; WCTV (CBS, MNT) Thomasville; WFSU-TV (PBS) Tallahassee; WPCH-TV (IND) Atlanta; WTLH (CW, FOX) Bainbridge; WTWC-TV (NBC) Tallahassee; WTXL-TV (ABC) Tallahassee; WVUP-CD Tallahassee.
Programming (via satellite): ABC Family Channel; AMC; Animal Planet; Arts & Entertainment; BET Networks; Bravo; Cartoon Network; CNBC; CNN; Comcast Sports Net Southeast; Comedy Central; Country Music TV; C-SPAN; C-SPAN 2; Discovery Channel; Disney Channel; E! Entertainment Television; ESPN; FX; Headline News; Lifetime; Nickelodeon; QVC; Speed Channel; Spike TV; Syfy; The Learning Channel; Travel Channel; Trinity Broadcasting Network; Turner Network TV; TV Land; USA Network; VH1; WE tv; Weather Channel; WGN America.
Fee: $29.95 installation; $39.95 monthly.

Pay Service 1
Pay Units: 9.
Programming (via satellite): HBO.
Fee: $10.95 monthly.

Pay Service 2
Pay Units: 6.
Programming (via satellite): Showtime.
Fee: $10.95 monthly.

Pay Service 3
Pay Units: 3.
Programming (via satellite): The Movie Channel.
Fee: $10.95 monthly.

Internet Service
Operational: No.

Telephone Service
None

Miles of Plant: 16.0 (coaxial); None (fiber optic). Homes passed: 425.

Chief Executive Officer: Joseph A. Sheehan. General Manager East: Mark Miller. General Manager West: Vance Johnson.

Ownership: KLiP Interactive LLC (MSO).

WILEY ACRES—Citizens Cable TV, PO Box 465, Leslie, GA 31764. Phones: 229-268-2288; 229-853-1600; 229-853-1600. Web Site: http://www.citizenscatv.com. ICA: GA0297.

TV Market Ranking: Below 100 (WILEY ACRES). Franchise award date: N.A. Franchise expiration date: N.A. Began: N.A.

Channel capacity: 65 (not 2-way capable). Channels available but not in use: 32.

Basic Service
Subscribers: 162.
Programming (received off-air): WACS-TV (PBS) Dawson; WALB (NBC) Albany; WFXL (FOX) Albany; WMAZ-TV (CBS) Macon; WPCH-TV (IND) Atlanta; WSST-TV (IND) Cordele; WTVM (ABC) Columbus.
Programming (via satellite): ABC Family Channel; AMC; Animal Planet; Arts & Entertainment; Bravo; CNBC; CNN; Comedy Central; Country Music TV; Discovery Channel; Disney Channel; ESPN; ESPN 2; Fox News Channel; Headline News; History Channel; Lifetime; Nickelodeon; QVC; Spike TV; The Learning Channel; Travel Channel; Turner Network TV; USA Network; Weather Channel; WGN America.
Fee: $29.95 installation; $33.55 monthly.

Pay Service 1
Pay Units: 19.
Programming (via satellite): HBO.
Fee: $10.95 monthly.

Pay Service 2
Pay Units: 12.
Programming (via satellite): Showtime.
Fee: $10.95 monthly.

Internet Service
Operational: No.

Telephone Service
None

Miles of Plant: 42.0 (coaxial); None (fiber optic). Homes passed: 535.

Chief Executive Officer: Joseph A. Sheehan. General Manager East: Mark Miller. General Manager West: Vance Johnson.

Ownership: Citizens Cable TV (MSO).

WILKINSON COUNTY (portions)—Windstream, 2000 Communications Blvd, Baldwin, GA 30511. Phones: 800-345-3874; 706-335-6640. Fax: 706-896-5170. Web Site: http://www.windstreamcable.com. ICA: GA0312.

TV Market Ranking: Below 100 (WILKINSON COUNTY (PORTIONS)).

Channel capacity: 100 (not 2-way capable). Channels available but not in use: 60.

Basic Service
Subscribers: 1,215.
Programming (received off-air): WGNM (IND) Macon; WGXA (FOX, MNT) Macon; WMAZ-TV (CBS) Macon; WMGT-TV (MNT, NBC) Macon; WMUM-TV (PBS) Cochran; WPCH-TV (IND) Atlanta; WPGA-TV (ABC) Perry.
Programming (via satellite): Arts & Entertainment; BET Networks; Cartoon Network; CNN; Comedy Central; Country Music TV; Discovery Channel; ESPN; ESPN 2; ESPN Classic Sports; Fox News Channel; Hallmark Channel; Headline News; HGTV; Lifetime; MTV; Nickelodeon; QVC; Spike TV; The Learning Channel; Trinity Broadcasting Network; truTV; Turner Network TV; TV Land; USA Network; Weather Channel.
Fee: $27.25 monthly.

Expanded Basic Service 1
Subscribers: 1,205.
Programming (via satellite): ABC Family Channel; AMC; Boomerang; CNBC; C-SPAN; C-SPAN 2; Encore; Food Network; Fox Sports Net; FX; History Channel; Home Shopping Network; MSNBC; National Geographic Channel; Outdoor Channel; Speed Channel; SportSouth; Syfy; TV Guide Network; VH1; WE tv.
Fee: $15.00 monthly.

Pay Service 1
Pay Units: 160.
Programming (via satellite): Cinemax.
Fee: $10.95 monthly.

Pay Service 2
Pay Units: 280.
Programming (via satellite): HBO.
Fee: $12.95 monthly.

Pay Service 3
Pay Units: 175.
Programming (via satellite): Showtime.
Fee: $10.95 monthly.

Pay Service 4
Pay Units: 180.
Programming (via satellite): Starz.
Fee: $9.95 monthly.

Video-On-Demand: No

Pay-Per-View
iN DEMAND (delivered digitally).

Internet Service
Operational: No, Both DSL & dial-up.

Telephone Service
None

President & Chief Executive Officer: Jeff Gardner. Executive Vice President & Chief Financial Officer: Brent Whittington. Executive Vice President, Network Operations: Grant Raney. Executive Vice President & Chief Marketing Officer: Ric Crane. Senior Vice President, Network Services: Frank Schueneman. Senior Vice President, Information Technology: Cindy Nash. Senior Vice President, Consumer Sales: Gregg Richey. Senior Vice President, Customer Services: Joe Marano.

Ownership: Windstream Communications Inc. (MSO).

WILLIAMSON—Georgia Broadband, 16018 Barnesville St, Zebulon, GA 30295. Phone: 770-567-5979. Web Site: http://www.georgia-broadband.com. ICA: GA0320.

TV Market Ranking: Outside TV Markets (WILLIAMSON).
Channel capacity: N.A. Channels available but not in use: N.A.

Basic Service

Subscribers: N.A.
Programming (received off-air): WAGA-TV (FOX) Atlanta; WGCL-TV (CBS) Atlanta; WGTV (PBS) Athens; WPBA (PBS) Atlanta; WSB-TV (ABC) Atlanta; WUPA (CW) Atlanta; WUVG-DT (UNV) Athens; WXIA-TV (NBC) Atlanta.
Programming (via satellite): TBS Superstation; WGN America.
Current originations: Leased Access.
Fee: $29.95 installation; $11.95 monthly.

Expanded Basic Service 1

Subscribers: N.A.
Programming (via satellite): ABC Family Channel; AMC; Animal Planet; Arts & Entertainment; BET Networks; Cartoon Network; CNN; Comcast Sports Net Southeast; Comcast/Charter Sports Southeast (CSS); Comedy Central; Country Music TV; C-SPAN; Discovery Channel; Disney Channel; E! Entertainment Television; ESPN; ESPN 2; Fox News Channel; FX; G4; Headline News; HGTV; History Channel; Home Shopping Network; INSP; MTV; Nickelodeon; Oxygen; Spike TV; Syfy; The Learning Channel; Travel Channel; Turner Network TV; Turner South; TV Land; USA Network; VH1; Weather Channel.
Fee: $11.95 monthly.

Digital Basic Service

Subscribers: N.A.
Programming (via satellite): BBC America; Bio; Bloomberg Television; CMT Pure Country; Discovery en Espanol; Discovery Health Channel; Discovery Kids Channel; Discovery Military Channel; Discovery Planet Green; DMX Music; Do-It-Yourself; Fuse; GSN; History Channel International; ID Investigation Discovery; MTV Hits; MTV Jams; MTV Tres; Nick Jr.; Nick Too; NickToons TV; Science Channel; Style Network; Sundance Channel; TeenNick; VH1 Classic; VH1 Soul.
Fee: $11.95 monthly.

Digital Pay Service 1

Pay Units: N.A.
Programming (via satellite): Cinemax (multiplexed); Encore (multiplexed); HBO (multiplexed); Showtime (multiplexed); Starz (multiplexed); The Movie Channel (multiplexed).

Video-On-Demand: Yes

Pay-Per-View

iN DEMAND (delivered digitally).

Internet Service

Operational: Yes.
Fee: $19.95 installation; $24.95 monthly.

Telephone Service

Digital: Operational
Fee: $29.95 monthly
Chief Executive Officer: Michelle Oneil. General Manager: Jerry Oneil.
Ownership: Georgia Broadband LLC (MSO).

WINDER—Comcast Cable. Now served by ATLANTA (perimeter north), GA [GA0033]. ICA: GA0066.

WOODBINE—Comcast Cable, 6805 Southpoint Pkwy, Jacksonville, FL 32216. Phone: 904-374-8000. Fax: 904-374-7622. Web Site: http://www.comcast.com. Also serves Harrietts Bluff. ICA: GA0111.
TV Market Ranking: Below 100 (Harrietts Bluff, WOODBINE). Franchise award date: N.A. Franchise expiration date: N.A. Began: January 1, 1980.
Channel capacity: N.A. Channels available but not in use: N.A.

Basic Service

Subscribers: 997.
Programming (received off-air): WAWS (FOX, MNT) Jacksonville; WCWJ (CW) Jacksonville; WJCT (PBS) Jacksonville; WJEB-TV (ETV) Jacksonville; WJXT (IND) Jacksonville; WJXX (ABC) Orange Park; WTEV-TV (CBS) Jacksonville; WTLV (NBC) Jacksonville; WTOC-TV (CBS) Savannah; WXGA-TV (PBS) Waycross.
Programming (via satellite): Discovery Health Channel; Home Shopping Network; QVC; TBS Superstation; Weather Channel; WGN America.

Expanded Basic Service 1

Subscribers: 929.
Programming (via satellite): ABC Family Channel; AMC; Animal Planet; Arts & Entertainment; BET Networks; Cartoon Network; CNBC; CNN; Comcast Sports Net Southeast; Comcast/Charter Sports Southeast (CSS); Comedy Central; Country Music TV; Discovery Channel; Disney Channel; E! Entertainment Television; ESPN; ESPN 2; Food Network; Fox News Channel; FX; Golf Channel; GSN; Headline News; HGTV; History Channel; Lifetime; MTV; Nickelodeon; Product Information Network; Speed Channel; Spike TV; Syfy; The Learning Channel; truTV; Turner Network TV; Turner South; TV Land; USA Network; Versus.
Fee: $49.95 installation; $49.99 monthly.

Digital Basic Service

Subscribers: N.A.
Programming (via satellite): Encore; Flix; GAS; MTV Networks Digital Suite; Music Choice; Nick Jr.; Nick Too.

Pay Service 1

Pay Units: 93.
Programming (via satellite): Encore.
Fee: $15.95 monthly.

Pay Service 2

Pay Units: 167.
Programming (via satellite): HBO.
Fee: $15.95 monthly.

Pay Service 3

Pay Units: 179.
Programming (via satellite): Showtime.
Fee: $15.95 monthly.

Pay Service 4

Pay Units: 128.
Programming (via satellite): The Movie Channel.
Fee: $15.95 monthly.

Digital Pay Service 1

Pay Units: N.A.
Programming (via satellite): Cinemax (multiplexed); HBO (multiplexed); Showtime (multiplexed); Starz (multiplexed); The Movie Channel (multiplexed).
Fee: $15.95 monthly (each).

Video-On-Demand: No

Pay-Per-View

iN DEMAND (delivered digitally); Hot Choice (delivered digitally).

Internet Service

Operational: Yes.

Telephone Service

Digital: Operational
Miles of Plant: 48.0 (coaxial); 12.0 (fiber optic). Homes passed: 2,219.
Vice President & General Manager: Doug McMillan. Vice President, Marketing: Vic Scarborough. Engineering Director: Mike Humphrey. Government Affairs Director: Bill Ferry.
Ownership: Comcast Cable Communications Inc. (MSO).

WOODBURY—Formerly served by Almega Cable. No longer in operation. ICA: GA0318.

WOODBURY—Georgia Broadband, 118 W Main St, Manchester, GA 31816. Phone: 706-846-4568. E-mail: dianne@georgia-broadband.com. Web Site: http://www.georgia-broadband.com. ICA: GA0322.
Note: This system is an overbuild.
TV Market Ranking: Outside TV Markets (WOODBURY).
Channel capacity: N.A. Channels available but not in use: N.A.

Basic Service

Subscribers: N.A.
Programming (received off-air): WAGA-TV (FOX) Atlanta; WATL (MNT) Atlanta; WGCL-TV (CBS) Atlanta; WLTZ (CW, NBC) Columbus; WRBL (CBS) Columbus; WSB-TV (ABC) Atlanta; WUPA (CW) Atlanta; WXIA-TV (NBC) Atlanta; WXTX (FOX) Columbus.
Programming (via satellite): Trinity Broadcasting Network; TV Guide Network; WGN America.
Fee: $11.95 monthly.

Expanded Basic Service 1

Subscribers: N.A.
Programming (via satellite): ABC Family Channel; AMC; Animal Planet; Arts & Entertainment; BET Networks; Cartoon Network; CNBC; CNN; Comcast Sports Net Southeast; Comcast/Charter Sports Southeast (CSS); Comedy Central; Country Music TV; C-SPAN; C-SPAN 2; Discovery Channel; Discovery Health Channel; Disney Channel; E! Entertainment Television; ESPN; ESPN 2; Fox News Channel; FX; G4; Golf Channel; GSN; Hallmark Channel; Headline News; HGTV; History Channel; Home Shopping Network; INSP; Lifetime; MTV; Nickelodeon; Oxygen; QVC; Spike TV; Syfy; TBS Superstation; The Learning Channel; The Sportsman Channel; Travel Channel; truTV; Turner Classic Movies; Turner Network TV; TV Land; USA Network; VH1; WE tv; Weather Channel.
Fee: $28.00 monthly.

Digital Basic Service

Subscribers: N.A.
Programming (via satellite): BBC America; Bio; Bloomberg Television; CMT Pure Country; Discovery en Espanol; Discovery Health Channel; Discovery Kids Channel; Discovery Military Channel; Discovery Planet Green; DMX Music; Do-It-Yourself; Fuse; GSN; History Channel International; ID Investigation Discovery; MTV Hits; MTV Jams; MTV Tres; MTV2; Nick Jr.; Nick Too; NickToons TV; Science Channel; Style Network; Sundance Channel; TeenNick; VH1 Classic; VH1 Soul.

Pay Service 1

Pay Units: N.A.
Programming (via satellite): HBO.

Digital Pay Service 1

Pay Units: N.A.
Programming (via satellite): Cinemax (multiplexed); Encore (multiplexed); HBO (multiplexed); Showtime (multiplexed); Starz (multiplexed); The Movie Channel (multiplexed).

Video-On-Demand: Yes

Pay-Per-View

iN DEMAND (delivered digitally).

Internet Service

Operational: Yes.
Fee: $19.95 installation; $24.95 monthly.

Telephone Service

Digital: Operational
Fee: $29.95 monthly
Chief Executive Officer: Michelle Oneil. General Manager: Jerry Oneil.
Ownership: Georgia Broadband LLC (MSO).

WRENS—KLiP Interactive, 455 Gees Mill Business Court, Conyers, GA 30013. Phone: 678-727-7100. Fax: 678-727-7002. E-mail: jsheehan@klipia.com. Web Site: http://www.klipia.com. ICA: GA0118.
TV Market Ranking: Below 100 (WRENS). Franchise award date: N.A. Franchise expiration date: N.A. Began: N.A.
Channel capacity: 65 (not 2-way capable). Channels available but not in use: 9.

Basic Service

Subscribers: 417.
Programming (received off-air): WAGT (CW, NBC) Augusta; WCES-TV (PBS) Wrens; WFXG (FOX) Augusta; WJBF (ABC) Augusta; WPCH-TV (IND) Atlanta; WRDW-TV (CBS, MNT) Augusta.
Programming (via satellite): ABC Family Channel; AMC; Animal Planet; Arts & Entertainment; BET Networks; Boomerang; Cartoon Network; CNN; Comcast Sports Net Southeast; Country Music TV; C-SPAN; CW+; Discovery Channel; Disney Channel; E! Entertainment Television; ESPN; ESPN 2; Food Network; Fox News Channel; FX; Hallmark Channel; Headline News; HGTV; History Channel; INSP; Lifetime; Lifetime Movie Network; MTV; Nickelodeon; ShopNBC; Speed Channel; Spike TV; SportSouth; Syfy; The Learning Channel; The Sportsman Channel; Travel Channel; Turner Classic Movies; Turner Network TV; TV Guide Network; TV Land; USA Network; VH1; Weather Channel; WGN America.
Current originations: Leased Access.
Fee: $29.95 installation; $39.95 monthly.

Pay Service 1

Pay Units: 32.
Programming (via satellite): Cinemax.
Fee: $10.95 monthly.

Pay Service 2

Pay Units: 72.
Programming (via satellite): HBO.
Fee: $10.95 monthly.

Internet Service

Operational: Yes.
Fee: $34.95 monthly.

Telephone Service

None
Miles of Plant: 20.0 (coaxial); None (fiber optic). Homes passed: 1,575. Total homes in franchised area: 1,575.
Chief Executive Officer: Joseph A. Sheehan. General Manager East: Mark Miller. General Manager West: Vance Johnson.
Ownership: KLiP Interactive LLC (MSO).

WRIGHTSVILLE—Comcast Cable, 141 Park of Commerce Dr, Savannah, GA 31405. Phone: 912-356-3113. Web Site: http://www.comcast.com. ICA: GA0265.

TV Market Ranking: Outside TV Markets (WRIGHTSVILLE). Franchise award date: August 17, 1979. Franchise expiration date: N.A. Began: January 16, 1981.

Channel capacity: N.A. Channels available but not in use: N.A.

Basic Service

Subscribers: N.A. Included in Savannah

Programming (received off-air): WGXA (FOX, MNT) Macon; WJBF (ABC) Augusta; WMAZ-TV (CBS) Macon; WMGT-TV (MNT, NBC) Macon; WMUM-TV (PBS) Cochran; WPGA-TV (ABC) Perry.

Programming (via satellite): TBS Superstation; Trinity Broadcasting Network; WGN America.

Fee: $47.99 installation; $7.67 monthly.

Expanded Basic Service 1

Subscribers: N.A.

Programming (via satellite): ABC Family Channel; Animal Planet; Arts & Entertainment; BET Networks; Cartoon Network; CNBC; CNN; Comcast/Charter Sports Southeast (CSS); Country Music TV; C-SPAN; CW+; Discovery Channel; Discovery Health Channel; Disney Channel; E! Entertainment Television; ESPN; ESPN 2; Food Network; Fox News Channel; Fox Sports Net; FX; Golf Channel; Great American Country; Hallmark Channel; Headline News; HGTV; History Channel; Lifetime; Nickelodeon; QVC; Speed Channel; Spike TV; SportSouth; Style Network; Syfy; The Learning Channel; truTV; Turner Classic Movies; Turner Network TV; TV Land; USA Network; Versus; Weather Channel.

Fee: $34.32 monthly.

Digital Basic Service

Subscribers: N.A.

Programming (via satellite): BBC America; Discovery Digital Networks; DMX Music; Encore (multiplexed); Flix; GAS; MTV Networks Digital Suite; Nick Jr.; Nick Too; WAM! America's Kidz Network.

Fee: $9.95 monthly.

Digital Pay Service 1

Pay Units: N.A.

Programming (via satellite): Cinemax (multiplexed); HBO (multiplexed); Showtime (multiplexed); Starz (multiplexed); The Movie Channel (multiplexed).

Fee: $7.95 monthly (each).

Video-On-Demand: No

Pay-Per-View

iN DEMAND (delivered digitally); Hot Choice (delivered digitally).

Internet Service

Operational: Yes.

Telephone Service

Digital: Operational

Homes passed & miles of plant (coax & fiber) included in Savannah

General Manager: Michael Daves. Technical Operations Director: Joel Godsen. Marketing Director: Jerry Avery. Marketing Manager: Ken Torres.

City fee: 2% of gross.

Ownership: Comcast Cable Communications Inc. (MSO).

YATESVILLE—Flint Cable TV, PO Box 669, 105 W Marion, Reynolds, GA 31076-0669. Phones: 888-593-7782; 478-847-3101. Fax: 478-847-2010. Web Site: http://www.flintcatv.com. Also serves Culloden. ICA: GA0289.

TV Market Ranking: Below 100 (Culloden, YATESVILLE). Franchise award date: September 19, 1991. Franchise expiration date: N.A. Began: N.A.

Channel capacity: 40 (not 2-way capable). Channels available but not in use: 8.

Basic Service

Subscribers: 153.

Programming (received off-air): WAGA-TV (FOX) Atlanta; WATL (MNT) Atlanta; WGCL-TV (CBS) Atlanta; WGNM (IND) Macon; WJSP-TV (PBS) Columbus; WMAZ-TV (CBS) Macon; WSB-TV (ABC) Atlanta; WTVM (ABC) Columbus; WXIA-TV (NBC) Atlanta.

Programming (via satellite): ABC Family Channel; AMC; Arts & Entertainment; BET Networks; CNN; Comcast Sports Net Southeast; Discovery Channel; Disney Channel; ESPN; HGTV; History Channel; Lifetime; Spike TV; Syfy; Trinity Broadcasting Network; Turner Classic Movies; Turner Network TV; Turner South; TV Land; USA Network; Weather Channel; WPCH-TV (IND) Atlanta.

Current originations: Religious Access; Educational Access; Public Access.

Fee: $35.00 installation; $29.99 monthly.

Pay Service 1

Pay Units: N.A.

Programming (via satellite): HBO.

Fee: $20.99 installation; $11.99 monthly (each).

Video-On-Demand: No

Internet Service

Operational: No.

Telephone Service

None

Miles of Plant: 12.0 (coaxial); None (fiber optic). Homes passed: 316. Total homes in franchised area: 316.

Manager: James L. Bond. Marketing: Laurie Long.

Ownership: Flint Cable Television Inc. (MSO).

ZEBULON—Georgia Broadband, 16018 Barnesville St, Zebulon, GA 30295. Phone: 770-567-5979. Web Site: http://www.georgia-broadband.com. Also serves Pike County (unincorporated areas). ICA: GA0316.

TV Market Ranking: Outside TV Markets (Pike County (unincorporated areas), ZEBULON).

Channel capacity: N.A. Channels available but not in use: N.A.

Basic Service

Subscribers: N.A.

Programming (received off-air): WAGA-TV (FOX) Atlanta; WATL (MNT) Atlanta; WGCL-TV (CBS) Atlanta; WGTV (PBS) Athens; WPBA (PBS) Atlanta; WSB-TV (ABC) Atlanta; WUPA (CW) Atlanta; WXIA-TV (NBC) Atlanta.

Programming (via satellite): FX; INSP; MyNetworkTV Inc.; PetCARE Television Network; TV Guide Network; WGN America.

Fee: $29.95 installation; $15.95 monthly.

Expanded Basic Service 1

Subscribers: N.A.

Programming (via satellite): ABC Family Channel; AMC; Animal Planet; Arts & Entertainment; BET Networks; Cartoon Network; CNBC; CNN; Comcast Sports Net Southeast; Comcast/Charter Sports Southeast (CSS); Comedy Central; Country Music TV; C-SPAN; C-SPAN 2; Discovery Channel; Disney Channel; E! Entertainment Television; ESPN; ESPN 2; Food Network; Fox News Channel; Fox Soccer; G4; Golf Channel; Hallmark Channel; Headline News; HGTV; History Channel; Home Shopping Network; Lifetime; MSNBC; MTV; NFL Network; Nickelodeon; Oxygen; QVC; RFD-TV; SoapNet; Spike TV; SportSouth; Syfy; TBS Superstation; The Learning Channel; The Sportsman Channel; Toon Disney; Travel Channel; Trinity Broadcasting Network; truTV; Turner Classic Movies; Turner Network TV; TV Land; USA Network; VH1; WE tv; Weather Channel.

Fee: $24.00 monthly.

Digital Basic Service

Subscribers: N.A.

Programming (via satellite): BBC America; Bio; Bloomberg Television; Discovery en Espanol; Discovery Home Channel; Discovery Kids Channel; Discovery Military Channel; DMX Music; Do-It-Yourself; Fuse; GAS; GSN; History Channel International; ID Investigation Discovery; MTV Hits; MTV Jams; MTV Latin America; MTV2; Nick Jr.; Nick Too; NickToons TV; Science Channel; Style Network; Sundance Channel; VH1 Classic; VH1 Country; VH1 Soul.

Fee: $12.49 monthly.

Pay Service 1

Pay Units: N.A.

Programming (via satellite): HBO.

Digital Pay Service 1

Pay Units: N.A.

Programming (via satellite): Cinemax (multiplexed); HBO (multiplexed); Showtime (multiplexed); Starz (multiplexed).

Pay-Per-View

iN DEMAND (delivered digitally).

Internet Service

Operational: Yes.

Fee: $19.95 installation; $24.95 monthly.

Telephone Service

Digital: Operational

Fee: $29.95 monthly

Ownership: Georgia Broadband LLC (MSO).

HAWAII

Total Systems: 6
Total Communities Served: 128
Franchises Not Yet Operating: 0
Applications Pending: 0
Communities with Applications: 0
Number of Basic Subscribers: 350,115
Number of Expanded Basic Subscribers: 0
Number of Pay Units: 0

Top 100 Markets Represented: N.A.

For a list of cable communities in this section, see the Cable Community Index located in the back of Cable Volume 2.
For explanation of terms used in cable system listings, see p. D-11.

BELLOWS AFB—Oceanic Time Warner Cable, 200 Akamainui St, Mililani, HI 96789-3999. Phone: 808-625-2100. Fax: 808-625-5888. Web Site: http://www.oceanic.com. ICA: HI0008.

TV Market Ranking: Below 100 (BELLOWS AFB). Franchise award date: N.A. Franchise expiration date: N.A. Began: N.A.

Channel capacity: N.A. Channels available but not in use: N.A.

Basic Service

Subscribers: 115.

Programming (received off-air): KAAH-TV (TBN) Honolulu; KALO (ETV) Honolulu; KBFD-DT (IND) Honolulu; KFVE (MNT) Honolulu; KGMB (CBS) Honolulu; KHNL (NBC) Honolulu; KHON-TV (CW, FOX) Honolulu; KITV (ABC) Honolulu; KPXO-TV (ION) Kaneohe; KWBN (ETV) Honolulu; KWHE (IND) Honolulu.

Programming (via satellite): C-SPAN; KHET (PBS) Honolulu; KIKU (IND) Honolulu; TBS Superstation.

Current originations: Public Access.

Fee: $29.95 installation; $43.60 monthly.

Digital Basic Service

Subscribers: N.A.

Programming (received off-air): KBFD-DT (IND) Honolulu; KFVE (MNT) Honolulu; KGMB (CBS) Honolulu; KHNL (NBC) Honolulu; KIKU (IND) Honolulu; KITV (ABC) Honolulu.

Programming (via satellite): ABC Family Channel; AMC; AmericanLife TV Network; America's Store; Animal Planet; Arts & Entertainment; BBC America; Bio; Boomerang; Bravo; Cartoon Network; CBS College Sports Network; Chinese Television Network; CNBC; CNN; CNN en Espanol; Comedy Central; Cooking Channel; Country Music TV; C-SPAN 2; C-SPAN 3; Discovery Channel; Discovery Digital Networks; Discovery en Espanol; Discovery HD Theater; Disney Channel; Do-It-Yourself; E! Entertainment Television; Encore; ESPN; ESPN 2; ESPN Classic Sports; ESPNews; Filipino Channel; FitTV; Flix; Food Network; Fox College Sports Central; Fox College Sports Pacific; Fox Movie Channel; Fox News Channel; Fox Sports en Espanol; Fox Sports Net West; Fox Sports Net West 2; Fox Sports World; Fuel TV; Fuse; FX; G4; GalaVision; GAS; Golf Channel; Great American Country; GSN; Hallmark Channel; HDNet; HDNet Movies; Headline News; HGTV; History Channel; History Channel International; Home Shopping Network; ImaginAsian TV; Independent Film Channel; INHD; INHD2; INSP; Jewelry Television; Lifetime; Lifetime Movie Network; Lifetime Real Women; MSNBC; MTV Networks Digital Suite; Music Choice; National Geographic Channel; NBA TV; Nick Jr.; Nickelodeon; Nippon Golden Network; Nippon Golden Network 2; Nippon Golden Network 3; Outdoor Channel; Ovation; Oxygen; PBS Kids Channel; Pentagon Channel; QVC; ShopNBC; Showtime HD; Sleuth; SoapNet; Speed Channel; Spike TV; Style Network; Sundance Channel; Syfy; Tennis Channel; The Learning Channel; Toon Disney; Travel Channel; truTV; Turner Classic Movies; Turner Network TV; Turner Network TV HD; TV Guide SPOT; TV Land; Universal HD; USA Network; Versus; WE tv.

Fee: $11.00 monthly.

Digital Pay Service 1

Pay Units: N.A.

Programming (via satellite): Cinemax (multiplexed); HBO (multiplexed); Showtime (multiplexed); Starz (multiplexed); The Movie Channel.

Pay-Per-View

Addressable homes: 115.

Movies (delivered digitally), Fee: $3.99-$9.99, Addressable: Yes; special events (delivered digitally); Hot Choice (delivered digitally); Playboy TV (delivered digitally); NBA League Pass (delivered digitally); MLB Extra Innings (delivered digitally); ESPN Full Court (delivered digitally); ESPN Gameplan (delivered digitally).

Internet Service

Operational: Yes. Began: July 1, 2003.

Broadband Service: In-house.

Fee: $75.00 installation; $39.95 monthly.

Miles of Plant: 2.0 (coaxial); None (fiber optic). Additional miles planned: 2.0 (fiber optic). Homes passed: 120. Total homes in franchised area: 120.

President: Nate Smith. Vice President, Engineering: Mike Goodish. Marketing Director: Allan Pollack. Controller: Ann Butak.

Ownership: Time Warner Cable (MSO).

HAWAII KAI—Oceanic Time Warner Cable. Now served by MILILANI (formerly HONOLULU), HI [HI0001]. ICA: HI0009.

HAWI—Oceanic Time Warner Cable. Now served by KONA (formerly KAILUA KONA), HI [HI0011]. ICA: HI0010.

HICKAM AFB—Formerly served by Cable TV Services. No longer in operation. ICA: HI0006.

HILO—Oceanic Time Warner Cable, 1257 Kilauea Ave, Hilo, HI 96720-4205. Phone: 808-625-2100 (Administrative office). Fax: 808-625-5888. Web Site: http://www.oceanic.com. Also serves Honokaa, Kilauea Military Camp, Pahoa, Puna, Volcano Village & Waiohinu. ICA: HI0002.

TV Market Ranking: Below 100 (HILO, Kilauea Military Camp, Pahoa, Puna, Volcano Village, Waiohinu); Outside TV Markets (Honokaa). Franchise award date: January 1, 1996. Franchise expiration date: N.A. Began: June 13, 1974.

Channel capacity: N.A. Channels available but not in use: N.A.

Basic Service

Subscribers: N.A. Included in Mililani

Programming (received off-air): KFVE (MNT) Honolulu; KGMB (CBS) Honolulu; KHET (PBS) Honolulu; KHNL (NBC) Honolulu; KHON-TV (CW, FOX) Honolulu; KIKU (IND) Honolulu; KITV (ABC) Honolulu; KWHE (IND) Honolulu; KWHH (IND) Hilo; 6 FMs.

Programming (via satellite): C-SPAN; C-SPAN 2; GSN; Product Information Network; QVC.

Fee: $40.00 installation; $18.00 additional installation.

Expanded Basic Service 1

Subscribers: N.A.

Programming (via satellite): ABC Family Channel; AMC; Animal Planet; Arts & Entertainment; Bravo; Cartoon Network; CNBC; CNN; Comedy Central; Discovery Channel; Disney Channel; E! Entertainment Television; ESPN; ESPN 2; FitTV; Food Network; Fox News Channel; Fox Sports Net West; Fox Sports Net West 2; FX; Golf Channel; GSN; Hallmark Channel; Headline News; HGTV; History Channel; Home Shopping Network; Lifetime; Lifetime Movie Network; MSNBC; MTV; National Geographic Channel; Nickelodeon; Oxygen; QVC; ShopNBC; SoapNet; Spike TV; Style Network; Syfy; TBS Superstation; The Learning Channel; Travel Channel; truTV; Turner Classic Movies; Turner Network TV; TV Land; USA Network; Versus; VH1; WE tv.

Fee: $43.60 monthly.

Digital Basic Service

Subscribers: N.A.

Programming (via satellite): America's Store; BBC America; Bio; Canales N; Comcast Sports Net Bay Area; Cooking Channel; Discovery Digital Networks; Do-It-Yourself; ESPN Classic Sports; ESPNews; Fox Sports World; Fuse; G4; Great American Country; History Channel International; INSP; Lifetime Real Women; MTV Networks Digital Suite; Music Choice; Nick Jr.; Outdoor Channel; Ovation; PBS Kids Channel; Science Television; Speed Channel; Toon Disney.

Fee: $11.00 monthly.

Digital Pay Service 1

Pay Units: N.A.

Programming (via satellite): Cinemax (multiplexed); Encore (multiplexed); HBO (multiplexed); Showtime (multiplexed); Sundance Channel; The Movie Channel (multiplexed).

Fee: $13.95 monthly (each).

Video-On-Demand: Yes

Pay-Per-View

Hot Choice (delivered digitally); iN DEMAND (delivered digitally); Playboy TV (delivered digitally); Sports PPV (delivered digitally).

Internet Service

Operational: Yes.

Broadband Service: AOL for Broadband, EarthLink, Road Runner.

Fee: $69.95 installation; $44.95 monthly.

Telephone Service

Digital: Operational

Note: Homes passed and miles of plant (coax & fiber) included in Mililani

President: Nate Smith. Vice President, Operations: Norman Santos. Vice President, Engineering: Mike Goodish. Marketing Director: Allan Pollack. Chief Technician: Met LeBar. Controller: Ann Butack.

State fee: 4% of gross.

Ownership: Time Warner Cable (MSO).

HONOLULU—Formerly served by Craig Wireless Honolulu Inc. No longer in operation. ICA: HI0017.

KAUAI ISLAND—Oceanic Time Warner Cable, 3022 Peleke St, Lihue, HI 96766-2100. Phone: 808-625-2100 (Administrative office). Fax: 808-625-5888. Web Site: http://www.oceanic.com. Also serves Anahola, Barking Sands Naval Base, Eleele, Hanalei, Hanamaulu, Hanapepe, Kalaheo, Kapaa, Kaumakani, Kealia, Kekaha, Kilauea, Koloa, Lawai, Lihue, Omao, Princeville, Wailua, Wailua Homesteads & Waimea. ICA: HI0004.

TV Market Ranking: Outside TV Markets (Anahola, Barking Sands Naval Base, Eleele, Hanalei, Hanamaulu, Hanapepe, Kalaheo, Kapaa, KAUAI ISLAND, Kaumakani, Kealia, Kekaha, Kilauea, Koloa, Lawai, Lihue, Omao, Princeville, Wailua, Wailua Homesteads, Waimea). Franchise award date: August 4, 1981. Franchise expiration date: N.A. Began: August 4, 1981.

Channel capacity: N.A. Channels available but not in use: N.A.

Basic Service

Subscribers: N.A. Included in Mililani

Programming (received off-air): KFVE (MNT) Honolulu; KGMB (CBS) Honolulu; KHET (PBS) Honolulu; KHNL (NBC) Honolulu; KHON-TV (CW, FOX) Honolulu; KIKU (IND) Honolulu; KITV (ABC) Honolulu; 12 FMs.

Programming (via satellite): C-SPAN; C-SPAN 2; GSN; Trinity Broadcasting Network.

Current originations: Leased Access; Government Access; Educational Access; Public Access.

Fee: $43.00 installation.

Expanded Basic Service 1

Subscribers: N.A.

Programming (via satellite): ABC Family Channel; AMC; Animal Planet; Arts & Entertainment; Bravo; Cartoon Network; CNBC; CNN; Comedy Central; Discovery Channel; Disney Channel; E! Entertainment Television; ESPN; ESPN 2; FitTV; Food Network; Fox News Channel; Fox Sports Net West;

Fox Sports Net West 2; FX; Golf Channel; GSN; Hallmark Channel; Headline News; HGTV; History Channel; Home Shopping Network; Lifetime; Lifetime Movie Network; MSNBC; MTV; National Geographic Channel; Nickelodeon; Oxygen; QVC; ShopNBC; SoapNet; Spike TV; Style Network; Syfy; TBS Superstation; The Learning Channel; Travel Channel; truTV; Turner Classic Movies; Turner Network TV; TV Land; USA Network; Versus; VH1; WE tv.
Fee: $43.60 monthly.

Digital Basic Service
Subscribers: N.A.
Programming (via satellite): America's Store; BBC America; Bio; Canales N; Cooking Channel; Country Music TV; Discovery Digital Networks; Do-It-Yourself; ESPN Classic Sports; ESPNews; Fox Sports World; Fuse; Great American Country; History Channel International; INSP; Lifetime Real Women; MTV Networks Digital Suite; Music Choice; Nick Jr.; Outdoor Channel; Ovation; Science Television; Speed Channel; Toon Disney.
Fee: $11.00 monthly.

Digital Pay Service 1
Pay Units: N.A.
Programming (taped): Nippon Golden Network.
Programming (via satellite): Cinemax (multiplexed); Encore (multiplexed); Filipino Channel; HBO (multiplexed); Showtime (multiplexed); Sundance Channel; The Movie Channel (multiplexed).
Fee: $13.95 monthly each.

Video-On-Demand: Yes

Pay-Per-View
iN DEMAND (delivered digitally); Hot Choice (delivered digitally); Playboy TV (delivered digitally).

Internet Service
Operational: Yes.
Broadband Service: EarthLink, Road Runner, AOL.
Fee: $69.95 installation; $44.95 monthly.

Telephone Service
Digital: Operational
Fee: $44.95 monthly

Note: Homes passed and miles of plant (coax & fiber) included in Mililani
President: Nate Smith. Vice President, Operations: Norman Santos. Vice President, Engineering: Mike Goodish. Marketing Director: Allan Pollack. Controller: Ann Butack.
State fee: 5% of gross.
Ownership: Time Warner Cable (MSO).

KONA—Oceanic Time Warner Cable, 74-5605 Luhia St, Ste B1, Kona, HI 96740-1678. Phone: 202-625-2100 (Administrative office). Fax: 808-625-5888. Web Site: http://www.oceanic.com. Also serves Captain Cook, Hawi, Holualoa, Honaunau, Kainaliu, Kalaoa, Kamuela, Kapaau, Kawaihae, Kealakekua, Keauhou, Kohala, Mauna Kea, Mauna Lani, Naalehu, North Kohala District, Puako, South Kona, Waikoloa Resort & Waikoloa Village. ICA: HI0011.
TV Market Ranking: Below 100 (Captain Cook, Holualoa, Honaunau, Kainaliu, Kalaoa, Kamuela, Kawaihae, Kealakekua, Keauhou, Kohala, KONA, Mauna Kea, Mauna Lani, Puako, South Kona, Waikoloa Resort, Waikoloa Village); Outside TV Markets (Hawi, Kapaau, Naalehu, North Kohala District). Franchise award date: January 1, 1973. Franchise expiration date: N.A. Began: October 1, 1974.
Channel capacity: N.A. Channels available but not in use: N.A.

Basic Service
Subscribers: N.A. Included in Mililani
Programming (received off-air): KFVE (MNT) Honolulu; KGMB (CBS) Honolulu; KHET (PBS) Honolulu; KHNL (NBC) Honolulu; KHON-TV (CW, FOX) Honolulu; KITV (ABC) Honolulu; KWHE (IND) Honolulu; 16 FMs.
Programming (via satellite): ABC Family Channel; AMC; Arts & Entertainment; Bravo; Cartoon Network; CNBC; CNN; Comedy Central; C-SPAN; C-SPAN 2; Discovery Channel; Disney Channel; E! Entertainment Television; ESPN; ESPN 2; FitTV; Food Network; Fox News Channel; Fox Sports Net West; Fox Sports Net West 2; FX; Golf Channel; GSN; Hallmark Channel; Headline News; HGTV; Home Shopping Network; Lifetime; Lifetime Movie Network; MSNBC; MTV; National Geographic Channel; Nickelodeon; Oxygen; Product Information Network; QVC; ShopNBC; SoapNet; Spike TV; Style Network; Syfy; TBS Superstation; The Learning Channel; Travel Channel; truTV; Turner Classic Movies; Turner Network TV; TV Land; USA Network; Versus; VH1; WE tv.
Current originations: Leased Access; Government Access; Educational Access; Public Access.
Fee: $50.00 installation; $43.60 monthly; $18.00 additional installation.

Digital Basic Service
Subscribers: N.A.
Programming (via satellite): America's Store; BBC America; Bio; Cooking Channel; Country Music TV; Discovery Digital Networks; Do-It-Yourself; ESPN Classic Sports; ESPNews; Fox Sports Net (multiplexed); Fox Sports World; Fuel TV; Fuse; G4; Great American Country; Halogen Network; Lifetime Real Women; MTV2; Music Choice; Nick Jr.; Outdoor Channel; Ovation; PBS Kids Channel; Speed Channel; Tennis Channel; Toon Disney; VH1 Classic.
Fee: $33.00 installation; $11.00 monthly.

Digital Pay Service 1
Pay Units: N.A.
Programming (via satellite): Canales N; Chinese Television Network; Cinemax (multiplexed); Encore; Filipino Channel; HBO (multiplexed); Showtime (multiplexed); Sundance Channel; The Movie Channel (multiplexed).
Fee: $33.00 installation; $14.95 monthly (each).

Video-On-Demand: Yes

Pay-Per-View
Hot Choice (delivered digitally); Playboy TV (delivered digitally); iN DEMAND (delivered digitally).

Internet Service
Operational: Yes. Began: December 31, 2001.
Broadband Service: EarthLink, Road Runner, AOL.
Fee: $69.95 installation; $44.95 monthly.

Telephone Service
Digital: Operational
Fee: $44.95 monthly

Note: Homes passed and miles of plant (coax & fiber) included in Mililani
President: Nate Smith. Vice President, Operations: Norman Santos. Vice President, Engineering: Mike Goodish. Marketing Director: Allan Pollack. Chief Technician: Met LeBar. Controller: Ann Butak.
State fee: 2% of basic & installation.
Ownership: Time Warner Cable (MSO).

MAUI—Formerly served by Maui Cablevision Corp. No longer in operation. ICA: HI0016.

MAUI—Hawaiian Cablevision. Now served by MAUI (formerly KIHEI), HI [HI0013]. ICA: HI0003.

MAUI—Oceanic Time Warner Cable, 350 Hoohana St, Kahului, HI 96732-2931. Phone: 808-625-2100 (Administrative office). Fax: 808-625-5888. Web Site: http://www.oceanic.com. Also serves Haiku, Haliimaile, Hana, Honokowai, Kaanapali, Kahana, Kahului, Kalaupapa, Kapalua, Kaunakakai, Kihei, Kula, Lahaina, Lanai City, Lower Paia, Maalaea, Mahinahina, Makawao, Maui Island, Napili, Pukalani, Spreckelsville, Waihee, Waikapu, Wailea & Wailuku. ICA: HI0013.
TV Market Ranking: Below 100 (Haiku, Haliimaile, Hana, Honokowai, Kaanapali, Kahana, Kahului, Kapalua, Kaunakakai, Kihei, Kula, Lahaina, Lanai City, Lower Paia, Maalaea, Mahinahina, Makawao, MAUI, Maui Island, Napili, Pukalani, Spreckelsville, Waihee, Waikapu, Wailea, Wailuku); Outside TV Markets (Kalaupapa). Franchise award date: N.A. Franchise expiration date: N.A. Began: May 3, 1978.
Channel capacity: N.A. Channels available but not in use: N.A.

Basic Service
Subscribers: N.A. Included in Mililani
Programming (received off-air): KAAH-TV (TBN) Honolulu; KFVE (MNT) Honolulu; KGMB (CBS) Honolulu; KHNL (NBC) Honolulu; KIKU (IND) Honolulu; allband FM.
Programming (via microwave): KFVE (MNT) Honolulu; KGMB (CBS) Honolulu; KHET (PBS) Honolulu; KHON-TV (CW, FOX) Honolulu; KIKU (IND) Honolulu; KITV (ABC) Honolulu; KWHM (IND) Wailuku.
Programming (via satellite): ABC Family Channel; Cartoon Network; CNBC; CNN; C-SPAN; C-SPAN 2; Disney Channel; ESPN; Headline News; Home Shopping Network; Lifetime; MTV; Nickelodeon; Product Information Network; QVC; TBS Superstation; The Learning Channel; Travel Channel; Turner Network TV; USA Network; VH1.
Current originations: Educational Access; Public Access.
Fee: $50.00 installation; $43.60 monthly; $3.00 converter; $18.00 additional installation.

Digital Basic Service
Subscribers: N.A.
Programming (via satellite): AMC; America's Store; Animal Planet; Arts & Entertainment; Asian Television Network; BBC America; Bio; Bravo; Chinese Television Network; CNBC; Comedy Central; Cooking Channel; Country Music TV; Discovery Digital Networks; DMX Music; Do-It-Yourself; E! Entertainment Television; ESPN 2; ESPN Classic Sports; ESPNews; Flix; Food Network; Fox College Sports Pacific; Fox Movie Channel; Fox News Channel; Fox Sports Net West; Fox Sports Net West 2; Fox Sports World; Fuel TV; Fuse; FX; G4; Golf Channel; Great American Country; GSN; Hallmark Channel; HGTV; History Channel; History Channel International; Independent Film Channel; INSP; Lifetime Movie Network; Lifetime Real Women; MSNBC; National Geographic Channel; NBA TV; Nick Jr.; Outdoor Channel; Ovation; Oxygen; PBS Kids Channel; ShopNBC; SoapNet; Speed Channel; Spike TV; Style Network; Syfy; Tennis Channel; Toon Disney; truTV; Turner Classic Movies; TV Land; Versus; VH1 Classic; WE tv.
Fee: $33.00 installation; $11.00 monthly.

Digital Pay Service 1
Pay Units: N.A.
Programming (taped): Nippon Golden Network.
Programming (via satellite): Canales N; Cinemax (multiplexed); Encore (multiplexed); Filipino Channel; HBO (multiplexed); Showtime; Sundance Channel; The Movie Channel (multiplexed).
Fee: $14.95 monthly (each).

Video-On-Demand: Yes

Pay-Per-View
Addressable homes: 9,277.
iN DEMAND (delivered digitally), Addressable: Yes; UH Football PPV (delivered digitally); PPV Highlights (delivered digitally); Hot Choice (delivered digitally); Playboy TV (delivered digitally).

Internet Service
Operational: Yes.
Broadband Service: Road Runner, EarthLink, Internet.
Fee: $69.95 installation; $44.95 monthly.

Telephone Service
Analog: Not Operational
Digital: Operational
Fee: $44.95 monthly

Note: Homes passed and miles of plant (coax & fiber) included in Mililani
President: Nate Smith. Vice President, Operations: Norman Santos. Vice President, Engineering: Mike Goodish. Marketing Director: Allan Pollack. Chief Technician: Met LeBar. Controller: Ann Butack.
Franchise fee: 1% of gross.
Ownership: Time Warner Cable (MSO).

MILILANI—Oceanic Time Warner Cable, 200 Akamainui St, Mililani, HI 96789-3999. Phone: 808-625-2100 (Administrative office). Fax: 808-625-5888. Web Site: http://www.oceanic.com. Also serves Ahuimanu, Aiea, Aliamanu Government Reserve, Diamond Head/Wilhelmina, Enchanted Hills, Ewa, Ewa Beach, Foster Village, Halawa Heights, Haleiwa, Hauula, Hawaii Kai, Honolulu, Kaaawa, Kahaluu, Kahuku, Kaimuki, Kapahulu, Kapalama, Kapiolani, Kuliouou Valley, Laie, Maili, Makaha, Makakilo City, Makiki, Manoa, Maunawili, McCully, Moanalua, Moiliili, Mokuleia, Nanakuli, North Shore, Nuuanu, Pacific Heights, Pauoa, Pearl City, Pearl Harbor Government Reserve, Punchbowl, Pupukea, St. Louis Heights, Sunset Beach, Wahiawa, Waialua, Waianae, Waikiki, Waimanalo, Waipahu & Waipio. ICA: HI0001.
TV Market Ranking: Below 100 (Ahuimanu, Aiea, Aliamanu Government Reserve, Diamond Head/Wilhelmina, Enchanted Hills, Ewa, Ewa Beach, Foster Village, Halawa Heights, Haleiwa, Hauula, Hawaii Kai, Honolulu, Kaaawa, Kahaluu, Kahuku, Kaimuki, Kapahulu, Kapalama, Kapiolani, Kuliouou Valley, Laie, Maili, Makaha, Makakilo City, Makiki, Manoa, Maunawili, McCully, MILILANI, Moanalua, Moiliili, Mokuleia, Nanakuli, North Shore, Nuuanu, Pacific Heights, Pauoa, Pearl City, Pearl Harbor Government Reserve, Punchbowl, Pupukea, St. Louis Heights, Sunset Beach, Wahiawa, Waialua, Waianae, Waikiki, Waimanalo, Waipahu, Waipio). Franchise award date: January 1, 1970. Franchise expiration date: N.A. Began: September 1, 1968.
Channel capacity: N.A. Channels available but not in use: N.A.

Basic Service
Subscribers: 350,000 Includes Hilo, Kauai Island, Kona, & Maui.
Programming (received off-air): KAAH-TV (TBN) Honolulu; KALO (ETV) Honolulu; KBFD-DT (IND) Honolulu; KFVE (MNT) Honolulu; KGMB (CBS) Honolulu; KHET (PBS) Honolulu; KHNL (NBC) Honolulu; KHON-TV (CW, FOX) Honolulu; KIKU (IND)

Honolulu; KITV (ABC) Honolulu; KWHE (IND) Honolulu; 13 FMs.
Programming (via satellite): America's Store; CNBC; CNN; C-SPAN; Fox News Channel; Headline News; Home Shopping Network; Lifetime; QVC; ShopNBC; TBS Superstation.
Current originations: Educational Access; Public Access.
Fee: $43.00 installation; $18.00 additional installation.

Expanded Basic Service 1
Subscribers: N.A.
Programming (via satellite): ABC Family Channel; AMC; Animal Planet; Arts & Entertainment; BBC America; Bravo; Cartoon Network; Comedy Central; Cooking Channel; Country Music TV; C-SPAN 2; Discovery Channel; Discovery Health Channel; Discovery Kids Channel; Discovery Military Channel; Disney Channel; Do-It-Yourself; E! Entertainment Television; ESPN; ESPN 2; ESPN Classic Sports; ESPNews; FitTV; Flix; Food Network; Fox Sports Net West; Fox Sports Net West 2; Fox Sports World; Fuel TV; Golf Channel; Hallmark Channel; HGTV; History Channel; History Channel International; MSNBC; MTV; National Geographic Channel; NBA TV; Nickelodeon; Outdoor Channel; Science Television; Speed Channel; Spike TV; Tennis Channel; The Learning Channel; Travel Channel; truTV; Turner Classic Movies; Turner Network TV; USA Network; Versus; VH1.
Fee: $43.60 monthly.

Digital Basic Service
Subscribers: N.A.
Programming (via satellite): Bio; DMX Music; Fox College Sports Pacific; Fox Movie Channel; Fox Sports Net (multiplexed); Fuse; FX; G4; Great American Country; GSN; Independent Film Channel; INSP; Lifetime Movie Network; Lifetime Real Women; MTV2; Nick Jr.; Ovation; Oxygen; PBS Kids Channel; SoapNet; Style Network; Sundance Channel; Syfy; Toon Disney; TV Land; VH1 Classic; WAM! America's Kidz Network; WE tv.
Fee: $11.00 monthly.

Digital Pay Service 1
Pay Units: N.A.
Programming (taped): Nippon Golden Network.
Programming (via satellite): Asian Television Network; Canales N; Cinemax (multiplexed); Filipino Channel; HBO (multiplexed); Playboy TV; Showtime (multiplexed); The Movie Channel (multiplexed).

Fee: $13.95 monthly (each).
Video-On-Demand: Yes

Pay-Per-View
Addressable homes: 160,000.
iN DEMAND, Fee: $3.95, Addressable: Yes; special events; Hot Choice (delivered digitally); Playboy TV (delivered digitally); UH Football PPV (delivered digitally); ESPN Gameplan (delivered digitally); NBA (delivered digitally).

Internet Service
Operational: Yes.
Subscribers: 100,000.
Broadband Service: AOL for Broadband; EarthLink; Road Runner.
Fee: $69.95 installation; $44.95 monthly.

Telephone Service
Digital: Operational
Fee: $44.95 monthly
Miles of Plant: 4,900.0 (coaxial); None (fiber optic). Homes passed: 563,000. Homes passed and miles of plant (coax & fiber) include Hilo, Kauai Island, Kona, & Maui
President: Nate Smith. Vice President, Operations: Norman Santos. Vice President, Engineering: Mike Goodish. Marketing Director: Allan Pollack. Chief Technician: Met LeBar. Controller: Ann Butak.
City fee: 5% of gross.
Ownership: Time Warner Cable (MSO).

PAHALA—Formerly served by Time Warner Cable. No longer in operation. ICA: HI0015.

IDAHO

Total Systems: **38**
Total Communities Served: **189**
Franchises Not Yet Operating: **0**
Applications Pending: **0**
Communities with Applications: **0**
Number of Basic Subscribers: **284,174**
Number of Expanded Basic Subscribers: **66,460**
Number of Pay Units: **15,240**

Top 100 Markets Represented: Spokane, WA (76).

**For a list of cable communities in this section, see the Cable Community Index located in the back of Cable Volume 2.
For explanation of terms used in cable system listings, see p. D-11.**

ABERDEEN—Direct Communications, PO Box 270, 150 S Main St, Rockland, ID 83271. Phone: 208-548-2345. Web Site: http://www.directcom.com. ICA: ID0099.

TV Market Ranking: Below 100 (ABERDEEN). Franchise award date: N.A. Franchise expiration date: N.A. Began: January 1, 2006.

Channel capacity: 48 (2-way capable). Channels available but not in use: N.A.

Basic Service

Subscribers: 120.

Programming (received off-air): KFXP (FOX) Pocatello; KIDK (CBS) Idaho Falls; KIFI-TV (ABC) Idaho Falls; KISU-TV (PBS) Pocatello; KPVI-DT (NBC) Pocatello; KUWB-LP Bloomington.

Programming (via satellite): ABC Family Channel; Animal Planet; Arts & Entertainment; CNN; Country Music TV; Discovery Channel; Disney Channel; ESPN; Fox News Channel; Fox Sports Net Rocky Mountain; FX; Headline News; HGTV; History Channel; Home Shopping Network; ION Television; Lifetime; MTV; Nickelodeon; Spike TV; Syfy; TBS Superstation; Telemundo; The Learning Channel; Turner Classic Movies; Turner Network TV; TV Land; Univision; USA Network; VH1; Weather Channel; WGN America.

Fee: $37.50 monthly.

Pay Service 1

Pay Units: N.A.

Programming (via satellite): Cinemax; Encore; HBO; Starz.

Fee: $7.99 monthly (Starz & Encore), $14.95 monthly (HBO orShowtime).

Internet Service

Operational: No.

Telephone Service

None

General Manager: Jeremy Smith.

Ownership: Direct Communications (MSO).

ADA COUNTY (unincorporated areas)—Formerly served by Ada Cable Vision Inc. No longer in operation. ICA: ID0056.

ALBION—Formerly served by Telsat Systems Inc. No longer in operation. ICA: ID0068.

AMERICAN FALLS—Cable One. Now served by POCATELLO, ID [ID0004]. ICA: ID0014.

ARCO—Independent Cable, PO Box 858, Soda Springs, ID 83276-0858. Phones: 208-547-4341; 800-295-3562. Fax: 208-547-4833. Web Site: http://www.icsofidaho.com. Also serves Mackay. ICA: ID0030.

TV Market Ranking: Outside TV Markets (ARCO, Mackay). Franchise award date: N.A. Franchise expiration date: N.A. Began: July 1, 1982.

Channel capacity: 54 (not 2-way capable). Channels available but not in use: N.A.

Basic Service

Subscribers: 250.

Programming (received off-air): KBYU-TV (PBS) Provo; KIDK (CBS) Idaho Falls; KIFI-TV (ABC) Idaho Falls; KISU-TV (PBS) Pocatello; KJZZ-TV (MNT) Salt Lake City; KPVI-DT (NBC) Pocatello; KSL-TV (NBC) Salt Lake City.

Programming (via satellite): ABC Family Channel; Animal Planet; Arts & Entertainment; Boomerang; Bravo; Cartoon Network; CNBC; CNN; C-SPAN; Discovery Channel; Disney Channel; ESPN; ESPN 2; Fox News Channel; Fox Sports Net West; FX; Golf Channel; Great American Country; Hallmark Channel; Headline News; HGTV; History Channel; INSP; Lifetime; MSNBC; Nickelodeon; Outdoor Channel; QVC; Speed Channel; Spike TV; Syfy; TBS Superstation; The Learning Channel; Travel Channel; Turner Classic Movies; Turner Network TV; TV Land; USA Network; VH1; Weather Channel; WGN America.

Fee: $32.45 monthly.

Pay Service 1

Pay Units: 48.

Programming (via satellite): Cinemax.

Fee: $9.00 monthly.

Pay Service 2

Pay Units: 30.

Programming (via satellite): HBO.

Fee: $9.00 monthly.

Video-On-Demand: No

Internet Service

Operational: No, Both DSL & dialup.

Telephone Service

None

Miles of Plant: 17.0 (coaxial); None (fiber optic). Homes passed: 523.

General Manager: Howard Wisenberger. Plant Manager: Dale Deno.

City fee: 5% of gross.

Ownership: Independent Cable Systems of Idaho LLC (MSO).

ASHTON—Independent Cable, PO Box 858, Soda Springs, ID 83276-0858. Phones: 208-547-4341; 800-295-3562. Fax: 208-547-4833. Web Site: http://www.icsofidaho.com. ICA: ID0040.

TV Market Ranking: Outside TV Markets (ASHTON-SANDY SPRING). Franchise award date: December 19, 1985. Franchise expiration date: N.A. Began: October 15, 1981.

Channel capacity: 45 (not 2-way capable). Channels available but not in use: 19.

Basic Service

Subscribers: 83.

Programming (received off-air): KIDK (CBS) Idaho Falls; KIFI-TV (ABC) Idaho Falls; KISU-TV (PBS) Pocatello; KPVI-DT (NBC) Pocatello.

Programming (via satellite): ABC Family Channel; AMC; Arts & Entertainment; Cartoon Network; CNN; Discovery Channel; Disney Channel; ESPN; ESPN 2; Fox News Channel; Fox Sports Net West; Great American Country; History Channel; Nickelodeon; QVC; Spike TV; TBS Superstation; Turner Network TV; TV Land; USA Network; WGN America.

Fee: $29.95 installation; $30.45 monthly.

Pay Service 1

Pay Units: 14.

Programming (via satellite): HBO.

Fee: $9.00 monthly.

Video-On-Demand: No

Internet Service

Operational: No.

Telephone Service

None

Miles of Plant: 6.0 (coaxial); None (fiber optic). Homes passed: 391.

General Manager: Jeremy Smith.

City fee: 1% of gross.

Ownership: Independent Cable Systems of Idaho LLC (MSO).

AVERY—Formerly served by Rapid Cable. No longer in operation. ICA: ID0093.

BOISE—Cable One, 8400 Westpark St, Boise, ID 83704-8365. Phones: 877-692-2253 (Technical support); 208-375-8288. Fax: 208-472-8330. E-mail: celynda.roach@cableone.net. Web Site: http://www.cableone.net. Also serves Ada County (portions) & Garden City. ICA: ID0001.

TV Market Ranking: Below 100 (Ada County (portions), BOISE, Garden City). Franchise award date: N.A. Franchise expiration date: N.A. Began: September 9, 1979.

Channel capacity: 68 (operating 2-way). Channels available but not in use: N.A.

Basic Service

Subscribers: 44,285.

Programming (received off-air): KAID (PBS) Boise; KBOI-TV (CBS) Boise; KIVI-TV (ABC) Nampa; KKJB (IND) Boise; KNIN-TV (CW) Caldwell; KTRV-TV (FOX) Nampa; KTVB (NBC) Boise; 11 FMs.

Programming (via satellite): C-SPAN; C-SPAN 2; Home Shopping Network; ION Television; QVC; Telefutura; Telemundo; TV Guide Network; Univision.

Current originations: Leased Access; Educational Access; Public Access; Leased Access.

Fee: $60.00 installation; $46.00 monthly; $60.00 additional installation.

Expanded Basic Service 1

Subscribers: N.A.

Programming (via satellite): 24/7 News Channel; ABC Family Channel; AMC; Animal Planet; Arts & Entertainment; Bravo; Cartoon Network; Celebrity Shopping Network; CNBC; CNN; Comcast Sports Net Northwest; Comedy Central; Country Music TV; Discovery Channel; Disney Channel; ESPN; ESPN 2; ESPN Classic Sports; Food Network; Fox News Channel; FX; Headline News; HGTV; History Channel; Lifetime; MSNBC; MTV; Nickelodeon; ShopNBC; Spike TV; Syfy; TBS Superstation; The Learning Channel; Travel Channel; truTV; Turner Classic Movies; Turner Network TV; TV Land; USA Network; VH1; Weather Channel.

Digital Basic Service

Subscribers: 14,090.

Programming (received off-air): KAID (PBS) Boise; KBOI-TV (CBS) Boise; KIVI-TV (ABC) Nampa; KNIN-TV (CW) Caldwell; KTRV-TV (FOX) Nampa; KTVB (NBC) Boise.

Programming (via satellite): 3 Angels Broadcasting Network; ABC Family HD; Arts & Entertainment HD; Bio; Boomerang; Boomerang en Espanol; BYU Television; Cine Mexicano; CNN en Espanol; Discovery Channel HD; Discovery HD Theater; Discovery Health Channel; Discovery Kids Channel; Discovery Military Channel; ESPN 2 HD; ESPN Classic Sports; ESPN Deportes; ESPN HD; ESPN U; ESPNews; FamilyNet; Food Network HD; Fox College Sports Atlantic; Fox College Sports Central; Fox College Sports Pacific; Fox Movie Channel; Fox Soccer; Fox Sports en Espanol; Fuel TV; Golf Channel; Great American Country; GSN; Hallmark Channel; HGTV HD; History Channel HD; History Channel International; INSP; La Familia Network; Latele Novela Network; Mountain West TV; Music Choice; National Geographic Channel; National Geographic Channel HD Network; Outdoor Channel; Science Channel; SoapNet; Speed Channel; TBS in HD; Telemundo; TLC HD; Toon Disney; Toon Disney en Espanol; Trinity Broadcasting Network; Turner Network TV HD; TVG Network; Universal HD; WE tv.

Fee: $9.95 monthly.

Digital Pay Service 1

Pay Units: N.A.

Programming (via satellite): Cinemax (multiplexed); Encore (multiplexed); Flix; HBO (multiplexed); HBO HD; HBO Latino; Showtime (multiplexed); Showtime HD; Starz (multiplexed); Sundance Channel; The Movie Channel (multiplexed); The Movie Channel HD.

Fee: $7.00 monthly (each).

Video-On-Demand: No

Pay-Per-View

Addressable homes: 11,995.

iN DEMAND (delivered digitally), Addressable: Yes; Penthouse TV (delivered digitally); ESPN (delivered digitally); Ten Clips (delivered digitally); Ten Blox (delivered digitally).

Internet Service

Operational: Yes.

Subscribers: 25,100.

Broadband Service: CableONE.net.

Fee: $75.00 installation; $43.00 monthly; $5.00 modem lease.

Telephone Service
Analog: Not Operational
Digital: Operational
Fee: $75.00 installation; $39.95 monthly
Miles of Plant: 1,308.0 (coaxial); None (fiber optic).
Manager: Celynda Roach. Marketing Director: Becky Trask. Chief Technician: Dave Reder. Office Manager: Bryan Klingelhoets.
City fee: 5% of gross.
Ownership: Cable One Inc. (MSO).

BOISE—Formerly served by Wireless Broadcasting Systems. No longer in operation. ICA: ID0086.

BONNERS FERRY—Windjammer Cable, 4400 PGA Blvd, Ste 902, Palm Beach Gardens, FL 33410. Phones: 877-450-5558; 561-775-1208. Fax: 561-775-7811. Web Site: http://www.windjammercable.com. Also serves Boundary County. ICA: ID0027.
TV Market Ranking: Outside TV Markets (BONNERS FERRY, Boundary County). Franchise award date: January 1, 1981. Franchise expiration date: N.A. Began: November 1, 1981.
Channel capacity: N.A. Channels available but not in use: N.A.
Basic Service
Subscribers: N.A. Included in Coeur d'Alene
Programming (received off-air): KAYU-TV (FOX) Spokane; KHQ-TV (NBC) Spokane; KREM (CBS) Spokane; KSPS-TV (PBS) Spokane; KUID-TV (PBS) Moscow; KXLY-TV (ABC, MNT) Spokane.
Programming (via satellite): ABC Family Channel; CNN; Comcast Sports Net Northwest; C-SPAN; E! Entertainment Television; Nickelodeon; Northwest Cable News; QVC; TBS Superstation; WGN America.
Fee: $39.95 installation; $26.32 monthly.
Expanded Basic Service 1
Subscribers: N.A. Included in Coeur d'Alene
Programming (via satellite): AMC; Animal Planet; Arts & Entertainment; Discovery Channel; Disney Channel; ESPN; Fox News Channel; Headline News; MTV; Spike TV; The Learning Channel; truTV; Turner Network TV; USA Network; VH1; Weather Channel.
Fee: $27.23 monthly.
Digital Basic Service
Subscribers: N.A.
Programming (via satellite): BBC America; Bloomberg Television; Bravo; Discovery Digital Networks; ESPN Classic Sports; ESPNews; FitTV; Fox Sports World; G4; Golf Channel; GSN; HGTV; History Channel; INSP; Outdoor Channel; Trinity Broadcasting Network; Versus; WE tv.
Digital Expanded Basic Service
Subscribers: N.A.
Programming (via satellite): DMX Music; Fox Movie Channel; Independent Film Channel; Nick Jr.; Turner Classic Movies.
Fee: $11.49 monthly.
Digital Pay Service 1
Pay Units: 64.
Programming (via satellite): Cinemax (multiplexed); Encore (multiplexed); HBO (multiplexed); Showtime (multiplexed); Starz (multiplexed).
Fee: $15.95 monthly (each).
Video-On-Demand: No
Pay-Per-View
Shorteez (delivered digitally); Fresh (delivered digitally); Urban Extra (delivered digitally); Hot Choice (delivered digitally); Playboy TV (delivered digitally); HITS PPV (delivered digitally).
Internet Service
Operational: Yes.
Broadband Service: Road Runner.
Fee: $19.95-$49.99 monthly.
Telephone Service
Digital: Operational
Fee: $49.95 monthly
Homes passed & miles of plant included in Coeur d'Alene
General Manager: Timothy Evard. Operations Director: Belinda Graham. Engineering Director: Mike Earehart. Finance & Accounting Director: Cindy Johnson.
City fee: 3% of gross.
Ownership: Windjammer Communications LLC (MSO).

BOVILL—Elk River TV Cable Co., PO Box 154, 411 S Main St, Troy, ID 83871. Phones: 208-835-5654; 877-874-4900. Fax: 208-835-5573. Web Site: http://www.elkrivertv.net. ICA: ID0095.
TV Market Ranking: Outside TV Markets (BOVILL).
Channel capacity: N.A. Channels available but not in use: N.A.
Basic Service
Subscribers: 16.
Programming (received off-air): KAYU-TV (FOX) Spokane; KHQ-TV (NBC) Spokane; KREM (CBS) Spokane; KSKN (CW) Spokane; KSPS-TV (PBS) Spokane; KXLY-TV (ABC, MNT) Spokane.
Programming (via satellite): ABC Family Channel; Arts & Entertainment; Cartoon Network; CNN; Country Music TV; Discovery Channel; Disney Channel; Encore; ESPN; ESPN 2; Fox News Channel; Fox Sports Net North; HGTV; History Channel; Lifetime; MTV; Nickelodeon; Northwest Cable News; Outdoor Channel; Spike TV; TBS Superstation; The Learning Channel; Trinity Broadcasting Network; Turner Classic Movies; Turner Network TV; USA Network; Weather Channel; WGN America.
Fee: $36.83 monthly.
Pay Service 1
Pay Units: 1.
Programming (via satellite): HBO.
Fee: $10.95 monthly.
Internet Service
Operational: No.
Telephone Service
None
Manager: Dave McGraw.; Leslie McGraw. Chief Technician: Justin McGraw.
Ownership: Elk River TV Cable Co.

BOVILL—Formerly served by Adelphia Communications. No longer in operation. ICA: ID0065.

BUHL—Millennium Digital Media. Now served by TWIN FALLS, ID [ID0088]. ICA: ID0019.

CALDWELL—Cable One, 2101 E Karcher Rd, Nampa, ID 83687. Phones: 208-455-5579 (Administrative office); 208-455-5555 (Customer service). Fax: 208-455-1797. Web Site: http://www.cableone.net. Also serves Cascade, Donnelly, Eagle, Emmett, Fruitland, Greenleaf, Homedale, Kuna, Marsing, McCall, Meridian, Middleton, Nampa, New Meadows, New Plymouth, Notus, Parma, Payette, Purple Sage, Star, Weiser & Wilder, ID; Nyssa, Ontario & Vale, OR. ICA: ID0008.
TV Market Ranking: Below 100 (CALDWELL, Eagle, Emmett, Fruitland, Greenleaf, Homedale, Kuna, Marsing, Meridian, Middleton, Nampa, New Plymouth, Notus, Nyssa, Ontario, Parma, Payette, Purple Sage, Star, Wilder); Outside TV Markets (Cascade, Donnelly, McCall, New Meadows, Vale, Weiser). Franchise award date: N.A. Franchise expiration date: N.A. Began: March 1, 1981.
Channel capacity: 98 (operating 2-way). Channels available but not in use: None.
Basic Service
Subscribers: 45,000.
Programming (received off-air): KAID (PBS) Boise; KBOI-TV (CBS) Boise; KIVI-TV (ABC) Nampa; KKJB (IND) Boise; KTRV-TV (FOX) Nampa; KTVB (NBC) Boise; allband FM.
Programming (via microwave): KOPB-TV (PBS) Portland.
Programming (via satellite): Azteca America; C-SPAN; C-SPAN 2; Home Shopping Network; ION Television; KIDK (CBS) Idaho Falls; QVC; Telefutura; Telemundo; TV Guide Network; Univision.
Current originations: Educational Access; Leased Access; Government Access; Public Access.
Fee: $46.00 monthly.
Expanded Basic Service 1
Subscribers: N.A.
Programming (via satellite): 24/7 News Channel; ABC Family Channel; AMC; Animal Planet; Arts & Entertainment; Bio; Bravo; Cartoon Network; CNBC; CNN; Comedy Central; Country Music TV; Discovery Channel; Disney Channel; E! Entertainment Television; ESPN; ESPN 2; ESPN Classic Sports; Food Network; Fox News Channel; Fox Sports Net Rocky Mountain; FX; Headline News; HGTV; History Channel; Jewelry Television; Lifetime; MSNBC; MTV; Nickelodeon; Product Information Network; ShopNBC; Spike TV; Syfy; TBS Superstation; The Learning Channel; Travel Channel; Turner Classic Movies; Turner Network TV; TV Land; USA Network; VH1; Weather Channel.
Digital Basic Service
Subscribers: 15,000.
Programming (received off-air): KAID (PBS) Boise; KBOI-TV (CBS) Boise; KIVI-TV (ABC) Nampa; KTVB (NBC) Boise.
Programming (via satellite): 3 Angels Broadcasting Network; Boomerang; BYU Television; Canales N; Discovery Digital Networks; ESPNews; FamilyNet; Fox College Sports Atlantic; Fox College Sports Central; Fox College Sports Pacific; Fox HD; Fox Movie Channel; Fox Soccer; Fuel TV; G4; Golf Channel; GSN; Hallmark Channel; History Channel International; INSP; National Geographic Channel; Outdoor Channel; PBS Kids Channel; SoapNet; Speed Channel; the mtn; Toon Disney; Trinity Broadcasting Network; truTV; Turner Network TV HD; Universal HD.
Fee: $46.44 monthly.
Digital Pay Service 1
Pay Units: N.A.
Programming (via satellite): Cinemax (multiplexed); Encore (multiplexed); Flix; HBO (multiplexed); Showtime (multiplexed); Showtime HD; Starz (multiplexed); Sundance Channel; The Movie Channel (multiplexed); The Movie Channel HD.
Video-On-Demand: No
Pay-Per-View
iN DEMAND; Pleasure; Ten Clips; Ten Blox; Ten Blue.
Internet Service
Operational: Yes.
Subscribers: 23,000.
Broadband Service: CableONE.net.
Fee: $75.00 installation; $43.00 monthly.
Telephone Service
Analog: Not Operational
Digital: Operational
Fee: $75.00 installation; $39.95 monthly
Miles of Plant: 3,000.0 (coaxial); None (fiber optic).
Manager: Michelle Cameron. Marketing Director: Nanci Doucet.
Ownership: Cable One Inc. (MSO).

CAMBRIDGE—Cambridge Cable TV, PO Box 88, 130 N Superior St, Cambridge, ID 83610. Phone: 208-257-3314. Fax: 208-257-3310. E-mail: jpiper@ctctele.com. Web Site: http://www.ctcweb.net. ICA: ID0075.
TV Market Ranking: Outside TV Markets (CAMBRIDGE). Franchise award date: N.A. Franchise expiration date: N.A. Began: January 1, 1984.
Channel capacity: 45 (not 2-way capable). Channels available but not in use: 3.
Basic Service
Subscribers: 104.
Programming (received off-air): KAID (PBS) Boise; KBOI-TV (CBS) Boise; KIVI-TV (ABC) Nampa; KTRV-TV (FOX) Nampa; KTVB (NBC) Boise.
Programming (via satellite): ABC Family Channel; AMC; Arts & Entertainment; Cartoon Network; CNBC; CNN; Country Music TV; C-SPAN; Discovery Channel; Disney Channel; ESPN; ESPN 2; Hallmark Channel; History Channel; Lifetime; MSNBC; Nickelodeon; Northwest Cable News; Outdoor Channel; QVC; Spike TV; Syfy; TBS Superstation; Trinity Broadcasting Network; Turner Classic Movies; Turner Network TV; TV Land; USA Network; VH1; WGN America.
Fee: $22.50 installation; $21.50 monthly.
Pay Service 1
Pay Units: 54.
Programming (via satellite): Starz (multiplexed).
Fee: $6.00 monthly.
Pay Service 2
Pay Units: 58.
Programming (via satellite): Encore; Starz.
Fee: $2.50 monthly (Encore), $7.50 monthly (Encore & Starz).
Video-On-Demand: No
Internet Service
Operational: No, Both DSL & dial-up.
Telephone Service
None
Manager: Richard Wiggins. Chief Technician: Gordon Huff. Marketing Director: Jerry Piper. Customer Service: Dana Munden.
Ownership: CTC Telecom.

CASCADE—Cable One. Now served by CALDWELL, ID [ID0008]. ICA: ID0035.

CASTLEFORD—Formerly served by WDB Communications. No longer in operation. ICA: ID0070.

CATALDO—Formerly served by Cebridge Connections. Now served by OSBURN, ID [ID0015]. ICA: ID0076.

CHALLIS—Independent Cable, PO Box 858, Soda Springs, ID 83276-0858. Phones: 208-547-4341; 800-295-3562. Fax: 208-547-4833. Web Site: http://www.icsofidaho.com. ICA: ID0077.
TV Market Ranking: Outside TV Markets (CHALLIS). Franchise award date: N.A. Franchise expiration date: N.A. Began: N.A.
Channel capacity: 45 (not 2-way capable). Channels available but not in use: 19.
Basic Service
Subscribers: 83.
Programming (received off-air): KIDK (CBS) Idaho Falls; KIFI-TV (ABC) Idaho

Falls; KISU-TV (PBS) Pocatello; KPVI-DT (NBC) Pocatello.
Programming (via satellite): ABC Family Channel; Arts & Entertainment; Cartoon Network; CNN; Country Music TV; Discovery Channel; Disney Channel; ESPN; Fox News Channel; Fox Sports Net West; INSP; KUSA (NBC) Denver; QVC; Spike TV; TBS Superstation; Turner Classic Movies; Turner Network TV; USA Network; WGN America.
Fee: $29.95 installation; $29.45 monthly.
Pay Service 1
Pay Units: 28.
Programming (via satellite): HBO.
Fee: $9.00 monthly.
Video-On-Demand: No
Internet Service
Operational: No.
Telephone Service
None
Miles of Plant: 16.0 (coaxial); None (fiber optic). Homes passed: 520.
General Manager: Jeremy Smith.
City fee: 3% of basic.
Ownership: Independent Cable Systems of Idaho LLC (MSO).

COEUR D'ALENE—Time Warner Cable, 2305 W Kathleen Ave, Coeur D'Alene, ID 83815-9402. Phone: 208-665-5002. Fax: 208-666-0488. Web Site: http://www.timewarnercable.com/northwest. Also serves Athol, Bayview, Dalton Gardens, Fernan Lake, Hauser Lake, Hayden, Hayden Lake, Huetter, Post Falls & Rathdrum. ICA: ID0003.
TV Market Ranking: 76 (COEUR D'ALENE, Dalton Gardens, Fernan Lake, Hauser Lake, Hayden, Hayden Lake, Huetter, Post Falls, Rathdrum); Outside TV Markets (Athol, Bayview). Franchise award date: January 26, 1979. Franchise expiration date: N.A. Began: September 15, 1970.
Channel capacity: N.A. Channels available but not in use: N.A.
Basic Service
Subscribers: 50,000 Includes Bonners Ferry, Moscow, Mountain Home, Libby MT, Troy MT, & Friday Harbor WA.
Programming (received off-air): KAYU-TV (FOX) Spokane; KHQ-TV (NBC) Spokane; KREM (CBS) Spokane; KSKN (CW) Spokane; KSPS-TV (PBS) Spokane; KUID-TV (PBS) Moscow; KXLY-TV (ABC, MNT) Spokane.
Programming (via satellite): Comcast Sports Net Northwest; C-SPAN; C-SPAN 2; E! Entertainment Television; Home Shopping Network; ION Television; MSNBC; Northwest Cable News; QVC; TV Guide Network; Weather Channel.
Current originations: Government Access; Educational Access.
Fee: $35.80 installation; $22.69 monthly.
Expanded Basic Service 1
Subscribers: 37,000 Includes Bonners Ferry, Moscow, Mountain Home, Libby MT, Troy MT, & Friday Harbor WA.
Programming (via satellite): ABC Family Channel; AMC; Animal Planet; Arts & Entertainment; Bravo; Cartoon Network; CNBC; CNN; Comedy Central; Country Music TV; Discovery Channel; Disney Channel; ESPN; ESPN 2; ESPN Classic Sports; Eternal Word TV Network; Food Network; Fox News Channel; FX; Golf Channel; Great American Country; Hallmark Channel; Headline News; HGTV; History Channel; Lifetime; MTV; Nickelodeon; Oxygen; Product Information Network; ShopNBC; Spike TV; Style Network; Syfy; TBS Superstation; The Learning Channel; Toon Disney; Travel Channel; truTV; Turner Network TV; TV Land; USA Network; Versus; VH1; WE tv; WGN America.
Fee: $28.29 monthly.
Digital Basic Service
Subscribers: N.A.
Programming (via satellite): American-Life TV Network; BBC America; Bio; Black Family Channel; Bloomberg Television; Canales N; Discovery Digital Networks; Do-It-Yourself; Encore (multiplexed); ESPNews; Fox College Sports Atlantic; Fox College Sports Central; Fox College Sports Pacific; Fox Movie Channel; Fox Sports World; Fuse; G4; GAS; GSN; Halogen Network; History Channel International; Independent Film Channel; Lifetime Movie Network; MTV Networks Digital Suite; Music Choice; National Geographic Channel; Nick Jr.; NickToons TV; Outdoor Channel; SoapNet; Speed Channel; Sundance Channel; Trinity Broadcasting Network; Turner Classic Movies.
Fee: $1.97 monthly access, $6.00 monthly (each tier).
Digital Pay Service 1
Pay Units: N.A.
Programming (via satellite): ART America; CCTV-4; Chinese Television Network; Cinemax (multiplexed); Filipino Channel; HBO (multiplexed); RAI International; Russian Television Network; Showtime (multiplexed); Starz (multiplexed); The Movie Channel (multiplexed); TV Asia; TV Japan; TV5, La Television International; Zee TV USA.
Fee: $12.00 monthly (HBO, Cinemax, Showtime, TMC or Starz).
Video-On-Demand: Planned
Pay-Per-View
iN DEMAND (delivered digitally); sports (delivered digitally).
Internet Service
Operational: Yes.
Broadband Service: Road Runner.
Fee: $39.95 installation; $45.95 monthly.
Telephone Service
Digital: Operational
Fee: $49.95 monthly
Miles of Plant: 1,300.0 (coaxial); None (fiber optic). Homes passed: 79,000. Homes passed & miles of plant (coax & fiber combined) include Bonners Ferry, Moscow, Mountain Home, Libby MT, Troy MT, & Friday Harbor WA
Area Manager: Correen Stauffer. Area Marketing Manager: Jody Veeder. Business Manager: Kirk Hobson. Technical Operations Manager: Tom Tantriella.
City fee: 5% of gross.
Ownership: Time Warner Cable (MSO).

COUNCIL—Cable One, 2101 E Karcher Rd, Nampa, ID 83687. Phones: 208-455-5579 (Administrative office); 208-455-5555 (Customer service). Fax: 208-455-1797. Web Site: http://www.cableone.net. ICA: ID0032.
TV Market Ranking: Outside TV Markets (COUNCIL). Franchise award date: February 5, 1985. Franchise expiration date: N.A. Began: January 1, 1984.
Channel capacity: 37 (not 2-way capable). Channels available but not in use: None.
Basic Service
Subscribers: 292.
Programming (received off-air): KAID (PBS) Boise; KBOI-TV (CBS) Boise; KIVI-TV (ABC) Nampa; KTRV-TV (FOX) Nampa; KTVB (NBC) Boise.
Programming (via satellite): ABC Family Channel; CNN; Country Music TV; ESPN; Headline News; Home Shopping Network; Lifetime; Nickelodeon; QVC; TBS Superstation; The Learning Channel; Trinity Broadcasting Network; Turner Network TV; WGN America.
Fee: $35.00 installation; $46.00 monthly.
Expanded Basic Service 1
Subscribers: 289.
Programming (via satellite): AMC; Arts & Entertainment; Discovery Channel; Disney Channel; Northwest Cable News; Spike TV; Syfy; USA Network.
Fee: $3.07 monthly.
Digital Basic Service
Subscribers: N.A.
Programming (via satellite): AmericanLife TV Network; BBC America; Bio; Bloomberg Television; Bravo; Discovery Digital Networks; DMX Music; ESPN 2; ESPN Classic Sports; FitTV; Fox Movie Channel; Fox Soccer; Fuse; G4; GAS; Golf Channel; GSN; Halogen Network; HGTV; History Channel; History Channel International; Independent Film Channel; Lifetime Movie Network; MTV Networks Digital Suite; Nick Jr.; Outdoor Channel; ShopNBC; Speed Channel; Toon Disney; Turner Classic Movies; Versus; WE tv.
Pay Service 1
Pay Units: 44.
Programming (via satellite): HBO.
Fee: $11.95 monthly.
Pay Service 2
Pay Units: 40.
Programming (via satellite): Showtime.
Fee: $10.95 monthly.
Digital Pay Service 1
Pay Units: N.A.
Programming (via satellite): Cinemax (multiplexed); Encore (multiplexed); Flix; HBO (multiplexed); Showtime (multiplexed); Starz (multiplexed); The Movie Channel (multiplexed).
Video-On-Demand: No
Pay-Per-View
iN DEMAND (delivered digitally); Hot Choice (delivered digitally); Playboy TV (delivered digitally); Fresh (delivered digitally); Shorteez (delivered digitally).
Internet Service
Operational: Yes.
Broadband Service: CableONE.net.
Fee: $75.00 installation; $43.00 monthly.
Telephone Service
Digital: Operational
Fee: $75.00 installation; $39.95 monthly
Miles of Plant: 12.0 (coaxial); None (fiber optic). Homes passed: 330.
General Manager: Michelle Cameron. Technical Operations Manager: Mark Campbell.
Franchise fee: 3% of gross.
Ownership: Cable One Inc. (MSO).

CULDESAC—Formerly served by Rapid Cable. No longer in operation. ICA: ID0066.

DEARY—Elk River TV Cable Co., PO Box 154, 411 S Main St, Troy, ID 83871. Phones: 208-835-5654; 877-874-4900. Fax: 208-835-5573. Web Site: http://www.elkrivertv.net. ICA: ID0058.
TV Market Ranking: Below 100 (DEARY). Franchise award date: N.A. Franchise expiration date: N.A. Began: September 1, 1953.
Channel capacity: 22 (not 2-way capable). Channels available but not in use: N.A.
Basic Service
Subscribers: 118.
Programming (received off-air): KHQ-TV (NBC) Spokane; KLEW-TV (CBS) Lewiston; KREM (CBS) Spokane; KUID-TV (PBS) Moscow; KXLY-TV (ABC, MNT) Spokane.
Fee: $25.00 installation; $28.00 monthly.
Pay Service 1
Pay Units: 23.
Programming (via satellite): HBO.
Fee: $9.95 monthly.
Internet Service
Operational: No.
Telephone Service
None
Miles of Plant: 3.0 (coaxial); None (fiber optic). Homes passed: 210.
Manager: Dave McGraw.; Leslie McGraw. Chief Technician: Justin McGraw.
Ownership: Elk River TV Cable Co.

DONNELLY—Cable One. Now served by CALDWELL, ID [ID0008]. ICA: ID0053.

DOWNEY—Independent Cable. Now served by SODA SPRINGS, ID [ID0022]. ICA: ID0055.

DRIGGS—Independent Cable. Now served by VICTOR, ID [ID0062]. ICA: ID0038.

ELK RIVER—Elk River TV Cable Co., PO Box 154, 411 S Main St, Troy, ID 83871. Phones: 877-874-4900; 208-835-5654. Fax: 208-538-5573. E-mail: leslie@elkrivertv.net. Web Site: http://www.elkrivertv.net. ICA: ID0069.
TV Market Ranking: Outside TV Markets (ELK RIVER). Franchise award date: October 10, 1953. Franchise expiration date: N.A. Began: November 25, 1953.
Channel capacity: 12 (not 2-way capable). Channels available but not in use: 1.
Basic Service
Subscribers: 19.
Programming (received off-air): KHQ-TV (NBC) Spokane; KLEW-TV (CBS) Lewiston; KREM (CBS) Spokane; KUID-TV (PBS) Moscow; KWSU-TV (PBS) Pullman; KXLY-TV (ABC, MNT) Spokane.
Programming (via satellite): Discovery Channel; ESPN; TBS Superstation; Turner Network TV.
Fee: $31.65 monthly.
Pay Service 1
Pay Units: N.A.
Programming (via satellite): HBO.
Fee: $10.00 monthly.
Video-On-Demand: No
Internet Service
Operational: No.
Telephone Service
None
Miles of Plant: 2.0 (coaxial); None (fiber optic). Homes passed: 110. Total homes in franchised area: 120.
Manager: Dave McGraw.; Leslie McGraw. Chief Technician: Justin McGraw.
Ownership: Elk River TV Cable Co. (MSO).

EMMETT—Cable One. Now served by CALDWELL, ID [ID0008]. Also serves EMMETT. ICA: ID0017.

FISH HAVEN—Independent Cable, 550 E 2nd St, Soda Springs, ID 83276. Phone: 208-547-4341. Fax: 208-547-4833. Web Site: http://www.icsofidaho.com. Also serves Bear Lake County, Franklin County & St. Charles, ID; Garden City, UT. ICA: ID0073.
TV Market Ranking: Below 100 (Bear Lake County, FISH HAVEN, Franklin County, Garden City, St. Charles).
Channel capacity: N.A. Channels available but not in use: N.A.
Basic Service
Subscribers: N.A. Included in Salt Lake City
Programming (received off-air): KJZZ-TV (MNT) Salt Lake City; KSL-TV (NBC) Salt Lake City; KSTU (FOX) Salt Lake City; KTVX

(ABC) Salt Lake City; KUED (PBS) Salt Lake City; KUTV (CBS) Salt Lake City.
Programming (via satellite): ABC Family Channel; Animal Planet; Arts & Entertainment; Cartoon Network; CNN; Discovery Channel; Disney Channel; Encore; ESPN; Lifetime; MoviePlex; Nickelodeon; Spike TV; Turner Network TV; USA Network; VH1.
Fee: $53.55 monthly.

Pay Service 1
Pay Units: N.A.
Programming (via satellite): Cinemax; HBO; Starz.

Internet Service
Operational: Yes.
Fee: $42.95 monthly.

Telephone Service
None

Miles of plant & homes passed included in Salt Lake City
General Manager: Howard Wisenberger.
Ownership: Independent Cable Systems of Idaho LLC (MSO).

GLENNS FERRY—Rural Telephone Co., 892 W Madison Ave, Glenns Ferry, ID 83623-2374. Phone: 208-366-2614. Fax: 208-366-2615. E-mail: mark@rtci.net. Web Site: http://www.rtci.net. ICA: ID0029.
TV Market Ranking: Outside TV Markets (GLENNS FERRY). Franchise award date: July 16, 1981. Franchise expiration date: N.A. Began: May 1, 1981.
Channel capacity: 65 (operating 2-way). Channels available but not in use: 26.

Basic Service
Subscribers: 350.
Programming (received off-air): KAID (PBS) Boise; KBOI-TV (CBS) Boise; KIVI-TV (ABC) Nampa; KMVT (CBS) Twin Falls; KNIN-TV (CW) Caldwell; KTRV-TV (FOX) Nampa; KTVB (NBC) Boise.
Programming (via satellite): ABC Family Channel; AMC; Animal Planet; Arts & Entertainment; Cartoon Network; CNN; Comedy Central; Country Music TV; C-SPAN; Discovery Channel; Disney Channel; Do-It-Yourself; ESPN; ESPN 2; Food Network; Fox News Channel; Fox Sports Net Rocky Mountain; FX; GalaVision; GSN; Headline News; HGTV; History Channel; Home Shopping Network; MoviePlex; MSNBC; MTV; Nickelodeon; Outdoor Channel; Spike TV; Syfy; TBS Superstation; The Learning Channel; Travel Channel; Turner Classic Movies; Turner Network TV; TV Guide Network; TV Land; Univision; USA Network; VH1; Weather Channel; WGN America.
Fee: $45.00 installation; $30.99 monthly; $8.00 converter; $45.00 additional installation.

Digital Basic Service
Subscribers: N.A.
Programming (via satellite): AmericanLife TV Network; BBC America; Bio; Bloomberg Television; Bravo; Cine Latino; Cine Mexicano; CNN en Espanol; Current; Daystar TV Network; Discovery en Espanol; Discovery Home Channel; Discovery Kids Channel; Discovery Military Channel; Discovery Planet Green; DMX Music; ESPN Classic Sports; ESPNews; FitTV; Fox Movie Channel; Fox Soccer; Fox Sports en Espanol; FSN Digital Atlantic; FSN Digital Central; FSN Digital Pacific; Fuse; G4; Golf Channel; Great American Country; History Channel International; ID Investigation Discovery; Independent Film Channel; INSP; MTV Hits; MTV2; Newsworld International; Nick Jr.; NickToons TV; Outdoor Channel; Ovation; Science Channel; ShopNBC; Speed Channel; Style Network; Sundance Channel; Syfy; TeenNick; The Word Network; Toon Disney; Trinity Broadcasting Network; Trio; TVE Internacional; TVG Network; Versus; VH1 Classic; VH1 Country; VH1 Soul; WE tv.
Fee: $15.00 monthly.

Digital Pay Service 1
Pay Units: N.A.
Programming (via satellite): Cinemax (multiplexed); Encore (multiplexed); Flix; HBO (multiplexed); HBO Latino; Showtime (multiplexed); Starz (multiplexed); The Movie Channel (multiplexed).
Fee: $12.99 monthly (each).

Internet Service
Operational: Yes. Began: January 1, 1996.
Subscribers: 67.
Broadband Service: WildBlue Satellite Internet.
Fee: $25.00 installation; $24.95-$39.95 monthly.

Telephone Service
None

Miles of Plant: 10.0 (coaxial); None (fiber optic). Homes passed: 600.
Manager: Mark R. Martell. Assistant Manager: Susan Case.
Ownership: Rural Telephone Co.

HARRISON—Formerly served by Rapid Cable. No longer in operation. ICA: ID0096.

HAZELTON—Formerly served by WDB Communications. No longer in operation. ICA: ID0061.

IDAHO CITY—Idaho City Cable TV, PO Box 70, 215 Montgomery St, Idaho City, ID 83631-0070. Phone: 208-392-4954. Fax: 208-392-4505. E-mail: cable78910@aol.com. ICA: ID0067.
TV Market Ranking: Below 100 (IDAHO CITY). Franchise award date: N.A. Franchise expiration date: N.A. Began: N.A.
Channel capacity: 78 (2-way capable). Channels available but not in use: 37.

Basic Service
Subscribers: 174.
Programming (received off-air): KAID (PBS) Boise; KBOI-TV (CBS) Boise; KIVI-TV (ABC) Nampa; KNIN-TV (CW) Caldwell; KTRV-TV (FOX) Nampa; KTVB (NBC) Boise.
Programming (via satellite): ABC Family Channel; AMC; Arts & Entertainment; CNN; Country Music TV; Discovery Channel; Disney Channel; ESPN; ESPN 2; Headline News; History Channel; Lifetime; MTV; Nickelodeon; Northwest Cable News; Outdoor Channel; QVC; Spike TV; Syfy; TBS Superstation; The Learning Channel; Trinity Broadcasting Network; Turner Classic Movies; Turner Network TV; TV Land; USA Network; VH1; Weather Channel; WGN America.
Current originations: Government Access; Educational Access; Public Access.
Fee: $25.00 installation; $21.95 monthly; $2.00 converter.

Pay Service 1
Pay Units: 33.
Programming (via satellite): Cinemax.
Fee: $8.95 monthly.

Pay Service 2
Pay Units: 60.
Programming (via satellite): HBO.
Fee: $9.95 monthly.

Pay Service 3
Pay Units: 17.
Programming (via satellite): The Movie Channel.
Fee: $8.95 monthly.

Pay Service 4
Pay Units: 15.
Programming (via satellite): Showtime.

Fee: $9.95 monthly.

Video-On-Demand: No

Internet Service
Operational: No.

Telephone Service
Analog: Not Operational
Digital: Planned

Miles of Plant: 4.0 (coaxial); None (fiber optic). Additional miles planned: 3.0 (coaxial). Homes passed: 215. Total homes in franchised area: 225.
Manager: Don Campbell.
Ownership: Idaho City Cable TV.

IDAHO FALLS—Cable One, PO Box 1827, 1480 Lincoln Rd, Idaho Falls, ID 83403-1827. Phone: 208-523-4567. Fax: 208-524-9983. E-mail: brett.young@cableone.net. Web Site: http://www.cableone.net. Also serves Ammon, Basalt, Bingham County, Blackfoot, Bonneville County, Firth, Fremont County (southern portion), Groveland, Iona, Jefferson County, Lemhi County (southern portion), Madison County (northern portion), Moreland, Rexburg, Rigby, Ririe, Riverside, Shelley, St. Anthony, Sugar City & Ucon. ICA: ID0002.
TV Market Ranking: Below 100 (Ammon, Basalt, Bingham County, Blackfoot, Bonneville County, Firth, Fremont County (portions), Groveland, IDAHO FALLS, Iona, Jefferson County, Madison County (northern portion), Moreland, Rexburg, Rigby, Ririe, Riverside, Shelley, Sugar City, Ucon); Outside TV Markets (Fremont County (portions), Lemhi County (southern portion), St. Anthony). Franchise award date: N.A. Franchise expiration date: N.A. Began: December 15, 1970.
Channel capacity: 120 (operating 2-way). Channels available but not in use: None.

Basic Service
Subscribers: 26,746.
Programming (received off-air): KFXP (FOX) Pocatello; KIDK (CBS) Idaho Falls; KIFI-TV (ABC) Idaho Falls; KISU-TV (PBS) Pocatello; KPIF (IND) Pocatello; KPVI-DT (NBC) Pocatello.
Programming (via microwave): KBYU-TV (PBS) Provo; KSL-TV (NBC) Salt Lake City.
Programming (via satellite): C-SPAN; C-SPAN 2; Home Shopping Network; ION Television; QVC; Telemundo; TV Guide Network; Univision.
Current originations: Government Access; Educational Access; Public Access.
Fee: $60.00 installation; $46.00 monthly; $15.00 additional installation.

Expanded Basic Service 1
Subscribers: 19,980.
Programming (via satellite): ABC Family Channel; AMC; Animal Planet; Arts & Entertainment; Bravo; Cartoon Network; CNBC; CNN; Comedy Central; Country Music TV; Discovery Channel; Disney Channel; ESPN; ESPN 2; Food Network; Fox News Channel; Fox Sports Net Rocky Mountain; FX; Headline News; HGTV; History Channel; Jewelry Television; Lifetime; MSNBC; MTV; Nickelodeon; ShopNBC; Spike TV; Syfy; TBS Superstation; The Learning Channel; Travel Channel; Turner Classic Movies; Turner Network TV; TV Land; USA Network; VH1; Weather Channel.
Fee: $1.80 monthly.

Digital Basic Service
Subscribers: 2,500.
Programming (received off-air): KISU-TV (PBS) Pocatello; KPVI-DT (NBC) Pocatello.
Programming (via satellite): 3 Angels Broadcasting Network; Bio; Boomerang; Boomerang en Espanol; BYU Television; Cine Latino; CNN en Espanol; Discovery Health Channel; Discovery Military Channel; ESPN Classic Sports; ESPN Deportes; ESPN HD; ESPNews; FamilyNet; Fox College Sports Atlantic; Fox College Sports Central; Fox College Sports Pacific; Fox Movie Channel; Fox Soccer; Fox Sports en Espanol; Fuel TV; Golf Channel; Great American Country; GSN; Hallmark Channel; History Channel International; INSP; La Familia Network; Latin Television (LTV); Mountain West TV; Music Choice; National Geographic Channel; Outdoor Channel; Puma TV; Science Channel; SoapNet; Speed Channel; Toon Disney; Toon Disney en Espanol; Trinity Broadcasting Network; TVG Network; Universal HD; WE tv.

Digital Pay Service 1
Pay Units: N.A.
Programming (via satellite): Cinemax (multiplexed); Encore (multiplexed); Flix; HBO (multiplexed); HBO HD; HBO Latino; Showtime (multiplexed); Showtime HD; Starz (multiplexed); Sundance Channel; The Movie Channel (multiplexed); The Movie Channel HD.
Fee: $20.00 installation; $10.00 monthly (each).

Video-On-Demand: No

Pay-Per-View
iN DEMAND (delivered digitally); Ten Clips (delivered digitally); Ten Blox (delivered digitally); Ten Blue (delivered digitally).

Internet Service
Operational: Yes. Began: March 1, 2001.
Subscribers: 1,000.
Broadband Service: CableONE.net.
Fee: $75.00 installation; $43.00 monthly; $5.00 modem lease.

Telephone Service
Digital: Operational
Fee: $75.00 installation; $39.95 monthly

Miles of Plant: 568.0 (coaxial); None (fiber optic). Homes passed: 37,754.
Manager: Dean Jones. Chief Technician: Brett Young. Marketing Director: Penny Schultz.
City fee: 3% of gross.
Ownership: Cable One Inc. (MSO).

KOOSKIA—Formerly served by Rapid Cable. No longer in operation. ICA: ID0060.

KOOTENAI COUNTY (portions)—Formerly served by Rapid Cable. No longer in operation. ICA: ID0100.

LAVA HOT SPRINGS—Independent Cable. Now served by SODA SPRINGS, ID [ID0022]. ICA: ID0043.

LEWISTON—Cable One, 2360 Nez Perce Dr, Lewiston, ID 83501. Phone: 208-746-3325. Fax: 208-746-0290. E-mail: les.shriver@cableone.net. Web Site: http://www.cableone.net. Also serves Nez Perce County (portions), ID; Asotin, Asotin County & Clarkston, WA. ICA: ID0007.

TV Market Ranking: Below 100 (Asotin, Asotin County, Clarkston, LEWISTON, Nez Perce County (portions)). Franchise award date: N.A. Franchise expiration date: N.A. Began: July 1, 1953.

Channel capacity: 212 (operating 2-way). Channels available but not in use: 39.

Basic Service

Subscribers: 13,704.

Programming (received off-air): KHQ-TV (NBC) Spokane; KREM (CBS) Spokane; KSPS-TV (PBS) Spokane; KWSU-TV (PBS) Pullman; KXLY-TV (ABC, MNT) Spokane; 9 FMs.

Programming (via microwave): KLEW-TV (CBS) Lewiston.

Programming (via satellite): AMC; Animal Planet; Arts & Entertainment; Bravo; Cartoon Network; CNBC; CNN; Comcast Sports Net Northwest; Comedy Central; Country Music TV; C-SPAN; C-SPAN 2; Discovery Channel; Disney Channel; ESPN; ESPN 2; ESPN Classic Sports; Eternal Word TV Network; Food Network; Fox News Channel; FX; Headline News; HGTV; History Channel; Home Shopping Network; Lifetime; MSNBC; MTV; Nickelodeon; QVC; Shop at Home; ShopNBC; Syfy; TBS Superstation; The Learning Channel; Travel Channel; Turner Classic Movies; Turner Network TV; TV Guide Network; TV Land; USA Network; VH1; Weather Channel.

Programming (via translator): KAYU-TV (FOX) Spokane.

Current originations: Leased Access; Public Access; Government Access.

Fee: $60.00 installation; $46.00 monthly; $1.44 converter; $60.00 additional installation.

Digital Basic Service

Subscribers: 6,720.

Programming (via satellite): ABC Family Channel; Bio; Boomerang; Canales N (multiplexed); Discovery Digital Networks; ESPN Classic Sports; ESPNews; Fox College Sports Atlantic; Fox College Sports Central; Fox College Sports Pacific; Fox Movie Channel; Fox Sports World; Fuel TV; G4; Golf Channel; Great American Country; GSN; Hallmark Channel; History Channel International; INSP; Lifetime Movie Network; Military History Channel; Music Choice; National Geographic Channel; Outdoor Channel; SoapNet; Speed Channel; Toon Disney; Trinity Broadcasting Network; truTV.

Fee: $9.95 monthly.

Digital Pay Service 1

Pay Units: N.A.

Programming (via satellite): Cinemax (multiplexed); Encore (multiplexed); HBO (multiplexed); Showtime (multiplexed); Starz (multiplexed); The Movie Channel (multiplexed).

Fee: $15.00 monthly for first premium channel, $7.00 for each additional premium channel.

Video-On-Demand: No

Pay-Per-View

Addressable homes: 3,358.

TEN (delivered digitally), Addressable: Yes; iN DEMAND (delivered digitally); ESPN (delivered digitally); Sports PPV (delivered digitally); Pleasure (delivered digitally); ETC (delivered digitally); Playboy TV (delivered digitally); Fresh (delivered digitally); Shorteez (delivered digitally).

Internet Service

Operational: Yes. Began: October 1, 1999.

Subscribers: 2,793.

Broadband Service: CableONE.net.

Fee: $75.00 installation; $43.00 monthly; $10.00 modem lease.

Telephone Service

Digital: Operational

Fee: $75.00 installation; $39.95 monthly

Miles of Plant: 237.0 (coaxial); None (fiber optic). Homes passed: 23,912. Total homes in franchised area: 23,912.

Manager: Jerry Giedt. Chief Technician: Les Shriver.

City fee: 3% of gross.

Ownership: Cable One Inc. (MSO).

MACKAY—Independent Cable. Now served by ARCO, ID [ID0030]. ICA: ID0047.

MALAD CITY—Independent Cable, PO Box 858, Soda Springs, ID 83276-0858. Phones: 208-547-4341; 800-295-3562. Fax: 208-547-3657. Web Site: http://www.icsofidaho.com. ICA: ID0028.

TV Market Ranking: Outside TV Markets (MALAD CITY). Franchise award date: N.A. Franchise expiration date: N.A. Began: January 1, 1983.

Channel capacity: 45 (not 2-way capable). Channels available but not in use: 13.

Basic Service

Subscribers: 192.

Programming (received off-air): KBYU-TV (PBS) Provo; KIDK (CBS) Idaho Falls; KIFI-TV (ABC) Idaho Falls; KJZZ-TV (MNT) Salt Lake City; KSL-TV (NBC) Salt Lake City; KSTU (FOX) Salt Lake City; KTVX (ABC) Salt Lake City; KUCW (CW) Ogden; KUTV (CBS) Salt Lake City.

Programming (via satellite): ABC Family Channel; Arts & Entertainment; CNBC; CNN; Comedy Central; Country Music TV; C-SPAN; Discovery Channel; Disney Channel; ESPN; ESPN 2; Fox News Channel; Fox Sports Net West; HGTV; Lifetime; QVC; Spike TV; TBS Superstation; Turner Classic Movies; Turner Network TV; TV Land; USA Network; Versus; WGN America.

Fee: $31.45 monthly.

Pay Service 1

Pay Units: 16.

Programming (via satellite): Cinemax.

Fee: $9.00 monthly.

Pay Service 2

Pay Units: 39.

Programming (via satellite): HBO.

Fee: $9.00 monthly.

Video-On-Demand: No

Internet Service

Operational: No, Both DSL & dialup.

Telephone Service

None

Miles of Plant: 17.0 (coaxial); None (fiber optic). Homes passed: 720.

General Manager: Jeremy Smith.

City fee: 3% of gross.

Ownership: Independent Cable Systems of Idaho LLC (MSO).

McCALL—Cable One. Now served by CALDWELL, ID [ID0008]. ICA: ID0023.

McCAMMON—Independent Cable. Now served by SODA SPRINGS, ID [ID0022]. ICA: ID0052.

MIDVALE—Midvale Telephone Exchange Inc., 2205 Keithley Creek Rd, Midvale, ID 83645-5019. Phone: 208-355-2211. Fax: 208-355-2222. ICA: ID0080.

TV Market Ranking: Outside TV Markets (MIDVALE). Franchise award date: N.A. Franchise expiration date: N.A. Began: N.A.

Channel capacity: N.A. Channels available but not in use: N.A.

Basic Service

Subscribers: 61.

Programming (received off-air): KAID (PBS) Boise; KBOI-TV (CBS) Boise; KIVI-TV (ABC) Nampa; KTRV-TV (FOX) Nampa; KTVB (NBC) Boise.

Programming (via satellite): ABC Family Channel; Cartoon Network; CNN; Country Music TV; C-SPAN; Discovery Channel; Disney Channel; ESPN; Headline News; History Channel; Nickelodeon; Northwest Cable News; QVC; Spike TV; TBS Superstation; The Learning Channel; Trinity Broadcasting Network; Turner Classic Movies; Turner Network TV; USA Network; Versus; WGN America.

Fee: $16.00 monthly.

Pay Service 1

Pay Units: 6.

Programming (via satellite): Cinemax.

Fee: $9.00 monthly.

Pay Service 2

Pay Units: 8.

Programming (via satellite): HBO.

Fee: $9.00 monthly.

Internet Service

Operational: No.

Telephone Service

None

Miles of Plant: 4.0 (coaxial); None (fiber optic).

Manager: John Stuart.

Ownership: Midvale Telephone Exchange Inc. (MSO).

MOSCOW—Time Warner Cable, 828 W Pullman Rd, Moscow, ID 83843. Phones: 866-489-2669; 208-882-2832. Web Site: http://www.timewarnercable.com. Also serves Genesee, Juliaetta, Kendrick, Latah County, Onaway & Potlatch, ID; Albion, Colton, Palouse, Princeton, Pullman, Uniontown & Whitman County (southeastern portion), WA. ICA: ID0081.

TV Market Ranking: Below 100 (Albion, Colton, Genesee, Juliaetta, Kendrick, Latah County (portions), MOSCOW, Onaway, Palouse, Potlatch, Princeton, Pullman, Uniontown, Whitman County (southeastern portion)); Outside TV Markets (Latah County (portions)). Franchise award date: N.A. Franchise expiration date: N.A. Began: May 1, 1953.

Channel capacity: N.A. Channels available but not in use: N.A.

Basic Service

Subscribers: N.A. Included in Coeur d'Alene

Programming (received off-air): KAYU-TV (FOX) Spokane; KHQ-TV (NBC) Spokane; KLEW-TV (CBS) Lewiston; KREM (CBS) Spokane; KSKN (CW) Spokane; KSPS-TV (PBS) Spokane; KUID-TV (PBS) Moscow; KWSU-TV (PBS) Pullman; KXLY-TV (ABC, MNT) Spokane.

Programming (via satellite): C-SPAN; Eternal Word TV Network; INSP; International Television (ITV); ION Television; QVC.

Current originations: Religious Access; Government Access; Educational Access; Public Access.

Fee: $35.80 installation; $13.28 monthly; $1.14 converter.

Expanded Basic Service 1

Subscribers: N.A. Included in Coeur d'Alene

Programming (via satellite): ABC Family Channel; AMC; Animal Planet; Arts & Entertainment; Bravo; Cartoon Network; CNBC; CNN; Comcast Sports Net Northwest; Comedy Central; Country Music TV; Discovery Channel; Disney Channel; E! Entertainment Television; ESPN; ESPN 2; Fox News Channel; FX; Hallmark Channel; Headline News; HGTV; History Channel; Lifetime; MTV; Nickelodeon; Northwest Cable News; Spike TV; Syfy; TBS Superstation; The Learning Channel; Travel Channel; truTV; Turner Network TV; TV Land; USA Network; VH1; Weather Channel.

Fee: $35.73 monthly.

Digital Basic Service

Subscribers: N.A.

Programming (via satellite): American-Life TV Network; BBC America; Bio; Black Family Channel; Bloomberg Television; Discovery Digital Networks; DMX Music; Do-It-Yourself; ESPN Classic Sports; ESPNews; FitTV; Fox College Sports Atlantic; Fox College Sports Central; Fox College Sports Pacific; Fox Movie Channel; Fox Sports World; G4; GAS; Golf Channel; Great American Country; GSN; Halogen Network; History Channel International; Independent Film Channel; MTV Networks Digital Suite; MuchMusic Network; National Geographic Channel; Nick Jr.; Outdoor Channel; SoapNet; Speed Channel; Style Network; Sundance Channel; The Word Network; Toon Disney; Trinity Broadcasting Network; Turner Classic Movies; Versus; WE tv.

Fee: $6.00 monthly (each tier).

Digital Pay Service 1

Pay Units: N.A.

Programming (via satellite): Arabic Channel; Canales N; CCTV-4; Cinemax (multiplexed); Encore (multiplexed); Filipino Channel; Flix; HBO (multiplexed); RAI International; Russian Television Network; Showtime (multiplexed); Starz (multiplexed); The Movie Channel (multiplexed); TV Asia; TV Japan; TV5, La Television International; Zee TV USA; Zhong Tian Channel.

Fee: $12.00 monthly (each).

Video-On-Demand: Planned

Pay-Per-View

Urban Extra (delivered digitally); Fresh (delivered digitally); Hot Choice (delivered digitally); Playboy TV (delivered digitally); HITS PPV 1-30 (delivered digitally).

Internet Service

Operational: Yes.

Broadband Service: RoadRunner.

Fee: $24.95 monthly.

Telephone Service

Digital: Operational

Fee: $24.95 monthly

Homes passed & miles of plant included in Coeur d'Alene

City fee: 3% of gross.

Ownership: Time Warner Cable (MSO).

MOUNTAIN HOME—Windjammer Cable, 4400 PGA Blvd, Ste 902, Palm Beach Gardens, FL 33410. Phones: 877-450-5558; 561-775-1208. Fax: 561-775-7811. Web Site: http://www.windjammercable.com. Also serves Elmore County & Mountain Home AFB. ICA: ID0010.

TV Market Ranking: Below 100 (Elmore County (portions)); Outside TV Markets (Elmore County (portions), MOUNTAIN HOME, Mountain Home AFB). Franchise award date: January 1, 1964. Franchise expiration date: N.A. Began: April 1, 1968.

Channel capacity: N.A. Channels available but not in use: N.A.

Basic Service

Subscribers: N.A. Included in Coeur d'Alene

Programming (received off-air): KAID (PBS) Boise; KBOI-TV (CBS) Boise; KIVI-TV (ABC) Nampa; KNIN-TV (CW) Caldwell; KTRV-TV (FOX) Nampa; KTVB (NBC) Boise.

Programming (via satellite): AMC; Animal Planet; Arts & Entertainment; BET Networks; Cartoon Network; CNN; Comedy Central; C-SPAN; Discovery Channel; Disney Channel; ESPN; ESPN 2; FX; Headline News; History Channel; Lifetime; MSNBC; MTV; Nickelodeon; Northwest Cable News; QVC; Spike TV; Style Network; Syfy; The Learning Channel; Travel Channel; truTV; Turner Network TV; TV Land; USA Network; VH1; Weather Channel; WGN America.

Current originations: Public Access.

Fee: $29.95 installation; $54.92 monthly.

Expanded Basic Service 1

Subscribers: N.A. Included in Coeur d'Alene

Programming (via satellite): ABC Family Channel; Country Music TV; Fox Sports Net Rocky Mountain; HGTV; TBS Superstation.

Fee: $7.44 monthly.

Digital Basic Service

Subscribers: N.A.

Programming (via satellite): AmericanLife TV Network; BBC America; Bio; Bloomberg Television; Canales N; Discovery Digital Networks; DMX Music; Do-It-Yourself; ESPN Classic Sports; ESPNews; Fox Movie Channel; Fuse; G4; Golf Channel; GSN; History Channel International; INSP; MTV Networks Digital Suite; National Geographic Channel; Nick Jr.; NickToons TV; Outdoor Channel; SoapNet; Speed Channel; Toon Disney; Trinity Broadcasting Network; Versus; WE tv.

Fee: $63.99 monthly.

Digital Pay Service 1

Pay Units: N.A.

Programming (via satellite): ART America; CCTV-4; Cinemax (multiplexed); Encore (multiplexed); Filipino Channel; Flix; HBO (multiplexed); RAI International; Showtime (multiplexed); Starz (multiplexed); The Movie Channel (multiplexed); TV Asia; TV Japan; TV5, La Television International; Zee TV USA; Zhong Tian Channel.

Fee: $12.00 monthly (HBO, Cinemax, Showtime/TMC or Starz), $15.00 monthly (TV Japan, Zhong Tian, CCTV, TV Asia, TV5, Filipino, RAI, or ART).

Video-On-Demand: No

Pay-Per-View

Shorteez (delivered digitally); Fresh (delivered digitally); Urban Extra (delivered digitally); Hot Choice (delivered digitally); Playboy TV (delivered digitally); HITS PPV 1-30 (delivered digitally).

Internet Service

Operational: Yes.

Broadband Service: Road Runner.

Fee: 20.79-$49.99 installation; $44.95 monthly.

Telephone Service

Digital: Operational

Fee: $74.95 installation; $49.95 monthly

Homes passed & miles of plant included in Coeur d'Alene

General Manager: Timothy Evard. Operations Director: Belinda Graham. Engineering Director: Mike Earehart. Finance & Accounting Director: Cindy Johnson.

City fee: 5% of gross.

Ownership: Windjammer Communications LLC (MSO).

MULLAN—Mullan Cable TV, Inc., PO Box 615, 202 N Second St, Mullan, ID 83846-0615. Phone: 208-744-1223. Fax: 208-744-7326. E-mail: jamesdahl@mctvusa.tv. Web Site: http://www.mullan.mctvusa.tv. ICA: ID0033.

TV Market Ranking: Outside TV Markets (MULLAN). Franchise award date: May 16, 2005. Franchise expiration date: N.A. Began: August 25, 1954.

Channel capacity: 60 (operating 2-way). Channels available but not in use: 12.

Basic Service

Subscribers: 219.

Programming (received off-air): KHQ-TV (NBC) Spokane; KREM (CBS) Spokane; allband FM.

Programming (via satellite): ABC Family Channel; Animal Planet; Arts & Entertainment; Bravo; Cartoon Network; Church Channel; CNN; Comedy Central; Country Music TV; C-SPAN; Discovery Channel; Disney Channel; ESPN; ESPN 2; Food Network; Headline News; HGTV; History Channel; JCTV; KAYU-TV (FOX) Spokane; KSPS-TV (PBS) Spokane; KXLY-TV (ABC, MNT) Spokane; Lifetime; Lifetime Movie Network; MTV; Nickelodeon; Outdoor Channel; QVC; Spike TV; Syfy; TBS Superstation; The Learning Channel; Toon Disney; Travel Channel; Trinity Broadcasting Network; Turner Classic Movies; Turner Network TV; TV Land; USA Network; VH1; Weather Channel; WGN America.

Current originations: Educational Access.

Fee: $15.00 installation; $41.00 monthly.

Pay Service 1

Pay Units: 96.

Programming (via satellite): Cinemax; HBO; The Movie Channel.

Video-On-Demand: No

Internet Service

Operational: Yes. Began: September 14, 2005.

Fee: $25.00 installation; $44.95 monthly; $30.00 modem purchase.

Telephone Service

None

Miles of Plant: 9.0 (coaxial); None (fiber optic). Homes passed: 420. Total homes in franchised area: 420.

Manager & Chief Technician: James R. Dahl.

Ownership: Mullan Cable TV Inc.

MURRAY—Formerly served by Rapid Cable. No longer in operation. ICA: ID0097.

NEW MEADOWS—Cable One. Now served by CALDWELL, ID [ID0008]. ICA: ID0082.

OROFINO—Suddenlink Communications, 227 Johnson Ave, Orofino, ID 83544. Phones: 314-965-2020; 800-326-8206; 208-476-5111. Fax: 208-752-9733. Web Site: http://www.suddenlink.com. Also serves Cottonwood, Craigmont, Grangeville, Headquarters, Kamiah, Nezperce, Peck, Pierce, Weippe & Winchester. ICA: ID0016.

TV Market Ranking: Below 100 (Craigmont, OROFINO, Peck, Winchester); Outside TV Markets (Cottonwood, Grangeville, Headquarters, Kamiah, Nezperce, Pierce, Weippe). Franchise award date: October 25, 1988. Franchise expiration date: N.A. Began: January 1, 1954.

Channel capacity: 150 (operating 2-way). Channels available but not in use: N.A.

Basic Service

Subscribers: 1,231.

Programming (received off-air): KAYU-TV (FOX) Spokane; KHQ-TV (NBC) Spokane; KLEW-TV (CBS) Lewiston; KREM (CBS) Spokane; KUID-TV (PBS) Moscow; KXLY-TV (ABC, MNT) Spokane; allband FM.

Programming (via satellite): ABC Family Channel; C-SPAN; Fox News Channel; Headline News; Northwest Cable News; WGN America.

Fee: $39.95 installation; $19.95 monthly.

Expanded Basic Service 1

Subscribers: N.A.

Programming (via satellite): AMC; Animal Planet; Arts & Entertainment; Cartoon Network; CNBC; CNN; Comcast Sports Net Northwest; Comedy Central; Discovery Channel; Disney Channel; ESPN; ESPN 2; Eternal Word TV Network; Great American Country; History Channel; Lifetime; MTV; Nickelodeon; Outdoor Channel; QVC; Spike TV; Style Network; TBS Superstation; The Learning Channel; Toon Disney; Turner Network TV; USA Network; VH1; Weather Channel.

Fee: $39.95 installation; $15.04 monthly.

Digital Basic Service

Subscribers: N.A.

Programming (via satellite): BBC America; Bravo; Discovery Digital Networks; DMX Music; Encore; ESPN Classic Sports; ESPNews; Fox Sports World; Golf Channel; GSN; HGTV; Independent Film Channel; Nick Jr.; Speed Channel; Starz (multiplexed); Syfy; Turner Classic Movies; Versus; VH1 Classic; VH1 Country; WE tv.

Fee: $3.95 monthly.

Pay Service 1

Pay Units: 286.

Programming (via satellite): Cinemax.

Fee: $15.00 installation; $10.00 monthly.

Pay Service 2

Pay Units: 411.

Programming (via satellite): HBO (multiplexed).

Fee: $15.00 installation; $11.00 monthly.

Pay Service 3

Pay Units: 325.

Programming (via satellite): The Movie Channel.

Fee: $9.95 monthly.

Pay Service 4

Pay Units: 382.

Programming (via satellite): Showtime.

Fee: $9.95 monthly.

Pay Service 5

Pay Units: 259.

Programming (via satellite): Encore; Starz.

Fee: $5.95 monthly.

Digital Pay Service 1

Pay Units: N.A.

Programming (via satellite): Cinemax (multiplexed); Flix; HBO (multiplexed); Showtime (multiplexed); The Movie Channel.

Video-On-Demand: No

Internet Service

Operational: Yes.

Broadband Service: Cebridge High Speed Cable Internet.

Fee: $99.99 installation; $24.95 monthly.

Telephone Service

None

Miles of Plant: 23.0 (coaxial); None (fiber optic). Additional miles planned: 7.0 (coaxial).

Manager: Sam Richardson. Chief Technician: Josh Kellburg. Marketing Director: Theresa Richardson.

City fee: 2% of gross & $500 annually.

Ownership: Cequel Communications LLC (MSO).

OSBURN—Suddenlink Communications, PO Box 868, 816 E Mullan St, Osburn, ID 83849. Phones: 800-326-8206; 208-752-1151. Fax: 208-752-9733. Web Site: http://www.suddenlink.com. Also serves Big Creek, Burke, Cataldo (portions), Elk Creek, Gem, Kellogg, Kingston, Kootenai County (portions), Page, Pinehurst, Silverton, Smelterville, Wallace, Wardner & Woodland Park. ICA: ID0015.

TV Market Ranking: Outside TV Markets (Big Creek, Burke, Cataldo (portions), Elk Creek, Gem, Kellogg, Kingston, Kootenai County (portions), OSBURN, Page, Pinehurst, Silverton, Smelterville, Wallace, Wardner, Woodland Park). Franchise award date: December 1, 1953. Franchise expiration date: N.A. Began: December 1, 1953.

Channel capacity: 49 (operating 2-way). Channels available but not in use: 1.

Basic Service

Subscribers: 3,898.

Programming (received off-air): KAYU-TV (FOX) Spokane; KHQ-TV (NBC) Spokane; KREM (CBS) Spokane; KSPS-TV (PBS) Spokane; KUID-TV (PBS) Moscow; KXLY-TV (ABC, MNT) Spokane; allband FM.

Programming (via satellite): ABC Family Channel; AMC; Animal Planet; Arts & Entertainment; Cartoon Network; CNBC; CNN; Comcast Sports Net Northwest; Comedy Central; C-SPAN; Discovery Channel; Disney Channel; E! Entertainment Television; ESPN; ESPN 2; Eternal Word TV Network; Fox News Channel; FX; Great American Country; Headline News; HGTV; History Channel; Lifetime; MTV; Nickelodeon; Northwest Cable News; Outdoor Channel; QVC; Spike TV; Style Network; Syfy; TBS Superstation; The Learning Channel; Toon Disney; Trinity Broadcasting Network; Turner Network TV; TV Land; USA Network; VH1; Weather Channel; WGN America.

Fee: $39.95 installation; $19.95 monthly.

Digital Basic Service

Subscribers: N.A.

Programming (via satellite): BBC America; Bravo; Discovery Digital Networks; Discovery Kids Channel; DMX Music; ESPN Classic Sports; ESPNews; Fox Sports World; Golf Channel; GSN; Nick Jr.; Speed Channel; Versus; VH1 Classic; VH1 Country; WE tv.

Fee: $3.95 monthly.

Pay Service 1

Pay Units: 328.

Programming (via satellite): Cinemax.

Fee: $10.00 monthly.

Pay Service 2

Pay Units: 459.

Programming (via satellite): HBO.

Fee: $35.00 installation; $11.00 monthly.

Pay Service 3
Pay Units: 305.
Programming (via satellite): The Movie Channel.
Fee: $20.00 installation; $9.95 monthly.

Pay Service 4
Pay Units: 349.
Programming (via satellite): Showtime.
Fee: $9.95 monthly.

Pay Service 5
Pay Units: 232.
Programming (via satellite): Encore; Starz.
Fee: $5.95 monthly (package).

Digital Pay Service 1
Pay Units: N.A.
Programming (via satellite): Cinemax (multiplexed); Encore (multiplexed); Flix; HBO (multiplexed); Independent Film Channel; Showtime (multiplexed); The Movie Channel (multiplexed); Turner Classic Movies.

Video-On-Demand: No

Pay-Per-View
Special events (delivered digitally).

Internet Service
Operational: Yes. Began: January 1, 2002.
Subscribers: 319.
Broadband Service: Cebridge High Speed Cable Internet.
Fee: $99.99 installation; $24.95 monthly; $10.00 modem lease.

Telephone Service
None

Miles of Plant: 150.0 (coaxial); None (fiber optic). Homes passed: 6,970.
Marketing Director: Teresa Richardson. Manager: Sam Richardson. Chief Technician: Josh Kellberg.
City fee: 3% of gross.
Ownership: Cequel Communications LLC (MSO).

POCATELLO—Cable One, 204 W Alameda Rd, Pocatello, ID 83201-4463. Phone: 208-232-1784. Fax: 208-234-4756. Web Site: http://www.cableone.net. Also serves American Falls, Bannock County, Chubbock & Inkom. ICA: ID0004.
TV Market Ranking: Below 100 (American Falls, Bannock County, Chubbock, Inkom, POCATELLO). Franchise award date: January 1, 1954. Franchise expiration date: N.A. Began: January 1, 1954.
Channel capacity: N.A. Channels available but not in use: N.A.

Basic Service
Subscribers: 13,572.
Programming (received off-air): KFXP (FOX) Pocatello; KIDK (CBS) Idaho Falls; KIFI-TV (ABC) Idaho Falls; KISU-TV (PBS) Pocatello; KPIF (IND) Pocatello; KPVI-DT (NBC) Pocatello; 14 FMs.
Programming (via microwave): KBYU-TV (PBS) Provo; KSL-TV (NBC) Salt Lake City.
Programming (via satellite): Cartoon Network; Disney Channel; ION Television; QVC; TV Guide Network.
Current originations: Government Access; Educational Access; Leased Access; Public Access.
Fee: $60.00 installation; $46.00 monthly; $.64 converter; $60.00 additional installation.

Expanded Basic Service 1
Subscribers: N.A.
Programming (via satellite): ABC Family Channel; AMC; Animal Planet; Arts & Entertainment; Bravo; CNBC; CNN; Comedy Central; Country Music TV; C-SPAN; C-SPAN 2; Discovery Channel; E! Entertainment Television; ESPN; ESPN 2; Fox News Channel; Fox Sports Net Rocky Mountain; FX; Headline News; HGTV; History Channel; Home Shopping Network; Jewelry Television; Lifetime; MSNBC; MTV; Nickelodeon; ShopNBC; Spike TV; Syfy; TBS Superstation; Telemundo; The Learning Channel; Travel Channel; Turner Classic Movies; Turner Network TV; TV Land; Univision; USA Network; VH1; Weather Channel.

Digital Basic Service
Subscribers: 7,114.
Programming (received off-air): KISU-TV (PBS) Pocatello.
Programming (via satellite): 3 Angels Broadcasting Network; Bio; Boomerang; BYU Television; Canales N; Discovery Digital Networks; ESPN Classic Sports; ESPNews; FamilyNet; Fox College Sports Atlantic; Fox College Sports Central; Fox College Sports Pacific; Fox Movie Channel; Fox Soccer; Fuel TV; G4; Golf Channel; GSN; Hallmark Channel; History Channel International; INSP; National Geographic Channel; Outdoor Channel; SoapNet; Speed Channel; Toon Disney; Trinity Broadcasting Network; truTV; Turner Network TV HD; Universal HD.
Fee: $45.95 monthly.

Digital Pay Service 1
Pay Units: 1,804.
Programming (via satellite): HBO (multiplexed).
Fee: $16.95 monthly.

Digital Pay Service 2
Pay Units: 1,036.
Programming (via satellite): Showtime (multiplexed); Showtime HD.
Fee: $15.15 monthly.

Digital Pay Service 3
Pay Units: 1,600.
Programming (via satellite): Cinemax (multiplexed).

Digital Pay Service 4
Pay Units: 982.
Programming (via satellite): Flix; Sundance Channel; The Movie Channel (multiplexed); The Movie Channel HD.

Digital Pay Service 5
Pay Units: 1,406.
Programming (via satellite): Encore (multiplexed).

Digital Pay Service 6
Pay Units: 1,363.
Programming (via satellite): Starz.

Video-On-Demand: No

Pay-Per-View
Addressable homes: 3,982.
iN Demand, Fee: $3.95, Fee: $8.95; Pleasure (delivered digitally); Ten Clips (delivered digitally); Ten Blox (delivered digitally); Ten Blue (delivered digitally); ESPN Now (delivered digitally); ESPN (delivered digitally).

Internet Service
Operational: Yes. Began: December 31, 2001.
Subscribers: 1,860.
Broadband Service: CableONE.net.
Fee: $75.00 installation; $43.00 monthly; $5.00 modem lease.

Telephone Service
Analog: Not Operational
Digital: Operational
Fee: $75.00 installation; $39.95 monthly

Miles of Plant: 277.0 (coaxial); None (fiber optic). Homes passed: 29,817. Total homes in franchised area: 29,817.
Manager: Judy Drennen. Chief Technician: Neil Ransbottom. Marketing Director: Nadine Singleton.
City fee: 3% of gross.
Ownership: Cable One Inc. (MSO).

PRESTON—Direct Communications, PO Box 270, 150 S Main St, Rockland, ID 83271. Phones: 866-675-1639; 208-547-4341. Fax: 208-548-9911. E-mail: marketing@directcom.com. Web Site: http://www.directcom.com. ICA: ID0094.
TV Market Ranking: 48 (PRESTON); Below 100 (PRESTON).
Channel capacity: N.A. Channels available but not in use: N.A.

Basic Service
Subscribers: 300.
Programming (received off-air): KBYU-TV (PBS) Provo; KIDK (CBS) Idaho Falls; KJZZ-TV (MNT) Salt Lake City; KSL-TV (NBC) Salt Lake City; KSTU (FOX) Salt Lake City; KTVX (ABC) Salt Lake City; KUED (PBS) Salt Lake City; KUTV (CBS) Salt Lake City.
Programming (via satellite): ABC Family Channel; AMC; Animal Planet; Arts & Entertainment; Cartoon Network; CNBC; CNN; Country Music TV; C-SPAN; Discovery Channel; Disney Channel; ESPN; Fox News Channel; Fox Sports Net Rocky Mountain; FX; Hallmark Channel; Lifetime; Nickelodeon; QVC; Spike TV; TBS Superstation; The Learning Channel; Turner Network TV; USA Network; Weather Channel.
Fee: $37.50 installation; $43.60 monthly.

Pay Service 1
Pay Units: N.A.
Programming (via satellite): Encore; HBO; Showtime; Starz.
Fee: $14.95 monthly.

Internet Service
Operational: Yes.
Fee: $35.95 monthly.

Telephone Service
None

General Manager: Howard Wisenberger.
Ownership: Independent Cable Systems of Idaho LLC (MSO).

PRICHARD—Formerly served by Rapid Cable. No longer in operation. ICA: ID0083.

RICHFIELD—Formerly served by WDB Communications. No longer in operation. ICA: ID0084.

RIGGINS—Elk River TV Cable Co., PO Box 154, 411 S Main St, Troy, ID 83871. Phones: 877-874-4900; 208-835-5654. Fax: 877-874-4900. Web Site: http://www.elkrivertv.net. Also serves Pollock. ICA: ID0037.
TV Market Ranking: Outside TV Markets (Pollock, RIGGINS). Franchise award date: January 8, 1980. Franchise expiration date: N.A. Began: January 1, 1963.
Channel capacity: 30 (not 2-way capable). Channels available but not in use: N.A.

Basic Service
Subscribers: 140.
Programming (received off-air): KAID (PBS) Boise; KBOI-TV (CBS) Boise; KIVI-TV (ABC) Nampa; KTVB (NBC) Boise; KXLY-TV (ABC, MNT) Spokane.
Programming (via satellite): ABC Family Channel; Arts & Entertainment; Discovery Channel; Disney Channel; Fox Sports Net West; Great American Country; Headline News; HGTV; History Channel; Northwest Cable News; Outdoor Channel; USA Network.
Fee: $39.95 installation; $15.95 monthly.

Expanded Basic Service 1
Subscribers: 77.
Programming (received off-air): KHQ-TV (NBC) Spokane; KREM (CBS) Spokane.
Programming (via satellite): AMC; CNN; ESPN; KAYU-TV (FOX) Spokane; Spike TV; TBS Superstation; Turner Network TV; WGN America.
Fee: $39.95 installation; $26.90 monthly.

Pay Service 1
Pay Units: 45.
Programming (via satellite): HBO.
Fee: $11.00 monthly.

Pay Service 2
Pay Units: 10.
Programming (via satellite): Showtime.
Fee: $9.95 monthly.

Internet Service
Operational: No.

Telephone Service
None

Miles of Plant: 18.0 (coaxial); None (fiber optic). Homes passed: 413.
Manager: Dave McGraw.; Leslie McGraw. Chief Technician: Justin McGraw.
City fee: None.
Ownership: Elk River TV Cable Co. (MSO).

SALMON—Independent Cable, 550 E 2nd S, Soda Springs, ID 83276. Phone: 208-547-4341. Fax: 208-547-4833. Web Site: http://www.icsofidaho.com. ICA: ID0098.
TV Market Ranking: Outside TV Markets (SALMON). Franchise award date: N.A. Franchise expiration date: N.A. Began: December 1, 2005.
Channel capacity: 58 (2-way capable). Channels available but not in use: N.A.

Basic Service
Subscribers: 410.
Programming (received off-air): KECI-TV (NBC) Missoula; KIDK (CBS) Idaho Falls; KIFI-TV (ABC) Idaho Falls; KISU-TV (PBS) Pocatello; KSL-TV (NBC) Salt Lake City.
Programming (via satellite): ABC Family Channel; AMC; Animal Planet; Arts & Entertainment; Bravo; BYU Television; Cartoon Network; CNBC; CNN; Comedy Central; Country Music TV; C-SPAN; C-SPAN 2; CW+; Discovery Channel; Disney Channel; ESPN; ESPN 2; Food Network; Fox News Channel; Fox Sports Net Rocky Mountain; FX; Hallmark Channel; Headline News; HGTV; History Channel; Home Shopping Network; ION Television; Lifetime; MSNBC; MTV; Nickelodeon; QVC; Spike TV; Syfy; TBS Superstation; The Learning Channel; Travel Channel; Turner Classic Movies; Turner Network TV; TV Guide Network; TV Land; USA Network; VH1; Weather Channel.
Fee: $39.25 monthly; $15.00 additional installation.

Digital Basic Service
Subscribers: N.A.
Programming (via satellite): Bio; Discovery Digital Networks; DMX Music; ESPN Classic Sports; ESPNews; Fox Movie Channel; Fox Sports World; G4; Golf Channel; History Channel International; National Geographic Channel; Outdoor Channel; Speed Channel; Toon Disney.
Fee: $4.50 monthly.

Digital Pay Service 1
Pay Units: N.A.
Programming (via satellite): Cinemax (multiplexed); Encore (multiplexed); HBO (multiplexed); Starz (multiplexed).
Fee: $9.95 monthly (Starz or Encore), $11.95 monthly (Cinemax), $14.95 monthly (HBO).

Pay-Per-View
iN DEMAND (delivered digitally).

Internet Service
Operational: Yes.
Fee: $19.95 monthly; $5.00 modem lease.

General Manager: Howard Wisenberger. Plant Manager: Dale Deno.
Ownership: Independent Cable Systems of Idaho LLC (MSO).

SANDPOINT—Northland Cable Television, PO Box 1488, 1305 Highway 2, Sandpoint, ID 83864. Phones: 208-263-4070; 800-233-4070. Fax: 208-263-1713. E-mail: sandpoint@northlandcabletv.com. Web Site: http://www.northlandcabletv.com. Also serves Dover, Kootenai, Ponderay, Sagle & Sandpoint (unincorporated areas). ICA: ID0012.
TV Market Ranking: Outside TV Markets (Dover, Kootenai, Ponderay, Sagle, SANDPOINT, Sandpoint (unincorporated areas)). Franchise award date: April 1, 1974. Franchise expiration date: N.A. Began: May 1, 1975.
Channel capacity: 45 (operating 2-way). Channels available but not in use: None.
Basic Service
Subscribers: 2,000.
Programming (received off-air): KAYU-TV (FOX) Spokane; KCDT (PBS) Coeur d'Alene; KHQ-TV (NBC) Spokane; KQUP (IND) Pullman; KREM (CBS) Spokane; KSPS-TV (PBS) Spokane; KXLY-TV (ABC, MNT) Spokane.
Programming (via satellite): Animal Planet; Arts & Entertainment; Cartoon Network; CNBC; CNN; Comcast Sports Net Northwest; Comedy Central; C-SPAN; CW+; Discovery Channel; ESPN; ESPN 2; Food Network; Fox Movie Channel; Fox News Channel; Great American Country; Hallmark Channel; Headline News; HGTV; History Channel; Lifetime; National Geographic Channel; Nickelodeon; Northwest Cable News; Outdoor Channel; QVC; Syfy; TBS Superstation; The Learning Channel; Travel Channel; Trinity Broadcasting Network; Turner Classic Movies; Turner Network TV; TV Land; USA Network; VH1; Weather Channel; WGN America.
Fee: $40.00 installation; $49.99 monthly.
Digital Basic Service
Subscribers: 200.
Programming (received off-air): KXLY-TV (ABC, MNT) Spokane.
Programming (via satellite): BBC America; Bloomberg Television; Bravo; Discovery Health Channel; Discovery Home Channel; Discovery Kids Channel; Discovery Military Channel; Discovery Times Channel; DMX Music; ESPNews; FitTV; Fox Soccer; G4; Golf Channel; Independent Film Channel; Science Television; Speed Channel; WE tv.
Fee: $5.00 monthly.
Pay Service 1
Pay Units: 155.
Programming (via satellite): Cinemax; HBO.
Fee: $20.00 installation; $14.00 monthly (HBO).
Digital Pay Service 1
Pay Units: N.A.
Programming (via satellite): Cinemax (multiplexed); Encore (multiplexed); Flix; HBO (multiplexed); Showtime (multiplexed); Starz (multiplexed); The Movie Channel (multiplexed).
Fee: $14.75 monthly (HBO, Cinemax, Starz/Encore or Showtime/TMC/Flix).
Video-On-Demand: Yes
Pay-Per-View
iN DEMAND (delivered digitally); Fresh (delivered digitally); Playboy TV (delivered digitally); Hot Choice (delivered digitally).
Internet Service
Operational: Yes.
Fee: $42.99 monthly.
Telephone Service
None
Miles of Plant: 76.0 (coaxial); None (fiber optic). Additional miles planned: 8.0 (coaxial). Homes passed: 4,000.
General Manager: Mary Strickley. Chief Technician: Justin Custis.
City fee: 5% of gross.
Ownership: Northland Communications Corp. (MSO).

SHOSHONE—Millennium Digital Media. Now served by TWIN FALLS, ID [ID0088]. ICA: ID0031.

SODA SPRINGS—Direct Communications, PO Box 270, 150 S Main St, Rockland, ID 83271. Phone: 208-547-4833. Fax: 208-548-9911. E-mail: marketing@directcom.com. Web Site: http://www.directcom.com. Also serves Bancroft, Downey, Georgetown, Grace, Lava Hot Springs, McCammon, Montpelier & Paris. ICA: ID0022.
TV Market Ranking: Below 100 (Bancroft, Lava Hot Springs, McCammon); Outside TV Markets (Downey, Georgetown, Grace, Montpelier, Paris, SODA SPRINGS). Franchise award date: N.A. Franchise expiration date: N.A. Began: January 1, 1955.
Channel capacity: 65 (not 2-way capable). Channels available but not in use: 7.
Basic Service
Subscribers: 1,619.
Programming (received off-air): KBYU-TV (PBS) Provo; KFXP (FOX) Pocatello; KIDK (CBS) Idaho Falls; KIFI-TV (ABC) Idaho Falls; KISU-TV (PBS) Pocatello; KJZZ-TV (MNT) Salt Lake City; KPNZ (IND) Ogden; KPVI-DT (NBC) Pocatello; KSL-TV (NBC) Salt Lake City; KTVX (ABC) Salt Lake City; KUCW (CW) Ogden; KUTV (CBS) Salt Lake City; 14 FMs.
Programming (via satellite): BYU Television; CNN; Discovery Channel; Fox News Channel; Lifetime; QVC; The Learning Channel; Travel Channel; TV Guide Network; Weather Channel; WGN America.
Current originations: Government Access; Educational Access; Public Access.
Fee: $19.00 monthly.
Expanded Basic Service 1
Subscribers: 1,243.
Programming (via satellite): ABC Family Channel; AMC; Animal Planet; Arts & Entertainment; BBC America; Boomerang; Bravo; Cartoon Network; CNBC; Comedy Central; Country Music TV; C-SPAN; Discovery Health Channel; Disney Channel; Do-It-Yourself; E! Entertainment Television; ESPN; ESPN 2; ESPN Classic Sports; Food Network; Fox Movie Channel; Fox Sports Net Rocky Mountain; FX; Gospel Music Channel; Great American Country; GSN; Hallmark Channel; Headline News; HGTV; History Channel; MoviePlex; MSNBC; MTV; National Geographic Channel; NFL Network; Nickelodeon; Outdoor Channel; RFD-TV; SoapNet; Speed Channel; Spike TV; Syfy; TBS Superstation; The Sportsman Channel; truTV; Turner Classic Movies; Turner Network TV; TV Land; USA Network; Versus; VH1; WE tv.
Fee: $18.95 monthly.
Video-On-Demand: No
Internet Service
Operational: Yes.
Subscribers: 320.
Fee: $23.95 monthly.
Telephone Service
None
Miles of Plant: 92.0 (coaxial); None (fiber optic).
General Manager: Howard Wisenberger.
City fee: 3% of basic gross.
Ownership: Independent Cable Systems of Idaho LLC (MSO).

SPIRIT LAKE—Formerly served by Cebridge Connections. Now served byTWIN LAKES, ID [ID0092]. ICA: ID0050.

ST. MARIES—Suddenlink Communications, PO Box 868, 816 E Mullan St, Osburn, ID 83849. Phones: 314-965-2020; 800-326-8206; 208-752-1151. Fax: 208-752-9733. Web Site: http://www.suddenlink.com. Also serves Milltown. ICA: ID0085.
TV Market Ranking: Outside TV Markets (Milltown, ST. MARIES). Franchise award date: N.A. Franchise expiration date: N.A. Began: March 1, 1959.
Channel capacity: 44 (operating 2-way). Channels available but not in use: None.
Basic Service
Subscribers: 830.
Programming (received off-air): KAYU-TV (FOX) Spokane; KHQ-TV (NBC) Spokane; KREM (CBS) Spokane; KSPS-TV (PBS) Spokane; KXLY-TV (ABC, MNT) Spokane; allband FM.
Programming (via satellite): C-SPAN; C-SPAN 2; KSKN (CW) Spokane; Northwest Cable News; WGN America.
Fee: $44.95 installation; $19.95 monthly.
Expanded Basic Service 1
Subscribers: N.A.
Programming (via satellite): ABC Family Channel; AMC; Arts & Entertainment; Cartoon Network; CNBC; CNN; Comcast Sports Net Northwest; Comedy Central; Discovery Channel; Disney Channel; E! Entertainment Television; ESPN; ESPN 2; Fox News Channel; Great American Country; Headline News; History Channel; Lifetime; MSNBC; MTV; Nickelodeon; Outdoor Channel; QVC; SoapNet; Spike TV; Style Network; Syfy; TBS Superstation; The Learning Channel; Toon Disney; Turner Network TV; USA Network; VH1; Weather Channel.
Fee: $39.95 installation; $16.04 monthly.
Digital Basic Service
Subscribers: N.A.
Programming (via satellite): BBC America; Bio; Bravo; Discovery Digital Networks; DMX Music; ESPN Classic Sports; ESPNews; Fox Soccer; Fuse; GAS; Golf Channel; GSN; HGTV; History Channel International; Independent Film Channel; Lifetime Movie Network; MTV Networks Digital Suite; Nick Jr.; Sleuth; Speed Channel; Turner Classic Movies; Versus; WE tv.
Pay Service 1
Pay Units: 154.
Programming (via satellite): Cinemax.
Fee: $15.00 installation; $10.00 monthly.
Pay Service 2
Pay Units: 92.
Programming (via satellite): HBO.
Fee: $11.00 monthly.
Pay Service 3
Pay Units: 136.
Programming (via satellite): The Movie Channel.
Fee: $9.95 monthly.
Pay Service 4
Pay Units: 232.
Programming (via satellite): Showtime.
Fee: $9.95 monthly.
Pay Service 5
Pay Units: 81.
Programming (via satellite): Encore; Starz.
Fee: $5.95 monthly.
Digital Pay Service 1
Pay Units: N.A.
Programming (via satellite): Cinemax (multiplexed); Encore (multiplexed); Flix; HBO (multiplexed); Showtime (multiplexed); Starz (multiplexed); The Movie Channel (multiplexed).
Video-On-Demand: No
Pay-Per-View
iN DEMAND (delivered digitally); Playboy TV (delivered digitally).
Internet Service
Operational: Yes.
Broadband Service: Cebridge High Speed Cable Internet.
Fee: $99.99 installation; $24.95 monthly.
Telephone Service
None
Miles of Plant: 50.0 (coaxial); None (fiber optic). Homes passed: 1,729.
Manager: Sam Richardson. Chief Technician: Josh Kellberg. Marketing Director: Teresa Richardson.
City fee: None.
Ownership: Cequel Communications LLC (MSO).

SUN VALLEY—Cox Communications, PO Box 537, 105 Lewis St, Ketchum, ID 83340-0537. Phone: 208-726-6041. Fax: 208-726-0178. Web Site: http://www.cox.com/idaho. Also serves Bellevue, Blaine County, Hailey & Ketchum. ICA: ID0079.
TV Market Ranking: Below 100 (Bellevue, Blaine County (portions), Hailey, Ketchum, SUN VALLEY); Outside TV Markets (Blaine County (portions)). Franchise award date: N.A. Franchise expiration date: N.A. Began: January 1, 1954.
Channel capacity: N.A. Channels available but not in use: N.A.
Basic Service
Subscribers: 10,600.
Programming (received off-air): KIPT (PBS) Twin Falls; KMVT (CBS) Twin Falls; KSAW-LD (ABC) Twin Falls; KSVT-LD (IND) Ketchum; KSVX-CD (ION) Hailey; KTFT-LP Twin Falls; KXTF (FOX) Twin Falls; allband FM.
Programming (via satellite): C-SPAN; C-SPAN 2; CW+; Headline News; Home Shopping Network; QVC; TBS Superstation; The Learning Channel; Travel Channel; TV Guide Network; Weather Channel; WGN America.
Fee: $38.00 installation; $23.50 monthly.
Expanded Basic Service 1
Subscribers: 6,000.
Programming (via satellite): ABC Family Channel; AMC; Animal Planet; Arts & Entertainment; Bravo; Cartoon Network; CNBC; CNN; Comedy Central; Country Music TV; C-SPAN 2; Discovery Channel; Disney Channel; E! Entertainment Television; ESPN; ESPN 2; Food Network; Fox News Channel; Fox Sports Net Rocky Mountain; FX; GalaVision; HGTV; History Channel; Lifetime; MSNBC; MTV; Nickelodeon; Speed Channel; Spike TV; Syfy; truTV; Turner Classic Movies; Turner Network TV; TV Land; Univision; USA Network; Versus; VH1.
Fee: $26.29 monthly.
Digital Basic Service
Subscribers: N.A.
Programming (received off-air): KIPT (PBS) Twin Falls.
Programming (via satellite): Animal Planet HD; Arts & Entertainment HD; Bandamax; BBC America; Bio; Bloomberg Television; Boomerang en Espanol; Bravo HD; Canal D; Canal Sur; Cine Latino; Cine Mexicano;

CMT Pure Country; CNBC HD+; CNN en Espanol; CNN HD; Cooking Channel; De Pelicula; De Pelicula Clasico; Discovery Channel HD; Discovery en Espanol; Discovery HD Theater; Discovery Health Channel; Discovery Kids Channel; Discovery Military Channel; Discovery Planet Green; Do-It-Yourself; Encore (multiplexed); ESPN 2 HD; ESPN Classic Sports; ESPN Deportes; ESPN HD; ESPN U; ESPNews; EWTN en Espanol; FitTV; Food Network HD; Fox Reality Channel; Fox Soccer; Fox Sports en Espanol; FSN HD; Fuel TV; Fuse; G4; GalaVision; Gol TV; Golf Channel; GSN; Hallmark Channel; Halogen Network; HGTV HD; History Channel en Espanol; History Channel HD; History Channel International; ID Investigation Discovery; Independent Film Channel; Lifetime Movie Network; Lifetime Television HD; MTV Hits; MTV Jams; MTV Tres; mun2 television; Music Choice; National Geographic Channel; National Geographic Channel HD Network; NBA TV; NFL Network; NFL Network HD; NHL Network; Nick Jr.; NickToons en Espanol; NickToons TV; Oxygen; Palladia; Ritmoson Latino; Science Channel; Science Channel HD; SoapNet; Sorpresa; Style Network; Sundance Channel; Syfy HD; TBN Enlace USA; TBS in HD; TeenNick; Telefutura; Telehit; Telemundo; Tennis Channel; TLC HD; Toon Disney; Travel Channel HD; Trinity Broadcasting Network; Turner Network TV HD; Universal HD; Univision; USA Network HD; Versus HD; VH1 Classic; Video Rola.
Fee: $25.49 monthly.

Digital Pay Service 1
Pay Units: N.A.
Programming (via satellite): Cinemax (multiplexed); Cinemax HD; Flix; HBO (multiplexed); HBO HD; HBO Latino; Showtime (multiplexed); Showtime HD; Starz; Starz HDTV; The Movie Channel (multiplexed).
Fee: $12.99 monthly (HBO, Cinemax, Starz or Showtime/TMC/Flix.

Video-On-Demand: No

Pay-Per-View
NHL Center Ice (delivered digitally); MLB Extra Innings (delivered digitally); MLS Direct Kick (delivered digitally); NBA League Pass (delivered digitally); Club Jenna (delivered digitally); iN DEMAND (delivered digitally); Playboy TV (delivered digitally); Hot Choice (delivered digitally); Fresh (delivered digitally); ESPN Gameplan (delivered digitally); ESPN Now (delivered digitally).

Internet Service
Operational: Yes. Began: December 31, 2000.
Broadband Service: Cox High Speed Internet.
Fee: $29.99-$56.99 monthly.

Telephone Service
Digital: Operational
Fee: $10.35-$49.95 monthly

Miles of Plant: 286.0 (coaxial); 33.0 (fiber optic). Homes passed: 15,498.

Vice President: Percy Kick. Vice President, Public & Government Affairs: Kristin Peck. Director of Operations: Dan Wherry. General Manager: Guy Cherp.

City fee: 3% of gross.

Ownership: Cox Communications Inc. (MSO).

TROY—Troy TV Cable Inc., PO Box 37, Troy, ID 83871-0037. Phone: 208-835-5624. Fax: 208-835-5573. ICA: ID0044.

TV Market Ranking: Below 100 (TROY). Franchise award date: June 1, 1953. Franchise expiration date: N.A. Began: September 1, 1953.

Channel capacity: 70 (operating 2-way). Channels available but not in use: 30.

Basic Service
Subscribers: 141.
Programming (received off-air): KAYU-TV (FOX) Spokane; KHQ-TV (NBC) Spokane; KLEW-TV (CBS) Lewiston; KREM (CBS) Spokane; KSKN (CW) Spokane; KUID-TV (PBS) Moscow; KWSU-TV (PBS) Pullman; KXLY-TV (ABC, MNT) Spokane; allband FM.
Programming (via satellite): AMC; Animal Planet; Arts & Entertainment; BYU Television; CNN; Comcast Sports Net Northwest; Comedy Central; Country Music TV; Discovery Channel; ESPN; ESPN 2; Eternal Word TV Network; HGTV; History Channel; Lifetime; National Geographic Channel; Nickelodeon; Northwest Cable News; Outdoor Channel; Spike TV; Syfy; TBS Superstation; The Learning Channel; Travel Channel; Turner Network TV; TV Land; USA Network; VH1.
Current originations: Educational Access.
Fee: $25.00 installation; $28.00 monthly; $2.00 converter; $15.00 additional installation.

Pay Service 1
Pay Units: N.A.
Programming (via satellite): The Movie Channel.
Fee: $25.00 installation; $10.00 monthly.

Video-On-Demand: No

Internet Service
Operational: Yes.
Subscribers: 110.
Fee: $112.00 installation; $32.00 monthly.

Telephone Service
Analog: Operational

Miles of Plant: 10.0 (coaxial); None (fiber optic). Homes passed: 350. Total homes in franchised area: 350.

President: Ellis Anderson. Chief Engineer: Dave McGraw.

City fee: None.

Ownership: Troy Television Co. Inc.

TWIN FALLS—Cable One, 261 Eastland Dr, Twin Falls, ID 83301. Phone: 208-733-6230. Fax: 208-733-6296. E-mail: russ.young@cableone.net. Web Site: http://www.cableone.net. Also serves Buhl, Burley, Cassia County (northern portion), Filer, Gooding, Gooding County (portions), Hagerman, Hansen, Heyburn, Jerome, Kimberly, Minidoka County (southern portion), Paul, Rupert, Shoshone, Twin Falls County (portions) & Wendell. ICA: ID0088.

TV Market Ranking: Below 100 (Buhl, Burley, Cassia County (portions), Filer, Gooding, Gooding County (portions), Hagerman, Hansen, Jerome, Kimberly, Minidoka County (portions), Paul, Shoshone, TWIN FALLS, Twin Falls County (portions), Wendell); Outside TV Markets (Cassia County (portions), Gooding County (portions), Heyburn, Minidoka County (portions), Rupert). Franchise award date: January 1, 1954. Franchise expiration date: N.A. Began: N.A.

Channel capacity: 78 (operating 2-way). Channels available but not in use: 10.

Basic Service
Subscribers: 16,600.
Programming (received off-air): KIPT (PBS) Twin Falls; KIVI-TV (ABC) Nampa; KMVT (CBS) Twin Falls; KSL-TV (NBC) Salt Lake City; KTFT-LP Twin Falls; KTRV-TV (FOX) Nampa; KXTF (FOX) Twin Falls.
Programming (via satellite): ABC Family Channel; AMC; Animal Planet; Arts & Entertainment; Bravo; Cartoon Network; CNBC; CNN; Comedy Central; Country Music TV; C-SPAN; C-SPAN 2; Discovery Channel; Disney Channel; E! Entertainment Television; ESPN; ESPN 2; ESPN Classic Sports; Food Network; Fox News Channel; Fox Sports Net Rocky Mountain; FX; GalaVision; Headline News; HGTV; History Channel; Home Shopping Network; INSP; Lifetime; MSNBC; MTV; Nickelodeon; QVC; ShopNBC; Spike TV; Syfy; TBS Superstation; Telefutura; Telemundo; The Learning Channel; Travel Channel; Turner Classic Movies; Turner Network TV; TV Guide Network; TV Land; Univision; USA Network; VH1; Weather Channel.
Fee: $44.95 installation; $46.00 monthly.

Digital Basic Service
Subscribers: 4,000.
Programming (via satellite): Bio; Boomerang; Discovery Digital Networks; ESPN Classic Sports; ESPNews; Fox College Sports Atlantic; Fox College Sports Central; Fox College Sports Pacific; Fox Movie Channel; Fox Soccer; Fuel TV; G4; Golf Channel; Great American Country; GSN; Hallmark Channel; History Channel International; INSP; Military History Channel; Music Choice (multiplexed); National Geographic Channel; Outdoor Channel; SoapNet; Speed Channel; Toon Disney; Trinity Broadcasting Network; truTV.
Fee: $49.44 monthly.

Digital Expanded Basic Service
Subscribers: 1,871.
Programming (via satellite): Canales N.
Fee: $4.00 installation; $4.00 monthly.

Digital Pay Service 1
Pay Units: 1,926.
Programming (via satellite): Cinemax (multiplexed); Encore (multiplexed); HBO (multiplexed); Showtime (multiplexed); Starz (multiplexed); The Movie Channel (multiplexed).

Video-On-Demand: No

Pay-Per-View
Addressable homes: 4,171.
ETC (delivered digitally); iN DEMAND; Playboy TV (delivered digitally); Fresh (delivered digitally); Shorteez (delivered digitally).

Internet Service
Operational: Yes. Began: April 1, 2002.
Subscribers: 7,200.
Broadband Service: CableONE.net.
Fee: $75.00 installation; $43.00 monthly; $5.00 modem lease.

Telephone Service
Analog: Not Operational
Digital: Operational
Fee: $75.00 installation; $39.95 monthly

Miles of Plant: 580.0 (coaxial); None (fiber optic). Homes passed: 41,500. Total homes in franchised area: 57,731.

Manager: Russ Young. Chief Technician: Todd Garcia.; Jay Preskek. Marketing Director: Mark Wolfe. Customer Service Manager: Eddy Cordova.

Ownership: Cable One Inc. (MSO).

TWIN LAKES—Suddenlink Communications, PO Box 868, 816 E Mullan St, Osburn, ID 83849. Phones: 800-326-8206; 314-965-2020; 208-752-1151. Fax: 208-752-9733. Web Site: http://www.suddenlink.com. Also serves Spirit Lake. ICA: ID0092.

TV Market Ranking: 76 (Spirit Lake); Below 100 (TWIN LAKES). Franchise award date: N.A. Franchise expiration date: N.A. Began: N.A.

Channel capacity: 43 (not 2-way capable). Channels available but not in use: None.

Basic Service
Subscribers: 1,065.
Programming (received off-air): KAYU-TV (FOX) Spokane; KHQ-TV (NBC) Spokane; KREM (CBS) Spokane; KSKN (CW) Spokane; KSPS-TV (PBS) Spokane; KUID-TV (PBS) Moscow; KXLY-TV (ABC, MNT) Spokane.
Programming (via satellite): ABC Family Channel; Animal Planet; Arts & Entertainment; Cartoon Network; CNBC; CNN; Comcast Sports Net Northwest; Comedy Central; C-SPAN; Discovery Channel; Disney Channel; E! Entertainment Television; ESPN; ESPN 2; Food Network; Fox News Channel; FX; Golf Channel; Great American Country; Headline News; HGTV; History Channel; INSP; Lifetime; MTV; Nickelodeon; Northwest Cable News; Outdoor Channel; QVC; Spike TV; Style Network; Syfy; TBS Superstation; The Learning Channel; Travel Channel; Turner Classic Movies; Turner Network TV; TV Land; USA Network; VH1; Weather Channel; WGN America.
Current originations: Educational Access.
Fee: $39.95 installation; $32.99 monthly.

Digital Basic Service
Subscribers: N.A.
Programming (via satellite): BBC America; Bio; Bravo; Discovery Digital Networks; DMX Music; ESPN Classic Sports; ESPNews; Fox Soccer; Fuse; GAS; GSN; History Channel International; Independent Film Channel; Lifetime Movie Network; MTV Networks Digital Suite; Nick Jr.; Sleuth; Speed Channel; Toon Disney; Versus; WE tv.

Pay Service 1
Pay Units: N.A.
Programming (via satellite): Showtime.
Fee: $10.00 monthly.

Pay Service 2
Pay Units: 70.
Programming (via satellite): HBO.
Fee: $11.00 monthly.

Pay Service 3
Pay Units: 33.
Programming (via satellite): The Movie Channel.
Fee: $10.00 monthly.

Digital Pay Service 1
Pay Units: N.A.
Programming (via satellite): Cinemax (multiplexed); Encore (multiplexed); Flix; HBO (multiplexed); Showtime (multiplexed); Starz (multiplexed); The Movie Channel (multiplexed).

Video-On-Demand: No

Pay-Per-View
iN DEMAND (delivered digitally); Playboy TV (delivered digitally).

Internet Service
Operational: Yes.

Telephone Service
Digital: Operational

Miles of Plant: 131.0 (coaxial); None (fiber optic). Homes passed: 1,484.

Marketing Director: Teresa Richardson. Manager: Sam Richardson. Chief Technician: Josh Kellberg.

Ownership: Cequel Communications LLC (MSO).

VICTOR—Independent Cable, PO Box 858, Soda Springs, ID 83276-0858. Phone: 800-295-3562. Fax: 208-547-4833. Web Site: http://www.icsofidaho.com. Also serves Driggs. ICA: ID0062.

TV Market Ranking: Below 100 (Driggs, VICTOR). Franchise award date: N.A. Franchise expiration date: N.A. Began: N.A.

Channel capacity: 53 (not 2-way capable). Channels available but not in use: N.A.

Basic Service
Subscribers: 134.
Programming (received off-air): KIDK (CBS) Idaho Falls; KIFI-TV (ABC) Idaho

Falls; KISU-TV (PBS) Pocatello; KPVI-DT (NBC) Pocatello.
Programming (via satellite): ABC Family Channel; Arts & Entertainment; Cartoon Network; CNBC; CNN; Discovery Channel; Disney Channel; ESPN; FX; HGTV; Spike TV; TBS Superstation; Turner Classic Movies; Turner Network TV; USA Network; WGN America.
Fee: $29.95 installation; $32.45 monthly.
Pay Service 1
Pay Units: 46.
Programming (via satellite): HBO.
Fee: $10.00 installation; $9.00 monthly.
Video-On-Demand: No
Internet Service
Operational: No.
Telephone Service
None
Miles of Plant: 5.0 (coaxial); None (fiber optic). Homes passed: 440.
General Manager: Howard Wisenberger. Plant Manager: Dale Deno.
City fee: 5% of gross annually.
Ownership: Independent Cable Systems of Idaho LLC (MSO).

WEISER—Cable One. Now served by CALDWELL, ID [ID0008]. ICA: ID0018.

WORLEY—Elk River TV Cable Co., PO Box 154, 411 S Main St, Troy, ID 83871. Phones: 877-874-4900; 208-835-5654. Fax: 208-835-5573. E-mail: leslie@elkrivertv.net. Web Site: http://www.elkrivertv.net. Also serves Plummer. ICA: ID0046.
TV Market Ranking: 76 (Plummer, WORLEY). Franchise award date: N.A. Franchise expiration date: N.A. Began: November 26, 1984.
Channel capacity: 42 (operating 2-way). Channels available but not in use: N.A.
Basic Service
Subscribers: 194.
Programming (received off-air): KAYU-TV (FOX) Spokane; KGPX-TV (ION) Spokane; KHQ-TV (NBC) Spokane; KREM (CBS) Spokane; KSKN (CW) Spokane; KSPS-TV (PBS) Spokane; KXLY-TV (ABC, MNT) Spokane.
Programming (via satellite): ABC Family Channel; Arts & Entertainment; Cartoon Network; CNN; Comcast Sports Net Northwest; Country Music TV; Discovery Channel; Disney Channel; ESPN; ESPN 2; History Channel; Lifetime; Nickelodeon; Northwest Cable News; Outdoor Channel; QVC; Spike TV; Syfy; TBS Superstation; The Learning Channel; Turner Classic Movies; Turner Network TV; TV Land; USA Network; Weather Channel; WGN America.
Fee: $35.00 installation; $34.75 monthly.
Pay Service 1
Pay Units: 39.
Programming (via satellite): HBO.
Fee: $10.00 installation; $10.95 monthly.
Video-On-Demand: No
Internet Service
Operational: No.
Telephone Service
None
Miles of Plant: 18.0 (coaxial); None (fiber optic). Additional miles planned: 2.0 (coaxial). Homes passed: 320. Total homes in franchised area: 340.
Manager: Dave McGraw.; Leslie McGraw. Chief Technician: Justin McGraw.
City fee: 3% of gross.
Ownership: Elk River TV Cable Co. (MSO).

ILLINOIS

Total Systems:	**280**	**Communities with Applications:**	**0**
Total Communities Served:	**1,301**	**Number of Basic Subscribers:**	**2,611,290**
Franchises Not Yet Operating:	**0**	**Number of Expanded Basic Subscribers:**	**602,683**
Applications Pending:	**0**	**Number of Pay Units:**	**312,275**

Top 100 Markets Represented: St. Louis (11); Chicago (3); Davenport, IA-Rock Island-Moline, IL (60); Springfield-Decatur-Champaign (64); Cape Girardeau, MO-Paducah, KY-Harrisburg, IL (69); Peoria (83); Evansville, IN (86); Rockford-Freeport (97).

For a list of cable communities in this section, see the Cable Community Index located in the back of Cable Volume 2.
For explanation of terms used in cable system listings, see p. D-11.

ABINGDON—Mediacom, PO Box 334, 609 S 4th St, Chillicothe, IL 61523. Phone: 309-274-4500. Fax: 309-274-3188. Web Site: http://www.mediacomcable.com. Also serves Avon & Maquon. ICA: IL0186.

TV Market Ranking: 83 (Maquon); Outside TV Markets (ABINGDON, Avon). Franchise award date: N.A. Franchise expiration date: N.A. Began: March 1, 1980.

Channel capacity: N.A. Channels available but not in use: N.A.

Basic Service

Subscribers: 1,343.

Programming (received off-air): KLJB (CW, FOX) Davenport; WAOE (MNT) Peoria; WEEK-TV (NBC) Peoria; WHOI (ABC, CW) Peoria; WMBD-TV (CBS) Peoria; WQAD-TV (ABC) Moline; WTVP (PBS) Peoria; WYZZ-TV (FOX) Bloomington.

Programming (via satellite): WGN America.

Fee: $45.00 installation; $20.95 monthly.

Expanded Basic Service 1

Subscribers: 866.

Programming (via satellite): ABC Family Channel; AMC; AmericanLife TV Network; Animal Planet; Arts & Entertainment; BET Networks; Bravo; Cartoon Network; CNBC; CNN; Comcast SportsNet Chicago; Comedy Central; Country Music TV; C-SPAN; C-SPAN 2; CW+; Discovery Channel; Disney Channel; E! Entertainment Television; ESPN; ESPN 2; Eternal Word TV Network; FitTV; Food Network; Fox News Channel; FX; Hallmark Channel; Headline News; HGTV; History Channel; Home Shopping Network; INSP; ION Television; Jewelry Television; Lifetime; Lifetime Movie Network; MSNBC; MTV; Nickelodeon; Product Information Network; QVC; Radar Channel; ShopNBC; SoapNet; Speed Channel; Spike TV; Syfy; TBS Superstation; The Learning Channel; Travel Channel; Trinity Broadcasting Network; truTV; Turner Network TV; TV Guide Network; TV Land; Univision; USA Network; VH1; WE tv; Weather Channel.

Fee: $34.00 monthly.

Digital Basic Service

Subscribers: N.A.

Programming (received off-air): WEEK-TV (NBC) Peoria; WHOI (ABC, CW) Peoria; WMBD-TV (CBS) Peoria; WTVP (PBS) Peoria; WYZZ-TV (FOX) Bloomington.

Programming (via satellite): ABC News Now; BBC America; Bio; Bloomberg Television; CCTV-9 (CCTV International); College Sports Television; Discovery Health Channel; Discovery Kids Channel; Discovery Military Channel; Discovery Planet Green; Discovery Times Channel; ESPN U; ESPNews; Fox College Sports Atlantic; Fox College Sports Central; Fox College Sports Pacific; Fox Movie Channel; Fox Reality Channel; Fox Soccer; Fuel TV; Fuse; G4; Gol TV; Golf Channel; GSN; History Channel International; Independent Film Channel; ION Life; Lifetime Movie Network; MTV Hits; MTV2; Music Choice; National Geographic Channel; Nick Jr.; NickToons TV; Outdoor Channel; Qubo; ReelzChannel; Science Channel; Sleuth; Style Network; Sundance Channel; TeenNick; Tennis Channel; The Sportsman Channel; Turner Classic Movies; TVG Network; Versus; VH1 Classic.

Fee: $9.00 monthly.

Digital Expanded Basic Service

Subscribers: N.A.

Programming (via satellite): Discovery HD Theater; ESPN 2 HD; ESPN HD; HDNet; HDNet Movies; Universal HD.

Fee: $6.95 monthly.

Digital Pay Service 1

Pay Units: N.A.

Programming (via satellite): Cinemax (multiplexed); Cinemax On Demand; Encore (multiplexed); Flix; HBO (multiplexed); HBO HD; HBO On Demand; Showtime (multiplexed); Showtime HD; Showtime On Demand; Starz (multiplexed); Starz HDTV; Starz On Demand; Sundance Channel; The Movie Channel (multiplexed); The Movie Channel HD; The Movie Channel On Demand.

Fee: $11.95 monthly (HBO, Cinemax, Starz/Encore or Showtime/TMC).

Video-On-Demand: Yes

Pay-Per-View

iN DEMAND (delivered digitally); Playboy TV (delivered digitally); Ten Clips (delivered digitally); Sports PPV (delivered digitally).

Internet Service

Operational: Yes.

Broadband Service: Mediacom High Speed Internet.

Fee: $59.95 installation; $45.95 monthly.

Telephone Service

Digital: Operational

Fee: $39.95 installation; $39.95 monthly

Miles of Plant: 123.0 (coaxial); None (fiber optic). Homes passed: 2,122.

Vice President: Don Hagwell. Operations Director: Gary Wightman. Technical Operations Manager: Larry Brackman. Marketing Director: Stephanie Law.

City fee: 5% of gross.

Ownership: Mediacom LLC (MSO).

ADAIR (unincorporated areas)—Formerly served by CableDirect. No longer in operation. ICA: IL0439.

ADDIEVILLE—Charter Communications. Now served by WOODLAWN, IL [IL0067]. ICA: IL0633.

ALBION—NewWave Communications, One Montgomery Plaza, 4th Fl, Sikeston, MO 63801. Phones: 888-863-9928 (Customer service); 573-472-9500. Fax: 573-481-9809. E-mail: info@newwavecom.com. Web Site: http://www.newwavecom.com. ICA: IL0457.

TV Market Ranking: Outside TV Markets (ALBION). Franchise award date: September 3, 1981. Franchise expiration date: N.A. Began: N.A.

Channel capacity: 136 (operating 2-way). Channels available but not in use: N.A.

Basic Service

Subscribers: 371.

Programming (received off-air): KFVS-TV (CBS, CW) Cape Girardeau; WEHT (ABC) Evansville; WEVV-TV (CBS, MNT) Evansville; WFIE (NBC) Evansville; WNIN (PBS) Evansville; WPXS (IND) Mount Vernon; WSIL-TV (ABC) Harrisburg; WTVW (FOX) Evansville; WUSI-TV (PBS) Olney.

Programming (via satellite): C-SPAN; C-SPAN 2 (multiplexed); Home Shopping Network; INSP; QVC; Spike TV; Trinity Broadcasting Network; WGN America.

Current originations: Educational Access.

Fee: $41.11 installation; $25.20 monthly.

Expanded Basic Service 1

Subscribers: 349.

Programming (via satellite): ABC Family Channel; AMC; Animal Planet; Arts & Entertainment; Big Ten Network; Bravo; Cartoon Network; CNBC; CNN; Comedy Central; Country Music TV; Discovery Channel; Disney Channel; E! Entertainment Television; ESPN; ESPN 2; ESPN Classic Sports; Eternal Word TV Network; Food Network; Fox News Channel; Fox Sports Net Midwest; FX; Golf Channel; GSN; Hallmark Channel; Headline News; HGTV; History Channel; Lifetime; MSNBC; MTV; National Geographic Channel; Nickelodeon; Outdoor Channel; Oxygen; ShopNBC; SoapNet; Speed Channel; Syfy; TBS Superstation; The Learning Channel; Toon Disney; Travel Channel; truTV; Turner Classic Movies; Turner Network TV; TV Land; USA Network; Versus; VH1; Weather Channel.

Digital Basic Service

Subscribers: 33.

Programming (received off-air): WEHT (ABC) Evansville; WEVV-TV (CBS, MNT) Evansville; WFIE (NBC) Evansville; WSIL-TV (ABC) Harrisburg; WTVW (FOX) Evansville.

Programming (via satellite): BBC America; Bio; Bloomberg Television; CMT Pure Country; Cooking Channel; Discovery HD Theater; Discovery Health Channel; Discovery Home Channel; Discovery Kids Channel; Discovery Military Channel; Do-It-Yourself; ESPN 2 HD; ESPN HD; ESPNews; FitTV; Fox College Sports Atlantic; Fox College Sports Central; Fox College Sports Pacific; Fox Movie Channel; FSN HD; G4; Great American Country; Halogen Network; HDNet; HDNet Movies; History Channel International; ID Investigation Discovery; Independent Film Channel; Lifetime Movie Network; MTV Hits; MTV Jams; MTV2; Music Choice; Nick Jr.; Nick Too; NickToons TV; RFD-TV; Science Channel; Sleuth; Style Network; TeenNick; Turner Network TV HD; Universal HD; VH1 Classic; VH1 Soul.

Digital Pay Service 1

Pay Units: N.A.

Programming (via satellite): Cinemax (multiplexed); Cinemax HD; Encore (multiplexed); Flix; HBO (multiplexed); HBO HD; Showtime (multiplexed); Starz (multiplexed); Starz HDTV; The Movie Channel (multiplexed).

Video-On-Demand: No

Pay-Per-View

iN DEMAND (delivered digitally); Spice: Xcess (delivered digitally); Club Jenna (delivered digitally); Playboy TV (delivered digitally); Fresh (delivered digitally); Shorteez (delivered digitally).

Internet Service

Operational: Yes.

Fee: $40.00 installation; $31.99 monthly.

Telephone Service

None

Miles of Plant: 21.0 (coaxial); None (fiber optic). Homes passed: 1,182.

General Manager: Bill Flowers. Technical Operations Manager: Chris Mooday.

City fee: 3% of gross.

Ownership: NewWave Communications (MSO).

ALEXANDER COUNTY (portions)—Galaxy Cablevision, 7155 US Hwy 45 S, Carrier Mills, IL 62917. Phone: 618-994-2261. Fax: 618-994-2261. Web Site: http://www.galaxycable.com. Also serves East Cape Girardeau, Honey School Lookout, McClure, Olive Branch, Pankeyville, Pulaski, Pulaski County, Thebes & Ullin. ICA: IL0458.

TV Market Ranking: 69 (ALEXANDER COUNTY (PORTIONS), East Cape Girardeau, Honey School Lookout, McClure, Olive Branch, Pankeyville, Pulaski, Pulaski County, Thebes, Ullin). Franchise award date: N.A. Franchise expiration date: N.A. Began: N.A.

Channel capacity: 61 (not 2-way capable). Channels available but not in use: None.

Basic Service

Subscribers: 259.

Programming (received off-air): KBSI (FOX) Cape Girardeau; KFVS-TV (CBS, CW) Cape Girardeau; WDKA (MNT) Paducah; WKPD (PBS) Paducah; WPSD-TV (NBC) Paducah; WSIL-TV (ABC) Harrisburg; WTCT (IND) Marion.

Programming (via satellite): ABC Family Channel; AMC; Animal Planet; Arts & Entertainment; BET Networks; Cartoon Network; CNN; Comedy Central; C-SPAN; Discovery Channel; Disney Channel; E! Entertainment Television; ESPN; ESPN 2; Fox News Channel; Fuse; FX; Great American Country; Headline News; HGTV; History Chan-

nel; Lifetime; Outdoor Channel; QVC; TBS Superstation; The Learning Channel; Toon Disney; Turner Classic Movies; Turner Network TV; USA Network; Weather Channel; WGN America.
Fee: $41.70 monthly.

Digital Basic Service
Subscribers: 43.

Pay Service 1
Pay Units: N.A.
Programming (via satellite): Encore; HBO; Showtime; The Movie Channel.

Internet Service
Operational: No.

Telephone Service
None

Miles of Plant: 45.0 (coaxial); None (fiber optic). Homes passed: 1,375.
State Manager: Ward Webb. Customer Service Manager: Malynda Walker. Engineer: John Stewart. Technical Manager: Audie Murphy.
Ownership: Galaxy Cable Inc. (MSO).

ALEXIS—Mediacom. Now served by MINERAL, IL [IL0170]. ICA: IL0302.

ALHAMBRA—Madison Communications. Now served by STAUNTON, IL [IL0171]. ICA: IL0367.

ALPHA—Diverse Communications Inc., PO Box 117, 246 N Division St, Woodhull, IL 61490-0117. Phone: 309-334-2150. Fax: 309-334-2989. E-mail: woodhulltel@yahoo.com. Web Site: http://www.woodhulltel.com. Also serves New Windsor, Ophiem & Woodhull. ICA: IL0459.
TV Market Ranking: 60 (ALPHA, New Windsor, Ophiem, Woodhull). Franchise award date: N.A. Franchise expiration date: N.A. Began: July 1, 1984.
Channel capacity: 65 (not 2-way capable). Channels available but not in use: 1.

Basic Service
Subscribers: 369.
Programming (received off-air): KIIN (PBS) Iowa City; KLJB (CW, FOX) Davenport; KWQC-TV (NBC) Davenport; WAOE (MNT) Peoria; WCIU-TV (IND) Chicago; WEEK-TV (NBC) Peoria; WHBF-TV (CBS) Rock Island; WHOI (ABC, CW) Peoria; WMBD-TV (CBS) Peoria; WQAD-TV (ABC) Moline; WQPT-TV (PBS) Moline; WTVP (PBS) Peoria.
Programming (via satellite): ABC Family Channel; AMC; Animal Planet; Arts & Entertainment; CNBC; CNN; Comcast SportsNet Chicago; Comedy Central; Country Music TV; Discovery Channel; Disney Channel; ESPN; ESPN 2; ESPN Classic Sports; ESPNews; Fox News Channel; Fox Sports Net Midwest; FX; Headline News; HGTV; History Channel; Lifetime; MSNBC; MTV; National Geographic Channel; Nickelodeon; QVC; RFD-TV; Spike TV; Syfy; TBS Superstation; The Learning Channel; Travel Channel; Turner Network TV; TV Land; USA Network; VH1; Weather Channel; WGN America.
Current originations: Public Access.
Fee: $35.00 installation; $30.00 monthly; $2.00 converter.

Digital Basic Service
Subscribers: 141.
Programming (via satellite): BBC America; Big Ten Network; Bio; Bloomberg Television; Boomerang; Bravo; Cartoon Network; CMT Pure Country; Court TV; C-SPAN; C-SPAN 2; Discovery Health Channel; Discovery Home Channel; Discovery Kids Channel; Discovery Military Channel; Discovery Times Channel; Do-It-Yourself; E! Entertainment Television; Eternal Word TV Network; Food Network; Fox Movie Channel; Fox Soccer; FSN Digital Atlantic; FSN Digital Central; FSN Digital Pacific; Fuse; G4; Golf Channel; Great American Country; GSN; Hallmark Channel; History Channel International; Independent Film Channel; ION Television; Lifetime Movie Network; Lifetime Real Women; MTV Hits; MTV2; Music Choice; NFL Network; Nick Jr.; NickToons TV; Outdoor Channel; Oxygen; Science Channel; ShopNBC; SoapNet; Speed Channel; TeenNick; Toon Disney; Trinity Broadcasting Network; Turner Classic Movies; Versus; VH1 Classic; VH1 Soul; WE tv.
Fee: $44.95 monthly.

Pay Service 1
Pay Units: 50.
Programming (via satellite): Cinemax; HBO.
Fee: $40.00 installation; $10.00 monthly (Cinemax), $12.00 monthly (HBO).

Digital Pay Service 1
Pay Units: N.A.
Programming (via satellite): Cinemax (multiplexed); Encore (multiplexed); HBO (multiplexed); Showtime (multiplexed); Starz (multiplexed).
Fee: $10.00 monthly (Cinemax, Showtime, or Starz & Encore), $12.00 monthly (HBO).

Internet Service
Operational: No, DSL & dial-up.

Telephone Service
None

Miles of Plant: 22.0 (coaxial); None (fiber optic).
Manager: George Wirt. Chief Technician: Jeremy Hand.
Ownership: Diverse Communications Inc.

ALSEY TWP.—Formerly served by Longview Communications. No longer in operation. ICA: IL0454.

ALTAMONT—Mediacom, PO Box 288, 4290 Blue Stem Rd, Charleston, IL 61920. Phone: 217-348-5533. Fax: 217-345-7074. Web Site: http://www.mediacomcable.com. Also serves St. Elmo. ICA: IL0160.
TV Market Ranking: Outside TV Markets (ALTAMONT, St. Elmo). Franchise award date: N.A. Franchise expiration date: N.A. Began: January 1, 1968.
Channel capacity: N.A. Channels available but not in use: N.A.

Basic Service
Subscribers: 1,477.
Programming (received off-air): KMOV (CBS) St. Louis; KPLR-TV (CW) St. Louis; KSDK (NBC) St. Louis; WAND (NBC) Decatur; WBUI (CW) Decatur; WCCU (FOX) Urbana; WCFN (MNT) Springfield; WCIA (CBS) Champaign; WEIU-TV (PBS) Charleston; WICS (ABC) Springfield; WILL-TV (PBS) Urbana; WPXS (IND) Mount Vernon; WSIU-TV (PBS) Carbondale; WTHI-TV (CBS) Terre Haute; WTWO (NBC) Terre Haute; allband FM.
Programming (via satellite): C-SPAN; Home Shopping Network; QVC; WGN America.
Fee: $45.00 installation; $20.95 monthly.

Expanded Basic Service 1
Subscribers: N.A.
Programming (via satellite): ABC Family Channel; American Movie Classics; Animal Planet; Arts & Entertainment; Cartoon Network; CNBC; CNN; Comedy Central; Country Music TV; C-SPAN 2; Discovery Channel; Disney Channel; E! Entertainment Television; ESPN; ESPN 2; ESPN Classic Sports; Eternal Word TV Network; Food Network; Fox News Channel; Fox Sports Net Midwest; Fuse; FX; Hallmark Channel; Headline News; HGTV; History Channel; INSP; ION Television; Jewelry Television; Lifetime; Lifetime Movie Network; MSNBC; MTV; Nickelodeon; Outdoor Channel; Product Information Network; ShopNBC; Speed Channel; Spike TV; Syfy; TBS Superstation; The Learning Channel; Travel Channel; Trinity Broadcasting Network; truTV; Turner Network TV; TV Guide Network; TV Land; USA Network; VH1; WE tv; Weather Channel.
Fee: $34.00 monthly.

Digital Basic Service
Subscribers: N.A.
Programming (received off-air): WAND (NBC) Decatur; WCCU (FOX) Urbana; WCIA (CBS) Champaign; WICS (ABC) Springfield; WILL-TV (PBS) Urbana; WTHI-TV (CBS) Terre Haute.
Programming (via satellite): ABC News Now; AmericanLife TV Network; BBC America; Bio; Bloomberg Television; Bravo; CCTV-Entertainment; CMT Pure Country; Discovery Digital Networks; Discovery HD Theater; ESPN 2 HD; ESPN HD; ESPNews; FitTV; Fox Movie Channel; Fox Reality Channel; Fox Soccer; G4; Golf Channel; GSN; HDNet; HDNet Movies; History Channel International; Independent Film Channel; ION Life; Lifetime Real Women; Military History Channel; MTV Hits; MTV2; Music Choice; National Geographic Channel; Nick Jr.; NickToons TV; Qubo; ReelzChannel; Science Channel; Sleuth; Style Network; TeenNick; Turner Classic Movies; Universal HD; Versus; VH1 Classic.
Fee: $9.00 monthly.

Digital Expanded Basic Service
Subscribers: N.A.
Programming (via satellite): College Sports Television; ESPN U; Fox College Sports Atlantic; Fox College Sports Central; Fox College Sports Pacific; Fuel TV; Gol TV; Tennis Channel; The Sportsman Channel; TVG Network.
Fee: $3.95 monthly.

Digital Pay Service 1
Pay Units: N.A.
Programming (via satellite): Cinemax (multiplexed); Encore (multiplexed); HBO (multiplexed); HBO HD; Showtime (multiplexed); Showtime HD; Starz (multiplexed); Starz HDTV; The Movie Channel (multiplexed); The Movie Channel HD.
Fee: $11.95 monthly (each).

Video-On-Demand: Yes

Pay-Per-View
iN DEMAND (delivered digitally); Playboy TV (delivered digitally); Ten Clips (delivered digitally); Ten Blox (delivered digitally); ESPN (delivered digitally); HDNet (delivered digitally).

Internet Service
Operational: Yes.
Broadband Service: Mediacom High Speed Internet.
Fee: $59.95 installation; $40.95 monthly.

Telephone Service
Digital: Operational
Fee: $39.95 installation; $39.95 monthly

Miles of Plant: 38.0 (coaxial); None (fiber optic). Homes passed: 1,832. Total homes in franchised area: 1,859.
Area Operations Director: Todd Acker. Technical Operations Manager: Jerry Ferguson.
City fee: 2% of gross.
Ownership: Mediacom LLC (MSO).

ALTONA—Mediacom. Now served by MINERAL, IL [IL0170]. ICA: IL0369.

AMBOY—Comcast Cable, 4450 Kishwaukee St, Rockford, IL 61101. Phone: 815-395-8890. Fax: 815-395-8901. Web Site: http://www.comcast.com. Also serves Lee County (southern portion). ICA: IL0689.
TV Market Ranking: Below 100 (AMBOY, Lee County (southern portion)).
Channel capacity: N.A. Channels available but not in use: N.A.

Basic Service
Subscribers: N.A. Included in Rockford
Programming (received off-air): KWQC-TV (NBC) Davenport; WHBF-TV (CBS) Rock Island; WIFR (CBS) Freeport; WQAD-TV (ABC) Moline; WQPT-TV (PBS) Moline; WQRF-TV (FOX) Rockford; WREX (CW, NBC) Rockford; WTTW (PBS) Chicago; WTVO (ABC, MNT) Rockford.
Programming (via satellite): C-SPAN; C-SPAN 2; CW+; Eternal Word TV Network; Home Shopping Network; QVC; TV Guide Network; WGN America.
Fee: $44.00 installation; $8.00 monthly.

Digital Basic Service
Subscribers: N.A.
Programming (received off-air): KWQC-TV (NBC) Davenport; WHBF-TV (CBS) Rock Island; WQAD-TV (ABC) Moline (multiplexed); WQRF-TV (FOX) Rockford; WTTW (PBS) Chicago.
Programming (via satellite): ABC Family HD; Animal Planet HD; Arts & Entertainment HD; BBC America; Bio; Bloomberg Television; CMT Pure Country; CNN HD; Cooking Channel; C-SPAN 3; Discovery Channel HD; Discovery HD Theater; Discovery Health Channel; Discovery Kids Channel; Discovery Military Channel; Discovery Planet Green; Disney Channel HD; Do-It-Yourself; Encore (multiplexed); ESPN 2 HD; ESPN Classic Sports; ESPN HD; ESPNews; FitTV; Flix; Food Network HD; Fox Business Channel; Fox Movie Channel; Fox Reality Channel; Fox Soccer; Fuse; G4; Golf Channel; GSN; HGTV HD; History Channel HD; History Channel International; ID Investigation Discovery; Independent Film Channel; Lifetime Movie Network; Mojo Mix; MTV Hits; MTV Jams; MTV Tres; MTV2; National Geographic Channel HD Network; NFL Network HD; Nick Jr.; Nick Too; NickToons TV; Outdoor Channel; PBS Kids Sprout; Science Channel; Si TV; SoapNet; Style Network; Sundance Channel; Syfy HD; TBS in HD; TeenNick; Tennis Channel; TLC HD; Toon Disney; Trinity Broadcasting Network; Turner Classic Movies; Turner Network TV HD; TV Land; USA Network HD; Versus; Versus HD; VH1 Classic; VH1 Soul; WE tv.
Fee: $15.95 monthly.

Digital Expanded Basic Service
Subscribers: N.A.
Programming (via satellite): CBS College Sports Network; Fox College Sports Atlantic; Fox College Sports Central; Fox College Sports Pacific; Fox Movie Channel; Fox Soccer; Gol TV; HorseRacing TV; NBA TV; NFL Network; NHL Network; Outdoor Channel; Tennis Channel; The Sportsman Channel; TVG Network.
Fee: $4.00 monthly.

Digital Expanded Basic Service 2
Subscribers: N.A.
Programming (via satellite): HDNet; HDNet Movies.
Fee: $6.99 monthly.

Digital Pay Service 1
Pay Units: N.A.
Programming (via satellite): Cinemax; Cinemax HD; HBO (multiplexed); HBO HD; Playgirl TV; Showtime (multiplexed); Showtime

HD; Starz (multiplexed); Starz HDTV; The Movie Channel (multiplexed).
Fee: $10.00 monthly (HBO, Cinemax, Starz, Showtime/TMC or Playboy).
Video-On-Demand: Yes
Pay-Per-View
iN DEMAND (delivered digitally); Penthouse TV (delivered digitally); Spice: Xcess (delivered digitally); Fresh (delivered digitally); Playboy TV (delivered digitally); Club Jenna (delivered digitally); ESPN (delivered digitally).
Internet Service
Operational: Yes.
Broadband Service: Comcast High Speed Internet.
Fee: $44.95 monthly.
Telephone Service
Digital: Operational
Homes passed & miles of plant included in Rockford
District Director: Joseph Browning. Technical Operations Manager: Lyle Matejewski. Program Director: Janice Schultz. Community & Government Affairs Manager: Joan Sage.
Ownership: Comcast Cable Communications Inc. (MSO).

ANDERSONVILLE—RCN Corp. Formerly served by Chicago (portions), IL [IL0661]. This cable system has converted to IPTV, 196 Van Buren St, Herndon, VA 20170. Phone: 703-434-8200. Web Site: http://www.rcn.com. ICA: IL5237.
TV Market Ranking: 3 (ANDERSONVILLE).
Channel capacity: N.A. Channels available but not in use: N.A.
Basic Service
Subscribers: N.A.
Fee: $59.94 monthly.
Expanded Basic Service 1
Subscribers: N.A.
Fee: $74.89 monthly.
Expanded Basic Service 2
Subscribers: N.A.
Fee: $8.99 monthly.
Pay Service 1
Pay Units: N.A.
Fee: $11.95 monthly (Cinemaz or Starz!); $16.95 monthly (Showtime/The Movie Channel); $17.95 monthly (HBO).
Internet Service
Operational: Yes.
Fee: $23.00 monthly.
Telephone Service
Digital: Operational
Fee: $30.00 monthly
Chairman: Steven J. Simmons. Chief Executive Officer: Jim Holanda.
Ownership: RCN Corp.

ANNA—NewWave Communications, One Montgomery Plaza, 4th Fl, Sikeston, MO 63801. Phones: 888-863-9928 (Customer service); 573-472-9500. Fax: 573-481-9809. E-mail: info@newwavecom.com. Web Site: http://www.newwavecom.com. Also serves Jonesboro & Union County (portions). ICA: IL0127.
TV Market Ranking: 69 (ANNA, Jonesboro, Union County (portions)). Franchise award date: N.A. Franchise expiration date: N.A. Began: December 15, 1977.
Channel capacity: 118 (operating 2-way). Channels available but not in use: N.A.
Basic Service
Subscribers: 841.
Programming (received off-air): KBSI (FOX) Cape Girardeau; KFVS-TV (CBS, CW) Cape Girardeau; WDKA (MNT) Paducah; WPSD-TV (NBC) Paducah; WSIL-TV (ABC) Harrisburg; WSIU-TV (PBS) Carbondale; WTCT (IND) Marion.
Programming (via satellite): C-SPAN; Home Shopping Network; QVC; WGN America.
Current originations: Government Access; Educational Access; Public Access.
Fee: $45.00 installation; $20.15 monthly; $.98 converter.
Expanded Basic Service 1
Subscribers: 752.
Programming (via satellite): ABC Family Channel; AMC; Animal Planet; Arts & Entertainment; Cartoon Network; CNBC; CNN; Comedy Central; Country Music TV; Discovery Channel; Disney Channel; E! Entertainment Television; ESPN; ESPN 2; Food Network; Fox News Channel; Fox Sports Net Midwest; FX; G4; Headline News; HGTV; History Channel; Lifetime; MSNBC; MTV; National Geographic Channel; Nickelodeon; Oxygen; Speed Channel; Spike TV; Syfy; TBS Superstation; The Learning Channel; Travel Channel; truTV; Turner Network TV; TV Land; USA Network; VH1; Weather Channel.
Fee: $24.80 monthly.
Digital Basic Service
Subscribers: 263.
Programming (via satellite): BBC America; Bio; Bloomberg Television; Discovery Digital Networks; Do-It-Yourself; GAS; GSN; History Channel International; Independent Film Channel; MTV Networks Digital Suite; Music Choice; Nick Jr.; Nick Too; NickToons TV; Science Television; SoapNet; Style Network; Sundance Channel; Toon Disney; TV Guide Interactive Inc.; WE tv.
Digital Pay Service 1
Pay Units: 889.
Programming (via satellite): Cinemax (multiplexed); Encore; Flix; HBO (multiplexed); LOGO; Showtime (multiplexed); Starz (multiplexed); The Movie Channel (multiplexed).
Fee: $9.50 monthly (each).
Video-On-Demand: No
Pay-Per-View
iN DEMAND (delivered digitally); Pleasure (delivered digitally); ETC (delivered digitally).
Internet Service
Operational: Yes.
Fee: $40.00 installation; $31.99 monthly.
Telephone Service
None
Miles of Plant: 66.0 (coaxial); None (fiber optic). Homes passed: 3,134.
General Manager: Bill Flowers. Technical Operations Manager: Chris Mooday.
City fee: 3% of gross.
Ownership: NewWave Communications (MSO).

APOLLO ACRES—Mediacom, PO Box 334, 609 S 4th St, Chillicothe, IL 61523. Phones: 800-874-2924; 309-274-4500. Fax: 309-274-3188. Web Site: http://www.mediacomcable.com. Also serves Danvers, Deer Creek, Goodfield, Hopedale, Hudson, Mackinaw, Mackinaw Trailer Park, Minier & Stanford. ICA: IL0340.
TV Market Ranking: 83 (Danvers, Deer Creek, Goodfield, Hopedale, Hudson, Mackinaw, Mackinaw Trailer Park, Minier, Stanford); Below 100 (APOLLO ACRES). Franchise award date: July 1, 1983. Franchise expiration date: N.A. Began: May 1, 1984.
Channel capacity: 134 (operating 2-way). Channels available but not in use: 9.
Basic Service
Subscribers: 3,091.
Programming (received off-air): WAOE (MNT) Peoria; WEEK-TV (NBC) Peoria; WHOI (ABC, CW) Peoria; WILL-TV (PBS) Urbana; WMBD-TV (CBS) Peoria; WTVP (PBS) Peoria; WYZZ-TV (FOX) Bloomington.
Programming (via satellite): ABC Family Channel; WGN America.
Fee: $45.00 installation; $20.95 monthly.
Expanded Basic Service 1
Subscribers: N.A.
Programming (via satellite): AMC; Animal Planet; Arts & Entertainment; Bravo; Cartoon Network; CNN; Comcast SportsNet Chicago; Comedy Central; Country Music TV; C-SPAN; C-SPAN 2; Disney Channel; E! Entertainment Television; ESPN; ESPN 2; Food Network; Fox News Channel; Hallmark Channel; Headline News; HGTV; History Channel; Home Shopping Network; Lifetime; MTV; Nickelodeon; Product Information Network; QVC; Speed Channel; Spike TV; Syfy; TBS Superstation; The Learning Channel; Travel Channel; Trinity Broadcasting Network; Turner Network TV; TV Guide Network; TV Land; USA Network; VH1; Weather Channel.
Fee: $34.00 monthly.
Digital Basic Service
Subscribers: N.A.
Programming (received off-air): WEEK-TV (NBC) Peoria; WHOI (ABC, CW) Peoria; WMBD-TV (CBS) Peoria; WTVP (PBS) Peoria; WYZZ-TV (FOX) Bloomington.
Programming (via satellite): ABC News Now; BBC America; Bio; Bloomberg Television; CCTV-9 (CCTV International); College Sports Television; Discovery Channel; Discovery Health Channel; Discovery Kids Channel; Discovery Military Channel; Discovery Planet Green; Discovery Times Channel; ESPN 2 HD; ESPN HD; ESPN U; ESPNews; Fox College Sports Atlantic; Fox College Sports Central; Fox College Sports Pacific; Fox Movie Channel; Fox Reality Channel; Fox Soccer; Fuel TV; Fuse; G4; Gol TV; Golf Channel; GSN; History Channel International; Independent Film Channel; ION Life; Lifetime Real Women; MTV Hits; MTV2; Music Choice; National Geographic Channel; Nick Jr.; NickToons TV; Outdoor Channel; Qubo; ReelzChannel; Science Channel; Sleuth; Style Network; Sundance Channel; TeenNick; Tennis Channel; The Sportsman Channel; Turner Classic Movies; TVG Network; Versus; VH1 Classic.
Fee: $9.00 monthly.
Digital Expanded Basic Service
Subscribers: N.A.
Programming (via satellite): Discovery HD Theater; HDNet; HDNet Movies; Universal HD.
Fee: $6.95 monthly.
Digital Pay Service 1
Pay Units: N.A.
Programming (via satellite): Cinemax (multiplexed); Cinemax On Demand; Flix; HBO (multiplexed); HBO HD; HBO On Demand; Showtime (multiplexed); Showtime HD; Showtime On Demand; Starz (multiplexed); Starz HDTV; Starz On Demand; Sundance Channel; The Movie Channel (multiplexed); The Movie Channel HD; The Movie Channel On Demand.
Fee: $11.95 monthly (HBO, Cinemax, Starz/Encore or Showtime/TMC).
Video-On-Demand: Yes
Internet Service
Operational: Yes.
Broadband Service: Mediacom High Speed Internet.
Fee: $59.95 installation; $45.95 monthly.
Telephone Service
Analog: Not Operational
Digital: Operational
Fee: $39.95 installation; $39.95 monthly
Miles of Plant: None (coaxial); 8.0 (fiber optic). Homes passed: 5,169. Miles of plant (coax) included in Roanoke
Vice President: Don Hagwell. Operations Director: Gary Wightman. Technical Operations Manager: Larry Brackman. Chief Technician: Scott Rocke. Marketing Director: Stephanie Law.
Ownership: Mediacom LLC (MSO).

ARENZVILLE—Mediacom, PO Box 288, 4290 Blue Stem Rd, Charleston, IL 61920. Phone: 217-348-5533. Fax: 217-345-7074. Web Site: http://www.mediacomcable.com. ICA: IL0391.
TV Market Ranking: Outside TV Markets (ARENZVILLE). Franchise award date: N.A. Franchise expiration date: N.A. Began: March 1, 1984.
Channel capacity: 121 (not 2-way capable). Channels available but not in use: 87.
Basic Service
Subscribers: 116.
Programming (received off-air): KHQA-TV (ABC, CBS) Hannibal; WAND (NBC) Decatur; WGEM-TV (CW, NBC) Quincy; WHOI (ABC, CW) Peoria; WICS (ABC) Springfield; WRSP-TV (FOX) Springfield; WSEC (PBS) Jacksonville; WTVP (PBS) Peoria.
Programming (via satellite): ABC Family Channel; Arts & Entertainment; CNN; Country Music TV; C-SPAN; Discovery Channel; ESPN; ESPN 2; Food Network; HGTV; History Channel; Home Shopping Network; Lifetime; Nickelodeon; Speed Channel; Spike TV; Syfy; TBS Superstation; Travel Channel; truTV; Turner Classic Movies; Turner Network TV; USA Network; Weather Channel; WGN America.
Fee: $45.00 installation; $47.95 monthly.
Pay Service 1
Pay Units: 33.
Programming (via satellite): Cinemax; HBO.
Fee: $1.95 monthly (Cinemax), $13.50 monthly (HBO).
Video-On-Demand: No
Internet Service
Operational: No.
Telephone Service
None
Miles of Plant: 4.0 (coaxial); 1.0 (fiber optic). Homes passed: 193.
Area Operations Director: Todd Acker. Technical Operations Manager: Jerry Ferguson.
City fee: 3% of gross.
Ownership: Mediacom LLC (MSO).

ARGENTA—Suddenlink Communications, PO Box 218, Poplar Bluff, MO 63901. Phones: 314-965-2020; 573-686-6387. Web Site: http://www.suddenlink.com. Also serves Oreana. ICA: IL0228.
TV Market Ranking: 64 (ARGENTA, Oreana). Franchise award date: January 8, 1980. Franchise expiration date: N.A. Began: March 1, 1982.
Channel capacity: 40 (operating 2-way). Channels available but not in use: 5.
Basic Service
Subscribers: 596.
Programming (received off-air): WAND (NBC) Decatur; WBUI (CW) Decatur; WCFN (MNT) Springfield; WCIA (CBS) Champaign; WICS (ABC) Springfield; WILL-TV (PBS) Urbana; WRSP-TV (FOX) Springfield.
Programming (via satellite): C-SPAN; Home Shopping Network; WGN America.
Fee: $45.00 installation; $15.95 monthly.

Expanded Basic Service 1
Subscribers: N.A.
Programming (via satellite): ABC Family Channel; AMC; Animal Planet; Arts & Entertainment; CNN; Comcast SportsNet Chicago; C-SPAN 2; Discovery Channel; Disney Channel; ESPN; ESPN 2; Fox News Channel; Fox Sports Net Midwest; FX; Great American Country; Hallmark Channel; HGTV; History Channel; Lifetime; MTV; Nickelodeon; Radar Channel; Speed Channel; Spike TV; Syfy; TBS Superstation; The Learning Channel; Toon Disney; Trinity Broadcasting Network; Turner Network TV; TV Land; USA Network; VH1; Weather Channel.
Fee: $25.00 monthly.

Digital Basic Service
Subscribers: N.A.
Programming (via satellite): BBC America; Bio; Bloomberg Television; Discovery Digital Networks; ESPN Classic Sports; ESPNews; Fox College Sports Atlantic; Fox College Sports Central; Fox College Sports Pacific; Fox Movie Channel; Fox Soccer; Fuse; Golf Channel; GSN; History Channel International; Independent Film Channel; Lifetime Movie Network; Military History Channel; National Geographic Channel; Outdoor Channel; Science Television; ShopNBC; Turner Classic Movies; Versus; WE tv.
Fee: $3.95 monthly.

Pay Service 1
Pay Units: 58.
Programming (via satellite): Cinemax; Encore; HBO.
Fee: $25.00 installation; $3.99 monthly (Encore), $7.95 monthly (Cinemax), $11.99 monthly (HBO).

Digital Pay Service 1
Pay Units: N.A.
Programming (via satellite): Cinemax (multiplexed); Encore (multiplexed); Flix; HBO (multiplexed); Showtime (multiplexed); Starz (multiplexed); The Movie Channel (multiplexed).

Video-On-Demand: No

Pay-Per-View
iN DEMAND (delivered digitally); Playboy TV (delivered digitally); Fresh (delivered digitally).

Internet Service
Operational: Yes. Began: November 1, 2004.
Fee: $99.99 installation; $24.95 monthly.

Telephone Service
None

Miles of Plant: 31.0 (coaxial); None (fiber optic). Homes passed: 892.
Manager: James Robinson. Chief Technician: Chris Marsh.
City fee: 3% of basic.
Ownership: Cequel Communications LLC (MSO).

ARMINGTON (village)—Heartland Cable Inc., PO Box 7, 167 W 5th St, Minonk, IL 61760. Phones: 800-448-4320; 309-432-2075. Fax: 309-432-2500. Web Site: http://www.heartlandcable.com. ICA: IL0419.
TV Market Ranking: 83 (ARMINGTON (VILLAGE)). Franchise award date: July 1, 1987. Franchise expiration date: N.A. Began: January 1, 1988.
Channel capacity: 60 (2-way capable). Channels available but not in use: 20.

Basic Service
Subscribers: 80.
Programming (received off-air): WEEK-TV (NBC) Peoria; WHOI (ABC, CW) Peoria; WMBD-TV (CBS) Peoria; WTVP (PBS) Peoria; WYZZ-TV (FOX) Bloomington.
Programming (via satellite): ABC Family Channel; CNN; Discovery Channel; Disney Channel; ESPN; Spike TV; Syfy; TBS Superstation; Turner Network TV; USA Network; Weather Channel; WGN America.
Fee: $39.00 installation; $32.90 monthly.

Pay Service 1
Pay Units: 10.
Programming (via satellite): HBO.
Fee: $10.95 monthly.

Pay Service 2
Pay Units: N.A.
Programming (via satellite): Showtime.
Fee: $8.95 monthly.

Video-On-Demand: Yes

Internet Service
Operational: No.

Telephone Service
None

Miles of Plant: 3.0 (coaxial); None (fiber optic). Homes passed: 140. Total homes in franchised area: 140.
Manager: Steve Allen.
Ownership: Heartland Cable Inc. (Illinois) (MSO).

ARMSTRONG—Park TV & Electronics Inc., PO Box 9, 205 E Fire Ln, Cissna Park, IL 60924. Phone: 815-457-2659. Fax: 815-457-2735. ICA: IL0678.
TV Market Ranking: 64 (ARMSTRONG). Franchise award date: N.A. Franchise expiration date: N.A. Began: N.A.
Channel capacity: N.A. Channels available but not in use: N.A.

Basic Service
Subscribers: N.A. Included in Cissna Park
Programming (received off-air): WAND (NBC) Decatur; WBUI (CW) Decatur; WCCU (FOX) Urbana; WCIA (CBS) Champaign; WICD (ABC) Champaign; WILL-TV (PBS) Urbana.
Programming (via satellite): ABC Family Channel; Animal Planet; Arts & Entertainment; CNN; Country Music TV; Discovery Channel; E! Entertainment Television; ESPN; ESPN 2; History Channel; Lifetime; Nickelodeon; QVC; Spike TV; TBS Superstation; Travel Channel; Trinity Broadcasting Network; Turner Network TV; USA Network; WGN America.
Fee: $35.00 installation; $23.50 monthly.

Pay Service 1
Pay Units: N.A.
Programming (via satellite): HBO.
Fee: $10.50 monthly.

Video-On-Demand: No

Internet Service
Operational: Yes.
Broadband Service: West Michigan Internet Service.
Fee: $99.00 installation; $39.95 monthly.

Telephone Service
None

Homes passed & miles of plant included in Cissna Park
Manager: Joe Young.
Ownership: Park TV & Electronics Inc. (MSO).

ASTORIA—Mediacom, PO Box 334, 609 S 4th St, Chillicothe, IL 61523. Phone: 309-274-4500. Fax: 309-274-3188. Web Site: http://www.mediacomcable.com. ICA: IL0258.
TV Market Ranking: Outside TV Markets (ASTORIA). Franchise award date: N.A. Franchise expiration date: N.A. Began: November 1, 1981.
Channel capacity: N.A. Channels available but not in use: N.A.

Basic Service
Subscribers: 234.
Programming (received off-air): WEEK-TV (NBC) Peoria; WHOI (ABC, CW) Peoria; WMBD-TV (CBS) Peoria; WRSP-TV (FOX) Springfield; WTVP (PBS) Peoria.
Programming (via satellite): ABC Family Channel; AMC; Animal Planet; Arts & Entertainment; Cartoon Network; CNN; Comedy Central; Country Music TV; Discovery Channel; ESPN; ESPN 2; Fox Sports Net; Headline News; HGTV; History Channel; Home Shopping Network; INSP; Lifetime; Nickelodeon; Speed Channel; Spike TV; Syfy; TBS Superstation; The Learning Channel; Trinity Broadcasting Network; Turner Network TV; TV Land; USA Network; Weather Channel; WGN America.
Fee: $45.00 installation; $47.95 monthly.

Pay Service 1
Pay Units: 88.
Programming (via satellite): Cinemax; HBO.
Fee: $7.95 monthly (Cinemax), $13.50 monthly (HBO).

Video-On-Demand: No

Internet Service
Operational: No.

Telephone Service
None

Miles of Plant: 7.0 (coaxial); None (fiber optic). Homes passed: 596.
Vice President: Don Hagwell. Operations Director: Gary Wightman. Technical Operations Manager: Larry Brackman. Marketing Director: Stephanie Law.
City fee: None.
Ownership: Mediacom LLC (MSO).

ATLANTA—Mediacom, PO Box 334, 609 S 4th St, Chillicothe, IL 61523. Phone: 309-274-4500. Fax: 309-274-3188. Web Site: http://www.mediacomcable.com. Also serves McLean & Waynesville. ICA: IL0197.
TV Market Ranking: 64 (McLean, Waynesville); 64,83 (ATLANTA). Franchise award date: N.A. Franchise expiration date: N.A. Began: September 1, 1982.
Channel capacity: 134 (operating 2-way). Channels available but not in use: 3.

Basic Service
Subscribers: 675.
Programming (received off-air): WAND (NBC) Decatur; WAOE (MNT) Peoria; WCCU (FOX) Urbana; WCIA (CBS) Champaign; WEEK-TV (NBC) Peoria; WHOI (ABC, CW) Peoria; WICS (ABC) Springfield; WILL-TV (PBS) Urbana; WMBD-TV (CBS) Peoria; WPXU-TV (ION, MNT) Jacksonville; WYZZ-TV (FOX) Bloomington.
Programming (via satellite): WGN America.
Fee: $45.00 installation; $20.95 monthly.

Expanded Basic Service 1
Subscribers: 605.
Programming (via satellite): ABC Family Channel; AMC; AmericanLife TV Network; Animal Planet; Arts & Entertainment; BET Networks; Bravo; Cartoon Network; CNBC; CNN; Comcast SportsNet Chicago; Comedy Central; Country Music TV; C-SPAN; C-SPAN 2; Discovery Channel; Disney Channel; E! Entertainment Television; ESPN; ESPN 2; Eternal Word TV Network; Food Network; Fox News Channel; Fuse; FX; Hallmark Channel; Halogen Network; Headline News; HGTV; History Channel; Home Shopping Network; ION Television; Lifetime; MSNBC; MTV; Nickelodeon; Product Information Network; QVC; ShopNBC; Speed Channel; Spike TV; Syfy; TBS Superstation; The Learning Channel; Travel Channel; Trinity Broadcasting Network; truTV; Turner Network TV; TV Guide Network; TV Land; Univision; USA Network; VH1; WE tv; Weather Channel; Weatherscan.
Fee: $34.00 monthly.

Digital Basic Service
Subscribers: N.A.
Programming (via satellite): BBC America; Bio; Bloomberg Television; Discovery Digital Networks; ESPNews; Fox Movie Channel; Fox Soccer; G4; GAS; Golf Channel; GSN; History Channel International; Independent Film Channel; Lifetime Movie Network; Lime; MTV Networks Digital Suite; Music Choice; National Geographic Channel; Nick Jr.; NickToons TV; Outdoor Channel; Sleuth; Style Network; Sundance Channel (multiplexed); Turner Classic Movies; Versus.
Fee: $9.00 monthly.

Digital Expanded Basic Service
Subscribers: N.A.
Programming (via satellite): Discovery HD Theater; ESPN 2 HD; ESPN HD; HDNet; HDNet Movies; INHD (multiplexed); Universal HD.
Fee: $6.95 monthly.

Digital Pay Service 1
Pay Units: N.A.
Programming (via satellite): Cinemax (multiplexed); Encore (multiplexed); Flix (multiplexed); HBO (multiplexed); HBO HD; Showtime (multiplexed); Showtime HD; Starz (multiplexed); Starz HDTV; The Movie Channel (multiplexed); The Movie Channel HD.

Video-On-Demand: Yes

Pay-Per-View
iN DEMAND (delivered digitally); Playboy TV (delivered digitally); ESPN (delivered digitally); Fox Sports Net (delivered digitally).

Internet Service
Operational: Yes, DSL only.
Broadband Service: Mediacom High Speed Internet.
Fee: $59.95 installation; $45.95 monthly.

Telephone Service
Analog: Not Operational
Digital: Operational
Fee: $39.95 installation; $39.95 monthly

Miles of Plant: 37.0 (coaxial); None (fiber optic). Homes passed: 1,316.
Vice President: Don Hagwell. Operations Director: Gary Wightman. Technical Operations Manager: Lary Brackman. Marketing Director: Stephanie Law.
City fee: 1% of gross.
Ownership: Mediacom LLC (MSO).

AUGUSTA—Adams Telephone. This cable system has converted to IPTV. See Augusta, IL [IL5282]. ICA: IL0356.

AUGUSTA (village)—Adams Telecom. Formerly [IL0356]. This cable system has converted to IPTV, PO Box 248, 405 Emminga Rd, Golden, IL 62339. Phone: 217-696-4411. E-mail: service@adams.net. Web Site: http://www.adams.net. ICA: IL5282.
Channel capacity: N.A. Channels available but not in use: N.A.

Internet Service
Operational: Yes.

Ownership: Adams Telephone Co-Operative.

AURORA—Comcast Cable. Now served by OAK BROOK, IL [IL0006]. ICA: IL0017.

AVA—Longview Communications, 12007 Sunrise Valley Dr, Ste 375, Reston, VA 20191. Phones: 866-611-6565 (Customer service); 703-476-9101. Fax: 703-476-9107. Web Site: http://www.longviewcomm.com. Also serves Campbell Hill, Cutler & Willisville. ICA: IL0461.
TV Market Ranking: Below 100 (AVA, Campbell Hill); Outside TV Markets (Cutler,

Willisville). Franchise award date: N.A. Franchise expiration date: N.A. Began: N.A.

Channel capacity: 36 (not 2-way capable). Channels available but not in use: 1.

Basic Service

Subscribers: 92.

Programming (received off-air): KBSI (FOX) Cape Girardeau; KDNL-TV (ABC) St. Louis; KFVS-TV (CBS, CW) Cape Girardeau; WBII-CD Holly Springs; WPSD-TV (NBC) Paducah; WPXS (IND) Mount Vernon; WSIL-TV (ABC) Harrisburg; WSIU-TV (PBS) Carbondale; WTCT (IND) Marion.

Programming (via satellite): C-SPAN; QVC.

Fee: $17.98 monthly.

Expanded Basic Service 1

Subscribers: N.A.

Programming (via satellite): ABC Family Channel; AMC; Animal Planet; Arts & Entertainment; CNN; Comedy Central; Discovery Channel; Disney Channel; E! Entertainment Television; ESPN; ESPN 2; Headline News; History Channel; Lifetime; TBS Superstation; The Learning Channel; Travel Channel; Turner Network TV; USA Network; Weather Channel; WGN America.

Fee: $17.97 monthly.

Pay Service 1

Pay Units: N.A.

Programming (via satellite): Showtime; The Movie Channel.

Fee: $8.95 monthly (TMC), $10.95 monthly (Showtime).

Video-On-Demand: No

Internet Service

Operational: No.

Telephone Service

None

Miles of Plant: 30.0 (coaxial); None (fiber optic). Homes passed: 958.

President: John Long. Senior Vice President: Marc W. Cohen. General Manager: Brandon Dickey. Technical Manager: Steve Boss.

Ownership: Longview Communications (MSO).

AVON—Mediacom. Now served by ABINGDON, IL [IL0186]. ICA: IL0300.

BARDOLPH—Formerly served by CableDirect. No longer in operation. ICA: IL0462.

BARRINGTON HILLS—Comcast Cable. Now served by SCHAUMBURG, IL [IL0036]. ICA: IL0110.

BARRY—Crystal Broadband Networks, PO Box 180336, Chicago, IL 60618. Phones: 877-319-0328; 630-206-0447. E-mail: info@crystalbn.com. Web Site: http://crystalbn.com. ICA: IL0262.

TV Market Ranking: Below 100 (BARRY). Franchise award date: September 2, 1980. Franchise expiration date: N.A. Began: February 1, 1982.

Channel capacity: 62 (operating 2-way). Channels available but not in use: 1.

Basic Service

Subscribers: 193.

Programming (received off-air): KETC (PBS) St. Louis; KHQA-TV (ABC, CBS) Hannibal; KMOV (CBS) St. Louis; KPLR-TV (CW) St. Louis; KSDK (NBC) St. Louis; KTVI (FOX) St. Louis; WABC-TV (ABC) New York; WGEM-TV (CW, NBC) Quincy; WTJR (IND) Quincy.

Programming (via satellite): Home Shopping Network; Weather Channel; WGN America.

Fee: $29.99 installation; $19.95 monthly.

Expanded Basic Service 1

Subscribers: N.A.

Programming (via satellite): ABC Family Channel; AMC; Animal Planet; Arts & Entertainment; CNN; Discovery Channel; Disney Channel; ESPN; ESPN 2; Fox Sports Net Midwest; FX; G4; Golf Channel; Great American Country; GSN; Halogen Network; HGTV; History Channel; Lifetime; Lifetime Movie Network; MTV; National Geographic Channel; Nickelodeon; Outdoor Channel; ShopNBC; Speed Channel; Spike TV; Syfy; TBS Superstation; The Learning Channel; Toon Disney; Turner Classic Movies; Turner Network TV; USA Network; Versus; WE tv.

Fee: $23.00 monthly.

Digital Basic Service

Subscribers: N.A.

Programming (via satellite): BBC America; Bio; Black Family Channel; Bloomberg Television; Discovery Digital Networks; Discovery Kids Channel; DMX Music; ESPN Classic Sports; ESPNews; Fox Movie Channel; Fox Sports World; FSN Digital Atlantic; FSN Digital Central; FSN Digital Pacific; History Channel International; Lime; Style Network.

Fee: $13.95 monthly.

Digital Pay Service 1

Pay Units: N.A.

Programming (via satellite): Cinemax (multiplexed); Encore (multiplexed); HBO (multiplexed); Showtime (multiplexed); Starz (multiplexed).

Fee: $3.99 monthly (Encore), $9.49 monthly (Cinemax), $13.49 monthly (HBO, Starz or Showtime).

Video-On-Demand: No

Pay-Per-View

Fresh; Playboy TV; iN DEMAND.

Internet Service

Operational: Yes.

Telephone Service

Digital: Operational

Miles of Plant: 9.0 (coaxial); None (fiber optic). Homes passed: 633.

General Manager: Nidhin Johnson. Program Manager: Shawn Smith.

City fee: 3% of gross.

Ownership: Crystal Broadband Networks (MSO).

BARTELSO—Formerly served by CableDirect. No longer in operation. ICA: IL0463.

BATAVIA—Comcast Cable. Now served by OAK BROOK, IL [IL0006]. ICA: IL0080.

BAYLIS (village)—Formerly served by Cass Cable TV Inc. No longer in operation. ICA: IL0464.

BEAVERVILLE TWP.—Formerly served by CableDirect. No longer in operation. ICA: IL0449.

BEECHER CITY—Clearvision Cable Systems Inc., 1785 US Rte 40, Greenup, IL 62428-3501. Phone: 217-923-5594. Fax: 217-923-5681. E-mail: mbct@rr1.net. ICA: IL0279.

TV Market Ranking: Outside TV Markets (BEECHER CITY). Franchise award date: N.A. Franchise expiration date: N.A. Began: August 25, 1989.

Channel capacity: 40 (not 2-way capable). Channels available but not in use: 22.

Basic Service

Subscribers: 50.

Programming (received off-air): WAND (NBC) Decatur; WBUI (CW) Decatur; WCIA (CBS) Champaign; WEIU-TV (PBS) Charleston; WICS (ABC) Springfield; WPXS (IND) Mount Vernon; WRSP-TV (FOX) Springfield; WUSI-TV (PBS) Olney.

Programming (via satellite): ABC Family Channel; AMC; Arts & Entertainment; Bravo; Cartoon Network; CNBC; CNN; Comedy Central; Country Music TV; C-SPAN; Discovery Channel; Disney Channel; ESPN; Fox News Channel; G4; Headline News; History Channel; Lifetime; MSNBC; MTV; Nickelodeon; QVC; Spike TV; Syfy; TBS Superstation; The Learning Channel; Trinity Broadcasting Network; Turner Network TV; USA Network; VH1; Weather Channel; WGN America.

Fee: $42.50 installation; $29.95 monthly.

Pay Service 1

Pay Units: N.A.

Programming (via satellite): Cinemax; HBO.

Fee: $6.50 monthly (Cinemax), $9.50 monthly (HBO), or $14.00 monthly (Cinemax & HBO).

Video-On-Demand: No

Internet Service

Operational: No.

Telephone Service

None

Miles of Plant: 6.0 (coaxial); None (fiber optic). Homes passed: 192.

Manager: Michael Bauguss.

Ownership: Clearvision Cable Systems Inc. (MSO).

BELLE RIVE—Formerly served by Longview Communications. No longer in operation. ICA: IL0668.

BELLEVILLE—Charter Communications, 941 Charter Commons Dr, Saint Louis, MO 63017. Phone: 636-207-7044. Fax: 636-230-7034. Web Site: http://www.charter.com. Also serves Fairview Heights, O'Fallon, St. Clair County, St. Clair Twp., Stookey Twp. & Swansea. ICA: IL0020.

TV Market Ranking: 11 (BELLEVILLE, Fairview Heights, O'Fallon, St. Clair County, St. Clair Twp., Stookey Twp., Swansea). Franchise award date: November 29, 1979. Franchise expiration date: N.A. Began: July 29, 1980.

Channel capacity: N.A. Channels available but not in use: N.A.

Basic Service

Subscribers: 32,137.

Programming (received off-air): KDNL-TV (ABC) St. Louis; KETC (PBS) St. Louis; KMOV (CBS) St. Louis; KNLC (IND) St. Louis; KPLR-TV (CW) St. Louis; KSDK (NBC) St. Louis; KTVI (FOX) St. Louis; WPXS (IND) Mount Vernon; WRBU (MNT) East St. Louis; WSIU-TV (PBS) Carbondale; allband FM.

Programming (via satellite): C-SPAN; C-SPAN 2; Eternal Word TV Network; GRTV Network; Home Shopping Network; INSP; Jewelry Television; QVC; ShopNBC; TBS Superstation; Trinity Broadcasting Network; TV Guide Network; Univision; Weatherscan; WGN America.

Current originations: Government Access; Educational Access; Public Access.

Fee: $29.99 installation.

Expanded Basic Service 1

Subscribers: N.A.

Programming (via satellite): ABC Family Channel; AMC; Animal Planet; Arts & Entertainment; BET Networks; Bravo; Cartoon Network; CNBC; CNN; Comedy Central; Country Music TV; Discovery Channel; Disney Channel; E! Entertainment Television; ESPN; ESPN 2; Food Network; Fox Movie Channel; Fox News Channel; Fox Sports Net Midwest; FX; G4; Golf Channel; GSN; Hallmark Channel; Headline News; HGTV; History Channel; Lifetime; Lifetime Movie Network; MSNBC; MTV; National Geographic Channel; Nickelodeon; Oxygen; SoapNet; Speed Channel; Spike TV; Style Network; Syfy; The Learning Channel; Toon Disney; Travel Channel; truTV; Turner Classic Movies; Turner Network TV; TV Land; USA Network; Versus; VH1; WE tv; Weather Channel.

Fee: $49.99 monthly.

Digital Basic Service

Subscribers: N.A.

Programming (via satellite): BBC America; Bio; Bloomberg Television; Discovery Digital Networks; Do-It-Yourself; Encore Action; ESPN Classic Sports; FitTV; Fox College Sports Atlantic; Fox College Sports Central; Fox College Sports Pacific; Fox Sports World; Fuel TV; Fuse; GAS; Great American Country; History Channel International; Independent Film Channel; MTV Networks Digital Suite; Music Choice; NFL Network; Nick Jr.; Nick Too; NickToons TV; Sundance Channel.

Digital Pay Service 1

Pay Units: N.A.

Programming (via satellite): Cinemax (multiplexed); HBO (multiplexed); Showtime (multiplexed); Starz (multiplexed); The Movie Channel (multiplexed).

Video-On-Demand: Yes

Pay-Per-View

iN DEMAND (delivered digitally); Playboy TV (delivered digitally); Fresh (delivered digitally); Shorteez (delivered digitally); Sports PPV (delivered digitally); ESPN Now (delivered digitally).

Internet Service

Operational: Yes.

Broadband Service: Charter Pipeline.

Fee: $29.99 monthly; $10.00 modem lease.

Telephone Service

Digital: Operational

Fee: $29.99 monthly

Miles of Plant: 644.0 (coaxial); None (fiber optic). Homes passed: 50,734.

Vice President & General Manager: Steve Trippe. Operations Director: Tom Williams. Marketing Director: Beverly Wall.

City fee: 3% of gross.

Ownership: Charter Communications Inc. (MSO).

BELLMONT—Formerly served by CableDirect. No longer in operation. ICA: IL0400.

BELVIDERE—Insight Communications. Now served by ROCKFORD, IL [IL0010]. ICA: IL0097.

BELVIDERE TWP.—Mediacom. Now served by POPLAR GROVE, IL [IL0282]. ICA: IL0663.

BETHANY—Suddenlink Communications, PO Box 218, Poplar Bluff, MO 63901. Phones: 314-965-2020; 573-686-6387. Web Site: http://www.suddenlink.com. Also serves Dalton City. ICA: IL0245.

TV Market Ranking: 64 (BETHANY, Dalton City). Franchise award date: August 12, 1982. Franchise expiration date: N.A. Began: September 1, 1983.

Channel capacity: 42 (operating 2-way). Channels available but not in use: 3.

Basic Service

Subscribers: 449.

Programming (received off-air): WAND (NBC) Decatur; WBUI (CW) Decatur; WCIA (CBS) Champaign; WICS (ABC) Springfield; WILL-TV (PBS) Urbana; WRSP-TV (FOX) Springfield.

Programming (via satellite): Home Shopping Network; WCFN (MNT) Springfield; WGN America.
Fee: $45.00 installation; $15.95 monthly.

Expanded Basic Service 1
Subscribers: N.A.
Programming (via satellite): ABC Family Channel; AMC; Animal Planet; Arts & Entertainment; Cartoon Network; CNN; Comcast SportsNet Chicago; Country Music TV; C-SPAN; C-SPAN 2; Discovery Channel; Disney Channel; E! Entertainment Television; ESPN; ESPN 2; ESPN Classic Sports; Fox News Channel; Fox Sports Net Midwest; FX; Great American Country; Headline News; HGTV; History Channel; INSP; Lifetime; MSNBC; MTV; National Geographic Channel; Nickelodeon; Radar Channel; SoapNet; Speed Channel; Spike TV; Syfy; TBS Superstation; The Learning Channel; Travel Channel; Trinity Broadcasting Network; Turner Classic Movies; Turner Network TV; TV Land; USA Network; VH1; WE tv; Weather Channel.
Fee: $25.00 monthly.

Digital Basic Service
Subscribers: N.A.
Programming (via satellite): BBC America; Bio; Bloomberg Television; Discovery Digital Networks; DMX Music; ESPNews; Fox College Sports Atlantic; Fox College Sports Central; Fox College Sports Pacific; Fox Movie Channel; Fox Soccer; Fuse; G4; Golf Channel; GSN; History Channel International; Independent Film Channel; Lifetime Movie Network; Military History Channel; Outdoor Channel; Science Television; ShopNBC; Toon Disney; Versus.
Fee: $3.95 monthly.

Pay Service 1
Pay Units: 42.
Programming (via satellite): Cinemax; Encore; HBO; Showtime; The Movie Channel.
Fee: $25.00 installation; $7.95 monthly (Cinemax), $11.99 monthly (HBO).

Digital Pay Service 1
Pay Units: N.A.
Programming (via satellite): Cinemax (multiplexed); Encore (multiplexed); HBO (multiplexed); Showtime (multiplexed); Starz (multiplexed); The Movie Channel (multiplexed).

Video-On-Demand: No

Pay-Per-View
iN DEMAND (delivered digitally); Playboy TV (delivered digitally); Fresh (delivered digitally).

Internet Service
Operational: Yes. Began: April 26, 2004.
Broadband Service: Cebridge High Speed Cable Internet.
Fee: $49.95 installation; $20.95 monthly.

Telephone Service
None

Miles of Plant: 14.0 (coaxial); None (fiber optic). Homes passed: 842.
Manager: James Robinson. Chief Technician: Chris Moody.
City fee: 3% of basic.
Ownership: Cequel Communications LLC (MSO).

BIGGSVILLE—Formerly served by CableDirect. No longer in operation. ICA: IL0466.

BIRDS—Park TV & Electronics Inc., PO Box 9, 205 E Fire Ln, Cissna Park, IL 60924. Phone: 815-457-2659. Fax: 815-457-2735. Also serves Flat Rock & Pinkstaff. ICA: IL0499.
TV Market Ranking: Outside TV Markets (BIRDS, Flat Rock, Pinkstaff). Franchise award date: N.A. Franchise expiration date: N.A. Began: May 1, 1988.
Channel capacity: 41 (not 2-way capable). Channels available but not in use: 34.

Basic Service
Subscribers: 84.
Programming (received off-air): WEHT (ABC) Evansville; WFXW (FOX) Terre Haute; WTHI-TV (CBS) Terre Haute; WTWO (NBC) Terre Haute; WUSI-TV (PBS) Olney.
Programming (via satellite): ABC Family Channel; AMC; Animal Planet; CNN; Comedy Central; C-SPAN; C-SPAN 2; Discovery Channel; Disney Channel; E! Entertainment Television; ESPN; ESPN 2; Fox News Channel; Headline News; Home Shopping Network; INSP; Lifetime; QVC; TBS Superstation; The Learning Channel; The Movie Channel; Travel Channel; Trinity Broadcasting Network; Turner Network TV; USA Network; Weather Channel; WGN America.
Fee: $22.95 monthly.

Pay Service 1
Pay Units: 44.
Programming (via satellite): Showtime.
Fee: $11.00 monthly.

Video-On-Demand: No

Internet Service
Operational: No.

Telephone Service
None

Miles of Plant: 20.0 (coaxial); None (fiber optic). Homes passed: 463.
Manager: Joe Young.
Ownership: Park TV & Electronics Inc. (MSO).

BISMARCK—Park TV & Electronics Inc., PO Box 9, 205 E Fire Ln, Cissna Park, IL 60924. Phone: 815-457-2659. Fax: 815-457-2735. ICA: IL0669.
TV Market Ranking: Below 100 (BISMARCK). Franchise award date: N.A. Franchise expiration date: N.A. Began: N.A.
Channel capacity: 31 (not 2-way capable). Channels available but not in use: 2.

Basic Service
Subscribers: 38.
Programming (received off-air): WAND (NBC) Decatur; WBUI (CW) Decatur; WCCU (FOX) Urbana; WCIA (CBS) Champaign; WICD (ABC) Champaign; WILL-TV (PBS) Urbana; WLFI-TV (CBS) Lafayette.
Programming (via satellite): ABC Family Channel; Arts & Entertainment; CNN; Comedy Central; Discovery Channel; Disney Channel; ESPN; Headline News; Lifetime; MTV; Nickelodeon; QVC; Spike TV; TBS Superstation; The Learning Channel; Travel Channel; Turner Network TV; USA Network; VH1; Weather Channel; WGN America.
Fee: $24.95 monthly.

Pay Service 1
Pay Units: N.A.
Programming (via satellite): Showtime; The Movie Channel.
Fee: $9.95 monthly (each).

Video-On-Demand: No

Internet Service
Operational: No.

Telephone Service
None

Miles of Plant: 27.0 (coaxial); None (fiber optic). Homes passed: 601.
Manager: Joe Young.
Ownership: Park TV & Electronics Inc. (MSO).

BLOOMINGTON—Comcast Cable, 3517 N Dries Ln, Peoria, IL 61604. Phone: 309-686-2600. Fax: 309-688-9828. Web Site: http://www.comcast.com. Also serves McLean County & Normal. ICA: IL0026.
TV Market Ranking: 83,64 (McLean County (portions)); Below 100 (BLOOMINGTON, Normal, McLean County (portions)). Franchise award date: N.A. Franchise expiration date: N.A. Began: September 10, 1969.
Channel capacity: 90 (operating 2-way). Channels available but not in use: 3.

Basic Service
Subscribers: N.A. Included in Peoria
Programming (received off-air): WAOE (MNT) Peoria; WEEK-TV (NBC) Peoria; WHOI (ABC, CW) Peoria; WILL-TV (PBS) Urbana; WMBD-TV (CBS) Peoria; WTVP (PBS) Peoria; WYZZ-TV (FOX) Bloomington; allband FM.
Programming (via satellite): C-SPAN; C-SPAN 2; Eternal Word TV Network; Home Shopping Network; ION Television; QVC; ShopNBC; Trinity Broadcasting Network; TV Guide Network; Weather Channel; WGN America; WHOI (ABC, CW) Peoria.
Current originations: Government Access; Educational Access.
Fee: $25.00 installation; $14.60 monthly.

Expanded Basic Service 1
Subscribers: 14,000.
Programming (via satellite): ABC Family Channel; AMC; Animal Planet; Arts & Entertainment; BET Networks; Bravo; Cartoon Network; CNBC; CNN; Comcast SportsNet Chicago; Comedy Central; Country Music TV; Discovery Channel; Disney Channel; E! Entertainment Television; ESPN; ESPN 2; Food Network; Fox News Channel; Fox Sports Net Midwest; FX; Golf Channel; Great American Country; Hallmark Channel; Headline News; HGTV; History Channel; Lifetime; MSNBC; MTV; MTV2; National Geographic Channel; Nickelodeon; Oxygen; SoapNet; Speed Channel; Spike TV; Style Network; Syfy; TBS Superstation; The Learning Channel; Toon Disney; Travel Channel; truTV; Turner Network TV; Univision; USA Network; VH1.
Fee: $37.15 monthly.

Digital Basic Service
Subscribers: 6,640.
Programming (via satellite): AmericanLife TV Network; BBC America; Bio; Bloomberg Television; CBS College Sports Network; CMT Pure Country; Cooking Channel; C-SPAN 3; Discovery Digital Networks; Discovery HD Theater; DMX Music; Do-It-Yourself; Encore (multiplexed); ESPN 2 HD; ESPN Classic Sports; ESPN HD; ESPN U; ESPNews; Fox College Sports Atlantic; Fox College Sports Central; Fox College Sports Pacific; Fox Movie Channel; Fox Reality Channel; Fox Soccer; Fuse; G4; GAS; GSN; Halogen Network; HDNet; HDNet Movies; History Channel International; HorseRacing TV; Independent Film Channel; Lifetime Movie Network; Lifetime Real Women; MTV Networks Digital Suite; NFL Network; Nick Jr.; Nick Too; NickToons TV; Outdoor Channel; Ovation; Palladia; PBS Kids Sprout; Si TV; Sleuth; Sundance Channel; Tennis Channel; Toon Disney; Turner Classic Movies; Turner Network TV HD; TV Land; TVG Network; Universal HD; Versus; WE tv.
Fee: $17.00 monthly.

Digital Pay Service 1
Pay Units: N.A.
Programming (via satellite): Cinemax (multiplexed); Flix; HBO (multiplexed); HBO HD; Showtime (multiplexed); Showtime HD; Starz (multiplexed); The Movie Channel (multiplexed).
Fee: $10.00 monthly (Cinemax or Starz), $13.00 monthly (HBO or Showtime/TMC).

Video-On-Demand: Yes

Pay-Per-View
ESPN (delivered digitally); iN DEMAND (delivered digitally); Playboy TV (delivered digitally); Special events (delivered digitally).

Internet Service
Operational: Yes.
Subscribers: 3,320.
Broadband Service: Comcast High Speed Internet.
Fee: $99.95 installation; $44.95 monthly; $10.00 modem lease; $99.95 modem purchase.

Telephone Service
Digital: Operational

Homes passed: Included in Peoria
General Manager: John Nieber. Chief Technician: Mike Vandergraft.
Ownership: Comcast Cable Communications Inc. (MSO).

BLUE GRASS—Mediacom. Now served by MOLINE, IL [IL0011]. ICA: IA0071.

BLUE MOUND—Suddenlink Communications, PO Box 218, Poplar Bluff, MO 63901. Phones: 314-965-2020; 573-686-6387. Web Site: http://www.suddenlink.com. Also serves Stonington. ICA: IL0229.
TV Market Ranking: 64 (BLUE MOUND, Stonington). Franchise award date: December 3, 1979. Franchise expiration date: N.A. Began: May 1, 1981.
Channel capacity: 42 (operating 2-way). Channels available but not in use: 2.

Basic Service
Subscribers: 501.
Programming (received off-air): WAND (NBC) Decatur; WBUI (CW) Decatur; WCIA (CBS) Champaign; WICS (ABC) Springfield; WILL-TV (PBS) Urbana; WRSP-TV (FOX) Springfield.
Programming (via satellite): Home Shopping Network; WCFN (MNT) Springfield; WGN America.
Fee: $45.00 installation; $16.95 monthly.

Expanded Basic Service 1
Subscribers: N.A.
Programming (via satellite): ABC Family Channel; AMC; Animal Planet; Arts & Entertainment; Cartoon Network; CNN; Comcast SportsNet Chicago; Country Music TV; C-SPAN; C-SPAN 2; Discovery Channel; Disney Channel; E! Entertainment Television; ESPN; ESPN 2; ESPN Classic Sports; Fox News Channel; Fox Sports Net Midwest; FX; Great American Country; Headline News; HGTV; History Channel; INSP; Lifetime; MSNBC; MTV; National Geographic Channel; Nickelodeon; Radar Channel; SoapNet; Speed Channel; Spike TV; Syfy; TBS Superstation; The Learning Channel; Travel Channel; Trinity Broadcasting Network; Turner Classic Movies; Turner Network TV; TV Land; USA Network; VH1; WE tv; Weather Channel.
Fee: $23.00 monthly.

Digital Basic Service
Subscribers: N.A.
Programming (via satellite): BBC America; Bio; Bloomberg Television; Discovery Digital Networks; DMX Music; ESPNews; Fox College Sports Atlantic; Fox College Sports Central; Fox College Sports Pacific; Fox Movie Channel; Fox Soccer; Fuse; G4; Golf Channel; GSN; History Channel International; Independent Film Channel; Lifetime Movie Network; Military History Channel; Outdoor Channel; Science Television; ShopNBC; Toon Disney; Versus.
Fee: $3.95 monthly.

Pay Service 1
Pay Units: 96.
Programming (via satellite): Cinemax; Encore; HBO; Showtime; The Movie Channel.
Fee: $25.00 installation; $3.99 monthly (Encore), $7.95 monthly (Cinemax), $11.99 monthly (HBO).
Digital Pay Service 1
Pay Units: N.A.
Programming (via satellite): Cinemax (multiplexed); Encore (multiplexed); HBO (multiplexed); Showtime (multiplexed); Starz (multiplexed); The Movie Channel (multiplexed).
Video-On-Demand: No
Pay-Per-View
iN DEMAND (delivered digitally); Playboy TV (delivered digitally); Fresh (delivered digitally).
Internet Service
Operational: Yes. Began: November 1, 2004.
Broadband Service: Cebridge High Speed Cable Internet.
Fee: $49.95 installation; $20.95 monthly.
Telephone Service
None
Miles of Plant: 17.0 (coaxial); None (fiber optic). Homes passed: 958.
Manager: James Robinson. Chief Technician: Chris Moody.
Ownership: Cequel Communications LLC (MSO).

BLUFFS—Crystal Broadband Networks, PO Box 180336, Chicago, IL 60618. Phones: 877-319-0328; 630-206-0447. E-mail: info@crystalbn.com. Web Site: http://crystalbn.com. Also serves Meredosia. ICA: IL0227.
TV Market Ranking: Outside TV Markets (BLUFFS, Meredosia). Franchise award date: N.A. Franchise expiration date: N.A. Began: August 10, 1981.
Channel capacity: 62 (not 2-way capable). Channels available but not in use: None.
Basic Service
Subscribers: 274.
Programming (received off-air): KDNL-TV (ABC) St. Louis; KETC (PBS) St. Louis; KHQA-TV (ABC, CBS) Hannibal; KPLR-TV (CW) St. Louis; KSDK (NBC) St. Louis; KTVI (FOX) St. Louis; WGEM-TV (CW, NBC) Quincy; WHOI (ABC, CW) Peoria; WICS (ABC) Springfield.
Programming (via satellite): Home Shopping Network; INSP; WGN America.
Fee: $45.00 installation; $25.16 monthly.
Expanded Basic Service 1
Subscribers: N.A.
Programming (via satellite): ABC Family Channel; AMC; Arts & Entertainment; CNN; Discovery Channel; Disney Channel; ESPN; ESPN 2; Fox Sports Net Midwest; Great American Country; History Channel; Lifetime; MTV; Nickelodeon; Spike TV; Syfy; TBS Superstation; Trinity Broadcasting Network; Turner Network TV; USA Network; Weather Channel; WTJR (IND) Quincy.
Pay Service 1
Pay Units: 80.
Programming (via satellite): Cinemax; Encore; HBO; Showtime; The Movie Channel.
Fee: $25.00 installation; $7.95 monthly (Cinemax), $11.99 monthly (HBO or Showtime).
Video-On-Demand: No
Internet Service
Operational: Yes.
Telephone Service
Digital: Operational
Miles of Plant: 23.0 (coaxial); None (fiber optic). Homes passed: 982.
Regional Manager: Paul Broseman. Plant Manager: Tony Gilbert.
Ownership: Crystal Broadband Networks (MSO).

BLUFORD—Formerly served by Longview Communications. No longer in operation. ICA: IL0360.

BONE GAP—Formerly served by CableDirect. No longer in operation. ICA: IL0418.

BONFIELD (village)—Formerly served by CableDirect. No longer in operation. ICA: IL0467.

BONNIE—Longview Communications. Now served by INA, IL [IL0392]. ICA: IL0395.

BOODY—Formerly served by CableDirect. No longer in operation. ICA: IL0468.

BOWEN (village)—Adams Telecom. Formerly served by Golden, IL [IL0257]. This cable system has converted to IPTV, PO Box 248, 405 Emminga Rd, Golden, IL 62339. Phone: 217-696-4411. E-mail: service@adams.net. Web Site: http://www.adams.net. ICA: IL5312.
Channel capacity: N.A. Channels available but not in use: N.A.
Internet Service
Operational: Yes.
Ownership: Adams Telephone Co-Operative.

BRADFORD—Mediacom. Now served by MINERAL, IL [IL0170]. ICA: IL0323.

BREESE—Charter Communications, 941 Charter Commons Dr, Saint Louis, MO 63017. Phone: 636-207-7044. Fax: 636-230-7034. Web Site: http://www.charter.com. Also serves Beckemeyer, Clinton County & Germantown. ICA: IL0149.
TV Market Ranking: Below 100 (Beckemeyer, Clinton County); Outside TV Markets (BREESE, Germantown). Franchise award date: N.A. Franchise expiration date: N.A. Began: March 1, 1982.
Channel capacity: N.A. Channels available but not in use: N.A.
Basic Service
Subscribers: 1,395.
Programming (received off-air): KDNL-TV (ABC) St. Louis; KETC (PBS) St. Louis; KMOV (CBS) St. Louis; KNLC (IND) St. Louis; KPLR-TV (CW) St. Louis; KSDK (NBC) St. Louis; KTVI (FOX) St. Louis; WPXS (IND) Mount Vernon; WRBU (MNT) East St. Louis; WSIU-TV (PBS) Carbondale.
Programming (via satellite): C-SPAN; C-SPAN 2; Eternal Word TV Network; GRTV Network; Home Shopping Network; INSP; Jewelry Television; QVC; ShopNBC; TBS Superstation; Trinity Broadcasting Network; TV Guide Network; Univision; Weatherscan; WGN America.
Current originations: Government Access; Educational Access; Public Access.
Fee: $29.99 installation.
Expanded Basic Service 1
Subscribers: N.A.
Programming (via satellite): ABC Family Channel; AMC; Animal Planet; Arts & Entertainment; BET Networks; Bravo; Cartoon Network; CNBC; CNN; Comedy Central; Country Music TV; Discovery Channel; Disney Channel; E! Entertainment Television; ESPN; ESPN 2; Food Network; Fox Movie Channel; Fox News Channel; Fox Sports Net Midwest; FX; G4; Golf Channel; GSN; Hallmark Channel; Headline News; HGTV; History Channel; Lifetime; MSNBC; MTV; National Geographic Channel; Nickelodeon; Oxygen; SoapNet; Speed Channel; Spike TV; Style Network; Syfy; The Learning Channel; Toon Disney; Travel Channel; truTV; Turner Classic Movies; Turner Network TV; TV Land; USA Network; Versus; VH1; WE tv; Weather Channel.
Fee: $49.99 monthly.
Digital Basic Service
Subscribers: N.A.
Programming (via satellite): BBC America; Bio; Bloomberg Television; Discovery Digital Networks; Do-It-Yourself; Encore Action; ESPN Classic Sports; FitTV; Fox College Sports Atlantic; Fox College Sports Central; Fox College Sports Pacific; Fox Sports World; Fuel TV; Fuse; GAS; Great American Country; History Channel International; Independent Film Channel; International Television (ITV); Lifetime Movie Network; MTV Networks Digital Suite; Music Choice; NFL Network; Nick Jr.; Nick Too; NickToons TV; Sundance Channel; TV Guide Interactive Inc.
Digital Pay Service 1
Pay Units: 970.
Programming (via satellite): Cinemax (multiplexed); HBO (multiplexed); Showtime (multiplexed); Starz (multiplexed); The Movie Channel (multiplexed).
Fee: $9.95 monthly (Cinemax or HBO).
Video-On-Demand: Yes
Pay-Per-View
iN DEMAND (delivered digitally); Playboy TV (delivered digitally); Shorteez (delivered digitally); Sports PPV (delivered digitally); ESPN Now (delivered digitally); Fresh (delivered digitally).
Internet Service
Operational: Yes. Began: January 1, 2002.
Broadband Service: Charter Pipeline.
Fee: $29.99 monthly; $5.00 modem lease; $99.99 modem purchase.
Telephone Service
Digital: Operational
Fee: $29.99 monthly
Miles of Plant: 47.0 (coaxial); None (fiber optic). Homes passed: 2,362.
Vice President & General Manager: Steve Trippe. Operations Director: Tom Williams. Marketing Director: Beverly Wall.
City fee: 5% of gross.
Ownership: Charter Communications Inc. (MSO).

BRIGHTON—BrightGreen Cable, PO Box 127, Gillespie, IL 62033. Phone: 817-685-9588. E-mail: support@brightgreencable.com. Web Site: http://www.brightgreencable.com. ICA: IL0210.
TV Market Ranking: 11 (BRIGHTON). Franchise award date: August 2, 1982. Franchise expiration date: N.A. Began: April 15, 1983.
Channel capacity: 52 (operating 2-way). Channels available but not in use: N.A.
Basic Service
Subscribers: 349.
Programming (received off-air): KDNL-TV (ABC) St. Louis; KETC (PBS) St. Louis; KMOV (CBS) St. Louis; KPLR-TV (CW) St. Louis; KSDK (NBC) St. Louis; KTVI (FOX) St. Louis.
Programming (via satellite): C-SPAN; Home Shopping Network; INSP; Trinity Broadcasting Network; WGN America.
Fee: $29.95 installation; $19.95 monthly.
Expanded Basic Service 1
Subscribers: N.A.
Programming (via satellite): ABC Family Channel; AMC; Arts & Entertainment; CNN; Discovery Channel; Disney Channel; ESPN; ESPN 2; Fox Sports Net Midwest; Great American Country; Headline News; History Channel; Lifetime; MTV; National Geographic Channel; Nickelodeon; SoapNet; Spike TV; Syfy; TBS Superstation; The Learning Channel; Toon Disney; Travel Channel; Turner Network TV; TV Land; USA Network; VH1; Weather Channel.
Fee: $23.00 monthly.
Digital Basic Service
Subscribers: N.A.
Programming (via satellite): Bio; Discovery Digital Networks; Discovery Kids Channel; DMX Music; ESPNews; G4; History Channel International; Lifetime Movie Network; Outdoor Channel; Speed Channel; Turner Classic Movies; WE tv.
Fee: $13.95 monthly.
Digital Pay Service 1
Pay Units: N.A.
Programming (via satellite): Cinemax (multiplexed); Encore (multiplexed); HBO (multiplexed); Showtime (multiplexed); Starz (multiplexed); The Movie Channel (multiplexed).
Fee: $3.99 monthly (Encore), $9.49 monthly (Cinemax), $13.49 monthly (HBO, Showtime or TMC), $13.95 monthly (Starz).
Video-On-Demand: No
Pay-Per-View
Fresh (delivered digitally); Playboy TV (delivered digitally); iN DEMAND (delivered digitally).
Internet Service
Operational: Yes. Began: November 1, 2004.
Broadband Service: Rapid High Speed Internet.
Fee: $39.95 monthly.
Telephone Service
None
Miles of Plant: 19.0 (coaxial); None (fiber optic). Homes passed: 1,079.
President & General Manager: Phil Claro.
City fee: 3% of gross.
Ownership: BrightGreen Communications (MSO).

BRIMFIELD—Mediacom, 3900 26th Ave, Moline, IL 61265. Phone: 309-797-2580. Fax: 309-797-2414. Web Site: http://www.mediacomcable.com. Also serves Bureau, Dunlap, Granville, Hennepin, Mark, Oak Park Estates, Princeville & Standard. ICA: IL0201.
TV Market Ranking: 83 (BRIMFIELD, Dunlap, Princeville); Below 100 (Bureau, Granville, Hennepin, Mark, Oak Park Estates, Standard). Franchise award date: N.A. Franchise expiration date: N.A. Began: N.A.
Channel capacity: 134 (operating 2-way). Channels available but not in use: None.
Basic Service
Subscribers: 2,108.
Programming (received off-air): WAOE (MNT) Peoria; WEEK-TV (NBC) Peoria; WHOI (ABC, CW) Peoria; WMBD-TV (CBS) Peoria; WTVP (PBS) Peoria; WYZZ-TV (FOX) Bloomington.
Programming (via satellite): Hallmark Channel; ION Television; QVC; WGN America.
Fee: $45.00 installation; $20.95 monthly.
Expanded Basic Service 1
Subscribers: 1,229.
Programming (via satellite): ABC Family Channel; AMC; Animal Planet; Arts & Entertainment; Bravo; Cartoon Network; CNBC; CNN; Comcast SportsNet Chicago; Comedy Central; Country Music TV; C-SPAN; CW+; Discovery Channel; Disney Channel; E! Entertainment Televi-

sion; ESPN; ESPN 2; ESPN Classic Sports; Eternal Word TV Network; Food Network; Fox News Channel; FX; Halogen Network; Headline News; HGTV; History Channel; Home Shopping Network; Lifetime; MSNBC; MTV; Nickelodeon; Product Information Network; SoapNet; Speed Channel; Spike TV; Syfy; TBS Superstation; The Learning Channel; Travel Channel; Trinity Broadcasting Network; truTV; Turner Network TV; TV Guide Network; TV Land; USA Network; VH1; WE tv; Weather Channel.
Fee: $34.00 monthly.

Digital Basic Service
Subscribers: N.A.
Programming (received off-air): WEEK-TV (NBC) Peoria; WHOI (ABC, CW) Peoria; WMBD-TV (CBS) Peoria; WTVP (PBS) Peoria; WYZZ-TV (FOX) Bloomington.
Programming (via satellite): ABC News Now; AmericanLife TV Network; BBC America; Bio; Bloomberg Television; CCTV-Entertainment; Discovery Digital Networks; ESPN 2 HD; ESPN HD; ESPNews; FitTV; Fox Movie Channel; Fox Reality Channel; Fox Soccer; Fuse; G4; Golf Channel; GSN; History Channel International; ID Investigation Discovery; Independent Film Channel; ION Life; Lifetime Movie Network; Lifetime Real Women; Military History Channel; MTV Hits; MTV2; Music Choice; National Geographic Channel; Nick Jr.; NickToons TV; Outdoor Channel; Qubo; ReelzChannel; RFD-TV; Science Channel; Style Network; Sundance Channel; TeenNick; Turner Classic Movies; VH1 Classic.
Fee: $9.00 monthly.

Digital Expanded Basic Service
Subscribers: N.A.
Programming (via satellite): College Sports Television; ESPN U; Fox College Sports Atlantic; Fox College Sports Central; Fox College Sports Pacific; Fuel TV; Gol TV; Tennis Channel; The Sportsman Channel; TVG Network.
Fee: $3.95 monthly.

Digital Expanded Basic Service 2
Subscribers: N.A.
Programming (via satellite): Discovery HD Theater; HDNet; HDNet Movies; Universal HD.
Fee: $6.95 monthly.

Digital Pay Service 1
Pay Units: N.A.
Programming (via satellite): Cinemax (multiplexed); Encore (multiplexed); Flix; HBO (multiplexed); HBO HD; Showtime (multiplexed); Showtime HD; Starz; Starz (multiplexed); The Movie Channel (multiplexed); The Movie Channel HD.
Fee: $11.95 monthly (HBO, Cinemax, Showtime/TMC, or Starz/Encore).

Video-On-Demand: No

Pay-Per-View
M/C Venture Partners (delivered digitally); Playboy TV (delivered digitally); Ten Clips (delivered digitally); TENReal (delivered digitally); ESPN On Demand (delivered digitally).

Internet Service
Operational: Yes.
Broadband Service: Mediacom High Speed Internet.
Fee: $59.95 installation; $45.95 monthly.

Telephone Service
Digital: Operational
Fee: $39.95 installation; $39.95 monthly

Homes passed: 3,673.
Regional Vice President: Cari Fenzel. Marketing Director: Greg Evans. Area Manager: Don DeMay. Engineering Director: Mitch Carlson. Technical Operations Manager: Chris Toalson.
City fee: 5% of gross.
Ownership: Mediacom LLC (MSO).

BRIMFIELD—Mediacom. Now served by BRIMFIELD, IL [IL0201]. ICA: IL0330.

BROCTON—Clearvision Cable Systems Inc., 1785 US Rte 40, Greenup, IL 62428-3501. Phone: 217-923-5594. Fax: 217-923-5681. ICA: IL0666.
TV Market Ranking: 64 (BROCTON). Franchise award date: N.A. Franchise expiration date: N.A. Began: N.A.
Channel capacity: 36 (not 2-way capable). Channels available but not in use: 13.

Basic Service
Subscribers: 55.
Programming (received off-air): WAND (NBC) Decatur; WBUI (CW) Decatur; WCFN (MNT) Springfield; WCIA (CBS) Champaign; WEIU-TV (PBS) Charleston; WICD (ABC) Champaign; WILL-TV (PBS) Urbana.
Programming (via satellite): ABC Family Channel; AMC; Arts & Entertainment; Bravo; Cartoon Network; CNBC; CNN; Comedy Central; C-SPAN; Discovery Channel; Disney Channel; ESPN; ESPN 2; Fox News Channel; G4; Great American Country; Headline News; History Channel; Lifetime; MSNBC; MTV; Nickelodeon; QVC; Spike TV; Syfy; TBS Superstation; The Learning Channel; Trinity Broadcasting Network; Turner Network TV; USA Network; VH1; Weather Channel; WGN America.
Fee: $22.50 monthly.

Pay Service 1
Pay Units: N.A.
Programming (via satellite): Showtime; The Movie Channel.
Fee: $9.45 monthly (each).

Video-On-Demand: No

Internet Service
Operational: No.

Telephone Service
None

Miles of Plant: 4.0 (coaxial); None (fiber optic). Homes passed: 188.
Manager: Michael Bauguss.
Ownership: Clearvision Cable Systems Inc. (MSO).

BRYANT (village)—Formerly served by CableDirect. No longer in operation. ICA: IL0472.

BUCKLEY (village)—Park TV & Electronics Inc., PO Box 9, 205 E Fire Ln, Cissna Park, IL 60924. Phone: 815-457-2659. Fax: 815-457-2735. ICA: IL0473.
TV Market Ranking: Below 100 (BUCKLEY (VILLAGE)). Franchise award date: N.A. Franchise expiration date: N.A. Began: December 1, 1983.
Channel capacity: 60 (operating 2-way). Channels available but not in use: 25.

Basic Service
Subscribers: N.A. Included in Cisna Park
Programming (received off-air): WAND (NBC) Decatur; WBUI (CW) Decatur; WCCU (FOX) Urbana; WCIA (CBS) Champaign; WICD (ABC) Champaign; WILL-TV (PBS) Urbana.
Programming (via satellite): ABC Family Channel; AMC; Animal Planet; Arts & Entertainment; Big Ten Network; Cartoon Network; CNBC; CNN; Comedy Central; Country Music TV; Discovery Channel; Disney Channel; E! Entertainment Television; ESPN; ESPN 2; Food Network; Fox News Channel; FX; GSN; Hallmark Channel; HGTV; History Channel; Lifetime; MTV; Nickelodeon; Outdoor Channel; Oxygen; QVC; Speed Channel; Spike TV; Syfy; TBS Superstation; The Learning Channel; Travel Channel; Trinity Broadcasting Network; Turner Classic Movies; Turner Network TV; TV Land; USA Network; VH1; Weather Channel; WGN America.

Pay Service 1
Pay Units: N.A.
Programming (via satellite): Cinemax; HBO; Showtime; The Movie Channel.

Video-On-Demand: No

Internet Service
Operational: Yes.
Broadband Service: West Michigan Internet Service.
Fee: $29.95 monthly.

Telephone Service
None

Homes passed & miles of plant included in Cissna Park
Manager: Joe Young.
Ownership: Park TV & Electronics Inc. (MSO).

BUFFALO—Mediacom. Now served by KINCAID, IL [IL0176]. ICA: IL0259.

BUNCOMBE—Galaxy Cablevision, 7155 US Hwy 45 S, Carrier Mills, IL 62917. Phone: 618-994-2261. Fax: 618-994-2261. Web Site: http://www.galaxycable.com. Also serves Johnson County (portions) & Vienna. ICA: IL0266.
TV Market Ranking: 69 (BUNCOMBE, Vienna). Franchise award date: N.A. Franchise expiration date: N.A. Began: September 1, 1982.
Channel capacity: 41 (not 2-way capable). Channels available but not in use: None.

Basic Service
Subscribers: 205.
Programming (received off-air): KBSI (FOX) Cape Girardeau; KFVS-TV (CBS, CW) Cape Girardeau; WDKA (MNT) Paducah; WPSD-TV (NBC) Paducah; WSIL-TV (ABC) Harrisburg; WSIU-TV (PBS) Carbondale; WTCT (IND) Marion.
Programming (via satellite): ABC Family Channel; AMC; Arts & Entertainment; Cartoon Network; CNN; Comedy Central; Discovery Channel; Disney Channel; E! Entertainment Television; ESPN; ESPN 2; Fox News Channel; Fuse; FX; Great American Country; Headline News; HGTV; History Channel; Home Shopping Network; Lifetime; Outdoor Channel; TBS Superstation; The Learning Channel; Turner Classic Movies; Turner Network TV; USA Network; Weather Channel; WGN America.
Fee: $30.00 installation; $40.20 monthly.

Pay Service 1
Pay Units: N.A.
Programming (via satellite): Encore; HBO; Showtime.
Fee: $12.00 monthly.

Internet Service
Operational: No.

Telephone Service
None

Miles of Plant: 13.0 (coaxial); None (fiber optic). Homes passed: 897.
State Manager: Ward Webb. Customer Service Manager: Malynda Walker. Engineer: John Stewart. Technical Manager: Audie Murphy.
City fee: 3% of gross.
Ownership: Galaxy Cable Inc. (MSO).

BUREAU—Mediacom. Now served by BRIMFIELD, IL [IL0201]. ICA: IL0388.

BURLINGTON (village)—Mediacom, 3900 26th Ave, Moline, IL 61265. Phone: 309-797-2580. Fax: 309-797-2414. Web Site: http://www.mediacomcable.com. ICA: IL0474.
TV Market Ranking: 97 (BURLINGTON (VILLAGE)). Franchise award date: N.A. Franchise expiration date: N.A. Began: N.A.
Channel capacity: 134 (not 2-way capable). Channels available but not in use: 88.

Basic Service
Subscribers: 43.
Programming (received off-air): WBBM-TV (CBS) Chicago; WCPX-TV (ION) Chicago; WFLD (FOX) Chicago; WGN-TV (CW, IND) Chicago; WIFR (CBS) Freeport; WLS-TV (ABC) Chicago; WMAQ-TV (NBC) Chicago; WPWR-TV (MNT) Gary; WQRF-TV (FOX) Rockford; WREX (CW, NBC) Rockford; WTTW (PBS) Chicago; WTVO (ABC, MNT) Rockford; WYCC (PBS) Chicago.
Programming (via satellite): ABC Family Channel; CNBC; CNN; Comedy Central; C-SPAN; Discovery Channel; Disney Channel; ESPN; ESPN 2; History Channel; Lifetime; Nickelodeon; QVC; TBS Superstation; The Learning Channel; Trinity Broadcasting Network; Turner Network TV; USA Network; Weather Channel.
Fee: $45.00 installation; $54.95 monthly.

Pay Service 1
Pay Units: N.A.
Programming (via satellite): Showtime.
Fee: $10.95 monthly.

Video-On-Demand: No

Internet Service
Operational: No.

Telephone Service
None

Homes passed: 256. Miles of plant (coax & fiber) included in Moline
Regional Vice President: Cari Fenzel. Engineering Director: Mitch Carlson. Technical Operations Manager: Chris Toalson. Marketing Director: Greg Evans.
City fee: 5% of gross.
Ownership: Mediacom LLC (MSO).

BUSHNELL—Insight Communications. Now served by MACOMB, IL [IL0076]. ICA: IL0190.

CAHOKIA—Charter Communications, 941 Charter Commons Dr, Saint Louis, MO 63017. Phone: 636-207-7044. Fax: 636-230-7034. Web Site: http://www.charter.com. Also serves Sauget. ICA: IL0088.
TV Market Ranking: 11 (CAHOKIA, Sauget). Franchise award date: N.A. Franchise expiration date: N.A. Began: April 1, 1982.
Channel capacity: N.A. Channels available but not in use: N.A.

Basic Service
Subscribers: 3,297.
Programming (received off-air): KDNL-TV (ABC) St. Louis; KETC (PBS) St. Louis; KMOV (CBS) St. Louis; KNLC (IND) St. Louis; KPLR-TV (CW) St. Louis; KSDK (NBC) St. Louis; KTVI (FOX) St. Louis; WPXS (IND) Mount Vernon; WRBU (MNT) East St. Louis; 1 FM.
Programming (via satellite): C-SPAN; Discovery Channel; QVC; TBS Superstation; Weather Channel; WGN America.
Current originations: Government Access.
Fee: $29.99 installation.

Expanded Basic Service 1
Subscribers: 3,288.
Programming (via satellite): ABC Family Channel; AMC; Animal Planet; Arts & Entertainment; BET Networks; Cartoon Network; CNN; Comedy Central; Disney Channel; ESPN; Fox News Channel; Fox Sports Net Midwest; FX; Hallmark Channel; Headline News; Lifetime; MTV; Nickelodeon; Spike TV; The Learning Channel; truTV; Turner Network TV; TV Land; USA Network; VH1.
Fee: $49.99 monthly.

Digital Basic Service
Subscribers: N.A.
Programming (via satellite): BBC America; Bravo; Discovery Digital Networks; DMX Music; ESPN 2; ESPN Classic Sports; ESPNews; Fox Sports World; Golf Channel; GSN; HGTV; History Channel; Independent Film Channel; MTV Networks Digital Suite; National Geographic Channel; Nick Jr.; Speed Channel; Syfy; Turner Classic Movies; TV Guide Interactive Inc.; Versus; WE tv.

Digital Pay Service 1
Pay Units: 762.
Programming (via satellite): Cinemax (multiplexed); Encore (multiplexed); HBO (multiplexed); Showtime (multiplexed); Starz (multiplexed); The Movie Channel (multiplexed).
Fee: $1.75 monthly (Encore), $12.60 monthly (Showtime), $13.40 monthly (Cinemax), $13.50 monthly (HBO).

Video-On-Demand: Yes

Pay-Per-View
iN DEMAND (delivered digitally); Playboy TV (delivered digitally).

Internet Service
Operational: Yes.
Broadband Service: Charter Pipeline.
Fee: $29.99 monthly.

Telephone Service
Digital: Operational
Fee: $29.99 monthly

Miles of Plant: 69.0 (coaxial); None (fiber optic). Homes passed: 6,105. Total homes in franchised area: 6,105.
Vice President & General Manager: Steve Trippe. Operations Director: Tom Williams. Marketing Director: Beverly Wall.
Ownership: Charter Communications Inc. (MSO).

CAIRO—NewWave Communications, One Montgomery Plaza, 4th Fl, Sikeston, MO 63801. Phones: 888-863-9928 (Customer service); 573-472-9500. Fax: 573-481-9809. E-mail: info@newwavecom.com. Web Site: http://www.newwavecom.com. ICA: IL0136.
TV Market Ranking: 69 (CAIRO). Franchise award date: N.A. Franchise expiration date: N.A. Began: August 1, 1981.
Channel capacity: 61 (operating 2-way). Channels available but not in use: 11.

Basic Service
Subscribers: 368.
Programming (received off-air): KBSI (FOX) Cape Girardeau; KFVS-TV (CBS, CW) Cape Girardeau; WDKA (MNT) Paducah; WPSD-TV (NBC) Paducah; WSIL-TV (ABC) Harrisburg; WSIU-TV (PBS) Carbondale; WTCT (IND) Marion.
Programming (via satellite): C-SPAN; C-SPAN 2; Hallmark Channel; Home Shopping Network; QVC; TBS Superstation; The Learning Channel; Weather Channel; WGN America.
Current originations: Government Access; Educational Access; Public Access.
Fee: $17.45 monthly.

Expanded Basic Service 1
Subscribers: 327.
Programming (via satellite): ABC Family Channel; AMC; Arts & Entertainment; BET Networks; Bravo; Cartoon Network; CNN; Comedy Central; Country Music TV; Discovery Channel; Disney Channel; E! Entertainment Television; ESPN; ESPN 2; ESPN Classic Sports; Eternal Word TV Network; Fox News Channel; Fox Sports Net Midwest; Headline News; HGTV; Lifetime; MTV; Nickelodeon; Speed Channel; Spike TV; Syfy; Toon Disney; Travel Channel; truTV; Turner Network TV; TV Land; USA Network; Versus; VH1.
Fee: $12.95 monthly.

Pay Service 1
Pay Units: 623.
Programming (via satellite): HBO (multiplexed); Showtime; The Movie Channel.
Fee: $7.95 monthly (TMC), $9.95 monthly (HBO or Showtime).

Pay Service 2
Pay Units: 243.
Programming (via satellite): Cinemax.
Fee: $8.95 monthly.

Video-On-Demand: No

Internet Service
Operational: Yes.

Telephone Service
Digital: Operational

Miles of Plant: 25.0 (coaxial); None (fiber optic). Homes passed: 2,365.
General Manager: Bill Flowers. Technical Operations Manager: Chris Mooday.
City fee: 5% of gross.
Ownership: NewWave Communications (MSO).

CALEDONIA—Mediacom, 3900 26th Ave, Moline, IL 61265. Phone: 309-797-2580. Fax: 309-797-2414. Web Site: http://www.mediacomcable.com. Also serves Argyle & Candlewick Lake. ICA: IL0465.
TV Market Ranking: 97 (Argyle, CALEDONIA, Candlewick Lake). Franchise award date: N.A. Franchise expiration date: N.A. Began: N.A.
Channel capacity: N.A. Channels available but not in use: N.A.

Basic Service
Subscribers: 649.
Programming (received off-air): WFLD (FOX) Chicago; WIFR (CBS) Freeport; WPWR-TV (MNT) Gary; WQRF-TV (FOX) Rockford; WREX (CW, NBC) Rockford; WTTW (PBS) Chicago; WTVO (ABC, MNT) Rockford.
Programming (via satellite): CW+; QVC; WGN America.
Fee: $45.00 installation; $20.95 monthly.

Expanded Basic Service 1
Subscribers: N.A.
Programming (via satellite): ABC Family Channel; AMC; Animal Planet; Arts & Entertainment; Bravo; Cartoon Network; CNBC; CNN; Comcast SportsNet Chicago; Comedy Central; Country Music TV; C-SPAN; Discovery Channel; Disney Channel; E! Entertainment Television; ESPN; ESPN 2; FitTV; Food Network; Headline News; HGTV; History Channel; Home Shopping Network; Lifetime; MSNBC; MTV; Nickelodeon; Speed Channel; Spike TV; Syfy; TBS Superstation; The Learning Channel; Travel Channel; truTV; Turner Network TV; TV Land; USA Network; VH1; Weather Channel.
Fee: $34.00 monthly.

Digital Basic Service
Subscribers: N.A.
Programming (via satellite): AmericanLife TV Network; BBC America; Bio; Bloomberg Television; Discovery Health Channel; Discovery Kids Channel; Discovery Military Channel; Discovery Planet Green; ESPNews; Fox Movie Channel; Fox Soccer; Fuse; G4; Golf Channel; History Channel International; ID Investigation Discovery; Independent Film Channel; Lifetime Movie Network; MTV Hits; MTV2; Music Choice; National Geographic Channel; Nick Jr.; NickToons TV; Outdoor Channel; Science Channel; Sleuth; Style Network; TeenNick; Turner Classic Movies; TVG Network; VH1 Classic.
Fee: $9.00 monthly.

Digital Pay Service 1
Pay Units: N.A.
Programming (via satellite): Cinemax (multiplexed); Encore (multiplexed); HBO (multiplexed); Showtime (multiplexed); Starz (multiplexed); The Movie Channel (multiplexed).
Fee: $11.95 monthly (HBO, Cinemax, Showtime/TMC or Starz/Encore).

Video-On-Demand: No

Pay-Per-View
iN DEMAND (delivered digitally); Playboy TV (delivered digitally); Ten Clips (delivered digitally).

Internet Service
Operational: Yes.
Broadband Service: Mediacom High Speed Internet.
Fee: $59.95 installation; $40.95 monthly.

Telephone Service
Analog: Not Operational
Digital: Operational
Fee: $39.95 installation; $39.95 monthly

Homes passed: 1,297. Mile of plant (coax & fiber) included in Moline
Regional Vice President: Cari Fenzel. Engineering Director: Mitch Carlson. Technical Operations Manager: Chris Toalson. Marketing Director: Greg Evans.
City fee: 5% of gross.
Ownership: Mediacom LLC (MSO).

CALHOUN—Formerly served by CableDirect. No longer in operation. ICA: IL0438.

CAMERON—Nova Cablevision Inc., PO Box 1412, 677 W Main St, Galesburg, IL 61401. Phone: 309-342-9681. Fax: 309-342-4408. Web Site: http://novacablevision.com. ICA: IL0444.
TV Market Ranking: Below 100 (CAMERON). Franchise award date: N.A. Franchise expiration date: N.A. Began: September 16, 1989.
Channel capacity: 60 (not 2-way capable). Channels available but not in use: N.A.

Basic Service
Subscribers: 49.
Programming (received off-air): KGCW (CW) Burlington; KIIN (PBS) Iowa City; KLJB (CW, FOX) Davenport; KWQC-TV (NBC) Davenport; WEEK-TV (NBC) Peoria; WHBF-TV (CBS) Rock Island; WHOI (ABC, CW) Peoria; WMBD-TV (CBS) Peoria; WQAD-TV (ABC) Moline; WQPT-TV (PBS) Moline; WTVP (PBS) Peoria.
Programming (via satellite): ABC Family Channel; AMC; Animal Planet; Arts & Entertainment; Cartoon Network; CNBC; CNN; Comedy Central; Country Music TV; Discovery Channel; Disney Channel; ESPN; ESPN 2; Food Network; HGTV; History Channel; Lifetime; MTV; Nickelodeon; QVC; Spike TV; Syfy; TBS Superstation; The Learning Channel; Turner Network TV; TV Land; USA Network; Weather Channel; WGN America.
Fee: $60.00 installation; $53.95 monthly.

Digital Basic Service
Subscribers: N.A.
Programming (via satellite): Bio; Bloomberg Television; CMT Pure Country; Discovery Health Channel; Discovery Kids Channel; Discovery Military Channel; Discovery Planet Green; Disney XD; DMX Music; ESPN 2; ESPN Classic Sports; ESPNews; Fox Movie Channel; Fox Soccer; FSN Digital Atlantic; FSN Digital Central; FSN Digital Pacific; Fuse; G4; Golf Channel; Great American Country; GSN; HGTV; History Channel; History Channel International; ID Investigation Discovery; Independent Film Channel; Lifetime Movie Network; MTV Hits; MTV2; NickToons TV; Noggin; Outdoor Channel; Science Channel; ShopNBC; Speed Channel; Style Network; Syfy; The N; Trinity Broadcasting Network; Turner Classic Movies; Versus; VH1 Classic; VH1 Soul; WE tv.
Fee: $16.95 monthly.

Pay Service 1
Pay Units: 4.
Programming (via satellite): HBO.
Fee: $12.85 monthly.

Pay Service 2
Pay Units: 2.
Programming (via satellite): Cinemax.
Fee: $12.85 monthly.

Digital Pay Service 1
Pay Units: N.A.
Programming (via satellite): Cinemax (multiplexed); Encore (multiplexed); Flix; HBO (multiplexed); Showtime (multiplexed); Starz (multiplexed); Sundance Channel; The Movie Channel (multiplexed).
Fee: $12.85 monthly (HBO, Showtime/TMC/Flix/Sundance), Cinemax, or Starz/Encore).

Video-On-Demand: No

Pay-Per-View
Hot Choice (delivered digitally); Playboy TV (delivered digitally); Fresh (delivered digitally); Spice: Xcess (delivered digitally); Club Jenna (delivered digitally).

Internet Service
Operational: Yes. Began: January 1, 2005.
Fee: $30.00 installation; $39.95 monthly; $3.95 modem lease.

Telephone Service
None

Miles of Plant: 2.0 (coaxial); None (fiber optic). Homes passed: 97.
Manager: Robert G. Fischer Jr. Office Manager: Hazel Harden.
Ownership: Nova Cablevision Inc. (MSO).

CAMP POINT—Adams Telephone. This cable system has converted to IPTV. See Camp Point, IL [IL5313]. ICA: IL0206.

CAMP POINT (village)—Adams Telecom. Formerly [IL0206]. This cable system has converted to IPTV, PO Box 248, 405 Em-

minga Rd, Golden, IL 62339. Phone: 217-696-4411. E-mail: service@adams.net. Web Site: http://www.adams.net. ICA: IL5313.
Channel capacity: N.A. Channels available but not in use: N.A.
Internet Service
Operational: Yes.
Ownership: Adams Telephone Co-Operative.

CAMPTON TWP.—Comcast Cable. Now served by OAK BROOK, IL [IL0006]. ICA: IL0108.

CANTON—Comcast Cable, 3517 N Dries Ln, Peoria, IL 61604. Phone: 309-686-2600. Fax: 309-686-9828. Web Site: http://www.comcast.com. Also serves Brereton, Cuba, Fulton County, Lewistown & Norris. ICA: IL0087.
TV Market Ranking: 83 (Brereton, CANTON, Fulton County (portions), Norris); Below 100 (Cuba, Lewistown); Outside TV Markets (Fulton County (portions)). Franchise award date: N.A. Franchise expiration date: N.A. Began: August 1, 1974.
Channel capacity: N.A. Channels available but not in use: N.A.
Basic Service
Subscribers: N.A. Included in Peoria
Programming (received off-air): WAOE (MNT) Peoria; WEEK-TV (NBC) Peoria; WHOI (ABC, CW) Peoria; WMBD-TV (CBS) Peoria; WTVP (PBS) Peoria; WYZZ-TV (FOX) Bloomington; 1 FM.
Programming (via satellite): C-SPAN; C-SPAN 2; Discovery Channel; Eternal Word TV Network; Home Shopping Network; ION Television; QVC; Trinity Broadcasting Network; TV Guide Network; Weather Channel; WGN America.
Current originations: Educational Access; Leased Access.
Planned originations: Public Access.
Fee: $25.00 installation; $14.60 monthly; $3.85 converter.
Expanded Basic Service 1
Subscribers: 3,648.
Programming (via satellite): ABC Family Channel; AMC; Animal Planet; Arts & Entertainment; BET Networks; Bravo; Cartoon Network; CNBC; CNN; Comcast SportsNet Chicago; Comedy Central; Country Music TV; Disney Channel; E! Entertainment Television; ESPN; ESPN 2; Food Network; Fox News Channel; Fox Sports Net Midwest; FX; Golf Channel; Great American Country; Hallmark Channel; Headline News; HGTV; History Channel; Lifetime; MSNBC; MTV; MTV2; National Geographic Channel; Nickelodeon; Oxygen; ShopNBC; SoapNet; Speed Channel; Spike TV; Style Network; Syfy; TBS Superstation; The Learning Channel; Toon Disney; Travel Channel; truTV; Turner Network TV; USA Network; VH1.
Fee: $37.15 monthly.
Digital Basic Service
Subscribers: 913.
Programming (received off-air): WEEK-TV (NBC) Peoria; WHOI (ABC, CW) Peoria; WMBD-TV (CBS) Peoria; WTVP (PBS) Peoria; WYZZ-TV (FOX) Bloomington.
Programming (via satellite): AmericanLife TV Network; BBC America; Bio; Bloomberg Television; CBS College Sports Network; Cooking Channel; C-SPAN 3; Discovery Digital Networks; Discovery HD Theater; DMX Music; Do-It-Yourself; Encore (multiplexed); ESPN 2 HD; ESPN Classic Sports; ESPN HD; ESPN U; ESPNews; Fox College Sports Atlantic; Fox College Sports Central; Fox College Sports Pacific; Fox Movie Channel; Fox Reality Channel; Fox Soccer; G4; GAS; GSN; Halogen Network; HDNet; HDNet Movies; History Channel International; HorseRacing TV; Independent Film Channel; Lifetime Movie Network; Lifetime Real Women; MTV Networks Digital Suite; NFL Network; Nick Jr.; Nick Too; NickToons TV; Outdoor Channel; Ovation; Palladia; PBS Kids Sprout; Si TV; Sleuth; Sundance Channel; Tennis Channel; Toon Disney; Turner Classic Movies; Turner Network TV HD; TV Land; TVG Network; Universal HD; Versus; WE tv.
Fee: $17.00 monthly.
Digital Pay Service 1
Pay Units: 324.
Programming (via satellite): Cinemax (multiplexed); Flix; HBO (multiplexed); HBO HD; Showtime (multiplexed); Showtime HD; Starz (multiplexed); The Movie Channel (multiplexed).
Fee: $10.00 monthly (Cinemax or Starz), $13.00 monthly (HBO or Showtime/TMC).
Video-On-Demand: Yes
Pay-Per-View
Addressable homes: 913.
iN DEMAND (delivered digitally), Fee: $3.95, Addressable: Yes; Playboy TV (delivered digitally); ESPN (delivered digitally).
Internet Service
Operational: Yes.
Subscribers: 500.
Broadband Service: Comcast High Speed Internet.
Fee: $99.95 installation; $44.95 monthly; $10.00 modem lease; $99.95 modem purchase.
Telephone Service
None
Homes passed, total homes in franchised area and miles of plant incuded in Peoria
General Manager: John Nieber. Chief Technician: Mike Vandergraft.
City fee: 5% of gross.
Ownership: Comcast Cable Communications Inc. (MSO).

CANTRALL—Mediacom. Now served by DELEVAN, IL [IL0172]. ICA: IL0308.

CARLINVILLE—NewWave Communications, 1176 E 1500 North Rd, Taylorville, IL 62568. Phone: 217-287-7992. Fax: 217-287-7034. E-mail: info@newwavecom.com. Web Site: http://www.newwavecom.com. ICA: IL0081.
TV Market Ranking: Outside TV Markets (CARLINVILLE). Franchise award date: N.A. Franchise expiration date: N.A. Began: July 27, 1979.
Channel capacity: N.A. Channels available but not in use: N.A.
Basic Service
Subscribers: 952.
Programming (received off-air): KDNL-TV (ABC) St. Louis; KETC (PBS) St. Louis; KMOV (CBS) St. Louis; KNLC (IND) St. Louis; KPLR-TV (CW) St. Louis; KSDK (NBC) St. Louis; KTVI (FOX) St. Louis; WICS (ABC) Springfield; WRBU (MNT) East St. Louis; allband FM.
Programming (via satellite): ABC Family Channel; C-SPAN; ESPN; Home Shopping Network; INSP; MTV; QVC; WGN America.
Fee: $29.99 installation.
Expanded Basic Service 1
Subscribers: 880.
Programming (via satellite): AMC; Animal Planet; Arts & Entertainment; Bravo; Cartoon Network; CNBC; CNN; Comedy

Central; Country Music TV; Discovery Channel; Disney Channel; E! Entertainment Television; ESPN 2; Food Network; Fox News Channel; Fox Sports Net Midwest; G4; Headline News; HGTV; History Channel; Lifetime; MSNBC; Nickelodeon; Oxygen; Spike TV; Syfy; TBS Superstation; The Learning Channel; Travel Channel; Turner Network TV; USA Network; VH1; Weather Channel.
Fee: $42.99 monthly.
Digital Basic Service
Subscribers: 56.
Fee: $15.00 installation; $8.45 monthly.
Video-On-Demand: No
Internet Service
Operational: Yes.
Telephone Service
Digital: Operational
Miles of Plant: 32.0 (coaxial); None (fiber optic). Homes passed: 3,234.
General Manager: Bill Flowers. Technical Operations Manager: Larry Harmon.
Ownership: NewWave Communications (MSO).

CARLOCK—Formerly served by CableDirect. No longer in operation. ICA: IL0670.

CARLYLE—Charter Communications, 941 Charter Commons Dr, Saint Louis, MO 63017. Phone: 636-207-7044. Fax: 636-230-7034. Web Site: http://www.charter.com. ICA: IL0184.
TV Market Ranking: Below 100 (CARLYLE). Franchise award date: N.A. Franchise expiration date: N.A. Began: June 1, 1983.
Channel capacity: N.A. Channels available but not in use: N.A.
Basic Service
Subscribers: 901.
Programming (received off-air): KDNL-TV (ABC) St. Louis; KETC (PBS) St. Louis; KNLC (IND) St. Louis; KPLR-TV (CW) St. Louis; KSDK (NBC) St. Louis; KTVI (FOX) St. Louis; WPXS (IND) Mount Vernon; WRBU (MNT) East St. Louis; WSIU-TV (PBS) Carbondale; allband FM.
Programming (via satellite): C-SPAN; C-SPAN 2; Eternal Word TV Network; GRTV Network; Home Shopping Network; INSP; Jewelry Television; QVC; ShopNBC; TBS Superstation; Trinity Broadcasting Network; TV Guide Network; Univision; Weatherscan; WGN America.
Current originations: Government Access; Public Access.
Fee: $29.99 installation.
Expanded Basic Service 1
Subscribers: N.A.
Programming (via satellite): ABC Family Channel; AMC; Animal Planet; Arts & Entertainment; BET Networks; Bravo; Cartoon Network; CNBC; CNN; Comedy Central; Country Music TV; Discovery Channel; Disney Channel; E! Entertainment Television; ESPN; ESPN 2; Food Network; Fox Movie Channel; Fox News Channel; Fox Sports Net Midwest; FX; G4; Golf Channel; GSN; Hallmark Channel; Headline News; HGTV; History Channel; Lifetime; MSNBC; MTV; National Geographic Channel; Nickelodeon; Oxygen; SoapNet; Speed Channel; Spike TV; Style Network; Syfy; The Learning Channel; Toon Disney; Travel Channel; truTV; Turner Classic Movies; Turner Network TV; TV Land; USA Network; Versus; VH1; WE tv; Weather Channel.
Fee: $49.99 monthly.
Digital Basic Service
Subscribers: N.A.
Programming (received off-air): KMOV (CBS) St. Louis.
Programming (via satellite): BBC America; Bio; Bloomberg Television; Discovery Digital Networks; Do-It-Yourself; Encore Action; ESPN Classic Sports; FitTV; Fox College Sports Atlantic; Fox College Sports Central; Fox College Sports Pacific; Fox Sports World; Fuel TV; Fuse; GAS; Great American Country; History Channel International; Independent Film Channel; International Television (ITV); Lifetime Movie Network; MTV Networks Digital Suite; Music Choice; NFL Network; Nick Jr.; Nick Too; NickToons TV; Sundance Channel; TV Guide Interactive Inc.
Digital Pay Service 1
Pay Units: 71.
Programming (via satellite): Cinemax (multiplexed); HBO (multiplexed); Showtime (multiplexed); Starz (multiplexed); The Movie Channel (multiplexed).
Fee: $1.75 monthly (Encore), $13.40 monthly (Showtime), $14.05 monthly (HBO).
Video-On-Demand: Yes
Pay-Per-View
iN DEMAND (delivered digitally); Playboy TV (delivered digitally); Shorteez (delivered digitally); Sports PPV (delivered digitally); ESPN Now (delivered digitally); Fresh (delivered digitally).
Internet Service
Operational: Yes. Began: January 1, 2002.
Broadband Service: Charter Pipeline.
Fee: $29.99 monthly; $5.00 modem lease; $99.99 modem purchase.
Telephone Service
Digital: Operational
Miles of Plant: 19.0 (coaxial); None (fiber optic). Homes passed: 1,362. Total homes in franchised area: 1,372.
Vice President & General Manager: Steve Trippe. Operations Director: Tom Williams. Marketing Director: Beverly Wall.
City fee: 3% of gross.
Ownership: Charter Communications Inc. (MSO).

CARMI—Formerly served by Charter Communications. No longer in operation. ICA: IL0126.

CARPENTERSVILLE—Comcast Cable. Now served by SCHAUMBURG, IL [IL0036]. ICA: IL0023.

CARRIER MILLS—Galaxy Cablevision, 7155 US Hwy 45 S, Carrier Mills, IL 62917. Phone: 573-472-8200. Fax: 618-991-2261. Web Site: http://www.galaxycable.com. Also serves Saline County (portions). ICA: IL0195.

TV Market Ranking: 69 (CARRIER MILLS, Saline County (portions)). Franchise award date: N.A. Franchise expiration date: N.A. Began: August 1, 1982.

Channel capacity: 116 (operating 2-way). Channels available but not in use: None.

Basic Service

Subscribers: 573.

Programming (received off-air): KBSI (FOX) Cape Girardeau; KFVS-TV (CBS, CW) Cape Girardeau; WDKA (MNT) Paducah; WPSD-TV (NBC) Paducah; WPXS (IND) Mount Vernon; WQWQ-LP (CW) Paducah; WSIL-TV (ABC) Harrisburg; WSIU-TV (PBS) Carbondale; WTCT (IND) Marion.

Programming (via satellite): ABC Family Channel; AMC; Animal Planet; Arts & Entertainment; BET Networks; Cartoon Network; CNBC; CNN; Comedy Central; C-SPAN; Discovery Channel; Disney Channel; E! Entertainment Television; ESPN; ESPN 2; ESPN Classic Sports; Food Network; Fox News Channel; Fox Sports Net; Fuse; FX; Great American Country; Headline News; HGTV; History Channel; Home Shopping Network; INSP; Lifetime; National Geographic Channel; Outdoor Channel; QVC; Syfy; TBS Superstation; The Learning Channel; Toon Disney; Travel Channel; truTV; Turner Classic Movies; Turner Network TV; USA Network; Weather Channel; WGN America.

Fee: $30.00 installation; $42.50 monthly; $3.00 converter.

Digital Basic Service

Subscribers: 123.

Programming (via satellite): AmericanLife TV Network; BBC America; Bio; Bloomberg Television; Discovery Health Channel; Discovery Kids Channel; Discovery Military Channel; Discovery Planet Green; ESPN Classic Sports; ESPNews; FitTV; Fox College Sports Atlantic; Fox College Sports Central; Fox College Sports Pacific; Fox Movie Channel; Fuse; G4; Golf Channel; Gospel Music Channel; GSN; Halogen Network; History Channel International; ID Investigation Discovery; Lifetime Movie Network; National Geographic Channel; Outdoor Channel; Science Channel; Sleuth; SoapNet; Speed Channel; Style Network; Toon Disney; Turner Classic Movies; WE tv.

Pay Service 1

Pay Units: N.A.

Programming (via satellite): Encore; HBO; Showtime; The Movie Channel.

Fee: $12.00 monthly (each).

Digital Pay Service 1

Pay Units: N.A.

Programming (via satellite): Cinemax (multiplexed); Encore (multiplexed); Flix; HBO (multiplexed); Showtime (multiplexed); Starz (multiplexed); The Movie Channel (multiplexed).

Pay-Per-View

iN DEMAND (delivered digitally); Hot Choice (delivered digitally); Playboy TV (delivered digitally); Spice: Xcess (delivered digitally).

Internet Service

Operational: Yes.

Subscribers: 164.

Broadband Service: Galaxy Cable Internet.

Fee: $49.95 installation; $35.00 monthly.

Telephone Service

None

Miles of Plant: 41.0 (coaxial); 12.0 (fiber optic). Homes passed: 1,419.

State Manager: Ward Webb. Technical Manager: Audie Murphy. Engineer: John Stewarr. Customer Service Manager: Malynda Walker.

Ownership: Galaxy Cable Inc. (MSO).

CARROLLTON—Greene County Partners Inc., PO Box 200, 100 Redbud Rd, Virginia, IL 62691. Phones: 800-252-1799; 217-452-7725. Fax: 217-452-7797. E-mail: solutions@casscomm.com. Web Site: http://www.casscomm.com. Also serves Roodhouse & White Hall. ICA: IL0221.

TV Market Ranking: Outside TV Markets (CARROLLTON, Roodhouse, White Hall). Franchise award date: N.A. Franchise expiration date: N.A. Began: August 1, 1981.

Channel capacity: 83 (operating 2-way). Channels available but not in use: 29.

Basic Service

Subscribers: 1,172.

Programming (received off-air): KDNL-TV (ABC) St. Louis; KETC (PBS) St. Louis; KMOV (CBS) St. Louis; KNLC (IND) St. Louis; KPLR-TV (CW) St. Louis; KSDK (NBC) St. Louis; KTVI (FOX) St. Louis; WICS (ABC) Springfield; WRBU (MNT) East St. Louis; WRSP-TV (FOX) Springfield.

Programming (via satellite): ABC Family Channel; AMC; AmericanLife TV Network; Animal Planet; Arts & Entertainment; Bravo; Cartoon Network; CNBC; CNN; Comedy Central; Country Music TV; C-SPAN; Discovery Channel; Disney Channel; E! Entertainment Television; ESPN; ESPN 2; ESPN Classic Sports; ESPNews; Food Network; Fox News Channel; Fox Sports Net Midwest; FX; Great American Country; Headline News; HGTV; History Channel; Home Shopping Network; Lifetime; MSNBC; MTV; Nickelodeon; Outdoor Channel; QVC; ShopNBC; Spike TV; Syfy; TBS Superstation; The Learning Channel; Travel Channel; Trinity Broadcasting Network; truTV; Turner Network TV; TV Guide Network; TV Land; USA Network; VH1; Weather Channel; WGN America.

Fee: $45.00 installation; $49.95 monthly.

Digital Basic Service

Subscribers: 75.

Programming (via satellite): BBC America; Bio; Bloomberg Television; Bravo; Discovery Digital Networks; DMX Music; ESPN Classic Sports; Fox College Sports Atlantic; Fox College Sports Central; Fox College Sports Pacific; Fox Movie Channel; Fox Soccer; GAS; Golf Channel; GSN; Halogen Network; History Channel; History Channel International; Independent Film Channel; Lifetime Movie Network; MTV Networks Digital Suite; National Geographic Channel; Nick Jr.; NickToons TV; Ovation; Speed Channel; Sundance Channel; Trio; Turner Classic Movies; Versus; WE tv.

Fee: $11.95 monthly.

Digital Pay Service 1

Pay Units: 319.

Programming (via satellite): Cinemax (multiplexed); Encore; HBO.

Fee: $20.00 installation; $11.95 monthly.

Pay-Per-View

iN DEMAND (delivered digitally).

Internet Service

Operational: Yes.

Subscribers: 586.

Fee: $30.00-$99.00 installation; $29.95-$99.95 monthly.

Telephone Service

Digital: Operational

Subscribers: 44.

Miles of Plant: 49.0 (coaxial); 26.0 (fiber optic). Total homes in franchised area: 2,283.

General Manager: Chad Winters. Chief Technician: Lance Allen. Marketing Director: Erynn Snedeker.

Ownership: Green County Partners Inc. (MSO).

CARTHAGE—Mediacom, PO Box 334, 609 S 4th St, Chillicothe, IL 61523. Phone: 309-274-4500. Fax: 309-274-3188. Web Site: http://www.mediacomcable.com. ICA: IL0183.

TV Market Ranking: Below 100 (CARTHAGE). Franchise award date: May 8, 1969. Franchise expiration date: N.A. Began: April 1, 1970.

Channel capacity: N.A. Channels available but not in use: N.A.

Basic Service

Subscribers: 1,035.

Programming (received off-air): KHQA-TV (ABC, CBS) Hannibal; KIIN (PBS) Iowa City; KTVO (ABC) Kirksville; KWQC-TV (NBC) Davenport; KYOU-TV (FOX) Ottumwa; WGEM-TV (CW, NBC) Quincy; WHBF-TV (CBS) Rock Island; WMEC (PBS) Macomb; WQAD-TV (ABC) Moline; WTJR (IND) Quincy.

Programming (via microwave): KPLR-TV (CW) St. Louis.

Programming (via satellite): WGN America.

Fee: $45.00 installation; $20.95 monthly.

Expanded Basic Service 1

Subscribers: 981.

Programming (via satellite): ABC Family Channel; AMC; Animal Planet; Arts & Entertainment; Cartoon Network; CNN; C-SPAN; C-SPAN 2; Discovery Channel; Disney Channel; E! Entertainment Television; ESPN; ESPN 2; Food Network; Fox News Channel; FX; Headline News; HGTV; History Channel; Home Shopping Network; Lifetime; MSNBC; MTV; Nickelodeon; QVC; ShopNBC; Speed Channel; Spike TV; TBS Superstation; The Learning Channel; Turner Network TV; TV Guide Network; USA Network; Versus; Weather Channel.

Fee: $34.00 monthly.

Digital Basic Service

Subscribers: N.A.

Programming (via satellite): AmericanLife TV Network; BBC America; Bio; Bloomberg Television; Discovery Digital Networks; ESPNews; Fox Movie Channel; Fox Soccer; Fuse; G4; GAS; Golf Channel; History Channel International; Independent Film Channel; Lifetime Movie Network; Lime; MTV Networks Digital Suite; Music Choice; National Geographic Channel; Nick Jr.; NickToons TV; Outdoor Channel; Sleuth; Style Network; Sundance Channel; Turner Classic Movies; TVG Network; Versus.

Fee: $9.00 monthly.

Digital Expanded Basic Service

Subscribers: N.A.

Programming (via satellite): Discovery HD Theater; ESPN 2 HD; ESPN HD; HDNet; HDNet Movies.

Fee: $6.95 monthly.

Digital Pay Service 1

Pay Units: N.A.

Programming (via satellite): Cinemax (multiplexed); Encore (multiplexed); Flix; HBO (multiplexed); HBO HD; Showtime (multiplexed); Showtime HD; Starz (multiplexed); Starz HDTV; The Movie Channel (multiplexed); The Movie Channel HD.

Fee: $11.95 monthly (HBO, Cinemax, Showtime/TMC or Starz/Encore).

Video-On-Demand: Yes

Pay-Per-View

iN DEMAND (delivered digitally); Playboy TV (delivered digitally); TEN Clip, TEN, & TEN BLOX (delivered digitally).

Internet Service

Operational: Yes.

Broadband Service: Mediacom High Speed Internet.

Fee: $59.95 installation; $45.95 monthly.

Telephone Service

Digital: Operational

Fee: $39.95 installation; $39.95 monthly

Miles of Plant: 22.0 (coaxial); None (fiber optic). Homes passed: 1,422.

Vice President: Don Hagwell. Operations Director: Gary Wightman. Technical Operations Manager: Larry Brackman. Marketing Director: Stephanie Law.

City fee: 3% of gross.

Ownership: Mediacom LLC (MSO).

CASEY—Mediacom. Now served by MARTINSVILLE, IL [IL0217]. ICA: IL0477.

CAVE-IN-ROCK—Windjammer Cable, 4400 PGA Blvd, Ste 902, Palm Beach Gardens, FL 33410. Phones: 877-450-5558; 561-775-1208. Fax: 561-775-7811. Web Site: http://www.windjammercable.com. ICA: IL0662.

TV Market Ranking: 69 (CAVE-IN-ROCK). Franchise award date: N.A. Franchise expiration date: N.A. Began: N.A.

Channel capacity: N.A. Channels available but not in use: N.A.

Basic Service

Subscribers: 179.

Programming (received off-air): KBSI (FOX) Cape Girardeau; KFVS-TV (CBS, CW) Cape Girardeau; WDKA (MNT) Paducah; WKMA-TV (PBS) Madisonville; WPSD-TV (NBC) Paducah; WSIL-TV (ABC) Harrisburg.

Programming (via satellite): ABC Family Channel; Arts & Entertainment; CNN; Country Music TV; Discovery Channel; Disney Channel; ESPN; ESPN 2; Great American Country; Headline News; Nickelodeon; QVC; Spike TV; Syfy; TBS Superstation; The Learning Channel; Trinity Broadcasting Network; Turner Network TV; TV Land; USA Network; VH1; WGN America.

Fee: $39.95 installation; $27.30 monthly.

Pay Service 1

Pay Units: N.A.

Programming (via satellite): HBO; Showtime.

Fee: $15.95 monthly (each).

Video-On-Demand: No

Internet Service

Operational: No.

Telephone Service

None

Miles of Plant: 15.0 (coaxial); None (fiber optic).

Ownership: Windjammer Communications LLC (MSO).

CEDAR POINT—McNabb Cable & Satellite Inc., PO Box 218, 308 W Main St, Mc Nabb, IL 61335-0218. Phone: 815-882-2202. Fax: 815-882-2141. ICA: IL0434.

TV Market Ranking: Below 100 (CEDAR POINT). Franchise award date: September 22, 1986. Franchise expiration date: N.A. Began: February 1, 1987.

Channel capacity: N.A. Channels available but not in use: N.A.

Basic Service

Subscribers: 42.

Programming (received off-air): WAOE (MNT) Peoria; WCIU-TV (IND) Chicago; WEEK-TV (NBC) Peoria; WGN-TV (CW, IND) Chicago; WHOI (ABC, CW) Peoria; WMBD-TV (CBS) Peoria; WTVP (PBS) Peoria; WYZZ-TV (FOX) Bloomington.

Programming (via satellite): ABC Family Channel; American Movie Classics; CNN; Comedy Central; Country Music TV; Discovery Channel; Disney Channel; ESPN; ESPN 2; Fox News Channel; FX; ION Television; Nickelodeon; QVC; Speed Channel; Spike TV; TBS Superstation; Turner Network TV; TV Land; USA Network; Weather Channel.

Fee: $35.00 installation; $18.95 monthly.

Pay Service 1

Pay Units: 1.

Programming (via satellite): Cinemax.

Fee: $9.00 monthly.

Pay Service 2

Pay Units: 8.

Programming (via satellite): HBO.

Fee: $11.47 monthly.

Video-On-Demand: No

Internet Service

Operational: No.

Telephone Service

None

Miles of Plant: 5.0 (coaxial); None (fiber optic). Homes passed: 109. Total homes in franchised area: 109.

Manager: Jackie Smith. Marketing Director: Bertie Soeder. Chief Technician: David Haworth.

City fee: 3% of gross.

Ownership: McNabb Cable & Satellite Inc. (MSO).

CERRO GORDO—Mediacom. Now served by TUSCOLA, IL [IL0135]. ICA: IL0478.

CHAPIN—Mediacom. Now served by JACKSONVILLE, IL [IL0065]. ICA: IL0366.

CHARLESTON—Mediacom, PO Box 288, 4290 Blue Stem Rd, Charleston, IL 61920. Phones: 217-348-5533; 309-274-4500 (Chillicothe regional office). Fax: 217-345-7074. Web Site: http://www.mediacomcable.com. Also serves Ashmore, Kansas & Westfield. ICA: IL0064.

TV Market Ranking: Below 100 (Ashmore, Kansas, Westfield); Outside TV Markets (CHARLESTON). Franchise award date: N.A. Franchise expiration date: N.A. Began: July 1, 1967.

Channel capacity: N.A. Channels available but not in use: N.A.

Basic Service

Subscribers: 5,937.

Programming (received off-air): WAND (NBC) Decatur; WBUI (CW) Decatur; WCCU (FOX) Urbana; WCFN (MNT) Springfield; WCIA (CBS) Champaign; WEIU-TV (PBS) Charleston; WICD (ABC) Champaign; WILL-TV (PBS) Urbana; WSIU-TV (PBS) Carbondale; WTHI-TV (CBS) Terre Haute; WTWO (NBC) Terre Haute; 5 FMs.

Programming (via satellite): C-SPAN; Disney Channel; Home Shopping Network; INSP; QVC; TV Guide Network.

Fee: $45.00 installation; $20.95 monthly.

Expanded Basic Service 1

Subscribers: N.A.

Programming (via satellite): ABC Family Channel; AMC; Animal Planet; Arts & Entertainment; BET Networks; Cartoon Network; CNBC; CNN; Comcast SportsNet Chicago; Comedy Central; Country Music TV; C-SPAN 2; Discovery Channel; E! Entertainment Television; ESPN; ESPN 2; ESPN Classic Sports; Eternal Word TV Network; FitTV; Food Network; Fox News Channel; Fox Sports Net Midwest; FX; Hallmark Channel; Headline News; HGTV; History Channel; ION Television; Jewelry Television; Lifetime; Lifetime Movie Network; MSNBC; MTV; Nickelodeon; Outdoor Channel; Oxygen; Product Information Network; ShopNBC; Speed Channel; Spike TV; Syfy; TBS Superstation; The Learning Channel; Travel Channel; Trinity Broadcasting Network; truTV; Turner Network TV; USA Network; VH1; WE tv; Weather Channel; WGN America.

Fee: $34.00 monthly.

Digital Basic Service

Subscribers: N.A.

Programming (received off-air): WAND (NBC) Decatur; WCCU (FOX) Urbana; WCIA (CBS) Champaign; WICD (ABC) Champaign; WILL-TV (PBS) Urbana; WTHI-TV (CBS) Terre Haute.

Programming (via satellite): ABC News Now; AmericanLife TV Network; BBC America; Bio; Bloomberg Television; Bravo; CBS College Sports Network; CCTV-9 (CCTV International); CMT Pure Country; Discovery HD Theater; Discovery Health Channel; Discovery Kids Channel; Discovery Military Channel; Discovery Planet Green; Discovery Times Channel; ESPN 2 HD; ESPN HD; ESPN U; ESPNews; FitTV; Fox College Sports Atlantic; Fox College Sports Central; Fox College Sports Pacific; Fox Movie Channel; Fox Reality Channel; Fox Soccer; Fuel TV; Fuse; G4; Gol TV; Golf Channel; GSN; HDNet; HDNet Movies; History Channel International; Independent Film Channel; ION Television; Lifetime Real Women; MTV Hits; MTV2; Music Choice; National Geographic Channel; Nick Jr.; NickToons TV; Qubo; ReelzChannel; Science Channel; Sleuth; Style Network; TeenNick; Tennis Channel; The Sportsman Channel; Toon Disney; Turner Classic Movies; TV Land; TVG Network; Universal HD; Versus; VH1 Classic.

Fee: $9.00 monthly.

Digital Pay Service 1

Pay Units: N.A.

Programming (via satellite): Cinemax (multiplexed); Cinemax On Demand; Encore (multiplexed); HBO (multiplexed); HBO HD; HBO On Demand; Showtime (multiplexed); Showtime HD; Showtime On Demand; Starz (multiplexed); Starz HDTV; Starz On Demand; The Movie Channel (multiplexed); The Movie Channel HD; The Movie Channel On Demand.

Fee: $11.95 monthly (HBO, Cinemax, Showtime/TMC or Starz/Encore.

Video-On-Demand: Yes

Pay-Per-View

iN DEMAND (delivered digitally); Playboy TV (delivered digitally); Ten Clips (delivered digitally); Ten Blox (delivered digitally); ESPN (delivered digitally).

Internet Service

Operational: Yes. Began: December 1, 2002.

Broadband Service: Mediacom High Speed Internet.

Fee: $59.95 installation; $40.95 monthly.

Telephone Service

Analog: Not Operational

Digital: Operational

Fee: $39.95 installation; $39.95 monthly

Miles of Plant: 137.0 (coaxial); None (fiber optic). Homes passed: 10,544. Total homes in franchised area: 10,544.

Vice President: Don Hagwell. Area Operations Director: Todd Acker. Technical Operations Manager: Jerry Ferguson. Sales & Marketing Director: Stephanie Law. Customer Service Manager: Angie McHenry.

City fee: 4% of gross.

Ownership: Mediacom LLC (MSO).

CHATHAM—Insight Communications. Now served by SPRINGFIELD, IL [IL0016]. ICA: IL0114.

CHEMUNG—Mediacom. Now served by POPLAR GROVE, IL [IL0282]. ICA: IL0479.

CHESTER—Charter Communications. Now served by SPARTA, IL [IL0147]. ICA: IL0144.

CHESTERFIELD (village)—Formerly served by CableDirect. No longer in operation. ICA: IL0480.

CHICAGO—Comcast Cable, 1500 McConnor Pkwy, Schaumburg, IL 60173-4399. Phones: 773-394-8796; 847-585-6300 (Regional office). Fax: 773-486-2847. Web Site: http://www.comcast.com. ICA: IL0001.

TV Market Ranking: 3 (CHICAGO). Franchise award date: March 16, 1984. Franchise expiration date: N.A. Began: March 1, 1984.

Channel capacity: N.A. Channels available but not in use: N.A.

Basic Service

Subscribers: 323,189.

Programming (received off-air): WBBM-TV (CBS) Chicago; WCIU-TV (IND) Chicago; WCPX-TV (ION) Chicago; WFLD (FOX) Chicago; WGBO-DT (UNV) Joliet; WGN-TV (CW, IND) Chicago; WJYS (IND) Hammond; WLS-TV (ABC) Chicago; WMAQ-TV (NBC) Chicago; WPWR-TV (MNT) Gary; WSNS-TV (TMO) Chicago; WTTW (PBS) Chicago; WXFT-DT (TEL) Aurora; WYCC (PBS) Chicago; WYIN (PBS) Gary; 28 FMs.

Programming (via satellite): BET Networks; C-SPAN; C-SPAN 2; Home Shopping Network; TBS Superstation; TV Guide Network.

Current originations: Leased Access; Government Access; Educational Access; Public Access.

Fee: $48.99 installation; $25.49 monthly.

Expanded Basic Service 1

Subscribers: N.A.

Programming (via satellite): ABC Family Channel; AMC; Animal Planet; Arts & Entertainment; Bravo; Cartoon Network; Chicagoland Television News; CNBC; CNN; Comcast SportsNet Chicago; Comedy Central; Discovery Channel; Disney Channel; E! Entertainment Television; ESPN; ESPN 2; Eternal Word TV Network; Food Network; Fox News Channel; FX; GalaVision; Golf Channel; Headline News; HGTV; History Channel; Lifetime; MoviePlex; MSNBC; MTV; MTV2; Nickelodeon; Oxygen; QVC; Spike TV; Style Network; The Learning Channel; Toon Disney; Total Living Network; Travel Channel; truTV; Turner Network TV; TV Land; USA Network; Versus; VH1; Weather Channel.

Fee: $34.00 monthly.

Digital Basic Service

Subscribers: 42,023.

Programming (received off-air): WBBM-TV (CBS) Chicago; WFLD (FOX) Chicago; WGN-TV (CW, IND) Chicago; WLS-TV (ABC) Chicago; WMAQ-TV (NBC) Chicago; WTTW (PBS) Chicago.

Programming (via satellite): BBC America; Bio; Bloomberg Television; Canales N; CMT Pure Country; Cooking Channel; Country Music TV; Current; Discovery Digital Networks; Discovery HD Theater; Do-It-Yourself; Encore (multiplexed); ESPN 2 HD; ESPN Classic Sports; ESPN HD; ESPNews; Flix; Fox College Sports Atlantic; Fox College Sports Central; Fox College Sports Pacific; Fox Movie Channel; Fox Reality Channel; Fox Soccer; Fuse; G4; GAS; Gol TV; Gospel Music Channel; Great American Country; GSN; Hallmark Channel; History Channel International; Independent Film Channel; Lifetime Movie Network; LOGO; MTV Networks Digital Suite; Music Choice; National Geographic Channel; NFL Network; Nick Jr.; Nick Too; NickToons TV; Outdoor Channel; Ovation; Palladia; PBS Kids Sprout; ShopNBC; Si TV; SoapNet; Speed Channel; Sundance Channel; Syfy; The Word Network; Toon Disney; Trinity Broadcasting Network; Turner Classic Movies; Turner Network TV HD; TVG Network; Universal HD; Versus HD; WE tv; Weatherscan.

Fee: $30.99 monthly.

Digital Pay Service 1

Pay Units: N.A.

Programming (via satellite): Cinemax (multiplexed); Cinemax HD; Flix; HBO (multiplexed); HBO HD; Showtime (multiplexed); Showtime HD; Starz (multiplexed); Starz HDTV; The Movie Channel (multiplexed); TV Polonia.

Fee: $16.00 monthly (each).

Video-On-Demand: Yes

Pay-Per-View

Addressable homes: 42,023.

Playboy TV (delivered digitally), Fee: $3.95-$6.95; Fresh (delivered digitally); iN DEMAND; ESPN (delivered digitally); Sports PPV (delivered digitally); NBA TV (delivered digitally); Shorteez (delivered digitally); iN DEMAND (delivered digitally).

Internet Service

Operational: Yes.

Subscribers: 28,140.

Broadband Service: Comcast High Speed Internet.

Fee: $99.00 installation; $42.95 monthly.

Telephone Service
Digital: Operational
Fee: $44.95 monthly
Miles of Plant: 1,005.0 (coaxial); 30.0 (fiber optic). Additional miles planned: 2.0 (coaxial). Homes passed: 1,103,594. Total homes in franchised area: 1,149,236.
Regional Senior Vice President: Steve Reimer. Area Vice President: Mark Allen. Vice President, Technical Operations: Bob Curtis. Vice President, Marketing & Sales: Eric Schaefer. Vice President, Communications: Rich Ruggiero.
City fee: 5% of gross.
Ownership: Comcast Cable Communications Inc. (MSO).

CHICAGO—Formerly served by Preferred Entertainment of Chicago. No longer in operation. ICA: IL0615.

CHICAGO (area 4)—Comcast Cable. Now served by CHICAGO, IL [IL0001]. ICA: IL0003.

CHICAGO (area 5)—Comcast Cable. Now served by CHICAGO, IL [IL0001]. ICA: IL0005.

CHICAGO (areas 1, 4 & 5)—Comcast Cable. Now served by CHICAGO, IL [IL0001]. ICA: IL0002.

CHICAGO (portions)—RCN Corp. Formerly [IL0661]. This cable system has converted to IPTV, 196 Van Buren St, Herndon, VA 20170. Phone: 703-434-8200. Web Site: http://www.rcn.com. ICA: IL5236.
TV Market Ranking: 3 (CHICAGO (PORTIONS)). Franchise award date: N.A. Franchise expiration date: N.A. Began: N.A.
Channel capacity: N.A. Channels available but not in use: N.A.
Video-On-Demand: Yes
Internet Service
Operational: Yes.
Broadband Service: RCN.
Fee: $23.00 monthly.
Telephone Service
Digital: Operational
Fee: $30.00 monthly
Chairman: Steven J. Simmons. Chief Executive Officer: Jim Holanda.
Ownership: RCN Corp. (MSO).

CHICAGO (portions)—RCN Corp. This cable system has converted to IPTV. See Chicago (portions), IL [IL5236], IL. ICA: IL0661.

CHICAGO (southern portion)—WOW! Internet Cable & Phone, 7887 E Belleview Ave, Ste 1000, Englewood, CO 80111. Phones: 720-479-3500; 866-496-9669 (Customer service). Fax: 720-479-3585. Web Site: http://www1.wowway.com. ICA: IL0680.
Note: This system is an overbuild.
TV Market Ranking: 3 (CHICAGO). Franchise award date: N.A. Franchise expiration date: N.A. Began: N.A.
Channel capacity: N.A. Channels available but not in use: N.A.
Basic Service
Subscribers: 350,000 Includes Naperville, Detroit MI, Cleveland OH, & Columbus OH.
Programming (received off-air): WBBM-TV (CBS) Chicago; WCIU-TV (IND) Chicago; WCPX-TV (ION) Chicago; WFLD (FOX) Chicago; WGBO-DT (UNV) Joliet; WJYS (IND) Hammond; WLS-TV (ABC) Chicago; WMAQ-TV (NBC) Chicago; WPWR-TV (MNT) Gary; WSNS-TV (TMO) Chicago; WTTW (PBS) Chicago; WXFT-DT (TEL) Aurora; WYCC (PBS) Chicago.
Programming (via satellite): C-SPAN; CW+; Home Shopping Network; INSP; QVC; V-me TV.
Current originations: Public Access; Government Access.
Fee: $39.99 installation; $16.99 monthly.
Expanded Basic Service 1
Subscribers: N.A.
Programming (via satellite): ABC Family Channel; AMC; Animal Planet; Arts & Entertainment; BET Networks; Big Ten Network; Cartoon Network; CNBC; CNN; Comcast SportsNet Chicago; Comedy Central; Country Music TV; Discovery Channel; Discovery Health Channel; Disney Channel; E! Entertainment Television; ESPN; ESPN 2; ESPN Classic Sports; Food Network; Fox News Channel; FX; GalaVision; GSN; Headline News; HGTV; History Channel; Lifetime; MSNBC; MTV; MTV2; Nickelodeon; NickToons TV; Oxygen; ShopNBC; Speed Channel; Spike TV; Syfy; TBS Superstation; The Learning Channel; Toon Disney; Travel Channel; Turner Classic Movies; Turner Network TV; TV Land; USA Network; VH1; Weather Channel.
Fee: $34.76 monthly.
Digital Basic Service
Subscribers: N.A.
Programming (via satellite): ABC News Now; BBC America; Big Ten Network; Bio; Bloomberg Television; Bridges TV; CMT Pure Country; Cooking Channel; Discovery Kids Channel; Discovery Military Channel; Discovery Planet Green; DMX Music; Do-It-Yourself; Encore (multiplexed); ESPN U; ESPNews; Eternal Word TV Network; Fox Business Channel; Fox Movie Channel; Fox Reality Channel; Fox Soccer; G4; GemsTV; here! On Demand; History Channel International; ID Investigation Discovery; Jewelry Television; Lifetime Movie Network; Lifetime Real Women; MTV Hits; National Geographic Channel; NFL Network; Nick Jr.; Nick Too; PBS Kids Sprout; Science Channel; SoapNet; Starz (multiplexed); Starz HDTV; Style Network; Sundance Channel; TeenNick; The Word Network; This TV; Trinity Broadcasting Network; Universal Sports; VH1 Classic.
Fee: $25.23 monthly.
Digital Expanded Basic Service
Subscribers: N.A.
Programming (via satellite): Fox College Sports Atlantic; Fox College Sports Central; Fox College Sports Pacific; Outdoor Channel; Tennis Channel.
Fee: $4.99 monthly.
Digital Expanded Basic Service 2
Subscribers: N.A.
Programming (received off-air): WBBM-TV (CBS) Chicago; WCIU-TV (IND) Chicago; WFLD (FOX) Chicago; WLS-TV (ABC) Chicago; WMAQ-TV (NBC) Chicago; WPWR-TV (MNT) Gary.
Programming (via satellite): ABC Family HD; Animal Planet HD; Arts & Entertainment HD; Discovery Channel HD; Discovery HD Theater; Disney Channel HD; ESPN 2 HD; ESPN HD; Food Network HD; Fox News HD; FX HD; HDNet; HDNet Movies; HGTV HD; History Channel HD; National Geographic Channel HD Network; NFL Network HD; PBS HD; TLC HD; Turner Network TV HD; WealthTV HD.
Fee: $13.00 monthly.
Digital Pay Service 1
Pay Units: N.A.
Programming (via satellite): Cinemax (multiplexed); Cinemax HD; Cinemax On Demand; Flix; HBO (multiplexed); HBO HD; HBO On Demand; Showtime (multiplexed); Showtime HD; Showtime On Demand; The Movie Channel (multiplexed); The Movie Channel On Demand.
Fee: $15.00 monthly (HBO, Cinemax, Starz or Showtime/TMC/Flix).
Video-On-Demand: Yes
Pay-Per-View
ETC (delivered digitally), Addressable: Yes; iN DEMAND (delivered digitally); Pleasure (delivered digitally); Playboy TV (delivered digitally); Sports PPV (delivered digitally).
Internet Service
Operational: Yes.
Broadband Service: WOW! Internet.
Fee: $40.99-$72.99 monthly; $2.50 modem lease.
Telephone Service
Digital: Operational
Fee: $30.00 monthly
Vice President & General Manager: Kelvin Fee. Vice President, Sales & Marketing: Cathy Kuo. Chief Technician: Cash Hagen.
Ownership: WideOpenWest LLC (MSO).

CHICAGO (southern suburbs)—Comcast Cable, 7720 W 98th St, Hickory Hills, IL 60457. Phones: 708-237-3260; 847-585-6300 (Schaumberg regional office). Fax: 708-237-3292. Web Site: http://www.comcast.com. Also serves Alsip, Aroma Park, Aroma Twp., Ashkum, Beecher, Bloom Twp., Blue Island, Bourbonais, Bradley, Burnham, Calumet City, Calumet Park, Chebanse, Chicago Heights, Chicago Ridge, Clifton, Country Club Hills, Crestwood, Crete, Custer Park, Dixmoor, Dolton, East Hazel Crest, Evergreen Park, Flossmoor, Ford Heights, Ganeer Twp., Glenwood, Harvey, Hazel Crest, Hickory Hills, Hometown, Homewood, Indian Head Park, Kankakee County (unincorporated areas), La Grange, La Grange Park, Lansing, Limestone Twp., Manteno, Markham, Matteson, Merrionette Park, Midlothian, Monee, Oak Forest, Oak Lawn, Olympia Fields, Orland Hills, Orland Park, Otto Twp., Palos Heights, Palos Hills, Palos Park, Palos Twp., Park Forest, Peotone, Phoenix, Posen, Rich Twp., Richton Park, Ritchie, Riverdale, Riverside, Robbins (village), Sauk Village, South Chicago Heights, South Holland, St. Anne, Steger, Sun River Twp., Thornton, Tinley Park, University Park, Western Springs, Will County (portions) & Worth, IL; Burns Harbor, Cedar Lake, Crown Point, Demotte, Dyer, East Chicago, Gary, Griffith, Hammond, Hebron, Hobart, Lake County (unincorporated areas), Lake of the Four Seasons, Lake Station, Lowell, Merrillville, Munster, New Chicago, Ogden Dunes, Portage, Schererville, St. John, Whiting & Winfield, IN. ICA: IL0008.
TV Market Ranking: 3 (Alsip, Beecher, Bloom Twp., Blue Island, Blue Island, Burnham, Burns Harbor, Calumet City, Calumet Park, CHICAGO (SOUTHERN SUBURBS), Chicago Heights, Chicago Ridge, Country Club Hills, Crestwood, Crete, Crown Point, Demotte, Dixmoor, Dolton, Dyer, East Chicago, East Hazel Crest, Evergreen Park, Flossmoor, Ford Heights, Gary, Glenwood, Griffith, Hammond, Harvey, Hazel Crest, Hazel Crest, Hickory Hills, Highland, Hobart, Hometown, Homewood, Indian Head Park, La Grange, La Grange Park, Lake County (unincorporated areas) (portions), Lake of the Four Seasons, Lake Station, Lansing, Manteno, Markham, Matteson, Merrillville, Merrionette Park, Midlothian, Monee, Munster, New Chicago, Oak Forest, Oak Lawn, Ogden Dunes, Olympia Fields, Orland Hills, Orland Park, Palos Heights, Palos Hills, Palos Park, Palos Twp., Park Forest, Park Forest, Peotone, Phoenix, Portage, Posen, Rich Twp., Richton Park, Riverdale, Riverside, Robbins (village), Sauk Village, Schererville, South Chicago Heights, South Holland, St. John, Steger, Thornton, Tinley Park, University Park, Western Springs, Whiting, Winfield, Worth); Below 100 (Aroma Park, Aroma Twp., Bourbonais, Bradley, Cedar Lake, Custer Park, Ganeer Twp., Hebron, Kankakee County (unincorporated areas), Limestone Twp., Lowell, Otto Twp., Ritchie, Sun River Twp., Will County (portions), Lake County (unincorporated areas) (portions)); Outside TV Markets (Ashkum, Chebanse, Clifton, St. Anne). Franchise award date: N.A. Franchise expiration date: N.A. Began: May 1, 1980.
Channel capacity: 69 (operating 2-way). Channels available but not in use: N.A.

Basic Service
Subscribers: 50,167.
Programming (received off-air): WBBM-TV (CBS) Chicago; WCIU-TV (IND) Chicago; WCPX-TV (ION) Chicago; WFLD (FOX) Chicago; WGBO-DT (UNV) Joliet; WGN-TV (CW, IND) Chicago; WJYS (IND) Hammond; WLS-TV (ABC) Chicago; WMAQ-TV (NBC) Chicago; WPWR-TV (MNT) Gary; WSNS-TV (TMO) Chicago; WTTW (PBS) Chicago; WXFT-DT (TEL) Aurora; WYCC (PBS) Chicago; WYIN (PBS) Gary.
Programming (via satellite): CNBC; C-SPAN; C-SPAN 2; Home Shopping Network 2; MTV; QVC; TV Guide Network; VH1.
Current originations: Government Access.
Fee: $48.99 installation; $17.24 monthly; $2.50 converter.

Expanded Basic Service 1
Subscribers: N.A.
Programming (via satellite): ABC Family Channel; AMC; Animal Planet; Arts & Entertainment; BET Networks; Cartoon Network; Chicagoland Television News; CNN; Comcast SportsNet Chicago; Comedy Central; Discovery Channel; Disney Channel; E! Entertainment Television; ESPN; ESPN 2; ESPN Classic Sports; Eternal Word TV Network; Food Network; Fox Movie Channel; Fox News Channel; FX; Headline News; History Channel; Lifetime; MSNBC; mun2 television; Nickelodeon; Oxygen; Spike TV; TBS Superstation; The Learning Channel; Total Living Network; truTV; Turner Network TV; TV Land; USA Network; Weather Channel.
Fee: $35.25 monthly.

Digital Basic Service
Subscribers: 17,007.
Programming (via satellite): AmericanLife TV Network; BBC America; Bio; Black Family Channel; Bloomberg Television; Bravo; Country Music TV; Discovery Digital Networks; ESPNews; FitTV; Fox College Sports Atlantic; Fox College Sports Central; Fox College Sports Pacific; Fox Sports World; Fuse; GAS; Golf Channel; Great American Country; GSN; Halogen Network; HGTV; History Channel International; Independent Film Channel; Lifetime Movie Network; Lime; MTV Networks Digital Suite; Music Choice; National Geographic Channel; Nick Jr.; NickToons TV; Outdoor Channel; Ovation; ShopNBC; Speed Channel; Style Network; Sundance Channel; Syfy; The Word Network; Toon Disney; Trinity Broadcasting Network; Turner Classic Movies; WE tv; Weatherscan.
Fee: $11.99 monthly.

Pay Service 1
Pay Units: 8,509.
Programming (via satellite): Cinemax; HBO; Showtime; The Movie Channel.
Fee: $6.95 monthly (each).
Digital Pay Service 1
Pay Units: N.A.
Programming (via satellite): Cinemax (multiplexed); Encore (multiplexed); Flix; HBO (multiplexed); Showtime (multiplexed); Starz (multiplexed); The Movie Channel (multiplexed).
Fee: $16.00 monthly (each).
Video-On-Demand: Yes
Pay-Per-View
Addressable homes: 45,000.
ESPN Now (delivered digitally), Addressable: Yes; iN DEMAND; Sports PPV (delivered digitally); iN DEMAND (delivered digitally); Fresh (delivered digitally); Shorteez (delivered digitally); Playboy TV (delivered digitally); Hot Choice (delivered digitally).
Internet Service
Operational: Yes.
Subscribers: 11,388.
Broadband Service: Comcast High Speed Internet.
Fee: $99.00 installation; $42.95 monthly.
Telephone Service
Digital: Operational
Miles of Plant: 746.0 (coaxial); None (fiber optic). Homes passed: 106,308.
Senior Regional Vice President: Steve Reiner. Area Vice President: Sandy Weicher. Vice President, Technical Operations: Bob Curtis. Vice President, Sales & Marketing: Eric Schaefer. Vice President, Communications: Rich Ruggiero. Marketing Director: Ron Knutson. Technical Operations Director: John Collucci.
City fee: 3% of gross.
Ownership: Comcast Cable Communications Inc. (MSO).

CHILLICOTHE—Mediacom, 3900 26th Ave, Moline, IL 61265. Phones: 309-797-2580 (Moline regional office); 309-274-4500 (Chillicothe office). Fax: 309-797-2414. Web Site: http://www.mediacomcable.com. Also serves Henry, Hopewell, Peoria County, Rome & Sparland. ICA: IL0118.
TV Market Ranking: 83 (CHILLICOTHE, Henry, Hopewell, Peoria County, Rome, Sparland). Franchise award date: January 15, 1980. Franchise expiration date: N.A. Began: February 1, 1980.
Channel capacity: N.A. Channels available but not in use: N.A.
Basic Service
Subscribers: 3,956.
Programming (received off-air): WAOE (MNT) Peoria; WEEK-TV (NBC) Peoria; WHOI (ABC, CW) Peoria; WMBD-TV (CBS) Peoria; WTVP (PBS) Peoria; WYZZ-TV (FOX) Bloomington.
Programming (via satellite): Eternal Word TV Network; Home Shopping Network; TBS Superstation; Trinity Broadcasting Network; WGN America.
Fee: $45.00 installation; $20.95 monthly.
Expanded Basic Service 1
Subscribers: 3,363.
Programming (via satellite): ABC Family Channel; AMC; AmericanLife TV Network; Animal Planet; Arts & Entertainment; Bio; Bloomberg Television; Cartoon Network; CNBC; CNN; Comcast SportsNet Chicago; Comedy Central; Country Music TV; C-SPAN; Discovery Channel; Disney Channel; E! Entertainment Television; ESPN; ESPN 2; Food Network; Fox Movie Channel; Fox News Channel; Fox Sports Net; FX; G4; Headline News; HGTV; History Channel; History Channel International; Lifetime; Lifetime Movie Network; MSNBC; MTV; Nickelodeon; QVC; Speed Channel; Spike TV; Style Network; Syfy; The Learning Channel; Turner Network TV; TV Guide Network; TV Land; USA Network; VH1; Weather Channel.
Fee: $34.00 monthly.
Digital Basic Service
Subscribers: 699.
Programming (via satellite): BBC America; Discovery Digital Networks; DMX Music; Fox Sports World; Golf Channel; GSN; Independent Film Channel; Turner Classic Movies; Versus.
Fee: $9.00 monthly.
Digital Pay Service 1
Pay Units: 2,384.
Programming (via satellite): Cinemax (multiplexed); HBO (multiplexed); Showtime (multiplexed); Starz (multiplexed); The Movie Channel (multiplexed).
Fee: $11.95 monthly (HBO, Cinemax, Showtime/TMC or Starz/Encore).
Video-On-Demand: No
Pay-Per-View
Addressable homes: 1,723.
Hot Choice, Addressable: Yes; Hot Choice (delivered digitally); iN DEMAND; iN DEMAND (delivered digitally); Playboy TV; Playboy TV (delivered digitally); Pleasure (delivered digitally); Fresh; Fresh (delivered digitally); Shorteez (delivered digitally).
Internet Service
Operational: Yes.
Subscribers: 769.
Broadband Service: Mediacom High Speed Internet.
Fee: $59.95 installation; $40.95 monthly.
Telephone Service
Analog: Not Operational
Digital: Operational
Fee: $39.95 installation; $39.95 monthly
Homes passed: 5,348. Miles of plant (coax & fiber) included in Moline
Regional Vice President: Cari Fenzel. Area Manager: Don DeMay. Engineering Director: Mitch Carlson. Technical Operations Manager: Chris Toalson. Marketing Director: Greg Evans.
City fee: 5% of gross.
Ownership: Mediacom LLC (MSO).

CISCO (village)—Formerly served by Longview Communications. No longer in operation. ICA: IL0481.

CISNE—Wabash Independent Networks, PO Box 719, 113 Hagen Dr, Flora, IL 62839. Phones: 877-878-2120; 618-665-9946. Fax: 618-665-3400. E-mail: winita@wabash.net. Web Site: http://www.wabash.net. ICA: IL0320.
TV Market Ranking: Below 100 (CISNE). Franchise award date: N.A. Franchise expiration date: N.A. Began: January 1, 1984.
Channel capacity: 37 (not 2-way capable). Channels available but not in use: 7.
Basic Service
Subscribers: 109.
Programming (received off-air): KFVS-TV (CBS, CW) Cape Girardeau; KMOV (CBS) St. Louis; KSDK (NBC) St. Louis; WEHT (ABC) Evansville; WFIE (NBC) Evansville; WSIL-TV (ABC) Harrisburg; WSIU-TV (PBS) Carbondale; WTHI-TV (CBS) Terre Haute; WTVW (FOX) Evansville; WTWO (NBC) Terre Haute.
Programming (via satellite): C-SPAN; C-SPAN 2; CW+; Eternal Word TV Network; Home Shopping Network; ION Television; QVC; ShopNBC; TBS Superstation; Trinity Broadcasting Network; Weather Channel; WGN America.
Fee: $15.00 installation; $19.95 monthly.
Expanded Basic Service 1
Subscribers: 101.
Programming (via satellite): ABC Family Channel; American Movie Classics; Animal Planet; Arts & Entertainment; Big Ten Network; Boomerang; Cartoon Network; CNN; Comedy Central; Country Music TV; Discovery Channel; Disney Channel; Do-It-Yourself; E! Entertainment Television; ESPN; ESPN 2; ESPN Classic Sports; FamilyNet; Food Network; Fox News Channel; Fox Sports Net; FX; G4; Gospel Music Channel; Hallmark Channel; Headline News; History Channel; INSP; Lifetime; MSNBC; MTV; National Geographic Channel; Nickelodeon; Outdoor Channel; Oxygen; Spike TV; The Learning Channel; Travel Channel; truTV; Turner Classic Movies; Turner Network TV; TV Land; USA Network; VH1.
Fee: $19.00 monthly.
Digital Basic Service
Subscribers: N.A.
Programming (via satellite): AZ TV; BBC America; Bio; Bloomberg Television; Bravo; CMT Pure Country; Current; Discovery Digital Networks; DMX Music; ESPNews; FitTV; Flix; Fox College Sports Atlantic; Fox College Sports Central; Fox College Sports Pacific; Fox Movie Channel; Fox Soccer; Fuse; Golf Channel; Great American Country; GSN; HGTV; History Channel International; Independent Film Channel; Lifetime Movie Network; Military History Channel; MTV Networks Digital Suite; Nick Jr.; Ovation; RFD-TV; Sleuth; SoapNet; Speed Channel; Style Network; Syfy; TeenNick; The Word Network; Toon Disney; Versus; WE tv.
Fee: $15.00 monthly.
Pay Service 1
Pay Units: N.A.
Programming (via satellite): Showtime; The Movie Channel.
Fee: $11.95 monthly (TMC), $12.95 monthly (Showtime).
Pay Service 2
Pay Units: 57.
Programming (via satellite): HBO.
Fee: $13.95 monthly.
Digital Pay Service 1
Pay Units: N.A.
Programming (via satellite): Cinemax (multiplexed); Encore (multiplexed); HBO (multiplexed); Showtime (multiplexed); Starz (multiplexed); The Movie Channel (multiplexed).
Fee: $11.95 monthly (Cinemax or Starz/Encore), $12.95 monthly (Showtime & TMC, or HBO).
Video-On-Demand: Planned
Pay-Per-View
Club Jenna (delivered digitally); Fresh (delivered digitally); Spice: Xcess (delivered digitally); Playboy TV (delivered digitally).
Internet Service
Operational: Yes.
Fee: $35.00-$50.00 monthly.
Telephone Service
None
Miles of Plant: 8.0 (coaxial); None (fiber optic). Homes passed: 501.
General Manager: Dave Grahn. Assistant General Manager: Jeff Williams. Marketing Director: Carol Oestreich. TV/Video Administrator: Don Ross. Controller: Tanya Wells.
Ownership: Wabash Independent Networks (MSO).

CISSNA PARK (village)—Park TV & Electronics Inc., PO Box 9, 205 E Fire Ln, Cissna Park, IL 60924. Phone: 815-457-2659. Fax: 815-457-2735. ICA: IL0482.
TV Market Ranking: Outside TV Markets (CISSNA PARK (VILLAGE)). Franchise award date: N.A. Franchise expiration date: N.A. Began: April 1, 1984.
Channel capacity: N.A. Channels available but not in use: N.A.
Basic Service
Subscribers: 625 Includes Armstrong, Buckley, Potomac & Rankin.
Programming (received off-air): WAND (NBC) Decatur; WBUI (CW) Decatur; WCCU (FOX) Urbana; WCIA (CBS) Champaign; WICD (ABC) Champaign; WILL-TV (PBS) Urbana.
Programming (via satellite): ABC Family Channel; AMC; Animal Planet; Arts & Entertainment; Big Ten Network; Cartoon Network; CNBC; CNN; Comedy Central; Country Music TV; Discovery Channel; Disney Channel; E! Entertainment Television; ESPN; ESPN 2; Food Network; Fox News Channel; FX; GSN; Hallmark Channel; HGTV; History Channel; Lifetime; MTV; Nickelodeon; Outdoor Channel; Oxygen; QVC; Speed Channel; Spike TV; Syfy; TBS Superstation; The Learning Channel; Travel Channel; Trinity Broadcasting Network; Turner Classic Movies; Turner Network TV; TV Land; USA Network; VH1; Weather Channel; WGN America.
Pay Service 1
Pay Units: N.A.
Programming (via satellite): Cinemax; HBO.
Video-On-Demand: No
Internet Service
Operational: Yes.
Broadband Service: West Michigan Internet Service.
Fee: $29.95 monthly.
Telephone Service
None
Miles of Plant: 15.0 (coaxial); None (fiber optic). Homes passed: 900. Miles of plant & homes passed includes Armstrong, Buckley, Potomac & Rankin
Manager: Joe Young.
Ownership: Park TV & Electronics Inc. (MSO).

CLAREMONT—Formerly served by CableDirect. No longer in operation. ICA: IL0437.

CLAY CITY—Mediacom, PO Box 288, 4290 Blue Stem Rd, Charleston, IL 61920. Phone: 217-348-5533. Fax: 217-348-5533. Web

Site: http://www.mediacomcable.com. ICA: IL0686.
TV Market Ranking: Outside TV Markets (CLAY CITY).
Channel capacity: N.A. Channels available but not in use: N.A.
Internet Service
Operational: Yes.
Telephone Service
None
Operations Director: Todd Acker. Technical Operations Manager: Jerry Ferguson.
Ownership: Mediacom LLC (MSO).

CLAYTON (village)—Adams Telecom. Formerly served by Camp Point, IL [IL0206]. This cable system has converted to IPTV, PO Box 248, 405 Emminga Rd, Golden, IL 62339. Phone: 217-696-4411. E-mail: service@adams.net. Web Site: http://www.adams.net. ICA: IL5314.
Channel capacity: N.A. Channels available but not in use: N.A.
Internet Service
Operational: Yes.
Ownership: Adams Telephone Co-Operative.

CLINTON—Mediacom, PO Box 334, 609 S 4th St, Chillicothe, IL 61523. Phone: 309-274-4500. Fax: 309-274-3188. Web Site: http://www.mediacomcable.com. Also serves Wapella. ICA: IL0113.
TV Market Ranking: 64 (CLINTON, Wapella). Franchise award date: July 13, 1972. Franchise expiration date: N.A. Began: December 13, 1975.
Channel capacity: 121 (operating 2-way). Channels available but not in use: None.
Basic Service
Subscribers: 2,802.
Programming (received off-air): WAND (NBC) Decatur; WBUI (CW) Decatur; WCCU (FOX) Urbana; WCFN (MNT) Springfield; WCIA (CBS) Champaign; WICS (ABC) Springfield; WILL-TV (PBS) Urbana.
Programming (via satellite): ABC Family Channel; INSP; Radar Channel; WGN America.
Current originations: Public Access.
Fee: $45.00 installation; $20.95 monthly.
Expanded Basic Service 1
Subscribers: 2,499.
Programming (via satellite): AMC; AmericanLife TV Network; Animal Planet; Arts & Entertainment; BET Networks; Bravo; Cartoon Network; CNBC; CNN; Comcast SportsNet Chicago; Comedy Central; Country Music TV; C-SPAN; C-SPAN 2; Discovery Channel; Disney Channel; E! Entertainment Television; ESPN; ESPN 2; Eternal Word TV Network; FitTV; Food Network; Fox News Channel; FX; Hallmark Channel; Headline News; HGTV; History Channel; Home Shopping Network; ION Television; Jewelry Television; Lifetime; Lifetime Movie Network; MSNBC; MTV; Nickelodeon; Product Information Network; QVC; ShopNBC; SoapNet; Speed Channel; Spike TV; Syfy; TBS Superstation; The Learning Channel; Toon Disney; Travel Channel; Trinity Broadcasting Network; truTV; Turner Network TV; TV Guide Network; TV Land; Univision; USA Network; VH1; WE tv; Weather Channel.
Fee: $34.00 monthly.
Digital Basic Service
Subscribers: 194.
Programming (received off-air): WAND (NBC) Decatur; WCCU (FOX) Urbana; WCIA (CBS) Champaign; WICS (ABC) Springfield; WILL-TV (PBS) Urbana.
Programming (via satellite): ABC News Now; BBC America; Bio; Bloomberg Television; CCTV-Entertainment; Discovery Digital Networks; ESPN 2 HD; ESPN HD; ESPNews; Fox Movie Channel; Fox Reality Channel; Fox Soccer; Fuse; G4; Golf Channel; GSN; History Channel International; Independent Film Channel; ION Life; Lifetime Real Women; Military History Channel; MTV Hits; MTV2; Music Choice; National Geographic Channel; Nick Jr.; NickToons TV; Outdoor Channel; Qubo; ReelzChannel; Science Television; Sleuth; Style Network; Sundance Channel; TeenNick; Turner Classic Movies; Versus; VH1 Classic.
Fee: $9.00 monthly.
Digital Expanded Basic Service
Subscribers: N.A.
Programming (via satellite): College Sports Television; ESPN U; Fox College Sports Atlantic; Fox College Sports Central; Fox College Sports Pacific; Fuel TV; Gol TV; Tennis Channel; The Sportsman Channel; TVG Network.
Fee: $3.95 monthly.
Digital Expanded Basic Service 2
Subscribers: N.A.
Programming (via satellite): Discovery HD Theater; HDNet; HDNet Movies; Universal HD.
Fee: $6.95 monthly.
Digital Pay Service 1
Pay Units: 546.
Programming (via satellite): Cinemax (multiplexed); Encore (multiplexed); Flix; HBO (multiplexed); HBO HD; Showtime (multiplexed); Showtime HD; Starz (multiplexed); Starz HDTV; The Movie Channel (multiplexed); The Movie Channel HD.
Fee: $11.95 monthly (HBO, Cinemax, Showtime/TMC, or Starz/Encore).
Video-On-Demand: Yes
Pay-Per-View
Addressable homes: 528.
ESPN On Demand (delivered digitally), Addressable: Yes; Ten Clips (delivered digitally); iN DEMAND (delivered digitally); Playboy TV (delivered digitally); Ten Blox (delivered digitally); Fox Sports Net (delivered digitally).
Internet Service
Operational: Yes.
Broadband Service: Mediacom High Speed Internet.
Fee: $59.95 installation; $45.95 monthly.
Telephone Service
Digital: Operational
Fee: $39.95 installation; $39.95 monthly
Miles of Plant: 41.0 (coaxial); 5.0 (fiber optic). Homes passed: 4,273.
Vice President: Don Hagwell. Marketing Director: Stephanie Law. Technical Operations Manager: Larry Brackman. Operations Director: Gary Wightman.
City fee: 5% of gross.
Ownership: Mediacom LLC (MSO).

COATSBURG (village)—Adams Telecom. Formerly served by Golden, IL [IL0257]. This cable system has converted to IPTV, PO Box 248, 405 Emminga Rd, Golden, IL 62339. Phone: 217-696-4411. E-mail: service@adams.net. Web Site: http://www.adams.net. ICA: IL5315.
Channel capacity: N.A. Channels available but not in use: N.A.
Internet Service
Operational: Yes.
Ownership: Adams Telephone Co-Operative.

COBDEN—Mediacom. Now served by ZEIGLER, IL [IL0123]. ICA: IL0260.

COFFEEN—Mediacom, PO Box 288, 4290 Blue Stem Rd, Charleston, IL 61920. Phone: 217-348-5533. Fax: 217-345-7074. Web Site: http://www.mediacomcable.com. ICA: IL0344.
TV Market Ranking: Outside TV Markets (COFFEEN). Franchise award date: N.A. Franchise expiration date: N.A. Began: December 15, 1983.
Channel capacity: N.A. Channels available but not in use: N.A.
Basic Service
Subscribers: 110.
Programming (received off-air): KDNL-TV (ABC) St. Louis; KETC (PBS) St. Louis; KMOV (CBS) St. Louis; KPLR-TV (CW) St. Louis; WAND (NBC) Decatur; WICS (ABC) Springfield; WRSP-TV (FOX) Springfield.
Programming (via satellite): ABC Family Channel; AMC; Animal Planet; Arts & Entertainment; Bravo; Cartoon Network; CNN; Comedy Central; Country Music TV; Discovery Channel; ESPN; ESPN 2; HGTV; History Channel; Home Shopping Network; Lifetime; MTV; Nickelodeon; Spike TV; Syfy; TBS Superstation; The Learning Channel; Turner Network TV; TV Land; USA Network; Weather Channel; WGN America.
Fee: $45.00 installation; $47.95 monthly.
Pay Service 1
Pay Units: 48.
Programming (via satellite): Cinemax; HBO.
Fee: $25.00 installation; $7.95 monthly (Cinemax), $13.50 monthly (HBO).
Video-On-Demand: No
Internet Service
Operational: No.
Telephone Service
None
Miles of Plant: 9.0 (coaxial); None (fiber optic). Homes passed: 315.
Area Operations Director: Todd Acker. Technical Operations Manager: Jerry Ferguson.
City fee: 3% of gross.
Ownership: Mediacom LLC (MSO).

COLFAX—Mediacom. Now served by LE ROY, IL [IL0539]. ICA: IL0319.

COMPTON—Formerly served by Compton Cable TV Co. No longer in operation. ICA: IL0483.

COMPTON—Heartland Cable Broadband, PO Box 254, Shabbona, IL 60550. Phone: 866-428-0490. Fax: 815-780-1328. Web Site: http://www.heartlandcable.com. ICA: IL0685.
TV Market Ranking: Below 100 (COMPTON).
Channel capacity: N.A. Channels available but not in use: N.A.
Basic Service
Subscribers: N.A.
Programming (received off-air): WBBM-TV (CBS) Chicago; WCIU-TV (IND) Chicago; WFLD (FOX) Chicago; WGN-TV (CW, IND) Chicago; WIFR (CBS) Freeport; WLS-TV (ABC) Chicago; WMAQ-TV (NBC) Chicago; WPWR-TV (MNT) Gary; WQRF-TV (FOX) Rockford; WREX (CW, NBC) Rockford; WTTW (PBS) Chicago; WTVO (ABC, MNT) Rockford.
Fee: $39.00 installation; $15.00 monthly.
Expanded Basic Service 1
Subscribers: N.A.
Programming (via satellite): ABC Family Channel; AMC; Animal Planet; Arts & Entertainment; Cartoon Network; CNBC; CNN; Comcast SportsNet Chicago; Comedy Central; Country Music TV; Discovery Channel; Disney Channel; E! Entertainment Television; ESPN; ESPN 2; ESPNews; Food Network; Fox News Channel; FX; G4; Headline News; HGTV; History Channel; Lifetime; MTV; Nickelodeon; QVC; Speed Channel; Spike TV; Syfy; TBS Superstation; The Learning Channel; Travel Channel; truTV; Turner Network TV; TV Land; USA Network; VH1; Weather Channel.
Fee: $19.99 monthly.
Pay Service 1
Pay Units: N.A.
Programming (via satellite): HBO; Showtime.
Fee: $10.99 monthly (each).
Internet Service
Operational: Yes.
Fee: $45.00 monthly; $5.00 modem lease.
Telephone Service
None
Manager: Steve Allen.
Ownership: Heartland Cable Inc. (Illinois) (MSO).

CONGERVILLE—Formerly served by Tel-Star Cablevision Inc. No longer in operation. ICA: IL0484.

CORNELL—Mediacom. Now served by PONTIAC, IL [IL0109]. ICA: IL0374.

CORTLAND (village)—Mediacom, 3900 26th Ave, Moline, IL 61265. Phone: 309-797-2580. Fax: 309-797-2414. Web Site: http://www.mediacomcable.com. Also serves Gilberts, Hampshire & Maple Park (village). ICA: IL0485.
TV Market Ranking: 97 (CORTLAND (VILLAGE), Hampshire, Maple Park (village)); Below 100 (Gilberts). Franchise award date: November 25, 1985. Franchise expiration date: N.A. Began: N.A.
Channel capacity: 134 (operating 2-way). Channels available but not in use: None.
Basic Service
Subscribers: 1,090.
Programming (received off-air): WBBM-TV (CBS) Chicago; WCIU-TV (IND) Chicago; WCPX-TV (ION) Chicago; WFLD (FOX) Chicago; WGBO-DT (UNV) Joliet; WGN-TV (CW, IND) Chicago; WIFR (CBS) Freeport; WLS-TV (ABC) Chicago; WMAQ-TV (NBC) Chicago; WPWR-TV (MNT) Gary; WQRF-TV (FOX) Rockford; WREX (CW, NBC) Rockford; WSNS-TV (TMO) Chicago; WTTW (PBS) Chicago; WWTO-TV (TBN) La Salle; WYCC (PBS) Chicago.
Programming (via satellite): TBS Superstation.
Current originations: Leased Access; Educational Access.
Fee: $45.00 installation; $20.95 monthly.
Expanded Basic Service 1
Subscribers: N.A.
Programming (via satellite): ABC Family Channel; AMC; Animal Planet; Arts & Entertainment; Bravo; Cartoon Network; CNBC; CNN; Comcast SportsNet Chicago; Comedy Central; Country Music TV; C-SPAN; C-SPAN 2; Discovery Channel; Disney Channel; E! Entertainment Television; ESPN; ESPN 2; Eternal Word TV Network; Food Network; Fox News Channel; FX; Hallmark Channel; Halogen Network; Headline News; HGTV; History Channel; Home Shopping Network; Lifetime; Lifetime Movie Network; MSNBC; MTV; Nickelodeon; QVC; ShopNBC; SoapNet; Speed Channel; Spike TV; Syfy; The Learning Channel; Travel Channel; Trinity Broadcasting Network; truTV; Turner Classic Movies; Turner Network TV; TV Guide Network; TV Land; USA Network; VH1; Weather Channel.
Fee: $34.00 monthly.

Digital Basic Service
Subscribers: N.A.
Programming (via satellite): ABC News Now; AmericanLife TV Network; BBC America; Bio; Bloomberg Television; CCTV-9 (CCTV International); Discovery Health Channel; Discovery Kids Channel; Discovery Military Channel; Discovery Planet Green; ESPN 2 HD; ESPN HD; ESPN U; ESPNews; FitTV; Fox Movie Channel; Fox Reality Channel; Fox Soccer; Fuel TV; Fuse; G4; Golf Channel; GSN; History Channel International; ID Investigation Discovery; Independent Film Channel; ION Life; Lifetime Real Women; MTV Hits; MTV2; Music Choice; National Geographic Channel; Nick Jr.; NickToons TV; Outdoor Channel; Qubo; ReelzChannel; Science Channel; Sleuth; Style Network; Sundance Channel; TeenNick; TVG Network; VH1 Classic; WE tv.
Fee: $9.00 monthly.

Digital Expanded Basic Service
Subscribers: N.A.
Programming (via satellite): College Sports Television; Fox College Sports Atlantic; Fox College Sports Central; Fox College Sports Pacific; Gol TV; Tennis Channel; The Sportsman Channel.
Fee: $3.95 monthly.

Digital Expanded Basic Service 2
Subscribers: N.A.
Programming (via satellite): Discovery HD Theater; HDNet; HDNet Movies; Universal HD.
Fee: $6.95 monthly.

Digital Pay Service 1
Pay Units: N.A.
Programming (via satellite): Cinemax (multiplexed); Encore (multiplexed); Flix; HBO (multiplexed); HBO HD; Showtime (multiplexed); Showtime HD; Starz (multiplexed); Starz HDTV; Sundance Channel; The Movie Channel (multiplexed); The Movie Channel HD.
Fee: $11.95 monthly (HBO, Cinemax, Showtime/TMC or Starz/Encore).

Video-On-Demand: Yes

Pay-Per-View
iN DEMAND (delivered digitally); Playboy TV (delivered digitally); Ten Clips (delivered digitally); ESPN (delivered digitally).

Internet Service
Operational: Yes, DSL only.
Broadband Service: Mediacom High Speed Internet.
Fee: $59.95 installation; $45.95 monthly.

Telephone Service
Digital: Operational
Fee: $39.95 installation; $39.95 monthly

Homes passed: 2,420. Miles of plant included in Moline

Regional Vice President: Cari Fenzel. Engineering Director: Mitch Carlson. Technical Operations Manager: Chris Toalson. Marketing Director: Greg Evans.

City fee: 3% of gross.

Ownership: Mediacom LLC (MSO).

COULTERVILLE—Mediacom, 90 Main St, Benton, KY 42025-1132. Phones: 417-875-5560 (Springfield regional office); 270-527-9939. Fax: 270-527-0813. Web Site: http://www.mediacomcable.com. Also serves Hecker, Monroe County (portions), Red Bud, Smithton & Tilden. ICA: IL0152.

TV Market Ranking: 11 (Hecker, Monroe County (portions), Red Bud, Smithton); Outside TV Markets (COULTERVILLE, Tilden). Franchise award date: October 1, 1982. Franchise expiration date: N.A. Began: December 1, 1983.

Channel capacity: N.A. Channels available but not in use: N.A.

Basic Service
Subscribers: 1,559.
Programming (received off-air): KDNL-TV (ABC) St. Louis; KETC (PBS) St. Louis; KFVS-TV (CBS, CW) Cape Girardeau; KMOV (CBS) St. Louis; KNLC (IND) St. Louis; KPLR-TV (CW) St. Louis; KSDK (NBC) St. Louis; KTVI (FOX) St. Louis; WRBU (MNT) East St. Louis; WSIU-TV (PBS) Carbondale.
Programming (via satellite): C-SPAN; QVC; TV Guide Network; WGN America.
Fee: $36.95 installation; $19.31 monthly.

Expanded Basic Service 1
Subscribers: N.A.
Programming (via satellite): ABC Family Channel; AMC; Animal Planet; Arts & Entertainment; BET Networks; Bravo; Cartoon Network; CNBC; CNN; Comedy Central; Country Music TV; C-SPAN 2; Discovery Channel; Disney Channel; E! Entertainment Television; ESPN; ESPN 2; FitTV; Food Network; Fox News Channel; Fox Sports Net Midwest; FX; Great American Country; GRTV Network; Hallmark Channel; Headline News; HGTV; History Channel; Home Shopping Network; INSP; Lifetime; MSNBC; MTV; Nickelodeon; Outdoor Channel; ShopNBC; SoapNet; Speed Channel; Spike TV; Syfy; TBS Superstation; The Learning Channel; Travel Channel; Trinity Broadcasting Network; truTV; Turner Network TV; TV Land; USA Network; VH1; WE tv; Weather Channel.

Digital Basic Service
Subscribers: N.A.
Programming (via satellite): BBC America; Bio; Bloomberg News Radio; Discovery Health Channel; Discovery Home Channel; Discovery Kids Channel; Discovery Times Channel; Fox Movie Channel; Fox Soccer; Fuse; G4; GAS; Golf Channel; History Channel International; Independent Film Channel; Lifetime Movie Network; MTV Networks Digital Suite; Music Choice; National Geographic Channel; Nick Jr.; NickToons TV; Science Television; Style Network; Turner Classic Movies; Versus.

Digital Pay Service 1
Pay Units: N.A.
Programming (via satellite): Cinemax (multiplexed); Encore; Flix; HBO (multiplexed); Showtime (multiplexed); Starz (multiplexed); Sundance Channel; The Movie Channel (multiplexed).

Video-On-Demand: Yes

Internet Service
Operational: Yes.
Broadband Service: Mediacom High Speed Internet.

Telephone Service
Digital: Operational

Miles of Plant: 77.0 (coaxial); None (fiber optic). Homes passed: 2,763. Total homes in franchised area: 10,818.

Regional Vice President: Bill Copeland. General Manager: Dale Haney. Regional Technical Operations Director: Alan Freedman. Marketing Director: Will Kuebler. Marketing Manager: Melanie Westerman. Technical Operations Manager: Jeff Brown.

City fee: 3% of basic.

Ownership: Mediacom LLC (MSO).

COULTERVILLE—Mediacom. Now served by COULTERVILLE (formerly Red Bud), IL [IL0152]. ICA: IL0234.

COWDEN—Clearvision Cable Systems Inc., 1785 US Rte 40, Greenup, IL 62428-3501. Phone: 217-923-5594. Fax: 217-923-5681. E-mail: mbct@rr1.net. ICA: IL0337.

TV Market Ranking: Outside TV Markets (COWDEN). Franchise award date: N.A. Franchise expiration date: N.A. Began: April 1, 1985.

Channel capacity: 40 (not 2-way capable). Channels available but not in use: 24.

Basic Service
Subscribers: 36.
Programming (received off-air): WAND (NBC) Decatur; WICS (ABC) Springfield; WPXS (IND) Mount Vernon; WRSP-TV (FOX) Springfield; WTOL (CBS) Toledo; WUSI-TV (PBS) Olney.
Programming (via satellite): ABC Family Channel; CNN; Country Music TV; Discovery Channel; Disney Channel; ESPN; HGTV; MTV; Nickelodeon; Spike TV; TBS Superstation; Turner Classic Movies; Turner Network TV; USA Network; VH1; WGN America.
Fee: $42.50 installation; $36.07 monthly.

Pay Service 1
Pay Units: 27.
Programming (via satellite): Cinemax; HBO.

Video-On-Demand: No

Internet Service
Operational: No.

Telephone Service
None

Miles of Plant: 7.0 (coaxial); None (fiber optic). Homes passed: 277.

Manager: Michael Bauguss.

City fee: 3% of gross.

Ownership: Clearvision Cable Systems Inc. (MSO).

CULLOM—Mediacom. Now served by PONTIAC, IL [IL0109]. ICA: IL0289.

CUSTER PARK—Comcast Cable. Now served by CHICAGO (southern suburbs), IL [IL0008]. ICA: IL0487.

DAHLGREN—Hamilton County Communications Inc., PO Box 40, Hwy 142, Dahlgren, IL 62828. Phones: 800-447-8725; 618-736-2242. Fax: 618-736-2616. Web Site: http://www.hamiltoncom.net. ICA: IL0381.

TV Market Ranking: 69 (DAHLGREN). Franchise award date: N.A. Franchise expiration date: N.A. Began: June 1, 1988.

Channel capacity: 41 (not 2-way capable). Channels available but not in use: 13.

Basic Service
Subscribers: 15.
Programming (received off-air): KBSI (FOX) Cape Girardeau; KFVS-TV (CBS, CW) Cape Girardeau; KSDK (NBC) St. Louis; WSIL-TV (ABC) Harrisburg; WSIU-TV (PBS) Carbondale.
Programming (via satellite): CNN; C-SPAN; Discovery Channel; ESPN; MTV; Nickelodeon; TBS Superstation; Turner Network TV; WGN America.
Fee: $31.95 monthly.

Pay Service 1
Pay Units: 17.
Programming (via satellite): Showtime; The Movie Channel.
Fee: $8.95 monthly (TMC), $10.95 monthly (Showtime).

Video-On-Demand: No

Internet Service
Operational: No, DSL & dial-up.

Telephone Service
None

Miles of Plant: 6.0 (coaxial); None (fiber optic). Additional miles planned: 6.0 (coaxial). Homes passed: 170.

Manager: Bob Thomas.

Ownership: Hamilton County Communications Inc. (MSO).

DALLAS CITY—Mediacom. Now served by ROSEVILLE, IL [IL0274]. ICA: IL0230.

DANVERS—Mediacom. Now served by APOLLO ACRES, IL [IL0340]. ICA: IL0303.

DANVILLE—Insight Communications. Now served by URBANA, IL [IL0019]. ICA: IL0041.

DECATUR—Insight Communications. Now served by SPRINGFIELD, IL [IL0016]. ICA: IL0024.

DEER CREEK—Mediacom. Now served by APOLLO ACRES, IL [IL0340]. ICA: IL0306.

DEKALB—Comcast Cable. Now served by SCHAUMBURG, IL [IL0036]. ICA: IL0046.

DELAVAN—Mediacom, PO Box 288, 4290 Blue Stem Rd, Charleston, IL 61920. Phone: 217-348-5533. Fax: 217-345-7074. Web Site: http://www.mediacomcable.com. Also serves Cantrall, Delavan, Elkhart, Emden, Green Valley, Hartsburg, Middletown, New Holland, San Jose & Sangamon County (portions). ICA: IL0172.

TV Market Ranking: 64 (Cantrall, Elkhart, Greenview, Hartsburg, Middletown, New Holland, Sangamon County (portions)); 64,83 (Emden, Green Valley, San Jose); 83,83 (DELAVAN). Franchise award date: N.A. Franchise expiration date: N.A. Began: September 1, 1982.

Channel capacity: N.A. Channels available but not in use: N.A.

Basic Service
Subscribers: 1,230.
Programming (received off-air): WAND (NBC) Decatur; WAOE (MNT) Peoria; WBUI (CW) Decatur; WCFN (MNT) Springfield; WCIA (CBS) Champaign; WEEK-TV (NBC) Peoria; WHOI (ABC, CW) Peoria; WICS (ABC) Springfield; WILL-TV (PBS) Urbana; WMBD-TV (CBS) Peoria; WRSP-TV (FOX) Springfield; WSEC (PBS) Jacksonville; WTVP (PBS) Peoria; WYZZ-TV (FOX) Bloomington.
Programming (via satellite): ABC Family Channel; AMC; Animal Planet; Arts & Entertainment; BET Networks; Bravo; Cartoon Network; CNBC; CNN; Comcast SportsNet Chicago; Comedy Central; Country Music TV; C-SPAN; C-SPAN 2; Discovery Channel; Disney Channel; E! Entertainment Television; ESPN; ESPN 2; Eternal Word TV Network; FitTV; Food Network; Fox News Channel; FX; Hallmark Channel; Headline News; HGTV; History Channel; Home Shopping Network; INSP; ION Television; Lifetime; MoviePlex; MSNBC; MTV; Nickelodeon; Product Information Network; QVC; RFD-TV; ShopNBC; SoapNet; Speed Channel; Spike TV; Syfy; TBS Superstation; The Learning Channel; Travel Channel; Trinity Broadcasting Network; truTV; Turner Network TV; TV Guide Network; TV Land; USA Network; VH1; WE tv; Weather Channel; WGN America.
Fee: $45.00 installation; $54.95 monthly.

Digital Basic Service
Subscribers: N.A.
Programming (via satellite): ABC News Now; AmericanLife TV Network; BBC America; Bio; Bloomberg Television; CCTV-9 (CCTV International); Discovery HD Theater; Discovery Health Channel;

Discovery Kids Channel; Discovery Military Channel; Discovery Planet Green; Discovery Times Channel; ESPN 2 HD; ESPN HD; ESPNews; Fox Movie Channel; Fox Reality Channel; Fox Soccer; Fuse; G4; Golf Channel; GSN; HDNet; HDNet Movies; History Channel International; Independent Film Channel; ION Life; Lifetime Movie Network; Lifetime Real Women; MTV Hits; MTV2; Music Choice; National Geographic Channel; Nick Jr.; NickToons TV; Outdoor Channel; Qubo; ReelzChannel; Science Channel; Sleuth; Style Network; TeenNick; Turner Classic Movies; TVG Network; Universal HD; Versus; VH1 Classic.
Fee: $9.00 monthly.

Digital Expanded Basic Service
Subscribers: N.A.
Programming (via satellite): College Sports Television; ESPN U; Fox College Sports Atlantic; Fox College Sports Central; Fox College Sports Pacific; Fuel TV; Gol TV; Tennis Channel; The Sportsman Channel.
Fee: $3.95 monthly.

Digital Pay Service 1
Pay Units: N.A.
Programming (via satellite): Cinemax (multiplexed); Cinemax On Demand; Encore (multiplexed); HBO (multiplexed); HBO HD; HBO On Demand; Showtime (multiplexed); Showtime HD; Showtime On Demand; Starz (multiplexed); Starz HDTV; Starz On Demand; The Movie Channel (multiplexed); The Movie Channel HD; The Movie Channel On Demand.
Fee: $11.95 monthly (each).

Video-On-Demand: Yes

Pay-Per-View
iN DEMAND (delivered digitally); Ten Blox (delivered digitally); Playboy TV (delivered digitally); Ten Clips (delivered digitally).

Internet Service
Operational: Yes.
Broadband Service: Mediacom High Speed Internet.
Fee: $59.95 installation; $40.95 monthly.

Telephone Service
Digital: Operational
Fee: $39.95 installation; $39.95 monthly

Miles of Plant: 46.0 (coaxial); 19.0 (fiber optic). Homes passed: 2,179.
Area Operations Director: Todd Acker. Technical Operations Manager: Jerry Ferguson.
City fee: 1% of gross.
Ownership: Mediacom LLC (MSO).

DIX—Formerly served by Beck's Cable Systems. No longer in operation. ICA: IL0490.

DIXON—Comcast Cable, 4450 Kishwaukee St, Rockford, IL 61101. Phone: 815-395-8890. Fax: 815-395-8901. Web Site: http://www.comcast.com. Also serves Lee County (western portion) & Ogle County (portions). ICA: IL0082.
TV Market Ranking: 97 (DIXON (VILLAGE), Lee County (western portion) (portions), Ogle County (portions)); Below 100 (Lee County (western portion) (portions)). Franchise award date: N.A. Franchise expiration date: N.A. Began: October 1, 1970.
Channel capacity: N.A. Channels available but not in use: N.A.

Basic Service
Subscribers: N.A. Included in Rockford
Programming (received off-air): KWQC-TV (NBC) Davenport; WHBF-TV (CBS) Rock Island; WIFR (CBS) Freeport; WQAD-TV (ABC) Moline; WQPT-TV (PBS) Moline; WQRF-TV (FOX) Rockford; WREX (CW, NBC) Rockford; WTTW (PBS) Chicago; WTVO (ABC, MNT) Rockford; 14 FMs.
Programming (via satellite): C-SPAN; C-SPAN 2; Eternal Word TV Network; Home Shopping Network; ION Television; QVC; TV Guide Network; WGN America.
Current originations: Public Access.
Fee: $44.00 installation; $8.00 monthly; $2.00 converter.

Expanded Basic Service 1
Subscribers: 5,219.
Programming (via satellite): ABC Family Channel; AMC; Animal Planet; Arts & Entertainment; BET Networks; Bravo; Cartoon Network; CNBC; CNN; Comcast SportsNet Chicago; Comedy Central; Country Music TV; Discovery Channel; Disney Channel; E! Entertainment Television; ESPN; ESPN 2; Food Network; Fox News Channel; Fox Sports Net Midwest; FX; Great American Country; Hallmark Channel; Headline News; HGTV; History Channel; Lifetime; MSNBC; MTV; National Geographic Channel; Nickelodeon; Oxygen; Speed Channel; Spike TV; Syfy; TBS Superstation; The Learning Channel; Total Living Network; Travel Channel; truTV; Turner Network TV; Univision; USA Network; VH1; Weather Channel.
Fee: $43.75 monthly.

Digital Basic Service
Subscribers: N.A.
Programming (via satellite): AmericanLife TV Network; BBC America; Bio; Bloomberg Television; CBS College Sports Network; CMT Pure Country; Cooking Channel; C-SPAN 3; Discovery Digital Networks; Discovery HD Theater; DMX Music; Do-It-Yourself; Encore (multiplexed); ESPN 2 HD; ESPN Classic Sports; ESPN HD; ESPN U; ESPNews; Fox Movie Channel; Fox Soccer; Fuse; G4; GAS; Golf Channel; GSN; Halogen Network; HDNet; HDNet Movies; History Channel International; HorseRacing TV; Independent Film Channel; Lifetime Movie Network; Lifetime Real Women; MTV Networks Digital Suite; NFL Network; Nick Jr.; Nick Too; NickToons TV; Outdoor Channel; Palladia; PBS Kids Sprout; Si TV; SoapNet; Style Network; Sundance Channel; Tennis Channel; Toon Disney; Trinity Broadcasting Network; Turner Classic Movies; Turner Network TV HD; TV Land; TVG Network; Universal HD; Versus; WE tv.
Fee: $15.95 monthly.

Digital Pay Service 1
Pay Units: N.A.
Programming (via satellite): Cinemax; Flix; HBO (multiplexed); HBO HD; Showtime (multiplexed); Showtime HD; Starz (multiplexed); The Movie Channel (multiplexed).
Fee: $10.00 monthly (each).

Video-On-Demand: Yes

Pay-Per-View
ESPN (delivered digitally); iN DEMAND (delivered digitally); Playboy TV (delivered digitally); Special events (delivered digitally).

Internet Service
Operational: Yes.
Broadband Service: Comcast High Speed Internet.
Fee: $99.95 installation; $44.95 monthly; $10.00 modem lease; $99.99 modem purchase.

Telephone Service
Digital: Operational

Total homes in franchised area: 6,682. Homes passed & miles of plant included in Rockford
District Director: Joseph Browning. Technical Operations Manager: Lyle Matejewski. Program Director: Janice Schultz. Community & Government Affairs Manager: Joan Sage.
City fee: 3% of gross.
Ownership: Comcast Cable Communications Inc. (MSO).

DOLTON—Comcast Cable. Now served by CHICAGO (southern suburbs), IL [IL0008]. ICA: IL0030.

DONGOLA—Longview Communications, 12007 Sunrise Valley Dr, Ste 375, Reston, VA 20191. Phone: 703-476-9101. Fax: 703-476-9107. Web Site: http://www.longviewcomm.com. ICA: IL0328.
TV Market Ranking: 69 (DONGOLA). Franchise award date: N.A. Franchise expiration date: N.A. Began: June 6, 1983.
Channel capacity: 41 (not 2-way capable). Channels available but not in use: 1.

Basic Service
Subscribers: 23.
Programming (received off-air): KBSI (FOX) Cape Girardeau; KFVS-TV (CBS, CW) Cape Girardeau; WDKA (MNT) Paducah; WKPD (PBS) Paducah; WPSD-TV (NBC) Paducah; WSIL-TV (ABC) Harrisburg; WTCT (IND) Marion.
Programming (via satellite): C-SPAN; C-SPAN 2; QVC; Trinity Broadcasting Network.
Fee: $30.00 installation; $17.98 monthly.

Expanded Basic Service 1
Subscribers: N.A.
Programming (via satellite): ABC Family Channel; American Movie Classics; Animal Planet; Arts & Entertainment; CNN; Discovery Channel; Disney Channel; E! Entertainment Television; ESPN; ESPN 2; Fox News Channel; Great American Country; Headline News; History Channel; Lifetime; MSNBC; Speed Channel; TBS Superstation; The Learning Channel; Turner Network TV; USA Network; Weather Channel; WGN America.
Fee: $17.97 monthly.

Pay Service 1
Pay Units: N.A.
Programming (via satellite): Cinemax; HBO; Showtime; The Movie Channel.
Fee: $8.95 monthly (TMC), $10.95 monthly (Cinemax or Showtime), $12.95 monthly (HBO).

Video-On-Demand: No

Internet Service
Operational: No.

Telephone Service
None

Miles of Plant: 6.0 (coaxial); None (fiber optic). Homes passed: 313.
President: John Long. Senior Vice President: Marc W. Cohen. General Manager: Brandon Dickey. Technical Manager: Steve Boss.
Ownership: Longview Communications (MSO).

DONOVAN TWP.—Formerly served by CableDirect. No longer in operation. ICA: IL0405.

DU QUOIN—Comcast Cable, 19 S Mulberry St, Du Quoin, IL 62832-1814. Phone: 618-542-5437. Fax: 618-542-9222. Web Site: http://www.comcast.com. Also serves Benton, Buckner, Christopher, Coello/North City, Ewing, Mulkeytown, Pinckneyville, St. Johns, Tamaroa, West City & Whittington. ICA: IL0117.
TV Market Ranking: 69 (Benton, Buckner, Christopher, Coello/North City, Ewing, Mulkeytown, West City, Whittington); Below 100 (DU QUOIN, Mulkeytown, Pinckneyville, St. Johns, Tamaroa). Franchise award date: January 1, 1975. Franchise expiration date: N.A. Began: October 1, 1976.
Channel capacity: 61 (operating 2-way). Channels available but not in use: None.

Basic Service
Subscribers: 7,118.
Programming (received off-air): KBSI (FOX) Cape Girardeau; KFVS-TV (CBS, CW) Cape Girardeau; KSDK (NBC) St. Louis; WDKA (MNT) Paducah; WPSD-TV (NBC) Paducah; WPXS (IND) Mount Vernon; WQWQ-LP (CW) Paducah; WSIL-TV (ABC) Harrisburg; WSIU-TV (PBS) Carbondale; WTCT (IND) Marion.
Programming (via satellite): ABC Family Channel; AMC; Animal Planet; Arts & Entertainment; BET Networks; Cartoon Network; CNBC; CNN; Comedy Central; Country Music TV; C-SPAN; Discovery Channel; Discovery Health Channel; Disney Channel; E! Entertainment Television; ESPN; ESPN 2; ESPN Classic Sports; ESPNews; Eternal Word TV Network; Food Network; Fox News Channel; Fox Sports Net Midwest; FX; GSN; Hallmark Channel; Headline News; HGTV; History Channel; Lifetime; MSNBC; MTV; Nickelodeon; QVC; ShopNBC; SoapNet; Spike TV; Syfy; TBS Superstation; The Learning Channel; Toon Disney; Travel Channel; truTV; Turner Network TV; TV Guide Network; TV Land; USA Network; VH1; Weather Channel; WGN America.
Fee: $14.99 monthly.

Digital Basic Service
Subscribers: 1,252.
Programming (via satellite): BBC America; Discovery Digital Networks; GAS; Lifetime Movie Network; MTV Networks Digital Suite; Music Choice; NFL Network; Nick Jr.; Nick Too; NickToons TV; Speed Channel.
Fee: $12.95 monthly.

Pay Service 1
Pay Units: N.A.
Programming (via satellite): Cinemax; HBO; Showtime.

Digital Pay Service 1
Pay Units: N.A.
Programming (via satellite): Cinemax (multiplexed); Encore (multiplexed); HBO (multiplexed); Showtime (multiplexed); Starz (multiplexed); The Movie Channel (multiplexed); WAM! America's Kidz Network.
Fee: $11.95 monthly (each).

Video-On-Demand: No

Pay-Per-View
Fresh (delivered digitally).

Internet Service
Operational: Yes.
Subscribers: 2,200.
Broadband Service: Comcast High Speed Internet.
Fee: $42.95 monthly.

Telephone Service
Digital: Operational

Miles of Plant: 302.0 (coaxial); None (fiber optic). Homes passed: 13,281.
General Manager: Don Richey. Technical Operations Director: Richard Ring. Technical Supervisor: Floyd Cairns.
City fee: 5% of gross.
Ownership: Comcast Cable Communications Inc. (MSO).

DUNLAP—Mediacom. Now served by BRIMFIELD, IL [IL0201]. ICA: IL0313.

DURAND—Formerly served by Mediacom. No longer in operation. ICA: IL0179.

DWIGHT—Mediacom. Now served by PONTIAC, IL [IL0109]. ICA: IL0163.

EAST DUBUQUE—Mediacom. Now served by DUBUQUE, IA [IA0007]. ICA: IL0188.

EAST ROGERS PARK—RCN Corp. Formerly served by Chicago (portions), IL [IL0661]. This cable system has converted to IPTV, 196 Van Buren St, Herndon, VA 20170. Phone: 703-434-8200. Web Site: http://www.rcn.com. ICA: IL5227.

TV Market Ranking: 3 (EAST ROGERS PARK).

Channel capacity: N.A. Channels available but not in use: N.A.

Internet Service

Operational: Yes.

Fee: $23.00 monthly.

Telephone Service

Digital: Operational

Fee: $30.00 monthly

Chairman: Steven J. Simmons. Chief Executive Officer: Jim Holanda.

Ownership: RCN Corp.

EAST ST. LOUIS—Charter Communications, 941 Charter Commons Dr, Saint Louis, MO 63017. Phone: 636-207-7044. Fax: 636-230-7034. Web Site: http://www.charter.com. Also serves Alorton & Centreville. ICA: IL0062.

TV Market Ranking: 11 (Alorton, Centreville, EAST ST. LOUIS). Franchise award date: N.A. Franchise expiration date: N.A. Began: October 1, 1981.

Channel capacity: N.A. Channels available but not in use: N.A.

Basic Service

Subscribers: 4,980.

Programming (received off-air): KDNL-TV (ABC) St. Louis; KETC (PBS) St. Louis; KMOV (CBS) St. Louis; KNLC (IND) St. Louis; KPLR-TV (CW) St. Louis; KSDK (NBC) St. Louis; KTVI (FOX) St. Louis; WPXS (IND) Mount Vernon; WRBU (MNT) East St. Louis.

Programming (via satellite): C-SPAN; Discovery Channel; QVC; TBS Superstation; WGN America.

Current originations: Government Access; Educational Access.

Fee: $29.99 installation.

Expanded Basic Service 1

Subscribers: 4,929.

Programming (via satellite): ABC Family Channel; AMC; Animal Planet; Arts & Entertainment; BET Networks; Cartoon Network; CNN; Comedy Central; Disney Channel; ESPN; ESPN 2; Fox News Channel; Fox Sports Net Midwest; FX; Hallmark Channel; Lifetime; MTV; Nickelodeon; Spike TV; The Learning Channel; truTV; Turner Network TV; TV Land; USA Network.

Fee: $49.99 monthly.

Digital Basic Service

Subscribers: N.A.

Programming (via satellite): BBC America; Bravo; Discovery Digital Networks; DMX Music; ESPN Classic Sports; ESPNews; Fox Sports World; Golf Channel; GSN; HGTV; History Channel; Independent Film Channel; MTV Hits; Nick Jr.; Sundance Channel; Syfy; Turner Classic Movies; TV Guide Interactive Inc.; Versus; VH1 Soul; WE tv.

Digital Pay Service 1

Pay Units: 2,225.

Programming (via satellite): Cinemax (multiplexed); Encore (multiplexed); HBO (multiplexed); Showtime (multiplexed); Starz (multiplexed); The Movie Channel (multiplexed).

Fee: $12.55 monthly (Cinemax, HBO or Showtime).

Video-On-Demand: Yes

Pay-Per-View

iN DEMAND (delivered digitally); Shorteez (delivered digitally); Playboy TV (delivered digitally).

Internet Service

Operational: Yes.

Broadband Service: Charter Pipeline.

Fee: $29.99 monthly.

Telephone Service

Digital: Operational

Fee: $29.99 monthly

Miles of Plant: 164.0 (coaxial); None (fiber optic). Homes passed: 10,780. Total homes in franchised area: 13,600.

Vice President & General Manager: Steve Trippe. Operations Director: Tom Williams. Marketing Director: Beverly Wall.

Ownership: Charter Communications Inc. (MSO).

EDGEWOOD—Clearvision Cable Systems Inc., 1785 US Rte 40, Greenup, IL 62428-3501. Phone: 217-923-5594. Fax: 217-923-5681. E-mail: mbct@rr1.net. Also serves Mason. ICA: IL0495.

TV Market Ranking: Outside TV Markets (EDGEWOOD, Mason). Franchise award date: N.A. Franchise expiration date: N.A. Began: N.A.

Channel capacity: 40 (not 2-way capable). Channels available but not in use: 20.

Basic Service

Subscribers: 55.

Programming (received off-air): WAND (NBC) Decatur; WBUI (CW) Decatur; WCFN (MNT) Springfield; WCIA (CBS) Champaign; WICS (ABC) Springfield; WPXS (IND) Mount Vernon; WRSP-TV (FOX) Springfield; WTHI-TV (CBS) Terre Haute; WUSI-TV (PBS) Olney.

Programming (via satellite): ABC Family Channel; Arts & Entertainment; Bravo; Cartoon Network; CNBC; CNN; Comedy Central; Country Music TV; C-SPAN; Discovery Channel; Disney Channel; Fox Sports Net; FX; G4; Hallmark Channel; Headline News; History Channel; Lifetime; MTV; National Geographic Channel; Nickelodeon; Oxygen; QVC; Spike TV; Syfy; TBS Superstation; The Learning Channel; Trinity Broadcasting Network; Turner Network TV; TV Land; USA Network; VH1; Weather Channel; WGN America.

Fee: $42.50 installation; $29.95 monthly.

Pay Service 1

Pay Units: N.A.

Programming (via satellite): Cinemax; HBO.

Fee: $11.00 monthly (each).

Video-On-Demand: No

Internet Service

Operational: No.

Telephone Service

None

Miles of Plant: 6.0 (coaxial); None (fiber optic). Homes passed: 390.

Manager: Michael Bauguss.

Ownership: Clearvision Cable Systems Inc. (MSO).

EDWARDS—Tel-Star Cablevision Inc., 1295 Lourdes Rd, Metamora, IL 61548-7710. Phone: 309-383-2677. Fax: 309-383-2657. E-mail: cdecker@telstar-online.net. Web Site: http://www.telstar-online.net. Also serves Brimfield, Fox Creek, Hanna City, Heritage Lake, Kickapoo, Lake Camelot, Lake Windermere, Mapleton & Peoria County (portions). ICA: IL0326.

TV Market Ranking: 83 (Brimfield, EDWARDS, Fox Creek, Hanna City, Heritage Lake, Kickapoo, Lake Camelot, Lake Windermere, Mapleton, Peoria County (portions)). Franchise award date: July 1, 1989. Franchise expiration date: N.A. Began: July 1, 1989.

Channel capacity: 40 (operating 2-way). Channels available but not in use: None.

Basic Service

Subscribers: 1,118.

Programming (received off-air): WAOE (MNT) Peoria; WEEK-TV (NBC) Peoria; WHOI (ABC, CW) Peoria; WMBD-TV (CBS) Peoria; WTVP (PBS) Peoria; WYZZ-TV (FOX) Bloomington.

Programming (via satellite): ABC Family Channel; AMC; Animal Planet; Arts & Entertainment; Cartoon Network; CNN; Comedy Central; Country Music TV; C-SPAN; Discovery Channel; Disney Channel; ESPN; ESPN 2; Fox News Channel; FX; Hallmark Channel; Headline News; HGTV; History Channel; Home Shopping Network; INSP; Lifetime; MTV; National Geographic Channel; Nickelodeon; QVC; Speed Channel; Spike TV; Syfy; TBS Superstation; The Learning Channel; Travel Channel; Turner Network TV; TV Land; USA Network; VH1; Weather Channel; WGN America.

Fee: $39.95 installation; $37.95 monthly; $2.95 converter.

Digital Basic Service

Subscribers: 116.

Programming (via satellite): BBC America; Bio; Bloomberg Television; Discovery Digital Networks; DMX Music; ESPN Classic Sports; ESPN Now; ESPNews; FitTV; Fox Movie Channel; Fox Sports World; G4; GAS; Golf Channel; GSN; History Channel International; Lifetime Movie Network; MTV Networks Digital Suite; Nick Jr.; NickToons TV; Outdoor Channel; Style Network; Toon Disney; Trinity Broadcasting Network; Turner Classic Movies; Versus; WE tv.

Fee: $50.95 monthly.

Digital Pay Service 1

Pay Units: N.A.

Programming (via satellite): Cinemax (multiplexed); Encore; HBO (multiplexed); Showtime; Starz (multiplexed); The Movie Channel.

Fee: $11.00 monthly (each).

Pay-Per-View

iN DEMAND (delivered digitally); Playboy TV (delivered digitally); Fresh (delivered digitally); Sports PPV (delivered digitally).

Internet Service

Operational: Yes.

Subscribers: 720.

Broadband Service: Tel-Star High Speed Internet.

Fee: $24.95-$49.95 monthly; $5.00 modem lease.

Telephone Service

Digital: Operational

Fee: $29.95-$59.95 monthly

Miles of Plant: 48.0 (coaxial); 27.0 (fiber optic).

General Manager: John Gregory. Network Operations Manager: Chris Decker. Customer Service Manager: Patti Sanders.

Franchise fee: 5% of gross.

Ownership: Tel-Star Cablevision Inc. (MSO).

EFFINGHAM—Mediacom, PO Box 288, 4290 Blue Stem Rd, Charleston, IL 61920. Phones: 217-348-5533 (Local office); 217-347-7454 (Effingham). Fax: 217-345-7074. Web Site: http://www.mediacomcable.com. Also serves Effingham County (unincorporated areas), Lake Sara, Sigel & Teutopolis. ICA: IL0094.

TV Market Ranking: Outside TV Markets (EFFINGHAM, Effingham County (unincorporated areas), Lake Sara, Sigel, Teutopolis). Franchise award date: N.A. Franchise expiration date: N.A. Began: August 19, 1962.

Channel capacity: N.A. Channels available but not in use: N.A.

Basic Service

Subscribers: 6,059.

Programming (received off-air): KPLR-TV (CW) St. Louis; KSDK (NBC) St. Louis; WAND (NBC) Decatur; WBUI (CW) Decatur; WCCU (FOX) Urbana; WCFN (MNT) Springfield; WCIA (CBS) Champaign; WEIU-TV (PBS) Charleston; WICS (ABC) Springfield; WILL-TV (PBS) Urbana; WPXS (IND) Mount Vernon; WTHI-TV (CBS) Terre Haute; WTWO (NBC) Terre Haute; WUSI-TV (PBS) Olney; 5 FMs.

Programming (via satellite): C-SPAN 2; Discovery Digital Networks; Home Shopping Network; Nick Jr.; QVC; WGN America.

Fee: $45.00 installation; $20.95 monthly; $1.18 converter.

Expanded Basic Service 1

Subscribers: N.A.

Programming (via satellite): ABC Family Channel; AMC; Animal Planet; Arts & Entertainment; Cartoon Network; CNBC; CNN; Comedy Central; Country Music TV; C-SPAN 2; Discovery Channel; Disney Channel; E! Entertainment Television; ESPN; ESPN 2; ESPN Classic Sports; Eternal Word TV Network; Food Network; Fox News Channel; Fox Sports Net Midwest; Fuse; FX; Hallmark Channel; Headline News; HGTV; History Channel; INSP; ION Television; Jewelry Television; Lifetime; Lifetime Movie Network; MSNBC; MTV; Nickelodeon; Outdoor Channel; Product Information Network; ShopNBC; Speed Channel; Spike TV; Syfy; TBS Superstation; The Learning Channel; Travel Channel; Trinity Broadcasting Network; truTV; Turner Network TV; TV Guide Network; TV Land; USA Network; VH1; WE tv; Weather Channel.

Fee: $34.00 monthly.

Digital Basic Service

Subscribers: N.A.

Programming (received off-air): WAND (NBC) Decatur; WCCU (FOX) Urbana; WCIA (CBS) Champaign; WICS (ABC) Springfield; WILL-TV (PBS) Urbana; WTHI-TV (CBS) Terre Haute.

Programming (via satellite): ABC News Now; AmericanLife TV Network; BBC America; Bio; Bloomberg Television; Bravo; CCTV-Entertainment; CMT Pure Country; Discovery HD Theater; ESPN 2 HD; ESPN HD; ESPNews; FitTV; Fox Movie Channel; Fox Reality Channel; Fox Soccer; Fuse; G4; Golf Channel; GSN; HDNet; HDNet Movies; History Channel International; Independent Film Channel; ION Life; Lifetime Real Women; Military History Channel; MTV Hits; MTV2; Music Choice; National Geographic Channel; NickToons TV; Qubo; ReelzChannel; Science Channel; Sleuth; Style Network; TeenNick; Toon Dis-

ney; Turner Classic Movies; Universal HD; Versus; VH1 Classic.
Fee: $9.00 monthly.

Digital Expanded Basic Service
Subscribers: N.A.
Programming (via satellite): College Sports Television; ESPN U; Fox College Sports Atlantic; Fox College Sports Central; Fox College Sports Pacific; Fuel TV; Gol TV; Tennis Channel; The Sportsman Channel; TVG Network.
Fee: $3.95 monthly.

Digital Pay Service 1
Pay Units: N.A.
Programming (via satellite): Cinemax (multiplexed); Encore (multiplexed); HBO (multiplexed); HBO HD; Showtime (multiplexed); Showtime HD; Starz (multiplexed); Starz HDTV; The Movie Channel (multiplexed); The Movie Channel HD.
Fee: $11.95 monthly (each).

Video-On-Demand: Yes

Pay-Per-View
iN DEMAND (delivered digitally); Playboy TV (delivered digitally); Ten Clips (delivered digitally); Ten Blox (delivered digitally); ESPN (delivered digitally); HDNet (delivered digitally).

Internet Service
Operational: Yes.
Broadband Service: Mediacom High Speed Internet.
Fee: $59.95 installation; $40.95 monthly.

Telephone Service
Analog: Not Operational
Digital: Operational
Fee: $39.95 installation; $39.95 monthly

Miles of Plant: 111.0 (coaxial); None (fiber optic). Additional miles planned: 2.0 (coaxial).
Area Operations Director: Todd Acker. Technical Operations Manager: Jerry Ferguson.
City fee: 5% of gross.
Ownership: Mediacom LLC (MSO).

EFFINGHAM COUNTY—Clearvision Cable Systems Inc., 1785 US Rte 40, Greenup, IL 62428-3501. Phone: 543-472-9500. Fax: 217-923-5681. Also serves Heartville & Watson. ICA: IL0349.
TV Market Ranking: Outside TV Markets (EFFINGHAM COUNTY, Heartville, Watson). Franchise award date: N.A. Franchise expiration date: N.A. Began: N.A.
Channel capacity: 41 (not 2-way capable). Channels available but not in use: N.A.

Basic Service
Subscribers: 204.
Programming (received off-air): WAND (NBC) Decatur; WBUI (CW) Decatur; WICS (ABC) Springfield; WPXS (IND) Mount Vernon; WRSP-TV (FOX) Springfield; WTHI-TV (CBS) Terre Haute; WTWO (NBC) Terre Haute; WUSI-TV (PBS) Olney.
Programming (via satellite): ESPN; QVC; TBS Superstation; WGN America.
Fee: $30.00 installation; $19.57 monthly.

Expanded Basic Service 1
Subscribers: 184.
Programming (via satellite): ABC Family Channel; Arts & Entertainment; CNN; C-SPAN; Discovery Channel; Disney Channel; ESPN 2; Eternal Word TV Network; Fox News Channel; Fox Sports Net Midwest; History Channel; Lifetime; MTV; Nickelodeon; Spike TV; Trinity Broadcasting Network; Turner Network TV; USA Network; Weather Channel.
Fee: $13.09 monthly.

Digital Basic Service
Subscribers: 14.
Programming (via satellite): BBC America; Bio; Bloomberg Television; Discovery Channel; DMX Music; Fox Movie Channel; G4; GAS; Golf Channel; GSN; Halogen Network; HGTV; History Channel International; Independent Film Channel; Lifetime Movie Network; MTV Networks Digital Suite; MuchMusic Network; Nick Jr.; Outdoor Channel; ShopNBC; Speed Channel; Style Network; Syfy; Toon Disney; Trinity Broadcasting Network; Turner Classic Movies; Versus; WE tv.

Pay Service 1
Pay Units: 47.
Programming (via satellite): HBO; Showtime; The Movie Channel.
Fee: $9.50 monthly (Showtime).

Digital Pay Service 1
Pay Units: N.A.
Programming (via satellite): Cinemax (multiplexed); Encore (multiplexed); Flix; HBO (multiplexed); Showtime (multiplexed); Starz (multiplexed); The Movie Channel (multiplexed).

Video-On-Demand: No

Pay-Per-View
sports (delivered digitally); Shorteez (delivered digitally); Fresh (delivered digitally); Playboy TV (delivered digitally); iN DEMAND (delivered digitally); Hot Choice (delivered digitally); ESPN Now (delivered digitally).

Internet Service
Operational: No.

Telephone Service
None

Additional miles planned: 10.0 (coaxial). Homes passed: 613.
General Manager: Michael Bauguss.
Ownership: Clearvision Cable Systems Inc. (MSO).

ELDRED—Formerly served by Longview Communications. No longer in operation. ICA: IL0626.

ELGIN—Comcast Cable. Now served by OAK BROOK, IL [IL0006]. ICA: IL0032.

ELIZABETH—Formerly served by Mediacom. No longer in operation. ICA: IL0305.

ELKHART TWP.—Formerly served by Mediacom. No longer in operation. ICA: IL0398.

ELMWOOD—Mediacom, PO Box 334, 609 S 4th St, Chillicothe, IL 61523. Phone: 309-274-4500. Fax: 309-274-3188. Web Site: http://www.mediacomcable.com. Also serves Dumferline, Fairview, Farmington, Glasford, Hanna City, London Mills, Smithville, St. David & Yates City. ICA: IL0205.
TV Market Ranking: 83 (Dumferline, ELMWOOD, Fairview, Farmington, Glasford, Hanna City, London Mills, Smithville, St. David, Yates City). Franchise award date: N.A. Franchise expiration date: N.A. Began: N.A.
Channel capacity: 121 (operating 2-way). Channels available but not in use: 66.

Basic Service
Subscribers: 2,675.
Programming (received off-air): WAOE (MNT) Peoria; WEEK-TV (NBC) Peoria; WHOI (ABC, CW) Peoria; WMBD-TV (CBS) Peoria; WTVP (PBS) Peoria; WYZZ-TV (FOX) Bloomington.
Programming (via satellite): WGN America.
Fee: $45.00 installation; $20.95 monthly.

Expanded Basic Service 1
Subscribers: 1,436.
Programming (via satellite): ABC Family Channel; AMC; Animal Planet; Arts & Entertainment; Cartoon Network; CNBC; CNN; Comcast SportsNet Chicago; Comedy Central; Country Music TV; C-SPAN; CW+; Discovery Channel; Disney Channel; E! Entertainment Television; ESPN; ESPN 2; ESPN Classic Sports; FitTV; Food Network; Fox News Channel; FX; Great American Country; Hallmark Channel; Headline News; HGTV; History Channel; Home Shopping Network; INSP; ION Television; Lifetime; Lifetime Movie Network; MSNBC; MTV; Nickelodeon; Product Information Network; QVC; ShopNBC; SoapNet; Speed Channel; Spike TV; Syfy; TBS Superstation; The Learning Channel; Travel Channel; Trinity Broadcasting Network; truTV; Turner Network TV; TV Land; TVG Network; USA Network; VH1; WE tv; Weather Channel.
Fee: $34.00 monthly.

Digital Basic Service
Subscribers: N.A.
Programming (via satellite): ABC News Now; AmericanLife TV Network; BBC America; Bio; Bloomberg Television; CBS College Sports Network; CCTV-9 (CCTV International); Discovery Health Channel; Discovery Home Channel; Discovery Kids Channel; Discovery Military Channel; ESPN 2 HD; ESPN HD; ESPN U; ESPNews; Fox College Sports Atlantic; Fox College Sports Central; Fox College Sports Pacific; Fox Movie Channel; Fox Soccer; Fuse; G4; Gol TV; Golf Channel; History Channel International; ID Investigation Discovery; Independent Film Channel; ION Life; MTV Hits; MTV2; National Geographic Channel; Nick Jr.; NickToons TV; Outdoor Channel; Qubo; Science Channel; Sleuth; Style Network; TeenNick; Tennis Channel; The Sportsman Channel; Turner Classic Movies; TVG Network; Versus; VH1 Classic.
Fee: $9.00 monthly.

Digital Expanded Basic Service
Subscribers: N.A.
Programming (via satellite): CNN HD; Discovery HD Theater; HDNet; HDNet Movies; TBS in HD; Turner Network TV HD.
Fee: $6.95 monthly.

Digital Pay Service 1
Pay Units: N.A.
Programming (via satellite): Cinemax (multiplexed); Encore (multiplexed); Flix; HBO (multiplexed); HBO HD; Showtime (multiplexed); Showtime HD; Starz (multiplexed); Starz HDTV; Sundance Channel; The Movie Channel (multiplexed); The Movie Channel HD.
Fee: $11.95 monthly (HBO, Cinemax, Showtime/TMC or Starz/Encore).

Video-On-Demand: Yes

Pay-Per-View
iN DEMAND (delivered digitally); Playboy TV (delivered digitally); Penthouse TV (delivered digitally); Ten Clips (delivered digitally); Ten Blox (delivered digitally).

Internet Service
Operational: Yes.
Broadband Service: Mediacom High Speed Internet.
Fee: $59.95 installation; $45.95 monthly.

Telephone Service
Digital: Operational
Fee: $39.95 installation; $39.95 monthly

Miles of Plant: 58.0 (coaxial); 8.0 (fiber optic). Homes passed: 4,396.
Vice President: Don Hagwell. Operations Director: Gary Wightman. Technical Operations Manager: Larry Brackman. Marketing Director: Stephanie Law.
City fee: 3% of basic gross.
Ownership: Mediacom LLC (MSO).

ENFIELD—NewWave Communications, 1176 E 1500 North Rd, Taylorville, IL 62568. Phone: 217-287-7992. Fax: 217-287-7304. E-mail: info@newwavecom.com. Web Site: http://www.newwavecom.com. ICA: IL0321.
TV Market Ranking: 69 (ENFIELD). Franchise award date: N.A. Franchise expiration date: N.A. Began: March 22, 1984.
Channel capacity: 136 (not 2-way capable). Channels available but not in use: N.A.

Basic Service
Subscribers: 45.
Programming (received off-air): KBSI (FOX) Cape Girardeau; KFVS-TV (CBS, CW) Cape Girardeau; WDKA (MNT) Paducah; WEVV-TV (CBS, MNT) Evansville; WPSD-TV (NBC) Paducah; WPXS (IND) Mount Vernon; WSIL-TV (ABC) Harrisburg; WSIU-TV (PBS) Carbondale; WTCT (IND) Marion; WTVW (FOX) Evansville.
Programming (via satellite): C-SPAN; Home Shopping Network; INSP; QVC; Trinity Broadcasting Network; WGN America.
Fee: $40.00 installation; $16.95 monthly; $40.00 additional installation.

Expanded Basic Service 1
Subscribers: 42.
Programming (via satellite): ABC Family Channel; AMC; Animal Planet; Arts & Entertainment; Big Ten Network; Bravo; Cartoon Network; CNBC; CNN; Comedy Central; Country Music TV; Discovery Channel; Disney Channel; E! Entertainment Television; ESPN; ESPN 2; ESPN Classic Sports; Eternal Word TV Network; Food Network; Fox News Channel; Fox Sports Net Midwest; FX; Golf Channel; GSN; Hallmark Channel; Headline News; HGTV; History Channel; Lifetime; MSNBC; MTV; National Geographic Channel; Nickelodeon; Outdoor Channel; Oxygen; ShopNBC; SoapNet; Speed Channel; Spike TV; Syfy; TBS Superstation; The Learning Channel; Toon Disney; Travel Channel; truTV; Turner Classic Movies; Turner Network TV; TV Land; USA Network; Versus; VH1; Weather Channel.

Digital Basic Service
Subscribers: 2.
Programming (received off-air): KBSI (FOX) Cape Girardeau; KFVS-TV (CBS, CW) Cape Girardeau; WPSD-TV (NBC) Paducah; WSIL-TV (ABC) Harrisburg; WSIU-TV (PBS) Carbondale.
Programming (via satellite): BBC America; Bio; Bloomberg Television; CMT Pure Country; Cooking Channel; Discovery HD Theater; Discovery Health Channel; Discovery Kids Channel; Discovery Military Channel; Discovery Planet Green; Do-It-Yourself;

ESPN 2 HD; ESPN HD; ESPNews; FitTV; Fox College Sports Atlantic; Fox College Sports Central; Fox College Sports Pacific; Fox Movie Channel; FSN HD; G4; Great American Country; Halogen Network; HD-Net; HDNet Movies; History Channel International; ID Investigation Discovery; Independent Film Channel; Lifetime Movie Network; MTV Hits; MTV Jams; MTV2; Music Choice; Nick Jr.; Nick Too; NickToons TV; Science Television; Sleuth; Style Network; TeenNick; Turner Network TV HD; Universal HD; USA Network HD; VH1 Classic; VH1 Soul; WE tv.

Digital Pay Service 1
Pay Units: N.A.
Programming (via satellite): Cinemax (multiplexed); Cinemax HD; Encore (multiplexed); Flix; HBO (multiplexed); HBO HD; Showtime (multiplexed); Starz (multiplexed); Starz HDTV; The Movie Channel (multiplexed).

Video-On-Demand: No

Pay-Per-View
iN DEMAND (delivered digitally); Shorteez (delivered digitally); Fresh (delivered digitally); Playboy TV (delivered digitally); Club Jenna (delivered digitally); Spice: Xcess (delivered digitally).

Internet Service
Operational: Yes.
Fee: $40.00 installation; $31.99 monthly.

Telephone Service
None

Miles of Plant: 8.0 (coaxial); None (fiber optic). Homes passed: 293. Total homes in franchised area: 362.
General Manager: Bill Flowers. Technical Operations Manager: Chris Mooday.
Ownership: NewWave Communications (MSO).

EVANSVILLE—NewWave Communications, One Montgomery Plaza, 4th Fl, Sikeston, MO 63801. Phone: 573-472-9500. Fax: 573-481-9809. E-mail: info@newwavecom.com. Web Site: http://www.newwavecom.com. Also serves Prairie du Rocher & Ruma. ICA: IL0237.
TV Market Ranking: Outside TV Markets (EVANSVILLE, Prairie du Rocher, Ruma). Franchise award date: October 1, 1987. Franchise expiration date: N.A. Began: June 13, 1988.
Channel capacity: N.A. Channels available but not in use: N.A.

Basic Service
Subscribers: 112.
Programming (received off-air): KDNL-TV (ABC) St. Louis; KETC (PBS) St. Louis; KFVS-TV (CBS, CW) Cape Girardeau; KMOV (CBS) St. Louis; KPLR-TV (CW) St. Louis; KSDK (NBC) St. Louis; KTVI (FOX) St. Louis; WRBU (MNT) East St. Louis; WSIL-TV (ABC) Harrisburg; WSIU-TV (PBS) Carbondale.
Programming (via satellite): AMC; C-SPAN; TBS Superstation; The Learning Channel; Trinity Broadcasting Network; Weather Channel; WGN America.
Current originations: Government Access; Educational Access; Public Access.
Fee: $17.45 monthly.

Expanded Basic Service 1
Subscribers: 100.
Programming (via satellite): ABC Family Channel; CNN; Comedy Central; Country Music TV; Discovery Channel; Disney Channel; ESPN; ESPN 2; Fox News Channel; Fox Sports Net Midwest; Headline News; Lifetime; MTV; Nickelodeon; Spike TV; Syfy; Turner Network TV; TV Land; USA Network; VH1.
Fee: $12.95 monthly.

Digital Basic Service
Subscribers: N.A.
Programming (via satellite): AmericanLife TV Network; BBC America; Bio; Bloomberg Television; Bravo; Discovery Digital Networks; DMX Music; Fox Movie Channel; G4; GAS; Golf Channel; GSN; Halogen Network; HGTV; History Channel; History Channel International; Independent Film Channel; Lifetime Movie Network; MTV Networks Digital Suite; MuchMusic Network; Nick Jr.; Outdoor Channel; ShopNBC; Speed Channel; Style Network; Toon Disney; Turner Classic Movies; Versus; WE tv.
Fee: $19.55 monthly.

Pay Service 1
Pay Units: 58.
Programming (via satellite): Cinemax.
Fee: $8.95 monthly.

Pay Service 2
Pay Units: 30.
Programming (via satellite): Showtime.
Fee: $9.95 monthly.

Pay Service 3
Pay Units: 87.
Programming (via satellite): HBO (multiplexed).
Fee: $9.95 monthly.

Digital Pay Service 1
Pay Units: N.A.
Programming (via satellite): Cinemax (multiplexed); Encore (multiplexed); Flix; HBO (multiplexed); Showtime (multiplexed); Starz (multiplexed); The Movie Channel (multiplexed).

Video-On-Demand: No

Pay-Per-View
iN DEMAND (delivered digitally); Hot Choice (delivered digitally); ESPN Extra (delivered digitally); ESPN Now (delivered digitally); Playboy TV (delivered digitally); Fresh (delivered digitally); Shorteez (delivered digitally).

Internet Service
Operational: Yes.
Fee: $40.00 installation; $31.99 monthly.

Telephone Service
None

Miles of Plant: 25.0 (coaxial); None (fiber optic). Homes passed: 777.
General Manager: Bill Flowers. Technical Operations Manager: Chris Mooday.
Ownership: NewWave Communications (MSO).

FAIRBURY—Mediacom, PO Box 334, 609 S 4th St, Chillicothe, IL 61523. Phone: 309-274-4500. Fax: 309-274-3188. Web Site: http://www.mediacomcable.com. Also serves Chatsworth, Chenoa, Forrest, Lamplighter, Lexington, Timber Ridge & Towanda. ICA: IL0346.
TV Market Ranking: Below 100 (Chenoa, FAIRBURY, Lamplighter, Lexington, Timber Ridge, Towanda); Outside TV Markets (Chatsworth, Forrest). Franchise award date: N.A. Franchise expiration date: N.A. Began: September 1, 1982.
Channel capacity: 134 (operating 2-way). Channels available but not in use: 6.

Basic Service
Subscribers: 3,691.
Programming (received off-air): WAOE (MNT) Peoria; WCIA (CBS) Champaign; WEEK-TV (NBC) Peoria; WHOI (ABC, CW) Peoria; WILL-TV (PBS) Urbana; WMBD-TV (CBS) Peoria; WTVP (PBS) Peoria; WYZZ-TV (FOX) Bloomington.

Programming (via satellite): ABC Family Channel; WGN America.
Fee: $45.00 installation; $20.95 monthly.

Expanded Basic Service 1
Subscribers: N.A.
Programming (via satellite): AMC; AmericanLife TV Network; Animal Planet; Arts & Entertainment; BET Networks; Bravo; Cartoon Network; CNBC; CNN; Comcast SportsNet Chicago; Comedy Central; Country Music TV; C-SPAN; C-SPAN 2; Discovery Channel; Disney Channel; E! Entertainment Television; ESPN; ESPN 2; Eternal Word TV Network; FitTV; Food Network; Fox News Channel; Fuse; FX; Hallmark Channel; Headline News; HGTV; History Channel; Home Shopping Network; INSP; ION Television; Lifetime; MSNBC; MTV; Nickelodeon; Product Information Network; QVC; ShopNBC; SoapNet; Speed Channel; Spike TV; Syfy; TBS Superstation; The Learning Channel; Travel Channel; Trinity Broadcasting Network; truTV; Turner Network TV; TV Guide Network; TV Land; Univision; USA Network; VH1; WE tv; Weather Channel; Weatherscan.
Fee: $34.00 monthly.

Digital Basic Service
Subscribers: 288.
Programming (received off-air): WEEK-TV (NBC) Peoria; WHOI (ABC, CW) Peoria; WTVP (PBS) Peoria.
Programming (via satellite): BBC America; Bio; Bloomberg Television; Discovery Digital Networks; Discovery HD Theater; DMX Music; ESPN; Fox Movie Channel; Fox Soccer; G4; GAS; Golf Channel; GSN; HD-Net; HDNet Movies; History Channel International; Independent Film Channel; Lifetime Movie Network; Lime; MTV Networks Digital Suite; National Geographic Channel; Nick Jr.; NickToons TV; Outdoor Channel; Style Network; Sundance Channel (multiplexed); Turner Classic Movies; Universal HD; Versus.
Fee: $9.00 monthly.

Digital Pay Service 1
Pay Units: 42.
Programming (via satellite): Cinemax (multiplexed); Encore (multiplexed); Flix (multiplexed); HBO (multiplexed); Showtime (multiplexed); Starz (multiplexed); Starz HDTV; The Movie Channel (multiplexed).
Fee: $11.95 monthly (each).

Video-On-Demand: Yes

Pay-Per-View
iN DEMAND (delivered digitally); Playboy TV (delivered digitally); TEN, TEN Clips, & TEN Blox (delivered digitally); iN DEMAND; ESPN Gameplan (delivered digitally).

Internet Service
Operational: Yes.
Broadband Service: Mediacom High Speed Internet.
Fee: $59.95 installation; $45.95 monthly.

Telephone Service
Digital: Operational
Fee: $39.95 installation; $39.95 monthly

Miles of Plant: 65.0 (coaxial); 2.0 (fiber optic). Homes passed: 4,971.
Vice President: Don Hagwell. Marketing Director: Stephanie Law. Operations Director: Gary Wightman. Technical Operations Manager: Larry Brackman.
City fee: 1% of gross.
Ownership: Mediacom LLC (MSO).

FAIRBURY—Mediacom. Now served by FAIRBURY, IL [IL0346]. ICA: IL0116.

FAIRFIELD—NewWave Communications, 1176 E 1500 North Rd, Taylorville, IL 62568. Phone: 217.287.7992. Fax: 217.287.7304. E-mail: info@newwavecom.com. Web Site: http://www.newwavecom.com. Also serves Wayne County (portions). ICA: IL0148.
TV Market Ranking: Below 100 (FAIRFIELD, Wayne County (portions)); Outside TV Markets (Wayne County (portions)). Franchise award date: N.A. Franchise expiration date: N.A. Began: September 1, 1965.
Channel capacity: N.A. Channels available but not in use: N.A.

Basic Service
Subscribers: 1,196.
Programming (received off-air): KFVS-TV (CBS, CW) Cape Girardeau; WAZE-LP (CW) Evansville; WEHT (ABC) Evansville; WEVV-TV (CBS, MNT) Evansville; WFIE (NBC) Evansville; WNIN (PBS) Evansville; WPXS (IND) Mount Vernon; WSIL-TV (ABC) Harrisburg; WTVW (FOX) Evansville; WUSI-TV (PBS) Olney; 1 FM.
Programming (via satellite): C-SPAN; C-SPAN 2; Home Shopping Network; INSP; QVC; Trinity Broadcasting Network; WGN America.
Fee: $25.00 installation; $22.84 monthly; $15.00 additional installation.

Expanded Basic Service 1
Subscribers: 1,004.
Programming (via satellite): ABC Family Channel; AMC; Animal Planet; Arts & Entertainment; Big Ten Network; Bravo; Cartoon Network; CNBC; CNN; Comedy Central; Country Music TV; Discovery Channel; Disney Channel; E! Entertainment Television; ESPN; ESPN 2; ESPN Classic Sports; Eternal Word TV Network; Food Network; Fox News Channel; Fox Sports Net Midwest; FX; G4; Golf Channel; GSN; Hallmark Channel; Headline News; HGTV; History Channel; Lifetime; MSNBC; MTV; National Geographic Channel; Nickelodeon; Outdoor Channel; Oxygen; ShopNBC; SoapNet; Speed Channel; Spike TV; Syfy; TBS Superstation; The Learning Channel; Toon Disney; Travel Channel; truTV; Turner Classic Movies; Turner Network TV; TV Land; USA Network; Versus; VH1; Weather Channel.
Fee: $6.03 monthly.

Digital Basic Service
Subscribers: 582.
Programming (received off-air): WEHT (ABC) Evansville; WEVV-TV (CBS, MNT) Evansville; WFIE (NBC) Evansville; WTVW (FOX) Evansville.
Programming (via satellite): BBC America; Bio; Bloomberg Television; CMT Pure Country; Cooking Channel; Discovery HD Theater; Discovery Health Channel; Discov-

ery Kids Channel; Discovery Military Channel; Discovery Planet Green; Do-It-Yourself; ESPN 2 HD; ESPN HD; ESPNews; FitTV; Fox College Sports Atlantic; Fox College Sports Central; Fox College Sports Pacific; Fox Movie Channel; FSN HD; Great American Country; Halogen Network; HDNet; HDNet Movies; History Channel International; ID Investigation Discovery; Independent Film Channel; Lifetime Movie Network; MTV Hits; MTV Jams; MTV2; Music Choice; Nick Jr.; Nick Too; NickToons TV; RFD-TV; Science Television; Sleuth; Style Network; TeenNick; Turner Network TV HD; Universal HD; VH1 Classic; VH1 Soul; WSIL-TV (ABC) Harrisburg.

Digital Pay Service 1

Pay Units: 127.

Programming (via satellite): Cinemax (multiplexed); Cinemax HD; Encore (multiplexed); Flix; HBO (multiplexed); HBO HD; Showtime (multiplexed); Starz (multiplexed); Starz HDTV; The Movie Channel (multiplexed).

Fee: $10.95 monthly.

Video-On-Demand: No

Pay-Per-View

iN DEMAND (delivered digitally); Playboy TV (delivered digitally); Fresh (delivered digitally); Shorteez (delivered digitally); Club Jenna (delivered digitally); Spice: Xcess (delivered digitally).

Internet Service

Operational: Yes.

Broadband Service: Charter Pipeline.

Fee: $40.00 installation; $31.99 monthly; $3.00 modem lease; $45.00 modem purchase.

Telephone Service

None

Miles of Plant: 59.0 (coaxial); None (fiber optic). Homes passed: 4,038.

General Manager: Bill Flowers. Technical Operations Manager: Chris Mooday.

City fee: 3% of gross.

Ownership: NewWave Communications (MSO).

FAIRVIEW—Mediacom. Now served by ELMWOOD, IL [IL0205]. ICA: IL0385.

FARMER CITY—Mediacom, PO Box 334, 609 S 4th St, Chillicothe, IL 61523. Phone: 309-274-4500. Fax: 309-274-3188. Web Site: http://www.mediacomcable.com. Also serves Bayles Lake, De Land, Loda, Mansfield, Melvin, Paxton & Weldon. ICA: IL0231.

TV Market Ranking: 64 (Bayles Lake, De Land, FARMER CITY, Loda, Mansfield, Melvin, Paxton, Weldon). Franchise award date: December 31, 1979. Franchise expiration date: N.A. Began: July 17, 1981.

Channel capacity: 134 (operating 2-way). Channels available but not in use: None.

Basic Service

Subscribers: 1,374.

Programming (received off-air): WAND (NBC) Decatur; WBUI (CW) Decatur; WCCU (FOX) Urbana; WCFN (MNT) Springfield; WCIA (CBS) Champaign; WICD (ABC) Champaign; WILL-TV (PBS) Urbana.

Programming (via satellite): ABC Family Channel; INSP; Radar Channel; WGN America.

Fee: $45.00 installation; $20.95 monthly.

Expanded Basic Service 1

Subscribers: 582.

Programming (via satellite): AMC; AmericanLife TV Network; Animal Planet; Arts & Entertainment; BET Networks; Bravo; Cartoon Network; CNBC; CNN; Comcast SportsNet Chicago; Comedy Central; Country Music TV; C-SPAN; C-SPAN 2; Discovery Channel; Disney Channel; E! Entertainment Television; ESPN; ESPN 2; Eternal Word TV Network; FitTV; Food Network; Fox News Channel; FX; Hallmark Channel; Headline News; HGTV; History Channel; Home Shopping Network; ION Television; Jewelry Television; Lifetime; Lifetime Movie Network; MSNBC; MTV; Nickelodeon; Product Information Network; QVC; ShopNBC; SoapNet; Speed Channel; Spike TV; Syfy; TBS Superstation; The Learning Channel; Toon Disney; Travel Channel; Trinity Broadcasting Network; truTV; Turner Network TV; TV Guide Network; TV Land; Univision; USA Network; VH1; WE tv; Weather Channel.

Fee: $34.00 monthly.

Digital Basic Service

Subscribers: 53.

Programming (received off-air): WAND (NBC) Decatur; WCCU (FOX) Urbana; WCIA (CBS) Champaign; WICD (ABC) Champaign; WILL-TV (PBS) Urbana.

Programming (via satellite): ABC News Now; BBC America; Bio; Bloomberg Television; CCTV-9 (CCTV International); Discovery Health Channel; Discovery Kids Channel; Discovery Military Channel; Discovery Planet Green; Discovery Times Channel; ESPN 2 HD; ESPN HD; ESPN U; ESPNews; Fox Movie Channel; Fox Reality Channel; Fox Soccer; Fuel TV; Fuse; G4; Golf Channel; GSN; History Channel International; Independent Film Channel; ION Life; Lifetime Real Women; MTV Hits; MTV2; Music Choice; National Geographic Channel; Nick Jr.; NickToons TV; Outdoor Channel; Qubo; ReelzChannel; Science Channel; Sleuth; Style Network; Sundance Channel; TeenNick; Turner Classic Movies; TVG Network; Versus; VH1 Classic.

Fee: $9.00 monthly.

Digital Expanded Basic Service

Subscribers: N.A.

Programming (via satellite): College Sports Television; Fox College Sports Atlantic; Fox College Sports Central; Fox College Sports Pacific; Gol TV; Tennis Channel; The Sportsman Channel.

Fee: $3.95 monthly.

Digital Expanded Basic Service 2

Subscribers: N.A.

Programming (via satellite): Discovery HD Theater; HDNet; HDNet Movies; Universal HD.

Fee: $6.95 monthly.

Digital Pay Service 1

Pay Units: 131.

Programming (via satellite): Cinemax (multiplexed); Cinemax On Demand; Encore (multiplexed); HBO (multiplexed); HBO HD; HBO On Demand; Showtime (multiplexed); Showtime HD; Showtime On Demand; Starz (multiplexed); Starz HDTV; Starz On Demand; The Movie Channel (multiplexed); The Movie Channel HD; The Movie Channel On Demand.

Fee: $11.95 monthly (HBO, Cinemax, Starz/Encore or Showtime/TMC/Flix/Sundance).

Video-On-Demand: Yes

Pay-Per-View

Addressable homes: 680.

iN DEMAND, Addressable: Yes; iN DEMAND (delivered digitally); Playboy TV (delivered digitally); Fresh (delivered digitally); Shorteez (delivered digitally).

Internet Service

Operational: Yes.

Broadband Service: Mediacom High Speed Internet.

Fee: $59.95 installation; $45.95 monthly.

Telephone Service

Digital: Operational

Fee: $39.95 installation; $39.95 monthly

Miles of Plant: 39.0 (coaxial); None (fiber optic). Additional miles planned: 7.0 (coaxial). Homes passed: 2,112.

Vice President: Don Hagwell. Operations Director: Gary Wightman. Technical Operations Manager: Larry Brackman. Marketing Director: Stephanie Law.

City fee: 5% of gross.

Ownership: Mediacom LLC (MSO).

FARMERSVILLE—Charter Communications, 11 Clearing, Taylorville, IL 62568-9279. Phones: 636-207-7044 (St Louis office); 217-287-7992. Fax: 217-287-7304. Web Site: http://www.charter.com. ICA: IL0370.

TV Market Ranking: 64 (FARMERSVILLE). Franchise award date: N.A. Franchise expiration date: N.A. Began: November 1, 1982.

Channel capacity: N.A. Channels available but not in use: N.A.

Basic Service

Subscribers: 135.

Programming (received off-air): KMOV (CBS) St. Louis; KPLR-TV (CW) St. Louis; WAND (NBC) Decatur; WICS (ABC) Springfield; WILL-TV (PBS) Urbana; WRSP-TV (FOX) Springfield.

Programming (via satellite): QVC; Trinity Broadcasting Network; Weather Channel; WGN America.

Fee: $29.99 installation.

Expanded Basic Service 1

Subscribers: 122.

Programming (via satellite): ABC Family Channel; AMC; Animal Planet; Arts & Entertainment; CNN; Country Music TV; Discovery Channel; Disney Channel; ESPN; ESPN 2; Fox Sports Net Midwest; Headline News; HGTV; History Channel; Lifetime; MSNBC; MTV; Nickelodeon; Spike TV; Syfy; TBS Superstation; The Learning Channel; Turner Network TV; TV Land; USA Network.

Fee: $42.99 monthly.

Pay Service 1

Pay Units: 38.

Programming (via satellite): Cinemax.

Fee: $10.50 monthly.

Pay Service 2

Pay Units: 62.

Programming (via satellite): HBO.

Fee: $10.50 monthly.

Video-On-Demand: No

Internet Service

Operational: No.

Telephone Service

None

Miles of Plant: 6.0 (coaxial); None (fiber optic). Homes passed: 407.

Vice President & General Manager: Steve Trippe. Operations Director: Dave Miller. Chief Technician: Larry Harmon. Marketing Director: Beverly Wall. Office Manager: Melinda Sincavage.

Ownership: Charter Communications Inc. (MSO).

FAYETTEVILLE—Formerly served by CableDirect. No longer in operation. ICA: IL0422.

FIELDON—Formerly served by CableDirect. No longer in operation. ICA: IL0451.

FILLMORE—Formerly served by CableDirect. No longer in operation. ICA: IL0498.

FINDLAY—Formerly served by Almega Cable. No longer in operation. ICA: IL0364.

FLANAGAN—Heartland Cable Inc., PO Box 7, 167 W 5th St, Minonk, IL 61760. Phones: 800-448-4320; 309-432-2075. Fax: 309-432-2500. Web Site: http://www.heartlandcable.com. Also serves Rutland. ICA: IL0304.

TV Market Ranking: 83 (Rutland); Below 100 (FLANAGAN). Franchise award date: January 1, 1971. Franchise expiration date: N.A. Began: March 1, 1972.

Channel capacity: 41 (operating 2-way). Channels available but not in use: 19.

Basic Service

Subscribers: 350.

Programming (received off-air): WEEK-TV (NBC) Peoria; WHOI (ABC, CW) Peoria; WMBD-TV (CBS) Peoria; WTVP (PBS) Peoria; WYZZ-TV (FOX) Bloomington.

Programming (via satellite): ABC Family Channel; Arts & Entertainment; CNN; Discovery Channel; Disney Channel; ESPN; Lifetime; Nickelodeon; Spike TV; TBS Superstation; Turner Network TV; VH1; Weather Channel; WGN America.

Current originations: Public Access.

Fee: $39.00 installation; $31.90 monthly.

Pay Service 1

Pay Units: 40.

Programming (via satellite): HBO.

Fee: $10.95 monthly.

Pay Service 2

Pay Units: N.A.

Programming (via satellite): Showtime.

Fee: $8.95 monthly.

Video-On-Demand: Yes

Pay-Per-View

Addressable homes: 30.

Movies, Addressable: Yes; special events.

Internet Service

Operational: Yes.

Subscribers: 50.

Fee: $39.00 installation; $29.99 monthly.

Telephone Service

None

Miles of Plant: 10.0 (coaxial); None (fiber optic). Homes passed: 450. Total homes in franchised area: 450.

Manager: Steve Allen.

City fee: None.

Ownership: Heartland Cable Inc. (Illinois) (MSO).

FLORA—Wabash Independent Networks, PO Box 719, 113 Hagen Dr, Flora, IL 62839. Phones: 800-228-9824; 877-878-2120; 618-665-9946. Fax: 618-665-3400. E-mail: winita@wabash.net. Web Site: http://www.wabash.net. Also serves Clay County (portions). ICA: IL0140.

TV Market Ranking: Below 100 (Clay County (portions), FLORA); Outside TV Markets (Clay County (portions)). Franchise award date: N.A. Franchise expiration date: N.A. Began: December 1, 1963.

Channel capacity: 38 (not 2-way capable). Channels available but not in use: None.

Basic Service

Subscribers: 512.

Programming (received off-air): KFVS-TV (CBS, CW) Cape Girardeau; KMOV (CBS) St. Louis; KPLR-TV (CW) St. Louis; KSDK (NBC) St. Louis; WEHT (ABC) Evansville; WFIE (NBC) Evansville; WSIL-TV (ABC) Harrisburg; WTHI-TV (CBS) Terre Haute; WTVW (FOX) Evansville; WTWO (NBC) Terre Haute; WUSI-TV (PBS) Olney.

Programming (via satellite): C-SPAN; C-SPAN 2; Eternal Word TV Network; Home Shopping Network; ION Television; MSNBC; QVC; ShopNBC; TBS Superstation; Trinity Broadcasting Network; Weather Channel; WGN America.
Current originations: Government Access; Educational Access; Public Access.
Fee: free installation; $19.95 monthly; $5.00 additional installation.

Expanded Basic Service 1
Subscribers: 491.
Programming (via satellite): ABC Family Channel; AMC; Animal Planet; Arts & Entertainment; Big Ten Network; Boomerang; Cartoon Network; CNN; Comedy Central; Country Music TV; Discovery Channel; Disney Channel; Do-It-Yourself; E! Entertainment Television; ESPN; ESPN 2; ESPN Classic Sports; FamilyNet; Food Network; Fox News Channel; Fox Sports Net; FX; Gospel Music Channel; Hallmark Channel; Halogen Network; Headline News; History Channel; Lifetime; MTV; National Geographic Channel; Nickelodeon; Outdoor Channel; Oxygen; Spike TV; The Learning Channel; Travel Channel; truTV; Turner Classic Movies; Turner Network TV; TV Land; USA Network; VH1.
Fee: $19.00 monthly.

Digital Basic Service
Subscribers: N.A.
Programming (via satellite): AZ TV; BBC America; Bio; Bloomberg Television; Bravo; CMT Pure Country; Current; Discovery Health Channel; Discovery Home Channel; Discovery Kids Channel; Discovery Military Channel; DMX Music; ESPNews; FitTV; Fox Movie Channel; Fox Soccer; FSN Digital Atlantic; FSN Digital Central; FSN Digital Pacific; Fuse; G4; Golf Channel; Great American Country; GSN; HGTV; History Channel International; ID Investigation Discovery; Independent Film Channel; Lifetime Movie Network; MTV Hits; MTV2; National Geographic Channel; Nick Jr.; Outdoor Channel; Ovation; RFD-TV; Science Channel; Sleuth; SoapNet; Speed Channel; Style Network; Syfy; TeenNick; The Word Network; Toon Disney; Versus; VH1 Classic; VH1 Soul; WE tv.
Fee: $15.00 monthly.

Pay Service 1
Pay Units: N.A.
Programming (via satellite): HBO; Showtime; The Movie Channel.
Fee: $15.00 installation; $11.95 monthly (TMC), $12.95 monthly (Showtime), $13.95 monthly (HBO).

Digital Pay Service 1
Pay Units: N.A.
Programming (via satellite): Cinemax (multiplexed); Encore (multiplexed); Flix; HBO (multiplexed); Showtime (multiplexed); Starz (multiplexed); The Movie Channel (multiplexed).
Fee: $11.95 monthly (Cinemax or Starz/Encore), $12.95 monthly (Showtime/TMC/Flix), $13.95 monthly (HBO).

Video-On-Demand: Planned

Pay-Per-View
iN DEMAND (delivered digitally); Playboy TV (delivered digitally); Fresh (delivered digitally); Club Jenna (delivered digitally); Spice: Xcess (delivered digitally).

Internet Service
Operational: Yes.
Fee: $35.00-$50.00 monthly.

Telephone Service
None

Miles of Plant: 57.0 (coaxial); None (fiber optic). Homes passed: 3,823.
General Manager: Dave Grahn. Marketing Director: Carol Oestreich. Technical Operations Manager: Farron Frutiger. Controller: Tanya Wells.
City fee: 3% of gross.
Ownership: Wabash Independent Networks (MSO).

FOWLER—Adams Telecom. Formerly served by Golden, IL [IL0257]. This cable system has converted to IPTV, PO Box 248, 405 Emminga Rd, Golden, IL 62339. Phone: 217-696-4411. E-mail: service@adams.net. Web Site: http://www.adams.net. ICA: IL5316.
Channel capacity: N.A. Channels available but not in use: N.A.

Internet Service
Operational: Yes.

Ownership: Adams Telephone Co-Operative.

FRANKLIN GROVE—Comcast Cable, 4450 Kishwaukee St, Rockford, IL 61101. Phone: 815-395-8890. Fax: 815-395-8901. Web Site: http://www.comcast.com. Also serves Ashton & Forreston. ICA: IL0690.
TV Market Ranking: 97 (Ashton, Forreston, FRANKLIN GROVE).
Channel capacity: N.A. Channels available but not in use: N.A.

Basic Service
Subscribers: N.A. Included in Rockford
Programming (received off-air): WHA-TV (PBS) Madison; WIFR (CBS) Freeport; WQPT-TV (PBS) Moline; WQRF-TV (FOX) Rockford; WREX (CW, NBC) Rockford; WTVO (ABC, MNT) Rockford.
Programming (via satellite): C-SPAN; Discovery Channel; Fox News Channel; QVC; TBS Superstation; WGN America.
Fee: $44.00 installation; $14.81 monthly; $10.00 additional installation.

Expanded Basic Service 1
Subscribers: N.A.
Programming (via satellite): ABC Family Channel; AMC; Animal Planet; Arts & Entertainment; Cartoon Network; CNN; Disney Channel; ESPN; FX; Headline News; Lifetime; Nickelodeon; Spike TV; Turner Network TV; USA Network.
Fee: $21.68 monthly.

Pay Service 1
Pay Units: N.A.
Programming (via satellite): Encore; HBO; Showtime; Starz.
Fee: $7.75 monthly (Starz & Encore), $14.90 monthly (Showtime), $15.05 monthly (HBO).

Internet Service
Operational: Yes.

Telephone Service
Digital: Operational

Homes passed & miles of plant included in Rockford
District Director: Joseph Browning. Technical Operations Manager: Lyle Matejewski. Program Director: Janice Schultz. Community & Government Affairs Manager: Joan Sage.
Ownership: Comcast Cable Communications Inc. (MSO).

FREEMAN SPUR—Galaxy Cablevision, 7155 US Hwy 45 S, Carrier Mills, IL 62917. Phone: 618-994-2261. Fax: 618-994-2261. Web Site: http://www.galaxycable.com. Also serves Cedar Grove, Franklin County, Orient & Spillertown. ICA: IL0232.
TV Market Ranking: 69 (Cedar Grove, Franklin County, FREEMAN SPUR, Orient, Spillertown). Franchise award date: N.A. Franchise expiration date: N.A. Began: September 26, 1989.
Channel capacity: 54 (not 2-way capable). Channels available but not in use: None.

Basic Service
Subscribers: 224.
Programming (received off-air): KBSI (FOX) Cape Girardeau; KFVS-TV (CBS, CW) Cape Girardeau; WDKA (MNT) Paducah; WPSD-TV (NBC) Paducah; WSIL-TV (ABC) Harrisburg; WSIU-TV (PBS) Carbondale; WTCT (IND) Marion.
Programming (via satellite): ABC Family Channel; AMC; Arts & Entertainment; Cartoon Network; CNN; Comedy Central; C-SPAN; Discovery Channel; Disney Channel; E! Entertainment Television; ESPN; ESPN 2; Fox News Channel; Fuse; FX; Great American Country; Headline News; HGTV; History Channel; Home Shopping Network; Lifetime; Outdoor Channel; TBS Superstation; The Learning Channel; Turner Network TV; USA Network; Weather Channel; WGN America.
Fee: $30.00 installation; $40.75 monthly.

Digital Basic Service
Subscribers: 39.

Pay Service 1
Pay Units: 15.
Programming (via satellite): Encore; HBO; Showtime.
Fee: $12.00 monthly (each).

Internet Service
Operational: No.

Telephone Service
None

Miles of Plant: 20.0 (coaxial); None (fiber optic). Homes passed: 755.
State Manager: Ward Webb. Technical Manager: Audie Murphy. Engineer: John Stewart. Customer Service Manager: Malynda Walker.
Ownership: Galaxy Cable Inc. (MSO).

FREEPORT—Comcast Cable, 4450 Kishwaukee St, Rockford, IL 61101. Phone: 815-395-8890. Fax: 815-395-8901. Web Site: http://www.comcast.com. Also serves Cedarville & Stephenson County. ICA: IL0049.
TV Market Ranking: 97 (Cedarville, FREEPORT, Stephenson County). Franchise award date: November 1, 1965. Franchise expiration date: N.A. Began: March 28, 1972.
Channel capacity: N.A. Channels available but not in use: N.A.

Basic Service
Subscribers: N.A. Included in Rockford
Programming (received off-air): WHA-TV (PBS) Madison; WIFR (CBS) Freeport; WISC-TV (CBS, MNT) Madison; WMSN-TV (FOX) Madison; WQRF-TV (FOX) Rockford; WREX (CW, NBC) Rockford; WTTW (PBS) Chicago; WTVO (ABC, MNT) Rockford; 13 FMs.
Programming (via satellite): AMC; CNBC; CNN; ESPN; Lifetime; TV Guide Network; Weather Channel; WGN America.
Current originations: Government Access; Educational Access; Public Access.
Fee: $44.00 installation; $8.40 monthly.

Expanded Basic Service 1
Subscribers: N.A.
Programming (received off-air): WREX (CW, NBC) Rockford.
Programming (via satellite): ABC Family Channel; Animal Planet; Arts & Entertainment; BET Networks; Bravo; Cartoon Network; Comcast SportsNet Chicago; Comedy Central; Country Music TV; C-SPAN; C-SPAN 2; Discovery Channel; Disney Channel; E! Entertainment Television; ESPN 2; Eternal Word TV Network; Food Network; Fox News Channel; FX; Golf Channel; Headline News; HGTV; History Channel; Home Shopping Network; Jewelry Television; MSNBC; MTV; National Geographic Channel; Nickelodeon; Oxygen; QVC; ShopNBC; SoapNet; Speed Channel; Spike TV; TBS Superstation; The Learning Channel; Travel Channel; truTV; Turner Network TV; TV Land; TV One; USA Network; VH1.
Fee: $43.35 monthly.

Digital Basic Service
Subscribers: N.A.
Programming (received off-air): WHA-TV (PBS) Madison; WIFR (CBS) Freeport; WQRF-TV (FOX) Rockford; WREX (CW, NBC) Rockford; WTVO (ABC, MNT) Rockford.
Programming (via satellite): ABC Family HD; Animal Planet HD; Arts & Entertainment HD; BBC America; Bio; Bloomberg Television; CBS College Sports Network; Cine Latino; Cine Mexicano; CMT Pure Country; CNN en Espanol; CNN HD; Cooking Channel; C-SPAN 3; Discovery Channel HD; Discovery en Espanol; Discovery HD Theater; Discovery Health Channel; Discovery Home Channel; Discovery Kids Channel; Discovery Military Channel; Disney Channel HD; Do-It-Yourself; Encore (multiplexed); ESPN 2 HD; ESPN Classic Sports; ESPN Deportes; ESPN HD; ESPNews; Flix; Food Network HD; Fox Business Channel; Fox College Sports Atlantic; Fox College Sports Central; Fox College Sports Pacific; Fox Movie Channel; Fox Reality Channel; Fox Soccer; Fox Sports en Espanol; Fuse; G4; Gol TV; Great American Country; GSN; HDNet; HDNet Movies; HGTV HD; History Channel en Espanol; History Channel HD; History Channel International; HorseRacing TV; ID Investigation Discovery; Independent Film Channel; La Familia Network; Latele Novela Network; Lifetime Movie Network; MTV Hits; MTV Jams; MTV Tres; MTV2; mun2 television; Music Choice; National Geographic Channel HD Network; NBA TV; NFL Network; NFL Network HD; NHL Network; Nick Jr.; Nick Too; NickToons TV; Outdoor Channel; Palladia; PBS Kids Sprout; Puma TV; Science Channel; Si TV; Style Network; Sundance Channel; Syfy; Syfy HD; TBN Enlace USA; TBS in HD; TeenNick; Telemundo; Tennis Channel; The Sportsman Channel; TLC HD; Toon Disney; Trinity Broadcasting Network; Turner Classic Movies; Turner Network TV HD; TV Chile; TVG Network; Universal HD; USA Network HD; VeneMovies; Versus; Versus HD; VH1 Classic; VH1 Soul; WE tv.
Fee: $4.00 monthly (Sports Entertainment Pkg.), $6.99 monthly (HDNet & HDNet Movies), $10.00 monthly (Selecto), $15.95 (Classic & Preferred).

Digital Pay Service 1
Pay Units: N.A.
Programming (via satellite): Cinemax (multiplexed); Cinemax HD; HBO (multiplexed); HBO HD; Playboy TV; Showtime (multiplexed); Showtime HD; Starz (multiplexed); Starz HDTV; The Movie Channel (multiplexed).
Fee: $11.00 monthly (Cinemax or Starz), $14.00 monthly (HBO or Showtime/TMC), $19.99 monthly (Playboy).
Video-On-Demand: Yes
Pay-Per-View
iN DEMAND (delivered digitally), Fee: $3.95, Addressable: Yes; ESPN (delivered digitally); Sports PPV (delivered digitally); Playboy TV (delivered digitally); Spice: Xcess (delivered digitally); Penthouse TV (delivered digitally).
Internet Service
Operational: Yes.
Broadband Service: Comcast High Speed Internet.
Fee: $99.95 installation; $44.95 monthly; $15.00 modem lease; $149.95 modem purchase.
Telephone Service
Analog: Not Operational
Digital: Operational
Fee: $39.95 monthly
Homes passed & miles of plant included in Rockford
District Director: Joseph Browning. Technical Operations Manager: Lyle Matejewski. Program Director: Janice Schultz. Community & Government Affairs Manager: Joan Sage.
City fee: 3% of gross.
Ownership: Comcast Cable Communications Inc. (MSO).

GALENA—Mediacom. Now served by DUBUQUE, IA [IA0007]. ICA: IL0657.

GALESBURG—Comcast Cable, 3517 N Dries Ln, Peoria, IL 61604. Phone: 309-686-2600. Fax: 309-686-9828. Web Site: http://www.comcast.com. Also serves East Galesburg & Knoxville. ICA: IL0038.
TV Market Ranking: Outside TV Markets (East Galesburg, GALESBURG, Knoxville). Franchise award date: January 1, 1968. Franchise expiration date: N.A. Began: February 11, 1971.
Channel capacity: 80 (operating 2-way). Channels available but not in use: N.A.
Basic Service
Subscribers: N.A. Included in Peoria
Programming (received off-air): KLJB (CW, FOX) Davenport; KWQC-TV (NBC) Davenport; WEEK-TV (NBC) Peoria; WHBF-TV (CBS) Rock Island; WHOI (ABC, CW) Peoria; WMBD-TV (CBS) Peoria; WQAD-TV (ABC) Moline; WQPT-TV (PBS) Moline; WTVP (PBS) Peoria.
Programming (via satellite): C-SPAN; C-SPAN 2; Eternal Word TV Network; Home Shopping Network; ION Television; QVC; Trinity Broadcasting Network; TV Guide Network; Weather Channel; WGN America.
Programming (via translator): WBQD-LP Davenport.
Current originations: Government Access; Public Access.
Fee: $25.00 installation; $14.60 monthly; $1.05 converter.
Expanded Basic Service 1
Subscribers: N.A.
Programming (via satellite): ABC Family Channel; AMC; Animal Planet; Arts & Entertainment; BET Networks; Bravo; Cartoon Network; CNBC; CNN; Comcast SportsNet Chicago; Comedy Central; Country Music TV; Discovery Channel; Disney Channel; E! Entertainment Television; ESPN; ESPN 2; Food Network; Fox News Channel; Fox Sports Net Midwest; FX; Golf Channel; Great American Country; Hallmark Channel; Headline News; HGTV; History Channel; Lifetime; MSNBC; MTV; MTV2; National Geographic Channel; Nickelodeon; Oxygen; ShopNBC; SoapNet; Speed Channel; Spike TV; Style Network; Syfy; TBS Superstation; The Learning Channel; Toon Disney; Travel Channel; truTV; Turner Network TV; USA Network; VH1.
Fee: $37.15 monthly.
Digital Basic Service
Subscribers: 2,350.
Programming (via satellite): AmericanLife TV Network; BBC America; Bio; Bloomberg Television; CBS College Sports Network; CMT Pure Country; Cooking Channel; C-SPAN 3; Discovery Digital Networks; Discovery HD Theater; DMX Music; Do-It-Yourself; Encore (multiplexed); ESPN Classic Sports; ESPN U; ESPNews; Fox College Sports Atlantic; Fox College Sports Central; Fox College Sports Pacific; Fox Movie Channel; Fox Reality Channel; Fox Soccer; Fuse; G4; GAS; GSN; Halogen Network; HDNet; HDNet Movies; History Channel International; HorseRacing TV; Independent Film Channel; Lifetime Movie Network; Lifetime Real Women; MTV Networks Digital Suite; NFL Network; Nick Jr.; Nick Too; NickToons TV; Outdoor Channel; Ovation; Palladia; PBS Kids Sprout; Si TV; Sleuth; Sundance Channel; Tennis Channel; Toon Disney; Turner Classic Movies; Turner Network TV HD; TV Land; TVG Network; Universal HD; Versus; WE tv.
Fee: $17.00 monthly.
Digital Pay Service 1
Pay Units: N.A.
Programming (via satellite): Cinemax (multiplexed); ESPN HD; ESPN U; Flix; HBO (multiplexed); HBO HD; Showtime (multiplexed); Showtime HD; Starz (multiplexed); The Movie Channel.
Fee: $10.00 monthly (Cinemax or Starz), $13.00 monthly (HBO or Showtime/TMC).
Video-On-Demand: Yes
Pay-Per-View
ESPN (delivered digitally); iN DEMAND (delivered digitally), Fee: $3.95; Playboy TV (delivered digitally); Special events (delivered digitally).
Internet Service
Operational: Yes.
Subscribers: 1,175.
Broadband Service: Comcast High Speed Internet.
Fee: $99.95 installation; $44.95 monthly; $10.00 modem lease; $99.95 modem purchase.
Telephone Service
None
Homes passed: Included in Peoria
General Manager: John Nieber. Chief Technician: Mike Vandergraft.
City fee: 3% of gross.
Ownership: Comcast Cable Communications Inc. (MSO).

GARDEN PRAIRIE—Mediacom. Now served by POPLAR GROVE, IL [IL0282]. ICA: IL0428.

GARDNER—Kraus Electronics Systems Inc., 305 State St, Manhattan, IL 60442-0011. Phones: 815-478-4000; 815-478-4444. Fax: 815-478-3386. Web Site: http://www.krausonline.com. ICA: IL0269.
TV Market Ranking: Below 100 (GARDNER). Franchise award date: August 27, 1984. Franchise expiration date: N.A. Began: October 1, 1985.
Channel capacity: 40 (operating 2-way). Channels available but not in use: N.A.
Basic Service
Subscribers: 476.
Programming (received off-air): WBBM-TV (CBS) Chicago; WCIU-TV (IND) Chicago; WCPX-TV (ION) Chicago; WFLD (FOX) Chicago; WGBO-DT (UNV) Joliet; WGN-TV (CW, IND) Chicago; WJYS (IND) Hammond; WLS-TV (ABC) Chicago; WMAQ-TV (NBC) Chicago; WPWR-TV (MNT) Gary; WSNS-TV (TMO) Chicago; WTTW (PBS) Chicago; WWTO-TV (TBN) La Salle; WYCC (PBS) Chicago; WYIN (PBS) Gary.
Programming (via satellite): Headline News; QVC.
Fee: $35.00 installation; $38.00 monthly.
Expanded Basic Service 1
Subscribers: N.A.
Programming (via satellite): ABC Family Channel; AMC; Animal Planet; Arts & Entertainment; Cartoon Network; CNBC; CNN; Comcast SportsNet Chicago; Comedy Central; Country Music TV; C-SPAN; C-SPAN 2; Discovery Channel; Disney Channel; ESPN; ESPN 2; ESPN Classic Sports; Eternal Word TV Network; Food Network; Fox News Channel; FX; GSN; Hallmark Channel; HGTV; History Channel; Lifetime; ME Television; MTV; National Geographic Channel; Nickelodeon; Spike TV; Syfy; TBS Superstation; The Learning Channel; truTV; Turner Network TV; TV Land; USA Network; VH1; Weather Channel.
Digital Basic Service
Subscribers: N.A.
Programming (via satellite): AmericanLife TV Network; BBC America; Bio; Bloomberg Television; Bravo; Discovery Digital Networks; DMX Music; ESPNews; Fox College Sports Atlantic; Fox College Sports Central; Fox College Sports Pacific; Fox Movie Channel; Fox Sports World; Fuse; G4; GAS; Golf Channel; Great American Country; GSN; History Channel; History Channel International; Independent Film Channel; Lifetime Movie Network; MTV Networks Digital Suite; Nick Jr.; NickToons TV; Outdoor Channel; Speed Channel; Style Network; Toon Disney; Trio; Turner Classic Movies; WE tv.
Pay Service 1
Pay Units: N.A.
Programming (via satellite): Cinemax; HBO.
Digital Pay Service 1
Pay Units: N.A.
Programming (via satellite): Cinemax (multiplexed); Encore (multiplexed); HBO (multiplexed); Showtime (multiplexed); Starz (multiplexed); The Movie Channel (multiplexed).
Video-On-Demand: No
Pay-Per-View
Playboy TV (delivered digitally); Fresh (delivered digitally); Shorteez (delivered digitally).
Internet Service
Operational: Yes.
Broadband Service: In-house.
Fee: $9.95-$49.95 monthly.
Telephone Service
Digital: Operational
Fee: $26.95-$34.95 monthly
Miles of Plant: 8.0 (coaxial); None (fiber optic). Homes passed: 525. Total homes in franchised area: 525.
Manager: Mike Bordeaux. Chief Technician: Skip Kraus.
City fee: $1.00 per subscriber annually.
Ownership: Arthur J. Kraus (MSO).

GAYS (village)—Formerly served by CableDirect. No longer in operation. ICA: IL0502.

GEFF—Wabash Independent Networks, PO Box 719, 113 Hagen Dr, Flora, IL 62839. Phone: 618-665-9946. Fax: 618-665-3400. Web Site: http://www.wabash.net. ICA: IL0683.
TV Market Ranking: Outside TV Markets (GEFF).
Channel capacity: N.A. Channels available but not in use: N.A.
Basic Service
Subscribers: N.A.
Programming (received off-air): KFVS-TV (CBS, CW) Cape Girardeau; KMOV (CBS) St. Louis; KSDK (NBC) St. Louis; WEHT (ABC) Evansville; WFIE (NBC) Evansville; WSIU-TV (PBS) Carbondale; WTHI-TV (CBS) Terre Haute; WTVW (FOX) Evansville; WTWO (NBC) Terre Haute.
Programming (via satellite): C-SPAN; C-SPAN 2; CW11 New York; Eternal Word TV Network; Home Shopping Network; ION Television; QVC; ShopNBC; TBS Superstation; Trinity Broadcasting Network; Weather Channel; WGN America.
Fee: $19.95 monthly.
Expanded Basic Service 1
Subscribers: N.A.
Programming (via satellite): ABC Family Channel; AMC; Animal Planet; Arts & Entertainment; Boomerang; Cartoon Network; CNN; Comedy Central; Country Music TV; Court TV; Discovery Channel; Disney Channel; Do-It-Yourself; E! Entertainment Television; ESPN; ESPN 2; ESPN Classic Sports; FamilyNet; Food Network; Fox News Channel; Fox Sports Net Midwest; FX; G4; Gospel Music TV; Hallmark Channel; Headline News; History Channel; Lifetime; MSNBC; MTV; National Geographic Channel; Nickelodeon; Outdoor Channel; Oxygen; Spike TV; The Learning Channel; Travel Channel; Turner Classic Movies; Turner Network TV; TV Land; USA Network; VH1.
Fee: $19.00 monthly.
Digital Basic Service
Subscribers: N.A.
Programming (via satellite): BBC America; Bio; Black Family Channel; Bloomberg Television; Bravo; Current; Discovery Health Channel; Discovery Home Channel; Discovery Kids Channel; Discovery Military Channel; Discovery Times Channel; DMX Music; ESPN 2; ESPN Classic Sports; ESPN Now; ESPNews; FitTV; Flix; Fox Movie Channel; Fox Soccer; FSN Digital Atlantic; FSN Digital Central; FSN Digital Pacific; Fuse; G4; GAS; Golf Channel; Great American Country; GSN; Halogen Network; HGTV; History Channel International; Independent Film Channel; Lifetime Movie Network; Lime; MTV Jams; MTV2; Nick Jr.; Outdoor Channel; Ovation; RFD-TV; Science Channel; Sleuth; Speed Channel; Style Network; Syfy; The Word Network; Toon Disney; Trinity Broadcasting Network; Turner Classic Movies; Versus; VH1 Classic; VH1 Country; VH1 Soul; WE tv.
Fee: $15.00 monthly.
Digital Pay Service 1
Pay Units: N.A.
Programming (via satellite): Cinemax (multiplexed); Encore (multiplexed); HBO (multiplexed); Showtime (multiplexed); Starz (multiplexed); The Movie Channel (multiplexed).

Fee: $11.95 monthly (Starz/Encore or Cinemax), $12.95 monthly (Showtiime/TMC/Flix), $13.95 monthly (HBO).

Video-On-Demand: Planned

Pay-Per-View

Shorteez (delivered digitally); Fresh (delivered digitally); Playboy TV (delivered digitally).

Internet Service

Operational: Yes.

Broadband Service: In-house.

Fee: $35.00-$50.00 monthly.

Telephone Service

None

General Manager: Dave Grahn. Assistant General Manager: Jeff Williams. Marketing Director: Carol Oestreich. TV/Video Administrator: Don Ross. Controller: Tanya Wells.

Ownership: Wabash Independent Networks (MSO).

GEM SUBURBAN MOBILE HOME PARK—Packerland Broadband, PO Box 885, 105 Kent St, Iron Mountain, MI 49801. Phones: 800-236-8434; 906-774-6621. Fax: 906-776-2811. E-mail: inquiries@plbb.us. Web Site: http://www.packerlandbroadband.com. ICA: IL0503.

TV Market Ranking: 97 (GEM SUBURBAN MOBILE HOME PARK). Franchise award date: N.A. Franchise expiration date: N.A. Began: April 1, 1988.

Channel capacity: 40 (not 2-way capable). Channels available but not in use: 10.

Basic Service

Subscribers: 82.

Programming (received off-air): WHA-TV (PBS) Madison; WIFR (CBS) Freeport; WQRF-TV (FOX) Rockford; WREX (CW, NBC) Rockford; WTVO (ABC, MNT) Rockford.

Programming (via satellite): ABC Family Channel; AMC; Arts & Entertainment; CNN; Comedy Central; Discovery Channel; Disney Channel; ESPN; ESPN 2; Lifetime; MTV; Nickelodeon; QVC; Spike TV; Syfy; TBS Superstation; The Learning Channel; Turner Network TV; TV Land; USA Network; VH1; Weather Channel; WGN America.

Fee: $24.95 installation; $33.95 monthly; $2.00 converter.

Pay Service 1

Pay Units: 26.

Programming (via satellite): HBO.

Fee: $14.95 installation; $10.95 monthly.

Internet Service

Operational: No.

Telephone Service

None

Miles of Plant: 1.0 (coaxial); None (fiber optic). Total homes in franchised area: 200.

General Manager: Dan Plante. Technical Supervisor: Chad Kay.

Ownership: Cable Constructors Inc. (MSO).

GENOA—Charter Communications. Now served by HARVARD, IL [IL0073]. ICA: IL0200.

GERMAN VALLEY—Mediacom, 3900 26th Ave, Moline, IL 61265. Phones: 309-797-2580 (Moline regional office); 563-557-8025. Fax: 309-797-2414. Web Site: http://www.mediacomcable.com. Also serves Ridott Twp. ICA: IL0505.

TV Market Ranking: 97 (GERMAN VALLEY, Ridott Twp.). Franchise award date: N.A. Franchise expiration date: N.A. Began: November 1, 1988.

Channel capacity: N.A. Channels available but not in use: N.A.

Basic Service

Subscribers: 101.

Programming (received off-air): WHA-TV (PBS) Madison; WIFR (CBS) Freeport; WQRF-TV (FOX) Rockford; WREX (CW, NBC) Rockford; WTVO (ABC, MNT) Rockford.

Programming (via satellite): ABC Family Channel; AMC; Animal Planet; Arts & Entertainment; CNN; Comedy Central; Country Music TV; C-SPAN; Discovery Channel; ESPN; ESPN 2; Fox Sports Net; History Channel; Lifetime; Nickelodeon; QVC; Spike TV; TBS Superstation; The Learning Channel; Travel Channel; Turner Network TV; USA Network; VH1; Weather Channel; WGN America.

Fee: $45.00 installation; $29.95 monthly.

Pay Service 1

Pay Units: 40.

Programming (via satellite): Encore; Starz.

Fee: $9.95 monthly.

Internet Service

Operational: No.

Telephone Service

None

Miles of Plant: 12.0 (coaxial); None (fiber optic). Homes passed: 310. Total homes in franchised area: 311. Miles of plant (coax & fiber) included in Moline

Regional Vice President: Cari Fenzel. Area Manager: Kathleen McMullen. Engineering Director: Mitch Carlson. Technical Operations Manager: Darren Dean. Marketing Director: Greg Evans.

Ownership: Mediacom LLC (MSO).

GIBSON CITY—Mediacom, PO Box 334, 609 S 4th St, Chillicothe, IL 61523. Phone: 309-274-4500. Fax: 309-274-3188. Web Site: http://www.mediacomcable.com. Also serves Braceville (village), East Brooklyn (village), Essex (village), Godley (village) & South Wilmington (village). ICA: IL0164.

TV Market Ranking: 64 (GIBSON CITY); Below 100 (Braceville (village), East Brooklyn (village), Essex (village), Godley (village), South Wilmington (village)). Franchise award date: N.A. Franchise expiration date: N.A. Began: March 15, 1972.

Channel capacity: 134 (operating 2-way). Channels available but not in use: 6.

Basic Service

Subscribers: 3,859.

Programming (received off-air): WAND (NBC) Decatur; WBUI (CW) Decatur; WCCU (FOX) Urbana; WCIA (CBS) Champaign; WICD (ABC) Champaign; WILL-TV (PBS) Urbana; WRSP-TV (FOX) Springfield; 12 FMs.

Programming (via satellite): ABC Family Channel; INSP; Radar Channel; WGN America.

Fee: $45.00 installation; $20.95 monthly.

Expanded Basic Service 1

Subscribers: 1,048.

Programming (received off-air): WCFN (MNT) Springfield.

Programming (via satellite): AMC; AmericanLife TV Network; Animal Planet; Arts & Entertainment; BET Networks; Bravo; Cartoon Network; CNBC; CNN; Comcast SportsNet Chicago; Comedy Central; Country Music TV; C-SPAN; C-SPAN 2; Discovery Channel; Disney Channel; E! Entertainment Television; ESPN; ESPN 2; Eternal Word TV Network; FitTV; Food Network; Fox News Channel; FX; Hallmark Channel; Headline News; HGTV; History Channel; Home Shopping Network; ION Television; Jewelry Television; Lifetime; Lifetime Movie Network; MSNBC; MTV; Nickelodeon; Product Information Network; QVC; ShopNBC; Speed Channel; Spike TV; Syfy; TBS Superstation; The Learning Channel; Travel Channel; Trinity Broadcasting Network; truTV; Turner Network TV; TV Guide Network; TV Land; Univision; USA Network; VH1; WE tv; Weather Channel.

Fee: $34.00 monthly.

Digital Basic Service

Subscribers: 78.

Programming (received off-air): WAND (NBC) Decatur; WCCU (FOX) Urbana; WCIA (CBS) Champaign; WICD (ABC) Champaign; WILL-TV (PBS) Urbana.

Programming (via satellite): ABC News Now; BBC America; Bio; Bloomberg Television; CCTV-4; Discovery HD Theater; Discovery Health Channel; Discovery Kids Channel; Discovery Military Channel; Discovery Planet Green; Discovery Times Channel; ESPN 2 HD; ESPN HD; ESPN U; Fox Movie Channel; Fox Reality Channel; Fox Soccer; Fuel TV; Fuse; G4; Golf Channel; GSN; HDNet; HDNet Movies; History Channel International; Independent Film Channel; ION Life; Lifetime Real Women; MTV Hits; MTV2; Music Choice; National Geographic Channel; Nick Jr.; NickToons TV; Outdoor Channel; Qubo; ReelzChannel; Science Channel; Sleuth; Style Network; Sundance Channel; TeenNick; Turner Classic Movies; TVG Network; Universal HD; Versus; VH1 Classic.

Fee: $9.00 monthly.

Digital Expanded Basic Service

Subscribers: N.A.

Programming (via satellite): CBS College Sports Network; ESPN U; Fox College Sports Atlantic; Fox College Sports Central; Fox College Sports Pacific; Fuel TV; Gol TV; Tennis Channel; The Sportsman Channel; TVG Network.

Fee: $3.95 monthly.

Digital Pay Service 1

Pay Units: 206.

Programming (via satellite): Cinemax (multiplexed); Cinemax On Demand; Encore (multiplexed); Flix; HBO (multiplexed); HBO HD; HBO On Demand; Showtime (multiplexed); Showtime HD; Showtime On Demand; Starz (multiplexed); Starz HDTV; Starz On Demand; Sundance Channel; The Movie Channel (multiplexed); The Movie Channel HD; The Movie Channel On Demand.

Fee: $11.95 monthly (HBO, Cinemax, Showtime/TMC/Sundance/Flix or Starz/Encore).

Video-On-Demand: Yes

Pay-Per-View

Ten Blox (delivered digitally); iN DEMAND (delivered digitally); Playboy TV (delivered digitally); Ten Clips (delivered digitally); ESPN (delivered digitally); Fox Sports Net (delivered digitally).

Internet Service

Operational: Yes.

Broadband Service: Mediacom High Speed Internet.

Fee: $59.95 installation; $45.95 monthly.

Telephone Service

Digital: Operational

Fee: $39.95 installation; $39.95 monthly

Miles of Plant: 83.0 (coaxial); 21.0 (fiber optic). Homes passed: 4,626.

Vice President: Don Hagwell. Operations Director: Gary Wightman. Technical Operations Manager: Larry Brackman. Marketing Director: Stephanie Law.

City fee: 3% of gross.

Ownership: Mediacom LLC (MSO).

GILBERTS—Mediacom. Now served by CORTLAND (village), IL [IL0485]. ICA: IL0507.

GILLESPIE—Charter Communications, 11 Clearing, Taylorville, IL 62568-9279. Phones: 636-207-7044 (St Louis office); 217-287-7992. Fax: 217-287-7304. Web Site: http://www.charter.com. Also serves Macoupin County (portions). ICA: IL0610.

TV Market Ranking: Outside TV Markets (GILLESPIE, Macoupin County (portions)). Franchise award date: N.A. Franchise expiration date: N.A. Began: N.A.

Channel capacity: 37 (not 2-way capable). Channels available but not in use: 1.

Basic Service

Subscribers: N.A. Included in Litchfield

Programming (received off-air): KDNL-TV (ABC) St. Louis; KETC (PBS) St. Louis; KMOV (CBS) St. Louis; KPLR-TV (CW) St. Louis; KSDK (NBC) St. Louis; KTVI (FOX) St. Louis; WICS (ABC) Springfield; WPXS (IND) Mount Vernon; WRBU (MNT) East St. Louis.

Programming (via satellite): Home Shopping Network; QVC; WGN America.

Fee: $29.99 installation.

Expanded Basic Service 1

Subscribers: 974.

Programming (via satellite): ABC Family Channel; AMC; Arts & Entertainment; Cartoon Network; CNBC; CNN; Comedy Central; Country Music TV; Discovery Channel; Disney Channel; E! Entertainment Television; ESPN; ESPN 2; ESPN Classic Sports; Fox News Channel; Fox Sports Net Midwest; FX; G4; Headline News; HGTV; History Channel; Lifetime; MTV; Nickelodeon; Oxygen; Spike TV; Syfy; TBS Superstation; The Learning Channel; Turner Network TV; TV Land; USA Network; VH1; Weather Channel.

Fee: $42.99 monthly.

Digital Basic Service

Subscribers: N.A.

Programming (via satellite): BBC America; Bio; Bloomberg Television; Discovery Digital Networks; DMX Music; Do-It-Yourself; FitTV; Fox Movie Channel; GAS; GSN; History Channel International; Independent Film Channel; MTV Networks Digital Suite; Nick Jr.; Nick Too; NickToons TV; Science Television; Style Network; Sundance Channel; Toon Disney; TV Guide Interactive Inc.; WE tv.

Digital Expanded Basic Service

Subscribers: N.A.

Programming (via satellite): Fox College Sports Atlantic; Fox College Sports Central; Fox College Sports Pacific; Fox Soccer.

Digital Pay Service 1
Pay Units: N.A.
Programming (via satellite): Cinemax (multiplexed); Encore (multiplexed); Flix; HBO (multiplexed); Showtime (multiplexed); Starz (multiplexed).
Video-On-Demand: No
Pay-Per-View
iN DEMAND (delivered digitally); Fresh (delivered digitally); Shorteez (delivered digitally); iN DEMAND (delivered digitally); Playboy TV (delivered digitally).
Internet Service
Operational: No.
Telephone Service
None
Miles of Plant: 22.0 (coaxial); None (fiber optic). Homes passed included in Litchfield
Vice President & General Manager: Steve Trippe. Operations Director: Dave Miller. Chief Technician: Larry Harman. Marketing Director: Beverly Wall.
Ownership: Charter Communications Inc. (MSO).

GINGER RIDGE—Formerly served by Universal Cable Inc. No longer in operation. ICA: IL0508.

GLADSTONE—Nova Cablevision Inc., PO Box 1412, 677 W Main St, Galesburg, IL 61401. Phone: 309-342-9681. Fax: 309-342-4408. Web Site: http://www.novacablevision.com. ICA: IL0415.
TV Market Ranking: Below 100 (GLADSTONE). Franchise award date: N.A. Franchise expiration date: N.A. Began: April 1, 1989.
Channel capacity: 117 (operating 2-way). Channels available but not in use: N.A.
Basic Service
Subscribers: 148.
Programming (received off-air): KGCW (CW) Burlington; KIIN (PBS) Iowa City; KLJB (CW, FOX) Davenport; KWQC-TV (NBC) Davenport; WEEK-TV (NBC) Peoria; WHBF-TV (CBS) Rock Island; WHOI (ABC, CW) Peoria; WMBD-TV (CBS) Peoria; WQAD-TV (ABC) Moline; WQPT-TV (PBS) Moline; WTVP (PBS) Peoria.
Programming (via satellite): ABC Family Channel; AMC; Animal Planet; Arts & Entertainment; Big Ten Network; Cartoon Network; CNBC; CNN; Comcast SportsNet Chicago; Comedy Central; Country Music TV; C-SPAN; C-SPAN 2; Discovery Channel; Disney Channel; Do-It-Yourself; E! Entertainment Television; ESPN; ESPN 2; ESPN U; Eternal Word TV Network; Food Network; Fox News Channel; Fox Sports Net Midwest; FX; Golf Channel; Great American Country; Hallmark Channel; Headline News; HGTV; History Channel; Home Shopping Network; HorseRacing TV; INSP; Lifetime; MSNBC; MTV; National Geographic Channel; Nickelodeon; QVC; RFD-TV; SoapNet; Speed Channel; Spike TV; Syfy; TBS Superstation; The Learning Channel; The Sportsman Channel; Travel Channel; truTV; Turner Network TV; TV Land; USA Network; VH1; Weather Channel; WGN America.
Fee: $60.00 installation; $53.95 monthly.
Digital Basic Service
Subscribers: N.A.
Programming (via satellite): Bio; Bloomberg Television; CMT Pure Country; Discovery Health Channel; Discovery Kids Channel; Discovery Military Channel; Discovery Planet Green; Disney XD; DMX Music; ESPN 2; ESPN Classic Sports; ESPNews; Fox Movie Channel; FSN Digital Atlantic; FSN Digital Central; FSN Digital Pacific; Fuse; G4; Golf Channel; Great American Country; GSN; HGTV; History Channel; History Channel International; ID Investigation Discovery; Independent Film Channel; Lifetime Movie Network; MTV Hits; MTV2; NickToons TV; Noggin; Outdoor Channel; Science Channel; ShopNBC; Speed Channel; Style Network; Syfy; The N; Trinity Broadcasting Network; Turner Classic Movies; Versus; VH1 Classic; VH1 Soul; WE tv.
Fee: $16.95 monthly.
Pay Service 1
Pay Units: 20.
Programming (via satellite): Cinemax.
Fee: $12.85 monthly.
Pay Service 2
Pay Units: 5.
Programming (via satellite): HBO.
Fee: $12.85 monthly.
Digital Pay Service 1
Pay Units: N.A.
Programming (via satellite): Cinemax (multiplexed); Encore (multiplexed); Flix; HBO (multiplexed); Showtime (multiplexed); Starz (multiplexed); Sundance Channel; The Movie Channel (multiplexed).
Fee: $12.85 monthly (HBO, Cinemax, Showtime/TMC/Flix/Sundance or Starz/Encore).
Video-On-Demand: No
Pay-Per-View
Hot Choice (delivered digitally); Playboy TV (delivered digitally); Fresh (delivered digitally); Spice: Xcess (delivered digitally); Club Jenna (delivered digitally).
Internet Service
Operational: Yes. Began: January 1, 2005.
Subscribers: 53.
Fee: $30.00 installation; $39.95 monthly; $3.95 modem lease.
Telephone Service
None
Miles of Plant: 11.0 (coaxial); None (fiber optic). Homes passed: 285.
Manager: Robert G. Fischer Jr. Office Manager: Hazel Harden.
Ownership: Nova Cablevision Inc. (MSO).

GLASFORD—Mediacom. Now served by ELMWOOD, IL [IL0205]. ICA: IL0214.

GLENDALE HEIGHTS—Comcast Cable. Now served by OAK BROOK, IL [IL0006]. ICA: IL0022.

GLENVIEW—Comcast Cable. Now served by SCHAUMBURG, IL [IL0036]. ICA: IL0236.

GOLCONDA—Galaxy Cablevision, 7155 US Hwy 45 S, Carrier Mills, IL 62917. Phone: 618-994-2261. Fax: 618-994-2261. Web Site: http://www.galaxycable.com. ICA: IL0297.
TV Market Ranking: 69 (GOLCONDA). Franchise award date: N.A. Franchise expiration date: N.A. Began: July 1, 1985.
Channel capacity: 36 (not 2-way capable). Channels available but not in use: None.
Basic Service
Subscribers: 81.
Programming (received off-air): KBSI (FOX) Cape Girardeau; KFVS-TV (CBS, CW) Cape Girardeau; WDKA (MNT) Paducah; WKPD (PBS) Paducah; WPSD-TV (NBC) Paducah; WSIL-TV (ABC) Harrisburg; WTCT (IND) Marion.
Programming (via satellite): ABC Family Channel; AMC; Animal Planet; Arts & Entertainment; Cartoon Network; CNN; Comedy Central; Discovery Channel; Disney Channel; E! Entertainment Television; ESPN; ESPN 2; Food Network; Fox News Channel; Fuse; Great American Country; HGTV; Home Shopping Network; Lifetime; Outdoor Channel; TBS Superstation; The Learning Channel; Turner Network TV; USA Network; Weather Channel; WGN America.
Fee: $30.00 installation; $40.90 monthly.
Pay Service 1
Pay Units: N.A.
Programming (via satellite): HBO; Showtime; The Movie Channel.
Fee: $12.00 monthly.
Internet Service
Operational: No.
Telephone Service
None
Miles of Plant: 7.0 (coaxial); None (fiber optic). Homes passed: 345. Total homes in franchised area: 432.
State Manager: Ward Webb. Technical Manager: Audie Murphy. Engineer: John Stewart. Customer Service Manager: Malynda Walker.
Ownership: Galaxy Cable Inc. (MSO).

GOLD COAST—RCN Corp. Formerly served by Chicago (portions), IL [IL0661]. This cable system has converted to IPTV, 196 Van Buren St, Herndon, VA 20170. Phone: 703-434-8200. Web Site: http://www.rcn.com. ICA: IL5235.
TV Market Ranking: 3 (GOLD COAST).
Channel capacity: N.A. Channels available but not in use: N.A.
Internet Service
Operational: Yes.
Fee: $23.00 monthly.
Telephone Service
Digital: Operational
Fee: $30.00 monthly
Chairman: Steven J. Simmons. Chief Executive Officer: Jim Holanda.
Ownership: RCN Corp.

GOLDEN—Adams Telephone. This cable system has converted to IPTV. See Golden, IL [IL5317]. ICA: IL0257.

GOLDEN (village)—Adams Telecom. Formerly [IL0257]. This cable system has converted to IPTV, PO Box 248, 405 Emminga Rd, Golden, IL 62339. Phone: 217-696-4411. E-mail: service@adams.net. Web Site: http://www.adams.net. ICA: IL5317.
Channel capacity: N.A. Channels available but not in use: N.A.
Internet Service
Operational: Yes.
Ownership: Adams Telephone Co-Operative.

GOOD HOPE—Mediacom, PO Box 334, 609 S 4th St, Chillicothe, IL 61523. Phone: 309-274-4500. Fax: 309-274-3188. Web Site: http://www.mediacomcable.com. Also serves Prairie City. ICA: IL0396.
TV Market Ranking: Below 100 (GOOD HOPE, Prairie City). Franchise award date: N.A. Franchise expiration date: N.A. Began: January 1, 1985.
Channel capacity: 42 (operating 2-way). Channels available but not in use: 5.
Basic Service
Subscribers: 106.
Programming (received off-air): KHQA-TV (ABC, CBS) Hannibal; WEEK-TV (NBC) Peoria; WGEM-TV (CW, NBC) Quincy; WMBD-TV (CBS) Peoria; WMEC (PBS) Macomb; WQAD-TV (ABC) Moline; WRSP-TV (FOX) Springfield; WTVP (PBS) Peoria.
Programming (via satellite): ABC Family Channel; AMC; Animal Planet; Arts & Entertainment; Cartoon Network; CNN; Comcast SportsNet Chicago; Discovery Channel; Disney Channel; ESPN; ESPN 2; Food Network; Fox Sports Net; Headline News; HGTV; History Channel; Home Shopping Network; Lifetime; Nickelodeon; Spike TV; Syfy; TBS Superstation; The Learning Channel; Turner Network TV; USA Network; Weather Channel; WGN America.
Fee: $45.00 installation; $29.95 monthly.
Digital Basic Service
Subscribers: N.A.
Programming (via satellite): AmericanLife TV Network; BBC America; Bio; Bloomberg Television; Discovery Digital Networks; ESPNews; Fox Movie Channel; Fuse; G4; GAS; Golf Channel; History Channel International; Independent Film Channel; Lifetime Movie Network; Lime; MTV Networks Digital Suite; National Geographic Channel; Nick Jr.; NickToons TV; Outdoor Channel; Sleuth; Style Network; Turner Classic Movies; TVG Network; Versus.
Digital Expanded Basic Service
Subscribers: N.A.
Programming (via satellite): Discovery HD Theater; ESPN; ESPN 2; HDNet; HDNet Movies; Universal HD.
Digital Pay Service 1
Pay Units: N.A.
Programming (via satellite): Cinemax (multiplexed); Encore (multiplexed); Flix (multiplexed); HBO (multiplexed); Showtime (multiplexed); Starz (multiplexed); Sundance Channel (multiplexed); The Movie Channel (multiplexed).
Digital Pay Service 2
Pay Units: N.A.
Programming (via satellite): HBO; Showtime; Starz HDTV; The Movie Channel.
Video-On-Demand: No
Pay-Per-View
iN DEMAND (delivered digitally); Playboy TV (delivered digitally).
Internet Service
Operational: Yes.
Broadband Service: Mediacom High Speed Internet.
Telephone Service
None
Miles of Plant: 3.0 (coaxial); None (fiber optic). Homes passed: 229.
Vice President: Jim Waldo. Technical Operations Manager: Larry Brackman. Operations Director: Gary Wightman.
City fee: 5% of gross.
Ownership: Mediacom LLC (MSO).

GORHAM TWP.—Formerly served by CableDirect. No longer in operation. ICA: IL0511.

GRAFTON—Formerly served by Almega Cable. No longer in operation. ICA: IL0315.

GRAND RIDGE—Grand Ridge Cable Co. Inc., PO Box 657, 730 Burlington Ave, Grand Ridge, IL 61325. Phone: 815-249-5517. Also serves Ransom. ICA: IL0325.
TV Market Ranking: Below 100 (GRAND RIDGE, Ransom). Franchise award date: January 1, 1960. Franchise expiration date: N.A. Began: November 1, 1960.
Channel capacity: 36 (not 2-way capable). Channels available but not in use: 4.
Basic Service
Subscribers: 140.
Programming (received off-air): WCIU-TV (IND) Chicago; WEEK-TV (NBC) Peoria; WFLD (FOX) Chicago; WGN-TV (CW, IND) Chicago; WHOI (ABC, CW) Peoria; WLS-TV (ABC) Chicago; WMBD-TV (CBS) Peoria; WPWR-TV (MNT) Gary; WTTW

(PBS) Chicago; WWTO-TV (TBN) La Salle; WYZZ-TV (FOX) Bloomington.
Programming (via satellite): ABC Family Channel; AMC; Arts & Entertainment; CNN; C-SPAN; Discovery Channel; Disney Channel; ESPN; ESPN 2; Headline News; HGTV; History Channel; Home Shopping Network; ION Television; QVC; Speed Channel; Spike TV; Syfy; TBS Superstation; The Learning Channel; Turner Network TV; TV Land; USA Network; Weather Channel; WGN America.
Fee: $30.00 installation; $32.00 monthly; $20.00 additional installation.

Pay Service 1
Pay Units: 15.
Programming (via satellite): HBO.
Fee: $10.00 monthly.

Internet Service
Operational: No.

Telephone Service
None

Miles of Plant: 5.0 (coaxial); None (fiber optic). Homes passed: 350. Total homes in franchised area: 350.
Manager: Ken Douvia.
City fee: $500 per year.
Ownership: Ken Douvia.

GRAND TOWER (village)—Formerly served by CableDirect. No longer in operation. ICA: IL0514.

GRANT PARK (village)—Mediacom. Now served by ROSELAWN, IN [IN0316]. ICA: IL0516.

GRANTFORK (village)—Clearvision Cable Systems Inc., 1785 US Rte 40, Greenup, IL 62428-3501. Phones: 866-923-5594; 217-923-5594. Fax: 217-923-5681. ICA: IL0517.
TV Market Ranking: 11 (GRANTFORK (VILLAGE)). Franchise award date: N.A. Franchise expiration date: N.A. Began: N.A.
Channel capacity: 42 (not 2-way capable). Channels available but not in use: 12.

Basic Service
Subscribers: 20.
Programming (received off-air): KDNL-TV (ABC) St. Louis; KETC (PBS) St. Louis; KMOV (CBS) St. Louis; KPLR-TV (CW) St. Louis; KSDK (NBC) St. Louis; KTVI (FOX) St. Louis.
Programming (via satellite): ABC Family Channel; AMC; Animal Planet; Arts & Entertainment; CNN; Country Music TV; C-SPAN; Discovery Channel; Disney Channel; ESPN; ESPN 2; G4; Headline News; History Channel; Home Shopping Network; Lifetime; Spike TV; Syfy; TBS Superstation; The Learning Channel; Travel Channel; Turner Network TV; USA Network; WGN America.
Fee: $42.50 installation; $29.95 monthly.

Pay Service 1
Pay Units: N.A.
Programming (via satellite): Showtime; The Movie Channel.

Video-On-Demand: No

Internet Service
Operational: No.

Telephone Service
None

Miles of Plant: 4.0 (coaxial); None (fiber optic). Homes passed: 118. Total homes in franchised area: 118.
Manager: Michael Bauguss.
Ownership: Clearvision Cable Systems Inc. (MSO).

GRAYVILLE—NewWave Communications, 1176 E 1500 North Rd, Taylorville, IL 62568. Phone: 217-287-7992. Fax: 217.287.7304. E-mail: info@newwavecom.com. Web Site: http://www.newwavecom.com. ICA: IL0211.
TV Market Ranking: 86 (GRAYVILLE). Franchise award date: N.A. Franchise expiration date: N.A. Began: January 15, 1982.
Channel capacity: 136 (operating 2-way). Channels available but not in use: N.A.

Basic Service
Subscribers: 382.
Programming (received off-air): KFVS-TV (CBS, CW) Cape Girardeau; WAZE-LP (CW) Evansville; WEHT (ABC) Evansville; WEVV-TV (CBS, MNT) Evansville; WFIE (NBC) Evansville; WNIN (PBS) Evansville; WPXS (IND) Mount Vernon; WSIL-TV (ABC) Harrisburg; WTVW (FOX) Evansville; WUSI-TV (PBS) Olney.
Programming (via satellite): C-SPAN; C-SPAN 2; Home Shopping Network; INSP; QVC; Trinity Broadcasting Network; WGN America.
Fee: $13.00 monthly.

Expanded Basic Service 1
Subscribers: 338.
Programming (via satellite): ABC Family Channel; AMC; Animal Planet; Arts & Entertainment; Big Ten Network; Bravo; Cartoon Network; CNBC; CNN; Comedy Central; Country Music TV; Discovery Channel; Disney Channel; E! Entertainment Television; ESPN; ESPN 2; ESPN Classic Sports; Eternal Word TV Network; Food Network; Fox News Channel; Fox Sports Net Midwest; FX; Golf Channel; GSN; Hallmark Channel; Headline News; HGTV; History Channel; Lifetime; MSNBC; MTV; National Geographic Channel; Nickelodeon; Outdoor Channel; Oxygen; ShopNBC; SoapNet; Speed Channel; Spike TV; Syfy; TBS Superstation; The Learning Channel; Toon Disney; Travel Channel; truTV; Turner Classic Movies; Turner Network TV; TV Land; USA Network; Versus; VH1; Weather Channel.
Fee: $15.90 monthly.

Digital Basic Service
Subscribers: N.A.
Programming (received off-air): WEHT (ABC) Evansville; WEVV-TV (CBS, MNT) Evansville; WFIE (NBC) Evansville; WSIL-TV (ABC) Harrisburg; WTVW (FOX) Evansville.
Programming (via satellite): BBC America; Bio; Bloomberg Television; CMT Pure Country; Cooking Channel; Discovery HD Theater; Discovery Health Channel; Discovery Kids Channel; Discovery Military Channel; Discovery Planet Green; Do-It-Yourself; ESPN 2 HD; ESPN HD; ESPNews; FitTV; Fox College Sports Atlantic; Fox College Sports Central; Fox College Sports Pacific; Fox Movie Channel; FSN HD; G4; Great American Country; Halogen Network; HDNet; HDNet Movies; History Channel International; ID Investigation Discovery; Independent Film Channel; Lifetime Movie Network; MTV Hits; MTV Jams; MTV2; Music Choice; Nick Jr.; Nick Too; NickToons TV; RFD-TV; Science Channel; Sleuth; Style Network; TeenNick; Turner Network TV HD; Universal HD; VH1 Classic; VH1 Soul.
Fee: $49.95 monthly.

Digital Pay Service 1
Pay Units: N.A.
Programming (via satellite): Cinemax (multiplexed); Cinemax HD; Encore (multiplexed); Flix; HBO (multiplexed); HBO HD; Showtime (multiplexed); Starz (multiplexed); Starz HDTV; The Movie Channel (multiplexed).

Video-On-Demand: No

Pay-Per-View
iN DEMAND (delivered digitally); Spice: Xcess (delivered digitally); Club Jenna (delivered digitally); Playboy TV (delivered digitally); Fresh (delivered digitally); Shorteez (delivered digitally).

Internet Service
Operational: Yes.
Broadband Service: Charter Pipeline.
Fee: $40.00 installation; $31.99 monthly; $5.00 modem lease; $99.99 modem purchase.

Telephone Service
None

Miles of Plant: 21.0 (coaxial); None (fiber optic). Homes passed: 1,017.
General Manager: Bill Flowers. Technical Operations Manager: Chris Mooday.
City fee: 3% of gross.
Ownership: NewWave Communications (MSO).

GREAT LAKES NAVAL TRAINING CENTER—Comcast Cable. Now served by SCHAUMBURG, IL [IL0036]. ICA: IL0518.

GREENFIELD—BrightGreen Cable, PO Box 127, Gillespie, IL 62033. Phones: 217-839-3732; 217-839-1498. E-mail: support@brightgreencable.com. Web Site: http://www.brightgreencable.com. ICA: IL0284.
TV Market Ranking: Outside TV Markets (GREENFIELD). Franchise award date: N.A. Franchise expiration date: N.A. Began: April 1, 1983.
Channel capacity: 36 (not 2-way capable). Channels available but not in use: 14.

Basic Service
Subscribers: 123.
Programming (received off-air): KDNL-TV (ABC) St. Louis; KETC (PBS) St. Louis; KMOV (CBS) St. Louis; KPLR-TV (CW) St. Louis; KSDK (NBC) St. Louis; KTVI (FOX) St. Louis; WICS (ABC) Springfield.
Programming (via satellite): Home Shopping Network; INSP; Weather Channel; WGN America.
Fee: $29.95 installation; $19.95 monthly.

Expanded Basic Service 1
Subscribers: N.A.
Programming (via satellite): ABC Family Channel; AMC; Arts & Entertainment; CNN; Country Music TV; Discovery Channel; ESPN; ESPN 2; Fox Sports Net Midwest; HGTV; History Channel; Lifetime; MTV; Nickelodeon; Spike TV; TBS Superstation; Trinity Broadcasting Network; Turner Network TV; TV Land; USA Network; VH1.
Fee: $22.00 monthly.

Pay Service 1
Pay Units: 35.
Programming (via satellite): Cinemax; HBO.
Fee: $9.49 monthly (Cinemax), $13.49 monthly (HBO).

Video-On-Demand: No

Internet Service
Operational: No.

Telephone Service
None

Miles of Plant: 7.0 (coaxial); None (fiber optic). Homes passed: 327.
President & General Manager: Phil Claro.
Ownership: BrightGreen Communications (MSO).

GREENUP—Mediacom, PO Box 288, 4290 Blue Stem Rd, Charleston, IL 61920. Phone: 217-348-5533. Fax: 217-345-7074. Web Site: http://www.mediacomcable.com. Also serves Toledo. ICA: IL0192.
TV Market Ranking: Outside TV Markets (GREENUP, Toledo). Franchise award date: January 1, 1981. Franchise expiration date: N.A. Began: February 25, 1981.
Channel capacity: N.A. Channels available but not in use: N.A.

Basic Service
Subscribers: 1,041.
Programming (received off-air): WAND (NBC) Decatur; WBUI (CW) Decatur; WCCU (FOX) Urbana; WCFN (MNT) Springfield; WCIA (CBS) Champaign; WEIU-TV (PBS) Charleston; WICD (ABC) Champaign; WILL-TV (PBS) Urbana; WSIU-TV (PBS) Carbondale; WTHI-TV (CBS) Terre Haute; WTWO (NBC) Terre Haute; 7 FMs.
Programming (via satellite): C-SPAN; Home Shopping Network; INSP; QVC; TV Guide Network; WGN America.
Fee: $45.00 installation; $20.95 monthly.

Expanded Basic Service 1
Subscribers: N.A.
Programming (via satellite): ABC Family Channel; AMC; Animal Planet; Arts & Entertainment; BET Networks; Cartoon Network; CNBC; CNN; Comedy Central; Country Music TV; C-SPAN 2; Discovery Channel; Disney Channel; E! Entertainment Television; ESPN; ESPN 2; ESPN Classic Sports; Eternal Word TV Network; FitTV; Food Network; Fox News Channel; Fox Sports Net Midwest; FX; Hallmark Channel; Headline News; HGTV; History Channel; ION Television; Jewelry Television; Lifetime; Lifetime Movie Network; MSNBC; MTV; Nickelodeon; Outdoor Channel; Oxygen; Product Information Network; ShopNBC; Speed Channel; Spike TV; Syfy; TBS Superstation; The Learning Channel; Travel Channel; Trinity Broadcasting Network; truTV; Turner Network TV; TV Land; USA Network; VH1; WE tv; Weather Channel.
Fee: $34.00 monthly.

Digital Basic Service
Subscribers: N.A.
Programming (received off-air): WAND (NBC) Decatur; WCCU (FOX) Urbana; WCIA (CBS) Champaign; WICD (ABC) Champaign; WILL-TV (PBS) Urbana; WTHI-TV (CBS) Terre Haute.
Programming (via satellite): ABC News Now; AmericanLife TV Network; BBC America; Bio; Bloomberg Television; Bravo; CBS College Sports Network; CCTV-9 (CCTV International); CMT Pure Country; Discovery HD Theater; Discovery Health Channel; Discovery Kids Channel; Discovery Military Channel; Discovery Planet Green; Discovery Times Channel; ESPN 2 HD; ESPN HD; ESPN U; ESPNews; FitTV; Fox College Sports Atlantic; Fox College Sports Central; Fox College Sports Pacific; Fox Movie Channel; Fox Reality Channel; Fox Soccer; Fuel TV; Fuse; G4; Gol TV; Golf Channel; GSN; HDNet; HDNet Movies; History Channel; Independent Film Channel; ION Life; Lifetime Real Women; MTV Hits; MTV2; Music Choice; National Geographic Channel; Nick Jr.; NickToons TV; Qubo; ReelzChannel; Science Channel; Sleuth; Style Network; TeenNick; Tennis Channel; The Sportsman Channel; Toon Disney; Turner Classic Movies; TVG Network; Universal HD; Versus; VH1 Classic.
Fee: $9.00 monthly.

Digital Pay Service 1
Pay Units: N.A.
Programming (via satellite): Cinemax (multiplexed); Cinemax On Demand; Encore (multiplexed); HBO (multiplexed); HBO HD; HBO On Demand; Showtime (multiplexed); Showtime HD; Showtime On Demand; Starz (multiplexed); Starz HDTV; Starz On Demand; The Movie Channel (multiplexed); The Movie Channel HD; The Movie Channel On Demand.

Fee: $11.95 monthly (HBO, Cinemax, Showtime/TMC or Starz/Encore).

Video-On-Demand: Yes

Internet Service

Operational: Yes.

Broadband Service: Mediacom High Speed Internet.

Fee: $59.95 installation; $40.95 monthly.

Telephone Service

Digital: Operational

Fee: $39.95 installation; $39.95 monthly

Miles of Plant: 27.0 (coaxial); None (fiber optic). Homes passed: 1,281. Total homes in franchised area: 1,281.

Area Operations Director: Todd Acker. Technical Operations Manager: Jerry Ferguson.

City fee: 3% of gross.

Ownership: Mediacom LLC (MSO).

GREENVIEW—Formerly served by Mediacom. No longer in operation. ICA: IL0331.

GREENVILLE—NewWave Communications, 318 N 4th St, Vandalia, IL 62471. Phones: 888-863-9928; 618-283-3567. Fax: 618-283-4483. E-mail: info@newwavecom.com. Web Site: http://www.newwavecom.com. Also serves Bond County. ICA: IL0137.

TV Market Ranking: Outside TV Markets (Bond County, GREENVILLE). Franchise award date: July 10, 1979. Franchise expiration date: N.A. Began: December 1, 1981.

Channel capacity: 83 (operating 2-way). Channels available but not in use: 32.

Basic Service

Subscribers: 1,072.

Programming (received off-air): KDNL-TV (ABC) St. Louis; KETC (PBS) St. Louis; KMOV (CBS) St. Louis; KNLC (IND) St. Louis; KPLR-TV (CW) St. Louis; KSDK (NBC) St. Louis; KTVI (FOX) St. Louis; WICS (ABC) Springfield; WPXS (IND) Mount Vernon; WRBU (MNT) East St. Louis; WSIU-TV (PBS) Carbondale; allband FM.

Programming (via satellite): ABC Family Channel; AMC; AmericanLife TV Network; Animal Planet; Arts & Entertainment; BET Networks; Bravo; Cartoon Network; CNBC; CNN; Comedy Central; Country Music TV; Discovery Channel; Disney Channel; ESPN; ESPN 2; ESPN Classic Sports; ESPNews; Eternal Word TV Network; Food Network; Fox News Channel; Fox Sports Net Midwest; FX; Great American Country; Headline News; HGTV; History Channel; Home Shopping Network; Lifetime; MSNBC; MTV; Nickelodeon; Outdoor Channel; QVC; ShopNBC; Spike TV; Syfy; TBS Superstation; Travel Channel; Trinity Broadcasting Network; Turner Network TV; TV Land; Univision; USA Network; VH1; Weather Channel; WGN America.

Fee: $30.82 installation; $33.67 monthly; $1.17 converter.

Digital Basic Service

Subscribers: 87.

Programming (via satellite): BBC America; Bio; Bloomberg Television; Bravo; Current; Discovery Digital Networks; DMX Music; ESPN Classic Sports; Fox College Sports Atlantic; Fox College Sports Central; Fox College Sports Pacific; Fox Movie Channel; Fox Soccer; G4; GAS; Golf Channel; GSN; Halogen Network; History Channel International; Independent Film Channel; Lifetime Movie Network; Lime; MTV Networks Digital Suite; National Geographic Channel; Nick Jr.; NickToons TV; Ovation; ShopNBC; Speed Channel; Sundance Channel; Trio; Turner Classic Movies; Versus; WE tv.

Fee: $12.05 monthly.

Digital Pay Service 1

Pay Units: N.A.

Programming (via satellite): Cinemax (multiplexed); Encore (multiplexed); Flix; HBO; Showtime (multiplexed); Starz (multiplexed); The Movie Channel (multiplexed).

Video-On-Demand: Planned

Pay-Per-View

iN DEMAND (delivered digitally); Hot Choice (delivered digitally); Playboy TV (delivered digitally); Fresh (delivered digitally); Shorteez (delivered digitally).

Internet Service

Operational: Yes.

Subscribers: 288.

Broadband Service: In-house.

Fee: $40.00 installation; $31.99 monthly.

Telephone Service

None

Miles of Plant: 39.0 (coaxial); 10.0 (fiber optic). Homes passed: 2,446. Total homes in franchised area: 2,446.

General Manager: Bill Flowers. Technical Operations Manager: Chris Mooday.

City fee: 3% of gross.

Ownership: NewWave Communications (MSO).

GRIDLEY—Gridley Cable, 108 E Third St, Gridley, IL 61744. Phones: 309-747-2221; 309-747-2324. Fax: 309-747-2888. E-mail: info@gridcom.net. Web Site: http://www.gridtel.com. Also serves Meadows. ICA: IL0280.

TV Market Ranking: Below 100 (GRIDLEY, Meadows). Franchise award date: N.A. Franchise expiration date: N.A. Began: September 1, 1982.

Channel capacity: 117 (not 2-way capable). Channels available but not in use: N.A.

Basic Service

Subscribers: 580.

Programming (received off-air): WAOE (MNT) Peoria; WEEK-TV (NBC) Peoria; WHOI (ABC, CW) Peoria; WMBD-TV (CBS) Peoria; WTVP (PBS) Peoria; WYZZ-TV (FOX) Bloomington.

Programming (via satellite): Big Ten Network; Cartoon Network; CNN; ESPN; Fox Sports Net Midwest; Hallmark Channel; Home Shopping Network; NFL Network; SoapNet; TBS Superstation; Toon Disney; Travel Channel; WGN America.

Fee: $39.95 monthly.

Expanded Basic Service 1

Subscribers: 517.

Programming (via satellite): ABC Family Channel; AMC; Animal Planet; Arts & Entertainment; Bravo; Cartoon Network; CNBC; Comcast SportsNet Chicago; Comedy Central; Country Music TV; C-SPAN; Discovery Channel; Disney Channel; ESPN 2; ESPN Classic Sports; Food Network; Fox News Channel; FX; Great American Country; HGTV; History Channel; Lifetime; MTV; National Geographic Channel; Nickelodeon; Spike TV; Syfy; The Learning Channel; Turner Classic Movies; Turner Network TV; TV Land; USA Network; VH1; Weather Channel.

Fee: $21.00 monthly.

Digital Basic Service

Subscribers: 62.

Programming (received off-air): WAOE (MNT) Peoria; WEEK-TV (NBC) Peoria; WHOI (ABC, CW) Peoria; WMBD-TV (CBS) Peoria; WTVP (PBS) Peoria; WYZZ-TV (FOX) Bloomington.

Programming (via satellite): AmericanLife TV Network; BBC America; Bio; Bloomberg Television; Bravo; CMT Pure Country; Current; Discovery Health Channel; Discovery Kids Channel; Discovery Military Channel; Discovery Planet Green; DMX Music; ESPN 2; ESPN Classic Sports; ESPN U; ESPNews; FitTV; Fox Movie Channel; Fox Soccer; Fuse; G4; Golf Channel; Great American Country; GSN; Halogen Network; HGTV; History Channel; History Channel International; ID Investigation Discovery; Independent Film Channel; Lifetime Movie Network; MTV Hits; MTV2; National Geographic Channel; Nick Jr.; NickToons TV; Outdoor Channel; Ovation; Science Channel; Speed Channel; Style Network; Syfy; TeenNick; Trinity Broadcasting Network; Turner Classic Movies; VH1 Classic; VH1 Soul; WE tv.

Fee: $9.00 monthly.

Pay Service 1

Pay Units: 319.

Programming (via satellite): Encore.

Fee: $1.95 monthly.

Pay Service 2

Pay Units: 49.

Programming (via satellite): HBO.

Fee: $10.95 monthly.

Digital Pay Service 1

Pay Units: N.A.

Programming (via satellite): Cinemax (multiplexed).

Fee: $8.95 monthly.

Digital Pay Service 2

Pay Units: 17.

Programming (via satellite): HBO (multiplexed).

Fee: $9.95 monthly.

Digital Pay Service 3

Pay Units: 6.

Programming (via satellite): Encore (multiplexed); Starz (multiplexed).

Fee: $12.95 monthly.

Digital Pay Service 4

Pay Units: 1.

Programming (via satellite): Flix; Showtime (multiplexed); The Movie Channel (multiplexed).

Fee: $9.95 monthly.

Video-On-Demand: No

Pay-Per-View

iN DEMAND (delivered digitally).

Internet Service

Operational: No, Both DSL & dial-up.

Telephone Service

None

Miles of Plant: 9.0 (coaxial); None (fiber optic).

General Manager: Herbert Flesher.

Ownership: American Broadband Communications Inc. (MSO).

GRIGGSVILLE—Crystal Broadband Networks, PO Box 180366, Chicago, IL 60618. Phones: 877-319-0328; 630-206-0447. E-mail: info@crystalbn.com. Web Site: http://crystalbn.com. Also serves Perry Twp. ICA: IL0246.

TV Market Ranking: Below 100 (GRIGGSVILLE, Perry Twp.). Franchise award date: N.A. Franchise expiration date: N.A. Began: N.A.

Channel capacity: 62 (not 2-way capable). Channels available but not in use: None.

Basic Service

Subscribers: 290.

Programming (received off-air): KETC (PBS) St. Louis; KHQA-TV (ABC, CBS) Hannibal; KMOV (CBS) St. Louis; KPLR-TV (CW) St. Louis; KSDK (NBC) St. Louis; WGEM-TV (CW, NBC) Quincy; WKRN-TV (ABC) Nashville; WRSP-TV (FOX) Springfield; WTJR (IND) Quincy.

Programming (via satellite): C-SPAN; Home Shopping Network; INSP; Weather Channel; WGN America.

Fee: $29.95 installation; $19.95 monthly.

Expanded Basic Service 1

Subscribers: N.A.

Programming (via satellite): ABC Family Channel; AMC; Arts & Entertainment; Boomerang; Cartoon Network; CNN; CNN International; Comedy Central; C-SPAN 2; Discovery Channel; Disney Channel; Do-It-Yourself; E! Entertainment Television; ESPN; Food Network; Fox Sports Net Midwest; FX; G4; Great American Country; GSN; Hallmark Channel; Headline News; HGTV; History Channel; Lifetime; Lifetime Movie Network; MSNBC; MTV; Nickelodeon; ShopNBC; Speed Channel; Spike TV; TBS Superstation; Toon Disney; Turner Network TV; USA Network.

Fee: $23.00 monthly.

Digital Basic Service

Subscribers: N.A.

Programming (via satellite): BBC America; Bio; Black Family Channel; Bloomberg Television; Discovery Digital Networks; Discovery Kids Channel; DMX Music; ESPN 2; ESPN Classic Sports; ESPNews; Fox Movie Channel; Fox Sports World; Golf Channel; Halogen Network; History Channel International; Lime; National Geographic Channel; Outdoor Channel; Style Network; Turner Classic Movies; Versus; WE tv.

Fee: $13.95 monthly.

Digital Pay Service 1

Pay Units: N.A.

Programming (via satellite): Cinemax (multiplexed); Encore (multiplexed); HBO (multiplexed); Showtime (multiplexed); Starz (multiplexed).

Fee: $9.49 monthly (Cinemax), $9.95 monthly (Starz/Encore), $13.49 monthly (HBO or Showtime).

Video-On-Demand: No

Pay-Per-View

Fresh (delivered digitally); Playboy TV (delivered digitally); iN DEMAND (delivered digitally).

Internet Service

Operational: Yes.

Telephone Service

Digital: Operational

Miles of Plant: 18.0 (coaxial); None (fiber optic). Homes passed: 802.

General Manager: Nidhin Johnson. Program Manager: Shawn Smith.

Ownership: Crystal Broadband Networks (MSO).

HAMEL—Madison Communications. Now served by STAUNTON, IL [IL0171]. ICA: IL0393.

HAMPSHIRE—Mediacom. Now served by CORTLAND (village), IL [IL0485]. ICA: IL0253.

HANOVER—Mediacom. Now served by LENA, IL [IL0223]. ICA: IL0285.

HARDIN—BrightGreen Cable, PO Box 127, Gillespie, IL 62033. Phone: 817-685-9588. E-mail: support@brightgreencable.com. Web Site: http://www.brightgreencable.com. ICA: IL0333.

TV Market Ranking: Outside TV Markets (HARDIN). Franchise award date: November 7, 1983. Franchise expiration date: N.A. Began: August 1, 1984.

Channel capacity: 62 (not 2-way capable). Channels available but not in use: N.A.

Basic Service

Subscribers: 130.

Programming (received off-air): KDNL-TV (ABC) St. Louis; KETC (PBS) St. Louis; KMOV (CBS) St. Louis; KPLR-TV (CW) St. Louis; KSDK (NBC) St. Louis; KTVI (FOX) St. Louis.

Programming (via satellite): Home Shopping Network; INSP; Trinity Broadcasting Network; Weather Channel; WGN America.

Fee: $29.95 installation; $19.95 monthly.

Expanded Basic Service 1

Subscribers: N.A.

Programming (via satellite): ABC Family Channel; AMC; Arts & Entertainment; CNN; C-SPAN; C-SPAN 2; Discovery Channel; Disney Channel; ESPN; ESPN 2; Fox Sports Net Midwest; G4; Golf Channel; Great American Country; GSN; Halogen Network; Headline News; History Channel; Lifetime; Lifetime Movie Network; MTV; National Geographic Channel; Nickelodeon; Outdoor Channel; ShopNBC; Speed Channel; Spike TV; Syfy; TBS Superstation; Toon Disney; Turner Classic Movies; Turner Network TV; TV Land; USA Network; Versus; WE tv.

Fee: $23.00 monthly.

Digital Basic Service

Subscribers: N.A.

Programming (via satellite): BBC America; Bio; Black Family Channel; Bloomberg Television; Discovery Digital Networks; Discovery Kids Channel; DMX Music; ESPN Classic Sports; ESPNews; Fox Movie Channel; Fox Sports World; HGTV; History Channel International; Lime; Style Network.

Fee: $13.95 monthly.

Digital Pay Service 1

Pay Units: N.A.

Programming (via satellite): Cinemax (multiplexed); Encore (multiplexed); HBO (multiplexed); Showtime (multiplexed).

Fee: $3.99 monthly (Encore), $9.49 monthly (Cinemax), $13.49 monthly (HBO, Starz or Showtime).

Video-On-Demand: No

Pay-Per-View

Fresh (delivered digitally); Playboy TV (delivered digitally); iN DEMAND (delivered digitally).

Internet Service

Operational: No.

Telephone Service

None

Miles of Plant: 6.0 (coaxial); None (fiber optic). Homes passed: 335.

President & General Manager: Phil Claro.

City fee: 3% of basic.

Ownership: BrightGreen Communications (MSO).

HARRISBURG—Mediacom. Now served by MARION, IL [IL0083]. ICA: IL0086.

HARTSBURG—Mediacom. Now served by DELAVAN, IL [IL0172]. ICA: IL0413.

HARVARD—Charter Communications, 2701 Daniels St, Madison, WI 53718. Phone: 608-274-3822. Fax: 608-274-1436. Web Site: http://www.charter.com. Also serves Genoa & Marengo, IL; Fontana, Linn (town), Sharon, Walworth & Williams Bay, WI. ICA: IL0073.

TV Market Ranking: 97 (Fontana, Genoa, HARVARD, Linn (town), Marengo, Sharon, Walworth, Williams Bay). Franchise award date: N.A. Franchise expiration date: N.A. Began: December 1, 1980.

Channel capacity: N.A. Channels available but not in use: N.A.

Basic Service

Subscribers: 6,348.

Programming (received off-air): WBBM-TV (CBS) Chicago; WBUW (CW) Janesville; WCGV-TV (MNT) Milwaukee; WDJT-TV (CBS) Milwaukee; WFLD (FOX) Chicago; WGN-TV (CW, IND) Chicago; WISN-TV (ABC) Milwaukee; WITI (FOX) Milwaukee; WLS-TV (ABC) Chicago; WMAQ-TV (NBC) Chicago; WMLW-CA (IND) Milwaukee; WMVS (PBS) Milwaukee; WMVT (PBS) Milwaukee; WTMJ-TV (NBC) Milwaukee; WTTW (PBS) Chicago; WTVO (ABC, MNT) Rockford.

Programming (via satellite): C-SPAN; Home Shopping Network; QVC; TV Guide Network.

Current originations: Educational Access; Public Access.

Fee: $28.59 installation; $13.95 monthly.

Expanded Basic Service 1

Subscribers: 4,792.

Programming (via satellite): ABC Family Channel; AMC; Animal Planet; Arts & Entertainment; BET Networks; Bravo; Cartoon Network; CNBC; CNN; Comedy Central; Country Music TV; Discovery Channel; Disney Channel; E! Entertainment Television; ESPN; ESPN 2; ESPN Classic Sports; Food Network; Fox News Channel; FX; G4; Golf Channel; GSN; Hallmark Channel; Headline News; HGTV; History Channel; Lifetime; Lifetime Movie Network; MSNBC; MTV; National Geographic Channel; Nickelodeon; Oxygen; SoapNet; Speed Channel; Spike TV; Style Network; Syfy; TBS Superstation; The Learning Channel; Travel Channel; truTV; Turner Classic Movies; Turner Network TV; TV Land; Univision; USA Network; Versus; VH1; Weather Channel.

Fee: $18.55 monthly.

Digital Basic Service

Subscribers: N.A.

Programming (received off-air): WSNS-TV (TMO) Chicago.

Programming (via satellite): 3 Angels Broadcasting Network; Arts & Entertainment HD; BBC America; Bio; BYU Television; Canal D; Cartoon Network Tambien en Espanol; CBS College Sports Network; CMT Pure Country; CNN en Espanol; CNN International; Cooking Channel; Daystar TV Network; Discovery en Espanol; Discovery Health Channel; Discovery Home Channel; Discovery Kids Channel; Discovery Military Channel; Do-It-Yourself; ESPN 2 HD; ESPN Deportes; ESPN U; ESPNews; Eternal Word TV Network; FamilyNet; Fox College Sports Atlantic; Fox College Sports Central; Fox College Sports Pacific; Fox Movie Channel; Fox Soccer; Fuse; Gol TV; Halogen Network; History Channel International; ID Investigation Discovery; Independent Film Channel; INSP; JCTV; La Familia Network; Lifetime Movie Network; Mexicanal; MTV Hits; MTV Jams; MTV Tres; MTV2; mtvU; mun2 television; Music Choice; NHL Network; Nick Jr.; Nick Too; NickToons TV; Palladia; ReelzChannel; Science Channel; Smile of a Child; TeenNick; Toon Disney; Toon Disney en Espanol; Trinity Broadcasting Network; Versus HD; VH1 Classic; VH1 Soul; WE tv.

Fee: $5.95 monthly.

Digital Pay Service 1

Pay Units: N.A.

Programming (via satellite): Cinemax (multiplexed); Encore (multiplexed); Flix; HBO (multiplexed); Showtime (multiplexed); Starz (multiplexed); Starz HDTV; The Movie Channel (multiplexed).

Fee: $13.95 monthly (Cinemax, HBO, Showtime/TMC, or Starz/Encore).

Video-On-Demand: Yes

Pay-Per-View

Addressable homes: 1,046.

NHL Center Ice/MLB Extra Innings (delivered digitally), Addressable: Yes; iN DEMAND (delivered digitally); Fresh (delivered digitally); NBA League Pass/WNBA (delivered digitally); Playboy TV (delivered digitally); Shorteez (delivered digitally).

Internet Service

Operational: Yes. Began: September 1, 2002.

Broadband Service: Charter Pipeline.

Fee: $39.99 monthly; $4.95 modem lease.

Telephone Service

Digital: Operational

Miles of Plant: 38.0 (coaxial); None (fiber optic). Homes passed: 11,917.

Vice President & General Manager: Lisa Washa. Technical Operations Director: Bruce Hummel. Engineering Director: Tim Sanderson. Marketing Director: Traci Loonstra. Government Relations Director: Tim Vowell.

Ownership: Charter Communications Inc. (MSO).

HARVEL—Mediacom. Now served by KINCAID, IL [IL0176]. ICA: IL0433.

HARVEY—Comcast Cable. Now served by CHICAGO (southern suburbs), IL [IL0008]. ICA: IL0055.

HEBRON (village)—Mediacom, 3900 26th Ave, Moline, IL 61265. Phone: 309-797-2580. Fax: 309-797-2414. Web Site: http://www.mediacomcable.com. ICA: IL0519.

TV Market Ranking: Below 100 (HEBRON (VILLAGE)). Franchise award date: October 7, 1985. Franchise expiration date: N.A. Began: N.A.

Channel capacity: N.A. Channels available but not in use: N.A.

Basic Service

Subscribers: 111.

Programming (received off-air): WBBM-TV (CBS) Chicago; WCIU-TV (IND) Chicago; WCPX-TV (ION) Chicago; WFLD (FOX) Chicago; WGN-TV (CW, IND) Chicago; WIFR (CBS) Freeport; WLS-TV (ABC) Chicago; WMAQ-TV (NBC) Chicago; WPWR-TV (MNT) Gary; WTTW (PBS) Chicago; WTVO (ABC, MNT) Rockford; WYCC (PBS) Chicago.

Fee: $20.95 installation; $45.00 monthly.

Expanded Basic Service 1

Subscribers: N.A.

Programming (via satellite): ABC Family Channel; AMC; Animal Planet; Arts & Entertainment; Bravo; Cartoon Network; CNBC; CNN; Comcast SportsNet Chicago; Comedy Central; Country Music TV; C-SPAN; Discovery Channel; Disney Channel; E! Entertainment Television; ESPN; ESPN 2; FitTV; Food Network; Hallmark Channel; Headline News; HGTV; History Channel; Home Shopping Network; Lifetime; MSNBC; MTV; Nickelodeon; QVC; Speed Channel; Spike TV; Syfy; TBS Superstation; The Learning Channel; Travel Channel; Trinity Broadcasting Network; truTV; Turner Network TV; TV Land; USA Network; VH1; Weather Channel.

Fee: $34.00 monthly.

Digital Basic Service

Subscribers: N.A.

Programming (via satellite): AmericanLife TV Network; BBC America; Bio; Bloomberg Television; Discovery Health Channel; Discovery Kids Channel; Discovery Military Channel; Discovery Planet Green; ESPNews; Fox Movie Channel; Fox Soccer; Fuse; G4; Golf Channel; History Channel International; ID Investigation Discovery; Independent Film Channel; Lifetime Movie Network; MTV Hits; MTV2; Music Choice; National Geographic Channel; Nick Jr.; NickToons TV; Outdoor Channel; Science Channel; Sleuth; Style Network; TeenNick; Turner Classic Movies; TVG Network; VH1 Classic.

Fee: $9.00 monthly.

Digital Pay Service 1

Pay Units: N.A.

Programming (via satellite): Cinemax (multiplexed); Encore (multiplexed); HBO (multiplexed); Showtime (multiplexed); Starz (multiplexed); The Movie Channel (multiplexed).

Fee: $11.95 monthly (HBO, Cinemax, Showtime/TMC or Starz/Encore).

Video-On-Demand: No

Pay-Per-View

iN DEMAND (delivered digitally); Playboy TV (delivered digitally); Ten Clips (delivered digitally).

Internet Service

Operational: Yes.

Broadband Service: Mediacom High Speed Internet.

Fee: $59.95 installation; $40.95 monthly.

Telephone Service

Digital: Operational

Fee: $39.95 installation; $39.95 monthly

Homes passed: 423. Miles of plant (coax & fiber) included in Moline

Regional Vice President: Cari Fenzel. Engineering Director: Mitch Carlson. Technical Operations Manager: Chris Toalson. Marketing Director: Greg Evans.

City fee: 3% of gross.

Ownership: Mediacom LLC (MSO).

HENNING—Formerly served by CableDirect. No longer in operation. ICA: IL0453.

HERITAGE LAKE—Tel-Star Cablevision Inc. Now served by EDWARDS, IL [IL0326]. ICA: IL0520.

HERRICK—Mediacom, PO Box 288, 4290 Blue Stem Rd, Charleston, IL 61920. Phones: 217-348-5533; 309-274-4500. Fax: 217-345-7074. Web Site: http://www.mediacomcable.com. ICA: IL0368.

TV Market Ranking: Outside TV Markets (HERRICK). Franchise award date: N.A. Franchise expiration date: N.A. Began: N.A.

Channel capacity: N.A. Channels available but not in use: N.A.

Basic Service

Subscribers: 99.

Programming (received off-air): WAND (NBC) Decatur; WCIA (CBS) Champaign; WICS (ABC) Springfield; WILL-TV (PBS) Urbana; WPXS (IND) Mount Vernon; WRSP-TV (FOX) Springfield.

Programming (via satellite): ABC Family Channel; AMC; Animal Planet; Arts & Entertainment; CNN; Comedy Central; Discovery Channel; ESPN; ESPN 2; Headline News; HGTV; History Channel; Home Shopping Network; Lifetime; MTV; Nickelodeon; Speed Channel; Spike TV; Syfy; TBS Superstation; The Learning Channel; Travel Channel; Turner Network TV; USA Network; Weather Channel; WGN America.

Fee: $45.00 installation; $47.95 monthly.

Pay Service 1

Pay Units: 39.

Programming (via satellite): Cinemax; HBO.

Fee: $7.95 monthly (Cinemax), $13.50 monthly (HBO).

Video-On-Demand: No

Internet Service

Operational: No.

Telephone Service

None

Miles of Plant: 5.0 (coaxial); None (fiber optic). Homes passed: 244.

Area Operations Director: Todd Acker. Technical Operations Manager: Jerry Ferguson.

City fee: 3% of gross.

Ownership: Mediacom LLC (MSO).

HERRIN—Mediacom. Now served by MARION, IL [IL0083]. ICA: IL0063.

HERSCHER—Formerly served by Comcast Cable. No longer in operation. ICA: IL0298.

HETTICK (village)—Formerly served by CableDirect. No longer in operation. ICA: IL0521.

HEYWORTH—Mediacom, PO Box 334, 609 S 4th St, Chillicothe, IL 61523. Phone: 309-274-4500. Fax: 309-274-3188. Web Site: http://www.mediacomcable.com. ICA: IL0226.

TV Market Ranking: 64 (HEYWORTH). Franchise award date: N.A. Franchise expiration date: N.A. Began: December 1, 1980.

Channel capacity: 134 (operating 2-way). Channels available but not in use: None.

Basic Service

Subscribers: 762.

Programming (received off-air): WAND (NBC) Decatur; WAOE (MNT) Peoria; WCIA (CBS) Champaign; WEEK-TV (NBC) Peoria; WHOI (ABC, CW) Peoria; WICS (ABC) Springfield; WILL-TV (PBS) Urbana; WMBD-TV (CBS) Peoria; WRSP-TV (FOX) Springfield; WTVP (PBS) Peoria; WYZZ-TV (FOX) Bloomington.

Programming (via satellite): WGN America.

Fee: $45.00 installation; $20.95 monthly.

Expanded Basic Service 1

Subscribers: 682.

Programming (via satellite): ABC Family Channel; AMC; AmericanLife TV Network; Animal Planet; Arts & Entertainment; BET Networks; Bravo; Cartoon Network; CNN; Comcast SportsNet Chicago; Comedy Central; Country Music TV; C-SPAN; C-SPAN 2; Discovery Channel; Disney Channel; E! Entertainment Television; ESPN; ESPN 2; Eternal Word TV Network; Food Network; Fox News Channel; FX; Hallmark Channel; Headline News; HGTV; History Channel; Home Shopping Network; INSP; ION Television; Jewelry Television; Lifetime; Lifetime Movie Network; MSNBC; MTV; Nickelodeon; Product Information Network; QVC; ShopNBC; Speed Channel; Spike TV; Syfy; TBS Superstation; The Learning Channel; Travel Channel; Trinity Broadcasting Network; truTV; Turner Network TV; TV Guide Network; TV Land; Univision; USA Network; VH1; WE tv; Weather Channel; Weatherscan.

Fee: $34.00 monthly.

Digital Basic Service

Subscribers: 94.

Programming (received off-air): WAND (NBC) Decatur; WEEK-TV (NBC) Peoria; WHOI (ABC, CW) Peoria; WILL-TV (PBS) Urbana; WMBD-TV (CBS) Peoria; WYZZ-TV (FOX) Bloomington.

Programming (via satellite): ABC News Now; BBC America; Bio; Bloomberg Television; CCTV-Entertainment; Discovery Digital Networks; ESPN 2 HD; ESPN HD; ESPNews; Fox Movie Channel; Fox Reality Channel; Fox Soccer; Fuse; G4; Golf Channel; GSN; History Channel International; Independent Film Channel; ION Life; Lifetime Real Women; Military History Channel; MTV Hits; MTV2; Music Choice; National Geographic Channel; Nick Jr.; NickToons TV; Outdoor Channel; Qubo; ReelzChannel; Science Channel; Sleuth; Style Network; Sundance Channel; TeenNick; Turner Classic Movies; Versus; VH1 Classic.

Fee: $9.00 monthly.

Digital Expanded Basic Service

Subscribers: N.A.

Programming (via satellite): College Sports Television; ESPN U; Fox College Sports Atlantic; Fox College Sports Central; Fox College Sports Pacific; Fuel TV; Gol TV; Tennis Channel; The Sportsman Channel; TVG Network.

Fee: $3.95 monthly.

Digital Expanded Basic Service 2

Subscribers: N.A.

Programming (via satellite): Discovery HD Theater; HDNet; HDNet Movies; Universal HD.

Fee: $6.95 monthly.

Digital Pay Service 1

Pay Units: 318.

Programming (via satellite): Cinemax (multiplexed); Encore (multiplexed); Flix; HBO (multiplexed); Showtime (multiplexed); Showtime HD; Starz (multiplexed); Starz HDTV; The Movie Channel (multiplexed); The Movie Channel HD.

Fee: $11.95 monthly (HBO, Cinemax, Showtime/TMC, or Starz/Encore).

Video-On-Demand: Yes

Pay-Per-View

Ten Clips (delivered digitally); iN DEMAND (delivered digitally); Playboy TV (delivered digitally); Ten Blox (delivered digitally); ESPN On Demand (delivered digitally); Fox Sports Net (delivered digitally).

Internet Service

Operational: Yes.

Broadband Service: Mediacom High Speed Internet.

Fee: $59.95 installation; $45.95 monthly.

Telephone Service

Digital: Operational

Fee: $39.95 installation; $39.95 monthly

Miles of Plant: 27.0 (coaxial); 9.0 (fiber optic). Homes passed: 1,330.

Vice President: Don Hagwell. Marketing Director: Stephanie Law. Technical Operations Manager: Larry Brackman. Operations Director: Gary Wightman.

City fee: 1% of gross.

Ownership: Mediacom LLC (MSO).

HIGHLAND PARK—Comcast Cable. Now served by SCHAUMBURG, IL [IL0036]. ICA: IL0031.

HILLSBORO—NewWave Communications, 1176 E 1500 North Rd, Taylorville, IL 62568. Phone: 217-287-7992. Fax: 217-287-7304. E-mail: info@newwavecom.com. Web Site: http://www.newwavecom.com. Also serves Schram City & Taylor Springs. ICA: IL0143.

TV Market Ranking: Outside TV Markets (HILLSBORO, Schram City, Taylor Springs). Franchise award date: N.A. Franchise expiration date: N.A. Began: September 1, 1974.

Channel capacity: 60 (not 2-way capable). Channels available but not in use: 16.

Basic Service

Subscribers: 843.

Programming (received off-air): KDNL-TV (ABC) St. Louis; KETC (PBS) St. Louis; KMOV (CBS) St. Louis; KPLR-TV (CW) St. Louis; KSDK (NBC) St. Louis; KTVI (FOX) St. Louis; WAND (NBC) Decatur; WICS (ABC) Springfield; WPXV-TV (ION) Norfolk.

Programming (via satellite): AMC; Arts & Entertainment; Bravo; CNBC; Country Music TV; C-SPAN; E! Entertainment Television; ESPN; FX; Home Shopping Network; Lifetime; MTV; QVC; Spike TV; Syfy; Trinity Broadcasting Network; Turner Network TV; USA Network.

Current originations: Government Access; Educational Access; Public Access.

Fee: $29.99 installation.

Expanded Basic Service 1

Subscribers: 790.

Programming (via satellite): ABC Family Channel; Animal Planet; Cartoon Network; CNN; Discovery Channel; Disney Channel; ESPN 2; Fox News Channel; Fox Sports Net Midwest; Headline News; HGTV; History Channel; MSNBC; Nickelodeon; TBS Superstation; The Learning Channel; Travel Channel; Weather Channel; WGN America.

Fee: $42.99 monthly.

Digital Basic Service

Subscribers: N.A.

Programming (via satellite): AmericanLife TV Network; BBC America; Bio; Discovery Digital Networks; DMX Music; Fox Movie Channel; G4; GAS; Golf Channel; GSN; Halogen Network; History Channel; History Channel International; Independent Film Channel; Lifetime Movie Network; MTV Networks Digital Suite; MuchMusic Network; Nick Jr.; Outdoor Channel; ShopNBC; Speed Channel; Style Network; Toon Disney; Turner Classic Movies; Versus; WE tv.

Pay Service 1

Pay Units: 131.

Programming (via satellite): Cinemax.

Fee: $15.00 installation; $9.45 monthly.

Pay Service 2

Pay Units: 305.

Programming (via satellite): HBO.

Fee: $15.00 installation; $11.00 monthly.

Pay Service 3

Pay Units: 71.

Programming (via satellite): Showtime.

Fee: $15.00 installation; $10.45 monthly.

Pay Service 4

Pay Units: N.A.

Programming (via satellite): The Movie Channel.

Digital Pay Service 1

Pay Units: N.A.

Programming (via satellite): Cinemax (multiplexed); Encore (multiplexed); Flix; HBO (multiplexed); Showtime (multiplexed); Starz (multiplexed); The Movie Channel (multiplexed).

Video-On-Demand: No

Pay-Per-View

iN DEMAND (delivered digitally); Hot Choice (delivered digitally); ESPN Now (delivered digitally); ESPN Extra (delivered digitally); Playboy TV (delivered digitally); Fresh (delivered digitally); Shorteez (delivered digitally).

Internet Service

Operational: Yes.

Telephone Service

Digital: Operational

Miles of Plant: 51.0 (coaxial); None (fiber optic). Homes passed: 2,365. Total homes in franchised area: 3,261.

Vice President, Operations: Larry Eby. General Manager: Bill Flowers. Technical Operations Manager: Larry Harmon.

City fee: 3% of gross.

Ownership: NewWave Communications (MSO).

HOFFMAN—Formerly served by CableDirect. No longer in operation. ICA: IL0622.

HOMEWOOD—Comcast Cable. Now served by CHICAGO (southern suburbs), IL [IL0008]. ICA: IL0052.

HOOPESTON—Avenue Broadband Communications, 2603 Hart St, Vincennes, IN 47591. Phones: 800-882-7185; 812-895-7676. Fax: 812-886-5017. Web Site: http://www.avenuebroadband.com. Also serves Milford, Rossville & Wellington. ICA: IL0112.

TV Market Ranking: Below 100 (Rossville); Outside TV Markets (HOOPESTON, Milford, Wellington). Franchise award date: N.A. Franchise expiration date: N.A. Began: May 1, 1964.

Channel capacity: 60 (not 2-way capable). Channels available but not in use: N.A.

Basic Service

Subscribers: 2,696.

Programming (received off-air): WAND (NBC) Decatur; WCCU (FOX) Urbana; WCIA (CBS) Champaign; WFLD (FOX) Chicago; WGN-TV (CW, IND) Chicago; WICD (ABC) Champaign; WILL-TV (PBS) Urbana; WLFI-TV (CBS) Lafayette; WLS-TV (ABC) Chicago; WTTV (CW) Bloomington; allband FM.

Current originations: Government Access; Educational Access; Public Access.

Fee: $29.99 installation.

Expanded Basic Service 1

Subscribers: N.A.

Programming (via satellite): ABC Family Channel; AMC; AmericanLife TV Network; Animal Planet; Arts & Entertainment; Bravo; Cartoon Network; CNBC; CNN; Comedy Central; Country Music TV; C-SPAN; C-SPAN 2; Discovery Channel;

Disney Channel; E! Entertainment Television; ESPN; ESPN 2; Eternal Word TV Network; FitTV; Food Network; Fox News Channel; FX; G4; Golf Channel; Hallmark Channel; Headline News; HGTV; History Channel; Home Shopping Network; ION Television; Lifetime; MSNBC; MTV; National Geographic Channel; Nickelodeon; Outdoor Channel; Oxygen; QVC; SoapNet; Speed Channel; Spike TV; Syfy; TBS Superstation; The Learning Channel; Toon Disney; Travel Channel; Trinity Broadcasting Network; truTV; Turner Classic Movies; Turner Network TV; TV Land; USA Network; Versus; VH1; WE tv; Weather Channel.
Fee: $49.99 monthly.

Digital Basic Service
Subscribers: 533.
Programming (via satellite): BBC America; Bio; Discovery Digital Networks; Do-It-Yourself; GAS; History Channel International; Independent Film Channel; Lifetime Movie Network; MTV Networks Digital Suite; Music Choice; Nick Jr.; Nick Too; NickToons TV; Sundance Channel; TV Guide Interactive Inc.
Fee: $49.95 monthly.

Digital Pay Service 1
Pay Units: 220.
Programming (via satellite): Cinemax (multiplexed); Encore (multiplexed); Flix; HBO (multiplexed); Showtime (multiplexed); Starz (multiplexed); The Movie Channel (multiplexed).
Fee: $15.00 installation; $8.50 monthly (HBO).

Video-On-Demand: No

Pay-Per-View
iN DEMAND (delivered digitally); NHL Center Ice/MLB Extra Innings (delivered digitally); Hot Choice (delivered digitally); Playboy TV (delivered digitally); Fresh (delivered digitally); Shorteez (delivered digitally).

Internet Service
Operational: Yes.

Telephone Service
Digital: Operational

Miles of Plant: 54.0 (coaxial); 40.0 (fiber optic). Homes passed: 4,486. Total homes in franchised area: 4,486.
Chief Executive Officer: Steve Lowe. Vice President & General Manager: Mary Iafrate. Vice President, Engineering: Jeff Spence. System Engineer: Bart Cotter.
City fee: 3% of gross.
Ownership: Buford Media Group LLC (MSO).

HOOPPOLE—Formerly served by CableDirect. No longer in operation. ICA: IL0429.

HOYLETON—Formerly served by CableDirect. No longer in operation. ICA: IL0430.

HUDSON—Mediacom. Now served by APOLLO ACRES, IL [IL0340]. ICA: IL0342.

HUME (village)—Clearvision Cable Systems Inc., 1785 US Rte 40, Greenup, IL 62428-3501. Phone: 217-923-5594. Fax: 217-923-5681. Also serves Metcalf (village). ICA: IL0526.
TV Market Ranking: 64 (HUME (VILLAGE), Metcalf (village)). Franchise award date: N.A. Franchise expiration date: N.A. Began: May 1, 1983.
Channel capacity: 36 (not 2-way capable). Channels available but not in use: 10.

Basic Service
Subscribers: 70.
Programming (received off-air): WAND (NBC) Decatur; WBUI (CW) Decatur; WCCU (FOX) Urbana; WCFN (MNT) Springfield; WCIA (CBS) Champaign; WEIU-TV (PBS) Charleston; WICD (ABC) Champaign; WILL-TV (PBS) Urbana.
Programming (via satellite): AMC; Arts & Entertainment; Bravo; Cartoon Network; CNBC; CNN; Comedy Central; Country Music TV; C-SPAN; C-SPAN 2; Discovery Channel; Disney Channel; ESPN; ESPN 2; Fox News Channel; G4; Headline News; History Channel; Lifetime; MSNBC; MTV; Nickelodeon; QVC; Spike TV; Syfy; TBS Superstation; The Learning Channel; Trinity Broadcasting Network; Turner Classic Movies; Turner Network TV; TV Land; USA Network; VH1; Weather Channel; WGN America.
Fee: $22.45 monthly.

Pay Service 1
Pay Units: N.A.
Programming (via satellite): Showtime; The Movie Channel.
Fee: $11.95 monthly (each).

Video-On-Demand: No

Internet Service
Operational: No.

Telephone Service
None

Miles of Plant: 9.0 (coaxial); None (fiber optic). Homes passed: 314.
Manager: Michael Bauguss.
Ownership: Clearvision Cable Systems Inc. (MSO).

HYDE PARK—RCN Corp. Formerly served by Chicago (portions), IL [IL0661]. This cable system has converted to IPTV, 196 Van Buren St, Herndon, VA 20170. Phone: 703-434-8200. Web Site: http://www.rcn.com. ICA: IL5240.
TV Market Ranking: 3 (HYDE PARK).
Channel capacity: N.A. Channels available but not in use: N.A.

Internet Service
Operational: Yes.
Fee: $23.00 monthly.

Telephone Service
Digital: Operational
Fee: $30.00 monthly

Chairman: Steven J. Simmons. Chief Executive Officer: Jim Holanda.
Ownership: RCN Corp.

INA—Longview Communications, 12007 Sunrise Valley Dr, Ste 375, Reston, VA 20191. Phones: 866-611-6565 (Customer service); 703-476-9101. Fax: 703-476-9107. Web Site: http://www.longviewcomm.com. Also serves Bonnie. ICA: IL0392.
TV Market Ranking: 69 (INA); Below 100 (Bonnie). Franchise award date: N.A. Franchise expiration date: N.A. Began: November 1, 1984.
Channel capacity: 40 (not 2-way capable). Channels available but not in use: None.

Basic Service
Subscribers: 134.
Programming (received off-air): KBSI (FOX) Cape Girardeau; KFVS-TV (CBS, CW) Cape Girardeau; WPSD-TV (NBC) Paducah; WPXS (IND) Mount Vernon; WSIL-TV (ABC) Harrisburg; WSIU-TV (PBS) Carbondale; WTCT (IND) Marion.
Programming (via satellite): ABC Family Channel; American Movie Classics; Animal Planet; Arts & Entertainment; BET Networks; CNN; Comedy Central; Country Music TV; Discovery Channel; Disney Channel; E! Entertainment Television; ESPN; Fox News Channel; FX; Headline News; HGTV; Lifetime; Nickelodeon; QVC; Spike TV; Syfy; TBS Superstation; The Learning Channel; Travel Channel; Turner Network TV; USA Network; Weather Channel; WGN America.
Fee: $35.95 monthly.

Pay Service 1
Pay Units: 59.
Programming (via satellite): Showtime; Starz; The Movie Channel; The New Encore.
Fee: $8.95 monthly (TMC), $9.95 monthly (Starz/Encore), $10.95 monthly (Showtime).

Video-On-Demand: No

Internet Service
Operational: No.

Telephone Service
None

Miles of Plant: 17.0 (coaxial); None (fiber optic). Homes passed: 647.
President: John Long. Senior Vice President: Marc W. Cohen. General Manager: Brandon Dickey. Technical Manager: Steve Boss.
City fee: 3% of gross.
Ownership: Longview Communications (MSO).

INDUSTRY—Mediacom, PO Box 334, 609 S 4th St, Chillicothe, IL 61523. Phone: 309-274-4500. Fax: 309-274-3188. Web Site: http://www.mediacomcable.com. ICA: IL0365.
TV Market Ranking: Outside TV Markets (INDUSTRY). Franchise award date: N.A. Franchise expiration date: N.A. Began: December 1, 1983.
Channel capacity: N.A. Channels available but not in use: N.A.

Basic Service
Subscribers: 101.
Programming (received off-air): KHQA-TV (ABC, CBS) Hannibal; WGEM-TV (CW, NBC) Quincy; WHOI (ABC, CW) Peoria; WRSP-TV (FOX) Springfield; WTVP (PBS) Peoria.
Programming (via satellite): ABC Family Channel; AMC; Arts & Entertainment; Cartoon Network; CNN; Comedy Central; Discovery Channel; ESPN; HGTV; History Channel; Home Shopping Network; Lifetime; Nickelodeon; Spike TV; TBS Superstation; The Learning Channel; Trinity Broadcasting Network; Turner Network TV; TV Land; USA Network; Weather Channel; WGN America.
Fee: $45.00 installation; $46.95 monthly.

Pay Service 1
Pay Units: 34.
Programming (via satellite): Cinemax; HBO.
Fee: $7.95 monthly (Cinemax), $13.50 monthly (HBO).

Video-On-Demand: No

Internet Service
Operational: No.

Telephone Service
None

Miles of Plant: 5.0 (coaxial); None (fiber optic). Homes passed: 260.
Vice President: Don Hagwell. Operations Director: Gary Wightman. Technical Operations Manager: Larry Brackman. Marketing Director: Stephanie Law.
City fee: None.
Ownership: Mediacom LLC (MSO).

IPAVA—Mediacom, PO Box 334, 609 S 4th St, Chillicothe, IL 61523. Phone: 309-274-4500. Fax: 309-274-3188. Web Site: http://www.mediacomcable.com. ICA: IL0357.
TV Market Ranking: Outside TV Markets (IPAVA). Franchise award date: N.A. Franchise expiration date: N.A. Began: March 1, 1984.
Channel capacity: N.A. Channels available but not in use: N.A.

Basic Service
Subscribers: 88.
Programming (received off-air): WEEK-TV (NBC) Peoria; WHOI (ABC, CW) Peoria; WMBD-TV (CBS) Peoria; WRSP-TV (FOX) Springfield; WTVP (PBS) Peoria.
Programming (via satellite): ABC Family Channel; AMC; Animal Planet; Arts & Entertainment; Cartoon Network; CNN; Comedy Central; Country Music TV; Discovery Channel; ESPN; ESPN 2; HGTV; Home Shopping Network; Lifetime; Nickelodeon; Spike TV; Syfy; TBS Superstation; Turner Network TV; USA Network; VH1; WGN America.
Fee: $45.00 installation; $47.95 monthly.

Pay Service 1
Pay Units: 17.
Programming (via satellite): HBO.
Fee: $12.00 monthly.

Video-On-Demand: No

Internet Service
Operational: No.

Telephone Service
None

Miles of Plant: 3.0 (coaxial); None (fiber optic). Homes passed: 230.
Vice President: Don Hagwell. Operations Director: Gary Wightman. Technical Operations Manager: Larry Brackman. Marketing Director: Stephanie Law.
Ownership: Mediacom LLC (MSO).

IROQUOIS (village)—Formerly served by CableDirect. No longer in operation. ICA: IL0527.

IRVING—Mediacom, PO Box 288, 4290 Blue Stem Rd, Charleston, IL 61920. Fax: 217-345-7074. Web Site: http://www.mediacomcable.com. ICA: IL0390.

IUKA—Formerly served by Advanced Technologies & Technical Resources Inc. No longer in operation. ICA: IL0528.

JACKSON COUNTY—Galaxy Cablevision, 7155 US Hwy 45 S, Carrier Mills, IL 62917. Phone: 618-994-2261. Fax: 618-994-2261. Web Site: http://www.galaxycable.com. Also serves Tantara Mobile Home Park. ICA: IL0634.
TV Market Ranking: 69 (JACKSON COUNTY (portions), Tantara Mobile Home Park); Below 100 (JACKSON COUNTY (portions)); Outside TV Markets (JACKSON COUNTY (portions)). Franchise award date: N.A. Franchise expiration date: N.A. Began: N.A.
Channel capacity: 54 (not 2-way capable). Channels available but not in use: None.

Basic Service
Subscribers: 407.
Programming (received off-air): KBSI (FOX) Cape Girardeau; KFVS-TV (CBS, CW) Cape Girardeau; WDKA (MNT) Paducah; WPSD-TV (NBC) Paducah; WSIL-TV (ABC) Harrisburg; WSIU-TV (PBS) Carbondale; WTCT (IND) Marion.
Programming (via satellite): ABC Family Channel; AMC; Animal Planet; Arts & Entertainment; Cartoon Network Tambien en Espanol; CNBC; CNN; Comedy Central; C-SPAN; Discovery Channel; Disney Channel; E! Entertainment Television; ESPN; ESPN 2; Food Network; Fox News Channel; Fuse; FX; Great American Country; Headline News; HGTV; History Channel; Home Shopping Network; Lifetime; Outdoor Channel; TBS Superstation; The Learning Channel; Turner Classic Movies; Turner Network TV; USA Network; Weather Channel; WGN America.
Fee: $43.50 monthly.
Digital Basic Service
Subscribers: 154.
Programming (via satellite): AmericanLife TV Network; BBC America; Bio; Bloomberg Television; Discovery Digital Networks; DMX Music; ESPN Classic Sports; ESPNews; FitTV; Fox Sports World; G4; Golf Channel; GSN; Halogen Network; History Channel International; National Geographic Channel; Style Network; Syfy; Toon Disney; WE tv.
Fee: $13.95 monthly.
Digital Expanded Basic Service
Subscribers: N.A.
Programming (via satellite): DMX Music; Encore; Fox Movie Channel; Lifetime Movie Network.
Fee: $13.95 monthly.
Pay Service 1
Pay Units: N.A.
Programming (via satellite): Encore; HBO; Showtime.
Digital Pay Service 1
Pay Units: N.A.
Programming (via satellite): Cinemax (multiplexed); Flix; HBO (multiplexed); Showtime (multiplexed); The Movie Channel (multiplexed).
Fee: $14.30 monthly.
Pay-Per-View
Addressable homes: 111.
ESPN Now (delivered digitally), Fee: $3.99, Addressable: Yes; Hot Choice (delivered digitally); Movies (delivered digitally); Playboy TV (delivered digitally); Fresh (delivered digitally); Shorteez (delivered digitally); sports (delivered digitally); Urban Xtra (delivered digitally).
Internet Service
Operational: Yes.
Subscribers: 273.
Fee: $49.95 installation; $35.00 monthly.
Telephone Service
None
Miles of Plant: 53.0 (coaxial); None (fiber optic). Homes passed: 1,295.
State Manager: Ward Webb. Technical Manager: Audie Murphy. Engineer: John Stewart. Customer Service Manager: Malynda Walker.
Ownership: Galaxy Cable Inc. (MSO).

JACKSONVILLE—Mediacom, PO Box 288, 4290 Blue Stem Rd, Charleston, IL 61920. Phone: 217-348-5533. Fax: 217-345-7074. Web Site: http://www.mediacomcable.com. Also serves Chapin & South Jacksonville. ICA: IL0065.
TV Market Ranking: 64 (JACKSONVILLE, South Jacksonville); Outside TV Markets (Chapin). Franchise award date: October 19, 1964. Franchise expiration date: N.A. Began: October 14, 1964.
Channel capacity: 83 (operating 2-way). Channels available but not in use: 2.
Basic Service
Subscribers: 8,618.
Programming (received off-air): KETC (PBS) St. Louis; KHQA-TV (ABC, CBS) Hannibal; KPLR-TV (CW) St. Louis; KTVI (FOX) St. Louis; WAND (NBC) Decatur; WBUI (CW) Decatur; WCFN (MNT) Springfield; WCIA (CBS) Champaign; WICS (ABC) Springfield; WILL-TV (PBS) Urbana; WRSP-TV (FOX) Springfield; WSEC (PBS) Jacksonville; allband FM.
Programming (via satellite): ABC Family Channel; Home Shopping Network; QVC; TBS Superstation; WGN America.
Current originations: Religious Access; Government Access; Educational Access; Public Access.
Fee: $45.00 installation; $20.95 monthly.
Expanded Basic Service 1
Subscribers: 7,417.
Programming (via satellite): AMC; Animal Planet; Arts & Entertainment; BET Networks; Bravo; Cartoon Network; CNBC; CNN; Comedy Central; Country Music TV; C-SPAN; C-SPAN 2; Discovery Channel; Disney Channel; E! Entertainment Television; ESPN; ESPN 2; ESPNews; Eternal Word TV Network; Food Network; Fox News Channel; Fox Sports Net Midwest; FX; Golf Channel; Hallmark Channel; Headline News; HGTV; History Channel; INSP; Lifetime; MoviePlex; MSNBC; MTV; Nickelodeon; Product Information Network; Speed Channel; Spike TV; Syfy; The Learning Channel; Toon Disney; Travel Channel; Trinity Broadcasting Network; truTV; Turner Classic Movies; Turner Network TV; TV Guide Network; TV Land; USA Network; VH1; WE tv; Weather Channel.
Fee: $34.00 monthly.
Digital Basic Service
Subscribers: 692.
Programming (via satellite): AmericanLife TV Network; BBC America; Bio; Bloomberg Television; Discovery Health Channel; Discovery Home Channel; Discovery Kids Channel; Discovery Military Channel; DMX Music; ESPNews; Fox Movie Channel; Fox Soccer; Fuse; G4; Golf Channel; GSN; History Channel International; ID Investigation Discovery; Independent Film Channel; Lifetime Movie Network; MTV2; National Geographic Channel; Nick Jr.; NickToons TV; Outdoor Channel; Science Channel; Sleuth; Style Network; Turner Classic Movies; TVG Network; Versus.
Fee: $9.00 monthly.
Digital Pay Service 1
Pay Units: 1,975.
Programming (via satellite): Cinemax (multiplexed); Encore (multiplexed); HBO (multiplexed); Showtime (multiplexed); Starz (multiplexed); The Movie Channel (multiplexed).
Fee: $11.95 monthly (HBO, Cinemax, Showtime/TMC or Starz/Encore).
Video-On-Demand: Yes
Pay-Per-View
Addressable homes: 1,168.
iN DEMAND (delivered digitally), Fee: $3.95-$7.95, Addressable: Yes; Playboy TV (delivered digitally); Pleasure (delivered digitally); Fresh (delivered digitally); Shorteez (delivered digitally).
Internet Service
Operational: Yes.
Subscribers: 248.
Broadband Service: Mediacom High Speed Internet.
Fee: $59.95 installation; $40.95 monthly.
Telephone Service
Digital: Operational
Fee: $39.95 installation; $39.95 monthly
Miles of Plant: 148.0 (coaxial); 18.0 (fiber optic). Homes passed: 9,875.
Area Operations Director: Todd Acker. Technical Operations Manager: Jerry Ferguson.
City fee: 3% of gross.
Ownership: Mediacom LLC (MSO).

JERSEYVILLE—Greene County Partners Inc., PO Box 200, 100 Redbud Rd, Virginia, IL 62691. Phones: 800-252-1799; 217-452-7725. Fax: 217-452-7797. E-mail: solutions@casscomm.com. Web Site: http://www.casscomm.com. Also serves Jersey County (portions). ICA: IL0130.
TV Market Ranking: 11 (Jersey County (portions), JERSEYVILLE). Franchise award date: May 1, 1979. Franchise expiration date: N.A. Began: May 29, 1980.
Channel capacity: N.A. Channels available but not in use: N.A.
Basic Service
Subscribers: 1,037.
Programming (received off-air): KDNL-TV (ABC) St. Louis; KETC (PBS) St. Louis; KMOV (CBS) St. Louis; KPLR-TV (CW) St. Louis; KSDK (NBC) St. Louis; KTVI (FOX) St. Louis.
Programming (via satellite): C-SPAN; Home Shopping Network; QVC; WGN America.
Fee: $45.00 installation; $49.95 monthly; $15.00 additional installation.
Expanded Basic Service 1
Subscribers: N.A.
Programming (via satellite): ABC Family Channel; AMC; Animal Planet; Arts & Entertainment; Bravo; Cartoon Network; CNBC; CNN; Comedy Central; Country Music TV; Discovery Channel; Disney Channel; E! Entertainment Television; ESPN; ESPN 2; Food Network; Fox News Channel; Fox Sports Net Midwest; FX; G4; Hallmark Channel; Headline News; HGTV; History Channel; Lifetime; MSNBC; MTV; National Geographic Channel; Nickelodeon; Outdoor Channel; SoapNet; Spike TV; Syfy; TBS Superstation; The Learning Channel; Travel Channel; Turner Network TV; TV Guide Network; TV Land; USA Network; VH1; Weather Channel.
Fee: $30.40 monthly.
Digital Basic Service
Subscribers: 82.
Programming (received off-air): KDNL-TV (ABC) St. Louis; KETC (PBS) St. Louis; KMOV (CBS) St. Louis; KSDK (NBC) St. Louis; KTIV (CW, NBC) Sioux City.
Programming (via satellite): BET Networks; Bio; Bloomberg Television; CMT Pure Country; Current; CW+; Discovery Channel HD; Discovery Health Channel; Discovery Kids Channel; Discovery Military Channel; Discovery Planet Green; Disney XD; ESPN Classic Sports; ESPN HD; ESPNews; FitTV; Food Network HD; Fox Movie Channel; Fox Soccer; Fuse; Golf Channel; Halogen Network; HDNet; HDNet Movies; HGTV HD; History Channel; ID Investigation Discovery; Independent Film Channel; Lifetime Movie Network; MTV Hits; MTV2; Nick Jr.; Nick Too; NickToons TV; Outdoor Channel 2 HD; Science Channel; ShopNBC; Speed Channel; Style Network; Trinity Broadcasting Network; Turner Classic Movies; Universal HD; Versus; VH1 Classic; VH1 Soul; WE tv.
Digital Pay Service 1
Pay Units: 204 Subs for all pay channels.
Programming (via satellite): Cinemax (multiplexed); Cinemax HD; Encore (multiplexed); Flix; HBO (multiplexed); HBO HD; Showtime (multiplexed); Showtime HD; Starz (multiplexed); The Movie Channel (multiplexed); The Movie Channel HD.
Video-On-Demand: No
Pay-Per-View
iN DEMAND (delivered digitally); Shorteez (delivered digitally); Hot Choice (delivered digitally); ESPN Now (delivered digitally); Playboy TV (delivered digitally); Fresh (delivered digitally).
Internet Service
Operational: Yes.
Subscribers: 295.
Fee: $29.95-$99.95 monthly.
Telephone Service
Digital: Operational
Subscribers: 60.
Fee: $34.95 monthly
Miles of Plant: 48.0 (coaxial); None (fiber optic). Homes passed: 4,123.
General Manager: Chad Winters. Chief Technician: Lance Allen. Marketing Director: Erynn Snedeker.
City fee: 3% of gross.
Ownership: Green County Partners Inc. (MSO).

KAMPSVILLE (village)—Cass Cable TV Inc. No longer in operation. ICA: IL0397.

KANKAKEE—Comcast Cable. Now served by CHICAGO (southern suburbs), IL [IL0008]. ICA: IL0035.

KARNAK—Longview Communications, 12007 Sunrise Valley Dr, Ste 375, Reston, VA 20191. Phones: 866-611-6565 (Customer service); 703-476-9101. Fax: 703-476-9107. Web Site: http://www.longviewcomm.com. ICA: IL0358.
TV Market Ranking: 69 (KARNAK). Franchise award date: N.A. Franchise expiration date: N.A. Began: January 1, 1985.
Channel capacity: 40 (not 2-way capable). Channels available but not in use: N.A.
Basic Service
Subscribers: 18.
Programming (received off-air): KBSI (FOX) Cape Girardeau; KFVS-TV (CBS, CW) Cape Girardeau; WDKA (MNT) Paducah; WKPD (PBS) Paducah; WPSD-TV (NBC) Paducah; WSIL-TV (ABC) Harrisburg; WTCT (IND) Marion.
Programming (via satellite): C-SPAN; C-SPAN 2; Eternal Word TV Network; QVC; WGN America.
Fee: $30.00 installation; $17.98 monthly.
Expanded Basic Service 1
Subscribers: N.A.
Programming (via satellite): ABC Family Channel; AMC; Animal Planet; Arts & Entertainment; CNN; Discovery Channel; Disney Channel; E! Entertainment Television; ESPN; ESPN 2; Fox News Channel; Fox Sports Net Midwest; Great American Country; Headline News; History Channel; Lifetime; MSNBC; Speed Channel; TBS Superstation; The Learning Channel; Turner Network TV; USA Network; Weather Channel.
Fee: $17.97 monthly.
Pay Service 1
Pay Units: N.A.
Programming (via satellite): Cinemax; HBO; Showtime; The Movie Channel.
Fee: $8.95 monthly (TMC), $10.95 monthly (Showtime or Cinemax), $12.95 monthly (HBO).
Video-On-Demand: No

Internet Service
Operational: No.

Telephone Service
None

Miles of Plant: 5.0 (coaxial); None (fiber optic). Homes passed: 274.

President: John Long. Senior Vice President: Marc W Cohen. General Manager: Brandon Dickey. Technical Manager: Steve Boss.

Ownership: Longview Communications (MSO).

KEITHSBURG—Nova Cablevision Inc., PO Box 1412, 677 W Main St, Galesburg, IL 61401. Phones: 800-397-6682; 309-342-9681. Fax: 309-342-4408. Web Site: http://www.novacablevision.com. ICA: IL0318.

TV Market Ranking: 60 (KEITHSBURG). Franchise award date: N.A. Franchise expiration date: N.A. Began: September 7, 1984.

Channel capacity: 31 (operating 2-way). Channels available but not in use: 9.

Basic Service
Subscribers: 40.
Programming (received off-air): KGCW (CW) Burlington; KIIN (PBS) Iowa City; KWQC-TV (NBC) Davenport; WEEK-TV (NBC) Peoria; WHBF-TV (CBS) Rock Island; WHOI (ABC, CW) Peoria; WMBD-TV (CBS) Peoria; WQAD-TV (ABC) Moline; WQPT-TV (PBS) Moline; WTVP (PBS) Peoria.
Programming (via satellite): ABC Family Channel; AMC; Animal Planet; Arts & Entertainment; Big Ten Network; Cartoon Network; CNBC; CNN; Comcast SportsNet Chicago; Comedy Central; Country Music TV; C-SPAN; C-SPAN 2; Discovery Channel; Disney Channel; Do-It-Yourself; E! Entertainment Television; ESPN; ESPN 2; ESPN U; Eternal Word TV Network; Food Network; Fox News Channel; Fox Sports Net Midwest; FX; Golf Channel; Hallmark Channel; Headline News; HGTV; History Channel; Home Shopping Network; HorseRacing TV; INSP; Lifetime; MSNBC; MTV; National Geographic Channel; Nickelodeon; QVC; RFD-TV; SoapNet; Speed Channel; Spike TV; Syfy; TBS Superstation; The Learning Channel; The Sportsman Channel; Travel Channel; truTV; Turner Network TV; TV Land; USA Network; VH1; Weather Channel; WGN America.
Fee: $60.00 installation; $48.95 monthly.

Digital Basic Service
Subscribers: N.A.
Programming (via satellite): Bio; Bloomberg Television; CMT Pure Country; Discovery Health Channel; Discovery Kids Channel; Discovery Military Channel; Discovery Planet Green; Disney XD; DMX Music; ESPN 2; ESPN Classic Sports; ESPNews; Fox Movie Channel; Fox Soccer; FSN Digital Atlantic; FSN Digital Central; FSN Digital Pacific; Fuse; G4; Golf Channel; Great American Country; GSN; HGTV; History Channel; History Channel International; ID Investigation Discovery; Independent Film Channel; Lifetime Movie Network; MTV Hits; MTV2; NickToons TV; Noggin; Outdoor Channel; Science Channel; ShopNBC; Speed Channel; Style Network; Syfy; The N; Trinity Broadcasting Network; Turner Classic Movies; Versus; VH1 Classic; VH1 Soul; WE tv.
Fee: $16.95 monthly.

Pay Service 1
Pay Units: N.A.
Programming (via satellite): Cinemax; HBO.
Fee: $11.95 monthly (each).

Digital Pay Service 1
Pay Units: N.A.
Programming (via satellite): Cinemax (multiplexed); Encore (multiplexed); Flix; HBO (multiplexed); Showtime (multiplexed); Starz (multiplexed); Sundance Channel; The Movie Channel (multiplexed).
Fee: $12.85 monthly (HBO, Cinemax, Starz/Encore or Showtime/TMC/Flix/Sundance).

Video-On-Demand: No

Internet Service
Operational: Yes.
Fee: $30.00 installation; $39.95 monthly; $3.95 modem lease.

Telephone Service
None

Miles of Plant: 10.0 (coaxial); None (fiber optic). Homes passed: 323. Total homes in franchised area: 375.

Manager: Robert G. Fischer Jr. Office Manager: Hazel Harden.

Ownership: Nova Cablevision Inc. (MSO).

KENNEY—Heartland Cable Inc., PO Box 7, 167 W 5th St, Minonk, IL 61760. Phones: 800-448-4320; 309-432-2075. Fax: 309-432-2500. Web Site: http://www.heartlandcable.com. ICA: IL0531.

TV Market Ranking: 64 (KENNEY). Franchise award date: August 1, 1987. Franchise expiration date: N.A. Began: January 1, 1988.

Channel capacity: 60 (2-way capable). Channels available but not in use: 20.

Basic Service
Subscribers: 100.
Programming (received off-air): WAND (NBC) Decatur; WCCU (FOX) Urbana; WCIA (CBS) Champaign; WICD (ABC) Champaign; WILL-TV (PBS) Urbana.
Programming (via satellite): ABC Family Channel; Arts & Entertainment; CNN; Discovery Channel; Disney Channel; ESPN; Spike TV; TBS Superstation; Turner Network TV; USA Network; WGN America.
Fee: $39.00 installation; $32.90 monthly.

Pay Service 1
Pay Units: 10.
Programming (via satellite): HBO.
Fee: $10.95 monthly.

Pay Service 2
Pay Units: N.A.
Programming (via satellite): Showtime.
Fee: $8.95 monthly.

Video-On-Demand: Yes

Internet Service
Operational: Yes.
Subscribers: 30.
Fee: $39.00 installation; $29.99 monthly.

Telephone Service
None

Miles of Plant: 3.0 (coaxial); None (fiber optic).

Manager: Steve Allen.

Ownership: Heartland Cable Inc. (Illinois) (MSO).

KEWANEE—Comcast Cable, 4450 Kishwaukee St, Rockford, IL 61101. Phone: 815-395-8890. Fax: 815-395-8901. Web Site: http://www.comcast.com. Also serves Henry County. ICA: IL0085.

TV Market Ranking: 60 (Henry County (portions), KEWANEE); Outside TV Markets (Henry County (portions)). Franchise award date: October 13, 1969. Franchise expiration date: N.A. Began: August 2, 1971.

Channel capacity: N.A. Channels available but not in use: N.A.

Basic Service
Subscribers: N.A. Included in Rockford
Programming (received off-air): KGCW (CW) Burlington; KLJB (CW, FOX) Davenport; KWQC-TV (NBC) Davenport; WBQD-LP Davenport; WEEK-TV (NBC) Peoria; WHBF-TV (CBS) Rock Island; WHOI (ABC, CW) Peoria; WMBD-TV (CBS) Peoria; WQAD-TV (ABC) Moline; WQPT-TV (PBS) Moline; WTVP (PBS) Peoria.
Programming (via satellite): C-SPAN; C-SPAN 2; Eternal Word TV Network; Home Shopping Network; ION Television; QVC; TV Guide Network; WGN America.
Current originations: Public Access.
Fee: $44.00 installation; $8.00 monthly.

Expanded Basic Service 1
Subscribers: N.A.
Programming (via satellite): ABC Family Channel; AMC; Animal Planet; Arts & Entertainment; BET Networks; Bravo; Cartoon Network; CNBC; CNN; Comcast SportsNet Chicago; Comedy Central; Country Music TV; Discovery Channel; Disney Channel; E! Entertainment Television; ESPN; ESPN 2; Food Network; Fox News Channel; Fox Sports Net Midwest; FX; Great American Country; Hallmark Channel; Headline News; HGTV; History Channel; Lifetime; MSNBC; MTV; National Geographic Channel; Nickelodeon; Oxygen; Speed Channel; Spike TV; Syfy; TBS Superstation; The Learning Channel; Total Living Network; Travel Channel; truTV; Turner Network TV; Univision; USA Network; VH1; Weather Channel.
Fee: $43.75 monthly.

Digital Basic Service
Subscribers: 550.
Programming (via satellite): AmericanLife TV Network; BBC America; Bio; Bloomberg Television; CBS College Sports Network; CMT Pure Country; Cooking Channel; C-SPAN 3; Discovery Digital Networks; Discovery HD Theater; DMX Music; Do-It-Yourself; Encore (multiplexed); ESPN 2 HD; ESPN Classic Sports; ESPN HD; ESPN U; ESPNews; Fox Movie Channel; Fox Soccer; Fuse; G4; GAS; Golf Channel; GSN; Halogen Network; HDNet; HDNet Movies; History Channel International; HorseRacing TV; Independent Film Channel; Lifetime Movie Network; Lifetime Real Women; MTV Networks Digital Suite; NFL Network; Nick Jr.; Nick Too; NickToons TV; Outdoor Channel; Palladia; PBS Kids Sprout; Si TV; SoapNet; Style Network; Sundance Channel; Tennis Channel; Toon Disney; Trinity Broadcasting Network; Turner Classic Movies; Turner Network TV HD; TV Land; TVG Network; Universal HD; Versus; WE tv.
Fee: $15.95 monthly.

Digital Pay Service 1
Pay Units: N.A.
Programming (via satellite): Cinemax (multiplexed); Flix; HBO (multiplexed); HBO HD; Showtime (multiplexed); Showtime HD; Starz (multiplexed); The Movie Channel (multiplexed).
Fee: $15.00 installation; $10.00 monthly (Cinemax or Starz), $13.00 monthly (HBO or Showtime/TMC).

Video-On-Demand: Yes

Pay-Per-View
ESPN (delivered digitally); iN DEMAND (delivered digitally); Special events (delivered digitally); Playboy TV (delivered digitally).

Internet Service
Operational: Yes.
Broadband Service: Comcast High Speed Internet.
Fee: $99.95 installation; $44.95 monthly; $10.00 modem lease; $40.00 modem purchase.

Telephone Service
Digital: Operational
Fee: $39.95 monthly

Total homes in franchised area: 6,839. Homes passed & miles of plant included in Rockford

District Director: Joseph Browning. Technical Operations Manager: Lyle Matejewski. Program Director: Janice Schultz. Community & Government Affairs Manager: Joan Sage.

City fee: 3% of gross.

Ownership: Comcast Cable Communications Inc. (MSO).

KEYESPORT—Formerly served by CableDirect. No longer in operation. ICA: IL0348.

KINCAID—Mediacom, PO Box 288, 4290 Blue Stem Rd, Charleston, IL 61920. Phone: 217-348-5533. Fax: 217-345-7074. Web Site: http://www.mediacomcable.com. Also serves Buffalo, Bulpitt, Clear Lake (village), Dawson, Edinburg, Harvel, Jeisyville, Laomi, Mechanicsburg, Morrisonville, Mount Auburn, New Berlin, Palmer, River Oaks (village) & Tovey. ICA: IL0176.

TV Market Ranking: 64 (Buffalo, Bulpitt, Clear Lake (village), Dawson, Edinburg, Harvel, Jeisyville, KINCAID, Laomi, Mechanicsburg, Morrisonville, Mount Auburn, New Berlin, Palmer, River Oaks (village), Tovey). Franchise award date: N.A. Franchise expiration date: N.A. Began: March 1, 1983.

Channel capacity: 121 (operating 2-way). Channels available but not in use: None.

Basic Service
Subscribers: 2,715.
Programming (received off-air): WAND (NBC) Decatur; WBUI (CW) Decatur; WCFN (MNT) Springfield; WCIA (CBS) Champaign; WICS (ABC) Springfield; WILL-TV (PBS) Urbana; WRSP-TV (FOX) Springfield; WSEC (PBS) Jacksonville.
Programming (via satellite): ABC Family Channel; Home Shopping Network; QVC; TBS Superstation; Weatherscan; WGN America.
Fee: $45.00 installation; $20.95 monthly.

Expanded Basic Service 1
Subscribers: 1,756.
Programming (via satellite): AMC; Animal Planet; Arts & Entertainment; BET Networks; Bravo; Cartoon Network; CNBC; CNN; Comcast SportsNet Chicago; Comedy Central; Country Music TV; C-SPAN; C-SPAN 2; Discovery Channel; Disney Channel; E! Entertainment Television; ESPN; ESPN 2; Eternal Word TV Network; FitTV; Food Network; Fox News Channel; FX; Hallmark Channel; Headline News;

HGTV; History Channel; INSP; ION Television; Lifetime; MoviePlex; MSNBC; MTV; Nickelodeon; Product Information Network; RFD-TV; ShopNBC; SoapNet; Speed Channel; Spike TV; Syfy; The Learning Channel; Travel Channel; Trinity Broadcasting Network; truTV; Turner Network TV; TV Guide Network; TV Land; USA Network; VH1; WE tv; Weather Channel.
Fee: $34.00 monthly.

Digital Basic Service
Subscribers: N.A.
Programming (received off-air): WAND (NBC) Decatur; WCIA (CBS) Champaign; WICD (ABC) Champaign; WILL-TV (PBS) Urbana; WRSP-TV (FOX) Springfield.
Programming (via satellite): ABC News Now; AmericanLife TV Network; BBC America; Bio; Bloomberg Television; CCTV-9 (CCTV International); Discovery HD Theater; Discovery Health Channel; Discovery Kids Channel; Discovery Military Channel; Discovery Planet Green; Discovery Times Channel; ESPN 2 HD; ESPN HD; ESPNews; Fox Movie Channel; Fox Reality Channel; Fox Soccer; Fuse; G4; Golf Channel; GSN; HDNet; HDNet Movies; History Channel International; Independent Film Channel; ION Life; Lifetime Movie Network; Lifetime Real Women; MTV Hits; MTV2; Music Choice; National Geographic Channel; Nick Jr.; NickToons TV; Outdoor Channel; Qubo; ReelzChannel; Science Channel; Sleuth; Style Network; TeenNick; Turner Classic Movies; TVG Network; Universal HD; Versus; VH1 Classic.
Fee: $9.00 monthly.

Digital Expanded Basic Service
Subscribers: N.A.
Programming (via satellite): College Sports Television; ESPN U; Fox College Sports Atlantic; Fox College Sports Central; Fox College Sports Pacific; Fuel TV; Gol TV; Tennis Channel; The Sportsman Channel.
Fee: $3.95 monthly.

Digital Pay Service 1
Pay Units: N.A.
Programming (via satellite): Cinemax (multiplexed); Cinemax On Demand; Encore (multiplexed); HBO (multiplexed); HBO HD; HBO On Demand; Showtime (multiplexed); Showtime HD; Showtime On Demand; Starz (multiplexed); Starz HDTV; Starz On Demand; The Movie Channel (multiplexed); The Movie Channel HD; The Movie Channel On Demand.
Fee: $11.95 monthly (each).

Video-On-Demand: Yes

Pay-Per-View
iN DEMAND (delivered digitally); Playboy TV (delivered digitally); Ten Clips (delivered digitally); Ten Blox (delivered digitally).

Internet Service
Operational: Yes.
Broadband Service: Mediacom High Speed Internet.
Fee: $59.95 installation; $40.95 monthly.

Telephone Service
Digital: Operational
Fee: $39.95 installation; $39.95 monthly

Miles of Plant: 127.0 (coaxial); 26.0 (fiber optic). Homes passed: 5,747. Homes passed & miles of plant include Irving
Area Operations Director: Todd Acker. Technical Operations Manager: Jerry Ferguson. Customer Service Manager: Angie McHenry.
City fee: 3% of gross.
Ownership: Mediacom LLC (MSO).

KINDERHOOK—Formerly served by Almega Cable. No longer in operation. ICA: IL0276.

KINGSTON—Formerly served by Kingston Cable TV Co. No longer in operation. ICA: IL0532.

KINGSTON MINES—KMHC Inc., PO Box 107, 207 Third St, Kingston Mines, IL 61539-0107. Phone: 309-389-5782. ICA: IL0440.
TV Market Ranking: 83 (KINGSTON MINES). Franchise award date: October 1, 1983. Franchise expiration date: N.A. Began: October 1, 1983.
Channel capacity: N.A. Channels available but not in use: N.A.

Basic Service
Subscribers: 60.
Programming (received off-air): WEEK-TV (NBC) Peoria; WHOI (ABC, CW) Peoria; WMBD-TV (CBS) Peoria; WTVP (PBS) Peoria; WYZZ-TV (FOX) Bloomington.
Programming (via satellite): ABC Family Channel; Comedy Central; Country Music TV; Discovery Channel; Disney Channel; ESPN; ESPN 2; Spike TV; Syfy; TBS Superstation; Turner Network TV; USA Network; WGN America.
Fee: $10.00 installation; $17.00 monthly.

Pay Service 1
Pay Units: 28.
Programming (via satellite): HBO; Showtime.
Fee: $6.50 monthly (each).

Internet Service
Operational: No.

Telephone Service
None

Miles of Plant: 2.0 (coaxial); None (fiber optic). Homes passed: 100. Total homes in franchised area: 100.
Manager: Tom Hedge.
Ownership: KMHC Inc. (MSO).

KINMUNDY—Clearvision Cable Systems Inc., 1785 US Rte 40, Greenup, IL 62428-3501. Phone: 217-923-5594. Fax: 217-923-5681. Also serves Alma. ICA: IL0338.
TV Market Ranking: Below 100 (Alma, KINMUNDY). Franchise award date: N.A. Franchise expiration date: N.A. Began: January 1, 1984.
Channel capacity: N.A. Channels available but not in use: N.A.

Basic Service
Subscribers: 192.
Programming (received off-air): KDNL-TV (ABC) St. Louis; KMOV (CBS) St. Louis; KPLR-TV (CW) St. Louis; KSDK (NBC) St. Louis; WPXS (IND) Mount Vernon; WSIU-TV (PBS) Carbondale.
Programming (via satellite): ABC Family Channel; AMC; Arts & Entertainment; CNN; Country Music TV; Discovery Channel; Disney Channel; ESPN; Fox News Channel; Fox Sports Net; History Channel; Lifetime; Nickelodeon; Spike TV; TBS Superstation; The Learning Channel; Trinity Broadcasting Network; Turner Network TV; TV Land; USA Network; WABC-TV (ABC) New York; Weather Channel; WGN America; WNBC (NBC) New York; WRAL-TV (CBS) Raleigh.
Fee: $15.00 installation; $19.34 monthly.

Pay Service 1
Pay Units: 32.
Programming (via satellite): HBO.
Fee: $10.75 monthly.

Video-On-Demand: No

Internet Service
Operational: No.

Telephone Service
None

Miles of Plant: 6.0 (coaxial); None (fiber optic). Homes passed: 719.
General Manager: Michael Bauguss.
Ownership: Clearvision Cable Systems Inc. (MSO).

KIRKLAND—Mediacom, 3900 26th Ave, Moline, IL 61265. Phone: 309-797-2580. Fax: 309-797-2414. Web Site: http://www.mediacomcable.com. Also serves Davis Junction, Malta, Monroe Center & Rolling Meadows Mobile Home Park. ICA: IL0277.
TV Market Ranking: 97 (Davis Junction, KIRKLAND, Malta, Monroe Center, Rolling Meadows Mobile Home Park). Franchise award date: N.A. Franchise expiration date: N.A. Began: February 1, 1985.
Channel capacity: 134 (operating 2-way). Channels available but not in use: N.A.

Basic Service
Subscribers: 644.
Programming (received off-air): WBBM-TV (CBS) Chicago; WCIU-TV (IND) Chicago; WCPX-TV (ION) Chicago; WFLD (FOX) Chicago; WGBO-DT (UNV) Joliet; WGN-TV (CW, IND) Chicago; WIFR (CBS) Freeport; WLS-TV (ABC) Chicago; WMAQ-TV (NBC) Chicago; WPWR-TV (MNT) Gary; WQRF-TV (FOX) Rockford; WREX (CW, NBC) Rockford; WSNS-TV (TMO) Chicago; WTTW (PBS) Chicago; WWTO-TV (TBN) La Salle; WYCC (PBS) Chicago.
Current originations: Educational Access.
Fee: $45.00 installation; $20.95 monthly.

Expanded Basic Service 1
Subscribers: 262.
Programming (via satellite): ABC Family Channel; AMC; Animal Planet; Arts & Entertainment; Bravo; Cartoon Network; CNBC; CNN; Comcast SportsNet Chicago; Comedy Central; Country Music TV; C-SPAN; C-SPAN 2; CW+; Discovery Channel; Disney Channel; E! Entertainment Television; ESPN; ESPN 2; Eternal Word TV Network; Food Network; Fox News Channel; FX; Hallmark Channel; Halogen Network; Headline News; HGTV; History Channel; Home Shopping Network; Lifetime; Lifetime Movie Network; MSNBC; MTV; Nickelodeon; QVC; ShopNBC; SoapNet; Speed Channel; Spike TV; Syfy; TBS Superstation; The Learning Channel; Travel Channel; Trinity Broadcasting Network; truTV; Turner Classic Movies; Turner Network TV; TV Guide Network; TV Land; USA Network; VH1; Weather Channel.
Fee: $34.00 monthly.

Digital Basic Service
Subscribers: N.A.
Programming (received off-air): WBBM-TV (CBS) Chicago; WFLD (FOX) Chicago; WMAQ-TV (NBC) Chicago.
Programming (via satellite): ABC News Now; AmericanLife TV Network; BBC America; Bio; Bloomberg Television; CCTV-9 (CCTV International); Discovery Health Channel; Discovery Kids Channel; Discovery Military Channel; Discovery Planet Green; ESPN 2 HD; ESPN HD; ESPN U; ESPNews; FitTV; Fox News Channel; Fox Reality Channel; Fox Soccer; Fuel TV; Fuse; G4; Golf Channel; GSN; History Channel International; ID Investigation Discovery; Independent Film Channel; ION Life; Lifetime Real Women; MTV Hits; MTV2; Music Choice; National Geographic Channel; Nick Jr.; NickToons TV; Outdoor Channel; Qubo; ReelzChannel; Science Channel; Sleuth; Style Network; Sundance Channel; TeenNick; TVG Network; VH1 Classic; WE tv; WLS-TV (ABC) Chicago.
Fee: $9.00 monthly.

Digital Expanded Basic Service
Subscribers: N.A.
Programming (via satellite): College Sports Television; Fox College Sports Atlantic; Fox College Sports Central; Fox College Sports Pacific; Gol TV; Tennis Channel; The Sportsman Channel.
Fee: $3.95 monthly.

Digital Expanded Basic Service 2
Subscribers: N.A.
Programming (via satellite): Discovery HD Theater; HDNet; HDNet Movies; Universal HD.
Fee: $6.95 monthly.

Digital Pay Service 1
Pay Units: N.A.
Programming (via satellite): Cinemax (multiplexed); Encore (multiplexed); Flix; HBO (multiplexed); HBO HD; Showtime (multiplexed); Showtime HD; Starz (multiplexed); Starz HDTV; Sundance Channel; The Movie Channel (multiplexed); The Movie Channel HD.
Fee: $11.95 monthly (HBO, Cinemax, Showtime/TMC or Starz/Encore).

Video-On-Demand: Yes

Pay-Per-View
iN DEMAND (delivered digitally); Playboy TV (delivered digitally); Ten Clips (delivered digitally); ESPN (delivered digitally).

Internet Service
Operational: Yes.
Broadband Service: Mediacom High Speed Internet.
Fee: $59.95 installation; $45.95 monthly.

Telephone Service
Digital: Operational
Fee: $39.95 installation; $39.95 monthly

Homes passed: 1,664. Miles of plant included in Moline
Regional Vice President: Cari Fenzel. Engineering Director: Mitch Carlson. Technical Operations Manager: Chris Toalson. Marketing Director: Greg Evans.
City fee: 3% of gross.
Ownership: Mediacom LLC (MSO).

KIRKWOOD—Nova Cablevision Inc., PO Box 1412, 677 W Main St, Galesburg, IL 61401. Phones: 800-397-6682; 309-342-9681. Fax: 309-342-4408. Web Site: http://www.novacablevision.com. ICA: IL0327.
TV Market Ranking: Below 100 (KIRKWOOD). Franchise award date: N.A. Franchise expiration date: N.A. Began: June 1, 1984.
Channel capacity: 31 (operating 2-way). Channels available but not in use: 23.

Basic Service
Subscribers: 20.
Programming (received off-air): KGCW (CW) Burlington; KIIN (PBS) Iowa City; KLJB (CW, FOX) Davenport; KWQC-TV (NBC) Davenport; WHBF-TV (CBS) Rock Island; WHOI (ABC, CW) Peoria; WMBD-TV (CBS) Peoria; WQAD-TV (ABC) Moline; WQPT-TV (PBS) Moline; WTVP (PBS) Peoria.
Programming (via satellite): ABC Family Channel; AMC; Animal Planet; Arts & Entertainment HD; Big Ten Network HD; Cartoon Network; CNBC; CNN; Comcast SportsNet Chicago; Comedy Central; Country Music TV; C-SPAN; C-SPAN 2; Discovery Channel; Disney Channel; Do-It-Yourself; E! Entertainment Television; ESPN 2; ESPN HD; ESPN U; Eternal Word TV Network; Food Network; Fox News Channel; Fox Sports Net Midwest; FX; Golf Channel; Great American Country; Hallmark Channel; Headline News; HGTV; History Channel; Home Shopping Network; HorseRacing TV; INSP; Lifetime; MSNBC; MTV; National Geographic Chan-

nel; Nickelodeon; QVC; RFD-TV; SoapNet; Speed Channel; Spike TV; Syfy; TBS Superstation; The Learning Channel; The Sportsman Channel; Travel Channel; truTV; Turner Network TV; TV Land; USA Network; VH1; Weather Channel; WEEK-TV (NBC) Peoria; WGN America.
Fee: $30.00 installation; $15.98 monthly.

Digital Basic Service
Subscribers: N.A.
Programming (via satellite): Bio; Bloomberg Television; CMT Pure Country; Discovery Health Channel; Discovery Kids Channel; Discovery Military Channel; Discovery Planet Green; Disney XD; DMX Music; ESPN 2; ESPN Classic Sports; ESPNews; Fox Movie Channel; Fox Soccer; FSN Digital Atlantic; FSN Digital Central; FSN Digital Pacific; Fuse; G4; Golf Channel; Great American Country; GSN; HGTV; History Channel; History Channel International; ID Investigation Discovery; Independent Film Channel; Lifetime Movie Network; MTV Hits; MTV2; NickToons TV; Noggin; Outdoor Channel; Science Channel; ShopNBC; Speed Channel; Style Network; Syfy; The N; Trinity Broadcasting Network; Turner Classic Movies; Versus; VH1 Classic; VH1 Soul; WE tv.
Fee: $16.95 monthly.

Pay Service 1
Pay Units: N.A.
Programming (via satellite): Cinemax; HBO.
Fee: $12.85 monthly (each).

Digital Pay Service 1
Pay Units: N.A.
Programming (via satellite): Cinemax (multiplexed); Encore (multiplexed); Flix; HBO (multiplexed); Showtime (multiplexed); Starz (multiplexed); Sundance Channel; The Movie Channel (multiplexed).
Fee: $12.95 monthly (HBO, Showtime/TMC/Flix/Sundance), Cinemax, or Starz/Encore).

Video-On-Demand: No

Pay-Per-View
Hot Choice (delivered digitally); Playboy TV (delivered digitally); Fresh (delivered digitally); Spice: Xcess (delivered digitally); Club Jenna (delivered digitally).

Internet Service
Operational: Yes.
Fee: $30.00 installation; $39.95 monthly; $3.95 modem lease.

Telephone Service
None

Miles of Plant: 7.0 (coaxial); None (fiber optic). Homes passed: 346. Total homes in franchised area: 346.
Manager: Robert G. Fischer Jr. Office Manager: Hazel Harden.
Ownership: Nova Cablevision Inc. (MSO).

LA HARPE—Insight Communications. Now served by MACOMB, IL [IL0076]. ICA: IL0222.

LA MOILLE (village)—Formerly served by CableDirect. No longer in operation. ICA: IL0533.

LA PLACE—Formerly served by Longview Communications. No longer in operation. ICA: IL0534.

LA ROSE—Formerly served by Tel-Star Cablevision Inc. No longer in operation. ICA: IL0535.

LACON—Mediacom, PO Box 334, 609 S 4th St, Chillicothe, IL 61523. Phones: 309-274-4500; 309-923-6061 (Roanoke office). Fax: 309-274-3188. Web Site: http://www.mediacomcable.com. Also serves Varna. ICA: IL0394.
TV Market Ranking: 83 (LACON, Varna). Franchise award date: March 5, 1984. Franchise expiration date: N.A. Began: April 23, 1984.
Channel capacity: N.A. Channels available but not in use: N.A.

Basic Service
Subscribers: 753.
Programming (received off-air): WAOE (MNT) Peoria; WEEK-TV (NBC) Peoria; WHOI (ABC, CW) Peoria; WILL-TV (PBS) Urbana; WMBD-TV (CBS) Peoria; WTVP (PBS) Peoria; WYZZ-TV (FOX) Bloomington.
Programming (via satellite): ABC Family Channel; WGN America.
Fee: $45.00 installation; $20.95 monthly.

Expanded Basic Service 1
Subscribers: N.A.
Programming (via satellite): AMC; AmericanLife TV Network; Animal Planet; Arts & Entertainment; BET Networks; Bravo; Cartoon Network; CNBC; CNN; Comcast SportsNet Chicago; Comedy Central; Country Music TV; C-SPAN; C-SPAN 2; Discovery Channel; Disney Channel; E! Entertainment Television; ESPN; ESPN 2; Eternal Word TV Network; Food Network; Fox News Channel; Fuse; FX; Hallmark Channel; Halogen Network; Headline News; HGTV; History Channel; Home Shopping Network; ION Television; Lifetime; MSNBC; MTV; Nickelodeon; Product Information Network; QVC; Radar Channel; ShopNBC; SoapNet; Speed Channel; Spike TV; Syfy; The Learning Channel; Travel Channel; Trinity Broadcasting Network; truTV; Turner Network TV; TV Guide Network; TV Land; Univision; USA Network; VH1; WE tv; Weather Channel.
Fee: $34.00 monthly.

Digital Basic Service
Subscribers: N.A.
Programming (via satellite): BBC America; Bio; Bloomberg Television; Discovery Digital Networks; ESPNews; Fox Movie Channel; Fox Sports World; G4; GAS; Golf Channel; GSN; History Channel International; Independent Film Channel; Lifetime Movie Network; Lime; MTV Networks Digital Suite; Music Choice; National Geographic Channel; Nick Jr.; NickToons TV; Outdoor Channel; Style Network; Sundance Channel; Trio; Turner Classic Movies; Versus.
Fee: $9.00 monthly.

Digital Expanded Basic Service
Subscribers: N.A.
Programming (received off-air): WCCU (FOX) Urbana; WEEK-TV (NBC) Peoria; WHOI (ABC, CW) Peoria; WTVP (PBS) Peoria.
Programming (via satellite): Discovery HD Theater; HDNet; HDNet Movies; INHD (multiplexed); Universal HD.
Fee: $6.95 monthly.

Digital Pay Service 1
Pay Units: N.A.
Programming (via satellite): Cinemax (multiplexed); Encore (multiplexed); Flix (multiplexed); HBO (multiplexed); Showtime (multiplexed); Starz (multiplexed); The Movie Channel (multiplexed).

Video-On-Demand: Yes

Pay-Per-View
iN DEMAND (delivered digitally); Playboy TV (delivered digitally); ESPN (delivered digitally); Fox Sports Net (delivered digitally).

Internet Service
Operational: Yes.
Broadband Service: Mediacom High Speed Internet.
Fee: $59.95 installation; $45.95 monthly.

Telephone Service
Digital: Operational
Fee: $39.95 installation; $39.95 monthly

Homes passed: 1,207. Miles of plant (coax) included in Roanoke
Vice President: Don Hagwell. Marketing Director: Stephanie Law. Operations Director: Gary Wightman. Technical Operations Manager: Larry Brackman. Chief Technician: Scott Rocke.
City fee: 5% of gross.
Ownership: Mediacom LLC (MSO).

LACON—Mediacom. Now served by LACON, IL [IL0394]. ICA: IL0225.

LADD—Comcast Cable, 4450 Kishwaukee St, Rockford, IL 61101. Phone: 815-395-8890. Fax: 815-395-8901. Web Site: http://www.comcast.com. Also serves Cherry, Dalzell & Depue. ICA: IL0161.
TV Market Ranking: Below 100 (Cherry, Dalzell, Depue, LADD). Franchise award date: N.A. Franchise expiration date: N.A. Began: April 1, 1981.
Channel capacity: N.A. Channels available but not in use: N.A.

Basic Service
Subscribers: N.A. Included in Rockford
Programming (received off-air): KGCW (CW) Burlington; KLJB (CW, FOX) Davenport; KWQC-TV (NBC) Davenport; WBBM-TV (CBS) Chicago; WEEK-TV (NBC) Peoria; WFLD (FOX) Chicago; WHBF-TV (CBS) Rock Island; WHOI (ABC, CW) Peoria; WQAD-TV (ABC) Moline; WTTW (PBS) Chicago; WWTO-TV (TBN) La Salle.
Programming (via satellite): C-SPAN; C-SPAN 2; Eternal Word TV Network; Home Shopping Network; ION Television; QVC; TV Guide Network; WGN America.
Fee: $44.00 installation; $8.00 monthly; $2.00 converter.

Expanded Basic Service 1
Subscribers: N.A.
Programming (via satellite): ABC Family Channel; AMC; Animal Planet; Arts & Entertainment; BET Networks; Bravo; Cartoon Network; CNBC; CNN; Comcast SportsNet Chicago; Comedy Central; Country Music TV; Discovery Channel; Disney Channel; E! Entertainment Television; ESPN; ESPN 2; Food Network; Fox News Channel; Fox Sports Net Midwest; FX; Great American Country; Hallmark Channel; Headline News; HGTV; History Channel; Lifetime; Lifetime Real Women; MSNBC; MTV; National Geographic Channel; Nickelodeon; Oxygen; Speed Channel; Spike TV; Syfy; TBS Superstation; The Learning Channel; Total Living Network; Travel Channel; truTV; Turner Network TV; Univision; USA Network; VH1; Weather Channel.
Fee: $43.75 monthly.

Digital Basic Service
Subscribers: N.A.
Programming (received off-air): KWQC-TV (NBC) Davenport; WFLD (FOX) Chicago; WHBF-TV (CBS) Rock Island; WQAD-TV (ABC) Moline; WTTW (PBS) Chicago.
Programming (via satellite): AmericanLife TV Network; BBC America; Bio; Bloomberg Television; CBS College Sports Network; CMT Pure Country; Cooking Channel; C-SPAN 3; Discovery Digital Networks; Discovery HD Theater; DMX Music; Do-It-Yourself; Encore (multiplexed); ESPN 2 HD; ESPN Classic Sports; ESPN HD; ESPN U; ESPNews; Fox Movie Channel; Fox Soccer; Fuse; G4; GAS; Golf Channel; GSN; Halogen Network; HDNet; HDNet Movies; History Channel International; HorseRacing TV; Independent Film Channel; Lifetime Movie Network; Lifetime Real Women; MTV Networks Digital Suite; NFL Network; Nick Jr.; Nick Too; NickToons TV; Outdoor Channel; Palladia; PBS Kids Sprout; Si TV; SoapNet; Style Network; Sundance Channel; Tennis Channel; Toon Disney; Trinity Broadcasting Network; Turner Classic Movies; Turner Network TV HD; TV Land; TVG Network; Universal HD; Versus; WE tv.
Fee: $15.95 monthly.

Digital Pay Service 1
Pay Units: N.A.
Programming (via satellite): Cinemax; Flix; HBO (multiplexed); Showtime (multiplexed); Starz (multiplexed); The Movie Channel (multiplexed).
Fee: $40.00 installation; $10.00 monthly (each).

Video-On-Demand: Yes

Pay-Per-View
ESPN (delivered digitally), Fee: $3.95; iN DEMAND (delivered digitally); Playboy TV (delivered digitally); Special events (delivered digitally).

Internet Service
Operational: Yes.
Broadband Service: Comcast High Speed Internet.
Fee: $99.95 installation; $44.95 monthly; $10.00 modem lease; $99.95 modem purchase.

Telephone Service
Digital: Operational
Fee: $39.95 monthly

Homes passed & miles of plant included in Rockford
District Director: Joseph Browning. Technical Operations Manager: Lyle Matejewski. Program Director: Janice Schultz. Community & Government Affairs Manager: Joan Sage.
Ownership: Comcast Cable Communications Inc. (MSO).

LAKE BRACKEN—Nova Cablevision Inc., PO Box 1412, 677 W Main St, Galesburg, IL 61401. Phone: 309-342-9681. Fax: 309-342-4408. E-mail: novariocable@hotmail.com. Web Site: http://www.novacablevision.com. ICA: IL0611.
TV Market Ranking: Outside TV Markets (LAKE BRACKEN). Franchise award date:

N.A. Franchise expiration date: N.A. Began: January 1, 1990.

Channel capacity: 40 (operating 2-way). Channels available but not in use: 15.

Basic Service

Subscribers: 200.

Programming (received off-air): KGCW (CW) Burlington; KIIN (PBS) Iowa City; KLJB (CW, FOX) Davenport; KWQC-TV (NBC) Davenport; WEEK-TV (NBC) Peoria; WHBF-TV (CBS) Rock Island; WHOI (ABC, CW) Peoria; WMBD-TV (CBS) Peoria; WQAD-TV (ABC) Moline; WQPT-TV (PBS) Moline; WTVP (PBS) Peoria.

Programming (via satellite): ABC Family Channel; AMC; Animal Planet; Arts & Entertainment; Big Ten Network; CNBC; CNN; Comcast SportsNet Chicago; Comedy Central; Country Music TV; C-SPAN; C-SPAN 2; Discovery Channel; Disney Channel; E! Entertainment Television; ESPN; ESPN 2; Eternal Word TV Network; Food Network; Fox News Channel; Fox Sports Net Midwest; Golf Channel; Great American Country; Hallmark Channel; Headline News; HGTV; History Channel; Home Shopping Network; HorseRacing TV; INSP; Lifetime; MSNBC; MTV; National Geographic Channel; Nickelodeon; QVC; RFD-TV; SoapNet; Speed Channel; Spike TV; Syfy; TBS Superstation; The Learning Channel; The Sportsman Channel; Travel Channel; truTV; Turner Network TV; TV Land; USA Network; VH1; Weather Channel; WGN America.

Fee: $60.00 installation; $44.95 monthly.

Digital Basic Service

Subscribers: N.A.

Programming (via satellite): Bio; Blackbelt TV; Bloomberg Television; CMT Pure Country; Discovery Health Channel; Discovery Kids Channel; Discovery Military Channel; Discovery Planet Green; DMX Music; ESPN 2; ESPN Classic Sports; ESPNews; Fox Movie Channel; Fox Soccer; FSN Digital Atlantic; FSN Digital Central; FSN Digital Pacific; Fuse; G4; Golf Channel; Great American Country; GSN; History Channel; History Channel International; ID Investigation Discovery; Independent Film Channel; Lifetime Movie Network; MTV Hits; MTV2; Nick Jr.; NickToons TV; Outdoor Channel; Science Channel; ShopNBC; Speed Channel; Style Network; Syfy; TeenNick; Toon Disney; Trinity Broadcasting Network; Turner Classic Movies; Versus; VH1 Classic; VH1 Soul; WE tv.

Fee: $16.95 monthly.

Pay Service 1

Pay Units: 4.

Programming (via satellite): Cinemax.

Fee: $11.95 monthly.

Pay Service 2

Pay Units: 19.

Programming (via satellite): HBO.

Fee: $11.95 monthly.

Digital Pay Service 1

Pay Units: N.A.

Programming (via satellite): Cinemax (multiplexed); Encore (multiplexed); Flix; HBO (multiplexed); Showtime (multiplexed); Starz (multiplexed); Sundance Channel; The Movie Channel (multiplexed).

Fee: $12.95 monthly (HBO, Cinemax, Showtime/TMC/Sundance/Flix or Starz/Encore).

Video-On-Demand: No

Pay-Per-View

Club Jenna (delivered digitally); Hot Choice (delivered digitally); iN DEMAND (delivered digitally), Addressable: Yes; Playboy TV (delivered digitally); Fresh (delivered digitally); Spice: Xcess (delivered digitally); sports (delivered digitally).

Internet Service

Operational: Yes. Began: January 1, 2005.

Subscribers: 59.

Fee: $25.00 installation; $34.95-$39.95 monthly.

Telephone Service

None

Miles of Plant: 8.0 (coaxial); None (fiber optic). Homes passed: 271. Total homes in franchised area: 271.

Manager & Chief Technician: Robert G. Fischer Jr.

Ownership: Nova Cablevision Inc. (MSO).

LAKE CAMELOT—Tel-Star Cablevision Inc. Now served by EDWARDS, IL [IL0326]. ICA: IL0536.

LAKE HOLIDAY—Formerly served by Comcast Cable. No longer in operation. ICA: IL0486.

LAKE OF EGYPT—Galaxy Cablevision, 7155 US Hwy 45 S, Carrier Mills, IL 62917. Phone: 618-994-2261. Fax: 618-994-2261. Web Site: http://www.galaxycable.com. Also serves Creal Springs, Goreville, Johnson County (northern portion) & Williamson County (southern portion). ICA: IL0510.

TV Market Ranking: 69 (Creal Springs, Goreville, Johnson County, LAKE OF EGYPT, Williamson County). Franchise award date: N.A. Franchise expiration date: N.A. Began: June 1, 1986.

Channel capacity: 54 (not 2-way capable). Channels available but not in use: None.

Basic Service

Subscribers: 447.

Programming (received off-air): KBSI (FOX) Cape Girardeau; KFVS-TV (CBS, CW) Cape Girardeau; WDKA (MNT) Paducah; WPSD-TV (NBC) Paducah; WSIL-TV (ABC) Harrisburg; WSIU-TV (PBS) Carbondale; WTCT (IND) Marion.

Programming (via satellite): ABC Family Channel; AMC; Animal Planet; Arts & Entertainment; Cartoon Network; CNBC; CNN; Comedy Central; Discovery Channel; Disney Channel; E! Entertainment Television; ESPN; ESPN 2; Fox News Channel; Fuse; FX; Great American Country; Headline News; HGTV; History Channel; Home Shopping Network; Lifetime; Outdoor Channel; TBS Superstation; The Learning Channel; Toon Disney; Turner Classic Movies; Turner Network TV; USA Network; Weather Channel; WGN America.

Fee: $30.00 installation; $39.50 monthly.

Digital Basic Service

Subscribers: 75.

Pay Service 1

Pay Units: N.A.

Programming (via satellite): Cinemax; Encore Action; HBO; Showtime; The Movie Channel.

Video-On-Demand: No

Internet Service

Operational: No.

Telephone Service

None

Miles of Plant: 54.0 (coaxial); None (fiber optic). Homes passed: 1,869.

State Manager: Ward Webb. Technical Manager: Audie Murphy. Customer Service Manager: Malynda Walker. Engineer: John Stewart.

Ownership: Galaxy Cable Inc. (MSO).

LAKE ZURICH—Comcast Cable. Now served by SCHAUMBURG, IL [IL0036]. ICA: IL0047.

LAKEVIEW—RCN Corp. Formerly served by Chicago (portions), IL [IL0061]. This cable system has converted to IPTV, 196 Van Buren St, Herndon, VA 20170. Phone: 703-434-8200. Web Site: http://www.rcn.com. ICA: IL5229.

TV Market Ranking: 3 (LAKEVIEW).

Channel capacity: N.A. Channels available but not in use: N.A.

Internet Service

Operational: Yes.

Fee: $23.00 monthly.

Telephone Service

Digital: Operational

Fee: $30.00 monthly

Chairman: Steven J. Simmons. Chief Executive Officer: Jim Holanda.

Ownership: RCN Corp.

LANSING—Comcast Cable. Now served by CHICAGO (southern suburbs), IL [IL0008]. ICA: IL0060.

LAWRENCEVILLE—Charter Communications. Now served by VINCENNES, IN [IN0035]. ICA: IL0119.

LE ROY—Mediacom, PO Box 334, 609 S 4th St, Chillicothe, IL 61523. Phone: 309-274-4500. Fax: 309-274-3188. Web Site: http://www.mediacomcable.com. Also serves Bellflower, Colfax, Downs, McLean County (portions) & Saybrook. ICA: IL0539.

TV Market Ranking: 64 (Bellflower, LE ROY, McLean County (portions), Saybrook); Below 100 (Colfax, Downs). Franchise award date: N.A. Franchise expiration date: N.A. Began: December 4, 1981.

Channel capacity: 134 (operating 2-way). Channels available but not in use: 12.

Basic Service

Subscribers: 2,206.

Programming (received off-air): WAND (NBC) Decatur; WAOE (MNT) Peoria; WCIA (CBS) Champaign; WEEK-TV (NBC) Peoria; WHOI (ABC, CW) Peoria; WILL-TV (PBS) Urbana; WMBD-TV (CBS) Peoria; WTVP (PBS) Peoria; WYZZ-TV (FOX) Bloomington.

Programming (via satellite): ABC Family Channel; WGN America.

Fee: $45.00 installation; $20.95 monthly.

Expanded Basic Service 1

Subscribers: 1,369.

Programming (via satellite): AMC; AmericanLife TV Network; Animal Planet; Arts & Entertainment; BET Networks; Bravo; Cartoon Network; CNBC; CNN; Comcast SportsNet Chicago; Comedy Central; Country Music TV; C-SPAN; C-SPAN 2; CW+; Discovery Channel; Disney Channel; E! Entertainment Television; ESPN; ESPN 2; Eternal Word TV Network; FitTV; Food Network; Fox News Channel; FX; Hallmark Channel; Headline News; HGTV; History Channel; Home Shopping Network; INSP; ION Television; Jewelry Television; Lifetime; Lifetime Movie Network; MSNBC; MTV; Nickelodeon; Product Information Network; QVC; Radar Channel; ShopNBC; SoapNet; Speed Channel; Spike TV; Syfy; TBS Superstation; The Learning Channel; Travel Channel; Trinity Broadcasting Network; truTV; Turner Network TV; TV Guide Network; TV Land; Univision; USA Network; VH1; WE tv; Weather Channel.

Fee: $34.00 monthly.

Digital Basic Service

Subscribers: 136.

Programming (received off-air): WAND (NBC) Decatur; WEEK-TV (NBC) Peoria; WHOI (ABC, CW) Peoria; WMBD-TV (CBS) Peoria; WTVP (PBS) Peoria; WYZZ-TV (FOX) Bloomington.

Programming (via satellite): ABC News Now; BBC America; Bio; Bloomberg Television; CCTV-9 (CCTV International); College Sports Television; Discovery Health Channel; Discovery Kids Channel; Discovery Military Channel; Discovery Planet Green; Discovery Times Channel; ESPN 2 HD; ESPN HD; ESPN U; ESPNews; Fox College Sports Atlantic; Fox College Sports Central; Fox College Sports Pacific; Fox Movie Channel; Fox Reality Channel; Fox Soccer; Fuel TV; Fuse; G4; Gol TV; Golf Channel; GSN; History Channel International; Independent Film Channel; ION Life; Lifetime Real Women; MTV Hits; MTV2; Music Choice; National Geographic Channel; Nick Jr.; NickToons TV; Outdoor Channel; Qubo; ReelzChannel; Science Channel; Sleuth; Style Network; Sundance Channel; TeenNick; Tennis Channel; The Sportsman Channel; Turner Classic Movies; TVG Network; Versus; VH1 Classic.

Fee: $9.00 monthly.

Digital Expanded Basic Service

Subscribers: N.A.

Programming (via microwave): Universal HD.

Programming (via satellite): Discovery HD Theater; HDNet; HDNet Movies.

Fee: $6.95 monthly.

Digital Pay Service 1

Pay Units: 385.

Programming (via satellite): Cinemax (multiplexed); Cinemax On Demand; Encore (multiplexed); Flix; HBO (multiplexed); HBO HD; HBO on Broadband; Showtime (multiplexed); Showtime HD; Showtime On Demand; Starz (multiplexed); Starz HDTV; Starz On Demand; Sundance Channel; The Movie Channel (multiplexed); The Movie Channel HD; The Movie Channel On Demand.

Fee: $11.95 monthly (HBO, Cinemax, Starz/Encore or Showtime/TMC).

Video-On-Demand: Yes

Pay-Per-View

Addressable homes: 779.

iN DEMAND (delivered digitally), Fee: $3.95, Addressable: Yes; Playboy TV (delivered digitally); Sports PPV (delivered digitally); Ten Clips (delivered digitally); Ten Blox (delivered digitally).

Internet Service

Operational: Yes.

Broadband Service: Mediacom High Speed Internet.

Fee: $59.95 installation; $45.95 monthly.

Telephone Service
Digital: Operational
Miles of Plant: 63.0 (coaxial); 11.0 (fiber optic). Homes passed: 3,652.
Vice President: Don Hagwell. Operations Director: Gary Wightman. Technical Operations Manager: Larry Brackman. Marketing Director: Stephanie Law.
Ownership: Mediacom LLC (MSO).

LEAF RIVER—Grand River Cablevision, PO Box 249, 102 West 2nd St, Leaf River, IL 61047. Phone: 815-738-2225. Fax: 815-738-6060. E-mail: grc@lrnet1.com. Web Site: http://www.grcblvsn.com. ICA: IL0540.
TV Market Ranking: 97 (LEAF RIVER). Franchise award date: N.A. Franchise expiration date: N.A. Began: February 1, 1989.
Channel capacity: 51 (not 2-way capable). Channels available but not in use: N.A.
Basic Service
Subscribers: 120.
Programming (received off-air): WHA-TV (PBS) Madison; WIFR (CBS) Freeport; WMSN-TV (FOX) Madison; WQRF-TV (FOX) Rockford; WREX (CW, NBC) Rockford; WTVO (ABC, MNT) Rockford.
Programming (via satellite): ABC Family Channel; AMC; Arts & Entertainment; CNN; Country Music TV; Discovery Channel; Disney Channel; ESPN; FX; Headline News; MTV; Nickelodeon; Outdoor Channel; SoapNet; Speed Channel; Spike TV; TBS Superstation; The Learning Channel; Toon Disney; Turner Network TV; TV Land; USA Network; VH1; Weather Channel; WGN America.
Fee: $30.00 installation; $25.00 monthly.
Pay Service 1
Pay Units: 12.
Programming (via satellite): Showtime.
Fee: $8.95 monthly.
Pay Service 2
Pay Units: N.A.
Programming (via satellite): Flix; Sundance Channel; The Movie Channel.
Fee: $12.95 monthly.
Video-On-Demand: No
Internet Service
Operational: No.
Telephone Service
None
Miles of Plant: 8.0 (coaxial); 2.0 (fiber optic). Homes passed: 240. Total homes in franchised area: 240.
Manager: K. L. Barney. Chief Technician: Eugene Barney. Customer Service Manager: Peggy Schelling.
Ownership: Grand River Cablevision (MSO).

LENA—Mediacom, 3033 Asbury Rd, Dubuque, IA 52001. Phone: 563-557-8024. Fax: 563-557-7413. Web Site: http://www.mediacomcable.com. Also serves Apple River, Chadwick, Hanover, Lanark, Milledgeville, Mount Carroll, Orangeville, Pecatonica, Shannon, Stephenson County, Stockton, Warren & Winslow, IL; Albany, Albany Twp., Argyle, Blanchardville, Browntown, Martintown & South Wayne, WI. ICA: IL0223.
TV Market Ranking: 93 (Albany, Albany Twp., Blanchardville); 97 (Apple River, Browntown, Chadwick, Hanover, Lanark, LENA, Martintown, Milledgeville, Mount Carroll, Orangeville, Pecatonica, Shannon, South Wayne, Stephenson County, Stockton, Warren, Winslow); Outside TV Markets (Argyle). Franchise award date: January 1, 1982. Franchise expiration date: N.A. Began: January 28, 1983.
Channel capacity: 121 (operating 2-way). Channels available but not in use: 1.
Basic Service
Subscribers: 784.
Programming (received off-air): WHA-TV (PBS) Madison; WIFR (CBS) Freeport; WISC-TV (CBS, MNT) Madison; WMSN-TV (FOX) Madison; WQRF-TV (FOX) Rockford; WREX (CW, NBC) Rockford; WTVO (ABC, MNT) Rockford.
Programming (via satellite): Home Shopping Network; TBS Superstation; Trinity Broadcasting Network; WGN America.
Current originations: Public Access.
Fee: $45.00 installation; $13.95 monthly.
Expanded Basic Service 1
Subscribers: 695.
Programming (via satellite): ABC Family Channel; AMC; Animal Planet; Arts & Entertainment; Cartoon Network; CNBC; CNN; Comcast SportsNet Chicago; Comedy Central; Country Music TV; C-SPAN; Discovery Channel; Disney Channel; E! Entertainment Television; ESPN; ESPN 2; Eternal Word TV Network; Fox News Channel; Fox Sports Net; FX; Hallmark Channel; Halogen Network; Headline News; HGTV; History Channel; Lifetime; MTV; Nickelodeon; QVC; Speed Channel; Spike TV; Syfy; The Learning Channel; Travel Channel; Turner Network TV; TV Land; USA Network; VH1; Weather Channel.
Fee: $24.00 monthly.
Pay Service 1
Pay Units: 332.
Programming (via satellite): Cinemax; Encore; HBO; Showtime; Starz.
Fee: $3.99 monthly (Encore), $5.99 monthly (Starz & Encore), $7.95 monthly (Cinemax), $11.99 monthly (HBO or Showtime).
Video-On-Demand: Yes
Internet Service
Operational: Yes.
Broadband Service: Mediacom High Speed Internet.
Telephone Service
Digital: Operational
Miles of Plant: 6.0 (coaxial); None (fiber optic). Homes passed: 3,684.
Vice President: Scott Westerman. Area Manager: Kathleen McMullen. Chief Technician: Darren Dean.
City fee: 5% of gross.
Ownership: Mediacom LLC (MSO).

LERNA—Formerly served by CableDirect. No longer in operation. ICA: IL0450.

LEWISTOWN—Insight Communications. Now served by CANTON, IL [IL0087]. ICA: IL0156.

LEXINGTON—Mediacom. Now served by FAIRBURY, IL [IL0346]. ICA: IL0240.

LIBERTY—Adams Telephone. This cable system has converted to IPTV. See Liberty, IL [IL5318]. ICA: IL0379.

LIBERTY (village)—Adams Telecom. Formerly [IL0379]. This cable system has converted to IPTV, PO Box 248, 405 Emminga Rd, Golden, IL 62339. Phone: 217-696-4411. E-mail: service@adams.net. Web Site: http://www.adams.net. ICA: IL5318.
Channel capacity: N.A. Channels available but not in use: N.A.
Internet Service
Operational: Yes.
Ownership: Adams Telephone Co-Operative.

LIBERTYVILLE—Comcast Cable. Now served by SCHAUMBURG, IL [IL0036]. ICA: IL0044.

LIMA (village)—Adams Telecom. Formerly served by Golden, IL [IL0257]. This cable system has converted to IPTV, PO Box 248, 405 Emminga Rd, Golden, IL 62339. Phone: 217-696-4411. E-mail: service@adams.net. Web Site: http://www.adams.net. ICA: IL5290.
Channel capacity: N.A. Channels available but not in use: N.A.
Internet Service
Operational: Yes.
Ownership: Adams Telephone Co-Operative.

LINCOLN—Insight Communications. Now served by SPRINGFIELD, IL [IL0016]. ICA: IL0078.

LINCOLN PARK—RCN Corp. Formerly served by Chicago (portions), IL [IL0661]. This cable system has converted to IPTV, 196 Van Buren St, Herndon, VA 20170. Phone: 703-434-8200. Web Site: http://www.rcn.com. ICA: IL5230.
TV Market Ranking: 3 (LINCOLN PARK).
Channel capacity: N.A. Channels available but not in use: N.A.
Internet Service
Operational: Yes.
Fee: $23.00 monthly.
Telephone Service
Digital: Operational
Fee: $30.00 monthly
Chairman: Steven J. Simmons. Chief Executive Officer: Jim Holanda.
Ownership: RCN Corp.

LISLE—Comcast Cable. Now served by OAK BROOK, IL [IL0006]. ICA: IL0054.

LITCHFIELD—NewWave Communications, 1176 E 1500 North Rd, Taylorville, IL 62568. Phones: 573-472-9500 (Corporate Office); 217-287-7992. Fax: 573.481.9809. E-mail: info@newwavecom.com. Web Site: http://www.newwavecom.com. Also serves Montgomery County (portions). ICA: IL0101.
TV Market Ranking: Outside TV Markets (LITCHFIELD, Montgomery County (portions)). Franchise award date: September 1, 1978. Franchise expiration date: N.A. Began: December 1, 1979.
Channel capacity: 118 (not 2-way capable). Channels available but not in use: N.A.
Basic Service
Subscribers: 1,123 Includes Gillespie.
Programming (received off-air): KDNL-TV (ABC) St. Louis; KETC (PBS) St. Louis; KMOV (CBS) St. Louis; KPLR-TV (CW) St. Louis; KSDK (NBC) St. Louis; KTVI (FOX) St. Louis; WICS (ABC) Springfield.
Programming (via satellite): ABC Family Channel; AMC; Arts & Entertainment; CNBC; Country Music TV; ESPN; Lifetime; MTV; Nickelodeon; QVC; Spike TV; Syfy; Turner Network TV; USA Network; VH1.
Current originations: Government Access; Educational Access; Public Access.
Fee: $29.99 installation.
Expanded Basic Service 1
Subscribers: 1,068.
Programming (via satellite): CNN; Comedy Central; Discovery Channel; Disney Channel; Fox News Channel; Fox Sports Net Midwest; Headline News; Home Shopping Network; TBS Superstation; Weather Channel; WGN America.
Fee: $42.99 monthly.
Digital Basic Service
Subscribers: N.A.
Programming (via satellite): AmericanLife TV Network; BBC America; Bio; Bloomberg Television; Bravo; Discovery Digital Networks; DMX Music; FitTV; Fox Movie Channel; Fuse; G4; GAS; Golf Channel; GSN; Halogen Network; HGTV; History Channel; History Channel International; Independent Film Channel; Lifetime Movie Network; MTV Networks Digital Suite; Nick Jr.; Outdoor Channel; Speed Channel; Style Network; Toon Disney; Trinity Broadcasting Network; Turner Classic Movies; Versus; WE tv.
Pay Service 1
Pay Units: 71.
Programming (via satellite): Cinemax.
Fee: $15.00 installation; $11.95 monthly.
Pay Service 2
Pay Units: 122.
Programming (via satellite): HBO.
Fee: $15.00 installation; $11.95 monthly.
Pay Service 3
Pay Units: 77.
Programming (via satellite): Showtime.
Fee: $11.95 monthly.
Pay Service 4
Pay Units: 183.
Programming (via satellite): The Movie Channel.
Fee: $15.00 installation; $11.95 monthly.
Digital Pay Service 1
Pay Units: N.A.
Programming (via satellite): Cinemax (multiplexed); Encore (multiplexed); Flix; HBO (multiplexed); Showtime (multiplexed); Starz (multiplexed); The Movie Channel (multiplexed).
Video-On-Demand: No
Pay-Per-View
iN DEMAND (delivered digitally); Shorteez (delivered digitally); Hot Choice (delivered digitally); ESPN Now (delivered digitally); Playboy TV (delivered digitally); Fresh (delivered digitally).
Internet Service
Operational: No.
Telephone Service
None
Miles of Plant: 41.0 (coaxial); None (fiber optic). Homes passed: 5,855. Total homes in franchised area: 5,274. Homes passed includes Gillespie
Vice President, Operations: Larry Eby. General Manager: Bill Flowers. Technical Operations Manager: Larry Harmon.
City fee: 3% of gross.
Ownership: NewWave Communications (MSO).

LITTLE YORK—Nova Cablevision Inc., PO Box 1412, 677 W Main St, Galesburg, IL 61401. Phone: 309-342-9681. Fax: 309-342-4408. Web Site: http://www.novacablevision.com. ICA: IL0414.

TV Market Ranking: 60 (LITTLE YORK). Franchise award date: N.A. Franchise expiration date: N.A. Began: July 29, 1988.
Channel capacity: 41 (not 2-way capable). Channels available but not in use: N.A.

Basic Service
Subscribers: 46.
Programming (received off-air): Eternal Word TV Network; HorseRacing TV; KGCW (CW) Burlington; KIIN (PBS) Iowa City; KLJB (CW, FOX) Davenport; KWQC-TV (NBC) Davenport; WEEK-TV (NBC) Peoria; WHBF-TV (CBS) Rock Island; WHOI (ABC, CW) Peoria; WMBD-TV (CBS) Peoria; WQAD-TV (ABC) Moline; WQPT-TV (PBS) Moline; WTVP (PBS) Peoria.
Programming (via satellite): ABC Family Channel; AMC; Animal Planet; Arts & Entertainment; Big Ten Network; Cartoon Network; CNBC; CNN; Comcast SportsNet Chicago; Comedy Central; Country Music TV; C-SPAN; C-SPAN 2; Discovery Channel; Disney Channel; Do-It-Yourself; E! Entertainment Television; ESPN; ESPN 2; ESPN U; Food Network; Fox News Channel; Fox Sports Net Midwest; FX; Golf Channel; Great American Country; Hallmark Channel; Headline News; HGTV; History Channel; Home Shopping Network; Lifetime; MSNBC; MTV; National Geographic Channel; Nickelodeon; QVC; RFD-TV; SoapNet; Speed Channel; Spike TV; Syfy; TBS Superstation; The Learning Channel; The Sportsman Channel; Travel Channel; truTV; Turner Network TV; TV Land; USA Network; VH1; Weather Channel; WGN America.
Fee: $60.00 installation; $53.95 monthly.

Digital Basic Service
Subscribers: N.A.
Programming (via satellite): Bio; Bloomberg Television; CMT Pure Country; Discovery Health Channel; Discovery Kids Channel; Discovery Military Channel; Discovery Planet Green; Disney XD; DMX Music; ESPN 2; ESPN Classic Sports; ESPNews; Fox Movie Channel; FSN Digital Atlantic; FSN Digital Central; FSN Digital Pacific; Fuse; G4; Golf Channel; Great American Country; GSN; HGTV; History Channel; History Channel International; ID Investigation Discovery; Independent Film Channel; Lifetime Movie Network; MTV Hits; MTV2; NickToons TV; Noggin; Outdoor Channel; Science Channel; ShopNBC; Speed Channel; Style Network; Syfy; The N; Trinity Broadcasting Network; Turner Classic Movies; Versus; VH1 Classic; VH1 Soul; WE tv.
Fee: $16.95 monthly.

Pay Service 1
Pay Units: 3.
Programming (via satellite): Cinemax; HBO.
Fee: $12.85 monthly (each).

Digital Pay Service 1
Pay Units: N.A.
Programming (via satellite): Cinemax (multiplexed); Encore (multiplexed); Flix; HBO (multiplexed); Showtime (multiplexed); Starz (multiplexed); Sundance Channel; The Movie Channel (multiplexed).
Fee: $12.85 monthly (HBO, Showtime/TMC/Flix/Sundance), Cinemax, or Starz/Encore).
Video-On-Demand: No

Pay-Per-View
Hot Choice (delivered digitally); Playboy TV (delivered digitally); Fresh (delivered digitally); Spice: Xcess (delivered digitally); Club Jenna (delivered digitally).

Internet Service
Operational: Yes. Began: January 1, 2005.
Fee: $30.00 installation; $39.95 monthly; $3.95 modem lease.

Telephone Service
None
Miles of Plant: 3.0 (coaxial); None (fiber optic). Homes passed: 142. Total homes in franchised area: 142.
Manager: Robert G. Fischer Jr. Office Manager: Hazel Harden.
Ownership: Nova Cablevision Inc. (MSO).

LOAMI—Mediacom. Now served by KINCAID, IL [IL0176]. ICA: IL0362.

LONDON MILLS—Mediacom. Now served by ELMWOOD, IL [IL0205]. ICA: IL0387.

LONG POINT (village)—Formerly served by Longview Communications. No longer in operation. ICA: IL0543.

LORAINE (village)—Adams Telecom. Formerly served by Golden, IL [IL0257]. This cable system has converted to IPTV, PO Box 248, 405 Emminga Rd, Golden, IL 62339. Phone: 217-696-4411. E-mail: service@adams.net. Web Site: http://www.adams.net. ICA: IL5319.
Channel capacity: N.A. Channels available but not in use: N.A.

Internet Service
Operational: Yes.
Ownership: Adams Telephone Co-Operative.

LOUISVILLE—Mediacom, PO Box 288, 4290 Blue Stem Rd, Charleston, IL 61920. Phone: 217-348-5533. Fax: 217-345-7074. Web Site: http://www.mediacomcable.com. Also serves Farina. ICA: IL0157.
TV Market Ranking: Outside TV Markets (Farina, LOUISVILLE). Franchise award date: January 1, 1976. Franchise expiration date: N.A. Began: June 15, 1977.
Channel capacity: N.A. Channels available but not in use: N.A.

Basic Service
Subscribers: 1,048.
Programming (received off-air): KDNL-TV (ABC) St. Louis; KMOV (CBS) St. Louis; KPLR-TV (CW) St. Louis; KSDK (NBC) St. Louis; WCIA (CBS) Champaign; WPXS (IND) Mount Vernon; WTHI-TV (CBS) Terre Haute; WTWO (NBC) Terre Haute; WUSI-TV (PBS) Olney.
Programming (via satellite): C-SPAN; Home Shopping Network; QVC; WGN America.
Current originations: Public Access.
Fee: $45.00 installation; $20.95 monthly.

Expanded Basic Service 1
Subscribers: N.A.
Programming (via satellite): ABC Family Channel; AMC; Animal Planet; Arts & Entertainment; BET Networks; Bravo; Cartoon Network; CNBC; CNN; Comedy Central; Country Music TV; C-SPAN 2; Discovery Channel; Disney Channel; E! Entertainment Television; ESPN; ESPN 2; ESPN Classic Sports; Food Network; Fox News Channel; Fox Sports Net Midwest; FX; Hallmark Channel; Headline News; HGTV; History Channel; ION Television; Jewelry Television; Lifetime; Lifetime Movie Network; MSNBC; MTV; Nickelodeon; Oxygen; ShopNBC; Speed Channel; Spike TV; Syfy; TBS Superstation; The Learning Channel; Travel Channel; Trinity Broadcasting Network; truTV; Turner Network TV; TV Land; USA Network; VH1; WE tv; Weather Channel.
Fee: $34.00 monthly.

Digital Basic Service
Subscribers: N.A.
Programming (received off-air): WAND (NBC) Decatur; WCCU (FOX) Urbana; WCIA (CBS) Champaign; WICD (ABC) Champaign; WILL-TV (PBS) Urbana.
Programming (via satellite): ABC News Now; AmericanLife TV Network; BBC America; Bio; Bloomberg Television; CCTV-Entertainment; CMT Pure Country; Discovery Digital Networks; ESPN 2 HD; ESPN HD; ESPNews; FitTV; Fox Movie Channel; Fox Reality Channel; Fox Soccer; Fuse; G4; Golf Channel; GSN; History Channel International; Independent Film Channel; ION Life; Lifetime Real Women; Military History Channel; MTV Hits; MTV2; Music Choice; National Geographic Channel; Nick Jr.; NickToons TV; Outdoor Channel; Qubo; ReelzChannel; Science Channel; Sleuth; Style Network; TeenNick; Toon Disney; Turner Classic Movies; Versus; VH1 Classic.
Fee: $9.00 monthly.

Digital Expanded Basic Service
Subscribers: N.A.
Programming (via satellite): College Sports Television; ESPN U; Fox College Sports Atlantic; Fox College Sports Central; Fox College Sports Pacific; Fuel TV; Gol TV; Tennis Channel; The Sportsman Channel; TVG Network.
Fee: $3.95 monthly.

Digital Expanded Basic Service 2
Subscribers: N.A.
Programming (via satellite): Discovery HD Theater; HDNet; HDNet Movies; Universal HD.
Fee: $6.95 monthly.

Digital Pay Service 1
Pay Units: N.A.
Programming (via satellite): Cinemax (multiplexed); Encore (multiplexed); HBO (multiplexed); HBO HD; Showtime (multiplexed); Showtime HD; Starz (multiplexed); Starz HDTV; The Movie Channel (multiplexed); The Movie Channel HD.
Fee: $11.95 monthly (each).
Video-On-Demand: Yes

Pay-Per-View
iN DEMAND (delivered digitally); Playboy TV (delivered digitally); Ten Clips (delivered digitally); Ten Blox (delivered digitally); ESPN (delivered digitally); HDNet (delivered digitally).

Internet Service
Operational: Yes.
Broadband Service: Mediacom High Speed Internet.
Fee: $59.95 installation; $40.95 monthly.

Telephone Service
Digital: Operational
Fee: $39.95 installation; $39.95 monthly
Miles of Plant: 46.0 (coaxial); None (fiber optic). Homes passed: 1,885. Total homes in franchised area: 1,885.
Area Operations Director: Todd Acker. Technical Operations Manager: Jerry Ferguson.
City fee: 3% of gross.
Ownership: Mediacom LLC (MSO).

LOUISVILLE—Wabash Independent Networks, PO Box 229, 210 S Church St, Louisville, IL 62858. Phones: 800-228-9824; 618-665-3311. Fax: 618-665-4188. E-mail: wabashtel@wabash.net. Web Site: http://www.wabash.net. ICA: IL0684. **Note:** This system is an overbuild.
TV Market Ranking: Outside TV Markets (LOUISVILLE). Franchise award date: N.A. Franchise expiration date: N.A. Began: January 1, 2003.
Channel capacity: N.A. Channels available but not in use: N.A.

Basic Service
Subscribers: 265.
Programming (received off-air): KFVS-TV (CBS, CW) Cape Girardeau; KMOV (CBS) St. Louis; KPLR-TV (CW) St. Louis; KSDK (NBC) St. Louis; ShopNBC; WEHT (ABC) Evansville; WFIE (NBC) Evansville; WSIL-TV (ABC) Harrisburg; WSIU-TV (PBS) Carbondale; WTHI-TV (CBS) Terre Haute; WTVW (FOX) Evansville; WTWO (NBC) Terre Haute.
Programming (via satellite): C-SPAN; C-SPAN 2; Eternal Word TV Network; Home Shopping Network; ION Television; QVC; TBS Superstation; Trinity Broadcasting Network; Weather Channel; WGN America.
Fee: free installation; $19.95 monthly.

Expanded Basic Service 1
Subscribers: N.A.
Programming (via satellite): ABC Family Channel; AMC; Animal Planet; Arts & Entertainment; Big Ten Network; Boomerang; Cartoon Network; CNN; Comedy Central; Country Music TV; Discovery Channel; Disney Channel; Do-It-Yourself; E! Entertainment Television; ESPN; ESPN 2; ESPN Classic Sports; FamilyNet; Food Network; Fox News Channel; Fox Sports Net Midwest; FX; G4; Gospel Music TV; Hallmark Channel; Halogen Network; Headline News; History Channel; Lifetime; MSNBC; MTV; National Geographic Channel; Nickelodeon; Outdoor Channel; Oxygen; Spike TV; The Learning Channel; Travel Channel; truTV; Turner Classic Movies; Turner Network TV; TV Land; USA Network; VH1.
Fee: $19.00 monthly.

Digital Basic Service
Subscribers: N.A.
Programming (via satellite): AZ TV; BBC America; Bio; Bloomberg Television; Bravo; CMT Pure Country; Current; Discovery Health Channel; Discovery Home Channel; Discovery Kids Channel; Discovery Military Channel; DMX Music; ESPNews; FitTV; Fox Movie Channel; Fox Soccer; FSN Digital Atlantic; FSN Digital Central; FSN Digital Pacific; Fuse; Golf Channel; Great American Country; GSN; HGTV; History Channel International; ID Investigation Discovery; Independent Film Channel; Lifetime Movie Network; MTV Hits; MTV2; Nick Jr.; Ovation; RFD-TV; Science Channel; Sleuth; SoapNet; Speed Channel; Style Network; Syfy; TeenNick; The Word Network; Toon Disney; Versus; VH1 Classic; VH1 Soul; WE tv.
Fee: $15.00 monthly.

Pay Service 1
Pay Units: N.A.
Programming (via satellite): HBO; Showtime; The Movie Channel.
Fee: $11.95 monthly (TMC), $12.95 monthly (Showtime), $13.95 monthly (HBO).

Digital Pay Service 1
Pay Units: N.A.
Programming (via satellite): Cinemax (multiplexed); Encore; Flix; HBO (multiplexed); Showtime (multiplexed); Starz (multiplexed); The Movie Channel (multiplexed).
Fee: $11.95 monthly (Cinemax or Starz/Encore), $12.95 monthly (Showtime/TMC/Flix), $13.95 monthly (HBO).
Video-On-Demand: Planned

Pay-Per-View
Club Jenna (delivered digitally); iN DEMAND (delivered digitally); Fresh (delivered digitally); Spice: Xcess (delivered digitally); Playboy TV (delivered digitally).
Internet Service
Operational: Yes.
Broadband Service: In-house.
Fee: $35.00-$50.00 monthly.
Telephone Service
None
General Manager: Dave Grahn. Assistant General Manager: Jeff Williams. Marketing Director: Carol Oestreich. TV/Video Administrator: Don Ross. Controller: Tanya Wells.
Ownership: Wabash Independent Networks (MSO).

LOVINGTON—Moultrie Telecommunications, PO Box 350, 111 State St & Broadway, Lovington, IL 61937. Phone: 217-873-5215. Fax: 217-873-4990. E-mail: dbowers@moultrie.com. Web Site: http://www.moultriemulticorp.com. ICA: IL0544.
TV Market Ranking: 64 (LOVINGTON). Franchise award date: October 13, 1980. Franchise expiration date: N.A. Began: June 26, 1982.
Channel capacity: 54 (operating 2-way). Channels available but not in use: None.
Basic Service
Subscribers: 455.
Programming (received off-air): WAND (NBC) Decatur; WBUI (CW) Decatur; WCIA (CBS) Champaign; WEIU-TV (PBS) Charleston; WICD (ABC) Champaign; WICS (ABC) Springfield; WILL-TV (PBS) Urbana; WRSP-TV (FOX) Springfield; allband FM.
Programming (via satellite): ABC Family Channel; AMC; Country Music TV; Disney Channel; ESPN; ESPN 2; History Channel; Syfy; TBS Superstation; The Learning Channel; Turner Classic Movies; Turner Network TV; Weather Channel; WGN America.
Planned originations: Leased Access; Religious Access; Government Access; Educational Access; Public Access.
Fee: $25.00 installation; $28.97 monthly; $2.00 converter.
Expanded Basic Service 1
Subscribers: 350.
Programming (via satellite): Arts & Entertainment; CNN; Comcast SportsNet Chicago; C-SPAN; Discovery Channel; Nickelodeon; Spike TV; USA Network; VH1.
Fee: $9.44 monthly.
Pay Service 1
Pay Units: 128.
Programming (via satellite): HBO.
Fee: $13.05 monthly.
Video-On-Demand: No
Internet Service
Operational: No, DSL only.
Telephone Service
None
Miles of Plant: 16.0 (coaxial); None (fiber optic). Homes passed: 626. Total homes in franchised area: 626.
Manager & Chief Technician: David A. Bowers. Customer Service Manager: Marcia Franklin.
City fee: 3% of basic.
Ownership: Moultrie Telecommunications Inc.

LOWPOINT—Formerly served by Tel-Star Cablevision Inc. No longer in operation. ICA: IL0545.

MACOMB—Comcast Cable, PO Box 487, 1504 E Jackson St, Macomb, IL 61455. Phone: 309-833-4539. Fax: 309-833-4539. Web Site: http://www.comcast.com. Also serves Blandinsville (village), Bushnell, Colchester, La Harpe & McDonough County. ICA: IL0076.
TV Market Ranking: Below 100 (Blandinsville (village), Colchester, La Harpe, MACOMB, McDonough County (portions)); Outside TV Markets (Bushnell, McDonough County (portions)). Franchise award date: N.A. Franchise expiration date: N.A. Began: June 1, 1966.
Channel capacity: N.A. Channels available but not in use: N.A.
Basic Service
Subscribers: 35,000 Includes Quincy.
Programming (received off-air): KHQA-TV (ABC, CBS) Hannibal; KLJB (CW, FOX) Davenport; WGEM-TV (CW, NBC) Quincy; WMEC (PBS) Macomb; WQAD-TV (ABC) Moline; WTJR (IND) Quincy; allband FM.
Programming (via satellite): C-SPAN; C-SPAN 2; G4; Home Shopping Network; ION Television; QVC; TV Guide Network; WGN America.
Current originations: Government Access; Educational Access.
Fee: $25.00 installation; $3.85 converter.
Expanded Basic Service 1
Subscribers: 4,850.
Programming (via satellite): ABC Family Channel; AMC; Animal Planet; Arts & Entertainment; BET Networks; Cartoon Network; CNBC; CNN; Comcast SportsNet Chicago; Comedy Central; Country Music TV; Discovery Channel; Disney Channel; E! Entertainment Television; ESPN; ESPN 2; Food Network; Fox News Channel; Fox Sports Net Midwest; FX; Hallmark Channel; Headline News; HGTV; History Channel; Lifetime; MSNBC; MTV; National Geographic Channel; Nickelodeon; Oxygen; Spike TV; Syfy; TBS Superstation; The Learning Channel; Travel Channel; Trinity Broadcasting Network; truTV; Turner Classic Movies; Turner Network TV; TV Land; USA Network; VH1; Weather Channel.
Fee: $40.00 monthly.
Digital Basic Service
Subscribers: 1,170.
Programming (via satellite): AmericanLife TV Network; BBC America; Bio; Bloomberg Television; Bravo; CBS College Sports Network; CMT Pure Country; Cooking Channel; Country Music TV; C-SPAN 3; Discovery Digital Networks; Discovery HD Theater; DMX Music; Do-It-Yourself; Encore (multiplexed); Encore Mystery; ESPN 2 HD; ESPN Classic Sports; ESPN HD; ESPN U; ESPNews; Fox College Sports Atlantic; Fox College Sports Central; Fox College Sports Pacific; Fox Movie Channel; Fox Reality Channel; Fox Soccer; Fuse; GAS; Golf Channel; GSN; Halogen Network; HDNet; HDNet Movies; History Channel International; HorseRacing TV; Independent Film Channel; Lifetime Movie Network; Lifetime Real Women; MTV Networks Digital Suite; NFL Network; Nick Jr.; Nick Too; NickToons TV; Outdoor Channel; Ovation; Palladia; PBS Kids Sprout; Si TV; Sleuth; Speed Channel; Style Network; Sundance Channel; Tennis Channel; Toon Disney; Turner Network TV HD; TVG Network; Universal HD; Versus; WE tv.
Fee: $17.00 monthly.
Digital Pay Service 1
Pay Units: N.A.
Programming (via satellite): Cinemax; HBO; HBO HD; Showtime; Showtime HD; Starz; The Movie Channel.

Fee: $10.00 monthly (Cinemax or Starz), $13.00 monthly (HBO or Showtime/TMC).
Video-On-Demand: Yes
Pay-Per-View
ESPN (delivered digitally); iN DEMAND (delivered digitally); Playboy TV (delivered digitally); Special events (delivered digitally).
Internet Service
Operational: Yes.
Broadband Service: Comcast High Speed Internet.
Fee: $99.95 installation; $44.95 monthly; $10.00 modem lease; $99.95 modem purchase.
Telephone Service
None
Miles of Plant: 125.0 (coaxial); 17.0 (fiber optic). Homes passed: 21,600.
General Manager: Dominick Ascone. Chief Technician: Gerry Salfen.
City fee: 5% of gross.
Ownership: Comcast Cable Communications Inc. (MSO).

MAHOMET—Mediacom, PO Box 334, 609 S 4th St, Chillicothe, IL 61523. Phone: 309-274-4500. Fax: 309-274-3188. Web Site: http://www.mediacomcable.com. Also serves Champaign County, Fisher & Lake of the Woods. ICA: IL0115.
TV Market Ranking: 64 (Champaign County, Fisher, Lake of the Woods, MAHOMET). Franchise award date: N.A. Franchise expiration date: N.A. Began: November 1, 1980.
Channel capacity: 134 (operating 2-way). Channels available but not in use: 1.
Basic Service
Subscribers: 3,219.
Programming (received off-air): WAND (NBC) Decatur; WBUI (CW) Decatur; WCCU (FOX) Urbana; WCFN (MNT) Springfield; WCIA (CBS) Champaign; WICD (ABC) Champaign; WILL-TV (PBS) Urbana.
Programming (via satellite): ABC Family Channel; INSP; Radar Channel; WGN America.
Fee: $45.00 installation; $20.95 monthly.
Expanded Basic Service 1
Subscribers: 2,925.
Programming (via satellite): AMC; AmeriCanLife TV Network; Animal Planet; Arts & Entertainment; BET Networks; Bravo; Cartoon Network; CNBC; CNN; Comcast SportsNet Chicago; Comedy Central; Country Music TV; C-SPAN; C-SPAN 2; Discovery Channel; Disney Channel; E! Entertainment Television; ESPN; ESPN 2; Eternal Word TV Network; FitTV; Food Network; Fox News Channel; FX; Hallmark Channel; Headline News; HGTV; History Channel; Home Shopping Network; ION Television; Jewelry Television; Lifetime; Lifetime Movie Network; MSNBC; MTV; Nickelodeon; Product Information Network; QVC; ShopNBC; SoapNet; Speed Channel; Spike TV; Syfy; TBS Superstation; The Learning Channel; Toon Disney; Travel Channel; Trinity Broadcasting Network; truTV; Turner Network TV; TV Guide Network; TV Land; Univision; USA Network; VH1; WE tv; Weather Channel.
Fee: $34.00 monthly.
Digital Basic Service
Subscribers: 255.
Programming (received off-air): WAND (NBC) Decatur; WCCU (FOX) Urbana; WCIA (CBS) Champaign; WICD (ABC) Champaign; WILL-TV (PBS) Urbana.
Programming (via satellite): ABC News Now; BBC America; Bio; Bloomberg Television; CCTV-Entertainment; Discovery Digital Networks; ESPN 2 HD; ESPN HD; ESPNews; Fox Movie Channel; Fox Reality Channel; Fox Soccer; Fuse; G4; Golf Channel; GSN; History Channel International; Independent Film Channel; ION Life; Lifetime Real Women; Military History Channel; MTV Hits; MTV2; Music Choice; National Geographic Channel; Nick Jr.; NickToons TV; Outdoor Channel; Qubo; ReelzChannel; Science Channel; Sleuth; Style Network; Sundance Channel; TeenNick; Turner Classic Movies; Versus; VH1 Classic.
Fee: $9.00 monthly.
Digital Expanded Basic Service
Subscribers: N.A.
Programming (via satellite): College Sports Television; ESPN U; Fox College Sports Atlantic; Fox College Sports Central; Fox College Sports Pacific; Fuel TV; Gol TV; Tennis Channel; The Sportsman Channel; TVG Network.
Fee: $3.95 monthly.
Digital Expanded Basic Service 2
Subscribers: N.A.
Programming (via satellite): Discovery HD Theater; HDNet; HDNet Movies; Universal HD.
Fee: $6.95 monthly.
Digital Pay Service 1
Pay Units: 686.
Programming (via satellite): Cinemax (multiplexed); Encore (multiplexed); Flix; HBO (multiplexed); HBO HD; Showtime (multiplexed); Showtime HD; Starz (multiplexed); Starz HDTV; The Movie Channel (multiplexed); The Movie Channel HD.
Fee: $11.95 monthly (each).
Video-On-Demand: Yes
Pay-Per-View
Addressable homes: 1,118.
Ten Clips (delivered digitally), Addressable: Yes; Ten Blox (delivered digitally); iN DEMAND (delivered digitally); ESPN (delivered digitally); Playboy TV (delivered digitally); Fox Sports Net (delivered digitally).
Internet Service
Operational: Yes.
Broadband Service: Mediacom High Speed Internet.
Fee: $59.95 installation; $45.95 monthly.
Telephone Service
Digital: Operational
Fee: $39.95 installation; $39.95 monthly
Miles of Plant: 86.0 (coaxial); 26.0 (fiber optic). Homes passed: 3,394.
Vice President: Don Hagwell. Marketing Director: Stephanie Law. Operations Director: Gary Wightman. Technical Operations Manager: Larry Brackman.

City fee: 3% of gross.
Ownership: Mediacom LLC (MSO).

MALDEN—HI Cablevision, 102 S Main St, Lostant, IL 61334. Phone: 815-368-3341. Fax: 815-368-3342. Web Site: http://www.hihart.net. ICA: IL0421.
TV Market Ranking: Below 100 (MALDEN). Franchise award date: August 1, 1985. Franchise expiration date: N.A. Began: February 1, 1986.
Channel capacity: 62 (not 2-way capable). Channels available but not in use: None.
Basic Service
Subscribers: 50.
Programming (received off-air): WEEK-TV (NBC) Peoria; WMBD-TV (CBS) Peoria; WQAD-TV (ABC) Moline; WTVP (PBS) Peoria; WYZZ-TV (FOX) Bloomington.
Programming (via satellite): ABC Family Channel; CNN; Country Music TV; Discovery Channel; Disney Channel; ESPN; Fox Sports Net Midwest; Nickelodeon; QVC; Spike TV; TBS Superstation; Turner Network TV; USA Network; WGN America.
Fee: $24.00 monthly.
Pay Service 1
Pay Units: 14.
Programming (via satellite): HBO; Showtime.
Fee: $8.45 installation; $10.45 monthly (Showtime or HBO).
Video-On-Demand: No
Internet Service
Operational: Yes.
Subscribers: 45.
Fee: $20.00 monthly.
Telephone Service
None
Homes passed: 134.
Manager: Fred Hartenbower.
City fee: 3% of gross.
Ownership: Hart Electric Inc. (MSO).

MALTA—Mediacom. Now served by KIRKLAND, IL [IL0277]. ICA: IL0296.

MANCHESTER (village)—Formerly served by Longview Communications. No longer in operation. ICA: IL0548.

MANHATTAN—Kraus Electronics Systems Inc., 305 State St, Manhattan, IL 60442-0011. Phones: 815-478-4444; 815-478-4000. Fax: 815-478-3386. Web Site: http://www.krausonline.com. ICA: IL0252.
TV Market Ranking: 3 (MANHATTAN). Franchise award date: N.A. Franchise expiration date: N.A. Began: September 1, 1981.
Channel capacity: 50 (operating 2-way). Channels available but not in use: N.A.
Basic Service
Subscribers: N.A.
Programming (received off-air): WBBM-TV (CBS) Chicago; WCIU-TV (IND) Chicago; WCPX-TV (ION) Chicago; WFLD (FOX) Chicago; WGBO-DT (UNV) Joliet; WGN-TV (CW, IND) Chicago; WJYS (IND) Hammond; WLS-TV (ABC) Chicago; WPWR-TV (MNT) Gary; WSNS-TV (TMO) Chicago; WTTW (PBS) Chicago; WWTO-TV (TBN) La Salle; WXFT-DT (TEL) Aurora; WYCC (PBS) Chicago; WYIN (PBS) Gary; allband FM.
Programming (via satellite): Headline News; QVC.
Fee: $35.00 installation; $38.00 monthly.
Expanded Basic Service 1
Subscribers: N.A.
Programming (via satellite): AMC; Animal Planet; Arts & Entertainment; Cartoon Network; CNBC; CNN; Comcast SportsNet Chicago; Comedy Central; Country Music TV; C-SPAN; C-SPAN 2; Discovery Channel; Disney Channel; ESPN; ESPN 2; ESPN Classic Sports; Eternal Word TV Network; FamilyNet; Food Network; Fox News Channel; FX; GSN; Hallmark Channel; HGTV; History Channel; Lifetime; MTV; National Geographic Channel; Nickelodeon; Spike TV; Syfy; TBS Superstation; The Learning Channel; truTV; Turner Network TV; TV Land; USA Network; VH1; Weather Channel.
Digital Basic Service
Subscribers: N.A.
Programming (via satellite): AmericanLife TV Network; BBC America; Bio; Bloomberg Television; Bravo; Discovery Home Channel; Discovery Kids Channel; Discovery Military Channel; Discovery Times Channel; DMX Music; ESPNews; FitTV; Fox Movie Channel; Fox Sports World; FSN Digital Atlantic; FSN Digital Central; FSN Digital Pacific; Fuse; G4; GAS; Golf Channel; Great American Country; History Channel; History Channel International; Independent Film Channel; Lifetime Movie Network; MTV Hits; MTV2; Nick Jr.; NickToons TV; Outdoor Channel; Science Television; Style Network; Toon Disney; Trio; Turner Classic Movies; VH1 Classic; VH1 Country; WE tv.
Digital Pay Service 1
Pay Units: N.A.
Programming (via satellite): Cinemax (multiplexed); Encore (multiplexed); HBO (multiplexed); Showtime (multiplexed); Starz (multiplexed); The Movie Channel (multiplexed).
Video-On-Demand: No
Pay-Per-View
Playboy TV (delivered digitally); Fresh (delivered digitally); Shorteez (delivered digitally).
Internet Service
Operational: Yes.
Broadband Service: In-house.
Fee: $9.95-$49.95 monthly.
Telephone Service
Digital: Operational
Fee: $26.95-$34.95 monthly
Miles of Plant: 10.0 (coaxial); None (fiber optic). Additional miles planned: 2.0 (coaxial). Homes passed: 625. Total homes in franchised area: 700.
Manager: Mike Bordeaux. Chief Technician: Skip Kraus.
Ownership: Arthur J. Kraus (MSO).

MANITO—Cass Cable TV Inc. Now served by VIRGINIA, IL [IL0598]. ICA: IL0220.

MANLIUS (village)—Mediacom. Now served by MINERAL, IL [IL0170]. ICA: IL0549.

MANSFIELD—Mediacom. Now served by FARMER CITY, IL [IL0231]. Also serves MANSFIELD. ICA: IL0322.

MAQUON—Mediacom. Now served by ABINGDON, IL [IL0186]. ICA: IL0406.

MARCELLINE—Adams Telecom. Formerly served by Golden, IL [IL0257]. This cable system has converted to IPTV, PO Box 248, 405 Emminga Rd, Golden, IL 62339. Phone: 217-696-4411. E-mail: service@adams.net. Web Site: http://www.adams.net. ICA: IL5320.
Channel capacity: N.A. Channels available but not in use: N.A.
Internet Service
Operational: Yes.
Ownership: Adams Telephone Co-Operative.

MARION—Mediacom, 90 Main St, Benton, KY 42025-1132. Phones: 417-875-5560 (Springfield regional office); 270-527-9939; 618-993-5216 (Local office). Fax: 270-527-0813. Web Site: http://www.mediacomcable.com. Also serves Carterville, Colp (village), Crainville, Eldorado, Energy, Harrisburg, Herrin, Johnston City, West Frankfort, Whiteash & Williamson County. ICA: IL0083.
TV Market Ranking: 60 (Eldorado); 69 (Carterville, Colp (village), Crainville, Energy, Harrisburg, Herrin, Johnston City, MARION, West Frankfort, Whiteash, Williamson County). Franchise award date: May 1, 1971. Franchise expiration date: N.A. Began: May 1, 1971.
Channel capacity: N.A. Channels available but not in use: N.A.
Basic Service
Subscribers: 17,719.
Programming (received off-air): KBSI (FOX) Cape Girardeau; KETC (PBS) St. Louis; KFVS-TV (CBS, CW) Cape Girardeau; WDKA (MNT) Paducah; WPSD-TV (NBC) Paducah; WPXS (IND) Mount Vernon; WQWQ-LP (CW) Paducah; WSIL-TV (ABC) Harrisburg; WSIU-TV (PBS) Carbondale; WTCT (IND) Marion.
Programming (via satellite): QVC; TV Guide Network; WGN America.
Current originations: Educational Access.
Fee: $37.50 installation; $11.72 monthly; $2.00 converter.
Expanded Basic Service 1
Subscribers: 15,652.
Programming (via satellite): ABC Family Channel; AMC; Animal Planet; Arts & Entertainment; BET Networks; Bravo; Cartoon Network; CNBC; CNN; Comedy Central; Country Music TV; C-SPAN; C-SPAN 2; Discovery Channel; Disney Channel; E! Entertainment Television; ESPN; ESPN 2; FitTV; Food Network; Fox News Channel; Fox Sports Net Midwest; FX; Great American Country; GRTV Network; Hallmark Channel; Headline News; HGTV; History Channel; Home Shopping Network; INSP; Lifetime; MSNBC; MTV; Nickelodeon; Outdoor Channel; ShopNBC; SoapNet; Speed Channel; Spike TV; Syfy; TBS Superstation; The Learning Channel; Travel Channel; Trinity Broadcasting Network; truTV; Turner Network TV; TV Land; USA Network; VH1; WE tv; Weather Channel.
Fee: $28.53 monthly.
Digital Basic Service
Subscribers: N.A.
Programming (via satellite): BBC America; Bio; Bloomberg Television; Discovery Health Channel; Discovery Home Channel; Discovery Kids Channel; Discovery Times Channel; Fox Movie Channel; Fox Soccer; Fuse; G4; GAS; Golf Channel; History Channel International; Independent Film Channel; Lifetime Movie Network; MTV Networks Digital Suite; Music Choice; National Geographic Channel; Nick Jr.; NickToons TV; Science Television; Style Network; Turner Classic Movies; Versus.
Digital Pay Service 1
Pay Units: N.A.
Programming (via satellite): Cinemax (multiplexed); Encore (multiplexed); Flix; HBO (multiplexed); Showtime (multiplexed); Starz (multiplexed); Sundance Channel; The Movie Channel (multiplexed).
Video-On-Demand: Yes
Pay-Per-View
Fresh.
Internet Service
Operational: Yes.
Broadband Service: Mediacom High Speed Internet.
Telephone Service
Analog: Not Operational
Digital: Operational
Miles of Plant: 420.0 (coaxial); None (fiber optic). Homes passed: 23,530. Total homes in franchised area: 24,850.
Regional Vice President: Bill Copeland. General Manager: Dale Haney. Regional Technical Operations Director: Alan Freedman. Marketing Director: Will Kuebler. Marketing Manager: Melanie Westerman. Technical Operations Manager: Jeff Brown.
City fee: 5% of gross.
Ownership: Mediacom LLC (MSO).

MAROA—Crystal Broadband Networks, PO Box 180336, Chicago, IL 60618. Phones: 877-319-0328; 630-206-0447. E-mail: techsupport.cbn@gmail.com. Web Site: http://crystalbn.com. ICA: IL0263.
TV Market Ranking: 64 (MAROA). Franchise award date: N.A. Franchise expiration date: N.A. Began: March 1, 1982.
Channel capacity: 42 (not 2-way capable). Channels available but not in use: N.A.
Basic Service
Subscribers: 293.
Programming (received off-air): WAND (NBC) Decatur; WBUI (CW) Decatur; WCFN (MNT) Springfield; WCIA (CBS) Champaign; WICS (ABC) Springfield; WILL-TV (PBS) Urbana; WRSP-TV (FOX) Springfield.
Programming (via satellite): C-SPAN; Home Shopping Network; WGN America.
Fee: $29.95 installation; $19.95 monthly.
Expanded Basic Service 1
Subscribers: N.A.
Programming (via satellite): ABC Family Channel; AMC; Arts & Entertainment; CNN; Country Music TV; Discovery Channel; Disney Channel; ESPN; ESPN 2; Fox Sports Net Midwest; INSP; Lifetime; MSNBC; MTV; Nickelodeon; Radar Channel; SoapNet; Spike TV; Syfy; TBS Superstation; The Learning Channel; Toon Disney; Trinity Broadcasting Network; Turner Network TV; TV Land; USA Network; VH1; Weather Channel.
Fee: $22.00 monthly.
Pay Service 1
Pay Units: 34.
Programming (via satellite): Cinemax; Encore; HBO.
Fee: $3.99 monthly (Encore), $9.49 monthly (Cinemax), $13.49 monthly (HBO).
Video-On-Demand: No
Internet Service
Operational: Yes.
Telephone Service
Digital: Operational
Miles of Plant: 8.0 (coaxial); None (fiber optic). Homes passed: 566.
General Manager: Nidhin Johnson. Program Manager: Shawn Smith.
City fee: 3% of gross.
Ownership: Crystal Broadband Networks (MSO).

MARTINSVILLE—Mediacom, PO Box 288, 4290 Blue Stem Rd, Charleston, IL 61920. Phone: 217-348-5533. Fax: 217-345-7074. Web Site: http://www.mediacomcable.com. Also serves Casey, Clark County & Marshall. ICA: IL0217.
TV Market Ranking: Below 100 (Casey, Clark County (portions), Marshall, MARTINSVILLE); Outside TV Markets (Clark County (portions)). Franchise award date:

January 1, 1982. Franchise expiration date: N.A. Began: January 11, 1982.
Channel capacity: N.A. Channels available but not in use: N.A.

Basic Service
Subscribers: 1,485.
Programming (received off-air): WBUI (CW) Decatur; WCFN (MNT) Springfield; WCIA (CBS) Champaign; WEIU-TV (PBS) Charleston; WFXW (FOX) Terre Haute; WICD (ABC) Champaign; WSIU-TV (PBS) Carbondale; WTHI-TV (CBS) Terre Haute; WTWO (NBC) Terre Haute; 6 FMs.
Programming (via satellite): C-SPAN; Home Shopping Network; INSP; QVC; TV Guide Network; WGN America.
Fee: $45.00 installation; $20.95 monthly.

Expanded Basic Service 1
Subscribers: N.A.
Programming (via satellite): ABC Family Channel; AMC; Animal Planet; Arts & Entertainment; BET Networks; Bravo; Cartoon Network; CNBC; CNN; Comedy Central; Country Music TV; C-SPAN 2; Discovery Channel; Disney Channel; E! Entertainment Television; ESPN; ESPN 2; ESPN Classic Sports; Eternal Word TV Network; FitTV; Food Network; Fox News Channel; Fox Sports Net Midwest; FX; Hallmark Channel; Headline News; HGTV; History Channel; ION Television; Jewelry Television; Lifetime; Lifetime Movie Network; MSNBC; MTV; Nickelodeon; Outdoor Channel; Oxygen; Product Information Network; ShopNBC; Speed Channel; Spike TV; Syfy; TBS Superstation; The Learning Channel; Travel Channel; Trinity Broadcasting Network; truTV; Turner Network TV; TV Land; USA Network; VH1; WE tv; Weather Channel.
Fee: $34.00 monthly.

Digital Basic Service
Subscribers: N.A.
Programming (received off-air): WAND (NBC) Decatur; WCCU (FOX) Urbana; WCIA (CBS) Champaign; WICD (ABC) Champaign; WILL-TV (PBS) Urbana.
Programming (via satellite): ABC News Now; AmericanLife TV Network; BBC America; Bio; Bloomberg Television; CCTV-9 (CCTV International); CMT Pure Country; Discovery Health Channel; Discovery Kids Channel; Discovery Military Channel; Discovery Planet Green; Discovery Times Channel; ESPN U; ESPNews; FitTV; Fox Movie Channel; Fox Reality Channel; Fox Soccer; Fuel TV; Fuse; G4; Golf Channel; GSN; History Channel International; Independent Film Channel; ION Life; Lifetime Real Women; MTV Hits; MTV2; Music Choice; National Geographic Channel; Nick Jr.; NickToons TV; Qubo; ReelzChannel; Science Channel; Sleuth; Style Network; TeenNick; Turner Classic Movies; TVG Network; Versus; VH1 Classic.
Fee: $9.00 monthly.

Digital Expanded Basic Service
Subscribers: N.A.
Programming (via satellite): College Sports Television; ESPN U; Fox College Sports Atlantic; Fox College Sports Central; Fox College Sports Pacific; Fuel TV; Gol TV; Tennis Channel; The Sportsman Channel; TVG Network.
Fee: $3.95 monthly.

Digital Expanded Basic Service 2
Subscribers: N.A.
Programming (via satellite): Discovery HD Theater; ESPN 2 HD; ESPN HD; HDNet; HDNet Movies; Universal HD.
Fee: $6.95 monthly.

Digital Pay Service 1
Pay Units: N.A.
Programming (via satellite): Cinemax (multiplexed); Cinemax On Demand; Encore (multiplexed); HBO (multiplexed); HBO HD; HBO On Demand; Showtime (multiplexed); Showtime HD; Showtime On Demand; Starz (multiplexed); Starz HDTV; Starz On Demand; The Movie Channel (multiplexed); The Movie Channel HD; The Movie Channel On Demand.
Fee: $11.95 monthly (each).

Video-On-Demand: Yes

Internet Service
Operational: Yes. Began: November 1, 2002.
Broadband Service: Mediacom High Speed Internet.
Fee: $59.95 installation; $40.95 monthly.

Telephone Service
Digital: Operational
Fee: $39.95 installation; $39.95 monthly
Miles of Plant: 42.0 (coaxial); None (fiber optic).
Area Operations Director: Todd Acker. Technical Operations Manager: Jerry Ferguson.
City fee: 3% of gross.
Ownership: Mediacom LLC (MSO).

MARTINTON (village)—Formerly served by CableDirect. No longer in operation. ICA: IL0552.

MARYVILLE—Charter Communications, 941 Charter Commons Dr, Saint Louis, MO 63017. Phone: 636-207-7044. Fax: 636-230-7034. Web Site: http://www.charter.com. Also serves Caseyville, Collinsville, Dupo, Edwardsville, Glen Carbon, Granite City, Highland, Hollywood Heights, Madison, Madison County, Marine, Millstadt (portions), Pontoon Beach, St. Clair County, St. Jacob, Troy & Venice. ICA: IL0018.
TV Market Ranking: 11 (Caseyville, Collinsville, Dupo, Edwardsville, Glen Carbon, Granite City, Highland, Hollywood Heights, Madison, Madison County (portions), Marine, MARYVILLE, Millstadt (portions), Pontoon Beach, St. Clair County, St. Jacob, Troy, Venice); Below 100 (Madison County (portions)). Franchise award date: N.A. Franchise expiration date: N.A. Began: December 1, 1979.
Channel capacity: 81 (operating 2-way). Channels available but not in use: None.

Basic Service
Subscribers: 38,449.
Programming (received off-air): KDNL-TV (ABC) St. Louis; KETC (PBS) St. Louis; KMOV (CBS) St. Louis; KNLC (IND) St. Louis; KPLR-TV (CW) St. Louis; KSDK (NBC) St. Louis; KTVI (FOX) St. Louis; WPXS (IND) Mount Vernon; WRBU (MNT) East St. Louis; 1 FM.
Programming (via satellite): C-SPAN; C-SPAN 2; Eternal Word TV Network; GRTV Network; Home Shopping Network; INSP; Jewelry Television; QVC; ShopNBC; TBS Superstation; Trinity Broadcasting Network; TV Guide Network; Univision; Weatherscan; WGN America.
Current originations: Leased Access; Religious Access; Government Access; Educational Access; Public Access.
Fee: $29.99 installation.

Expanded Basic Service 1
Subscribers: N.A.
Programming (via satellite): ABC Family Channel; AMC; Animal Planet; Arts & Entertainment; BET Networks; Bravo; Cartoon Network; CNBC; CNN; Comedy Central; Country Music TV; Discovery Channel; Disney Channel; E! Entertainment Television; ESPN; ESPN 2; Food Network; Fox Movie Channel; Fox News Channel; Fox Sports Net Midwest; FX; G4; Golf Channel; GSN; Hallmark Channel; Headline News; HGTV; History Channel; Lifetime; MSNBC; MTV; National Geographic Channel; Nickelodeon; Oxygen; SoapNet; Speed Channel; Spike TV; Style Network; Syfy; The Learning Channel; Toon Disney; Travel Channel; truTV; Turner Classic Movies; Turner Network TV; TV Land; USA Network; Versus; VH1; WE tv; Weather Channel.
Fee: $49.99 monthly.

Digital Basic Service
Subscribers: N.A.
Programming (via satellite): BBC America; Bio; Bloomberg Television; Discovery Digital Networks; Do-It-Yourself; Encore Action; ESPN Classic Sports; FitTV; Fox College Sports Atlantic; Fox College Sports Central; Fox College Sports Pacific; Fox Sports World; Fuel TV; Fuse; GAS; Great American Country; History Channel International; Independent Film Channel; International Television (ITV); Lifetime Movie Network; MTV Networks Digital Suite; Music Choice; NFL Network; Nick Jr.; Nick Too; NickToons TV; Sundance Channel; TV Guide Interactive Inc.

Digital Pay Service 1
Pay Units: 19,655.
Programming (via satellite): Cinemax (multiplexed); HBO (multiplexed); Showtime (multiplexed); Starz (multiplexed); The Movie Channel (multiplexed).
Fee: $10.95 monthly (HBO, Showtime or TMC).

Video-On-Demand: Yes

Pay-Per-View
Addressable homes: 25,400.
iN DEMAND (delivered digitally), Addressable: Yes; Fresh (delivered digitally); ESPN Now (delivered digitally); Sports PPV (delivered digitally); Playboy TV (delivered digitally); Shorteez (delivered digitally).

Internet Service
Operational: Yes.
Broadband Service: Charter Pipeline.
Fee: $39.99 monthly; $5.00 modem lease; $99.99 modem purchase.

Telephone Service
Digital: Operational
Fee: $29.99 monthly
Miles of Plant: 954.0 (coaxial); None (fiber optic). Homes passed: 64,666.
Vice President & General Manager: Steve Trippe. Operations Director: Tom Williams. Marketing Director: Beverly Wall.
City fee: 3% of gross.
Ownership: Charter Communications Inc. (MSO).

MASON—West Shore Cable TV Inc., 2358 Gatetree Ln SE, Grand Rapids, MI 49546. E-mail: westshorecabletv@yahoo.com. ICA: IL0242.
TV Market Ranking: Outside TV Markets (MASON). Franchise award date: N.A. Franchise expiration date: N.A. Began: N.A.
Channel capacity: N.A. Channels available but not in use: N.A.

Basic Service
Subscribers: 1,437.
Programming (received off-air): WFXW (FOX) Terre Haute; WPXS (IND) Mount Vernon; WTHI-TV (CBS) Terre Haute; WTWO (NBC) Terre Haute; WUSI-TV (PBS) Olney.
Programming (via satellite): ABC Family Channel; AMC; CNBC; CNN; C-SPAN; ESPN; Home Shopping Network; TBS Superstation; WGN America.
Current originations: Government Access; Educational Access; Public Access.
Fee: $29.95 installation; $19.95 monthly.

Expanded Basic Service 1
Subscribers: 827.
Programming (via satellite): Arts & Entertainment; History Channel International; Lifetime; MTV; National Geographic Channel; Nickelodeon; VH1.
Fee: $12.95 monthly.

Pay Service 1
Pay Units: N.A.
Programming (via satellite): Cinemax; HBO; Showtime.

Internet Service
Operational: No.
Miles of Plant: 26.0 (coaxial); None (fiber optic). Homes passed: 1,755.
Manager: Lisa Jenkins. Chief Technician: Todd Peterson. Marketing Manager: Mark Stevens.
City fee: 2% of gross.
Ownership: South Shore Cable TV Inc. (MSO).

MASON CITY—Greene County Cable. Now served by VIRGINIA, IL [IL0598]. ICA: IL0209.

MATTESON—Comcast Cable. Now served by CHICAGO (southern suburbs), IL [IL0008]. ICA: IL0028.

MATTOON—Mediacom, PO Box 288, 4290 Blue Stem Rd, Charleston, IL 61920. Phone: 217-348-5533. Fax: 217-345-7074. Web Site: http://www.mediacomcable.com. Also serves Coles County. ICA: IL0072.
TV Market Ranking: 64 (Coles County (portions)); Below 100 (Coles County (portions)); Outside TV Markets (MATTOON, Coles County (portions)). Franchise award date: N.A. Franchise expiration date: N.A. Began: May 1, 1967.
Channel capacity: N.A. Channels available but not in use: N.A.

Basic Service
Subscribers: 5,642.
Programming (received off-air): WAND (NBC) Decatur; WBUI (CW) Decatur; WCCU (FOX) Urbana; WCFN (MNT) Springfield; WCIA (CBS) Champaign; WEIU-TV (PBS) Charleston; WICD (ABC) Champaign; WILL-TV (PBS) Urbana; WSIU-TV (PBS) Carbondale; WTHI-TV (CBS) Terre Haute; WTWO (NBC) Terre Haute; 11 FMs.
Programming (via satellite): C-SPAN; Home Shopping Network; INSP; QVC; TV Guide Network; WGN America.
Fee: $45.00 installation; $20.95 monthly; $.91 converter.

Expanded Basic Service 1
Subscribers: N.A.
Programming (via satellite): ABC Family Channel; AMC; Animal Planet; Arts & Entertainment; BET Networks; Cartoon Network; CNBC; CNN; Comcast SportsNet Chicago; Country Music TV; C-SPAN 2; Discovery Channel; Disney Channel; E! Entertainment Television; ESPN; ESPN 2; ESPN Classic Sports; Eternal Word TV Network; FitTV; Food Network; Fox News Channel; Fox Sports Net Midwest; FX; Hallmark Channel; Headline News; HGTV; History Channel; ION Television; Jewelry Television; Lifetime; Lifetime Movie Network; MSNBC; MTV; Nickelodeon; Outdoor Channel; Oxygen; Product Information Network; ShopNBC; Speed Channel; Spike TV; Syfy; TBS Superstation; The Learning Channel; Travel Channel; Trinity Broadcasting Network; truTV; Turner Network TV; TV

Land; USA Network; VH1; WE tv; Weather Channel.
Fee: $34.00 monthly.

Digital Basic Service
Subscribers: N.A.
Programming (received off-air): WAND (NBC) Decatur; WCCU (FOX) Urbana; WCIA (CBS) Champaign; WICD (ABC) Champaign; WILL-TV (PBS) Urbana; WTHI-TV (CBS) Terre Haute.
Programming (via satellite): ABC News Now; AmericanLife TV Network; BBC America; Bio; Bloomberg Television; Bravo; CBS College Sports Network; CCTV-9 (CCTV International); CMT Pure Country; Discovery HD Theater; Discovery Health Channel; Discovery Kids Channel; Discovery Military Channel; Discovery Planet Green; Discovery Times Channel; ESPN 2 HD; ESPN HD; ESPN U; ESPNews; Fox College Sports Atlantic; Fox College Sports Central; Fox College Sports Pacific; Fox Movie Channel; Fox Reality Channel; Fox Soccer; Fuel TV; Fuse; G4; Gol TV; Golf Channel; GSN; HDNet; HDNet Movies; History Channel International; Independent Film Channel; ION Life; Lifetime Real Women; MTV Hits; MTV2; Music Choice; National Geographic Channel; Nick Jr.; NickToons TV; Qubo; ReelzChannel; Science Channel; Sleuth; Style Network; TeenNick; Tennis Channel; The Sportsman Channel; Toon Disney; Turner Classic Movies; TVG Network; Universal HD; Versus; VH1 Classic.
Fee: $9.00 monthly.

Digital Pay Service 1
Pay Units: N.A.
Programming (via satellite): Cinemax (multiplexed); Cinemax On Demand; Encore (multiplexed); HBO (multiplexed); HBO HD; HBO On Demand; Showtime (multiplexed); Showtime HD; Showtime On Demand; Starz (multiplexed); Starz HDTV; Starz On Demand; The Movie Channel (multiplexed); The Movie Channel HD; The Movie Channel On Demand.
Fee: $11.95 monthly (HBO, Cinemax, Showtime/TMC or Starz/Encore).

Video-On-Demand: Yes

Pay-Per-View
iN DEMAND (delivered digitally); Playboy TV (delivered digitally); Ten Clips (delivered digitally); Ten Blox (delivered digitally); ESPN (delivered digitally).

Internet Service
Operational: Yes. Began: December 1, 2002.
Subscribers: 988.
Broadband Service: Mediacom High Speed Internet.
Fee: $59.95 installation; $40.95 monthly.

Telephone Service
Digital: Operational
Fee: $39.95 installation; $39.95 monthly

Miles of Plant: 332.0 (coaxial); 18.0 (fiber optic). Homes passed: 8,385. Total homes in franchised area: 11,086.
Area Operations Manager: Todd Acker. Technical Operations Manager: Jerry Ferguson.
City fee: 5% of gross.
Ownership: Mediacom LLC (MSO).

MAYWOOD—Comcast Cable. Now served by OAK BROOK, IL [IL0006]. ICA: IL0071.

MAZON (village)—Formerly served by CableDirect. No longer in operation. ICA: IL0553.

McHENRY—Comcast Cable. Now served by SCHAUMBURG, IL [IL0036]. ICA: IL0034.

MCLEANSBORO—NewWave Communications, 318 N 4th St, Vandalia, IL 62471. Phone: 573-472-9500. Fax: 618.283.4483. E-mail: info@newwavecom.com. Web Site: http://www.newwavecom.com. ICA: IL0177.
TV Market Ranking: 69 (MCLEANSBORO). Franchise award date: N.A. Franchise expiration date: N.A. Began: October 1, 1980.
Channel capacity: 118 (not 2-way capable). Channels available but not in use: N.A.

Basic Service
Subscribers: 565.
Programming (received off-air): KBSI (FOX) Cape Girardeau; KFVS-TV (CBS, CW) Cape Girardeau; WDKA (MNT) Paducah; WEVV-TV (CBS, MNT) Evansville; WPSD-TV (NBC) Paducah; WPXS (IND) Mount Vernon; WSIL-TV (ABC) Harrisburg; WSIU-TV (PBS) Carbondale; WTCT (IND) Marion; WTVW (FOX) Evansville; 1 FM.
Programming (via satellite): C-SPAN; Home Shopping Network; INSP; QVC; Trinity Broadcasting Network; WGN America.
Fee: $17.45 monthly.

Expanded Basic Service 1
Subscribers: 502.
Programming (via satellite): ABC Family Channel; AMC; Animal Planet; Arts & Entertainment; Big Ten Network; Bravo; Cartoon Network; CNBC; CNN; Comedy Central; Country Music TV; Discovery Channel; Disney Channel; E! Entertainment Television; ESPN; ESPN 2; ESPN Classic Sports; Eternal Word TV Network; Food Network; Fox News Channel; Fox Sports Net Midwest; FX; Golf Channel; GSN; Hallmark Channel; Headline News; HGTV; History Channel; Lifetime; MSNBC; MTV; National Geographic Channel; Nickelodeon; Outdoor Channel; Oxygen; ShopNBC; SoapNet; Speed Channel; Spike TV; Syfy; TBS Superstation; The Learning Channel; Toon Disney; Travel Channel; truTV; Turner Classic Movies; Turner Network TV; TV Land; USA Network; Versus; VH1; Weather Channel.
Fee: $12.95 monthly.

Digital Basic Service
Subscribers: 49.
Programming (received off-air): KBSI (FOX) Cape Girardeau; KFVS-TV (CBS, CW) Cape Girardeau; WPSD-TV (NBC) Paducah; WSIL-TV (ABC) Harrisburg; WSIU-TV (PBS) Carbondale.
Programming (via satellite): BBC America; Bio; Bloomberg Television; CMT Pure Country; Cooking Channel; Discovery HD Theater; Discovery Health Channel; Discovery Kids Channel; Discovery Military Channel; Discovery Planet Green; Do-It-Yourself; ESPN 2 HD; ESPN HD; ESPNews; FitTV; Fox College Sports Atlantic; Fox College Sports Central; Fox College Sports Pacific; Fox Movie Channel; FSN HD; G4; Great American Country; Halogen Network; HDNet; HDNet Movies; History Channel International; ID Investigation Discovery; Independent Film Channel; Lifetime Movie Network; MTV Hits; MTV Jams; MTV2; Music Choice; Nick Jr.; Nick Too; NickToons TV; RFD-TV; Science Channel; Sleuth; Style Network; TeenNick; Turner Network TV HD; Universal HD; USA Network HD; VH1 Classic; VH1 Soul; WE tv.
Fee: $19.55 monthly.

Digital Pay Service 1
Pay Units: N.A.
Programming (via satellite): Cinemax (multiplexed); Cinemax HD; Encore (multiplexed); Flix; HBO (multiplexed); HBO HD; Showtime (multiplexed); Starz (multiplexed); Starz HDTV; The Movie Channel (multiplexed).

Video-On-Demand: No

Pay-Per-View
iN DEMAND (delivered digitally); Spice: Xcess (delivered digitally); Club Jenna (delivered digitally); Shorteez (delivered digitally); Playboy TV (delivered digitally); Fresh (delivered digitally).

Internet Service
Operational: Yes.

Telephone Service
Digital: Operational

Miles of Plant: 29.0 (coaxial); 2.0 (fiber optic). Homes passed: 1,738.
General Manager: Bill Flowers. Technical Operations Manager: Chris Mooday.
City fee: 3% of gross.
Ownership: NewWave Communications (MSO).

MCNABB—McNabb Cable & Satellite Inc., PO Box 218, 308 W Main St, Mc Nabb, IL 61335-0218. Phone: 815-882-2202. Fax: 815-882-2141. ICA: IL0431.
TV Market Ranking: Below 100 (MCNABB). Franchise award date: September 19, 1984. Franchise expiration date: N.A. Began: January 1, 1985.
Channel capacity: 36 (not 2-way capable). Channels available but not in use: 11.

Basic Service
Subscribers: 94.
Programming (received off-air): WAOE (MNT) Peoria; WEEK-TV (NBC) Peoria; WHOI (ABC, CW) Peoria; WMBD-TV (CBS) Peoria; WTVP (PBS) Peoria; WYZZ-TV (FOX) Bloomington.
Programming (via satellite): ABC Family Channel; AMC; Arts & Entertainment; Bravo; CNN; Comcast SportsNet Chicago; Comedy Central; Country Music TV; Discovery Channel; Disney Channel; ESPN; ESPN 2; Fox News Channel; History Channel; Lifetime; MSNBC; MTV; Nickelodeon; QVC; Spike TV; Syfy; TBS Superstation; The Learning Channel; Travel Channel; Turner Network TV; TV Land; USA Network; VH1; Weather Channel; WGN America.
Fee: $35.00 installation; $24.20 monthly.

Pay Service 1
Pay Units: 26.
Programming (via satellite): Cinemax.
Fee: $9.00 installation; $9.00 monthly.

Pay Service 2
Pay Units: N.A.
Programming (via satellite): HBO.
Fee: $9.00 monthly.

Video-On-Demand: No

Internet Service
Operational: No.

Telephone Service
None

Miles of Plant: 5.0 (coaxial); None (fiber optic). Homes passed: 114.
Manager: Jackie Smith. Chief Technician: David Haworth. Marketing Director: Bertie Soeder.
City fee: 3% of gross.
Ownership: McNabb Cable & Satellite Inc. (MSO).

MEDORA—Formerly served by CableDirect. No longer in operation. ICA: IL0441.

MELVIN—Mediacom. Now served by FARMER CITY, IL [IL0231]. ICA: IL0377.

MENDON (village)—Adams Telecom. Formerly served by Golden, IL [IL0257]. This cable system has converted to IPTV, PO Box 248, 405 Emminga Rd, Golden, IL 62339. Phone: 217-696-4411. E-mail: service@adams.net. Web Site: http://www.adams.net. ICA: IL5321.
Channel capacity: N.A. Channels available but not in use: N.A.

Internet Service
Operational: Yes.

Ownership: Adams Telephone Co-Operative.

MIDDLETOWN—Mediacom. Now served by DELAVAN, IL [IL0172]. ICA: IL0383.

MILL SHOALS—Formerly served by CableDirect. No longer in operation. ICA: IL0410.

MILLINGTON—Comcast Cable. Now served by OAK BROOK, IL [IL0006]. ICA: IL0556.

MILTON—Cass Cable TV Inc. No longer in operation. ICA: IL0417.

MINERAL—Mediacom, 3900 26th Ave, Moline, IL 61265. Phone: 309-797-2580. Fax: 309-797-2414. Web Site: http://www.mediacomcable.com. Also serves Aledo, Alexis, Altona, Andover, Annawan, Atkinson, Boden, Bradford, Buda, Cambridge, Cordova, Frye Lake, Galva, Geneseo, Henry County (unincorporated areas), Hillsdale, Manlius (village), Matherville, Mobet, Neponset, Port Bryon, Preemption, Rapids City, Reynolds, Sheffield, Sherrard, Viola & Walnut. ICA: IL0170.
TV Market Ranking: 60 (Aledo, Alexis, Altona, Andover, Annawan, Atkinson, Boden, Cambridge, Cordova, Frye Lake, Galva, Geneseo, Henry County (unincorporated areas), Hillsdale, Matherville, MINERAL, Mobet, Port Byron, Preemption, Rapids City, Reynolds, Sherrard, Viola); 83 (Bradford); Below 100 (Buda, Manlius (village), Sheffield, Walnut); Outside TV Markets (Neponset). Franchise award date: December 1, 1982. Franchise expiration date: N.A. Began: February 1, 1983.
Channel capacity: 83 (operating 2-way). Channels available but not in use: None.

Basic Service
Subscribers: 7,968.
Programming (received off-air): KGCW (CW) Burlington; KIIN (PBS) Iowa City; KLJB (CW, FOX) Davenport; KWQC-TV (NBC) Davenport; WBQD-LP Davenport; WHBF-TV (CBS) Rock Island; WQAD-TV (ABC) Moline; WQPT-TV (PBS) Moline.
Programming (via satellite): Home Shopping Network; TBS Superstation; Trinity Broadcasting Network; WGN America.
Fee: $45.00 installation; $13.95 monthly.

Expanded Basic Service 1
Subscribers: 6,674.
Programming (via satellite): ABC Family Channel; AMC; AmericanLife TV Network; Animal Planet; Arts & Entertainment; Bravo; Cartoon Network; CNBC; CNN; Comcast SportsNet Chicago; Comedy Central; Country Music TV; C-SPAN; C-SPAN 2; Discovery Channel; Disney Channel; E! Entertainment Television; ESPN; ESPN 2; Eternal Word TV Network; Food Network; Fox News Channel; Fox Sports Net Midwest; FX; Hallmark Channel; Headline News; HGTV; History Channel; INSP; Lifetime; MSNBC; MTV; Nickelodeon; Product Information Network; QVC; SoapNet; Speed Channel; Spike TV; Syfy; The Learning Channel; Travel Channel; truTV; Turner Network TV; TV Guide Network; TV Land; USA Network; VH1; WE tv; Weather Channel.
Fee: $24.00 monthly.

Digital Basic Service
Subscribers: 913.
Programming (via satellite): BBC America; Bio; Bloomberg Television; Discovery Digital Networks; DMX Music; Fox Movie Channel; Fox Sports World; G4; Golf Channel; GSN; History Channel International; Independent Film Channel; Lifetime Movie Network; Outdoor Channel; Style Network; Turner Classic Movies; Versus.
Fee: $11.00 monthly.
Pay Service 1
Pay Units: 1,169.
Programming (via satellite): Cinemax; Encore; HBO; Starz.
Fee: $3.99 monthly (Encore), $5.99 monthly (Starz/Encore), $7.95 monthly (Cinemax), $11.99 monthly (HBO).
Digital Pay Service 1
Pay Units: 2,086.
Programming (via satellite): Cinemax (multiplexed); Encore (multiplexed); Flix; HBO (multiplexed); Showtime (multiplexed); Starz (multiplexed); Sundance Channel; The Movie Channel (multiplexed).
Video-On-Demand: No
Pay-Per-View
Hot Choice (delivered digitally), Fee: $3.95; TVN Entertainment; sports (delivered digitally); Playboy TV (delivered digitally); Fresh (delivered digitally); Shorteez (delivered digitally).
Internet Service
Operational: Yes.
Subscribers: 539.
Broadband Service: Mediacom High Speed Internet.
Telephone Service
Analog: Not Operational
Digital: Planned
Miles of Plant: 496.0 (coaxial); 144.0 (fiber optic). Homes passed: 21,487.
Vice President: Scott Westerman. Technical Operations Manager: Mitch Carlson. Marketing Manager: Greg Evans. Business Operations Manager: Cari Venzell.
City fee: 3% of gross.
Ownership: Mediacom LLC (MSO).

MINIER—Mediacom. Now served by APOLLO ACRES, IL [IL0340]. ICA: IL0173.

MINOOKA—Comcast Cable. Now served by OAK BROOK, IL [IL0006]. ICA: IL0150.

MOLINE—Mediacom, 3900 26th Ave, Moline, IL 61265. Phone: 309-797-2580. Fax: 309-797-2414. Web Site: http://www.mediacomcable.com. Also serves Andalusia, Andalusia Twp., Barstow, Campbells Island, Carbon Cliff, Cleveland, Coal Valley, Colona, East Moline, Green Rock, Hampton, Henry County (northwestern portion), Milan, Oak Grove, Orion, Rock Island, Rock Island Arsenal, Rock Island County, Silvis & Taylor Ridge, IL; Bettendorf, Blue Grass, Buffalo, Davenport, Durant, Eldridge, Long Grove, Mount Joy, Panorama Park, Park View, Pleasant Valley, Riverdale, Scott County (portions), Walcott & Wilton, IA. ICA: IL0011.
TV Market Ranking: 60 (Andalusia, Andalusia Twp., Barstow, Bettendorf, Blue Grass, Buffalo, Campbells Island, Carbon Cliff, Cleveland, Coal Valley, Colona, Davenport, Durant, East Moline, Eldridge, Green Rock, Hampton, Henry County (northwestern portion), Long Grove, Milan, MOLINE, Mount Joy, Oak Grove, Orion, Panorama Park, Park View, Pleasant Valley, Riverdale, Rock Island, Rock Island Arsenal, Rock Island County, Scott County (portions), Silvis, Taylor Ridge, Walcott, Wilton). Franchise award date: November 18, 1969. Franchise expiration date: N.A. Began: December 1, 1972.
Channel capacity: 113 (operating 2-way). Channels available but not in use: 39.
Basic Service
Subscribers: 50,910.
Programming (received off-air): KDIN-TV (PBS) Des Moines; KGCW (CW) Burlington; KLJB (CW, FOX) Davenport; KWQC-TV (NBC) Davenport; WBQD-LP Davenport; WHBF-TV (CBS) Rock Island; WQAD-TV (ABC) Moline; WQPT-TV (PBS) Moline; allband FM.
Programming (via satellite): C-SPAN; Discovery Channel; Local Cable Weather; QVC; TBS Superstation; TV Guide Network; Univision; WGN America.
Current originations: Leased Access; Educational Access.
Fee: $45.00 installation; $20.95 monthly.
Expanded Basic Service 1
Subscribers: N.A.
Programming (via satellite): ABC Family Channel; AMC; Animal Planet; Arts & Entertainment; BET Networks; Bravo; Cartoon Network; CNBC; CNN; Comcast SportsNet Chicago; Comedy Central; Country Music TV; C-SPAN 2; Disney Channel; E! Entertainment Television; ESPN; ESPN 2; Eternal Word TV Network; FitTV; Food Network; Fox News Channel; FX; GalaVision; Hallmark Channel; Headline News; HGTV; History Channel; Home Shopping Network; INSP; ION Television; Lifetime; Lifetime Movie Network; MSNBC; MTV; National Geographic Channel; Nickelodeon; ShopNBC; SoapNet; Speed Channel; Spike TV; Syfy; Telefutura; The Learning Channel; Travel Channel; Trinity Broadcasting Network; truTV; Turner Classic Movies; Turner Network TV; TV Land; USA Network; Versus; VH1; WE tv; Weather Channel.
Fee: $34.00 monthly.
Digital Basic Service
Subscribers: 24,000.
Programming (received off-air): KDIN-TV (PBS) Des Moines; KLJB (CW, FOX) Davenport; KWQC-TV (NBC) Davenport; WHBF-TV (CBS) Rock Island; WQAD-TV (ABC) Moline; WQPT-TV (PBS) Moline.
Programming (via satellite): ABC News Now; AmericanLife TV Network; BBC America; Bio; Bloomberg Television; Canal 52MX; CCTV-9 (CCTV International); Cine Latino; Cine Mexicano; CMT Pure Country; CNN en Espanol; Discovery en Espanol; Discovery Health Channel; Discovery Kids Channel; Discovery Military Channel; Discovery Planet Green; ESPN 2 HD; ESPN Deportes; ESPN HD; ESPN U; ESPNews; Fox Movie Channel; Fox Reality Channel; Fox Soccer; Fuel TV; Fuse; G4; Golf Channel; GSN; Halogen Network; History Channel en Espanol; History Channel International; ID Investigation Discovery; Independent Film Channel; ION Life; Lifetime Real Women; MTV Hits; MTV Tres; MTV2; Music Choice; Nick Jr.; NickToons TV; Outdoor Channel; Ovation; Qubo; ReelzChannel; RFD-TV; Science Channel; Sleuth; Style Network; Sundance Channel; TeenNick; Toon Disney; TVG Network; VeneMovies; VH1 Classic; VH1 Soul.
Fee: $9.00 monthly.
Digital Expanded Basic Service
Subscribers: N.A.
Programming (via satellite): College Sports Television; Fox College Sports Atlantic; Fox College Sports Central; Fox College Sports Pacific; Gol TV; Tennis Channel; The Sportsman Channel.
Fee: $3.95 monthly.

Digital Expanded Basic Service 2
Subscribers: N.A.
Programming (via satellite): Discovery HD Theater; HDNet; HDNet Movies; Universal HD.
Fee: $6.95 monthly.
Digital Pay Service 1
Pay Units: 35,049.
Programming (via satellite): Cinemax (multiplexed); Encore (multiplexed); Flix; HBO (multiplexed); HBO HD; Showtime (multiplexed); Showtime HD; Starz (multiplexed); Starz HDTV; Sundance Channel; The Movie Channel (multiplexed); The Movie Channel HD.
Fee: $11.95 monthly (HBO, Cinemax, Showtime/TMC/Sundance/Flix or Starz/Encore).
Video-On-Demand: Yes
Pay-Per-View
iN DEMAND (delivered digitally); Ten Clips (delivered digitally); Playboy TV (delivered digitally); sports (delivered digitally).
Internet Service
Operational: Yes.
Broadband Service: Mediacom High Speed Internet.
Fee: $59.95 installation; $40.95 monthly.
Telephone Service
Digital: Operational
Fee: $39.95 installation; $39.95 monthly
Miles of Plant: 4,500.0 (coaxial); None (fiber optic). Homes passed: 125,910. Total homes in franchised area: 127,012. Miles of plant (coax & fiber combined) includes all Northern IL, Dobuque IA, Cuba City WI, Monticello WI, Orfordville WI & Sugar Creek WI)
Regional Vice President: Cari Fenzel. Business Operations Manager: Leonard Lipe. Technical Operations Manager: Chris Toalson. Engineering Director: Mitch Carlson. Marketing Director: Greg Evans. Government Affairs Manager: LeeAnn Herrera. Customer Service Manager: Jody Jones. Human Relations Manager: Hazel Butter.
City fee: 5% of gross. County fee: 5% of gross.
Ownership: Mediacom LLC (MSO).

MOMENCE—Mediacom. Now served by ROSELAWN, IN [IN0316]. ICA: IL0182.

MONMOUTH—Comcast Cable, 3517 N Dries Ln, Peoria, IL 61604. Phone: 309-686-2600. Fax: 309-686-9828. Web Site: http://www.comcast.com. Also serves Warren County. ICA: IL0557.
TV Market Ranking: 60 (Warren County (portions)); Below 100 (MONMOUTH, Warren County (portions)). Franchise award date: N.A. Franchise expiration date: N.A. Began: N.A.
Channel capacity: N.A. Channels available but not in use: N.A.
Basic Service
Subscribers: N.A. Included in Peoria
Programming (received off-air): KIIN (PBS) Iowa City; KLJB (CW, FOX) Davenport; KWQC-TV (NBC) Davenport; WEEK-TV (NBC) Peoria; WHBF-TV (CBS) Rock Island; WMBD-TV (CBS) Peoria; WMEC (PBS) Macomb; WQAD-TV (ABC) Moline; WQPT-TV (PBS) Moline.
Programming (via satellite): ABC Family Channel; AMC; Animal Planet; Arts & Entertainment; BET Networks; Cartoon Network; CNBC; CNN; Comedy Central; C-SPAN; C-SPAN 2; Discovery Channel; Disney Channel; E! Entertainment Television; ESPN; FitTV; Food Network; Fox News Channel; Fox Sports Net Midwest; FX; Great American Country; Hallmark Channel; Headline News; HGTV; Home Shopping Network; Lifetime; MoviePlex; MSNBC; MTV; Nickelodeon; Oxygen; QVC; Spike TV; Syfy; TBS Superstation; The Learning Channel; truTV; Turner Network TV; USA Network; Weather Channel; WGN America.
Current originations: Public Access.
Fee: $25.00 installation; $51.15 monthly.
Digital Basic Service
Subscribers: 600.
Programming (via satellite): BBC America; Bravo; Discovery Digital Networks; DMX Music; Encore (multiplexed); ESPN 2; ESPN Classic Sports; ESPNews; Fox Sports World; Golf Channel; GSN; History Channel International; Independent Film Channel; Nick Jr.; Speed Channel; Turner Classic Movies; TV Land; Versus; WE tv.
Fee: $17.00 monthly.
Digital Pay Service 1
Pay Units: N.A.
Programming (via satellite): Cinemax (multiplexed); HBO (multiplexed); Showtime (multiplexed); Starz (multiplexed); The Movie Channel.
Fee: $10.00 monthly (Cinemax or Starz), $13.00 monthly (HBO or Showtime/TMC).
Video-On-Demand: No
Pay-Per-View
Addressable homes: 600.
Hot Choice (delivered digitally), Addressable: Yes; Playboy TV (delivered digitally); iN DEMAND (delivered digitally); ESPN Now (delivered digitally); Sports PPV (delivered digitally); ESPN Extra (delivered digitally).
Internet Service
Operational: Yes.
Subscribers: 300.
Broadband Service: Comcast High Speed Internet.
Fee: $99.95 installation; $44.95 monthly; $10.00 modem lease; $99.95 modem purchase.
Telephone Service
None
Homes passed: Included in Peoria
General Manager: John Nieber. Chief Technician: Mike Vandergraft.
Ownership: Comcast Cable Communications Inc. (MSO).

MONROE CENTER—Mediacom. Now served by KIRKLAND, IL [IL0277]. ICA: IL0664.

MONTICELLO—Mediacom, PO Box 288, 4290 Blue Stem Rd, Charleston, IL 61920. Phone: 217-348-5533. Fax: 217-345-7074.

Web Site: http://www.mediacomcable.com. Also serves Bement. ICA: IL0133.

TV Market Ranking: 64 (Bement, MONTICELLO). Franchise award date: N.A. Franchise expiration date: N.A. Began: May 1, 1977.

Channel capacity: 134 (operating 2-way). Channels available but not in use: N.A.

Basic Service

Subscribers: 2,528.

Programming (received off-air): WAND (NBC) Decatur; WBUI (CW) Decatur; WCCU (FOX) Urbana; WCFN (MNT) Springfield; WCIA (CBS) Champaign; WEIU-TV (PBS) Charleston; WICD (ABC) Champaign; WICS (ABC) Springfield; WILL-TV (PBS) Urbana.

Programming (via satellite): C-SPAN; Home Shopping Network; INSP; QVC; TV Guide Network; Weatherscan; WGN America.

Current originations: Public Access.

Fee: $45.00 installation; $20.95 monthly.

Expanded Basic Service 1

Subscribers: N.A.

Programming (via satellite): ABC Family Channel; AMC; Animal Planet; Arts & Entertainment; BET Networks; Bravo; Cartoon Network; CNBC; CNN; Comcast SportsNet Chicago; Comedy Central; Country Music TV; C-SPAN 2; Discovery Channel; Disney Channel; E! Entertainment Television; ESPN; ESPN 2; ESPN Classic Sports; Eternal Word TV Network; FitTV; Food Network; Fox News Channel; Fox Sports Net Midwest; FX; Hallmark Movie Channel; Headline News; HGTV; History Channel; ION Television; Jewelry Television; Lifetime; Lifetime Movie Network; MSNBC; MTV; Nickelodeon; Outdoor Channel; Product Information Network; ShopNBC; Speed Channel; Spike TV; Syfy; TBS Superstation; The Learning Channel; Toon Disney; Travel Channel; Trinity Broadcasting Network; truTV; Turner Network TV; TV Land; USA Network; VH1; WE tv; Weather Channel.

Fee: $34.00 monthly.

Digital Basic Service

Subscribers: N.A.

Programming (received off-air): WAND (NBC) Decatur; WCCU (FOX) Urbana; WCIA (CBS) Champaign; WICD (ABC) Champaign; WILL-TV (PBS) Urbana.

Programming (via satellite): ABC News Now; AmericanLife TV Network; BBC America; Bio; Bloomberg Television; CCTV-Entertainment; Discovery Digital Networks; Discovery HD Theater; ESPN 2 HD; ESPN HD; Fox Movie Channel; Fox Reality Channel; Fox Soccer; Fuse; Golf Channel; GSN; HDNet; HDNet Movies; History Channel International; Independent Film Channel; ION Life; Lifetime Real Women; Military History Channel; MTV Hits; MTV2; Music Choice; National Geographic Channel; Nick Jr.; NickToons TV; Qubo; ReelzChannel; Science Channel; Sleuth; Style Network; TeenNick; Turner Classic Movies; Universal HD; Versus; VH1 Classic.

Fee: $9.00 monthly.

Digital Expanded Basic Service

Subscribers: N.A.

Programming (via satellite): College Sports Television; ESPN U; Fox College Sports Atlantic; Fox College Sports Central; Fox College Sports Pacific; Fuel TV; Gol TV; Tennis Channel; The Sportsman Channel; TVG Network.

Fee: $3.95 monthly.

Digital Pay Service 1

Pay Units: N.A.

Programming (via satellite): Cinemax (multiplexed); Encore (multiplexed); HBO (multiplexed); HBO HD; Showtime (multiplexed); Showtime HD; Starz (multiplexed); Starz HDTV; The Movie Channel (multiplexed); The Movie Channel HD.

Fee: $11.95 monthly (each).

Video-On-Demand: Yes

Pay-Per-View

iN DEMAND (delivered digitally); Playboy TV (delivered digitally); Ten Clips (delivered digitally); Ten Blox (delivered digitally); ESPN (delivered digitally); HDNet (delivered digitally).

Internet Service

Operational: Yes.

Broadband Service: Mediacom High Speed Internet.

Fee: $59.95 installation; $40.95 monthly.

Telephone Service

Digital: Operational

Fee: $39.95 installation; $39.95 monthly

Miles of Plant: 60.0 (coaxial); None (fiber optic). Homes passed: 3,299.

Area Operations Manager: Todd Acker. Technical Operations Manager: Jerry Ferguson.

City fee: 5% of gross.

Ownership: Mediacom LLC (MSO).

MONTROSE—Clearvision Cable Systems Inc., 1785 US Rte 40, Greenup, IL 62428-3501. Phone: 217-923-5594. Fax: 217-923-5681. E-mail: mbct@rr1.net. Also serves Dieterich & Shumway. ICA: IL0659.

TV Market Ranking: Outside TV Markets (Dieterich, MONTROSE, Shumway). Franchise award date: N.A. Franchise expiration date: N.A. Began: N.A.

Channel capacity: N.A. Channels available but not in use: N.A.

Basic Service

Subscribers: 239.

Programming (received off-air): WAND (NBC) Decatur; WBUI (CW) Decatur; WFXW (FOX) Terre Haute; WPXS (IND) Mount Vernon; WTHI-TV (CBS) Terre Haute; WTWO (NBC) Terre Haute; WUSI-TV (PBS) Olney.

Programming (via satellite): ABC Family Channel; AMC; Animal Planet; Arts & Entertainment; CNN; Country Music TV; C-SPAN; Discovery Channel; Disney Channel; ESPN; G4; History Channel; Home Shopping Network; Lifetime; Spike TV; Syfy; TBS Superstation; The Learning Channel; Travel Channel; Trinity Broadcasting Network; Turner Network TV; USA Network; WGN America.

Fee: $36.07 installation; $29.95 monthly.

Pay Service 1

Pay Units: N.A.

Programming (via satellite): Cinemax; HBO; Showtime; The Movie Channel.

Fee: $6.50 monthly (Cinemax), $11.50 monthly (HBO).

Video-On-Demand: No

Internet Service

Operational: No.

Telephone Service

None

Miles of Plant: 100.0 (coaxial); None (fiber optic).

Manager: Michael Bauguss.

Ownership: Clearvision Cable Systems Inc. (MSO).

MORRIS—Comcast Cable. Now served by OAK BROOK, IL [IL0006]. ICA: IL0084.

MORRIS—Mediacom, 3900 26th Ave, Moline, IL 61265. Phone: 309-797-2580. Fax: 309-797-2414. Web Site: http://www.mediacomcable.com. Also serves Minooka & Shady Oaks Trailer Park. ICA: IL0402.

TV Market Ranking: Below 100 (Minooka, MORRIS, Shady Oaks Trailer Park). Franchise award date: N.A. Franchise expiration date: N.A. Began: December 1, 1989.

Channel capacity: N.A. Channels available but not in use: N.A.

Basic Service

Subscribers: 179.

Programming (received off-air): WBBM-TV (CBS) Chicago; WCIU-TV (IND) Chicago; WFLD (FOX) Chicago; WGN-TV (CW, IND) Chicago; WLS-TV (ABC) Chicago; WMAQ-TV (NBC) Chicago; WPWR-TV (MNT) Gary; WTTW (PBS) Chicago; WYCC (PBS) Chicago.

Programming (via satellite): ABC Family Channel; AMC; Animal Planet; Arts & Entertainment; CNN; Comedy Central; Discovery Channel; Disney Channel; ESPN; ESPN 2; Eternal Word TV Network; Headline News; History Channel; Lifetime; MTV; Nickelodeon; Spike TV; TBS Superstation; The Learning Channel; Trinity Broadcasting Network; Turner Network TV; USA Network; Weather Channel.

Fee: $45.00 installation; $54.95 monthly.

Pay Service 1

Pay Units: 59.

Programming (via satellite): Showtime.

Fee: $10.95 monthly.

Video-On-Demand: No

Internet Service

Operational: No.

Telephone Service

None

Homes passed: 510. Miles of plant included in Moline

Marketing Director: Greg Evans. Technical Operations Manager: Mitch Carlson.

City fee: 5% of gross.

Ownership: Mediacom LLC (MSO).

MORRISONVILLE—Mediacom. Now served by KINCAID, IL [IL0176]. ICA: IL0286.

MORTON GROVE—Comcast Cable. Now served by SHAUMBURG, IL [IL0036]. ICA: IL0027.

MOUNDS—Mediacom. Now served by ZEIGLER, IL [IL0123]. ICA: IL0207.

MOUNT AUBURN—Mediacom. Now served by KINCAID, IL [IL0176]. ICA: IL0371.

MOUNT CARMEL—NewWave Communications, 318 N 4th St, Vandalia, IL 62471. Phone: 573-472-9500. Fax: 618.283.4483. E-mail: info@newwavecom.com. Web Site: http://www.newwavecom.com. Also serves Wabash County (portions). ICA: IL0124.

TV Market Ranking: 86 (MOUNT CARMEL, Wabash County (portions)). Franchise award date: N.A. Franchise expiration date: N.A. Began: June 1, 1975.

Channel capacity: 136 (not 2-way capable). Channels available but not in use: N.A.

Basic Service

Subscribers: 1,422.

Programming (received off-air): KFVS-TV (CBS, CW) Cape Girardeau; WAZE-LP (CW) Evansville; WEHT (ABC) Evansville; WEVV-TV (CBS, MNT) Evansville; WFIE (NBC) Evansville; WNIN (PBS) Evansville; WPXS (IND) Mount Vernon; WSIL-TV (ABC) Harrisburg; WTVW (FOX) Evansville; WUSI-TV (PBS) Olney; 9 FMs.

Programming (via satellite): C-SPAN; C-SPAN 2; Home Shopping Network; INSP; QVC; Trinity Broadcasting Network; WGN America.

Fee: $25.00 installation; $20.64 monthly; $15.00 additional installation.

Expanded Basic Service 1

Subscribers: 1,256.

Programming (via satellite): ABC Family Channel; AMC; Animal Planet; Arts & Entertainment; Big Ten Network; Bravo; Cartoon Network; CNBC; CNN; Comedy Central; Country Music TV; Discovery Channel; Disney Channel; E! Entertainment Television; ESPN; ESPN 2; ESPN Classic Sports; Eternal Word TV Network; Food Network; Fox News Channel; Fox Sports Net Midwest; FX; Golf Channel; GSN; Hallmark Channel; Headline News; HGTV; History Channel; Lifetime; MSNBC; MTV; National Geographic Channel; Nickelodeon; Outdoor Channel; Oxygen; ShopNBC; SoapNet; Speed Channel; Spike TV; Syfy; TBS Superstation; The Learning Channel; Toon Disney; Travel Channel; truTV; Turner Classic Movies; Turner Network TV; TV Land; USA Network; Versus; VH1; Weather Channel.

Digital Basic Service

Subscribers: 645.

Programming (received off-air): WEHT (ABC) Evansville; WEVV-TV (CBS, MNT) Evansville; WFIE (NBC) Evansville; WSIL-TV (ABC) Harrisburg; WTVW (FOX) Evansville.

Programming (via satellite): BBC America; Bio; Bloomberg Television; CMT Pure Country; Cooking Channel; Discovery HD Theater; Discovery Health Channel; Discovery Kids Channel; Discovery Military Channel; Discovery Planet Green; Do-It-Yourself; ESPN 2 HD; ESPN HD; ESPNews; FitTV; Fox College Sports Atlantic; Fox College Sports Central; Fox College Sports Pacific; Fox Movie Channel; FSN HD; G4; Great American Country; Halogen Network; HDNet; HDNet Movies; History Channel International; ID Investigation Discovery; Independent Film Channel; Lifetime Movie Network; MTV Hits; MTV Jams; MTV2; Music Choice; Nick Jr.; Nick Too; NickToons TV; RFD-TV; Science Channel; Sleuth; Style Network; TeenNick; Turner Network TV HD; Universal HD; VH1 Classic; VH1 Soul.

Digital Pay Service 1

Pay Units: 140.

Programming (via satellite): Cinemax (multiplexed); Cinemax HD; HBO HD; Starz HDTV.

Fee: $15.00 installation; $10.95 monthly.

Digital Pay Service 2
Pay Units: 395.
Programming (via satellite): HBO (multiplexed).
Fee: $15.00 installation; $11.95 monthly.
Digital Pay Service 3
Pay Units: 111.
Programming (via satellite): Flix; Showtime (multiplexed); The Movie Channel (multiplexed).
Fee: $15.00 installation; $10.95 monthly.
Digital Pay Service 4
Pay Units: N.A.
Programming (via satellite): Encore (multiplexed); Starz (multiplexed).
Video-On-Demand: No
Pay-Per-View
iN DEMAND (delivered digitally); Spice: Xcess (delivered digitally); Club Jenna (delivered digitally); Playboy TV (delivered digitally); Fresh (delivered digitally); Shorteez (delivered digitally).
Internet Service
Operational: Yes.
Telephone Service
Digital: Operational
Miles of Plant: 51.0 (coaxial); None (fiber optic). Homes passed: 4,462.
General Manager: Bill Flowers. Technical Operations Manager: Chris Mooday.
City fee: 3% of gross.
Ownership: NewWave Communications (MSO).

MOUNT CARROLL—Mediacom. Now served by LENA, IL [IL0223]. ICA: IL0141.

MOUNT PROSPECT—Comcast Cable. Now served by SCHAUMBURG, IL [IL0036]. ICA: IL0007.

MOUNT PULASKI—Insight Communications. Now served by SPRINGFIELD, IL [IL0016]. ICA: IL0090.

MOUNT STERLING—Cass Cable TV Inc. Now served by VIRGINIA, IL [IL0598]. ICA: IL0208.

MOWEAQUA—Suddenlink Communications, 12444 Powerscourt Dr, Saint Louis, MO 63131-3660. Phones: 314-965-2020; 573-686-6387. Web Site: http://www.suddenlink.com. Also serves Assumption & Macon. ICA: IL0185.
TV Market Ranking: 64 (Assumption, Macon, MOWEAQUA). Franchise award date: N.A. Franchise expiration date: N.A. Began: October 1, 1982.
Channel capacity: N.A. Channels available but not in use: N.A.
Basic Service
Subscribers: 1,318.
Programming (received off-air): WAND (NBC) Decatur; WBUI (CW) Decatur; WCFN (MNT) Springfield; WCIA (CBS) Champaign; WEIU-TV (PBS) Charleston; WICS (ABC) Springfield; WILL-TV (PBS) Urbana; WRSP-TV (FOX) Springfield.
Programming (via satellite): Home Shopping Network; WGN America.
Fee: $45.00 installation; $25.14 monthly.
Expanded Basic Service 1
Subscribers: N.A.
Programming (via satellite): ABC Family Channel; AMC; Animal Planet; Arts & Entertainment; Cartoon Network; CNN; Comcast SportsNet Chicago; Country Music TV; C-SPAN; C-SPAN 2; Discovery Channel; Disney Channel; E! Entertainment Television; ESPN; ESPN 2; ESPN Classic Sports; Fox News Channel; Fox Sports Net Midwest; FX; Great American Country; Headline News; HGTV; History Channel; INSP; Lifetime; MSNBC; MTV; National Geographic Channel; Nickelodeon; Radar Channel; SoapNet; Speed Channel; Spike TV; Syfy; TBS Superstation; The Learning Channel; Trinity Broadcasting Network; Turner Classic Movies; Turner Network TV; TV Land; USA Network; VH1; WE tv; Weather Channel.
Digital Basic Service
Subscribers: N.A.
Programming (via satellite): BBC America; Bio; Bloomberg Television; CMT Pure Country; Discovery Health Channel; Discovery Home Channel; Discovery Kids Channel; Discovery Military Channel; DMX Music; ESPNews; Fox College Sports Atlantic; Fox College Sports Central; Fox College Sports Pacific; Fox Movie Channel; Fox Soccer; Fuse; G4; Golf Channel; GSN; History Channel International; ID Investigation Discovery; Independent Film Channel; Lifetime Movie Network; MTV2; Nick Jr.; NickToons TV; Outdoor Channel; Science Channel; ShopNBC; Style Network; TeenNick; Toon Disney; Versus; VH1 Classic.
Pay Service 1
Pay Units: 178.
Programming (via satellite): Cinemax; Encore; HBO; Showtime; The Movie Channel.
Fee: $25.00 installation; $3.99 monthly (Encore), $7.95 monthly (Cinemax), $11.99 monthly (HBO, Showtime or TMC).
Digital Pay Service 1
Pay Units: N.A.
Programming (via satellite): Cinemax (multiplexed); Encore (multiplexed); HBO (multiplexed); Showtime (multiplexed); Starz (multiplexed); The Movie Channel.
Video-On-Demand: No
Pay-Per-View
iN DEMAND (delivered digitally); Playboy TV (delivered digitally); Fresh (delivered digitally); Club Jenna (delivered digitally).
Internet Service
Operational: Yes. Began: April 15, 2004.
Broadband Service: Cebridge High Speed Cable Internet.
Fee: $99.99 installation; $24.95 monthly.
Telephone Service
None
Miles of Plant: 35.0 (coaxial); None (fiber optic). Homes passed: 1,911.
Manager: James Robinson.
Ownership: Cequel Communications LLC (MSO).

MULBERRY GROVE—Clearvision Cable Systems Inc., 1785 US Rte 40, Greenup, IL 62428-3501. Phone: 217-923-5594. Fax: 217-923-5681. E-mail: mbct@rr1.net. ICA: IL0355.
TV Market Ranking: Outside TV Markets (MULBERRY GROVE). Franchise award date: N.A. Franchise expiration date: N.A. Began: April 1, 1986.
Channel capacity: 40 (not 2-way capable). Channels available but not in use: 22.
Basic Service
Subscribers: 45.
Programming (received off-air): KDNL-TV (ABC) St. Louis; KETC (PBS) St. Louis; KMOV (CBS) St. Louis; KPLR-TV (CW) St. Louis; KSDK (NBC) St. Louis; KTVI (FOX) St. Louis; WPXS (IND) Mount Vernon; WRBU (MNT) East St. Louis.
Programming (via satellite): ABC Family Channel; AMC; Arts & Entertainment; Bravo; Cartoon Network; CNBC; CNN; Comedy Central; Country Music TV; C-SPAN; Discovery Channel; Disney Channel; ESPN; Fox News Channel; Headline News; History Channel; Lifetime; MSNBC; MTV; Nickelodeon; QVC; Spike TV; Syfy; TBS Superstation; The Learning Channel; Trinity Broadcasting Network; Turner Network TV; USA Network; VH1; Weather Channel; WGN America.
Fee: $42.50 installation; $29.95 monthly.
Pay Service 1
Pay Units: 23.
Programming (via satellite): Showtime; The Movie Channel.
Video-On-Demand: No
Internet Service
Operational: No.
Telephone Service
None
Miles of Plant: 7.0 (coaxial); None (fiber optic). Homes passed: 292.
Manager: Michael Bauguss.
City fee: 3% of gross.
Ownership: Clearvision Cable Systems Inc. (MSO).

MURPHYSBORO—Mediacom, 90 Main St, Benton, KY 42025-1132. Phones: 417-875-5560 (Springfield regional office); 270-527-9939. Fax: 270-527-0813. Web Site: http://www.mediacomcable.com. Also serves Carbondale, Carbondale Twp., De Soto & Jackson County (portions). ICA: IL0059.
TV Market Ranking: 69 (Carbondale, Carbondale Twp., Jackson County (portions), MURPHYSBORO); Below 100 (De Soto, Jackson County (portions)). Franchise award date: N.A. Franchise expiration date: N.A. Began: July 1, 1971.
Channel capacity: N.A. Channels available but not in use: N.A.
Basic Service
Subscribers: 8,801.
Programming (received off-air): KBSI (FOX) Cape Girardeau; KETC (PBS) St. Louis; KFVS-TV (CBS, CW) Cape Girardeau; WPSD-TV (NBC) Paducah; WPXS (IND) Mount Vernon; WSIL-TV (ABC) Harrisburg; WSIU-TV (PBS) Carbondale; WTCT (IND) Marion; allband FM.
Programming (via satellite): ABC Family Channel; AMC; Animal Planet; Arts & Entertainment; BET Networks; Bravo; Cartoon Network; CNN; Comedy Central; Country Music TV; C-SPAN; C-SPAN 2; Discovery Channel; Disney Channel; E! Entertainment Television; ESPN; ESPN 2; Food Network; Fox News Channel; Fox Sports Net Midwest; FX; GRTV Network; Hallmark Channel; Headline News; HGTV; History Channel; Home Shopping Network; INSP; Lifetime; MSNBC; MTV; Nickelodeon; Outdoor Channel; QVC; SoapNet; Speed Channel; Spike TV; Syfy; TBS Superstation; The Learning Channel; Travel Channel; truTV; Turner Network TV; TV Guide Network; TV Land; USA Network; VH1; W Network; Weather Channel; WGN America; WQWQ-LP (CW) Paducah.
Fee: $43.64 installation; $9.03 monthly; $2.59 converter.
Digital Basic Service
Subscribers: N.A.
Programming (via satellite): BBC America; Bloomberg Television; Discovery Digital Networks; Fox Movie Channel; Fox Soccer; G4; GAS; Golf Channel; History Channel International; Independent Film Channel; Lifetime Movie Network; MTV Networks Digital Suite; National Geographic Channel; Nick Jr.; NickToons TV; Style Network; Turner Classic Movies; Versus.
Digital Pay Service 1
Pay Units: 1,137.
Programming (via satellite): Cinemax (multiplexed).
Fee: $13.60 monthly.
Digital Pay Service 2
Pay Units: 3,253.
Programming (via satellite): Encore (multiplexed).
Fee: $1.70 monthly.
Digital Pay Service 3
Pay Units: 2,202.
Programming (via satellite): HBO (multiplexed).
Fee: $14.55 installation; $14.30 monthly.
Digital Pay Service 4
Pay Units: 686.
Programming (via satellite): Showtime.
Fee: $14.10 monthly.
Digital Pay Service 5
Pay Units: N.A.
Programming (via satellite): DMX Music; Starz.
Fee: $4.75 monthly (Starz), $9.95 monthly (DMX).
Video-On-Demand: Yes
Pay-Per-View
152-156 (delivered digitally); Playboy Entertainment Group Inc. (delivered digitally); Pleasure (delivered digitally).
Internet Service
Operational: Yes.
Broadband Service: Mediacom High Speed Internet.
Telephone Service
Digital: Operational
Miles of Plant: 114.0 (coaxial); None (fiber optic). Homes passed: 11,088. Total homes in franchised area: 11,129.
General Manager: Dale Haney. Marketing Director: Will Kuebler. Marketing Manager: Melanie Westerman. Regional Vice President: Bill Copeland. Technical Operations Manager: Jeff Brown. Regional Technical Operations Director: Alan Freedman.
City fee: 3% of gross.
Ownership: Mediacom LLC (MSO).

MURRAYVILLE—Formerly served by Almega Cable. No longer in operation. ICA: IL0294.

NAPERVILLE—Comcast Cable. Now served by OAK BROOK, IL [IL0006]. ICA: IL0029.

NAPERVILLE—WOW! Internet Cable & Phone, 7887 E Belleview Ave, Ste 1000, Englewood, CO 80111. Phones: 720-479-3500; 630-536-3100 (Customer service). Fax: 720-479-3585. Web Site: http://www1.wowway.com. Also serves Arlington Heights, Bartlett, Calumet City, Chicago Heights, Crestwood, Des Plaines, DuPage County (portions), Elgin, Glen Ellyn, Glendale Heights, Glenview, Harvey, Mount Prospect, Oak Forest, Palos Park, Posen, Prospect Heights, Robbins, Schaumburg, South Holland, Streamwood, Vernon Hills & Wheeling. ICA: IL0655. **Note:** This system is an overbuild.

TV Market Ranking: 3 (Arlington Heights, Bartlett, Calumet City, Chicago Heights, Crestwood, Des Plaines, Dupage County (Portions), Elgin, Glen Ellyn, Glendale Heights, Glenview, Harvey, Mount Prospect, NAPERVILLE, Oak Forest, Palos Park, Posen, Prospect Heights, Robbins, Schaumburg, South Holland, Streamwood, Vernon Hills, Wheeling). Franchise award date: February 1, 1996. Franchise expiration date: N.A. Began: N.A.

Channel capacity: N.A. Channels available but not in use: N.A.

Basic Service

Subscribers: N.A. Included in Chicago

Programming (received off-air): WBBM-TV (CBS) Chicago; WCIU-TV (IND) Chicago; WCPX-TV (ION) Chicago; WFLD (FOX) Chicago; WGBO-DT (UNV) Joliet; WGN-TV (CW, IND) Chicago; WJYS (IND) Hammond; WLS-TV (ABC) Chicago; WMAQ-TV (NBC) Chicago; WPWR-TV (MNT) Gary; WSNS-TV (TMO) Chicago; WTTW (PBS) Chicago; WXFT-DT (TEL) Aurora; WYCC (PBS) Chicago.

Programming (via satellite): Home Shopping Network; INSP; TBS Superstation; V-me TV.

Current originations: Government Access; Educational Access; Public Access.

Fee: $39.99 installation; $16.99 monthly.

Expanded Basic Service 1

Subscribers: N.A.

Programming (via satellite): ABC Family Channel; AMC; Animal Planet; Arts & Entertainment; BET Networks; Big Ten Network; Bravo; Cartoon Network; CNBC; CNN; Comcast SportsNet Chicago; Comedy Central; Country Music TV; C-SPAN; Discovery Channel; Discovery Health Channel; Disney Channel; E! Entertainment Television; ESPN; ESPN 2; ESPN Classic Sports; Food Network; Fox News Channel; FX; Golf Channel; GSN; Hallmark Channel; Headline News; HGTV; History Channel; Lifetime; MSNBC; MTV; MTV2; Nickelodeon; NickToons TV; Oxygen; QVC; ShopNBC; Speed Channel; Spike TV; Syfy; The Learning Channel; Toon Disney; Travel Channel; truTV; Turner Classic Movies; Turner Network TV; TV Land; USA Network; VH1; Weather Channel.

Fee: $34.76 monthly.

Digital Basic Service

Subscribers: N.A.

Programming (via satellite): ABC News Now; BBC America; Big Ten Network; Bio; Bloomberg Television; Bridges TV; CMT Pure Country; Cooking Channel; Discovery Kids Channel; Discovery Military Channel; Discovery Planet Green; DMX Music; Do-It-Yourself; Encore (multiplexed); ESPN U; ESPNews; Eternal Word TV Network; Fox Business Channel; Fox College Sports Atlantic; Fox College Sports Central; Fox College Sports Pacific; Fox Movie Channel; Fox Reality Channel; Fox Soccer; G4; History Channel International; ID Investigation Discovery; Lifetime Movie Network; Lifetime Real Women; MTV Hits; National Geographic Channel; NFL Network; Nick Jr.; Nick Too; Outdoor Channel; PBS Kids Sprout; Science Channel; SoapNet; Starz (multiplexed); Style Network; Sundance Channel; TeenNick; Tennis Channel; The Word Network; VH1 Classic.

Fee: $25.23 monthly.

Digital Expanded Basic Service

Subscribers: N.A.

Programming (received off-air): WBBM-TV (CBS) Chicago; WCIU-TV (IND) Chicago; WFLD (FOX) Chicago; WGN-TV (CW, IND) Chicago; WLS-TV (ABC) Chicago; WMAQ-TV (NBC) Chicago; WPWR-TV (MNT) Gary; WYCC (PBS) Chicago.

Programming (via satellite): ABC Family HD; Animal Planet HD; Arts & Entertainment HD; Discovery Channel HD; Discovery HD Theater; Disney Channel HD; ESPN 2 HD; ESPN HD; Food Network HD; Fox News HD; FX HD; HDNet; HDNet Movies; HGTV HD; History Channel HD; National Geographic Channel HD Network; NFL Network HD; Starz HDTV; TLC HD; Turner Network TV HD; WealthTV HD.

Fee: $13.00 monthly.

Digital Pay Service 1

Pay Units: N.A.

Programming (via satellite): Cinemax (multiplexed); Cinemax HD; Cinemax On Demand; HBO (multiplexed); HBO HD; HBO On Demand; Showtime (multiplexed); Showtime HD; Showtime On Demand; The Movie Channel (multiplexed); The Movie Channel On Demand.

Fee: $15.00 monthly (HBO, Cinemax, Starz or Showtime/TMC/Flix).

Video-On-Demand: Yes

Pay-Per-View

ETC, Addressable: Yes; iN DEMAND (delivered digitally); Pleasure (delivered digitally); Playboy TV (delivered digitally); Sports PPV (delivered digitally).

Internet Service

Operational: Yes.

Broadband Service: WOW! Internet.

Fee: $40.99-$72.99 monthly; $2.50 modem lease.

Telephone Service

Digital: Operational

Total homes in franchised area: 165,150.

Vice President & General Manager: Kelvin Fee. Vice President, Sales & Marketing: Cathy Kuo. Chief Technician: Cash Hagan.

Ownership: WideOpenWest LLC (MSO).

NAUVOO—Mediacom, PO Box 334, 609 S 4th St, Chillicothe, IL 61523. Phone: 309-274-4500. Fax: 309-274-3188. Web Site: http://www.mediacomcable.com. ICA: IL0299.

TV Market Ranking: Below 100 (NAUVOO). Franchise award date: N.A. Franchise expiration date: N.A. Began: March 23, 1983.

Channel capacity: N.A. Channels available but not in use: N.A.

Basic Service

Subscribers: 236.

Programming (received off-air): KHQA-TV (ABC, CBS) Hannibal; KIIN (PBS) Iowa City; KTVO (ABC) Kirksville; KYOU-TV (FOX) Ottumwa; WGEM-TV (CW, NBC) Quincy; WQAD-TV (ABC) Moline.

Programming (via satellite): ABC Family Channel; AMC; Animal Planet; Arts & Entertainment; CNBC; CNN; Comcast SportsNet Chicago; Comedy Central; Country Music TV; C-SPAN; Discovery Channel; E! Entertainment Television; ESPN; ESPN 2; Hallmark Channel; History Channel; Home Shopping Network; Lifetime; Nickelodeon; ShopNBC; Speed Channel; Spike TV; Syfy; TBS Superstation; The Learning Channel; Travel Channel; Trinity Broadcasting Network; truTV; Turner Network TV; TV Land; USA Network; VH1; Weather Channel; WGN America.

Fee: $45.00 installation; $54.95 monthly.

Digital Basic Service

Subscribers: N.A.

Programming (via satellite): AmericanLife TV Network; BBC America; Bio; Bloomberg Television; Discovery Digital Networks; ESPNews; Fox Movie Channel; Fuse; G4; GAS; Golf Channel; History Channel International; Independent Film Channel; Lifetime Movie Network; Lime; MTV Networks Digital Suite; National Geographic Channel; Nick Jr.; NickToons TV; Outdoor Channel; Sleuth; Style Network; Sundance Channel; Turner Classic Movies; TVG Network; Versus.

Fee: $9.00 monthly.

Digital Expanded Basic Service

Subscribers: N.A.

Programming (via satellite): Discovery HD Theater; ESPN 2 HD; ESPN HD; HDNet; HDNet Movies; Universal HD.

Fee: $6.95 monthly.

Digital Pay Service 1

Pay Units: N.A.

Programming (via satellite): Cinemax (multiplexed); Encore (multiplexed); Flix (multiplexed); HBO (multiplexed); HBO HD; Showtime (multiplexed); Showtime HD; Starz (multiplexed); Starz HDTV; The Movie Channel (multiplexed); The Movie Channel HD.

Fee: $11.95 monthly (HBO, Cinemax, Showtime/TMC, or Starz/Encore).

Video-On-Demand: Yes

Pay-Per-View

iN DEMAND (delivered digitally); Playboy TV (delivered digitally).

Internet Service

Operational: Yes.

Broadband Service: Mediacom High Speed Internet.

Fee: $59.95 installation; $45.95 monthly.

Telephone Service

Digital: Operational

Fee: $39.95 installation; $39.95 monthly

Miles of Plant: 12.0 (coaxial); None (fiber optic). Homes passed: 476.

Vice President: Don Hagwell. Operations Director: Gary Wightman. Technical Operations Manager: Larry Brackman. Marketing Director: Stephanie Law.

City fee: 3% of gross.

Ownership: Mediacom LLC (MSO).

NEOGA—Mediacom, PO Box 288, 4290 Blue Stem Rd, Charleston, IL 61920. Phone: 217-348-5533. Fax: 217-345-7074. Web Site: http://www.mediacomcable.com. Also serves Stewardson, Strasburg & Windsor. ICA: IL0249.

TV Market Ranking: 64 (Windsor); Outside TV Markets (NEOGA, Stewardson, Strasburg). Franchise award date: January 1, 1981. Franchise expiration date: N.A. Began: May 26, 1981.

Channel capacity: N.A. Channels available but not in use: N.A.

Basic Service

Subscribers: 1,278.

Programming (received off-air): WAND (NBC) Decatur; WBUI (CW) Decatur; WCCU (FOX) Urbana; WCFN (MNT) Springfield; WCIA (CBS) Champaign; WEIU-TV (PBS) Charleston; WICD (ABC) Champaign; WILL-TV (PBS) Urbana; WSIU-TV (PBS) Carbondale; WTHI-TV (CBS) Terre Haute; WTWO (NBC) Terre Haute; 6 FMs.

Programming (via satellite): C-SPAN; Home Shopping Network; INSP; QVC; TV Guide Network; WGN America.

Fee: $45.00 installation; $20.95 monthly.

Expanded Basic Service 1

Subscribers: N.A.

Programming (via satellite): ABC Family Channel; AMC; Animal Planet; Arts & Entertainment; BET Networks; Cartoon Network; CNBC; CNN; Comedy Central; Country Music TV; C-SPAN 2; Discovery Channel; Disney Channel; E! Entertainment Television; ESPN; ESPN 2; ESPN Classic Sports; Eternal Word TV Network; FitTV; Food Network; Fox News Channel; Fox Sports Net Midwest; FX; Hallmark Channel; Headline News; HGTV; History Channel; ION Television; Jewelry Television; Lifetime; Lifetime Movie Network; MSNBC; MTV; Nickelodeon; Outdoor Channel; Oxygen; Product Information Network; ShopNBC; Speed Channel; Spike TV; Syfy; TBS Superstation; The Learning Channel; Travel Channel; Trinity Broadcasting Network; truTV; Turner Network TV; TV Land; USA Network; VH1; WE tv; Weather Channel.

Fee: $34.00 monthly.

Digital Basic Service

Subscribers: N.A.

Programming (received off-air): WAND (NBC) Decatur; WCCU (FOX) Urbana; WCIA (CBS) Champaign; WICD (ABC) Champaign; WILL-TV (PBS) Urbana; WTHI-TV (CBS) Terre Haute.

Programming (via satellite): ABC News Now; AmericanLife TV Network; BBC America; Bio; Bloomberg Television; CCTV-9 (CCTV International); CMT Pure Country; Discovery Health Channel; Discovery Kids Channel; Discovery Military Channel; Discovery Planet Green; Discovery Times Channel; ESPN 2 HD; ESPN HD; ESPN U; ESPNews; FitTV; Fox Movie Channel; Fox Reality Channel; Fox Soccer; Fuel TV; Fuse; G4; Golf Channel; GSN; History Channel International; Independent Film Channel; ION Life; Lifetime Real Women; MTV Hits; MTV2; Music Choice; National Geographic Channel; Nick Jr.; NickToons TV; Qubo; ReelzChannel; Science Channel; Sleuth; Speed Channel; Style Network; TeenNick; Toon Disney; Turner Classic Movies; TVG Network; Versus; VH1 Classic.

Fee: $9.00 monthly.

Digital Expanded Basic Service

Subscribers: N.A.

Programming (via satellite): College Sports Television; Fox College Sports Atlantic; Fox College Sports Central; Fox College Sports Pacific; Fox Soccer; Gol TV; Tennis Channel; The Sportsman Channel.

Fee: $3.95 monthly.

Digital Expanded Basic Service 2

Subscribers: N.A.

Programming (via satellite): Discovery HD Theater; HDNet; HDNet Movies; Universal HD.

Fee: $6.95 monthly.

Digital Pay Service 1

Pay Units: N.A.

Programming (via satellite): Cinemax (multiplexed); Cinemax On Demand; Encore; HBO (multiplexed); HBO HD; HBO on Broadband; Showtime (multiplexed); Showtime HD; Showtime On Demand; Starz (multiplexed); Starz HDTV; Starz On Demand; The Movie Channel (multiplexed); The Movie Channel HD; The Movie Channel On Demand.

Fee: $11.95 monthly (HBO, Cinemax, Showtime/TMC or Starz/Encore).

Video-On-Demand: Planned

Pay-Per-View
iN DEMAND (delivered digitally); Playboy TV (delivered digitally); Ten Clips (delivered digitally); Ten Blox (delivered digitally); ESPN (delivered digitally).
Internet Service
Operational: Yes.
Broadband Service: Mediacom High Speed Internet.
Fee: $59.95 installation; $40.95 monthly; $15.00 modem lease.
Telephone Service
Digital: Operational
Fee: $39.95 installation; $39.95 monthly
Miles of Plant: 33.0 (coaxial); None (fiber optic). Homes passed: 1,543.
Area Operations Director: Todd Acker. Technical Operations Manager: Jerry Ferguson.
City fee: 3% of gross.
Ownership: Mediacom LLC (MSO).

NEW BERLIN—Mediacom. Now served by KINCAID, IL [IL0176]. ICA: IL0334.

NEW BOSTON—Nova Cablevision Inc., PO Box 1412, 677 W Main St, Galesburg, IL 61401. Phones: 800-397-6682; 309-342-9681. Fax: 309-342-4408. Web Site: http://www.novacablevision.com. ICA: IL0558.
TV Market Ranking: 60 (NEW BOSTON). Franchise award date: N.A. Franchise expiration date: N.A. Began: October 1, 1984.
Channel capacity: 31 (not 2-way capable). Channels available but not in use: N.A.
Basic Service
Subscribers: 21.
Programming (received off-air): HGTV; KGCW (CW) Burlington; KIIN (PBS) Iowa City; KLJB (CW, FOX) Davenport; KWQC-TV (NBC) Davenport; RFD-TV; WEEK-TV (NBC) Peoria; WHBF-TV (CBS) Rock Island; WHOI (ABC, CW) Peoria; WMBD-TV (CBS) Peoria; WQAD-TV (ABC) Moline; WQPT-TV (PBS) Moline; WTVP (PBS) Peoria.
Programming (via satellite): ABC Family Channel; AMC; Animal Planet; Arts & Entertainment; Big Ten Network; Cartoon Network; CNBC; CNN; Comcast SportsNet Chicago; Comedy Central; Country Music TV; C-SPAN; C-SPAN 2; Discovery Channel; Disney Channel; Do-It-Yourself; E! Entertainment Television; ESPN; ESPN 2; ESPN U; Eternal Word TV Network; Food Network; Fox News Channel; Fox Sports Net Midwest; FX; Golf Channel; Great American Country; Hallmark Channel; Headline News; History Channel; Home Shopping Network; HorseRacing TV; Lifetime; MSNBC; MTV; National Geographic Channel; Nickelodeon; QVC; SoapNet; Spike TV; Syfy; TBS Superstation; The Learning Channel; The Sportsman Channel; Travel Channel; truTV; Turner Network TV; TV Land; USA Network; VH1; Weather Channel; WGN America.
Fee: $60.00 installation; $53.95 monthly.
Digital Basic Service
Subscribers: N.A.
Programming (via satellite): Bio; Bloomberg Television; CMT Pure Country; Discovery Health Channel; Discovery Kids Channel; Discovery Military Channel; Discovery Planet Green; Disney XD; DMX Music; ESPN 2; ESPN Classic Sports; ESPNews; Fox Movie Channel; Fox Soccer; FSN Digital Atlantic; FSN Digital Central; FSN Digital Pacific; Fuse; G4; Golf Channel; Great American Country; GSN; HGTV; History Channel; History Channel International; ID Investigation Discovery; Independent Film Channel; Lifetime Movie Network; MTV Hits; MTV2; NickToons TV; Noggin; Outdoor Channel; Science Channel; ShopNBC; Speed Channel; Style Network; Syfy; The N; Trinity Broadcasting Network; Turner Classic Movies; Versus; VH1 Classic; VH1 Soul; WE tv.
Fee: $16.95 monthly.
Pay Service 1
Pay Units: N.A.
Programming (via satellite): Cinemax; HBO.
Fee: $12.85 monthly (each).
Digital Pay Service 1
Pay Units: N.A.
Programming (via satellite): Cinemax (multiplexed); Encore (multiplexed); Flix; HBO (multiplexed); Showtime (multiplexed); Starz (multiplexed); Sundance Channel; The Movie Channel (multiplexed).
Fee: $12.85 monthly (HBO, Showtime/TMC/Flix/Sundance), Cinemax, or Starz/Encore).
Video-On-Demand: No
Pay-Per-View
Hot Choice (delivered digitally); Playboy TV (delivered digitally); Fresh (delivered digitally); Spice: Xcess (delivered digitally); Club Jenna (delivered digitally).
Internet Service
Operational: Yes.
Fee: $39.95 monthly; $3.95 modem lease.
Telephone Service
None
Miles of Plant: 8.0 (coaxial); None (fiber optic). Homes passed: 422.
Manager: Robert G. Fischer Jr. Office Manager: Hazel Harden.
Ownership: Nova Cablevision Inc. (MSO).

NEW DOUGLAS—Madison Communications. Now served by SORENTO/NEW DOUGLAS (formerly Sorento), IL [IL0354]. ICA: IL0404.

NEW HAVEN (village)—Formerly served by CableDirect. No longer in operation. ICA: IL0442.

NEW HOLLAND—Mediacom. Now served by DELAVAN, IL [IL0172]. ICA: IL0416.

NEWMAN—Comcast Cable, 303 E Fairlawn Dr, Urbana, IL 61801-5141. Phone: 217-384-2530. Fax: 217-384-2021. Web Site: http://www.comcast.com. Also serves Broadlands & Douglas County. ICA: IL0255.
TV Market Ranking: 64 (Broadlands, Douglas County, NEWMAN). Franchise award date: N.A. Franchise expiration date: N.A. Began: September 28, 1981.
Channel capacity: 36 (not 2-way capable). Channels available but not in use: N.A.
Basic Service
Subscribers: 458.
Programming (received off-air): WAND (NBC) Decatur; WBUI (CW) Decatur; WCCU (FOX) Urbana; WCIA (CBS) Champaign; WEIU-TV (PBS) Charleston; WICD (ABC) Champaign; WILL-TV (PBS) Urbana; 6 FMs.
Programming (via satellite): ABC Family Channel; Animal Planet; Arts & Entertainment; Cartoon Network; CNN; C-SPAN; C-SPAN 2; Discovery Channel; Disney Channel; ESPN; Fox News Channel; FX; Headline News; HGTV; Lifetime; MTV; Nickelodeon; QVC; Spike TV; TBS Superstation; The Learning Channel; Turner Network TV; USA Network; Weather Channel; WGN America.
Fee: $25.00 installation; $35.00 monthly.

Pay Service 1
Pay Units: 5.
Programming (via satellite): Cinemax; Encore; HBO; Starz.
Fee: $8.50 installation; $10.00 monthly (Cinemax, HBO or Starz & Encore).
Internet Service
Operational: Yes.
Telephone Service
Digital: Operational
Miles of Plant: 22.0 (coaxial); None (fiber optic). Homes passed: 620. Total homes in franchised area: 620.
District Director: Melody Brucker. Chief Technician: Jim Lee.
City fee: 3% of gross.
Ownership: Comcast Cable Communications Inc. (MSO).

NEWTON—NewWave Communications, 318 N 4th St, Vandalia, Il 62471. Phone: 573-472-9500. Fax: 618.283.4483. E-mail: info@newwavecom.com. Web Site: http://www.newwavecom.com. ICA: IL0559.
TV Market Ranking: Outside TV Markets (NEWTON). Franchise award date: N.A. Franchise expiration date: N.A. Began: October 1, 1964.
Channel capacity: N.A. Channels available but not in use: N.A.
Basic Service
Subscribers: 760.
Programming (received off-air): WEHT (ABC) Evansville; WFXW (FOX) Terre Haute; WPXS (IND) Mount Vernon; WTHI-TV (CBS) Terre Haute; WTWO (NBC) Terre Haute; WUSI-TV (PBS) Olney; allband FM.
Programming (via satellite): C-SPAN; QVC; Spike TV; Trinity Broadcasting Network; WGN America.
Fee: $15.00 installation; $13.34 monthly; $2.00 converter.
Expanded Basic Service 1
Subscribers: N.A.
Programming (via satellite): ABC Family Channel; AMC; Animal Planet; Arts & Entertainment; Bravo; Cartoon Network; CNBC; CNN; Comedy Central; Country Music TV; Court TV; Discovery Channel; Disney Channel; E! Entertainment Television; ESPN; ESPN 2; Food Network; Fox News Channel; Fox Sports Net Midwest; FX; GSN; Hallmark Channel; Headline News; HGTV; History Channel; Lifetime; MTV; MTV2; National Geographic Channel; Nickelodeon; Outdoor Channel; Speed Channel; Syfy; TBS Superstation; The Learning Channel; Travel Channel; Turner Classic Movies; Turner Network TV; TV Land; USA Network; VH1; Weather Channel.
Digital Basic Service
Subscribers: N.A.
Programming (via satellite): BBC America; Bio; Bloomberg Television; CMT Pure Country; Discovery Health Channel; Discovery Home Channel; Discovery Kids Channel; Discovery Military Channel; Discovery Times Channel; DMX Music; ESPNews; FitTV; Fox Movie Channel; G4; GAS; Golf Channel; Halogen Network; History Channel International; Independent Film Channel; Lifetime Movie Network; MTV Hits; Nick Jr.; Science Channel; ShopNBC; Style Network; Toon Disney; Versus; VH1 Classic; VH1 Soul; WE tv.
Pay Service 1
Pay Units: 226.
Programming (via satellite): Encore; HBO; Showtime; The Movie Channel.
Fee: $20.00 installation; $10.75 monthly (each).
Digital Pay Service 1
Pay Units: N.A.
Programming (via satellite): Cinemax (multiplexed); Encore (multiplexed); Flix; HBO (multiplexed); Showtime (multiplexed); Starz (multiplexed); The Movie Channel (multiplexed).
Video-On-Demand: No
Pay-Per-View
Hot Choice (delivered digitally); iN DEMAND (delivered digitally); Playboy TV (delivered digitally); Fresh (delivered digitally); Shorteez (delivered digitally).
Internet Service
Operational: No.
Telephone Service
None
Miles of Plant: 15.0 (coaxial); None (fiber optic).
General Manager: Bill Flowers. Technical Operations Manager: Chris Mooday.
City fee: 3% of gross.
Ownership: NewWave Communications (MSO).

NOBLE—Wabash Independent Networks, PO Box 719, 113 Hagen Dr, Flora, IL 62839. Phones: 877-878-2120; 618-665-9946. Fax: 618-665-3400. E-mail: winita@wabash.net. Web Site: http://www.wabash.net. ICA: IL0339.
TV Market Ranking: Outside TV Markets (NOBLE). Franchise award date: N.A. Franchise expiration date: N.A. Began: March 22, 1984.
Channel capacity: 37 (not 2-way capable). Channels available but not in use: 2.
Basic Service
Subscribers: 143.
Programming (received off-air): KFVS-TV (CBS, CW) Cape Girardeau; KMOV (CBS) St. Louis; KPLR-TV (CW) St. Louis; KSDK (NBC) St. Louis; WEHT (ABC) Evansville; WFIE (NBC) Evansville; WSIL-TV (ABC) Harrisburg; WSIU-TV (PBS) Carbondale; WTHI-TV (CBS) Terre Haute; WTVW (FOX) Evansville; WTWO (NBC) Terre Haute.
Programming (via satellite): C-SPAN; C-SPAN 2; Eternal Word TV Network; Home Shopping Network; ION Television; QVC; ShopNBC; TBS Superstation; Trinity Broadcasting Network; Weather Channel; WGN America.
Fee: free installation; $19.95 monthly.
Expanded Basic Service 1
Subscribers: 136.
Programming (via satellite): ABC Family Channel; AMC; Animal Planet; Arts & Entertainment; Big Ten Network; Boomerang; Cartoon Network; CNN; Comedy Central; Country Music TV; Discovery Channel; Disney Channel; Do-It-Yourself; E! Entertainment Television; ESPN; ESPN 2; ESPN Clas-

sic Sports; FamilyNet; Food Network; Fox News Channel; Fox Sports Net Midwest; FX; G4; Gospel Music Channel; Hallmark Channel; Halogen Network; Headline News; History Channel; Lifetime; MSNBC; MTV; National Geographic Channel; Nickelodeon; Outdoor Channel; Oxygen; Spike TV; The Learning Channel; Travel Channel; truTV; Turner Classic Movies; Turner Network TV; TV Land; USA Network; VH1.
Fee: $19.00 monthly.

Digital Basic Service
Subscribers: N.A.
Programming (via satellite): AZ TV; BBC America; Bio; Bloomberg Television; Bravo; CMT Pure Country; Current; Discovery Health Channel; Discovery Home Channel; Discovery Kids Channel; Discovery Military Channel; DMX Music; ESPNews; FitTV; Fox Movie Channel; Fox Soccer; FSN Digital Atlantic; FSN Digital Central; FSN Digital Pacific; Fuse; Golf Channel; Great American Country; GSN; HGTV; History Channel International; ID Investigation Discovery; Independent Film Channel; Lifetime Movie Network; MTV Hits; MTV2; Nick Jr.; Ovation; RFD-TV; Science Channel; Sleuth; SoapNet; Speed Channel; Style Network; TeenNick; The Word Network; Toon Disney; Versus; VH1 Classic; VH1 Soul; WE tv.
Fee: $15.00 monthly.

Pay Service 1
Pay Units: 42.
Programming (via satellite): HBO; Showtime; The Movie Channel.
Fee: $15.00 installation; $11.95 monthly (TMC), $12.95 monthly (Showtime), $13.95 monthly (HBO).

Digital Pay Service 1
Pay Units: N.A.
Programming (via satellite): Cinemax (multiplexed); Encore (multiplexed); Flix; HBO (multiplexed); Showtime (multiplexed); Starz (multiplexed); The Movie Channel (multiplexed).
Fee: $11.95 monthly (Cinemax or Starz/Encore), $12.95 monthly (Showtime/TMC/Flix), $13.95 monthly (HBO).

Video-On-Demand: Planned

Pay-Per-View
Club Jenna (delivered digitally); Fresh (delivered digitally); Spice: Xcess (delivered digitally); Playboy TV (delivered digitally).

Internet Service
Operational: Yes.
Broadband Service: In-house.
Fee: $35.00-$50.00 monthly.

Telephone Service
None

Miles of Plant: 9.0 (coaxial); None (fiber optic). Homes passed: 518.

General Manager: Dave Grahn. Assistant General Manager: Jeff Williams. Marketing Director: Carol Oestreich. Controller: Tanya Wells.

Ownership: Wabash Independent Networks (MSO).

NOKOMIS—Charter Communications, 11 Clearing, Taylorville, IL 62568-9279. Phones: 217-287-7992; 636-207-7044 (St Louis office). Fax: 217-287-7304. Web Site: http://www.charter.com. Also serves Coalton & Witt. ICA: IL0199.

TV Market Ranking: Outside TV Markets (Coalton, NOKOMIS, Witt). Franchise award date: N.A. Franchise expiration date: N.A. Began: May 1, 1974.

Channel capacity: 60 (not 2-way capable). Channels available but not in use: None.

Basic Service
Subscribers: 681.
Programming (received off-air): KDNL-TV (ABC) St. Louis; KETC (PBS) St. Louis; KMOV (CBS) St. Louis; KPLR-TV (CW) St. Louis; KSDK (NBC) St. Louis; WAND (NBC) Decatur; WICS (ABC) Springfield; WRSP-TV (FOX) Springfield.
Programming (via satellite): ABC Family Channel; AMC; Arts & Entertainment; Bravo; CNBC; Country Music TV; C-SPAN; E! Entertainment Television; ESPN; Home Shopping Network; Lifetime; MTV; QVC; Syfy; Trinity Broadcasting Network; Turner Network TV; USA Network.
Current originations: Government Access; Educational Access; Public Access.
Fee: $29.99 installation.

Expanded Basic Service 1
Subscribers: N.A.
Programming (via satellite): Animal Planet; CNN; Comedy Central; Discovery Channel; Disney Channel; ESPN 2; Food Network; Fox News Channel; Fox Sports Net Midwest; Headline News; HGTV; History Channel; MSNBC; Nickelodeon; Oxygen; Spike TV; TBS Superstation; The Learning Channel; Travel Channel; TV Land; VH1; Weather Channel; WGN America.
Fee: $42.99 monthly.

Pay Service 1
Pay Units: 59.
Programming (via satellite): Cinemax.
Fee: $15.00 installation; $9.45 monthly.

Pay Service 2
Pay Units: 152.
Programming (via satellite): HBO.
Fee: $15.00 installation; $11.00 monthly.

Pay Service 3
Pay Units: 25.
Programming (via satellite): Showtime.
Fee: $10.45 monthly.

Pay Service 4
Pay Units: 50.
Programming (via satellite): The Movie Channel.
Fee: $15.00 installation; $10.45 monthly.

Video-On-Demand: No

Internet Service
Operational: No.

Telephone Service
None

Miles of Plant: 38.0 (coaxial); None (fiber optic). Homes passed: 2,125.

Vice President & General Manager: Steve Trippe. Operations Director: Dave Miller. Chief Technician: Larry Harmon. Marketing Director: Beverly Wall. Office Manager: Melinda Sincavage.

City fee: 3% of gross.

Ownership: Charter Communications Inc. (MSO).

NORRIS—Insight Communications. Now served by CANTON, IL [IL0087]. ICA: IL0353.

NORRIS CITY—NewWave Communications, 318 N 4th St, Vandalia, IL 62471. Phone: 573-472-9500. Fax: 618.283.4483. E-mail: info@newwavecom.com. Web Site: http://www.newwavecom.com. ICA: IL0235.

TV Market Ranking: 69 (NORRIS CITY). Franchise award date: September 21, 1981. Franchise expiration date: N.A. Began: June 1, 1983.

Channel capacity: 136 (not 2-way capable). Channels available but not in use: N.A.

Basic Service
Subscribers: 149.
Programming (received off-air): KFVS-TV (CBS, CW) Cape Girardeau; WEHT (ABC) Evansville; WEVV-TV (CBS, MNT) Evansville; WFIE (NBC) Evansville; WNIN (PBS) Evansville; WPXS (IND) Mount Vernon; WSIL-TV (ABC) Harrisburg; WTVW (FOX) Evansville; WUSI-TV (PBS) Olney.
Programming (via satellite): C-SPAN; C-SPAN 2; Home Shopping Network; INSP; QVC; Trinity Broadcasting Network; WGN America.
Current originations: Educational Access.
Fee: $40.00 installation; $16.95 monthly; $40.00 additional installation.

Expanded Basic Service 1
Subscribers: 136.
Programming (via satellite): ABC Family Channel; AMC; Animal Planet; Arts & Entertainment; Big Ten Network; Bravo; Cartoon Network; CNBC; CNN; Comedy Central; Country Music TV; Discovery Channel; Disney Channel; E! Entertainment Television; ESPN; ESPN 2; ESPN Classic Sports; Eternal Word TV Network; Food Network; Fox News Channel; Fox Sports Net Midwest; FX; Golf Channel; GSN; Hallmark Channel; Headline News; HGTV; History Channel; Lifetime; MSNBC; MTV; National Geographic Channel; Nickelodeon; Outdoor Channel; Oxygen; ShopNBC; SoapNet; Speed Channel; Spike TV; Syfy; TBS Superstation; The Learning Channel; Toon Disney; Travel Channel; truTV; Turner Classic Movies; Turner Network TV; TV Land; USA Network; Versus; VH1; Weather Channel.

Digital Basic Service
Subscribers: N.A.
Programming (received off-air): WEHT (ABC) Evansville; WEVV-TV (CBS, MNT) Evansville; WFIE (NBC) Evansville; WSIL-TV (ABC) Harrisburg; WTVW (FOX) Evansville.
Programming (via satellite): BBC America; Bio; Bloomberg Television; CMT Pure Country; Cooking Channel; Discovery HD Theater; Discovery Health Channel; Discovery Home Channel; Discovery Kids Channel; Discovery Military Channel; Do-It-Yourself; ESPN 2 HD; ESPN HD; ESPNews; FitTV; Fox College Sports Atlantic; Fox College Sports Central; Fox College Sports Pacific; Fox Movie Channel; FSN HD; G4; Great American Country; Halogen Network; HDNet; HDNet Movies; History Channel International; ID Investigation Discovery; Lifetime Movie Network; MTV Hits; MTV Jams; MTV2; Music Choice; Nick Jr.; Nick Too; NickToons TV; Outdoor Channel; RFD-TV; Science Channel; Sleuth; Style Network; TeenNick; Turner Network TV HD; Universal HD; VH1 Classic; VH1 Soul.

Digital Pay Service 1
Pay Units: N.A.
Programming (via satellite): Cinemax (multiplexed); Cinemax HD; Encore (multiplexed); HBO (multiplexed); HBO HD; Showtime (multiplexed); Starz (multiplexed); Starz HDTV; The Movie Channel (multiplexed).

Video-On-Demand: No

Pay-Per-View
iN DEMAND (delivered digitally); Spice: Xcess (delivered digitally); Club Jenna (delivered digitally); Playboy TV (delivered digitally); Fresh (delivered digitally); Shorteez (delivered digitally).

Internet Service
Operational: Yes.

Telephone Service
Digital: Operational

Miles of Plant: 15.0 (coaxial); None (fiber optic). Homes passed: 798. Total homes in franchised area: 798.

General Manager: Bill Flowers. Technical Operations Manager: Chris Mooday.

City fee: 3% of gross.

Ownership: NewWave Communications (MSO).

OAK BROOK—Comcast Cable, 2001 York Rd, Oak Brook, IL 60523. Phones: 630-288-1000; 847-585-6300 (Schaumberg office). Fax: 630-288-1292. Web Site: http://www.comcast.com. Also serves Addison, Aurora, Bartlett, Batavia, Bedford Park, Bellwood, Bensenville, Berkeley, Berwyn, Bloomingdale, Bolingbrook, Boulder Hill, Bridgeview, Broadview, Brookfield, Burbank, Burr Ridge, Campton Twp., Carbon Hill, Carol Stream, Channahon, Cicero, Clarendon Hills, Coal City, Countryside, Crest Hill, Darien, Diamond, Downers Grove, Du Page County (unincorporated areas), Elgin, Elmhurst, Elmwood Park, Forest Park, Forest View, Frankfort, Franklin Park, Geneva, Glen Ellyn, Glendale Heights, Grundy County, Harwood Heights, Hasca, Hillside, Hinsdale, Hodgkins, Homer Glen, Joliet, Justice, Kane County, Keeneyville, Kendall County, Lemont, Leyden Twp., Lily Lake, Lisle, Lockport, Lombard, Lyons, Maywood, Mazon (village), McCook, Medinah, Melrose Park, Millington, Minooka, Mokena, Montgomery, Morris, Naperville, New Lenox, Norridge, North Aurora, North Riverside, Northlake, Oak Park, Oakbrook Terrace, Oswego, Plainfield, Plano, Plato Twp., Proviso Twp., River Forest, River Grove, Rockdale, Romeoville, Roselle, Rosemont, Sandwich, Schiller Park, Shorewood, South Elgin, St. Charles, Stickney, Stone Park, Summit, Villa Park, Warrenville, West Chicago, Westchester, Westmont, Wheatland, Wheaton, Will County, Willow Springs, Willowbrook, Wilmington, Winfield, Wood Dale, Woodridge & Yorkville. ICA: IL0006.

TV Market Ranking: 3 (Addison, Aurora, Bartlett, Batavia, Bedford Park, Bensenville, Berkeley, Bloomingdale, Bolingbrook, Bridgeview, Broadview, Burbank, Burr Ridge, Campton Twp., Carol Stream, Cicero, Clarendon Hills, Countryside, Crest Hill, Darien, Downers Grove, Du Page County (unincorporated areas), Elgin, Elmhurst, Elmwood Park, Forest Park, Forest View, Frankfort, Franklin Park, Geneva, Glen Ellyn, Glendale Heights, Hasca, Hillside, Hinsdale, Hodgkins, Homer Glen, Joliet, Justice, Kane County (portions), Keeneyville, Kendall County (portions), Lemont, Leyden Twp., Lisle, Lockport, Lombard, Lyons, Maywood, McCook, Medinah, Mokena, Montgomery, Naperville, New Lenox, North Aurora, North Riverside, OAK BROOK, Oak Park, Oakbrook Terrace, Plainfield, Plato Twp., Proviso Twp., River Forest, River Grove, Romeoville, Roselle, Roselle, Rosemont, Schiller Park, South Elgin, St. Charles, Stone Park, Summit, Villa Park, Warrenville, West Chicago, Westchester, Westmont, Wheatland, Wheaton, Will County (portions), Willow Springs, Willowbrook, Winfield, Wood Dale, Woodridge); Below 100 (Boulder Hill, Carbon Hill, Channahon, Coal City, Diamond, Grundy County, Lily Lake, Mazon (village), Millington, Minooka, Norris, Oswego, Plano, Rockdale, Sandwich, Shorewood, Wilmington, Yorkville, Kane County (portions), Kendall County (portions), Will County (portions)). Franchise award date: September 1, 1979. Franchise expiration date: N.A. Began: August 1, 1980.

Channel capacity: N.A. Channels available but not in use: N.A.

Basic Service

Subscribers: 347,230.

Programming (received off-air): WBBM-TV (CBS) Chicago; WCIU-TV (IND) Chicago; WCPX-TV (ION) Chicago; WFLD (FOX) Chicago; WGBO-DT (UNV) Joliet; WGN-TV (CW, IND) Chicago; WJYS (IND) Hammond; WLS-TV (ABC) Chicago; WMAQ-TV (NBC) Chicago; WPWR-TV (MNT) Gary; WSNS-TV (TMO) Chicago; WTTW (PBS) Chicago; WXFT-DT (TEL) Aurora; WYCC (PBS) Chicago; WYIN (PBS) Gary; 24 FMs.

Programming (via satellite): C-SPAN; Home Shopping Network; QVC; The Comcast Network; Total Living Network; TV Guide Network.

Current originations: Leased Access; Religious Access; Government Access; Educational Access; Public Access.

Fee: $48.99 installation; $15.49 monthly.

Expanded Basic Service 1

Subscribers: 337,631.

Programming (via satellite): ABC Family Channel; AMC; Animal Planet; Arts & Entertainment; BET Networks; Cartoon Network; Chicagoland Television News; CNBC; CNN; Comcast SportsNet Chicago; Comedy Central; Country Music TV; C-SPAN 2; Discovery Channel; Disney Channel; E! Entertainment Television; ESPN; ESPN 2; Eternal Word TV Network; Food Network; Fox News Channel; FX; Golf Channel; Hallmark Channel; Headline News; HGTV; History Channel; Lifetime; MoviePlex; MSNBC; MTV; Nickelodeon; Oxygen; Speed Channel; TBS Superstation; The Learning Channel; Travel Channel; truTV; Turner Network TV; TV Land; USA Network; Versus; VH1; Weather Channel.

Fee: $54.99 monthly.

Digital Basic Service

Subscribers: 117,711.

Programming (received off-air): WBBM-TV (CBS) Chicago; WFLD (FOX) Chicago; WGN-TV (CW, IND) Chicago; WLS-TV (ABC) Chicago; WMAQ-TV (NBC) Chicago; WPWR-TV (MNT) Gary; WTTW (PBS) Chicago.

Programming (via satellite): AmericanLife TV Network; BBC America; Bio; Black Family Channel; Bloomberg Television; Bravo; Canales N; Discovery Digital Networks; Discovery HD Theater; ESPN 2 HD; ESPN HD; ESPNews; Fox College Sports Atlantic; Fox College Sports Central; Fox College Sports Pacific; Fox Movie Channel; Fox Sports World; Fuse; G4; GAS; Great American Country; GSN; Halogen Network; History Channel International; Independent Film Channel; INHD; Lifetime Movie Network; Lime; MTV Networks Digital Suite; Music Choice; National Geographic Channel; NFL Network; Nick Jr.; NickToons TV; Outdoor Channel; Ovation; Palladia; ShopNBC; Style Network; Sundance Channel; Syfy; The Word Network; Toon Disney; Trinity Broadcasting Network; Turner Classic Movies; Turner Network TV HD; TVG Network; Versus HD; WE tv; Weatherscan.

Fee: $56.98 monthly.

Digital Pay Service 1

Pay Units: 148,062.

Programming (via satellite): Cinemax (multiplexed); Cinemax HD; Encore (multiplexed); Flix; HBO (multiplexed); HBO HD; Showtime (multiplexed); Showtime HD; Starz (multiplexed); Starz HDTV; The Movie Channel (multiplexed).

Fee: $16.00 monthly (each).

Video-On-Demand: Yes

Pay-Per-View

Addressable homes: 196,592.

iN DEMAND, Addressable: Yes; ESPN Now (delivered digitally); Playboy TV (delivered digitally); Hot Choice (delivered digitally); sports (delivered digitally); NBA TV (delivered digitally); NBA/WNBA League Pass (delivered digitally); NHL Center Ice/MLB Extra Innings (delivered digitally); iN DEMAND (delivered digitally); Fresh (delivered digitally); Shorteez (delivered digitally).

Internet Service

Operational: Yes.

Subscribers: 78,821.

Broadband Service: Comcast High Speed Internet.

Fee: $99.95 installation; $42.95 monthly.

Telephone Service

Digital: Operational

Fee: $44.95 monthly

Miles of Plant: 6,704.0 (coaxial); 315.0 (fiber optic). Homes passed: 672,088. Total homes in franchised area: 672,088.

Area Vice President: Leigh Anne Hughes. Senior Regional Vice President: Steve Reimer. Vice President, Technical Operations: Bob Curtis. Vice President, Sales & Marketing: Eric Schaefer. Vice President, Communications: Rich Ruggiero.

City fee: 5% of gross.

Ownership: Comcast Cable Communications Inc. (MSO).

OAK FOREST—Comcast Cable. Now served by CHICAGO (southern suburbs), IL [IL0008]. ICA: IL0050.

OAK LAWN—Comcast Cable. Now served by CHICAGO (southern suburbs), IL [IL0008]. ICA: IL0021.

OCONEE—Formerly served by Mediacom. No longer in operation. ICA: IL0447.

ODELL—Mediacom. Now served by PONTIAC, IL [IL0109]. ICA: IL0310.

OKAWVILLE—Charter Communications, 5111 Lake Terrace NE, Mount Vernon, IL 62864-9666. Phones: 636-207-7044 (St Louis office); 618-242-9512. Fax: 618-242-4156. Web Site: http://www.charter.com. Also serves Central City, Centralia, Clinton County, Marion County, Nashville, Wamac & Washington County. ICA: IL0075.

TV Market Ranking: 11 (Clinton County (portions)); Below 100 (Central City, Centralia, Marion County, Nashville, Wamac, Washington County, Clinton County (portions)); Outside TV Markets (OKAWVILLE, Clinton County (portions)). Franchise award date: N.A. Franchise expiration date: N.A. Began: March 1, 1968.

Channel capacity: N.A. Channels available but not in use: N.A.

Basic Service

Subscribers: 5,237.

Programming (received off-air): KDNL-TV (ABC) St. Louis; KETC (PBS) St. Louis; KFVS-TV (CBS, CW) Cape Girardeau; KMOV (CBS) St. Louis; KPLR-TV (CW) St. Louis; KSDK (NBC) St. Louis; KTVI (FOX) St. Louis; WPXS (IND) Mount Vernon; WSIU-TV (PBS) Carbondale; WTCT (IND) Marion.

Programming (via satellite): C-SPAN; C-SPAN 2; Home Shopping Network; INSP; Product Information Network; QVC; TBS Superstation; TV Guide Network; Weather Channel; WGN America.

Fee: $29.99 installation.

Expanded Basic Service 1

Subscribers: 4,559.

Programming (via satellite): ABC Family Channel; AMC; Animal Planet; Arts & Entertainment; BET Networks; Bravo; Cartoon Network; CNBC; CNN; Comedy Central; Country Music TV; Discovery Channel; Disney Channel; E! Entertainment Television; ESPN; ESPN 2; Eternal Word TV Network; FitTV; Food Network; Fox News Channel; Fox Sports Net Midwest; FX; G4; Golf Channel; GSN; Hallmark Channel; Headline News; HGTV; History Channel; Lifetime; MSNBC; MTV; National Geographic Channel; Nickelodeon; Oxygen; SoapNet; Speed Channel; Spike TV; Syfy; The Learning Channel; Toon Disney; Travel Channel; truTV; Turner Network TV; TV Land; USA Network; Versus; VH1.

Fee: $49.99 monthly.

Digital Basic Service

Subscribers: 1,887.

Programming (via satellite): AmericanLife TV Network; BBC America; BET Networks; Bio; Bloomberg Television; Discovery Digital Networks; DMX Music; ESPN Classic Sports; ESPNews; Fox Movie Channel; Fox Sports World; GAS; Halogen Network; History Channel International; Independent Film Channel; Lifetime Movie Network; MTV Networks Digital Suite; MuchMusic Network; Nick Jr.; Outdoor Channel; Ovation; Style Network; Sundance Channel; Trinity Broadcasting Network; Turner Classic Movies; WE tv.

Fee: $10.00 monthly.

Digital Pay Service 1

Pay Units: 1,412.

Programming (via satellite): Cinemax (multiplexed); Encore (multiplexed); HBO (multiplexed); Showtime (multiplexed); Starz (multiplexed); The Movie Channel (multiplexed).

Fee: $10.95 monthly (Cinemax), $11.95 monthly (HBO, Showtime or TMC).

Video-On-Demand: Yes

Pay-Per-View

iN DEMAND (delivered digitally); Playboy TV (delivered digitally); Fresh (delivered digitally); Shorteez (delivered digitally); sports (delivered digitally).

Internet Service

Operational: Yes.

Broadband Service: Charter Pipeline.

Fee: $39.99 monthly; $5.00 modem lease; $99.99 modem purchase.

Telephone Service

Digital: Operational

Fee: $29.99 monthly

Homes passed: 11,420. Miles of plant (coax) included in Woodlawn

Vice President & General Manager: Steve Trippe. Operations Director: Dave Miller. Technical Operations Manager: Eddie Prior. Marketing Director: Beverly Wall.

City fee: 5% of gross.

Ownership: Charter Communications Inc. (MSO).

OLNEY—Comcast Cable, PO Box T, 311A Whittle Ave, Olney, IL 62450-0918. Phones: 618-395-8663 (Customer service); 618-395-5298. Fax: 618-395-4131. Web Site: http://www.comcast.com. Also serves Dundas, Jasper County (southern portion) & West Liberty. ICA: IL0103.

TV Market Ranking: Outside TV Markets (Dundas, Jasper County (southern portion), OLNEY, West Liberty). Franchise award date: September 1, 1964. Franchise expiration date: N.A. Began: September 1, 1964.

Channel capacity: 63 (operating 2-way). Channels available but not in use: N.A.

Basic Service

Subscribers: 3,399.

Programming (received off-air): WEHT (ABC) Evansville; WFIE (NBC) Evansville; WTHI-TV (CBS) Terre Haute; WTVW (FOX) Evansville; WTWO (NBC) Terre Haute; WUSI-TV (PBS) Olney; 1 FM.

Programming (via microwave): KPLR-TV (CW) St. Louis.

Programming (via satellite): ABC Family Channel; AMC; Animal Planet; Arts & Entertainment; Cartoon Network; CNBC; CNN; Comedy Central; Country Music TV; C-SPAN; Discovery Channel; Discovery Health Channel; Disney Channel; E! Entertainment Television; ESPN; ESPN 2; ESPN Classic Sports; ESPNews; Food Network; Fox News Channel; Fox Sports Net Midwest; FX; GSN; Hallmark Channel; Headline News; HGTV; History Channel; ION Television; Lifetime; MSNBC; MTV; Nickelodeon; QVC; ShopNBC; SoapNet; Spike TV; Syfy; TBS Superstation; The Learning Channel; Toon Disney; Travel Channel; Trinity Broadcasting Network; truTV; Turner Network TV; TV Guide Network; TV Land; USA Network; VH1; Weather Channel; WGN America.

Fee: $14.99 monthly.

Expanded Basic Service 1

Subscribers: 2,200.

Fee: $30.00 monthly.

Digital Basic Service

Subscribers: 557.

Programming (via satellite): BBC America; Discovery Digital Networks; GAS; Lifetime Movie Network; MTV Networks Digital Suite; Music Choice; NFL Network; Nick Jr.; Nick Too; Speed Channel.

Fee: $12.95 monthly.

Pay Service 1

Pay Units: N.A.

Programming (via satellite): Cinemax; HBO; Showtime.

Digital Pay Service 1

Pay Units: N.A.

Programming (via satellite): Cinemax (multiplexed); Encore (multiplexed); HBO (multiplexed); Showtime (multiplexed); Starz (multiplexed); The Movie Channel (multiplexed); WAM! America's Kidz Network.

Video-On-Demand: No

Pay-Per-View

ESPN Full Court (delivered digitally), Addressable: Yes; ESPN Gameplan (delivered digitally), Addressable: Yes; Fresh (delivered digitally).

Internet Service

Operational: Yes.

Subscribers: 850.

Broadband Service: Comcast High Speed Internet.

Fee: $42.95 monthly.

Telephone Service

None

Miles of Plant: 83.0 (coaxial); 8.0 (fiber optic). Homes passed: 5,300.

General Manager: Don Richey. Technical Operations Director: Richard Ring. Plant Manager: Tom Rauch.

City fee: 3% of gross.

Ownership: Comcast Cable Communications Inc. (MSO).

OMAHA—Formerly served by CableDirect. No longer in operation. ICA: IL0624.

ONARGA—Comcast Cable, 7720 W 98th St, Hickory Hills, IL 60457. Phone: 847-585-6300 (Kankakee office). Fax: 708-237-3292. Web Site: http://www.comcast.com. Also serves Danforth & Gilman. ICA: IL0168.

TV Market Ranking: Outside TV Markets (Danforth, Gilman, ONARGA). Franchise award date: N.A. Franchise expiration date: N.A. Began: December 1, 1968.
Channel capacity: N.A. Channels available but not in use: N.A.
Basic Service
Subscribers: 1,269.
Programming (received off-air): WAND (NBC) Decatur; WCCU (FOX) Urbana; WCIA (CBS) Champaign; WFLD (FOX) Chicago; WGN-TV (CW, IND) Chicago; WICD (ABC) Champaign; WILL-TV (PBS) Urbana; WLS-TV (ABC) Chicago; WPWR-TV (MNT) Gary; WTTW (PBS) Chicago.
Programming (via satellite): C-SPAN; Discovery Channel; QVC; TBS Superstation.
Fee: $48.99 installation; $16.17 monthly.
Expanded Basic Service 1
Subscribers: 1,252.
Programming (via satellite): ABC Family Channel; AMC; Animal Planet; Cartoon Network; CNN; Comcast SportsNet Chicago; Country Music TV; Disney Channel; ESPN; Fox News Channel; FX; HGTV; Lifetime; MoviePlex; Nickelodeon; Spike TV; The Learning Channel; Turner Network TV; Univision; USA Network; Weather Channel.
Fee: $23.32 monthly.
Digital Basic Service
Subscribers: N.A.
Programming (via satellite): BBC America; Bravo; Discovery Digital Networks; Encore; ESPN Classic Sports; ESPNews; Fox Soccer; Golf Channel; GSN; Independent Film Channel; Nick Jr.; Syfy; Turner Classic Movies; TV Land; Versus; WE tv.
Fee: $11.99 monthly.
Digital Pay Service 1
Pay Units: N.A.
Programming (via satellite): Cinemax (multiplexed); Flix; HBO (multiplexed); Showtime (multiplexed); Starz (multiplexed); The Movie Channel (multiplexed).
Pay-Per-View
iN DEMAND (delivered digitally); Playboy TV (delivered digitally).
Internet Service
Operational: Yes.
Telephone Service
Digital: Operational
Miles of Plant: 51.0 (coaxial); None (fiber optic). Homes passed: 1,710. Total homes in franchised area: 1,710.
Area Vice President: Sandy Weicher. Vice President, Technical Operations: Bob Curtis. Vice President, Sales & Marketing: Eric Schaefer. Vice President, Communications: Rich Ruggiero.
City fee: 5% of gross.
Ownership: Comcast Cable Communications Inc. (MSO).

ONEIDA—Oneida Cablevision Inc., PO Box 445, 129 W Hwy, Oneida, IL 61467-0445. Phone: 309-483-3111. Fax: 309-483-7777. Web Site: http://www.winco.net. ICA: IL0361.
TV Market Ranking: 60 (ONEIDA). Franchise award date: N.A. Franchise expiration date: N.A. Began: September 1, 1985.
Channel capacity: N.A. Channels available but not in use: N.A.
Basic Service
Subscribers: 250.
Programming (received off-air): KGCW (CW) Burlington; KLJB (CW, FOX) Davenport; KWQC-TV (NBC) Davenport; WEEK-TV (NBC) Peoria; WHBF-TV (CBS) Rock Island; WHOI (ABC, CW) Peoria; WMBD-TV (CBS) Peoria; WQAD-TV (ABC) Moline; WQPT-TV (PBS) Moline; WTVP (PBS) Peoria.
Programming (via satellite): ABC Family Channel; AMC; Animal Planet; Arts & Entertainment; Cartoon Network; CNBC; CNN; Comedy Central; Country Music TV; C-SPAN; Discovery Channel; Disney Channel; ESPN; ESPN 2; Fox News Channel; FX; Headline News; HGTV; History Channel; Lifetime; MSNBC; MTV; National Geographic Channel; Nickelodeon; QVC; Spike TV; Syfy; TBS Superstation; The Learning Channel; Travel Channel; Turner Network TV; TV Land; USA Network; VH1; Weather Channel; WGN America.
Fee: $30.00 installation; $26.00 monthly; $1.50 converter.
Internet Service
Operational: No, Both DSL & dialup.
Telephone Service
None
Miles of Plant: 8.0 (coaxial); None (fiber optic).
Manager: David Olson.
Ownership: Oneida Cablevision.

OQUAWKA—Mediacom. Now served by ROSEVILLE, IL [IL0274]. ICA: IL0250.

OREGON—Formerly served by Insight Communications. No longer in operation. ICA: IL0074.

ORLAND PARK—Comcast Cable. Now served by CHICAGO (southern suburbs), IL [IL0008]. ICA: IL0048.

OTTAWA—Mediacom. Now served by STREATOR, IL [IL0069]. ICA: IL0058.

PALMER—Mediacom. Now served by KINCAID, IL [IL0176]. ICA: IL0435.

PALMYRA—Formerly served by Almega Cable. No longer in operation. ICA: IL0290.

PALOMA—Adams Telecom. Formerly served by Golden, IL [IL0257]. This cable system has converted to IPTV, PO Box 248, 405 Emminga Rd, Golden, IL 62339. Phone: 217-696-4411. E-mail: service@adams.net. Web Site: http://www.adams.net. ICA: IL5322.
Channel capacity: N.A. Channels available but not in use: N.A.
Internet Service
Operational: Yes.
Ownership: Adams Telephone Co-Operative.

PALOS PARK—Formerly served by TV Max. No longer in operation. ICA: IL0167.

PANA—Charter Communications, 11 Clearing, Taylorville, IL 62568-9279. Phones: 217-287-7992; 636-207-7044 (St Louis office). Fax: 217-287-7304. Web Site: http://www.charter.com. Also serves Christian County (portions). ICA: IL0562.
TV Market Ranking: 64 (Christian County (portions), PANA). Franchise award date: April 1, 1977. Franchise expiration date: N.A. Began: April 1, 1977.
Channel capacity: 60 (not 2-way capable). Channels available but not in use: 19.
Basic Service
Subscribers: N.A. Included in Taylorville
Programming (received off-air): KPLR-TV (CW) St. Louis; KSDK (NBC) St. Louis; WAND (NBC) Decatur; WBUI (CW) Decatur; WCFN (MNT) Springfield; WCIA (CBS) Champaign; WICS (ABC) Springfield; WILL-TV (PBS) Urbana; WRSP-TV (FOX) Springfield.
Programming (via satellite): C-SPAN; C-SPAN 2; Home Shopping Network; QVC; Weatherscan; WGN America.
Current originations: Government Access; Educational Access; Public Access.
Fee: $29.99 installation.
Expanded Basic Service 1
Subscribers: 1,684.
Programming (via satellite): ABC Family Channel; AMC; Animal Planet; Arts & Entertainment; Cartoon Network; CNBC; CNN; Comedy Central; Country Music TV; Discovery Channel; Disney Channel; E! Entertainment Television; ESPN; ESPN 2; Food Network; Fox News Channel; Fox Sports Net Midwest; FX; GSN; Headline News; HGTV; History Channel; Lifetime; MTV; Nickelodeon; Spike TV; Syfy; TBS Superstation; The Learning Channel; Turner Network TV; TV Guide Network; USA Network; VH1; Weather Channel.
Fee: $42.99 monthly.
Video-On-Demand: No
Internet Service
Operational: No.
Telephone Service
None
Miles of Plant: 46.0 (coaxial); None (fiber optic). Homes passed included in Taylorville
Vice President & General Manager: Steve Trippe. Operations Director: Dave Miller. Chief Technician: Larry Harmon. Marketing Director: Beverly Wall. Office Manager: Melinda Sincavage.
Ownership: Charter Communications Inc. (MSO).

PANAMA—Formerly served by Beck's Cable Systems. No longer in operation. ICA: IL0350.

PARIS—Avenue Broadband Communications, 2603 Hart St, Vincennes, IN 47591. Phones: 800-882-7185; 812-895-7676. Fax: 812-886-5017. Web Site: http://www.avenuebroadband.com. ICA: IL0122.
TV Market Ranking: Below 100 (PARIS). Franchise award date: July 1, 1962. Franchise expiration date: N.A. Began: July 1, 1965.
Channel capacity: N.A. Channels available but not in use: N.A.
Basic Service
Subscribers: 3,003.
Programming (received off-air): WAND (NBC) Decatur; WCCU (FOX) Urbana; WCIA (CBS) Champaign; WEIU-TV (PBS) Charleston; WFXW (FOX) Terre Haute; WICD (ABC) Champaign; WILL-TV (PBS) Urbana; WRTV (ABC) Indianapolis; WTHI-TV (CBS) Terre Haute; WTTV (CW) Bloomington; WTWO (NBC) Terre Haute; 24 FMs.
Current originations: Educational Access.
Fee: $29.99 installation.
Expanded Basic Service 1
Subscribers: N.A.
Programming (via satellite): ABC Family Channel; AMC; Animal Planet; Arts & Entertainment; Bravo; Cartoon Network; CNBC; CNN; Comedy Central; Country Music TV; C-SPAN; C-SPAN 2; Discovery Channel; Disney Channel; E! Entertainment Television; ESPN; ESPN 2; Eternal Word TV Network; FitTV; Food Network; Fox News Channel; FX; G4; Golf Channel; Hallmark Channel; Headline News; HGTV; History Channel; Home Shopping Network; ION Television; Lifetime; MSNBC; MTV; National Geographic Channel; Nickelodeon; Oxygen; QVC; SoapNet; Speed Channel; Spike TV; Syfy; TBS Superstation; The Learning Channel; Toon Disney; Travel Channel; Trinity Broadcasting Network; truTV; Turner Classic Movies; Turner Network TV; TV Land; USA Network; Versus; VH1; WE tv; Weather Channel; WGN America.
Fee: $49.99 monthly.
Digital Basic Service
Subscribers: 758.
Programming (via satellite): BBC America; Bio; Discovery Digital Networks; Do-It-Yourself; GAS; History Channel International; Independent Film Channel; Lifetime Movie Network; MTV Networks Digital Suite; Music Choice; Nick Jr.; Nick Too; NickToons TV; Sundance Channel; TV Guide Interactive Inc.
Fee: $49.95 monthly.
Digital Pay Service 1
Pay Units: 255.
Programming (via satellite): Cinemax (multiplexed).
Digital Pay Service 2
Pay Units: 555.
Programming (via satellite): Starz (multiplexed).
Digital Pay Service 3
Pay Units: 339.
Programming (via satellite): HBO (multiplexed).
Digital Pay Service 4
Pay Units: 154.
Programming (via satellite): Flix; Showtime (multiplexed).
Digital Pay Service 5
Pay Units: 94.
Programming (via satellite): The Movie Channel (multiplexed).
Digital Pay Service 6
Pay Units: 25.
Programming (via satellite): Encore (multiplexed).
Video-On-Demand: No
Pay-Per-View
iN DEMAND (delivered digitally); NHL Center Ice/MLB Extra Innings (delivered digitally); Hot Choice (delivered digitally); Playboy TV (delivered digitally); Fresh (delivered digitally); Shorteez (delivered digitally).
Internet Service
Operational: Yes.
Telephone Service
Digital: Operational
Miles of Plant: 61.0 (coaxial); 8.0 (fiber optic). Homes passed: 5,200. Total homes in franchised area: 5,200.
Chief Executive Officer: Steve Lowe. Vice President & General Manager: Mary Iafrate. Vice President, Engineering: Jeff Spence. System Engineer: Bart Cotter.
City fee: 5% of gross.
Ownership: Buford Media Group LLC (MSO).

PARK FOREST—Comcast Cable. Now served by CHICAGO (southern suburbs), IL [IL0008]. ICA: IL0066.

PARKERSBURG—Formerly served by CableDirect. No longer in operation. ICA: IL0424.

PATOKA—Clearvision Cable Systems Inc., 1785 US Rte 40, Greenup, IL 62428-3501. Phone: 217-923-5594. Fax: 217-923-5681. Also serves Vernon. ICA: IL0159.
TV Market Ranking: Below 100 (PATOKA, Vernon). Franchise award date: N.A. Franchise expiration date: N.A. Began: September 1, 1984.
Channel capacity: N.A. Channels available but not in use: N.A.

Basic Service
Subscribers: 130.
Programming (received off-air): KDNL-TV (ABC) St. Louis; KMOV (CBS) St. Louis; KPLR-TV (CW) St. Louis; KSDK (NBC) St. Louis; KTVI (FOX) St. Louis; WPXS (IND) Mount Vernon; WSIU-TV (PBS) Carbondale.
Programming (via satellite): TBS Superstation; Trinity Broadcasting Network; WGN America; WKRN-TV (ABC) Nashville.
Fee: $20.00 installation; $13.34 monthly; $2.00 converter.

Expanded Basic Service 1
Subscribers: 128.
Programming (via satellite): ABC Family Channel; AMC; Arts & Entertainment; CNBC; CNN; Country Music TV; Discovery Channel; Disney Channel; ESPN; Fox Sports Net Midwest; Headline News; History Channel; Lifetime; Nickelodeon; Spike TV; Syfy; Turner Network TV; USA Network; Weather Channel.
Fee: $20.00 installation; $6.00 monthly.

Digital Basic Service
Subscribers: 9.
Programming (via satellite): AmericanLife TV Network; BBC America; Bio; Bloomberg Television; Bravo; Discovery Digital Networks; DMX Music; FitTV; Fox Movie Channel; Fuse; G4; GAS; Golf Channel; GSN; Halogen Network; HGTV; History Channel International; Independent Film Channel; Lifetime Movie Network; MTV Networks Digital Suite; Nick Jr.; Outdoor Channel; ShopNBC; Speed Channel; Style Network; Toon Disney; Turner Classic Movies; Versus; WE tv.

Pay Service 1
Pay Units: 28.
Programming (via satellite): HBO.
Fee: $20.00 installation; $11.00 monthly.

Digital Pay Service 1
Pay Units: N.A.
Programming (via satellite): Cinemax (multiplexed); Encore (multiplexed); Flix; HBO (multiplexed); Showtime (multiplexed); Starz (multiplexed); The Movie Channel (multiplexed).

Video-On-Demand: No

Pay-Per-View
ESPN Now (delivered digitally); Hot Choice (delivered digitally); iN DEMAND (delivered digitally); Playboy TV (delivered digitally); Fresh (delivered digitally); Shorteez (delivered digitally).

Internet Service
Operational: No.

Telephone Service
None

Miles of Plant: 12.0 (coaxial); None (fiber optic). Homes passed: 437.
General Manager: Michael Bauguss.
Ownership: Clearvision Cable Systems Inc. (MSO).

PAYSON—Adams Telephone. This cable system has converted to IPTV. See Payson. IL [IL5323]. ICA: IL0288.

PAYSON (village)—Adams Telecom. Formerly [IL0288]. This cable system has converted to IPTV, PO Box 248, 405 Emminga Rd, Golden, IL 62339. Phone: 217-696-4411. E-mail: service@adams.net. Web Site: http://www.adams.net. ICA: IL5323.
Channel capacity: N.A. Channels available but not in use: N.A.

Internet Service
Operational: Yes.

Ownership: Adams Telephone Co-Operative.

PEARL CITY (village)—Mediacom, 3900 26th Ave, Moline, IL 61265. Phones: 309-797-2580 (Moline regional office); 563-557-8025. Fax: 309-797-2414. Web Site: http://www.mediacomcable.com. ICA: IL0565.
TV Market Ranking: 97 (PEARL CITY (VILLAGE)). Franchise award date: N.A. Franchise expiration date: N.A. Began: March 1, 1988.
Channel capacity: 42 (not 2-way capable). Channels available but not in use: N.A.

Basic Service
Subscribers: 172.
Programming (received off-air): WHA-TV (PBS) Madison; WIFR (CBS) Freeport; WQRF-TV (FOX) Rockford; WREX (CW, NBC) Rockford; WTVO (ABC, MNT) Rockford.
Programming (via satellite): ABC Family Channel; AMC; Animal Planet; Arts & Entertainment; CNN; Comedy Central; Country Music TV; C-SPAN; Discovery Channel; ESPN; ESPN 2; Fox Sports Net; History Channel; Lifetime; Nickelodeon; QVC; Spike TV; TBS Superstation; The Learning Channel; Travel Channel; Turner Network TV; USA Network; VH1; Weather Channel; WGN America.
Fee: $45.00 installation; $29.95 monthly.

Pay Service 1
Pay Units: 27.
Programming (via satellite): Encore; Starz.
Fee: $9.95 monthly.

Video-On-Demand: No

Internet Service
Operational: Yes.

Telephone Service
Digital: Operational

Homes passed: 319. Miles of plant (coax & fiber) included in Moline
Regional Vice President: Cari Fenzel. Area Manager: Kathleen McMullen. Engineering Director: Mitch Carlson. Technical Operations Manager: Darren Dean. Marketing Director: Greg Evans.
Ownership: Mediacom LLC (MSO).

PECATONICA—Mediacom. Now served by LENA, IL [IL0223]. ICA: IL0233.

PEKIN—Comcast Cable, 3517 N Dries Ln, Peoria, IL 61604. Phone: 309-686-2600. Fax: 309-686-9828. Web Site: http://www.comcast.com. Also serves Groveland, Marquette Heights, Morton, North Pekin, South Pekin, Tazewell County (portions) & Tremont. ICA: IL0045.
TV Market Ranking: 83 (Groveland, Marquette Heights, Morton, North Pekin, PEKIN, South Pekin, Tazewell County (portions), Tremont). Franchise award date: December 23, 1974. Franchise expiration date: N.A. Began: November 20, 1976.
Channel capacity: 94 (operating 2-way). Channels available but not in use: 6.

Basic Service
Subscribers: N.A. Included in Peoria
Programming (received off-air): WEEK-TV (NBC) Peoria; WHOI (ABC, CW) Peoria; WMBD-TV (CBS) Peoria; WTVP (PBS) Peoria; WYZZ-TV (FOX) Bloomington; allband FM.
Programming (via satellite): C-SPAN; C-SPAN 2; Eternal Word TV Network; Home Shopping Network; ION Television; QVC; ShopNBC; Trinity Broadcasting Network; TV Guide Network; WAOE (MNT) Peoria; Weather Channel; WGN America.
Current originations: Public Access; Government Access; Educational Access.
Fee: $25.00 installation; $14.60 monthly; $3.68 converter.

Expanded Basic Service 1
Subscribers: N.A.
Programming (via satellite): ABC Family Channel; AMC; Animal Planet; Arts & Entertainment; BET Networks; Bravo; Cartoon Network; CNBC; CNN; Comcast SportsNet Chicago; Comedy Central; Country Music TV; Discovery Channel; Disney Channel; E! Entertainment Television; ESPN; ESPN 2; Food Network; Fox News Channel; Fox Sports Net Midwest; FX; Great American Country; Hallmark Channel; Headline News; HGTV; History Channel; Lifetime; MSNBC; MTV; MTV2; National Geographic Channel; Nickelodeon; Oxygen; SoapNet; Speed Channel; Spike TV; Style Network; Syfy; TBS Superstation; The Learning Channel; Toon Disney; Travel Channel; truTV; Turner Network TV; USA Network; VH1.
Fee: $37.15 monthly.

Digital Basic Service
Subscribers: 5,000.
Programming (via satellite): AmericanLife TV Network; BBC America; Bio; Bloomberg Television; Bravo; CBS College Sports Network; CMT Pure Country; Cooking Channel; C-SPAN 3; Discovery Digital Networks; Discovery HD Theater; DMX Music; Encore (multiplexed); ESPN 2 HD; ESPN Classic Sports; ESPN HD; ESPN U; ESPNews; Fox College Sports Atlantic; Fox College Sports Central; Fox College Sports Pacific; Fox Movie Channel; Fox Reality Channel; Fox Soccer; Fuse; G4; GAS; Golf Channel; GSN; HDNet; HDNet Movies; History Channel International; HorseRacing TV; Independent Film Channel; Lifetime Movie Network; Lifetime Real Women; MTV Networks Digital Suite; NFL Network; Nick Jr.; Nick Too; NickToons TV; Outdoor Channel; Ovation; Palladia; PBS Kids Sprout; Si TV; Sleuth; Sundance Channel; Tennis Channel; Toon Disney; Turner Classic Movies; Turner Network TV HD; TV Land; TVG Network; Universal HD; Versus; WE tv.
Fee: $17.00 monthly.

Digital Pay Service 1
Pay Units: 4,002.
Programming (via satellite): Cinemax (multiplexed); Flix; HBO (multiplexed); Showtime (multiplexed); Starz (multiplexed); The Movie Channel (multiplexed).

Video-On-Demand: Yes

Pay-Per-View
Addressable homes: 5,000.
ESPN Now (delivered digitally), Fee: $3.95, Addressable: Yes; iN DEMAND (delivered digitally); Playboy TV (delivered digitally); Special events (delivered digitally).

Internet Service
Operational: Yes.
Subscribers: 1,930.
Broadband Service: Comcast High Speed Internet.
Fee: $99.95 installation; $44.95 monthly; $10.00 modem lease; $99.95 modem purchase.

Telephone Service
None

Homes passed: Included in Peoria
General Manager: John Nieber. Chief Technician: Mike Vandergraft.
City fee: 3% of gross.
Ownership: Comcast Cable Communications Inc. (MSO).

PENFIELD—Formerly served by CableDirect. No longer in operation. ICA: IL0456.

PEORIA—Comcast Cable, 3517 N Dries Ln, Peoria, IL 61604. Phone: 309-686-2600. Fax: 309-688-9828. Web Site: http://www.comcast.com. Also serves Bartonville, Bellevue, Creve Coeur, East Peoria, Hollis Twp., Kickapoo Twp., Limestone Twp. (Peoria County), Medina Twp., Norwood, Peoria Heights, Richwoods Twp., Tazewell Twp., Washington & West Peoria Twp. ICA: IL0012.
TV Market Ranking: 83 (Bartonville, Bellevue, Creve Coeur, East Peoria, Hollis Twp., Kickapoo Twp., Limestone Twp. (Peoria County), Medina Twp., Norwood, PEORIA, Peoria Heights, Richwoods Twp., Tazewell Twp., Washington, West Peoria Twp.). Franchise award date: N.A. Franchise expiration date: N.A. Began: April 16, 1973.
Channel capacity: 92 (operating 2-way). Channels available but not in use: 5.

Basic Service
Subscribers: 125,000 Includes Bloomington, Canton, Galesburg, Monmouth & Pekin.
Programming (received off-air): WAOE (MNT) Peoria; WEEK-TV (NBC) Peoria; WHOI (ABC, CW) Peoria; WMBD-TV (CBS) Peoria; WTVP (PBS) Peoria; WYZZ-TV (FOX) Bloomington; 18 FMs.
Programming (via satellite): C-SPAN 2; Discovery Channel; Eternal Word TV Network; Home Shopping Network; ION Television; QVC; Trinity Broadcasting Network; TV Guide Network; Weather Channel; WGN America.
Current originations: Religious Access; Government Access; Educational Access; Public Access.
Fee: $25.00 installation; $14.60 monthly; $1.06 converter.

Expanded Basic Service 1
Subscribers: N.A.
Programming (via satellite): ABC Family Channel; AMC; Animal Planet; Arts & Entertainment; BET Networks; Bravo; Cartoon Network; CNBC; CNN; Comcast SportsNet Chicago; Comedy Central; Country Music TV; Disney Channel; E! Entertainment Television; ESPN; ESPN 2; Food Network; Fox News Channel; Fox Sports Net Midwest; FX; Golf Channel; Great American Country; Hallmark Channel; Headline News; HGTV; History Channel; Lifetime; MSNBC; MTV; National Geographic Channel; Nickelodeon; Oxygen; ShopNBC; SoapNet; Speed Channel; Spike TV; Style Network; Syfy; TBS Superstation; The Learning Channel; Toon Disney; Travel Channel; truTV; Turner Network TV; USA Network; VH1.
Fee: $37.15 monthly.

Digital Basic Service
Subscribers: 23,000.
Programming (via satellite): AmericanLife TV Network; BBC America; Bio; Bloomberg Television; CBS College Sports Network;

CMT Pure Country; Cooking Channel; C-SPAN 3; Discovery Digital Networks; Discovery HD Theater; Do-It-Yourself; Encore (multiplexed); ESPN 2 HD; ESPN Classic Sports; ESPN HD; ESPN U; ESPNews; Fox College Sports Atlantic; Fox College Sports Central; Fox College Sports Pacific; Fox Movie Channel; Fox Reality Channel; Fox Soccer; Fuse; G4; GAS; GSN; Halogen Network; HDNet; HDNet Movies; History Channel International; HorseRacing TV; Independent Film Channel; Lifetime Movie Network; Lifetime Real Women; MTV Networks Digital Suite; NFL Network; Nick Jr.; Nick Too; NickToons TV; Outdoor Channel; Ovation; Palladia; PBS Kids Sprout; Si TV; Sleuth; Sundance Channel; Tennis Channel; Toon Disney; Turner Classic Movies; Turner Network TV HD; TV Land; TVG Network; Universal HD; Versus; WE tv.
Fee: $17.00 monthly.

Digital Pay Service 1
Pay Units: N.A.
Programming (via satellite): Cinemax (multiplexed); Flix; HBO (multiplexed); HBO HD; Showtime (multiplexed); Starz (multiplexed); The Movie Channel (multiplexed).
Fee: $10.00 monthly (Cinemax or Starz), $13.00 monthly (HBO or Showtime/TMC).

Video-On-Demand: Yes

Pay-Per-View
Addressable homes: 23,000.
ESPN Now (delivered digitally), Fee: $3.95, Addressable: Yes; iN DEMAND (delivered digitally); Playboy TV (delivered digitally); Special events (delivered digitally).

Internet Service
Operational: Yes.
Subscribers: 6,550.
Broadband Service: Comcast High Speed Internet.
Fee: $99.95 installation; $44.95 monthly; $10.00 modem lease; $99.95 modem purchase.

Telephone Service
Digital: Operational
Miles of Plant: 3,000.0 (coaxial); None (fiber optic). Homes passed: 275,000. Homes passed includes Bloomington, Canton, Galesburg, Monmouth & Pekin
General Manager: John Nieber. Chief Technician: Mike Vandergraft.
City fee: 5% of basic.
Ownership: Comcast Cable Communications Inc. (MSO).

PEOTONE—Comcast Cable. Now served by CHICAGO (southern suburbs), IL [IL0008]. ICA: IL0107.

PERU—Comcast Cable, 4450 Kishwaukee St, Rockford, IL 61101. Phone: 815-395-8890. Fax: 815-395-8901. Web Site: http://www.comcast.com. Also serves La Salle, Mendota, North Utica, Oglesby, Spring Valley & Utica Twp. ICA: IL0053.
TV Market Ranking: Below 100 (La Salle, Mendota, North Utica, Oglesby, PERU, Spring Valley, Utica Twp.). Franchise award date: N.A. Franchise expiration date: N.A. Began: June 1, 1951.
Channel capacity: N.A. Channels available but not in use: N.A.

Basic Service
Subscribers: N.A. Included in Rockford
Programming (received off-air): WBBM-TV (CBS) Chicago; WEEK-TV (NBC) Peoria; WFLD (FOX) Chicago; WGN-TV (CW, IND) Chicago; WLS-TV (ABC) Chicago; WMAQ-TV (NBC) Chicago; WPWR-TV (MNT) Gary; WQAD-TV (ABC) Moline; WTTW (PBS) Chicago; WWTO-TV (TBN) La Salle; WYZZ-TV (FOX) Bloomington; 9 FMs.
Programming (via satellite): C-SPAN; C-SPAN 2; Eternal Word TV Network; Home Shopping Network; ION Television; QVC; TV Guide Network; WHBF-TV (CBS) Rock Island; WPWR-TV (MNT) Gary.
Current originations: Public Access.
Fee: $44.00 installation; $8.00 monthly; $.56 converter.

Expanded Basic Service 1
Subscribers: 9,000.
Programming (via satellite): ABC Family Channel; AMC; Animal Planet; Arts & Entertainment; BET Networks; Bravo; Cartoon Network; CNBC; CNN; Comcast SportsNet Chicago; Comedy Central; Country Music TV; Discovery Channel; Disney Channel; E! Entertainment Television; ESPN; ESPN 2; Food Network; Fox News Channel; Fox Sports Net Midwest; FX; Great American Country; Hallmark Channel; Headline News; HGTV; History Channel; Lifetime; MSNBC; MTV; National Geographic Channel; Nickelodeon; Oxygen; Speed Channel; Spike TV; Syfy; TBS Superstation; The Learning Channel; Total Living Network; Travel Channel; truTV; Turner Network TV; Univision; USA Network; VH1; Weather Channel.
Fee: $43.75 monthly.

Digital Basic Service
Subscribers: N.A.
Programming (via satellite): AmericanLife TV Network; BBC America; Bio; Bloomberg Television; CBS College Sports Network; CMT Pure Country; Cooking Channel; C-SPAN 3; Discovery Digital Networks; Discovery HD Theater; DMX Music; Do-It-Yourself; Encore (multiplexed); ESPN 2 HD; ESPN Classic Sports; ESPN HD; ESPN U; ESPNews; Fox Movie Channel; Fox Soccer; Fox Sports World; Fuse; G4; GAS; Golf Channel; GSN; Halogen Network; HDNet; HDNet Movies; History Channel International; HorseRacing TV; Independent Film Channel; Lifetime Movie Network; Lifetime Real Women; MTV Networks Digital Suite; National Geographic Channel; NFL Network; Nick Jr.; Nick Too; NickToons TV; Outdoor Channel; Palladia; PBS Kids Sprout; Si TV; SoapNet; Speed Channel; Style Network; Sundance Channel; Syfy; Tennis Channel; Toon Disney; Trinity Broadcasting Network; Turner Classic Movies; Turner Network TV HD; TV Land; TVG Network; Universal HD; Versus; WE tv.
Fee: $15.95 monthly.

Digital Pay Service 1
Pay Units: N.A.
Programming (via satellite): Cinemax (multiplexed); Flix; HBO (multiplexed); HBO HD; Showtime (multiplexed); Showtime HD; Starz (multiplexed); The Movie Channel (multiplexed).
Fee: $10.00 monthly (each).

Video-On-Demand: Yes

Pay-Per-View
iN DEMAND (delivered digitally), Fee: $3.95; Playboy TV (delivered digitally); Fresh (delivered digitally); ESPN (delivered digitally); Barker (delivered digitally).

Internet Service
Operational: Yes.
Broadband Service: Comcast High Speed Internet.
Fee: $99.95 installation; $44.95 monthly; $10.00 modem lease; $99.95 modem purchase.

Telephone Service
Digital: Operational
Total homes in franchised area: 16,512. Homes passed & miles of plant included in Rockford
District Director: Joseph Browning. Technical Operations Manager: Lyle Matejewski. Program Director: Janice Schultz. Community & Government Affairs Manager: Joan Sage.
City fee: 3% of gross.
Ownership: Comcast Cable Communications Inc. (MSO).

PIERRON—Clearvision Cable Systems Inc., 1785 US Rte 40, Greenup, IL 62428-3501. Phone: 217-923-5594. Fax: 217-923-5681. E-mail: mbct@rr1.net. Also serves Pocahontas (unincorporated areas). ICA: IL0620.
TV Market Ranking: 11 (PIERRON); Outside TV Markets (Pocahontas (unincorporated areas)). Franchise award date: N.A. Franchise expiration date: N.A. Began: N.A.
Channel capacity: 36 (not 2-way capable). Channels available but not in use: 8.

Basic Service
Subscribers: 35.
Programming (received off-air): KDNL-TV (ABC) St. Louis; KETC (PBS) St. Louis; KMOV (CBS) St. Louis; KPLR-TV (CW) St. Louis; KSDK (NBC) St. Louis; KTVI (FOX) St. Louis; WPXS (IND) Mount Vernon.
Programming (via satellite): ABC Family Channel; AMC; Arts & Entertainment; Bravo; Cartoon Network; CNBC; CNN; Comedy Central; Country Music TV; C-SPAN; Discovery Channel; Disney Channel; ESPN; G4; Headline News; History Channel; Lifetime; MSNBC; MTV; Nickelodeon; QVC; Spike TV; Syfy; TBS Superstation; The Learning Channel; Trinity Broadcasting Network; Turner Network TV; USA Network; VH1; Weather Channel; WGN America.
Fee: $42.50 installation; $29.95 monthly.

Pay Service 1
Pay Units: N.A.
Programming (via satellite): Showtime; The Movie Channel.

Video-On-Demand: No

Internet Service
Operational: No.

Telephone Service
None
Homes passed: 253.
Manager: Michael Bauguss.
Ownership: Clearvision Cable Systems Inc. (MSO).

PIPER CITY—Comcast Cable, 7720 W 98th St, Hickory Hills, IL 60457. Phones: 847-585-6300 (Kanakee office); 708-237-3260. Fax: 708-237-3292. Web Site: http://www.comcast.com. ICA: IL0309.
TV Market Ranking: Outside TV Markets (PIPER CITY). Franchise award date: N.A. Franchise expiration date: N.A. Began: January 1, 1975.
Channel capacity: 37 (not 2-way capable). Channels available but not in use: None.

Basic Service
Subscribers: 277.
Programming (received off-air): WAND (NBC) Decatur; WCCU (FOX) Urbana; WCIA (CBS) Champaign; WFLD (FOX) Chicago; WGN-TV (CW, IND) Chicago; WICD (ABC) Champaign; WILL-TV (PBS) Urbana; WLS-TV (ABC) Chicago; allband FM.
Programming (via satellite): Discovery Channel; TBS Superstation.
Fee: $48.99 installation; $16.17 monthly; $3.00 converter.

Expanded Basic Service 1
Subscribers: 275.
Programming (via satellite): ABC Family Channel; AMC; Animal Planet; Cartoon Network; CNN; Comcast SportsNet Chicago; Disney Channel; ESPN; Fox News Channel; HGTV; Lifetime; Nickelodeon; QVC; The Learning Channel; Turner Network TV; USA Network.
Fee: $23.73 monthly.

Pay Service 1
Pay Units: 16.
Programming (via satellite): Encore; Showtime; Starz.
Fee: $1.75 monthly (Encore), $6.75 monthly (Starz), $13.10 monthly (Showtime).

Internet Service
Operational: Yes.

Telephone Service
Digital: Operational
Miles of Plant: 6.0 (coaxial); None (fiber optic). Homes passed: 393. Total homes in franchised area: 393.
Area Vice President: Sandy Weicher. Vice President, Technical Operations: Bob Curtis. Vice President, Sales & Marketing: Eric Schaefer. Vice President, Communications: Rich Ruggiero.
City fee: 3% of gross.
Ownership: Comcast Cable Communications Inc. (MSO).

PITTSFIELD—Cass Cable TV Inc., PO Box 200, 100 Redbud Rd, Virginia, IL 62691. Phones: 800-252-1799; 217-452-7725. Fax: 217-452-7030. E-mail: casscatv@casscomm.com. Web Site: http://www.casscomm.com. ICA: IL0158.
TV Market Ranking: Below 100 (PITTSFIELD). Franchise award date: N.A. Franchise expiration date: N.A. Began: February 1, 1980.
Channel capacity: 100 (operating 2-way). Channels available but not in use: None.

Basic Service
Subscribers: 1,365.
Programming (received off-air): KDNL-TV (ABC) St. Louis; KETC (PBS) St. Louis; KHQA-TV (ABC, CBS) Hannibal; KPLR-TV (CW) St. Louis; KSDK (NBC) St. Louis; KTVI (FOX) St. Louis; WGEM-TV (CW, NBC) Quincy; WKRN-TV (ABC) Nashville; WRSP-TV (FOX) Springfield; WSEC (PBS) Jacksonville; WTJR (IND) Quincy.
Programming (via satellite): Animal Planet; Toon Disney.
Fee: $45.00 installation; $14.95 monthly; $4.00 converter.

Expanded Basic Service 1
Subscribers: 1,245.
Programming (via satellite): ABC Family Channel; AMC; AmericanLife TV Network;

Arts & Entertainment; Cartoon Network; CNBC; CNN; Comcast SportsNet Chicago; Comedy Central; Country Music TV; C-SPAN; Discovery Channel; Disney Channel; E! Entertainment Television; ESPN; ESPN 2; ESPN Classic Sports; Food Network; Fox News Channel; Fox Sports Net Midwest; FX; Golf Channel; GSN; Headline News; HGTV; History Channel; Home Shopping Network; Lifetime; MSNBC; MTV; Nickelodeon; QVC; Speed Channel; Spike TV; Syfy; TBS Superstation; The Learning Channel; Travel Channel; Trinity Broadcasting Network; truTV; Turner Network TV; TV Land; USA Network; Versus; VH1; Weather Channel; WGN America.
Fee: $32.00 monthly.

Digital Basic Service
Subscribers: 97.
Programming (via satellite): AmericanLife TV Network; Arts & Entertainment; BBC America; Bloomberg Television; Bravo; Discovery Digital Networks; DMX Music; ESPNews; FitTV; Fox Sports World; Fuse; G4; GAS; Halogen Network; History Channel International; MTV2; National Geographic Channel; Nick Jr.; Outdoor Channel; Ovation; Style Network; Trinity Broadcasting Network; WE tv.
Fee: $8.04 monthly.

Pay Service 1
Pay Units: 77.
Programming (via satellite): Cinemax.
Fee: $20.00 installation; $11.35 monthly.

Pay Service 2
Pay Units: 44.
Programming (via satellite): Showtime; The Movie Channel.
Fee: $20.00 installation; $12.95 monthly.

Pay Service 3
Pay Units: 81.
Programming (via satellite): Encore; Starz.
Fee: $20.00 installation; $8.95 monthly.

Pay Service 4
Pay Units: 125.
Programming (via satellite): HBO.
Fee: $20.00 installation; $13.55 monthly.

Digital Pay Service 1
Pay Units: N.A.
Programming (via satellite): Cinemax (multiplexed); Encore (multiplexed); HBO (multiplexed); Showtime (multiplexed); Starz (multiplexed); The Movie Channel (multiplexed).
Fee: $8.95 monthly (Starz/Encore), $11.35 monthly (Cinemax), $12.95 monthly (Showtime/TMC), $13.55 monthly (HBO).

Video-On-Demand: No

Pay-Per-View
Addressable homes: 79.
iN DEMAND (delivered digitally); ESPN Now (delivered digitally); Playboy TV (delivered digitally); Fresh (delivered digitally); ESPN (delivered digitally); Sports PPV (delivered digitally).

Internet Service
Operational: Yes. Began: January 1, 2002.
Subscribers: 325.
Broadband Service: casscomm.com.
Fee: $39.95 monthly.

Telephone Service
Analog: Operational
Fee: $34.95 monthly
Digital: Operational
Subscribers: 3.
Fee: $34.95 monthly

Miles of Plant: 29.0 (coaxial); None (fiber optic). Homes passed: 1,941. Total homes in franchised area: 1,941.
Plant Manager: Lance Allen. Cable TV Services Manager: Chad Winters. Marketing Director: Erynn Snedeker. Advertising Director: Laymon Carter. Office Manager: Cindy Kilby.
Ownership: Cass Cable TV Inc. (MSO).

PLAINFIELD—Comcast Cable. Now served by OAK BROOK, IL [IL0006]. ICA: IL0351.

PLAINVILLE (village)—Adams Telecom. Formerly served by Payson, IL [IL0288] This cable system has converted to IPTV, PO Box 248, 405 Emminga Rd, Golden, IL 62339. Phone: 217-696-4411. E-mail: service@adams.net. Web Site: http://www.adams.net. ICA: IL5324.
Channel capacity: N.A. Channels available but not in use: N.A.

Internet Service
Operational: Yes.

Ownership: Adams Telephone Co-Operative.

PLANO—Comcast Cable. Now served by OAK BROOK, IL [IL0006]. ICA: IL0100.

PLEASANT HILL—Crystal Broadband Networks, PO Box 180336, Chicago, IL 60618. Phones: 877-319-0328; 630-206-0447. Fax: 817-685-6488. E-mail: info@crystalbn.com. Web Site: http://crystalbn.com. Also serves Nebo. ICA: IL0248.
TV Market Ranking: Below 100 (PLEASANT HILL); Outside TV Markets (Nebo). Franchise award date: March 17, 1981. Franchise expiration date: N.A. Began: February 1, 1983.
Channel capacity: 36 (not 2-way capable). Channels available but not in use: N.A.

Basic Service
Subscribers: 162.
Programming (received off-air): KDNL-TV (ABC) St. Louis; KETC (PBS) St. Louis; KHQA-TV (ABC, CBS) Hannibal; KMOV (CBS) St. Louis; KPLR-TV (CW) St. Louis; KSDK (NBC) St. Louis; KTVI (FOX) St. Louis; WGEM-TV (CW, NBC) Quincy; WTJR (IND) Quincy.
Programming (via satellite): ABC Family Channel; AMC; Arts & Entertainment; CNN; Discovery Channel; Disney Channel; ESPN; Fox Sports Net Midwest; Great American Country; History Channel; Home Shopping Network; INSP; Lifetime; Nickelodeon; Spike TV; Syfy; TBS Superstation; Toon Disney; Trinity Broadcasting Network; Turner Network TV; USA Network; VH1; Weather Channel; WGN America.
Fee: $29.95 installation; $41.95 monthly.

Pay Service 1
Pay Units: 42.
Programming (via satellite): Cinemax; HBO; Showtime.
Fee: $25.00 installation; $9.49 monthly (Cinemax), $13.49 monthly (HBO or Showtime).

Video-On-Demand: No

Internet Service
Operational: Yes.

Telephone Service
Digital: Operational

Miles of Plant: 15.0 (coaxial); None (fiber optic). Homes passed: 382.
General Manager: Nidhin Johnson. Program Manager: Shawn Smith.
City fee: 3% of gross.
Ownership: Crystal Broadband Networks (MSO).

PLYMOUTH (village)—Adams Telecom. Formerly served by Golden, IL [IL0257]. This cable system has converted to IPTV, PO Box 248, 405 Emminga Rd, Golden, IL 62339. Phone: 217-696-4411. E-mail: service@adams.net. Web Site: http://www.adams.net. ICA: IL5325.
Channel capacity: N.A. Channels available but not in use: N.A.

Internet Service
Operational: Yes.

Ownership: Adams Telephone Co-Operative.

POCAHONTAS—Clearvision Cable Systems Inc., 1785 US Rte 40, Greenup, IL 62428-3501. Phone: 217-923-5594. Fax: 217-923-5681. E-mail: mbct@rr1.net. ICA: IL0332.
TV Market Ranking: Outside TV Markets (POCAHONTAS). Franchise award date: N.A. Franchise expiration date: N.A. Began: August 1, 1985.
Channel capacity: 40 (not 2-way capable). Channels available but not in use: 16.

Basic Service
Subscribers: 66.
Programming (received off-air): KDNL-TV (ABC) St. Louis; KETC (PBS) St. Louis; KMOV (CBS) St. Louis; KPLR-TV (CW) St. Louis; KSDK (NBC) St. Louis; KTVI (FOX) St. Louis; WPXS (IND) Mount Vernon.
Programming (via satellite): ABC Family Channel; American Movie Classics; Arts & Entertainment; Bravo; Cartoon Network; CNBC; CNN; Comedy Central; Country Music TV; C-SPAN; Discovery Channel; Disney Channel; G4; Headline News; History Channel; Lifetime; MSNBC; MTV; Nickelodeon; QVC; Spike TV; Syfy; TBS Superstation; The Learning Channel; Trinity Broadcasting Network; Turner Network TV; USA Network; VH1; Weather Channel; WGN America.
Fee: $22.95 monthly.

Pay Service 1
Pay Units: 44.
Programming (via satellite): Showtime; The Movie Channel.
Fee: $11.00 monthly (each).

Video-On-Demand: No

Internet Service
Operational: No.

Telephone Service
None

Miles of Plant: 6.0 (coaxial); None (fiber optic). Homes passed: 322.
Manager: Michael Bauguss.
City fee: 3% of gross.
Ownership: Clearvision Cable Systems Inc. (MSO).

PONTIAC—Mediacom, 903 E Howard St, Pontiac, IL 61764. Phones: 309-274-4500 (Chillicothe office); 815-844-3142. Fax: 815-844-6755. Web Site: http://www.mediacomcable.com. Also serves Cornell, Cullom, Dwight, Odell & Saunemin. ICA: IL0109.
TV Market Ranking: Below 100 (Cornell, Dwight, PONTIAC); Outside TV Markets (Cullom, Odell, Saunemin). Franchise award date: October 1, 1964. Franchise expiration date: N.A. Began: April 1, 1964.
Channel capacity: 134 (2-way capable). Channels available but not in use: None.

Basic Service
Subscribers: 6,794.
Programming (received off-air): WCFN (MNT) Springfield; WCIA (CBS) Champaign; WEEK-TV (NBC) Peoria; WFLD (FOX) Chicago; WGN-TV (CW, IND) Chicago; WHOI (ABC, CW) Peoria; WILL-TV (PBS) Urbana; WLS-TV (ABC) Chicago; WMAQ-TV (NBC) Chicago; WMBD-TV (CBS) Peoria; WTTW (PBS) Chicago; WYZZ-TV (FOX) Bloomington; 22 FMs.
Fee: $45.00 installation; $20.95 monthly.

Expanded Basic Service 1
Subscribers: 5,949.
Programming (via satellite): ABC Family Channel; AMC; AmericanLife TV Network; Animal Planet; Arts & Entertainment; BET Networks; Bravo; Cartoon Network; CNBC; CNN; Comcast SportsNet Chicago; Comedy Central; Country Music TV; C-SPAN; C-SPAN 2; Discovery Channel; Disney Channel; E! Entertainment Television; ESPN; ESPN 2; Eternal Word TV Network; Food Network; Fox News Channel; Fuse; FX; Hallmark Channel; Headline News; HGTV; History Channel; Home Shopping Network; INSP; Lifetime; MSNBC; MTV; Nickelodeon; Product Information Network; QVC; ShopNBC; Speed Channel; Spike TV; Syfy; TBS Superstation; The Learning Channel; Travel Channel; Trinity Broadcasting Network; truTV; Turner Network TV; TV Guide Network; TV Land; Univision; USA Network; VH1; WE tv; Weather Channel.
Fee: $34.00 monthly.

Digital Basic Service
Subscribers: 212.
Programming (received off-air): WEEK-TV (NBC) Peoria; WHOI (ABC, CW) Peoria.
Programming (via satellite): BBC America; Bio; Bloomberg Television; Discovery Digital Networks; Discovery HD Theater; DMX Music; ESPN; Fox Movie Channel; Fox Soccer; G4; GAS; Golf Channel; GSN; HDNet; HDNet Movies; History Channel International; Independent Film Channel; Lifetime Movie Network; Lime; MTV Networks Digital Suite; National Geographic Channel; Nick Jr.; NickToons TV; Outdoor Channel; Style Network; Turner Classic Movies; Universal HD; Versus.
Fee: $9.00 monthly.

Digital Pay Service 1
Pay Units: 669.
Programming (via satellite): Cinemax (multiplexed); Encore (multiplexed); Flix (multiplexed); HBO (multiplexed); Showtime (multiplexed); Starz (multiplexed); Starz HDTV; Sundance Channel (multiplexed); The Movie Channel (multiplexed).
Fee: $11.95 monthly (HBO, Cinemax, Starz/Encore or Showtime/TMC).

Video-On-Demand: Yes

Pay-Per-View
ESPN Extra, Fee: $3.95, Addressable: Yes; Hot Choice; Playboy TV; Fresh; Shorteez.

Internet Service
Operational: Yes.
Broadband Service: Mediacom High Speed Internet.
Fee: $59.95 installation; $45.95 monthly.

Telephone Service
Digital: Operational
Fee: $39.95 installation; $39.95 monthly

Miles of Plant: 104.0 (coaxial); 7.0 (fiber optic). Homes passed: 9,108.

Vice President: Don Hagwell. Operations Director: Gary Wightman. Technical Operations Manager: Larry Brackman. Marketing Director: Stephanie Law.
City fee: 5% of gross.
Ownership: Mediacom LLC (MSO).

POPLAR GROVE—Mediacom, 3900 26th Ave, Moline, IL 61265. Phone: 309-797-2580. Fax: 309-797-2414. Web Site: http://www.mediacomcable.com. Also serves Belvidere Twp., Capron, Chemung, Garden Prairie & Rockford (unincorporated areas). ICA: IL0282.
TV Market Ranking: 97 (Belvidere Twp., Capron, Chemung, Garden Prairie, POPLAR GROVE, Rockford). Franchise award date: May 28, 1985. Franchise expiration date: N.A. Began: August 1, 1985.
Channel capacity: 134 (operating 2-way). Channels available but not in use: 8.

Basic Service
Subscribers: 596.
Programming (received off-air): WFLD (FOX) Chicago; WIFR (CBS) Freeport; WPWR-TV (MNT) Gary; WQRF-TV (FOX) Rockford; WREX (CW, NBC) Rockford; WTTW (PBS) Chicago; WTVO (ABC, MNT) Rockford.
Programming (via satellite): CW+; QVC; WGN America.
Fee: $45.00 installation; $20.95 monthly.

Expanded Basic Service 1
Subscribers: N.A.
Programming (via satellite): ABC Family Channel; AMC; Animal Planet; Arts & Entertainment; Bravo; Cartoon Network; CNBC; CNN; Comcast SportsNet Chicago; Comedy Central; Country Music TV; C-SPAN; Discovery Channel; Disney Channel; E! Entertainment Television; ESPN; ESPN 2; FitTV; Food Network; Headline News; HGTV; History Channel; Home Shopping Network; Lifetime; MSNBC; MTV; Nickelodeon; Speed Channel; Spike TV; Syfy; TBS Superstation; The Learning Channel; Travel Channel; Trinity Broadcasting Network; truTV; Turner Network TV; TV Land; USA Network; VH1; Weather Channel.
Fee: $34.00 monthly.

Digital Basic Service
Subscribers: N.A.
Programming (via satellite): AmericanLife TV Network; BBC America; Bio; Bloomberg Television; Discovery Health Channel; Discovery Kids Channel; Discovery Military Channel; Discovery Planet Green; ESPNews; Fox Movie Channel; Fox Soccer; Fuse; G4; Golf Channel; History Channel International; ID Investigation Discovery; Independent Film Channel; Lifetime Movie Network; MTV Hits; MTV2; Music Choice; National Geographic Channel; Nick Jr.; NickToons TV; Outdoor Channel; Science Channel; Sleuth; Style Network; TeenNick; Turner Classic Movies; TVG Network; VH1 Classic.
Fee: $9.00 monthly.

Digital Pay Service 1
Pay Units: N.A.
Programming (via satellite): Cinemax (multiplexed); Encore (multiplexed); HBO (multiplexed); Showtime (multiplexed); Starz (multiplexed); The Movie Channel (multiplexed).
Fee: $11.95 monthly (HBO, Cinemax, Starz/Encore or Showtime/TMC).
Video-On-Demand: No

Internet Service
Operational: Yes.
Broadband Service: Mediacom High Speed Internet.
Fee: $59.95 installation; $40.95 monthly.

Telephone Service
Digital: Operational
Fee: $39.95 installation; $39.95 monthly
Homes passed: 1,937. Miles of plant included in Moline
Regional Vice President: Cari Fenzel. Engineering Director: Mitch Carlson. Technical Operations Manager: Chris Toalson. Marketing Director: Greg Evans.
Ownership: Mediacom LLC (MSO).

POTOMAC (village)—Park TV & Electronics Inc., PO Box 9, 205 E Fire Ln, Cissna Park, IL 60924. Phone: 815-457-2659. Fax: 815-457-2735. ICA: IL0568.
TV Market Ranking: 64 (POTOMAC (VILLAGE)). Franchise award date: N.A. Franchise expiration date: N.A. Began: September 1, 1984.
Channel capacity: 60 (operating 2-way). Channels available but not in use: 27.

Basic Service
Subscribers: N.A. Included in Cissna Park
Programming (received off-air): WAND (NBC) Decatur; WBUI (CW) Decatur; WCCU (FOX) Urbana; WCIA (CBS) Champaign; WICD (ABC) Champaign; WILL-TV (PBS) Urbana.
Programming (via satellite): ABC Family Channel; AMC; Animal Planet; Arts & Entertainment; Big Ten Network; Cartoon Network; CNBC; CNN; Comedy Central; Country Music TV; Discovery Channel; Disney Channel; E! Entertainment Television; ESPN; ESPN 2; Food Network; Fox News Channel; FX; GSN; Hallmark Channel; HGTV; History Channel; Lifetime; MTV; Nickelodeon; Outdoor Channel; Oxygen; QVC; Speed Channel; Spike TV; Syfy; TBS Superstation; The Learning Channel; Travel Channel; Trinity Broadcasting Network; Turner Classic Movies; Turner Network TV; TV Land; USA Network; VH1; Weather Channel; WGN America.

Pay Service 1
Pay Units: N.A.
Programming (via satellite): Cinemax; HBO.
Video-On-Demand: No

Internet Service
Operational: Yes.
Broadband Service: West Michigan Internet Service.
Fee: $29.95 monthly.

Telephone Service
None
Homes passed & miles of plant included in Cissna Park
Manager: Joe Young.
Ownership: Park TV & Electronics Inc. (MSO).

PRAIRIE CITY—Formerly served by CableDirect. No longer in operation. ICA: IL0569.

PRINCETON—Comcast Cable, 4450 Kishwaukee St, Rockford, IL 61101. Phone: 815-395-8890. Fax: 815-395-8901. Web Site: http://www.comcast.com. Also serves Bureau County, Tiskilwa & Wyanet. ICA: IL0105.
TV Market Ranking: Below 100 (Bureau County (portions), PRINCETON, Tiskilwa, Wyanet). Franchise award date: N.A. Franchise expiration date: N.A. Began: January 1, 1977.
Channel capacity: N.A. Channels available but not in use: N.A.

Basic Service
Subscribers: N.A. Included in Rockford
Programming (received off-air): KGCW (CW) Burlington; KLJB (CW, FOX) Davenport; KWQC-TV (NBC) Davenport; WEEK-TV (NBC) Peoria; WHBF-TV (CBS) Rock Island; WHOI (ABC, CW) Peoria; WMBD-TV (CBS) Peoria; WQAD-TV (ABC) Moline; WTVP (PBS) Peoria; 9 FMs.
Programming (via microwave): WTTW (PBS) Chicago.
Programming (via satellite): C-SPAN; C-SPAN 2; Eternal Word TV Network; Home Shopping Network; ION Television; QVC; TV Guide Network; WGN America.
Fee: $44.00 installation; $8.00 monthly.

Expanded Basic Service 1
Subscribers: 3,533.
Programming (via satellite): ABC Family Channel; AMC; Animal Planet; Arts & Entertainment; BET Networks; Bravo; Cartoon Network; CNBC; CNN; Comcast SportsNet Chicago; Comedy Central; Country Music TV; Discovery Channel; Disney Channel; E! Entertainment Television; ESPN; ESPN 2; Food Network; Fox News Channel; Fox Sports Net Midwest; FX; Great American Country; Hallmark Channel; Headline News; HGTV; History Channel; Lifetime; MSNBC; MTV; National Geographic Channel; Nickelodeon; Oxygen; Speed Channel; Spike TV; Syfy; TBS Superstation; The Learning Channel; Total Living Network; Travel Channel; truTV; Turner Network TV; Univision; USA Network; VH1; Weather Channel.
Fee: $43.75 monthly.

Digital Basic Service
Subscribers: N.A.
Programming (via satellite): AmericanLife TV Network; BBC America; Bio; Bloomberg Television; CBS College Sports Network; CMT Pure Country; Cooking Channel; C-SPAN 3; Discovery Digital Networks; Discovery HD Theater; DMX Music; Do-It-Yourself; Encore (multiplexed); ESPN 2 HD; ESPN Classic Sports; ESPN HD; ESPN U; ESPNews; Fox Movie Channel; Fox Soccer; Fuse; G4; GAS; Golf Channel; GSN; Halogen Network; HDNet; HDNet Movies; History Channel International; HorseRacing TV; Independent Film Channel; Lifetime Movie Network; Lifetime Real Women; MTV Networks Digital Suite; NFL Network; Nick Jr.; Nick Too; NickToons TV; Outdoor Channel; Palladia; PBS Kids Sprout; Si TV; SoapNet; Style Network; Sundance Channel; Tennis Channel; Toon Disney; Trinity Broadcasting Network; Turner Classic Movies; Turner Network TV HD; TV Land; TVG Network; Universal HD; Versus; WE tv.
Fee: $15.95 monthly.

Digital Pay Service 1
Pay Units: N.A.
Programming (via satellite): Cinemax (multiplexed); Flix; HBO (multiplexed); HBO HD; Showtime; Showtime HD; Starz; The Movie Channel (multiplexed).
Fee: $10.00 monthly (each).
Video-On-Demand: Yes

Pay-Per-View
ESPN (delivered digitally); iN DEMAND (delivered digitally), Fee: $3.95; Playboy TV (delivered digitally); Special events (delivered digitally).

Internet Service
Operational: Yes.
Broadband Service: Comcast High Speed Internet.
Fee: $99.95 installation; $44.95 monthly; $10.00 modem lease; $149.95 modem purchase.

Telephone Service
Digital: Operational
Total homes in franchised area: 4,803. Homes passed & miles of plant included in Rockford
District Director: Joseph Browning. Technical Operations Manager: Lyle Matejewski. Program Director: Janice Schultz. Community & Government Affairs Manager: Joan Sage.
City fee: 5% of gross.
Ownership: Comcast Cable Communications Inc. (MSO).

PRINCEVILLE—Mediacom. Now served by BRIMFIELD, IL [IL0201]. ICA: IL0254.

QUINCY—Comcast Cable, 2930 State St, Quincy, IL 62301-5718. Phone: 217-222-5388. Fax: 217-224-9820. Web Site: http://www.comcast.com. Also serves Adams County. ICA: IL0039.
TV Market Ranking: Below 100 (Adams County, QUINCY). Franchise award date: August 1, 1965. Franchise expiration date: N.A. Began: March 16, 1968.
Channel capacity: 64 (operating 2-way). Channels available but not in use: None.

Basic Service
Subscribers: N.A. Included in Macomb
Programming (received off-air): KHQA-TV (ABC, CBS) Hannibal; KTVO (ABC) Kirksville; WGEM-TV (CW, NBC) Quincy; WQEC (PBS) Quincy; WTJR (IND) Quincy; 30 FMs.
Programming (via satellite): C-SPAN; C-SPAN 2; Eternal Word TV Network; Home Shopping Network; QVC; ShopNBC; TBS Superstation; TV Guide Network; Weather Channel; WGN America.
Fee: $25.00 installation; $1.35 converter.

Expanded Basic Service 1
Subscribers: N.A.
Programming (via satellite): ABC Family Channel; AMC; Animal Planet; Arts & Entertainment; BET Networks; Bravo; Cartoon Network; CNBC; CNN; Comcast SportsNet Chicago; Comedy Central; Country Music TV; Discovery Channel; Disney Channel; E! Entertainment Television; ESPN; ESPN 2; Food Network; Fox News Channel; Fox Sports Net Midwest; FX; Great American Country; Hallmark Channel; Headline News; HGTV; History Channel; Lifetime; MTV; National Geographic Channel; Nickelodeon; Oxygen; Spike TV; Syfy; The Learning Channel; Travel Channel; Trinity Broadcasting Network; truTV; Turner Network TV; TV Land; USA Network; Versus; VH1.
Fee: $40.00 monthly.

Digital Basic Service
Subscribers: 2,993.
Programming (via satellite): BBC America; Bio; Bloomberg Television; CMT Pure Country; Discovery Digital Networks; DMX Music; Encore (multiplexed); ESPN Classic Sports; ESPNews; Fox Movie Channel; GAS; Golf Channel; GSN; History Channel International; Independent Film Channel; Lifetime Movie Network; MTV Networks Digital Suite; Nick Jr.; NickToons TV; Outdoor Channel; Sleuth; Speed Channel; Style Network; Toon Disney; Turner Classic Movies; Versus; WE tv.
Fee: $17.00 monthly.

Digital Pay Service 1
Pay Units: 2,642.
Programming (via satellite): HBO (multiplexed).
Fee: $15.00 installation; $13.00 monthly.

Digital Pay Service 2
Pay Units: 2,433.
Programming (via satellite): Cinemax (multiplexed).
Fee: $15.00 installation; $10.00 monthly.
Digital Pay Service 3
Pay Units: 2,118.
Programming (via satellite): Flix; Showtime (multiplexed); The Movie Channel (multiplexed).
Fee: $15.00 installation; $13.00 monthly.
Digital Pay Service 4
Pay Units: 3,873.
Programming (via satellite): Starz (multiplexed).
Fee: $15.00 installation; $10.00 monthly.
Video-On-Demand: No
Pay-Per-View
Addressable homes: 2,993.
iN DEMAND (delivered digitally), Fee: $3.95, Addressable: Yes; Playboy TV (delivered digitally).
Internet Service
Operational: Yes.
Subscribers: 898.
Broadband Service: Comcast High Speed Internet.
Fee: $99.95 installation; $44.95 monthly; $10.00 modem lease; $99.99 modem purchase.
Telephone Service
Analog: Not Operational
Digital: Operational
Miles of Plant: 256.0 (coaxial); None (fiber optic). Homes passed: 22,430.
General Manager: Dominick Ascone. Chief Technician: Gerry Salfen.
City fee: 5% of gross.
Ownership: Comcast Cable Communications Inc. (MSO).

RAMSEY—NewWave Communications, 318 N 4th St, Vandalia, IL 62471. Phone: 573-472-9500. Fax: 618.283.4483. E-mail: info@newwavecom.com. Web Site: http://www.newwavecom.com. ICA: IL0316.
TV Market Ranking: Outside TV Markets (RAMSEY). Franchise award date: N.A. Franchise expiration date: N.A. Began: September 1, 1971.
Channel capacity: N.A. Channels available but not in use: N.A.
Basic Service
Subscribers: 178.
Programming (received off-air): KDNL-TV (ABC) St. Louis; KETC (PBS) St. Louis; KMOV (CBS) St. Louis; KPLR-TV (CW) St. Louis; KSDK (NBC) St. Louis; WAND (NBC) Decatur; WICS (ABC) Springfield; WPXS (IND) Mount Vernon; allband FM.
Programming (via satellite): Trinity Broadcasting Network; WGN America.
Fee: $20.00 installation; $13.34 monthly; $2.00 converter.
Expanded Basic Service 1
Subscribers: 162.
Programming (received off-air): WRSP-TV (FOX) Springfield.
Programming (via satellite): ABC Family Channel; AMC; Animal Planet; Arts & Entertainment; CNBC; CNN; Country Music TV; Court TV; Discovery Channel; Disney Channel; ESPN; Fox News Channel; Fox Sports Net Midwest; Headline News; Lifetime; Nickelodeon; Spike TV; Syfy; TBS Superstation; The Learning Channel; Turner Network TV; TV Land; USA Network; VH1; Weather Channel.
Fee: $15.00 installation; $6.00 monthly.
Pay Service 1
Pay Units: 11.
Programming (via satellite): HBO.
Fee: $20.00 installation; $11.00 monthly.
Video-On-Demand: No
Internet Service
Operational: No.
Telephone Service
None
Miles of Plant: 12.0 (coaxial); None (fiber optic). Additional miles planned: 1.0 (coaxial). Homes passed: 653.
General Manager: Bill Flowers. Technical Operations Manager: Chris Mooday.
City fee: 3% of gross.
Ownership: NewWave Communications (MSO).

RANKIN (village)—Park TV & Electronics Inc., PO Box 9, 205 E Fire Ln, Cissna Park, IL 60924. Phone: 815-457-2659. Fax: 815-457-2735. ICA: IL0571.
TV Market Ranking: 64 (RANKIN (VILLAGE)). Franchise award date: N.A. Franchise expiration date: N.A. Began: November 1, 1984.
Channel capacity: 60 (operating 2-way). Channels available but not in use: 25.
Basic Service
Subscribers: N.A. Included in Cissna Park
Programming (received off-air): WAND (NBC) Decatur; WBUI (CW) Decatur; WCCU (FOX) Urbana; WCIA (CBS) Champaign; WICD (ABC) Champaign; WILL-TV (PBS) Urbana.
Programming (via satellite): ABC Family Channel; AMC; Animal Planet; Arts & Entertainment; Big Ten Network; Cartoon Network; CNBC; CNN; Comcast SportsNet Chicago; Comedy Central; Country Music TV; Discovery Channel; Disney Channel; E! Entertainment Television; ESPN; ESPN 2; Food Network; Fox News Channel; FX; GSN; Hallmark Channel; HGTV; History Channel; Lifetime; MTV; Nickelodeon; Outdoor Channel; Oxygen; QVC; Speed Channel; Spike TV; Syfy; TBS Superstation; The Learning Channel; Travel Channel; Trinity Broadcasting Network; Turner Classic Movies; Turner Network TV; TV Land; USA Network; VH1; Weather Channel; WGN America.
Pay Service 1
Pay Units: N.A.
Programming (via satellite): Cinemax; HBO; Showtime; The Movie Channel.
Video-On-Demand: No
Internet Service
Operational: Yes.
Broadband Service: West Michigan Internet Service.
Fee: $29.95 monthly.
Telephone Service
None
Included in Cissna Park
Manager: Joe Young.
Ownership: Park TV & Electronics Inc. (MSO).

RANTOUL—Mediacom, PO Box 334, 609 S 4th St, Chillicothe, IL 61523. Phone: 309-274-4500. Fax: 309-274-3188. Web Site: http://www.mediacomcable.com. Also serves Champaign County (portions), Gifford (village), Ludlow (village) & Thomasboro. ICA: IL0089.
TV Market Ranking: 64 (Champaign County (portions), Gifford (village), Ludlow (village), RANTOUL, Thomasboro). Franchise award date: N.A. Franchise expiration date: N.A. Began: December 7, 1974.
Channel capacity: 121 (operating 2-way). Channels available but not in use: 1.
Basic Service
Subscribers: 5,836.
Programming (received off-air): WAND (NBC) Decatur; WBUI (CW) Decatur; WCCU (FOX) Urbana; WCFN (MNT) Springfield; WCIA (CBS) Champaign; WICD (ABC) Champaign; WILL-TV (PBS) Urbana; 14 FMs.
Programming (via satellite): ABC Family Channel; INSP; Radar Channel; WGN America.
Current originations: Educational Access; Public Access.
Fee: $45.00 installation; $20.95 monthly.
Expanded Basic Service 1
Subscribers: 5,335.
Programming (via satellite): AMC; AmericanLife TV Network; Animal Planet; Arts & Entertainment; BET Networks; Bravo; Cartoon Network; CNBC; CNN; Comcast SportsNet Chicago; Comedy Central; Country Music TV; C-SPAN; C-SPAN 2; Discovery Channel; Disney Channel; E! Entertainment Television; ESPN; ESPN 2; Eternal Word TV Network; FitTV; Food Network; Fox News Channel; FX; Hallmark Channel; Headline News; HGTV; History Channel; Home Shopping Network; ION Television; Jewelry Television; Lifetime; Lifetime Movie Network; MSNBC; MTV; Nickelodeon; Product Information Network; QVC; ShopNBC; SoapNet; Speed Channel; Spike TV; Syfy; TBS Superstation; The Learning Channel; Toon Disney; Travel Channel; Trinity Broadcasting Network; truTV; Turner Network TV; TV Land; Univision; USA Network; VH1; WE tv; Weather Channel.
Fee: $34.00 monthly.
Digital Basic Service
Subscribers: 417.
Programming (received off-air): WAND (NBC) Decatur; WCCU (FOX) Urbana; WCIA (CBS) Champaign; WICD (ABC) Champaign; WILL-TV (PBS) Urbana.
Programming (via satellite): ABC News Now; BBC America; Bio; Bloomberg Television; CCTV-Entertainment; Discovery Digital Networks; ESPN 2 HD; ESPN HD; ESPNews; Fox Movie Channel; Fox Reality Channel; Fox Soccer; Fuse; G4; Golf Channel; GSN; History Channel International; Independent Film Channel; ION Life; Lifetime Real Women; Military History Channel; MTV Hits; MTV2; Music Choice; National Geographic Channel; Nick Jr.; NickToons TV; Outdoor Channel; Qubo; ReelzChannel; Science Channel; Sleuth; Style Network; Sundance Channel; TeenNick; Turner Classic Movies; Versus; VH1 Classic.
Fee: $9.00 monthly.
Digital Expanded Basic Service
Subscribers: N.A.
Programming (via satellite): College Sports Television; ESPN U; Fox College Sports Atlantic; Fox College Sports Central; Fox College Sports Pacific; Fuel TV; Gol TV; Tennis Channel; The Sportsman Channel; TVG Network.
Fee: $3.95 monthly.
Digital Expanded Basic Service 2
Subscribers: N.A.
Programming (via satellite): Discovery HD Theater; HDNet; HDNet Movies; Universal HD.
Fee: $6.95 monthly.
Digital Pay Service 1
Pay Units: 1,532.
Programming (via satellite): Cinemax (multiplexed); Encore (multiplexed); Flix; HBO (multiplexed); HBO HD; Showtime (multiplexed); Showtime HD; Starz (multiplexed); Starz HDTV; The Movie Channel (multiplexed); The Movie Channel HD.
Fee: $11.95 monthly (HBO, Cinemax, Showtime/TMC or Starz/Encore).
Video-On-Demand: Yes
Pay-Per-View
Addressable homes: 3,300.
Ten Clips (delivered digitally), Fee: $3.95, Addressable: Yes; Ten Blox (delivered digitally); iN DEMAND (delivered digitally); Playboy TV (delivered digitally); ESPN (delivered digitally); Fox Sports Net (delivered digitally).
Internet Service
Operational: Yes.
Broadband Service: Mediacom High Speed Internet.
Fee: $59.95 installation; $45.95 monthly.
Telephone Service
Digital: Operational
Fee: $39.95 installation; $39.95 monthly
Miles of Plant: 84.0 (coaxial); 52.0 (fiber optic). Homes passed: 7,228.
Vice President: Don Hagwell. Marketing Director: Stephanie Law. Operations Director: Gary Wightman. Technical Operations Manager: Larry Brackman.
City fee: 5% of gross.
Ownership: Mediacom LLC (MSO).

RAYMOND—Charter Communications, 11 Clearing, Taylorville, IL 62568-9279. Phones: 636-207-7044 (St Louis office); 217-287-7992. Fax: 217-287-7304. Web Site: http://www.charter.com. ICA: IL0291.
TV Market Ranking: 64 (RAYMOND). Franchise award date: March 1, 1983. Franchise expiration date: N.A. Began: December 1, 1983.
Channel capacity: N.A. Channels available but not in use: N.A.
Basic Service
Subscribers: 171.
Programming (received off-air): KMOV (CBS) St. Louis; KPLR-TV (CW) St. Louis; WAND (NBC) Decatur; WICS (ABC) Springfield; WILL-TV (PBS) Urbana; WRSP-TV (FOX) Springfield.
Programming (via satellite): QVC; Trinity Broadcasting Network; Weather Channel; WGN America.
Fee: $29.99 installation.
Expanded Basic Service 1
Subscribers: N.A.
Programming (via satellite): ABC Family Channel; Animal Planet; Arts & Entertainment; Bravo; CNN; Country Music TV; Discovery Channel; Disney Channel; ESPN; ESPN 2; Fox Sports Net Midwest; Headline News; HGTV; History Channel; Lifetime; MSNBC; MTV; Nickelodeon; Spike TV; Syfy; TBS Superstation; The Learning Channel; Turner Classic Movies; Turner Network TV; TV Land; USA Network.
Fee: $42.99 monthly.

Pay Service 1
Pay Units: 41.
Programming (via satellite): Cinemax.
Fee: $10.50 monthly.
Pay Service 2
Pay Units: 60.
Programming (via satellite): HBO.
Fee: $10.50 monthly.
Video-On-Demand: No
Internet Service
Operational: No.
Telephone Service
None
Miles of Plant: 7.0 (coaxial); None (fiber optic). Homes passed: 481.
Vice President & General Manager: Steve Trippe. Operations Director: Dave Miller. Chief Technician: Larry Harmon. Marketing Director: Beverly Wall. Office Manager: Melinda Sincavage.
Ownership: Charter Communications Inc. (MSO).

REDMON—Formerly served by CableDirect. No longer in operation. ICA: IL0627.

RICHVIEW—Formerly served by CableDirect. No longer in operation. ICA: IL0425.

RIDGE FARM—Insight Communications. Now served by URBANA, IL [IL0019]. ICA: IL0215.

RIO—Nova Cablevision Inc., PO Box 1412, 677 W Main St, Galesburg, IL 61401. Phone: 309-342-9681. Fax: 309-342-4408. Web Site: http://www.novacablevision.com. Also serves North Henderson. ICA: IL0612.
TV Market Ranking: 60 (North Henderson, RIO). Franchise award date: N.A. Franchise expiration date: N.A. Began: December 15, 1989.
Channel capacity: 40 (operating 2-way). Channels available but not in use: 19.
Basic Service
Subscribers: 96.
Programming (received off-air): KGCW (CW) Burlington; KIIN (PBS) Iowa City; KLJB (CW, FOX) Davenport; KWQC-TV (NBC) Davenport; WEEK-TV (NBC) Peoria; WHBF-TV (CBS) Rock Island; WHOI (ABC, CW) Peoria; WMBD-TV (CBS) Peoria; WQAD-TV (ABC) Moline; WQPT-TV (PBS) Moline; WTVP (PBS) Peoria.
Programming (via satellite): ABC Family Channel; AMC; Animal Planet; Arts & Entertainment; Big Ten Network; Cartoon Network; CNBC; CNN; Comcast SportsNet Chicago; Comedy Central; Country Music TV; C-SPAN; C-SPAN 2; Discovery Channel; Disney Channel; E! Entertainment Television; ESPN; ESPN 2; Eternal Word TV Network; Food Network; Fox News Channel; Fox Sports Net Midwest; FX; Golf Channel; Great American Country; Hallmark Channel; Headline News; HGTV; History Channel; Home Shopping Network; HorseRacing TV; INSP; Lifetime; MSNBC; MTV; National Geographic Channel; Nickelodeon; QVC; RFD-TV; SoapNet; Speed Channel; Spike TV; Syfy; TBS Superstation; The Learning Channel; The Sportsman Channel; Travel Channel; truTV; Turner Network TV; TV Land; USA Network; VH1; Weather Channel; WGN America.
Fee: $60.00 installation; $44.95 monthly.
Digital Basic Service
Subscribers: 7.
Programming (received off-air): KGCW (CW) Burlington; KLJB (CW, FOX) Davenport; KWQC-TV (NBC) Davenport; WEEK-TV (NBC) Peoria; WHBF-TV (CBS) Rock Island; WHOI (ABC, CW) Peoria; WMBD-TV (CBS) Peoria; WQAD-TV (ABC) Moline; WQPT-TV (PBS) Moline; WTVP (PBS) Peoria.
Programming (via satellite): Bio; Blackbelt TV; Bloomberg Television; Discovery Health Channel; Discovery Kids Channel; Discovery Military Channel; Discovery Planet Green; ESPN 2; ESPN Classic Sports; ESPNews; Fox Movie Channel; Fox Soccer; FSN Digital Atlantic; FSN Digital Central; FSN Digital Pacific; Fuse; G4; Golf Channel; Great American Country; GSN; HGTV; History Channel; History Channel International; ID Investigation Discovery; Independent Film Channel; Lifetime Movie Network; MTV Hits; MTV2; Music Choice; Nick Jr.; NickToons TV; Outdoor Channel; Science Channel; ShopNBC; Speed Channel; Style Network; Syfy; TeenNick; Toon Disney; Trinity Broadcasting Network; Turner Classic Movies; Versus; VH1 Classic; VH1 Soul; WE tv.
Fee: $16.95 monthly.
Pay Service 1
Pay Units: 1.
Programming (via satellite): Cinemax.
Fee: $11.95 monthly.
Pay Service 2
Pay Units: 8.
Programming (via satellite): HBO.
Fee: $11.95 monthly.
Digital Pay Service 1
Pay Units: N.A.
Programming (via satellite): Cinemax (multiplexed); Encore (multiplexed); Flix; HBO (multiplexed); Showtime (multiplexed); Starz (multiplexed); Sundance Channel; The Movie Channel (multiplexed).
Fee: $12.95 monthly (HBO, Cinemax, Starz/Encore or Showtime/TMC/Flix/ Sundance).
Video-On-Demand: No
Pay-Per-View
ESPN Now (delivered digitally); Hot Choice (delivered digitally); iN DEMAND (delivered digitally), Addressable: Yes; Playboy TV (delivered digitally); Fresh (delivered digitally); Shorteez (delivered digitally); sports (delivered digitally).
Internet Service
Operational: Yes.
Fee: $35.95-$39.95 monthly.
Telephone Service
None
Miles of Plant: 9.0 (coaxial); None (fiber optic). Homes passed: 190.
Manager & Chief Technician: Robert G. Fischer Jr.
Ownership: Nova Cablevision Inc. (MSO).

RIVER OAKS (village)—Mediacom. Now served by KINCAID, IL [IL0176]. ICA: IL0251.

ROANOKE—Mediacom, PO Box 334, 609 S 4th St, Chillicothe, IL 61523. Phones: 309-274-4500; 309-923-6061. Fax: 309-274-3188. Web Site: http://www.mediacomcable.com. Also serves Bayview Gardens, Benson, El Paso, Eureka, Far Hills, Germantown Hills, Metamora, Minonk, Secor, Spring Bay, Toluca, Washburn, Wenona & Woodford County. ICA: IL0068.
TV Market Ranking: 83 (Bayview Gardens, Benson, El Paso, Eureka, Far Hills, Germantown Hills, Metamora, Minonk, ROANOKE, Secor, Spring Bay, Toluca, Washburn, Woodford County); Below 100 (Wenona). Franchise award date: N.A. Franchise expiration date: N.A. Began: N.A.
Channel capacity: 121 (operating 2-way). Channels available but not in use: None.
Basic Service
Subscribers: 7,082.
Programming (received off-air): WAOE (MNT) Peoria; WCIA (CBS) Champaign; WEEK-TV (NBC) Peoria; WHOI (ABC, CW) Peoria; WILL-TV (PBS) Urbana; WMBD-TV (CBS) Peoria; WTVP (PBS) Peoria; WYZZ-TV (FOX) Bloomington.
Programming (via satellite): ABC Family Channel; WGN America.
Fee: $45.00 installation; $20.95 monthly.
Expanded Basic Service 1
Subscribers: 6,318.
Programming (via satellite): AMC; AmericanLife TV Network; Animal Planet; Arts & Entertainment; BET Networks; Bravo; Cartoon Network; CNBC; CNN; Comcast SportsNet Chicago; Comedy Central; Country Music TV; C-SPAN; C-SPAN 2; CW+; Discovery Channel; Disney Channel; E! Entertainment Television; ESPN; ESPN 2; Eternal Word TV Network; FitTV; Food Network; Fox News Channel; FX; Hallmark Channel; Halogen Network; Headline News; HGTV; History Channel; Home Shopping Network; INSP; ION Television; Jewelry Television; Lifetime; Lifetime Movie Network; MSNBC; MTV; Nickelodeon; Product Information Network; QVC; Radar Channel; ShopNBC; SoapNet; Speed Channel; Spike TV; Syfy; TBS Superstation; The Learning Channel; Travel Channel; truTV; Turner Network TV; TV Guide Network; TV Land; Univision; USA Network; VH1; WE tv; Weather Channel.
Fee: $34.00 monthly.
Digital Basic Service
Subscribers: 842.
Programming (received off-air): WEEK-TV (NBC) Peoria; WHOI (ABC, CW) Peoria; WMBD-TV (CBS) Peoria; WTVP (PBS) Peoria; WYZZ-TV (FOX) Bloomington.
Programming (via satellite): ABC News Now; BBC America; Bio; Bloomberg Television; CCTV-4; Discovery Health Channel; Discovery Kids Channel; Discovery Military Channel; Discovery Planet Green; Discovery Times Channel; ESPN 2 HD; ESPN HD; ESPN U; ESPNews; Fox Movie Channel; Fox Reality Channel; Fox Soccer; Fuel TV; Fuse; G4; Golf Channel; GSN; History Channel International; Independent Film Channel; ION Life; Lifetime Real Women; MTV Hits; MTV2; National Geographic Channel; Nick Jr.; NickToons TV; Outdoor Channel; Qubo; ReelzChannel; Science Channel; Sleuth; Style Network; Sundance Channel; TeenNick; Turner Classic Movies; Versus; VH1 Classic.
Fee: $9.00 monthly.
Digital Expanded Basic Service
Subscribers: N.A.
Programming (via satellite): CBS College Sports Network; Discovery HD Theater; ESPN U; Fox College Sports Atlantic; Fox College Sports Central; Fox College Sports Pacific; Fuel TV; Gol TV; HDNet; HDNet Movies; Tennis Channel; The Sportsman Channel; TVG Network; Universal HD.
Fee: $3.95 monthly (Sports Pak), $6.95 monthly (HD Pac).
Digital Pay Service 1
Pay Units: 2,502.
Programming (via satellite): Cinemax (multiplexed); Cinemax On Demand; Encore (multiplexed); Flix; HBO (multiplexed); HBO HD; HBO On Demand; Showtime (multiplexed); Showtime HD; Showtime On Demand; Starz (multiplexed); Starz HDTV; Starz On Demand; Sundance Channel; The Movie Channel (multiplexed); The Movie Channel HD; The Movie Channel On Demand.
Fee: $11.95 monthly (HBO, Cinemax, Showtime/TMC/Sundance/Flix or Starz/ Encore).
Video-On-Demand: Yes
Pay-Per-View
ESPN Now (delivered digitally), Fee: $3.95; Hot Choice (delivered digitally); iN DEMAND; iN DEMAND (delivered digitally); Playboy TV (delivered digitally); Pleasure (delivered digitally); Fresh (delivered digitally); Shorteez (delivered digitally).
Internet Service
Operational: Yes.
Broadband Service: Mediacom High Speed Internet.
Fee: $59.95 installation; $45.95 monthly.
Telephone Service
Analog: Not Operational
Digital: Operational
Fee: $39.95 installation; $39.95 monthly
Miles of Plant: 350.0 (coaxial); None (fiber optic). Homes passed: 10,018. Miles of plant includes Apollo Acres & Lacon
Vice President: Don Hagwell. Operations Director: Gary Wightman. Technical Operations Manager: Larry Brackman. Chief Technician: Scott Rocke. Marketing Director: Stephanie Law.
City fee: 3% of gross.
Ownership: Mediacom LLC (MSO).

ROBBINS—Comcast Cable. Now served by CHICAGO (southern suburbs), IL [IL0008]. ICA: IL0146.

ROBINSON—Mediacom, PO Box 288, 4290 Blue Stem Rd, Charleston, IL 61920. Phone: 217-348-5533. Fax: 217-345-7074. Web Site: http://www.mediacomcable.com. Also serves Crawford County, Hutsonville, Oblong & Palestine. ICA: IL0106.
TV Market Ranking: Below 100 (Crawford County (portions), Hutsonville, Palestine); Outside TV Markets (Crawford County (portions), Oblong, ROBINSON). Franchise award date: N.A. Franchise expiration date: N.A. Began: N.A.
Channel capacity: N.A. Channels available but not in use: N.A.
Basic Service
Subscribers: 3,723.
Programming (received off-air): WAND (NBC) Decatur; WBUI (CW) Decatur; WCCU (FOX) Urbana; WCFN (MNT) Springfield; WCIA (CBS) Champaign; WEIU-TV (PBS) Charleston; WICD (ABC) Champaign; WILL-TV (PBS) Urbana; WSIU-TV (PBS) Carbondale; WTHI-TV (CBS) Terre Haute; WTWO (NBC) Terre Haute; 1 FM.
Programming (via satellite): C-SPAN; Home Shopping Network; INSP; QVC; TV Guide Network; WGN America.
Fee: $45.00 installation; $20.95 monthly.
Expanded Basic Service 1
Subscribers: 3,066.
Programming (via satellite): ABC Family Channel; AMC; Animal Planet; Arts & Entertainment; BET Networks; Cartoon Network; CNBC; CNN; Comcast SportsNet Chicago; Comedy Central; Country Music TV; C-SPAN 2; Discovery Channel; Disney Channel; E! Entertainment Television; ESPN; ESPN 2; ESPN Classic Sports; Eternal Word TV Network; FitTV; Food Network; Fox News Channel; Fox Sports Net Midwest; FX; Hallmark Channel; Headline News; HGTV; History Channel; ION Television; Jewelry Television; Lifetime; Lifetime Movie Network; MSNBC; MTV; Nickelodeon; Outdoor Channel; Oxygen; Product Information Network; ShopNBC;

Speed Channel; Spike TV; Syfy; TBS Superstation; The Learning Channel; Travel Channel; Trinity Broadcasting Network; truTV; Turner Network TV; TV Land; USA Network; VH1; WE tv; Weather Channel.
Fee: $34.00 monthly.

Digital Basic Service
Subscribers: 484.
Programming (received off-air): WAND (NBC) Decatur; WCCU (FOX) Urbana; WCIA (CBS) Champaign; WICD (ABC) Champaign; WILL-TV (PBS) Urbana; WTHI-TV (CBS) Terre Haute.
Programming (via satellite): ABC News Now; AmericanLife TV Network; BBC America; Bio; Bloomberg Television; Bravo; CBS College Sports Network; CCTV-9 (CCTV International); CMT Pure Country; Discovery HD Theater; Discovery Health Channel; Discovery Home Channel; Discovery Kids Channel; Discovery Military Channel; Discovery Planet Green; Discovery Times Channel; ESPN U; ESPNews; Fox College Sports Atlantic; Fox College Sports Central; Fox College Sports Pacific; Fox Movie Channel; Fox Reality Channel; Fox Soccer; Fuel TV; Fuse; G4; Gol TV; Golf Channel; GSN; HDNet; HDNet Movies; History Channel International; Independent Film Channel; ION Life; Lifetime Real Women; MTV Hits; MTV2; Music Choice; National Geographic Channel; Nick Jr.; NickToons TV; Qubo; ReelzChannel; Science Channel; Sleuth; Style Network; TeenNick; Tennis Channel; The Sportsman Channel; Toon Disney; Turner Classic Movies; TVG Network; Universal HD; Versus; VH1 Classic.
Fee: $9.00 monthly.

Digital Pay Service 1
Pay Units: 1,489.
Programming (via satellite): Cinemax (multiplexed); Cinemax On Demand; Encore (multiplexed); HBO (multiplexed); HBO HD; HBO On Demand; Showtime (multiplexed); Showtime HD; Showtime On Demand; Starz (multiplexed); Starz HDTV; Starz On Demand; The Movie Channel (multiplexed); The Movie Channel HD; The Movie Channel On Demand.
Fee: $11.95 monthly (HBO, Cinemax, Showtime/TMC or Starz/Encore).

Video-On-Demand: Yes

Pay-Per-View
iN DEMAND (delivered digitally); Playboy TV; Ten Clips (delivered digitally); Ten Blox (delivered digitally); ESPN (delivered digitally).

Internet Service
Operational: Yes.
Broadband Service: Mediacom High Speed Internet.
Fee: $59.95 installation; $40.95 monthly.

Telephone Service
Digital: Operational
Fee: $39.95 installation; $39.95 monthly

Miles of Plant: 88.0 (coaxial); 9.0 (fiber optic). Additional miles planned: 4.0 (coaxial). Homes passed: 5,691.
Area Operations Director: Todd Acker. Technical Operations Manager: Jerry Ferguson.
City fee: 5% of gross.
Ownership: Mediacom LLC (MSO).

ROCK ISLAND—Mediacom. Now served by MOLINE, IL [IL0011]. ICA: IL0042.

ROCKFORD—Comcast Cable, 4450 Kishwaukee St, Rockford, IL 61101. Phone: 815-395-8890. Fax: 815-395-8901. Web Site: http://www.comcast.com. Also serves Belvidere, Boone County, Byron, Cherry Valley, Loves Park, Machesney Park, Mount Morris, New Milford, Ogle County, Polo, Stillman Valley & Winnebago County (portions). ICA: IL0010.
TV Market Ranking: 97 (Belvidere, Boone County, Byron, Cherry Valley, Loves Park, Machesney Park, Mount Morris, New Milford, Ogle County, Polo, ROCKFORD, Stillman Valley, Winnebago County (portions)). Franchise award date: January 1, 1972. Franchise expiration date: N.A. Began: September 1, 1973.
Channel capacity: N.A. Channels available but not in use: N.A.

Basic Service
Subscribers: 120,000 Includes Amboy, Dixon, Franklin Grove, Freeport, Kewanee, Ladd, Peru, Princeton, & Sterling.
Programming (received off-air): WGN-TV (CW, IND) Chicago; WHA-TV (PBS) Madison; WIFR (CBS) Freeport; WQRF-TV (FOX) Rockford; WREX (CW, NBC) Rockford; WTTW (PBS) Chicago; WTVO (ABC, MNT) Rockford; 8 FMs.
Programming (via satellite): C-SPAN; TV Guide Network.
Current originations: Government Access; Educational Access.
Fee: $44.00 installation; $8.00 monthly; $.84 converter.

Expanded Basic Service 1
Subscribers: N.A.
Programming (via satellite): ABC Family Channel; AMC; Animal Planet; Arts & Entertainment; BET Networks; Bravo; Cartoon Network; CNBC; CNN; Comcast SportsNet Chicago; Comedy Central; Cooking Channel; Country Music TV; C-SPAN 2; Discovery Channel; Disney Channel; E! Entertainment Television; ESPN; ESPN 2; Eternal Word TV Network; Food Network; Fox News Channel; FX; Golf Channel; Hallmark Channel; Headline News; HGTV; History Channel; Home Shopping Network; Jewelry Television; Lifetime; MSNBC; MTV; National Geographic Channel; Nickelodeon; Oxygen; QVC; ShopNBC; SoapNet; Speed Channel; Spike TV; TBS Superstation; The Learning Channel; Travel Channel; truTV; Turner Network TV; TV Land; TV One; Univision; USA Network; VH1; Weather Channel.
Fee: $43.75 monthly.

Digital Basic Service
Subscribers: 21,000.
Programming (received off-air): WHA-TV (PBS) Madison; WIFR (CBS) Freeport; WQRF-TV (FOX) Rockford; WREX (CW, NBC) Rockford; WTVO (ABC, MNT) Rockford.
Programming (via satellite): ABC Family HD; Animal Planet HD; Arts & Entertainment HD; BBC America; Bloomberg Television; CNN HD; C-SPAN 3; Discovery HD Theater; Discovery Health Channel; Discovery Kids Channel; Disney Channel HD; Encore (multiplexed); ESPN 2 HD; ESPN Classic Sports; ESPN HD; ESPNews; Flix; Food Network HD; Fox Business Channel; Fuse; G4; Great American Country; GSN; HGTV HD; History Channel HD; Independent Film Channel; MTV Hits; MTV Jams; MTV Tres; MTV2; mun2 television; Music Choice; National Geographic Channel HD Network; NFL Network HD; Nick Jr.; NickToons TV; Palladia; PBS Kids Sprout; Science Channel; Si TV; Style Network; Syfy; Syfy HD; TBS in HD; TeenNick; TLC HD; Toon Disney; Trinity Broadcasting Network; Turner Classic Movies; Turner Network TV HD; Universal HD; USA Network HD; Versus; Versus HD; VH1 Classic; VH1 Soul; WE tv.
Fee: $15.95 monthly.

Digital Expanded Basic Service
Subscribers: N.A.
Programming (via satellite): Bio; CMT Pure Country; Discovery Planet Green; Do-It-Yourself; History Channel International; ID Investigation Discovery; Lifetime Movie Network; Nick Too; Sundance Channel.
Fee: $15.95 monthly.

Digital Expanded Basic Service 2
Subscribers: N.A.
Programming (via satellite): CBS College Sports Network; Cine Latino; Cine Mexicano; CNN en Espanol; Discovery en Espanol; ESPN Deportes; Fox College Sports Atlantic; Fox College Sports Central; Fox College Sports Pacific; Fox Movie Channel; Fox Soccer; Fox Sports en Espanol; Gol TV; HDNet; HDNet Movies; History Channel en Espanol; HorseRacing TV; La Familia Network; Latele Novela Network; mun2 television; NFL Network; Outdoor Channel; Puma TV; TBN Enlace USA; Telemundo; Tennis Channel; The Sportsman Channel; TV Chile; TVG Network; VeneMovies.
Fee: $4.00 monthly (Sports Entertainment), $6.99 monthly (HDNet & HDNet Movies), $10.00 monthly (Selecto).

Digital Pay Service 1
Pay Units: N.A.
Programming (via satellite): Cinemax (multiplexed); Cinemax HD; HBO (multiplexed); HBO HD; Playboy TV; Showtime (multiplexed); Showtime HD; Starz (multiplexed); Starz HDTV; The Movie Channel (multiplexed).
Fee: $13.00 monthly (HBO, Cinemax, Starz, Showtime/TMC or Playboy).

Video-On-Demand: Yes

Pay-Per-View
Addressable homes: 21,000.
Hot Choice (delivered digitally), Fee: $3.95, Addressable: Yes; ESPN (delivered digitally); iN DEMAND; Special events (delivered digitally).

Internet Service
Operational: Yes. Began: April 1, 2000.
Broadband Service: Comcast High Speed Internet.
Fee: $99.95 installation; $44.95 monthly; $15.00 modem lease; $149.95 modem purchase.

Telephone Service
Digital: Operational
Fee: $39.95 monthly

Miles of Plant: 3,165.0 (coaxial); 8.0 (fiber optic). Homes passed: 178,500. Homes passed & miles of plant include Amboy, Dixon, Franklin Grove, Freeport, Kewanee, Ladd, Peru, Princeton, Sterling
District Director: Joseph Browning. Technical Operations Manager: Lyle Matejewski.
City fee: 5% of gross.
Ownership: Comcast Cable Communications Inc. (MSO).; Insight Communications Co. (MSO).

ROCKFORD—Formerly served by Wireless Cable Systems Inc. No longer in operation. ICA: IL0617.

ROLLING MEADOWS—Comcast Cable. Now served by SCHAUMBURG, IL [IL0036]. ICA: IL0013.

ROMEOVILLE—Comcast Cable. Now served by OAK BROOK, IL [IL0006]. ICA: IL0009.

ROSAMOND—Formerly served by Beck's Cable Systems. No longer in operation. ICA: IL0681.

ROSEVILLE—Mediacom, PO Box 334, 609 S 4th St, Chillicothe, IL 61523. Phone: 309-274-4500. Fax: 309-274-3188. Web Site: http://www.mediacomcable.com. Also serves Dallas City, Lomax, Oquawka, Pontoosuc & Stronghurst. ICA: IL0274.
TV Market Ranking: Below 100 (Dallas City, Lomax, Oquawka, Pontoosuc, ROSEVILLE, Stronghurst). Franchise award date: N.A. Franchise expiration date: N.A. Began: N.A.
Channel capacity: 134 (operating 2-way). Channels available but not in use: 82.

Basic Service
Subscribers: 1,352.
Programming (received off-air): KIIN (PBS) Iowa City; KLJB (CW, FOX) Davenport; KWQC-TV (NBC) Davenport; WHBF-TV (CBS) Rock Island; WHOI (ABC, CW) Peoria; WQAD-TV (ABC) Moline.
Programming (via satellite): ABC Family Channel; INSP; Radar Channel; WGN America.
Fee: $45.00 installation; $20.95 monthly.

Digital Basic Service
Subscribers: N.A.
Programming (via satellite): ABC News Now; AmericanLife TV Network; BBC America; Bio; Bloomberg Television; CCTV-9 (CCTV International); College Sports Television; Discovery Health Channel; Discovery Kids Channel; Discovery Military Channel; Discovery Planet Green; Discovery Times Channel; ESPNews; Fox College Sports Atlantic; Fox College Sports Central; Fox College Sports Pacific; Fox Movie Channel; Fox Reality Channel; Fuse; G4; GAS; Gol TV; Golf Channel; History Channel International; Independent Film Channel; ION Life; Lifetime Movie Network; Lime; MTV Hits; MTV2; National Geographic Channel; Nick Jr.; NickToons TV; Outdoor Channel; Qubo; ReelzChannel; Science Channel; Sleuth; Style Network; Sundance Channel; Tennis Channel; The Sportsman Channel; Turner Classic Movies; TVG Network; Versus; VH1 Classic.
Fee: $9.00 monthly.

Digital Expanded Basic Service
Subscribers: N.A.
Programming (via satellite): Discovery HD Theater; ESPN 2 HD; ESPN HD; HDNet; HDNet Movies; Universal HD.
Fee: $6.95 monthly.

Digital Pay Service 1
Pay Units: N.A.
Programming (via satellite): Cinemax (multiplexed); Encore (multiplexed); Flix (multiplexed); HBO (multiplexed); HBO HD; Showtime (multiplexed); Showtime HD; Starz (multiplexed); Starz HDTV; The Movie

Channel (multiplexed); The Movie Channel HD.
Fee: $11.95 monthly (HBO, Cinemax, Starz/ Encore or Showtime/TMC).
Video-On-Demand: No
Pay-Per-View
iN DEMAND (delivered digitally); Playboy TV (delivered digitally).
Internet Service
Operational: Yes.
Broadband Service: Mediacom High Speed Internet.
Fee: $59.95 installation; $45.95 monthly.
Telephone Service
Digital: Operational
Fee: $39.95 installation; $39.95 monthly
Miles of Plant: 51.0 (coaxial); None (fiber optic). Homes passed: 2,697.
Vice President: Don Hagwell. Operations Director: Gary Wightman. Technical Operations Manager: Larry Brackman. Marketing Director: Stephanie Law.
City fee: 3% of gross.
Ownership: Mediacom LLC (MSO).

ROSICLARE—Galaxy Cablevision, 7155 US Hwy 45 S, Carrier Mills, IL 62917. Phone: 618-994-2261. Fax: 618-994-2261. Web Site: http://www.galaxycable.com. Also serves Elizabethtown & Hardin County. ICA: IL0216.
TV Market Ranking: 69 (Elizabethtown, Hardin County, ROSICLARE). Franchise award date: N.A. Franchise expiration date: N.A. Began: October 1, 1982.
Channel capacity: 41 (not 2-way capable). Channels available but not in use: None.
Basic Service
Subscribers: 263.
Programming (received off-air): KBSI (FOX) Cape Girardeau; KFVS-TV (CBS, CW) Cape Girardeau; WDKA (MNT) Paducah; WKPD (PBS) Paducah; WPSD-TV (NBC) Paducah; WSIL-TV (ABC) Harrisburg; WTCT (IND) Marion.
Programming (via satellite): ABC Family Channel; AMC; Animal Planet; Arts & Entertainment; Cartoon Network; CNBC; CNN; Comedy Central; C-SPAN; Discovery Channel; Disney Channel; E! Entertainment Television; ESPN; ESPN 2; Fox News Channel; Fuse; FX; Great American Country; Headline News; HGTV; History Channel; Home Shopping Network; Lifetime; Outdoor Channel; TBS Superstation; The Learning Channel; Travel Channel; Trinity Broadcasting Network; Turner Network TV; USA Network; Weather Channel; WGN America.
Fee: $30.00 installation; $44.00 monthly; $3.00 converter.
Pay Service 1
Pay Units: N.A.
Programming (via satellite): Cinemax; HBO; Showtime.
Fee: $12.00 monthly (each).
Internet Service
Operational: No.
Telephone Service
None
Miles of Plant: 16.0 (coaxial); None (fiber optic). Homes passed: 834.
State Manager: Ward Webb. Technical Manager: Audie Murphy. Engineer: John Stewart. Customer Service Manager: Malynda Ward.
Ownership: Galaxy Cable Inc. (MSO).

ROXANA—Charter Communications, 941 Charter Commons Dr, Saint Louis, MO 63017. Phone: 636-207-7044. Fax: 636-207-7034. Web Site: http://www.charter.com. Also serves Alton, Bethalto, Cottage Hills, East Alton, Godfrey, Hartford, Madison County, Moro Twp., Rosewood Heights, South Roxana & Wood River. ICA: IL0025.
TV Market Ranking: 11 (Alton, Bethalto, Cottage Hills, East Alton, Godfrey, Hartford, Madison County, Moro Twp., Rosewood Heights, ROXANA, South Roxana, Wood River). Franchise award date: N.A. Franchise expiration date: N.A. Began: January 1, 1975.
Channel capacity: N.A. Channels available but not in use: N.A.
Basic Service
Subscribers: 24,135.
Programming (received off-air): KDNL-TV (ABC) St. Louis; KETC (PBS) St. Louis; KMOV (CBS) St. Louis; KNLC (IND) St. Louis; KPLR-TV (CW) St. Louis; KSDK (NBC) St. Louis; KTVI (FOX) St. Louis; WPXS (IND) Mount Vernon; WRBU (MNT) East St. Louis; 20 FMs.
Programming (via satellite): C-SPAN; C-SPAN 2; Eternal Word TV Network; GRTV Network; Home Shopping Network; INSP; Jewelry Television; QVC; ShopNBC; TBS Superstation; Trinity Broadcasting Network; TV Guide Network; Univision; Weatherscan; WGN America.
Current originations: Public Access; Educational Access.
Fee: $29.99 installation.
Expanded Basic Service 1
Subscribers: 23,171.
Programming (via satellite): ABC Family Channel; AMC; Animal Planet; Arts & Entertainment; BET Networks; Bravo; Cartoon Network; CNBC; CNN; Comedy Central; Country Music TV; Discovery Channel; Disney Channel; E! Entertainment Television; ESPN; ESPN 2; Food Network; Fox Movie Channel; Fox News Channel; Fox Sports Net Midwest; FX; G4; GSN; Hallmark Channel; Headline News; HGTV; History Channel; Lifetime; MSNBC; MTV; Nickelodeon; Oxygen; SoapNet; Speed Channel; Spike TV; Style Network; Syfy; The Learning Channel; Toon Disney; Travel Channel; truTV; Turner Classic Movies; Turner Network TV; TV Land; USA Network; VH1; WE tv; Weather Channel.
Fee: $49.99 monthly.
Digital Basic Service
Subscribers: N.A.
Programming (via satellite): BBC America; Bio; Bloomberg Television; Discovery Digital Networks; Do-It-Yourself; Encore Action; ESPN Classic Sports; FitTV; Fox College Sports Atlantic; Fox College Sports Central; Fox College Sports Pacific; Fox Sports World; Fuel TV; Fuse; GAS; Golf Channel; Great American Country; History Channel International; Independent Film Channel; Lifetime Movie Network; MTV Networks Digital Suite; Music Choice; National Geographic Channel; NFL Network; Nick Jr.; Nick Too; NickToons TV; Style Network; Sundance Channel; TV Guide Interactive Inc.; Versus.
Digital Pay Service 1
Pay Units: 1,816.
Programming (via satellite): Cinemax (multiplexed).
Fee: $13.15 monthly.
Digital Pay Service 2
Pay Units: 6,713.
Programming (via satellite): Starz (multiplexed).
Fee: $6.75 monthly.
Digital Pay Service 3
Pay Units: 4,167.
Programming (via satellite): HBO (multiplexed).
Fee: $14.05 monthly.
Digital Pay Service 4
Pay Units: 4,305.
Programming (via satellite): Showtime (multiplexed); The Movie Channel (multiplexed).
Fee: $13.90 monthly.
Video-On-Demand: Yes
Pay-Per-View
iN DEMAND (delivered digitally); Playboy TV (delivered digitally); Fresh (delivered digitally); Shorteez (delivered digitally); Sports PPV (delivered digitally); ESPN Now (delivered digitally).
Internet Service
Operational: Yes.
Broadband Service: Charter Pipeline.
Fee: $29.99 monthly.
Telephone Service
Digital: Operational
Miles of Plant: 471.0 (coaxial); 77.0 (fiber optic). Homes passed: 44,136. Total homes in franchised area: 44,199.
Vice President & General Manager: Steve Trippe. Operations Director: Tom Williams. Marketing Director: Beverly Wall.
City fee: 5% of gross.
Ownership: Charter Communications Inc. (MSO).

ROYAL—Formerly served by CableDirect. No longer in operation. ICA: IL0640.

RUSHVILLE—Cass Cable TV Inc. Now served by VIRGINIA, IL [IL0598]. ICA: IL0191.

SADORUS—Formerly served by Longview Communications. No longer in operation. ICA: IL0575.

SALEM—Charter Communications, 5111 Lake Terrace NE, Mount Vernon, IL 62864-9666. Phones: 636-207-7044 (St Louis office); 618-242-9512. Fax: 618-242-4156. Web Site: http://www.charter.com. Also serves Junction City, Marion County (portions), Odin & Sandoval. ICA: IL0121.
TV Market Ranking: Below 100 (Junction City, Marion County (portions), Odin, SALEM, Sandoval). Franchise award date: N.A. Franchise expiration date: N.A. Began: December 1, 1964.
Channel capacity: N.A. Channels available but not in use: N.A.
Basic Service
Subscribers: 4,427.
Programming (received off-air): KDNL-TV (ABC) St. Louis; KMOV (CBS) St. Louis; KPLR-TV (CW) St. Louis; KSDK (NBC) St. Louis; KTVI (FOX) St. Louis; WPXS (IND) Mount Vernon; WSIU-TV (PBS) Carbondale.
Programming (via satellite): AMC; Arts & Entertainment; Home Shopping Network; Lifetime; MTV; Nickelodeon; QVC; Syfy; Trinity Broadcasting Network; Turner Network TV; VH1; Weather Channel.
Current originations: Government Access; Educational Access; Public Access.
Fee: $29.99 installation.
Expanded Basic Service 1
Subscribers: N.A.
Programming (via satellite): ABC Family Channel; Animal Planet; Bravo; Cartoon Network; CNBC; CNN; Comedy Central; Country Music TV; C-SPAN; Discovery Channel; Disney Channel; E! Entertainment Television; ESPN; ESPN 2; FitTV; Food Network; Fox News Channel; Fox Sports Net Midwest; FX; G4; Hallmark Channel; Headline News; HGTV; History Channel; MSNBC; National Geographic Channel; Oxygen; SoapNet; Spike TV; TBS Superstation; The Learning Channel; Toon Disney; Travel Channel; Turner Classic Movies; TV Guide Network; TV Land; USA Network; Versus; WGN America.
Fee: $49.99 monthly.
Digital Basic Service
Subscribers: 462.
Programming (via satellite): American-Life TV Network; BBC America; Bio; Bloomberg Television; Discovery Digital Networks; DMX Music; Fox Movie Channel; Fuse; GAS; Golf Channel; GSN; Halogen Network; History Channel International; Independent Film Channel; Lifetime Movie Network; MTV Networks Digital Suite; Nick Jr.; Outdoor Channel; Speed Channel; Style Network; WE tv.
Digital Pay Service 1
Pay Units: N.A.
Programming (via satellite): Cinemax (multiplexed); Encore (multiplexed); Flix; HBO (multiplexed); Showtime (multiplexed); Starz (multiplexed); The Movie Channel (multiplexed).
Video-On-Demand: No
Pay-Per-View
iN DEMAND (delivered digitally); ESPN Now (delivered digitally); Playboy TV (delivered digitally); Fresh (delivered digitally); Shorteez (delivered digitally); Hot Choice (delivered digitally).
Internet Service
Operational: Yes. Began: April 1, 2003.
Broadband Service: Charter Pipeline.
Fee: $29.99 monthly.
Telephone Service
Digital: Operational
Fee: $29.99 monthly
Homes passed: 5,062. Miles of plant (coax) included in Woodlawn
Vice President & General Manager: Steve Trippe. Operations Director: Dave Miller. Technical Operations Manager: Eddie Prior. Marketing Director: Beverly Wall.
City fee: 3% of gross.
Ownership: Charter Communications Inc. (MSO).

SALINE COUNTY (portions)—Galaxy Cablevision, 7155 US Hwy 45 S, Carrier Mills, IL 62917. Phone: 618-994-2261. Fax: 618-994-2261. E-mail: kmorris@galaxycable.com. Web Site: http://www.galaxycable.com. Also serves Galatia & Raleigh. ICA: IL0501.
TV Market Ranking: 69 (Raleigh, SALINE COUNTY (PORTIONS)). Franchise award date: N.A. Franchise expiration date: N.A. Began: November 1, 1986.
Channel capacity: 41 (not 2-way capable). Channels available but not in use: None.
Basic Service
Subscribers: 194.
Programming (received off-air): KBSI (FOX) Cape Girardeau; KFVS-TV (CBS, CW) Cape Girardeau; WDKA (MNT) Paducah; WPSD-TV (NBC) Paducah; WSIL-TV (ABC) Harrisburg; WSIU-TV (PBS) Carbondale; WTCT (IND) Marion.
Programming (via satellite): ABC Family Channel; Animal Planet; Arts & Entertainment; Cartoon Network; CNN; Comedy Central; Discovery Channel; Disney Channel; E! Entertainment Television; ESPN; ESPN 2; Fox News Channel; Fuse; FX; Great American Country; Headline News; HGTV; History Channel; Home Shopping Network; Lifetime; Outdoor Channel; TBS Superstation; The Learning Channel; Turner Classic Movies; Turner Network TV; USA Network; Weather Channel; WGN America.
Fee: $30.00 installation; $40.70 monthly.

Pay Service 1
Pay Units: N.A.
Programming (via satellite): Cinemax; Encore Action; HBO.
Internet Service
Operational: Yes.
Telephone Service
None
Miles of Plant: 22.0 (coaxial); None (fiber optic). Homes passed: 934.
State Manager: Ward Webb. Customer Service Manager: Malynda Walker. Engineer: John Stewart. Technical Manager: Audie Murphy.
Ownership: Galaxy Cable Inc. (MSO).

SAYBROOK—Mediacom. Now served by LE ROY, IL [IL0539]. ICA: IL0283.

SCALES MOUND—Mediacom, 3900 26th Ave, Moline, IL 61265. Phone: 309-797-2580. Fax: 309-797-2414. Web Site: http://www.mediacomcable.com. ICA: IL0688.
Channel capacity: N.A. Channels available but not in use: N.A.
Video-On-Demand: No
Internet Service
Operational: Yes.
Broadband Service: Mediacom High Speed Internet.
Fee: $59.95 installation; $49.95 monthly.
Telephone Service
Digital: Operational
Fee: $39.95 installation; $39.95 monthly
MIles of plant included with Moline
Regional Vice President: Cari Fenzel. Area Manager: Katherine McMullen. Engineering Director: Mitch Carlson. Marketing Director: Greg Evans. Technical Operations Manager: Darren Dean.
Ownership: Mediacom LLC (MSO).

SCHAUMBURG—Comcast Cable, 1500 McConnor Pkwy, Schaumburg, IL 60173-4399. Phone: 847-585-6300. Fax: 847-585-6733. Web Site: http://www.comcast.com. Also serves Algonquin, Arlington Heights, Bannockburn, Barrington, Barrington Hills, Bartlett, Beach Park, Buffalo Grove, Carpentersville, Cary, Cook County, Creston, Crystal Lake, Deer Park, Deerfield, DeKalb, Des Plaines, East Dundee, Elk Grove (village), Evanston, Fort Sheridan, Fox River Grove, Glencoe, Glenview, Glenview Naval Air Station, Golf, Great Lakes Naval Training Center, Hainesville, Hanover Park, Hawthorne Woods, Highland Park, Highwood, Hillcrest, Hoffman Estates, Holiday Hills, Huntley, Indian Creek, Inverness (village), Island Lake, Kane County (portions), Kenilworth (village), Kildeer, Lake Barrington, Lake Bluff, Lake County, Lake Forest, Lake in the Hills, Lake Zurich, Lakemoor, Lakewood Village, Libertyville, Lincolnshire, Lincolnwood, Long Grove, McCollum Lake, McHenry, Morton Grove, Mount Prospect, Mundelein, New Trier Twp., Niles, North Barrington (village), North Chicago, Northbrook, Northfield, Oakwood Hills, Palatine, Park Ridge, Prospect Heights, Riverwoods (village), Rochelle, Rolling Meadows, Round Lake, Round Lake Beach, Round Lake Heights, Round Lake Park, Skokie, Sleepy Hollow, South Barrington (village), Streamwood, Sunnyside, Sycamore, Tower Lakes, Vernon Hills, Wauconda, West Dundee, Wheeling, Wilmette, Winnetka, Wonder Lake & Woodstock. ICA: IL0036.
TV Market Ranking: 3 (Arlington Heights, Arlington Heights, Bannockburn, Barrington, Barrington Hills, Barrington Hills, Bartlett, Beach Park, Buffalo Grove, Buffalo Grove, Cook County, Cook County, Deer Park, Deerfield, Des Plaines, East Dundee, Elk Grove (village), Evanston, Fort Sheridan, Glencoe, Glenview, Glenview Naval Air Station, Golf, Great Lakes Naval Training Center, Hanover Park, Hawthorne Woods, Highland Park, Highwood, Hoffman Estates, Indian Creek, Inverness (village), Kane County (portions) (portions), Kenilworth (village), Kildeer, Lake Barrington, Lake Bluff, Lake County (portions), Lake Forest, Lake Zurich, Libertyville, Lincolnshire, Lincolnwood, Long Grove, Morton Grove, Mount Prospect, Mundelein, New Trier Twp., Niles, North Barrington (village), North Chicago, Northbrook, Northfield, Palatine, Park Ridge, Park Ridge, Prospect Heights, Riverwoods (village), Rolling Meadows, SCHAUMBURG, Skokie, South Barrington (village), Streamwood, Tower Lakes, Vernon Hills, Waukegan, Wheeling, Wilmette, Winnetka); 97 (Creston, De Kalb, Hillcrest, Huntley, Lakewood Village, Rochelle, Sycamore, Wonder Lake); Below 100 (Algonquin, Carpentersville, Cary, Crystal Lake, Fox River Grove, Hainesville, Holiday Hills, Island Lake, Island Lake, Lake in the Hills, Lakemoor, McCollum Lake, McHenry, Oakwood Hills, Round Lake, Round Lake Beach, Round Lake Heights, Round Lake Park, Sleepy Hollow, Sunnyside, Wauconda, West Dundee, Woodstock, Kane County (portions) (portions), Lake County (portions)). Franchise award date: N.A. Franchise expiration date: N.A. Began: August 1, 1982.
Channel capacity: N.A. Channels available but not in use: N.A.
Basic Service
Subscribers: 343,843.
Programming (received off-air): WBBM-TV (CBS) Chicago; WCIU-TV (IND) Chicago; WCPX-TV (ION) Chicago; WFLD (FOX) Chicago; WGBO-DT (UNV) Joliet; WGN-TV (CW, IND) Chicago; WJYS (IND) Hammond; WLS-TV (ABC) Chicago; WMAQ-TV (NBC) Chicago; WPWR-TV (MNT) Gary; WSNS-TV (TMO) Chicago; WTTW (PBS) Chicago; WXFT-DT (TEL) Aurora; WYCC (PBS) Chicago.
Programming (via satellite): C-SPAN; C-SPAN 2; Discovery Channel; QVC; TBS Superstation; The Learning Channel; Turner Classic Movies; TV Guide Network.
Current originations: Public Access.
Fee: $37.37 installation; $10.39 monthly.
Expanded Basic Service 1
Subscribers: N.A.
Programming (via satellite): ABC Family Channel; AMC; Animal Planet; Arts & Entertainment; BET Networks; Cartoon Network; Chicagoland Television News; CNBC; CNN; Comcast SportsNet Chicago; Comedy Central; Disney Channel; E! Entertainment Television; ESPN; ESPN 2; ESPN Classic Sports; Eternal Word TV Network; Food Network; Fox News Channel; FX; Golf Channel; Hallmark Channel; Headline News; HGTV; History Channel; Home Shopping Network 2; Lifetime; MSNBC; MTV; Nickelodeon; Oxygen; Spike TV; Syfy; Total Living Network; Travel Channel; truTV; Turner Network TV; TV Land; USA Network; VH1; Weather Channel.
Fee: $29.60 monthly.
Digital Basic Service
Subscribers: 7,406.
Programming (via satellite): AmericanLife TV Network; BBC America; Bio; Black Family Channel; Bloomberg Television; Bravo; Canales N; Discovery Digital Networks; ESPNews; FitTV; Fox College Sports Atlantic; Fox College Sports Central; Fox College Sports Pacific; Fox Movie Channel; Fox Sports World; Fuse; G4; GAS; Great American Country; GSN; Halogen Network; History Channel International; Independent Film Channel; Lifetime Movie Network; Lime; MTV Networks Digital Suite; Music Choice; National Geographic Channel; Nick Jr.; NickToons TV; Outdoor Channel; Ovation; ShopNBC; Speed Channel; Style Network; Sundance Channel; The Word Network; Toon Disney; Trinity Broadcasting Network; Versus; WE tv; Weatherscan.
Fee: $14.99 monthly.
Pay Service 1
Pay Units: 1,867.
Programming (via satellite): Cinemax; Encore; HBO; Showtime.
Digital Pay Service 1
Pay Units: N.A.
Programming (via satellite): Cinemax (multiplexed); Encore (multiplexed); Flix; HBO (multiplexed); Showtime (multiplexed); Starz (multiplexed); The Movie Channel (multiplexed).
Fee: $10.00 monthly (each).
Video-On-Demand: Yes
Pay-Per-View
Addressable homes: 7,406.
iN DEMAND, Addressable: Yes; ESPN Now (delivered digitally); Sports PPV (delivered digitally); iN DEMAND (delivered digitally); Fresh (delivered digitally); Shorteez (delivered digitally); Playboy TV (delivered digitally); Hot Choice (delivered digitally).
Internet Service
Operational: Yes.
Subscribers: 4,959.
Broadband Service: Comcast High Speed Internet.
Fee: $99.99 installation; $45.95 monthly.
Telephone Service
Digital: Operational
Fee: $44.95 monthly
Miles of Plant: 8,425.0 (coaxial); 161.0 (fiber optic). Homes passed: 603,594.
Regional Senior Vice President: Steve Reimer. Area Vice President: Brian Sullivan. Vice President, Technical Operations: Bob Curtis. Vice President, Sales & Marketing: Eric Schaefer. Vice President, Communications: Rich Ruggiero. Operations Director: Robert Rogola. Technical Operations Director: Bob Cole. Sales & Marketing Director: Lori Tybon.
Ownership: Comcast Cable Communications Inc. (MSO).

SCOTT AFB—Charter Communications, 941 Charter Commons Dr, Saint Louis, MO 63017. Phone: 626-207-7044. Fax: 636-230-7034. Web Site: http://www.charter.com. Also serves Albers, Aviston, Clinton County, Damiansville, Freeburg, Lebanon, Mascoutah, New Baden, Shiloh, St. Clair County, Summerfield & Trenton. ICA: IL0057.
TV Market Ranking: 11 (Albers, Aviston, Clinton County (portions), Damiansville, Freeburg, Lebanon, Mascoutah, New Baden, SCOTT AFB, Shiloh, St. Clair County, Summerfield, Trenton); Below 100 (Clinton County (portions)); Outside TV Markets (Clinton County (portions)). Franchise award date: August 21, 1980. Franchise expiration date: N.A. Began: January 1, 1981.
Channel capacity: N.A. Channels available but not in use: N.A.
Basic Service
Subscribers: 8,340.
Programming (received off-air): KDNL-TV (ABC) St. Louis; KETC (PBS) St. Louis; KMOV (CBS) St. Louis; KNLC (IND) St. Louis; KPLR-TV (CW) St. Louis; KSDK (NBC) St. Louis; KTVI (FOX) St. Louis; WPXS (IND) Mount Vernon; WRBU (MNT) East St. Louis; WSIU-TV (PBS) Carbondale.
Programming (via satellite): C-SPAN; C-SPAN 2; Eternal Word TV Network; GRTV Network; Home Shopping Network; INSP; Jewelry Television; QVC; ShopNBC; TBS Superstation; Trinity Broadcasting Network; TV Guide Network; Univision; Weatherscan; WGN America.
Current originations: Government Access; Educational Access; Public Access.
Fee: $29.95 installation.
Expanded Basic Service 1
Subscribers: N.A.
Programming (via satellite): ABC Family Channel; AMC; Animal Planet; Arts & Entertainment; BET Networks; Bravo; Cartoon Network; CNBC; CNN; Comedy Central; Country Music TV; Discovery Channel; Disney Channel; E! Entertainment Television; ESPN; ESPN 2; Food Network; Fox Movie Channel; Fox News Channel; Fox Sports Net Midwest; FX; G4; Golf Channel; GSN; Hallmark Channel; Headline News; HGTV; History Channel; Lifetime; MSNBC; MTV; National Geographic Channel; Nickelodeon; Oxygen; SoapNet; Speed Channel; Spike TV; Style Network; Syfy; The Learning Channel; Toon Disney; Travel Channel; truTV; Turner Classic Movies; Turner Network TV; TV Land; USA Network; Versus; VH1; WE tv; Weather Channel.
Fee: $49.99 monthly.
Digital Basic Service
Subscribers: N.A.
Programming (via satellite): BBC America; Bio; Bloomberg Television; Discovery Digital Networks; Do-It-Yourself; Encore Action; ESPN Classic Sports; FitTV; Fox College Sports Atlantic; Fox College Sports Central; Fox College Sports Pacific; Fox Sports World; Fuel TV; Fuse; GAS; Great American Country; History Channel International; Independent Film Channel; International Television (ITV); Lifetime Movie Network; MTV Networks Digital Suite; Music Choice; NFL Network; Nick Jr.; Nick Too; NickToons TV; Sundance Channel; TV Guide Interactive Inc.
Digital Pay Service 1
Pay Units: N.A.
Programming (via satellite): Cinemax (multiplexed); HBO (multiplexed); Showtime (multiplexed); Starz (multiplexed); The Movie Channel (multiplexed).
Video-On-Demand: Yes
Pay-Per-View
Sports PPV (delivered digitally); iN DEMAND (delivered digitally); Playboy TV (delivered digitally); Fresh (delivered digitally); Shorteez (delivered digitally); ESPN Now (delivered digitally).
Internet Service
Operational: Yes.
Broadband Service: Charter Pipeline.
Fee: $29.99 monthly.
Telephone Service
Digital: Operational
Fee: $29.99 monthly
Miles of Plant: 247.0 (coaxial); 9.0 (fiber optic). Homes passed: 12,900.
Vice President & General Manager: Steve Trippe. Operations Director: Tom Williams. Marketing Director: Beverly Wall.
City fee: 3% of gross.
Ownership: Charter Communications Inc. (MSO).

SEATONVILLE (village)—Formerly served by CableDirect. No longer in operation. ICA: IL0576.

SENECA & ELWOOD—Kraus Electronics Systems Inc., 305 State St, Manhattan, IL 60442-0011. Phones: 815-357-6678 (Customer service); 815-478-4000; 815-478-4444. Fax: 815-478-3386. Web Site: http://www.krausonline.com. ICA: IL0238.

TV Market Ranking: Below 100 (SENECA). Franchise award date: N.A. Franchise expiration date: N.A. Began: March 1, 1972.

Channel capacity: 12 (operating 2-way). Channels available but not in use: N.A.

Basic Service

Subscribers: 960.

Programming (received off-air): WBBM-TV (CBS) Chicago; WCIU-TV (IND) Chicago; WCPX-TV (ION) Chicago; WFLD (FOX) Chicago; WGBO-DT (UNV) Joliet; WGN-TV (CW, IND) Chicago; WJYS (IND) Hammond; WLS-TV (ABC) Chicago; WMAQ-TV (NBC) Chicago; WPWR-TV (MNT) Gary; WSNS-TV (TMO) Chicago; WTTW (PBS) Chicago; WWTO-TV (TBN) La Salle; WXFT-DT (TEL) Aurora; WYCC (PBS) Chicago; WYIN (PBS) Gary; allband FM.

Programming (via satellite): Headline News; QVC.

Fee: $35.00 installation; $38.00 monthly.

Expanded Basic Service 1

Subscribers: N.A.

Programming (via satellite): ABC Family Channel; AMC; Animal Planet; Arts & Entertainment; Cartoon Network; CNBC; CNN; Comcast SportsNet Chicago; Comedy Central; Country Music TV; Court TV; C-SPAN; C-SPAN 2; Discovery Channel; Disney Channel; ESPN; ESPN 2; ESPN Classic Sports; Eternal Word TV Network; Food Network; Fox News Channel; FX; GSN; Hallmark Channel; HGTV; History Channel; Lifetime; ME Television; MTV; National Geographic Channel; Nickelodeon; Spike TV; Syfy; TBS Superstation; The Learning Channel; Turner Network TV; TV Land; USA Network; VH1; Weather Channel.

Digital Basic Service

Subscribers: N.A.

Programming (via satellite): AmericanLife TV Network; BBC America; Bio; Bloomberg Television; Bravo; Discovery Home Channel; Discovery Kids Channel; Discovery Military Channel; Discovery Times Channel; DMX Music; ESPNews; FitTV; Fox Movie Channel; Fox Sports World; FSN Digital Atlantic; FSN Digital Central; FSN Digital Pacific; Fuse; G4; GAS; Golf Channel; Great American Country; History Channel; History Channel International; Independent Film Channel; Lifetime Movie Network; MTV Hits; MTV2; Nick Jr.; NickToons TV; Outdoor Channel; Science Television; Speed Channel; Style Network; Toon Disney; Trio; Turner Classic Movies; VH1 Classic; VH1 Country; WE tv.

Pay Service 1

Pay Units: N.A.

Programming (via satellite): Cinemax; HBO.

Fee: $10.00 monthly (Cinemax), $13.95 monthly (HBO).

Digital Pay Service 1

Pay Units: N.A.

Programming (via satellite): Cinemax (multiplexed); Encore (multiplexed); HBO (multiplexed); Showtime (multiplexed); Starz (multiplexed); The Movie Channel (multiplexed).

Video-On-Demand: No

Pay-Per-View

Playboy TV (delivered digitally); Fresh (delivered digitally); Shorteez (delivered digitally).

Internet Service

Operational: Yes.

Broadband Service: In-house.

Fee: $9.95-$49.95 monthly.

Telephone Service

Digital: Operational

Fee: $26.95-$34.95 monthly

Miles of Plant: 12.0 (coaxial); None (fiber optic). Additional miles planned: 3.0 (coaxial).

Manager: Mike Bordeaux. Chief Technician: Skip Kraus.

Ownership: Arthur J. Kraus (MSO).

SESSER—NewWave Communications, 318 N 4th St, Vandalia, IL 62471. Phone: 573-472-9500. Fax: 618.283.4483. E-mail: info@newwavecom.com. Web Site: http://www.newwavecom.com. Also serves Valier. ICA: IL0189.

TV Market Ranking: 69 (Valier); Below 100 (SESSER). Franchise award date: N.A. Franchise expiration date: N.A. Began: N.A.

Channel capacity: 60 (not 2-way capable). Channels available but not in use: 14.

Basic Service

Subscribers: 381.

Programming (received off-air): KBSI (FOX) Cape Girardeau; KFVS-TV (CBS, CW) Cape Girardeau; KPLR-TV (CW) St. Louis; WDKA (MNT) Paducah; WPSD-TV (NBC) Paducah; WPXS (IND) Mount Vernon; WSIL-TV (ABC) Harrisburg; WSIU-TV (PBS) Carbondale; WTCT (IND) Marion; allband FM.

Programming (via satellite): AMC; Arts & Entertainment; C-SPAN; Home Shopping Network; TBS Superstation; The Learning Channel; Weather Channel; WGN America.

Fee: $17.45 monthly.

Expanded Basic Service 1

Subscribers: 333.

Programming (via satellite): ABC Family Channel; Bravo; Cartoon Network; CNBC; CNN; Comedy Central; Discovery Channel; Disney Channel; E! Entertainment Television; ESPN; ESPN 2; Fox News Channel; Fox Sports Net Midwest; FX; G4; Great American Country; Hallmark Channel; Headline News; HGTV; History Channel; Lifetime; MTV; National Geographic Channel; Nickelodeon; QVC; Spike TV; Syfy; Toon Disney; Travel Channel; truTV; Turner Network TV; TV Land; USA Network; Versus; VH1.

Fee: $12.95 monthly.

Digital Basic Service

Subscribers: N.A.

Programming (via satellite): AmericanLife TV Network; BBC America; Bio; Bloomberg Television; Discovery Digital Networks; DMX Music; ESPN Classic Sports; ESPNews; Fox Movie Channel; GAS; Golf Channel; GSN; Halogen Network; HGTV; History Channel; History Channel International; Independent Film Channel; Lifetime Movie Network; MTV Networks Digital Suite; MuchMusic Network; Nick Jr.; Outdoor Channel; ShopNBC; Speed Channel; Style Network; Syfy; Toon Disney; Trinity Broadcasting Network; Turner Classic Movies; Versus; WE tv.

Fee: $19.95 monthly.

Digital Pay Service 1

Pay Units: N.A.

Programming (via satellite): Cinemax (multiplexed); Encore (multiplexed); Flix; HBO (multiplexed); Showtime (multiplexed); Starz (multiplexed); The Movie Channel (multiplexed).

Video-On-Demand: No

Pay-Per-View

iN DEMAND (delivered digitally); Hot Choice (delivered digitally); ESPN Extra (delivered digitally); ESPN Now (delivered digitally); Playboy TV (delivered digitally); Fresh (delivered digitally); Shorteez (delivered digitally).

Internet Service

Operational: Yes.

Telephone Service

Digital: Operational

Miles of Plant: 34.0 (coaxial); None (fiber optic). Homes passed: 2,072.

General Manager: Bill Flowers. Technical Operations Manager: Chris Mooday.

City fee: 3% of gross.

Ownership: NewWave Communications (MSO).

SHAWNEETOWN—Now served by OWENSBORO, KY [KY0004]. ICA: IL0198.

SHELBYVILLE—Charter Communications, 11 Clearing, Taylorville, IL 62568-9279. Phones: 636-207-7044 (St Louis office); 217-287-7992. Fax: 217-287-7304. Web Site: http://www.charter.com. Also serves Shelby County (portions). ICA: IL0162.

TV Market Ranking: 64 (Shelby County (portions), SHELBYVILLE). Franchise award date: N.A. Franchise expiration date: N.A. Began: March 27, 1979.

Channel capacity: N.A. Channels available but not in use: N.A.

Basic Service

Subscribers: N.A. Included in Taylorville

Programming (received off-air): KPLR-TV (CW) St. Louis; KSDK (NBC) St. Louis; WAND (NBC) Decatur; WBUI (CW) Decatur; WCFN (MNT) Springfield; WCIA (CBS) Champaign; WICS (ABC) Springfield; WILL-TV (PBS) Urbana; WRSP-TV (FOX) Springfield.

Programming (via satellite): C-SPAN; C-SPAN 2; Home Shopping Network; QVC; Weatherscan; WGN America.

Current originations: Religious Access; Government Access; Educational Access; Public Access.

Fee: $29.99 installation; $1.95 converter.

Expanded Basic Service 1

Subscribers: 1,526.

Programming (via satellite): ABC Family Channel; AMC; Animal Planet; Arts & Entertainment; Bravo; Cartoon Network; CNBC; CNN; Comedy Central; Country Music TV; Discovery Channel; Disney Channel; E! Entertainment Television; ESPN; ESPN 2; Food Network; Fox News Channel; Fox Sports Net Midwest; FX; G4; Golf Channel; GSN; Hallmark Channel; Headline News; HGTV; History Channel; Lifetime; MSNBC; MTV; National Geographic Channel; Nickelodeon; Oxygen; SoapNet; Speed Channel; Spike TV; Syfy; TBS Superstation; The Learning Channel; Toon Disney; Travel Channel; Trinity Broadcasting Network; truTV; Turner Network TV; TV Guide Network; TV Land; USA Network; VH1; Weather Channel.

Fee: $49.99 monthly.

Digital Pay Service 1

Pay Units: 170.

Programming (via satellite): Cinemax (multiplexed).

Fee: $15.00 installation; $9.50 monthly.

Digital Pay Service 2

Pay Units: 283.

Programming (via satellite): HBO (multiplexed).

Fee: $15.00 installation; $10.00 monthly.

Digital Pay Service 3

Pay Units: N.A.

Programming (via satellite): Encore (multiplexed); Flix; Showtime (multiplexed); Starz (multiplexed); The Movie Channel (multiplexed).

Video-On-Demand: Yes

Pay-Per-View

Playboy TV (delivered digitally); iN DEMAND (delivered digitally); NASCAR In Car (delivered digitally); NHL Center Ice (delivered digitally); MLB Extra Innings (delivered digitally); Fresh (delivered digitally); Shorteez (delivered digitally).

Internet Service

Operational: Yes.

Broadband Service: Charter Pipeline.

Fee: $29.99 monthly.

Telephone Service

Digital: Operational

Miles of Plant: 29.0 (coaxial); None (fiber optic). Total homes in franchised area: 2,000. Homes passed included in Taylorville

Vice President & General Manager: Steve Trippe. Operations Director: Dave Miller. Chief Technician: Larry Harmon. Marketing Director: Beverly Wall. Office Manager: Melinda Sincavage.

City fee: 3% of gross.

Ownership: Charter Communications Inc. (MSO).

SHERIDAN (village)—Mediacom. Now served by STREATOR, IL [IL0069]. ICA: IL0577.

SHIPMAN—Mediacom, PO Box 288, 4290 Blue Stem Rd, Charleston, IL 61920. Phone: 217-348-5533. Fax: 217-345-7074. Web Site: http://www.mediacomcable.com. ICA: IL0384.

TV Market Ranking: Outside TV Markets (SHIPMAN). Franchise award date: N.A. Franchise expiration date: N.A. Began: December 15, 1983.

Channel capacity: N.A. Channels available but not in use: N.A.

Basic Service

Subscribers: 62.

Programming (received off-air): KDNL-TV (ABC) St. Louis; KETC (PBS) St. Louis; KMOV (CBS) St. Louis; KPLR-TV (CW) St. Louis; KSDK (NBC) St. Louis; KTVI (FOX) St. Louis.

Programming (via satellite): ABC Family Channel; AMC; Arts & Entertainment; Cartoon Network; CNN; Comedy Central; Country Music TV; Discovery Channel; ESPN; ESPN 2; Home Shopping Net-

work; Lifetime; Nickelodeon; Spike TV; TBS Superstation; Travel Channel; Trinity Broadcasting Network; Turner Network TV; USA Network; WGN America.
Fee: $45.00 installation; $45.95 monthly.
Pay Service 1
Pay Units: 27.
Programming (via satellite): Cinemax; HBO.
Fee: $25.00 installation; $7.95 monthly (Cinemax), $13.50 monthly (HBO).
Video-On-Demand: No
Internet Service
Operational: No.
Telephone Service
None
Miles of Plant: 7.0 (coaxial); None (fiber optic). Homes passed: 216.
Area Operations Director: Todd Acker. Technical Operations Manager: Jerry Ferguson.
City fee: 3% of gross.
Ownership: Mediacom LLC (MSO).

SIBLEY (village)—Heartland Cable Inc., PO Box 7, 167 W 5th St, Minonk, IL 61760. Phones: 800-448-4320; 309-432-2075. Fax: 309-432-2500. Web Site: http://www.heartlandcable.com. Also serves Elliott & Ellsworth. ICA: IL0409.
TV Market Ranking: 64 (Elliott, Ellsworth, SIBLEY (VILLAGE)). Franchise award date: June 1, 1987. Franchise expiration date: N.A. Began: January 1, 1988.
Channel capacity: 60 (2-way capable). Channels available but not in use: 30.
Basic Service
Subscribers: 150.
Programming (received off-air): WAND (NBC) Decatur; WCIA (CBS) Champaign; WICD (ABC) Champaign; WILL-TV (PBS) Urbana; WYZZ-TV (FOX) Bloomington.
Programming (via satellite): ABC Family Channel; CNN; Discovery Channel; Disney Channel; ESPN; Spike TV; TBS Superstation; Turner Network TV; USA Network; WGN America.
Fee: $39.00 installation; $32.90 monthly.
Pay Service 1
Pay Units: 15.
Programming (via satellite): HBO.
Fee: $10.95 monthly.
Pay Service 2
Pay Units: N.A.
Programming (via satellite): Showtime.
Fee: $8.95 monthly.
Video-On-Demand: Yes
Pay-Per-View
Addressable homes: 20.
Movies, Addressable: Yes; special events.
Internet Service
Operational: Yes.
Subscribers: 30.
Fee: $39.00 installation; $29.99 monthly.
Telephone Service
None
Miles of Plant: 3.0 (coaxial); None (fiber optic).
Manager: Steve Allen.
Ownership: Heartland Cable Inc. (Illinois) (MSO).

SIDELL (village)—Clearvision Cable Systems Inc., 1785 US Rte 40, Greenup, IL 62428-3501. Phone: 217-923-5594. Fax: 217-923-5681. ICA: IL0578.
TV Market Ranking: 64 (SIDELL (VILLAGE)). Franchise award date: N.A. Franchise expiration date: N.A. Began: October 1, 1984.
Channel capacity: 36 (not 2-way capable). Channels available but not in use: 11.
Basic Service
Subscribers: 70.
Programming (received off-air): WAND (NBC) Decatur; WBUI (CW) Decatur; WCCU (FOX) Urbana; WCFN (MNT) Springfield; WCIA (CBS) Champaign; WEIU-TV (PBS) Charleston; WICD (ABC) Champaign; WILL-TV (PBS) Urbana.
Programming (via satellite): ABC Family Channel; AMC; Arts & Entertainment; Bravo; Cartoon Network; CNBC; CNN; Comedy Central; C-SPAN; Discovery Channel; Disney Channel; ESPN; ESPN 2; Fox News Channel; G4; Great American Country; Hallmark Channel; Headline News; HGTV; History Channel; Lifetime; MSNBC; MTV; Nickelodeon; QVC; Spike TV; Syfy; TBS Superstation; The Learning Channel; Trinity Broadcasting Network; Turner Classic Movies; Turner Network TV; TV Land; USA Network; VH1; Weather Channel; WGN America.
Fee: $22.45 monthly.
Pay Service 1
Pay Units: N.A.
Programming (via satellite): Showtime; The Movie Channel.
Fee: $12.95 monthly (each).
Video-On-Demand: No
Internet Service
Operational: No.
Telephone Service
None
Miles of Plant: 4.0 (coaxial); None (fiber optic). Homes passed: 267.
Manager: Michael Bauguss.
Ownership: Clearvision Cable Systems Inc. (MSO).

SIMS—Formerly served by CableDirect. No longer in operation. ICA: IL0420.

SKOKIE—Comcast Cable. Now served by SCHAUMBURG, IL [IL0036]. ICA: IL0040.

SKOKIE—Formerly served by RCN Corp. No longer in operation. ICA: IL0665.

SKOKIE (portions)—RCN Corp. Formerly served by Chicago (portions), IL [IL0661]. This cable system has converted to IPTV, 196 Van Buren St, Herndon, VA 20170. Phone: 703-434-8200. Web Site: http://www.rcn.com. ICA: IL5233.
TV Market Ranking: 3 (SKOKIE (PORTIONS)).
Channel capacity: N.A. Channels available but not in use: N.A.
Internet Service
Operational: Yes.
Fee: $23.00 monthly.
Telephone Service
Digital: Operational
Fee: $30.00 monthly
Chairman: Steven J. Simmons. Chief Executive Officer: Jim Holanda.
Ownership: RCN Corp.

SMITHFIELD—Formerly served by CableDirect. No longer in operation. ICA: IL0427.

SORENTO/NEW DOUGLAS—Madison Communications, 21668 Double Arch Rd, Staunton, IL 62088-4374. Phones: 800-422-4848; 618-635-5456. Fax: 618-633-2713. E-mail: infomtc@madisontelco.com. Web Site: http://www.gomadison.com. Also serves New Douglas. ICA: IL0354.
TV Market Ranking: Outside TV Markets (NEW DOUGLAS, SORENTO). Franchise award date: N.A. Franchise expiration date: N.A. Began: December 14, 1983.
Channel capacity: 72 (operating 2-way). Channels available but not in use: N.A.
Basic Service
Subscribers: 150.
Programming (received off-air): KDNL-TV (ABC) St. Louis; KETC (PBS) St. Louis; KMOV (CBS) St. Louis; KPLR-TV (CW) St. Louis; KSDK (NBC) St. Louis; KTVI (FOX) St. Louis.
Programming (via satellite): ABC Family Channel; Arts & Entertainment; Cartoon Network; CNN; C-SPAN; Discovery Channel; Do-It-Yourself; ESPN; ESPN 2; Great American Country; Hallmark Channel; Headline News; HGTV; History Channel; Lifetime; MSNBC; Spike TV; Syfy; TBS Superstation; The Learning Channel; Trinity Broadcasting Network; Turner Classic Movies; Turner Network TV; TV Land; USA Network; Weather Channel; WGN America.
Fee: $35.00 installation; $29.95 monthly.
Pay Service 1
Pay Units: 64.
Programming (via satellite): Cinemax; HBO; Showtime.
Fee: $15.00 installation; $8.00 monthly (each).
Video-On-Demand: No
Internet Service
Operational: Yes.
Telephone Service
None
Miles of Plant: 100.0 (coaxial); None (fiber optic). Homes passed: 463.
Manager: Mary Schwartz. Marketing Manager: Linda Prante. Chief Technician: Dave Black.
Ownership: Madison Communications Co. (MSO).

SOUTH HOLLAND—Comcast Cable. Now served by CHICAGO (southern suburbs), IL [IL0008]. ICA: IL0077.

SOUTH WILMINGTON (village)—Mediacom. Now served by GIBSON CITY, IL [IL0164]. ICA: IL0579.

SPARTA—NewWave Communications, 318 N 4th St, Vandalia, IL 62471. Phone: 573-472-9500. Fax: 618.283.4483. E-mail: info@newwavecom.com. Web Site: http://www.newwavecom.com. Also serves Chester, Lenzburg, Marissa, New Athens, Percy & Steeleville. ICA: IL0147.
TV Market Ranking: 11 (Lenzburg, New Athens); Outside TV Markets (Chester, Marissa, Percy, SPARTA, Steeleville). Franchise award date: N.A. Franchise expiration date: N.A. Began: October 1, 1981.
Channel capacity: N.A. Channels available but not in use: N.A.
Basic Service
Subscribers: 3,049.
Programming (received off-air): KBSI (FOX) Cape Girardeau; KDNL-TV (ABC) St. Louis; KETC (PBS) St. Louis; KFVS-TV (CBS, CW) Cape Girardeau; KMOV (CBS) St. Louis; KNLC (IND) St. Louis; KPLR-TV (CW) St. Louis; KSDK (NBC) St. Louis; KTVI (FOX) St. Louis; WPXS (IND) Mount Vernon; WRBU (MNT) East St. Louis.
Programming (via satellite): C-SPAN; C-SPAN 2; Eternal Word TV Network; Hallmark Channel; Home Shopping Network; Jewelry Television; QVC; TBS Superstation; Trinity Broadcasting Network; Weather Channel; WGN America.
Fee: $30.00 installation; $16.95 monthly.
Expanded Basic Service 1
Subscribers: 2,614.
Programming (via satellite): ABC Family Channel; AMC; Animal Planet; Arts & Entertainment; BET Networks; Big Ten Network; Bravo; Cartoon Network; CNBC; CNN; Comedy Central; Country Music TV; Discovery Channel; Disney Channel; E! Entertainment Television; ESPN; ESPN 2; Food Network; Fox News Channel; Fox Sports Net Midwest; FX; G4; Golf Channel; Great American Country; GSN; Headline News; HGTV; History Channel; Lifetime; MSNBC; MTV; MTV2; National Geographic Channel; Nickelodeon; Outdoor Channel; SoapNet; Speed Channel; Spike TV; Style Network; Syfy; The Learning Channel; Toon Disney; Travel Channel; truTV; Turner Network TV; TV Land; USA Network; Versus; VH1; WE tv.
Digital Basic Service
Subscribers: 600.
Programming (received off-air): KBSI (FOX) Cape Girardeau; KDNL-TV (ABC) St. Louis; KTVI (FOX) St. Louis.
Programming (via satellite): BBC America; Bio; CMT Pure Country; Discovery HD Theater; Discovery Health Channel; Discovery Kids Channel; Discovery Military Channel; Discovery Planet Green; Do-It-Yourself; ESPN 2 HD; ESPN HD; FitTV; Fox College Sports Atlantic; Fox College Sports Central; Fox College Sports Pacific; Fox Movie Channel; FSN HD; G4; HDNet; HDNet Movies; History Channel International; ID Investigation Discovery; Lifetime Movie Network; MTV Hits; MTV Jams; MTV Tres; Music Choice; Nick Jr.; Nick Too; NickToons TV; Science Channel; TeenNick; Turner Network TV HD; Universal HD; VH1 Classic; VH1 Soul.
Fee: $10.00 monthly.
Digital Pay Service 1
Pay Units: 1,400.
Programming (via satellite): Cinemax (multiplexed); Cinemax HD; Encore (multiplexed); HBO (multiplexed); HBO HD; Showtime (multiplexed); Starz (multiplexed); Starz HDTV; The Movie Channel (multiplexed).
Fee: $10.95 monthly (Cinemax, Showtime or TMC), $11.95 monthly (HBO).
Video-On-Demand: No
Pay-Per-View
iN DEMAND (delivered digitally); Playboy TV (delivered digitally); Fresh (delivered digitally); Shorteez (delivered digitally); Spice: Xcess (delivered digitally); Club Jenna (delivered digitally).
Internet Service
Operational: Yes.
Fee: $40.00 installation; $31.99 monthly.
Telephone Service
Digital: Operational
Fee: $34.99 monthly
Miles of Plant: 150.0 (coaxial); None (fiber optic). Homes passed: 8,937.
General Manager: Bill Flowers. Technical Operations Manager: Chris Mooday.
City fee: 3% of gross.
Ownership: NewWave Communications (MSO).

SPRING GROVE (village)—Mediacom, 3900 26th Ave, Moline, IL 61265. Phone: 309-797-2580. Fax: 3097972414. Web Site: http://www.mediacomcable.com. Also serves Richmond, Ringwood & Solon Mills. ICA: IL0574.
TV Market Ranking: Below 100 (Richmond, Ringwood, Solon Mills, SPRING GROVE (VILLAGE)). Franchise award date: N.A. Franchise expiration date: N.A. Began: N.A.
Channel capacity: 47 (operating 2-way). Channels available but not in use: 15.

Basic Service
Subscribers: 575.
Programming (received off-air): WBBM-TV (CBS) Chicago; WCPX-TV (ION) Chicago; WFLD (FOX) Chicago; WISN-TV (ABC) Milwaukee; WITI (FOX) Milwaukee; WLS-TV (ABC) Chicago; WMAQ-TV (NBC) Chicago; WPWR-TV (MNT) Gary; WTMJ-TV (NBC) Milwaukee; WTTW (PBS) Chicago.
Programming (via satellite): Cartoon Network; QVC; WGN America.
Fee: $45.00 installation; $20.95 monthly.

Expanded Basic Service 1
Subscribers: N.A.
Programming (via satellite): ABC Family Channel; AMC; Animal Planet; Arts & Entertainment; Bravo; CNBC; CNN; Comcast SportsNet Chicago; Comedy Central; Country Music TV; C-SPAN; Discovery Channel; Disney Channel; E! Entertainment Television; ESPN; ESPN 2; FitTV; Food Network; Hallmark Channel; Headline News; HGTV; History Channel; Home Shopping Network; Lifetime; MSNBC; MTV; Nickelodeon; Speed Channel; Spike TV; Syfy; TBS Superstation; The Learning Channel; Travel Channel; Trinity Broadcasting Network; truTV; Turner Network TV; TV Land; USA Network; VH1; Weather Channel.
Fee: $34.00 monthly.

Digital Basic Service
Subscribers: N.A.
Programming (via satellite): AmericanLife TV Network; BBC America; Bio; Bloomberg Television; Discovery Health Channel; Discovery Kids Channel; Discovery Military Channel; Discovery Planet Green; ESPNews; Fox Movie Channel; Fox Soccer; Fuse; G4; Golf Channel; History Channel International; ID Investigation Discovery; Independent Film Channel; Lifetime Movie Network; MTV Hits; MTV2; Music Choice; National Geographic Channel; Nick Jr.; NickToons TV; Outdoor Channel; Science Channel; Sleuth; Style Network; TeenNick; Turner Classic Movies; TVG Network; VH1 Classic.
Fee: $9.00 monthly.

Digital Pay Service 1
Pay Units: N.A.
Programming (via satellite): Cinemax (multiplexed); Encore (multiplexed); HBO (multiplexed); Showtime (multiplexed); Starz (multiplexed); The Movie Channel (multiplexed).
Fee: $11.95 monthly (HBO, Cinemax, Showtime/TMC or Starz/Encore).

Video-On-Demand: No

Pay-Per-View
iN DEMAND (delivered digitally); Playgirl TV (delivered digitally); Ten Clips (delivered digitally).

Internet Service
Operational: Yes.
Broadband Service: Mediacom High Speed Internet.
Fee: $59.95 installation; $40.95 monthly.

Telephone Service
Digital: Operational
Fee: $39.95 installation; $39.95 monthly

Homes passed: 1,045. Miles of plant (coax & fiber) included in Moline
Regional Vice President: Cari Fenzel. Technical Operations Manager: Chris Toalson.
City fee: 3% of gross.
Ownership: Mediacom LLC (MSO).

SPRINGFIELD—Comcast Cable, PO Box 3066, 701 S Dirksen Pkwy, Springfield, IL 62703. Phone: 217-788-5898. Fax: 217-788-8093. Web Site: http://www.comcast.com. Also serves Ball Twp., Berlin, Bissel, Chatham, Curran, Curran Twp., Decatur, Divernon, Forsyth, Gardner Twp., Glenarm, Grandview, Harristown, Illiopolis, Jerome, Leland Grove, Lincoln, Logan County (portions), Long Creek, Macon County, Mount Pulaski, Mount Zion, Niantic, Pawnee, Rochester, Sangamon County, Southern View, Spaulding, Springfield Twp. & Woodside Twp. ICA: IL0016.
TV Market Ranking: 64 (Ball Twp., Berlin, Bissel, Chatham, Curran, Curran Twp., Decatur, Divernon, Forsyth, Gardner Twp., Glenarm, Grandview, Harristown, Illiopolis, Jerome, Leland Grove, Lincoln, Logan County (portions), Long Creek, Macon County, Mount Pulaski, Mount Zion, Niantic, Pawnee, Rochester, Sangamon County, Southern View, Spaulding, SPRINGFIELD, Springfield Twp., Woodside Twp.). Franchise award date: October 20, 2003. Franchise expiration date: N.A. Began: February 1, 1967.
Channel capacity: N.A. Channels available but not in use: N.A.

Basic Service
Subscribers: 90,000.
Programming (received off-air): WAND (NBC) Decatur; WBUI (CW) Decatur; WCFN (MNT) Springfield; WCIA (CBS) Champaign; WICS (ABC) Springfield; WILL-TV (PBS) Urbana; WRSP-TV (FOX) Springfield; WSEC (PBS) Jacksonville; 22 FMs.
Programming (via satellite): C-SPAN; C-SPAN 2; Eternal Word TV Network; Home Shopping Network; ION Television; QVC; ShopNBC; TV Guide Network; WGN America.
Current originations: Public Access; Leased Access; Government Access; Educational Access.
Fee: $13.13 monthly; $1.75 converter.

Expanded Basic Service 1
Subscribers: N.A.
Programming (via satellite): ABC Family Channel; AMC; Animal Planet; Arts & Entertainment; BET Networks; Bravo; Cartoon Network; CNBC; CNN; Comcast SportsNet Chicago; Comedy Central; Country Music TV; Discovery Channel; Disney Channel; E! Entertainment Television; ESPN; ESPN 2; Food Network; Fox News Channel; Fox Sports Net Midwest; FX; Golf Channel; Hallmark Channel; Headline News; HGTV; History Channel; Lifetime; MSNBC; MTV; MTV2; National Geographic Channel; Nickelodeon; Oxygen; SoapNet; Speed Channel; Spike TV; Style Network; Syfy; TBS Superstation; The Learning Channel; Toon Disney; Travel Channel; truTV; Turner Network TV; TV Land; USA Network; VH1; Weather Channel.
Fee: $37.87 monthly.

Digital Basic Service
Subscribers: 9,076.
Programming (via satellite): AmericanLife TV Network; BBC America; Bio; Bloomberg Television; CBS College Sports Network; CMT Pure Country; Cooking Channel; C-SPAN 3; Discovery Digital Networks; Discovery HD Theater; DMX Music; Do-It-Yourself; Encore (multiplexed); ESPN 2 HD; ESPN Classic Sports; ESPN HD; ESPN U; ESPNews; Fox College Sports Atlantic; Fox College Sports Central; Fox College Sports Pacific; Fox Movie Channel; Fox Soccer; Fuse; G4; GAS; Great American Country; GSN; Halogen Network; HDNet; HDNet Movies; History Channel International; HorseRacing TV; Independent Film Channel; Lifetime Movie Network; MTV Networks Digital Suite; NFL Network; Nick Jr.; Nick Too; NickToons TV; Outdoor Channel; Ovation; Palladia; PBS Kids Sprout; Si TV; Sleuth; Sundance Channel; Tennis Channel; Toon Disney; Trinity Broadcasting Network; Turner Classic Movies; Turner Network TV HD; TVG Network; Universal HD; Versus; WE tv.
Fee: $17.00 monthly.

Digital Pay Service 1
Pay Units: N.A.
Programming (via satellite): Cinemax (multiplexed); Flix; HBO (multiplexed); Showtime (multiplexed); Starz (multiplexed); The Movie Channel (multiplexed).
Fee: $10.00 monthly (Cinemax or Starz), $13.00 monthly (HBO or Showtime/TMC).

Video-On-Demand: Yes

Pay-Per-View
ESPN (delivered digitally); iN DEMAND (delivered digitally); Playboy TV (delivered digitally); Special events (delivered digitally).

Internet Service
Operational: Yes.
Subscribers: 7,734.
Broadband Service: Comcast High Speed Internet.
Fee: $99.95 installation; $44.95 monthly; $10.00 modem lease; $39.99 modem purchase.

Telephone Service
Digital: Operational

Miles of Plant: 1,600.0 (coaxial); 400.0 (fiber optic). Homes passed: 170,000.
Chief Technician: Terry Blackwell. Community & Government Affairs Director: Libbie Stehn. Customer Service Manager: Holt Lisa.
City fee: 5% of gross.
Ownership: Comcast Cable Communications Inc. (MSO).

ST. DAVID—Mediacom. Now served by ELMWOOD, IL [IL0205]. ICA: IL0301.

ST. FRANCISVILLE—Avenue Broadband Communications, 2603 Hart St, Vincennes, IN 47591. Phones: 800-882-7185; 812-895-7676. Fax: 812-886-5017. Web Site: http://www.avenuebroadband.com. ICA: IL0317.
TV Market Ranking: Outside TV Markets (ST. FRANCISVILLE). Franchise award date: N.A. Franchise expiration date: N.A. Began: January 1, 1984.
Channel capacity: N.A. Channels available but not in use: N.A.

Basic Service
Subscribers: 137.
Programming (received off-air): WEHT (ABC) Evansville; WEVV-TV (CBS, MNT) Evansville; WFIE (NBC) Evansville; WTHI-TV (CBS) Terre Haute; WTVW (FOX) Evansville; WUSI-TV (PBS) Olney.
Programming (via satellite): Home Shopping Network; Weather Channel; WGN America.
Fee: $29.99 installation.

Expanded Basic Service 1
Subscribers: 119.
Programming (via satellite): ABC Family Channel; AMC; Animal Planet; Arts & Entertainment; CNN; Comedy Central; Discovery Channel; E! Entertainment Television; ESPN; ESPN 2; HGTV; Lifetime; Nickelodeon; Spike TV; TBS Superstation; The Learning Channel; truTV; Turner Network TV; TV Land; USA Network.
Fee: $49.99 monthly.

Digital Basic Service
Subscribers: N.A.
Programming (via satellite): AmericanLife TV Network; BBC America; Bio; Bloomberg Television; Bravo; Discovery Digital Networks; DMX Music; FitTV; Fox Movie Channel; Fuse; G4; GAS; Golf Channel; GSN; Halogen Network; HGTV; History Channel; History Channel International; Independent Film Channel; Lifetime Movie Network; MTV Networks Digital Suite; Nick Jr.; Outdoor Channel; ShopNBC; Speed Channel; Style Network; Syfy; Toon Disney; Trinity Broadcasting Network; Turner Classic Movies; Versus; WE tv.

Pay Service 1
Pay Units: N.A.
Programming (via satellite): Cinemax; HBO (multiplexed).
Fee: $40.00 installation; $8.95 monthly (Cinemax), $9.95 monthly (HBO).

Digital Pay Service 1
Pay Units: N.A.
Programming (via satellite): Cinemax (multiplexed); Encore (multiplexed); HBO (multiplexed); Showtime (multiplexed); Starz (multiplexed); The Movie Channel (multiplexed).

Video-On-Demand: No

Pay-Per-View
ESPN Now (delivered digitally); Hot Choice (delivered digitally); iN DEMAND (delivered digitally); Playboy TV (delivered digitally); Fresh (delivered digitally); Shorteez (delivered digitally).

Internet Service
Operational: No.

Telephone Service
None

Miles of Plant: 10.0 (coaxial); None (fiber optic). Homes passed: 457.
Chief Executive Officer: Steve Lowe. Vice President & General Manager: Mary Iafrate. Vice President, Engineering: Jeff Spence. System Engineer: Bart Kotter.
Ownership: Buford Media Group LLC (MSO).

ST. LIBORY—Formerly served by CableDirect. No longer in operation. ICA: IL0641.

ST. PETER—Clearvision Cable Systems Inc., 1785 US Rte 40, Greenup, IL 62428-3501. Phone: 217-923-5594. Fax: 217-923-5681. ICA: IL0667.
TV Market Ranking: Outside TV Markets (ST. PETER). Franchise award date: N.A. Franchise expiration date: N.A. Began: N.A.
Channel capacity: 42 (not 2-way capable). Channels available but not in use: 16.

Basic Service
Subscribers: 45.
Programming (received off-air): KMOV (CBS) St. Louis; WAND (NBC) Decatur; WICS (ABC) Springfield; WPXS (IND) Mount Vernon; WRSP-TV (FOX) Springfield; WUSI-TV (PBS) Olney.
Programming (via satellite): ABC Family Channel; AMC; Arts & Entertainment; CNBC; CNN; Country Music TV; Discovery Channel; Disney Channel; ESPN; Headline News; History Channel; Nickelodeon; QVC; Spike TV; TBS Superstation; Turner Network TV; USA Network; Weather Channel; WGN America.
Fee: $18.95 monthly.

Pay Service 1
Pay Units: N.A.
Programming (via satellite): Showtime; The Movie Channel.
Fee: $9.45 monthly.

Video-On-Demand: No

Internet Service
Operational: No.

Telephone Service
None

Miles of Plant: 3.0 (coaxial); None (fiber optic). Homes passed: 152.

Manager: Michael Bauguss.
Ownership: Clearvision Cable Systems Inc. (MSO).

STAUNTON—Madison Communications, 21668 Double Arch Rd, Staunton, IL 62088-4374. Phones: 618-633-2267 (Business office); 618-635-5456. Fax: 618-633-2713. E-mail: informtc@madisontelco.com. Web Site: http://www.gomadison.com. Also serves Alhambra, Benld, Bunker Hill, Hamel, Livingston, Mount Clare, Mount Olive, Sawyerville, Williamson & Worden. ICA: IL0171.
TV Market Ranking: 11 (Alhambra, Bunker Hill, Hamel, Livingston, Worden); Outside TV Markets (Benld, Mount Clare, Mount Olive, Sawyerville, STAUNTON, Williamson). Franchise award date: N.A. Franchise expiration date: N.A. Began: June 1, 1981.
Channel capacity: 26 (operating 2-way). Channels available but not in use: N.A.
Basic Service
Subscribers: 5,000.
Programming (received off-air): KDNL-TV (ABC) St. Louis; KETC (PBS) St. Louis; KMOV (CBS) St. Louis; KNLC (IND) St. Louis; KPLR-TV (CW) St. Louis; KSDK (NBC) St. Louis; KTVI (FOX) St. Louis; WPXS (IND) Mount Vernon; WRBU (MNT) East St. Louis.
Programming (via satellite): America's Store; Classic Arts Showcase; C-SPAN; C-SPAN 2; C-SPAN 3; ESPN Classic Sports; Eternal Word TV Network; INSP; Jewelry Television; QVC; Shop at Home; ShopNBC; Trinity Broadcasting Network; WGN America.
Current originations: Public Access.
Fee: $17.00 installation; $21.75 monthly.
Expanded Basic Service 1
Subscribers: N.A.
Programming (via satellite): ABC Family Channel; AMC; AmericanLife TV Network; Animal Planet; Arts & Entertainment; Boomerang; Bravo; Cartoon Network; CNBC; CNN; Comedy Central; Cooking Channel; Country Music TV; Discovery Channel; Disney Channel; Do-It-Yourself; E! Entertainment Television; ESPN; ESPN 2; FamilyNet; Food Network; Fox News Channel; Fox Sports Net Midwest; FX; Great American Country; Hallmark Channel; Headline News; HGTV; History Channel; Lifetime; MSNBC; MTV; National Geographic Channel; Nickelodeon; Oxygen; SoapNet; Speed Channel; Spike TV; Syfy; TBS Superstation; The Learning Channel; The Sportsman Channel; Travel Channel; truTV; Turner Network TV; TV Land; USA Network; VH1; Weather Channel.
Digital Basic Service
Subscribers: N.A.
Programming (received off-air): KDNL-TV (ABC) St. Louis; KETC (PBS) St. Louis; KMOV (CBS) St. Louis; KPLR-TV (CW) St. Louis; KTVI (FOX) St. Louis; WPXS (IND) Mount Vernon.
Programming (via satellite): AmericanLife TV Network; Barker; BBC America; Bio; Bloomberg Television; Bravo; Current; Discovery Digital Networks; Discovery HD Theater; DMX Music; ESPN; ESPN Classic Sports; ESPNews; Fox College Sports Atlantic; Fox College Sports Central; Fox College Sports Pacific; Fox Movie Channel; Fox Sports World; Fuse; G4; GAS; Golf Channel; GSN; Halogen Network; HDNet; HDNet Movies; History Channel International; Independent Film Channel; International Television (ITV); Lifetime Movie Network; Lime; MTV Networks Digital Suite; National Geographic Channel; Nick Jr.; NickToons TV; Outdoor Channel; Ovation; Speed Channel; Style Network; Trinity Broadcasting Network; Turner Classic Movies; Versus; WE tv.
Digital Pay Service 1
Pay Units: N.A.
Programming (via satellite): Cinemax (multiplexed); Cinemax HD; Encore (multiplexed); Flix; HBO (multiplexed); HBO HD; Showtime (multiplexed); Showtime HD; Starz (multiplexed); Starz HDTV; Sundance Channel; The Movie Channel (multiplexed).
Fee: $12.95 monthly (HBO), $10.95 monthly (Cinemax, Showtime, Encore, or TMC).
Video-On-Demand: No
Pay-Per-View
Movies (delivered digitally).
Internet Service
Operational: Yes, Dial-up only. Began: June 1, 2002.
Broadband Service: In-house.
Fee: $29.99 monthly.
Telephone Service
None
Miles of Plant: 200.0 (coaxial); None (fiber optic).
Manager: Mary Schwartz. Marketing Manager: Linda Prante. Chief Technician: Dave Black.
Ownership: Madison Communications Co. (MSO).

STE. MARIE TWP.—Formerly served by Advanced Technologies & Technical Resources Inc. No longer in operation. ICA: IL0583.

STERLING—Comcast Cable, 4450 Kishwaukee St, Rockford, IL 61101. Phone: 815-395-8890. Fax: 815-395-8901. Web Site: http://www.comcast.com. Also serves Coloma Twp., Hopkins Twp., Montmorency Twp., Rock Falls & Sterling Twp. ICA: IL0051.
TV Market Ranking: 97 (Hopkins Twp., STERLING, Sterling Twp.); Outside TV Markets (Coloma Twp., Montmorency Twp., Rock Falls). Franchise award date: February 1, 1966. Franchise expiration date: N.A. Began: June 1, 1968.
Channel capacity: 85 (operating 2-way). Channels available but not in use: None.
Basic Service
Subscribers: N.A. Included in Rockford
Programming (received off-air): KGCW (CW) Burlington; KLJB (CW, FOX) Davenport; KWQC-TV (NBC) Davenport; WBQD-LP Davenport; WEEK-TV (NBC) Peoria; WHBF-TV (CBS) Rock Island; WHOI (ABC, CW) Peoria; WMBD-TV (CBS) Peoria; WQAD-TV (ABC) Moline; WTVP (PBS) Peoria.
Programming (via satellite): C-SPAN; C-SPAN 2; Eternal Word TV Network; Home Shopping Network; ION Television; QVC; TV Guide Network; WGN America; WTTW (PBS) Chicago.
Fee: $44.00 installation; $8.00 monthly.
Expanded Basic Service 1
Subscribers: 9,712.
Programming (via satellite): ABC Family Channel; AMC; Animal Planet; Arts & Entertainment; BET Networks; Bravo; Cartoon Network; CNBC; CNN; Comcast SportsNet Chicago; Comedy Central; Country Music TV; Discovery Channel; Disney Channel; E! Entertainment Television; ESPN; ESPN 2; Food Network; Fox News Channel; Fox Sports Net Midwest; FX; Great American Country; Hallmark Channel; Headline News; HGTV; History Channel; Lifetime; MSNBC; MTV; National Geographic Channel; Nickelodeon; Oxygen; Speed Channel; Spike TV; Syfy; TBS Superstation; The Learning Channel; Total Living Network; Travel Channel; truTV; Turner Network TV; Univision; USA Network; VH1; Weather Channel.
Fee: $43.75 monthly.
Digital Basic Service
Subscribers: N.A.
Programming (via satellite): AmericanLife TV Network; BBC America; Bio; Bloomberg Television; CBS College Sports Network; CMT Pure Country; Cooking Channel; C-SPAN 3; Discovery Digital Networks; Discovery HD Theater; DMX Music; Do-It-Yourself; Encore (multiplexed); ESPN 2 HD; ESPN Classic Sports; ESPN HD; ESPN U; ESPNews; Fox Movie Channel; Fox Soccer; Fuse; G4; GAS; Golf Channel; GSN; Halogen Network; HDNet; HDNet Movies; History Channel International; HorseRacing TV; Independent Film Channel; Lifetime Movie Network; Lifetime Real Women; MTV Networks Digital Suite; NFL Network; Nick Jr.; Nick Too; NickToons TV; Outdoor Channel; Palladia; PBS Kids Sprout; Si TV; SoapNet; Style Network; Sundance Channel; Tennis Channel; Toon Disney; Trinity Broadcasting Network; Turner Classic Movies; Turner Network TV HD; TV Land; TVG Network; Universal HD; Versus; WE tv.
Fee: $15.95 monthly.
Digital Pay Service 1
Pay Units: N.A.
Programming (via satellite): Cinemax (multiplexed); Flix; HBO (multiplexed); HBO HD; Showtime (multiplexed); Showtime HD; Starz (multiplexed); The Movie Channel (multiplexed).
Fee: $10.00 monthly (each).
Video-On-Demand: Yes
Pay-Per-View
ESPN (delivered digitally); iN DEMAND (delivered digitally), Fee: $3.95; Playboy TV (delivered digitally); Special events (delivered digitally).
Internet Service
Operational: Yes.
Broadband Service: Comcast High Speed Internet.
Fee: $99.95 installation; $44.95 monthly; $10.00 modem lease; $99.99 modem purchase.
Telephone Service
Digital: Operational
Total homes in franchised area: 13,543. Homes passed & miles of plant included in Rockford
District Director: Joseph Browning. Technical Operations Manager: Lyle Matejewski. Program Director: Janice Schultz. Community & Government Affairs Manager: Joan Sage.
City fee: 3% of gross.
Ownership: Comcast Cable Communications Inc. (MSO).

STOCKTON—Mediacom. Now served by LENA, IL [IL0223]. ICA: IL0247.

STRASBURG—Mediacom. Now served by NEOGA, IL [IL0249]. ICA: IL0585.

STREAMWOOD—Comcast Cable. Now served by SCHAUMBURG, IL [IL0036]. ICA: IL0061.

STREATOR—Mediacom, 3900 26th Ave, Moline, IL 61265. Phones: 309-797-2580; 815-672-5071 (Streator office). Fax: 309-797-2414. Web Site: http://www.mediacomcable.com. Also serves Bruce Twp., Dayton Twp., Eagle Twp., Kangley, La Salle Twp., Marseilles, Naplate, Ottawa, Otter Creek Twp., Reading Twp., Sheridan & South Ottawa Twp. ICA: IL0069.
TV Market Ranking: Below 100 (Bruce Twp., Dayton Twp., Eagle Twp., Kangley, La Salle Twp., Marseilles, Naplate, Ottawa, Otter Creek Twp., Reading Twp., Sheridan, South Ottawa Twp., STREATOR). Franchise award date: February 1, 1963. Franchise expiration date: N.A. Began: February 1, 1963.
Channel capacity: 121 (operating 2-way). Channels available but not in use: None.
Basic Service
Subscribers: 15,562.
Programming (received off-air): WBBM-TV (CBS) Chicago; WCIU-TV (IND) Chicago; WCPX-TV (ION) Chicago; WEEK-TV (NBC) Peoria; WFLD (FOX) Chicago; WGN-TV (CW, IND) Chicago; WHOI (ABC, CW) Peoria; WLS-TV (ABC) Chicago; WMAQ-TV (NBC) Chicago; WMBD-TV (CBS) Peoria; WTTW (PBS) Chicago; WWTO-TV (TBN) La Salle; WYZZ-TV (FOX) Bloomington; 21 FMs.
Programming (via satellite): ABC Family Channel; C-SPAN; Home Shopping Network; QVC; TBS Superstation; TV Guide Network.
Fee: $45.00 installation; $20.95 monthly.
Expanded Basic Service 1
Subscribers: 15,200.
Programming (via satellite): AMC; Animal Planet; Arts & Entertainment; Bravo; Cartoon Network; CNBC; CNN; Comcast SportsNet Chicago; Comedy Central; Country Music TV; C-SPAN 2; Discovery Channel; Disney Channel; E! Entertainment Television; ESPN; ESPN 2; Eternal Word TV Network; Food Network; Fox News Channel; FX; Halogen Network; Headline News; HGTV; History Channel; Lifetime; MSNBC; MTV; Nickelodeon; ShopNBC; SoapNet; Speed Channel; Spike TV; Syfy; The Learning Channel; Travel Channel; Trinity Broadcasting Network; truTV; Turner Network TV; TV Land; USA Network; VH1; Weather Channel.
Fee: $34.00 monthly.
Digital Basic Service
Subscribers: 1,137.
Programming (via satellite): BBC America; Discovery Digital Networks; DMX Music; Fox Sports World; Golf Channel; GSN; Independent Film Channel; Turner Classic Movies.
Fee: $9.00 monthly.
Digital Pay Service 1
Pay Units: 3,327.
Programming (via satellite): Cinemax (multiplexed); Encore (multiplexed); HBO (multiplexed); Showtime (multiplexed);

Starz (multiplexed); The Movie Channel (multiplexed).
Fee: $11.95 monthly (HBO, Cinemax, Starz/Encore or Showtime/TMC.
Video-On-Demand: Yes
Pay-Per-View
Addressable homes: 2,855.
ESPN Now (delivered digitally), Fee: $3.95-$5.99, Addressable: Yes; Hot Choice (delivered digitally); iN DEMAND; iN DEMAND (delivered digitally); Playboy TV (delivered digitally); Pleasure (delivered digitally); Fresh (delivered digitally); Shorteez (delivered digitally).
Internet Service
Operational: Yes.
Subscribers: 1,859.
Broadband Service: Mediacom High Speed Internet.
Fee: $59.95 installation; $45.95 monthly.
Telephone Service
Analog: Not Operational
Digital: Operational
Fee: $39.95 installation; $39.95 monthly
Total homes in franchised area: 26,400. Miles of plant included in Moline
Vice President: Cari Fenzel. Engineering Director: Mitch Carlson. Technical Operations Manager: Chris Toalson. Lead Technician: Bobby Brown. Marketing Director: Greg Evans.
City fee: 3% of gross.
Ownership: Mediacom LLC (MSO).

STRONGHURST—Mediacom. Now served by ROSEVILLE, IL [IL0274]. ICA: IL0314.

SUBLETTE (village)—Heartland Cable Broadband, PO Box 254, Shabbona, IL 60550. Phone: 866-428-0490. Fax: 309-432-2500. Web Site: http://www.heartlandcable.com. ICA: IL0408.
TV Market Ranking: Below 100 (SUBLETTE (VILLAGE)). Franchise award date: May 1, 1989. Franchise expiration date: N.A. Began: January 1, 1990.
Channel capacity: 60 (2-way capable). Channels available but not in use: 30.
Basic Service
Subscribers: 100.
Programming (received off-air): WIFR (CBS) Freeport; WQRF-TV (FOX) Rockford; WREX (CW, NBC) Rockford; WTTW (PBS) Chicago; WTVO (ABC, MNT) Rockford.
Programming (via satellite): ABC Family Channel; Animal Planet; Arts & Entertainment; Cartoon Network; CNN; Comcast/Charter Sports Southeast (CSS); Comedy Central; Discovery Channel; Disney Channel; ESPN; ESPN 2; Food Network; Fox Movie Channel; Fox News Channel; FX; Great American Country; GSN; Headline News; HGTV; History Channel; Lifetime; MSNBC; MTV; Nickelodeon; Outdoor Channel; QVC; Speed Channel; Spike TV; Style Network; Syfy; TBS Superstation; The Learning Channel; Travel Channel; truTV; Turner Network TV; TV Land; USA Network; VH1; WE tv; Weather Channel; WGN America.
Fee: $39.00 installation; $32.90 monthly.
Pay Service 1
Pay Units: 10.
Programming (via satellite): HBO.
Fee: $10.90 monthly.
Video-On-Demand: Yes
Internet Service
Operational: Yes.
Subscribers: 40.
Fee: $39.00 installation; $45.00 monthly.
Telephone Service
None
Miles of Plant: 3.0 (coaxial); None (fiber optic). Homes passed: 160. Total homes in franchised area: 160.
Manager: Steve Allen.
Ownership: Heartland Cable Inc. (Illinois) (MSO).

SUGAR GROVE—Mediacom, 3900 26th Ave, Moline, IL 61265. Phones: 630-365-0045 (Local office); 309-797-2580. Fax: 309-797-2414. Web Site: http://www.mediacomcable.com. Also serves DeKalb County (portions), Earlville, Elburn, Hinckley, Kane County, Kaneville, Leland, Shabbona, Somonauk & Waterman. ICA: IL0131.
TV Market Ranking: 3,97 (Kane County (portions)); Below 100 (DeKalb County (portions), Earlville, Elburn, Hinckley, Kaneville, Leland, Shabbona, Somonauk, SUGAR GROVE, Waterman, Kane County (portions)). Franchise award date: N.A. Franchise expiration date: N.A. Began: December 12, 1984.
Channel capacity: N.A. Channels available but not in use: N.A.
Basic Service
Subscribers: 5,296.
Programming (received off-air): WBBM-TV (CBS) Chicago; WCIU-TV (IND) Chicago; WCPX-TV (ION) Chicago; WFLD (FOX) Chicago; WGBO-DT (UNV) Joliet; WGN-TV (CW, IND) Chicago; WJYS (IND) Hammond; WLS-TV (ABC) Chicago; WMAQ-TV (NBC) Chicago; WPWR-TV (MNT) Gary; WQRF-TV (FOX) Rockford; WREX (CW, NBC) Rockford; WSNS-TV (TMO) Chicago; WTTW (PBS) Chicago; WYCC (PBS) Chicago.
Programming (via satellite): TBS Superstation; TV Guide Network.
Current originations: Educational Access.
Fee: $45.00 installation; $20.95 monthly.
Expanded Basic Service 1
Subscribers: 4,794.
Programming (via satellite): ABC Family Channel; AMC; Animal Planet; Arts & Entertainment; Bravo; Cartoon Network; CNBC; CNN; Comcast SportsNet Chicago; Comedy Central; Country Music TV; C-SPAN; Discovery Channel; Disney Channel; E! Entertainment Television; ESPN; ESPN 2; Food Network; Fox News Channel; Fox Sports Net; HGTV; History Channel; Home Shopping Network; INSP; Lifetime; MSNBC; MTV; MuchMusic Network; Nickelodeon; Speed Channel; Spike TV; Syfy; The Learning Channel; Travel Channel; Trinity Broadcasting Network; Turner Network TV; TV Land; USA Network; VH1; Weather Channel.
Fee: $34.00 monthly.
Digital Basic Service
Subscribers: 688.
Programming (via satellite): BBC America; Discovery Digital Networks; DMX Music; Fox Sports World; Golf Channel; GSN; Independent Film Channel; Turner Classic Movies; Versus.
Fee: $9.00 monthly.
Digital Pay Service 1
Pay Units: 1,581.
Programming (via satellite): Cinemax (multiplexed); Encore (multiplexed); HBO (multiplexed); Showtime (multiplexed); Starz (multiplexed); The Movie Channel (multiplexed).
Fee: $11.95 monthly (each).
Video-On-Demand: Yes
Pay-Per-View
iN DEMAND, Addressable: Yes; iN DEMAND (delivered digitally); Playboy TV (delivered digitally); Fresh (delivered digitally); Shorteez (delivered digitally).
Internet Service
Operational: Yes.
Broadband Service: Mediacom High Speed Internet.
Fee: $59.95 installation; $45.95 monthly.
Telephone Service
Analog: Not Operational
Digital: Operational
Homes passed: 9,212. Miles of plant included in Moline
Vice President: Cari Fenzel. Area Manager: Don DeMay. Engineering Director: Mitch Carlson. Marketing Director: Greg Evans. Business Operations Manager: Leonard Lipe. Technical Operations Manager: Chris Toalson.
City fee: 5% of gross.
Ownership: Mediacom LLC (MSO).

SULLIVAN—Mediacom, PO Box 288, 4290 Blue Stem Rd, Charleston, IL 61920. Phones: 217-348-5533; 309-274-4500. Fax: 217-345-7074. Web Site: http://www.mediacomcable.com. ICA: IL0154.
TV Market Ranking: 64 (SULLIVAN). Franchise award date: N.A. Franchise expiration date: N.A. Began: January 1, 1980.
Channel capacity: N.A. Channels available but not in use: N.A.
Basic Service
Subscribers: 1,445.
Programming (received off-air): WAND (NBC) Decatur; WBUI (CW) Decatur; WCCU (FOX) Urbana; WCFN (MNT) Springfield; WCIA (CBS) Champaign; WEIU-TV (PBS) Charleston; WICD (ABC) Champaign; WILL-TV (PBS) Urbana; WSIU-TV (PBS) Carbondale; WTHI-TV (CBS) Terre Haute; WTWO (NBC) Terre Haute; 1 FM.
Programming (via satellite): C-SPAN; Home Shopping Network; INSP; QVC; TV Guide Network; WGN America.
Current originations: Educational Access.
Fee: $45.00 installation; $20.95 monthly.
Expanded Basic Service 1
Subscribers: 1,435.
Programming (via satellite): ABC Family Channel; AMC; Animal Planet; Arts & Entertainment; BET Networks; Cartoon Network; CNBC; CNN; Comcast SportsNet Chicago; Comedy Central; Country Music TV; C-SPAN 2; Discovery Channel; Disney Channel; E! Entertainment Television; ESPN; ESPN 2; ESPN Classic Sports; Eternal Word TV Network; FitTV; Food Network; Fox News Channel; Fox Sports Net Midwest; FX; Hallmark Channel; Headline News; HGTV; History Channel; ION Television; Jewelry Television; Lifetime; Lifetime Movie Network; MSNBC; MTV; Nickelodeon; Outdoor Channel; Oxygen; Product Information Network; ShopNBC; Speed Channel; Spike TV; Syfy; TBS Superstation; The Learning Channel; Travel Channel; Trinity Broadcasting Network; truTV; Turner Network TV; TV Land; USA Network; Versus; VH1; WE tv; Weather Channel.
Fee: $34.00 monthly.
Digital Basic Service
Subscribers: N.A.
Programming (received off-air): WAND (NBC) Decatur; WCCU (FOX) Urbana; WCIA (CBS) Champaign; WICD (ABC) Champaign; WILL-TV (PBS) Urbana; WTHI-TV (CBS) Terre Haute.
Programming (via satellite): ABC News Now; AmericanLife TV Network; BBC America; Bio; Bloomberg Television; Bravo; CBS College Sports Network; CCTV-9 (CCTV International); CMT Pure Country; Discovery HD Theater; Discovery Health Channel; Discovery Kids Channel; Discovery Military Channel; Discovery Planet Green; Discovery Times Channel; ESPN 2 HD; ESPN HD; ESPN U; ESPNews; FitTV; Fox College Sports Atlantic; Fox College Sports Central; Fox College Sports Pacific; Fox Movie Channel; Fox Reality Channel; Fox Soccer; Fuel TV; Fuse; G4; Gol TV; Golf Channel; GSN; HDNet; HDNet Movies; History Channel International; Independent Film Channel; ION Life; Lifetime Real Women; MTV Hits; MTV2; Music Choice; National Geographic Channel; Nick Jr.; NickToons TV; Qubo; ReelzChannel; Science Channel; Sleuth; Style Network; TeenNick; Tennis Channel; The Sportsman Channel; Toon Disney; Turner Classic Movies; TVG Network; Universal HD; Versus; VH1 Classic.
Fee: $9.00 monthly.
Digital Pay Service 1
Pay Units: N.A.
Programming (via satellite): Cinemax (multiplexed); Cinemax On Demand; Encore (multiplexed); HBO (multiplexed); HBO HD; HBO On Demand; Showtime (multiplexed); Showtime HD; Showtime On Demand; Starz (multiplexed); Starz HDTV; Starz On Demand; The Movie Channel (multiplexed); The Movie Channel HD; The Movie Channel On Demand.
Fee: $11.95 monthly (HBO, Cinemax, Showtime/TMC or Starz/Encore).
Video-On-Demand: Yes
Pay-Per-View
iN DEMAND (delivered digitally); Playboy TV (delivered digitally); Ten Clips (delivered digitally); Ten Blox (delivered digitally); ESPN (delivered digitally).
Internet Service
Operational: Yes.
Broadband Service: Mediacom High Speed Internet.
Fee: $59.95 installation; $40.95 monthly.
Telephone Service
Digital: Operational
Fee: $39.95 installation; $39.95 monthly
Miles of Plant: 23.0 (coaxial); None (fiber optic). Homes passed: 2,062.
Area Operations Director: Todd Acker. Technical Operations Manager: Jerry Ferguson.
City fee: 5% of gross.
Ownership: Mediacom LLC (MSO).

SUMNER—Avenue Broadband Communications, 2603 Hart St, Vincennes, IN 47591. Phones: 800-882-7185; 812-895-7676. Fax: 812-886-5017. Web Site: http://www.avenuebroadband.com. ICA: IL0268.
TV Market Ranking: Outside TV Markets (SUMNER). Franchise award date: N.A. Franchise expiration date: N.A. Began: January 1, 1984.
Channel capacity: 36 (not 2-way capable). Channels available but not in use: N.A.
Basic Service
Subscribers: 220.
Programming (received off-air): WIFR (CBS) Freeport; WTHI-TV (CBS) Terre Haute; WTWO (NBC) Terre Haute; WUSI-TV (PBS) Olney; WXYZ-TV (ABC) Detroit.
Programming (via microwave): WFXW (FOX) Terre Haute.
Programming (via satellite): QVC; WGN America.
Fee: $29.99 installation.

Expanded Basic Service 1
Subscribers: 204.
Programming (via satellite): ABC Family Channel; AMC; Animal Planet; Arts & Entertainment; CNN; Comedy Central; Country Music TV; Discovery Channel; Disney Channel; ESPN; ESPN 2; HGTV; History Channel; Lifetime; Nickelodeon; Spike TV; TBS Superstation; The Learning Channel; truTV; Turner Network TV; TV Land; USA Network; Weather Channel.
Fee: $49.99 monthly.
Digital Basic Service
Subscribers: N.A.
Programming (via satellite): AmericanLife TV Network; BBC America; Bio; Bloomberg Television; Bravo; Discovery Digital Networks; DMX Music; FitTV; Fox Movie Channel; G4; GAS; Golf Channel; GSN; Halogen Network; HGTV; History Channel; History Channel International; Independent Film Channel; Lifetime Movie Network; MTV Networks Digital Suite; MuchMusic Network; Nick Jr.; Outdoor Channel; Speed Channel; Style Network; Syfy; Toon Disney; Trinity Broadcasting Network; Turner Classic Movies; Versus; WE tv.
Pay Service 1
Pay Units: N.A.
Programming (via satellite): Cinemax; HBO (multiplexed).
Fee: $40.00 installation; $8.95 monthly (Cinemax), $9.95 monthly (HBO).
Digital Pay Service 1
Pay Units: N.A.
Programming (via satellite): Cinemax (multiplexed); Encore (multiplexed); HBO (multiplexed); Showtime (multiplexed); Starz (multiplexed); The Movie Channel (multiplexed).
Video-On-Demand: No
Pay-Per-View
ESPN Now (delivered digitally); Hot Choice (delivered digitally); iN DEMAND (delivered digitally); Playboy TV (delivered digitally); Fresh (delivered digitally); Shorteez (delivered digitally).
Internet Service
Operational: No.
Telephone Service
None
Miles of Plant: 8.0 (coaxial); None (fiber optic). Homes passed: 576.
Chief Executive Officer: Steve Lowe. Vice President & General Manager: Mary Iafrate. Vice President, Engineering: Jeff Spence. System Engineer: Bart Kotter.
Ownership: Buford Media Group LLC (MSO).

TABLE GROVE—Mid Century Telephone Cooperative. Formerly [IL0587]. This cable system has converted to IPTV., PO Box 390, 285 Mid Century Ln, Fairview, IL 61432-0380. Phones: 877-643-2368; 309-778-8611. Fax: 309-783-3297. Web Site: http://www.midcentury.com. ICA: IL5244.
Channel capacity: N.A. Channels available but not in use: N.A.
Internet Service
Operational: Yes.
Fee: $29.95 monthly.
Telephone Service
Digital: Operational
Fee: $20.93 monthly
General Manager: James Sherburne.
Ownership: Mid Century Telephone Cooperative.

TABLE GROVE—Mid Century Telephone Cooperative. This cable system has converted to IPTV. See Table Grove, IL [IL5244]. ICA: IL0587.

TAMMS—NewWave Communications, 318 N 4th St, Vandalia, IL 62471. Phone: 573-472-9500. Fax: 618.283.4483. E-mail: info@newwavecom.com. Web Site: http://www.newwavecom.com. ICA: IL0329.
TV Market Ranking: 69 (TAMMS). Franchise award date: N.A. Franchise expiration date: N.A. Began: January 27, 1988.
Channel capacity: 41 (not 2-way capable). Channels available but not in use: None.
Basic Service
Subscribers: 35.
Programming (received off-air): KBSI (FOX) Cape Girardeau; KFVS-TV (CBS, CW) Cape Girardeau; WDKA (MNT) Paducah; WPSD-TV (NBC) Paducah; WSIL-TV (ABC) Harrisburg; WSIU-TV (PBS) Carbondale; WTCT (IND) Marion.
Programming (via satellite): ABC Family Channel; AMC; Arts & Entertainment; BET Networks; Cartoon Network; CNN; Comedy Central; Country Music TV; C-SPAN; Discovery Channel; Disney Channel; ESPN; ESPN 2; Fox News Channel; Headline News; Home Shopping Network; Lifetime; MTV; Nickelodeon; Spike TV; Syfy; TBS Superstation; The Learning Channel; Turner Network TV; TV Land; USA Network; VH1; Weather Channel; WGN America.
Fee: $30.90 monthly.
Pay Service 1
Pay Units: 32.
Programming (via satellite): Cinemax.
Fee: $8.95 monthly.
Pay Service 2
Pay Units: 14.
Programming (via satellite): Showtime.
Fee: $9.95 monthly.
Pay Service 3
Pay Units: 60.
Programming (via satellite): HBO (multiplexed).
Fee: $9.95 monthly.
Video-On-Demand: No
Pay-Per-View
iN DEMAND (delivered digitally); Hot Choice (delivered digitally); ESPN Now (delivered digitally); ESPN Extra (delivered digitally); Playboy TV (delivered digitally); Fresh (delivered digitally); Shorteez (delivered digitally).
Internet Service
Operational: No.
Telephone Service
None
Miles of Plant: 8.0 (coaxial); None (fiber optic). Homes passed: 332.
Technical Operations Manager: Chris Mooday. General Manager: Bill Flowers.
Ownership: NewWave Communications (MSO).

TAMPICO—Mediacom, 3900 26th Ave, Moline, IL 61265. Phone: 309-797-2580. Fax: 309-797-2414. Web Site: http://www.mediacomcable.com. ICA: IL0347.
TV Market Ranking: Outside TV Markets (TAMPICO). Franchise award date: November 1, 1982. Franchise expiration date: N.A. Began: November 1, 1984.
Channel capacity: N.A. Channels available but not in use: N.A.
Basic Service
Subscribers: 182.
Programming (received off-air): KIIN (PBS) Iowa City; KLJB (CW, FOX) Davenport; KWQC-TV (NBC) Davenport; WHBF-TV (CBS) Rock Island; WQAD-TV (ABC) Moline.
Programming (via satellite): Home Shopping Network; TBS Superstation; Trinity Broadcasting Network; WGN America.
Fee: $45.00 installation; $20.95 monthly.

Expanded Basic Service 1
Subscribers: 163.
Programming (via satellite): ABC Family Channel; AMC; Animal Planet; Arts & Entertainment; Bravo; CNN; Comcast SportsNet Chicago; Country Music TV; Discovery Channel; Disney Channel; ESPN; ESPN 2; Fox Sports Net; History Channel; Lifetime; MTV; Nickelodeon; QVC; Speed Channel; Spike TV; Syfy; The Learning Channel; Travel Channel; Turner Network TV; TV Land; USA Network; Weather Channel.
Fee: $34.00 monthly.
Pay Service 1
Pay Units: 41.
Programming (via satellite): HBO; Showtime.
Fee: $11.99 monthly (each).
Video-On-Demand: No
Internet Service
Operational: No.
Telephone Service
None
Miles of Plant: 6.0 (coaxial); None (fiber optic). Homes passed: 364.
Regional Vice President: Cari Fenzel. Area Manager: Don DeMay. Engineering Director: Mitch Carlson. Technical Operations Manager: Chris Toalson. Marketing Director: Greg Evans.
Ownership: Mediacom LLC (MSO).

TAYLORVILLE—NewWave Communications, 1176 E 1500 North Rd, Taylorville, IL 62568. Phone: 217-287-7992. Fax: 217-287-7304. E-mail: info@newwavecom.com. Web Site: http://www.newwavecom.com. Also serves Christian County (portions), Hewittville & Owaneco. ICA: IL0098.
TV Market Ranking: 64 (Christian County (portions), Hewittville, Owaneco, TAYLORVILLE). Franchise award date: November 1, 1977. Franchise expiration date: N.A. Began: November 1, 1951.
Channel capacity: 118 (operating 2-way). Channels available but not in use: N.A.
Basic Service
Subscribers: 4,699 Includes Shelbyville & Pana.
Programming (received off-air): KPLR-TV (CW) St. Louis; KSDK (NBC) St. Louis; WAND (NBC) Decatur; WBUI (CW) Decatur; WCIA (CBS) Champaign; WICS (ABC) Springfield; WILL-TV (PBS) Urbana; WRSP-TV (FOX) Springfield.
Programming (via satellite): C-SPAN; C-SPAN 2; Home Shopping Network; QVC; WGN America.
Current originations: Government Access; Educational Access; Public Access.
Fee: $25.00 installation; $21.97 monthly; $15.00 additional installation.
Expanded Basic Service 1
Subscribers: 4,382.
Programming (via satellite): ABC Family Channel; AMC; Animal Planet; Arts & Entertainment; Bravo; Cartoon Network; CNBC; CNN; Comedy Central; Country Music TV; Discovery Channel; Disney Channel; E! Entertainment Television; ESPN; ESPN 2; Food Network; Fox News Channel; Fox Sports Net Midwest; FX; G4; Golf Channel; GSN; Hallmark Channel; Headline News; HGTV; History Channel; Lifetime; MSNBC; MTV; National Geographic Channel; Nickelodeon; Oxygen; SoapNet; Spike TV; Syfy; TBS Superstation; The Learning Channel; Toon Disney; Travel Channel; Trinity Broadcasting Network; truTV; Turner Network TV; TV Guide Network; TV Land; USA Network; VH1; Weather Channel.
Fee: $1.48 monthly.
Digital Basic Service
Subscribers: 1,347.
Programming (via satellite): BBC America; Bio; Discovery Digital Networks; Do-It-Yourself; GAS; History Channel International; Independent Film Channel; Lifetime Movie Network; MTV Networks Digital Suite; Nick Jr.; Nick Too; NickToons TV; Sundance Channel.
Digital Pay Service 1
Pay Units: 285.
Programming (via satellite): Cinemax (multiplexed).
Fee: $15.00 installation; $10.45 monthly.
Digital Pay Service 2
Pay Units: 476.
Programming (via satellite): HBO (multiplexed).
Fee: $15.00 installation; $11.00 monthly.
Digital Pay Service 3
Pay Units: 127.
Programming (via satellite): Showtime (multiplexed).
Fee: $10.45 monthly.
Digital Pay Service 4
Pay Units: 187.
Programming (via satellite): The Movie Channel (multiplexed).
Fee: $15.00 installation; $10.45 monthly.
Digital Pay Service 5
Pay Units: N.A.
Programming (via satellite): Encore (multiplexed); Flix; Starz (multiplexed).
Video-On-Demand: No
Pay-Per-View
iN DEMAND (delivered digitally); Hot Choice (delivered digitally); Fresh (delivered digitally); Shorteez (delivered digitally); Playboy TV (delivered digitally).
Internet Service
Operational: Yes. Began: July 1, 2004.
Subscribers: 174.
Broadband Service: Charter Pipeline.
Fee: $39.99 monthly.
Telephone Service
None
Miles of Plant: 84.0 (coaxial); None (fiber optic). Homes passed: 13,315. Homes passed includes Shelbyville & Pana
General Manager: Bill Flowers. Technical Operations Manager: Larry Harmon.
City fee: 3% of gross.
Ownership: NewWave Communications (MSO).

THAWVILLE—Formerly served by CableDirect. No longer in operation. ICA: IL0590.

TOLONO—Mediacom. Now served by TUSCOLA, IL [IL0135]. ICA: IL0592.

TONICA—Heartland Cable Inc., PO Box 7, 167 W 5th St, Minonk, IL 61760. Phones: 800-448-4320; 309-432-2075. Fax: 309-432-2500. Web Site: http://www.heartlandcable.com. ICA: IL0677.

TV Market Ranking: Below 100 (TONICA). Franchise award date: N.A. Franchise expiration date: N.A. Began: N.A.

Channel capacity: 60 (operating 2-way). Channels available but not in use: N.A.

Basic Service

Subscribers: 180.

Programming (received off-air): WEEK-TV (NBC) Peoria; WGN-TV (CW, IND) Chicago; WHOI (ABC, CW) Peoria; WMBD-TV (CBS) Peoria; WTVP (PBS) Peoria; WYZZ-TV (FOX) Bloomington.

Programming (via satellite): ABC Family Channel; Arts & Entertainment; CNN; Country Music TV; C-SPAN; Discovery Channel; Disney Channel; ESPN; ESPN 2; Fox Sports Net; Headline News; HGTV; History Channel; Lifetime; Nickelodeon; QVC; Spike TV; TBS Superstation; Turner Network TV; TV Land; USA Network; Weather Channel.

Current originations: Educational Access.

Fee: $39.00 installation; $31.90 monthly.

Pay Service 1

Pay Units: 15.

Programming (via satellite): HBO.

Fee: $10.95 monthly.

Pay Service 2

Pay Units: 10.

Programming (via satellite): Showtime.

Fee: $8.95 monthly.

Video-On-Demand: Yes

Pay-Per-View

Addressable homes: 30.

Movies, Addressable: Yes; special events.

Internet Service

Operational: Yes.

Subscribers: 40.

Fee: $39.00 installation; $29.99 monthly.

Telephone Service

None

Miles of Plant: 3.0 (coaxial); None (fiber optic). Homes passed: 350.

Manager: Steve Allen.

Ownership: Heartland Cable Inc. (Illinois) (MSO).

TOWER HILL—Mediacom, PO Box 288, 4290 Blue Stem Rd, Charleston, IL 61920. Phone: 217-348-5533. Fax: 217-345-7074. Web Site: http://www.mediacomcable.com. ICA: IL0363.

TV Market Ranking: 64 (TOWER HILL). Franchise award date: N.A. Franchise expiration date: N.A. Began: April 7, 1986.

Channel capacity: N.A. Channels available but not in use: N.A.

Basic Service

Subscribers: 66.

Programming (received off-air): WAND (NBC) Decatur; WCFN (MNT) Springfield; WICS (ABC) Springfield; WILL-TV (PBS) Urbana; WPXS (IND) Mount Vernon; WRSP-TV (FOX) Springfield.

Programming (via satellite): ABC Family Channel; AMC; Animal Planet; Arts & Entertainment; CNN; Discovery Channel; ESPN; Headline News; History Channel; Home Shopping Network; Lifetime; MTV; Nickelodeon; TBS Superstation; The Learning Channel; Turner Network TV; TV Land; USA Network; Weather Channel; WGN America.

Fee: $45.00 installation; $33.95 monthly.

Pay Service 1

Pay Units: 24.

Programming (via satellite): Cinemax.

Fee: $7.95 monthly.

Video-On-Demand: No

Internet Service

Operational: No.

Telephone Service

None

Miles of Plant: 6.0 (coaxial); None (fiber optic). Homes passed: 277.

Area Operations Director: Todd Acker. Technical Operations Manager: Jerry Ferguson.

City fee: 3% of gross.

Ownership: Mediacom LLC (MSO).

TRIVOLI—Nova Cablevision Inc., PO Box 1412, 677 W Main St, Galesburg, IL 61401. Phone: 309-342-9681. Fax: 309-342-4408. Web Site: http://www.novacablevision.com. ICA: IL0411.

TV Market Ranking: 83 (TRIVOLI). Franchise award date: N.A. Franchise expiration date: N.A. Began: June 18, 1989.

Channel capacity: 41 (operating 2-way). Channels available but not in use: 19.

Basic Service

Subscribers: 70.

Programming (received off-air): WEEK-TV (NBC) Peoria; WHOI (ABC, CW) Peoria; WICS (ABC) Springfield; WMBD-TV (CBS) Peoria; WRSP-TV (FOX) Springfield; WTVP (PBS) Peoria; WYZZ-TV (FOX) Bloomington.

Programming (via satellite): ABC Family Channel; Arts & Entertainment; CNN; Discovery Channel; Disney Channel; ESPN; Spike TV; Syfy; TBS Superstation; Turner Network TV; USA Network; WGN America.

Fee: $50.00 installation; $36.95 monthly.

Pay Service 1

Pay Units: 1.

Programming (via satellite): Cinemax.

Fee: $10.00 monthly.

Pay Service 2

Pay Units: 3.

Programming (via satellite): HBO.

Fee: $10.00 monthly.

Video-On-Demand: No

Internet Service

Operational: Yes. Began: January 1, 2005.

Subscribers: 16.

Fee: $30.00 installation; $39.95 monthly.

Telephone Service

None

Miles of Plant: 3.0 (coaxial); None (fiber optic). Homes passed: 150. Total homes in franchised area: 150.

Manager: Robert G. Fischer Jr. Office Manager: Hazel Harden.

Ownership: Nova Cablevision Inc. (MSO).

TROY GROVE (village)—Formerly served by CableDirect. No longer in operation. ICA: IL0594.

TUSCOLA—Mediacom, PO Box 288, 4290 Blue Stem Rd, Charleston, IL 61920. Phones: 217-348-5533; 217-253-9028 (Tuscola office). Fax: 217-345-7074. Web Site: http://www.mediacomcable.com. Also serves Arcola, Arthur, Atwood, Camargo, Cerro Gordo, Garrett, Hammond, Hindsboro, Humboldt, Ivesdale, Oakland, Pesotum, Pierson, Tolono & Villa Grove. ICA: IL0135.

TV Market Ranking: 64 (Arcola, Arthur, Atwood, Camargo, Cerro Gordo, Garrett, Hammond, Hindsboro, Ivesdale, Oakland, Pesotum, Pierson, Tolono, TUSCOLA, Villa Grove); Outside TV Markets (Humboldt). Franchise award date: February 12, 1979. Franchise expiration date: N.A. Began: May 1, 1980.

Channel capacity: 134 (operating 2-way). Channels available but not in use: None.

Basic Service

Subscribers: 6,300.

Programming (received off-air): WAND (NBC) Decatur; WBUI (CW) Decatur; WCCU (FOX) Urbana; WCFN (MNT) Springfield; WCIA (CBS) Champaign; WEIU-TV (PBS) Charleston; WICD (ABC) Champaign; WICS (ABC) Springfield; WILL-TV (PBS) Urbana.

Programming (via satellite): C-SPAN; Halogen Network; Home Shopping Network; QVC; Radar Channel; TV Guide Network; WGN America.

Fee: $45.00 installation; $20.45 monthly.

Expanded Basic Service 1

Subscribers: N.A.

Programming (via satellite): ABC Family Channel; AMC; Animal Planet; Arts & Entertainment; BET Networks; Bravo; Cartoon Network; CNBC; CNN; Comedy Central; Country Music TV; C-SPAN 2; Discovery Channel; Disney Channel; E! Entertainment Television; ESPN; ESPN 2; ESPN Classic Sports; Eternal Word TV Network; FitTV; Food Network; Fox News Channel; Fox Sports Net; FX; Hallmark Channel; Headline News; HGTV; History Channel; ION Television; Lifetime; Lifetime Movie Network; MSNBC; MTV; Nickelodeon; Outdoor Channel; Product Information Network; ShopNBC; SoapNet; Speed Channel; Spike TV; Syfy; TBS Superstation; The Learning Channel; Toon Disney; Travel Channel; Trinity Broadcasting Network; truTV; Turner Network TV; TV Land; USA Network; VH1; WE tv; Weather Channel.

Fee: $34.00 monthly.

Digital Basic Service

Subscribers: N.A.

Programming (via satellite): ABC News Now; AmericanLife TV Network; BBC America; Bio; Bloomberg Television; CBS College Sports Network; CCTV-9 (CCTV International); CNN HD; Discovery HD Theater; Discovery Health Channel; Discovery Home Channel; Discovery Kids Channel; Discovery Military Channel; ESPN 2 HD; ESPN HD; ESPN U; ESPNews; FitTV; Fox College Sports Atlantic; Fox College Sports Central; Fox College Sports Pacific; Fox Movie Channel; Fox Soccer; Fuse; G4; Gol TV; Golf Channel; GSN; HDNet; HDNet Movies; History Channel International; ID Investigation Discovery; Independent Film Channel; ION Life; Lifetime Movie Network; MTV Hits; MTV2; National Geographic Channel; Nick Jr.; NickToons TV; Qubo; ReelzChannel; Science Channel; Sleuth; Style Network; TBS in HD; TeenNick; Tennis Channel; The Sportsman Channel; Turner Classic Movies; Turner Network TV HD; TVG Network; Universal HD; Versus; VH1 Classic.

Fee: $9.00 monthly.

Digital Pay Service 1

Pay Units: N.A.

Programming (via satellite): Cinemax (multiplexed); Encore (multiplexed); HBO (multiplexed); HBO HD; Showtime (multiplexed); Showtime HD; Starz (multiplexed); The Movie Channel (multiplexed); The Movie Channel HD.

Fee: $11.95 monthly (HBO, Cinemax, Starz/Encore or Showtime/TMC).

Video-On-Demand: Yes

Pay-Per-View

iN DEMAND (delivered digitally); Playboy TV (delivered digitally); Ten Clips (delivered digitally); Penthouse TV (delivered digitally); Ten Blox (delivered digitally).

Internet Service

Operational: Yes.

Broadband Service: Mediacom High Speed Internet.

Fee: $59.95 installation; $40.95 monthly.

Telephone Service

Analog: Not Operational

Digital: Operational

Fee: $39.95 installation; $39.95 monthly

Miles of Plant: 154.0 (coaxial); None (fiber optic). Homes passed: 8,267.

Area Operations Director: Todd Acker. Technical Operations Manager: Jerry Ferguson. Office Manager: Karl McClelland.

City fee: 3% of basic gross.

Ownership: Mediacom LLC (MSO).

UNION—Packerland Broadband, PO Box 885, 105 Kent St, Iron Mountain, MI 49801. Phones: 800-236-8434; 906-774-6621. Fax: 906-776-2811. E-mail: inquiries@plbb.us. Web Site: http://www.packerlandbroadband.com. ICA: IL0380.

TV Market Ranking: 97 (UNION). Franchise award date: N.A. Franchise expiration date: N.A. Began: December 1, 1986.

Channel capacity: N.A. Channels available but not in use: N.A.

Basic Service

Subscribers: 52.

Programming (received off-air): WBBM-TV (CBS) Chicago; WCIU-TV (IND) Chicago; WFLD (FOX) Chicago; WGBO-DT (UNV) Joliet; WGN-TV (CW, IND) Chicago; WIFR (CBS) Freeport; WLS-TV (ABC) Chicago; WMAQ-TV (NBC) Chicago; WPWR-TV (MNT) Gary; WQRF-TV (FOX) Rockford; WREX (CW, NBC) Rockford; WSNS-TV (TMO) Chicago; WTTW (PBS) Chicago; WTVO (ABC, MNT) Rockford; WYCC (PBS) Chicago.

Programming (via satellite): ABC Family Channel; AMC; Animal Planet; Arts & Entertainment; Bravo; Cartoon Network; CNBC; CNN; Comcast SportsNet Chicago; Comedy Central; Country Music TV; C-SPAN; C-SPAN 2; Discovery Channel; E! Entertainment Television; ESPN; ESPN 2; Food Network; Hallmark Channel; Headline News; HGTV; History Channel; Home Shopping Network; Lifetime; MTV; Nickelodeon; Spike TV; Syfy; TBS Superstation; Telefutura; The Learning Channel; Travel Channel; truTV; Turner Network TV; USA Network; VH1; Weather Channel.

Fee: $25.00 installation; $18.20 monthly; $9.95 additional installation.

Expanded Basic Service 1

Subscribers: 51.

Fee: $20.50 monthly.

Pay Service 1

Pay Units: 16.

Programming (via satellite): Cinemax; HBO; Showtime; The Movie Channel.

Fee: $14.72 monthly.

Internet Service

Operational: No.

Telephone Service

None

Miles of Plant: 3.0 (coaxial); None (fiber optic). Homes passed: 160.

General Manager: Dan Plante. Technical Supervisor: Chad Kay.

Ownership: Cable Constructors Inc. (MSO).

URBANA—Comcast Cable, 303 E Fairlawn Dr, Urbana, IL 61801-5141. Phone: 217-384-2530. Fax: 217-384-2021. Web Site: http://www.comcast.com. Also serves Bondville (village), Cayuga, Champaign, Champaign County, Chrisman, Danville, Eugene, Fairmount, Fithian, Homer, Indianola, Lodi, Muncie, Oakwood, Ogden, Olivet, Philo, Ridge Farm, Savoy (village), Sidney, Silverwood, St. Joseph & Vermilion Grove, IL; Olivet, IN. ICA: IL0019.

TV Market Ranking: 64 (Bondville (village), Champaign, Champaign County, Danville, Fairmount, Fithian, Homer, Indianola, Muncie, Oakwood, Ogden, Olivet, Philo, Savoy (village), Sidney, St. Joseph, URBANA, Vermilion Grove); Below 100 (Cayuga, Chrisman, Eugene, Lodi, Ridge Farm, Silverwood). Franchise award date: April 1, 1979. Franchise expiration date: N.A. Began: April 1, 1979.

Channel capacity: 119 (operating 2-way). Channels available but not in use: 3.

Basic Service

Subscribers: 54,000.

Programming (received off-air): WAND (NBC) Decatur; WBUI (CW) Decatur; WCCU (FOX) Urbana; WCFN (MNT) Springfield; WCIA (CBS) Champaign; WEIU-TV (PBS) Charleston; WICD (ABC) Champaign; WILL-TV (PBS) Urbana.

Programming (via satellite): Comcast SportsNet Chicago; C-SPAN; C-SPAN 2; QVC; TBS Superstation; TV Guide Network; Weatherscan; WGN America.

Current originations: Educational Access.

Fee: $25.00 installation.

Expanded Basic Service 1

Subscribers: 34,427.

Programming (via satellite): ABC Family Channel; AMC; Animal Planet; Arts & Entertainment; BET Networks; Bravo; Cartoon Network; CNBC; CNN; Comcast SportsNet Chicago; Comedy Central; Country Music TV; Discovery Channel; Disney Channel; E! Entertainment Television; ESPN; ESPN 2; Eternal Word TV Network; Food Network; Fox News Channel; Fox Sports Net Midwest; FX; G4; Hallmark Channel; Headline News; HGTV; History Channel; Home Shopping Network; Lifetime; MSNBC; MTV; MTV2; National Geographic Channel; Nickelodeon; Oxygen; Speed Channel; Spike TV; Style Network; The Learning Channel; Travel Channel; Trinity Broadcasting Network; truTV; Turner Classic Movies; Turner Network TV; TV Land; USA Network; VH1; Weather Channel.

Fee: $40.00 monthly.

Digital Basic Service

Subscribers: 15,500.

Programming (via satellite): AmericanLife TV Network; BBC America; Bio; Bloomberg Television; CBS College Sports Network; CMT Pure Country; Cooking Channel; C-SPAN 3; Discovery Digital Networks; Discovery HD Theater; DMX Music; Do-It-Yourself; Encore (multiplexed); ESPN 2 HD; ESPN Classic Sports; ESPN HD; ESPN U; ESPNews; Fox Movie Channel; Fox Reality Channel; Fox Soccer; Fuse; GAS; Golf Channel; Great American Country; GSN; Halogen Network; HDNet; HDNet Movies; History Channel International; HorseRacing TV; Independent Film Channel; Lifetime Movie Network; LOGO; MTV Networks Digital Suite; NFL Network; Nick Jr.; Nick Too; NickToons TV; Outdoor Channel; Palladia; PBS Kids Sprout; Si TV; SoapNet; Sundance Channel; Syfy; Tennis Channel; Toon Disney; Turner Network TV HD; TVG Network; Universal HD; Versus; WE tv.

Fee: $17.00 monthly.

Digital Expanded Basic Service

Subscribers: N.A.

Programming (via satellite): Canales N.

Fee: $10.00 monthly.

Digital Pay Service 1

Pay Units: 7,540.

Programming (via satellite): Cinemax (multiplexed); Flix; HBO (multiplexed); Showtime (multiplexed); Showtime HD; Starz (multiplexed); The Movie Channel (multiplexed); The Movie Channel.

Fee: $10.00 monthly (Cinemax or Starz), $13.00 monthly (HBO or Showtime/TMC).

Video-On-Demand: Yes

Pay-Per-View

ESPN (delivered digitally); iN DEMAND (delivered digitally); Playboy TV (delivered digitally); Special events (delivered digitally).

Internet Service

Operational: Yes.

Subscribers: 6,000.

Broadband Service: Comcast High Speed Internet.

Fee: $99.95 installation; $44.95 monthly; $10.00 modem lease; $149.95 modem purchase.

Telephone Service

Digital: Operational

Miles of Plant: 890.0 (coaxial); 4.0 (fiber optic). Additional miles planned: 2.0 (fiber optic). Homes passed: 122,438. Total homes in franchised area: 123,085.

District Director: Melody Brucker. Chief Technician: Jim Lee.

City fee: 3% of gross.

Ownership: Comcast Cable Communications Inc. (MSO).

URSA (village)—Adams Telecom. Formerly served by Golden, IL [IL0257]. This cable system has converted to IPTV, PO Box 248, 405 Emminga Rd, Golden, IL 62339. Phone: 217-696-4411. E-mail: service@adams.net. Web Site: http://www.adams.net. ICA: IL5326.

Channel capacity: N.A. Channels available but not in use: N.A.

Internet Service

Operational: Yes.

Ownership: Adams Telephone Co-Operative.

VANDALIA—NewWave Communications, 318 N 4th St, Vandalia, IL 62471. Phone: 573-472-9500. Fax: 618-283-4483. Web Site: http://www.newwavecom.com. Also serves Bluff City, Brownstown & Vera. ICA: IL0596.

TV Market Ranking: Outside TV Markets (Bluff City, Brownstown, VANDALIA, Vera). Franchise award date: N.A. Franchise expiration date: N.A. Began: January 1, 1966.

Channel capacity: 54 (not 2-way capable). Channels available but not in use: N.A.

Basic Service

Subscribers: 1,349.

Programming (received off-air): KDNL-TV (ABC) St. Louis; KETC (PBS) St. Louis; KMOV (CBS) St. Louis; KPLR-TV (CW) St. Louis; KSDK (NBC) St. Louis; KTVI (FOX) St. Louis; WAND (NBC) Decatur; WICS (ABC) Springfield; WPXS (IND) Mount Vernon; WRSP-TV (FOX) Springfield; WSIU-TV (PBS) Carbondale.

Programming (via satellite): C-SPAN; QVC; WGN America.

Fee: $15.00 installation; $13.34 monthly.

Expanded Basic Service 1

Subscribers: 1,254.

Programming (via satellite): ABC Family Channel; AMC; Animal Planet; Arts & Entertainment; Big Ten Network; Cartoon Network; CNBC; CNN; Comedy Central; Country Music TV; Discovery Channel; Disney Channel; E! Entertainment Television; ESPN; ESPN 2; Food Network; Fox News Channel; Fox Sports Net Midwest; FX; Hallmark Channel; Headline News; HGTV; History Channel; Lifetime; MTV; National Geographic Channel; Nickelodeon; SoapNet; Spike TV; Syfy; TBS Superstation; The Learning Channel; Toon Disney; Travel Channel; Trinity Broadcasting Network; truTV; Turner Network TV; TV Land; USA Network; VH1; Weather Channel.

Digital Basic Service

Subscribers: 161.

Programming (via satellite): BBC America; Bloomberg Television; Bravo; CMT Pure Country; Discovery Health Channel; Discovery Home Channel; Discovery Kids Channel; Discovery Military Channel; DMX Music; ESPN 2; ESPN Classic Sports; ESPNews; FitTV; G4; Golf Channel; GSN; Halogen Network; ID Investigation Discovery; Independent Film Channel; Nick Jr.; Outdoor Channel; Science Channel; Speed Channel; Turner Classic Movies; TV Guide Interactive Inc.; Versus; VH1 Classic.

Digital Pay Service 1

Pay Units: 770.

Programming (via satellite): Cinemax (multiplexed); Encore (multiplexed); HBO (multiplexed); Showtime (multiplexed); Starz (multiplexed); The Movie Channel (multiplexed).

Fee: $10.75 monthly (each).

Video-On-Demand: No

Pay-Per-View

Club Jenna (delivered digitally); iN DEMAND (delivered digitally); Playboy TV (delivered digitally); Fresh (delivered digitally).

Internet Service

Operational: No.

Telephone Service

None

Miles of Plant: 43.0 (coaxial); None (fiber optic). Homes passed: 4,096.

General Manager: Bill Flowers. Technical Operations Manager: Chris Mooday.

Ownership: NewWave Communications (MSO).

VERGENNES—Formerly served by CableDirect. No longer in operation. ICA: IL0625.

VERMILLION (village)—Formerly served by CableDirect. No longer in operation. ICA: IL0597.

VERMONT—Mediacom, PO Box 334, 609 S 4th St, Chillicothe, IL 61523. Phone: 309-274-4500. Fax: 309-274-3188. Web Site: http://www.mediacomcable.com. ICA: IL0311.

TV Market Ranking: Outside TV Markets (VERMONT). Franchise award date: N.A. Franchise expiration date: N.A. Began: December 1, 1982.

Channel capacity: N.A. Channels available but not in use: N.A.

Basic Service

Subscribers: 116.

Programming (received off-air): WEEK-TV (NBC) Peoria; WHOI (ABC, CW) Peoria; WMBD-TV (CBS) Peoria; WRSP-TV (FOX) Springfield; WTVP (PBS) Peoria.

Programming (via satellite): ABC Family Channel; AMC; Arts & Entertainment; CNN; Comedy Central; Country Music TV; Discovery Channel; ESPN; ESPN 2; Headline News; History Channel; Home Shopping Network; Lifetime; Nickelodeon; Speed Channel; Spike TV; TBS Superstation; The Learning Channel; Travel Channel; Turner Network TV; USA Network; Weather Channel; WGN America.

Fee: $45.00 installation; $47.95 monthly.

Pay Service 1

Pay Units: 33.

Programming (via satellite): HBO.

Fee: $12.00 monthly.

Video-On-Demand: No

Internet Service

Operational: No.

Telephone Service

None

Miles of Plant: 8.0 (coaxial); None (fiber optic). Homes passed: 389.

Vice President: Don Hagwell. Operations Director: Gary Wightman. Technical Operations Manager: Larry Brackman. Marketing Director: Stephanie Law.

Ownership: Mediacom LLC (MSO).

VERSAILLES—Cass Cable TV Inc. Now served by VIRGINIA, IL [IL0598]. ICA: IL0382.

VICTORIA—Mediacom, 3900 26th Ave, Moline, IL 61265. Phone: 309-797-2580. Fax: 309-797-2414. Web Site: http://www.mediacomcable.com. ICA: IL0436.

TV Market Ranking: 83 (VICTORIA).

Channel capacity: N.A. Channels available but not in use: N.A.

Basic Service

Subscribers: N.A.

Fee: $45.00 installation; $54.95 monthly.

Pay Service 1

Pay Units: N.A.

Programming (via satellite): Cinemax; HBO.

Internet Service

Operational: No.

Telephone Service

None

Miles of plant included in Moline

Area Manager: Don DeMay. Engineering Director: Mitch Carlson. Technical Operations Manager: Chris Toalson. Marketing Director: Greg Evans.

Ownership: Mediacom LLC (MSO).

VILLA PARK—Comcast Cable. Now served by OAK BROOK, IL [IL0006]. ICA: IL0070.

VIRDEN—Charter Communications, 11 Clearing, Taylorville, IL 62568-9279. Phones: 217-287-7992; 636-207-7044 (St Louis office). Fax: 217-287-7304. Web Site: http://www.charter.com. Also serves Auburn, Girard, Nilwood, Sunset Lake & Thayer. ICA: IL0609.

TV Market Ranking: 64 (Auburn, Girard, Nilwood, Sunset Lake, Thayer, VIRDEN). Franchise award date: N.A. Franchise expiration date: N.A. Began: N.A.

Channel capacity: 38 (not 2-way capable). Channels available but not in use: None.

Basic Service

Subscribers: 2,846.

Programming (received off-air): KDNL-TV (ABC) St. Louis; KETC (PBS) St. Louis; KMOV (CBS) St. Louis; KPLR-TV (CW) St. Louis; KSDK (NBC) St. Louis; WAND (NBC) Decatur; WCFN (MNT) Springfield; WICS (ABC) Springfield; WRSP-TV (FOX) Springfield.

Programming (via satellite): AMC; Arts & Entertainment; Country Music TV; C-SPAN; E! Entertainment Television; ESPN; Home Shopping Network; INSP; Lifetime; MTV; Nickelodeon; QVC; Spike TV; USA Network; Weather Channel.
Fee: $29.99 installation.

Expanded Basic Service 1
Subscribers: 2,810.
Programming (via satellite): ABC Family Channel; CNN; Discovery Channel; Disney Channel; Fox News Channel; Headline News; TBS Superstation; Turner Network TV; WGN America.
Fee: $42.99 monthly.

Pay Service 1
Pay Units: 197.
Programming (via satellite): Cinemax.
Fee: $8.45 monthly.

Pay Service 2
Pay Units: 542.
Programming (via satellite): HBO.
Fee: $9.45 monthly.

Pay Service 3
Pay Units: 386.
Programming (via satellite): Showtime.
Fee: $8.45 monthly.

Pay Service 4
Pay Units: 119.
Programming (via satellite): The Movie Channel.
Fee: $8.45 monthly.

Video-On-Demand: No

Internet Service
Operational: No.

Telephone Service
None

Miles of Plant: 85.0 (coaxial); None (fiber optic).
Vice President & General Manager: Steve Trippe. Operations Director: Dave Miller. Chief Technician: Larry Harmon. Marketing Director: Beverly Wall. Office Manager: Melinda Sincavage.
Ownership: Charter Communications Inc. (MSO).

VIRGINIA—Cass Cable TV Inc., PO Box 200, 100 Redbud Rd, Virginia, IL 62691. Phones: 800-252-1799; 217-452-7725. Fax: 217-452-7030. E-mail: casscatv@casscomm.com. Web Site: http://www.casscomm.com. Also serves Ashland, Bath, Beardstown, Bluff Springs, Buzzville, Chandlerville, Easton, Forest City, Goofy Ridge, Havana, Hersman, Kilbourne, Manito, Mason City, Mount Sterling, Oakford (Village), Pleasant Plains, Quiver Twp., Rushville, Spring Lake, Talbott Addition, Tallula & Versailles. ICA: IL0598.
TV Market Ranking: 64 (Ashland, Chandlerville, Mason City, Oakford (Village), Pleasant Plains, Quiver Twp., Tallula, VIRGINIA); 83 (Easton, Forest City, Goofy Ridge, Kilbourne, Manito, Spring Lake, Talbott Addition); Below 100 (Buzzville, Havana, Hersman, Mount Sterling); Outside TV Markets (Bath, Beardstown, Bluff Springs, Rushville, Versailles). Franchise award date: N.A. Franchise expiration date: N.A. Began: June 1, 1976.
Channel capacity: 100 (operating 2-way). Channels available but not in use: None.

Basic Service
Subscribers: 6,835.
Programming (received off-air): KHQA-TV (ABC, CBS) Hannibal; WAND (NBC) Decatur; WCIA (CBS) Champaign; WGEM-TV (CW, NBC) Quincy; WHOI (ABC, CW) Peoria; WICS (ABC) Springfield; WMBD-TV (CBS) Peoria; WRSP-TV (FOX) Springfield; WSEC (PBS) Jacksonville; WTVP (PBS) Peoria.
Programming (via satellite): WGN America.
Fee: $45.00 installation; $14.95 monthly; $4.00 converter.

Expanded Basic Service 1
Subscribers: 6,337.
Programming (via satellite): ABC Family Channel; AMC; AmericanLife TV Network; Animal Planet; Arts & Entertainment; Cartoon Network; CNBC; CNN; Comcast SportsNet Chicago; Comedy Central; Country Music TV; C-SPAN; Discovery Channel; Disney Channel; E! Entertainment Television; ESPN; ESPN 2; ESPN Classic Sports; Food Network; Fox News Channel; Fox Sports Net Midwest; FX; Golf Channel; GSN; Hallmark Channel; Headline News; HGTV; History Channel; Home Shopping Network; ION Television; Lifetime; MSNBC; MTV; Nickelodeon; QVC; Speed Channel; Spike TV; Syfy; TBS Superstation; Telemundo; The Learning Channel; Toon Disney; Travel Channel; Trinity Broadcasting Network; truTV; Turner Network TV; TV Land; Univision; USA Network; Versus; VH1; Weather Channel.
Fee: $32.00 monthly.

Digital Basic Service
Subscribers: 533.
Programming (via satellite): AmericanLife TV Network; BBC America; Bio; Bloomberg Television; Bravo; Discovery Digital Networks; DMX Music; ESPNews; FitTV; Fox Movie Channel; Fox Sports World; G4; GAS; History Channel International; Independent Film Channel; INSP; Lifetime Movie Network; MuchMusic Network; National Geographic Channel; Nick Jr.; Outdoor Channel; Ovation; Style Network; Syfy; Trinity Broadcasting Network; Turner Classic Movies; WE tv; Weatherscan.
Fee: $8.04 monthly.

Pay Service 1
Pay Units: 536.
Programming (via satellite): Cinemax.
Fee: $20.00 installation; $11.35 monthly.

Pay Service 2
Pay Units: 429.
Programming (via satellite): Showtime; The Movie Channel.
Fee: $20.00 installation; $12.95 monthly.

Pay Service 3
Pay Units: 728.
Programming (via satellite): Encore; Starz.
Fee: $20.00 installation; $8.95 monthly.

Pay Service 4
Pay Units: 881.
Programming (via satellite): HBO.
Fee: $20.00 installation; $13.55 monthly.

Digital Pay Service 1
Pay Units: 46.
Programming (via satellite): Cinemax (multiplexed); DMX Music; Encore; HBO (multiplexed); Showtime (multiplexed); The Movie Channel (multiplexed).

Video-On-Demand: No

Pay-Per-View
Addressable homes: 700.
ESPN Extra, Addressable: Yes; ESPN Now; iN DEMAND; Playboy TV; Spice.

Internet Service
Operational: Yes. Began: January 1, 1999.
Subscribers: 4,499.
Broadband Service: casscomm.com.
Fee: $39.95 monthly.

Telephone Service
Analog: Operational
Fee: $34.95 monthly
Digital: Operational
Subscribers: 37.
Fee: $34.95 monthly

Miles of Plant: 240.0 (coaxial); 14.0 (fiber optic). Homes passed: 12,155.
Plant Manager: Lance Allen. Cable TV Services Manager: Chad Winters. Marketing Director: Erynn Snedeker. Advertising Director: Laymon Carter. Office Manager: Cindy Kilby.
City fee: 3% of gross/base basic service.
Ownership: Cass Cable TV Inc. (MSO).

WALNUT—Mediacom. Now served by MINERAL, IL [IL0170]. ICA: IL0600.

WALTONVILLE—Longview Communications, 12007 Sunrise Valley Dr, Ste 375, Reston, VA 20191. Phones: 866-611-6565 (Customer service); 703-476-9101. Fax: 703-476-9107. Web Site: http://www.longviewcomm.com. ICA: IL0623.
TV Market Ranking: Below 100 (WALTONVILLE). Franchise award date: N.A. Franchise expiration date: N.A. Began: N.A.
Channel capacity: 31 (not 2-way capable). Channels available but not in use: 3.

Basic Service
Subscribers: 24.
Programming (received off-air): KBSI (FOX) Cape Girardeau; KFVS-TV (CBS, CW) Cape Girardeau; KPLR-TV (CW) St. Louis; WPSD-TV (NBC) Paducah; WPXS (IND) Mount Vernon; WSIL-TV (ABC) Harrisburg; WUSI-TV (PBS) Olney.
Programming (via satellite): ABC Family Channel; AMC; Arts & Entertainment; CNN; Comedy Central; Country Music TV; C-SPAN; Discovery Channel; Disney Channel; ESPN; Lifetime; QVC; Spike TV; TBS Superstation; The Learning Channel; Trinity Broadcasting Network; Turner Network TV; TV Land; USA Network; WGN America.
Fee: $30.95 monthly.

Pay Service 1
Pay Units: N.A.
Programming (via satellite): Showtime; The Movie Channel.
Fee: $8.95 monthly (TMC), $10.95 monthly (Showtime).

Video-On-Demand: No

Internet Service
Operational: No.

Telephone Service
None

Miles of Plant: 4.0 (coaxial); None (fiber optic). Homes passed: 181.
President: John Long. Senior Vice President: Marc W. Cohen. General Manager: Brandon Dickey. Technical Manager: Steve Boss.
Ownership: Longview Communications (MSO).

WARREN—Mediacom. Now served by LENA, IL [IL0223]. ICA: IL0243.

WARRENSBURG—Crystal Broadcast Networks, PO Box 180336, Chicago, IL 60618. Phones: 877-319-0328; 630-206-0447. E-mail: info@crystalbn.com. Web Site: http://crystalbn.com. Also serves De Witt County (portions), Latham & Macon County (portions). ICA: IL0264.
TV Market Ranking: 64 (De Witt County (portions), Latham, Macon County (portions), WARRENSBURG). Franchise award date: N.A. Franchise expiration date: N.A. Began: June 1, 1981.
Channel capacity: 42 (not 2-way capable). Channels available but not in use: None.

Basic Service
Subscribers: 247.
Programming (received off-air): WAND (NBC) Decatur; WBUI (CW) Decatur; WCFN (MNT) Springfield; WCIA (CBS) Champaign; WICS (ABC) Springfield; WILL-TV (PBS) Urbana; WRSP-TV (FOX) Springfield.
Programming (via satellite): C-SPAN; Home Shopping Network; WGN America.
Fee: $29.95 installation; $19.95 monthly.

Expanded Basic Service 1
Subscribers: N.A.
Programming (via satellite): ABC Family Channel; AMC; Arts & Entertainment; CNN; Comedy Central; Country Music TV; Discovery Channel; Disney Channel; ESPN; ESPN 2; Fox News Channel; Fox Sports Net Midwest; FX; Lifetime; MSNBC; MTV; Nickelodeon; SoapNet; Spike TV; Syfy; TBS Superstation; Toon Disney; Trinity Broadcasting Network; Turner Classic Movies; Turner Network TV; TV Land; USA Network; VH1; Weather Channel.
Fee: $22.00 monthly.

Pay Service 1
Pay Units: 58.
Programming (via satellite): Cinemax; Encore; HBO.
Fee: $25.00 installation; $3.99 monthly (Encore), $13.49 monthly (Cinemax or HBO).

Video-On-Demand: No

Internet Service
Operational: Yes.

Telephone Service
Digital: Operational

Miles of Plant: 15.0 (coaxial); None (fiber optic). Homes passed: 813.
General Manager: Nidhin Johnson. Program Manager: Shawn Smith.
City fee: 3% of gross.
Ownership: Crystal Broadband Networks (MSO).

WASHINGTON PARK—Mediacom, PO Box 288, 4290 Blue Stem Rd, Charleston, IL 61920. Phone: 217-348-5533. Fax: 217-345-7074. Web Site: http://www.mediacomcable.com. Also serves Fairmont City, Madison County, St. Clair County (unincorporated portions) & St. Clair Twp. ICA: IL0093.
TV Market Ranking: 11 (Fairmont City, Madison County (portions), St. Clair County (unincorporated portions), St. Clair Twp., WASHINGTON PARK); Below 100 (Madison County (portions)). Franchise award date: N.A. Franchise expiration date: N.A. Began: June 23, 1983.
Channel capacity: 134 (not 2-way capable). Channels available but not in use: 1.

Basic Service
Subscribers: 1,553.
Programming (received off-air): KDNL-TV (ABC) St. Louis; KETC (PBS) St. Louis; KMOV (CBS) St. Louis; KNLC (IND) St. Louis; KPLR-TV (CW) St. Louis; KSDK (NBC) St. Louis; KTVI (FOX) St. Louis; WSIU-TV (PBS) Carbondale.

Programming (via satellite): Home Shopping Network; TBS Superstation; Trinity Broadcasting Network.
Fee: $45.00 installation; $20.95 monthly.
Expanded Basic Service 1
Subscribers: 1,427.
Programming (via satellite): ABC Family Channel; AMC; Animal Planet; Arts & Entertainment; BET Networks; Cartoon Network; CNN; Comedy Central; Country Music TV; Discovery Channel; Disney Channel; E! Entertainment Television; ESPN; ESPN 2; Fox Sports Net; History Channel; Lifetime; MTV; Nickelodeon; Spike TV; Syfy; Turner Network TV; TV Land; USA Network; VH1; Weather Channel; WGN America.
Fee: $27.00 monthly.
Pay Service 1
Pay Units: 1,361.
Programming (via satellite): Cinemax; HBO; Showtime; The Movie Channel.
Fee: $7.95 monthly (Cinemax), $11.99 monthly (Showtime or TMC), $13.50 monthly (HBO).
Video-On-Demand: No
Internet Service
Operational: No.
Telephone Service
None
Miles of Plant: 60.0 (coaxial); 8.0 (fiber optic). Homes passed: 6,018.
Area Operations Director: Todd Acker. Technical Operations Manager: Jerry Ferguson.
City fee: 5% of gross.
Ownership: Mediacom LLC (MSO).

WATAGA—Formerly served by Mediacom. No longer in operation. ICA: IL0261.

WATERLOO—Charter Communications, 941 Charter Commons Dr, Saint Louis, MO 63017. Phone: 636-207-7044. Fax: 636-230-7034. Web Site: http://www.charter.com. Also serves Columbia. ICA: IL0175.
TV Market Ranking: 11 (Columbia, WATERLOO). Franchise award date: N.A. Franchise expiration date: N.A. Began: January 1, 1981.
Channel capacity: N.A. Channels available but not in use: N.A.
Basic Service
Subscribers: 1,493.
Programming (received off-air): KDNL-TV (ABC) St. Louis; KETC (PBS) St. Louis; KMOV (CBS) St. Louis; KNLC (IND) St. Louis; KPLR-TV (CW) St. Louis; KSDK (NBC) St. Louis; KTVI (FOX) St. Louis; WPXS (IND) Mount Vernon; WRBU (MNT) East St. Louis.
Programming (via satellite): C-SPAN; C-SPAN 2; Eternal Word TV Network; GRTV Network; Home Shopping Network; INSP; Jewelry Television; QVC; TBS Superstation; Trinity Broadcasting Network; TV Guide Network; Univision; Weatherscan; WGN America.
Current originations: Government Access; Government Access; Public Access; Public Access; Educational Access.
Fee: $29.99 installation.
Expanded Basic Service 1
Subscribers: N.A.
Programming (via satellite): ABC Family Channel; AMC; Animal Planet; Arts & Entertainment; BET Networks; Bravo; Cartoon Network; CNBC; CNN; Comedy Central; Country Music TV; Discovery Channel; Disney Channel; E! Entertainment Television; ESPN; ESPN 2; Food Network; Fox Movie Channel; Fox News Channel; Fox Sports Net Midwest; FX; G4; Golf Channel; GSN; Hallmark Channel; Headline News; HGTV; History Channel; Lifetime; MSNBC; MTV; National Geographic Channel; Nickelodeon; Oxygen; ShopNBC; SoapNet; Speed Channel; Spike TV; Style Network; Syfy; The Learning Channel; Toon Disney; Travel Channel; truTV; Turner Classic Movies; Turner Network TV; TV Land; USA Network; Versus; VH1; WE tv; Weather Channel.
Fee: $49.99 monthly.
Digital Basic Service
Subscribers: N.A.
Programming (via satellite): BBC America; Bio; Bloomberg Television; Discovery Digital Networks; Do-It-Yourself; Encore Action; ESPN Classic Sports; FitTV; Fox College Sports Atlantic; Fox College Sports Central; Fox College Sports Pacific; Fox Sports World; Fuel TV; Fuse; GAS; Great American Country; History Channel International; Independent Film Channel; International Television (ITV); Lifetime Movie Network; MTV Networks Digital Suite; Music Choice; NFL Network; Nick Jr.; Nick Too; NickToons TV; Sundance Channel; TV Guide Interactive Inc.
Digital Pay Service 1
Pay Units: 246.
Programming (via satellite): Cinemax (multiplexed); HBO (multiplexed); Showtime (multiplexed); Starz (multiplexed); The Movie Channel (multiplexed).
Video-On-Demand: Yes
Pay-Per-View
iN DEMAND (delivered digitally); Playboy TV (delivered digitally); Fresh (delivered digitally); Shorteez (delivered digitally); Sports PPV (delivered digitally); ESPN Now (delivered digitally).
Internet Service
Operational: Yes.
Broadband Service: Charter Pipeline.
Fee: $29.99 monthly; $5.00 modem lease; $99.99 modem purchase.
Telephone Service
None
Miles of Plant: 27.0 (coaxial); None (fiber optic). Homes passed: 2,537.
Vice President & General Manager: Steve Trippe. Operations Director: Tom Williams. Marketing Director: Beverly Wall.
City fee: 3% of gross.
Ownership: Charter Communications Inc. (MSO).

WATSEKA—Mediacom, Suite A, 109 E 5th St, Auburn, IN 46706. Phone: 260-927-3015. Fax: 260-347-4433. Web Site: http://www.mediacomcable.com. Also serves Crescent City, Sheldon & Woodland (village). ICA: IL0092.
TV Market Ranking: Outside TV Markets (Crescent City, Sheldon, WATSEKA, Woodland (village)). Franchise award date: January 1, 1966. Franchise expiration date: N.A. Began: June 1, 1966.
Channel capacity: N.A. Channels available but not in use: N.A.
Basic Service
Subscribers: 2,867.
Programming (received off-air): WAND (NBC) Decatur; WBBM-TV (CBS) Chicago; WCCU (FOX) Urbana; WCFN (MNT) Springfield; WCIA (CBS) Champaign; WFLD (FOX) Chicago; WGN-TV (CW, IND) Chicago; WICD (ABC) Champaign; WILL-TV (PBS) Urbana; WLS-TV (ABC) Chicago; WMAQ-TV (NBC) Chicago; WPWR-TV (MNT) Gary; WPXU-TV (ION, MNT) Jacksonville; WTTW (PBS) Chicago; allband FM.
Fee: $45.00 installation; $20.95 monthly.

Expanded Basic Service 1
Subscribers: 2,568.
Programming (via satellite): ABC Family Channel; AMC; Animal Planet; Arts & Entertainment; Cartoon Network; CNBC; CNN; Comcast SportsNet Chicago; Comedy Central; Country Music TV; C-SPAN; C-SPAN 2; Discovery Channel; Disney Channel; E! Entertainment Television; ESPN; ESPN 2; FitTV; Food Network; Fox News Channel; FX; Great American Country; Hallmark Channel; Headline News; HGTV; History Channel; Home Shopping Network; ION Television; Lifetime; MSNBC; MTV; Nickelodeon; Outdoor Channel; QVC; RFD-TV; ShopNBC; Speed Channel; Spike TV; Syfy; TBS Superstation; The Learning Channel; Travel Channel; Trinity Broadcasting Network; truTV; Turner Network TV; TV Guide Network; TV Land; USA Network; VH1; WE tv; Weather Channel.
Fee: $33.00 monthly.
Digital Basic Service
Subscribers: N.A.
Programming (via satellite): AmericanLife TV Network; BBC America; Bio; Bloomberg Television; Discovery Digital Networks; Discovery Kids Channel; ESPNews; Fox Movie Channel; Fox Sports World; Fuse; G4; GAS; Golf Channel; GSN; Halogen Network; History Channel International; Independent Film Channel; Lifetime Movie Network; Lime; MTV Networks Digital Suite; Music Choice; National Geographic Channel; Nick Jr.; NickToons TV; Outdoor Channel; Style Network; Trio; Turner Classic Movies; TVG Network; Versus.
Fee: $9.00 monthly.
Digital Expanded Basic Service
Subscribers: N.A.
Programming (via satellite): Discovery HD Theater; ESPN; ESPN 2; HDNet; HDNet Movies; iN DEMAND.
Digital Pay Service 1
Pay Units: N.A.
Programming (via satellite): Cinemax (multiplexed); Encore (multiplexed); Flix (multiplexed); HBO (multiplexed); Showtime (multiplexed); Starz (multiplexed); Sundance Channel (multiplexed); The Movie Channel (multiplexed).
Fee: $11.95 monthly (each).
Video-On-Demand: Yes
Pay-Per-View
iN DEMAND (delivered digitally); Playboy TV (delivered digitally); TENClips, TEN by the Movie, TEN Blox (delivered digitally).
Internet Service
Operational: Yes.
Broadband Service: Mediacom High Speed Internet.
Fee: $59.95 installation; $40.95 monthly.
Telephone Service
Digital: Operational
Fee: $39.95 installation; $39.95 monthly
Miles of plant included in Kendallville, IN
Technical Operations Manager: Craig Grey. Operations Director: Joe Poffenberger.
City fee: 1% of gross.
Ownership: Mediacom LLC (MSO).

WAUKEGAN—Formerly served by Comcast Cable. No longer in operation. ICA: IL0014.

WAVERLY—Crystal Broadband Networks, PO Box 180336, Chicago, IL 60618. Phones: 817-319-0328; 630-206-0447. E-mail: info@crystalbn.com. Web Site: http://crystalbn.com. Also serves Franklin. ICA: IL0218.
TV Market Ranking: 64 (Franklin, WAVERLY). Franchise award date: N.A. Franchise expiration date: N.A. Began: March 1, 1982.
Channel capacity: 62 (not 2-way capable). Channels available but not in use: N.A.
Basic Service
Subscribers: 319.
Programming (received off-air): KETC (PBS) St. Louis; KMOV (CBS) St. Louis; KSDK (NBC) St. Louis; KTVI (FOX) St. Louis; WAND (NBC) Decatur; WBUI (CW) Decatur; WCFN (MNT) Springfield; WICS (ABC) Springfield; WRSP-TV (FOX) Springfield.
Programming (via satellite): C-SPAN; Home Shopping Network; INSP; Trinity Broadcasting Network; Weather Channel; WGN America.
Fee: $29.95 installation; $19.95 monthly.
Expanded Basic Service 1
Subscribers: N.A.
Programming (via satellite): ABC Family Channel; AMC; Arts & Entertainment; Boomerang; Cartoon Network; CNN; CNN International; Comedy Central; C-SPAN 2; Discovery Channel; Disney Channel; Do-It-Yourself; E! Entertainment Television; ESPN; Food Network; Fox Sports Net Midwest; FX; G4; Great American Country; GSN; Hallmark Channel; Headline News; HGTV; History Channel; Lifetime; Lifetime Movie Network; MSNBC; MTV; Nickelodeon; ShopNBC; Speed Channel; Spike TV; TBS Superstation; Toon Disney; Turner Network TV; USA Network.
Fee: $23.00 monthly.
Digital Basic Service
Subscribers: N.A.
Programming (via satellite): BBC America; Bio; Black Family Channel; Bloomberg Television; Discovery Digital Networks; Discovery Kids Channel; DMX Music; ESPN 2; ESPN Classic Sports; ESPNews; FitTV; Fox Movie Channel; Fox Sports World; Golf Channel; Halogen Network; History Channel International; Lime; National Geographic Channel; Outdoor Channel; Style Network; Turner Classic Movies; Versus; WE tv.
Fee: $13.95 monthly.
Digital Pay Service 1
Pay Units: N.A.
Programming (via satellite): Cinemax (multiplexed); Encore; Encore Action; HBO The Works; Showtime (multiplexed); The Movie Channel (multiplexed).
Fee: $3.99 monthly (Encore), $9.49 monthly (Cinemax), $13.49 monthly (HBO, Starz or Showtime).
Video-On-Demand: No
Pay-Per-View
Fresh (delivered digitally); Playboy TV (delivered digitally); iN DEMAND (delivered digitally).

Internet Service
Operational: Yes.
Telephone Service
Digital: Operational
Miles of Plant: 19.0 (coaxial); None (fiber optic). Homes passed: 853.
General Manager: Nidhin Johnson. Program Manager: Shawn Smith.
Ownership: Crystal Broadband Networks (MSO).

WAYNE CITY—NewWave Communications, 318 N 4th St, Vandalia, IL 62471. Phone: 573-472-9500. Fax: 618-283-4483. Web Site: http://www.newwavecom.com. ICA: IL0270.
TV Market Ranking: Below 100 (WAYNE CITY). Franchise award date: N.A. Franchise expiration date: N.A. Began: August 1, 1980.
Channel capacity: 136 (not 2-way capable). Channels available but not in use: N.A.
Basic Service
Subscribers: 197.
Programming (received off-air): KFVS-TV (CBS, CW) Cape Girardeau; WAZE-LP (CW) Evansville; WEHT (ABC) Evansville; WEVV-TV (CBS, MNT) Evansville; WFIE (NBC) Evansville; WNIN (PBS) Evansville; WPXS (IND) Mount Vernon; WSIL-TV (ABC) Harrisburg; WTVW (FOX) Evansville; WUSI-TV (PBS) Olney; allband FM.
Programming (via satellite): C-SPAN; C-SPAN 2; Home Shopping Network; INSP; QVC; Trinity Broadcasting Network; WGN America.
Fee: $17.45 monthly.
Expanded Basic Service 1
Subscribers: 174.
Programming (via satellite): ABC Family Channel; AMC; Animal Planet; Arts & Entertainment; Big Ten Network; Bravo; Cartoon Network; CNBC; CNN; Comedy Central; Country Music TV; Discovery Channel; Disney Channel; E! Entertainment Television; ESPN; ESPN 2; ESPN Classic Sports; Eternal Word TV Network; Food Network; Fox News Channel; Fox Sports Net Midwest; FX; Golf Channel; GSN; Hallmark Channel; Headline News; HGTV; History Channel; Lifetime; MSNBC; MTV; National Geographic Channel; Nickelodeon; Outdoor Channel; Oxygen; ShopNBC; SoapNet; Speed Channel; Spike TV; Syfy; TBS Superstation; The Learning Channel; Toon Disney; Travel Channel; truTV; Turner Classic Movies; Turner Network TV; TV Land; USA Network; Versus; VH1; Weather Channel.
Fee: $12.45 monthly.
Digital Basic Service
Subscribers: N.A.
Programming (received off-air): WEHT (ABC) Evansville; WEVV-TV (CBS, MNT) Evansville; WFIE (NBC) Evansville; WSIL-TV (ABC) Harrisburg; WTVW (FOX) Evansville.
Programming (via satellite): BBC America; Bio; Bloomberg Television; CMT Pure Country; Cooking Channel; Discovery HD Theater; Discovery Health Channel; Discovery Kids Channel; Discovery Military Channel; Discovery Planet Green; Do-It-Yourself; ESPN 2 HD; ESPN HD; ESPNews; FitTV; Fox College Sports Atlantic; Fox College Sports Central; Fox College Sports Pacific; Fox Movie Channel; FSN HD; G4; Great American Country; Halogen Network; HDNet; HDNet Movies; History Channel International; ID Investigation Discovery; Independent Film Channel; Lifetime Movie Network; MTV Hits; MTV Jams; MTV2; Music Choice; Nick Jr.; Nick Too; NickToons TV; RFD-TV; Science Channel; Sleuth; Style Network; TeenNick; Turner Network TV HD; Universal HD; VH1 Classic; VH1 Soul.
Fee: $49.95 monthly.
Digital Pay Service 1
Pay Units: N.A.
Programming (via satellite): Cinemax (multiplexed); Cinemax HD; Encore (multiplexed); Flix; HBO (multiplexed); HBO HD; Showtime (multiplexed); Starz (multiplexed); Starz HDTV; The Movie Channel (multiplexed).
Video-On-Demand: No
Pay-Per-View
iN DEMAND (delivered digitally); Spice: Xcess (delivered digitally); Club Jenna (delivered digitally); Shorteez (delivered digitally); Playboy TV (delivered digitally); Fresh (delivered digitally).
Internet Service
Operational: Yes.
Telephone Service
Digital: Operational
Miles of Plant: 11.0 (coaxial); None (fiber optic). Homes passed: 632.
General Manager: Bill Flowers. Technical Operations Manager: Chris Mooday.
City fee: 3% of gross.
Ownership: NewWave Communications (MSO).

WEE-MA-TUK HILLS—Nova Cablevision Inc., PO Box 1412, 677 W Main St, Galesburg, IL 61401. Phone: 309-342-9681. Fax: 309-342-4408. Web Site: http://www.novacablevision.com. Also serves Fiatt. ICA: IL0603.
TV Market Ranking: 83 (Fiatt, WEE-MA-TUK HILLS). Franchise award date: N.A. Franchise expiration date: N.A. Began: October 1, 1990.
Channel capacity: 40 (operating 2-way). Channels available but not in use: N.A.
Basic Service
Subscribers: 153.
Programming (received off-air): KGCW (CW) Burlington; KIIN (PBS) Iowa City; KLJB (CW, FOX) Davenport; KWQC-TV (NBC) Davenport; WAOE (MNT) Peoria; WEEK-TV (NBC) Peoria; WHOI (ABC, CW) Peoria; WMBD-TV (CBS) Peoria; WQAD-TV (ABC) Moline; WQPT-TV (PBS) Moline; WTVP (PBS) Peoria.
Programming (via satellite): ABC Family Channel; AMC; Animal Planet; Arts & Entertainment; Big Ten Network; Cartoon Network; CNBC; CNN; Comcast SportsNet Chicago; Comedy Central; Country Music TV; C-SPAN; C-SPAN 2; Discovery Channel; Disney Channel; E! Entertainment Television; ESPN; ESPN 2; Eternal Word TV Network; Food Network; Fox News Channel; Fox Sports Net Midwest; FX; Golf Channel; Great American Country; Hallmark Channel; Headline News; HGTV; History Channel; Home Shopping Network; HorseRacing TV; INSP; Lifetime; MSNBC; MTV; National Geographic Channel; Nickelodeon; QVC; RFD-TV; SoapNet; Speed Channel; Spike TV; Syfy; TBS Superstation; The Learning Channel; The Sportsman Channel; Travel Channel; truTV; Turner Network TV; TV Land; USA Network; VH1; Weather Channel; WGN America.
Fee: $60.00 installation; $44.95 monthly.
Digital Basic Service
Subscribers: N.A.
Programming (received off-air): KGCW (CW) Burlington; KLJB (CW, FOX) Davenport; KWQC-TV (NBC) Davenport; WEEK-TV (NBC) Peoria; WHBF-TV (CBS) Rock Island; WHOI (ABC, CW) Peoria; WMBD-TV (CBS) Peoria; WQAD-TV (ABC) Moline; WQPT-TV (PBS) Moline; WTVP (PBS) Peoria.
Programming (via satellite): Bio; Blackbelt TV; Bloomberg Television; CMT Pure Country; Discovery Health Channel; Discovery Kids Channel; Discovery Military Channel; Discovery Planet Green; ESPN 2; ESPN Classic Sports; ESPNews; Fox Movie Channel; Fox Soccer; FSN Digital Atlantic; FSN Digital Central; FSN Digital Pacific; Fuse; G4; Golf Channel; Great American Country; GSN; HGTV; History Channel; History Channel International; ID Investigation Discovery; Independent Film Channel; Lifetime Movie Network; MTV Hits; MTV2; Music Choice; Nick Jr.; NickToons TV; Outdoor Channel; Science Channel; ShopNBC; Speed Channel; Style Network; Syfy; TeenNick; Toon Disney; Trinity Broadcasting Network; Turner Classic Movies; Versus; VH1 Classic; VH1 Soul; WE tv.
Fee: $16.95 monthly.
Pay Service 1
Pay Units: 1.
Programming (via satellite): Cinemax.
Fee: $11.95 monthly.
Pay Service 2
Pay Units: 14.
Programming (via satellite): HBO.
Fee: $11.95 monthly.
Digital Pay Service 1
Pay Units: N.A.
Programming (via satellite): Cinemax (multiplexed); Encore (multiplexed); Flix; HBO (multiplexed); Showtime (multiplexed); Starz (multiplexed); Sundance Channel; The Movie Channel (multiplexed).
Fee: $12.95 monthly (HBO, Cinemax, Showtime/TMC/Flix/Sundance or Starz/Encore).
Video-On-Demand: No
Pay-Per-View
Hot Choice (delivered digitally); Fresh (delivered digitally); Spice: Xcess (delivered digitally); Club Jenna (delivered digitally).
Internet Service
Operational: Yes. Began: January 1, 2005.
Subscribers: 92.
Fee: $25.00 installation; $35.95-$39.95 monthly.
Telephone Service
None
Miles of Plant: 12.0 (coaxial); None (fiber optic). Homes passed: 285.
Manager & Chief Technician: Robert G. Fischer Jr.
Ownership: Nova Cablevision Inc. (MSO).

WELDON—Mediacom. Now served by FARMER CITY, IL [IL0231]. ICA: IL0295.

WEST CHICAGO—Comcast Cable. Now served by OAK BROOK, IL [IL0006]. ICA: IL0015.

WEST SALEM—Full Choice Communications, PO Box 9, 205 E Fire Ln, Cissna Park, IL 60924. Phone: 815-457-2659. Fax: 815-457-2735. ICA: IL0275.
TV Market Ranking: Outside TV Markets (WEST SALEM). Franchise award date: N.A. Franchise expiration date: N.A. Began: May 1, 1984.
Channel capacity: 41 (not 2-way capable). Channels available but not in use: 6.
Basic Service
Subscribers: 67.
Programming (received off-air): WEHT (ABC) Evansville; WEVV-TV (CBS, MNT) Evansville; WFIE (NBC) Evansville; WNIN (PBS) Evansville; WPXS (IND) Mount Vernon; WTVW (FOX) Evansville; WUSI-TV (PBS) Olney.
Programming (via satellite): ABC Family Channel; AMC; Animal Planet; Arts & Entertainment; Cartoon Network; CNN; C-SPAN; C-SPAN 2; Discovery Channel; Disney Channel; ESPN; ESPN 2; Headline News; HGTV; INSP; Lifetime; Nickelodeon; QVC; TBS Superstation; The Learning Channel; Travel Channel; Trinity Broadcasting Network; Turner Network TV; USA Network; Weather Channel; WGN America.
Fee: $22.95 monthly.
Pay Service 1
Pay Units: 158.
Programming (via satellite): Showtime; The Movie Channel.
Fee: $11.00 monthly (each).
Video-On-Demand: No
Internet Service
Operational: No.
Telephone Service
None
Miles of Plant: 10.0 (coaxial); None (fiber optic). Homes passed: 484.
Manager: Joe Young.
City fee: 3% of gross.
Ownership: Park TV & Electronics Inc. (MSO).

WEST UNION—Formerly served by Longview Communications. No longer in operation. ICA: IL0619.

WESTERN SPRINGS—Comcast Cable. Now served by CHICAGO (southern suburbs), IL [IL0008]. ICA: IL0043.

WESTVILLE—Charter Communications, 1209 N State St, Westville, IL 61883-1129. Phones: 217-267-3196; 636-207-7044 (St Louis office). Fax: 217-267-7650. Web Site: http://www.charter.com. Also serves Belgium, Catlin, Georgetown, Hegeler, Home Gardens & Tilton. ICA: IL0079.
TV Market Ranking: 64 (Belgium, Catlin, Georgetown, Hegeler, Home Gardens, Tilton, WESTVILLE). Franchise award date: N.A. Franchise expiration date: N.A. Began: December 27, 1965.
Channel capacity: N.A. Channels available but not in use: N.A.
Basic Service
Subscribers: 5,511.
Programming (received off-air): WAND (NBC) Decatur; WBUI (CW) Decatur; WCCU (FOX) Urbana; WCIA (CBS) Champaign; WICD (ABC) Champaign; WILL-TV (PBS) Urbana; WRTV (ABC) Indianapolis; WTHI-TV (CBS) Terre Haute; WTTV (CW) Bloomington; WTWO (NBC) Terre Haute; allband FM.
Programming (via satellite): G4; TV Guide Network; WGN America.
Current originations: Public Access.
Fee: $29.99 installation.
Expanded Basic Service 1
Subscribers: N.A.
Programming (via satellite): ABC Family Channel; AMC; AmericanLife TV Network; Animal Planet; Arts & Entertainment; Bravo; Cartoon Network; CNBC; CNN; Comedy Central; Country Music TV; C-SPAN; C-SPAN 2; Discovery Channel; Disney Channel; E! Entertainment Television; ESPN; ESPN 2; Eternal Word TV Network; FitTV; Food Network; Fox News Channel; FX; Golf Channel; Hallmark Channel; Headline News; HGTV; History Channel; Home Shopping Network; ION Television; Lifetime; MSNBC; MTV; National Geographic Channel; Nickelodeon; Outdoor Channel; Oxygen; QVC; SoapNet;

Speed Channel; Spike TV; Syfy; TBS Superstation; The Learning Channel; Toon Disney; Travel Channel; Trinity Broadcasting Network; truTV; Turner Classic Movies; Turner Network TV; TV Land; USA Network; Versus; VH1; WE tv; Weather Channel.
Fee: $49.99 monthly.

Digital Basic Service
Subscribers: 1,449.
Programming (via satellite): BBC America; Bio; Discovery Digital Networks; Do-It-Yourself; GAS; History Channel International; Independent Film Channel; Lifetime Movie Network; MTV Networks Digital Suite; Music Choice; Nick Jr.; Nick Too; NickToons TV; Sundance Channel; TV Guide Interactive Inc.
Fee: $49.95 monthly.

Digital Pay Service 1
Pay Units: 557.
Programming (via satellite): Cinemax (multiplexed); Encore (multiplexed); Flix; HBO (multiplexed); Showtime (multiplexed); Starz (multiplexed); The Movie Channel (multiplexed).
Fee: $2.95 monthly (Encore), $8.95 monthly (Cinemax or Showtime), $10.95 monthly (HBO).

Video-On-Demand: Yes

Pay-Per-View
iN DEMAND (delivered digitally); NHL Center Ice/MLB Extra Innings (delivered digitally); Hot Choice (delivered digitally); Playboy TV (delivered digitally); Fresh (delivered digitally); Shorteez (delivered digitally).

Internet Service
Operational: Yes. Began: July 1, 2001.
Subscribers: 1,195.
Broadband Service: Charter Pipeline.
Fee: $50.00 installation; $29.99 monthly.

Telephone Service
Digital: Operational

Miles of Plant: 125.0 (coaxial); 31.0 (fiber optic). Homes passed: 8,076. Total homes in franchised area: 8,076.
Vice President & General Manager: Steve Trippe. Operations Director: Dave Miller. Plant Manager: Kevin Goetz. Chief Technician: Frank Lemezis. Marketing Director: Beverly Wall.
City fee: 3% of gross (Catlin & Georgetown).
Ownership: Charter Communications Inc. (MSO).

WHITE HEATH—Full Choice Communications, PO Box 9, 205 E Fire Ln, Cissna Park, IL 60924. Phone: 815-457-2659. Fax: 815-457-2735. Also serves Monticello (unincorporated areas), Piatt County (eastern portion) & Seymour (village). ICA: IL0642.
TV Market Ranking: 64 (Monticello (unincorporated areas), Piatt County (eastern portion), Seymour (village), WHITE HEATH). Franchise award date: N.A. Franchise expiration date: N.A. Began: N.A.
Channel capacity: N.A. Channels available but not in use: N.A.

Basic Service
Subscribers: 36.
Programming (received off-air): WAND (NBC) Decatur; WBUI (CW) Decatur; WCCU (FOX) Urbana; WCIA (CBS) Champaign; WICD (ABC) Champaign; WILL-TV (PBS) Urbana.
Programming (via satellite): ABC Family Channel; AMC; Animal Planet; Arts & Entertainment; CNN; Comedy Central; Country Music TV; C-SPAN; Discovery Channel; Disney Channel; E! Entertainment Television; ESPN; ESPN 2; Fox News Channel; Headline News; History Channel; Lifetime; MSNBC; Nickelodeon; QVC; Speed Channel; Spike TV; TBS Superstation; The Learning Channel; Trinity Broadcasting Network; Turner Network TV; USA Network; Weather Channel; WGN America.
Fee: $33.95 monthly.

Pay Service 1
Pay Units: N.A.
Programming (via satellite): Cinemax; HBO; Showtime; The Movie Channel.
Fee: $8.95 monthly (TMC), $10.95 monthly (Cinemax or Showtime), $12.95 monthly (HBO).

Video-On-Demand: No

Internet Service
Operational: No.

Telephone Service
None

Miles of Plant: 4.0 (coaxial); None (fiber optic). Homes passed: 400.
Manager: Joe Young.
Ownership: Park TV & Electronics Inc. (MSO).

WILLIAMSFIELD—Mediacom. Now served by WYOMING, IL [IL0196]. ICA: IL0389.

WILLIAMSON COUNTY—Galaxy Cablevision, 7155 US Hwy 45 S, Carrier Mills, IL 62917. Phone: 618-994-2261. Fax: 618-994-2261. Web Site: http://www.galaxycable.com. Also serves Pittsburg. ICA: IL0372.
TV Market Ranking: 69 (Pittsburg, WILLIAMSON COUNTY (PORTIONS)). Franchise award date: N.A. Franchise expiration date: N.A. Began: June 1, 1986.
Channel capacity: 36 (not 2-way capable). Channels available but not in use: None.

Basic Service
Subscribers: 99.
Programming (received off-air): KBSI (FOX) Cape Girardeau; KFVS-TV (CBS, CW) Cape Girardeau; WDKA (MNT) Paducah; WPSD-TV (NBC) Paducah; WSIL-TV (ABC) Harrisburg; WSIU-TV (PBS) Carbondale; WTCT (IND) Marion.
Programming (via satellite): ABC Family Channel; AMC; Cartoon Network; CNN; Comedy Central; Discovery Channel; Disney Channel; E! Entertainment Television; Encore; ESPN; ESPN 2; Fox News Channel; Fuse; FX; Great American Country; Headline News; HGTV; History Channel; Home Shopping Network; Lifetime; Outdoor Channel; TBS Superstation; The Learning Channel; Turner Classic Movies; Turner Network TV; USA Network; Weather Channel; WGN America.
Fee: $30.00 installation; $40.20 monthly.

Pay Service 1
Pay Units: N.A.
Programming (via satellite): HBO; Starz.

Internet Service
Operational: No.

Telephone Service
None

Miles of Plant: 32.0 (coaxial); None (fiber optic). Homes passed: 592.
State Manager: Ward Webb. Technical Manager: Audie Murphy. Customer Service Manager: Malynda Walker. Engineer: John Stewart.
Ownership: Galaxy Cable Inc. (MSO).

WILLIAMSVILLE—Greene County Partners Inc., PO Box 200, 100 Redbud Rd, Virginia, IL 62691. Phones: 800-274-5789; 217-452-7725. Fax: 217-452-7797. E-mail: solutions@casscomm.com. Web Site: http://www.casscomm.com. Also serves Athens, Lake Petersburg, Menard County, Petersburg, Riverton & Sherman. ICA: IL0244.
TV Market Ranking: 64 (Athens, Lake Petersburg, Menard County, Petersburg, Riverton, Sherman, WILLIAMSVILLE). Franchise award date: N.A. Franchise expiration date: N.A. Began: April 1, 1980.
Channel capacity: 83 (operating 2-way). Channels available but not in use: None.

Basic Service
Subscribers: 3,809.
Programming (received off-air): WAND (NBC) Decatur; WBUI (CW) Decatur; WCFN (MNT) Springfield; WCIA (CBS) Champaign; WICS (ABC) Springfield; WILL-TV (PBS) Urbana; WRSP-TV (FOX) Springfield; WSEC (PBS) Jacksonville.
Programming (via satellite): ABC Family Channel; AMC; AmericanLife TV Network; Animal Planet; Arts & Entertainment; Bravo; Cartoon Network; CNBC; CNN; Comedy Central; Country Music TV; C-SPAN; C-SPAN 2; Discovery Channel; Disney Channel; E! Entertainment Television; ESPN; ESPN 2; ESPN Classic Sports; ESPNews; Eternal Word TV Network; Food Network; Fox Movie Channel; Fox News Channel; Fox Sports Net Midwest; FX; Golf Channel; Great American Country; Headline News; HGTV; History Channel; Home Shopping Network; Lifetime; MSNBC; MTV; National Geographic Channel; Nickelodeon; Outdoor Channel; QVC; ShopNBC; Spike TV; Syfy; TBS Superstation; The Learning Channel; Travel Channel; Trinity Broadcasting Network; truTV; Turner Classic Movies; Turner Network TV; TV Guide Network; TV Land; USA Network; VH1; WE tv; Weather Channel; WGN America.
Fee: $45.00 installation; $49.95 monthly; $2.00 converter; $25.00 additional installation.

Digital Basic Service
Subscribers: 543.
Programming (via satellite): BBC America; Discovery Digital Networks; DMX Music; Fox College Sports Atlantic; Fox College Sports Central; Fox College Sports Pacific; Fox Soccer; G4; GSN; Halogen Network; Independent Film Channel; National Geographic Channel; Nick Jr.; NickToons TV; Speed Channel; Versus; VH1 Classic; VH1 Country.
Fee: $11.95 monthly.

Pay Service 1
Pay Units: N.A.
Programming (via satellite): Cinemax; Encore; HBO.
Fee: $40.00 installation; $4.95 monthly (Encore), $10.95 monthly (Cinemax), $11.95 monthly (HBO).

Digital Pay Service 1
Pay Units: 1,761 Includes all pay subs.
Programming (via satellite): Cinemax; Encore (multiplexed); HBO (multiplexed); Showtime (multiplexed); Starz (multiplexed); The Movie Channel (multiplexed).

Video-On-Demand: No

Pay-Per-View
iN DEMAND (delivered digitally); Fresh (delivered digitally); Playboy TV (delivered digitally); Hot Choice (delivered digitally).

Internet Service
Operational: Yes. Began: June 1, 1999.
Subscribers: 3,096.
Broadband Service: Netlink.
Fee: $30.00-$99.00 installation; $29.95-$99.95 monthly.

Telephone Service
Digital: Operational
Subscribers: 349.

Miles of Plant: 147.0 (coaxial); 37.0 (fiber optic). Homes passed: 4,657.
General Manager: Chad Winters. Chief Technician: Lance Allen. Marketing Director: Erynn Snedeker.
Ownership: Green County Partners Inc. (MSO).

WILLOW HILL TWP.—Formerly served by Advanced Technologies & Technical Resources Inc. No longer in operation. ICA: IL0605.

WILMINGTON—Comcast Cable. Now served by OAK BROOK, IL [IL0006]. ICA: IL0099.

WILSONVILLE—Mediacom, PO Box 288, 4290 Blue Stem Rd, Charleston, IL 61920. Phones: 217-348-5533; 309-274-4500. Fax: 217-345-7074. Web Site: http://www.mediacomcable.com. ICA: IL0359.
TV Market Ranking: Outside TV Markets (WILSONVILLE). Franchise award date: N.A. Franchise expiration date: N.A. Began: November 3, 1983.
Channel capacity: N.A. Channels available but not in use: N.A.

Basic Service
Subscribers: 74.
Programming (received off-air): KDNL-TV (ABC) St. Louis; KETC (PBS) St. Louis; KMOV (CBS) St. Louis; KPLR-TV (CW) St. Louis; KSDK (NBC) St. Louis; KTVI (FOX) St. Louis.
Programming (via satellite): ABC Family Channel; Arts & Entertainment; CNN; Country Music TV; Discovery Channel; ESPN; ESPN 2; Lifetime; Nickelodeon; QVC; Spike TV; TBS Superstation; Trinity Broadcasting Network; Turner Network TV; USA Network; WGN America.
Fee: $45.00 installation; $45.95 monthly.

Pay Service 1
Pay Units: 34.
Programming (via satellite): Cinemax; HBO.
Fee: $11.95 monthly (Cinemax), $12.99 monthly (HBO).

Video-On-Demand: No

Internet Service
Operational: No.

Telephone Service
None

Miles of Plant: 7.0 (coaxial); None (fiber optic). Homes passed: 227.
Area Operations Director: Todd Acker. Technical Operations Manager: Jerry Ferguson.
City fee: 3% of gross.
Ownership: Mediacom LLC (MSO).

WINCHESTER—Crystal Broadband Networks, PO Box 180336, Chicago, LA 60618. Phones: 877-319-0328; 630-206-0447. E-mail: info@crystalbn.com. Web Site: http://crystalbn.com. ICA: IL0241.
TV Market Ranking: Outside TV Markets (WINCHESTER). Franchise award date: N.A. Franchise expiration date: N.A. Began: March 1, 1981.
Channel capacity: 36 (not 2-way capable). Channels available but not in use: None.

Basic Service
Subscribers: 371.
Programming (received off-air): KDNL-TV (ABC) St. Louis; KETC (PBS) St. Louis; KHQA-TV (ABC, CBS) Hannibal; KPLR-TV (CW) St. Louis; KSDK (NBC) St. Louis; KTVI (FOX) St. Louis; WGEM-TV (CW, NBC) Quincy; WICS (ABC) Springfield; WRSP-TV (FOX) Springfield; WSEC (PBS) Jacksonville.
Programming (via satellite): Home Shopping Network; WGN America.
Fee: $29.95 installation; $19.95 monthly.

Expanded Basic Service 1
Subscribers: N.A.
Programming (received off-air): WTJR (IND) Quincy.
Programming (via satellite): ABC Family Channel; AMC; Arts & Entertainment; CNN; Discovery Channel; Disney Channel; ESPN; Fox Sports Net Midwest; Great American Country; History Channel; Lifetime; MTV; Nickelodeon; Syfy; TBS Superstation; Trinity Broadcasting Network; Turner Network TV; USA Network.
Fee: $22.00 monthly.
Pay Service 1
Pay Units: 77.
Programming (via satellite): Cinemax; HBO; Showtime; The Movie Channel.
Fee: $25.00 installation; $9.49 monthly (Cinemax), $13.49 monthly (HBO, Showtime or TMC).
Video-On-Demand: No
Internet Service
Operational: Yes.
Telephone Service
Digital: Operational
Miles of Plant: 10.0 (coaxial); None (fiber optic). Homes passed: 890.
General Manager: Nidhin Johnson. Program Manager: Shawn Smith.
Ownership: Crystal Broadband Networks (MSO).

WINDSOR—Mediacom. Now served by NEOGA, IL [IL0249]. ICA: IL0271.

WINSLOW—Mediacom. Now served by LENA, IL [IL0223]. ICA: IL0606.

WOLF LAKE—Formerly served by CableDirect. No longer in operation. ICA: IL0607.

WOODLAND HEIGHTS—Tel-Star Cablevision Inc., 1295 Lourdes Rd, Metamora, IL 61548-7710. Phones: 888-842-0258; 309-383-2677. Fax: 309-383-2657. E-mail: cdecker@telstar-online.net. Web Site: http://www.telstar-online.net. ICA: IL0448.
TV Market Ranking: 83 (WOODLAND HEIGHTS). Franchise award date: July 1, 1989. Franchise expiration date: N.A. Began: July 11, 1989.
Channel capacity: 37 (operating 2-way). Channels available but not in use: 1.
Basic Service
Subscribers: 25.
Programming (received off-air): WAOE (MNT) Peoria; WEEK-TV (NBC) Peoria; WHOI (ABC, CW) Peoria; WMBD-TV (CBS) Peoria; WTVP (PBS) Peoria; WYZZ-TV (FOX) Bloomington.
Programming (via satellite): ABC Family Channel; AMC; Animal Planet; Arts & Entertainment; CNN; Country Music TV; Discovery Channel; Disney Channel; ESPN; ESPN 2; Food Network; Hallmark Channel; HGTV; History Channel; Lifetime; MSNBC; National Geographic Channel; Nickelodeon; QVC; Speed Channel; Spike TV; Syfy; TBS Superstation; The Learning Channel; Travel Channel; Turner Network TV; USA Network; Weather Channel; WGN America.
Current originations: Public Access.
Fee: $49.95 installation; $28.95 monthly; $2.95 converter.
Pay Service 1
Pay Units: 4.
Programming (via satellite): HBO.
Fee: $10.95 monthly.
Video-On-Demand: No
Internet Service
Operational: Yes.
Subscribers: 56.
Broadband Service: Tel-Star High Speed Internet.
Fee: $44.95 monthly; $5.00 modem lease.
Telephone Service
Digital: Operational
Fee: $24.95-$54.95 monthly
Miles of Plant: 4.0 (coaxial); None (fiber optic). Homes passed: 80. Total homes in franchised area: 80.
General Manager: John Gregory. Network Operations Manager: Chris Decker. Customer Service Manager: Patti Sanders.
Ownership: Tel-Star Cablevision Inc. (MSO).

WOODLAWN—Charter Communications, 5111 Lake Terrace NE, Mount Vernon, IL 62864-9666. Phones: 636-207-7044 (St. Louis office); 618-242-9512. Fax: 618-242-4156. Web Site: http://www.charter.com. Also serves Addieville, Ashley, Beaucoup, Jefferson County & Mount Vernon. ICA: IL0067.
TV Market Ranking: 69 (Jefferson County (portions)); Below 100 (Addieville, Ashley, Beaucoup, Mount Vernon, WOODLAWN, Jefferson County (portions)). Franchise award date: N.A. Franchise expiration date: N.A. Began: September 1, 1964.
Channel capacity: N.A. Channels available but not in use: N.A.
Basic Service
Subscribers: 6,366.
Programming (received off-air): KBSI (FOX) Cape Girardeau; KFVS-TV (CBS, CW) Cape Girardeau; KMOV (CBS) St. Louis; KPLR-TV (CW) St. Louis; KSDK (NBC) St. Louis; KTVI (FOX) St. Louis; WPXS (IND) Mount Vernon; WSIL-TV (ABC) Harrisburg; WSIU-TV (PBS) Carbondale; WTCT (IND) Marion; 1 FM.
Programming (via satellite): C-SPAN; C-SPAN 2; E! Entertainment Television; Home Shopping Network; INSP; Product Information Network; QVC; TBS Superstation; TV Guide Network; Weather Channel; WGN America.
Fee: $29.99 installation; $17.45 monthly.
Expanded Basic Service 1
Subscribers: 5,632.
Programming (via satellite): ABC Family Channel; AMC; Animal Planet; Arts & Entertainment; BET Networks; Bravo; Cartoon Network; CNBC; CNN; Comedy Central; Country Music TV; Discovery Channel; Disney Channel; ESPN; ESPN 2; Eternal Word TV Network; Food Network; Fox News Channel; Fox Sports Net Midwest; FX; G4; Golf Channel; GSN; Hallmark Channel; Headline News; HGTV; History Channel; Lifetime; MSNBC; MTV; National Geographic Channel; Nickelodeon; Oxygen; SoapNet; Speed Channel; Spike TV; Syfy; The Learning Channel; Toon Disney; Travel Channel; truTV; Turner Network TV; TV Land; USA Network; Versus; VH1.
Fee: $49.99 monthly.
Digital Basic Service
Subscribers: 2,769.
Programming (via satellite): AmericanLife TV Network; BBC America; Bio; Bloomberg Television; Discovery Digital Networks; DMX Music; ESPN Classic Sports; ESPNews; Fox Movie Channel; Fox Sports World; GAS; Halogen Network; History Channel International; Independent Film Channel; Lifetime Movie Network; MTV Networks Digital Suite; MuchMusic Network; Nick Jr.; Outdoor Channel; Ovation; Style Network; Sundance Channel; Trinity Broadcasting Network; Turner Classic Movies; WE tv.
Fee: $10.00 monthly.
Digital Pay Service 1
Pay Units: 753.
Programming (via satellite): Cinemax (multiplexed).
Fee: $8.95 monthly.
Digital Pay Service 2
Pay Units: 1,935.
Programming (via satellite): HBO (multiplexed).
Fee: $9.95 monthly.
Digital Pay Service 3
Pay Units: 485.
Programming (via satellite): Encore (multiplexed); Starz (multiplexed).
Fee: $7.95 monthly.
Digital Pay Service 4
Pay Units: 617.
Programming (via satellite): Showtime (multiplexed); The Movie Channel (multiplexed).
Fee: $9.95 monthly.
Video-On-Demand: No
Pay-Per-View
Addressable homes: 2,500.
iN DEMAND (delivered digitally); Playboy TV (delivered digitally); Fresh (delivered digitally); Shorteez (delivered digitally); sports (delivered digitally).
Internet Service
Operational: Yes.
Subscribers: 3,100.
Broadband Service: Charter Pipeline.
Fee: $29.99 monthly; $5.00 modem lease; $99.99 modem purchase.
Telephone Service
Digital: Operational
Fee: $29.99 monthly
Miles of Plant: 474.0 (coaxial); 18.0 (fiber optic). Homes passed: 12,172. Miles of plant (coax) includes Salem & Okawville
Vice President & General Manager: Steve Trippe. Operations Director: Dave Miller. Chief Technician: Eddie Prior. Marketing Director: Beverly Wall.
City fee: 3% of gross.
Ownership: Charter Communications Inc. (MSO).

WOODLAWN—Charter Communications. Now served by WOODLAWN, IL [IL0067]. ICA: IL0256.

WOODSTOCK—Comcast Cable. Now served by SCHAUMBURG, IL [IL0036]. ICA: IL0608.

WORDEN—Madison Communications. Now served by STAUNTON, IL [IL0171]. ICA: IL0312.

WYOMING—Mediacom, 3900 26th Ave, Moline, IL 61265. Phone: 309-797-2580. Fax: 309-797-2414. Web Site: http://www.mediacomcable.com. Also serves Bradford, Toulon & Williamsfield. ICA: IL0196.
TV Market Ranking: 60 (Williamsfield); 83 (Bradford, Toulon, WYOMING). Franchise award date: N.A. Franchise expiration date: N.A. Began: October 1, 1982.
Channel capacity: 134 (operating 2-way). Channels available but not in use: None.
Basic Service
Subscribers: 1,104.
Programming (received off-air): KLJB (CW, FOX) Davenport; KWQC-TV (NBC) Davenport; WAOE (MNT) Peoria; WEEK-TV (NBC) Peoria; WHBF-TV (CBS) Rock Island; WHOI (ABC, CW) Peoria; WMBD-TV (CBS) Peoria; WQAD-TV (ABC) Moline; WTVP (PBS) Peoria; WYZZ-TV (FOX) Bloomington.
Programming (via satellite): WGN America.
Fee: $45.00 installation; $20.95 monthly.
Digital Basic Service
Subscribers: N.A.
Programming (received off-air): WEEK-TV (NBC) Peoria; WHOI (ABC, CW) Peoria; WMBD-TV (CBS) Peoria; WTVP (PBS) Peoria; WYZZ-TV (FOX) Bloomington.
Programming (via satellite): ABC News Now; AmericanLife TV Network; BBC America; Bio; Bloomberg Television; CCTV-9 (CCTV International); Discovery Health Channel; Discovery Kids Channel; Discovery Military Channel; Discovery Planet Green; ESPN 2 HD; ESPN HD; ESPN U; ESPNews; FitTV; Fox Movie Channel; Fox Reality Channel; Fox Soccer; Fuel TV; Fuse; G4; Golf Channel; GSN; History Channel International; ID Investigation Discovery; Independent Film Channel; ION Life; Lifetime Movie Network; Lifetime Real Women; MTV Hits; MTV2; Music Choice; National Geographic Channel; Nick Jr.; NickToons TV; Outdoor Channel; Qubo; ReelzChannel; RFD-TV; Science Channel; Sleuth; Style Network; Sundance Channel; TeenNick; Turner Classic Movies; TVG Network; VH1 Classic.
Fee: $9.00 monthly.
Digital Expanded Basic Service
Subscribers: N.A.
Programming (via satellite): College Sports Television; Fox College Sports Atlantic; Fox College Sports Central; Fox College Sports Pacific; Gol TV; Tennis Channel; The Sportsman Channel.
Fee: $6.95 monthly.
Digital Expanded Basic Service 2
Subscribers: N.A.
Programming (via satellite): Discovery HD Theater; HDNet; HDNet Movies; Universal HD.
Fee: $3.95 monthly.
Digital Pay Service 1
Pay Units: N.A.
Programming (via satellite): Cinemax (multiplexed); Encore (multiplexed); Flix; HBO (multiplexed); HBO HD; Showtime (multiplexed); Showtime HD; Starz (multiplexed); Starz HDTV; Sundance Channel; The Movie Channel (multiplexed); The Movie Channel HD.
Fee: $11.95 monthly (HBO, Cinemax, Starz/Encore or Showtime/TMC).
Video-On-Demand: No
Pay-Per-View
ESPN (delivered digitally); Playboy TV (delivered digitally); Ten Clips (delivered digitally).
Internet Service
Operational: Yes.
Broadband Service: Mediacom High Speed Internet.
Fee: $59.95 installation; $45.95 monthly.
Telephone Service
Digital: Operational
Fee: $39.95 installation; $39.95 monthly
Homes passed: 2,304. Miles of plant (coax & fiber) included in Moline
Regional Vice President: Cari Fenzel. Area Manager: Don DeMay. Engineering Director: Mitch Carlson. Technical Operations Manager: Chris Toalson. Marketing Director: Greg Evans.
City fee: 3% of gross.
Ownership: Mediacom LLC (MSO).

XENIA—Wabash Independent Networks, PO Box 719, 113 Hagen Dr, Flora, IL 62839. Phone: 618-665-9946. Fax: 618-665-3400. E-mail: winita@wabash.net. Web Site: http://www.wabash.net. ICA: IL0373.

TV Market Ranking: Below 100 (XENIA). Franchise award date: N.A. Franchise expiration date: N.A. Began: March 15, 1983.
Channel capacity: N.A. Channels available but not in use: N.A.

Basic Service
Subscribers: 133.
Programming (received off-air): KFVS-TV (CBS, CW) Cape Girardeau; KMOV (CBS) St. Louis; KPLR-TV (CW) St. Louis; KSDK (NBC) St. Louis; WEHT (ABC) Evansville; WFIE (NBC) Evansville; WSIL-TV (ABC) Harrisburg; WSIU-TV (PBS) Carbondale; WTHI-TV (CBS) Terre Haute; WTVW (FOX) Evansville; WTWO (NBC) Terre Haute.
Programming (via satellite): C-SPAN; C-SPAN 2; Eternal Word TV Network; Home Shopping Network; ION Television; QVC; ShopNBC; TBS Superstation; Trinity Broadcasting Network; Weather Channel; WGN America.
Fee: $19.95 monthly.

Expanded Basic Service 1
Subscribers: N.A.
Programming (via satellite): ABC Family Channel; AMC; Animal Planet; Arts & Entertainment; Big Ten Network; Boomerang; Cartoon Network; CNN; Comedy Central; Country Music TV; Discovery Channel; Disney Channel; Do-It-Yourself; E! Entertainment Television; ESPN; ESPN 2; ESPN Classic Sports; FamilyNet; Food Network; Fox News Channel; Fox Sports Net; FX; G4; Gospel Music Channel; Hallmark Channel; Halogen Network; Headline News; History Channel; Lifetime; MSNBC; MTV; National Geographic Channel; Nickelodeon; Outdoor Channel; Oxygen; Spike TV; The Learning Channel; Travel Channel; truTV; Turner Classic Movies; Turner Network TV; TV Land; USA Network; VH1.
Fee: $19.00 monthly.

Digital Basic Service
Subscribers: N.A.
Programming (via satellite): BBC America; Bio; Bloomberg Television; Bravo; CMT Pure Country; Current; Discovery Health Channel; Discovery Home Channel; Discovery Kids Channel; Discovery Military Channel; DMX Music; ESPN 2; ESPN Classic Sports; ESPNews; FitTV; Flix; Fox Movie Channel; Fox Soccer; FSN Digital Atlantic; FSN Digital Central; FSN Digital Pacific; Fuse; G4; Golf Channel; Gospel Music Channel; Great American Country; GSN; Halogen Network; HGTV; History Channel International; ID Investigation Discovery; Independent Film Channel; Lifetime Movie Network; MTV Hits; MTV2; National Geographic Channel; Nick Jr.; Outdoor Channel; Ovation; RFD-TV; Science Channel; Sleuth; SoapNet; Speed Channel; Style Network; Syfy; TeenNick; The Word Network; Toon Disney; Trinity Broadcasting Network; Turner Classic Movies; Versus; VH1 Classic; VH1 Soul; WE tv.
Fee: $15.00 monthly.

Pay Service 1
Pay Units: 23.
Programming (via satellite): HBO; Showtime; The Movie Channel.
Fee: $15.00 installation; $11.95 monthly (TMC), $12.95 monthly (Showtime), $13.95 monthly (HBO).

Digital Pay Service 1
Pay Units: N.A.
Programming (via satellite): Cinemax (multiplexed); Encore (multiplexed); Flix; HBO (multiplexed); Showtime (multiplexed); Starz (multiplexed); The Movie Channel (multiplexed).
Fee: $11.95 monthly (Cinemax or Starz/Encore), $12.95 monthly (Showtime/TMC/Flix), $13.95 monthly (HBO).

Pay-Per-View
Club Jenna (delivered digitally); Fresh (delivered digitally); Spice: Xcess (delivered digitally); Playboy TV (delivered digitally).

Internet Service
Operational: Yes.
Broadband Service: In-house.
Fee: $35.00-$50.00 monthly.

Telephone Service
None
Miles of Plant: 7.0 (coaxial); None (fiber optic). Homes passed: 200.
General Manager: Dave Grahn. Assistant General Manager: Jeff Williams. Marketing Director: Carol Oestreich. TV/Video Administrator: Don Ross. Controller: Tanya Wells.
Ownership: Wabash Independent Networks (MSO).

ZEIGLER—Mediacom, 90 Main St, Benton, KY 42025-1132. Phones: 417-875-5560 (Springfield regional office); 270-527-9939. Fax: 270-527-0813. Web Site: http://www.mediacomcable.com. Also serves Alto Pass, Blairsville, Bush, Cambria, Cobden, Dowell, Elkville, Franklin County, Hurst, Jackson County (portions), Mound City, Mounds, Perry County, Pulaski County (portions), Royalton & Williamson County. ICA: IL0123.
TV Market Ranking: 69 (Alto Pass, Blairsville, Bush, Cambria, Cobden, Franklin County, Hurst, Jackson County (portions), Mound City, Mounds, Pulaski County (portions), Royalton, Williamson County, ZEIGLER); Below 100 (Dowell, Elkville, Perry County (portions), Jackson County (portions)); Outside TV Markets (Perry County (portions), Jackson County (portions)). Franchise award date: N.A. Franchise expiration date: N.A. Began: January 1, 1982.
Channel capacity: N.A. Channels available but not in use: N.A.

Basic Service
Subscribers: 2,951.
Programming (received off-air): KBSI (FOX) Cape Girardeau; KFVS-TV (CBS, CW) Cape Girardeau; WDKA (MNT) Paducah; WPSD-TV (NBC) Paducah; WPXS (IND) Mount Vernon; WQWQ-LP (CW) Paducah; WSIL-TV (ABC) Harrisburg; WSIU-TV (PBS) Carbondale; WTCT (IND) Marion.
Programming (via satellite): ABC Family Channel; C-SPAN; TV Guide Network; WGN America.
Fee: $36.95 installation; $19.22 monthly.

Expanded Basic Service 1
Subscribers: N.A.
Programming (via satellite): AMC; Animal Planet; Arts & Entertainment; BET Networks; Bravo; Cartoon Network; CNBC; CNN; Comedy Central; Country Music TV; C-SPAN 2; Discovery Channel; Disney Channel; E! Entertainment Television; ESPN; ESPN 2; FitTV; Food Network; Fox News Channel; Fox Sports Net Midwest; FX; Great American Country; GRTV Network; Hallmark Channel; Headline News; HGTV; History Channel; Home Shopping Network; INSP; Lifetime; MSNBC; MTV; Nickelodeon; Outdoor Channel; QVC; ShopNBC; SoapNet; Speed Channel; Spike TV; Syfy; TBS Superstation; The Learning Channel; Travel Channel; Trinity Broadcasting Network; Turner Network TV; TV Land; USA Network; VH1; WE tv; Weather Channel.

Digital Basic Service
Subscribers: N.A.
Programming (via satellite): BBC America; Bio; Bloomberg News Radio; Discovery Health Channel; Discovery Home Channel; Discovery Kids Channel; Discovery Times Channel; DMX Music; Fox Movie Channel; Fox Soccer; Fuse; G4; GAS; Golf Channel; History Channel International; Independent Film Channel; Lifetime Movie Network; MTV Networks Digital Suite; National Geographic Channel; Nick Jr.; NickToons TV; Science Television; Style Network; Trio; Turner Classic Movies; Versus.

Digital Pay Service 1
Pay Units: N.A.
Programming (via satellite): Cinemax (multiplexed); Encore (multiplexed); Flix; HBO; Showtime (multiplexed); Starz (multiplexed); Sundance Channel; The Movie Channel (multiplexed).

Video-On-Demand: Yes

Internet Service
Operational: Yes.
Broadband Service: Mediacom High Speed Internet.

Telephone Service
Digital: Operational
Miles of Plant: 116.0 (coaxial); None (fiber optic). Homes passed: 5,142.
Regional Vice President: Bill Copeland. General Manager: Dale Haney. Regional Technical Operations Director: Alan Freedman. Technical Operations Manager: Jeff Brown. Marketing Director: Will Kuebler. Marketing Manager: Melanie Westerman.
City fee: 3% of gross.
Ownership: Mediacom LLC (MSO).

INDIANA

Total Systems: **143**
Total Communities Served: **727**
Franchises Not Yet Operating: **0**
Applications Pending: **0**
Communities with Applications: **0**
Number of Basic Subscribers: **1,422,829**
Number of Expanded Basic Subscribers: **373,353**
Number of Pay Units: **101,499**

Top 100 Markets Represented: Indianapolis-Bloomington (16); Cincinnati, OH-Newport, KY (17); Louisville, KY (38); Chicago (3); Dayton-Kettering, OH (41); Cape Girardeau, MO-Paducah, KY-Harrisburg, IL (69); South Bend-Elkhart (80); Fort Wayne-Roanoke (82); Evansville (86).

For a list of cable communities in this section, see the Cable Community Index located in the back of Cable Volume 2.
For explanation of terms used in cable system listings, see p. D-11.

AKRON—Comcast Cable. Now served by SOUTH BEND, IN [IN0005]. ICA: IN0170.

ALLEN COUNTY—Mediacom. Now served by KENDALLVILLE, IN [IN0066]. ICA: IN0087.

AMBOY—Formerly served by CableDirect. No longer in operation. ICA: IN0222.

ANDERSON—Comcast Cable, 5330 E 65th St, Indianapolis, IN 46220. Phone: 317-275-6370. Fax: 317-275-6340. Web Site: http://www.comcast.com. Also serves Alexandria, Blountsville, Cadiz, Carthage, Chesterfield, Dunreith, Edgewood, Elwood, Greensboro, Henry County (portions), Huntsville, Knightstown, Lewisville, Losantville, Madison County (portions), Markleville, Middletown, Modoc, Moonville, Mooreland, Mount Summit, New Castle, Orestes, Pendleton, Rush County (portions), Spiceland, Springport, Straughn, Tipton County (portions) & Wayne County (northwestern portion). ICA: IN0012.

TV Market Ranking: 16 (ANDERSON, Carthage, Edgewood, Henry County (portions) (portions), Huntsville, Knightstown, Madison County (portions), Markleville, Pendleton, Rush County (portions) (portions)); Below 100 (Alexandria, Blountsville, Cadiz, Chesterfield, Dunreith, Elwood, Greensboro, Lewisville, Losantville, Middletown, Modoc, Moonville, Mooreland, Mount Summit, New Castle, Orestes, Spiceland, Springport, Straughn, Sulphur Springs, Tipton County (portions), Wayne County (northwestern portion), Henry County (portions) (portions), Madison County (portions), Rush County (portions) (portions)). Franchise award date: January 12, 1967. Franchise expiration date: N.A. Began: March 28, 1972.

Channel capacity: N.A. Channels available but not in use: N.A.

Basic Service

Subscribers: 120,000 Includes Hartford City, Noblesville, Portland, Richmond, Winchester, & Fort Recovery (village) OH.

Programming (received off-air): WFYI (PBS) Indianapolis; WHMB-TV (IND) Indianapolis; WIPB (PBS) Muncie; WISH-TV (CBS) Indianapolis; WNDY-TV (MNT) Marion; WRTV (ABC) Indianapolis; WTHR (NBC) Indianapolis; WTTV (CW) Bloomington; WXIN (FOX) Indianapolis.

Programming (via satellite): C-SPAN; C-SPAN 2; Home Shopping Network; QVC; Trinity Broadcasting Network; WGN America.

Planned originations: Public Access.

Fee: $1.19 converter.

Expanded Basic Service 1

Subscribers: N.A.

Programming (via satellite): ABC Family Channel; AMC; Animal Planet; Arts & Entertainment; BET Networks; Bravo; Cartoon Network; CNBC; CNN; Comedy Central; Country Music TV; Discovery Channel; Disney Channel; E! Entertainment Television; ESPN; ESPN 2; Eternal Word TV Network; Food Network; Fox News Channel; Fox Sports Net Midwest; Headline News; HGTV; History Channel; Lifetime; MSNBC; MTV; Nickelodeon; Oxygen; Speed Channel; Spike TV; Syfy; TBS Superstation; The Learning Channel; Travel Channel; Turner Network TV; TV Guide Network; TV Land; USA Network; VH1; Weather Channel.

Fee: $51.74 monthly.

Digital Basic Service

Subscribers: 6,918.

Programming (via satellite): BBC America; Bio; Bloomberg Television; C-SPAN 3; Discovery Digital Networks; DMX Music; Do-It-Yourself; Encore; ESPN Classic Sports; ESPNews; Fox Sports World; G4; GAS; Golf Channel; GSN; History Channel International; Independent Film Channel; INSP; Lifetime Movie Network; MTV2; National Geographic Channel; Nick Jr.; Nick Too; Ovation; SoapNet; Style Network; Sundance Channel; Toon Disney; truTV; Turner Classic Movies; Versus; WE tv.

Fee: $17.00 monthly.

Digital Pay Service 1

Pay Units: N.A.

Programming (via satellite): Cinemax (multiplexed); Flix; HBO (multiplexed); Showtime (multiplexed); Starz (multiplexed); The Movie Channel (multiplexed).

Fee: $10.00 monthly (Cinemax or Starz), $13.00 monthly (HBO or Showtime/TMC).

Video-On-Demand: Yes

Pay-Per-View

Addressable homes: 6,918.

iN DEMAND, Fee: $3.99, Addressable: Yes; Playboy TV (delivered digitally); Fresh (delivered digitally); iN DEMAND (delivered digitally).

Internet Service

Operational: Yes.

Subscribers: 3,008.

Broadband Service: Comcast High Speed Internet.

Fee: $99.95 installation; $44.95 monthly; $15.00 modem lease; $99.95 modem purchase.

Telephone Service

Digital: Operational

Fee: $39.95 monthly

Miles of Plant: 1,173.0 (coaxial); None (fiber optic). Homes passed: 61,781.

Regional Vice President: Scott Tenney. Regional Vice President, Technical Operations: Max Woolsey. Regional Vice President, Marketing: Aaron Geisel. Marketing Manager: Marci Hefley. Regional Vice President, Communications: Mark Apple.

City fee: 5% of gross.

Ownership: Comcast Cable Communications Inc. (MSO).

ANDERSON—Formerly served by Broadcast Cable Inc. No longer in operation. ICA: IN0344.

ANDREWS—Longview Communications, 12007 Sunrise Valley Dr, Ste 375, Reston, VA 20191. Phones: 866-611-6565 (Customer service); 703-476-9101. Fax: 703-476-9107. Web Site: http://www.longviewcomm.com. ICA: IN0223.

TV Market Ranking: 82 (ANDREWS). Franchise award date: N.A. Franchise expiration date: N.A. Began: November 1, 1986.

Channel capacity: 31 (not 2-way capable). Channels available but not in use: 12.

Basic Service

Subscribers: 24.

Programming (received off-air): WANE-TV (CBS) Fort Wayne; WFFT-TV (FOX) Fort Wayne; WFWA (PBS) Fort Wayne; WISE-TV (MNT, NBC) Fort Wayne; WNDY-TV (MNT) Marion; WPTA (ABC, CW) Fort Wayne; WTHR (NBC) Indianapolis; WTTK (IND) Kokomo.

Programming (via satellite): 3 Angels Broadcasting Network; QVC; Weather Channel.

Fee: $39.90 installation; $16.98 monthly.

Expanded Basic Service 1

Subscribers: N.A.

Programming (via satellite): AMC; Arts & Entertainment; CNN; Discovery Channel; ESPN; Headline News; Lifetime; TBS Superstation; Turner Network TV.

Fee: $16.97 monthly.

Video-On-Demand: No

Internet Service

Operational: No.

Telephone Service

None

Miles of Plant: 7.0 (coaxial); None (fiber optic). Homes passed: 519.

President: John Long. Senior Vice President: Marc W. Cohen. General Manager: Brandon Dickey. Technical Manager: Steve Boss.

Ownership: Longview Communications (MSO).

ANGOLA—Mediacom, 109 E 5th St, Ste A, Auburn, IN 46706. Phones: 260-927-3015; 260-665-3035 (Angola office). Fax: 260-347-4433. Web Site: http://www.mediacomcable.com. Also serves Clear Lake, Fremont, Hamilton, Pleasant Lake & Steuben County (portions). ICA: IN0034.

TV Market Ranking: 82 (Hamilton, Steuben County (portions) (portions)); Below 100 (ANGOLA, Clear Lake, Fremont, Pleasant Lake, Steuben County (portions) (portions)). Franchise award date: N.A. Franchise expiration date: N.A. Began: September 1, 1966.

Channel capacity: 83 (operating 2-way). Channels available but not in use: 21.

Basic Service

Subscribers: 5,780.

Programming (received off-air): WANE-TV (CBS) Fort Wayne; WFFT-TV (FOX) Fort Wayne; WFWA (PBS) Fort Wayne; WHME-TV (IND) South Bend; WINM (IND) Angola; WISE-TV (MNT, NBC) Fort Wayne; WNIT (PBS) South Bend; WPTA (ABC, CW) Fort Wayne; 20 FMs.

Programming (via satellite): ABC Family Channel; AMC; Animal Planet; Arts & Entertainment; Bravo!; Cartoon Network; CNBC; CNN; Comedy Central; Country Music TV; C-SPAN; Discovery Channel; Disney Channel; E! Entertainment Television; ESPN; ESPN 2; Food Network; Fox News Channel; Fox Sports Net Midwest; FX; Hallmark Channel; Headline News; HGTV; History Channel; Home Shopping Network; Lifetime; MSNBC; MTV; Nickelodeon; QVC; Speed Channel; Spike TV; Syfy; TBS Superstation; The Learning Channel; Travel Channel; Trinity Broadcasting Network; Turner Network TV; TV Guide Network; TV Land; Univision; USA Network; VH1; WE tv; Weather Channel; WGN America.

Fee: $45.00 installation; $20.95 monthly.

Expanded Basic Service 1

Subscribers: 4,570.

Fee: $34.00 monthly.

Digital Basic Service

Subscribers: 812.

Programming (via satellite): AmericanLife TV Network; BBC America; Bio; Bloomberg Television; Canales N; Discovery Digital Networks; DMX Music; Fox Sports World; G4; Golf Channel; GSN; History Channel International; Independent Film Channel; Lifetime Movie Network; Style Network; Turner Classic Movies; Versus.

Fee: $9.00 monthly.

Digital Pay Service 1

Pay Units: N.A.

Programming (via satellite): Cinemax (multiplexed); Encore (multiplexed); HBO (multiplexed); Showtime (multiplexed); The Movie Channel (multiplexed).

Fee: $11.95 monthly (each).

Video-On-Demand: Yes

Pay-Per-View

Playboy TV (delivered digitally).

Internet Service

Operational: Yes.

Subscribers: 73.

Broadband Service: Mediacom High Speed Internet.

Fee: $59.95 installation; $40.95 monthly.

Telephone Service
Analog: Not Operational
Digital: Operational
Fee: $39.95 installation; $39.95 monthly
Homes passed: 11,515. Total homes in franchised area: 12,000.
Technical Operations Manager: Craig Grey. Chief Technician: Mike Parr. Operations Director: Joe Poffenberger.
City fee: None.
Ownership: Mediacom LLC (MSO).

ARGOS—Mediacom. Now served by NORTH WEBSTER, IN [IN0038]. ICA: IN0154.

ASHLEY—Formerly served by Longview Communications. No longer in operation. ICA: IN0225.

ATTICA—Comcast Cable, 5330 E 65th St, Indianapolis, IN 46220. Phone: 317-275-6370. Fax: 317-275-6340. Web Site: http://www.comcast.com. Also serves Benton County, Fountain County, Fowler, Warren County & Williamsport. ICA: IN0091.
TV Market Ranking: Below 100 (ATTICA, Benton County (portions), Fountain County (portions), Fowler, Warren County (portions), Williamsport); Outside TV Markets (Benton County (portions), Fountain County (portions), Warren County (portions)). Franchise award date: January 1, 1962. Franchise expiration date: N.A. Began: May 1, 1963.
Channel capacity: N.A. Channels available but not in use: N.A.
Basic Service
Subscribers: N.A. Included in Lafayette
Programming (received off-air): WFYI (PBS) Indianapolis; WHMB-TV (IND) Indianapolis; WILL-TV (PBS) Urbana; WLFI-TV (CBS) Lafayette; WNDY-TV (MNT) Marion; WRTV (ABC) Indianapolis; WTHR (NBC) Indianapolis; WTTV (CW) Bloomington; WXIN (FOX) Indianapolis; 1 FM.
Programming (via satellite): C-SPAN; C-SPAN 2; Hallmark Channel; Home Shopping Network; Iowa Communications Network; MarketConnect Network; QVC; Weatherscan; WGN America.
Current originations: Educational Access.
Fee: $13.55 monthly; $2.00 converter.
Expanded Basic Service 1
Subscribers: 85.
Programming (via satellite): ABC Family Channel; AMC; Animal Planet; Arts & Entertainment; BET Networks; Bravo; Cartoon Network; CNBC; CNN; Comedy Central; Country Music TV; Discovery Channel; Disney Channel; E! Entertainment Television; ESPN; ESPN 2; Eternal Word TV Network; Food Network; Fox News Channel; FX; Headline News; HGTV; History Channel; Lifetime; MSNBC; MTV; Nickelodeon; Spike TV; Syfy; TBS Superstation; The Learning Channel; Travel Channel; Turner Network TV; TV Guide Network; TV Land; USA Network; VH1; Weather Channel.
Fee: $30.00 monthly.
Digital Basic Service
Subscribers: N.A.
Programming (via satellite): BBC America; Bio; Bloomberg Television; Canales N; C-SPAN 3; Discovery Digital Networks; DMX Music; Do-It-Yourself; Encore (multiplexed); ESPN Classic Sports; ESPNews; Fox Sports World; G4; GAS; Golf Channel; GSN; Halogen Network; History Channel International; Independent Film Channel; Lifetime Movie Network; MTV2; National Geographic Channel; Nick Jr.; Nick Too; Ovation; SoapNet; Speed Channel; Style Network; Sundance Channel; Toon Disney; truTV; Turner Classic Movies; Versus; WE tv.
Fee: $17.00 monthly.
Digital Pay Service 1
Pay Units: N.A.
Programming (via satellite): Cinemax (multiplexed); Flix; HBO (multiplexed); Showtime (multiplexed); Starz (multiplexed); The Movie Channel (multiplexed).
Fee: $10.00 monthly (Cinemax or Starz), $13.00 monthly (HBO or Showtime/TMC/Flix).
Video-On-Demand: Yes
Pay-Per-View
iN DEMAND; Adult (delivered digitally); iN DEMAND (delivered digitally).
Internet Service
Operational: Yes. Began: September 1, 2002.
Broadband Service: Comcast High Speed Internet.
Fee: $99.95 installation; $44.95 monthly; $15.00 modem lease; $129.95 modem purchase.
Telephone Service
Analog: Not Operational
Digital: Operational
Fee: $39.95 monthly
Miles of Plant: 66.0 (coaxial); None (fiber optic). Homes passed: 2,390. Total homes in franchised area: 2,720.
Regional Vice President: Scott Tenney. Regional Vice President, Technical Operations: Max Woolsey. Regional Vice President, Marketing: Aaron Geisel. Regional Vice President, Communications: Mark Apple.
City fee: 2% of gross.
Ownership: Comcast Cable Communications Inc. (MSO).

AVILLA—Comcast Cable, 720 Taylor St, Fort Wayne, IN 46802-5144. Phones: 260-458-5103; 317-275-6370 (Indianapolis office). Fax: 260-458-5138. Web Site: http://www.comcast.com. Also serves Noble County (portions). ICA: IN0357.
TV Market Ranking: 82 (AVILLA); Below 100 (Noble County (portions)). Franchise award date: June 1, 1981. Franchise expiration date: N.A. Began: N.A.
Channel capacity: 41 (operating 2-way). Channels available but not in use: None.
Basic Service
Subscribers: N.A. Included in Indianapolis
Programming (received off-air): WANE-TV (CBS) Fort Wayne; WFFT-TV (FOX) Fort Wayne; WFWA (PBS) Fort Wayne; WINM (IND) Angola; WISE-TV (MNT, NBC) Fort Wayne; WPTA (ABC, CW) Fort Wayne.
Programming (via satellite): ABC Family Channel.
Fee: $50.99 installation.
Expanded Basic Service 1
Subscribers: 425.
Programming (via satellite): AMC; Arts & Entertainment; CNBC; CNN; Country Music TV; C-SPAN; Discovery Channel; Disney Channel; E! Entertainment Television; ESPN; ESPN 2; Eternal Word TV Network; Headline News; Lifetime; MTV; Nickelodeon; QVC; Spike TV; Syfy; TBS Superstation; Turner Network TV; USA Network; VH1; WGN America.
Fee: $39.98 monthly.
Pay Service 1
Pay Units: N.A.
Programming (via satellite): Cinemax; HBO; Showtime.
Fee: $15.95 monthly (each).
Internet Service
Operational: Yes.
Telephone Service
Digital: Operational
Miles of plant included in Fort Wayne
Regional Vice President: Scott Tenney. Technical Operations Director: Bennie Logan. Engineering Manager: Tom Struckholz. Vice President, Marketing: Aaron Geisel. Marketing Manager: Marci Hefley. Vice President, Communications: Mark Apple.
Ownership: Comcast Cable Communications Inc. (MSO).

BAINBRIDGE—Global Com Inc., 3410 S 7th St, Terre Haute, IN 47802. Phone: 866-382-2253. Fax: 812-235-5554. ICA: IN0205.
TV Market Ranking: Outside TV Markets (BAINBRIDGE). Franchise award date: June 9, 1984. Franchise expiration date: N.A. Began: N.A.
Channel capacity: 36 (not 2-way capable). Channels available but not in use: None.
Basic Service
Subscribers: 23.
Programming (received off-air): WCLJ-TV (TBN) Bloomington; WFYI (PBS) Indianapolis; WHMB-TV (IND) Indianapolis; WISH-TV (CBS) Indianapolis; WRTV (ABC) Indianapolis; WTHR (NBC) Indianapolis; WTTV (CW) Bloomington; WXIN (FOX) Indianapolis.
Programming (via satellite): Home Shopping Network; WGN America.
Fee: $61.50 installation; $12.16 monthly.
Expanded Basic Service 1
Subscribers: N.A.
Programming (via satellite): ABC Family Channel; AMC; Animal Planet; Arts & Entertainment; CNBC; CNN; Country Music TV; Discovery Channel; Disney Channel; ESPN; Fox Sports Net Midwest; FX; HGTV; Lifetime; MTV; Nickelodeon; Speed Channel; Spike TV; TBS Superstation; Turner Network TV; USA Network.
Fee: $18.91 monthly.
Pay Service 1
Pay Units: N.A.
Programming (via satellite): Cinemax; HBO.
Fee: $17.50 installation; $8.99 monthly (Cinemax), $12.99 monthly (HBO).
Video-On-Demand: No
Internet Service
Operational: No.
Telephone Service
None
Miles of Plant: 5.0 (coaxial); None (fiber optic). Homes passed: 272.
Quality Manager: John Van Sandt.
City fee: 3% of basic.
Ownership: Global Com Inc. (MSO).

BATESVILLE—Comcast Cable, 10778 Randall Ave, Aurora, IN 47001. Phones: 317-275-6370 (Indianapolis office); 812-926-2297. Fax: 812-926-1269. Web Site: http://www.comcast.com. Also serves Morris & Oldenburg. ICA: IN0078.
TV Market Ranking: Outside TV Markets (BATESVILLE, Morris, Oldenburg). Franchise award date: N.A. Franchise expiration date: N.A. Began: September 1, 1982.
Channel capacity: 80 (not 2-way capable). Channels available but not in use: 4.
Basic Service
Subscribers: N.A. Included in Indianapolis
Programming (received off-air): WCET (PBS) Cincinnati; WCPO-TV (ABC) Cincinnati; WKRC-TV (CBS, CW) Cincinnati; WLWT (NBC) Cincinnati; WRTV (ABC) Indianapolis; WSTR-TV (MNT) Cincinnati; WTTV (CW) Bloomington; WXIX-TV (FOX) Newport; allband FM.
Programming (via satellite): Bravo; C-SPAN; C-SPAN 2; Home Shopping Network; WGN America.
Fee: $50.99 installation.
Expanded Basic Service 1
Subscribers: 1,400.
Programming (via satellite): ABC Family Channel; Animal Planet; Arts & Entertainment; CNN; Country Music TV; Discovery Channel; Disney Channel; ESPN; ESPN 2; FX; Golf Channel; GSN; Headline News; History Channel; Lifetime; MSNBC; MTV; Nickelodeon; Speed Channel; Spike TV; Syfy; TBS Superstation; The Learning Channel; Toon Disney; Travel Channel; Turner Network TV; TV Land; USA Network; VH1; Weather Channel.
Fee: $35.98 monthly.
Pay Service 1
Pay Units: 91.
Programming (via satellite): Cinemax; HBO; Showtime; The Movie Channel.
Fee: $12.95 monthly (each).
Video-On-Demand: No
Pay-Per-View
iN DEMAND (delivered digitally), Fee: $3.99, Addressable: Yes; Adult (delivered digitally).
Internet Service
Operational: Yes.
Telephone Service
Digital: Operational
Miles of Plant: 40.0 (coaxial); None (fiber optic). Homes passed: 2,975. Total homes in franchised area: 2,975.
Regional Vice President: Scott Tenney. Technical Operations Director: Richard Ring. Marketing Director: Damon Miller.
City fee: 3% of gross.
Ownership: Comcast Cable Communications Inc. (MSO).

BEDFORD—Comcast Cable, 2450 S Henderson St, Bloomington, IN 47401-4540. Phone: 812-332-9486. Fax: 812-332-0129. Web Site: http://www.comcast.com. Also serves Avoca, Lawrence County (portions), Medora, Oolitic & Vallonia. ICA: IN0033.
TV Market Ranking: 16 (Avoca, BEDFORD, Lawrence County (portions), Medora, Oolitic, Vallonia). Franchise award date: September 20, 1965. Franchise expiration date: N.A. Began: December 31, 1966.
Channel capacity: 90 (operating 2-way). Channels available but not in use: N.A.
Basic Service
Subscribers: N.A. Included in Bloomington
Programming (received off-air): WAVE (NBC) Louisville; WCLJ-TV (TBN) Bloomington; WDRB (FOX) Louisville; WHAS-TV (ABC) Louisville; WHMB-TV (IND) Indianapolis; WIPX-TV (ION) Bloomington; WISH-TV (CBS) Indianapolis; WLKY-TV (CBS) Louisville; WNDY-TV (MNT) Marion; WRTV (ABC) Indianapolis; WTHI-TV (CBS) Terre Haute; WTHR (NBC) Indianapolis; WTIU (PBS) Bloomington; WTTV (CW) Bloomington; WXIN (FOX) Indianapolis; 21 FMs.
Programming (via satellite): ABC Family Channel; CNBC; CNN; Country Music TV; C-SPAN; Discovery Channel; Headline News; Lifetime; MTV; Nickelodeon; QVC; TBS Superstation; Turner Network TV; WGN America.
Fee: $24.99 installation; $.71 converter.
Expanded Basic Service 1
Subscribers: 5,467.
Programming (via satellite): AMC; Animal Planet; Arts & Entertainment; BET Networks; Cartoon Network; Comedy Central; C-SPAN 2; Disney Channel; E! Entertain-

ment Television; ESPN; Food Network; Fox News Channel; Fox Sports Net Midwest; FX; HGTV; History Channel; Home Shopping Network; LWS Local Weather Station; MSNBC; Spike TV; The Learning Channel; Travel Channel; TV Guide Network; TV Land; USA Network; VH1; Weather Channel.
Fee: $40.00 monthly.

Digital Basic Service
Subscribers: N.A.
Programming (via satellite): AmericanLife TV Network; BBC America; Bio; Bloomberg Television; Bravo; C-SPAN 3; Discovery Digital Networks; DMX Music; Do-It-Yourself; Encore; ESPN Classic Sports; ESPNews; Eternal Word TV Network; Fox Movie Channel; Fox Sports World; Fuse; G4; GAS; Golf Channel; GSN; Halogen Network; History Channel International; Independent Film Channel; Lifetime Movie Network; National Geographic Channel; Nick Jr.; Nick Too; SoapNet; Speed Channel; Style Network; Sundance Channel; Syfy; Toon Disney; truTV; Turner Classic Movies; Versus; WE tv.
Fee: $17.00 monthly.

Digital Pay Service 1
Pay Units: N.A.
Programming (via satellite): Cinemax (multiplexed); Flix; HBO (multiplexed); Showtime (multiplexed); Starz (multiplexed); The Movie Channel (multiplexed).
Fee: $10.00 monthly (Cinemax or Starz), $13.00 monthly (HBO or Showtime).

Video-On-Demand: Yes

Pay-Per-View
iN DEMAND (delivered digitally); Adult (delivered digitally); iN DEMAND.

Internet Service
Operational: Yes.
Broadband Service: Comcast High Speed Internet.
Fee: $99.95 installation; $44.95 monthly; $15.00 modem lease; $99.95 modem purchase.

Telephone Service
Digital: Operational
Miles of Plant: 103.0 (coaxial); None (fiber optic). Homes passed: 9,618. Total homes in franchised area: 9,618.
Area Director: Wendy Henry. Chief Technician: Jeff Harrington. Customer Service Manager: Jennifer Lane.
City fee: $25.00 annually.
Ownership: Comcast Cable Communications Inc. (MSO).

BICKNELL—Charter Communications. Now served by VINCENNES, IN [IN0035]. ICA: IN0092.

BIRDSEYE—Formerly served by CableDirect. No longer in operation. ICA: IN0319.

BLOOMFIELD—Insight Communications. Now served by LINTON, IN [IN0052]. ICA: IN0228.

BLOOMINGTON—Comcast Cable, 5330 E 65th St, Indianapolis, IN 46220. Phones: 317-275-6370 (Indianapolis regional office); 812-332-9486 (Customer service). Fax: 812-332-0129. Web Site: http://www.comcast.com. Also serves Brown County (western portion), Clear Creek, Ellettsville, Gosport, Green County (eastern portion), Lawrence County (northern portion), Lyons, Monroe County (portions), Owen County (portions), Smithville, Spencer, Stanford, Stinesville, Switz City & Unionville. ICA: IN0016.
TV Market Ranking: 16 (BLOOMINGTON, Brown County (western portion), Clear Creek, Ellettsville, Gosport, Green County (eastern portion), Lawrence County (northern portion), Lyons, Monroe County (portions), Owen County (portions), Smithville, Spencer, Stanford, Stinesville, Switz City, Unionville). Franchise award date: N.A. Franchise expiration date: N.A. Began: November 1, 1966.
Channel capacity: 100 (operating 2-way). Channels available but not in use: N.A.

Basic Service
Subscribers: 79,000 Includes Bedford, Columbus, Greencastle, Greensburg, Greenwood, Linton, Martinsville, & Seymour.
Programming (received off-air): WCLJ-TV (TBN) Bloomington; WHMB-TV (IND) Indianapolis; WIPX-TV (ION) Bloomington; WISH-TV (CBS) Indianapolis; WNDY-TV (MNT) Marion; WRTV (ABC) Indianapolis; WTHI-TV (CBS) Terre Haute; WTHR (NBC) Indianapolis; WTIU (PBS) Bloomington; WTTV (CW) Bloomington; WXIN (FOX) Indianapolis; 13 FMs.
Programming (via satellite): AMC; Animal Planet; CNN; C-SPAN; C-SPAN 2; Disney Channel; ESPN; ESPN 2; Headline News; Home Shopping Network; MTV; Nickelodeon; QVC; USA Network; WGN America.
Fee: $24.95 installation; $2.00 converter.

Expanded Basic Service 1
Subscribers: 20,000.
Programming (via satellite): ABC Family Channel; Arts & Entertainment; BET Networks; Cartoon Network; CNBC; Comedy Central; Country Music TV; Discovery Channel; E! Entertainment Television; Food Network; Fox News Channel; Fox Sports Net Midwest; FX; HGTV; History Channel; Lifetime; MSNBC; Spike TV; TBS Superstation; The Learning Channel; Travel Channel; Turner Network TV; TV Guide Network; TV Land; VH1; Weather Channel.
Fee: $40.00 monthly.

Digital Basic Service
Subscribers: N.A.
Programming (via satellite): AmericanLife TV Network; BBC America; Bio; Bloomberg Television; Bravo; C-SPAN 3; Discovery Digital Networks; DMX Music; Do-It-Yourself; Encore (multiplexed); ESPN Classic Sports; ESPNews; Eternal Word TV Network; Fox Movie Channel; Fox Sports World; Fuse; G4; GAS; Golf Channel; GSN; Halogen Network; History Channel International; Independent Film Channel; Lifetime Movie Network; National Geographic Channel; Nick Jr.; Nick Too; SoapNet; Speed Channel; Style Network; Sundance Channel; Syfy; Toon Disney; truTV; Turner Classic Movies; Versus; WE tv.
Fee: $17.00 monthly.

Digital Pay Service 1
Pay Units: N.A.
Programming (via satellite): Cinemax (multiplexed); Flix; HBO (multiplexed); Showtime (multiplexed); Starz (multiplexed); The Movie Channel (multiplexed).
Fee: $10.00 monthly (Cinemax or Starz), $13.00 monthly (HBO or Showtime/TMC).

Video-On-Demand: Yes

Pay-Per-View
iN DEMAND; iN DEMAND (delivered digitally).

Internet Service
Operational: Yes.
Broadband Service: Comcast High Speed Internet.
Fee: $99.95 installation; $44.95 monthly; $15.00 modem lease; $99.95 modem purchase.

Telephone Service
Digital: Operational
Miles of Plant: 631.0 (coaxial); None (fiber optic). Homes passed: 40,992.
Regional Vice President: Scott Tenney. Area Director: Wendy Henry. Chief Technician: Jeff Harrington. Human Resources Manager: Shirley Gibson. Customer Service Manager: Jennifer Lane.
City fee: 3% of gross.
Ownership: Comcast Cable Communications Inc. (MSO).

BLUFFTON—Mediacom, 109 E 5th St, Ste A, Auburn, IN 46706. Phone: 260-927-3015. Fax: 260-347-4433. Web Site: http://www.mediacomcable.com. Also serves Craigville, Decatur, Kingsland, Liberty Center, Monroe, Murray, Poneto, Tocsin, Uniondale, Vera Cruz & Wells County. ICA: IN0059.
TV Market Ranking: 82 (BLUFFTON, Craigville, Decatur, Kingsland, Liberty Center, Monroe, Murray, Poneto, Tocsin, Uniondale, Vera Cruz, Wells County). Franchise award date: January 1, 1975. Franchise expiration date: N.A. Began: February 1, 1976.
Channel capacity: 121 (operating 2-way). Channels available but not in use: None.

Basic Service
Subscribers: 7,590.
Programming (received off-air): WANE-TV (CBS) Fort Wayne; WFFT-TV (FOX) Fort Wayne; WFWA (PBS) Fort Wayne; WHME-TV (IND) South Bend; WINM (IND) Angola; WIPB (PBS) Muncie; WISE-TV (MNT, NBC) Fort Wayne; WPTA (ABC, CW) Fort Wayne; WTTK (IND) Kokomo; allband FM.
Programming (via satellite): Bravo; CW+; WGN America.
Current originations: Public Access.
Fee: $45.00 installation; $20.95 monthly; $2.75 converter.

Expanded Basic Service 1
Subscribers: 6,778.
Programming (via satellite): ABC Family Channel; AMC; Animal Planet; Arts & Entertainment; Cartoon Network; CNBC; CNN; Comedy Central; Country Music TV; C-SPAN; Discovery Channel; Disney Channel; E! Entertainment Television; ESPN; ESPN 2; Food Network; Fox News Channel; Fox Sports Net; FX; Hallmark Channel; Headline News; HGTV; History Channel; Home Shopping Network; Lifetime; MSNBC; MTV; MyNetworkTV Inc.; Nickelodeon; Product Information Network; QVC; Radar Channel; Speed Channel; Spike TV; Syfy; TBS Superstation; The Learning Channel; Travel Channel; Trinity Broadcasting Network; Turner Network TV; TV Land; Univision; USA Network; VH1; WE tv; Weather Channel.
Fee: $34.00 monthly.

Digital Basic Service
Subscribers: N.A.
Programming (received off-air): WANE-TV (CBS) Fort Wayne; WFFT-TV (FOX) Fort Wayne; WFWA (PBS) Fort Wayne; WPTA (ABC, CW) Fort Wayne.
Programming (via satellite): ABC News Now; AmericanLife TV Network; BBC America; Bio; Bloomberg Television; CBS College Sports Network; CCTV-9 (CCTV International); Cine Latino; CNN en Espanol; CNN HD; Discovery en Espanol; Discovery HD Theater; Discovery Health Channel; Discovery Home Channel; Discovery Kids Channel; Discovery Military Channel; Discovery Times Channel; ESPN 2 HD; ESPN HD; ESPN U; ESPNews; FitTV; Fox College Sports Atlantic; Fox College Sports Central; Fox College Sports Pacific; Fox Movie Channel; Fox Soccer; Fox Sports en Espanol; FSN HD; G4; Gol TV; Golf Channel; GSN; Halogen Network; HDNet; HDNet Movies; History Channel International; Independent Film Channel; ION Life; Lifetime Movie Network; MTV Hits; MTV Tres; MTV2; National Geographic Channel; Nick Jr.; NickToons TV; Outdoor Channel; ReelzChannel; Science Channel; Sleuth; Style Network; TBS in HD; TeenNick; Tennis Channel; The Sportsman Channel; Toon Disney en Espanol; Turner Classic Movies; Turner Network TV HD; TVE Internacional; TVG Network; Universal HD; Utilisima; Versus; VH1 Classic.
Fee: $9.00 monthly.

Digital Pay Service 1
Pay Units: N.A.
Programming (via satellite): Cinemax (multiplexed); Encore (multiplexed); Flix; HBO (multiplexed); HBO HD; Showtime (multiplexed); Showtime HD; Starz (multiplexed); Sundance Channel; The Movie Channel (multiplexed); The Movie Channel HD.
Fee: $11.95 monthly (HBO, Cinemax, Showtime/TMC or Starz/Encore).

Video-On-Demand: Yes

Pay-Per-View
Movies, Addressable: Yes; special events; iN DEMAND.

Internet Service
Operational: Yes.
Subscribers: 380.
Broadband Service: Mediacom High Speed Internet.
Fee: $40.95 monthly.

Telephone Service
Analog: Not Operational
Digital: Operational
Fee: $39.95 monthly
Miles of Plant: 262.0 (coaxial); 44.0 (fiber optic). Homes passed: 12,482.
Operations Director: Joe Poffenberger. Technical Operations Manager: Craig Grey.
Franchise fee: 3% of gross.
Ownership: Mediacom LLC (MSO).

BOONVILLE—Now served by EVANSVILLE, IN [IN0006]. ICA: IN0086.

BOSWELL—Indiana Communications, PO Box 617, Boswell, IN 47921. Phone: 888-610-1119. Web Site: http://www.indcomm.net. ICA: IN0229.
TV Market Ranking: Below 100 (BOSWELL). Franchise award date: N.A. Franchise expiration date: N.A. Began: N.A.
Channel capacity: 36 (not 2-way capable). Channels available but not in use: 22.

Basic Service
Subscribers: 64.
Programming (received off-air): WAND (NBC) Decatur; WCCU (FOX) Urbana; WCIA (CBS) Champaign; WHMB-TV (IND) Indianapolis; WILL-TV (PBS) Urbana; WLFI-TV (CBS) Lafayette; WRTV (ABC) Indianapolis; WTHR (NBC) Indianapolis; WTTV (CW) Bloomington; WXIN (FOX) Indianapolis.
Programming (via satellite): QVC; Trinity Broadcasting Network; Weather Channel.
Fee: $32.50 installation; $15.98 monthly.

Video-On-Demand: No

Internet Service
Operational: No.

Telephone Service
None
Miles of Plant: 5.0 (coaxial); None (fiber optic). Homes passed: 356. Total homes in franchised area: 356.
Manager: Joe Young.
Ownership: Park TV & Electronics Inc. (MSO).

BOURBON—Mediacom. Now served by NORTH WEBSTER, IN [IN0038]. ICA: IN0128.

BRAZIL—Avenue Broadband Communications, 2603 Hart St, Vincennes, IN 47591. Phones: 800-882-7185; 812-895-7676. Fax: 812-886-5017. Web Site: http://www.avenuebroadband.com. Also serves Clay County (north central portion), Lost Creek Twp. (northeastern portion), Seelyville, Staunton, Terre Haute City & Vigo County (portions). ICA: IN0027.
TV Market Ranking: Below 100 (BRAZIL, Clay County (north central portion), Lost Creek Twp. (northeastern portion), Seelyville, Staunton, Terre Haute City, Vigo County (portions)). Franchise award date: July 1, 1971. Franchise expiration date: N.A. Began: March 31, 1972.
Channel capacity: N.A. Channels available but not in use: N.A.

Basic Service
Subscribers: 6,520.
Programming (received off-air): WFXW (FOX) Terre Haute; WFYI (PBS) Indianapolis; WHMB-TV (IND) Indianapolis; WISH-TV (CBS) Indianapolis; WRTV (ABC) Indianapolis; WTHI-TV (CBS) Terre Haute; WTHR (NBC) Indianapolis; WTIU (PBS) Bloomington; WTTV (CW) Bloomington; WTWO (NBC) Terre Haute; 14 FMs.
Programming (via satellite): C-SPAN; Home Shopping Network; ION Television; QVC; WGN America.
Current originations: Educational Access.
Fee: $34.95 installation; $22.95 monthly; $2.75 converter.

Expanded Basic Service 1
Subscribers: N.A.
Programming (via satellite): ABC Family Channel; AMC; Animal Planet; Arts & Entertainment; BET Networks; Cartoon Network; CNBC; CNN; Comedy Central; Country Music TV; Discovery Channel; Disney Channel; E! Entertainment Television; ESPN; ESPN 2; Food Network; Fox News Channel; Fox Sports Net Midwest; FX; G4; Golf Channel; Headline News; HGTV; History Channel; Lifetime; MSNBC; MTV; Nickelodeon; Outdoor Channel; Oxygen; Speed Channel; Spike TV; Syfy; TBS Superstation; The Learning Channel; Toon Disney; truTV; Turner Network TV; TV Land; USA Network; VH1; Weather Channel.

Digital Basic Service
Subscribers: N.A.
Programming (via satellite): BBC America; Bio; Bloomberg Television; Discovery Digital Networks; Do-It-Yourself; Fox College Sports Atlantic; Fox College Sports Central; Fox College Sports Pacific; Fox Movie Channel; Fox Sports World; GAS; GSN; History Channel International; Lifetime Movie Network; MTV Networks Digital Suite; Music Choice; Nick Jr.; Nick Too; NickToons TV; Sundance Channel; TV Guide Interactive Inc.; WE tv.

Digital Pay Service 1
Pay Units: 548.
Programming (via satellite): Cinemax (multiplexed).
Fee: $14.00 installation; $8.00 monthly.

Digital Pay Service 2
Pay Units: 1,169.
Programming (via satellite): HBO (multiplexed).
Fee: $14.00 installation; $9.95 monthly.

Digital Pay Service 3
Pay Units: 315.
Programming (via satellite): The Movie Channel (multiplexed).
Fee: $14.00 installation; $7.00 monthly.

Digital Pay Service 4
Pay Units: 776.
Programming (via satellite): Showtime (multiplexed).
Fee: $14.00 installation; $7.00 monthly.

Digital Pay Service 5
Pay Units: N.A.
Programming (via satellite): Encore (multiplexed); Flix; Starz (multiplexed).

Video-On-Demand: No

Pay-Per-View
Playboy TV (delivered digitally); Fresh (delivered digitally); Shorteez (delivered digitally); iN DEMAND (delivered digitally); NHL Center Ice (delivered digitally); MLB Extra Innings (delivered digitally).

Internet Service
Operational: Yes.

Telephone Service
Digital: Operational
Miles of Plant: 250.0 (coaxial); 35.0 (fiber optic). Homes passed: 13,330. Total homes in franchised area: 19,513.
Chief Executive Officer: Steve Lowe. Vice President & General Manager: Mary Iafrate. Vice President, Engineering: Jeff Spence. System Engineer: Bart Cotter.
City fee: 5% of gross.
Ownership: Buford Media Group LLC (MSO).

BREMEN—Mediacom. Now served by NORTH WEBSTER, IN [IN0038]. ICA: IN0067.

BRISTOL—Comcast Cable. Now served by SOUTH BEND, IN [IN0005]. ICA: IN0231.

BROOKLYN—Formerly served by CableDirect. No longer in operation. ICA: IN0232.

BROOKVILLE—Comcast Cable, 10778 Randall Ave, Aurora, IN 47001. Phones: 317-275-6370 (Indianapolis office); 812-926-2297. Fax: 812-926-1269. Web Site: http://www.comcast.com. Also serves Franklin County. ICA: IN0108.
TV Market Ranking: 17 (BROOKVILLE, Franklin County (portions)); Below 100 (Franklin County (portions)); Outside TV Markets (Franklin County (portions)). Franchise award date: N.A. Franchise expiration date: N.A. Began: January 1, 1982.
Channel capacity: 90 (not 2-way capable). Channels available but not in use: 27.

Basic Service
Subscribers: N.A. Included in Indianapolis
Programming (received off-air): WCET (PBS) Cincinnati; WCPO-TV (ABC) Cincinnati; WKRC-TV (CBS, CW) Cincinnati; WLWT (NBC) Cincinnati; WPTD (PBS) Dayton; WPTO (PBS) Oxford; WSTR-TV (MNT) Cincinnati; WTTV (CW) Bloomington; WXIX-TV (FOX) Newport.
Programming (via satellite): C-SPAN; Home Shopping Network; Trinity Broadcasting Network; WGN America.
Fee: $50.99 installation; $11.74 monthly.

Expanded Basic Service 1
Subscribers: N.A.
Programming (via satellite): ABC Family Channel; AMC; Animal Planet; Arts & Entertainment; CNBC; CNN; Country Music TV; C-SPAN 2; Discovery Channel; Disney Channel; E! Entertainment Television; ESPN; ESPN 2; ESPNews; Eternal Word TV Network; Fox News Channel; FX; GSN; Hallmark Channel; Headline News; HGTV; History Channel; Lifetime; MSNBC; MTV; Nickelodeon; Spike TV; Syfy; TBS Superstation; The Learning Channel; Toon Disney; Travel Channel; Turner Network TV; TV Land; USA Network; Versus; VH1; Weather Channel.
Fee: $37.98 monthly.

Pay Service 1
Pay Units: 421.
Programming (via satellite): Cinemax; HBO; iN DEMAND; Showtime; The Movie Channel.
Fee: $12.95 monthly (each).

Video-On-Demand: No

Internet Service
Operational: Yes.

Telephone Service
Digital: Operational
Miles of Plant: 21.0 (coaxial); None (fiber optic). Homes passed: 1,520.
Regional Vice President: Scott Tenney. Technical Operations Director: Richard Ring.
Ownership: Comcast Cable Communications Inc. (MSO).

BROWNSTOWN—Comcast Cable, 2450 S Henderson St, Bloomington, IN 47401-4540. Phones: 812-275-6370 (Regional office); 812-332-9486. Fax: 812-332-0129. Web Site: http://www.comcast.com. ICA: IN0127.
TV Market Ranking: 16 (BROWNSTOWN). Franchise award date: November 1, 1981. Franchise expiration date: N.A. Began: August 13, 1982.
Channel capacity: N.A. Channels available but not in use: N.A.

Basic Service
Subscribers: N.A.
Programming (received off-air): WAVE (NBC) Louisville; WBKI-TV (CW) Campbellsville; WBNA (ION) Louisville; WDRB (FOX) Louisville; WHAS-TV (ABC) Louisville; WISH-TV (CBS) Indianapolis; WLKY-TV (CBS) Louisville; WMYO (MNT) Salem; WRTV (ABC) Indianapolis; WTHR (NBC) Indianapolis; WTIU (PBS) Bloomington; WTTV (CW) Bloomington; 1 FM.
Programming (via satellite): C-SPAN; C-SPAN 2; Home Shopping Network; QVC; Trinity Broadcasting Network; WGN America.
Current originations: Public Access.
Fee: $24.95 installation.

Expanded Basic Service 1
Subscribers: N.A.
Programming (via satellite): ABC Family Channel; AMC; Animal Planet; Arts & Entertainment; BET Networks; Bravo; Cartoon Network; CNBC; CNN; Comedy Central; Country Music TV; Discovery Channel; Disney Channel; E! Entertainment Television; ESPN; ESPN 2; Food Network; Fox News Channel; Fox Sports Net Midwest; FX; Hallmark Channel; Headline News; HGTV; History Channel; Lifetime; MSNBC; MTV; MTV2; Nickelodeon; Oxygen; SoapNet; Speed Channel; Spike TV; Syfy; TBS Superstation; The Learning Channel; Travel Channel; truTV; Turner Network TV; TV Land; USA Network; VH1; Weather Channel.
Fee: $40.00 monthly.

Digital Basic Service
Subscribers: N.A.
Programming (received off-air): WISH-TV (CBS) Indianapolis; WRTV (ABC) Indianapolis; WTHR (NBC) Indianapolis; WTIU (PBS) Bloomington; WTTV (CW) Bloomington.
Programming (via satellite): AmericanLife TV Network; BBC America; Bio; Bloomberg Television; CBS College Sports Network; CMT Pure Country; Cooking Channel; C-SPAN 3; Discovery Digital Networks; Discovery HD Theater; Do-It-Yourself; Encore (multiplexed); ESPN 2 HD; ESPN Classic Sports; ESPN HD; ESPN U; ESPNews; Eternal Word TV Network; Fox College Sports Atlantic; Fox College Sports Central; Fox College Sports Pacific; Fox Movie Channel; Fox Soccer; Fuse; G4; GAS; Golf Channel; Great American Country; GSN; Halogen Network; HDNet; HDNet Movies; History Channel International; HorseRacing TV; Independent Film Channel; Lifetime Movie Network; Lifetime Real Women; LOGO; MTV Networks Digital Suite; Music Choice; National Geographic Channel; NFL Network; Nick Jr.; Nick Too; NickToons TV; Outdoor Channel; Palladia; PBS Kids Sprout; Si TV; Style Network; Sundance Channel; Tennis Channel; Toon Disney; Turner Classic Movies; Turner Network TV HD; TVG Network; Universal HD; Versus; WE tv.
Fee: $17.00 monthly.

Digital Pay Service 1
Pay Units: N.A.
Programming (via satellite): Cinemax (multiplexed); Flix; HBO (multiplexed); HBO HD; Showtime (multiplexed); Showtime HD; Starz (multiplexed); The Movie Channel (multiplexed).
Fee: $10.00 monthly (Cinemax or Starz), $13.00 monthly (HBO or Showtime/TMC).

Video-On-Demand: No

Pay-Per-View
Fresh (delivered digitally); ESPN; iN DEMAND (delivered digitally).

Internet Service
Operational: Yes.
Broadband Service: Comcast High Speed Internet.
Fee: $99.95 installation; $44.95 monthly; $15.00 modem lease; $59.95 modem purchase.

Telephone Service
Digital: Operational
Miles of Plant: 24.0 (coaxial); None (fiber optic). Homes passed: 1,025. Total homes in franchised area: 1,200.
Regional Vice President: Scott Tenney. Area Director: Wendy Henry. Regional Vice President, Technical Operations: Max Woolsey. Regional Vice President, Marketing: Aaron Geisel. Regional Vice President, Communications: Mark Apple.
City fee: 3% of gross.
Ownership: Comcast Cable Communications Inc. (MSO).

BUTLER—Mediacom, 109 E 5th St, Ste A, Auburn, IN 46706. Phone: 260-927-3015. Fax: 260-927-4433. Web Site: http://www.mediacomcable.com. ICA: IN0359.
TV Market Ranking: 82 (BUTLER). Franchise award date: N.A. Franchise expiration date: N.A. Began: November 3, 1980.
Channel capacity: 134 (operating 2-way). Channels available but not in use: N.A.

Basic Service
Subscribers: 697.
Programming (received off-air): WANE-TV (CBS) Fort Wayne; WFFT-TV (FOX) Fort Wayne; WFWA (PBS) Fort Wayne; WHME-TV (IND) South Bend; WINM (IND) Angola; WISE-TV (MNT, NBC) Fort Wayne; WNIT (PBS) South Bend; WPTA (ABC, CW) Fort Wayne.

Programming (via satellite): WGN America.
Fee: $45.00 installation; $20.95 monthly.

Expanded Basic Service 1
Subscribers: 558.
Programming (via satellite): ABC Family Channel; AMC; Animal Planet; Arts & Entertainment; Bravo; Cartoon Network; CNBC; CNN; Comedy Central; Country Music TV; C-SPAN; Discovery Channel; Disney Channel; E! Entertainment Television; ESPN; ESPN 2; Food Network; Fox News Channel; Fox Sports Net; FX; Hallmark Channel; Headline News; HGTV; History Channel; Home Shopping Network; Lifetime; MSNBC; MTV; MyNetworkTV Inc.; Nickelodeon; Product Information Network; QVC; Speed Channel; Spike TV; Syfy; TBS Superstation; The Learning Channel; Travel Channel; Trinity Broadcasting Network; Turner Network TV; TV Guide Network; TV Land; Univision; USA Network; VH1; WE tv; Weather Channel.
Fee: $34.00 monthly.

Digital Basic Service
Subscribers: N.A.
Programming (received off-air): Discovery Kids Channel.
Programming (via satellite): AmericanLife TV Network; BBC America; Bio; Bloomberg Television; CBS College Sports Network; CCTV-9 (CCTV International); Discovery Health Channel; Discovery Home Channel; Discovery Military Channel; ESPN U; ESPNews; FitTV; Fox College Sports Atlantic; Fox College Sports Central; Fox College Sports Pacific; Fox Movie Channel; Fox Soccer; G4; Gol TV; Golf Channel; GSN; Halogen Network; History Channel International; ID Investigation Discovery; Independent Film Channel; Lifetime Movie Network; MTV Hits; MTV2; National Geographic Channel; Nick Jr.; NickToons TV; Outdoor Channel; Science Channel; Sleuth; Style Network; TeenNick; Tennis Channel; The Sportsman Channel; Turner Classic Movies; TVG Network; Versus; VH1 Classic.
Fee: $9.00 monthly.

Digital Pay Service 1
Pay Units: N.A.
Programming (via satellite): Cinemax (multiplexed); Encore (multiplexed); HBO (multiplexed); Showtime (multiplexed); Starz; The Movie Channel (multiplexed).
Fee: $11.95 monthly (HBO, Cinemax, Showtime/TMC or Starz/Encore).

Video-On-Demand: Yes

Internet Service
Operational: Yes.
Broadband Service: Mediacom High Speed Internet.
Fee: $40.95 monthly.

Telephone Service
Digital: Operational
Fee: $39.95 monthly

Miles of Plant: 13.0 (coaxial); None (fiber optic). Homes passed: 1,123.
Operations Director: Joe Poffenberger. Technical Operations Manager: Craig Grey.
City fee: None.
Ownership: Mediacom LLC (MSO).

CAMPBELLSBURG—Insight Communications. Now served by LOUISVILLE, KY [KY0001]. ICA: IN0233.

CARBON—Avenue Broadband Communications, 2603 Hart St, Vincennes, IN 47591. Phones: 800-882-7185; 812-895-7676. Fax: 812-886-5017. Web Site: http://www.avenuebroadband.com. ICA: IN0374.
TV Market Ranking: Below 100 (CARBON).
Channel capacity: N.A. Channels available but not in use: N.A.

Basic Service
Subscribers: N.A.
Programming (received off-air): WFXW (FOX) Terre Haute; WFYI (PBS) Indianapolis; WHMB-TV (IND) Indianapolis; WRTV (ABC) Indianapolis; WTHI-TV (CBS) Terre Haute; WTHR (NBC) Indianapolis; WTIU (PBS) Bloomington; WTTV (CW) Bloomington; WTWO (NBC) Terre Haute.
Programming (via satellite): C-SPAN; Home Shopping Network; ION Television; QVC; WGN America.
Current originations: Public Access.

Expanded Basic Service 1
Subscribers: N.A.
Programming (via satellite): ABC Family Channel; AMC; Animal Planet; Arts & Entertainment; BET Networks; Big Ten Network; Bravo; Cartoon Network; CNBC; CNN; Comedy Central; Country Music TV; Discovery Channel; Disney Channel; Disney XD; E! Entertainment Television; ESPN; ESPN 2; Food Network; Fox News Channel; Fox Sports Net Midwest; FX; G4; Golf Channel; Hallmark Channel; Headline News; HGTV; History Channel; Lifetime; MSNBC; MTV; National Geographic Channel; Nickelodeon; Outdoor Channel; Oxygen; SoapNet; Speed Channel; Spike TV; Syfy; TBS Superstation; The Learning Channel; Travel Channel; truTV; Turner Network TV; TV Land; USA Network; VH1; Weather Channel.

Digital Basic Service
Subscribers: N.A.
Programming (via satellite): BBC America; Bio; Bloomberg Television; Boomerang; CMT Pure Country; Discovery en Espanol; Discovery Health Channel; Discovery Kids Channel; Discovery Military Channel; Discovery Planet Green; DMX Music; Do-It-Yourself; ESPN U; Fox Business Channel; Fox Movie Channel; GSN; History Channel International; ID Investigation Discovery; Lifetime Movie Network; MTV Jams; MTV Tres; MTV2; mtvU; Nick Jr.; Nick Too; NickToons TV; PBS Kids Sprout; RFD-TV; Science Channel; Style Network; Sundance Channel; TeenNick; VH1 Classic; VH1 Soul; WE tv.

Digital Expanded Basic Service
Subscribers: N.A.
Programming (via satellite): Encore (multiplexed); Flix; Showtime (multiplexed); The Movie Channel.

Digital Expanded Basic Service 2
Subscribers: N.A.
Programming (via satellite): Fox College Sports Atlantic; Fox College Sports Central; Fox College Sports Pacific; Fox Soccer.

Digital Expanded Basic Service 3
Subscribers: N.A.
Programming (received off-air): WFYI (PBS) Indianapolis; WRTV (ABC) Indianapolis; WTHI-TV (CBS) Terre Haute; WTWO (NBC) Terre Haute.
Programming (via satellite): ABC Family HD; Animal Planet HD; Arts & Entertainment HD; Big Ten Network HD; Discovery Channel HD; Discovery HD Theater; Disney Channel HD; ESPN 2 HD; ESPN HD; Food Network HD; Fox News HD; FX HD; HDNet; HDNet Movies; HGTV HD; History Channel HD; Lifetime Movie Network HD; National Geographic Channel HD Network; Outdoor Channel 2 HD; Science Channel HD; Speed HD; Syfy HD; Travel Channel HD; Universal HD; USA Network HD.

Digital Pay Service 1
Pay Units: N.A.
Programming (via satellite): Cinemax (multiplexed); HBO (multiplexed); Starz (multiplexed); Starz HDTV.

Pay-Per-View
iN DEMAND (delivered digitally); Spice: Xcess (delivered digitally); Club Jenna (delivered digitally); Playboy TV (delivered digitally); Fresh (delivered digitally); Shorteez (delivered digitally).

Chief Executive Officer: Steve Lowe. Vice President & General Manager: Mary Iafrate. Vice President, Engineering: Jeff Spence. System Engineer: Bart Cotter.
Ownership: Buford Media Group LLC (MSO).

CARLISLE—Formerly served by Almega Cable. No longer in operation. ICA: IN0199.

CATARACT LAKE—Formerly served by Longview Communications. No longer in operation. ICA: IN0235.

CENTER POINT—Formerly served by CableDirect. No longer in operation. ICA: IN0236.

CENTERTON—Avenue Broadband Communications, 2603 Hart St, Vincennes, IN 47591. Phones: 800-882-7185; 812-895-7676. Fax: 812-886-5017. Web Site: http://www.avenuebroadband.com. Also serves Morgan County (northern portion). ICA: IN0367.
TV Market Ranking: 16 (CENTERTON, Morgan County (northern portion)).
Channel capacity: N.A. Channels available but not in use: N.A.

Basic Service
Subscribers: 917.
Programming (received off-air): WCLJ-TV (TBN) Bloomington; WFYI (PBS) Indianapolis; WIPX-TV (ION) Bloomington; WISH-TV (CBS) Indianapolis; WNDY-TV (MNT) Marion; WRTV (ABC) Indianapolis; WTHR (NBC) Indianapolis; WTTV (CW) Bloomington; WXIN (FOX) Indianapolis.
Programming (via satellite): QVC; TBS Superstation; WGN America.

Expanded Basic Service 1
Subscribers: 894.
Programming (received off-air): WREP-LD Martinsville.
Programming (via satellite): ABC Family Channel; AMC; Arts & Entertainment; CNN; Country Music TV; C-SPAN; Discovery Channel; Disney Channel; E! Entertainment Television; ESPN; ESPN 2; Fox Sports Net Midwest; FX; Headline News; History Channel; Home Shopping Network; Lifetime; MTV; Nickelodeon; Spike TV; Syfy; The Learning Channel; Turner Network TV; USA Network; VH1; Weather Channel.

Pay Service 1
Pay Units: N.A.
Programming (via satellite): Cinemax; HBO; Showtime.

Video-On-Demand: No

Internet Service
Operational: No.

Telephone Service
None

Miles of Plant: 92.0 (coaxial); None (fiber optic). Homes passed: 2,913.
Chief Executive Officer: Steve Lowe. Vice President & General Manager: Mary Iafrate. Vice President, Engineering: Jeff Spence. System Engineer: Bart Cotter.
Ownership: Buford Media Group LLC (MSO).

CHRISNEY—Formerly served by CableDirect. No longer in operation. ICA: IN0237.

CLAY CITY—Global Com Inc., 3410 S 7th St, Terre Haute, IN 47802. Phone: 866-382-2253. Fax: 812-235-5554. ICA: IN0174.
TV Market Ranking: 16 (CLAY CITY). Franchise award date: January 16, 1984. Franchise expiration date: N.A. Began: June 1, 1985.
Channel capacity: 36 (2-way capable). Channels available but not in use: 4.

Basic Service
Subscribers: 123.
Programming (received off-air): WFXW (FOX) Terre Haute; WRTV (ABC) Indianapolis; WTHI-TV (CBS) Terre Haute; WTTV (CW) Bloomington; WTWO (NBC) Terre Haute; WVUT (PBS) Vincennes.
Programming (via satellite): C-SPAN; Home Shopping Network; INSP; TBS Superstation; Trinity Broadcasting Network; Weather Channel; WGN America.
Fee: $61.50 installation; $13.20 monthly.

Expanded Basic Service 1
Subscribers: N.A.
Programming (via satellite): ABC Family Channel; AMC; Arts & Entertainment; CNBC; CNN; Discovery Channel; Disney Channel; ESPN; ESPN 2; Fox Sports Net Midwest; FX; History Channel; Lifetime; MTV; Nickelodeon; Speed Channel; Spike TV; Syfy; The Learning Channel; Turner Network TV; USA Network.
Fee: $21.11 monthly.

Pay Service 1
Pay Units: 118.
Programming (via satellite): Cinemax; Encore; HBO.
Fee: $3.99 monthly (Encore), $8.99 monthly (Cinemax), $12.99 monthly (HBO).

Video-On-Demand: No

Internet Service
Operational: No.

Telephone Service
None

Miles of Plant: 9.0 (coaxial); None (fiber optic). Homes passed: 523.
Quality Manager: John Van Sandt.
City fee: 3% of basic.
Ownership: Global Com Inc. (MSO).

CLEAR LAKE—Longview Communications. Now served by ANGOLA, IN [IN0034]. ICA: IN0239.

CLINTON—Avenue Broadband Communications, 2603 Hart St, Vincennes, IN 47591. Phones: 800-882-7185; 812-895-7676. Fax: 812-886-5017. Web Site: http://www.avenuebroadband.com. Also serves Fairview Park, Parke County (portions), Rosedale, Universal, Vermillion County (portions) & Vigo County (portions). ICA: IN0049.
TV Market Ranking: Below 100 (CLINTON, Fairview Park, Parke County (portions), Rosedale, Universal, Vermillion County (portions), Vigo County (portions)). Franchise award date: January 1, 1965. Franchise expiration date: N.A. Began: October 4, 1965.
Channel capacity: N.A. Channels available but not in use: N.A.

Basic Service
Subscribers: 4,003.
Programming (received off-air): WCIA (CBS) Champaign; WFXW (FOX) Terre Haute; WRTV (ABC) Indianapolis; WTHI-TV (CBS) Terre Haute; WTIU (PBS) Bloomington; WTTV (CW) Bloomington; WTWO (NBC) Terre Haute.

Programming (via satellite): ABC Family Channel; AMC; AmericanLife TV Network; Animal Planet; Arts & Entertainment; Cartoon Network; CNN; Comedy Central; Country Music TV; C-SPAN; C-SPAN 2; Discovery Channel; Disney Channel; Do-It-Yourself; ESPN; ESPN 2; ESPN Classic Sports; Food Network; Fox News Channel; Fox Sports Net; FX; Great American Country; Hallmark Channel; Headline News; HGTV; History Channel; INSP; Lifetime; MSNBC; MTV; National Geographic Channel; Nickelodeon; QVC; Spike TV; Syfy; TBS Superstation; The Learning Channel; Travel Channel; Turner Network TV; TV Land; USA Network; VH1; Weather Channel; WGN America.
Fee: $29.95 installation; $38.00 monthly; $10.00 additional installation.

Digital Basic Service
Subscribers: N.A.
Programming (via satellite): BBC America; Bio; Bloomberg Television; CMT Pure Country; Current; Discovery Health Channel; Discovery Kids Channel; Discovery Military Channel; Discovery Planet Green; DMX Music; ESPNews; Fox Movie Channel; Fox Soccer; G4; Golf Channel; GSN; History Channel International; ID Investigation Discovery; Lifetime Movie Network; MTV Jams; MTV2; Nick Jr.; NickToons TV; Outdoor Channel; Ovation; Science Channel; Sleuth; Speed Channel; Style Network; Sundance Channel; TeenNick; Turner Classic Movies; Versus; VH1 Classic; VH1 Soul.
Fee: $12.95 monthly.

Digital Pay Service 1
Pay Units: N.A.
Programming (via satellite): Cinemax (multiplexed); Encore (multiplexed); HBO (multiplexed); Showtime (multiplexed); Starz (multiplexed); The Movie Channel (multiplexed).
Fee: $8.35 monthly (Starz), $9.50 monthly (Cinemax), $11.00 monthly (HBO).

Video-On-Demand: No

Pay-Per-View
iN DEMAND (delivered digitally); Playboy TV (delivered digitally); Fresh (delivered digitally); Shorteez (delivered digitally).

Internet Service
Operational: Yes.
Broadband Service: Rapid High Speed Internet.
Fee: $29.95 installation; $39.95 monthly.

Telephone Service
None

Miles of Plant: 175.0 (coaxial); None (fiber optic). Homes passed: 14,430.
Chief Executive Officer: Steve Lowe. Vice President & General Manager: Mary lafrate. Vice President, Engineering: Jeff Spence. System Engineer: Bart Cotter.
Ownership: Buford Media Group LLC.

CLOVERDALE—Indiana Communications, PO Box 617, Boswell, IN 47921. Phone: 888-610-1119. Web Site: http://www.indcomm.net. ICA: IN0240.
TV Market Ranking: 16 (CLOVERDALE). Franchise award date: N.A. Franchise expiration date: N.A. Began: January 1, 1985.
Channel capacity: 38 (not 2-way capable). Channels available but not in use: None.

Basic Service
Subscribers: 168.
Programming (received off-air): WCLJ-TV (TBN) Bloomington; WFXW (FOX) Terre Haute; WFYI (PBS) Indianapolis; WIPX-TV (ION) Bloomington; WISH-TV (CBS) Indianapolis; WNDY-TV (MNT) Marion; WRTV (ABC) Indianapolis; WTHI-TV (CBS) Terre Haute; WTHR (NBC) Indianapolis; WTTV (CW) Bloomington; WTWO (NBC) Terre Haute; WXIN (FOX) Indianapolis.
Programming (via satellite): ABC Family Channel; AMC; Arts & Entertainment; CNN; Comedy Central; Country Music TV; C-SPAN; Discovery Channel; Disney Channel; E! Entertainment Television; ESPN; ESPN 2; Headline News; History Channel; Lifetime; Nickelodeon; QVC; Spike TV; TBS Superstation; The Learning Channel; Turner Network TV; USA Network; Weather Channel; WGN America.
Fee: $39.90 installation; $33.95 monthly.

Pay Service 1
Pay Units: N.A.
Programming (via satellite): Cinemax; HBO; Showtime; The Movie Channel.
Fee: $8.95 monthly (TMC), $10.95 monthly (Cinemax or Showtime), $12.95 monthly (HBO).

Video-On-Demand: No

Internet Service
Operational: No.

Telephone Service
None

Miles of Plant: 14.0 (coaxial); None (fiber optic). Homes passed: 918.
Manager: Joe Young.
City fee: 3% of gross.
Ownership: Park TV & Electronics Inc. (MSO).

COAL CITY—Formerly served by CableDirect. No longer in operation. ICA: IN0241.

COATESVILLE—Avenue Broadband Communications, 2603 Hart St, Vincennes, IN 47591. Phones: 800-882-7185; 812-895-7676. Fax: 812-886-5017. Web Site: http://www.avenuebroadband.com. Also serves Amo, Clayton, Hendricks County (southern portion) & Stilesville. ICA: IN0261.
TV Market Ranking: 16 (Amo, Clayton, COATESVILLE, Hendricks County (southern portion), Stilesville). Franchise award date: N.A. Franchise expiration date: N.A. Began: February 1, 1986.
Channel capacity: N.A. Channels available but not in use: N.A.

Basic Service
Subscribers: 482.
Programming (received off-air): WFYI (PBS) Indianapolis; WHMB-TV (IND) Indianapolis; WIPX-TV (ION) Bloomington; WISH-TV (CBS) Indianapolis; WNDY-TV (MNT) Marion; WRTV (ABC) Indianapolis; WTHR (NBC) Indianapolis; WTTV (CW) Bloomington; WXIN (FOX) Indianapolis.
Programming (via satellite): Home Shopping Network; QVC; WGN America.
Fee: $49.95 installation; $29.15 monthly.

Expanded Basic Service 1
Subscribers: N.A.
Programming (via satellite): ABC Family Channel; AMC; Animal Planet; Arts & Entertainment; CNBC; CNN; Country Music TV; C-SPAN; Discovery Channel; Disney Channel; E! Entertainment Television; ESPN; ESPN 2; Food Network; Fox News Channel; Fox Sports Net Midwest; FX; Headline News; HGTV; History Channel; Lifetime; MSNBC; MTV; Nickelodeon; SoapNet; Spike TV; Syfy; TBS Superstation; The Learning Channel; Toon Disney; Travel Channel; truTV; Turner Network TV; TV Land; USA Network; Versus; VH1; Weather Channel.

Pay Service 1
Pay Units: N.A.
Programming (via satellite): Cinemax; HBO; Showtime.
Fee: $40.00 installation; $9.95 monthly (each).

Video-On-Demand: No

Internet Service
Operational: No.

Telephone Service
None

Miles of Plant: 42.0 (coaxial); None (fiber optic). Homes passed: 1,706.
Chief Executive Officer: Steve Lowe. Vice President & General Manager: Mary lafrate. Vice President, Engineering: Jeff Spence. System Engineer: Bart Cotter.
Ownership: Buford Media Group LLC (MSO).

COLUMBUS—Comcast Cable, 10778 Randall Ave, Aurora, IN 47001. Phones: 317-275-6370 (Indianapolis office); 812-926-2297. Fax: 812-926-1269. Web Site: http://www.comcast.com. Also serves Bartholomew County, Clifford, Elizabethtown, Garden City, Hartsville, Jonesville, Newbern, Ogilville, Petersville, Rosstown, Taylorsville, Walesboro, Waynesville & Westport. ICA: IN0022.
TV Market Ranking: 16 (Bartholomew County (portions), COLUMBUS, Garden City, Jonesville, Ogilville, Rosstown, Taylorsville, Walesboro, Waynesville); Outside TV Markets (Clifford, Elizabethtown, Hartsville, Newbern, Petersville, Westport, Bartholomew County (portions)). Franchise award date: January 1, 1967. Franchise expiration date: N.A. Began: July 15, 1967.
Channel capacity: 80 (operating 2-way). Channels available but not in use: None.

Basic Service
Subscribers: N.A. Included in Bloomington
Programming (received off-air): WCLJ-TV (TBN) Bloomington; WFYI (PBS) Indianapolis; WHMB-TV (IND) Indianapolis; WIPX-TV (ION) Bloomington; WISH-TV (CBS) Indianapolis; WNDY-TV (MNT) Marion; WRTV (ABC) Indianapolis; WTHR (NBC) Indianapolis; WTIU (PBS) Bloomington; WTTV (CW) Bloomington; WXIN (FOX) Indianapolis.
Programming (via satellite): C-SPAN; QVC; TBS Superstation; WGN America.
Current originations: Government Access; Educational Access; Public Access.
Fee: $50.99 installation.

Expanded Basic Service 1
Subscribers: N.A.
Programming (via satellite): ABC Family Channel; AMC; Animal Planet; Arts & Entertainment; BET Networks; Bravo; Cartoon Network; CNBC; CNN; Comedy Central; Country Music TV; C-SPAN 2; Discovery Channel; Disney Channel; E! Entertainment Television; ESPN; ESPN 2; ESPN Classic Sports; ESPNews; Food Network; Fox News Channel; Fox Sports Net Midwest; FX; Golf Channel; GSN; Headline News; HGTV; History Channel; Home Shopping Network; Lifetime; LWS Local Weather Station; MSNBC; MTV; Nickelodeon; Speed Channel; Spike TV; Style Network; Syfy; The Learning Channel; Toon Disney; Travel Channel; truTV; Turner Classic Movies; Turner Network TV; TV Japan; TV Land; USA Network; Versus; VH1; Weather Channel.
Fee: $50.98 monthly.

Digital Basic Service
Subscribers: N.A.
Programming (via satellite): BBC America; Bio; Canales N; CBS College Sports Network; C-SPAN 3; Discovery Digital Networks; DMX Music; Encore (multiplexed); ESPNews; Flix; Fox College Sports Atlantic; Fox College Sports Central; Fox College Sports Pacific; Fox Soccer; G4; GAS; Gol TV; Hallmark Channel; History Channel International; MTV Networks Digital Suite; National Geographic Channel; NBA TV; NFL Network; Nick Jr.; Nick Too; NickToons TV; SoapNet; Sundance Channel (multiplexed); TVG Network; Weatherscan.
Fee: $14.95 monthly.

Digital Pay Service 1
Pay Units: N.A.
Programming (via satellite): Cinemax (multiplexed); HBO (multiplexed); Showtime (multiplexed); Starz (multiplexed); The Movie Channel (multiplexed); TV Japan.
Fee: $16.99 monthly (HBO, Cinemax, Starz, Showtime or TMC), $25.00 monthly (TV Japan).

Video-On-Demand: No

Pay-Per-View
iN DEMAND (delivered digitally); Hot Choice (delivered digitally); Playboy TV (delivered digitally); Fresh (delivered digitally); Shorteez (delivered digitally); Pleasure (delivered digitally); Sports PPV (delivered digitally); NBA TV (delivered digitally).

Internet Service
Operational: Yes.
Broadband Service: Comcast High Speed Internet.
Fee: $42.95 monthly; $15.00 modem lease; $99.95 modem purchase.

Telephone Service
Digital: Operational
Fee: $44.95 monthly

Miles of Plant: 333.0 (coaxial); None (fiber optic). Homes passed: 22,000.
Vice President: William (Rusty) Robertson. General Manager: Don Richey. Technical Operations Director: Richard Ring. Chief Technician: Mike Kesterman.
Ownership: Comcast Cable Communications Inc. (MSO).

CONNERSVILLE—Comcast Cable, 5330 E 65th St, Indianapolis, IN 46220. Phone: 317-275-6370. Fax: 317-275-6340. Web Site: http://www.comcast.com. Also serves Everton & Fayette County (portions). ICA: IN0040.
TV Market Ranking: Below 100 (CONNERSVILLE, Everton, Fayette County (portions)). Franchise award date: N.A. Franchise expiration date: N.A. Began: August 18, 1972.
Channel capacity: 100 (operating 2-way). Channels available but not in use: 26.

Basic Service
Subscribers: N.A. Included in Indianapolis
Programming (received off-air): WCPO-TV (ABC) Cincinnati; WFYI (PBS) Indianapolis; WHMB-TV (IND) Indianapolis; WIPX-TV (ION) Bloomington; WISH-TV (CBS) Indianapolis; WKRC-TV (CBS, CW) Cincinnati; WLWT (NBC) Cincinnati; WNDY-TV (MNT) Marion; WPTD (PBS) Dayton; WPTO (PBS) Oxford; WRTV (ABC) Indianapolis; WTTV (CW) Bloomington; WXIN (FOX) Indianapolis.
Programming (via satellite): C-SPAN; C-SPAN 2; The Comcast Network; Trinity Broadcasting Network; WGN America.
Fee: $31.99 installation.

Expanded Basic Service 1
Subscribers: N.A.
Programming (via satellite): ABC Family Channel; AMC; Animal Planet; Arts & Entertainment; Bravo; Cartoon Network; CNN; Comedy Central; Country Music TV; Discovery Channel; Disney Channel; E! Entertainment Television; ESPN; ESPN 2; ESPNews; Food Network; Fox News Channel; Fox Sports Net Midwest; FX; G4; Golf Channel; GSN; Hallmark Channel; Head-

line News; HGTV; History Channel; Home Shopping Network; Lifetime; MSNBC; MTV; Nickelodeon; Speed Channel; Spike TV; Syfy; TBS Superstation; The Learning Channel; Toon Disney; Travel Channel; truTV; Turner Network TV; TV Land; USA Network; Versus; VH1; Weather Channel.
Fee: $50.98 monthly.

Digital Basic Service
Subscribers: N.A.
Programming (via satellite): BBC America; Bio; Canales N; CMT Pure Country; Cooking Channel; C-SPAN 3; Current; Discovery Digital Networks; Do-It-Yourself; Encore; ESPNews; Flix; Fox Reality Channel; GAS; History Channel International; Lifetime Movie Network; LOGO; MoviePlex; MTV Networks Digital Suite; Music Choice; National Geographic Channel; Nick Jr.; Nick Too; NickToons TV; Oxygen; PBS Kids Sprout; SoapNet; Sundance Channel; Toon Disney; TV One.
Fee: $17.32 monthly.

Digital Pay Service 1
Pay Units: N.A.
Programming (via satellite): Cinemax (multiplexed); HBO (multiplexed); Playboy TV; Showtime (multiplexed); Starz (multiplexed); The Movie Channel (multiplexed).

Video-On-Demand: No

Pay-Per-View
Addressable homes: 1,610.
Sports PPV, Fee: $3.95, Addressable: Yes.

Internet Service
Operational: Yes.
Subscribers: 700.
Broadband Service: Comcast High Speed Internet.
Fee: $42.95 monthly; $15.00 modem lease; $99.95 modem purchase.

Telephone Service
Digital: Operational

Miles of Plant: 116.0 (coaxial); None (fiber optic). Additional miles planned: 4.0 (coaxial). Homes passed: 9,752.
Vice President & General Manager: William Robertson. Vice President, Technical Operations: Mark Woolsey. Vice President, Communications: Mark Apple. Marketing Director: Damian Miller.
City fee: None.
Ownership: Comcast Cable Communications Inc. (MSO).

CORUNNA—Formerly served by CableDirect. No longer in operation. ICA: IN0242.

COVINGTON—Comcast Cable, 5330 E 65th St, Indianapolis, IN 46220. Phone: 317-275-6370. Fax: 317-275-6340. Web Site: http://www.comcast.com. ICA: IN0124.
TV Market Ranking: Below 100 (COVINGTON). Franchise award date: N.A. Franchise expiration date: N.A. Began: September 1, 1965.
Channel capacity: 52 (operating 2-way). Channels available but not in use: 23.

Basic Service
Subscribers: N.A. Included in Indianapolis
Programming (received off-air): WCIA (CBS) Champaign; WHMB-TV (IND) Indianapolis; WILL-TV (PBS) Urbana; WISH-TV (CBS) Indianapolis; WLFI-TV (CBS) Lafayette; WRTV (ABC) Indianapolis; WTHR (NBC) Indianapolis; WTTV (CW) Bloomington; WTWO (NBC) Terre Haute; WXIN (FOX) Indianapolis.
Programming (via satellite): C-SPAN; C-SPAN 2; Home Shopping Network; WGN America.
Fee: $31.99 installation; $39.98 monthly.

Expanded Basic Service 1
Subscribers: 1,142.
Programming (via satellite): ABC Family Channel; AMC; Animal Planet; Arts & Entertainment; CNBC; CNN; Comedy Central; Country Music TV; Discovery Channel; Disney Channel; E! Entertainment Television; ESPN; ESPN 2; ESPNews; Food Network; FX; Golf Channel; HGTV; History Channel; Lifetime; MSNBC; MTV; Nickelodeon; Spike TV; TBS Superstation; The Learning Channel; Turner Network TV; USA Network; Versus; VH1; Weather Channel.

Digital Basic Service
Subscribers: N.A.
Programming (via satellite): BBC America; Bio; CMT Pure Country; Discovery Digital Networks; Encore; Flix; Fuse; G4; GAS; GSN; Halogen Network; History Channel International; Lifetime Movie Network; MTV Networks Digital Suite; Music Choice; National Geographic Channel; Nick Jr.; NickToons TV; Outdoor Channel; PBS Kids Sprout; SoapNet; Style Network; Sundance Channel; Syfy; Toon Disney; Trinity Broadcasting Network; Turner Classic Movies; TV Land; WE tv.

Digital Pay Service 1
Pay Units: N.A.
Programming (via satellite): Cinemax (multiplexed); HBO (multiplexed); Showtime (multiplexed); Starz (multiplexed); The Movie Channel (multiplexed).

Video-On-Demand: No

Pay-Per-View
iN DEMAND (delivered digitally); Playboy TV (delivered digitally).

Internet Service
Operational: Yes.

Telephone Service
Digital: Operational

Miles of Plant: 27.0 (coaxial); None (fiber optic). Homes passed: 1,371.
Vice President & General Manager: William (Rusty) Robertson. Vice President, Technical Operations: Max Woolsey. Marketing Director: Damian Miller. Vice President, Communications: Mark Apple.
Ownership: Comcast Cable Communications Inc. (MSO).

CRAWFORD COUNTY—Charter Communications. Now served by MARENGO, IL [IL0370]. ICA: IN0134.

CRAWFORDSVILLE—Comcast Cable, 5330 E 65th St, Indianapolis, IN 46220. Phone: 317-275-6370. Fax: 317-275-6340. Web Site: http://www.comcast.com. Also serves Montgomery County (portions). ICA: IN0043.
TV Market Ranking: Below 100 (CRAWFORDSVILLE (PORTIONS), Montgomery County (portions)). Franchise award date: N.A. Franchise expiration date: N.A. Began: April 5, 1969.
Channel capacity: 60 (operating 2-way). Channels available but not in use: 22.

Basic Service
Subscribers: N.A. Included in Indianapolis
Programming (received off-air): WFYI (PBS) Indianapolis; WHMB-TV (IND) Indianapolis; WIPX-TV (ION) Bloomington; WISH-TV (CBS) Indianapolis; WLFI-TV (CBS) Lafayette; WNDY-TV (MNT) Marion; WRTV (ABC) Indianapolis; WTHR (NBC) Indianapolis; WTTV (CW) Bloomington; WTWO (NBC) Terre Haute; WXIN (FOX) Indianapolis; allband FM.
Programming (via satellite): ABC Family Channel; AMC; Animal Planet; Arts & Entertainment; Bravo; Cartoon Network; CNBC; CNN; Comedy Central; Country Music TV; C-SPAN; C-SPAN 2; Discovery Channel; Disney Channel; E! Entertainment Television; ESPN; ESPN 2; ESPNews; Eternal Word TV Network; Food Network; Fox News Channel; Fox Sports Net Midwest; FX; Golf Channel; GSN; Hallmark Channel; Headline News; HGTV; History Channel; Home Shopping Network; Lifetime; MSNBC; MTV; NASA TV; Nickelodeon; Speed Channel; Spike TV; Style Network; Syfy; TBS Superstation; The Learning Channel; Toon Disney; Travel Channel; Trinity Broadcasting Network; truTV; Turner Network TV; TV Guide Network; TV Land; USA Network; Versus; VH1; Weather Channel; WGN America.
Fee: $31.99 installation; $47.98 monthly; $2.00 converter.

Digital Basic Service
Subscribers: N.A.
Programming (via satellite): BBC America; Discovery Digital Networks; DMX Music; Encore; Flix; GAS; MTV Networks Digital Suite; Nick Jr.; Nick Too; NickToons TV; Science Television; Sundance Channel.

Digital Pay Service 1
Pay Units: N.A.
Programming (via satellite): Canales N; Cinemax (multiplexed); HBO (multiplexed); Showtime (multiplexed); Starz (multiplexed); The Movie Channel (multiplexed).

Video-On-Demand: Planned

Pay-Per-View
iN DEMAND (delivered digitally); Hot Choice (delivered digitally); Playboy TV (delivered digitally); Fresh (delivered digitally); Shorteez (delivered digitally); Pleasure (delivered digitally).

Internet Service
Operational: Yes.
Broadband Service: Comcast High Speed Internet.
Fee: $42.95 monthly.

Telephone Service
Analog: Not Operational
Digital: Operational

Miles of Plant: 121.0 (coaxial); None (fiber optic). Homes passed: 10,460.
Vice President & General Manager: William (Rusty) Roberson. Vice President, Technical Operations: Max Woolsey. Vice President, Communications: Mark Apple. Marketing Director: Damian Miller.
City fee: 2% of basic gross.
Ownership: Comcast Cable Communications Inc. (MSO).

CYNTHIANA—Now served by EVANSVILLE, IN [IN0006]. ICA: IN0201.

DARLINGTON—Indiana Communications, PO Box 617, Boswell, IN 47921. Phone: 888-610-1119. Web Site: http://www.indcomm.net. ICA: IN0195.
TV Market Ranking: Below 100 (DARLINGTON). Franchise award date: January 1, 1981. Franchise expiration date: N.A. Began: January 8, 1982.
Channel capacity: 31 (not 2-way capable). Channels available but not in use: 17.

Basic Service
Subscribers: 69.
Programming (received off-air): WFYI (PBS) Indianapolis; WHMB-TV (IND) Indianapolis; WIPX-TV (ION) Bloomington; WISH-TV (CBS) Indianapolis; WLFI-TV (CBS) Lafayette; WNDY-TV (MNT) Marion; WRTV (ABC) Indianapolis; WTHR (NBC) Indianapolis; WTTK (IND) Kokomo; WXIN (FOX) Indianapolis.
Programming (via satellite): QVC; Trinity Broadcasting Network.
Fee: $25.00 installation; $17.98 monthly; $3.50 converter.

Expanded Basic Service 1
Subscribers: N.A.
Programming (via satellite): ABC Family Channel; AMC; Animal Planet; Arts & Entertainment; CNN; Discovery Channel; Disney Channel; E! Entertainment Television; ESPN; ESPN 2; Fox News Channel; Great American Country; Headline News; History Channel; Lifetime; MSNBC; Speed Channel; TBS Superstation; The Learning Channel; Turner Network TV; USA Network; Weather Channel; WGN.
Fee: $17.97 monthly.

Pay Service 1
Pay Units: N.A.
Programming (via satellite): Cinemax; HBO; Showtime; The Movie Channel.
Fee: $10.00 installation; $8.95 monthly (TMC), $10.95 monthly (Cinemax or Showtime), $12.95 monthly (HBO).

Video-On-Demand: No

Internet Service
Operational: No.

Telephone Service
None

Miles of Plant: 6.0 (coaxial); None (fiber optic). Homes passed: 356. Total homes in franchised area: 356.
Manager: Joe Young.
City fee: 3% of basic gross.
Ownership: Park TV & Electronics Inc. (MSO).

DECKER—Formerly served by CableDirect. No longer in operation. ICA: IN0244.

DESOTO—Comcast Cable. Now served by MUNCIE, IN [IN0014]. ICA: IN0187.

DISTRICT OF SWEETWATER—Avenue Broadband Communications, 2603 Hart St, Vincennes, IN 47591. Phones: 800-882-7185; 812-895-7676. Fax: 812-886-5017. Web Site: http://www.avenuebroadband.com. ICA: IN0373.
TV Market Ranking: 16 (DISTRICT OF SWEETWATER).
Channel capacity: N.A. Channels available but not in use: N.A.

Basic Service
Subscribers: N.A.
Programming (received off-air): WCLJ-TV (TBN) Bloomington; WFYI (PBS) Indianapolis; WHMB-TV (IND) Indianapolis; WIPX-TV (ION) Bloomington; WISH-TV (CBS) Indianapolis; WNDY-TV (MNT) Marion; WRTV (ABC) Indianapolis; WTHR (NBC) Indianapolis; WTIU (PBS) Bloomington; WTTV (CW) Bloomington; WXIN (FOX) Indianapolis.
Programming (via satellite): Home Shopping Network; QVC; WGN America.
Current originations: Public Access.

Expanded Basic Service 1
Subscribers: N.A.
Programming (via satellite): ABC Family Channel; AMC; Animal Planet; Arts & Entertainment; Big Ten Network; Bravo; Cartoon Network; CNBC; CNN; Comedy Central; Country Music TV; C-SPAN; C-SPAN 2; Discovery Channel; Disney Channel; E! Entertainment Television; ESPN; ESPN 2; Food Network; Fox News Channel; Fox Sports Net Midwest; FX; Hallmark Channel; Headline News; HGTV; History Channel; Lifetime; MTV; National Geographic Channel; Nickelodeon; Outdoor Channel; Oxygen; SoapNet; Speed Channel; Spike TV; Syfy; TBS Superstation; The Learning Channel; Travel

Channel; truTV; Turner Network TV; TV Land; USA Network; Versus; VH1; Weather Channel.

Digital Basic Service

Subscribers: N.A.

Programming (via satellite): AmericanLife TV Network; BBC America; Bio; Bloomberg Television; Bravo; CMT Pure Country; Cooking Channel; Discovery Health Channel; Discovery Kids Channel; Discovery Military Channel; Discovery Planet Green; Disney XD; DMX Music; ESPN Classic Sports; ESPNews; FitTV; Fox Business Channel; Fox College Sports Atlantic; Fox College Sports Central; Fox College Sports Pacific; Fox Movie Channel; Fox Soccer; Fuse; G4; Golf Channel; Gospel Music Channel; GSN; Halogen Network; History Channel; ID Investigation Discovery; Independent Film Channel; Lifetime Movie Network; MTV2; mtvU; National Geographic Channel; Nick Jr.; NickToons TV; Outdoor Channel; PBS Kids Sprout; RFD-TV; Science Channel; ShopNBC; Speed Channel; Style Network; TeenNick; Trinity Broadcasting Network; Turner Classic Movies; Versus; VH1 Classic; VH1 Soul; WE tv.

Digital Expanded Basic Service

Subscribers: N.A.

Programming (via satellite): Encore (multiplexed); Flix; Showtime (multiplexed); Starz IndiePlex; Starz RetroPlex; The Movie Channel (multiplexed).

Digital Pay Service 1

Pay Units: N.A.

Programming (via satellite): Cinemax (multiplexed); HBO (multiplexed); Starz (multiplexed).

Pay-Per-View

iN DEMAND (delivered digitally); Hot Choice (delivered digitally); Playboy TV (delivered digitally); Fresh (delivered digitally); Spice: Xcess (delivered digitally); Club Jenna (delivered digitally).

Chief Executive Officer: Steve Lowe. Vice President & General Manager: Mary lafrate. Vice President, Engineering: Jeff Spence. System Engineer: Bart Cotter.

Ownership: Buford Media Group LLC (MSO).

DUBOIS COUNTY—Formerly served by CableDirect. No longer in operation. ICA: IN0247.

DUPONT—Formerly served by CableDirect. No longer in operation. ICA: IN0248.

ECONOMY—Formerly served by CableDirect. No longer in operation. ICA: IN0219.

EDINBURGH—Avenue Broadband Communications, 2603 Hart St, Vincennes, IN 47591. Phones: 800-882-7185; 812-895-7676. Fax: 812-886-5017. Web Site: http://www.avenuebroadband.com. ICA: IN0105.

TV Market Ranking: 16 (EDINBURGH). Franchise award date: January 1, 1981. Franchise expiration date: N.A. Began: May 1, 1981.

Channel capacity: 37 (not 2-way capable). Channels available but not in use: 18.

Basic Service

Subscribers: 1,057.

Programming (received off-air): WCLJ-TV (TBN) Bloomington; WFYI (PBS) Indianapolis; WHMB-TV (IND) Indianapolis; WIPX-TV (ION) Bloomington; WISH-TV (CBS) Indianapolis; WNDY-TV (MNT) Marion; WRTV (ABC) Indianapolis; WTHR (NBC) Indianapolis; WTIU (PBS) Bloomington; WTTV (CW) Bloomington; WXIN (FOX) Indianapolis.

Programming (via satellite): QVC; WGN America.

Current originations: Educational Access.

Fee: $40.00 installation; $16.95 monthly.

Expanded Basic Service 1

Subscribers: N.A.

Programming (via satellite): ABC Family Channel; AMC; Animal Planet; Arts & Entertainment; CNN; Country Music TV; C-SPAN; C-SPAN 2; Discovery Channel; Disney Channel; E! Entertainment Television; ESPN; ESPN 2; Food Network; Fox News Channel; Fox Sports Net Midwest; FX; Hallmark Channel; Headline News; HGTV; History Channel; Lifetime; MTV; Nickelodeon; Oxygen; SoapNet; Speed Channel; Spike TV; Syfy; TBS Superstation; The Learning Channel; Travel Channel; truTV; Turner Network TV; TV Land; USA Network; Versus; VH1; Weather Channel.

Pay Service 1

Pay Units: 504.

Programming (via satellite): Cinemax; HBO; Showtime.

Fee: $10.00 installation; $8.95 monthly (Cinemax), $9.95 monthly (HBO or Showtime).

Video-On-Demand: No

Internet Service

Operational: No.

Telephone Service

None

Miles of Plant: 30.0 (coaxial); None (fiber optic). Homes passed: 2,187.

Chief Executive Officer: Steve Lowe. Vice President & General Manager: Mary lafrate. Vice President, Engineering: Jeff Spence. System Engineer: Bart Cotter.

City fee: 2% of gross.

Ownership: Buford Media Group LLC (MSO).

ELBERFELD—Avenue Broadband Communications, 2603 Hart St, Vincennes, IN 47591. Phones: 800-882-7185; 812-895-7676. Fax: 812-886-5017. Web Site: http://www.avenuebroadband.com. ICA: IN0190.

TV Market Ranking: 86 (ELBERFELD). Franchise award date: September 10, 1981. Franchise expiration date: N.A. Began: January 1, 1982.

Channel capacity: 35 (not 2-way capable). Channels available but not in use: None.

Basic Service

Subscribers: 322.

Programming (received off-air): WAZE-TV (CW) Madisonville; WEHT (ABC) Evansville; WEVV-TV (CBS, MNT) Evansville; WFIE (NBC) Evansville; WNIN (PBS) Evansville; WTVW (FOX) Evansville.

Programming (via satellite): QVC; TBS Superstation; WGN America.

Current originations: Government Access; Educational Access; Public Access.

Fee: $45.25 installation; $12.40 monthly; $1.81 converter.

Expanded Basic Service 1

Subscribers: 319.

Programming (via satellite): ABC Family Channel; Animal Planet; Arts & Entertainment; CNN; Comedy Central; Discovery Channel; Disney Channel; ESPN; ESPN 2; Fox News Channel; Headline News; HGTV; Lifetime; MTV; Nickelodeon; Spike TV; Syfy; Turner Classic Movies; Turner Network TV; TV Land; USA Network; VH1; Weather Channel.

Fee: $9.31 monthly.

Pay Service 1

Pay Units: 66.

Programming (via satellite): HBO.

Fee: $20.00 installation; $9.50 monthly.

Pay Service 2

Pay Units: 20.

Programming (via satellite): Cinemax.

Fee: $20.00 installation; $9.50 monthly.

Video-On-Demand: No

Internet Service

Operational: No.

Telephone Service

None

Miles of Plant: 12.0 (coaxial); None (fiber optic). Homes passed: 521.

Chief Executive Officer: Steve Lowe. Vice President & General Manager: Mary lafrate. Vice President, Engineering: Jeff Spence. System Engineer: Bart Cotter.

City fee: 3% of gross.

Ownership: Charter Communications Inc. (MSO).

ELIZABETH—Windjammer Cable, 4400 PGA Blvd, Ste 902, Palm Beach Gardens, FL 33410. Phones: 877-450-5558; 561-775-1208. Fax: 561-775-7811. Web Site: http://www.windjammercable.com. Also serves New Middletown. ICA: IN0249.

TV Market Ranking: 38 (ELIZABETH, New Middletown). Franchise award date: N.A. Franchise expiration date: N.A. Began: N.A.

Channel capacity: N.A. Channels available but not in use: N.A.

Basic Service

Subscribers: 28.

Programming (received off-air): WAVE (NBC) Louisville; WBNA (ION) Louisville; WDRB (FOX) Louisville; WHAS-TV (ABC) Louisville; WKPC-TV (PBS) Louisville; WLKY-TV (CBS) Louisville; WMYO (MNT) Salem.

Programming (via satellite): ABC Family Channel; AMC; Arts & Entertainment; CNN; Discovery Channel; Disney Channel; ESPN; Spike TV; TBS Superstation; The Learning Channel; Trinity Broadcasting Network; Turner Network TV; USA Network; WGN America.

Fee: $39.95 installation; $35.65 monthly; $10.00 additional installation.

Digital Basic Service

Subscribers: N.A.

Programming (via satellite): BBC America; Bloomberg Television; Discovery Health Channel; Discovery Kids Channel; ESPN Classic Sports; ESPNews; FitTV; Fox Movie Channel; Fox Sports World; G4; Golf Channel; GSN; INSP; Music Choice; Nick Jr.; NickToons TV; Outdoor Channel; Science Channel; truTV; Versus; WE tv.

Fee: $8.45 monthly.

Digital Pay Service 1

Pay Units: N.A.

Programming (via satellite): Cinemax (multiplexed); Encore (multiplexed); HBO (multiplexed); Showtime (multiplexed); Starz (multiplexed); The Movie Channel (multiplexed).

Fee: $15.95 monthly (each).

Video-On-Demand: No

Pay-Per-View

HITS PPV (delivered digitally).

Internet Service

Operational: No.

Telephone Service

None

Homes passed: 431. Miles of plant (coax) included in Willisburg, KY

Ownership: Windjammer Communications LLC (MSO).

ELKHART—Comcast Cable. No longer in operation. ICA: IN0010.

ENGLISH—Avenue Broadband Communications, 2603 Hart St, Vincennes, IN 47591. Phones: 800-882-7185; 812-895-7676. Fax: 812-886-5017. Web Site: http://www.avenuebroadband.com. ICA: IN0379.

TV Market Ranking: Below 100 (ENGLISH).

Channel capacity: N.A. Channels available but not in use: N.A.

Basic Service

Subscribers: N.A.

Programming (received off-air): WAVE (NBC) Louisville; WDRB (FOX) Louisville; WHAS-TV (ABC) Louisville; WKPC-TV (PBS) Louisville; WLKY-TV (CBS) Louisville; WMYO (MNT) Salem; WTTV (CW) Bloomington.

Programming (via satellite): ION Television; QVC; Trinity Broadcasting Network; WGN America.

Current originations: Educational Access.

Expanded Basic Service 1

Subscribers: N.A.

Programming (via satellite): ABC Family Channel; AMC; Animal Planet; Arts & Entertainment; CNN; Comedy Central; Country Music TV; Discovery Channel; Disney Channel; E! Entertainment Television; ESPN; ESPN 2; Fox News Channel; Fox Sports Net Midwest; Hallmark Channel; Headline News; HGTV; History Channel; Home Shopping Network; Lifetime; MTV; Nickelodeon; Oxygen; Spike TV; Syfy; TBS Superstation; The Learning Channel; Turner Classic Movies; Turner Network TV; USA Network; VH1; Weather Channel.

Digital Basic Service

Subscribers: N.A.

Programming (via satellite): BBC America; Bio; Bloomberg Television; Bravo; CMT Pure Country; Cooking Channel; Discovery Health Channel; Discovery Kids Channel; Discovery Military Channel; Discovery Planet Green; Disney XD; DMX Music; ESPN Classic Sports; ESPNews; FitTV; Fox Movie Channel; Fox Soccer; Fuse; G4; Golf Channel; GSN; Halogen Network; History Channel International; ID Investigation Discovery; Independent Film Channel; Lifetime Movie Network; MTV2; National Geographic Channel; Nick Jr.; NickToons TV; Outdoor Channel; Science Channel; Sleuth; SoapNet; Speed Channel; Style Network; TeenNick; Trinity Broadcasting Network; Turner Classic Movies; VH1 Classic.

Digital Expanded Basic Service

Subscribers: N.A.

Programming (via satellite): Encore (multiplexed); HBO Signature; Showtime (multiplexed); Starz (multiplexed); The Movie Channel (multiplexed).

Digital Pay Service 1

Pay Units: N.A.

Programming (via satellite): Cinemax (multiplexed); HBO (multiplexed); Starz (multiplexed).

Pay-Per-View

Playboy TV (delivered digitally); Fresh (delivered digitally).

Chief Executive Officer: Steve Lowe. Vice President & General Manager: Mary lafrate. Vice President, Engineering: Jeff Spence. System Engineer: Bart Cotter.

Ownership: Buford Media Group LLC (MSO).

EVANSVILLE—Insight Communications, 1900 N Fares Ave, Evansville, IN 47711. Phones: 800-824-4003; 812-838-2044; 812-422-1167. Fax: 812-428-2427. Web Site: http://www.myinsight.com. Also serves Armstrong Twp., Boonville, Center Twp. (Vanderburgh County), Cynthiana, Darmstadt, Fort Branch, German Twp. (Vanderburgh

County), Gibson County, Haubstadt, Knight Twp., Mount Vernon, Ohio Twp. (western portion), Owensville, Perry Twp., Posey County, Poseyville, Princeton, Union Twp. (Vanderburgh County), Vanderburgh County (portions) & Warrick County, IN; Henderson & Henderson County (unincorporated areas), KY. ICA: IN0006.

TV Market Ranking: 86 (Boonville, Center Twp. (Vanderburgh County), Cynthiana, Darmstadt, EVANSVILLE, Fort Branch, German Twp. (Vanderburgh County), Gibson County, Haubstadt, Henderson, Henderson County (unincorporated areas), Knight Twp., Mount Vernon, Ohio Twp. (western portion), Owensville, Perry Twp., Posey County, Poseyville, Princeton, Princeton, Vanderburgh County (portions), Warrick County); 98 (Armstrong Twp., Union Twp. (Vanderburgh County)). Franchise award date: March 14, 1976. Franchise expiration date: N.A. Began: March 1, 1979.

Channel capacity: 80 (operating 2-way). Channels available but not in use: None.

Basic Service

Subscribers: 60,458 Includes Jasper.

Programming (received off-air): WAZE-TV (CW) Madisonville; WEHT (ABC) Evansville; WEVV-TV (CBS, MNT) Evansville; WFIE (NBC) Evansville; WNIN (PBS) Evansville; WTVW (FOX) Evansville; WYYW-LP Evansville.

Programming (via satellite): C-SPAN; C-SPAN 2; Discovery Channel; Eternal Word TV Network; QVC; TBS Superstation; Trinity Broadcasting Network; WGN America.

Current originations: Government Access; Educational Access; Public Access.

Fee: $35.00 installation; $1.01 converter.

Expanded Basic Service 1

Subscribers: 57,412.

Programming (via satellite): ABC Family Channel; AMC; Animal Planet; Arts & Entertainment; BET Networks; Bravo; Cartoon Network; CNBC; CNN; Comedy Central; Country Music TV; Disney Channel; E! Entertainment Television; ESPN; ESPN 2; Food Network; Fox News Channel; Fox Sports Net Midwest; Fox Sports Net Ohio; FX; G4; Golf Channel; Hallmark Channel; Headline News; HGTV; History Channel; Home Shopping Network; Lifetime; MSNBC; MTV; National Geographic Channel; Nickelodeon; Oxygen; SoapNet; Speed Channel; Spike TV; Syfy; The Learning Channel; Toon Disney; Travel Channel; truTV; Turner Network TV; TV Guide Network; TV Land; USA Network; VH1; Weather Channel.

Fee: $40.00 monthly.

Digital Basic Service

Subscribers: N.A.

Programming (received off-air): WEHT (ABC) Evansville; WFIE (NBC) Evansville; WNIN (PBS) Evansville.

Programming (via satellite): BBC America; Big Ten Network; Bio; Bloomberg Television; CBS College Sports Network; Cooking Channel; Discovery Digital Networks; Discovery HD Theater; Do-It-Yourself; Encore (multiplexed); ESPN; ESPN Classic Sports; ESPN U; ESPNews; Fox Movie Channel; Fox Soccer; Fuse; GAS; GSN; HDNet; HDNet Movies; History Channel International; Independent Film Channel; Lifetime Movie Network; MTV Networks Digital Suite; Music Choice; NFL Network; Nick Jr.; Nick Too; NickToons TV; Outdoor Channel; PBS Kids Sprout; Sleuth; Style Network; Sundance Channel; Turner Classic Movies; Universal HD; Versus; WE tv.

Fee: $17.00 monthly.

Digital Pay Service 1

Pay Units: N.A.

Programming (via satellite): Cinemax (multiplexed); Flix; HBO (multiplexed); HBO HD; Showtime (multiplexed); Showtime HD; Starz (multiplexed); The Movie Channel (multiplexed).

Fee: $10.00 monthly (Cinemax or Starz), $13.00 monthly (HBO or Showtime/TMC).

Video-On-Demand: Yes

Pay-Per-View

iN DEMAND (delivered digitally); ESPN (delivered digitally).

Internet Service

Operational: Yes.

Broadband Service: InsightBB.com.

Fee: $99.95 installation; $40.00 monthly; $10.00 modem lease; $99.00 modem purchase.

Telephone Service

Digital: Operational

Fee: $40.00 monthly

Miles of Plant: 1,215.0 (coaxial); None (fiber optic). Homes passed: 130,023. Homes passed includes Jasper

President & Chief Operating Officer: Dinni Jain. Senior Vice President, Operations: John Hutton. District Vice President: Lanae Juffer. Technical Operations Manager: Don Baumholser. Customer Service Manager: Kyle Hamilton.

Franchise fee: 5% of gross split between city & county.

Ownership: Insight Communications Co. (MSO).

EVANSVILLE—WOW! Internet Cable & Phone, 6045 Wedeking Ave, Evansville, IN 47715. Phones: 866-496-9669; 812-437-0345. Fax: 812-437-0317. Web Site: http://www1.wowway.com. Also serves Newburgh. ICA: IN0365. **Note:** This system is an overbuild.

TV Market Ranking: 86 (EVANSVILLE, Newburgh). Franchise award date: N.A. Franchise expiration date: N.A. Began: April 1, 1999.

Channel capacity: N.A. Channels available but not in use: N.A.

Basic Service

Subscribers: 27,000.

Programming (received off-air): WEHT (ABC) Evansville; WEVV-TV (CBS, MNT) Evansville; WFIE (NBC) Evansville; WNIN (PBS) Evansville; WTVW (FOX) Evansville; WYYW-LP Evansville.

Programming (via satellite): ABC Family Channel; AMC; Animal Planet; Arts & Entertainment; BET Networks; Big Ten Network; Bio; Bloomberg Television; Bravo; Cartoon Network; CNBC; CNN; Comedy Central; Country Music TV; C-SPAN; C-SPAN 2; Discovery Channel; Discovery Health Channel; Disney Channel; E! Entertainment Television; ESPN; ESPN 2; ESPN Classic Sports; ESPNews; Eternal Word TV Network; Food Network; Fox News Channel; Fox Sports Net Midwest; FX; Golf Channel; Great American Country; Hallmark Channel; Headline News; HGTV; History Channel; Home Shopping Network; Lifetime; MSNBC; MTV; National Geographic Channel; Nickelodeon; Oxygen; QVC; ShopNBC; SoapNet; Speed Channel; Spike TV; Style Network; Syfy; TBS Superstation; The Learning Channel; Toon Disney; Travel Channel; truTV; Turner Network TV; TV Land; USA Network; VH1; Weather Channel; WGN America.

Fee: $39.99 installation; $50.00 monthly.

Digital Basic Service

Subscribers: 9,000.

Programming (received off-air): WEHT (ABC) Evansville; WEVV-TV (CBS, MNT) Evansville; WFIE (NBC) Evansville.

Programming (via satellite): ABC News Now; AmericanLife TV Network; Animal Planet HD; Arts & Entertainment HD; BBC America; Big Ten Network; Big Ten Network HD; Boomerang; BYU Television; CBS College Sports Network; Church Channel; CMT Pure Country; CNBC World; Cooking Channel; Daystar TV Network; Discovery Channel; Discovery Channel HD; Discovery HD Theater; Discovery Kids Channel; Discovery Military Channel; Discovery Planet Green; Do-It-Yourself; Encore (multiplexed); ESPN 2 HD; ESPN HD; ESPN U; FitTV; Food Network HD; Fox Business Channel; Fox College Sports Atlantic; Fox College Sports Central; Fox College Sports Pacific; Fox HD; Fox Movie Channel; Fox News HD; Fox Soccer; FX HD; G4; HD-Net; HDNet Movies; here! On Demand; HGTV HD; History Channel HD; History Channel International; HorseRacing TV; ID Investigation Discovery; Independent Film Channel; Lifetime Movie Network; Lifetime Real Women; MTV Hits; MTV Jams; MTV Tres; MTV2; mun2 television; National Geographic Channel HD Network; NFL Network; NFL Network HD; Nick Jr.; Nick Too; NickToons TV; Outdoor Channel; PBS HD; PBS Kids Sprout; Science Channel; Starz (multiplexed); Starz On Demand; Sundance Channel; TeenNick; Tennis Channel; The Sportsman Channel; TLC HD; Trinity Broadcasting Network; Turner Classic Movies; Turner Network TV HD; TVG Network; Universal HD; VH1 Classic; VH1 Soul; WAM! America's Kidz Network.

Fee: $26.98 monthly.

Digital Pay Service 1

Pay Units: N.A. Included in Pay Service 1

Programming (via satellite): Cinemax (multiplexed); Cinemax On Demand; Flix; HBO (multiplexed); HBO HD; HBO On Demand; Showtime (multiplexed); Showtime HD; Showtime On Demand; Starz HDTV; The Movie Channel (multiplexed); The Movie Channel On Demand.

Fee: $15.00 monthly (HBO, Cinemax, Showtime/TMC/Flix or Showtime).

Video-On-Demand: Yes

Pay-Per-View

Addressable homes: 10,000.

Playboy TV (delivered digitally), Addressable: Yes; Fresh (delivered digitally); Shorteez (delivered digitally); Hustler TV (delivered digitally); Hot Choice (delivered digitally); Penthouse TV (delivered digitally); ESPN (delivered digitally); iN DEMAND (delivered digitally).

Internet Service

Operational: Yes.

Subscribers: 42,860.

Broadband Service: In-house.

Fee: $40.99-$72.99 monthly.

Telephone Service

Digital: Operational

Miles of Plant: 1,300.0 (coaxial); 200.0 (fiber optic). Homes passed: 76,000. Total homes in franchised area: 88,000.

Vice President & General Manager: Kelvin Fee. Vice President, Sales & Marketing: Cathy Kuo. Chief Technician: Cash Hagen.

Ownership: WideOpenWest LLC (MSO).

FERDINAND—Avenue Broadband Communications, 2603 Hart St, Vincennes, IN 47591. Phones: 800-882-7185; 812-895-7676. Fax: 812-886-5017. Web Site: http://www.avenuebroadband.com. ICA: IN0378.

TV Market Ranking: Outside TV Markets (FERDINAND).

Channel capacity: N.A. Channels available but not in use: N.A.

Basic Service

Subscribers: N.A.

Programming (received off-air): WAVE (NBC) Louisville; WAZE-TV (CW) Madisonville; WDRB (FOX) Louisville; WEHT (ABC) Evansville; WEVV-TV (CBS, MNT) Evansville; WFIE (NBC) Evansville; WHAS-TV (ABC) Louisville; WJTS-LD (IND) Jasper; WNIN (PBS) Evansville; WTVW (FOX) Evansville.

Programming (via satellite): Eternal Word TV Network; QVC; WGN America.

Expanded Basic Service 1

Subscribers: N.A.

Programming (received off-air): The Learning Channel.

Programming (via satellite): ABC Family Channel; Animal Planet; Arts & Entertainment; CNN; Comedy Central; Discovery Channel; Disney Channel; E! Entertainment Television; ESPN; ESPN 2; Headline News; MTV; Nickelodeon; Spike TV; Syfy; TBS Superstation; Turner Classic Movies; Turner Network TV; USA Network; VH1; Weather Channel.

Pay Service 1

Pay Units: N.A.

Programming (via satellite): Cinemax; HBO; Showtime.

Chief Executive Officer: Steve Lowe. Vice President & General Manager: Mary Iafrate. Vice President, Engineering: Jeff Spence. System Engineer: Bart Cotter.

Ownership: Buford Media Group LLC (MSO).

FILLMORE—Global Com Inc., 3410 S 7th St, Terre Haute, IN 47802. Phones: 866-382-2253; 812-242-2253. Fax: 812-235-5554. ICA: IN0210.

TV Market Ranking: 16 (FILLMORE). Franchise award date: November 1, 1989. Franchise expiration date: N.A. Began: November 1, 1989.

Channel capacity: 35 (not 2-way capable). Channels available but not in use: 5.

Basic Service

Subscribers: 44.

Programming (received off-air): WFYI (PBS) Indianapolis; WHMB-TV (IND) Indianapolis; WISH-TV (CBS) Indianapolis; WNDY-TV (MNT) Marion; WRTV (ABC) Indianapolis; WTHI-TV (CBS) Terre Haute; WTHR (NBC) Indianapolis; WTTV (CW) Bloomington; WXIN (FOX) Indianapolis.

Programming (via satellite): ABC Family Channel; AMC; CNBC; CNN; Comedy Central; Country Music TV; C-SPAN; Discovery Channel; Disney Channel; ESPN; History Channel; Home Shopping Network; MTV; Nickelodeon; Spike TV; TBS Superstation; The Learning Channel; Turner Network TV; USA Network; WGN America.

Fee: $35.00 installation; $31.07 monthly.

Pay Service 1

Pay Units: 12.

Programming (via satellite): HBO.

Fee: $11.00 installation; $11.00 monthly.

Video-On-Demand: No

Internet Service

Operational: No.

Telephone Service

None

Miles of Plant: 7.0 (coaxial); None (fiber optic). Homes passed: 250. Total homes in franchised area: 260.

Franchise fee: 3% of gross.

Ownership: Global Com Inc. (MSO).

FISH LAKE—Formerly served by CableDirect. No longer in operation. ICA: IN0317.

FLAT ROCK—Suscom. Now served by SHELBYVILLE, IN [IN0042]. ICA: IN0252.

FLORA—Comcast Cable, 5330 E 65th St, Indianapolis, IN 46220. Phone: 317-275-6370. Fax: 317-275-6340. Web Site: http://www.comcast.com. ICA: IN0371.

TV Market Ranking: Below 100 (FLORA).

Channel capacity: N.A. Channels available but not in use: N.A.

Basic Service

Subscribers: N.A. Included in Indianapolis

Programming (received off-air): WFYI (PBS) Indianapolis; WHMB-TV (IND) Indianapolis; WISH-TV (CBS) Indianapolis; WLFI-TV (CBS) Lafayette; WNDY-TV (MNT) Marion; WRTV (ABC) Indianapolis; WTHR (NBC) Indianapolis; WTTK (IND) Kokomo; WXIN (FOX) Indianapolis.

Programming (via satellite): C-SPAN; C-SPAN 2; Home Shopping Network; QVC; TV Guide Network; WGN America.

Fee: $50.99 installation; $50.48 monthly.

Expanded Basic Service 1

Subscribers: N.A.

Programming (via satellite): ABC Family Channel; AMC; Animal Planet; Arts & Entertainment; Bravo; Cartoon Network; CNBC; CNN; Comedy Central; Country Music TV; Discovery Channel; Disney Channel; Disney XD; E! Entertainment Television; ESPN; ESPN 2; ESPNews; Food Network; Fox News Channel; Fox Sports Net Midwest; FX; GalaVision; Golf Channel; Headline News; HGTV; History Channel; Lifetime; MSNBC; MTV; Nickelodeon; Speed Channel; Spike TV; Syfy; TBS Superstation; The Learning Channel; Travel Channel; Trinity Broadcasting Network; truTV; Turner Classic Movies; Turner Network TV; TV Land; Univision; USA Network; Versus; VH1; Weather Channel.

Digital Basic Service

Subscribers: N.A.

Programming (via satellite): BBC America; Bio; CMT Pure Country; Discovery Health Channel; Discovery Kids Channel; Discovery Military Channel; Discovery Planet Green; Encore; Flix; Fuse; G4; Halogen Network; History Channel International; ID Investigation Discovery; Lifetime Movie Network; MTV Hits; MTV2; National Geographic Channel; Nick Jr.; NickToons TV; Outdoor Channel; PBS Kids Sprout; Science Channel; SoapNet; Style Network; Sundance Channel; Syfy; TeenNick; Toon Disney; Trinity Broadcasting Network; Turner Classic Movies; TV Land; TVG Network; VH1 Classic; VH1 Soul; WAM! America"s Kidz Network.

Digital Pay Service 1

Pay Units: N.A.

Programming (via satellite): Cinemax (multiplexed); HBO (multiplexed); Showtime (multiplexed); Starz (multiplexed); The Movie Channel (multiplexed).

Pay-Per-View

iN DEMAND (delivered digitally); Playboy TV (delivered digitally); Fresh (delivered digitally); Spice: Xcess (delivered digitally).

Internet Service

Operational: Yes.

Telephone Service

Digital: Operational

Vice President & General Manager: William Robertson. Vice President, Technical Operations: Max Woolsey. Vice President, Communications: Mark Apple. Marketing Director: Damian Miller.

Ownership: Comcast Cable Communications Inc. (MSO).

FORT BRANCH—Now served by EVANSVILLE, IN [IN0006]. ICA: IN0088.

FORT WAYNE—Comcast Cable, 720 Taylor St, Fort Wayne, IN 46802-5144. Phones: 260-458-5103; 317-275-6370 (Indianapolis office). Fax: 260-458-5138. Web Site: http://www.comcast.com. Also serves Adams Twp., Allen County, Canterbury Green, Huntertown, Huntington County (portions), Marion Twp., New Haven, Noble County, Ossian (town), Perry Twp., Pleasant Twp., Roanoke, St. Joseph Twp., Wayne Twp., Wells County, Whitley County (portions) & Woodburn. ICA: IN0003.

TV Market Ranking: 82 (Adams Twp., Allen County, Canterbury Green, FORT WAYNE (PORTIONS), Huntertown, Huntington County (portions), Marion Twp., New Haven, Noble County, Ossian (town), Perry Twp., Pleasant Twp., Roanoke, St. Joseph Twp., Wayne Twp., Wells County (portions), Whitley County (portions), Woodburn). Franchise award date: July 19, 1978. Franchise expiration date: N.A. Began: August 15, 1979.

Channel capacity: N.A. Channels available but not in use: N.A.

Basic Service

Subscribers: N.A. Included in Indianapolis

Programming (received off-air): WANE-TV (CBS) Fort Wayne; WFFT-TV (FOX) Fort Wayne; WFWA (PBS) Fort Wayne; WINM (IND) Angola; WISE-TV (MNT, NBC) Fort Wayne; WPTA (ABC, CW) Fort Wayne; allband FM.

Programming (via satellite): ABC Family Channel; CityTV; C-SPAN; QVC; Radar Channel; TV Guide Network; WGN America.

Current originations: Leased Access; Government Access; Educational Access; Public Access.

Fee: $50.99 installation.

Expanded Basic Service 1

Subscribers: 71,674.

Programming (via satellite): AMC; Animal Planet; Arts & Entertainment; BET Networks; Cartoon Network; CNBC; CNN; Comcast SportsNet Chicago; Comedy Central; Country Music TV; C-SPAN 2; Discovery Channel; Discovery Health Channel; Disney Channel; E! Entertainment Television; ESPN; ESPN 2; ESPN Classic Sports; Eternal Word TV Network; Food Network; Fox News Channel; FX; Golf Channel; Great American Country; GSN; Headline News; HGTV; History Channel; Home Shopping Network; INSP; ION Television; Lifetime; MSNBC; MTV; MTV2; Nickelodeon; Speed Channel; Spike TV; Style Network; Syfy; TBS Superstation; The Learning Channel; Travel Channel (multiplexed); Turner Classic Movies; Turner Network TV; TV Land; Univision; USA Network; Versus; VH1; Weather Channel.

Fee: $51.98 monthly.

Digital Basic Service

Subscribers: N.A.

Programming (received off-air): WANE-TV (CBS) Fort Wayne; WFWA (PBS) Fort Wayne; WISE-TV (MNT, NBC) Fort Wayne; WPTA (ABC, CW) Fort Wayne.

Programming (via satellite): Arts & Entertainment HD; BBC America; Bio; Canales N; CBS College Sports Network; Cooking Channel; Country Music TV; C-SPAN 3; Current; Discovery Digital Networks; Discovery HD Theater; Do-It-Yourself; Encore (multiplexed); ESPN 2 HD; ESPN HD; ESPNews; Eternal Word TV Network; Flix; Fox Reality Channel; Fox Soccer; G4; GAS; Gol TV; Hallmark Channel; Halogen Network; History Channel International; INHD; Lifetime Movie Network; LOGO; MoviePlex; MTV Networks Digital Suite; Music Choice; National Geographic Channel; National Geographic Channel HD Network; NBA TV; NFL Network; Nick Jr.; Nick Too; NickToons TV; Oxygen; Palladia; PBS Kids Sprout; SoapNet; Sundance Channel; Tennis Channel; The Word Network; Toon Disney; Turner Network TV HD; TV One; TVG Network; Universal HD; Versus HD; Weatherscan.

Fee: $14.95 monthly.

Digital Pay Service 1

Pay Units: N.A.

Programming (via satellite): Cinemax (multiplexed); Cinemax HD; HBO (multiplexed); HBO HD; Showtime (multiplexed); Showtime HD; Starz (multiplexed); Starz HDTV; The Movie Channel (multiplexed).

Fee: $18.95 monthly (each).

Video-On-Demand: Yes

Pay-Per-View

Addressable homes: 22,447.

iN DEMAND, Addressable: Yes; iN DEMAND (delivered digitally); Playboy TV (delivered digitally); MLS Direct Kick (delivered digitally); NHL Center Ice (delivered digitally); MLB Extra Innings (delivered digitally); ESPN Gameplan (delivered digitally); NBA TV (delivered digitally).

Internet Service

Operational: Yes.

Broadband Service: Comcast High Speed Internet.

Fee: $149.00 installation; $42.95 monthly; $7.00 modem lease; $199.00 modem purchase.

Telephone Service

Digital: Operational

Fee: $44.95 monthly

Miles of Plant: 2,061.0 (coaxial); 422.0 (fiber optic). Homes passed: 151,414. Miles of plant (coax & fiber) include Avilla, Frankfort, Huntington, Logansport, Monroeville, Peru, Wabash, Convoy OH, & Payne OH

Regional Vice President: Scott Tenney. Technical Operations Director: Bennie Logan. Engineering Manager: Tom Stuckholz. Vice President, Marketing: Aaron Geisel. Marketing Manager: Marci Hefley. Vice President, Communications: Mark Apple.

Ownership: Comcast Cable Communications Inc. (MSO).

FRANCESVILLE—Mediacom. Now served by SAN PIERRE, IN [IN0221]. ICA: IN0253.

FRANCISCO—Formerly served by Almega Cable. No longer in operation. ICA: IN0152.

FRANKFORT—Comcast Cable, 720 Taylor St, Fort Wayne, IN 46802-5144. Phones: 317-275-6370 (Indianapolis office); 260-458-5103. Fax: 260-458-5138. Web Site: http://www.comcast.com. Also serves Antioch, Clinton County & Jefferson. ICA: IN0048.

TV Market Ranking: 16 (Clinton County (portions)); Below 100 (Antioch, FRANKFORT, Jefferson, Clinton County (portions)). Franchise award date: September 1, 1974. Franchise expiration date: N.A. Began: September 7, 1976.

Channel capacity: 77 (operating 2-way). Channels available but not in use: None.

Basic Service

Subscribers: N.A. Included in Indianapolis

Programming (received off-air): WCLJ-TV (TBN) Bloomington; WFYI (PBS) Indianapolis; WHMB-TV (IND) Indianapolis; WIPX-TV (ION) Bloomington; WISH-TV (CBS) Indianapolis; WLFI-TV (CBS) Lafayette; WNDY-TV (MNT) Marion; WRTV (ABC) Indianapolis; WTHR (NBC) Indianapolis; WTTK (IND) Kokomo; WXIN (FOX) Indianapolis; 25 FMs.

Programming (via satellite): Bravo; C-SPAN; C-SPAN 2; TV Guide Network; WGN America.

Current originations: Religious Access; Educational Access.

Fee: $31.99 installation.

Expanded Basic Service 1

Subscribers: 4,653.

Programming (via satellite): ABC Family Channel; AMC; Animal Planet; Arts & Entertainment; Cartoon Network; CNBC; CNN; Comedy Central; Country Music TV; Discovery Channel; Disney Channel; E! Entertainment Television; ESPN; ESPN 2; ESPN Classic Sports; ESPNews; Food Network; Fox Sports Net; Fox Sports Net Midwest; FX; G4; GalaVision; Golf Channel; GSN; Headline News; HGTV; History Channel; Home Shopping Network; Lifetime; MSNBC; MTV; Nickelodeon; QVC; Speed Channel; Spike TV; Syfy; TBS Superstation; The Learning Channel; Toon Disney; Travel Channel; truTV; Turner Classic Movies; Turner Network TV; TV Land; Univision; USA Network; Versus; VH1; Weather Channel.

Fee: $50.48 monthly.

Digital Basic Service

Subscribers: N.A.

Programming (via satellite): BBC America; Discovery Digital Networks; DMX Music; Encore (multiplexed); Flix (multiplexed); GAS; Nick Jr.; Nick Too; NickToons TV; Sundance Channel.

Fee: $14.95 monthly.

Digital Pay Service 1

Pay Units: N.A.

Programming (via satellite): Canales N; Cinemax (multiplexed); HBO (multiplexed); Showtime (multiplexed); Starz (multiplexed); The Movie Channel (multiplexed).

Fee: $16.99 monthly each.

Video-On-Demand: No

Pay-Per-View

iN DEMAND (delivered digitally); Hot Choice (delivered digitally); Playboy TV (delivered digitally); Fresh (delivered digitally); Shorteez (delivered digitally); Pleasure (delivered digitally).

Internet Service

Operational: Yes.

Broadband Service: Comcast High Speed Internet.

Fee: $42.95 monthly; $15.00 modem lease; $129.95 modem purchase.

Telephone Service

Digital: Operational

Homes passed: 5,917. Total homes in franchised area: 6,000. Miles of plant included in Fort Wayne

Regional Vice President: Scott Tenney. Technical Operations Director: Bennie Logan. Engineering Manager: Tom Stuckholz. Vice President, Marketing: Aaron Geisel. Marketing Manager: Marci Hefley. Vice President, Communications: Mark Apple.

Franchise fee: 3% of gross.

Ownership: Comcast Cable Communications Inc.

FRANKLIN—Insight Communications. Now served by GREENWOOD, IN [IN0023]. ICA: IN0062.

FRANKTON—Longview Communications, 1923 N Main, Higginsville, MO 64037. Phone: 866-611-6565. Fax: 866-329-4790. Web Site: http://www.longviewcomm.com. Also serves Madison County (portions). ICA: IN0143.

TV Market Ranking: 16 (Madison County (portions)); Below 100 (FRANKTON, Madison County (portions)). Franchise award date: September 1, 1982. Franchise expiration date: N.A. Began: September 19, 1983.

Channel capacity: N.A. Channels available but not in use: N.A.

Basic Service

Subscribers: 184.

Programming (received off-air): WFYI (PBS) Indianapolis; WHMB-TV (IND) Indianapolis; WIPX-TV (ION) Bloomington; WISH-TV (CBS) Indianapolis; WLFI-TV (CBS) Lafayette; WRTV (ABC) Indianapolis; WTHR (NBC) Indianapolis; WTTK (IND) Kokomo; WTTV (CW) Bloomington; WXIN (FOX) Indianapolis.

Programming (via satellite): QVC.

Fee: $35.00 installation; $18.98 monthly.

Expanded Basic Service 1

Subscribers: N.A.

Programming (via satellite): ABC Family Channel; AMC; Animal Planet; Arts & Entertainment; Bravo; CBS College Sports Network; CNBC; CNN; Comedy Central; Discovery Channel; Disney Channel; E! Entertainment Television; ESPN; ESPN 2; Food Network; Fox News Channel; FX; Great American Country; Hallmark Channel; Hallmark Movie Channel; Headline News; HGTV; History Channel; Lifetime; MSNBC; National Geographic Channel; Syfy; TBS Superstation; The Learning Channel; Travel Channel; Trinity Broadcasting Network; truTV; Turner Network TV; USA Network; WE tv; Weather Channel; WGN America.

Fee: $19.97 monthly.

Digital Basic Service

Subscribers: 22.

Programming (via satellite): AmericanLife TV Network; BBC America; Bio; Bloomberg Television; Discovery Digital Networks; Encore (multiplexed); ESPN Classic Sports; ESPNews; Fox Movie Channel; G4; Golf Channel; GSN; Halogen Network; History Channel International; Independent Film Channel; Lifetime Movie Network; Outdoor Channel; Speed Channel; Style Network; Toon Disney; Turner Classic Movies.

Fee: $16.00 monthly.

Pay Service 1

Pay Units: N.A.

Programming (via satellite): Cinemax; HBO; Showtime; The Movie Channel.

Fee: $8.95 monthly (TMC), $10.95 monthly (Cinemax or Showtime), $12.95 monthly (HBO).

Digital Pay Service 1

Pay Units: N.A.

Programming (via satellite): Cinemax (multiplexed); Flix; HBO (multiplexed); Showtime (multiplexed); Starz (multiplexed); The Movie Channel (multiplexed).

Fee: $8.95 monthly (TMC), $10.95 monthly (Showtime or Cinemax), $12.95 monthly (HBO).

Video-On-Demand: No

Pay-Per-View

iN DEMAND (delivered digitally); Hot Choice (delivered digitally); Playboy TV (delivered digitally); Fresh (delivered digitally); Shorteez (delivered digitally).

Internet Service

Operational: Yes.

Subscribers: 62.

Broadband Service: IBBS.

Telephone Service

None

Miles of Plant: 17.0 (coaxial); None (fiber optic). Homes passed: 894. Total homes in franchised area: 894.

President: John Long. Senior Vice President: Marc W. Cohen. General Manager: Brandon Dickey. Technical Manager: Steve Boss.

City fee: 3% of gross.

Ownership: Longview Communications (MSO).

FREETOWN—Formerly served by CableDirect. No longer in operation. ICA: IN0254.

FRENCH LICK—Avenue Broadband Communications, 2603 Hart St, Vincennes, IN 47591. Phones: 800-882-7185; 812-895-7676. Fax: 812-886-5017. Web Site: http://www.avenuebroadband.com. Also serves West Baden Springs. ICA: IN0117.

TV Market Ranking: Below 100 (FRENCH LICK, West Baden Springs). Franchise award date: May 21, 1981. Franchise expiration date: N.A. Began: March 1, 1980.

Channel capacity: N.A. Channels available but not in use: N.A.

Basic Service

Subscribers: 518.

Programming (received off-air): WAVE (NBC) Louisville; WBKI-TV (CW) Campbellsville; WDRB (FOX) Louisville; WHAS-TV (ABC) Louisville; WLKY-TV (CBS) Louisville; WMYO (MNT) Salem; WTHI-TV (CBS) Terre Haute; WTTV (CW) Bloomington; WTVW (FOX) Evansville; WVUT (PBS) Vincennes.

Programming (via satellite): QVC; WGN America.

Fee: $32.25 installation; $8.70 monthly; $1.27 converter.

Expanded Basic Service 1

Subscribers: 454.

Programming (via satellite): ABC Family Channel; Animal Planet; CNN; Comedy Central; Country Music TV; Discovery Channel; Disney Channel; E! Entertainment Television; ESPN; ESPN 2; Fox News Channel; Fox Sports Net Midwest; Hallmark Channel; Headline News; HGTV; History Channel; Lifetime; MTV; National Geographic Channel; Nickelodeon; Oxygen; Spike TV; Syfy; TBS Superstation; The Learning Channel; Travel Channel; Turner Network TV; TV Land; USA Network; VH1; Weather Channel.

Fee: $2.61 monthly.

Pay Service 1

Pay Units: 161.

Programming (via satellite): HBO.

Fee: $25.00 installation; $9.50 monthly.

Pay Service 2

Pay Units: 161.

Programming (via satellite): The Movie Channel.

Fee: $9.50 monthly.

Pay Service 3

Pay Units: 113.

Programming (via satellite): Showtime.

Video-On-Demand: No

Internet Service

Operational: Yes.

Telephone Service

Digital: Operational

Miles of Plant: 38.0 (coaxial); None (fiber optic). Homes passed: 1,749.

Chief Executive Officer: Steve Lowe. Vice President & General Manager: Mary Iafrate. Vice President, Engineering: Jeff Spence. System Engineer: Bart Cotter.

City fee: 3% of basic.

Ownership: Buford Media Group LLC (MSO).

GARY—Comcast Cable. Now served by CHICAGO (southern suburbs), IL [IL0008]. ICA: IN0013.

GASTON—Longview Communications, 12007 Sunrise Valley Dr, Ste 375, Reston, VA 20191. Phones: 866-611-6565 (Customer service); 703-476-9101. Fax: 703-476-9107. Web Site: http://www.longviewcomm.com. Also serves Matthews. ICA: IN0191.

TV Market Ranking: Below 100 (GASTON, Matthews). Franchise award date: July 1, 1984. Franchise expiration date: N.A. Began: June 1, 1986.

Channel capacity: 36 (not 2-way capable). Channels available but not in use: N.A.

Basic Service

Subscribers: 38.

Programming (received off-air): WHMB-TV (IND) Indianapolis; WIPB (PBS) Muncie; WISH-TV (CBS) Indianapolis; WNDY-TV (MNT) Marion; WRTV (ABC) Indianapolis; WTHR (NBC) Indianapolis; WTTK (IND) Kokomo; WXIN (FOX) Indianapolis.

Programming (via satellite): C-SPAN; QVC; Trinity Broadcasting Network.

Fee: $39.90 installation; $19.98 monthly.

Expanded Basic Service 1

Subscribers: N.A.

Programming (via satellite): ABC Family Channel; AMC; Animal Planet; Arts & Entertainment; CNN; Comedy Central; Discovery Channel; Disney Channel; E! Entertainment Television; ESPN; ESPN 2; Headline News; History Channel; Lifetime; TBS Superstation; The Learning Channel; Travel Channel; truTV; Turner Network TV; USA Network; Weather Channel; WGN America.

Fee: $17.97 monthly.

Pay Service 1

Pay Units: N.A.

Programming (via satellite): Showtime; The Movie Channel.

Fee: $8.95 monthly (TMC), $10.95 monthly (Showtime).

Video-On-Demand: No

Internet Service

Operational: No.

Telephone Service

None

Miles of Plant: 29.0 (coaxial); None (fiber optic). Homes passed: 731.

President: John Long. Senior Vice President: Marc W. Cohen. General Manager: Brandon Dickey. Technical Manager: Steve Boss.

Ownership: Longview Communications (MSO).

GLENWOOD—Formerly served by CableDirect. No longer in operation. ICA: IN0256.

GOLDEN LAKE—Formerly served by CableDirect. No longer in operation. ICA: IN0362.

GOSPORT—Insight Communications. Now served by BLOOMINGTON, IN [IN0016]. ICA: IN0189.

GREENCASTLE—Comcast Cable, 2450 S Henderson St, Bloomington, IN 47401-4540. Phones: 317-275-6370 (Indianapolis regional office); 812-332-9486 (Customer service). Fax: 812-332-0129. Web Site: http://www.comcast.com. Also serves Putnam County (portions). ICA: IN0079.

TV Market Ranking: 16 (Putnam County (portions)); Below 100 (GREENCASTLE, Putnam County (portions)); Outside TV Markets (Putnam County (portions)). Franchise award date: N.A. Franchise expiration date: N.A. Began: March 1, 1969.

Channel capacity: 80 (operating 2-way). Channels available but not in use: None.

Basic Service

Subscribers: N.A. Included in Bloomington

Programming (received off-air): WHMB-TV (IND) Indianapolis; WIPX-TV (ION) Bloomington; WISH-TV (CBS) Indianapolis; WNDY-TV (MNT) Marion; WRTV (ABC) Indianapolis; WTHI-TV (CBS) Terre Haute; WTHR (NBC) Indianapolis; WTIU (PBS) Bloomington; WTTV (CW) Bloomington; WXIN (FOX) Indianapolis; allband FM.

Programming (via satellite): C-SPAN; C-SPAN 2; FX; QVC; TBS Superstation; Turner Network TV; WGN America.

Current originations: Public Access.

Fee: $24.95 installation.

Expanded Basic Service 1

Subscribers: 2,278.

Programming (via satellite): ABC Family Channel; AMC; Animal Planet; Arts & Entertainment; BET Networks; Cartoon Network; CNBC; CNN; Comedy Central; Country Music TV; Discovery Channel; Disney Channel; ESPN; ESPN 2; ESPNews; Fox News Channel; Fox Sports Net Midwest; Headline News; HGTV; History Channel; Lifetime; MSNBC; MTV; Nickelodeon; Spike TV; The Learning Channel; Travel Channel; truTV; USA Network; VH1; Weather Channel.

Fee: $40.00 monthly.

Digital Basic Service

Subscribers: N.A.

Programming (via satellite): BBC America; Bio; Bravo; Discovery Digital Networks; DMX Music; Encore (multiplexed); ESPN Classic Sports; Fox Sports World; Fuse; GAS; Golf Channel; GSN; History Channel International; Independent Film Channel; Lifetime Movie Network; MTV Networks Digital Suite; National Geographic Channel; Nick Jr.; Speed Channel; Style Network; Syfy; Toon Disney; Turner Classic Movies; TV Land; Versus; WE tv.

Fee: $17.00 monthly.

Digital Pay Service 1

Pay Units: N.A.

Programming (via satellite): Cinemax (multiplexed); Flix; HBO (multiplexed); Showtime (multiplexed); Starz (multiplexed); The Movie Channel (multiplexed).

Fee: $10.00 monthly (Cinemax or Starz), $13.00 monthly (HBO or Showtime).

Video-On-Demand: Yes

Pay-Per-View

iN DEMAND (delivered digitally); Playboy TV (delivered digitally).

Internet Service

Operational: Yes.

Broadband Service: Comcast High Speed Internet.

Fee: $99.95 installation; $44.95 monthly; $15.00 modem lease; $99.95 modem purchase.

Telephone Service

Digital: Operational

Miles of Plant: 52.0 (coaxial); 7.0 (fiber optic). Homes passed: 2,887. Total homes in franchised area: 3,150.

Regional Vice President: Scott Tenney. Area Director: Wendy Henry. Chief Technician: Jeff Harrington. Customer Service Manager: Jennifer Lane.

City fee: 3% of gross.

Ownership: Comcast Cable Communications Inc. (MSO).

GREENS FORK—Formerly served by CableDirect. No longer in operation. ICA: IN0258.

GREENSBURG—Comcast Cable, 2450 S Henderson St, Bloomington, IN 47401-4540. Phone: 812-332-9486. Fax: 812-332-0129. Web Site: http://www.comcast.com. Also serves Decatur County (portions). ICA: IN0072.

TV Market Ranking: Outside TV Markets (Decatur County (portions), GREENSBURG). Franchise award date: N.A. Franchise expiration date: N.A. Began: June 1, 1975.

Channel capacity: N.A. Channels available but not in use: N.A.

Basic Service

Subscribers: N.A. Included in Bloomington

Programming (received off-air): WCLJ-TV (TBN) Bloomington; WFYI (PBS) Indianapolis; WHMB-TV (IND) Indianapolis; WIPX-TV (ION) Bloomington; WISH-TV (CBS) Indianapolis; WNDY-TV (MNT) Marion; WRTV (ABC) Indianapolis; WTHR (NBC) Indianapolis; WTTV (CW) Bloomington; WXIN (FOX) Indianapolis; allband FM.

Programming (via satellite): Discovery Channel; FX; TBS Superstation; WGN America.

Fee: $60.00 installation; $2.00 converter.

Expanded Basic Service 1

Subscribers: 2,426.

Programming (via satellite): ABC Family Channel; AMC; Animal Planet; Arts & Entertainment; BET Networks; Cartoon Network; CNBC; CNN; Comedy Central; Country Music TV; Disney Channel; E! Entertainment Television; ESPN; ESPN 2; Food Network; Fox News Channel; Fox Sports Net Midwest; Headline News; HGTV; History Channel; Home Shopping Network; Lifetime; MoviePlex; MTV; Nickelodeon; QVC; Spike TV; The Learning Channel; Travel Channel; truTV; Turner Network TV; TV Land; USA Network; VH1; Weather Channel.

Fee: $40.00 monthly.

Digital Basic Service

Subscribers: N.A.

Programming (via satellite): American-Life TV Network; BBC America; Bio; Bloomberg Television; Bravo; C-SPAN 3; Discovery Digital Networks; DMX Music; Do-It-Yourself; Encore (multiplexed); ESPN Classic Sports; ESPNews; Eternal Word TV Network; Fox Movie Channel; Fox Sports World; Fuse; G4; GAS; Golf Channel; GSN; Halogen Network; History Channel International; Independent Film Channel; Lifetime Movie Network; National Geographic Channel; Nick Jr.; Nick Too; SoapNet; Speed Channel; Style Network; Sundance Channel; Syfy; Toon Disney; Turner Classic Movies; Versus; WE tv.

Fee: $17.00 monthly.

Digital Pay Service 1

Pay Units: N.A.

Programming (via satellite): Cinemax (multiplexed); Flix; HBO (multiplexed); Showtime (multiplexed); Starz (multiplexed); The Movie Channel (multiplexed).

Fee: $10.00 monthly (Cinemax or Starz), $13.00 monthly (HBO or Showtime).

Video-On-Demand: Yes

Pay-Per-View

iN DEMAND (delivered digitally); Adult (delivered digitally).

Internet Service

Operational: Yes.

Broadband Service: Comcast High Speed Internet.

Fee: $99.95 installation; $44.95 monthly; $15.00 modem lease; $99.95 modem purchase.

Telephone Service

Analog: Not Operational

Digital: Operational

Miles of Plant: 63.0 (coaxial); None (fiber optic). Homes passed: 3,472. Total homes in franchised area: 3,750.

Area Director: Wendy Henry. Chief Technician: Jeff Harrington. Customer Service Manager: Jennifer Lane.

City fee: 3% of gross.

Ownership: Comcast Cable Communications Inc. (MSO).

GREENWOOD—Comcast Cable, 2450 S Henderson St, Bloomington, IN 47401-4540. Phone: 812-332-9486. Fax: 812-332-0129. Web Site: http://www.comcast.com. Also serves Bargersville, Franklin, Johnson County, New Whiteland & Whiteland. ICA: IN0023.

TV Market Ranking: 16 (Bargersville, Franklin, GREENWOOD, Johnson County, New Whiteland, Whiteland). Franchise award date: May 17, 1976. Franchise expiration date: N.A. Began: May 28, 1981.

Channel capacity: N.A. Channels available but not in use: N.A.

Basic Service

Subscribers: N.A. Included in Bloomington

Programming (received off-air): WCLJ-TV (TBN) Bloomington; WDTI (IND) Indianapolis; WFYI (PBS) Indianapolis; WHMB-TV (IND) Indianapolis; WIPX-TV (ION) Bloomington; WISH-TV (CBS) Indianapolis; WNDY-TV (MNT) Marion; WRTV (ABC) Indianapolis; WTHR (NBC) Indianapolis; WTTV (CW) Bloomington; WXIN (FOX) Indianapolis; 18 FMs.

Programming (via satellite): ABC Family Channel; AMC; Animal Planet; Arts & Entertainment; BET Networks; Cartoon Network; CNBC; CNN; Comedy Central; Country Music TV; C-SPAN; C-SPAN 2; Discovery Channel; Disney Channel; E! Entertainment Television; ESPN; ESPN 2; Eternal Word TV Network; Food Network; Fox News Channel; Fox Sports Net Midwest; FX; Headline News; HGTV; History Channel; Lifetime; MSNBC; MTV; Nickelodeon; QVC; Spike TV; TBS Superstation; The Learning Channel; Travel Channel; Turner Network TV; TV Land; USA Network; VH1; Weather Channel; Weatherscan; WGN America.

Fee: $40.00 installation; $40.00 monthly; $1.00 converter.

Digital Basic Service

Subscribers: 1,370.

Programming (via satellite): American-Life TV Network; BBC America; Bio; Bloomberg Television; Bravo; C-SPAN 3; Discovery Digital Networks; DMX Music; Do-It-Yourself; Encore (multiplexed); ESPN Classic Sports; ESPNews; Eternal Word TV Network; Fox Movie Channel; Fox Sports World; Fuse; G4; GAS; Golf Channel; GSN; Halogen Network; History Channel International; Independent Film Channel; Lifetime Movie Network; National Geographic Channel; Nick Jr.; Nick Too; SoapNet; Speed Channel; Style Network; Sundance Channel; Syfy; Toon Disney; truTV; Turner Classic Movies; Versus; WE tv.

Fee: $17.00 monthly.

Digital Pay Service 1

Pay Units: N.A.

Programming (via satellite): Cinemax (multiplexed); Flix; HBO (multiplexed); Showtime (multiplexed); Starz (multiplexed); The Movie Channel (multiplexed).

Fee: $10.00 monthly (Cinemax or Starz), $13.00 monthly (HBO or Showtime/TMC/Flix).

Video-On-Demand: Yes

Pay-Per-View

Addressable homes: 1,370.

Hot Choice, Fee: $3.95-$5.95, Addressable: Yes; iN DEMAND; Fresh; iN DEMAND (delivered digitally); Adult (delivered digitally).

Internet Service

Operational: Yes.

Broadband Service: Comcast High Speed Internet.

Fee: $99.95 installation; $44.95 monthly; $15.00 modem lease; $99.95 modem purchase.

Telephone Service

Digital: Operational

Miles of Plant: 491.0 (coaxial); None (fiber optic). Homes passed: 30,089.

Area Director: Wendy Henry. Chief Engineer: Jeff Harrington. Customer Service Manager: Jennifer Lane.

City fee: 3% of gross.

Ownership: Comcast Cable Communications Inc. (MSO).

GRIFFIN—Formerly served by CableDirect. No longer in operation. ICA: IN0259.

HAMLET—Formerly served by CableDirect. No longer in operation. ICA: IN0202.

HAMMOND—Comcast Cable. Now served by CHICAGO (southern suburbs), IL [IL0008]. ICA: IN0008.

HAMMOND—WOW! Internet Cable & Phone, 7887 E Belleview Ave, Ste 1000, Englewood, CO 80111. Phones: 866-496-9669; 720-479-3500. Fax: 720-479-3585. Web Site: http://www1.wowway.com. ICA: IN0366.

Note: This system is an overbuild.

TV Market Ranking: 3 (HAMMOND). Franchise award date: N.A. Franchise expiration date: N.A. Began: N.A.

Channel capacity: N.A. Channels available but not in use: N.A.

Basic Service

Subscribers: N.A. Included in Chicago

Programming (received off-air): WBBM-TV (CBS) Chicago; WCIU-TV (IND) Chicago; WCPX-TV (ION) Chicago; WFLD (FOX) Chicago; WGBO-DT (UNV) Joliet; WGN-TV (CW, IND) Chicago; WJYS (IND) Hammond; WLS-TV (ABC) Chicago; WMAQ-TV (NBC) Chicago; WPWR-TV (MNT) Gary; WSNS-TV (TMO) Chicago; WTTW (PBS) Chicago; WXFT-DT (TEL) Aurora; WYCC (PBS) Chicago.

Programming (via satellite): Home Shopping Network; INSP; TBS Superstation; V-me TV.

Current originations: Government Access; Educational Access; Public Access.

Fee: $39.99 installation; $16.99 monthly.

Expanded Basic Service 1

Subscribers: N.A.

Programming (via satellite): ABC Family Channel; AMC; Animal Planet; Arts & Entertainment; BET Networks; Big Ten Network; Bravo; Cartoon Network; CNBC; CNN; Comcast SportsNet Chicago; Comedy Central; Country Music TV; C-SPAN; Discovery Channel; Discovery Health Channel; Disney Channel; E! Entertainment Television; ESPN; ESPN 2; ESPN Classic Sports; Food Network; Fox News Channel; FX; Golf Channel; GSN; Hallmark Channel; Headline News; HGTV; History Channel; Lifetime; MSNBC; MTV; MTV2; Nickelodeon; NickToons TV; Oxygen; QVC; ShopNBC; Speed Channel; Spike TV; Syfy; The Learning Channel; Toon Disney; Travel Channel; truTV; Turner Classic Movies; Turner Network TV; TV Land; USA Network; VH1; Weather Channel.

Fee: $34.76 monthly.

Digital Basic Service

Subscribers: N.A.

Programming (via satellite): ABC News Now; BBC America; Big Ten Network; Bio; Bloomberg Television; Bridges TV; CMT Pure Country; Cooking Channel; Discovery Kids Channel; Discovery Military Channel; Discovery Planet Green; DMX Music; Do-It-Yourself; Encore (multiplexed); ESPN U; ESPNews; Eternal Word TV Network; Fox Business Channel; Fox Movie Channel; Fox Reality Channel; Fox Soccer; G4; GemsTV; here! On Demand; History Channel International; ID Investigation Discovery; Jewelry Television; Lifetime Movie Network; Lifetime Real Women; MTV Hits; National Geographic Channel; NFL Network; Nick Jr.; Nick Too; PBS Kids Sprout; Science Channel; SoapNet; Starz (multiplexed); Style Network; Sundance Channel; TeenNick; The Word Network; This TV; Trinity Broadcasting Network; Universal Sports; VH1 Classic.

Fee: $25.23 monthly.

Digital Expanded Basic Service

Subscribers: N.A.

Programming (via satellite): Fox College Sports Atlantic; Fox College Sports Central; Fox College Sports Pacific; Outdoor Channel; Tennis Channel.

Fee: $4.99 monthly.

Digital Expanded Basic Service 2

Subscribers: N.A.

Programming (received off-air): WBBM-TV (CBS) Chicago; WCIU-TV (IND) Chicago; WFLD (FOX) Chicago; WGN-TV (CW, IND) Chicago; WLS-TV (ABC) Chicago; WMAQ-TV (NBC) Chicago; WPWR-TV (MNT) Gary.

Programming (via satellite): ABC Family HD; Animal Planet HD; Arts & Entertainment HD; Discovery Channel HD; Discovery HD Theater; Disney Channel HD; ESPN 2 HD; ESPN HD; Food Network HD; Fox News HD; FX HD; HDNet; HDNet Movies; HGTV HD; History Channel HD; National Geographic Channel HD Network; NFL Network HD; PBS HD; Starz HDTV; TLC HD; Turner Network TV HD; WealthTV HD.

Fee: $13.00 monthly.

Digital Pay Service 1

Pay Units: N.A.

Programming (via satellite): Cinemax (multiplexed); Cinemax HD; Cinemax On Demand; Flix; HBO (multiplexed); HBO HD; HBO On Demand; Showtime (multiplexed);

Showtime HD; Showtime On Demand; The Movie Channel (multiplexed); The Movie Channel On Demand.
Fee: $15.00 monthly (HBO, Cinemax, Starz or Showtime/TMC/Flix).
Video-On-Demand: Yes
Pay-Per-View
ETC (delivered digitally), Addressable: Yes; iN DEMAND (delivered digitally); Pleasure (delivered digitally); Playboy TV (delivered digitally); Sports PPV (delivered digitally).
Internet Service
Operational: Yes.
Broadband Service: WOW! Internet.
Fee: $40.99-$72.99 monthly; $2.50 modem lease.
Telephone Service
Digital: Operational
Vice President & General Manager: Kelvin Fee. Vice President, Sales & Marketing: Cathy Kuo. Chief Technician: Cash Hagen.
Ownership: WideOpenWest LLC (MSO).

HARDINSBURG—Formerly served by CableDirect. No longer in operation. ICA: IN0260.

HARMONY—Avenue Broadband Communications, 2603 Hart St, Vincennes, IN 47591. Phones: 800-882-7185; 812-895-7676. Fax: 812-886-5017. Web Site: http://www.avenuebroadband.com. ICA: IN0377.
TV Market Ranking: Below 100 (HARMONY).
Channel capacity: N.A. Channels available but not in use: N.A.
Basic Service
Subscribers: N.A.
Programming (received off-air): WFXW (FOX) Terre Haute; WFYI (PBS) Indianapolis; WHMB-TV (IND) Indianapolis; WRTV (ABC) Indianapolis; WTHI-TV (CBS) Terre Haute; WTHR (NBC) Indianapolis; WTIU (PBS) Bloomington; WTTV (CW) Bloomington; WTWO (NBC) Terre Haute.
Programming (via satellite): C-SPAN; Home Shopping Network; ION Television; QVC; WGN America.
Current originations: Public Access.
Expanded Basic Service 1
Subscribers: N.A.
Programming (via satellite): ABC Family Channel; AMC; Animal Planet; Arts & Entertainment; BET Networks; Big Ten Network; Bravo; Cartoon Network; CNBC; CNN; Comedy Central; Country Music TV; Discovery Channel; Disney Channel; Disney XD; E! Entertainment Television; ESPN; ESPN 2; Food Network; Fox News Channel; Fox Sports Net Midwest; FX; G4; Golf Channel; Hallmark Channel; Headline News; HGTV; History Channel; Lifetime; MSNBC; MTV; National Geographic Channel; Nickelodeon; Outdoor Channel; Oxygen; SoapNet; Speed Channel; Spike TV; Syfy; TBS Superstation; The Learning Channel; Travel Channel; truTV; Turner Network TV; TV Land; USA Network; VH1; Weather Channel.
Digital Basic Service
Subscribers: N.A.
Programming (via satellite): BBC America; Bio; Bloomberg Television; Boomerang; CMT Pure Country; Discovery en Espanol; Discovery Health Channel; Discovery Kids Channel; Discovery Military Channel; Discovery Planet Green; DMX Music; Do-It-Yourself; ESPN U; Fox Business Channel; Fox Movie Channel; GSN; History Channel International; ID Investigation Discovery; Lifetime Movie Network; MTV Jams; MTV Tres; MTV2; mtvU; Nick Jr.; Nick Too; NickToons TV; PBS Kids Sprout; RFD-TV; Science Channel; Style Network; Sundance Channel; TeenNick; VH1 Classic; VH1 Soul; WE tv.
Digital Expanded Basic Service
Subscribers: N.A.
Programming (via satellite): Encore (multiplexed); Flix; Showtime (multiplexed); The Movie Channel (multiplexed).
Digital Expanded Basic Service 2
Subscribers: N.A.
Programming (via satellite): Fox College Sports Atlantic; Fox College Sports Central; Fox College Sports Pacific; Fox Soccer.
Digital Expanded Basic Service 3
Subscribers: N.A.
Programming (received off-air): HGTV HD; WFYI (PBS) Indianapolis; WRTV (ABC) Indianapolis; WTHI-TV (CBS) Terre Haute; WTWO (NBC) Terre Haute.
Programming (via satellite): ABC Family HD; Animal Planet HD; Arts & Entertainment HD; Big Ten Network HD; Discovery Channel HD; Discovery HD Theater; Disney Channel HD; ESPN 2 HD; ESPN HD; Food Network HD; Fox News HD; FX HD; HDNet; HDNet Movies; History Channel HD; Lifetime Movie Network HD; National Geographic Channel HD Network; Outdoor Channel 2 HD; Science Channel HD; Speed HD; Syfy HD; Travel Channel HD; Universal HD; USA Network HD.
Digital Pay Service 1
Pay Units: N.A.
Programming (via satellite): Cinemax (multiplexed); HBO (multiplexed); Starz (multiplexed); Starz HDTV.
Pay-Per-View
iN DEMAND (delivered digitally); Spice: Xcess (delivered digitally); Club Jenna (delivered digitally); Playboy TV (delivered digitally); Fresh (delivered digitally); Shorteez (delivered digitally).
Chief Executive Officer: Steve Lowe. Vice President & General Manager: Mary Iafrate. Vice President, Engineering: Jeff Spence. System Engineer: Bart Cotter.
Ownership: Buford Media Group LLC (MSO).

HARTFORD CITY—Comcast Cable, 5330 E 65th St, Indianapolis, IN 46220. Phone: 317-275-6370. Web Site: http://www.comcast.com. Also serves Blackford County, Delaware County, Eaton, Fairmount, Fowlerton, Grant County, Shamrock & Upland. ICA: IN0047.
TV Market Ranking: 82 (Blackford County (portions), Grant County (portions), HARTFORD CITY, Upland); Below 100 (Delaware County, Eaton, Fairmount, Fowlerton, Shamrock, Blackford County (portions), Grant County (portions)). Franchise award date: May 1, 1969. Franchise expiration date: N.A. Began: May 1, 1970.
Channel capacity: N.A. Channels available but not in use: N.A.
Basic Service
Subscribers: N.A. Included in Anderson
Programming (received off-air): WANE-TV (CBS) Fort Wayne; WFFT-TV (FOX) Fort Wayne; WHMB-TV (IND) Indianapolis; WIPB (PBS) Muncie; WISE-TV (MNT, NBC) Fort Wayne; WISH-TV (CBS) Indianapolis; WNDY-TV (MNT) Marion; WPTA (ABC, CW) Fort Wayne; WRTV (ABC) Indianapolis; WTHR (NBC) Indianapolis; WTTK (IND) Kokomo; WXIN (FOX) Indianapolis; 27 FMs.
Programming (via satellite): C-SPAN; C-SPAN 2; Home Shopping Network; QVC; Trinity Broadcasting Network; WGN America.
Fee: $2.00 converter.
Expanded Basic Service 1
Subscribers: 1,014.
Programming (via satellite): ABC Family Channel; AMC; Animal Planet; Arts & Entertainment; BET Networks; Bravo; Cartoon Network; CNBC; CNN; Comedy Central; Country Music TV; Discovery Channel; Disney Channel; E! Entertainment Television; ESPN; ESPN 2; Eternal Word TV Network; Food Network; Fox News Channel; Fox Sports Net Midwest; Headline News; HGTV; History Channel; Lifetime; MSNBC; MTV; Nickelodeon; Oxygen; Speed Channel; Spike TV; Syfy; TBS Superstation; The Learning Channel; Travel Channel; Turner Network TV; TV Guide Network; TV Land; USA Network; VH1; Weather Channel.
Fee: $51.74 monthly.
Digital Basic Service
Subscribers: 1,142.
Programming (via satellite): BBC America; Bio; Bloomberg Television; C-SPAN 3; Discovery Digital Networks; DMX Music; Do-It-Yourself; Encore (multiplexed); ESPN Classic Sports; ESPNews; Fox Sports World; G4; GAS; Golf Channel; GSN; Halogen Network; History Channel International; Independent Film Channel; Lifetime Movie Network; MTV2; National Geographic Channel; Nick Jr.; Nick Too; Ovation; SoapNet; Style Network; Sundance Channel; Toon Disney; truTV; Turner Classic Movies; Versus; WE tv.
Fee: $17.00 monthly.
Digital Pay Service 1
Pay Units: N.A.
Programming (via satellite): Cinemax (multiplexed); HBO (multiplexed); Showtime (multiplexed); Starz (multiplexed); The Movie Channel (multiplexed).
Fee: $10.00 monthly (Cinemax or Starz), $13.00 monthly (HBO or Showtime).
Video-On-Demand: Yes
Pay-Per-View
Addressable homes: 1,142.
iN DEMAND, Addressable: Yes; iN DEMAND (delivered digitally); Fresh (delivered digitally); Playboy TV (delivered digitally).
Internet Service
Operational: Yes.
Subscribers: 496.
Broadband Service: Comcast High Speed Internet.
Fee: $99.95 installation; $44.95 monthly; $15.00 modem lease; $99.95 modem purchase.
Telephone Service
Analog: Not Operational
Digital: Operational
Fee: $39.95 monthly
Miles of Plant: 217.0 (coaxial); None (fiber optic). Homes passed: 6,100. Total homes in franchised area: 6,897.
Regional Vice President: Scott Tenney. Regional Vice President, Technical Operations: Max Woolsey. Regional Vice President, Marketing: Aaron Geisel. Regional Vice President, Communications: Mark Apple.
City fee: 5% of gross.
Ownership: Comcast Cable Communications Inc. (MSO).

HATFIELD—Now served by OWENSBORO, KY [KY0004]. ICA: IN0179.

HAYDEN—Formerly served by CableDirect. No longer in operation. ICA: IN0351.

HEBRON—Comcast Cable. Now served by CHICAGO (southern suburbs), IL [IL0008]. ICA: IN0070.

HERITAGE LAKE—Global Com Inc., 3410 S 7th St, Terre Haute, IN 47802. Phones: 866-382-2253; 812-242-2253. Fax: 812-235-5554. ICA: IN0188.
TV Market Ranking: 16 (HERITAGE LAKE). Franchise award date: December 1, 1989. Franchise expiration date: N.A. Began: December 1, 1989.
Channel capacity: 35 (not 2-way capable). Channels available but not in use: 5.
Basic Service
Subscribers: 401.
Programming (received off-air): WFYI (PBS) Indianapolis; WHMB-TV (IND) Indianapolis; WISH-TV (CBS) Indianapolis; WNDY-TV (MNT) Marion; WRTV (ABC) Indianapolis; WTHI-TV (CBS) Terre Haute; WTHR (NBC) Indianapolis; WTTV (CW) Bloomington; WXIN (FOX) Indianapolis.
Programming (via satellite): AMC; Arts & Entertainment; CNBC; CNN; Comedy Central; Country Music TV; C-SPAN; Discovery Channel; Disney Channel; ESPN; ESPN 2; Home Shopping Network; MTV; Nickelodeon; Spike TV; TBS Superstation; The Learning Channel; Turner Network TV; USA Network; WGN America.
Fee: $35.00 installation; $27.50 monthly.
Pay Service 1
Pay Units: 228.
Programming (via satellite): HBO.
Fee: $35.00 installation.
Internet Service
Operational: No.
Telephone Service
None
Miles of Plant: 30.0 (coaxial); None (fiber optic). Homes passed: 700. Total homes in franchised area: 750.
Ownership: Global Com Inc. (MSO).

HILLSBORO—Formerly served by Longview Communications. No longer in operation. ICA: IN0265.

HILLSDALE—Formerly served by CableDirect. No longer in operation. ICA: IN0266.

HOAGLAND—Formerly served by CableDirect. No longer in operation. ICA: IN0267.

HOLLAND—Formerly served by CableDirect. No longer in operation. ICA: IN0268.

HOLTON—Formerly served by CableDirect. No longer in operation. ICA: IN0269.

HUNTINGTON—Comcast Cable, 720 Taylor St, Fort Wayne, IN 46802-5144. Phones: 260-458-5103; 317-275-6370 (Indianapolis office). Fax: 260-458-5138. Web Site: http://www.comcast.com. Also serves Huntington County. ICA: IN0051.
TV Market Ranking: 82 (HUNTINGTON, Huntington County). Franchise award date: N.A. Franchise expiration date: N.A. Began: October 15, 1976.
Channel capacity: N.A. Channels available but not in use: N.A.
Basic Service
Subscribers: N.A. Included in Indianapolis
Programming (received off-air): WANE-TV (CBS) Fort Wayne; WFFT-TV (FOX) Fort Wayne; WGN-TV (CW, IND) Chicago; WHME-TV (IND) South Bend; WISE-TV (MNT, NBC) Fort Wayne; WPTA (ABC, CW) Fort Wayne; allband FM.
Programming (via satellite): CNN; C-SPAN; Discovery Channel; ESPN; Spike TV; TBS Superstation; Weather Channel.
Fee: $31.99 installation.

Expanded Basic Service 1
Subscribers: N.A.
Programming (received off-air): WINM (IND) Angola.
Programming (via satellite): ABC Family Channel; AMC; Arts & Entertainment; Bravo; CNBC; Comedy Central; Country Music TV; C-SPAN 2; Discovery Health Channel; Disney Channel; E! Entertainment Television; Food Network; Golf Channel; Headline News; HGTV; History Channel; Home Shopping Network; Lifetime; MSNBC; Nickelodeon; Syfy; TBS Superstation; The Learning Channel; Turner Classic Movies; Turner Network TV; USA Network; VH1.
Fee: $51.98 monthly.
Digital Basic Service
Subscribers: N.A.
Programming (via satellite): BBC America; Discovery Digital Networks; ESPN Extra; ESPN Now; GAS; MTV Networks Digital Suite; Music Choice; Nick Jr.; Nick Too; Science Television; Sundance Channel (multiplexed); WAM! America's Kidz Network; Weatherscan.
Fee: $14.95 monthly.
Digital Pay Service 1
Pay Units: N.A.
Programming (via satellite): Cinemax (multiplexed); Encore (multiplexed); Flix; HBO (multiplexed); Showtime (multiplexed); The Movie Channel.
Fee: $18.95 monthly each.
Video-On-Demand: No
Pay-Per-View
iN DEMAND (delivered digitally); Playboy TV (delivered digitally); Pleasure (delivered digitally); Fresh (delivered digitally); Shorteez (delivered digitally).
Internet Service
Operational: Yes.
Broadband Service: Comcast High Speed Internet.
Fee: $57.95 monthly.
Telephone Service
Digital: Operational
Fee: $44.95 monthly
Homes passed: 5,400. Total homes in franchised area: 5,700. Miles of plant included in Fort Wayne
Regional Vice President: Scott Tenney. Technical Operations Director: Bennie Logan. Engineering Manager: Tom Stuckholz. Vice President, Marketing: Aaron Geisel. Marketing Manager: Marci Hefley. Vice President, Communications: Mark Apple.
City fee: 3% of gross.
Ownership: Comcast Cable Communications Inc. (MSO).

INDIANAPOLIS—Comcast Cable, 5330 E 65th St, Indianapolis, IN 46220. Phone: 317-275-6370. Fax: 317-275-6340. Web Site: http://www.comcast.com. Also serves Beech Grove, Brownsburg (town), Clermont, Crows Nest, Cumberland, Danville (town), Fort Benjamin Harrison, Hamilton County, Hancock County, Homecroft, Lake Hart (town), Lawrence, Marion County, Meridian Hills, Mooresville, Morgan County, North Crows Nest, Paragon (town), Plainfield, Ravenswood, Shelby County, Southport, Speedway, Warren Park, Williams Creek & Wynnedale. ICA: IN0001.
TV Market Ranking: 16 (Beech Grove, Brownsburg (town), Clermont, Crows Nest, Cumberland, Danville (town), Fort Benjamin Harrison, Hamilton County, Hancock County, Homecroft, INDIANAPOLIS, Lake Hart (town), Lawrence, Marion County, Meridian Hills, Mooresville, Morgan County, North Crows Nest, Paragon (town), Plainfield, Ravenswood, Shelby County (portions), Southport, Speedway, Warren Park, Williams Creek, Wynnedale). Franchise award date: May 19, 1967. Franchise expiration date: N.A. Began: August 1, 1979.
Channel capacity: N.A. Channels available but not in use: N.A.
Basic Service
Subscribers: 460,600 Includes all Indianapolis, Fort Wayne, and Aurora area systems.
Programming (received off-air): WFYI (PBS) Indianapolis; WHMB-TV (IND) Indianapolis; WIPB (PBS) Muncie; WIPX-TV (ION) Bloomington; WISH-TV (CBS) Indianapolis; WMUN-LP (TBN) Muncie; WNDY-TV (MNT) Marion; WRTV (ABC) Indianapolis; WTHR (NBC) Indianapolis; WTTV (CW) Bloomington; WXIN (FOX) Indianapolis.
Programming (via satellite): ABC Family Channel; AMC; AmericanLife TV Network; Animal Planet; Arts & Entertainment; BET Networks; Cartoon Network; CNBC; CNN; Comedy Central; Country Music TV; C-SPAN; C-SPAN 2; Discovery Channel; Disney Channel; E! Entertainment Television; ESPN; ESPN 2; Food Network; Fox News Channel; Fox Sports Net Midwest; FX; G4; Golf Channel; GSN; Headline News; HGTV; History Channel; Home Shopping Network; Lifetime; MSNBC; MTV; Nickelodeon; QVC; Speed Channel; Spike TV; Style Network; Syfy; TBS Superstation; The Learning Channel; Travel Channel; truTV; Turner Classic Movies; Turner Network TV; TV Guide Network; TV Land; USA Network; Versus; VH1; Weather Channel; WGN America.
Current originations: Government Access; Educational Access; Public Access.
Fee: $50.99 installation.
Expanded Basic Service 1
Subscribers: N.A.
Fee: $54.48 monthly.
Digital Basic Service
Subscribers: 31,800.
Programming (via satellite): BBC America; Discovery Digital Networks; Encore Action; Flix; GAS; MTV Networks Digital Suite; Nick Jr.; Nick Too; Sundance Channel.
Fee: $14.95 monthly.
Digital Pay Service 1
Pay Units: N.A.
Programming (via satellite): Cinemax (multiplexed); DMX Music; Flix; HBO (multiplexed); Showtime (multiplexed); Starz (multiplexed); The Movie Channel (multiplexed).
Video-On-Demand: Yes
Pay-Per-View
iN DEMAND (delivered digitally), Addressable: Yes; Playboy TV (delivered digitally); Fresh (delivered digitally); Fresh; iN DEMAND (delivered digitally); Shorteez (delivered digitally); Pleasure (delivered digitally).
Internet Service
Operational: Yes.
Subscribers: 30,501.
Broadband Service: Comcast High Speed Internet.
Fee: $42.95 monthly; $7.00 modem lease.
Telephone Service
Digital: Operational
Fee: $39.95 monthly
Miles of Plant: 3,145.0 (coaxial); None (fiber optic). Homes passed: 238,723. Total homes in franchised area: 245,000.
Regional Vice President: Scott Tenney. Regional Vice President, Technical Operations: Max Woolsey. Vice President, Marketing: Aaron Geisel. Marketing Manager: Marci Hefley. Regional Vice President, Communications: Mark Apple.
Ownership: Comcast Cable Communications Inc. (MSO).

INDIANAPOLIS—Formerly served by Sprint Corp. No longer in operation. ICA: IN0348.

INDIANAPOLIS (portions)—Bright House Networks, 3030 Roosevelt Ave, Indianapolis, IN 46218-3755. Phones: 317-972-9700 (Customer service); 317-632-9077 (Administrative office). Fax: 317-632-5311. E-mail: customersupport.indiana@mybrighthouse.com. Web Site: http://indiana.brighthouse.com/default.aspx. Also serves Avon, Brownsburg, Carmel, Clay Twp., Danville, Fortville, Ingalls, Lizton, McCordsville, Pittsboro, Plainfield, Whitestown & Zionsville. ICA: IN0002.
TV Market Ranking: 16 (Avon, Brownsburg, Carmel, Clay Twp., Danville, Fortville, INDIANAPOLIS (PORTIONS), Ingalls, Lizton, McCordsville, Pittsboro, Plainfield, Whitestown, Zionsville). Franchise award date: February 7, 1981. Franchise expiration date: N.A. Began: December 7, 1981.
Channel capacity: 78 (operating 2-way). Channels available but not in use: None.
Basic Service
Subscribers: 100,686.
Programming (received off-air): WCLJ-TV (TBN) Bloomington; WDNI-CD Indianapolis; WFYI (PBS) Indianapolis; WHMB-TV (IND) Indianapolis; WIPX-TV (ION) Bloomington; WISH-TV (CBS) Indianapolis; WNDY-TV (MNT) Marion; WRTV (ABC) Indianapolis; WTHR (NBC) Indianapolis; WTTV (CW) Bloomington; WXIN (FOX) Indianapolis; 7 FMs.
Programming (via satellite): C-SPAN 2; QVC; Weather Channel; WGN America.
Current originations: Government Access; Educational Access.
Fee: $12.55 monthly.
Expanded Basic Service 1
Subscribers: N.A.
Programming (via satellite): ABC Family Channel; AMC; Animal Planet; Arts & Entertainment; BET Networks; Bravo; Cartoon Network; CNBC; CNN; Comedy Central; Country Music TV; C-SPAN; Discovery Channel; E! Entertainment Television; ESPN; ESPN 2; ESPN Classic Sports; Food Network; Fox News Channel; Fox Sports Net Midwest; FX; Golf Channel; GSN; Hallmark Channel; Headline News; HGTV; History Channel; Home Shopping Network; Independent Film Channel; Lifetime; MSNBC; MTV; Nickelodeon; Oxygen; QVC; ShopNBC; Speed Channel; Spike TV; Syfy; TBS Superstation; The Learning Channel; Travel Channel; truTV; Turner Classic Movies; Turner Network TV; TV Land; Univision; USA Network; Versus; VH1; WE tv.
Fee: $34.95 monthly.
Digital Basic Service
Subscribers: 40,615.
Programming (via satellite): America's Store; BBC America; C-SPAN 3; Discovery Digital Networks; Disney Channel; DMX Music; Do-It-Yourself; ESPNews; Fox Sports World; Lifetime Movie Network; MTV2; MuchMusic Network; National Geographic Channel; Nick Jr.; Outdoor Channel; Style Network; Toon Disney; VH1 Classic.
Fee: $10.50 monthly.
Digital Pay Service 1
Pay Units: 52,258.
Programming (via satellite): Cinemax (multiplexed); Encore (multiplexed); Fox Movie Channel; HBO (multiplexed); Independent Film Channel; Showtime (multiplexed); Starz (multiplexed); Sundance Channel; The Movie Channel (multiplexed).
Fee: $9.00 monthly (Starz), $13.00 monthly (Cinemax, HBO or Showtime/TMC).
Video-On-Demand: No
Pay-Per-View
Shorteez (delivered digitally); Fresh (delivered digitally); Pleasure (delivered digitally); Playboy TV (delivered digitally); NHL Center Ice (delivered digitally); NBA League Pass (delivered digitally); MLB Extra Innings (delivered digitally); Pay-Per-View movies, sports, events (delivered digitally).
Internet Service
Operational: Yes.
Subscribers: 43,765.
Broadband Service: Road Runner.
Fee: $24.95 installation; $44.95 monthly.
Telephone Service
Digital: Operational
Fee: $24.95 installation; $49.95 monthly
Miles of Plant: 2,578.0 (coaxial); 225.0 (fiber optic). Homes passed: 242,430.
Division President: Buz Nesbit. Vice President, Engineering: Kerry Fouts. Vice President, Marketing & Customer Service: Wayde Klein. Vice President, Finance: Rick Langhals. Vice President, Sales & Area Operations: Ray Pawulich. Digital Services Director: Doug Murray. Public Affairs Director: Al Aldridge. Customer Service Director: Anita Hendricks. General Manager: Cal Blumharst.
County fee: 3% of gross.
Ownership: Bright House Networks LLC (MSO).

JAMESTOWN—Indiana Communications, PO Box 617, Boswell, IN 47921. Phone: 815-457-2659. Web Site: http://www.indcomm.net. Also serves Advance, Boone County (portions), Hendricks County (portions), New Ross & North Salem. ICA: IN0132.
TV Market Ranking: 16 (Advance, Boone County (portions), Hendricks County (portions), JAMESTOWN, New Ross, North Salem); Below 100 (Boone County (portions)). Franchise award date: March 1, 1981. Franchise expiration date: N.A. Began: March 14, 1982.
Channel capacity: N.A. Channels available but not in use: N.A.

Basic Service
Subscribers: 178.
Programming (received off-air): WCLJ-TV (TBN) Bloomington; WFYI (PBS) Indianapolis; WHMB-TV (IND) Indianapolis; WIPX-TV (ION) Bloomington; WISH-TV (CBS) Indianapolis; WNDY-TV (MNT) Marion; WRTV (ABC) Indianapolis; WTHR (NBC) Indianapolis; WTTV (CW) Bloomington; WXIN (FOX) Indianapolis; 1 FM.
Programming (via satellite): ABC Family Channel; AMC; Animal Planet; Arts & Entertainment; CBS College Sports Network; CNN; Comedy Central; Country Music TV; C-SPAN; Discovery Channel; Disney Channel; Do-It-Yourself; ESPN; ESPN 2; ESPN Classic Sports; Food Network; Fox News Channel; FX; Hallmark Channel; Hallmark Movie Channel; Headline News; HGTV; History Channel; Lifetime; MSNBC; Nickelodeon; QVC; Spike TV; Syfy; TBS Superstation; The Learning Channel; Travel Channel; Turner Network TV; USA Network; Weather Channel; WGN America.
Fee: $25.00 installation; $19.98 monthly.

Expanded Basic Service 1
Subscribers: N.A.
Fee: $19.97 monthly.

Digital Basic Service
Subscribers: 13.
Programming (via satellite): AmericanLife TV Network; BBC America; Bio; Bloomberg Television; Discovery Health Channel; Discovery Kids Channel; Discovery Military Channel; Discovery Planet Green; DMX Music; Encore (multiplexed); ESPNews; FitTV; Fox Movie Channel; Fox Soccer; Fuse; G4; Golf Channel; GSN; Halogen Network; History Channel International; ID Investigation Discovery; Independent Film Channel; Lifetime Movie Network; Outdoor Channel; Science Channel; Speed Channel; Style Network; Sundance Channel; Toon Disney; Turner Classic Movies; Versus.
Fee: $17.00 monthly.

Pay Service 1
Pay Units: N.A.
Programming (via satellite): Cinemax; HBO; Showtime; The Movie Channel.
Fee: $10.00 installation; $10.50 monthly (each).

Digital Pay Service 1
Pay Units: N.A.
Programming (via satellite): Cinemax (multiplexed); Flix; HBO (multiplexed); Showtime (multiplexed); Starz (multiplexed); The Movie Channel (multiplexed).
Fee: $8.95 monthly (TMC), $10.95 monthly (Cinemax & Showtime), $12.95 monthly (HBO.

Video-On-Demand: No

Pay-Per-View
iN DEMAND (delivered digitally); Hot Choice (delivered digitally); Playboy TV (delivered digitally); Fresh (delivered digitally); Shorteez (delivered digitally).

Internet Service
Operational: Yes.
Subscribers: 81.
Broadband Service: West Michigan Internet Service.
Fee: $29.95 monthly.

Telephone Service
None
Miles of Plant: 28.0 (coaxial); None (fiber optic). Homes passed: 1,112. Total homes in franchised area: 1,112.
Manager: Joe Young.
City fee: 3% of gross.
Ownership: Park TV & Electronics Inc. (MSO).

JASONVILLE—Suddenlink Communications, PO Box 218, Poplar Bluff, MO 63901. Phones: 314-965-2020; 800-255-8389. Web Site: http://www.suddenlink.com. Also serves Coalmont, Dugger, Farmersburg, Greene County (western portion), Hymera, Midland, Shelburn & Wilfred. ICA: IN0106.
TV Market Ranking: Below 100 (Coalmont, Dugger, Farmersburg, Greene County (western portion), Hymera, JASONVILLE, Midland, Shelburn, Wilfred). Franchise award date: March 16, 1981. Franchise expiration date: N.A. Began: November 1, 1981.
Channel capacity: 39 (operating 2-way). Channels available but not in use: None.

Basic Service
Subscribers: 1,748.
Programming (received off-air): WFXW (FOX) Terre Haute; WRTV (ABC) Indianapolis; WTHI-TV (CBS) Terre Haute; WTTV (CW) Bloomington; WTWO (NBC) Terre Haute; WVUT (PBS) Vincennes.
Programming (via satellite): Home Shopping Network; INSP; Trinity Broadcasting Network; Weather Channel; WGN America.
Fee: $61.50 installation; $16.95 monthly.

Expanded Basic Service 1
Subscribers: N.A.
Programming (via satellite): ABC Family Channel; AMC; Animal Planet; Arts & Entertainment; Cartoon Network; CNN; Comedy Central; Discovery Channel; Disney Channel; E! Entertainment Television; ESPN; ESPN 2; Food Network; Fox News Channel; Fox Sports Net Midwest; FX; Great American Country; Hallmark Channel; Headline News; HGTV; History Channel; Lifetime; MSNBC; MTV; National Geographic Channel; Nickelodeon; Speed Channel; Spike TV; Syfy; TBS Superstation; The Learning Channel; Travel Channel; Turner Network TV; TV Land; USA Network; VH1.
Fee: $25.00 monthly.

Digital Basic Service
Subscribers: N.A.
Programming (via satellite): BBC America; Bio; Bloomberg Television; Discovery Digital Networks; DMX Music; ESPN Classic Sports; ESPNews; Fox College Sports Atlantic; Fox College Sports Central; Fox College Sports Pacific; Fox Movie Channel; Fox Soccer; Fuse; G4; Golf Channel; GSN; History Channel International; Lifetime Movie Network; Outdoor Channel; ShopNBC; Style Network; Toon Disney; Turner Classic Movies; Versus; WE tv.
Fee: $3.95 monthly.

Pay Service 1
Pay Units: 985.
Programming (via satellite): Cinemax; Encore; HBO; Showtime; The Movie Channel.
Fee: $10.00 installation; $3.99 monthly (Encore), $8.99 monthly (Cinemax), $12.99 monthly (HBO), $13.99 monthly (Showtime & TMC).

Digital Pay Service 1
Pay Units: N.A.
Programming (via satellite): Cinemax (multiplexed); Encore (multiplexed); HBO (multiplexed); Showtime (multiplexed); Starz (multiplexed); The Movie Channel (multiplexed).

Pay-Per-View
iN DEMAND (delivered digitally); Playboy TV (delivered digitally); Fresh (delivered digitally).

Internet Service
Operational: Yes. Began: April 15, 2004.
Broadband Service: Cebridge High Speed Cable Internet.
Fee: $49.95 installation; $20.95 monthly.

Telephone Service
None
Miles of Plant: 127.0 (coaxial); None (fiber optic). Homes passed: 4,144.
Regional Manager: James Robinson. Chief Technician: Chris Mooday. Customer Service Manager: Sandra Baker.
City fee: 3% of gross.
Ownership: Cequel Communications LLC (MSO).

JASPER—Avenue Broadband Communications, 2603 Hart St, Vincennes, IN 47591. Phones: 800-882-7185; 812-895-7676. Fax: 812-886-5017. Web Site: http://www.avenuebroadband.com. Also serves Dubois County (portions) & Ireland. ICA: IN0368.
Note: This system is an overbuild.
TV Market Ranking: 86 (Dubois County (portions) (portions)); Outside TV Markets (Indiana, JASPER, Dubois County (portions) (portions)).
Channel capacity: N.A. Channels available but not in use: N.A.

Basic Service
Subscribers: N.A.
Programming (received off-air): WEHT (ABC) Evansville; WEVV-TV (CBS, MNT) Evansville; WFIE (NBC) Evansville; WJTS-LD (IND) Jasper; WNIN (PBS) Evansville; WTVW (FOX) Evansville.
Programming (via satellite): Eternal Word TV Network; QVC; WGN America.

Expanded Basic Service 1
Subscribers: N.A.
Programming (via satellite): ABC Family Channel; Animal Planet; Arts & Entertainment; CNN; Comedy Central; Discovery Channel; Disney Channel; ESPN; ESPN 2; Fox News Channel; Headline News; Lifetime; MTV; Nickelodeon; Spike TV; Syfy; TBS Superstation; Turner Network TV; USA Network; VH1; Weather Channel.

Pay Service 1
Pay Units: N.A.
Programming (via satellite): Cinemax; HBO.

Pay-Per-View
iN DEMAND (delivered digitally); Hot Choice (delivered digitally); Playboy TV (delivered digitally); Fresh (delivered digitally); Shorteez (delivered digitally).

Internet Service
Operational: No.

Telephone Service
None
Miles of Plant: 37.0 (coaxial); None (fiber optic).
Chief Executive Officer: Steve Lowe. Vice President & General Manager: Mary Iafrate. Vice President, Engineering: Jeff Spence. System Engineer: Bart Cotter.
Ownership: Buford Media Group LLC (MSO).

JASPER—Insight Communications, 2856 Cathy Ln, Jasper, IN 47546-9400. Phone: 812-482-4588. Fax: 812-482-4589. Web Site: http://www.myinsight.com. Also serves Dubois County & Huntingburg. ICA: IN0044.
TV Market Ranking: 86 (Dubois County (portions)); Outside TV Markets (Huntingburg, JASPER, Dubois County (portions)). Franchise award date: N.A. Franchise expiration date: N.A. Began: November 1, 1965.
Channel capacity: N.A. Channels available but not in use: N.A.

Basic Service
Subscribers: N.A. Included in Evansville
Programming (received off-air): WAZE-TV (CW) Madisonville; WEHT (ABC) Evansville; WEVV-TV (CBS, MNT) Evansville; WFIE (NBC) Evansville; WHAS-TV (ABC) Louisville; WJTS-LD (IND) Jasper; WLKY-TV (CBS) Louisville; WNIN (PBS) Evansville; WTTV (CW) Bloomington; WTVW (FOX) Evansville; WVUT (PBS) Vincennes; WYYW-LP Evansville; 4 FMs.
Programming (via satellite): C-SPAN; C-SPAN 2; Discovery Channel; QVC; TBS Superstation; Trinity Broadcasting Network; WGN America.
Current originations: Leased Access.
Fee: $24.95 installation; $2.00 converter.

Expanded Basic Service 1
Subscribers: 5,332.
Programming (via satellite): ABC Family Channel; AMC; Animal Planet; Arts & Entertainment; BET Networks; Bravo; Cartoon Network; CNBC; CNN; Comedy Central; Country Music TV; Disney Channel; E! Entertainment Television; ESPN; ESPN 2; Eternal Word TV Network; Food Network; Fox News Channel; Fox Sports Net Midwest; FX; G4; Golf Channel; Hallmark Channel; Halogen Network; Headline News; HGTV; History Channel; Home Shopping Network; Lifetime; MSNBC; MTV; National Geographic Channel; Nickelodeon; Oxygen; SoapNet; Speed Channel; Spike TV; Syfy; The Learning Channel; Toon Disney; Travel Channel; truTV; Turner Network TV; TV Guide Network; TV Land; Univision; USA Network; VH1; Weather Channel.
Fee: $40.00 monthly.

Digital Basic Service
Subscribers: N.A.
Programming (received off-air): WEHT (ABC) Evansville; WFIE (NBC) Evansville; WNIN (PBS) Evansville.
Programming (via satellite): BBC America; Bio; Bloomberg Television; CBS College Sports Network; Cooking Channel; Discovery Digital Networks; Discovery HD Theater; Do-It-Yourself; ESPN Classic Sports; ESPN HD; ESPN U; ESPNews; Fox Movie Channel; Fox Soccer; Fuse; GAS; GSN; HDNet; HDNet Movies; History Channel International; Independent Film Channel; Lifetime Movie Network; MTV Networks Digital Suite; Music Choice; NFL Network; Nick Jr.; Nick Too; NickToons TV; Outdoor Channel; PBS Kids Sprout; Style Network; Sundance Channel; Trio; Turner Classic Movies; Universal HD; Versus; WE tv.
Fee: $17.00 monthly.

Digital Pay Service 1
Pay Units: N.A.
Programming (via satellite): Cinemax (multiplexed); Encore (multiplexed); Flix; HBO (multiplexed); HBO HD; Showtime (multiplexed); Showtime HD; Starz (multiplexed); The Movie Channel (multiplexed).
Fee: $10.00 monthly (Cinemax or Starz), $13.00 monthly (HBO or Showtime).

Video-On-Demand: Yes

Pay-Per-View
ESPN (delivered digitally); iN DEMAND (delivered digitally).

Internet Service
Operational: Yes.
Broadband Service: InsightBB.com.
Fee: $99.95 installation; $44.95 monthly; $10.00 modem lease; $39.99 modem purchase.

Telephone Service
None
Miles of Plant: 155.0 (coaxial); None (fiber optic). Total homes in franchised area: 6,760. Homes passes included in Evansville
President & Chief Operating Officer: Dinni Jain. Senior Vice President, Operations: John Hutton. District Vice President: Lanae Juffer. Technical Operations Manager: Don Baumholser.
Ownership: Insight Communications Co. (MSO).

JEFFERSON TWP. (Elkhart County)—Comcast Cable. Now served by SOUTH BEND, IN [IN0005]. ICA: IN0159.

JEFFERSONVILLE—Insight Communications. Now served by LOUISVILLE, KY [KY0001]. ICA: IN0015.

KEMPTON—Formerly served by Country Cablevision. No longer in operation. ICA: IN0273.

KENDALLVILLE—Mediacom, 109 E 5th St, Ste A, Auburn, IN 46706. Phones: 309-274-4500 (Chillicothe regional office); 260-927-3015. Fax: 260-347-4433. Web Site: http://www.mediacomcable.com. Also serves Allen County, Auburn, Cedarville, Columbia City, De Kalb County, Garrett, Grabill, Harlan, Laotto, Leo, Noble County (portions), Spencerville, St. Joe & Waterloo. ICA: IN0066.

TV Market Ranking: 82 (Allen County, Auburn, Cedarville, Columbia City, De Kalb County, Garrett, Grabill, Harlan, KENDALLVILLE, Laotto, Leo, Noble County (portions), Spencerville, St. Joe, Waterloo). Franchise award date: N.A. Franchise expiration date: N.A. Began: May 1, 1975.

Channel capacity: N.A. Channels available but not in use: N.A.

Basic Service

Subscribers: 14,647.

Programming (received off-air): WANE-TV (CBS) Fort Wayne; WFFT-TV (FOX) Fort Wayne; WFWA (PBS) Fort Wayne; WHME-TV (IND) South Bend; WINM (IND) Angola; WISE-TV (MNT, NBC) Fort Wayne; WNIT (PBS) South Bend; WPTA (ABC, CW) Fort Wayne; WTTK (IND) Kokomo; 1 FM.

Programming (via satellite): WGN America.

Fee: $45.00 installation; $20.95 monthly.

Expanded Basic Service 1

Subscribers: 10,849.

Programming (via satellite): ABC Family Channel; AMC; Animal Planet; Arts & Entertainment; Bravo; Cartoon Network; CNBC; CNN; Comedy Central; Country Music TV; C-SPAN; CW+; Discovery Channel; Disney Channel; E! Entertainment Television; ESPN; ESPN 2; Food Network; Fox News Channel; Fox Sports Net; FX; Hallmark Channel; Headline News; HGTV; History Channel; Home Shopping Network; Lifetime; MSNBC; MTV; Nickelodeon; Product Information Network; QVC; Radar Channel; Speed Channel; Spike TV; Syfy; TBS Superstation; The Learning Channel; Travel Channel; Trinity Broadcasting Network; Turner Network TV; TV Guide Network; TV Land; Univision; USA Network; VH1; WE tv; Weather Channel.

Fee: $34.00 monthly.

Digital Basic Service

Subscribers: 1,738.

Programming (via satellite): AmericanLife TV Network; BBC America; Bio; Bloomberg Television; Cine Latino; CNN en Espanol; Discovery en Espanol; Discovery Health Channel; Discovery Home Channel; Discovery Kids Channel; Discovery Military Channel; FitTV; Fox Movie Channel; Fox Soccer; Fox Sports en Espanol; G4; Golf Channel; GSN; Halogen Network; History Channel International; ID Investigation Discovery; Independent Film Channel; Lifetime Movie Network; MTV Hits; MTV Tres; National Geographic Channel; Outdoor Channel; Science Channel; Style Network; Toon Disney en Espanol; Turner Classic Movies; TVE Internacional; Utilisima; Versus.

Fee: $9.00 monthly.

Pay Service 1

Pay Units: N.A.

Programming (via satellite): Cinemax; Encore; HBO; Showtime; Starz.

Digital Pay Service 1

Pay Units: 3,984.

Programming (via satellite): Cinemax (multiplexed); Encore (multiplexed); HBO (multiplexed); Showtime (multiplexed); Starz (multiplexed); The Movie Channel (multiplexed).

Fee: $11.95 monthly (HBO, Cinemax, Starz/Encore or Showtime/TMC).

Video-On-Demand: Yes

Pay-Per-View

Addressable homes: 1,009.

Movies, Fee: $3.95-$5.99, Addressable: Yes.

Internet Service

Operational: Yes.

Subscribers: 250.

Broadband Service: Mediacom High Speed Internet.

Fee: $59.95 installation; $40.95 monthly.

Telephone Service

Analog: Not Operational

Digital: Operational

Fee: $39.95 installation; $39.95 monthly

Miles of Plant: 2,248.0 (coaxial); None (fiber optic). Homes passed: 120,810. Homes passed & miles of plant (coax & fiber combined) includes all of Indiana & Michigan, Hicksville, OH & Wateka, IL)

Vice President: Don Hagwell. Operations Manager: Joe Poffenberger. Technical Operations Manager: Craig Grey. Sales & Marketing Director: Stephanie Law.

City fee: 5% of gross.

Ownership: Mediacom LLC (MSO).

KENTLAND—Mediacom, Suite A, 109 E 5th St, Auburn, IN 46706. Phone: 260-927-3015. Fax: 260-347-4433. Web Site: http://www.mediacomcable.com. Also serves Brook & Goodland. ICA: IN0097.

TV Market Ranking: Below 100 (Goodland); Outside TV Markets (Brook, KENTLAND). Franchise award date: October 1, 1967. Franchise expiration date: N.A. Began: October 1, 1967.

Channel capacity: N.A. Channels available but not in use: N.A.

Basic Service

Subscribers: 1,609.

Programming (received off-air): WBBM-TV (CBS) Chicago; WCIA (CBS) Champaign; WCPX-TV (ION) Chicago; WFLD (FOX) Chicago; WGBO-DT (UNV) Joliet; WGN-TV (CW, IND) Chicago; WJYS (IND) Hammond; WLFI-TV (CBS) Lafayette; WLS-TV (ABC) Chicago; WMAQ-TV (NBC) Chicago; WPWR-TV (MNT) Gary; WSNS-TV (TMO) Chicago; WTTW (PBS) Chicago; WWTO-TV (TBN) La Salle; WYCC (PBS) Chicago; WYIN (PBS) Gary.

Programming (via satellite): QVC; TV Guide Network.

Fee: $45.00 installation; $20.95 monthly.

Expanded Basic Service 1

Subscribers: N.A.

Programming (via satellite): ABC Family Channel; AMC; Animal Planet; Arts & Entertainment; Cartoon Network; CNBC; CNN; Comcast SportsNet Chicago; Comedy Central; Country Music TV; C-SPAN; C-SPAN 2; Discovery Channel; Disney Channel; E! Entertainment Television; ESPN; ESPN 2; FitTV; Food Network; Fox News Channel; FX; Great American Country; Hallmark Channel; Headline News; HGTV; History Channel; Home Shopping Network; Lifetime; MSNBC; MTV; Nickelodeon; Outdoor Channel; RFD-TV; ShopNBC; Speed Channel; Spike TV; Syfy; TBS Superstation; The Learning Channel; Travel Channel; Trinity Broadcasting Network; truTV; Turner Network TV; TV Land; USA Network; VH1; WE tv; Weather Channel.

Fee: $34.00 monthly.

Digital Basic Service

Subscribers: N.A.

Programming (via satellite): AmericanLife TV Network; BBC America; Bio; Bloomberg Television; Discovery Digital Networks; ESPNews; Fox Movie Channel; Fox Sports World; Fuse; G4; GAS; Golf Channel; GSN; Halogen Network; History Channel International; Independent Film Channel; Lifetime Movie Network; Lime; MTV Networks Digital Suite; Music Choice; National Geographic Channel; Nick Jr.; NickToons TV; Outdoor Channel; Style Network; Trio; Turner Classic Movies; TVG Network; Versus.

Fee: $9.00 monthly.

Digital Expanded Basic Service

Subscribers: N.A.

Programming (via satellite): Discovery HD Theater; ESPN; ESPN 2; HDNet; HDNet Movies; INHD (multiplexed); Universal HD.

Digital Pay Service 1

Pay Units: N.A.

Programming (via satellite): Cinemax (multiplexed); Encore (multiplexed); Flix (multiplexed); HBO (multiplexed); Showtime (multiplexed); Starz (multiplexed); Sundance Channel (multiplexed); The Movie Channel (multiplexed).

Digital Pay Service 2

Pay Units: N.A.

Programming (via satellite): HBO; Showtime; Starz; The Movie Channel.

Video-On-Demand: Yes

Pay-Per-View

iN DEMAND (delivered digitally); Playboy TV (delivered digitally).

Internet Service

Operational: Yes.

Broadband Service: Mediacom High Speed Internet.

Fee: $59.95 installation; $40.95 monthly.

Telephone Service

Digital: Operational

Fee: $39.95 installation; $39.95 monthly

Operations Director: Joe Poffenberger. Technical Operations Director: Craig Grey.

City fee: 5% of basic.

Ownership: Mediacom LLC (MSO).

KEWANNA—Formerly served by CableDirect. No longer in operation. ICA: IN0274.

KIMMEL—Formerly served by CableDirect. No longer in operation. ICA: IN0275.

KINGMAN—Formerly served by CableDirect. No longer in operation. ICA: IN0276.

KNIGHTSTOWN—Insight Communications. Now served by ANDERSON, IN [IN0012]. ICA: IN0077.

KNIGHTSVILLE—Avenue Broadband Communications, 2603 Hart St, Vincennes, IN 47591. Phones: 800-882-7185; 812-895-7676. Fax: 812-886-5017. Web Site: http://www.avenuebroadband.com. ICA: IN0376.

TV Market Ranking: Below 100 (KNIGHTSVILLE).

Channel capacity: N.A. Channels available but not in use: N.A.

Basic Service

Subscribers: N.A.

Programming (received off-air): WFXW (FOX) Terre Haute; WFYI (PBS) Indianapolis; WHMB-TV (IND) Indianapolis; WRTV (ABC) Indianapolis; WTHI-TV (CBS) Terre Haute; WTHR (NBC) Indianapolis; WTIU (PBS) Bloomington; WTTV (CW) Bloomington; WTWO (NBC) Terre Haute.

Programming (via satellite): C-SPAN; Home Shopping Network; ION Television; QVC; WGN America.

Current originations: Public Access.

Expanded Basic Service 1

Subscribers: N.A.

Programming (via satellite): ABC Family Channel; AMC; Animal Planet; Arts & Entertainment; BET Networks; Big Ten Network; Bravo; Cartoon Network; CNBC; CNN; Comedy Central; Country Music TV; Discovery Channel; Disney Channel; Disney XD; E! Entertainment Television; ESPN; ESPN 2; Food Network; Fox News Channel; Fox Sports Net Midwest; FX; G4; Golf Channel; Hallmark Channel; Headline News; HGTV; History Channel; Lifetime; MSNBC; MTV; National Geographic Channel; Nickelodeon; Outdoor Channel; Oxygen; SoapNet; Speed Channel; Spike TV; Syfy; TBS Superstation; The Learning Channel; Travel Channel; truTV; Turner Network TV; TV Land; USA Network; VH1; Weather Channel.

Digital Basic Service

Subscribers: N.A.

Programming (via satellite): BBC America; Bio; Bloomberg Television; Boomerang; CMT Pure Country; Discovery en Espanol; Discovery Health Channel; Discovery Kids Channel; Discovery Military Channel; Discovery Planet Green; DMX Music; Do-It-Yourself; ESPN U; Fox Business Channel; Fox Movie Channel; GSN; History Channel International; ID Investigation Discovery; Lifetime Movie Network; MTV Jams; MTV Tres; MTV2; mtvU; Nick Jr.; Nick Too; NickToons TV; PBS Kids Sprout; RFD-TV; Science Channel; Style Network; Sundance Channel; TeenNick; VH1 Classic; VH1 Soul; WE tv.

Digital Expanded Basic Service

Subscribers: N.A.

Programming (via satellite): Encore (multiplexed); Flix; Showtime (multiplexed); The Movie Channel (multiplexed).

Digital Expanded Basic Service 2

Subscribers: N.A.

Programming (via satellite): Fox College Sports Atlantic; Fox College Sports Central; Fox College Sports Pacific; Fox Soccer.

Digital Expanded Basic Service 3
Subscribers: N.A.
Programming (received off-air): WFYI (PBS) Indianapolis; WRTV (ABC) Indianapolis; WTHI-TV (CBS) Terre Haute; WTWO (NBC) Terre Haute.
Programming (via satellite): ABC Family HD; Animal Planet HD; Arts & Entertainment HD; Big Ten Network HD; Discovery Channel HD; Discovery HD Theater; Disney Channel HD; ESPN 2 HD; ESPN HD; Food Network HD; Fox News HD; FX HD; HDNet; HDNet Movies; HGTV HD; History Channel HD; Lifetime Movie Network HD; National Geographic Channel HD Network; Outdoor Channel 2 HD; Science Channel HD; Speed HD; Syfy HD; Travel Channel HD; Universal HD; USA Network HD.

Digital Pay Service 1
Pay Units: N.A.
Programming (via satellite): Cinemax (multiplexed); HBO (multiplexed); Starz (multiplexed); Starz HDTV.

Pay-Per-View
iN DEMAND (delivered digitally); Spice: Xcess (delivered digitally); Club Jenna (delivered digitally); Playboy TV (delivered digitally); Fresh (delivered digitally); Shorteez (delivered digitally).

Chief Executive Officer: Steve Lowe. Vice President & General Manager: Mary lafrate. Vice President, Engineering: Jeff Spence. System Engineer: Bart Cotter.
Ownership: Buford Media Group LLC (MSO).

KNOX—Mediacom, 109 E 5th St, Ste A, Auburn, IN 46706. Phone: 260-927-3015. Fax: 260-347-4433. Web Site: http://www.mediacomcable.com. Also serves Culver, North Judson & Starke County. ICA: IN0060.
TV Market Ranking: 80 (Culver, KNOX, Starke County (portions)); Outside TV Markets (North Judson, Starke County (portions)). Franchise award date: N.A. Franchise expiration date: N.A. Began: August 1, 1983.
Channel capacity: 83 (operating 2-way). Channels available but not in use: 20.

Basic Service
Subscribers: 2,800.
Programming (received off-air): WBND-LP South Bend; WCWW-LP (CW) South Bend; WFLD (FOX) Chicago; WHME-TV (IND) South Bend; WNDU-TV (NBC) South Bend; WNIT (PBS) South Bend; WSBT-TV (CBS, IND) South Bend; WSJV (FOX) Elkhart; WYIN (PBS) Gary.
Programming (via satellite): WGN America.
Planned originations: Public Access.
Fee: $45.00 installation; $20.95 monthly.

Expanded Basic Service 1
Subscribers: 2,298.
Programming (via satellite): ABC Family Channel; AMC; Animal Planet; Arts & Entertainment; Cartoon Network; CNBC; CNN; Comcast SportsNet Chicago; Comedy Central; Country Music TV; C-SPAN; C-SPAN 2; Discovery Channel; Disney Channel; E! Entertainment Television; ESPN; ESPN 2; Food Network; Fox News Channel; FX; Great American Country; Hallmark Channel; Headline News; HGTV; History Channel; Home Shopping Network; Lifetime; MSNBC; MTV; Nickelodeon; QVC; RFD-TV; Speed Channel; Spike TV; Syfy; TBS Superstation; The Learning Channel; Travel Channel; Trinity Broadcasting Network; truTV; Turner Network TV; TV Guide Network; TV Land; USA Network; VH1; WE tv; Weather Channel.
Fee: $34.00 monthly.

Digital Basic Service
Subscribers: 320.
Programming (via satellite): AmericanLife TV Network; BBC America; Bio; Bloomberg Television; Discovery Digital Networks; Discovery HD Theater; ESPN 2 HD; ESPN HD; ESPNews; Fox Movie Channel; Fox Soccer; Fuse; G4; GAS; Golf Channel; GSN; Halogen Network; HDNet; HDNet Movies; History Channel International; Independent Film Channel; INHD (multiplexed); Lifetime Movie Network; Lime; MTV Networks Digital Suite; Music Choice; National Geographic Channel; Nick Jr.; NickToons TV; Outdoor Channel; Sleuth; Style Network; Turner Classic Movies; TVG Network; Universal HD; Versus.
Fee: $9.00 monthly.

Digital Pay Service 1
Pay Units: 840.
Programming (via satellite): Cinemax (multiplexed); Encore (multiplexed); Flix (multiplexed); HBO (multiplexed); HBO HD; Showtime (multiplexed); Showtime HD; Starz (multiplexed); Starz HDTV; Sundance Channel (multiplexed); The Movie Channel (multiplexed); The Movie Channel HD.
Fee: $11.95 monthly (HBO, Cinemax, Showtime/TMC/Flix/Sundance or Starz/Encore.

Video-On-Demand: Yes

Pay-Per-View
Addressable homes: 836.
iN DEMAND (delivered digitally), Addressable: Yes; Playboy TV (delivered digitally).

Internet Service
Operational: Yes.
Broadband Service: Mediacom High Speed Internet.
Fee: $59.95 installation; $40.95 monthly.

Telephone Service
Digital: Operational
Fee: $39.95 installation; $39.95 monthly

Miles of Plant: 270.0 (coaxial); 43.0 (fiber optic). Additional miles planned: 5.0 (coaxial). Homes passed: 4,843.
Operations Director: Joe Poffenberger. Technical Operations Manager: Craig Grey.
City fee: 3% of gross.
Ownership: Mediacom LLC (MSO).

KOKOMO—Comcast Cable, 5330 E 65th St, Indianapolis, IN 46220. Phone: 317-275-6370. Fax: 317-275-6340. Web Site: http://www.comcast.com. Also serves Cass County, Galveston, Greentown, Howard County, Miami County, Russiaville, Sharpsville, Tipton County & Windfall. ICA: IN0017.
TV Market Ranking: 16 (Tipton County (portions)); 82 (Miami County (portions)); Below 100 (Cass County, Galveston, Greentown, Howard County, KOKOMO, Russiaville, Sharpsville, Windfall, Tipton County (portions), Miami County (portions)). Franchise award date: N.A. Franchise expiration date: N.A. Began: August 28, 1970.
Channel capacity: N.A. Channels available but not in use: N.A.

Basic Service
Subscribers: N.A. Included in Lafayette
Programming (received off-air): WFYI (PBS) Indianapolis; WHMB-TV (IND) Indianapolis; WIPB (PBS) Muncie; WISH-TV (CBS) Indianapolis; WLFI-TV (CBS) Lafayette; WNDY-TV (MNT) Marion; WRTV (ABC) Indianapolis; WTHR (NBC) Indianapolis; WTTK (IND) Kokomo; WXIN (FOX) Indianapolis; allband FM.
Programming (via microwave): WGN-TV (CW, IND) Chicago.
Programming (via satellite): C-SPAN; C-SPAN 2; Home Shopping Network; ION Television; MarketConnect Network; QVC; Trinity Broadcasting Network; Weatherscan.
Fee: $13.55 monthly.

Expanded Basic Service 1
Subscribers: 18,430.
Programming (via satellite): ABC Family Channel; AMC; Animal Planet; Arts & Entertainment; BET Networks; Bravo; Cartoon Network; CNBC; CNN; Comedy Central; Country Music TV; Discovery Channel; Disney Channel; E! Entertainment Television; ESPN; ESPN 2; Eternal Word TV Network; Food Network; Fox News Channel; Fox Sports Net Midwest; FX; Headline News; HGTV; History Channel; Lifetime; MSNBC; MTV; Nickelodeon; Oxygen; Spike TV; Syfy; TBS Superstation; The Learning Channel; Travel Channel; Turner Network TV; TV Guide Network; USA Network; VH1; Weather Channel.
Fee: $30.00 monthly.

Digital Basic Service
Subscribers: N.A.
Programming (via satellite): BBC America; Bio; Bloomberg Television; Canales N; C-SPAN 3; Discovery Digital Networks; DMX Music; Do-It-Yourself; Encore; ESPN Classic Sports; ESPNews; Fox Sports World; G4; GAS; Golf Channel; GSN; Halogen Network; History Channel International; Independent Film Channel; Lifetime Movie Network; MTV2; National Geographic Channel; Nick Jr.; Nick Too; Ovation; SoapNet; Speed Channel; Style Network; Sundance Channel; Toon Disney; truTV; Turner Classic Movies; Versus; WE tv.
Fee: $17.00 monthly.

Digital Pay Service 1
Pay Units: N.A.
Programming (via satellite): Cinemax (multiplexed); Flix; HBO (multiplexed); Showtime (multiplexed); Starz (multiplexed); The Movie Channel (multiplexed).
Fee: $10.00 monthly (Cinemax or Starz), $13.00 monthly (HBO or Showtime/TMC).

Video-On-Demand: Yes

Pay-Per-View
iN DEMAND, Addressable: Yes; iN DEMAND (delivered digitally); Adult (delivered digitally).

Internet Service
Operational: Yes.
Subscribers: 4,325.
Broadband Service: Comcast High Speed Internet.
Fee: $99.95 installation; $44.95 monthly; $15.00 modem lease; $129.95 modem purchase.

Telephone Service
Digital: Operational
Fee: $39.95 monthly

Miles of Plant: 530.0 (coaxial); 95.0 (fiber optic). Homes passed: 30,584. Total homes in franchised area: 41,834.
Regional Vice President: Scott Tenney. Regional Vice President, Technical Operations: Max Woolsey. Regional Vice President, Marketing: Aaron Geisel. Regional Vice President, Communications: Mark Apple.
City fee: None.
Ownership: Comcast Cable Communications Inc. (MSO).

KOUTS—Mediacom. Now served by ROSELAWN, IN [IN0316]. ICA: IN0277.

LA FONTAINE—Longview Communications, 12007 Sunrise Valley Dr, Ste 375, Reston, VA 20191. Phones: 866-611-6565 (Customer service); 703-476-9101. Fax: 703-476-9107. Web Site: http://www.longviewcomm.com. ICA: IN0196.
TV Market Ranking: 82 (LA FONTAINE). Franchise award date: April 1, 1984. Franchise expiration date: N.A. Began: August 1, 1986.
Channel capacity: 31 (not 2-way capable). Channels available but not in use: None.

Basic Service
Subscribers: 154.
Programming (received off-air): WANE-TV (CBS) Fort Wayne; WFFT-TV (FOX) Fort Wayne; WIPB (PBS) Muncie; WISE-TV (MNT, NBC) Fort Wayne; WISH-TV (CBS) Indianapolis; WNDY-TV (MNT) Marion; WPTA (ABC, CW) Fort Wayne; WRTV (ABC) Indianapolis; WTHR (NBC) Indianapolis; WTTK (IND) Kokomo.
Programming (via satellite): QVC; Trinity Broadcasting Network.
Fee: $39.90 installation; $19.98 monthly.

Expanded Basic Service 1
Subscribers: N.A.
Programming (via satellite): ABC Family Channel; AMC; Arts & Entertainment; CNN; C-SPAN; Discovery Channel; Disney Channel; E! Entertainment Television; ESPN; ESPN 2; Headline News; History Channel; Lifetime; Nickelodeon; TBS Superstation; The Learning Channel; Travel Channel; Turner Network TV; USA Network; Weather Channel; WGN America.
Fee: $17.97 monthly.

Pay Service 1
Pay Units: N.A.
Programming (via satellite): Showtime; The Movie Channel.
Fee: $10.00 installation; $8.95 monthly (TMC), $10.95 monthly (Showtime).

Video-On-Demand: No

Internet Service
Operational: No.

Telephone Service
None

Miles of Plant: 7.0 (coaxial); None (fiber optic). Homes passed: 530.
President: John Long. Senior Vice President: Marc W. Cohen. General Manager: Brandon Dickey. Technical Manager: Steve Boss.
Ownership: Longview Communications (MSO).

LA PORTE—Comcast Cable, 7720 W 98th St, Hickory Hills, IL 60457. Phone: 219-872-9306 (Michigan City office). Web Site: http://www.comcast.com. Also serves Chesterton, Dune Acres, Kingsbury, Kingsford Heights, Porter & Valparaiso. ICA: IN0009.
TV Market Ranking: 3 (Dune Acres, Porter); 80 (Kingsbury, Kingsford Heights, LA PORTE); Below 100 (Chesterton, Valparaiso). Franchise award date: April 12, 1983. Franchise expiration date: N.A. Began: November 28, 1983.
Channel capacity: N.A. Channels available but not in use: N.A.

Basic Service
Subscribers: 28,402.
Programming (received off-air): WBBM-TV (CBS) Chicago; WCIU-TV (IND) Chicago; WCPX-TV (ION) Chicago; WFLD (FOX) Chicago; WGBO-DT (UNV) Joliet; WGN-TV (CW, IND) Chicago; WHME-TV (IND) South Bend; WJYS (IND) Hammond; WLS-TV (ABC) Chicago; WMAQ-TV (NBC) Chicago; WNDU-TV (NBC) South Bend; WNIT (PBS) South Bend; WPWR-TV (MNT) Gary; WSBT-TV (CBS, IND) South Bend; WSJV

(FOX) Elkhart; WSNS-TV (TMO) Chicago; WTTW (PBS) Chicago; WXFT-DT (TEL) Aurora; WYCC (PBS) Chicago; WYIN (PBS) Gary; allband FM.
Programming (via satellite): Home Shopping Network; QVC.
Current originations: Religious Access; Educational Access.
Planned originations: Leased Access; Government Access; Public Access.
Fee: $48.99 installation; $18.04 monthly.

Expanded Basic Service 1
Subscribers: 28,400.
Programming (via microwave): Chicagoland Television News.
Programming (via satellite): ABC Family Channel; AMC; Animal Planet; Arts & Entertainment; Bravo; Cartoon Network; CNBC; CNN; Comcast SportsNet Chicago; Comedy Central; Country Music TV; C-SPAN; C-SPAN 2; Discovery Channel; Disney Channel; E! Entertainment Television; ESPN; ESPN 2; ESPN Classic Sports; Eternal Word TV Network; Food Network; Fox News Channel; FX; Golf Channel; Hallmark Channel; Headline News; HGTV; History Channel; Lifetime; MoviePlex; MSNBC; MTV; Nickelodeon; Oxygen; Spike TV; TBS Superstation; The Learning Channel; Total Living Network; Travel Channel; truTV; Turner Classic Movies; Turner Network TV; TV Guide Network; TV Land; USA Network; Versus; VH1; Weather Channel.
Fee: $34.45 monthly.

Digital Basic Service
Subscribers: 9,628.
Programming (received off-air): WBBM-TV (CBS) Chicago; WFLD (FOX) Chicago; WGN-TV (CW, IND) Chicago; WLS-TV (ABC) Chicago; WMAQ-TV (NBC) Chicago; WTTW (PBS) Chicago.
Programming (via satellite): BBC America; Bio; Bloomberg Television; Canales N; CMT Pure Country; Cooking Channel; Current; Discovery Digital Networks; Discovery HD Theater; Do-It-Yourself; Encore (multiplexed); ESPN 2 HD; ESPN HD; ESPNews; Fox College Sports Atlantic; Fox College Sports Central; Fox College Sports Pacific; Fox Movie Channel; Fox Reality Channel; Fox Soccer; Fuse; G4; GAS; Gospel Music Channel; Great American Country; GSN; History Channel International; Independent Film Channel; Jewelry Television; Lifetime Movie Network; LOGO; MTV Networks Digital Suite; Music Choice; National Geographic Channel; NBA TV; NFL Network; Nick Jr.; Nick Too; NickToons TV; Outdoor Channel; Ovation; Palladia; PBS Kids Sprout; ShopNBC; SoapNet; Speed Channel; Style Network; Sundance Channel; Syfy; The Word Network; Toon Disney; Trinity Broadcasting Network; Turner Classic Movies; Turner Network TV HD; TV One; TVG Network; Universal HD; Versus HD; WE tv; Weatherscan.
Fee: $11.99 monthly.

Digital Pay Service 1
Pay Units: N.A.
Programming (via satellite): Cinemax (multiplexed); Cinemax HD; Flix; HBO (multiplexed); HBO HD; Showtime (multiplexed); Showtime HD; Starz (multiplexed); Starz HDTV; The Movie Channel (multiplexed).
Fee: $16.90 monthly (each).

Video-On-Demand: Yes

Pay-Per-View
iN DEMAND (delivered digitally); ESPN (delivered digitally); NBA League Pass (delivered digitally); Sports PPV (delivered digitally); iN DEMAND (delivered digitally); Fresh (delivered digitally); Shorteez (delivered digitally); Playboy TV (delivered digitally).

Internet Service
Operational: Yes.
Subscribers: 472.
Broadband Service: Comcast High Speed Internet.
Fee: $150.00 installation; $39.95 monthly.

Telephone Service
Digital: Operational
Fee: $44.95 monthly

Miles of Plant: 820.0 (coaxial); None (fiber optic). Homes passed: 48,007.
Area Vice President: Sandy Weicher. Vice President, Technical Operations: Bob Curtis. Vice President, Sales & Marketing: Eric Schaefer. Vice President, Communications: Rich Ruggiero. Technical Operations Manager: Karl Braun. Marketing Director: Ron Knutson.
City fee: 3% of gross.
Ownership: Comcast Cable Communications Inc. (MSO).

LA PORTE MOBILE HOME PARK—North American Cablevision. Now served by LA PORTE, IN [IN0009]. ICA: IN0278.

LAFAYETTE—Comcast Cable, 5330 E 65th St, Indianapolis, IN 46220. Phone: 317-275-6370. Fax: 317-275-6340. Web Site: http://www.comcast.com. Also serves Americus, Battle Ground, Buck Creek, Clinton County (northwestern portion), Dayton, Mulberry, Otterbein, Shadeland, Tippecanoe County & West Lafayette. ICA: IN0007.
TV Market Ranking: Below 100 (Americus, Battle Ground, Buck Creek, Clinton County (northwestern portion), Dayton, LAFAYETTE, Mulberry, Otterbein, Shadeland, Tippecanoe County, West Lafayette). Franchise award date: January 1, 1963. Franchise expiration date: N.A. Began: March 1, 1965.
Channel capacity: N.A. Channels available but not in use: N.A.

Basic Service
Subscribers: 69,000 Includes Attica & Kokomo.
Programming (received off-air): WFYI (PBS) Indianapolis; WISH-TV (CBS) Indianapolis; WLFI-TV (CBS) Lafayette; WNDY-TV (MNT) Marion; WRTV (ABC) Indianapolis; WTHR (NBC) Indianapolis; WTTK (IND) Kokomo; WXIN (FOX) Indianapolis; 8 FMs.
Programming (via microwave): WHMB-TV (IND) Indianapolis; WTTW (PBS) Chicago.
Programming (via satellite): C-SPAN; C-SPAN 2; Hallmark Channel; Home Shopping Network; Iowa Communications Network; QVC; Weatherscan; WGN America.
Current originations: Leased Access; Educational Access.
Fee: $13.55 monthly.

Expanded Basic Service 1
Subscribers: 38,872.
Programming (via satellite): ABC Family Channel; AMC; Animal Planet; Arts & Entertainment; BET Networks; Bravo; Cartoon Network; CNBC; CNN; Comcast SportsNet Chicago; Comedy Central; Country Music TV; Discovery Channel; Disney Channel; E! Entertainment Television; ESPN; ESPN 2; Eternal Word TV Network; Food Network; Fox News Channel; FX; Headline News; HGTV; History Channel; Lifetime; MSNBC; MTV; MTV2; National Geographic Channel; Nickelodeon; Oxygen; Speed Channel; Spike TV; Syfy; TBS Superstation; The Learning Channel; Travel Channel; truTV; Turner Network TV; TV Guide Network; TV Land; USA Network; VH1; Weather Channel.
Fee: $30.00 monthly.

Digital Basic Service
Subscribers: 15,000.
Programming (received off-air): WFYI (PBS) Indianapolis; WISH-TV (CBS) Indianapolis; WRTV (ABC) Indianapolis; WTHR (NBC) Indianapolis; WTTV (CW) Bloomington; WXIN (FOX) Indianapolis.
Programming (via satellite): BBC America; Bio; Bloomberg Television; Canales N; CBS College Sports Network; Cooking Channel; C-SPAN 3; Discovery Digital Networks; Discovery HD Theater; DMX Music; Do-It-Yourself; Encore; ESPN; ESPN Classic Sports; ESPN U; ESPNews; Fox College Sports Atlantic; Fox College Sports Central; Fox College Sports Pacific; Fox Movie Channel; Fox Soccer; Fuse; G4; GAS; Golf Channel; GSN; Halogen Network; HDNet; HDNet Movies; History Channel International; Independent Film Channel; Lifetime Movie Network; Lifetime Real Women; MTV Networks Digital Suite; mun2 television; NFL Network; Nick Jr.; Nick Too; NickToons TV; Outdoor Channel; Ovation; PBS Kids Sprout; SoapNet; Style Network; Sundance Channel; Telemundo; Toon Disney; Turner Classic Movies; Universal HD; Versus; WE tv.
Fee: $17.00 monthly.

Digital Pay Service 1
Pay Units: N.A.
Programming (via satellite): Cinemax (multiplexed); Flix; HBO (multiplexed); HBO HD; Showtime (multiplexed); Showtime HD; Starz (multiplexed); The Movie Channel (multiplexed).
Fee: $10.00 monthly (Cinemax or Starz), $13.00 monthly (HBO or Showtime/TMC).

Video-On-Demand: Yes

Pay-Per-View
Addressable homes: 15,000.
iN DEMAND (delivered digitally), Addressable: Yes; Playboy TV (delivered digitally); Fresh (delivered digitally); ESPN (delivered digitally).

Internet Service
Operational: Yes. Began: May 15, 1999.
Broadband Service: Comcast High Speed Internet.
Fee: $99.95 installation; $44.95 monthly; $15.00 modem lease; $129.95 modem purchase.

Telephone Service
Digital: Operational
Fee: $39.95 monthly

Miles of Plant: 660.0 (coaxial); 80.0 (fiber optic). Additional miles planned: 20.0 (coaxial); 40.0 (fiber optic).
Regional Vice President: Scott Tenney. Regional Vice President, Technical Operations: Max Woolsey. Regional Vice President, Marketing: Aaron Geisel. Regional Vice President, Communications: Mark Apple.
City fee: 3% of gross.
Ownership: Comcast Cable Communications Inc. (MSO).

LAGRANGE—Mediacom, 109 E 5th St, Ste A, Auburn, IN 46706. Phone: 260-927-3015. Fax: 260-347-4433. Web Site: http://www.mediacomcable.com. Also serves Howe. ICA: IN0123.
TV Market Ranking: 80 (Howe, LAGRANGE). Franchise award date: N.A. Franchise expiration date: N.A. Began: June 1, 1981.
Channel capacity: 131 (operating 2-way). Channels available but not in use: None.

Basic Service
Subscribers: 878.
Programming (received off-air): WANE-TV (CBS) Fort Wayne; WBND-LP South Bend; WCWW-LP (CW) South Bend; WFWA (PBS) Fort Wayne; WHME-TV (IND) South Bend; WISE-TV (MNT, NBC) Fort Wayne; WNDU-TV (NBC) South Bend; WNIT (PBS) South Bend; WSBT-TV (CBS, IND) South Bend; WSJV (FOX) Elkhart.
Programming (via satellite): C-SPAN; Trinity Broadcasting Network.
Fee: $45.00 installation; $20.95 monthly.

Expanded Basic Service 1
Subscribers: 727.
Programming (via satellite): ABC Family Channel; AMC; AmericanLife TV Network; Animal Planet; Arts & Entertainment; Bio; Bloomberg Television; Cartoon Network; CNBC; CNN; Comedy Central; Country Music TV; Discovery Channel; Disney Channel; E! Entertainment Television; ESPN; ESPN 2; Fox Movie Channel; Fox News Channel; FX; G4; Hallmark Channel; Headline News; HGTV; History Channel; History Channel International; Home Shopping Network; Lifetime; Lifetime Movie Network; MSNBC; MTV; Nickelodeon; Product Information Network; QVC; Speed Channel; Spike TV; Style Network; Syfy; TBS Superstation; The Learning Channel; Travel Channel; Turner Network TV; TV Guide Network; TV Land; USA Network; Versus; VH1; Weather Channel; WGN America.
Fee: $34.00 monthly.

Digital Basic Service
Subscribers: 93.
Programming (via satellite): BBC America; Discovery Digital Networks; DMX Music; ESPN Classic Sports; Fox Sports World; Golf Channel; GSN; Independent Film Channel; Turner Classic Movies.
Fee: $9.00 monthly.

Digital Pay Service 1
Pay Units: 264.
Programming (via satellite): Cinemax (multiplexed); Encore (multiplexed); HBO (multiplexed); Showtime (multiplexed); Starz (multiplexed); The Movie Channel (multiplexed).
Fee: $11.95 monthly (HBO, Cinemax, Showtime/TMC or Starz/Encore).

Video-On-Demand: Yes

Pay-Per-View
iN DEMAND, Fee: $3.95, Addressable: Yes; iN DEMAND (delivered digitally); Playboy TV (delivered digitally); Pleasure (delivered digitally); Fresh (delivered digitally); Shorteez (delivered digitally).

Internet Service
Operational: Yes.
Broadband Service: Mediacom High Speed Internet.
Fee: $59.95 installation; $40.95 monthly.
Telephone Service
Digital: Operational
Fee: $39.95 installation; $39.95 monthly
Miles of Plant: 29.0 (coaxial); 8.0 (fiber optic). Homes passed: 2,041.
Operations Director: Joe Poffenberger. Technical Operations Manager: Craig Grey.
City fee: 5% of gross.
Ownership: Mediacom LLC (MSO).

LAGRO—Formerly served by CableDirect. No longer in operation. ICA: IN0279.

LAKE CICOTT—Insight Communications. Now served by LOGANSPORT, IN [IN0037]. ICA: IN0171.

LAKE OF THE FOUR SEASONS—Comcast Cable. Now served by CHICAGO (southern suburbs), IL [IL0008]. ICA: IN0280.

LAKE SANTEE—Formerly served by CableDirect. No longer in operation. ICA: IN0281.

LAKEVILLE—Mediacom. Now served by WALKERTON, IN [IN0081]. ICA: IN0115.

LAPEL—Longview Communications, 1923 N Main, Higginsville, MO 64037. Phone: 866-611-6565. Fax: 866-329-4790. Web Site: http://www.longviewcomm.com. Also serves Fishersburg. ICA: IN0144.
TV Market Ranking: 16 (Fishersburg, LAPEL). Franchise award date: N.A. Franchise expiration date: N.A. Began: November 1, 1982.
Channel capacity: N.A. Channels available but not in use: N.A.
Basic Service
Subscribers: 200.
Programming (received off-air): WFYI (PBS) Indianapolis; WHMB-TV (IND) Indianapolis; WISH-TV (CBS) Indianapolis; WNDY-TV (MNT) Marion; WRTV (ABC) Indianapolis; WTTV (CW) Bloomington; WXIN (FOX) Indianapolis.
Programming (via satellite): C-SPAN; QVC; Trinity Broadcasting Network; WTHR (NBC) Indianapolis.
Fee: $35.00 installation; $20.98 monthly.
Expanded Basic Service 1
Subscribers: N.A.
Programming (via satellite): ABC Family Channel; AMC; Animal Planet; Arts & Entertainment; Bravo; Cartoon Network; CNBC; CNN; Comedy Central; Discovery Channel; Disney Channel; Do-It-Yourself; E! Entertainment Television; ESPN; ESPN 2; Food Network; Fox News Channel; FX; Great American Country; Hallmark Channel; Headline News; HGTV; History Channel; INSP; Lifetime; MSNBC; Nickelodeon; Sleuth; Syfy; TBS Superstation; The Learning Channel; Travel Channel; truTV; Turner Network TV; USA Network; WE tv; Weather Channel; WGN America.
Fee: $19.97 monthly.
Digital Basic Service
Subscribers: 22.
Programming (via satellite): AmericanLife TV Network; BBC America; Bio; Bloomberg Television; Discovery Digital Networks; Encore (multiplexed); ESPN Classic Sports; ESPNews; Fox Movie Channel; Fox Soccer; G4; Golf Channel; GSN; Halogen Network; History Channel International; Independent Film Channel; Lifetime Movie Network; MTV2; Outdoor Channel; Speed Channel; Style Network; Toon Disney; Turner Classic Movies.
Fee: $17.00 monthly.
Pay Service 1
Pay Units: 60.
Programming (via satellite): Cinemax; HBO; Showtime; The Movie Channel.
Fee: $8.95 monthly (TMC), $10.95 monthly (Cinemax or Showtime), $12.95 monthly (HBO).
Digital Pay Service 1
Pay Units: N.A.
Programming (via satellite): Cinemax (multiplexed); Flix; HBO (multiplexed); Showtime (multiplexed); Starz (multiplexed); The Movie Channel (multiplexed).
Fee: $8.95 monthly (TMC), $10.95 monthly (Showtime or Cinemax), $12.95 monthly (HBO).
Video-On-Demand: No
Pay-Per-View
iN DEMAND (delivered digitally); Hot Choice (delivered digitally); Playboy TV (delivered digitally); Fresh (delivered digitally).
Internet Service
Operational: Yes.
Subscribers: 83.
Broadband Service: IBBS.
Telephone Service
None
Miles of Plant: 12.0 (coaxial); None (fiber optic). Homes passed: 910.
President: John Long. Senior Vice President: Marc W. Cohen. General Manager: Brandon Dickey. Technical Manager: Steve Boss.
Ownership: Longview Communications (MSO).

LARWILL—Formerly served by CableDirect. No longer in operation. ICA: IN0282.

LAUREL TWP.—Formerly served by CableDirect. No longer in operation. ICA: IN0213.

LAWRENCEBURG—Comcast Cable, 10778 Randall Ave, Aurora, IN 47001. Phone: 812-926-2297. Fax: 812-926-1269. Web Site: http://www.comcast.com. Also serves Aurora, Bright, Dearborn County (unincorporated areas), Dillsboro, Greendale, Guilford, Hidden Valley Lake, Milan, Moores Hill, Ohio County (portions), Osgood, Ripley County, Rising Sun, Sunman (portions), Versailles & West Harrison. ICA: IN0050.
TV Market Ranking: 17 (Aurora, Bright, Dearborn County (unincorporated areas), Dillsboro, Greendale, Guilford, Hidden Valley Lake, LAWRENCEBURG, Milan, Moores Hill, Ohio County (portions), Ripley County, Rising Sun, Sunman (portions), West Harrison); Outside TV Markets (Osgood, Versailles, Ripley County). Franchise award date: January 18, 1971. Franchise expiration date: N.A. Began: October 1, 1971.
Channel capacity: N.A. Channels available but not in use: N.A.
Basic Service
Subscribers: N.A. Included in Indianapolis
Programming (received off-air): WCET (PBS) Cincinnati; WCPO-TV (ABC) Cincinnati; WKRC-TV (CBS, CW) Cincinnati; WLWT (NBC) Cincinnati; WSTR-TV (MNT) Cincinnati; WTTV (CW) Bloomington; WXIX-TV (FOX) Newport.
Programming (via satellite): QVC; WGN America; WOTH-CA (IND) Cincinnati.
Current originations: Religious Access.
Fee: $31.99 installation.
Expanded Basic Service 1
Subscribers: 10,755.
Programming (via satellite): ABC Family Channel; AMC; Animal Planet; Arts & Entertainment; BET Networks; Cartoon Network; CNBC; CNN; Comedy Central; Country Music TV; C-SPAN; Discovery Channel; Discovery Health Channel; Disney Channel; E! Entertainment Television; ESPN; ESPN 2; ESPN Classic Sports; ESPNews; Eternal Word TV Network; Food Network; Fox News Channel; Fox Sports Net Ohio; FX; GSN; Hallmark Channel; Headline News; HGTV; History Channel; Home Shopping Network; ION Television; Lifetime; MSNBC; MTV; Nickelodeon; ShopNBC; SoapNet; Spike TV; Syfy; TBS Superstation; The Learning Channel; Toon Disney; Travel Channel; Trinity Broadcasting Network; truTV; Turner Classic Movies; Turner Network TV; TV Guide Network; TV Land; USA Network; VH1; Weather Channel.
Fee: $45.94 monthly.
Digital Basic Service
Subscribers: 2,206.
Programming (received off-air): WXIX-TV (FOX) Newport.
Programming (via satellite): BBC America; Discovery Digital Networks; Discovery HD Theater; ESPN; GAS; HDNet; HDNet Movies; Lifetime Movie Network; MTV Networks Digital Suite; Music Choice; NFL Network; Nick Jr.; Nick Too; NickToons TV; WCET (PBS) Cincinnati; WCPO-TV (ABC) Cincinnati; WKRC-TV (CBS, CW) Cincinnati; WLWT (NBC) Cincinnati.
Fee: $12.94 monthly.
Digital Pay Service 1
Pay Units: N.A.
Programming (via satellite): Cinemax (multiplexed); Encore (multiplexed); HBO (multiplexed); Showtime (multiplexed); Starz (multiplexed); The Movie Channel (multiplexed).
Fee: $11.95 monthly (each).
Video-On-Demand: No
Pay-Per-View
ESPN Full Court (delivered digitally), Addressable: Yes; ESPN Gameplan (delivered digitally); Fresh (delivered digitally).
Internet Service
Operational: Yes.
Subscribers: 3,171.
Broadband Service: Comcast High Speed Internet.
Telephone Service
Digital: Operational
Miles of Plant: 258.0 (coaxial); 35.0 (fiber optic). Homes passed: 21,066.
Regional Vice President: Scott Tenney. Vice President, Communications: Mark Apple. Technical Operations Director: Richard Ring. Chief Technician: Dan Snow.
City fee: 3% of gross.
Ownership: Comcast Cable Communications Inc. (MSO).

LEAVENWORTH—Formerly served by CableDirect. No longer in operation. ICA: IN0283.

LEBANON—Now served by NOBLESVILLE, IN [IN0020]. ICA: IN0056.

LEITERS FORD—Formerly served by CableDirect. No longer in operation. ICA: IN0245.

LIBERTY—Comcast Cable, 10778 Randall Ave, Aurora, IN 47001. Phones: 317-275-6370 (Indianapolis office); 812-926-2297 (Indianapolis office). Fax: 812-926-1269. Web Site: http://www.comcast.com. ICA: IN0137.
TV Market Ranking: Below 100 (LIBERTY (VILLAGE)). Franchise award date: N.A. Franchise expiration date: N.A. Began: January 1, 1982.
Channel capacity: 90 (operating 2-way). Channels available but not in use: None.
Basic Service
Subscribers: N.A. Included in Indianapolis
Programming (received off-air): WCPO-TV (ABC) Cincinnati; WISH-TV (CBS) Indianapolis; WKRC-TV (CBS, CW) Cincinnati; WLWT (NBC) Cincinnati; WPTD (PBS) Dayton; WPTO (PBS) Oxford; WRGT-TV (FOX, MNT) Dayton; WSTR-TV (MNT) Cincinnati; WTTV (CW) Bloomington; WXIX-TV (FOX) Newport.
Programming (via satellite): C-SPAN; C-SPAN 2; Home Shopping Network; WGN America.
Fee: $50.99 installation; $11.74 monthly.
Expanded Basic Service 1
Subscribers: N.A.
Programming (via satellite): ABC Family Channel; AMC; Animal Planet; Arts & Entertainment; CNN; Country Music TV; Discovery Channel; Disney Channel; ESPN; ESPN 2; ESPNews; Fox Sports Net Midwest; FX; GSN; Hallmark Channel; Headline News; HGTV; History Channel; Lifetime; MSNBC; MTV; Nickelodeon; Spike TV; Syfy; TBS Superstation; The Learning Channel; Toon Disney; Turner Network TV; TV Land; USA Network; Versus; VH1; Weather Channel.
Fee: $37.98 monthly.
Pay Service 1
Pay Units: 251.
Programming (via satellite): Cinemax; HBO; Showtime; The Movie Channel.
Fee: $12.95 monthly (each).
Internet Service
Operational: Yes.
Telephone Service
Digital: Operational
Miles of Plant: 15.0 (coaxial); None (fiber optic). Homes passed: 1,061. Total homes in franchised area: 1,061.
Regional Vice President: Scott Tenney. Technical Operations Director: Richard Ring.
Ownership: Comcast Cable Communications Inc. (MSO).

LIBERTY MILLS—Formerly served by CableDirect. No longer in operation. ICA: IN0284.

LIGONIER—Lig TV, 414 S Cavin St, Ligonier, IN 46767. Phone: 260-894-7161. E-mail: support@ligtvonline.com. Web Site: http://www.ligtvonline.com. ICA: IN0372.
Note: This system is an overbuild.
TV Market Ranking: 80 (LIGONIER).
Channel capacity: N.A. Channels available but not in use: N.A.
Digital Basic Service
Subscribers: 218.
Programming (received off-air): WANE-TV (CBS) Fort Wayne; WBND-LP South Bend; WFWA (PBS) Fort Wayne; WHME-TV (IND) South Bend; WINM (IND) Angola; WISE-TV (MNT, NBC) Fort Wayne; WNDU-TV (NBC) South Bend; WNIT (PBS) South Bend; WPTA (ABC, CW) Fort Wayne; WSJV (FOX) Elkhart; WTTV (CW) Bloomington.
Programming (via satellite): ABC Family Channel; AMC; Animal Planet; Arts & Entertainment; BBC America; Boomerang; Bravo; Cartoon Network; CMT Pure Country; CNBC; CNN; Comedy Central; Country Music TV; C-SPAN; C-SPAN 2; Discov-

ery Channel; Discovery Health Channel; Discovery Kids Channel; Disney Channel; E! Entertainment Television; ESPN; ESPN 2; ESPN Classic Sports; ESPNews; Eternal Word TV Network; Food Network; Fox News Channel; Fox Soccer; Fox Sports Net Midwest; FX; GAS; Hallmark Channel; Headline News; HGTV; History Channel; Home Shopping Network; Lifetime; Lifetime Movie Network; Lifetime Real Women; MTV; MTV Hits; MTV2; Music Choice; National Geographic Channel; Nick Jr.; Nickelodeon; NickToons TV; Outdoor Channel; Oxygen; QVC; Radar Channel; ShopNBC; Speed Channel; Spike TV; Syfy; TBS Superstation; The Learning Channel; The Word Network; Toon Disney; Travel Channel; Turner Network TV; TV Land; Univision; USA Network; VH1; VH1 Classic; WE tv; Weather Channel; WGN America.
Fee: $45.95 monthly.

Digital Expanded Basic Service
Subscribers: N.A.
Programming (via satellite): AmericanLife TV Network; Bio; Bloomberg Television; Daystar TV Network; Discovery Home Channel; Discovery Military Channel; Discovery Times Channel; Do-It-Yourself; Encore (multiplexed); FitTV; Fox Movie Channel; FSN Digital Atlantic; FSN Digital Central; FSN Digital Pacific; Golf Channel; Great American Country; GSN; History Channel International; MSNBC; Science Channel; SoapNet; Turner Classic Movies; Versus.
Fee: $11.00 monthly.

Digital Expanded Basic Service 2
Subscribers: N.A.
Programming (via satellite): Cine Latino; Fox Sports en Espanol; GalaVision; HITN; MTV Tres; mun2 television; Telefutura; TVE Internacional.

Digital Pay Service 1
Pay Units: N.A.
Programming (via satellite): Cinemax (multiplexed); Flix; HBO (multiplexed); Starz (multiplexed); Sundance Channel; The Movie Channel (multiplexed).

Video-On-Demand: Planned

Pay-Per-View
Playboy TV (delivered digitally); Spice 2 (delivered digitally); Spice (delivered digitally).

Internet Service
Operational: Yes.

Telephone Service
Digital: Operational
General Manager: Don Johnson.
Ownership: Ligonier Telephone Co. (MSO).

LIGONIER—Mediacom, 109 E 5th St, Ste A, Auburn, IN 46706. Phone: 260-927-3015. Fax: 260-347-4433. Web Site: http://www.mediacomcable.com. Also serves Albion, Churubusco, Cromwell, Skinner Lake, South Whitley & Tri-Lakes. ICA: IN0156.
TV Market Ranking: 80 (Cromwell, LIGONIER); 80,82 (Albion, Skinner Lake); 82 (Churubusco, South Whitley, Tri-Lakes). Franchise award date: N.A. Franchise expiration date: N.A. Began: December 20, 1981.
Channel capacity: N.A. Channels available but not in use: N.A.

Basic Service
Subscribers: 859.
Programming (received off-air): WANE-TV (CBS) Fort Wayne; WFFT-TV (FOX) Fort Wayne; WFWA (PBS) Fort Wayne; WHME-TV (IND) South Bend; WINM (IND) Angola; WISE-TV (MNT, NBC) Fort Wayne; WNIT (PBS) South Bend; WPTA (ABC, CW) Fort Wayne; WTTK (IND) Kokomo.
Programming (via satellite): WGN America.
Fee: $45.00 installation; $20.95 monthly.

Expanded Basic Service 1
Subscribers: 690.
Programming (via satellite): ABC Family Channel; AMC; Animal Planet; Arts & Entertainment; Bravo; Cartoon Network; CNBC; CNN; Comedy Central; Country Music TV; C-SPAN; Discovery Channel; Disney Channel; E! Entertainment Television; ESPN; ESPN 2; Food Network; Fox News Channel; Fox Sports Net; FX; Hallmark Channel; Headline News; HGTV; History Channel; Home Shopping Network; Lifetime; MSNBC; MTV; MyNetworkTV Inc.; Nickelodeon; Product Information Network; QVC; Radar Channel; Speed Channel; Spike TV; Syfy; TBS Superstation; The Learning Channel; Travel Channel; Trinity Broadcasting Network; Turner Network TV; TV Guide Network; TV Land; Univision; USA Network; VH1; WE tv; Weather Channel.
Fee: $34.00 monthly.

Digital Basic Service
Subscribers: N.A.
Programming (received off-air): WANE-TV (CBS) Fort Wayne; WFFT-TV (FOX) Fort Wayne; WFWA (PBS) Fort Wayne; WPTA (ABC, CW) Fort Wayne.
Programming (via satellite): ABC News Now; AmericanLife TV Network; BBC America; Bio; Bloomberg Television; Cartoon Network Tambien en Espanol; CCTV-9 (CCTV International); Cine Latino; Cine Mexicano; CNN en Espanol; CNN HD; Discovery en Espanol; Discovery HD Theater; Discovery Health Channel; Discovery Home Channel; Discovery Kids Channel; Discovery Military Channel; ESPN 2 HD; ESPN HD; ESPNews; FitTV; Fox Movie Channel; Fox Soccer; Fox Sports en Espanol; G4; Golf Channel; GSN; Halogen Network; HDNet; HDNet Movies; History Channel International; ID Investigation Discovery; Independent Film Channel; ION Life; Lifetime Movie Network; MTV Hits; MTV Tres; MTV2; National Geographic Channel; Nick Jr.; NickToons TV; Outdoor Channel; Qubo; ReelzChannel; Science Channel; Sleuth; Style Network; TBS in HD; TeenNick; Turner Classic Movies; Turner Network TV HD; TVE Internacional; TVG Network; Universal HD; Versus; VH1 Classic.
Fee: $9.00 monthly.

Digital Expanded Basic Service
Subscribers: N.A.
Programming (via satellite): CBS College Sports Network; ESPN U; Fox College Sports Atlantic; Fox College Sports Central; Fox College Sports Pacific; Gol TV; Tennis Channel; The Sportsman Channel.
Fee: $3.95 monthly.

Digital Pay Service 1
Pay Units: N.A.
Programming (via satellite): Cinemax (multiplexed); Encore (multiplexed); Flix; HBO (multiplexed); HBO HD; Showtime (multiplexed); Showtime HD; Starz (multiplexed); Sundance Channel; The Movie Channel (multiplexed); The Movie Channel HD.
Fee: $11.95 monthly (HBO, Cinemax, Starz/Encore or Showtime/TMC).

Video-On-Demand: Yes

Internet Service
Operational: Yes.
Broadband Service: Mediacom High Speed Internet.
Fee: $59.95 installation; $40.95 monthly.

Telephone Service
Digital: Operational
Fee: $39.95 installation; $39.95 monthly
Homes passed & miles of plant included in Kendallville
Operations Director: Joe Poffenberger. Technical Operations Manager: Craig Grey.
City fee: 3% of gross.
Ownership: Mediacom LLC (MSO).

LINDEN—TDS Cable Services, PO Box 186, 117 E Washington St, New Richmond, IN 47967. Phone: 765-339-4651. Fax: 765-339-7999. Web Site: http://www.tdstelecom.com. Also serves Colfax, New Richmond, Romney, Tippecanoe County (southern portion) & Wingate. ICA: IN0103.
TV Market Ranking: Below 100 (Colfax, LINDEN, New Richmond, Romney, Tippecanoe County (southern portion), Wingate). Franchise award date: N.A. Franchise expiration date: N.A. Began: February 1, 1982.
Channel capacity: 60 (operating 2-way). Channels available but not in use: 5.

Basic Service
Subscribers: 1,700.
Programming (received off-air): WFYI (PBS) Indianapolis; WHMB-TV (IND) Indianapolis; WISH-TV (CBS) Indianapolis; WLFI-TV (CBS) Lafayette; WNDY-TV (MNT) Marion; WRTV (ABC) Indianapolis; WTHR (NBC) Indianapolis; WTTK (IND) Kokomo; WXIN (FOX) Indianapolis.
Programming (via satellite): ABC Family Channel; AMC; Animal Planet; Arts & Entertainment; Big Ten Network; CNBC; CNN; Comedy Central; Country Music TV; C-SPAN; Discovery Channel; Disney Channel; Do-It-Yourself; ESPN; ESPN 2; Eternal Word TV Network; FitTV; Food Network; Fox News Channel; Fox Sports Net Midwest; FX; Great American Country; GSN; Hallmark Channel; Headline News; HGTV; History Channel; Home Shopping Network; Lifetime; MTV; National Geographic Channel; Nickelodeon; QVC; Speed Channel; Spike TV; Syfy; TBS Superstation; The Learning Channel; Toon Disney; Travel Channel; truTV; Turner Classic Movies; Turner Network TV; TV Guide Network; TV Land; USA Network; Versus; VH1; Weather Channel; WGN America.
Fee: $43.00 installation; $41.80 monthly; $1.38 converter.

Pay Service 1
Pay Units: 300.
Programming (via satellite): Cinemax; HBO; Showtime.
Fee: $10.00 installation; $11.00 monthly (Cinemax or Showtime), $13.00 monthly (HBO).

Video-On-Demand: No

Pay-Per-View
Addressable homes: 133.
iN DEMAND, Fee: $3.75, Addressable: No.

Internet Service
Operational: No, DSL & dialup.

Telephone Service
None
Miles of Plant: 30.0 (coaxial); 29.0 (fiber optic). Homes passed: 1,945. Total homes in franchised area: 1,945.
Chief Technician: Mark Grote. Customer Service Manager: Myra Goings.
Ownership: TDS Telecom (MSO).

LINTON—Comcast Cable, 2450 S Henderson St, Bloomington, IN 47401-4540. Phones: 317-275-6370 (Indianapolis regional office); 812-332-9486 (Customer service). Fax: 812-332-0129. Web Site: http://www.comcast.com. Also serves Bloomfield, Greene County, Sullivan & Sullivan County (portions). ICA: IN0052.
TV Market Ranking: 16 (Bloomfield, Greene County (portions)); Below 100 (LINTON, Sullivan, Sullivan County (portions) (portions), Greene County (portions)); Outside TV Markets (Sullivan, Sullivan County (portions) (portions), Greene County (portions)). Franchise award date: N.A. Franchise expiration date: N.A. Began: May 1, 1968.
Channel capacity: N.A. Channels available but not in use: N.A.

Basic Service
Subscribers: N.A. Included in Bloomington
Programming (received off-air): WCLJ-TV (TBN) Bloomington; WFXW (FOX) Terre Haute; WRTV (ABC) Indianapolis; WTHI-TV (CBS) Terre Haute; WTHR (NBC) Indianapolis; WTIU (PBS) Bloomington; WTTV (CW) Bloomington; WTWO (NBC) Terre Haute; WVUT (PBS) Vincennes; allband FM.
Programming (via satellite): C-SPAN; C-SPAN 2; QVC; WGN America.
Fee: $24.95 installation.

Expanded Basic Service 1
Subscribers: 1,834.
Programming (via satellite): ABC Family Channel; AMC; Animal Planet; Arts & Entertainment; BET Networks; Cartoon Network; CNBC; CNN; Comedy Central; Country Music TV; Discovery Channel; Disney Channel; E! Entertainment Television; ESPN; ESPN 2; Food Network; Fox News Channel; Fox Sports Net Midwest; FX; HGTV; History Channel; Home Shopping Network; Lifetime; MSNBC; MTV; Nickelodeon; Spike TV; TBS Superstation; The Learning Channel; Travel Channel; Turner Network TV; TV Land; USA Network; VH1; Weather Channel.
Fee: $40.00 monthly.

Digital Basic Service
Subscribers: N.A.
Programming (via satellite): AmericanLife TV Network; BBC America; Bio; Bloomberg Television; Bravo; C-SPAN 3; Discovery Digital Networks; DMX Music; Do-It-Yourself; Encore (multiplexed); ESPN Classic Sports; ESPNews; Eternal Word TV Network; Fox Movie Channel; Fox Sports World; Fuse; G4; GAS; Golf Channel; GSN; Halogen Network; History Channel International; Independent Film Channel; Lifetime Movie Network; National Geographic Channel; Nick Jr.; Nick Too; SoapNet; Speed Channel; Style Network; Sundance Channel; Syfy; Toon Disney; truTV; Turner Classic Movies; Versus; WE tv.
Fee: $17.00 monthly.

Digital Pay Service 1
Pay Units: N.A.
Programming (via satellite): Cinemax (multiplexed); Flix; HBO (multiplexed); Showtime (multiplexed); Starz (multiplexed); The Movie Channel (multiplexed).
Fee: $10.00 monthly (Cinemax or Starz), $13.00 monthly (HBO or Showtime).

Video-On-Demand: Yes

Pay-Per-View
iN DEMAND; iN DEMAND (delivered digitally); Adult (delivered digitally).

Internet Service
Operational: Yes.
Broadband Service: Comcast High Speed Internet.
Fee: $99.95 installation; $44.95 monthly; $15.00 modem lease; $99.95 modem purchase.

Telephone Service
Analog: Not Operational
Digital: Operational
Miles of Plant: 101.0 (coaxial); None (fiber optic). Homes passed: 5,138. Total homes in franchised area: 8,168.

Regional Vice President: Scott Tenney. Area Director: Wendy Henry. Chief Technician: Jeff Harrington. Customer Service Manager: Jennifer Lane.
City fee: 3% of gross.
Ownership: Comcast Cable Communications Inc. (MSO).

LOGANSPORT—Comcast Cable, 720 Taylor St, Fort Wayne, IN 46802-5144. Phone: 260-458-5103. Fax: 260-458-5138. Web Site: http://www.comcast.com. Also serves Adamsboro, Cass County & Lake Cicott. ICA: IN0037.
TV Market Ranking: Below 100 (Adamsboro, Cass County, Lake Cicott, LOGANSPORT). Franchise award date: December 1, 1963. Franchise expiration date: N.A. Began: December 1, 1963.
Channel capacity: 80 (operating 2-way). Channels available but not in use: 15.

Basic Service
Subscribers: N.A. Included in Indianapolis
Programming (received off-air): WISH-TV (CBS) Indianapolis; WLFI-TV (CBS) Lafayette; WNDU-TV (NBC) South Bend; WNDY-TV (MNT) Marion; WRTV (ABC) Indianapolis; WTHR (NBC) Indianapolis; WTTK (IND) Kokomo; WXIN (FOX) Indianapolis.
Programming (via microwave): WTTW (PBS) Chicago.
Programming (via satellite): Bravo; C-SPAN; C-SPAN 2; Home Shopping Network; QVC; Spike TV; TV Guide Network; WGN America.
Fee: $35.00 installation; $11.76 monthly.

Expanded Basic Service 1
Subscribers: N.A.
Programming (via satellite): ABC Family Channel; AMC; Animal Planet; Arts & Entertainment; Cartoon Network; CNBC; CNN; Comedy Central; Country Music TV; Discovery Channel; Disney Channel; E! Entertainment Television; ESPN; ESPN 2; ESPN Classic Sports; Food Network; Fox Sports Net Midwest; GalaVision; Golf Channel; GSN; Headline News; HGTV; History Channel; Lifetime; MSNBC; MTV; Nickelodeon; Speed Channel; Syfy; TBS Superstation; The Learning Channel; Toon Disney; Travel Channel; Trinity Broadcasting Network; Turner Classic Movies; Turner Network TV; TV Land; USA Network; Versus; VH1; Weather Channel.
Fee: $24.20 monthly.

Digital Basic Service
Subscribers: 3,600.
Programming (via satellite): BBC America; Bio; Bloomberg Television; Canales N; C-SPAN 3; Discovery Digital Networks; DMX Music; Do-It-Yourself; Encore Action; ESPNews; Fox Sports World; G4; GAS; Halogen Network; History Channel International; Independent Film Channel; Lifetime Movie Network; MTV2; National Geographic Channel; Nick Jr.; Nick Too; Ovation; SoapNet; Style Network; Sundance Channel; truTV; WE tv.
Fee: $7.95 monthly.

Pay Service 1
Pay Units: 1,034.
Programming (via satellite): Cinemax (multiplexed).
Fee: $2.00 installation; $12.95 monthly.

Pay Service 2
Pay Units: 953.
Programming (via satellite): HBO (multiplexed).
Fee: $12.95 monthly.

Pay Service 3
Pay Units: 113.
Programming (via satellite): Showtime (multiplexed).
Fee: $12.95 monthly.

Pay Service 4
Pay Units: 28.
Programming (via satellite): The Movie Channel.
Fee: $12.95 monthly.

Digital Pay Service 1
Pay Units: N.A.
Programming (via satellite): Cinemax (multiplexed); Flix; HBO (multiplexed); Showtime (multiplexed); Starz (multiplexed); The Movie Channel (multiplexed).
Fee: $10.00 monthly (Cinemax, HBO, Starz or Flix, Showtime & TMC).

Video-On-Demand: Yes

Pay-Per-View
Addressable homes: 3,600.
iN DEMAND (delivered digitally), Fee: $3.99, Addressable: Yes; Adult (delivered digitally).

Internet Service
Operational: Yes.
Broadband Service: Comcast High Speed Internet.
Fee: $99.95 installation; $42.95 monthly; $15.00 modem lease; $129.95 modem purchase.

Telephone Service
Analog: Not Operational
Digital: Operational
Miles of plant included in Fort Wayne
Regional Vice President: Scott Tenney. Technical Operations Director: Bennie Logan. Engineering Manager: Tom Stuckholz. Vice President, Marketing: Aaron Geisel. Marketing Director: Marci Hefley. Vice President, Communications: Mark Apple.
City fee: 3% of gross.
Ownership: Comcast Cable Communications Inc. (MSO).

LOOGOOTEE—Avenue Broadband Communications, 2603 Hart St, Vincennes, VT 47591. Phones: 800-882-7185; 812-895-7676. Fax: 812-886-5017. Web Site: http://www.avenuebroadband.com. Also serves Daviess County (eastern portion). ICA: IN0102.
TV Market Ranking: Outside TV Markets (Daviess County (eastern portion), LOOGOOTEE). Franchise award date: August 19, 1977. Franchise expiration date: N.A. Began: March 12, 1980.
Channel capacity: N.A. Channels available but not in use: N.A.

Basic Service
Subscribers: 930.
Programming (received off-air): WCLJ-TV (TBN) Bloomington; WEHT (ABC) Evansville; WEVV-TV (CBS, MNT) Evansville; WFXW (FOX) Terre Haute; WNIN (PBS) Evansville; WTHI-TV (CBS) Terre Haute; WTTV (CW) Bloomington; WTVW (FOX) Evansville; WTWO (NBC) Terre Haute; WVUT (PBS) Vincennes; allband FM.
Programming (via satellite): Eternal Word TV Network; Home Shopping Network; WGN America.
Current originations: Government Access; Educational Access; Public Access.
Fee: $27.75 installation; $9.22 monthly; $1.05 converter.

Expanded Basic Service 1
Subscribers: 855.
Programming (via satellite): ABC Family Channel; AMC; Animal Planet; Arts & Entertainment; Bravo; CNN; Comedy Central; Country Music TV; Discovery Channel; Disney Channel; E! Entertainment Television; ESPN; ESPN 2; Food Network; Fox News Channel; Fox Sports Net Midwest; FX; Hallmark Channel; Headline News; HGTV; History Channel; Lifetime; MTV; Nickelodeon; Oxygen; QVC; Spike TV; Syfy; TBS Superstation; The Learning Channel; Travel Channel; truTV; Turner Classic Movies; Turner Network TV; TV Land; USA Network; Versus; VH1; Weather Channel.
Fee: $2.51 monthly.

Pay Service 1
Pay Units: 178.
Programming (via satellite): Cinemax; HBO; Showtime.
Fee: $25.00 installation; $9.50 monthly.

Video-On-Demand: No

Internet Service
Operational: Yes.

Telephone Service
Digital: Operational
Miles of Plant: 39.0 (coaxial); None (fiber optic). Homes passed: 2,196.
Chief Executive Officer: Steve Lowe. Vice President & General Manager: Mary lafrate. Vice President, Engineering: Jeff Spence. System Engineer: Bart Cotter.
City fee: 3% of basic.
Ownership: Buford Media Group LLC (MSO).

LOON LAKE—Formerly served by CableDirect. No longer in operation. ICA: IN0286.

LYNNVILLE—Avenue Broadband Communications, 2603 Hart St, Vincennes, IN 47591. Phones: 800-882-7185; 812-895-7676. Fax: 812-886-5017. Web Site: http://www.avenuebroadband.com. ICA: IN0209.
TV Market Ranking: 86 (LYNNVILLE). Franchise award date: August 1, 1982. Franchise expiration date: N.A. Began: January 1, 1984.
Channel capacity: N.A. Channels available but not in use: N.A.

Basic Service
Subscribers: 48.
Programming (received off-air): WEHT (ABC) Evansville; WEVV-TV (CBS, MNT) Evansville; WFIE (NBC) Evansville; WNIN (PBS) Evansville; WTVW (FOX) Evansville.
Programming (via satellite): C-SPAN; TBS Superstation; WGN America.
Current originations: Government Access; Educational Access; Public Access.
Fee: $45.00 installation; $6.99 monthly; $2.07 converter.

Expanded Basic Service 1
Subscribers: 43.
Programming (via satellite): ABC Family Channel; Animal Planet; CNN; Country Music TV; Discovery Channel; E! Entertainment Television; ESPN; Fox News Channel; History Channel; Lifetime; Nickelodeon; Spike TV; Syfy; Travel Channel; Turner Network TV; TV Land; USA Network; VH1; Weather Channel.
Fee: $9.79 monthly.

Pay Service 1
Pay Units: 36.
Programming (via satellite): The Movie Channel.
Fee: $25.00 installation; $10.00 monthly.

Pay Service 2
Pay Units: 33.
Programming (via satellite): Showtime.
Fee: $10.00 monthly.

Video-On-Demand: No

Internet Service
Operational: No.

Telephone Service
None
Miles of Plant: 8.0 (coaxial); None (fiber optic). Homes passed: 339.
Chief Executive Officer: Steve Lowe. Vice President & General Manager: Mary lafrate. Vice President, Engineering: Jeff Spence. System Engineer: Bart Cotter.
City fee: 3% of gross.
Ownership: Buford Media Group LLC (MSO).

LYONS—Insight Communications. Now served by BLOOMINGTON, IN [IN0016]. ICA: IN0186.

MACY—Longview Communications, 12007 Sunrise Valley Dr, Ste 375, Reston, VA 20191. Phones: 866-611-6565 (Customer service); 703-476-9101. Fax: 703-476-9107. Web Site: http://www.longviewcomm.com. Also serves Fulton, Fulton County (portions) & Liberty Twp. (Fulton County). ICA: IN0349.
TV Market Ranking: Below 100 (Fulton, Fulton County (portions), Liberty Twp. (Fulton County), MACY). Franchise award date: N.A. Franchise expiration date: N.A. Began: N.A.
Channel capacity: 36 (not 2-way capable). Channels available but not in use: N.A.

Basic Service
Subscribers: 87.
Programming (received off-air): WHME-TV (IND) South Bend; WLFI-TV (CBS) Lafayette; WNDU-TV (NBC) South Bend; WNDY-TV (MNT) Marion; WNIT (PBS) South Bend; WPTA (ABC, CW) Fort Wayne; WSBT-TV (CBS, IND) South Bend; WSJV (FOX) Elkhart; WTTK (IND) Kokomo.
Programming (via satellite): INSP; QVC.
Fee: $17.98 monthly.

Expanded Basic Service 1
Subscribers: N.A.
Programming (via satellite): ABC Family Channel; AMC; Animal Planet; Arts & Entertainment; Cartoon Network; CNN; C-SPAN; Discovery Channel; Disney Channel; ESPN; ESPN 2; Headline News; HGTV; Lifetime; Nickelodeon; TBS Superstation; The Learning Channel; Travel Channel; Turner Network TV; USA Network; Weather Channel; WGN America.
Fee: $17.97 monthly.

Pay Service 1
Pay Units: N.A.
Programming (via satellite): Showtime; The Movie Channel.
Fee: $8.95 monthly (TMC), $10.95 monthly (Showtime).

Video-On-Demand: No

Internet Service
Operational: No.

Telephone Service
None
Miles of Plant: 15.0 (coaxial); None (fiber optic). Homes passed: 770.
President: John Long. Senior Vice President: Marc W. Cohen. Engineering Director: Joe Ferrell. Technical Manager: Steve Boss. Marketing Director: Brandon Dickey.
Ownership: Longview Communications (MSO).

MADISON—Time Warner Cable, 1615 Foxhaven Dr, Richmond, KY 40475. Phones: 859-626-4800; 859-624-9666; 812-265-5499 (Local office). Fax: 859-624-0060. Web Site: http://www.timewarnercable.com. Also serves Hanover, Jefferson County (portions) & Vevay. ICA: IN0046.
TV Market Ranking: 38 (Jefferson County (portions)); Below 100 (Hanover); Outside TV Markets (MADISON, Vevay, Jefferson County (portions)). Franchise award date: N.A. Franchise expiration date: N.A. Began: June 3, 1951.
Channel capacity: N.A. Channels available but not in use: N.A.

Basic Service
Subscribers: 6,778.
Programming (received off-air): WAVE (NBC) Louisville; WBKI-TV (CW) Campbellsville; WBNA (ION) Louisville; WCPO-TV (ABC) Cincinnati; WDRB (FOX) Louisville; WHAS-TV (ABC) Louisville; WKPC-TV (PBS) Louisville; WLKY-TV (CBS) Louisville; WLWT (NBC) Cincinnati; WMYO (MNT) Salem; WTTV (CW) Bloomington; WXIX-TV (FOX) Newport; allband FM.
Programming (via satellite): ABC Family Channel; C-SPAN; C-SPAN 2; Disney Channel; Home Shopping Network; QVC; TBS Superstation; Turner Network TV; TV Guide Network; WGN America.
Fee: $39.95 installation; $12.15 monthly; $25.00 additional installation.
Expanded Basic Service 1
Subscribers: N.A.
Programming (via satellite): AMC; Animal Planet; Arts & Entertainment; BET Networks; Bravo; Cartoon Network; CNBC; CNN; Comedy Central; Country Music TV; Discovery Channel; E! Entertainment Television; ESPN; ESPN 2; Eternal Word TV Network; Food Network; Fox News Channel; Fox Sports Net Ohio; FX; Great American Country; Hallmark Channel; Headline News; HGTV; History Channel; INSP; MSNBC; MTV; Oxygen; Spike TV; Syfy; The Learning Channel; Travel Channel; Trinity Broadcasting Network; truTV; Turner Classic Movies; TV Land; USA Network; VH1; Weather Channel.
Fee: $38.20 monthly.
Digital Basic Service
Subscribers: 1,580.
Programming (via satellite): AmericanLife TV Network; BBC America; Bio; Black Family Channel; Bloomberg Television; Canales N; CNBC; Discovery Digital Networks; Do-It-Yourself; ESPN Classic Sports; ESPNews; FitTV; Fox College Sports Atlantic; Fox College Sports Central; Fox College Sports Pacific; Fox Sports World; G4; Golf Channel; GSN; Independent Film Channel; INSP; Outdoor Channel; Speed Channel; Toon Disney; Versus; WE tv.
Fee: $6.00 monthly.
Digital Expanded Basic Service
Subscribers: 324.
Programming (via satellite): FX; GAS; History Channel International; Lifetime; MTV Networks Digital Suite; National Geographic Channel; Nick Jr.; Nick Too; Nickelodeon; NickToons TV; SoapNet; Style Network; Sundance Channel.
Fee: $6.00 monthly.
Digital Pay Service 1
Pay Units: 160.
Programming (via satellite): ART America; CCTV-4; Cinemax (multiplexed); DMX Music; Encore (multiplexed); Filipino Channel; Flix; HBO (multiplexed); RAI International; Russian Television Network; Showtime (multiplexed); Starz (multiplexed); The Movie Channel (multiplexed); TV Asia; TV Japan; TV5, La Television International; Zee TV USA; Zhong Tian Channel.
Fee: $12.00 monthly (HBO, Cinemax, Showtime/TMC or Starz), $15.00 monthly (CCTV, TV Asia, TV5, Filipino, RAI, ART, TV Russia or TV Japan).
Video-On-Demand: No
Pay-Per-View
Urban Extra (delivered digitally); Hot Choice (delivered digitally); Fresh (delivered digitally); Playboy TV (delivered digitally); HITS PPV 1-30 (delivered digitally).
Internet Service
Operational: Yes.
Subscribers: 1,165.
Broadband Service: Road Runner.
Fee: $44.95 monthly.
Telephone Service
Digital: Operational
Fee: $44.95 monthly
Miles of Plant: 154.0 (coaxial); 65.0 (fiber optic). Homes passed: 11,239.
General Manager: Robert Trott. Technical Operations Manager: Dennis Lester. Chief Technician: Mardy Osterman. Marketing Director: Betrina Morse. Government & Public Affairs Manager: Carla Deaton.
City fee: 5% of gross.
Ownership: Time Warner Cable (MSO).

MANILLA—Formerly served by CableDirect. No longer in operation. ICA: IN0270.

MARENGO—Avenue Broadband Communications, 2603 Hart St, Vincennes, IN 47591. Phones: 800-882-7185; 812-895-7676. Fax: 812-886-5017. Web Site: http://www.avenuebroadband.com. Also serves Crawford County, Eckerty, Grantsburg & Taswell. ICA: IN0370.
TV Market Ranking: 38 (Crawford County (portions), MARENGO); Below 100 (Eckerty, Grantsburg, Taswell, Crawford County (portions)); Outside TV Markets (Crawford County (portions)). Franchise award date: August 11, 1980. Franchise expiration date: N.A. Began: May 15, 1980.
Channel capacity: N.A. Channels available but not in use: N.A.
Basic Service
Subscribers: 649.
Programming (received off-air): WBBM-TV (CBS) Chicago; WCIU-TV (IND) Chicago; WCPX-TV (ION) Chicago; WFLD (FOX) Chicago; WGBO-DT (UNV) Joliet; WGN-TV (CW, IND) Chicago; WIFR (CBS) Freeport; WLS-TV (ABC) Chicago; WMAQ-TV (NBC) Chicago; WPWR-TV (MNT) Gary; WREX (CW, NBC) Rockford; WSNS-TV (TMO) Chicago; WTTW (PBS) Chicago; WTVO (ABC, MNT) Rockford; WWTO-TV (TBN) La Salle; WXFT-DT (TEL) Aurora; allband FM.
Programming (via satellite): C-SPAN; C-SPAN 2; Eternal Word TV Network; Home Shopping Network; QVC; TV Guide Network.
Fee: $42.95 installation; $23.50 monthly.
Expanded Basic Service 1
Subscribers: 487.
Programming (via satellite): ABC Family Channel; AMC; Animal Planet; Arts & Entertainment; BET Networks; Bravo; Cartoon Network; CNBC; CNN; Comedy Central; Country Music TV; Discovery Channel; Disney Channel; E! Entertainment Television; ESPN; ESPN 2; ESPN Classic Sports; Food Network; Fox News Channel; FX; G4; Golf Channel; GSN; Hallmark Channel; Headline News; HGTV; History Channel; INSP; Lifetime; MSNBC; MTV; MTV2; National Geographic Channel; Nickelodeon; Oxygen; SoapNet; Speed Channel; Spike TV; Style Network; Syfy; TBS Superstation; The Learning Channel; Toon Disney; Travel Channel; truTV; Turner Classic Movies; Turner Network TV; TV Land; USA Network; Versus; VH1; WE tv; Weather Channel.
Video-On-Demand: No
Internet Service
Operational: No.
Telephone Service
None
Miles of Plant: 58.0 (coaxial); None (fiber optic). Homes passed: 2,377. Miles of plant (coax) includes Crawford Co.
Chief Executive Officer: Steve Lowe. Vice President & General Manager: Mary Iafrate.

Vice President, Engineering: Jeff Spence. System Engineer: Bart Cotter.
City fee: 3% of gross.
Ownership: Buford Media Group LLC (MSO).

MARION—Bright House Networks, 2923 S Western Ave, Indianapolis, IN 46953. Phones: 765-662-0071 (Customer service); 765-668-5456 (Administrative office). Fax: 317-632-5311. E-mail: customersupport.indiana@mybrighthouse.com. Web Site: http://indiana.brighthouse.com/default.aspx. Also serves Gas City, Grant County & Jonesboro. ICA: IN0021.
TV Market Ranking: 82 (Grant County (portions), MARION); Below 100 (Gas City, Jonesboro, Grant County (portions)). Franchise award date: January 4, 1966. Franchise expiration date: N.A. Began: May 1, 1966.
Channel capacity: 70 (operating 2-way). Channels available but not in use: None.
Basic Service
Subscribers: 16,000.
Programming (received off-air): WANE-TV (CBS) Fort Wayne; WFFT-TV (FOX) Fort Wayne; WFWA (PBS) Fort Wayne; WHMB-TV (IND) Indianapolis; WIPB (PBS) Muncie; WISE-TV (MNT, NBC) Fort Wayne; WISH-TV (CBS) Indianapolis; WIWU-CD (IND) Marion; WNDY-TV (MNT) Marion; WPTA (ABC, CW) Fort Wayne; WRTV (ABC) Indianapolis; WSOT-LP Marion; WTHR (NBC) Indianapolis; WTTK (IND) Kokomo; WXIN (FOX) Indianapolis.
Programming (via satellite): C-SPAN; C-SPAN 2; Hallmark Channel; Home Shopping Network; ION Television; QVC; ShopNBC; TBS Superstation; Travel Channel; Trinity Broadcasting Network; TV Guide Network; WGN America.
Current originations: Government Access; Educational Access; Public Access.
Fee: $67.67 installation; $16.20 monthly; $6.95 converter.
Expanded Basic Service 1
Subscribers: 12,384.
Programming (via satellite): ABC Family Channel; AMC; AmericanLife TV Network; Animal Planet; Arts & Entertainment; BET Networks; Cartoon Network; CNBC; CNN; Country Music TV; Discovery Channel; Disney Channel; E! Entertainment Television; ESPN; ESPN 2; Food Network; Fox News Channel; Fox Sports Net Midwest; FX; Golf Channel; Headline News; HGTV; History Channel; Lifetime; MSNBC; MTV; Nickelodeon; Oxygen; Spike TV; The Learning Channel; Turner Network TV; USA Network; Versus; VH1; WE tv; Weather Channel.
Fee: $31.30 monthly.
Digital Basic Service
Subscribers: 5,280.
Programming (via satellite): America's Store; BBC America; Comedy Central; C-SPAN 3; Discovery Digital Networks; Disney Channel; DMX Music; Do-It-Yourself; ESPN Classic Sports; ESPNews; Flix; Fox Sports World; GSN; Lifetime Movie Network; MTV2; MuchMusic Network; National Geographic Channel; Nick Jr.; Outdoor Channel; Speed Channel; Style Network; Syfy; Toon Disney; truTV; TV Land; VH1 Classic.
Fee: $10.50 monthly.
Digital Pay Service 1
Pay Units: 8,032.
Programming (via satellite): Cinemax (multiplexed); Encore (multiplexed); HBO (multiplexed); Showtime (multiplexed); Starz (multiplexed); The Movie Channel (multiplexed).
Fee: $9.00 monthly (Starz), $13.00 monthly (Cinemax, HBO or Showtime/TMC).
Video-On-Demand: Yes
Pay-Per-View
iN DEMAND (delivered digitally); MLB Extra Innings (delivered digitally); NBA League Pass (delivered digitally); NHL Center Ice (delivered digitally); Playboy TV (delivered digitally); Pleasure (delivered digitally); Fresh (delivered digitally); Shorteez (delivered digitally).
Internet Service
Operational: Yes. Began: April 1, 2001.
Subscribers: 1,183.
Broadband Service: Road Runner.
Fee: $19.95 installation; $44.95 monthly.
Telephone Service
Digital: Operational
Fee: $19.95 installation; $44.95 monthly
Miles of Plant: 322.0 (coaxial); 25.0 (fiber optic). Homes passed: 25,572.
Division President: Buz Nesbit. General Manager: Cal Blumhorst. Technical Operations Manager: Michael Buckles. Public Affairs Director: Al Aldridge. Community Program Director: Inge Harte-North.
City fee: 3% Franchise Fee.
Ownership: Bright House Networks LLC (MSO).

MARKLE—Longview Communications, 1923 N Main, Higginsville, MO 64037. Phone: 703-476-9101. Fax: 866-329-4790. Web Site: http://www.longviewcomm.com. ICA: IN0192.
TV Market Ranking: 82 (MARKLE). Franchise award date: July 17, 1985. Franchise expiration date: N.A. Began: October 1, 1986.
Channel capacity: N.A. Channels available but not in use: N.A.
Basic Service
Subscribers: 153.
Programming (received off-air): WANE-TV (CBS) Fort Wayne; WFFT-TV (FOX) Fort Wayne; WFWA (PBS) Fort Wayne; WIPB (PBS) Muncie; WISE-TV (MNT, NBC) Fort Wayne; WNDY-TV (MNT) Marion; WPTA (ABC, CW) Fort Wayne; WSOT-LP Marion; WTTK (IND) Kokomo.
Programming (via satellite): ABC Family Channel; AMC; Animal Planet; Arts & Entertainment; CBS College Sports Network; CNN; C-SPAN; Discovery Channel; Disney Channel; Do-It-Yourself; E! Entertainment Television; ESPN; ESPN 2; ESPN Classic Sports; Flix; Food Network; Fox News Channel; FX; Great American Country; Hallmark Channel; Hallmark Movie Channel; Headline News; HGTV; History Channel; Home Shopping Network; Lifetime; MSNBC; Nick-

elodeon; QVC; Spike TV; TBS Superstation; The Learning Channel; Travel Channel; Trinity Broadcasting Network; truTV; Turner Network TV; USA Network; Weather Channel; WGN America.
Fee: $35.95 installation; $41.95 monthly.

Digital Basic Service
Subscribers: 14.
Programming (via satellite): AmericanLife TV Network; BBC America; Bio; Bloomberg Television; Discovery Digital Networks; Encore (multiplexed); ESPNews; Fox Movie Channel; Fox Soccer; Fuse; G4; Golf Channel; GSN; Halogen Network; History Channel International; Independent Film Channel; Lifetime Movie Network; Outdoor Channel; Speed Channel; Style Network; Sundance Channel; Toon Disney; Turner Classic Movies; Versus.
Fee: $18.00 monthly.

Pay Service 1
Pay Units: 217.
Programming (via satellite): Cinemax; HBO; Showtime; The Movie Channel.
Fee: $8.95 monthly (TMC), $10.95 monthly (Cinemax or Showtime), $12.95 monthly (HBO).

Digital Pay Service 1
Pay Units: N.A.
Programming (via satellite): Cinemax (multiplexed); Flix; HBO (multiplexed); Showtime (multiplexed); Starz (multiplexed); The Movie Channel (multiplexed).
Fee: $8.95 monthly (TMC), $10.95 monthly (Showtime or Cinemax), $12.95 monthly (HBO).

Video-On-Demand: No

Pay-Per-View
iN DEMAND (delivered digitally); Hot Choice (delivered digitally); Playboy TV (delivered digitally); Fresh (delivered digitally); Shorteez (delivered digitally).

Internet Service
Operational: Yes.
Subscribers: 61.
Broadband Service: IBBS.

Telephone Service
None

Miles of Plant: 6.0 (coaxial); None (fiber optic). Homes passed: 513.
President: John Long. Senior Vice President: Marc W. Cohen. General Manager: Brandon Dickey. Technical Manager: Steve Boss.
Ownership: Longview Communications (MSO).

MARSHALL COUNTY—Windjammer Cable, 4400 PGA Blvd, Ste 902, Palm Beach Gardens, FL 33410. Phones: 877-450-5558; 561-775-1208. Fax: 561-775-7811. Web Site: http://www.windjammercable.com. Also serves Donaldson, Greene Twp., Penn Twp., South Bend (eastern portion) & Tyner, IN; Eau Claire, Galien & Galien Twp., MI. ICA: IN0341.
TV Market Ranking: 80 (Donaldson, Eau Claire, Galien, Galien Twp., Greene Twp., MARSHALL COUNTY, Penn Twp., South Bend (eastern portion), Tyner). Franchise award date: N.A. Franchise expiration date: N.A. Began: N.A.
Channel capacity: N.A. Channels available but not in use: N.A.

Basic Service
Subscribers: 700.
Programming (received off-air): WBND-LP South Bend; WHME-TV (IND) South Bend; WNDU-TV (NBC) South Bend; WNIT (PBS) South Bend; WSBT-TV (CBS, IND) South Bend; WSJV (FOX) Elkhart.
Programming (via satellite): Home Shopping Network; QVC; TV Guide Network; WGN America.
Fee: $45.86 installation; $9.45 monthly.

Expanded Basic Service 1
Subscribers: N.A.
Programming (via satellite): ABC Family Channel; AMC; Animal Planet; Arts & Entertainment; BET Networks; Cartoon Network; CNBC; CNN; Country Music TV; C-SPAN; Discovery Channel; Disney Channel; E! Entertainment Television; ESPN; ESPN 2; Food Network; Fox News Channel; Fox Sports Net Detroit; Headline News; HGTV; History Channel; INSP; Lifetime; MTV; Nickelodeon; Spike TV; TBS Superstation; The Learning Channel; Travel Channel; Turner Network TV; USA Network; Versus; VH1; Weather Channel.
Fee: $27.05 monthly.

Pay Service 1
Pay Units: N.A.
Programming (via satellite): HBO; Showtime.
Fee: $10.95 monthly (each).

Video-On-Demand: No

Internet Service
Operational: No.

Telephone Service
None

Ownership: Windjammer Communications LLC (MSO).

MARTINSVILLE—Comcast Cable, 2450 S Henderson St, Bloomington, IN 47401-4540. Phone: 812-332-9486. Fax: 812-332-0129. Web Site: http://www.comcast.com. Also serves Morgan County. ICA: IN0054.
TV Market Ranking: 16 (MARTINSVILLE, Morgan County). Franchise award date: N.A. Franchise expiration date: N.A. Began: July 1, 1974.
Channel capacity: N.A. Channels available but not in use: N.A.

Basic Service
Subscribers: N.A. Included in Bloomington
Programming (received off-air): WCLJ-TV (TBN) Bloomington; WFYI (PBS) Indianapolis; WHMB-TV (IND) Indianapolis; WIPX-TV (ION) Bloomington; WISH-TV (CBS) Indianapolis; WNDY-TV (MNT) Marion; WREP-LD Martinsville; WRTV (ABC) Indianapolis; WTHR (NBC) Indianapolis; WTIU (PBS) Bloomington; WTTV (CW) Bloomington; 1 FM.
Programming (via microwave): WGN-TV (CW, IND) Chicago.
Programming (via satellite): C-SPAN; C-SPAN 2; QVC.
Current originations: Government Access.
Fee: $24.95 installation.

Expanded Basic Service 1
Subscribers: 4,101.
Programming (via satellite): ABC Family Channel; AMC; Animal Planet; Arts & Entertainment; BET Networks; Cartoon Network; CNBC; CNN; Comedy Central; Country Music TV; Discovery Channel; Disney Channel; E! Entertainment Television; ESPN; ESPN 2; Food Network; Fox News Channel; Fox Sports Net Midwest; FX; Headline News; HGTV; History Channel; Home Shopping Network; Lifetime; MSNBC; MTV; Nickelodeon; Spike TV; TBS Superstation; The Learning Channel; Travel Channel; Turner Network TV; TV Guide Network; USA Network; VH1; Weather Channel.
Fee: $40.00 monthly.

Digital Basic Service
Subscribers: N.A.
Programming (via satellite): AmericanLife TV Network; Bio; Bloomberg Television; Bravo; C-SPAN 3; Discovery Digital Networks; DMX Music; Do-It-Yourself; Encore (multiplexed); ESPN Classic Sports; ESPNews; Eternal Word TV Network; Fox Movie Channel; Fox Sports World; Fuse; G4; GAS; Golf Channel; GSN; Halogen Network; History Channel International; Independent Film Channel; Lifetime Movie Network; National Geographic Channel; Nick Jr.; Nick Too; SoapNet; Speed Channel; Style Network; Sundance Channel; Syfy; Toon Disney; truTV; Turner Classic Movies; Versus; WE tv.
Fee: $17.00 monthly.

Digital Pay Service 1
Pay Units: N.A.
Programming (via satellite): Cinemax (multiplexed); Flix; HBO (multiplexed); Showtime (multiplexed); Starz (multiplexed); The Movie Channel (multiplexed).
Fee: $10.00 monthly (Cinemax or Starz), $13.00 monthly (HBO or Showtime).

Video-On-Demand: Yes

Pay-Per-View
iN DEMAND; iN DEMAND (delivered digitally); Adult (delivered digitally).

Internet Service
Operational: Yes.
Broadband Service: Comcast High Speed Internet.
Fee: $99.95 installation; $44.95 monthly; $15.00 modem lease; $99.95 modem purchase.

Telephone Service
Analog: Not Operational
Digital: Operational

Miles of Plant: 113.0 (coaxial); 11.0 (fiber optic). Homes passed: 5,226.
Area Director: Wendy Henry. Chief Technician: Jeff Harrington. Customer Service Manager: Jennifer Lane.
City fee: 3% of gross.
Ownership: Comcast Cable Communications Inc. (MSO).

MEDORA—Insight Communications. Now served by BEDFORD, IN [IN0033]. ICA: IN0291.

MENTONE—Longview Communications, 12007 Sunrise Valley Dr, Ste 375, Reston, VA 20191. Phones: 866-611-6565 (Customer service); 703-476-9101. Fax: 703-476-9107. Web Site: http://www.longviewcomm.com. ICA: IN0193.
TV Market Ranking: Outside TV Markets (MENTONE). Franchise award date: N.A. Franchise expiration date: N.A. Began: January 1, 1986.
Channel capacity: 42 (not 2-way capable). Channels available but not in use: None.

Basic Service
Subscribers: 32.
Programming (received off-air): WFWA (PBS) Fort Wayne; WHME-TV (IND) South Bend; WNDU-TV (NBC) South Bend; WNIT (PBS) South Bend; WPTA (ABC, CW) Fort Wayne; WSBT-TV (CBS, IND) South Bend; WSJV (FOX) Elkhart; WTTK (IND) Kokomo.
Programming (via satellite): ABC Family Channel; AMC; Arts & Entertainment; CNN; Country Music TV; C-SPAN; C-SPAN 2; Discovery Channel; Disney Channel; E! Entertainment Television; ESPN; ESPN 2; Flix; Hallmark Channel; Hallmark Movie Channel; Headline News; HGTV; History Channel; Lifetime; Nickelodeon; QVC; Spike TV; TBS Superstation; The Learning Channel; Trinity Broadcasting Network; Turner Network TV; USA Network; Weather Channel; WGN America.
Fee: $39.90 installation; $37.95 monthly.

Pay Service 1
Pay Units: N.A.
Programming (via satellite): Showtime; The Movie Channel.
Fee: $10.00 installation; $8.95 monthly (TMC), $10.95 monthly (Showtime).

Video-On-Demand: No

Internet Service
Operational: No.

Telephone Service
None

Miles of Plant: 5.0 (coaxial); None (fiber optic). Homes passed: 392.
President: John Long. Senior Vice President: Marc W. Cohen. General Manager: Brandon Dickey. Technical Manager: Steve Boss.
Ownership: Longview Communications (MSO).

MEROM—Formerly served by CableDirect. No longer in operation. ICA: IN0217.

MERRILLVILLE—Comcast Cable. Now served by CHICAGO (southern suburbs), IL [IL0008]. ICA: IN0004.

METAMORA—Formerly served by CableDirect. No longer in operation. ICA: IN0293.

MIAMI—Formerly served by CableDirect. No longer in operation. ICA: IN0214.

MICHIANA—Formerly served by Sprint Corp. No longer in operation. ICA: IN0342.

MICHIGAN CITY—Comcast Cable, 7720 W 98th St, Hickory Hills, IL 60457. Phone: 219-872-9306 (Local office). Web Site: http://www.comcast.com. Also serves Beverly Shores, Duneland Beach, La Porte County (unincorporated areas), Long Beach, Michiana Shores, Porter County (unincorporated areas), Pottawattomie Park & Trail Creek, IN; Grand Beach (village), Michiana (village) & New Buffalo Twp., MI. ICA: IN0024.
TV Market Ranking: 3 (Porter County (unincorporated areas) (portions)); 80 (Duneland Beach, Grand Beach (village), La Porte County (unincorporated areas) (portions), Long Beach, Michiana (village), Michiana Shores, MICHIGAN CITY, New Buffalo Twp., Pottawattomie Park, Trail Creek); Below 100 (Beverly Shores, Porter County (unincorporated areas) (portions), La Porte County (unincorporated areas) (portions)). Franchise award date: July 18, 1980. Franchise expiration date: N.A. Began: December 16, 1981.
Channel capacity: N.A. Channels available but not in use: N.A.

Basic Service
Subscribers: 12,819.
Programming (received off-air): WBBM-TV (CBS) Chicago; WCIU-TV (IND) Chicago; WCPX-TV (ION) Chicago; WFLD (FOX) Chicago; WGBO-DT (UNV) Joliet; WGN-TV (CW, IND) Chicago; WHME-TV (IND) South Bend; WJYS (IND) Hammond; WLS-TV (ABC) Chicago; WMAQ-TV (NBC) Chicago; WNDU-TV (NBC) South Bend; WNIT (PBS) South Bend; WPWR-TV (MNT) Gary; WSBT-TV (CBS, IND) South Bend; WSJV (FOX) Elkhart; WSNS-TV (TMO) Chicago; WTTW (PBS) Chicago; WXFT-DT (TEL) Aurora; WYCC (PBS) Chicago; WYIN (PBS) Gary.
Programming (via satellite): Home Shopping Network; QVC.
Current originations: Government Access; Educational Access; Public Access.
Fee: $48.99 installation; $18.04 monthly.

Expanded Basic Service 1
Subscribers: N.A.
Programming (via satellite): ABC Family Channel; AMC; Animal Planet; Arts & Entertainment; BET Networks; Bravo; Cartoon Network; CNBC; CNN; Comcast SportsNet Chicago; Comedy Central; Country Music TV; C-SPAN; C-SPAN 2; Discovery Channel; Disney Channel; E! Entertainment Television; ESPN; ESPN 2; Eternal Word TV Network; Food Network; Fox News Channel; FX; Golf Channel; Hallmark Channel; Headline News; HGTV; History Channel; Lifetime; MSNBC; MTV; Nickelodeon; Oxygen; Spike TV; TBS Superstation; The Learning Channel; Total Living Network; truTV; Turner Network TV; TV Guide Network; USA Network; Versus; VH1; Weather Channel.
Fee: $34.45 monthly.

Digital Basic Service
Subscribers: 4,346.
Programming (received off-air): WBBM-TV (CBS) Chicago; WFLD (FOX) Chicago; WGN-TV (CW, IND) Chicago; WLS-TV (ABC) Chicago; WMAQ-TV (NBC) Chicago; WTTW (PBS) Chicago.
Programming (via satellite): BBC America; Bio; Bloomberg Television; Canales N; CMT Pure Country; Cooking Channel; Current; Discovery Digital Networks; Discovery HD Theater; Do-It-Yourself; Encore (multiplexed); ESPN 2 HD; ESPN Classic Sports; ESPN HD; ESPNews; Fox College Sports Atlantic; Fox College Sports Central; Fox College Sports Pacific; Fox Movie Channel; Fox Reality Channel; Fox Soccer; Fuse; G4; GAS; Gol TV; Gospel Music Channel; Great American Country; GSN; History Channel; History Channel International; Independent Film Channel; Jewelry Television; Lifetime Movie Network; LOGO; MTV Networks Digital Suite; Music Choice; National Geographic Channel; NBA TV; NFL Network; Nick Jr.; Nick Too; NickToons TV; Outdoor Channel; Ovation; Palladia; PBS Kids Sprout; ShopNBC; SoapNet; Speed Channel; Style Network; Sundance Channel; Syfy; The Word Network; Toon Disney; Trinity Broadcasting Network; Turner Classic Movies; Turner Network TV HD; TV Land; TV One; TVG Network; Universal HD; Versus HD; WE tv; Weatherscan.
Fee: $11.99 monthly.

Digital Pay Service 1
Pay Units: N.A.
Programming (via satellite): Arabic Channel; CCTV-4; Cinemax (multiplexed); Cinemax HD; Filipino Channel; Flix; HBO (multiplexed); HBO HD; RAI International; Russian Television Network; Saigon Broadcasting TV Network; Showtime (multiplexed); Showtime HD; Starz (multiplexed); Starz HDTV; The Movie Channel (multiplexed); TV Asia; TV Japan; TV5, La Television International; Zhong Tian Channel.
Fee: $16.99 monthly (each).

Video-On-Demand: Yes

Pay-Per-View
Addressable homes: 4,346.
iN DEMAND (delivered digitally), Addressable: Yes; Sports PPV (delivered digitally), Addressable: Yes; ESPN Now (delivered digitally), Addressable: Yes; Fresh (delivered digitally), Addressable: Yes; Shorteez (delivered digitally), Addressable: Yes; Playboy TV (delivered digitally), Addressable: Yes, Addressable: Yes, Addressable: Yes.

Internet Service
Operational: Yes.
Subscribers: 2,910.
Broadband Service: Comcast High Speed Internet.
Fee: $99.00 installation; $45.95 monthly.

Telephone Service
Digital: Operational
Fee: $44.95 monthly

Miles of Plant: 265.0 (coaxial); None (fiber optic). Additional miles planned: 1.0 (coaxial); 15.0 (fiber optic). Homes passed: 17,219. Total homes in franchised area: 17,850.

Area Vice President: Sandy Weicher. Vice President, Technical Operations: Bob Curtis. Vice President, Sales & Marketing: Eric Schaefer. Vice President, Communications: Rich Ruggiero. Technical Operations Manager: Karl Braun. Marketing Director: Ron Knutson.

City fee: 3% of gross.

Ownership: Comcast Cable Communications Inc. (MSO).

MICHIGANTOWN—Formerly served by Country Cablevision. No longer in operation. ICA: IN0294.

MIDDLEBURY—Comcast Cable. Now served by SOUTH BEND, IN [IN0005]. ICA: IN0114.

MIDDLETOWN—Insight Communications. Now served by ANDERSON, IN [IN0012]. ICA: IN0121.

MILROY—Formerly served by CableDirect. No longer in operation. ICA: IN0295.

MITCHELL—Avenue Broadband Communications, 2603 Hart St, Vincennes, IN 47591. Phones: 800-882-7185; 812-895-7676. Fax: 812-886-5017. Web Site: http://www.avenuebroadband.com. Also serves Lawrence County (unincorporated areas), Orange County (unincorporated areas), Orleans & Paoli. ICA: IN0061.

TV Market Ranking: 16 (Lawrence County (unincorporated areas), MITCHELL, Orange County (unincorporated areas) (portions), Orleans); Below 100 (Paoli, Orange County (unincorporated areas) (portions)). Franchise award date: N.A. Franchise expiration date: N.A. Began: December 6, 1968.

Channel capacity: N.A. Channels available but not in use: N.A.

Basic Service
Subscribers: 2,789.
Programming (received off-air): WAVE (NBC) Louisville; WCLJ-TV (TBN) Bloomington; WDRB (FOX) Louisville; WHAS-TV (ABC) Louisville; WIPX-TV (ION) Bloomington; WISH-TV (CBS) Indianapolis; WLKY-TV (CBS) Louisville; WMYO (MNT) Salem; WTIU (PBS) Bloomington; WTTV (CW) Bloomington; WTWO (NBC) Terre Haute.
Programming (via satellite): C-SPAN; C-SPAN 2; Home Shopping Network; QVC; WGN America.
Fee: $39.95 installation; $16.45 monthly.

Expanded Basic Service 1
Subscribers: N.A.
Programming (via satellite): ABC Family Channel; AMC; Animal Planet; Arts & Entertainment; Cartoon Network; CNBC; CNN; Comedy Central; Country Music TV; Discovery Channel; Disney Channel; E! Entertainment Television; ESPN; ESPN 2; Food Network; Fox News Channel; Fox Sports Net Midwest; FX; G4; Golf Channel; Headline News; HGTV; History Channel; Lifetime; MSNBC; MTV; Nickelodeon; Outdoor Channel; Oxygen; Speed Channel; Spike TV; Syfy; TBS Superstation; The Learning Channel; Travel Channel; truTV; Turner Network TV; TV Land; USA Network; VH1; Weather Channel.

Digital Basic Service
Subscribers: N.A.
Programming (via satellite): BBC America; Bio; Bloomberg Television; Discovery Health Channel; Discovery Home Channel; Discovery Kids Channel; Discovery Times Channel; Do-It-Yourself; FitTV; Fox Movie Channel; GAS; GSN; History Channel International; Independent Film Channel; MTV Networks Digital Suite; Nick Jr.; Nick Too; NickToons TV; Science Television; SoapNet; Sundance Channel; Toon Disney; TV Guide Interactive Inc.; WE tv.

Digital Expanded Basic Service
Subscribers: N.A.
Programming (via satellite): Music Choice.

Digital Pay Service 1
Pay Units: N.A.
Programming (via satellite): Cinemax (multiplexed); Fox College Sports Atlantic (multiplexed); Fox College Sports Central; Fox College Sports Pacific; Fox Soccer; HBO (multiplexed); Starz (multiplexed).

Video-On-Demand: No

Pay-Per-View
Playboy TV (delivered digitally); Fresh (delivered digitally); Shorteez (delivered digitally); iN DEMAND (delivered digitally).

Internet Service
Operational: Yes.

Telephone Service
Digital: Operational

Miles of Plant: 134.0 (coaxial); None (fiber optic). Homes passed: 6,659.

Chief Executive Officer: Steve Lowe. Vice President & General Manager: Mary Iafrate. Vice President, Engineering: Jeff Spence. System Engineer: Bart Cotter.

City fee: None.

Ownership: Buford Media Group LLC (MSO).

MONROE CITY—Formerly served by Cebridge Connections. Now served by VINCENNES, IN [IN0035]. ICA: IN0177.

MONROEVILLE (town)—Comcast Cable, 720 Taylor St, Fort Wayne, IN 46802-5144. Phones: 317-275-6370 (Indianapolis office); 260-458-5103. Fax: 260-458-5138. Web Site: http://www.comcast.com. ICA: IN0358.

TV Market Ranking: Below 100 (MONROEVILLE (TOWN)). Franchise award date: May 20, 1981. Franchise expiration date: N.A. Began: N.A.

Channel capacity: 41 (not 2-way capable). Channels available but not in use: None.

Basic Service
Subscribers: N.A. Included in Indianapolis
Programming (received off-air): WANE-TV (CBS) Fort Wayne; WFFT-TV (FOX) Fort Wayne; WFWA (PBS) Fort Wayne; WINM (IND) Angola; WISE-TV (MNT, NBC) Fort Wayne; WPTA (ABC, CW) Fort Wayne.
Programming (via satellite): ABC Family Channel.
Fee: $50.99 installation.

Expanded Basic Service 1
Subscribers: 344.
Programming (via satellite): AMC; Arts & Entertainment; Big Ten Network; Cartoon Network; CNBC; CNN; C-SPAN; Discovery Channel; Disney Channel; E! Entertainment Television; ESPN; ESPN 2; Eternal Word TV Network; Great American Country; Headline News; HGTV; History Channel; ION Television; Lifetime; MSNBC; MTV; Nickelodeon; QVC; Speed Channel; Spike TV; Syfy; TBS Superstation; Turner Network TV; TV Land; USA Network; VH1; WGN America.
Fee: $37.98 monthly.

Pay Service 1
Pay Units: 344.
Programming (via satellite): Cinemax; HBO; Showtime.
Fee: $15.95 monthly (each).

Internet Service
Operational: Yes.

Telephone Service
Digital: Operational

Total homes in franchised area: 643. Miles of plant included in Fort Wayne

Regional Vice President: Scott Tenney. Technical Operations Director: Bennie Logan. Engineering Manager: Tom Stuckholz. Vice President, Marketing: Aaron Geisel. Marketing Manager: Marci Hefley. Vice President, Communications: Mark Apple.

Ownership: Comcast Cable Communications Inc. (MSO).

MONROVIA—Comcast Cable, 5330 E 65th St, Indianapolis, IN 46220. Phone: 317-275-6370. Fax: 317-275-6340. Web Site: http://www.comcast.com. Also serves Hendricks County (portions), Morgan County (portions) & Paragon. ICA: IN0098.

TV Market Ranking: 16 (Hendricks County (portions), MONROVIA, Morgan County (portions), Paragon). Franchise award date: N.A. Franchise expiration date: N.A. Began: N.A.

Channel capacity: 50 (operating 2-way). Channels available but not in use: None.

Basic Service
Subscribers: N.A. Included in Indianapolis
Programming (received off-air): WFYI (PBS) Indianapolis; WHMB-TV (IND) Indianapolis; WISH-TV (CBS) Indianapolis; WNDY-TV (MNT) Marion; WRTV (ABC) Indianapolis; WTHR (NBC) Indianapolis; WTTV (CW) Bloomington; WXIN (FOX) Indianapolis.
Programming (via satellite): ABC Family Channel; AMC; Arts & Entertainment; Cartoon Network; CNBC; CNN; Comedy Central; C-SPAN; C-SPAN 2; Discovery Channel; E! Entertainment Television; ESPN; ESPN 2; ESPN Classic Sports; Food Network; Fox Sports Net Midwest; Golf Channel; Great American Country; GSN; Headline News; HGTV; History Channel; Lifetime; MSNBC; MTV; Nickelodeon; QVC; Speed Channel; Spike TV; Syfy; TBS Superstation; The Learning Channel; Trinity Broadcasting Network; Turner Network TV; TV Land; USA Network; VH1; Weather Channel; WPIX (CW, IND) New York.
Fee: $50.99 installation; $54.48 monthly.

Digital Basic Service
Subscribers: 341.
Programming (via satellite): BBC America; Canales N; C-SPAN 3; Discovery Digital Networks; Disney Channel; ESPNews; GAS; MTV Networks Digital Suite; Nick Jr.; Nick Too; SoapNet; Toon Disney; Weatherscan.
Fee: $14.95 monthly.
Digital Pay Service 1
Pay Units: N.A.
Programming (via satellite): Cinemax (multiplexed); Encore (multiplexed); Flix; HBO (multiplexed); Showtime (multiplexed); Starz (multiplexed); Sundance Channel; The Movie Channel (multiplexed).
Fee: $9.95 monthly (each).
Pay-Per-View
iN DEMAND (delivered digitally); Playboy TV (delivered digitally); Fresh (delivered digitally); Shorteez (delivered digitally); Pleasure (delivered digitally); ESPN Extra (delivered digitally); ESPN Now (delivered digitally); NBA TV (delivered digitally).
Internet Service
Operational: Yes.
Telephone Service
Digital: Operational
Miles of Plant: 17.0 (coaxial); None (fiber optic). Homes passed: 2,000.
Regional Vice President & General Manager: William (Rusty) Robertson. Regional Vice President, Technical Operations: Max Woolsey. Regional Vice President, Communications & Public Affairs: Mark Apple. Marketing Director: Damion Miller.
Ownership: Comcast Cable Communications Inc. (MSO).

MONTEREY—Formerly served by CableDirect. No longer in operation. ICA: IN0298.

MONTEZUMA—Indiana Communications, PO Box 617, Boswell, IN 47921. Phone: 815-457-2659. Web Site: http://www.indcomm.net. Also serves Parke County. ICA: IN0136.
TV Market Ranking: Below 100 (MONTEZUMA, Parke County). Franchise award date: June 1, 1983. Franchise expiration date: N.A. Began: June 2, 1984.
Channel capacity: N.A. Channels available but not in use: N.A.
Basic Service
Subscribers: 207.
Programming (received off-air): WCCU (FOX) Urbana; WICD (ABC) Champaign; WILL-TV (PBS) Urbana; WRTV (ABC) Indianapolis; WTHI-TV (CBS) Terre Haute; WTTV (CW) Bloomington; WTWO (NBC) Terre Haute; 1 FM.
Programming (via satellite): ABC Family Channel; AMC; Animal Planet; Arts & Entertainment; CNBC; CNN; Country Music TV; C-SPAN; Discovery Channel; Disney Channel; E! Entertainment Television; ESPN; ESPN 2; ESPN Classic Sports; Food Network; Fox News Channel; Headline News; HGTV; History Channel; Lifetime; MSNBC; Nickelodeon; QVC; Spike TV; TBS Superstation; The Learning Channel; Travel Channel; Trinity Broadcasting Network; truTV; Turner Network TV; USA Network; Weather Channel; WGN America.
Fee: $35.00 installation; $35.95 monthly; $3.50 converter.
Digital Basic Service
Subscribers: 11.
Programming (via satellite): AmericanLife TV Network; BBC America; Bio; Bloomberg Television; Discovery Digital Networks; Encore (multiplexed); ESPNews; Fox Movie Channel; G4; Golf Channel; GSN; Halogen Network; History Channel International; Independent Film Channel; Lifetime Movie Network; Outdoor Channel; Speed Channel; Style Network; Toon Disney; Turner Classic Movies.
Fee: $17.00 monthly.
Pay Service 1
Pay Units: N.A.
Programming (via satellite): Cinemax; HBO; Showtime; The Movie Channel.
Fee: $10.00 installation; $12.50 monthly (each).
Digital Pay Service 1
Pay Units: N.A.
Programming (via satellite): Cinemax (multiplexed); Flix; HBO (multiplexed); Showtime; Starz (multiplexed); The Movie Channel (multiplexed).
Fee: $40.00 monthly.
Video-On-Demand: No
Pay-Per-View
iN DEMAND (delivered digitally); Hot Choice (delivered digitally); Playboy TV (delivered digitally); Fresh (delivered digitally); Shorteez (delivered digitally).
Internet Service
Operational: Yes.
Subscribers: 41.
Broadband Service: IBBS.
Fee: $29.95 monthly.
Telephone Service
None
Miles of Plant: 9.0 (coaxial); None (fiber optic). Homes passed: 610.
Manager: Joe Young.
City fee: 3% of gross.
Ownership: Park TV & Electronics Inc. (MSO).

MONTGOMERY—Formerly served by CableDirect. No longer in operation. ICA: IN0204.

MONTICELLO—Comcast Cable, 5330 E 65th St, Indianapolis, IN 46220. Phone: 317-275-6370. Fax: 317-275-6340. Web Site: http://www.comcast.com. Also serves Bringhurst, Brookston, Buffalo, Burlington, Burnettsville, Camden, Carroll County, Chalmers, Delphi, Idaville, Jasper County, Monon, Norway, Patton, Pittsburg, Remington, Reynolds, Rockfield, Rossville, White County, Wolcott & Yeoman. ICA: IN0025.
TV Market Ranking: Below 100 (Bringhurst, Brookston, Buffalo, Burlington, Burnettsville, Camden, Carroll County, Chalmers, Delphi, Idaville, Jasper County (portions), Monon, MONTICELLO, Norway, Patton, Pittsburg, Remington, Reynolds, Rockfield, Rossville, White County, Wolcott, Yeoman); Outside TV Markets (Jasper County (portions)). Franchise award date: January 1, 1967. Franchise expiration date: N.A. Began: September 1, 1968.
Channel capacity: 82 (operating 2-way). Channels available but not in use: N.A.
Basic Service
Subscribers: N.A. Included in Indianapolis
Programming (received off-air): WANE-TV (CBS) Fort Wayne; WFFT-TV (FOX) Fort Wayne; WFWA (PBS) Fort Wayne; WISE-TV (MNT, NBC) Fort Wayne; WISH-TV (CBS) Indianapolis; WNDU-TV (NBC) South Bend; WNDY-TV (MNT) Marion; WPTA (ABC, CW) Fort Wayne; WRTV (ABC) Indianapolis; WTHR (NBC) Indianapolis; WTTK (IND) Kokomo; 1 FM.
Programming (via satellite): Bravo; C-SPAN; C-SPAN 2; Home Shopping Network; QVC; The Comcast Network (multiplexed); TV Guide Network; WGN America.
Planned originations: Educational Access; Public Access.
Fee: $31.99 installation; $7.00 monthly.
Expanded Basic Service 1
Subscribers: 12,201.
Programming (via satellite): ABC Family Channel; AMC; Animal Planet; Arts & Entertainment; Cartoon Network; CNBC; CNN; Comedy Central; Country Music TV; Discovery Channel; Disney Channel; E! Entertainment Television; ESPN; ESPN 2; Food Network; Fox News Channel (multiplexed); Fox Sports Net Midwest; FX; G4; GalaVision; Golf Channel; GSN; Hallmark Channel; Headline News; HGTV; History Channel; Lifetime; MSNBC; MTV; Nickelodeon; Speed Channel; Spike TV; Style Network (multiplexed); Syfy; TBS Superstation; The Learning Channel; Toon Disney; Travel Channel; Trinity Broadcasting Network; truTV; Turner Classic Movies; Turner Network TV; TV Land; USA Network; Versus; VH1; Weather Channel.
Fee: $43.48 monthly.
Digital Basic Service
Subscribers: N.A.
Programming (via satellite): Arts & Entertainment HD; BBC America; Bio; Canales N; CBS College Sports Network; CMT Pure Country; Cooking Channel; C-SPAN 3; Current; Discovery Digital Networks; Discovery HD Theater; Do-It-Yourself; Encore; ESPN 2 HD; ESPN HD; ESPNews; Eternal Word TV Network; Flix; Fox Reality Channel; Fox Soccer; G4; GAS; Gol TV; History Channel International; INHD; Lifetime Movie Network; LOGO; MoviePlex; MTV Networks Digital Suite; Music Choice; National Geographic Channel; National Geographic Channel HD Network; NFL Network; Nick Jr.; Nick Too; NickToons TV; Oxygen; Palladia; PBS Kids Channel; SoapNet; Sundance Channel; Tennis Channel; The Word Network; Turner Network TV HD; TV One; TVG Network; Universal HD; Versus HD; Weatherscan.
Fee: $17.82 monthly.
Digital Pay Service 1
Pay Units: N.A.
Programming (via satellite): Cinemax (multiplexed); Cinemax HD; HBO (multiplexed); HBO HD; Playboy TV; Showtime (multiplexed); Showtime HD; Starz (multiplexed); Starz HDTV; The Movie Channel (multiplexed).
Fee: $16.99 monthly (each).
Video-On-Demand: Yes
Pay-Per-View
iN DEMAND (delivered digitally), Addressable: Yes; Playboy TV (delivered digitally); Sports PPV (delivered digitally); NBA League Pass (delivered digitally).
Internet Service
Operational: Yes.
Broadband Service: Comcast High Speed Internet.
Fee: $42.95 monthly; $15.00 modem lease; $129.95 modem purchase.
Telephone Service
Digital: Operational
Fee: $44.95 monthly
Miles of Plant: 404.0 (coaxial); 115.0 (fiber optic). Additional miles planned: 4.0 (coaxial). Homes passed: 19,000. Total homes in franchised area: 20,000.
Vice President & General Manager: William (Rusty) Robertson. Vice President, Technical Operations: Max Woolsey. Vice President, Communications: Mark Apple. Marketing Director: Damion Miller.
City fee: 5% of gross.
Ownership: Comcast Cable Communications Inc. (MSO).

MORGANTOWN—Avenue Broadband Communications, 2603 Hart St, Vincennes, IN 47591. Phones: 800-882-7185; 812-895-7676. Fax: 812-886-5017. Web Site: http://www.avenuebroadband.com. ICA: IN0369.
TV Market Ranking: 16 (MORGANTOWN).
Channel capacity: N.A. Channels available but not in use: N.A.
Basic Service
Subscribers: 166.
Programming (received off-air): WCLJ-TV (TBN) Bloomington; WFYI (PBS) Indianapolis; WHMB-TV (IND) Indianapolis; WIPX-TV (ION) Bloomington; WNDY-TV (MNT) Marion; WRTV (ABC) Indianapolis; WTHR (NBC) Indianapolis; WTTV (CW) Bloomington; WXIN (FOX) Indianapolis.
Programming (via satellite): TBS Superstation; WGN America; WISH-TV (CBS) Indianapolis.
Expanded Basic Service 1
Subscribers: N.A.
Programming (via satellite): ABC Family Channel; AMC; Arts & Entertainment; CNN; Country Music TV; C-SPAN; Discovery Channel; Disney Channel; ESPN; ESPN 2; Fox Sports Net Midwest; Headline News; History Channel; Home Shopping Network; Lifetime; MTV; Nickelodeon; Spike TV; The Learning Channel; Turner Network TV; USA Network; VH1; Weather Channel.
Pay Service 1
Pay Units: N.A.
Programming (via satellite): Cinemax; HBO; Showtime.
Video-On-Demand: No
Internet Service
Operational: No.
Telephone Service
None
Miles of Plant: None (coaxial); 10.0 (fiber optic). Homes passed: 485.
Chief Executive Officer: Steve Lowe. Vice President & General Manager: Mary Iafrate. Vice President, Engineering: Jeff Spence. System Engineer: Bart Cotter.
Ownership: Buford Media Group LLC (MSO).

MOROCCO—TV Cable of Rensselaer Inc., PO Box 319, 215 W Kellner Blvd, Ste 19, Rensselaer, IN 47978-2665. Phone: 800-621-2344. Fax: 219-866-5785. E-mail: tvcable@rensselaer.tv. Web Site: http://www.rensselaer.tv. ICA: IN0162.
TV Market Ranking: Outside TV Markets (MOROCCO). Franchise award date: N.A. Franchise expiration date: N.A. Began: May 1, 1984.
Channel capacity: 65 (operating 2-way). Channels available but not in use: 5.
Basic Service
Subscribers: 245.
Programming (received off-air): WCIU-TV (IND) Chicago; WCPX-TV (ION) Chicago; WFLD (FOX) Chicago; WGBO-DT (UNV) Joliet; WGN-TV (CW, IND) Chicago; WJYS (IND) Hammond; WLFI-TV (CBS) Lafayette; WLS-TV (ABC) Chicago; WMAQ-TV (NBC) Chicago; WNDU-TV (NBC) South Bend; WPWR-TV (MNT) Gary; WSBT-TV (CBS, IND) South Bend; WSNS-TV (TMO) Chicago; WTTK (IND) Kokomo; WTTW (PBS) Chicago; WXFT-DT (TEL) Aurora; WYIN (PBS) Gary.
Programming (via satellite): ABC Family Channel; AMC; Animal Planet; Arts & Entertainment; Cartoon Network; CNBC; CNN; Comcast SportsNet Mid-Atlantic; Comedy Central; Country Music TV; C-SPAN; Discovery Channel; Discovery Health Channel; Disney Channel; E! Entertainment Television; ESPN; ESPN 2; ESPN Classic Sports;

Food Network; Fox Movie Channel; Fox News Channel; FX; Golf Channel; Hallmark Channel; Headline News; HGTV; History Channel; Home Shopping Network; Lifetime; MSNBC; MTV; National Geographic Channel; Nickelodeon; Outdoor Channel; QVC; ShopNBC; SoapNet; Speed Channel; Spike TV; Syfy; TBS Superstation; The Learning Channel; The Sportsman Channel; Toon Disney; Travel Channel; truTV; Turner Classic Movies; Turner Network TV; TV Guide Network; TV Land; USA Network; VH1; WE tv; Weather Channel.
Fee: $10.00 installation; $37.93 monthly; $2.30 converter.

Pay Service 1
Pay Units: 21.
Programming (via satellite): HBO.
Fee: $5.00 installation; $12.65 monthly.

Pay Service 2
Pay Units: 19.
Programming (via satellite): Cinemax.
Fee: $5.00 installation; $8.20 monthly.

Pay Service 3
Pay Units: 6.
Programming (via satellite): Encore; Starz.
Fee: $5.00 installation; $9.95 monthly.

Video-On-Demand: No

Pay-Per-View
Addressable homes: 245.
iN DEMAND, Addressable: Yes.

Internet Service
Operational: No.

Telephone Service
None

Miles of Plant: 10.0 (coaxial); 17.0 (fiber optic). Homes passed: 500.
Vice President, Operations: Eric Galbreath. Headend Technician: Eric Sampson. Office Manager: Sue Shuey. Customer Service Representative: Lisa Cawby.
Ownership: Theodore W. Filson (MSO).

MORRISTOWN—Formerly served by Longview Communications. No longer in operation. ICA: IN0299.

MOUNT SUMMIT—Now served by ANDERSON, IN [IN0012]. ICA: IN0111.

MOUNT VERNON—Now served by EVANSVILLE, IN [IN0006]. ICA: IN0074.

MUNCIE—Comcast Cable, 5330 E 65th St, Indianapolis, IN 46220. Phone: 317-275-6370. Fax: 317-275-6340. Web Site: http://www.comcast.com. Also serves Cowan, Daleville, De Soto, Delaware County, Farmland, Hamilton Twp., Harrison Twp., Liberty Twp., Monroe Twp., Mount Pleasant Twp., Oakville, Parker City, Randolph County, Salem Twp., Selma & Yorktown. ICA: IN0014.
TV Market Ranking: Below 100 (Cowan, Daleville, De Soto, Delaware County, Farmland, Hamilton Twp., Harrison Twp., Liberty Twp., Monroe Twp., Mount Pleasant Twp., MUNCIE, Oakville, Parker City, Randolph County, Salem Twp., Selma, Yorktown). Franchise award date: February 1, 1972. Franchise expiration date: N.A. Began: February 1, 1972.
Channel capacity: N.A. Channels available but not in use: N.A.

Basic Service
Subscribers: N.A. Included in Indianapolis
Programming (received off-air): WDNI-CD Indianapolis; WDTI (IND) Indianapolis; WHMB-TV (IND) Indianapolis; WIPB (PBS) Muncie; WIPX-TV (ION) Bloomington; WISH-TV (CBS) Indianapolis; WNDY-TV (MNT) Marion; WRTV (ABC) Indianapolis; WTHR (NBC) Indianapolis; WTTV (CW) Bloomington; WXIN (FOX) Indianapolis; 19 FMs.
Programming (via satellite): ABC Family Channel; AMC; Animal Planet; Arts & Entertainment; BET Networks; Bravo; Cartoon Network; CNBC; CNN; Comedy Central; Country Music TV; C-SPAN; C-SPAN 2; Discovery Channel; Discovery Health Channel; E! Entertainment Television; ESPN; ESPN 2; Food Network; Fox News Channel; Fox Sports Net Midwest; FX; Golf Channel; Great American Country; GSN; Headline News; HGTV; History Channel; Home Shopping Network; Lifetime; MSNBC; MTV; Nickelodeon; QVC; Speed Channel; Spike TV; Style Network; Syfy; TBS Superstation; The Learning Channel; Trinity Broadcasting Network; truTV; Turner Classic Movies; Turner Network TV; TV Guide Network; TV Land; USA Network; Versus; VH1; WE tv; Weather Channel; Weatherscan; WGN America.
Current originations: Government Access; Educational Access; Public Access.
Fee: $50.99 installation; $52.48 monthly.

Digital Basic Service
Subscribers: 8,280.
Programming (via satellite): BBC America; Canales N; C-SPAN 3; Discovery Digital Networks; Disney Channel; DMX Music; ESPNews; G4; MTV Networks Digital Suite; National Geographic Channel; Nick Jr.; Nick Too; SoapNet; Weatherscan.
Fee: $14.95 monthly.

Digital Pay Service 1
Pay Units: N.A.
Programming (via satellite): Cinemax (multiplexed); Encore (multiplexed); Flix (multiplexed); HBO (multiplexed); Showtime (multiplexed); Starz (multiplexed); Sundance Channel (multiplexed); The Movie Channel (multiplexed).

Video-On-Demand: Yes; Yes

Pay-Per-View
Addressable homes: 8,280.
ESPN Extra (delivered digitally), Addressable: Yes; ESPN Now (delivered digitally); iN DEMAND; iN DEMAND (delivered digitally); Playboy TV (delivered digitally); Pleasure (delivered digitally); NBA TV (delivered digitally); Fresh (delivered digitally); Shorteez (delivered digitally).

Internet Service
Operational: Yes. Began: April 1, 1999.
Subscribers: 1,269.
Broadband Service: Comcast High Speed Internet.
Fee: $42.95 monthly; $9.95 modem lease; $264.99 modem purchase.

Telephone Service
Digital: Operational
Fee: $44.95 monthly

Miles of Plant: 647.0 (coaxial); 72.0 (fiber optic). Homes passed: 50,000. Total homes in franchised area: 50,000.
Vice President & General Manager: William (Rusty) Roberson. Vice President, Technical Operations: Max Woolsey. Vice President, Communications: Mark Apple. Marketing Director: Damion Miller.
Ownership: Comcast Cable Communications Inc. (MSO).

NASHVILLE—Avenue Broadband Communications, 2603 Hart St, Vincennes, MO 47591. Phones: 800-882-7185; 812-895-7676. Fax: 812-886-5017. Web Site: http://www.avenuebroadband.com. Also serves Brown County & Cordry Lake. ICA: IN0099.
TV Market Ranking: 16 (Brown County, Cordry Lake, NASHVILLE). Franchise award date: June 1, 1985. Franchise expiration date: N.A. Began: May 1, 1985.
Channel capacity: 70 (not 2-way capable). Channels available but not in use: 35.

Basic Service
Subscribers: 1,270.
Programming (received off-air): WCLJ-TV (TBN) Bloomington; WFYI (PBS) Indianapolis; WHMB-TV (IND) Indianapolis; WIPX-TV (ION) Bloomington; WISH-TV (CBS) Indianapolis; WNDY-TV (MNT) Marion; WRTV (ABC) Indianapolis; WTHR (NBC) Indianapolis; WTIU (PBS) Bloomington; WTTV (CW) Bloomington; WXIN (FOX) Indianapolis.
Programming (via satellite): QVC; WGN America.
Current originations: Government Access; Educational Access.
Fee: $29.95 installation; $28.27 monthly.

Expanded Basic Service 1
Subscribers: N.A.
Programming (via satellite): ABC Family Channel; AMC; Arts & Entertainment; CNBC; CNN; Comedy Central; Country Music TV; C-SPAN; Discovery Channel; Disney Channel; E! Entertainment Television; ESPN; ESPN 2; Fox News Channel; Fox Sports Net Midwest; FX; Headline News; HGTV; History Channel; Lifetime; MTV; Nickelodeon; Outdoor Channel; Spike TV; Syfy; TBS Superstation; truTV; Turner Network TV; USA Network; Weather Channel.

Pay Service 1
Pay Units: N.A.
Programming (via satellite): Cinemax; Encore; HBO; Showtime; The Movie Channel.

Video-On-Demand: No

Internet Service
Operational: Yes.

Telephone Service
Digital: Operational

Miles of Plant: 66.0 (coaxial); None (fiber optic). Homes passed: 5,305.
Chief Executive Officer: Steve Lowe. Vice President & General Manager: Mary Iafrate. Vice President, Engineering: Jeff Spence. System Engineer: Bart Cotter.
Ownership: Buford Media Group LLC (MSO).

NEW CASTLE—Insight Communications. Now served by ANDERSON, IN [IN0012]. ICA: IN0031.

NEW MARKET—Indiana Communications, PO Box 617, Boswell, IN 47921. Phone: 888-610-1119. Web Site: http://www.indcomm.net. Also serves Montgomery County (portions). ICA: IN0185.
TV Market Ranking: 16 (Montgomery County (portions)); Below 100 (NEW MARKET, Montgomery County (portions)); Outside TV Markets (Montgomery County (portions)). Franchise award date: February 1, 1982. Franchise expiration date: N.A. Began: February 1, 1983.
Channel capacity: 31 (not 2-way capable). Channels available but not in use: 16.

Basic Service
Subscribers: 49.
Programming (received off-air): WFYI (PBS) Indianapolis; WHMB-TV (IND) Indianapolis; WIPX-TV (ION) Bloomington; WISH-TV (CBS) Indianapolis; WLFI-TV (CBS) Lafayette; WNDY-TV (MNT) Marion; WRTV (ABC) Indianapolis; WTHR (NBC) Indianapolis; WTTV (CW) Bloomington; WXIN (FOX) Indianapolis; 1 FM.
Programming (via satellite): QVC; Trinity Broadcasting Network.
Fee: $25.00 installation; $17.98 monthly.

Expanded Basic Service 1
Subscribers: N.A.
Programming (via satellite): ABC Family Channel; AMC; Animal Planet; Arts & Entertainment; CNN; Discovery Channel; Disney Channel; E! Entertainment Television; ESPN; ESPN 2; Fox News Channel; Great American Country; Headline News; History Channel; Lifetime; MSNBC; Speed Channel; TBS Superstation; The Learning Channel; Turner Network TV; USA Network; Weather Channel; WGN America.
Fee: $17.97 monthly.

Pay Service 1
Pay Units: N.A.
Programming (via satellite): Cinemax; HBO; Showtime; The Movie Channel.
Fee: $10.00 installation; $8.95 monthly (TMC), $10.95 monthly (Showtime or Cinemax), $12.95 monthly (HBO).

Video-On-Demand: No

Internet Service
Operational: No.

Telephone Service
None

Miles of Plant: 16.0 (coaxial); None (fiber optic). Homes passed: 604. Total homes in franchised area: 604.
Manager: Joe Young.
City fee: 3% of gross.
Ownership: Park TV & Electronics Inc. (MSO).

NEW PARIS—Quality Cablevision, PO Box 7, New Paris, IN 46553-0007. Phones: 260-768-9152; 574-831-2225. Fax: 219-574-7125. E-mail: qualcabl@bnin.net. Web Site: http://qc.bnin.net. Also serves Goshen & Millersburg. ICA: IN0100. **Note:** This system is an overbuild.
TV Market Ranking: 80 (Goshen, Millersburg, NEW PARIS). Franchise award date: May 1, 1986. Franchise expiration date: N.A. Began: October 24, 1986.
Channel capacity: 71 (operating 2-way). Channels available but not in use: None.

Basic Service
Subscribers: 2,209.
Programming (received off-air): WBND-LP South Bend; WHME-TV (IND) South Bend; WNDU-TV (NBC) South Bend; WNIT (PBS) South Bend; WSBT-TV (CBS, IND) South Bend; WSJV (FOX) Elkhart.
Programming (via satellite): ABC Family Channel; AMC; CNBC; CNN; Comedy Central; Country Music TV; Discovery Channel; Disney Channel; ESPN; ESPN 2; ESPN Classic Sports; Fox News Channel; Fox Sports Net; Headline News; HGTV; History Channel; Lifetime; Lifetime Movie Network;

Nickelodeon; QVC; Speed Channel; Spike TV; Syfy; TBS Superstation; Trinity Broadcasting Network; Turner Network TV; TV Land; USA Network; VH1; Weather Channel; WGN America.
Current originations: Educational Access; Public Access.
Fee: $19.95 installation; $31.95 monthly; $3.35 converter; $15.00 additional installation.

Expanded Basic Service 1
Subscribers: N.A.
Programming (received off-air): WCWW-LP (CW) South Bend; WSBT-TV (CBS, IND) South Bend.
Programming (via satellite): Animal Planet; Arts & Entertainment; Cartoon Network; C-SPAN; C-SPAN 2; E! Entertainment Television; Flix; Food Network; Fox Movie Channel; FX; GSN; Hallmark Channel; ION Television; MSNBC; MTV; Outdoor Channel; Sports Network; Telemundo; The Learning Channel; Toon Disney; Travel Channel; truTV; Turner Classic Movies; WE tv.
Fee: $13.00 monthly.

Pay Service 1
Pay Units: 29.
Programming (via satellite): HBO.
Fee: $9.25 monthly.

Pay Service 2
Pay Units: 16.
Programming (via satellite): Cinemax.
Fee: $7.75 monthly.

Pay Service 3
Pay Units: 6.
Programming (via satellite): Showtime.
Fee: $8.75 monthly.

Pay Service 4
Pay Units: 1.
Programming (via satellite): The Movie Channel.
Fee: $7.75 monthly.

Video-On-Demand: No

Internet Service
Operational: Yes.
Subscribers: 435.
Broadband Service: Brightnet.
Fee: $29.95 installation; $19.95-$74.95 monthly; $10.00 modem lease; $69.95 modem purchase.

Telephone Service
Analog: Not Operational
Digital: Operational

Miles of Plant: 63.0 (coaxial); None (fiber optic). Homes passed: 5,315.
Manager: Mark Grady. Chief Technician: Dan Cox. Plant Manager: Robin Loucks.
County fee: $300 flat fee.
Ownership: New Paris Telephone Co.

NEWBURGH—Time Warner Cable, 100 Industrial Dr, Owensboro, KY 42301-8711. Phones: 270-685-2991; 270-852-2000. Fax: 270-688-8228. Web Site: http://www.timewarnercable.com/westernky.
Also serves Chandler, Ohio Twp. (eastern portion) & Warrick County. ICA: IN0032.
TV Market Ranking: 86 (Chandler, NEWBURGH, Ohio Twp. (eastern portion), Warrick County). Franchise award date: June 14, 1979. Franchise expiration date: N.A. Began: April 8, 1980.
Channel capacity: N.A. Channels available but not in use: N.A.

Basic Service
Subscribers: N.A. Included in Owensboro, KY
Programming (received off-air): WEHT (ABC) Evansville; WEVV-TV (CBS, MNT) Evansville; WFIE (NBC) Evansville; WNIN (PBS) Evansville; WTVW (FOX) Evansville; WYYW-LP Evansville.
Programming (via satellite): ABC Family Channel; AMC; Animal Planet; Arts & Entertainment; BET Networks; Bravo; Cartoon Network; CNBC; CNN; Comedy Central; Country Music TV; C-SPAN; C-SPAN 2; Discovery Channel; Disney Channel; E! Entertainment Television; ESPN; ESPN 2; ESPN Classic Sports; Eternal Word TV Network; Food Network; Fox News Channel; Fox Sports Net Midwest; FX; Golf Channel; Hallmark Channel; Headline News; HGTV; History Channel; Home Shopping Network; Lifetime; MSNBC; MTV; Nickelodeon; Oxygen; Product Information Network; QVC; ShopNBC; Spike TV; Style Network; Syfy; TBS Superstation; The Learning Channel; Travel Channel; Trinity Broadcasting Network; truTV; Turner Classic Movies; Turner Network TV; TV Land; USA Network; VH1; WE tv; Weather Channel; WGN America.
Planned originations: Public Access.
Fee: $49.95 installation; $30.92 monthly; $1.00 converter.

Digital Basic Service
Subscribers: N.A.
Programming (via satellite): American-Life TV Network; BBC America; Bio; Black Family Channel; Bloomberg Television; Discovery Digital Networks; Do-It-Yourself; ESPNews; FitTV; Fox Sports World; G4; Great American Country; GSN; History Channel International; INSP; MuchMusic Network; Outdoor Channel; Speed Channel; The Word Network; Versus.
Fee: $5.98 monthly.

Digital Expanded Basic Service
Subscribers: N.A.
Programming (via satellite): Fox College Sports Atlantic; Fox College Sports Central; Fox College Sports Pacific; Fox Movie Channel; GAS; Independent Film Channel; MTV Networks Digital Suite; National Geographic Channel; Nick Jr.; Nick Too; NickToons TV; Sundance Channel.
Fee: $6.00 monthly (per tier).

Digital Pay Service 1
Pay Units: N.A.
Programming (via satellite): ART America; Canales N; CCTV-4; Cinemax (multiplexed); DMX Music; Encore (multiplexed); Filipino Channel; Flix; HBO (multiplexed); RAI International; Russian Television Network; Showtime (multiplexed); Starz (multiplexed); The Movie Channel (multiplexed); TV Asia; TV Japan; TV5, La Television International; Zee TV USA; Zhong Tian Channel.
Fee: $12.00 monthly (HBO, Cinemax, Starz or Showtime Unlimited), $15.00 monthly (CCTV, TV Asia, TV5, Filipino, RAI, ART, TV Russia or TV Japan).

Video-On-Demand: Planned

Pay-Per-View
Urban Extra (delivered digitally); Hot Choice (delivered digitally); Shorteez (delivered digitally); Fresh (delivered digitally); Playboy TV (delivered digitally); HITS PPV 1-30 (delivered digitally).

Internet Service
Operational: Yes.
Broadband Service: Road Runner.
Fee: $44.95 monthly.

Telephone Service
Digital: Operational
Fee: $49.95 monthly

Miles of Plant: 1,349.0 (coaxial); None (fiber optic). Miles of plant (coax) & homes passed included in Owensboro, KY
General Manager: Chris Poynter. Marketing Manager: Doug Rodgers. Technical Operations Director: Don Collins.
City fee: 5% of gross.
Ownership: Time Warner Cable (MSO).

NEWPORT—Indiana Communications, PO Box 617, Boswell, IN 47921. Phone: 888-610-1119. Web Site: http://www.indcomm.net. ICA: IN0304.
TV Market Ranking: Below 100 (NEWPORT). Franchise award date: N.A. Franchise expiration date: N.A. Began: October 1, 1984.
Channel capacity: 31 (not 2-way capable). Channels available but not in use: 20.

Basic Service
Subscribers: 79.
Programming (received off-air): WFXW (FOX) Terre Haute; WRTV (ABC) Indianapolis; WTHI-TV (CBS) Terre Haute; WTTV (CW) Bloomington; WTWO (NBC) Terre Haute.
Programming (via satellite): C-SPAN; C-SPAN 2; Home Shopping Network; INSP; QVC; Trinity Broadcasting Network; WGN America.
Fee: $17.98 monthly.

Expanded Basic Service 1
Subscribers: N.A.
Programming (via satellite): ABC Family Channel; AMC; Animal Planet; Arts & Entertainment; CNN; Discovery Channel; Disney Channel; E! Entertainment Television; ESPN; ESPN 2; Fox News Channel; G4; Great American Country; Headline News; History Channel; Lifetime; MSNBC; Speed Channel; TBS Superstation; The Learning Channel; Turner Network TV; USA Network; Weather Channel.
Fee: $17.97 monthly.

Pay Service 1
Pay Units: N.A.
Programming (via satellite): Cinemax; HBO; Showtime; The Movie Channel.
Fee: $8.95 monthly (TMC), $10.95 monthly (Cinemax or Showtime), $12.95 monthly (HBO).

Video-On-Demand: No

Internet Service
Operational: No.

Telephone Service
None

Miles of Plant: 4.0 (coaxial); None (fiber optic). Homes passed: 270.
Manager: Joe Young.
Ownership: Park TV & Electronics Inc. (MSO).

NOBLESVILLE—Comcast Cable, 5330 E 65th St, Indianapolis, IN 46220. Phone: 317-275-6370. Fax: 317-275-6340. Web Site: http://www.comcast.com. Also serves Arcadia, Atlanta, Boone County, Cicero, Fishers, Geist Lake, Greenfield, Hamilton County, Hancock County (portions), Kennard, Lebanon, McCordsville, New Palestine, Philadelphia, Spring Lake, Tipton, Ulen, Westfield & Wilkenson. ICA: IN0020.
TV Market Ranking: 16 (Arcadia, Atlanta, Boone County, Cicero, Fishers, Geist Lake, Greenfield, Hamilton County, Hancock County (portions), Kennard, Lebanon, McCordsville, New Palestine, NOBLESVILLE, Philadelphia, Spring Lake, Ulen, Westfield, Wilkenson); Below 100 (Tipton). Franchise award date: July 21, 1978. Franchise expiration date: N.A. Began: September 2, 1980.
Channel capacity: N.A. Channels available but not in use: N.A.

Basic Service
Subscribers: N.A. Included in Anderson
Programming (received off-air): WALV-CA Indianapolis; WCLJ-TV (TBN) Bloomington; WDTI (IND) Indianapolis; WFYI (PBS) Indianapolis; WHMB-TV (IND) Indianapolis; WIPB (PBS) Muncie; WIPX-TV (ION) Bloomington; WISH-TV (CBS) Indianapolis; WNDY-TV (MNT) Marion; WRTV (ABC) Indianapolis; WTHR (NBC) Indianapolis; WTTV (CW) Bloomington; WXIN (FOX) Indianapolis.
Programming (via satellite): C-SPAN; C-SPAN 2; Home Shopping Network; QVC; WGN America.
Current originations: Leased Access; Public Access.
Fee: $1.46 converter.

Expanded Basic Service 1
Subscribers: N.A.
Programming (via satellite): ABC Family Channel; AMC; Animal Planet; Arts & Entertainment; BET Networks; Bravo; Cartoon Network; CNBC; CNN; Comedy Central; Country Music TV; Discovery Channel; Disney Channel; E! Entertainment Television; ESPN; ESPN 2; Eternal Word TV Network; Food Network; Fox News Channel; Fox Sports Net Midwest; FX; Headline News; HGTV; History Channel; Lifetime; MSNBC; MTV; Nickelodeon; Oxygen; Speed Channel; Spike TV; Syfy; TBS Superstation; The Learning Channel; Travel Channel; Turner Network TV; TV Guide Network; TV Land; USA Network; VH1; Weather Channel.
Fee: $51.74 monthly.

Digital Basic Service
Subscribers: 7,227.
Programming (via satellite): BBC America; Bio; Bloomberg Television; C-SPAN 3; Discovery Digital Networks; DMX Music; Do-It-Yourself; Encore; ESPN Classic Sports; ESPNews; Fox Sports World; G4; GAS; Golf Channel; GSN; Halogen Network; History Channel International; Independent Film Channel; Lifetime Movie Network; MTV2; National Geographic Channel; Nick Jr.; Nick Too; Ovation; SoapNet; Style Network; Sundance Channel; Toon Disney; truTV; Turner Classic Movies; Versus; WE tv.
Fee: $17.00 monthly.

Digital Pay Service 1
Pay Units: 1,589.
Programming (via satellite): Cinemax (multiplexed); Flix; HBO (multiplexed); Showtime (multiplexed); Starz (multiplexed); The Movie Channel (multiplexed).
Fee: $10.00 monthly (Cinemax or Starz), $13.00 monthly (HBO or Showtime/TMC).

Video-On-Demand: Yes

Pay-Per-View
Addressable homes: 9,643.
iN DEMAND, Addressable: Yes; Fresh (delivered digitally); Playboy TV (delivered digitally); iN DEMAND (delivered digitally).

Internet Service
Operational: Yes.
Subscribers: 3,142.
Broadband Service: Comcast High Speed Internet.
Fee: $99.95 installation; $44.95 monthly; $15.00 modem lease; $99.95 modem purchase.

Telephone Service
Digital: Operational
Fee: $39.95 monthly

Miles of Plant: 1,092.0 (coaxial); 15.0 (fiber optic). Homes passed: 38,899.
Regional Vice President: Scott Tenney. Regional Vice President, Technical Operations: Max Woolsey. Regional Vice President, Marketing: Aaron Geisel. Regional Vice President, Communications: Mark Apple.
City fee: 3% of gross.
Ownership: Comcast Cable Communications Inc. (MSO).

NORTH MANCHESTER—Mediacom, 109 E 5th St, Ste A, Auburn, IN 46706. Phone: 260-927-3015. Fax: 260-347-4433. Web Site: http://www.mediacomcable.com. Also serves Laketon. ICA: IN0093.

TV Market Ranking: 82 (Laketon, NORTH MANCHESTER). Franchise award date: N.A. Franchise expiration date: N.A. Began: July 1, 1979.

Channel capacity: 83 (operating 2-way). Channels available but not in use: 24.

Basic Service

Subscribers: 1,588.

Programming (received off-air): WANE-TV (CBS) Fort Wayne; WFFT-TV (FOX) Fort Wayne; WFWA (PBS) Fort Wayne; WHME-TV (IND) South Bend; WINM (IND) Angola; WISE-TV (MNT, NBC) Fort Wayne; WNDU-TV (NBC) South Bend; WNIT (PBS) South Bend; WPTA (ABC, CW) Fort Wayne; WTTK (IND) Kokomo.

Programming (via satellite): TBS Superstation; WGN America.

Current originations: Public Access.

Fee: $45.00 installation; $20.95 monthly.

Expanded Basic Service 1

Subscribers: 1,304.

Programming (via satellite): ABC Family Channel; AMC; AmericanLife TV Network; Animal Planet; Arts & Entertainment; Bio; Bloomberg Television; Cartoon Network; CNBC; CNN; Comedy Central; Country Music TV; C-SPAN; Discovery Channel; Disney Channel; E! Entertainment Television; ESPN; ESPN 2; Food Network; Fox Movie Channel; Fox News Channel; Fox Sports Net Midwest; FX; G4; Hallmark Channel; Headline News; HGTV; History Channel; History Channel International; Home Shopping Network; Lifetime; Lifetime Movie Network; MSNBC; MTV; Nickelodeon; Product Information Network; QVC; Speed Channel; Spike TV; Style Network; Syfy; The Learning Channel; Travel Channel; Trinity Broadcasting Network; Turner Network TV; TV Guide Network; TV Land; USA Network; VH1; Weather Channel.

Fee: $34.00 monthly.

Digital Basic Service

Subscribers: 157.

Programming (via satellite): BBC America; Discovery Digital Networks; DMX Music; ESPN Classic Sports; Fox Sports World; Golf Channel; GSN; Independent Film Channel; Turner Classic Movies.

Fee: $9.00 monthly.

Digital Pay Service 1

Pay Units: 353.

Programming (via satellite): Cinemax (multiplexed); Encore (multiplexed); HBO (multiplexed); Showtime (multiplexed); Starz (multiplexed); The Movie Channel (multiplexed).

Fee: $11.95 monthly (HBO, Cinemax, Showtime/TMC or Starz/Encore).

Video-On-Demand: Yes

Pay-Per-View

Addressable homes: 600.

iN DEMAND, Addressable: Yes; iN DEMAND (delivered digitally); Playboy TV (delivered digitally); Pleasure (delivered digitally); Fresh (delivered digitally); Shorteez (delivered digitally).

Internet Service

Operational: Yes.

Broadband Service: Mediacom High Speed Internet.

Fee: $59.95 installation; $40.95 monthly.

Telephone Service

Digital: Operational

Fee: $39.95 installation; $39.95 monthly

Miles of Plant: 53.0 (coaxial); 7.0 (fiber optic). Homes passed: 2,892.

Operations Director: Joe Poffenberger. Technical Operations Manager: Craig Grey.

City fee: 3% of gross.

Ownership: Mediacom LLC (MSO).

NORTH VERNON—Now served by SEYMOUR, IN [IN0039]. ICA: IN0069.

NORTH WEBSTER—Mediacom, 109 E 5th St, Ste A, Auburn, IN 46706. Phone: 260-927-3015. Fax: 260-347-4433. Web Site: http://www.mediacomcable.com. Also serves Argos, Bourbon, Bremen, Kosciusko County, Leesburg, Milford, Nappanee, Pierceton, Syracuse & Tippecanoe. ICA: IN0038.

TV Market Ranking: 80 (Argos, Bourbon, Bremen, Milford, Nappanee, Syracuse, Tippecanoe); 80,82 (Kosciusko County (portions), Leesburg, NORTH WEBSTER); 82 (Pierceton); Outside TV Markets (Kosciusko County (portions)). Franchise award date: N.A. Franchise expiration date: N.A. Began: January 1, 1984.

Channel capacity: 134 (operating 2-way). Channels available but not in use: 4.

Basic Service

Subscribers: 10,841.

Programming (received off-air): WBND-LP South Bend; WCWW-LP (CW) South Bend; WFFT-TV (FOX) Fort Wayne; WHME-TV (IND) South Bend; WISE-TV (MNT, NBC) Fort Wayne; WNDU-TV (NBC) South Bend; WNIT (PBS) South Bend; WPTA (ABC, CW) Fort Wayne; WSBT-TV (CBS, IND) South Bend; WSJV (FOX) Elkhart; WTTW (PBS) Chicago.

Programming (via satellite): TBS Superstation; WGN America.

Fee: $45.00 installation; $20.95 monthly.

Expanded Basic Service 1

Subscribers: 3,833.

Programming (via satellite): ABC Family Channel; AMC; Animal Planet; Arts & Entertainment; Cartoon Network; CNBC; CNN; Comedy Central; Country Music TV; C-SPAN; Discovery Channel; Disney Channel; E! Entertainment Television; ESPN; ESPN 2; Fox News Channel; FX; Headline News; HGTV; History Channel; Home Shopping Network; Lifetime; MTV; Nickelodeon; QVC; Speed Channel; Spike TV; Syfy; The Learning Channel; Travel Channel; Trinity Broadcasting Network; Turner Network TV; TV Guide Network; TV Land; USA Network; VH1; Weather Channel.

Fee: $34.00 monthly.

Digital Basic Service

Subscribers: 36.

Programming (via satellite): BBC America; Discovery Digital Networks; DMX Music; Fox Sports World; Golf Channel; GSN; Independent Film Channel; Turner Classic Movies; Versus.

Fee: $9.00 monthly.

Digital Pay Service 1

Pay Units: 116.

Programming (via satellite): Cinemax (multiplexed); Encore (multiplexed); HBO (multiplexed); Showtime (multiplexed); Starz (multiplexed); The Movie Channel (multiplexed).

Fee: $11.95 monthly (HBO, Cinemax, Starz/Encore or Showtime/TMC).

Video-On-Demand: Yes

Pay-Per-View

iN DEMAND, Fee: $3.95, Addressable: Yes; iN DEMAND (delivered digitally); Playboy TV (delivered digitally); Pleasure (delivered digitally); Fresh (delivered digitally); Shorteez (delivered digitally).

Internet Service

Operational: Yes.

Broadband Service: Mediacom High Speed Internet.

Fee: $59.95 installation; $40.95 monthly.

Telephone Service

Digital: Operational

Fee: $39.95 installation; $39.95 monthly

Homes passed and miles of plant included in Kendallville

Operations Director: Joe Poffenberger. Technical Operations Manager: Craig Grey.

City fee: 3% of gross.

Ownership: Mediacom LLC (MSO).

OAKLAND CITY—Charter Communications. Now served by WINSLOW (formerly Petersburg), IN [IN0118]. ICA: IN0122.

OAKTOWN—Formerly served by Almega Cable. No longer in operation. ICA: IN0203.

ODON—Suddenlink Communications, 12444 Powerscourt Dr, Saint Louis, MO 63131-3660. Phones: 314-965-2020; 573-686-6387. Web Site: http://www.suddenlink.com. Also serves Daviess County (portions), Elnora, Knox County (portions), Newberry, Plainville, Sandborn & Westphalia. ICA: IN0107.

TV Market Ranking: 16 (Daviess County (portions), Newberry, ODON); Outside TV Markets (Elnora, Knox County (portions), Plainville, Sandborn, Westphalia, Daviess County (portions)). Franchise award date: January 10, 1984. Franchise expiration date: N.A. Began: December 1, 1984.

Channel capacity: 36 (operating 2-way). Channels available but not in use: None.

Basic Service

Subscribers: 655.

Programming (received off-air): WEHT (ABC) Evansville; WFXW (FOX) Terre Haute; WTHI-TV (CBS) Terre Haute; WTTV (CW) Bloomington; WTWO (NBC) Terre Haute; WVUT (PBS) Vincennes.

Programming (via satellite): Home Shopping Network; INSP; Trinity Broadcasting Network; Weather Channel; WGN America.

Fee: $61.50 installation; $16.95 monthly.

Expanded Basic Service 1

Subscribers: N.A.

Programming (via satellite): ABC Family Channel; AMC; Animal Planet; Arts & Entertainment; CNBC; CNN; Discovery Channel; Disney Channel; E! Entertainment Television; ESPN; ESPN 2; Fox News Channel; Fox Sports Net Midwest; FX; Great American Country; Hallmark Channel; Headline News; HGTV; History Channel; Lifetime; MTV; Nickelodeon; Outdoor Channel; Spike TV; Syfy; TBS Superstation; The Learning Channel; Turner Network TV; USA Network.

Fee: $23.00 monthly.

Digital Basic Service

Subscribers: N.A.

Programming (via satellite): BBC America; Bio; Black Family Channel; Bloomberg Television; Discovery Digital Networks; DMX Music; ESPN Classic Sports; ESPNews; Fox College Sports Atlantic; Fox College Sports Central; Fox College Sports Pacific; Fox Movie Channel; Fox Soccer; Golf Channel; Halogen Network; History Channel International; Lifetime Movie Network; Lime; National Geographic Channel; ShopNBC; Sleuth; Speed Channel; Toon Disney; Turner Classic Movies; Versus; WE tv.

Fee: $3.95 monthly.

Pay Service 1

Pay Units: 313.

Programming (via satellite): Cinemax; Encore; HBO; Showtime; The Movie Channel.

Fee: $3.99 monthly (Encore), $8.99 monthly (Cinemax), $12.99 monthly (HBO).

Digital Pay Service 1

Pay Units: N.A.

Programming (via satellite): Cinemax (multiplexed); Encore (multiplexed); Flix; HBO (multiplexed); Showtime (multiplexed); Starz (multiplexed); The Movie Channel (multiplexed).

Pay-Per-View

iN DEMAND (delivered digitally); Playboy TV (delivered digitally); Fresh (delivered digitally).

Internet Service

Operational: Yes. Began: August 23, 2004.

Broadband Service: Cebridge High Speed Cable Internet.

Fee: $49.95 installation; $20.95 monthly.

Telephone Service

None

Miles of Plant: 3.0 (coaxial); None (fiber optic). Homes passed: 1,676.

Regional Manager: James Robinson. Chief Technician: Chris Mooday. Customer Service Manager: Sandra Baker.

City fee: 3% of basic.

Ownership: Cequel Communications LLC (MSO).

OLIVER LAKE—Formerly served by CableDirect. No longer in operation. ICA: IN0306.

OTTER LAKE—Formerly served by CableDirect. No longer in operation. ICA: IN0363.

OTWELL—Formerly served by CableDirect. No longer in operation. ICA: IN0309.

OWENSBURG—Formerly served by CableDirect. No longer in operation. ICA: IN0310.

OWENSVILLE—Sigecom. Now served by EVANSVILLE, IN [IN0006]. ICA: IN0178.

OXFORD—Indiana Communications, PO Box 617, Boswell, IN 47921. Phone: 888-610-1119. Web Site: http://www.indcomm.net. ICA: IN0176.

TV Market Ranking: Below 100 (OXFORD). Franchise award date: January 1, 1984. Franchise expiration date: N.A. Began: January 4, 1985.

Channel capacity: 31 (not 2-way capable). Channels available but not in use: None.

Basic Service

Subscribers: 112.

Programming (received off-air): WCIA (CBS) Champaign; WICD (ABC) Champaign; WLFI-TV (CBS) Lafayette; WRTV

(ABC) Indianapolis; WTHR (NBC) Indianapolis; 1 FM.
Programming (via satellite): ABC Family Channel; CNN; ESPN; Headline News; Lifetime; Nickelodeon; TBS Superstation; Turner Network TV; USA Network; WGN America.
Fee: $25.00 installation; $15.98 monthly.
Pay Service 1
Pay Units: N.A.
Programming (via satellite): Showtime; The Movie Channel.
Fee: $10.00 installation; $10.95 monthly (Showtime), $8.95 monthly (TMC).
Video-On-Demand: No
Internet Service
Operational: No.
Telephone Service
None
Miles of Plant: 9.0 (coaxial); None (fiber optic). Homes passed: 463. Total homes in franchised area: 463.
Manager: Joe Young.
City fee: 3% of basic gross.
Ownership: Park TV & Electronics Inc. (MSO).

PAINT MILL LAKE—Formerly served by CableDirect. No longer in operation. ICA: IN0311.

PATOKA—Formerly served by Almega Cable. No longer in operation. ICA: IN0173.

PATRICKSBURG—Formerly served by CableDirect. No longer in operation. ICA: IN0312.

PEKIN—Now served by LOUISVILLE, KY [KY0001]. ICA: IN0164.

PERRYSVILLE—Indiana Communications, PO Box 617, Boswell, IN 47921. Phone: 888-610-1119. Web Site: http://www.indcomm.net. ICA: IN0314.
TV Market Ranking: Outside TV Markets (PERRYSVILLE). Franchise award date: N.A. Franchise expiration date: N.A. Began: August 1, 1989.
Channel capacity: 31 (not 2-way capable). Channels available but not in use: 17.
Basic Service
Subscribers: 62.
Programming (received off-air): WAND (NBC) Decatur; WCCU (FOX) Urbana; WCIA (CBS) Champaign; WFXW (FOX) Terre Haute; WICD (ABC) Champaign; WILL-TV (PBS) Urbana; WLFI-TV (CBS) Lafayette; WTHI-TV (CBS) Terre Haute; WTHR (NBC) Indianapolis; WTTV (CW) Bloomington; WTWO (NBC) Terre Haute.
Programming (via satellite): Trinity Broadcasting Network.
Fee: $17.98 monthly.
Expanded Basic Service 1
Subscribers: N.A.
Programming (via satellite): ABC Family Channel; AMC; Animal Planet; Arts & Entertainment; CNN; Discovery Channel; Disney Channel; E! Entertainment Television; ESPN; ESPN 2; Fox News Channel; Great American Country; Headline News; History Channel; Lifetime; MSNBC; Speed Channel; TBS Superstation; The Learning Channel; Turner Network TV; USA Network; Weather Channel; WGN America.
Fee: $17.97 monthly.
Pay Service 1
Pay Units: N.A.
Programming (via satellite): Cinemax; HBO; Showtime; The Movie Channel.
Fee: $8.95 monthly (TMC), $10.95 monthly (Cinemax or Showtime), $12.95 monthly (HBO).
Video-On-Demand: No
Internet Service
Operational: No.
Telephone Service
None
Miles of Plant: 3.0 (coaxial); None (fiber optic). Homes passed: 243.
Manager: Joe Young.
Ownership: Park TV & Electronics Inc. (MSO).

PERU—Comcast Cable, 720 Taylor St, Fort Wayne, IN 46802-5144. Phones: 317-275-6370 (Indianapolis office); 260-458-5103. Fax: 206-458-5138. Web Site: http://www.comcast.com. Also serves Bunker Hill, Denver, Grissom AFB, Mexico, Montpelier & New Waverly. ICA: IN0029.
TV Market Ranking: 82 (Montpelier); Below 100 (Bunker Hill, Denver, Grissom AFB, Mexico, New Waverly, PERU). Franchise award date: August 1, 1962. Franchise expiration date: N.A. Began: March 1, 1963.
Channel capacity: 80 (operating 2-way). Channels available but not in use: None.
Basic Service
Subscribers: N.A. Included in Indianapolis
Programming (received off-air): WFYI (PBS) Indianapolis; WHMB-TV (IND) Indianapolis; WISH-TV (CBS) Indianapolis; WLFI-TV (CBS) Lafayette; WNDU-TV (NBC) South Bend; WPTA (ABC, CW) Fort Wayne; WRTV (ABC) Indianapolis; WTHR (NBC) Indianapolis; WXIN (FOX) Indianapolis; allband FM.
Programming (via microwave): WTTV (CW) Bloomington.
Programming (via satellite): Bravo; C-SPAN; C-SPAN 2; Home Shopping Network; QVC; TV Guide Network; WGN America.
Planned originations: Public Access.
Fee: $50.99 installation.
Expanded Basic Service 1
Subscribers: N.A.
Programming (via satellite): ABC Family Channel; AMC; Animal Planet; Arts & Entertainment; BET Networks; Cartoon Network; CNN; Comedy Central; Country Music TV; Discovery Channel; Disney Channel; E! Entertainment Television; ESPN; ESPN 2; ESPNews; Food Network; Fox News Channel; Fox Sports Net Midwest; GalaVision; Golf Channel; GSN; Headline News; HGTV; History Channel; Lifetime; MTV; Nickelodeon; Speed Channel; Spike TV; Syfy; TBS Superstation; The Learning Channel; Toon Disney; Travel Channel; Trinity Broadcasting Network; Turner Classic Movies; Turner Network TV; TV Land; USA Network; Versus; VH1; Weather Channel.
Fee: $47.98 monthly.
Digital Basic Service
Subscribers: N.A.
Programming (via satellite): BBC America; Bio; Bloomberg Television; Canales N; C-SPAN 3; Discovery Digital Networks; DMX Music; Do-It-Yourself; Encore Action; ESPN Classic Sports; Fox Sports World; G4; GAS; Halogen Network; History Channel International; Independent Film Channel; Lifetime Movie Network; MTV2; National Geographic Channel; Nick Jr.; Nick Too; Ovation; SoapNet; Style Network; Sundance Channel; truTV; WE tv.
Fee: $14.95 monthly.
Digital Pay Service 1
Pay Units: N.A.
Programming (via satellite): Cinemax (multiplexed); Flix; HBO (multiplexed); Showtime (multiplexed); Starz (multiplexed); The Movie Channel (multiplexed).
Fee: $16.99 monthly (each).
Video-On-Demand: No
Pay-Per-View
iN DEMAND (delivered digitally), Fee: $3.99, Addressable: Yes; Adult (delivered digitally).
Internet Service
Operational: Yes.
Broadband Service: Comcast High Speed Internet.
Fee: $42.95 monthly; $15.00 modem lease; $129.95 modem purchase.
Telephone Service
Digital: Operational
Fee: $44.95 monthly
Homes passed: 12,000. Miles of plant included in Fort Wayne
Regional Vice President: Scott Tenney. Technical Operations Director: Bennie Logan. Engineering Manager: Tom Stuckholz. Vice President, Marketing: Aaron Geisel. Marketing Manager: Marci Hefley. Vice President, Communications: Mark Apple.
City fee: 4% of gross.
Ownership: Comcast Cable Communications Inc. (MSO).

PINE VILLAGE—Formerly served by CableDirect. No longer in operation. ICA: IN0218.

PORTAGE—Comcast Cable. Now served by CHICAGO (southern suburbs), IL [IL0008]. ICA: IN0028.

PORTLAND—Comcast Cable, 5330 E 65th St, Indianapolis, IN 46220. Phone: 317-275-6370. Fax: 317-275-6340. Web Site: http://www.comcast.com. Also serves Adams County, Albany, Berne, Bryant, Ceylon, Dunkirk, Geneva, Jay County, Pennville, Randolph County & Redkey. ICA: IN0083.
TV Market Ranking: 82 (Adams County (portions), Berne, Ceylon, Geneva, Jay County (portions), Pennville); Below 100 (Albany, Dunkirk, Randolph County, Redkey, Jay County (portions)); Outside TV Markets (Bryant, PORTLAND, Adams County (portions), Jay County (portions)). Franchise award date: June 1, 1990. Franchise expiration date: N.A. Began: April 1, 1991.
Channel capacity: N.A. Channels available but not in use: N.A.
Basic Service
Subscribers: N.A. Included in Anderson
Programming (received off-air): WANE-TV (CBS) Fort Wayne; WFFT-TV (FOX) Fort Wayne; WFWA (PBS) Fort Wayne; WIPB (PBS) Muncie; WISE-TV (MNT, NBC) Fort Wayne; WISH-TV (CBS) Indianapolis; WNDY-TV (MNT) Marion; WPTA (ABC, CW) Fort Wayne; WRGT-TV (FOX, MNT) Dayton; WTTK (IND) Kokomo.
Programming (via satellite): C-SPAN; C-SPAN 2; Home Shopping Network; QVC; Trinity Broadcasting Network; WGN America.
Current originations: Religious Access; Public Access.
Expanded Basic Service 1
Subscribers: N.A.
Programming (via satellite): ABC Family Channel; AMC; Animal Planet; Arts & Entertainment; BET Networks; Bravo; Cartoon Network; CNBC; CNN; Comedy Central; Country Music TV; Discovery Channel; Disney Channel; E! Entertainment Television; ESPN; ESPN 2; Eternal Word TV Network; Food Network; Fox Movie Channel; Fox News Channel; Fox Sports Net Midwest; Headline News; HGTV; History Channel; Lifetime; MSNBC; MTV; Nickelodeon; Oxygen; Speed Channel; Spike TV; Syfy; TBS Superstation; The Learning Channel; Travel Channel; Turner Network TV; TV Guide Network; TV Land; USA Network; VH1; Weather Channel.
Fee: $51.74 monthly.
Digital Basic Service
Subscribers: 2,300.
Programming (via satellite): BBC America; Bio; Bloomberg Television; C-SPAN 3; Discovery Digital Networks; DMX Music; Do-It-Yourself; Encore (multiplexed); ESPN Classic Sports; ESPNews; Fox Sports World; G4; GAS; Golf Channel; GSN; Halogen Network; History Channel International; Independent Film Channel; Lifetime Movie Network; MTV2; National Geographic Channel; Nick Jr.; Nick Too; Ovation; SoapNet; Style Network; Sundance Channel; Toon Disney; truTV; Turner Classic Movies; Versus; WE tv.
Fee: $17.00 monthly.
Digital Pay Service 1
Pay Units: N.A.
Programming (via satellite): Cinemax (multiplexed); Flix; HBO (multiplexed); Showtime (multiplexed); Starz (multiplexed); The Movie Channel (multiplexed).
Fee: $10.00 monthly (Cinemax or Starz), $13.00 monthly (HBO or Showtime).
Video-On-Demand: Yes
Pay-Per-View
Addressable homes: 2,300.
iN DEMAND, Addressable: Yes; Fresh (delivered digitally); Playboy TV (delivered digitally); iN DEMAND (delivered digitally).
Internet Service
Operational: Yes.
Subscribers: 1,000.
Broadband Service: InsightBB.com.
Fee: $99.95 installation; $44.95 monthly; $15.00 modem lease; $99.95 modem purchase.
Telephone Service
Digital: Operational
Miles of Plant: 206.0 (coaxial); 72.0 (fiber optic). Homes passed: 12,806.
Regional Vice President: Scott Tenney. Regional Vice President, Technical Operations: Max Woolsey. Regional Vice President, Marketing: Aaron Geisel. Regional Vice President, Communications: Mark Apple.
Ownership: Comcast Cable Communications Inc. (MSO).

POSEYVILLE—Now served by EVANSVILLE, IN [IN0006]. ICA: IN0180.

PRETTY LAKE—Formerly served by Longview Communications. No longer in operation. ICA: IN0227.

PRINCES LAKES—Avenue Broadband Communications, 2603 Hart St, Vincennes, IN 47591. Phones: 800-882-7185; 812-895-7676. Fax: 812-886-5017. Web Site: http://www.avenuebroadband.com. ICA: IN0147.
TV Market Ranking: 16 (PRINCES LAKES).
Channel capacity: N.A. Channels available but not in use: N.A.
Basic Service
Subscribers: N.A.
Programming (received off-air): WCLJ-TV (TBN) Bloomington; WFYI (PBS) Indianapolis; WHMB-TV (IND) Indianapolis; WIPX-TV (ION) Bloomington; WISH-TV (CBS) Indianapolis; WNDY-TV (MNT) Marion; WRTV (ABC) Indianapolis; WTHR

(NBC) Indianapolis; WTIU (PBS) Bloomington; WTTV (CW) Bloomington; WXIN (FOX) Indianapolis.
Programming (via satellite): Home Shopping Network; QVC; WGN America.
Current originations: Educational Access.

Expanded Basic Service 1
Subscribers: N.A.
Programming (via satellite): ABC Family Channel; AMC; Animal Planet; Arts & Entertainment; Big Ten Network; Bravo; Cartoon Network; CNBC; CNN; Comedy Central; Country Music TV; C-SPAN; C-SPAN 2; Discovery Channel; Disney Channel; E! Entertainment Television; ESPN; ESPN 2; Food Network; Fox News Channel; Fox Sports Net Midwest; FX; Hallmark Channel; Headline News; HGTV; History Channel; Lifetime; MTV; National Geographic Channel; Nickelodeon; Outdoor Channel; Oxygen; SoapNet; Speed Channel; Spike TV; Syfy; TBS Superstation; The Learning Channel; Travel Channel; truTV; Turner Network TV; TV Land; USA Network; Versus; VH1; Weather Channel.

Digital Basic Service
Subscribers: N.A.
Programming (via satellite): American-Life TV Network; BBC America; Bio; Bloomberg Television; Bravo; CMT Pure Country; Cooking Channel; Discovery Health Channel; Discovery Kids Channel; Discovery Military Channel; Discovery Planet Green; Disney XD; DMX Music; ESPN Classic Sports; ESPNews; FitTV; Fox Business Channel; Fox College Sports Atlantic; Fox College Sports Central; Fox College Sports Pacific; Fox Movie Channel; Fox Soccer; Fuse; G4; Golf Channel; Gospel Music Channel; GSN; History Channel; History Channel International; ID Investigation Discovery; Independent Film Channel; INSP; Lifetime Movie Network; MTV2; mtvU; National Geographic Channel; Nick Jr.; NickToons TV; Outdoor Channel; PBS Kids Sprout; RFD-TV; Science Channel; ShopNBC; Speed Channel; Style Network; TeenNick; Trinity Broadcasting Network; Turner Classic Movies; Versus; VH1 Classic; VH1 Soul; WE tv.

Digital Expanded Basic Service
Subscribers: N.A.
Programming (via satellite): Encore (multiplexed); Flix; Showtime (multiplexed); Starz IndiePlex; Starz RetroPlex; The Movie Channel (multiplexed).

Digital Pay Service 1
Pay Units: N.A.
Programming (via satellite): Cinemax (multiplexed); HBO (multiplexed); Starz (multiplexed).

Pay-Per-View
iN DEMAND (delivered digitally); Hot Choice (delivered digitally); Playboy TV (delivered digitally); Fresh (delivered digitally); Spice: Xcess (delivered digitally); Club Jenna (delivered digitally).

Chief Executive Officer: Steve Lowe. Vice President & General Manager: Mary Iafrate. Vice President, Engineering: Jeff Spence. System Engineer: Bart Cotter.
Ownership: Buford Media Group LLC (MSO).

PRINCETON—Now served by EVANSVILLE, IN [IN0006]. ICA: IN0071.

RENSSELAER—TV Cable of Rensselaer Inc., PO Box 319, 215 W Kellner Blvd, Ste 19, Rensselaer, IN 47978-2665. Phone: 219-866-7101. Fax: 219-866-5785. E-mail: tvcable@rensselaer.tv. Web Site: http://www.rensselaer.tv. Also serves Jasper County (portions). ICA: IN0082.
TV Market Ranking: Outside TV Markets (Jasper County (portions), RENSSELAER). Franchise award date: N.A. Franchise expiration date: N.A. Began: January 1, 1966.
Channel capacity: 64 (operating 2-way). Channels available but not in use: 14.

Basic Service
Subscribers: 1,983.
Programming (received off-air): WCIU-TV (IND) Chicago; WCPX-TV (ION) Chicago; WFLD (FOX) Chicago; WGBO-DT (UNV) Joliet; WGN-TV (CW, IND) Chicago; WJYS (IND) Hammond; WLFI-TV (CBS) Lafayette; WLS-TV (ABC) Chicago; WMAQ-TV (NBC) Chicago; WNDU-TV (NBC) South Bend; WPWR-TV (MNT) Gary; WSBT-TV (CBS, IND) South Bend; WSNS-TV (TMO) Chicago; WTTK (IND) Kokomo; WTTW (PBS) Chicago; WXFT-DT (TEL) Aurora; WYIN (PBS) Gary.
Programming (via satellite): ABC Family Channel; AMC; Animal Planet; Arts & Entertainment; Cartoon Network; CNBC; CNN; Comcast SportsNet Chicago; Comedy Central; Country Music TV; C-SPAN; Discovery Channel; Discovery Health Channel; Disney Channel; E! Entertainment Television; ESPN; ESPN 2; ESPN Classic Sports; Food Network; Fox Movie Channel; Fox News Channel; FX; Golf Channel; Hallmark Channel; Headline News; HGTV; History Channel; Home Shopping Network; Lifetime; MSNBC; MTV; National Geographic Channel; Nickelodeon; Outdoor Channel; QVC; ShopNBC; SoapNet; Speed Channel; Spike TV; Syfy; TBS Superstation; The Learning Channel; The Sportsman Channel; Toon Disney; Travel Channel; truTV; Turner Classic Movies; Turner Network TV; TV Guide Network; TV Land; USA Network; VH1; WE tv; Weather Channel.
Current originations: Public Access.
Fee: $10.00 installation; $37.93 monthly (city); $41.13 monthly (rural areas); $2.30 converter.

Pay Service 1
Pay Units: 234.
Programming (via satellite): HBO.
Fee: $5.00 installation; $12.65 monthly.

Pay Service 2
Pay Units: 121.
Programming (via satellite): Cinemax.
Fee: $5.00 installation; $8.20 monthly.

Pay Service 3
Pay Units: N.A.
Programming (via satellite): Encore; Starz.

Video-On-Demand: No

Pay-Per-View
Addressable homes: 1,983.
special events, Addressable: Yes; iN DEMAND, Addressable: Yes.

Internet Service
Operational: Yes. Began: December 31, 2002.
Subscribers: 400.
Broadband Service: Northwest Internet Services.
Fee: $30.00 installation; $39.95 monthly; $4.95 modem lease; $69.95 modem purchase.

Telephone Service
None

Miles of Plant: 21.0 (coaxial); 5.0 (fiber optic). Homes passed: 2,800. Total homes in franchised area: 2,800.
Vice President, Operations: Eric Galbreath. Office Manager: Sue Shuey.
City fee: None.
Ownership: Theodore W. Filson (MSO).

RICHLAND—Formerly served by Time Warner Cable. No longer in operation. ICA: IN0315.

RICHMOND—Comcast Cable, 5330 E 65th St, Indianapolis, IN 46220. Phone: 317-275-6370. Fax: 317-275-6340. Web Site: http://www.comcast.com. Also serves Cambridge City, Centerville, Dublin, East Germantown, Fountain City, Hagerstown, Milton, Mount Auburn, Pershing, Spring Grove & Wayne County. ICA: IN0018.
TV Market Ranking: Below 100 (Cambridge City, Centerville, Dublin, East Germantown, Fountain City, Hagerstown, Milton, Mount Auburn, Pershing, RICHMOND, Spring Grove, Wayne County). Franchise award date: December 28, 1966. Franchise expiration date: N.A. Began: February 1, 1971.
Channel capacity: N.A. Channels available but not in use: N.A.

Basic Service
Subscribers: N.A. Included in Anderson
Programming (received off-air): WDTN (NBC) Dayton; WHIO-TV (CBS) Dayton; WIPB (PBS) Muncie; WISH-TV (CBS) Indianapolis; WKEF (ABC) Dayton; WKOI-TV (TBN) Richmond; WLWT (NBC) Cincinnati; WPTD (PBS) Dayton; WPTO (PBS) Oxford; WRGT-TV (FOX, MNT) Dayton; WRTV (ABC) Indianapolis; WTHR (NBC) Indianapolis; WTTV (CW) Bloomington; WXIX-TV (FOX) Newport; 1 FM.
Programming (via satellite): C-SPAN; C-SPAN 2; Home Shopping Network; LWS Local Weather Station; QVC; WGN America.
Current originations: Educational Access; Government Access; Public Access.
Fee: $1.60 converter.

Expanded Basic Service 1
Subscribers: 14,000.
Programming (via satellite): ABC Family Channel; AMC; Animal Planet; Arts & Entertainment; BET Networks; Bravo; Cartoon Network; CNBC; CNN; Comedy Central; Country Music TV; Discovery Channel; Disney Channel; E! Entertainment Television; ESPN; ESPN 2; Eternal Word TV Network; Food Network; Fox Movie Channel; Fox News Channel; Fox Sports Net Midwest; Headline News; HGTV; History Channel; Lifetime; MSNBC; MTV; Nickelodeon; Oxygen; Speed Channel; Spike TV; Syfy; TBS Superstation; The Learning Channel; Travel Channel; Turner Network TV; TV Guide Network; TV Land; USA Network; VH1; Weather Channel.
Fee: $51.74 monthly.

Digital Basic Service
Subscribers: 4,103.
Programming (via satellite): BBC America; Bio; Bloomberg Television; C-SPAN 3; Discovery Digital Networks; DMX Music; Do-It-Yourself; Encore (multiplexed); ESPN Classic Sports; ESPNews; Fox Sports World; G4; GAS; Golf Channel; GSN; Halogen Network; History Channel International; Independent Film Channel; Lifetime Movie Network; MTV2; National Geographic Channel; Nick Too; Ovation; SoapNet; Style Network; Sundance Channel; Toon Disney; truTV; Turner Classic Movies; Versus; WE tv.
Fee: $17.00 monthly.

Digital Pay Service 1
Pay Units: N.A.
Programming (via satellite): Cinemax (multiplexed); Flix; HBO (multiplexed); Showtime (multiplexed); Starz (multiplexed); The Movie Channel (multiplexed).
Fee: $10.00 monthly (Cinemax or Starz), $13.00 monthly (HBO or Showtime/TMC).

Video-On-Demand: Yes

Pay-Per-View
Addressable homes: 4,103.
iN DEMAND, Fee: $3.99, Addressable: Yes; Playboy TV (delivered digitally); Fresh (delivered digitally); iN DEMAND (delivered digitally).

Internet Service
Operational: Yes.
Subscribers: 1,784.
Broadband Service: Comcast High Speed Internet.
Fee: $99.95 installation; $44.95 monthly; $15.00 modem lease; $99.95 modem purchase.

Telephone Service
Digital: Operational
Fee: $39.95 monthly

Miles of Plant: 531.0 (coaxial); None (fiber optic). Homes passed: 26,420. Total homes in franchised area: 30,000.
Regional Vice President: Scott Tenney. Regional Vice President, Technical Operations: Max Wolsey. Regional Vice President, Marketing: Aaron Geisel. Regional Vice President, Communications: Mark Apple.
City fee: 3% of gross.
Ownership: Comcast Cable Communications Inc. (MSO).

ROACHDALE—Indiana Communications, PO Box 617, Boswell, IN 47921. Phone: 888-610-1119. Web Site: http://www.indcomm.net. Also serves Ladoga. ICA: IN0163.
TV Market Ranking: Below 100 (Ladoga); Outside TV Markets (ROACHDALE). Franchise award date: April 1, 1983. Franchise expiration date: N.A. Began: April 2, 1984.
Channel capacity: 35 (not 2-way capable). Channels available but not in use: N.A.

Basic Service
Subscribers: 114.
Programming (received off-air): WCLJ-TV (TBN) Bloomington; WFYI (PBS) Indianapolis; WHMB-TV (IND) Indianapolis; WIPX-TV (ION) Bloomington; WLFI-TV (CBS) Lafayette; WNDY-TV (MNT) Marion; WTHR (NBC) Indianapolis; WTTV (CW) Bloomington; WXIN (FOX) Indianapolis.
Programming (via satellite): ABC Family Channel; AMC; Animal Planet; Cartoon Network; CNN; Comedy Central; Country Music TV; C-SPAN; Discovery Channel; Disney Channel; E! Entertainment Television; Encore; ESPN; ESPN 2; Headline News; HGTV; History Channel; Lifetime; Nickelodeon; QVC; Spike TV; TBS Superstation; The Learning Channel; Turner Network TV; USA Network; WGN America.
Fee: $25.00 installation; $32.95 monthly; $3.50 converter.

Pay Service 1
Pay Units: N.A.
Programming (via satellite): Showtime; The Movie Channel.
Fee: $10.00 installation; $8.95 monthly (TMC), $10.95 monthly (Showtime).

Video-On-Demand: No

Internet Service
Operational: No.

Telephone Service
None

Miles of Plant: 12.0 (coaxial); None (fiber optic). Homes passed: 600. Total homes in franchised area: 600.
Manager: Joe Young.
City fee: 3% of basic gross.
Ownership: Park TV & Electronics Inc. (MSO).

ROANN—Formerly served by CableDirect. No longer in operation. ICA: IN0350.

ROCKPORT—Now served by OWENSBORO, KY [KY0004]. ICA: IN0120.

ROCKVILLE—Suddenlink Communications, 12444 Powerscourt Dr, Saint Louis, MO 63131-3660. Phones: 314-965-2020; 573-686-6387. Web Site: http://www.suddenlink.com. Also serves Bloomingdale, Marshall, Mecca & Parke County (unincorporated areas). ICA: IN0101.

TV Market Ranking: Below 100 (Bloomingdale, Marshall, Mecca, Parke County (unincorporated areas), ROCKVILLE). Franchise award date: July 17, 1979. Franchise expiration date: N.A. Began: May 1, 1980.

Channel capacity: 54 (operating 2-way). Channels available but not in use: 1.

Basic Service

Subscribers: 1,362.

Programming (received off-air): WFXW (FOX) Terre Haute; WFYI (PBS) Indianapolis; WHMB-TV (IND) Indianapolis; WRTV (ABC) Indianapolis; WTHI-TV (CBS) Terre Haute; WTHR (NBC) Indianapolis; WTTV (CW) Bloomington; WTWO (NBC) Terre Haute.

Programming (via satellite): Home Shopping Network; WGN America.

Fee: $61.50 installation; $16.95 monthly.

Expanded Basic Service 1

Subscribers: 1,231.

Programming (via satellite): ABC Family Channel; AMC; Arts & Entertainment; CNN; C-SPAN; Discovery Channel; Disney Channel; ESPN; ESPN 2; Fox Sports Net Midwest; G4; Great American Country; GSN; Headline News; History Channel; Lifetime; MSNBC; MTV; National Geographic Channel; Nickelodeon; SoapNet; Speed Channel; Spike TV; TBS Superstation; The Learning Channel; Toon Disney; Trinity Broadcasting Network; Turner Network TV; TV Land; USA Network; Versus; VH1; WE tv; Weather Channel.

Fee: $21.00 monthly.

Digital Basic Service

Subscribers: N.A.

Programming (via satellite): BBC America; Black Family Channel; Bloomberg Television; Discovery Digital Networks; DMX Music; ESPN Classic Sports; ESPNews; Fox College Sports Atlantic; Fox College Sports Central; Fox College Sports Pacific; Fox Movie Channel; Fox Sports World; Golf Channel; Halogen Network; HGTV; Outdoor Channel; ShopNBC; Syfy; Turner Classic Movies.

Fee: $3.95 monthly.

Pay Service 1

Pay Units: 470.

Programming (via satellite): Cinemax; HBO; Showtime; The Movie Channel.

Fee: $8.99 monthly (Cinemax), $12.99 monthly (HBO), $13.99 monthly (Showtime or TMC).

Digital Pay Service 1

Pay Units: N.A.

Programming (via satellite): Cinemax (multiplexed); Encore (multiplexed); HBO (multiplexed); Showtime (multiplexed); Starz (multiplexed); The Movie Channel (multiplexed).

Pay-Per-View

Fresh; Playboy TV; iN DEMAND.

Internet Service

Operational: Yes. Began: May 19, 2004.

Broadband Service: Cebridge High Speed Cable Internet.

Fee: $49.95 installation; $20.95 monthly.

Telephone Service

None

Miles of Plant: 50.0 (coaxial); None (fiber optic). Homes passed: 1,835. Total homes in franchised area: 1,835.

Regional Manager: James Robinson. Chief Technician: Chris Mooday. Customer Service Manager: Sandra Baker.

City fee: 2% of gross.

Ownership: Cequel Communications LLC (MSO).

ROME CITY—Mediacom, 109 E 5th St, Ste A, Auburn, IN 46706. Phones: 800-874-2924 (Customer service); 260-927-3015. Fax: 260-347-4433. Web Site: http://www.mediacomcable.com. Also serves Adams Lake & Wolcottville. ICA: IN0095.

TV Market Ranking: 80,82 (Adams Lake, ROME CITY, Wolcottville). Franchise award date: N.A. Franchise expiration date: N.A. Began: August 1, 1984.

Channel capacity: 121 (operating 2-way). Channels available but not in use: None.

Basic Service

Subscribers: 1,390.

Programming (received off-air): WANE-TV (CBS) Fort Wayne; WFFT-TV (FOX) Fort Wayne; WFWA (PBS) Fort Wayne; WHME-TV (IND) South Bend; WINM (IND) Angola; WISE-TV (MNT, NBC) Fort Wayne; WNDU-TV (NBC) South Bend; WNIT (PBS) South Bend; WPTA (ABC, CW) Fort Wayne; WSBT-TV (CBS, IND) South Bend; WSJV (FOX) Elkhart.

Programming (via satellite): TBS Superstation; TV Guide Network; WGN America.

Fee: $45.00 installation; $20.95 monthly.

Expanded Basic Service 1

Subscribers: 1,032.

Programming (via satellite): ABC Family Channel; AMC; AmericanLife TV Network; Animal Planet; Arts & Entertainment; Bio; Bloomberg Television; Cartoon Network; CNBC; CNN; Comedy Central; Country Music TV; C-SPAN; Discovery Channel; Disney Channel; E! Entertainment Television; ESPN; ESPN 2; Fox Movie Channel; Fox News Channel; FX; G4; Hallmark Channel; Headline News; HGTV; History Channel; History Channel International; Home Shopping Network; Lifetime; Lifetime Movie Network; MSNBC; MTV; Nickelodeon; Product Information Network; QVC; Speed Channel; Spike TV; Style Network; Syfy; The Learning Channel; Travel Channel; Trinity Broadcasting Network; Turner Network TV; TV Land; USA Network; Versus; VH1; Weather Channel.

Fee: $34.00 monthly.

Digital Basic Service

Subscribers: 175.

Programming (via satellite): BBC America; Discovery Digital Networks; DMX Music; ESPN Classic Sports; Fox Sports World; Golf Channel; GSN; Independent Film Channel; Turner Classic Movies; WE tv.

Fee: $9.00 monthly.

Digital Pay Service 1

Pay Units: 417.

Programming (via satellite): Cinemax (multiplexed); Encore (multiplexed); HBO (multiplexed); Showtime (multiplexed); Starz (multiplexed); The Movie Channel (multiplexed).

Fee: $11.95 monthly (HBO, Cinemax, Showtime/TMC or Starz/Encore).

Video-On-Demand: Yes

Pay-Per-View

iN DEMAND, Fee: $3.95, Addressable: Yes; iN DEMAND (delivered digitally); Playboy TV (delivered digitally); Pleasure (delivered digitally); Fresh (delivered digitally); Shorteez (delivered digitally).

Internet Service

Operational: Yes.

Subscribers: 1.

Broadband Service: Mediacom High Speed Internet.

Fee: $59.95 installation; $40.95 monthly.

Telephone Service

Analog: Not Operational

Digital: Operational

Fee: $39.95 installation; $39.95 monthly

Miles of Plant: 42.0 (coaxial); 20.0 (fiber optic). Homes passed: 2,867.

Operations Director: Joe Poffenberger. Technical Operations Manager: Craig Grey.

City fee: 3% of gross.

Ownership: Mediacom LLC (MSO).

ROSEDALE—Rapid Cable. Now served by CLINTON, IN [IN0049]. ICA: IN0200.

ROSELAWN—Mediacom, 109 E 5th St, Ste A, Auburn, IN 46706. Phone: 260-927-3015. Fax: 260-347-4433. Web Site: http://www.mediacomcable.com. Also serves Grant Park (village), Kankakee County & Momence, IL; Jasper County (western portion), Kouts, La Crosse, Lake County (southern portion), Lake Village, Malden, New Durham Twp., Newton County (northern portion), Rosewood Manor, Schneider, Shelby, Sumava Resorts, Thayer, Wanatah, Westville & Wheatfield, IN. ICA: IN0316.

TV Market Ranking: 80 (New Durham Twp., Westville); Below 100 (Grant Park (village), Jasper County (western portion), Kankakee County (portions), Kouts, La Crosse, Lake County (southern portion), Lake Village, Malden, Momence, Newton County (northern portion), ROSELAWN, Rosewood Manor, Schneider, Shelby, Sumava Resorts, Thayer, Wanatah, Wheatfield); Outside TV Markets (Kankakee County (portions)). Franchise award date: N.A. Franchise expiration date: N.A. Began: May 1, 1989.

Channel capacity: N.A. Channels available but not in use: N.A.

Basic Service

Subscribers: 3,377.

Programming (received off-air): WBBM-TV (CBS) Chicago; WCIU-TV (IND) Chicago; WCPX-TV (ION) Chicago; WFLD (FOX) Chicago; WGBO-DT (UNV) Joliet; WGN-TV (CW, IND) Chicago; WJYS (IND) Hammond; WLS-TV (ABC) Chicago; WMAQ-TV (NBC) Chicago; WPWR-TV (MNT) Gary; WSNS-TV (TMO) Chicago; WTTW (PBS) Chicago; WWTO-TV (TBN) La Salle; WYCC (PBS) Chicago; WYIN (PBS) Gary.

Fee: $45.00 installation; $20.95 monthly; $4.00 converter.

Expanded Basic Service 1

Subscribers: 1,391.

Programming (via satellite): ABC Family Channel; AMC; Animal Planet; Arts & Entertainment; Cartoon Network; CNBC; CNN; Comcast SportsNet Chicago; Comedy Central; Country Music TV; C-SPAN; C-SPAN 2; Discovery Channel; Disney Channel; E! Entertainment Television; ESPN; ESPN 2; FitTV; Food Network; Fox News Channel; FX; Great American Country; Hallmark Channel; Headline News; HGTV; History Channel; Home Shopping Network; Lifetime; MSNBC; MTV; Nickelodeon; QVC; RFD-TV; ShopNBC; Speed Channel; Spike TV; Syfy; TBS Superstation; The Learning Channel; Travel Channel; Trinity Broadcasting Network; truTV; Turner Network TV; TV Guide Network; TV Land; USA Network; VH1; WE tv; Weather Channel.

Fee: $34.00 monthly.

Digital Basic Service

Subscribers: N.A.

Programming (via satellite): AmericanLife TV Network; BBC America; Bio; Bloomberg Television; Discovery Digital Networks; Discovery HD Theater; ESPN 2 HD; ESPN HD; ESPNews; Fox Movie Channel; Fox Sports World; Fuse; G4; GAS; Golf Channel; GSN; Halogen Network; HDNet; HDNet Movies; History Channel International; Independent Film Channel; INHD (multiplexed); Lifetime Movie Network; Lime; MTV Networks Digital Suite; National Geographic Channel; Nick Jr.; NickToons TV; Outdoor Channel; Sleuth; Style Network; Turner Classic Movies; TVG Network; Universal HD; Versus.

Fee: $9.00 monthly.

Digital Pay Service 1

Pay Units: N.A.

Programming (via satellite): Cinemax (multiplexed); Encore; Flix (multiplexed); HBO (multiplexed); HBO HD; Showtime (multiplexed); Showtime HD; Starz (multiplexed); Starz HDTV; Sundance Channel (multiplexed); The Movie Channel (multiplexed); The Movie Channel HD.

Fee: $11.95 monthly (HBO, Cinemax, Starz/Encore or Showtime/TMC/Flix/Sundance).

Video-On-Demand: Yes

Pay-Per-View

iN DEMAND (delivered digitally); Playboy TV (delivered digitally).

Internet Service

Operational: Yes.

Broadband Service: Mediacom High Speed Internet.

Fee: $59.95 installation; $40.95 monthly.

Telephone Service

Digital: Operational

Fee: $39.95 installation; $39.95 monthly

Homes passed: 3,005. Miles of plant included in Kendallville

Operations Director: Joe Poffenberger. Technical Operations Manager: Craig Grey.

Ownership: Mediacom LLC (MSO).

ROYAL CENTER—Longview Communications, 12007 Sunrise Valley Dr, Ste 375, Reston, VA 20191. Phones: 866-611-6565 (Customer service); 703-476-9101. Fax: 703-476-9107. Web Site: http://www.longviewcomm.com. ICA: IN0194.

TV Market Ranking: Below 100 (ROYAL CENTER). Franchise award date: June 1, 1984. Franchise expiration date: N.A. Began: October 1, 1985.

Channel capacity: 40 (not 2-way capable). Channels available but not in use: N.A.

Basic Service

Subscribers: 67.

Programming (received off-air): WFYI (PBS) Indianapolis; WLFI-TV (CBS) Lafayette; WNDU-TV (NBC) South Bend; WNDY-TV (MNT) Marion; WRTV (ABC) Indianapolis; WSBT-TV (CBS, IND) South Bend; WSJV (FOX) Elkhart; WTHR (NBC) Indianapolis; WTTK (IND) Kokomo; WXIN (FOX) Indianapolis.

Programming (via satellite): C-SPAN; Trinity Broadcasting Network.

Fee: $39.90 installation; $17.98 monthly.

Expanded Basic Service 1

Subscribers: N.A.

Programming (via satellite): ABC Family Channel; AMC; Animal Planet; Arts & Entertainment; CNN; Discovery Channel; Dis-

ney Channel; E! Entertainment Television; ESPN; ESPN 2; Fox News Channel; Great American Country; Headline News; History Channel; Lifetime; MSNBC; Nickelodeon; Speed Channel; Spike TV; TBS Superstation; The Learning Channel; Turner Network TV; USA Network; Weather Channel; WGN America.
Fee: $17.97 monthly.
Pay Service 1
Pay Units: N.A.
Programming (via satellite): Cinemax; HBO; Showtime; The Movie Channel.
Fee: $8.95 monthly (TMC), $10.95 monthly (Cinemax or Showtime), $12.95 monthly (HBO).
Video-On-Demand: No
Internet Service
Operational: No.
Telephone Service
None
Miles of Plant: 5.0 (coaxial); None (fiber optic). Homes passed: 355.
President: John Long. Senior Vice President: Marc W. Cohen. General Manager: Brandon Dickey. Technical Manager: Steve Boss.
Ownership: Longview Communications (MSO).

RUSHVILLE—Comcast Cable, 5330 E 65th St, Indianapolis, IN 46220. Phone: 317-275-6370. Fax: 317-275-6340. Web Site: http://www.comcast.com. Also serves Circleville. ICA: IN0076.
TV Market Ranking: Below 100 (Circleville, RUSHVILLE). Franchise award date: October 12, 1976. Franchise expiration date: N.A. Began: March 1, 1977.
Channel capacity: 99 (operating 2-way). Channels available but not in use: 4.
Basic Service
Subscribers: N.A. Included in Indianapolis
Programming (received off-air): WCLJ-TV (TBN) Bloomington; WFYI (PBS) Indianapolis; WHMB-TV (IND) Indianapolis; WIPX-TV (ION) Bloomington; WISH-TV (CBS) Indianapolis; WNDY-TV (MNT) Marion; WRTV (ABC) Indianapolis; WTHR (NBC) Indianapolis; WTTV (CW) Bloomington; WXIN (FOX) Indianapolis.
Programming (via satellite): C-SPAN; QVC; The Comcast Network; WGN America.
Fee: $31.99 installation.
Expanded Basic Service 1
Subscribers: N.A.
Programming (via satellite): ABC Family Channel; AMC; Animal Planet; Arts & Entertainment; Bravo; CNBC; CNN; Country Music TV; C-SPAN 2; Discovery Channel; Disney Channel; E! Entertainment Television; ESPN; ESPN 2; ESPNews; Fox News Channel; Fox Sports Net Midwest; FX; G4; Golf Channel; GSN; Hallmark Channel; Headline News; HGTV; History Channel; Lifetime; MSNBC; MTV; Nickelodeon; Speed Channel; Spike TV; Syfy; TBS Superstation; The Learning Channel; Toon Disney; Travel Channel; truTV; Turner Network TV; TV Land; USA Network; Versus; VH1; Weather Channel.
Fee: $47.98 monthly.
Digital Basic Service
Subscribers: N.A.
Programming (via satellite): BBC America; Bio; Canales N; CMT Pure Country; Cooking Channel; C-SPAN 3; Current; Discovery Digital Networks; Do-It-Yourself; Encore; ESPNews; Flix; Fox Reality Channel; GAS; History Channel International; Lifetime Movie Network; LOGO; MTV Networks Digital Suite; Music Choice; National Geographic Channel; Nick Jr.; Nick Too; NickToons TV; Oxygen; PBS Kids Sprout; SoapNet; Sundance Channel; Toon Disney; TV One; Weatherscan.
Digital Pay Service 1
Pay Units: N.A.
Programming (via satellite): Cinemax (multiplexed); HBO (multiplexed); Playboy TV; Showtime (multiplexed); Starz (multiplexed); The Movie Channel (multiplexed).
Video-On-Demand: No
Pay-Per-View
iN DEMAND (delivered digitally); Playboy TV (delivered digitally).
Internet Service
Operational: Yes.
Broadband Service: Comcast High Speed Internet.
Fee: $42.95 monthly.
Telephone Service
Digital: Operational
Miles of Plant: 44.0 (coaxial); None (fiber optic). Additional miles planned: 10.0 (coaxial). Homes passed: 3,692.
Vice President & General Manager: William (Rusty) Robertson. Vice President, Technical Operations: Max Woolsey. Vice President, Communications: Mark Apple. Marketing Director: Damion Miller.
City fee: 3% of gross.
Ownership: Comcast Cable Communications Inc. (MSO).

RUSSELLVILLE—Formerly served by CableDirect. No longer in operation. ICA: IN0364.

SALEM—Insight Communications. Now served by LOUISVILLE, KY [KY0001]. ICA: IN0084.

SAN PIERRE—Mediacom, 109 E 5th St, Ste A, Auburn, IN 46706. Phone: 260-927-3015. Fax: 260- 347-4433. Web Site: http://www.mediacomcable.com. Also serves Francesville, Grovertown, Koontz Lake & Medaryville. ICA: IN0221.
TV Market Ranking: 80 (Grovertown, Koontz Lake); Outside TV Markets (Francesville, Medaryville, SAN PIERRE). Franchise award date: N.A. Franchise expiration date: N.A. Began: November 1, 1989.
Channel capacity: N.A. Channels available but not in use: N.A.
Basic Service
Subscribers: 243.
Programming (received off-air): WBND-LP South Bend; WFLD (FOX) Chicago; WHME-TV (IND) South Bend; WNDU-TV (NBC) South Bend; WNIT (PBS) South Bend; WSBT-TV (CBS, IND) South Bend; WSJV (FOX) Elkhart; WYIN (PBS) Gary.
Programming (via satellite): TV Guide Network; WCWW-LP (CW) South Bend; WGN America.
Fee: $45.00 installation; $20.95 monthly.
Expanded Basic Service 1
Subscribers: N.A.
Programming (via satellite): ABC Family Channel; AMC; Animal Planet; Arts & Entertainment; Cartoon Network; CNBC; CNN; Comcast SportsNet Chicago; Comedy Central; Country Music TV; C-SPAN; C-SPAN 2; Discovery Channel; Disney Channel; E! Entertainment Television; ESPN; ESPN 2; Food Network; Fox News Channel; FX; Great American Country; Hallmark Channel; Headline News; HGTV; History Channel; Home Shopping Network; Lifetime; MSNBC; MTV; Nickelodeon; QVC; RFD-TV; Speed Channel; Spike TV; Syfy; TBS Superstation; The Learning Channel; Travel Channel; Trinity Broadcasting Network; truTV; Turner Network TV; TV Land; USA Network; VH1; WE tv; Weather Channel.
Fee: $34.00 monthly.
Digital Basic Service
Subscribers: N.A.
Programming (received off-air): WBBM-TV (CBS) Chicago; WFLD (FOX) Chicago; WLS-TV (ABC) Chicago; WMAQ-TV (NBC) Chicago; WTTW (PBS) Chicago.
Programming (via satellite): ABC News Now; AmericanLife TV Network; BBC America; Bio; Bloomberg News Radio; CNN HD; Discovery Health Channel; Discovery Home Channel; Discovery Kids Channel; Discovery Military Channel; ESPN U; ESPNews; Fox Movie Channel; Fox Soccer; Fuse; G4; Golf Channel; GSN; Halogen Network; History Channel International; ID Investigation Discovery; Independent Film Channel; International Television (ITV); ION Life; Lifetime Movie Network; MTV2; National Geographic Channel; Nick Jr.; NickToons TV; Outdoor Channel; Qubo; ReelzChannel; Science Channel; Sleuth; Style Network; TBS in HD; Turner Classic Movies; Turner Network TV HD; TVG Network; Versus.
Fee: $9.00 monthly.
Digital Pay Service 1
Pay Units: N.A.
Programming (via satellite): Cinemax (multiplexed); Encore (multiplexed); Flix; HBO (multiplexed); Showtime (multiplexed); Starz (multiplexed); Sundance Channel; The Movie Channel (multiplexed).
Fee: $11.95 monthly (HBO, Cinemax, Starz/Encore or Showtime/TMC).
Video-On-Demand: Yes
Pay-Per-View
iN DEMAND (delivered digitally); Playboy TV (delivered digitally); Ten Clips (delivered digitally); Penthouse TV (delivered digitally); Pleasure (delivered digitally).
Internet Service
Operational: Yes.
Broadband Service: Mediacom High Speed Internet.
Fee: $59.95 installation; $40.95 monthly.
Telephone Service
Digital: Operational
Fee: $39.95 installation; $39.95 monthly
Homes passed & miles of plant included in Kendallville
Operations Director: Joe Poffenberger. Technical Operations Manager: Craig Grey.
City fee: 3% of gross.
Ownership: Mediacom LLC (MSO).

SANTA CLAUS—Avenue Broadband Communications, 2603 Hart St, Vincennes, IN 47591. Phones: 800-882-7185; 812-895-7676. Fax: 812-886-5017. Web Site: http://www.avenuebroadband.com. Also serves Chrisney, Christmas Lake Village, Dale, Mariah Hill & Spencer County. ICA: IN0089.
TV Market Ranking: 86 (Chrisney, Christmas Lake Village, Dale, SANTA CLAUS, Spencer County (portions)); Outside TV Markets (Mariah Hill, Spencer County (portions)). Franchise award date: September 10, 1981. Franchise expiration date: N.A. Began: April 19, 1982.
Channel capacity: 35 (not 2-way capable). Channels available but not in use: None.
Basic Service
Subscribers: 1,260.
Programming (received off-air): WAVE (NBC) Louisville; WAZE-TV (CW) Madisonville; WDRB (FOX) Louisville; WEHT (ABC) Evansville; WEVV-TV (CBS, MNT) Evansville; WFIE (NBC) Evansville; WHAS-TV (ABC) Louisville; WJTS-LD (IND) Jasper; WNIN (PBS) Evansville; WTVW (FOX) Evansville.
Programming (via satellite): Eternal Word TV Network; QVC; WGN America.
Current originations: Government Access; Educational Access; Public Access.
Fee: $36.50 installation; $10.03 monthly; $1.46 converter.
Expanded Basic Service 1
Subscribers: 1,252.
Programming (via satellite): ABC Family Channel; Animal Planet; Arts & Entertainment; CNN; Comedy Central; Discovery Channel; Disney Channel; E! Entertainment Television; ESPN; ESPN 2; Headline News; MTV; Nickelodeon; Spike TV; Syfy; TBS Superstation; The Learning Channel; Turner Classic Movies; Turner Network TV; USA Network; VH1; Weather Channel.
Fee: $11.71 monthly.
Pay Service 1
Pay Units: 237.
Programming (via satellite): HBO.
Fee: $9.50 monthly.
Pay Service 2
Pay Units: 254.
Programming (via satellite): The Movie Channel.
Fee: $9.50 monthly.
Pay Service 3
Pay Units: 209.
Programming (via satellite): Showtime.
Fee: $9.50 monthly.
Video-On-Demand: No
Internet Service
Operational: No.
Telephone Service
None
Miles of Plant: 84.0 (coaxial); None (fiber optic). Homes passed: 2,144. Total homes in franchised area: 3,150.
Chief Executive Officer: Steve Lowe.; Mary Iafrate. Vice President, Engineering: Jeff Spence. System Engineer: Bart Cotter.
City & county fee: 3% of gross.
Ownership: Buford Media Group LLC (MSO).

SCOTTSBURG—Insight Communications. Now served by LOUISVILLE, KY [KY0001]. ICA: IN0053.

SEYMOUR—Comcast Cable, 10778 Randall Ave, Aurora, IN 47001. Phones: 317-275-6370 (Indianapolis office); 812-926-2297. Fax: 812-926-1269. Web Site: http://www.comcast.com. Also serves Butlerville, Crawford, Jackson County, Jennings County, North Vernon, Queensville, Reddington, Rockford, Scipio & Vernon. ICA: IN0039.

TV Market Ranking: 16 (Jackson County (portions)); Below 100 (Reddington, Rockford, SEYMOUR, Jackson County (portions)); Outside TV Markets (Butlerville, Crawford, Jennings County, North Vernon, Queensville, Scipio, Vernon). Franchise award date: N.A. Franchise expiration date: N.A. Began: January 1, 1973.

Channel capacity: 78 (operating 2-way). Channels available but not in use: 2.

Basic Service

Subscribers: N.A. Included in Bloomington

Programming (received off-air): WAVE (NBC) Louisville; WBKI-TV (CW) Campbellsville; WBNA (ION) Louisville; WHAS-TV (ABC) Louisville; WHMB-TV (IND) Indianapolis; WISH-TV (CBS) Indianapolis; WLKY-TV (CBS) Louisville; WMYO (MNT) Salem; WRTV (ABC) Indianapolis; WTHR (NBC) Indianapolis; WTIU (PBS) Bloomington; WTTV (CW) Bloomington; WXIN (FOX) Indianapolis; allband FM.

Programming (via satellite): CNN; C-SPAN; QVC; Trinity Broadcasting Network; WGN America.

Fee: $31.99 installation; $7.00 monthly.

Expanded Basic Service 1

Subscribers: N.A.

Programming (via satellite): ABC Family Channel; AMC; Animal Planet; Arts & Entertainment; BET Networks; Bravo; Cartoon Network; CNBC; Comedy Central; Country Music TV; C-SPAN 2; Discovery Channel; Disney Channel; E! Entertainment Television; ESPN; ESPN 2; ESPN Classic Sports; ESPNews; Food Network; Fox News Channel; Fox Sports Net Midwest; FX; Golf Channel; Headline News; HGTV; History Channel; Home Shopping Network; Lifetime; LWS Local Weather Station; MSNBC; MTV; Nickelodeon; Speed Channel; Spike TV; Style Network; Syfy; TBS Superstation; The Learning Channel; Toon Disney; Travel Channel; truTV; Turner Classic Movies; Turner Network TV; TV Japan; TV Land; USA Network; Versus; VH1; Weather Channel.

Fee: $43.98 monthly.

Digital Basic Service

Subscribers: N.A.

Programming (via satellite): BBC America; Bio; Canales N; CBS College Sports Network; C-SPAN 3; Discovery Digital Networks; DMX Music; Encore (multiplexed); ESPN Classic Sports; ESPNews; Eternal Word TV Network; Flix (multiplexed); Fox College Sports Central; Fox College Sports Pacific; Fox Soccer; G4; GAS; Gol TV; History Channel International; MTV Networks Digital Suite; National Geographic Channel; NBA TV; NFL Network; Nick Jr.; Nick Too; NickToons TV; SoapNet; Sundance Channel (multiplexed); Toon Disney; TV One; TVG Network; Weatherscan.

Fee: $17.82 monthly.

Digital Pay Service 1

Pay Units: N.A.

Programming (via satellite): Cinemax (multiplexed); HBO (multiplexed); Showtime (multiplexed); Starz (multiplexed); The Movie Channel (multiplexed).

Fee: $16.99 monthly (each).

Video-On-Demand: No

Pay-Per-View

iN DEMAND (delivered digitally); Hot Choice (delivered digitally); Playboy TV (delivered digitally); Fresh (delivered digitally); Shorteez (delivered digitally); Pleasure (delivered digitally); Sports PPV (delivered digitally); NBA League Pass (delivered digitally).

Internet Service

Operational: Yes. Began: December 1, 2002.

Broadband Service: Comcast High Speed Internet.

Fee: $42.95 monthly.

Telephone Service

Digital: Operational

Miles of Plant: 216.0 (coaxial); None (fiber optic). Homes passed: 12,206.

Vice President: William (Rusty) Robertson. General Manager: Don Richey. Technical Operations Director: Richard Ring.

City fee: 3% of gross.

Ownership: Comcast Cable Communications Inc. (MSO).

SHELBYVILLE—Comcast Cable, 24 E Hendricks St, Shelbyville, IN 46176-2125. Phones: 317-398-6681; 317-392-3695. Fax: 317-398-3553. Web Site: http://www.comcast.com. Also serves Fairland, Flat Rock, Hope & New Palestine (portions). ICA: IN0042.

TV Market Ranking: 16 (Fairland, Flat Rock, New Palestine (portions), SHELBYVILLE); Outside TV Markets (Hope). Franchise award date: November 1, 1973. Franchise expiration date: N.A. Began: December 1, 1973.

Channel capacity: N.A. Channels available but not in use: N.A.

Basic Service

Subscribers: 6,684.

Programming (received off-air): WCLJ-TV (TBN) Bloomington; WDTI (IND) Indianapolis; WFYI (PBS) Indianapolis; WHMB-TV (IND) Indianapolis; WIPX-TV (ION) Bloomington; WISH-TV (CBS) Indianapolis; WNDY-TV (MNT) Marion; WRTV (ABC) Indianapolis; WTHR (NBC) Indianapolis; WTTV (CW) Bloomington; WXIN (FOX) Indianapolis.

Programming (via satellite): ABC Family Channel; AMC; Animal Planet; Arts & Entertainment; BET Networks; Cartoon Network; CNBC; CNN; Comedy Central; Country Music TV; C-SPAN; Discovery Channel; Discovery Health Channel; Disney Channel; E! Entertainment Television; ESPN; ESPN 2; ESPN Classic Sports; ESPNews; Food Network; Fox News Channel; Fox Sports Net Midwest; FX; GSN; Hallmark Channel; Headline News; HGTV; History Channel; Lifetime; MSNBC; MTV; Nickelodeon; QVC; ShopNBC; SoapNet; Spike TV; Syfy; TBS Superstation; The Learning Channel; Toon Disney; Travel Channel; truTV; Turner Network TV; TV Guide Network; TV Land; Univision; USA Network; VH1; Weather Channel; WGN America.

Fee: $30.00 monthly.

Digital Basic Service

Subscribers: 1,703.

Programming (via satellite): BBC America; Discovery Digital Networks; GAS; Lifetime Movie Network; MTV Networks Digital Suite; Music Choice; Nick Jr.; Nick Too.

Fee: $12.95 monthly.

Pay Service 1

Pay Units: N.A.

Programming (via satellite): Cinemax; HBO (multiplexed); Showtime.

Digital Pay Service 1

Pay Units: N.A.

Programming (via satellite): Cinemax (multiplexed); Encore (multiplexed); HBO (multiplexed); Showtime (multiplexed); Starz (multiplexed); The Movie Channel (multiplexed).

Video-On-Demand: Yes

Pay-Per-View

ESPN Full Court (delivered digitally), Addressable: Yes; ESPN Gameplan (delivered digitally), Addressable: Yes; Fresh (delivered digitally).

Internet Service

Operational: Yes.

Subscribers: 1,406.

Broadband Service: Comcast High Speed Internet.

Fee: $42.95 monthly.

Telephone Service

Digital: Operational

Fee: $44.95 monthly

Miles of Plant: 260.0 (coaxial); None (fiber optic). Homes passed: 13,498.

General Manager: Don Richey. Technical Operations Director: Richard Ring. Technical Supervisor: Jeff Weaver.

City fee: None.

Ownership: Comcast Cable Communications Inc. (MSO).

SHERIDAN—Longview Communications, 1923 N Main, Higginsville, MO 64037. Phone: 866-611-6565. Fax: 866-329-4790. Web Site: http://www.longviewcomm.com. Also serves Kirklin & Terhune. ICA: IN0116.

TV Market Ranking: 16 (Kirklin, SHERIDAN, Terhune). Franchise award date: October 1, 1981. Franchise expiration date: N.A. Began: October 1, 1981.

Channel capacity: N.A. Channels available but not in use: N.A.

Basic Service

Subscribers: 327.

Programming (received off-air): WCLJ-TV (TBN) Bloomington; WFYI (PBS) Indianapolis; WHMB-TV (IND) Indianapolis; WIPX-TV (ION) Bloomington; WISH-TV (CBS) Indianapolis; WNDY-TV (MNT) Marion; WRTV (ABC) Indianapolis; WTHR (NBC) Indianapolis; WTTK (IND) Kokomo; WXIN (FOX) Indianapolis; 1 FM.

Programming (via satellite): ABC Family Channel; AMC; Animal Planet; Arts & Entertainment; Cartoon Network; CNN; Comedy Central; Country Music TV; C-SPAN; Discovery Channel; Disney Channel; E! Entertainment Television; ESPN; ESPN 2; Food Network; Fox News Channel; Fox Sports Net Midwest; FX; Hallmark Channel; Hallmark Movie Channel; Headline News; HGTV; History Channel; Home Shopping Network; INSP; Lifetime; Nickelodeon; QVC; Spike TV; Syfy; TBS Superstation; The Learning Channel; Travel Channel; truTV; Turner Network TV; USA Network; Weather Channel; WGN America; WISH-TV (CBS) Indianapolis.

Fee: $35.95 installation; $40.95 monthly.

Digital Basic Service

Subscribers: 51.

Programming (via satellite): AmericanLife TV Network; BBC America; Bio; Bloomberg Television; Discovery Digital Networks; Encore (multiplexed); ESPN Classic Sports; ESPNews; Fox Movie Channel; Fox Soccer; G4; Golf Channel; GSN; Halogen Network; History Channel International; Independent Film Channel; Lifetime Movie Network; Outdoor Channel; Speed Channel; Style Network; Toon Disney; Turner Classic Movies.

Fee: $17.00 monthly.

Pay Service 1

Pay Units: N.A.

Programming (via satellite): Cinemax; HBO; Showtime; The Movie Channel.

Fee: $10.00 installation; $8.95 monthly (TMC), $10.95 monthly (Cinemax or Showtime), $12.95 monthly (HBO).

Digital Pay Service 1

Pay Units: N.A.

Programming (via satellite): Cinemax (multiplexed); Flix; HBO (multiplexed); Showtime (multiplexed); Starz (multiplexed); The Movie Channel (multiplexed).

Fee: $8.95 monthly (TMC), $10.95 monthly (Cinemax or Showtime), $12.95 monthly (HBO).

Video-On-Demand: No

Pay-Per-View

iN DEMAND (delivered digitally); Hot Choice (delivered digitally); Playboy TV (delivered digitally); Fresh (delivered digitally); Shorteez (delivered digitally).

Internet Service

Operational: Yes.

Subscribers: 98.

Broadband Service: IBBS.

Fee: $29.95 monthly.

Telephone Service

None

Miles of Plant: 26.0 (coaxial); None (fiber optic). Homes passed: 1,597. Total homes in franchised area: 1,597.

President: John Long. Senior Vice President: Marc W. Cohen. General Manager: Brandon Dickey. Technical Manager: Steve Boss.

City fee: 3% of gross.

Ownership: Longview Communications (MSO).

SHIPSHEWANA—Formerly served by Longview Communications. No longer in operation. ICA: IN0320.

SHOALS—Formerly served by Almega Cable. No longer in operation. ICA: IN0168.

TV Market Ranking: 16 (Martin County (portions)); Outside TV Markets (Martin County (portions)).

SILVER LAKE—Comcast Cable. Now served by SOUTH BEND, IN [IN0005]. ICA: IN0165.

SOMERSET—Formerly served by CableDirect. No longer in operation. ICA: IN0321.

SOUTH BEND—Comcast Cable, 7720 W 98th St, Hickory Hills, IL 60457. Phones: 708-237-3260; 574-259-2112 (Mishawaka office). Fax: 708-237-3292. Web Site: http://www.comcast.com. Also serves Akron, Bristol, Burket, Etna Green, Fulton County, Goshen, Jefferson Twp., Kosciusko County, Marshall County, Middlebury, Mishawaka, Osceola, Plymouth, Rochester, Roseland, Silver Lake, St. Joseph County, Wakarusa, Warsaw & Winona Lake, IN; Park Twp. & Sherman Twp. (St. Joseph County), MI. ICA: IN0005.

TV Market Ranking: 37 (Park Twp., Sherman Twp. (St. Joseph County)); 80 (Bristol, Burket, Cass County, Etna Green, Goshen, Jefferson Twp., Kosciusko County (portions), Marshall County, Mason Twp., Middlebury, Mishawaka, Osceola, Plymouth, Roseland, SOUTH BEND, St. Joseph County, Wakarusa); 82 (Akron, Silver Lake); Below 100 (Fulton County (portions)); Outside TV Markets (Fulton County (portions), Rochester, Kosciusko County (portions)). Franchise award date: N.A. Franchise expiration date: N.A. Began: May 1, 1971.

Channel capacity: N.A. Channels available but not in use: N.A.

Basic Service

Subscribers: 133,804.

Programming (received off-air): WBND-LP South Bend; WCWW-LP (CW) South Bend; WGN-TV (CW, IND) Chicago; WHME-TV

(IND) South Bend; WNDU-TV (NBC) South Bend; WNIT (PBS) South Bend; WSBT-TV (CBS, IND) South Bend; WSJV (FOX) Elkhart.
Programming (via satellite): C-SPAN; Discovery Channel; Fox News Channel; Home Shopping Network 2; QVC; Shop at Home; TBS Superstation.
Current originations: Government Access; Educational Access; Public Access.
Fee: $48.99 installation; $15.69 monthly.

Expanded Basic Service 1
Subscribers: N.A.
Programming (via satellite): ABC Family Channel; AMC; Animal Planet; Arts & Entertainment; BET Networks; Cartoon Network; CNBC; CNN; Comcast SportsNet Chicago; Comedy Central; Country Music TV; C-SPAN 2; Disney Channel; E! Entertainment Television; ESPN; ESPN 2; Eternal Word TV Network; Food Network; FX; Golf Channel; Hallmark Channel; Headline News; HGTV; History Channel; Lifetime; MSNBC; MTV; Nickelodeon; Oxygen; Spike TV; Telemundo; The Learning Channel; Travel Channel; truTV; Turner Network TV; TV Land; Univision; USA Network; Versus; VH1; Weather Channel.
Fee: $34.80 monthly.

Digital Basic Service
Subscribers: N.A.
Programming (via satellite): AmericanLife TV Network; BBC America; Bio; Black Family Channel; Bloomberg Television; Bravo; Canales N; Discovery Digital Networks; DMX Music; Encore Action; ESPN Classic Sports; ESPNews; FitTV; Fox College Sports Atlantic; Fox College Sports Central; Fox College Sports Pacific; Fox Movie Channel; Fox Sports World; Fuse; G4; GAS; Great American Country; GSN; Halogen Network; History Channel International; Independent Film Channel; International Television (ITV); Lifetime Movie Network; Lime; MTV Networks Digital Suite; NBA TV; Nick Jr.; NickToons TV; Outdoor Channel; Ovation; ShopNBC; Speed Channel; Style Network; Sundance Channel; Syfy; The Word Network; Toon Disney; Trinity Broadcasting Network; Turner Classic Movies; WE tv.
Fee: $11.99 monthly.

Digital Pay Service 1
Pay Units: 20,056.
Programming (via satellite): Cinemax (multiplexed); Flix; HBO (multiplexed); Showtime (multiplexed); Starz (multiplexed); The Movie Channel (multiplexed).
Fee: $10.00 installation; $16.99 monthly (each).

Video-On-Demand: Yes

Pay-Per-View
ESPN Now (delivered digitally); Sports PPV (delivered digitally); iN DEMAND (delivered digitally); Barker (delivered digitally); Urban Xtra (delivered digitally); Fresh (delivered digitally); Shorteez (delivered digitally); Playboy TV (delivered digitally); Hot Choice (delivered digitally).

Internet Service
Operational: Yes.
Broadband Service: Comcast High Speed Internet.
Fee: $42.95 monthly.

Telephone Service
Digital: Operational

Miles of Plant: 3,435.0 (coaxial); None (fiber optic). Total homes in franchised area: 197,523.
Area Vice President: Sandy Weicher. Vice President, Technical Operations: Bob Curtis. Vice President, Marketing & Sales: Eric Schaefer. Office Manager: Lynette Hoyt. Technical Operations Manager: John Collucci. Marketing Director: Ron Knutson.
City fee: 3% of gross.
Ownership: Comcast Cable Communications Inc. (MSO).

SOUTH BEND—Formerly served by Sprint Corp. No longer in operation. ICA: IN0355.

SOUTH WHITLEY—Mediacom. Now served by LIGONIER, IN [IN0156]. ICA: IN0146.

SPENCER—Insight Communications. Now served by BLOOMINGTON, IN [IN0016]. ICA: IN0104.

SPURGEON—Formerly served by CableDirect. No longer in operation. ICA: IN0353.

ST. PAUL—Formerly served by Longview Communications. No longer in operation. ICA: IN0157.

SULLIVAN—Insight Communications. Now served by LINTON, IN [IN0052]. ICA: IN0090.

SUMMITVILLE—Longview Communications, 1923 N Main, Higginsville, MO 64037. Phone: 703-476-9101. Fax: 866-329-4790. Web Site: http://www.longviewcomm.com. ICA: IN0175.
TV Market Ranking: Below 100 (SUMMITVILLE). Franchise award date: N.A. Franchise expiration date: N.A. Began: April 1, 1984.
Channel capacity: N.A. Channels available but not in use: N.A.

Basic Service
Subscribers: 121.
Programming (received off-air): WCLJ-TV (TBN) Bloomington; WFYI (PBS) Indianapolis; WHMB-TV (IND) Indianapolis; WISH-TV (CBS) Indianapolis; WRTV (ABC) Indianapolis; WTHR (NBC) Indianapolis; WTTK (IND) Kokomo; WTTV (CW) Bloomington; WXIN (FOX) Indianapolis.
Programming (via satellite): C-SPAN; QVC.
Fee: $35.95 installation; $19.98 monthly.

Expanded Basic Service 1
Subscribers: N.A.
Programming (via satellite): ABC Family Channel; AMC; Animal Planet; Arts & Entertainment; CBS College Sports Network; CNN; Discovery Channel; Disney Channel; Do-It-Yourself; E! Entertainment Television; ESPN; ESPN 2; ESPN Classic Sports; Food Network; Fox News Channel; FX; Great American Country; Hallmark Channel; Hallmark Movie Channel; Headline News; HGTV; History Channel; INSP; Lifetime; MSNBC; National Geographic Channel; Nickelodeon; Syfy; TBS Superstation; The Learning Channel; Travel Channel; truTV; Turner Network TV; USA Network; Weather Channel; WGN America.
Fee: $21.97 monthly.

Digital Basic Service
Subscribers: 13.
Programming (via satellite): AmericanLife TV Network; BBC America; Bio; Bloomberg Television; Discovery Digital Networks; Encore (multiplexed); ESPNews; Fox Movie Channel; Fox Soccer; Fuse; G4; Golf Channel; GSN; Halogen Network; History Channel International; Independent Film Channel; Lifetime Movie Network; Outdoor Channel; Speed Channel; Style Network; Sundance Channel; Toon Disney; Turner Classic Movies; Versus.
Fee: $18.00 monthly.

Pay Service 1
Pay Units: 22.
Programming (via satellite): Cinemax; HBO; Showtime; The Movie Channel.
Fee: $8.95 monthly (TMC), $10.95 monthly (Cinemax or Showtime), $12.95 monthly (HBO).

Digital Pay Service 1
Pay Units: N.A.
Programming (via satellite): Cinemax (multiplexed); Flix; HBO (multiplexed); Showtime (multiplexed); Starz (multiplexed); The Movie Channel (multiplexed).
Fee: $8.95 monthly (TMC), $10.95 monthly (Cinemax or Showtime), $12.95 monthly (HBO).

Video-On-Demand: No

Pay-Per-View
iN DEMAND (delivered digitally); Hot Choice (delivered digitally); Playboy TV (delivered digitally); Fresh (delivered digitally); Shorteez (delivered digitally).

Internet Service
Operational: Yes.
Subscribers: 20.
Broadband Service: IBBS.

Telephone Service
None

Miles of Plant: 10.0 (coaxial); None (fiber optic). Homes passed: 507.
President: John Long. Senior Vice President: Marc W. Cohen. General Manager: Brandon Dickey. Technical Manager: Steve Boss.
Ownership: Longview Communications (MSO).

SUNMAN—Enhanced Telecommunications Corp., PO Box 145, 123 Nieman St, Sunman, IN 47041-0145. Phones: 812-932-1000; 812-623-2122. Fax: 812-623-4159. E-mail: afledderman@etc1.net. Web Site: http://www.etc1.net. Also serves Napoleon, New Point & St. Leon. ICA: IN0183.
TV Market Ranking: 17 (BATESVILLE (PORTIONS), Napoleon, St. Leon); Outside TV Markets (New Point). Franchise award date: May 24, 1984. Franchise expiration date: N.A. Began: May 1, 1984.
Channel capacity: 50 (operating 2-way). Channels available but not in use: 16.

Basic Service
Subscribers: 529.
Programming (received off-air): WCET (PBS) Cincinnati; WCPO-TV (ABC) Cincinnati; WISH-TV (CBS) Indianapolis; WKOI-TV (TBN) Richmond; WKRC-TV (CBS, CW) Cincinnati; WLWT (NBC) Cincinnati; WNDY-TV (MNT) Marion; WPTO (PBS) Oxford; WRTV (ABC) Indianapolis; WSTR-TV (MNT) Cincinnati; WTHR (NBC) Indianapolis; WTTV (CW) Bloomington; WXIN (FOX) Indianapolis; WXIX-TV (FOX) Newport.
Programming (via satellite): ABC Family Channel; Arts & Entertainment; Cartoon Network; CNN; Comedy Central; Country Music TV; Discovery Channel; Disney Channel; E! Entertainment Television; ESPN; ESPN 2; Eternal Word TV Network; Food Network; Fox News Channel; Fox Sports Net; Headline News; History Channel; Lifetime; MSNBC; MTV; Nickelodeon; QVC; Spike TV; TBS Superstation; The Learning Channel; Turner Classic Movies; Turner Network TV; USA Network; VH1; Weather Channel; WGN America.
Fee: $32.00 installation; $42.95 monthly; $2.00 converter; $15.00 additional installation.

Digital Basic Service
Subscribers: 289.
Programming (via satellite): Bloomberg Television; Discovery Digital Networks; ESPN Classic Sports; ESPNews; FitTV; Fox Sports World; G4; GAS; Golf Channel; GSN; HGTV; Lifetime Movie Network; National Geographic Channel; Nick Jr.; Outdoor Channel; Speed Channel; Syfy.
Fee: $49.95 installation; $51.95 monthly.

Digital Expanded Basic Service
Subscribers: 45.
Programming (via satellite): BBC America; Bio; Bravo; DMX Music; Encore; Fox Movie Channel; History Channel International; Independent Film Channel; MTV Networks Digital Suite; Ovation; Style Network; Sundance Channel; Versus; WE tv.
Fee: $49.95 installation; $19.00 monthly.

Digital Pay Service 1
Pay Units: 44.
Programming (via satellite): Cinemax (multiplexed); HBO (multiplexed); Showtime (multiplexed); The Movie Channel (multiplexed).
Fee: $49.95 installation; $11.00 monthly.

Video-On-Demand: No

Pay-Per-View
Addressable homes: 426.

Internet Service
Operational: No, Both DSL & dial-up.

Telephone Service
None

Miles of Plant: 100.0 (coaxial); 26.0 (fiber optic). Additional miles planned: 12.0 (coaxial); 23.0 (fiber optic). Homes passed: 2,000. Total homes in franchised area: 5,000.
President & Chief Executive Officer: Chad Miles. Vice President, Operations: Mike Fledderman. Chief Technician: Brian Appleton. Program Director & Marketing Director: Anita Fledderman. Customer Service & Sales Manager: Becky Brashear.
Ownership: Enhanced Telecommunications Corp. (MSO).

SWAYZEE—The Swayzee Telephone Co., PO Box 97, 214 S Washington St, Swayzee, IN 46986-0097. Phones: 800-435-8353; 765-922-7916. Fax: 765-922-4545. E-mail: swayzee@swayzee.com. Web Site: http://www.swayzee.com. Also serves Herbst & Sims. ICA: IN0323.
TV Market Ranking: Below 100 (Herbst, Sims, SWAYZEE). Franchise award date: N.A. Franchise expiration date: N.A. Began: January 1, 1983.
Channel capacity: 53 (not 2-way capable). Channels available but not in use: N.A.

Basic Service
Subscribers: 315.
Programming (received off-air): WHMB-TV (IND) Indianapolis; WIPB (PBS) Muncie; WISH-TV (CBS) Indianapolis; WNDY-TV (MNT) Marion; WRTV (ABC) Indianapolis;

WSOT-LP Marion; WTHR (NBC) Indianapolis; WTTV (CW) Bloomington; WXIN (FOX) Indianapolis.
Programming (via satellite): ABC Family Channel; AMC; Animal Planet; Arts & Entertainment; Big Ten Network; Boomerang; Cartoon Network; CNN; Comedy Central; Country Music TV; Discovery Channel; Disney Channel; Do-It-Yourself; ESPN; ESPN 2; Food Network; Fox News Channel; FX; Great American Country; Hallmark Channel; Headline News; HGTV; History Channel; Lifetime; MSNBC; MTV; National Geographic Channel; Nickelodeon; Oxygen; QVC; Speed Channel; Spike TV; Syfy; TBS Superstation; The Learning Channel; Travel Channel; Turner Classic Movies; Turner Network TV; TV Land; USA Network; VH1; Weather Channel; WGN America.
Current originations: Government Access.
Fee: $20.00 installation; $34.95 monthly; $4.00 converter.

Pay Service 1
Pay Units: 18.
Programming (via satellite): Cinemax.
Fee: $13.00 monthly.

Pay Service 2
Pay Units: 22.
Programming (via satellite): HBO.
Fee: $13.00 monthly.

Video-On-Demand: No

Internet Service
Operational: No, Both DSL & dial-up.

Telephone Service
None

Miles of Plant: 15.0 (coaxial); None (fiber optic). Homes passed: 650. Total homes in franchised area: 650.
General Manager: Tim Miles. Plant Manager & Chief Technician: Jeff Duncan. Customer Service Manager: Sue Whitlow.
Ownership: Swayzee Tele Broadband.

SWEETSER—Oak Hill Cablevision Inc., PO Box 200, 206 N Main St, Sweetser, IN 46987. Phone: 765-384-5444. Fax: 765-384-7002. E-mail: billing@comteck.com. Also serves Converse & Jalapa. ICA: IN0129.
TV Market Ranking: 82 (Jalapa, SWEETSER); Below 100 (Converse). Franchise award date: March 24, 1983. Franchise expiration date: N.A. Began: July 1, 1983.
Channel capacity: 38 (operating 2-way). Channels available but not in use: 2.

Basic Service
Subscribers: 819.
Programming (received off-air): WFFT-TV (FOX) Fort Wayne; WFTC (MNT) Minneapolis; WHMB-TV (IND) Indianapolis; WIPB (PBS) Muncie; WISE-TV (MNT, NBC) Fort Wayne; WISH-TV (CBS) Indianapolis; WLFI-TV (CBS) Lafayette; WNDY-TV (MNT) Marion; WPTA (ABC, CW) Fort Wayne; WRTV (ABC) Indianapolis; WSOT-LP Marion; WTHR (NBC) Indianapolis; WXIN (FOX) Indianapolis.
Programming (via satellite): ABC Family Channel; Arts & Entertainment; Cartoon Network; CNN; Country Music TV; C-SPAN; Discovery Channel; Disney Channel; ESPN; ESPN 2; HGTV; History Channel; Nickelodeon; QVC; Spike TV; TBS Superstation; The Learning Channel; Turner Classic Movies; Turner Network TV; USA Network; VH1; Weather Channel; WGN America.
Current originations: Public Access.
Fee: $20.00 installation; $25.50 monthly; $1.00 converter.

Pay Service 1
Pay Units: 213.
Programming (via satellite): Cinemax.
Fee: $11.95 monthly.

Pay Service 2
Pay Units: 109.
Programming (via satellite): HBO.
Fee: $11.95 monthly.

Video-On-Demand: No

Internet Service
Operational: No.

Telephone Service
None

Miles of Plant: 51.0 (coaxial); None (fiber optic). Homes passed: 1,275.
Manager: Rocky Bradshaw.
City fee: 3% of gross.
Ownership: Scott Winger.

SYRACUSE—Mediacom. Now served by NORTH WEBSTER, IN [IN0038]. ICA: IN0340.

TALMA—Formerly served by CableDirect. No longer in operation. ICA: IN0324.

TELL CITY—Comcast Cable, 2919 Ring Rd, Elizabethtown, KY 42701. Phone: 270-737-2731. Fax: 270-737-3379. E-mail: tim_hagen@cable.comcast.com. Web Site: http://www.comcast.com. Also serves Cannelton. ICA: IN0063.
TV Market Ranking: Outside TV Markets (Cannelton, TELL CITY). Franchise award date: July 1, 1965. Franchise expiration date: N.A. Began: September 1, 1965.
Channel capacity: N.A. Channels available but not in use: N.A.

Basic Service
Subscribers: 3,670.
Programming (received off-air): WAVE (NBC) Louisville; WDRB (FOX) Louisville; WEHT (ABC) Evansville; WEVV-TV (CBS, MNT) Evansville; WFIE (NBC) Evansville; WHAS-TV (ABC) Louisville; WKOH (PBS) Owensboro; WLKY-TV (CBS) Louisville; WNIN (PBS) Evansville; WTVW (FOX) Evansville.
Programming (via satellite): ABC Family Channel; CNN; Country Music TV; Discovery Channel; Disney Channel; ESPN; Food Network; Fox Sports Net Ohio; Headline News; HGTV; Lifetime; MSNBC; MTV; Nickelodeon; Spike TV; Syfy; TBS Superstation; Turner Network TV; USA Network; VH1; WGN America.
Fee: $54.99 installation; $46.99 monthly.

Digital Basic Service
Subscribers: N.A.
Programming (via satellite): BBC America; CMT Pure Country; C-SPAN 3; Discovery Digital Networks; Encore (multiplexed); ESPNews; Flix; GAS; Lifetime Movie Network; MoviePlex; MTV Networks Digital Suite; Music Choice; National Geographic Channel; NFL Network; Nick Jr.; Nick Too; NickToons TV; PBS Kids Sprout; SoapNet; Sundance Channel; Toon Disney.
Fee: $14.95 monthly.

Digital Pay Service 1
Pay Units: N.A.
Programming (via satellite): Cinemax (multiplexed); HBO (multiplexed); Showtime (multiplexed); Starz (multiplexed); The Movie Channel (multiplexed).
Fee: $13.05 monthly (each).

Video-On-Demand: No

Pay-Per-View
iN DEMAND (delivered digitally); Hot Choice (delivered digitally); Playboy TV (delivered digitally).

Internet Service
Operational: Yes.
Broadband Service: Comcast High Speed Internet.
Fee: $42.95 monthly.

Telephone Service
None

Miles of Plant: 65.0 (coaxial); None (fiber optic). Homes passed: 4,000.
General Manager: Tim Hagan. Technical Operations Director: Bob Tharp. Marketing Director: Laurie Nicholson.
City fee: 5% of gross.
Ownership: Comcast Cable Communications Inc. (MSO).

TERRE HAUTE—Time Warner Cable, 1605 Wabash Ave, Terre Haute, IN 47807. Phone: 812-232-5808. Fax: 812-232-7453. Web Site: http://www.timewarnercable.com/Terrehaute. Also serves Riley & West Terre Haute. ICA: IN0011.
TV Market Ranking: Below 100 (Riley, TERRE HAUTE, West Terre Haute). Franchise award date: N.A. Franchise expiration date: N.A. Began: October 18, 1966.
Channel capacity: N.A. Channels available but not in use: N.A.

Basic Service
Subscribers: 23,638.
Programming (received off-air): WFXW (FOX) Terre Haute; WFYI (PBS) Indianapolis; WRTV (ABC) Indianapolis; WTHI-TV (CBS) Terre Haute; WTIU (PBS) Bloomington; WTTV (CW) Bloomington; WTWO (NBC) Terre Haute; WXIN (FOX) Indianapolis; 22 FMs.
Programming (via satellite): Boomerang; C-SPAN; C-SPAN 2; Discovery Health Channel; FitTV; Food Network; Fox News Channel; FX; INSP; Lifetime Movie Network; Oxygen; ShopNBC; TBS Superstation; WE tv; WGN America.
Fee: $49.45 installation; $9.91 monthly.

Expanded Basic Service 1
Subscribers: N.A.
Programming (via satellite): ABC Family Channel; AMC; Animal Planet; Arts & Entertainment; BET Networks; Bravo; Cartoon Network; CNBC; CNN; Comedy Central; Country Music TV; Discovery Channel; Disney Channel; E! Entertainment Television; ESPN; ESPN 2; Eternal Word TV Network; Fox Sports Net Midwest; Fox Sports Net Ohio; Headline News; HGTV; History Channel; Home Shopping Network; ION Television; Lifetime; MSNBC; MTV; Nickelodeon; QVC; Spike TV; The Learning Channel; Travel Channel; Trinity Broadcasting Network; Turner Classic Movies; Turner Network TV; TV Guide Network; TV Land; USA Network; VH1; Weather Channel.
Fee: $39.96 monthly.

Digital Basic Service
Subscribers: N.A.
Programming (via satellite): AmericanLife TV Network; BBC America; Bio; Bloomberg Television; Cooking Channel; Discovery Digital Networks; Do-It-Yourself; ESPN Now; ESPNews; Fox College Sports Atlantic; Fox College Sports Central; Fox College Sports Pacific; Fox Movie Channel; Fox Sports World; Fuse; G4; GAS; Golf Channel; Great American Country; GSN; History Channel International; Independent Film Channel; MTV Hits; MTV2; Music Choice; National Geographic Channel; NBA TV; Nick Jr.; NickToons TV; Outdoor Channel; Ovation; Speed Channel; Style Network; Sundance Channel; Toon Disney; Versus; VH1 Classic.
Fee: $6.00 monthly (per tier).

Digital Pay Service 1
Pay Units: N.A.
Programming (via satellite): Cinemax (multiplexed); Encore (multiplexed); Flix (multiplexed); HBO (multiplexed); Showtime (multiplexed); The Movie Channel (multiplexed).
Fee: $12.00 monthly (each).

Video-On-Demand: Yes

Pay-Per-View
NASCAR In Car (delivered digitally); MLB Extra Innings (delivered digitally); Fresh (delivered digitally); Shorteez (delivered digitally); Playboy TV (delivered digitally); Hot Choice (delivered digitally).

Internet Service
Operational: Yes.
Broadband Service: Road Runner.
Fee: $99.00 installation; $44.95 monthly.

Telephone Service
Digital: Operational
Fee: $74.95 installation; $44.95 monthly

Miles of Plant: 470.0 (coaxial); 71.0 (fiber optic). Homes passed: 39,150.
General Manager: Irene Christopher. Business Manager: Terry Goodman. Technical Operations Manager: Patrick Rafferty.
City fee: 5% of basic; 3% of pay service.
Ownership: Time Warner Cable (MSO).

THORNTOWN—Comcast Cable, 5330 E 65th St, Indianapolis, IN 46220. Phones: 765-832-6053; 765-832-3586. Fax: 317-275-6340. Web Site: http://www.comcast.com. Also serves Clarks Hill & Tippecanoe County (portions). ICA: IN0325.
TV Market Ranking: 16 (THORNTOWN); Below 100 (Clarks Hill, Tippecanoe County (portions)). Franchise award date: N.A. Franchise expiration date: N.A. Began: November 1, 1982.
Channel capacity: 78 (operating 2-way). Channels available but not in use: 17.

Basic Service
Subscribers: 800.
Programming (received off-air): WFYI (PBS) Indianapolis; WHMB-TV (IND) Indianapolis; WISH-TV (CBS) Indianapolis; WLFI-TV (CBS) Lafayette; WNDY-TV (MNT) Marion; WRTV (ABC) Indianapolis; WTHR (NBC) Indianapolis; WTTV (CW) Bloomington; WXIN (FOX) Indianapolis.
Programming (via satellite): ABC Family Channel; AMC; Animal Planet; Arts & Entertainment; Cartoon Network; CNN; Comedy Central; Country Music TV; Discovery Channel; ESPN; ESPN 2; ESPN Classic Sports; Food Network; Fox News Channel; Fox Sports Net; Hallmark Channel; Headline News; HGTV; History Channel; INSP; Lifetime; MSNBC; MTV; National Geographic Channel; Nickelodeon; QVC; Spike TV; Syfy; TBS Superstation; The Learning Channel; Travel Channel; Turner Classic Movies; Turner Network TV; TV Land; USA Network; VH1; Weather Channel; WGN America.
Fee: $29.95 installation; $36.95 monthly.

Digital Basic Service
Subscribers: N.A.
Programming (via satellite): BBC America; Bio; Bloomberg Television; Discovery Digital Networks; Discovery Kids Channel; DMX Music; ESPNews; Fox Movie Channel; Fox Sports World; G4; GAS; Golf Channel; GSN; History Channel International; Lifetime Movie Network; MTV Networks Digital Suite; Nick Jr.; NickToons TV; Outdoor Channel; Ovation; Speed Channel; Sundance Channel.

Pay Service 1
Pay Units: N.A.
Programming (via satellite): Cinemax; HBO.
Fee: $10.95 monthly (each).

Digital Pay Service 1
Pay Units: N.A.
Programming (via satellite): Cinemax (multiplexed); Encore; HBO (multiplexed);

Showtime (multiplexed); Starz (multiplexed); The Movie Channel (multiplexed).
Video-On-Demand: No
Internet Service
Operational: Yes.
Telephone Service
Digital: Operational
Miles of Plant: 29.0 (coaxial); None (fiber optic). Homes passed: 1,210.
City fee: 2% of basic gross.
Ownership: Comcast Cable Communications Inc. (MSO).

TIPTON (portions)—Formerly served by Country Cablevision. No longer in operation. ICA: IN0326.

TOPEKA—Lig TV, 414 S Cavin St, Ligonier, IN 46767. Phone: 260-894-7161. E-mail: support@ligtvonline.com. Web Site: http://www.ligtvonline.com. ICA: IN0198.
TV Market Ranking: 80 (TOPEKA). Franchise award date: N.A. Franchise expiration date: N.A. Began: May 1, 1987.
Channel capacity: 37 (not 2-way capable). Channels available but not in use: N.A.
Basic Service
Subscribers: 26.
Programming (received off-air): WANE-TV (CBS) Fort Wayne; WFFT-TV (FOX) Fort Wayne; WHME-TV (IND) South Bend; WISE-TV (MNT, NBC) Fort Wayne; WNDU-TV (NBC) South Bend; WNIT (PBS) South Bend; WPTA (ABC, CW) Fort Wayne; WSBT-TV (CBS, IND) South Bend; WSJV (FOX) Elkhart.
Programming (via satellite): ABC Family Channel; AMC; Arts & Entertainment; CNN; C-SPAN; Discovery Channel; ESPN; Lifetime; Nickelodeon; Spike TV; TBS Superstation; Turner Network TV; USA Network; VH1; Weather Channel; WGN America.
Fee: $15.98 monthly.
Pay Service 1
Pay Units: N.A.
Programming (via satellite): HBO; Showtime; The Movie Channel.
Fee: $10.00 installation; $8.95 monthly (TMC), $10.95 monthly (Showime), $12.95 monthly (HBO).
Video-On-Demand: No
Internet Service
Operational: No.
Telephone Service
Analog: Operational
Miles of Plant: 6.0 (coaxial); None (fiber optic). Homes passed: 511.
General Manager: Don Johnson.
Ownership: Ligonier Telephone Co. (MSO).

TRAFALGAR—Formerly served by CableDirect. No longer in operation. ICA: IN0327.

TROY—Avenue Broadband Communications, 2603 Hart St, Vincennes, IN 47591. Phones: 800-882-7185; 812-895-7676. Fax: 812-886-5017. Web Site: http://www.avenuebroadband.com. ICA: IN0207.
TV Market Ranking: Outside TV Markets (TROY). Franchise award date: February 16, 1983. Franchise expiration date: N.A. Began: September 1, 1983.
Channel capacity: 35 (not 2-way capable). Channels available but not in use: 5.
Basic Service
Subscribers: 55.
Programming (received off-air): WAZE-TV (CW) Madisonville; WDRB (FOX) Louisville; WEHT (ABC) Evansville; WEVV-TV (CBS, MNT) Evansville; WFIE (NBC) Evansville; WNIN (PBS) Evansville; WTVW (FOX) Evansville.
Programming (via satellite): TBS Superstation; WGN America.
Current originations: Government Access; Educational Access; Public Access.
Fee: $45.50 installation; $18.50 monthly; $1.79 converter.
Expanded Basic Service 1
Subscribers: 54.
Programming (via satellite): Animal Planet; Arts & Entertainment; CNN; Country Music TV; Discovery Channel; ESPN; ESPN 2; Headline News; History Channel; Lifetime; Nickelodeon; Spike TV; Syfy; Turner Classic Movies; Turner Network TV; TV Land; USA Network; VH1; Weather Channel.
Fee: $8.22 monthly.
Pay Service 1
Pay Units: 41.
Programming (via satellite): HBO.
Fee: $25.00 installation; $9.00 monthly.
Video-On-Demand: No
Internet Service
Operational: No.
Telephone Service
None
Miles of Plant: 5.0 (coaxial); None (fiber optic). Homes passed: 329.
Chief Executive Officer: Steve Lowe. Vice President & General Manager: Mary Iafrate. Vice President, Engineering: Jeff Spence. System Engineer: Bart Cotter.
City fee: 3% of gross.
Ownership: Buford Media Group LLC (MSO).

TWELVE MILE—Formerly served by CableDirect. No longer in operation. ICA: IN0328.

TWIN LAKES—Formerly served by CableDirect. No longer in operation. ICA: IN0329.

UNION CITY—Time Warner Cable. Now served by DAYTON, OH [OH0011]. ICA: IN0080.

URBANA—Formerly served by CableDirect. No longer in operation. ICA: IN0330.

VAN BUREN—Longview Communications, 12007 Sunrise Valley Dr, Ste 375, Reston, VA 20191. Phones: 866-611-6565 (Customer service); 703-476-9101. Fax: 703-476-9107. Web Site: http://www.longviewcomm.com. ICA: IN0331.
TV Market Ranking: 82 (VAN BUREN). Franchise award date: N.A. Franchise expiration date: N.A. Began: October 1, 1986.
Channel capacity: 40 (not 2-way capable). Channels available but not in use: N.A.
Basic Service
Subscribers: 60.
Programming (received off-air): WANE-TV (CBS) Fort Wayne; WFFT-TV (FOX) Fort Wayne; WIPB (PBS) Muncie; WISE-TV (MNT, NBC) Fort Wayne; WNDY-TV (MNT) Marion; WPTA (ABC, CW) Fort Wayne; WSOT-LP Marion; WTTV (CW) Bloomington.
Programming (via satellite): C-SPAN; C-SPAN 2; INSP; QVC.
Fee: $39.90 installation; $19.98 monthly.
Expanded Basic Service 1
Subscribers: N.A.
Programming (via satellite): ABC Family Channel; AMC; Animal Planet; Arts & Entertainment; CNN; Discovery Channel; Disney Channel; E! Entertainment Television; ESPN; ESPN 2; Fox News Channel; Great American Country; Headline News; History Channel; Lifetime; MSNBC; Speed Channel; TBS Superstation; The Learning Channel; Turner Network TV; USA Network; Weather Channel; WGN America.
Fee: $17.97 monthly.
Pay Service 1
Pay Units: N.A.
Programming (via satellite): Cinemax; HBO; Showtime; The Movie Channel.
Fee: $8.95 monthly (TMC), $10.95 monthly (Cinemax or Showtime), $12.95 monthly (HBO).
Video-On-Demand: No
Internet Service
Operational: No.
Telephone Service
None
Miles of Plant: 6.0 (coaxial); None (fiber optic). Homes passed: 429.
President: John Long. Senior Vice President: Marc W. Cohen. General Manager: Brandon Dickey. Technical Manager: Steve Boss.
Ownership: Longview Communications (MSO).

VEEDERSBURG—Comcast Cable, 5330 E 65th St, Indianapolis, IN 46220. Phone: 317-275-6370. Fax: 317-275-6340. Web Site: http://www.comcast.com. ICA: IN0145.
TV Market Ranking: Below 100 (VEEDERSBURG). Franchise award date: January 1, 1969. Franchise expiration date: N.A. Began: December 31, 1969.
Channel capacity: 36 (operating 2-way). Channels available but not in use: 7.
Basic Service
Subscribers: N.A. Included in Indianapolis
Programming (received off-air): WCIA (CBS) Champaign; WFYI (PBS) Indianapolis; WICD (ABC) Champaign; WISH-TV (CBS) Indianapolis; WLFI-TV (CBS) Lafayette; WRTV (ABC) Indianapolis; WTHR (NBC) Indianapolis; WTTK (IND) Kokomo; WXIN (FOX) Indianapolis.
Programming (via satellite): C-SPAN; C-SPAN 2; Home Shopping Network; WGN America.
Fee: $39.98 installation; $39.98 monthly.
Expanded Basic Service 1
Subscribers: N.A.
Programming (via satellite): ABC Family Channel; AMC; Animal Planet; Arts & Entertainment; CNBC; CNN; Comedy Central; Country Music TV; Discovery Channel; Disney Channel; E! Entertainment Television; ESPN; ESPN 2; ESPNews; Food Network; Golf Channel; HGTV; History Channel; Lifetime; MSNBC; MTV; Nickelodeon; Spike TV; TBS Superstation; The Learning Channel; Turner Network TV; USA Network; VH1; Weather Channel.
Digital Basic Service
Subscribers: N.A.
Programming (via satellite): BBC America; Bio; CMT Pure Country; Discovery Digital Networks; Encore; Flix; Fuse; G4; GAS; GSN; Halogen Network; History Channel International; Lifetime Movie Network; MTV Networks Digital Suite; Music Choice; National Geographic Channel; Nick Jr.; NickToons TV; Outdoor Channel; PBS Kids Sprout; SoapNet; Style Network; Sundance Channel; Syfy; Toon Disney; Trinity Broadcasting Network; Turner Classic Movies; TV Land.
Digital Pay Service 1
Pay Units: N.A.
Programming (via satellite): Cinemax (multiplexed); HBO (multiplexed); Showtime (multiplexed); Starz (multiplexed); The Movie Channel (multiplexed).
Pay-Per-View
iN DEMAND (delivered digitally); Playboy TV (delivered digitally); Fresh (delivered digitally); Shorteez (delivered digitally).
Internet Service
Operational: Yes.
Telephone Service
Digital: Operational
Miles of Plant: 15.0 (coaxial); None (fiber optic). Homes passed: 894. Total homes in franchised area: 900.
Vice President & General Manager: William (Rusty) Robertson. Vice President, Technical Operations: Max Woolsey. Vice President, Communications: Mark Apple. Marketing Director: Damion Miller.
City fee: 2% of basic.
Ownership: Comcast Cable Communications Inc. (MSO).

VEVAY—Formerly served by Adelphia Communications. Now served by LIGONIER, IN [IN0156]. ICA: IN0153.

VINCENNES—Avenue Broadband Communications, 2603 Hart St, Vincennes, IN 47591. Phones: 800-882-7185; 812-895-7676. Fax: 812-886-5017. Web Site: http://www.avenuebroadband.com. Also serves Bridgeport, Lawrence County (portions) & Lawrenceville, IL; Bicknell, Bruceville, Daviess County, Edwardsport, Freelandville, Knox County, Monroe City & Washington, IN. ICA: IN0035.
TV Market Ranking: Outside TV Markets (Bicknell, Bridgeport, Bruceville, Daviess County, Edwardsport, Freelandville, Knox County, Lawrence County (portions), Lawrenceville, Monroe City, VINCENNES, Washington).
Channel capacity: N.A. Channels available but not in use: N.A.
Basic Service
Subscribers: 13,070.
Programming (received off-air): WEHT (ABC) Evansville; WEVV-TV (CBS, MNT) Evansville; WFIE (NBC) Evansville; WFXW (FOX) Terre Haute; WNIN (PBS) Evansville; WTHI-TV (CBS) Terre Haute; WTTV (CW) Bloomington; WTWO (NBC) Terre Haute; WVUT (PBS) Vincennes; allband FM.
Programming (via satellite): C-SPAN; C-SPAN 2; Eternal Word TV Network; Home Shopping Network; INSP; Jewelry Television; QVC; ShopNBC; Trinity Broadcasting Network; WGN America.
Current originations: Public Access.
Fee: $29.95 installation; $17.20 monthly.
Expanded Basic Service 1
Subscribers: 11,893.
Programming (via satellite): ABC Family Channel; AMC; Animal Planet; Arts & Entertainment; BET Networks; Bravo; Car-

toon Network; CNBC; CNN; Comedy Central; Country Music TV; Discovery Channel; Disney Channel; E! Entertainment Television; ESPN; ESPN 2; FitTV; Food Network; Fox Sports Net Midwest; FX; G4; Golf Channel; GSN; Hallmark Channel; Headline News; HGTV; History Channel; ION Television; Lifetime; MSNBC; MTV; National Geographic Channel; Nickelodeon; Oxygen; Sci-Fi Channel; SoapNet; Speed Channel; Spike TV; TBS Superstation; The Learning Channel; Toon Disney; Travel Channel; truTV; Turner Classic Movies; Turner Network TV; TV Land; Univision; USA Network; Versus; VH1; Weather Channel.
Fee: $49.99 monthly.

Digital Basic Service
Subscribers: 4,280.
Programming (via satellite): BBC America; Bio; Discovery Digital Networks; Do-It-Yourself; ESPN Classic Sports; ESPNews; Fox Soccer; Fuse; History Channel International; Independent Film Channel; Lifetime Movie Network; MTV Networks Digital Suite; Music Choice; Nick Jr.; Nick Too; NickToons TV; Sundance Channel; TeenNick; TV Guide Interactive Inc.; WE tv.

Digital Pay Service 1
Pay Units: 897.
Programming (via satellite): Cinemax (multiplexed); HBO (multiplexed); Showtime (multiplexed).
Fee: $6.95 monthly (Cinemax or HBO).

Digital Pay Service 2
Pay Units: N.A.
Programming (via satellite): Encore (multiplexed); Flix; Starz (multiplexed); The Movie Channel (multiplexed).

Video-On-Demand: No

Pay-Per-View
iN DEMAND (delivered digitally); NHL Center Ice (delivered digitally); MLB Extra Innings (delivered digitally); Hot Choice (delivered digitally); Playboy TV (delivered digitally); Fresh (delivered digitally); Shorteez (delivered digitally).

Internet Service
Operational: Yes.
Subscribers: 5,888.
Broadband Service: In-house.
Fee: $46.95 installation; $33.99 monthly.

Telephone Service
Digital: Operational
Subscribers: 1,982.
Fee: $25.99 monthly

Miles of Plant: 481.0 (coaxial); None (fiber optic). Homes passed: 27,032.
Chief Executive Officer: Steve Lowe. Vice President & General Manager: Mary Iafrate. Vice President, Engineering: Jeff Spence. System Engineer: Bart Cotter.
City fee: 2% of gross.
Ownership: Buford Media Group LLC (MSO).

WABASH—Comcast Cable, 720 Taylor St, Fort Wayne, IN 46802-5144. Phones: 317-275-6370 (Indianapolis office); 260-458-5103. Fax: 206-458-5138. Web Site: http://www.comcast.com. Also serves Wabash County (portions). ICA: IN0045.
TV Market Ranking: 82 (WABASH, Wabash County (portions)). Franchise award date: August 1, 1962. Franchise expiration date: N.A. Began: April 1, 1963.
Channel capacity: 76 (operating 2-way). Channels available but not in use: None.

Basic Service
Subscribers: N.A. Included in Indianapolis
Programming (received off-air): WANE-TV (CBS) Fort Wayne; WFFT-TV (FOX) Fort Wayne; WFWA (PBS) Fort Wayne; WFYI (PBS) Indianapolis; WISE-TV (MNT, NBC) Fort Wayne; WISH-TV (CBS) Indianapolis; WNDU-TV (NBC) South Bend; WNDY-TV (MNT) Marion; WPTA (ABC, CW) Fort Wayne; WRTV (ABC) Indianapolis; WTHR (NBC) Indianapolis; WTTK (IND) Kokomo.
Programming (via microwave): WGN-TV (CW, IND) Chicago.
Programming (via satellite): C-SPAN; C-SPAN 2; Home Shopping Network; QVC; The Comcast Network; TV Guide Network.
Current originations: Educational Access; Public Access.
Fee: $31.99 installation.

Expanded Basic Service 1
Subscribers: N.A.
Programming (via satellite): ABC Family Channel; AMC; Animal Planet; Arts & Entertainment; Cartoon Network; CNBC; CNN; Comedy Central; Country Music TV; Discovery Channel; Disney Channel; E! Entertainment Television; ESPN; ESPN 2; Food Network; Fox News Channel; Fox Sports Net Midwest; FX; G4; GalaVision; Golf Channel; GSN; Hallmark Channel; Headline News; HGTV; History Channel; Lifetime; MSNBC; MTV; Nickelodeon; Speed Channel; Spike TV; Style Network; Syfy; TBS Superstation; The Learning Channel; Toon Disney; Travel Channel; Trinity Broadcasting Network; truTV; Turner Classic Movies; Turner Network TV; TV Land; USA Network; Versus; VH1; Weather Channel.
Fee: $47.98 monthly.

Digital Basic Service
Subscribers: N.A.
Programming (via satellite): Arts & Entertainment HD; BBC America; Bio; CBS College Sports Network; CMT Pure Country; Cooking Channel; C-SPAN 3; Current; Discovery Digital Networks; Discovery HD Theater; Do-It-Yourself; Encore (multiplexed); ESPN 2 HD; ESPN HD; ESPNews; Eternal Word TV Network; Flix; Fox Reality Channel; Fox Soccer; G4; GAS; Gol TV; History Channel International; INHD; Lifetime Movie Network; MTV Networks Digital Suite; Music Choice; National Geographic Channel; National Geographic Channel HD Network; NFL Network; Nick Jr.; Nick Too; NickToons TV; Oxygen; Palladia; PBS Kids Sprout; SoapNet; Sundance Channel; Tennis Channel; The Word Network; Turner Network TV HD; TV One; TVG Network; Universal HD; Versus HD; Weatherscan.
Fee: $14.95 monthly.

Digital Pay Service 1
Pay Units: N.A.
Programming (via satellite): Canales N; Cinemax (multiplexed); Cinemax HD; HBO (multiplexed); HBO HD; Playboy TV; Showtime (multiplexed); Showtime HD; Starz (multiplexed); Starz HDTV; The Movie Channel (multiplexed).
Fee: $16.99 monthly (each).

Video-On-Demand: No

Pay-Per-View
Addressable homes: 1,143.
iN DEMAND, Addressable: Yes; iN DEMAND (delivered digitally); Playboy TV (delivered digitally); Sports PPV (delivered digitally); NBA League Pass (delivered digitally).

Internet Service
Operational: Yes.
Broadband Service: Comcast High Speed Internet.
Fee: $42.95 monthly; $15.00 modem lease; $129.95 modem purchase.

Telephone Service
Digital: Operational
Fee: $44.95 monthly

Homes passed: 7,070. Miles of plant included in Fort Wayne
Regional Vice President: Scott Tenney. Technical Operations Director: Bennie Logan. Engineering Manager: Tom Stuckholz. Vice President, Marketing: Aaron Geisel. Marketing Manager: Marci Hefley. Vice President, Communications: Mark Apple.
City fee: 3% of gross.
Ownership: Comcast Cable Communications Inc. (MSO).

WADESVILLE—NewWave Communications, 318 N 4th St, Vandalia, IL 62471. Phone: 573-472-9500. Fax: 618-283-4483. Web Site: http://www.newwavecom.com. Also serves White County, IL; New Harmony, Posey County & Vanderburgh County (western portion), IN. ICA: IN0301.
TV Market Ranking: 69 (Carmi, White County (portions)); 86 (Crossville, New Harmony, Posey County, Vanderburgh County (western portion), WADESVILLE); Below 100 (White County (portions)); Outside TV Markets (White County (portions)). Franchise award date: N.A. Franchise expiration date: N.A. Began: November 1, 1984.
Channel capacity: 41 (not 2-way capable). Channels available but not in use: 6.

Basic Service
Subscribers: 447.
Programming (received off-air): WEHT (ABC) Evansville; WEVV-TV (CBS, MNT) Evansville; WFIE (NBC) Evansville; WNIN (PBS) Evansville; WTVW (FOX) Evansville.
Programming (via satellite): C-SPAN; Eternal Word TV Network; History Channel; QVC; TBS Superstation; Trinity Broadcasting Network; WGN America.
Fee: $41.11 installation; $20.74 monthly.

Expanded Basic Service 1
Subscribers: 398.
Programming (via satellite): ABC Family Channel; AMC; Arts & Entertainment; Bravo; CNN; Comedy Central; Discovery Channel; Disney Channel; E! Entertainment Television; ESPN; Fox News Channel; Fox Sports Net Midwest; FX; HGTV; Lifetime; Nickelodeon; Spike TV; Turner Network TV; USA Network; VH1; Weather Channel.

Digital Basic Service
Subscribers: N.A.
Programming (via satellite): BBC America; Bloomberg Television; Discovery Digital Networks; ESPN 2; ESPN Classic Sports; ESPNews; FitTV; Fox Sports World; G4; GAS; Golf Channel; GSN; Halogen Network; Independent Film Channel; MTV Networks Digital Suite; Music Choice; National Geographic Channel; Nick Jr.; Nick Too; NickToons TV; Outdoor Channel; Speed Channel; Sundance Channel; Syfy; Turner Classic Movies; TV Guide Interactive Inc.; Versus; WE tv.

Digital Pay Service 1
Pay Units: N.A.
Programming (via satellite): Cinemax (multiplexed); Encore (multiplexed); Flix; HBO (multiplexed); Showtime (multiplexed); Starz; The Movie Channel (multiplexed).

Video-On-Demand: No

Pay-Per-View
iN DEMAND (delivered digitally); Playboy TV (delivered digitally); Fresh (delivered digitally); Shorteez (delivered digitally).

Internet Service
Operational: No.

Telephone Service
None

Miles of Plant: 172.0 (coaxial); None (fiber optic). Homes passed: 2,482.
General Manager: Bill Flowers. Technical Operations Manager: Chris Mooday.
Ownership: NewWave Communications (MSO).

WAKARUSA—Comcast Cable. Now served by SOUTH BEND, IN [IN0005]. ICA: IN0149.

WALKERTON—Mediacom, 109 E 5th St, Ste A, Auburn, IN 46706. Phone: 260-927-3015. Fax: 260-347-4433. Web Site: http://www.mediacomcable.com. Also serves Koontz Lake, La Paz, Lakeville, Marshall County, North Liberty & St. Joseph County. ICA: IN0081.
TV Market Ranking: 80 (Koontz Lake, La Paz, Lakeville, Marshall County, North Liberty, St. Joseph County, WALKERTON). Franchise award date: N.A. Franchise expiration date: N.A. Began: July 20, 1996.
Channel capacity: N.A. Channels available but not in use: N.A.

Basic Service
Subscribers: 1,571.
Programming (received off-air): WBND-LP South Bend; WCWW-LP (CW) South Bend; WFLD (FOX) Chicago; WHME-TV (IND) South Bend; WNDU-TV (NBC) South Bend; WNIT (PBS) South Bend; WSBT-TV (CBS, IND) South Bend; WSJV (FOX) Elkhart; WYIN (PBS) Gary.
Programming (via satellite): TBS Superstation; WGN America.
Fee: $45.00 installation; $20.95 monthly.

Expanded Basic Service 1
Subscribers: 985.
Programming (via satellite): ABC Family Channel; AMC; Animal Planet; Arts & Entertainment; Cartoon Network; CNBC; CNN; Comcast SportsNet Chicago; Comedy Central; Country Music TV; C-SPAN; C-SPAN 2; Discovery Channel; Disney Channel; ESPN; ESPN 2; Food Network; Fox News Channel; FX; Hallmark Channel; Headline News; HGTV; History Channel; Home Shopping Network; Lifetime; MSNBC; MTV; Nickelodeon; QVC; Speed Channel; Spike TV; Syfy; The Learning Channel; Travel Channel; Trinity Broadcasting Network; truTV; Turner Network TV; TV Guide Network; TV Land; USA Network; VH1; Weather Channel.
Fee: $34.00 monthly.

Digital Basic Service
Subscribers: N.A.
Programming (via satellite): ABC News Now; AmericanLife TV Network; BBC America; Bio; Bloomberg Television; CCTV-9 (CCTV International); Discovery Health Channel; Discovery Home Channel; Discovery Kids Channel; Discovery Military Channel; ESPN 2 HD; ESPN HD; ESPN U; ESPNews; Fox Movie Channel; Fox Soccer; Fuse; G4; Golf Channel; GSN; Halogen Network; History Channel International; Independent Film Channel; ION Life; Lifetime Movie Network; Music Choice; National Geographic Channel; Nick Jr.; Outdoor Channel; Qubo; ReelzChannel; Science Channel; Style Network; TeenNick; Turner Classic Movies; TVG Network; Versus; WE tv.
Fee: $9.00 monthly.

Digital Expanded Basic Service
Subscribers: N.A.
Programming (via satellite): CNN HD; Discovery HD Theater; HDNet; HDNet Movies; TBS in HD; Turner Network TV HD.
Fee: $6.95 monthly.

Digital Pay Service 1
Pay Units: N.A.
Programming (via satellite): Cinemax (multiplexed); Encore (multiplexed); Flix; HBO (multiplexed); HBO HD; Showtime (multiplexed); Showtime HD; Starz (multiplexed); Starz HDTV; Sundance Channel; The Movie Channel (multiplexed); The Movie Channel HD.

Fee: $11.95 monthly (HBO, Cinemax, Starz/ Encore or Showtime/TMC).
Video-On-Demand: Yes
Pay-Per-View
IN DEMAND (delivered digitally); TenClips, Ten by the Movie & Ten BLOX (delivered digitally).
Internet Service
Operational: Yes.
Broadband Service: Mediacom High Speed Internet.
Fee: $59.95 installation; $40.95 monthly.
Telephone Service
Digital: Operational
Fee: $39.95 installation; $39.95 monthly
Homes passed & miles of plant included in Kendallville, IN
Operations Director: Joe Poffenberger. Technical Operations Manager: Craig Grey.
City fee: 3% of gross.
Ownership: Mediacom LLC (MSO).

WALTON—Longview Communications, 12007 Sunrise Valley Dr, Ste 375, Reston, VA 20191. Phones: 866-611-6565 (Customer service); 703-476-9101. Fax: 703-476-9107. Web Site: http://www.longviewcomm.com. ICA: IN0181.
TV Market Ranking: Below 100 (WALTON). Franchise award date: June 1, 1984. Franchise expiration date: N.A. Began: N.A.
Channel capacity: 31 (not 2-way capable). Channels available but not in use: None.
Basic Service
Subscribers: 41.
Programming (received off-air): WFYI (PBS) Indianapolis; WISH-TV (CBS) Indianapolis; WLFI-TV (CBS) Lafayette; WRTV (ABC) Indianapolis; WTHR (NBC) Indianapolis; WTTK (IND) Kokomo; WXIN (FOX) Indianapolis.
Programming (via satellite): C-SPAN; C-SPAN 2; QVC; Trinity Broadcasting Network.
Fee: $39.90 installation; $17.98 monthly.
Expanded Basic Service 1
Subscribers: N.A.
Programming (via satellite): ABC Family Channel; AMC; Animal Planet; Arts & Entertainment; CNN; Discovery Channel; Disney Channel; E! Entertainment Television; ESPN; ESPN 2; Headline News; History Channel; Lifetime; Nickelodeon; Spike TV; TBS Superstation; The Learning Channel; Travel Channel; Turner Network TV; USA Network; Weather Channel; WGN America.
Fee: $17.97 monthly.
Pay Service 1
Pay Units: N.A.
Programming (via satellite): Showtime; The Movie Channel.
Fee: $8.95 monthly (TMC), $10.95 monthly (Showtime).
Video-On-Demand: No
Internet Service
Operational: No.
Telephone Service
None
Miles of Plant: 5.0 (coaxial); None (fiber optic). Homes passed: 524.
President: John Long. Senior Vice President: Marc W. Cohen. General Manager: Brandon Dickey. Technical Manager: Steve Boss.
Ownership: Longview Communications (MSO).

WANATAH—Mediacom. Now served by ROSELAWN, IN [IN0316]. ICA: IN0333.

WARREN—Warren Cable, PO Box 330, 426 N Wayne St, Warren, IN 46792. Phones: 260-375-2111; 260-375-2115. Fax: 260-375-2244. Web Site: http://www.citznet.com. ICA: IN0172.
TV Market Ranking: 82 (WARREN). Franchise award date: November 22, 1983. Franchise expiration date: N.A. Began: July 1, 1985.
Channel capacity: 36 (operating 2-way). Channels available but not in use: 1.
Basic Service
Subscribers: 775.
Programming (received off-air): WANE-TV (CBS) Fort Wayne; WFFT-TV (FOX) Fort Wayne; WFWA (PBS) Fort Wayne; WIPB (PBS) Muncie; WISH-TV (CBS) Indianapolis; WNDY-TV (MNT) Marion; WPTA (ABC, CW) Fort Wayne; WTHR (NBC) Indianapolis; WTTK (IND) Kokomo.
Programming (via satellite): ABC Family Channel; AMC; Arts & Entertainment; CNN; Country Music TV; C-SPAN; Discovery Channel; Disney Channel; ESPN; ESPN 2; Fox News Channel; HGTV; History Channel; Lifetime; Nickelodeon; Spike TV; TBS Superstation; The Learning Channel; Travel Channel; Turner Network TV; USA Network; Weather Channel; WGN America.
Fee: $15.00 installation; $18.00 monthly; $1.00 converter; $7.00 additional installation.
Pay Service 1
Pay Units: 189.
Programming (via satellite): HBO; Showtime.
Fee: $5.00 installation; $10.00 monthly (HBO or Showtime), $15.00 monthly (HBO & Showtime).
Internet Service
Operational: No.
Telephone Service
None
Miles of Plant: 28.0 (coaxial); 705.0 (fiber optic). Homes passed: 893. Total homes in franchised area: 893.
Manager: Gordon Layman. Marketing Director: Ellen Layman. Chief Technician: Jack Roberts.
Ownership: Citizens Telephone Corp.

WARSAW—Comcast Cable. Now served by SOUTH BEND, IN [IN0005]. ICA: IN0030.

WASHINGTON—Charter Communications. Now served by VINCENNES, IN [IN0035]. ICA: IN0055.

WAVELAND—Formerly served by CableDirect. No longer in operation. ICA: IN0332.

WAYNETOWN—Indiana Communications, PO Box 617, Boswell, IN 47921. Phone: 888-610-1119. Web Site: http://www.indcomm.net. ICA: IN0184.
TV Market Ranking: Below 100 (WAYNETOWN). Franchise award date: May 1, 1981. Franchise expiration date: N.A. Began: May 17, 1982.
Channel capacity: 36 (not 2-way capable). Channels available but not in use: 1.
Basic Service
Subscribers: 62.
Programming (received off-air): WFYI (PBS) Indianapolis; WHMB-TV (IND) Indianapolis; WICD (ABC) Champaign; WISH-TV (CBS) Indianapolis; WLFI-TV (CBS) Lafayette; WNDY-TV (MNT) Marion; WRTV (ABC) Indianapolis; WTHR (NBC) Indianapolis; WTTK (IND) Kokomo; WTTV (CW) Bloomington; WXIN (FOX) Indianapolis; 1 FM.
Programming (via satellite): Trinity Broadcasting Network.
Fee: $25.00 installation; $17.98 monthly.

Expanded Basic Service 1
Subscribers: N.A.
Programming (via satellite): ABC Family Channel; AMC; Animal Planet; Arts & Entertainment; Cartoon Network; CNN; Discovery Channel; Disney Channel; ESPN; ESPN 2; Headline News; HGTV; Lifetime; Nickelodeon; TBS Superstation; The Learning Channel; Travel Channel; Turner Network TV; USA Network; Weather Channel; WGN America.
Fee: $17.97 monthly.
Pay Service 1
Pay Units: N.A.
Programming (via satellite): Showtime; The Movie Channel.
Fee: $10.00 installation; $9.95 monthly (TMC), $10.95 monthly (Showtime).
Video-On-Demand: No
Internet Service
Operational: No.
Telephone Service
None
Miles of Plant: 13.0 (coaxial); None (fiber optic). Homes passed: 458. Total homes in franchised area: 458.
Manager: Joe Young.
City fee: 3% of basic gross.
Ownership: Park TV & Electronics Inc. (MSO).

WEST LEBANON—Indiana Communications, PO Box 617, Boswell, IN 47921. Phone: 888-610-1119. Web Site: http://www.indcomm.net. ICA: IN0197.
TV Market Ranking: Below 100 (WEST LEBANON). Franchise award date: N.A. Franchise expiration date: N.A. Began: November 1, 1988.
Channel capacity: 31 (not 2-way capable). Channels available but not in use: N.A.
Basic Service
Subscribers: 96.
Programming (received off-air): WCCU (FOX) Urbana; WCIA (CBS) Champaign; WICD (ABC) Champaign; WILL-TV (PBS) Urbana; WLFI-TV (CBS) Lafayette; WRTV (ABC) Indianapolis; WTHR (NBC) Indianapolis; WTTV (CW) Bloomington.
Fee: $39.90 installation; $15.98 monthly.
Expanded Basic Service 1
Subscribers: N.A.
Programming (via satellite): ABC Family Channel; CNN; Discovery Channel; Disney Channel; ESPN; Headline News; MTV; Nickelodeon; TBS Superstation; Turner Network TV; VH1; WGN America.
Fee: $17.97 monthly.
Pay Service 1
Pay Units: N.A.
Programming (via satellite): Cinemax; HBO; Showtime; The Movie Channel.
Fee: $8.95 monthly (TMC), $10.95 monthly (Cinemax or Showtime), $12.95 monthly (HBO).
Video-On-Demand: No
Internet Service
Operational: No.
Telephone Service
None
Miles of Plant: 4.0 (coaxial); None (fiber optic). Additional miles planned: 1.0 (coaxial). Homes passed: 340.
Manager: Joe Young.
Ownership: Park TV & Electronics Inc. (MSO).

WESTPORT—Now served by COLUMBUS, IN [IN0022]. ICA: IN0166.

WHEATFIELD—Mediacom. Now served by ROSELAWN, IN [IN0316]. ICA: IN0334.

WHITESTOWN—Formerly served by Longview Communications. No longer in operation. ICA: IN0160.

WILKINSON—Insight Communications. Now served by NOBLESVILLE, IN [IN0020]. ICA: IN0148.

WILLIAMSBURG—Formerly served by CableDirect. No longer in operation. ICA: IN0335.

WILLIAMSBURG—Windjammer Cable, 4400 PGA Blvd, Ste 902, Palm Beach Gardens, FL 33410. Phones: 877-450-5558; 561-775-1208. Fax: 561-775-7811. Web Site: http://www.windjammercable.com. ICA: IN0360.
TV Market Ranking: Below 100 (WILLIAMSBURG). Franchise award date: N.A. Franchise expiration date: N.A. Began: N.A.
Channel capacity: 37 (not 2-way capable). Channels available but not in use: N.A.
Basic Service
Subscribers: N.A. Included in Dayton, OH
Programming (received off-air): WDTN (NBC) Dayton; WHIO-TV (CBS) Dayton; WISH-TV (CBS) Indianapolis; WKEF (ABC) Dayton; WKOI-TV (TBN) Richmond; WPTO (PBS) Oxford; WRGT-TV (FOX, MNT) Dayton; WSTR-TV (MNT) Cincinnati; WTTV (CW) Bloomington; WXIX-TV (FOX) Newport.
Programming (via satellite): C-SPAN; QVC; TBS Superstation; WGN America.
Fee: $45.86 installation; $13.57 monthly; $31.81 additional installation.
Expanded Basic Service 1
Subscribers: N.A.
Programming (via satellite): ABC Family Channel; AMC; Arts & Entertainment; CNN; Country Music TV; Discovery Channel; Disney Channel; E! Entertainment Television; ESPN; ESPN 2; Headline News; History Channel; Lifetime; Nickelodeon; Spike TV; The Learning Channel; Turner Network TV; USA Network; VH1; Weather Channel.
Fee: $18.34 monthly.
Pay Service 1
Pay Units: N.A.
Programming (via satellite): HBO; Showtime.
Fee: $10.95 monthly (each).
Internet Service
Operational: No.
Telephone Service
None
Homes passed and miles of plant (coax) included in Dayton, OH
General Manager: Timothy Evard. Operations Director: Belinda Graham. Engineering Di-

rector: Mike Earehart. Finance & Accounting Director: Cindy Johnson.
Ownership: Windjammer Communications LLC (MSO).

WINAMAC—TV Cable of Rensselaer Inc., PO Box 319, 215 W Kellner Blvd, Ste 19, Rensselaer, IN 47978-2665. Phones: 800-621-2344; 219-866-7101. Fax: 219-866-5785. E-mail: tvcable@winamac.tv. Web Site: http://www.winamac.tv. Also serves Bruce Lake, Fulton County (western portion), Pulaski County (southern portion) & Star City. ICA: IN0130.
TV Market Ranking: Below 100 (Fulton County (western portion) (portions), Pulaski County (southern portion) (portions)); Outside TV Markets (Bruce Lake, Fulton County (western portion) (portions), Pulaski County (southern portion) (portions), Star City, WINAMAC). Franchise award date: March 1, 1970. Franchise expiration date: N.A. Began: March 1, 1971.
Channel capacity: 78 (operating 2-way). Channels available but not in use: 14.

Basic Service
Subscribers: 1,297.
Programming (received off-air): WBND-LP South Bend; WCIU-TV (IND) Chicago; WCWW-LP (CW) South Bend; WGN-TV (CW, IND) Chicago; WHME-TV (IND) South Bend; WLFI-TV (CBS) Lafayette; WLS-TV (ABC) Chicago; WNDU-TV (NBC) South Bend; WNIT (PBS) South Bend; WSBT-TV (CBS, IND) South Bend; WSJV (FOX) Elkhart; WTHR (NBC) Indianapolis; WTTK (IND) Kokomo; WTTW (PBS) Chicago.
Programming (via satellite): ABC Family Channel; AMC; Animal Planet; Arts & Entertainment; Cartoon Network; CNBC; CNN; Comcast SportsNet Chicago; Comedy Central; Country Music TV; C-SPAN; Discovery Channel; Discovery Health Channel; Disney Channel; E! Entertainment Television; ESPN; ESPN 2; ESPN Classic Sports; Food Network; Fox Movie Channel; Fox News Channel; FX; Hallmark Channel; Headline News; HGTV; History Channel; Home Shopping Network; Lifetime; MSNBC; MTV; National Geographic Channel; Nickelodeon; QVC; ShopNBC; SoapNet; Speed Channel; Spike TV; Syfy; TBS Superstation; The Learning Channel; The Sportsman Channel; Toon Disney; truTV; Turner Classic Movies; Turner Network TV; TV Land; USA Network; VH1; WE tv; Weather Channel.
Current originations: Public Access.
Fee: $10.00 installation; $37.62 monthly; $2.30 converter.

Pay Service 1
Pay Units: 91.
Programming (via satellite): HBO.
Fee: $5.00 installation; $12.65 monthly.

Pay Service 2
Pay Units: 47.
Programming (via satellite): Cinemax.
Fee: $5.00 installation; $8.20 monthly.

Pay Service 3
Pay Units: 51.
Programming (via satellite): Encore; Starz.
Fee: $5.00 installation; $9.95 monthly.

Video-On-Demand: No

Pay-Per-View
Addressable homes: 1,297.
iN DEMAND, Addressable: Yes; special events, Addressable: Yes.

Internet Service
Operational: Yes. Began: January 1, 2004.
Subscribers: 5.
Broadband Service: Nortwest Indiana Internet Services (NWIIS).
Fee: $30.00 installation; $19.95-$39.95 monthly; $4.95 modem lease; $69.95 modem purchase.

Telephone Service
None
Miles of Plant: 30.0 (coaxial); None (fiber optic). Homes passed: 1,650.
Vice President: Eric Galbreath. Chief Technician: Jason Crissinger. Customer Service Representative: Lisa Cawby.
Ownership: Theodore W. Filson (MSO).

WINCHESTER—Comcast Cable, 5330 E 65th St, Indianapolis, IN 46220. Phone: 317-275-6370. Fax: 317-275-6340. Web Site: http://www.comcast.com. Also serves Lynn, Ridgeville & Saratoga. ICA: IN0068.
TV Market Ranking: Below 100 (Lynn, Ridgeville, Saratoga, WINCHESTER). Franchise award date: N.A. Franchise expiration date: N.A. Began: April 1, 1967.
Channel capacity: N.A. Channels available but not in use: N.A.

Basic Service
Subscribers: N.A. Included in Anderson
Programming (received off-air): WDTN (NBC) Dayton; WFFT-TV (FOX) Fort Wayne; WHIO-TV (CBS) Dayton; WIPB (PBS) Muncie; WISH-TV (CBS) Indianapolis; WKOI-TV (TBN) Richmond; WNDY-TV (MNT) Marion; WRTV (ABC) Indianapolis; WTHR (NBC) Indianapolis; WTTV (CW) Bloomington; WXIN (FOX) Indianapolis; allband FM.
Programming (via satellite): C-SPAN; C-SPAN 2; Home Shopping Network; LWS Local Weather Station; QVC; WGN America.
Fee: $1.55 converter.

Expanded Basic Service 1
Subscribers: 2,219.
Programming (via satellite): ABC Family Channel; AMC; Animal Planet; Arts & Entertainment; BET Networks; Bravo; Cartoon Network; CNBC; CNN; Comedy Central; Country Music TV; Discovery Channel; Disney Channel; E! Entertainment Television; ESPN; ESPN 2; Eternal Word TV Network; Food Network; Fox News Channel; Fox Sports Net Midwest; Headline News; HGTV; History Channel; Lifetime; MSNBC; MTV; Nickelodeon; Oxygen; Speed Channel; Spike TV; Syfy; TBS Superstation; The Learning Channel; Travel Channel; Turner Network TV; TV Guide Network; TV Land; USA Network; VH1; Weather Channel.
Fee: $51.74 monthly.

Digital Basic Service
Subscribers: 641.
Programming (via satellite): BBC America; Bio; Bloomberg Television; CNBC; C-SPAN 3; Discovery Digital Networks; DMX Music; Do-It-Yourself; Encore; ESPN Classic Sports; ESPNews; Fox Sports World; G4; GAS; Golf Channel; GSN; Halogen Network; History Channel International; Independent Film Channel; Lifetime Movie Network; MTV2; National Geographic Channel; Nick Jr.; Nick Too; Ovation; SoapNet; Style Network; Sundance Channel; Toon Disney; truTV; Turner Classic Movies; Versus; WE tv.
Fee: $17.00 monthly.

Digital Pay Service 1
Pay Units: N.A.
Programming (via satellite): Cinemax (multiplexed); Flix; HBO (multiplexed); Showtime (multiplexed); Starz (multiplexed); The Movie Channel (multiplexed).
Fee: $10.00 monthly (Cinemax or Starz), $13.00 monthly (HBO or Showtime).

Video-On-Demand: No

Pay-Per-View
Addressable homes: 641.
iN DEMAND, Fee: $3.99, Addressable: Yes; Playboy TV (delivered digitally); Fresh (delivered digitally); iN DEMAND (delivered digitally).

Internet Service
Operational: Yes.
Subscribers: 279.
Broadband Service: Comcast High Speed Internet.
Fee: $99.95 installation; $44.95 monthly; $15.00 modem lease; $99.95 modem purchase.

Telephone Service
Analog: Not Operational
Digital: Operational
Miles of Plant: 94.0 (coaxial); None (fiber optic). Additional miles planned: 27.0 (coaxial). Homes passed: 4,500. Total homes in franchised area: 4,875.
Regional Vice President: Scott Tenney. Regional Vice President, Technical Operations: Max Woolsey. Regional Vice President, Marketing: Aaron Geisel. Regional Vice President, Communications: Mark Apple.
City fee: 1% of gross.
Ownership: Comcast Cable Communications Inc. (MSO).

WINSLOW—Avenue Broadband Communications, 2603 Hart St, Vincennes, IN 47591. Phones: 800-882-7185; 812-895-7676. Fax: 812-886-5017. Web Site: http://www.avenuebroadband.com. Also serves Arthur, Oakland City & Petersburg. ICA: IN0118.
TV Market Ranking: 86 (Arthur, Oakland City, WINSLOW); Outside TV Markets (Petersburg). Franchise award date: December 4, 1979. Franchise expiration date: N.A. Began: March 1, 1980.
Channel capacity: N.A. Channels available but not in use: N.A.

Basic Service
Subscribers: 1,818 Includes Oakland.
Programming (received off-air): WEHT (ABC) Evansville; WEVV-TV (CBS, MNT) Evansville; WFIE (NBC) Evansville; WNIN (PBS) Evansville; WTVW (FOX) Evansville; WVUT (PBS) Vincennes.
Programming (via satellite): C-SPAN; Home Shopping Network; QVC; Trinity Broadcasting Network; WGN America.
Fee: $29.99 installation; $1.30 converter.

Expanded Basic Service 1
Subscribers: 1,727.
Programming (via satellite): ABC Family Channel; AMC; Animal Planet; Arts & Entertainment; CNBC; Country Music TV; Disney Channel; E! Entertainment Television; ESPN 2; Food Network; Fox News Channel; Fox Sports Net Midwest; HGTV; History Channel; Lifetime; MTV; National Geographic Channel; Oxygen; SoapNet; Speed Channel; Syfy; TBS Superstation; The Learning Channel; Toon Disney; truTV; Turner Classic Movies; TV Land; Versus; VH1; Weather Channel.
Fee: $49.99 monthly.

Expanded Basic Service 2
Subscribers: 1,514.
Programming (via satellite): CNN; Comedy Central; Discovery Channel; ESPN; Headline News; Nickelodeon; Spike TV; Turner Network TV; USA Network.
Fee: $8.90 monthly.

Digital Basic Service
Subscribers: N.A.
Programming (via satellite): American-Life TV Network; BBC America; Bio; Bloomberg Television; Bravo; Discovery Digital Networks; DMX Music; FitTV; Fox Movie Channel; Fox Sports World; Fuse; G4; GAS; Golf Channel; GSN; Halogen Network; History Channel International; Independent Film Channel; Lifetime Movie Network; MTV Networks Digital Suite; Nick Jr.; Outdoor Channel; ShopNBC; TV Guide Interactive Inc.; WE tv.

Pay Service 1
Pay Units: 236.
Programming (via satellite): HBO.
Fee: $20.00 installation; $9.50 monthly.

Pay Service 2
Pay Units: N.A.
Programming (via satellite): Cinemax.

Pay Service 3
Pay Units: 279.
Programming (via satellite): Showtime.
Fee: $25.00 installation; $9.50 monthly.

Digital Pay Service 1
Pay Units: N.A.
Programming (via satellite): Cinemax (multiplexed); Encore (multiplexed); Flix; HBO (multiplexed); Showtime (multiplexed); Starz (multiplexed); The Movie Channel (multiplexed).

Video-On-Demand: No

Pay-Per-View
iN DEMAND (delivered digitally); Hot Choice (delivered digitally); Playboy TV (delivered digitally); Fresh (delivered digitally); Shorteez (delivered digitally).

Internet Service
Operational: Yes.

Telephone Service
Digital: Operational
Miles of Plant: 96.0 (coaxial); None (fiber optic). Homes passed: 6,097.
Chief Executive Officer: Steve Lowe. Vice President & General Manager: Mary Iafrate. Vice President, Engineering: Jeff Spence. System Engineer: Bart Cotter.
City fee: 3% of basic.
Ownership: Buford Media Group LLC (MSO).

WORTHINGTON—Indiana Communications, PO Box 617, Boswell, IN 47921. Phone: 888-610-1119. Web Site: http://www.indcomm.net. ICA: IN0138.
TV Market Ranking: 16 (WORTHINGTON). Franchise award date: N.A. Franchise expiration date: N.A. Began: June 1, 1984.
Channel capacity: N.A. Channels available but not in use: N.A.

Basic Service
Subscribers: 225.
Programming (received off-air): WFXW (FOX) Terre Haute; WRTV (ABC) Indianapolis; WTHI-TV (CBS) Terre Haute; WTHR (NBC) Indianapolis; WTIU (PBS) Bloomington; WTTV (CW) Bloomington; WTWO (NBC) Terre Haute; WVUT (PBS) Vincennes.
Programming (via satellite): C-SPAN; QVC; Trinity Broadcasting Network.
Fee: $35.95 installation; $19.98 monthly; $10.00 additional installation.

Expanded Basic Service 1
Subscribers: N.A.
Programming (via satellite): ABC Family Channel; AMC; Animal Planet; Arts & Entertainment; Bravo; Cartoon Network; CNBC; CNN; Comedy Central; Discovery Channel; Disney Channel; E! Entertainment Television; ESPN; ESPN 2; Food Network; Fox News Channel; Fox Sports Net Midwest; FX; Great American Country; Hallmark Channel;

Hallmark Movie Channel; Headline News; HGTV; History Channel; Lifetime; MSNBC; Nickelodeon; Syfy; TBS Superstation; The Learning Channel; Travel Channel; truTV; Turner Network TV; USA Network; WE tv; Weather Channel; WGN America.
Fee: $20.97 monthly.

Digital Basic Service
Subscribers: N.A.
Programming (via satellite): AmericanLife TV Network; BBC America; Bio; Bloomberg Television; Discovery Health Channel; Discovery Military Channel; Discovery Planet Green; DMX Music; Encore (multiplexed); ESPN Classic Sports; ESPNews; FitTV; Fox Movie Channel; G4; Golf Channel; GSN; Halogen Network; History Channel International; ID Investigation Discovery; Independent Film Channel; Lifetime Movie Network; Outdoor Channel; Science Channel; Speed Channel; Style Network; Toon Disney; Turner Classic Movies.
Fee: $49.95 installation; $17.00 monthly.

Pay Service 1
Pay Units: N.A.
Programming (via satellite): Cinemax; HBO; Showtime; The Movie Channel.
Fee: $10.00 installation; $8.95 monthly (TMC), $10.95 monthly (Cinemax or Showtime), $12.95 monthly (HBO).

Digital Pay Service 1
Pay Units: N.A.
Programming (via satellite): Cinemax (multiplexed); Flix; HBO (multiplexed); Showtime (multiplexed); Starz (multiplexed); The Movie Channel (multiplexed).
Fee: $40.00 monthly (HBO, Cinemax, Showtime, TMC, Flix, and Starz).

Video-On-Demand: No

Pay-Per-View
iN DEMAND (delivered digitally); Hot Choice (delivered digitally); Playboy TV (delivered digitally); Fresh (delivered digitally); Shorteez (delivered digitally).

Internet Service
Operational: Yes.
Subscribers: 76.
Broadband Service: IBBS.
Fee: $29.95 monthly.

Telephone Service
None

Miles of Plant: 10.0 (coaxial); None (fiber optic). Homes passed: 677.
Manager: Joe Young.
Ownership: Park TV & Electronics Inc. (MSO).

YANKEETOWN—Formerly served by Time Warner Cable. No longer in operation. ICA: IN0336.

YOUNG AMERICA—Formerly served by CableDirect. No longer in operation. ICA: IN0338.

ZANESVILLE—Formerly served by CableDirect. No longer in operation. ICA: IN0339.

IOWA

Total Systems: 245
Total Communities Served: 756
Franchises Not Yet Operating: 0
Applications Pending: 0
Communities with Applications: 0
Number of Basic Subscribers: 696,880
Number of Expanded Basic Subscribers: 349,108
Number of Pay Units: 151,223

Top 100 Markets Represented: Omaha (53); Davenport, IA-Rock Island-Moline, IL (60); Cedar Rapids-Waterloo (65); Des Moines-Ames (66); Sioux Falls-Mitchell, SD (85); Rockford-Freeport (97).

For a list of cable communities in this section, see the Cable Community Index located in the back of Cable Volume 2.
For explanation of terms used in cable system listings, see p. D-11.

ADAIR—B & L Technologies LLC, 3329 270th St, Lenox, IA 50851. Phones: 800-798-5488; 641-348-2240. Fax: 641-348-2240. ICA: IA0216.
TV Market Ranking: Outside TV Markets (ADAIR). Franchise award date: N.A. Franchise expiration date: N.A. Began: September 1, 1984.
Channel capacity: 41 (not 2-way capable). Channels available but not in use: 6.
Basic Service
Subscribers: 108.
Programming (received off-air): KCCI (CBS) Des Moines; KDIN-TV (PBS) Des Moines; KDSM-TV (FOX) Des Moines; WHO-DT (NBC) Des Moines; WOI-DT (ABC) Ames.
Programming (via satellite): ABC Family Channel; CNN; C-SPAN; Discovery Channel; Disney Channel; ESPN; Nickelodeon; Spike TV; TBS Superstation; Turner Network TV; USA Network; Weather Channel; WGN America.
Fee: $24.10 monthly.
Pay Service 1
Pay Units: 130.
Programming (via satellite): Cinemax; HBO; Showtime; The Movie Channel.
Fee: $11.00 monthly (Cinemax), $12.95 monthly (HBO, Showtime or TMC).
Video-On-Demand: No
Internet Service
Operational: No.
Telephone Service
None
Miles of Plant: 7.0 (coaxial); None (fiber optic). Homes passed: 389.
President & General Manager: Robert Hintz. Office Manager: Linda Hintz.
City fee: 3% of gross.
Ownership: B & L Technologies LLC (MSO).

ADEL—Mediacom. Now served by DES MOINES, IA [IA0001]. ICA: IA0030.

AFTON—B & L Technologies LLC, 3329 270th St, Lenox, IA 50851. Phones: 800-798-5488; 641-348-2240. Fax: 641-348-2240. ICA: IA0222.
TV Market Ranking: Outside TV Markets (AFTON). Franchise award date: N.A. Franchise expiration date: N.A. Began: September 1, 1982.
Channel capacity: 41 (not 2-way capable). Channels available but not in use: 5.
Basic Service
Subscribers: 100.
Programming (received off-air): KCCI (CBS) Des Moines; KDIN-TV (PBS) Des Moines; KDSM-TV (FOX) Des Moines; WHO-DT (NBC) Des Moines; WOI-DT (ABC) Ames.
Programming (via satellite): ABC Family Channel; Arts & Entertainment; CNN; Discovery Channel; Disney Channel; ESPN; Nickelodeon; Spike TV; TBS Superstation; Turner Network TV; USA Network; Weather Channel; WGN America.
Fee: $25.00 installation; $24.10 monthly.
Pay Service 1
Pay Units: 122.
Programming (via satellite): Cinemax; HBO; Showtime; The Movie Channel.
Fee: $15.00 installation; $11.00 monthly (Cinemax), $12.95 monthly (HBO, Showtime or TMC).
Video-On-Demand: No
Internet Service
Operational: No.
Telephone Service
None
Miles of Plant: 8.0 (coaxial); None (fiber optic). Homes passed: 305. Total homes in franchised area: 305.
President & General Manager: Robert Hintz. Office Manager: Linda Hintz.
Ownership: B & L Technologies LLC (MSO).

AINSWORTH—Starwest Inc., 15235 235th St, Milton, IA 52570-8016. Phones: 319-293-6336; 319-397-2283. ICA: IA0614.
TV Market Ranking: Below 100 (AINSWORTH).
Channel capacity: N.A. Channels available but not in use: N.A.
Basic Service
Subscribers: N.A.
Programming (received off-air): KCRG-TV (ABC) Cedar Rapids; KGAN (CBS) Cedar Rapids; KIIN (PBS) Iowa City; KWKB (CW, MNT) Iowa City; KWWL (NBC) Waterloo; KYOU-TV (FOX) Ottumwa.
Programming (via satellite): ABC Family Channel; AMC; CNN; Discovery Channel; Disney Channel; ESPN; ESPN 2; Headline News; HGTV; Lifetime; MTV; Nickelodeon; Spike TV; Syfy; TBS Superstation; Turner Network TV; VH1; WGN America.
Pay Service 1
Pay Units: N.A.
Programming (via satellite): Showtime.
Internet Service
Operational: No.
Manager & Chief Technician: John Stooksberry.
Ownership: Starwest Inc. (MSO).

AKRON—Premier Communications. Now served by SIOUX CENTER, IA [IA0076]. ICA: IA0150.

ALBION—Heart of Iowa Telecommunications. Formerly [IA0623]. This cable system has converted to IPTV, PO Box 130, 502 Main St, Union, IA 50258-0130. Phones: 800-806-4482; 641-486-2211. Fax: 641-486-2205. E-mail: customerservice@heartofiowa.coop. Web Site: http://www.heartofiowa.net. ICA: IA5000.
TV Market Ranking: Below 100 (ALBION). Franchise award date: N.A. Franchise expiration date: N.A. Began: N.A.
Channel capacity: N.A. Channels available but not in use: N.A.
Internet Service
Operational: Yes.
Broadband Service: Netins.
Fee: $39.95 monthly.
Telephone Service
Digital: Operational
General Manager: David Schmidt. Plant Manager: Jay Duncan. Customer Service Manager: Heidi Mitchell.
Ownership: Heart of Iowa Communications Cooperative.

ALBION—Heart of Iowa Telecommunications. This cable system has converted to IPTV. See Albion, IA [IA5000], IA. ICA: IA0623.

ALDEN—Formerly served by Latimer/Coulter Cablevision. No longer in operation. ICA: IA0389.

ALEXANDER—Formerly served by CableDirect. No longer in operation. ICA: IA0390.

ALGONA—Algona Municipal Utilities, PO Box 10, 104 W Call St, Algona, IA 50511. Phone: 515-295-3584. Fax: 515-295-3364. E-mail: info@netamu.com. Web Site: http://www.netamu.com. ICA: IA0598. **Note:** This system is an overbuild.
TV Market Ranking: Outside TV Markets (ALGONA).
Channel capacity: 77 (operating 2-way). Channels available but not in use: N.A.
Basic Service
Subscribers: 1,804.
Programming (received off-air): KAAL (ABC) Austin; KCCI (CBS) Des Moines; KCWI-TV (CW) Ames; KDSM-TV (FOX) Des Moines; KEYC-TV (CBS, FOX) Mankato; KIMT (CBS, MNT) Mason City; KTIN (PBS) Fort Dodge; WHO-DT (NBC) Des Moines; WOI-DT (ABC) Ames.
Programming (via satellite): C-SPAN; C-SPAN 2; Eternal Word TV Network; QVC; TBS Superstation; Trinity Broadcasting Network; Weather Channel; WGN America.
Current originations: Public Access.
Fee: $14.95 monthly.
Expanded Basic Service 1
Subscribers: 832.
Programming (via satellite): ABC Family Channel; AMC; AmericanLife TV Network; Animal Planet; Arts & Entertainment; Big Ten Network; Bravo; Cartoon Network; CNBC; CNN; Comedy Central; Country Music TV; Discovery Channel; Discovery Health Channel; Disney Channel; Disney XD; Do-It-Yourself; E! Entertainment Television; ESPN; ESPN 2; ESPN Classic Sports; Food Network; Fox Movie Channel; Fox News Channel; Fox Sports Net North; FX; Golf Channel; Hallmark Channel; Headline News; HGTV; History Channel; Lifetime; Lifetime Movie Network; MoviePlex; MSNBC; MTV; NFL Network; Nickelodeon; Speed Channel; Spike TV; Syfy; The Learning Channel; Travel Channel; truTV; Turner Classic Movies; Turner Network TV; TV Land; USA Network; VH1.
Fee: $34.95 monthly.
Digital Basic Service
Subscribers: 805.
Programming (received off-air): KDMI (MNT, IND) Des Moines.
Programming (via satellite): BBC America; CMT Pure Country; Discovery Kids Channel; Discovery Military Channel; Discovery Planet Green; DMX Music; ESPN U; ESPNews; Fox College Sports Atlantic; Fox College Sports Central; Fox College Sports Pacific; G4; GSN; ID Investigation Discovery; Lifetime Real Women; MTV2; National Geographic Channel; Nick Jr.; NickToons TV; Outdoor Channel; PBS World; RFD-TV; Russian Television Network; Science Channel; SoapNet; TeenNick; Versus; VH1 Classic; VH1 Soul; WE tv.
Fee: $38.95 monthly.
Digital Expanded Basic Service
Subscribers: N.A.
Programming (received off-air): KAAL (ABC) Austin; KCCI (CBS) Des Moines; KDIN-TV (PBS) Des Moines; KDSM-TV (FOX) Des Moines; KEYC-TV (CBS, FOX) Mankato; KIMT (CBS, MNT) Mason City; WHO-DT (NBC) Des Moines; WOI-DT (ABC) Ames.
Programming (via satellite): Big Ten Network HD.
Digital Expanded Basic Service 2
Subscribers: N.A.
Programming (via satellite): Discovery Channel HD; ESPN 2 HD; ESPN HD; HDNet; HDNet Movies; NFL Network HD.
Digital Pay Service 1
Pay Units: 150.
Programming (via satellite): HBO (multiplexed); HBO HD.
Fee: $14.95 monthly.
Digital Pay Service 2
Pay Units: 98.
Programming (via satellite): Cinemax (multiplexed); Cinemax HD.
Fee: $14.95 monthly.
Digital Pay Service 3
Pay Units: 91.
Programming (via satellite): Flix; Independent Film Channel; Showtime (multiplexed); Showtime HD; Sundance Channel; The Movie Channel (multiplexed); The Movie Channel HD.
Fee: $16.95 monthly.

Digital Pay Service 4
Pay Units: 142.
Programming (via satellite): Encore (multiplexed); Starz (multiplexed); Starz HDTV.
Fee: $12.95 monthly.
Pay-Per-View
iN DEMAND (delivered digitally); Movies (delivered digitally).
Internet Service
Operational: Yes.
Subscribers: 1,422.
Broadband Service: In-house.
Fee: $22.95 monthly.
Telephone Service
None
Miles of Plant: 63.0 (coaxial); None (fiber optic). Homes passed: 3,100.
General Manager: John Bilsten. Information Director: Bob Jennings. Communications Supervisor: Lowell Roethler.
Ownership: Algona Municipal Utilities.

ALGONA—Mediacom. Now served by FORT DODGE, IA [IA0011]. ICA: IA0045.

ALLEMAN—Formerly served by Huxley Communications Corp. No longer in operation. ICA: IA0391.

ALLERTON—Formerly served by Longview Communications. No longer in operation. ICA: IA0297.

ALTA—ALTA-TEC, 223 Main St, Alta, IA 51002-1345. Phone: 712-200-1122. E-mail: altatec@alta-tec.net. Web Site: http://www.alta-tec.net. ICA: IA0599. **Note:** This system is an overbuild.
TV Market Ranking: Outside TV Markets (ALTA).
Channel capacity: 72 (operating 2-way). Channels available but not in use: N.A.
Basic Service
Subscribers: 600.
Programming (received off-air): KCAU-TV (ABC) Sioux City; KCCI (CBS) Des Moines; KDSM-TV (FOX) Des Moines; KMEG (CBS) Sioux City; KPTH (FOX, MNT) Sioux City; KSIN-TV (PBS) Sioux City; KTIV (CW, NBC) Sioux City; WOI-DT (ABC) Ames.
Current originations: Public Access.
Fee: $18.15 monthly.
Expanded Basic Service 1
Subscribers: N.A.
Programming (via satellite): ABC Family Channel; AMC; Animal Planet; Arts & Entertainment; Cartoon Network; CNBC; CNN; Comedy Central; Country Music TV; C-SPAN; C-SPAN 2; CW+; Discovery Channel; Disney Channel; Do-It-Yourself; Encore; ESPN; ESPN 2; ESPN Classic Sports; ESPN Deportes; ESPNews; Food Network; Fox News Channel; Fox Sports Net North; FX; Hallmark Channel; Headline News; HGTV; History Channel; Lifetime; MoviePlex; MSNBC; MTV; Nickelodeon; Outdoor Channel; QVC; RFD-TV; SoapNet; Speed Channel; Spike TV; Syfy; TBS Superstation; The Learning Channel; Travel Channel; Trinity Broadcasting Network; truTV; Turner Classic Movies; Turner Network TV; TV Land; Univision; USA Network; VH1; Weather Channel; WGN America.
Fee: $28.00 monthly.
Digital Basic Service
Subscribers: N.A.
Programming (via satellite): BBC America; Bio; Cooking Channel; Discovery Health Channel; Discovery Kids Channel; Discovery Military Channel; Discovery Planet Green; Disney XD; Do-It-Yourself; ESPN U; ESPNews; FitTV; Fox College Sports Atlantic; Fox College Sports Central; Fox College Sports Pacific; Fox Movie Channel; Fox Soccer; G4; Great American Country; GSN; History Channel International; ID Investigation Discovery; i-Lifetv; Independent Film Channel; Lifetime Real Women; RFD-TV; Science Channel; SoapNet; Versus; WE tv.
Fee: $12.95 monthly.
Digital Expanded Basic Service
Subscribers: N.A.
Programming (received off-air): KCAU-TV (ABC) Sioux City; KCSD-TV (PBS) Sioux Falls; KMEG (CBS) Sioux City; KSIN-TV (PBS) Sioux City; KTIV (CW, NBC) Sioux City.
Programming (via satellite): Big Ten Network HD; Discovery Channel HD; ESPN 2 HD; ESPN HD; Fox HD; Fuse HD; HDNet; HDNet Movies.
Fee: $9.95 monthly.
Digital Expanded Basic Service 2
Subscribers: N.A.
Programming (via satellite): Bandamax; De Pelicula; De Pelicula Clasico; Discovery en Espanol; ESPN Deportes; Fox Sports en Espanol; Ritmoson Latino; Telehit.
Fee: $2.99 monthly.
Pay Service 1
Pay Units: N.A.
Programming (via satellite): Cinemax (multiplexed); Flix; HBO (multiplexed); Showtime; Starz; The Movie Channel.
Fee: $12.00 monthly (Showtime/TMC/Flix), $14.00 monthly (HBO or Cinemax).
Digital Pay Service 1
Pay Units: N.A.
Programming (via satellite): Cinemax (multiplexed); Encore (multiplexed); HBO (multiplexed); Starz (multiplexed).
Fee: $7.10 monthly (Starz/Encore), $14.00 monthly (HBO or Cinemax).
Internet Service
Operational: Yes.
Subscribers: 212.
Broadband Service: In-house.
Fee: $39.95-$59.95 monthly; $150.00 modem purchase.
Telephone Service
None
Miles of Plant: 11.0 (coaxial); None (fiber optic). Homes passed: 750.
Telecommunications Clerk: April Meyer. Utilities Superintendent: Ron Chapman.
Ownership: Altatec.

ALTA VISTA (town)—Alta Vista Municipal Cable, PO Box 115, Alta Vista, IA 50603. Phone: 614-364-2975. Fax: 614-364-2975. ICA: IA0392.
TV Market Ranking: Outside TV Markets (ALTA VISTA (TOWN)). Franchise award date: N.A. Franchise expiration date: N.A. Began: January 1, 2002.
Channel capacity: 36 (not 2-way capable). Channels available but not in use: 14.
Basic Service
Subscribers: 30.
Programming (received off-air): KAAL (ABC) Austin; KCRG-TV (ABC) Cedar Rapids; KFXA (FOX) Cedar Rapids; KGAN (CBS) Cedar Rapids; KIMT (CBS, MNT) Mason City; KWWL (NBC) Waterloo; KYIN (PBS) Mason City.
Programming (via satellite): ABC Family Channel; CNN; Discovery Channel; Disney Channel; ESPN; TBS Superstation; Travel Channel; Trinity Broadcasting Network; Turner Network TV; USA Network; WGN America.
Fee: $39.90 installation; $22.00 monthly.
Internet Service
Operational: No.
Miles of Plant: 3.0 (coaxial); None (fiber optic). Homes passed: 151.
Ownership: Alta Vista Municipal Cable.

AMES—Mediacom, 2205 Ingersoll Ave, Des Moines, IA 50312. Phone: 515-246-1890. Fax: 515-246-2211. Web Site: http://www.mediacomcable.com. Also serves Boone, Boone County (eastern portion), Boone County (southern portion), Dysart, Greene County, Huxley, Jefferson, Madrid, Marshall County, Marshalltown, Nevada, Polk City, Polk County (northwestern portion), Randall, Sheldahl, Slater, Story City, Story County, Tama, Toledo, Traer & Woodward. ICA: IA0008.
TV Market Ranking: 65 (Dysart, Marshall County (portions), Traer); 66 (AMES, Boone, Boone County (eastern portion), Boone County (southern portion), Greene County (portions), Huxley, Madrid, Nevada, Polk City, Polk County (northwestern portion), Randall, Sheldahl, Slater, Story City, Story County, Woodward); Below 100 (Green Mountain, Marshalltown, Tama, Toledo, Marshall County (portions)); Outside TV Markets (Jefferson, Greene County (portions)). Franchise award date: January 1, 1983. Franchise expiration date: N.A. Began: January 1, 1980.
Channel capacity: N.A. Channels available but not in use: N.A.
Basic Service
Subscribers: 11,175.
Programming (received off-air): KCCI (CBS) Des Moines; KCWI-TV (CW) Ames; KDIN-TV (PBS) Des Moines; KDSM-TV (FOX) Des Moines; KFPX-TV (ION) Newton; WHO-DT (NBC) Des Moines; WOI-DT (ABC) Ames.
Programming (via satellite): CNN; C-SPAN; Discovery Channel; Home Shopping Network; QVC; TBS Superstation; WGN America.
Current originations: Government Access; Educational Access; Public Access.
Fee: $60.00 installation; $9.49 monthly.
Expanded Basic Service 1
Subscribers: 10,504.
Programming (via satellite): ABC Family Channel; AMC; Animal Planet; Arts & Entertainment; BET Networks; Bravo; Cartoon Network; CNBC; Comedy Central; Country Music TV; C-SPAN 2; Disney Channel; E! Entertainment Television; ESPN; ESPN 2; Eternal Word TV Network; Food Network; Fox News Channel; FX; Hallmark Channel; Headline News; HGTV; History Channel; INSP; Lifetime; Lifetime Movie Network; MoviePlex; MSNBC; MTV; Nickelodeon; RFD-TV; ShopNBC; SoapNet; Speed Channel; Spike TV; Syfy; Telemundo; The Learning Channel; Travel Channel; Trinity Broadcasting Network; truTV; Turner Classic Movies; Turner Network TV; TV Guide Network; TV Land; Univision; USA Network; VH1; WE tv; Weather Channel.
Fee: $31.46 monthly.
Digital Basic Service
Subscribers: 9,616.
Programming (via satellite): American-Life TV Network; BBC America; Bio; Bloomberg Television; Discovery Digital Networks; DMX Music; Fox Movie Channel; Fox Sports World; Fuse; G4; GAS; Golf Channel; GSN; Halogen Network; History Channel International; Independent Film Channel; Lime; MTV Networks Digital Suite; National Geographic Channel; Nick Jr.; Outdoor Channel; Ovation; Style Network; Toon Disney; Versus.
Fee: $12.00 monthly.
Digital Pay Service 1
Pay Units: 2,803.
Programming (via satellite): Cinemax (multiplexed); Encore (multiplexed); Flix; HBO (multiplexed); Showtime (multiplexed); Starz (multiplexed); Sundance Channel; The Movie Channel (multiplexed).
Fee: $9.95 monthly (Cinemax, HBO, Showtime, Flix/Sundance/TMC, or Starz/Encore).
Video-On-Demand: Yes
Pay-Per-View
Addressable homes: 9,616.
ESPN Now (delivered digitally), Addressable: Yes; ETC (delivered digitally); Playboy TV (delivered digitally); Pleasure (delivered digitally); Fresh (delivered digitally); Shorteez (delivered digitally); TVN Entertainment (delivered digitally); sports (delivered digitally).
Internet Service
Operational: Yes.
Subscribers: 2,384.
Broadband Service: Mediacom High Speed Internet.
Fee: $49.95 installation; $29.95 monthly; $10.00 modem lease.
Telephone Service
Analog: Not Operational
Digital: Operational
Miles of Plant: 633.0 (coaxial); None (fiber optic). Homes passed: 54,079.
Vice President: Steve Purcell. Marketing Director: LeAnn Treloar. Technical Operations Manager: Cliff Waggener. Government & Media Relations Manager: Bill Peard.
City fee: 3% of gross.
Ownership: Mediacom LLC (MSO).

ANDREW—Andrew Telephone Co. Inc., PO Box 259, Andrew, IA 52030-0259. Phones: 641-765-4201 (Truro office); 712-824-7231 (Emerson office); 563-672-3277. Fax: 563-672-9511. E-mail: andrtel@netins.net. Web Site: http://www.interstatecom.com. ICA: IA0351.
TV Market Ranking: Below 100 (ANDREW). Franchise award date: July 1, 1985. Franchise expiration date: N.A. Began: October 1, 1985.
Channel capacity: 30 (operating 2-way). Channels available but not in use: 12.
Basic Service
Subscribers: 93.
Programming (received off-air): KCRG-TV (ABC) Cedar Rapids; KIIN (PBS) Iowa City; KLJB (CW, FOX) Davenport; KWQC-TV (NBC) Davenport; KWWL (NBC) Waterloo; WHBF-TV (CBS) Rock Island; WQAD-TV (ABC) Moline.
Programming (via satellite): ABC Family Channel; Arts & Entertainment; CNN; Disney Channel; ESPN; Spike TV; TBS Superstation; Turner Classic Movies; Turner Network TV; WGN America.
Current originations: Educational Access.
Fee: $18.85 monthly.
Video-On-Demand: No
Internet Service
Operational: No.
Telephone Service
None
Miles of Plant: 3.0 (coaxial); None (fiber optic). Homes passed: 155. Total homes in franchised area: 155.
Manager & Chief Technician: Milt Cornelius. Customer Service: Carla Ehlers.
Ownership: Interstate Communications.

ANITA—WesTel Systems, PO Box 330, 012 E 3rd St, Remsen, IA 51050. Phone: 712-786-1181. Fax: 712-786-2400. E-mail: acctinfo@westelsystems.com. Web Site: http://www.westelsystems.com. ICA: IA0188.

TV Market Ranking: Outside TV Markets (ANITA). Franchise award date: N.A. Franchise expiration date: N.A. Began: March 1, 1983.

Channel capacity: 30 (not 2-way capable). Channels available but not in use: N.A.

Basic Service

Subscribers: 329.

Programming (received off-air): KCCI (CBS) Des Moines; KDIN-TV (PBS) Des Moines; KDSM-TV (FOX) Des Moines; KETV (ABC) Omaha; KMTV-TV (CBS) Omaha; WHO-DT (NBC) Des Moines; WOI-DT (ABC) Ames; WOWT-TV (IND, NBC) Omaha.

Programming (via satellite): ABC Family Channel; Animal Planet; Arts & Entertainment; Big Ten Network; CNBC; CNN; Comedy Central; Country Music TV; CW+; Discovery Channel; Disney Channel; Do-It-Yourself; ESPN; ESPN 2; Food Network; Fox News Channel; FX; Headline News; HGTV; History Channel; Lifetime; MTV; Nickelodeon; Speed Channel; Spike TV; Syfy; TBS Superstation; The Learning Channel; Travel Channel; Turner Classic Movies; Turner Network TV; TV Land; USA Network; Versus; VH1; WE tv; Weather Channel; WGN America.

Fee: $24.15 installation; $21.62 monthly.

Digital Basic Service

Subscribers: N.A.

Programming (via satellite): BBC America; Bio; Bloomberg Television; CMT Pure Country; Discovery Health Channel; Discovery Kids Channel; Discovery Military Channel; Discovery Planet Green; DMX Music; ESPN Classic Sports; ESPNews; FitTV; Fox Movie Channel; Fox Soccer; Fuse; Golf Channel; Great American Country; GSN; History Channel International; ID Investigation Discovery; Lifetime Movie Network; MTV Hits; MTV2; Nick Jr.; NickToons TV; Outdoor Channel; RFD-TV; Science Channel; ShopNBC; SoapNet; Style Network; TeenNick; The Word Network; Toon Disney; Trinity Broadcasting Network; VH1 Classic; VH1 Soul.

Pay Service 1

Pay Units: 31.

Programming (via satellite): Cinemax.

Fee: $11.00 monthly.

Pay Service 2

Pay Units: 28.

Programming (via satellite): HBO.

Fee: $12.95 monthly.

Digital Pay Service 1

Pay Units: N.A.

Programming (via satellite): Cinemax (multiplexed); Encore (multiplexed); Flix; HBO (multiplexed); Showtime (multiplexed); Starz (multiplexed); The Movie Channel (multiplexed).

Pay-Per-View

iN DEMAND (delivered digitally).

Internet Service

Operational: No.

Telephone Service

None

Miles of Plant: 10.0 (coaxial); None (fiber optic). Homes passed: 477.

Chief Executive Officer: Jim Sherburne. Chief Technician: Rich Barnholdt.

City fee: 3% of gross.

Ownership: West Iowa Telephone Co.

ANTHON—Long Lines, 501 4th St, Sergeant Bluff, IA 51054-8509. Phone: 712-271-4000. Fax: 712-271-2727. E-mail: info@longlines.com. Web Site: http://www.longlines.com. Also serves Ida Grove. ICA: IA0243.

TV Market Ranking: Below 100 (ANTHON); Outside TV Markets (Ida Grove). Franchise award date: N.A. Franchise expiration date: N.A. Began: June 1, 1984.

Channel capacity: 75 (not 2-way capable). Channels available but not in use: N.A.

Basic Service

Subscribers: 1,494.

Programming (received off-air): KCAU-TV (ABC) Sioux City; KMEG (CBS) Sioux City; KPTH (FOX, MNT) Sioux City; KSIN-TV (PBS) Sioux City; KTIV (CW, NBC) Sioux City.

Programming (via satellite): ABC Family Channel; AMC; AmericanLife TV Network; Animal Planet; Arts & Entertainment; Big Ten Network; Cartoon Network; CNBC; CNN; Comedy Central; Country Music TV; C-SPAN; C-SPAN 2; CW+; Discovery Channel; Disney Channel; E! Entertainment Television; ESPN; ESPN 2; ESPN Classic Sports; Eternal Word TV Network; Food Network; Fox News Channel; Fox Sports Net North; FX; Golf Channel; Hallmark Channel; Headline News; HGTV; History Channel; Home Shopping Network; INSP; Lifetime; Lifetime Movie Network; MSNBC; MTV; Nickelodeon; QVC; Speed Channel; Spike TV; Syfy; TBS Superstation; The Learning Channel; The Sportsman Channel; Travel Channel; Trinity Broadcasting Network; truTV; Turner Classic Movies; Turner Network TV; TuTv; TV Guide Network; TV Land; USA Network; VH1; Weather Channel; WGN America.

Fee: $45.00 installation; $41.99 monthly.

Digital Basic Service

Subscribers: N.A.

Programming (via satellite): BBC America; Bio; Cooking Channel; Discovery Health Channel; Discovery Kids Channel; Discovery Planet Green; Do-It-Yourself; ESPN U; ESPNews; FitTV; Fox College Sports Atlantic; Fox College Sports Central; Fox College Sports Pacific; Fox Movie Channel; Fox Soccer; G4; Great American Country; GSN; Halogen Network; History Channel International; ID Investigation Discovery; Independent Film Channel; Lifetime Real Women; Military Channel; MTV Hits; MTV Jams; MTV2; Music Choice; Nick Jr.; NickToons TV; Outdoor Channel; Science Channel; SoapNet; TeenNick; Toon Disney; Versus; VH1 Classic; VH1 Country; VH1 Soul; WE tv.

Fee: $9.99 monthly.

Digital Expanded Basic Service

Subscribers: N.A.

Programming (via satellite): Bandamax; De Pelicula; De Pelicula Clasico; Discovery en Espanol; ESPN Deportes; Fox Sports en Espanol; Ritmoson Latino; Telehit.

Fee: $2.95 monthly.

Digital Expanded Basic Service 2

Subscribers: N.A.

Programming (received off-air): KCAU-TV (ABC) Sioux City; KMEG (CBS) Sioux City; KPTH (FOX, MNT) Sioux City; KSIN-TV (PBS) Sioux City; KTIV (CW, NBC) Sioux City.

Programming (via satellite): Big Ten Network HD; Discovery Channel HD; ESPN 2 HD; ESPN HD; HDNet; HDNet Movies; Outdoor Channel 2 HD.

Fee: $9.95 monthly.

Pay Service 1

Pay Units: N.A.

Programming (via satellite): Flix; Showtime (multiplexed); The Movie Channel.

Fee: $11.00 monthly (each).

Pay Service 2

Pay Units: 8.

Programming (via satellite): HBO (multiplexed).

Fee: $12.00 monthly.

Digital Pay Service 1

Pay Units: N.A.

Programming (via satellite): Cinemax (multiplexed); Cinemax HD; Encore (multiplexed); Flix; HBO (multiplexed); HBO HD; Showtime (multiplexed); Starz (multiplexed); Starz HDTV; The Movie Channel (multiplexed).

Fee: $11.95 monthly (Cinemax), $13.95 monthly (Starz/Encore), $14.45 monthly (Showtime/Flix/TMC), $14.95 monthly (HBO).

Video-On-Demand: Yes

Internet Service

Operational: No.

Manager: Paul Bergmann. Chief Technician: Tony Seubert. Marketing Director: Denise Moberg.

City fee: 3% of gross.

Ownership: Long Lines (MSO).

ARLINGTON—Alpine Communications LC, PO Box 1008, 923 Humphrey St, Elkader, IA 52043. Phones: 800-635-1059; 563-245-4000. Fax: 563-245-2887. Web Site: http://www.alpinecom.net. Also serves Clermont, Volga & Wadena (village). ICA: IA0393.

TV Market Ranking: Outside TV Markets (ARLINGTON, Clermont, Volga, Wadena (village)). Franchise award date: N.A. Franchise expiration date: N.A. Began: N.A.

Channel capacity: 38 (not 2-way capable). Channels available but not in use: 19.

Basic Service

Subscribers: 222.

Programming (received off-air): KCRG-TV (ABC) Cedar Rapids; KFXA (FOX) Cedar Rapids; KGAN (CBS) Cedar Rapids; KPXR-TV (ION) Cedar Rapids; KRIN (PBS) Waterloo; KWWL (NBC) Waterloo.

Programming (via satellite): ABC Family Channel; AMC; Arts & Entertainment; Cartoon Network; CNN; Discovery Channel; ESPN; ESPN 2; HGTV; Lifetime; Nickelodeon; Outdoor Channel; QVC; Spike TV; TBS Superstation; The Learning Channel; Trinity Broadcasting Network; Turner Network TV; USA Network; Weather Channel; WGN America.

Fee: $29.95 monthly.

Pay Service 1

Pay Units: N.A.

Programming (via satellite): Flix; Showtime; The Movie Channel.

Fee: $9.95 monthly (each).

Video-On-Demand: No

Internet Service

Operational: No.

Telephone Service

None

Miles of Plant: 3.0 (coaxial); None (fiber optic).

General Manager: Chris Hopp. Network Operations Manager: Dirk Buckman. Chief Technician: Jerry Schroeder. Sales & Marketing Manager: Sara Hertrampf. Finance Manager: Margaret Corlett. Customer Service Manager: Lori Keppler.

Ownership: Alpine Communications LC (MSO).

ARTHUR—Sac County Mutual Telco, PO Box 488, 108 S Maple, Odebolt, IA 51458. Phone: 712-668-2200. Fax: 712-668-2100. E-mail: odetelco@netins.net. Web Site: http://www.odebolt.net/sac_co__mutual_telco.html. ICA: IA0361.

TV Market Ranking: Outside TV Markets (ARTHUR). Franchise award date: August 1, 1988. Franchise expiration date: N.A. Began: January 1, 1989.

Channel capacity: 40 (not 2-way capable). Channels available but not in use: 1.

Basic Service

Subscribers: 63.

Programming (received off-air): KCAU-TV (ABC) Sioux City; KMEG (CBS) Sioux City; KPTH (FOX, MNT) Sioux City; KTIV (CW, NBC) Sioux City.

Programming (via satellite): ABC Family Channel; Arts & Entertainment; Cartoon Network; CNN; Country Music TV; C-SPAN; C-SPAN 2; Discovery Channel; Disney Channel; ESPN; ESPN 2; Food Network; Fox News Channel; FX; Hallmark Channel; HGTV; History Channel; ION Television; Nickelodeon; Speed Channel; Spike TV; TBS Superstation; The Learning Channel; truTV; Turner Classic Movies; Turner Network TV; TV Land; USA Network; Versus; WE tv; Weather Channel; WGN America.

Fee: $15.00 installation; $25.72 monthly; $2.00 converter.

Pay Service 1

Pay Units: 4.

Programming (via satellite): Cinemax; HBO.

Fee: $15.00 installation; $11.00 monthly (Cinemax), $12.95 monthly (HBO).

Internet Service

Operational: No, DSL & dialup.

Telephone Service

None

Miles of Plant: 2.0 (coaxial); None (fiber optic). Homes passed: 110. Total homes in franchised area: 110.

Manager: Dale Schaefer.

Ownership: Sac County Mutual Telephone Co. (MSO).

ASHTON—Premier Communications. Now served by SHELDON, IA [IA0060]. ICA: IA0300.

ATKINS—Atkins Cablevision Inc., PO Box 157, 85 Main Ave, Atkins, IA 52206-9750. Phone: 319-446-7331. Fax: 319-446-9100. E-mail: jtraut@atkinstelephone.com. Web Site: http://www.atkinstelephone.com. ICA: IA0269.

TV Market Ranking: 65 (ATKINS). Franchise award date: N.A. Franchise expiration date: N.A. Began: November 1, 1981.

Channel capacity: 68 (operating 2-way). Channels available but not in use: None.

Basic Service

Subscribers: 372.

Programming (received off-air): KCRG-TV (ABC) Cedar Rapids; KFXA (FOX) Cedar Rapids; KGAN (CBS) Cedar Rapids; KIIN (PBS) Iowa City; KPXR-TV (ION) Cedar Rapids; KWKB (CW, MNT) Iowa City; KWWL (NBC) Waterloo.

Programming (via satellite): ABC Family Channel; AMC; Animal Planet; Arts & Entertainment; Cartoon Network; CNBC; CNN; Comedy Central; Country Music TV; C-SPAN; Discovery Channel; Disney Channel; E! Entertainment Television; ESPN; ESPN 2; Eternal Word TV Network; Food Network; Fox News Channel; FX; Headline News; HGTV; History Channel; Lifetime; MTV; Nickelodeon; QVC; Speed Channel; Spike TV; TBS Superstation; The Learning

Channel; Travel Channel; Trinity Broadcasting Network; truTV; Turner Classic Movies; Turner Network TV; TV Land; USA Network; VH1; Weather Channel; WGN America.
Current originations: Educational Access.
Fee: $10.00 installation; $36.00 monthly.

Pay Service 1
Pay Units: 59.
Programming (via satellite): HBO.
Fee: $10.00 monthly.

Pay Service 2
Pay Units: 6.
Programming (via satellite): Showtime.
Fee: $10.00 monthly.

Pay Service 3
Pay Units: 2.
Programming (via satellite): Cinemax.
Fee: $10.00 monthly.

Video-On-Demand: No

Internet Service
Operational: No, Both DSL & dial-up.

Telephone Service
None

Miles of Plant: 6.0 (coaxial); None (fiber optic). Homes passed: 383. Total homes in franchised area: 1,000.

General Manager: Jerry Spaight. Chief Technician: Chad Carlson. Cable Administrator: Jody Traut.

Ownership: Atkins Telephone Co.

ATLANTIC—Mediacom, 2205 Ingersoll Ave, Des Moines, IA 50312. Phone: 515-246-1890. Fax: 515-246-2211. Web Site: http://www.mediacomcable.com. Also serves Audubon, Avoca, Bedford, Carroll, Clarinda, Corning, Crawford County (southern portion), Denison, Essex, Glenwood, Glidden, Harlan, Mills County (eastern portion), Red Oak, Shenandoah & Villisca. ICA: IA0032.

TV Market Ranking: 53 (Glenwood, Mills County (eastern portion)); Outside TV Markets (ATLANTIC, Audubon, Avoca, Bedford, Carroll, Clarinda, Corning, Crawford County (southern portion), Denison, Essex, Glidden, Harlan, Red Oak, Shenandoah, Villisca). Franchise award date: April 27, 1972. Franchise expiration date: N.A. Began: October 15, 1973.

Channel capacity: N.A. Channels available but not in use: N.A.

Basic Service
Subscribers: 7,077.
Programming (received off-air): KCCI (CBS) Des Moines; KDIN-TV (PBS) Des Moines; KDSM-TV (FOX) Des Moines; KETV (ABC) Omaha; KMTV-TV (CBS) Omaha; KPTM (FOX, MNT) Omaha; KXVO (CW) Omaha; WHO-DT (NBC) Des Moines; WOI-DT (ABC) Ames; WOWT-TV (IND, NBC) Omaha.
Programming (via satellite): C-SPAN; C-SPAN 2; Home Shopping Network; ION Television; QVC; TV Guide Network; Weather Channel; WGN America.
Current originations: Religious Access; Public Access.
Fee: $9.51 monthly; $2.31 converter.

Expanded Basic Service 1
Subscribers: 6,830.
Programming (via satellite): ABC Family Channel; AMC; Animal Planet; Arts & Entertainment; Cartoon Network; CNBC; CNN; Country Music TV; Discovery Channel; Disney Channel; ESPN; ESPN 2; Fox News Channel; Fox Sports Net Midwest; FX; Hallmark Channel; Headline News; HGTV; History Channel; Lifetime; MSNBC; MTV; Nickelodeon; RFD-TV; Speed Channel; Spike TV; Syfy; TBS Superstation; Telemundo; The Learning Channel; truTV; Turner Network TV; Univision; USA Network; WE tv; Weather Channel.
Fee: $19.78 monthly.

Digital Basic Service
Subscribers: N.A.
Programming (via satellite): AmericanLife TV Network; BBC America; Bio; Bloomberg Television; Bravo; Discovery Digital Networks; DMX Music; Fox Movie Channel; Fox Sports World; Fuse; G4; GAS; Golf Channel; GSN; Halogen Network; History Channel International; Independent Film Channel; Lifetime Movie Network; Lime; MTV Networks Digital Suite; National Geographic Channel; Nick Jr.; Outdoor Channel; Ovation; Style Network; TV Land; Versus.

Digital Pay Service 1
Pay Units: 689.
Programming (via satellite): Cinemax (multiplexed); Encore (multiplexed); Flix; HBO (multiplexed); Showtime (multiplexed); Starz (multiplexed); Sundance Channel; The Movie Channel (multiplexed).
Fee: $20.00 installation; $9.50 monthly (Cinemax, HBO, Showtime, Flix/Sundance/TMC, or Starz/Encore).

Video-On-Demand: Yes

Pay-Per-View
ESPN Now (delivered digitally); ETC (delivered digitally); Playboy TV (delivered digitally); Pleasure (delivered digitally); TVN Entertainment (delivered digitally); sports (delivered digitally).

Internet Service
Operational: Yes. Began: September 1, 2002.
Broadband Service: Mediacom High Speed Internet.
Fee: $45.95 monthly.

Telephone Service
Analog: Not Operational
Digital: Operational

Miles of Plant: 324.0 (coaxial); None (fiber optic). Homes passed: 9,228. Total homes in franchised area: 9,228.

Vice President: Steve Purcell. Technical Operations Manager: Cliff Waggoner. Marketing Director: LeAnn Treloar. Government & Media Relations Manager: Bill Peard.

City fee: 3% of gross.

Ownership: Mediacom LLC (MSO).

AURELIA—NU-Telecom. Formerly [IA0212]. This cable system has converted to IPTV, PO Box 697, 27 N Minnesota, New Ulm, MN 56073-0697. Phone: 712-434-5989. Fax: 712-434-5555. Web Site: http://www.nutelecom.net. ICA: IA5021.

TV Market Ranking: Outside TV Markets (AURELIA). Franchise award date: N.A. Franchise expiration date: N.A. Began: N.A.

Channel capacity: N.A. Channels available but not in use: N.A.

Internet Service
Operational: Yes.

Telephone Service
Digital: Operational

President: Bill Otis. Chief Technician: Rick Wegner.

City fee: 3% of gross.

Ownership: NU-Telecom (MSO).

AURELIA—NU-Telecom. This cable system has converted to IPTV. See Aurelia, IL [IA5021], IA. ICA: IA0212.

AURORA—Formerly served by Alpine Communications LC. No longer in operation. ICA: IA0395.

AYRSHIRE—ATC Cablevision, PO Box 248, 1405 Silver Lake Ave, Ayrshire, IA 50515-0248. Phones: 712-426-2800; 800-642-2884; 712-426-2815. Fax: 712-426-2008. E-mail: info@ayrshireia.com. Web Site: http://www.ayrshireia.com. ICA: IA0368.

TV Market Ranking: Outside TV Markets (AYRSHIRE). Franchise award date: May 1, 1984. Franchise expiration date: N.A. Began: N.A.

Channel capacity: 36 (operating 2-way). Channels available but not in use: 12.

Basic Service
Subscribers: 58.
Programming (received off-air): KCAU-TV (ABC) Sioux City; KELO-TV (CBS, MNT) Sioux Falls; KEYC-TV (CBS, FOX) Mankato; KMEG (CBS) Sioux City; KPTH (FOX, MNT) Sioux City; KSFY-TV (ABC) Sioux Falls; KTIN (PBS) Fort Dodge; KTIV (CW, NBC) Sioux City; WOI-DT (ABC) Ames.
Programming (via satellite): ABC Family Channel; AMC; AmericanLife TV Network; Animal Planet; Arts & Entertainment; Cartoon Network; CNBC; CNN; Comedy Central; Country Music TV; C-SPAN; C-SPAN 2; Discovery Channel; Disney Channel; E! Entertainment Television; ESPN; ESPN 2; ESPN Classic Sports; Food Network; Fox News Channel; FX; Hallmark Channel; Headline News; HGTV; History Channel; ION Television; Lifetime; MTV; Nickelodeon; Outdoor Channel; QVC; Spike TV; Syfy; TBS Superstation; The Learning Channel; Travel Channel; Turner Classic Movies; Turner Network TV; TV Guide Network; TV Land; USA Network; VH1; Weather Channel; WGN America.
Fee: $30.00 installation; $43.40 monthly.

Digital Basic Service
Subscribers: N.A.
Programming (via satellite): BBC America; Bio; Discovery Digital Networks; DMX Music; ESPNews; FitTV; Fox Movie Channel; G4; GAS; Golf Channel; GSN; History Channel; Independent Film Channel; MTV2; National Geographic Channel; Nick Jr.; NickToons TV; Outdoor Channel; Speed Channel; Toon Disney; VH1 Classic; VH1 Country.
Fee: $11.00 monthly.

Digital Pay Service 1
Pay Units: 5.
Programming (via satellite): Cinemax (multiplexed); Encore (multiplexed); Flix; HBO (multiplexed); Showtime (multiplexed); Starz (multiplexed); Sundance Channel; The Movie Channel (multiplexed).
Fee: $9.50 monthly (Cinemax), $11.00 monthly (Showtime/TMC or Starz/Encore), $12.00 monthly (HBO).

Digital Pay Service 2
Pay Units: 2.
Programming (via satellite): Showtime; The Movie Channel.

Video-On-Demand: No

Pay-Per-View
Movies (delivered digitally), Fee: $3.95; Special events (delivered digitally); Sports PPV (delivered digitally).

Internet Service
Operational: No, Dialup only.

Telephone Service
None

Miles of Plant: 3.0 (coaxial); 12.0 (fiber optic). Homes passed: 106. Total homes in franchised area: 106.

Manager: Don Miller. Plant Manager: Chase Cox. Chief Technician: Derek Franker. Customer Service: Lonna Hess. Accounting Manager: Robin Dietrich. Executive Secretary: Kelly Otto.

Ownership: Ayrshire Communications (MSO).

BADGER—Goldfield Communication Services Corp., PO Box 67, 536 N Main St, Goldfield, IA 50542. Phones: 515-825-3996; 800-825-9753; 515-825-3888. Fax: 515-825-3801. E-mail: gold@goldfieldaccess.net. Web Site: http://www.goldfieldaccess.net. ICA: IA0396.

TV Market Ranking: Outside TV Markets (BADGER). Franchise award date: N.A. Franchise expiration date: N.A. Began: October 1, 1984.

Channel capacity: 45 (not 2-way capable). Channels available but not in use: 23.

Basic Service
Subscribers: N.A.
Programming (received off-air): KCCI (CBS) Des Moines; KDIN-TV (PBS) Des Moines; KDSM-TV (FOX) Des Moines; WHO-DT (NBC) Des Moines; WOI-DT (ABC) Ames.
Programming (via satellite): ABC Family Channel; AMC; Arts & Entertainment; CNN; Discovery Channel; Disney Channel; ESPN; Lifetime; Nickelodeon; Spike TV; TBS Superstation; Turner Network TV; USA Network; WGN America.
Fee: $10.00 installation; $19.95 monthly; $.50 converter.

Pay Service 1
Pay Units: N.A.
Programming (via satellite): HBO; Showtime.
Fee: $9.85 monthly (each).

Video-On-Demand: No

Internet Service
Operational: No.

Telephone Service
None

Miles of Plant: 3.0 (coaxial); None (fiber optic). Homes passed: 220.

Manager: Darrell L. Seaba. Chief Technician: Dean Schipull. Operations Director: Ron Massingill.

Ownership: Goldfield Communication Services Corp. (MSO).

BAGLEY—Panora Cooperative Cablevision Assn. Inc., PO Box 189, 114 E Main St, Panora, IA 50216. Phone: 641-755-2424. Fax: 641-755-2425. E-mail: panora@netins.net. Web Site: http://www.panoratelco.com. ICA: IA0356.

TV Market Ranking: Outside TV Markets (BAGLEY). Franchise award date: March 1, 1988. Franchise expiration date: N.A. Began: May 15, 1988.

Channel capacity: 36 (operating 2-way). Channels available but not in use: None.

Basic Service
Subscribers: 84.
Programming (received off-air): KCCI (CBS) Des Moines; KDIN-TV (PBS) Des Moines; KDSM-TV (FOX) Des Moines; WHO-DT (NBC) Des Moines; WOI-DT (ABC) Ames.
Programming (via satellite): ABC Family Channel; AMC; Animal Planet; Arts & Entertainment; CNBC; CNN; Country Music TV; C-SPAN; Discovery Channel; Disney Channel; ESPN; ESPN 2; Fox News Channel; FX; Headline News; HGTV; History Channel; INSP; ION Television; Lifetime; Nickelodeon; Outdoor Channel; Spike TV; TBS Superstation; The Learning Channel; Toon Disney; Travel Channel; Turner Network TV; TV Guide Network; USA Network; Weather Channel; WGN America.
Fee: $20.00 installation; $33.00 monthly.

Digital Basic Service
Subscribers: N.A.
Programming (via satellite): BBC America; Bio; Bloomberg Television; Bravo;

Discovery Digital Networks; DMX Music; ESPN Classic Sports; ESPNews; Fox College Sports Atlantic; Fox College Sports Central; Fox College Sports Pacific; Fox Movie Channel; Fox Sports World; G4; GAS; Golf Channel; Great American Country; GSN; History Channel International; Independent Film Channel; Lifetime Movie Network; Lime; MBC America; National Geographic Channel; Nick Jr.; NickToons TV; ShopNBC; Speed Channel; Style Network; The Word Network; Trio; Turner Classic Movies; Versus; WE tv.
Fee: $16.95 monthly.

Pay Service 1
Pay Units: 13.
Programming (via satellite): Encore; HBO; Starz.
Fee: $12.00 monthly (Starz/Encore), $13.00 monthly (HBO).

Digital Pay Service 1
Pay Units: N.A.
Programming (via satellite): Cinemax (multiplexed); Encore (multiplexed); Flix; HBO (multiplexed); Showtime (multiplexed); Starz (multiplexed); The Movie Channel (multiplexed).
Fee: $13.00 monthly (Starz/Encore or Cinemax), $15.00 monthly (HBO or Showtime/TMC/Flix).

Video-On-Demand: No

Pay-Per-View
Movies (delivered digitally); Special events (delivered digitally); ESPN Now (delivered digitally); Sports PPV (delivered digitally).

Internet Service
Operational: No, DSL & dial-up.

Telephone Service
Analog: Operational
Digital: Planned

Miles of Plant: 3.0 (coaxial); None (fiber optic). Homes passed: 120. Total homes in franchised area: 120.
General Manager: Andy Randol. Plant Manager: Bill Dorsett. Marketing Director: Douglas Pals. Office Manager: Cheryl Castile.
City fee: 1% of basic.
Ownership: Panora Cooperative Cablevision Assn. Inc. (MSO).

BATAVIA—Formerly served by Westcom. No longer in operation. ICA: IA0398.

BATTLE CREEK—Sac County Mutual Telco, PO Box 488, 108 S Maple, Odebolt, IA 51458. Phone: 712-668-2200. Fax: 712-668-2100. E-mail: odetelco@netins.net. Web Site: http://www.odebolt.net/sac_co_mutual_telco.html. ICA: IA0238.
TV Market Ranking: Outside TV Markets (BATTLE CREEK). Franchise award date: N.A. Franchise expiration date: N.A. Began: October 1, 1984.
Channel capacity: 41 (operating 2-way). Channels available but not in use: N.A.

Basic Service
Subscribers: 236.
Programming (received off-air): KCAU-TV (ABC) Sioux City; KMEG (CBS) Sioux City; KSIN-TV (PBS) Sioux City; KTIV (CW, NBC) Sioux City.
Programming (via satellite): ABC Family Channel; Arts & Entertainment; Cartoon Network; CNN; Country Music TV; Discovery Channel; Disney Channel; Encore; Encore Westerns; ESPN; ESPN 2; Food Network; Fox News Channel; FX; Hallmark Channel; HGTV; History Channel; Nickelodeon; Speed Channel; Spike TV; TBS Superstation; truTV; Turner Classic Movies; Turner Network TV; TV Land; USA Network; Versus; WE tv; Weather Channel; WGN America.
Fee: $15.00 installation; $25.72 monthly.

Pay Service 1
Pay Units: 9.
Programming (via satellite): Cinemax; HBO.
Fee: $15.00 installation; $11.00 monthly (Cinemax), $12.95 monthly (HBO).

Pay Service 2
Pay Units: 22.
Programming (via satellite): Flix; Showtime; The Movie Channel.
Fee: $12.75 monthly.

Internet Service
Operational: No.

Telephone Service
None

Miles of Plant: 6.0 (coaxial); None (fiber optic). Homes passed: 347. Total homes in franchised area: 347.
Manager: Dale Schaefer.
City fee: 3% of gross.
Ownership: Sac County Mutual Telephone Co. (MSO).

BAYARD—Formerly served by Tele-Services Ltd. No longer in operation. ICA: IA0260.

BELLEVUE—IVUE Network. Formerly [IA0553]. This cable system has converted to IPTV, 106 N Third St, Bellevue, IA 52031. Phone: 563-872-4456. Web Site: http://www.ivuenet.com. ICA: IA5033.
Channel capacity: N.A. Channels available but not in use: N.A.

Internet Service
Operational: Yes.

Ownership: City of Bellevue.

BELLEVUE—IVUE Network. This cable system has converted to IPTV. See Bellevue, IA [IA5033]. ICA: IA0553.

BENNETT—F & B Cablevision, PO Box 309, 103 Main St N, Wheatland, IA 52777-0309. Phone: 563-374-1236. Fax: 563-374-1930. E-mail: info@fbc.bz. Web Site: http://www.fbc.bz. ICA: IA0400.
TV Market Ranking: 60 (BENNETT). Franchise award date: N.A. Franchise expiration date: N.A. Began: July 1, 1989.
Channel capacity: N.A. Channels available but not in use: N.A.

Digital Basic Service
Subscribers: N.A.
Programming (received off-air): KCRG-TV (ABC) Cedar Rapids; KFXA (FOX) Cedar Rapids; KGAN (CBS) Cedar Rapids; KGCW (CW) Burlington; KIIN (PBS) Iowa City; KLJB (CW, FOX) Davenport; KWKB (CW, MNT) Iowa City; KWQC-TV (NBC) Davenport; KWWL (NBC) Waterloo; WHBF-TV (CBS) Rock Island; WQAD-TV (ABC) Moline; WQPT-TV (PBS) Moline.
Programming (via satellite): Bloomberg Television; CNN International; C-SPAN 2; Headline News; History Channel International; Home Shopping Network; INSP; Local Cable Weather; QVC; ShopNBC; SoapNet; Trinity Broadcasting Network.
Fee: $23.99 monthly.

Digital Expanded Basic Service
Subscribers: N.A.
Programming (received off-air): KPXR-TV (ION) Cedar Rapids; KWWF (IND) Waterloo [LICENSED & SILENT].
Programming (via satellite): ABC Family Channel; AMC; Animal Planet; Arts & Entertainment; Big Ten Network; Bio; Boomerang; Bravo; Cartoon Network; CNBC; CNN; Comcast Sports Net Northwest; Comedy Central; Cooking Channel; Country Music TV; C-SPAN; Discovery Channel; Discovery Health Channel; Disney Channel; Do-It-Yourself; E! Entertainment Television; ESPN; ESPN 2; ESPN Classic Sports; ESPNews; Food Network; Fox News Channel; FX; G4; Golf Channel; Great American Country; GSN; Hallmark Channel; HGTV; History Channel; Lifetime; Lifetime Movie Network; MSNBC; MTV; Music Choice; National Geographic Channel; Nickelodeon; Outdoor Channel; Oxygen; RFD-TV; Speed Channel; Spike TV; Syfy; TBS Superstation; The Learning Channel; Toon Disney; Travel Channel; truTV; Turner Classic Movies; Turner Network TV; TV Land; USA Network; VH1; WE tv; Weather Channel; WGN America.
Fee: $26.00 monthly.

Digital Pay Service 1
Pay Units: N.A.
Programming (via satellite): Cinemax (multiplexed); Encore (multiplexed); Flix; HBO; Showtime (multiplexed); Starz (multiplexed); Sundance Channel; The Movie Channel (multiplexed).
Fee: $15.00 monthly (HBO, Cinemax, Showtime/TMC/Flix/Sundance or Starz/Encore).

Pay-Per-View
Special events (delivered digitally); ESPN (delivered digitally).

Internet Service
Operational: No.
Broadband Service: Offers dial-up and DSL only; no cable modem service.

Telephone Service
None

Miles of Plant: 4.0 (coaxial); None (fiber optic).
General Manager: Ken Laursen. Plant Manager: Jan Muhl. Marketing Manager: Aaron Horman. Office Manager: Julie Steines.
Ownership: Farmers' & Businessmen's Telephone Co. (MSO).

BIRMINGHAM—Starwest Inc. Now served by KEOSAUQUA, IA [IA0186]. ICA: IA0401.

BLAIRSBURG—Milford Cable TV, PO Box 163, 806 Okoboji Ave, Milford, IA 51351. Phone: 712-338-4967. Fax: 712-338-4719. Web Site: http://www.milfordcable.net. ICA: IA0545.
TV Market Ranking: 66 (BLAIRSBURG). Franchise award date: N.A. Franchise expiration date: N.A. Began: January 1, 1990.
Channel capacity: 60 (not 2-way capable). Channels available but not in use: 24.

Basic Service
Subscribers: 30.
Programming (received off-air): KCCI (CBS) Des Moines; KCWI-TV (CW) Ames; KDIN-TV (PBS) Des Moines; KDSM-TV (FOX) Des Moines; KPXD-TV (ION) Arlington; WHO-DT (NBC) Des Moines; WOI-DT (ABC) Ames.
Programming (via satellite): ABC Family Channel; Arts & Entertainment; Bravo; CNBC; CNN; Country Music TV; Discovery Channel; Disney Channel; ESPN; HGTV; History Channel; Home Shopping Network; Lifetime; MSNBC; MTV; Nickelodeon; Spike TV; TBS Superstation; Turner Network TV; USA Network; VH1; WGN America.
Fee: $35.00 installation; $17.45 monthly.

Digital Basic Service
Subscribers: N.A.
Programming (via satellite): BBC America; Bio; Bloomberg Television; Current; Discovery Digital Networks; DMX Music; ESPN 2; ESPN Classic Sports; ESPNews; FitTV; Fox Movie Channel; Fox Sports Net; G4; GAS; Golf Channel; GSN; Halogen Network; HGTV; History Channel; History Channel International; Lifetime Movie Network; Lime; MTV Networks Digital Suite; National Geographic Channel; Nick Jr.; NickToons TV; Outdoor Channel; Speed Channel; Style Network; Sundance Channel; Toon Disney; Trinity Broadcasting Network; Turner Classic Movies; WE tv.

Pay Service 1
Pay Units: N.A.
Programming (via satellite): HBO (multiplexed).
Fee: $10.00 monthly.

Digital Pay Service 1
Pay Units: N.A.
Programming (via satellite): Cinemax (multiplexed); Encore (multiplexed); Flix; HBO (multiplexed); Showtime; Starz (multiplexed); The Movie Channel (multiplexed).

Internet Service
Operational: Yes.

Telephone Service
None

Miles of Plant: 1.0 (coaxial); None (fiber optic). Homes passed: 90.
General Manager & Chief Technician: Matt Plagman.
Ownership: Milford Cable TV (MSO).

BLAIRSTOWN—Coon Creek Telephone & Cablevision, PO Box 150, 312 Locust St, Blairstown, IA 52209-0150. Phones: 888-823-6234; 319-454-6234. Fax: 319-454-6480. E-mail: cooncrek@netins.net. Web Site: http://www.cooncreektelephone.com. ICA: IA0402.
TV Market Ranking: 65 (BLAIRSTOWN). Franchise award date: N.A. Franchise expiration date: N.A. Began: January 1, 1984.
Channel capacity: N.A. Channels available but not in use: N.A.

Digital Basic Service
Subscribers: 250.
Programming (received off-air): KCRG-TV (ABC) Cedar Rapids; KGAN (CBS) Cedar Rapids; KIIN (PBS) Iowa City; KWWL (NBC) Waterloo.
Programming (via satellite): ABC Family Channel; Arts & Entertainment; CNN; Discovery Channel; Disney Channel; ESPN; ESPN 2; Home Shopping Network; Lifetime; Nickelodeon; Syfy; TBS Superstation; The Learning Channel; Trinity Broadcasting Network; truTV; Turner Network TV; USA Network; WGN America.
Fee: $39.95 monthly.

Digital Pay Service 1
Pay Units: 72.
Programming (via satellite): HBO; Showtime.
Fee: $9.50 monthly.

Digital Pay Service 2
Pay Units: 43.
Programming (via satellite): Cinemax; Starz.
Fee: $9.50 monthly.

Internet Service
Operational: No, DSL only.

Telephone Service
None

Manager: Duane Andrew. Office Manager: Kami Thenhaus. Plant Superintendent: Craig Von Scoyoc.
Ownership: Coon Creek Telephone & Cablevision.

BLAKESBURG—Formerly served by Telnet South LC. No longer in operation. ICA: IA0303.

BLENCOE—Formerly served by Sky Scan Cable Co. No longer in operation. ICA: IA0352.

BLENCOE—Long Lines, 501 4th St, Sergeant Bluff, IA 51054-8509. Phones: 712-884-2203; 712-271-4000. Fax: 712-271-2727. Web Site: http://www.longlines.com. ICA: IA0604.

TV Market Ranking: Outside TV Markets (BLENCOE).

Channel capacity: N.A. Channels available but not in use: N.A.

Basic Service

Subscribers: 33.

Programming (received off-air): KCAU-TV (ABC) Sioux City; KMEG (CBS) Sioux City; KPTH (FOX, MNT) Sioux City; KSIN-TV (PBS) Sioux City; KTIV (CW, NBC) Sioux City; KXVO (CW) Omaha.

Programming (via satellite): ABC Family Channel; AMC; AmericanLife TV Network; Animal Planet; Arts & Entertainment; Big Ten Network; Cartoon Network; CNBC; CNN; Comedy Central; Country Music TV; C-SPAN; C-SPAN 2; Discovery Channel; Disney Channel; E! Entertainment Television; ESPN; ESPN 2; ESPN Classic Sports; Eternal Word TV Network; Food Network; Fox News Channel; Fox Sports Net North; FX; Golf Channel; Hallmark Channel; Headline News; HGTV; History Channel; Home Shopping Network; INSP; Lifetime; Lifetime Movie Network; MSNBC; MTV; Nickelodeon; QVC; Speed Channel; Spike TV; Syfy; TBS Superstation; The Learning Channel; The Sportsman Channel; Travel Channel; Trinity Broadcasting Network; truTV; Turner Classic Movies; Turner Network TV; TuTv; TV Guide Network; TV Land; USA Network; VH1; Weather Channel; WGN America.

Fee: $41.99 monthly.

Digital Basic Service

Subscribers: N.A.

Programming (via satellite): BBC America; Bio; Cooking Channel; Discovery Health Channel; Discovery Kids Channel; Discovery Military Channel; Discovery Planet Green; DMX Music; Do-It-Yourself; ESPN U; ESPNews; FitTV; Fox College Sports Atlantic; Fox College Sports Central; Fox College Sports Pacific; Fox Movie Channel; Fox Soccer; G4; Great American Country; GSN; Halogen Network; History Channel International; ID Investigation Discovery; Independent Film Channel; Lifetime Real Women; MTV Hits; MTV Jams; MTV2; Nick Jr.; NickToons TV; Outdoor Channel; RFD-TV; Science Channel; SoapNet; TeenNick; Toon Disney; Versus; VH1 Classic; VH1 Country; VH1 Soul; WE tv.

Fee: $9.99 monthly.

Digital Expanded Basic Service

Subscribers: N.A.

Programming (via satellite): Bandamax; De Pelicula; De Pelicula Clasico; Discovery en Espanol; ESPN Deportes; Fox Sports en Espanol; Ritmoson Latino; Telehit.

Fee: $2.99 monthly.

Digital Expanded Basic Service 2

Subscribers: N.A.

Programming (received off-air): KCAU-TV (ABC) Sioux City; KMEG (CBS) Sioux City; KPTH (FOX, MNT) Sioux City; KSIN-TV (PBS) Sioux City; KTIV (CW, NBC) Sioux City.

Programming (via satellite): Big Ten Network HD; Discovery Channel HD; ESPN 2 HD; ESPN HD; HDNet; HDNet Movies; Outdoor Channel 2 HD.

Fee: $9.95 monthly.

Pay Service 1

Pay Units: 3.

Programming (via satellite): HBO (multiplexed).

Fee: $14.95 monthly.

Pay Service 2

Pay Units: 2.

Programming (via satellite): Flix; Showtime (multiplexed); The Movie Channel.

Fee: $14.45 monthly.

Digital Pay Service 1

Pay Units: N.A.

Programming (via satellite): Cinemax (multiplexed); Cinemax HD; Encore (multiplexed); Flix; HBO (multiplexed); HBO HD; Showtime (multiplexed); Starz (multiplexed); Starz HDTV; The Movie Channel (multiplexed).

Fee: $11.95 monthly (Cinemax), $13.95 monthly (Starz/Encore), $14.45 monthly (Showtime/TMC/Flix), $14.95 monthly (HBO).

Video-On-Demand: Yes

Internet Service

Operational: No.

Miles of Plant: 109.0 (coaxial); None (fiber optic).

Manager: Paul Bergmann. System Engineer: Tony Seubert. Marketing Manager: Pat McElroy. Office Manager: Denise Moberg.

Ownership: Long Lines (MSO).

BLOCKTON—B & L Technologies LLC, 3329 270th St, Lenox, IA 50851. Phones: 800-798-5488; 641-348-2240. Fax: 641-348-2240. ICA: IA0357.

TV Market Ranking: Outside TV Markets (BLOCKTON). Franchise award date: February 1, 1988. Franchise expiration date: N.A. Began: August 1, 1988.

Channel capacity: 36 (not 2-way capable). Channels available but not in use: 14.

Basic Service

Subscribers: 13.

Programming (received off-air): KCCI (CBS) Des Moines; KDIN-TV (PBS) Des Moines; KDSM-TV (FOX) Des Moines; WHO-DT (NBC) Des Moines; WOI-DT (ABC) Ames.

Programming (via satellite): ABC Family Channel; AMC; Arts & Entertainment; CNN; Discovery Channel; ESPN; History Channel; KARE (NBC) Minneapolis; Nickelodeon; Spike TV; TBS Superstation; Turner Network TV; USA Network; VH1; WCCO-TV (CBS) Minneapolis; WGN America.

Fee: $25.00 installation; $30.50 monthly.

Pay Service 1

Pay Units: 2.

Programming (via satellite): HBO.

Fee: $12.00 monthly.

Video-On-Demand: No

Internet Service

Operational: No.

Telephone Service

None

Miles of Plant: 3.0 (coaxial); None (fiber optic). Homes passed: 120.

Manager & Chief Technician: Robert Hintz. Office Manager: Linda Hintz.

Ownership: B & L Technologies LLC (MSO).

BODE—Video Services Ltd., PO Box 23, Livermore, IA 50558-0099. Phone: 515-379-1471. Fax: 515-379-1472. ICA: IA0329.

TV Market Ranking: Outside TV Markets (BODE). Franchise award date: N.A. Franchise expiration date: N.A. Began: October 1, 1969.

Channel capacity: 30 (not 2-way capable). Channels available but not in use: 2.

Basic Service

Subscribers: N.A.

Programming (received off-air): KCCI (CBS) Des Moines; KDIN-TV (PBS) Des Moines; KDSM-TV (FOX) Des Moines; KEYC-TV (CBS, FOX) Mankato; KTIN (PBS) Fort Dodge; KTTC (CW, NBC) Rochester; WHO-DT (NBC) Des Moines; WOI-DT (ABC) Ames.

Programming (via satellite): ABC Family Channel; Discovery Channel; Disney Channel; TBS Superstation; WABC-TV (ABC) New York; WXIA-TV (NBC) Atlanta.

Fee: $30.00 installation; $8.00 monthly.

Expanded Basic Service 1

Subscribers: 55.

Programming (via satellite): Arts & Entertainment; CNN; ESPN; Lifetime; Nickelodeon; QVC; Spike TV; Travel Channel; Turner Network TV; USA Network; WGN America.

Fee: $21.00 monthly.

Pay Service 1

Pay Units: 5.

Programming (via satellite): HBO; Showtime.

Fee: $9.00 monthly (Showtime), $10.00 monthly (HBO).

Miles of Plant: 3.0 (coaxial); None (fiber optic).

Manager: Mark Steil.

City fee: None.

Ownership: Video Services Ltd.

BONAPARTE—Mediacom. Now served by KEOSAUQUA, IA [IA0186]. ICA: IA0278.

BOYDEN—Premier Communications. Now served by SIOUX CENTER, IA [IA0076]. ICA: IA0307.

BRADDYVILLE—Formerly served by CableDirect. No longer in operation. ICA: IA0582.

BRANDON—Formerly served by New Path Communications LC. No longer in operation. ICA: IA0579.

BREDA—Western Iowa Networks, PO Box 190, 112 E Main St, Breda, IA 51436-0190. Phone: 712-673-2311. Fax: 712-673-2800. Web Site: http://www.westIANet.com. Also serves Arcadia & Auburn. ICA: IA0318.

TV Market Ranking: Outside TV Markets (Arcadia, Auburn, BREDA). Franchise award date: N.A. Franchise expiration date: N.A. Began: January 1, 1983.

Channel capacity: 35 (not 2-way capable). Channels available but not in use: N.A.

Basic Service

Subscribers: 2,000 Includes Churdan, Farragut, Grand Junction, Hamburg, Malvern, Oakland, Sidney, Tabor, Treynor, Westside, & Beaver Lake NE.

Programming (received off-air): KCCI (CBS) Des Moines; KDIN-TV (PBS) Des Moines; KDSM-TV (FOX) Des Moines; KPTH (FOX, MNT) Sioux City; KTIV (CW, NBC) Sioux City; WHO-DT (NBC) Des Moines; WOI-DT (ABC) Ames.

Programming (via satellite): AMC; CNN; Country Music TV; Discovery Channel; Disney Channel; ESPN; HGTV; Lifetime; Nickelodeon; Spike TV; TBS Superstation; Turner Network TV; TV Land; USA Network; WGN America.

Fee: $20.00 installation; $25.45 monthly.

Pay Service 1

Pay Units: 35.

Programming (via satellite): HBO.

Fee: $10.95 monthly.

Video-On-Demand: No

Internet Service

Operational: No, DSL.

Telephone Service

None

Miles of Plant: 4.0 (coaxial); None (fiber optic).

Chief Executive Officer: Steve Frickenstein. Marketing & Sales Manager: Megan Badding. Chief Technician: Mike Ludwig.

Ownership: Tele-Services Ltd. (MSO).

BRIGHTON—Starwest Inc., 15235 235th St, Milton, IA 52570-8016. Phones: 319-397-2283; 319-293-6336. ICA: IA0403.

TV Market Ranking: Below 100 (BRIGHTON). Franchise award date: N.A. Franchise expiration date: N.A. Began: N.A.

Channel capacity: N.A. Channels available but not in use: N.A.

Basic Service

Subscribers: N.A.

Programming (received off-air): KCRG-TV (ABC) Cedar Rapids; KGAN (CBS) Cedar Rapids; KWWL (NBC) Waterloo.

Programming (via satellite): ABC Family Channel; CNN; Discovery Channel; ESPN; Headline News; MTV; Nickelodeon; TBS Superstation; USA Network; VH1; WGN America.

Fee: $30.00 installation; $14.50 monthly.

Pay Service 1

Pay Units: N.A.

Programming (via satellite): Showtime.

Fee: $10.00 monthly.

Internet Service

Operational: No.

Manager & Chief Technician: John Stooksberry.

Ownership: Starwest Inc. (MSO).

BRISTOW—Dumont Cablevision. Now served by DUMONT, IA [IA0250]. ICA: IA0371.

BRONSON—TelePartners. Now served by LAWTON, IA [IA0330]. ICA: IA0372.

BROOKLYN—Inter-County Cable Co., PO Box 513, 129 Jackson St, Brooklyn, IA 52211. Phones: 641-522-9211; 641-522-7000. Fax: 641-522-5001. E-mail: icc@netins.net. Web Site: http://www.showcase.netins.net/web/brooktelco/index.html. Also serves Malcom. ICA: IA0158.

TV Market Ranking: Below 100 (BROOKLYN, Malcom). Franchise award date: July 29, 1982. Franchise expiration date: N.A. Began: July 29, 1982.

Channel capacity: 31 (not 2-way capable). Channels available but not in use: N.A.

Basic Service

Subscribers: 953.

Programming (received off-air): KCCI (CBS) Des Moines; KCRG-TV (ABC) Cedar Rapids; KDIN-TV (PBS) Des Moines; KDSM-TV (FOX) Des Moines; KGAN (CBS) Cedar Rapids; KWWL (NBC) Waterloo; WHO-DT (NBC) Des Moines; WOI-DT (ABC) Ames.

Programming (via satellite): ABC Family Channel; AMC; AmericanLife TV Network; Animal Planet; Arts & Entertainment; Cartoon Network; CNN; Comedy Central; Country Music TV; C-SPAN; Discovery Channel; Disney Channel; E! Entertainment Television; ESPN; ESPN 2; ESPNews; Food Network; Fox News Channel; Fox Sports Net Midwest; FX; Golf Channel; Great American Country; GSN; Hallmark Channel; HGTV; History Channel; Home Shopping Network; INSP; Lifetime; MTV;

Nickelodeon; Outdoor Channel; Paxson Communications Corp.; QVC; SoapNet; Spike TV; Syfy; TBS Superstation; The Learning Channel; Travel Channel; Trinity Broadcasting Network; truTV; Turner Classic Movies; Turner Network TV; TV Land; USA Network; VH1; WE tv; Weather Channel; WGN America.
Fee: $25.00 installation; $29.90 monthly.

Digital Basic Service
Subscribers: 65.
Programming (via satellite): Bio; Bloomberg Television; Bravo; DMX Music; ESPN Classic Sports; Fox College Sports Atlantic; Fox College Sports Central; Fox College Sports Pacific; Fox Sports World; GAS; History Channel International; Lifetime Movie Network; MTV Networks Digital Suite; National Geographic Channel; Nick Jr.; ShopNBC; Style Network; Trio; Versus.
Fee: $15.95 monthly.

Pay Service 1
Pay Units: 204.
Programming (via satellite): Cinemax; HBO.
Fee: $9.95 monthly (each).

Digital Pay Service 1
Pay Units: N.A.
Programming (via satellite): Cinemax (multiplexed); Encore (multiplexed); HBO (multiplexed); Showtime (multiplexed); Starz (multiplexed); The Movie Channel (multiplexed).

Pay-Per-View
Addressable homes: 65.
ActionMax (delivered digitally), Addressable: Yes; Sports PPV (delivered digitally); Hot Choice (delivered digitally); Playboy TV (delivered digitally); Fresh (delivered digitally); Shorteez (delivered digitally); ESPN Now (delivered digitally); ESPN Extra (delivered digitally).

Internet Service
Operational: No, DSL.

Telephone Service
None

Miles of Plant: 26.0 (coaxial); 8.0 (fiber optic).
General Manager: Tim Atkinson. Plant Manager: Don Gepner. Office Manager: Martina Korns.
City fee: 3% of gross.
Ownership: Inter-County Cable Co.

BUFFALO CENTER—Mediacom, PO Box 110, 1504 2nd St SE, Waseca, MN 56093. Phone: 507-835-2356. Fax: 507-835-4567. Web Site: http://www.mediacomcable.com. Also serves Bancroft & Burt. ICA: IA0179.
TV Market Ranking: Outside TV Markets (Bancroft, BUFFALO CENTER, Burt). Franchise award date: N.A. Franchise expiration date: N.A. Began: N.A.
Channel capacity: N.A. Channels available but not in use: N.A.

Basic Service
Subscribers: 791.
Programming (received off-air): KAAL (ABC) Austin; KELO-TV (CBS, MNT) Sioux Falls; KEYC-TV (CBS, FOX) Mankato; KIMT (CBS, MNT) Mason City; KPTH (FOX, MNT) Sioux City; KTIN (PBS) Fort Dodge; KTTC (CW, NBC) Rochester; WHO-DT (NBC) Des Moines.
Programming (via microwave): WFTC (MNT) Minneapolis.
Programming (via satellite): ABC Family Channel; AMC; Animal Planet; Arts & Entertainment; Bravo; Cartoon Network; CNBC; CNN; Comedy Central; Country Music TV; C-SPAN; C-SPAN 2; CW+; Discovery Channel; Disney Channel; E! Entertainment Television; ESPN; ESPN 2; ESPN Classic Sports; ESPNews; Eternal Word TV Network; Food Network; Fox Movie Channel; Fox News Channel; Fox Sports Net North; FX; Hallmark Channel; Headline News; HGTV; History Channel; Home Shopping Network; INSP; Lifetime; MoviePlex; MSNBC; MTV; Nickelodeon; Oxygen; QVC; Radar Channel; SoapNet; Speed Channel; Spike TV; Syfy; TBS Superstation; Telemundo; The Learning Channel; Toon Disney; Travel Channel; Trinity Broadcasting Network; truTV; Turner Classic Movies; Turner Network TV; TV Guide Network; TV Land; Univision; USA Network; Versus; VH1; WE tv; Weather Channel; WGN America.
Fee: $24.90 monthly.

Digital Basic Service
Subscribers: N.A.
Programming (via satellite): AmericanLife TV Network; BBC America; Bio; Bloomberg Television; Canal 52MX; CBS College Sports Network; CCTV-9 (CCTV International); Cine Latino; CMT Pure Country; CNN en Espanol; Discovery en Espanol; Discovery Health Channel; Discovery Home Channel; Discovery Kids Channel; Discovery Military Channel; Discovery Times Channel; DMX Music; ESPN 2 HD; ESPN Deportes; ESPN HD; ESPN U; ESPNews; FitTV; Fox College Sports Atlantic; Fox College Sports Central; Fox College Sports Pacific; Fox Reality Channel; Fox Soccer; Fox Sports en Espanol; Fuel TV; Fuse; G4; Gol TV; Golf Channel; GSN; Halogen Network; HDNet; HDNet Movies; History Channel en Espanol; History Channel International; Independent Film Channel; Lifetime Movie Network; Lifetime Real Women; MTV Hits; MTV Tres; MTV2; National Geographic Channel; Nick Jr.; NickToons TV; Outdoor Channel; Ovation; Science Channel; Sleuth; Style Network; TeenNick; Tennis Channel; The Sportsman Channel; TV Guide Network; Universal HD; VeneMovies; VH1 Classic; VH1 Soul.

Digital Pay Service 1
Pay Units: N.A.
Programming (via satellite): Cinemax (multiplexed); Encore (multiplexed); Flix; HBO (multiplexed); HBO HD; Showtime (multiplexed); Showtime HD; Starz (multiplexed); Starz HDTV; Sundance Channel; The Movie Channel (multiplexed); The Movie Channel HD.
Fee: $9.95 monthly (Cinemax, HBO, Showtime or Flix, Sundance & TMC or Starz & Encore).

Video-On-Demand: Yes

Pay-Per-View
ESPN Now (delivered digitally); Hot Choice (delivered digitally); Playboy TV (delivered digitally); Fresh (delivered digitally); Shorteez (delivered digitally); TVN Entertainment (delivered digitally); sports (delivered digitally).

Internet Service
Operational: Yes.
Broadband Service: Mediacom High Speed Internet.
Fee: $99.00 installation; $40.95 monthly.

Telephone Service
Digital: Operational

Miles of Plant: 18.0 (coaxial); None (fiber optic). Homes passed: 1,087.
Vice President: Bill Jensen. Engineering Manager: Kraig Kaiser. Marketing & Sales Director: Lori Huberty.
Ownership: Mediacom LLC (MSO).

BUFFALO CENTER—Winnebago Cooperative Telephone Assn., 704 E Main St, Lake Mills, IA 50450-1420. Phones: 641-592-6105; 800-592-6105. Fax: 641-592-6102. E-mail: wcta@wctatel.net. Web Site: http://www.wctatel.net. ICA: IA0588. **Note:** This system is an overbuild.
TV Market Ranking: Outside TV Markets (BUFFALO CENTER). Franchise award date: N.A. Franchise expiration date: N.A. Began: N.A.
Channel capacity: N.A. Channels available but not in use: N.A.

Basic Service
Subscribers: 319.
Programming (received off-air): KAAL (ABC) Austin; KEYC-TV (CBS, FOX) Mankato; KFPX-TV (ION) Newton; KIMT (CBS, MNT) Mason City; KTTC (CW, NBC) Rochester; KXLT-TV (FOX) Rochester; KYIN (PBS) Mason City.
Fee: $20.00 installation; $19.95 monthly.

Expanded Basic Service 1
Subscribers: N.A.
Programming (via satellite): ABC Family Channel; AMC; Animal Planet; Arts & Entertainment; Bravo; Cartoon Network; CNBC; CNN; Comedy Central; Country Music TV; C-SPAN; CW+; Discovery Channel; Disney Channel; Do-It-Yourself; E! Entertainment Television; Encore (multiplexed); ESPN; ESPN 2; ESPN Classic Sports; Food Network; Fox News Channel; Fox Sports Net North; FX; G4; Golf Channel; Hallmark Channel; Headline News; HGTV; History Channel; Home Shopping Network; INSP; Lifetime; MSNBC; MTV; Nickelodeon; Outdoor Channel; Speed Channel; Spike TV; Syfy; TBS Superstation; The Learning Channel; Travel Channel; Trinity Broadcasting Network; Turner Classic Movies; Turner Network TV; TV Land; USA Network; VH1; Weather Channel; WGN America.
Fee: $18.30 monthly.

Video-On-Demand: No

Internet Service
Operational: No.

Telephone Service
None

General Manager: Don Whipple. Assistant Manager: John Kroger. Chief Engineer: Neal Sletten. Marketing Manager: David Taft.
Ownership: Winnebago Cooperative Telephone Assn. (MSO).

BURLINGTON—Mediacom, 6300 Council St NE, Ste A, Cedar Rapids, IA 52402. Phones: 319-395-9699 (Cedar Rapids office); 319-753-6576 (Local office). Fax: 319-393-7017. Web Site: http://www.mediacomcable.com. Also serves Carthage, IL; Columbus City, Columbus Junction, Danville, Fredonia, Iowa Army Munitions Plant, Lee County (northern portion), Louisa County, Middletown, Morning Sun, Wapello & West Burlington, IA. ICA: IA0405.
TV Market Ranking: Below 100 (BURLINGTON, Carthage, Columbus City, Columbus Junction, Danville, Fredonia, Iowa Army Munitions Plant, Lee County (northern portion), Louisa County, Middletown, Morning Sun, Wapello, West Burlington). Franchise award date: N.A. Franchise expiration date: N.A. Began: December 31, 1979.
Channel capacity: N.A. Channels available but not in use: N.A.

Basic Service
Subscribers: 27,864.
Programming (received off-air): KGCW (CW) Burlington; KIIN (PBS) Iowa City; KLJB (CW, FOX) Davenport; KWQC-TV (NBC) Davenport; KYOU-TV (FOX) Ottumwa; WGEM-TV (CW, NBC) Quincy; WHBF-TV (CBS) Rock Island; WQAD-TV (ABC) Moline; 18 FMs.
Programming (via satellite): C-SPAN; C-SPAN 2; Home Shopping Network; ION Television; Local Cable Weather; QVC; TV Guide Network; WGN America.
Current originations: Government Access; Educational Access; Public Access.
Fee: $10.10 monthly.

Expanded Basic Service 1
Subscribers: 26,583.
Programming (via satellite): ABC Family Channel; AMC; Animal Planet; Arts & Entertainment; BET Networks; Bravo; Cartoon Network; CNBC; CNN; Comedy Central; Country Music TV; Discovery Channel; Disney Channel; E! Entertainment Television; ESPN; ESPN 2; Eternal Word TV Network; FitTV; Food Network; Fox News Channel; Fox Sports Net Midwest; FX; Hallmark Channel; Headline News; HGTV; History Channel; INSP; Lifetime; Lifetime Movie Network; MSNBC; MTV; National Geographic Channel; Nickelodeon; SoapNet; Speed Channel; Spike TV; Syfy; TBS Superstation; Telemundo; The Learning Channel; Travel Channel; Trinity Broadcasting Network; truTV; Turner Network TV; TV Land; Univision; USA Network; Versus; VH1; WE tv; Weather Channel.
Fee: $21.31 monthly.

Digital Basic Service
Subscribers: 2,980.
Programming (received off-air): KLJB (CW, FOX) Davenport; WQAD-TV (ABC) Moline.
Programming (via satellite): AmericanLife TV Network; BBC America; Bio; Bloomberg Television; Discovery Digital Networks; Discovery HD Theater; ESPN 2 HD; ESPN HD; ESPNews; Fox Movie Channel; Fox Soccer; Fuse; G4; GAS; Golf Channel; GSN; Halogen Network; HDNet; HDNet Movies; History Channel International; Independent Film Channel; Lime; MTV Networks Digital Suite; Music Choice; Nick Jr.; NickToons TV; Outdoor Channel; Ovation; Sleuth; Style Network; Toon Disney; Turner Classic Movies; TVG Network; Universal HD.

Digital Pay Service 1
Pay Units: 4,673.
Programming (via satellite): Cinemax (multiplexed); Encore (multiplexed); Flix (multiplexed); HBO (multiplexed); HBO HD; Showtime (multiplexed); Showtime HD; Starz (multiplexed); Starz HDTV; Sundance Channel (multiplexed); The Movie Channel (multiplexed); The Movie Channel HD.
Fee: $10.00 installation; $8.95 monthly (Cinemax, HBO, Showtime, Flix/Sundance/TMC, or Starz/Encore).

Video-On-Demand: No

Pay-Per-View
Addressable homes: 2,890.
ESPN Now (delivered digitally); ETC (delivered digitally); Playboy TV (delivered digitally); Pleasure (delivered digitally); TVN Entertainment (delivered digitally); sports (delivered digitally).

Internet Service
Operational: Yes.
Broadband Service: Mediacom High Speed Internet.
Fee: $49.95 installation; $45.95 monthly; $10.00 modem lease.

Telephone Service
Digital: Operational
Fee: $39.95 monthly

Miles of Plant: 250.0 (coaxial); None (fiber optic). Homes passed: 32,911. Total homes in franchised area: 34,508. Miles of plant is fiber and coax combined.

Sales & Marketing Director: Michelle Harper. Technical Operations Manager: Joel Hanger.
City fee: 3% of gross.
Ownership: Mediacom LLC (MSO).

CALHOUN COUNTY (portions)—Gowrie Cablevision, PO Box 415, Gowrie, IA 50543. Phones: 800-292-8989; 515-352-5227. Fax: 515-352-5226. E-mail: gocabletv@lvcta.com. Web Site: http://www.gowrie.org/utilities/gowrie_catv.htm. ICA: IA0609.
TV Market Ranking: Outside TV Markets (CALHOUN COUNTY (PORTIONS)).
Channel capacity: 30 (not 2-way capable). Channels available but not in use: N.A.
Basic Service
Subscribers: 125.
Programming (received off-air): KCCI (CBS) Des Moines; KCWI-TV (CW) Ames; KDIN-TV (PBS) Des Moines; KDSM-TV (FOX) Des Moines; WHO-DT (NBC) Des Moines; WOI-DT (ABC) Ames.
Programming (via satellite): ABC Family Channel; AMC; CNBC; CNN; Comedy Central; Discovery Channel; ESPN; ESPN 2; Fox News Channel; Headline News; HGTV; History Channel; Nickelodeon; Spike TV; TBS Superstation; Turner Classic Movies; Turner Network TV; TV Land; USA Network; Weather Channel; WGN America.
Fee: $22.00 monthly.
Internet Service
Operational: No, Both DSL & dialup.
Telephone Service
None
Miles of Plant: 6.0 (coaxial); None (fiber optic). Homes passed: 330.
Manager: Paul Johnson.
Ownership: Gowrie Cablevision Inc. (MSO).

CAMBRIDGE—Huxley Communications Corp., PO Box 70, 102 N Main Ave, Huxley, IA 50124-0070. Phones: 800-231-4922; 515-597-2281. Fax: 515-597-2899. E-mail: huxtel@huxcomm.net. Web Site: http://www.huxcomm.net. ICA: IA0406.
TV Market Ranking: 66 (CAMBRIDGE). Franchise award date: N.A. Franchise expiration date: N.A. Began: January 1, 1985.
Channel capacity: 44 (operating 2-way). Channels available but not in use: None.
Basic Service
Subscribers: 163.
Programming (received off-air): KCCI (CBS) Des Moines; KDIN-TV (PBS) Des Moines; KDSM-TV (FOX) Des Moines; WHO-DT (NBC) Des Moines; WOI-DT (ABC) Ames.
Programming (via satellite): ABC Family Channel; AMC; Animal Planet; Arts & Entertainment; Big Ten Network; Cartoon Network; CNBC; CNN; Comedy Central; Cooking Channel; Country Music TV; Discovery Channel; Disney Channel; Do-It-Yourself; E! Entertainment Television; ESPN; ESPN 2; ESPN Classic Sports; ESPN U; ESPNews; Food Network; Fox Movie Channel; Fox News Channel; Fox Sports Net Midwest; FX; G4; Golf Channel; Hallmark Channel; Headline News; HGTV; History Channel; Home Shopping Network; ION Television; Lifetime; MSNBC; MTV; National Geographic Channel; Nickelodeon; Outdoor Channel; RFD-TV; Speed Channel; Spike TV; Syfy; TBS Superstation; The Learning Channel; Toon Disney; Travel Channel; Trinity Broadcasting Network; truTV; Turner Classic Movies; Turner Network TV; TV Land; USA Network; VH1; Weather Channel; WGN America.
Current originations: Public Access.
Fee: $30.00 installation; $40.00 monthly.
Digital Basic Service
Subscribers: N.A.
Programming (via satellite): AmericanLife TV Network; BBC America; Bio; Bloomberg Television; Bravo; Current; Discovery Health Channel; Discovery Home Channel; Discovery Kids Channel; Discovery Military Channel; Discovery Times Channel; DMX Music; ESPN 2; ESPN Classic Sports; ESPNews; FitTV; Fox College Sports Atlantic; Fox College Sports Central; Fox College Sports Pacific; Fox Movie Channel; Fox Soccer; Fuse; G4; Golf Channel; Gospel Music Channel; Great American Country; GSN; HGTV; History Channel; History Channel International; Independent Film Channel; INSP; International Television (ITV); Lifetime Movie Network; Lime; MTV Hits; MTV2; National Geographic Channel; Nick Jr.; NickToons TV; Outdoor Channel; Ovation; Science Channel; ShopNBC; Sleuth; Speed Channel; Style Network; Sundance Channel; TeenNick; The Word Network; Toon Disney; Trinity Broadcasting Network; Turner Classic Movies; Versus; VH1 Classic; VH1 Country; VH1 Soul; WE tv.
Fee: $10.00 monthly.
Pay Service 1
Pay Units: 13.
Programming (via satellite): HBO.
Fee: $15.00 monthly.
Pay Service 2
Pay Units: 16.
Programming (via satellite): Showtime.
Fee: $10.00 monthly.
Pay Service 3
Pay Units: 25.
Programming (via satellite): Cinemax.
Fee: $10.00 monthly.
Pay Service 4
Pay Units: 33.
Programming (via satellite): Encore; Starz.
Fee: $10.00 monthly.
Digital Pay Service 1
Pay Units: N.A.
Programming (via satellite): Cinemax (multiplexed); Encore (multiplexed); Flix; HBO (multiplexed); Showtime (multiplexed); Starz; The Movie Channel (multiplexed).
Fee: $10.00 monthly (Cinemax, Showtime or Starz/Encore), $15.00 monthly (HBO).
Video-On-Demand: Planned
Pay-Per-View
iN DEMAND (delivered digitally); Spice (delivered digitally); Spice 2 (delivered digitally); Playboy TV (delivered digitally).
Internet Service
Operational: No, DSL.
Telephone Service
None
Homes passed: 304.
General Manager: Gary Clark. Operations Director: Terry Ferguson. Plant Manager: Brant Strumpfer.
City fee: 3% of gross.
Ownership: Huxley Communications Corp. (MSO).

CARROLL—Mediacom. Now served by ATLANTIC, IA [IA0032]. ICA: IA0025.

CARSON—Interstate Communications, PO Box 229, 105 N West St, Truro, IA 50257-0229. Phones: 641-765-4201; 712-824-7227. Fax: 641-765-4204. Web Site: http://www.interstatecom.com. Also serves Macedonia. ICA: IA0198.
TV Market Ranking: 53 (CARSON, Macedonia). Franchise award date: N.A. Franchise expiration date: N.A. Began: November 1, 1983.
Channel capacity: 54 (not 2-way capable). Channels available but not in use: N.A.
Basic Service
Subscribers: 308.
Programming (received off-air): KETV (ABC) Omaha; KMTV-TV (CBS) Omaha; KPTM (FOX, MNT) Omaha; KXVO (CW) Omaha; WOWT-TV (IND, NBC) Omaha.
Programming (via satellite): ABC Family Channel; AMC; Animal Planet; Arts & Entertainment; Cartoon Network; CNN; Country Music TV; C-SPAN; C-SPAN 2; Discovery Channel; Disney Channel; ESPN; ESPN 2; Hallmark Channel; HGTV; History Channel; Iowa Communications Network; Lifetime; Nickelodeon; Spike TV; Syfy; TBS Superstation; The Learning Channel; Turner Network TV; USA Network; Weather Channel; WGN America.
Fee: $35.00 installation; $23.50 monthly.
Pay Service 1
Pay Units: 140.
Programming (via satellite): Cinemax; HBO.
Fee: $9.00 monthly (each).
Video-On-Demand: No
Internet Service
Operational: No.
Telephone Service
None
Miles of Plant: 6.0 (coaxial); None (fiber optic). Homes passed: 420.
Manager: Mike Weis. Chief Technician: Rick Lunn.
Ownership: Interstate Communications (MSO).

CASCADE—Cascade Communications, PO Box 250, 106 Taylor St, Cascade, IA 52033. Phone: 563-852-3710. Fax: 563-852-9935. E-mail: info@cascadecomm.com. Web Site: http://www.cascadecomm.com. ICA: IA0608.
TV Market Ranking: Below 100 (CASCADE).
Channel capacity: N.A. Channels available but not in use: N.A.
Basic Service
Subscribers: N.A.
Programming (received off-air): KCRG-TV (ABC) Cedar Rapids; KFXA (FOX) Cedar Rapids; KFXB-TV (IND) Dubuque; KGAN (CBS) Cedar Rapids; KPXR-TV (ION) Cedar Rapids; KRIN (PBS) Waterloo; KWKB (CW, MNT) Iowa City; KWWL (NBC) Waterloo.
Programming (via satellite): C-SPAN; Home Shopping Network; QVC; ShopNBC; TV Guide Network.
Fee: $18.99 monthly.
Expanded Basic Service 1
Subscribers: N.A.
Programming (via satellite): ABC Family Channel; AMC; Animal Planet; Arts & Entertainment; BET Networks; Bravo; Cartoon Network; CNBC; CNN; Comcast SportsNet Chicago; Comedy Central; Country Music TV; Discovery Channel; Disney Channel; E! Entertainment Television; ESPN; ESPN 2; ESPN Classic Sports; Eternal Word TV Network; Food Network; Fox News Channel; FX; Great American Country; Hallmark Channel; Headline News; HGTV; History Channel; INSP; Lifetime; MSNBC; MTV; National Geographic Channel; Nickelodeon; Speed Channel; Spike TV; Syfy; TBS Superstation; The Learning Channel; Travel Channel; Trinity Broadcasting Network; truTV; Turner Classic Movies; Turner Network TV; TV Land; USA Network; VH1; WE tv; Weather Channel; WGN America.
Fee: $49.95 monthly.
Pay Service 1
Pay Units: N.A.
Programming (via satellite): Cinemax; HBO; Showtime.
Internet Service
Operational: No, DSL only.
Telephone Service
None
Homes passed: 1,000.
General Manager: Dave Gibson. Technical Operations Manager: Marcus Behnken.
Ownership: Cascade Communications Co.

CASEY—Casey Cable Co., 108 E Logan St, Casey, IA 50048-1012. Phone: 641-746-2222. Fax: 641-746-2221. ICA: IA0286.
TV Market Ranking: Outside TV Markets (CASEY). Franchise award date: February 1, 1984. Franchise expiration date: N.A. Began: February 1, 1984.
Channel capacity: 45 (not 2-way capable). Channels available but not in use: N.A.
Basic Service
Subscribers: 142.
Programming (received off-air): KCCI (CBS) Des Moines; KDSM-TV (FOX) Des Moines; WHO-DT (NBC) Des Moines; WOI-DT (ABC) Ames.
Programming (via satellite): ABC Family Channel; AMC; Arts & Entertainment; CNN; Country Music TV; Discovery Channel; Disney Channel; ESPN; ESPN 2; Headline News; Nickelodeon; Spike TV; Syfy; TBS Superstation; The Learning Channel; Turner Network TV; USA Network; WGN America.
Fee: $20.00 monthly.
Pay Service 1
Pay Units: 42.
Programming (via satellite): HBO.
Fee: $10.00 monthly.
Pay Service 2
Pay Units: 28.
Programming (via satellite): Flix; Showtime; The Movie Channel.
Fee: $10.95 monthly.
Internet Service
Operational: No, DSL only.
Telephone Service
None
Miles of Plant: 6.0 (coaxial); None (fiber optic). Homes passed: 228. Total homes in franchised area: 228.
Manager & Chief Technician: John Breining. Customer Service Manager: Traci Clarke.
Ownership: Casey Mutual Telephone Co.

CEDAR FALLS—Cedar Falls Municipal Communications Utility, PO Box 769, Utility Parkway, Cedar Falls, IA 50613. Phone: 319-266-1761. Fax: 319-266-8158. E-mail: cfu@cfunet.net. Web Site: http://www.cfunet.net. ICA: IA0564.
TV Market Ranking: 65 (CEDAR FALLS). Franchise award date: N.A. Franchise expiration date: N.A. Began: March 1, 1996.
Channel capacity: 78 (operating 2-way). Channels available but not in use: None.
Basic Service
Subscribers: 7,800.
Programming (received off-air): KCRG-TV (ABC) Cedar Rapids; KFXA (FOX) Cedar Rapids; KGAN (CBS) Cedar Rapids; KPXR-TV (ION) Cedar Rapids; KRIN (PBS) Waterloo; KWKB (CW, MNT) Iowa City; KWWL (NBC) Waterloo.
Programming (via satellite): Church Channel; C-SPAN; C-SPAN 2; QVC; TBS Superstation; Toon Disney; Weather Channel; WGN America.

Current originations: Religious Access; Educational Access; Public Access.
Fee: $25.00 installation; $11.00 monthly; $2.00 converter; $5.00 additional installation.

Expanded Basic Service 1
Subscribers: 6,290.
Programming (via satellite): ABC Family Channel; AMC; AmericanLife TV Network; Animal Planet; Arts & Entertainment; BET Networks; Bravo; Cartoon Network; CNBC; CNN; Comcast SportsNet Chicago; Comedy Central; Country Music TV; Discovery Channel; Disney Channel; E! Entertainment Television; ESPN; ESPN 2; ESPN Classic Sports; ESPN U; ESPNews; Food Network; Fox News Channel; FX; Golf Channel; Hallmark Channel; Headline News; HGTV; History Channel; Lifetime; MoviePlex; MSNBC; MTV; National Geographic Channel; Nickelodeon; Oxygen; Speed Channel; Spike TV; Syfy; The Learning Channel; Travel Channel; truTV; Turner Classic Movies; Turner Network TV; TV Land; USA Network; Versus; VH1; WE tv.
Fee: $28.00 monthly.

Digital Basic Service
Subscribers: 3,600.
Programming (received off-air): KCRG-TV (ABC) Cedar Rapids; KGAN (CBS) Cedar Rapids; KWWL (NBC) Waterloo.
Programming (via satellite): BBC America; Bio; Bloomberg Television; CBS College Sports Network; Current; Discovery Digital Networks; Discovery HD Theater; DMX Music; Encore (multiplexed); ESPN 2 HD; ESPN U; Fox HD; Fox Movie Channel; Fox Sports World; Fuse; G4; GAS; Golf Channel; GSN; Hallmark Movie Channel; Halogen Network; HDNet; HDNet Movies; History Channel International; Independent Film Channel; INHD; MTV Networks Digital Suite; NFL Network; Nick Jr.; Outdoor Channel; Ovation; RFD-TV; Style Network; The Sportsman Channel; Trinity Broadcasting Network.
Fee: $17.50 monthly; $7.00 converter.

Pay Service 1
Pay Units: N.A.
Programming (via satellite): Encore.

Pay Service 2
Pay Units: 589.
Programming (via satellite): Starz.
Fee: $6.00 monthly.

Pay Service 3
Pay Units: 1,571.
Programming (via satellite): HBO.
Fee: $12.00 monthly.

Digital Pay Service 1
Pay Units: N.A.
Programming (via satellite): Cinemax (multiplexed); HBO (multiplexed); Showtime (multiplexed); Starz (multiplexed); Sundance Channel; The Movie Channel (multiplexed).
Fee: $6.00 monthly (Starz/Encore), $10.00 monthly (Cinemax or Showtime/TMC), $12.00 monthly (HBO).

Video-On-Demand: No

Pay-Per-View
iN DEMAND (delivered digitally); Urban Xtra PPV (delivered digitally); Hot Choice (delivered digitally); Playboy TV (delivered digitally); Fresh (delivered digitally); Shorteez (delivered digitally); ESPN Now (delivered digitally); Sports PPV (delivered digitally).

Internet Service
Operational: Yes. Began: January 9, 1997.
Subscribers: 4,000.
Broadband Service: In-house.
Fee: $25.00 installation; $40.00 monthly.

Telephone Service
None

Miles of Plant: 150.0 (coaxial); 50.0 (fiber optic). Homes passed: 12,848. Total homes in franchised area: 13,681.
Manager: Jim Krieg. Marketing Manager: Betty Zeman. Chief Engineer: Dave Schilling.
Ownership: Cedar Falls Municipal Communications Utility (MSO).

CEDAR RAPIDS—Mediacom, 6300 Council St NE, Ste A, Cedar Rapids, IA 52402. Phones: 800-332-0245; 319-395-9699. Fax: 319-393-7017. Web Site: http://www.mediacomcable.com. Also serves Amana, Anamosa, Atalissa, Belle Plaine, Bertram, Coralville, Fairfax, Hiawatha, Hills, Iowa City, Johnson County, Jones County (portions), Kalona, Keota, Linn County (unincorporated areas), Lisbon, Lone Tree, Marengo, Marion, Monticello, Mount Vernon, Newhall, North English, North Liberty, Norway, Oxford, Oxford Junction, Riverside, Sigourney, Solon Mills, Swisher, Tiffin, Tipton, Toddville, University Heights, Vinton, Washington, Wellman, West Branch, West Liberty, What Cheer, Williamsburg & Wyoming. ICA: IA0002.
TV Market Ranking: 60 (Atalissa, West Liberty); 65 (Amana, Anamosa, Belle Plain, Bertram, CEDAR RAPIDS, Coralville, Fairfax, Hiawatha, Hills, Iowa City, Johnson County, Kalona, Linn County (unincorporated areas), Lisbon, Marengo, Marion, Monticello, Mount Vernon, Newhall, Oxford, Oxford Junction, Riverside, Swisher, Tiffin, Toddville, University Heights, Vinton, West Branch, Williamsburg, Wyoming); Below 100 (Keota, Lone Tree, North English, Sigourney, Washington, What Cheer, Wellman). Franchise award date: June 21, 1978. Franchise expiration date: N.A. Began: April 30, 1979.
Channel capacity: 110 (operating 2-way). Channels available but not in use: 30.

Basic Service
Subscribers: 90,229.
Programming (received off-air): KCRG-TV (ABC) Cedar Rapids; KFXA (FOX) Cedar Rapids; KGAN (CBS) Cedar Rapids; KIIN (PBS) Iowa City; KPXR-TV (ION) Cedar Rapids; KWKB (CW, MNT) Iowa City; KWWF (IND) Waterloo [LICENSED & SILENT]; KWWL (NBC) Waterloo.
Programming (via satellite): C-SPAN; C-SPAN 2; Home Shopping Network; QVC; ShopNBC; TBS Superstation; TV Guide Network; WGN America.
Current originations: Educational Access; Public Access.
Fee: $25.00 installation; $9.40 monthly; $3.50 converter.

Expanded Basic Service 1
Subscribers: 83,598.
Programming (via satellite): ABC Family Channel; AMC; Animal Planet; Arts & Entertainment; BET Networks; Bravo; Cartoon Network; CNBC; CNN; Comedy Central; Country Music TV; Discovery Channel; Disney Channel; E! Entertainment Television; ESPN; ESPN 2; Eternal Word TV Network; FitTV; Food Network; Fox News Channel; FX; Great American Country; Hallmark Channel; Headline News; HGTV; History Channel; INSP; Lifetime; MSNBC; MTV; National Geographic Channel; Nickelodeon; SoapNet; Speed Channel; Spike TV; Syfy; The Learning Channel; Travel Channel; Trinity Broadcasting Network; truTV; Turner Network TV; TV Land; Univision; USA Network; Versus; VH1; WE tv; Weather Channel.
Fee: $45.95 monthly.

Digital Basic Service
Subscribers: 18,244.
Programming (via satellite): AmericanLife TV Network; BBC America; Bio; Bloomberg Television; Current; Discovery Digital Networks; Discovery HD Theater; DMX Music; ESPN; Fox Movie Channel; Fox Soccer; Fuse; G4; GAS; Golf Channel; GSN; Halogen Network; HDNet; HDNet Movies; History Channel International; Independent Film Channel; KFXA (FOX) Cedar Rapids; KWWL (NBC) Waterloo; Lifetime Movie Network; Lime; MTV Networks Digital Suite; Nick Jr.; Outdoor Channel; Ovation; Science Television; Sleuth; Style Network; Toon Disney; Turner Classic Movies; Universal HD.
Fee: $12.00 monthly.

Digital Pay Service 1
Pay Units: 9,713.
Programming (via satellite): Cinemax (multiplexed).
Fee: $10.00 installation; $10.50 monthly.

Digital Pay Service 2
Pay Units: 8,476.
Programming (via satellite): HBO (multiplexed).

Digital Pay Service 3
Pay Units: 6,159.
Programming (via satellite): Showtime (multiplexed).
Fee: $10.50 monthly.

Digital Pay Service 4
Pay Units: 11,693.
Programming (via satellite): Starz (multiplexed).
Fee: $7.10 monthly.

Digital Pay Service 5
Pay Units: 4,385.
Programming (via satellite): Flix; Sundance Channel; The Movie Channel (multiplexed).
Fee: $9.50 monthly.

Digital Pay Service 6
Pay Units: 23,636.
Programming (via satellite): Encore (multiplexed).
Fee: $2.10 monthly.

Video-On-Demand: Yes

Pay-Per-View
Addressable homes: 18,244.
ESPN Now (delivered digitally), Fee: $3.95, Addressable: Yes; Playboy TV (delivered digitally); Pleasure (delivered digitally); Fresh (delivered digitally); Shorteez (delivered digitally); Ten Clips (delivered digitally).

Internet Service
Operational: Yes. Began: November 24, 1998.
Subscribers: 4,219.
Broadband Service: Mediacom High Speed Internet.
Fee: $150.00 installation; $39.95 monthly; $10.00 modem lease.

Telephone Service
Digital: Operational

Miles of Plant: 1,487.0 (coaxial); 90.0 (fiber optic). Additional miles planned: 1.0 (fiber optic). Homes passed: 132,993.
Regional Vice President: Doug Frank. Marketing & Sales Director: Steve Schuh. Technical Operations Director: Greg Nank.
City fee: 5% of gross.
Ownership: Mediacom LLC (MSO).

CENTER JUNCTION—Center Junction Telephone Co., PO Box 67, 513 Main St, Center Junction, IA 52212-0067. Phone: 563-487-2631. Fax: 563-487-3701. ICA: IA0407.
TV Market Ranking: 65 (CENTER JUNCTION). Franchise award date: May 2, 1990. Franchise expiration date: N.A. Began: November 1, 1990.
Channel capacity: 60 (not 2-way capable). Channels available but not in use: 1.

Basic Service
Subscribers: 45.
Programming (received off-air): KCRG-TV (ABC) Cedar Rapids; KFXA (FOX) Cedar Rapids; KGAN (CBS) Cedar Rapids; KIIN (PBS) Iowa City; KLJB (CW, FOX) Davenport; KWKB (CW, MNT) Iowa City; KWQC-TV (NBC) Davenport; KWWL (NBC) Waterloo; WHBF-TV (CBS) Rock Island; WQAD-TV (ABC) Moline.
Programming (via satellite): ABC Family Channel; AMC; AmericanLife TV Network; Animal Planet; Arts & Entertainment; Cartoon Network; CNBC; CNN; Comedy Central; Country Music TV; C-SPAN; Discovery Channel; Disney Channel; E! Entertainment Television; ESPN; ESPN 2; Food Network; Fox News Channel; FX; Great American Country; GSN; HGTV; History Channel; Home Shopping Network; INSP; Lifetime; MTV; Nickelodeon; Outdoor Channel; QVC; Speed Channel; Spike TV; Syfy; TBS Superstation; The Learning Channel; Travel Channel; Trinity Broadcasting Network; Turner Classic Movies; Turner Network TV; TV Land; USA Network; VH1; Weather Channel; WGN America.
Fee: $12.50 installation; $25.45 monthly.

Pay Service 1
Pay Units: N.A.
Programming (via satellite): Cinemax; HBO; Showtime.
Fee: $9.95 monthly (each).

Internet Service
Operational: No.

Telephone Service
None

Homes passed: 72. Total homes in franchised area: 72.
Manager: John Heiken. Chief Technician: Jim Petersen.
Ownership: Center Junction Telephone Co.

CENTERVILLE—Mediacom, 6300 Council St NE, Ste A, Cedar Rapids, IA 52402. Phones: 319-395-9699; 641-682-1695 (Ottumwa office). Fax: 319-393-7017. Web Site: http://www.mediacomcable.com. Also serves Albia, Appanoose County, Bloomfield, Eddyville, Eldon & Monroe County (portions). ICA: IA0039.
TV Market Ranking: Below 100 (Albia, Appanoose County (portions), Bloomfield, CENTERVILLE, Eddyville, Eldon, Monroe County (portions)); Outside TV Markets (Appanoose County (portions)). Franchise award date: N.A. Franchise expiration date: N.A. Began: April 1, 1970.
Channel capacity: N.A. Channels available but not in use: N.A.

Basic Service
Subscribers: 5,350.
Programming (received off-air): KCCI (CBS) Des Moines; KCWI-TV (CW) Ames; KDSM-TV (FOX) Des Moines; KFPX-TV (ION) Newton; KIIN (PBS) Iowa City; KTVO (ABC) Kirksville; KYOU-TV (FOX) Ottumwa; WHO-DT (NBC) Des Moines; WOI-DT (ABC) Ames; allband FM.
Programming (via satellite): C-SPAN; C-SPAN 2; Home Shopping Network; QVC; Weather Channel; WGN America.
Fee: $9.87 monthly; $1.01 converter.

Expanded Basic Service 1
Subscribers: 4,455.
Programming (via satellite): ABC Family Channel; AMC; Animal Planet; Arts & Entertainment; BET Networks; Bravo;

Cartoon Network; CNBC; CNN; Comedy Central; Country Music TV; Discovery Channel; Disney Channel; E! Entertainment Television; ESPN; ESPN 2; Eternal Word TV Network; FitTV; Food Network; Fox News Channel; Fox Sports Net Midwest; FX; Hallmark Channel; Headline News; HGTV; History Channel; INSP; Lifetime; Lifetime Movie Network; MSNBC; MTV; National Geographic Channel; Nickelodeon; Oxygen; RFD-TV; Speed Channel; Spike TV; Syfy; TBS Superstation; Telemundo; The Learning Channel; Travel Channel; Trinity Broadcasting Network; truTV; Turner Network TV; TV Land; Univision; USA Network; Versus; VH1; WE tv; Weather Channel.
Fee: $17.57 monthly.

Digital Basic Service
Subscribers: N.A.
Programming (via satellite): AmericanLife TV Network; BBC America; Bio; Bloomberg Television; CBS College Sports Network; CMT Pure Country; Discovery HD Theater; Discovery Health Channel; Discovery Home Channel; Discovery Kids Channel; Discovery Military Channel; Discovery Times Channel; DMX Music; ESPN 2 HD; ESPN HD; ESPN U; ESPNews; Fox College Sports Atlantic; Fox College Sports Central; Fox College Sports Pacific; Fox Movie Channel; Fox Reality Channel; Fox Soccer; Fuel TV; Fuse; G4; Gol TV; Golf Channel; GSN; Halogen Network; HDNet; HDNet Movies; History Channel International; Independent Film Channel; Lifetime Real Women; MTV Hits; MTV2; Nick Jr.; NickToons TV; Outdoor Channel; Ovation; Science Channel; Sleuth; Style Network; TeenNick; Tennis Channel; The Sportsman Channel; Toon Disney; Turner Classic Movies; TVG Network; Universal HD; VH1 Classic; VH1 Soul.

Digital Pay Service 1
Pay Units: 577.
Programming (via satellite): Cinemax (multiplexed); Encore (multiplexed); Flix; HBO (multiplexed); HBO HD; Showtime (multiplexed); Showtime HD; Starz (multiplexed); Starz HDTV; Sundance Channel; The Movie Channel (multiplexed); The Movie Channel HD.
Fee: $10.00 installation; $9.50 monthly (Cinemax, HBO, Showtime/Flix/Sundance/TMC, or Starz/Encore).

Video-On-Demand: Yes

Pay-Per-View
ESPN Now (delivered digitally); ETC (delivered digitally); Playboy TV (delivered digitally); Pleasure (delivered digitally); Fresh (delivered digitally); Shorteez (delivered digitally); TVN Entertainment (delivered digitally); sports (delivered digitally).

Internet Service
Operational: Yes.
Subscribers: 13,500.
Broadband Service: Mediacom High Speed Internet.

Telephone Service
Digital: Operational

Miles of Plant: 112.0 (coaxial); None (fiber optic). Homes passed: 7,335. Total homes in franchised area: 7,359.
Regional Vice President: Doug Frank. Technical Operations Director: Greg Nank. Technical Operations Manager: Steve Angren. Marketing Director: Steve Schuh.
Ownership: Mediacom LLC (MSO).

CENTRAL CITY—USA Communications. Now served by SHELLSBURG, IA [IA0255]. ICA: IA0200.

CHARLES CITY—Mediacom, 4010 Alexandra Dr, Waterloo, IA 50702. Phone: 319-235-2197. Fax: 319-232-7841. Web Site: http://www.mediacomcable.com. Also serves Floyd County (portions). ICA: IA0037.
TV Market Ranking: Below 100 (CHARLES CITY, Floyd County (portions)). Franchise award date: August 3, 1979. Franchise expiration date: N.A. Began: August 3, 1981.
Channel capacity: N.A. Channels available but not in use: N.A.

Basic Service
Subscribers: 3,041.
Programming (received off-air): KAAL (ABC) Austin; KCRG-TV (ABC) Cedar Rapids; KGAN (CBS) Cedar Rapids; KIMT (CBS, MNT) Mason City; KTTC (CW, NBC) Rochester; KWWL (NBC) Waterloo; KXLT-TV (FOX) Rochester; KYIN (PBS) Mason City.
Programming (via satellite): C-SPAN; C-SPAN 2; QVC; WGN America.
Current originations: Educational Access; Public Access.
Fee: $40.95 installation; $10.05 monthly.

Expanded Basic Service 1
Subscribers: 2,541.
Programming (via satellite): ABC Family Channel; AMC; Animal Planet; Arts & Entertainment; Bravo; Cartoon Network; CNBC; CNN; Comcast SportsNet Chicago; Comedy Central; Country Music TV; Discovery Channel; Disney Channel; E! Entertainment Television; ESPN; ESPN 2; Eternal Word TV Network; Fox News Channel; FX; HGTV; History Channel; Home Shopping Network; INSP; ION Television; Lifetime; MSNBC; MTV; Nickelodeon; Oxygen; Speed Channel; Spike TV; Syfy; TBS Superstation; The Learning Channel; Travel Channel; Trinity Broadcasting Network; truTV; Turner Network TV; TV Guide Network; TV Land; USA Network; VH1; WE tv; Weather Channel.
Fee: $21.91 monthly.

Digital Basic Service
Subscribers: 375.
Programming (via satellite): AmericanLife TV Network; BBC America; Bio; Bloomberg Television; Discovery Digital Networks; DMX Music; Fox Movie Channel; Fox Sports World; Fuse; G4; GAS; Golf Channel; GSN; Halogen Network; History Channel International; Independent Film Channel; Lifetime Movie Network; Lime; MTV Networks Digital Suite; National Geographic Channel; Nick Jr.; Outdoor Channel; Ovation; Style Network; Toon Disney; Turner Classic Movies; Versus.
Fee: $12.00 monthly.

Digital Pay Service 1
Pay Units: 150.
Programming (via satellite): Cinemax (multiplexed).
Fee: $12.95 monthly.

Digital Pay Service 2
Pay Units: 575.
Programming (via satellite): Encore (multiplexed).
Fee: $2.10 monthly.

Digital Pay Service 3
Pay Units: 250.
Programming (via satellite): HBO (multiplexed).
Fee: $13.95 monthly.

Digital Pay Service 4
Pay Units: 150.
Programming (via satellite): Showtime (multiplexed).
Fee: $12.95 monthly.

Digital Pay Service 5
Pay Units: 400.
Programming (via satellite): Starz (multiplexed).
Fee: $7.10 monthly.

Digital Pay Service 6
Pay Units: 62.
Programming (via satellite): Sundance Channel; The Movie Channel (multiplexed).

Video-On-Demand: Yes

Pay-Per-View
Addressable homes: 375.
ESPN Now (delivered digitally), Addressable: Yes; ETC (delivered digitally); Playboy TV (delivered digitally); Pleasure (delivered digitally); TVN Entertainment (delivered digitally); sports (delivered digitally).

Internet Service
Operational: Yes.
Broadband Service: Mediacom High Speed Internet.

Telephone Service
Analog: Not Operational
Digital: Operational

Miles of Plant: 64.0 (coaxial); 2.0 (fiber optic). Homes passed: 4,163. Total homes in franchised area: 4,230.
Regional Vice President: Doug Frank. General Manager: Doug Nix. Technical Operations Director: Greg Nank. Marketing Director: Steve Schuh. Marketing Coordinator: Joni Lindauer.
Ownership: Mediacom LLC (MSO).

CHARTER OAK—Tip Top Communication. Now served by SCHLESWIG, IA [IA0231]. ICA: IA0237.

CHESTER—Formerly served by CableDirect. No longer in operation. ICA: IA0410.

CHURDAN—Western Iowa Networks. No longer in operation. ICA: IA0616.

CINCINNATI—B & L Technologies LLC, 3329 270th St, Lenox, IA 50851. Phones: 800-798-5488; 641-348-2240. Fax: 641-348-2240. ICA: IA0301.
TV Market Ranking: Below 100 (CINCINNATI). Franchise award date: December 14, 1982. Franchise expiration date: N.A. Began: N.A.
Channel capacity: 23 (not 2-way capable). Channels available but not in use: 2.

Basic Service
Subscribers: 46.
Programming (received off-air): KCCI (CBS) Des Moines; KDIN-TV (PBS) Des Moines; KDSM-TV (FOX) Des Moines; KTVO (ABC) Kirksville; KYOU-TV (FOX) Ottumwa; WHO-DT (NBC) Des Moines; WOI-DT (ABC) Ames.
Programming (via satellite): ABC Family Channel; Arts & Entertainment; CNN; Discovery Channel; ESPN; Nickelodeon; TBS Superstation; Turner Network TV; USA Network; WGN America.
Fee: $41.11 installation; $19.86 monthly.

Pay Service 1
Pay Units: 37.
Programming (via satellite): HBO.
Fee: $23.49 installation; $11.00 monthly.

Video-On-Demand: No

Internet Service
Operational: No.

Telephone Service
None

Miles of Plant: 4.0 (coaxial); None (fiber optic). Homes passed: 197. Total homes in franchised area: 197.
President & General Manager: Robert Hintz. Office Manager: Linda Hintz.
Ownership: B & L Technologies LLC (MSO).

CLARENCE—Clarence Cablevision, PO Box 246, 608 Lombard St, Clarence, IA 52216-0246. Phone: 563-452-3852. Fax: 563-452-3883. E-mail: clarence@netins.net. Web Site: http://www.clarencetelinc.com. ICA: IA0213.
TV Market Ranking: 65 (CLARENCE). Franchise award date: July 15, 1983. Franchise expiration date: N.A. Began: January 1, 1984.
Channel capacity: 82 (not 2-way capable). Channels available but not in use: 19.

Basic Service
Subscribers: 385.
Programming (received off-air): KCRG-TV (ABC) Cedar Rapids; KFXA (FOX) Cedar Rapids; KGAN (CBS) Cedar Rapids; KIIN (PBS) Iowa City; KLJB (CW, FOX) Davenport; KWKB (CW, MNT) Iowa City; KWQC-TV (NBC) Davenport; KWWL (NBC) Waterloo; WHBF-TV (CBS) Rock Island; WQAD-TV (ABC) Moline.
Programming (via satellite): ABC Family Channel; AMC; AmericanLife TV Network; Animal Planet; Arts & Entertainment; Cartoon Network; CNBC; CNN; Comcast/Charter Sports Southeast (CSS); Comedy Central; Country Music TV; C-SPAN; Discovery Channel; Disney Channel; E! Entertainment Television; ESPN; ESPN 2; Food Network; Fox News Channel; FX; Great American Country; GSN; HGTV; History Channel; Home Shopping Network; INSP; Lifetime; MTV; Nickelodeon; Outdoor Channel; Paxson Communications Corp.; QVC; Speed Channel; Spike TV; Syfy; TBS Superstation; The Learning Channel; Travel Channel; Trinity Broadcasting Network; Turner Classic Movies; Turner Network TV; TV Land; USA Network; VH1; Weather Channel; WGN America.
Fee: $20.00 installation; $26.95 monthly.

Pay Service 1
Pay Units: 56.
Programming (via satellite): Cinemax.
Fee: $9.00 monthly.

Pay Service 2
Pay Units: 76.
Programming (via satellite): HBO.
Fee: $9.00 monthly.

Pay Service 3
Pay Units: N.A.
Programming (via satellite): Showtime.
Fee: $8.50 monthly.

Video-On-Demand: No

Internet Service
Operational: No, DSL only.

Telephone Service
None
Miles of Plant: 8.0 (coaxial); None (fiber optic). Homes passed: 400. Total homes in franchised area: 400.
Manager & Chief Technician: Curtis Eldred.
Ownership: Clarence Telephone Co. Inc.

CLEARFIELD—B & L Technologies LLC, 3329 270th St, Lenox, IA 50851. Phones: 800-798-5488; 641-348-2240. Fax: 641-348-2240. ICA: IA0341.
TV Market Ranking: Outside TV Markets (CLEARFIELD). Franchise award date: N.A. Franchise expiration date: N.A. Began: November 1, 1987.
Channel capacity: 36 (not 2-way capable). Channels available but not in use: 8.
Basic Service
Subscribers: 48.
Programming (received off-air): KCCI (CBS) Des Moines; KDIN-TV (PBS) Des Moines; KDSM-TV (FOX) Des Moines; WHO-DT (NBC) Des Moines; WOI-DT (ABC) Ames.
Programming (via satellite): ABC Family Channel; AMC; Arts & Entertainment; CNN; Discovery Channel; ESPN; History Channel; Nickelodeon; Spike TV; TBS Superstation; Turner Network TV; USA Network; VH1; WGN America.
Fee: $25.00 installation; $30.50 monthly.
Pay Service 1
Pay Units: 4.
Programming (via satellite): HBO.
Fee: $12.00 monthly.
Video-On-Demand: No
Internet Service
Operational: No.
Telephone Service
None
Miles of Plant: 3.0 (coaxial); None (fiber optic). Homes passed: 150.
Manager & Chief Technician: Robert Hintz. Office Manager: Linda Hintz.
Ownership: B & L Technologies LLC (MSO).

CLEGHORN—Wetherell Cable TV System, PO Box 188, 407 W Grace St, Cleghorn, IA 51014-0188. Phone: 712-436-2266. Fax: 712-436-2672. Also serves Early, Galva, Marathon, Meriden, Pierson, Rembrandt & Washta. ICA: IA0132.
TV Market Ranking: Below 100 (Pierson, Washta); Outside TV Markets (CLEGHORN, Early, Galva, Marathon, Meriden, Rembrandt). Franchise award date: June 1, 1983. Franchise expiration date: N.A. Began: December 1, 1983.
Channel capacity: 36 (not 2-way capable). Channels available but not in use: N.A.
Basic Service
Subscribers: 450.
Programming (received off-air): KCAU-TV (ABC) Sioux City; KELO-TV (CBS, MNT) Sioux Falls; KMEG (CBS) Sioux City; KPTH (FOX, MNT) Sioux City; KSFY-TV (ABC) Sioux Falls; KSIN-TV (PBS) Sioux City; KTIV (CW, NBC) Sioux City.
Programming (via satellite): ABC Family Channel; Arts & Entertainment; Cartoon Network; CNN; Discovery Channel; ESPN; ESPN 2; Food Network; Fox Business Channel; Fox News Channel; FX; Great American Country; HGTV; History Channel; Home Shopping Network; Lifetime; MoviePlex; MTV; Nickelodeon; Speed Channel; Spike TV; TBS Superstation; The Learning Channel; truTV; Turner Classic Movies; Turner Network TV; USA Network; Weather Channel; WGN America.
Fee: $25.00 installation; $30.95 monthly.
Pay Service 1
Pay Units: 75.
Programming (via satellite): The Movie Channel.
Fee: $7.00 monthly.
Internet Service
Operational: No.
Telephone Service
None
Miles of Plant: 16.0 (coaxial); None (fiber optic).
Manager: Ronald Wetherell. Chief Technician: Boyd White.
City fee: None.
Ownership: Wetherell Cable TV System.

CLERMONT—Alpine Communications LC. Now served by ARLINGTON, IA [IA0393]. ICA: IA0412.

CLINTON—Mediacom, 3900 26th Ave, Moline, IL 61265. Phone: 309-797-2580. Fax: 309-797-2414. Web Site: http://www.mediacomcable.com. Also serves Albany, Erie, Fulton, Lyndon, Morrison, Prophetstown, Savanna, Thomson & Whiteside County (portions), IL; Camanche, Charlotte, Clinton County, De Witt, Goose Lake, Jackson County, Low Moor, Maquoketa, McCausland, Miles, Preston & Sabula, IA. ICA: IA0006.
TV Market Ranking: 60 (Albany, Camanche, Charlotte, CLINTON, Clinton County, De Witt, Erie, Fulton, Goose Lake, Low Moor, Lyndon, McCausland, Prophetstown, Whiteside County (portions)); 97 (Sabula, Savanna, Thomson); Below 100 (Jackson County, Maquoketa, Miles, Preston); Outside TV Markets (Morrison). Franchise award date: June 1, 1963. Franchise expiration date: N.A. Began: October 16, 1974.
Channel capacity: N.A. Channels available but not in use: N.A.
Basic Service
Subscribers: 22,205.
Programming (received off-air): KGCW (CW) Burlington; KIIN (PBS) Iowa City; KLJB (CW, FOX) Davenport; KWQC-TV (NBC) Davenport; WBQD-LP Davenport; WHBF-TV (CBS) Rock Island; WQAD-TV (ABC) Moline; WQPT-TV (PBS) Moline.
Programming (via satellite): C-SPAN; Discovery Channel; QVC; TBS Superstation; Trinity Broadcasting Network; TV Guide Network; Univision; WGN America.
Current originations: Government Access; Public Access.
Fee: $45.00 installation; $20.95 monthly.
Expanded Basic Service 1
Subscribers: 20,832.
Programming (via satellite): ABC Family Channel; AMC; Animal Planet; Arts & Entertainment; BET Networks; Bravo; Cartoon Network; CNBC; CNN; Comcast SportsNet Chicago; Comedy Central; Country Music TV; C-SPAN 2; Disney Channel; E! Entertainment Television; ESPN; ESPN 2; Eternal Word TV Network; Food Network; Fox News Channel; Fuse; FX; Hallmark Channel; Headline News; HGTV; History Channel; Home Shopping Network; INSP; ION Television; Lifetime; MSNBC; MTV; Nickelodeon; Shop at Home; SoapNet; Speed Channel; Spike TV; Syfy; The Learning Channel; Travel Channel; truTV; Turner Network TV; TV Land; USA Network; VH1; WE tv; Weather Channel.
Fee: $34.00 monthly.
Digital Basic Service
Subscribers: 6,380.
Programming (via satellite): BBC America; Bio; Canales N; Discovery Digital Networks; DMX Music; ESPN Classic Sports; ESPNews; Fox Sports World; GAS; Golf Channel; GSN; History Channel International; Independent Film Channel; Lifetime Movie Network; Lime; MTV Networks Digital Suite; National Geographic Channel; Nick Jr.; Outdoor Channel; Ovation; Style Network; Sundance Channel; Toon Disney; Turner Classic Movies; Versus.
Fee: $9.00 monthly.
Digital Pay Service 1
Pay Units: 3,695.
Programming (via satellite): Cinemax (multiplexed).
Fee: $11.95 monthly.
Digital Pay Service 2
Pay Units: 6,825.
Programming (via satellite): Encore (multiplexed); Starz (multiplexed).
Fee: $11.95 monthly.
Digital Pay Service 3
Pay Units: 5,785.
Programming (via satellite): HBO (multiplexed).
Fee: $11.95 monthly.
Digital Pay Service 4
Pay Units: 515.
Programming (via satellite): Showtime (multiplexed); The Movie Channel (multiplexed).
Fee: $11.95 monthly.
Video-On-Demand: Yes
Pay-Per-View
Addressable homes: 6,380.
ESPN Now (delivered digitally), Addressable: Yes; ETC (delivered digitally); Playboy TV (delivered digitally); Pleasure (delivered digitally); TVN Entertainment (delivered digitally); sports (delivered digitally).
Internet Service
Operational: Yes.
Broadband Service: Mediacom High Speed Internet.
Fee: $59.95 installation; $40.95 monthly.
Telephone Service
Analog: Not Operational
Digital: Operational
Fee: $39.95 installation; $39.95 monthly
Homes passed: 32,005. Total homes in franchised area: 33,618. Miles of plant included in Moline
Regional Vice President: Cari Fenzel. Marketing Director: Greg Evans. Engineering Director: Mitch Carlson. Technical Operations Manager: Chris Toalson.
City fee: 3% of basic.
Ownership: Mediacom LLC (MSO).

CLUTIER—Farmers Cooperative Telephone Co. Formerly [IA0413]. This cable system has converted to IPTV, PO Box 280, 332 Main St, Dysart, IA 52224. Phone: 319-476-7911. Fax: 319-476-7911. Web Site: http://www.fctc.coop. ICA: IA5077.
Channel capacity: N.A. Channels available but not in use: N.A.
Internet Service
Operational: Yes.
Ownership: Farmers Cooperative Telephone Co.

CLUTIER—Farmers Cooperative Telephone Co. This cable system has converted to IPTV. See Clutier, IA [IA5077]. ICA: IA0413.

COGGON—USA Communications, PO Box 389, 124 Main St, Shellsburg, IA 52332. Phones: 800-248-8007; 319-436-2224. Fax: 319-436-2228. E-mail: frmutshe@fmtcs.com. Web Site: http://www.usacomm.coop. ICA: IA0287.
TV Market Ranking: 65 (COGGON). Franchise award date: N.A. Franchise expiration date: N.A. Began: March 1, 1984.
Channel capacity: 35 (not 2-way capable). Channels available but not in use: 3.
Basic Service
Subscribers: 153.
Programming (received off-air): KCRG-TV (ABC) Cedar Rapids; KFXA (FOX) Cedar Rapids; KGAN (CBS) Cedar Rapids; KPXR-TV (ION) Cedar Rapids; KRIN (PBS) Waterloo; KWKB (CW, MNT) Iowa City; KWWL (NBC) Waterloo.
Programming (via satellite): ABC Family Channel; AMC; Animal Planet; Arts & Entertainment; Cartoon Network; CNBC; CNN; Comcast SportsNet West; Comedy Central; Country Music TV; C-SPAN; Discovery Channel; Disney Channel; Do-It-Yourself; E! Entertainment Television; ESPN; ESPN 2; ESPN Classic Sports; Eternal Word TV Network; Food Network; Fox News Channel; FX; Gospel Music Channel; Great American Country; Hallmark Channel; Hallmark Movie Channel; Headline News; HGTV; History Channel; Home Shopping Network; Lifetime; MTV; National Geographic Channel; Nickelodeon; QVC; SoapNet; Speed Channel; Spike TV; Syfy; TBS Superstation; The Learning Channel; The Sportsman Channel; Travel Channel; Trinity Broadcasting Network; truTV; Turner Classic Movies; Turner Network TV; TV Land; USA Network; VH1; Weather Channel; WGN America.
Fee: $25.00 installation; $37.95 monthly.
Pay Service 1
Pay Units: 6.
Programming (via satellite): Cinemax.
Fee: $10.00 monthly.
Pay Service 2
Pay Units: 16.
Programming (via satellite): HBO.
Fee: $12.00 monthly.
Pay Service 3
Pay Units: 5.
Programming (via satellite): Showtime.
Fee: $10.00 monthly.
Internet Service
Operational: No.
Telephone Service
None
Homes passed: 225.
Manager: Mark Harrison. Plant Manager: Mitch Kuhn. Marketing Administrator: Marnie Burkey. Office Manager: Nancy Seely.
Ownership: Shellsburg Cablevision Inc. (MSO).

COLESBURG—Formerly served by Alpine Communications LC. No longer in operation. ICA: IA0414.

COLLINS—Formerly served by Huxley Communications Corp. No longer in operation. ICA: IA0415.

COLO—Colo Telephone Co. Formerly [IA0416]. This cable system has converted to IPTV, PO Box 315, 303 Main St, Colo, IA 50056. Phone: 641-377-2202. Fax: 641-377-2209. E-mail: colo@netins.net. Web Site: http://www.colotel.org. ICA: IA5003.
TV Market Ranking: 66 (COLO).
Channel capacity: N.A. Channels available but not in use: N.A.
Internet Service
Operational: Yes, Both DSL & dial-up.

Telephone Service
Digital: Operational
President: Keith McKinney. Vice President: Joe Harper. Secretary: Fred Cerka. Manager: Larry Springer.
Ownership: Colo Telephone Co.

COLO—Colo Telephone Co. This cable system has converted to IPTV. See COLO, IA [IA5003]. ICA: IA0416.

COLUMBUS JUNCTION—Mediacom. Now served by BURLINGTON, IA [IA0405]. ICA: IA0111.

COON RAPIDS—Coon Rapids Municipal Cable System, PO Box 207, 123 3rd Ave S, Coon Rapids, IA 50058. Phone: 712-999-2225. Fax: 712-999-5148. ICA: IA0172.
TV Market Ranking: Outside TV Markets (COON RAPIDS). Franchise award date: N.A. Franchise expiration date: N.A. Began: October 1, 1982.
Channel capacity: 35 (operating 2-way). Channels available but not in use: None.
Basic Service
Subscribers: 536.
Programming (received off-air): KCCI (CBS) Des Moines; KDIN-TV (PBS) Des Moines; WHO-DT (NBC) Des Moines; WOI-DT (ABC) Ames; allband FM.
Programming (via satellite): ABC Family Channel; CNN; Hallmark Channel; Headline News; Home Shopping Network; LWS Local Weather Station; Weather Channel; WGN America.
Fee: $15.00 installation; $44.95 monthly; $3.00 converter.
Digital Basic Service
Subscribers: N.A.
Programming (received off-air): KCCI (CBS) Des Moines; KDIN-TV (PBS) Des Moines; KDSM-TV (FOX) Des Moines; WHO-DT (NBC) Des Moines; WOI-DT (ABC) Ames.
Programming (via satellite): Discovery HD Theater; ESPN; ESPN 2; HDNet; HDNet Movies; Outdoor Channel 2 HD.
Fee: $12.95 monthly.
Pay Service 1
Pay Units: 104.
Programming (via satellite): Cinemax.
Fee: $5.00 installation; $12.95 monthly.
Pay Service 2
Pay Units: 90.
Programming (via satellite): HBO.
Fee: $5.00 installation; $12.95 monthly.
Internet Service
Operational: Yes.
Broadband Service: In-house.
Fee: $49.95 installation; $49.95 monthly.
Telephone Service
Analog: Operational
Fee: $13.95 monthly
Miles of Plant: 11.0 (coaxial); None (fiber optic). Homes passed: 555. Total homes in franchised area: 572.
Manager: Bradley A. Hunold. Chief Technician: Kevin Dorpinghaus.
Ownership: Coon Rapids Municipal Cable System.

CORWITH—Communications 1 Cablevision. Now served by KANAWHA, IA [IA0229]. ICA: IA0417.

COULTER—Formerly served by Latimer/Coulter Cablevision. No longer in operation. ICA: IA0418.

CRESCO—Mediacom. Now served by OSAGE, IA [IA0085]. ICA: IA0081.

CRESTON—Mediacom. Now served by DES MOINES, IA [IA0001]. ICA: IA0028.

CYLINDER—Formerly served by ATC Cablevision. No longer in operation. ICA: IA0384.

DANBURY—Long Lines, 501 4th St, Sergeant Bluff, IA 51054-8509. Phones: 712-884-2203; 712-271-4000. Fax: 712-271-2727. Web Site: http://www.longlines.com. ICA: IA0316.
TV Market Ranking: Outside TV Markets (DANBURY). Franchise award date: N.A. Franchise expiration date: N.A. Began: February 1, 1984.
Channel capacity: 37 (not 2-way capable). Channels available but not in use: 16.
Basic Service
Subscribers: 126.
Programming (received off-air): KCAU-TV (ABC) Sioux City; KMEG (CBS) Sioux City; KPTH (FOX, MNT) Sioux City; KSIN-TV (PBS) Sioux City; KTIV (CW, NBC) Sioux City.
Programming (via satellite): ABC Family Channel; AMC; AmericanLife TV Network; Animal Planet; Arts & Entertainment; Big Ten Network; Cartoon Network; CNBC; CNN; Comedy Central; Country Music TV; C-SPAN; C-SPAN 2; CW+; Discovery Channel; Disney Channel; E! Entertainment Television; ESPN; ESPN 2; ESPN Classic Sports; Eternal Word TV Network; Food Network; Fox News Channel; Fox Sports Net North; FX; Golf Channel; Hallmark Channel; Headline News; HGTV; History Channel; Home Shopping Network; INSP; Lifetime; Lifetime Movie Network; MSNBC; MTV; Nickelodeon; QVC; Speed Channel; Spike TV; Syfy; TBS Superstation; The Learning Channel; The Sportsman Channel; Travel Channel; Trinity Broadcasting Network; truTV; Turner Classic Movies; Turner Network TV; TuTv; TV Guide Network; TV Land; USA Network; VH1; Weather Channel; WGN America.
Current originations: Public Access.
Fee: $25.00 installation; $41.99 monthly.
Digital Basic Service
Subscribers: N.A.
Programming (via satellite): BBC America; Bio; Cooking Channel; Discovery Health Channel; Discovery Kids Channel; Discovery Military Channel; Discovery Planet Green; DMX Music; Do-It-Yourself; ESPN U; ESPNews; FitTV; Fox College Sports Atlantic; Fox College Sports Central; Fox College Sports Pacific; Fox Movie Channel; Fox Soccer; G4; Great American Country; GSN; Halogen Network; History Channel International; ID Investigation Discovery; Independent Film Channel; Lifetime Real Women; MTV Hits; MTV Jams; MTV2; Nick Jr.; NickToons TV; Outdoor Channel; RFD-TV; Science Channel; SoapNet; TeenNick; Toon Disney; Versus; VH1 Classic; VH1 Country; VH1 Soul; WE tv.
Fee: $9.99 monthly.
Digital Expanded Basic Service
Subscribers: N.A.
Programming (via satellite): Bandamax; De Pelicula; De Pelicula Clasico; Discovery en Espanol; ESPN Deportes; Fox Sports en Espanol; Ritmoson Latino; Telehit.
Fee: $2.95 monthly.
Digital Expanded Basic Service 2
Subscribers: N.A.
Programming (received off-air): KCAU-TV (ABC) Sioux City; KMEG (CBS) Sioux City; KPTM (FOX, MNT) Omaha; KSIN-TV (PBS) Sioux City; KTIV (CW, NBC) Sioux City.
Programming (via satellite): Big Ten Network HD; Discovery Channel HD; ESPN 2 HD; ESPN HD; HDNet; HDNet Movies; Outdoor Channel 2 HD.
Fee: $9.95 monthly.
Pay Service 1
Pay Units: 14.
Programming (via satellite): HBO (multiplexed).
Fee: $15.00 installation; $14.95 monthly.
Pay Service 2
Pay Units: 5.
Programming (via satellite): Flix; Showtime (multiplexed); The Movie Channel (multiplexed).
Fee: $14.45 monthly.
Digital Pay Service 1
Pay Units: N.A.
Programming (via satellite): Cinemax (multiplexed); Cinemax HD; Encore (multiplexed); Flix; HBO (multiplexed); HBO HD; Showtime (multiplexed); Starz (multiplexed); Starz HDTV; The Movie Channel (multiplexed).
Fee: $11.95 monthly (Cinemax), $13.95 monthly (Starz/Encore), $14.45 monthly (Showtime/TMC/Flix), $14.95 monthly (HBO).
Video-On-Demand: Yes
Internet Service
Operational: No, Both DSL & dial-up.
Telephone Service
None
Miles of Plant: 3.0 (coaxial); None (fiber optic). Homes passed: 189.
Manager: Paul Bergmann. Chief Technician: Dennis Swenson. Customer Service Manager: Barb Johnson.
City fee: 3% of gross.
Ownership: Long Lines (MSO).

DAVIS CITY—Formerly served by Telnet South LC. No longer in operation. ICA: IA0373.

DAYTON—Lehigh Services Inc. Now served by LEHIGH, IA [IA0464]. ICA: IA0232.

DECATUR—Telnet South LC. Now served by DES MOINES, IA [IA0001]. ICA: IA0383.

DECORAH—Mediacom, 4010 Alexandra Dr, Waterloo, IA 50702. Phones: 319-232-7841; 563-387-0825 (Decorah office). Fax: 319-232-7841. Web Site: http://www.mediacomcable.com. ICA: IA0034.
TV Market Ranking: Outside TV Markets (DECORAH). Franchise award date: January 1, 1957. Franchise expiration date: N.A. Began: January 1, 1957.
Channel capacity: N.A. Channels available but not in use: N.A.
Basic Service
Subscribers: 3,035.
Programming (received off-air): KAAL (ABC) Austin; KCRG-TV (ABC) Cedar Rapids; KFXA (FOX) Cedar Rapids; KGAN (CBS) Cedar Rapids; KIMT (CBS, MNT) Mason City; KRIN (PBS) Waterloo; KTTC (CW, NBC) Rochester; KWKB (CW, MNT) Iowa City; KWWF (IND) Waterloo [LICENSED & SILENT]; KWWL (NBC) Waterloo; KXLT-TV (FOX) Rochester; WHLA-TV (PBS) La Crosse; WLAX (FOX) La Crosse; allband FM.
Programming (via satellite): C-SPAN; Home Shopping Network; ION Television; QVC; TV Guide Network; WGN America.
Current originations: Religious Access; Public Access.
Fee: $15.00 installation; $20.50 monthly.
Expanded Basic Service 1
Subscribers: 1,663.
Programming (via satellite): ABC Family Channel; AMC; Animal Planet; Arts & Entertainment; BET Networks; Bravo; Cartoon Network; CNBC; CNN; Comcast SportsNet Northwest; Comedy Central; Country Music TV; C-SPAN 2; Discovery Channel; Disney Channel; E! Entertainment Television; ESPN; ESPN 2; ESPN Classic Sports; Eternal Word TV Network; FitTV; Food Network; Fox News Channel; FX; Hallmark Channel; Headline News; HGTV; History Channel; INSP; Lifetime; Lifetime Movie Network; MSNBC; MTV; Nickelodeon; Outdoor Channel; RFD-TV; Speed Channel; Spike TV; Syfy; TBS Superstation; Telemundo; The Learning Channel; Travel Channel; Trinity Broadcasting Network; truTV; Turner Classic Movies; Turner Network TV; TV Land; USA Network; Versus; VH1; WE tv; Weather Channel.
Fee: $10.00 installation; $4.45 monthly.
Digital Basic Service
Subscribers: N.A.
Programming (received off-air): KCRG-TV (ABC) Cedar Rapids; KFXA (FOX) Cedar Rapids; KGAN (CBS) Cedar Rapids; KWWL (NBC) Waterloo.
Programming (via satellite): ABC News Now; AmericanLife TV Network; BBC America; Bio; Bloomberg Television; CMT Pure Country; Discovery Channel HD; Discovery Health Channel; Discovery Kids Channel; Discovery Military Channel; Discovery Planet Green; ESPN 2 HD; ESPN HD; ESPN U; ESPNews; Fox Movie Channel; Fox Reality Channel; Fox Soccer; Fuel TV; Fuse; G4; Golf Channel; GSN; Halogen Network; HDNet; HDNet Movies; History Channel International; ID Investigation Discovery; Independent Film Channel; ION Life; MTV Hits; MTV2; National Geographic Channel; Nick Jr.; NickToons TV; Ovation; Qubo; ReelzChannel; Science Channel; Sleuth; Style Network; TeenNick; Turner Network TV HD; TVG Network; Universal HD; VH1 Classic; VH1 Soul.
Digital Expanded Basic Service
Subscribers: N.A.
Programming (via satellite): CBS College Sports Network; ESPN U; Fox College Sports Atlantic; Fox College Sports Central; Fox College Sports Pacific; Fuel TV; Gol TV; Tennis Channel; The Sportsman Channel; TVG Network.
Digital Pay Service 1
Pay Units: N.A.
Programming (via satellite): Cinemax (multiplexed); Encore (multiplexed); Flix; HBO (multiplexed); HBO HD; Showtime (multiplexed); Showtime HD; Starz (multiplexed); Starz HDTV; Sundance Channel; The Movie

Channel (multiplexed); The Movie Channel HD.

Video-On-Demand: Yes

Pay-Per-View

iN DEMAND (delivered digitally); ESPN (delivered digitally); Fresh (delivered digitally); Spice: Xcess (delivered digitally); Playboy TV (delivered digitally); Penthouse TV (delivered digitally); Ten Clips (delivered digitally).

Internet Service

Operational: Yes.

Broadband Service: Mediacom High Speed Internet.

Telephone Service

Digital: Operational

Miles of Plant: 63.0 (coaxial); None (fiber optic). Additional miles planned: 10.0 (coaxial). Homes passed: 3,600.

Regional Vice President: Doug Frank. General Manager: Doug Nix. Technical Operations Director: Greg Nank. Technical Operations Manager: Chip Piper. Marketing Director: Steve Schuh. Marketing Coordinator: Joni Lindauer.

City fee: None.

Ownership: Mediacom LLC (MSO).

DEDHAM—Templeton Telephone Co. Now served by TEMPLETON, IA [IA0338]. ICA: IA0362.

DEEP RIVER—Montezuma Mutual Telephone & Cable Co., PO Box 10, 107 N 4th St, Montezuma, IA 50171. Phone: 641-623-5654. Fax: 641-623-2199. E-mail: motel1@netins.net. Also serves Barnes City & Montezuma. ICA: IA0419.

TV Market Ranking: Below 100 (Barnes City, Montezuma); Outside TV Markets (DEEP RIVER). Franchise award date: N.A. Franchise expiration date: N.A. Began: September 1, 1989.

Channel capacity: 78 (operating 2-way). Channels available but not in use: 10.

Basic Service

Subscribers: 172.

Programming (received off-air): KCCI (CBS) Des Moines; KCRG-TV (ABC) Cedar Rapids; KCWI-TV (CW) Ames; KDIN-TV (PBS) Des Moines; KDSM-TV (FOX) Des Moines; KFXA (FOX) Cedar Rapids; KGAN (CBS) Cedar Rapids; KWWL (NBC) Waterloo; KYOU-TV (FOX) Ottumwa; WHO-DT (NBC) Des Moines; WOI-DT (ABC) Ames.

Programming (via satellite): ABC Family Channel; AMC; Animal Planet; Arts & Entertainment; Cartoon Network; CNBC; CNN; Comedy Central; Country Music TV; C-SPAN; C-SPAN 2; Discovery Channel; Disney Channel; Do-It-Yourself; ESPN; ESPN 2; ESPN Classic Sports; Food Network; Fox News Channel; Fox Sports Net; FX; G4; Hallmark Channel; HGTV; History Channel; Home Shopping Network; ION Television; Lifetime; MTV; Nickelodeon; Spike TV; Syfy; TBS Superstation; The Learning Channel; The Sportsman Channel; Travel Channel; Trinity Broadcasting Network; truTV; Turner Network TV; TV Land; USA Network; VH1; Weather Channel; WGN America.

Fee: $10.00 installation; $17.00 monthly.

Digital Basic Service

Subscribers: 1,300.

Programming (via satellite): Bio; Bravo; CMT Pure Country; Discovery Health Channel; Discovery Kids Channel; Discovery Military Channel; Discovery Planet Green; ESPN Classic Sports; Golf Channel; History Channel International; ID Investigation Discovery; Lifetime Movie Network; MTV2; National Geographic Channel; Nick Jr.; Outdoor Channel; Science Channel; Speed Channel; Style Network; Teen-Nick; Toon Disney; Turner Classic Movies; Versus; VH1 Classic.

Fee: $20.00 installation; $19.00 monthly.

Pay Service 1

Pay Units: N.A.

Programming (via satellite): Cinemax; Encore; HBO; Showtime; Starz; The Movie Channel.

Digital Pay Service 1

Pay Units: N.A.

Programming (via satellite): Cinemax (multiplexed); Encore (multiplexed); Flix; HBO (multiplexed); Showtime (multiplexed); Starz (multiplexed); The Movie Channel (multiplexed).

Internet Service

Operational: Yes.

Subscribers: 255.

Broadband Service: Netins.

Fee: $29.95 monthly.

Telephone Service

None

Miles of Plant: 35.0 (coaxial); 14.0 (fiber optic).

Manager: Dave Stevenson.

Ownership: Montezuma Mutual Telephone Co.

DEFIANCE—Farmers Mutual Telephone Co. Now served by EARLING, IA [IA0302]. ICA: IA0280.

DELHI—New Century Communications, 3588 Kennebec Dr, Eagan, MN 55122-1001. Phones: 800-247-1566; 651-688-2623. Fax: 651-688-2624. E-mail: tanderson@cablesystemservices.com. ICA: IA0420.

TV Market Ranking: Below 100 (DELHI). Franchise award date: October 13, 1987. Franchise expiration date: N.A. Began: July 1, 1988.

Channel capacity: 35 (not 2-way capable). Channels available but not in use: 3.

Basic Service

Subscribers: 107.

Programming (received off-air): KCRG-TV (ABC) Cedar Rapids; KFXA (FOX) Cedar Rapids; KGAN (CBS) Cedar Rapids; KIIN (PBS) Iowa City; KPXR-TV (ION) Cedar Rapids; KWKB (CW, MNT) Iowa City; KWWL (NBC) Waterloo.

Programming (via satellite): ABC Family Channel; AMC; Arts & Entertainment; CNN; Discovery Channel; Disney Channel; Do-It-Yourself; ESPN; ESPN 2; Headline News; History Channel; Lifetime; MTV; Nickelodeon; QVC; Spike TV; TBS Superstation; The Learning Channel; Turner Classic Movies; Turner Network TV; USA Network; VH1; Weather Channel; WGN America.

Current originations: Public Access.

Fee: $30.00 installation; $23.45 monthly.

Pay Service 1

Pay Units: 22.

Programming (via satellite): Cinemax.

Fee: $10.00 monthly.

Pay Service 2

Pay Units: 31.

Programming (via satellite): HBO.

Fee: $10.00 monthly.

Pay Service 3

Pay Units: 8.

Programming (via satellite): Showtime.

Fee: $10.00 monthly.

Video-On-Demand: No

Internet Service

Operational: No.

Telephone Service

None

Miles of Plant: 4.0 (coaxial); None (fiber optic). Homes passed: 213.

Executive Vice President: Marty Walch. General Manager & Chief Technician: Todd Anderson.

Ownership: New Century Communications (MSO).

DELMAR—F & B Cablevision, PO Box 309, 103 Main St N, Wheatland, IA 52777-0309. Phone: 563-374-1236. Fax: 563-374-1930. E-mail: info@fbc.bz. Web Site: http://www.fbc.bz. ICA: IA0421.

TV Market Ranking: 60 (DELMAR). Franchise award date: N.A. Franchise expiration date: N.A. Began: August 1, 1989.

Channel capacity: N.A. Channels available but not in use: N.A.

Digital Basic Service

Subscribers: N.A.

Programming (received off-air): KCRG-TV (ABC) Cedar Rapids; KFXA (FOX) Cedar Rapids; KGAN (CBS) Cedar Rapids; KGCW (CW) Burlington; KIIN (PBS) Iowa City; KLJB (CW, FOX) Davenport; KWKB (CW, MNT) Iowa City; KWQC-TV (NBC) Davenport; KWWL (NBC) Waterloo; WHBF-TV (CBS) Rock Island; WQAD-TV (ABC) Moline; WQPT-TV (PBS) Moline.

Programming (via satellite): Bloomberg Television; CNN International; C-SPAN 2; Headline News; History Channel International; Home Shopping Network; INSP; Local Cable Weather; QVC; ShopNBC; SoapNet; Trinity Broadcasting Network.

Fee: $23.99 monthly.

Digital Expanded Basic Service

Subscribers: N.A.

Programming (received off-air): KPXR-TV (ION) Cedar Rapids; KWWF (IND) Waterloo [LICENSED & SILENT].

Programming (via satellite): ABC Family Channel; AMC; Animal Planet; Arts & Entertainment; Big Ten Network; Bio; Boomerang; Bravo; Cartoon Network; CNBC; CNN; Comcast SportsNet Chicago; Comedy Central; Cooking Channel; Country Music TV; C-SPAN; Discovery Channel; Discovery Health Channel; Disney Channel; Do-It-Yourself; E! Entertainment Television; ESPN; ESPN 2; ESPN Classic Sports; ESPNews; Food Network; Fox News Channel; Fox Sports Net Midwest; FX; G4; Golf Channel; Great American Country; GSN; Hallmark Channel; HGTV; History Channel; Lifetime; Lifetime Movie Network; MSNBC; MTV; Music Choice; National Geographic Channel; Nickelodeon; Outdoor Channel; Oxygen; RFD-TV; SoapNet; Speed Channel; Spike TV; Syfy; TBS Superstation; The Learning Channel; Toon Disney; Travel Channel; truTV; Turner Classic Movies; Turner Network TV; TV Land; USA Network; VH1; WE tv; Weather Channel; WGN America.

Fee: $26.00 monthly.

Digital Pay Service 1

Pay Units: N.A.

Programming (via satellite): Cinemax (multiplexed); Encore (multiplexed); Flix; HBO (multiplexed); Showtime (multiplexed); Starz (multiplexed); Sundance Channel; The Movie Channel (multiplexed).

Fee: $15.00 monthly (HBO, Cinemax, Showtime/TMC/Flix/Sundance or Starz/Encore).

Pay-Per-View

Special events (delivered digitally); ESPN (delivered digitally).

Internet Service

Operational: No, Both DSL & dial-up.

Telephone Service

None

Miles of Plant: 4.0 (coaxial); None (fiber optic).

General Manager: Ken Laursen. Plant Manager: Jan Muhl. Marketing Manager: Aaron Horman. Office Manager: Julie Steines.

Ownership: Farmers' & Businessmen's Telephone Co. (MSO).

DELOIT—Tip Top Communication, PO Box 7, 200 W Center St, Arcadia, IA 51430. Phones: 800-290-0986; 712-689-2238. Fax: 712-689-2600. Also serves Vail. ICA: IA0422.

TV Market Ranking: Outside TV Markets (DELOIT, Vail). Franchise award date: N.A. Franchise expiration date: N.A. Began: December 1, 1988.

Channel capacity: 32 (not 2-way capable). Channels available but not in use: N.A.

Basic Service

Subscribers: 114.

Programming (received off-air): KCAU-TV (ABC) Sioux City; KETV (ABC) Omaha; KHIN (PBS) Red Oak; KMTV-TV (CBS) Omaha; KPTH (FOX, MNT) Sioux City; KTIV (CW, NBC) Sioux City; KXVO (CW) Omaha; WOWT-TV (IND, NBC) Omaha.

Programming (via satellite): CNN; Country Music TV; Discovery Channel; Disney Channel; ESPN; ESPN 2; Eternal Word TV Network; Fox Movie Channel; G4; Headline News; HGTV; History Channel; Lifetime; Lifetime Movie Network; Nickelodeon; Speed Channel; Spike TV; TBS Superstation; Turner Network TV; USA Network; WGN America.

Fee: $20.00 installation; $25.36 monthly.

Pay Service 1

Pay Units: N.A.

Programming (via satellite): Cinemax; HBO.

Fee: $12.95 monthly (Cinemax), $13.95 monthly (HBO).

Video-On-Demand: No

Internet Service

Operational: No.

Telephone Service

None

Miles of Plant: 7.0 (coaxial); None (fiber optic). Homes passed: 127.

Manager: Sheila Griffin. Chief Engineer: Mike Ahart.

Ownership: Tip Top Communication (MSO).

DELTA—Formerly served by Longview Communications. No longer in operation. ICA: IA0540.

DENMARK—Formerly served by Longview Communications. No longer in operation. ICA: IA0424.

DES MOINES—Mediacom, 2205 Ingersoll Ave, Des Moines, IA 50312. Phone: 515-246-1890. Fax: 515-246-2211. Web Site: http://www.mediacomcable.com. Also serves Ackworth, Adel, Altoona, Ankeny, Bondurant, Booneville, Bussey, Carlisle, Chariton, Clive, Colfax, Corydon, Creston, Dallas, Dallas Center, Dallas County, Decatur, Desoto, Dexter, Earlham, Granger, Greenfield, Grimes, Grinnell, Guthrie, Hamilton, Hartford, Indianola, Jasper County (central portion), Johnston, Kellerton, Knoxville, Knoxville (unincorporated areas), Lakewood, Lambs Grove, Lamoni, Leon, Lovilia, Lucas, Lynnville, Marion County, Melcher, Mitchellville, Monroe, Mount Ayr, Newton, Norwalk, Ortonville, Osceola, Pella, Perry, Pershing, Pleasant Hill, Pleasantville, Polk, Prairie City, Redfield, Saylorville, Stuart, Sully, Summerset, Urbandale, Van Meter, Warren County (portions), Waukee, Waukee (eastern portion), West Des Moines, Windsor Heights, Winterset & Woodburn. ICA: IA0001.

TV Market Ranking: 66 (Ackworth, Adel, Altoona, Ankeny, Bondurant, Booneville, Carlisle, Clive, Colfax, Dallas, Dallas Center, Dallas County, DES MOINES, Desoto, Dexter, Earlham, Granger, Grimes, Hartford, Indianola, Jasper County (central portion), Johnston, Knoxville, Knoxville (unincorporated areas), Lakewood, Lambs Grove, Marion County (portions), Melcher, Mitchellville, Monroe, Newton, Norwalk, Ortonville, Perry, Pleasant Hill, Pleasantville, Polk, Prairie City, Redfield, Saylorville, Summerset, Urbandale, Van Meter, Warren County (portions), Waukee, Waukee (eastern portion), West Des Moines, Windsor Heights); Below 100 (Bussey, Grinnell, Hamilton, Lovilia, Lynnville, Pella, Pershing, Sully, Marion County (portions)); Outside TV Markets (Chariton, Corydon, Creston, Decatur, Greenfield, Guthrie Center, Kellerton, Lamoni, Leon, Lucas, Mount Ayr, Osceola, Stuart, Winterset, Woodburn, Marion County (portions)). Franchise award date: January 1, 1972. Franchise expiration date: N.A. Began: June 1, 1974.

Channel capacity: N.A. Channels available but not in use: N.A.

Basic Service

Subscribers: 155,400.

Programming (received off-air): KCCI (CBS) Des Moines; KCWI-TV (CW) Ames; KDIN-TV (PBS) Des Moines; KDSM-TV (FOX) Des Moines; KFPX-TV (ION) Newton; WHO-DT (NBC) Des Moines; WOI-DT (ABC) Ames; 14 FMs.

Programming (via satellite): CNN; C-SPAN; Discovery Channel; Nickelodeon; QVC; TBS Superstation; WGN America.

Current originations: Religious Access; Government Access; Educational Access; Public Access.

Fee: $39.02 installation; $9.72 monthly.

Expanded Basic Service 1

Subscribers: 116,092.

Programming (via satellite): ABC Family Channel; AMC; Animal Planet; Arts & Entertainment; BET Networks; Bravo; Cartoon Network; CNBC; Comedy Central; Country Music TV; C-SPAN 2; Disney Channel; E! Entertainment Television; ESPN; ESPN 2; Eternal Word TV Network; Food Network; Fox News Channel; FX; Hallmark Channel; Headline News; HGTV; History Channel; Home Shopping Network; Lifetime; MSNBC; MTV; RFD-TV; Shop at Home; SoapNet; Speed Channel; Spike TV; Syfy; Telemundo; The Learning Channel; Trinity Broadcasting Network; truTV; Turner Network TV; TV Guide Network; TV Land; Univision; USA Network; VH1; WE tv; Weather Channel.

Fee: $31.23 monthly.

Digital Basic Service

Subscribers: 36,117.

Programming (via satellite): American-Life TV Network; BBC America; Bio; Bloomberg Television; Discovery Digital Networks; DMX Music; Fox Movie Channel; Fox Sports World; Fuse; G4; GAS; Golf Channel; GSN; Halogen Network; History Channel International; Independent Film Channel; Lifetime Movie Network; Lime; MTV Networks Digital Suite; National Geographic Channel; Nick Jr.; Outdoor Channel; Ovation; Style Network; Toon Disney; Turner Classic Movies; Versus.

Fee: $12.00 monthly.

Digital Pay Service 1

Pay Units: 24,482.

Programming (via satellite): Cinemax (multiplexed); Flix; HBO (multiplexed); Showtime (multiplexed); Starz (multiplexed); Sundance Channel; The Movie Channel (multiplexed).

Fee: $15.00 installation; $9.95 monthly (Cinemax, HBO, Showtime, Flix/Sundance/TMC, or Starz/Encore).

Video-On-Demand: Yes

Pay-Per-View

Addressable homes: 25,827.

ESPN Now (delivered digitally); ETC (delivered digitally); Playboy TV (delivered digitally); Pleasure (delivered digitally); Fresh (delivered digitally); Shorteez (delivered digitally); TVN Entertainment (delivered digitally); sports (delivered digitally).

Internet Service

Operational: Yes.

Subscribers: 25,526.

Broadband Service: Mediacom High Speed Internet.

Fee: $55.95 installation; $29.95 monthly; $10.00 modem lease.

Telephone Service

Digital: Operational

Miles of Plant: 2,441.0 (coaxial); None (fiber optic). Homes passed: 312,800. Total homes in franchised area: 312,800.

Regional Vice President: Steve Purcell. Division Vice President: Ed Pardini. Technical Operations Manager: Cliff Waggoner. Marketing Director: LeAnn Treloar. Government & Media Relations Manager: Bill Peard.

City fee: 3% of basic & net pay.

Ownership: Mediacom LLC (MSO).

DIAGONAL—B & L Technologies LLC, 3329 270th St, Lenox, IA 50851. Phones: 800-798-5488; 641-348-2240. Fax: 641-348-2240. ICA: IA0353.

TV Market Ranking: Outside TV Markets (DIAGONAL). Franchise award date: N.A. Franchise expiration date: N.A. Began: October 1, 1987.

Channel capacity: 36 (not 2-way capable). Channels available but not in use: 6.

Basic Service

Subscribers: 30.

Programming (received off-air): KCCI (CBS) Des Moines; KCWI-TV (CW) Ames; KDIN-TV (PBS) Des Moines; KDSM-TV (FOX) Des Moines; WHO-DT (NBC) Des Moines; WOI-DT (ABC) Ames.

Programming (via satellite): ABC Family Channel; AMC; Arts & Entertainment; CNN; Discovery Channel; ESPN; ESPN 2; History Channel; Home Shopping Network; Lifetime; Nickelodeon; Spike TV; TBS Superstation; Turner Network TV; USA Network; VH1; WGN America.

Fee: $25.00 installation; $30.50 monthly.

Pay Service 1

Pay Units: 3.

Programming (via satellite): HBO.

Fee: $12.00 monthly.

Video-On-Demand: No

Internet Service

Operational: No.

Telephone Service

None

Miles of Plant: 3.0 (coaxial); None (fiber optic). Homes passed: 124.

Manager & Chief Technician: Robert Hintz. Office Manager: Linda Hintz.

Ownership: B & L Technologies LLC (MSO).

DICKENS—Premier Communications, PO Box 200, 339 1st Ave NE, Sioux Center, IA 51250. Phones: 800-642-4088; 712-722-3451. Fax: 712-722-1113. E-mail: dboone@mtcnet.net. Web Site: http://www.mypremieronline.com. Also serves Webb. ICA: IA0379.

TV Market Ranking: Outside TV Markets (DICKENS, Webb). Franchise award date: March 5, 1985. Franchise expiration date: N.A. Began: February 1, 1987.

Channel capacity: N.A. Channels available but not in use: N.A.

Basic Service

Subscribers: N.A.

Programming (received off-air): KCAU-TV (ABC) Sioux City; KELO-TV (CBS, MNT) Sioux Falls; KMEG (CBS) Sioux City; KPTH (FOX, MNT) Sioux City; KSFY-TV (ABC) Sioux Falls; KTIN (PBS) Fort Dodge; KTIV (CW, NBC) Sioux City; WOI-DT (ABC) Ames.

Programming (via satellite): KEYC-TV (CBS, FOX) Mankato; Paxson Communications Corp.; Weather Channel.

Fee: $12.95 monthly.

Expanded Basic Service 1

Subscribers: 105.

Programming (via satellite): ABC Family Channel; AMC; AmericanLife TV Network; Animal Planet; Arts & Entertainment; Cartoon Network; CNBC; CNN; Comedy Central; Country Music TV; C-SPAN; C-SPAN 2; Discovery Channel; Disney Channel; E! Entertainment Television; ESPN; ESPN 2; ESPN Classic Sports; Food Network; Fox News Channel; FX; Hallmark Channel; Headline News; HGTV; History Channel; Home Shopping Network; Lifetime; MTV; National Geographic Channel; Nickelodeon; Outdoor Channel; Spike TV; Syfy; TBS Superstation; The Learning Channel; Travel Channel; Turner Classic Movies; Turner Network TV; TV Guide Network; TV Land; USA Network; VH1; WGN America.

Fee: $16.00 installation; $29.95 monthly.

Digital Basic Service

Subscribers: N.A.

Programming (via satellite): BBC America; Bio; Discovery Digital Networks; ESPNews; FitTV; Fox Movie Channel; G4; GAS; Golf Channel; GSN; History Channel International; Independent Film Channel; MTV Networks Digital Suite; Music Choice; National Geographic Channel; Nick Jr.; NickToons TV; Outdoor Channel; Speed Channel; Toon Disney; Uth TV.

Fee: $14.95 monthly.

Digital Pay Service 1

Pay Units: N.A.

Programming (via satellite): Cinemax (multiplexed); Encore (multiplexed); Flix; HBO (multiplexed); Showtime (multiplexed); Starz (multiplexed); Sundance Channel; The Movie Channel (multiplexed).

Fee: $8.95 monthly (Cinemax or Showtime/TMC), $12.95 monthly (HBO or Starz/Encore).

Video-On-Demand: No

Pay-Per-View

iN DEMAND (delivered digitally).

Internet Service

Operational: Yes, Both DSL & dial-up.

Broadband Service: Premier Internet.

Fee: $50.00 installation; $47.50 monthly.

Telephone Service

Digital: Operational

Miles of Plant: 7.0 (coaxial); None (fiber optic). Homes passed: 176.

Chief Executive Officer: Douglas A. Boone. Chief Technician: Leslie Sybesma. Marketing Director: Scott Te Stroete.

Ownership: Premier Communications Inc. (MSO).

DIXON—Dixon Telephone Co., PO Box 10, 608 Davenport St, Dixon, IA 52745-0010. Phone: 563-843-2901. Fax: 563-843-2481. E-mail: dixontel@netins.net. Also serves Donahue, Maysville & New Liberty. ICA: IA0358.

TV Market Ranking: 60 (DIXON (VILLAGE), Donahue, Maysville, New Liberty). Franchise award date: N.A. Franchise expiration date: N.A. Began: September 1, 1990.

Channel capacity: N.A. Channels available but not in use: N.A.

Basic Service

Subscribers: 500.

Programming (received off-air): KIIN (PBS) Iowa City; KLJB (CW, FOX) Davenport; KWQC-TV (NBC) Davenport; WHBF-TV (CBS) Rock Island; WQAD-TV (ABC) Moline.

Programming (via satellite): ABC Family Channel; AMC; Animal Planet; Arts & Entertainment; Big Ten Network; Cartoon Network; CNN; Country Music TV; Discovery Channel; Disney Channel; E! Entertainment Television; ESPN; ESPN 2; ESPN Classic Sports; Fox News Channel; Fox Sports Net; FX; Headline News; HGTV; History Channel; Lifetime; MTV; Nickelodeon; Outdoor Channel; RFD-TV; Speed Channel; Spike TV; Syfy; TBS Superstation; Turner Classic Movies; Turner Network TV; TV Guide Network; USA Network; VH1; Weather Channel; WGN America.

Fee: $10.00 installation; $25.95 monthly.

Digital Basic Service

Subscribers: 25.

Fee: $12.95 monthly.

Pay Service 1

Pay Units: N.A.

Programming (via satellite): Cinemax; HBO; Showtime.

Fee: $9.95 monthly (each).

Digital Pay Service 1

Pay Units: N.A.

Programming (via satellite): Cinemax (multiplexed); HBO (multiplexed); Showtime (multiplexed); Starz (multiplexed).

Fee: $9.95 monthly (each).

Video-On-Demand: No

Internet Service

Operational: Yes. Began: April 1, 2002.

Subscribers: 230.

Broadband Service: Netins.

Fee: $39.45 monthly.

Telephone Service

None

Miles of Plant: 65.0 (coaxial); 30.0 (fiber optic). Homes passed: 750.

Manager & Chief Technician: Howard Hunt.

Ownership: Dixon Telephone Co.

DONAHUE—Dixon Telephone Co. Now served by DIXON, IA [IA0358]. ICA: IA0425.

DONNELLSON—Formerly served by Longview Communications. No longer in operation. ICA: IA0426.

DOW CITY—Tip Top Communication, PO Box 7, 200 W Center St, Arcadia, IA 51430. Phone: 712-689-2238. Fax: 712-689-2600. E-mail: sheilag@netins.net. Also serves Arion. ICA: IA0272.

TV Market Ranking: Outside TV Markets (Arion, DOW CITY). Franchise award date: N.A. Franchise expiration date: N.A. Began: December 1, 1983.

Channel capacity: 33 (not 2-way capable). Channels available but not in use: N.A.

Basic Service

Subscribers: 163.

Programming (received off-air): KCAU-TV (ABC) Sioux City; KETV (ABC) Omaha; KHIN (PBS) Red Oak; KMEG (CBS) Sioux City; KMTV-TV (CBS) Omaha; KPTM (FOX, MNT) Omaha; KTIV (CW, NBC) Sioux City; KXVO (CW) Omaha; WOWT-TV (IND, NBC) Omaha.

Programming (via satellite): ABC Family Channel; CNN; Country Music TV; Discovery Channel; Disney Channel; ESPN; ESPN 2; Fox Movie Channel; G4; Headline News; HGTV; History Channel; Lifetime; Lifetime Movie Network; Nickelodeon; Speed Channel; Spike TV; TBS Superstation; Turner Network TV; USA Network; WGN America.

Fee: $20.00 installation; $25.36 monthly.

Pay Service 1

Pay Units: 64.

Programming (via satellite): Cinemax; HBO.

Fee: $12.95 monthly (Cinemax), $13.95 monthly (HBO).

Video-On-Demand: No

Internet Service

Operational: No.

Telephone Service

None

Miles of Plant: 4.0 (coaxial); None (fiber optic). Homes passed: 302.

Manager: Sheila Griffin. Chief Engineer: Mike Ahart.

City fee: 3% of gross.

Ownership: Tip Top Communication (MSO).

DOWS—Dows Cablevision. No longer in operation. ICA: IA0427.

DUBUQUE—Mediacom, 3033 Asbury Rd, Dubuque, IA 52001. Phone: 563-557-8025 (Local office). Fax: 563-557-7413. Web Site: http://www.mediacomcable.com. Also serves East Dubuque, Galena & Jo Daviess County, IL; Asbury, Dubuque County, Dyersville, Epworth, Farley & Sageville, IA. ICA: IA0007.

TV Market Ranking: 97 (Jo Daviess County (portions)); Below 100 (Asbury, DUBUQUE, Dubuque County, Dyersville, East Dubuque, Epworth, Farley, Galena, Sageville, Jo Daviess County (portions)). Franchise award date: January 1, 1954. Franchise expiration date: N.A. Began: April 1, 1954.

Channel capacity: N.A. Channels available but not in use: N.A.

Basic Service

Subscribers: 29,542.

Programming (received off-air): KCRG-TV (ABC) Cedar Rapids; KFXB-TV (IND) Dubuque; KGAN (CBS) Cedar Rapids; KIIN (PBS) Iowa City; KPXR-TV (ION) Cedar Rapids; KWKB (CW, MNT) Iowa City; KWQC-TV (NBC) Davenport; KWWL (NBC) Waterloo; WHA-TV (PBS) Madison; WISC-TV (CBS, MNT) Madison; WQAD-TV (ABC) Moline; 25 FMs.

Programming (via satellite): ABC Family Channel; AMC; Animal Planet; Arts & Entertainment; BET Networks; Bravo; Cartoon Network; CNBC; CNN; Comedy Central; Country Music TV; C-SPAN; C-SPAN 2; Discovery Channel; Disney Channel; E! Entertainment Television; ESPN; ESPN 2; Eternal Word TV Network; Food Network; Fox News Channel; FX; Hallmark Channel; Headline News; HGTV; History Channel; Home Shopping Network; Lifetime; MoviePlex; MSNBC; MTV; Nickelodeon; QVC; Shop at Home; SoapNet; Spike TV; Syfy; TBS Superstation; The Learning Channel; Travel Channel; Trinity Broadcasting Network; truTV; Turner Classic Movies; Turner Network TV; TV Guide Network; TV Land; USA Network; Versus; VH1; WE tv; Weather Channel; WGN America.

Current originations: Government Access; Educational Access; Public Access.

Fee: $45.00 installation; $54.95 monthly; $2.00 converter.

Digital Basic Service

Subscribers: N.A.

Programming (via satellite): BBC America; Bio; Discovery Digital Networks; DMX Music; Fox Sports World; Fuse; GAS; Golf Channel; GSN; History Channel International; Independent Film Channel; Lifetime Movie Network; Lime; MTV Networks Digital Suite; National Geographic Channel; Nick Jr.; Outdoor Channel; Speed Channel; Style Network; Toon Disney.

Fee: $9.00 monthly.

Digital Pay Service 1

Pay Units: N.A.

Programming (via satellite): Cinemax (multiplexed); Encore (multiplexed); Flix; HBO (multiplexed); Showtime (multiplexed); Starz (multiplexed); Sundance Channel; The Movie Channel (multiplexed).

Fee: $11.95 monthly (each).

Video-On-Demand: Yes

Pay-Per-View

Playboy TV (delivered digitally); Pleasure (delivered digitally).

Internet Service

Operational: Yes. Began: December 31, 2001.

Broadband Service: Mediacom High Speed Internet.

Fee: $59.95 installation; $45.95 monthly.

Telephone Service

Digital: Operational

Fee: $39.95 installation; $39.95 monthly

Homes passed: 30,073.

Regional Vice President: Cari Fenzel. Marketing Director: Greg Evans. Area Manager: Kathleen McMullen. Technical Operations Manager: Darren Dean. Engineering Director: Mitch Carlson.

City fee: 5% of gross.

Ownership: Mediacom LLC (MSO).

DUMONT—Dumont Cablevision, PO Box 349, 506 Pine St, Dumont, IA 50625-0349. Phones: 800-328-6543; 641-857-3213. Fax: 641-857-3300. E-mail: dumontel@netins.net. Web Site: http://www.dumonttelephone.com. Also serves Allison & Bristow. ICA: IA0250.

TV Market Ranking: 65 (Allison, Bristow); Below 100 (DUMONT). Franchise award date: N.A. Franchise expiration date: N.A. Began: August 5, 1983.

Channel capacity: N.A. Channels available but not in use: N.A.

Digital Basic Service

Subscribers: 496.

Programming (received off-air): KCRG-TV (ABC) Cedar Rapids; KFXA (FOX) Cedar Rapids; KGAN (CBS) Cedar Rapids; KIMT (CBS, MNT) Mason City; KWKB (CW, MNT) Iowa City; KWWF (IND) Waterloo [LICENSED & SILENT]; KWWL (NBC) Waterloo; KYIN (PBS) Mason City.

Programming (via satellite): ABC Family Channel; AMC; Animal Planet; Arts & Entertainment; Big Ten Network; Bloomberg Television; Cartoon Network; CNN; CNN International; Comedy Central; Country Music TV; C-SPAN; C-SPAN 2; CW+; Discovery Channel; Disney Channel; E! Entertainment Television; ESPN; ESPN 2; ESPN Classic Sports; ESPN U; ESPNews; Food Network; Fox News Channel; Fox Sports Net Midwest; Fox Sports Net North; FX; GAS; Golf Channel; GSN; Hallmark Channel; Headline News; HGTV; History Channel; ION Television; Lifetime; Lifetime Movie Network; Lifetime Real Women; MTV; MTV Hits; MTV2; Music Choice; Nick Jr.; Nickelodeon; NickToons TV; Outdoor Channel; QVC; RFD-TV; SoapNet; Speed Channel; Spike TV; Syfy; TBS Superstation; The Learning Channel; Toon Disney; Travel Channel; Trinity Broadcasting Network; Turner Classic Movies; Turner Network TV; TV Land; USA Network; VH1; VH1 Classic; Weather Channel; WGN America.

Current originations: Public Access.

Fee: $25.00 installation; $54.56 monthly.

Digital Pay Service 1

Pay Units: 20.

Programming (via satellite): Cinemax (multiplexed); HBO (multiplexed).

Fee: $10.00 installation; $14.95 monthly.

Digital Pay Service 2

Pay Units: 30.

Fee: $10.00 installation; $14.95 monthly.

Pay-Per-View

Movies (delivered digitally); Special events (delivered digitally); Playboy TV (delivered digitally); Fresh (delivered digitally); Club Jenna (delivered digitally).

Internet Service

Operational: No, DSL & dialup.

Telephone Service

None

Miles of Plant: 6.0 (coaxial); None (fiber optic). Homes passed: 399.

Manager: Roger Kregel. Office Manager: Lorraine Ubben. Operations Manager: Terry Arenholz. Plant Manager: Burdette Janssen.

Ownership: Dumont Telephone Co. (MSO).

DUNKERTON—Dunkerton Telephone Coop. Formerly [IA0428]. This cable system has converted to IPTV, PO Box 188, 701 S Canfield St, Dunkerton, IA 50626. Phone: 319-822-4512. Fax: 319-822-2206. Web Site: http://www.dunkerton.net. ICA: IA5032.

TV Market Ranking: Franchise award date: N.A. Franchise expiration date: N.A. Began: January 1, 2009.

Channel capacity: N.A. Channels available but not in use: N.A.

Internet Service

Operational: Yes.

Fee: $55.00 monthly.

Telephone Service

Digital: Operational

Fee: $79.00 installation; $13.50 monthly

General Manager: Sue Bruns. Plant Supervisor: Hans Arwine.

Ownership: Dunkerton Telephone Cooperative.

DUNKERTON—Dunkerton Telephone Coop. This cable system has converted to IPTV. See Dunkerton, IA [IA5032]. ICA: IA0428.

DUNLAP—Tip Top Communication, PO Box 7, 200 W Center St, Arcadia, IA 51430. Phones: 800-290-0986; 712-689-2238. Fax: 712-689-2600. E-mail: sheilag@netins.net. ICA: IA0184.

TV Market Ranking: Outside TV Markets (DUNLAP). Franchise award date: N.A. Franchise expiration date: N.A. Began: April 1, 1984.

Channel capacity: 36 (not 2-way capable). Channels available but not in use: N.A.

Basic Service

Subscribers: 189.

Programming (received off-air): KCAU-TV (ABC) Sioux City; KETV (ABC) Omaha; KHIN (PBS) Red Oak; KMTV-TV (CBS) Omaha; KPTM (FOX, MNT) Omaha; KTIV (CW, NBC) Sioux City; KXVO (CW) Omaha; WOWT-TV (IND, NBC) Omaha.

Programming (via satellite): ABC Family Channel; CNN; Country Music TV; Discovery Channel; Disney Channel; ESPN; ESPN 2; Fox Movie Channel; G4; HGTV; History Channel; Lifetime; Lifetime Movie Network; MTV; Nickelodeon; Speed Channel; Spike TV; TBS Superstation; Turner Network TV; USA Network; WGN America.

Fee: $20.00 installation; $25.86 monthly.

Pay Service 1

Pay Units: 130.

Programming (via satellite): Cinemax; HBO.

Fee: $12.95 monthly (Cinemax), $13.95 monthly (HBO).

Pay Service 2

Pay Units: 11.

Programming (via satellite): Showtime; The Movie Channel.

Fee: $8.95 monthly (each).

Video-On-Demand: No

Internet Service

Operational: No.

Telephone Service

None

Miles of Plant: 8.0 (coaxial); None (fiber optic). Homes passed: 505.

Manager: Sheila Griffin. Chief Engineer: Mike Ahart.

City fee: 3% of gross.

Ownership: Tip Top Communication (MSO).

EARLING—Mutual Communications Services, PO Box 311, 801 19th St, Harlan, IA 51537. Phone: 712-744-3131. Fax: 712-744-3100. E-mail: fmctc@fmctc.com. Web Site: http://www.fmctc.com. Also serves Corley, Defiance, Hancock, Irwin, Jacksonville, Kirkman, Manilla, Panama, Tennant & Westphalia. ICA: IA0302.

TV Market Ranking: 53 (Hancock); Outside TV Markets (Corley, Defiance, EARLING, Irwin, Jacksonville, Kirkman, Manilla, Panama, Tennant, Westphalia). Franchise award date: May 24, 1988. Franchise expiration date: N.A. Began: January 1, 1989.

Channel capacity: 62 (not 2-way capable). Channels available but not in use: 44.

Basic Service

Subscribers: 1,022.

Programming (received off-air): KCAU-TV (ABC) Sioux City; KCCI (CBS) Des Moines; KETV (ABC) Omaha; KHIN (PBS) Red Oak; KMEG (CBS) Sioux City; KMTV-TV (CBS) Omaha; KPTM (FOX, MNT) Omaha; KTIV (CW, NBC) Sioux City; KXVO (CW) Omaha; KYNE-TV (PBS) Omaha; WHO-DT (NBC) Des Moines; WOI-DT (ABC) Ames; WOWT-TV (IND, NBC) Omaha.

Programming (via satellite): ABC Family Channel; AMC; Arts & Entertainment;

Cartoon Network; CNN; Comedy Central; Country Music TV; C-SPAN; C-SPAN 2; Discovery Channel; Disney Channel; ESPN; ESPN 2; ESPN Classic Sports; Eternal Word TV Network; Fox News Channel; G4; Headline News; HGTV; History Channel; Lifetime; Lifetime Movie Network; MTV; NASA TV; Nickelodeon; Outdoor Channel; RFD-TV; Spike TV; TBS Superstation; The Learning Channel; Turner Classic Movies; Turner Network TV; TV Land; USA Network; VH1; Weather Channel; WGN America.
Fee: $20.00 installation; $27.25 monthly.

Pay Service 1
Pay Units: 56.
Programming (via satellite): Cinemax.
Fee: $9.00 monthly.

Pay Service 2
Pay Units: 154.
Programming (via satellite): HBO.
Fee: $10.00 monthly.

Pay Service 3
Pay Units: 25.
Programming (via satellite): Showtime.
Fee: $9.00 monthly.

Internet Service
Operational: No, Both DSL & dial-up.

Telephone Service
None

Miles of Plant: 4.0 (coaxial); 26.0 (fiber optic).
Manager: Thomas Conry. Chief Technician: Mark Davis.
Ownership: Farmers Mutual Cooperative Telephone Co.

EARLVILLE—Formerly served by Alpine Communications LC. No longer in operation. ICA: IA0429.

EDDYVILLE—Mediacom. Now served by CENTERVILLE, IA [IA0039]. ICA: IA0203.

ELDON—Mediacom. Now served by CENTERVILLE, IA [IA0039]. ICA: IA0183.

ELK HORN—Marne & Elk Horn Telephone Co., PO Box 120, 4242 Main St, Elk Horn, IA 51531-0120. Phones: 712-764-6161; 888-764-6141. E-mail: metc@metc.net. Web Site: http://www.metc.net. Also serves Brayton, Exira, Kimballton & Marne. ICA: IA0123.
TV Market Ranking: Outside TV Markets (Brayton, ELK HORN, Exira, Kimballton, Marne). Franchise award date: N.A. Franchise expiration date: N.A. Began: January 1, 1984.
Channel capacity: 55 (not 2-way capable). Channels available but not in use: 2.

Basic Service
Subscribers: 909.
Programming (received off-air): KCCI (CBS) Des Moines; KDIN-TV (PBS) Des Moines; KDSM-TV (FOX) Des Moines; KETV (ABC) Omaha; KMTV-TV (CBS) Omaha; KPTM (FOX, MNT) Omaha; KXVO (CW) Omaha; WHO-DT (NBC) Des Moines; WOI-DT (ABC) Ames; WOWT-TV (IND, NBC) Omaha.
Programming (via satellite): ABC Family Channel; Animal Planet; Arts & Entertainment; Big Ten Network; Bloomberg Television; CNN; Country Music TV; C-SPAN; C-SPAN 2; Discovery Channel; Disney Channel; ESPN; ESPN 2; ESPN Classic Sports; Eternal Word TV Network; Food Network; Fox News Channel; Fox Sports Net Midwest; FX; Golf Channel; Hallmark Channel; Hallmark Movie Channel; Headline News; HGTV; History Channel; Home Shopping Network; Lifetime; Lifetime Movie Network; MTV; NASA TV; Nickelodeon; Outdoor Channel; Radar Channel; RFD-TV; Speed Channel; Spike TV; Syfy; TBS Superstation; The Learning Channel; Travel Channel; Turner Classic Movies; Turner Network TV; TV Land; USA Network; VH1; Weather Channel; WGN America.
Current originations: Public Access.
Fee: $10.00 installation; $29.95 monthly; $2.00 converter.

Pay Service 1
Pay Units: 59.
Programming (via satellite): Cinemax.
Fee: $12.00 monthly.

Pay Service 2
Pay Units: 26.
Programming (via satellite): Showtime.
Fee: $12.00 monthly.

Pay Service 3
Pay Units: 119.
Programming (via satellite): HBO (multiplexed).
Fee: $12.00 monthly.

Internet Service
Operational: No, Both DSL & dialup.

Telephone Service
None

Miles of Plant: 19.0 (coaxial); None (fiber optic). Homes passed: 1,200.
General Manager: Janell Hansen. Plant Manager: Bruce Poldberg. Chief Technician: Kennard Mertz. Office Manager: Jill Madsen.
Ownership: Marne & Elk Horn Telephone Co.

ELKHART—Huxley Communications Corp., PO Box 70, 102 N Main Ave, Huxley, IA 50124-0070. Phones: 800-231-4922; 515-597-2281. Fax: 515-597-2899. E-mail: huxtel@huxcomm.net. Web Site: http://www.huxcomm.net. ICA: IA0594.
TV Market Ranking: 66 (ELKHART). Franchise award date: N.A. Franchise expiration date: N.A. Began: N.A.
Channel capacity: 44 (not 2-way capable). Channels available but not in use: None.

Basic Service
Subscribers: 44.
Programming (received off-air): KCCI (CBS) Des Moines; KCWI-TV (CW) Ames; KDIN-TV (PBS) Des Moines; KDSM-TV (FOX) Des Moines; KFPX-TV (ION) Newton; WHO-DT (NBC) Des Moines; WOI-DT (ABC) Ames.
Programming (via satellite): ABC Family Channel; AMC; Animal Planet; Arts & Entertainment; Cartoon Network; CNBC; CNN; Comedy Central; Cooking Channel; Country Music TV; Discovery Channel; Disney Channel; Do-It-Yourself; E! Entertainment Television; ESPN; ESPN 2; ESPN Classic Sports; ESPNews; Food Network; Fox Movie Channel; Fox News Channel; Fox Sports Net Midwest; FX; G4; Golf Channel; Hallmark Channel; Headline News; HGTV; History Channel; Home Shopping Network; Lifetime; MSNBC; MTV; National Geographic Channel; Nickelodeon; Outdoor Channel; RFD-TV; Shop at Home; Speed Channel; Spike TV; TBS Superstation; The Learning Channel; Toon Disney; Travel Channel; Trinity Broadcasting Network; truTV; Turner Classic Movies; Turner Network TV; TV Land; USA Network; VH1; Weather Channel; WGN America.
Fee: $30.00 installation.

Digital Basic Service
Subscribers: N.A.
Programming (via satellite): AmericanLife TV Network; BBC America; Bio; Black Family Channel; Bloomberg Television; Bravo; Current; Discovery Digital Networks; DMX Music; ESPN 2; ESPN Classic Sports; ESPNews; FitTV; Fox College Sports Atlantic; Fox College Sports Central; Fox College Sports Pacific; Fox Movie Channel; Fox Soccer; Fuse; G4; GAS; Golf Channel; Great American Country; GSN; Halogen Network; HGTV; History Channel; History Channel International; Independent Film Channel; International Television (ITV); Lifetime Movie Network; Lime; MTV Networks Digital Suite; National Geographic Channel; Nick Jr.; NickToons TV; Outdoor Channel; Ovation; ShopNBC; Speed Channel; Style Network; Sundance Channel; The Word Network; Toon Disney; Trinity Broadcasting Network; Trio; Turner Classic Movies; Versus; WE tv.
Fee: $10.00 monthly.

Pay Service 1
Pay Units: 7.
Programming (via satellite): Cinemax.
Fee: $10.00 monthly.

Pay Service 2
Pay Units: 11.
Programming (via satellite): HBO.
Fee: $15.00 monthly.

Pay Service 3
Pay Units: 3.
Programming (via satellite): Showtime.
Fee: $10.00 monthly.

Pay Service 4
Pay Units: 6.
Programming (via satellite): Encore; Starz.
Fee: $10.00 monthly.

Digital Pay Service 1
Pay Units: N.A.
Programming (via satellite): Cinemax (multiplexed); Encore (multiplexed); Flix; HBO (multiplexed); Showtime (multiplexed); Starz (multiplexed); The Movie Channel (multiplexed).
Fee: $10.00 monthly (Cinemax, Showtime/TMC or Starz/Encore), $15.00 monthly (HBO).

Video-On-Demand: Planned

Pay-Per-View
iN DEMAND (delivered digitally); Playboy TV (delivered digitally); Fresh (delivered digitally); Shorteez (delivered digitally).

Internet Service
Operational: No, DSL.

Telephone Service
None

Homes passed: 127.
General Manager: Billy L. Hotchkiss. Operations Director: Terry Ferguson. Plant Manager: Brant Strumpfer.
City fee: 3% of gross.
Ownership: Huxley Communications Corp. (MSO).

ELY—South Slope Coop. Communications Co. Formerly served by North Liberty, IA [IA0432]. This cable system has converted to IPTV, PO Box 19, 980 N Front St, North Liberty, IA 52317. Phones: 800-272-6449; 319-626-2211. Fax: 319-665-7000. E-mail: info@southslope.com. Web Site: http://www.southslope.com. ICA: IA5004.
TV Market Ranking: 65 (Ely). Franchise award date: January 12, 2004. Franchise expiration date: N.A. Began: N.A.
Channel capacity: N.A. Channels available but not in use: N.A.

Basic Service
Subscribers: N.A.
Fee: $25.00 installation; $41.95 monthly.

Expanded Basic Service 1
Subscribers: N.A.
Fee: $25.00 installation; $54.95 monthly.

Expanded Basic Service 2
Subscribers: N.A.
Fee: $25.00 installation; $10.00 monthly.

Limited Basic Service
Subscribers: N.A.
Fee: $14.95 monthly.

Pay Service 1
Pay Units: N.A.
Fee: $10.95 monthy (Starz); $11.95 monthly (Cinemax); $12.95 monthly (Showtime); $13.95 monthy (HBO); $15.95 monthly (Adult).

Internet Service
Operational: Yes.
Fee: $39.95 monthly; $10.00 modem lease; $130.00 modem purchase.

Telephone Service
Digital: Operational
Fee: $14.50 monthly

Ownership: South Slope Cooperative Communications Co.

EMERSON—Interstate Communications, PO Box 229, 105 N West St, Truro, IA 50257-0229. Phones: 712-824-7231; 712-824-7227. Fax: 641-765-4204. Web Site: http://www.interstatecom.com. ICA: IA0288.
TV Market Ranking: Outside TV Markets (EMERSON). Franchise award date: January 1, 1982. Franchise expiration date: N.A. Began: January 1, 1983.
Channel capacity: N.A. Channels available but not in use: N.A.

Digital Basic Service
Subscribers: 129.
Programming (received off-air): KETV (ABC) Omaha; KFPX-TV (ION) Newton; KMTV-TV (CBS) Omaha; KPTM (FOX, MNT) Omaha; KXVO (CW) Omaha; WOWT-TV (IND, NBC) Omaha.
Programming (via satellite): ABC Family Channel; AMC; AmericanLife TV Network; Animal Planet; Arts & Entertainment; BBC America; Big Ten Network; Bio; Bloomberg Television; Boomerang; Bravo; Cartoon Network; CNBC; CNN; CNN International; Comcast SportsNet West; Comedy Central; Country Music TV; C-SPAN; C-SPAN 2; Discovery Channel; Discovery Health Channel; Discovery Home Channel; Discovery Kids Channel; Discovery Military Channel; Discovery Times Channel; Disney Channel; Do-It-Yourself; E! Entertainment Television; ESPN; ESPN 2; ESPN Classic Sports; ESPN U; ESPNews; Eternal Word TV Network; Food Network; Fox News Channel; Fox Sports Net Midwest; FX; G4; GalaVision; GAS; Golf Channel; GSN; Hallmark Channel; Headline News; HGTV; History Channel; History Channel International; Home Shopping Network; Lifetime; Lifetime Movie Network; Lifetime Real Women; MSNBC; MTV; MTV Hits; MTV2; Music Choice; National Geographic Channel; Nick Jr.; Nickelodeon; NickToons TV; Outdoor Channel; Oxygen; QVC; RFD-TV; Science Channel; SoapNet; Speed Channel; Spike TV; Style Network; Syfy; TBS Superstation; The Learning Channel; Travel Channel; Trinity Broadcasting Network; truTV; Turner Classic Movies; Turner Network TV; TV Land; Univision; USA Network; Versus; VH1; VH1 Classic; WE tv; Weather Channel; WGN America.
Fee: $35.00 installation; $39.95 monthly.

Digital Pay Service 1
Pay Units: 14.
Programming (via satellite): Cinemax (multiplexed); Encore (multiplexed); HBO (multiplexed); Starz (multiplexed).
Fee: $9.00 monthly (each).

Video-On-Demand: No

Internet Service
Operational: Yes.
Telephone Service
None
Miles of Plant: 3.0 (coaxial); None (fiber optic). Homes passed: 225. Total homes in franchised area: 260.
Manager: Mike Weis. Chief Technician: Rick Lunn.
Ownership: Interstate Communications (MSO).

EXIRA—Marne & Elk Horn Telephone Co. Now served by ELK HORN, IA [IA0123]. ICA: IA0433.

FAIRBANK—Mediacom. Now served by WAVERLY, IA [IA0021]. Also serves FAIRBANK. ICA: IA0217.

FAIRFAX—Formerly served by Starwest Inc. No longer in operation. ICA: IA0284.

FARMINGTON—Starwest Inc., 15235 235th St, Milton, IA 52570-8016. Phones: 319-397-2283; 319-293-6336. ICA: IA0228.
TV Market Ranking: Below 100 (FARMINGTON). Franchise award date: N.A. Franchise expiration date: N.A. Began: December 1, 1982.
Channel capacity: N.A. Channels available but not in use: N.A.
Basic Service
Subscribers: N.A.
Programming (via satellite): ESPN; TBS Superstation; WGN America.
Fee: $30.00 installation; $10.50 monthly.
Pay Service 1
Pay Units: N.A.
Programming (via satellite): Showtime.
Fee: $6.95 monthly.
Internet Service
Operational: No.
Miles of Plant: 6.0 (coaxial); None (fiber optic). Homes passed: 350.
Manager & Chief Technician: John Stooksberry.
Ownership: Starwest Inc. (MSO).

FARRAGUT—Western Iowa Networks, PO Box 190, 112 E Main St, Breda, IA 51436-0190. Phone: 712-673-2311. Fax: 712-673-2880. Web Site: http://www.westIAnet.com. ICA: IA0434.
TV Market Ranking: Outside TV Markets (FARRAGUT). Franchise award date: N.A. Franchise expiration date: N.A. Began: N.A.
Channel capacity: N.A. Channels available but not in use: N.A.
Basic Service
Subscribers: N.A. Included in Breda
Programming (received off-air): KETV (ABC) Omaha; KHIN (PBS) Red Oak; KMTV-TV (CBS) Omaha; KPTM (FOX, MNT) Omaha; KUON-TV (PBS) Lincoln; KXVO (CW) Omaha; WOWT-TV (IND, NBC) Omaha.
Programming (via satellite): ABC Family Channel; AMC; Arts & Entertainment; CNN; Country Music TV; Discovery Channel; Disney Channel; ESPN; ESPN 2; Headline News; HGTV; History Channel; Lifetime; Nickelodeon; Spike TV; Syfy; TBS Superstation; Turner Network TV; TV Land; USA Network; VH1; Weather Channel; WGN America.
Fee: $20.00 installation; $25.95 monthly.
Pay Service 1
Pay Units: N.A.
Programming (via satellite): HBO; The Movie Channel.
Fee: $10.95 monthly (HBO or TMC).
Video-On-Demand: No
Internet Service
Operational: No, DSL.
Telephone Service
None
Chief Executive Officer: Steve Frickenstein. Marketing & Sales Manager: Megan Badding. Chief Technician: Mike Ludwig.
Ownership: Tele-Services Ltd. (MSO).

FENTON—Fenton Cablevision, PO Box 77, 300 2nd St, Fenton, IA 50539-0077. Phone: 515-889-2785. Fax: 515-889-2255. E-mail: fntn@netins.net. ICA: IA0327.
TV Market Ranking: Outside TV Markets (FENTON). Franchise award date: N.A. Franchise expiration date: N.A. Began: August 1, 1967.
Channel capacity: 35 (operating 2-way). Channels available but not in use: N.A.
Basic Service
Subscribers: 142.
Programming (received off-air): KAAL (ABC) Austin; KCAU-TV (ABC) Sioux City; KCCI (CBS) Des Moines; KEYC-TV (CBS, FOX) Mankato; KIMT (CBS, MNT) Mason City; KTIN (PBS) Fort Dodge; KTTC (CW, NBC) Rochester; WHO-DT (NBC) Des Moines; WOI-DT (ABC) Ames; allband FM.
Programming (via satellite): ABC Family Channel; CNN; Discovery Channel; ESPN; Headline News; Spike TV; TBS Superstation; Turner Network TV; USA Network; WGN America.
Fee: $10.00 installation; $25.95 monthly.
Pay Service 1
Pay Units: 18.
Programming (via satellite): Cinemax.
Fee: $9.00 monthly.
Pay Service 2
Pay Units: 20.
Programming (via satellite): HBO.
Fee: $9.00 monthly.
Internet Service
Operational: No.
Broadband Service: DSL service only.
Telephone Service
None
Miles of Plant: 3.0 (coaxial); None (fiber optic). Homes passed: 175. Total homes in franchised area: 175.
Manager: Steven Longhenry.
City fee: None.
Ownership: Fenton Cooperative Telephone Co.

FERTILE—Formerly served by Westcom. No longer in operation. ICA: IA0580.

FONDA—Formerly served by TelePartners. No longer in operation. ICA: IA0219.

FONTANELLE—B & L Technologies LLC, 3329 270th St, Lenox, IA 50851. Phones: 800-798-5488; 641-348-2240. Fax: 641-348-2240. ICA: IA0246.
TV Market Ranking: Outside TV Markets (FONTANELLE). Franchise award date: October 1, 1984. Franchise expiration date: N.A. Began: November 30, 1984.
Channel capacity: 36 (not 2-way capable). Channels available but not in use: 1.
Basic Service
Subscribers: 46.
Programming (received off-air): KCCI (CBS) Des Moines; KDIN-TV (PBS) Des Moines; KDSM-TV (FOX) Des Moines; WHO-DT (NBC) Des Moines; WOI-DT (ABC) Ames.
Programming (via satellite): ABC Family Channel; AMC; CNN; Discovery Channel; ESPN; Lifetime; Nickelodeon; Spike TV; TBS Superstation; Turner Network TV; USA Network; Weather Channel; WGN America.
Fee: $19.43 monthly.
Pay Service 1
Pay Units: 36.
Programming (via satellite): HBO.
Fee: $11.00 monthly.
Video-On-Demand: No
Internet Service
Operational: No.
Telephone Service
None
Miles of Plant: 6.0 (coaxial); None (fiber optic). Homes passed: 365.
President & General Manager: Robert Hintz. Office Manager: Linda Hintz.
City fee: 3% of gross.
Ownership: B & L Technologies LLC (MSO).

FOREST CITY—Winnebago Cooperative Telephone Assn., 704 E Main St, Lake Mills, IA 50450-1420. Phones: 800-592-6105; 641-592-6105. Fax: 641-592-6102. E-mail: wcta@wctatel.net. Web Site: http://www.wctatel.net. ICA: IA0589. **Note:** This system is an overbuild.
TV Market Ranking: Below 100 (FOREST CITY). Franchise award date: N.A. Franchise expiration date: N.A. Began: N.A.
Channel capacity: N.A. Channels available but not in use: N.A.
Basic Service
Subscribers: 720.
Programming (received off-air): KAAL (ABC) Austin; KIMT (CBS, MNT) Mason City; KTTC (CW, NBC) Rochester; KXLT-TV (FOX) Rochester; KYIN (PBS) Mason City.
Current originations: Leased Access; Educational Access.
Fee: $20.00 installation; $19.95 monthly.
Expanded Basic Service 1
Subscribers: N.A.
Programming (via satellite): ABC Family Channel; AMC; Animal Planet; Arts & Entertainment; Bravo; Cartoon Network; CNBC; CNN; Comedy Central; Country Music TV; C-SPAN; CW+; Discovery Channel; Disney Channel; Do-It-Yourself; E! Entertainment Television; ESPN; ESPN 2; ESPN Classic Sports; Food Network; Fox News Channel; Fox Sports Net; FX; G4; Golf Channel; Hallmark Channel; Headline News; HGTV; History Channel; Home Shopping Network; INSP; ION Television; Lifetime; MSNBC; MTV; Nickelodeon; Outdoor Channel; Speed Channel; Spike TV; Syfy; TBS Superstation; The Learning Channel; Travel Channel; Trinity Broadcasting Network; Turner Classic Movies; Turner Network TV; TV Land; USA Network; VH1; Weather Channel; WGN America.
Fee: $18.30 monthly.
Video-On-Demand: No
Internet Service
Operational: No.
Telephone Service
None
General Manager: Don Whipple. Assistant Manager: John Kroger. Chief Engineer: Neal Sletten. Marketing Manager: David Taft.
Ownership: Winnebago Cooperative Telephone Assn. (MSO).

FORT DODGE—Mediacom, 2205 Ingersoll Ave, Des Moines, IA 50312. Phone: 515-246-1890. Fax: 515-246-2211. Web Site: http://www.mediacomcable.com. Also serves Algona, Alta, Barnum, Belmond, Buena Vista County, Cherokee, Clare, Clarion, Coalville, Cornelia, Dakota City, Eagle Grove, Hamilton County, Humboldt, Lake City, Lakeside, Laurens, Manson, Moorland, Pocahontas, Rockwell City, Sac City, Storm Lake, Webster City, Webster County & Wright County (central portion). ICA: IA0011.
TV Market Ranking: 66 (Hamilton County, Webster City, Webster County (portions)); Below 100 (Belmond); Outside TV Markets (Algona, Alta, Barnum, Buena Vista County, Cherokee, Clare, Clarion, Coalville, Cornelia, Dakota City, Eagle Grove, FORT DODGE, Humboldt, Lake City, Lakeside, Laurens, Manson, Moorland, Pocahontas, Rockwell City, Sac City, Storm Lake, Wright County (central portion), Webster County (portions)). Franchise award date: June 11, 1977. Franchise expiration date: N.A. Began: November 1, 1978.
Channel capacity: N.A. Channels available but not in use: N.A.
Basic Service
Subscribers: 29,920.
Programming (received off-air): KCCI (CBS) Des Moines; KCWI-TV (CW) Ames; KDIN-TV (PBS) Des Moines; KDSM-TV (FOX) Des Moines; WHO-DT (NBC) Des Moines; WOI-DT (ABC) Ames; allband FM.
Programming (via satellite): C-SPAN; C-SPAN 2; MyNetworkTV Inc.; QVC; TV Guide Network; Weather Channel; WGN America.
Current originations: Leased Access; Educational Access.
Fee: $41.99 installation; $10.99 monthly; $1.60 converter.
Expanded Basic Service 1
Subscribers: 21,110.
Programming (via satellite): ABC Family Channel; AMC; Animal Planet; Arts & Entertainment; Bravo; Cartoon Network; CNBC; CNN; Comedy Central; Country Music TV; Discovery Channel; Disney Channel; E! Entertainment Television; ESPN; ESPN 2; ESPN Classic Sports; Eternal Word TV Network; Food Network; Fox Movie Channel; Fox News Channel; Fox Sports Net North; FX; Hallmark Channel; Headline News; HGTV; History Channel; Home Shopping Network; INSP; Lifetime; MoviePlex; MSNBC; MTV; National Geographic Channel; Nickelodeon; Oxygen; RFD-TV; SoapNet; Speed Channel; Spike TV; Syfy; TBS Superstation; Telemundo; The Learning Channel; Travel Channel; Trinity Broadcasting Network; truTV; Turner Classic Movies; Turner Network TV; TV Land; Univision; USA Network; Versus; VH1; WE tv.
Fee: $13.95 installation; $29.96 monthly.
Digital Basic Service
Subscribers: 7,302.
Programming (via satellite): AmericanLife TV Network; BBC America; Bio; Bloomberg Television; Canal 52MX; CBS College Sports Network; Cine Latino; CMT Pure Country; CNN en Espanol; Discovery en Espanol; Discovery HD Theater; Discovery Health Channel; Discovery Home Channel; Discovery Kids Channel; Discovery Military Channel; DMX Music; ESPN 2 HD; ESPN HD; ESPN U; ESPNews; FitTV; Fox College Sports Atlantic; Fox College Sports Central; Fox College Sports Pacific; Fox Soccer; Fox Sports en Espanol; Fuel TV; Fuse; G4; Gol TV; Golf Channel; GSN; Halogen Network; HDNet; HDNet Movies; History Channel en Espanol; History Channel International; ID Investigation Discovery; Independent Film Channel; Lifetime Movie Network; Lifetime Real Women; MTV Hits; MTV Tres; MTV2; Nick Jr.; NickToons TV; Outdoor Channel; Ovation; Science Channel; Sleuth; Style Network; TeenNick; Tennis Channel; The

Sportsman Channel; Toon Disney; TVG Network; Universal HD; VeneMovies; VH1 Classic; VH1 Soul.
Fee: $12.00 monthly.

Digital Pay Service 1
Pay Units: 2,676.
Programming (via satellite): Cinemax (multiplexed).
Fee: $13.95 installation; $14.00 monthly.

Digital Pay Service 2
Pay Units: 3,618.
Programming (via satellite): Encore (multiplexed).
Fee: $13.95 installation; $2.52 monthly.

Digital Pay Service 3
Pay Units: 3,500.
Programming (via satellite): HBO (multiplexed); HBO HD.
Fee: $13.95 installation; $14.00 monthly.

Digital Pay Service 4
Pay Units: 1,064.
Programming (via satellite): Showtime (multiplexed); Showtime HD.
Fee: $13.95 installation; $14.00 monthly.

Digital Pay Service 5
Pay Units: 2,947.
Programming (via satellite): Starz (multiplexed); Starz HDTV.
Fee: $13.95 installation; $8.52 monthly.

Digital Pay Service 6
Pay Units: 871.
Programming (via satellite): Flix; Sundance Channel; The Movie Channel (multiplexed); The Movie Channel HD.
Fee: $1.99 installation; $9.54 monthly.

Video-On-Demand: Yes

Pay-Per-View
Addressable homes: 6,574.
ESPN Now (delivered digitally), Addressable: Yes; ETC (delivered digitally); Playboy TV (delivered digitally); Pleasure (delivered digitally); Fresh (delivered digitally); Shorteez (delivered digitally); TVN Entertainment (delivered digitally); sports (delivered digitally).

Internet Service
Operational: Yes.
Subscribers: 4,646.
Broadband Service: Mediacom High Speed Internet.
Fee: $55.95 monthly.

Telephone Service
Digital: Operational

Miles of Plant: 594.0 (coaxial); 123.0 (fiber optic). Homes passed: 39,662. Total homes in franchised area: 39,662.
Vice President: Steve Purcell. Technical Operations Manager: Cliff Waggoner. Marketing Director: LeAnn Treloar. Government & Media Relations Manager: Bill Peard.
City fee: 3% of basic & expanded basic.
Ownership: Mediacom LLC (MSO).

FREMONT—Starwest Inc., 15235 235th St, Milton, IA 52570-8016. Phones: 319-397-2283; 319-293-6336. ICA: IA0291.
TV Market Ranking: Below 100 (FREMONT). Franchise award date: N.A. Franchise expiration date: N.A. Began: August 1, 1984.
Channel capacity: 35 (not 2-way capable). Channels available but not in use: N.A.

Basic Service
Subscribers: N.A.
Programming (received off-air): KCCI (CBS) Des Moines; KDIN-TV (PBS) Des Moines; KTVO (ABC) Kirksville; WHO-DT (NBC) Des Moines; WOI-DT (ABC) Ames.
Programming (via satellite): ESPN; TBS Superstation; WGN America.

Pay Service 1
Pay Units: N.A.
Programming (via satellite): Showtime.
Fee: $8.95 monthly.

Internet Service
Operational: No.

Miles of Plant: 4.0 (coaxial); None (fiber optic). Homes passed: 220.
Manager & Chief Technician: John Stooksberry.
Ownership: Starwest Inc. (MSO).

GARBER—Formerly served by Alpine Communications LC. No longer in operation. ICA: IA0435.

GARNAVILLO—Mediacom. Now served by PRAIRIE DU CHIEN, WI [WI0066]. ICA: IA0547.

GENEVA—Dumont Cablevision, PO Box 349, 506 Pine St, Dumont, IA 50625-0349. Phones: 800-328-6543; 641-857-3211. E-mail: dumontel@netins.net. Web Site: http://www.dumonttelephone.com. ICA: IA0382.
TV Market Ranking: Below 100 (GENEVA). Franchise award date: February 27, 1990. Franchise expiration date: N.A. Began: August 1, 1990.
Channel capacity: 28 (not 2-way capable). Channels available but not in use: N.A.

Basic Service
Subscribers: 47.
Programming (received off-air): KCCI (CBS) Des Moines; KDSM-TV (FOX) Des Moines; KIMT (CBS, MNT) Mason City; KWWL (NBC) Waterloo; KYIN (PBS) Mason City; WHO-DT (NBC) Des Moines; WOI-DT (ABC) Ames.
Programming (via satellite): ABC Family Channel; AMC; Animal Planet; Arts & Entertainment; Cartoon Network; CNN; Comedy Central; Country Music TV; Discovery Channel; Disney Channel; ESPN; ESPN 2; FX; GSN; Hallmark Channel; HGTV; History Channel; Lifetime; Nickelodeon; Outdoor Channel; QVC; Speed Channel; Spike TV; TBS Superstation; The Learning Channel; Trinity Broadcasting Network; Turner Network TV; TV Land; USA Network; VH1; Weather Channel; WGN America.
Fee: $35.00 installation; $27.00 monthly.

Pay Service 1
Pay Units: 4.
Programming (via satellite): Cinemax.
Fee: $10.00 installation; $9.50 monthly.

Pay Service 2
Pay Units: 4.
Programming (via satellite): HBO.
Fee: $10.00 installation; $9.50 monthly.

Internet Service
Operational: No, DSL & dialup.

Telephone Service
None

Miles of Plant: 2.0 (coaxial); None (fiber optic). Homes passed: 79.
Manager: Roger Kregel. Office Manager: Lorraine Ubben. Operations Manager: Terry Arenholz. Plant Manager: Burdette Janssen.
Ownership: Dumont Telephone Co. (MSO).

GEORGE—Siebring Cable TV. Now served by SIOUX CENTER, IA [IA0076]. ICA: IA0199.

GILLETT GROVE—ATC Cablevision, PO Box 248, 1405 Silver Lake Ave, Ayrshire, IA 50515-0248. Phones: 712-426-2800; 800-642-2884; 712-426-2815. Fax: 712-426-4008. E-mail: info@ayrshireia.com. Web Site: http://www.ayrshireia.com. ICA: IA0386.
TV Market Ranking: Outside TV Markets (GILLETT GROVE). Franchise award date: N.A. Franchise expiration date: N.A. Began: April 1, 1987.
Channel capacity: 36 (not 2-way capable). Channels available but not in use: 13.

Basic Service
Subscribers: 20.
Programming (received off-air): KCAU-TV (ABC) Sioux City; KELO-TV (CBS, MNT) Sioux Falls; KEYC-TV (CBS, FOX) Mankato; KMEG (CBS) Sioux City; KPTH (FOX, MNT) Sioux City; KSFY-TV (ABC) Sioux Falls; KTIN (PBS) Fort Dodge; KTIV (CW, NBC) Sioux City; WOI-DT (ABC) Ames.
Programming (via satellite): ABC Family Channel; AmericanLife TV Network; Animal Planet; Arts & Entertainment; Cartoon Network; CNBC; CNN; Comedy Central; Country Music TV; C-SPAN; C-SPAN 2; Discovery Channel; Disney Channel; E! Entertainment Television; ESPN; ESPN 2; ESPN Classic Sports; Food Network; Fox News Channel; FX; Hallmark Channel; Headline News; HGTV; History Channel; ION Television; Lifetime; MTV; Nickelodeon; Outdoor Channel; QVC; Spike TV; Syfy; TBS Superstation; The Learning Channel; Travel Channel; Turner Classic Movies; Turner Network TV; TV Guide Network; TV Land; USA Network; VH1; Weather Channel; WGN America.
Fee: $30.00 installation; $43.40 monthly.

Digital Basic Service
Subscribers: N.A.
Programming (via satellite): BBC America; Bio; Discovery Digital Networks; DMX Music; ESPNews; FitTV; Fox Movie Channel; G4; GAS; Golf Channel; GSN; History Channel; Independent Film Channel; MTV2; National Geographic Channel; Nick Jr.; NickToons TV; Outdoor Channel; Speed Channel; Toon Disney; VH1 Classic; VH1 Country.
Fee: $7.00 monthly.

Digital Pay Service 1
Pay Units: 3.
Programming (via satellite): Cinemax (multiplexed); Encore (multiplexed); Flix; HBO (multiplexed); Showtime (multiplexed); Starz (multiplexed); Sundance Channel; The Movie Channel (multiplexed).
Fee: $9.50 monthly (Cinemax), $11.00 monthly (Showtime/TMC or Starz/Encore), $12.00 monthly (HBO).

Digital Pay Service 2
Pay Units: 2.
Programming (via satellite): Showtime HD; The Movie Channel HD.

Video-On-Demand: No

Pay-Per-View
Movies (delivered digitally), Fee: $3.95; Sports PPV (delivered digitally), Fee: $3.95; Special events (delivered digitally), Fee: $3.95.

Internet Service
Operational: No, Dial-up only.

Telephone Service
None

Miles of Plant: 2.0 (coaxial); None (fiber optic). Homes passed: 41. Total homes in franchised area: 41.
Manager: Don Miller. Plant Manager: Chase Cox. Chief Technician: Derek Franker. Customer Service: Lonna Hess. Accounting Manager: Robin Dietrich. Executive Secretary: Kelly Otto.
Ownership: Ayrshire Communications (MSO).

GILMAN—Partner Cable TV, PO Box 8, 101 East Church St, Gilman, IA 50106. Phones: 800-647-2355; 641-498-7701. Fax: 641-498-7308. E-mail: custsvc@partnercom.net. Web Site: http://www.pcctel.net. Also serves Baxter, Harvester Community, Kellogg, Laurel, Melbourne, Montour, Oakland Acres, Rhodes, Rock Creek Lake & State Center. ICA: IA0128.
TV Market Ranking: 66 (Baxter, Melbourne, Rhodes, State Center); Below 100 (GILMAN, Harvester Community, Kellogg, Laurel, Montour, Oakland Acres, Rock Creek Lake). Franchise award date: N.A. Franchise expiration date: N.A. Began: January 1, 1984.
Channel capacity: 62 (operating 2-way). Channels available but not in use: 1.

Basic Service
Subscribers: 1,150.
Programming (received off-air): KCCI (CBS) Des Moines; KDIN-TV (PBS) Des Moines; KDSM-TV (FOX) Des Moines; KFPX-TV (ION) Newton; WHO-DT (NBC) Des Moines; WOI-DT (ABC) Ames.
Programming (via satellite): ABC Family Channel; Animal Planet; Arts & Entertainment; Cartoon Network; CNN; Comcast SportsNet Chicago; Comedy Central; Country Music TV; C-SPAN; C-SPAN 2; Discovery Channel; Disney Channel; Do-It-Yourself; ESPN; ESPN 2; ESPN Classic Sports; ESPN U; Fox News Channel; Fox Sports Net Midwest; FX; Hallmark Channel; Headline News; HGTV; History Channel; Home Shopping Network; INSP; Lifetime; MTV; National Geographic Channel; NFL Network; Nickelodeon; SoapNet; Speed Channel; Spike TV; Syfy; TBS Superstation; The Learning Channel; Travel Channel; Trinity Broadcasting Network; truTV; Turner Classic Movies; Turner Network TV; TV Land; USA Network; VH1; Weather Channel; WGN America.
Current originations: Public Access.
Fee: $26.95 installation; $37.95 monthly.

Digital Basic Service
Subscribers: 338.
Programming (via satellite): BBC America; Bio; Bloomberg Television; Discovery Digital Networks; DMX Music; ESPN 2; ESPN Classic Sports; ESPNews; Fox Movie Channel; Fox Sports World; FSN Digital Atlantic; FSN Digital Central; FSN Digital Pacific; G4; GAS; Golf Channel; GSN; Halogen Network; HGTV; History Channel; History Channel International; Lifetime Movie Network; MTV Networks Digital Suite; National Geographic Channel; Nick Jr.; NickToons TV; Outdoor Channel; Speed Channel; Style Network; Syfy; Toon Disney; Trinity Broadcasting Network; Turner Classic Movies; Versus.
Fee: $5.00 monthly.

Pay Service 1
Pay Units: N.A.
Programming (via satellite): Encore (multiplexed); HBO (multiplexed); Showtime (multiplexed); Starz (multiplexed).
Fee: $12.95 monthly (each).

Digital Pay Service 1
Pay Units: 146.
Programming (via satellite): HBO (multiplexed).
Fee: $10.00 monthly.

Digital Pay Service 2
Pay Units: 29.
Programming (via satellite): Showtime (multiplexed); The Movie Channel (multiplexed).
Fee: $10.00 monthly.

Digital Pay Service 3
Pay Units: 57.
Programming (via satellite): Encore (multiplexed); Starz (multiplexed).
Fee: $10.00 monthly.

Video-On-Demand: Planned

Pay-Per-View
Addressable homes: 317.
ESPN Extra (delivered digitally), Addressable: Yes; Hot Choice (delivered digitally); iN DEMAND (delivered digitally); ESPN Classic Sports (delivered digitally); ESPN Gameplan (delivered digitally); Hot Choice (delivered digitally); iN DEMAND (delivered digitally).

Internet Service
Operational: Yes, DSL.
Fee: $39.95-$79.95 monthly.

Telephone Service
None

Miles of Plant: 52.0 (coaxial); None (fiber optic). Homes passed: 2,390.
Manager: Donald S. Jennings. Chief Technician: Dave Grewell. Marketing Coordinator: Deb Heater. Customer Service Manager: Dot Burgess.
Ownership: Partner Communications Cooperative.

GILMORE CITY—Mediacom, 2205 Ingersoll Ave, Des Moines, IA 50312. Phone: 515-246-1890. Fax: 515-246-2211. Web Site: http://www.mediacomcable.com. ICA: IA0251.
TV Market Ranking: Outside TV Markets (GILMORE CITY). Franchise award date: N.A. Franchise expiration date: N.A. Began: January 1, 1983.
Channel capacity: N.A. Channels available but not in use: N.A.

Basic Service
Subscribers: 200.
Programming (received off-air): KCCI (CBS) Des Moines; KDSM-TV (FOX) Des Moines; KTIN (PBS) Fort Dodge; WHO-DT (NBC) Des Moines; WOI-DT (ABC) Ames.
Programming (via satellite): ABC Family Channel; Animal Planet; Arts & Entertainment; CNBC; CNN; Country Music TV; Discovery Channel; ESPN; ESPN 2; Fox News Channel; HGTV; Lifetime; Nickelodeon; QVC; Spike TV; Syfy; TBS Superstation; Turner Classic Movies; Turner Network TV; TV Land; USA Network; VH1; Weather Channel; WGN America.
Fee: $19.95 installation; $9.50 monthly.

Pay Service 1
Pay Units: N.A.
Programming (via satellite): Cinemax; HBO.
Fee: $10.00 installation; $9.95 monthly (each).

Video-On-Demand: No

Internet Service
Operational: No.

Telephone Service
None

Miles of Plant: 5.0 (coaxial); None (fiber optic). Homes passed: 300. Total homes in franchised area: 300.
Division Vice President: Ed Pardini. Regional Vice President: Steve Purcell. Technical Operations Director: Cliff Waggoner. Marketing Director: LeAnn Treloar. Government Relations Manager: Bill Peard.
City fee: None.
Ownership: Mediacom LLC (MSO).

GLADBROOK—Mediacom, 2205 Ingersoll Ave, Des Moines, IA 50312. Phone: 515-246-1890. Fax: 515-246-2211. Web Site: http://www.mediacomcable.com. Also serves Beaman, Conrad & Garwin. ICA: IA0087.
TV Market Ranking: 65 (Beaman, Conrad, Garwin, GLADBROOK). Franchise award date: N.A. Franchise expiration date: N.A. Began: October 1, 1984.
Channel capacity: N.A. Channels available but not in use: N.A.

Basic Service
Subscribers: 882.
Programming (received off-air): KCCI (CBS) Des Moines; KCRG-TV (ABC) Cedar Rapids; KCWI-TV (CW) Ames; KDIN-TV (PBS) Des Moines; KDSM-TV (FOX) Des Moines; KFPX-TV (ION) Newton; KFXA (FOX) Cedar Rapids; KGAN (CBS) Cedar Rapids; KPXR-TV (ION) Cedar Rapids; KWKB (CW, MNT) Iowa City; KWWL (NBC) Waterloo; WHO-DT (NBC) Des Moines; WOI-DT (ABC) Ames.
Programming (via satellite): ABC Family Channel; AMC; Animal Planet; Arts & Entertainment; Bravo; Cartoon Network; CNBC; CNN; Comedy Central; Country Music TV; C-SPAN; C-SPAN 2; Discovery Channel; Disney Channel; E! Entertainment Television; ESPN; ESPN 2; Eternal Word TV Network; Food Network; Fox News Channel; Fox Sports Net; FX; Hallmark Channel; Headline News; HGTV; History Channel; Home Shopping Network; Lifetime; MSNBC; MTV; Nickelodeon; Speed Channel; Spike TV; Syfy; TBS Superstation; The Learning Channel; Travel Channel; Trinity Broadcasting Network; truTV; Turner Classic Movies; Turner Network TV; TV Guide Network; TV Land; USA Network; VH1; Weather Channel; WGN America.
Fee: $40.95 monthly.

Digital Basic Service
Subscribers: 263.
Programming (via satellite): AmericanLife TV Network; BBC America; Bio; Bloomberg Television; Discovery Digital Networks; Fox Movie Channel; Fox Sports World; Fuse; G4; GAS; Golf Channel; GSN; Halogen Network; History Channel International; Independent Film Channel; Lifetime Movie Network; Lime; MTV2; Music Choice; National Geographic Channel; Nick Jr.; Outdoor Channel; Ovation; Style Network; Toon Disney; Versus.

Digital Pay Service 1
Pay Units: 108.
Programming (via satellite): Cinemax (multiplexed); Encore; HBO (multiplexed); Showtime (multiplexed); Starz; The Movie Channel.
Fee: $9.95 monthly (each).

Video-On-Demand: Yes

Pay-Per-View
Addressable homes: 263.
Sports PPV (delivered digitally), Addressable: Yes.

Internet Service
Operational: Yes.
Subscribers: 186.
Broadband Service: Mediacom High Speed Internet.
Fee: $99.00 installation; $55.95 monthly.

Telephone Service
Digital: Operational

Miles of Plant: 40.0 (coaxial); None (fiber optic). Homes passed: 1,335.
Regional Vice President: Steve Purcell. Technical Operations Director: Cliff Waggoner. Marketing Director: LeAnn Treloar. Government & Media Relations Manager: Bill Peard.
Ownership: Mediacom LLC (MSO).

GOLDFIELD—Goldfield Communication Services Corp., PO Box 67, 536 N Main St, Goldfield, IA 50542. Phones: 800-825-9753; 515-825-3996; 515-825-3888. Fax: 515-825-3801. E-mail: gold@goldfieldaccess.net. Web Site: http://www.goldfieldaccess.net. Also serves Renwick (portions). ICA: IA0252.
TV Market Ranking: Outside TV Markets (GOLDFIELD). Franchise award date: March 31, 1980. Franchise expiration date: N.A. Began: December 30, 1982.
Channel capacity: 35 (2-way capable). Channels available but not in use: 6.

Basic Service
Subscribers: N.A.
Programming (received off-air): KCCI (CBS) Des Moines; KIMT (CBS, MNT) Mason City; WHO-DT (NBC) Des Moines; WOI-DT (ABC) Ames; allband FM.
Programming (via satellite): ABC Family Channel; CNN; TBS Superstation; USA Network; WGN America.
Current originations: Government Access; Educational Access; Public Access.
Fee: $10.00 installation; $12.35 monthly; $.50 converter; $10.00 additional installation.

Expanded Basic Service 1
Subscribers: N.A.
Programming (via satellite): AMC; Arts & Entertainment; Bravo; Discovery Channel; Disney Channel; ESPN; ESPN 2; Fox News Channel; Headline News; Lifetime; MTV; Nickelodeon; Spike TV; Turner Network TV; VH1; Weather Channel.
Fee: $10.00 installation; $10.14 monthly.

Pay Service 1
Pay Units: N.A.
Programming (via satellite): HBO.
Fee: $9.85 monthly.

Pay Service 2
Pay Units: N.A.
Programming (via satellite): Cinemax; Flix; Showtime; Sundance Channel; The Movie Channel.
Fee: $7.00 monthly (Cinemax), $12.95 monthly (Flix, Showtime, Sundance & TMC).

Video-On-Demand: No

Internet Service
Operational: No, Both DSL & dialup.

Telephone Service
None

Miles of Plant: 50.0 (coaxial); None (fiber optic). Additional miles planned: 2.0 (coaxial). Homes passed: 450. Total homes in franchised area: 450.
Manager: Darrell L. Seaba. Operations Director: Ron Massingill. Chief Technician: Dean Schipull.
City fee: None.
Ownership: Goldfield Communication Services Corp. (MSO).

GOODELL (village)—Formerly served by New Path Communications LC. No longer in operation. ICA: IA0438.

GOWRIE—Gowrie Cablevision, PO Box 415, Gowrie, IA 50543. Phones: 800-292-8989; 515-352-5227. Fax: 515-352-5226. Web Site: http://www.gowrie.org/utilities/gowrie_catv.htm. ICA: IA0439.
TV Market Ranking: Outside TV Markets (GOWRIE). Franchise award date: N.A. Franchise expiration date: N.A. Began: December 1, 1983.
Channel capacity: 42 (not 2-way capable). Channels available but not in use: N.A.

Basic Service
Subscribers: 340.
Programming (received off-air): KCCI (CBS) Des Moines; KDIN-TV (PBS) Des Moines; KDSM-TV (FOX) Des Moines; WHO-DT (NBC) Des Moines; WOI-DT (ABC) Ames.
Programming (via satellite): CNN; ESPN; Headline News; Nickelodeon; Spike TV; TBS Superstation; WGN America.
Fee: $25.00 installation; $27.50 monthly.

Pay Service 1
Pay Units: N.A.
Programming (via satellite): HBO; Showtime.
Fee: $10.00 monthly (each).

Video-On-Demand: No

Internet Service
Operational: No, Both DSL & dialup.

Telephone Service
None

Miles of Plant: 8.0 (coaxial); None (fiber optic). Homes passed: 425.
Manager: Paul Johnson.
Ownership: Gowrie Cablevision Inc. (MSO).

GRAFTON—Formerly served by Westcom. No longer in operation. ICA: IA0568.

GRAND JUNCTION—Jefferson Telephone & Cablevision, 105 W Harrison St, Jefferson, IA 50129. Phone: 515-386-4141. Fax: 515-386-2600. Web Site: http://www.jeffersontelephone.com. ICA: IA0440.
TV Market Ranking: 66 (GRAND JUNCTION). Franchise award date: N.A. Franchise expiration date: N.A. Began: January 1, 1985.
Channel capacity: N.A. Channels available but not in use: N.A.

Basic Service
Subscribers: N.A. Included in Breda
Programming (received off-air): KCCI (CBS) Des Moines; KCWI-TV (CW) Ames; KDIN-TV (PBS) Des Moines; KDSM-TV (FOX) Des Moines; WHO-DT (NBC) Des Moines; WOI-DT (ABC) Ames.
Programming (via satellite): ABC Family Channel; Arts & Entertainment; CNN; Country Music TV; Discovery Channel; Disney Channel; ESPN; ESPN 2; Headline News; HGTV; Lifetime; Nickelodeon; Spike TV; TBS Superstation; The Learning Channel; Turner Network TV; TV Land; USA Network; WGN America.
Fee: $20.00 installation; $25.45 monthly; $4.00 additional installation.

Pay Service 1
Pay Units: N.A.
Programming (via satellite): Showtime.
Fee: $10.95 monthly.

Video-On-Demand: No

Internet Service
Operational: No.

Telephone Service
None

General Manager: Jim Daubendick.
Ownership: Jefferson Telephone & Cablevision (MSO).

GRAND MOUND—Grand Mound Cooperative Telephone, PO Box 316, 705 Clinton St, Grand Mound, IA 52751-0316. Phones: 888-732-1378; 563-847-3000. Fax: 563-847-3001. E-mail: grmd@gmcta.coop. Web Site: http://www.gmcta.coop. Also serves De Witt. ICA: IA0557. **Note:** This system is an overbuild.

TV Market Ranking: 60 (De Witt, GRAND MOUND). Franchise award date: N.A. Franchise expiration date: N.A. Began: January 17, 1994.

Channel capacity: 66 (operating 2-way). Channels available but not in use: 14.

Basic Service

Subscribers: 270.

Programming (received off-air): KCRG-TV (ABC) Cedar Rapids; KGAN (CBS) Cedar Rapids; KIIN (PBS) Iowa City; KLJB (CW, FOX) Davenport; KWQC-TV (NBC) Davenport; KWWL (NBC) Waterloo; WHBF-TV (CBS) Rock Island; WQAD-TV (ABC) Moline.

Programming (via satellite): ABC Family Channel; AMC; Arts & Entertainment; Cartoon Network; CNN; Country Music TV; C-SPAN; Discovery Channel; ESPN; MTV; Nickelodeon; Spike TV; Syfy; TBS Superstation; Turner Network TV; USA Network; VH1; WGN America.

Fee: $28.95 monthly.

Pay Service 1

Pay Units: 30.

Programming (via satellite): Cinemax; HBO; Showtime.

Fee: $9.95 monthly (each).

Video-On-Demand: No; No

Internet Service

Operational: No.

Telephone Service

None

General Manager: Mark Harvey. Office Manager: Terri Bumann.

Ownership: Grand Mound Cooperative Telephone Assn.

GRAND RIVER—B & L Technologies LLC, 3329 270th St, Lenox, IA 50851. Phones: 800-798-5488; 641-348-2240. Fax: 641-348-2240. ICA: IA0364.

TV Market Ranking: Outside TV Markets (GRAND RIVER). Franchise award date: December 7, 1987. Franchise expiration date: N.A. Began: July 1, 1988.

Channel capacity: 36 (not 2-way capable). Channels available but not in use: 9.

Basic Service

Subscribers: 31.

Programming (received off-air): KCCI (CBS) Des Moines; KDIN-TV (PBS) Des Moines; KDSM-TV (FOX) Des Moines; WHO-DT (NBC) Des Moines; WOI-DT (ABC) Ames.

Programming (via satellite): ABC Family Channel; AMC; Arts & Entertainment; CNN; Discovery Channel; ESPN; History Channel; Nickelodeon; Spike TV; TBS Superstation; Turner Network TV; USA Network; VH1; WGN America.

Fee: $25.00 installation; $30.50 monthly.

Pay Service 1

Pay Units: 5.

Programming (via satellite): HBO.

Fee: $12.00 monthly.

Video-On-Demand: No

Internet Service

Operational: No.

Telephone Service

None

Miles of Plant: 2.0 (coaxial); None (fiber optic). Homes passed: 103.

Manager & Chief Technician: Robert Hintz. Office Manager: Linda Hintz.

Ownership: B & L Technologies LLC (MSO).

GRANVILLE—Premier Communications. Now served by SIOUX CENTER, IA [IA0076]. ICA: IA0597.

GRAVITY—Formerly served by CableDirect. No longer in operation. ICA: IA0558.

GREELEY—Formerly served by Alpine Communications LC. No longer in operation. ICA: IA0441.

GREENE—Mediacom. Now served by DES MOINES, IA [IA0001]. ICA: IA0162.

GRISWOLD—Griswold Cable TV, PO Box 640, 607 Main St, Griswold, IA 51535-0640. Phone: 712-778-2121. Fax: 712-778-2500. E-mail: gctc@netins.net. Web Site: http://www.griswoldtelco.com. Also serves Elliot, Grant, Lewis & Lyman. ICA: IA0442.

TV Market Ranking: Outside TV Markets (Elliott, Grant, GRISWOLD, Lewis, LYMAN). Franchise award date: N.A. Franchise expiration date: N.A. Began: January 1, 1985.

Channel capacity: 35 (not 2-way capable). Channels available but not in use: None.

Digital Basic Service

Subscribers: N.A.

Programming (received off-air): KCCI (CBS) Des Moines; KDSM-TV (FOX) Des Moines; KETV (ABC) Omaha; KHIN (PBS) Red Oak; KMTV-TV (CBS) Omaha; KPTM (FOX, MNT) Omaha; KXVO (CW) Omaha; WHO-DT (NBC) Des Moines; WOI-DT (ABC) Ames; WOWT-TV (IND, NBC) Omaha.

Programming (via satellite): ABC Family Channel; AMC; Animal Planet; Arts & Entertainment; BBC America; Big Ten Network; Boomerang; Cartoon Network; CNN; CNN International; Country Music TV; C-SPAN; C-SPAN 2; Discovery Channel; Discovery Health Channel; Discovery Kids Channel; Discovery Military Channel; Discovery Planet Green; Disney Channel; Disney XD; ESPN; ESPN 2; ESPN Classic Sports; ESPNews; Food Network; Fox News Channel; Fox Sports Net Midwest; FX; Hallmark Channel; Headline News; HGTV; History Channel; Home Shopping Network; ID Investigation Discovery; Lifetime; Lifetime Movie Network; Lifetime Real Women; MTV; MTV Jams; MTV2; National Geographic Channel; Nick Jr.; Nickelodeon; NickToons TV; Outdoor Channel; Oxygen; QVC; RFD-TV; Science Channel; Speed Channel; Spike TV; Syfy; TBS Superstation; The Learning Channel; Travel Channel; Turner Classic Movies; Turner Network TV; TV Land; USA Network; Versus; VH1; VH1 Classic; Weather Channel; WGN America.

Fee: $30.00 installation; $34.99 monthly.

Digital Pay Service 1

Pay Units: N.A.

Programming (via satellite): Cinemax; Encore; HBO; Playboy TV; Starz.

Fee: $20.00 installation; $11.00 monthly (HBO, Cinemax, Starz/Encore or Playboy).

Video-On-Demand: No

Internet Service

Operational: Yes, dial-up.

Fee: $44.95-$99.95 monthly.

Telephone Service

None

Miles of Plant: 30.0 (coaxial); None (fiber optic).

Executive Vice President & General Manager: Robert A. Drogo. Chief Technician: Mark Gronewold. Marketing Director: Amy Carlisle.

Ownership: Griswold Co-op Telephone Co. (MSO).

GRUNDY CENTER—Grundy Center Municipal Utilities, PO Box 307, 706 6th St, Grundy Center, IA 50638-0307. Phone: 319-825-5207. E-mail: grunmuni@gcmuni.net. Web Site: http://www.gcmuni.net. ICA: IA0600. **Note:** This system is an overbuild.

TV Market Ranking: 65 (GRUNDY CENTER).

Channel capacity: 52 (operating 2-way). Channels available but not in use: N.A.

Basic Service

Subscribers: 1,221.

Programming (received off-air): KCCI (CBS) Des Moines; KCRG-TV (ABC) Cedar Rapids; KFXA (FOX) Cedar Rapids; KGAN (CBS) Cedar Rapids; KPXR-TV (ION) Cedar Rapids; KRIN (PBS) Waterloo; KWWL (NBC) Waterloo; WHO-DT (NBC) Des Moines; WOI-DT (ABC) Ames.

Programming (via satellite): ABC Family Channel; AMC; Animal Planet; Arts & Entertainment; Cartoon Network; CNN; Comedy Central; Country Music TV; Discovery Channel; Disney Channel; E! Entertainment Television; ESPN; ESPN 2; Fox News Channel; Fox Sports Net Midwest; G4; Golf Channel; HGTV; History Channel; Lifetime; MSNBC; MTV; Nickelodeon; QVC; Syfy; TBS Superstation; The Learning Channel; Travel Channel; truTV; Turner Classic Movies; Turner Network TV; TV Land; USA Network; VH1; Weather Channel; WGN America.

Current originations: Educational Access.

Fee: $26.95 monthly.

Pay Service 1

Pay Units: N.A.

Programming (via satellite): Encore; HBO; Showtime; Starz; The Movie Channel.

Fee: $10.00 monthly (each).

Internet Service

Operational: Yes, dial-up.

Broadband Service: In-house.

Fee: $39.95 monthly; $15.00 modem lease.

Telephone Service

None

Miles of Plant: 16.0 (coaxial); None (fiber optic).

General Manager: Jeff Carson. Chief Technician: Darrel Shuey.

Ownership: Grundy Center Municipal Light & Power.

HAMBURG—Our Cable, PO Box 190, 112 E Main St, Breda, IA 51436-0190. Phone: 877-873-8715. E-mail: info@ourcableia.com. Web Site: http://ourcableia.com. ICA: IA0443.

TV Market Ranking: Outside TV Markets (HAMBURG). Franchise award date: N.A. Franchise expiration date: N.A. Began: July 1, 1981.

Channel capacity: N.A. Channels available but not in use: N.A.

Basic Service

Subscribers: N.A. Included in Breda

Programming (received off-air): KETV (ABC) Omaha; KHIN (PBS) Red Oak; KMTV-TV (CBS) Omaha; KPTM (FOX, MNT) Omaha; KUON-TV (PBS) Lincoln; KXVO (CW) Omaha; WOWT-TV (IND, NBC) Omaha.

Programming (via satellite): ABC Family Channel; AMC; Arts & Entertainment; CNN; Comedy Central; Discovery Channel; Disney Channel; ESPN; ESPN 2; Headline News; History Channel; Lifetime; Nickelodeon; Spike TV; Syfy; TBS Superstation; Turner Network TV; TV Land; USA Network; Weather Channel; WGN America.

Fee: $20.00 installation; $25.45 monthly.

Pay Service 1

Pay Units: N.A.

Programming (via satellite): HBO; The Movie Channel.

Fee: $10.95 monthly (HBO or TMC).

Video-On-Demand: No

Internet Service

Operational: No.

Telephone Service

None

Chief Executive Officer: Steve Frickenstein. Marketing & Sales Manager: Megan Badding. Chief Technician: Mike Ludwig.

City fee: 3% of gross.

Ownership: Our Cable (MSO).

HAMPTON—Mediacom, 4010 Alexandra Dr, Waterloo, IA 50702. Phone: 319-235-2197. Fax: 319-232-7841. Web Site: http://www.mediacomcable.com. Also serves Rockwell & Sheffield. ICA: IA0070.

TV Market Ranking: Below 100 (HAMPTON, Rockwell, Sheffield). Franchise award date: N.A. Franchise expiration date: N.A. Began: December 1, 1981.

Channel capacity: N.A. Channels available but not in use: N.A.

Basic Service

Subscribers: 1,940.

Programming (received off-air): KAAL (ABC) Austin; KCCI (CBS) Des Moines; KCRG-TV (ABC) Cedar Rapids; KCWI-TV (CW) Ames; KFPX-TV (ION) Newton; KFXA (FOX) Cedar Rapids; KIMT (CBS, MNT) Mason City; KTTC (CW, NBC) Rochester; KWWL (NBC) Waterloo; KYIN (PBS) Mason City; WHO-DT (NBC) Des Moines; WOI-DT (ABC) Ames.

Programming (via satellite): CNBC; CNN; Country Music TV; C-SPAN; Discovery Channel; Headline News; Lifetime; MTV; Nickelodeon; TBS Superstation; Turner Network TV; Weather Channel; WGN America.

Current originations: Educational Access.

Fee: $60.00 installation; $20.28 monthly; $.69 converter; $50.00 additional installation.

Expanded Basic Service 1

Subscribers: 1,768.

Programming (via satellite): ABC Family Channel; AMC; Animal Planet; Arts & Entertainment; Bravo; Cartoon Network; Comedy Central; Disney Channel; E! Entertainment Television; ESPN; ESPN 2; Eternal Word TV

Network; Fox News Channel; Fox Sports Net Midwest; FX; HGTV; History Channel; Home Shopping Network; INSP; Speed Channel; Spike TV; Syfy; Telemundo; The Learning Channel; Trinity Broadcasting Network; TV Guide Network; TV Land; USA Network; VH1; WE tv.
Fee: $11.45 monthly.

Digital Basic Service
Subscribers: N.A.
Programming (via satellite): American-Life TV Network; BBC America; Bio; Bloomberg Television; Discovery Digital Networks; DMX Music; Fox Movie Channel; Fox Sports World; Fuse; G4; GAS; Golf Channel; GSN; Halogen Network; History Channel International; Independent Film Channel; Lifetime Movie Network; Lime; MTV Networks Digital Suite; National Geographic Channel; Nick Jr.; Outdoor Channel; Ovation; Style Network; Toon Disney; Turner Classic Movies; Versus.

Digital Pay Service 1
Pay Units: 297.
Programming (via satellite): Cinemax (multiplexed); Encore (multiplexed); HBO (multiplexed); Showtime (multiplexed); Starz (multiplexed); Sundance Channel; The Movie Channel (multiplexed).
Fee: $9.95 monthly (Cinemax, HBO, Showtime, Starz/Encore, or Sundance/TMC).

Video-On-Demand: Yes

Pay-Per-View
ESPN Now (delivered digitally); ETC (delivered digitally); Hot Choice (delivered digitally); Playboy TV (delivered digitally); Pleasure (delivered digitally); Fresh (delivered digitally); TVN Entertainment (delivered digitally); sports (delivered digitally).

Internet Service
Operational: Yes.
Broadband Service: Mediacom High Speed Internet.
Fee: $49.95 installation; $55.95 monthly.

Telephone Service
Digital: Operational
Miles of Plant: 48.0 (coaxial); None (fiber optic). Homes passed: 2,458. Total homes in franchised area: 2,458.
Regional Vice President: Doug Frank. General Manager: Doug Nix. Technical Operations Director: Greg Nank. Marketing Director: Steve Schuh. Marketing Coordinator: Joni Lindauer.
Ownership: Mediacom LLC (MSO).

HARLAN—Harlan Municipal Utilities, PO Box 71, 405 Chatburn Ave, Harlan, IA 51537. Phone: 712-755-5182. Fax: 712-755-2320. E-mail: hmu@harlannet.com. Web Site: http://www.har-tel.com. ICA: IA0586. **Note:** This system is an overbuild.
TV Market Ranking: Outside TV Markets (HARLAN).
Channel capacity: N.A. Channels available but not in use: N.A.

Basic Service
Subscribers: 1,500.
Programming (received off-air): KCCI (CBS) Des Moines; KETV (ABC) Omaha; KHIN (PBS) Red Oak; KMTV-TV (CBS) Omaha; KPTM (FOX, MNT) Omaha; KXVO (CW) Omaha; WHO-DT (NBC) Des Moines; WOI-DT (ABC) Ames; WOWT-TV (IND, NBC) Omaha.
Programming (via satellite): C-SPAN.
Fee: $10.99 monthly; $15.00 converter.

Expanded Basic Service 1
Subscribers: N.A.
Programming (via satellite): ABC Family Channel; AMC; Animal Planet; Arts & Entertainment; Big Ten Network; Bravo!; Cartoon Network; CNBC; CNN; Comedy Central; Country Music TV; C-SPAN 2; Discovery Channel; Disney Channel; E! Entertainment Television; ESPN; ESPN 2; ESPN Classic Sports; ESPNews; Food Network; Fox News Channel; Fox Sports Net Midwest; FX; G4; GSN; Hallmark Movie Channel; Headline News; HGTV; History Channel; Lifetime; Lifetime Movie Network; MSNBC; MTV; MyNetworkTV Inc.; National Geographic Channel; Nickelodeon; Outdoor Channel; QVC; RFD-TV; Speed Channel; Spike TV; Syfy; TBS Superstation; The Learning Channel; Toon Disney; Travel Channel; Turner Classic Movies; Turner Network TV; TV Land; USA Network; VH1; Weather Channel; WGN America.
Fee: $39.95 monthly.

Digital Basic Service
Subscribers: N.A.
Programming (received off-air): KAZO-LP Omaha; KETV (ABC) Omaha; KHIN (PBS) Red Oak; KMTV-TV (CBS) Omaha; KPTM (FOX, MNT) Omaha; KXVO (CW) Omaha; WOWT-TV (IND, NBC) Omaha.
Programming (via satellite): Animal Planet HD; Arts & Entertainment HD; BBC America; Big Ten Network HD; Bio; Bloomberg Television; Chiller; CMT Pure Country; CNN HD; Discovery Channel HD; Discovery Health Channel; Discovery Kids Channel; Discovery Planet Green; ESPN 2 HD; ESPN U; FitTV; Fox Business Channel; Fox College Sports Atlantic; Fox College Sports Central; Fox College Sports Pacific; Fox News HD; Fox Sports Net Midwest; FX HD; Golf Channel; History Channel HD; History Channel International; ID Investigation Discovery; Lifetime Movie Network HD; Lifetime Real Women; Military Channel; MTV Hits; MTV2; National Geographic Channel HD Network; Nick Jr.; NickToons TV; Oxygen; Science Channel; ShopNBC; Sleuth; SoapNet; Speed HD; Syfy HD; TBS in HD; TeenNick; TLC HD; Turner Network TV HD; USA Network HD; Versus; VH1 Classic; VH1 Soul.
Fee: $9.95 monthly.

Digital Pay Service 1
Pay Units: N.A.
Programming (via satellite): Cinemax (multiplexed); Cinemax HD; Encore (multiplexed); HBO (multiplexed); HBO HD; Showtime (multiplexed); Showtime HD; Starz (multiplexed); Starz HDTV.
Fee: $10.00 monthly (Cinemax, Showtime or Starz/Encore), $14.00 monthly (HBO).

Video-On-Demand: No

Pay-Per-View
iN DEMAND (delivered digitally); Club Jenna (delivered digitally); Fresh (delivered digitally); Playboy TV (delivered digitally); Spice: Xcess (delivered digitally).

Internet Service
Operational: Yes.
Subscribers: 862.
Broadband Service: In-house.
Fee: $42.95-$52.95 monthly.

Telephone Service
Digital: Operational
Miles of Plant: 44.0 (coaxial); 9.0 (fiber optic).
Operations Manager: Tim Hodapp. Chief Technician: Dan Murray. Customer Service Director: John Doonan.
Ownership: Harlan Municipal Utilities.

HARTFORD—Telnet South LC. Now served by DES MOINES, IA [IA0001]. ICA: IA0445.

HAVELOCK—Northwest Communications Inc., PO Box 186, 844 Wood St, Havelock, IA 50546. Phones: 800-249-5251; 712-776-2612. Fax: 712-776-4444. E-mail: nis@ncn.net. Web Site: http://www.ncn.net. Also serves Curlew, Mallard, Plover, Rolfe & West Bend. ICA: IA0365.
TV Market Ranking: Outside TV Markets (Curlew, HAVELOCK, Mallard, Plover, Rolfe, West Bend). Franchise award date: N.A. Franchise expiration date: N.A. Began: January 1, 1987.
Channel capacity: N.A. Channels available but not in use: N.A.

Basic Service
Subscribers: 824.
Programming (received off-air): KCAU-TV (ABC) Sioux City; KCCI (CBS) Des Moines; KCWI-TV (CW) Ames; KDSM-TV (FOX) Des Moines; KEYC-TV (CBS, FOX) Mankato; KMEG (CBS) Sioux City; KPTH (FOX, MNT) Sioux City; KTIN (PBS) Fort Dodge; KTIV (CW, NBC) Sioux City; WHO-DT (NBC) Des Moines; WOI-DT (ABC) Ames; 10 FMs.
Programming (via satellite): ABC Family Channel; AMC; AmericanLife TV Network; Animal Planet; Arts & Entertainment; Bravo; Cartoon Network; CNN; Comedy Central; Country Music TV; C-SPAN; C-SPAN 2; Discovery Channel; Discovery Health Channel; Disney Channel; Do-It-Yourself; E! Entertainment Television; ESPN; ESPN 2; ESPN Classic Sports; ESPN U; Eternal Word TV Network; Food Network; Fox Movie Channel; Fox News Channel; FX; Golf Channel; Hallmark Channel; Headline News; HGTV; History Channel; Home Shopping Network; INSP; ION Television; Lifetime; MSNBC; MTV; Nickelodeon; Outdoor Channel; QVC; Radar Channel; Speed Channel; Spike TV; Syfy; TBS Superstation; The Learning Channel; Travel Channel; Trinity Broadcasting Network; truTV; Turner Classic Movies; Turner Network TV; TV Guide Network; TV Land; USA Network; VH1; Weather Channel; WGN America.
Current originations: Public Access.
Fee: $30.00 installation; $29.45 monthly.

Digital Basic Service
Subscribers: N.A.
Programming (received off-air): KCCI (CBS) Des Moines; KDSM-TV (FOX) Des Moines; KTIN (PBS) Fort Dodge; WHO-DT (NBC) Des Moines; WOI-DT (ABC) Ames.
Programming (via satellite): BBC America; Bio; CMT Pure Country; Discovery HD Theater; Discovery Home Channel; Discovery Kids Channel; Discovery Military Channel; Discovery Times Channel; ESPN 2 HD; ESPN HD; ESPNews; FitTV; Fox Soccer; G4; GSN; HDNet; HDNet Movies; History Channel; Independent Film Channel; Lifetime Movie Network; MTV2; National Geographic Channel; Nick Jr.; NickToons TV; Science Channel; TeenNick; Universal HD; VH1 Classic.

Digital Pay Service 1
Pay Units: N.A.
Programming (via satellite): Cinemax (multiplexed); Cinemax HD; Encore (multiplexed); Flix; HBO (multiplexed); HBO HD; Showtime (multiplexed); Showtime HD; Starz (multiplexed); Starz HDTV; Sundance Channel; The Movie Channel (multiplexed); The Movie Channel HD.

Video-On-Demand: No

Internet Service
Operational: No, DSL only.

Telephone Service
None
Miles of Plant: 17.0 (coaxial); None (fiber optic). Homes passed: 966.
Chief Executive Officer & General Manager: Donald D. Miller. Customer Service Supervisor: Sharon O'Donnell.
Ownership: Northwest Communications Inc.

HAWARDEN—HiTec Cable, 1150 Central Ave, Hawarden, IA 51023-0231. Phone: 712-551-2565. Fax: 712-551-1117. E-mail: jasonm@cityofhawarden.com. Web Site: http://www.cityofhawarden.com. ICA: IA0566.
TV Market Ranking: Below 100 (HAWARDEN). Franchise award date: N.A. Franchise expiration date: N.A. Began: November 1, 1997.
Channel capacity: N.A. Channels available but not in use: N.A.

Basic Service
Subscribers: 838.
Programming (received off-air): KCAU-TV (ABC) Sioux City; KDLT-TV (NBC) Sioux Falls; KELO-TV (CBS, MNT) Sioux Falls; KMEG (CBS) Sioux City; KPTH (FOX, MNT) Sioux City; KSFY-TV (ABC) Sioux Falls; KSIN-TV (PBS) Sioux City; KTIV (CW, NBC) Sioux City; KTTW (FOX) Sioux Falls; KUSD-TV (PBS) Vermillion.
Programming (via satellite): C-SPAN; National Geographic Channel.
Current originations: Educational Access.
Fee: $27.50 monthly.

Expanded Basic Service 1
Subscribers: N.A.
Programming (via satellite): ABC Family Channel; AMC; Animal Planet; Arts & Entertainment; Cartoon Network; CNN; Comedy Central; Country Music TV; CW+; Discovery Channel; Disney Channel; ESPN; ESPN 2; ESPN Classic Sports; ESPN U; Food Network; Fox News Channel; FX; Hallmark Channel; Headline News; HGTV; History Channel; Home Shopping Network; Lifetime; MTV; NASA TV; Nickelodeon; Outdoor Channel; QVC; Spike TV; Syfy; TBS Superstation; The Learning Channel; Turner Classic Movies; Turner Network TV; TV Land; USA Network; VH1; Weather Channel; WGN America.
Fee: $27.50 monthly.

Digital Basic Service
Subscribers: 47.
Programming (via satellite): AmericanLife TV Network; BBC America; Bio; Bloomberg Television; Bravo; Canales N; Discovery Digital Networks; DMX Music; ESPN Classic Sports; ESPNews; FitTV; Fox College Sports Atlantic; Fox College Sports Central; Fox College Sports Pacific; Fox Movie Channel; Fox Sports World; Golf Channel; Great American Country; GSN; Halogen Network; History Channel International; Independent Film Channel; International Television (ITV); MTV Networks Digital Suite; MuchMusic Network; Nick Jr.; NickToons TV; Ovation; Speed Channel; Style Network; Sundance Channel; TeenNick; Toon Disney; Trio; Urban American Television Network; Versus; WE tv.
Fee: $16.00 monthly.

Pay Service 1
Pay Units: N.A.
Programming (via satellite): Cinemax; Flix; HBO; Showtime; Sundance Channel; The Movie Channel.
Fee: $7.50 monthly (Cinemax) $9.95 monthly (HBO), $10.95 monthly (Flix, Showtime, Sundance or TMC).

Digital Pay Service 1
Pay Units: N.A.
Programming (via satellite): Cinemax (multiplexed); Encore (multiplexed); Flix; HBO (multiplexed); Showtime (multiplexed);

Starz (multiplexed); The Movie Channel (multiplexed).
Fee: $10.00 monthly (Cinemax), $12.50 monthly (HBO, Starz/Encore or Showtime/TMC).
Video-On-Demand: No
Pay-Per-View
Addressable homes: 47.
iN DEMAND (delivered digitally); Hot Choice (delivered digitally); Playboy TV (delivered digitally); Spice (delivered digitally); Spice 2 (delivered digitally); ESPN Now (delivered digitally); ESPN Extra (delivered digitally).
Internet Service
Operational: Yes.
Subscribers: 510.
Fee: $100.00 installation; $14.95 monthly.
Telephone Service
Digital: Operational
Subscribers: 838.
Fee: $36.10 monthly
Miles of Plant: 35.0 (coaxial); 4.0 (fiber optic). Homes passed: 1,214. Total homes in franchised area: 1,214.
City Administrator: Jason Metten. Telecommunications Assistant: Kristi Hansman.
Ownership: City of Hawarden.

HAWARDEN—Mediacom. Now served by ORANGE CITY, IA [IA0488]. ICA: IA0092.

HAWKEYE—Hawkeye TV Co., PO Box 250, Hawkeye, IA 52147-0250. Phone: 563-427-3222. Fax: 563-427-7553. ICA: IA0298.
TV Market Ranking: Outside TV Markets (HAWKEYE). Franchise award date: N.A. Franchise expiration date: N.A. Began: January 1, 1985.
Channel capacity: 35 (not 2-way capable). Channels available but not in use: 15.
Basic Service
Subscribers: 125.
Programming (received off-air): KCRG-TV (ABC) Cedar Rapids; KGAN (CBS) Cedar Rapids; KIIN (PBS) Iowa City; KWWL (NBC) Waterloo.
Programming (via satellite): ABC Family Channel; AMC; Arts & Entertainment; CNN; Discovery Channel; Disney Channel; ESPN; ESPN 2; HGTV; History Channel; Nickelodeon; Outdoor Channel; Spike TV; TBS Superstation; Turner Network TV; USA Network; WGN America.
Fee: $10.00 installation; $22.00 monthly; $2.00 converter.
Pay Service 1
Pay Units: 11.
Programming (via satellite): Cinemax.
Fee: $9.50 monthly.
Pay Service 2
Pay Units: 9.
Programming (via satellite): HBO.
Fee: $10.00 monthly.
Video-On-Demand: No
Internet Service
Operational: No.
Telephone Service
None
Miles of Plant: 4.0 (coaxial); None (fiber optic). Homes passed: 215.
Manager: Aaron Loucks.
Ownership: Hawkeye TV Co.

HEDRICK—Starwest Inc., 15235 235th St, Milton, IA 52570-8016. Phones: 319-293-6336; 319-397-2283; 319-446-7331. ICA: IA0270.
TV Market Ranking: Below 100 (HEDRICK). Franchise award date: N.A. Franchise expiration date: N.A. Began: January 1, 1984.
Channel capacity: 35 (not 2-way capable). Channels available but not in use: N.A.
Basic Service
Subscribers: N.A.
Programming (received off-air): KCCI (CBS) Des Moines; KDIN-TV (PBS) Des Moines; WHO-DT (NBC) Des Moines; WOI-DT (ABC) Ames.
Programming (via satellite): TBS Superstation; WGN America.
Internet Service
Operational: No.
Miles of Plant: 4.0 (coaxial); None (fiber optic). Homes passed: 260.
Manager & Chief Technician: John Stooksberry.
Ownership: Starwest Inc. (MSO).

HINTON—Premier Communications. Now served by SIOUX CENTER, IA [IA0076]. ICA: IA0309.

HOLLAND—Formerly served by CableDirect. No longer in operation. ICA: IA0446.

HOPKINTON—New Century Communications, 3588 Kennebec Dr, Eagan, MN 55122-1001. Phone: 651-688-2623. Fax: 651-688-2624. E-mail: tanderson@cablesystemservices.com. ICA: IA0447.
TV Market Ranking: 65 (HOPKINTON). Franchise award date: N.A. Franchise expiration date: N.A. Began: March 1, 1988.
Channel capacity: 35 (not 2-way capable). Channels available but not in use: 3.
Basic Service
Subscribers: 81.
Programming (received off-air): KCRG-TV (ABC) Cedar Rapids; KFXA (FOX) Cedar Rapids; KGAN (CBS) Cedar Rapids; KIIN (PBS) Iowa City; KPXR-TV (ION) Cedar Rapids; KWKB (CW, MNT) Iowa City; KWWL (NBC) Waterloo.
Programming (via satellite): ABC Family Channel; AMC; Arts & Entertainment; CNN; Discovery Channel; Disney Channel; Do-It-Yourself; ESPN; ESPN 2; Headline News; History Channel; Lifetime; MTV; Nickelodeon; QVC; Spike TV; TBS Superstation; The Learning Channel; Turner Classic Movies; Turner Network TV; USA Network; VH1; Weather Channel; WGN America.
Current originations: Public Access.
Fee: $30.00 installation; $23.45 monthly.
Pay Service 1
Pay Units: 30.
Programming (via satellite): Cinemax.
Fee: $10.00 monthly.
Pay Service 2
Pay Units: 28.
Programming (via satellite): HBO.
Fee: $10.00 monthly.
Pay Service 3
Pay Units: 10.
Programming (via satellite): Showtime.
Fee: $10.00 monthly.
Video-On-Demand: No
Internet Service
Operational: No.
Telephone Service
None
Miles of Plant: 7.0 (coaxial); None (fiber optic). Homes passed: 322.
Executive Vice President: Marty Walch. General Manager & Chief Technician: Todd Anderson.
Ownership: New Century Communications (MSO).

HORNICK—Telepartners. Now served by LAWTON, IA [IA0330]. ICA: IA0363.

HOSPERS—HTC Cablecom. Now served by SHELDON, IA [IA0060]. ICA: IA0275.

HUBBARD—Hubbard Co-op Cable, PO Box 428, 306 E Maple St, Hubbard, IA 50122. Phone: 641-864-2216. Fax: 641-864-2666. E-mail: hubbard@netins.net. Web Site: http://www.hubbardtelephone.com. ICA: IA0448.
TV Market Ranking: 66 (HUBBARD (VILLAGE)). Franchise award date: N.A. Franchise expiration date: N.A. Began: January 1, 1985.
Channel capacity: 36 (not 2-way capable). Channels available but not in use: N.A.
Basic Service
Subscribers: 253.
Programming (received off-air): KCCI (CBS) Des Moines; KDIN-TV (PBS) Des Moines; KDSM-TV (FOX) Des Moines; WHO-DT (NBC) Des Moines; WOI-DT (ABC) Ames.
Programming (via satellite): ABC Family Channel; AMC; Arts & Entertainment; CNN; Country Music TV; Discovery Channel; Disney Channel; ESPN; ESPN 2; History Channel; ION Television; Nickelodeon; Spike TV; TBS Superstation; The Learning Channel; Travel Channel; Turner Network TV; USA Network; Weather Channel; WGN America.
Fee: $10.00 installation; $22.95 monthly.
Pay Service 1
Pay Units: 39.
Programming (via satellite): HBO.
Fee: $8.95 monthly.
Video-On-Demand: No
Internet Service
Operational: No, DSL & dial-up.
Telephone Service
None
Miles of Plant: 6.0 (coaxial); None (fiber optic).
Manager: Larry Kielsmeier. Chief Technician: Ken Kissinger.
City fee: 3% of gross.
Ownership: Hubbard Co-op Cable.

HUDSON—Mediacom. Now served by INDEPENDENCE, IA [IA0059]. ICA: IA0130.

HUMESTON—B & L Technologies LLC, 3329 270th St, Lenox, IA 50851. Phones: 800-798-5488; 641-348-2240. Fax: 641-348-2240. ICA: IA0268.
TV Market Ranking: Outside TV Markets (HUMESTON). Franchise award date: September 7, 1982. Franchise expiration date: N.A. Began: N.A.
Channel capacity: 23 (not 2-way capable). Channels available but not in use: None.
Basic Service
Subscribers: 69.
Programming (received off-air): KCCI (CBS) Des Moines; KDIN-TV (PBS) Des Moines; KDSM-TV (FOX) Des Moines; KTVO (ABC) Kirksville; WHO-DT (NBC) Des Moines; WOI-DT (ABC) Ames.
Programming (via satellite): ABC Family Channel; CNN; Discovery Channel; ESPN; TBS Superstation; Turner Network TV; USA Network; WGN America.
Fee: $41.11 installation; $19.01 monthly.
Pay Service 1
Pay Units: 44.
Programming (via satellite): HBO.
Fee: $23.49 installation; $11.00 monthly.
Video-On-Demand: No
Internet Service
Operational: No.
Telephone Service
None
Miles of Plant: 6.0 (coaxial); None (fiber optic). Homes passed: 277. Total homes in franchised area: 277.
President & General Manager: Robert Hintz. Office Manager: Linda Hintz.
City fee: None.
Ownership: B & L Technologies LLC (MSO).

HUXLEY—Huxley Communications Corp., PO Box 70, 102 N Main Ave, Huxley, IA 50124-0070. Phones: 800-231-4922; 515-597-2281. Fax: 515-597-2899. E-mail: huxtel@huxcomm.net. Web Site: http://www.huxcomm.net. ICA: IA0595.
Note: This system is an overbuild.
TV Market Ranking: 66 (HUXLEY). Franchise award date: N.A. Franchise expiration date: N.A. Began: N.A.
Channel capacity: 102 (operating 2-way). Channels available but not in use: None.
Basic Service
Subscribers: 599.
Programming (received off-air): KCCI (CBS) Des Moines; KDSM-TV (FOX) Des Moines; WHO-DT (NBC) Des Moines; WOI-DT (ABC) Ames.
Programming (via satellite): ABC Family Channel; AMC; Animal Planet; Arts & Entertainment; Cartoon Network; CNBC; CNN; Comedy Central; Cooking Channel; Country Music TV; Discovery Channel; Disney Channel; Do-It-Yourself; E! Entertainment Television; ESPN; ESPN 2; ESPN Classic Sports; ESPNews; Food Network; Fox Movie Channel; Fox News Channel; Fox Sports Net Midwest; FX; G4; Golf Channel; Hallmark Channel; Headline News; HGTV; History Channel; Home Shopping Network; ION Television; Lifetime; MSNBC; MTV; Nickelodeon; Outdoor Channel; RFD-TV; Shop at Home; Speed Channel; Spike TV; The Learning Channel; Toon Disney; Travel Channel; Trinity Broadcasting Network; truTV; Turner Classic Movies; Turner Network TV; TV Land; USA Network; VH1; Weather Channel; WGN America; WPCH-TV (IND) Atlanta.
Current originations: Educational Access.
Fee: $30.00 installation; $40.00 monthly.
Digital Basic Service
Subscribers: 75.
Programming (via satellite): American-Life TV Network; BBC America; Bio; Black Family Channel; Bloomberg Television; Bravo; Discovery Digital Networks; DMX Music; ESPN 2; ESPN Classic Sports; ESPNews; Fox College Sports Atlantic; Fox College Sports Central; Fox College Sports Pacific; Fox Movie Channel; Fox Soccer; Fuse; G4; GAS; Golf Channel; Great American Country; GSN; HGTV; History Channel; History Channel International; Independent Film Channel; INSP; International Televi-

sion (ITV); Lifetime Movie Network; Lime; MTV Networks Digital Suite; National Geographic Channel; Nick Jr.; NickToons TV; Outdoor Channel; Ovation; ShopNBC; Speed Channel; Style Network; Sundance Channel; The Word Network; Toon Disney; Trinity Broadcasting Network; Turner Classic Movies; Versus; WE tv.
Fee: $10.00 monthly.

Pay Service 1
Pay Units: 92.
Programming (via satellite): HBO (multiplexed).
Fee: $15.00 monthly.

Pay Service 2
Pay Units: 14.
Programming (via satellite): Showtime (multiplexed).
Fee: $10.00 monthly.

Pay Service 3
Pay Units: 57.
Programming (via satellite): Cinemax (multiplexed).
Fee: $10.00 monthly.

Pay Service 4
Pay Units: 75.
Programming (via satellite): Encore (multiplexed); Starz (multiplexed).
Fee: $10.00 monthly.

Digital Pay Service 1
Pay Units: 20.
Programming (via satellite): Cinemax (multiplexed); Encore (multiplexed); HBO (multiplexed); Showtime (multiplexed); Starz (multiplexed); The Movie Channel.
Fee: $10.00 monthly (Cinemax, Showtime or Starz/Encore), $15.00 monthly (HBO).

Video-On-Demand: Planned

Pay-Per-View
Playboy TV (delivered digitally); Fresh (delivered digitally); Shorteez (delivered digitally); ESPN Now (delivered digitally); Sports PPV (delivered digitally); iN DEMAND (delivered digitally).

Internet Service
Operational: No, DSL.

Telephone Service
None

Homes passed: 977.
Manager: Billy L. Hotchkiss. Operations Director: Terry Ferguson. Plant Manager: Brant Strumpfer.
Ownership: Huxley Communications Corp. (MSO).

INDEPENDENCE—Independence Light & Power Telecommunications, PO Box 754, 700 7th Ave NE, Independence, IA 50644-0754. Phones: 319-332-3880; 319-332-0100. Fax: 319-332-0101. E-mail: darrel@indytel.com. Web Site: http://www.indytel.com. ICA: IA0591. **Note:** This system is an overbuild.
TV Market Ranking: 65 (INDEPENDENCE). Franchise award date: N.A. Franchise expiration date: N.A. Began: May 1, 2000.
Channel capacity: N.A. Channels available but not in use: N.A.

Basic Service
Subscribers: 1,683.
Programming (received off-air): KCRG-TV (ABC) Cedar Rapids; KFXA (FOX) Cedar Rapids; KGAN (CBS) Cedar Rapids; KPXR-TV (ION) Cedar Rapids; KRIN (PBS) Waterloo; KWKB (CW, MNT) Iowa City; KWWF (IND) Waterloo [LICENSED & SILENT]; KWWL (NBC) Waterloo.
Programming (via satellite): C-SPAN; C-SPAN 2; Eternal Word TV Network; NickToons TV; QVC; Trinity Broadcasting Network; TV Guide Network; Weather Channel; WGN America.
Current originations: Government Access; Educational Access.
Fee: $20.00 installation; $12.95 monthly.

Expanded Basic Service 1
Subscribers: N.A.
Programming (via satellite): ABC Family Channel; AMC; Animal Planet; Arts & Entertainment; Big Ten Network; Cartoon Network; CNBC; CNN; Comcast SportsNet Chicago; Comedy Central; Country Music TV; Discovery Channel; Disney Channel; Do-It-Yourself; E! Entertainment Television; ESPN 2; ESPN Classic Sports; Food Network; Fox News Channel; FX; G4; Golf Channel; GSN; Hallmark Channel; Headline News; HGTV; History Channel; Lifetime; MoviePlex; MTV; National Geographic Channel; NFL Network; Outdoor Channel; RFD-TV; Speed Channel; Spike TV; Syfy; TBS Superstation; The Learning Channel; Travel Channel; truTV; Turner Classic Movies; Turner Network TV; TV Land; USA Network; VH1; WE tv.
Fee: $23.00 monthly.

Digital Basic Service
Subscribers: N.A.
Programming (received off-air): KCRG-TV (ABC) Cedar Rapids; KFXA (FOX) Cedar Rapids; KGAN (CBS) Cedar Rapids; KPXR-TV (ION) Cedar Rapids; KRIN (PBS) Waterloo; KWKB (CW, MNT) Iowa City; KWWL (NBC) Waterloo.
Programming (via satellite): AmericanLife TV Network; BBC America; Big Ten Network HD; Bio; Bloomberg Television; Discovery HD Theater; Discovery Health Channel; Discovery Kids Channel; Discovery Military Channel; Discovery Planet Green; DMX Music; ESPN 2 HD; ESPN HD; ESPN U; ESPNews; FitTV; Fox Movie Channel; Fox Soccer; Halogen Network; HDNet; HDNet Movies; History Channel; ID Investigation Discovery; INHD; International Television (ITV); Lifetime Movie Network; MTV Hits; MTV2; Nick Jr.; Science Channel; SoapNet; Style Network; TeenNick; Toon Disney; Versus; VH1 Classic; VH1 Country; VH1 Soul.
Fee: $16.00 monthly.

Pay Service 1
Pay Units: N.A.
Programming (via satellite): Cinemax (multiplexed); Encore; HBO (multiplexed); Starz.
Fee: $1.75 monthly (Encore), $6.95 monthly (Starz), $12.95 monthly (HBO-multiplexed).

Digital Pay Service 1
Pay Units: N.A.
Programming (via satellite): Cinemax (multiplexed); Cinemax HD; Encore (multiplexed); HBO (multiplexed); HBO HD; Showtime (multiplexed); Starz (multiplexed); Sundance Channel; The Movie Channel (multiplexed).
Fee: $7.95 monthly (Starz & Encore), $12.95 monthly (HBO, Cinemax, or Showtime, TMC & Sundance).

Video-On-Demand: No

Pay-Per-View
iN DEMAND (delivered digitally), Fee: $3.95-$9.95, Addressable: Yes; Fresh (delivered digitally); Shorteez (delivered digitally); Playboy TV (delivered digitally).

Internet Service
Operational: Yes. Began: May 1, 2001.
Subscribers: 1,030.
Broadband Service: In-house.
Fee: $50.00 installation; $21.95 monthly.

Telephone Service
Analog: Not Operational
Digital: Operational

General Manager: Darrel L Wenzel. Chief Technician: Ron Curry.
Ownership: Independence Light & Power Telecommunications.

INDEPENDENCE—Mediacom, 4010 Alexandra Dr, Waterloo, IA 50702. Phone: 319-235-2197. Fax: 319-232-7841. Web Site: http://www.mediacomcable.com. Also serves Hudson. ICA: IA0059.
TV Market Ranking: 65 (Hudson, INDEPENDENCE). Franchise award date: April 23, 1979. Franchise expiration date: N.A. Began: May 1, 1986.
Channel capacity: N.A. Channels available but not in use: N.A.

Basic Service
Subscribers: 2,001.
Programming (received off-air): KCRG-TV (ABC) Cedar Rapids; KFXA (FOX) Cedar Rapids; KGAN (CBS) Cedar Rapids; KPXR-TV (ION) Cedar Rapids; KRIN (PBS) Waterloo; KWKB (CW, MNT) Iowa City; KWWL (NBC) Waterloo.
Programming (via satellite): TBS Superstation.
Current originations: Government Access; Public Access.
Fee: $40.95 installation; $24.39 monthly.

Expanded Basic Service 1
Subscribers: 1,127.
Programming (via satellite): ABC Family Channel; AMC; Animal Planet; Arts & Entertainment; BET Networks; Bravo; Cartoon Network; CNBC; CNN; Comedy Central; Country Music TV; C-SPAN; C-SPAN 2; Discovery Channel; Disney Channel; E! Entertainment Television; ESPN; ESPN 2; Eternal Word TV Network; Food Network; Fox News Channel; Fox Sports Net Midwest; FX; Golf Channel; Hallmark Channel; Headline News; HGTV; History Channel; Home Shopping Network; Lifetime; MoviePlex; MSNBC; MTV; mun2 television; Nickelodeon; QVC; Speed Channel; Spike TV; Syfy; The Learning Channel; Travel Channel; Trinity Broadcasting Network; truTV; Turner Classic Movies; Turner Network TV; TV Guide Network; TV Land; USA Network; VH1; WE tv; Weather Channel; WGN America.
Fee: $60.00 installation; $7.04 monthly.

Digital Basic Service
Subscribers: 150.
Programming (via satellite): AmericanLife TV Network; BBC America; Bio; Bloomberg Television; Discovery Digital Networks; DMX Music; Fox Movie Channel; Fox Sports World; Fuse; G4; GAS; GSN; Halogen Network; History Channel International; Independent Film Channel; Lifetime Movie Network; Lime; MTV Networks Digital Suite; National Geographic Channel; Nick Jr.; Outdoor Channel; Ovation; Style Network; Sundance Channel; Toon Disney; Versus.
Fee: $12.00 monthly.

Digital Pay Service 1
Pay Units: 50.
Programming (via satellite): Cinemax (multiplexed); Encore (multiplexed); HBO (multiplexed); Showtime (multiplexed); Starz (multiplexed); The Movie Channel (multiplexed).
Fee: $8.95 monthly (each).

Video-On-Demand: Yes

Pay-Per-View
Addressable homes: 150.
TVN Entertainment (delivered digitally), Addressable: Yes; Shorteez (delivered digitally); Fresh (delivered digitally); Playboy TV (delivered digitally); Pleasure (delivered digitally); ETC (delivered digitally); ESPN Now (delivered digitally); Sports PPV (delivered digitally).

Internet Service
Operational: Yes.
Broadband Service: Mediacom High Speed Internet.

Telephone Service
Digital: Operational

Miles of Plant: 62.0 (coaxial); 3.0 (fiber optic). Homes passed: 2,765.
Regional Vice President: Doug Frank. General Manager: Doug Nix. Technical Operations Director: Greg Nank. Marketing Director: Steve Schuh. Marketing Coordinator: Joni Lindauer.
Ownership: Mediacom LLC (MSO).

INWOOD—Alliance Communications, PO Box 349, 612 3rd St, Garretson, SD 57030-0349. Phones: 800-701-4980; 605-594-3411. Fax: 605-594-6776. E-mail: email@alliancecom.net. Web Site: http://www.alliancecom.net. ICA: IA0449.
TV Market Ranking: 85 (INWOOD). Franchise award date: November 1, 1982. Franchise expiration date: N.A. Began: January 1, 1984.
Channel capacity: 36 (not 2-way capable). Channels available but not in use: 8.

Basic Service
Subscribers: 191.
Programming (received off-air): KCAU-TV (ABC) Sioux City; KDLT-TV (NBC) Sioux Falls; KELO-TV (CBS, MNT) Sioux Falls; KMEG (CBS) Sioux City; KSFY-TV (ABC) Sioux Falls; KSIN-TV (PBS) Sioux City; KTIV (CW, NBC) Sioux City; KTTW (FOX) Sioux Falls; KUSD-TV (PBS) Vermillion.
Programming (via satellite): ABC Family Channel; AMC; Animal Planet; Arts & Entertainment; Bloomberg Television; Cartoon Network; CNN; Comedy Central; Country Music TV; C-SPAN; Discovery Channel; Disney Channel; ESPN; ESPN 2; ESPN Classic Sports; Eternal Word TV Network; Food Network; Fox News Channel; Fox Sports Net; FX; Golf Channel; Great American Country; Headline News; HGTV; History Channel; Home Shopping Network; Lifetime; LWS Local Weather Station; MTV; Nickelodeon; Outdoor Channel; QVC; Speed Channel; Spike TV; Syfy; TBS Superstation; The Learning Channel; Travel Channel; truTV; Turner Classic Movies; Turner Network TV; TV Land; Univision; USA Network; VH1; Weather Channel; WGN America.
Fee: $30.00 installation; $26.95 monthly.

Pay Service 1
Pay Units: 57.
Programming (via satellite): HBO.
Fee: $13.00 installation; $9.95 monthly.

Pay Service 2
Pay Units: 12.
Programming (via satellite): Showtime; The Movie Channel.
Fee: $13.00 installation; $9.95 monthly.

Internet Service
Operational: Yes, DSL.

Telephone Service
None

Miles of Plant: 8.0 (coaxial); None (fiber optic). Homes passed: 325. Total homes in franchised area: 380.
Manager: Don Synders. Chief Technician: Bob Stiefvater. Marketing Director: Amy Ahlers. Executive Assistant: Chris Frerk.
City fee: 2% of gross.
Ownership: Alliance Communications (MSO).

IONIA—Formerly served by Mid-American Cable Systems. No longer in operation. ICA: IA0450.

IOWA FALLS—Mediacom, 4010 Alexandra Dr, Waterloo, IA 50702. Phone: 319-235-2197. Fax: 319-232-7841. Web Site: http://www.mediacomcable.com. Also serves Ackley, Eldora, Grundy Center & Hardin County. ICA: IA0053.

TV Market Ranking: 65 (Eldora, Grundy Center); 65,66 (Hardin County (portions)); Outside TV Markets (Ackley, IOWA FALLS, Hardin County (portions)). Franchise award date: October 12, 1979. Franchise expiration date: N.A. Began: N.A.

Channel capacity: N.A. Channels available but not in use: N.A.

Basic Service

Subscribers: 3,754.

Programming (received off-air): KCCI (CBS) Des Moines; KCRG-TV (ABC) Cedar Rapids; KCWI-TV (CW) Ames; KDIN-TV (PBS) Des Moines; KDSM-TV (FOX) Des Moines; KFPX-TV (ION) Newton; KFXA (FOX) Cedar Rapids; KGAN (CBS) Cedar Rapids; KPXR-TV (ION) Cedar Rapids; KWKB (CW, MNT) Iowa City; KWWL (NBC) Waterloo; WHO-DT (NBC) Des Moines; WOI-DT (ABC) Ames.

Programming (via satellite): C-SPAN; Home Shopping Network; QVC; TV Guide Network; WGN America.

Current originations: Public Access.

Fee: $40.95 installation; $11.19 monthly.

Expanded Basic Service 1

Subscribers: 3,410.

Programming (via satellite): ABC Family Channel; AMC; Animal Planet; Arts & Entertainment; Bravo; Cartoon Network; CNBC; CNN; Comcast SportsNet Chicago; Comedy Central; Country Music TV; C-SPAN 2; Discovery Channel; Disney Channel; E! Entertainment Television; ESPN; ESPN 2; Eternal Word TV Network; Food Network; Fox News Channel; FX; Hallmark Channel; Headline News; HGTV; History Channel; Lifetime; MSNBC; Nickelodeon; Speed Channel; Spike TV; Syfy; TBS Superstation; The Learning Channel; Travel Channel; Trinity Broadcasting Network; truTV; Turner Classic Movies; Turner Network TV; TV Land; USA Network; VH1; WE tv; Weather Channel.

Fee: $29.76 monthly.

Digital Basic Service

Subscribers: 1,116.

Programming (via satellite): AmericanLife TV Network; BBC America; Bio; Bloomberg Television; Discovery Digital Networks; DMX Music; ESPN Classic Sports; ESPNews; Fox Movie Channel; Fox Sports World; Fuse; G4; GAS; Golf Channel; GSN; Halogen Network; History Channel International; Independent Film Channel; Lifetime Movie Network; Lime; MTV Networks Digital Suite; Nick Jr.; Outdoor Channel; Ovation; Style Network; Toon Disney; Versus.

Fee: $12.00 monthly.

Digital Pay Service 1

Pay Units: 377.

Programming (via satellite): Cinemax (multiplexed).

Fee: $12.95 monthly.

Digital Pay Service 2

Pay Units: 427.

Programming (via satellite): HBO (multiplexed).

Fee: $13.95 monthly.

Digital Pay Service 3

Pay Units: 236.

Programming (via satellite): Encore (multiplexed).

Fee: $2.10 monthly.

Digital Pay Service 4

Pay Units: 146.

Programming (via satellite): Showtime (multiplexed); Sundance Channel; The Movie Channel (multiplexed).

Fee: $12.95 monthly (Showtime).

Digital Pay Service 5

Pay Units: 527.

Programming (via satellite): Starz (multiplexed).

Fee: $7.10 monthly.

Video-On-Demand: Yes

Pay-Per-View

Addressable homes: 1,116.

ESPN Now (delivered digitally); ETC (delivered digitally); Playboy TV (delivered digitally); Pleasure (delivered digitally); Fresh (delivered digitally); Shorteez (delivered digitally); TVN Entertainment (delivered digitally); sports (delivered digitally).

Internet Service

Operational: Yes.

Subscribers: 789.

Broadband Service: Mediacom High Speed Internet.

Fee: $55.95 monthly.

Telephone Service

Analog: Not Operational

Digital: Not Operational

Digital: Operational

Miles of Plant: 94.0 (coaxial); None (fiber optic). Homes passed: 5,883. Total homes in franchised area: 5,883.

Regional Vice President: Doug Frank. General Manager: Doug Nix. Technical Operations Director: Greg Nank. Marketing Director: Steve Schuh. Marketing Coordinator: Joni Lindauer.

Ownership: Mediacom LLC (MSO).

IRETON—Premier Communications. Now served by SIOUX CENTER, IA [IA0076]. ICA: IA0451.

JAMAICA—Panora Cooperative Cablevision Assn. Inc., PO Box 189, 114 E Main St, Panora, IA 50216. Phone: 641-755-2424. Fax: 641-755-2425. E-mail: panora@netins.net. Web Site: http://www.panoratelco.com. ICA: IA0380.

TV Market Ranking: Outside TV Markets (JAMAICA). Franchise award date: April 1, 1988. Franchise expiration date: N.A. Began: June 20, 1988.

Channel capacity: 36 (operating 2-way). Channels available but not in use: N.A.

Basic Service

Subscribers: 70.

Programming (received off-air): KCCI (CBS) Des Moines; KDIN-TV (PBS) Des Moines; KDSM-TV (FOX) Des Moines; WHO-DT (NBC) Des Moines; WOI-DT (ABC) Ames.

Programming (via satellite): ABC Family Channel; AMC; Animal Planet; Arts & Entertainment; CNBC; CNN; Comcast SportsNet Chicago; Country Music TV; C-SPAN; Discovery Channel; Disney Channel; ESPN; ESPN 2; Fox News Channel; FX; Headline News; HGTV; History Channel; INSP; ION Television; Lifetime; Nickelodeon; Outdoor Channel; Spike TV; TBS Superstation; The Learning Channel; Toon Disney; Travel Channel; Turner Network TV; TV Guide Network; USA Network; Weather Channel; WGN America.

Fee: $20.00 installation; $33.00 monthly.

Digital Basic Service

Subscribers: N.A.

Programming (via satellite): BBC America; Bio; Bloomberg Television; Bravo; Discovery Digital Networks; DMX Music; ESPN Classic Sports; ESPNews; Fox College Sports Atlantic; Fox College Sports Central; Fox College Sports Pacific; Fox Movie Channel; Fox Sports World; G4; GAS; Golf Channel; Great American Country; GSN; History Channel International; Independent Film Channel; Lifetime Movie Network; Lime; MBC America; National Geographic Channel; Nick Jr.; NickToons TV; ShopNBC; Speed Channel; Style Network; The Word Network; Trio; Turner Classic Movies; Versus; WE tv.

Fee: $16.95 monthly.

Pay Service 1

Pay Units: 31.

Programming (via satellite): Encore; HBO; Starz.

Fee: $12.00 monthly (Starz & Encore), 13.00 monthly (HBO).

Digital Pay Service 1

Pay Units: N.A.

Programming (via satellite): Cinemax (multiplexed); Encore (multiplexed); Flix; HBO (multiplexed); Showtime (multiplexed); Starz (multiplexed); The Movie Channel (multiplexed).

Fee: $13.00 monthly (Starz/Encore or Cinemax), $15.00 monthly (HBO or Showtime/TMC/Flix).

Video-On-Demand: No

Pay-Per-View

Movies (delivered digitally); Special events (delivered digitally); ESPN Now (delivered digitally); Sports PPV (delivered digitally).

Internet Service

Operational: No, DSL & dial-up.

Telephone Service

Analog: Operational

Miles of Plant: 3.0 (coaxial); None (fiber optic). Homes passed: 80. Total homes in franchised area: 80.

General Manager: Andy Randol. Plant Manager: Bill Dorsett. Marketing Director: Douglas Pals. Office Manager: Cheryl Castile.

City fee: 1% of gross.

Ownership: Panora Cooperative Cablevision Assn. Inc. (MSO).

JEFFERSON—Mediacom. Now served by AMES, IA [IA0008]. ICA: IA0054.

JESUP—Jesup Cablevision, PO Box 249, 541 Young St, Jesup, IA 50648-0249. Phones: 319-827-1151; 319-827-3434. Fax: 319-827-1110. Web Site: http://www.jtt.net/. Also serves Littleton. ICA: IA0116.

TV Market Ranking: 65 (JESUP, Littleton). Franchise award date: January 1, 1982. Franchise expiration date: N.A. Began: December 1, 1982.

Channel capacity: 77 (2-way capable). Channels available but not in use: N.A.

Basic Service

Subscribers: 814.

Programming (received off-air): KCRG-TV (ABC) Cedar Rapids; KFXA (FOX) Cedar Rapids; KGAN (CBS) Cedar Rapids; KPXR-TV (ION) Cedar Rapids; KRIN (PBS) Waterloo; KWWF (IND) Waterloo [LICENSED & SILENT]; KWWL (NBC) Waterloo.

Programming (via satellite): ABC Family Channel; AMC; Animal Planet; Arts & Entertainment; Big Ten Network; Bloomberg Television; Cartoon Network; CNBC; CNN; Comcast SportsNet Northwest; Comedy Central; Country Music TV; C-SPAN; C-SPAN 2; Discovery Channel; Disney Channel; Do-It-Yourself; E! Entertainment Television; ESPN; ESPN 2; ESPN Classic Sports; ESPN U; Eternal Word TV Network; Food Network; Fox News Channel; FX; G4; Golf Channel; GSN; Hallmark Channel; Headline News; HGTV; History Channel; KWKB (CW, MNT) Iowa City; Lifetime; MoviePlex; MTV; National Geographic Channel; Nickelodeon; Outdoor Channel; QVC; RFD-TV; Speed Channel; Spike TV; Syfy; TBS Superstation; The Learning Channel; Travel Channel; Trinity Broadcasting Network; truTV; Turner Classic Movies; Turner Network TV; TV Guide Network; TV Land; USA Network; VH1; WE tv; Weather Channel; WGN America.

Current originations: Public Access.

Fee: $18.00 installation; $38.00 monthly; $.75 converter.

Pay Service 1

Pay Units: 1.

Programming (via satellite): Cinemax (multiplexed).

Fee: $16.00 installation; $8.50 monthly.

Pay Service 2

Pay Units: 2.

Programming (via satellite): Encore; Starz.

Fee: $16.00 installation; $8.50 monthly.

Pay Service 3

Pay Units: 125.

Programming (via satellite): HBO (multiplexed).

Fee: $16.00 installation; $10.00 monthly.

Internet Service

Operational: No, Dial-up only.

Telephone Service

None

Miles of Plant: 20.0 (coaxial); None (fiber optic). Homes passed: 1,800.

Manager: Jim Alberts. Chief Technician: Ben Wehrspamn.

City fee: 3% of gross minus programming costs.

Ownership: Jesup Farmer's Mutual Telephone Co.

JOICE (village)—Formerly served by Westcom. No longer in operation. ICA: IA0452.

KANAWHA—Communications 1 Cablevision, PO Box 20, 105 S Main, Kanawha, IA 50447-0020. Phones: 800-469-3772; 641-762-3772. Fax: 641-762-8201. E-mail: comm1net@comm1net.net. Web Site: http://www.comm1net.net. Also serves Corwith, Klemme & Wesley. ICA: IA0229.

TV Market Ranking: Below 100 (KANAWHA, Klemme); Outside TV Markets (Corwith, Wesley). Franchise award date: December 14, 1982. Franchise expiration date: N.A. Began: February 2, 1984.

Channel capacity: 40 (operating 2-way). Channels available but not in use: None.

Digital Basic Service

Subscribers: N.A.

Programming (received off-air): KAAL (ABC) Austin; KCCI (CBS) Des Moines; KCWI-TV (CW) Ames; KDIN-TV (PBS) Des Moines; KDMI (MNT, IND) Des Moines; KDSM-TV (FOX) Des Moines; KIMT (CBS, MNT) Mason City; WHO-DT (NBC) Des Moines; WOI-DT (ABC) Ames.

Programming (via satellite): ABC Family Channel; American Movie Classics; AmericanLife TV Network; Animal Planet; Arts & Entertainment; BBC America; Big Ten Network; Bio; Bloomberg Television; Boomerang; Bravo; Cartoon Network; CNBC; CNBC World; CNN; CNN International; Comedy Central; Country Music TV; C-SPAN; C-SPAN 2; Discovery Channel; Discovery Health Channel; Discovery Kids

Channel; Discovery Military Channel; Disney Channel; Disney XD; Do-It-Yourself; E! Entertainment Television; ESPN; ESPN 2; Eternal Word TV Network; Food Network; Fox Movie Channel; Fox News Channel; Fox Sports Net North; FX; Golf Channel; Great American Country; GSN; Hallmark Channel; Headline News; HGTV; History Channel; History Channel International; Home Shopping Network; ID Investigation Discovery; Independent Film Channel; Lifetime; Lifetime Movie Network; Lifetime Real Women; MSNBC; MTV; Music Choice; National Geographic Channel; NFL Network; Nick Jr.; Nick Too; Nickelodeon; NickToons TV; Outdoor Channel; Oxygen; QVC; RFD-TV; Science Channel; ShopNBC; SoapNet; Speed Channel; Spike TV; Sundance Channel; Syfy; TBS Superstation; TeenNick; The Learning Channel; Travel Channel; Trinity Broadcasting Network; truTV; Turner Classic Movies; Turner Network TV; TV Land; USA Network; Versus; VH1; VH1 Classic; WE tv; Weather Channel; WGN America.

Fee: $32.00 installation; $49.95 monthly.

Digital Pay Service 1

Pay Units: N.A.

Programming (via satellite): Cinemax (multiplexed); Encore (multiplexed); Flix; HBO (multiplexed); Showtime (multiplexed); Starz (multiplexed); The Movie Channel (multiplexed).

Fee: $12.95 monthly (HBO, Cinemax, Showtime/TMC/Flix or Starz/Encore).

Internet Service

Operational: No, DSL only.

Telephone Service

None

Miles of Plant: 16.0 (coaxial); None (fiber optic). Homes passed: 1,035. Total homes in franchised area: 1,035.

Manager: Randolph Yeakel. Chief Technician: Jayson Keiper.

Ownership: Communications 1 Network Inc. (MSO).

KELLERTON—Telnet South LC. Now served by DES MOINES, IA [IA0001]. ICA: IA0349.

KELLEY—Huxley Communications Corp., PO Box 70, 102 N Main Ave, Huxley, IA 50124-0070. Phones: 800-231-4922; 515-597-2281. Fax: 515-597-2899. E-mail: huxtel@huxcomm.net. Web Site: http://www.huxcomm.net. ICA: IA0560.

TV Market Ranking: 66 (KELLEY). Franchise award date: N.A. Franchise expiration date: N.A. Began: N.A.

Channel capacity: 102 (operating 2-way). Channels available but not in use: None.

Basic Service

Subscribers: 69.

Programming (received off-air): KCCI (CBS) Des Moines; KDSM-TV (FOX) Des Moines; WHO-DT (NBC) Des Moines; WOI-DT (ABC) Ames.

Programming (via satellite): ABC Family Channel; AMC; Animal Planet; Arts & Entertainment; Big Ten Network; Cartoon Network; CNBC; CNN; Comedy Central; Cooking Channel; Country Music TV; Discovery Channel; Disney Channel; Do-It-Yourself; E! Entertainment Television; ESPN; ESPN 2; ESPN Classic Sports; ESPN U; ESPNews; Food Network; Fox Movie Channel; Fox News Channel; Fox Sports Net Midwest; FX; G4; Golf Channel; Hallmark Channel; Headline News; HGTV; History Channel; Home Shopping Network; ION Television; KDIN-TV (PBS) Des Moines; Lifetime; MSNBC; MTV; National Geographic Channel; Nickelodeon; Outdoor Channel; RFD-TV; Speed Channel; Spike TV; Syfy; TBS Superstation; The Learning Channel; Toon Disney; Travel Channel; Trinity Broadcasting Network; truTV; Turner Classic Movies; Turner Network TV; TV Land; USA Network; VH1; Weather Channel; WGN America.

Current originations: Educational Access.

Fee: $30.00 installation; $40.00 monthly.

Digital Basic Service

Subscribers: 3.

Programming (via satellite): AmericanLife TV Network; BBC America; Bio; Bloomberg Television; Bravo; Current; Discovery Health Channel; Discovery Home Channel; Discovery Kids Channel; Discovery Military Channel; Discovery Times Channel; DMX Music; ESPN 2; ESPN Classic Sports; ESPNews; FitTV; Fox Movie Channel; Fox Soccer; FSN Digital Atlantic; FSN Digital Central; FSN Digital Pacific; Fuse; G4; Golf Channel; Gospel Music Channel; Great American Country; GSN; HGTV; History Channel; History Channel International; Independent Film Channel; INSP; International Television (ITV); Lifetime Movie Network; Lime; MTV Hits; MTV2; National Geographic Channel; Nick Jr.; NickToons TV; Outdoor Channel; Ovation; Science Channel; ShopNBC; Sleuth; Speed Channel; Style Network; Sundance Channel; TeenNick; The Word Network; Toon Disney; Trinity Broadcasting Network; Turner Classic Movies; Versus; VH1 Classic; VH1 Country; VH1 Soul; WE tv.

Fee: $10.00 monthly.

Pay Service 1

Pay Units: 8.

Programming (via satellite): HBO.

Fee: $13.00 monthly.

Pay Service 2

Pay Units: 5.

Programming (via satellite): Showtime.

Fee: $13.00 monthly.

Pay Service 3

Pay Units: 1.

Programming (via satellite): Cinemax.

Fee: $10.00 monthly.

Pay Service 4

Pay Units: 9.

Programming (via satellite): Encore; Starz.

Fee: $10.00 monthly.

Digital Pay Service 1

Pay Units: N.A.

Programming (via satellite): Cinemax (multiplexed); Encore (multiplexed); Flix; HBO (multiplexed); Showtime (multiplexed); Starz (multiplexed); The Movie Channel (multiplexed).

Fee: $10.00 monthly (CInemax, Showtime/TMC or Starz/Encore), $15.00 monthly (HBO).

Video-On-Demand: Planned

Pay-Per-View

iN DEMAND (delivered digitally); Spice (delivered digitally); Spice 2 (delivered digitally); Playboy TV (delivered digitally).

Internet Service

Operational: No, DSL.

Telephone Service

None

Homes passed: 90.

General Manager: Gary Clark. Operations Director: Terry Ferguson. Plant Manager: Brant Strumpfer.

City fee: 3% of gross.

Ownership: Huxley Communications Corp. (MSO).

KEOKUK—Mediacom, 6300 Council St NE, Ste A, Cedar Rapids, IA 52402. Phones: 319-753-6576 (Burlington office); 319-395-9699. Fax: 319-393-7017. Web Site: http://www.mediacomcable.com. Also serves Hamilton, Hancock County (portions) & Warsaw, IL; Hamilton County (portions), Lee County (portions) & Montrose, IA. ICA: IA0612.

TV Market Ranking: Below 100 (Hamilton, Hamilton County (portions), Hancock County (portions), KEOKUK, Lee County (portions), Montrose, Warsaw).

Channel capacity: N.A. Channels available but not in use: N.A.

Basic Service

Subscribers: N.A.

Programming (received off-air): KHQA-TV (ABC, CBS) Hannibal; KIIN (PBS) Iowa City; KTVO (ABC) Kirksville; KWQC-TV (NBC) Davenport; KYOU-TV (FOX) Ottumwa; WGEM-TV (CW, NBC) Quincy; WQAD-TV (ABC) Moline; WTJR (IND) Quincy.

Programming (via satellite): C-SPAN; C-SPAN 2; Home Shopping Network; ION Television; QVC; TV Guide Network; Weather Channel; WGN America.

Current originations: Government Access; Educational Access; Public Access.

Expanded Basic Service 1

Subscribers: N.A.

Programming (via satellite): ABC Family Channel; AMC; Animal Planet; Arts & Entertainment; BET Networks; Cartoon Network; CNBC; CNN; Comedy Central; Country Music TV; Discovery Channel; Disney Channel; E! Entertainment Television; ESPN; ESPN 2; Eternal Word TV Network; Food Network; Fox News Channel; Fox Sports Net Midwest; FX; Hallmark Channel; Headline News; HGTV; History Channel; INSP; Lifetime; MSNBC; MTV; National Geographic Channel; Nickelodeon; SoapNet; Speed Channel; Spike TV; Syfy; TBS Superstation; Telemundo; The Learning Channel; truTV; Turner Network TV; TV Land; Univision; USA Network; VH1; WE tv.

Digital Basic Service

Subscribers: N.A.

Programming (via satellite): AmericanLife TV Network; BBC America; Bio; Bloomberg Television; Bravo; Discovery Digital Networks; DMX Music; Fox Movie Channel; Fox Sports World; Fuse; G4; GAS; Golf Channel; GSN; Halogen Network; History Channel International; Independent Film Channel; Lifetime Movie Network; Lime; MTV Networks Digital Suite; Nick Jr.; Outdoor Channel; Ovation; Style Network; Trinity Broadcasting Network; Turner Classic Movies; Versus.

Digital Pay Service 1

Pay Units: N.A.

Programming (via satellite): Cinemax (multiplexed); Encore (multiplexed); Flix; HBO (multiplexed); Showtime (multiplexed); Starz (multiplexed); Sundance Channel; The Movie Channel (multiplexed).

Video-On-Demand: Yes

Pay-Per-View

ETC (delivered digitally); Playboy TV (delivered digitally); Pleasure (delivered digitally); TVN Entertainment (delivered digitally); Sports PPV (delivered digitally).

Internet Service

Operational: Yes.

Broadband Service: Mediacom High Speed Internet.

Fee: $45.95 monthly.

Telephone Service

Digital: Operational

Fee: $39.95 monthly

Miles of Plant: 210.0 (coaxial); None (fiber optic). Miles of plant (fiber) included in miles of plant (coax)

Regional Vice President: Doug Frank. Technical Operations Director: Greg Nank. Technical Operations Manager: Joel Hanger. Marketing Director: Steve Schuh.

Ownership: Mediacom LLC (MSO).

KEOSAUQUA—Starwest Inc., 15235 235th St, Milton, IA 52570-8016. Phones: 319-397-2283; 319-293-6336. Also serves Birmingham, Bonaparte, Cantril, Milton & Stockport. ICA: IA0186.

TV Market Ranking: Below 100 (Birmingham, Bonaparte, Cantril, KEOSAUQUA, Milton, Stockport). Franchise award date: N.A. Franchise expiration date: N.A. Began: N.A.

Channel capacity: N.A. Channels available but not in use: N.A.

Basic Service

Subscribers: 379.

Programming (via satellite): Cartoon Network.

Fee: $30.00 installation; $14.50 monthly.

Pay Service 1

Pay Units: N.A.

Programming (via satellite): Showtime.

Fee: $14.95 monthly.

Internet Service

Operational: No.

Miles of Plant: 5.0 (coaxial); None (fiber optic). Homes passed: 490.

Manager & Chief Technician: John Stooksberry.

City fee: None.

Ownership: Starwest Inc. (MSO).

KESWICK—Formerly served by Longview Communications. No longer in operation. ICA: IA0359.

KEYSTONE—Keystone Communications, PO Box 277, 86 Main St, Keystone, IA 52249. Phones: 800-568-9584; 319-442-3241. Fax: 319-442-3210. E-mail: keystone@netins.net. Web Site: http://www.keystonecommunications.com. Also serves Elberon & Garrison. ICA: IA0187.

TV Market Ranking: 65 (Elberon, Garrison, KEYSTONE). Franchise award date: N.A. Franchise expiration date: N.A. Began: January 1, 1985.

Channel capacity: 33 (operating 2-way). Channels available but not in use: N.A.

Basic Service

Subscribers: 402.

Programming (received off-air): KCRG-TV (ABC) Cedar Rapids; KFXA (FOX) Cedar Rapids; KGAN (CBS) Cedar Rapids; KPXR-TV (ION) Cedar Rapids; KWBK-LP Pine Bluff; KWWL (NBC) Waterloo; WOI-DT (ABC) Ames.

Programming (via satellite): ABC Family Channel; Cartoon Network; CNBC; CNN; Country Music TV; Discovery Channel; Disney Channel; ESPN; ESPN 2; Headline News; History Channel; Lifetime; MTV; Nickelodeon; Outdoor Channel; Spike TV; Syfy; TBS Superstation; The Learning Channel; Turner Classic Movies; Turner Network TV; USA Network; VH1; Weather Channel; WGN America.

Current originations: Public Access.

Fee: $20.00 installation; $29.95 monthly.

Pay Service 1

Pay Units: 117.

Programming (via satellite): HBO.

Fee: $10.00 monthly.

Pay Service 2

Pay Units: 96.

Programming (via satellite): Showtime.

Fee: $10.00 monthly.

Video-On-Demand: No

Internet Service
Operational: No, dial-up.
Telephone Service
None
Miles of Plant: 7.0 (coaxial); 8.0 (fiber optic). Homes passed: 475. Total homes in franchised area: 586.
General Manager: Byran Kim.
Ownership: Keystone Farmers Cooperative Telephone Co.

KINGSLEY—Evertek Inc., PO Box 270, 216 N Main, Everly, IA 51338. Phone: 712-834-2255. Fax: 712-834-2214. E-mail: internet@evertek.net. Web Site: http://www.evertek.net. ICA: IA0197.
TV Market Ranking: Below 100 (KINGSLEY). Franchise award date: N.A. Franchise expiration date: N.A. Began: February 1, 1984.
Channel capacity: 35 (not 2-way capable). Channels available but not in use: N.A.
Basic Service
Subscribers: 250.
Programming (received off-air): KCAU-TV (ABC) Sioux City; KMEG (CBS) Sioux City; KSIN-TV (PBS) Sioux City; KTIV (CW, NBC) Sioux City.
Programming (via satellite): ABC Family Channel; Animal Planet; Arts & Entertainment; CNN; Country Music TV; C-SPAN; Discovery Channel; Disney Channel; ESPN; ESPN 2; Headline News; History Channel; Lifetime; Nickelodeon; Spike TV; Syfy; TBS Superstation; The Learning Channel; Turner Classic Movies; Turner Network TV; USA Network; VH1; Weather Channel; WGN America.
Fee: $45.00 installation; $26.95 monthly.
Pay Service 1
Pay Units: 6.
Programming (via satellite): Cinemax.
Fee: $11.00 monthly.
Pay Service 2
Pay Units: 15.
Programming (via satellite): HBO.
Fee: $11.00 monthly.
Pay Service 3
Pay Units: 16.
Programming (via satellite): Showtime; The Movie Channel.
Fee: $15.95 monthly.
Video-On-Demand: No
Internet Service
Operational: No.
Telephone Service
None
Miles of Plant: 6.0 (coaxial); None (fiber optic). Homes passed: 440.
General Manager: Roxanne White. Chief Technician: Fred Gibson.
City fee: 5% of gross.
Ownership: Evertek Inc. (MSO).

KLEMME—Communications 1 Cablevision. Now served by KANAWHA, IA [IA0229]. ICA: IA0454.

KNOXVILLE—Mediacom. Now served by DES MOINES, IA [IA0001]. ICA: IA0029.

KNOXVILLE (unincorporated areas)—Telnet South LC. Now served by DES MOINES, IA [IA0001]. ICA: IA0578.

LACONA—Formerly served by Telnet South LC. No longer in operation. ICA: IA0456.

LAKE MILLS—Winnebago Cooperative Telephone Assn., 704 E Main St, Lake Mills, IA 50450-1420. Phones: 641-592-6105; 800-592-6105. Fax: 641-592-6102. E-mail: wcta@wctatel.net. Web Site: http://www.wctatel.net. ICA: IA0590.
TV Market Ranking: Below 100 (LAKE MILLS). Franchise award date: N.A. Franchise expiration date: N.A. Began: N.A.
Channel capacity: 35 (operating 2-way). Channels available but not in use: N.A.
Basic Service
Subscribers: N.A.
Programming (received off-air): KAAL (ABC) Austin; KIMT (CBS, MNT) Mason City; KTTC (CW, NBC) Rochester; KXLT-TV (FOX) Rochester; KYIN (PBS) Mason City.
Programming (via satellite): KFPX-TV (ION) Newton.
Fee: $20.00 installation; $19.95 monthly.
Expanded Basic Service 1
Subscribers: N.A.
Programming (via satellite): ABC Family Channel; AMC; Arts & Entertainment; CNN; Country Music TV; C-SPAN; CW+; Discovery Channel; ESPN; ESPN 2; ESPN Classic Sports; Food Network; Fox Sports Net North; Headline News; HGTV; History Channel; Home Shopping Network; Lifetime; MTV; Nickelodeon; Spike TV; TBS Superstation; The Learning Channel; Turner Network TV; TV Land; USA Network; VH1; Weather Channel; WGN America.
Fee: $17.55 monthly.
Pay Service 1
Pay Units: N.A.
Programming (via satellite): HBO.
Fee: $12.95 monthly.
Video-On-Demand: No
Internet Service
Operational: No.
Telephone Service
None
Homes passed: 1,250. Total homes in franchised area: 1,250.
General Manager: Don Whipple. Assistant Manager: John Kroger. Chief Engineer: Neal Sletten. Marketing Manager: David Taft.
Ownership: Winnebago Cooperative Telephone Assn. (MSO).

LAKE PARK—Mediacom. Now served by SPIRIT LAKE, IA [IA0036]. ICA: IA0457.

LAKE VIEW—Corn Belt Telephone Co., PO Box 445, 108 Main St, Wall Lake, IA 51466. Phone: 712-664-2221. Fax: 712-664-2083. E-mail: cbtelco@netins.net. ICA: IA0159.
TV Market Ranking: Outside TV Markets (LAKE VIEW). Franchise award date: N.A. Franchise expiration date: N.A. Began: November 1, 1984.
Channel capacity: 40 (not 2-way capable). Channels available but not in use: 4.
Basic Service
Subscribers: 400.
Programming (received off-air): KCAU-TV (ABC) Sioux City; KCCI (CBS) Des Moines; KPTH (FOX, MNT) Sioux City; KTIV (CW, NBC) Sioux City; WHO-DT (NBC) Des Moines; WOI-DT (ABC) Ames.
Programming (via satellite): ABC Family Channel; AMC; Animal Planet; Arts & Entertainment; CNN; Country Music TV; Discovery Channel; Disney Channel; ESPN; ESPN 2; ESPN Classic Sports; Fox News Channel; Headline News; HGTV; History Channel; Lifetime; Nickelodeon; Spike TV; Syfy; TBS Superstation; The Learning Channel; Turner Network TV; TV Land; USA Network; VH1; Weather Channel; WGN America.
Fee: $30.00 installation; $25.95 monthly.
Pay Service 1
Pay Units: 9.
Programming (via satellite): Cinemax; HBO.
Fee: $12.00 monthly (each).

Internet Service
Operational: No, DSL only.
Telephone Service
None
Miles of Plant: 11.0 (coaxial); None (fiber optic). Homes passed: 600.
Manager: Larry Neppl. Chief Technician: Bill Cates.
City fee: fee: None.
Ownership: Corn Belt Telephone Co. (MSO).

LAKOTA—Heck's TV & Cable, PO Box 517, 601 7th St, Armstrong, IA 50514-0517. Phone: 712-864-3431. Fax: 712-864-3431. ICA: IA0458.
TV Market Ranking: Outside TV Markets (LAKOTA). Franchise award date: N.A. Franchise expiration date: N.A. Began: N.A.
Channel capacity: N.A. Channels available but not in use: N.A.
Basic Service
Subscribers: N.A.
Programming (received off-air): KAAL (ABC) Austin; KEYC-TV (CBS, FOX) Mankato; KIMT (CBS, MNT) Mason City; KTIN (PBS) Fort Dodge; KTTC (CW, NBC) Rochester.
Programming (via satellite): ABC Family Channel; CNN; ESPN; Spike TV; TBS Superstation; WGN America.
Video-On-Demand: No
Internet Service
Operational: No.
Telephone Service
None
Manager: Steven Heck.
Ownership: Steven Heck (MSO).

LAMONI—Telnet South LC. Now served by DES MOINES, IA [IA0001]. ICA: IA0143.

LAMONT—Formerly served by Alpine Communications LC. No longer in operation. ICA: IA0459.

LANSING—Mediacom, 4010 Alexandra Dr, Waterloo, IA 50702. Phone: 319-235-2197. Fax: 319-232-7841. Web Site: http://www.mediacomcable.com. Also serves Harpers Ferry & Waukon Junction. ICA: IA0177.
TV Market Ranking: Below 100 (LANSING); Outside TV Markets (Harpers Ferry, Waukon Junction). Franchise award date: N.A. Franchise expiration date: N.A. Began: February 1, 1966.
Channel capacity: 56 (operating 2-way). Channels available but not in use: N.A.
Basic Service
Subscribers: 481.
Programming (received off-air): KCRG-TV (ABC) Cedar Rapids; KFXB-TV (IND) Dubuque; KGAN (CBS) Cedar Rapids; KRIN (PBS) Waterloo; KWWL (NBC) Waterloo; WHLA-TV (PBS) La Crosse; WKBT-DT (CBS, MNT) La Crosse; WLAX (FOX) La Crosse; WMTV-TV (NBC) Madison; WXOW (ABC, CW) La Crosse.
Programming (via satellite): KWKB (CW, MNT) Iowa City.
Current originations: Educational Access.
Fee: $45.00 installation; $18.95 monthly; $15.00 additional installation.
Expanded Basic Service 1
Subscribers: N.A.
Programming (via satellite): ABC Family Channel; AMC; Arts & Entertainment; Cartoon Network; CNBC; CNN; Country Music TV; C-SPAN; Discovery Channel; Disney Channel; ESPN; ESPN 2; Eternal Word TV Network; Fox Movie Channel; Fox Sports Net Midwest; Hallmark Channel; Headline News; HGTV; History Channel; Lifetime; MSNBC; Nickelodeon; Outdoor Channel; Spike TV; Syfy; TBS Superstation; The Learning Channel; Trinity Broadcasting Network; Turner Classic Movies; Turner Network TV; TV Guide Network; USA Network; VH1; Weather Channel; WGN America.
Digital Basic Service
Subscribers: N.A.
Programming (via satellite): Music Choice.
Pay Service 1
Pay Units: N.A.
Programming (via satellite): Cinemax; Encore; HBO (multiplexed); Showtime (multiplexed); Starz.
Fee: $20.00 installation; $9.95 monthly (each).
Digital Pay Service 1
Pay Units: N.A.
Programming (via satellite): Cinemax (multiplexed); Encore (multiplexed); HBO (multiplexed); Showtime (multiplexed); Starz (multiplexed); The Movie Channel (multiplexed).
Video-On-Demand: Planned
Pay-Per-View
TVN Entertainment (delivered digitally); Fresh (delivered digitally); Shorteez (delivered digitally); Playboy TV (delivered digitally).
Internet Service
Operational: Yes.
Broadband Service: Mediacom High Speed Internet.
Telephone Service
Analog: Planned
Digital: Planned
Miles of Plant: 8.0 (coaxial); None (fiber optic). Additional miles planned: 1.0 (coaxial). Homes passed: 609.
Manager: Doug Nix. Chief Engineer: Greg Nank. Marketing Coordinator: Johnnie Lindauer.
City fee: None.
Ownership: Mediacom LLC (MSO).

LARCHWOOD—Alliance Communications, PO Box 349, 612 3rd St, Garretson, SD 57030-0349. Phones: 800-701-4980; 605-594-3411. Fax: 605-594-6776. E-mail: email@alliancecom.net. Web Site: http://www.alliancecom.net. ICA: IA0271.
TV Market Ranking: 85 (LARCHWOOD). Franchise award date: January 1, 1983. Franchise expiration date: N.A. Began: January 1, 1984.
Channel capacity: 36 (not 2-way capable). Channels available but not in use: 8.

Basic Service
Subscribers: 179.
Programming (received off-air): K53EG Sioux Falls; KCAU-TV (ABC) Sioux City; KDLT-TV (NBC) Sioux Falls; KELO-TV (CBS, MNT) Sioux Falls; KMEG (CBS) Sioux City; KSFY-TV (ABC) Sioux Falls; KSIN-TV (PBS) Sioux City; KTIV (CW, NBC) Sioux City; KTTW (FOX) Sioux Falls; KUSD-TV (PBS) Vermillion.
Programming (via satellite): ABC Family Channel; AMC; Animal Planet; Arts & Entertainment; Bloomberg Television; Cartoon Network; CNN; Comedy Central; Country Music TV; C-SPAN; Discovery Channel; Disney Channel; ESPN; ESPN 2; ESPN Classic Sports; Eternal Word TV Network; Food Network; Fox News Channel; Fox Sports Net; FX; Golf Channel; Great American Country; Headline News; HGTV; History Channel; Home Shopping Network; Lifetime; MTV; Nickelodeon; Outdoor Channel; QVC; Speed Channel; Spike TV; Syfy; TBS Superstation; The Learning Channel; Travel Channel; truTV; Turner Classic Movies; Turner Network TV; TV Land; USA Network; VH1; Weather Channel; WGN America.
Current originations: Educational Access.
Fee: $30.00 installation; $26.95 monthly.
Pay Service 1
Pay Units: 29.
Programming (via satellite): HBO.
Fee: $13.00 installation; $9.95 monthly.
Pay Service 2
Pay Units: 11.
Programming (via satellite): Showtime.
Fee: $13.00 installation; $9.95 monthly.
Pay Service 3
Pay Units: N.A.
Programming (via satellite): The Movie Channel.
Fee: $13.00 installation; $9.95 monthly.
Video-On-Demand: No
Internet Service
Operational: Yes, DSL.
Telephone Service
None
Miles of Plant: 8.0 (coaxial); None (fiber optic). Homes passed: 298. Total homes in franchised area: 349.
Manager: Dan Synder. Chief Technician: Bob Stietvater. Marketing Director: Amy Ahlers. Executive Assistant: Chris Frerk.
City fee: 3% of gross.
Ownership: Alliance Communications (MSO).

LATIMER—Formerly served by Latimer/Coulter Cablevision. No longer in operation. ICA: IA0460.

LAURENS—Laurens Municipal Power & Communications, PO Box 148, 272 N 3rd St, Laurens, IA 50554-0148. Phone: 712-841-4610. E-mail: chadc@laurens-ia.com. Web Site: http://www.laurens-ia.com/businesses/AnalogCable.html. ICA: IA0601. **Note:** This system is an overbuild.
TV Market Ranking: Outside TV Markets (LAURENS).
Channel capacity: 110 (operating 2-way). Channels available but not in use: 20.
Basic Service
Subscribers: 542.
Programming (received off-air): KCAU-TV (ABC) Sioux City; KCCI (CBS) Des Moines; KCWI-TV (CW) Ames; KDSM-TV (FOX) Des Moines; KEYC-TV (CBS, FOX) Mankato; KMEG (CBS) Sioux City; KPTH (FOX, MNT) Sioux City; KTIN (PBS) Fort Dodge; KTIV (CW, NBC) Sioux City; WHO-DT (NBC) Des Moines; WOI-DT (ABC) Ames.
Programming (via satellite): Home Shopping Network; QVC; TV Guide Network; Weather Channel.
Current originations: Public Access.
Fee: $20.00 monthly.
Expanded Basic Service 1
Subscribers: 535.
Programming (via satellite): ABC Family Channel; AMC; AmericanLife TV Network; Animal Planet; Arts & Entertainment; Cartoon Network; CNBC; CNN; Comedy Central; Country Music TV; C-SPAN; C-SPAN 2; Discovery Channel; Disney Channel; Do-It-Yourself; E! Entertainment Television; ESPN; ESPN 2; ESPN Classic Sports; Eternal Word TV Network; Food Network; Fox News Channel; Fox Sports Net North; FX; G4; Hallmark Channel; Hallmark Movie Channel; Headline News; HGTV; History Channel; INSP; Lifetime; LWS Local Weather Station; MSNBC; MTV; National Geographic Channel; NFL Network; Nickelodeon; Outdoor Channel; Oxygen; Speed Channel; Spike TV; Syfy; TBS Superstation; The Learning Channel; Travel Channel; truTV; Turner Classic Movies; Turner Network TV; TV Land; USA Network; Versus; VH1; WE tv; WGN America.
Fee: $40.00 monthly.
Digital Basic Service
Subscribers: 117.
Programming (via satellite): BBC America; Bio; Discovery Health Channel; Discovery Kids Channel; Discovery Military Channel; Discovery Planet Green; DMX Music; ESPNews; FitTV; Fox Movie Channel; Golf Channel; GSN; History Channel International; ID Investigation Discovery; Independent Film Channel; Lifetime Movie Network; MTV2; Nick Jr.; NickToons TV; Science Channel; TeenNick; VH1 Classic; VH1 Country.
Fee: $10.00 monthly.
Digital Pay Service 1
Pay Units: 46.
Programming (via satellite): Cinemax (multiplexed).
Digital Pay Service 2
Pay Units: 54.
Programming (via satellite): HBO (multiplexed).
Digital Pay Service 3
Pay Units: 64.
Programming (via satellite): Encore (multiplexed); Starz (multiplexed).
Internet Service
Operational: Yes.
Subscribers: 400.
Broadband Service: Future Net.
Fee: $50.00 monthly.
Homes passed: 750. Total homes in franchised area: 750.
General Manager: Chad Cleveland. Operations Manager: Tom Schmidt.
Ownership: Laurens Municipal Power & Communications.

LAWLER—Alpine Communications LC, PO Box 1008, 923 Humphrey St, Elkader, IA 52043. Phones: 800-635-1059; 563-245-4000. Fax: 563-245-2887. Web Site: http://www.alpinecom.net. Also serves St. Lucas. ICA: IA0462.
TV Market Ranking: Outside TV Markets (LAWLER, St. Lucas). Franchise award date: N.A. Franchise expiration date: N.A. Began: N.A.
Channel capacity: 38 (not 2-way capable). Channels available but not in use: 15.
Basic Service
Subscribers: 55.
Programming (received off-air): KCRG-TV (ABC) Cedar Rapids; KFXA (FOX) Cedar Rapids; KGAN (CBS) Cedar Rapids; KIMT (CBS, MNT) Mason City; KRIN (PBS) Waterloo; KTTC (CW, NBC) Rochester; KWWL (NBC) Waterloo.
Programming (via satellite): ABC Family Channel; AMC; Arts & Entertainment; Cartoon Network; CNN; Country Music TV; Discovery Channel; E! Entertainment Television; ESPN; ESPN 2; HGTV; History Channel; Lifetime; MTV; Nickelodeon; Outdoor Channel; QVC; Spike TV; TBS Superstation; The Learning Channel; Trinity Broadcasting Network; Turner Network TV; TV Land; USA Network; VH1; Weather Channel; WGN America.
Fee: $20.00 installation; $29.95 monthly.
Pay Service 1
Pay Units: N.A.
Programming (via satellite): Showtime.
Fee: $9.95 monthly.
Video-On-Demand: No
Internet Service
Operational: No.
Telephone Service
None
General Manager: Chris Hopp. Network Operations Manager: Dirk Buckman. Chief Technician: Jerry Schroeder. Sales & Marketing Manager: Sara Hertranpf. Finance Manager: Margaret Corlett. Customer Service Manager: Lori Kepplen.
Ownership: Alpine Communications LC (MSO).

LAWTON—Western Iowa Telephone, PO Box 38, 202 Cedar St, Lawton, IA 51030. Phone: 712-944-5711. Fax: 712-944-5272. E-mail: wiatel@wiatel.com. Web Site: http://www.westerniowatelephone.com. Also serves Bronson, Hornick, Oto, Rodney & Smithland. ICA: IA0330.
TV Market Ranking: Below 100 (Bronson, Hornick, LAWTON, Oto, Rodney, Smithland). Franchise award date: N.A. Franchise expiration date: N.A. Began: February 1, 1984.
Channel capacity: 42 (not 2-way capable). Channels available but not in use: N.A.
Basic Service
Subscribers: 600.
Programming (received off-air): KCAU-TV (ABC) Sioux City; KELO-TV (CBS, MNT) Sioux Falls; KETV (ABC) Omaha; KMEG (CBS) Sioux City; KPTH (FOX, MNT) Sioux City; KSFY-TV (ABC) Sioux Falls; KSIN-TV (PBS) Sioux City; KTIV (CW, NBC) Sioux City; KUSD-TV (PBS) Vermillion.
Programming (via microwave): KAZS-LP South Sioux City.
Programming (via satellite): ABC Family Channel; AMC; AmericanLife TV Network; Animal Planet; Arts & Entertainment; Big Ten Network; Cartoon Network; CNBC; CNN; Comedy Central; Country Music TV; C-SPAN; C-SPAN 2; CW+; Discovery Channel; Disney Channel; E! Entertainment Television; ESPN; ESPN 2; ESPN Classic Sports; Eternal Word TV Network; Food Network; Fox News Channel; Fox Sports Net North; FX; Golf Channel; Hallmark Channel; Halogen Network; Headline News; HGTV; History Channel; Home Shopping Network; Lifetime; Lifetime Movie Network; MSNBC; MTV; Nickelodeon; QVC; Speed Channel; Spike TV; Syfy; TBS Superstation; The Learning Channel; The Sportsman Channel; Travel Channel; Trinity Broadcasting Network; truTV; Turner Classic Movies; Turner Network TV; TV Guide Network; TV Land; USA Network; VH1; Weather Channel; WGN America.
Fee: $25.00 installation; $37.95 monthly.
Digital Basic Service
Subscribers: N.A.
Programming (received off-air): KCAU-TV (ABC) Sioux City; KMEG (CBS) Sioux City; KPTH (FOX, MNT) Sioux City; KSIN-TV (PBS) Sioux City; KTIV (CW, NBC) Sioux City.
Programming (via satellite): BBC America; Big Ten Network HD; Bio; Cooking Channel; Discovery Channel HD; Discovery Health Channel; Discovery Home Channel; Discovery Kids Channel; Discovery Military Channel; Do-It-Yourself; ESPN 2 HD; ESPN HD; ESPN U; ESPNews; FitTV; Fox Movie Channel; Fox Soccer; FSN Digital Atlantic; FSN Digital Central; FSN Digital Pacific; G4; Great American Country; GSN; HDNet; HDNet Movies; History Channel International; ID Investigation Discovery; Independent Film Channel; Lifetime Real Women; MTV Hits; MTV Jams; MTV2; Music Choice; Nick Jr.; NickToons TV; Outdoor Channel; Outdoor Channel 2 HD; RFD-TV; Science Channel; SoapNet; TeenNick; Toon Disney; Versus; VH1 Classic; VH1 Country; VH1 Soul; WE tv.
Fee: $18.95 monthly.
Digital Expanded Basic Service
Subscribers: N.A.
Programming (via satellite): Bandamax; De Pelicula; De Pelicula Clasico; Discovery en Espanol; ESPN Deportes; Fox Sports en Espanol; Ritmoson Latino; Telehit.
Fee: $2.99 monthly.
Digital Pay Service 1
Pay Units: N.A.
Programming (via satellite): Cinemax (multiplexed); Cinemax HD; Encore (multiplexed); Flix; HBO (multiplexed); HBO HD; Showtime (multiplexed); Starz (multiplexed); Starz HDTV; The Movie Channel (multiplexed).
Fee: $11.95 monthly (Cinemax), 13.95 monthly (Starz/Encore), $14.95 monthly (HBO or Showtime, Flix & TMC).
Video-On-Demand: Yes
Internet Service
Operational: No, DSL & dialup.
Telephone Service
None
Homes passed: 1,360.
Manager: Heath Mallory. Operations Manager: Phil Robinson. Chief Technician: Mark Livermore. Marketing & Sales Manager: Pam Clark.
City fee: 3% of gross.
Ownership: Western Iowa Telephone (MSO).

LE MARS—Mediacom, 1504 2nd St SE, Waseca, MN 56093. Phone: 507-835-2356. Fax: 507-835-4567. Web Site: http://www.mediacomcable.com. Also serves Oyens & Plymouth County. ICA: IA0027.
TV Market Ranking: Below 100 (LE MARS, Oyens, Plymouth County (portions)); Outside TV Markets (Plymouth County (portions)). Franchise award date: April 30, 1979. Franchise expiration date: N.A. Began: January 31, 1980.
Channel capacity: 50 (operating 2-way). Channels available but not in use: None.
Basic Service
Subscribers: 2,543.
Programming (received off-air): KCAU-TV (ABC) Sioux City; KELO-TV (CBS, MNT) Sioux Falls; KMEG (CBS) Sioux City; KPTH (FOX, MNT) Sioux City; KSIN-TV (PBS) Sioux City; KTIV (CW, NBC) Sioux City; KUSD-TV (PBS) Vermillion; allband FM.

Programming (via satellite): C-SPAN; Discovery Channel; TBS Superstation; Weather Channel; WGN America.
Fee: $39.95 installation; $9.31 monthly; $1.60 converter.

Expanded Basic Service 1
Subscribers: N.A.
Programming (via satellite): ABC Family Channel; AMC; Animal Planet; Arts & Entertainment; Cartoon Network; CNN; Comedy Central; Country Music TV; Disney Channel; E! Entertainment Television; ESPN; ESPN 2; Eternal Word TV Network; Fox News Channel; FX; Headline News; History Channel; INSP; Lifetime; MSNBC; MTV; Nickelodeon; QVC; RFD-TV; Spike TV; Syfy; Telemundo; The Learning Channel; Travel Channel; truTV; Turner Network TV; TV Guide Network; TV Land; USA Network; VH1; WE tv.
Fee: $18.47 monthly.

Digital Basic Service
Subscribers: N.A.
Programming (via satellite): BBC America; Bravo; Discovery Digital Networks; Fox Sports World; G4; Golf Channel; GSN; HGTV; Independent Film Channel; Lime; Music Choice; National Geographic Channel; Nick Jr.; Speed Channel; Turner Classic Movies; Versus; VH1 Classic; VH1 Country.

Digital Pay Service 1
Pay Units: 222.
Programming (via satellite): Cinemax (multiplexed).
Fee: $13.95 installation; $14.00 monthly.

Digital Pay Service 2
Pay Units: 767.
Programming (via satellite): Encore (multiplexed).
Fee: $13.95 installation; $2.52 monthly.

Digital Pay Service 3
Pay Units: 461.
Programming (via satellite): HBO (multiplexed).
Fee: $13.95 installation; $14.00 monthly.

Digital Pay Service 4
Pay Units: 107.
Programming (via satellite): Showtime (multiplexed).
Fee: $13.95 installation; $14.00 monthly.

Digital Pay Service 5
Pay Units: 363.
Programming (via satellite): Starz (multiplexed).
Fee: $13.95 installation; $8.52 monthly.

Digital Pay Service 6
Pay Units: 3.
Programming (via satellite): Sundance Channel; The Movie Channel (multiplexed).
Fee: $9.54 monthly.

Video-On-Demand: Planned

Pay-Per-View
Addressable homes: 246.
TVN Entertainment (delivered digitally), Fee: $3.99, Addressable: Yes; Fresh (delivered digitally), Fee: $8.99; Shorteez (delivered digitally); Playboy TV (delivered digitally).

Internet Service
Operational: Yes.
Broadband Service: Mediacom High Speed Internet.

Telephone Service
Digital: Planned

Miles of Plant: 53.0 (coaxial); None (fiber optic). Homes passed: 5,051. Total homes in franchised area: 5,379.
Vice President: Bill Jenson. Engineering Director: Scott Walters. Sales & Marketing Director: Lori Huberty.
City fee: 5% of gross (LeMars); 3% of basic (Remsen).
Ownership: Mediacom LLC (MSO).

LEDYARD (village)—Formerly served by New Path Communications LC. No longer in operation. ICA: IA0463.

LEHIGH—Lehigh Services Inc., PO Box 137, 9090 Taylor Rd, Lehigh, IA 50557-0137. Phone: 515-359-2211. Fax: 515-359-2424. E-mail: lvcta@mail.lvcta.com. Web Site: http://www.lvcta.net. Also serves Boxholm, Callender, Dayton, Duncombe, Harcourt, Otho & Pilot Mound. ICA: IA0464.
TV Market Ranking: 66 (Boxholm, Harcourt, Lehigh, LEHIGH, Pilot Mound); Outside TV Markets (Callender, Duncombe, Otho). Franchise award date: N.A. Franchise expiration date: N.A. Began: September 1, 1984.
Channel capacity: 78 (operating 2-way). Channels available but not in use: 21.

Basic Service
Subscribers: 1,300.
Programming (received off-air): KCCI (CBS) Des Moines; KCWI-TV (CW) Ames; KDIN-TV (PBS) Des Moines; KDSM-TV (FOX) Des Moines; KFPX-TV (ION) Newton; WHO-DT (NBC) Des Moines; WOI-DT (ABC) Ames.
Programming (via satellite): ABC Family Channel; AMC; Animal Planet; Arts & Entertainment; Cartoon Network; CNN; CNN International; Country Music TV; Discovery Channel; Discovery Health Channel; Disney Channel; E! Entertainment Television; ESPN; ESPN 2; ESPN Classic Sports; Food Network; Fox News Channel; Fox Sports Net; FX; Great American Country; Hallmark Channel; Headline News; HGTV; History Channel; Home Shopping Network; Lifetime; Lifetime Movie Network; Lifetime Real Women; MTV; National Geographic Channel; Nickelodeon; Spike TV; Syfy; TBS Superstation; The Learning Channel; The Sportsman Channel; Travel Channel; Trinity Broadcasting Network; Turner Classic Movies; Turner Network TV; TV Land; USA Network; VH1; Weather Channel; WGN America.
Current originations: Public Access.
Fee: $25.00 installation; $32.00 monthly.

Digital Basic Service
Subscribers: 150.
Programming (via satellite): BBC America; Discovery Health Channel; Discovery Kids Channel; Discovery Military Channel; Discovery Planet Green; DMX Music; ESPN Classic Sports; ESPNews; Fox Movie Channel; Fox Soccer; FSN Digital Atlantic; FSN Digital Central; FSN Digital Pacific; Golf Channel; GSN; ID Investigation Discovery; Independent Film Channel; MTV Hits; MTV2; Nick Jr.; NickToons TV; Outdoor Channel; Science Channel; Speed Channel; TeenNick; TV Land; Versus; VH1 Soul; WE tv.
Fee: $14.95 monthly.

Digital Pay Service 1
Pay Units: N.A.
Programming (via satellite): Cinemax (multiplexed); Encore (multiplexed); Flix; HBO (multiplexed); Showtime (multiplexed); Starz (multiplexed); The Movie Channel (multiplexed).

Pay-Per-View
Movies (delivered digitally).

Internet Service
Operational: Yes.
Subscribers: 21.
Broadband Service: Lehigh Valley Co-op Telephone Assoc..
Fee: $29.95-$49.95 monthly.

Telephone Service
None

Miles of Plant: 18.0 (coaxial); 34.0 (fiber optic).
Manager: James Suchan. Chief Technician: Kurt DeVries.
Ownership: Lehigh Services Inc.

LENOX—Lenox Municipal Cablevision, 205 S Main St, Lenox, IA 50851-0096. Phone: 641-333-2550. Web Site: http://lenoxia.com/cityoflenox.htm. ICA: IA0180.
TV Market Ranking: Outside TV Markets (LENOX). Franchise award date: N.A. Franchise expiration date: N.A. Began: September 1, 1976.
Channel capacity: 36 (not 2-way capable). Channels available but not in use: 2.

Basic Service
Subscribers: 426.
Programming (received off-air): KCCI (CBS) Des Moines; KDIN-TV (PBS) Des Moines; KDMI (MNT, IND) Des Moines; KDSM-TV (FOX) Des Moines; KETV (ABC) Omaha; KMTV-TV (CBS) Omaha; KPTM (FOX, MNT) Omaha; WHO-DT (NBC) Des Moines; WOI-DT (ABC) Ames; WOWT-TV (IND, NBC) Omaha; allband FM.
Programming (via satellite): ABC Family Channel; AMC; Arts & Entertainment; CNN; Comedy Central; Country Music TV; Discovery Channel; Disney Channel; ESPN; ESPN 2; History Channel; Lifetime; Lifetime Movie Network; MTV; Nickelodeon; Spike TV; TBS Superstation; Turner Network TV; TV Land; USA Network; VH1; Weather Channel; WGN America.
Fee: $20.00 installation; $19.95 monthly.

Pay Service 1
Pay Units: 100.
Programming (via satellite): Cinemax; HBO.
Fee: $10.00 monthly (each).

Internet Service
Operational: No.

Telephone Service
None

Miles of Plant: 7.0 (coaxial); None (fiber optic). Homes passed: 535. Total homes in franchised area: 535.
Manager: David Ferris. Chief Technician: John Borland.
City fee: None.
Ownership: Lenox Municipal Cablevision.

LIBERTYVILLE—Formerly served by Westcom. No longer in operation. ICA: IA0570.

LISCOMB—Formerly served by New Path Communications LC. No longer in operation. ICA: IA0571.

LITTLE ROCK—Premier Communications, PO Box 200, 339 1st Ave NE, Sioux Center, IA 51250. Phones: 800-642-4088; 712-722-3451. Fax: 712-722-1113. E-mail: dboone@mtcnet.net. Web Site: http://www.mypremieronline.com. ICA: IA0292.
TV Market Ranking: Outside TV Markets (LITTLE ROCK). Franchise award date: N.A. Franchise expiration date: N.A. Began: January 1, 1984.
Channel capacity: N.A. Channels available but not in use: N.A.

Basic Service
Subscribers: 117.
Programming (received off-air): KCAU-TV (ABC) Sioux City; KDLT-TV (NBC) Sioux Falls; KELO-TV (CBS, MNT) Sioux Falls; KPTH (FOX, MNT) Sioux City; KSFY-TV (ABC) Sioux Falls; KSIN-TV (PBS) Sioux City; KTIV (CW, NBC) Sioux City.
Programming (via satellite): ABC Family Channel; Arts & Entertainment; CNN; C-SPAN; Discovery Channel; Disney Channel; ESPN; ESPN 2; Fox News Channel; Great American Country; Hallmark Channel; Headline News; HGTV; History Channel; Lifetime; Nickelodeon; Speed Channel; Spike TV; TBS Superstation; The Learning Channel; Trinity Broadcasting Network; Turner Network TV; TV Land; USA Network; Weather Channel; WGN America.
Current originations: Public Access.
Fee: $16.00 installation; $21.95 monthly.

Pay Service 1
Pay Units: 13.
Programming (via satellite): HBO; Showtime.
Fee: $16.00 installation; $8.95 monthly (each).

Video-On-Demand: No

Internet Service
Operational: Yes, Both DSL & dial-up.
Broadband Service: Premier Internet.
Fee: $50.00 installation; $47.50 monthly.

Telephone Service
Digital: Operational

Miles of Plant: 4.0 (coaxial); None (fiber optic). Homes passed: 253.
Chief Executive Officer: Douglas A. Boone. Chief Technician: Leslie Sybesma. Marketing Director: Scott Te Stroete.
Ownership: Premier Communications Inc. (MSO).

LITTLE SIOUX—Formerly served by TelePartners. No longer in operation. ICA: IA0333.

LITTLETON—Farmers Mutual Cooperative Telephone Co. Now served by JESUP, IA [IA0116]. ICA: IA0467.

LIVERMORE—Milford Cable TV, PO Box 163, 806 Okoboji Ave, Milford, IA 51351. Phone: 712-338-4967. Fax: 712-338-4719. E-mail: mplagman@milfordcable.net. Web Site: http://www.milfordcable.net. ICA: IA0320.
TV Market Ranking: Outside TV Markets (LIVERMORE). Franchise award date: November 2, 1980. Franchise expiration date: N.A. Began: February 1, 1981.
Channel capacity: 52 (operating 2-way). Channels available but not in use: 19.

Basic Service
Subscribers: 105.
Programming (received off-air): KCCI (CBS) Des Moines; KCWI-TV (CW) Ames;

KDSM-TV (FOX) Des Moines; KEYC-TV (CBS, FOX) Mankato; KTIN (PBS) Fort Dodge; WHO-DT (NBC) Des Moines; WOI-DT (ABC) Ames.
Programming (via satellite): C-SPAN; C-SPAN 2; Eternal Word TV Network; Home Shopping Network; MyNetworkTV Inc.; QVC; Trinity Broadcasting Network; Weather Channel.
Fee: $25.00 installation; $26.50 monthly; $2.00 converter.

Expanded Basic Service 1
Subscribers: 95.
Programming (via satellite): ABC Family Channel; Animal Planet; Arts & Entertainment; Big Ten Network; Bravo; Cartoon Network; CNBC; CNN; Comedy Central; Country Music TV; Discovery Channel; Discovery Health Channel; Do-It-Yourself; ESPN; ESPN 2; Food Network; Fox Movie Channel; Fox News Channel; Fox Sports Net North; FX; G4; Great American Country; Hallmark Channel; HGTV; History Channel; ION Television; Lifetime; MSNBC; MTV; National Geographic Channel; Nickelodeon; Radar Channel; RFD-TV; Speed Channel; Spike TV; Syfy; TBS Superstation; The Learning Channel; Travel Channel; Turner Classic Movies; Turner Network TV; TV Land; USA Network; VH1; WGN America.
Fee: $17.25 monthly.

Pay Service 1
Pay Units: N.A.
Programming (via satellite): Cinemax; Encore; HBO; Showtime; Starz.
Fee: $10.00 installation; $9.63 monthly each (Cinemax & Starz/Encore), $10.17 monthly (Showtime), $10.70 monthly (HBO).

Video-On-Demand: No

Internet Service
Operational: Yes.
Broadband Service: Milford Cable.
Fee: $25.95-$45.00 monthly.

Telephone Service
None
Miles of Plant: 5.0 (coaxial); None (fiber optic). Additional miles planned: 8.0 (coaxial). Homes passed: 186. Total homes in franchised area: 189.
General Manager & Chief Technician: Matt Plagman.
Ownership: Livermore Cable.

LOCKRIDGE—Formerly served by Westcom. No longer in operation. ICA: IA0572.

LOGAN—Long Lines, 501 4th St, Sergeant Bluff, IA 51054-8509. Phones: 712-884-2203; 712-271-4000. Fax: 712-271-2727. Web Site: http://www.longlines.com. Also serves Magnolia & Woodbine. ICA: IA0155.
TV Market Ranking: 53 (LOGAN, Magnolia); Outside TV Markets (Woodbine). Franchise award date: May 1, 1982. Franchise expiration date: N.A. Began: November 27, 1982.
Channel capacity: 54 (not 2-way capable). Channels available but not in use: N.A.

Basic Service
Subscribers: 613.
Programming (received off-air): KCAU-TV (ABC) Sioux City; KMEG (CBS) Sioux City; KPTH (FOX, MNT) Sioux City; KSIN-TV (PBS) Sioux City; KTIV (CW, NBC) Sioux City; KXVO (CW) Omaha.
Programming (via satellite): ABC Family Channel; AMC; AmericanLife TV Network; Animal Planet; Arts & Entertainment; Big Ten Network; Cartoon Network; CNBC; CNN; Comedy Central; Country Music TV; C-SPAN; C-SPAN 2; Discovery Channel; Disney Channel; E! Entertainment Television; ESPN; ESPN 2; ESPN Classic Sports; Eternal Word TV Network; Food Network; Fox News Channel; Fox Sports Net North; FX; Golf Channel; Hallmark Channel; Headline News; HGTV; History Channel; Home Shopping Network; INSP; Lifetime; Lifetime Movie Network; MSNBC; MTV; Nickelodeon; QVC; Speed Channel; Spike TV; Syfy; TBS Superstation; The Learning Channel; The Sportsman Channel; Travel Channel; Trinity Broadcasting Network; truTV; Turner Classic Movies; Turner Network TV; TuTv; TV Guide Network; TV Land; USA Network; VH1; Weather Channel; WGN America.
Current originations: Religious Access; Public Access.
Fee: $39.00 installation; $41.99 monthly; $10.00 additional installation.

Digital Basic Service
Subscribers: N.A.
Programming (via satellite): BBC America; Bio; Cooking Channel; Discovery Health Channel; Discovery Kids Channel; Discovery Military Channel; Discovery Planet Green; DMX Music; Do-It-Yourself; ESPN U; ESPNews; FitTV; Fox College Sports Atlantic; Fox College Sports Central; Fox College Sports Pacific; Fox Movie Channel; Fox Soccer; G4; Great American Country; GSN; Halogen Network; History Channel International; ID Investigation Discovery; Independent Film Channel; Lifetime Real Women; MTV Hits; MTV Jams; MTV2; Nick Jr.; NickToons TV; Outdoor Channel; RFD-TV; Science Channel; SoapNet; TeenNick; Toon Disney; Versus; VH1 Classic; VH1 Country; VH1 Soul; WE tv.
Fee: $9.99 monthly.

Digital Expanded Basic Service
Subscribers: N.A.
Programming (via satellite): Bandamax; De Pelicula; De Pelicula Clasico; Discovery en Espanol; ESPN Deportes; Fox Sports en Espanol; Ritmoson Latino; Telehit.
Fee: $2.95 monthly.

Digital Expanded Basic Service 2
Subscribers: N.A.
Programming (received off-air): KCAU-TV (ABC) Sioux City; KMTV-TV (CBS) Omaha; KPTM (FOX, MNT) Omaha; KTIV (CW, NBC) Sioux City; KYNE-TV (PBS) Omaha.
Programming (via satellite): Big Ten Network HD; Discovery Channel HD; ESPN 2 HD; ESPN HD; HDNet; HDNet Movies; Outdoor Channel 2 HD.
Fee: $9.95 monthly.

Pay Service 1
Pay Units: 43.
Programming (via satellite): Flix; Showtime (multiplexed); The Movie Channel.
Fee: $14.45 monthly.

Pay Service 2
Pay Units: 23.
Programming (via satellite): HBO (multiplexed).
Fee: $14.95 monthly.

Digital Pay Service 1
Pay Units: N.A.
Programming (via satellite): Cinemax (multiplexed); Cinemax HD; Encore (multiplexed); Flix; HBO (multiplexed); HBO HD; Showtime (multiplexed); Starz (multiplexed); Starz HDTV; The Movie Channel (multiplexed).
Fee: $11.95 monthly (Cinemax), $13.95 monthly (Starz/Encore), $14.45 monthly (Showtime/TMC/Flix), $14.95 monthly (HBO).

Video-On-Demand: Yes

Internet Service
Operational: No.
Miles of Plant: 24.0 (coaxial); None (fiber optic). Homes passed: 1,198.
Chief Executive Officer: Jon Winkel. Chief Operating Officer: Paul Bergmann. Vice President, Sales: Bill Gaukel.
City fee: 3% of gross.
Ownership: Long Lines (MSO).

LOHRVILLE—Formerly served by Tele-Services Ltd. No longer in operation. ICA: IA0468.

LOST NATION—LN Satellite Communications Co., PO Box 97, 304 Long Ave, Lost Nation, IA 52254-0097. Phone: 563-678-2470. Fax: 563-678-2300. E-mail: lnation@netins.net. Web Site: http://www.lnetelco.com. Also serves Elwood & Oxford Junction. ICA: IA0279. **Note:** This system is an overbuild.
TV Market Ranking: 60 (Elwood, LOST NATION, Oxford Junction). Franchise award date: August 22, 1983. Franchise expiration date: N.A. Began: January 15, 1984.
Channel capacity: 64 (not 2-way capable). Channels available but not in use: N.A.

Basic Service
Subscribers: 500.
Programming (received off-air): KCRG-TV (ABC) Cedar Rapids; KFXA (FOX) Cedar Rapids; KGAN (CBS) Cedar Rapids; KIIN (PBS) Iowa City; KLJB (CW, FOX) Davenport; KWKB (CW, MNT) Iowa City; KWQC-TV (NBC) Davenport; KWWL (NBC) Waterloo; WHBF-TV (CBS) Rock Island; WQAD-TV (ABC) Moline.
Programming (via satellite): ABC Family Channel; AMC; AmericanLife TV Network; Animal Planet; Arts & Entertainment; Cartoon Network; CNBC; CNN; Comedy Central; Country Music TV; C-SPAN; Discovery Channel; Disney Channel; E! Entertainment Television; ESPN; ESPN 2; ESPN Classic Sports; Food Network; Fox News Channel; FX; Great American Country; GSN; Hallmark Channel; HGTV; History Channel; Home Shopping Network; INSP; ION Television; Lifetime; MTV; Nickelodeon; Outdoor Channel; QVC; Speed Channel; Spike TV; Syfy; TBS Superstation; The Learning Channel; Travel Channel; Trinity Broadcasting Network; Turner Classic Movies; Turner Network TV; TV Land; USA Network; VH1; Weather Channel; WGN America.
Current originations: Government Access; Public Access.
Fee: $10.00 installation; $34.95 monthly.

Pay Service 1
Pay Units: 51.
Programming (via satellite): Cinemax.
Fee: $7.00 monthly.

Pay Service 2
Pay Units: 44.
Programming (via satellite): HBO.
Fee: $12.50 monthly.

Pay Service 3
Pay Units: 27.
Programming (via satellite): Showtime.
Fee: $7.00 monthly.

Internet Service
Operational: No, DSL.

Telephone Service
None
Miles of Plant: 17.0 (coaxial); None (fiber optic). Homes passed: 602.
President: Alvin Weirup. General Manager: Glenn Short.
Ownership: Lost Nation-Elwood Telephone Co.

LOWDEN—F & B Cablevision, PO Box 309, 103 Main St N, Wheatland, IA 52777-0309. Phone: 563-374-1236. Fax: 563-374-1930. E-mail: info@fbc.bz. Web Site: http://www.fbc.bz. ICA: IA0556.
TV Market Ranking: 60,65 (LOWDEN). Franchise award date: N.A. Franchise expiration date: N.A. Began: April 1, 1994.
Channel capacity: N.A. Channels available but not in use: N.A.

Digital Basic Service
Subscribers: N.A.
Programming (received off-air): KCRG-TV (ABC) Cedar Rapids; KGAN (CBS) Cedar Rapids; KGCW (CW) Burlington; KIIN (PBS) Iowa City; KLJB (CW, FOX) Davenport; KPXR-TV (ION) Cedar Rapids; KWKB (CW, MNT) Iowa City; KWQC-TV (NBC) Davenport; KWWF (IND) Waterloo [LICENSED & SILENT]; KWWL (NBC) Waterloo; WHBF-TV (CBS) Rock Island; WQAD-TV (ABC) Moline; WQPT-TV (PBS) Moline.
Programming (via satellite): Bloomberg Television; CNN International; C-SPAN 2; Headline News; History Channel International; Home Shopping Network; INSP; KFXA (FOX) Cedar Rapids; QVC; Radar Channel; ShopNBC; SoapNet; Trinity Broadcasting Network; WGN America.
Fee: $23.99 monthly.

Digital Expanded Basic Service
Subscribers: N.A.
Programming (via satellite): ABC Family Channel; AMC; Animal Planet; Arts & Entertainment; Big Ten Network; Bio; Boomerang; Bravo; Cartoon Network; CNBC; CNN; Comcast SportsNet Chicago; Comedy Central; Cooking Channel; Country Music TV; C-SPAN; Discovery Channel; Discovery Health Channel; Disney Channel; Do-It-Yourself; E! Entertainment Television; ESPN; ESPN 2; ESPN Classic Sports; ESPNews; Food Network; Fox News Channel; Fox Sports Net Midwest; FX; G4; Golf Channel; Great American Country; GSN; Hallmark Channel; HGTV; History Channel; Lifetime; Lifetime Movie Network; MSNBC; MTV; Music Choice; National Geographic Channel; Nickelodeon; Outdoor Channel; Oxygen; RFD-TV; Speed Channel; Spike TV; Syfy; TBS Superstation; The Learning Channel; Travel Channel; truTV; Turner Classic Movies; Turner Network TV; TV Land; USA Network; VH1; WE tv; Weather Channel.
Fee: $26.00 monthly.

Digital Pay Service 1
Pay Units: N.A.
Programming (via satellite): Cinemax (multiplexed); Encore (multiplexed); Flix; HBO (multiplexed); Showtime (multiplexed); Starz (multiplexed); Sundance Channel; The Movie Channel (multiplexed).
Fee: $15.00 monthly (each).

Pay-Per-View
Movies (delivered digitally); Special events (delivered digitally); ESPN (delivered digitally).

Internet Service
Operational: No, Both DSL & dial-up.

Telephone Service
None
Miles of Plant: 4.0 (coaxial); 16.0 (fiber optic). Homes passed: 350.
Manager: Ken Laursen. Plant Manager: Jan Muhl. Marketing Manager: Aaron Horman. Office Manager: Julie Steines.
Ownership: Farmers' & Businessmen's Telephone Co. (MSO).

LU VERNE—Signal Inc., PO Box 435, West Bend, IA 50597. Phone: 515-887-4591. E-mail: msignal@ncn.net. ICA: IA0342.

TV Market Ranking: Outside TV Markets (LU VERNE). Franchise award date: N.A. Franchise expiration date: N.A. Began: September 1, 1968.

Channel capacity: 78 (operating 2-way). Channels available but not in use: N.A.

Basic Service

Subscribers: 90.

Programming (received off-air): KAAL (ABC) Austin; KCCI (CBS) Des Moines; KCWI-TV (CW) Ames; KDIN-TV (PBS) Des Moines; KDSM-TV (FOX) Des Moines; KEYC-TV (CBS, FOX) Mankato; KIMT (CBS, MNT) Mason City; KTTC (CW, NBC) Rochester; WHO-DT (NBC) Des Moines; WOI-DT (ABC) Ames; allband FM.

Fee: $50.00 installation; $50.00 monthly.

Pay Service 1

Pay Units: 1.

Programming (via satellite): HBO.

Miles of Plant: 3.0 (coaxial); None (fiber optic). Homes passed: 110.

Manager: Michael Steil.

City fee: None.

Ownership: Signal Inc.

LUCAS—Telnet South LC. Now served by DES MOINES, IA [IA0001]. ICA: IA0573.

LUXEMBURG—New Century Communications, 3588 Kennebec Dr, Eagan, MN 55122-1001. Phone: 651-688-2623. Fax: 651-688-2624. E-mail: tanderson@cablesystemservices.com. Also serves Holy Cross & New Vienna. ICA: IA0554.

TV Market Ranking: Below 100 (Holy Cross, LUXEMBURG, New Vienna). Franchise award date: February 6, 1989. Franchise expiration date: N.A. Began: November 14, 1989.

Channel capacity: 35 (not 2-way capable). Channels available but not in use: 3.

Basic Service

Subscribers: 237.

Programming (received off-air): KCRG-TV (ABC) Cedar Rapids; KFXA (FOX) Cedar Rapids; KGAN (CBS) Cedar Rapids; KIIN (PBS) Iowa City; KPXR-TV (ION) Cedar Rapids; KWKB (CW, MNT) Iowa City; KWWL (NBC) Waterloo.

Programming (via satellite): ABC Family Channel; AMC; Arts & Entertainment; CNN; Discovery Channel; Disney Channel; Do-It-Yourself; ESPN; ESPN 2; Eternal Word TV Network; Headline News; History Channel; Lifetime; MTV; Nickelodeon; QVC; Spike TV; TBS Superstation; The Learning Channel; Turner Classic Movies; Turner Network TV; USA Network; VH1; Weather Channel; WGN America.

Current originations: Public Access.

Fee: $30.00 installation; $23.45 monthly.

Pay Service 1

Pay Units: 17.

Programming (via satellite): Cinemax.

Fee: $10.00 monthly.

Pay Service 2

Pay Units: 15.

Programming (via satellite): HBO.

Fee: $10.00 monthly.

Pay Service 3

Pay Units: 8.

Programming (via satellite): Showtime.

Fee: $10.00 monthly.

Video-On-Demand: No

Internet Service

Operational: No.

Telephone Service

None

Miles of Plant: 19.0 (coaxial); None (fiber optic). Homes passed: 378.

Executive Vice President: Marty Walch. General Manager & Chief Technician: Todd Anderson.

Ownership: New Century Communications (MSO).

LYTTON—Formerly served by TelePartners. No longer in operation. ICA: IA0328.

MALVERN—Our Cable, PO Box 190, 112 E Main St, Breda, IA 51436-0190. Phone: 877-873-8715. E-mail: info@ourcableia.com. Web Site: http://ourcableia.com. ICA: IA0471.

TV Market Ranking: 53 (MALVERN). Franchise award date: N.A. Franchise expiration date: N.A. Began: January 1, 1985.

Channel capacity: N.A. Channels available but not in use: N.A.

Basic Service

Subscribers: N.A. Included in Breda

Programming (received off-air): KETV (ABC) Omaha; KHIN (PBS) Red Oak; KMTV-TV (CBS) Omaha; KPTM (FOX, MNT) Omaha; KXVO (CW) Omaha; KYNE-TV (PBS) Omaha; WOWT-TV (IND, NBC) Omaha.

Programming (via satellite): ABC Family Channel; Arts & Entertainment; CNN; Country Music TV; Discovery Channel; Disney Channel; ESPN; ESPN 2; Headline News; HGTV; Lifetime; Spike TV; Syfy; TBS Superstation; The Learning Channel; Trinity Broadcasting Network; Turner Network TV; TV Land; USA Network; WGN America.

Fee: $20.00 installation; $26.45 monthly.

Pay Service 1

Pay Units: N.A.

Programming (via satellite): Showtime.

Fee: $10.95 monthly.

Video-On-Demand: No

Internet Service

Operational: No.

Telephone Service

None

Chief Executive Officer: Steve Frickenstein. Chief Technician: Mike Ludwig. Marketing & Sales Manager: Megan Badding.

City fee: 3% of gross.

Ownership: Our Cable (MSO).

MANILLA—Manilla Municipal Cable. Now served by EARLING, IA [IA0302]. ICA: IA0202.

MANNING—Manning Municipal Cable TV, PO Box 386, 719 3rd St, Manning, IA 51455. Phone: 712-655-2660. Fax: 712-655-3304. E-mail: info@mmctsu.com. Web Site: http://www.mmctsu.com. ICA: IA0145.

TV Market Ranking: Outside TV Markets (MANNING). Franchise award date: N.A. Franchise expiration date: N.A. Began: October 1, 1982.

Channel capacity: 69 (operating 2-way). Channels available but not in use: N.A.

Basic Service

Subscribers: 562.

Programming (received off-air): KCCI (CBS) Des Moines; KDIN-TV (PBS) Des Moines; KDSM-TV (FOX) Des Moines; KETV (ABC) Omaha; KMTV-TV (CBS) Omaha; KPTM (FOX, MNT) Omaha; KTVO (ABC) Kirksville; WHO-DT (NBC) Des Moines; WOI-DT (ABC) Ames; WOWT-TV (IND, NBC) Omaha; allband FM.

Programming (via satellite): ABC Family Channel; AMC; Animal Planet; Arts & Entertainment; CNN; Comedy Central; Country Music TV; Discovery Channel; Disney Channel; Encore Westerns; ESPN; ESPN 2; ESPN Classic Sports; Eternal Word TV Network; Food Network; Fox News Channel; Fox Sports Net; FX; Golf Channel; Hallmark Channel; Headline News; HGTV; History Channel; Lifetime; MSNBC; MTV; Nickelodeon; Outdoor Channel; QVC; RFD-TV; SoapNet; Speed Channel; Spike TV; Syfy; TBS Superstation; The Learning Channel; Toon Disney; Travel Channel; Trinity Broadcasting Network; Turner Classic Movies; Turner Network TV; TV Guide Network; TV Land; USA Network; Versus; VH1; Weather Channel; WGN America.

Current originations: Leased Access; Religious Access; Government Access; Educational Access; Public Access.

Fee: $15.00 installation; $34.95 monthly.

Pay Service 1

Pay Units: 97.

Programming (via satellite): Cinemax.

Fee: $9.50 monthly.

Pay Service 2

Pay Units: 77.

Programming (via satellite): HBO (multiplexed).

Fee: $9.50 monthly.

Pay Service 3

Pay Units: N.A.

Programming (via satellite): Showtime; Starz; The Movie Channel.

Video-On-Demand: No

Internet Service

Operational: Yes.

Broadband Service: Long Lines Internet.

Fee: $33.00 installation; $29.95-$79.95 monthly.

Telephone Service

None

Miles of Plant: 18.0 (coaxial); 3.0 (fiber optic). Homes passed: 670. Total homes in franchised area: 670.

Manager: Wendel Kahl.

Ownership: Manning Municipal Communication & TV System Utility.

MAPLETON—Long Lines, 501 4th St, Sergeant Bluff, IA 51054-8509. Phones: 712-884-2203; 712-271-4000. Fax: 712-271-2727. E-mail: info@longlines.com. Web Site: http://www.longlines.com. ICA: IA0153.

TV Market Ranking: Outside TV Markets (MAPLETON). Franchise award date: N.A. Franchise expiration date: N.A. Began: November 15, 1983.

Channel capacity: 36 (2-way capable). Channels available but not in use: 19.

Basic Service

Subscribers: 522.

Programming (received off-air): KCAU-TV (ABC) Sioux City; KMEG (CBS) Sioux City; KPTH (FOX, MNT) Sioux City; KSIN-TV (PBS) Sioux City; KTIV (CW, NBC) Sioux City; KXVO (CW) Omaha.

Programming (via satellite): ABC Family Channel; AMC; AmericanLife TV Network; Animal Planet; Arts & Entertainment; Big Ten Network; Cartoon Network; CNBC; CNN; Comedy Central; Country Music TV; C-SPAN; C-SPAN 2; Discovery Channel; Disney Channel; E! Entertainment Television; ESPN; ESPN 2; ESPN Classic Sports; Eternal Word TV Network; Food Network; Fox News Channel; Fox Sports Net North; FX; Golf Channel; Hallmark Channel; Headline News; HGTV; History Channel; Home Shopping Network; INSP; Lifetime; Lifetime Movie Network; MSNBC; MTV; Nickelodeon; QVC; Speed Channel; Spike TV; Syfy; TBS Superstation; The Learning Channel; The Sportsman Channel; Travel Channel; Trinity Broadcasting Network; truTV; Turner Classic Movies; Turner Network TV; TuTv; TV Guide Network; TV Land; USA Network; VH1; Weather Channel; WGN America.

Current originations: Public Access.

Fee: $15.00 installation; $41.99 monthly.

Digital Basic Service

Subscribers: N.A.

Programming (via satellite): BBC America; Bio; Cooking Channel; Discovery Health Channel; Discovery Kids Channel; Discovery Military Channel; Discovery Planet Green; DMX Music; Do-It-Yourself; ESPN U; ESPNews; FitTV; Fox College Sports Atlantic; Fox College Sports Central; Fox College Sports Pacific; Fox Movie Channel; Fox Soccer; G4; Great American Country; GSN; Halogen Network; History Channel International; ID Investigation Discovery; Independent Film Channel; Lifetime Real Women; MTV Hits; MTV Jams; MTV2; Nick Jr.; NickToons TV; Outdoor Channel; RFD-TV; Science Channel; SoapNet; TeenNick; Toon Disney; Versus; VH1 Classic; VH1 Country; VH1 Soul; WE tv.

Fee: $9.99 monthly.

Digital Expanded Basic Service

Subscribers: N.A.

Programming (via satellite): Bandamax; De Pelicula; De Pelicula Clasico; Discovery en Espanol; ESPN Deportes; Fox Sports en Espanol; Ritmoson Latino; Telehit.

Fee: $2.95 monthly.

Digital Expanded Basic Service 2

Subscribers: N.A.

Programming (received off-air): KCAU-TV (ABC) Sioux City; KMEG (CBS) Sioux City; KPTM (FOX, MNT) Omaha; KSIN-TV (PBS) Sioux City; KTIV (CW, NBC) Sioux City.

Programming (via satellite): Big Ten Network HD; Discovery Channel HD; ESPN 2 HD; ESPN HD; HDNet; HDNet Movies; Outdoor Channel 2 HD.

Fee: $9.95 monthly.

Pay Service 1

Pay Units: 5.

Programming (via satellite): Flix; Showtime (multiplexed); The Movie Channel (multiplexed).

Fee: $14.45 monthly.

Pay Service 2

Pay Units: 63.

Programming (via satellite): HBO (multiplexed).

Fee: $14.95 monthly.

Digital Pay Service 1

Pay Units: N.A.

Programming (via satellite): Cinemax (multiplexed); Cinemax HD; Encore (mul-

tiplexed); Flix; HBO (multiplexed); HBO HD; Showtime (multiplexed); Starz (multiplexed); Starz HDTV; The Movie Channel (multiplexed).
Fee: $11.95 monthly (Cinemax), $13.95 monthly (Starz/Encore), $14.45 monthly (Showtime/TMC/Flix), $14.95 monthly (HBO).
Video-On-Demand: Yes
Internet Service
Operational: No, Both DSL & dialup.
Telephone Service
None
Miles of Plant: 8.0 (coaxial); None (fiber optic). Homes passed: 650.
Manager: Paul Bergmann. Marketing Manager: Pat McElry. System Engineer: Tony Seubert. Office Manager: Denise Mobery.
Ownership: Mapleton Communications Inc.; Long Lines (MSO).

MARBLE ROCK—Omnitel Communications. Now served by RUDD, IA [IA0503]. ICA: IA0473.

MARCUS—WesTel Systems, PO Box 330, 012 E 3rd St, Remsen, IA 51050. Phone: 712-786-1181. Fax: 712-786-2400. E-mail: acctinfo@westelsystems.com. Web Site: http://www.westelsystems.com. Also serves Calumet, Larrabee, Peterson, Remsen, Sioux Rapids & Sutherland. ICA: IA0171.
TV Market Ranking: Below 100 (Remsen); Outside TV Markets (Calumet, Larrabee, MARCUS, Peterson, Peterson, Sioux Rapids, Sutherland). Franchise award date: N.A. Franchise expiration date: N.A. Began: October 1, 1982.
Channel capacity: N.A. Channels available but not in use: N.A.
Basic Service
Subscribers: 329.
Programming (received off-air): KCAU-TV (ABC) Sioux City; KELO-TV (CBS, MNT) Sioux Falls; KMEG (CBS) Sioux City; KPTH (FOX, MNT) Sioux City; KSFY-TV (ABC) Sioux Falls; KSIN-TV (PBS) Sioux City; KTIV (CW, NBC) Sioux City.
Programming (via satellite): ABC Family Channel; AMC; Animal Planet; Arts & Entertainment; Big Ten Network; CNN; Comedy Central; Country Music TV; CW+; Discovery Channel; Disney Channel; Do-It-Yourself; ESPN; ESPN 2; ESPN Classic Sports; Food Network; Fox News Channel; FX; Great American Country; GSN; HGTV; History Channel; Lifetime; MTV; Nickelodeon; QVC; Speed Channel; Spike TV; Syfy; TBS Superstation; The Learning Channel; Travel Channel; Turner Network TV; TV Guide Network; TV Land; USA Network; Versus; VH1; WE tv; Weather Channel; WGN America.
Fee: $19.95 installation; $9.50 monthly.
Digital Basic Service
Subscribers: N.A.
Programming (received off-air): KCAU-TV (ABC) Sioux City; KMEG (CBS) Sioux City; KPTH (FOX, MNT) Sioux City; KTIV (CW, NBC) Sioux City.
Programming (via satellite): BBC America; Bio; Bloomberg Television; CMT Pure Country; Discovery Health Channel; Discovery Kids Channel; Discovery Military Channel; Discovery Planet Green; DMX Music; ESPN Classic Sports; ESPNews; FitTV; Fox Movie Channel; Fox Soccer; Fuse; Golf Channel; History Channel International; ID Investigation Discovery; Lifetime Movie Network; MTV Hits; MTV2; Nick Jr.; NickToons TV; Outdoor Channel; PBS HD; RFD-TV; Science Channel; ShopNBC; Sleuth; SoapNet; Style Network; TeenNick; The Word Network; Toon Disney; Trinity Broadcasting Network; Turner Classic Movies; VH1 Classic; VH1 Soul.
Pay Service 1
Pay Units: N.A.
Programming (via satellite): HBO.
Fee: $10.00 installation; $9.95 monthly.
Digital Pay Service 1
Pay Units: N.A.
Programming (via satellite): Cinemax (multiplexed); Encore (multiplexed); Flix; HBO (multiplexed); Showtime (multiplexed); Starz (multiplexed); The Movie Channel (multiplexed).
Video-On-Demand: No
Pay-Per-View
iN DEMAND (delivered digitally).
Internet Service
Operational: Yes.
Telephone Service
None
Miles of Plant: 8.0 (coaxial); None (fiber optic). Additional miles planned: 1.0 (coaxial). Homes passed: 556.
Manager & Chief Executive Officer: Jim Sherburn. Chief Technician: Rich Barnholdt.
City fee: None.
Ownership: West Iowa Telephone Co. (MSO).

MARSHALLTOWN—Mediacom. Now served by AMES, IA [IA0008]. ICA: IA0012.

MARTELLE—Martelle Communications Co-op, PO Box 128, 204 South St, Martelle, IA 52305-0128. Phone: 319-482-2381. Fax: 319-482-3018. E-mail: martelle@netins.net. Also serves Fairview, Morley & Stone City. ICA: IA0262.
TV Market Ranking: 65 (Fairview, MARTELLE, Morley, Stone City). Franchise award date: February 1, 1990. Franchise expiration date: N.A. Began: February 1, 1990.
Channel capacity: 36 (not 2-way capable). Channels available but not in use: 1.
Basic Service
Subscribers: 500.
Programming (received off-air): KCRG-TV (ABC) Cedar Rapids; KFXA (FOX) Cedar Rapids; KGAN (CBS) Cedar Rapids; KIIN (PBS) Iowa City; KPXR-TV (ION) Cedar Rapids; KWWL (NBC) Waterloo.
Programming (via satellite): ABC Family Channel; AMC; Arts & Entertainment; CNN; Comedy Central; Country Music TV; Discovery Channel; Disney Channel; ESPN; ESPN 2; Fox Sports Net Midwest; HGTV; History Channel; National Geographic Channel; Nickelodeon; Spike TV; Syfy; TBS Superstation; The Learning Channel; Turner Classic Movies; Turner Network TV; TV Land; USA Network; WGN America.
Current originations: Educational Access.
Planned originations: Government Access; Public Access.
Fee: $30.00 installation; $27.00 monthly.
Pay Service 1
Pay Units: 200.
Programming (via satellite): HBO.
Fee: $10.00 monthly.
Pay Service 2
Pay Units: 60.
Programming (via satellite): Showtime.
Fee: $9.95 monthly.
Internet Service
Operational: Yes, Both DSL & dial-up.
Subscribers: 525.
Fee: $30.00 installation; $27.00 monthly.
Miles of Plant: 65.0 (coaxial); None (fiber optic). Homes passed: 1,500. Total homes in franchised area: 1,500.
Manager: Sandra M. Davis. Chief Technician & Program Director: Allen H. Heefner.
Ownership: Martelle Cooperative Telephone Association.

MARTENSDALE—Interstate Communications. Now served by TRURO, IA [IA0344]. ICA: IA0474.

MASON CITY—Mediacom, 4010 Alexandra Dr, Waterloo, IA 50702. Phone: 319-235-2197. Fax: 319-232-7841. Web Site: http://www.mediacomcable.com. Also serves Britt, Cerro Gordo, Clear Lake, Duncan, Forest City, Garner, Kensett, Leland, Manly, Northwood & Ventura. ICA: IA0010.
TV Market Ranking: Below 100 (Britt, Cerro Gordo, Clear Lake, Duncan, Forest City, Garner, Kensett, Leland, Manly, MASON CITY, Northwood, Ventura). Franchise award date: N.A. Franchise expiration date: N.A. Began: November 1, 1980.
Channel capacity: N.A. Channels available but not in use: N.A.
Basic Service
Subscribers: 18,229.
Programming (received off-air): KAAL (ABC) Austin; KIMT (CBS, MNT) Mason City; KSMQ-TV (PBS) Austin; KTTC (CW, NBC) Rochester; KXLT-TV (FOX) Rochester; KYIN (PBS) Mason City.
Programming (via satellite): CNBC; Country Music TV; C-SPAN; Discovery Channel; Headline News; MTV; TBS Superstation; Weather Channel; WGN America.
Current originations: Public Access.
Fee: $60.00 installation; $10.57 monthly; $.70 converter; $50.00 additional installation.
Expanded Basic Service 1
Subscribers: 15,331.
Programming (via satellite): ABC Family Channel; AMC; Animal Planet; Arts & Entertainment; Bravo; Cartoon Network; CNN; Comedy Central; C-SPAN 2; Disney Channel; E! Entertainment Television; ESPN; Eternal Word TV Network; FitTV; Fox News Channel; Fox Sports Net North; FX; Golf Channel; Hallmark Channel; HGTV; History Channel; Home Shopping Network; INSP; ION Television; Lifetime; MoviePlex; MSNBC; Nickelodeon; Oxygen; Speed Channel; Spike TV; Syfy; Telemundo; The Learning Channel; Travel Channel; Trinity Broadcasting Network; truTV; Turner Classic Movies; Turner Network TV; TV Guide Network; TV Land; USA Network; VH1; WE tv.
Fee: $28.27 monthly.
Digital Basic Service
Subscribers: N.A.
Programming (via satellite): American-Life TV Network; BBC America; Bio; Bloomberg Television; Discovery Digital Networks; DMX Music; Fox Movie Channel; Fox Sports World; Fuse; G4; GAS; GSN; Halogen Network; History Channel International; Independent Film Channel; Lifetime Movie Network; Lime; MTV Networks Digital Suite; National Geographic Channel; Nick Jr.; Outdoor Channel; Ovation; Style Network; Toon Disney; Turner Classic Movies; Versus.
Digital Pay Service 1
Pay Units: 2,296.
Programming (via satellite): Cinemax (multiplexed); Encore (multiplexed); HBO (multiplexed); Showtime (multiplexed); Starz (multiplexed); The Movie Channel (multiplexed).
Fee: $9.95 monthly (Cinemax, HBO, Showtime, TMC, or Starz/Encore).
Video-On-Demand: Yes
Pay-Per-View
ESPN Now (delivered digitally); ETC (delivered digitally); Playboy TV (delivered digitally); Pleasure (delivered digitally); Fresh (delivered digitally); Shorteez (delivered digitally); TVN Entertainment (delivered digitally); sports (delivered digitally).
Internet Service
Operational: Yes.
Broadband Service: Mediacom High Speed Internet.
Fee: $49.95 installation; $29.95 monthly; $10.00 modem lease.
Telephone Service
Analog: Not Operational
Digital: Operational
Miles of Plant: 312.0 (coaxial); None (fiber optic). Homes passed: 23,034.
Regional Vice President: Doug Frank. General Manager: Doug Nix. Technical Operations Director: Greg Nank. Marketing Director: Steve Schuh. Marketing Coordinator: Joni Lindauer.
Ownership: Mediacom LLC (MSO).

MASSENA—B & L Technologies LLC, 3329 270th St, Lenox, IA 50851. Phones: 800-798-5488; 641-348-2240. Fax: 641-348-2240. ICA: IA0306.
TV Market Ranking: Outside TV Markets (MASSENA). Franchise award date: N.A. Franchise expiration date: N.A. Began: May 1, 1983.
Channel capacity: 36 (not 2-way capable). Channels available but not in use: 24.
Basic Service
Subscribers: 62.
Programming (received off-air): KCCI (CBS) Des Moines; KDIN-TV (PBS) Des Moines; KDSM-TV (FOX) Des Moines; KETV (ABC) Omaha; KXVO (CW) Omaha; WHO-DT (NBC) Des Moines; WOI-DT (ABC) Ames; WOWT-TV (IND, NBC) Omaha.
Programming (via satellite): CNN; ESPN; Nickelodeon; TBS Superstation; Turner Network TV; WGN America.
Fee: $15.00 installation; $22.31 monthly.
Pay Service 1
Pay Units: 50.
Programming (via satellite): Cinemax; HBO.
Fee: $11.00 monthly (Cinemax), $12.95 monthly (HBO).
Video-On-Demand: No
Internet Service
Operational: No.
Telephone Service
None
Miles of Plant: 3.0 (coaxial); None (fiber optic). Homes passed: 204.
President & General Manager: Robert Hintz. Office Manager: Linda Hintz.
City fee: 3% of gross.
Ownership: B & L Technologies LLC (MSO).

MAURICE—Premier Communications. Now served by SIOUX CENTER, IA [IA0076]. ICA: IA0475.

MAXWELL—Formerly served by Huxley Communications Corp. No longer in operation. ICA: IA0476.

MAYNARD—Mediacom. Now served by WAVERLY, IA [IA0021]. ICA: IA0293.

MAYSVILLE—Dixon Telephone Co. Now served by DIXON, IA [IA0358]. ICA: IA0477.

MECHANICSVILLE—Mechanicsville Cablevision, PO Box 159, 107 N John, Mechanicsville, IA 52306. Phone: 563-432-7221.

Fax: 563-432-7721. E-mail: mtco@netins.net. Web Site: http://www.mechanicsvilletel.com. ICA: IA0194.
TV Market Ranking: 65 (MECHANICSVILLE). Franchise award date: N.A. Franchise expiration date: N.A. Began: October 1, 1983.
Channel capacity: 60 (operating 2-way). Channels available but not in use: 2.

Basic Service
Subscribers: 419.
Programming (received off-air): KCRG-TV (ABC) Cedar Rapids; KFXA (FOX) Cedar Rapids; KGAN (CBS) Cedar Rapids; KIIN (PBS) Iowa City; KLJB (CW, FOX) Davenport; KWKB (CW, MNT) Iowa City; KWQC-TV (NBC) Davenport; KWWL (NBC) Waterloo; WHBF-TV (CBS) Rock Island; WQAD-TV (ABC) Moline.
Programming (via satellite): ABC Family Channel; AMC; AmericanLife TV Network; Arts & Entertainment; Big Ten Network; Cartoon Network; CNBC; CNN; Comcast SportsNet Chicago; Comedy Central; Country Music TV; C-SPAN; Discovery Channel; Disney Channel; ESPN; ESPN 2; ESPN Classic Sports; Food Network; Fox News Channel; FX; Great American Country; GSN; Hallmark Channel; HGTV; History Channel; Home Shopping Network; INSP; ION Television; Lifetime; Nickelodeon; Outdoor Channel; QVC; Speed Channel; Spike TV; Syfy; TBS Superstation; The Learning Channel; Travel Channel; Trinity Broadcasting Network; Turner Classic Movies; Turner Network TV; TV Land; USA Network; VH1; Weather Channel; WGN America.
Fee: $12.00 installation; $24.00 monthly.

Digital Basic Service
Subscribers: N.A.
Programming (received off-air): KCRG-TV (ABC) Cedar Rapids; KFXA (FOX) Cedar Rapids; KGAN (CBS) Cedar Rapids; KIIN (PBS) Iowa City; KLJB (CW, FOX) Davenport; KWKB (CW, MNT) Iowa City; KWQC-TV (NBC) Davenport; KWWL (NBC) Waterloo; WHBF-TV (CBS) Rock Island; WQAD-TV (ABC) Moline.
Programming (via satellite): ABC Family Channel; ABC Family HD; AMC HD; American Movie Classics; AmericanLife TV Network; Animal Planet; Animal Planet HD; Arts & Entertainment; Arts & Entertainment HD; Big Ten Network; Big Ten Network HD; Cartoon Network; Cartoon Network HD; CMT HD; CNBC; CNBC HD+; CNN; CNN HD; Comcast SportsNet Chicago; Comedy Central; Country Music TV; C-SPAN; Discovery Channel; Discovery Channel HD; Disney Channel; Disney Channel HD; E! Entertainment Television; E! Entertainment Television HD; ESPN; ESPN 2; ESPN 2 HD; ESPN Classic Sports; ESPN HD; ESPN U; ESPNews; ESPNews HD; ESPNU HD; Food Network; Food Network HD; Fox News Channel; Fox News HD; FX; FX HD; FX Preview Channel; Great American Country; GSN; Hallmark Channel; HGTV; HGTV HD; History Channel; History Channel HD; Home Shopping Network; INSP; ION Television; Lifetime; Lifetime Television HD; MTV; MTV Networks HD; National Geographic Channel; National Geographic Channel HD Network; Nick HD; Nickelodeon; Outdoor Channel; Outdoor Channel 2 HD; QVC; QVC HD; RFD HD; RFD-TV; Speed Channel; Speed HD; Spike TV; Spike TV HD; Superstation WGN; Syfy; Syfy HD; TBN HD; TBS in HD; TBS Superstation; The Learning Channel; TLC HD; Travel Channel; Travel Channel HD; Turner Classic Movies; Turner Network TV; Turner Network TV HD; TV Land; USA Network; USA Network HD; VH1; VH1 HD; Weather Channel; Weather Channel HD.

Pay Service 1
Pay Units: 174.
Programming (via satellite): Cinemax; HBO.
Fee: $9.50 monthly.

Pay Service 2
Pay Units: N.A.
Programming (via satellite): Showtime.

Digital Pay Service 1
Pay Units: N.A.
Programming (via satellite): Cinemax (multiplexed); Cinemax HD; Flix; HBO (multiplexed); HBO HD; Showtime (multiplexed); Showtime HD; Sundance Channel; The Movie Channel (multiplexed); The Movie Channel HD.

Internet Service
Operational: No, Both DSL & dialup.

Telephone Service
None
Miles of Plant: 8.0 (coaxial); None (fiber optic). Homes passed: 450. Total homes in franchised area: 450.
Manager: Jason Best.
Ownership: Mechanicsville Telephone Co.

MEDIAPOLIS—Mediapolis Cablevision, PO Box 398, 652 Main St, Mediapolis, IA 52637-0398. Phones: 800-762-1527; 319-394-3456; 319-394-3996. Fax: 319-394-9155. E-mail: office@mtctech.net. Web Site: http://www.mtctech.net. ICA: IA0142.
TV Market Ranking: Below 100 (MEDIAPOLIS). Franchise award date: N.A. Franchise expiration date: N.A. Began: June 15, 1984.
Channel capacity: 35 (operating 2-way). Channels available but not in use: N.A.

Basic Service
Subscribers: 657.
Programming (received off-air): KGCW (CW) Burlington; KIIN (PBS) Iowa City; KLJB (CW, FOX) Davenport; KWQC-TV (NBC) Davenport; KYOU-TV (FOX) Ottumwa; WBQD-LP Davenport; WHBF-TV (CBS) Rock Island; WQAD-TV (ABC) Moline; WQPT-TV (PBS) Moline.
Programming (via satellite): Jewish Television (JTV); Weather Channel; WGN America.
Planned originations: Public Access.
Fee: $15.00 installation; $12.95 monthly; $1.00 converter.

Expanded Basic Service 1
Subscribers: N.A.
Programming (via satellite): ABC Family Channel; AMC; Animal Planet; Arts & Entertainment; BET Networks; Big Ten Network; Bravo; Cartoon Network; CNBC; CNN; Comcast SportsNet Chicago; Comedy Central; Country Music TV; C-SPAN; C-SPAN 2; Discovery Channel; Discovery Health Channel; Disney Channel; E! Entertainment Television; ESPN; ESPN 2; ESPN Classic Sports; Eternal Word TV Network; FitTV; Food Network; Fox Movie Channel; Fox News Channel; Fox Sports en Espanol; Fox Sports Net Midwest; FX; GalaVision; Golf Channel; Hallmark Channel; Headline News; HGTV; History Channel; Home Shopping Network; INSP; Lifetime; MSNBC; MTV; National Geographic Channel; Nickelodeon; Outdoor Channel; QVC; Speed Channel; Spike TV; Syfy; TBS Superstation; The Learning Channel; Toon Disney; Travel Channel; truTV; Turner Classic Movies; Turner Network TV; TV Guide Network; TV Land; Univision; USA Network; VH1.
Fee: $23.50 monthly.

Digital Basic Service
Subscribers: N.A.
Programming (received off-air): KGCW (CW) Burlington; KIIN (PBS) Iowa City; KLJB (CW, FOX) Davenport; KWQC-TV (NBC) Davenport; WHBF-TV (CBS) Rock Island; WQAD-TV (ABC) Moline; WQPT-TV (PBS) Moline.
Programming (via satellite): BBC America; Discovery Digital Networks; Discovery HD Theater; ESPN 2 HD; ESPN HD; ESPN U; ESPNews; Fox Soccer; GAS; GSN; HDNet; HDNet Movies; Independent Film Channel; MTV Networks Digital Suite; Music Choice; Nick Jr.; Nick Too; NickToons TV; SoapNet; Speed Channel; Versus; WE tv.
Fee: $10.00 monthly.

Pay Service 1
Pay Units: 56.
Programming (via satellite): Cinemax.

Pay Service 2
Pay Units: 125.
Programming (via satellite): HBO.
Fee: $15.00 installation.

Pay Service 3
Pay Units: 67.
Programming (via satellite): Showtime.
Fee: $15.00 installation.

Digital Pay Service 1
Pay Units: N.A.
Programming (via satellite): Cinemax (multiplexed); Encore (multiplexed); Flix; HBO (multiplexed); HBO HD; Starz (multiplexed); Starz HDTV; The Movie Channel (multiplexed).
Fee: $10.00 monthly (each).

Video-On-Demand: Yes

Internet Service
Operational: No.
Subscribers: 200.
Broadband Service: Offers dial-up and DSL only; no cable modem service.

Telephone Service
None
Miles of Plant: 20.0 (coaxial); None (fiber optic). Homes passed: 800. Total homes in franchised area: 1,200.
General Manager: Bill Malcom. Office Manager: Angie Rupe. Customer Service Manager: Rhonda Klenk.
City fee: None.
Ownership: Mediapolis Cablevision Co.

MELVIN—Premier Communications, PO Box 200, 339 1st Ave NE, Sioux Center, IA 51250. Phones: 800-642-4088; 712-722-3451. Fax: 712-722-1113. E-mail: dboone@mtcnet.net. Web Site: http://www.mypremieronline.com. ICA: IA0354.
TV Market Ranking: Outside TV Markets (MELVIN). Franchise award date: N.A. Franchise expiration date: N.A. Began: June 1, 1985.
Channel capacity: 54 (not 2-way capable). Channels available but not in use: N.A.

Basic Service
Subscribers: 72.
Programming (received off-air): KCAU-TV (ABC) Sioux City; KDLT-TV (NBC) Sioux Falls; KELO-TV (CBS, MNT) Sioux Falls; KPTH (FOX, MNT) Sioux City; KSFY-TV (ABC) Sioux Falls; KSIN-TV (PBS) Sioux City; KTIV (CW, NBC) Sioux City.
Programming (via satellite): ABC Family Channel; Arts & Entertainment; CNN; C-SPAN; Discovery Channel; Disney Channel; ESPN; ESPN 2; Fox News Channel; Great American Country; Hallmark Channel; Headline News; HGTV; History Channel; Lifetime; Nickelodeon; Speed Channel; Spike TV; TBS Superstation; The Learning Channel; Turner Network TV; TV Land; USA Network; Weather Channel; WGN America.
Fee: $16.00 installation; $21.95 monthly.

Pay Service 1
Pay Units: N.A.
Programming (via satellite): HBO; Showtime.
Fee: $8.95 monthly (each).

Internet Service
Operational: No.
Miles of Plant: 3.0 (coaxial); None (fiber optic). Homes passed: 139.
Chief Executive Officer: Douglas A. Boone. Chief Technician: Leslie Sybesma. Marketing Director: Scott Te Stroete.
Ownership: Premier Communications Inc. (MSO).

MENLO—Coon Valley Cooperative Telephone, PO Box 108, 516 Sherman St, Menlo, IA 50164. Phone: 641-524-2111. Fax: 641-524-2112. Web Site: http://www.coonvalleytelco.com. ICA: IA0340.
TV Market Ranking: Outside TV Markets (MENLO). Franchise award date: May 1, 1988. Franchise expiration date: N.A. Began: July 15, 1988.
Channel capacity: 36 (operating 2-way). Channels available but not in use: 24.

Basic Service
Subscribers: 80.
Programming (received off-air): KCCI (CBS) Des Moines; KCWI-TV (CW) Ames; KDIN-TV (PBS) Des Moines; KDSM-TV (FOX) Des Moines; WHO-DT (NBC) Des Moines; WOI-DT (ABC) Ames.
Programming (via satellite): ABC Family Channel; AMC; Arts & Entertainment; CNN; Comedy Central; Country Music TV; Discovery Channel; Disney Channel; ESPN; ESPN 2; Headline News; History Channel; Lifetime; Nickelodeon; Outdoor Channel; Syfy; TBS Superstation; The Learning Channel; Turner Network TV; USA Network; Weather Channel; WGN America.
Fee: $30.00 installation; $19.95 monthly; $1.50 converter; $10.00 additional installation.

Pay Service 1
Pay Units: 24.
Programming (via satellite): Flix; Showtime (multiplexed); The Movie Channel.
Fee: $10.00 installation; $10.95 monthly each (HBO or Showtime/TMC/Flix).

Pay Service 2
Pay Units: 38.
Programming (via satellite): HBO.
Fee: $10.00 installation; $10.95 monthly.

Internet Service
Operational: No, DSL only.

Telephone Service
None
Miles of Plant: 3.0 (coaxial); None (fiber optic). Homes passed: 152. Total homes in franchised area: 152.
General Manager: Jim Nelson. Chief Technician: Jonathon Skeens.
City fee: 1% of gross.
Ownership: Coon Valley Cablevision.

MERRILL—Premier Communications. Now served by SIOUX CENTER, IA [IA0076]. ICA: IA0311.

MESERVEY—Rockwell Communications Systems Inc., PO Box 416, 111 N 4th St, Rockwell, IA 50469. Phone: 641-822-3211. Fax: 641-822-3550. E-mail: rockwell@netins.net. Web Site: http://www.rockwellcoop.com. ICA: IA0478.

TV Market Ranking: Below 100 (MESERVEY). Franchise award date: N.A. Franchise expiration date: N.A. Began: January 1, 1990.
Channel capacity: N.A. Channels available but not in use: N.A.

Basic Service
Subscribers: N.A. Included in Thornton
Video-On-Demand: No
Pay-Per-View
ESPN (delivered digitally).
Internet Service
Operational: No, DSL & dialup.
Telephone Service
None
General Manager: David Severin. Chief Technician: Jason Dick.
Ownership: Rockwell Cooperative Telephone Association (MSO).

MILFORD—Milford Cable TV, PO Box 163, 806 Okoboji Ave, Milford, IA 51351. Phone: 712-338-4967. Fax: 712-338-4719. E-mail: mplagman@milfordcable.net. Web Site: http://www.milfordcable.net. Also serves Fostoria. ICA: IA0109.
TV Market Ranking: Outside TV Markets (Fostoria, MILFORD). Franchise award date: N.A. Franchise expiration date: N.A. Began: January 1, 1982.
Channel capacity: 90 (operating 2-way). Channels available but not in use: N.A.

Basic Service
Subscribers: 1,000.
Programming (received off-air): KCAU-TV (ABC) Sioux City; KDLT-TV (NBC) Sioux Falls; KELO-TV (CBS, MNT) Sioux Falls; KEYC-TV (CBS, FOX) Mankato; KMEG (CBS) Sioux City; KPTH (FOX, MNT) Sioux City; KSFY-TV (ABC) Sioux Falls; KTIN (PBS) Fort Dodge; KTIV (CW, NBC) Sioux City; KTTW (FOX) Sioux Falls.
Programming (via satellite): ABC Family Channel; Animal Planet; Arts & Entertainment; Bravo; CNBC; CNN; Comedy Central; Cooking Channel; Country Music TV; C-SPAN; C-SPAN 2; Discovery Channel; Discovery Health Channel; Disney Channel; Do-It-Yourself; ESPN; ESPN 2; ESPN Classic Sports; Eternal Word TV Network; Food Network; Fox Movie Channel; Fox News Channel; Fox Sports Net; FX; Great American Country; Hallmark Channel; Headline News; HGTV; History Channel; Home Shopping Network; ION Television; Lifetime; MSNBC; MTV; National Geographic Channel; Nickelodeon; Outdoor Channel; QVC; RFD-TV; SoapNet; Spike TV; Syfy; TBS Superstation; The Learning Channel; Toon Disney; Travel Channel; Trinity Broadcasting Network; truTV; Turner Classic Movies; Turner Network TV; TV Land; USA Network; VH1; Weather Channel; WGN America.
Current originations: Public Access.
Fee: $49.95 installation; $44.45 monthly.
Digital Basic Service
Subscribers: 90.
Programming (via satellite): BBC America; Bio; Bloomberg Television; Current; Discovery Digital Networks; DMX Music; ESPN 2; ESPN Classic Sports; ESPNews; Fox College Sports Atlantic; Fox College Sports Central; Fox College Sports Pacific; Fox Movie Channel; G4; GAS; Golf Channel; GSN; Halogen Network; HGTV; History Channel; History Channel International; Lifetime Movie Network; Lime; MTV Networks Digital Suite; National Geographic Channel; Nick Jr.; NickToons TV; Outdoor Channel; Speed Channel; Style Network; Sundance Channel; Toon Disney; Trinity Broadcasting Network; Turner Classic Movies; WE tv.
Fee: $7.15 monthly.
Pay Service 1
Pay Units: N.A.
Programming (via satellite): Cinemax; Encore; HBO; Starz.
Fee: $9.65 monthly (Starz/Encore), $10.70 monthly (Cinemax or HBO).
Digital Pay Service 1
Pay Units: N.A.
Programming (via satellite): Cinemax (multiplexed); Encore (multiplexed); Flix; HBO (multiplexed); Showtime (multiplexed); Starz (multiplexed); The Movie Channel (multiplexed).
Fee: $10.70 monthly (each).
Video-On-Demand: No
Internet Service
Operational: Yes, DSL only. Began: January 1, 2001.
Subscribers: 600.
Broadband Service: Milford Cable.
Fee: $25.95-$45.00 monthly; $6.42 modem lease; $80.00 modem purchase.
Telephone Service
None
Miles of Plant: 17.0 (coaxial); 7.0 (fiber optic). Homes passed: 1,300. Total homes in franchised area: 1,300.
Manager & Chief Technician: Matt Plagman.
City fee: 3% of gross.
Ownership: Milford Cable TV.

MILO—Formerly served by Telnet South LC. No longer in operation. ICA: IA0479.

MILTON—Starwest Inc. Now served by KEOSAUQUA, IA [IA0186]. ICA: IA0480.

MINBURN—Minburn Cablevision Inc., PO Box 206, 416 Chestnut St, Minburn, IA 50167. Phones: 515-677-2264; 515-677-2100. Fax: 515-677-2007. E-mail: minbrntl@netins.net. ICA: IA0339.
TV Market Ranking: 66 (MINBURN). Franchise award date: May 1, 1989. Franchise expiration date: N.A. Began: December 20, 1989.
Channel capacity: 72 (not 2-way capable). Channels available but not in use: 54.
Basic Service
Subscribers: 75.
Programming (received off-air): KCCI (CBS) Des Moines; KDIN-TV (PBS) Des Moines; KDSM-TV (FOX) Des Moines; WHO-DT (NBC) Des Moines; WOI-DT (ABC) Ames.
Programming (via satellite): ABC Family Channel; AMC; CNN; Country Music TV; Discovery Channel; Disney Channel; ESPN; ESPN 2; History Channel; ION Television; Lifetime; Spike TV; Syfy; TBS Superstation; The Learning Channel; Turner Network TV; USA Network; Weather Channel; WGN America.
Fee: $15.00 installation; $23.00 monthly.
Pay Service 1
Pay Units: 57.
Programming (via satellite): HBO; Showtime.
Fee: $15.00 installation; $9.50 monthly (each).
Internet Service
Operational: No.
Miles of Plant: 3.0 (coaxial); None (fiber optic). Homes passed: 161. Total homes in franchised area: 161.
Manager: R. N. (Ron) Flam.
Ownership: Minburn Cablevision Inc.

MINDEN—Walnut Telephone. Now served by WALNUT, IA [IA0241]. ICA: IA0304.

MINGO—Formerly served by Huxley Communications Corp. No longer in operation. ICA: IA0593.

MISSOURI VALLEY—Long Lines, 501 4th St, Sergeant Bluff, IA 51054-8509. Phones: 712-884-2203; 712-271-4000. Fax: 712-271-2727. Web Site: http://www.longlines.com. Also serves Harrison County (unincorporated areas). ICA: IA0096.
TV Market Ranking: 53 (Harrison County (unincorporated areas) (portions), MISSOURI VALLEY). Franchise award date: N.A. Franchise expiration date: N.A. Began: June 1, 1981.
Channel capacity: 42 (not 2-way capable). Channels available but not in use: N.A.
Basic Service
Subscribers: 541.
Programming (received off-air): KCAU-TV (ABC) Sioux City; KETV (ABC) Omaha; KMEG (CBS) Sioux City; KMTV-TV (CBS) Omaha; KPTM (FOX, MNT) Omaha; KSIN-TV (PBS) Sioux City; KTIV (CW, NBC) Sioux City; KXVO (CW) Omaha; KYNE-TV (PBS) Omaha; WOWT-TV (IND, NBC) Omaha.
Programming (via satellite): ABC Family Channel; AMC; AmericanLife TV Network; Animal Planet; Arts & Entertainment; Big Ten Network; Cartoon Network; CNBC; CNN; Comedy Central; Country Music TV; C-SPAN; C-SPAN 2; Discovery Channel; Disney Channel; E! Entertainment Television; ESPN; ESPN 2; ESPN Classic Sports; Eternal Word TV Network; Food Network; Fox News Channel; Fox Sports Net Midwest; FX; Golf Channel; Hallmark Channel; Headline News; HGTV; History Channel; Home Shopping Network; INSP; Lifetime; Lifetime Movie Network; MSNBC; MTV; Nickelodeon; QVC; Speed Channel; Spike TV; Syfy; TBS Superstation; The Learning Channel; The Sportsman Channel; Travel Channel; Trinity Broadcasting Network; truTV; Turner Classic Movies; Turner Network TV; TuTv; TV Guide Network; TV Land; USA Network; VH1; Weather Channel; WGN America.
Fee: $39.00 installation; $41.99 monthly.
Digital Basic Service
Subscribers: N.A.
Programming (via satellite): BBC America; Bio; Cooking Channel; Discovery Health Channel; Discovery Kids Channel; Discovery Military Channel; Discovery Planet Green; DMX Music; Do-It-Yourself; ESPN U; ESPNews; FitTV; Fox College Sports Atlantic; Fox College Sports Central; Fox College Sports Pacific; Fox Movie Channel; Fox Soccer; G4; Great American Country; GSN; Halogen Network; History Channel International; ID Investigation Discovery; Independent Film Channel; Lifetime Real Women; MTV Hits; MTV Jams; MTV2; Nick Jr.; NickToons TV; Outdoor Channel; RFD-TV; Science Channel; SoapNet; TeenNick; Toon Disney; Versus; VH1 Classic; VH1 Country; VH1 Soul; WE tv.
Fee: $9.99 monthly.
Digital Expanded Basic Service
Subscribers: N.A.
Programming (received off-air): KCAU-TV (ABC) Sioux City; KMTV-TV (CBS) Omaha; KPTM (FOX, MNT) Omaha; KSIN-TV (PBS) Sioux City; KTIV (CW, NBC) Sioux City.
Programming (via satellite): Big Ten Network HD; Discovery Channel HD; ESPN 2 HD; ESPN HD; HDNet; HDNet Movies; Outdoor Channel 2 HD.
Fee: $9.95 monthly.
Digital Expanded Basic Service 2
Subscribers: N.A.
Programming (via satellite): Bandamax; De Pelicula; De Pelicula Clasico; Discovery en Espanol; ESPN Deportes; Fox Sports en Espanol; Ritmoson Latino; Telehit.
Fee: $2.95 monthly.
Pay Service 1
Pay Units: 23.
Programming (via satellite): Flix; Showtime (multiplexed); The Movie Channel.
Fee: $15.00 installation; $11.10 monthly.
Pay Service 2
Pay Units: 41.
Programming (via satellite): HBO (multiplexed).
Fee: $13.35 monthly.
Digital Pay Service 1
Pay Units: N.A.
Programming (via satellite): Cinemax (multiplexed); Cinemax HD; Encore (multiplexed); Flix; HBO (multiplexed); HBO HD; Showtime (multiplexed); Starz (multiplexed); Starz HDTV; Starz On Demand; The Movie Channel (multiplexed).
Fee: $11.95 monthly (Cinemax), $13.95 monthly (Starz/Encore), $14.45 monthly (Showtime/TMC/Flix), $14.95 monthly (HBO).
Video-On-Demand: Yes
Internet Service
Operational: No.
Telephone Service
None
Miles of Plant: 17.0 (coaxial); None (fiber optic). Additional miles planned: 1.0 (coaxial). Homes passed: 1,155. Total homes in franchised area: 1,155.
Manager & Chief Operations Officer: Paul Bergmann. Marketing Manager: Paul McElry. System Engineer: Tony Seubert. Office Manager: Denise Mobery.
City fee: 3% of gross.
Ownership: Long Lines (MSO).

MODALE—Formerly served by TelePartners. No longer in operation. ICA: IA0574.

MONDAMIN—Formerly served by TelePartners. No longer in operation. ICA: IA0315.

MONONA—Northeast Iowa Telephone Co., 800 S Main St, Monona, IA 52159. Phone: 563-539-2122. Fax: 563-539-2003. E-mail: neitel@neitel.com. Web Site: http://www.neitel.com. Also serves Farmersburg, Luana & St. Olaf. ICA: IA0122.
TV Market Ranking: Outside TV Markets (Farmersburg, Luana, MONONA, St. Olaf). Franchise award date: January 1, 1983. Franchise expiration date: N.A. Began: March 1, 1983.
Channel capacity: N.A. Channels available but not in use: N.A.
Basic Service
Subscribers: 850.
Programming (received off-air): KCRG-TV (ABC) Cedar Rapids; KFXA (FOX) Cedar Rapids; KFXB-TV (IND) Dubuque; KGAN (CBS) Cedar Rapids; KPXR-TV (ION) Cedar Rapids; KRIN (PBS) Waterloo; KWKB (CW, MNT) Iowa City; KWWL (NBC) Waterloo.
Programming (via satellite): ABC Family Channel; AMC; Arts & Entertainment; Big Ten Network; CNBC; CNN; Country Music TV; Discovery Channel; ESPN; Fox News Channel; Fox Sports Net Midwest; FX; Hallmark Channel; HGTV; History Channel; MTV; Nickelodeon; Outdoor Channel; Spike TV; Syfy; TBS Superstation; The Learning Channel; Turner Network TV; TV Land; USA

Network; VH1; Weather Channel; WGN America.
Current originations: Public Access.
Fee: $10.00 installation; $28.75 monthly.

Digital Basic Service
Subscribers: N.A.
Programming (via satellite): BBC America; Bio; Discovery Health Channel; Discovery Kids Channel; Discovery Military Channel; Discovery Planet Green; DMX Music; ESPN Classic Sports; ESPNews; FitTV; Fox College Sports Atlantic; Fox College Sports Central; Fox College Sports Pacific; Fox Soccer; Fuse; Great American Country; GSN; History Channel International; ID Investigation Discovery; MTV2; Nick Jr.; NickToons TV; Science Channel; Speed Channel; TeenNick; Trinity Broadcasting Network; VH1 Classic; VH1 Country.
Fee: $9.95 monthly.

Pay Service 1
Pay Units: 365.
Programming (via satellite): Cinemax; HBO.
Fee: $10.00 installation; $11.00 monthly (Cinemax), $12.00 monthly (HBO).

Digital Pay Service 1
Pay Units: N.A.
Programming (via satellite): Cinemax (multiplexed); Encore (multiplexed); Flix; HBO (multiplexed); Showtime (multiplexed); Starz (multiplexed); The Movie Channel (multiplexed).
Fee: $11.00 monthly (Cinemax), $12.00 monthly (HBO), $13.50 monthly (Showtime/TMC/Flix), $14.50 monthly (Starz/Encore).

Internet Service
Operational: No, DSL & dial-up.

Telephone Service
None

Miles of Plant: 17.0 (coaxial); None (fiber optic).
General Manager: David Byers. Marketing Manager: Steve Hanson. Plant Manager: Dennis Landt.
Ownership: Northeast Iowa Telephone Co.

MONROE—Telnet South LC. Now served by DES MOINES, IA [IA0001]. ICA: IA0139.

MONTROSE—Mediacom. Now served by KEOKUK, IA [IA0612]. ICA: IA0192.

MOORHEAD—Long Lines, 501 4th St, Sergeant Bluff, IA 51054-8509. Phones: 712-884-2203; 712-271-4000. Fax: 712-271-2727. Web Site: http://www.longlines.com. ICA: IA0602.
TV Market Ranking: Outside TV Markets (MOORHEAD).
Channel capacity: N.A. Channels available but not in use: N.A.

Basic Service
Subscribers: 74.
Programming (received off-air): KCAU-TV (ABC) Sioux City; KMEG (CBS) Sioux City; KPTH (FOX, MNT) Sioux City; KSIN-TV (PBS) Sioux City; KTIV (CW, NBC) Sioux City; KXVO (CW) Omaha.
Programming (via satellite): ABC Family Channel; AMC; AmericanLife TV Network; Animal Planet; Arts & Entertainment; Big Ten Network; Cartoon Network; CNBC; CNN; Comedy Central; Country Music TV; C-SPAN; C-SPAN 2; Discovery Channel; Disney Channel; E! Entertainment Television; ESPN; ESPN 2; ESPN Classic Sports; Eternal Word TV Network; Food Network; Fox News Channel; Fox Sports Net North; FX; Golf Channel; Hallmark Channel; Headline News; HGTV; History Channel; Home Shopping Network; INSP; Lifetime; Lifetime Movie Network; MSNBC; MTV; Nickelodeon; QVC; Speed Channel; Spike TV; Syfy; TBS Superstation; The Learning Channel; The Sportsman Channel; Travel Channel; Trinity Broadcasting Network; truTV; Turner Classic Movies; Turner Network TV; TuTv; TV Guide Network; TV Land; USA Network; VH1; Weather Channel; WGN America.
Fee: $41.99 monthly.

Digital Basic Service
Subscribers: N.A.
Programming (via satellite): BBC America; Bio; Cooking Channel; Discovery Health Channel; Discovery Kids Channel; Discovery Military Channel; Discovery Planet Green; DMX Music; Do-It-Yourself; ESPN U; ESPNews; FitTV; Fox College Sports Atlantic; Fox College Sports Central; Fox College Sports Pacific; Fox Movie Channel; Fox Soccer; G4; Great American Country; GSN; Halogen Network; History Channel International; ID Investigation Discovery; Independent Film Channel; Lifetime Real Women; MTV Hits; MTV Jams; MTV2; Nick Jr.; NickToons TV; Outdoor Channel; RFD-TV; Science Channel; SoapNet; TeenNick; Toon Disney; Versus; VH1 Classic; VH1 Country; VH1 Soul; WE tv.
Fee: $9.99 monthly.

Digital Expanded Basic Service
Subscribers: N.A.
Programming (received off-air): KCAU-TV (ABC) Sioux City; KMEG (CBS) Sioux City; KPTH (FOX, MNT) Sioux City; KSIN-TV (PBS) Sioux City; KTIV (CW, NBC) Sioux City.
Programming (via satellite): Big Ten Network HD; Discovery Channel HD; ESPN 2 HD; ESPN HD; HDNet; HDNet Movies; Outdoor Channel 2 HD.
Fee: $9.95 monthly.

Digital Expanded Basic Service 2
Subscribers: N.A.
Programming (via satellite): Bandamax; De Pelicula; De Pelicula Clasico; Discovery en Espanol; ESPN Deportes; Fox Sports en Espanol; Ritmoson Latino; Telehit.
Fee: $2.95 monthly.

Pay Service 1
Pay Units: 10.
Programming (via satellite): HBO (multiplexed).
Fee: $14.95 monthly.

Pay Service 2
Pay Units: 2.
Programming (via satellite): Flix; Showtime (multiplexed); The Movie Channel.
Fee: $14.45 monthly.

Digital Pay Service 1
Pay Units: N.A.
Programming (via satellite): Cinemax (multiplexed); Cinemax HD; Encore (multiplexed); Flix; HBO (multiplexed); HBO HD; Showtime (multiplexed); Starz (multiplexed); Starz HDTV; Starz On Demand; The Movie Channel (multiplexed).
Fee: $11.95 monthly (Cinemax), $13.95 monthly (Starz/Encore), $14.45 monthly (Showtime/TMC/Flix), $14.95 monthly (HBO).

Video-On-Demand: Yes

Internet Service
Operational: No, Both DSL & dial-up.

Homes passed: 118.
Manager & Chief Operations Officer: Paul Bergmann. System Engineer: Tony Seubert. Marketing Manager: Pat Melvoy. Office Manager: Denise Moberg.
Ownership: Long Lines (MSO).

MOORHEAD—Soldier Valley Telephone. Now served by SALIX, IA [IA0510]. Also serves MOORHEAD. ICA: IA0347.

MORAVIA—B & L Technologies LLC, 3329 270th St, Lenox, IA 50851. Phones: 800-798-5488; 641-348-2240. Fax: 641-348-2240. ICA: IA0273.
TV Market Ranking: Below 100 (MORAVIA). Franchise award date: August 2, 1984. Franchise expiration date: N.A. Began: September 1, 1985.
Channel capacity: 23 (not 2-way capable). Channels available but not in use: None.

Basic Service
Subscribers: 52.
Programming (received off-air): KCCI (CBS) Des Moines; KDIN-TV (PBS) Des Moines; KDSM-TV (FOX) Des Moines; KTVO (ABC) Kirksville; KYOU-TV (FOX) Ottumwa; WHO-DT (NBC) Des Moines; WOI-DT (ABC) Ames.
Programming (via satellite): ABC Family Channel; CNN; Discovery Channel; ESPN; Nickelodeon; Spike TV; TBS Superstation; Turner Network TV; USA Network; WGN America.
Fee: $41.11 installation; $20.05 monthly.

Pay Service 1
Pay Units: 61.
Programming (via satellite): HBO.
Fee: $23.49 installation; $11.00 monthly.

Video-On-Demand: No

Internet Service
Operational: No.

Telephone Service
None

Miles of Plant: 5.0 (coaxial); None (fiber optic). Homes passed: 361. Total homes in franchised area: 361.
President & General Manager: Robert Hintz. Office Manager: Linda Hintz.
City fee: None.
Ownership: B & L Technologies LLC (MSO).

MOULTON—B & L Technologies LLC, 3329 270th St, Lenox, IA 50851. Phones: 800-798-5488; 641-348-2240. Fax: 641-348-2240. ICA: IA0535.
TV Market Ranking: Below 100 (MOULTON). Franchise award date: N.A. Franchise expiration date: N.A. Began: N.A.
Channel capacity: 36 (not 2-way capable). Channels available but not in use: 24.

Basic Service
Subscribers: 127.
Programming (received off-air): KCCI (CBS) Des Moines; KDIN-TV (PBS) Des Moines; KTVO (ABC) Kirksville; KYOU-TV (FOX) Ottumwa; WHO-DT (NBC) Des Moines.
Programming (via satellite): ABC Family Channel; Bravo; CNN; Discovery Channel; Disney Channel; ESPN; QVC; Spike TV; TBS Superstation; Turner Network TV; USA Network; WGN America.
Fee: $15.98 monthly.

Pay Service 1
Pay Units: N.A.
Programming (via satellite): Showtime; The Movie Channel.
Fee: $8.95 monthly (TMC), $10.95 monthly (Showtime).

Video-On-Demand: No

Internet Service
Operational: No.

Telephone Service
None

Miles of Plant: 4.0 (coaxial); None (fiber optic). Homes passed: 298.
President & General Manager: Robert Hintz. Office Manager: Linda Hintz.
Ownership: B & L Technologies LLC (MSO).

MOUNT PLEASANT—Mediacom, 6300 Council St NE, Ste A, Cedar Rapids, IA 52402. Phones: 319-395-9699; 319-753-6576 (Burlington office). Fax: 319-393-9017. Web Site: http://www.mediacomcable.com. Also serves Fort Madison, Henry County, Lee County (portions), New London, West Point & Westwood. ICA: IA0611.
TV Market Ranking: Below 100 (Fort Madison, Henry County, Lee County (portions), MOUNT PLEASANT, New London, West Point, Westwood).
Channel capacity: N.A. Channels available but not in use: N.A.

Basic Service
Subscribers: N.A.
Programming (received off-air): KCRG-TV (ABC) Cedar Rapids; KIIN (PBS) Iowa City; KLJB (CW, FOX) Davenport; KTVO (ABC) Kirksville; KWQC-TV (NBC) Davenport; KYOU-TV (FOX) Ottumwa; WHBF-TV (CBS) Rock Island; WQAD-TV (ABC) Moline.
Programming (via satellite): C-SPAN; C-SPAN 2; Home Shopping Network; ION Television; QVC; TV Guide Network; Weather Channel; WGN America.
Current originations: Government Access; Educational Access; Public Access.

Expanded Basic Service 1
Subscribers: N.A.
Programming (via satellite): ABC Family Channel; AMC; Animal Planet; Arts & Entertainment; BET Networks; Cartoon Network; CNBC; CNN; Comedy Central; Country Music TV; Discovery Channel; Disney Channel; E! Entertainment Television; ESPN; ESPN 2; Eternal Word TV Network; Food Network; Fox News Channel; Fox Sports Net Midwest; FX; Hallmark Channel; Headline News; HGTV; History Channel; INSP; Lifetime; MSNBC; MTV; National Geographic Channel; Nickelodeon; SoapNet; Speed Channel; Spike TV; Syfy; TBS Superstation; Telemundo; The Learning Channel; truTV; Turner Network TV; TV Land; Univision; USA Network; VH1; WE tv.

Digital Basic Service
Subscribers: N.A.
Programming (via satellite): AmericanLife TV Network; BBC America; Bio; Bloomberg Television; Bravo; Discovery Digital Networks; DMX Music; Fox Movie Channel; Fox Sports World; Fuse; G4; GAS; Golf Channel; GSN; Halogen Network; History Channel International; Independent Film Channel; Lifetime Movie Network; Lime; MTV Networks Digital Suite; Nick Jr.; Outdoor Chan-

nel; Ovation; Style Network; Trinity Broadcasting Network; Turner Classic Movies; Versus.

Digital Pay Service 1

Pay Units: N.A.

Programming (via satellite): Cinemax (multiplexed); Encore (multiplexed); Flix; HBO (multiplexed); Showtime (multiplexed); Starz (multiplexed); Sundance Channel; The Movie Channel (multiplexed).

Video-On-Demand: Yes

Pay-Per-View

ETC (delivered digitally); Playboy TV (delivered digitally); Pleasure (delivered digitally); TVN Entertainment (delivered digitally); Sports PPV (delivered digitally).

Internet Service

Operational: Yes.

Broadband Service: Mediacom High Speed Internet.

Fee: $45.95 monthly.

Telephone Service

Digital: Operational

Fee: $39.95 monthly

Miles of Plant: 210.0 (coaxial); None (fiber optic). Miles of plant (fiber) included in miles of plant (coax)

Regional Vice President: Doug Frank. Technical Operations Director: Greg Nank. Technical Operations Manager: Joel Hanger. Marketing Director: Steve Schuh.

Ownership: Mediacom LLC (MSO).

MOVILLE—Evertek Inc., PO Box 270, 216 N Main, Everly, IA 51338. Phone: 712-834-2255. Fax: 712-834-2214. E-mail: internet@evertek.net. Web Site: http://www.evertek.net. ICA: IA0189.

TV Market Ranking: Below 100 (MOVILLE). Franchise award date: N.A. Franchise expiration date: N.A. Began: February 1, 1984.

Channel capacity: 35 (not 2-way capable). Channels available but not in use: N.A.

Basic Service

Subscribers: 51.

Programming (received off-air): KCAU-TV (ABC) Sioux City; KMEG (CBS) Sioux City; KSIN-TV (PBS) Sioux City; KTIV (CW, NBC) Sioux City.

Programming (via satellite): ABC Family Channel; AMC; Animal Planet; Arts & Entertainment; CNN; Country Music TV; C-SPAN; Discovery Channel; Disney Channel; ESPN; ESPN 2; Headline News; History Channel; Lifetime; Nickelodeon; Spike TV; Syfy; TBS Superstation; The Learning Channel; Turner Network TV; USA Network; VH1; Weather Channel; WGN America.

Fee: $45.00 installation; $26.95 monthly.

Pay Service 1

Pay Units: 4.

Programming (via satellite): Cinemax.

Fee: $11.00 monthly.

Pay Service 2

Pay Units: 7.

Programming (via satellite): HBO.

Fee: $11.00 monthly.

Pay Service 3

Pay Units: 34.

Programming (via satellite): Showtime; The Movie Channel.

Fee: $12.95 monthly.

Video-On-Demand: No

Internet Service

Operational: No.

Telephone Service

None

Miles of Plant: 7.0 (coaxial); None (fiber optic). Homes passed: 467.

General Manager: Roxanne White. Chief Technician: Fred Gibson.

City fee: 5% of gross.

Ownership: Evertek Inc. (MSO).

MURRAY—Interstate Communications, PO Box 229, 105 N West St, Truro, IA 50257-0229. Phones: 712-824-7227; 641-765-4201. Fax: 641-765-4204. Web Site: http://www.interstatecom.com. Also serves Lorimor. ICA: IA0257.

TV Market Ranking: Outside TV Markets (Lorimor, MURRAY). Franchise award date: N.A. Franchise expiration date: N.A. Began: October 1, 1985.

Channel capacity: N.A. Channels available but not in use: N.A.

Basic Service

Subscribers: 193.

Programming (received off-air): KCCI (CBS) Des Moines; KCWI-TV (CW) Ames; KDSM-TV (FOX) Des Moines; WHO-DT (NBC) Des Moines; WOI-DT (ABC) Ames.

Programming (via satellite): ABC Family Channel; AMC; Animal Planet; Arts & Entertainment; Cartoon Network; CNN; Country Music TV; C-SPAN; Discovery Channel; Disney Channel; ESPN; ESPN 2; HGTV; History Channel; Home Shopping Network; ION Television; Iowa Communications Network; Nickelodeon; Spike TV; Syfy; TBS Superstation; Turner Network TV; USA Network; WGN America.

Fee: $35.00 installation; $23.50 monthly.

Pay Service 1

Pay Units: 89.

Programming (via satellite): Cinemax; HBO.

Fee: $7.50 installation; $9.00 monthly (each).

Video-On-Demand: No

Internet Service

Operational: No.

Telephone Service

None

Miles of Plant: 3.0 (coaxial); None (fiber optic). Homes passed: 295.

Manager: Mike Weis. Chief Technician: Rick Lunn.

Ownership: Interstate Communications (MSO).

MUSCATINE—Mediacom. Now served by MUSCATINE, IA [IA0587]. ICA: IA0014.

MUSCATINE—MPW Cable, PO Box 899, 3205 Cedar St, Muscatine, IA 52761. Phone: 563-262-2631. E-mail: webmaster@mpw.org. Web Site: http://www.mpw.org. Also serves Fruitland, Louisa County & Muscatine County. ICA: IA0587.

TV Market Ranking: 60 (Fruitland, Louisa County (portions), MUSCATINE, Muscatine County); Below 100 (Louisa County (portions)); Outside TV Markets (Louisa County (portions)). Franchise award date: N.A. Franchise expiration date: N.A. Began: N.A.

Channel capacity: 73 (operating 2-way). Channels available but not in use: N.A.

Basic Service

Subscribers: 8,735.

Programming (received off-air): KGCW (CW) Burlington; KIIN (PBS) Iowa City; KLJB (CW, FOX) Davenport; KWQC-TV (NBC) Davenport; WBQD-LP Davenport; WHBF-TV (CBS) Rock Island; WQAD-TV (ABC) Moline; WQPT-TV (PBS) Moline.

Programming (via satellite): C-SPAN; C-SPAN 2; Eternal Word TV Network; Headline News; Home Shopping Network; INSP; TV Guide Network; Univision; Weather Channel; WGN America.

Current originations: Leased Access; Government Access; Educational Access; Public Access.

Fee: $25.00 installation; $17.50 monthly; $25.00 additional installation.

Expanded Basic Service 1

Subscribers: N.A.

Programming (via satellite): ABC Family Channel; AMC; Animal Planet; Arts & Entertainment; BET Networks; Big Ten Network; Bravo; Cartoon Network; CNBC; CNN; Comcast SportsNet Chicago; Comedy Central; Country Music TV; Discovery Channel; Disney Channel; E! Entertainment Television; ESPN; ESPN 2; ESPN Classic Sports; FitTV; Food Network; Fox Movie Channel; Fox News Channel; Fox Sports Net Midwest; Fox Sports World; FX; GalaVision; Golf Channel; Hallmark Channel; HGTV; History Channel; Lifetime; MSNBC; MTV; Nickelodeon; Outdoor Channel; QVC; Spike TV; Syfy; TBS Superstation; The Learning Channel; Toon Disney; Travel Channel; truTV; Turner Network TV; TV Land; USA Network; VH1.

Fee: $32.39 monthly.

Digital Basic Service

Subscribers: N.A.

Programming (received off-air): KGCW (CW) Burlington; KIIN (PBS) Iowa City; KLJB (CW, FOX) Davenport; KWQC-TV (NBC) Davenport; WHBF-TV (CBS) Rock Island; WQAD-TV (ABC) Moline; WQPT-TV (PBS) Moline.

Programming (via satellite): BBC America; CMT Pure Country; Discovery Digital Networks; Discovery HD Theater; DMX Music; ESPN 2 HD; ESPN HD; ESPN U; ESPNews; Fox Soccer; GAS; GSN; HDNet; HDNet Movies; Independent Film Channel; MTV Networks Digital Suite; Nick Jr.; Nick Too; NickToons TV; SoapNet; Speed Channel; Turner Classic Movies; Versus; WE tv.

Fee: $15.99 monthly.

Pay Service 1

Pay Units: N.A.

Programming (via satellite): Cinemax; Encore; HBO; Showtime; Starz; The Movie Channel.

Fee: $9.00 monthly (Starz/Encore), $11.50 monthly (Cinemax or Showtime/TMC), $14.50 monthly (HBO).

Digital Pay Service 1

Pay Units: N.A.

Programming (via satellite): Cinemax (multiplexed); Encore (multiplexed); HBO (multiplexed); HBO HD; Showtime (multiplexed); Starz (multiplexed); Starz HDTV; The Movie Channel (multiplexed).

Video-On-Demand: Yes

Pay-Per-View

Movies, Fee: $3.95.

Internet Service

Operational: Yes.

Subscribers: 3,897.

Broadband Service: In-house.

Fee: $40.00 installation; $21.95 monthly.

Telephone Service

None

Miles of Plant: 240.0 (coaxial); 81.0 (fiber optic). Homes passed: 12,400.

General Manager: Salvatore L. LoBianco. Marketing Manager: Tina Campbell. Sales Manager: Terry Curry. Communications Manager: David Fyffe.

Ownership: Muscatine Power & Water.

MYSTIC—B & L Technologies LLC, 3329 270th St, Lenox, IA 50851. Phones: 800-798-5488; 641-348-2240. Fax: 641-348-2240. ICA: IA0263.

TV Market Ranking: Below 100 (MYSTIC). Franchise award date: September 1, 1982. Franchise expiration date: N.A. Began: April 1, 1984.

Channel capacity: 23 (not 2-way capable). Channels available but not in use: None.

Basic Service

Subscribers: 42.

Programming (received off-air): KCCI (CBS) Des Moines; KDIN-TV (PBS) Des Moines; KDSM-TV (FOX) Des Moines; KTVO (ABC) Kirksville; KYOU-TV (FOX) Ottumwa; WHO-DT (NBC) Des Moines; WOI-DT (ABC) Ames.

Programming (via satellite): ABC Family Channel; CNN; Country Music TV; Discovery Channel; ESPN; MTV; Nickelodeon; Spike TV; TBS Superstation; Turner Network TV; USA Network; WGN America.

Fee: $41.11 installation; $15.95 monthly.

Video-On-Demand: No

Internet Service

Operational: No.

Telephone Service

None

Miles of Plant: 7.0 (coaxial); None (fiber optic). Homes passed: 266. Total homes in franchised area: 266.

President & General Manager: Robert Hintz. Office Manager: Linda Hintz.

City fee: None.

Ownership: B & L Technologies LLC (MSO).

NEOLA—Walnut Communications, PO Box 346, 510 Highland St, Walnut, IA 51577-0346. Phone: 712-784-2211. Fax: 712-784-2010. E-mail: info@walnutel.net. Web Site: http://www.walnutcommunications.com. ICA: IA0481.

TV Market Ranking: 53 (NEOLA). Franchise award date: N.A. Franchise expiration date: N.A. Began: November 1, 1984.

Channel capacity: N.A. Channels available but not in use: N.A.

Basic Service

Subscribers: N.A. Included in Walnut

Programming (received off-air): KCCI (CBS) Des Moines; KETV (ABC) Omaha; KHIN (PBS) Red Oak; KMTV-TV (CBS) Omaha; KPTM (FOX, MNT) Omaha; KXVO (CW) Omaha; WHO-DT (NBC) Des Moines; WOI-DT (ABC) Ames; WOWT-TV (IND, NBC) Omaha.

Programming (via satellite): ABC Family Channel; AMC; Arts & Entertainment; Big Ten Network; Bravo; Cartoon Network; CNBC; CNN; Comedy Central; Country Music TV; C-SPAN; C-SPAN 2; Discovery Channel; Disney Channel; E! Entertainment Television; ESPN; ESPN 2; ESPN Classic Sports; ESPNews; Eternal Word TV Network; Food Network; Fox News Channel; Fox Sports Net Midwest; FX; G4; GSN; Hallmark Channel; Hallmark Movie Channel; Headline News; HGTV; History Channel; Lifetime; Lifetime Movie Network; MSNBC; MTV; MyNetworkTV Inc.; National Geographic Channel; Nickelodeon; Outdoor Channel; QVC; RFD-TV; Speed Channel; Spike TV; Syfy; TBS Superstation; The Learning Channel; Toon Disney; Travel Channel; Turner Classic Movies; Turner Network TV; TV Land; USA Network; VH1; Weather Channel; WGN America.

Fee: $25.00 installation; $44.95 monthly.

Digital Basic Service

Subscribers: N.A.

Programming (received off-air): KETV (ABC) Omaha; KHIN (PBS) Red Oak; KMTV-TV (CBS) Omaha; KPTM (FOX, MNT) Omaha; KXVO (CW) Omaha; WOWT-TV (IND, NBC) Omaha.

Programming (via satellite): Animal Planet HD; Arts & Entertainment HD; Azteca America; BBC America; Big Ten Network HD; Bio; Bloomberg Television; Chiller; CMT Pure Country; CNN HD; Discovery Channel HD; Discovery HD Theater; Discovery Health Channel; Discovery Kids Channel; Discovery Military Channel; Discovery Planet Green; DMX Music; ESPN 2 HD; ESPN HD; ESPN U; FitTV; Fox Business Channel; Fox News HD; FSN Digital Atlantic; FSN Digital Central; FSN Digital Pacific; FSN HD; FX HD; Golf Channel; HDNet; HDNet Movies; History Channel HD; History Channel International; ID Investigation Discovery; Lifetime Movie Network HD; Lifetime Real Women; MTV Hits; MTV2; National Geographic Channel HD Network; Nick Jr.; NickToons TV; Oxygen; Science Channel; ShopNBC; Sleuth; SoapNet; Speed HD; Syfy HD; TBS in HD; TeenNick; TLC HD; Turner Network TV HD; Universal HD; USA Network HD; Versus; VH1 Classic; VH1 Soul.

Digital Pay Service 1
Pay Units: N.A.
Programming (via satellite): Cinemax (multiplexed); Cinemax HD; Encore (multiplexed); HBO (multiplexed); HBO HD; Showtime (multiplexed); Showtime HD; Starz (multiplexed); Starz HDTV.
Fee: $12.95 monthly (HBO, Cinemax, Starz/Encore or Showtime).

Video-On-Demand: No

Pay-Per-View
iN DEMAND (delivered digitally); ESPN (delivered digitally).

Internet Service
Operational: No, DSL only.

Telephone Service
None

Miles of Plant: 5.0 (coaxial); None (fiber optic). Homes passed & total homes in franchised area included in Walnut

General Manager: Bruce Heyne. Plant Manager: Denny Book. Marketing Manager: Leanne Blotzer. Office Manager: Rachel Becorra.

Ownership: Walnut Communications (MSO).

NEW ALBIN—Mediacom, 4010 Alexandra Dr, Waterloo, IA 50702. Phone: 319-235-2197. Fax: 319-232-7841. Web Site: http://www.mediacomcable.com. ICA: IA0482.

TV Market Ranking: Below 100 (NEW ALBIN). Franchise award date: N.A. Franchise expiration date: N.A. Began: January 1, 1967.

Channel capacity: N.A. Channels available but not in use: N.A.

Basic Service
Subscribers: 227.
Programming (received off-air): KAAL (ABC) Austin; KGAN (CBS) Cedar Rapids; KIMT (CBS, MNT) Mason City; KPXM-TV (ION) St. Cloud; KTTC (CW, NBC) Rochester; KXLT-TV (FOX) Rochester; WEAU-TV (NBC) Eau Claire; WHLA-TV (PBS) La Crosse; WKBT-DT (CBS, MNT) La Crosse; WLAX (FOX) La Crosse; WXOW (ABC, CW) La Crosse.
Fee: $10.00 installation; $9.00 monthly.

Expanded Basic Service 1
Subscribers: N.A.
Programming (via satellite): ABC Family Channel; AMC; Animal Planet; Arts & Entertainment; Bravo; Cartoon Network; CNBC; CNN; Comedy Central; Country Music TV; C-SPAN; Discovery Channel; Disney Channel; E! Entertainment Television; ESPN; ESPN 2; Fox News Channel; Fox Sports Net Midwest; FX; Headline News; HGTV; History Channel; Home Shopping Network; Lifetime; MTV; Nickelodeon; QVC; Speed Channel; Spike TV; Syfy; TBS Superstation; The Learning Channel; truTV; Turner Network TV; TV Land; USA Network; VH1; Weather Channel; WGN America.

Digital Basic Service
Subscribers: N.A.
Programming (via satellite): AmericanLife TV Network; BBC America; Bio; Bloomberg Television; Discovery Digital Networks; Fox Movie Channel; Fox Sports World; Fuse; G4; Golf Channel; GSN; Halogen Network; History Channel International; Independent Film Channel; Lifetime Movie Network; Music Choice; Outdoor Channel; Style Network.

Digital Pay Service 1
Pay Units: N.A.
Programming (via satellite): Cinemax (multiplexed); Encore (multiplexed); Flix; HBO (multiplexed); Showtime (multiplexed); Starz (multiplexed); Sundance Channel; The Movie Channel (multiplexed).
Fee: $20.00 installation; $10.00 monthly (each).

Video-On-Demand: Yes

Pay-Per-View
TVN Entertainment (delivered digitally); ESPN Now (delivered digitally); Sports PPV (delivered digitally); Fresh (delivered digitally); Shorteez (delivered digitally); Playboy TV (delivered digitally); Pleasure (delivered digitally); ETC (delivered digitally).

Internet Service
Operational: Yes.
Broadband Service: Mediacom High Speed Internet.

Telephone Service
Digital: Operational

Miles of Plant: 4.0 (coaxial); None (fiber optic). Homes passed: 480.

Regional Vice President: Doug Frank. General Manager: Doug Nix. Technical Operations Director: Greg Nank. Marketing Director: Steve Schuh. Marketing Coordinator: Joni Lindauer.

Ownership: Mediacom LLC (MSO).

NEW HAMPTON—Mediacom, 4010 Alexandra Dr, Waterloo, IA 50702. Phone: 319-235-2197. Fax: 319-232-7841. Web Site: http://www.mediacomcable.com. Also serves Calmar, Elgin, Fayette, Fort Atkinson, Fredericksburg, Ossian, Spillville, Sumner & West Union. ICA: IA0074.

TV Market Ranking: 65 (Fredericksburg, Sumner); Outside TV Markets (Calmar, Elgin, Fayette, Fort Atkinson, NEW HAMPTON, Ossian, Spillville, West Union). Franchise award date: N.A. Franchise expiration date: N.A. Began: January 1, 1982.

Channel capacity: N.A. Channels available but not in use: N.A.

Basic Service
Subscribers: 3,467.
Programming (received off-air): KAAL (ABC) Austin; KCRG-TV (ABC) Cedar Rapids; KFXA (FOX) Cedar Rapids; KGAN (CBS) Cedar Rapids; KIMT (CBS, MNT) Mason City; KRIN (PBS) Waterloo; KTTC (CW, NBC) Rochester; KWKB (CW, MNT) Iowa City; KWWL (NBC) Waterloo; KXLT-TV (FOX) Rochester.
Programming (via satellite): C-SPAN; Home Shopping Network; INSP; Nickelodeon; QVC; Sneak Prevue; TV Guide Network.
Fee: $20.00 installation; $8.77 monthly; $10.00 additional installation.

Expanded Basic Service 1
Subscribers: 2,664.
Programming (via satellite): ABC Family Channel; AMC; Animal Planet; Arts & Entertainment; Bravo; Cartoon Network; CNBC; CNN; Comcast SportsNet Chicago; Comedy Central; Country Music TV; C-SPAN 2; Discovery Channel; Disney Channel; E! Entertainment Television; ESPN; ESPN 2; Eternal Word TV Network; Food Network; Fox News Channel; FX; Hallmark Channel; Headline News; HGTV; History Channel; Lifetime; MSNBC; MTV; RFD-TV; Speed Channel; Spike TV; Syfy; TBS Superstation; Telemundo; The Learning Channel; Travel Channel; Trinity Broadcasting Network; truTV; Turner Classic Movies; Turner Network TV; TV Land; USA Network; VH1; WE tv; Weather Channel; WGN America.
Fee: $10.00 installation; $29.95 monthly.

Digital Basic Service
Subscribers: N.A.
Programming (via satellite): AmericanLife TV Network; BBC America; Bio; Bloomberg Television; Discovery Digital Networks; DMX Music; Fox Movie Channel; Fox Sports World; Fuse; G4; GAS; Golf Channel; GSN; Halogen Network; History Channel International; Independent Film Channel; Lifetime Movie Network; Lime; MTV Networks Digital Suite; National Geographic Channel; Nick Jr.; Outdoor Channel; Ovation; Style Network; Toon Disney; Versus.

Digital Pay Service 1
Pay Units: 520.
Programming (via satellite): Cinemax (multiplexed); Encore (multiplexed); Flix; HBO (multiplexed); Showtime (multiplexed); Starz (multiplexed); Sundance Channel; The Movie Channel (multiplexed).
Fee: $10.00 installation; $9.95 monthly (Cinemax, HBO, Showtime, Flix/Sundance/TMC, or Starz/Encore).

Video-On-Demand: Yes

Pay-Per-View
ESPN Now (delivered digitally); ETC (delivered digitally); Playboy TV (delivered digitally); Pleasure (delivered digitally); Fresh (delivered digitally); Shorteez (delivered digitally); TVN Entertainment (delivered digitally); sports (delivered digitally).

Internet Service
Operational: Yes.
Broadband Service: Mediacom High Speed Internet.
Fee: $99.00 installation; $40.00 monthly.

Telephone Service
Digital: Operational

Miles of Plant: 105.0 (coaxial); None (fiber optic). Homes passed: 5,650.

Regional Vice President: Doug Frank. General Manager: Doug Nix. Technical Operations Director: Greg Nank. Marketing Director: Steve Schuh. Marketing Coordinator: Joni Lindauer.

City fee: 3% of gross.

Ownership: Mediacom LLC (MSO).

NEW LIBERTY—Dixon Telephone Co. Now served by DIXON, IA [IA0358]. ICA: IA0483.

NEW MARKET—Farmers Mutual Telephone Co. Now served by STANTON, IA [IA0264]. ICA: IA0294.

NEW VIRGINIA—Interstate Communications. Now served by TRURO, IA [IA0344]. ICA: IA0343.

NEWELL—Formerly served by TelePartners. No longer in operation. ICA: IA0205.

NEWTON—Mediacom. Now served by DES MOINES, IA [IA0001]. ICA: IA0016.

NICHOLS—PEC Cablevision, 1700 S 1st Ave, Ste 1, Iowa City, IA 52240-6077. Phone: 319-351-2297. Fax: 319-358-5810. E-mail: joepeter@aol.com. ICA: IA0485.

TV Market Ranking: Below 100 (NICHOLS). Franchise award date: April 5, 1989. Franchise expiration date: N.A. Began: August 1, 1989.

Channel capacity: 35 (not 2-way capable). Channels available but not in use: 5.

Basic Service
Subscribers: 70.
Programming (received off-air): KCRG-TV (ABC) Cedar Rapids; KGAN (CBS) Cedar Rapids; KIIN (PBS) Iowa City; KLJB (CW, FOX) Davenport; KWKB (CW, MNT) Iowa City; KWQC-TV (NBC) Davenport; KWWL (NBC) Waterloo; WHBF-TV (CBS) Rock Island; WQAD-TV (ABC) Moline.
Programming (via satellite): ABC Family Channel; Arts & Entertainment; CNBC; CNN; Country Music TV; Discovery Channel; Disney Channel; ESPN; ESPN 2; GalaVision; Spike TV; TBS Superstation; Turner Network TV; WGN America.
Fee: $25.00 installation; $25.23 monthly.

Pay Service 1
Pay Units: 57.
Programming (via satellite): HBO; Showtime.
Fee: $10.95 monthly (each).

Video-On-Demand: No

Internet Service
Operational: No.

Telephone Service
None

Miles of Plant: 2.0 (coaxial); None (fiber optic). Homes passed: 144. Total homes in franchised area: 144.

Manager & Chief Technician: Joe Peterson.

Ownership: PEC Cable.

NORTH LIBERTY—South Slope Communications Co. This cable system has converted to IPTV. See North Liberty, IA [IA5007], IA. ICA: IA0432.

NORTH LIBERTY—South Slope Coop. Communications Co. Formerly [IA0432]. This cable system has converted to IPTV, PO Box 19, 980 N Front St, North Liberty, IA 52317. Phones: 800-272-6449; 319-626-2211. Fax: 319-665-7000. E-mail: info@southslope.com. Web Site: http://www.southslope.com. ICA: IA5007.

TV Market Ranking: 65 (NORTH LIBERTY). Franchise award date: N.A. Franchise expiration date: N.A. Began: January 1, 2005.

Channel capacity: N.A. Channels available but not in use: N.A.

Basic Service
Subscribers: N.A.
Fee: $25.00 installation; $41.95 monthly.
Expanded Basic Service 1
Subscribers: N.A.
Fee: $25.00 installation; $54.95 monthly.
Expanded Basic Service 2
Subscribers: N.A.
Fee: $25.00 installation; $10.00 monthly.
Limited Basic Service
Subscribers: N.A.
Fee: $25.00 installation; $14.95 monthly.
Pay Service 1
Pay Units: N.A.
Fee: $25.00 installation; $10.95 monthy (Starz); $11.95 monthly (Cinemax); $12.95 monthly (Showtime); $13.95 monthy (HBO); $15.95 monthly (Adult).
Internet Service
Operational: Yes.
Fee: $39.95 monthly; $10.00 modem lease; $130.00 modem purchase.
Telephone Service
Digital: Operational
Fee: $14.50 monthly
Manager: J. R. Brumley.
Ownership: South Slope Cooperative Communications Co. (MSO).

NORTHWOOD—Mediacom. Now served by MASON CITY, IA [IA0010]. ICA: IA0131.

OAKLAND—Our Cable, PO Box 190, 112 E Main St, Breda, IA 51436-0190. Phone: 877-873-8715. E-mail: info@ourcableia.com. Web Site: http://ourcableia.com. ICA: IA0486.
TV Market Ranking: 53 (OAKLAND). Franchise award date: N.A. Franchise expiration date: N.A. Began: January 1, 1985.
Channel capacity: N.A. Channels available but not in use: N.A.
Basic Service
Subscribers: N.A. Included in Breda
Programming (received off-air): KETV (ABC) Omaha; KHIN (PBS) Red Oak; KMTV-TV (CBS) Omaha; KPTM (FOX, MNT) Omaha; KUON-TV (PBS) Lincoln; KXVO (CW) Omaha; WOWT-TV (IND, NBC) Omaha.
Programming (via satellite): ABC Family Channel; Arts & Entertainment; CNN; Country Music TV; Discovery Channel; Disney Channel; ESPN; ESPN 2; Headline News; HGTV; Lifetime; Nickelodeon; Spike TV; TBS Superstation; Turner Network TV; TV Land; USA Network; WGN America.
Fee: $20.00 installation; $26.45 monthly.
Pay Service 1
Pay Units: N.A.
Programming (via satellite): Showtime.
Fee: $10.95 monthly.
Video-On-Demand: No
Internet Service
Operational: No.
Telephone Service
None
Ownership: Our Cable (MSO).

OAKVILLE—Formerly served by Longview Communications. No longer in operation. ICA: IA0323.

OCHEYEDAN—Premier Communications, PO Box 200, 339 1st Ave NE, Sioux Center, IA 51250. Phones: 800-642-4088; 712-722-3451. Fax: 712-722-1113. E-mail: dboone@mtcnet.net. Web Site: http://www.mypremieronline.com. ICA: IA0276.
TV Market Ranking: Outside TV Markets (OCHEYEDAN). Franchise award date: N.A. Franchise expiration date: N.A. Began: January 1, 1984.
Channel capacity: 36 (not 2-way capable). Channels available but not in use: 14.
Basic Service
Subscribers: 127.
Programming (received off-air): KCAU-TV (ABC) Sioux City; KDLT-TV (NBC) Sioux Falls; KELO-TV (CBS, MNT) Sioux Falls; KPTH (FOX, MNT) Sioux City; KSFY-TV (ABC) Sioux Falls; KSIN-TV (PBS) Sioux City; KTIV (CW, NBC) Sioux City.
Programming (via satellite): ABC Family Channel; Arts & Entertainment; CNN; C-SPAN; Discovery Channel; Disney Channel; ESPN; ESPN 2; Fox News Channel; Great American Country; Hallmark Channel; Headline News; HGTV; History Channel; Lifetime; Nickelodeon; Speed Channel; Spike TV; TBS Superstation; The Learning Channel; Turner Network TV; TV Land; USA Network; Weather Channel; WGN America.
Current originations: Public Access.
Fee: $16.00 installation; $21.95 monthly.
Pay Service 1
Pay Units: 15.
Programming (via satellite): HBO; Showtime.
Fee: $16.00 installation; $8.95 monthly (each).
Internet Service
Operational: No.
Fee: $50.00 installation; $47.50 monthly.
Miles of Plant: 4.0 (coaxial); None (fiber optic). Homes passed: 247.
Chief Executive Officer: Douglas A. Boone. Chief Technician: Leslie Sybesna. Marketing Director: Scott Te Stroete.
Ownership: Premier Communications Inc. (MSO).

OELWEIN—Mediacom. Now served by WAVERLY, IA [IA0021]. ICA: IA0044.

OGDEN—Ogden Telephone Co. Cablevision, PO Box 457, 202 W Walnut St, Ogden, IA 50212. Phone: 515-275-2050. Fax: 515-275-2599. E-mail: ogdentel@netins.net. ICA: IA0126.
TV Market Ranking: 66 (OGDEN). Franchise award date: N.A. Franchise expiration date: N.A. Began: July 1, 1983.
Channel capacity: N.A. Channels available but not in use: N.A.
Basic Service
Subscribers: 478.
Programming (received off-air): KCCI (CBS) Des Moines; KCWI-TV (CW) Ames; KDIN-TV (PBS) Des Moines; KDSM-TV (FOX) Des Moines; KFPX-TV (ION) Newton; WHO-DT (NBC) Des Moines; WOI-DT (ABC) Ames.
Programming (via satellite): Home Shopping Network; Trinity Broadcasting Network; WGN America.
Fee: $15.75 installation; $13.10 monthly.
Expanded Basic Service 1
Subscribers: 455.
Programming (via satellite): ABC Family Channel; AMC; Animal Planet; Arts & Entertainment; Cartoon Network; CNN; C-SPAN; C-SPAN 2; Discovery Channel; Disney Channel; Encore; ESPN; Eternal Word TV Network; Fox Sports Net Midwest; FX; Great American Country; Hallmark Channel; Headline News; HGTV; History Channel; Lifetime; MTV; National Geographic Channel; Nickelodeon; Spike TV; Syfy; The Learning Channel; Travel Channel; Turner Network TV; TV Land; USA Network; Versus; Weather Channel.
Fee: $31.75 monthly.
Pay Service 1
Pay Units: 71.
Programming (via satellite): Cinemax; HBO; Showtime; Starz; The Movie Channel.
Fee: $6.95 monthly (Starz), $8.95 monthly (Cinemax), $11.95 monthly (HBO, Showtime or TMC).
Video-On-Demand: No
Internet Service
Operational: No, DSL only.
Telephone Service
None
Miles of Plant: 13.0 (coaxial); None (fiber optic). Homes passed: 800.
Manager: John P. Ellis.
Ownership: Ogden Telephone Co.

OLDS—Farmers & Merchants Mutual Telephone. Formerly served by Wayland, IA [IA0525]. This cable system has converted to IPTV., PO Box 247, 210 W Main St, Wayland, IA 52654. Phone: 319-256-2736. Fax: 319-256-7210. E-mail: manager@farmtel.com. Web Site: http://www.farmtel.net. ICA: IA5075.
Channel capacity: N.A. Channels available but not in use: N.A.
Internet Service
Operational: Yes.
Telephone Service
Digital: Operational
Ownership: Farmers & Merchants Mutual Telephone Co.

OLIN—Olin Telephone & Cablevision Co., 318 Jackson St, Olin, IA 52320. Phone: 319-484-2200. Fax: 319-484-2800. E-mail: olintel@netins.net. Web Site: http://www.olintelephone.com. ICA: IA0615.
TV Market Ranking: 65 (OLIN). Franchise award date: N.A. Franchise expiration date: N.A. Began: December 31, 1996.
Channel capacity: N.A. Channels available but not in use: N.A.
Basic Service
Subscribers: 235.
Programming (received off-air): KCRG-TV (ABC) Cedar Rapids; KFXA (FOX) Cedar Rapids; KGAN (CBS) Cedar Rapids; KIIN (PBS) Iowa City; KLJB (CW, FOX) Davenport; KWKB (CW, MNT) Iowa City; KWQC-TV (NBC) Davenport; KWWL (NBC) Waterloo; WHBF-TV (CBS) Rock Island; WQAD-TV (ABC) Moline.
Programming (via satellite): ABC Family Channel; AMC; AmericanLife TV Network; Animal Planet; Arts & Entertainment; Big Ten Network; Cartoon Network; CNBC; CNN; Comcast SportsNet Chicago; Comedy Central; Country Music TV; C-SPAN; Discovery Channel; Disney Channel; E! Entertainment Television; ESPN; ESPN 2; ESPN Classic Sports; Food Network; Fox News Channel; FX; Great American Country; GSN; Hallmark Channel; HGTV; History Channel; Home Shopping Network; INSP; ION Television; Lifetime; MTV; Nickelodeon; Outdoor Channel; QVC; Speed Channel; Spike TV; Syfy; TBS Superstation; The Learning Channel; Travel Channel; Trinity Broadcasting Network; Turner Classic Movies; Turner Network TV; TV Land; USA Network; VH1; Weather Channel; WGN America.
Fee: $34.95 monthly.
Pay Service 1
Pay Units: N.A.
Programming (via satellite): Cinemax; HBO; Showtime.
Fee: $9.50 monthly (each).
Video-On-Demand: No
Internet Service
Operational: No, DSL & dial-up.
Telephone Service
None
Miles of Plant: 5.0 (coaxial); None (fiber optic). Homes passed: 250. Total homes in franchised area: 250.
Manager: Rodney Cozart. Chief Technician: Frank Wood. Office Manager: Sheila Rouse.
Ownership: Olin Telephone & Cablevision Co.

ONAWA—Long Lines, 501 4th St, Sergeant Bluff, IA 51054-8509. Phones: 712-884-2203; 712-271-4000. Fax: 712-271-2727. Web Site: http://www.longlines.com. ICA: IA0090.
TV Market Ranking: Outside TV Markets (ONAWA). Franchise award date: N.A. Franchise expiration date: N.A. Began: November 1, 1982.
Channel capacity: 35 (not 2-way capable). Channels available but not in use: N.A.
Basic Service
Subscribers: 1,035.
Programming (received off-air): KCAU-TV (ABC) Sioux City; KMEG (CBS) Sioux City; KPTH (FOX, MNT) Sioux City; KSIN-TV (PBS) Sioux City; KTIV (CW, NBC) Sioux City.
Programming (via satellite): ABC Family Channel; AMC; AmericanLife TV Network; Animal Planet; Arts & Entertainment; Big Ten Network; Cartoon Network; CNBC; CNN; Comedy Central; Country Music TV; C-SPAN; C-SPAN 2; CW+; Discovery Channel; Disney Channel; E! Entertainment Television; ESPN; ESPN 2; ESPN Classic Sports; Eternal Word TV Network; Food Network; Fox News Channel; Fox Sports Net North; FX; Golf Channel; Hallmark Channel; Headline News; HGTV; History Channel; Home Shopping Network; INSP; Lifetime; Lifetime Movie Network; MSNBC; MTV; Nickelodeon; QVC; Speed Channel; Spike TV; Syfy; TBS Superstation; The Learning Channel; The Sportsman Channel; Travel Channel; Trinity Broadcasting Network; truTV; Turner Classic Movies; Turner Network TV; TuTv; TV Guide Network; TV Land; USA Network; VH1; Weather Channel; WGN America.
Fee: $37.80 installation; $41.99 monthly.
Digital Basic Service
Subscribers: N.A.
Programming (via satellite): BBC America; Bio; Cooking Channel; Discovery Health Channel; Discovery Kids Channel; Discovery Military Channel; Discovery Planet Green; DMX Music; Do-It-Yourself; ESPN U; ESPNews; FitTV; Fox College Sports Atlantic; Fox College Sports Central; Fox College Sports Pacific; Fox Movie Channel; Fox Soccer; G4; Great American Country; GSN; Halogen Network; History Channel International; ID Investigation Discovery; Independent Film Channel; Lifetime Real Women; MTV Hits; MTV Jams; MTV2; Nick Jr.; NickToons TV; Outdoor Channel; RFD-TV; Science Channel; SoapNet; TeenNick; Toon Disney; Versus; VH1 Classic; VH1 Country; VH1 Soul; WE tv.
Fee: $9.99 monthly.
Digital Expanded Basic Service
Subscribers: N.A.
Programming (received off-air): KCAU-TV (ABC) Sioux City; KMEG (CBS) Sioux City; KPTH (FOX, MNT) Sioux City; KSIN-TV (PBS) Sioux City; KTIV (CW, NBC) Sioux City.
Programming (via satellite): Big Ten Network HD; Discovery Channel HD; ESPN 2 HD; ESPN HD; HDNet; HDNet Movies; Outdoor Channel 2 HD.
Fee: $9.95 monthly.

Digital Expanded Basic Service 2
Subscribers: N.A.
Programming (via satellite): Bandamax; De Pelicula; De Pelicula Clasico; Discovery en Espanol; ESPN Deportes; Fox Sports en Espanol; Ritmoson Latino; Telehit.
Fee: $2.95 monthly.
Pay Service 1
Pay Units: 152.
Programming (via satellite): HBO (multiplexed).
Fee: $15.00 installation; $14.95 monthly.
Pay Service 2
Pay Units: 82.
Programming (via satellite): Flix; Showtime (multiplexed); The Movie Channel.
Fee: $14.45 monthly.
Digital Pay Service 1
Pay Units: N.A.
Programming (via satellite): Cinemax (multiplexed); Cinemax HD; Encore (multiplexed); Flix; HBO (multiplexed); HBO HD; Showtime (multiplexed); Starz (multiplexed); Starz HDTV; Starz On Demand; The Movie Channel (multiplexed).
Fee: $11.95 monthly (Cinemax), $13.95 monthly (Starz/Encore), $14.45 (Showtime/TMC/Flix), $14.95 monthly (HBO).
Video-On-Demand: Yes
Internet Service
Operational: No, Both DSL & dial-up.
Telephone Service
Analog: Operational
Fee: $18.50 monthly
Miles of Plant: 18.0 (coaxial); None (fiber optic). Additional miles planned: 1.0 (coaxial). Homes passed: 1,192. Total homes in franchised area: 1,200.
Manager: O. H. Boeckman. Chief Technician: Dennis Swenson. Customer Service Manager: Barb Johnson.
City fee: 3% of gross.
Ownership: Long Lines (MSO).

ONSLOW—Onslow Cooperative Telephone Assn., PO Box 6, 102 Anamosa Ave, Onslow, IA 52321. Phone: 563-485-2833. Fax: 563-485-3891. Web Site: http://www.yourclosestconnection.com/membership.asp?id=154. ICA: IA0487.
TV Market Ranking: 65 (ONSLOW). Franchise award date: N.A. Franchise expiration date: N.A. Began: October 1, 1990.
Channel capacity: 56 (not 2-way capable). Channels available but not in use: None.
Basic Service
Subscribers: 84.
Programming (received off-air): KCRG-TV (ABC) Cedar Rapids; KFXA (FOX) Cedar Rapids; KGAN (CBS) Cedar Rapids; KIIN (PBS) Iowa City; KLJB (CW, FOX) Davenport; KWQC-TV (NBC) Davenport; KWWL (NBC) Waterloo; WHBF-TV (CBS) Rock Island; WQAD-TV (ABC) Moline.
Programming (via satellite): ABC Family Channel; AMC; AmericanLife TV Network; Animal Planet; Arts & Entertainment; Cartoon Network; CNBC; CNN; Comedy Central; Country Music TV; C-SPAN; Discovery Channel; Disney Channel; E! Entertainment Television; ESPN; ESPN 2; Food Network; FX; Great American Country; GSN; HGTV; History Channel; Home Shopping Network; INSP; Lifetime; MTV; Nickelodeon; Outdoor Channel; QVC; Speed Channel; Spike TV; Syfy; TBS Superstation; The Learning Channel; Travel Channel; Trinity Broadcasting Network; Turner Classic Movies; Turner Network TV; TV Land; USA Network; VH1; Weather Channel; WGN America.
Fee: $21.95 monthly.
Pay Service 1
Pay Units: N.A.
Programming (via satellite): HBO.
Fee: $9.95 monthly.
Pay Service 2
Pay Units: 3.
Programming (via satellite): Cinemax.
Fee: $9.95 monthly.
Video-On-Demand: No
Internet Service
Operational: No, DSL & dial-up.
Telephone Service
None
Manager: Russ Benke.
Ownership: Onslow Cooperative Telephone Association.

ORANGE CITY—Long Lines, 501 4th St, Sergeant Bluff, IA 51054-8509. Phones: 712-884-2203; 712-271-4000. Fax: 712-271-2727. Web Site: http://www.longlines.com. ICA: IA0605. **Note:** This system is an overbuild.
TV Market Ranking: Outside TV Markets (ORANGE CITY).
Channel capacity: N.A. Channels available but not in use: N.A.
Basic Service
Subscribers: 137.
Programming (received off-air): KCAU-TV (ABC) Sioux City; KMEG (CBS) Sioux City; KPTH (FOX, MNT) Sioux City; KSIN-TV (PBS) Sioux City; KTIV (CW, NBC) Sioux City; KXVO (CW) Omaha.
Programming (via satellite): ABC Family Channel; AMC; AmericanLife TV Network; Animal Planet; Arts & Entertainment; Big Ten Network; Cartoon Network; CNBC; CNN; Comedy Central; Country Music TV; C-SPAN; C-SPAN 2; Discovery Channel; Disney Channel; E! Entertainment Television; ESPN; ESPN 2; ESPN Classic Sports; Eternal Word TV Network; Food Network; Fox News Channel; Fox Sports Net North; FX; Golf Channel; Hallmark Channel; Headline News; HGTV; History Channel; Home Shopping Network; INSP; Lifetime; Lifetime Movie Network; MSNBC; MTV; Nickelodeon; QVC; Speed Channel; Spike TV; Syfy; TBS Superstation; The Learning Channel; The Sportsman Channel; Travel Channel; Trinity Broadcasting Network; truTV; Turner Classic Movies; Turner Network TV; TuTv; TV Guide Network; TV Land; USA Network; VH1; Weather Channel; WGN America.
Fee: $41.99 monthly.
Digital Basic Service
Subscribers: N.A.
Programming (via satellite): BBC America; Bio; Cooking Channel; Discovery Health Channel; Discovery Kids Channel; Discovery Military Channel; Discovery Planet Green; DMX Music; Do-It-Yourself; ESPN U; ESPNews; FitTV; Fox College Sports Atlantic; Fox College Sports Central; Fox College Sports Pacific; Fox Movie Channel; Fox Soccer; G4; Great American Country; GSN; Halogen Network; History Channel International; ID Investigation Discovery; Independent Film Channel; Lifetime Real Women; MTV Hits; MTV Jams; MTV2; Nick Jr.; NickToons TV; Outdoor Channel; RFD-TV; Science Channel; SoapNet; TeenNick; Toon Disney; Versus; VH1 Classic; VH1 Country; VH1 Soul; WE tv.
Fee: $9.99 monthly.
Digital Expanded Basic Service
Subscribers: N.A.
Programming (received off-air): KCAU-TV (ABC) Sioux City; KMEG (CBS) Sioux City; KPTH (FOX, MNT) Sioux City; KTIV (CW, NBC) Sioux City; KUSD-TV (PBS) Vermillion.
Programming (via satellite): Big Ten Network HD; Discovery Channel HD; ESPN 2 HD; ESPN HD; HDNet; HDNet Movies; Outdoor Channel 2 HD.
Fee: $9.95 monthly.
Digital Expanded Basic Service 2
Subscribers: N.A.
Programming (via satellite): Bandamax; De Pelicula; De Pelicula Clasico; Discovery en Espanol; ESPN Deportes; Fox Sports en Espanol; Ritmoson Latino; Telehit.
Fee: $2.95 monthly.
Pay Service 1
Pay Units: 24.
Programming (via satellite): HBO (multiplexed).
Fee: $14.95 monthly.
Pay Service 2
Pay Units: 18.
Programming (via satellite): Flix; Showtime (multiplexed); The Movie Channel.
Fee: $14.45 monthly.
Digital Pay Service 1
Pay Units: N.A.
Programming (via satellite): Cinemax (multiplexed); Cinemax HD; Encore (multiplexed); Flix; HBO (multiplexed); HBO HD; Showtime (multiplexed); Starz (multiplexed); Starz HDTV; Starz On Demand; The Movie Channel (multiplexed).
Fee: $11.95 monthly (Cinemax), $13.95 monthly (Starz/Encore), $14.45 monthly (Showtime/TMC/Flix), $14.95 monthly (HBO).
Video-On-Demand: Yes
Internet Service
Operational: No, Both DSL & dial-up.
Homes passed: 1,646.
System Engineer: Tony Seubert. Marketing Manager: Pat McElroy. Office Manager: Denise Moberg.
Ownership: Long Lines (MSO).

ORANGE CITY—Mediacom, PO Box 110, 1504 2nd St SE, Waseca, MN 56093. Phone: 507-835-2356. Fax: 507-835-4567. Web Site: http://www.mediacomcable.com. Also serves Alton, Hawarden & Sioux County. ICA: IA0488.
TV Market Ranking: 85 (Sioux County (portions)); Below 100 (Hawarden, Sioux County (portions)); Outside TV Markets (Alton, ORANGE CITY, Sioux County (portions)). Franchise award date: N.A. Franchise expiration date: N.A. Began: December 31, 1981.
Channel capacity: N.A. Channels available but not in use: N.A.
Basic Service
Subscribers: 1,152.
Programming (received off-air): KCAU-TV (ABC) Sioux City; KELO-TV (CBS, MNT) Sioux Falls; KMEG (CBS) Sioux City; KPTH (FOX, MNT) Sioux City; KSFY-TV (ABC) Sioux Falls; KSIN-TV (PBS) Sioux City; KTIV (CW, NBC) Sioux City; KUSD-TV (PBS) Vermillion.
Programming (via satellite): C-SPAN; C-SPAN 2; Eternal Word TV Network; Home Shopping Network; ION Television; QVC; ShopNBC; TV Guide Network; WGN America.
Fee: $25.00 installation; $6.95 monthly.
Expanded Basic Service 1
Subscribers: 552.
Programming (via satellite): ABC Family Channel; AMC; Animal Planet; Arts & Entertainment; BET Networks; Bravo; Cartoon Network; CNBC; CNN; Comedy Central; Country Music TV; Discovery Channel; Disney Channel; E! Entertainment Television; ESPN; ESPN 2; ESPN Classic Sports; Food Network; Fox News Channel; Fox Sports Net Midwest; FX; Hallmark Channel; Headline News; HGTV; History Channel; INSP; Lifetime; MSNBC; MTV; Nickelodeon; Outdoor Channel; RFD-TV; Speed Channel; Spike TV; Syfy; TBS Superstation; Telemundo; The Learning Channel; Travel Channel; Trinity Broadcasting Network; truTV; Turner Network TV; TV Land; Univision; USA Network; Versus; VH1; WE tv; Weather Channel.
Fee: $14.00 monthly.
Digital Basic Service
Subscribers: N.A.
Programming (via satellite): AmericanLife TV Network; BBC America; Bio; Bloomberg Television; Discovery Digital Networks; DMX Music; ESPN 2; FitTV; Fox Movie Channel; Fox Soccer; Fuse; G4; GAS; Golf Channel; GSN; Halogen Network; History Channel International; Independent Film Channel; Lifetime Movie Network; Lime; MTV Networks Digital Suite; National Geographic Channel; Nick Jr.; NickToons TV; Style Network; Turner Classic Movies.
Digital Pay Service 1
Pay Units: N.A.
Programming (via satellite): Cinemax (multiplexed); Encore (multiplexed); Flix (multiplexed); HBO (multiplexed); Showtime (multiplexed); Starz (multiplexed); Sundance Channel (multiplexed); The Movie Channel (multiplexed).
Video-On-Demand: Planned
Pay-Per-View
iN DEMAND (delivered digitally); Fresh (delivered digitally); Shorteez (delivered digitally); Playboy TV (delivered digitally); Pleasure (delivered digitally).
Internet Service
Operational: Yes.
Broadband Service: Mediacom High Speed Internet.
Telephone Service
Analog: Planned
Miles of Plant: 31.0 (coaxial); None (fiber optic). Total homes in franchised area: 2,100.
Vice President: Bill Jenson. Marketing & Sales Director: Lori Huberty. Engineering Manager: Craig Kaiser. Engineering Director: Scott Walter.
City fee: 6% of gross.
Ownership: Mediacom LLC (MSO).

OSAGE—Mediacom, 4010 Alexandra Dr, Waterloo, IA 50702. Phone: 319-235-2197. Fax: 319-232-7841. Web Site: http://www.mediacomcable.com. Also serves Cresco, Elma & Lime Springs. ICA: IA0085.
TV Market Ranking: Below 100 (OSAGE); Outside TV Markets (Cresco, Elma, Lime

Springs). Franchise award date: N.A. Franchise expiration date: N.A. Began: January 1, 1981.
Channel capacity: N.A. Channels available but not in use: N.A.

Basic Service
Subscribers: 2,421.
Programming (received off-air): KAAL (ABC) Austin; KCRG-TV (ABC) Cedar Rapids; KGAN (CBS) Cedar Rapids; KIMT (CBS, MNT) Mason City; KTTC (CW, NBC) Rochester; KWWL (NBC) Waterloo; KXLT-TV (FOX) Rochester; KYIN (PBS) Mason City.
Programming (via satellite): ABC Family Channel; CNN; C-SPAN; Discovery Channel; Headline News; Lifetime; MTV; Nickelodeon; TBS Superstation; Turner Network TV; Weather Channel; WGN America.
Current originations: Public Access.
Fee: $60.00 installation; $17.56 monthly; $.69 converter.

Expanded Basic Service 1
Subscribers: 877.
Programming (via satellite): AMC; Animal Planet; Arts & Entertainment; Bravo; Cartoon Network; CNBC; Comedy Central; Country Music TV; C-SPAN 2; Disney Channel; E! Entertainment Television; ESPN; ESPN 2; Eternal Word TV Network; Food Network; Fox News Channel; Fox Sports Net Midwest; FX; Golf Channel; Hallmark Channel; HGTV; History Channel; Home Shopping Network; INSP; ION Television; MoviePlex; MSNBC; Outdoor Channel; Oxygen; QVC; Speed Channel; Spike TV; Syfy; The Learning Channel; Travel Channel; Trinity Broadcasting Network; truTV; Turner Classic Movies; TV Guide Network; TV Land; USA Network; VH1; WE tv.
Fee: $10.45 monthly.

Digital Basic Service
Subscribers: N.A.
Programming (via satellite): AmericanLife TV Network; BBC America; Bio; Bloomberg Television; Discovery Digital Networks; ESPN Classic Sports; ESPNews; Fox Sports World; Fuse; G4; GSN; Halogen Network; History Channel International; Independent Film Channel; Lifetime Movie Network; Music Choice; National Geographic Channel; Nick Jr.; Style Network; Versus.

Digital Pay Service 1
Pay Units: 137.
Programming (via satellite): Cinemax (multiplexed); Encore (multiplexed); HBO (multiplexed); Showtime (multiplexed); Starz (multiplexed); The Movie Channel (multiplexed).
Fee: $9.95 monthly (each).

Video-On-Demand: Yes

Pay-Per-View
TVN Entertainment (delivered digitally); iN DEMAND (delivered digitally); Fresh (delivered digitally); Shorteez (delivered digitally); Playboy TV (delivered digitally); Hot Choice (delivered digitally); ESPN Now (delivered digitally); Sports PPV (delivered digitally).

Internet Service
Operational: Yes.
Broadband Service: Mediacom High Speed Internet.
Fee: $49.95 installation; $55.95 monthly.

Telephone Service
Analog: Not Operational
Digital: Operational
Miles of Plant: 64.0 (coaxial); None (fiber optic). Homes passed: 3,191.
Regional Vice President: Doug Frank. Manager: Doug Nix. Technical Operations Director: Greg Nank. Marketing Director: Steve Schuh. Marketing Coordinator: Joni Lindauer.
City fee: 3% of gross.
Ownership: Mediacom LLC (MSO).

OSKALOOSA—Mediacom, 6300 Council St NE, Ste A, Cedar Rapids, IA 52402. Phones: 641-682-1695 (Ottumwa office); 319-395-9699. Fax: 319-393-7017. Web Site: http://www.mediacomcable.com. Also serves Beacon, New Sharon & University Park. ICA: IA0026.
TV Market Ranking: Below 100 (Beacon, New Sharon, OSKALOOSA, University Park). Franchise award date: N.A. Franchise expiration date: N.A. Began: January 1, 1980.
Channel capacity: N.A. Channels available but not in use: N.A.

Basic Service
Subscribers: 4,188.
Programming (received off-air): KCCI (CBS) Des Moines; KCRG-TV (ABC) Cedar Rapids; KDSM-TV (FOX) Des Moines; KIIN (PBS) Iowa City; KYOU-TV (FOX) Ottumwa; WHO-DT (NBC) Des Moines; WOI-DT (ABC) Ames.
Programming (via satellite): C-SPAN; C-SPAN 2; Home Shopping Network; QVC; WGN America.
Current originations: Government Access.
Fee: $33.59 installation; $8.98 monthly; $2.00 converter.

Expanded Basic Service 1
Subscribers: 3,913.
Programming (via satellite): ABC Family Channel; AMC; Animal Planet; Arts & Entertainment; BET Networks; Bravo; Cartoon Network; CNBC; CNN; Comcast SportsNet Chicago; Comedy Central; Country Music TV; Discovery Channel; Disney Channel; E! Entertainment Television; ESPN; ESPN 2; Eternal Word TV Network; Food Network; Fox News Channel; FX; Hallmark Channel; Headline News; HGTV; History Channel; INSP; Lifetime; Lifetime Movie Network; MSNBC; MTV; National Geographic Channel; Nickelodeon; RFD-TV; Speed Channel; Spike TV; Syfy; TBS Superstation; Telemundo; The Learning Channel; Travel Channel; Trinity Broadcasting Network; truTV; Turner Network TV; TV Land; Univision; USA Network; Versus; VH1; WE tv; Weather Channel.
Fee: $31.97 monthly.

Digital Basic Service
Subscribers: 1,245.
Programming (via satellite): AmericanLife TV Network; BBC America; Bio; Bloomberg Television; CBS College Sports Network; CMT Pure Country; Discovery HD Theater; Discovery Health Channel; Discovery Home Channel; Discovery Kids Channel; Discovery Military Channel; DMX Music; ESPN 2 HD; ESPN HD; ESPN U; ESPNews; Fox College Sports Atlantic; Fox College Sports Central; Fox College Sports Pacific; Fox Movie Channel; Fox Reality Channel; Fox Soccer; Fuel TV; Fuse; G4; Gol TV; Golf Channel; GSN; Halogen Network; HDNet; HDNet Movies; History Channel International; ID Investigation Discovery; Independent Film Channel; Lifetime Real Women; MTV Hits; MTV2; Nick Jr.; NickToons TV; Outdoor Channel; Ovation; Science Channel; Sleuth; Style Network; TeenNick; Tennis Channel; The Sportsman Channel; Toon Disney; Turner Classic Movies; TVG Network; Universal HD; VH1 Classic; VH1 Soul.
Fee: $12.00 monthly.

Digital Pay Service 1
Pay Units: N.A.
Programming (via satellite): Cinemax (multiplexed); Encore (multiplexed); Flix; HBO (multiplexed); HBO HD; Showtime (multiplexed); Showtime HD; Starz (multiplexed); Starz HDTV; Sundance Channel; The Movie Channel (multiplexed); The Movie Channel HD.
Fee: $9.95 monthly (Cinemax, HBO, Showtime, Flix/Sundance/TMC, or Starz/Encore).

Video-On-Demand: Yes

Pay-Per-View
Addressable homes: 1,245.
ESPN Now (delivered digitally), Addressable: Yes; ETC (delivered digitally); Playboy TV (delivered digitally); Pleasure (delivered digitally); Fresh (delivered digitally); Shorteez (delivered digitally); TVN Entertainment (delivered digitally); sports (delivered digitally).

Internet Service
Operational: Yes.
Subscribers: 880.
Broadband Service: Mediacom High Speed Internet.
Fee: $55.95 monthly.

Telephone Service
Digital: Operational
Miles of Plant: 112.0 (coaxial); None (fiber optic). Homes passed: 6,036. Total homes in franchised area: 6,036.
Regional Vice President: Doug Frank. Technical Operations Director: Greg Nank. Technical Operations Manager: Steve Angren. Marketing Director: Steve Schuh.
Ownership: Mediacom LLC (MSO).

OTTUMWA—Mediacom, 6300 Council St NE, Ste A, Cedar Rapids, IA 52402. Phone: 319-395-9699. Fax: 319-393-7017. Web Site: http://www.mediacomcable.com. Also serves Agency, Batavia, Fairfield, Jefferson County & Wapello County. ICA: IA0013.
TV Market Ranking: Below 100 (Agency, Batavia, Fairfield, Jefferson County, OTTUMWA, Wapello County). Franchise award date: N.A. Franchise expiration date: N.A. Began: July 27, 1971.
Channel capacity: N.A. Channels available but not in use: N.A.

Basic Service
Subscribers: 6,471.
Programming (received off-air): KCCI (CBS) Des Moines; KDSM-TV (FOX) Des Moines; KFPX-TV (ION) Newton; KIIN (PBS) Iowa City; KTVO (ABC) Kirksville; KYOU-TV (FOX) Ottumwa; WHO-DT (NBC) Des Moines; WOI-DT (ABC) Ames; allband FM.
Programming (via satellite): ABC Family Channel; Arts & Entertainment; Cartoon Network; CNBC; CNN; Comedy Central; C-SPAN; Discovery Channel; Hallmark Channel; Headline News; Home Shopping Network; ION Television; Lifetime; Nickelodeon; QVC; TBS Superstation; Turner Network TV; VH1; Weather Channel; WGN America.
Current originations: Government Access.
Fee: $60.00 installation; $20.40 monthly; $2.00 converter.

Expanded Basic Service 1
Subscribers: 6,212.
Programming (via satellite): AMC; Animal Planet; BET Networks; Bravo; Comcast SportsNet Chicago; Country Music TV; Disney Channel; E! Entertainment Television; ESPN; ESPN 2; Eternal Word TV Network; FitTV; Food Network; Fox News Channel; FX; HGTV; History Channel; INSP; MSNBC; MTV; National Geographic Channel; Speed Channel; Spike TV; Syfy; Telemundo; The Learning Channel; Travel Channel; Trinity Broadcasting Network; truTV; TV Land; USA Network; WE tv.
Fee: $21.16 monthly.

Digital Basic Service
Subscribers: N.A.
Programming (via satellite): American-Life TV Network; BBC America; Bio; Bloomberg Television; Discovery Digital Networks; DMX Music; Fox Movie Channel; Fox Sports World; Fuse; G4; GAS; Golf Channel; GSN; Halogen Network; History Channel International; Independent Film Channel; Lifetime Movie Network; Lime; MTV Networks Digital Suite; Nick Jr.; Outdoor Channel; Ovation; Style Network; Toon Disney; Versus.

Digital Pay Service 1
Pay Units: 842.
Programming (via satellite): Cinemax (multiplexed); Encore (multiplexed); Flix; HBO (multiplexed); Showtime (multiplexed); Starz (multiplexed); Sundance Channel; The Movie Channel (multiplexed).
Fee: $9.95 monthly (Cinemax, HBO, Showtime, Flix/Sundance/TMC, or Starz/Encore).

Video-On-Demand: Yes

Pay-Per-View
ESPN Now (delivered digitally); ETC (delivered digitally); Playboy TV (delivered digitally); Pleasure (delivered digitally); Fresh (delivered digitally); Shorteez (delivered digitally); TVN Entertainment (delivered digitally); sports (delivered digitally).

Internet Service
Operational: Yes. Began: January 1, 2003.
Broadband Service: Mediacom High Speed Internet.
Fee: $50.95 monthly.

Telephone Service
Analog: Not Operational
Digital: Operational
Miles of Plant: 295.0 (coaxial); None (fiber optic). Additional miles planned: 5.0 (coaxial). Homes passed: 16,717. Total homes in franchised area: 16,784.
Regional Vice President: Doug Frank. Technical Operations Director: Greg Nank. Technical Operations Manager: Steve Angren. Marketing Director: Steve Schuh.
Ownership: Mediacom LLC (MSO).

OXFORD—South Slope Coop. Communications Co. Formerly served by North Liberty, IA [IA0432]. This cable system has converted to IPTV, PO Box 19, 980 N Front St, North Liberty, IA 52317. Phones: 800-272-6449; 319-626-2211. Fax: 319-665-7000. E-mail: info@southslope.com. Web Site: http://www.southslope.com. ICA: IA5010.
TV Market Ranking: 65 (Oxford). Franchise award date: July 13, 2004. Franchise expiration date: N.A. Began: December 1, 2005.
Channel capacity: N.A. Channels available but not in use: N.A.

Basic Service
Subscribers: N.A.
Fee: $25.00 installation; $41.95 monthly.

Expanded Basic Service 1
Subscribers: N.A.
Fee: $25.00 installation; $54.95 monthly.

Expanded Basic Service 2
Subscribers: N.A.
Fee: $25.00 installation; $10.00 monthly.

Limited Basic Service
Subscribers: N.A.
Fee: $25.00 installation; $14.95 monthly.

Pay Service 1
Pay Units: N.A.
Fee: $10.95 monthy (Starz); $11.95 monthly (Cinemax); $12.95 monthly (Showtime); $13.95 monthy (HBO); $15.95 monthly (Adult).
Internet Service
Operational: Yes.
Fee: $39.95 monthly; $10.00 modem lease; $130.00 modem purchase.
Telephone Service
Digital: Operational
Fee: $14.50 monthly
Ownership: South Slope Cooperative Communications Co.

OXFORD JUNCTION—Mediacom. Now served by CEDAR RAPIDS [IA0002]. ICA: IA0163.

PALMER—Palmer Mutual Telephone Co., PO Box 155, 306 Main St, Palmer, IA 50571-0155. Phone: 712-359-2411. E-mail: palmerone@palmerone.com. Web Site: http://www.palmerone.com. ICA: IA0490.
TV Market Ranking: Outside TV Markets (PALMER). Franchise award date: February 13, 1990. Franchise expiration date: N.A. Began: September 15, 1990.
Channel capacity: N.A. Channels available but not in use: N.A.
Basic Service
Subscribers: 75.
Programming (received off-air): KCAU-TV (ABC) Sioux City; KCCI (CBS) Des Moines; KDSM-TV (FOX) Des Moines; KEYC-TV (CBS, FOX) Mankato; KMEG (CBS) Sioux City; KPTH (FOX, MNT) Sioux City; KTIN (PBS) Fort Dodge; KTIV (CW, NBC) Sioux City; WHO-DT (NBC) Des Moines; WOI-DT (ABC) Ames; 2 FMs.
Programming (via satellite): ABC Family Channel; AMC; AmericanLife TV Network; Animal Planet; Arts & Entertainment; Bravo; Cartoon Network; CNBC; CNN; Comedy Central; Country Music TV; Court TV; C-SPAN; C-SPAN 2; Discovery Channel; Discovery Health Channel; Disney Channel; Do-It-Yourself; E! Entertainment Television; ESPN; ESPN 2; ESPN Classic Sports; ESPN U; Eternal Word TV Network; Food Network; Fox Movie Channel; Fox News Channel; FX; Golf Channel; Hallmark Channel; Headline News; HGTV; History Channel; Home Shopping Network; INSP; ION Television; Lifetime; Lifetime Movie Network; MSNBC; MTV; NFL Network; Nickelodeon; Outdoor Channel; QVC; Radar Channel; Speed Channel; Spike TV; Syfy; TBS Superstation; The Learning Channel; Travel Channel; Trinity Broadcasting Network; Turner Classic Movies; Turner Network TV; TV Guide Network; TV Land; USA Network; VH1; Weather Channel; WGN America.
Fee: $30.00 installation; $45.00 monthly.
Digital Basic Service
Subscribers: N.A.
Programming (received off-air): KCCI (CBS) Des Moines; KDSM-TV (FOX) Des Moines; KMEG (CBS) Sioux City; KPTH (FOX, MNT) Sioux City; KTIN (PBS) Fort Dodge; KTIV (CW, NBC) Sioux City; WHO-DT (NBC) Des Moines; WOI-DT (ABC) Ames.
Programming (via satellite): BBC America; Bio; Discovery HD Theater; Discovery Kids Channel; Discovery Military Channel; Discovery Planet Green; ESPN 2 HD; ESPN HD; ESPNews; FitTV; Fox Soccer; G4; GSN; HDNet; HDNet Movies; History Channel; ID Investigation Discovery; Independent Film Channel; Lifetime Movie Network; MTV2; Music Choice; National Geographic Channel; Nick Jr.; NickToons TV; Outdoor Channel; RFD-TV; Science Channel; SoapNet; TeenNick; Toon Disney; Universal HD; Versus; VH1 Classic; VH1 Country.
Fee: $8.00 monthly.
Digital Pay Service 1
Pay Units: N.A.
Programming (via satellite): Cinemax (multiplexed); Cinemax HD; Encore; HBO (multiplexed); HBO HD; Starz (multiplexed); Starz HDTV.
Fee: $10.00 monthly (Cinemax), $11.00 monthly (Starz/Encore), $14.00 monthly (HBO).
Internet Service
Operational: No, DSL & dial-up.
Telephone Service
None
Miles of Plant: 3.0 (coaxial); 3.0 (fiber optic). Homes passed: 100. Total homes in franchised area: 100.
General Manager: Steve Trimble. Office Manager: Pauline Schultz.
Ownership: Palmer Mutual Telephone Co.

PALO—Palo Cooperative Telephone Association. Formerly [IA0319]. This cable system has converted to IPTV, PO Box 169, 807 Second St, Palo, IA 52324. Phone: 319-851-3431. Fax: 319-851-6970. E-mail: palocoop@netins.net. ICA: IA5066.
Channel capacity: N.A. Channels available but not in use: N.A.
Internet Service
Operational: Yes.
Ownership: Palo Cooperative Telephone Assn.

PALO—Palo Cooperative Telephone Association. This cable system has converted to IPTV. See Palo, IA [IA5066]. ICA: IA0319.

PANORA—Panora Cooperative Cablevision Assn. Inc., PO Box 189, 114 E Main St, Panora, IA 50216. Phones: 800-622-5726; 641-755-2424. Fax: 641-755-2425. E-mail: panora@netins.net. Web Site: http://www.panoratelco.com. Also serves Lake Panorama, Linden & Yale. ICA: IA0108.
TV Market Ranking: 66 (Linden); Outside TV Markets (Lake Panorama, PANORA, Yale). Franchise award date: January 1, 1981. Franchise expiration date: N.A. Began: January 1, 1981.
Channel capacity: N.A. Channels available but not in use: N.A.
Basic Service
Subscribers: 1,262.
Programming (received off-air): KCCI (CBS) Des Moines; KCWI-TV (CW) Ames; KDIN-TV (PBS) Des Moines; KDSM-TV (FOX) Des Moines; WHO-DT (NBC) Des Moines; WOI-DT (ABC) Ames.
Programming (via satellite): ABC Family Channel; AMC; Animal Planet; Arts & Entertainment; Big Ten Network; CNBC; CNN; Comcast SportsNet Chicago; Country Music TV; C-SPAN; Discovery Channel; Disney Channel; ESPN; ESPN 2; Fox News Channel; FX; Headline News; HGTV; History Channel; INSP; ION Television; Lifetime; Nickelodeon; Outdoor Channel; Spike TV; TBS Superstation; The Learning Channel; Toon Disney; Travel Channel; Turner Network TV; TV Guide Network; USA Network; Weather Channel; WGN America.
Fee: $20.00 installation; $33.00 monthly; $1.50 converter.
Digital Basic Service
Subscribers: N.A.
Programming (via satellite): BBC America; Bio; Bloomberg Television; Bravo; Discovery Health Channel; Discovery Kids Channel; Discovery Military Channel; Discovery Planet Green; DMX Music; ESPN Classic Sports; ESPNews; Fox College Sports Atlantic; Fox College Sports Central; Fox College Sports Pacific; Fox Movie Channel; Fox Soccer; G4; Golf Channel; Great American Country; GSN; History Channel International; ID Investigation Discovery; Independent Film Channel; Lifetime Movie Network; Nick Jr.; NickToons TV; ShopNBC; Sleuth; Speed Channel; Style Network; TeenNick; The Word Network; Turner Classic Movies; Versus; WE tv.
Fee: $16.95 monthly.
Pay Service 1
Pay Units: 301.
Programming (via satellite): HBO.
Fee: $13.00 monthly.
Pay Service 2
Pay Units: 257.
Programming (via satellite): Encore; Starz.
Fee: $12.00 monthly.
Digital Pay Service 1
Pay Units: N.A.
Programming (via satellite): Cinemax (multiplexed); Encore (multiplexed); Flix; HBO (multiplexed); Showtime (multiplexed); Starz (multiplexed); The Movie Channel (multiplexed).
Fee: $13.00 monthly (Cinemax or Starz/Encore), $15 monthly (HBO or Showtime/TMC/Flix).
Video-On-Demand: No
Pay-Per-View
Special events (delivered digitally); Movies (delivered digitally).
Internet Service
Operational: No, DSL only.
Telephone Service
None
Miles of Plant: 49.0 (coaxial); 56.0 (fiber optic). Homes passed: 1,385. Total homes in franchised area: 1,400.
General Manager: Andy Randol. Plant Manager: Bill Dorsett. Marketing Director: Douglas Pals. Office Manager: Cheryl Castile.
Ownership: Panora Cooperative Cablevision Assn. Inc. (MSO).

PATON—Gowrie Cablevision, PO Box 415, Gowrie, IA 50543. Phones: 800-292-8989; 515-352-5227. Fax: 515-352-5226. Web Site: http://www.gowrie.org/utilities/gowrie_catv.htm. ICA: IA0492.
TV Market Ranking: 66 (PATON). Franchise award date: N.A. Franchise expiration date: N.A. Began: March 1, 1986.
Channel capacity: 42 (not 2-way capable). Channels available but not in use: N.A.
Basic Service
Subscribers: 80.
Programming (received off-air): KCCI (CBS) Des Moines; KDIN-TV (PBS) Des Moines; KDSM-TV (FOX) Des Moines; WHO-DT (NBC) Des Moines; WOI-DT (ABC) Ames.
Programming (via satellite): ABC Family Channel; CNN; ESPN; Spike TV; TBS Superstation; WGN America.
Fee: $25.00 installation; $27.50 monthly.
Pay Service 1
Pay Units: N.A.
Programming (via satellite): HBO; Showtime.
Fee: $10.00 monthly (each).
Video-On-Demand: No
Internet Service
Operational: No, Both DSL & dialup.
Telephone Service
None
Miles of Plant: 3.0 (coaxial); None (fiber optic). Homes passed: 140.
Manager: Paul Johnson.
Ownership: Gowrie Cablevision Inc. (MSO).

PAULINA—WesTel Systems. Now served by SANBORN, IA [IA0104]. ICA: IA0164.

PERSIA—TelePartners. Now served by WALNUT, IA [IA0241]. ICA: IA0575.

PETERSON—WesTel Systems. Now served by MARCUS, IA [IA0171]. ICA: IA0312.

PISGAH—Formerly served by TelePartners. No longer in operation. ICA: IA0494.

PLYMOUTH—Omnitel Communications, 608 E Congress St, Nora Springs, IA 50458-8634. Phone: 641-749-2531. Fax: 641-749-9510. E-mail: question@omnitel.biz. Web Site: http://www.omnitel.biz. ICA: IA0495.
TV Market Ranking: Below 100 (PLYMOUTH (VILLAGE)). Franchise award date: N.A. Franchise expiration date: N.A. Began: July 1, 1989.
Channel capacity: N.A. Channels available but not in use: N.A.
Basic Service
Subscribers: 129.
Programming (received off-air): KAAL (ABC) Austin; KCRG-TV (ABC) Cedar Rapids; KGAN (CBS) Cedar Rapids; KIMT (CBS, MNT) Mason City; KSMQ-TV (PBS) Austin; KTTC (CW, NBC) Rochester; KWWL (NBC) Waterloo; KXLT-TV (FOX) Rochester; KYIN (PBS) Mason City.
Programming (via satellite): ABC Family Channel; AMC; Animal Planet; Arts & Entertainment; Big Ten Network; Bravo; Cartoon Network; CNBC; CNN; Comedy Central; Country Music TV; C-SPAN; Discovery Channel; Disney Channel; Do-It-Yourself; E! Entertainment Television; ESPN; ESPN 2; ESPN Classic Sports; ESPN U; Eternal Word TV Network; Food Network; Fox News Channel; Fox Sports Net; FX; Golf Channel; Hallmark Channel; Headline News; HGTV; History Channel; Lifetime; MoviePlex; MSNBC; MTV; National Geographic Channel; Nickelodeon; Outdoor Channel; QVC; Radar Channel; RFD-TV; Speed Channel; Spike TV; Syfy; TBS Superstation; The Learning Channel; Travel Channel; truTV; Turner Classic Movies; Turner Network TV; TV Guide Network; TV Land; USA Network; VH1; Weather Channel; WGN America.
Fee: $25.00 installation; $39.95 monthly; $20.00 additional installation.
Digital Basic Service
Subscribers: N.A.
Programming (received off-air): KAAL (ABC) Austin; KIMT (CBS, MNT) Mason City; KTTC (CW, NBC) Rochester.
Programming (via satellite): BBC America; Bloomberg Television; Bravo; Current; Discovery Digital Networks; Discovery HD Theater; DMX Music; ESPN Classic Sports; ESPN HD; ESPNews; Fox Movie Channel; Fox Soccer; G4; GSN; Halogen Network; HDNet; HDNet Movies; Independent Film Channel; KXLT-TV (FOX) Rochester; MTV Networks Digital Suite; National Geographic Channel; Nick Jr.; NickToons TV; Ovation; Trinity Broadcasting Network; Versus; WE tv.
Fee: $10.00 monthly.

Pay Service 1
Pay Units: N.A.
Programming (via satellite): Cinemax; Encore; HBO; Showtime; Starz.
Fee: $10.00 monthly (Starz/Encore), $12.00 monthly each (HBO, Showtime, & Cinemax).
Digital Pay Service 1
Pay Units: N.A.
Programming (via satellite): Cinemax (multiplexed); Encore; HBO (multiplexed); HBO HD; Showtime (multiplexed); Starz (multiplexed); Sundance Channel; The Movie Channel (multiplexed).
Fee: $10.00 monthly (Starz/Encore), $12.00 monthly (HBO, Showtime, TMC or Cinemax).
Pay-Per-View
iN DEMAND (delivered digitally); Fresh (delivered digitally); Playboy TV (delivered digitally); Shorteez (delivered digitally).
Internet Service
Operational: Yes, Both DSL & dial-up. Began: June 1, 2002.
Broadband Service: Omnitel Communications.
Fee: $25.00 installation; $39.95 monthly.
Telephone Service
None
Manager: Ron Laudner.
Ownership: Farmers Mutual Telephone Co. (MSO).

POMEROY—Formerly served by TelePartners. No longer in operation. ICA: IA0220.

POSTVILLE—CenturyTel, 205 5th Ave S, La Cross, WI 54601. Phones: 608-796-7447 (Regional office); 318-388-9000 (Corporate office); 888-835-2485. E-mail: mary.gotstein@centurytel.com. Web Site: http://www.centurytel.com. ICA: IA0161.
TV Market Ranking: Outside TV Markets (POSTVILLE). Franchise award date: February 27, 1982. Franchise expiration date: N.A. Began: December 1, 1983.
Channel capacity: 60 (not 2-way capable). Channels available but not in use: 4.
Basic Service
Subscribers: 489.
Programming (received off-air): KCRG-TV (ABC) Cedar Rapids; KGAN (CBS) Cedar Rapids; KPXR-TV (ION) Cedar Rapids; KRIN (PBS) Waterloo; KWWL (NBC) Waterloo; WLAX (FOX) La Crosse.
Programming (via satellite): ABC Family Channel; AMC; Animal Planet; Arts & Entertainment; Cartoon Network; CNN; Comedy Central; Country Music TV; Discovery Channel; Disney Channel; ESPN; ESPN 2; Food Network; Fox News Channel; FX; Hallmark Channel; HGTV; History Channel; Home Shopping Network; Lifetime; MTV; Nickelodeon; QVC; Spike TV; Syfy; TBS Superstation; The Learning Channel; Travel Channel; Turner Classic Movies; Turner Network TV; TV Land; Univision; USA Network; VH1; Weather Channel; WGN America.
Fee: $35.00 installation; $27.95 monthly.
Digital Basic Service
Subscribers: 30.
Programming (via satellite): BBC America; Bio; Bloomberg Television; Bravo; Discovery Digital Networks; DMX Music; ESPN Classic Sports; ESPNews; FitTV; Fox Movie Channel; Fox Sports World; GAS; Golf Channel; GSN; Halogen Network; Independent Film Channel; International Television (ITV); Lifetime Movie Network; MTV Networks Digital Suite; Nick Jr.; NickToons TV; Outdoor Channel; Ovation; Speed Channel; Style Network; Toon Disney; Trinity Broadcasting Network; Versus; WE tv.
Fee: $12.95 monthly.
Digital Expanded Basic Service
Subscribers: N.A.
Programming (via satellite): CNN en Espanol; Fox Sports en Espanol; History Channel en Espanol; MTV Latin America; TVE Internacional.
Fee: $5.00 monthly.
Digital Pay Service 1
Pay Units: N.A.
Programming (via satellite): Cinemax (multiplexed); Encore (multiplexed); HBO (multiplexed); Showtime (multiplexed); Starz (multiplexed).
Fee: $10.95 monthly (Cinemax or Starz & Encore), $11.95 monthly (HBO or Showtime), $15.95 monthly (Cinemax & HBO).
Pay-Per-View
iN DEMAND (delivered digitally), Fee: $3.99-$42.95, Addressable: Yes.
Internet Service
Operational: No.
Telephone Service
None
Miles of Plant: 13.0 (coaxial); None (fiber optic). Homes passed: 800. Total homes in franchised area: 800.
Manager: Mary Gotstein. Chief Technician: Bob Jacob.
City fee: 1% of gross.
Ownership: CenturyLink (MSO).

PRESTON—Telnet of Preston. Now served by CLINTON, IA [IA0006]. ICA: IA0148.

PROTIVIN—Protivin Cablevision, PO Box 53, 117 N Main St, Protivin, IA 52163. Phone: 563-569-8401. Fax: 563-569-8401. ICA: IA0561.
TV Market Ranking: Outside TV Markets (PROTIVIN). Franchise award date: N.A. Franchise expiration date: N.A. Began: N.A.
Channel capacity: 35 (not 2-way capable). Channels available but not in use: None.
Basic Service
Subscribers: 124.
Programming (received off-air): KCRG-TV (ABC) Cedar Rapids; KIMT (CBS, MNT) Mason City; KTTC (CW, NBC) Rochester; KWWL (NBC) Waterloo; KYIN (PBS) Mason City; WLAX (FOX) La Crosse.
Programming (via satellite): ABC Family Channel; CNN; Discovery Channel; ESPN; Eternal Word TV Network; Nickelodeon; Spike TV; TBS Superstation; Turner Classic Movies; Turner Network TV; USA Network; WGN America.
Current originations: Public Access.
Fee: $17.36 monthly.
Pay Service 1
Pay Units: 23.
Programming (via satellite): Cinemax.
Fee: $7.50 monthly.
Pay Service 2
Pay Units: 17.
Programming (via satellite): HBO.
Fee: $7.50 monthly.
Internet Service
Operational: No.
Telephone Service
None
Miles of Plant: 2.0 (coaxial); None (fiber optic). Homes passed: 150. Total homes in franchised area: 150.
Manager: Michael Pecinovsky.
Ownership: City of Protivin.

RADCLIFFE—Radcliffe Cablevision. Formerly [IA0265]. This cable system has converted to IPTV, PO Box 140, Radcliffe, IA 50230-0140. Phone: 515-899-2341. Fax: 515-899-2499. ICA: IA5020.
TV Market Ranking: 66 (RADCLIFFE). Franchise award date: N.A. Franchise expiration date: N.A. Began: N.A.
Channel capacity: N.A. Channels available but not in use: N.A.
Video-On-Demand: Planned
Internet Service
Operational: Yes, DSL only.
Subscribers: 30.
Broadband Service: In-house.
Telephone Service
Digital: Operational
Manager & Chief Technician: Ed Drake.
Ownership: Radcliffe Cablevision Inc.

RADCLIFFE—Radcliffe Cablevision. This cable system has converted to IPTV. See Radcliffe, IA [IA5020], IA. ICA: IA0265.

RANDOLPH—Formerly served by Westcom. No longer in operation. ICA: IA0366.

READLYN—Readlyn Telephone Co., PO Box 159, 121 Main St, Readlyn, IA 50668. Phones: 800-590-7747; 319-279-3375. Fax: 319-279-7575. E-mail: readlyn@netins.net. Web Site: http://www.readlyntelco.com. ICA: IA0245.
TV Market Ranking: 65 (READLYN). Franchise award date: December 1, 1983. Franchise expiration date: N.A. Began: January 1, 1984.
Channel capacity: 60 (operating 2-way). Channels available but not in use: 22.
Basic Service
Subscribers: 272.
Programming (received off-air): KCRG-TV (ABC) Cedar Rapids; KFXA (FOX) Cedar Rapids; KGAN (CBS) Cedar Rapids; KIMT (CBS, MNT) Mason City; KPXR-TV (ION) Cedar Rapids; KRIN (PBS) Waterloo; KWWL (NBC) Waterloo.
Programming (via satellite): ABC Family Channel; AMC; Animal Planet; Arts & Entertainment; Big Ten Network; Cartoon Network; CNN; Comcast SportsNet Northwest; Comedy Central; Country Music TV; Discovery Channel; Discovery Health Channel; Disney Channel; Do-It-Yourself; E! Entertainment Television; ESPN; ESPN 2; ESPN Classic Sports; Food Network; Fox News Channel; FX; Golf Channel; GSN; Hallmark Channel; Hallmark Movie Channel; Headline News; HGTV; History Channel; Lifetime; MSNBC; MTV; National Geographic Channel; Nickelodeon; Outdoor Channel; QVC; RFD-TV; SoapNet; Speed Channel; Spike TV; Syfy; TBS Superstation; The Learning Channel; Toon Disney; Travel Channel; truTV; Turner Classic Movies; Turner Network TV; TV Guide Network; TV Land; USA Network; VH1; WE tv; Weather Channel; WGN America.
Current originations: Public Access; Educational Access.
Fee: $20.00 installation; $24.95 monthly.
Pay Service 1
Pay Units: 20.
Programming (via satellite): Cinemax; Encore; HBO; Starz.
Fee: $10.00 monthly (HBO, Cinemax or Starz/Encore).
Video-On-Demand: No
Internet Service
Operational: No, DSL only.
Telephone Service
None
Miles of Plant: 5.0 (coaxial); None (fiber optic). Homes passed: 320. Total homes in franchised area: 320.
Manager: Sharon K. Huck. Chief Technician: Clinton Watts.
Franchise fee: None.
Ownership: Readlyn Telephone Co.

RED OAK—Mediacom. Now served by ATLANTIC, IA [IA0032]. ICA: IA0040.

RENWICK—Heck's TV & Cable, PO Box 517, 601 7th St, Armstrong, IA 50514-0517. Phone: 712-864-3431. Fax: 712-864-3431. ICA: IA0497.
TV Market Ranking: Outside TV Markets (RENWICK). Franchise award date: N.A. Franchise expiration date: N.A. Began: December 1, 1987.
Channel capacity: 12 (not 2-way capable). Channels available but not in use: N.A.
Basic Service
Subscribers: 111.
Programming (received off-air): KCCI (CBS) Des Moines; KDSM-TV (FOX) Des Moines; KTIN (PBS) Fort Dodge; WHO-DT (NBC) Des Moines; WOI-DT (ABC) Ames.
Programming (via satellite): ABC Family Channel; CNN; ESPN; Headline News; Spike TV; TBS Superstation; WGN America.
Fee: $12.00 monthly.
Pay Service 1
Pay Units: 58.
Programming (via satellite): The Movie Channel.
Fee: $10.00 monthly.
Video-On-Demand: No
Internet Service
Operational: No.
Telephone Service
None
Manager: Steven Heck.
Ownership: Steven Heck (MSO).

RICHLAND—Starwest Inc., 15235 235th St, Milton, IA 52570-8016. Phones: 319-397-2283; 319-293-6336. ICA: IA0498.
TV Market Ranking: Below 100 (RICHLAND). Franchise award date: N.A. Franchise expiration date: N.A. Began: N.A.
Channel capacity: N.A. Channels available but not in use: N.A.
Basic Service
Subscribers: N.A.
Programming (received off-air): KCRG-TV (ABC) Cedar Rapids; KGAN (CBS) Cedar Rapids; KWWL (NBC) Waterloo.
Programming (via satellite): ABC Family Channel; ESPN; TBS Superstation; USA Network; WGN America.
Fee: $30.00 installation; $10.50 monthly.
Pay Service 1
Pay Units: N.A.
Programming (via satellite): Showtime.
Fee: $9.95 monthly.
Internet Service
Operational: No.
Manager & Chief Technician: John Stooksberry.
City fee: None.
Ownership: Starwest Inc. (MSO).

RINGSTED—Ringsted Cablevision, PO Box 187, 19 W Maple St, Ringsted, IA 50578-0187. Phones: 712-866-8000; 712-866-1456. Fax: 712-866-0002. Web Site: http://www.ringstedtelephone.com. ICA: IA0285.
TV Market Ranking: Outside TV Markets (RINGSTED). Franchise award date: N.A. Franchise expiration date: N.A. Began: September 1, 1973.
Channel capacity: N.A. Channels available but not in use: N.A.

Basic Service

Subscribers: 148.

Programming (received off-air): KAAL (ABC) Austin; KCAU-TV (ABC) Sioux City; KEYC-TV (CBS, FOX) Mankato; KIMT (CBS, MNT) Mason City; KMEG (CBS) Sioux City; KPTH (FOX, MNT) Sioux City; KSFY-TV (ABC) Sioux Falls; KTIN (PBS) Fort Dodge; KTIV (CW, NBC) Sioux City; WHO-DT (NBC) Des Moines; allband FM.

Programming (via satellite): ABC Family Channel; AMC; AmericanLife TV Network; Animal Planet; Arts & Entertainment; Cartoon Network; CNBC; CNN; Comedy Central; Country Music TV; C-SPAN; C-SPAN 2; Disney Channel; E! Entertainment Television; ESPN; ESPN 2; ESPN Classic Sports; ESPN U; Food Network; Fox News Channel; Fox Sports Net; FX; Hallmark Channel; Headline News; HGTV; History Channel; ION Television; KARE (NBC) Minneapolis; Lifetime; MTV; National Geographic Channel; Nickelodeon; Outdoor Channel; QVC; Spike TV; Syfy; TBS Superstation; The Learning Channel; Travel Channel; Turner Classic Movies; Turner Network TV; TV Land; USA Network; VH1; Weather Channel; WGN America.

Fee: $40.95 monthly.

Digital Basic Service

Subscribers: 18.

Programming (received off-air): KELO-TV (CBS, MNT) Sioux Falls; KSFY-TV (ABC) Sioux Falls.

Programming (via satellite): BBC America; Bio; CMT Pure Country; Discovery Health Channel; Discovery Home Channel; Discovery Kids Channel; Discovery Military Channel; ESPNews; FitTV; Fox Movie Channel; G4; Golf Channel; GSN; History Channel International; ID Investigation Discovery; Independent Film Channel; MTV2; National Geographic Channel; Nick Jr.; NickToons TV; Outdoor Channel; Science Channel; Speed Channel; TeenNick; Toon Disney; VH1 Classic.

Fee: $11.00 monthly.

Digital Pay Service 1

Pay Units: 14.

Programming (via satellite): HBO (multiplexed).

Fee: $11.00 monthly.

Digital Pay Service 2

Pay Units: 4.

Programming (via satellite): Cinemax (multiplexed).

Fee: $11.00 monthly.

Digital Pay Service 3

Pay Units: 7.

Programming (via satellite): Encore (multiplexed); Starz (multiplexed).

Fee: $11.00 monthly.

Video-On-Demand: No

Internet Service

Operational: No, DSL & dialup.

Telephone Service

None

Miles of Plant: 4.0 (coaxial); None (fiber optic). Homes passed: 230. Total homes in franchised area: 230.

General Manager: Tim Johnson. Technician: Travis Neilson. Customer Service Manager: Suzanne Bonnicksen.

Ownership: Ringsted Telephone Co.

ROCK RAPIDS—Modern Communications, PO Box 229, 202 Briar Ln, Rock Rapids, IA 51246. Phone: 712-472-2941. ICA: IA0100.

TV Market Ranking: 85 (ROCK RAPIDS). Franchise award date: June 1, 1981. Franchise expiration date: N.A. Began: December 23, 1981.

Channel capacity: N.A. Channels available but not in use: N.A.

Basic Service

Subscribers: 970.

Programming (received off-air): KCAU-TV (ABC) Sioux City; KDLT-TV (NBC) Sioux Falls; KELO-TV (CBS, MNT) Sioux Falls; KMEG (CBS) Sioux City; KSFY-TV (ABC) Sioux Falls; KSIN-TV (PBS) Sioux City; KTTW (FOX) Sioux Falls; KUSD-TV (PBS) Vermillion; KWSD (CW) Sioux Falls; allband FM.

Programming (via satellite): ABC Family Channel; Animal Planet; Arts & Entertainment; CNN; C-SPAN; Discovery Channel; Disney Channel; ESPN; ESPN 2; Food Network; Fox News Channel; FX; G4; Great American Country; HGTV; History Channel; Lifetime; MyNetworkTV Inc.; Nickelodeon; Outdoor Channel; QVC; Speed Channel; Spike TV; TBS Superstation; The Learning Channel; Turner Classic Movies; Turner Network TV; TV Land; USA Network; Weather Channel; WGN America.

Current originations: Government Access; Educational Access; Public Access.

Fee: $20.00 installation; $14.95 monthly; $2.25 converter.

Pay Service 1

Pay Units: 105.

Programming (via satellite): Cinemax.

Fee: $15.00 installation; $9.00 monthly.

Pay Service 2

Pay Units: 220.

Programming (via satellite): HBO.

Fee: $9.00 monthly.

Internet Service

Operational: No.

Telephone Service

None

Miles of Plant: 20.0 (coaxial); None (fiber optic). Homes passed: 1,045. Total homes in franchised area: 1,130.

Manager & Chief Technician: Carl DeJongh.

City fee: 4% of gross.

Ownership: C.E.D. Enterprises Inc.

ROWLEY (village)—Formerly served by New Path Communications LC. No longer in operation. ICA: IA0502.

ROYAL—Royal Telephone Co., PO Box 80, 307 Main St, Royal, IA 51357. Phone: 712-933-2615. Fax: 712-933-0015. E-mail: info@royaltelco.com. Web Site: http://www.royaltelco.com. ICA: IA0299.

TV Market Ranking: Outside TV Markets (ROYAL). Franchise award date: N.A. Franchise expiration date: N.A. Began: March 1, 1983.

Channel capacity: 35 (operating 2-way). Channels available but not in use: N.A.

Basic Service

Subscribers: 186.

Programming (received off-air): KCAU-TV (ABC) Sioux City; KELO-TV (CBS, MNT) Sioux Falls; KEYC-TV (CBS, FOX) Mankato; KMEG (CBS) Sioux City; KPTH (FOX, MNT) Sioux City; KSFY-TV (ABC) Sioux Falls; KTIN (PBS) Fort Dodge; KTIV (CW, NBC) Sioux City; WOI-DT (ABC) Ames.

Programming (via satellite): CW+; ION Television; Radar Channel; Weather Channel; WGN America.

Fee: $14.75 monthly.

Expanded Basic Service 1

Subscribers: N.A.

Programming (via satellite): ABC Family Channel; AMC; AmericanLife TV Network; Animal Planet; Arts & Entertainment;

Bravo; Cartoon Network; CNBC; CNN; Comedy Central; Country Music TV; C-SPAN; C-SPAN 2; Discovery Channel; Discovery Health Channel; Disney Channel; Do-It-Yourself; E! Entertainment Television; ESPN; ESPN 2; ESPN Classic Sports; Eternal Word TV Network; Food Network; Fox Movie Channel; Fox News Channel; Fox Sports Net North; FX; Golf Channel; Hallmark Channel; Headline News; HGTV; History Channel; Home Shopping Network; INSP; Lifetime; MSNBC; MTV; Nickelodeon; Outdoor Channel; Speed Channel; Spike TV; Syfy; TBS Superstation; The Learning Channel; Travel Channel; Trinity Broadcasting Network; truTV; Turner Classic Movies; Turner Network TV; TV Guide Network; TV Land; USA Network; VH1.

Fee: $26.75 monthly.

Digital Basic Service

Subscribers: 70.

Programming (received off-air): KELO-TV (CBS, MNT) Sioux Falls; KSFY-TV (ABC) Sioux Falls.

Programming (via satellite): BBC America; Bio; Discovery Kids Channel; Discovery Military Channel; Discovery Planet Green; ESPNews; FitTV; G4; GSN; History Channel International; ID Investigation Discovery; Independent Film Channel; MTV2; mtvU; Music Choice; National Geographic Channel; Nick Jr.; NickToons TV; Science Channel; TeenNick; VH1 Classic; VH1 Country.

Fee: $31.75 monthly.

Digital Expanded Basic Service

Subscribers: N.A.

Programming (via satellite): Bravo; Discovery Channel HD; ESPN HD; HDNet; HDNet Movies.

Fee: $8.50 monthly.

Digital Pay Service 1

Pay Units: N.A.

Programming (via satellite): Cinemax (multiplexed); Cinemax HD; Encore (multiplexed); Flix; HBO (multiplexed); HBO HD; Showtime (multiplexed); Showtime HD; Starz (multiplexed); Starz HDTV; Sundance Channel; The Movie Channel (multiplexed); The Movie Channel HD.

Fee: $9.00 monthly (each).

Pay-Per-View

Movies (delivered digitally); Sports PPV (delivered digitally).

Internet Service

Operational: No.

Telephone Service

None

Miles of Plant: 3.0 (coaxial); None (fiber optic). Homes passed: 215.

Manager: Doug Nelson. Chief Technician: Rob Wassom. Marketing Director: Sherry Toft.

Ownership: Royal Telephone Co.

RUDD—Omnitel Communications, 608 E Congress St, Nora Springs, IA 50458-8634. Phones: 877-OMNITEL; 641-749-2531. Fax: 641-749-9510. E-mail: question@omnitelcom.com. Web Site: http://www.omnitel.biz. Also serves Greene, Marble Rock, Nora Springs, Plymouth, Riceville, Rockford, St. Ansgar & Staceyville. ICA: IA0503.

TV Market Ranking: Below 100 (Greene, Marble Rock, Nora Springs, Plymouth, Riceville, Rockford, RUDD, St. Ansgar, Staceyville). Franchise award date: N.A. Franchise expiration date: N.A. Began: October 1, 1989.

Channel capacity: 125 (operating 2-way). Channels available but not in use: N.A.

Basic Service

Subscribers: 2,869.

Programming (received off-air): KAAL (ABC) Austin; KCRG-TV (ABC) Cedar Rapids; KGAN (CBS) Cedar Rapids; KIMT (CBS, MNT) Mason City; KSMQ-TV (PBS) Austin; KTTC (CW, NBC) Rochester; KWWL (NBC) Waterloo; KXLT-TV (FOX) Rochester; KYIN (PBS) Mason City.

Programming (via satellite): ABC Family Channel; AMC; Animal Planet; Arts & Entertainment; Big Ten Network; Bravo!; Cartoon Network; CNBC; CNN; Comedy Central; Country Music TV; C-SPAN; Discovery Channel; Disney Channel; Do-It-Yourself; E! Entertainment Television; ESPN; ESPN 2; ESPN Classic Sports; ESPN U; Eternal Word TV Network; Food Network; Fox News Channel; Fox Sports Net; FX; Golf Channel; Hallmark Channel; Headline News; HGTV; History Channel; Lifetime; MoviePlex; MSNBC; MTV; National Geographic Channel; Nickelodeon; Outdoor Channel; QVC; Radar Channel; RFD-TV; Speed Channel; Spike TV; Syfy; TBS Superstation; The Learning Channel; Travel Channel; truTV; Turner Classic Movies; Turner Network TV; TV Guide Network; TV Land; USA Network; VH1; Weather Channel; WGN America.

Fee: $25.00 installation; $39.95 monthly; $20.00 additional installation.

Digital Basic Service

Subscribers: 482.

Programming (received off-air): KAAL (ABC) Austin; KIMT (CBS, MNT) Mason City; KTTC (CW, NBC) Rochester; KXLT-TV (FOX) Rochester.

Programming (via satellite): BBC America; Bloomberg Television; Bravo; Current; Discovery Digital Networks; Discovery HD Theater; DMX Music; ESPN Classic Sports; ESPN HD; ESPNews; Fox Movie Channel; Fox Soccer; G4; GSN; Halogen Network; HDNet; HDNet Movies; Independent Film Channel; MTV Networks Digital Suite; National Geographic Channel; Nick Jr.; NickToons TV; Ovation; Trinity Broadcasting Network; Versus; WE tv.

Fee: $10.00 monthly.

Pay Service 1

Pay Units: N.A.

Programming (via satellite): Cinemax; Encore; HBO; Showtime; Starz.

Fee: $10.00 monthly (Starz/Encore), $12.00 monthly each (HBO, Showtime, & Cinemax).

Digital Pay Service 1

Pay Units: N.A.

Programming (via satellite): Cinemax (multiplexed); Encore (multiplexed); HBO (multiplexed); HBO HD; Showtime (mul-

tiplexed); Starz (multiplexed); Sundance Channel; The Movie Channel (multiplexed).
Fee: $10.00 monthly (Starz/Encore), $12.00 monthly (HBO, Showtime, TMC or Cinemax).

Pay-Per-View

iN DEMAND (delivered digitally); Playboy TV (delivered digitally); Fresh (delivered digitally); Shorteez (delivered digitally).

Internet Service

Operational: No, DSL only.

Telephone Service

None

Miles of Plant: 82.0 (coaxial); 105.0 (fiber optic).

General Manager: Ronald Laudner.

Ownership: Farmers Mutual Telephone Co. (MSO).

RUNNELLS—Formerly served by Telnet South LC. No longer in operation. ICA: IA0504.

RUSSELL—Longview Communications, 12007 Sunrise Valley Dr, Ste 375, Reston, VA 20191. Phones: 866-611-6565; 703-476-9101. Fax: 703-476-9107. Web Site: http://www.longviewcomm.com. ICA: IA0283.

TV Market Ranking: Outside TV Markets (RUSSELL). Franchise award date: June 20, 1983. Franchise expiration date: N.A. Began: June 1, 1986.

Channel capacity: N.A. Channels available but not in use: N.A.

Basic Service

Subscribers: 41.

Programming (received off-air): KCCI (CBS) Des Moines; KCWI-TV (CW) Ames; KDIN-TV (PBS) Des Moines; KDSM-TV (FOX) Des Moines; KTVO (ABC) Kirksville; KYOU-TV (FOX) Ottumwa; WHO-DT (NBC) Des Moines; WOI-DT (ABC) Ames.

Programming (via satellite): C-SPAN; QVC; Trinity Broadcasting Network.

Fee: $41.11 installation; $17.98 monthly.

Expanded Basic Service 1

Subscribers: N.A.

Programming (via satellite): ABC Family Channel; AMC; Animal Planet; Arts & Entertainment; CNN; Discovery Channel; Disney Channel; E! Entertainment Television; ESPN; ESPN 2; Fox News Channel; G4; Great American Country; Headline News; History Channel; Lifetime; MSNBC; Speed Channel; Spike TV; TBS Superstation; The Learning Channel; Turner Network TV; USA Network; Weather Channel.

Fee: $17.97 monthly.

Pay Service 1

Pay Units: 59.

Programming (via satellite): Cinemax; HBO; Showtime; The Movie Channel.

Fee: $23.49 installation; $8.95 monthly (TMC), $10.95 monthly (Cinemax or Showtime), $12.95 monthly (HBO).

Video-On-Demand: No

Internet Service

Operational: No.

Telephone Service

None

Miles of Plant: 4.0 (coaxial); None (fiber optic). Homes passed: 231. Total homes in franchised area: 231.

President: John Long. Senior Vice President: Marc W. Cohen. General Manager: Brandon Dickey. Operations Manager: Perry Scarborough.

Ownership: Longview Communications (MSO).

RUTHVEN—Formerly served by Terril Cable Systems. No longer in operation. ICA: IA0551.

RYAN—USA Communications, PO Box 389, 124 Main St, Shellsburg, IA 52332. Phones: 800-248-8007; 319-436-2224. Fax: 319-436-2228. E-mail: frmutshe@fmtcs.com. Web Site: http://www.usacomm.coop. ICA: IA0346.

TV Market Ranking: 65 (RYAN). Franchise award date: May 1, 1985. Franchise expiration date: N.A. Began: November 15, 1985.

Channel capacity: 35 (not 2-way capable). Channels available but not in use: 3.

Basic Service

Subscribers: 69.

Programming (received off-air): KCRG-TV (ABC) Cedar Rapids; KFXA (FOX) Cedar Rapids; KGAN (CBS) Cedar Rapids; KPXR-TV (ION) Cedar Rapids; KRIN (PBS) Waterloo; KWKB (CW, MNT) Iowa City; KWWL (NBC) Waterloo.

Programming (via satellite): ABC Family Channel; AMC; Animal Planet; Arts & Entertainment; Cartoon Network; CNBC; CNN; Comcast SportsNet Chicago; Comedy Central; Country Music TV; C-SPAN; Discovery Channel; Disney Channel; Do-It-Yourself; E! Entertainment Television; ESPN; ESPN 2; ESPN Classic Sports; ESPN U; Eternal Word TV Network; Food Network; Fox News Channel; FX; Gospel Music Channel; Great American Country; Hallmark Channel; Hallmark Movie Channel; Headline News; HGTV; History Channel; Home Shopping Network; Lifetime; MTV; National Geographic Channel; Nickelodeon; QVC; SoapNet; Speed Channel; Spike TV; Syfy; TBS Superstation; The Learning Channel; The Sportsman Channel; Travel Channel; Trinity Broadcasting Network; truTV; Turner Classic Movies; Turner Network TV; TV Land; USA Network; VH1; Weather Channel; WGN America.

Fee: $25.00 installation; $37.95 monthly.

Pay Service 1

Pay Units: 3.

Programming (via satellite): Cinemax.

Fee: $10.00 monthly.

Pay Service 2

Pay Units: 6.

Programming (via satellite): HBO.

Fee: $12.00 monthly.

Pay Service 3

Pay Units: 2.

Programming (via satellite): Showtime.

Fee: $10.00 monthly.

Internet Service

Operational: No.

Telephone Service

None

Miles of Plant: 3.0 (coaxial); None (fiber optic). Homes passed: 171.

General Manager: Mark Harrison. Plant Manager: Mitch Kuhn. Marketing Administrator: Marnie Burkey. Office Manager: Nancy Seely.

City fee: None.

Ownership: Shellsburg Cablevision Inc. (MSO).

SALEM—Formerly served by Longview Communications. No longer in operation. ICA: IA0505.

SALIX—Long Lines, 501 4th St, Sergeant Bluff, IA 51054-8509. Phone: 712-271-4000. Fax: 712-271-2727. E-mail: info@longlines.com. Web Site: http://www.longlines.com. Also serves Correctionville, Holstein & Sloan, IA; Jefferson, SD. ICA: IA0510.

TV Market Ranking: Below 100 (Correctionville, Jefferson, SALIX, Sloan); Outside TV Markets (Holstein). Franchise award date: N.A. Franchise expiration date: N.A. Began: N.A.

Channel capacity: 41 (not 2-way capable). Channels available but not in use: None.

Basic Service

Subscribers: 521.

Programming (received off-air): KCAU-TV (ABC) Sioux City; KMEG (CBS) Sioux City; KPTH (FOX, MNT) Sioux City; KSIN-TV (PBS) Sioux City; KTIV (CW, NBC) Sioux City.

Programming (via satellite): ABC Family Channel; AMC; AmericanLife TV Network; Animal Planet; Arts & Entertainment; Big Ten Network; Cartoon Network; CNBC; CNN; Comedy Central; Country Music TV; C-SPAN; C-SPAN 2; CW+; Discovery Channel; Disney Channel; E! Entertainment Television; ESPN; ESPN 2; ESPN Classic Sports; Eternal Word TV Network; Food Network; Fox News Channel; Fox Sports Net North; FX; Golf Channel; Hallmark Channel; Headline News; HGTV; History Channel; Home Shopping Network; INSP; Lifetime; Lifetime Movie Network; MSNBC; MTV; Nickelodeon; QVC; Speed Channel; Spike TV; Syfy; TBS Superstation; The Learning Channel; The Sportsman Channel; Travel Channel; Trinity Broadcasting Network; truTV; Turner Classic Movies; Turner Network TV; TuTv; TV Guide; TV Land; USA Network; VH1; Weather Channel; WGN America.

Fee: $15.00 installation; $41.99 monthly.

Digital Basic Service

Subscribers: N.A.

Programming (via satellite): BBC America; Bio; Cooking Channel; Discovery Health Channel; Discovery Kids Channel; Discovery Military Channel; Discovery Planet Green; DMX Music; Do-It-Yourself; ESPN U; ESPNews; FitTV; Fox College Sports Atlantic; Fox College Sports Central; Fox College Sports Pacific; Fox Movie Channel; Fox Soccer; G4; Great American Country; GSN; Halogen Network; History Channel International; ID Investigation Discovery; Independent Film Channel; Lifetime Real Women; MTV Hits; MTV Jams; MTV2; Nick Jr.; NickToons TV; Outdoor Channel; RFD-TV; Science Channel; SoapNet; TeenNick; Toon Disney; Versus; VH1 Classic; VH1 Country; VH1 Soul; WE tv.

Fee: $9.99 monthly.

Digital Expanded Basic Service

Subscribers: N.A.

Programming (received off-air): KCAU-TV (ABC) Sioux City; KMEG (CBS) Sioux City; KPTH (FOX, MNT) Sioux City; KSIN-TV (PBS) Sioux City; KTIV (CW, NBC) Sioux City.

Programming (via satellite): Big Ten Network HD; Discovery Channel HD; ESPN 2 HD; ESPN HD; HDNet; HDNet Movies; Outdoor Channel 2 HD.

Fee: $9.95 monthly.

Digital Expanded Basic Service 2

Subscribers: N.A.

Programming (via satellite): Bandamax; De Pelicula; De Pelicula Clasico; Discovery en Espanol; ESPN Deportes; Fox Sports en Espanol; Ritmoson Latino; Telehit.

Fee: $2.95 monthly.

Pay Service 1

Pay Units: 92.

Programming (via satellite): HBO (multiplexed).

Fee: $14.95 monthly.

Pay Service 2

Pay Units: 40.

Programming (via satellite): Flix; Showtime (multiplexed); The Movie Channel.

Fee: $14.45 monthly.

Digital Pay Service 1

Pay Units: N.A.

Programming (via satellite): Cinemax (multiplexed); Cinemax HD; Encore (multiplexed); Flix; HBO (multiplexed); HBO HD; Showtime (multiplexed); Starz (multiplexed); Starz HDTV; Starz On Demand; The Movie Channel (multiplexed).

Fee: $11.95 monthly (Cinemax), $13.95 monthly (Starz/Encore), $14.45 monthly (Showtime/TMC/Flix), $14.95 monthly (HBO).

Video-On-Demand: Yes

Internet Service

Operational: No.

Telephone Service

None

Miles of Plant: 8.0 (coaxial); None (fiber optic). Homes passed: 725.

Manager & Chief Operations Officer: Paul Bergmann. Chief Technician: Tony Seubert. Marketing Director: Denise Moberg.

Ownership: Long Lines (MSO).

SANBORN—Community Cable TV Agency of O'Brien County, PO Box 489, 102 S Eastern St, Sanborn, IA 51248. Phone: 712-930-5593. Fax: 712-930-5595. E-mail: tca@tcaexpress.net. Web Site: http://www.tcaexpress.net. Also serves Hartley, Paulina & Primghar. ICA: IA0104.

TV Market Ranking: Outside TV Markets (Hartley, Paulina, Primghar, SANBORN). Franchise award date: N.A. Franchise expiration date: N.A. Began: April 1, 1982.

Channel capacity: 78 (operating 2-way). Channels available but not in use: 13.

Basic Service

Subscribers: 1,950.

Programming (received off-air): KCAU-TV (ABC) Sioux City; KDLT-TV (NBC) Sioux Falls; KELO-TV (CBS, MNT) Sioux Falls; KMEG (CBS) Sioux City; KPTH (FOX, MNT) Sioux City; KSFY-TV (ABC) Sioux Falls; KSIN-TV (PBS) Sioux City; KTIV (CW, NBC) Sioux City.

Programming (via satellite): C-SPAN; Home Shopping Network; QVC; TBS Superstation; Trinity Broadcasting Network; TV Guide Network; Weather Channel; WGN America.

Current originations: Religious Access; Government Access; Educational Access.

Fee: $30.00 installation; $17.00 monthly.

Expanded Basic Service 1

Subscribers: N.A.

Programming (via satellite): ABC Family Channel; AMC; Animal Planet; Arts & Entertainment; Big Ten Network; Bravo; Cartoon Network; CNBC; CNN; Comedy Central; Country Music TV; Discovery Channel; Disney Channel; Do-It-Yourself; ESPN; ESPN 2; ESPN Classic Sports; FitTV; Food Network; Fox News Channel; Fox Sports Net North; FX; G4; Great American Country; Hallmark Channel; HGTV; History Channel; Lifetime; MSNBC; MTV; National Geographic Channel; NFL Network; Nickelodeon; Outdoor Channel; Oxygen; RFD-TV; Speed Channel; Spike TV; Syfy; The Learning Channel; Travel Channel; Turner Classic Movies; Turner Network TV; TV Land; USA Network; VH1.

Fee: $21.95 monthly.

Digital Basic Service

Subscribers: N.A.

Programming (received off-air): KCAU-TV (ABC) Sioux City; KDLT-TV (NBC) Sioux Falls; KELO-TV (CBS, MNT) Sioux Falls; KMEG (CBS) Sioux City; KPTH (FOX, MNT) Sioux City; KSFY-TV (ABC) Sioux Falls;

KSIN-TV (PBS) Sioux City; KTIV (CW, NBC) Sioux City.
Programming (via satellite): AmericanLife TV Network; AZN Television; BBC America; BET J; Bio; Bloomberg Television; Bravo; Church Channel; CMT Pure Country; Current; Discovery Health Channel; Discovery Kids Channel; Discovery Military Channel; Discovery Planet Green; Disney XD; DMX Music; ESPN 2; ESPN Classic Sports; ESPN U; ESPNews; FitTV; Fox Business Channel; Fox College Sports Atlantic; Fox College Sports Central; Fox College Sports Pacific; Fox Movie Channel; Fox Soccer; Fuse; G4; Golf Channel; Great American Country; GSN; HGTV; History Channel; History Channel International; ID Investigation Discovery; i-Lifetv; Independent Film Channel; JCTV; Lifetime Movie Network; MTV Hits; MTV Jams; MTV2; National Geographic Channel; Nick Jr.; NickToons TV; Outdoor Channel; Ovation; Science Channel; ShopNBC; Sleuth; SoapNet; Speed Channel; Style Network; Syfy; The N; Trinity Broadcasting Network; Turner Classic Movies; Versus; VH1 Classic; VH1 Soul; WE tv.
Fee: $10.00 installation; $11.95 monthly; $4.00 converter.

Digital Expanded Basic Service
Subscribers: N.A.
Programming (via satellite): Arts & Entertainment HD; Big Ten Network HD; Discovery Channel HD; ESPN 2 HD; ESPN HD; Food Network HD; HDNet; HDNet Movies; HGTV HD; Lifetime Television HD; National Geographic Channel HD Network; NFL Network HD; Outdoor Channel 2 HD; Travel Channel HD; Turner Network TV HD; Universal HD.
Fee: $5.95 monthly; $8.00 converter.

Pay Service 1
Pay Units: 19.
Programming (via satellite): Cinemax.
Fee: $9.95 monthly.

Pay Service 2
Pay Units: 228.
Programming (via satellite): HBO (multiplexed).
Fee: $12.95 monthly.

Pay Service 3
Pay Units: 4.
Programming (via satellite): Showtime; The Movie Channel.
Fee: $11.95 monthly.

Digital Pay Service 1
Pay Units: N.A.
Programming (via satellite): Cinemax (multiplexed); Encore (multiplexed); Flix; HBO (multiplexed); Showtime (multiplexed); Showtime HD; Starz (multiplexed); Starz HDTV; The Movie Channel (multiplexed).
Fee: $9.95 monthly (Cinemax), $10.00 monthly (Starz/Encore), $11.95 monthly (Showtime/TMC), $12.95 monthly (HBO).

Video-On-Demand: No

Pay-Per-View
Addressable homes: 1,904.
iN DEMAND, Fee: $3.50, Addressable: Yes; Fresh, Fee: $5.95; Event Entertainment (delivered digitally); Movies (delivered digitally).

Internet Service
Operational: Yes.
Broadband Service: In-house.
Fee: $40.00 installation; $18.95-$62.95 monthly; $10.00 modem lease; $180.00 modem purchase.

Telephone Service
None

Miles of Plant: 50.0 (coaxial); 50.0 (fiber optic). Homes passed: 2,600.
Manager: Denny Weber.
Ownership: Community Cable TV Corp.

SCHALLER—Comserv Ltd., PO Box 9, 111 W 2nd St, Schaller, IA 51053. Phones: 800-469-9099; 712-275-4211. Fax: 712-275-4121. Web Site: http://www.schallertel.net. Also serves Cushing, Kiron & Odebolt. ICA: IA0253.

TV Market Ranking: Outside TV Markets (Cushing, Kiron, Odebolt, SCHALLER). Franchise award date: N.A. Franchise expiration date: N.A. Began: December 1, 1983.

Channel capacity: 75 (not 2-way capable). Channels available but not in use: 20.

Basic Service
Subscribers: 613.
Programming (received off-air): KCAU-TV (ABC) Sioux City; KMEG (CBS) Sioux City; KSIN-TV (PBS) Sioux City; KTIV (CW, NBC) Sioux City.
Programming (via satellite): ABC Family Channel; AMC; Animal Planet; Arts & Entertainment; CNN; Comedy Central; Country Music TV; C-SPAN; C-SPAN 2; Discovery Channel; Disney Channel; ESPN; ESPN 2; ESPN Classic Sports; ESPNews; Fox News Channel; FX; Golf Channel; GSN; Headline News; HGTV; History Channel; Home Shopping Network; Lifetime; MTV; Nickelodeon; Outdoor Channel; SoapNet; Spike TV; Syfy; TBS Superstation; The Learning Channel; The Sportsman Channel; Toon Disney; Travel Channel; truTV; Turner Classic Movies; Turner Network TV; TV Land; USA Network; VH1; WE tv; Weather Channel; WGN America.
Current originations: Religious Access; Educational Access.
Fee: $30.00 installation; $28.95 monthly.

Pay Service 1
Pay Units: 34.
Programming (via satellite): Showtime.
Fee: $11.00 monthly.

Pay Service 2
Pay Units: 39.
Programming (via satellite): The Movie Channel.
Fee: $11.00 monthly.

Pay Service 3
Pay Units: 31.
Programming (via satellite): HBO.
Fee: $12.00 monthly.

Pay Service 4
Pay Units: 15.
Programming (via satellite): Cinemax.
Fee: $12.00 monthly.

Pay Service 5
Pay Units: 15.
Programming (via satellite): Encore; Starz.
Fee: $11.00 monthly.

Video-On-Demand: No

Internet Service
Operational: No, DSL only.

Telephone Service
None

Miles of Plant: 46.0 (coaxial); None (fiber optic).
Manager: Missy Kestel. Marketing Director: Diana Myrtue. Chief Technician: Doug Thomas.
City fee: None.
Ownership: Comserv Ltd.

SCHLESWIG—Tip Top Communication, PO Box 7, 200 W Center St, Arcadia, IA 51430. Phones: 800-290-0986; 712-689-2238. Fax: 712-689-2600. E-mail: sheilag@netins.net. Also serves Charter Oak & Ricketts. ICA: IA0231.

TV Market Ranking: Outside TV Markets (Charter Oak, Ricketts, SCHLESWIG). Franchise award date: N.A. Franchise expiration date: N.A. Began: January 1, 1985.

Channel capacity: 37 (not 2-way capable). Channels available but not in use: N.A.

Basic Service
Subscribers: 351.
Programming (received off-air): KCAU-TV (ABC) Sioux City; KETV (ABC) Omaha; KMEG (CBS) Sioux City; KMTV-TV (CBS) Omaha; KPTH (FOX, MNT) Sioux City; KSIN-TV (PBS) Sioux City; KTIV (CW, NBC) Sioux City; KXVO (CW) Omaha; WOWT-TV (IND, NBC) Omaha.
Programming (via satellite): ABC Family Channel; AMC; CNN; Country Music TV; Discovery Channel; Disney Channel; ESPN; ESPN 2; Fox Movie Channel; G4; Headline News; HGTV; History Channel; Lifetime; Lifetime Movie Network; Nickelodeon; Speed Channel; Spike TV; TBS Superstation; Turner Network TV; USA Network; WGN America.
Fee: $20.00 installation; $25.36 monthly.

Pay Service 1
Pay Units: N.A.
Programming (via satellite): Cinemax; HBO.
Fee: $12.95 monthly (Cinemax) $13.95 monthly (HBO).

Pay Service 2
Pay Units: 11.
Programming (via satellite): Showtime; The Movie Channel.
Fee: $8.95 monthly (each).

Video-On-Demand: No

Internet Service
Operational: No.

Telephone Service
None

Miles of Plant: 11.0 (coaxial); None (fiber optic).
Manager: Sheila Griffin. Chief Engineer: Mike Ahart.
City fee: 3% of gross.
Ownership: Tip Top Communication (MSO).

SCRANTON—Scranton Community Antenna Television, PO Box 8, 1200 Main St, Scranton, IA 51462. Phone: 712-652-3355. Fax: 712-652-3777. E-mail: jingles@netins.net. ICA: IA0254.

TV Market Ranking: Outside TV Markets (SCRANTON). Franchise award date: January 4, 1983. Franchise expiration date: N.A. Began: November 1, 1983.

Channel capacity: 86 (operating 2-way). Channels available but not in use: None.

Basic Service
Subscribers: 210.
Programming (received off-air): KCCI (CBS) Des Moines; KDIN-TV (PBS) Des Moines; KDSM-TV (FOX) Des Moines; WHO-DT (NBC) Des Moines; WOI-DT (ABC) Ames.
Programming (via satellite): ABC Family Channel; Arts & Entertainment; CNN; Comedy Central; Country Music TV; Discovery Channel; Disney Channel; Encore; ESPN; ESPN 2; Fox Sports Net; HGTV; History Channel; Lifetime; Nickelodeon; Spike TV; Syfy; TBS Superstation; Turner Network TV; TV Land; USA Network; Weather Channel; WGN America.
Current originations: Religious Access; Educational Access; Public Access.
Fee: $25.00 monthly.

Pay Service 1
Pay Units: 20.
Programming (via satellite): Cinemax.
Fee: $7.50 monthly.

Pay Service 2
Pay Units: N.A.
Programming (via satellite): Starz.
Fee: $7.50 monthly.

Pay Service 3
Pay Units: 18.
Programming (via satellite): HBO.
Fee: $7.50 monthly.

Internet Service
Operational: No, DSL only.

Telephone Service
None

Miles of Plant: 7.0 (coaxial); None (fiber optic). Homes passed: 270. Total homes in franchised area: 270.
Manager: Sam Fengel.
City fee: None.
Ownership: Scranton Telephone Co.

SEYMOUR—Longview Communications, 12007 Sunrise Valley Dr, Ste 375, Reston, VA 20191. Phones: 866-611-6565 (Customer service); 703-476-9101. Fax: 703-476-9107. Web Site: http://www.longviewcomm.com. ICA: IA0207.

TV Market Ranking: Outside TV Markets (SEYMOUR). Franchise award date: August 18, 1982. Franchise expiration date: N.A. Began: August 1, 1983.

Channel capacity: 41 (not 2-way capable). Channels available but not in use: None.

Basic Service
Subscribers: 110.
Programming (received off-air): KCCI (CBS) Des Moines; KCWI-TV (CW) Ames; KDIN-TV (PBS) Des Moines; KDSM-TV (FOX) Des Moines; KTVO (ABC) Kirksville; KYOU-TV (FOX) Ottumwa; WHO-DT (NBC) Des Moines; WOI-DT (ABC) Ames.
Programming (via satellite): C-SPAN; Home Shopping Network; QVC; Trinity Broadcasting Network.
Fee: $41.11 installation; $17.98 monthly.

Expanded Basic Service 1
Subscribers: N.A.
Programming (via satellite): ABC Family Channel; AMC; Animal Planet; Arts & Entertainment; Cartoon Network; CNN; Comedy Central; Discovery Channel; Disney Channel; ESPN; ESPN 2; Food Network; Fox News Channel; G4; Great American Country; Hallmark Channel; Headline News; HGTV; Lifetime; TBS Superstation; The Learning Channel; Travel Channel; Turner Network TV; USA Network; Weather Channel; WGN America.
Fee: $17.97 monthly.

Pay Service 1
Pay Units: N.A.
Programming (via satellite): Showtime; The Movie Channel.

Fee: $8.95 monthly (TMC), $10.95 monthly (Showtime).
Video-On-Demand: No
Internet Service
Operational: No.
Telephone Service
None
Miles of Plant: 8.0 (coaxial); None (fiber optic). Homes passed: 410. Total homes in franchised area: 410.
President: John Long. Senior Vice President: Marc W. Cohen. General Manager: Brandon Dickey. Operations Manager: Perry Scarborough.
Ownership: Longview Communications (MSO).

SHELBY—Walnut Telephone Co. Now served by WALNUT, IA [IA0241]. ICA: IA0537.

SHELDON—HTC Cablecom, PO Box 142, 107 2nd Ave S, Hospers, IA 51238-0142. Phones: 712-752-8100; 712-752-8500. Fax: 712-752-8280. E-mail: htc@hosperstel.com. Web Site: http://www.hosperstel.com. Also serves Ashton, Hospers & Sibley. ICA: IA0060.
TV Market Ranking: Outside TV Markets (Ashton, Hospers, SHELDON, Sibley). Franchise award date: N.A. Franchise expiration date: N.A. Began: August 1, 1979.
Channel capacity: 58 (operating 2-way). Channels available but not in use: N.A.
Basic Service
Subscribers: 2,800.
Programming (received off-air): KCAU-TV (ABC) Sioux City; KDLT-TV (NBC) Sioux Falls; KELO-TV (CBS, MNT) Sioux Falls; KMEG (CBS) Sioux City; KPTH (FOX, MNT) Sioux City; KSFY-TV (ABC) Sioux Falls; KSIN-TV (PBS) Sioux City; KTIV (CW, NBC) Sioux City.
Programming (via satellite): C-SPAN; CW+; Home Shopping Network; QVC; TV Guide Network.
Current originations: Government Access; Educational Access; Public Access.
Fee: $25.00 installation; $13.00 monthly.
Expanded Basic Service 1
Subscribers: N.A.
Programming (via satellite): ABC Family Channel; Animal Planet; Arts & Entertainment; Big Ten Network; Bloomberg Television; Cartoon Network; CNN; Comedy Central; Country Music TV; Discovery Channel; Discovery Health Channel; Disney Channel; ESPN; ESPN 2; ESPN Classic Sports; Food Network; Fox News Channel; Fox Sports Net North; FX; Gospel Music TV; Great American Country; Hallmark Channel; HGTV; History Channel; ION Television; Lifetime; MTV; Nickelodeon; Outdoor Channel; Speed Channel; Spike TV; Syfy; TBS Superstation; The Learning Channel; Travel Channel; Trinity Broadcasting Network; Turner Classic Movies; Turner Network TV; TV Land; USA Network; VH1; Weather Channel; WGN America.
Fee: $32.95 monthly.
Digital Basic Service
Subscribers: N.A.
Programming (via satellite): DMX Music; Fuse; Halogen Network.
Fee: $5.95 monthly.
Digital Expanded Basic Service
Subscribers: N.A.
Programming (via satellite): AmericanLife TV Network; BBC America; Bio; Bravo; CMT Pure Country; College Sports Television; Discovery Digital Networks; Do-It-Yourself; ESPN U; ESPNews; Fox College Sports Atlantic; Fox College Sports Central; Fox College Sports Pacific; Fox Movie Channel; Fox Soccer; G4; Golf Channel; GSN; History Channel International; Independent Film Channel; Lifetime Movie Network; MTV Networks Digital Suite; National Geographic Channel; Nick Jr.; NickToons TV; RFD-TV; Science Channel; ShopNBC; Sleuth; Style Network; TeenNick; Versus.
Fee: $14.95 monthly.
Digital Expanded Basic Service 2
Subscribers: N.A.
Programming (received off-air): KELO-TV (CBS, MNT) Sioux Falls; KPTH (FOX, MNT) Sioux City; KSFY-TV (ABC) Sioux Falls; KTIV (CW, NBC) Sioux City; KUSD-TV (PBS) Vermillion.
Programming (via satellite): Arts & Entertainment HD; Big Ten Network HD; Canales N; Discovery HD Theater; ESPN 2 HD; ESPN HD; Food Network HD; Fox Sports Net North; HDNet; HDNet Movies; HGTV HD; National Geographic Channel HD Network; Outdoor Channel 2 HD; Universal HD.
Fee: $7.95 monthly (spanish channels), $17.95 monthly (high-definition channels).
Pay Service 1
Pay Units: 175.
Programming (via satellite): HBO.
Fee: $10.95 monthly.
Digital Pay Service 1
Pay Units: N.A.
Programming (via satellite): Encore (multiplexed); Flix; HBO (multiplexed); Showtime (multiplexed); Starz (multiplexed); The Movie Channel (multiplexed).
Fee: $7.95 monthly (Encore), $12.95 monthly (HBO, Starz/Encore, or Showtime/TMC/Flix).
Video-On-Demand: No
Pay-Per-View
World Wrestling Entertainment Inc., Addressable: Yes.
Internet Service
Operational: Yes, DSL & dial-up.
Subscribers: 971.
Broadband Service: In-house.
Fee: $39.95 installation; $23.95 monthly.
Telephone Service
None
Miles of Plant: 16.0 (coaxial); None (fiber optic). Homes passed: 3,724.
Manager: David Raak. Chief Technician: Gregg Andringa.
City fee: 3% of gross.
Ownership: HTC Cablecom.

SHELLSBURG—USA Communications, PO Box 389, 124 Main St, Shellsburg, IA 52332. Phones: 800-248-8007; 319-436-2224. Fax: 319-436-2228. Web Site: http://www.usacomm.coop. Also serves Alburnett, Center Point, Central City, Robins & Urbana. ICA: IA0255.
TV Market Ranking: 65 (Alburnett, Center Point, Central City, Robins, SHELLSBURG, Urbana). Franchise award date: N.A. Franchise expiration date: N.A. Began: November 1, 1984.
Channel capacity: 35 (operating 2-way). Channels available but not in use: 3.
Basic Service
Subscribers: 1,553.
Programming (received off-air): KCRG-TV (ABC) Cedar Rapids; KFXA (FOX) Cedar Rapids; KGAN (CBS) Cedar Rapids; KPXR-TV (ION) Cedar Rapids; KRIN (PBS) Waterloo; KWKB (CW, MNT) Iowa City; KWWF (IND) Waterloo [LICENSED & SILENT]; KWWL (NBC) Waterloo.
Programming (via satellite): ABC Family Channel; AMC; Animal Planet; Arts & Entertainment; Big Ten Network; Cartoon Network; CNBC; CNN; Comcast SportsNet Chicago; Comedy Central; Country Music TV; C-SPAN; Discovery Channel; Disney Channel; Do-It-Yourself; E! Entertainment Television; ESPN; ESPN 2; ESPN Classic Sports; ESPN U; Eternal Word TV Network; Food Network; Fox News Channel; FX; Gospel Music Channel; Great American Country; Hallmark Channel; Hallmark Movie Channel; Headline News; HGTV; History Channel; Home Shopping Network; Lifetime; MTV; National Geographic Channel; Nickelodeon; QVC; RFD-TV; SoapNet; Speed Channel; Spike TV; Syfy; TBS Superstation; The Learning Channel; The Sportsman Channel; Travel Channel; Trinity Broadcasting Network; truTV; Turner Classic Movies; Turner Network TV; TV Land; USA Network; VH1; Weather Channel; WGN America.
Current originations: Public Access.
Fee: $40.00 installation; $37.95 monthly; $30.00 additional installation.
Digital Basic Service
Subscribers: N.A.
Programming (via satellite): Bio; Bloomberg Television; Bravo; Cooking Channel; Discovery Health Channel; Discovery Kids Channel; Discovery Military Channel; Discovery Planet Green; DMX Music; ESPN Classic Sports; ESPNews; FitTV; Fox Movie Channel; G4; Golf Channel; GSN; Halogen Network; History Channel International; ID Investigation Discovery; Lifetime Movie Network; MTV2; Nick Jr.; NickToons TV; Outdoor Channel; Science Channel; Sleuth; Style Network; TeenNick; Toon Disney; Versus; WE tv.
Fee: $30.00 installation; $10.00 monthly.
Digital Expanded Basic Service
Subscribers: N.A.
Programming (received off-air): KCRG-TV (ABC) Cedar Rapids; KFXA (FOX) Cedar Rapids; KPXR-TV (ION) Cedar Rapids; KRIN (PBS) Waterloo; KWKB (CW, MNT) Iowa City.
Programming (via satellite): Arts & Entertainment HD; Discovery Channel HD; ESPN 2 HD; ESPN HD; HDNet; HDNet Movies; KGAN (CBS) Cedar Rapids; KWWL (NBC) Waterloo; Turner Network TV HD; Universal HD.
Fee: $15.00 monthly.
Pay Service 1
Pay Units: N.A.
Programming (via satellite): Cinemax; HBO; Showtime.
Fee: $10.00 monthly (Cinemax), $12.00 monthly (HBO or Showtime).
Digital Pay Service 1
Pay Units: N.A.
Programming (via satellite): Cinemax (multiplexed); Encore (multiplexed); HBO (multiplexed); Showtime (multiplexed); Starz (multiplexed).
Fee: $10.00 monthly (HBO, Showtime or Starz/Encore), $12.00 monthly (Cinemax).
Internet Service
Operational: Yes, Both DSL & dial-up.
Broadband Service: In-house.
Fee: $44.95 monthly; $3.95 modem lease; $80.00 modem purchase.
Telephone Service
None
Miles of Plant: 12.0 (coaxial); None (fiber optic).
General Manager: Mark Harrison. Marketing Administrator: Marnie Burkey. Plant Manager: Mitch Kuhn. Office Manager: Nancy Seely.
City fee: 3% of gross.
Ownership: Shellsburg Cablevision Inc. (MSO).

SHERRILL—Formerly served by Alpine Communications LC. No longer in operation. ICA: IA0507.

SHUEYVILLE—South Slope Coop. Communications Co. Formerly served by North Liberty, IA [IA0432]. This cable system has converted to IPTV, PO Box 19, 980 N Front St, North Liberty, IA 52317. Phones: 800-272-6449; 319-626-2211. Fax: 319-665-7000. E-mail: info@southslopw.com. Web Site: http://www.southslope.com. ICA: IA5011.
TV Market Ranking: 65 (Shueyville).
Channel capacity: N.A. Channels available but not in use: N.A.
Basic Service
Subscribers: N.A.
Fee: $25.00 installation; $41.95 monthly.
Expanded Basic Service 1
Subscribers: N.A.
Fee: $25.00 installation; $54.95 monthly.
Expanded Basic Service 2
Subscribers: N.A.
Fee: $25.00 installation; $10.00 monthly.
Limited Basic Service
Subscribers: N.A.
Fee: $25.00 installation; $14.95 monthly.
Pay Service 1
Pay Units: N.A.
Fee: $25.00 installation; $10.95 monthy (Starz); $11.95 monthly (Cinemax); $12.95 monthly (Showtime); $13.95 monthy (HBO); $15.95 monthly (Adult).
Internet Service
Operational: Yes.
Fee: $39.95 monthly; $10.00 modem lease; $130.00 modem purchase.
Telephone Service
Digital: Operational
Fee: $14.50 monthly
Ownership: South Slope Cooperative Communications Co.

SIBLEY—HTC Cablecom. Now served by SHELDON, IA [IA0060]. ICA: IA0097.

SIDNEY—Our Cable, PO Box 190, 112 E Main St, Breda, IA 51436-0190. Phone: 877-873-8715. E-mail: info@ourcableia.com. Web Site: http://ourcableia.com. ICA: IA0508.
TV Market Ranking: Outside TV Markets (SIDNEY). Franchise award date: N.A. Franchise expiration date: N.A. Began: November 2, 1981.
Channel capacity: N.A. Channels available but not in use: N.A.
Basic Service
Subscribers: N.A. Included in Breda
Programming (received off-air): KETV (ABC) Omaha; KHIN (PBS) Red Oak; KMTV-TV (CBS) Omaha; KPTM (FOX, MNT) Omaha; KUON-TV (PBS) Lincoln; KXVO (CW) Omaha; WOWT-TV (IND, NBC) Omaha.
Programming (via satellite): ABC Family Channel; AMC; Arts & Entertainment; CNN; Discovery Channel; Disney Channel; ESPN; ESPN 2; Headline News; History Channel; Lifetime; Nickelodeon; Spike TV; Syfy; TBS Superstation; Turner Network TV; TV Land; USA Network; VH1; Weather Channel; WGN America.
Fee: $20.00 installation; $25.45 monthly.
Pay Service 1
Pay Units: N.A.
Programming (via satellite): HBO; The Movie Channel.

Fee: $10.95 monthly (each).
Video-On-Demand: No
Internet Service
Operational: No.
Telephone Service
None
City fee: 3% of gross.
Ownership: Our Cable (MSO).

SIGOURNEY—Mediacom. Now served by CEDAR RAPIDS, IA [IA0002]. ICA: IA0107.
Video-On-Demand: Yes

SILVER CITY—Formerly served by Interstate Communications. No longer in operation. ICA: IA0509.

SIOUX CENTER—Premier Communications, PO Box 200, 339 1st Ave NE, Sioux Center, IA 51250. Phones: 800-741-8351; 712-722-3451. Fax: 712-722-1113. E-mail: carolr@mypremieronline.com. Web Site: http://www.mypremieronline.com. Also serves Akron, Boyden, Doon, George, Granville, Hinton, Hull, Ireton, Maurice, Merrill, Rock Valley & Sanborn. ICA: IA0076.
TV Market Ranking: 85 (Doon, Rock Valley); Below 100 (Akron, Hinton, Ireton, Maurice, Merrill); Outside TV Markets (Boyden, George, Granville, Hull, Sanborn, SIOUX CENTER). Franchise award date: March 1, 1982. Franchise expiration date: N.A. Began: N.A.
Channel capacity: 116 (2-way capable). Channels available but not in use: None.
Basic Service
Subscribers: 5,513.
Programming (received off-air): KCAU-TV (ABC) Sioux City; KELO-TV (CBS, MNT) Sioux Falls; KMEG (CBS) Sioux City; KPTH (FOX, MNT) Sioux City; KSFY-TV (ABC) Sioux Falls; KSIN-TV (PBS) Sioux City; KTIV (CW, NBC) Sioux City; KUSD-TV (PBS) Vermillion; 11 FMs.
Programming (via satellite): ABC Family Channel; Disney Channel; TBS Superstation; TV Guide Network; Weather Channel.
Current originations: Public Access.
Fee: $29.95 installation; $12.95 monthly; $2.95 converter.
Expanded Basic Service 1
Subscribers: N.A.
Programming (via satellite): Animal Planet; Arts & Entertainment; Bloomberg Television; CNN; Comedy Central; Country Music TV; C-SPAN; CW+; Discovery Channel; ESPN; ESPN 2; ESPN Classic Sports; Food Network; Fox News Channel; Fox Sports Net Midwest; FX; Global Village Network; Great American Country; Hallmark Channel; Headline News; HGTV; History Channel; Lifetime; MSNBC; MTV; Nickelodeon; Outdoor Channel; QVC; Speed Channel; Spike TV; The Learning Channel; Toon Disney; Travel Channel; Trinity Broadcasting Network; truTV; Turner Classic Movies; Turner Network TV; TV Land; Univision; USA Network; VH1; WGN America.
Fee: $28.95 monthly.
Digital Basic Service
Subscribers: N.A.
Programming (received off-air): KELO-TV (CBS, MNT) Sioux Falls; KSFY-TV (ABC) Sioux Falls; KTIV (CW, NBC) Sioux City; KUSD-TV (PBS) Vermillion.
Programming (via satellite): AmericanLife TV Network; BBC America; Bio; Bravo; Canales N; CBS College Sports Network; Discovery Digital Networks; DMX Music; Do-It-Yourself; ESPN U; ESPNews; Fox College Sports Atlantic; Fox College Sports Central; Fox College Sports Pacific; Fox Movie Channel; G4; GAS; Golf Channel; GSN; HDNet; HDNet Movies; History Channel International; Lifetime Movie Network; MTV Networks Digital Suite; National Geographic Channel; Nick Jr.; NickToons TV; RFD-TV; ShopNBC; Style Network; Versus.
Fee: $14.95 monthly.
Pay Service 1
Pay Units: 316.
Programming (via satellite): HBO.
Fee: $20.00 installation; $8.00 monthly.
Digital Pay Service 1
Pay Units: N.A.
Programming (via satellite): Cinemax; Encore (multiplexed); HBO (multiplexed); Starz (multiplexed); The Movie Channel.
Fee: $7.95 (Encore), $8.95 monthly (Cinemax or TMC), $12.95 monthly (HBO or Starz/Encore).
Video-On-Demand: Yes
Internet Service
Operational: Yes, Both DSL & dial-up.
Fee: $21.95 monthly.
Telephone Service
Analog: Operational
Fee: $25.00 installation; $21.00 monthly
Miles of Plant: 115.0 (coaxial); 8,181.0 (fiber optic). Homes passed: 6,824.
Chief Executive Officer: Douglas A. Boone. Marketing Director: Scott Te Stroete. Chief Technician: Les Sybesma.
City fee: 3% of gross.
Ownership: Premier Communications Inc.

SIOUX CITY—Cable One, 900 Steuben St, Sioux City, IA 51101-2049. Phone: 712-233-2000. Fax: 712-233-2235. Web Site: http://www.cableone.net. Also serves Sergeant Bluff & Woodbury County, IA; Dakota City, Dakota County (portions), Freeway Mobile Home Park, Lake Village Mobile Home Park, South Sioux City & Tompkins Mobile Home Park, NE; Dakota Dunes, North Sioux City & Union County (portions), SD. ICA: IA0004.
TV Market Ranking: Below 100 (Dakota City, Dakota County (portions), Freeway Mobile Home Park, Lake Village Mobile Home Park, North Sioux City, Sergeant Bluff, SIOUX CITY, South Sioux City, Tompkins Mobile Home Park, Union County (portions), Woodbury County (portions)); Outside TV Markets (Dakota Dunes, Woodbury County (portions)). Franchise award date: December 16, 1978. Franchise expiration date: N.A. Began: July 1, 1979.
Channel capacity: 78 (operating 2-way). Channels available but not in use: 7.
Basic Service
Subscribers: 24,558.
Programming (received off-air): KCAU-TV (ABC) Sioux City; KMEG (CBS) Sioux City; KPTH (FOX, MNT) Sioux City; KSIN-TV (PBS) Sioux City; KTIV (CW, NBC) Sioux City.
Programming (via satellite): ABC Family Channel; AMC; Animal Planet; Arts & Entertainment; Azteca America; Cartoon Network; CNBC; CNN; Comedy Central; Country Music TV; C-SPAN; C-SPAN 2; CW+; Discovery Channel; Disney Channel; ESPN; ESPN 2; Food Network; Fox News Channel; Fox Sports Net North; FX; Headline News; HGTV; History Channel; Home Shopping Network; INSP; Lifetime; MSNBC; MTV; Nickelodeon; Product Information Network; QVC; ShopNBC; Spike TV; Syfy; The Learning Channel; Travel Channel; Turner Classic Movies; Turner Network TV; TV Guide Network; TV Land; USA Network; VH1; Weather Channel; WGN America.
Current originations: Educational Access.
Fee: $75.00 installation; $46.00 monthly.

Digital Basic Service
Subscribers: 7,400.
Programming (received off-air): KCAU-TV (ABC) Sioux City; KSIN-TV (PBS) Sioux City; KTIV (CW, NBC) Sioux City.
Programming (via satellite): 3 Angels Broadcasting Network; Bio; Boomerang; BYU Television; Canales N; Discovery Digital Networks; DMX Music; ESPN Classic Sports; ESPNews; FamilyNet; Fox College Sports Atlantic; Fox College Sports Central; Fox College Sports Pacific; Fox Movie Channel; Fox Soccer; Fuel TV; G4; Golf Channel; Great American Country; Hallmark Channel; History Channel International; INSP; National Geographic Channel; Outdoor Channel; SoapNet; Speed Channel; Toon Disney; Trinity Broadcasting Network; truTV; Turner Network TV HD; TVG Network; Universal HD.
Fee: $9.95 monthly.
Digital Pay Service 1
Pay Units: N.A.
Programming (via satellite): Cinemax (multiplexed); Encore (multiplexed); Flix; HBO (multiplexed); Showtime (multiplexed); Showtime HD; Starz (multiplexed); Sundance Channel; The Movie Channel (multiplexed); The Movie Channel HD.
Fee: $15.00 monthly.
Video-On-Demand: No
Pay-Per-View
Movies (delivered digitally); Ten Blox (delivered digitally); Ten Blue (delivered digitally); Pleasure (delivered digitally); Ten Clips (delivered digitally).
Internet Service
Operational: Yes. Began: October 1, 2000.
Subscribers: 8,900.
Broadband Service: CableONE.net.
Fee: $75.00 installation; $43.00 monthly.
Telephone Service
Digital: Operational
Fee: $75.00 installation; $39.95 monthly
Miles of Plant: 577.0 (coaxial); 85.0 (fiber optic). Homes passed: 47,677. Total homes in franchised area: 47,677.
Manager: Cheryl Goettsche. Chief Technician: Robert Wignes. Marketing Director: Paula Todd.
City fee: 3% of gross.
Ownership: Cable One Inc. (MSO).

SIOUX RAPIDS—WesTel Systems. Now served by MARCUS, IA [IA0171]. ICA: IA0209.

SMITHLAND—TelePartners. Now served by LAWTON, IA [IA0330]. ICA: IA0350.

SOLDIER—Long Lines, 501 4th St, Sergeant Bluff, IA 51054-8509. Phones: 712-884-2203; 712-271-4000. Fax: 712-271-2727. Web Site: http://www.longlines.com. ICA: IA0603.
TV Market Ranking: Outside TV Markets (SOLDIER).
Channel capacity: N.A. Channels available but not in use: N.A.
Basic Service
Subscribers: 69.
Programming (received off-air): KCAU-TV (ABC) Sioux City; KMEG (CBS) Sioux City; KPTH (FOX, MNT) Sioux City; KSIN-TV (PBS) Sioux City; KTIV (CW, NBC) Sioux City; KXVO (CW) Omaha.
Programming (via satellite): ABC Family Channel; AMC; AmericanLife TV Network; Animal Planet; Arts & Entertainment; Big Ten Network; Cartoon Network; CNBC; CNN; Comedy Central; Country Music TV; C-SPAN; C-SPAN 2; Discovery Channel; Disney Channel; E! Entertainment Television; ESPN; ESPN 2; ESPN Classic Sports; Eternal Word TV Network; Food Network; Fox News Channel; Fox Sports Net North; FX; Golf Channel; Hallmark Channel; Headline News; HGTV; History Channel; Home Shopping Network; INSP; Lifetime; Lifetime Movie Network; MSNBC; MTV; Nickelodeon; QVC; Speed Channel; Spike TV; Syfy; TBS Superstation; The Learning Channel; The Sportsman Channel; Travel Channel; Trinity Broadcasting Network; truTV; Turner Classic Movies; Turner Network TV; TuTv; TV Guide Network; TV Land; USA Network; VH1; Weather Channel; WGN America.
Fee: $41.99 monthly.
Digital Basic Service
Subscribers: N.A.
Programming (via satellite): BBC America; Bio; Cooking Channel; Discovery Health Channel; Discovery Kids Channel; Discovery Military Channel; Discovery Planet Green; DMX Music; Do-It-Yourself; ESPN U; ESPNews; FitTV; Fox College Sports Atlantic; Fox College Sports Central; Fox College Sports Pacific; Fox Movie Channel; Fox Soccer; G4; Great American Country; GSN; Halogen Network; History Channel International; ID Investigation Discovery; Independent Film Channel; Lifetime Real Women; MTV Hits; MTV Jams; MTV2; Nick Jr.; NickToons TV; Outdoor Channel; RFD-TV; Science Channel; SoapNet; TeenNick; Toon Disney; Versus; VH1 Classic; VH1 Country; VH1 Soul; WE tv.
Fee: $9.99 monthly.
Digital Expanded Basic Service
Subscribers: N.A.
Programming (received off-air): KCAU-TV (ABC) Sioux City; KMEG (CBS) Sioux City; KPTH (FOX, MNT) Sioux City; KSIN-TV (PBS) Sioux City; KTIV (CW, NBC) Sioux City.
Programming (via satellite): Big Ten Network HD; Discovery Channel HD; ESPN 2 HD; ESPN HD; HDNet; HDNet Movies; Outdoor Channel 2 HD.
Fee: $9.95 monthly.
Digital Expanded Basic Service 2
Subscribers: N.A.
Programming (via satellite): Bandamax; De Pelicula; De Pelicula Clasico; Discovery en Espanol; ESPN Deportes; Fox Sports en Espanol; Ritmoson Latino; Telehit.
Fee: $2.95 monthly.

Pay Service 1
Pay Units: 5.
Programming (via satellite): HBO (multiplexed).
Fee: $14.95 monthly.
Pay Service 2
Pay Units: 2.
Programming (via satellite): Flix; Showtime (multiplexed); The Movie Channel.
Fee: $14.45 monthly.
Digital Pay Service 1
Pay Units: N.A.
Programming (via satellite): Cinemax (multiplexed); Cinemax HD; Encore (multiplexed); Flix; HBO (multiplexed); HBO HD; Showtime; Starz (multiplexed); Starz HDTV; Starz On Demand; The Movie Channel (multiplexed).
Fee: $11.95 monthly (Cinemax), $13.95 monthly (Starz/Encore), $14.45 monthly (Showtime/TMC/Flix), $14.95 monthly (HBO).
Video-On-Demand: Yes
Internet Service
Operational: No, Both DSL & dial-up.
Homes passed: 99.
Manager & Chief Operations Officer: Paul Bergmann. System Engineer: Tony Seubert. Marketing Manager: Pat McElroy. Office Manager: Denise Moberg.
Ownership: Long Lines (MSO).

SOLDIER—Soldier Valley Telephone. Now served by SALIX, IA [IA0510]. ICA: IA0360.

SOLON—South Slope Coop. Communications Co. Formerly served by North Liberty, IA [IA0432]. This cable system has converted to IPTV, PO Box 19, 980 N Front St, North Liberty, IA 52317. Phones: 800-272-6449; 319-626-2211. Fax: 319-665-7000. E-mail: info@southslope.com. Web Site: http://www.southslope.com. ICA: IA5012.
TV Market Ranking: 65 (Solon). Franchise award date: April 15, 2004. Franchise expiration date: N.A. Began: September 1, 2005.
Channel capacity: N.A. Channels available but not in use: N.A.
Basic Service
Subscribers: N.A.
Fee: $25.00 installation; $41.95 monthly.
Expanded Basic Service 1
Subscribers: N.A.
Fee: $25.00 installation; $54.95 monthly.
Expanded Basic Service 2
Subscribers: N.A.
Fee: $25.00 installation; $10.00 monthly.
Limited Basic Service
Subscribers: N.A.
Fee: $25.00 installation; $14.95 monthly.
Pay Service 1
Pay Units: N.A.
Fee: $25.00 installation; $10.95 monthy (Starz); $11.95 monthly (Cinemax); $12.95 monthly (Showtime); $13.95 monthy (HBO); $15.95 monthly (Adult).
Internet Service
Operational: Yes.
Fee: $39.95 monthly; $10.00 modem lease; $130.00 modem purchase.
Telephone Service
Digital: Operational
Fee: $14.50 monthly
Ownership: South Slope Cooperative Communications Co.

SPENCER—Mediacom, PO Box 110, 1504 2nd St SE, Waseca, MN 56093. Phone: 507-835-2356. Fax: 507-835-4567. Web Site: http://www.mediacomcable.com. Also serves Armstrong, Emmetsburg, Esterville, Graettinger & Wallingford. ICA: IA0022.
TV Market Ranking: Outside TV Markets (Armstrong, Emmetsburg, Estherville, Graettinger, SPENCER, Wallingford). Franchise award date: July 8, 1958. Franchise expiration date: N.A. Began: December 24, 1968.
Channel capacity: N.A. Channels available but not in use: N.A.
Basic Service
Subscribers: 8,909.
Programming (received off-air): KCAU-TV (ABC) Sioux City; KELO-TV (CBS, MNT) Sioux Falls; KEYC-TV (CBS, FOX) Mankato; KMEG (CBS) Sioux City; KPTH (FOX, MNT) Sioux City; KSFY-TV (ABC) Sioux Falls; KTIN (PBS) Fort Dodge; KTIV (CW, NBC) Sioux City; WHO-DT (NBC) Des Moines; 11 FMs.
Programming (via satellite): ABC Family Channel; AMC; AmericanLife TV Network; Animal Planet; Arts & Entertainment; Big Ten Network; Bravo; Cartoon Network; CNBC; CNN; Comedy Central; Country Music TV; C-SPAN; C-SPAN 2; CW+; Discovery Channel; Discovery Health Channel; Disney Channel; Do-It-Yourself; E! Entertainment Television; ESPN; ESPN 2; ESPN Classic Sports; ESPN U; Eternal Word TV Network; Food Network; Fox Movie Channel; Fox News Channel; Fox Sports Net North; FX; Golf Channel; Hallmark Channel; Headline News; HGTV; History Channel; Home Shopping Network; INSP; ION Television; Lifetime; MSNBC; MTV; NFL Network; Nickelodeon; Radar Channel; Speed Channel; Spike TV; Syfy; TBS Superstation; The Learning Channel; Travel Channel; Trinity Broadcasting Network; truTV; Turner Classic Movies; Turner Network TV; TV Guide Network; TV Land; USA Network; VH1; Weather Channel; WGN America.
Current originations: Government Access; Educational Access; Public Access.
Fee: $20.00 installation; $24.90 monthly; $2.38 converter; $10.00 additional installation.
Digital Basic Service
Subscribers: 1,258.
Programming (received off-air): KELO-TV (CBS, MNT) Sioux Falls; KMEG (CBS) Sioux City; KPTH (FOX, MNT) Sioux City; KSFY-TV (ABC) Sioux Falls; KSIN-TV (PBS) Sioux City.
Programming (via satellite): BBC America; Bio; Discovery Home Channel; Discovery Kids Channel; Discovery Military Channel; Discovery Times Channel; DMX Music; ESPN 2 HD; ESPN Deportes; ESPN HD; ESPNews; FitTV; Fox Business Channel; Fox Soccer; G4; Golf Channel; GSN; HDNet; HDNet Movies; History Channel International; Independent Film Channel; Lifetime Movie Network; MTV Hits; mun2 television; MyNetworkTV Inc.; Nick Jr.; Outdoor Channel; RFD-TV; Science Channel; SoapNet; Speed Channel; Telemundo; Toon Disney; Universal HD; VH1 Soul.
Digital Pay Service 1
Pay Units: N.A.
Programming (via satellite): Cinemax (multiplexed); Encore (multiplexed); Flix; HBO (multiplexed); Showtime (multiplexed); Starz (multiplexed); Sundance Channel; The Movie Channel (multiplexed).
Fee: $9.95 monthly (Cinemax, HBO, Showtime, Flix/Sundance/TMC, or Starz/Encore).
Video-On-Demand: Yes
Pay-Per-View
Addressable homes: 1,258.
ESPN Now (delivered digitally); Hot Choice (delivered digitally); Playboy TV (delivered digitally); Fresh (delivered digitally); Shorteez (delivered digitally); TVN Entertainment (delivered digitally); sports (delivered digitally).
Internet Service
Operational: Yes.
Broadband Service: Mediacom High Speed Internet.
Fee: $99.00 installation; $40.00 monthly.
Telephone Service
Digital: Operational
Miles of Plant: 926.0 (coaxial); 123.0 (fiber optic). Homes passed: 10,775. Total homes in franchised area: 10,782.
Vice President: Bill Jensen. Engineering Manager: Kraig Kaiser. Marketing & Sales Manager: Lori Huberty.
City fee: 5% of gross.
Ownership: Mediacom LLC (MSO).

SPENCER—SMU Cable TV, PO Box 222, 712 N Grand Ave, Spencer, IA 51301. Phone: 712-580-5800. Fax: 712-580-5888. E-mail: smu@smunet.net. Web Site: http://www.smunet.net. ICA: IA0592. **Note:** This system is an overbuild.
TV Market Ranking: Outside TV Markets (SPENCER). Franchise award date: May 1, 1999. Franchise expiration date: N.A. Began: December 1, 2000.
Channel capacity: 78 (not 2-way capable). Channels available but not in use: 7.
Basic Service
Subscribers: 3,600.
Programming (received off-air): KCAU-TV (ABC) Sioux City; KELO-TV (CBS, MNT) Sioux Falls; KMEG (CBS) Sioux City; KPTH (FOX, MNT) Sioux City; KSFY-TV (ABC) Sioux Falls; KTIN (PBS) Fort Dodge; KTIV (CW, NBC) Sioux City.
Programming (via satellite): ION Television; MSNBC; TBS Superstation; TV Guide Network; Weather Channel; WGN America.
Fee: $9.99 monthly.
Expanded Basic Service 1
Subscribers: 3,400.
Programming (via satellite): ABC Family Channel; AMC; AmericanLife TV Network; Animal Planet; Arts & Entertainment; Bravo; Cartoon Network; CNBC; CNN; Comedy Central; Country Music TV; C-SPAN; C-SPAN 2; Discovery Channel; Discovery Health Channel; Disney Channel; E! Entertainment Television; ESPN; ESPN 2; Eternal Word TV Network; Food Network; Fox Movie Channel; Fox News Channel; Fox Sports Net North; FX; Headline News; HGTV; History Channel; Home Shopping Network; INSP; Lifetime; MTV; Nickelodeon; Outdoor Channel; Spike TV; Syfy; The Learning Channel; Travel Channel; Trinity Broadcasting Network; Turner Classic Movies; Turner Network TV; TV Land; USA Network; VH1.
Fee: $18.00 monthly.
Digital Basic Service
Subscribers: 1,000.
Programming (via satellite): BBC America; Bio; Discovery Digital Networks; DMX Music; ESPNews; FitTV; Fox Sports World; G4; Golf Channel; GSN; History Channel International; Independent Film Channel; Nick Jr.; Science Television; Speed Channel; VH1 Classic; VH1 Country.
Fee: $4.00 monthly; $3.00 converter.
Digital Pay Service 1
Pay Units: N.A.
Programming (via satellite): Cinemax (multiplexed); Encore (multiplexed); Flix; HBO (multiplexed); Showtime (multiplexed); Starz (multiplexed); Sundance Channel; The Movie Channel (multiplexed).
Fee: $8.00 monthly (each package).
Video-On-Demand: No
Pay-Per-View
Playboy TV (delivered digitally), Fee: $3.95, Addressable: Yes; Fresh (delivered digitally), Fee: $3.95, Fee: $3.95.
Internet Service
Operational: Yes.
Subscribers: 2,000.
Fee: $29.99 monthly.
Telephone Service
None
Miles of Plant: 330.0 (coaxial); 21.0 (fiber optic). Homes passed: 5,100. Total homes in franchised area: 5,100.
General Manager: Steve Pick. Telecom Manager: Jeff Rezabek. Marketing Director: Curtis Dean.
Ownership: Spencer Municipal Utilities.

SPIRIT LAKE—Mediacom, PO Box 110, 1504 2nd St SE, Waseca, MN 56093. Phone: 507-835-2356. Fax: 507-835-4567. Web Site: http://www.mediacomcable.com. Also serves Arnolds Park, Harris, Lake Park, Okoboji, Orleans, Wahpeton & West Okoboji. ICA: IA0036.
TV Market Ranking: Outside TV Markets (Arnolds Park, Harris, Lake Park, Okoboji, Orleans, SPIRIT LAKE, Wahpeton, West Okoboji). Franchise award date: N.A. Franchise expiration date: N.A. Began: October 1, 1976.
Channel capacity: N.A. Channels available but not in use: N.A.
Basic Service
Subscribers: 1,000.
Programming (received off-air): KCAU-TV (ABC) Sioux City; KELO-TV (CBS, MNT) Sioux Falls; KMEG (CBS) Sioux City; KPTH (FOX, MNT) Sioux City; KSFY-TV (ABC) Sioux Falls; KTIN (PBS) Fort Dodge; KTIV (CW, NBC) Sioux City; WOI-DT (ABC) Ames.
Programming (via satellite): ABC Family Channel; AMC; Animal Planet; Arts & Entertainment; Bravo; Cartoon Network; CNBC; CNN; Comedy Central; Country Music TV; C-SPAN; C-SPAN 2; Discovery Channel; Disney Channel; E! Entertainment Television; ESPN; ESPN 2; ESPN Classic Sports; Eternal Word TV Network; Fox Movie Channel; Fox News Channel; Fox Sports Net Midwest; FX; Hallmark Channel; Headline News; HGTV; History Channel; Home Shopping Network; Lifetime; MoviePlex; MSNBC; MTV; Nickelodeon; Oxygen; Radar Channel; SoapNet; Speed Channel; Spike TV; Syfy; TBS Superstation; Telemundo; The Learning Channel; Toon Disney; Travel Channel; Trinity Broadcasting Network; truTV; Turner Classic Movies; Turner Network TV; TV Guide Network; TV Land; Univision; USA Network; VH1; Weather Channel; WGN America.
Fee: $20.00 installation; $23.95 monthly; $5.00 additional installation.
Digital Basic Service
Subscribers: N.A.
Programming (received off-air): KDIN-TV (PBS) Des Moines.
Programming (via satellite): ABC News Now; AmericanLife TV Network; BBC America; Bio; Bloomberg Television; Canal 52MX; CBS College Sports Network; CCTV-9 (CCTV International); Cine Latino; CMT Pure Country; CNN en Espanol; CNN HD; Discovery en Espanol; Discovery HD Theater; Discovery Health Channel; Discovery Home Channel; Discovery Kids Channel; Discovery Military Channel; ESPN 2 HD; ESPN Deportes; ESPN HD; ESPN U; ESPNews; FitTV; Fox College Sports

Atlantic; Fox College Sports Central; Fox College Sports Pacific; Fox Reality Channel; Fox Soccer; Fox Sports en Espanol; Fuel TV; Fuse; G4; Gol TV; Golf Channel; GSN; Halogen Network; HDNet; HDNet Movies; History Channel en Espanol; History Channel International; ID Investigation Discovery; Independent Film Channel; ION Life; Lifetime Movie Network; Lifetime Real Women; MTV Hits; MTV Tres; MTV2; Music Choice; National Geographic Channel; Nick Jr.; NickToons TV; Outdoor Channel; Ovation; Qubo; ReelzChannel; Science Channel; Sleuth; Style Network; TBS in HD; TeenNick; Tennis Channel; The Sportsman Channel; Turner Network TV HD; TVG Network; Universal HD; VeneMovies; VH1 Classic; VH1 Soul.

Digital Pay Service 1

Pay Units: 406.

Programming (via satellite): Cinemax (multiplexed); Encore (multiplexed); Flix; HBO (multiplexed); HBO HD; Showtime (multiplexed); Showtime HD; Starz (multiplexed); Starz HDTV; Sundance Channel; The Movie Channel (multiplexed); The Movie Channel HD.

Fee: $10.00 monthly (each).

Video-On-Demand: Yes

Pay-Per-View

iN DEMAND (delivered digitally); Ten Clips (delivered digitally); Playboy TV (delivered digitally); Penthouse TV (delivered digitally); Spice: Xcess (delivered digitally).

Internet Service

Operational: Yes.

Broadband Service: Mediacom High Speed Internet.

Telephone Service

Digital: Operational

Miles of Plant: 121.0 (coaxial); None (fiber optic). Homes passed: 3,861.

Vice President: Bill Jensen. Engineering Manager: Kraig Kaiser. Marketing & Sales Manager: Lori Huberty.

City fee: 3% of gross.

Ownership: Mediacom LLC (MSO).

SPRINGVILLE—Springville Co-operative Telephone Assn Inc, PO Box 9, 207 Broadway, Springville, IA 52336-0009. Phone: 319-854-6500. Fax: 319-854-9010. E-mail: springvl@netins.net. Also serves Paralta, Viola & Whittier. ICA: IA0144.

TV Market Ranking: 65 (Paralta, SPRINGVILLE, Viola, Whittier). Franchise award date: January 1, 1983. Franchise expiration date: N.A. Began: January 1, 1983.

Channel capacity: 59 (not 2-way capable). Channels available but not in use: 10.

Basic Service

Subscribers: 537.

Programming (received off-air): KCRG-TV (ABC) Cedar Rapids; KFXA (FOX) Cedar Rapids; KGAN (CBS) Cedar Rapids; KIIN (PBS) Iowa City; KPXR-TV (ION) Cedar Rapids; KWKB (CW, MNT) Iowa City; KWWL (NBC) Waterloo.

Programming (via satellite): ABC Family Channel; AMC; Animal Planet; Arts & Entertainment; Big Ten Network; Cartoon Network; CNN; Comedy Central; Country Music TV; Discovery Channel; Disney Channel; ESPN; ESPN 2; FitTV; Food Network; Fox News Channel; FX; Great American Country; Hallmark Channel; HGTV; History Channel; Home Shopping Network; Lifetime; MTV; Nickelodeon; Speed Channel; Spike TV; Syfy; TBS Superstation; The Learning Channel; Turner Classic Movies; Turner Network TV; TV Land; USA Network; Versus; VH1; Weather Channel; WGN America.

Current originations: Public Access.

Fee: $30.00 installation; $32.00 monthly.

Pay Service 1

Pay Units: 55.

Programming (via satellite): HBO.

Fee: $30.00 installation; $14.75 monthly.

Pay Service 2

Pay Units: 42.

Programming (via satellite): Cinemax.

Fee: $10.75 monthly.

Internet Service

Operational: No.

Telephone Service

None

Miles of Plant: 33.0 (coaxial); None (fiber optic). Homes passed: 813. Total homes in franchised area: 813.

Manager: Jim Teig. Chief Technician: Todd McWherter.

City fee: None.

Ownership: Springville Cooperative Telephone Assn. Inc.

ST. CHARLES—Interstate Communications. Now served by TRURO, IA [IA0344]. ICA: IA0295.

ST. LUCAS—Alpine Communications LC. Now served by LAWLER, IA [IA0462]. ICA: IA0559.

STANTON—Farmers Mutual Telephone Co, PO Box 220, 410 Broad Ave, Stanton, IA 51573-0220. Phone: 712-829-2111. Fax: 712-829-2509. E-mail: customerservices@fmtcnet.com. Web Site: http://www.myfmtc.com. Also serves New Market. ICA: IA0264.

TV Market Ranking: Outside TV Markets (New Market, STANTON). Franchise award date: N.A. Franchise expiration date: N.A. Began: August 1, 1983.

Channel capacity: 39 (not 2-way capable). Channels available but not in use: None.

Basic Service

Subscribers: 377.

Programming (received off-air): KETV (ABC) Omaha; KHIN (PBS) Red Oak; KMTV-TV (CBS) Omaha; KPTM (FOX, MNT) Omaha; KXVO (CW) Omaha; WHO-DT (NBC) Des Moines; WOWT-TV (IND, NBC) Omaha.

Programming (via satellite): ABC Family Channel; AMC; Animal Planet; Arts & Entertainment; CNN; Comedy Central; Discovery Channel; Disney Channel; ESPN; ESPN 2; Fox News Channel; Fox Sports Net Midwest; Great American Country; Hallmark Channel; Headline News; HGTV; History Channel; Lifetime; Nickelodeon; Speed Channel; Spike TV; TBS Superstation; The Learning Channel; Travel Channel; Turner Network TV; TV Land; USA Network; WGN America.

Fee: $20.00 installation; $24.95 monthly; $1.00 converter.

Pay Service 1

Pay Units: 46.

Programming (via satellite): HBO.

Fee: $20.00 installation; $12.00 monthly.

Pay Service 2

Pay Units: 20.

Programming (via satellite): Cinemax.

Fee: $20.00 installation; $12.00 monthly.

Internet Service

Operational: No, DSL & dial-up.

Telephone Service

None

General Manager: Kevin Cabbage. Assistant Manager: Dennis Crawford. Central Office Manager: Scott Boatman. Outside Plant Manager: Brad Sunderman. Customer Service Manager: Kathie Bell.

Ownership: Farmers Mutual Cooperative Telephone Co. (MSO).

STANWOOD—Cedar Communications LLC, PO Box 246, 608 Lombard St, Clarence, IA 52216-0246. Phones: 800-695-3896; 563-452-3852. Fax: 563-452-3883. E-mail: clarence@netins.net. Web Site: http://www.clarencetelinc.com. ICA: IA0174.

TV Market Ranking: 65 (STANWOOD). Franchise award date: N.A. Franchise expiration date: N.A. Began: November 1, 1984.

Channel capacity: 82 (operating 2-way). Channels available but not in use: 20.

Basic Service

Subscribers: 200.

Programming (received off-air): KCRG-TV (ABC) Cedar Rapids; KFXA (FOX) Cedar Rapids; KGAN (CBS) Cedar Rapids; KIIN (PBS) Iowa City; KLJB (CW, FOX) Davenport; KWKB (CW, MNT) Iowa City; KWQC-TV (NBC) Davenport; KWWL (NBC) Waterloo; WHBF-TV (CBS) Rock Island; WQAD-TV (ABC) Moline.

Programming (via satellite): ABC Family Channel; AMC; AmericanLife TV Network; Animal Planet; Arts & Entertainment; Cartoon Network; CNBC; CNN; Comcast SportsNet Chicago; Comedy Central; Country Music TV; C-SPAN; Discovery Channel; Disney Channel; E! Entertainment Television; ESPN; ESPN 2; Food Network; Fox News Channel; FX; Great American Country; GSN; HGTV; History Channel; Home Shopping Network; INSP; Lifetime; MTV; Nickelodeon; Outdoor Channel; QVC; Speed Channel; Spike TV; Syfy; TBS Superstation; The Learning Channel; Travel Channel; Trinity Broadcasting Network; Turner Classic Movies; Turner Network TV; TV Land; USA Network; VH1; Weather Channel; WGN America.

Fee: $25.00 installation; $26.95 monthly.

Pay Service 1

Pay Units: N.A.

Programming (via satellite): Cinemax (multiplexed); HBO; Showtime (multiplexed).

Fee: $8.50 monthly (Showtime), $9 monthly (Cinemax or HBO).

Video-On-Demand: No

Pay-Per-View

ESPN Now (delivered digitally); Hot Choice (delivered digitally); Playboy TV (delivered digitally); Fresh (delivered digitally); Shorteez (delivered digitally); TVN Entertainment (delivered digitally); sports (delivered digitally).

Internet Service

Operational: No.

Telephone Service

None

Manager & Chief Technician: Curtis Eldred.

Ownership: Clarence Telephone Co. Inc. (MSO).

STATE CENTER—Partner Communications. Now served by GILMAN, IA [IA0128]. ICA: IA0513.

STEAMBOAT ROCK—Formerly served by Steamboat Rock Cablevision. No longer in operation. ICA: IA0514.

STORM LAKE—Knology, 5100 S Broadband Ln, Sioux Falls, SD 57108-2207. Phone: 605-965-9393. Fax: 605-965-7867. Web Site: http://www.knology.com. ICA: IA0596. **Note:** This system is an overbuild.

TV Market Ranking: Outside TV Markets (STORM LAKE).

Channel capacity: N.A. Channels available but not in use: N.A.

Basic Service

Subscribers: N.A. Included in Viborg

Programming (received off-air): KCAU-TV (ABC) Sioux City; KCCI (CBS) Des Moines; KDSM-TV (FOX) Des Moines; KMEG (CBS) Sioux City; KPTH (FOX, MNT) Sioux City; KSIN-TV (PBS) Sioux City; KTIV (CW, NBC) Sioux City.

Programming (via satellite): ABC Family Channel; AMC; Animal Planet; Arts & Entertainment; Bravo; Cartoon Network; CNBC; CNN; Comedy Central; Country Music TV; C-SPAN; CW+; Discovery Channel; Disney Channel; E! Entertainment Television; ESPN; ESPN 2; ESPN Classic Sports; Food Network; Fox News Channel; Fox Sports Net North; FX; G4; GalaVision; Golf Channel; Hallmark Channel; Headline News; HGTV; History Channel; Lifetime; Lifetime Movie Network; MSNBC; MTV; MyNetworkTV Inc.; National Geographic Channel; NFL Network; Nickelodeon; QVC; Speed Channel; Spike TV; Syfy; TBS Superstation; Telefutura; Telemundo; The Learning Channel; Toon Disney; Travel Channel; truTV; Turner Classic Movies; Turner Network TV; TV Guide Network; TV Land; Univision; USA Network; VH1; Weather Channel; WGN America.

Fee: $50.00 installation; $32.95 monthly.

Digital Basic Service

Subscribers: N.A.

Programming (received off-air): KMEG (CBS) Sioux City; KPTH (FOX, MNT) Sioux City; KSIN-TV (PBS) Sioux City; KTIV (CW, NBC) Sioux City.

Programming (via satellite): Bandamax; BBC America; Bio; Bloomberg Television; Boomerang; CMT Pure Country; Cooking Channel; De Pelicula; De Pelicula Clasico; Discovery en Espanol; Discovery HD Theater; Discovery Health Channel; Discovery Kids Channel; Discovery Military Channel; Discovery Planet Green; Do-It-Yourself; ESPN 2 HD; ESPN Deportes; ESPN Deportes On Demand; ESPN HD; ESPN On Demand; ESPN U; ESPN U On Demand; ESPNews; Eternal Word TV Network; FitTV; Flix; Fox College Sports Atlantic; Fox College Sports Central; Fox College Sports Pacific; Fox Movie Channel; Fox Reality Channel; Fox Soccer; Fox Sports en Espanol; Fuse; G4; Gospel Music Channel; GSN; HDNet; HDNet Movies; History Channel International; ID Investigation Discovery; Independent Film Channel; INSP; Lifetime Real Women; MTV Hits; MTV Jams; MTV2; Music Choice; National Geographic Channel; National Geographic Channel HD Network; National Geographic Channel On Demand; NFL Network HD; Nick Jr.; NickToons TV; Outdoor Channel; Outdoor Channel 2 HD; Outdoor Channel On Demand; QVC HD; RFD-TV; Ritmoson Latino; Science Channel; Sleuth; Sleuth On Demand; SoapNet; Speed On Demand; Style Network; Sundance Channel; TBS in HD; TeenNick; Telehit; Turner Network TV HD; TV Guide SPOT; Universal HD; Versus; Versus HD; Versus On Demand; VH1 Classic; VH1 Soul; WAM! America's Kidz Network; WE tv.

Pay Service 1

Pay Units: N.A.

Programming (via satellite): HBO; Showtime.

Fee: $10.00 installation; $9.85 monthly (HBO or Showtime).

Digital Pay Service 1
Pay Units: N.A.
Programming (via satellite): Cinemax (multiplexed); Cinemax HD; Cinemax On Demand; Encore (multiplexed); HBO (multiplexed); HBO HD; HBO On Demand; Showtime (multiplexed); Showtime HD; Showtime On Demand; Starz (multiplexed); Starz HDTV; Starz On Demand; The Movie Channel (multiplexed); The Movie Channel On Demand.
Video-On-Demand: Yes
Pay-Per-View
iN DEMAND (delivered digitally); Hot Choice (delivered digitally).
Internet Service
Operational: Yes.
Broadband Service: Knology.Net.
Telephone Service
Digital: Operational
Homes passed included in Viborg
General Manager: Scott Schroeder. Technical Operations Manager: Daryl Elcock. Marketing Manager: Scott Determan.
Ownership: Knology Inc. (MSO).

STORM LAKE—Mediacom. Now served by FORT DODGE, IA [IA0011]. ICA: IA0020.

STRATFORD—Complete Communications Service, PO Box 438, 1001 Tennyson Ave, Stratford, IA 50249. Phone: 515-838-2390. Fax: 515-838-9998. E-mail: info@globalccs.net. Web Site: http://www.globalccs.net. Also serves Ellsworth, Gilbert, Jewell, Kamrar, Roland & Stanhope. ICA: IA0248.
TV Market Ranking: 66 (Ellsworth, Gilbert, Jewell, Kamrar, Roland, Stanhope, STRATFORD). Franchise award date: July 11, 1983. Franchise expiration date: N.A. Began: January 1, 1983.
Channel capacity: 51 (operating 2-way). Channels available but not in use: None.
Basic Service
Subscribers: 1,207.
Programming (received off-air): KCCI (CBS) Des Moines; KCWI-TV (CW) Ames; KDIN-TV (PBS) Des Moines; KDSM-TV (FOX) Des Moines; KFPX-TV (ION) Newton; WHO-DT (NBC) Des Moines; WOI-DT (ABC) Ames.
Programming (via satellite): ABC Family Channel; AMC; Animal Planet; Arts & Entertainment; CNN; Comedy Central; Country Music TV; Discovery Channel; Disney Channel; E! Entertainment Television; ESPN; ESPN 2; Food Network; Fox News Channel; Fox Sports Net; FX; Great American Country; Hallmark Channel; Headline News; HGTV; History Channel; Home Shopping Network; Lifetime; MTV; Nickelodeon; RFD-TV; Spike TV; Syfy; TBS Superstation; The Learning Channel; Travel Channel; Trinity Broadcasting Network; Turner Network TV; TV Land; USA Network; VH1; Weather Channel; WGN America.
Fee: $25.00 installation; $34.95 monthly.
Pay Service 1
Pay Units: 76.
Programming (via satellite): Cinemax; Flix; HBO; Showtime; The Movie Channel.
Fee: $15.00 installation; $10.95 monthly (Cinemax, Showtime or TMC), $11.95 monthly (HBO).
Video-On-Demand: No
Internet Service
Operational: No, DSL.
Telephone Service
None
Miles of Plant: 35.0 (coaxial); None (fiber optic). Homes passed: 2,248. Total homes in franchised area: 2,248.
General Manager: Randall Baker. Technical Operations Manager: Josh Angove. Office Manager: Elaine Ubben.
Ownership: Stratford Mutual Telephone (MSO).

STRAWBERRY POINT—Mediacom. Now served by WAVERLY, IA [IA0021]. ICA: IA0168.

SUN VALLEY LAKE—Interstate Communications, PO Box 229, 105 N West St, Truro, IA 50257-0229. Phones: 641-765-4201; 712-824-7227. Fax: 641-765-4204. Web Site: http://www.interstatecom.com. ICA: IA0515.
TV Market Ranking: Outside TV Markets (SUN VALLEY LAKE). Franchise award date: N.A. Franchise expiration date: N.A. Began: N.A.
Channel capacity: N.A. Channels available but not in use: N.A.
Basic Service
Subscribers: 133.
Programming (received off-air): KCCI (CBS) Des Moines; KCWI-TV (CW) Ames; KDSM-TV (FOX) Des Moines; WHO-DT (NBC) Des Moines; WOI-DT (ABC) Ames.
Programming (via satellite): ABC Family Channel; AMC; Animal Planet; Arts & Entertainment; Cartoon Network; CNN; Country Music TV; C-SPAN; Discovery Channel; Disney Channel; ESPN; ESPN 2; HGTV; History Channel; Home Shopping Network; Iowa Communications Network; Nickelodeon; Spike TV; Syfy; TBS Superstation; The Learning Channel; Turner Network TV; USA Network; Weather Channel; WGN America.
Fee: $35.00 installation; $23.50 monthly.
Pay Service 1
Pay Units: N.A.
Programming (via satellite): HBO.
Fee: $9.00 monthly (each).
Internet Service
Operational: No.
Telephone Service
None
Miles of Plant: 3.0 (coaxial); None (fiber optic). Homes passed: 160.
Manager: Mike Weis. Chief Technician: Rick Lunn.
Ownership: Interstate Communications (MSO).

SUTHERLAND—WesTel Systems. Now served by MARCUS, IA [IA0171]. ICA: IA0208.

SWALEDALE (village)—Formerly served by New Path Communications LC. No longer in operation. ICA: IA0516.

SWEA CITY—Mediacom, PO Box 110, 1504 2nd St SE, Waseca, MN 56093. Phone: 507-835-2356. Fax: 507-835-4567. Web Site: http://www.mediacomcable.com. ICA: IA0226.
TV Market Ranking: Outside TV Markets (SWEA CITY). Franchise award date: N.A. Franchise expiration date: N.A. Began: October 1, 1974.
Channel capacity: N.A. Channels available but not in use: N.A.
Basic Service
Subscribers: 223.
Programming (received off-air): KAAL (ABC) Austin; KELO-TV (CBS, MNT) Sioux Falls; KEYC-TV (CBS, FOX) Mankato; KIMT (CBS, MNT) Mason City; KPTH (FOX, MNT) Sioux City; KTIN (PBS) Fort Dodge; KTTC (CW, NBC) Rochester; WFTC (MNT) Minneapolis; WHO-DT (NBC) Des Moines; allband FM.
Programming (via satellite): ABC Family Channel; AMC; Animal Planet; Arts & Entertainment; Bravo; Cartoon Network; CNBC; CNN; Comedy Central; Country Music TV; C-SPAN; C-SPAN 2; CW+; Discovery Channel; Disney Channel; E! Entertainment Television; ESPN; ESPN 2; ESPN Classic Sports; Eternal Word TV Network; Food Network; Fox Movie Channel; Fox News Channel; Fox Sports Net Midwest; FX; Hallmark Channel; Headline News; HGTV; History Channel; Home Shopping Network; INSP; Lifetime; MoviePlex; MSNBC; MTV; Nickelodeon; Oxygen; QVC; Radar Channel; SoapNet; Speed Channel; Spike TV; Syfy; TBS Superstation; Telemundo; The Learning Channel; Toon Disney; Travel Channel; Trinity Broadcasting Network; truTV; Turner Classic Movies; Turner Network TV; TV Guide Network; TV Land; Univision; USA Network; Versus; VH1; WE tv; Weather Channel; WGN America.
Fee: $9.95 installation; $9.00 monthly.
Digital Basic Service
Subscribers: N.A.
Programming (via satellite): AmericanLife TV Network; BBC America; Bio; Bloomberg Television; Canal 52MX; CBS College Sports Network; CCTV-9 (CCTV International); Cine Latino; CMT Pure Country; CNN en Espanol; Discovery en Espanol; Discovery Health Channel; Discovery Home Channel; Discovery Kids Channel; Discovery Military Channel; ESPN 2 HD; ESPN HD; ESPN U; ESPNews; FitTV; Fox College Sports Atlantic; Fox College Sports Central; Fox College Sports Pacific; Fox Reality Channel; Fox Soccer; Fox Sports en Espanol; Fuel TV; Fuse; G4; Gol TV; Golf Channel; GSN; Halogen Network; HDNet; HDNet Movies; History Channel en Espanol; History Channel International; ID Investigation Discovery; Independent Film Channel; Lifetime Movie Network; Lifetime Real Women; MTV Hits; MTV Tres; MTV2; Music Choice; National Geographic Channel; Nick Jr.; NickToons TV; Outdoor Channel; Ovation; Science Channel; Sleuth; Style Network; TeenNick; Tennis Channel; The Sportsman Channel; Toon Disney en Espanol; TVG Network; Universal HD; VeneMovies; VH1 Classic; VH1 Soul.
Digital Pay Service 1
Pay Units: N.A.
Programming (via satellite): Cinemax (multiplexed); Encore (multiplexed); Flix; HBO (multiplexed); HBO HD; Showtime (multiplexed); Showtime HD; Starz (multiplexed); Starz HDTV; Sundance Channel; The Movie Channel (multiplexed); The Movie Channel HD.
Video-On-Demand: Yes
Pay-Per-View
TVN Entertainment (delivered digitally); Playboy TV (delivered digitally); Fresh (delivered digitally); Shorteez (delivered digitally); Hot Choice (delivered digitally); ESPN Now (delivered digitally); Sports PPV (delivered digitally).
Internet Service
Operational: Yes.
Broadband Service: Mediacom High Speed Internet.
Fee: $99.00 installation; $40.00 monthly.
Telephone Service
Digital: Operational
Miles of Plant: 8.0 (coaxial); None (fiber optic). Homes passed: 360. Total homes in franchised area: 360.
Vice President: Bill Jensen. Engineering Manager: Kraig Kaiser. Marketing & Sales Manager: Lori Huberty.
City fee: None.
Ownership: Mediacom LLC (MSO).

TABOR—Our Cable, PO Box 190, 112 E Main St, Breda, IA 51436-0190. Phone: 877-873-8715. E-mail: info@ourcableia.com. Web Site: http://ourcableia.com. ICA: IA0517.
TV Market Ranking: 53 (TABOR). Franchise award date: N.A. Franchise expiration date: N.A. Began: January 1, 1985.
Channel capacity: N.A. Channels available but not in use: N.A.
Basic Service
Subscribers: N.A. Included in Breda
Programming (received off-air): KBIN-TV (PBS) Council Bluffs; KETV (ABC) Omaha; KMTV-TV (CBS) Omaha; KPTM (FOX, MNT) Omaha; KUON-TV (PBS) Lincoln; KXVO (CW) Omaha; WOWT-TV (IND, NBC) Omaha.
Programming (via satellite): ABC Family Channel; America's Store; Arts & Entertainment; CNN; Country Music TV; Discovery Channel; Disney Channel; ESPN; ESPN 2; Headline News; History Channel; Lifetime; Spike TV; TBS Superstation; The Learning Channel; Trinity Broadcasting Network; truTV; Turner Network TV; TV Land; USA Network; WGN America.
Fee: $20.00 installation; $26.45 monthly.
Pay Service 1
Pay Units: N.A.
Programming (via satellite): Showtime.
Fee: $10.95 monthly.
Video-On-Demand: No
Internet Service
Operational: No.
Telephone Service
None
Ownership: Our Cable (MSO).

TEMPLETON—Templeton Telephone Co., PO Box 77, 115 N Main St, Templeton, IA 51463. Phones: 888-669-3311; 712-669-3311. Fax: 712-669-3312. Web Site: http://www.templetoniowa.com. Also serves Dedham. ICA: IA0338.
TV Market Ranking: Outside TV Markets (Dedham, TEMPLETON). Franchise award date: July 1, 1988. Franchise expiration date: N.A. Began: January 1, 1989.
Channel capacity: 72 (operating 2-way). Channels available but not in use: N.A.
Basic Service
Subscribers: 200.
Programming (received off-air): KCAU-TV (ABC) Sioux City; KCCI (CBS) Des Moines; KDSM-TV (FOX) Des Moines; KETV (ABC) Omaha; KHIN (PBS) Red Oak; KMTV-TV (CBS) Omaha; KPTM (FOX, MNT) Omaha; KTIV (CW, NBC) Sioux City; KTVO (ABC) Kirksville; WHO-DT (NBC) Des Moines; WOI-DT (ABC) Ames; WOWT-TV (IND, NBC) Omaha.
Programming (via satellite): ABC Family Channel; AMC; Animal Planet; Arts & Entertainment; CNN; Comedy Central; Country Music TV; Discovery Channel; Disney Channel; Encore Westerns; ESPN; ESPN 2; ESPN Classic Sports; Eternal Word TV Network; Food Network; Fox News Channel; Fox Sports Net; FX; Golf Channel; Hallmark Channel; Headline News; HGTV; History Channel; Lifetime; MSNBC; MTV; Nickelodeon; Outdoor Channel; QVC; RFD-TV; Speed Channel; Spike TV; Syfy; TBS Superstation; The Learning Channel; The Movie Channel; Toon Disney; Travel Channel; Trinity Broadcasting Network; Turner Classic

Movies; Turner Network TV; TV Guide Network; TV Land; USA Network; Versus; VH1; Weather Channel; WGN America.
Fee: $10.00 installation; $27.95 monthly.
Pay Service 1
Pay Units: 40.
Programming (via satellite): Cinemax; Encore; HBO (multiplexed); Showtime; Starz.
Fee: $9.50 monthly (each).
Internet Service
Operational: No, DSL & dialup.
Telephone Service
None
Miles of Plant: 5.0 (coaxial); None (fiber optic). Homes passed: 294. Total homes in franchised area: 294.
Manager: Patricia Snyder.
Ownership: Templeton Telephone Co.

TERRIL—Terril Cable Systems, PO Box 100, Terril, IA 51364-0100. Phone: 712-853-6121. Fax: 712-853-6185. E-mail: dloring@terril.com. Web Site: http://www.terril.com. ICA: IA0317.
TV Market Ranking: Outside TV Markets (TERRIL). Franchise award date: N.A. Franchise expiration date: N.A. Began: March 1, 1983.
Channel capacity: N.A. Channels available but not in use: N.A.
Basic Service
Subscribers: 150.
Programming (received off-air): KCAU-TV (ABC) Sioux City; KDIN-TV (PBS) Des Moines; KELO-TV (CBS, MNT) Sioux Falls; KEYC-TV (CBS, FOX) Mankato; KMEG (CBS) Sioux City; KPTH (FOX, MNT) Sioux City; KSFY-TV (ABC) Sioux Falls; KTIV (CW, NBC) Sioux City; WOI-DT (ABC) Ames.
Programming (via satellite): ABC Family Channel; AMC; AmericanLife TV Network; Animal Planet; Arts & Entertainment; Cartoon Network; CNBC; CNN; Comedy Central; Country Music TV; C-SPAN; C-SPAN 2; CW+; Discovery Channel; Disney Channel; E! Entertainment Television; ESPN; ESPN 2; ESPN Classic Sports; Food Network; Fox News Channel; FX; Hallmark Channel; Headline News; HGTV; History Channel; ION Television; Lifetime; MTV; National Geographic Channel; Nickelodeon; Outdoor Channel; QVC; Spike TV; Syfy; TBS Superstation; The Learning Channel; Travel Channel; Turner Classic Movies; Turner Network TV; TV Guide Network; TV Land; USA Network; VH1; Weather Channel; WGN America.
Fee: $20.00 installation; $30.00 monthly.
Digital Basic Service
Subscribers: N.A.
Programming (received off-air): KELO-TV (CBS, MNT) Sioux Falls; KPTH (FOX, MNT) Sioux City; KSFY-TV (ABC) Sioux Falls; KTIV (CW, NBC) Sioux City.
Programming (via satellite): BBC America; Bio; Discovery Health Channel; Discovery Home Channel; Discovery Kids Channel; Discovery Military Channel; Discovery Times Channel; ESPN HD; ESPNews; FitTV; Fox Movie Channel; G4; Golf Channel; GSN; History Channel International; Independent Film Channel; MTV2; Music Choice; Nick Jr.; NickToons TV; Outdoor Channel; Science Channel; Speed Channel; TeenNick; Toon Disney; Univision; VH1 Classic; VH1 Country.
Fee: $8.00 monthly.
Digital Pay Service 1
Pay Units: N.A.
Programming (via satellite): Cinemax (multiplexed); Encore (multiplexed); HBO (multiplexed); Starz (multiplexed).
Fee: $11.00 monthly (each).
Video-On-Demand: No
Pay-Per-View
iN DEMAND (delivered digitally); Spice (delivered digitally); Playboy TV (delivered digitally); Spice (delivered digitally).
Internet Service
Operational: No.
Telephone Service
None
Miles of Plant: 9.0 (coaxial); None (fiber optic). Homes passed: 545.
Manager: Douglas Nelson.
City fee: 1% of gross.
Ownership: Ter Tel Enterprises (MSO).

THOR—Milford Cable TV, PO Box 163, 806 Okoboji Ave, Milford, IA 51351. Phone: 712-338-4967. Fax: 712-338-4719. Web Site: http://www.milfordcable.net. Also serves Vincent. ICA: IA0541.
TV Market Ranking: Outside TV Markets (THOR, Vincent). Franchise award date: N.A. Franchise expiration date: N.A. Began: January 1, 1990.
Channel capacity: 60 (not 2-way capable). Channels available but not in use: 25.
Basic Service
Subscribers: 50.
Programming (received off-air): KCCI (CBS) Des Moines; KCWI-TV (CW) Ames; KDIN-TV (PBS) Des Moines; KDSM-TV (FOX) Des Moines; WHO-DT (NBC) Des Moines; WOI-DT (ABC) Ames.
Programming (via satellite): ABC Family Channel; Arts & Entertainment; Bravo; CNBC; CNN; Country Music TV; Discovery Channel; Disney Channel; ESPN; HGTV; History Channel; Home Shopping Network; Lifetime; MSNBC; MTV; Nickelodeon; Spike TV; TBS Superstation; Turner Network TV; USA Network; VH1; WGN America.
Fee: $35.00 installation; $32.25 monthly.
Digital Basic Service
Subscribers: 5.
Programming (via satellite): BBC America; Bio; Bloomberg Television; Current; Discovery Digital Networks; DMX Music; ESPN 2; ESPN Classic Sports; ESPNews; FitTV; Fox Movie Channel; Fox Soccer; G4; GAS; Golf Channel; GSN; Halogen Network; HGTV; History Channel; History Channel International; Lifetime Movie Network; Lime; MTV Networks Digital Suite; National Geographic Channel; Nick Jr.; NickToons TV; Outdoor Channel; Speed Channel; Style Network; Sundance Channel; Toon Disney; Trinity Broadcasting Network; Turner Classic Movies; WE tv.
Fee: $12.10 monthly.
Pay Service 1
Pay Units: N.A.
Programming (via satellite): HBO (multiplexed).
Fee: $10.70 monthly.
Digital Pay Service 1
Pay Units: N.A.
Programming (via satellite): Cinemax (multiplexed); Encore (multiplexed); Flix; HBO (multiplexed); Showtime (multiplexed); Starz (multiplexed); The Movie Channel (multiplexed).
Fee: $10.70 monthly (each).
Internet Service
Operational: Yes.
Telephone Service
None
Miles of Plant: 1.0 (coaxial); None (fiber optic). Homes passed: 160.
General Manager & Chief Technician: Matt Plagman.
Ownership: Milford Cable TV (MSO).

THORNTON—Rockwell Communications Systems Inc., PO Box 416, 111 N 4th St, Rockwell, IA 50469. Phone: 641-822-3211. Fax: 641-822-3550. E-mail: rockwell@netins.net. Web Site: http://www.rockwellcoop.com. ICA: IA0518.
TV Market Ranking: Below 100 (THORNTON). Franchise award date: N.A. Franchise expiration date: N.A. Began: July 1, 1985.
Channel capacity: N.A. Channels available but not in use: N.A.
Basic Service
Subscribers: 97 Includes Meservey.
Video-On-Demand: No
Pay-Per-View
ESPN (delivered digitally).
Internet Service
Operational: No, DSL & dialup.
Telephone Service
None
General Manager: David Severin. Chief Technician: Jason Dick.
Ownership: Rockwell Cooperative Telephone Association (MSO).

THURMAN—Formerly served by Tele-Services Ltd. No longer in operation. ICA: IA0519.

TIFFIN—South Slope Coop. Communications Co. Formerly served by North Liberty, IA [IA0432]. This cable system has converted to IPTV, PO Box 19, 980 N Front St, North Liberty, IA 52317. Phones: 800-272-6449; 319-626-2211. Fax: 319-665-7000. E-mail: info@slouthslope.com. Web Site: http://www.southslope.com. ICA: IA5013.
TV Market Ranking: 65 (Tiffin). Franchise award date: August 23, 2004. Franchise expiration date: N.A. Began: November 1, 2005.
Channel capacity: N.A. Channels available but not in use: N.A.
Basic Service
Subscribers: N.A.
Fee: $25.00 installation; $41.95 monthly.
Expanded Basic Service 1
Subscribers: N.A.
Fee: $25.00 installation; $54.95 monthly.
Expanded Basic Service 2
Subscribers: N.A.
Fee: $25.00 installation; $10.00 monthly.
Limited Basic Service
Subscribers: N.A.
Fee: $25.00 installation; $14.95 monthly.
Pay Service 1
Pay Units: N.A.
Fee: $25.00 installation; $10.95 monthy (Starz); $11.95 monthly (Cinemax); $12.95 monthly (Showtime); $13.95 monthy (HBO); $15.95 monthly (Adult).
Internet Service
Operational: Yes.
Fee: $39.96 monthly; $10.00 modem lease; $130.00 modem purchase.
Telephone Service
Digital: Operational
Fee: $14.50 monthly
Ownership: South Slope Cooperative Communications Co.

TITONKA—Titonka-Burt Communications, PO Box 321, 247 Main St N, Titonka, IA 50480-0321. Phones: 515-928-2110; 515-928-2120. Fax: 515-928-2897. E-mail: titonka@tbctel.com. Web Site: http://www.tbctel.com. ICA: IA0249.
TV Market Ranking: Outside TV Markets (TITONKA). Franchise award date: January 1, 1982. Franchise expiration date: N.A. Began: January 1, 1983.
Channel capacity: 37 (operating 2-way). Channels available but not in use: N.A.
Basic Service
Subscribers: 221.
Programming (received off-air): KAAL (ABC) Austin; KEYC-TV (CBS, FOX) Mankato; KIMT (CBS, MNT) Mason City; KTIN (PBS) Fort Dodge; KTTC (CW, NBC) Rochester; KXLT-TV (FOX) Rochester; WHO-DT (NBC) Des Moines; allband FM.
Programming (via satellite): ABC Family Channel; Arts & Entertainment; CNN; Country Music TV; Discovery Channel; Disney Channel; ESPN; ESPN 2; Food Network; Fox Sports Net North; Headline News; HGTV; History Channel; Home Shopping Network; ION Television; Lifetime; MTV; Nickelodeon; Spike TV; TBS Superstation; The Learning Channel; Turner Classic Movies; Turner Network TV; TV Land; USA Network; VH1; Weather Channel; WGN America.
Current originations: Public Access.
Fee: $10.00 installation; $25.00 monthly.
Pay Service 1
Pay Units: 20.
Programming (via satellite): HBO.
Fee: $10.00 installation; $11.00 monthly.
Video-On-Demand: No
Internet Service
Operational: No, DSL & dialup.
Telephone Service
None
Miles of Plant: 5.0 (coaxial); None (fiber optic). Homes passed: 301. Total homes in franchised area: 301.
General Manager: Jim Mayland. Secretary: Denise Heyer. Secretary & Treasurer: Vicky Nelson.
Ownership: Titonka Telephone Co.

TOLEDO—Mediacom. Now served by AMES, IA [IA0008]. ICA: IA0052.

TORONTO—F & B Cablevision, PO Box 309, 103 Main St, Wheatland, IA 52777. Phone: 563-374-1236. Web Site: http://www.fbc.bz. ICA: IA0617.
TV Market Ranking: 60 (TORONTO).
Channel capacity: N.A. Channels available but not in use: N.A.
Digital Basic Service
Subscribers: N.A.
Programming (received off-air): KCRG-TV (ABC) Cedar Rapids; KGCW (CW) Burlington; KLJB (CW, FOX) Davenport; KPXR-TV (ION) Cedar Rapids; KQIN (PBS) Davenport; KWQC-TV (NBC) Davenport; KWWF (IND) Waterloo [LICENSED & SILENT]; KWWL (NBC) Waterloo; WHBF-TV (CBS) Rock Island; WQAD-TV (ABC) Moline; WQPT-TV (PBS) Moline.

Programming (via satellite): ABC Family Channel; AMC; Animal Planet; Arts & Entertainment; Big Ten Network; Bio; Bloomberg Television; Boomerang; Bravo; Cartoon Network; Chiller; CNBC; CNBC World; CNN; CNN International; Comcast SportsNet Chicago; Comedy Central; Cooking Channel; Country Music TV; C-SPAN; C-SPAN 2; Discovery Channel; Discovery Health Channel; Disney Channel; Do-It-Yourself; E! Entertainment Television; ESPN; ESPN 2; ESPN Classic Sports; ESPN U; ESPNews; Food Network; Fox News Channel; Fox Sports Net Midwest; FX; G4; Golf Channel; Great American Country; GSN; Hallmark Channel; Headline News; HGTV; History Channel; History Channel International; Home Shopping Network; INSP; KWKB (CW, MNT) Iowa City; Lifetime; Lifetime Movie Network; Lifetime Real Women; MSNBC; MTV; Music Choice; National Geographic Channel; Nickelodeon; Outdoor Channel; Oxygen; QVC; RFD-TV; ShopNBC; Sleuth; SoapNet; Speed Channel; Spike TV; Syfy; TBS Superstation; The Learning Channel; Toon Disney; Travel Channel; Trinity Broadcasting Network; truTV; Turner Classic Movies; Turner Network TV; TV Land; USA Network; VH1; WE tv; Weather Channel; WGN America.
Fee: $54.99 monthly.

Digital Expanded Basic Service
Subscribers: N.A.
Programming (via satellite): Arts & Entertainment HD; Big Ten Network HD; Bio HD; Bravo HD; CNBC HD+; Discovery HD Theater; ESPN 2 HD; ESPN HD; Food Network HD; FSN HD; FX HD; HDNet; HDNet Movies; HGTV HD; History Channel HD; Lifetime Movie Network HD; Lifetime Television HD; National Geographic Channel HD Network; Outdoor Channel 2 HD; Speed HD; Syfy HD; Universal HD; USA Network HD.
Fee: $11.00 monthly.

Digital Pay Service 1
Pay Units: N.A.
Programming (via satellite): Cinemax (multiplexed); Encore (multiplexed); Flix; HBO (multiplexed); Showtime (multiplexed); Showtime HD; Starz (multiplexed); Sundance Channel; The Movie Channel (multiplexed); The Movie Channel HD.
Fee: $15.00 monthly (HBO, Cinemax, Showtime/MTC/Sundance/Flix or Starz/Encore).

Internet Service
Operational: No, Both DSL & dialup.

Telephone Service
None

General Manager: Ken Laursen. Marketing Manager: Aaron Horman.
Ownership: Farmers' & Businessmen's Telephone Co. (MSO).

TRAER—Mediacom. Now served by AMES, IA [IA0008]. ICA: IA0083.

TREYNOR—Our Cable, PO Box 190, 112 E Main St, Breda, IA 51436-0190. Phone: 877-873-8715. E-mail: info@ourcableia.com. Web Site: http://ourcableia.com. ICA: IA0520.
TV Market Ranking: 53 (TREYNOR). Franchise award date: N.A. Franchise expiration date: N.A. Began: November 1, 1984.
Channel capacity: N.A. Channels available but not in use: N.A.

Basic Service
Subscribers: N.A. Included in Breda
Programming (received off-air): KBIN-TV (PBS) Council Bluffs; KETV (ABC) Omaha; KMTV-TV (CBS) Omaha; KPTM (FOX, MNT) Omaha; KUON-TV (PBS) Lincoln; KXVO (CW) Omaha; WOWT-TV (IND, NBC) Omaha.
Programming (via satellite): ABC Family Channel; Arts & Entertainment; CNN; Country Music TV; Disney Channel; ESPN; ESPN 2; Headline News; HGTV; Lifetime; Spike TV; TBS Superstation; The Learning Channel; Trinity Broadcasting Network; Turner Network TV; TV Land; USA Network; Weather Channel; WGN America.
Fee: $20.00 installation; $26.45 monthly.

Pay Service 1
Pay Units: N.A.
Programming (via satellite): Showtime.
Fee: $10.45 monthly.

Video-On-Demand: No

Internet Service
Operational: No.

Telephone Service
None

Ownership: Our Cable (MSO).

TRIPOLI—Butler-Bremer Communications, PO Box 99, 715 Main St, Plainfield, IA 50666. Phone: 319-276-4458. Fax: 319-276-7530. E-mail: comments@butler-bremer.com. Web Site: http://www.butler-bremer.com. Also serves Clarksville, Frederika, Nashua & Plainfield. ICA: IA0127.
TV Market Ranking: 65 (Clarksville, Frederika, Nashua, Plainfield, TRIPOLI). Franchise award date: September 1, 1983. Franchise expiration date: N.A. Began: September 1, 1983.
Channel capacity: 59 (operating 2-way). Channels available but not in use: None.

Basic Service
Subscribers: 1,450.
Programming (received off-air): KCRG-TV (ABC) Cedar Rapids; KFXA (FOX) Cedar Rapids; KIMT (CBS, MNT) Mason City; KPXR-TV (ION) Cedar Rapids; KRIN (PBS) Waterloo; KWWL (NBC) Waterloo.
Programming (via satellite): ABC Family Channel; AMC; Animal Planet; Arts & Entertainment; Cartoon Network; CNN; Comedy Central; Country Music TV; Discovery Channel; Discovery Health Channel; Disney Channel; Do-It-Yourself; E! Entertainment Television; ESPN; ESPN 2; ESPN Classic Sports; Food Network; Fox News Channel; FX; Golf Channel; GSN; Hallmark Channel; Headline News; HGTV; History Channel; Lifetime; MSNBC; MTV; Nickelodeon; Outdoor Channel; QVC; RFD-TV; Speed Channel; Spike TV; Syfy; TBS Superstation; The Learning Channel; Toon Disney; Travel Channel; truTV; Turner Classic Movies; Turner Network TV; TV Guide Network; TV Land; USA Network; VH1; WE tv; Weather Channel; WGN America.
Current originations: Educational Access.
Fee: $25.00 installation; $45.00 monthly.

Digital Basic Service
Subscribers: N.A.
Programming (received off-air): KCRG-TV (ABC) Cedar Rapids; KFXA (FOX) Cedar Rapids; KIMT (CBS, MNT) Mason City; KPXR-TV (ION) Cedar Rapids; KRIN (PBS) Waterloo; KWKB (CW, MNT) Iowa City.
Programming (via satellite): ABC Family Channel; American Movie Classics; Animal Planet; Arts & Entertainment; Arts & Entertainment HD; Big Ten Network; Big Ten Network HD; Bio; Cartoon Network; CNN; Comcast SportsNet Northwest; Comedy Central; Country Music TV; C-SPAN; C-SPAN 2; Discovery Channel; Discovery Health Channel; Disney Channel; Disney XD; Do-It-Yourself; E! Entertainment Television; ESPN; ESPN 2; ESPN 2 HD; ESPN Classic Sports; ESPN HD; ESPN U; ESPNews; Food Network; Food Network HD; Fox News Channel; FX; FX HD; Golf Channel; GSN; Hallmark Channel; Headline News; HGTV; HGTV HD; History Channel; History Channel HD; History Channel International; KWWL (NBC) Waterloo; Lifetime; Lifetime Movie Network; Lifetime Movie Network HD; Lifetime Real Women; Lifetime Television HD; MSNBC; MTV; Music Choice; National Geographic Channel; National Geographic Channel HD Network; Nickelodeon; Outdoor Channel; Outdoor Channel 2 HD; QVC; RFD-TV; SoapNet; Speed Channel; Speed HD; Spike TV; Syfy; TBS Superstation; The Learning Channel; Travel Channel; truTV; Turner Classic Movies; Turner Network TV; Turner Network TV HD; TV Land; USA Network; Versus; VH1; WE tv; Weather Channel; WGN America.
Fee: $49.00 monthly.

Pay Service 1
Pay Units: 85.
Programming (via satellite): Cinemax.
Fee: $10.00 monthly.

Pay Service 2
Pay Units: 72.
Programming (via satellite): HBO.
Fee: $12.00 monthly.

Pay Service 3
Pay Units: 52.
Programming (via satellite): Encore; Starz.
Fee: $10.00 monthly.

Digital Pay Service 1
Pay Units: N.A.
Programming (via satellite): Cinemax (multiplexed); Cinemax HD; Encore (multiplexed); HBO (multiplexed); HBO HD; Starz (multiplexed); Starz Comedy HD; Starz Edge HD; Starz HDTV; Starz Kids & Family HD.
Fee: $12.00 monthly (Cinemax or Starz/Encore), $15.00 monthly (HBO).

Internet Service
Operational: Yes.
Fee: $25.00 installation; $45.00 monthly.

Telephone Service
None

Miles of Plant: 14.0 (coaxial); 32.0 (fiber optic).
General Manager: Richard McBurney. Chief Technician: James Chesnut.
Ownership: Butler-Bremer Communications.

TRURO—Interstate Communications, PO Box 229, 105 N West St, Truro, IA 50257-0229. Phones: 712-824-7227; 641-765-4201. Fax: 641-765-4204. Web Site: http://www.interstatecom.com. Also serves Martensdale, New Virginia, St. Charles & St. Marys. ICA: IA0344.
TV Market Ranking: 66 (Martensdale, New Virginia, St. Charles, St. Marys, TRURO). Franchise award date: N.A. Franchise expiration date: N.A. Began: N.A.
Channel capacity: N.A. Channels available but not in use: N.A.

Basic Service
Subscribers: 1,700.
Programming (received off-air): KCCI (CBS) Des Moines; KDIN-TV (PBS) Des Moines; KDSM-TV (FOX) Des Moines; KOFY-TV (IND) San Francisco; WHO-DT (NBC) Des Moines; WOI-DT (ABC) Ames.
Programming (via satellite): ABC Family Channel; AMC; Animal Planet; Arts & Entertainment; Cartoon Network; CNN; Country Music TV; C-SPAN; Discovery Channel; Disney Channel; ESPN; ESPN 2; Fox Sports Net; FX; HGTV; History Channel; Home Shopping Network; ION Television; Iowa Communications Network; Lifetime; Nickelodeon; Spike TV; Syfy; TBS Superstation; The Learning Channel; Turner Network TV; TV Land; USA Network; Weather Channel; WGN America.
Fee: $35.00 installation; $23.50 monthly.

Pay Service 1
Pay Units: 39.
Programming (via satellite): Cinemax; HBO.
Fee: $9.00 monthly (each).

Video-On-Demand: No

Internet Service
Operational: Yes.

Telephone Service
None

Miles of Plant: 36.0 (coaxial); 13.0 (fiber optic). Homes passed: 2,874.
Manager: Mike Weis. Chief Technician: Rick Lunn.
Ownership: Interstate Communications (MSO).

UNDERWOOD—TelePartners. Now served by WALNUT, IA [IA0241]. ICA: IA0296.

UNION—Heart of Iowa Telecommunications. Formerly [IA0521]. This cable system has converted to IPTV., PO Box 130, 502 Main St, Union, IA 50258-0130. Phones: 641-486-2211; 800-806-4482; 641-486-2302 (Union office). Fax: 641-486-2205. E-mail: jsquires@heartofiowa.coop. Web Site: http://www.heartofiowa.net. ICA: IA5001.
TV Market Ranking: 66 (UNION). Franchise award date: N.A. Franchise expiration date: N.A. Began: N.A.
Channel capacity: N.A. Channels available but not in use: N.A.

Internet Service
Operational: Yes.

Telephone Service
Digital: Operational

General Manager: David Schmidt. Plant Manager: Jay Duncan. Customer Service Manager: Heidi Mitchell.
Ownership: Heart of Iowa Communications Cooperative.

UNION GROVE VILLAGE—Heart of Iowa Telecommunications. This cable system has converted to IPTV. See Union, IA [IA5001], IA. ICA: IA0521.

UTE—Long Lines, 501 4th St, Sergeant Bluff, IA 51054-8509. Phone: 712-884-2203. Fax: 712-884-2205. E-mail: info@longlines.com. Web Site: http://www.longlines.com. ICA: IA0289.
TV Market Ranking: Outside TV Markets (UTE). Franchise award date: N.A. Franchise expiration date: N.A. Began: March 1, 1984.
Channel capacity: 35 (not 2-way capable). Channels available but not in use: 13.

Basic Service
Subscribers: 93.
Programming (received off-air): KCAU-TV (ABC) Sioux City; KMEG (CBS) Sioux City; KPTH (FOX, MNT) Sioux City; KSIN-TV (PBS) Sioux City; KTIV (CW, NBC) Sioux City.
Programming (via satellite): ABC Family Channel; AMC; AmericanLife TV Network; Animal Planet; Arts & Entertainment; Big Ten Network; Cartoon Network; CNBC; CNN; Comedy Central; Country Music TV; C-SPAN; C-SPAN 2; CW+; Discovery Channel; Disney Channel; E! Entertainment Television; ESPN; ESPN 2; ESPN Classic Sports; Eternal Word TV Network; Food Network; Fox News Channel; Fox Sports Net North; FX; Golf Channel; Hallmark Channel; Headline News; HGTV; History

Channel; Home Shopping Network; INSP; Lifetime; Lifetime Movie Network; MSNBC; MTV; Nickelodeon; QVC; Speed Channel; Spike TV; Syfy; TBS Superstation; The Learning Channel; The Sportsman Channel; Travel Channel; Trinity Broadcasting Network; truTV; Turner Classic Movies; Turner Network TV; TuTv; TV Guide Network; TV Land; USA Network; VH1; Weather Channel; WGN America.
Fee: $41.99 monthly.

Digital Basic Service
Subscribers: N.A.
Programming (via satellite): BBC America; Bio; Cooking Channel; Discovery Health Channel; Discovery Kids Channel; Discovery Military Channel; Discovery Planet Green; DMX Music; Do-It-Yourself; ESPN U; ESPNews; FitTV; Fox College Sports Atlantic; Fox College Sports Central; Fox College Sports Pacific; Fox Movie Channel; Fox Soccer; G4; Great American Country; GSN; Halogen Network; History Channel International; ID Investigation Discovery; Independent Film Channel; Lifetime Real Women; MTV Hits; MTV Jams; MTV2; Nick Jr.; NickToons TV; Outdoor Channel; RFD-TV; Science Channel; SoapNet; TeenNick; Toon Disney; Versus; VH1 Classic; VH1 Country; VH1 Soul; WE tv.
Fee: $9.99 monthly.

Digital Expanded Basic Service
Subscribers: N.A.
Programming (received off-air): KCAU-TV (ABC) Sioux City; KMEG (CBS) Sioux City; KPTH (FOX, MNT) Sioux City; KSIN-TV (PBS) Sioux City; KTIV (CW, NBC) Sioux City.
Programming (via satellite): Big Ten Network HD; Discovery Channel HD; ESPN 2 HD; ESPN HD; HDNet; HDNet Movies; Outdoor Channel 2 HD.
Fee: $9.95 monthly.

Digital Expanded Basic Service 2
Subscribers: N.A.
Programming (via satellite): Bandamax; De Pelicula; De Pelicula Clasico; Discovery en Espanol; ESPN Deportes; Fox Sports en Espanol; Ritmoson Latino; Telehit.
Fee: $2.95 monthly.

Pay Service 1
Pay Units: 6.
Programming (via satellite): Flix; Showtime (multiplexed); The Movie Channel.
Fee: $14.45 monthly.

Pay Service 2
Pay Units: 5.
Programming (via satellite): HBO (multiplexed).
Fee: $14.95 monthly.

Digital Pay Service 1
Pay Units: N.A.
Programming (via satellite): Cinemax (multiplexed); Cinemax HD (multiplexed); Encore (multiplexed); Flix; HBO (multiplexed); HBO HD; Showtime (multiplexed); Starz (multiplexed); Starz HDTV; Starz On Demand; The Movie Channel (multiplexed).
Fee: $11.95 monthly (Cinemax), $13.95 monthly (Starz/Encore), $14.45 monthly (Showtime/TMC/Flix) $14.95 monthly (HBO).

Video-On-Demand: Yes

Internet Service
Operational: No.

Telephone Service
Analog: Operational
Digital: Not Operational

Miles of Plant: 4.0 (coaxial); None (fiber optic). Homes passed: 192.
Manager & Chief Operations Officer: Paul Bergmann. Plant Supervisor: Randy L. Olson.
City fee: 3% of gross.
Ownership: Long Lines (MSO).

VAIL—Tip Top Communications. Now served by DELOIT, IA [IA0422]. ICA: IA0322.

VAN HORNE—Van Horne Telephone Co., 204 Main St, Van Horne, IA 52346-9712. Phone: 319-228-8791. Fax: 319-228-8784. ICA: IA0261.
TV Market Ranking: 65 (VAN HORNE). Franchise award date: February 8, 1983. Franchise expiration date: N.A. Began: N.A.
Channel capacity: 60 (not 2-way capable). Channels available but not in use: N.A.

Basic Service
Subscribers: 240.
Programming (received off-air): KCRG-TV (ABC) Cedar Rapids; KFXA (FOX) Cedar Rapids; KGAN (CBS) Cedar Rapids; KPXR-TV (ION) Cedar Rapids; KRIN (PBS) Waterloo; KWKB (CW, MNT) Iowa City; KWWF (IND) Waterloo [LICENSED & SILENT]; KWWL (NBC) Waterloo.
Programming (via satellite): ABC Family Channel; AMC; Animal Planet; Arts & Entertainment; Big Ten Network; Cartoon Network; CNBC; CNN; Comcast SportsNet Chicago; Comedy Central; Country Music TV; C-SPAN; Discovery Channel; Disney Channel; Do-It-Yourself; E! Entertainment Television; ESPN; ESPN 2; ESPN Classic Sports; ESPN U; Eternal Word TV Network; Food Network; Fox News Channel; FX; Gospel Music Channel; Great American Country; Hallmark Channel; Hallmark Movie Channel; Headline News; HGTV; History Channel; Home Shopping Network; Lifetime; MTV; National Geographic Channel; Nickelodeon; QVC; RFD-TV; SoapNet; Speed Channel; Spike TV; Syfy; TBS Superstation; The Learning Channel; The Sportsman Channel; Travel Channel; Trinity Broadcasting Network; truTV; Turner Classic Movies; Turner Network TV; TV Land; USA Network; VH1; Weather Channel; WGN America.
Fee: $20.00 installation; $38.00 monthly.

Pay Service 1
Pay Units: 17.
Programming (via satellite): HBO.
Fee: $10.00 installation; $10.95 monthly.

Pay Service 2
Pay Units: 9.
Programming (via satellite): Showtime.
Fee: $10.00 installation; $9.95 monthly.

Pay Service 3
Pay Units: 7.
Programming (via satellite): Cinemax.
Fee: $10.00 installation; $9.95 monthly.

Video-On-Demand: No

Pay-Per-View
Addressable homes: 5.
Movies (delivered digitally), Addressable: Yes; special events (delivered digitally).

Internet Service
Operational: No.

Telephone Service
None

Miles of Plant: 5.0 (coaxial); None (fiber optic). Homes passed: 275. Total homes in franchised area: 275.
Manager: Donald Whipple. Chief Technician: Ronald Schnor.
Ownership: Van Horne Telephone Co.

VAN WERT—B & L Technologies LLC, 3329 270th St, Lenox, IA 50851. Phones: 800-798-5488; 641-348-2240. Fax: 641-348-2240. Also serves Weldon. ICA: IA0555.
TV Market Ranking: Outside TV Markets (VAN WERT, Weldon). Franchise award date: April 7, 1992. Franchise expiration date: N.A. Began: January 1, 1994.
Channel capacity: 36 (not 2-way capable). Channels available but not in use: 7.

Basic Service
Subscribers: 54.
Programming (received off-air): KCCI (CBS) Des Moines; KDIN-TV (PBS) Des Moines; KDSM-TV (FOX) Des Moines; WHO-DT (NBC) Des Moines; WOI-DT (ABC) Ames.
Programming (via satellite): ABC Family Channel; AMC; Arts & Entertainment; CNN; Country Music TV; Discovery Channel; Disney Channel; ESPN; History Channel; Spike TV; TBS Superstation; Turner Network TV; USA Network; WGN America.
Fee: $40.00 installation; $30.50 monthly.

Pay Service 1
Pay Units: 9.
Programming (via satellite): HBO.
Fee: $12.00 monthly.

Video-On-Demand: No

Internet Service
Operational: No.

Telephone Service
None

Miles of Plant: 9.0 (coaxial); None (fiber optic). Homes passed: 220.
Manager & Chief Technician: Robert Hintz. Office Manager: Linda Hintz.
Ownership: B & L Technologies LLC (MSO).

VOLGA—Alpine Communications LC. Now served by ARLINGTON, IA [IA0393]. ICA: IA0522.

WADENA (village)—Alpine Communications LC. Now served by ARLINGTON, IA [IA0393]. ICA: IA0523.

WALFORD—South Slope Coop. Communications Inc. Formerly served by North Liberty, IA [IA0432]. This cable system has converted to IPTV, PO Box 19, 980 N Front St, North Liberty, IA 52317. Phones: 800-272-6449; 319-626-2211. Fax: 319-665-7000. E-mail: info@southslope.com. Web Site: http://www.southslope.com. ICA: IA5016.
TV Market Ranking: 65 (Walford).
Channel capacity: N.A. Channels available but not in use: N.A.

Basic Service
Subscribers: N.A.
Fee: $25.00 installation; $41.95 monthly.

Expanded Basic Service 1
Subscribers: N.A.
Fee: $25.00 installation; $54.95 monthly.

Expanded Basic Service 2
Subscribers: N.A.
Fee: $25.00 installation; $10.00 monthly.

Limited Basic Service
Subscribers: N.A.
Fee: $25.00 installation; $14.95 monthly.

Pay Service 1
Pay Units: N.A.
Fee: $25.00 installation; $10.95 monthy (Starz); $11.95 monthly (Cinemax); $12.95 monthly (Showtime); $13.95 monthy (HBO); $15.95 monthly (Adult).

Internet Service
Operational: Yes.
Fee: $39.95 monthly; $10.00 modem lease; $130.00 modem purchase.

Telephone Service
Digital: Operational
Fee: $14.50 monthly

Ownership: South Slope Cooperative Communications Co.

WALKER—Formerly served by Mid American Cable Systems. No longer in operation. ICA: IA0581.

WALL LAKE—Corn Belt Telephone Co., PO Box 445, 108 Main St, Wall Lake, IA 51466. Phone: 712-664-2221. Fax: 712-664-2083. ICA: IA0256.
TV Market Ranking: Outside TV Markets (WALL LAKE). Franchise award date: N.A. Franchise expiration date: N.A. Began: February 1, 1984.
Channel capacity: 36 (operating 2-way). Channels available but not in use: None.

Basic Service
Subscribers: 300.
Programming (received off-air): KCAU-TV (ABC) Sioux City; KCCI (CBS) Des Moines; KDIN-TV (PBS) Des Moines; KDSM-TV (FOX) Des Moines; KMEG (CBS) Sioux City; KPTH (FOX, MNT) Sioux City; KTIV (CW, NBC) Sioux City; WHO-DT (NBC) Des Moines; WOI-DT (ABC) Ames.
Programming (via satellite): AMC; Arts & Entertainment; CNN; Discovery Channel; Disney Channel; ESPN; ESPN 2; Fox Sports Net Midwest; HGTV; History Channel; Nickelodeon; Spike TV; Syfy; TBS Superstation; The Learning Channel; Turner Network TV; TV Land; USA Network; VH1; Weather Channel; WGN America.
Fee: $26.00 monthly.

Pay Service 1
Pay Units: N.A.
Programming (via satellite): Cinemax; HBO.
Fee: $12.00 monthly (each).

Internet Service
Operational: No, DSL only.

Telephone Service
None

Miles of Plant: 5.0 (coaxial); None (fiber optic). Total homes in franchised area: 350.
Manager: Larry Neppl. Secretary: Shelli Harms.
Ownership: Corn Belt Telephone Co. (MSO).

WALNUT—Walnut Communications, PO Box 346, 510 Highland St, Walnut, IA 51577-0346. Phone: 712-784-2211. Fax: 712-784-2010. E-mail: info@walnutel.net. Web Site: http://www.walnutcommunications.com. Also serves Avoca, Minden, Persia, Shelby & Underwood. ICA: IA0241. **Note:** This system is an overbuild.
TV Market Ranking: 53 (Minden, Persia, Shelby, Underwood); Outside TV Markets (Avoca, WALNUT). Franchise award date: N.A. Franchise expiration date: N.A. Began: October 1, 1983.
Channel capacity: N.A. Channels available but not in use: N.A.

Basic Service

Subscribers: 1,328 Includes Neola.

Programming (received off-air): KCCI (CBS) Des Moines; KETV (ABC) Omaha; KHIN (PBS) Red Oak; KMTV-TV (CBS) Omaha; KPTM (FOX, MNT) Omaha; KXVO (CW) Omaha; WHO-DT (NBC) Des Moines; WOI-DT (ABC) Ames; WOWT-TV (IND, NBC) Omaha; allband FM.

Programming (via satellite): ABC Family Channel; AMC; Animal Planet; Arts & Entertainment; Big Ten Network; Bravo; Cartoon Network; CNBC; CNN; Comedy Central; Country Music TV; C-SPAN; C-SPAN 2; Discovery Channel; Disney Channel; E! Entertainment Television; ESPN; ESPN 2; ESPN Classic Sports; ESPNews; Eternal Word TV Network; Food Network; Fox News Channel; Fox Sports Net Midwest; FX; G4; GSN; Hallmark Channel; Hallmark Movie Channel; Headline News; HGTV; History Channel; Lifetime; Lifetime Movie Network; MSNBC; MTV; MyNetworkTV Inc.; National Geographic Channel; Nickelodeon; Outdoor Channel; QVC; RFD-TV; Speed Channel; Spike TV; Syfy; TBS Superstation; The Learning Channel; Toon Disney; Travel Channel; Turner Classic Movies; Turner Network TV; TV Land; USA Network; VH1; Weather Channel; WGN America.

Fee: $25.00 installation; $27.50 monthly.

Video-On-Demand: No

Pay-Per-View

iN DEMAND (delivered digitally); ESPN (delivered digitally).

Internet Service

Operational: No, DSL only.

Telephone Service

None

Miles of Plant: 34.0 (coaxial); None (fiber optic). Homes passed: 2,227. Total homes in franchised area: 2,227. Homes passed and total homes in franchised area includes Neola

General Manager: Bruce Heyne. Plant Manager: Denny Book. Marketing Manager: Leanne Blotzer. Office Manager: Rachel Becorra.

City fee: 1% of gross.

Ownership: Walnut Communications (MSO).

WATERLOO—Formerly served by Wireless Cable TV of Waterloo. No longer in operation. ICA: IA0562.

WATERLOO—Mediacom, 4010 Alexandra Dr, Waterloo, IA 50702. Phones: 319-395-9699 (Cedar Rapids regional office); 319-235-2197. Fax: 319-232-7841. Web Site: http://www.mediacomcable.com. Also serves Black Hawk County (portions), Cedar Falls, Dewar, Elk Run Heights, Evansdale, Gilbertville, Raymond & Washburn. ICA: IA0003.

TV Market Ranking: 65 (Black Hawk County (portions), Cedar Falls, Dewar, Elk Run Heights, Evansdale, Gilbertville, Raymond, Washburn, WATERLOO). Franchise award date: March 20, 1978. Franchise expiration date: N.A. Began: June 7, 1979.

Channel capacity: N.A. Channels available but not in use: N.A.

Basic Service

Subscribers: 23,500.

Programming (received off-air): KCRG-TV (ABC) Cedar Rapids; KFXA (FOX) Cedar Rapids; KGAN (CBS) Cedar Rapids; KPXR-TV (ION) Cedar Rapids; KRIN (PBS) Waterloo; KWKB (CW, MNT) Iowa City; KWWF (IND) Waterloo [LICENSED & SILENT]; KWWL (NBC) Waterloo.

Programming (via satellite): ABC Family Channel; AMC; Animal Planet; Arts & Entertainment; BET Networks; Bravo; Cartoon Network; CNBC; CNN; Comcast SportsNet Chicago; Comedy Central; Country Music TV; C-SPAN; C-SPAN 2; Discovery Channel; Disney Channel; E! Entertainment Television; ESPN; ESPN 2; ESPN Classic Sports; Eternal Word TV Network; Food Network; Fox News Channel; Fox Sports Net Midwest; FX; Golf Channel; Hallmark Channel; Headline News; HGTV; History Channel; Home Shopping Network; INSP; Lifetime; MoviePlex; MSNBC; MTV; mun2 television; Nickelodeon; Outdoor Channel; QVC; RFD-TV; Speed Channel; Spike TV; Syfy; TBS Superstation; The Learning Channel; Travel Channel; Trinity Broadcasting Network; truTV; Turner Classic Movies; Turner Network TV; TV Guide Network; TV Land; USA Network; Versus; VH1; Weather Channel; WGN America.

Current originations: Government Access; Educational Access; Public Access.

Fee: $40.95 installation; $8.93 monthly.

Digital Basic Service

Subscribers: 4,500.

Programming (received off-air): KCRG-TV (ABC) Cedar Rapids; KFXA (FOX) Cedar Rapids; KRIN (PBS) Waterloo; KWWL (NBC) Waterloo.

Programming (via satellite): AmericanLife TV Network; BBC America; Bio; Bloomberg Television; Discovery Digital Networks; Discovery HD Theater; ESPN; ESPN 2; ESPNews; Fox Movie Channel; Fox Soccer; Fuse; G4; GAS; GSN; Halogen Network; HDNet; HDNet Movies; History Channel International; Independent Film Channel; INHD (multiplexed); Lifetime Movie Network; Lime; MTV Networks Digital Suite; Music Choice; National Geographic Channel; Nick Jr.; NickToons TV; Ovation; Sleuth; Style Network; Toon Disney; TVG Network; Universal HD.

Fee: $12.00 monthly.

Digital Pay Service 1

Pay Units: N.A.

Programming (via satellite): Cinemax (multiplexed); Encore (multiplexed); Flix (multiplexed); HBO (multiplexed); HBO HD; Showtime (multiplexed); Showtime HD; Starz (multiplexed); Sundance Channel (multiplexed); The Movie Channel (multiplexed); The Movie Channel HD.

Video-On-Demand: Yes

Pay-Per-View

Ten Clips (delivered digitally); ESPN (delivered digitally); Playboy TV (delivered digitally); Fresh (delivered digitally); Shorteez (delivered digitally); Pleasure (delivered digitally).

Internet Service

Operational: Yes.

Subscribers: 3,400.

Broadband Service: Mediacom High Speed Internet.

Fee: $49.95 installation; $39.95 monthly; $10.00 modem lease.

Telephone Service

Digital: Operational

Fee: $49.95 monthly

Miles of Plant: 370.0 (coaxial); 25.0 (fiber optic). Homes passed: 33,725. Total homes in franchised area: 34,205.

Regional Vice President: Doug Frank. General Manager: Doug Nix. Technical Operations Director: Greg Nank. Marketing Director: Steve Schuh. Marketing Coordinator: Joni Lindauer.

City fee: 3% of gross.

Ownership: Mediacom LLC (MSO).

WAVERLY—Mediacom, 4010 Alexandra Dr, Waterloo, IA 50702. Phone: 319-235-2197. Fax: 319-232-7841. Web Site: http://www.mediacomcable.com. Also serves Aplington, Delaware County (portions), Denver, Dike, Edgewood, Fairbank, Fayette County (portions), Hazleton, Janesville, La Porte, Manchester, Maynard, New Hartford, Oelwein, Parkersburg, Reinbeck, Shell Rock & Strawberry Point. ICA: IA0021.

TV Market Ranking: 65 (Aplington, Delaware County, Denver, Dike, Fairbank, Fayette County, Hazleton, Janesville, La Porte, Maynard, New Hartford, Oelwein, Parkersburg, Reinbeck, Shell Rock, WAVERLY); Outside TV Markets (Edgewood, Manchester, Strawberry Point, Delaware County, Fayette County). Franchise award date: N.A. Franchise expiration date: N.A. Began: September 1, 1982.

Channel capacity: 62 (operating 2-way). Channels available but not in use: None.

Basic Service

Subscribers: 8,514.

Programming (received off-air): KCRG-TV (ABC) Cedar Rapids; KFXA (FOX) Cedar Rapids; KGAN (CBS) Cedar Rapids; KPXR-TV (ION) Cedar Rapids; KRIN (PBS) Waterloo; KWKB (CW, MNT) Iowa City; KWWL (NBC) Waterloo.

Programming (via satellite): C-SPAN; C-SPAN 2; Home Shopping Network; INSP; Nickelodeon; QVC; TV Guide Network; WGN America.

Current originations: Government Access; Educational Access; Public Access.

Fee: $60.00 installation; $10.20 monthly; $.70 converter; $50.00 additional installation.

Expanded Basic Service 1

Subscribers: 7,279.

Programming (via satellite): ABC Family Channel; AMC; Animal Planet; Arts & Entertainment; Bravo; Cartoon Network; CNBC; CNN; Comcast SportsNet Chicago; Comedy Central; Country Music TV; Discovery Channel; Disney Channel; E! Entertainment Television; ESPN; ESPN 2; Eternal Word TV Network; Food Network; Fox News Channel; FX; Hallmark Channel; Headline News; HGTV; History Channel; Lifetime; MSNBC; MTV; RFD-TV; Speed Channel; Spike TV; Syfy; TBS Superstation; Telemundo; The Learning Channel; Travel Channel; Trinity Broadcasting Network; truTV; Turner Classic Movies; Turner Network TV; TV Land; USA Network; VH1; WE tv; Weather Channel.

Fee: $22.08 monthly.

Digital Basic Service

Subscribers: N.A.

Programming (via satellite): AmericanLife TV Network; BBC America; Bio; Bloomberg Television; Discovery Digital Networks; DMX Music; Fox Movie Channel; Fox Sports World; Fuse; G4; GAS; Golf Channel; GSN; Halogen Network; History Channel International; Independent Film Channel; Lifetime Movie Network; Lime; National Geographic Channel; Nick Jr.; Outdoor Channel; Ovation; Style Network; Toon Disney; Turner Classic Movies; Versus.

Digital Pay Service 1

Pay Units: 614.

Programming (via satellite): Cinemax (multiplexed); Encore (multiplexed); HBO (multiplexed); Showtime (multiplexed); Starz (multiplexed); Sundance Channel; The Movie Channel (multiplexed).

Fee: $9.95 monthly (Cinemax, HBO, Showtime, Starz/Encore, or Sundance/TMC).

Video-On-Demand: Yes

Pay-Per-View

ESPN Now (delivered digitally); ETC (delivered digitally); Playboy TV (delivered digitally); Pleasure (delivered digitally); Fresh (delivered digitally); Shorteez (delivered digitally); TVN Entertainment (delivered digitally); sports (delivered digitally).

Internet Service

Operational: Yes.

Broadband Service: Mediacom High Speed Internet.

Telephone Service

Digital: Operational

Fee: $39.95 monthly

Miles of Plant: 235.0 (coaxial); 7.0 (fiber optic). Homes passed: 13,787.

Regional Vice President: Doug Frank. General Manager: Doug Nix. Technical Operations Director: Greg Nank. Marketing Director: Steve Schuh. Marketing Coordinator: Joni Lindauer.

Ownership: Mediacom LLC (MSO).

WAYLAND—Farmers & Merchants Mutual Telephone. Formerly [IA0525]. This cable system has converted to IPTV., PO Box 247, 210 W Main St, Wayland, IA 52654. Phone: 319-256-2736. Fax: 319-256-7210. E-mail: manager@farmtel.com. Web Site: http://www.farmtel.net. ICA: IA5076.

Channel capacity: N.A. Channels available but not in use: N.A.

Internet Service

Operational: Yes.

Ownership: Farmers & Merchants Mutual Telephone Co.

WAYLAND—Farmers & Merchants Mutual Telephone. This cable system has converted to IPTV. See Olds, IA [IA5075] & Wayland, IA [IA5076]. ICA: IA0525.

WELLSBURG—Formerly served by Union Cablevision. No longer in operation. ICA: IA0526.

WESLEY—Communications 1 Cablevision. Now served by KANAWHA, IA [IA0229]. ICA: IA0527.

WESTGATE (village)—Formerly served by Alpine Communications LC. No longer in operation. ICA: IA0528.

WESTSIDE—Western Iowa Networks, PO Box 190, 112 E Main St, Breda, IA 51436-0190. Phone: 712-673-2311. Fax: 712-673-2800. Web Site: http://www.westIAnet.com. Also serves Arcadia. ICA: IA0242.

TV Market Ranking: Outside TV Markets (Arcadia, WESTSIDE). Franchise award date: July 1, 1984. Franchise expiration date: N.A. Began: March 1, 1985.

Channel capacity: 35 (operating 2-way). Channels available but not in use: N.A.

Basic Service

Subscribers: N.A. Included in Breda

Programming (received off-air): KCAU-TV (ABC) Sioux City; KCCI (CBS) Des Moines; KDSM-TV (FOX) Des Moines; KHIN (PBS) Red Oak; KTIV (CW, NBC) Sioux City; WHO-DT (NBC) Des Moines.

Programming (via satellite): ABC Family Channel; AMC; Cartoon Network; CNN; Country Music TV; Discovery Channel; Disney Channel; ESPN; ESPN 2; Eternal Word TV Network; Food Network; Fox College Sports Atlantic; Fox College Sports Central; Fox College Sports Pacific; Fox Movie Channel; Fox Sports Net; Headline News; HGTV; History Channel; Home

Shopping Network; Lifetime; Nickelodeon; Spike TV; TBS Superstation; Turner Network TV; TV Land; USA Network; Weather Channel; WGN America.
Fee: $20.00 installation; $25.45 monthly.

Pay Service 1
Pay Units: N.A.
Programming (via satellite): HBO.
Fee: $10.95 monthly.

Video-On-Demand: No

Internet Service
Operational: No, DSL.

Telephone Service
None

Miles of Plant: 11.0 (coaxial); None (fiber optic). Homes passed: 325. Total homes in franchised area: 480.

Chief Executive Officer: Steve Frickenstein. Chief Technician: Mike Ludwig. Marketing & Sales Manager: Megan Badding.

Ownership: Tele-Services Ltd. (MSO).

WHEATLAND—F & B Cablevision, PO Box 309, 103 Main St N, Wheatland, IA 52777-0309. Phone: 563-374-1236. Fax: 563-374-1930. E-mail: info@fbc.bz. Web Site: http://www.fbc.bz. Also serves Calamus. ICA: IA0529.

TV Market Ranking: 60 (Calamus, WHEATLAND). Franchise award date: N.A. Franchise expiration date: N.A. Began: January 1, 1983.

Channel capacity: N.A. Channels available but not in use: N.A.

Digital Basic Service
Subscribers: N.A.
Programming (received off-air): KCRG-TV (ABC) Cedar Rapids; KFXA (FOX) Cedar Rapids; KGAN (CBS) Cedar Rapids; KGCW (CW) Burlington; KIIN (PBS) Iowa City; KLJB (CW, FOX) Davenport; KPXR-TV (ION) Cedar Rapids; KWQC-TV (NBC) Davenport; KWWL (NBC) Waterloo; WHBF-TV (CBS) Rock Island; WQAD-TV (ABC) Moline; WQPT-TV (PBS) Moline.
Programming (via satellite): Bloomberg Television; CNN International; C-SPAN 2; Headline News; History Channel International; Home Shopping Network; INSP; KWKB (CW, MNT) Iowa City; QVC; Radar Channel; ShopNBC; SoapNet; Trinity Broadcasting Network; WGN America.
Fee: $23.99 monthly.

Digital Expanded Basic Service
Subscribers: N.A.
Programming (via satellite): ABC Family Channel; AMC; Animal Planet; Arts & Entertainment; Big Ten Network; Bio; Bloomberg Television; Bravo; Cartoon Network; CNBC; CNN; Comcast SportsNet Chicago; Comedy Central; Cooking Channel; Country Music TV; C-SPAN; Discovery Channel; Discovery Health Channel; Disney Channel; Do-It-Yourself; E! Entertainment Television; ESPN; ESPN 2; ESPN Classic Sports; ESPNews; Food Network; Fox News Channel; Fox Sports Net Midwest; FX; G4; Golf Channel; Great American Country; GSN; Hallmark Channel; HGTV; History Channel; Lifetime; Lifetime Movie Network; MSNBC; MTV; Music Choice; National Geographic Channel; Nickelodeon; Outdoor Channel; Oxygen; RFD-TV; Speed Channel; Spike TV; Syfy; TBS Superstation; The Learning Channel; Toon Disney; Travel Channel; truTV; Turner Classic Movies; Turner Network TV; TV Land; USA Network; VH1; WE tv; Weather Channel.
Fee: $26.00 monthly.

Digital Pay Service 1
Pay Units: N.A.
Programming (via satellite): Cinemax (multiplexed); Encore (multiplexed); Flix; HBO (multiplexed); Showtime (multiplexed); Starz (multiplexed); Sundance Channel; The Movie Channel (multiplexed).
Fee: $15.00 monthly (HBO, Cinemax, Showtime/TMC/Flix/Sundance or Starz/Encore).

Pay-Per-View
Special events (delivered digitally); Movies (delivered digitally); ESPN (delivered digitally).

Internet Service
Operational: No, DSL & Dialup.

Telephone Service
None

Miles of Plant: 5.0 (coaxial); None (fiber optic). Homes passed: 590.

Manager: Ken Laursen. Plant Manager: Jan Muhl. Marketing Manager: Aaron Horman. Office Manager: Julie Steines.

Ownership: Farmers' & Businessmen's Telephone Co. (MSO).

WHITING—Long Lines, 501 4th St, Sergeant Bluff, IA 51054-8509. Phones: 712-884-2203; 712-271-4000. Fax: 712-271-2727. Web Site: http://www.longlines.com. ICA: IA0267.

TV Market Ranking: Below 100 (WHITING). Franchise award date: N.A. Franchise expiration date: N.A. Began: February 1, 1984.

Channel capacity: 37 (not 2-way capable). Channels available but not in use: 19.

Basic Service
Subscribers: 212.
Programming (received off-air): KCAU-TV (ABC) Sioux City; KMEG (CBS) Sioux City; KPTH (FOX, MNT) Sioux City; KSIN-TV (PBS) Sioux City; KTIV (CW, NBC) Sioux City.
Programming (via satellite): ABC Family Channel; AMC; AmericanLife TV Network; Animal Planet; Arts & Entertainment; Big Ten Network; Cartoon Network; CNBC; CNN; Comedy Central; Country Music TV; C-SPAN; C-SPAN 2; CW+; Discovery Channel; Disney Channel; E! Entertainment Television; ESPN; ESPN 2; ESPN Classic Sports; Eternal Word TV Network; Food Network; Fox News Channel; Fox Sports Net North; FX; Golf Channel; Hallmark Channel; Headline News; HGTV; History Channel; Home Shopping Network; INSP; Lifetime; Lifetime Movie Network; MSNBC; MTV; Nickelodeon; QVC; Speed Channel; Spike TV; Syfy; TBS Superstation; The Learning Channel; The Sportsman Channel; Travel Channel; Trinity Broadcasting Network; truTV; Turner Classic Movies; Turner Network TV; TuTv; TV Guide Network; TV Land; USA Network; VH1; Weather Channel; WGN America.
Fee: $25.00 installation; $41.99 monthly.

Digital Basic Service
Subscribers: N.A.
Programming (via satellite): BBC America; Bio; Cooking Channel; Discovery Health Channel; Discovery Kids Channel; Discovery Military Channel; Discovery Planet Green; DMX Music; Do-It-Yourself; ESPN U; ESPNews; FitTV; Fox College Sports Atlantic; Fox College Sports Central; Fox College Sports Pacific; Fox Movie Channel; Fox Soccer; G4; Great American Country; GSN; Halogen Network; History Channel International; ID Investigation Discovery; Independent Film Channel; Lifetime Real Women; MTV Hits; MTV Jams; MTV2; Nick Jr.; NickToons TV; Outdoor Channel; RFD-TV; Science Channel; SoapNet; TeenNick; Toon Disney; Versus; VH1 Classic; VH1 Country; VH1 Soul; WE tv.
Fee: $9.99 monthly.

Digital Expanded Basic Service
Subscribers: N.A.
Programming (received off-air): KCAU-TV (ABC) Sioux City; KMEG (CBS) Sioux City; KPTH (FOX, MNT) Sioux City; KSIN-TV (PBS) Sioux City; KTIV (CW, NBC) Sioux City.
Programming (via satellite): Big Ten Network HD; Discovery Channel HD; ESPN 2 HD; ESPN HD; HDNet; HDNet Movies; Outdoor Channel 2 HD.
Fee: $9.95 monthly.

Digital Expanded Basic Service 2
Subscribers: N.A.
Programming (via satellite): Bandamax; De Pelicula; De Pelicula Clasico; Discovery en Espanol; ESPN Deportes; Fox Sports en Espanol; Ritmoson Latino; Telehit.
Fee: $2.95 monthly.

Pay Service 1
Pay Units: 62.
Programming (via satellite): Flix; HBO (multiplexed); Showtime (multiplexed); The Movie Channel.
Fee: $15.00 installation; $14.45 monthly (Showtime, TMC & Flix), $14.95 monthly (HBO).

Digital Pay Service 1
Pay Units: N.A.
Programming (via satellite): Cinemax (multiplexed); Cinemax HD; Encore (multiplexed); Flix; HBO (multiplexed); HBO HD; Showtime (multiplexed); Starz (multiplexed); Starz HDTV; Starz On Demand; The Movie Channel (multiplexed).
Fee: $11.95 monthly (Cinemax), $13.95 monthly (Starz/Encore), $14.45 monthly (Showtime/TMC/Flix), $14.95 monthly (HBO).

Video-On-Demand: Yes

Internet Service
Operational: Yes.
Broadband Service: Long Lines Internet.
Fee: $39.95 monthly.

Telephone Service
Analog: Operational
Fee: $18.50 monthly

Miles of Plant: 5.0 (coaxial); None (fiber optic). Homes passed: 272.

Manager: Paul Bergmann. Chief Technician: Dennis Swenson. Customer Service Manager: Barb Johnson.

City fee: 3% of gross.

Ownership: Long Lines (MSO).

WHITTEMORE—ATC Cablevision, PO Box 248, 1405 Silver Lake Ave, Ayrshire, IA 50515-0248. Phones: 712-776-2222; 800-642-2884; 712-426-2815. Fax: 712-426-2008. E-mail: info@ayrshireia.com. Web Site: http://www.ayrshireia.com. ICA: IA0266.

TV Market Ranking: Outside TV Markets (WHITTEMORE). Franchise award date: N.A. Franchise expiration date: N.A. Began: N.A.

Channel capacity: 36 (operating 2-way). Channels available but not in use: 8.

Basic Service
Subscribers: 186.
Programming (received off-air): KCAU-TV (ABC) Sioux City; KCCI (CBS) Des Moines; KCWI-TV (CW) Ames; KDSM-TV (FOX) Des Moines; KEYC-TV (CBS, FOX) Mankato; KMEG (CBS) Sioux City; KPTH (FOX, MNT) Sioux City; KTIN (PBS) Fort Dodge; KTIV (CW, NBC) Sioux City; WHO-DT (NBC) Des Moines; WOI-DT (ABC) Ames.
Programming (via satellite): ABC Family Channel; AMC; AmericanLife TV Network; Animal Planet; Arts & Entertainment; Cartoon Network; CNBC; CNN; Comedy Central; Country Music TV; C-SPAN; C-SPAN 2; Discovery Channel; Disney Channel; E! Entertainment Television; ESPN; ESPN 2; ESPN Classic Sports; Eternal Word TV Network; Food Network; Fox News Channel; FX; Hallmark Channel; Headline News; HGTV; History Channel; Home Shopping Network; ION Television; Lifetime; MTV; National Geographic Channel; Nickelodeon; Outdoor Channel; QVC; Speed Channel; Spike TV; Syfy; TBS Superstation; The Learning Channel; Travel Channel; Turner Classic Movies; Turner Network TV; TV Guide Network; TV Land; USA Network; VH1; Weather Channel; WGN America.
Fee: $30.00 installation; $37.30 monthly.

Digital Basic Service
Subscribers: 16.
Programming (received off-air): KCCI (CBS) Des Moines; KDIN-TV (PBS) Des Moines; KDSM-TV (FOX) Des Moines; WHO-DT (NBC) Des Moines.
Programming (via satellite): BBC America; Bio; Discovery Digital Networks; DMX Music; ESPNews; FitTV; Fox Movie Channel; G4; GAS; Golf Channel; GSN; History Channel; Independent Film Channel; MTV Networks Digital Suite; National Geographic Channel; Nick Jr.; NickToons TV; Outdoor Channel; Speed Channel; Toon Disney.
Fee: $11.00 monthly.

Digital Pay Service 1
Pay Units: 26.
Programming (via satellite): Cinemax (multiplexed); Encore (multiplexed); Flix; HBO (multiplexed); Showtime (multiplexed); Showtime HD; Starz (multiplexed); Sundance Channel; The Movie Channel (multiplexed).
Fee: $9.50 monthly (Cinemax), $11.00 monthly (Showtime/TMC or Starz/Encore), $12.00 monthly (HBO),.

Video-On-Demand: No

Pay-Per-View
Movies (delivered digitally); Sports (delivered digitally); Events (delivered digitally).

Internet Service
Operational: No, DSL only.

Telephone Service
None

Miles of Plant: 5.0 (coaxial); None (fiber optic). Homes passed: 270. Total homes in franchised area: 270.

General Manager: Don Miller. Plant Manager: Chase Cox. Chief Technician: Derek Franker. Accounting Manager: Robin Dietrich. Customer Service Manager: Lonna Hess. Executive Secretary: Kelly Otto.

Ownership: Ayrshire Communications (MSO).

WILLIAMS—Formerly served by Williams Cablevision. No longer in operation. ICA: IA0530.

WILLIAMSBURG—Mediacom. Now served by CEDAR RAPIDS, IA [IA0002]. ICA: IA0124.

WINFIELD—Formerly served by Longview Communications. No longer in operation. ICA: IA0201.

WINTHROP—East Buchanan Telephone Cooperative, PO Box 100, 214 Third St N, Winthrop, IA 50682-0100. Phone: 319-935-3011. Fax: 319-935-3010. E-mail: ebtccw@netins.net. Web Site: http://www.eastbuchanan.com. Also serves Quasqueton. ICA: IA0531.

TV Market Ranking: 65 (Quasqueton, WINTHROP). Franchise award date: January 1, 1981. Franchise expiration date: N.A. Began: January 1, 1983.

Channel capacity: N.A. Channels available but not in use: N.A.

Basic Service

Subscribers: 355.

Programming (received off-air): KCRG-TV (ABC) Cedar Rapids; KFXA (FOX) Cedar Rapids; KGAN (CBS) Cedar Rapids; KRIN (PBS) Waterloo; KWKB (CW, MNT) Iowa City; KWWL (NBC) Waterloo.

Programming (via satellite): ABC Family Channel; AMC; Animal Planet; Arts & Entertainment; Cartoon Network; CNBC; CNN; Comedy Central; Country Music TV; C-SPAN; C-SPAN 2; Discovery Channel; Disney Channel; Do-It-Yourself; E! Entertainment Television; ESPN; ESPN 2; ESPN Classic Sports; Eternal Word TV Network; Food Network; Fox News Channel; FX; G4; Golf Channel; GSN; Hallmark Channel; Headline News; HGTV; History Channel; ION Television; Lifetime; MoviePlex; MTV; National Geographic Channel; NFL Network; Nickelodeon; Outdoor Channel; QVC; RFD-TV; Speed Channel; Spike TV; Syfy; TBS Superstation; The Learning Channel; Travel Channel; Trinity Broadcasting Network; truTV; Turner Classic Movies; Turner Network TV; TV Guide Network; TV Land; USA Network; VH1; WE tv; Weather Channel; WGN America.

Fee: $25.00 installation; $35.95 monthly.

Pay Service 1

Pay Units: 78.

Programming (via satellite): HBO (multiplexed).

Fee: $15.00 installation; $13.49 monthly (each).

Internet Service

Operational: No, DSL & dial-up.

Telephone Service

Digital: Operational

Miles of Plant: 5.0 (coaxial); None (fiber optic). Homes passed: 500. Total homes in franchised area: 500.

Manager: Butch Rorabaugh. Plant Manager: Roger Olsen. Office Manager: Karen Kremer.

Ownership: East Buchanan Telephone Cooperative (MSO).

WODEN—Heck's TV & Cable, PO Box 517, 601 7th St, Armstrong, IA 50514-0517. Phone: 712-864-3431. Fax: 712-864-3431. Also serves Crystal Lake. ICA: IA0355.

TV Market Ranking: Below 100 (Crystal Lake); Outside TV Markets (WODEN). Franchise award date: N.A. Franchise expiration date: N.A. Began: August 1, 1985.

Channel capacity: N.A. Channels available but not in use: N.A.

Basic Service

Subscribers: N.A.

Programming (received off-air): KAAL (ABC) Austin; KEYC-TV (CBS, FOX) Mankato; KIMT (CBS, MNT) Mason City; KTIN (PBS) Fort Dodge; KTTC (CW, NBC) Rochester.

Programming (via satellite): ABC Family Channel; CNN; ESPN; Spike TV; TBS Superstation; WGN America.

Video-On-Demand: No

Internet Service

Operational: No.

Telephone Service

None

Miles of Plant: 3.0 (coaxial); None (fiber optic). Homes passed: 121.

Manager: Steven Heck.

Ownership: Steven Heck (MSO).

WOODBURN—Telnet South LC. Now served by DES MOINES, IA [IA0001]. ICA: IA0577.

WOOLSTOCK—Goldfield Communication Services Corp., PO Box 67, 536 N Main St, Goldfield, IA 50542. Phones: 515-825-3996; 800-825-9753; 515-825-3888. Fax: 515-825-3801. E-mail: gold@goldfieldaccess.net. Web Site: http://www.goldfieldaccess.net. ICA: IA0552.

TV Market Ranking: Outside TV Markets (WOOLSTOCK). Franchise award date: N.A. Franchise expiration date: N.A. Began: December 1, 1990.

Channel capacity: 35 (not 2-way capable). Channels available but not in use: 13.

Basic Service

Subscribers: N.A.

Programming (received off-air): KCCI (CBS) Des Moines; KDIN-TV (PBS) Des Moines; KDSM-TV (FOX) Des Moines; KIMT (CBS, MNT) Mason City; WHO-DT (NBC) Des Moines; WOI-DT (ABC) Ames.

Programming (via satellite): ABC Family Channel; AMC; Arts & Entertainment; CNN; Discovery Channel; Disney Channel; ESPN; Lifetime; Nickelodeon; Spike TV; TBS Superstation; Turner Network TV; USA Network; WGN America.

Fee: $10.00 installation; $18.85 monthly; $.50 converter.

Pay Service 1

Pay Units: N.A.

Programming (via satellite): HBO; Showtime.

Fee: $9.85 monthly (each).

Video-On-Demand: No

Internet Service

Operational: No.

Telephone Service

None

Miles of Plant: 2.0 (coaxial); None (fiber optic). Homes passed: 100.

General Manager: Darrell L. Seaba. Chief Technician: Dean Schipull. Operations Director: Ron Massingill.

Ownership: Goldfield Communication Services Corp. (MSO).

WORTHINGTON—New Century Communications, 3588 Kennebec Dr, Eagan, MN 55122-1001. Phone: 651-688-2623. Fax: 651-688-2624. E-mail: tanderson@cablesystemservices.com. ICA: IA0613.

TV Market Ranking: Below 100 (WORTHINGTON). Franchise award date: February 6, 1989. Franchise expiration date: N.A. Began: February 6, 1989.

Channel capacity: 42 (not 2-way capable). Channels available but not in use: N.A.

Basic Service

Subscribers: 89.

Programming (received off-air): KCRG-TV (ABC) Cedar Rapids; KFXA (FOX) Cedar Rapids; KGAN (CBS) Cedar Rapids; KIIN (PBS) Iowa City; KPXR-TV (ION) Cedar Rapids; KWKB (CW, MNT) Iowa City; KWWL (NBC) Waterloo.

Programming (via satellite): ABC Family Channel; AMC; Arts & Entertainment; CNN; Discovery Channel; Disney Channel; Do-It-Yourself; ESPN; ESPN 2; Eternal Word TV Network; Headline News; History Channel; Lifetime; MTV; Nickelodeon; QVC; Spike TV; TBS Superstation; The Learning Channel; Turner Classic Movies; Turner Network TV; USA Network; VH1; Weather Channel; WGN America.

Current originations: Public Access.

Fee: $23.45 monthly.

Pay Service 1

Pay Units: N.A.

Programming (via satellite): Cinemax; HBO; Showtime.

Fee: $10.00 monthly (each).

Video-On-Demand: No

Internet Service

Operational: No.

Telephone Service

None

Homes passed: 175.

Executive Vice President: Marty Walch. General Manager & Chief Technician: Todd Anderson.

Ownership: New Century Communications (MSO).

WORTHINGTON—New Century Communications. Now served by LUXEMBURG, IA [IA0554]. ICA: IA0532.

ZEARING—Minerva Valley Cablevision, PO Box 176, 104 N Pine St, Zearing, IA 50278. Phone: 641-487-7399. Fax: 641-487-7599. E-mail: minerva@netins.net. Web Site: http://www.minervavalley.com. Also serves Clemons, McCallsburg & St. Anthony. ICA: IA0533.

TV Market Ranking: 66 (Clemons, McCallsburg, St. Anthony, ZEARING). Franchise award date: N.A. Franchise expiration date: N.A. Began: April 1, 1985.

Channel capacity: 37 (operating 2-way). Channels available but not in use: N.A.

Basic Service

Subscribers: 300.

Programming (received off-air): KCCI (CBS) Des Moines; KCWI-TV (CW) Ames; KDIN-TV (PBS) Des Moines; KDSM-TV (FOX) Des Moines; KFPX-TV (ION) Newton; WHO-DT (NBC) Des Moines; WOI-DT (ABC) Ames.

Programming (via satellite): ABC Family Channel; AMC; Animal Planet; Arts & Entertainment; Big Ten Network; Bravo; CNBC; CNN; Comedy Central; Country Music TV; Discovery Channel; Disney Channel; ESPN; ESPN 2; Flix; Food Network; Fox News Channel; FX; G4; Hallmark Channel; Headline News; Home Shopping Network; Lifetime; Lifetime Movie Network; MSNBC; MTV; Nickelodeon; Spike TV; Syfy; TBS Superstation; The Learning Channel; Trinity Broadcasting Network; Turner Network TV; TV Land; USA Network; VH1; Weather Channel; WGN America.

Fee: $20.00 installation; $24.95 monthly.

Digital Basic Service

Subscribers: 15.

Programming (via satellite): American-Life TV Network; BBC America; Bio; Bloomberg Television; Bravo; Current; Discovery Health Channel; Discovery Kids Channel; Discovery Military Channel; Discovery Planet Green; DMX Music; ESPN 2; ESPN Classic Sports; ESPNews; FitTV; Fox Movie Channel; Fuse; Golf Channel; Great American Country; GSN; Halogen Network; HGTV; History Channel; History Channel International; ID Investigation Discovery; Independent Film Channel; Lifetime Movie Network; Lime; MBC America; MTV Hits; MTV2; Nick Jr.; NickToons TV; Outdoor Channel; Ovation; RFD-TV; Science Channel; Speed Channel; Style Network; Sundance Channel; Syfy; TeenNick; Toon Disney; Trinity Broadcasting Network; Trio; Turner Classic Movies; Versus; VH1 Classic; VH1 Country; VH1 Soul; WE tv.

Fee: $25.05 monthly.

Pay Service 1

Pay Units: N.A.

Programming (via satellite): HBO.

Fee: $10.25 monthly.

Digital Pay Service 1

Pay Units: N.A.

Programming (via satellite): Cinemax (multiplexed); Encore (multiplexed); Flix; HBO (multiplexed); Showtime (multiplexed); Starz (multiplexed); The Movie Channel (multiplexed).

Fee: $10.00 monthly (Cinemax), $12.95 monthly (Starz & Encore), $14.00 monthly (HBO or Showtime).

Internet Service

Operational: No.

Broadband Service: Offers dial-up and DSL only; no cable modem service.

Telephone Service

None

Miles of Plant: 8.0 (coaxial); None (fiber optic).

Manager: Levi Bappe. Office Manager: Mary Phillips.

Ownership: Minerva Valley Cablevision Inc.

KANSAS

Total Systems: 203
Total Communities Served: 462
Franchises Not Yet Operating: 0
Applications Pending: 0
Communities with Applications: 0
Number of Basic Subscribers: 650,750
Number of Expanded Basic Subscribers: 295,029
Number of Pay Units: 78,936

Top 100 Markets Represented: Kansas City (22); Wichita-Hutchinson (67).

**For a list of cable communities in this section, see the Cable Community Index located in the back of Cable Volume 2.
For explanation of terms used in cable system listings, see p. D-11.**

ABBYVILLE—Formerly served by Cox Communications. No longer in operation. ICA: KS0359.

ABILENE—Eagle Communications, 406 NE 14th St, Abilene, KS 67410. Phones: 785-625-4000 (Corporate office); 785-263-2529. Fax: 865-625-8030. Web Site: http://www.eaglecom.net. Also serves Dickinson County. ICA: KS0034.
TV Market Ranking: Below 100 (ABILENE, Dickinson County (portions)); Outside TV Markets (Dickinson County (portions)). Franchise award date: September 2, 1962. Franchise expiration date: N.A. Began: September 1, 1962.
Channel capacity: 51 (operating 2-way). Channels available but not in use: None.

Basic Service
Subscribers: 2,183.
Programming (received off-air): KAAS-TV (FOX) Salina; KAKE-TV (ABC) Wichita; KSNT (FOX, NBC) Topeka; KSNW (NBC) Wichita; KTWU (PBS) Topeka; KWCH-DT (CBS) Hutchinson; WIBW-TV (CBS, MNT) Topeka.
Programming (via microwave): KCTV (CBS) Kansas City; KSCW-DT (CW) Wichita; WDAF-TV (FOX) Kansas City.
Programming (via satellite): Home Shopping Network.
Fee: $24.95 installation; $19.95 monthly.

Expanded Basic Service 1
Subscribers: N.A.
Programming (via satellite): ABC Family Channel; AMC; Arts & Entertainment; Cartoon Network; CNBC; CNN; Comedy Central; C-SPAN; Discovery Channel; Disney Channel; E! Entertainment Television; ESPN; ESPN 2; Eternal Word TV Network; Food Network; Fox News Channel; Fox Sports Net Midwest; FX; Great American Country; Headline News; HGTV; History Channel; INSP; Lifetime; MSNBC; MTV; National Geographic Channel; NFL Network; Nickelodeon; Outdoor Channel; Spike TV; Syfy; TBS Superstation; The Learning Channel; Travel Channel; Turner Network TV; TV Land; USA Network; VH1; Weather Channel.
Fee: $25.50 monthly.

Digital Basic Service
Subscribers: N.A.
Programming (via satellite): BBC America; Bio; Bloomberg Television; Discovery Health Channel; Discovery Kids Channel; Discovery Military Channel; Discovery Planet Green; ESPN Classic Sports; ESPNews; Fox Soccer; Fuse; G4; Golf Channel; GSN; History Channel International; ID Investigation Discovery; Independent Film Channel; Lifetime Movie Network; Science Channel; Sleuth; Speed Channel; Style Network; Toon Disney; Trinity Broadcasting Network; Turner Classic Movies; Versus; WE tv.
Fee: $4.95 monthly (Discovery, Entertainment or Sports Package).

Digital Pay Service 1
Pay Units: N.A.
Programming (via satellite): Cinemax (multiplexed); Encore (multiplexed); HBO (multiplexed); Showtime (multiplexed); Starz; The Movie Channel (multiplexed).
Fee: $11.95 monthly (HBO, Cinemax, Starz/Encore or Showtime/TMC).

Video-On-Demand: No

Pay-Per-View
iN DEMAND; Playboy TV (delivered digitally); Club Jenna (delivered digitally); Fresh (delivered digitally).

Internet Service
Operational: Yes. Began: January 2, 2004.
Subscribers: 876.
Broadband Service: Eagle Internet.
Fee: $22.95 monthly.

Telephone Service
Analog: Not Operational
Digital: Operational
Fee: $16.00 monthly
Miles of Plant: 55.0 (coaxial); None (fiber optic). Homes passed: 3,100.
President & Chief Executive Officer: Gary Shorman. General Manager: Rex Skiles. Chief Technician: Les Libal.
City fee: 3% of gross.
Ownership: Eagle Communications Inc. (KS) (MSO).

ALMA—Galaxy Cablevision, 1928 S Lincoln Ave, Ste 200, York, NE 68467. Phone: 408-362-3332. Fax: 402-362-4890. Web Site: http://www.galaxycable.com. ICA: KS0181.
TV Market Ranking: Below 100 (ALMA). Franchise award date: N.A. Franchise expiration date: N.A. Began: March 1, 1981.
Channel capacity: 36 (not 2-way capable). Channels available but not in use: None.

Basic Service
Subscribers: 56.
Programming (received off-air): KSNT (FOX, NBC) Topeka; KTKA-TV (ABC, CW) Topeka; KTWU (PBS) Topeka; WIBW-TV (CBS, MNT) Topeka.
Programming (via satellite): ABC Family Channel; AMC; Animal Planet; Arts & Entertainment; Cartoon Network; CNN; Discovery Channel; Disney Channel; ESPN; Food Network; Fox News Channel; Fuse; FX; Great American Country; Headline News; HGTV; History Channel; Lifetime; MSNBC; Outdoor Channel; TBS Superstation; The Learning Channel; Turner Network TV; USA Network; Weather Channel; WGN America.
Current originations: Public Access.
Fee: $40.10 monthly.

Pay Service 1
Pay Units: N.A.
Programming (via satellite): Cinemax; HBO; Showtime; The Movie Channel.
Fee: $11.00 monthly (each).

Internet Service
Operational: No.

Telephone Service
None
Miles of Plant: 5.0 (coaxial); None (fiber optic). Homes passed: 323.
State Manager: Cheyenne Wohlford. Technical Manager: John Davidshofer. Sales Manager: Mike Thomas. Customer Service Manager: Michael Debermardin.
City fee: 1% of gross.
Ownership: Galaxy Cable Inc. (MSO).

ALMENA—Nex-Tech. Now served by EDMOND, KS [KS0450]. ICA: KS0360.

ALTA VISTA—Formerly served by Galaxy Cablevision. No longer in operation. ICA: KS0219.

ALTAMONT—Altamont Cable TV, PO Box 921, Parsons, KS 67357. Phone: 620-784-5612. Fax: 620-784-5882. Web Site: http://www.wavewls.com. ICA: KS0170.
TV Market Ranking: Outside TV Markets (ALTAMONT). Franchise award date: N.A. Franchise expiration date: N.A. Began: October 21, 1983.
Channel capacity: 38 (not 2-way capable). Channels available but not in use: None.

Basic Service
Subscribers: 367.
Programming (received off-air): KOAM-TV (CBS) Pittsburg; KODE-TV (ABC) Joplin; KOED-TV (PBS) Tulsa; KOKI-TV (FOX) Tulsa; KSNF (NBC) Joplin.
Programming (via satellite): ABC Family Channel; AmericanLife TV Network; Arts & Entertainment; Cartoon Network; CNN; Comedy Central; Country Music TV; C-SPAN; Discovery Channel; Disney Channel; ESPN; ESPN 2; Fox Sports Net Midwest; Hallmark Channel; Hallmark Movie Channel; History Channel; Lifetime; MTV; Nickelodeon; QVC; Spike TV; TBS Superstation; The Learning Channel; Travel Channel; Trinity Broadcasting Network; Turner Classic Movies; Turner Network TV; TV Land; USA Network; VH1; Weather Channel; WGN America.
Fee: $20.00 installation; $25.50 monthly.

Pay Service 1
Pay Units: 123.
Programming (via satellite): Cinemax; HBO.
Fee: $10.95 monthly (each).

Video-On-Demand: No

Internet Service
Operational: No.

Telephone Service
None
Miles of Plant: 1.0 (coaxial); None (fiber optic). Homes passed: 429.
Ownership: Wave Wireless LLC.

ALTOONA—Mediacom, 901 N College Ave, Columbia, MO 65201. Phones: 417-875-5560 (Springfield regional office); 573-443-1536. Fax: 417-883-0265. Web Site: http://www.mediacomcable.com. ICA: KS0266.
TV Market Ranking: Outside TV Markets (ALTOONA). Franchise award date: February 21, 1984. Franchise expiration date: N.A. Began: January 1, 1985.
Channel capacity: N.A. Channels available but not in use: N.A.

Basic Service
Subscribers: 119.
Programming (received off-air): KOAM-TV (CBS) Pittsburg; KODE-TV (ABC) Joplin; KSNF (NBC) Joplin; KTWU (PBS) Topeka.
Programming (via satellite): ABC Family Channel; Arts & Entertainment; CNBC; CNN; Country Music TV; Discovery Channel; ESPN; ESPN 2; Headline News; Nickelodeon; QVC; Spike TV; TBS Superstation; Turner Network TV; USA Network; Weather Channel; WGN America.
Fee: $35.00 installation; $25.25 monthly.

Pay Service 1
Pay Units: N.A.
Programming (via satellite): Flix; HBO; The Movie Channel.
Fee: $10.50 monthly (each).

Video-On-Demand: No

Internet Service
Operational: No.

Telephone Service
None
Miles of Plant: 12.0 (coaxial); None (fiber optic). Homes passed: 232.
Regional Vice President: Bill Copeland. Operations Director: Bryan Gann. Regional Technical Operations Director: Alan Freedman. Technical Operations Manager: Roger Shearer. Marketing Director: Will Kuebler.
City fee: 3% of gross.
Ownership: Mediacom LLC (MSO).

AMERICUS—Galaxy Cablevision, 1928 S Lincoln Ave, Ste 200, York, NE 68467. Phone: 402-362-3332. Fax: 402-362-4890. Web Site: http://www.galaxycable.com. ICA: KS0183.
TV Market Ranking: Outside TV Markets (AMERICUS). Franchise award date: N.A. Franchise expiration date: N.A. Began: November 1, 1976.
Channel capacity: 78 (not 2-way capable). Channels available but not in use: None.

Basic Service
Subscribers: 96.
Programming (received off-air): KSNT (FOX, NBC) Topeka; KTKA-TV (ABC, CW)

Topeka; KTWU (PBS) Topeka; WIBW-TV (CBS, MNT) Topeka.
Programming (via satellite): ABC Family Channel; AMC; Arts & Entertainment; Cartoon Network; CNN; Comedy Central; Discovery Channel; Disney Channel; ESPN; ESPN 2; Fox News Channel; Fuse; FX; Great American Country; Headline News; HGTV; History Channel; Lifetime; MSNBC; Outdoor Channel; QVC; TBS Superstation; The Learning Channel; Turner Network TV; USA Network; Weather Channel; WGN America.
Planned originations: Educational Access.
Fee: $25.00 installation; $39.40 monthly.

Pay Service 1
Pay Units: 130.
Programming (via satellite): Cinemax; HBO; Showtime; Starz; The Movie Channel.
Fee: $25.00 installation; $11.00 monthly.

Internet Service
Operational: No.

Telephone Service
None

Miles of Plant: 6.0 (coaxial); None (fiber optic). Additional miles planned: 1.0 (coaxial). Homes passed: 344.
State Manager: Cheyenne Wohlford. Technical Manager: John Davidshofer. Sales Manager: Mike Thomas. Customer Service Manager: Michael Debermardin.
Ownership: Galaxy Cable Inc. (MSO).

ANDALE—Formerly served by Almega Cable. No longer in operation. ICA: KS0264.

ANTHONY—Suddenlink Communications, 12444 Powerscourt Dr, Saint Louis, MO 63131-3660. Phones: 314-965-2020; 800-999-6845 (Customer service). Fax: 903-561-5485. Web Site: http://www.suddenlink.com. ICA: KS0362.
TV Market Ranking: Outside TV Markets (ANTHONY). Franchise award date: N.A. Franchise expiration date: N.A. Began: June 1, 1977.
Channel capacity: 41 (operating 2-way). Channels available but not in use: N.A.

Basic Service
Subscribers: 786.
Programming (received off-air): KAKE-TV (ABC) Wichita; KETA-TV (PBS) Oklahoma City; KPTS (PBS) Hutchinson; KSAS-TV (FOX) Wichita; KSCW-DT (CW) Wichita; KSNW (NBC) Wichita; KWCH-DT (CBS) Hutchinson.
Programming (via satellite): Eternal Word TV Network; National Geographic Channel; QVC; TV Land.
Fee: $35.00 installation; $19.95 monthly.

Expanded Basic Service 1
Subscribers: N.A.
Programming (via satellite): ABC Family Channel; Animal Planet; Arts & Entertainment; CNN; C-SPAN; Discovery Channel; Disney Channel; E! Entertainment Television; ESPN; Fox News Channel; Fox Sports Net Midwest; FX; Great American Country; Headline News; HGTV; History Channel; Nickelodeon; Spike TV; TBS Superstation; The Learning Channel; Turner Classic Movies; Turner Network TV; USA Network; VH1; Weather Channel.
Fee: $24.00 monthly.

Pay Service 1
Pay Units: 112.
Programming (via satellite): HBO.
Fee: $35.00 installation; $10.95 monthly.

Pay Service 2
Pay Units: 61.
Programming (via satellite): Showtime.
Fee: $9.95 monthly.

Pay Service 3
Pay Units: 67.
Programming (via satellite): The Movie Channel.
Fee: $5.95 monthly.

Video-On-Demand: No

Pay-Per-View
Fresh (delivered digitally); Playboy TV (delivered digitally); iN DEMAND (delivered digitally).

Internet Service
Operational: Yes. Began: May 26, 2003.
Broadband Service: Cebridge High Speed Cable Internet.
Fee: $49.95 installation; $26.95 monthly.

Telephone Service
None

Miles of Plant: 14.0 (coaxial); None (fiber optic). Homes passed: 798.
Regional Manager: Todd Cruthird. Chief Technician: Norm Schwatken. Marketing Director: Beverly Gambell.
City fee: 3% of gross.
Ownership: Cequel Communications LLC (MSO).

ARCADIA—Formerly served by National Cable Inc. No longer in operation. ICA: KS0257.

ARGONIA—Formerly served by Almega Cable. No longer in operation. ICA: KS0260.

ARLINGTON—Formerly served by Almega Cable. No longer in operation. ICA: KS0231.

ASHLAND—Formerly served by Cebridge Connections. Now served by CIMARRON, KS [KS0126]. ICA: KS0148.

ASSARIA—Home Communications Inc. Formerly [KS0363]. This cable system has converted to IPTV, PO Box 8, 211 S Main, Galva, KS 67443. Phones: 800-362-9336; 620-654-3381. Fax: 620-654-3122. E-mail: hciservice@homecomminc.com. Web Site: http://www.hometelco.net. ICA: KS5061.
TV Market Ranking: Below 100 (ASSARIA). Franchise award date: N.A. Franchise expiration date: N.A. Began: N.A.
Channel capacity: N.A. Channels available but not in use: N.A.

Basic Service
Subscribers: N.A.
Fee: $18.99 installation; $44.99 monthly; $5.99 converter.

Expanded Basic Service 1
Subscribers: N.A.
Fee: $4.99 monthly.

Expanded Basic Service 2
Subscribers: N.A.
Fee: $4.00 monthly.

Pay Service 1
Pay Units: N.A.
Fee: $12.99 monthly.

Pay Service 2
Pay Units: N.A.
Fee: $12.99 monthly.

Video-On-Demand: No

Internet Service
Operational: Yes.
Fee: $39.95 monthly; $2.00 modem lease.

Telephone Service
Analog: Not Operational
Digital: Operational
Fee: $23.76 monthly

President: Carla Shearer. Customer Service Manager: Tina Anderson. Central Manager: Chuck Fairchild.
Ownership: Home Communications Inc (MSO).

ASSARIA—Home Communications Inc. This cable system has converted to IPTV. See Assaria, KS [KS5062]. ICA: KS0363.

ATCHISON—Allegiance Communications, 707 W Saratoga St, Shawnee, OK 74804. Phones: 405-395-1131; 405-275-6923. Web Site: http://www.allegiance.tv. Also serves Atchison County (portions) & Lancaster, KS; Buchanan County, Lewis & Clark Village, Platte County & Rushville, MO. ICA: KS0026.
TV Market Ranking: 22 (Buchanan County, Platte County); Below 100 (ATCHISON, Atchison County (portions), Lancaster, Lewis & Clark Village, Rushville). Franchise award date: N.A. Franchise expiration date: N.A. Began: April 5, 1968.
Channel capacity: 78 (operating 2-way). Channels available but not in use: None.

Basic Service
Subscribers: 3,643.
Programming (received off-air): KCPT (PBS) Kansas City; KCTV (CBS) Kansas City; KCWE (CW) Kansas City; KMBC-TV (ABC) Kansas City; KMCI-TV (IND) Lawrence; KPXE-TV (ION) Kansas City; KQTV (ABC) St. Joseph; KSHB-TV (NBC) Kansas City; KSMO-TV (MNT) Kansas City; KTWU (PBS) Topeka; WDAF-TV (FOX) Kansas City; WIBW-TV (CBS, MNT) Topeka; allband FM.
Programming (via satellite): C-SPAN; Eternal Word TV Network; Home Shopping Network; Trinity Broadcasting Network; TV Guide Network; WGN America.
Current originations: Public Access; Educational Access.
Fee: $20.00 installation; $21.95 monthly.

Expanded Basic Service 1
Subscribers: 2,086.
Programming (via satellite): ABC Family Channel; AMC; Animal Planet; Arts & Entertainment; BET Networks; Bravo; Cartoon Network; CNBC; CNN; Comedy Central; Country Music TV; C-SPAN 2; Discovery Channel; Disney Channel; E! Entertainment Television; ESPN; ESPN 2; FitTV; Food Network; Fox News Channel; Fox Sports Net Midwest; FX; G4; Golf Channel; Hallmark Channel; Headline News; HGTV; History Channel; Lifetime; MSNBC; MTV; National Geographic Channel; Nickelodeon; Oxygen; RFD-TV; SoapNet; Speed Channel; Spike TV; Syfy; TBS Superstation; The Learning Channel; Travel Channel; truTV; Turner Classic Movies; Turner Network TV; TV Land; USA Network; Versus; VH1; Weather Channel.
Fee: $10.00 installation; $3.50 monthly.

Digital Basic Service
Subscribers: N.A.
Programming (via satellite): Arts & Entertainment HD; BBC America; Bio; Bloomberg Television; Chiller; CMT Pure Country; Current; Discovery HD Theater; Discovery Health Channel; Discovery Kids Channel; Discovery Military Channel; Discovery Planet Green; Encore (multiplexed); ESPN 2 HD; ESPN Classic Sports; ESPN HD; ESPN U; ESPNews; Flix; Food Network HD; Fox College Sports Atlantic; Fox College Sports Central; Fox College Sports Pacific; Fox Movie Channel; Fox Soccer; Fuse; Gospel Music Channel; Great American Country; GSN; HDNet; HDNet Movies; HGTV HD; History Channel International; ID Investigation Discovery; Independent Film Channel; Lifetime Movie Network; MTV Hits; MTV2; Music Choice; National Geographic Channel HD Network; Nick Jr.; NickToons TV; Outdoor Channel; Outdoor Channel 2 HD; Science Channel; ShopNBC; Sleuth; Style Network; Sundance Channel; TeenNick; The Word Network; Toon Disney; Universal HD; VH1 Classic; VH1 Soul; WE tv.

Digital Pay Service 1
Pay Units: N.A.
Programming (via satellite): Cinemax (multiplexed); Encore (multiplexed); Flix; HBO (multiplexed); HBO HD; Showtime (multiplexed); Showtime HD; Starz (multiplexed); Starz HDTV; The Movie Channel (multiplexed).

Video-On-Demand: No

Pay-Per-View
Fresh (delivered digitally); iN DEMAND (delivered digitally); Club Jenna (delivered digitally); Spice: Xcess (delivered digitally); Playboy TV (delivered digitally).

Internet Service
Operational: Yes.
Broadband Service: Charter Pipeline.
Fee: $24.95 installation; $39.99 monthly.

Telephone Service
None

Miles of Plant: 63.0 (coaxial); 53.0 (fiber optic). Total homes in franchised area: 5,139.
Chief Executive Officer: Bill Haggarty. Regional Vice President: Andrew Dearth. Vice President, Marketing: Tracy Bass.
Ownership: Allegiance Communications (MSO).

ATTICA—Formerly served by Almega Cable. No longer in operation. ICA: KS0205.

ATWOOD—Atwood Cable Systems Inc., 423 State St, Atwood, KS 67730-1928. Phone: 785-626-3261. Fax: 785-626-9005. E-mail: dunkertv@atwoodtv.net. ICA: KS0135.
TV Market Ranking: Below 100 (ATWOOD). Franchise award date: May 1, 1982. Franchise expiration date: N.A. Began: May 1, 1982.
Channel capacity: 65 (not 2-way capable). Channels available but not in use: N.A.

Basic Service
Subscribers: 450.
Programming (received off-air): KBSL-DT (CBS) Goodland; KLBY (ABC) Colby; KOOD (PBS) Hays; KPNE-TV (PBS) North Platte; KSNK (NBC) McCook; KWNB-TV (ABC) Hayes Center; 5 FMs.
Programming (via satellite): ABC Family Channel; Arts & Entertainment; CNN; Comedy Central; Discovery Channel; Disney Channel; ESPN; ESPN 2; Eternal Word TV Network; Great American Country; Headline News; HGTV; History Channel; ION Television; MTV; Nickelodeon; Outdoor Channel; QVC; Spike TV; Syfy; TBS Superstation; The Learning Channel; Turner Classic Movies; Turner Network TV; TV Land; USA Network; VH1; Weather Channel; WGN America.
Current originations: Public Access.
Fee: $20.00 installation; $39.00 monthly.

Digital Basic Service
Subscribers: N.A.
Programming (via satellite): AmericanLife TV Network; BBC America; Bio; Bloomberg Television; Bravo; Discovery Digital Networks; DMX Music; ESPN 2; ESPN Classic Sports; ESPNews; FitTV; Fox Movie Channel; Fox Sports World; G4; GAS; Golf Channel; GSN; Halogen Network; History Channel International; Independent Film Channel; MTV Networks Digital Suite; MuchMusic Network; National Geographic Channel; Nick Jr.; Ovation; Speed Channel; Style Network; Trinity Broadcasting Network; Versus; WE tv.
Fee: $4.00 monthly.

Pay Service 1
Pay Units: N.A.
Programming (via satellite): HBO; The Movie Channel.
Fee: $12.95 monthly (each).

Digital Pay Service 1
Pay Units: 33.
Programming (via satellite): HBO (multiplexed).
Fee: $10.00 installation; $10.95 monthly.

Digital Pay Service 2
Pay Units: 20.
Programming (via satellite): Showtime (multiplexed); The Movie Channel (multiplexed).
Fee: $10.00 installation; $12.95 monthly.

Digital Pay Service 3
Pay Units: N.A.
Programming (via satellite): Cinemax (multiplexed).
Fee: $9.00 monthly.

Digital Pay Service 4
Pay Units: 3.
Programming (via satellite): Encore (multiplexed); Starz (multiplexed).
Fee: $12.95 monthly.

Video-On-Demand: No

Pay-Per-View
Sports PPV (delivered digitally); Shorteez (delivered digitally); Fresh (delivered digitally); Playboy TV (delivered digitally); iN DEMAND (delivered digitally); Hot Choice (delivered digitally); ESPN Now (delivered digitally).

Internet Service
Operational: Yes.
Subscribers: 124.
Fee: $39.99 monthly.

Telephone Service
Analog: Not Operational
Digital: Operational

Miles of Plant: 12.0 (coaxial); None (fiber optic). Homes passed: 625. Total homes in franchised area: 625.
Manager: Robert Dunker. Chief Technician: Kerry Dunker.
City fee: 3% of basic gross.
Ownership: Atwood Cable Systems Inc.

AXTELL—Blue Valley Telecommunications. Formerly [KS0242]. This cable system has converted to IPTV, 1557 Pony Express Hwy, Home, KS 66438. Phones: 877-876-1228; 785-799-3311. E-mail: info@bluevalley.net. Web Site: http://www.bluevalley.net. ICA: KS5019.
TV Market Ranking: Outside TV Markets (AXTELL). Franchise award date: N.A. Franchise expiration date: N.A. Began: N.A.
Channel capacity: N.A. Channels available but not in use: N.A.

Internet Service
Operational: Yes.

Telephone Service
Digital: Operational

General Manager: Dennis Doyle.
City fee: 1% of basic after 60% penetration.
Ownership: Blue Valley Telecommunications (MSO).

AXTELL—Blue Valley Telecommunications. This cable system has converted to IPTV. See Axtell, KS [KS5019]. ICA: KS0242.

BAILEYVILLE—Rainbow Communications, PO Box 147, Everest, KS 66424. Phones: 800-892-0163; 785-866-2390. Fax: 785-548-7517. Web Site: http://www.rainbowtel.net. ICA: KS0451.
TV Market Ranking: Outside TV Markets (BAILEYVILLE). Franchise award date: N.A. Franchise expiration date: N.A. Began: N.A.
Channel capacity: 36 (operating 2-way). Channels available but not in use: 20.

Basic Service
Subscribers: 4.
Programming (received off-air): KOLN (CBS, MNT) Lincoln; KPTM (FOX, MNT) Omaha; KSNT (FOX, NBC) Topeka; KTKA-TV (ABC, CW) Topeka; KTWU (PBS) Topeka; WIBW-TV (CBS, MNT) Topeka.
Programming (via satellite): ABC Family Channel; Cartoon Network; CNN; Discovery Channel; Eternal Word TV Network; Headline News; TBS Superstation; Trinity Broadcasting Network; USA Network.
Fee: $29.95 installation; $23.95 monthly; $4.00 converter.

Video-On-Demand: No

Internet Service
Operational: No.

Telephone Service
None

Miles of Plant: 3.0 (coaxial); None (fiber optic). Homes passed: 67. Total homes in franchised area: 67.
Plant Manager: Jim Streeter. General Manager: James Lednicky. Marketing Manager: Jackie Petersen. Network Engineer: Scott Wheeler.
Ownership: Rainbow Communications (MSO).

BALDWIN CITY—Mediacom, 901 N College Ave, Columbia, MO 65201. Phone: 417-875-5560 (Springfield regional office). Fax: 417-883-0265. Web Site: http://www.mediacomcable.com. Also serves Edgerton & Wellsville. ICA: KS0055.
TV Market Ranking: Below 100 (BALDWIN CITY, Edgerton, Wellsville). Franchise award date: N.A. Franchise expiration date: N.A. Began: April 13, 1981.
Channel capacity: N.A. Channels available but not in use: N.A.

Basic Service
Subscribers: 1,536.
Programming (received off-air): KCPT (PBS) Kansas City; KCTV (CBS) Kansas City; KCWE (CW) Kansas City; KMBC-TV (ABC) Kansas City; KMCI-TV (IND) Lawrence; KPXE-TV (ION) Kansas City; KSHB-TV (NBC) Kansas City; KSMO-TV (MNT) Kansas City; KSNT (FOX, NBC) Topeka; KTKA-TV (ABC, CW) Topeka; KTWU (PBS) Topeka; WDAF-TV (FOX) Kansas City; WIBW-TV (CBS, MNT) Topeka.
Programming (via satellite): TV Guide Network; WGN America.
Fee: $35.00 installation; $23.95 monthly; $10.00 additional installation.

Expanded Basic Service 1
Subscribers: N.A.
Programming (via satellite): ABC Family Channel; AMC; Animal Planet; Arts & Entertainment; BET Networks; Bravo; Cartoon Network; CNBC; CNN; Comedy Central; Country Music TV; C-SPAN; Discovery Channel; Disney Channel; E! Entertainment Television; ESPN; ESPN 2; Food Network; Fox News Channel; Fox Sports Net Midwest; FX; Hallmark Channel; Headline News; HGTV; History Channel; Home Shopping Network; Lifetime; MSNBC; MTV; Nickelodeon; Outdoor Channel; QVC; ShopNBC; SoapNet; Speed Channel; Spike TV; Syfy; TBS Superstation; The Learning Channel; Travel Channel; Trinity Broadcasting Network; truTV; Turner Network TV; TV Land; USA Network; VH1; WE tv; Weather Channel.

Digital Basic Service
Subscribers: N.A.
Programming (via satellite): AmericanLife TV Network; BBC America; Bio; Bloomberg Television; Discovery Digital Networks; Fox Movie Channel; Fox Soccer; Fuse; G4; GAS; Golf Channel; GSN; Halogen Network; History Channel International; Independent Film Channel; Lifetime Movie Network; Lime; MTV Networks Digital Suite; Music Choice; National Geographic Channel; Nick Jr.; NickToons TV; Style Network; Turner Classic Movies; Versus.

Digital Pay Service 1
Pay Units: N.A.
Programming (via satellite): Cinemax (multiplexed); Encore (multiplexed); Flix (multiplexed); HBO (multiplexed); Showtime (multiplexed); Starz (multiplexed); Sundance Channel (multiplexed); The Movie Channel (multiplexed).

Video-On-Demand: No

Pay-Per-View
Mediacom PPV & Events PPv (delivered digitally); Playboy TV (delivered digitally); TEN Clips (delivered digitally); Pleasure (delivered digitally); Hot Body (delivered digitally).

Internet Service
Operational: Yes.
Broadband Service: Mediacom High Speed Internet.

Telephone Service
None

Miles of Plant: 37.0 (coaxial); None (fiber optic). Homes passed: 2,411. Total homes in franchised area: 2,562.
Regional Vice President: Bill Copeland. Operations Director: Bryan Gann. Regional Technical Operations Director: Alan Freedman. Technical Operations Manager: Roger Shearer. Marketing Director: Will Kuebler.
City fee: 3% of gross.
Ownership: Mediacom LLC (MSO).

BARNARD—Twin Valley Communications. Formerly served by Bennington, KS [KS0214]. This cable system has converted to IPTV, PO Box 515, Clay Center, KS 67432. Phones: 800-515-3311; 785-427-2288. Fax: 785-427-2216. E-mail: tvinc@twinvalley.net. Web Site: http://www.twinvalley.net. ICA: KS5024.
Channel capacity: N.A. Channels available but not in use: N.A.

Internet Service
Operational: Yes.

Telephone Service
Digital: Operational

Ownership: Twin Valley Communications Inc.

BARNES—Formerly served by Eagle Communications. No longer in operation. ICA: KS0365.

BASEHOR—Sunflower Broadband. Now served by LAWRENCE, KS [KS0004]. ICA: KS0164.

BAXTER SPRINGS—City of Baxter Springs, PO Box 577, 1445 Military Ave, Baxter Springs, KS 66713. Phone: 620-856-2114. Fax: 620-856-2460. ICA: KS0042.
TV Market Ranking: Below 100 (BAXTER SPRINGS). Franchise award date: N.A. Franchise expiration date: N.A. Began: February 1, 1980.
Channel capacity: 42 (not 2-way capable). Channels available but not in use: None.

Basic Service
Subscribers: 1,355.
Programming (received off-air): KOAM-TV (CBS) Pittsburg; KODE-TV (ABC) Joplin; KOED-TV (PBS) Tulsa; KOKI-TV (FOX) Tulsa; KOZJ (PBS) Joplin; KSNF (NBC) Joplin.
Programming (via satellite): ABC Family Channel; CNN; Discovery Channel; ESPN; QVC; TBS Superstation; Travel Channel; Trinity Broadcasting Network; Turner Network TV; USA Network; WGN America.
Fee: $10.00 installation; $12.14 monthly.

Expanded Basic Service 1
Subscribers: 1,200.
Programming (via satellite): AMC; AmericanLife TV Network; Arts & Entertainment; Cartoon Network; Country Music TV; C-SPAN; Disney Channel; ESPN 2; Headline News; HGTV; History Channel; Lifetime; MTV; Nickelodeon; Outdoor Channel; Spike TV; Syfy; The Learning Channel; Turner Classic Movies; VH1; Weather Channel.
Fee: $15.95 monthly.

Pay Service 1
Pay Units: 417.
Programming (via satellite): Cinemax.
Fee: $4.00 monthly.

Pay Service 2
Pay Units: 423.
Programming (via satellite): HBO.
Fee: $8.00 monthly.

Video-On-Demand: No

Internet Service
Operational: No. Began: November 30, 2008.

Telephone Service
None

Miles of Plant: 34.0 (coaxial); None (fiber optic). Homes passed: 1,451. Total homes in franchised area: 2,200.
Manager: Jim Thiele. Marketing Director: Donna Wickson.
Ownership: City of Baxter Springs.

BAZINE—Formerly served by Cebridge Connections. Now served by RUSH CENTER, KS [KS0418]. ICA: KS0288.

BEATTIE—Allegiance Communications, 707 W Saratoga St, Shawnee, OK 74804. Phones: 405-395-1131; 405-275-6923. Web Site: http://www.allegiance.tv. ICA: KS0278.
TV Market Ranking: Outside TV Markets (BEATTIE). Franchise award date: N.A. Franchise expiration date: N.A. Began: August 1, 1985.
Channel capacity: 40 (operating 2-way). Channels available but not in use: N.A.

Basic Service
Subscribers: 93.
Programming (received off-air): KOLN (CBS, MNT) Lincoln; KPTM (FOX, MNT) Omaha; KSNT (FOX, NBC) Topeka; KTKA-TV (ABC, CW) Topeka; KTWU (PBS) Topeka; KUON-TV (PBS) Lincoln; WIBW-TV (CBS, MNT) Topeka.
Programming (via satellite): ABC Family Channel; Animal Planet; Arts & Entertainment; Cartoon Network; CNN; Country Music TV; Discovery Channel; Disney Channel; E! Entertainment Television; ESPN; ESPN 2; Fox News Channel; FX; History Channel; MTV; Nickelodeon; Spike TV; TBS Superstation; The Learning Channel; Travel Channel; Turner Network TV; TV Land; USA Network; Weather Channel; WGN America.
Fee: $37.50 installation; $21.95 monthly.

Pay Service 1
Pay Units: 3.
Programming (via satellite): Cinemax.
Fee: $12.50 installation; $11.50 monthly.

Pay Service 2
Pay Units: 17.
Programming (via satellite): HBO.
Fee: $12.15 installation; $11.95 monthly.

Video-On-Demand: No

Pay-Per-View
Hot Choice (delivered digitally); Fresh (delivered digitally); Playboy TV (delivered digitally); Shorteez (delivered digitally); iN DEMAND (delivered digitally).
Internet Service
Operational: No.
Telephone Service
None
Miles of Plant: 3.0 (coaxial); None (fiber optic). Homes passed: 169. Total homes in franchised area: 169.
Chief Executive Officer: Bill Haggarty. Regional Vice President: Andrew Dearth. Vice President, Marketing: Tracy Bass.
Ownership: Allegiance Communications (MSO).

BELLE PLAINE—SKT Entertainment. Now served by CLEARWATER, KS [KS0136]. ICA: KS0128.

BELLEVILLE—Cunningham Cable TV. Now served by WASHINGTON (formerly Glen Elder), KS [KS0228]. ICA: KS0073.

BELOIT—Cunningham Cable TV. Now served by WASHINGTON (formerly Glen Elder), KS [KS0228]. ICA: KS0046.

BELVUE—Formerly served by Giant Communications. No longer in operation. ICA: KS0443.

BENNINGTON—Twin Valley Communications. Formerly [KS0214]. This cable system has converted to IPTV, PO Box 515, Clay Center, KS 67432. Phones: 800-515-3311; 785-427-2288. Fax: 785-427-2216. E-mail: tvinc@twinvalley.net. Web Site: http://www.twinvalley.net. ICA: KS5025.
TV Market Ranking: Below 100 (BENNINGTON). Franchise award date: N.A. Franchise expiration date: N.A. Began: N.A.
Channel capacity: N.A. Channels available but not in use: N.A.
Video-On-Demand: No
Internet Service
Operational: Yes.
Telephone Service
Digital: Operational
City fee: 1% of gross.
Ownership: Twin Valley Communications Inc.

BENNINGTON—Twin Valley Communications. This system has converted to IPTV. See Bennington, KS [KS5025], KS. ICA: KS0214.

BENTLEY—Blue Sky Cable LLC, 412 W Blackwell Rd, Blackwell, OK 74631. Phones: 800-342-0099; 580-262-2800. Web Site: http://www.marquetteks.us/blueskycable/index.html. ICA: KS0282.
TV Market Ranking: 67 (BENTLEY). Franchise award date: December 1, 1988. Franchise expiration date: N.A. Began: July 15, 1989.
Channel capacity: 47 (operating 2-way). Channels available but not in use: 1.
Basic Service
Subscribers: 25.
Programming (received off-air): KAKE-TV (ABC) Wichita; KMTW (MNT) Hutchinson; KPTS (PBS) Hutchinson; KSAS-TV (FOX) Wichita; KSNW (NBC) Wichita; KWCH-DT (CBS) Hutchinson.
Programming (via satellite): ABC Family Channel; American Movie Classics; Arts & Entertainment; CNBC; CNN; Country Music TV; C-SPAN; C-SPAN 2; Discovery Channel; Disney Channel; ESPN; ESPN 2; Great American Country; HGTV; History Channel; Lifetime; Nickelodeon; Outdoor Channel; QVC; Spike TV; Syfy; TBS Superstation; The Learning Channel; Trinity Broadcasting Network; Turner Network TV; TV Land; USA Network; Weather Channel; WGN America.
Fee: $25.00 installation; $30.60 monthly.
Pay Service 1
Pay Units: N.A.
Programming (via satellite): Cinemax (multiplexed); HBO (multiplexed); MoviePlex; Showtime; Starz; The Movie Channel.
Fee: $15.00 monthly (each).
Internet Service
Operational: Yes.
Subscribers: 50.
Broadband Service: In-house.
Fee: $55.00 installation; $29.95 monthly.
Telephone Service
None
Miles of Plant: 4.0 (coaxial); None (fiber optic). Homes passed: 153.
Manager: Julie Hodges.
Ownership: Blue Sky Cable LLC (MSO).

BERN—Formerly served by Rainbow Communications. No longer in operation. ICA: KS0366.

BEVERLY—Twin Valley Communications. Formerly served by Bennington, KS [KS0214]. This cable system has converted to IPTV, PO Box 515, Clay Center, KS 67432. Phones: 800-515-3311; 785-427-2288. Fax: 785-427-2216. E-mail: tvinc@twinvalley.net. Web Site: http://www.twinvalley.net. ICA: KS5026.
Channel capacity: N.A. Channels available but not in use: N.A.
Internet Service
Operational: Yes.
Telephone Service
Digital: Operational
Ownership: Twin Valley Communications Inc.

BLUE MOUND—Formerly served by National Cable Inc. No longer in operation. ICA: KS0292.

BLUE RAPIDS—Galaxy Cablevision, 1928 S Lincoln Ave, Ste 200, York, NE 68467. Phone: 402-362-4890. Fax: 402-362-4890. Web Site: http://www.galaxycable.com. ICA: KS0096.
TV Market Ranking: Outside TV Markets (BLUE RAPIDS). Franchise award date: N.A. Franchise expiration date: N.A. Began: May 1, 1978.
Channel capacity: 41 (not 2-way capable). Channels available but not in use: None.
Basic Service
Subscribers: 168.
Programming (received off-air): KOLN (CBS, MNT) Lincoln; KSAS-TV (FOX) Wichita; KSNT (FOX, NBC) Topeka; KTKA-TV (ABC, CW) Topeka; KTWU (PBS) Topeka; WIBW-TV (CBS, MNT) Topeka.
Programming (via satellite): ABC Family Channel; AMC; Arts & Entertainment; Cartoon Network; CNN; Discovery Channel; Disney Channel; E! Entertainment Television; ESPN; ESPN 2; Fox News Channel; Fox Sports Net Midwest; FX; Great American Country; Headline News; History Channel; Home Shopping Network; Lifetime; MSNBC; Outdoor Channel; TBS Superstation; Trinity Broadcasting Network; Turner Network TV; USA Network; Weather Channel; WGN America.
Fee: $35.00 installation; $38.55 monthly; $1.00 converter; $15.00 additional installation.
Digital Basic Service
Subscribers: 30.
Programming (via satellite): BBC America; Bio; Bloomberg Television; Discovery Digital Networks; DMX Music; ESPN Classic Sports; ESPNews; FitTV; Fox Sports World; Fuse; G4; Golf Channel; GSN; HGTV; History Channel International; INSP; National Geographic Channel; Style Network; Toon Disney; WE tv.
Fee: $13.95 monthly.
Digital Expanded Basic Service
Subscribers: N.A.
Programming (via satellite): DMX Music; Encore; Fox Movie Channel; Lifetime Movie Network; Turner Classic Movies.
Fee: $13.95 monthly.
Pay Service 1
Pay Units: N.A.
Programming (via satellite): Cinemax; HBO; Showtime; The Movie Channel.
Fee: $25.00 installation; $13.00 monthly (each).
Digital Pay Service 1
Pay Units: N.A.
Programming (via satellite): Cinemax (multiplexed); Flix; HBO (multiplexed); Showtime (multiplexed); The Movie Channel (multiplexed).
Fee: $16.55 monthly.
Pay-Per-View
Addressable homes: 54.
Addressable: Yes; Movies (delivered digitally); Playboy TV (delivered digitally); Fresh (delivered digitally).
Internet Service
Operational: No.
Telephone Service
None
Miles of Plant: 11.0 (coaxial); None (fiber optic). Homes passed: 550. Total homes in franchised area: 900.
State Manager: Cheyenne Wohlford. Technical Manager: John Debermardin. Sales Manager: Mike Thomas. Customer Service Manager: Michael Debermardin.
City fee: 0% of gross.
Ownership: Galaxy Cable Inc. (MSO).

BREWSTER—S&T Cable, PO Box 99, 320 Kansas Ave, Brewster, KS 67732-0099. Phones: 800-432-8294; 785-694-2256; 785-694-2000. Fax: 785-694-2750. Web Site: http://www.sttelcom.com. Also serves Grinnell, Kanorado, Levant, Russell Springs & Winona. ICA: KS0315.
TV Market Ranking: Below 100 (BREWSTER, Grinnell, Kanorado, Levant, Russell Springs, Winona). Franchise award date: N.A. Franchise expiration date: N.A. Began: January 1, 1984.
Channel capacity: 169 (not 2-way capable). Channels available but not in use: 30.
Basic Service
Subscribers: 378.
Programming (received off-air): KBSL-DT (CBS) Goodland; KLBY (ABC) Colby; KOOD (PBS) Hays; KSAS-TV (FOX) Wichita; KSCW-DT (CW) Wichita; KSNK (NBC) McCook; KUSA (NBC) Denver; KWGN-TV (CW) Denver.
Programming (via satellite): LWS Local Weather Station; QVC.
Current originations: Public Access.
Fee: $20.00 installation; $13.00 monthly.
Expanded Basic Service 1
Subscribers: N.A.
Programming (received off-air): KMTW (MNT) Hutchinson.
Programming (via satellite): ABC Family Channel; AMC; Animal Planet; Arts & Entertainment; Bravo; Cartoon Network; CNBC; CNN; Comedy Central; Country Music TV; C-SPAN; C-SPAN 2; Daystar TV Network; Discovery Channel; Discovery Kids Channel; Disney Channel; Do-It-Yourself; E! Entertainment Television; ESPN; ESPN 2; ESPN Classic Sports; Eternal Word TV Network; Food Network; Fox News Channel; Fox Sports Net; FX; Golf Channel; Hallmark Channel; Headline News; HGTV; History Channel; Home Shopping Network; Lifetime; MSNBC; MTV; National Geographic Channel; NFL Network; Nickelodeon; Oxygen; RFD-TV; Speed Channel; Spike TV; Syfy; TBS Superstation; The Learning Channel; The Sportsman Channel; Travel Channel; Trinity Broadcasting Network; truTV; Turner Classic Movies; Turner Network TV; TV Guide Network; TV Land; Univision; USA Network; Versus; VH1; WE tv; Weather Channel; WGN America.
Fee: $21.95 monthly.
Digital Basic Service
Subscribers: 50.
Programming (received off-air): KAKE-TV (ABC) Wichita; KMTW (MNT) Hutchinson; KSAS-TV (FOX) Wichita; KSNK (NBC) McCook; KWCH-DT (CBS) Hutchinson.
Programming (via satellite): AmericanLife TV Network; BBC America; Bio; Bloomberg Television; CMT Pure Country; Discovery Health Channel; Discovery Kids Channel; Discovery Military Channel; Discovery Planet Green; Encore (multiplexed); ESPN U; ESPNews; FitTV; FSN Digital Atlantic; FSN Digital Central; FSN Digital Pacific; Fuse; G4; Gospel Music Channel; Great American Country; GSN; Halogen Network; History Channel International; ID Investigation Discovery; Independent Film Channel; Lifetime Movie Network; Lime; MTV Hits; MTV Jams; MTV Tres; MTV2; Music Choice; Nick Jr.; Nick Too; NickToons TV; Outdoor Channel; Science Channel; SoapNet; Style Network; TeenNick; The Word Network; Toon Disney; VH1 Classic; VH1 Soul.
Fee: $17.95 monthly.
Digital Expanded Basic Service
Subscribers: N.A.
Programming (via satellite): Cine Latino; CNN en Espanol; Discovery en Espanol; ESPN Deportes; Fox Sports en Espanol; History Channel en Espanol.
Fee: $15.95 monthly.
Digital Expanded Basic Service 2
Subscribers: N.A.
Programming (via satellite): Arts & Entertainment HD; Discovery Channel HD; ESPN 2 HD; ESPN HD; HDNet; HDNet Movies; NFL Network HD; Universal HD.
Fee: $14.95 monthly.
Digital Pay Service 1
Pay Units: N.A.
Programming (via satellite): Cinemax (multiplexed); Cinemax HD; Flix; Fox Movie Channel; HBO (multiplexed); HBO HD; Showtime (multiplexed); Showtime HD; Starz (multiplexed); Starz HDTV; Sundance Channel (multiplexed); The Movie Channel.
Fee: $11.75 monthly (each).
Video-On-Demand: No
Pay-Per-View
special events (delivered digitally).
Internet Service
Operational: No, Both DSL & dial-up.
Telephone Service
None
Miles of Plant: 11.0 (coaxial); 100.0 (fiber optic). Homes passed: 461. Total homes in franchised area: 461.

General Manager: Steve Richards. Cable TV Manager: Clint Felzien. Chief Technician: Craig Grantz.
Ownership: S & T Communications Inc. (MSO).

BROOKVILLE—Wilson Communications, PO Box 508, 2504 Ave D, Wilson, KS 67490-0508. Phones: 785-658-2111; 800-432-7607. Fax: 785-658-3344. Web Site: http://www.wilsoncommunications.us. ICA: KS0368.
TV Market Ranking: Below 100 (BROOKVILLE). Franchise award date: N.A. Franchise expiration date: N.A. Began: August 1, 1988.
Channel capacity: N.A. Channels available but not in use: N.A.

Basic Service
Subscribers: 67.
Programming (received off-air): KAKE-TV (ABC) Wichita; KMTW (MNT) Hutchinson; KOOD (PBS) Hays; KSAS-TV (FOX) Wichita; KSNC (NBC) Great Bend; KWCH-DT (CBS) Hutchinson.
Programming (via satellite): ABC Family Channel; AMC; AmericanLife TV Network; Arts & Entertainment; CNN; Country Music TV; C-SPAN; C-SPAN 2; CW+; Discovery Channel; Disney Channel; ESPN; ESPN 2; ESPN Classic Sports; ESPNews; Eternal Word TV Network; Food Network; Fox News Channel; Fox Sports Net Rocky Mountain; FX; Hallmark Channel; Headline News; HGTV; Home Shopping Network; ION Television; KPTS (PBS) Hutchinson; Lifetime; MTV; National Geographic Channel; Nickelodeon; Spike TV; Syfy; TBS Superstation; The Learning Channel; Turner Network TV; TV Land; USA Network; VH1; Weather Channel; WGN America.
Current originations: Public Access.
Fee: $25.00 installation; $39.95 monthly.

Digital Basic Service
Subscribers: N.A.
Programming (received off-air): KAKE-TV (ABC) Wichita; KMTV-TV (CBS) Omaha; KOOD (PBS) Hays; KPTS (PBS) Hutchinson; KSAS-TV (FOX) Wichita; KSCW-DT (CW) Wichita; KSNC (NBC) Great Bend; KWCH-DT (CBS) Hutchinson.
Programming (via satellite): Arts & Entertainment HD; BBC America; Bio; Bravo; CMT Pure Country; Discovery HD Theater; Discovery Health Channel; Discovery Kids Channel; Discovery Military Channel; Discovery Planet Green; DMX Music; ESPN 2 HD; ESPN HD; ESPN U; ESPNU HD; Food Network HD; Fox Soccer; Fuse; Golf Channel; GSN; HGTV HD; History Channel; History Channel HD; History Channel International; ID Investigation Discovery; Independent Film Channel; Lifetime Movie Network; MTV2; Nick Jr.; RFD-TV; Science Channel; Sleuth; Speed Channel; Style Network; TeenNick; Turner Classic Movies; Universal HD; Versus; VH1 Classic; WE tv.
Fee: $49.95 installation; $12.00 monthly.

Digital Pay Service 1
Pay Units: N.A.
Programming (via satellite): Cinemax (multiplexed); Encore (multiplexed); HBO (multiplexed); Showtime (multiplexed); Starz (multiplexed); Starz HDTV; The Movie Channel (multiplexed).
Fee: $13.95 monthly (Showtime & TMC or Starz & Encore), $18.95 monthly (Cinemax & HBO).

Internet Service
Operational: No, DSL & dial-up.

Telephone Service
None
Miles of Plant: 4.0 (coaxial); None (fiber optic). Homes passed: 126.
Vice President, Marketing: Scott Grauer. General Manager: Brian Boisvert. Plant Supervisor: Dan Steinike. Controller: Gary Everett. Customer Service Manager: Mary Zorn.
Ownership: Wilson Communications (MSO).

BUCKLIN—United Communications Assn. Inc., PO Box 117, 1107 McArtor Rd, Dodge City, KS 67801. Phone: 620-227-8645. Fax: 620-855-4009. Web Site: http://www.unitedtelcom.net. ICA: KS0369.
TV Market Ranking: Below 100 (BUCKLIN). Franchise award date: N.A. Franchise expiration date: N.A. Began: January 1, 1973.
Channel capacity: N.A. Channels available but not in use: N.A.

Basic Service
Subscribers: 140.
Programming (received off-air): KBSD-DT (CBS) Ensign; KSAS-TV (FOX) Wichita; KSNG (NBC) Garden City; KUPK-TV (ABC) Garden City.
Programming (via satellite): ABC Family Channel; AMC; Animal Planet; CNN; Country Music TV; Discovery Channel; Disney Channel; E! Entertainment Television; ESPN; Fox Sports Net Rocky Mountain; Hallmark Channel; Headline News; KMGH-TV (ABC) Denver; KRMA-TV (PBS) Denver; KUSA (NBC) Denver; QVC; Spike TV; Syfy; TBS Superstation; The Learning Channel; Turner Network TV; TV Land; USA Network; Weather Channel; WGN America.
Fee: $39.95 installation; $49.98 monthly.

Digital Basic Service
Subscribers: N.A.
Programming (received off-air): KBSD-DT (CBS) Ensign; KOOD (PBS) Hays; KSNG (NBC) Garden City; KUPK-TV (ABC) Garden City.
Programming (via satellite): ABC Family HD; Animal Planet HD; Arts & Entertainment HD; BBC America; Bio; Bravo; Chiller; CMT Pure Country; Discovery Channel HD; Discovery HD Theater; Discovery Health Channel; Discovery Kids Channel; Discovery Military Channel; Discovery Planet Green; Discovery Planet Green HD; Disney Channel HD; Disney XD; DMX Music; ESPN 2; ESPN 2 HD; ESPN Classic Sports; ESPN HD; ESPN U; ESPNews; Fine Living Network; FitTV; Food Network HD; Fox Business Channel; Fox College Sports Atlantic; Fox College Sports Central; Fox College Sports Pacific; Fox Movie Channel; Fox News HD; Fox Soccer; FX HD; G4; Golf Channel; Great American Country; GSN; Halogen Network; HGTV; HGTV HD; History Channel; History Channel HD; History Channel International; ID Investigation Discovery; Independent Film Channel; Lifetime Movie Network; Lifetime Movie Network HD; Lifetime Real Women; MTV Hits; MTV2; National Geographic Channel; National Geographic Channel HD Network; Nick Jr.; NickToons TV; Outdoor Channel; Outdoor Channel 2 HD; PBS Kids Sprout; RFD-TV; Science Channel; Science Channel HD; Sleuth; SoapNet; Speed Channel; Speed HD; Style Network; Syfy; Syfy HD; TLC HD; Travel Channel HD; Turner Classic Movies; Universal HD; USA Network HD; Versus; VH1 Classic; VH1 Soul; WE tv; Weather Channel HD.
Fee: $16.00 monthly.

Digital Expanded Basic Service
Subscribers: N.A.
Programming (via satellite): Cine Latino; Cine Mexicano; CNN en Espanol; Discovery en Espanol; ESPN Deportes; Fox Sports en Espanol; History Channel en Espanol; MTV Tres; VeneMovies.
Fee: $5.00 monthly.

Digital Pay Service 1
Pay Units: N.A.
Programming (via satellite): Cinemax HD; HBO (multiplexed); Showtime (multiplexed); Starz (multiplexed); Starz HDTV.
Fee: $11.95 monthly (HBO, Showtime, Cinemax or Starz).

Internet Service
Operational: Yes.
Fee: $55.48-$85.48 monthly.

Telephone Service
None
Miles of Plant: 6.0 (coaxial); None (fiber optic). Homes passed: 370.
General Manager: Craig Mock. Chief Technician: Keith Brack. Customer Service Manager: Jeannie Linnebur.
City fee: 3% of gross.
Ownership: United Communications Assn. Inc. (MSO).

BUFFALO—Formerly served by National Cable Inc. No longer in operation. ICA: KS0283.

BUHLER—Allegiance Communications, 707 W Saratoga St, Shawnee, OK 74804. Phones: 405-395-1131; 405-275-6923. Web Site: http://www.allegiance.tv. Also serves Inman. ICA: KS0160.
TV Market Ranking: 67 (BUHLER, Inman). Franchise award date: N.A. Franchise expiration date: N.A. Began: August 25, 1981.
Channel capacity: 30 (not 2-way capable). Channels available but not in use: 5.

Basic Service
Subscribers: 516.
Programming (received off-air): KAKE-TV (ABC) Wichita; KPTS (PBS) Hutchinson; KSAS-TV (FOX) Wichita; KSNW (NBC) Wichita; KWCH-DT (CBS) Hutchinson.
Programming (via satellite): ABC Family Channel; AMC; Arts & Entertainment; CNN; Country Music TV; C-SPAN; CW+; Discovery Channel; ESPN; ESPN 2; Hallmark Channel; Lifetime; MTV; Nickelodeon; Spike TV; TBS Superstation; The Learning Channel; Turner Network TV; TV Land; USA Network; Weather Channel; WGN America.
Fee: $36.80 installation; $24.00 monthly.

Pay Service 1
Pay Units: 59.
Programming (via satellite): Encore.
Fee: $2.00 monthly.

Pay Service 2
Pay Units: 69.
Programming (via satellite): HBO.
Fee: $12.82 monthly.

Pay Service 3
Pay Units: 58.
Programming (via satellite): Showtime.
Fee: $12.82 monthly.

Internet Service
Operational: No.

Telephone Service
None
Miles of Plant: 13.0 (coaxial); None (fiber optic). Homes passed: 1,066. Total homes in franchised area: 1,066.
Chief Executive Officer: Bill Haggarty. Regional Vice President: Andrew Dearth. Vice President, Marketing: Tracy Bass.
Ownership: Allegiance Communications (MSO).

BURDEN—SKT Entertainment. Now served by CLEARWATER, KS [KS0136]. ICA: KS0370.

BURLINGTON—Mediacom, 901 N College Ave, Columbia, MO 65201. Phones: 417-875-5560 (Springfield regional office); 573-443-1536. Fax: 417-883-0265. Web Site: http://www.mediacomcable.com. Also serves Burlingame, Carbondale, Gridley, Le Roy, Lebo, Lyndon, New Strawn, Osage City & Scranton. ICA: KS0064.
TV Market Ranking: Below 100 (Burlingame, Carbondale, Lyndon, Osage City, Scranton); Outside TV Markets (BURLINGTON, Gridley, Le Roy, Lebo, New Strawn). Franchise award date: N.A. Franchise expiration date: N.A. Began: January 1, 1966.
Channel capacity: N.A. Channels available but not in use: N.A.

Basic Service
Subscribers: 4,279.
Programming (received off-air): KAKE-TV (ABC) Wichita; KCTV (CBS) Kansas City; KMBC-TV (ABC) Kansas City; KSHB-TV (NBC) Kansas City; KSNT (FOX, NBC) Topeka; KTKA-TV (ABC, CW) Topeka; KTMJ-CA Topeka; KTWU (PBS) Topeka; WDAF-TV (FOX) Kansas City; WIBW-TV (CBS, MNT) Topeka; allband FM.
Programming (via satellite): C-SPAN; TV Guide Network; WGN America.
Fee: $35.00 installation; $27.95 monthly.

Expanded Basic Service 1
Subscribers: 543.
Programming (via satellite): ABC Family Channel; AMC; Animal Planet; Arts & Entertainment; BET Networks; Bravo; Cartoon Network; CNBC; CNN; Comedy Central; Country Music TV; Discovery Channel; Disney Channel; E! Entertainment Television; ESPN; ESPN 2; Food Network; Fox News Channel; Fox Sports Net; FX; Hallmark Channel; Headline News; HGTV; History Channel; Home Shopping Network; Lifetime; MSNBC; MTV; Nickelodeon; Outdoor Channel; QVC; ShopNBC; SoapNet; Speed Channel; Spike TV; Syfy; TBS Superstation; The Learning Channel; Travel Channel; Trinity Broadcasting Network; truTV; Turner Network TV; TV Land; USA Network; VH1; WE tv; Weather Channel.
Fee: $3.95 monthly.

Digital Basic Service
Subscribers: N.A.
Programming (via satellite): Barker; BBC America; Bio; Bloomberg Television; Discovery Health Channel; Discovery Home Channel; Discovery Kids Channel; Discovery Military Channel; ESPNews; Fox Movie Channel; Fox Soccer; Fuse; Golf Channel; GSN; Halogen Network; History Channel International; ID Investigation Discovery; Independent Film Channel; Lifetime Movie Network; MTV Hits; MTV2; Music Choice; National Geographic Channel; Nick Jr.; NickToons TV; RFD-TV; Science Channel; Sleuth; Style Network; TeenNick; Turner Classic Movies; TVG Network; Versus; VH1 Classic.

Digital Pay Service 1
Pay Units: N.A.
Programming (via satellite): Cinemax (multiplexed); Encore (multiplexed); Flix; HBO (multiplexed); Showtime (multiplexed); Starz (multiplexed); Sundance Channel; The Movie Channel (multiplexed).

Video-On-Demand: No

Pay-Per-View
iN DEMAND (delivered digitally); Playboy TV (delivered digitally); Ten Clips (delivered digitally); Penthouse TV (delivered digitally); Ten Blox (delivered digitally).

Internet Service
Operational: Yes.
Broadband Service: Mediacom High Speed Internet.

Telephone Service
None
Miles of Plant: 49.0 (coaxial); None (fiber optic). Homes passed: 6,013.
Regional Vice President: Bill Copeland. Operations Director: Bryan Gann. Regional Technical Operations Director: Alan Freedman. Technical Operations Manager: Roger Shearer. Marketing Director: Will Kuebler.
City fee: 2% of gross.
Ownership: Mediacom LLC (MSO).

BURNS—Formerly served by Blue Sky Cable LLC. No longer in operation. ICA: KS0311.

BURR OAK—Nex-Tech. Formerly [KS0265]. This cable system has converted to IPTV, PO Box 158, 145 N Main St, Lenora, KS 67645-0158. Phones: 877-567-7872; 785-567-4281. Fax: 785-567-4401. E-mail: webmaster@nex-tech.com. Web Site: http://www.nex-tech.com. ICA: KS5042.
Channel capacity: N.A. Channels available but not in use: N.A.
Internet Service
Operational: Yes.
Telephone Service
Digital: Operational
Ownership: Rural Telephone Co.

BURR OAK—Nex-Tech. This cable system has converted to IPTV. See Burr Oak, KS [KS5042]. ICA: KS0265.

BURRTON—Formerly served by Cebridge Connections. No longer in operation. ICA: KS0195.

CALDWELL—Formerly served by Almega Cable. No longer in operation. ICA: KS0151.

CANTON—Formerly served by Cox Communications. No longer in operation. ICA: KS0371.

CANTON—Home Communications Inc., PO Box 8, 211 S Main, Galva, KS 67443. Phones: 800-362-9336; 620-654-3381; 620-654-3673. Fax: 620-65-3122. E-mail: service@hometelephone.com. Web Site: http://www.hometelephone.com. ICA: KS0472.
TV Market Ranking: 67 (CANTON).
Channel capacity: 36 (not 2-way capable). Channels available but not in use: 9.
Basic Service
Subscribers: N.A.
Programming (received off-air): KAKE-TV (ABC) Wichita; KPTS (PBS) Hutchinson; KSNW (NBC) Wichita; KWCH-DT (CBS) Hutchinson.
Programming (via satellite): ESPN; HBO; Showtime; WGN America.
Fee: $26.95 installation; $9.59 monthly.
Pay Service 1
Pay Units: N.A.
Fee: $7.95 monthly (Showtime), $10.00 monthly (HBO).
Internet Service
Operational: No, DSL.
Telephone Service
None
President: Carol Baldwin Shearer.
Ownership: Galva Cable Co. Inc. (MSO).

CAWKER CITY—City of Cawker City. Now served by WASHINGTON, KS [KS0228]. ICA: KS0202.

CENTRALIA—Blue Valley Tele-Communications, 1559 Pony Express Hwy, Home, KS 66438. Phones: 877-876-1228; 785-799-3311. E-mail: info@bluevalley.net. Web Site: http://www.bluevalley.net. ICA: KS0230.
TV Market Ranking: Outside TV Markets (CENTRALIA). Franchise award date: N.A. Franchise expiration date: N.A. Began: December 1, 1981.
Channel capacity: N.A. Channels available but not in use: N.A.
Basic Service
Subscribers: 119.
Programming (received off-air): KSNT (FOX, NBC) Topeka; KTKA-TV (ABC, CW) Topeka; KTMJ-CA Topeka; KTWU (PBS) Topeka; WIBW-TV (CBS, MNT) Topeka.
Programming (via satellite): ABC Family Channel; AMC; Animal Planet; Arts & Entertainment; Cartoon Network; CNN; Comedy Central; C-SPAN; Discovery Channel; Disney Channel; ESPN; ESPN 2; Eternal Word TV Network; Food Network; Fox News Channel; Fox Sports Net; FX; Great American Country; Hallmark Channel; Headline News; HGTV; History Channel; Lifetime; Nickelodeon; QVC; Spike TV; Syfy; TBS Superstation; The Learning Channel; Travel Channel; Trinity Broadcasting Network; Turner Classic Movies; Turner Network TV; TV Land; USA Network; VH1; Weather Channel; WGN America.
Fee: $29.95 installation; $37.95 monthly; $5.00 converter; $22.50 additional installation.
Pay Service 1
Pay Units: 12.
Programming (via satellite): Cinemax.
Fee: $10.95 monthly.
Pay Service 2
Pay Units: 12.
Programming (via satellite): HBO.
Fee: $13.95 monthly.
Pay Service 3
Pay Units: 12.
Programming (via satellite): Showtime; The Movie Channel.
Fee: $12.95 monthly.
Video-On-Demand: No
Internet Service
Operational: Yes.
Telephone Service
Digital: Operational
Miles of Plant: 5.0 (coaxial); None (fiber optic). Homes passed: 225. Total homes in franchised area: 250.
General Manager: Dennis Doyle. Operations Manager: Andy Torrey. Marketing Manager: Angie Armstrong. Customer Service Supervisor: Deb Runnebaum.
City fee: None.
Ownership: Blue Valley Telecommunications (MSO).

CHANUTE—Cable One, PO Box 503, 1716 S Santa Fe St, Chanute, KS 66720. Phone: 620-431-2440. Fax: 620-431-3855. Web Site: http://www.cableone.net. ICA: KS0027.
TV Market Ranking: Outside TV Markets (CHANUTE). Franchise award date: N.A. Franchise expiration date: N.A. Began: April 1, 1964.
Channel capacity: 61 (operating 2-way). Channels available but not in use: 2.
Basic Service
Subscribers: 3,000.
Programming (received off-air): KFJX (FOX) Pittsburg; KOAM-TV (CBS) Pittsburg; KODE-TV (ABC) Joplin; KSNF (NBC) Joplin; KTWU (PBS) Topeka.
Programming (via microwave): KJRH-TV (NBC) Tulsa; KMBC-TV (ABC) Kansas City; WIBW-TV (CBS, MNT) Topeka.
Programming (via satellite): ABC Family Channel; Animal Planet; Arts & Entertainment; Bravo; Cartoon Network; CNBC; CNN; Comedy Central; C-SPAN; C-SPAN 2; Discovery Channel; Disney Channel; ESPN; ESPN 2; ESPN Classic Sports; Food Network; Fox News Channel; Fox Sports Net Midwest; FX; Great American Country; Hallmark Channel; Headline News; HGTV; History Channel; Lifetime; MoviePlex; MSNBC; MTV; Nickelodeon; Outdoor Channel; Oxygen; QVC; ShopNBC; Spike TV; Syfy; TBS Superstation; The Learning Channel; Travel Channel; Trinity Broadcasting Network; Turner Classic Movies; Turner Network TV; TV Guide Network; TV Land; USA Network; WE tv; Weather Channel.
Current originations: Government Access; Educational Access.
Fee: $50.00 installation; $46.00 monthly.
Digital Basic Service
Subscribers: 425.
Programming (via satellite): Bio; Boomerang; BYU Television; Canales N (multiplexed); Discovery Digital Networks; DMX Music; ESPN Classic Sports; ESPNews; FamilyNet; Fox College Sports Atlantic; Fox College Sports Central; Fox College Sports Pacific; Fox Movie Channel; Fox Soccer; Fuel TV; G4; Golf Channel; Hallmark Channel; History Channel International; INSP; Military History Channel; National Geographic Channel; Outdoor Channel; Science Television; SoapNet; Speed Channel; Toon Disney; Trinity Broadcasting Network; truTV.
Fee: $14.95 monthly.
Digital Pay Service 1
Pay Units: N.A.
Programming (via satellite): Cinemax (multiplexed); Encore; HBO (multiplexed); Showtime (multiplexed); Sundance Channel; The Movie Channel (multiplexed).
Fee: $15.00 monthly (each).
Video-On-Demand: No
Pay-Per-View
Shorteez (delivered digitally); Fresh (delivered digitally); Hot Choice (delivered digitally); sports (delivered digitally); Movies (delivered digitally).
Internet Service
Operational: Yes.
Subscribers: 1,000.
Broadband Service: CableONE.net.
Fee: $75.00 installation; $43.00 monthly.
Telephone Service
Digital: Operational
Fee: $75.00 installation; $39.95 monthly
Miles of Plant: 63.0 (coaxial); None (fiber optic). Homes passed: 4,800.
Manager: Clarence Matlock. Chief Technician: B. A. Swalley.
City fee: 3% of gross.
Ownership: Cable One Inc. (MSO).

CHAPMAN—Eagle Communications, 406 NE 14th St, Abilene, KS 67410. Phones: 785-625-4000; 785-625-5910. Fax: 785-625-8030. Web Site: http://www.eaglecom.net. Also serves Detroit & Enterprise. ICA: KS0074.
TV Market Ranking: Below 100 (CHAPMAN, Detroit, Enterprise). Franchise award date: January 5, 1984. Franchise expiration date: N.A. Began: January 1, 1974.
Channel capacity: 78 (operating 2-way). Channels available but not in use: None.
Basic Service
Subscribers: 310.
Programming (received off-air): KAAS-TV (FOX) Salina; KAKE-TV (ABC) Wichita; KSNT (FOX, NBC) Topeka; KTKA-TV (ABC, CW) Topeka; KTMJ-CA Topeka; KTWU (PBS) Topeka; KWCH-DT (CBS) Hutchinson; WIBW-TV (CBS, MNT) Topeka; allband FM.
Programming (via satellite): ABC Family Channel; AMC; Animal Planet; Arts & Entertainment; Cartoon Network; CNN; Comedy Central; Country Music TV; Discovery Channel; Disney Channel; E! Entertainment Television; ESPN; ESPN 2; Food Network; Fox News Channel; Fox Sports Net Midwest; Fuse; FX; Great American Country; Headline News; HGTV; History Channel; INSP; Lifetime; LWS Local Weather Station; MSNBC; MTV; National Geographic Channel; Nickelodeon; Outdoor Channel; QVC; Speed Channel; Syfy; TBS Superstation; The Learning Channel; Toon Disney; Trinity Broadcasting Network; Turner Network TV; USA Network; VH1; Weather Channel; WGN America.
Fee: $24.95 installation; $45.95 monthly.
Digital Basic Service
Subscribers: 67.
Programming (via satellite): AmericanLife TV Network; BBC America; Bio; Bloomberg Television; Discovery Health Channel; Discovery Kids Channel; Discovery Military Channel; Discovery Planet Green; DMX Music; ESPN Classic Sports; ESPNews; FitTV; Fox Movie Channel; Fox Soccer; Fuse; G4; Golf Channel; GSN; Halogen Network; History Channel International; ID Investigation Discovery; Lifetime Movie Network; National Geographic Channel; Science Channel; Sleuth; Speed Channel; Style Network; Turner Classic Movies; WE tv.
Fee: $13.95 monthly.
Pay Service 1
Pay Units: N.A.
Programming (via satellite): HBO; Showtime; The Movie Channel.
Fee: $11.95 monthly (each).
Digital Pay Service 1
Pay Units: N.A.
Programming (via satellite): Cinemax (multiplexed); Encore; Flix; HBO (multiplexed); Showtime (multiplexed); Starz (multiplexed); The Movie Channel (multiplexed).
Fee: $11.95 monthly (HBO, Cinemax, Showtime/TMC/Flix or Starz/Encore).
Pay-Per-View
iN DEMAND (delivered digitally); Spice: Xcess (delivered digitally); Club Jenna (delivered digitally); Playboy TV (delivered digitally); Fresh (delivered digitally).
Internet Service
Operational: Yes.
Subscribers: 92.
Broadband Service: Eagle Internet.
Fee: $22.95 monthly; $5.00 modem lease.
Telephone Service
None
Miles of Plant: 13.0 (coaxial); 2.0 (fiber optic). Homes passed: 721.
President: Gary Shorman. Regional Manager: Dennis Weese. General Manager: Rex Skiles.
City fee: 3% of gross.
Ownership: Eagle Communications Inc. (KS) (MSO).

CHETOPA—Allegiance Communications, 707 W Saratoga St, Shawnee, OK 74804. Phones: 405-395-1131; 405-275-6923. Web Site: http://www.allegiance.tv. ICA: KS0131.
TV Market Ranking: Below 100 (CHETOPA). Franchise award date: N.A. Franchise expiration date: N.A. Began: N.A.
Channel capacity: N.A. Channels available but not in use: N.A.

Basic Service
Subscribers: 292.
Programming (received off-air): KFJX (FOX) Pittsburg; KOAM-TV (CBS) Pittsburg; KOED-TV (PBS) Tulsa; KSNF (NBC) Joplin.
Programming (via satellite): ABC Family Channel; AMC; Animal Planet; Arts & Entertainment; Cartoon Network; CNBC; CNN; Comedy Central; Country Music TV; Discovery Channel; Disney Channel; ESPN; ESPN 2; Food Network; Hallmark Channel; Headline News; HGTV; History Channel; KODE-TV (ABC) Joplin; MSNBC; Nickelodeon; Spike TV; TBS Superstation; The Learning Channel; truTV; Turner Network TV; TV Land; USA Network; Weather Channel.
Fee: $20.00 installation; $22.49 monthly; $2.00 converter; $7.50 additional installation.

Digital Basic Service
Subscribers: N.A.
Programming (via satellite): BBC America; Bio; Bloomberg Television; Bravo; Chiller; CMT Pure Country; Current; Discovery Health Channel; Discovery Kids Channel; Discovery Military Channel; Discovery Planet Green; Encore (multiplexed); ESPN Classic Sports; ESPNews; FitTV; Flix; Fox Movie Channel; Fox Soccer; Fuse; G4; Golf Channel; GSN; History Channel International; ID Investigation Discovery; Independent Film Channel; Lifetime Movie Network; MTV Hits; MTV2; National Geographic Channel; Nick Jr.; NickToons TV; Outdoor Channel; RFD-TV; Science Channel; Sleuth; SoapNet; Speed Channel; Style Network; Sundance Channel; Syfy; TeenNick; Toon Disney; Trinity Broadcasting Network; Turner Classic Movies; Versus; VH1 Classic; VH1 Soul; WE tv.

Pay Service 1
Pay Units: N.A.
Programming (via satellite): Cinemax; Encore; HBO; Showtime; Starz.
Fee: $15.00 installation; $9.95 monthly (HBO or Showtime).

Digital Pay Service 1
Pay Units: N.A.
Programming (via satellite): Cinemax (multiplexed); HBO (multiplexed); Showtime (multiplexed); Starz (multiplexed); The Movie Channel (multiplexed).

Pay-Per-View
iN DEMAND (delivered digitally); Playboy TV (delivered digitally); Fresh (delivered digitally); Spice: Xcess (delivered digitally); Club Jenna (delivered digitally).

Internet Service
Operational: No.

Telephone Service
None

Miles of Plant: 11.0 (coaxial); None (fiber optic). Homes passed: 668. Total homes in franchised area: 675.
Chief Executive Officer: Bill Haggarty. Regional Vice President: Andrew Dearth. Vice President, Marketing: Tracy Bass.
Ownership: Allegiance Communications (MSO).

CIMARRON—United Communications Assn. Inc., PO Box 117, 1107 McArtor Rd, Dodge City, KS 67801. Phones: 800-794-9999; 620-227-8645. Fax: 620-855-4009. Web Site: http://www.unitedtelcom.net. Also serves Ashland, Bucklin, Copeland, Ensign, Ford, Hanston, Ingalls, Jetmore, Montezuma & Spearville. ICA: KS0126.
TV Market Ranking: Below 100 (Bucklin, CIMARRON, Copeland, Ensign, Ford, Ingalls, Jetmore, Montezuma, Spearville); Outside TV Markets (Ashland, Hanston). Franchise award date: March 2, 1983. Franchise expiration date: N.A. Began: November 1, 1981.
Channel capacity: 116 (2-way capable). Channels available but not in use: 43.

Basic Service
Subscribers: 1,800.
Programming (received off-air): KBSD-DT (CBS) Ensign; KMTW (MNT) Hutchinson; KOOD (PBS) Hays; KSAS-TV (FOX) Wichita; KSCW-DT (CW) Wichita; KSNG (NBC) Garden City; KUPK-TV (ABC) Garden City.
Programming (via satellite): ION Television; TBS Superstation; TV Guide Network; Weather Channel.
Fee: $36.00 installation.

Expanded Basic Service 1
Subscribers: N.A.
Programming (via satellite): ABC Family Channel; AMC; Animal Planet; Arts & Entertainment; Bloomberg Television; Cartoon Network; CNBC; CNN; Comedy Central; Country Music TV; Court TV; C-SPAN; C-SPAN 2; Discovery Channel; Disney Channel; Do-It-Yourself; E! Entertainment Television; Encore; ESPN; ESPN 2; ESPN Classic Sports; Eternal Word TV Network; Food Network; Fox Movie Channel; Fox News Channel; Fox Sports Net Midwest; FX; G4; GalaVision; Golf Channel; Great American Country; GSN; Hallmark Channel; Headline News; HGTV; History Channel; Home Shopping Network; INSP; Lifetime; MSNBC; MTV; NFL Network; Nickelodeon; Outdoor Channel; Oxygen; QVC; RFD-TV; Science Channel; Speed Channel; Spike TV; Syfy; The Learning Channel; Toon Disney; Travel Channel; Trinity Broadcasting Network; Turner Classic Movies; Turner Network TV; TV Land; Univision; USA Network; Versus; VH1; WGN America.
Fee: $48.98 monthly.

Digital Basic Service
Subscribers: N.A.
Programming (received off-air): KBSD-DT (CBS) Ensign; KOOD (PBS) Hays; KSNG (NBC) Garden City; KUPK-TV (ABC) Garden City.
Programming (via satellite): ABC Family HD; Animal Planet HD; Arts & Entertainment HD; BBC America; Bio; Bravo; Chiller; CMT Pure Country; Discovery Channel HD; Discovery HD Theater; Discovery Health Channel; Discovery Kids Channel; Discovery Military Channel; Discovery Planet Green; Discovery Planet Green HD; Disney Channel HD; Disney XD; DMX Music; Encore (multiplexed); ESPN 2; ESPN 2 HD; ESPN Classic Sports; ESPN HD; ESPN U; ESPNews; Fine Living Network; FitTV; Food Network HD; Fox Business Channel; Fox College Sports Atlantic; Fox College Sports Central; Fox College Sports Pacific; Fox Movie Channel; Fox News HD; Fox Soccer; FX HD; G4; Golf Channel; Great American Country; GSN; Halogen Network; HGTV; HGTV HD; History Channel; History Channel HD; History Channel International; ID Investigation Discovery; Independent Film Channel; Lifetime Movie Network; Lifetime Movie Network HD; Lifetime Real Women; MTV Hits; MTV2; National Geographic Channel; National Geographic Channel HD Network; Nick Jr.; NickToons TV; Outdoor Channel; Outdoor Channel 2 HD; PBS Kids Sprout; RFD-TV; Science Channel; Science Channel HD; Sleuth; SoapNet; Speed Channel; Speed HD; Style Network; Syfy; Syfy HD; TLC HD; Travel Channel HD; Turner Classic Movies; Universal HD; USA Network HD; Versus; VH1 Classic; VH1 Soul; WE tv; Weather Channel HD.
Fee: $16.00 monthly.

Digital Expanded Basic Service
Subscribers: N.A.
Programming (via satellite): Cine Latino; Cine Mexicano; CNN en Espanol; Discovery en Espanol; ESPN Deportes; Fox Sports en Espanol; History Channel en Espanol; MTV Tres; VeneMovies.
Fee: $5.00 monthly.

Digital Pay Service 1
Pay Units: N.A.
Programming (via satellite): Cinemax (multiplexed); HBO (multiplexed); Showtime (multiplexed); Starz (multiplexed); Starz HDTV.
Fee: $11.95 monthly (HBO, Cinemax, Showtime or Starz).

Video-On-Demand: No

Internet Service
Operational: Yes.
Fee: $57.48-$87.98 monthly.

Telephone Service
None

Miles of Plant: 62.0 (coaxial); 141.0 (fiber optic). Homes passed: 2,215. Total homes in franchised area: 2,215.
General Manager: Craig Mock. Chief Technician: Keith Brack. Customer Service Manager: Jeannie Linnebur.
City fee: 3% of basic.
Ownership: United Communications Assn. Inc. (MSO).

CLAY CENTER—Eagle Communications, 430 Court St, Clay Center, KS 67432. Phones: 785-632-3118; 785-625-4000 (Corporate office). Fax: 785-625-8030. Web Site: http://www.eaglecom.net. Also serves Clay County (portions). ICA: KS0043.
TV Market Ranking: Below 100 (Clay County (portions) (portions)); Outside TV Markets (CLAY CENTER, Clay County (portions) (portions)). Franchise award date: August 5, 1958. Franchise expiration date: N.A. Began: June 1, 1962.
Channel capacity: 50 (operating 2-way). Channels available but not in use: None.

Basic Service
Subscribers: 1,417.
Programming (received off-air): KSNT (FOX, NBC) Topeka; KTKA-TV (ABC, CW) Topeka; KTWU (PBS) Topeka; WIBW-TV (CBS, MNT) Topeka; 5 FMs.
Programming (via microwave): KCTV (CBS) Kansas City; KSHB-TV (NBC) Kansas City; WDAF-TV (FOX) Kansas City.
Programming (via satellite): C-SPAN; Eternal Word TV Network; INSP; QVC.
Fee: $24.95 installation; $19.95 monthly; $.68 converter.

Expanded Basic Service 1
Subscribers: N.A.
Programming (via satellite): ABC Family Channel; AMC; Animal Planet; Arts & Entertainment; Cartoon Network; CNBC; CNN; Comedy Central; Country Music TV; Discovery Channel; Disney Channel; E! Entertainment Television; ESPN; ESPN 2; Food Network; Fox News Channel; Fox Sports Net Midwest; FX; Great American Country; Hallmark Channel; Headline News; HGTV; History Channel; Lifetime; MSNBC; MTV; National Geographic Channel; NFL Network; Nickelodeon; Outdoor Channel; Speed Channel; Spike TV; Syfy; TBS Superstation; The Learning Channel; Travel Channel; Turner Classic Movies; Turner Network TV; TV Land; USA Network; VH1; Weather Channel.
Fee: $25.50 monthly.

Digital Basic Service
Subscribers: N.A.
Programming (via satellite): BBC America; Bio; Bloomberg Television; CMT Pure Country; Cooking Channel; Current; Discovery Health Channel; Discovery Kids Channel; Discovery Military Channel; Discovery Planet Green; DMX Music; ESPN Classic Sports; ESPNews; FitTV; Fox Movie Channel; Fox Soccer; Fuse; G4; Golf Channel; GSN; Halogen Network; History Channel International; ID Investigation Discovery; Independent Film Channel; Lifetime Movie Network; MTV Hits; MTV2; Nick Jr.; NickToons TV; PBS Kids Sprout; RFD-TV; Science Channel; Sleuth; SoapNet; Style Network; Sundance Channel; TeenNick; Toon Disney; Trinity Broadcasting Network; VH1 Classic; VH1 Soul.
Fee: $3.95 monthly (entertainment or variety package), $5.95 monthly (basic).

Digital Pay Service 1
Pay Units: N.A.
Programming (via satellite): Cinemax (multiplexed); Encore (multiplexed); Flix; HBO (multiplexed); Showtime; Starz (multiplexed); The Movie Channel (multiplexed).
Fee: $11.95 monthly (HBO, Cinemax, Showtime/TMC/Flix or Starz/Encore).

Video-On-Demand: No

Internet Service
Operational: Yes. Began: May 1, 2002.
Subscribers: 496.
Broadband Service: Eagle Internet.
Fee: $22.95 monthly.

Telephone Service
Analog: Not Operational
Digital: Operational
Fee: $16.00 monthly

Miles of Plant: 33.0 (coaxial); None (fiber optic). Homes passed: 2,085.
President & Chief Executive Officer: Gary Shorman. General Manager: Rex Skiles. Chief Technician: Les Libal.
City fee: 5% of gross.
Ownership: Eagle Communications Inc. (KS) (MSO).

CLEARWATER—SKT Entertainment, PO Box 800, 128 N Gorin St, Clearwater, KS 67026. Phones: 800-362-2396; 620-584-2077. Fax: 620-584-2260. Web Site: http://www.sktmainstreet.com. Also serves Atlanta, Belle Plaine, Burden, Cedar Vale, Dexter, Elk County, Grenola, Howard, Leon, Longton, Moline, Severy & Viola. ICA: KS0136.
TV Market Ranking: 67 (Belle Plaine, CLEARWATER (VILLAGE), Leon, Viola); Outside TV Markets (Atlanta, Burden, Cedar Vale, Dexter, Elk County, Grenola, Howard, Longton, Moline, Severy). Franchise award date: N.A. Franchise expiration date: N.A. Began: February 1, 1981.
Channel capacity: 62 (operating 2-way). Channels available but not in use: 16.

Basic Service
Subscribers: 3,000.
Programming (received off-air): KAKE-TV (ABC) Wichita; KMTW (MNT) Hutchinson; KPTS (PBS) Hutchinson; KSAS-TV (FOX) Wichita; KSCW-DT (CW) Wichita; KSNW (NBC) Wichita; KWCH-DT (CBS) Hutchinson.
Programming (via satellite): ABC Family Channel; AMC; Animal Planet; Arts & Entertainment; Cartoon Network; CNBC; CNN; Comedy Central; Country Music TV; C-SPAN; C-SPAN 2; Discovery Channel; Disney Channel; ESPN; ESPN 2; ESPN Classic Sports; Eternal Word TV Network; FitTV; Food Network; Fox News Channel; Fox Sports Net; FX; Hallmark Channel; Headline News; HGTV; History Channel;

INSP; Lifetime; MTV; National Geographic Channel; NFL Network; Nickelodeon; Outdoor Channel; QVC; Speed Channel; Spike TV; Syfy; TBS Superstation; The Learning Channel; Travel Channel; truTV; Turner Classic Movies; Turner Network TV; TV Guide Network; TV Land; USA Network; VH1; Weather Channel; WGN America.
Current originations: Public Access; Educational Access.
Fee: $42.00 monthly.

Digital Basic Service
Subscribers: N.A.
Programming (received off-air): KAKE-TV (ABC) Wichita; KMTW (MNT) Hutchinson; KPTS (PBS) Hutchinson; KSAS-TV (FOX) Wichita; KSCW-DT (CW) Wichita; KSNW (NBC) Wichita; KWCH-DT (CBS) Hutchinson.
Programming (via satellite): Animal Planet HD; Arts & Entertainment HD; BBC America; Bio; Bravo; CMT Pure Country; CNN HD; Current; Discovery Channel HD; Discovery HD Theater; Discovery Health Channel; Discovery Kids Channel; Discovery Military Channel; Discovery Planet Green; DMX Music; ESPN HD; FitTV; Food Network HD; Fox Soccer; HGTV HD; History Channel International; ID Investigation Discovery; Independent Film Channel; Lifetime Movie Network; MTV Hits; MTV2; National Geographic Channel; National Geographic Channel HD Network; Nick Jr.; NickToons TV; Outdoor Channel 2 HD; RFD-TV; Science Channel; Science Channel HD; Sleuth; Speed Channel; TBS in HD; TeenNick; TLC HD; Toon Disney; Turner Network TV HD; Versus; VH1 Classic; VH1 Soul; WE tv.
Fee: $16.25 monthly.

Digital Expanded Basic Service
Subscribers: N.A.
Programming (via satellite): AmericanLife TV Network; Bloomberg Television; ESPN Classic Sports; ESPNews; Fox College Sports Atlantic; Fox College Sports Central; Fox College Sports Pacific; Fox Movie Channel; Fuse; G4; Golf Channel; Great American Country; GSN; Halogen Network; Outdoor Channel; Sleuth; Style Network; Trinity Broadcasting Network.
Fee: $9.95 monthly.

Pay Service 1
Pay Units: N.A.
Programming (via satellite): Cinemax; HBO; Showtime; The Movie Channel.
Fee: $11.00 monthly (Cinemax), $12.95 monthly (HBO or Showtime/TMC).

Digital Pay Service 1
Pay Units: N.A.
Programming (via satellite): Cinemax (multiplexed); Cinemax HD; Encore (multiplexed); Flix; HBO (multiplexed); HBO HD; Showtime (multiplexed); Showtime HD; Starz (multiplexed); Starz HDTV; Sundance Channel; The Movie Channel (multiplexed); The Movie Channel HD.
Fee: $11.00 monthly (Cinemax), $12.95 monthly (HBO, Showtime/TMC or Starz/Encore).
Video-On-Demand: No

Internet Service
Operational: Yes, DSL only.
Broadband Service: TurboLink.
Fee: $30.00 monthly.
Telephone Service
None
Miles of Plant: 72.0 (coaxial); None (fiber optic).
Cable TV Services Manager: Philip Brown. Marketing Manager: Doug McQueary.
City fee: 3% of gross.
Ownership: Southern Kansas Telephone Co.

CLIFTON—Galaxy Cablevision, 1928 S Lincoln Ave, Ste 200, York, NE 68467. Phone: 402-362-3332. Fax: 402-362-4890. Web Site: http://www.galaxycable.com. Also serves Clay County, Clyde & Vining. ICA: KS0120.
TV Market Ranking: Outside TV Markets (Clay County, CLIFTON, Clyde, Vining). Franchise award date: November 24, 1976. Franchise expiration date: N.A. Began: February 1, 1977.
Channel capacity: 31 (not 2-way capable). Channels available but not in use: None.
Basic Service
Subscribers: 108.
Programming (received off-air): KAAS-TV (FOX) Salina; KOLN (CBS, MNT) Lincoln; KSNT (FOX, NBC) Topeka; KTKA-TV (ABC, CW) Topeka; KTWU (PBS) Topeka; WIBW-TV (CBS, MNT) Topeka; allband FM.
Programming (via satellite): ABC Family Channel; Arts & Entertainment; Cartoon Network; CNN; Discovery Channel; Disney Channel; ESPN; ESPN 2; Eternal Word TV Network; Fox News Channel; Fuse; FX; History Channel; Lifetime; Outdoor Channel; QVC; TBS Superstation; Trinity Broadcasting Network; Turner Network TV; USA Network; Weather Channel; WGN America.
Fee: $35.00 installation; $37.80 monthly.
Pay Service 1
Pay Units: N.A.
Programming (via satellite): HBO; Showtime; The Movie Channel.
Internet Service
Operational: No.
Telephone Service
None
Miles of Plant: 25.0 (coaxial); 7.0 (fiber optic). Homes passed: 683. Total homes in franchised area: 717.
State Manager: Cheyenne Wohlford. Technical Manager: John Davidshofer. Sales Manager: Mike Thomas. Customer Service Manager: Michael Debermardin.
City fee: 1% of gross.
Ownership: Galaxy Cable Inc. (MSO).

COFFEYVILLE—Cox Communications, PO Box 189, 102 W 11th St, Coffeyville, KS 67337. Phones: 316-260-7000 (Wichita office); 620-251-6261. Fax: 620-251-4064. Web Site: http://www.cox.com/kansas. Also serves Caney, Cherryvale, Dearing, Montgomery County (portions) & Tyro (portions), KS; South Coffeyville, OK. ICA: KS0016.
TV Market Ranking: Below 100 (Caney, COFFEYVILLE, Dearing, Montgomery County (portions), South Coffeyville, Tyro (portions)); Outside TV Markets (Cherryvale, Montgomery County (portions)). Franchise award date: January 1, 1967. Franchise expiration date: N.A. Began: November 1, 1968.
Channel capacity: N.A. Channels available but not in use: N.A.
Basic Service
Subscribers: N.A. Included in Wichita
Programming (received off-air): KJRH-TV (NBC) Tulsa; KOAM-TV (CBS) Pittsburg; KODE-TV (ABC) Joplin; KOKI-TV (FOX) Tulsa; KOTV-DT (CBS) Tulsa; KSNF (NBC) Joplin; KTUL (ABC) Tulsa; KTWU (PBS) Topeka; allband FM.
Programming (via satellite): C-SPAN; C-SPAN 2; CW+; Kansas Now 22; TV Guide Network; Weather Channel; WGN America.
Current originations: Government Access; Educational Access; Public Access.
Fee: $29.95 installation; $15.95 monthly.
Expanded Basic Service 1
Subscribers: N.A.
Programming (via satellite): ABC Family Channel; AMC; Animal Planet; Arts & Entertainment; BET Networks; Bravo; Cartoon Network; CNBC; CNN; Comedy Central; Country Music TV; Discovery Channel; Discovery Health Channel; Disney Channel; E! Entertainment Television; ESPN; ESPN 2; Eternal Word TV Network; Food Network; Fox News Channel; Fox Sports Net Midwest; FX; Hallmark Channel; Headline News; HGTV; History Channel; Home Shopping Network; INSP; Jewelry Television; Lifetime; MSNBC; MTV; MTV2; Nickelodeon; QVC; Speed Channel; Spike TV; Syfy; TBS Superstation; The Learning Channel; Travel Channel; Trinity Broadcasting Network; truTV; Turner Classic Movies; Turner Network TV; TV Land; Univision; USA Network; VH1.
Fee: $27.20 monthly.
Digital Basic Service
Subscribers: N.A.
Programming (received off-air): KOAM-TV (CBS) Pittsburg.
Programming (via satellite): American-Life TV Network; Anime Network; Arts & Entertainment HD; BBC America; Bio; Bloomberg Television; Boomerang; CBS College Sports Network; CMT Pure Country; Cooking Channel; Daystar TV Network; Discovery Digital Networks; Discovery HD Theater; Do-It-Yourself; ESPN 2 HD; ESPN Classic Sports; ESPN HD; ESPN U; ESPNews; FamilyNet; Fox Reality Channel; Fox Soccer; Fuel TV; Fuse; G4; GAS; Golf Channel; Gospel Music Channel; Great American Country; GSN; Hallmark Channel; Halogen Network; History Channel International; Howard TV; Independent Film Channel; Lifetime Movie Network; MTV Networks Digital Suite; NASA TV; National Geographic Channel; National Geographic Channel HD Network; NBA TV; NFL Network; Nick Jr.; Nick Too; NickToons TV; Outdoor Channel; Oxygen; Palladia; PBS Kids Sprout; Pentagon Channel; Si TV; SoapNet; Style Network; Sundance Channel; Tennis Channel; The Sportsman Channel; Toon Disney; Trinity Broadcasting Network; Turner Network TV HD; TV One; Universal HD; Versus; WE tv.
Fee: $14.00 monthly.
Digital Pay Service 1
Pay Units: N.A.
Programming (via satellite): Canales N; Cinemax (multiplexed); Cinemax On Demand; DMX Music; Encore (multiplexed); Flix; HBO (multiplexed); HBO HD; HBO On Demand; Showtime (multiplexed); Showtime HD; Showtime On Demand; Starz (multiplexed); Starz HDTV; Starz On Demand; The Movie Channel (multiplexed).
Video-On-Demand: Planned
Pay-Per-View
iN DEMAND (delivered digitally); Fresh (delivered digitally); MLS Direct Kick (delivered digitally); MLB Extra Innings (delivered digitally); NHL Center Ice (delivered digitally); Playboy TV (delivered digitally); Shorteez (delivered digitally); Ten Clips (delivered digitally); Ten Blox (delivered digitally); ESPN (delivered digitally); NBA League Pass (delivered digitally).
Internet Service
Operational: Yes.
Subscribers: 889.
Broadband Service: Cox High Speed Internet.
Fee: $19.99-$59.99 monthly.
Telephone Service
Digital: Operational
Fee: 15.95-$48.95 monthly
Miles of Plant: 155.0 (coaxial); None (fiber optic). Homes passed included in Wichita
Vice President & General Manager: Kimberly Edmonds. Vice President, Engineering: Nick DiPonzio. Vice President, Marketing: Tony Matthews. Field Operations Regional Manager: Joe Michael. Technical Operations Manager: David Sanders. Marketing Director: Tina Gabbard. Public Affairs Director: Sarah Kauffman.
City fee: 3% of gross.
Ownership: Cox Communications Inc. (MSO).

COLBY—S&T Cable, PO Box 345, 755 Davis Ave, Colby, KS 67701. Phones: 866-790-0241 (Goodland office); 785-460-7300. Fax: 785-460-7301. Web Site: http://www.sttelcom.com. ICA: KS0039.
TV Market Ranking: Below 100 (COLBY). Franchise award date: September 1, 1967. Franchise expiration date: N.A. Began: September 1, 1967.
Channel capacity: N.A. Channels available but not in use: N.A.
Basic Service
Subscribers: 1,721.
Programming (received off-air): KBSL-DT (CBS) Goodland; KLBY (ABC) Colby; KOOD (PBS) Hays; KSAS-TV (FOX) Wichita; KSCW-DT (CW) Wichita; KSNK (NBC) McCook; KUSA (NBC) Denver; KWGN-TV (CW) Denver.
Programming (via satellite): QVC.
Current originations: Government Access; Educational Access; Public Access.
Fee: $20.00 installation; $13.00 monthly; $.57 converter.
Expanded Basic Service 1
Subscribers: N.A.
Programming (received off-air): KMTW (MNT) Hutchinson.
Programming (via satellite): ABC Family Channel; AMC; Animal Planet; Arts & Entertainment; Bravo!; Cartoon Network; CNBC; CNN; Comedy Central; Country Music TV; C-SPAN; C-SPAN 2; Daystar TV Network; Discovery Channel; Discovery Kids Channel; Disney Channel; Do-It-Yourself; E! Entertainment Television; ESPN; ESPN 2; ESPN Classic Sports; Eternal Word TV Network; Food Network; Fox News Channel; Fox Sports Net Midwest; FX; Golf Channel; Hallmark Channel; Headline News; HGTV; History Channel; Home Shopping Network; Lifetime; MSNBC; MTV; National Geographic Channel; NFL Network; Nickelodeon; Oxygen; RFD-TV; Speed Channel; Spike TV; Syfy; TBS Superstation; The Learning Channel; The Sportsman Channel; Travel Channel; Trinity Broadcasting Network; truTV; Turner Classic Movies;

Turner Network TV; TV Guide Network; TV Land; Univision; USA Network; Versus; VH1; WE tv; Weather Channel; WGN America.
Fee: $21.95 monthly.

Digital Basic Service
Subscribers: N.A.
Programming (received off-air): KAKE-TV (ABC) Wichita; KMTW (MNT) Hutchinson; KSAS-TV (FOX) Wichita; KSNK (NBC) McCook; KWCH-DT (CBS) Hutchinson.
Programming (via satellite): AmericanLife TV Network; BBC America; Bio; Bloomberg Television; CMT Pure Country; Discovery Health Channel; Discovery Kids Channel; Discovery Military Channel; Discovery Planet Green; Encore (multiplexed); ESPN U; ESPNews; FitTV; FSN Digital Atlantic; FSN Digital Central; FSN Digital Pacific; Fuse; G4; Gospel Music Channel; Great American Country; GSN; Halogen Network; History Channel International; ID Investigation Discovery; Independent Film Channel; Lifetime Movie Network; Lime; MTV Hits; MTV Jams; MTV Tres; MTV2; Music Choice; Nick Jr.; Nick Too; NickToons TV; Outdoor Channel; Science Channel; SoapNet; Style Network; TeenNick; The Word Network; Toon Disney; VH1 Classic; VH1 Soul.
Fee: $12.75 monthly.

Digital Expanded Basic Service
Subscribers: N.A.
Programming (via satellite): Cine Latino; CNN en Espanol; Discovery en Espanol; ESPN Deportes; Fox Sports en Espanol; History Channel en Espanol.
Fee: $9.95 monthly.

Digital Expanded Basic Service 2
Subscribers: N.A.
Programming (via satellite): Arts & Entertainment HD; Discovery Channel HD; ESPN 2 HD; ESPN HD; HDNet; HDNet Movies; NFL Network HD; Universal HD.

Digital Pay Service 1
Pay Units: N.A.
Programming (via satellite): Cinemax (multiplexed); Cinemax HD; Flix; Fox Movie Channel; HBO (multiplexed); HBO HD; Showtime (multiplexed); Showtime HD; Starz (multiplexed); Starz HDTV; Sundance Channel; The Movie Channel (multiplexed).
Fee: $11.75 monthly (each).

Video-On-Demand: No

Pay-Per-View
iN DEMAND (delivered digitally); HITS (Headend In The Sky) (delivered digitally); Sports PPV (delivered digitally); Fresh (delivered digitally); Shorteez (delivered digitally); Hot Choice (delivered digitally).

Internet Service
Operational: No, Both DSL & dial-up.

Telephone Service
None

Miles of Plant: 34.0 (coaxial); 7.0 (fiber optic). Homes passed: 2,988. Total homes in franchised area: 2,988.
General Manager: Steve Richards. Cable Manager: Clint Felzien. Manager: Pat Mabry.
City fee: 3% of gross.
Ownership: S & T Communications Inc. (MSO).

COLDWATER—United Communications Assn. Inc., PO Box 117, 1107 McArtor Rd, Dodge City, KS 67801. Phone: 620-227-8645. Fax: 620-855-4009. Web Site: http://www.unitedtelcom.net. ICA: KS0169.
TV Market Ranking: Outside TV Markets (COLDWATER). Franchise award date: N.A. Franchise expiration date: N.A. Began: April 1, 1963.
Channel capacity: 38 (operating 2-way). Channels available but not in use: N.A.

Basic Service
Subscribers: 145.
Programming (received off-air): KAKE-TV (ABC) Wichita; KMTW (MNT) Hutchinson; KOOD (PBS) Hays; KSAS-TV (FOX) Wichita; KSCW-DT (CW) Wichita; 1 FM.
Programming (via satellite): Fox News Channel; HGTV; KSNW (NBC) Wichita; KWCH-DT (CBS) Hutchinson; National Geographic Channel; Trinity Broadcasting Network.
Fee: $39.95 installation; $16.48 monthly.

Expanded Basic Service 1
Subscribers: N.A.
Programming (via satellite): ABC Family Channel; AMC; Cartoon Network; CNN; C-SPAN; Discovery Channel; Disney Channel; E! Entertainment Television; ESPN; Food Network; Fox Sports Net Midwest; Great American Country; Headline News; History Channel; Lifetime; NFL Network; Nickelodeon; QVC; Spike TV; TBS Superstation; The Learning Channel; Turner Classic Movies; Turner Network TV; TV Land; USA Network; VH1; Weather Channel.
Fee: $44.81 monthly.

Pay Service 1
Pay Units: 51.
Programming (via satellite): HBO.
Fee: $11.00 monthly.

Pay Service 2
Pay Units: 24.
Programming (via satellite): Showtime.
Fee: $9.00 monthly.

Internet Service
Operational: No, DSL & dialup.

Telephone Service
None

Miles of Plant: 9.0 (coaxial); None (fiber optic). Homes passed: 625.
General Manager: Craig Mock. Chief Technician: Keith Brack. Customer Service Manager: Jeannie Linnebur.
City fee: 2% of gross.
Ownership: United Communications Assn. Inc. (MSO).

COLUMBUS—Columbus Telephone Co. Formerly [KS0056]. This cable system has converted to IPTV, 224 S Kansas Ave, Columbus, KS 66725. Phone: 620-429-3132. Fax: 620-429-1159. E-mail: columbus@columbus-ks.com. Web Site: http://www.columbus-ks.com. ICA: KS5041.
TV Market Ranking: Below 100 (COLUMBUS). Franchise award date: N.A. Franchise expiration date: N.A. Began: N.A.
Channel capacity: N.A. Channels available but not in use: N.A.

Internet Service
Operational: Yes, Both DSL & dial-up.

Telephone Service
Digital: Operational
Fee: $7.00 installation; $23.00 monthly

City fee: None.
Ownership: Columbus Telephone Co.

COLUMBUS—Columbus Telephone Co. This cable system has converted to IPTV. See Columbus, KS [KS5041], KS. ICA: KS0056.

COLWICH—Formerly served by Almega Cable. No longer in operation. ICA: KS0211.

CONCORDIA—Cunningham Cable TV, 407 W 6th St, Concordia, KS 66901. Phone: 785-243-4068. Fax: 785-545-3277. E-mail: brent@ctctelephony.tv. Web Site: http://www.cunninghamtelephoneandcable.com. Also serves Cloud County (portions). ICA: KS0035.
TV Market Ranking: Outside TV Markets (Cloud County (portions), CONCORDIA). Franchise award date: July 1, 1959. Franchise expiration date: N.A. Began: July 1, 1959.
Channel capacity: 77 (operating 2-way). Channels available but not in use: 3.

Basic Service
Subscribers: 1,662.
Programming (received off-air): KAAS-TV (FOX) Salina; KAKE-TV (ABC) Wichita; KBSH-DT (CBS) Hays; KHGI-TV (ABC) Kearney; KOOD (PBS) Hays; KSHB-TV (NBC) Kansas City; KSNT (FOX, NBC) Topeka.
Programming (via microwave): WIBW-TV (CBS, MNT) Topeka.
Programming (via satellite): Eternal Word TV Network; Weather Channel.
Fee: $16.95 monthly; $.40 converter.

Expanded Basic Service 1
Subscribers: N.A.
Programming (received off-air): KSCW-DT (CW) Wichita; KSNC (NBC) Great Bend.
Programming (via satellite): ABC Family Channel; AMC; AmericanLife TV Network; Animal Planet; Arts & Entertainment; Bravo; Cartoon Network; CNBC; CNN; Comedy Central; Country Music TV; C-SPAN; Discovery Channel; Disney Channel; Do-It-Yourself; E! Entertainment Television; ESPN; ESPN 2; ESPN Classic Sports; Food Network; Fox News Channel; Fox Sports Net Midwest; FX; Great American Country; GSN; Hallmark Channel; Hallmark Movie Channel; Headline News; HGTV; History Channel; Home Shopping Network; INSP; ION Television; Lifetime; MSNBC; MTV; National Geographic Channel; NFL Network; Nickelodeon; Outdoor Channel; Oxygen; QVC; RFD-TV; SoapNet; Speed Channel; Spike TV; Syfy; TBS Superstation; The Learning Channel; The Sportsman Channel; Travel Channel; Trinity Broadcasting Network; truTV; Turner Classic Movies; Turner Network TV; TV Land; USA Network; VH1; WGN America.
Fee: $20.00 monthly.

Digital Basic Service
Subscribers: 103.
Programming (via satellite): AmericanLife TV Network; BBC America; Bio; Bloomberg Television; Bravo; Discovery Digital Networks; DMX Music; ESPN 2; ESPN Classic Sports; ESPNews; Fox Movie Channel; Fox Soccer; FSN Digital Atlantic; FSN Digital Central; FSN Digital Pacific; Fuse; G4; GAS; Golf Channel; Great American Country; GSN; Halogen Network; HGTV; History Channel; History Channel International; Independent Film Channel; Lifetime Movie Network; Lime; MTV Networks Digital Suite; National Geographic Channel; Nick Jr.; NickToons TV; Outdoor Channel; ShopNBC; Sleuth; Speed Channel; Style Network; Syfy; Toon Disney; Trinity Broadcasting Network; Turner Classic Movies; Versus; WE tv.
Fee: $15.95 monthly.

Digital Pay Service 1
Pay Units: N.A.
Programming (via satellite): Cinemax (multiplexed); Encore (multiplexed); Flix; HBO (multiplexed); Showtime (multiplexed); Starz (multiplexed); The Movie Channel (multiplexed).
Fee: $7.95 monthly (Cinemax), $9.95 monthly (Starz/Encore), $10.95 monthly (Showtime/TMC/Flix), $12.95 monthly (HBO).

Video-On-Demand: No

Pay-Per-View
Addressable homes: 196.
Playboy TV (delivered digitally); Fresh (delivered digitally); Sports PPV (delivered digitally); Hot Choice, Fee: $2.99, Addressable: Yes; iN DEMAND.

Internet Service
Operational: Yes. Began: May 1, 2002.
Subscribers: 626.
Fee: $25.00 installation; $29.95 monthly; $3.00 modem lease; $49.95 modem purchase.

Telephone Service
None

Miles of Plant: 35.0 (coaxial); None (fiber optic). Homes passed: 2,578. Total homes in franchised area: 2,635.
Manager: Brent Cunningham.
City fee: 5% of gross.
Ownership: Cunningham Communications (MSO).

CONWAY SPRINGS—Allegiance Communications, 707 W Saratoga St, Shawnee, OK 74804. Phones: 405-395-1131; 405-275-6923. Web Site: http://www.allegiance.tv. ICA: KS0161.
TV Market Ranking: 67 (CONWAY SPRINGS). Franchise award date: March 3, 1981. Franchise expiration date: N.A. Began: January 1, 1982.
Channel capacity: N.A. Channels available but not in use: N.A.

Basic Service
Subscribers: 232.
Programming (received off-air): KAKE-TV (ABC) Wichita; KMTW (MNT) Hutchinson; KPTS (PBS) Hutchinson; KSAS-TV (FOX) Wichita; KSCW-DT (CW) Wichita; KSNW (NBC) Wichita; KWCH-DT (CBS) Hutchinson.
Programming (via satellite): ABC Family Channel; AMC; Arts & Entertainment; CNN; Country Music TV; Discovery Channel; Disney Channel; ESPN; ESPN 2; Food Network; Fox News Channel; Fox Sports Net Midwest; FX; Hallmark Channel; Headline News; History Channel; Home Shopping Network; Lifetime; MTV; Nickelodeon; Spike TV; TBS Superstation; The Learning Channel; Turner Network TV; TV Land; USA Network; VH1; Weather Channel; WGN America.
Fee: $41.11 installation; $21.95 monthly.

Digital Basic Service
Subscribers: N.A.
Programming (via satellite): BBC America; Bio; Bloomberg Television; Bravo; Chiller; CMT Pure Country; Current; Discovery Health Channel; Discovery Kids Chan-

nel; Discovery Military Channel; Discovery Planet Green; DMX Music; Encore (multiplexed); ESPN Classic Sports; ESPNews; FitTV; Flix; Fox College Sports Atlantic; Fox College Sports Central; Fox College Sports Pacific; Fox Movie Channel; Fox Soccer; Fuse; G4; Golf Channel; Great American Country; GSN; HGTV; History Channel International; ID Investigation Discovery; Independent Film Channel; Lifetime Movie Network; MTV Hits; MTV2; National Geographic Channel; Nick Jr.; NickToons TV; Outdoor Channel; RFD-TV; Science Channel; ShopNBC; Sleuth; SoapNet; Speed Channel; Style Network; Sundance Channel; Syfy; TeenNick; Toon Disney; Trinity Broadcasting Network; Turner Classic Movies; Versus; VH1 Classic; VH1 Soul; WE tv.

Digital Pay Service 1

Pay Units: N.A.

Programming (via satellite): Cinemax (multiplexed); HBO (multiplexed); Showtime (multiplexed); Starz (multiplexed); The Movie Channel (multiplexed).

Video-On-Demand: No

Pay-Per-View

iN DEMAND (delivered digitally); Club Jenna (delivered digitally); Spice: Xcess (delivered digitally); Playboy TV (delivered digitally); Fresh (delivered digitally).

Internet Service

Operational: No.

Telephone Service

None

Miles of Plant: 11.0 (coaxial); None (fiber optic). Homes passed: 461. Total homes in franchised area: 461.

Chief Executive Officer: Bil Haggarty. Regional Vice President: Andrew Dearth. Vice President, Marketing: Tracy Bass.

City fee: 3% of gross.

Ownership: Allegiance Communications (MSO).

COPELAND—United Communications Assn. Inc. Now served by CIMARRON, KS [KS0126]. ICA: KS0318.

COUNCIL GROVE—Council Grove Telecommunications Inc., 1410 Lilac Ln, Wamego, KS 66547-1220. Web Site: http://www.councilgrove.cablerocket.com. Also serves Morris County (portions). ICA: KS0079.

TV Market Ranking: Outside TV Markets (COUNCIL GROVE, Morris County (portions)). Franchise award date: June 1, 2002. Franchise expiration date: N.A. Began: October 1, 1964.

Channel capacity: 52 (2-way capable). Channels available but not in use: 3.

Basic Service

Subscribers: 820.

Programming (received off-air): KCTV (CBS) Kansas City; KSHB-TV (NBC) Kansas City; KSNT (FOX, NBC) Topeka; KTKA-TV (ABC, CW) Topeka; KTLJ-CA (FOX) Junction City; KTWU (PBS) Topeka; WDAF-TV (FOX) Kansas City; WIBW-TV (CBS, MNT) Topeka; allband FM.

Programming (via satellite): ABC Family Channel; AMC; Arts & Entertainment; CNBC; CNN; Country Music TV; C-SPAN; Discovery Channel; E! Entertainment Television; ESPN; ESPN 2; Food Network; Fox Movie Channel; Fox News Channel; Fox Sports Net; FX; G4; Golf Channel; HGTV; History Channel; Lifetime; National Geographic Channel; Nickelodeon; Outdoor Channel; QVC; Speed Channel; Spike TV; Syfy; TBS Superstation; The Learning Channel; Trinity Broadcasting Network; Turner Classic Movies; Turner Network TV; TV Land; USA Network; VH1; Weather Channel; WGN America.

Fee: $32.00 monthly.

Pay Service 1

Pay Units: 43.

Programming (via satellite): Showtime.

Fee: $7.95 monthly.

Internet Service

Operational: Yes.

Subscribers: 360.

Fee: $20.00 installation; $25.95 monthly.

Telephone Service

None

Miles of Plant: 26.0 (coaxial); None (fiber optic). Homes passed: 1,100. Total homes in franchised area: 1,100.

Manager & Chief Technician: R.H. Morse, Jr.

City fee: 3% of gross.

Ownership: Council Grove Telecommunications (MSO).

COURTLAND—Nex-Tech. Formerly [KS0271]. This cable system has converted to IPTV, PO Box 158, 145 N Main St, Lenora, KS 67645-0158. Phones: 877-567-7872; 785-567-4281. Fax: 785-567-4401. E-mail: webmaster@nex-tech.com. Web Site: http://www.nex-tech.com. ICA: KS5043.

Channel capacity: N.A. Channels available but not in use: N.A.

Internet Service

Operational: Yes.

Telephone Service

Digital: Operational

Ownership: Rural Telephone Co.

COURTLAND—Nex-Tech. This cable system has converted to IPTV. See Courtland, KS [KS5043]. ICA: KS0271.

CUBA—Eagle Communications, 406 NE 14th St, Abilene, KS 67410. Phones: 785-625-4000 (Corporate office); 785-263-2529. Fax: 865-625-8030. Web Site: http://www.eaglecom.net. ICA: KS0372.

TV Market Ranking: Outside TV Markets (CUBA). Franchise award date: N.A. Franchise expiration date: N.A. Began: May 1, 1988.

Channel capacity: 36 (not 2-way capable). Channels available but not in use: 16.

Basic Service

Subscribers: 37.

Programming (received off-air): KAAS-TV (FOX) Salina; KHNE-TV (PBS) Hastings; KMGH-TV (ABC) Denver; KOLN (CBS, MNT) Lincoln; KSNT (FOX, NBC) Topeka.

Programming (via satellite): ABC Family Channel; Arts & Entertainment; CNN; Discovery Channel; ESPN; Outdoor Channel; TBS Superstation; The Learning Channel; Turner Network TV; USA Network; Weather Channel; WGN America.

Fee: $20.00 installation; $30.35 monthly.

Pay Service 1

Pay Units: N.A.

Programming (via satellite): Cinemax; HBO.

Fee: $11.95 monthly (each).

Internet Service

Operational: No.

Telephone Service

None

Miles of Plant: 4.0 (coaxial); None (fiber optic). Homes passed: 140.

President: Gary Shorman. General Manager: Rex Skiles.

Ownership: Eagle Communications Inc. (KS) (MSO).

CUNNINGHAM—Cox Communications. Now served by WICHITA, KS [KS0001]. ICA: KS0223.

DEARING—SKT Entertainment. Now served by COFFEYVILLE, KS [KS0016]. ICA: KS0255.

DELPHOS—Cunningham Cable TV. No longer in operation. ICA: KS0374.

DENISON—Rainbow Communications, PO Box 147, Everest, KS 66424. Phones: 800-892-0163; 785-866-2390. Fax: 785-548-7517. Web Site: http://www.rainbowtel.net. ICA: KS0324.

TV Market Ranking: Below 100 (DENISON). Franchise award date: N.A. Franchise expiration date: N.A. Began: August 1, 1989.

Channel capacity: 36 (operating 2-way). Channels available but not in use: 22.

Basic Service

Subscribers: 10.

Programming (received off-air): KCTV (CBS) Kansas City; KCWE (CW) Kansas City; KMBC-TV (ABC) Kansas City; KMCI-TV (IND) Lawrence; KPXE-TV (ION) Kansas City; KSHB-TV (NBC) Kansas City; KSMO-TV (MNT) Kansas City; KSNT (FOX, NBC) Topeka; KTKA-TV (ABC, CW) Topeka; KTWU (PBS) Topeka; WDAF-TV (FOX) Kansas City; WIBW-TV (CBS, MNT) Topeka.

Programming (via satellite): CNN; C-SPAN; Headline News; Trinity Broadcasting Network; Weather Channel; WGN America.

Fee: $29.95 installation; $13.95 monthly.

Pay Service 1

Pay Units: N.A.

Programming (via satellite): Cinemax.

Fee: $9.00 installation; $9.95 monthly.

Pay Service 2

Pay Units: 3.

Programming (via satellite): Showtime; The Movie Channel.

Fee: $8.95 monthly (each).

Video-On-Demand: No

Internet Service

Operational: Yes.

Broadband Service: Lighting Jack High Speed.

Fee: $39.95 monthly.

Telephone Service

None

Miles of Plant: 3.0 (coaxial); None (fiber optic). Homes passed: 96.

General Manager: James Lednicky. Network Engineer: Scott Wheeler. Marketing Manager: Jackie Petersen. Plant Manager: Jim Streeter.

Ownership: Rainbow Communications (MSO).

DIGHTON—S&T Cable, PO Box 99, 320 Kansas Ave, Brewster, KS 67732-0099. Phones: 620-397-2111 (Dighton office); 800-432-8294 (Brewster office); 785-694-2256. Fax: 785-694-2750. Web Site: http://www.sttelcom.com. ICA: KS0144.

TV Market Ranking: Outside TV Markets (DIGHTON). Franchise award date: N.A. Franchise expiration date: N.A. Began: N.A.

Channel capacity: N.A. Channels available but not in use: N.A.

Basic Service

Subscribers: 425.

Programming (received off-air): KSAS-TV (FOX) Wichita; KSCW-DT (CW) Wichita; KSNG (NBC) Garden City; KSWK (PBS) Lakin; KUPK-TV (ABC) Garden City; KUSA (NBC) Denver; KWGN-TV (CW) Denver.

Programming (via satellite): QVC.

Current originations: Public Access; Educational Access.

Fee: $20.00 installation; $13.00 monthly.

Expanded Basic Service 1

Subscribers: N.A.

Programming (received off-air): KMTW (MNT) Hutchinson.

Programming (via satellite): ABC Family Channel; AMC; Animal Planet; Arts & Entertainment; Bravo; Cartoon Network; CNBC; CNN; Comedy Central; Country Music TV; C-SPAN; C-SPAN 2; Daystar TV Network; Discovery Channel; Discovery Kids Channel; Disney Channel; Do-It-Yourself; E! Entertainment Television; ESPN; ESPN 2; ESPN Classic Sports; Eternal Word TV Network; Food Network; Fox News Channel; Fox Sports Net Rocky Mountain; FX; Golf Channel; Hallmark Channel; Headline News; HGTV; History Channel; Home Shopping Network; Lifetime; MSNBC; MTV; National Geographic Channel; NFL Network; Nickelodeon; Oxygen; RFD-TV; Speed Channel; Spike TV; Syfy; TBS Superstation; The Learning Channel; The Sportsman Channel; Travel Channel; Trinity Broadcasting Network; truTV; Turner Classic Movies; Turner Network TV; TV Guide Network; TV Land; Univision; USA Network; Versus; VH1; WE tv; Weather Channel; WGN America.

Fee: $21.95 monthly.

Digital Basic Service

Subscribers: 57.

Programming (received off-air): KAKE-TV (ABC) Wichita; KMTW (MNT) Hutchinson; KOOD (PBS) Hays; KSAS-TV (FOX) Wichita; KSNG (NBC) Garden City; KWCH-DT (CBS) Hutchinson.

Programming (via satellite): AmericanLife TV Network; BBC America; Bio; Bloomberg Television; CMT Pure Country; Discovery Health Channel; Discovery Kids Channel; Discovery Military Channel; Discovery Planet Green; Encore (multiplexed); ESPN U; ESPNews; FitTV; FSN Digital Atlantic; FSN Digital Central; FSN Digital Pacific; Fuse; G4; Gospel Music Channel; Great American Country; GSN; Halogen Network; History Channel International; ID Investigation Discovery; Independent Film Channel; Lifetime Movie Network; Lime; MTV Hits; MTV Jams; MTV Tres; MTV2; Music Choice; Nick Jr.; Nick Too; NickToons TV; Outdoor Channel; Science Channel; SoapNet; Style Network; TeenNick; The Word Network; Toon Disney; VH1 Classic; VH1 Soul.

Fee: $17.95 monthly.

Digital Expanded Basic Service

Subscribers: N.A.

Programming (via satellite): Cine Latino; CNN en Espanol; Discovery en Espanol; ESPN Deportes; Fox Sports en Espanol; History Channel en Espanol.

Fee: $15.95 monthly.

Digital Pay Service 1

Pay Units: N.A.

Programming (via satellite): Cinemax (multiplexed); Flix; Fox Movie Channel; HBO (multiplexed); Showtime (multiplexed); Starz (multiplexed); Sundance Channel; The Movie Channel (multiplexed).

Fee: $11.75 monthly (each).

Video-On-Demand: No

Pay-Per-View

special events (delivered digitally), Addressable: Yes.

Internet Service

Operational: No, Both DSL & dial-up.

Telephone Service
None
General Manager: Steve Richards. Cable TV Manager: Clint Felzien. Office Manager: Malinda Bradstreet.
Ownership: S & T Communications Inc. (MSO).

DODGE CITY—Cox Communications, 1109 College Dr, Garden City, KS 67846. Phones: 316-260-7000 (Wichita office); 620-275-2003. Fax: 620-275-2061. Web Site: http://www.cox.com/kansas. Also serves Ford County. ICA: KS0015.
TV Market Ranking: Below 100 (DODGE CITY, Ford County). Franchise award date: N.A. Franchise expiration date: N.A. Began: June 1, 1970.
Channel capacity: N.A. Channels available but not in use: N.A.
Basic Service
Subscribers: N.A. Included in Wichita
Programming (received off-air): KBSD-DT (CBS) Ensign; KDCK (PBS) Dodge City; KMTW (MNT) Hutchinson; KSAS-TV (FOX) Wichita; KSCW-DT (CW) Wichita; KSNG (NBC) Garden City; KUPK-TV (ABC) Garden City.
Programming (via satellite): C-SPAN; C-SPAN 2; ShopNBC; TV Guide Network; TVN Entertainment; Univision; Weather Channel; WGN America.
Current originations: Educational Access.
Fee: $29.95 installation; $10.35 monthly.
Expanded Basic Service 1
Subscribers: 9,077.
Programming (via satellite): ABC Family Channel; AMC; Animal Planet; Arts & Entertainment; BET Networks; Bravo; Cartoon Network; CNBC; CNN; Comedy Central; Country Music TV; Discovery Channel; Discovery Health Channel; Disney Channel; E! Entertainment Television; ESPN; ESPN 2; Eternal Word TV Network; Food Network; Fox News Channel; Fox Sports Net Midwest; FX; GalaVision; Hallmark Channel; Headline News; HGTV; History Channel; Home Shopping Network; INSP; Jewelry Television; Lifetime; MSNBC; MTV; MTV2; Nickelodeon; QVC; Speed Channel; Spike TV; Syfy; TBS Superstation; Telemundo; The Learning Channel; Travel Channel; truTV; Turner Classic Movies; Turner Network TV; TV Land; USA Network; VH1.
Fee: $43.15 monthly.
Digital Basic Service
Subscribers: N.A.
Programming (received off-air): KBSD-DT (CBS) Ensign; KDCK (PBS) Dodge City; KSAS-TV (FOX) Wichita; KSMI-LP Wichita; KSNG (NBC) Garden City; KUPK-TV (ABC) Garden City.
Programming (via satellite): AmericanLife TV Network; BBC America; Bio; Bloomberg Television; Boomerang; Canales N; CBS College Sports Network; Cooking Channel; Daystar TV Network; Discovery HD Theater; Do-It-Yourself; ESPN Classic Sports; ESPN HD; ESPNews; FamilyNet; FitTV; Fox Reality Channel; Fox Soccer; Fuel TV; Fuse; G4; GAS; Golf Channel; Gospel Music TV; Great American Country; GSN; Hallmark Movie Channel; Halogen Network; HBO HD; History Channel International; Independent Film Channel; INHD; INHD2; Lifetime Movie Network; Military History Channel; MTV Networks Digital Suite; Music Choice; NASA TV; National Geographic Channel; NBA TV; NFL Network; Nick Jr.; Nick Too; NickToons TV; Outdoor Channel; Oxygen; Palladia; PBS Kids Sprout; Pentagon Channel; Showtime HD; Si TV; SoapNet; Starz HDTV; Sundance Channel; Tennis Channel; The Sportsman Channel; Toon Disney; Trinity Broadcasting Network; TV One; Universal HD; Versus; WE tv.
Fee: $15.00 monthly.
Digital Pay Service 1
Pay Units: N.A.
Programming (via satellite): Cinemax (multiplexed); Encore (multiplexed); Flix; HBO (multiplexed); Showtime (multiplexed); Starz (multiplexed); The Movie Channel (multiplexed).
Fee: $11.50 monthly (each).
Video-On-Demand: Planned
Pay-Per-View
iN DEMAND, Addressable: Yes; iN DEMAND (delivered digitally); ESPN (delivered digitally); NBA/WNBA League Pass (delivered digitally); NHL Center Ice/MLB Extra Innings (delivered digitally); NASCAR In Car (delivered digitally); NBA TV (delivered digitally); Adult Swim (delivered digitally).
Internet Service
Operational: Yes.
Subscribers: 824.
Broadband Service: Cox High Speed Internet.
Fee: $19.99-$59.99 monthly.
Telephone Service
Digital: Operational
Fee: 15.95-$48.95 monthly
Miles of Plant: 126.0 (coaxial); 27.0 (fiber optic). Homes passed included in Wichita
Vice President & General Manager: Kimberly Edmonds. Vice President, Engineering: Nick DiPonzio. Vice President, Marketing: Tony Matthews. Field Operations Regional Manager: Jim Fronk. Marketing Director: Tina Gabbard. Public Affairs Director: Sarah Kauffman. Office Manager: Edgar Cardenas.
City fee: 5% of gross.
Ownership: Cox Communications Inc. (MSO).

DOUGLASS—Allegiance Communications, 707 W Saratoga St, Shawnee, OK 74804. Phones: 405-275-6923; 405-395-1131. Web Site: http://www.allegiance.tv. ICA: KS0129.
TV Market Ranking: 67 (DOUGLASS). Franchise award date: July 7, 1980. Franchise expiration date: N.A. Began: N.A.
Channel capacity: N.A. Channels available but not in use: N.A.
Basic Service
Subscribers: 390.
Programming (received off-air): KAKE-TV (ABC) Wichita; KARK-TV (NBC) Little Rock; KMTW (MNT) Hutchinson; KPTS (PBS) Hutchinson; KSAS-TV (FOX) Wichita; KSCW-DT (CW) Wichita; KSNW (NBC) Wichita; KWCH-DT (CBS) Hutchinson.
Programming (via satellite): E! Entertainment Television; Home Shopping Network; WGN America.
Current originations: Educational Access.
Fee: $41.11 installation; $23.70 monthly.
Expanded Basic Service 1
Subscribers: N.A.
Programming (via satellite): ABC Family Channel; AMC; Arts & Entertainment; CNBC; CNN; Comedy Central; Country Music TV; Discovery Channel; Disney Channel; E! Entertainment Television; ESPN; ESPN 2; Food Network; Fox News Channel; Fox Sports Net Midwest; FX; Hallmark Channel; Headline News; History Channel; Lifetime; MSNBC; MTV; Nickelodeon; Oxygen; Spike TV; Syfy; TBS Superstation; The Learning Channel; Travel Channel; Turner Network TV; TV Land; USA Network; VH1; Weather Channel.

Digital Basic Service
Subscribers: N.A.
Programming (via satellite): BBC America; Bio; Bloomberg Television; Bravo; Chiller; CMT Pure Country; Current; Discovery Health Channel; Discovery Kids Channel; Discovery Military Channel; Discovery Planet Green; DMX Music; Encore (multiplexed); ESPN Classic Sports; ESPNews; FitTV; Flix; Fox College Sports Atlantic; Fox College Sports Central; Fox College Sports Pacific; Fox Movie Channel; Fox Soccer; Fuse; G4; Golf Channel; GSN; HGTV; History Channel International; ID Investigation Discovery; Independent Film Channel; Lifetime Movie Network; MTV Hits; MTV2; National Geographic Channel; Nick Jr.; NickToons TV; Outdoor Channel; RFD-TV; Science Channel; ShopNBC; Sleuth; SoapNet; Speed Channel; Style Network; Sundance Channel; Syfy; TeenNick; Toon Disney; Trinity Broadcasting Network; Turner Classic Movies; Versus; VH1 Classic; VH1 Soul; WE tv.
Digital Pay Service 1
Pay Units: N.A.
Programming (via satellite): Cinemax (multiplexed); HBO (multiplexed); Showtime (multiplexed); Starz (multiplexed); The Movie Channel (multiplexed).
Video-On-Demand: No
Pay-Per-View
iN DEMAND (delivered digitally); Club Jenna (delivered digitally); Hot Choice (delivered digitally); Spice: Xcess (delivered digitally); Playboy TV (delivered digitally); Fresh (delivered digitally).
Internet Service
Operational: No.
Telephone Service
None
Miles of Plant: 13.0 (coaxial); None (fiber optic). Homes passed: 680. Total homes in franchised area: 680.
Chief Executive Officer: Bill Haggarty. Regional Vice President: Andrew Dearth. Vice President, Marketing: Tracy Bass.
City fee: 3% of gross.
Ownership: Allegiance Communications (MSO).

DOWNS—Cunningham Cable TV. Now served by WASHINGTON (formerly Glen Elder), KS [KS0228]. ICA: KS0463.

DOWNS—Formerly served by Cebridge Connections. Now served by GLEN ELDER, KS [KS0228]. ICA: KS0154.

DURHAM—Formerly served by Eagle Communications. No longer in operation. ICA: KS0431.

DWIGHT—Formerly served by Eagle Communications. No longer in operation. ICA: KS0289.

EASTON—Formerly served by Giant Communications. No longer in operation. ICA: KS0276.

EDMOND—Nex-Tech, PO Box 158, 145 N Main St, Lenora, KS 67645-0158. Phones: 785-567-4281; 785-567-9226. Fax: 785-567-4401. Web Site: http://www.nex-tech.com. Also serves Agra, Almena, Alton, Bogue, Gaylord, Gorham, Grainfield, Hill City, Jennings, Kensington, Lenora, Logan, Morland, Natoma, Osborne, Palco, Park, Quinter, Selden, Victoria & Woodston. ICA: KS0450.
TV Market Ranking: Below 100 (Gorham, Natoma, Palco, Selden, Victoria); Outside TV Markets (Agra, Almena, Alton, Bogue, EDMOND, Gaylord, Grainfield, Hill City, Jennings, Kensington, Lenora, Logan, Morland, Osborne, Park, Quinter, Woodston). Franchise award date: N.A. Franchise expiration date: N.A. Began: N.A.
Channel capacity: N.A. Channels available but not in use: N.A.
Basic Service
Subscribers: 4,396.
Programming (received off-air): KAKE-TV (ABC) Wichita; KBSH-DT (CBS) Hays; KGIN (CBS, MNT) Grand Island; KHGI-TV (ABC) Kearney; KLNE-TV (PBS) Lexington; KMTW (MNT) Hutchinson; KOOD (PBS) Hays; KSAS-TV (FOX) Wichita; KSCW-DT (CW) Wichita; KSNC (NBC) Great Bend; KSNK (NBC) McCook.
Programming (via satellite): C-SPAN; Eternal Word TV Network; QVC; Weather Channel; WGN America.
Current originations: Educational Access.
Expanded Basic Service 1
Subscribers: N.A.
Programming (via satellite): ABC Family Channel; AMC; Animal Planet; Arts & Entertainment; Bio; Cartoon Network; CNBC; CNN; Comedy Central; Country Music TV; Discovery Channel; Disney Channel; E! Entertainment Television; ESPN; ESPN 2; ESPN Classic Sports; Food Network; Fox News Channel; Fox Sports Net Rocky Mountain; FX; G4; Great American Country; GSN; Hallmark Channel; Headline News; HGTV; History Channel; History Channel International; ION Television; Lifetime; MSNBC; MTV; National Geographic Channel; NFL Network; Nickelodeon; Outdoor Channel; RFD-TV; Speed Channel; Spike TV; Syfy; TBS Superstation; The Learning Channel; Travel Channel; Trinity Broadcasting Network; truTV; Turner Classic Movies; Turner Network TV; TV Land; USA Network; Versus; VH1.
Digital Basic Service
Subscribers: N.A.
Programming (via satellite): AmericanLife TV Network; BBC America; Bloomberg Television; CMT Pure Country; Current; Discovery Health Channel; Discovery Home Channel; Discovery Kids Channel; Discovery Military Channel; ESPN Classic Sports; ESPNews; Fox College Sports Atlantic; Fox College Sports Central; Fox College Sports Pacific; Fox Movie Channel; Fox Soccer; Golf Channel; ID Investigation Discovery; Independent Film Channel; INSP; Lifetime Movie Network; MTV Hits; MTV2; National Geographic Channel; Nick Jr.; Science Channel; ShopNBC; Sleuth;

Style Network; Sundance Channel; TeenNick; Toon Disney; Versus; VH1 Classic; VH1 Soul; WE tv.

Digital Pay Service 1

Pay Units: N.A.

Programming (via satellite): Cinemax (multiplexed); Encore (multiplexed); Flix; HBO (multiplexed); Showtime (multiplexed); Starz (multiplexed); The Movie Channel (multiplexed).

Internet Service

Operational: No.

Telephone Service

None

Manager: Brent Fine.

Ownership: Rural Telephone Co. (MSO).

EDNA—Formerly served by Craw-Kan Telephone Co-op. No longer in operation.. ICA: KS0244.

EDNA—Formerly served by GIRARD, KS [KS0446]. Craw-Kan Telephone Co-op. This cable system has converted to IPTV, PO Box 100, 200 N Ozark St, Girard, KS 66743. Phones: 800-362-0316; 620-724-8235. Fax: 620-724-4099. E-mail: webmaster@ckt.net. Web Site: http://www.ckt.net. ICA: KS5102.

TV Market Ranking: Outside TV Markets (EDNA).

Channel capacity: N.A. Channels available but not in use: N.A.

Internet Service

Operational: Yes.

Internet Service

Operational: Yes.

Telephone Service

Digital: Operational

Ownership: Craw-Kan Telephone Cooperative.

EFFINGHAM—Rainbow Communications, PO Box 147, Everest, KS 66424. Phones: 800-892-0163; 785-866-2390. Fax: 785-866-2393. Web Site: http://www.rainbowtel.net. ICA: KS0209.

TV Market Ranking: Below 100 (EFFINGHAM). Franchise award date: N.A. Franchise expiration date: N.A. Began: May 1, 1983.

Channel capacity: 62 (operating 2-way). Channels available but not in use: 35.

Basic Service

Subscribers: 118.

Programming (received off-air): KCTV (CBS) Kansas City; KCWE (CW) Kansas City; KMBC-TV (ABC) Kansas City; KMCI-TV (IND) Lawrence; KPXE-TV (ION) Kansas City; KSHB-TV (NBC) Kansas City; KSMO-TV (MNT) Kansas City; KTWU (PBS) Topeka; WDAF-TV (FOX) Kansas City; WIBW-TV (CBS, MNT) Topeka.

Programming (via satellite): ABC Family Channel; AMC; Animal Planet; Arts & Entertainment; Cartoon Network; CNN; Comedy Central; C-SPAN; Discovery Channel; Disney Channel; ESPN; ESPN 2; Eternal Word TV Network; Food Network; Fox News Channel; Fox Sports Net; FX; Great American Country; Hallmark Channel; Headline News; HGTV; History Channel; Lifetime; Nickelodeon; QVC; Speed Channel; Spike TV; Syfy; TBS Superstation; The Learning Channel; Travel Channel; Trinity Broadcasting Network; Turner Network TV; TV Land; USA Network; VH1; Weather Channel; WGN America.

Fee: $35.00 installation; $28.00 monthly.

Digital Basic Service

Subscribers: N.A.

Programming (via satellite): AmericanLife TV Network; BBC America; Bio; Bloomberg Television; Country Music TV; Discovery Digital Networks; DMX Music; ESPN Classic Sports; ESPNews; Fox Movie Channel; G4; GAS; Golf Channel; GSN; History Channel International; Lifetime Movie Network; MTV Networks Digital Suite; National Geographic Channel; Nick Jr.; NickToons TV; Outdoor Channel; Speed Channel; Style Network; Toon Disney; WE tv.

Fee: $12.95 monthly.

Digital Pay Service 1

Pay Units: N.A.

Programming (via satellite): Cinemax (multiplexed); Encore (multiplexed); Flix; HBO (multiplexed); Showtime (multiplexed); Starz (multiplexed); The Movie Channel (multiplexed).

Fee: $12.95 monthly (each).

Pay-Per-View

iN DEMAND (delivered digitally); Hot Choice (delivered digitally); Playboy TV (delivered digitally).

Internet Service

Operational: Yes.

Fee: $39.95 monthly.

Telephone Service

None

Miles of Plant: 5.0 (coaxial); None (fiber optic). Homes passed: 270.

General Manager: James Lednicky. Assistant Manager: Jason Smith. Plant Manager: Jim Streeter. Marketing Manager: Jackie Petersen.

Ownership: Rainbow Communications (MSO).

ELK CITY—Formerly served by SKT Entertainment. No longer in operation. ICA: KS0258.

ELKHART—Epic Touch Co., PO Box 1260, 610 S Cosmos, Elkhart, KS 67950-1260. Phone: 620-697-2111. Fax: 620-697-4262. E-mail: etc@elkhart.com. Web Site: http://www.epictouch.com. Also serves Keyes. ICA: KS0068.

TV Market Ranking: Outside TV Markets (ELKHART, Keyes). Franchise award date: N.A. Franchise expiration date: N.A. Began: July 1, 1960.

Channel capacity: 43 (operating 2-way). Channels available but not in use: 4.

Basic Service

Subscribers: 1,133.

Programming (received off-air): KAKE-TV (ABC) Wichita; KAMR-TV (NBC) Amarillo; KCIT (FOX) Amarillo; KETA-TV (PBS) Oklahoma City; KMTW (MNT) Hutchinson; KSAS-TV (FOX) Wichita; KSCW-DT (CW) Wichita; KSNW (NBC) Wichita; KVII-TV (ABC, CW) Amarillo.

Programming (via microwave): KFDA-TV (CBS) Amarillo.

Programming (via satellite): ABC Family Channel; AMC; Animal Planet; Arts & Entertainment; Bravo; Cartoon Network; CNBC; CNN; Comedy Central; Country Music TV; C-SPAN; Discovery Channel; Discovery Health Channel; Disney Channel; E! Entertainment Television; ESPN; ESPN 2; Food Network; Fox News Channel; Fox Sports Net; FX; Golf Channel; Hallmark Channel; HGTV; History Channel; Home Shopping Network; Lifetime; MTV; NFL Network; Nickelodeon; Outdoor Channel; Spike TV; Syfy; TBS Superstation; Telemundo; The Learning Channel; Toon Disney; Travel Channel; Turner Classic Movies; Turner Network TV; TV Land; Univision; USA Network; VH1; Weather Channel; WGN America.

Current originations: Government Access; Public Access; Educational Access.

Fee: $29.00 installation; $40.99 monthly.

Pay Service 1

Pay Units: 96.

Programming (via satellite): Showtime.

Fee: $20.00 installation; $10.95 monthly.

Pay Service 2

Pay Units: 257.

Programming (via satellite): HBO.

Fee: $20.00 installation; $10.95 monthly.

Video-On-Demand: Planned

Internet Service

Operational: No, DSL & dialup.

Telephone Service

None

Miles of Plant: 38.0 (coaxial); None (fiber optic). Homes passed: 1,378.

President: Bob Boaldin. Vice President, Operations: Trent Boaldin. Marketing & Advertising Director: Linda Ward. Economic Development Manager: Mike Shannon.

City fee: 3% of gross.

Ownership: Bob Boaldin.

ELLINWOOD—Allegiance Communications, 707 W Saratoga St, Shawnee, OK 74804. Phones: 405-275-6923; 405-395-1131. Web Site: http://www.allegiance.tv. ICA: KS0080.

TV Market Ranking: Below 100 (ELLINWOOD). Franchise award date: N.A. Franchise expiration date: N.A. Began: September 1, 1976.

Channel capacity: N.A. Channels available but not in use: N.A.

Basic Service

Subscribers: 1,223.

Programming (received off-air): KAKE-TV (ABC) Wichita; KMTW (MNT) Hutchinson; KOOD (PBS) Hays; KPTS (PBS) Hutchinson; KSAS-TV (FOX) Wichita; KSCW-DT (CW) Wichita; KSNC (NBC) Great Bend; KWCH-DT (CBS) Hutchinson; allband FM.

Programming (via satellite): Comedy Central; C-SPAN; Food Network; Hallmark Channel; Home Shopping Network; QVC; truTV; WGN America.

Fee: $35.00 installation; $18.85 monthly.

Expanded Basic Service 1

Subscribers: N.A.

Programming (via satellite): ABC Family Channel; AMC; Animal Planet; Arts & Entertainment; Cartoon Network; CNBC; CNN; Comedy Central; Country Music TV; Discovery Channel; Disney Channel; E! Entertainment Television; ESPN; ESPN 2; Eternal Word TV Network; Fox News Channel; Fox Sports Net Midwest; FX; Headline News; HGTV; History Channel; Lifetime; MSNBC; MTV; National Geographic Channel; Nickelodeon; Oxygen; Speed Channel; Spike TV; Syfy; TBS Superstation; The Learning Channel; Travel Channel; Turner Classic Movies; Turner Network TV; TV Land; USA Network; VH1; Weather Channel.

Digital Basic Service

Subscribers: N.A.

Programming (via satellite): BBC America; Bio; Bloomberg Television; Bravo; Chiller; CMT Pure Country; Current; Discovery Health Channel; Discovery Kids Channel; Discovery Military Channel; Discovery Planet Green; DMX Music; Encore (multiplexed); ESPN Classic Sports; ESPNews; FitTV; Flix; Fox College Sports Atlantic; Fox College Sports Central; Fox College Sports Pacific; Fox Movie Channel; Fox Soccer; Fuse; G4; Golf Channel; Great American Country; GSN; History Channel International; ID Investigation Discovery; Independent Film Channel; Lifetime Movie Network; MTV Hits; MTV2; Nick Jr.; NickToons TV; Outdoor Channel; RFD-TV; Science Channel; ShopNBC; Sleuth; SoapNet; Style Network; Sundance Channel; TeenNick; Toon Disney; Trinity Broadcasting Network; Versus; VH1 Classic; VH1 Soul; WE tv.

Digital Pay Service 1

Pay Units: N.A.

Programming (via satellite): Cinemax (multiplexed); HBO (multiplexed); Showtime (multiplexed); Starz (multiplexed); The Movie Channel (multiplexed).

Video-On-Demand: No

Pay-Per-View

iN DEMAND (delivered digitally); Club Jenna (delivered digitally); Spice: Xcess (delivered digitally); Playboy TV (delivered digitally); Fresh (delivered digitally).

Internet Service

Operational: Yes.

Fee: $24.95 installation; $39.99 monthly.

Telephone Service

None

Miles of Plant: 14.0 (coaxial); None (fiber optic).

Chief Executive Officer: Bill Haggarty. Regional Vice President: Andrew Dearth. Vice President, Marketing: Tracy Bass.

City fee: 3% of gross.

Ownership: Allegiance Communications (MSO).

ELLSWORTH—Eagle Communications, 406 NE 14th St, Abilene, Ks 67410. Phones: 785-263-2529; 785-625-4000 (Corporate office). Fax: 785-625-8030. Web Site: http://www.eaglecom.net. Also serves Kanopolis. ICA: KS0069.

TV Market Ranking: Below 100 (ELLSWORTH, Kanopolis). Franchise award date: November 1, 1976. Franchise expiration date: N.A. Began: November 1, 1976.

Channel capacity: N.A. Channels available but not in use: N.A.

Basic Service

Subscribers: 864.

Programming (received off-air): KAKE-TV (ABC) Wichita; KMTW (MNT) Hutchinson; KOOD (PBS) Hays; KPTS (PBS) Hutchinson; KSAS-TV (FOX) Wichita; KSCW-DT (CW) Wichita; KSNC (NBC) Great Bend; KWCH-DT (CBS) Hutchinson; allband FM.

Programming (via satellite): C-SPAN; QVC; Trinity Broadcasting Network; Weather Channel; WGN America.

Current originations: Religious Access.

Fee: $24.95 installation; $19.95 monthly.

Expanded Basic Service 1

Subscribers: N.A.

Programming (via satellite): ABC Family Channel; AMC; Animal Planet; Arts & Entertainment; Bravo; Cartoon Network; CNBC; CNN; Comedy Central; Country Music TV; Discovery Channel; Disney Channel; E! Entertainment Television;

ESPN; ESPN 2; ESPN Classic Sports; Food Network; Fox News Channel; Fox Sports Net Midwest; FX; Great American Country; Hallmark Channel; Headline News; HGTV; History Channel; Home Shopping Network; Lifetime; MSNBC; MTV; National Geographic Channel; NFL Network; Nickelodeon; Outdoor Channel; Spike TV; Syfy; TBS Superstation; The Learning Channel; Travel Channel; Turner Classic Movies; Turner Network TV; TV Land; USA Network; VH1.
Fee: $25.50 monthly.

Digital Basic Service
Subscribers: N.A.
Programming (via satellite): BBC America; Bio; Bloomberg Television; CMT Pure Country; Cooking Channel; Current; Discovery Health Channel; Discovery Military Channel; DMX Music; ESPNews; FitTV; Fox Movie Channel; Fox Soccer; Fuse; G4; Golf Channel; GSN; Halogen Network; ID Investigation Discovery; Independent Film Channel; Lifetime Movie Network; MTV Hits; MTV2; Nick Jr.; NickToons TV; PBS Kids Sprout; RFD-TV; Sleuth; SoapNet; Speed Channel; Style Network; Sundance Channel; TeenNick; Toon Disney; VH1 Classic; VH1 Soul.
Fee: $3.95 monthly (entertainment or variety tier), $5.95 monthly (basic).

Pay Service 1
Pay Units: 166.
Programming (via satellite): HBO.
Fee: $11.95 monthly.

Pay Service 2
Pay Units: 70.
Programming (via satellite): Showtime.
Fee: $11.95 monthly.

Pay Service 3
Pay Units: 80.
Programming (via satellite): The Movie Channel.
Fee: $11.95 monthly.

Digital Pay Service 1
Pay Units: N.A.
Programming (via satellite): Cinemax (multiplexed); Encore (multiplexed); Flix; HBO (multiplexed); Showtime (multiplexed); Starz (multiplexed); The Movie Channel.
Fee: $11.95 monthly (HOB, Cinemax, Starz/Encore or Showtime/TMC/Flix).

Video-On-Demand: No

Pay-Per-View
iN DEMAND (delivered digitally); Playboy TV (delivered digitally); Fresh (delivered digitally).

Internet Service
Operational: Yes. Began: May 15, 2003.
Subscribers: 343.
Broadband Service: Eagle Internet.
Fee: $22.95 monthly.

Telephone Service
Analog: Not Operational
Digital: Operational
Fee: $16.00 monthly

Miles of Plant: 29.0 (coaxial); None (fiber optic). Homes passed: 1,355. Total homes in franchised area: 1,386.
President & Chief Executive Officer: Gary Shorman. Regional Manager: Dennis Weese. General Manager: Rex Skiles. Chief Technician: Les Libal.
City fee: $100.00.
Ownership: Eagle Communications Inc. (KS) (MSO).

EMMETT—Rainbow Communications, PO Box 147, Everest, KS 66424. Phones: 800-548-7517; 785-866-2390. Fax: 785-548-7517. Web Site: http://www.rainbowtel.net. ICA: KS0346.
TV Market Ranking: Below 100 (EMMETT). Franchise award date: N.A. Franchise expiration date: N.A. Began: June 30, 1989.
Channel capacity: 36 (operating 2-way). Channels available but not in use: 22.

Basic Service
Subscribers: 9.
Programming (received off-air): KSNT (FOX, NBC) Topeka; KTKA-TV (ABC, CW) Topeka; KTMJ-CA Topeka; KTWU (PBS) Topeka; WIBW-TV (CBS, MNT) Topeka.
Programming (via satellite): ABC Family Channel; CNN; Discovery Channel; ESPN; TBS Superstation; Trinity Broadcasting Network.
Fee: $29.95 installation; $23.95 monthly.

Pay Service 1
Pay Units: 3.
Programming (via satellite): Cinemax.
Fee: $9.95 monthly.

Video-On-Demand: No

Internet Service
Operational: Yes.
Broadband Service: Lighting Jack High Speed.
Fee: $39.95 monthly.

Telephone Service
None

Miles of Plant: 3.0 (coaxial); None (fiber optic). Homes passed: 96.
General Manager: James Lednicky. Network Engineer: Scott Wheeler. Marketing Manager: Jackie Petersen. Plant Manager: Jim Streeter.
Ownership: Rainbow Communications (MSO).

EMPORIA—Cable One, PO Box 867, 714 Commercial St, Emporia, KS 66801. Phone: 620-342-3535. Fax: 620-342-3620. Web Site: http://www.cableone.net. Also serves Lyon County. ICA: KS0009.
TV Market Ranking: Below 100 (Lyon County); Outside TV Markets (EMPORIA). Franchise award date: N.A. Franchise expiration date: N.A. Began: February 1, 1961.
Channel capacity: 79 (operating 2-way). Channels available but not in use: None.

Basic Service
Subscribers: 7,915.
Programming (received off-air): KAKE-TV (ABC) Wichita; KSHB-TV (NBC) Kansas City; KSNT (FOX, NBC) Topeka; KTKA-TV (ABC, CW) Topeka; KTMJ-CA Topeka; KTWU (PBS) Topeka; WIBW-TV (CBS, MNT) Topeka; 14 FMs.
Programming (via microwave): KMBC-TV (ABC) Kansas City; KSNW (NBC) Wichita; KWCH-DT (CBS) Hutchinson; WDAF-TV (FOX) Kansas City.
Programming (via satellite): ABC Family Channel; AMC; Animal Planet; Arts & Entertainment; BET Networks; Bravo; Cartoon Network; CNBC; CNN; Comedy Central; C-SPAN; C-SPAN 2; CW+; Discovery Channel; Disney Channel; ESPN; ESPN 2; Food Network; Fox News Channel; Fox Sports Net Midwest; FX; Great American Country; Headline News; HGTV; History Channel; Home Shopping Network; Lifetime; MSNBC; MTV; Nickelodeon; QVC; Spike TV; Syfy; TBS Superstation; The Learning Channel; Travel Channel; Trinity Broadcasting Network; Turner Classic Movies; Turner Network TV; TV Land; Univision; USA Network; Weather Channel; WGN America.
Current originations: Government Access; Educational Access.
Fee: $30.00 installation; $46.00 monthly.

Digital Basic Service
Subscribers: N.A.
Programming (received off-air): WIBW-TV (CBS, MNT) Topeka.
Programming (via satellite): 3 Angels Broadcasting Network; Bio; Boomerang; BYU Television; Canales N; Discovery Digital Networks; ESPN Classic Sports; ESPNews; FamilyNet; Fox College Sports Atlantic; Fox College Sports Central; Fox College Sports Pacific; Fox Movie Channel; Fuel TV; G4; Golf Channel; Hallmark Channel; History Channel International; INSP; National Geographic Channel; Outdoor Channel; SoapNet; Speed Channel; Toon Disney; Trinity Broadcasting Network; truTV; Turner Network TV HD; Universal HD.

Digital Pay Service 1
Pay Units: N.A.
Programming (via satellite): Cinemax (multiplexed); Encore (multiplexed); Flix; HBO (multiplexed); Showtime (multiplexed); Showtime HD; Starz (multiplexed); Sundance Channel; The Movie Channel HD.
Fee: $14.95 monthly (each).

Video-On-Demand: No

Pay-Per-View
Movies (delivered digitally); Pleasure (delivered digitally); Ten Clips (delivered digitally); Ten Blox (delivered digitally); Ten Blue (delivered digitally).

Internet Service
Operational: Yes.
Subscribers: 3,500.
Broadband Service: CableONE.net.
Fee: $75.00 installation; $43.00 monthly.

Telephone Service
Digital: Operational
Fee: $75.00 installation; $39.95 monthly

Miles of Plant: 123.0 (coaxial); None (fiber optic). Homes passed: 13,400.
Manager: Joe Michaels. Marketing Director: Chris Harris. Technical Operations Manager: Ron Davis.
City fee: 3% of gross.
Ownership: Cable One Inc. (MSO).

ENSIGN—United Communications Assn. Inc. Now served by CIMARRON, KS [KS0126]. ICA: KS0312.

ESBON—Nex-Tech. Formerly served by Lebanon, KS [KS0397]. This cable system has converted to IPTV, PO Box 158, 145 N Main St, Lenora, KS 67645-0158. Phones: 877-567-7872; 785-567-4281. Fax: 785-567-4401. E-mail: webmaster@nex-tech.com. Web Site: http://www.nex-tech.com. ICA: KS5046.
Channel capacity: N.A. Channels available but not in use: N.A.

Internet Service
Operational: Yes.

Telephone Service
Digital: Operational

Ownership: Rural Telephone Co.

ESKRIDGE—Galaxy Cablevision, 1928 S Lincoln Ave, Ste 200, York, NE 68467. Phone: 402-362-3332. Fax: 402-362-4890. Web Site: http://www.galaxycable.com. ICA: KS0206.
TV Market Ranking: Below 100 (ESKRIDGE). Franchise award date: April 1, 1982. Franchise expiration date: N.A. Began: N.A.
Channel capacity: 31 (not 2-way capable). Channels available but not in use: 5.

Basic Service
Subscribers: 42.
Programming (received off-air): KSNT (FOX, NBC) Topeka; KTKA-TV (ABC, CW) Topeka; KTWU (PBS) Topeka; WIBW-TV (CBS, MNT) Topeka.
Programming (via satellite): ABC Family Channel; AMC; Animal Planet; Arts & Entertainment; CNN; Discovery Channel; Disney Channel; ESPN; ESPN 2; Great American Country; Headline News; History Channel; Lifetime; Outdoor Channel; TBS Superstation; Toon Disney; Turner Network TV; USA Network; WGN America.
Fee: $36.95 monthly.

Pay Service 1
Pay Units: N.A.
Programming (via satellite): Cinemax; HBO.
Fee: $11.00 monthly (each).

Internet Service
Operational: No.

Telephone Service
None

Miles of Plant: 7.0 (coaxial); None (fiber optic). Homes passed: 259.
State Manager: Cheyenne Wohlford. Technical Manager: John Davidshofer. Sales Manager: Mike Thomas. Customer Service Manager: Michael Debermardin.
City fee: 2% of gross.
Ownership: Galaxy Cable Inc. (MSO).

EUREKA—Mediacom, 901 N College Ave, Columbia, MO 65201. Phones: 417-875-5560 (Customer service); 573-443-1536. Fax: 417-883-0265. Web Site: http://www.mediacomcable.com. Also serves Hamilton & Madison. ICA: KS0058.
TV Market Ranking: Outside TV Markets (EUREKA, Hamilton, Madison). Franchise award date: N.A. Franchise expiration date: N.A. Began: May 1, 1981.
Channel capacity: N.A. Channels available but not in use: N.A.

Basic Service
Subscribers: 1,779.
Programming (received off-air): KAKE-TV (ABC) Wichita; KSAS-TV (FOX) Wichita; KSCW-DT (CW) Wichita; KSNT (FOX, NBC) Topeka; KSNW (NBC) Wichita; KTKA-TV (ABC, CW) Topeka; KTWU (PBS) Topeka; KWCH-DT (CBS) Hutchinson; WIBW-TV (CBS, MNT) Topeka.
Programming (via satellite): C-SPAN; GRTV Network; TV Guide Network; WGN America.
Planned originations: Public Access.
Fee: $35.00 installation; $27.95 monthly.

Expanded Basic Service 1
Subscribers: 303.
Programming (via satellite): ABC Family Channel; AMC; Animal Planet; Arts & Entertainment; BET Networks; Bravo; Cartoon Network; CNBC; CNN; Comedy Central; Country Music TV; Discovery Channel; E! Entertainment Television; ESPN; ESPN

2; FitTV; Food Network; Fox News Channel; Fox Sports Net; FX; Hallmark Channel; Headline News; HGTV; History Channel; Home Shopping Network; INSP; Lifetime; MSNBC; MTV; Nickelodeon; Outdoor Channel; QVC; ShopNBC; SoapNet; Speed Channel; Spike TV; Syfy; TBS Superstation; The Learning Channel; Travel Channel; Trinity Broadcasting Network; truTV; Turner Network TV; TV Land; USA Network; VH1; WE tv; Weather Channel.
Fee: $3.95 monthly.

Digital Basic Service
Subscribers: N.A.
Programming (via satellite): Barker; BBC America; Bio; Bloomberg Television; Discovery Health Channel; Discovery Home Channel; Discovery Kids Channel; Discovery Military Channel; DMX Music; ESPNews; Eternal Word TV Network; Fox Movie Channel; Fox Soccer; Fuse; G4; Golf Channel; GSN; Halogen Network; History Channel International; ID Investigation Discovery; Independent Film Channel; Lifetime Movie Network; MTV Hits; MTV2; National Geographic Channel; Nick Jr.; NickToons TV; RFD-TV; Science Channel; Sleuth; Style Network; TeenNick; Turner Classic Movies; TVG Network; Versus.

Digital Pay Service 1
Pay Units: 137.
Programming (via satellite): Cinemax (multiplexed).
Fee: $10.50 monthly.

Digital Pay Service 2
Pay Units: 330.
Programming (via satellite): Showtime.
Fee: $10.50 monthly.

Digital Pay Service 3
Pay Units: 29.
Programming (via satellite): Flix; Sundance Channel.
Fee: $2.95 monthly.

Digital Pay Service 4
Pay Units: 334.
Programming (via satellite): HBO (multiplexed).
Fee: $10.50 monthly.

Digital Pay Service 5
Pay Units: 159.
Programming (via satellite): The Movie Channel.
Fee: $10.50 monthly.

Digital Pay Service 6
Pay Units: N.A.
Programming (via satellite): Encore (multiplexed); Starz (multiplexed).

Video-On-Demand: No

Pay-Per-View
Events (delivered digitally); Playboy TV (delivered digitally); TEN Clips; Pleasure (delivered digitally).

Internet Service
Operational: Yes.
Broadband Service: Mediacom High Speed Internet.

Telephone Service
None

Miles of Plant: 40.0 (coaxial); None (fiber optic). Homes passed: 2,573.
Regional Vice President: Bill Copeland. Operations Director: Bryan Gann. Regional Technical Operations Director: Alan Freedman. Technical Operations Director: Roger Shearer. Marketing Director: Will Kuebler.
City fee: 3% of gross.
Ownership: Mediacom LLC (MSO).

FAIRVIEW—Carson Communications. Now served by HIAWATHA, KS [KS0059]. ICA: KS0293.

FORD—United Communications Assn. Inc. Now served by CIMARRON, KS [KS0126]. ICA: KS0307.

FORMOSO—Cunningham Cable TV. Now served by WASHINGTON (formerly Glen Elder), KS [KS0228]. ICA: KS0344.

FORT RILEY—Allegiance Communications, 707 W Saratoga St, Shawnee, OK 74804. Phones: 405-275-6923; 405-395-1131. Web Site: http://www.allegiance.tv. ICA: KS0023.
TV Market Ranking: Outside TV Markets (FORT RILEY). Franchise award date: N.A. Franchise expiration date: N.A. Began: January 1, 1980.
Channel capacity: N.A. Channels available but not in use: N.A.

Basic Service
Subscribers: 3,200.
Programming (received off-air): KSNT (FOX, NBC) Topeka; KTKA-TV (ABC, CW) Topeka; KTMJ-CA Topeka; KTWU (PBS) Topeka; WIBW-TV (CBS, MNT) Topeka.
Programming (via satellite): C-SPAN; CW+; Home Shopping Network; ION Television; QVC; TBS Superstation; Weather Channel; WGN America.
Fee: $25.00 installation; $19.95 monthly.

Expanded Basic Service 1
Subscribers: 3,115.
Programming (via satellite): ABC Family Channel; AMC; Animal Planet; Arts & Entertainment; BET Networks; Bravo; Cartoon Network; CNBC; CNN; Comedy Central; Country Music TV; Discovery Channel; Disney Channel; E! Entertainment Television; ESPN; ESPN 2; ESPN U; Food Network; Fox News Channel; Fox Sports Net Midwest; FX; G4; Golf Channel; GSN; Hallmark Channel; Halogen Network; Headline News; HGTV; History Channel; Lifetime; MSNBC; MTV; National Geographic Channel; Nickelodeon; Oxygen; Sleuth; SoapNet; Spike TV; Syfy; The Learning Channel; Toon Disney; Travel Channel; truTV; Turner Classic Movies; Turner Network TV; TV Guide Network; TV Land; Univision; USA Network; VH1.
Fee: $17.19 monthly.

Digital Basic Service
Subscribers: N.A.
Programming (via satellite): Arts & Entertainment HD; BBC America; Bio; Bloomberg Television; Chiller; Cine Latino; Cine Mexicano; CMT Pure Country; CNN en Espanol; Current; Discovery en Espanol; Discovery HD Theater; Discovery Health Channel; Discovery Kids Channel; Discovery Military Channel; Discovery Planet Green; Encore (multiplexed); ESPN 2 HD; ESPN Classic Sports; ESPN Deportes; ESPN HD; ESPNews; FitTV; Flix; Food Network HD; Fox College Sports Atlantic; Fox College Sports Central; Fox College Sports Pacific; Fox Movie Channel; Fox Soccer; Fox Sports en Espanol; Fuse; Gospel Music Channel; Great American Country; HDNet; HDNet Movies; HGTV HD; History Channel en Espanol; History Channel International; ID Investigation Discovery; Independent Film Channel; Lifetime Movie Network; MTV Hits; MTV Tres; MTV2; mun2 television; Music Choice; National Geographic Channel; National Geographic Channel HD Network; Nick Jr.; NickToons TV; Outdoor Channel; Outdoor Channel 2 HD; Science Channel; ShopNBC; Speed Channel; Style Network; Sundance Channel; TeenNick; The Word Network; Trinity Broadcasting Network; Universal HD; VeneMovies; Versus; VH1 Classic; VH1 Soul; WE tv.

Digital Pay Service 1
Pay Units: N.A.
Programming (via satellite): Cinemax (multiplexed); Encore (multiplexed); HBO (multiplexed); HBO HD; HBO Latino; Showtime (multiplexed); Showtime HD; Starz (multiplexed); Starz HDTV; The Movie Channel (multiplexed).

Video-On-Demand: No

Pay-Per-View
iN DEMAND (delivered digitally); Spice: Xcess (delivered digitally); Fresh (delivered digitally); Playboy TV (delivered digitally); Club Jenna (delivered digitally).

Internet Service
Operational: Yes. Began: January 1, 2003.
Broadband Service: Charter Pipeline.
Fee: $24.95 installation; $39.99 monthly.

Telephone Service
None

Miles of Plant: 55.0 (coaxial); None (fiber optic). Homes passed: 6,600. Total homes in franchised area: 6,600.
Chief Executive Officer: Bill Haggarty. Regional Vice President: Andrew Dearth. Vice President, Marketing: Tracy Bass.
Ownership: Allegiance Communications (MSO).

FORT SCOTT—Suddenlink Communications, 14 E 2nd St, Fort Scott, KS 66701. Phones: 620-223-1804; 314-965-2020. Web Site: http://www.suddenlink.com. Also serves Bourbon County (unincorporated areas). ICA: KS0028.
TV Market Ranking: Below 100 (Bourbon County (unincorporated areas) (portions), FORT SCOTT); Outside TV Markets (Bourbon County (unincorporated areas) (portions)). Franchise award date: N.A. Franchise expiration date: N.A. Began: October 1, 1966.
Channel capacity: 61 (operating 2-way). Channels available but not in use: N.A.

Basic Service
Subscribers: 2,906.
Programming (received off-air): K30AL-D (PBS) Iola; KCPT (PBS) Kansas City; KCTV (CBS) Kansas City; KCWE (CW) Kansas City; KMBC-TV (ABC) Kansas City; KOAM-TV (CBS) Pittsburg; KODE-TV (ABC) Joplin; KSHB-TV (NBC) Kansas City; KSMO-TV (MNT) Kansas City; KSNF (NBC) Joplin; WDAF-TV (FOX) Kansas City; allband FM.
Programming (via satellite): ABC Family Channel; Arts & Entertainment; BET Networks; CNBC; CNN; C-SPAN; C-SPAN 2; Discovery Channel; Disney Channel; ESPN; Food Network; Fox Sports Net Midwest; Great American Country; Headline News; HGTV; History Channel; Lifetime; National Geographic Channel; Nickelodeon; QVC; Spike TV; TBS Superstation; The Learning Channel; Travel Channel; Trinity Broadcasting Network; Turner Classic Movies; Turner Network TV; TV Land; USA Network; Weather Channel.
Current originations: Government Access; Educational Access.
Fee: $39.95 installation; $19.95 monthly.

Expanded Basic Service 1
Subscribers: N.A.
Programming (via satellite): Eternal Word TV Network; Fox News Channel; ION Television; VH1.
Fee: $25.00 monthly.

Digital Basic Service
Subscribers: N.A.
Programming (via satellite): AmericanLife TV Network; BBC America; Bio; Bloomberg Television; Discovery Digital Networks; DMX Music; ESPN 2; ESPN Classic Sports; ESPNews; Fox Sports World; Fuse; G4; Golf Channel; GSN; Halogen Network; HGTV; History Channel; History Channel International; Independent Film Channel; Lifetime Movie Network; Outdoor Channel; Ovation; ShopNBC; Speed Channel; Style Network; Syfy; Trinity Broadcasting Network; Turner Classic Movies; Versus; WE tv.
Fee: $3.99 monthly.

Pay Service 1
Pay Units: 326.
Programming (via satellite): HBO.
Fee: $9.00 installation; $10.95 monthly.

Pay Service 2
Pay Units: 259.
Programming (via satellite): Showtime.
Fee: $9.95 monthly.

Pay Service 3
Pay Units: 188.
Programming (via satellite): The Movie Channel.
Fee: $7.95 monthly.

Digital Pay Service 1
Pay Units: N.A.
Programming (via satellite): Cinemax (multiplexed); Encore Action; HBO (multiplexed); Showtime (multiplexed); Starz; The Movie Channel.

Video-On-Demand: No

Pay-Per-View
Sports PPV (delivered digitally); ESPN Extra (delivered digitally); ESPN Now (delivered digitally); Shorteez (delivered digitally); Fresh (delivered digitally); Playboy TV (delivered digitally); iN DEMAND (delivered digitally).

Internet Service
Operational: Yes. Began: June 23, 2002.
Broadband Service: Cebridge High Speed Cable Internet.
Fee: $49.95 installation; $26.95 monthly.

Telephone Service
None

Miles of Plant: 93.0 (coaxial); None (fiber optic). Additional miles planned: 5.0 (coaxial). Homes passed: 4,400.
Regional Manager: Todd Cruthird. Plant Manager: Lee Mott. Regional Marketing Manager: Beverly Gambell.
City fee: 3% of gross.
Ownership: Cequel Communications LLC (MSO).

FRANKFORT—Blue Valley Tele-Communications, 1559 Pony Express Hwy, Home, KY 66438. Phones: 877-876-1228; 785-799-3311. E-mail: info@bluevalley.net. Web Site: http://www.bluevalley.net. ICA: KS0167.
TV Market Ranking: Outside TV Markets (FRANKFORT). Franchise award date:

N.A. Franchise expiration date: N.A. Began: May 1, 1980.
Channel capacity: 30 (operating 2-way). Channels available but not in use: 6.

Basic Service

Subscribers: 260.
Programming (received off-air): KSNT (FOX, NBC) Topeka; KTKA-TV (ABC, CW) Topeka; KTMJ-CA Topeka; KTWU (PBS) Topeka; WIBW-TV (CBS, MNT) Topeka.
Programming (via satellite): ABC Family Channel; AMC; Animal Planet; Arts & Entertainment; Cartoon Network; CNN; Comedy Central; C-SPAN; Discovery Channel; Disney Channel; ESPN; ESPN 2; Great American Country; Headline News; HGTV; History Channel; Lifetime; Nickelodeon; QVC; Spike TV; Syfy; TBS Superstation; The Learning Channel; Travel Channel; Trinity Broadcasting Network; Turner Classic Movies; Turner Network TV; USA Network; VH1; Weather Channel; WGN America.
Fee: $29.95 installation; $27.95 monthly.

Digital Basic Service

Subscribers: N.A.
Programming (via satellite): AmericanLife TV Network; Arts & Entertainment; BBC America; Bloomberg Television; Discovery Digital Networks; ESPN Classic Sports; ESPNews; Fox Movie Channel; GAS; Golf Channel; GSN; History Channel International; Lifetime Movie Network; National Geographic Channel; Nick Jr.; Outdoor Channel; Speed Channel; Style Network; Toon Disney; WE tv.

Pay Service 1

Pay Units: 19.
Programming (via satellite): HBO.
Fee: $11.95 monthly.

Pay Service 2

Pay Units: 44.
Programming (via satellite): Showtime.
Fee: $8.95 monthly.

Pay Service 3

Pay Units: N.A.
Programming (via satellite): Cinemax.
Fee: $8.95 monthly.

Pay Service 4

Pay Units: 38.
Programming (via satellite): The Movie Channel.
Fee: $8.95 monthly.

Digital Pay Service 1

Pay Units: N.A.
Programming (via satellite): Cinemax (multiplexed); Encore (multiplexed); Flix; HBO (multiplexed); Showtime (multiplexed); Starz (multiplexed); The Movie Channel.

Video-On-Demand: No

Internet Service

Operational: Yes.

Telephone Service

Digital: Planned
Miles of Plant: 6.0 (coaxial); None (fiber optic). Homes passed: 444.
General Manager: Dennis Doyle. Operations Manager: Andy Torrey. Marketing Manager: Angie Armstrong. Customer Service Supervisor: Deb Runnebaum.
City fee: 2% of basic.
Ownership: Blue Valley Telecommunications (MSO).

FREDONIA—Allegiance Communications, 707 W Saratoga St, Shawnee, OK 74804. Phones: 405-395-1131; 405-275-6923. Web Site: http://www.allegiance.tv. Also serves Wilson County. ICA: KS0052.
TV Market Ranking: Outside TV Markets (FREDONIA, Wilson County). Franchise award date: N.A. Franchise expiration date: N.A. Began: N.A.
Channel capacity: 60 (not 2-way capable). Channels available but not in use: 13.

Basic Service

Subscribers: 1,122.
Programming (received off-air): KAKE-TV (ABC) Wichita; KFJX (FOX) Pittsburg; KOAM-TV (CBS) Pittsburg; KODE-TV (ABC) Joplin; KOED-TV (PBS) Tulsa; KSNF (NBC) Joplin; WIBW-TV (CBS, MNT) Topeka.
Programming (via satellite): CNN; C-SPAN; C-SPAN 2; CW+; QVC; ShopNBC; TV Guide Network; Weather Channel; WGN America.
Fee: $10.00 installation; $21.95 monthly; $2.00 converter; $9.95 additional installation.

Expanded Basic Service 1

Subscribers: N.A.
Programming (via satellite): ABC Family Channel; AMC; Animal Planet; Arts & Entertainment; Bravo; Cartoon Network; CNBC; Comedy Central; Country Music TV; Court TV; Discovery Channel; Disney Channel; ESPN; ESPN 2; Food Network; Fox News Channel; Fox Sports Net Midwest; FX; Great American Country; Hallmark Channel; Headline News; HGTV; History Channel; Lifetime; MSNBC; MTV; NFL Network; Nickelodeon; Outdoor Channel; Spike TV; Syfy; TBS Superstation; The Learning Channel; Travel Channel; Turner Network TV; TV Land; USA Network; VH1.

Digital Basic Service

Subscribers: N.A.
Programming (via satellite): AmericanLife TV Network; BBC America; Bio; Bloomberg Television; Bravo; Cine Latino; Cine Mexicano; CMT Pure Country; CNN en Espanol; Current; Discovery en Espanol; Discovery Health Channel; Discovery Kids Channel; Discovery Military Channel; Discovery Planet Green; DMX Music; Encore (multiplexed); ESPN 2; ESPN Classic Sports; ESPN Deportes; ESPNews; FitTV; Flix; Fox College Sports Atlantic; Fox College Sports Central; Fox College Sports Pacific; Fox Movie Channel; Fox Soccer; Fox Sports en Espanol; Fuse; G4; Golf Channel; Gospel Music Channel; Great American Country; GSN; Halogen Network; HGTV; History Channel; History Channel en Espanol; History Channel International; ID Investigation Discovery; Independent Film Channel; Lifetime Movie Network; MTV Hits; MTV Tres; MTV2; mun2 television; National Geographic Channel; Nick Jr.; NickToons TV; Outdoor Channel; Ovation; Science Channel; ShopNBC; Sleuth; Speed Channel; Style Network; Sundance Channel; Syfy; TeenNick; The Word Network; Toon Disney; Trinity Broadcasting Network; Turner Classic Movies; VeneMovies; Versus; VH1 Classic; VH1 Soul; WE tv.

Pay Service 1

Pay Units: N.A.
Programming (via satellite): Cinemax; Encore; HBO; Showtime; Starz.
Fee: $10.00 installation; $11.95 monthly (Cinemax or HBO).

Digital Pay Service 1

Pay Units: N.A.
Programming (via satellite): Cinemax (multiplexed); HBO (multiplexed); HBO Latino; Showtime (multiplexed); Starz (multiplexed); The Movie Channel (multiplexed).

Video-On-Demand: No

Pay-Per-View

iN DEMAND (delivered digitally); Hot Choice (delivered digitally); Playboy TV (delivered digitally); Fresh (delivered digitally); Club Jenna (delivered digitally); Spice: Xcess (delivered digitally).

Internet Service

Operational: Yes.

Telephone Service

Digital: Operational
Miles of Plant: 29.0 (coaxial); None (fiber optic). Homes passed: 1,732.
Chief Executive Officer: Bill Haggarty. Regional Vice President: Andrew Dearth. Vice President, Marketing: Tracy Bass.
Ownership: Allegiance Communications (MSO).

FRONTENAC—Formerly served by Almega Cable. No longer in operation. ICA: KS0037.

GALVA—Home Telephone Co., PO Box 8, 211 S Main, Galva, KS 67443. Phones: 620-654-3381; 620-654-3673. Fax: 620-654-3122. E-mail: hciservice@homecomminc.com. Web Site: http://www.hometelephone.com. ICA: KS0378.
TV Market Ranking: 67 (GALVA). Franchise award date: N.A. Franchise expiration date: N.A. Began: July 1, 1982.
Channel capacity: 24 (operating 2-way). Channels available but not in use: N.A.

Basic Service

Subscribers: 184.
Programming (received off-air): KAKE-TV (ABC) Wichita; KMTW (MNT) Hutchinson; KPTS (PBS) Hutchinson; KSAS-TV (FOX) Wichita; KSNW (NBC) Wichita; KWCH-DT (CBS) Hutchinson.
Programming (via satellite): ABC Family Channel; CNN; Discovery Channel; ESPN; Spike TV; TBS Superstation; Turner Network TV; USA Network; WGN America.
Fee: $34.95 monthly.

Pay Service 1

Pay Units: 43.
Programming (via satellite): HBO; Showtime.
Fee: $12.50 monthly (each).

Video-On-Demand: No

Internet Service

Operational: No, DSL & dial-up.

Telephone Service

None
Miles of Plant: 4.0 (coaxial); None (fiber optic). Homes passed: 285. Total homes in franchised area: 285.
President: Carla Shearer. Operations Manager: Brian Williams. Chief Technology Officer: Richard Baldwin. Customer Service Supervisor: Tina Anderson.
City fee: 2% of basic gross.
Ownership: Galva Cable Co. Inc. (MSO).

GARDEN CITY—Cox Communications, 1109 College Dr, Garden City, KS 67846. Phone: 316-260-7000 (Wichita office). Fax: 620-275-2061. Web Site: http://www.cox.com/kansas. Also serves Finney County. ICA: KS0010.
TV Market Ranking: Below 100 (Finney County, GARDEN CITY). Franchise award date: December 1, 1969. Franchise expiration date: N.A. Began: September 1, 1971.
Channel capacity: N.A. Channels available but not in use: N.A.

Basic Service

Subscribers: N.A. Included in Wichita
Programming (received off-air): KDCK (PBS) Dodge City; KMTW (MNT) Hutchinson; KSAS-TV (FOX) Wichita; KSCW-DT (CW) Wichita; KSNG (NBC) Garden City; KUPK-TV (ABC) Garden City; 4 FMs.
Programming (via microwave): KBSD-DT (CBS) Ensign.
Programming (via satellite): C-SPAN; C-SPAN 2; ShopNBC; TV Guide Network; TVN Entertainment; Univision; Weather Channel; WGN America.
Current originations: Educational Access; Public Access.
Fee: $29.95 installation; $11.00 monthly; $2.00 converter.

Expanded Basic Service 1

Subscribers: 5,999.
Programming (via satellite): ABC Family Channel; AMC; Animal Planet; Arts & Entertainment; BET Networks; Bravo; Cartoon Network; CNBC; CNN; Comedy Central; Country Music TV; Discovery Channel; Discovery Health Channel; Disney Channel; E! Entertainment Television; ESPN; ESPN 2; Eternal Word TV Network; Food Network; Fox News Channel; Fox Sports Net Midwest; FX; GalaVision; Hallmark Channel; Headline News; HGTV; History Channel; Home Shopping Network; INSP; Lifetime; MSNBC; MTV; MTV2; Nickelodeon; QVC; Speed Channel; Spike TV; Syfy; TBS Superstation; Telemundo; The Learning Channel; Travel Channel; truTV; Turner Classic Movies; Turner Network TV; TV Land; USA Network; VH1.
Fee: $43.15 monthly.

Digital Basic Service

Subscribers: N.A.
Programming (received off-air): KBSD-DT (CBS) Ensign; KSNG (NBC) Garden City; KUPK-TV (ABC) Garden City; KWCH-DT (CBS) Hutchinson.
Programming (via satellite): AmericanLife TV Network; Azteca America; BBC America; Bio; Bloomberg Television; Boomerang; Canales N; CBS College Sports Network; Cooking Channel; Country Music TV; Daystar TV Network; Discovery Digital Networks; Discovery HD Theater; Do-It-Yourself; ESPN Classic Sports; ESPN HD; ESPN U; ESPNews; FamilyNet; Fox HD; Fox Reality Channel; Fox Soccer; Fuel TV; Fuse; G4; GAS; Golf Channel; Gospel Music Channel; Great American Country; GSN; Halogen Network; History Channel International; Independent Film Channel; INHD; INHD2; Lifetime Movie Network; MTV Networks Digital Suite; Music Choice; NASA TV; National Geographic Channel; NBA League Pass; NBA TV; NFL Network; Nick Jr.; Nick Too; NickToons TV; Outdoor Channel; Oxygen; Palladia; PBS HD; PBS Kids Sprout; Pentagon Channel; Si TV; SoapNet; Sundance Channel; Tennis Channel; The Sportsman Channel; Toon Disney; Trinity Broadcasting Network; TV One; Universal HD; Versus; WE tv.
Fee: $15.00 monthly.

Digital Pay Service 1
Pay Units: N.A.
Programming (via satellite): Cinemax (multiplexed); Encore (multiplexed); Flix; HBO (multiplexed); HBO HD; Showtime (multiplexed); Showtime HD; Starz (multiplexed); Starz HDTV; The Movie Channel (multiplexed).
Fee: $11.50 monthly (each).
Video-On-Demand: Planned
Pay-Per-View
Fresh (delivered digitally); iN DEMAND (delivered digitally); MLB Extra Innings (delivered digitally); ESPN (delivered digitally); NASCAR In Car (delivered digitally); Playboy TV (delivered digitally); Ten Clips (delivered digitally); Ten Blox (delivered digitally); NBA League Pass (delivered digitally); MLS Direct Kick (delivered digitally); NHL Center Ice (delivered digitally).
Internet Service
Operational: Yes.
Subscribers: 1,048.
Broadband Service: Cox High Speed Internet.
Fee: $19.99-$59.99 monthly; $15.00 modem lease; $199.95 modem purchase.
Telephone Service
Digital: Operational
Fee: 15.95-$48.95 monthly
Miles of Plant: 124.0 (coaxial); None (fiber optic). Homes passed included in Wichita
Vice President & General Manager: Kimberly Edmonds. Vice President, Engineering: Nick DiPonzio. Vice President, Marketing: Tony Matthews. Field Operations Regional Manager: Jim Fronk. Marketing Director: Tina Gabbard. Public Affairs Director: Sarah Kauffman. Office Manager: Edgar Cardenas.
City fee: 5% of gross.
Ownership: Cox Communications Inc. (MSO).

GARDEN PLAIN—Formerly served by Cebridge Connections. No longer in operation. ICA: KS0218.

GENESEO—Formerly served by Eagle Communications. No longer in operation. ICA: KS0251.

GIRARD—Craw-Kan Telephone Co-op. This cable system has converted to IPTV. See GIRARD, KS [KS5099]. ICA: KS0446.

GIRARD—Formerly [KS0446]. Craw-Kan Telephone Coop. This cable system has converted to IPTV, PO Box 100, 200 N Ozark St, Girard, KS 66743. Phones: 800-362-0316; 620-724-8235. Fax: 620-724-4099. E-mail: webmaster@ckt.net. Web Site: http://www.ckt.net. ICA: KS5099.
TV Market Ranking: Below 100 (GIRARD).
Channel capacity: N.A. Channels available but not in use: N.A.
Internet Service
Operational: Yes.
Telephone Service
Digital: Operational
Ownership: Craw-Kan Telephone Cooperative.

GIRARD—Formerly served by Craw-Kan Telephone Co-op. No longer in operation. ICA: KS0470.

GLASCO—Cunningham Cable TV. No longer in operation. ICA: KS0186.

GOESSEL—Mid-Kansas Cable Services Inc., PO Box 960, 109 N Christian Ave, Moundridge, KS 67107-0960. Phone: 620-345-2831. Fax: 620-345-6106. ICA: KS0379.
TV Market Ranking: 67 (GOESSEL). Franchise award date: N.A. Franchise expiration date: N.A. Began: December 1, 1988.
Channel capacity: 40 (not 2-way capable). Channels available but not in use: 24.
Basic Service
Subscribers: 94.
Programming (received off-air): KAKE-TV (ABC) Wichita; KPTS (PBS) Hutchinson; KSAS-TV (FOX) Wichita; KSCW-DT (CW) Wichita; KSNW (NBC) Wichita; KWCH-DT (CBS) Hutchinson; WMTW (ABC) Poland Spring.
Programming (via satellite): ABC Family Channel; AMC; Arts & Entertainment; Country Music TV; C-SPAN; Discovery Channel; Disney Channel; ESPN; ESPN 2; Fox News Channel; Fox Sports Net; HGTV; History Channel; Lifetime; Nickelodeon; Spike TV; TBS Superstation; Turner Classic Movies; Turner Network TV; TV Land; USA Network; Weather Channel; WGN America.
Fee: $15.89 installation; $17.95 monthly.
Pay Service 1
Pay Units: 25.
Programming (via satellite): HBO.
Fee: $10.50 monthly.
Video-On-Demand: No
Internet Service
Operational: No, DSL only.
Telephone Service
None
Miles of Plant: 6.0 (coaxial); None (fiber optic). Homes passed: 180.
Manager: Reiny Wedel.
Ownership: Mid-Kansas Cable Services Inc. (MSO).

GOFF—Rainbow Communications, PO Box 147, Everest, KS 66424. Phones: 800-892-0163; 785-866-2390. Fax: 785-548-7517. Web Site: http://www.rainbowtel.net. ICA: KS0340.
TV Market Ranking: Outside TV Markets (GOFF). Franchise award date: N.A. Franchise expiration date: N.A. Began: August 1, 1989.
Channel capacity: 36 (operating 2-way). Channels available but not in use: 22.
Basic Service
Subscribers: 13.
Programming (received off-air): KSNT (FOX, NBC) Topeka; KTKA-TV (ABC, CW) Topeka; KTWU (PBS) Topeka; WIBW-TV (CBS, MNT) Topeka.
Programming (via satellite): CNN; C-SPAN; Headline News; Trinity Broadcasting Network; Weather Channel; WGN America.
Fee: $29.95 installation; $13.95 monthly.
Pay Service 1
Pay Units: 1.
Programming (via satellite): Cinemax.
Fee: $9.95 monthly.
Pay Service 2
Pay Units: 1.
Programming (via satellite): Showtime; The Movie Channel.
Fee: $11.95 monthly.
Video-On-Demand: No
Internet Service
Operational: Yes.
Broadband Service: Lighting Jack High Speed.
Fee: $39.95 monthly.
Telephone Service
None
Miles of Plant: 2.0 (coaxial); None (fiber optic). Homes passed: 79.
General Manager: James Lednicky. Plant Manager: Jim Streeter. Network Engineer: Scott Wheeler. Marketing Manager: Jackie Petersen.
Ownership: Rainbow Communications (MSO).

GOODLAND—Eagle Communications, PO Box 336, 114 W 11th St, Goodland, KS 67735. Phones: 785-625-4000 (Corporate office); 785-899-3371. Fax: 785-899-3299. Web Site: http://www.eaglecom.net. ICA: KS0045.
TV Market Ranking: Below 100 (GOODLAND). Franchise award date: October 5, 1965. Franchise expiration date: N.A. Began: November 1, 1966.
Channel capacity: 64 (operating 2-way). Channels available but not in use: 12.
Basic Service
Subscribers: 548.
Programming (received off-air): KBSL-DT (CBS) Goodland; KLBY (ABC) Colby; KOOD (PBS) Hays; KSAS-TV (FOX) Wichita; KSCW-DT (CW) Wichita; KSNK (NBC) McCook; KUSA (NBC) Denver; 10 FMs.
Programming (via satellite): C-SPAN; Home Shopping Network; KWGN-TV (CW) Denver; QVC; Weather Channel; WGN America.
Fee: $24.95 installation; $14.95 monthly.
Expanded Basic Service 1
Subscribers: 539.
Programming (via satellite): ABC Family Channel; Animal Planet; Arts & Entertainment; Bravo; CNBC; CNN; Comedy Central; Country Music TV; Discovery Channel; Disney Channel; E! Entertainment Television; ESPN; ESPN 2; ESPNews; Eternal Word TV Network; FitTV; Food Network; Fox Movie Channel; Fox News Channel; Fox Sports Net Rocky Mountain; FX; Hallmark Channel; Headline News; HGTV; History Channel; Lifetime; MSNBC; MTV; NFL Network; Nickelodeon; Spike TV; Syfy; TBS Superstation; The Learning Channel; Toon Disney; Travel Channel; Turner Network TV; TV Land; Univision; USA Network; VH1.
Fee: $20.50 monthly.
Digital Basic Service
Subscribers: 70.
Programming (via satellite): AmericanLife TV Network; BBC America; Bio; Bloomberg Television; Bravo; CMT Pure Country; Discovery Health Channel; Discovery Kids Channel; Discovery Military Channel; Discovery Planet Green; DMX Music; ESPN Classic Sports; ESPNews; Fox Soccer; Fuse; G4; Golf Channel; GSN; Halogen Network; HGTV; History Channel International; ID Investigation Discovery; Independent Film Channel; Lifetime Movie Network; MTV2; National Geographic Channel; Nick Jr.; NickToons TV; Outdoor Channel; Science Channel; Sleuth; Speed Channel; Style Network; TeenNick; Trinity Broadcasting Network; Turner Classic Movies; Versus; VH1 Classic; WE tv.
Fee: $3.95 monthly (Entertainment, Variety, Discovery or Sports tier).
Pay Service 1
Pay Units: 93.
Programming (via satellite): HBO.
Fee: $11.95 monthly.
Digital Pay Service 1
Pay Units: N.A.
Programming (via satellite): Cinemax (multiplexed); Encore (multiplexed); HBO (multiplexed); Showtime; Starz (multiplexed); The Movie Channel (multiplexed).
Fee: $11.95 monthly (Cinemax, Showtime/TMC, HBO, or Starz/Encore).
Video-On-Demand: No
Pay-Per-View
iN DEMAND (delivered digitally); Spice: Xcess (delivered digitally); Fresh (delivered digitally); Playboy TV (delivered digitally); Club Jenna (delivered digitally).
Internet Service
Operational: Yes.
Subscribers: 331.
Broadband Service: Eagle Internet.
Fee: $13.00 monthly.
Telephone Service
Analog: Not Operational
Digital: Operational
Fee: $23.00 monthly
Miles of Plant: 35.0 (coaxial); None (fiber optic). Homes passed: 2,745.
President: Gary Shorman. General Manager: Rex Skiles. Chief Technician: Les Libal.
City fee: 3% of gross.
Ownership: Eagle Communications Inc. (KS) (MSO).

GOODLAND—S&T Cable, PO Box 90, 1318 Main St, Goodland, KS 67735. Phones: 866-790-0243; 785-694-2256 (Brewster office); 785-890-7400. Fax: 785-890-7404. Web Site: http://www.sttelcom.com. ICA: KS0471. **Note:** This system is an overbuild.
TV Market Ranking: Below 100 (GOODLAND).
Channel capacity: N.A. Channels available but not in use: N.A.
Basic Service
Subscribers: 1,000.
Programming (received off-air): KBSL-DT (CBS) Goodland; KLBY (ABC) Colby; KOOD (PBS) Hays; KSAS-TV (FOX) Wichita; KSCW-DT (CW) Wichita; KSNK (NBC) McCook; KUSA (NBC) Denver; KWGN-TV (CW) Denver; LWS Local Weather Station.
Programming (via satellite): QVC.
Fee: $20.00 installation; $13.00 monthly.
Expanded Basic Service 1
Subscribers: N.A.
Programming (received off-air): KMTW (MNT) Hutchinson.
Programming (via satellite): ABC Family Channel; AMC; Animal Planet; Arts & Entertainment; Bravo; Cartoon Network; CNBC; CNN; Comedy Central; Country Music TV; C-SPAN; C-SPAN 2; Daystar TV Network; Discovery Channel; Discovery Kids Channel; Disney Channel; Do-It-Yourself; E! Entertainment Television; ESPN; ESPN 2; ESPN Classic Sports; Eternal Word TV Network; Food Network; Fox News Channel; Fox Sports Net; FX; Golf Channel; Hallmark Channel; Headline News; HGTV; History Channel; Home Shopping Network; Lifetime; MSNBC; MTV; National Geographic Channel; NFL Network; Nickelodeon; Oxygen; RFD-TV; Speed Channel; Spike TV; Syfy; TBS Superstation; The Learning Channel; The Sportsman Channel; Travel Channel; Trinity Broadcasting Network; truTV; Turner Classic Movies; Turner Network TV; TV Guide Network; TV Land; Univision; USA Network; Versus; VH1; WE tv; Weather Channel; WGN America.
Fee: $21.95 monthly.
Digital Basic Service
Subscribers: N.A.
Programming (received off-air): KAKE-TV (ABC) Wichita; KMTW (MNT) Hutchinson; KSAS-TV (FOX) Wichita; KSNK (NBC) McCook; KWCH-DT (CBS) Hutchinson.
Programming (via satellite): AmericanLife TV Network; BBC America; Bio; Bloomberg Television; CMT Pure Country; Discovery Health Channel; Discovery Military Channel; Discovery Planet Green; Encore (multiplexed); ESPN U; ESPNews; FitTV; FSN Digital Atlantic; FSN Digital Central; FSN Digi-

tal Pacific; Fuse; G4; Gospel Music Channel; Great American Country; GSN; Halogen Network; History Channel International; ID Investigation Discovery; Independent Film Channel; Lifetime Movie Network; Lime; MTV Hits; MTV Jams; MTV Tres; MTV2; Music Choice; Nick Jr.; Nick Too; NickToons TV; Outdoor Channel; Science Channel; SoapNet; Style Network; TeenNick; The Word Network; Toon Disney; VH1 Classic; VH1 Soul.
Fee: $12.75 monthly.

Digital Expanded Basic Service
Subscribers: N.A.
Programming (via satellite): Cine Latino; CNN en Espanol; Discovery en Espanol; ESPN Deportes; Fox Sports en Espanol; History Channel en Espanol.

Digital Expanded Basic Service 2
Subscribers: N.A.
Programming (via satellite): Arts & Entertainment HD; Discovery Channel HD; ESPN 2 HD; ESPN HD; HDNet; HDNet Movies; NFL Network HD; Universal HD.

Digital Pay Service 1
Pay Units: N.A.
Programming (via satellite): Cinemax; Cinemax HD; Flix; Fox Movie Channel; HBO (multiplexed); HBO HD; Showtime (multiplexed); Showtime; Showtime HD; Starz (multiplexed); Starz HDTV; Sundance Channel; The Movie Channel (multiplexed).
Fee: $11.75 monthly (each).

Video-On-Demand: No

Pay-Per-View
iN DEMAND (delivered digitally).

Internet Service
Operational: No, Both DSL & dial-up.

Telephone Service
None

General Manager: Steve Richards. Manager: Don Newell. Cable TV Manager: Clint Felzien.
Ownership: S & T Communications Inc. (MSO).

GORHAM—Nex-Tech. Now served by EDMOND, KS [KS0450]. ICA: KS0380.

GRAINFIELD—Nex-Tech. Now served by EDMOND, KS [KS0450]. ICA: KS0381.

GRANTVILLE—SCI Cable, PO Box 67235, 6700 SW Topeka Blvd, Topeka, KS 66619-0241. Phone: 785-862-1950. Fax: 785-862-2423. E-mail: scicable@sbcglobal.net. Also serves Meriden (portions). ICA: KS0224.
TV Market Ranking: Below 100 (GRANTVILLE, Meriden (portions)). Franchise award date: January 1, 1988. Franchise expiration date: N.A. Began: January 1, 1990.
Channel capacity: 40 (not 2-way capable). Channels available but not in use: N.A.

Basic Service
Subscribers: 160.
Programming (received off-air): KCTV (CBS) Kansas City; KMBC-TV (ABC) Kansas City; KSHB-TV (NBC) Kansas City; KSNT (FOX, NBC) Topeka; KTKA-TV (ABC, CW) Topeka; KTMJ-CA Topeka; KTWU (PBS) Topeka; WDAF-TV (FOX) Kansas City; WIBW-TV (CBS, MNT) Topeka.
Programming (via satellite): ABC Family Channel; AMC; Animal Planet; Arts & Entertainment; CNBC; CNN; Comedy Central; Country Music TV; Discovery Channel; Disney Channel; E! Entertainment Television; ESPN; ESPN 2; Food Network; Fox News Channel; Fox Sports Net; FX; Headline News; HGTV; History Channel; Lifetime; MTV; Nickelodeon; Speed Channel; Spike TV; Syfy; TBS Superstation; The Learning Channel; Travel Channel; Trinity Broadcasting Network; Turner Network TV; TV Land; USA Network; Versus; VH1; Weather Channel; WGN America.
Fee: $35.00 installation; $20.95 monthly.

Pay Service 1
Pay Units: N.A.
Programming (via satellite): Cinemax; HBO (multiplexed).
Fee: $10.95 monthly (HBO).

Internet Service
Operational: Yes.

Telephone Service
None

Miles of Plant: 21.0 (coaxial); 1.0 (fiber optic). Homes passed: 215.
Manager: Kirt Keberlein.
Ownership: SCI Cable Inc. (MSO).

GREAT BEND—Cox Communications, PO Box 3027, 701 E Douglas Ave, Wichita, KS 67202. Phones: 888-566-7751 (Wichita corporate office); 316-858-1730 (Customer service); 316-262-0661 (Customer service); 316-260-7000. Fax: 316-262-2330. Web Site: http://www.cox.com/kansas. Also serves Barton County, Hoisington, Larned, Lyons, Rice County & Sterling. ICA: KS0012.
Note: This system is an overbuild.
TV Market Ranking: 67 (Lyons, Rice County, Sterling); Below 100 (Barton County, GREAT BEND, Hoisington, Larned). Franchise award date: January 18, 1968. Franchise expiration date: N.A. Began: January 18, 1968.
Channel capacity: 120 (operating 2-way). Channels available but not in use: 49.

Basic Service
Subscribers: N.A. Included in Wichita
Programming (received off-air): KAKE-TV (ABC) Wichita; KBSH-DT (CBS) Hays; KOOD (PBS) Hays; KPTS (PBS) Hutchinson; KSAS-TV (FOX) Wichita; KSCW-DT (CW) Wichita; KSNC (NBC) Great Bend; KWCH-DT (CBS) Hutchinson; 12 FMs.
Programming (via satellite): C-SPAN; C-SPAN 2; TV Guide Network; Weather Channel; WGN America.
Current originations: Government Access; Educational Access; Public Access.
Fee: $29.95 installation; $12.49 monthly.

Expanded Basic Service 1
Subscribers: N.A.
Programming (via satellite): ABC Family Channel; AMC; Animal Planet; Arts & Entertainment; BET Networks; Cartoon Network; CNBC; CNN; Comedy Central; Country Music TV; Discovery Channel; Disney Channel; E! Entertainment Television; ESPN; ESPN 2; Eternal Word TV Network; FitTV; Food Network; Fox News Channel; Fox Sports Net Midwest; FX; Hallmark Channel; Headline News; HGTV; History Channel; Home Shopping Network; INSP; ION Television; Lifetime; MSNBC; MTV; Nickelodeon; QVC; ShopNBC; Speed Channel; Spike TV; Syfy; TBS Superstation; The Learning Channel; Travel Channel; truTV; Turner Classic Movies; Turner Network TV; TV Land; Univision; USA Network; VH1.
Fee: $33.68 monthly.

Digital Basic Service
Subscribers: N.A.
Programming (via satellite): BBC America; Bio; Bloomberg Television; Canales N; Discovery Digital Networks; DMX Music; ESPN Classic Sports; ESPNews; Fox Sports World; G4; GAS; Golf Channel; Great American Country; GSN; History Channel International; Independent Film Channel; Lifetime Movie Network; MTV Networks Digital Suite; MuchMusic Network; NBA TV; Nick Jr.; Nick Too; Outdoor Channel; Oxygen; SoapNet; Sundance Channel; Toon Disney; Versus.
Fee: $15.00 monthly.

Digital Pay Service 1
Pay Units: N.A.
Programming (via satellite): Cinemax (multiplexed); DMX Music; Encore (multiplexed); HBO (multiplexed); Showtime (multiplexed); Starz (multiplexed).
Fee: $12.95 monthly (each).

Video-On-Demand: No

Pay-Per-View
iN DEMAND (delivered digitally).

Internet Service
Operational: Yes.
Broadband Service: Cox High Speed Internet.
Fee: $19.99-$59.99 monthly; $15.00 modem lease; $259.00 modem purchase.

Telephone Service
Digital: Operational
Fee: 15.95-$48.95 monthly

Miles of Plant: 124.0 (coaxial); 45.0 (fiber optic). Homes passed included in Wichita
Vice President & General Manager: Kimberly Edmonds. Vice President, Engineering: Nick DiPonzio. Vice President, Marketing: Tony Matthews. Marketing Director: Tina Gabbard. Public Affairs Director: Sarah Kauffman.
City fee: 5% of gross.
Ownership: Cox Communications Inc. (MSO).

GREEN—Formerly served by Eagle Communications. No longer in operation. ICA: KS0464.

GREENLEAF—Allegiance Communications, 707 W Saratoga St, Shawnee, OK 74804. Phones: 405-275-6923; 405-395-1131. Web Site: http://www.allegiance.tv. ICA: KS0246.
TV Market Ranking: Outside TV Markets (GREENLEAF). Franchise award date: N.A. Franchise expiration date: N.A. Began: June 1, 1984.
Channel capacity: 40 (not 2-way capable). Channels available but not in use: N.A.

Basic Service
Subscribers: 160.
Programming (received off-air): KLKN (ABC) Lincoln; KOLN (CBS, MNT) Lincoln; KSNT (FOX, NBC) Topeka; KTKA-TV (ABC, CW) Topeka; KTWU (PBS) Topeka; WIBW-TV (CBS, MNT) Topeka.
Programming (via microwave): KSAS-TV (FOX) Wichita.
Programming (via satellite): ABC Family Channel; Animal Planet; Arts & Entertainment; Cartoon Network; CMT Pure Country; CNN; Discovery Channel; Disney Channel; E! Entertainment Television; ESPN; ESPN 2; Fox News Channel; FX; History Channel; MTV; Nickelodeon; Spike TV; TBS Superstation; The Learning Channel; Travel Channel; Turner Network TV; TV Land; USA Network; Weather Channel; WGN America.
Fee: $44.95 installation; $21.95 monthly.

Pay Service 1
Pay Units: 4.
Programming (via satellite): Cinemax.
Fee: $12.95 installation; $11.50 monthly.

Pay Service 2
Pay Units: 5.
Programming (via satellite): HBO.
Fee: $12.95 installation; $11.95 monthly.

Pay-Per-View
iN DEMAND (delivered digitally); Hot Choice (delivered digitally); Playboy TV (delivered digitally); Fresh (delivered digitally); Shorteez (delivered digitally).

Internet Service
Operational: No.

Telephone Service
None

Miles of Plant: 5.0 (coaxial); None (fiber optic). Homes passed: 213. Total homes in franchised area: 213.
Chief Executive Officer: Bill Haggarty. Regional Vice President: Andrew Dearth. Vice President, Marketing: Tracy Bass.
Ownership: Allegiance Communications (MSO).

GYPSUM—Home Telephone Co., PO Box 8, 211 S Main, Galva, KS 67443. Phones: 620-654-3673; 800-362-9336; 620-654-3381. Fax: 620-654-3122. E-mail: hciservice@homecomminc.com. Web Site: http://www.hometelephone.com. ICA: KS0383.
TV Market Ranking: Below 100 (GYPSUM). Franchise award date: N.A. Franchise expiration date: N.A. Began: N.A.
Channel capacity: 36 (operating 2-way). Channels available but not in use: 19.

Basic Service
Subscribers: 99.
Programming (received off-air): KAKE-TV (ABC) Wichita; KPTS (PBS) Hutchinson; KSNW (NBC) Wichita; KWCH-DT (CBS) Hutchinson.
Programming (via satellite): ESPN; WGN America.
Fee: $9.95 installation; $26.95 monthly.

Pay Service 1
Pay Units: 19.
Programming (via satellite): HBO; Showtime.
Fee: $9.95 installation; $7.95 monthly (Showtime), $10.00 monthly (HBO).

Video-On-Demand: No

Internet Service
Operational: No, DSL & dial-up.

Telephone Service
None

President: Carla Baldwin Shearer. Operations Manager: Brian Williams. Chief Technology Officer: Richard Baldwin. Customer Service Manager: Tina Anderson.
Ownership: Galva Cable Co. Inc. (MSO).

HADDAM—Formerly served by Westcom. No longer in operation. ICA: KS0303.

HAMILTON—Mediacom. Now served by EUREKA, KS [KS0058]. ICA: KS0273.

HANOVER—Blue Valley Tele-Communications, 1559 Pony Express Hwy, Home, KS 66438. Phones: 877-876-1228; 785-799-3311.

E-mail: info@bluevalley.net. Web Site: http://www.bluevalley.net. ICA: KS0179.
TV Market Ranking: Outside TV Markets (HANOVER). Franchise award date: June 9, 1980. Franchise expiration date: N.A. Began: May 1, 1982.
Channel capacity: 35 (not 2-way capable). Channels available but not in use: N.A.

Basic Service
Subscribers: 245.
Programming (received off-air): KLKN (ABC) Lincoln; KOLN (CBS, MNT) Lincoln; KSNT (FOX, NBC) Topeka; KUON-TV (PBS) Lincoln; WIBW-TV (CBS, MNT) Topeka.
Programming (via satellite): ABC Family Channel; Animal Planet; Arts & Entertainment; Cartoon Network; CNN; Discovery Channel; Disney Channel; E! Entertainment Television; ESPN; Fox News Channel; FX; History Channel; Nickelodeon; Spike TV; TBS Superstation; The Learning Channel; Travel Channel; Turner Network TV; TV Land; USA Network; Weather Channel; WGN America.
Fee: $37.50 installation; $22.63 monthly.

Pay Service 1
Pay Units: 17.
Programming (via satellite): Cinemax.
Fee: $12.50 installation; $11.50 monthly.

Pay Service 2
Pay Units: 22.
Programming (via satellite): HBO.
Fee: $12.50 installation; $11.95 monthly.

Video-On-Demand: No

Pay-Per-View
iN DEMAND (delivered digitally); Hot Choice (delivered digitally); Playboy TV (delivered digitally); Fresh (delivered digitally); Shorteez (delivered digitally).

Internet Service
Operational: Yes.

Telephone Service
None

Miles of Plant: 7.0 (coaxial); None (fiber optic). Homes passed: 391. Total homes in franchised area: 391.
General Manager: Dennis Doyle. Operations Manager: Andy Torrey. Marketing Manager: Angie Armstrong. Customer Service Supervisor: Deb Runnebaum.
City fee: 0.5% of basic.
Ownership: Blue Valley Telecommunications (MSO).

HANSTON—United Communications Assn. Inc. Now served by CIMARRON, KS [KS0126]. ICA: KS0291.

HARPER—Allegiance Communications, 707 W Saratoga St, Shawnee, OK 74804. Phones: 405-395-1131; 405-275-6923. Web Site: http://www.allegiance.tv. ICA: KS0121.
TV Market Ranking: Outside TV Markets (HARPER). Franchise award date: N.A. Franchise expiration date: N.A. Began: July 1, 1982.
Channel capacity: 34 (operating 2-way). Channels available but not in use: N.A.

Basic Service
Subscribers: 405.
Programming (received off-air): KAKE-TV (ABC) Wichita; KPTS (PBS) Hutchinson; KSAS-TV (FOX) Wichita; KSNW (NBC) Wichita; KWCH-DT (CBS) Hutchinson.
Programming (via satellite): ABC Family Channel; AMC; Arts & Entertainment; Cartoon Network; CNN; Comedy Central; Country Music TV; C-SPAN; CW+; Discovery Channel; Disney Channel; ESPN; ESPN 2; Headline News; HGTV; Lifetime; MTV; Nickelodeon; Spike TV; Syfy; TBS Superstation; Turner Network TV; TV Land; USA Network; Weather Channel; WGN America.
Fee: $29.95 installation; $32.95 monthly.

Pay Service 1
Pay Units: 109.
Programming (via satellite): Encore.
Fee: $8.95 monthly.

Pay Service 2
Pay Units: 101.
Programming (via satellite): HBO.
Fee: $8.95 monthly.

Pay Service 3
Pay Units: 89.
Programming (via satellite): Showtime.
Fee: $8.95 monthly.

Video-On-Demand: No

Internet Service
Operational: No.

Telephone Service
None

Miles of Plant: 12.0 (coaxial); None (fiber optic). Homes passed: 797. Total homes in franchised area: 797.
Chief Executive Officer: Bill Haggarty. Regional Vice President: Andrew Dearth. Vice President, Marketing: Tracy Bass.
City fee: 5% of gross.
Ownership: Allegiance Communications (MSO).

HARTFORD—Galaxy Cablevision, 1928 S Lincoln Ave, Ste 200, York, NE 68467. Phone: 402-362-3332. Fax: 402-362-4890. Web Site: http://www.galaxycable.com. ICA: KS0245.
TV Market Ranking: Outside TV Markets (HARTFORD). Franchise award date: April 1, 1982. Franchise expiration date: N.A. Began: N.A.
Channel capacity: 31 (not 2-way capable). Channels available but not in use: 7.

Basic Service
Subscribers: 30.
Programming (received off-air): KSNT (FOX, NBC) Topeka; KTKA-TV (ABC, CW) Topeka; KTWU (PBS) Topeka; WIBW-TV (CBS, MNT) Topeka.
Programming (via satellite): ABC Family Channel; Arts & Entertainment; CNN; Discovery Channel; Disney Channel; ESPN; ESPN 2; Headline News; HGTV; Lifetime; Outdoor Channel; TBS Superstation; Toon Disney; Turner Classic Movies; Turner Network TV; USA Network; WGN America.
Fee: $35.30 monthly.

Pay Service 1
Pay Units: N.A.
Programming (via satellite): Cinemax; HBO.
Fee: $11.00 monthly (each).

Internet Service
Operational: No.

Telephone Service
None

Miles of Plant: 6.0 (coaxial); None (fiber optic). Homes passed: 221.
State Manager: Cheyenne Wohlford. Technical Manager: John Davidshofer. Sales Manager: Mike Thomas. Customer Service Manager: Michael Debermardin.
City fee: 3% of basic gross.
Ownership: Galaxy Cable Inc. (MSO).

HARVEYVILLE—Formerly served by Galaxy Cablevision. No longer in operation. ICA: KS0297.

HAVEN—Allegiance Communications, 707 W Saratoga St, Shawnee, OK 74804. Phones: 405-395-1131; 405-275-6923. Web Site: http://www.allegiance.tv. ICA: KS0163.
TV Market Ranking: 67 (HAVEN). Franchise award date: N.A. Franchise expiration date: N.A. Began: July 1, 1982.
Channel capacity: 32 (not 2-way capable). Channels available but not in use: N.A.

Basic Service
Subscribers: 240.
Programming (received off-air): KAKE-TV (ABC) Wichita; KMTW (MNT) Hutchinson; KPTS (PBS) Hutchinson; KSAS-TV (FOX) Wichita; KSNW (NBC) Wichita; KWCH-DT (CBS) Hutchinson.
Programming (via satellite): ABC Family Channel; AMC; Arts & Entertainment; CNN; Country Music TV; C-SPAN; CW+; Discovery Channel; Disney Channel; ESPN; ESPN 2; Lifetime; MTV; Nickelodeon; Spike TV; TBS Superstation; The Learning Channel; Turner Network TV; TV Land; USA Network; Weather Channel; WGN America.
Current originations: Public Access.
Fee: $29.95 installation; $31.00 monthly.

Pay Service 1
Pay Units: 65.
Programming (via satellite): Encore.
Fee: $14.95 monthly.

Pay Service 2
Pay Units: 57.
Programming (via satellite): HBO.
Fee: $14.95 monthly.

Pay Service 3
Pay Units: 49.
Programming (via satellite): Showtime.
Fee: $14.95 monthly.

Video-On-Demand: No

Internet Service
Operational: No.

Telephone Service
None

Miles of Plant: 6.0 (coaxial); None (fiber optic). Homes passed: 539. Total homes in franchised area: 539.
Chief Executive Officer: Bill Haggarty. Regional Vice President: Andrew Dearth. Vice President, Marketing: Tracy Bass.
City fee: 3% of gross.
Ownership: Allegiance Communications (MSO).

HAVENSVILLE—Blue Valley Telecommunications. Formerly served by Onaga, KS [KS0407]. This cable system has converted to IPTV, 1557 Pony Express Hwy, Home, KS 66438. E-mail: info@bluevalley.net. Web Site: http://www.bluevalley.net. ICA: KS5058.
TV Market Ranking: Outside TV Markets (HAVENSVILLE).
Channel capacity: N.A. Channels available but not in use: N.A.

Internet Service
Operational: Yes.

Telephone Service
Digital: Operational

General Manager: Dennis Doyle.
Ownership: Blue Valley Telecommunications.

HAVENSVILLE—Rainbow Communications, PO Box 147, Everest, KS 66424. Phones: 785-866-2390; 800-892-0163. Fax: 785-548-7517. Web Site: http://www.rainbowtel.net. ICA: KS0465.
TV Market Ranking: Outside TV Markets (HAVENSVILLE). Franchise award date: June 27, 1989. Franchise expiration date: N.A. Began: N.A.
Channel capacity: 36 (not 2-way capable). Channels available but not in use: 30.

Basic Service
Subscribers: 7.
Programming (received off-air): KSNT (FOX, NBC) Topeka; KTKA-TV (ABC, CW) Topeka; KTWU (PBS) Topeka; WIBW-TV (CBS, MNT) Topeka.
Programming (via satellite): Weather Channel.

Internet Service
Operational: No.

Telephone Service
None

Miles of Plant: 2.0 (coaxial); None (fiber optic). Homes passed: 86.
General Manager: James Lednicky. Network Engineer: Scott Wheeler. Plant Manager: Jim Streeter. Marketing Manager: Jackie Petersen.
Ownership: Rainbow Communications (MSO).

HAVILAND—Haviland Cable-Vision, PO Box 308, 104 N Main St, Haviland, KS 67059-0308. Phones: 800-339-8052; 620-862-5211. Fax: 620-862-5204. E-mail: steve@havilandtelco.com. Web Site: http://www.havilandtelco.com. ICA: KS0235.
TV Market Ranking: Outside TV Markets (HAVILAND). Franchise award date: N.A. Franchise expiration date: N.A. Began: April 1, 1975.
Channel capacity: 43 (operating 2-way). Channels available but not in use: N.A.

Basic Service
Subscribers: 183.
Programming (received off-air): KAKE-TV (ABC) Wichita; KPTS (PBS) Hutchinson; KSAS-TV (FOX) Wichita; KSNC (NBC) Great Bend; KWCH-DT (CBS) Hutchinson; allband FM.
Programming (via satellite): ABC Family Channel; CNN; Discovery Channel; Disney Channel; ESPN; Hallmark Channel; Local Cable Weather; Nickelodeon; Spike TV; Syfy; TBS Superstation; The Learning Channel; Travel Channel; Turner Network TV; TV Land; USA Network.
Fee: $10.00 installation; $18.00 monthly.

Video-On-Demand: No

Internet Service
Operational: No, DSL.

Telephone Service
None

Miles of Plant: 6.0 (coaxial); None (fiber optic). Homes passed: 224.
President: Gene Morris. General Manager: Mark Wade. Chief Technician: Dan King.
City fee: 1% of gross.
Ownership: Haviland Telephone Co.

HAYS—Eagle Communications, PO Box 817, 2703 Hall St, Ste 13, Hays, KS 67601. Phones: 785-625-4000 (Corporate office); 785-625-5910. Fax: 785-625-3465. E-mail: gary.shorman@eaglecom.net. Web Site: http://www.eaglecom.net. Also serves Ellis. ICA: KS0384.
TV Market Ranking: Below 100 (Ellis, HAYS). Franchise award date: February 1, 1967. Franchise expiration date: N.A. Began: February 1, 1967.
Channel capacity: 65 (operating 2-way). Channels available but not in use: 5.

Basic Service
Subscribers: 6,908.
Programming (received off-air): KAKE-TV (ABC) Wichita; KBSH-DT (CBS) Hays; KMTW (MNT) Hutchinson; KOOD (PBS) Hays; KSAS-TV (FOX) Wichita; KSCW-DT (CW) Wichita; KSNC (NBC) Great Bend; 11 FMs.
Programming (via satellite): C-SPAN; Home Shopping Network; QVC; TV Guide Network; Weather Channel; WGN America.

Current originations: Public Access; Government Access; Educational Access.
Fee: $24.95 installation; $14.95 monthly.

Expanded Basic Service 1
Subscribers: 6,556.
Programming (via satellite): ABC Family Channel; AMC; Animal Planet; Arts & Entertainment; Boomerang; Bravo; Cartoon Network; CNBC; CNN; Comedy Central; Country Music TV; Discovery Channel; Disney Channel; Do-It-Yourself; E! Entertainment Television; ESPN; ESPN 2; ESPN Classic Sports; ESPNews; Eternal Word TV Network; FitTV; Food Network; Fox Movie Channel; Fox News Channel; Fox Sports Net Midwest; FX; Hallmark Channel; Headline News; HGTV; History Channel; Lifetime; MSNBC; MTV; National Geographic Channel; NFL Network; Nickelodeon; Spike TV; Syfy; TBS Superstation; The Learning Channel; The Sportsman Channel; Toon Disney; Travel Channel; truTV; Turner Network TV; TV Land; USA Network; VH1.
Fee: $30.00 monthly.

Digital Basic Service
Subscribers: 621.
Programming (received off-air): KAKE-TV (ABC) Wichita; KMTW (MNT) Hutchinson; KOOD (PBS) Hays; KSAS-TV (FOX) Wichita; KSNC (NBC) Great Bend (multiplexed).
Programming (via satellite): AmericanLife TV Network; BBC America; Bio; Bloomberg Television; Bravo; Church Channel; CMT Pure Country; Cooking Channel; Current; Discovery Health Channel; Discovery Kids Channel; Discovery Military Channel; Discovery Planet Green; DMX Music; ESPN 2; ESPN Classic Sports; ESPN U; ESPNews; Fox Business Channel; Fox College Sports Atlantic; Fox College Sports Central; Fox College Sports Pacific; Fox Movie Channel; Fox Soccer; Fuse; G4; Golf Channel; Gospel Music Channel; Great American Country; GSN; Halogen Network; HGTV; History Channel; History Channel International; ID Investigation Discovery; Independent Film Channel; JCTV; Lifetime Movie Network; MTV Hits; MTV Jams; MTV2; National Geographic Channel; Nick Jr.; NickToons TV; Outdoor Channel; PBS Kids Sprout; RFD-TV; Science Channel; Sleuth; SoapNet; Speed Channel; Style Network; Syfy; TeenNick; The Sportsman Channel; The Word Network; Toon Disney; Trinity Broadcasting Network; Turner Classic Movies; Versus; VH1 Classic; VH1 Soul; WE tv.
Fee: $3.95 monthly (Sports, Variety or Entertainment package), $5.95 monthly (Basic).

Digital Expanded Basic Service
Subscribers: N.A.
Programming (via satellite): Animal Planet HD; Arts & Entertainment HD; Discovery Channel HD; Discovery HD Theater; ESPN HD; Food Network HD; HGTV HD; History Channel HD; National Geographic Channel HD Network; NFL Network HD; Science Channel HD; TBS in HD; TLC HD; Turner Network TV HD; Universal HD.
Fee: $9.95 monthly.

Pay Service 1
Pay Units: 360.
Programming (via satellite): Cinemax.
Fee: $11.95 monthly.

Pay Service 2
Pay Units: 746.
Programming (via satellite): HBO.
Fee: $11.95 monthly.

Digital Pay Service 1
Pay Units: N.A.
Programming (via satellite): Cinemax; Cinemax HD; Encore (multiplexed); HBO (multiplexed); HBO HD; Showtime (multiplexed); Showtime HD; Starz (multiplexed); Starz HDTV; The Movie Channel (multiplexed); The Movie Channel HD.
Fee: $11.95 monthly (HBO, Cinemax, Starz/Encore or Showtime/TMC/Flix).

Video-On-Demand: No

Pay-Per-View
iN DEMAND (delivered digitally); Playboy TV (delivered digitally); Fresh (delivered digitally); Hot Choice (delivered digitally); Club Jenna (delivered digitally); Spice: Xcess (delivered digitally).

Internet Service
Operational: Yes.
Subscribers: 3,036.
Broadband Service: Eagle Internet.
Fee: $19.95 monthly.

Telephone Service
Analog: Not Operational
Digital: Operational
Fee: $16.00 monthly

Miles of Plant: 110.0 (coaxial); 9.0 (fiber optic). Homes passed: 10,459. Total homes in franchised area: 10,975.
President: Gary Shorman. General Manager: Rex Skiles. Chief Technician: Les Libal.
City fee: 2% of basic gross; 5% of premium.
Ownership: Eagle Communications Inc. (KS) (MSO).

HEALY—S&T Cable, PO Box 99, 320 Kansas Ave, Brewster, KS 67732-0099. Phones: 800-432-8294 (Brewster office); 785-694-2256. Fax: 785-694-2750. Web Site: http://www.sttelcom.com. ICA: KS0385.
TV Market Ranking: Outside TV Markets (HEALY). Franchise award date: N.A. Franchise expiration date: N.A. Began: January 1, 1988.
Channel capacity: N.A. Channels available but not in use: N.A.

Basic Service
Subscribers: 52.
Programming (received off-air): KBSD-DT (CBS) Ensign; KSAS-TV (FOX) Wichita; KSCW-DT (CW) Wichita; KSNG (NBC) Garden City; KSWK (PBS) Lakin; KUPK-TV (ABC) Garden City; KUSA (NBC) Denver.
Programming (via satellite): QVC.
Current originations: Educational Access; Public Access.
Fee: $20.00 installation; $13.00 monthly.

Expanded Basic Service 1
Subscribers: 43.
Programming (via satellite): ABC Family Channel; AMC; Animal Planet; Arts & Entertainment; Bravo; Cartoon Network; CNBC; CNN; Comedy Central; Country Music TV; C-SPAN; C-SPAN 2; Daystar TV Network; Discovery Channel; Discovery Kids Channel; Disney Channel; Do-It-Yourself; E! Entertainment Television; ESPN; ESPN 2; ESPN Classic Sports; Eternal Word TV Network; Food Network; Fox News Channel; Fox Sports Net; FX; Golf Channel; Hallmark Channel; Headline News; HGTV; History Channel; Home Shopping Network; KWGN-TV (CW) Denver; Lifetime; MSNBC; MTV; National Geographic Channel; NFL Network; Nickelodeon; Oxygen; RFD-TV; Speed Channel; Spike TV; Syfy; TBS Superstation; The Learning Channel; The Sportsman Channel; Travel Channel; Trinity Broadcasting Network; truTV; Turner Classic Movies; Turner Network TV; TV Guide Network; TV Land; Univision; USA Network; Versus; VH1; WE tv; Weather Channel; WGN America.
Fee: $21.95 monthly.

Digital Basic Service
Subscribers: N.A.
Programming (received off-air): KAKE-TV (ABC) Wichita; KMTW (MNT) Hutchinson; KOOD (PBS) Hays; KSAS-TV (FOX) Wichita; KSNG (NBC) Garden City; KWCH-DT (CBS) Hutchinson.
Programming (via satellite): AmericanLife TV Network; BBC America; Bio; Bloomberg Television; CMT Pure Country; Discovery Health Channel; Discovery Kids Channel; Discovery Military Channel; Discovery Planet Green; Encore (multiplexed); ESPN U; ESPNews; FitTV; FSN Digital Atlantic; FSN Digital Central; FSN Digital Pacific; Fuse; G4; Gospel Music Channel; Great American Country; GSN; Halogen Network; History Channel International; ID Investigation Discovery; Independent Film Channel; Lifetime Movie Network; Lime; MTV Hits; MTV Jams; MTV Tres; MTV2; Music Choice; Nick Jr.; Nick Too; NickToons TV; Outdoor Channel; Science Channel; SoapNet; Style Network; TeenNick; The Word Network; Toon Disney; VH1 Classic; VH1 Soul.
Fee: $17.95 monthly.

Digital Expanded Basic Service
Subscribers: N.A.
Programming (via satellite): Cine Latino; CNN en Espanol; Discovery en Espanol; ESPN Deportes; Fox Sports en Espanol; History Channel en Espanol.
Fee: $15.95 monthly.

Digital Pay Service 1
Pay Units: N.A.
Programming (via satellite): Cinemax (multiplexed); Flix (multiplexed); Fox Movie Channel; HBO (multiplexed); Showtime (multiplexed); Starz (multiplexed); Sundance Channel (multiplexed); The Movie Channel (multiplexed).
Fee: $11.75 monthly (each).

Video-On-Demand: No

Pay-Per-View
iN DEMAND (delivered digitally).

Internet Service
Operational: No, Both DSL & dial-up.

Telephone Service
None

Miles of Plant: 2.0 (coaxial); None (fiber optic).
Manager: Steve Richards. Technician: Ken Schroller. Cable TV Manager: Clint Felzien. Chief Technician: Craig Grantz.
Ownership: S & T Communications Inc. (MSO).

HERINGTON—Allegiance Communications, 707 W Saratoga St, Shawnee, OK 74804. Phones: 405-395-1131; 405-275-6923. Web Site: http://www.allegiance.tv. Also serves Dickinson County. ICA: KS0054.
TV Market Ranking: Below 100 (Dickinson County (portions)); Outside TV Markets (Dickinson County (portions), HERINGTON). Franchise award date: May 14, 1968. Franchise expiration date: N.A. Began: April 1, 1969.
Channel capacity: 48 (operating 2-way). Channels available but not in use: N.A.

Basic Service
Subscribers: 1,013.
Programming (received off-air): KAKE-TV (ABC) Wichita; KPTS (PBS) Hutchinson; KSAS-TV (FOX) Wichita; KSNW (NBC) Wichita; KTKA-TV (ABC, CW) Topeka; KWCH-DT (CBS) Hutchinson; WIBW-TV (CBS, MNT) Topeka; 7 FMs.
Programming (via satellite): ABC Family Channel; AMC; Animal Planet; Arts & Entertainment; Cartoon Network; CMT Pure Country; CNN; Comedy Central; C-SPAN; CW+; Discovery Channel; Disney Channel; ESPN; ESPN 2; ESPN Classic Sports; Food Network; Fox News Channel; Fox Sports Net Midwest; Hallmark Channel; Headline News; HGTV; History Channel; Home Shopping Network; Lifetime; Lifetime Movie Network; MTV; NFL Network; Nickelodeon; Spike TV; Syfy; TBS Superstation; The Learning Channel; Travel Channel; Turner Network TV; TV Land; USA Network; Weather Channel; WGN America.
Fee: $29.95 installation; $39.95 monthly.

Digital Basic Service
Subscribers: N.A.
Programming (via satellite): AmericanLife TV Network; BBC America; Bio; Black Family Channel; Bloomberg Television; Bravo; Canal 52MX; Cine Latino; Cine Mexicano; CMT Pure Country; CNN en Espanol; Current; Discovery en Espanol; Discovery Health Channel; Discovery Home Channel; Discovery Kids Channel; Discovery Military Channel; Discovery Times Channel; DMX Music; Encore (multiplexed); ESPN 2; ESPN Classic Sports; ESPNews; FitTV; Flix; Fox College Sports Atlantic; Fox College Sports Central; Fox College Sports Pacific; Fox Movie Channel; Fox Soccer; Fox Sports en Espanol; Fuse; G4; GAS; Golf Channel; Great American Country; GSN; Halogen Network; HGTV; History Channel; History Channel en Espanol; History Channel International; Independent Film Channel; Lifetime Movie Network; MTV Hits; MTV Networks Digital Suite; MTV Tres; MTV2; National Geographic Channel; Nick Jr.; NickToons TV; Outdoor Channel; Ovation; Science Channel; ShopNBC; Sleuth; Speed Channel; Style Network; Sundance Channel; Syfy; The Word Network; Toon Disney; Toon Disney en Espanol; Trinity Broadcasting Network; Turner Classic Movies; Versus; VH1 Classic; VH1 Soul; WE tv.

Pay Service 1
Pay Units: 171.
Programming (via satellite): Cinemax.
Fee: $14.95 installation; $8.95 monthly.

Pay Service 2
Pay Units: 219.
Programming (via satellite): HBO.
Fee: $14.95 installation; $8.95 monthly.

Digital Pay Service 1
Pay Units: N.A.
Programming (via satellite): Cinemax (multiplexed); HBO (multiplexed); Showtime (multiplexed); Starz (multiplexed); The Movie Channel (multiplexed).

Video-On-Demand: No

Pay-Per-View
iN DEMAND (delivered digitally); Hot Choice (delivered digitally); Playboy TV (delivered digitally); Fresh (delivered digitally); Shorteez (delivered digitally).

Internet Service
Operational: Yes.
Broadband Service: Cox High Speed Internet.
Fee: $24.95 installation; $39.95 monthly.
Telephone Service
None
Miles of Plant: 21.0 (coaxial); None (fiber optic). Homes passed: 1,633. Total homes in franchised area: 1,633.
Chief Executive Officer: Bill Haggarty. Regional Vice President: Andrew Dearth. Vice President, Marketing: Tracy Bass.
City fee: 3% of gross.
Ownership: Allegiance Communications (MSO).

HERNDON—Formerly served by Pinpoint Cable TV. No longer in operation. ICA: KS0304.

HIAWATHA—Rainbow Communications, 628 Oregon St, Hiawatha, KS 66434. Phones: 800-892-0163; 785-742-8200. Fax: 785-742-2628. Web Site: http://www.rainbowtel.net. Also serves Elwood, Everest, Fairview, Highland, Horton, Robinson, Sabetha, Seneca, Troy & Wathena. ICA: KS0059.
TV Market Ranking: Below 100 (Elwood, Everest, Highland, Robinson, Troy, Wathena); Outside TV Markets (Fairview, HIAWATHA, Horton, Sabetha, Seneca). Franchise award date: January 1, 1965. Franchise expiration date: N.A. Began: November 1, 1966.
Channel capacity: N.A. Channels available but not in use: N.A.
Basic Service
Subscribers: 2,922.
Programming (received off-air): KCPT (PBS) Kansas City; KCTV (CBS) Kansas City; KMBC-TV (ABC) Kansas City; KPXE-TV (ION) Kansas City; KQTV (ABC) St. Joseph; KSHB-TV (NBC) Kansas City; KSNT (FOX, NBC) Topeka; KTKA-TV (ABC, CW) Topeka; KTWU (PBS) Topeka; WDAF-TV (FOX) Kansas City; WIBW-TV (CBS, MNT) Topeka; allband FM.
Programming (via satellite): Home Shopping Network; QVC; Weather Channel.
Fee: $18.75 monthly.
Expanded Basic Service 1
Subscribers: 2,656.
Programming (via satellite): ABC Family Channel; AMC; Animal Planet; Arts & Entertainment; CNN; Comedy Central; C-SPAN; Discovery Channel; Disney Channel; ESPN; ESPN 2; Food Network; Fox Sports Net; Great American Country; Headline News; HGTV; History Channel; Lifetime; MTV; Nickelodeon; Spike TV; Syfy; TBS Superstation; The Learning Channel; Trinity Broadcasting Network; Turner Network TV; USA Network; VH1; WGN America.
Fee: $13.20 monthly.
Digital Basic Service
Subscribers: 471.
Programming (via satellite): AmericanLife TV Network; BBC America; Bio; Bloomberg Television; Discovery Digital Networks; DMX Music; ESPN Classic Sports; ESPNews; Fox Movie Channel; GAS; Golf Channel; GSN; History Channel; Lifetime Movie Network; National Geographic Channel; Nick Jr.; Outdoor Channel; Speed Channel; WE tv.
Pay Service 1
Pay Units: 287.
Programming (via satellite): HBO.
Fee: $11.95 monthly.
Pay Service 2
Pay Units: 168.
Programming (via satellite): The Movie Channel.
Fee: $8.95 monthly.
Pay Service 3
Pay Units: 245.
Programming (via satellite): Showtime.
Fee: $8.95 monthly.
Pay Service 4
Pay Units: 70.
Programming (via satellite): Cinemax.
Fee: $9.95 monthly.
Digital Pay Service 1
Pay Units: 52.
Programming (via satellite): Cinemax (multiplexed); Encore (multiplexed); HBO (multiplexed); Showtime (multiplexed); Starz (multiplexed); The Movie Channel (multiplexed).
Video-On-Demand: No
Pay-Per-View
Addressable homes: 471.
ESPN Extra (delivered digitally); ESPN Now (delivered digitally); Hot Choice (delivered digitally); iN DEMAND (delivered digitally); Playboy TV (delivered digitally); Fresh (delivered digitally); sports (delivered digitally).
Internet Service
Operational: Yes.
Subscribers: 143.
Broadband Service: Lighting Jack High Speed.
Fee: $39.95 monthly.
Telephone Service
Analog: Operational
Digital: Operational
Miles of Plant: 74.0 (coaxial); 2.0 (fiber optic). Homes passed: 4,891.
General Manager: James Lednicky. Assistant Manager: Jason Smith. Plant Manager: Jim Streeter. Marketing Manager: Jackie Petersen.
Franchise fee: 5% of gross.
Ownership: Rainbow Communications (MSO).

HILL CITY—Nex-Tech. Now served by EDMOND, KS [KS0450]. ICA: KS0447.

HOLTON—Giant Communications, 418 W 5th St, Ste C, Holton, KS 66436-1506. Phones: 800-346-9084; 785-364-9331. Fax: 785-866-2144. E-mail: billbarton@giantcomm.net. Web Site: http://www.giantcomm.net. Also serves Circleville. ICA: KS0066.
TV Market Ranking: Below 100 (Circleville, HOLTON). Franchise award date: N.A. Franchise expiration date: N.A. Began: May 15, 1979.
Channel capacity: 40 (operating 2-way). Channels available but not in use: 8.
Basic Service
Subscribers: 977.
Programming (received off-air): KCWE (CW) Kansas City; KSNT (FOX, NBC) Topeka; KTKA-TV (ABC, CW) Topeka; KTMJ-CA Topeka; KTWU (PBS) Topeka; WDAF-TV (FOX) Kansas City; WIBW-TV (CBS, MNT) Topeka.
Programming (via satellite): ABC Family Channel; AMC; Animal Planet; Arts & Entertainment; CNN; Comedy Central; Country Music TV; Discovery Channel; Disney Channel; Do-It-Yourself; ESPN 2; ESPN Classic Sports; Eternal Word TV Network; Food Network; Fox News Channel; Fox Sports Net Midwest; Great American Country; Hallmark Channel; Headline News; HGTV; History Channel; Home Shopping Network; Lifetime; MSNBC; MTV; National Geographic Channel; Nickelodeon; Speed Channel; Spike TV; Syfy; TBS Superstation; The Learning Channel; Toon Disney; Travel Channel; Trinity Broadcasting Network; truTV; Turner Classic Movies; Turner Network TV; TV Land; USA Network; VH1; Weather Channel; WGN America.
Fee: $40.00 installation; $35.95 monthly; $4.00 converter.
Digital Basic Service
Subscribers: N.A.
Programming (via satellite): BBC America; Bio; Bloomberg Television; Discovery Digital Networks; DMX Music; ESPN Classic Sports; ESPNews; FitTV; Fox Movie Channel; Fox Soccer; Fuse; G4; GAS; Golf Channel; GSN; Halogen Network; History Channel International; Independent Film Channel; MTV Networks Digital Suite; National Geographic Channel; Nick Jr.; NickToons TV; Style Network; Syfy; Turner Classic Movies; Versus; WE tv.
Fee: $14.00 monthly.
Pay Service 1
Pay Units: 11.
Programming (via satellite): Cinemax.
Fee: $8.95 monthly.
Pay Service 2
Pay Units: 103.
Programming (via satellite): HBO.
Fee: $11.95 monthly.
Pay Service 3
Pay Units: 151.
Programming (via satellite): Showtime.
Fee: $11.95 monthly.
Pay Service 4
Pay Units: 135.
Programming (via satellite): The Movie Channel.
Fee: $11.95 monthly.
Digital Pay Service 1
Pay Units: N.A.
Programming (via satellite): Cinemax (multiplexed); Encore (multiplexed); HBO (multiplexed); Showtime (multiplexed); Starz (multiplexed); The Movie Channel (multiplexed).
Video-On-Demand: No
Pay-Per-View
Addressable homes: 17.
Movies (delivered digitally), Fee: $3.99-$100.00, Addressable: Yes; special events (delivered digitally).
Internet Service
Operational: Yes, Dial-up only.
Broadband Service: WildBlue Satellite Internet.
Fee: $39.95 monthly.
Telephone Service
None
Miles of Plant: 22.0 (coaxial); None (fiber optic). Homes passed: 1,324.
Manager: Bill Barton. Headend Technician: Jay Stewart.; Julian Rodriguez.
City fee: 1% of gross.
Ownership: Giant Communications (MSO).

HOLYROOD—H & B Cable Service Inc., PO Box 108, 108 N Main, Holyrood, KS 67450. Phones: 800-432-8296; 785-252-4000. Fax: 785-252-3229. E-mail: commentsquestions@hbcomm.net. Web Site: http://www.hbcomm.net. Also serves Bushton, Chase, Claflin, Dorrance, Little River & Lorraine. ICA: KS0097.
TV Market Ranking: 67 (Chase, HOLYROOD, Little River); Below 100 (Bushton, Claflin, Dorrance, Lorraine, HOLYROOD). Franchise award date: January 1, 1982. Franchise expiration date: N.A. Began: October 1, 1982.
Channel capacity: N.A. Channels available but not in use: N.A.
Basic Service
Subscribers: 1,048.
Programming (received off-air): KAKE-TV (ABC) Wichita; KMTW (MNT) Hutchinson; KOOD (PBS) Hays; KPTS (PBS) Hutchinson; KSAS-TV (FOX) Wichita; KSCW-DT (CW) Wichita; KSNC (NBC) Great Bend; KWCH-DT (CBS) Hutchinson.
Programming (via satellite): ABC Family Channel; AMC; AmericanLife TV Network; Arts & Entertainment; CNN; Country Music TV; C-SPAN; C-SPAN 2; Discovery Channel; Disney Channel; ESPN; Eternal Word TV Network; Food Network; Fox Sports Net Rocky Mountain; Hallmark Channel; Headline News; HGTV; Home Shopping Network; ION Television; Lifetime; Nickelodeon; Spike TV; TBS Superstation; The Learning Channel; Turner Network TV; TV Land; USA Network; VH1; Weather Channel; WGN America.
Fee: $25.00 installation; $30.99 monthly.
Digital Basic Service
Subscribers: 233.
Programming (via satellite): BBC America; Bio; Bravo; Discovery Digital Networks; ESPN 2; ESPN Classic Sports; ESPNews; Fox Sports World; Fuse; GAS; Golf Channel; GSN; History Channel; History Channel International; Independent Film Channel; Lifetime Movie Network; Music Choice; National Geographic Channel; Nick Jr.; Speed Channel; Style Network; Syfy; Turner Classic Movies; Versus; WE tv.
Fee: $11.00 monthly.
Digital Pay Service 1
Pay Units: 210.
Programming (via satellite): Showtime (multiplexed); The Movie Channel (multiplexed).
Fee: $10.95 monthly.
Digital Pay Service 2
Pay Units: 100.
Programming (via satellite): Cinemax (multiplexed); HBO (multiplexed).
Fee: $10.95 monthly.
Digital Pay Service 3
Pay Units: N.A.
Programming (via satellite): Encore (multiplexed); Starz (multiplexed).
Fee: $10.95 monthly.
Video-On-Demand: No
Internet Service
Operational: Yes, DSL.
Telephone Service
None
Miles of Plant: 38.0 (coaxial); 48.0 (fiber optic). Homes passed: 1,125.
President & General Manager: Robert Koch. Marketing Director: D.J. Nash. Chief Technician: Tim Herber.

Franchise fee: $50.00 annually (Claflin), $1.00 annually (Bushton & Holyrood).
Ownership: H & B Cable Service Inc.

HOME—Blue Valley Telecommunications. Formerly [KS0424]. This cable system has converted to IPTV, 1557 Pony Express Hwy, Home, KS 66438. Phones: 877-876-1228; 785-799-3311. Fax: 402-793-5139. E-mail: bvtc@bluevalley.net. Web Site: http://www.bluevalley.net. ICA: KS5022.
TV Market Ranking: Outside TV Markets (HOME). Franchise award date: N.A. Franchise expiration date: N.A. Began: N.A.
Channel capacity: N.A. Channels available but not in use: N.A.
Internet Service
Operational: Yes.
Telephone Service
Digital: Operational
General Manager: Dennis Doyle.
Ownership: Blue Valley Telecommunications (MSO).

HOME—Blue Valley Telecommunications. Formerly [KS0424]. This cable system has converted to IPTV. See Home, KS [K5022], KS. ICA: KS0424.

HOPE—Eagle Communications, 406 NE 14th St, Abilene, KS 67410. Phones: 785-263-2529; 785-625-4000 (Corporate office). Fax: 785-625-8030. Web Site: http://www.eaglecom.net. ICA: KS0386.
TV Market Ranking: Below 100 (HOPE). Franchise award date: N.A. Franchise expiration date: N.A. Began: N.A.
Channel capacity: 31 (not 2-way capable). Channels available but not in use: 1.
Basic Service
Subscribers: 53.
Programming (received off-air): KAAS-TV (FOX) Salina; KAKE-TV (ABC) Wichita; KPTS (PBS) Hutchinson; KSNT (FOX, NBC) Topeka; KSNW (NBC) Wichita; KTKA-TV (ABC, CW) Topeka; KWCH-DT (CBS) Hutchinson; WIBW-TV (CBS, MNT) Topeka.
Programming (via satellite): ABC Family Channel; AMC; Animal Planet; Arts & Entertainment; CNN; Discovery Channel; Disney Channel; E! Entertainment Television; ESPN; Great American Country; History Channel; Home Shopping Network; Outdoor Channel; TBS Superstation; The Learning Channel; The Movie Channel; Turner Network TV; USA Network; Weather Channel; WGN America.
Fee: $24.95 installation; $38.95 monthly.
Pay Service 1
Pay Units: N.A.
Programming (via satellite): HBO; Showtime; The Movie Channel.
Fee: $11.95 monthly (each).
Internet Service
Operational: No.
Telephone Service
None
Miles of Plant: 3.0 (coaxial); None (fiber optic). Homes passed: 188.
President: Gary Shorman. Regional Manager: Dennis Weese. General Manager: Rex Skiles.
City fee: 3% of gross.
Ownership: Eagle Communications Inc. (KS) (MSO).

HOXIE—Eagle Communications, PO Box 426, 415 Barclay Ave, Wakeeney, KS 67672. Phones: 785-743-5616 (WaKeeney office); 785-625-4000 (Corporate office); 785-675-2310. Fax: 785-743-2694. Web Site: http://www.eaglecom.net. ICA: KS0137.
TV Market Ranking: Below 100 (HOXIE). Franchise award date: N.A. Franchise expiration date: N.A. Began: October 10, 1988.
Channel capacity: 50 (operating 2-way). Channels available but not in use: N.A.
Basic Service
Subscribers: 414.
Programming (received off-air): KBSL-DT (CBS) Goodland; KLBY (ABC) Colby; KMTW (MNT) Hutchinson; KOOD (PBS) Hays; KSAS-TV (FOX) Wichita; KSCW-DT (CW) Wichita; KSNK (NBC) McCook.
Programming (via satellite): C-SPAN; Home Shopping Network; Weather Channel; WGN America.
Current originations: Leased Access.
Fee: $24.95 installation; $14.95 monthly.
Expanded Basic Service 1
Subscribers: N.A.
Programming (via satellite): ABC Family Channel; AMC; Animal Planet; Arts & Entertainment; CNBC; CNN; Comedy Central; Country Music TV; Discovery Channel; Disney Channel; Do-It-Yourself; ESPN; ESPN 2; ESPNews; Eternal Word TV Network; Food Network; Fox Movie Channel; Fox News Channel; Fox Sports Net Midwest; FX; Great American Country; Hallmark Channel; Headline News; HGTV; History Channel; Lifetime; MTV; NFL Network; Nickelodeon; Outdoor Channel; Spike TV; Syfy; TBS Superstation; The Learning Channel; Toon Disney; Travel Channel; Trinity Broadcasting Network; Turner Network TV; TV Land; USA Network; VH1.
Fee: $27.20 monthly.
Digital Basic Service
Subscribers: 53.
Programming (via satellite): BBC America; Bio; Bloomberg Television; CMT Pure Country; Discovery Digital Networks; DMX Music; ESPN 2; ESPN Classic Sports; ESPNews; Fox Movie Channel; Fox Soccer; Fuse; GAS; Golf Channel; Halogen Network; HGTV; History Channel; History Channel International; Independent Film Channel; Lifetime Movie Network; MTV Networks Digital Suite; National Geographic Channel; Nick Jr.; NickToons TV; Outdoor Channel; Sleuth; Speed Channel; Style Network; Toon Disney; Trinity Broadcasting Network; Turner Classic Movies; Versus; WE tv.
Fee: $3.95 monthly (Discovery, Variety, Movies & Arts, or Sports & Information); $4.95 converter.
Digital Pay Service 1
Pay Units: N.A.
Programming (via satellite): Cinemax (multiplexed); Encore (multiplexed); HBO (multiplexed); Showtime (multiplexed); Starz (multiplexed); The Movie Channel (multiplexed).
Fee: $11.95 monthly (HBO, Cinemax, Showtime/TMC, or Starz/Encore).
Video-On-Demand: No
Pay-Per-View
iN DEMAND (delivered digitally); Playboy TV (delivered digitally); Fresh (delivered digitally); Spice: Xcess (delivered digitally).
Internet Service
Operational: Yes. Began: December 31, 2004.
Subscribers: 102.
Broadband Service: Eagle Internet.
Fee: $19.95 monthly.
Telephone Service
None
Miles of Plant: 12.0 (coaxial); None (fiber optic). Homes passed: 605.
President: Gary Shorman. General Manager: Rex Skiles.
Ownership: Eagle Communications Inc. (KS) (MSO).

HOYT—Giant Communications, 418 W 5th St, Ste C, Holton, KS 66436-1506. Phones: 800-346-9084; 785-364-9331. Fax: 785-866-2144. E-mail: billbarton@giantcomm.net. Web Site: http://www.giantcomm.net. ICA: KS0281.
TV Market Ranking: Below 100 (HOYT). Franchise award date: N.A. Franchise expiration date: N.A. Began: September 1, 1982.
Channel capacity: 30 (operating 2-way). Channels available but not in use: 8.
Basic Service
Subscribers: 67.
Programming (received off-air): KCWE (CW) Kansas City; KSMO-TV (MNT) Kansas City; KSNT (FOX, NBC) Topeka; KTKA-TV (ABC, CW) Topeka; KTMJ-CA Topeka; KTWU (PBS) Topeka; WIBW-TV (CBS, MNT) Topeka.
Programming (via satellite): ABC Family Channel; AMC; Animal Planet; Arts & Entertainment; Bloomberg Television; Bravo; Cartoon Network; CNN; Comedy Central; Country Music TV; C-SPAN; Discovery Channel; Discovery Health Channel; Disney Channel; Disney XD; Do-It-Yourself; E! Entertainment Television; ESPN; ESPN 2; ESPN Classic Sports; Eternal Word TV Network; Food Network; Fox News Channel; Fox Sports Net Midwest; FX; Great American Country; Hallmark Channel; Headline News; HGTV; History Channel; Home Shopping Network; KPXE-TV (ION) Kansas City; Lifetime; Lifetime Movie Network; MSNBC; MTV; National Geographic Channel; NFL Network; Nickelodeon; Outdoor Channel; QVC; RFD-TV; Speed Channel; Spike TV; Syfy; TBS Superstation; The Learning Channel; Travel Channel; Trinity Broadcasting Network; truTV; Turner Classic Movies; Turner Network TV; TV Land; USA Network; VH1; Weather Channel; WGN America.
Fee: $35.00 installation; $28.00 monthly; $4.00 converter.
Digital Basic Service
Subscribers: N.A.
Programming (via satellite): BBC America; Bio; Bloomberg Television; Country Music TV; Discovery Health Channel; Discovery Kids Channel; Discovery Military Channel; Discovery Planet Green; DMX Music; ESPN Classic Sports; ESPN U; ESPNews; FitTV; Fox Movie Channel; Fox Soccer; Fuse; G4; Golf Channel; GSN; Halogen Network; History Channel International; ID Investigation Discovery; Independent Film Channel; Lifetime Movie Network; MTV2; National Geographic Channel; Nick Jr.; NickToons TV; Science Channel; Style Network; Syfy; TeenNick; Turner Classic Movies; Versus; VH1 Classic; WE tv.
Fee: $15.95 monthly.
Digital Expanded Basic Service
Subscribers: N.A.
Programming (via satellite): Encore (multiplexed); Fox Movie Channel; Starz (multiplexed); Starz HDTV; Starz Kids & Family HD; Turner Classic Movies.
Fee: $13.95 monthly.
Digital Expanded Basic Service 2
Subscribers: N.A.
Programming (via satellite): ABC Family HD; Animal Planet HD; Arts & Entertainment HD; CNN HD; Discovery Channel HD; Discovery HD Theater; Discovery Planet Green HD; Disney Channel HD; ESPN 2 HD; ESPN HD; Food Network HD; Fox News HD; FSN HD; FX HD; HGTV HD; History Channel HD; Lifetime Movie Network HD; Lifetime Television HD; National Geographic Channel HD Network; Outdoor Channel 2 HD; QVC HD; Science Channel HD; Speed HD; Syfy HD; TBS in HD; TLC HD; Travel Channel HD; Turner Network TV HD; USA Network HD.
Fee: $10.95 monthly.
Pay Service 1
Pay Units: 24.
Programming (via satellite): HBO.
Fee: $11.95 monthly.
Pay Service 2
Pay Units: 3.
Programming (via satellite): Cinemax.
Fee: $8.95 monthly.
Pay Service 3
Pay Units: N.A.
Programming (via satellite): The Movie Channel.
Digital Pay Service 1
Pay Units: N.A.
Programming (via satellite): Cinemax (multiplexed); Cinemax HD; Flix; HBO (multiplexed); HBO HD; Showtime (multiplexed); Showtime HD; The Movie Channel (multiplexed); The Movie Channel HD.
Fee: $11.95 monthly (Cinemax), $14.95 monthly (HBO or Showtime/TMC/Flix).
Video-On-Demand: No
Pay-Per-View
iN DEMAND (delivered digitally); Hot Choice (delivered digitally).
Internet Service
Operational: Yes, Dial-up only.
Broadband Service: WildBlue Satellite Internet.
Fee: $39.95 monthly.
Telephone Service
None
Miles of Plant: 5.0 (coaxial); None (fiber optic). Homes passed: 143.
Manager: Bill Barton. Headend Technician: Jay Stewart.; Julian Rodriguez.
City fee: 2% of basic.
Ownership: Giant Communications (MSO).

HUTCHINSON—Cox Communications. Now served by WICHITA, KS [KS0001]. ICA: KS0388.

INDEPENDENCE—Cable One, PO Box 427, 309 N Penn Ave, Independence, KS 67301. Phones: 620-331-3699 (Advertising sales); 800-794-9128; 620-331-3630. Fax: 620-331-8170. E-mail: mike.flood@cableone.net. Web Site: http://www.cableone.net. Also serves Montgomery County (portions) & Neodesha. ICA: KS0022.

TV Market Ranking: Below 100 (Montgomery County (portions)); Outside TV Markets (INDEPENDENCE, Montgomery County (portions), Neodesha). Franchise award date: N.A. Franchise expiration date: N.A. Began: October 1, 1961.

Channel capacity: 80 (operating 2-way). Channels available but not in use: N.A.

Basic Service

Subscribers: 4,800.

Programming (received off-air): KDOR-TV (TBN) Bartlesville; KFJX (FOX) Pittsburg; KJRH-TV (NBC) Tulsa; KOAM-TV (CBS) Pittsburg; KOED-TV (PBS) Tulsa; KOKI-TV (FOX) Tulsa; KOTV-DT (CBS) Tulsa; KSNT (FOX, NBC) Topeka; KTUL (ABC) Tulsa; KTWU (PBS) Topeka.

Programming (via microwave): KMBC-TV (ABC) Kansas City; WIBW-TV (CBS, MNT) Topeka.

Programming (via satellite): BET Networks; C-SPAN; C-SPAN 2; QVC; TV Guide Network.

Current originations: Government Access; Educational Access.

Fee: $75.00 installation; $46.00 monthly.

Expanded Basic Service 1

Subscribers: N.A.

Programming (via satellite): ABC Family Channel; AMC; Animal Planet; Arts & Entertainment; Bravo; Cartoon Network; CNBC; CNN; Comedy Central; Country Music TV; Discovery Channel; Disney Channel; ESPN; ESPN 2; Eternal Word TV Network; Food Network; Fox News Channel; Fox Sports Net Midwest; FX; Headline News; HGTV; History Channel; Lifetime; MSNBC; MTV; Nickelodeon; Oxygen; ShopNBC; Spike TV; Syfy; TBS Superstation; The Learning Channel; Travel Channel; Turner Classic Movies; Turner Network TV; TV Land; USA Network; WE tv; Weather Channel.

Digital Basic Service

Subscribers: 922.

Programming (received off-air): KJRH-TV (NBC) Tulsa; KMBC-TV (ABC) Kansas City; KOTV-DT (CBS) Tulsa.

Programming (via satellite): 3 Angels Broadcasting Network; Bio; Boomerang; BYU Television; Canales N; Discovery Digital Networks; ESPN Classic Sports; ESPNews; FamilyNet; Fox College Sports Atlantic; Fox College Sports Central; Fox College Sports Pacific; Fox HD; Fox Movie Channel; Fox Soccer; Fuel TV; G4; Golf Channel; Hallmark Channel; History Channel International; INSP; Music Choice; National Geographic Channel; Outdoor Channel; SoapNet; Speed Channel; Toon Disney; Trinity Broadcasting Network; truTV; Turner Network TV HD; Universal HD.

Fee: $52.45 monthly.

Digital Pay Service 1

Pay Units: N.A.

Programming (via satellite): Cinemax (multiplexed); Encore; Flix; HBO (multiplexed); Showtime (multiplexed); Showtime HD; Starz (multiplexed); Sundance Channel; The Movie Channel (multiplexed); The Movie Channel HD.

Fee: $15.00 monthly (each).

Video-On-Demand: No

Pay-Per-View

Shorteez (delivered digitally); Fresh (delivered digitally); Hot Choice (delivered digitally); sports (delivered digitally); Movies (delivered digitally).

Internet Service

Operational: Yes.

Subscribers: 1,400.

Broadband Service: CableONE.net.

Fee: $75.00 installation; $43.00 monthly.

Telephone Service

Digital: Operational

Fee: $75.00 installation; $39.95 monthly

Miles of Plant: 93.0 (coaxial); None (fiber optic).

General Manager: Mike Flood. Technical Operations Manager: Jerry Millis.

City fee: 5% of gross.

Ownership: Cable One Inc. (MSO).

INGALLS—United Communications Assn. Inc. Now served by CIMARRON, KS [KS0126]. ICA: KS0313.

IOLA—Cox Communications, 602 N State St, Iola, KS 66749-2204. Phones: 316-260-7000 (Wichita office); 620-365-5975. Fax: 620-365-7862. Web Site: http://www.cox.com/kansas. Also serves Allen County (portions), Erie, Gas, Humboldt, Neosho County (portions) & Yates Center. ICA: KS0030.

TV Market Ranking: Below 100 (Erie, Neosho County (portions)); Outside TV Markets (Allen County (portions), Gas, Humboldt, IOLA, Yates Center). Franchise award date: N.A. Franchise expiration date: N.A. Began: January 1, 1961.

Channel capacity: N.A. Channels available but not in use: N.A.

Basic Service

Subscribers: N.A. Included in Wichita

Programming (received off-air): K30AL-D (PBS) Iola; KMBC-TV (ABC) Kansas City; KOAM-TV (CBS) Pittsburg; KODE-TV (ABC) Joplin; KSHB-TV (NBC) Kansas City; KSNF (NBC) Joplin; WDAF-TV (FOX) Kansas City; WIBW-TV (CBS, MNT) Topeka.

Programming (via satellite): C-SPAN; C-SPAN 2; CW+; TV Guide Network; Weather Channel; WGN America.

Current originations: Leased Access; Educational Access; Public Access.

Fee: $29.95 installation; $10.35 monthly; $2.00 converter.

Expanded Basic Service 1

Subscribers: 4,409.

Programming (via satellite): ABC Family Channel; AMC; Animal Planet; Arts & Entertainment; BET Networks; Cartoon Network; CNBC; CNN; Comedy Central; Country Music TV; Discovery Channel; Disney Channel; E! Entertainment Television; ESPN; ESPN 2; Eternal Word TV Network; Food Network; Fox News Channel; Fox Sports Net Midwest; FX; Hallmark Channel; Headline News; HGTV; History Channel; Home Shopping Network; INSP; Lifetime; MSNBC; MTV; Nickelodeon; QVC; Speed Channel; Spike TV; Syfy; TBS Superstation; The Learning Channel; Travel Channel; Trinity Broadcasting Network; truTV; Turner Classic Movies; Turner Network TV; TV Land; Univision; USA Network; VH1.

Fee: $43.15 monthly.

Digital Basic Service

Subscribers: N.A.

Programming (via satellite): BBC America; Bio; Bloomberg Television; Canales N; Discovery Digital Networks; DMX Music; ESPN Classic Sports; ESPN Now; ESPNews; Fox Sports World; G4; GAS; Golf Channel; Great American Country; GSN; History Channel International; Independent Film Channel; Lifetime Movie Network; MTV Networks Digital Suite; MuchMusic Network; NBA TV; Nick Jr.; Nick Too; Outdoor Channel; Oxygen; SoapNet; Sundance Channel; Toon Disney; Versus.

Fee: $15.00 monthly.

Digital Pay Service 1

Pay Units: 705.

Programming (via satellite): Cinemax (multiplexed); Encore; HBO (multiplexed); Showtime (multiplexed).

Fee: $11.50 monthly (each).

Video-On-Demand: Planned

Pay-Per-View

ESPN (delivered digitally); iN DEMAND (delivered digitally); NBA/WNBA League Pass (delivered digitally); NHL Center Ice/MLB Extra Innings (delivered digitally).

Internet Service

Operational: Yes.

Subscribers: 850.

Broadband Service: Cox High Speed Internet.

Fee: $19.99-$59.99 monthly; $15.00 modem lease; $199.95 modem purchase.

Telephone Service

Digital: Operational

Miles of Plant: 105.0 (coaxial); None (fiber optic). Homes passed included in Wichita

Vice President & General Manager: Kimberly Edmonds. Vice President, Engineering: Nick DiPonzio. Vice President, Marketing: Tony Matthews. Field Operations Regional Manager: Joseph Michael. Technical Operations Manager: Mark Manbeck. Marketing Director: Tina Gabbard. Public Affairs Director: Sarah Kauffman.

City fee: 3% of gross.

Ownership: Cox Communications Inc. (MSO).

IUKA—Formerly served by Cox Communications. No longer in operation. ICA: KS0389.

JAMESTOWN—Cunningham Cable TV. Now served by WASHINGTON (formerly Glen Elder), KS [KS0228]. ICA: KS0256.

JETMORE—United Communications Assn. Inc. Now served by CIMARRON, KS [KS0126]. ICA: KS0185.

JEWELL—Cunningham Cable TV. Now served by WASHINGTON (formerly Glen Elder), KS [KS0228]. ICA: KS0220.

JUNCTION CITY—Cox Communications, 931 SW Henderson Rd, Topeka, KS 66615. Phones: 316-260-7000 (Wichita office); 785-215-6700. Fax: 785-215-6127. Web Site: http://www.cox.com/kansas. Also serves Grandview Plaza, Kansas State University, Manhattan, Milford (portions), Ogden, Pottawatomie County (southeastern portion) & Riley County (southern portion). ICA: KS0006.

TV Market Ranking: Outside TV Markets (Grandview Plaza, JUNCTION CITY, Kansas State University, Manhattan, Milford (portions), Ogden, Pottawatomie County (southeastern portion), Riley County (southern portion)). Franchise award date: June 1, 1987. Franchise expiration date: N.A. Began: December 1, 1961.

Channel capacity: N.A. Channels available but not in use: N.A.

Basic Service

Subscribers: 23,132.

Programming (received off-air): KCTV (CBS) Kansas City; KMBC-TV (ABC) Kansas City; KSNT (FOX, NBC) Topeka; KTKA-TV (ABC, CW) Topeka; KTMJ-CA Topeka; KTWU (PBS) Topeka; WIBW-TV (CBS, MNT) Topeka.

Programming (via satellite): C-SPAN; C-SPAN 2; TV Guide Network; Weather Channel; WGN America.

Current originations: Public Access; Educational Access.

Fee: $29.95 installation; $10.35 monthly.

Expanded Basic Service 1

Subscribers: 14,719.

Programming (via satellite): ABC Family Channel; AMC; Animal Planet; Arts & Entertainment; BET Networks; CNBC; CNN; Comedy Central; Country Music TV; Discovery Channel; Disney Channel; E! Entertainment Television; ESPN; ESPN 2; Eternal Word TV Network; Food Network; Fox News Channel; Fox Sports Net Midwest; FX; Hallmark Channel; Headline News; HGTV; History Channel; Home Shopping Network; INSP; Lifetime; MSNBC; MTV; Nickelodeon; QVC; Speed Channel; Spike TV; Syfy; TBS Superstation; The Learning Channel; Travel Channel; truTV; Turner Classic Movies; Turner Network TV; TV Land; USA Network; VH1.

Fee: $43.15 monthly.

Digital Basic Service

Subscribers: N.A.

Programming (via satellite): BBC America; Bio; Bloomberg Television; Canales N; Discovery Digital Networks; DMX Music; ESPN Classic Sports; ESPNews; Fox Sports World; G4; GAS; Golf Channel; Great American Country; GSN; History Channel International; Independent Film Channel; International Television (ITV); Lifetime Movie Network; MTV Networks Digital Suite; MuchMusic Network; NBA TV; Nick Jr.; Nick Too; Outdoor Channel; Oxygen; SoapNet; Sundance Channel; Toon Disney; Versus.

Fee: $15.00 monthly.

Digital Pay Service 1

Pay Units: 2,801.

Programming (via satellite): Cinemax (multiplexed); Encore (multiplexed); HBO (multiplexed); Showtime (multiplexed); Starz (multiplexed).

Fee: $11.50 monthly (each).

Video-On-Demand: No

Pay-Per-View

Addressable homes: 1,000.

Addressable: Yes; iN DEMAND (delivered digitally); ESPN Now (delivered digitally); NBA/WNBA League Pass (delivered digitally); NHL Center Ice/MLB Extra Innings (delivered digitally).

Internet Service

Operational: Yes.

Subscribers: 3,454.

Broadband Service: Cox High Speed Internet.

Fee: $19.99-$59.99 monthly; $15.00 modem lease; $199.95 modem purchase.

Telephone Service

Digital: Operational

Fee: 15.95-$48.95 monthly

Miles of Plant: 334.0 (coaxial); 27.0 (fiber optic). Additional miles planned: 4.0 (coaxial); 3.0 (fiber optic). Total homes in franchised area: 34,810.

Vice President & General Manager: Kimberly Edmunds. Vice President, Engineering: Nick DiPonzio. Vice President, Marketing: Tony Matthews. Field Operations Regional Manager: Scott Terry. Marketing Director: Tina Gabbard. Public Affairs Director: Sarah Kauffman.

City fee: 3% of gross.

Ownership: Cox Communications Inc. (MSO).

KANSAS CITY (unincorporated areas)—Charter Communications. Now served by LAWRENCE, KS [KS0004]. ICA: KS0390.

KENSINGTON—Cunningham Cable TV. Now served by EDMOND, KS [KS0450]. ICA: KS0392.

KINSLEY—Cox Communications, PO Box 3027, 701 E Douglas Ave, Wichita, KS 67202. Phone: 316-260-7000. Fax: 316-262-2330. Web Site: http://www.cox.com/kansas. ICA: KS0093.

TV Market Ranking: Outside TV Markets (KINSLEY). Franchise award date: N.A. Franchise expiration date: N.A. Began: March 15, 1972.

Channel capacity: N.A. Channels available but not in use: N.A.

Basic Service

Subscribers: N.A. Included in Wichita

Programming (received off-air): KBSD-DT (CBS) Ensign; KDCK (PBS) Dodge City; KMTW (MNT) Hutchinson; KSAS-TV (FOX) Wichita; KSCW-DT (CW) Wichita; KSNG (NBC) Garden City; KUPK-TV (ABC) Garden City; allband FM.

Programming (via satellite): C-SPAN; C-SPAN 2; ShopNBC; TV Guide Network; TVN Entertainment; Univision; Weather Channel; WGN America.

Fee: $29.95 installation; $27.76 monthly; $1.55 converter.

Expanded Basic Service 1

Subscribers: N.A.

Programming (via satellite): ABC Family Channel; AMC; Animal Planet; Arts & Entertainment; BET Networks; Bravo; Cartoon Network; CNBC; CNN; Comedy Central; Country Music TV; Discovery Channel; Discovery Health Channel; Disney Channel; E! Entertainment Television; ESPN; ESPN 2; Eternal Word TV Network; Food Network; Fox News Channel; Fox Sports Net Midwest; FX; GalaVision; Hallmark Channel; Headline News; HGTV; History Channel; Home Shopping Network; INSP; Jewelry Television; Lifetime; MSNBC; MTV; MTV2; Nickelodeon; QVC; Speed Channel; Spike TV; Syfy; TBS Superstation; Telemundo; The Learning Channel; Travel Channel; truTV; Turner Classic Movies; Turner Network TV; TV Land; USA Network; VH1.

Fee: $43.15 monthly.

Digital Basic Service

Subscribers: N.A.

Programming (received off-air): KBSD-DT (CBS) Ensign; KDCK (PBS) Dodge City; KSAS-TV (FOX) Wichita; KSMI-LP Wichita; KSNG (NBC) Garden City; KUPK-TV (ABC) Garden City.

Programming (via satellite): AmericanLife TV Network; BBC America; Bio; Bloomberg Television; CBS College Sports Network; Cooking Channel; Daystar TV Network; Discovery Digital Networks; Discovery HD Theater; Do-It-Yourself; ESPN Classic Sports; ESPN HD; ESPNews; FamilyNet; FitTV; Fox Reality Channel; Fox Soccer; Fuel TV; Fuse; G4; GAS; Golf Channel; Gospel Music Channel; Great American Country; GSN; Hallmark Movie Channel; Halogen Network; HBO HD; History Channel International; Independent Film Channel; INHD; INHD2; Lifetime Movie Network; Military History Channel; MTV Networks Digital Suite; NASA TV; National Geographic Channel; NBA TV; NFL Network; Nick Jr.; Nick Too; NickToons TV; Outdoor Channel; Oxygen; Palladia; PBS Kids Sprout; Pentagon Channel; Showtime HD; Si TV; SoapNet; Starz HDTV; Sundance Channel; Tennis Channel; The Sportsman Channel; Toon Disney; Trinity Broadcasting Network; TV One; Universal HD; Versus; WE tv.

Fee: $15.00 monthly.

Digital Expanded Basic Service

Subscribers: N.A.

Programming (via satellite): Canales N; DMX Music.

Digital Pay Service 1

Pay Units: N.A.

Programming (via satellite): Cinemax (multiplexed); Encore (multiplexed); Flix; HBO (multiplexed); Showtime (multiplexed); Starz (multiplexed); The Movie Channel (multiplexed).

Fee: $11.50 monthly (each).

Video-On-Demand: Planned

Pay-Per-View

iN DEMAND (delivered digitally); Adult Swim (delivered digitally); ESPN On Demand (delivered digitally); MLS Direct Kick (delivered digitally); NBA League Pass (delivered digitally); MLB Extra Innings (delivered digitally); NHL Center Ice (delivered digitally); NASCAR In Car (delivered digitally).

Internet Service

Operational: Yes.

Fee: $19.99-$59.99 monthly.

Telephone Service

Digital: Operational

Fee: 15.95-$48.95 monthly

Miles of Plant: 14.0 (coaxial); None (fiber optic). Homes passed included in Wichita

Vice President & General Manager: Kimberly Edmonds. Vice President, Engineering: Nick DiPonzio. Vice President, Marketing: Tony Matthews. Marketing Director: Tina Gabbard. Public Affairs Director: Sarah Kauffman.

City fee: 3% of gross.

Ownership: Cox Communications Inc. (MSO).

KIOWA—Formerly served by Almega Cable. No longer in operation. ICA: KS0115.

KIRWIN—Nex-Tech. Formerly [KS0287]. This cable system has converted to IPTV, Rural Telephone Co, PO Box 158, 145 N Main St, Lenora, KS 67645-0158. Phones: 877-567-7872; 785-567-4281. Fax: 785-567-4401. E-mail: webmaster@nex-tech.com. Web Site: http://www.nex-tech.com. ICA: KS5075.

TV Market Ranking: Franchise award date: April 27, 2007. Franchise expiration date: N.A. Began: N.A.

Channel capacity: N.A. Channels available but not in use: N.A.

Internet Service

Operational: No.

Ownership: Rural Telephone Co.

KIRWIN—Nex-Tech. This cable system has converted to IPTV. See Kirwin, KS [KS5075]. ICA: KS0287.

LA CROSSE—Cox Communications. Now served by RUSH CENTER, KS [KS0418]. ICA: KS0132.

LA CYGNE—Formerly served by Almega Cable. No longer in operation. ICA: KS0153.

LA HARPE—Formerly served by CableDirect. No longer in operation. ICA: KS0393.

LAKE DABINAWA—Rainbow Communications, PO Box 147, Everest, KS 66424. Phones: 800-892-0163; 785-866-2390. Fax: 785-548-0163. Web Site: http://www.rainbowtel.net. Also serves Lakewood Hills. ICA: KS0308.

TV Market Ranking: Below 100 (LAKE DABINAWA, Lakewood Hills). Franchise award date: N.A. Franchise expiration date: N.A. Began: April 3, 1990.

Channel capacity: 35 (operating 2-way). Channels available but not in use: 15.

Basic Service

Subscribers: 77.

Programming (received off-air): KCTV (CBS) Kansas City; KMBC-TV (ABC) Kansas City; KMCI-TV (IND) Lawrence; KSHB-TV (NBC) Kansas City; KSMO-TV (MNT) Kansas City; KSNT (FOX, NBC) Topeka; KTKA-TV (ABC, CW) Topeka; KTWU (PBS) Topeka; WDAF-TV (FOX) Kansas City; WIBW-TV (CBS, MNT) Topeka.

Programming (via satellite): ABC Family Channel; Arts & Entertainment; CNN; Country Music TV; Discovery Channel; Disney Channel; ESPN; Spike TV; TBS Superstation; WGN America.

Fee: $23.95 monthly.

Pay Service 1

Pay Units: N.A.

Programming (via satellite): Cinemax.

Fee: $9.95 monthly.

Video-On-Demand: No

Internet Service

Operational: Yes.

Broadband Service: Lighting Jack High Speed.

Fee: $39.95 monthly.

Telephone Service

None

Miles of Plant: 10.0 (coaxial); None (fiber optic). Homes passed: 258.

General Manager: James Lednicky. Network Engineer: Scott Wheeler. Marketing Manager: Jackie Petersen. Plant Manager: Jim Streeter.

Ownership: Rainbow Communications (MSO).

LAKE OF THE FOREST—Time Warner Cable. Now served by KANSAS CITY, MO [MO0001]. ICA: KS0394.

LAKE WABAUNSEE—Formerly served by Galaxy Cablevision. No longer in operation. ICA: KS0241.

LANE—Formerly served by National Cable Inc. No longer in operation. ICA: KS0338.

LAWRENCE—Sunflower Broadband, 1 Riverfront Plz, Ste 301, Lawrence, KS 66044-4700. Phones: 800-869-1214; 785-841-2100; 785-841-2720. Fax: 785-312-2100. E-mail: rkutemeier@sunflowerbroadband.com. Web Site: http://www.sunflowerbroadband.com. Also serves Basehor, Douglas County (unincorporated areas), Eudora, Kansas City (unincorporated areas), Leavenworth County (unincorporated areas), Linwood, Tonganoxie & Wyandotte County (portions). ICA: KS0004.

TV Market Ranking: 22 (Basehor, Douglas County (unincorporated areas) (portions), Eudora, Kansas City (unincorporated areas), Leavenworth County (unincorporated areas), Linwood, Tonganoxie, Wyandotte County (portions)); Below 100 (LAWRENCE, Douglas County (unincorporated areas) (portions)). Franchise award date: January 1, 1971. Franchise expiration date: N.A. Began: January 1, 1972.

Channel capacity: 77 (operating 2-way). Channels available but not in use: None.

Basic Service

Subscribers: 30,350.

Programming (received off-air): KCPT (PBS) Kansas City; KCTV (CBS) Kansas City; KCWE (CW) Kansas City; KMBC-TV (ABC) Kansas City; KMCI-TV (IND) Lawrence; KPXE-TV (ION) Kansas City; KSHB-TV (NBC) Kansas City; KSMO-TV (MNT) Kansas City; KSNT (FOX, NBC) Topeka; KTKA-TV (ABC, CW) Topeka; KTWU (PBS) Topeka; KUKC-LP Kansas City; WDAF-TV (FOX) Kansas City; WIBW-TV (CBS, MNT) Topeka.

Programming (via satellite): C-SPAN; C-SPAN 2; C-SPAN 3; Home Shopping Network; Jewelry Television; QVC; ShopNBC; TV Guide Network; WGN America.

Current originations: Leased Access; Government Access; Educational Access; Public Access.

Fee: $39.00 installation; $19.95 monthly.

Expanded Basic Service 1

Subscribers: 28,000.

Programming (via satellite): ABC Family Channel; ABC News Now; AMC; AmericanLife TV Network; Animal Planet; Arts & Entertainment; BET Networks; BlueHighways TV; Bravo; Cartoon Network; CNBC; CNN; Comedy Central; Country Music TV; Discovery Channel; Disney Channel; E! Entertainment Television; ESPN; ESPN 2; ESPN Classic Sports; Eternal Word TV Network; FamilyNet; Food Network; Fox News Channel; Fox Sports Net Midwest; FX; Great American Country; Hallmark Channel; Halogen Network; Headline News; HGTV; History Channel; INSP; Lifetime; Lifetime Movie Network; Metro Sports; MSNBC; MTV; MTV2; National Geographic Channel; Nick Jr.; Nickelodeon; NickToons TV; Oxygen; PBS Kids Sprout; Retirement Living; Spike TV; Syfy; TBS Superstation; TeenNick; The Learning Channel; Toon Disney; Travel Channel; Trinity Broadcasting Network; truTV; Turner Network TV; TV Land; USA Network; Versus; VH1; Weather Channel.

Fee: $28.00 monthly.

Digital Basic Service

Subscribers: 18,600.

Programming (received off-air): KCTV (CBS) Kansas City; KCWE (CW) Kansas City; KMBC-TV (ABC) Kansas City; KMCI-TV (IND) Lawrence; KSHB-TV (NBC) Kansas City; KTWU (PBS) Topeka; WDAF-TV (FOX) Kansas City.

Programming (via satellite): ABC Family HD; Animal Planet HD; Arts & Entertainment HD; BBC America; Big Ten Network; Big Ten Network HD; Bio; Bio HD; Bloomberg Television; Boomerang; Bravo HD; Cartoon Network HD; CBS College Sports Network; CBS College Sports Network HD; Chiller; CMT HD; CMT Pure Country; CNBC HD+; CNN HD; Cooking Channel; Crime & Investigation Network; Discovery Channel HD; Discovery Health Channel; Discovery Kids Channel; Discovery Military Channel; Discovery Planet Green; Disney Channel HD; Do-It-Yourself; ESPN 2 HD; ESPN HD; ESPN U; ESPNews; ESPNews HD; FitTV; Flix; Food Network HD; Fox College Sports Atlantic; Fox College Sports Central; Fox College Sports Pacific; Fox Movie Channel; Fox News HD; Fox Soccer; FSN HD; FX HD; G4; Golf Channel; GSN; Hallmark Movie Channel; Hallmark Movie Channel HD; HGTV HD; History Channel HD; History Channel International; ID Investigation Discovery; Independent Film Channel; Lifetime Movie Network HD; Lifetime Real Women; Lifetime Television HD; Military History Channel; MTV Hits; MTV Jams; MTV Networks HD; Music Choice; NFL Network; Nick HD; Outdoor Channel; Outdoor Channel 2 HD; QVC HD; Science Channel; Science Channel HD; Sleuth; SoapNet; Speed Channel; Spike TV HD; Style Network; Sundance Channel; Syfy HD; TBS in HD; Tennis Channel; Tennis Channel HD; The Sportsman Channel; TLC HD; Toon Disney HD; Travel Channel HD; Turner Classic Movies; Turner Network TV HD; USA Network HD; Versus HD; VH1 Classic; VH1 HD; VH1 Soul; WE tv; WealthTV; Weather Channel HD.

Fee: $15.90 monthly; $5.00 converter.

Digital Expanded Basic Service

Subscribers: 13,800.

Programming (via satellite): Discovery HD Theater; HDNet; HDNet Movies; National Geographic Channel HD Network; NFL Network HD; Smithsonian Channel HD; Speed HD; Universal HD; WealthTV HD.

Fee: $39.00 installation; $9.95 monthly; $5.00 converter.

Digital Pay Service 1

Pay Units: 4,900.

Programming (via satellite): HBO (multiplexed); HBO HD.

Fee: $15.95 monthly; $5.00 converter.

Digital Pay Service 2

Pay Units: 2,600.

Programming (via satellite): Cinemax (multiplexed); Cinemax HD.

Fee: $9.95 monthly; $5.00 converter.

Digital Pay Service 3

Pay Units: 2,200.

Programming (via satellite): Showtime (multiplexed); Showtime HD; The Movie Channel (multiplexed).

Fee: $13.95 monthly; $5.00 converter.

Digital Pay Service 4

Pay Units: 2,200.

Programming (via satellite): Encore (multiplexed); Starz (multiplexed); Starz HDTV.

Fee: $13.95 monthly; $5.00 converter.

Video-On-Demand: Yes

Pay-Per-View

Addressable homes: 7,801.

Hot Choice (delivered digitally), Addressable: Yes; iN DEMAND (delivered digitally); Playboy TV (delivered digitally); Shorteez (delivered digitally); Fresh (delivered digitally); Sports PPV (delivered digitally).

Internet Service

Operational: Yes. Began: September 1, 1996.

Subscribers: 21,500.

Broadband Service: Sprint/UUNET.

Fee: $39.00 installation; $17.95-$59.95 monthly; $5.00 modem lease; $79.95 modem purchase.

Telephone Service

Analog: Operational

Subscribers: 3,000.

Fee: $39.00 installation; $12.95 monthly

Digital: Operational

Fee: $18.95 monthly

Miles of Plant: 600.0 (coaxial); 250.0 (fiber optic). Homes passed: 54,000. Total homes in franchised area: 54,000.

General Manager: Rod Kutemeier. Operations Director: Stephen Schneider. Engineering Director: Jim Day. Marketing Manager: Christina Phelps. Customer Service Manager: Tiffany Cody.

Lawrence fee: 3.25% of gross.

Ownership: Sunflower Broadband.

LEBANON—Nex-Tech. Formerly [KS0397]. This cable system has converted to IPTV, PO Box 158, 145 N Main St, Lenora, KS 67645-0158. Phones: 877-567-7872; 785-567-4281. Fax: 785-567-4401. E-mail: webmaster@nex-tech.com. Web Site: http://www.nex-tech.com. ICA: KS5049.

Channel capacity: N.A. Channels available but not in use: N.A.

Internet Service

Operational: Yes.

Telephone Service

Digital: Operational

Ownership: Rural Telephone Co.

LEBANON—Nex-Tech. This cable system has converted to IPTV. See Lebanon, KS [KS5049]. ICA: KS0397.

LEHIGH—Formerly served by Eagle Communications. No longer in operation. ICA: KS0466.

LENEXA—Formerly [KS0462]. SureWest Broadband. This cable system has converted to IPTV, 9647 Lackman Rd, Lenexa, KS 66219. Phones: 913-825-2800; 913-825-3000. Fax: 913-322-9901. Web Site: http://www.surewest.com. ICA: KS5122.

TV Market Ranking: 22 (LENEXA).

Channel capacity: N.A. Channels available but not in use: N.A.

Video-On-Demand: Yes

Internet Service

Operational: Yes.

Subscribers: 32,000.

Telephone Service

Digital: Operational

Ownership: SureWest Broadband.

LENEXA—SureWest Broadband. This cable system has converted to IPTV. See Lenexa, KS [KS5122]. ICA: KS0462.

LEONARDVILLE—Formerly served by Giant Communications. No longer in operation. ICA: KS0263.

LEOTI—Formerly served by Cebridge Connections. Now served by ULYSSES, KS [KS0044]. ICA: KS0122.

LIBERAL—Windjammer Cable, 4400 PGA Blvd, Ste 902, Palm Beach Gardens, FL 33410. Phones: 877-450-5558; 561-775-1208. Fax: 561-775-7811. Web Site: http://www.windjammercable.com. ICA: KS0017.

TV Market Ranking: Outside TV Markets (LIBERAL). Franchise award date: February 24, 1956. Franchise expiration date: N.A. Began: February 24, 1956.

Channel capacity: N.A. Channels available but not in use: N.A.

Basic Service

Subscribers: 4,260.

Programming (received off-air): KAMR-TV (NBC) Amarillo; KBSD-DT (CBS) Ensign; KCIT (FOX) Amarillo; KFDA-TV (CBS) Amarillo; KSNG (NBC) Garden City; KSWK (PBS) Lakin; KUPK-TV (ABC) Garden City; KWET (PBS) Cheyenne; WCVB-TV (ABC) Boston.

Programming (via satellite): ABC Family Channel; AMC; Animal Planet; Arts & Entertainment; BET Networks; Bravo; Cartoon Network; CNBC; CNN; Comedy Central; Country Music TV; C-SPAN; C-SPAN 2; Discovery Channel; E! Entertainment Television; ESPN; ESPN 2; Eternal Word TV Network; Food Network; Fox News Channel; Fox Sports en Espanol; Fox Sports Net Midwest; Fox Sports Net Rocky Mountain; FX; GalaVision; Hallmark Channel; Headline News; HGTV; History Channel; Home Shopping Network; INSP; Lifetime; MSNBC; MTV; Nickelodeon; Oxygen; QVC; ShopNBC; Spike TV; Syfy; The Learning Channel; Travel Channel; Trinity Broadcasting Network; truTV; Turner Classic Movies; TV Guide Network; TV Land; USA Network; VH1; Weather Channel; WGN America.

Current originations: Public Access; Government Access; Educational Access.

Fee: $49.95 installation; $49.34 monthly.

Expanded Basic Service 1

Subscribers: 4,200.

Programming (via satellite): Disney Channel; TBS Superstation; Turner Network TV.

Fee: $7.91 monthly.

Digital Basic Service

Subscribers: 1,387.

Programming (via satellite): AmericanLife TV Network; BBC America; Bio; Black Family Channel; Bloomberg Television; Canales N; Discovery Digital Networks; Do-It-Yourself; ESPN Classic Sports; ESPNews; Fox College Sports Atlantic; Fox College Sports Central; Fox College Sports Pacific; Fox Movie Channel; Fox Sports World; Fuse; G4; GAS; Golf Channel; Great American Country; GSN; Halogen Network; History Channel International; Independent Film Channel; MTV Networks Digital Suite; Music Choice; National Geographic Channel; Nick Jr.; Nick Too; Outdoor Channel; SoapNet; Speed Channel; Style Network; Sundance Channel; Toon Disney; Versus; WE tv.

Fee: $53.99 monthly.

Digital Pay Service 1

Pay Units: N.A.

Programming (via satellite): ART America; CCTV-4; Cinemax (multiplexed); Encore (multiplexed); Filipino Channel; Flix; HBO (multiplexed); RAI International; Russian Television Network; Showtime (multiplexed); Starz (multiplexed); The Movie Channel (multiplexed); TV Asia; TV5, La Television International; Zee TV USA; Zhong Tian Channel.

Fee: $12.00 monthly (HBO, Cinemax, Showtime Unlimited or Starz), $15.00 monthly (CCTV, TV Asia, TV5, Filipino, RAI, ART or TV Russia).

Video-On-Demand: No

Pay-Per-View

Playboy TV (delivered digitally); Urban American Television Network (delivered digitally); Shorteez (delivered digitally); Fresh (delivered digitally); Hot Choice (delivered digitally); Playboy TV (delivered digitally); HITS PPV (delivered digitally).

Internet Service

Operational: Yes.

Broadband Service: In-house.

Fee: $19.95-$49.99 installation; $44.95 monthly.

Telephone Service

Digital: Operational

Fee: $74.95 installation; $49.95 monthly

Miles of Plant: 95.0 (coaxial); 14.0 (fiber optic). Homes passed: 7,785.

General Manager: Timothy Evard. Operations Director: Belinda Graham. Engineering Director: Mike Earehart. Finance & Accounting Director: Cindy Johnson.

City fee: 3% of gross.

Ownership: Windjammer Communications LLC (MSO).

LINCOLN—Eagle Communications, 406 NE 14th St, Abilene, KS 67410. Phones: 785-263-2529; 785-625-4000 (Corporate access). Fax: 785-625-8030. Web Site: http://www.eaglecom.net. ICA: KS0134.

TV Market Ranking: Below 100 (LINCOLN). Franchise award date: N.A. Franchise expiration date: N.A. Began: October 1, 1975.

Channel capacity: 41 (operating 2-way). Channels available but not in use: N.A.

Basic Service

Subscribers: 231.

Programming (received off-air): KAAS-TV (FOX) Salina; KAKE-TV (ABC) Wichita; KBSH-DT (CBS) Hays; KOOD (PBS) Hays; KSNC (NBC) Great Bend; KWCH-DT (CBS) Hutchinson; 1 FM.

Programming (via satellite): Eternal Word TV Network; KMGH-TV (ABC) Denver; QVC; Weather Channel.

Current originations: Educational Access.

Fee: $24.95 installation; $19.95 monthly.

Expanded Basic Service 1

Subscribers: N.A.

Programming (via satellite): ABC Family Channel; Animal Planet; Arts & Entertainment; CNN; C-SPAN; Discovery Channel; Disney Channel; ESPN; ESPN 2; Fox News Channel; Fox Sports Net Midwest; Great American Country; Headline News; History Channel; Lifetime; National Geographic Channel; Nickelodeon; Spike TV; TBS Superstation; The Learning Channel; Turner Network TV; TV Land; USA Network; VH1.

Fee: $21.50 monthly.

Pay Service 1

Pay Units: 78.

Programming (via satellite): HBO.

Fee: $11.95 monthly.

Pay Service 2

Pay Units: 52.

Programming (via satellite): Showtime.

Fee: $11.95 monthly.

Pay Service 3

Pay Units: 56.

Programming (via satellite): The Movie Channel.

Fee: $11.95 monthly.

Video-On-Demand: No

Pay-Per-View

iN DEMAND (delivered digitally); Playboy TV (delivered digitally); Fresh (delivered digitally); Shorteez (delivered digitally).

Internet Service

Operational: Yes.

Fee: $34.95-$54.95 monthly.

Telephone Service

None

Miles of Plant: 12.0 (coaxial); None (fiber optic). Homes passed: 640.

President & Chief Executive Officer: Gary Shorman. General Manager: Rex Skiles. Chief Technician: Les Libal.

City fee: 1% of gross.

Ownership: Eagle Communications Inc. (KS) (MSO).

LINN—Allegiance Communications, 707 W Saratoga St, Shawnee, OK 74804. Phones: 405-275-6923; 405-395-1131. Web Site: http://www.allegiance.tv. ICA: KS0253.

TV Market Ranking: Outside TV Markets (LINN). Franchise award date: N.A. Franchise expiration date: N.A. Began: October 1, 1983.

Channel capacity: 40 (not 2-way capable). Channels available but not in use: N.A.

Basic Service

Subscribers: 135.

Programming (received off-air): KLKN (ABC) Lincoln; KOLN (CBS, MNT) Lincoln; KSAS-TV (FOX) Wichita; KSNT (FOX, NBC) Topeka; KTKA-TV (ABC, CW) Topeka; KTWU (PBS) Topeka; WIBW-TV (CBS, MNT) Topeka.

Programming (via satellite): ABC Family Channel; Animal Planet; Arts & Entertainment; Cartoon Network; CNN; Country Music TV; Discovery Channel; Disney Channel; E! Entertainment Television; ESPN; ESPN 2; Fox News Channel; FX; History Channel; MTV; Nickelodeon; Spike TV; TBS Superstation; The Learning Channel; Travel Channel; Turner Network TV; TV Land; USA Network; Weather Channel; WGN America.

Fee: $44.95 installation; $21.98 monthly.

Pay Service 1

Pay Units: 7.

Programming (via satellite): Cinemax.

Fee: $12.95 installation; $11.50 monthly.

Pay Service 2

Pay Units: 10.

Programming (via satellite): HBO.

Fee: $12.95 installation; $11.95 monthly.

Video-On-Demand: No

Pay-Per-View

iN DEMAND (delivered digitally); Hot Choice (delivered digitally); Playboy TV (delivered digitally); Fresh (delivered digitally); Shorteez (delivered digitally).

Internet Service

Operational: No.

Telephone Service

None

Miles of Plant: 4.0 (coaxial); None (fiber optic). Homes passed: 219. Total homes in franchised area: 219.

Chief Executive Officer: Bill Haggarty. Regional Vice President: Andrew Dearth. Vice President, Marketing: Tracy Bass.

Ownership: Allegiance Communications (MSO).

LINSBORG—Cox Communications. Now served by WICHITA, KS [KS0001]. ICA: KS0070.

LOUISBURG—Formerly served by Almega Cable. No longer in operation. ICA: KS0123.

LOUISVILLE—WTC Communications. Formerly served by Wamego, KS [KS0057]. This cable system has converted to IPTV, 1009 Lincoln St, Wamego, KS 66547. Phones: 877-492-6835; 785-456-1000. Fax: 785-456-9903. E-mail: support@wamego.net. Web Site: http://www.wamtelco.com. ICA: KS5040.

TV Market Ranking: Outside TV Markets (Louisville).

Channel capacity: N.A. Channels available but not in use: N.A.

Telephone Service

Digital: Operational

President & General Manager: Steve Tackrider. Plant Manager: Ken Blew.

Ownership: WTC Communications Inc.

LOWELL—Formerly served by Riverton-Lowell Cablevision. No longer in operation. ICA: KS0399.

LUCAS—Wilson Communications, PO Box 508, 2504 Ave D, Wilson, KS 67490-0508. Phones: 800-432-7607; 785-658-2111. Fax: 785-658-3344. Web Site: http://www.wilsoncommunications.us. ICA: KS0216.

TV Market Ranking: Outside TV Markets (LUCAS). Franchise award date: N.A. Franchise expiration date: N.A. Began: October 1, 1981.

Channel capacity: N.A. Channels available but not in use: N.A.

Basic Service

Subscribers: 153.

Programming (received off-air): KAKE-TV (ABC) Wichita; KMTW (MNT) Hutchinson; KOOD (PBS) Hays; KPTS (PBS) Hutchinson; KSAS-TV (FOX) Wichita; KSNC (NBC) Great Bend; KWCH-DT (CBS) Hutchinson.

Programming (via satellite): ABC Family Channel; AMC; AmericanLife TV Network; Arts & Entertainment; CNN; Country Music TV; C-SPAN; C-SPAN 2; CW+; Discovery Channel; Disney Channel; ESPN; ESPN 2; ESPN Classic Sports; ESPNews; Eternal Word TV Network; Food Network; Fox News Channel; Fox Sports Net Rocky Mountain; FX; Hallmark Channel; Headline News; HGTV; Home Shopping Network; ION Television; Lifetime; MTV; National Geographic Channel; Nickelodeon; Spike TV; Syfy; TBS Superstation; The Learning Channel; Turner Network TV; TV Land; USA Network; VH1; Weather Channel; WGN America.

Current originations: Public Access.

Fee: $25.00 installation; $39.95 monthly.

Digital Basic Service

Subscribers: N.A.

Programming (received off-air): KAKE-TV (ABC) Wichita; KHAS-TV (NBC) Hastings; KMTV-TV (CBS) Omaha; KOOD (PBS) Hays; KSCW-DT (CW) Wichita; KSNC (NBC) Great Bend; KWCH-DT (CBS) Hutchinson.

Programming (via satellite): Arts & Entertainment HD; BBC America; Bio; Bravo; CMT Pure Country; Discovery HD Theater; Discovery Health Channel; Discovery Kids Channel; Discovery Military Channel; Discovery Planet Green; DMX Music; ESPN 2 HD; ESPN HD; ESPN U; ESPNU HD; Food Network HD; Fox Soccer; Fuse; Golf Channel; GSN; HGTV HD; History Channel; History Channel HD; History Channel International; ID Investigation Discovery; Independent Film Channel; KPTS (PBS) Hutchinson; Lifetime Movie Network; MTV2; Nick Jr.; RFD-TV; Science Channel; Sleuth; Speed Channel; Style Network; TeenNick; Turner Classic Movies; Universal HD; Versus; VH1 Classic; WE tv.

Fee: $49.95 installation; $12.00 monthly.

Digital Pay Service 1

Pay Units: N.A.

Programming (via satellite): Cinemax (multiplexed); Encore (multiplexed); HBO (multiplexed); Showtime (multiplexed); Starz (multiplexed); Starz HDTV; The Movie Channel (multiplexed).

Fee: $13.95 monthly (Showtime/TMC or Starz/Encore), $18.95 monthly (HBO or Cinemax).

Internet Service

Operational: No, DSL & dial-up.

Telephone Service

None

Miles of Plant: 5.0 (coaxial); None (fiber optic). Homes passed: 307.

Vice President, Marketing: Scott Grauer. General Manager: Brian Boisvert. Plant Supervisor: Dan Steinike. Controller: Gary Everett. Customer Service Manager: Mary Zorn.

City fee: 3% of gross.

Ownership: Wilson Communications (MSO).

LURAY—Gorham Telephone Co. Formerly [KS0298]. This cable system has converted to IPTV, PO Box 235, 100 Market St, Gorham, KS 67640-0235. Phone: 785-637-5300. Fax: 785-637-5590. E-mail: gtc@gorhamtel.com. Web Site: http://www.gorhamtel.com. ICA: KS5094.

TV Market Ranking: Outside TV Markets (LURAY).

Channel capacity: N.A. Channels available but not in use: N.A.

Internet Service

Operational: Yes.

Telephone Service

Digital: Operational

Ownership: Gorham Telephone Co.

LURAY—Gorham Telephone Co. This cable system has converted to IPTV. See Luray, KS [KS5094]. ICA: KS0298.

LYON COUNTY—Formerly served by Galaxy Cablevision. No longer in operation. ICA: KS0467.

LYONS—Cox Communications. Now served by GREAT BEND, KS [KS0012]. ICA: KS0047.

MACKSVILLE—Formerly served by Almega Cable. No longer in operation. ICA: KS0225.

MADISON—Mediacom. Now served by EUREKA, KS [KS0058]. ICA: KS0155.

MAHASKA—Formerly served by Westcom. No longer in operation. ICA: KS0348.

MANKATO—Cunningham Cable TV. Now served by WASHINGTON (formerly Glen Elder), KS [KS0228]. ICA: KS0156.

MAPLE HILL—Galaxy Cablevision, 1928 S Lincoln Ave, Ste 200, York, NE 68467. Phone: 402-362-3332. Fax: 402-362-4890. Web Site: http://www.galaxycable.com. ICA: KS0275.

TV Market Ranking: Below 100 (MAPLE HILL). Franchise award date: N.A. Franchise expiration date: N.A. Began: N.A.

Channel capacity: 36 (not 2-way capable). Channels available but not in use: 3.

Basic Service

Subscribers: 51.

Programming (received off-air): KSNT (FOX, NBC) Topeka; KTKA-TV (ABC, CW) Topeka; KTWU (PBS) Topeka; WDAF-TV (FOX) Kansas City; WIBW-TV (CBS, MNT) Topeka.

Programming (via satellite): ABC Family Channel; AMC; Arts & Entertainment; Cartoon Network; CNN; Comedy Central; Discovery Channel; Disney Channel; E! Entertainment Television; Encore; ESPN; ESPN 2; Food Network; Great American Country; Headline News; HGTV; History Channel; Lifetime; Outdoor Channel; TBS Superstation; The Learning Channel; Turner Network TV; USA Network; Weather Channel.

Fee: $60.00 installation; $34.85 monthly; $3.00 converter.

Pay Service 1

Pay Units: N.A.

Programming (via satellite): Cinemax; HBO; Starz.

Internet Service

Operational: No.

Telephone Service

None

Miles of Plant: 4.0 (coaxial); None (fiber optic). Homes passed: 196. Total homes in franchised area: 196.

State Manager: Cheyenne Wohlford. Technical Manager: John Davidshofer. Sales Manager: Mike Thomas. Customer Service Manager: Michael Debermardin.

Ownership: Galaxy Cable Inc. (MSO).

MARION—Eagle Communications, 406 NE 14th St, Abilene, KS 67410. Phones: 785-625-4000 (Corporate office); 785-263-2529. Fax: 785-625-8030. Web Site: http://www.eaglecom.net. Also serves Florence, Hillsboro, Lincolnville & Marion County. ICA: KS0089.

TV Market Ranking: Outside TV Markets (Florence, Hillsboro, Lincolnville, MARION, Marion County). Franchise award date: N.A. Franchise expiration date: N.A. Began: July 15, 1978.

Channel capacity: 78 (operating 2-way). Channels available but not in use: None.

Basic Service

Subscribers: 1,089.

Programming (received off-air): KAKE-TV (ABC) Wichita; KMTW (MNT) Hutchinson; KPTS (PBS) Hutchinson; KSAS-TV (FOX) Wichita; KSCW-DT (CW) Wichita; KSNW (NBC) Wichita; KWCH-DT (CBS) Hutchinson; WIBW-TV (CBS, MNT) Topeka; allband FM.

Programming (via satellite): ABC Family Channel; AMC; Animal Planet; Arts & Entertainment; Cartoon Network; CNN; Comedy Central; Country Music TV; C-SPAN; Discovery Channel; Disney Channel; E! Entertainment Television; ESPN; ESPN 2; Food Network; Fox News Channel; Fox Sports Net Midwest; Fuse; FX; Great American Country; Halogen Network; Headline News; HGTV; History Channel; Lifetime; LWS Local Weather Station; MTV; NFL Network; Nickelodeon; Outdoor Channel; QVC; Speed Channel; Syfy; TBS Superstation; The Learning Channel; Toon Disney; Trinity Broadcasting Network; Turner Classic Movies; Turner Network TV; TV Land; USA Network; VH1; Weather Channel; WGN America.

Current originations: Government Access; Educational Access; Public Access.

Fee: $24.95 installation; $45.95 monthly.

Digital Basic Service

Subscribers: 198.

Programming (via satellite): AmericanLife TV Network; BBC America; Bio; Bloomberg Television; Discovery Health Channel; Discovery Kids Channel; Discovery Military Channel; Discovery Planet Green; DMX Music; ESPN Classic Sports; ESPNews; FitTV; Fox College Sports Atlantic; Fox College Sports Central; Fox College Sports Pacific; Fox Movie Channel; Fox Soccer; Fuse;

G4; Golf Channel; GSN; Halogen Network; HGTV; History Channel; History Channel International; ID Investigation Discovery; Lifetime Movie Network; National Geographic Channel; Outdoor Channel; Science Channel; Sleuth; Speed Channel; Style Network; Syfy; Toon Disney; Turner Classic Movies; WE tv.
Fee: $13.95 monthly.

Pay Service 1
Pay Units: N.A.
Programming (via satellite): Cinemax; HBO; Showtime; The Movie Channel.
Fee: $11.95 monthly (each).

Digital Pay Service 1
Pay Units: N.A.
Programming (via satellite): Cinemax (multiplexed); Encore (multiplexed); Flix; HBO (multiplexed); Showtime (multiplexed); Starz (multiplexed); The Movie Channel (multiplexed).
Fee: $11.95 monthly (HBO, Cinemax, Starz/Encore or Showtime/TMC/Flix).

Pay-Per-View
Club Jenna (delivered digitally); Hot Choice (delivered digitally); iN DEMAND (delivered digitally); Playboy TV (delivered digitally); Fresh (delivered digitally).

Internet Service
Operational: Yes.
Subscribers: 362.
Broadband Service: Eagle Internet.
Fee: $22.95 monthly.

Telephone Service
None
Miles of Plant: 35.0 (coaxial); None (fiber optic). Homes passed: 2,836.
President: Gary Shorman. Regional Manager: Dennis Weese. General Manager: Rex Skiles.
Ownership: Eagle Communications Inc. (KS) (MSO).

MARQUETTE—Blue Sky Cable LLC, 412 W Blackwell Rd, Blackwell, OK 74631. Phones: 800-342-0099; 580-262-2800. Web Site: http://www.marquetteks.us/blueskycable/index.html. ICA: KS0212.
TV Market Ranking: 67 (MARQUETTE). Franchise award date: January 1, 1982. Franchise expiration date: N.A. Began: June 1, 1983.
Channel capacity: 47 (operating 2-way). Channels available but not in use: 1.

Basic Service
Subscribers: 55.
Programming (received off-air): KAKE-TV (ABC) Wichita; KMTW (MNT) Hutchinson; KPTS (PBS) Hutchinson; KSAS-TV (FOX) Wichita; KSNW (NBC) Wichita; KWCH-DT (CBS) Hutchinson.
Programming (via satellite): ABC Family Channel; American Movie Classics; Arts & Entertainment; CNBC; CNN; Country Music TV; C-SPAN; C-SPAN 2; Discovery Channel; Disney Channel; ESPN; ESPN 2; Great American Country; HGTV; History Channel; Lifetime; Nickelodeon; Outdoor Channel; QVC; Spike TV; Syfy; TBS Superstation; The Learning Channel; Trinity Broadcasting Network; Turner Network TV; TV Land; USA Network; Weather Channel; WGN America.
Fee: $15.00 monthly.

Pay Service 1
Pay Units: 5.
Programming (via satellite): Cinemax (multiplexed); HBO (multiplexed); MoviePlex; Showtime; Starz; The Movie Channel.
Fee: $10.00 monthly.

Internet Service
Operational: Yes.
Subscribers: 30.
Broadband Service: In-house.
Fee: $25.00 installation; $29.95 monthly.

Telephone Service
None
Miles of Plant: 5.0 (coaxial); None (fiber optic). Homes passed: 262. Total homes in franchised area: 262.
Manager: Julie Hodges.
City fee: 3% of basic.
Ownership: Blue Sky Cable LLC (MSO).

MARYSVILLE—Great Plains Communications, PO Box 500, 1600 Great Plains Centre, Blair, NE 68008. Phones: 877-876-1228; 785-799-3311. Fax: 402-456-6550. Web Site: http://www.gpcom.com. Also serves Marshall County (portions). ICA: KS0048.
TV Market Ranking: Outside TV Markets (Marshall County (portions), MARYSVILLE). Franchise award date: N.A. Franchise expiration date: N.A. Began: November 1, 1965.
Channel capacity: 65 (operating 2-way). Channels available but not in use: N.A.

Basic Service
Subscribers: 1,454.
Programming (received off-air): KLKN (ABC) Lincoln; KOLN (CBS, MNT) Lincoln; KPTM (FOX, MNT) Omaha; KSNT (FOX, NBC) Topeka; KTKA-TV (ABC, CW) Topeka; KTWU (PBS) Topeka; WIBW-TV (CBS, MNT) Topeka; WOWT-TV (IND, NBC) Omaha.
Programming (via satellite): C-SPAN; C-SPAN 2; Eternal Word TV Network; Fox Sports Net Midwest; Home Shopping Network; WGN America.
Current originations: Public Access.
Fee: $37.50 installation; $11.56 monthly; $18.75 additional installation.

Expanded Basic Service 1
Subscribers: N.A.
Programming (via satellite): ABC Family Channel; AMC; Animal Planet; Arts & Entertainment; Cartoon Network; CNBC; CNN; Comedy Central; Country Music TV; Discovery Channel; Disney Channel; E! Entertainment Television; ESPN; ESPN 2; Food Network; Fox News Channel; FX; G4; Golf Channel; Hallmark Channel; Headline News; HGTV; History Channel; Lifetime; MSNBC; MTV; Nickelodeon; Oxygen; Speed Channel; Spike TV; TBS Superstation; The Learning Channel; Toon Disney; Travel Channel; truTV; Turner Network TV; TV Land; USA Network; VH1; Weather Channel.

Digital Basic Service
Subscribers: N.A.
Programming (via satellite): BBC America; Bio; Bravo; Discovery Digital Networks; DMX Music; ESPN Classic Sports; ESPNews; Fox Sports World; GAS; GSN; History Channel International; Independent Film Channel; Lifetime Movie Network; MTV Networks Digital Suite; Nick Jr.; NickToons TV; Syfy; Trinity Broadcasting Network; Turner Classic Movies; TV Guide Interactive Inc.; Versus; WE tv.

Pay Service 1
Pay Units: 148.
Programming (via satellite): Cinemax.
Fee: $12.50 installation; $11.50 monthly.

Pay Service 2
Pay Units: 238.
Programming (via satellite): HBO.
Fee: $12.50 installation; $11.95 monthly.

Pay Service 3
Pay Units: 68.
Programming (via satellite): Showtime.
Fee: $11.50 monthly.

Pay Service 4
Pay Units: 289.
Programming (via satellite): Encore.
Fee: $1.75 monthly.

Pay Service 5
Pay Units: 232.
Programming (via satellite): Starz (multiplexed).
Fee: $6.75 monthly.

Digital Pay Service 1
Pay Units: N.A.
Programming (via satellite): Cinemax (multiplexed); Encore (multiplexed); Flix; HBO (multiplexed); Showtime (multiplexed); Starz (multiplexed); The Movie Channel (multiplexed).

Video-On-Demand: No

Pay-Per-View
Addressable homes: 26.
iN DEMAND (delivered digitally), Addressable: Yes; Playboy TV (delivered digitally); Fresh (delivered digitally); Shorteez (delivered digitally).

Internet Service
Operational: Yes.

Telephone Service
Digital: Planned
Miles of Plant: 29.0 (coaxial); None (fiber optic). Homes passed: 1,959. Total homes in franchised area: 1,959.
General Manager: Dennis Doyle. Chief Technician: Mark Stottler. Marketing Manager: Angie Armstrong. Customer Service Supervisor: Deb Runnebaum.
City fee: 3% of gross.
Ownership: Blue Valley Telecommunications (MSO).

MAYETTA—Giant Communications, 418 W 5th St, Ste C, Holton, KS 66436-1506. Phones: 785-364-9331; 800-346-9084; 785-866-2133. Fax: 785-866-2144. E-mail: billbarton@giantcomm.net. Web Site: http://www.giantcomm.net. ICA: KS0321.
TV Market Ranking: Below 100 (MAYETTA). Franchise award date: N.A. Franchise expiration date: N.A. Began: July 1, 1984.
Channel capacity: 40 (operating 2-way). Channels available but not in use: 17.

Basic Service
Subscribers: 32.
Programming (received off-air): KPXE-TV (ION) Kansas City; KSNT (FOX, NBC) Topeka; KTKA-TV (ABC, CW) Topeka; KTMJ-CA Topeka; KTWU (PBS) Topeka; WIBW-TV (CBS, MNT) Topeka.
Programming (via satellite): ABC Family Channel; AMC; Animal Planet; Arts & Entertainment; Bloomberg Television; Bravo; Cartoon Network; CNN; Comedy Central; Country Music TV; C-SPAN; Discovery Channel; Discovery Health Channel; Disney Channel; Disney XD; Do-It-Yourself; E! Entertainment Television; ESPN; ESPN 2; ESPN Classic Sports; Eternal Word TV Network; Food Network; Fox News Channel; Fox Soccer; FX; Great American Country; Hallmark Channel; Headline News; HGTV; History Channel; Home Shopping Network; Lifetime; Lifetime Movie Network; MSNBC; MTV; National Geographic Channel; NFL Network; Nickelodeon; Outdoor Channel; RFD-TV; Speed Channel; Spike TV; Syfy; TBS Superstation; The Learning Channel; Travel Channel; Trinity Broadcasting Network; truTV; Turner Classic Movies; Turner Network TV; TV Land; USA Network; VH1; Weather Channel; WGN America.
Fee: $35.00 installation; $46.95 monthly; $5.00 converter.

Digital Basic Service
Subscribers: N.A.
Programming (via satellite): BBC America; Bio; Bloomberg Television; Country Music TV; Discovery Health Channel; Discovery Kids Channel; Discovery Military Channel; Discovery Planet Green; DMX Music; ESPN Classic Sports; ESPN U; ESPNews; FitTV; Fox Movie Channel; Fox Soccer; Fuse; G4; Golf Channel; GSN; Halogen Network; History Channel International; ID Investigation Discovery; Independent Film Channel; Lifetime Movie Network; MTV2; National Geographic Channel; Nick Jr.; NickToons TV; Science Channel; Style Network; Syfy; TeenNick; Turner Classic Movies; Versus; VH1 Classic; WE tv.
Fee: $15.95 monthly.

Digital Expanded Basic Service
Subscribers: N.A.
Programming (via satellite): Encore (multiplexed); Fox Movie Channel; Starz (multiplexed); Starz HDTV; Starz Kids & Family HD; Turner Classic Movies.
Fee: $13.95 monthly.

Digital Expanded Basic Service 2
Subscribers: N.A.
Programming (via satellite): Cinemax; Cinemax HD; Flix; HBO (multiplexed); HBO HD; Showtime; Showtime HD; The Movie Channel (multiplexed); The Movie Channel HD.
Fee: $10.95 monthly.

Pay Service 1
Pay Units: 4.
Programming (via satellite): Cinemax.
Fee: $8.95 monthly.

Pay Service 2
Pay Units: 16.
Programming (via satellite): HBO.
Fee: $11.95 monthly.

Pay Service 3
Pay Units: N.A.
Programming (via satellite): The Movie Channel.

Video-On-Demand: No

Pay-Per-View
iN DEMAND (delivered digitally); Hot Choice (delivered digitally).

Internet Service
Operational: Yes.

Telephone Service
None
Miles of Plant: 3.0 (coaxial); None (fiber optic). Homes passed: 125.
Manager: Bill Barton. Headend Technician: Jay Stewart.; Julian Rodriguez.
City fee: 3% of basic.
Ownership: Giant Communications (MSO).

McCUNE—Formerly served by Craw-Kan Telephone Co-op. No longer in operation.. ICA: KS0213.

MCCUNE—Formerly served by GIRARD, KS [KS0446]. Craw-Kan Telephone Co-op. This cable system has converted to IPTV, PO Box 100, 200 N Ozark St, Girard, KS 66743. Phones: 800-362-0316; 620-724-8235. Fax: 620-724-4099. E-mail: webmaster@ckt.net. Web Site: http://www.ckt.net. ICA: KS5126.
TV Market Ranking: Below 100 (MCCUNE).
Channel capacity: N.A. Channels available but not in use: N.A.

Internet Service
Operational: Yes.

Telephone Service
Digital: Operational
Ownership: Craw-Kan Telephone Cooperative.

McDONALD—Eagle Communications, PO Box 336, 114 W 11th St, Goodland, KS 67735. Phones: 785-899-3371; 785-625-

4000 (Corporate office). Fax: 785-899-3299. Web Site: http://www.eaglecom.net. Also serves Bird City. ICA: KS0084.

TV Market Ranking: Below 100 (Bird City, MCDONALD). Franchise award date: N.A. Franchise expiration date: N.A. Began: December 1, 1976.

Channel capacity: 62 (operating 2-way). Channels available but not in use: N.A.

Basic Service

Subscribers: 132.

Programming (received off-air): KBSL-DT (CBS) Goodland; KLBY (ABC) Colby; KSAS-TV (FOX) Wichita; KSNK (NBC) McCook; 1 FM.

Programming (via microwave): KOOD (PBS) Hays.

Programming (via satellite): Great American Country; KCNC-TV (CBS) Denver; KMGH-TV (ABC) Denver; KUSA (NBC) Denver; KWGN-TV (CW) Denver; National Geographic Channel; QVC; TV Land; Weather Channel.

Fee: $24.95 installation; $19.95 monthly.

Expanded Basic Service 1

Subscribers: N.A.

Programming (via satellite): ABC Family Channel; Animal Planet; Arts & Entertainment; CNN; Discovery Channel; Disney Channel; ESPN; Fox Sports Net Midwest; Headline News; HGTV; History Channel; Nickelodeon; Spike TV; Style Network; TBS Superstation; The Learning Channel; Turner Network TV; USA Network.

Fee: $21.50 monthly.

Pay Service 1

Pay Units: 14.

Programming (via satellite): HBO.

Fee: $11.95 monthly.

Pay Service 2

Pay Units: 38.

Programming (via satellite): Showtime.

Fee: $11.95 monthly.

Pay Service 3

Pay Units: 34.

Programming (via satellite): The Movie Channel.

Fee: $11.95 monthly.

Video-On-Demand: No

Internet Service

Operational: Yes.

Fee: $34.95-$54.95 monthly.

Telephone Service

None

Miles of Plant: 22.0 (coaxial); None (fiber optic). Homes passed: 373.

President & Chief Executive Officer: Gary Shorman. General Manager: Rex Skiles. Chief Technician: Les Libal.

City fee: 3% of gross.

Ownership: Eagle Communications Inc. (KS) (MSO).

McFARLAND—Formerly served by Galaxy Cablevision. No longer in operation. ICA: KS0327.

McLOUTH—Giant Communications, 418 W 5th St, Ste C, Holton, KS 66436-1506. Phones: 800-346-9084; 785-364-9331. Fax: 785-866-2144. E-mail: billbarton@giantcomm.net. Web Site: http://www.giantcomm.net. Also serves Oskaloosa. ICA: KS0191.

TV Market Ranking: Below 100 (MCLOUTH, Oskaloosa). Franchise award date: N.A. Franchise expiration date: N.A. Began: June 1, 1984.

Channel capacity: 60 (operating 2-way). Channels available but not in use: 35.

Basic Service

Subscribers: 268.

Programming (received off-air): KCPT (PBS) Kansas City; KCTV (CBS) Kansas City; KCWE (CW) Kansas City; KPXE-TV (ION) Kansas City; KSMO-TV (MNT) Kansas City; KSNT (FOX, NBC) Topeka; KTKA-TV (ABC, CW) Topeka; KTMJ-CA Topeka; KTWU (PBS) Topeka; WIBW-TV (CBS, MNT) Topeka.

Programming (via satellite): ABC Family Channel; AMC; Animal Planet; Arts & Entertainment; Bloomberg Television; Bravo; Cartoon Network; CNN; Comedy Central; Country Music TV; C-SPAN; Discovery Channel; Discovery Health Channel; Disney Channel; Disney XD; Do-It-Yourself; E! Entertainment Television; ESPN; ESPN 2; ESPN Classic Sports; Eternal Word TV Network; Food Network; Fox News Channel; Fox Soccer; FX; Great American Country; Hallmark Channel; Headline News; HGTV; History Channel; Home Shopping Network; Lifetime; Lifetime Movie Network; MSNBC; MTV; National Geographic Channel; NFL Network; Nickelodeon; Outdoor Channel; QVC; RFD-TV; Speed Channel; Spike TV; Syfy; TBS Superstation; The Learning Channel; Travel Channel; Trinity Broadcasting Network; truTV; Turner Classic Movies; Turner Network TV; TV Land; USA Network; VH1; Weather Channel; WGN America.

Fee: $35.00 installation; $30.95 monthly; $5.00 converter.

Digital Basic Service

Subscribers: N.A.

Programming (via satellite): BBC America; Bio; Bloomberg Television; Country Music TV; Discovery Health Channel; Discovery Kids Channel; Discovery Military Channel; Discovery Planet Green; DMX Music; ESPN Classic Sports; ESPN U; ESPNews; FitTV; Fox Movie Channel; Fox Soccer; Fuse; G4; Golf Channel; GSN; Halogen Network; History Channel International; ID Investigation Discovery; Independent Film Channel; Lifetime Movie Network; MTV2; National Geographic Channel; Nick Jr.; NickToons TV; Science Channel; Style Network; Syfy; TeenNick; Turner Classic Movies; Versus; VH1 Classic; WE tv.

Fee: $15.95 monthly.

Digital Expanded Basic Service

Subscribers: N.A.

Programming (via satellite): Encore (multiplexed); Fox Movie Channel; Starz (multiplexed); Starz HDTV; Starz Kids & Family HD; Turner Classic Movies.

Fee: $13.95 monthly.

Digital Expanded Basic Service 2

Subscribers: N.A.

Programming (via satellite): ABC Family HD; Animal Planet HD; Arts & Entertainment HD; CNN HD; Discovery Channel HD; Discovery HD Theater; Discovery Planet Green HD; Disney Channel HD; ESPN 2 HD; ESPN HD; Food Network HD; Fox News HD; FSN HD; FX HD; HGTV HD; History Channel HD; Lifetime Movie Network HD; Lifetime Television HD; National Geographic Channel HD Network; Outdoor Channel 2 HD; QVC HD; Science Channel HD; Speed HD; Syfy HD; TBS in HD; TLC HD; Travel Channel HD; Turner Network TV HD; USA Network HD.

Fee: $10.95 monthly.

Pay Service 1

Pay Units: 6.

Programming (via satellite): Cinemax.

Fee: $8.95 monthly.

Pay Service 2

Pay Units: 23.

Programming (via satellite): The Movie Channel.

Fee: $11.95 monthly.

Pay Service 3

Pay Units: 21.

Programming (via satellite): HBO.

Fee: $11.95 monthly.

Digital Pay Service 1

Pay Units: N.A.

Programming (via satellite): Cinemax (multiplexed); Cinemax HD; Flix; HBO (multiplexed); HBO HD; Showtime (multiplexed); Showtime HD; The Movie Channel (multiplexed); The Movie Channel HD.

Fee: $11.95 monthly (Cinemax), $14.95 monthly (HBO or Showtime/TMC/Flix).

Video-On-Demand: No

Pay-Per-View

iN DEMAND (delivered digitally); Hot Choice (delivered digitally).

Internet Service

Operational: Yes.

Fee: $39.95 monthly.

Telephone Service

None

Miles of Plant: 5.0 (coaxial); None (fiber optic). Homes passed: 310.

Manager: Bill Barton. Headend Technician: Jay Stewart.; Julian Rodriquez.

City fee: 3% of basic.

Ownership: Giant Communications (MSO).

McPHERSON—Cox Communications. Now served by WICHITA, KS [KS0001]. ICA: KS0019.

MEADE—Allegiance Communications, 707 W Saratoga St, Shawnee, OK 74804. Phones: 405-395-1131; 405-275-6923. Web Site: http://www.allegiance.tv. Also serves Fowler, Kismet, Minneola, Plains & Seward County (portions). ICA: KS0124.

TV Market Ranking: Below 100 (Fowler, MEADE, Minneola, Plains); Outside TV Markets (Kismet, Seward County (portions)). Franchise award date: N.A. Franchise expiration date: N.A. Began: February 1, 1976.

Channel capacity: 60 (operating 2-way). Channels available but not in use: None.

Basic Service

Subscribers: 1,176.

Programming (received off-air): KBSD-DT (CBS) Ensign; KSAS-TV (FOX) Wichita; KSNG (NBC) Garden City; KSWK (PBS) Lakin; KUPK-TV (ABC) Garden City; 7 FMs.

Programming (via satellite): C-SPAN; Eternal Word TV Network; Home Shopping Network; Product Information Network; QVC; ShopNBC; Trinity Broadcasting Network; WGN America.

Current originations: Public Access; Educational Access.

Fee: $49.95 installation; $21.95 monthly.

Expanded Basic Service 1

Subscribers: N.A.

Programming (via satellite): ABC Family Channel; AMC; Animal Planet; Arts & Entertainment; Bravo; Cartoon Network; CNBC; CNN; Comedy Central; Country Music TV; Court TV; Discovery Channel; Disney Channel; E! Entertainment Television; ESPN; ESPN 2; Food Network; Fox News Channel; Fox Sports Net Midwest; FX; Golf Channel; Hallmark Channel; Headline News; HGTV; History Channel; Lifetime; MSNBC; MTV; National Geographic Channel; Nickelodeon; Outdoor Channel; Oxygen; Speed Channel; Spike TV; Syfy; TBS Superstation; Telemundo; The Learning Channel; Travel Channel; Turner Classic Movies; Turner Network TV; TV Land; Univision; USA Network; VH1; Weather Channel.

Digital Basic Service

Subscribers: N.A.

Programming (via satellite): BBC America; Bio; Black Family Channel; Bloomberg Television; CMT Pure Country; Current; Discovery Health Channel; Discovery Home Channel; Discovery Kids Channel; Discovery Military Channel; Discovery Times Channel; DMX Music; Encore (multiplexed); ESPN Classic Sports; ESPNews; FitTV; Flix; Fox College Sports Atlantic; Fox College Sports Central; Fox College Sports Pacific; Fox Movie Channel; Fox Soccer; Fuse; G4; GAS; Great American Country; GSN; History Channel International; Independent Film Channel; Lifetime Movie Network; MTV Hits; MTV2; Nick Jr.; Nickelodeon; NickToons TV; Ovation; Science Channel; ShopNBC; Sleuth; SoapNet; Style Network; Sundance Channel; The Word Network; Toon Disney; Versus; VH1 Classic; VH1 Soul; WE tv.

Digital Pay Service 1

Pay Units: N.A.

Programming (via satellite): Cinemax (multiplexed); Encore (multiplexed); Flix; HBO (multiplexed); Showtime (multiplexed); Starz (multiplexed); The Movie Channel (multiplexed).

Video-On-Demand: No

Pay-Per-View

Addressable homes: 198.

Shorteez (delivered digitally); iN DEMAND (delivered digitally), Addressable: Yes; Playboy TV (delivered digitally); Fresh (delivered digitally).

Internet Service

Operational: Yes.

Telephone Service

Digital: Operational

Miles of Plant: 37.0 (coaxial); 56.0 (fiber optic). Homes passed: 2,439.

Chief Executive Officer: Bil Haggarty. Regional Vice President: Andrew Dearth. Vice President, Marketing: Tracy Bass.

City fee: 2% of gross.

Ownership: Allegiance Communications (MSO).

MEDICINE LODGE—Allegiance Communications, 707 W Saratoga St, Shawnee, OK 74804. Phones: 405-395-1131; 405-275-6923. Web Site: http://www.allegiance.tv. Also serves Barber County (portions). ICA: KS0067.

TV Market Ranking: Outside TV Markets (Barber County (portions), MEDICINE LODGE). Franchise award date: N.A. Franchise ex-

piration date: N.A. Began: December 1, 1968.

Channel capacity: 34 (operating 2-way). Channels available but not in use: N.A.

Basic Service

Subscribers: 787.

Programming (received off-air): ESPN Classic Sports; KAKE-TV (ABC) Wichita; KPTS (PBS) Hutchinson; KSAS-TV (FOX) Wichita; KSNW (NBC) Wichita; KWCH-DT (CBS) Hutchinson; 9 FMs.

Programming (via satellite): ABC Family Channel; Animal Planet; Arts & Entertainment; Cartoon Network; CNN; Comedy Central; Country Music TV; C-SPAN; CW+; Discovery Channel; Disney Channel; ESPN; ESPN 2; Food Network; Fox News Channel; Fox Sports Net Midwest; FX; Hallmark Channel; Headline News; HGTV; History Channel; Home Shopping Network; Lifetime; MSNBC; MTV; NFL Network; Nickelodeon; Speed Channel; Spike TV; Syfy; TBS Superstation; The Learning Channel; Travel Channel; Turner Network TV; TV Guide Network; TV Land; USA Network; Weather Channel; WGN America.

Current originations: Public Access.

Fee: $29.95 installation; $39.95 monthly.

Digital Basic Service

Subscribers: N.A.

Programming (via satellite): AmericanLife TV Network; BBC America; Bio; Black Family Channel; Bloomberg Television; Bravo; Canales N; CMT Pure Country; Current; Discovery Digital Networks; DMX Music; Encore (multiplexed); ESPN 2; ESPN Classic Sports; ESPNews; Flix; Fox College Sports Atlantic; Fox College Sports Central; Fox College Sports Pacific; Fox Movie Channel; Fox Soccer; Fuse; G4; GAS; Golf Channel; Great American Country; GSN; Halogen Network; HGTV; History Channel; History Channel International; Independent Film Channel; Lifetime Movie Network; MTV Networks Digital Suite; National Geographic Channel; Nick Jr.; NickToons TV; Outdoor Channel; Ovation; ShopNBC; Sleuth; Speed Channel; Style Network; Sundance Channel; Syfy; The Word Network; Toon Disney; Trinity Broadcasting Network; Turner Classic Movies; Versus; WE tv.

Pay Service 1

Pay Units: 122.

Programming (via satellite): Cinemax.

Fee: $14.95 installation; $8.95 monthly.

Pay Service 2

Pay Units: 152.

Programming (via satellite): HBO.

Fee: $14.95 installation; $8.95 monthly.

Digital Pay Service 1

Pay Units: N.A.

Programming (via satellite): Cinemax (multiplexed); HBO (multiplexed); Showtime (multiplexed); Starz (multiplexed); The Movie Channel (multiplexed).

Pay-Per-View

iN DEMAND (delivered digitally); Hot Choice (delivered digitally); Playboy TV (delivered digitally); Fresh (delivered digitally); Shorteez (delivered digitally).

Internet Service

Operational: Yes.

Fee: $24.95 installation; $39.95 monthly.

Telephone Service

None

Miles of Plant: 22.0 (coaxial); None (fiber optic). Homes passed: 1,437. Total homes in franchised area: 1,437.

Chief Executive Officer: Bill Haggarty. Regional Vice President: Andrew Dearth. Vice President, Marketing: Tracy Bass.

City fee: 3% of gross.

Ownership: Allegiance Communications (MSO).

MELVERN—Galaxy Cablevision, 1928 S Lincoln Ave, Ste 200, York, NE 68467. Phone: 402-362-3332. Fax: 402-362-4890. Web Site: http://www.galaxycable.com. ICA: KS0400.

TV Market Ranking: Outside TV Markets (MELVERN). Franchise award date: N.A. Franchise expiration date: N.A. Began: January 1, 1983.

Channel capacity: 36 (not 2-way capable). Channels available but not in use: 8.

Basic Service

Subscribers: 36.

Programming (received off-air): KCTV (CBS) Kansas City; KMBC-TV (ABC) Kansas City; KSHB-TV (NBC) Kansas City; KSMO-TV (MNT) Kansas City; KSNT (FOX, NBC) Topeka; KTKA-TV (ABC, CW) Topeka; KTWU (PBS) Topeka; WDAF-TV (FOX) Kansas City; WIBW-TV (CBS, MNT) Topeka.

Programming (via satellite): ABC Family Channel; Arts & Entertainment; CNN; Discovery Channel; Disney Channel; ESPN; ESPN 2; HGTV; Lifetime; Outdoor Channel; TBS Superstation; Toon Disney; Trinity Broadcasting Network; Turner Classic Movies; Turner Network TV; USA Network; WGN America.

Fee: $35.00 installation; $36.80 monthly.

Pay Service 1

Pay Units: N.A.

Programming (via satellite): Cinemax; HBO.

Internet Service

Operational: No.

Telephone Service

None

Miles of Plant: 5.0 (coaxial); None (fiber optic). Homes passed: 210.

State Manager: Cheyenne Wohlford. Technical Manager: John Davidshofer. Sales Manager: Mike Thomas. Customer Service Manager: Michael Debermardin.

Ownership: Galaxy Cable Inc. (MSO).

MERIDEN—SCI Cable, PO Box 67235, 6700 SW Topeka Blvd, Topeka, KS 66619-0241. Phone: 785-862-4141. Fax: 785-862-2423. Web Site: http://www.scibroadband.com. ICA: KS0221.

TV Market Ranking: Below 100 (MERIDEN). Franchise award date: N.A. Franchise expiration date: N.A. Began: July 1, 1983.

Channel capacity: 36 (operating 2-way). Channels available but not in use: None.

Basic Service

Subscribers: 89.

Programming (received off-air): KCPT (PBS) Kansas City; KCTV (CBS) Kansas City; KPXE-TV (ION) Kansas City; KSMO-TV (MNT) Kansas City; KSNT (FOX, NBC) Topeka; KTKA-TV (ABC, CW) Topeka; KTWU (PBS) Topeka; WIBW-TV (CBS, MNT) Topeka.

Programming (via satellite): ABC Family Channel; AMC; Animal Planet; Arts & Entertainment; Cartoon Network; CNN; Discovery Channel; Disney Channel; ESPN; ESPN 2; Fox News Channel; Fuse; FX; HGTV; History Channel; Lifetime; Outdoor Channel; TBS Superstation; The Learning Channel; Turner Network TV; USA Network; Weather Channel; WGN America.

Current originations: Public Access.

Fee: $40.00 installation; $39.80 monthly.

Pay Service 1

Pay Units: N.A.

Programming (via satellite): Cinemax; HBO; Showtime; The Movie Channel.

Fee: $11.00 monthly (each).

Internet Service

Operational: No.

Telephone Service

None

Miles of Plant: 8.0 (coaxial); None (fiber optic). Homes passed: 339.

Manager: Kirk Keberlein.

City fee: 3% of gross.

Ownership: SCI Cable Inc. (MSO).

MILFORD—Eagle Communications, 406 NE 14th St, Abilene, KS 67410. Phones: 785-625-4000 (Corporate office); 785-263-2529. Fax: 785-625-8030. Web Site: http://www.eaglecom.net. ICA: KS0239.

TV Market Ranking: Outside TV Markets (MILFORD). Franchise award date: N.A. Franchise expiration date: N.A. Began: June 1, 1976.

Channel capacity: 36 (not 2-way capable). Channels available but not in use: None.

Basic Service

Subscribers: 113.

Programming (received off-air): KAAS-TV (FOX) Salina; KSNT (FOX, NBC) Topeka; KTKA-TV (ABC, CW) Topeka; KTWU (PBS) Topeka; KUSA (NBC) Denver; KWCH-DT (CBS) Hutchinson; WIBW-TV (CBS, MNT) Topeka.

Programming (via satellite): ABC Family Channel; AMC; Arts & Entertainment; Cartoon Network; CNN; Comedy Central; Discovery Channel; Disney Channel; E! Entertainment Television; ESPN; ESPN 2; Fox Sports Net Midwest; Fuse; Great American Country; Headline News; History Channel; Lifetime; Outdoor Channel; QVC; Syfy; TBS Superstation; The Learning Channel; Turner Network TV; USA Network; Weather Channel; WGN America.

Fee: $24.95 installation; $41.45 monthly.

Pay Service 1

Pay Units: 14.

Programming (via satellite): HBO.

Fee: $11.95 monthly.

Pay Service 2

Pay Units: N.A.

Programming (via satellite): Showtime; The Movie Channel.

Fee: $11.95 monthly (each).

Internet Service

Operational: No.

Telephone Service

None

Miles of Plant: 5.0 (coaxial); None (fiber optic). Homes passed: 260.

President: Gary Shorman. Regional Manager: Dennis Weese. General Manager: Rex Skiles.

City fee: 5% of gross.

Ownership: Eagle Communications Inc. (KS) (MSO).

MILTONVALE—Twin Valley Communications. Formerly served by Bennington, KS [KS0214]. This cable system has converted to IPTV, PO Box 515, Clay Center, KS 67432. Phones: 800-515-3311; 785-427-2288. Fax: 785-427-2216. E-mail: tvinc@twinvalley.net. Web Site: http://www.twinvalley.net. ICA: KS5032.

Channel capacity: N.A. Channels available but not in use: N.A.

Internet Service

Operational: Yes.

Telephone Service

Digital: Operational

Ownership: Twin Valley Communications Inc.

MINNEAPOLIS—Eagle Communications, 406 NE 14th St, Abilene, KS 67410. Phones: 785-625-4000 (Corporate office); 785-625-5910. Fax: 785-625-8030. Web Site: http://www.eaglecom.net. ICA: KS0117.

TV Market Ranking: Below 100 (MINNEAPOLIS). Franchise award date: May 1, 1974. Franchise expiration date: N.A. Began: September 1, 1975.

Channel capacity: N.A. Channels available but not in use: N.A.

Basic Service

Subscribers: 279.

Programming (received off-air): KAAS-TV (FOX) Salina; KAKE-TV (ABC) Wichita; KMGH-TV (ABC) Denver; KMTW (MNT) Hutchinson; KOOD (PBS) Hays; KSCW-DT (CW) Wichita; KSNC (NBC) Great Bend; KUSA (NBC) Denver; WIBW-TV (CBS, MNT) Topeka; allband FM.

Programming (via satellite): C-SPAN; Home Shopping Network; QVC; Weather Channel.

Current originations: Religious Access.

Planned originations: Public Access.

Fee: $35.00 installation; $19.95 monthly.

Expanded Basic Service 1

Subscribers: N.A.

Programming (via satellite): ABC Family Channel; AMC; Animal Planet; Arts & Entertainment; Bravo; CNBC; CNN; C-SPAN 2; Discovery Channel; Disney Channel; E! Entertainment Television; ESPN; ESPN 2; ESPN Classic Sports; ESPNews; FitTV; Food Network; Fox Movie Channel; Fox News Channel; Fox Sports Net Midwest; Fuse; FX; Great American Country; Hallmark Channel; HGTV; History Channel; Jewelry Television; Lifetime; MSNBC; National Geographic Channel; NFL Network; Nickelodeon; Outdoor Channel; RFD-TV; Syfy; TBS Superstation; The Learning Channel; Toon Disney; Travel Channel; Trinity Broadcasting Network; truTV; Turner Network TV; TV Land; USA Network; WGN America.

Fee: $21.50 monthly.

Digital Basic Service

Subscribers: N.A.

Programming (via satellite): AmericanLife TV Network; BBC America; Bio; Bloomberg Television; Church Channel; Cooking Channel; Current; Discovery Health Channel; Discovery Kids Channel; Discovery Military Channel; Discovery Planet Green; DMX Music; Do-It-Yourself; Eternal Word TV Network; Fox College Sports Atlantic; Fox College Sports Central; Fox College Sports Pacific; Fox Soccer; G4; Golf Channel; Gospel Music Channel; GSN; Hallmark

Movie Channel; Halogen Network; History Channel International; ID Investigation Discovery; Independent Film Channel; INSP; JCTV; Lifetime Movie Network; Science Channel; Sleuth; SoapNet; Speed Channel; Style Network; Sundance Channel; The Word Network; Turner Classic Movies; Versus; WE tv.

Fee: $3.95 monthly (sports, variety or entertainment package), $5.95 monthly (basic).

Digital Pay Service 1

Pay Units: N.A.

Programming (via satellite): Cinemax (multiplexed); Encore (multiplexed); Flix; HBO (multiplexed); Showtime (multiplexed); Starz (multiplexed); The Movie Channel (multiplexed).

Fee: $11.95 monthly (HBO, Cinemax, Starz/Encore or Showtime/TMC/Flix).

Pay-Per-View

iN DEMAND (delivered digitally); Playboy TV (delivered digitally); Fresh (delivered digitally); Spice 2 (delivered digitally); Club Jenna (delivered digitally).

Internet Service

Operational: Yes.

Fee: $22.95 monthly.

Telephone Service

Digital: Operational

Fee: $16.00 monthly

Miles of Plant: 14.0 (coaxial); None (fiber optic). Homes passed: 859.

President: Gary Shorman. Regional Manager: Dennis Weese. General Manager: Rex Skiles.

City fee: 3% of gross.

Ownership: Eagle Communications Inc. (KS) (MSO).

MONTEZUMA—United Communications Assn. Inc. Now served by CIMARRON, KS [KS0126]. ICA: KS0259.

MORGANVILLE—Formerly served by Eagle Communications. No longer in operation. ICA: KS0401.

MORRILL—Rainbow Communications, PO Box 147, Everest, KS 66424. Phones: 800-892-0163; 785-866-2390. Fax: 785-866-2393. Web Site: http://www.rainbowtel.net. ICA: KS0402.

TV Market Ranking: Outside TV Markets (MORRILL). Franchise award date: N.A. Franchise expiration date: N.A. Began: N.A.

Channel capacity: 36 (operating 2-way). Channels available but not in use: N.A.

Basic Service

Subscribers: 31.

Programming (received off-air): KPTM (FOX, MNT) Omaha; KQTV (ABC) St. Joseph; KSNT (FOX, NBC) Topeka; KTKA-TV (ABC, CW) Topeka; KTWU (PBS) Topeka; KUON-TV (PBS) Lincoln; KXVO (CW) Omaha; WIBW-TV (CBS, MNT) Topeka.

Programming (via satellite): CNN; ESPN; Headline News; Lifetime; QVC; Spike TV; TBS Superstation; Turner Network TV; USA Network; Weather Channel; WGN America.

Fee: $29.95 installation; $18.95 monthly.

Expanded Basic Service 1

Subscribers: 26.

Programming (via satellite): ABC Family Channel; Arts & Entertainment; Discovery Channel; Disney Channel; Great American Country; History Channel; Nickelodeon; The Learning Channel; VH1.

Fee: $14.00 monthly.

Digital Basic Service

Subscribers: 3.

Programming (via satellite): AmericanLife TV Network; BBC America; Bio; Bloomberg Television; Discovery Digital Networks; DMX Music; ESPN Classic Sports; ESPNews; Fox Movie Channel; G4; GAS; Golf Channel; GSN; History Channel International; Lifetime Movie Network; National Geographic Channel; Nick Jr.; Outdoor Channel; Speed Channel; Style Network; Toon Disney; WE tv.

Fee: $12.95 monthly.

Digital Pay Service 1

Pay Units: 1.

Programming (via satellite): Cinemax (multiplexed); Encore (multiplexed); Flix; HBO (multiplexed); Showtime (multiplexed); Starz (multiplexed); The Movie Channel (multiplexed).

Fee: $12.95 monthly (each).

Video-On-Demand: No

Pay-Per-View

iN DEMAND (delivered digitally); Hot Choice (delivered digitally); Playboy TV (delivered digitally).

Internet Service

Operational: Yes.

Broadband Service: Lighting Jack High Speed.

Fee: $39.95 monthly.

Telephone Service

None

Miles of Plant: 3.0 (coaxial); None (fiber optic). Homes passed: 131.

General Manager: James Lednicky. Plant Manager: Jim Streeter. Marketing Manager: Jackie Petersen. Network Engineer: Scott Wheeler.

Ownership: Rainbow Communications (MSO).

MORROWVILLE—Formerly served by Diode Cable Co. No longer in operation. ICA: KS0350.

MOUND VALLEY—Formerly served by National Cable Inc. No longer in operation. ICA: KS0274.

MOUNDRIDGE—Mid-Kansas Cable Services Inc., PO Box 960, 109 N Christian Ave, Moundridge, KS 67107-0960. Phone: 620-345-2831. Fax: 620-345-6106. ICA: KS0133.

TV Market Ranking: 67 (MOUNDRIDGE). Franchise award date: April 15, 1980. Franchise expiration date: N.A. Began: April 1, 1981.

Channel capacity: 36 (2-way capable). Channels available but not in use: N.A.

Basic Service

Subscribers: 559.

Programming (received off-air): KAKE-TV (ABC) Wichita; KMTW (MNT) Hutchinson; KPTS (PBS) Hutchinson; KSAS-TV (FOX) Wichita; KSCW-DT (CW) Wichita; KSNW (NBC) Wichita; KWCH-DT (CBS) Hutchinson.

Programming (via satellite): ABC Family Channel; AMC; Arts & Entertainment; Country Music TV; C-SPAN; Discovery Channel; Disney Channel; ESPN; ESPN 2; Fox News Channel; Fox Sports Net; HGTV; History Channel; Lifetime; Nickelodeon; Spike TV; TBS Superstation; Turner Classic Movies; Turner Network TV; TV Land; USA Network; Weather Channel; WGN America.

Fee: $20.00 installation; $16.70 monthly; $3.00 converter; $5.00 additional installation.

Pay Service 1

Pay Units: 92.

Programming (via satellite): HBO.

Fee: $20.00 installation; $10.50 monthly.

Video-On-Demand: No

Internet Service

Operational: No, DSL only.

Telephone Service

None

Miles of Plant: 15.0 (coaxial); None (fiber optic). Homes passed: 646. Total homes in franchised area: 646.

Manager: Reiny Wedel. Marketing Director: Kay Koehn. Chief Technician: Tom Stucky.

City fee: 3% of gross.

Ownership: Mid-Kansas Cable Services Inc. (MSO).

MOUNT HOPE—Formerly served by Almega Cable. No longer in operation. ICA: KS0208.

MULLINVILLE—Formerly served by Mullinville Cable TV. No longer in operation. ICA: KS0309.

MULVANE—Cox Communications. Now served by WICHITA, KS [KS0001]. ICA: KS0095.

MULVANE (unincorporated areas)—Formerly served by CableDirect. No longer in operation. ICA: KS0403.

MUNDEN—Formerly served by Westcom. No longer in operation. ICA: KS0354.

MUNJOR—Nex-Tech, PO Box 158, 145 N Main St, Lenora, KS 67645-0158. Phones: 785-567-9226; 785-567-4281. Fax: 785-567-7872. Web Site: http://www.nex-tech.com. ICA: KS0473.

TV Market Ranking: Below 100 (MUNJOR). Channel capacity: N.A. Channels available but not in use: N.A.

Basic Service

Subscribers: N.A.

Programming (received off-air): KAKE-TV (ABC) Wichita; KBSH-DT (CBS) Hays; KGIN (CBS, MNT) Grand Island; KHGI-TV (ABC) Kearney; KLNE-TV (PBS) Lexington; KMTW (MNT) Hutchinson; KOOD (PBS) Hays; KSAS-TV (FOX) Wichita; KSCW-DT (CW) Wichita; KSNC (NBC) Great Bend; KSNK (NBC) McCook.

Programming (via satellite): C-SPAN; Eternal Word TV Network; QVC; TV Guide Network; Weather Channel; WGN America.

Current originations: Public Access.

Fee: $34.95 monthly.

Digital Basic Service

Subscribers: N.A.

Programming (via satellite): AmericanLife TV Network; BBC America; Bloomberg Television; CMT Pure Country; Current; Discovery Health Channel; Discovery Kids Channel; Discovery Military Channel; Discovery Planet Green; DMX Music; ESPN Classic Sports; ESPNews; Fox College Sports Atlantic; Fox College Sports Central; Fox College Sports Pacific; Fox Movie Channel; Fox Soccer; Golf Channel; Halogen Network; ID Investigation Discovery; Independent Film Channel; Lifetime Movie Network; MTV Hits; MTV2; National Geographic Channel; Nick Jr.; Science Channel; ShopNBC; Style Network; TeenNick; Toon Disney; Versus; VH1 Classic; VH1 Soul; WE tv.

Fee: $5.00 monthly (digital access), $6.95 monthly (sports), $10.95 monthly (variety).

Pay Service 1

Pay Units: N.A.

Fee: $11.45 monthly.

Digital Pay Service 1

Pay Units: N.A.

Programming (via satellite): Cinemax (multiplexed); Encore (multiplexed); Flix; HBO (multiplexed); Showtime (multiplexed); Starz (multiplexed); Sundance Channel; The Movie Channel (multiplexed).

Fee: $6.95 monthly (Cinemax), $9.95 monthly (Starz/Encore), $11.95 monthly (HBO), $13.45 monthly (Showtime/TMC).

Pay-Per-View

Movies (delivered digitally); Hot Choice (delivered digitally); Playboy TV (delivered digitally); Fresh (delivered digitally); Club Jenna (delivered digitally).

Chief Operating Officer: Jeff Wick. Manager: Brent Fine.

Ownership: Rural Telephone Co. (MSO).

MUSCOTAH—Rainbow Communications, PO Box 147, Everest, KS 66424. Phones: 800-892-0163; 785-866-2390. Fax: 785-548-7517. E-mail: carsoncomm@carsoncomm.net. Web Site: http://www.rainbowtel.net. ICA: KS0345.

TV Market Ranking: Outside TV Markets (MUSCOTAH). Franchise award date: N.A. Franchise expiration date: N.A. Began: March 15, 1989.

Channel capacity: 36 (operating 2-way). Channels available but not in use: None.

Basic Service

Subscribers: 13.

Programming (received off-air): KCTV (CBS) Kansas City; KCWE (CW) Kansas City; KMBC-TV (ABC) Kansas City; KMCI-TV (IND) Lawrence; KPXE-TV (ION) Kansas City; KSHB-TV (NBC) Kansas City; KSMO-TV (MNT) Kansas City; KSNT (FOX, NBC) Topeka; KTKA-TV (ABC, CW) Topeka; KTWU (PBS) Topeka; WDAF-TV (FOX) Kansas City; WIBW-TV (CBS, MNT) Topeka.

Programming (via satellite): CNN; Hallmark Channel; Headline News; Weather Channel; WGN America.

Fee: $29.95 installation; $13.95 monthly.

Pay Service 1

Pay Units: N.A.

Programming (via satellite): Showtime; The Movie Channel.

Fee: $8.95 monthly.

Video-On-Demand: No

Internet Service

Operational: Yes.

Broadband Service: Lighting Jack High Speed.

Fee: $39.95 monthly.

Telephone Service
None
Miles of Plant: 3.0 (coaxial); None (fiber optic). Homes passed: 98.
General Manager: James Lednicky. Chief Technician: Brian McQueen. Plant Manager: Jim Streeter. Operations Director: Chris Wardman.
Ownership: Rainbow Communications (MSO).

NARKA—Formerly served by Westcom. No longer in operation. ICA: KS0460.

NATOMA—Eagle Communications. Now served by EDMOND, KS [KS0450]. ICA: KS0222.

NEODESHA—Cable One. Now served by INDEPENDENCE, KS [KS0022]. ICA: KS0063.

NEOSHO RAPIDS—Galaxy Cablevision, 1928 S Lincoln Ave, Ste 200, York, NE 68467. Phone: 402-362-3332. Fax: 402-362-4890. Web Site: http://www.galaxycable.com. ICA: KS0433.
TV Market Ranking: Outside TV Markets (NEOSHO RAPIDS). Franchise award date: N.A. Franchise expiration date: N.A. Began: N.A.
Channel capacity: 31 (not 2-way capable). Channels available but not in use: 15.
Basic Service
Subscribers: 22.
Programming (received off-air): KSNT (FOX, NBC) Topeka; KTKA-TV (ABC, CW) Topeka; KTWU (PBS) Topeka; WIBW-TV (CBS, MNT) Topeka.
Programming (via satellite): ABC Family Channel; Arts & Entertainment; CNN; Discovery Channel; ESPN; ESPN 2; Outdoor Channel; TBS Superstation; USA Network; WGN America.
Fee: $26.80 monthly.
Pay Service 1
Pay Units: N.A.
Programming (via satellite): HBO.
Internet Service
Operational: No.
Telephone Service
None
Miles of Plant: 5.0 (coaxial); None (fiber optic). Homes passed: 134.
State Manager: Cheyenne Wohlford. Technical Manager: John Davidshofer. Sales Manager: Mike Thomas. Customer Service Manager: Michael Debermardin.
Ownership: Galaxy Cable Inc. (MSO).

NESS CITY—Formerly served by Cebridge Connections. Now served by RUSH CENTER, KS [KS0418]. ICA: KS0109.

NEWTON—Cox Communications. Now served by WICHITA, KS [KS0001]. ICA: KS0018.

NORCATUR—Formerly served by Pinpoint Cable TV. No longer in operation. ICA: KS0314.

NORTON—Nex-Tech. Formerly [KS0050]. This cable system has converted to IPTV, PO Box 158, 145 N Main St, Lenora, KS 67645-0158. Phones: 877-567-7872; 785-567-4281. Fax: 785-567-4401. E-mail: webmaster@nex-tech.com. Web Site: http://www.nex-tech.com. ICA: KS5050.
Channel capacity: N.A. Channels available but not in use: N.A.
Internet Service
Operational: Yes.
Telephone Service
Digital: Operational
Ownership: Rural Telephone Co.

NORTON—Nex-Tech. This cable system has converted to IPTV. See Norton, KS [KS5050]. ICA: KS0050.

NORTONVILLE—Giant Communications, 418 W 5th St, Ste C, Holton, KS 66436-1506. Phones: 800-346-9084; 785-364-9331. Fax: 785-866-2144. E-mail: billbarton@giantcomm.net. Web Site: http://www.giantcomm.net. ICA: KS0196.
TV Market Ranking: Below 100 (NORTONVILLE). Franchise award date: N.A. Franchise expiration date: N.A. Began: February 10, 1984.
Channel capacity: 40 (operating 2-way). Channels available but not in use: 14.
Basic Service
Subscribers: 90.
Programming (received off-air): KCPT (PBS) Kansas City; KCTV (CBS) Kansas City; KCWE (CW) Kansas City; KSMO-TV (MNT) Kansas City; KSNT (FOX, NBC) Topeka; KTKA-TV (ABC, CW) Topeka; KTMJ-CA Topeka; KTWU (PBS) Topeka; WIBW-TV (CBS, MNT) Topeka.
Programming (via satellite): ABC Family Channel; AMC; Animal Planet; Arts & Entertainment; Bloomberg Television; Bravo; Cartoon Network; CNN; Comedy Central; Country Music TV; C-SPAN; Discovery Channel; Discovery Health Channel; Disney Channel; Disney XD; Do-It-Yourself; E! Entertainment Television; ESPN; ESPN 2; ESPN Classic Sports; Eternal Word TV Network; Food Network; Fox News Channel; Fox Soccer; FX; Great American Country; Hallmark Channel; Headline News; HGTV; Home Shopping Network; Lifetime; Lifetime Movie Network; MSNBC; MTV; National Geographic Channel; NFL Network; Nickelodeon; Outdoor Channel; QVC; RFD-TV; Speed Channel; Spike TV; Syfy; TBS Superstation; The Learning Channel; Travel Channel; Trinity Broadcasting Network; truTV; Turner Classic Movies; Turner Network TV; TV Land; USA Network; VH1; Weather Channel; WGN America.
Fee: $35.00 installation; $46.95 monthly; $5.00 converter.
Digital Basic Service
Subscribers: N.A.
Programming (via satellite): BBC America; Bio; Bloomberg Television; Country Music TV; Discovery Health Channel; Discovery Kids Channel; Discovery Military Channel; Discovery Planet Green; DMX Music; ESPN Classic Sports; ESPN U; ESPNews; FitTV; Fox Movie Channel; Fox Soccer; Fuse; G4; Golf Channel; GSN; Halogen Network; History Channel International; ID Investigation Discovery; Independent Film Channel; Lifetime Movie Network; MTV2; National Geographic Channel; Nick Jr.; NickToons TV; Science Channel; Style Network; Syfy; TeenNick; Turner Classic Movies; Versus; VH1 Classic; WE tv.
Fee: $15.95 monthly.
Digital Expanded Basic Service
Subscribers: N.A.
Programming (via satellite): Encore (multiplexed); Fox Movie Channel; Starz (multiplexed); Starz HDTV; Starz Kids & Family HD; Turner Classic Movies.
Fee: $13.95 monthly.
Digital Expanded Basic Service 2
Subscribers: N.A.
Programming (via satellite): ABC Family HD; Animal Planet HD; Arts & Entertainment HD; CNN HD; Discovery Channel HD; Discovery HD Theater; Discovery Planet Green HD; Disney Channel HD; ESPN 2 HD; ESPN HD; Food Network HD; Fox News HD; FSN HD; FX HD; HGTV HD; History Channel HD; Lifetime Movie Network HD; Lifetime Television HD; National Geographic Channel HD Network; Outdoor Channel 2 HD; QVC HD; Science Channel HD; Speed HD; Syfy HD; TBS in HD; TLC HD; Travel Channel HD; Turner Network TV HD; USA Network HD.
Fee: $10.95 monthly.
Pay Service 1
Pay Units: 2.
Programming (via satellite): Cinemax.
Fee: $8.95 monthly.
Pay Service 2
Pay Units: 19.
Programming (via satellite): The Movie Channel.
Fee: $11.95 monthly.
Pay Service 3
Pay Units: 14.
Programming (via satellite): HBO.
Fee: $11.95 monthly.
Digital Pay Service 1
Pay Units: N.A.
Programming (via satellite): Cinemax (multiplexed); Cinemax HD; Flix; HBO (multiplexed); HBO HD; Showtime (multiplexed); Showtime HD; The Movie Channel (multiplexed); The Movie Channel HD.
Fee: $11.95 monthly (Cinemax), $14.95 monthly (HBO or Showtime/TMC/Flix).
Video-On-Demand: No
Pay-Per-View
iN DEMAND (delivered digitally); Hot Choice (delivered digitally).
Internet Service
Operational: Yes.
Telephone Service
None
Miles of Plant: 5.0 (coaxial); None (fiber optic). Homes passed: 320.
Manager: Bill Barton. Headend Technician: Jay Stewart.; Julian Rodriguez.
City fee: 3% of basic gross.
Ownership: Giant Communications (MSO).

NORWICH—Formerly served by Almega Cable. No longer in operation. ICA: KS0247.

OAKLEY—S&T Cable, 211 Center Ave, Oakley, KS 67748. Phones: 866-790-0241; 785-694-2256; 785-671-8930. Fax: 785-671-8960. Web Site: http://www.sttelcom.com. ICA: KS0099.
TV Market Ranking: Below 100 (OAKLEY). Franchise award date: April 1, 1976. Franchise expiration date: N.A. Began: May 1, 1976.
Channel capacity: 165 (2-way capable). Channels available but not in use: None.
Basic Service
Subscribers: 812.
Programming (received off-air): KBSL-DT (CBS) Goodland; KLBY (ABC) Colby; KOOD (PBS) Hays; KSAS-TV (FOX) Wichita; KSNK (NBC) McCook; KWGN-TV (CW) Denver.
Programming (via satellite): C-SPAN 2; LWS Local Weather Station; QVC.
Current originations: Government Access; Educational Access; Public Access.
Fee: $20.00 installation; $13.00 monthly; $.57 converter.
Expanded Basic Service 1
Subscribers: 796.
Programming (via satellite): ABC Family Channel; AMC; Animal Planet; Arts & Entertainment; Bravo; Cartoon Network; CNBC; CNN; Comedy Central; Country Music TV; C-SPAN; Daystar TV Network; Discovery Channel; Disney Channel; E! Entertainment Television; ESPN; ESPN 2; Eternal Word TV Network; FitTV; Food Network; Fox News Channel; Fox Sports Net; FX; Hallmark Channel; Headline News; HGTV; History Channel; Home Shopping Network; Lifetime; Lifetime Movie Network; MSNBC; MTV; NFL Network; Nickelodeon; Oxygen; RFD-TV; Speed Channel; Spike TV; Syfy; TBS Superstation; The Learning Channel; The Sportsman Channel; Travel Channel; Trinity Broadcasting Network; truTV; Turner Classic Movies; Turner Network TV; TV Land; USA Network; VH1; WE tv; Weather Channel; WGN America.
Fee: $22.33 monthly.
Digital Basic Service
Subscribers: N.A.
Programming (via satellite): AmericanLife TV Network; BBC America; Bio; Bloomberg Television; Current; Discovery Health Channel; Discovery Kids Channel; Discovery Military Channel; Discovery Planet Green; ESPN Classic Sports; ESPN U; ESPNews; G4; Golf Channel; GSN; History Channel International; ID Investigation Discovery; MTV2; Music Choice; National Geographic Channel; Nick Jr.; Outdoor Channel; Ovation; Science Channel; Style Network; TeenNick; Toon Disney; Versus; VH1 Classic.
Fee: $14.95 monthly.
Digital Expanded Basic Service
Subscribers: N.A.
Programming (via satellite): Encore (multiplexed); Fox Movie Channel; Independent Film Channel; Sundance Channel.
Digital Pay Service 1
Pay Units: N.A.
Programming (via satellite): Cinemax (multiplexed); HBO (multiplexed); Showtime (multiplexed); Starz (multiplexed); The Movie Channel (multiplexed).
Fee: $11.75 monthly (HBO, Cinemax, Showtime/TMC or Starz/Encore).
Video-On-Demand: No
Pay-Per-View
iN DEMAND (delivered digitally); Hot Choice (delivered digitally); Pleasure (delivered digitally).
Internet Service
Operational: No, Both DSL & dial-up.
Telephone Service
None
Miles of Plant: 14.0 (coaxial); None (fiber optic). Homes passed: 900. Total homes in franchised area: 900.
General Manager: Steve Richards. Cable Manager: Clint Felzien. Manager: Pat Mallory.

Franchise fee: None.
Ownership: S & T Communications Inc. (MSO).

OBERLIN—Eagle Communications, PO Box 426, 415 Barclay Ave, WaKeeney, KS 67672. Phones: 785-743-5616; 785-625-4000 (Corporate office). Fax: 785-743-2694. Web Site: http://www.eaglecom.net. ICA: KS0090.
TV Market Ranking: Below 100 (OBERLIN). Franchise award date: N.A. Franchise expiration date: N.A. Began: April 1, 1970.
Channel capacity: 61 (operating 2-way). Channels available but not in use: 10.

Basic Service
Subscribers: 503.
Programming (received off-air): KBSL-DT (CBS) Goodland; KLBY (ABC) Colby; KMTW (MNT) Hutchinson; KOOD (PBS) Hays; KSAS-TV (FOX) Wichita; KSNK (NBC) McCook; KWNB-TV (ABC) Hayes Center; 4 FMs.
Programming (via satellite): Eternal Word TV Network; KWGN-TV (CW) Denver; QVC; Trinity Broadcasting Network; Weather Channel.
Current originations: Educational Access.
Fee: $24.95 installation; $19.95 monthly.

Expanded Basic Service 1
Subscribers: N.A.
Programming (received off-air): KSCW-DT (CW) Wichita.
Programming (via satellite): ABC Family Channel; AMC; Animal Planet; Arts & Entertainment; Cartoon Network; CNBC; CNN; Comedy Central; Country Music TV; Discovery Channel; Disney Channel; E! Entertainment Television; ESPN; ESPN 2; Food Network; Fox News Channel; Fox Sports Net Midwest; FX; Great American Country; Hallmark Channel; Headline News; HGTV; History Channel; Lifetime; MSNBC; MTV; National Geographic Channel; NFL Network; Nickelodeon; Outdoor Channel; Speed Channel; Spike TV; Syfy; TBS Superstation; The Learning Channel; Travel Channel; Turner Classic Movies; Turner Network TV; TV Land; USA Network; VH1.
Fee: $25.50 monthly.

Pay Service 1
Pay Units: 57.
Programming (via satellite): The Movie Channel.
Fee: $11.95 monthly.

Pay Service 2
Pay Units: 40.
Programming (via satellite): Showtime.
Fee: $11.95 monthly.

Pay Service 3
Pay Units: 74.
Programming (via satellite): HBO.
Fee: $11.95 monthly.

Video-On-Demand: No

Internet Service
Operational: Yes. Began: June 23, 2002.
Subscribers: 176.
Broadband Service: Eagle Internet.
Fee: $22.95 monthly.

Telephone Service
Analog: Not Operational
Digital: Operational
Fee: $16.00 monthly
Miles of Plant: 14.0 (coaxial); None (fiber optic). Homes passed: 954. Total homes in franchised area: 977.
President & Chief Executive Officer: Gary Shorman. General Manager: Rex Skiles. Chief Technician: Les Libal.
City fee: 2% of gross.
Ownership: Eagle Communications Inc. (KS) (MSO).

OFFERLE—GBT Communications Inc., PO Box 229, 103 Lincoln St, Rush Center, KS 67575-0229. Phones: 800-432-7965; 785-372-4236. Fax: 785-372-4210. Web Site: http://www.gbta.net. ICA: KS0405.
TV Market Ranking: Outside TV Markets (OFFERLE). Franchise award date: N.A. Franchise expiration date: N.A. Began: January 1, 1977.
Channel capacity: N.A. Channels available but not in use: N.A.

Basic Service
Subscribers: 60.
Programming (received off-air): KBSD-DT (CBS) Ensign; KOOD (PBS) Hays; KSAS-TV (FOX) Wichita; KSNC (NBC) Great Bend; KUPK-TV (ABC) Garden City; LWS Local Weather Station; allband FM.
Programming (via satellite): C-SPAN; C-SPAN 2; Eternal Word TV Network; TBS Superstation; WGN America.
Fee: $15.00 installation; $9.95 monthly.

Expanded Basic Service 1
Subscribers: N.A.
Programming (via satellite): ABC Family Channel; AMC; Animal Planet; Arts & Entertainment; Cartoon Network; CNN; Comedy Central; Country Music TV; Discovery Channel; Disney Channel; E! Entertainment Television; ESPN; ESPN 2; ESPN Classic Sports; ESPNews; Food Network; Fox News Channel; FX; Hallmark Channel; Headline News; HGTV; History Channel; INSP; Lifetime; MSNBC; MTV; NFL Network; Nickelodeon; Outdoor Channel; QVC; Speed Channel; Spike TV; Syfy; The Learning Channel; TLC; Travel Channel; Trinity Broadcasting Network; truTV; Turner Classic Movies; Turner Network TV; TV Land; USA Network; VH1; Weather Channel.
Fee: $23.45 monthly.

Pay Service 1
Pay Units: N.A.
Programming (via satellite): Cinemax; Flix; HBO; Showtime; The Movie Channel.
Fee: $7.00 monthly (Cinemax), $10.00 monthly (HBO), $10.95 monthly (Showtime).

Internet Service
Operational: No.

Telephone Service
None
Miles of Plant: 2.0 (coaxial); None (fiber optic).
General Manager: Gerald Washburn. Chief Technician: Rick Dechant. Marketing Director: Steve Miller. Customer Service Manager: Janice Rein.
City fee: 0% of gross.
Ownership: Golden Belt Telephone Association Inc. (MSO).

OKETO—Blue Valley Tele-Communications. Formerly served by Home, KS [KS0424]. This cable system has converted to IPTV, 1557 Pony Express Hwy, Home, KS 66438. Phones: 877-876-1228; 785-799-3311. E-mail: info@bluevalley.net. Web Site: http://www.bluevalley.net. ICA: KS5012.
TV Market Ranking: Outside TV Markets (Oketo).
Channel capacity: N.A. Channels available but not in use: N.A.

Internet Service
Operational: Yes.

Telephone Service
Digital: Operational
General Manager: Dennis Doyle.
Ownership: Blue Valley Telecommunications.

OLATHE—Comcast Cable, PO Box 2000, 4700 Little Blue Pkwy, Independence, MO 64057. Phone: 816-795-8377. Fax: 816-795-0946. Web Site: http://www.comcast.com. Also serves Johnson County. ICA: KS0005.
TV Market Ranking: 22 (Johnson County, OLATHE). Franchise award date: N.A. Franchise expiration date: N.A. Began: N.A.
Channel capacity: 110 (operating 2-way). Channels available but not in use: 35.

Basic Service
Subscribers: 26,620.
Programming (received off-air): KCPT (PBS) Kansas City; KCTV (CBS) Kansas City; KCWE (CW) Kansas City; KMBC-TV (ABC) Kansas City; KMCI-TV (IND) Lawrence; KPXE-TV (ION) Kansas City; KSHB-TV (NBC) Kansas City; KSMO-TV (MNT) Kansas City; WDAF-TV (FOX) Kansas City.
Programming (via satellite): C-SPAN; Home Shopping Network; Product Information Network; QVC; TBS Superstation; TV Guide Network; WGN America.
Current originations: Leased Access; Government Access; Educational Access.
Fee: $40.00 installation; $10.94 monthly; $1.05 converter; $15.00 additional installation.

Expanded Basic Service 1
Subscribers: N.A.
Programming (via satellite): ABC Family Channel; AMC; Animal Planet; Arts & Entertainment; BET Networks; Bravo; Cartoon Network; CNBC; CNN; Comedy Central; C-SPAN 2; Discovery Channel; Discovery Health Channel; Disney Channel; E! Entertainment Television; ESPN; ESPN 2; ESPN Classic Sports; Eternal Word TV Network; Food Network; Fox News Channel; Fox Sports Net Rocky Mountain; FX; Golf Channel; Great American Country; GSN; Hallmark Channel; Headline News; HGTV; History Channel; Lifetime; Metro Sports; MSNBC; MTV; MTV2; Nickelodeon; Speed Channel; Spike TV; Style Network; Syfy; The Learning Channel; Travel Channel; truTV; Turner Classic Movies; Turner Network TV; TV Land; Univision; USA Network; Versus; VH1; WE tv; Weather Channel.

Digital Basic Service
Subscribers: N.A.
Programming (via satellite): BBC America; Cable in the Classroom; C-SPAN 3; Discovery Digital Networks; DMX Music; Encore Action; ESPNews; Flix; G4; GAS; MTV Networks Digital Suite; National Geographic Channel; Nick Jr.; Nick Too; SoapNet; Sundance Channel; Toon Disney; Weatherscan.

Pay Service 1
Pay Units: N.A.
Programming (via satellite): Cinemax; HBO; Showtime; The Movie Channel.
Fee: $10.95 monthly (each).

Digital Pay Service 1
Pay Units: N.A.
Programming (via satellite): Cinemax (multiplexed); HBO (multiplexed); Showtime (multiplexed); Starz (multiplexed); The Movie Channel (multiplexed).
Fee: $19.99 monthly (each).

Video-On-Demand: Yes

Pay-Per-View
Addressable homes: 1,775.
iN DEMAND (delivered digitally), Fee: $3.95-$5.95, Addressable: Yes; iN DEMAND; Fresh (delivered digitally); Playboy TV (delivered digitally); Shorteez (delivered digitally); Pleasure (delivered digitally); ESPN Extra (delivered digitally); ESPN Now (delivered digitally); NBA TV (delivered digitally).

Internet Service
Operational: Yes.
Broadband Service: Comcast High Speed Internet.
Fee: $42.95 monthly; $7.00 modem lease; $199.00 modem purchase.

Telephone Service
Digital: Operational
Fee: $44.95 monthly
Miles of Plant: 502.0 (coaxial); 104.0 (fiber optic). Homes passed: 46,680.
General Manager: Kandice Wepler. Chief Technician: Ken Covey. Marketing Director: Bill Rougdley. Customer Service Manager: Dana Price.
Ownership: Comcast Cable Communications Inc. (MSO).

OLPE—Galaxy Cablevision, 1928 S Lincoln Ave, Ste 200, York, NE 68467. Phone: 402-362-3332. Fax: 402-362-4890. Web Site: http://www.galaxycable.com. ICA: KS0233.
TV Market Ranking: Outside TV Markets (OLPE). Franchise award date: April 1, 1982. Franchise expiration date: N.A. Began: N.A.
Channel capacity: 31 (not 2-way capable). Channels available but not in use: 7.

Basic Service
Subscribers: 61.
Programming (received off-air): KSNT (FOX, NBC) Topeka; KTKA-TV (ABC, CW) Topeka; KTWU (PBS) Topeka; WIBW-TV (CBS, MNT) Topeka.
Programming (via satellite): ABC Family Channel; Arts & Entertainment; CNN; Discovery Channel; Disney Channel; ESPN; ESPN 2; Headline News; History Channel; Outdoor Channel; TBS Superstation; Toon Disney; Turner Classic Movies; Turner Network TV; USA Network; Weather Channel; WGN America.
Fee: $33.80 monthly.

Pay Service 1
Pay Units: N.A.
Programming (via satellite): Cinemax; HBO.
Fee: $11.00 monthly (each).

Internet Service
Operational: No.

Telephone Service
None
Miles of Plant: 7.0 (coaxial); None (fiber optic). Homes passed: 194.
State Manager: Cheyenne Wohlford. Technical Manager: John Davidshofer. Sales Manager: Mike Thomas. Customer Service Manager: Michael Debermardin.
City fee: 3% of basic.
Ownership: Galaxy Cable Inc. (MSO).

OLSBURG—Formerly served by Giant Communications. No longer in operation. ICA: KS0436.

ONAGA—Blue Valley Tele-communications, 1559 Pony Express Hwy, Home, KS 66438. Phones: 877-876-1228; 785-799-3311. E-mail: info@bluevalley.net. Web Site: http://www.bluevalley.net. Also serves ONAGA. ICA: KS0407.

TV Market Ranking: Outside TV Markets (ONAGA). Franchise award date: N.A. Franchise expiration date: N.A. Began: N.A.

Channel capacity: N.A. Channels available but not in use: N.A.

Digital Basic Service

Subscribers: N.A.

Programming (received off-air): KLKN (ABC) Lincoln; KOLN (CBS, MNT) Lincoln; KPTM (FOX, MNT) Omaha; KSNT (FOX, NBC) Topeka; KTKA-TV (ABC, CW) Topeka; KTWU (PBS) Topeka; WIBW-TV (CBS, MNT) Topeka.

Programming (via satellite): ABC Family Channel; American Movie Classics; Animal Planet; Arts & Entertainment; Bravo; Cartoon Network; Church Channel; CNBC; CNN; Country Music TV; C-SPAN; C-SPAN 2; Discovery Channel; Disney Channel; Do-It-Yourself; E! Entertainment Television; ESPN; ESPN 2; ESPN Classic Sports; Eternal Word TV Network; Food Network; Fox News Channel; Fox Sports Net Midwest; FX; Hallmark Channel; Hallmark Movie Channel; Headline News; HGTV; History Channel; Home Shopping Network; ION Television; JCTV; Lifetime; Lifetime Movie Network; MSNBC; MTV; Music Choice; National Geographic Channel; NFL Network; Nickelodeon; Oxygen; QVC; RFD-TV; Smile of a Child; Spike TV; Syfy; TBS Superstation; The Learning Channel; The Sportsman Channel; Travel Channel; Trinity Broadcasting Network; truTV; Turner Network TV; TV Land; USA Network; VH1; Weather Channel; WGN America.

Fee: $51.95 monthly.

Digital Expanded Basic Service

Subscribers: N.A.

Programming (via satellite): BBC America; Bio; Bloomberg Television; Boomerang; CMT Pure Country; Comedy Central; Discovery Health Channel; Discovery Kids Channel; Discovery Military Channel; Discovery Planet Green; Disney XD; ESPN U; ESPNews; FitTV; Fox College Sports Atlantic; Fox College Sports Central; Fox College Sports Pacific; Fox Movie Channel; Fox Soccer; Fuse; G4; Golf Channel; Great American Country; GSN; History Channel International; ID Investigation Discovery; Independent Film Channel; Lifetime Real Women; MTV2; Noggin; Outdoor Channel; Science Channel; Sleuth; Speed Channel; Style Network; TeenNick; Turner Classic Movies; Versus; VH1 Classic; WE tv.

Fee: $12.95 monthly.

Digital Expanded Basic Service 2

Subscribers: N.A.

Programming (via satellite): Animal Planet HD; Arts & Entertainment HD; Discovery Channel HD; Discovery Planet Green HD; Disney Channel HD; ESPN 2 HD; ESPN HD; ESPNews HD; ESPNU HD; History Channel HD; NFL Network HD; Outdoor Channel 2 HD; Palladia; Science Channel HD; TLC HD; Travel Channel HD; Universal HD; Weather Channel HD.

Fee: $10.00 monthly.

Digital Pay Service 1

Pay Units: N.A.

Programming (via satellite): Cinemax (multiplexed); Encore (multiplexed); Flix; HBO (multiplexed); Showtime (multiplexed); Showtime HD; Starz (multiplexed); Starz HDTV; The Movie Channel (multiplexed); The Movie Channel HD.

Fee: $12.95 monthly (HBO, Cinemax, Showtime/TMC/Flix or Starz/Encore).

Internet Service

Operational: Yes, DSL.

Fee: $39.95-$74.95 monthly.

Telephone Service

Digital: Operational

Fee: $23.25 monthly

General Manager: Dennis Doyle. Operations Manager: Andy Torrey. Marketing Manager: Angie Armstrong. Customer Service Supervisor: Deb Runnebaum.

Ownership: Blue Valley Telecommunications (MSO).

OSAGE CITY—Mediacom. Now served by BURLINGTON, KS [KS0064]. ICA: KS0072.

OSAGE COUNTY—Formerly served by Galaxy Cablevision. No longer in operation. ICA: KS0269.

OSKALOOSA—Giant Communications. Now served by McLOUTH, KS [KS0191]. ICA: KS0175.

OSWEGO—Mediacom, 1533 S Enterprise Ave, Springfield, MO 65804. Phone: 417-875-5560. Fax: 417-883-0265. Web Site: http://www.mediacomcable.com. ICA: KS0103.

TV Market Ranking: Below 100 (OSWEGO). Franchise award date: N.A. Franchise expiration date: N.A. Began: October 27, 1980.

Channel capacity: 35 (not 2-way capable). Channels available but not in use: None.

Basic Service

Subscribers: 557.

Programming (received off-air): KOAM-TV (CBS) Pittsburg; KODE-TV (ABC) Joplin; KOED-TV (PBS) Tulsa; KOKI-TV (FOX) Tulsa; KSNF (NBC) Joplin.

Programming (via satellite): ABC Family Channel; AMC; Animal Planet; Arts & Entertainment; CNN; Country Music TV; C-SPAN; Discovery Channel; Disney Channel; ESPN; ESPN 2; Headline News; Lifetime; MTV; Nickelodeon; QVC; Spike TV; Syfy; TBS Superstation; The Learning Channel; Turner Network TV; TV Land; USA Network; Weather Channel; WGN America.

Fee: $35.00 installation; $25.25 monthly.

Pay Service 1

Pay Units: 48.

Programming (via satellite): Cinemax.

Fee: $10.50 monthly.

Pay Service 2

Pay Units: 49.

Programming (via satellite): The Movie Channel.

Fee: $15.00 installation; $10.50 monthly.

Pay Service 3

Pay Units: 123.

Programming (via satellite): Showtime.

Fee: $15.00 installation; $10.50 monthly.

Pay Service 4

Pay Units: 128.

Programming (via satellite): HBO.

Fee: $10.50 monthly.

Video-On-Demand: No

Internet Service

Operational: No.

Telephone Service

None

Miles of Plant: 17.0 (coaxial); None (fiber optic). Homes passed: 1,001.

Vice President: Bill Copeland. Technical Operations Director: Alan Freedman. Technical Operations Manager: Glen Parrish. Sales & Marketing Manager: Will Kuebler.

City fee: 3% of basic.

Ownership: Mediacom LLC (MSO).

OTTAWA—Allegiance Communications, 707 W Saratoga St, Shawnee, OK 74804. Phones: 405-275-6923; 405-395-1131. Web Site: http://www.allegiance.tv. Also serves Garnett. ICA: KS0025.

TV Market Ranking: Below 100 (OTTAWA); Outside TV Markets (Garnett). Franchise award date: N.A. Franchise expiration date: N.A. Began: January 1, 1972.

Channel capacity: N.A. Channels available but not in use: N.A.

Basic Service

Subscribers: 5,272.

Programming (received off-air): KCPT (PBS) Kansas City; KCTV (CBS) Kansas City; KCWE (CW) Kansas City; KMBC-TV (ABC) Kansas City; KMCI-TV (IND) Lawrence; KSHB-TV (NBC) Kansas City; KSMO-TV (MNT) Kansas City; KSNT (FOX, NBC) Topeka; KTKA-TV (ABC, CW) Topeka; KTWU (PBS) Topeka; WDAF-TV (FOX) Kansas City; WIBW-TV (CBS, MNT) Topeka; allband FM.

Programming (via satellite): C-SPAN; ION Television; TV Guide Network; Weather Channel.

Current originations: Public Access.

Fee: $29.95 installation; $21.95 monthly; $2.00 converter; $14.95 additional installation.

Expanded Basic Service 1

Subscribers: 4,784.

Programming (via satellite): ABC Family Channel; AMC; Animal Planet; Arts & Entertainment; Cartoon Network; CNBC; CNN; Comedy Central; Country Music TV; C-SPAN 2; Discovery Channel; Discovery Health Channel; Disney Channel; E! Entertainment Television; Encore (multiplexed); ESPN; ESPN 2; Eternal Word TV Network; Food Network; Fox News Channel; Fox Sports Net Midwest; FX; Hallmark Channel; Headline News; HGTV; History Channel; Home Shopping Network; Lifetime; MSNBC; MTV; Nickelodeon; QVC; Speed Channel; Spike TV; Syfy; TBS Superstation; The Learning Channel; Travel Channel; truTV; Turner Classic Movies; Turner Network TV; TV Land; USA Network; Versus; VH1; WGN America.

Fee: $29.95 installation; $18.02 monthly; $14.95 additional installation.

Digital Basic Service

Subscribers: N.A.

Programming (via satellite): BBC America; Bravo!; Canales N; Discovery Digital Networks; DMX Music; ESPN Classic Sports; ESPNews; Fox Sports World; Fuse; G4; Golf Channel; GSN; Independent Film Channel; Lifetime Movie Network; Sundance Channel; Toon Disney.

Digital Pay Service 1

Pay Units: 500.

Programming (via satellite): Cinemax (multiplexed); HBO (multiplexed); Starz (multiplexed); The Movie Channel (multiplexed).

Video-On-Demand: No

Pay-Per-View

iN DEMAND (delivered digitally), Addressable: Yes; ESPN (delivered digitally).

Internet Service

Operational: Yes.

Fee: $24.95 installation; $39.95 monthly.

Telephone Service

None

Miles of Plant: 88.0 (coaxial); None (fiber optic). Homes passed: 6,558. Total homes in franchised area: 6,558.

Chief Executive Officer: Bill Haggarty. Regional Vice President: Andrew Dearth. Vice President, Marketing: Tracy Bass.

City fee: 5% of gross.

Ownership: Allegiance Communications (MSO).

OVERBROOK—Galaxy Cablevision, 1928 S Lincoln Ave, Ste 200, York, NE 68467. Phone: 402-362-3332. Fax: 402-362-4890. Web Site: http://www.galaxycable.com. ICA: KS0408.

TV Market Ranking: Below 100 (OVERBROOK). Franchise award date: N.A. Franchise expiration date: N.A. Began: February 1, 1982.

Channel capacity: 36 (not 2-way capable). Channels available but not in use: None.

Basic Service

Subscribers: 98.

Programming (received off-air): KCTV (CBS) Kansas City; KMBC-TV (ABC) Kansas City; KSHB-TV (NBC) Kansas City; KSMO-TV (MNT) Kansas City; KSNT (FOX, NBC) Topeka; KTKA-TV (ABC, CW) Topeka; KTWU (PBS) Topeka; WDAF-TV (FOX) Kansas City; WIBW-TV (CBS, MNT) Topeka.

Programming (via satellite): ABC Family Channel; Arts & Entertainment; CNN; Discovery Channel; Disney Channel; ESPN; ESPN 2; Fox News Channel; Fox Sports Net Midwest; FX; Great American Country; Home Shopping Network; Lifetime; Outdoor Channel; TBS Superstation; The Learning Channel; Toon Disney; Turner Network TV; USA Network; Weather Channel; WGN America.

Current originations: Public Access.

Fee: $35.00 installation; $36.70 monthly.

Digital Basic Service

Subscribers: 7.

Programming (via satellite): AmericanLife TV Network; BBC America; Bio; Bloomberg Television; Discovery Digital Networks; DMX Music; ESPN Classic Sports; ESPNews; FitTV; Fox College Sports Atlantic; Fox College Sports Central; Fox College Sports Pacific; Fox Sports World; G4; Golf Channel; GSN; Halogen Network; History Channel; Style Network; WE tv.

Fee: $16.00 monthly.

Digital Expanded Basic Service

Subscribers: N.A.

Programming (via satellite): DMX Music; Encore; Fox Movie Channel; Lifetime Movie Network; Turner Classic Movies.

Fee: $16.00 monthly.

Pay Service 1

Pay Units: 20.

Programming (via satellite): Cinemax; HBO; Showtime; The Movie Channel.

Fee: $7.95 monthly (TMC), $9.95 monthly (Showtime), $10.95 monthly (Cinemax), $13.95 monthly (HBO).

Digital Pay Service 1

Pay Units: N.A.

Programming (via satellite): Cinemax (multiplexed); Flix; HBO (multiplexed); Showtime (multiplexed); The Movie Channel (multiplexed).

Fee: $15.50 monthly.

Pay-Per-View

Addressable homes: 11.

ESPN Now (delivered digitally), Addressable: Yes; sports (delivered digitally); Urban Xtra (delivered digitally).

Internet Service

Operational: No.

Telephone Service

None

Miles of Plant: 8.0 (coaxial); None (fiber optic). Homes passed: 396.

State Manager: Cheyenne Wohlford. Technical Manager: John Davidshofer. Sales Manager: Mike Thomas. Customer Service Manager: Michael Debermardin.
Ownership: Galaxy Cable Inc. (MSO).

OVERLAND PARK—Formerly served by LENEXA, KS [KS0462]. SureWest Broadband. This cable system has converted to IPTV, 9647 Lackman Rd, Lenexa, KS 66219. Phones: 913-825-3000; 913-825-2800. Fax: 913-322-9901. Web Site: http://www.surewest.com. ICA: KS5123.
TV Market Ranking: 22 (OVERLAND PARK).
Channel capacity: N.A. Channels available but not in use: N.A.
Video-On-Demand: Yes
Internet Service
Operational: Yes.
Telephone Service
Digital: Operational
Ownership: SureWest Broadband.

OVERLAND PARK—Time Warner Cable of Johnson County. No longer in operation. ICA: KS0003.

OXFORD—Allegiance Communications, 707 W Saratoga St, Shawnee, OK 74804. Phones: 405-395-1131; 405-275-6923. Web Site: http://www.allegiance.tv. ICA: KS0158.
TV Market Ranking: 67 (OXFORD). Franchise award date: N.A. Franchise expiration date: N.A. Began: May 1, 1982.
Channel capacity: N.A. Channels available but not in use: N.A.
Basic Service
Subscribers: 342.
Programming (received off-air): KAKE-TV (ABC) Wichita; KMTW (MNT) Hutchinson; KPTS (PBS) Hutchinson; KSAS-TV (FOX) Wichita; KSNW (NBC) Wichita; KWCH-DT (CBS) Hutchinson.
Programming (via satellite): C-SPAN; Home Shopping Network; WGN America.
Fee: $41.11 installation; $21.95 monthly.
Expanded Basic Service 1
Subscribers: N.A.
Programming (via satellite): ABC Family Channel; AMC; Animal Planet; Arts & Entertainment; Cartoon Network; CMT Pure Country; CNBC; CNN; Comedy Central; Discovery Channel; Disney Channel; ESPN; ESPN 2; Food Network; Fox News Channel; Fox Sports Net Midwest; FX; Hallmark Channel; Headline News; History Channel; Lifetime; MSNBC; MTV; National Geographic Channel; Nickelodeon; Oxygen; Spike TV; TBS Superstation; The Learning Channel; Travel Channel; Turner Network TV; TV Land; USA Network; VH1; Weather Channel.
Digital Basic Service
Subscribers: N.A.
Programming (via satellite): AmericanLife TV Network; BBC America; Bio; Bloomberg Television; Bravo; Discovery Health Channel; Discovery Home Channel; Discovery Kids Channel; Discovery Military Channel; Discovery Times Channel; DMX Music; Encore (multiplexed); ESPN Classic Sports; ESPNews; FitTV; Flix; Fox Movie Channel; Fox Soccer; G4; GAS; Golf Channel; GSN; Halogen Network; HGTV; History Channel International; Independent Film Channel; Lifetime Movie Network; MTV Hits; MTV2; Nick Jr.; Outdoor Channel; Science Channel; ShopNBC; Speed Channel; Style Network; Syfy; Toon Disney; Trinity Broadcasting Network; Turner Classic Movies; Versus; VH1 Classic; VH1 Country; VH1 Soul; WE tv.
Digital Pay Service 1
Pay Units: N.A.
Programming (via satellite): Cinemax (multiplexed); Encore (multiplexed); HBO (multiplexed); Showtime (multiplexed); Starz (multiplexed); The Movie Channel (multiplexed).
Video-On-Demand: No; No
Pay-Per-View
Movies (delivered digitally); Special events (delivered digitally); Hot Choice (delivered digitally); Playboy TV (delivered digitally); Fresh (delivered digitally); Shorteez (delivered digitally).
Internet Service
Operational: No.
Telephone Service
None
Miles of Plant: 9.0 (coaxial); None (fiber optic). Homes passed: 481. Total homes in franchised area: 481.
Chief Executive Officer: Bill Haggarty. Regional Vice President: Andrew Dearth. Vice President, Marketing: Tracy Bass.
City fee: 2% of gross.
Ownership: Allegiance Communications (MSO).

OZAWKIE—Giant Communications, 418 W 5th St, Ste C, Holton, KS 66436-1506. Phones: 800-346-9084; 785-364-9331. Fax: 785-866-2144. E-mail: billbarton@giantcomm.net. Web Site: http://www.giantcomm.net. ICA: KS0409.
TV Market Ranking: Below 100 (OZAWKIE). Franchise award date: N.A. Franchise expiration date: N.A. Began: May 1, 1983.
Channel capacity: 40 (2-way capable). Channels available but not in use: 14.
Basic Service
Subscribers: 72.
Programming (received off-air): KCPT (PBS) Kansas City; KCTV (CBS) Kansas City; KCWE (CW) Kansas City; KPXE-TV (ION) Kansas City; KSMO-TV (MNT) Kansas City; KSNT (FOX, NBC) Topeka; KTKA-TV (ABC, CW) Topeka; KTMJ-CA Topeka; KTWU (PBS) Topeka; WIBW-TV (CBS, MNT) Topeka.
Programming (via satellite): ABC Family Channel; American Movie Classics; Animal Planet; Arts & Entertainment; Bloomberg Television; Bravo; Cartoon Network; CNN; Comedy Central; Country Music TV; C-SPAN; Discovery Channel; Discovery Health Channel; Disney Channel; Disney XD; Do-It-Yourself; E! Entertainment Television; ESPN; ESPN 2; ESPN Classic Sports; Eternal Word TV Network; Food Network; Fox News Channel; Fox Sports Net; FX; Great American Country; Hallmark Channel; Headline News; HGTV; History Channel; Home Shopping Network; Lifetime; Lifetime Movie Network; MSNBC; MTV; National Geographic Channel; NFL Network; Nickelodeon; Outdoor Channel; QVC; RFD-TV; Speed Channel; Spike TV; Syfy; TBS Superstation; The Learning Channel; Travel Channel; Trinity Broadcasting Network; truTV; Turner Classic Movies; Turner Network TV; TV Land; USA Network; VH1; Weather Channel; WGN America.
Fee: $35.00 installation; $46.95 monthly; $5.00 converter.
Digital Basic Service
Subscribers: N.A.
Programming (via satellite): BBC America; Bio; Bloomberg Television; Country Music TV; Discovery Health Channel; Discovery Kids Channel; Discovery Military Channel; Discovery Planet Green; DMX Music; ESPN Classic Sports; ESPN U; ESPNews; FitTV; Fox Movie Channel; Fox Soccer; Fuse; G4; Golf Channel; GSN; Halogen Network; History Channel International; ID Investigation Discovery; Independent Film Channel; Lifetime Movie Network; MTV2; National Geographic Channel; Nick Jr.; NickToons TV; Science Channel; Style Network; Syfy; TeenNick; Turner Classic Movies; Versus; VH1 Classic; WE tv.
Fee: $15.95 monthly.
Digital Expanded Basic Service
Subscribers: N.A.
Programming (via satellite): Encore (multiplexed); Fox Movie Channel; Starz (multiplexed); Starz HDTV; Starz Kids & Family HD; Turner Classic Movies.
Fee: $13.95 monthly.
Digital Expanded Basic Service 2
Subscribers: N.A.
Programming (via satellite): ABC Family HD; Animal Planet HD; Arts & Entertainment HD; CNN HD; Discovery Channel HD; Discovery HD Theater; Discovery Planet Green HD; Disney Channel HD; ESPN 2 HD; ESPN HD; Food Network HD; Fox News HD; FSN HD; FX HD; HGTV HD; History Channel HD; Lifetime Movie Network HD; Lifetime Television HD; National Geographic Channel HD Network; Outdoor Channel 2 HD; QVC HD; Science Channel HD; Speed HD; Syfy HD; TBS in HD; TLC HD; Travel Channel HD; Turner Network TV HD; USA Network HD.
Fee: $10.95 monthly.
Pay Service 1
Pay Units: 9.
Programming (via satellite): Cinemax.
Fee: $8.95 monthly.
Pay Service 2
Pay Units: 31.
Programming (via satellite): HBO.
Fee: $11.95 monthly.
Digital Pay Service 1
Pay Units: N.A.
Programming (via satellite): Cinemax (multiplexed); Cinemax HD; Flix; HBO (multiplexed); HBO HD; Showtime (multiplexed); Showtime HD; The Movie Channel (multiplexed); The Movie Channel HD.
Fee: $11.95 monthly (Cinemax), $14.95 monthly (HBO or Showtime/TMC/Flix).
Video-On-Demand: No
Pay-Per-View
iN DEMAND (delivered digitally); Hot Choice (delivered digitally).
Internet Service
Operational: Yes.
Telephone Service
None
Miles of Plant: 5.0 (coaxial); None (fiber optic). Homes passed: 183.
Manager: Bill Barton. Headend Technician: Jay Stewart.; Julian Rodriguez.
City fee: 0.5% of basic gross.
Ownership: Giant Communications (MSO).

PALMER—Formerly served by Eagle Communications. No longer in operation. ICA: KS0468.

PAOLA—Suddenlink Communications, 12444 Powerscourt Dr, Saint Louis, MO 63131-3660. Phones: 800-999-6845 (Customer service); 314-965-2020. Fax: 913-294-9284. Web Site: http://www.suddenlink.com. Also serves Johnson County (southern portion), Miami County (unincorporated areas), Osawatomie & Spring Hill. ICA: KS0029.
TV Market Ranking: 22 (Johnson County (southern portion), Miami County (unincorporated areas) (portions), Spring Hill); Below 100 (PAOLA, Miami County (unincorporated areas) (portions)); Outside TV Markets (Osawatomie, Miami County (unincorporated areas) (portions)). Franchise award date: N.A. Franchise expiration date: N.A. Began: August 1, 1974.
Channel capacity: 78 (operating 2-way). Channels available but not in use: N.A.
Basic Service
Subscribers: 5,180.
Programming (received off-air): KCPT (PBS) Kansas City; KCTV (CBS) Kansas City; KCWE (CW) Kansas City; KMBC-TV (ABC) Kansas City; KMCI-TV (IND) Lawrence; KPXE-TV (ION) Kansas City; KSHB-TV (NBC) Kansas City; KSMO-TV (MNT) Kansas City; KSNT (FOX, NBC) Topeka; KTWU (PBS) Topeka; WDAF-TV (FOX) Kansas City; WIBW-TV (CBS, MNT) Topeka; 14 FMs.
Programming (via satellite): ABC Family Channel; Arts & Entertainment; Cartoon Network; CNN; C-SPAN; Discovery Channel; Disney Channel; ESPN; Eternal Word TV Network; Headline News; History Channel; Lifetime; MuchMusic Network; Nickelodeon; QVC; Spike TV; TBS Superstation; The Learning Channel; Turner Classic Movies; Turner Network TV; TV Land; USA Network; Weather Channel; WGN America.
Current originations: Public Access.
Fee: $39.95 installation; $19.95 monthly.
Expanded Basic Service 1
Subscribers: N.A.
Programming (via satellite): Fox News Channel; Fox Sports Net Rocky Mountain; FX; Great American Country; HGTV; MSNBC; VH1.
Fee: $25.00 monthly.
Digital Basic Service
Subscribers: N.A.
Programming (via satellite): BBC America; Discovery Digital Networks; DMX Music; Encore Action; ESPN 2; ESPN Classic Sports; Golf Channel; Outdoor Channel; Speed Channel; Versus.
Fee: $3.99 monthly.
Pay Service 1
Pay Units: 838.
Programming (via satellite): HBO.
Fee: $10.95 monthly.
Pay Service 2
Pay Units: 585.
Programming (via satellite): Showtime.
Fee: $9.95 monthly.
Pay Service 3
Pay Units: 493.
Programming (via satellite): The Movie Channel.
Fee: $7.95 monthly.
Pay Service 4
Pay Units: 65.
Programming (via satellite): Cinemax.
Digital Pay Service 1
Pay Units: N.A.
Programming (via satellite): Cinemax (multiplexed); HBO (multiplexed); Showtime (multiplexed); The Movie Channel (multiplexed).
Video-On-Demand: No
Pay-Per-View
Addressable: Yes; iN DEMAND (delivered digitally); Fresh (delivered digitally).
Internet Service
Operational: Yes. Began: June 23, 2002.
Broadband Service: Cebridge High Speed Cable Internet.
Fee: $49.95 installation; $26.95 monthly.
Telephone Service
None
Miles of Plant: 97.0 (coaxial); None (fiber optic). Total homes in franchised area: 5,553.
Regional Manager: Todd Cruthird. Plant Manager: Lee Mott. Regional Marketing Manager: Beverly Gambell.

City fee: 3% of gross.
Ownership: Cequel Communications LLC (MSO).

PARKER—Formerly served by National Cable Inc. No longer in operation. ICA: KS0316.

PARSONS—Cable One, 2229 Broadway St, Ste 200, Parsons, KS 67357. Phone: 620-421-2510. Fax: 620-421-2719. Web Site: http://www.cableone.net. ICA: KS0024.
TV Market Ranking: Below 100 (PARSONS). Franchise award date: N.A. Franchise expiration date: N.A. Began: January 1, 1966.
Channel capacity: 53 (operating 2-way). Channels available but not in use: N.A.

Basic Service
Subscribers: 2,900.
Programming (received off-air): KFJX (FOX) Pittsburg; KJRH-TV (NBC) Tulsa; KOAM-TV (CBS) Pittsburg; KODE-TV (ABC) Joplin; KOED-TV (PBS) Tulsa; KSNF (NBC) Joplin; 12 FMs.
Programming (via microwave): KMBC-TV (ABC) Kansas City; WIBW-TV (CBS, MNT) Topeka.
Programming (via satellite): ABC Family Channel; Animal Planet; Arts & Entertainment; BET Networks; Bravo; Cartoon Network; CNBC; CNN; Comedy Central; Country Music TV; C-SPAN; C-SPAN 2; CW+; Discovery Channel; Disney Channel; Encore; ESPN; ESPN 2; ESPN Classic Sports; Eternal Word TV Network; Food Network; Fox News Channel; Fox Sports Net Midwest; FX; Hallmark Channel; Headline News; HGTV; History Channel; Lifetime; MSNBC; MTV; Nickelodeon; Outdoor Channel; Oxygen; QVC; ShopNBC; Spike TV; Syfy; TBS Superstation; The Learning Channel; Travel Channel; Trinity Broadcasting Network; Turner Classic Movies; Turner Network TV; TV Guide Network; TV Land; USA Network; WE tv; Weather Channel; WGN America.
Current originations: Government Access; Educational Access; Public Access.
Fee: $50.00 installation; $46.00 monthly; $.23 converter; $7.50 additional installation.

Digital Basic Service
Subscribers: 450.
Programming (received off-air): WIBW-TV (CBS, MNT) Topeka.
Programming (via satellite): 3 Angels Broadcasting Network; Bio; Boomerang; BYU Television; Canales N; Discovery Digital Networks; ESPN Classic Sports; ESPNews; FamilyNet; Fox College Sports Atlantic; Fox College Sports Central; Fox College Sports Pacific; Fox Movie Channel; Fox Soccer; Fuel TV; G4; Golf Channel; Hallmark Channel; History Channel International; INSP; Music Choice; National Geographic Channel; Outdoor Channel; SoapNet; Speed Channel; Toon Disney; Trinity Broadcasting Network; truTV; Turner Network TV HD; Universal HD.
Fee: $9.95 monthly.

Digital Pay Service 1
Pay Units: 2,400.
Programming (via satellite): Cinemax (multiplexed); Encore (multiplexed); Flix; HBO (multiplexed); Showtime (multiplexed); Showtime HD; Starz (multiplexed); Sundance Channel; The Movie Channel (multiplexed); The Movie Channel HD.
Fee: $7.50 installation; $15.00 monthly (each package).

Video-On-Demand: No

Pay-Per-View
iN DEMAND (delivered digitally); Sports PPV (delivered digitally); Fresh (delivered digitally); Shorteez (delivered digitally); Hot Choice (delivered digitally).

Internet Service
Operational: Yes.
Subscribers: 800.
Fee: $75.00 installation; $43.00 monthly.

Telephone Service
Analog: Not Operational
Digital: Operational
Fee: $75.00 installation; $39.95 monthly

Miles of Plant: 72.0 (coaxial); None (fiber optic). Homes passed: 5,071. Total homes in franchised area: 5,835.
Manager: Clarence Matlock. Marketing Director: Chris Harris. Chief Technician: Roger Lee.
City fee: 3% of gross.
Ownership: Cable One Inc. (MSO).

PARTRIDGE—Formerly served by CableDirect. No longer in operation. ICA: KS0410.

PAWNEE ROCK—Golden Belt Telephone Association Inc. Now served by RUSH CENTER, KS [KS0418]. ICA: KS0412.

PAXICO—Galaxy Cablevision, 1928 S Lincoln Ave, Ste 200, York, NE 68467. Phone: 402-362-3332. Fax: 402-362-4890. Web Site: http://www.galaxycable.com. ICA: KS0347.
TV Market Ranking: Below 100 (PAXICO). Franchise award date: N.A. Franchise expiration date: N.A. Began: December 1, 1988.
Channel capacity: 31 (not 2-way capable). Channels available but not in use: 12.

Basic Service
Subscribers: 5.
Programming (received off-air): KSNT (FOX, NBC) Topeka; KTKA-TV (ABC, CW) Topeka; KTWU (PBS) Topeka; WIBW-TV (CBS, MNT) Topeka.
Programming (via satellite): ABC Family Channel; Arts & Entertainment; CNN; Discovery Channel; Disney Channel; ESPN; Headline News; Outdoor Channel; TBS Superstation; Turner Network TV; USA Network.
Fee: $32.85 monthly.

Pay Service 1
Pay Units: N.A.
Programming (via satellite): HBO.
Fee: $11.00 monthly.

Internet Service
Operational: No.

Telephone Service
None

Miles of Plant: 3.0 (coaxial); None (fiber optic). Homes passed: 96.
State Manager: Cheyenne Wohlford. Technical Manager: John Davidshofer. Sales Manager: Mike Thomas. Customer Service Manager: Michael Debermardin.
Ownership: Galaxy Cable Inc. (MSO).

PEABODY—Allegiance Communications, 707 W Saratoga St, Shawnee, OK 74804. Phones: 405-395-1131; 405-275-6923. Web Site: http://www.allegiance.tv. ICA: KS0141.
TV Market Ranking: Outside TV Markets (PEABODY). Franchise award date: N.A. Franchise expiration date: N.A. Began: N.A.
Channel capacity: 48 (operating 2-way). Channels available but not in use: None.

Basic Service
Subscribers: 330.
Programming (received off-air): KAKE-TV (ABC) Wichita; KPTS (PBS) Hutchinson; KSAS-TV (FOX) Wichita; KSNW (NBC) Wichita; KWCH-DT (CBS) Hutchinson.
Programming (via satellite): ABC Family Channel; AMC; Animal Planet; Arts & Entertainment; Cartoon Network; CMT Pure Country; CNN; Court TV; C-SPAN; CW+; Discovery Channel; Disney Channel; ESPN; ESPN 2; Food Network; Fox News Channel; Fox Sports Net Midwest; FX; Great American Country; Hallmark Channel; Headline News; HGTV; History Channel; Lifetime; MSNBC; MTV; NFL Network; Nickelodeon; Outdoor Channel; QVC; Spike TV; Syfy; TBS Superstation; The Learning Channel; Turner Network TV; TV Land; USA Network; VH1; Weather Channel; WGN America.
Fee: $24.95 installation; $34.00 monthly.

Digital Basic Service
Subscribers: N.A.
Programming (via satellite): AmericanLife TV Network; BBC America; Bio; Bloomberg Television; Bravo; Cine Latino; Cine Mexicano; CMT Pure Country; CNN en Espanol; Current; Discovery en Espanol; Discovery Health Channel; Discovery Kids Channel; Discovery Military Channel; Discovery Planet Green; DMX Music; Encore (multiplexed); ESPN 2; ESPN Classic Sports; ESPN Deportes; ESPNews; Flix; Fox College Sports Atlantic; Fox College Sports Central; Fox College Sports Pacific; Fox Movie Channel; Fox Soccer; Fox Sports en Espanol; Fuse; G4; GAS; Golf Channel; Gospel Music Channel; Great American Country; GSN; Halogen Network; HGTV; History Channel; History Channel en Espanol; History Channel International; ID Investigation Discovery; Independent Film Channel; Lifetime Movie Network; MTV Tres; mun2 television; National Geographic Channel; Nick Jr.; NickToons TV; Outdoor Channel; Ovation; Science Channel; ShopNBC; Sleuth; Speed Channel; Style Network; Sundance Channel; Syfy; The Word Network; Toon Disney; Trinity Broadcasting Network; Turner Classic Movies; VeneMovies; Versus; WE tv.

Pay Service 1
Pay Units: N.A.
Programming (via satellite): Cinemax.
Fee: $11.95 monthly.

Pay Service 2
Pay Units: 67.
Programming (via satellite): HBO.
Fee: $11.95 monthly.

Digital Pay Service 1
Pay Units: N.A.
Programming (via satellite): Cinemax (multiplexed); HBO (multiplexed); Showtime (multiplexed); Starz (multiplexed); The Movie Channel (multiplexed).

Pay-Per-View
iN DEMAND (delivered digitally); Hot Choice (delivered digitally); Playboy TV (delivered digitally); Fresh (delivered digitally); Spice: Xcess (delivered digitally); Spice: Xcess (delivered digitally).

Internet Service
Operational: No.

Telephone Service
None

Miles of Plant: 11.0 (coaxial); None (fiber optic). Homes passed: 723. Total homes in franchised area: 723.
Chief Executive Officer: Bill Haggarty. Regional Vice President: Andrew Dearth. Vice President, Marketing: Tracy Bass.
Ownership: Allegiance Communications (MSO).

PERRY—SCI Cable, PO Box 67235, 6700 SW Topeka Blvd, Topeka, KS 66619-0241. Phones: 785-862-1950; 800-879-9724. Fax: 785-862-2423. E-mail: scicable@sbcglobal.net. Also serves Lecompton. ICA: KS0147.
TV Market Ranking: Below 100 (Lecompton, PERRY). Franchise award date: N.A. Franchise expiration date: N.A. Began: April 1, 1982.
Channel capacity: 36 (2-way capable). Channels available but not in use: 16.

Basic Service
Subscribers: 490.
Programming (received off-air): KCPT (PBS) Kansas City; KCTV (CBS) Kansas City; KMBC-TV (ABC) Kansas City; KSHB-TV (NBC) Kansas City; KSMO-TV (MNT) Kansas City; KSNT (FOX, NBC) Topeka; KTKA-TV (ABC, CW) Topeka; KTWU (PBS) Topeka; WDAF-TV (FOX) Kansas City; WIBW-TV (CBS, MNT) Topeka.
Programming (via satellite): Arts & Entertainment; CNN; Discovery Channel; Disney Channel; ESPN; ESPN 2; History Channel; Lifetime; MTV; Nickelodeon; Spike TV; TBS Superstation; The Learning Channel; Turner Network TV; TV Land; USA Network; Weather Channel.
Fee: $25.00 installation; $26.00 monthly.

Pay Service 1
Pay Units: 155.
Programming (via satellite): HBO.
Fee: $11.95 monthly.

Pay Service 2
Pay Units: 61.
Programming (via satellite): Showtime.
Fee: $11.95 monthly.

Internet Service
Operational: Yes.
Broadband Service: SCI Broadband.
Fee: $19.95 monthly.

Telephone Service
None

Miles of Plant: 15.0 (coaxial); None (fiber optic). Homes passed: 544.
Manager: Kirk Keberlein.
Ownership: SCI Cable Inc. (MSO).

PHILLIPSBURG—Nex-Tech, PO Box 381, 770 4th St, Phillipsburg, KS 67661. Phones: 785-567-9226; 800-843-9874; 785-567-4281 (Lenora office); 785-543-6694. Fax: 785-543-5362. Web Site: http://www.nex-tech.com. ICA: KS0060.
TV Market Ranking: Outside TV Markets (PHILLIPSBURG). Franchise award date: N.A. Franchise expiration date: N.A. Began: August 1, 1966.
Channel capacity: 61 (operating 2-way). Channels available but not in use: 10.

Basic Service
Subscribers: 908.
Programming (received off-air): KBSH-DT (CBS) Hays; KGIN (CBS, MNT) Grand Island; KHAS-TV (NBC) Hastings; KHGI-TV (ABC) Kearney; KLNE-TV (PBS) Lexington; KOOD (PBS) Hays; KSNK (NBC) McCook; allband FM.
Programming (via satellite): National Geographic Channel.
Fee: $39.95 installation; $33.60 monthly.

Expanded Basic Service 1
Subscribers: N.A.
Programming (via satellite): ABC Family Channel; Animal Planet; Arts & Entertainment; Cartoon Network; CNN; C-SPAN; Discovery Channel; Disney Channel; ESPN; ESPN 2; Fox Sports Net Midwest; FX; Great American Country; HGTV; History Channel; INSP; ION Television; Nickelodeon; QVC; Spike TV; TBS Superstation; The Learning Channel; Turner Classic Movies; Turner Network TV; TV Land; USA Network; VH1; Weather Channel.

Digital Basic Service
Subscribers: N.A.
Programming (via satellite): AmericanLife TV Network; BBC America; Bio; Bloomberg Television; Discovery Digital Networks; DMX Music; ESPN 2; ESPN Classic Sports; ESPNews; Fox Sports World; G4; Golf Channel; GSN; Halogen Network; HGTV; History Channel; History Channel International; Lifetime Movie Network; MuchMusic Network; Outdoor Channel; Ovation; ShopNBC; Speed Channel; Style Network; Syfy; Trinity Broadcasting Network; Turner Classic Movies; Versus.

Pay Service 1
Pay Units: 102.
Programming (via satellite): The Movie Channel.
Fee: $7.95 monthly.

Pay Service 2
Pay Units: 32.
Programming (via satellite): Cinemax.
Fee: $9.95 monthly.

Pay Service 3
Pay Units: 89.
Programming (via satellite): Showtime.
Fee: $9.95 monthly.

Pay Service 4
Pay Units: 162.
Programming (via satellite): HBO.
Fee: $10.95 monthly.

Digital Pay Service 1
Pay Units: N.A.
Programming (via satellite): Cinemax; Encore; HBO; Showtime; Starz; The Movie Channel.

Video-On-Demand: No

Pay-Per-View
iN DEMAND (delivered digitally); Sports PPV (delivered digitally); Fresh (delivered digitally); Shorteez (delivered digitally).

Internet Service
Operational: Yes.

Telephone Service
None

Miles of Plant: 23.0 (coaxial); None (fiber optic). Homes passed: 1,566. Total homes in franchised area: 1,930.
Manager: Brent Fine.
City fee: 2% of gross.
Ownership: Rural Telephone Co. (MSO).

PITTSBURG—Cox Communications, 2802 N Joplin St, Pittsburg, KS 66762. Phones: 316-260-7000 (Wichita office); 620-231-2099. Fax: 620-231-8589. Web Site: http://www.cox.com/kansas. Also serves Arma, Cherokee County (northern portion), Chicopee, Crawford County (eastern portion), Franklin & Frontenac. ICA: KS0011.
Note: This system is an overbuild.
TV Market Ranking: Below 100 (Arma, Cherokee County (northern portion), Chicopee, Crawford County (eastern portion), Franklin, Frontenac, WILLIAMSON COUNTY). Franchise award date: May 10, 1966. Franchise expiration date: N.A. Began: September 1, 1967.
Channel capacity: N.A. Channels available but not in use: N.A.

Basic Service
Subscribers: N.A. Included in Wichita
Programming (received off-air): K30AL-D (PBS) Iola; KFJX (FOX) Pittsburg; KMBC-TV (ABC) Kansas City; KOAM-TV (CBS) Pittsburg; KODE-TV (ABC) Joplin; KOZJ (PBS) Joplin; KQCW-DT (CW) Muskogee; KSNF (NBC) Joplin; WDAF-TV (FOX) Kansas City.
Programming (via satellite): C-SPAN; C-SPAN 2; TV Guide Network; Weather Channel; WGN America.
Current originations: Leased Access; Government Access; Educational Access; Public Access.
Fee: $29.95 installation; $10.35 monthly; $14.95 additional installation.

Expanded Basic Service 1
Subscribers: 1,712.
Programming (via satellite): ABC Family Channel; AMC; Animal Planet; Arts & Entertainment; BET Networks; Bravo; Cartoon Network; CNBC; CNN; Comedy Central; Country Music TV; Cox Sports Television; Discovery Channel; Discovery Health Channel; Disney Channel; E! Entertainment Television; ESPN; ESPN 2; Eternal Word TV Network; Food Network; Fox News Channel; Fox Sports Net Midwest; FX; Hallmark Channel; Headline News; HGTV; History Channel; Home Shopping Network; INSP; Lifetime; MSNBC; MTV; MTV2; Nickelodeon; QVC; Speed Channel; Spike TV; Syfy; TBS Superstation; The Learning Channel; Travel Channel; Trinity Broadcasting Network; truTV; Turner Classic Movies; Turner Network TV; TV Land; Univision; USA Network; VH1.
Fee: $29.95 installation; $18.02 monthly; $14.95 additional installation.

Digital Basic Service
Subscribers: N.A.
Programming (via satellite): AmericanLife TV Network; BBC America; Bio; Bloomberg Television; Boomerang; Canales N; CBS College Sports Network; Cooking Channel; Daystar TV Network; Discovery Digital Networks; DMX Music; Do-It-Yourself; ESPN Classic Sports; ESPNews; FamilyNet; FitTV; Fox Reality Channel; Fox Soccer; Fuel TV; Fuse; G4; GAS; Golf Channel; Gospel Music Channel; Great American Country; GSN; Hallmark Movie Channel; Halogen Network; History Channel International; Independent Film Channel; Lifetime Movie Network; MTV Networks Digital Suite; NASA TV; National Geographic Channel; NBA League Pass; NFL Network; Nick Jr.; Nick Too; NickToons TV; Outdoor Channel; Oxygen; Pentagon Channel; Si TV; SoapNet; Style Network; Sundance Channel; Tennis Channel; The Sportsman Channel; Toon Disney; Trinity Broadcasting Network; TV One; Versus; WE tv; XY.tv.
Fee: $15.00 monthly.

Digital Expanded Basic Service
Subscribers: N.A.
Programming (via satellite): Discovery HD Theater; INHD (multiplexed).

Digital Pay Service 1
Pay Units: 311.
Programming (via satellite): Cinemax (multiplexed); Encore (multiplexed); Flix; HBO (multiplexed); Showtime (multiplexed); Starz (multiplexed).
Fee: $11.50 monthly (each).

Digital Pay Service 2
Pay Units: N.A.
Programming (via satellite): HBO; Showtime; Starz HDTV.

Video-On-Demand: Planned

Pay-Per-View
iN DEMAND (delivered digitally), Addressable: Yes; ESPN (delivered digitally); NBA/WNBA League Pass (delivered digitally); NHL Center Ice/MLB Extra Innings (delivered digitally).

Internet Service
Operational: Yes.
Subscribers: 383.
Broadband Service: Cox High Speed Internet.
Fee: $41.95 monthly; $15.00 modem lease; $199.95 modem purchase.

Telephone Service
Digital: Planned

Miles of Plant: 142.0 (coaxial); None (fiber optic). Homes passed included in Wichita
Vice President & General Manager: Kimberly Edmonds. Field Operations Regional Manager: Joe Michael. Vice President, Engineering: Nick DiPonzio. Vice President, Marketing: Tony Matthews. Technical Operations Manager: Rick Fox. Marketing Director: Tina Gabbard. Public Affairs Director: Sarah Kauffman.
City fee: 5% of gross.
Ownership: Cox Communications Inc. (MSO).

PLAINVILLE—Nex-Tech, PO Box 7, 112 S Main, Plainville, KS 67663. Phones: 785-434-4946; 800-843-9874; 785-567-9226. Fax: 785-434-2053. Web Site: http://www.nex-tech.com. ICA: KS0445.
TV Market Ranking: Below 100 (PLAINVILLE (VILLAGE)). Franchise award date: N.A. Franchise expiration date: N.A. Began: N.A.
Channel capacity: 61 (not 2-way capable). Channels available but not in use: N.A.

Basic Service
Subscribers: 616.
Programming (received off-air): KBSH-DT (CBS) Hays; KOOD (PBS) Hays; KSAS-TV (FOX) Wichita; KSNK (NBC) McCook.
Programming (via satellite): KMGH-TV (ABC) Denver; KUSA (NBC) Denver; QVC.
Current originations: Public Access.
Fee: $35.00 installation; $25.29 monthly.

Expanded Basic Service 1
Subscribers: N.A.
Programming (via satellite): ABC Family Channel; Animal Planet; Arts & Entertainment; CNN; Discovery Channel; Disney Channel; E! Entertainment Television; ESPN; Eternal Word TV Network; Fox Sports Net Rocky Mountain; FX; Great American Country; Headline News; HGTV; History Channel; Lifetime; MSNBC; Nickelodeon; Spike TV; TBS Superstation; Turner Network TV; TV Land; USA Network; VH1; Weather Channel.

Digital Basic Service
Subscribers: N.A.
Programming (via satellite): AmericanLife TV Network; BBC America; Bio; Bloomberg Television; Discovery Digital Networks; Discovery Kids Channel; DMX Music; ESPN 2; ESPN Classic Sports; ESPNews; Fox Sports World; G4; Golf Channel; GSN; Halogen Network; HGTV; History Channel; History Channel International; MuchMusic Network; Outdoor Channel; Ovation; ShopNBC; Speed Channel; Style Network; Syfy; Trinity Broadcasting Network; Turner Classic Movies; Versus.

Digital Pay Service 1
Pay Units: N.A.
Programming (via satellite): Cinemax; Encore; HBO; Showtime; Starz; The Movie Channel.

Video-On-Demand: No

Pay-Per-View
iN DEMAND (delivered digitally); Playboy TV (delivered digitally); Fresh (delivered digitally); Shorteez (delivered digitally); Sports PPV (delivered digitally).

Internet Service
Operational: Yes.

Telephone Service
None

Miles of Plant: 13.0 (coaxial); None (fiber optic). Homes passed: 1,011.
Manager: Brent Fine.
Ownership: Rural Telephone Co. (MSO).

PLEASANTON—Formerly served by Almega Cable. No longer in operation. ICA: KS0083.

POMONA—Galaxy Cablevision, 1928 S Lincoln Ave, Ste 200, York, NE 68467. Phone: 402-362-3332. Fax: 402-362-4890. Web Site: http://www.galaxycable.com. ICA: KS0414.
TV Market Ranking: Below 100 (POMONA). Franchise award date: N.A. Franchise expiration date: N.A. Began: January 1, 1981.
Channel capacity: 36 (not 2-way capable). Channels available but not in use: None.

Basic Service
Subscribers: 91.
Programming (received off-air): KCTV (CBS) Kansas City; KCWE (CW) Kansas City; KMBC-TV (ABC) Kansas City; KMCI-TV (IND) Lawrence; KSHB-TV (NBC) Kansas City; KSMO-TV (MNT) Kansas City; KSNT (FOX, NBC) Topeka; KTWU (PBS) Topeka; WDAF-TV (FOX) Kansas City; WIBW-TV (CBS, MNT) Topeka.
Programming (via satellite): ABC Family Channel; Animal Planet; Arts & Entertainment; CNN; Discovery Channel; Disney Channel; ESPN; ESPN 2; Fox News Channel; FX; Great American Country; Outdoor Channel; TBS Superstation; The Learning Channel; Toon Disney; Trinity Broadcasting Network; Turner Network TV; USA Network; Weather Channel; WGN America.
Fee: $35.00 installation; $36.80 monthly.

Digital Basic Service
Subscribers: 3.
Programming (via satellite): AmericanLife TV Network; BBC America; Bio; Bloomberg Television; Discovery Digital Networks; ESPN Classic Sports; ESPNews; FitTV; Fox Sports World; G4; Golf Channel; GSN; Halogen Network; History Channel International; National Geographic Channel; Style Network; WE tv.
Fee: $16.00 monthly.

Digital Expanded Basic Service
Subscribers: N.A.
Programming (via satellite): DMX Music; Encore; Fox Movie Channel; Lifetime Movie Network; Turner Classic Movies.
Fee: $16.00 monthly.

Pay Service 1
Pay Units: 52.
Programming (via satellite): Cinemax; HBO; Showtime; The Movie Channel.
Fee: $7.95 monthly (TMC), $9.95 monthly (Showtime), $10.95 monthly (Cinemax), $13.95 monthly (HBO).

Digital Pay Service 1
Pay Units: N.A.
Programming (via satellite): Cinemax (multiplexed); Flix; HBO (multiplexed);

Showtime (multiplexed); The Movie Channel (multiplexed).
Fee: $15.50 monthly.
Pay-Per-View
Addressable homes: 6.
ESPN Now (delivered digitally), Addressable: Yes; sports (delivered digitally); Urban Xtra (delivered digitally).
Internet Service
Operational: No.
Telephone Service
None
Miles of Plant: 9.0 (coaxial); None (fiber optic). Homes passed: 425.
State Manager: Cheyenne Wohlford. Technical Manager: John Davishofer. Sales Manager: Mike Thomas. Customer Service Manager: Michael Debermardin.
Ownership: Galaxy Cable Inc. (MSO).

POTTAWATOMIE COUNTY (portions)—WTC Communications. Formerly served by Wamego, KS [KS0057]. This cable system has converted to IPTV, 1009 Lincoln St, Wamego, KS 66547. Phones: 877-492-6835; 785-456-1000. Fax: 785-456-9903. E-mail: support@wamego.net. Web Site: http://www.wamtelco.com. ICA: KS5039.
TV Market Ranking: Outside TV Markets (Pottawatomie County (portions)).
Channel capacity: N.A. Channels available but not in use: N.A.
Telephone Service
Digital: Operational
President & General Manager: Steve Tackrider. Plant Manager: Ken Blew.
Ownership: WTC Communications Inc.

PRATT—Cox Communications. Now served by WICHITA, KS [KS0001]. ICA: KS0031.

PRESCOTT—Craw-Kan Telephone Co-op. This cable system has converted to IPTV. See PRESCOTT, KS [KS5101]. ICA: KS0341.

PRESCOTT—Formerly [KS0446]. Craw-Kan Telephone Coop. This cable system has converted to IPTV, PO Box 100, 200 N Ozark St, Girard, KS 66743. Phones: 800-362-0316; 620-724-8235. Fax: 620-724-4099. E-mail: webmaster@ckt.net. Web Site: http://www.ckt.net. ICA: KS5101.
TV Market Ranking: Outside TV Markets (PRESCOTT).
Channel capacity: N.A. Channels available but not in use: N.A.
Internet Service
Operational: Yes.
Ownership: Craw-Kan Telephone Cooperative.

PRETTY PRAIRIE—Formerly served by Almega Cable. No longer in operation. ICA: KS0194.

PRINCETON—Formerly served by CableDirect. No longer in operation. ICA: KS0325.

PROTECTION—United Communications Assn. Inc., PO Box 117, 1107 McArtor Rd, Dodge City, KS 67801. Phone: 620-227-8645. Fax: 620-855-4009. Web Site: http://www.unitedtelcom.net. ICA: KS0207.
TV Market Ranking: Outside TV Markets (PROTECTION). Franchise award date: N.A. Franchise expiration date: N.A. Began: November 24, 1964.
Channel capacity: N.A. Channels available but not in use: N.A.
Basic Service
Subscribers: 76.
Programming (received off-air): KBSD-DT (CBS) Ensign; KOOD (PBS) Hays; KSAS-TV (FOX) Wichita; KSNG (NBC) Garden City; KUPK-TV (ABC) Garden City; allband FM.
Programming (via satellite): Fox News Channel; National Geographic Channel; QVC; TBS Superstation; Trinity Broadcasting Network; Weather Channel.
Fee: $39.95 installation.
Expanded Basic Service 1
Subscribers: N.A.
Programming (received off-air): KMTW (MNT) Hutchinson; KSCW-DT (CW) Wichita.
Programming (via satellite): ABC Family Channel; AMC; Animal Planet; CNN; C-SPAN; Discovery Channel; Disney Channel; ESPN; Fox Sports Net Midwest; Great American Country; Headline News; HGTV; History Channel; NFL Network; Nickelodeon; Spike TV; The Learning Channel; Turner Network TV; TV Land; USA Network; VH1.
Fee: $48.98 monthly.
Digital Basic Service
Subscribers: N.A.
Programming (received off-air): KBSD-DT (CBS) Ensign; KOOD (PBS) Hays; KSNG (NBC) Garden City; KUPK-TV (ABC) Garden City.
Programming (via satellite): ABC Family HD; Animal Planet HD; Arts & Entertainment HD; BBC America; Bio; Bravo; Chiller; CMT Pure Country; Discovery Channel HD; Discovery HD Theater; Discovery Health Channel; Discovery Kids Channel; Discovery Military Channel; Discovery Planet Green; Discovery Planet Green HD; Disney Channel HD; Disney XD; Encore (multiplexed); ESPN 2; ESPN 2 HD; ESPN Classic Sports; ESPN HD; ESPN U; ESPNews; Fine Living Network; FitTV; Food Network HD; Fox Business Channel; Fox College Sports Atlantic; Fox College Sports Central; Fox College Sports Pacific; Fox Movie Channel; Fox News HD; Fox Soccer; FX HD; G4; Golf Channel; Great American Country; GSN; Halogen Network; HGTV; HGTV HD; History Channel; History Channel HD; History Channel International; ID Investigation Discovery; Independent Film Channel; Lifetime Movie Network; Lifetime Movie Network HD; Lifetime Real Women; MTV Hits; MTV2; National Geographic Channel; National Geographic Channel HD Network; Nick Jr.; NickToons TV; Outdoor Channel; Outdoor Channel 2 HD; PBS Kids Sprout; RFD-TV; Science Channel; Science Channel HD; Sleuth; SoapNet; Speed Channel; Speed HD; Style Network; Syfy; Syfy HD; TeenNick; TLC HD; Travel Channel HD; Turner Classic Movies; Universal HD; USA Network HD; Versus; VH1 Classic; VH1 Soul; WE tv; Weather Channel HD.
Fee: $16.00 monthly.
Digital Expanded Basic Service
Subscribers: N.A.
Programming (via satellite): Cine Latino; Cine Mexicano; CNN en Espanol; Discovery en Espanol; ESPN Deportes; Fox Sports en Espanol; History Channel en Espanol; MTV Tres; VeneMovies.
Fee: $5.00 monthly.
Digital Pay Service 1
Pay Units: N.A.
Programming (via satellite): Cinemax (multiplexed); HBO (multiplexed); Showtime (multiplexed); Starz (multiplexed); Starz HDTV.
Fee: $11.95 monthly (HBO, Cinemax, Showtime or Starz).
Internet Service
Operational: Yes.
Fee: $57.48-$87.98 monthly.
Telephone Service
None
Miles of Plant: 6.0 (coaxial); None (fiber optic). Homes passed: 305.
General Manager: Craig Mock. Chief Technician: Keith Brack. Customer Service Manager: Jeannie Linnebur.
City fee: 1% of gross.
Ownership: United Communications Assn. Inc. (MSO).

QUENEMO—Formerly served by Galaxy Cablevision. No longer in operation. ICA: KS0290.

QUINTER—Quinter Cable Co. Now served by EDMUND, KS [KS0450]. ICA: KS0415.

RANDALL—Cunningham Cable TV. Now served by WASHINGTON (formerly Glen Elder), KS [KS0228]. ICA: KS0351.

RANDOLPH—Rainbow Communications, PO Box 147, Everest, KS 66424. Phones: 800-892-0163; 785-866-2390. Fax: 785-548-7517. Web Site: http://www.rainbowtel.net. ICA: KS0352.
TV Market Ranking: Outside TV Markets (RANDOLPH). Franchise award date: N.A. Franchise expiration date: N.A. Began: September 18, 1989.
Channel capacity: 36 (not 2-way capable). Channels available but not in use: 15.
Basic Service
Subscribers: 8.
Programming (received off-air): KAAS-TV (FOX) Salina; KSNT (FOX, NBC) Topeka; KTKA-TV (ABC, CW) Topeka; KTLJ-CA (FOX) Junction City; KTWU (PBS) Topeka; WIBW-TV (CBS, MNT) Topeka.
Programming (via satellite): ABC Family Channel; AmericanLife TV Network; CNN; C-SPAN; Discovery Channel; ESPN; Hallmark Channel; Headline News; Nickelodeon; Spike TV; TBS Superstation; Trinity Broadcasting Network; Turner Network TV; USA Network; Weather Channel; WGN America.
Fee: $13.95 monthly.
Pay Service 1
Pay Units: 1.
Programming (via satellite): Cinemax.
Fee: $9.95 monthly.
Pay Service 2
Pay Units: 1.
Programming (via satellite): The Movie Channel.
Fee: $8.95 monthly.
Pay Service 3
Pay Units: 1.
Programming (via satellite): Showtime.
Fee: $8.95 monthly.
Internet Service
Operational: No.
Telephone Service
None
Miles of Plant: 2.0 (coaxial); None (fiber optic). Homes passed: 84.
General Manager: James Lednicky. Network Engineer: Scott Wheeler. Plant Manager: Jim Streeter. Marketing Manager: Jackie Petersen.
Ownership: Rainbow Communications (MSO).

READING—Formerly served by Galaxy Cablevision. No longer in operation. ICA: KS0301.

REPUBLIC—Formerly served by Diode Cable Co. No longer in operation. ICA: KS0349.

RESERVE—Rainbow Communications, PO Box 147, Everest, KS 66424. Phones: 800-892-0163; 785-866-2390. Fax: 785-548-7517. Web Site: http://www.rainbowtel.net. ICA: KS0356.
TV Market Ranking: Outside TV Markets (RESERVE). Franchise award date: N.A. Franchise expiration date: N.A. Began: October 20, 1989.
Channel capacity: 36 (operating 2-way). Channels available but not in use: 22.
Basic Service
Subscribers: 10.
Programming (received off-air): KPTM (FOX, MNT) Omaha; KQTV (ABC) St. Joseph; KSNT (FOX, NBC) Topeka; KTAJ-TV (TBN) St. Joseph; KTWU (PBS) Topeka; KUON-TV (PBS) Lincoln; WDAF-TV (FOX) Kansas City; WIBW-TV (CBS, MNT) Topeka.
Programming (via satellite): CNN; C-SPAN; Headline News; Weather Channel; WGN America.
Fee: $29.95 installation; $13.95 monthly; $5.00 converter; $22.50 additional installation.
Pay Service 1
Pay Units: 2.
Programming (via satellite): Showtime; The Movie Channel.
Fee: $8.95 monthly (each).
Video-On-Demand: No
Internet Service
Operational: Yes.
Broadband Service: Lighting Jack High Speed.
Fee: $39.95 monthly.
Telephone Service
None
Miles of Plant: 2.0 (coaxial); None (fiber optic). Homes passed: 63.
General Manager: James Lednicky. Marketing Manager: Jackie Petersen. Plant Manager: Jim Streeter. Network Engineer: Scott Wheeler.
Ownership: Rainbow Communications (MSO).

RICHMOND—Galaxy Cablevision, 1928 S Lincoln Ave, Ste 200, York, NE 68467. Phone: 402-362-3332. Fax: 402-362-4890. Web Site: http://www.galaxycable.com. ICA: KS0262.
TV Market Ranking: Outside TV Markets (RICHMOND). Franchise award date: N.A. Franchise expiration date: N.A. Began: October 1, 1983.
Channel capacity: 36 (not 2-way capable). Channels available but not in use: 13.

Basic Service
Subscribers: 23.
Programming (received off-air): KCTV (CBS) Kansas City; KMBC-TV (ABC) Kansas City; KSHB-TV (NBC) Kansas City; KTWU (PBS) Topeka; WDAF-TV (FOX) Kansas City; WIBW-TV (CBS, MNT) Topeka.
Programming (via satellite): ABC Family Channel; Arts & Entertainment; CNN; Discovery Channel; Disney Channel; ESPN; ESPN 2; Headline News; Lifetime; Outdoor Channel; QVC; TBS Superstation; Toon Disney; Turner Network TV; USA Network.
Fee: $35.30 monthly.

Pay Service 1
Pay Units: N.A.
Programming (via satellite): Cinemax; HBO.
Fee: $11.00 monthly (each).

Internet Service
Operational: No.

Telephone Service
None

Miles of Plant: 4.0 (coaxial); None (fiber optic). Homes passed: 187.
State Manager: Cheyenne Wohlford. Technical Manager: John Davidshofer. Sales Manager: Mike Thomas. Customer Service Manager: Michael Debermardin.
City fee: 3% of gross.
Ownership: Galaxy Cable Inc. (MSO).

RILEY—Eagle Communications, 430 Court St, Clay Center, KS 67432. Phones: 785-625-4000 (Corporate office); 785-632-3118. Fax: 785-625-8030. Web Site: http://www.eaglecom.net. ICA: KS0190.
TV Market Ranking: Outside TV Markets (RILEY). Franchise award date: March 1, 1977. Franchise expiration date: N.A. Began: June 1, 1978.
Channel capacity: 78 (operating 2-way). Channels available but not in use: 37.

Basic Service
Subscribers: 195.
Programming (received off-air): KAAS-TV (FOX) Salina; KSNT (FOX, NBC) Topeka; KTKA-TV (ABC, CW) Topeka; KTMJ-CA Topeka; KTWU (PBS) Topeka; WIBW-TV (CBS, MNT) Topeka; allband FM.
Programming (via satellite): ABC Family Channel; AMC; Animal Planet; Arts & Entertainment; Cartoon Network; CNN; Comedy Central; Discovery Channel; Disney Channel; E! Entertainment Television; ESPN; ESPN 2; Fox News Channel; Fox Sports Net Midwest; FX; Great American Country; Headline News; HGTV; History Channel; Home Shopping Network; INSP; Lifetime; MTV; Outdoor Channel; QVC; Speed Channel; Syfy; TBS Superstation; The Learning Channel; Toon Disney; Trinity Broadcasting Network; Turner Classic Movies; Turner Network TV; TV Land; USA Network; VH1; Weather Channel; WGN America.
Fee: $24.95 installation; $45.45 monthly.

Digital Basic Service
Subscribers: 60.
Programming (via satellite): AmericanLife TV Network; BBC America; Bio; Bloomberg Television; Discovery Health Channel; Discovery Kids Channel; Discovery Military Channel; Discovery Planet Green; DMX Music; ESPN Classic Sports; ESPNews; FitTV; Fox Movie Channel; Fox Soccer; Fuse; G4; Golf Channel; GSN; Halogen Network; History Channel International; ID Investigation Discovery; Independent Film Channel; Lifetime Movie Network; Outdoor Channel; Science Channel; Sleuth; Speed Channel; Style Network; Turner Classic Movies; Versus; WE tv.
Fee: $13.95 monthly.

Pay Service 1
Pay Units: N.A.
Programming (via satellite): HBO; Showtime; The Movie Channel.
Fee: $11.95 monthly (each).

Digital Pay Service 1
Pay Units: N.A.
Programming (via satellite): Cinemax (multiplexed); Encore (multiplexed); Flix; HBO (multiplexed); Showtime (multiplexed); Starz (multiplexed); The Movie Channel (multiplexed).
Fee: $11.95 monthly (HBO, Cinemax, Showtime/TMC or Starz/Encore).

Pay-Per-View
iN DEMAND (delivered digitally); Playboy TV (delivered digitally); Fresh (delivered digitally); Spice: Xcess (delivered digitally); Club Jenna (delivered digitally).

Internet Service
Operational: Yes.
Subscribers: 99.
Broadband Service: Eagle Internet.
Fee: $22.95 monthly.

Telephone Service
None

Miles of Plant: 6.0 (coaxial); None (fiber optic). Homes passed: 406.
President: Gary Shorman. Regional Manager: Dennis Weese. General Manager: Rex Skiles.
City fee: 1% of gross.
Ownership: Eagle Communications Inc. (KS) (MSO).

ROSALIA—Formerly served by CableDirect. No longer in operation. ICA: KS0353.

ROSSVILLE—Galaxy Cablevision, 1928 S Lincoln Ave, Ste 200, York, NE 68467. Phone: 402-362-3332. Fax: 402-362-4890. Web Site: http://www.galaxycable.com. Also serves Silver Lake. ICA: KS0417.
TV Market Ranking: Below 100 (ROSSVILLE, Silver Lake). Franchise award date: N.A. Franchise expiration date: N.A. Began: November 1, 1982.
Channel capacity: 36 (operating 2-way). Channels available but not in use: None.

Basic Service
Subscribers: 324.
Programming (received off-air): KCTV (CBS) Kansas City; KCWE (CW) Kansas City; KSHB-TV (NBC) Kansas City; KSNT (FOX, NBC) Topeka; KTKA-TV (ABC, CW) Topeka; KTWU (PBS) Topeka; WDAF-TV (FOX) Kansas City; WIBW-TV (CBS, MNT) Topeka.
Programming (via satellite): ABC Family Channel; AMC; Animal Planet; Arts & Entertainment; Cartoon Network; CNN; C-SPAN; Discovery Channel; Disney Channel; E! Entertainment Television; ESPN; ESPN 2; Fox News Channel; Fuse; Great American Country; Headline News; HGTV; Lifetime; Outdoor Channel; TBS Superstation; The Learning Channel; Turner Network TV; USA Network; Weather Channel; WGN America.
Current originations: Public Access.
Fee: $15.00 installation; $39.70 monthly.

Digital Basic Service
Subscribers: 52.
Programming (via satellite): AmericanLife TV Network; BBC America; Bio; Bloomberg Television; Discovery Digital Networks; DMX Music; ESPN Classic Sports; ESPNews; FitTV; Fox Sports World; G4; Golf Channel; GSN; Halogen Network; History Channel International; National Geographic Channel; Style Network; Toon Disney; WE tv; Weatherscan.
Fee: $15.00 monthly.

Digital Expanded Basic Service
Subscribers: N.A.
Programming (via satellite): DMX Music; Encore; Fox Movie Channel; Lifetime Movie Network; Turner Classic Movies.
Fee: $15.00 monthly.

Pay Service 1
Pay Units: 36.
Programming (via satellite): HBO.
Fee: $12.00 installation; $11.00 monthly.

Pay Service 2
Pay Units: N.A.
Programming (via satellite): Showtime; The Movie Channel.

Digital Pay Service 1
Pay Units: N.A.
Programming (via satellite): Cinemax (multiplexed); Flix; HBO (multiplexed); Showtime (multiplexed); The Movie Channel (multiplexed).
Fee: $15.50 monthly.

Pay-Per-View
Addressable homes: 37.
ESPN Now (delivered digitally), Addressable: Yes; Movies (delivered digitally); sports (delivered digitally); Urban Xtra (delivered digitally).

Internet Service
Operational: Yes.
Subscribers: 53.
Broadband Service: Galaxy Cable Internet.
Fee: $49.95 installation; $44.95 monthly.

Telephone Service
None

Miles of Plant: 16.0 (coaxial); None (fiber optic). Homes passed: 879.
State Manager: Cheyenne Wohlford. Technical Manager: John Davidshofer. Sales Manager: Mike Thomas. Customer Service Manager: Michael Debermardin.
City fee: 3% of gross.
Ownership: Galaxy Cable Inc. (MSO).

RUSH CENTER—GBT Communications Inc., PO Box 229, 103 Lincoln St, Rush Center, KS 67575-0229. Phones: 800-946-4282 (out-of-state); 785-372-4236. Fax: 785-372-4210. Web Site: http://www.gbta.net. Also serves Albert, Bazine, Bison, Burdett, Ellis, Garfield, La Crosse, Lewis, Liebenthal, McCracken, Ness City, Otis, Pawnee Rock, Ransom, Rozel, Schoenchen, Timken & Utica. ICA: KS0418. **Note:** This system is an overbuild.
TV Market Ranking: Below 100 (Albert, Bison, Ellis, Garfield, La Crosse, Liebenthal, McCracken, Otis, Pawnee Rock, Rozel, RUSH CENTER, Schoenchen, Timken); Outside TV Markets (Bazine, Burdett, Lewis, Ness City, Ransom, Utica). Franchise award date: N.A. Franchise expiration date: N.A. Began: March 1, 1982.
Channel capacity: N.A. Channels available but not in use: N.A.

Basic Service
Subscribers: 2,915.
Programming (received off-air): KAKE-TV (ABC) Wichita; KBSH-DT (CBS) Hays; KOOD (PBS) Hays; KSAS-TV (FOX) Wichita; KSNC (NBC) Great Bend.
Programming (via satellite): C-SPAN; Disney Channel; TBS Superstation; WGN America.
Fee: $9.95 monthly; $3.00 converter.

Expanded Basic Service 1
Subscribers: 2,761.
Programming (received off-air): KSCW-DT (CW) Wichita.
Programming (via satellite): ABC Family Channel; AMC; Animal Planet; Arts & Entertainment; Cartoon Network; CNN; Comedy Central; Country Music TV; C-SPAN 2; Discovery Channel; E! Entertainment Television; ESPN; ESPN 2; ESPN Classic Sports; Eternal Word TV Network; Food Network; Fox News Channel; Fox Sports Net Midwest; FX; GSN; Hallmark Channel; Headline News; HGTV; History Channel; Home Shopping Network; INSP; Lifetime; MSNBC; MTV; National Geographic Channel; NFL Network; Nickelodeon; Outdoor Channel; QVC; RFD-TV; Speed Channel; Spike TV; Syfy; The Learning Channel; Travel Channel; Trinity Broadcasting Network; truTV; Turner Classic Movies; Turner Network TV; TV Land; Univision; USA Network; VH1; Weather Channel.
Fee: $23.45 monthly.

Digital Basic Service
Subscribers: 152.
Programming (received off-air): KAKE-TV (ABC) Wichita; KOOD (PBS) Hays; KSAS-TV (FOX) Wichita; KSNW (NBC) Wichita.
Programming (via satellite): AmericanLife TV Network; BBC America; Bloomberg Television; Canal 52MX; Cine Latino; CNN en Espanol; Discovery Channel HD; Discovery en Espanol; Discovery Health Channel; Discovery Home Channel; Discovery Kids Channel; Discovery Military Channel; Discovery Times Channel; DMX Music; Encore (multiplexed); ESPN Deportes; ESPN HD; ESPNews; FitTV; Fox Movie Channel; Fox Soccer; Fox Sports en Espanol; G4; Golf Channel; Halogen Network; History Channel en Espanol; History Channel International; Independent Film Channel; Lifetime Movie Network; MTV Hits; MTV Tres; MTV2; MyNetworkTV Inc.; National Geographic Channel; NFL Network HD; Nick Jr.; Science Channel; Starz (multiplexed); TBS in HD; TeenNick; Toon Disney; Trinity Broadcasting Network; Turner Network TV HD; VeneMovies; Versus; VH1 Classic; VH1 Country; WE tv.
Fee: $10.95 monthly.

Pay Service 1
Pay Units: 233.
Programming (via satellite): Cinemax.
Fee: $7.00 monthly.

Pay Service 2
Pay Units: 342.
Programming (via satellite): HBO.
Fee: $10.00 monthly.

Pay Service 3
Pay Units: 314.
Programming (via satellite): Flix; Showtime; The Movie Channel.
Fee: $10.95 monthly.

Digital Pay Service 1
Pay Units: 81.
Programming (via satellite): Cinemax (multiplexed); Cinemax HD; Flix; HBO (multiplexed); HBO HD; HBO Latino; Showtime (multiplexed); Showtime HD; The Movie Channel (multiplexed); The Movie Channel HD.
Fee: $12.95 monthly (each).

Pay-Per-View
ESPN Now (delivered digitally); Hot Choice (delivered digitally); Playboy TV (delivered digitally); Fresh (delivered digitally); movies (delivered digitally); sports (delivered digitally).

Internet Service
Operational: No, DSL only.

Telephone Service
None

Miles of Plant: 50.0 (coaxial); 79.0 (fiber optic).
General Manager: Gerald Washburn. Chief Technician: Rick Dechant. Marketing Director: Steve Miller. Customer Service Manager: Janice Rein.
Ownership: Golden Belt Telephone Association Inc. (MSO).

RUSSELL—Eagle Communications, 336 E Wichita, Russell, KS 67665. Phones: 785-483-3244; 785-625-4000 (Corporate office). Fax: 785-483-2569. E-mail: gary.shorman@eaglecom.net. Web Site: http://www.eaglecom.net. ICA: KS0038.
TV Market Ranking: Below 100 (RUSSELL). Franchise award date: November 20, 1984. Franchise expiration date: N.A. Began: November 20, 1984.
Channel capacity: 64 (operating 2-way). Channels available but not in use: N.A.

Basic Service
Subscribers: 1,611.
Programming (received off-air): KAKE-TV (ABC) Wichita; KBSH-DT (CBS) Hays; KMTW (MNT) Hutchinson; KOOD (PBS) Hays; KSAS-TV (FOX) Wichita; KSCW-DT (CW) Wichita; KSNC (NBC) Great Bend; 2 FMs.
Programming (via satellite): C-SPAN; Home Shopping Network; QVC; TV Guide Network; Weather Channel; WGN America.
Current originations: Educational Access.
Fee: $24.95 installation; $14.95 monthly.

Expanded Basic Service 1
Subscribers: 1,539.
Programming (via satellite): ABC Family Channel; AMC; Animal Planet; Arts & Entertainment; Boomerang; Bravo; Cartoon Network; CNBC; CNN; Comedy Central; Country Music TV; Discovery Channel; Disney Channel; Do-It-Yourself; E! Entertainment Television; ESPN; ESPN 2; ESPN Classic Sports; ESPNews; Eternal Word TV Network; FitTV; Food Network; Fox Movie Channel; Fox News Channel; Fox Sports Net Midwest; FX; Hallmark Channel; Headline News; HGTV; History Channel; Lifetime; MSNBC; MTV; National Geographic Channel; NFL Network; Nickelodeon; Spike TV; Syfy; TBS Superstation; The Learning Channel; The Sportsman Channel; Toon Disney; Travel Channel; truTV; Turner Network TV; TV Land; USA Network; VH1.
Fee: $30.00 monthly.

Digital Basic Service
Subscribers: 183.
Programming (received off-air): KAKE-TV (ABC) Wichita; KMTW (MNT) Hutchinson; KOOD (PBS) Hays; KSAS-TV (FOX) Wichita; KSNC (NBC) Great Bend.
Programming (via satellite): AmericanLife TV Network; BBC America; Bio; Bloomberg Television; Bravo; Church Channel; CMT Pure Country; Cooking Channel; Current; Discovery Health Channel; Discovery Kids Channel; Discovery Military Channel; Discovery Planet Green; DMX Music; ESPN 2; ESPN Classic Sports; ESPN U; ESPNews; FitTV; Fox Business Channel; Fox College Sports Atlantic; Fox College Sports Central; Fox College Sports Pacific; Fox Movie Channel; Fox Soccer; Fuse; G4; Golf Channel; Gospel Music Channel; Great American Country; GSN; Halogen Network; HGTV; History Channel; History Channel International; ID Investigation Discovery; Independent Film Channel; JCTV; Lifetime Movie Network; MTV Hits; MTV Jams; MTV2; National Geographic Channel; Nick Jr.; NickToons TV; Outdoor Channel; PBS Kids Sprout; RFD-TV; Science Channel; Sleuth; SoapNet; Speed Channel; Style Network; Syfy; TeenNick; The Sportsman Channel; The Word Network; Toon Disney; Trinity Broadcasting Network; Turner Classic Movies; Versus; VH1 Classic; VH1 Soul; WE tv.
Fee: $3.95 monthly (sports, variety or entertainment packages), $5.95 monthly (basic package).

Digital Expanded Basic Service
Subscribers: N.A.
Programming (via satellite): Animal Planet HD; Arts & Entertainment HD; Discovery Channel HD; Discovery HD Theater; ESPN HD; Food Network HD; HGTV HD; History Channel HD; National Geographic Channel HD Network; NFL Network HD; Science Channel HD; TBS in HD; TLC HD; Turner Network TV HD; Universal HD.
Fee: $9.95 monthly.

Pay Service 1
Pay Units: 66.
Programming (via satellite): HBO.
Fee: $11.95 monthly.

Pay Service 2
Pay Units: 25.
Programming (via satellite): Cinemax.
Fee: $11.95 monthly.

Digital Pay Service 1
Pay Units: N.A.
Programming (via satellite): Cinemax (multiplexed); Cinemax HD; Encore (multiplexed); Flix; HBO (multiplexed); HBO HD; Showtime (multiplexed); Showtime HD; Starz (multiplexed); Starz HDTV; The Movie Channel (multiplexed); The Movie Channel HD.
Fee: $11.95 monthly (HBO, Cinemax, Showtime/TMC/Flix, or Starz/Encore).

Video-On-Demand: No

Pay-Per-View
Fresh (delivered digitally); Playboy TV (delivered digitally); iN DEMAND (delivered digitally); Spice: Xcess (delivered digitally); Club Jenna (delivered digitally).

Internet Service
Operational: Yes.
Subscribers: 717.
Broadband Service: Eagle Internet.
Fee: $19.95 monthly.

Telephone Service
Analog: Not Operational
Digital: Operational
Fee: $16.00 monthly

Miles of Plant: 42.0 (coaxial); None (fiber optic). Homes passed: 2,299. Total homes in franchised area: 2,450.
President: Gary Shorman. General Manager: Rex Skiles. Chief Technician: Les Libal.
City fee: 3% of gross.
Ownership: Eagle Communications Inc. (KS) (MSO).

SALINA—Cox Communications, PO Box 3027, 701 E Douglas Ave, Wichita, KS 67202. Phone: 316-260-7000. Fax: 316-262-2330. Web Site: http://www.cox.com/kansas. Also serves Saline County (portions). ICA: KS0007.
TV Market Ranking: Below 100 (SALINA, Saline County (portions)). Franchise award date: N.A. Franchise expiration date: N.A. Began: November 1, 1962.
Channel capacity: N.A. Channels available but not in use: N.A.

Basic Service
Subscribers: N.A. Included in Wichita
Programming (received off-air): KAAS-TV (FOX) Salina; KAKE-TV (ABC) Wichita; KMBC-TV (ABC) Kansas City; KMTW (MNT) Hutchinson; KOOD (PBS) Hays; KPTS (PBS) Hutchinson; KSCW-DT (CW) Wichita; KSNW (NBC) Wichita; KWCH-DT (CBS) Hutchinson; WIWB (CW) Suring.
Programming (via satellite): C-SPAN; C-SPAN 2; Home Shopping Network; QVC; TV Guide Network; Weather Channel; WGN America.
Current originations: Government Access; Educational Access; Public Access.
Fee: $29.95 installation; $10.35 monthly.

Expanded Basic Service 1
Subscribers: 16,289.
Programming (via satellite): ABC Family Channel; AMC; Animal Planet; Arts & Entertainment; BET Networks; Cartoon Network; CNBC; CNN; Comedy Central; Country Music TV; Discovery Channel; Disney Channel; E! Entertainment Television; ESPN; ESPN 2; Food Network; Fox News Channel; Fox Sports Net Midwest; FX; Hallmark Channel; Headline News; HGTV; Lifetime; MSNBC; MTV; Nickelodeon; Speed Channel; Spike TV; Syfy; TBS Superstation; The Learning Channel; truTV; Turner Network TV; TV Land; USA Network; VH1.
Fee: $43.15 monthly.

Digital Basic Service
Subscribers: N.A.
Programming (via satellite): BBC America; Bio; Bloomberg Television; Canales N; Discovery Digital Networks; DMX Music; ESPN Classic Sports; ESPNews; Fox Sports World; G4; Golf Channel; GSN; History Channel; History Channel International; Independent Film Channel; Lifetime Movie Network; MuchMusic Network; SoapNet; Sundance Channel; Toon Disney; Turner Classic Movies; Versus.
Fee: $15.00 monthly.

Digital Pay Service 1
Pay Units: 1,391.
Programming (via satellite): Cinemax (multiplexed); Encore (multiplexed); HBO (multiplexed); Showtime (multiplexed); Starz (multiplexed); The Movie Channel (multiplexed).
Fee: $29.95 installation; $11.50 monthly (each).

Video-On-Demand: Yes

Pay-Per-View
Addressable homes: 947.
iN DEMAND (delivered digitally), Fee: $3.95, Addressable: Yes.

Internet Service
Operational: Yes.
Subscribers: 2,649.
Broadband Service: Cox High Speed Internet.
Fee: $19.99-$59.99 monthly; $15.00 modem lease; $199.95 modem purchase.

Telephone Service
Digital: Operational
Fee: $15.95 monthly

Miles of Plant: 211.0 (coaxial); 26.0 (fiber optic). Homes passed included in Wichita
Vice President & General Manager: Kimberly Edmonds. Vice President, Engineering: Nick DiPonzio. Vice President, Marketing: Tony Matthews. Marketing Director: Tina Gabbard. Public Affairs Director: Sarah Kauffman.
City fee: 5% of gross.
Ownership: Cox Communications Inc. (MSO).

SALINA—Formerly served by TVCN. No longer in operation. ICA: KS0426.

SCANDIA—Cunningham Cable TV. Now served by WASHINGTON (formerly Glen Elder), KS [KS0228]. ICA: KS0227.

SCOTT CITY—Pioneer Communications. Now served by ULYSSES, KS [KS0044]. ICA: KS0053.

SEDAN—Allegiance Communications, 707 W Saratoga St, Shawnee, OK 74804. Phones: 405-395-1131; 405-275-6923. Web Site: http://www.allegiance.tv. ICA: KS0125.
TV Market Ranking: Below 100 (SEDAN). Franchise award date: November 1, 1979. Franchise expiration date: N.A. Began: August 1, 1981.
Channel capacity: N.A. Channels available but not in use: N.A.

Basic Service
Subscribers: 504.
Programming (received off-air): KJRH-TV (NBC) Tulsa; KMYT-TV (MNT) Tulsa; KOAM-TV (CBS) Pittsburg; KOED-TV (PBS) Tulsa; KOKI-TV (FOX) Tulsa; KOTV-DT (CBS) Tulsa; KSNF (NBC) Joplin; KTUL (ABC) Tulsa; KWHB (IND) Tulsa.
Programming (via satellite): C-SPAN; E! Entertainment Television; Home Shopping Network; Product Information Network; QVC; Trinity Broadcasting Network; WGN America.
Current originations: Leased Access.
Fee: $30.00 installation; $19.95 monthly.

Expanded Basic Service 1
Subscribers: N.A.
Programming (via satellite): ABC Family Channel; AMC; Animal Planet; Arts & Entertainment; Cartoon Network; CNBC; CNN; Comedy Central; Country Music TV; Discovery Channel; Disney Channel; ESPN; ESPN 2; Food Network; Fox News Channel; Fox Sports Net Midwest; FX; Headline News; HGTV; History Channel; Lifetime; Nickelodeon; Outdoor Channel; Oxygen; SoapNet; Speed Channel; Spike TV; Syfy; TBS Superstation; The Learning Channel; Travel Channel; Turner Classic Movies; Turner Network TV; TV Land; USA Network; Weather Channel.

Digital Basic Service
Subscribers: N.A.
Programming (via satellite): AmericanLife TV Network; BBC America; Bio; Bloomberg Television; Bravo; Discovery Digital Networks; DMX Music; ESPN Classic Sports; ESPNews; FitTV; Fox Movie Channel; Fox Soccer; Fuse; G4; GAS; Golf Channel; GSN; Halogen Network; History Channel International; Independent Film Channel; Lifetime Movie Network; MTV Networks Digital Suite; Nick Jr.; ShopNBC; Style Network; Toon Disney; TV Guide Network; Versus; WE tv.

Digital Pay Service 1
Pay Units: N.A.
Programming (via satellite): Cinemax (multiplexed); Encore (multiplexed); Flix; HBO (multiplexed); Showtime (multiplexed); Starz (multiplexed); The Movie Channel (multiplexed).

Video-On-Demand: No

Pay-Per-View
iN DEMAND (delivered digitally); Hot Choice (delivered digitally); Playboy TV (delivered digitally); Fresh (delivered digitally); Shorteez (delivered digitally).
Internet Service
Operational: Yes.
Telephone Service
None
Miles of Plant: 14.0 (coaxial); None (fiber optic). Homes passed: 700. Total homes in franchised area: 710.
Chief Executive Officer: Bill Haggarty. Regional Vice President: Andrew Dearth. Vice President, Marketing: Tracy Bass.
City fee: 3% of gross.
Ownership: Allegiance Communications (MSO).

SEDGWICK COUNTY (portions)—Formerly served by Westcom. No longer in operation. ICA: KS0420.

SENECA—Carson Communications. Now served by HIAWATHA, KS [KS0059]. ICA: KS0087.

SHARON—Allegiance Communications, 707 W Saratoga St, Shawnee, OK 74804. Phones: 405-395-1131; 405-275-6923. Fax: 620-873-2238. Web Site: http://www.allegiance.tv. ICA: KS0254.
TV Market Ranking: Outside TV Markets (SHARON). Franchise award date: January 1, 1989. Franchise expiration date: N.A. Began: January 1, 1989.
Channel capacity: N.A. Channels available but not in use: N.A.
Basic Service
Subscribers: 71.
Programming (received off-air): KAKE-TV (ABC) Wichita; KPTS (PBS) Hutchinson; KWCH-DT (CBS) Hutchinson.
Programming (via satellite): ABC Family Channel; CMT Pure Country; CNN; Discovery Channel; Disney Channel; ESPN; Lifetime; Nickelodeon; Spike TV; Syfy; TBS Superstation; The Learning Channel; Turner Network TV; TV Land; USA Network; Weather Channel; WGN America; WNBC (NBC) New York.
Fee: $29.95 installation; $31.00 monthly.
Pay Service 1
Pay Units: 21.
Programming (via satellite): HBO.
Fee: $9.95 monthly.
Video-On-Demand: No
Internet Service
Operational: No.
Telephone Service
None
Miles of Plant: 2.0 (coaxial); None (fiber optic). Homes passed: 131. Total homes in franchised area: 131.
Chief Executive Officer: Bill Haggarty. Regional Vice President: Andrew Dearth. Vice President, Marketing: Tracy Bass.
City fee: 3% gross.
Ownership: Allegiance Communications (MSO).

SHARON SPRINGS—Formerly served by Cebridge Connections. Now served by ULYSSES, KS [KS0044]. ICA: KS0178.

SHAWNEE—Formerly served by LENEXA, KS [KS0462]. SureWest Broadband. This cable system has converted to IPTV, 9647 Lackman Rd, Lenexa, KS 66219. Phones: 913-825-3000; 913-825-2800. Fax: 913-322-9901. Web Site: http://www.surewest.com. ICA: KS5124.
TV Market Ranking: 22 (SHAWNEE).
Channel capacity: N.A. Channels available but not in use: N.A.
Video-On-Demand: Yes
Internet Service
Operational: Yes.
Telephone Service
Digital: Operational
Ownership: SureWest Broadband.

SMITH CENTER—Nex-Tech, 705 North F, Smith Center, KS 66967. Phones: 785-567-9226; 800-843-9874; 785-567-4281 (Lenora office); 785-282-3535. Fax: 785-282-3539. Web Site: http://www.nex-tech.com. ICA: KS0102.
TV Market Ranking: Outside TV Markets (SMITH CENTER). Franchise award date: N.A. Franchise expiration date: N.A. Began: January 1, 1977.
Channel capacity: 61 (operating 2-way). Channels available but not in use: N.A.
Basic Service
Subscribers: 741.
Programming (received off-air): KBSH-DT (CBS) Hays; KGIN (CBS, MNT) Grand Island; KHAS-TV (NBC) Hastings; KHGI-TV (ABC) Kearney; KLNE-TV (PBS) Lexington; KOOD (PBS) Hays; KSNC (NBC) Great Bend.
Current originations: Educational Access.
Fee: $35.00 installation; $13.95 monthly.
Expanded Basic Service 1
Subscribers: N.A.
Programming (via satellite): ABC Family Channel; Animal Planet; Arts & Entertainment; Cartoon Network; CNN; Discovery Channel; Disney Channel; E! Entertainment Television; ESPN; Fox News Channel; Fox Sports Net Midwest; FX; Great American Country; Headline News; HGTV; History Channel; Lifetime; Nickelodeon; QVC; Spike TV; TBS Superstation; Turner Network TV; TV Land; USA Network; VH1; Weather Channel.
Digital Basic Service
Subscribers: N.A.
Programming (via satellite): AmericanLife TV Network; BBC America; Bio; Bloomberg Television; Discovery Digital Networks; Discovery Kids Channel; DMX Music; ESPN 2; ESPN Classic Sports; ESPNews; Fox Sports World; G4; Golf Channel; GSN; Halogen Network; HGTV; History Channel; History Channel International; Lifetime Movie Network; MuchMusic Network; Outdoor Channel; Ovation; ShopNBC; Speed Channel; Style Network; Syfy; Trinity Broadcasting Network; Turner Classic Movies; Versus; WE tv.
Fee: $15.95 monthly.
Pay Service 1
Pay Units: 103.
Programming (via satellite): HBO.
Fee: $10.95 monthly.
Digital Pay Service 1
Pay Units: N.A.
Programming (via satellite): Cinemax (multiplexed); Encore (multiplexed); HBO (multiplexed); Showtime (multiplexed); Starz (multiplexed); The Movie Channel (multiplexed).
Fee: $6.95 monthly (Cinemax), $9.95 monthly (Starz/Encore), $11.45 monthly (HBO), $13.45 monthly (Showtime/TMC).
Video-On-Demand: No
Pay-Per-View
Fresh (delivered digitally); Playboy TV (delivered digitally); iN DEMAND (delivered digitally); Sports PPV (delivered digitally); ESPN Extra (delivered digitally); ESPN Now (delivered digitally); Shorteez (delivered digitally).
Internet Service
Operational: Yes.
Telephone Service
None
Miles of Plant: 15.0 (coaxial); None (fiber optic). Homes passed: 896.
Manager: Brent Fine.
City fee: 1% of gross.
Ownership: Rural Telephone Co. (MSO).

SMOLAN—Home Telephone Co., PO Box 8, 211 S Main, Galva, KS 67443. Phones: 620-654-3381; 800-362-9336; 620-654-3673. Fax: 316-654-3122. E-mail: hciservice@homecomminc.com. Web Site: http://www.hometelephone.com. ICA: KS0355.
TV Market Ranking: Below 100 (SMOLAN). Franchise award date: January 1, 1989. Franchise expiration date: N.A. Began: October 20, 1989.
Channel capacity: 35 (operating 2-way). Channels available but not in use: 20.
Basic Service
Subscribers: 27.
Programming (received off-air): KAKE-TV (ABC) Wichita; KSAS-TV (FOX) Wichita; KSNW (NBC) Wichita; KWCH-DT (CBS) Hutchinson.
Programming (via satellite): ABC Family Channel; CNN; Discovery Channel; ESPN; TBS Superstation; Turner Network TV.
Fee: $26.95 monthly.
Pay Service 1
Pay Units: N.A.
Programming (via satellite): Cinemax.
Fee: $11.00 monthly.
Video-On-Demand: No
Internet Service
Operational: No, DSL & dial-up.
Telephone Service
None
Homes passed: 80.
President: Carla Shearer. Operations Manager: Brian Williams. Chief Technology Officer: Richard Baldwin. Customer Service Supervisor: Tina Anderson.
Ownership: Galva Cable Co. Inc. (MSO).

SOLOMON—Eagle Communications, 406 NE 14th St, Abilene, KS 67410. Phones: 785-263-2529; 785-625-4000 (Corporate office). Fax: 785-625-8030. Web Site: http://www.eaglecom.net. ICA: KS0177.
TV Market Ranking: Below 100 (SOLOMON). Franchise award date: March 19, 1973. Franchise expiration date: N.A. Began: January 1, 1974.
Channel capacity: 78 (operating 2-way). Channels available but not in use: 34.
Basic Service
Subscribers: 206.
Programming (received off-air): KAAS-TV (FOX) Salina; KAKE-TV (ABC) Wichita; KPTS (PBS) Hutchinson; KSNC (NBC) Great Bend; KUSA (NBC) Denver; KWCH-DT (CBS) Hutchinson; WIBW-TV (CBS, MNT) Topeka; allband FM.
Programming (via satellite): 3 Angels Broadcasting Network; ABC Family Channel; AMC; Animal Planet; Arts & Entertainment; Cartoon Network; CNN; Comedy Central; Discovery Channel; Disney Channel; E! Entertainment Television; ESPN; ESPN 2; Food Network; Fox News Channel; Fox Sports Net Midwest; FX; Great American Country; Headline News; HGTV; History Channel; Home Shopping Network; INSP; Lifetime; LWS Local Weather Station; MTV; Outdoor Channel; QVC; Speed Channel; Syfy; TBS Superstation; The Learning Channel; Toon Disney; Trinity Broadcasting Network; Turner Classic Movies; Turner Network TV; TV Land; USA Network; VH1; Weather Channel; WGN America.
Fee: $24.95 installation; $45.45 monthly.
Pay Service 1
Pay Units: N.A.
Programming (via satellite): Cinemax; HBO; Showtime; The Movie Channel.
Fee: $11.95 monthly (each).
Internet Service
Operational: Yes.
Subscribers: 79.
Broadband Service: Eagle Internet.
Fee: $22.95 monthly.
Telephone Service
None
Miles of Plant: 8.0 (coaxial); None (fiber optic). Homes passed: 399.
President: Gary Shorman. Regional Manager: Dennis Weese. General Manager: Rex Skiles.
City fee: 3% of gross.
Ownership: Eagle Communications Inc. (KS) (MSO).

SOUTH HAVEN—Formerly served by Almega Cable. No longer in operation. ICA: KS0270.

SPEARVILLE—United Communications Assn. Inc. Now served by CIMARRON, KS [KS0126]. ICA: KS0188.

SPRING HILL—Formerly served by Cebridge Connections. Now served by PAOLA, KS [KS0029]. ICA: KS0119.

ST. FRANCIS—Eagle Communications, PO Box 336, 114 W 11th St, Goodland, KS 67735. Phones: 785-899-3371; 785-625-4000 (Corporate office). Fax: 785-625-8030. Web Site: http://www.eaglecom.net. ICA: KS0444.
TV Market Ranking: Below 100 (ST. FRANCIS). Franchise award date: N.A. Franchise expiration date: N.A. Began: N.A.
Channel capacity: 36 (operating 2-way). Channels available but not in use: N.A.
Basic Service
Subscribers: 317.
Programming (received off-air): KLBY (ABC) Colby; KOOD (PBS) Hays; KSAS-TV (FOX) Wichita; KSNK (NBC) McCook; KUSA (NBC) Denver.
Programming (via satellite): CNBC; Comedy Central; FX; KCNC-TV (CBS) Denver; KMGH-TV (ABC) Denver; MSNBC; QVC.
Fee: $24.95 installation; $19.95 monthly.

Expanded Basic Service 1
Subscribers: N.A.
Programming (received off-air): KWGN-TV (CW) Denver.
Programming (via satellite): ABC Family Channel; Animal Planet; CNN; Discovery Channel; Disney Channel; ESPN; ESPN 2; Fox News Channel; Fox Sports Net Midwest; Great American Country; Headline News; HGTV; National Geographic Channel; Nickelodeon; Spike TV; TBS Superstation; The Learning Channel; Travel Channel; Turner Network TV; TV Land; USA Network; VH1; Weather Channel.
Fee: $24.50 monthly.
Pay Service 1
Pay Units: 60.
Programming (via satellite): The Movie Channel.
Fee: $11.95 monthly.
Pay Service 2
Pay Units: 62.
Programming (via satellite): Showtime.
Fee: $11.95 monthly.
Pay Service 3
Pay Units: 62.
Programming (via satellite): HBO.
Fee: $11.95 monthly.
Video-On-Demand: No
Internet Service
Operational: Yes.
Fee: $34.95-$54.95 monthly.
Telephone Service
None
Miles of Plant: 33.0 (coaxial); None (fiber optic). Homes passed: 793.
President & Chief Executive Officer: Gary Shorman. General Manager: Rex Skiles. Chief Technician: Les Libal.
Ownership: Eagle Communications Inc. (KS) (MSO).

ST. GEORGE—SCI Cable, PO Box 67235, 6700 SW Topeka Blvd, Topeka, KS 66619-0241. Phone: 785-862-1950. Fax: 785-862-2423. E-mail: scicable@sbcglobal.net. Also serves Manhattan (portions). ICA: KS0114.
TV Market Ranking: Outside TV Markets (Manhattan (portions), ST. GEORGE). Franchise award date: September 1, 1988. Franchise expiration date: N.A. Began: August 1, 1990.
Channel capacity: N.A. Channels available but not in use: N.A.
Basic Service
Subscribers: N.A.
Programming (received off-air): KSAS-TV (FOX) Wichita; KSNT (FOX, NBC) Topeka; KTKA-TV (ABC, CW) Topeka; KTMJ-CA Topeka; KTWU (PBS) Topeka; WIBW-TV (CBS, MNT) Topeka.
Programming (via satellite): CNN; CW+; Discovery Channel; Disney Channel; TBS Superstation; The Learning Channel; TV Guide Network; Weather Channel; WGN America.
Current originations: Leased Access; Public Access.
Fee: $35.00 installation; $11.95 monthly.
Expanded Basic Service 1
Subscribers: 620.
Programming (received off-air): KMCI-TV (IND) Lawrence.
Programming (via satellite): ABC Family Channel; AMC; Animal Planet; Arts & Entertainment; Cartoon Network; CNBC; Comedy Central; Country Music TV; C-SPAN; E! Entertainment Television; ESPN; ESPN 2; ESPN Classic Sports; ESPNews; Food Network; Fox News Channel; Fox Sports Net; FX; Golf Channel; GSN; Hallmark Channel; Halogen Network; Headline News; HGTV; History Channel; Home Shopping Network; Lifetime; MSNBC; MTV; National Geographic Channel; Nickelodeon; ShopNBC; Speed Channel; Spike TV; Syfy; Toon Disney; Travel Channel; truTV; Turner Classic Movies; Turner Network TV; TV Land; USA Network; Versus; VH1.
Fee: $35.00 installation; $24.95 monthly.
Digital Basic Service
Subscribers: N.A.
Programming (via satellite): AmericanLife TV Network; BBC America; Bio; Bloomberg Television; Bravo; CMT Pure Country; CNN en Espanol; Comedy Central; Current; Discovery Health Channel; Discovery Home Channel; Discovery Kids Channel; Discovery Military Channel; Discovery Times Channel; ESPN 2; ESPN Classic Sports; ESPNews; FitTV; Fox Movie Channel; Fox Soccer; Fox Sports en Espanol; Fuse; G4; Golf Channel; Gospel Music Channel; Great American Country; GSN; Halogen Network; HGTV; History Channel; History Channel International; Independent Film Channel; Lifetime Movie Network; MTV Jams; MTV2; National Geographic Channel; Nick Jr.; Outdoor Channel; Ovation; Science Channel; Speed Channel; Style Network; Sundance Channel; Syfy; TeenNick; The Word Network; Toon Disney; Trinity Broadcasting Network; Turner Classic Movies; TV Land; Versus; VH1 Classic; VH1 Soul; WE tv; Weatherscan.
Pay Service 1
Pay Units: N.A.
Programming (via satellite): Cinemax (multiplexed); HBO (multiplexed); Showtime.
Fee: $10.95 monthly (each).
Digital Pay Service 1
Pay Units: N.A.
Programming (via satellite): Cinemax (multiplexed); Encore (multiplexed); HBO (multiplexed); Showtime (multiplexed); The Movie Channel (multiplexed).
Pay-Per-View
Special events.
Internet Service
Operational: Yes.
Broadband Service: SCI Broadband.
Fee: $29.95 monthly.
Telephone Service
None
Miles of Plant: 40.0 (coaxial); None (fiber optic). Additional miles planned: 6.0 (coaxial). Homes passed: 780. Total homes in franchised area: 900.
Manager: Kirk Keberlein.
Ownership: SCI Cable Inc. (MSO).

ST. JOHN—GBT Communications Inc., PO Box 229, 103 Lincoln St, Rush Center, KS 67575-0229. Phone: 785-372-4236. Fax: 785-372-4201. Web Site: http://www.gbta.net. ICA: KS0127.
TV Market Ranking: Below 100 (ST. JOHN). Franchise award date: N.A. Franchise expiration date: N.A. Began: March 1, 1979.
Channel capacity: N.A. Channels available but not in use: N.A.
Basic Service
Subscribers: 258.
Programming (received off-air): KAKE-TV (ABC) Wichita; KOOD (PBS) Hays; KPTS (PBS) Hutchinson; KSAS-TV (FOX) Wichita; KSNC (NBC) Great Bend; KWCH-DT (CBS) Hutchinson; allband FM.
Programming (via satellite): C-SPAN; TBS Superstation; WGN America.
Current originations: Public Access.
Fee: $35.00 installation; $25.29 monthly.
Expanded Basic Service 1
Subscribers: N.A.
Programming (received off-air): KSCW-DT (CW) Wichita.
Programming (via satellite): ABC Family Channel; American Movie Classics; Animal Planet; Arts & Entertainment; Cartoon Network; CNN; Comedy Central; Country Music TV; C-SPAN 2; Discovery Channel; Disney Channel; E! Entertainment Television; ESPN; ESPN 2; ESPN Classic Sports; Eternal Word TV Network; Food Network; Fox News Channel; Fox Sports Net Midwest; FX; GSN; Hallmark Channel; Headline News; HGTV; History Channel; Home Shopping Network; INSP; Lifetime; MSNBC; MTV; National Geographic Channel; NFL Network; Nickelodeon; Outdoor Channel; QVC; RFD-TV; Speed Channel; Spike TV; Syfy; The Learning Channel; Travel Channel; Trinity Broadcasting Network; truTV; Turner Classic Movies; Turner Network TV; TV Land; Univision; USA Network; VH1; Weather Channel.
Digital Basic Service
Subscribers: N.A.
Programming (received off-air): KAKE-TV (ABC) Wichita; KOOD (PBS) Hays; KSAS-TV (FOX) Wichita; KSNW (NBC) Wichita; KWCH-DT (CBS) Hutchinson.
Programming (via satellite): Discovery Channel HD; ESPN HD; MyNetworkTV Inc.; NFL Network HD; TBS in HD; Turner Network TV HD.
Pay Service 1
Pay Units: 44.
Programming (via satellite): Cinemax; Flix (multiplexed); The Movie Channel.
Fee: $5.95 monthly (TMC), $9.95 monthly (Showtime), $10.95 monthly (HBO).
Digital Pay Service 1
Pay Units: N.A.
Programming (via satellite): Cinemax HD; HBO HD; Showtime HD; The Movie Channel HD.
Video-On-Demand: No
Pay-Per-View
Sports PPV (delivered digitally); ESPN Extra (delivered digitally); ESPN Now; Hot Choice (delivered digitally); Shorteez (delivered digitally); Fresh (delivered digitally); Playboy TV (delivered digitally); iN DEMAND (delivered digitally).
Internet Service
Operational: Yes.
Fee: $29.95 monthly.
Telephone Service
None
Miles of Plant: 14.0 (coaxial); None (fiber optic). Homes passed: 685. Total homes in franchised area: 900.
General Manager: Gerald Washburn. Chief Technician: Rick Dechant. Marketing Director: Steve Miller.
City fee: 3% of gross.
Ownership: Golden Belt Telephone Association Inc. (MSO).

ST. MARYS—WTC Communications. Formerly served by Wamego, KS [KS0057]. This cable system has converted to IPTV, 1009 Lincoln St, Wamego, KS 66547. Phones: 877-492-6835; 785-456-1000. Fax: 785-456-9903. E-mail: support@wamego.net. Web Site: http://www.wamtelco.com. ICA: KS5014.
TV Market Ranking: Outside TV Markets (St. Marys).
Channel capacity: N.A. Channels available but not in use: N.A.
Telephone Service
Digital: Operational
President & General Manager: Steve Tackrider. Plant Manager: Ken Blew.
Ownership: WTC Communications Inc.

ST. PAUL—Cable TV of St. Paul, PO Box 435, Parsons, KS 67357-0435. Phone: 620-421-2322. E-mail: mattox@par1.net. ICA: KS0240.
TV Market Ranking: Below 100 (ST. PAUL). Franchise award date: N.A. Franchise expiration date: N.A. Began: May 1, 1984.
Channel capacity: 35 (not 2-way capable). Channels available but not in use: N.A.
Basic Service
Subscribers: 185.
Programming (received off-air): KOAM-TV (CBS) Pittsburg; KODE-TV (ABC) Joplin; KOZJ (PBS) Joplin; KSNF (NBC) Joplin.
Programming (via satellite): ABC Family Channel; CNN; ESPN; Lifetime; TBS Superstation; Turner Network TV; USA Network; WGN America.
Fee: $10.00 installation; $25.95 monthly.
Pay Service 1
Pay Units: 20.
Programming (via satellite): The Movie Channel.
Fee: $9.95 monthly.
Internet Service
Operational: No.
Telephone Service
None
Miles of Plant: 6.0 (coaxial); None (fiber optic). Homes passed: 220.
Manager: Edward Mattox.
Ownership: Edward Mattox.

STAFFORD—Allegiance Communications, 707 W Saratoga St, Shawnee, OK 74804. Phones: 405-395-1131; 405-275-6923. Web Site: http://www.allegiance.tv. ICA: KS0469.
TV Market Ranking: Below 100 (STAFFORD).
Channel capacity: N.A. Channels available but not in use: N.A.
Basic Service
Subscribers: N.A.
Programming (received off-air): KAKE-TV (ABC) Wichita; KMTW (MNT) Hutchinson; KOOD (PBS) Hays; KPTS (PBS) Hutchinson; KSAS-TV (FOX) Wichita; KSCW-DT (CW) Wichita; KSNC (NBC) Great Bend; KWCH-DT (CBS) Hutchinson.
Programming (via satellite): E! Entertainment Television; Home Shopping Network; QVC; WGN America.
Expanded Basic Service 1
Subscribers: N.A.
Programming (via satellite): ABC Family Channel; AMC; Animal Planet; Arts & Entertainment; Cartoon Network; CNBC; CNN; Comedy Central; Country Music TV; Discovery Channel; Disney Channel; ESPN; ESPN 2; Food Network; Fox News Channel; Fox Sports Net Midwest; FX; Hallmark Channel; Headline News; HGTV; History Channel; Lifetime; MSNBC; MTV; National Geographic Channel; Nickelodeon; Oxygen; Speed Channel; Spike TV; Syfy; TBS Superstation; The Learning Channel; Travel Channel; Turner Network TV; TV Land; USA Network; VH1; Weather Channel.
Digital Basic Service
Subscribers: N.A.
Programming (via satellite): BBC America; Bio; Bloomberg Television; Bravo; Chiller; CMT Pure Country; Current; Discovery Health Channel; Discovery Kids Channel; Discovery Military Channel; Discovery Planet Green; DMX Music; Encore (multi-

plexed); ESPN Classic Sports; ESPNews; FitTV; Flix; Fox Movie Channel; Fox Soccer; Fuse; G4; Golf Channel; GSN; History Channel International; ID Investigation Discovery; Independent Film Channel; Lifetime Movie Network; MTV Hits; MTV2; Nick Jr.; NickToons TV; Outdoor Channel; RFD-TV; Science Channel; Sleuth; SoapNet; Style Network; Sundance Channel; TeenNick; Toon Disney; Trinity Broadcasting Network; Turner Classic Movies; Versus; VH1 Classic; VH1 Soul; WE tv.

Pay Service 1

Pay Units: N.A.

Programming (via satellite): Cinemax; HBO; Showtime; The Movie Channel.

Digital Pay Service 1

Pay Units: N.A.

Programming (via satellite): Cinemax (multiplexed); HBO (multiplexed); Showtime (multiplexed); Starz (multiplexed); The Movie Channel (multiplexed).

Video-On-Demand: No

Pay-Per-View

iN DEMAND (delivered digitally); Spice: Xcess (delivered digitally); Fresh (delivered digitally); Playboy TV (delivered digitally); Club Jenna (delivered digitally).

Internet Service

Operational: No.

Telephone Service

None

Miles of Plant: 12.0 (coaxial); None (fiber optic).

Chief Executive Officer: Bill Haggarty. Regional Vice President: Andrew Dearth. Vice President, Marketing: Tracy Bass.

Ownership: Allegiance Communications (MSO).

STERLING—Eagle Communications. Now served by GREAT BEND, KS [KS0012]. ICA: KS0091.

STOCKTON—Nex-Tech. Formerly [KS0051]. This cable system has converted to IPTV, PO Box 158, 145 N Main St, Lenora, KS 67645-0158. Phones: 877-567-7872; 785-567-4281. Fax: 785-567-4401. E-mail: webmaster@nex-tech.com. Web Site: http://www.nex-tech.com. ICA: KS5055.

Channel capacity: N.A. Channels available but not in use: N.A.

Internet Service

Operational: Yes.

Telephone Service

Digital: Operational

Ownership: Rural Telephone Co.

STOCKTON—Nex-Tech. This cable system has converted to IPTV. See Stockton, KS [KS5055]. ICA: KS0051.

STRONG CITY—Galaxy Cablevision, 1928 S Lincoln Ave, Ste 200, York, NE 68467. Phone: 402-362-3332. Fax: 402-362-4890. Web Site: http://www.galaxycable.com. Also serves Cottonwood Falls. ICA: KS0421.

TV Market Ranking: Outside TV Markets (Cottonwood Falls, STRONG CITY). Franchise award date: N.A. Franchise expiration date: N.A. Began: May 1, 1976.

Channel capacity: 31 (not 2-way capable). Channels available but not in use: None.

Basic Service

Subscribers: 148.

Programming (received off-air): KAKE-TV (ABC) Wichita; KMTW (MNT) Hutchinson; KSAS-TV (FOX) Wichita; KSCW-DT (CW) Wichita; KSNT (FOX, NBC) Topeka; KTKA-TV (ABC, CW) Topeka; KTWU (PBS) Topeka; KWCH-DT (CBS) Hutchinson; WIBW-TV (CBS, MNT) Topeka.

Programming (via satellite): ABC Family Channel; Arts & Entertainment; Cartoon Network; CNN; Discovery Channel; Disney Channel; ESPN; ESPN 2; Fox News Channel; Fuse; FX; Great American Country; HGTV; History Channel; Lifetime; Outdoor Channel; Starz; TBS Superstation; The Learning Channel; Trinity Broadcasting Network; Turner Network TV; USA Network; Weather Channel.

Current originations: Public Access.

Fee: $39.80 monthly.

Pay Service 1

Pay Units: N.A.

Programming (via satellite): Cinemax; HBO; Showtime; The Movie Channel.

Internet Service

Operational: No.

Telephone Service

None

Miles of Plant: 16.0 (coaxial); None (fiber optic). Homes passed: 719.

State Manager: Cheyenne Wohlford. Technical Manager: John Davidshofer. Sales Manager: Mike Thomas. Customer Service Manager: Michael Debermardin.

City fee: 0.5% of gross.

Ownership: Galaxy Cable Inc. (MSO).

SUMMERFIELD—Blue Valley Telecommunications. Formerly [KS0452]. This cable system has converted to IPTV, 1557 Pony Express Hwy, Home, KS 66438. Phones: 785-799-3311; 877-876-1228. E-mail: info@bluevalley.net. Web Site: http://www.bluevalley.net. ICA: KS5015.

TV Market Ranking: Outside TV Markets (SUMMERFIELD).

Channel capacity: N.A. Channels available but not in use: N.A.

Internet Service

Operational: Yes.

Telephone Service

Digital: Operational

General Manager: Dennis Doyle.

Ownership: Blue Valley Telecommunications.

SUMMERFIELD—Blue Valley Tele-Communications. This cable system has converted to IPTV. See Summerfield, KS [KS5015], KS. ICA: KS0452.

SYLVAN GROVE—Wilson Communications, PO Box 508, 2504 Ave D, Wilson, KS 67490-0508. Phones: 800-432-7607; 785-658-2111. Fax: 785-658-3344. Web Site: http://www.wilsoncommunications.us. ICA: KS0279.

TV Market Ranking: Outside TV Markets (SYLVAN GROVE). Franchise award date: N.A. Franchise expiration date: N.A. Began: January 1, 1983.

Channel capacity: N.A. Channels available but not in use: N.A.

Basic Service

Subscribers: 76.

Programming (received off-air): KAKE-TV (ABC) Wichita; KOOD (PBS) Hays; KPTS (PBS) Hutchinson; KSAS-TV (FOX) Wichita; KSNC (NBC) Great Bend; KWCH-DT (CBS) Hutchinson.

Programming (via satellite): ABC Family Channel; AMC; AmericanLife TV Network; Arts & Entertainment; CNN; Country Music TV; C-SPAN; C-SPAN 2; CW+; Discovery Channel; Disney Channel; ESPN; ESPN 2; ESPN Classic Sports; ESPNews; Eternal Word TV Network; Food Network; Fox News Channel; Fox Sports Net Rocky Mountain; FX; Hallmark Channel; Headline News; HGTV; Home Shopping Network; ION Television; KMGH-TV (ABC) Denver; Lifetime; MTV; National Geographic Channel; Nickelodeon; Spike TV; Syfy; TBS Superstation; The Learning Channel; Turner Network TV; TV Land; USA Network; VH1; Weather Channel; WGN America.

Fee: $25.00 installation; $35.95 monthly.

Digital Basic Service

Subscribers: N.A.

Programming (received off-air): KAKE-TV (ABC) Wichita; KMTV-TV (CBS) Omaha; KOOD (PBS) Hays; KPTS (PBS) Hutchinson; KSAS-TV (FOX) Wichita; KSCW-DT (CW) Wichita; KSNC (NBC) Great Bend; KWCH-DT (CBS) Hutchinson.

Programming (via satellite): Arts & Entertainment HD; BBC America; Bio; Bravo; CMT Pure Country; Discovery HD Theater; Discovery Health Channel; Discovery Kids Channel; Discovery Military Channel; Discovery Planet Green; DMX Music; ESPN 2 HD; ESPN HD; ESPN U; ESPNU HD; Food Network HD; Fox Soccer; Fuse; Golf Channel; GSN; HGTV HD; History Channel; History Channel HD; History Channel International; ID Investigation Discovery; Independent Film Channel; Lifetime Movie Network; MTV2; Nick Jr.; RFD-TV; Science Channel; Sleuth; Speed Channel; Style Network; TeenNick; Turner Classic Movies; Universal HD; Versus; VH1 Classic; WE tv.

Fee: $49.95 installation; $12.00 monthly.

Digital Pay Service 1

Pay Units: N.A.

Programming (via satellite): Cinemax (multiplexed); Encore (multiplexed); HBO (multiplexed); Showtime (multiplexed); Starz (multiplexed); Starz HDTV; The Movie Channel (multiplexed).

Fee: $13.95 monthly (Starz/Encore or Showtime/TMC) $16.95 monthly (HBO & Cinemax).

Video-On-Demand: No

Internet Service

Operational: No, DSL & dial-up.

Telephone Service

None

Miles of Plant: 5.0 (coaxial); None (fiber optic). Homes passed: 249.

Vice President, Marketing: Scott Grauer. Plant Supervisor: Dan Steinike. Controller: Gary Everett. Customer Service Manager: Mary Zorn.

Ownership: Wilson Communications (MSO).

SYLVIA—Formerly served by Cox Communications. No longer in operation. ICA: KS0280.

TAMPA—Formerly served by Eagle Communications. No longer in operation. ICA: KS0434.

TESCOTT—Twin Valley Communications. Formerly served by Bennington, KS [KS0214]. This cable system has converted to IPTV, PO Box 515, Clay Center, KS 67432. Phones: 800-515-3311; 785-427-2288. Fax: 785-427-2216. E-mail: tvinc@twinvalley.net. Web Site: http://www.twinvalley.net. ICA: KS5036.

Channel capacity: N.A. Channels available but not in use: N.A.

Internet Service

Operational: Yes.

Telephone Service

Digital: Operational

Ownership: Twin Valley Communications Inc.

THAYER—Mediacom, 901 N College Ave, Columbia, MO 65201. Phones: 417-875-5560 (Springfield regional office); 573-443-1536. Fax: 417-883-0255. Web Site: http://www.mediacomcable.com. ICA: KS0237.

TV Market Ranking: Outside TV Markets (THAYER). Franchise award date: N.A. Franchise expiration date: N.A. Began: December 1, 1985.

Channel capacity: N.A. Channels available but not in use: N.A.

Basic Service

Subscribers: 79.

Programming (received off-air): KOAM-TV (CBS) Pittsburg; KODE-TV (ABC) Joplin; KSNF (NBC) Joplin; KTWU (PBS) Topeka.

Programming (via satellite): ABC Family Channel; Arts & Entertainment; CNN; Country Music TV; Discovery Channel; ESPN; Headline News; Lifetime; Nickelodeon; QVC; Spike TV; TBS Superstation; Turner Network TV; USA Network; Weather Channel; WGN America.

Fee: $35.00 installation; $23.95 monthly.

Pay Service 1

Pay Units: 16.

Programming (via satellite): The Movie Channel.

Fee: $10.50 monthly.

Pay Service 2

Pay Units: 21.

Programming (via satellite): Showtime.

Fee: $10.50 monthly.

Video-On-Demand: No

Internet Service

Operational: No.

Telephone Service

None

Miles of Plant: 12.0 (coaxial); None (fiber optic). Homes passed: 240.

Regional Vice President: Bill Copeland. Operations Director: Bryan Gann. Regional Technical Operations Manager: Alan Freedman. Technical Operations Manager: Roger Shearer. Marketing Director: Will Kuebler.

City fee: 3% of basic.

Ownership: Mediacom LLC (MSO).

TIPTON—Wilson Communications, PO Box 508, 2504 Ave D, Wilson, KS 67490-0508. Phones: 800-432-7607; 785-658-2111. Fax: 785-658-3344. Web Site: http://www.wilsoncommunications.us. ICA: KS0326.

TV Market Ranking: Outside TV Markets (TIPTON). Franchise award date: April 1, 1982. Franchise expiration date: N.A. Began: N.A.

Channel capacity: N.A. Channels available but not in use: N.A.

Basic Service

Subscribers: 40.

Programming (received off-air): KAKE-TV (ABC) Wichita; KMTV-TV (CBS) Omaha; KOOD (PBS) Hays; KPTS (PBS) Hutchinson; KSAS-TV (FOX) Wichita; KSNC (NBC) Great Bend; KWCH-DT (CBS) Hutchinson.

Programming (via satellite): ABC Family Channel; AMC; AmericanLife TV Network; Arts & Entertainment; CNN; Country Music TV; C-SPAN; C-SPAN 2; CW+; Discovery Channel; Disney Channel; ESPN; ESPN 2; ESPN Classic Sports; ESPNews; Eternal Word TV Network; Food Network; Fox News Channel; Fox Sports Net Rocky Mountain; FX; Hallmark Channel; Headline News; HGTV; Home Shopping Network; ION Television; Lifetime; MTV; National Geographic Channel; Nickelodeon; Spike TV; Syfy; TBS Superstation; The Learning Channel; Turner Network TV; TV Land; USA Network; VH1; Weather Channel; WGN America.

Fee: $25.00 installation; $35.95 monthly.

Digital Basic Service

Subscribers: N.A.

Programming (received off-air): KAKE-TV (ABC) Wichita; KMTV-TV (CBS) Omaha;

KOOD (PBS) Hays; KSAS-TV (FOX) Wichita; KSCW-DT (CW) Wichita; KWCH-DT (CBS) Hutchinson.

Programming (via satellite): Arts & Entertainment HD; BBC America; Bio; Bravo; CMT Pure Country; Discovery HD Theater; Discovery Health Channel; Discovery Kids Channel; Discovery Military Channel; Discovery Planet Green; DMX Music; ESPN 2 HD; ESPN HD; ESPN U; Food Network HD; Fox Soccer; Fuse; Golf Channel; GSN; HGTV HD; History Channel; History Channel HD; History Channel International; ID Investigation Discovery; Independent Film Channel; KPTS (PBS) Hutchinson; KSNC (NBC) Great Bend; Lifetime Movie Network; MTV2; Nick Jr.; RFD-TV; Science Channel; Sleuth; Speed Channel; Style Network; TeenNick; Turner Classic Movies; Universal HD; Versus; VH1 Classic; WE tv.

Fee: $49.95 installation; $12.00 monthly.

Digital Pay Service 1

Pay Units: N.A.

Programming (via satellite): Cinemax (multiplexed); Encore (multiplexed); HBO (multiplexed); Showtime (multiplexed); Starz (multiplexed); Starz HDTV; The Movie Channel (multiplexed).

Fee: $13.95 monthly (Showtime/TMC or Starz/Encore) $16.95 monthly (HBO & Cinemax).

Video-On-Demand: No

Internet Service

Operational: No, DSL & dial-up.

Telephone Service

None

Miles of Plant: 3.0 (coaxial); None (fiber optic). Homes passed: 56.

Vice President, Marketing: Scott Grauer. Controller: Gary Everett. Customer Service Manager: Mary Zorn. Plant Supervisor: Dan Steinike.

City fee: 3% of basic gross.

Ownership: Wilson Communications (MSO).

TOPEKA—Cox Communications, 931 SW Henderson Rd, Topeka, KS 66615. Phones: 785-215-6700; 316-260-7000 (Wichita office). Fax: 785-215-6127. Web Site: http://www.cox.com/kansas. Also serves Auburn, Berryton, Pauline, Shawnee County & Tecumseh. ICA: KS0002.

TV Market Ranking: Below 100 (Auburn, Berryton, Pauline, Shawnee County, Tecumseh, TOPEKA). Franchise award date: N.A. Franchise expiration date: N.A. Began: December 12, 1977.

Channel capacity: N.A. Channels available but not in use: N.A.

Basic Service

Subscribers: N.A. Included in Wichita

Programming (received off-air): KCTV (CBS) Kansas City; KMBC-TV (ABC) Kansas City; KSHB-TV (NBC) Kansas City; KSNT (FOX, NBC) Topeka; KTKA-TV (ABC, CW) Topeka; KTWU (PBS) Topeka; WDAF-TV (FOX) Kansas City; WIBW-TV (CBS, MNT) Topeka; 15 FMs.

Programming (via satellite): C-SPAN; TV Guide Network; Weather Channel; WGN America.

Current originations: Government Access; Educational Access.

Fee: $29.95 installation; $10.35 monthly.

Expanded Basic Service 1

Subscribers: 50,265.

Programming (via satellite): ABC Family Channel; AMC; Animal Planet; Arts & Entertainment; BET Networks; Cartoon Network; CNBC; CNN; Comedy Central; Country Music TV; C-SPAN 2; Discovery Channel; Disney Channel; E! Entertainment Television; ESPN; ESPN 2; Eternal Word TV Network; Food Network; Fox News Channel; Fox Sports Net Midwest; FX; Hallmark Channel; Headline News; HGTV; History Channel; Home Shopping Network; INSP; Lifetime; MSNBC; MTV; Nickelodeon; QVC; ShopNBC; Speed Channel; Spike TV; Syfy; TBS Superstation; The Learning Channel; Travel Channel; truTV; Turner Classic Movies; Turner Network TV; TV Land; USA Network; VH1.

Fee: $43.15 monthly.

Digital Basic Service

Subscribers: N.A.

Programming (via satellite): BBC America; Bio; Bloomberg Television; Canales N; Discovery Digital Networks; DMX Music; ESPN Classic Sports; ESPNews; Fox Sports World; G4; GAS; Golf Channel; Great American Country; GSN; History Channel International; Independent Film Channel; Lifetime Movie Network; MTV Networks Digital Suite; MuchMusic Network; NBA TV; Nick Jr.; Nick Too; Outdoor Channel; Oxygen; SoapNet; Sundance Channel; Toon Disney; Versus.

Fee: $15.00 monthly.

Digital Pay Service 1

Pay Units: 10,317.

Programming (via satellite): Cinemax (multiplexed); Encore (multiplexed); HBO (multiplexed); Showtime (multiplexed); Starz (multiplexed); The Movie Channel (multiplexed).

Fee: $11.50 monthly (each).

Video-On-Demand: Yes

Pay-Per-View

iN DEMAND; ESPN (delivered digitally); NBA/WNBA League Pass (delivered digitally); NHL Center Ice/MLB Extra Innings (delivered digitally).

Internet Service

Operational: Yes.

Subscribers: 8,807.

Broadband Service: Cox High Speed Internet.

Fee: $19.99-$59.99 monthly; $15.00 modem lease; $199.95 modem purchase.

Telephone Service

Digital: Operational

Fee: $15.95 monthly

Miles of Plant: 1,429.0 (coaxial); None (fiber optic). Homes passed included in Wichita

Vice President & General Manager: Kimberly Edmonds. Field Operations Regional Manager: Scott Terry. Vice President, Engineering: Nick DiPonzio. Vice President, Marketing: Tony Matthews. Marketing Director: Tina Gabbard. Public Affairs Director: Sarah Kauffman.

City fee: 3% of gross.

Ownership: Cox Communications Inc. (MSO).

TORONTO—Mediacom, 901 N College Ave, Columbia, MO 65201. Phones: 417-875-5560 (Springfield regional office); 573-443-1536. Fax: 417-883-0265. Web Site: http://www.mediacomcable.com. ICA: KS0250.

TV Market Ranking: Outside TV Markets (TORONTO). Franchise award date: N.A. Franchise expiration date: N.A. Began: September 1, 1984.

Channel capacity: N.A. Channels available but not in use: N.A.

Basic Service

Subscribers: 114.

Programming (received off-air): KAKE-TV (ABC) Wichita; KOAM-TV (CBS) Pittsburg; KSNF (NBC) Joplin; KSNW (NBC) Wichita; KTWU (PBS) Topeka; WIBW-TV (CBS, MNT) Topeka.

Programming (via satellite): ABC Family Channel; Arts & Entertainment; CNN; Country Music TV; Discovery Channel; ESPN; Headline News; Nickelodeon; QVC; Spike TV; TBS Superstation; Turner Network TV; USA Network; Weather Channel; WGN America.

Fee: $35.00 installation; $23.95 monthly.

Pay Service 1

Pay Units: 22.

Programming (via satellite): Showtime.

Fee: $10.50 monthly.

Pay Service 2

Pay Units: N.A.

Programming (via satellite): HBO.

Fee: $10.50 monthly.

Video-On-Demand: No

Internet Service

Operational: No.

Telephone Service

None

Miles of Plant: 6.0 (coaxial); None (fiber optic). Homes passed: 251. Total homes in franchised area: 278.

Regional Vice President: Bill Copeland. Operations Director: Bryan Gann. Regional Technical Operations Director: Alan Freedman. Technical Operations Manager: Roger Shearer. Marketing Director: Will Kuebler.

City fee: 3% of basic.

Ownership: Mediacom LLC (MSO).

TRIBUNE—Formerly served by Cebridge Connections. Now served by ULYSSES, KS [KS0044]. ICA: KS0168.

TURON—Formerly served by Cox Communications. No longer in operation. ICA: KS0217.

UDALL—Wheat State Telecable Inc., PO Box 320, 106 W First St, Udall, KS 67146. Phone: 620-782-3347. Fax: 620-782-3302. E-mail: support@wheatstate.com. Web Site: http://www.wheatstate.com. ICA: KS0197.

TV Market Ranking: 67 (UDALL). Franchise award date: July 1, 1983. Franchise expiration date: N.A. Began: September 1, 1983.

Channel capacity: 60 (operating 2-way). Channels available but not in use: 6.

Basic Service

Subscribers: 210.

Programming (received off-air): KAKE-TV (ABC) Wichita; KMTW (MNT) Hutchinson; KPTS (PBS) Hutchinson; KSAS-TV (FOX) Wichita; KSCW-DT (CW) Wichita; KSNW (NBC) Wichita; KWCH-DT (CBS) Hutchinson.

Programming (via satellite): Arts & Entertainment; CNBC; C-SPAN; C-SPAN 2; Discovery Channel; Disney Channel; ESPN; ESPN 2; Eternal Word TV Network; Fox News Channel; G4; Headline News; HGTV; Home Shopping Network; INSP; Lifetime; MSNBC; MTV; Nickelodeon; Outdoor Channel; QVC; The Learning Channel; Trinity Broadcasting Network; TV Land; USA Network; VH1; Weather Channel.

Planned originations: Educational Access.

Fee: $25.00 installation; $21.95 monthly.

Expanded Basic Service 1

Subscribers: 155.

Programming (via satellite): CNN; Hallmark Channel; Spike TV; Syfy; TBS Superstation; Turner Network TV; WGN America.

Fee: $7.50 monthly.

Expanded Basic Service 2

Subscribers: N.A.

Programming (via satellite): ABC Family Channel; AMC; Animal Planet; Cartoon Network; Comedy Central; Country Music TV; History Channel; Speed Channel.

Fee: $7.00 monthly.

Pay Service 1

Pay Units: 12.

Programming (via satellite): Cinemax.

Fee: $11.00 monthly.

Pay Service 2

Pay Units: 20.

Programming (via satellite): HBO.

Fee: $11.00 monthly.

Pay Service 3

Pay Units: 12.

Programming (via satellite): Showtime.

Fee: $11.00 monthly.

Video-On-Demand: No

Internet Service

Operational: No, DSL only.

Telephone Service

None

Miles of Plant: 5.0 (coaxial); None (fiber optic). Homes passed: 275. Total homes in franchised area: 275.

Manager: Arturo Macias. Chief Technician: Bruce Cardwell.

City fee: 2% of gross.

Ownership: Wheat State Telecable Inc.

ULYSSES—Pioneer Communications, 120 W Kansas Ave, Ulysses, KS 67880-2036. Phone: 620-356-3211. Fax: 620-356-3242. E-mail: marketing@pioncomm.net. Web Site: http://www.pioncomm.net. Also serves Big Bow, Coolidge, Deerfield, Greeley County (portions), Holcomb, Hugoton, Johnson, Kendall, Lakin, Leoti, Manter, Marienthal, Moscow, Richfield, Rolla, Satanta, Scott City, Sharon Springs, Sublette, Syracuse & Tribune. ICA: KS0044.

TV Market Ranking: Below 100 (Deerfield, Holcomb, Lakin, Scott City, Sharon Springs, Sublette); Outside TV Markets (Big Bow, Coolidge, Greeley County (portions), Hugoton, Johnson, Kendall, Leoti, Manter, Marienthal, Moscow, Richfield, Rolla, Satanta, Syracuse, Tribune, ULYSSES). Franchise award date: N.A. Franchise expiration date: N.A. Began: February 1, 1975.

Channel capacity: 117 (operating 2-way). Channels available but not in use: 10.

Basic Service

Subscribers: 9,300.

Programming (received off-air): KBSD-DT (CBS) Ensign; KMTW (MNT) Hutchinson; KSAS-TV (FOX) Wichita; KSCW-DT (CW) Wichita; KSNG (NBC) Garden City; KSWK (PBS) Lakin; KUPK-TV (ABC) Garden City.

Programming (via satellite): ABC Family Channel; AMC; AmericanLife TV Network; Animal Planet; Arts & Entertainment; Bravo; Cartoon Network; CNBC; CNN; Comedy Central; Country Music TV; C-SPAN; C-SPAN 2; Discovery Channel; Disney Channel; E! Entertainment Television; ESPN; ESPN 2; ESPN Classic Sports; ESPNews; Eternal Word TV Network; Food Network; Fox News Channel; Fox Sports Net Midwest; FX; Golf Channel; Hallmark Channel; Headline News; HGTV; History Channel; Home Shopping Network; ION Television; Lifetime; Lifetime Movie Network; MSNBC; MTV; Nickelodeon; Ovation; QVC; ShopNBC; Spike TV; Syfy; TBS Superstation; Telemundo; The Learning Channel; Travel Channel; Trinity Broadcasting Network; truTV; Turner Classic Movies; Turner Network TV; TV Guide Network; TV Land; Univision; USA Network; VH1; Weather Channel; WGN America.

Current originations: Educational Access.

Fee: $35.00 installation; $40.95 monthly.

Digital Basic Service

Subscribers: 1,730.

Programming (via satellite): BBC America; Bloomberg Television; Discovery Dig-

ital Networks; DMX Music; FitTV; Fox College Sports Atlantic; Fox College Sports Central; Fox College Sports Pacific; Fox Movie Channel; G4; GAS; Great American Country; Halogen Network; MTV Networks Digital Suite; Nick Jr.; Nick Too; NickToons TV; Outdoor Channel; Speed Channel; Versus.
Fee: $12.95 monthly.

Digital Pay Service 1
Pay Units: 1,913.
Programming (via satellite): HBO (multiplexed).
Fee: $12.95 monthly.

Digital Pay Service 2
Pay Units: 845.
Programming (via satellite): Showtime (multiplexed); The Movie Channel.
Fee: $12.95 monthly.

Digital Pay Service 3
Pay Units: 644.
Programming (via satellite): Cinemax (multiplexed).
Fee: $10.95 monthly.

Digital Pay Service 4
Pay Units: 716.
Programming (via satellite): Encore (multiplexed); Starz (multiplexed).
Fee: $10.95 monthly.

Digital Pay Service 5
Pay Units: N.A.
Programming (via satellite): Canales N; Discovery HD Theater; HDNet; HDNet Movies; Turner Network TV HD.

Video-On-Demand: Planned

Pay-Per-View
Addressable homes: 2,970.
Movies (delivered digitally), Fee: $3.99, Addressable: Yes; special events (delivered digitally).

Internet Service
Operational: Yes, DSL.
Subscribers: 6,600.
Broadband Service: Pioneer.
Fee: $45.00 installation; $38.95 monthly; $6.00 modem lease; $50.00 modem purchase.

Telephone Service
None

Miles of Plant: 153.0 (coaxial); 11.0 (fiber optic). Homes passed: 13,000.
Manager: Richard K. Veach. Chief Engineer: Matt Schonlau. Marketing Director: Taylor R. Summers. Customer Service Manager: Doris Waldron.
City fee: 2% of gross.
Ownership: Pioneer Communications.

UNIONTOWN—Craw-Kan Telephone Co-op. This cable system has converted to IPTV, PO Box 100, 200 N Ozark St, Girard, KS 66743. Phones: 800-362-0316; 620-724-8235. Fax: 620-724-4099. E-mail: webmaster@ckt.net. Web Site: http://www.ckt.net. ICA: KS5100.
TV Market Ranking: Below 100 (UNIONTOWN).
Channel capacity: N.A. Channels available but not in use: N.A.

Internet Service
Operational: Yes.

Telephone Service
Digital: Operational

Ownership: Craw-Kan Telephone Cooperative.

UNIONTOWN—Craw-Kan Telephone Co-op. This cable system has converted to IPTV. See UNIONTOWN, KS [KS5100]. ICA: KS0310.

VALLEY FALLS—Giant Communications, 418 W 5th St, Ste C, Holton, KS 66436-1506. Phones: 800-346-9084; 785-364-9331. Fax: 785-866-2144. E-mail: billbarton@giantcomm.net. Web Site: http://www.giantcomm.net. ICA: KS0145.
TV Market Ranking: Below 100 (VALLEY FALLS). Franchise award date: N.A. Franchise expiration date: N.A. Began: January 1, 1983.
Channel capacity: 40 (operating 2-way). Channels available but not in use: 10.

Basic Service
Subscribers: 202.
Programming (received off-air): KCWE (CW) Kansas City; KSNT (FOX, NBC) Topeka; KTKA-TV (ABC, CW) Topeka; KTMJ-CA Topeka; KTWU (PBS) Topeka; WDAF-TV (FOX) Kansas City; WIBW-TV (CBS, MNT) Topeka.
Programming (via satellite): ABC Family Channel; AMC; Animal Planet; Arts & Entertainment; Bloomberg Television; Bravo; Cartoon Network; CNN; Comedy Central; Country Music TV; C-SPAN; Discovery Channel; Discovery Health Channel; Disney Channel; Disney XD; Do-It-Yourself; E! Entertainment Television; ESPN; ESPN 2; ESPN Classic Sports; Eternal Word TV Network; Food Network; Fox News Channel; Fox Sports Net; FX; Great American Country; Hallmark Channel; Headline News; HGTV; History Channel; Home Shopping Network; Lifetime; Lifetime Movie Network; MSNBC; MTV; National Geographic Channel; NFL Network; Nickelodeon; Outdoor Channel; QVC; RFD-TV; Speed Channel; Spike TV; Syfy; TBS Superstation; The Learning Channel; Travel Channel; Trinity Broadcasting Network; truTV; Turner Classic Movies; Turner Network TV; TV Land; USA Network; VH1; Weather Channel; WGN America.
Fee: $35.00 installation; $46.95 monthly; $5.00 converter.

Digital Basic Service
Subscribers: N.A.
Programming (via satellite): BBC America; Bio; Bloomberg Television; Country Music TV; Discovery Health Channel; Discovery Kids Channel; Discovery Military Channel; Discovery Planet Green; DMX Music; ESPN Classic Sports; ESPN U; ESPNews; FitTV; Fox Movie Channel; Fox Soccer; Fuse; G4; Golf Channel; GSN; Halogen Network; History Channel International; ID Investigation Discovery; Independent Film Channel; Lifetime Movie Network; MTV2; National Geographic Channel; Nick Jr.; NickToons TV; Science Channel; Style Network; Syfy; TeenNick; Turner Classic Movies; Versus; VH1 Classic; WE tv.
Fee: $15.95 monthly.

Digital Expanded Basic Service
Subscribers: N.A.
Programming (via satellite): Encore (multiplexed); Fox Movie Channel; Starz (multiplexed); Starz HDTV; Starz Kids & Family HD; Turner Classic Movies.
Fee: $13.95 monthly.

Digital Expanded Basic Service 2
Subscribers: N.A.
Programming (via satellite): ABC Family HD; Animal Planet HD; Arts & Entertainment HD; CNN HD; Discovery Channel HD; Discovery HD Theater; Discovery Planet Green HD; Disney Channel HD; ESPN 2 HD; ESPN HD; Food Network HD; Fox News HD; FSN HD; FX HD; HGTV HD; History Channel HD; Lifetime Movie Network HD; Lifetime Television HD; National Geographic Channel HD Network; Outdoor Channel 2 HD; QVC HD; Science Channel HD; Speed HD; Syfy HD; TBS in HD; TLC HD; Travel Channel HD; Turner Network TV HD; USA Network HD.
Fee: $10.95 monthly.

Pay Service 1
Pay Units: 34.
Programming (via satellite): HBO.
Fee: $11.95 monthly.

Pay Service 2
Pay Units: 46.
Programming (via satellite): The Movie Channel.
Fee: $11.95 monthly.

Digital Pay Service 1
Pay Units: N.A.
Programming (via satellite): Cinemax (multiplexed); Cinemax HD; Flix; HBO (multiplexed); HBO HD; Showtime (multiplexed); Showtime HD; The Movie Channel (multiplexed); The Movie Channel HD.
Fee: $11.95 monthly (Cinemax), $14.95 monthly (HBO or Showtime/TMC/Flix).

Video-On-Demand: No

Pay-Per-View
iN DEMAND (delivered digitally); Hot Choice (delivered digitally).

Internet Service
Operational: Yes.

Telephone Service
None

Miles of Plant: 7.0 (coaxial); None (fiber optic). Homes passed: 583.
Manager: Bill Barton. Headend Technician: Jay Stewart.; Julian Rodriguez.
City fee: 3% of basic gross.
Ownership: Giant Communications (MSO).

VERMILLION—Blue Valley Telecommunications. Formerly [KS0339]. This cable system has converted to IPTV, 1557 Pony Express Hwy, Home, KS 66438. Phones: 785-799-3311; 877-876-1228. E-mail: info@bluevalley.net. Web Site: http://www.bluevalley.net. ICA: KS5016.
TV Market Ranking: Outside TV Markets (VERMILLION).
Channel capacity: N.A. Channels available but not in use: N.A.

Internet Service
Operational: Yes.

Telephone Service
Digital: Operational

General Manager: Dennis Doyle.
Ownership: Blue Valley Telecommunications.

VERMILLION—Blue Valley Telecommunications. This cable system has converted to IPTV. See Vermillion, KS [KS5016], KS. ICA: KS0339.

VICTORIA—Nex-Tech. Now served by EDMOND, KS [KS0450]. ICA: KS0157.

WAKEENEY—Eagle Communications, PO Box 426, 415 Barclay Ave, Wakeeney, KS 67672. Phones: 785-625-4000 (Corporate office); 785-743-5616. Fax: 785-743-2694. Web Site: http://www.eaglecom.net. ICA: KS0100.
TV Market Ranking: Below 100 (WAKEENEY). Franchise award date: August 13, 1973. Franchise expiration date: N.A. Began: July 1, 1976.
Channel capacity: 62 (operating 2-way). Channels available but not in use: N.A.

Basic Service
Subscribers: 766.
Programming (received off-air): KAKE-TV (ABC) Wichita; KBSH-DT (CBS) Hays; KMTW (MNT) Hutchinson; KOOD (PBS) Hays; KSAS-TV (FOX) Wichita; KSCW-DT (CW) Wichita; KSNC (NBC) Great Bend; 4 FMs.
Programming (via satellite): C-SPAN; Home Shopping Network; QVC; TV Guide Network; Weather Channel; WGN America.
Current originations: Educational Access.
Fee: $24.95 installation; $14.95 monthly; $15.00 additional installation.

Expanded Basic Service 1
Subscribers: 700.
Programming (via satellite): ABC Family Channel; AMC; Animal Planet; Arts & Entertainment; Boomerang; Bravo; Cartoon Network; CNBC; CNN; Comedy Central; Country Music TV; Discovery Channel; Disney Channel; Do-It-Yourself; E! Entertainment Television; ESPN; ESPN 2; ESPN Classic Sports; ESPNews; Eternal Word TV Network; FitTV; Food Network; Fox Movie Channel; Fox News Channel; Fox Sports Net Midwest; FX; Hallmark Channel; Headline News; HGTV; History Channel; Lifetime; MSNBC; MTV; National Geographic Channel; NFL Network; Nickelodeon; Spike TV; Syfy; TBS Superstation; The Learning Channel; The Sportsman Channel; Toon Disney; Travel Channel; truTV; Turner Network TV; TV Land; USA Network; VH1.
Fee: $30.00 monthly.

Digital Basic Service
Subscribers: 80.
Programming (received off-air): KAKE-TV (ABC) Wichita; KMTW (MNT) Hutchinson; KOOD (PBS) Hays; KSAS-TV (FOX) Wichita; KSNC (NBC) Great Bend.
Programming (via satellite): AmericanLife TV Network; BBC America; Bio; Bloomberg Television; Bravo; Church Channel; CMT Pure Country; Cooking Channel; Current; Discovery Health Channel; Discovery Kids Channel; Discovery Military Channel; Discovery Planet Green; DMX Music; ESPN 2; ESPN Classic Sports; ESPN U; ESPNews; FitTV; Fox Business Channel; Fox College Sports Atlantic; Fox College Sports Central; Fox College Sports Pacific; Fox Movie Channel; Fox Soccer; Fuse; G4; Golf Channel; Gospel Music Channel; Great American Country; GSN; Halogen Network; HGTV; History Channel; History Channel International; ID Investigation Discovery; Independent Film Channel; JCTV; Lifetime Movie Network; MTV Hits; MTV Jams; MTV2; National Geographic Channel; Nick Jr.; NickToons TV; Outdoor Channel; PBS Kids Sprout; RFD-TV; Science Channel; Sleuth; SoapNet; Speed Channel; Style Network; Syfy; TeenNick; The Sportsman Channel; The Word Network; Toon Disney; Trinity Broadcasting Network; Turner Classic Movies; Versus; VH1 Classic; VH1 Soul; WE tv.
Fee: $3.95 monthly (sports, variety or entertainment package), $5.95 monthly (basic).

Digital Expanded Basic Service
Subscribers: N.A.
Programming (via satellite): Animal Planet HD; Arts & Entertainment HD; Discovery Channel HD; Discovery HD Theater; ESPN HD; Food Network HD; HGTV HD; History Channel HD; National Geographic Channel HD Network; NFL Network HD; Science Channel HD; TBS in HD; TLC HD; Turner Network TV HD; Universal HD.
Fee: $9.95 monthly.

Pay Service 1
Pay Units: 49.
Programming (via satellite): HBO.
Fee: $10.00 installation; $11.95 monthly.

Pay Service 2
Pay Units: 25.
Programming (via satellite): Cinemax.
Fee: $11.95 monthly.

Digital Pay Service 1
Pay Units: N.A.
Programming (via satellite): Cinemax (multiplexed); Cinemax HD; Encore (multiplexed); Flix; HBO (multiplexed); HBO HD; Showtime (multiplexed); Showtime HD; Starz (multiplexed); Starz HDTV; The Movie Channel (multiplexed); The Movie Channel HD.
Fee: $11.95 monthly (HBO, Cinemax, Showtime/TMC/Flix, or Starz/Encore).
Video-On-Demand: No
Pay-Per-View
Playboy TV (delivered digitally); iN DEMAND (delivered digitally); Fresh (delivered digitally); Club Jenna (delivered digitally); Hot Choice (delivered digitally); Spice: Xcess (delivered digitally).
Internet Service
Operational: Yes.
Subscribers: 200.
Broadband Service: Eagle Internet.
Fee: $19.95 monthly.
Telephone Service
Analog: Not Operational
Digital: Operational
Fee: $16.00 monthly
Miles of Plant: 21.0 (coaxial); None (fiber optic). Homes passed: 1,181.
President: Gary Shorman. General Manager: Rex Skiles. Chief Technician: Les Libal.
City fee: 2% of gross.
Ownership: Eagle Communications Inc. (KS) (MSO).

WAKEFIELD—Eagle Communications, 406 NE 14th St, Abilene, KS 67410. Phones: 785-625-4000 (Corporate office); 785-263-2529. Fax: 785-625-8030. Web Site: http://www.eaglecom.net. ICA: KS0200.
TV Market Ranking: Outside TV Markets (WAKEFIELD). Franchise award date: N.A. Franchise expiration date: N.A. Began: May 15, 1978.
Channel capacity: 78 (not 2-way capable). Channels available but not in use: 35.
Basic Service
Subscribers: 188.
Programming (received off-air): KAAS-TV (FOX) Salina; KSNT (FOX, NBC) Topeka; KTKA-TV (ABC, CW) Topeka; KTMJ-CA Topeka; KTWU (PBS) Topeka; KWCH-DT (CBS) Hutchinson; WIBW-TV (CBS, MNT) Topeka; allband FM.
Programming (via satellite): ABC Family Channel; AMC; Animal Planet; Arts & Entertainment; Cartoon Network; CNN; Comedy Central; Discovery Channel; Disney Channel; E! Entertainment Television; ESPN; ESPN 2; Fox Movie Channel; Fox News Channel; Fuse; FX; Great American Country; Halogen Network; Headline News; HGTV; History Channel; Home Shopping Network; Lifetime; MSNBC; MTV; Outdoor Channel; QVC; Speed Channel; Syfy; TBS Superstation; The Learning Channel; Toon Disney; Trinity Broadcasting Network; Turner Classic Movies; Turner Network TV; TV Land; USA Network; VH1; Weather Channel; WGN America.
Fee: $24.95 installation; $45.45 monthly.

Digital Basic Service
Subscribers: N.A.
Programming (via satellite): AmericanLife TV Network; BBC America; Bio; Bloomberg Television; Discovery Health Channel; Discovery Kids Channel; Discovery Military Channel; Discovery Planet Green; DMX Music; ESPN Classic Sports; ESPNews; FitTV; Fox Movie Channel; Fox Soccer; Fuse; G4; Golf Channel; GSN; Halogen Network; History Channel International; ID Investigation Discovery; Independent Film Channel; Lifetime Movie Network; Science Channel; Sleuth; Speed Channel; Style Network; Versus; WE tv.
Fee: $13.95 monthly.
Pay Service 1
Pay Units: N.A.
Programming (via satellite): HBO; Showtime; The Movie Channel.
Fee: $11.95 monthly (each).
Digital Pay Service 1
Pay Units: N.A.
Programming (via satellite): Cinemax (multiplexed); Encore (multiplexed); Flix; HBO (multiplexed); Showtime (multiplexed); Starz (multiplexed); The Movie Channel (multiplexed).
Fee: $11.95 monthly (HBO, Cinemax, Starz/Encore or Showtime/TMC/Flix).
Pay-Per-View
iN DEMAND (delivered digitally); Playboy TV (delivered digitally); Fresh (delivered digitally); Spice: Xcess (delivered digitally); Club Jenna (delivered digitally).
Internet Service
Operational: Yes.
Broadband Service: Eagle Internet.
Fee: $22.95 monthly.
Telephone Service
None
Miles of Plant: 6.0 (coaxial); None (fiber optic). Homes passed: 364.
President: Gary Shorman. Regional Manager: Dennis Weese. General Manager: Rex Skiles.
City fee: 1% of gross.
Ownership: Eagle Communications Inc. (KS) (MSO).

WALNUT—Craw-Kan Telephone Co-op. This cable system has converted to IPTV, PO Box 100, 200 N Ozark St, Girard, KS 66743. Phones: 800-362-0316; 620-724-8235. Fax: 620-724-4099. E-mail: webmaster@ckt.net. Web Site: http://www.ckt.net. ICA: KS5103.
TV Market Ranking: Below 100 (WALNUT).
Channel capacity: N.A. Channels available but not in use: N.A.
Internet Service
Operational: Yes.
Telephone Service
Digital: Operational
Ownership: Craw-Kan Telephone Cooperative.

WALNUT—Craw-Kan Telephone Co-op. This cable system has converted to IPTV. See WALNUT, KS [KS5103]. ICA: KS0343.

WALTON—Formerly served by Galaxy Cablevision. No longer in operation. ICA: KS0435.

WAMEGO—WTC Communications. Formerly [KS0057]. This cable system has converted to IPTV, 1009 Lincoln St, Wamego, KS 66547. Phones: 877-492-6835; 785-456-1000. Fax: 785-456-9903. E-mail: support@wamego.net. Web Site: http://www.wamtelco.com. ICA: KS5017.
TV Market Ranking: Outside TV Markets (Wamego).
Channel capacity: N.A. Channels available but not in use: N.A.
Telephone Service
Digital: Operational
President & General Manager: Steve Tackrider. Plant Manager: Ken Blew.
Ownership: WTC Communications Inc.

WAMEGO—WTC Communications. This cable system has converted to IPTV. See Wamego, KA [KS5017], KS. ICA: KS0057.

WASHINGTON—Blue Valley Tele-Communications, 1559 Pony Express Hwy, Home, KS 66438. Phones: 877-876-1228; 785-799-3311. E-mail: info@bluevalley.net. Web Site: http://www.bluevalley.net. Also serves Belleville, Beloit, Cawker City, Downs, Formoso, Glen Elder, Jamestown, Jewell, Mankato, Mitchell County (portions), Randall & Scandia. ICA: KS0228.
TV Market Ranking: Below 100 (Belleville, Formoso, Jamestown, Jewell, Mankato, Randall, Scandia); Outside TV Markets (Beloit, Cawker City, Downs, Glen Elder, Mitchell County (portions), WASHINGTON). Franchise award date: N.A. Franchise expiration date: N.A. Began: July 1, 1977.
Channel capacity: 77 (2-way capable). Channels available but not in use: 25.
Basic Service
Subscribers: 4,237.
Programming (received off-air): KAKE-TV (ABC) Wichita; KBSH-DT (CBS) Hays; KGIN (CBS, MNT) Grand Island; KHAS-TV (NBC) Hastings; KHGI-TV (ABC) Kearney; KOOD (PBS) Hays; KSHB-TV (NBC) Kansas City; KSNC (NBC) Great Bend; WIBW-TV (CBS, MNT) Topeka.
Programming (via satellite): Weather Channel.
Fee: $16.95 monthly.
Expanded Basic Service 1
Subscribers: N.A.
Programming (received off-air): KSAS-TV (FOX) Wichita.
Programming (via satellite): ABC Family Channel; AMC; AmericanLife TV Network; Animal Planet; Arts & Entertainment; Cartoon Network; CNBC; CNN; Comedy Central; Country Music TV; C-SPAN; Discovery Channel; Disney Channel; E! Entertainment Television; ESPN; ESPN 2; ESPN Classic Sports; Eternal Word TV Network; Food Network; Fox News Channel; Fox Sports Net Midwest; FX; Great American Country; Hallmark Channel; Hallmark Movie Channel; Headline News; HGTV; History Channel; Home Shopping Network; ION Television; Lifetime; MTV; MyNetworkTV Inc.; National Geographic Channel; Nickelodeon; Outdoor Channel; QVC; RFD-TV; Speed Channel; Spike TV; Syfy; TBS Superstation; The Learning Channel; The Sportsman Channel; Travel Channel; Trinity Broadcasting Network; Turner Classic Movies; Turner Network TV; TV Land; USA Network; VH1; WGN America.
Fee: $20.00 monthly.
Digital Basic Service
Subscribers: 325.
Programming (via satellite): AmericanLife TV Network; BBC America; Bio; Bloomberg Television; Bravo; Discovery Digital Networks; DMX Music; ESPN 2; ESPN Classic Sports; ESPNews; Fox Movie Channel; Fox Soccer; FSN Digital Atlantic; FSN Digital Central; FSN Digital Pacific; Fuse; G4; GAS; Golf Channel; Great American Country; GSN; Halogen Network; HGTV; History Channel; History Channel International; Independent Film Channel; Lifetime Movie Network; Lime; MTV Networks Digital Suite; National Geographic Channel; Nick Jr.; NickToons TV; Outdoor Channel; ShopNBC; Sleuth; Speed Channel; Style Network; Syfy; Toon Disney; Trinity Broadcasting Network; Turner Classic Movies; Versus; WE tv.
Fee: $15.95 monthly.
Pay Service 1
Pay Units: N.A.
Programming (via satellite): Cinemax; Encore; HBO; Showtime; The Movie Channel.
Fee: $7.95 monthly (Cinemax or Encore), $9.95 monthly (Showtime or TMC), $11.95 monthly (HBO).
Digital Pay Service 1
Pay Units: N.A.
Programming (via satellite): Cinemax (multiplexed); Encore (multiplexed); Flix; HBO (multiplexed); Showtime (multiplexed); Starz (multiplexed); The Movie Channel (multiplexed).
Fee: $7.95 monthly (Cinemax), $9.95 monthly (Starz/Encore), $10.95 monthly (Showtime/TMC/Flix), $12.95 monthly (HBO).
Pay-Per-View
ESPN Now (delivered digitally); Sports PPV (delivered digitally); iN DEMAND (delivered digitally).
Internet Service
Operational: Yes.
Telephone Service
Digital: Operational
Miles of Plant: 107.0 (coaxial); None (fiber optic). Homes passed: 4,738.
General Manager: Dennis Doyle. Operations Manager: Andy Torrey. Marketing Manager: Angie Armstrong. Customer Service Supervisor: Deb Runnebaum.
Ownership: Blue Valley Telecommunications (MSO).

WASHINGTON—Cunningham Cable TV. Now served by WASHINGTON (formerly Glen Elder), KS [KS0228]. ICA: KS0139.

WATERVILLE—Blue Valley Tele-Communications, 1559 Pony Express Hwy, Home, KS 66438. Phones: 877-876-1228; 785-799-3311. E-mail: info@bluevalley.net. Web Site: http://www.bluevalley.net. ICA: KS0193.
TV Market Ranking: Outside TV Markets (WATERVILLE). Franchise award date: May 11, 1987. Franchise expiration date: N.A. Began: May 1, 1987.
Channel capacity: N.A. Channels available but not in use: N.A.
Basic Service
Subscribers: 250.
Programming (received off-air): KAAS-TV (FOX) Salina; KOLN (CBS, MNT) Lincoln; KSNT (FOX, NBC) Topeka; KTKA-TV (ABC, CW) Topeka; KTWU (PBS) Topeka; KUON-TV (PBS) Lincoln; WIBW-TV (CBS, MNT) Topeka; WPIX (CW, IND) New York.
Programming (via satellite): ABC Family Channel; Arts & Entertainment; Cartoon Network; CNN; Discovery Channel; Disney Channel; ESPN; ESPN 2; Fox News Channel; Fox Sports Net; HGTV; History Channel; Lifetime; Outdoor Channel; QVC; Spike

TV; Syfy; TBS Superstation; The Learning Channel; Trinity Broadcasting Network; Turner Network TV; TV Land; USA Network; Weather Channel; WGN America.
Fee: $12.47 monthly.

Pay Service 1
Pay Units: 27.
Programming (via satellite): Cinemax; HBO.
Fee: $8.98 monthly (each).

Video-On-Demand: No

Internet Service
Operational: Yes.

Telephone Service
Analog: Not Operational
Digital: Planned

Miles of Plant: 7.0 (coaxial); None (fiber optic). Homes passed: 300. Total homes in franchised area: 300.
General Manager: Dennis Doyle. Operations Manager: Andy Torrey. Marketing Manager: Angie Armstrong. Customer Service Supervisor: Deb Runnebaum.
City fee: 2% of gross.
Ownership: Blue Valley Telecommunications (MSO).

WAVERLY—Galaxy Cablevision, 1928 S Lincoln Ave, Ste 200, York, NE 68467. Phone: 402-362-3332. Fax: 402-362-4890. Web Site: http://www.galaxycable.com. ICA: KS0210.
TV Market Ranking: Outside TV Markets (WAVERLY). Franchise award date: N.A. Franchise expiration date: N.A. Began: February 1, 1977.
Channel capacity: 36 (not 2-way capable). Channels available but not in use: 1.

Basic Service
Subscribers: 48.
Programming (received off-air): KCTV (CBS) Kansas City; KSNT (FOX, NBC) Topeka; KTKA-TV (ABC, CW) Topeka; KTWU (PBS) Topeka; WIBW-TV (CBS, MNT) Topeka; allband FM.
Programming (via satellite): ABC Family Channel; AMC; Animal Planet; Arts & Entertainment; CNN; Discovery Channel; Disney Channel; ESPN; ESPN 2; Fuse; Great American Country; HGTV; Lifetime; Nickelodeon; Outdoor Channel; TBS Superstation; The Learning Channel; Turner Network TV; USA Network; Weather Channel.
Planned originations: Educational Access.
Fee: $20.00 installation; $38.00 monthly.

Pay Service 1
Pay Units: N.A.
Programming (via satellite): Cinemax; Encore; HBO; Showtime; The Movie Channel.
Fee: $11.00 monthly (HBO).

Internet Service
Operational: No.

Telephone Service
None

Miles of Plant: 6.0 (coaxial); None (fiber optic). Homes passed: 298.
State Manager: Cheyenne Wohlford. Technical Manager: John Davidshofer. Sales Manager: Mike Thomas. Customer Service Manager: Michael Debermardin.
Ownership: Galaxy Cable Inc. (MSO).

WEIR—Formerly served by WSC Cablevision. No longer in operation. ICA: KS0422.

WELLINGTON—Sumner Cable TV Inc., 117 W Harvey Ave, Wellington, KS 67152-3840. Phone: 620-326-8989. Fax: 620-326-5332. E-mail: sumnertv@sutv.com. Web Site: http://www.sutv.com. ICA: KS0032.
TV Market Ranking: 67 (WELLINGTON). Franchise award date: September 1, 2005. Franchise expiration date: N.A. Began: April 5, 1977.
Channel capacity: N.A. Channels available but not in use: N.A.

Basic Service
Subscribers: 2,609.
Programming (received off-air): KAKE-TV (ABC) Wichita; KMTW (MNT) Hutchinson; KPTS (PBS) Hutchinson; KSAS-TV (FOX) Wichita; KSCW-DT (CW) Wichita; KSNW (NBC) Wichita; KWCH-DT (CBS) Hutchinson.
Programming (via satellite): ABC Family Channel; Bravo; C-SPAN; QVC; Weather Channel.
Fee: $16.25 monthly.

Expanded Basic Service 1
Subscribers: 2,526.
Programming (via satellite): AMC; Animal Planet; Cartoon Network; Country Music TV; Discovery Channel; Disney Channel; Do-It-Yourself; E! Entertainment Television; ESPN; ESPN 2; ESPN Classic Sports; Eternal Word TV Network; Food Network; Fox Sports Net; FX; Great American Country; Hallmark Channel; Hallmark Movie Channel; Headline News; HGTV; History Channel; Home Shopping Network; Lifetime; MSNBC; MTV; NFL Network; Nickelodeon; Spike TV; Syfy; TBS Superstation; Travel Channel; truTV; Turner Network TV; TV Land; USA Network; VH1; WE tv; WGN America.
Fee: $31.95 installation; $22.20 monthly.

Digital Basic Service
Subscribers: 242.
Programming (via satellite): AmericanLife TV Network; BBC America; Bio; Bloomberg Television; Bravo; CMT Pure Country; Comedy Central; C-SPAN 2; Current; Discovery Health Channel; Discovery Kids Channel; Discovery Military Channel; Discovery Planet Green; DMX Music; ESPN Classic Sports; ESPNews; FitTV; Fox Movie Channel; Fox Soccer; FSN Digital Atlantic; FSN Digital Central; FSN Digital Pacific; Fuse; G4; Golf Channel; Gospel Music Channel; Great American Country; GSN; HGTV; History Channel International; ID Investigation Discovery; Independent Film Channel; INSP; ION Television; Lifetime Movie Network; Lime; MTV Hits; MTV2; National Geographic Channel; Nick Jr.; NickToons TV; Outdoor Channel; Ovation; RFD-TV; Science Channel; Sleuth; SoapNet; Speed Channel; Style Network; Sundance Channel; Syfy; TeenNick; Telemundo; Toon Disney; Trinity Broadcasting Network; Turner Classic Movies; TV Guide Network; Versus; VH1 Soul; WE tv.
Fee: $16.50 monthly.

Digital Pay Service 1
Pay Units: N.A.
Programming (via satellite): Cinemax (multiplexed); Encore (multiplexed); Flix; HBO (multiplexed); Showtime (multiplexed); Starz (multiplexed); The Movie Channel (multiplexed).
Fee: $12.75 monthly (HBO or Cinemax), $13.75 monthly (Showtime/TMC/Flix), $14.35 monthly (Starz/Encore).

Video-On-Demand: No

Pay-Per-View
Movies (delivered digitally); Playboy TV (delivered digitally); Fresh (delivered digitally); Club Jenna (delivered digitally); Shorteez (delivered digitally).

Internet Service
Operational: Yes. Began: October 1, 1997.
Subscribers: 1,532.
Broadband Service: In-house.
Fee: $25.00 installation; $27.45 monthly; $135.00 modem purchase.

Telephone Service
Digital: Operational
Subscribers: 193.
Fee: $85.00 installation; $30.95 monthly

Miles of Plant: 60.0 (coaxial); None (fiber optic). Homes passed: 3,300. Total homes in franchised area: 4,500.
Manager & Chief Technician: David Steinbech. Marketing Director: Alda Boyd. Office Manager: Jill Bales.
City fee: 3% of gross.
Ownership: Sumner Communications.

WESTMORELAND—Formerly served by Giant Communications. No longer in operation. ICA: KS0198.

WETMORE—Rainbow Communications, PO Box 147, Everest, KS 66424. Phones: 785-548-7511; 800-892-0163. Fax: 785-548-7517. Web Site: http://www.rainbowtel.net. ICA: KS0285.
TV Market Ranking: Outside TV Markets (WETMORE). Franchise award date: N.A. Franchise expiration date: N.A. Began: March 1, 1984.
Channel capacity: 40 (operating 2-way). Channels available but not in use: 15.

Basic Service
Subscribers: 87.
Programming (received off-air): KCWE (CW) Kansas City; KSNT (FOX, NBC) Topeka; KTKA-TV (ABC, CW) Topeka; KTWU (PBS) Topeka; WDAF-TV (FOX) Kansas City; WIBW-TV (CBS, MNT) Topeka.
Programming (via satellite): ABC Family Channel; AMC; Animal Planet; Arts & Entertainment; Cartoon Network; CNN; Comedy Central; C-SPAN; Discovery Channel; Disney Channel; ESPN; ESPN 2; Eternal Word TV Network; Food Network; Fox News Channel; Fox Sports Net; FX; Great American Country; Hallmark Channel; Headline News; HGTV; History Channel; Lifetime; Nickelodeon; QVC; Speed Channel; Spike TV; Syfy; TBS Superstation; The Learning Channel; Travel Channel; Trinity Broadcasting Network; Turner Classic Movies; Turner Network TV; TV Land; USA Network; VH1; Weather Channel; WGN America.
Fee: $29.95 installation; $39.95 monthly; $5.00 converter; $22.50 additional installation.

Digital Basic Service
Subscribers: 7.
Programming (via satellite): AmericanLife TV Network; Bio; Bloomberg Television; Country Music TV; Discovery Digital Networks; DMX Music; ESPN Classic Sports; ESPNews; G4; GAS; Golf Channel; GSN; History Channel International; MTV Networks Digital Suite; National Geographic Channel; Nick Jr.; NickToons TV; Outdoor Channel; Speed Channel; Style Network; Toon Disney.
Fee: $12.95 monthly.

Digital Pay Service 1
Pay Units: N.A.
Programming (via satellite): Cinemax (multiplexed); Encore (multiplexed); Flix; HBO (multiplexed); Showtime (multiplexed); Starz (multiplexed); The Movie Channel (multiplexed).
Fee: $12.95 monthly (each).

Video-On-Demand: No

Pay-Per-View
iN DEMAND (delivered digitally); Hot Choice (delivered digitally); Playboy TV (delivered digitally).

Internet Service
Operational: Yes.
Broadband Service: Lighting Jack High Speed.
Fee: $34.95 monthly.

Telephone Service
None

Miles of Plant: 3.0 (coaxial); None (fiber optic). Homes passed: 149.
General Manager: James Lednicky. Network Engineer: Scott Wheeler. Plant Manager: Jim Streeter. Marketing Manager: Jackie Petersen.
City fee: 3% of basic.
Ownership: Rainbow Communications (MSO).

WHITE CITY—Eagle Communications, 406 NE 14th St, Abilene, KS 67410. Phones: 785-625-4000 (Corporate office); 785-263-2529. Fax: 785-625-8030. Web Site: http://www.eaglecom.net. ICA: KS0248.
TV Market Ranking: Outside TV Markets (WHITE CITY). Franchise award date: N.A. Franchise expiration date: N.A. Began: N.A.
Channel capacity: 31 (not 2-way capable). Channels available but not in use: 1.

Basic Service
Subscribers: 38.
Programming (received off-air): KAAS-TV (FOX) Salina; KSNT (FOX, NBC) Topeka; KTKA-TV (ABC, CW) Topeka; KTWU (PBS) Topeka; KWCH-DT (CBS) Hutchinson; WIBW-TV (CBS, MNT) Topeka.
Programming (via satellite): ABC Family Channel; Animal Planet; Arts & Entertainment; CNN; Discovery Channel; Disney Channel; E! Entertainment Television; ESPN; ESPN 2; Home Shopping Network; Lifetime; Outdoor Channel; TBS Superstation; The Learning Channel; Toon Disney; Trinity Broadcasting Network; Turner Network TV; USA Network; Weather Channel; WGN America.
Current originations: Public Access.
Fee: $24.95 installation; $38.95 monthly.

Pay Service 1
Pay Units: N.A.
Programming (via satellite): HBO; Showtime; The Movie Channel.
Fee: $11.95 monthly (each).

Internet Service
Operational: No.

Telephone Service
None

Miles of Plant: 6.0 (coaxial); None (fiber optic). Homes passed: 251.
President: Gary Shorman. General Manager: Rex Skiles.
City fee: 1% of gross.
Ownership: Eagle Communications Inc. (KS) (MSO).

WHITE CLOUD—Rainbow Communications, PO Box 242, Wetmore, KS 66550-0242. Phones: 800-892-0163; 785-866-2390. Fax: 785-866-2393. Web Site: http://www.rainbowtel.net. ICA: KS0302.

TV Market Ranking: Below 100 (WHITE CLOUD). Franchise award date: N.A. Franchise expiration date: N.A. Began: March 15, 1989.

Channel capacity: 36 (operating 2-way). Channels available but not in use: 21.

Basic Service

Subscribers: 43.

Programming (received off-air): KMBC-TV (ABC) Kansas City; KPTM (FOX, MNT) Omaha; KQTV (ABC) St. Joseph; KSNT (FOX, NBC) Topeka; KTAJ-TV (TBN) St. Joseph; KTWU (PBS) Topeka; KUON-TV (PBS) Lincoln; WIBW-TV (CBS, MNT) Topeka.

Programming (via satellite): CNN; C-SPAN; Headline News; Weather Channel; WGN America; WNBC (NBC) New York.

Fee: $29.95 installation; $13.95 monthly.

Pay Service 1

Pay Units: 3.

Programming (via satellite): Cinemax.

Fee: $24.95 installation; $9.95 monthly.

Pay Service 2

Pay Units: 3.

Programming (via satellite): Showtime; The Movie Channel.

Fee: $8.95 monthly (each).

Video-On-Demand: No

Internet Service

Operational: No, Dial-up only.

Telephone Service

None

Miles of Plant: 3.0 (coaxial); None (fiber optic). Homes passed: 103.

General Manager: James Lednicky. Assistant Manager: Jason Smith. Marketing Manager: Jackie Petersen. Plant Manager: Jim Streeter.

Ownership: Rainbow Communications (MSO).

WHITING—Rainbow Communications, PO Box 147, Everest, KS 66424. Phones: 800-892-0163; 785-866-2390. Fax: 785-548-7517. Web Site: http://www.rainbowtel.net. ICA: KS0358.

TV Market Ranking: Outside TV Markets (WHITING). Franchise award date: N.A. Franchise expiration date: N.A. Began: April 1, 1989.

Channel capacity: 36 (operating 2-way). Channels available but not in use: N.A.

Basic Service

Subscribers: 14.

Programming (received off-air): KCTV (CBS) Kansas City; KCWE (CW) Kansas City; KMBC-TV (ABC) Kansas City; KPXE-TV (ION) Kansas City; KSHB-TV (NBC) Kansas City; KSMO-TV (MNT) Kansas City; KSNT (FOX, NBC) Topeka; KTKA-TV (ABC, CW) Topeka; KTWU (PBS) Topeka; WDAF-TV (FOX) Kansas City; WIBW-TV (CBS, MNT) Topeka.

Programming (via satellite): CNN; C-SPAN; Hallmark Channel; Trinity Broadcasting Network; Weather Channel; WGN America.

Fee: $29.95 installation; $13.95 monthly.

Pay Service 1

Pay Units: 1.

Programming (via satellite): Cinemax.

Fee: $9.95 monthly.

Pay Service 2

Pay Units: 2.

Programming (via satellite): Showtime; The Movie Channel.

Fee: $8.95 monthly (each).

Video-On-Demand: No

Internet Service

Operational: Yes.

Broadband Service: Lighting Jack High Speed.

Fee: $39.95 monthly.

Telephone Service

None

Miles of Plant: 3.0 (coaxial); None (fiber optic). Homes passed: 98.

General Manager: James Lednicky. Chief Technician: Brian McQueen. Operations Director: Chris Wardman. Plant Manager: Jim Streeter.

Ownership: Rainbow Communications (MSO).

WICHITA—Cox Communications, PO Box 3027, 701 E Douglas Ave, Wichita, KS 67202. Phones: 316-260-7000; 316-262-4270. Fax: 316-262-2330. Web Site: http://www.cox.com/kansas. Also serves Andover, Arkansas City, Augusta, Bel Aire, Burrton, Butler County (portions), Cheney, Cunningham, Derby, Eastborough, El Dorado, Garden Plain (portions), Goddard, Halstead, Harvey County (unincorporated areas), Haysville, Hesston, Hutchinson, Kechi, Kingman, Kingman County, Linsborg, Maize, Marion County (southern portion), McConnell AFB, McPherson, McPherson County (portions), Mulvane, Newton, Nickerson, North Newton, Park City, Pratt, Pratt County, Reno County (portions), Rose Hill, Sedgwick, Sedgwick County (portions), South Hutchinson, Towanda, Valley Center, Willowbrook & Winfield. ICA: KS0001.

TV Market Ranking: 67 (Andover, Augusta, Bel Aire, Burrton, Butler County (portions), Cheney, Derby, Eastborough, El Dorado, Garden Plain (portions), Goddard, Halstead, Harvey County (unincorporated areas), Haysville, Hesston, Hutchinson, Kechi, Maize, Marion County (southern portion), McConnell AFB, McPherson, McPherson County (portions) (portions), Mulvane, Newton, Nickerson, North Newton, Park City, Reno County (portions), Rose Hill, Sedgwick, Sedgwick County (portions), South Hutchinson, Towanda, Valley Center, WICHITA, Willowbrook); Below 100 (Linsborg, McPherson County (portions) (portions)); Outside TV Markets (Arkansas City, Cunningham, Kingman, Kingman County, Pratt, Pratt County, Winfield). Franchise award date: December 1, 1978. Franchise expiration date: N.A. Began: January 1, 1979.

Channel capacity: N.A. Channels available but not in use: N.A.

Basic Service

Subscribers: 410,000 Includes all Cox Kansas & Arkansas systems.

Programming (received off-air): KAKE-TV (ABC) Wichita; KMTW (MNT) Hutchinson; KPTS (PBS) Hutchinson; KSAS-TV (FOX) Wichita; KSCW-DT (CW) Wichita; KSNW (NBC) Wichita; KWCH-DT (CBS) Hutchinson.

Programming (via satellite): C-SPAN; C-SPAN 2; TV Guide Network; Weather Channel; WGN America.

Current originations: Government Access; Educational Access.

Fee: $29.95 installation; $11.00 monthly; $3.00 converter.

Expanded Basic Service 1

Subscribers: 115,611.

Programming (via satellite): ABC Family Channel; AMC; Animal Planet; Arts & Entertainment; BET Networks; Cartoon Network; CNBC; CNN; Comedy Central; Country Music TV; Discovery Channel; Disney Channel; E! Entertainment Television; ESPN; ESPN 2; Eternal Word TV Network; FitTV; Food Network; Fox News Channel; Fox Sports Net Midwest; FX; Hallmark Channel; Headline News; HGTV; History Channel; Home Shopping Network; INSP; ION Television; Lifetime; MSNBC; MTV; Nickelodeon; QVC; ShopNBC; Speed Channel; Spike TV; Syfy; TBS Superstation; The Learning Channel; Travel Channel; truTV; Turner Classic Movies; Turner Network TV; TV Land; Univision; USA Network; VH1.

Fee: $29.95 installation; $43.15 monthly; $14.95 additional installation.

Digital Basic Service

Subscribers: N.A.

Programming (via satellite): BBC America; Bio; Bloomberg Television; Canales N; Discovery Digital Networks; DMX Music; ESPN Classic Sports; ESPNews; Fox Sports World; G4; GAS; Golf Channel; Great American Country; GSN; History Channel International; Independent Film Channel; Lifetime Movie Network; MTV Networks Digital Suite; MuchMusic Network; NBA TV; Nick Jr.; Nick Too; Outdoor Channel; Oxygen; SoapNet; Sundance Channel; Toon Disney; Versus.

Fee: $15.95 monthly.

Digital Pay Service 1

Pay Units: 29,614.

Programming (via satellite): Cinemax (multiplexed); Encore (multiplexed); HBO (multiplexed); Showtime (multiplexed); Starz (multiplexed).

Fee: $29.95 installation; $10.50 monthly (each).

Video-On-Demand: Yes

Pay-Per-View

Addressable homes: 20,575.

iN DEMAND, Addressable: Yes; ESPN Now (delivered digitally); NBA/WNBA League Pass (delivered digitally); NHL Center Ice/MLB Extra Innings (delivered digitally).

Internet Service

Operational: Yes.

Subscribers: 29,331.

Broadband Service: Cox High Speed Internet.

Fee: $41.95 monthly; $15.00 modem lease; $19.95 modem purchase.

Telephone Service

Digital: Operational

Fee: $15.95 monthly

Homes passed: 526,572. Homes passed includes all Cox Kansas systems

Vice President & General Manager: Kimberly Edmunds. Vice President, Engineering: Nick Difonzio. Vice President, Marketing: Tony Matthews. Marketing Director: Tina Gabbard. Public Affairs Director: Sarah Kauffman.

City fee: 5% of gross.

Ownership: Cox Communications Inc. (MSO).

WICHITA—Formerly served by Sprint Corp. No longer in operation. ICA: KS0428.

WILLIAMSBURG—Galaxy Cablevision, 1928 S Lincoln Ave, Ste 200, York, NE 68467. Phone: 402-362-3332. Fax: 402-362-4890. Web Site: http://www.galaxycable.com. ICA: KS0300.

TV Market Ranking: Outside TV Markets (WILLIAMSBURG). Franchise award date: N.A. Franchise expiration date: N.A. Began: December 1, 1988.

Channel capacity: 31 (not 2-way capable). Channels available but not in use: 11.

Basic Service

Subscribers: 7.

Programming (received off-air): KCWE (CW) Kansas City; KMCI-TV (IND) Lawrence; KSNT (FOX, NBC) Topeka; KTKA-TV (ABC, CW) Topeka; KTWU (PBS) Topeka; WIBW-TV (CBS, MNT) Topeka.

Programming (via satellite): ABC Family Channel; AMC; CNN; Discovery Channel; ESPN; KMCI-TV (IND) Lawrence; Lifetime; Outdoor Channel; TBS Superstation; Turner Network TV; USA Network; WGN America.

Fee: $35.80 monthly.

Pay Service 1

Pay Units: N.A.

Programming (via satellite): HBO.

Fee: $11.00 monthly.

Internet Service

Operational: No.

Telephone Service

None

Miles of Plant: 5.0 (coaxial); None (fiber optic). Homes passed: 170.

State Manager: Cheyenne Wohlford. Technical Manager: John Davidshofer. Sales Manager: Mike Thomas. Customer Service Manager: Michael Debermardin.

Ownership: Galaxy Cable Inc. (MSO).

WILSEY—Formerly served by CableDirect. No longer in operation. ICA: KS0335.

WILSON—Wilson Communications, PO Box 508, 2504 Ave D, Wilson, KS 67490-0508. Phones: 800-432-7607; 785-658-2111. Fax: 785-658-3344. Web Site: http://www.wilsoncommunications.us. ICA: KS0162.

TV Market Ranking: Below 100 (WILSON). Franchise award date: N.A. Franchise expiration date: N.A. Began: January 28, 1999.

Channel capacity: N.A. Channels available but not in use: N.A.

Basic Service

Subscribers: 254.

Programming (received off-air): KAKE-TV (ABC) Wichita; KMTW (MNT) Hutchinson; KOOD (PBS) Hays; KPTS (PBS) Hutchinson; KSAS-TV (FOX) Wichita; KSCW-DT (CW) Wichita; KSNC (NBC) Great Bend; KWCH-DT (CBS) Hutchinson; 15 FMs.

Programming (via satellite): ABC Family Channel; AMC; AmericanLife TV Network; Arts & Entertainment; CNN; Country Music TV; C-SPAN; C-SPAN 2; Discovery Channel; Disney Channel; ESPN 2; ESPN Classic Sports; ESPNews; Eternal Word TV Network; Food Network; Fox News Channel; Fox Sports Net Rocky Mountain; FX; Hallmark Channel; Headline News; HGTV; Home Shopping Network; ION Television; Lifetime; MTV; National Geographic Channel; Nickelodeon; Spike TV; Syfy; TBS Superstation; The Learning Channel; Turner Network TV; TV Land; USA Network; VH1; Weather Channel; WGN America.

Current originations: Educational Access.

Fee: $25.00 installation; $39.95 monthly.

Digital Basic Service

Subscribers: N.A.

Programming (received off-air): KAKE-TV (ABC) Wichita; KMTW (MNT) Hutchinson; KOOD (PBS) Hays; KPTS (PBS) Hutchinson; KSAS-TV (FOX) Wichita; KSCW-DT (CW) Wichita; KSNW (NBC) Wichita; KWCH-DT (CBS) Hutchinson.

Programming (via satellite): Arts & Entertainment HD; BBC America; Bio; Bravo; CMT Pure Country; Discovery HD Theater; Discovery Health Channel; Discovery Kids Channel; Discovery Military Channel; Discovery Planet Green; DMX Music; ESPN; ESPN 2 HD; ESPN HD; ESPN U; ESPNU HD; Food Network HD; Fox Soccer; Fuse; Golf Channel; GSN; HGTV HD; History Channel International; History Channel HD; History Channel International; ID Investigation Discovery; Independent Film Channel; Life-

time Movie Network; MTV2; Nick Jr.; RFD-TV; Science Channel; Sleuth; Speed Channel; Style Network; TeenNick; Turner Classic Movies; Universal HD; Versus; VH1 Classic; WE tv.
Fee: $49.95 installation; $12.00 monthly.

Digital Pay Service 1
Pay Units: N.A.
Programming (via satellite): Cinemax (multiplexed); Encore (multiplexed); HBO (multiplexed); Showtime (multiplexed); Starz (multiplexed); Starz HDTV; The Movie Channel (multiplexed).
Fee: $13.95 monthly (Showtime/TMC or Starz/Encore), $18.95 monthly (Cinemax or HBO).

Video-On-Demand: No

Internet Service
Operational: No, DSL & dial-up.

Telephone Service
None

Miles of Plant: 9.0 (coaxial); None (fiber optic). Homes passed: 440. Total homes in franchised area: 440.
Vice President, Marketing: Scott Grauer. General Manager: Brian Boisvert. Plant Supervisor: Dan Steinike. Controller: Gary Everett. Customer Service Manager: Mary Zorn.
City of Wilson fee: $100.00/Year Franchise Fee.
Ownership: Wilson Communications (MSO).

WINCHESTER—Giant Communications, 418 W 5th St, Ste C, Holton, KS 66436-1506. Phones: 785-866-2133; 800-346-9084; 785-364-9331. Fax: 785-866-2144. E-mail: billbarton@giantcomm.net. Web Site: http://www.giantcomm.net. ICA: KS0249.
TV Market Ranking: Below 100 (WINCHESTER). Franchise award date: N.A. Franchise expiration date: N.A. Began: July 1, 1983.
Channel capacity: 40 (operating 2-way). Channels available but not in use: 16.

Basic Service
Subscribers: 73.
Programming (received off-air): KCPT (PBS) Kansas City; KCTV (CBS) Kansas City; KCWE (CW) Kansas City; KMCI-TV (IND) Lawrence; KPXE-TV (ION) Kansas City; KSMO-TV (MNT) Kansas City; KSNT (FOX, NBC) Topeka; KTKA-TV (ABC, CW) Topeka; KTWU (PBS) Topeka; WDAF-TV (FOX) Kansas City; WIBW-TV (CBS, MNT) Topeka.
Programming (via satellite): ABC Family Channel; CNN; Discovery Channel; Disney Channel; ESPN; Lifetime; Nick At Nite; Nickelodeon; QVC; Spike TV; TBS Superstation; Turner Classic Movies; Turner Network TV; USA Network; VH1; Weather Channel; WGN America.
Fee: $35.00 installation; $46.95 monthly; $5.00 converter.

Digital Basic Service
Subscribers: N.A.
Programming (via satellite): BBC America; Bio; Bloomberg Television; Country Music TV; Discovery Health Channel; Discovery Kids Channel; Discovery Military Channel; Discovery Planet Green; DMX Music; ESPN Classic Sports; ESPN U; ESPNews; FitTV; Fox Movie Channel; Fox Soccer; Fuse; G4; Golf Channel; GSN; Halogen Network; History Channel International; ID Investigation Discovery; Independent Film Channel; Lifetime Movie Network; MTV2; National Geographic Channel; Nick Jr.; NickToons TV; Science Channel; Style Network; Syfy; TeenNick; Turner Classic Movies; Versus; VH1 Classic; WE tv.
Fee: $15.95 monthly.

Digital Expanded Basic Service
Subscribers: N.A.
Programming (via satellite): Encore (multiplexed); Fox Movie Channel; Starz (multiplexed); Starz HDTV; Starz Kids & Family HD; Turner Classic Movies.
Fee: $13.95 monthly.

Digital Expanded Basic Service 2
Subscribers: N.A.
Programming (via satellite): ABC Family HD; Animal Planet HD; Arts & Entertainment HD; CNN HD; Discovery Channel HD; Discovery HD Theater; Discovery Planet Green HD; Disney Channel HD; ESPN 2 HD; ESPN HD; Food Network HD; Fox News HD; FSN HD; FX HD; HGTV HD; History Channel HD; Lifetime Movie Network HD; Lifetime Television HD; National Geographic Channel HD Network; Outdoor Channel 2 HD; QVC HD; Science Channel HD; Speed HD; Syfy HD; TBS in HD; TLC HD; Travel Channel HD; Turner Network TV HD; USA Network HD.
Fee: $10.95 monthly.

Pay Service 1
Pay Units: 2.
Programming (via satellite): Cinemax.
Fee: $8.95 monthly.

Pay Service 2
Pay Units: 19.
Programming (via satellite): HBO.
Fee: $11.95 monthly.

Digital Pay Service 1
Pay Units: N.A.
Programming (via satellite): Cinemax (multiplexed); Cinemax HD; Flix; HBO (multiplexed); HBO HD; Showtime (multiplexed); Showtime HD; The Movie Channel (multiplexed); The Movie Channel HD.
Fee: $11.95 monthly (Cinemax), $14.95 monthly (HBO or Showtime/TMC/Flix).

Video-On-Demand: No

Pay-Per-View
iN DEMAND (delivered digitally); Hot Choice (delivered digitally).

Internet Service
Operational: Yes.

Telephone Service
None

Miles of Plant: 4.0 (coaxial); None (fiber optic). Homes passed: 214.
Manager: Bill Barton. Headend Technician: Jay Stewart.; Julian Rodriguez.
City fee: 1% of basic.
Ownership: Giant Communications (MSO).

WOODBINE—Eagle Communications, 406 NE 14th St, Abilene, KS 67410. Phones: 785-325-4000 (Corporate office); 785-263-2529. Fax: 785-625-8030. E-mail: comments@eablecom.net. Web Site: http://www.eaglecom.net. ICA: KS0423.
TV Market Ranking: Outside TV Markets (WOODBINE). Franchise award date: January 1, 1981. Franchise expiration date: N.A. Began: N.A.
Channel capacity: 31 (not 2-way capable). Channels available but not in use: 10.

Basic Service
Subscribers: 46.
Programming (received off-air): KAKE-TV (ABC) Wichita; KPTS (PBS) Hutchinson; KSAS-TV (FOX) Wichita; KSNT (FOX, NBC) Topeka; KSNW (NBC) Wichita; KTKA-TV (ABC, CW) Topeka; KWCH-DT (CBS) Hutchinson; WIBW-TV (CBS, MNT) Topeka.
Programming (via satellite): ABC Family Channel; Arts & Entertainment; CNN; C-SPAN; Disney Channel; ESPN; Great American Country; History Channel; Outdoor Channel; TBS Superstation; The Learning Channel; Turner Network TV; WGN America.
Fee: $24.95 installation; $28.55 monthly.

Pay Service 1
Pay Units: 14.
Programming (via satellite): HBO.
Fee: $11.95 monthly.

Internet Service
Operational: No.

Telephone Service
None

Miles of Plant: 2.0 (coaxial); None (fiber optic). Homes passed: 86.
President & Chief Executive Officer: Gary Shorman. Regional Manager: Dennis Weese. General Manager: Rex Skiles.
Ownership: Eagle Communications Inc. (KS).

WOODSTON—Nex-Tech. Now served by EDMOND, KS [KS0450]. ICA: KS0306.

KENTUCKY

Total Systems: 152
Total Communities Served: 1,001
Franchises Not Yet Operating: 0
Applications Pending: 0
Communities with Applications: 0
Number of Basic Subscribers: 1,017,578
Number of Expanded Basic Subscribers: 570,241
Number of Pay Units: 198,356

Top 100 Markets Represented: Cincinnati, OH-Newport, KY (17); Nashville, TN (30); Charleston-Huntington, WV (36); Louisville (38); Cape Girardeau, MO-Paducah, KY-Harrisburg, IL (69); Evansville, IN (86).

For a list of cable communities in this section, see the Cable Community Index located in the back of Cable Volume 2.
For explanation of terms used in cable system listings, see p. D-11.

ADAIRVILLE—Suddenlink Communications, 12444 Powerscourt Dr, Saint Louis, MO 63131-3660. Phones: 800-999-6845 (Customer service); 314-965-2020. Fax: 903-561-5485. Web Site: http://www.suddenlink.com. ICA: KY0197.

TV Market Ranking: 30 (ADAIRVILLE). Franchise award date: October 14, 1986. Franchise expiration date: N.A. Began: January 1, 1980.

Channel capacity: 32 (not 2-way capable). Channels available but not in use: None.

Basic Service

Subscribers: 151.

Programming (received off-air): WBKO (ABC, CW) Bowling Green; WKLE (PBS) Lexington; WKYU-TV (PBS) Bowling Green; WNAB (CW) Nashville; WNKY (CBS, NBC) Bowling Green; WNPT (PBS) Nashville; WNPX-TV (ION) Cookeville; WPGD-TV (IND) Hendersonville; WSMV-TV (NBC, TMO) Nashville; WTVF (CBS) Nashville; WUXP-TV (MNT) Nashville; WZTV (FOX) Nashville.

Programming (via satellite): TV Guide Network; WGN America.

Current originations: Government Access; Educational Access; Public Access.

Fee: $35.00 installation; $17.95 monthly.

Expanded Basic Service 1

Subscribers: 13.

Programming (via satellite): ABC Family Channel; AMC; Animal Planet; Arts & Entertainment; BET Networks; Cartoon Network; CNBC; CNN; Country Music TV; C-SPAN; Discovery Channel; Disney Channel; ESPN; ESPN 2; ESPN Classic Sports; Fox News Channel; FX; Headline News; HGTV; History Channel; Home Shopping Network; Lifetime; MTV; Nickelodeon; QVC; Spike TV; Syfy; TBS Superstation; The Learning Channel; Turner Classic Movies; Turner Network TV; TV Land; USA Network; VH1; Weather Channel.

Fee: $22.00 monthly.

Video-On-Demand: No

Pay-Per-View

iN DEMAND (delivered digitally); Playboy TV (delivered digitally); Fresh (delivered digitally).

Internet Service

Operational: Yes.

Telephone Service

None

Miles of Plant: 8.0 (coaxial); None (fiber optic). Homes passed: 411.

Manager: Wayne Harrison. Chief Technician: Jim Adkins. Vice President: Robert Herrald.

Ownership: Cequel Communications LLC (MSO).

ALBANY—Mediacom. Now served by TOMPKINSVILLE, KY [KY0092]. ICA: KY0108.

ALTRO—Formerly served by Altro TV Inc. No longer in operation. ICA: KY0115.

ANNVILLE—C & W Cable, PO Box 490, 7920 Hwy 30 W, Annville, KY 40402-9748. Phone: 606-364-5357. Fax: 606-364-2138. Also serves Clay County (portions), Jackson County (portions), Lauren County (portions), Manchester, Peoples & Tyner. ICA: KY0122.

TV Market Ranking: Below 100 (ANNVILLE, Clay County (portions), Jackson County (portions), Laurel County (portions), Manchester, Peoples, Tyner). Franchise award date: N.A. Franchise expiration date: N.A. Began: May 1, 1976.

Channel capacity: N.A. Channels available but not in use: N.A.

Basic Service

Subscribers: 750.

Programming (received off-air): WDKY-TV (FOX) Danville; WKLE (PBS) Lexington; WKYT-TV (CBS, CW) Lexington; WLEX-TV (NBC) Lexington; WTVQ-DT (ABC) Lexington; WYMT-TV (CBS, CW) Hazard.

Programming (via satellite): ABC Family Channel; AMC; AmericanLife TV Network; Animal Planet; Arts & Entertainment; Cartoon Network; CNN; Country Music TV; CW+; Discovery Channel; Disney Channel; Encore Westerns; ESPN; ESPN 2; Food Network; Fox News Channel; Fox Sports Net; FX; Golf Channel; Gospel Music Channel; Hallmark Channel; HGTV; History Channel; Home Shopping Network; ION Television; Lifetime; MTV; Nickelodeon; Outdoor Channel; QVC; RFD-TV; Speed Channel; Spike TV; Syfy; TBS Superstation; TLC; Toon Disney; Trinity Broadcasting Network; truTV; Turner Network TV; TV Land; USA Network; Versus; VH1; Weather Channel; WGN America.

Fee: $30.00 installation; $16.00 monthly.

Pay Service 1

Pay Units: N.A.

Programming (via satellite): Encore; HBO; Showtime.

Fee: $23.00 monthly.

Video-On-Demand: No

Internet Service

Operational: No.

Telephone Service

None

Miles of Plant: 37.0 (coaxial); None (fiber optic). Homes passed: 890.

Vice President & General Manager: Veola Williams. Chief Technician: Brett Williams.

Ownership: C & W Cable Inc.

ASHLAND—Formerly served by Adelphia Communications. Now served by HUNTINGTON, WV [WV0002]. ICA: KY0009.

ASHLAND—Time Warner Cable, 225 Russell Rd, Ashland, KY 41101. Phone: 606-329-2201. Fax: 606-329-9579. Web Site: http://www.timewarnercable.com. Also serves Bellefonte, Boyd County (portions), Flatwoods, Greenup County (portions), Raceland, Russell, Westwood & Worthington, KY; Coal Grove, Franklin Furnace, Hanging Rock, Ironton & Kitts Hill, OH. ICA: KY0326.

TV Market Ranking: 36 (ASHLAND, Bellefonte, Boyd County (portions), Coal Grove, Flatwoods, Franklin Furnace, Greenup County (portions), Hanging Rock, Ironton, Kitts Hill, Raceland, Russell, Westwood, Worthington).

Channel capacity: N.A. Channels available but not in use: N.A.

Basic Service

Subscribers: N.A.

Programming (received off-air): WCHS-TV (ABC) Charleston; WKAS (PBS) Ashland; WKYT-TV (CBS, CW) Lexington; WLPX-TV (ION) Charleston; WOWK-TV (CBS) Huntington; WPBY-TV (PBS) Huntington; WQCW (CW) Portsmouth; WSAZ-TV (MNT, NBC) Huntington; WTSF (IND) Ashland; WVAH-TV (FOX) Charleston.

Programming (via satellite): ABC Family Channel; C-SPAN; Eternal Word TV Network; Home Shopping Network; INSP; MyNetworkTV Inc.; QVC; TBS Superstation; TV Guide Network; Weather Channel; WGN America.

Current originations: Educational Access; Public Access.

Fee: $13.66 monthly.

Expanded Basic Service 1

Subscribers: N.A.

Programming (via satellite): AMC; Animal Planet; Arts & Entertainment; BET Networks; Bio; Bravo; Cartoon Network; CNBC; CNN; Comedy Central; Country Music TV; Court TV; C-SPAN 2; Discovery Channel; Disney Channel; E! Entertainment Television; ESPN; ESPN 2; Food Network; Fox News Channel; Fox Sports Net Ohio; FX; Golf Channel; Great American Country; Hallmark Channel; Headline News; HGTV; History Channel; Lifetime; MSNBC; MTV; MTV2; National Geographic Channel; Nickelodeon; Outdoor Channel; Oxygen; Product Information Network; ShopNBC; Speed Channel; Spike TV; SportsTime Ohio; Syfy; The Learning Channel; Toon Disney; Travel Channel; Turner Network TV; TV Land; USA Network; VH1.

Fee: $37.12 monthly.

Digital Basic Service

Subscribers: N.A.

Programming (received off-air): WCHS-TV (ABC) Charleston; WSAZ-TV (MNT, NBC) Huntington; WVAH-TV (FOX) Charleston.

Programming (via satellite): AmericanLife TV Network; BBC America; Bloomberg Television; Boomerang; Canal 52MX; CBS College Sports Network; Cine Latino; CNN en Espanol; Cooking Channel; C-SPAN 3; Current; Daystar TV Network; Discovery en Espanol; Discovery HD Theater; Discovery Health Channel; Discovery Home Channel; Discovery Kids Channel; Discovery Military Channel; Discovery Times Channel; Do-It-Yourself; Encore (multiplexed); ESPN 2 HD; ESPN Classic Sports; ESPN Deportes; ESPN HD; ESPN U; ESPNews; Eternal Word TV Network; EWTN en Espanol; FamilyNet; FitTV; Flix; Fox Business Channel; Fox College Sports Atlantic; Fox College Sports Central; Fox College Sports Pacific; Fox Movie Channel; Fox Reality Channel; Fox Soccer; Fox Sports en Espanol; Fuel TV; Fuse; G4; GAS; GSN; Halogen Network; HDNet; HDNet Movies; History Channel en Espanol; History Channel International; Independent Film Channel; Lifetime Movie Network; LOGO; MTV Hits; MTV Jams; MTV Tres; MTV2; Music Choice; NBA TV; Nick Jr.; Nick Too; NickToons TV; Outdoor Channel; Ovation; ReelzChannel; Science Channel; Sleuth; SoapNet; Style Network; Sundance Channel; Tennis Channel; The Sportsman Channel; The Word Network; Toon Disney en Espanol; Trinity Broadcasting Network; Turner Classic Movies; Turner Network TV HD; TVG Network; Universal HD; Versus; VH1 Classic; VH1 Country; VH1 Soul; WE tv.

Fee: $6.00 monthly (each tier).

Digital Pay Service 1

Pay Units: N.A.

Programming (via satellite): ART America; CCTV-4; Cinemax (multiplexed); Cinemax HD; Filipino Channel; HBO (multiplexed); HBO HD; RAI International; Russian Television Network; Showtime (multiplexed); Showtime HD; Starz (multiplexed); Starz HDTV; The Movie Channel (multiplexed); TV Asia; TV Japan; TV5, La Television International; Zhong Tian Channel.

Video-On-Demand: Yes

Pay-Per-View

iN DEMAND (delivered digitally); NHL Center Ice (delivered digitally); MLB Extra Innings (delivered digitally); ESPN (delivered digitally); Fresh (delivered digitally); Hot Choice (delivered digitally); Playboy TV (delivered digitally).

Internet Service

Operational: Yes.

Broadband Service: Road Runner.

Fee: $99.95 installation; $44.95 monthly.

Telephone Service

Digital: Operational

Fee: $74.95 installation; $49.95 monthly

Miles of Plant: 900.0 (coaxial); None (fiber optic). Homes passed: 50,000.

General Manager: Russ Pomfrey. Technical Operations Manager: Mike Jones. Marketing Manager: Mark Cole. Business Manager: Tracy Tackett. Technical Supervisor: Rod Frost.

Ownership: Time Warner Cable (MSO).

AUBURN—Formerly served by Cebridge Connections. Now served by RUSSELLVILLE, KY [KY0032]. ICA: KY0198.

AUGUSTA—Bracken County Cablevision Inc. Now served by MAYSVILLE, KY [KY0033]. ICA: KY0100.

BARBOURVILLE—Barbourville Utility Commission, PO Box 1600, 202 Daniel Boone Dr, Barbourville, KY 40906. Phones: 606-545-9205; 606-546-4127. Fax: 606-546-4848. Web Site: http://www.barbourville.com. Also serves Artemus, Boone Heights, Heidrick & Knox County. ICA: KY0057.

TV Market Ranking: Below 100 (Artemus, BARBOURVILLE, Boone Heights, Heidrick, Knox County (portions)). Franchise award date: September 8, 1952. Franchise expiration date: N.A. Began: October 1, 1952.

Channel capacity: 116 (operating 2-way). Channels available but not in use: 55.

Basic Service

Subscribers: 2,700.

Programming (received off-air): WAGV (IND) Harlan; WATE-TV (ABC) Knoxville; WBIR-TV (NBC) Knoxville; WBXX-TV (CW) Crossville; WDKY-TV (FOX) Danville; WKSO-TV (PBS) Somerset; WKYT-TV (CBS, CW) Lexington; WLEX-TV (NBC) Lexington; WLFG (IND) Grundy; WLJC-TV (TBN) Beattyville; WTVQ-DT (ABC) Lexington; WVLT-TV (CBS, MNT) Knoxville; WYMT-TV (CBS, CW) Hazard.

Programming (via satellite): ABC Family Channel; AMC; Animal Planet; Arts & Entertainment; Bravo; Cartoon Network; CNBC; CNN; Comcast Sports Net Southeast; Comedy Central; Cooking Channel; Country Music TV; C-SPAN; CW+; Discovery Channel; Disney Channel; Do-It-Yourself; E! Entertainment Television; ESPN; ESPN 2; ESPN Classic Sports; Food Network; Fox News Channel; FX; Golf Channel; Headline News; HGTV; History Channel; Lifetime; MSNBC; MTV; Nickelodeon; Outdoor Channel; Oxygen; QVC; Speed Channel; Spike TV; Syfy; TBS Superstation; The Learning Channel; Travel Channel; Turner Classic Movies; Turner Network TV; TV Guide Network; TV Land; USA Network; VH1; Weather Channel; WGN America.

Current originations: Public Access; Educational Access.

Fee: $20.00 installation; $35.00 monthly; $20.00 additional installation.

Digital Basic Service

Subscribers: N.A.

Programming (via satellite): BBC America; Bio; Bloomberg Television; CMT Pure Country; Discovery Health Channel; Discovery Kids Channel; Discovery Military Channel; Discovery Planet Green; DMX Music; E! Entertainment Television; ESPN U; ESPNews; FitTV; FX; G4; GSN; Halogen Network; History Channel International; ID Investigation Discovery; Lifetime Movie Network; MTV Hits; MTV2; Nick Jr.; NickToons TV; Ovation; PBS Kids Sprout; Science Channel; SoapNet; TeenNick; Toon Disney; Trinity Broadcasting Network; TVG Network; VH1 Classic; VH1 Soul; WE tv.

Fee: $12.00 monthly.

Digital Expanded Basic Service

Subscribers: N.A.

Programming (received off-air): WATE-TV (ABC) Knoxville; WBIR-TV (NBC) Knoxville; WBXX-TV (CW) Crossville; WDKY-TV (FOX) Danville; WKSO-TV (PBS) Somerset; WKYT-TV (CBS, CW) Lexington; WTVQ-DT (ABC) Lexington; WVLT-TV (CBS, MNT) Knoxville; WYMT-TV (CBS, CW) Hazard.

Programming (via satellite): ESPN 2 HD; ESPN HD; HDNet; HDNet Movies; Outdoor Channel 2 HD; Turner Network TV HD.

Fee: $12.00 monthly.

Digital Pay Service 1

Pay Units: N.A.

Programming (via satellite): Cinemax (multiplexed); Encore (multiplexed); Flix; HBO (multiplexed); Showtime (multiplexed); Showtime HD; Starz (multiplexed); Starz HDTV; The Movie Channel (multiplexed); The Movie Channel HD.

Fee: $9.00 monthly (Starz/Encore), $12.95 monthly (Showtime/TMC/Flix), $18.00 monthly (HBO/Cinemax).

Video-On-Demand: No

Pay-Per-View

iN DEMAND (delivered digitally).

Internet Service

Operational: Yes.

Broadband Service: In-house.

Fee: $103.00 installation; $29.95 monthly; $29.95 modem lease.

Telephone Service

None

Miles of Plant: 75.0 (coaxial); 30.0 (fiber optic). Homes passed: 3,000. Total homes in franchised area: 3,000.

Manager: Randall Young. Chief Technician: Ron Bowling.

City fee: None.

Ownership: Barbourville Utility Commission.

BARDSTOWN—Bardstown Cable TV, 220 N 5th St, Bardstown, KY 40004-1458. Phone: 502-348-5947. Fax: 502-348-2433. Web Site: http://www.cityofbardstown.org/cabletv/. Also serves Nelson County. ICA: KY0026.

TV Market Ranking: 38 (BARDSTOWN, Nelson County (portions)); Below 100 (Nelson County (portions)). Franchise award date: October 1, 1964. Franchise expiration date: N.A. Began: May 5, 1965.

Channel capacity: 60 (operating 2-way). Channels available but not in use: None.

Basic Service

Subscribers: 8,084.

Programming (received off-air): WAVE (NBC) Louisville; WBNA (ION) Louisville; WDRB (FOX) Louisville; WHAS-TV (ABC) Louisville; WKMJ-TV (PBS) Louisville; WKZT-TV (PBS) Elizabethtown; WLKY-TV (CBS) Louisville; WMYO (MNT) Salem.

Programming (via satellite): ABC Family Channel; AMC; Animal Planet; Arts & Entertainment; BET Networks; Cartoon Network; CNBC; CNN; Comcast Sports Net Southeast; Comedy Central; Country Music TV; C-SPAN; Discovery Channel; Disney Channel; E! Entertainment Television; ESPN; ESPN 2; Eternal Word TV Network; Food Network; Fox News Channel; FX; GSN; Hallmark Channel; Headline News; HGTV; History Channel; Lifetime; MTV; National Geographic Channel; Nickelodeon; Outdoor Channel; QVC; Spike TV; Syfy; TBS Superstation; The Learning Channel; Toon Disney; Travel Channel; Turner Classic Movies; Turner Network TV; TV Guide Network; TV Land; USA Network; VH1; Weather Channel; WGN America.

Fee: $80.00 installation; $12.95 monthly; $3.00 converter.

Digital Basic Service

Subscribers: 245.

Programming (received off-air): WAVE (NBC) Louisville; WBKI-TV (CW) Campbellsville; WBNA (ION) Louisville; WDRB (FOX) Louisville; WHAS-TV (ABC) Louisville; WKPC-TV (PBS) Louisville; WLKY-TV (CBS) Louisville; WMYO (MNT) Salem.

Programming (via satellite): Discovery Digital Networks; DMX Music; ESPN Classic Sports; Fox Soccer; GAS; Independent Film Channel; Lifetime Movie Network; MTV2; Nick Jr.; Sleuth; VH1 Classic.

Fee: $8.95 monthly.

Digital Expanded Basic Service

Subscribers: 151.

Programming (via satellite): AmericanLife TV Network; BBC America; Bio; Bloomberg Television; Current; ESPNews; Fox Movie Channel; Fuse; G4; Golf Channel; History Channel International; MTV Networks Digital Suite; Ovation; Speed Channel; Style Network; Versus; WebMD Television.

Fee: $3.95 monthly.

Pay Service 1

Pay Units: 1,330.

Programming (via satellite): HBO (multiplexed).

Fee: $10.95 monthly.

Pay Service 2

Pay Units: 708.

Programming (via satellite): Cinemax.

Fee: $8.95 monthly.

Pay Service 3

Pay Units: 519.

Programming (via satellite): Flix; Showtime; Sundance Channel; The Movie Channel.

Fee: $12.95 monthly.

Digital Pay Service 1

Pay Units: 69.

Programming (via satellite): Cinemax (multiplexed); Encore (multiplexed); Flix; HBO (multiplexed); Showtime (multiplexed); Starz (multiplexed); The Movie Channel (multiplexed); WE tv.

Fee: $9.00 monthly.

Video-On-Demand: No

Pay-Per-View

iN DEMAND (delivered digitally).

Internet Service

Operational: Yes. Began: December 1, 1999.

Subscribers: 1,076.

Broadband Service: Bardstown Cable Internet Service.

Fee: $39.95 installation; $24.95 monthly; $5.00 modem lease; $99.00 modem purchase.

Telephone Service

None

Miles of Plant: None (coaxial); 325.0 (fiber optic). Homes passed: 11,000. Total homes in franchised area: 12,000.

Manager: Dixie Hibbs. Marketing: Pam Bose. Chief Financial Officer: Mike Abell. System Engineer: Jeffrey C. Mills.

County fee: 3% of gross.

Ownership: City of Bardstown.

BEATTYVILLE—Windjammer Cable, 4400 PGA Blvd, Ste 902, Palm Beach Gardens, FL 33410. Phones: 877-450-5558; 561-775-1208. Fax: 561-775-7811. Web Site: http://www.windjammercable.com. Also serves Athol, Booneville, Congleton, Heidelberg, Lone, Primrose, Proctor, South Beattyville, St. Helens & Tallega. ICA: KY0141.

TV Market Ranking: Below 100 (Athol, BEATTYVILLE, Booneville, Congleton, Heidelberg, Lone, Primrose, Proctor, South Beattyville, St. Helens, Tallega). Franchise award date: N.A. Franchise expiration date: N.A. Began: January 1, 1958.

Channel capacity: 36 (not 2-way capable). Channels available but not in use: 3.

Basic Service

Subscribers: 1,681.

Programming (received off-air): WDKY-TV (FOX) Danville; WKHA (PBS) Hazard; WKYT-TV (CBS, CW) Lexington; WLEX-TV (NBC) Lexington; WLJC-TV (TBN) Beattyville; WTVQ-DT (ABC) Lexington; WUPX-TV (ION) Morehead; WYMT-TV (CBS, CW) Hazard.

Programming (via satellite): QVC; TBS Superstation; WGN America.

Fee: $39.95 installation; $14.56 monthly.

Expanded Basic Service 1

Subscribers: 1,666.

Programming (via satellite): ABC Family Channel; AMC; Arts & Entertainment; CNN; Country Music TV; Discovery Channel; Disney Channel; ESPN; ESPN 2; Fox News Channel; FX; Hallmark Channel; Headline News; Lifetime; Nickelodeon; Spike TV; The Learning Channel; Turner Network TV; USA Network; VH1; Weather Channel.

Fee: $31.95 monthly.

Digital Basic Service

Subscribers: N.A.

Programming (via satellite): BBC America; Bio; Black Family Channel; Bloomberg Television; Bravo; Canales N; Discovery Digital Networks; ESPN Classic Sports; ESPNews; Fox Sports World; FSN Digital Atlantic; FSN Digital Central; FSN Digital Pacific; G4; GAS; Golf Channel; Great American Country; GSN; Halogen Network; HGTV; History Channel; History Channel International; Independent Film Channel; MTV Networks Digital Suite; National Geographic Channel; Nick Too; NickToons TV; Outdoor Channel; ShopNBC; Speed Channel; Style Network; Syfy; Trinity Broadcasting Network; Turner Classic Movies; Versus; WE tv.

Fee: $55.21 monthly.

Digital Pay Service 1

Pay Units: N.A.

Programming (via satellite): Cinemax (multiplexed); Encore; Flix; HBO (multiplexed); Showtime (multiplexed); The Movie Channel (multiplexed).

Fee: $15.95 monthly (each).

Video-On-Demand: No

Pay-Per-View

HITS PPV (delivered digitally).

Internet Service

Operational: No.

Telephone Service

None

Miles of Plant: 139.0 (coaxial); None (fiber optic). Homes passed: 2,419. Total homes in franchised area: 3,458.

General Manager: Timothy Evard. Operations Director: Belinda Graham. Engineering Director: Mike Earehart. Finance & Accounting Director: Cindy Johnson.

City fee: None.

Ownership: Windjammer Communications LLC (MSO).

BEAVER DAM—NewWave Communications, 250 Madison Square Dr, Madisonville, KY 42431. Phone: 888.863.9928 (Customer service). Fax: 270.245.2022. Web Site: http://www.newwavecom.com. Also serves Centertown, Hartford, McHenry, Ohio County & Rockport. ICA: KY0054.

TV Market Ranking: Below 100 (BEAVER DAM, Centertown, Hartford, McHenry, Ohio County (portions), Rockport); Outside TV Markets (Ohio County (portions)). Franchise award date: N.A. Franchise expiration date: N.A. Began: January 1, 1976.

Channel capacity: 118 (not 2-way capable). Channels available but not in use: N.A.

Basic Service

Subscribers: 2,253.

Programming (received off-air): WAZE-TV (CW) Madisonville; WBKO (ABC, CW)

Bowling Green; WEHT (ABC) Evansville; WEVV-TV (CBS, MNT) Evansville; WFIE (NBC) Evansville; WKAG-CA Hopkinsville; WKMA-TV (PBS) Madisonville; WKYU-TV (PBS) Bowling Green; WNIN (PBS) Evansville; WPSD-TV (NBC) Paducah; WTVW (FOX) Evansville.
Programming (via satellite): C-SPAN; C-SPAN 2; Home Shopping Network; INSP; QVC; Trinity Broadcasting Network; TV Guide Network; WGN America.
Fee: $32.00 installation; $8.50 monthly; $.63 converter.

Expanded Basic Service 1
Subscribers: N.A.
Programming (via satellite): ABC Family Channel; AMC; Animal Planet; Arts & Entertainment; BET Networks; Bravo; Cartoon Network; CNBC; CNN; Comcast Sports Net Southeast; Comedy Central; Country Music TV; Discovery Channel; Disney Channel; E! Entertainment Television; ESPN; ESPN 2; ESPN Classic Sports; Food Network; Fox News Channel; FX; G4; Golf Channel; Great American Country; GSN; Hallmark Channel; Headline News; HGTV; History Channel; Lifetime; MSNBC; MTV; National Geographic Channel; Nickelodeon; Outdoor Channel; Oxygen; SoapNet; Speed Channel; Spike TV; Syfy; TBS Superstation; The Learning Channel; Toon Disney; Travel Channel; truTV; Turner Classic Movies; Turner Network TV; TV Land; USA Network; Versus; VH1; Weather Channel.
Fee: $25.39 monthly.

Digital Basic Service
Subscribers: N.A.
Programming (received off-air): WEHT (ABC) Evansville; WEVV-TV (CBS, MNT) Evansville; WFIE (NBC) Evansville; WTVW (FOX) Evansville.
Programming (via satellite): Arts & Entertainment HD; BBC America; Bio; CMT Pure Country; Cooking Channel; Discovery HD Theater; Discovery Health Channel; Discovery Kids Channel; Discovery Military Channel; Discovery Planet Green; Do-It-Yourself; ESPN 2 HD; ESPN HD; ESPN U; ESPNews; FitTV; Fox Movie Channel; FSN HD; Gospel Music Channel; Hallmark Movie Channel; HDNet; HDNet Movies; History Channel HD; History Channel International; HorseRacing TV; ID Investigation Discovery; Jewelry Television; Lifetime Movie Network; Lifetime Real Women; MTV Hits; MTV Jams; MTV2; Music Choice; Nick Jr.; Nick Too; NickToons TV; Palladia; RFD-TV; Science Channel; Style Network; TeenNick; Turner Network TV HD; USA Network HD; VH1 Classic; VH1 Soul; Weather Channel HD.

Digital Pay Service 1
Pay Units: N.A.
Programming (via satellite): Cinemax (multiplexed); Cinemax HD; Encore (multiplexed); Flix; HBO (multiplexed); HBO HD; Showtime (multiplexed); Starz (multiplexed); Starz HDTV; The Movie Channel (multiplexed).

Video-On-Demand: No

Pay-Per-View
Movies (delivered digitally); Special events (delivered digitally); Hot Choice (delivered digitally); Playboy TV (delivered digitally).

Internet Service
Operational: No.

Telephone Service
None

Miles of Plant: 110.0 (coaxial); None (fiber optic). Homes passed: 3,480.
General Manager: Mark Boyer. Technical Operations Director: Roy Hibbs.
City fee: 5% of gross.
Ownership: NewWave Communications (MSO).

BENHAM—Tri-Star Communications. No longer in operation. ICA: KY0176.

BENTON—Charter Communications. Now served by MAYFIELD, KY [KY0037]. ICA: KY0085.

BIG CLIFTY—Mediacom. Now served by CANEYVILLE, KY [KY0291]. ICA: KY0200.

BLACK MOUNTAIN—Zito Media, 106 S Main St, Edinburg, VA 22824. Phone: 814-260-9575. Web Site: http://www.zitomedia.com. Also serves Ages, Baxter, Bobs Creek, Brookside, Cawood, Chevrolet, Closplint, Coalgood, Coxton, Cranks, Crummies, Dione, Dizney, Holmes Mill, Kenvir, Laden, Lejunior, Louellen, Nolansburg, Putney, Redbud, Rosspoint, Totz & Verda. ICA: KY0042.
TV Market Ranking: Below 100 (Ages, Baxter, BLACK MOUNTAIN, Bobs Creek, Brookside, Cawood, Chevrolet, Closplint, Coalgood, Coxton, Cranks, Crummies, Dione, Dizney, Holmes Mill, Kenvir, Lejunior, Louellen, Nolansburg, Putney, Redbud, Rosspoint, Totz, Verda). Franchise award date: N.A. Franchise expiration date: N.A. Began: N.A.
Channel capacity: 37 (not 2-way capable). Channels available but not in use: None.

Basic Service
Subscribers: 2,746.
Programming (received off-air): WAGV (IND) Harlan; WATE-TV (ABC) Knoxville; WBIR-TV (NBC) Knoxville; WBXX-TV (CW) Crossville; WEMT (FOX) Greeneville; WETP-TV (PBS) Sneedville; WKHA (PBS) Hazard; WKYT-TV (CBS, CW) Lexington; WVLT-TV (CBS, MNT) Knoxville; WYMT-TV (CBS, CW) Hazard.
Programming (via satellite): Home Shopping Network; WGN America.
Fee: $29.95 installation; $19.95 monthly; $.73 converter.

Expanded Basic Service 1
Subscribers: N.A.
Programming (via satellite): ABC Family Channel; AMC; Arts & Entertainment; CNN; Country Music TV; C-SPAN; Discovery Channel; Disney Channel; E! Entertainment Television; ESPN; Lifetime; MTV; Nickelodeon; Outdoor Channel; Spike TV; Syfy; TBS Superstation; Trinity Broadcasting Network; Turner Network TV; USA Network; Weather Channel.
Fee: $16.89 monthly.

Digital Basic Service
Subscribers: N.A.
Programming (via satellite): AmericanLife TV Network; BBC America; Bio; Bloomberg Television; Bravo!; Discovery Digital Networks; DMX Music; ESPN 2; ESPN Classic Sports; FitTV; Fox Movie Channel; Fox Soccer; Fuse; G4; GAS; Golf Channel; GSN; HGTV; History Channel; History Channel International; Independent Film Channel; INSP; Lifetime Movie Network; MTV Networks Digital Suite; Nick Jr.; Outdoor Channel; Science Television; Speed Channel; Syfy; Toon Disney; Turner Classic Movies; Versus; WE tv.

Pay Service 1
Pay Units: 493.
Programming (via satellite): Cinemax; Encore; HBO; Showtime; The Movie Channel.
Fee: $3.99 monthly (Encore), $7.99 monthly (Cinemax), $11.99 monthly (HBO, Showtime or TMC).

Digital Pay Service 1
Pay Units: N.A.
Programming (via satellite): Cinemax (multiplexed); Encore (multiplexed); Flix; HBO (multiplexed); Showtime (multiplexed); Starz (multiplexed); The Movie Channel (multiplexed); WAM! America's Kidz Network.

Video-On-Demand: No

Pay-Per-View
iN DEMAND (delivered digitally); Hot Choice (delivered digitally); Playboy TV (delivered digitally); Fresh (delivered digitally); Shorteez (delivered digitally).

Internet Service
Operational: No.

Telephone Service
None

Miles of Plant: 116.0 (coaxial); None (fiber optic). Homes passed: 4,270.
Public Relations Manager: Mark Laver.
Ownership: Zito Media (MSO).

BLAINE—Formerly served by Lycom Communications. No longer in operation. ICA: KY0302.

BLOOMFIELD—Insight Communications, 4701 Commerce Crossings Dr, Louisville, KY 40229-2167. Phone: 502-357-4660. Fax: 502-357-4662. Web Site: http://www.myinsight.com. ICA: KY0160.
TV Market Ranking: 38 (BLOOMFIELD). Franchise award date: March 9, 1984. Franchise expiration date: N.A. Began: October 1, 1984.
Channel capacity: N.A. Channels available but not in use: N.A.

Basic Service
Subscribers: 206.
Programming (received off-air): WAVE (NBC) Louisville; WBKI-TV (CW) Campbellsville; WBNA (ION) Louisville; WDRB (FOX) Louisville; WHAS-TV (ABC) Louisville; WKYT-TV (CBS, CW) Lexington; WKZT-TV (PBS) Elizabethtown; WLKY-TV (CBS) Louisville; WMYO (MNT) Salem.
Programming (via satellite): C-SPAN; Discovery Channel; FX; Home Shopping Network; WGN America.
Fee: $35.00 installation.

Expanded Basic Service 1
Subscribers: N.A.
Programming (via satellite): ABC Family Channel; AMC; Arts & Entertainment; Cartoon Network; CNN; Country Music TV; Disney Channel; ESPN; ESPN 2; Fox News Channel; Hallmark Channel; Headline News; HGTV; MTV; Nickelodeon; Spike TV; TBS Superstation; The Learning Channel; Turner Network TV; USA Network; VH1; Weather Channel.
Fee: $30.82 monthly.

Internet Service
Operational: No.

Telephone Service
None

Miles of Plant: 10.0 (coaxial); None (fiber optic). Homes passed: 450. Total homes in franchised area: 450.
Vice President, Operations: Woody Hutton. Marketing Director: Shannon Likens. Community Relations Director: Reba Doutrick.
City fee: 3% of gross.
Ownership: Insight Communications Co. (MSO).

BONNYMAN—Bonnyman TV. Now served by HINDMAN, KY [KY0027]. ICA: KY0201.

BOONEVILLE—Peoples Telecom, PO Box 159, US Hwy 421 S, McKee, KY 40447. Phone: 606-287-7101. Fax: 606-287-8332. E-mail: prtccs@prtcnet.org. Web Site: http://www.prtcnet.org. Also serves Owsley County (portions). ICA: KY0328.
TV Market Ranking: Below 100 (BOONEVILLE, Owsley County).
Channel capacity: N.A. Channels available but not in use: N.A.

Basic Service
Subscribers: 400.
Programming (received off-air): WBKI-TV (CW) Campbellsville; WDKY-TV (FOX) Danville; WKLE (PBS) Lexington; WKYT-TV (CBS, CW) Lexington; WLEX-TV (NBC) Lexington; WLJC-TV (TBN) Beattyville; WTVQ-DT (ABC) Lexington; WUPX-TV (ION) Morehead; WYMT-TV (CBS, CW) Hazard.
Programming (via satellite): WGN-TV (CW, IND) Chicago.
Fee: $16.22 monthly.

Expanded Basic Service 1
Subscribers: N.A.
Programming (via satellite): ABC Family Channel; Animal Planet; Arts & Entertainment; Cartoon Network; CNN; Country Music TV; Discovery Channel; Disney Channel; ESPN; ESPN 2; Fox News Channel; Fox Sports Net Ohio; FX; HGTV; History Channel; Lifetime; Nickelodeon; QVC; Spike TV; TBS Superstation; The Learning Channel; Turner Network TV; TV Land; USA Network; VH1; Weather Channel.

Digital Basic Service
Subscribers: N.A. Included in McKee
Programming (via satellite): BBC America; Bio; Bloomberg Television; Bravo; CMT Pure Country; Discovery Health Channel; Discovery Kids Channel; Discovery Military Channel; Discovery Planet Green; DMX Music; ESPN 2; ESPN Classic Sports; ESPNews; FitTV; Fox Movie Channel; Fuse; G4; Golf Channel; Halogen Network; HGTV; History Channel; History Channel International; ID Investigation Discovery; Lifetime Movie Network; MTV Hits; MTV2; Nick Jr.; NickToons TV; Outdoor Channel; Ovation; PBS Kids Sprout; RFD-TV; Science Channel; SoapNet; Speed Channel; Style Network; TeenNick; Toon Disney; Trinity Broadcasting Network; Turner Classic Movies; VH1 Classic; VH1 Soul.
Fee: $7.75 monthly.

Digital Pay Service 1
Pay Units: N.A.
Programming (via satellite): Cinemax (multiplexed); Encore (multiplexed); Flix; HBO (multiplexed); Showtime (multiplexed); Starz (multiplexed); The Movie Channel (multiplexed).
Fee: $9.95 monthly (Cinemax or Starz/Encore), $11.95 monthly (HBO or Showtime/TMC/Flix).

Video-On-Demand: No

Internet Service
Operational: No.

Telephone Service
None

Homes passed: 1,000. Miles of plant included in McKee
General Manager: Keith Grabbard. Chief Technician: Jeff Bingham.
Ownership: Peoples Rural Telephone Cooperative (MSO).

BOWLING GREEN—Insight Communications, 515 Double Springs Rd, Bowling Green, KY 42101. Phone: 270-782-0903. Fax: 270-782-8355. Web Site: http://www.myinsight.com. Also serves Alvaton, Oakland, Plano, Plum Springs, Rockfield, Smiths Grove, Warren County & Woodburn. ICA: KY0007.

TV Market Ranking: Below 100 (Alvaton, BOWLING GREEN, Oakland, Plano, Plum Springs, Rockfield, Smiths Grove, Warren County, Woodburn). Franchise award date: September 1, 1980. Franchise expiration date: N.A. Began: July 21, 1981.
Channel capacity: N.A. Channels available but not in use: N.A.
Basic Service
Subscribers: 28,581.
Programming (received off-air): WBKO (ABC, CW) Bowling Green; WKGB-TV (PBS) Bowling Green; WKYU-TV (PBS) Bowling Green; WLKY-TV (CBS) Louisville; WNKY (CBS, NBC) Bowling Green; WPSD-TV (NBC) Paducah; WTVF (CBS) Nashville; 30 FMs.
Programming (via satellite): C-SPAN; C-SPAN 2; Home Shopping Network; INSP; QVC; Trinity Broadcasting Network; TV Guide Network; WGN America.
Current originations: Government Access; Educational Access; Public Access.
Fee: $35.00 installation.
Expanded Basic Service 1
Subscribers: N.A.
Programming (via satellite): ABC Family Channel; AMC; Animal Planet; Arts & Entertainment; BET Networks; Cartoon Network; CNBC; CNN; Comcast Sports Net Southeast; Comedy Central; Country Music TV; Discovery Channel; Disney Channel; E! Entertainment Television; ESPN; Eternal Word TV Network; Food Network; Fox News Channel; Fox Sports Net Ohio; FX; G4; Golf Channel; Hallmark Channel; Headline News; HGTV; History Channel; ION Television; Lifetime; MSNBC; MTV; National Geographic Channel; Nickelodeon; Oxygen; SoapNet; Spike TV; TBS Superstation; The Learning Channel; Travel Channel; truTV; Turner Network TV; Univision; USA Network; VH1; Weather Channel.
Fee: $40.00 monthly.
Digital Basic Service
Subscribers: 16,934.
Programming (received off-air): WBKO (ABC, CW) Bowling Green; WKGB-TV (PBS) Bowling Green; WKYU-TV (PBS) Bowling Green; WNKY (CBS, NBC) Bowling Green; WTVF (CBS) Nashville.
Programming (via satellite): AmericanLife TV Network; BBC America; Big Ten Network; Bio; Bloomberg Television; Bravo; CBS College Sports Network; CMT Pure Country; Cooking Channel; C-SPAN 3; Discovery Digital Networks; Discovery HD Theater; Do-It-Yourself; Encore (multiplexed); ESPN 2 HD; ESPN Classic Sports; ESPN HD; ESPN U; ESPNews; Fox College Sports Atlantic; Fox College Sports Central; Fox College Sports Pacific; Fox Movie Channel; Fox Soccer; Fuse; GAS; Great American Country; GSN; Halogen Network; HDNet; HDNet Movies; History Channel International; HorseRacing TV; Independent Film Channel; Lifetime Movie Network; MTV Networks Digital Suite; Music Choice; NFL Network; Nick Jr.; Nick Too; NickToons TV; Outdoor Channel; Ovation; Palladia; PBS Kids Sprout; Si TV; Sleuth; Speed Channel; Style Network; Sundance Channel; Syfy; Tennis Channel; Toon Disney; Turner Classic Movies; Turner Network TV HD; TV Land; TVG Network; Universal HD; Versus; WE tv.
Fee: $12.00 monthly.
Digital Pay Service 1
Pay Units: N.A.
Programming (via satellite): Cinemax (multiplexed); Flix; HBO (multiplexed); HBO HD; Showtime; Showtime HD; Starz (multiplexed); The Movie Channel (multiplexed).
Fee: $10.00 monthly (Cinemax or Starz), $13.00 monthly (HBO or Showtime/TMC).
Video-On-Demand: Yes
Pay-Per-View
iN DEMAND (delivered digitally); ESPN (delivered digitally); Playboy TV (delivered digitally); Fresh (delivered digitally).
Internet Service
Operational: Yes.
Subscribers: 16,766.
Broadband Service: InsightBB.com.
Fee: $99.95 installation; $44.95 monthly; $15.00 modem lease.
Telephone Service
Digital: Operational
Subscribers: 2,277.
Miles of Plant: 741.0 (coaxial); None (fiber optic). Homes passed: 41,517. Miles of plant includes both coax & fiber
President & Chief Operating Officer: Dinni Jain. Senior Vice President, Operations: John Hutton. District Vice President: Lanae Juffer. General Manager: Jerry Avery. Technical Operations Manager: Chris Bussell.
City fee: 3% of gross.
Ownership: Insight Communications Co. (MSO).

BRADFORDSVILLE—Formerly served by Charter Communications. No longer in operation. ICA: KY0298.

BREMEN—Windjammer Cable, 4400 PGA Blvd, Ste 902, Palm Beach Gardens, FL 33410. Phones: 877-450-5558; 561-775-1208. Fax: 561-775-7811. Web Site: http://www.windjammercable.com. Also serves Sacramento. ICA: KY0130.
TV Market Ranking: Below 100 (BREMEN, Sacramento). Franchise award date: N.A. Franchise expiration date: N.A. Began: N.A.
Channel capacity: N.A. Channels available but not in use: N.A.
Basic Service
Subscribers: N.A. Included in Owensboro
Programming (received off-air): WAZE-TV (CW) Madisonville; WBKO (ABC, CW) Bowling Green; WEHT (ABC) Evansville; WEVV-TV (CBS, MNT) Evansville; WFIE (NBC) Evansville; WKMA-TV (PBS) Madisonville; WNIN (PBS) Evansville; WTVW (FOX) Evansville.
Programming (via satellite): Nickelodeon; QVC; TBS Superstation; WGN America.
Fee: $39.95 installation; $18.12 monthly.
Expanded Basic Service 1
Subscribers: N.A.
Programming (via satellite): ABC Family Channel; AMC; Animal Planet; Arts & Entertainment; Bravo; Cartoon Network; CNBC; CNN; Comedy Central; Country Music TV; C-SPAN; Discovery Channel; E! Entertainment Television; ESPN; ESPN 2; FitTV; Food Network; Halogen Network; Headline News; HGTV; History Channel; Home Shopping Network; Lifetime; MTV; Outdoor Channel; Spike TV; Syfy; The Learning Channel; Travel Channel; truTV; Turner Network TV; TV Land; USA Network; Weather Channel.
Fee: $27.69 monthly.
Pay Service 1
Pay Units: 141.
Programming (via satellite): HBO (multiplexed).
Fee: $15.95 monthly.
Pay Service 2
Pay Units: 140.
Programming (via satellite): Showtime; The Movie Channel.
Fee: $15.95 monthly.
Pay Service 3
Pay Units: N.A.
Programming (via satellite): Cinemax.
Fee: $15.95 monthly.
Video-On-Demand: No
Internet Service
Operational: No.
Telephone Service
None
Miles of Plant: 32.0 (coaxial); None (fiber optic). Homes passed included in Owensboro
General Manager: Timothy Evard. Operations Director: Belinda Graham. Engineering Director: Mike Earehart. Finance & Accounting Director: Cindy Johnson.
City fee: 3% of basic.
Ownership: Windjammer Communications LLC (MSO).

BRODHEAD—Wilcop Cable TV, PO Box 558, 101 Pine Ave, Brodhead, KY 40409-0558. Phone: 606-758-8320. Fax: 606-758-8320. Also serves Crab Orchard. ICA: KY0173.
TV Market Ranking: Below 100 (BRODHEAD, Crab Orchard). Franchise award date: N.A. Franchise expiration date: N.A. Began: January 1, 1952.
Channel capacity: 40 (not 2-way capable). Channels available but not in use: 10.
Basic Service
Subscribers: 495.
Programming (received off-air): WDRB (FOX) Louisville; WKLE (PBS) Lexington; WKYT-TV (CBS, CW) Lexington; WLEX-TV (NBC) Lexington; WLKY-TV (CBS) Louisville; WTVQ-DT (ABC) Lexington.
Programming (via satellite): ESPN; TBS Superstation; WGN America.
Fee: $25.00 installation; $32.00 monthly.
Pay Service 1
Pay Units: 18.
Programming (via satellite): HBO (multiplexed).
Fee: $10.00 monthly.
Video-On-Demand: No
Internet Service
Operational: No.
Telephone Service
None
Miles of Plant: 20.0 (coaxial); None (fiber optic). Homes passed: 850. Total homes in franchised area: 850.
Manager: Johnny Wilcop.
City fee: None.
Ownership: Wilcop Cable TV (MSO).

BROOKS—Windjammer Cable, 4400 PGA Blvd, Ste 902, Palm Beach Gardens, FL 33410. Phones: 877-450-5558; 561-775-1208. Fax: 561-775-7811. Web Site: http://www.windjammercable.com. Also serves Barrallton, Shepherdsville & West Point. ICA: KY0199.
TV Market Ranking: 38 (Barrallton, BROOKS, Shepherdsville, West Point). Franchise award date: N.A. Franchise expiration date: N.A. Began: N.A.
Channel capacity: 42 (not 2-way capable). Channels available but not in use: 14.
Basic Service
Subscribers: 364.
Programming (received off-air): WAVE (NBC) Louisville; WDRB (FOX) Louisville; WHAS-TV (ABC) Louisville; WKPC-TV (PBS) Louisville; WLKY-TV (CBS) Louisville; WMYO (MNT) Salem; WUPX-TV (ION) Morehead.
Programming (via satellite): ABC Family Channel; AMC; Arts & Entertainment; CNN; Country Music TV; Discovery Channel; Disney Channel; ESPN; MTV; Nickelodeon; Spike TV; TBS Superstation; The Learning Channel; Trinity Broadcasting Network; Turner Network TV; USA Network; VH1; WGN America.
Fee: $29.95 installation; $24.52 monthly.
Pay Service 1
Pay Units: N.A.
Programming (via satellite): Flix; Showtime.
Digital Pay Service 1
Pay Units: N.A.
Programming (via satellite): Cinemax (multiplexed); Encore (multiplexed); HBO (multiplexed); Showtime (multiplexed); Starz (multiplexed); The Movie Channel (multiplexed).
Fee: $15.95 monthly (each).
Video-On-Demand: No
Pay-Per-View
iN DEMAND (delivered digitally); Fresh (delivered digitally); Playboy TV (delivered digitally).
Internet Service
Operational: No.
Telephone Service
None
Miles of Plant: 305.0 (coaxial); None (fiber optic). Homes passed: 445.
General Manager: Timothy Evard. Operations Director: Belinda Graham. Engineering Director: Mike Earehart. Finance & Accounting Director: Cindy Johnson.
Ownership: Windjammer Communications LLC (MSO).

BROOKSVILLE—Bracken County Cablevision Inc. Now served by MAYSVILLE, KY [KY0033]. ICA: KY0204.

BROWNSVILLE—Mediacom. Now served by MORGANTOWN, KY [KY0096]. ICA: KY0088.

BRYANTSVILLE—Formerly served by Charter Communications. No longer in operation. ICA: KY0205.

BULAN—NewWave Communications, 5026 S Hwy 27, Somerset, KY 42501. Phone: 606-678-9215. Fax: 606-679-7111. Web Site: http://www.newwavecom.com. Also serves Airport Gardens, Darfork, Fisty, Hardburly, Hardshell, Lost Creek, Lotts Creek, Rowdy, Second Creek & Tribbey. ICA: KY0062.
TV Market Ranking: Below 100 (Airport Gardens, BULAN, Darfork, Fisty, Hardburly, Hardshell, Lost Creek, Lotts Creek, Rowdy, Second Creek, Tribbey). Franchise award date: N.A. Franchise expiration date: N.A. Began: January 1, 1952.
Channel capacity: 136 (not 2-way capable). Channels available but not in use: N.A.
Basic Service
Subscribers: 1,632.
Programming (received off-air): WAGV (IND) Harlan; WDKY-TV (FOX) Danville; WKPI-TV (PBS) Pikeville; WKYT-TV (CBS, CW) Lexington; WLEX-TV (NBC) Lexington; WLJC-TV (TBN) Beattyville; WTVQ-DT (ABC) Lexington; WUPX-TV (ION) Morehead; WYMT-TV (CBS, CW) Hazard.
Programming (via satellite): C-SPAN; ESPN Classic Sports; QVC; Weather Channel; WGN America.
Fee: $35.57 installation; $9.26 monthly.
Expanded Basic Service 1
Subscribers: N.A.
Programming (via satellite): ABC Family Channel; AMC; Animal Planet; Arts & Entertainment; Bravo; Cartoon Network; CNBC; CNN; Comcast/Charter Sports Southeast (CSS); Comedy Central; Country Music TV; Court TV; Discovery Channel; Disney Channel; E! Entertainment Television;

ESPN; ESPN 2; Food Network; Fox News Channel; Fox Sports Net Ohio; FX; G4; Golf Channel; Hallmark Channel; Headline News; HGTV; History Channel; Home Shopping Network; INSP; Jewelry Television; Lifetime; MSNBC; MTV; National Geographic Channel; Nickelodeon; Oxygen; ShopNBC; SoapNet; Speed Channel; Spike TV; Style Network; Syfy; TBS Superstation; The Learning Channel; Toon Disney; Travel Channel; Trinity Broadcasting Network; Turner Classic Movies; Turner Network TV; TV Land; USA Network; Versus; VH1; WE tv.

Digital Basic Service
Subscribers: N.A.
Programming (via satellite): BBC America; Bio; Bloomberg Television; CMT Pure Country; Discovery en Espanol; Discovery Health Channel; Discovery Home Channel; Discovery Kids Channel; Discovery Military Channel; Discovery Times Channel; Do-It-Yourself; ESPN Classic Sports; ESPNews; FitTV; Fox College Sports Atlantic; Fox College Sports Central; Fox College Sports Pacific; Fox Movie Channel; GAS; Great American Country; History Channel International; Independent Film Channel; Lifetime Movie Network; Lifetime Real Women; MTV Hits; MTV Jams; MTV Tres; MTV2; Music Choice; Nick Jr.; Nick Too; NickToons TV; Science Channel; VH1 Classic; VH1 Soul.

Digital Pay Service 1
Pay Units: N.A.
Programming (via satellite): Cinemax (multiplexed); Encore (multiplexed); Flix; HBO (multiplexed); Showtime (multiplexed); Starz (multiplexed); The Movie Channel (multiplexed).

Video-On-Demand: No

Pay-Per-View
iN DEMAND (delivered digitally); Special events (delivered digitally); Movies (delivered digitally); Ten Clips (delivered digitally); Ten Blue (delivered digitally); Ten Blox (delivered digitally).

Internet Service
Operational: No.

Telephone Service
None

Miles of Plant: 154.0 (coaxial); None (fiber optic). Homes passed: 3,698. Total homes in franchised area: 2,902.
General Manager: Mark Bookout. Technical Operations Manager: Lynn McMahan.
Ownership: NewWave Communications (MSO).

BULLSKIN CREEK—Formerly served by Bullskin Cable TV. No longer in operation. ICA: KY0206.

BURKESVILLE—Mediacom, 90 Main St, Benton, KY 42025-1132. Phones: 417-875-5560 (Springfield regional office); 270-527-9939. Fax: 270-527-0813. Web Site: http://www.mediacomcable.com. Also serves Cumberland County (portions) & Marrowbone. ICA: KY0116.
TV Market Ranking: Below 100 (Cumberland County (portions), Marrowbone); Outside TV Markets (BURKESVILLE, Cumberland County (portions)). Franchise award date: N.A. Franchise expiration date: N.A. Began: September 1, 1961.
Channel capacity: N.A. Channels available but not in use: N.A.

Basic Service
Subscribers: 1,098.
Programming (received off-air): WAVE (NBC) Louisville; WBKO (ABC, CW) Bowling Green; WDRB (FOX) Louisville; WKSO-TV (PBS) Somerset; WKYU-TV (PBS) Bowling Green; WLKY-TV (CBS) Louisville; WNKY (CBS, NBC) Bowling Green; WSMV-TV (NBC, TMO) Nashville; WTVF (CBS) Nashville; allband FM.
Programming (via satellite): TV Guide Network; WGN America.
Fee: $36.95 installation; $18.49 monthly.

Digital Basic Service
Subscribers: N.A.
Programming (via satellite): BBC America; Bio; Bloomberg Television; Discovery Digital Networks; DMX Music; Fox Movie Channel; Fox Soccer; Fuse; G4; GAS; Golf Channel; GSN; History Channel International; Independent Film Channel; Lifetime Movie Network; Lime; MTV Networks Digital Suite; Nick Jr.; NickToons TV; Turner Classic Movies; Versus.

Digital Pay Service 1
Pay Units: N.A.
Programming (via satellite): Cinemax (multiplexed); Flix (multiplexed); HBO (multiplexed); Showtime (multiplexed); Starz (multiplexed); Sundance Channel (multiplexed); The Movie Channel (multiplexed).

Video-On-Demand: No

Pay-Per-View
Barker (delivered digitally); Mediacom PPV (delivered digitally); Playboy TV (delivered digitally); TEN Clips (delivered digitally); TEN (delivered digitally); TEN Blox (delivered digitally); Pleasure (delivered digitally); ESPN Gameplan (delivered digitally).

Internet Service
Operational: Yes, DSL only.
Broadband Service: Mediacom High Speed Internet.

Telephone Service
None

Miles of Plant: 53.0 (coaxial); None (fiber optic). Homes passed: 1,370.
Regional Vice President: Bill Copeland. General Manager: Dale Haney. Regional Technical Operations Director: Alan Freedman. Marketing Director: Will Kuebler. Technical Operations Manager: Jeff Brown. Chief Technician: Richard Hanning. Marketing Manager: Melanie Westerman.
City fee: 3% of gross.
Ownership: Mediacom LLC (MSO).

BURNSIDE—Charter Communications. Now served by SOMERSET, KY [KY0021]. ICA: KY0039.

CADIZ—Mediacom, 90 Main St, Benton, KY 42025-1132. Phones: 417-875-5560 (Springfield regional office); 270-527-9939. Fax: 270-527-0813. Web Site: http://www.mediacomcable.com. Also serves Trigg County. ICA: KY0079.
TV Market Ranking: 69 (Trigg County (portions)); Below 100 (Trigg County (portions)); Outside TV Markets (CADIZ, Trigg County (portions)). Franchise award date: August 1, 1977. Franchise expiration date: N.A. Began: January 1, 1980.
Channel capacity: N.A. Channels available but not in use: N.A.

Basic Service
Subscribers: 2,093.
Programming (received off-air): WEHT (ABC) Evansville; WKAG-CA Hopkinsville; WKMA-TV (PBS) Madisonville; WKRN-TV (ABC) Nashville; WNAB (CW) Nashville; WNPT (PBS) Nashville; WPSD-TV (NBC) Paducah; WSMV-TV (NBC, TMO) Nashville; WTVF (CBS) Nashville; WUXP-TV (MNT) Nashville; WZTV (FOX) Nashville.
Programming (via satellite): TV Guide Network; WGN America.
Fee: $36.95 installation; $19.13 monthly.

Expanded Basic Service 1
Subscribers: N.A.
Programming (via satellite): ABC Family Channel; AMC; Animal Planet; Arts & Entertainment; BET Networks; Bravo; Cartoon Network; CNBC; CNN; Comcast Sports Net Southeast; Comedy Central; Country Music TV; C-SPAN; Discovery Channel; Disney Channel; E! Entertainment Television; ESPN; ESPN 2; FitTV; Food Network; Fox News Channel; FX; GRTV Network; Hallmark Channel; Headline News; HGTV; History Channel; Home Shopping Network; INSP; Lifetime; MSNBC; MTV; Nickelodeon; Outdoor Channel; QVC; SoapNet; Speed Channel; Spike TV; Syfy; TBS Superstation; The Learning Channel; Travel Channel; Trinity Broadcasting Network; Turner Network TV; TV Land; Univision; USA Network; VH1; WE tv; Weather Channel.

Digital Basic Service
Subscribers: N.A.
Programming (via satellite): BBC America; Bio; Bloomberg Television; Discovery Digital Networks; Fox Movie Channel; Fox Soccer; Fuse; G4; GAS; Golf Channel; GSN; History Channel International; Independent Film Channel; Lifetime Movie Network; Lime; MTV Networks Digital Suite; Music Choice; National Geographic Channel; Nick Jr.; NickToons TV; Style Network; Turner Classic Movies; Versus.

Digital Pay Service 1
Pay Units: N.A.
Programming (via satellite): Cinemax (multiplexed); Encore (multiplexed); Flix (multiplexed); HBO (multiplexed); Showtime (multiplexed); Starz (multiplexed); Sundance Channel (multiplexed); The Movie Channel (multiplexed).

Video-On-Demand: No

Pay-Per-View
Barker (delivered digitally); Mediacom PPV (delivered digitally); Playboy TV (delivered digitally); TEN Clips (delivered digitally); TEN Blox (delivered digitally).

Internet Service
Operational: Yes.
Broadband Service: Mediacom High Speed Internet.

Telephone Service
Digital: Operational

Miles of Plant: 85.0 (coaxial); None (fiber optic). Homes passed: 2,200.
Regional Vice President: Bill Copeland. General Manager: Dale Haney. Regional Technical Operations Director: Alan Freedman. Technical Operations Manager: Jeff Brown. Marketing Director: Will Kuebler. Marketing Manager: Melanie Westerman.
City fee: 3% of basic.
Ownership: Mediacom LLC (MSO).

CALLOWAY COUNTY—Mediacom, 90 Main St, Benton, KY 42025-1132. Phones: 417-875-5560 (Springfield regional office); 270-527-9939. Fax: 270-527-0813. Web Site: http://www.mediacomcable.com. Also serves Almo, Dexter & Kirksey. ICA: KY0323.
TV Market Ranking: 69 (Almo, CALLOWAY COUNTY (portions), Dexter, Kirksey); Below 100 (CALLOWAY COUNTY (portions)); Outside TV Markets (CALLOWAY COUNTY (portions)).
Channel capacity: N.A. Channels available but not in use: N.A.

Basic Service
Subscribers: N.A.
Programming (received off-air): KBSI (FOX) Cape Girardeau; KFVS-TV (CBS, CW) Cape Girardeau; WDKA (MNT) Paducah; WKMU (PBS) Murray; WPSD-TV (NBC) Paducah; WQTV-LP (CW) Murray; WSIL-TV (ABC) Harrisburg; WTCT (IND) Marion.
Programming (via satellite): TV Guide Network.

Expanded Basic Service 1
Subscribers: N.A.
Programming (via satellite): ABC Family Channel; AMC; Animal Planet; Arts & Entertainment; Bravo; Cartoon Network; CNBC; CNN; Comcast Sports Net Southeast; Comedy Central; Country Music TV; C-SPAN; Discovery Channel; Disney Channel; E! Entertainment Television; ESPN; ESPN 2; FitTV; Food Network; Fox News Channel; FX; Golf Channel; GRTV Network; Hallmark Channel; Headline News; HGTV; History Channel; Home Shopping Network; INSP; Lifetime; MSNBC; MTV; Nickelodeon; Outdoor Channel; QVC; SoapNet; Speed Channel; Spike TV; Syfy; TBS Superstation; The Learning Channel; Travel Channel; Trinity Broadcasting Network; Turner Network TV; TV Land; Univision; USA Network; VH1; WE tv; Weather Channel.

Digital Basic Service
Subscribers: N.A.
Programming (via satellite): BBC America; Bio; Bloomberg Television; Discovery Health Channel; Discovery Home Channel; Discovery Kids Channel; Discovery Times Channel; DMX Music; Fox Movie Channel; Fox Soccer; Fuse; G4; GAS; Golf Channel; GSN; History Channel International; Independent Film Channel; Lifetime Movie Network; MTV Networks Digital Suite; National Geographic Channel; Nick Jr.; NickToons TV; Science Television; Style Network; Turner Classic Movies; Versus.

Digital Pay Service 1
Pay Units: N.A.
Programming (via satellite): Cinemax (multiplexed); Encore; Flix; HBO (multiplexed); Showtime (multiplexed); Starz; Sundance Channel; The Movie Channel (multiplexed).

Video-On-Demand: No

Internet Service
Operational: Yes.
Broadband Service: Mediacom High Speed Internet.

Telephone Service
Digital: Operational

Regional Vice President: Bill Copeland. General Manager: Dale Haney. Regional Technical Operations Director: Alan Freedman. Technical Operations Manager: Jeff Brown. Marketing Director: Will Kuebler. Marketing Manager: Melanie Westerman.
Ownership: Mediacom LLC (MSO).

CALVERT CITY—Charter Communications. Now served by MAYFIELD, KY [KY0037]. ICA: KY0117.

CAMPBELLSVILLE—Comcast Cablevision of the South. Now served by ELIZABETHTOWN, KY [KY0012]. ICA: KY0029.

CAMPTON—Windjammer Cable, 4400 PGA Blvd, Ste 902, Palm Beach Gardens, FL 33410. Phones: 877-450-5558; 561-775-1208. Fax: 561-775-7811. Web Site: http://www.windjammercable.com. Also serves Hazel Green, Landsaw, Menifee County (unincorporated areas), Morgan County & Wolfe County (unincorporated areas). ICA: KY0249.
TV Market Ranking: Below 100 (CAMPTON (portions), Hazel Green, Landsaw, Menifee County (unincorporated areas), Morgan

County, Wolfe County (unincorporated areas)). Franchise award date: N.A. Franchise expiration date: N.A. Began: January 1, 1987.

Channel capacity: 36 (not 2-way capable). Channels available but not in use: 3.

Basic Service

Subscribers: 939.

Programming (received off-air): WDKY-TV (FOX) Danville; WKMR (PBS) Morehead; WKYT-TV (CBS, CW) Lexington; WLEX-TV (NBC) Lexington; WLJC-TV (TBN) Beattyville; WTVQ-DT (ABC) Lexington; WUPX-TV (ION) Morehead; WYMT-TV (CBS, CW) Hazard.

Programming (via satellite): C-SPAN; QVC; TBS Superstation; WGN America.

Current originations: Public Access.

Fee: $39.95 installation; $16.91 monthly.

Expanded Basic Service 1

Subscribers: 792.

Programming (via satellite): ABC Family Channel; AMC; Arts & Entertainment; CNN; Country Music TV; Discovery Channel; Disney Channel; E! Entertainment Television; ESPN; ESPN 2; FX; Headline News; Lifetime; Nickelodeon; Spike TV; Syfy; The Learning Channel; Turner Network TV; USA Network; VH1; Weather Channel.

Fee: $28.05 monthly.

Digital Basic Service

Subscribers: N.A.

Programming (via satellite): BBC America; Bio; Black Family Channel; Bloomberg Television; Bravo; Discovery Digital Networks; ESPN Classic Sports; ESPNews; FitTV; Fox Movie Channel; Fox Soccer; Fuse; G4; GAS; Golf Channel; Great American Country; GSN; Halogen Network; HGTV; History Channel; History Channel International; Independent Film Channel; Lifetime Movie Network; MTV2; National Geographic Channel; Nick Jr.; NickToons TV; Outdoor Channel; Speed Channel; Style Network; The Word Network; Toon Disney; Trinity Broadcasting Network; Turner Classic Movies; Versus; VH1 Classic; VH1 Country; WE tv.

Fee: $56.91 monthly.

Digital Pay Service 1

Pay Units: N.A.

Programming (via satellite): Cinemax (multiplexed); Encore (multiplexed); HBO (multiplexed); Showtime (multiplexed); Starz (multiplexed); The Movie Channel (multiplexed).

Fee: $15.95 monthly (each).

Video-On-Demand: No

Pay-Per-View

HITS 1 (delivered digitally); HITS 2 (delivered digitally); HITS 3 (delivered digitally); HITS 4 (delivered digitally); Playboy TV (delivered digitally); Fresh (delivered digitally).

Internet Service

Operational: No.

Telephone Service

None

Miles of Plant: 72.0 (coaxial); None (fiber optic). Homes passed: 1,237.

General Manager: Timothy Evard. Operations Director: Belinda Graham. Engineering Director: Mike Earehart. Finance & Accounting Director: Cindy Johnson.

Ownership: Windjammer Communications LLC (MSO).

CANEYVILLE—Mediacom, 90 Main St, Benton, KY 42025-1132. Phones: 417-875-5560 (Springfield regional office); 270-527-9939. Fax: 270-527-0813. Web Site: http://www.mediacomcable.com. Also serves Big Clifty, Grayson County (portions), McDaniels, Millwood, Rough River Dam & St. Paul. ICA: KY0291.

TV Market Ranking: Below 100 (CANEYVILLE, Grayson County (portions), Millwood); Outside TV Markets (Big Clifty, McDaniels, Rough River Dam, St. Paul). Franchise award date: September 20, 1988. Franchise expiration date: N.A. Began: January 1, 1988.

Channel capacity: N.A. Channels available but not in use: N.A.

Basic Service

Subscribers: 1,077.

Programming (received off-air): WAVE (NBC) Louisville; WBKI-CA Louisville; WBKO (ABC, CW) Bowling Green; WDRB (FOX) Louisville; WHAS-TV (ABC) Louisville; WKYU-TV (PBS) Bowling Green; WKZT-TV (PBS) Elizabethtown; WMYO (MNT) Salem.

Fee: $29.95 installation; $24.95 monthly; $3.95 converter.

Expanded Basic Service 1

Subscribers: N.A.

Programming (via satellite): ABC Family Channel; AMC; Animal Planet; Arts & Entertainment; Bravo; Cartoon Network; CNBC; CNN; Comcast Sports Net Southeast; Comedy Central; Country Music TV; C-SPAN; Discovery Channel; Disney Channel; E! Entertainment Television; ESPN; ESPN 2; Food Network; Fox News Channel; FX; Great American Country; Hallmark Channel; Headline News; HGTV; History Channel; INSP; Lifetime; MSNBC; MTV; National Geographic Channel; Nickelodeon; Outdoor Channel; QVC; ShopNBC; SoapNet; Speed Channel; Spike TV; Syfy; TBS Superstation; The Learning Channel; Travel Channel; Trinity Broadcasting Network; truTV; Turner Classic Movies; Turner Network TV; TV Land; USA Network; VH1; WE tv; Weather Channel; WGN America.

Digital Basic Service

Subscribers: N.A.

Programming (via satellite): AmericanLife TV Network; BBC America; Bio; Bloomberg News Radio; Discovery Health Channel; Discovery Home Channel; Discovery Kids Channel; Discovery Times Channel; DMX Music; ESPN Classic Sports; ESPNews; FitTV; Fox Movie Channel; Fox Soccer; Fuse; G4; GAS; Golf Channel; GSN; History Channel International; Independent Film Channel; Lifetime Movie Network; MTV Networks Digital Suite; National Geographic Channel; Nick Jr.; NickToons TV; Outdoor Channel; Science Television; Style Network; Turner Classic Movies; Versus.

Digital Pay Service 1

Pay Units: N.A.

Programming (via satellite): Cinemax (multiplexed); Encore (multiplexed); HBO (multiplexed); Showtime (multiplexed); Starz (multiplexed); The Movie Channel (multiplexed).

Video-On-Demand: No

Internet Service

Operational: Yes.

Broadband Service: Mediacom High Speed Internet.

Telephone Service

None

Miles of Plant: 89.0 (coaxial); None (fiber optic). Homes passed: 2,054.

Regional Vice President: Bill Copeland. General Manager: Dale Haney. Regional Technical Operations Director: Alan Freedman. Technical Operations Manager: Jeff Brown. Marketing Director: Will Kuebler. Marketing Manager: Melanie Westerman.

Ownership: Mediacom LLC (MSO).

CARLISLE—Now served by MOUNT STERLING, KY [KY0046]. ICA: KY0208.

CASEY COUNTY (southwestern portion)—Mediacom, 90 Main St, Benton, KY 42025-1132. Phones: 417-875-5560 (Springfield regional office); 270-527-9939. Fax: 270-527-0813. Web Site: http://www.mediacomcable.com. ICA: KY0144.

TV Market Ranking: Below 100 (CASEY COUNTY (SOUTHWESTERN PORTION)). Franchise award date: April 17, 1989. Franchise expiration date: N.A. Began: October 1, 1990.

Channel capacity: N.A. Channels available but not in use: N.A.

Basic Service

Subscribers: 351.

Programming (received off-air): WBKI-TV (CW) Campbellsville; WDKY-TV (FOX) Danville; WDRB (FOX) Louisville; WKSO-TV (PBS) Somerset; WKYT-TV (CBS, CW) Lexington; WLEX-TV (NBC) Lexington; WLKY-TV (CBS) Louisville; WTVQ-DT (ABC) Lexington.

Programming (via satellite): ABC Family Channel; CNN; Country Music TV; Discovery Channel; Disney Channel; ESPN; Fox News Channel; History Channel; Lifetime; MTV; Nickelodeon; OpenTV; QVC; Spike TV; Syfy; TBS Superstation; Trinity Broadcasting Network; Turner Network TV; USA Network; Weather Channel; WGN America.

Fee: $29.95 installation; $24.95 monthly; $3.95 converter.

Pay Service 1

Pay Units: 54.

Programming (via satellite): HBO.

Fee: $10.00 monthly.

Pay Service 2

Pay Units: N.A.

Programming (via satellite): Cinemax; Encore; Starz.

Video-On-Demand: No

Internet Service

Operational: No.

Telephone Service

None

Miles of Plant: 40.0 (coaxial); None (fiber optic). Additional miles planned: 4.0 (coaxial). Homes passed: 587. Total homes in franchised area: 600.

Regional Vice President: Bill Copeland. General Manager: Dale Haney. Regional Technical Operations Director: Alan Freedman. Technical Operations Manager: Jeff Brown. Marketing Director: Will Kuebler. Marketing Manager: Melanie Westerman.

Ownership: Mediacom LLC (MSO).

CLAY—Now served by DIXON, KY [KY0218]. ICA: KY0133.

CLINTON COUNTY—Mediacom. Now served by TOMPKINSVILLE, KY [KY0092]. ICA: KY0212.

CLOVER BOTTOM—McKee TV Enterprises Inc. Now served by McKEE, KY [KY0113]. ICA: KY0179.

CLOVERPORT—Windjammer Cable, 4400 PGA Blvd, Ste 902, Palm Beach Gardens, FL 33410. Phones: 877-450-5558; 561-775-1208. Fax: 561-775-7811. Web Site: http://www.windjammercable.com. Also serves Breckinridge County (portions). ICA: KY0121.

TV Market Ranking: Outside TV Markets (Breckinridge County (portions), CLOVERPORT). Franchise award date: December 17, 1986. Franchise expiration date: N.A. Began: June 1, 1981.

Channel capacity: N.A. Channels available but not in use: N.A.

Basic Service

Subscribers: N.A. Included in Owensboro

Programming (received off-air): WAVE (NBC) Louisville; WDRB (FOX) Louisville; WEHT (ABC) Evansville; WFIE (NBC) Evansville; WHAS-TV (ABC) Louisville; WKZT-TV (PBS) Elizabethtown; WLKY-TV (CBS) Louisville; WNIN (PBS) Evansville; WTVW (FOX) Evansville.

Programming (via satellite): QVC; TBS Superstation; WGN America.

Current originations: Government Access; Educational Access; Public Access.

Fee: $39.95 installation; $24.52 monthly; $1.50 converter.

Expanded Basic Service 1

Subscribers: N.A.

Programming (via satellite): ABC Family Channel; AMC; CNN; Country Music TV; Discovery Channel; ESPN; MTV; Nickelodeon; Spike TV; Turner Network TV; USA Network.

Fee: $15.34 monthly.

Pay Service 1

Pay Units: 56.

Programming (via satellite): HBO.

Fee: $15.95 monthly.

Pay Service 2

Pay Units: 59.

Programming (via satellite): The Movie Channel.

Fee: $15.95 monthly.

Video-On-Demand: No

Internet Service

Operational: No.

Telephone Service

None

Miles of Plant: 15.0 (coaxial); None (fiber optic). Total homes in franchised area: 600. Homes passed included in Owensboro

General Manager: Timothy Evard. Operations Director: Belinda Graham. Engineering Director: Mike Earehart. Finance & Accounting Director: Cindy Johnson.

City fee: 3% of basic.

Ownership: Windjammer Communications LLC (MSO).

COLUMBIA—Duo County Telecom, PO Box 80, 2150 N Main St, Jamestown, KY 42629. Phones: 270-378-4141; 270-343-3131. Fax: 270-343-6500. Web Site: http://www.duocounty.com. Also serves Adair County (portions). ICA: KY0213.

TV Market Ranking: Below 100 (Adair County (portions), COLUMBIA). Franchise award date: August 5, 1996. Franchise expiration date: N.A. Began: May 1, 1960.

Channel capacity: 54 (not 2-way capable). Channels available but not in use: N.A.

Basic Service

Subscribers: 1,700.

Programming (received off-air): WBKI-TV (CW) Campbellsville; WBKO (ABC, CW) Bowling Green; WDRB (FOX) Louisville; WHAS-TV (ABC) Louisville; WKSO-TV (PBS) Somerset; WKYT-TV (CBS, CW) Lexington; WLKY-TV (CBS) Louisville; WNKY (CBS, NBC) Bowling Green.

Programming (via satellite): QVC; Trinity Broadcasting Network; WGN America.

Current originations: Public Access.

Fee: $20.00 installation; $22.90 monthly.

Expanded Basic Service 1

Subscribers: 1,425.

Programming (via satellite): ABC Family Channel; AMC; Animal Planet; Arts & Entertainment; BET Networks; Bravo; Cartoon Network; CNBC; CNN; Comedy Central; Country Music TV; C-SPAN; Discovery Channel; Disney Channel; E! Entertainment Television; ESPN; ESPN 2; Fox News Channel; FX; G4; Golf Channel; Gospel Music TV; Headline News; HGTV; History Channel; Home Shopping Network; Lifetime; MSNBC; MTV; Nickelodeon; Oxygen; Speed Channel; Spike TV; Style Network; Syfy; TBS Superstation; The Learning Channel; Turner Classic Movies; Turner Network TV; TV Land; USA Network; VH1; Weather Channel.

Fee: $21.05 monthly.

Digital Basic Service

Subscribers: N.A.

Programming (via satellite): BBC America; Bio; Bloomberg Television; Discovery Digital Networks; ESPN Classic Sports; Flix; Fox Movie Channel; Fuse; GAS; GSN; History Channel International; Independent Film Channel; Lifetime Movie Network; Lifetime Real Women; MTV Networks Digital Suite; Music Choice; Nick Jr.; Nick Too; NickToons TV; Showtime (multiplexed); SoapNet; Sundance Channel; The Movie Channel (multiplexed); Toon Disney; TV Guide Interactive Inc.; WE tv.

Fee: $7.95 monthly (family tier or movie tier).

Digital Pay Service 1

Pay Units: N.A.

Programming (via satellite): Cinemax (multiplexed); Encore; HBO (multiplexed); Starz (multiplexed).

Fee: $12.95 monthly (Cinemax, Showtime/TMC/Flix/Sundance or Starz/Encore), $13.95 monthly (HBO).

Video-On-Demand: Planned

Pay-Per-View

iN DEMAND (delivered digitally); Playboy TV (delivered digitally); Fresh (delivered digitally); Shorteez (delivered digitally).

Internet Service

Operational: Yes.

Fee: $24.95 monthly.

Telephone Service

None

Miles of Plant: 102.0 (coaxial); None (fiber optic). Homes passed: 6,000.

Vice President, Operations: Mark Henry. Marketing Director: Eric West. Plant Supervisor: Mike Bradshaw.

Ownership: Duo County Telephone Cooperative (MSO).

CORBIN—NewWave Communications, 5026 S Hwy 27, Somerset, KY 42501. Phone: 606-678-9215. Fax: 606-679-7111. Web Site: http://www.newwavecom.com. Also serves Knox County, Laurel County, Lily & Whitley County. ICA: KY0030.

TV Market Ranking: Below 100 (CORBIN, Knox County, Laurel County (portions), Lily, Whitley County); Outside TV Markets (Laurel County (portions)). Franchise award date: August 3, 1988. Franchise expiration date: N.A. Began: March 1, 1956.

Channel capacity: N.A. Channels available but not in use: N.A.

Basic Service

Subscribers: 7,916.

Programming (received off-air): WAGV (IND) Harlan; WATE-TV (ABC) Knoxville; WBIR-TV (NBC) Knoxville; WBXX-TV (CW) Crossville; WDKY-TV (FOX) Danville; WKSO-TV (PBS) Somerset; WKYT-TV (CBS, CW) Lexington; WLEX-TV (NBC) Lexington; WLJC-TV (TBN) Beattyville; WTVQ-DT (ABC) Lexington; WUPX-TV (ION) Morehead; WVTN-LP Corbin; WYMT-TV (CBS, CW) Hazard; 1 FM.

Programming (via satellite): Home Shopping Network; QVC; ShopNBC; TV Guide Network; WGN America.

Current originations: Government Access; Educational Access; Public Access.

Fee: $33.75 installation; $18.69 monthly.

Expanded Basic Service 1

Subscribers: 7,050.

Programming (via satellite): ABC Family Channel; AMC; Animal Planet; Arts & Entertainment; Bravo; Cartoon Network; CNBC; CNN; Comcast/Charter Sports Southeast (CSS); Comedy Central; Country Music TV; C-SPAN; C-SPAN 2; Discovery Channel; Disney Channel; E! Entertainment Television; ESPN; ESPN 2; FitTV; Food Network; Fox News Channel; Fox Sports Net Ohio; FX; Golf Channel; Hallmark Channel; Headline News; HGTV; History Channel; INSP; Lifetime; MSNBC; MTV; National Geographic Channel; Nickelodeon; Oxygen; SoapNet; Speed Channel; Spike TV; Style Network; Syfy; TBS Superstation; The Learning Channel; Toon Disney; Travel Channel; Trinity Broadcasting Network; truTV; Turner Classic Movies; Turner Network TV; TV Land; USA Network; Versus; VH1; WE tv; Weather Channel.

Fee: $1.64 monthly.

Digital Basic Service

Subscribers: N.A.

Programming (via satellite): BBC America; Bio; Bloomberg Television; Discovery Digital Networks; Do-It-Yourself; ESPN Classic Sports; ESPNews; Fox College Sports Atlantic; Fox College Sports Central; Fox College Sports Pacific; Fox Movie Channel; Fox Soccer; Fuel TV; Fuse; GAS; Great American Country; History Channel International; Independent Film Channel; Jewelry Television; Lifetime Movie Network; Lifetime Real Women; MTV Networks Digital Suite; Music Choice; NFL Network; Nick Jr.; Nick Too; NickToons TV; Sundance Channel; TV Guide Interactive Inc.

Digital Pay Service 1

Pay Units: N.A.

Programming (via satellite): Cinemax (multiplexed); Encore (multiplexed); Flix; HBO (multiplexed); Showtime (multiplexed); Starz (multiplexed); The Movie Channel (multiplexed).

Video-On-Demand: No

Pay-Per-View

iN DEMAND (delivered digitally); NHL Center Ice (delivered digitally); MLB Extra Innings (delivered digitally); Playboy TV (delivered digitally); Fresh (delivered digitally); Shorteez (delivered digitally).

Internet Service

Operational: Yes.

Fee: $40.00 installation; $23.95 monthly.

Telephone Service

None

Miles of Plant: 197.0 (coaxial); None (fiber optic). Homes passed: 9,285.

General Manager: Mark Bookout. Technical Operations Manager: Lynn McMahan.

Ownership: NewWave Communications (MSO).

CORINTH—Windjammer Cable, 4400 PGA Blvd, Ste 902, Palm Beach Gardens, FL 33410. Phones: 877-450-5558; 561-775-1208. Fax: 561-775-7811. Web Site: http://www.windjammercable.com. ICA: KY0307.

TV Market Ranking: Below 100 (CORINTH). Franchise award date: N.A. Franchise expiration date: N.A. Began: N.A.

Channel capacity: 36 (not 2-way capable). Channels available but not in use: 11.

Basic Service

Subscribers: 68.

Programming (received off-air): WCPO-TV (ABC) Cincinnati; WDKY-TV (FOX) Danville; WKON (PBS) Owenton; WKRC-TV (CBS, CW) Cincinnati; WKYT-TV (CBS, CW) Lexington; WLEX-TV (NBC) Lexington; WLWT (NBC) Cincinnati; WSTR-TV (MNT) Cincinnati; WTVQ-DT (ABC) Lexington; WXIX-TV (FOX) Newport.

Programming (via satellite): ABC Family Channel; AMC; Arts & Entertainment; CNN; Discovery Channel; Discovery Health Channel; Disney Channel; ESPN; Spike TV; TBS Superstation; The Learning Channel; Trinity Broadcasting Network; Turner Network TV; USA Network; WGN America.

Fee: $39.95 installation; $35.65 monthly.

Digital Basic Service

Subscribers: N.A.

Programming (via satellite): BBC America; Bloomberg Television; Discovery Digital Networks; DMX Music; ESPN Classic Sports; ESPNews; FitTV; Fox Movie Channel; G4; Golf Channel; GSN; Halogen Network; Nick Jr.; NickToons TV; Outdoor Channel; Trinity Broadcasting Network; Versus; WE tv.

Fee: $8.45 monthly.

Digital Pay Service 1

Pay Units: N.A.

Programming (via satellite): Cinemax (multiplexed); Encore; HBO (multiplexed); Showtime (multiplexed); The Movie Channel (multiplexed).

Fee: $15.95 monthly (each).

Video-On-Demand: No

Pay-Per-View

Fresh (delivered digitally); Playboy TV (delivered digitally).

Internet Service

Operational: No.

Homes passed: 395.

Ownership: Windjammer Communications LLC (MSO).

CORYDON—Now served by OWENSBORO, KY [KY0004]. ICA: KY0214.

COVINGTON—Insight Communications, 7906 Dixie Hwy, Florence, KY 41042. Phones: 888-735-0300; 859-431-0300. Fax: 859-431-3464. Web Site: http://www.myinsight.com. Also serves Alexandria, Bellevue, Boone County, Bromley, Burlington, Butler, Camp Springs, Campbell County, Claryville, Cold Spring, Crescent Park, Crescent Springs, Crestview Hills, Crittenden, Dry Ridge, Edgewood, Elsmere, Erlanger, Falmouth, Florence, Fort Mitchell, Fort Thomas, Fort Wright, Grant County, Hebron, Highland Heights, Independence, Kenton County, Kenton Vale, Lakeside Park, Latonia Lakes, Ludlow, Melbourne, Morning View, Newport, Park Hills, Ryland Heights, Silver Grove, Southgate, Taylor Mill, Union, Villa Hills, Visalia, Walton, Wilder & Woodlawn. ICA: KY0002.

TV Market Ranking: 17 (Alexandria, Bellevue, Boone County, Bromley, Burlington, Butler, Camp Springs, Campbell County, Claryville, Cold Spring, COVINGTON, Crescent Park, Crescent Springs, Crestview Hills, Crittenden, Dry Ridge, Edgewood, Elsmere, Erlanger, Falmouth, Florence, Fort Mitchell, Fort Thomas, Fort Wright, Grant County (portions), Hebron, Highland Heights, Independence, Kenton County, Kenton Vale, Lakeside Park, Latonia Lakes, Ludlow, Melbourne, Morning View, Newport, Park Hills, Ryland Heights, Silver Grove, Southgate, Taylor Mill, Union, Villa Hills, Visalia, Walton, Wilder, Woodlawn); Below 100 (Grant County (portions)). Franchise award date: December 1, 1980. Franchise expiration date: N.A. Began: January 1, 1981.

Channel capacity: 82 (operating 2-way). Channels available but not in use: 7.

Basic Service

Subscribers: 81,000 Includes Warsaw.

Programming (received off-air): WCET (PBS) Cincinnati; WCPO-TV (ABC) Cincinnati; WCVN-TV (PBS) Covington; WKRC-TV (CBS, CW) Cincinnati; WLWT (NBC) Cincinnati; WOTH-CA (IND) Cincinnati; WPTO (PBS) Oxford; WSTR-TV (MNT) Cincinnati; WXIX-TV (FOX) Newport.

Programming (via satellite): C-SPAN; C-SPAN 2; QVC; TV Guide Network; WGN America.

Current originations: Leased Access; Religious Access; Government Access; Educational Access; Public Access.

Fee: $35.00 installation; $15.00 monthly.

Expanded Basic Service 1

Subscribers: 68,250.

Programming (via satellite): ABC Family Channel; AMC; Animal Planet; Arts & Entertainment; BET Networks; Big Ten Network; Cartoon Network; CNBC; CNN; Comedy Central; Country Music TV; Discovery Channel; Disney Channel; E! Entertainment Television; ESPN; ESPN 2; Eternal Word TV Network; Food Network; Fox News Channel; Fox Sports Net Ohio; FX; Golf Channel; Hallmark Channel; Headline News; HGTV; History Channel; Home Shopping Network; ION Television; Lifetime; MSNBC; MTV; Nickelodeon; Spike TV; Syfy; TBS Superstation; The Learning Channel; Travel Channel; truTV; Turner Network TV; TV Land; Univision; USA Network; VH1; Weather Channel; Weatherscan.

Fee: $40.00 monthly.

Digital Basic Service

Subscribers: 55,000 Includes Warsaw.

Programming (via satellite): AmericanLife TV Network; BBC America; Bio; Bloomberg Television; Bravo; Discovery Digital Networks; DMX Music; Encore (multiplexed); ESPN Classic Sports; ESPNews; Fox Movie Channel; Fox Sports World; Fuse; G4; GAS; GSN; Halogen Network; History Channel International; Independent Film Channel; Lifetime Movie Network; MTV Networks Digital Suite; National Geographic Channel; Nick Jr.; Nick Too; Outdoor Channel; Ovation; Speed Channel; Style Network; Sundance Channel; Toon Disney; Trinity Broadcasting Network; Turner Classic Movies; Versus; WE tv.

Fee: $17.00 monthly.

Digital Pay Service 1
Pay Units: 7,053.
Programming (via satellite): Cinemax (multiplexed); Flix; HBO (multiplexed); Showtime (multiplexed); Starz (multiplexed); The Movie Channel (multiplexed).
Fee: $10.00 monthly (Cinemax or Starz), $13.00 monthly (HBO or Showtime/ TMC/Flix).
Video-On-Demand: Yes
Pay-Per-View
Addressable homes: 29,100.
Hot Choice (delivered digitally), Fee: $3.95, Addressable: Yes; iN DEMAND (delivered digitally); BET Action Pay-Per-View (delivered digitally); Shorteez (delivered digitally); Fresh (delivered digitally); Sports PPV (delivered digitally).
Internet Service
Operational: Yes.
Subscribers: 30,000.
Broadband Service: InsightBB.com.
Fee: $99.95 installation; $40.00 monthly; $10.00 modem lease; $140.00 modem purchase.
Telephone Service
Digital: Operational
Miles of Plant: 2,020.0 (coaxial); None (fiber optic). Homes passed: 165,000. Homes passed & miles of plant (coax & fiber combined) include Warsaw
President & Chief Operating Officer: Dinni Jain. Senior Vice President, Operations: John Hutton. District Vice President: Tim Klinefelter. Technical Operations Director: Bill Arnold. Marketing Coordinator: Maggie Woolf.
Ownership: Insight Communications Co. (MSO).

CRAB ORCHARD—Wilcop Cable TV. Now served by BRODHEAD, KY [KY0173]. ICA: KY0175.

CRITTENDEN—Insight Communications. Now served by COVINGTON, KY [KY0002]. ICA: KY0068.

CROMWELL—Windjammer Cable, 4400 PGA Blvd, Ste 902, Palm Beach Gardens, FL 33410. Phones: 877-450-5558; 561-775-1208. Fax: 561-775-7811. Web Site: http://www.windjammercable.com. ICA: KY0215.
TV Market Ranking: Below 100 (CROMWELL). Franchise award date: N.A. Franchise expiration date: N.A. Began: March 1, 1990.
Channel capacity: N.A. Channels available but not in use: N.A.
Basic Service
Subscribers: N.A. Included in Owensboro
Programming (received off-air): WBKO (ABC, CW) Bowling Green; WEHT (ABC) Evansville; WEVV-TV (CBS, MNT) Evansville; WFIE (NBC) Evansville; WKGB-TV (PBS) Bowling Green.
Programming (via satellite): ABC Family Channel; AMC; Arts & Entertainment; CNN; Country Music TV; Discovery Channel; ESPN; Showtime; TBS Superstation; Turner Network TV; USA Network; WGN America.
Fee: $39.95 installation; $24.10 monthly.
Pay Service 1
Pay Units: N.A.
Programming (via satellite): HBO; Showtime; The Movie Channel.
Fee: $15.95 monthly (each).
Video-On-Demand: No
Internet Service
Operational: No.
Telephone Service
None
Miles of Plant: 4.0 (coaxial); None (fiber optic). Homes passed included in Owensboro
Ownership: Windjammer Communications LLC (MSO).

CUMBERLAND—Access Cable Television Inc., 302 Enterprise Dr, Somerset, KY 42501. Phone: 606-677-2444. Fax: 606-677-2443. E-mail: cable@accesshsd.net. Also serves Blair, Harlan County & Hiram. ICA: KY0075.
TV Market Ranking: Below 100 (Blair, CUMBERLAND, Harlan County (portions), Hiram); Outside TV Markets (Harlan County (portions)). Franchise award date: N.A. Franchise expiration date: N.A. Began: N.A.
Channel capacity: 65 (operating 2-way). Channels available but not in use: None.
Basic Service
Subscribers: 982.
Programming (received off-air): WAGV (IND) Harlan; WATE-TV (ABC) Knoxville; WCYB-TV (CW, NBC) Bristol; WKHA (PBS) Hazard; WKPT-TV (ABC) Kingsport; WKYT-TV (CBS, CW) Lexington; WLEX-TV (NBC) Lexington; WTNZ (FOX) Knoxville; WTVQ-DT (ABC) Lexington; WVLT-TV (CBS, MNT) Knoxville; WYMT-TV (CBS, CW) Hazard; allband FM.
Programming (via satellite): AMC; Arts & Entertainment; Country Music TV; CW+; Discovery Channel; ESPN; ESPN 2; History Channel; Home Shopping Network; Lifetime; MTV; Nickelodeon; QVC; Syfy; TBS Superstation; Trinity Broadcasting Network; Turner Network TV; VH1; WGN America.
Current originations: Public Access.
Fee: $25.00 installation; $18.50 monthly; $3.00 converter; $15.00 additional installation.
Expanded Basic Service 1
Subscribers: 901.
Programming (via satellite): ABC Family Channel; Animal Planet; BET Networks; Cartoon Network; CNN; Disney Channel; Food Network; Fox News Channel; FX; Hallmark Channel; Headline News; HGTV; Outdoor Channel; Speed Channel; Spike TV; The Learning Channel; truTV; Turner Classic Movies; TV Land; USA Network; Weather Channel.
Fee: $9.50 monthly.
Pay Service 1
Pay Units: 58.
Programming (via satellite): Cinemax.
Fee: $15.00 installation; $11.95 monthly.
Pay Service 2
Pay Units: 58.
Programming (via satellite): HBO.
Fee: $15.00 installation; $11.95 monthly.
Video-On-Demand: No
Internet Service
Operational: Yes.
Telephone Service
Digital: Operational
Fee: $35.00 installation; $24.95 monthly
Miles of Plant: 48.0 (coaxial); None (fiber optic). Homes passed: 2,200.
President & Manager: Roy Baker.
Franchise fee: 5% of gross.
Ownership: Access Cable Television Inc. (MSO).

CUTSHIN—Craft Cable Service. Now served by HINDMAN, KY [KY0027]. ICA: KY0217.

CYNTHIANA—Time Warner Cable, 1615 Foxhaven Dr, Richmond, KY 40475. Phones: 859-626-4800; 859-624-9666. Fax: 859-624-0060. Web Site: http://www.timewarnercable.com. ICA: KY0051.

TV Market Ranking: Below 100 (CYNTHIANA). Franchise award date: N.A. Franchise expiration date: N.A. Began: March 13, 1972.
Channel capacity: N.A. Channels available but not in use: N.A.
Basic Service
Subscribers: 2,567.
Programming (received off-air): WCPO-TV (ABC) Cincinnati; WDKY-TV (FOX) Danville; WKLE (PBS) Lexington; WKRC-TV (CBS, CW) Cincinnati; WKYT-TV (CBS, CW) Lexington; WLEX-TV (NBC) Lexington; WTVQ-DT (ABC) Lexington; WUPX-TV (ION) Morehead; WXIX-TV (FOX) Newport.
Programming (via satellite): QVC; WGN America.
Fee: $39.95 installation; $20.35 monthly.
Expanded Basic Service 1
Subscribers: 2,355.
Programming (via satellite): ABC Family Channel; AMC; Animal Planet; Arts & Entertainment; BET Networks; Bravo; Cartoon Network; CNBC; CNN; Comedy Central; Country Music TV; C-SPAN; C-SPAN 2; Discovery Channel; Disney Channel; E! Entertainment Television; ESPN; ESPN 2; Eternal Word TV Network; Food Network; Fox News Channel; Fox Sports Net Ohio; FX; Headline News; HGTV; History Channel; Home Shopping Network; Lifetime; MSNBC; MTV; Nickelodeon; Product Information Network; ShopNBC; Spike TV; Syfy; TBS Superstation; The Learning Channel; Travel Channel; Trinity Broadcasting Network; truTV; Turner Network TV; TV Land; USA Network; VH1; Weather Channel.
Fee: $30.00 monthly.
Digital Basic Service
Subscribers: N.A.
Programming (via satellite): BBC America; Bloomberg Television; Canales N; CMT Pure Country; Discovery Digital Networks; Do-It-Yourself; ESPNews; Fox Movie Channel; Fox Soccer; Fuse; G4; GAS; GSN; Halogen Network; Lifetime Movie Network; MTV Networks Digital Suite; Music Choice; National Geographic Channel; Nick Jr.; NickToons TV; Speed Channel; Toon Disney; Turner Classic Movies; TV Guide Network; WE tv.
Fee: $6.00 monthly.
Digital Pay Service 1
Pay Units: N.A.
Programming (via satellite): Cinemax (multiplexed); Encore (multiplexed); Flix; HBO (multiplexed); Showtime (multiplexed); Starz (multiplexed); The Movie Channel (multiplexed).
Fee: $15.95 monthly (HBO, Cinemax, Showtime/TMC or Starz/Encore).
Video-On-Demand: No
Pay-Per-View
iN DEMAND (delivered digitally); Playboy TV (delivered digitally); Fresh (delivered digitally).
Internet Service
Operational: Yes.
Broadband Service: Road Runner.
Fee: $44.95 monthly.
Telephone Service
Digital: Planned
Miles of Plant: 55.0 (coaxial); None (fiber optic). Additional miles planned: 1.0 (coaxial). Homes passed: 3,846.
General Manager: Robert Trott. Technical Operations Manager: Dennis Lester. Marketing Director: Betrina Morse. Government & Public Affairs Manager: Carla Deaton. Office Manager: Laverne Farris.
Ownership: Time Warner Cable (MSO).

DANVILLE—Now served by HARRODSBURG, KY [KY0231]. ICA: KY0024.

DAWSON SPRINGS—Insight Communications, PO Box 190, 116 S Main St, Dawson Springs, KY 42408. Phone: 270-797-5061. Fax: 270-826-8242. Web Site: http://www.myinsight.com. Also serves Caldwell County, Hopkins County & St. Charles. ICA: KY0069.
TV Market Ranking: 69 (Caldwell County (portions)); 86 (Hopkins County (portions)); Below 100 (DAWSON SPRINGS, St. Charles, Caldwell County (portions), Hopkins County (portions)). Franchise award date: N.A. Franchise expiration date: N.A. Began: April 1, 1969.
Channel capacity: 42 (not 2-way capable). Channels available but not in use: N.A.
Basic Service
Subscribers: 1,854.
Programming (received off-air): WAZE-TV (CW) Madisonville; WEHT (ABC) Evansville; WEVV-TV (CBS, MNT) Evansville; WFIE (NBC) Evansville; WKAG-CA Hopkinsville; WKMA-TV (PBS) Madisonville; WNIN (PBS) Evansville; WPSD-TV (NBC) Paducah; WTVF (CBS) Nashville; WTVW (FOX) Evansville; allband FM.
Programming (via satellite): WGN America.
Fee: $35.00 installation; $13.02 monthly; $2.00 converter.
Expanded Basic Service 1
Subscribers: 1,655.
Programming (via satellite): ABC Family Channel; AMC; Cartoon Network; CNBC; CNN; C-SPAN; Discovery Channel; Disney Channel; ESPN; ESPN 2; Fox News Channel; FX; Headline News; Lifetime; MoviePlex; MTV; Nickelodeon; QVC; Spike TV; TBS Superstation; The Learning Channel; Turner Network TV; USA Network; Weather Channel.
Fee: $19.63 monthly.
Pay Service 1
Pay Units: 170.
Programming (via satellite): Cinemax; Encore; HBO; Showtime; Starz.
Fee: $10.00 monthly (Cinemax, HBO, Showtime, or Starz/Encore).
Video-On-Demand: No
Internet Service
Operational: No.
Telephone Service
None
Miles of Plant: 99.0 (coaxial); None (fiber optic). Homes passed: 2,444. Total homes in franchised area: 2,943.
President & Chief Operating Officer: Dinni Jain. Senior Vice President, Operations: John Hutton. District Vice President: Lanae

Juffer. Technical Operations Manager: Don Baumholser. Customer Service Manager: Kyle Hamilton.
City fee: 3% of gross.
Ownership: Insight Communications Co. (MSO).

DIXON—Time Warner Cable, 100 Industrial Dr, Owensboro, KY 42301-8711. Phones: 270-685-2991; 270-852-2000. Fax: 270-688-8228. Web Site: http://www.timewarnercable.com/westernky. Also serves Clay & Wheatcroft. ICA: KY0218.
TV Market Ranking: 86 (DIXON (VILLAGE)); Below 100 (Clay, Wheatcroft). Franchise award date: October 12, 1987. Franchise expiration date: N.A. Began: N.A.
Channel capacity: N.A. Channels available but not in use: N.A.

Basic Service
Subscribers: N.A. Included in Owensboro
Programming (received off-air): WAZE-TV (CW) Madisonville; WEHT (ABC) Evansville; WEVV-TV (CBS, MNT) Evansville; WFIE (NBC) Evansville; WKMA-TV (PBS) Madisonville; WNIN (PBS) Evansville; WPSD-TV (NBC) Paducah; WTVW (FOX) Evansville; WYYW-LP Evansville.
Programming (via satellite): ABC Family Channel; AMC; Animal Planet; Arts & Entertainment; Country Music TV; C-SPAN; Discovery Channel; E! Entertainment Television; ESPN; ESPN 2; Food Network; FX; Headline News; Home Shopping Network; Lifetime; MSNBC; MTV; Nickelodeon; QVC; ShopNBC; Spike TV; Syfy; The Learning Channel; Travel Channel; Trinity Broadcasting Network; truTV; Turner Network TV; TV Land; USA Network; VH1; Weather Channel; WGN America.
Current originations: Government Access; Educational Access; Public Access.
Fee: $39.95 installation; $38.06 monthly.

Expanded Basic Service 1
Subscribers: 623.
Programming (via satellite): CNN; Disney Channel; Fox News Channel; HGTV; History Channel; TBS Superstation.
Fee: $9.15 monthly.

Digital Basic Service
Subscribers: N.A.
Programming (via satellite): AmericanLife TV Network; BBC America; Bloomberg Television; Discovery Digital Networks; DMX Music; ESPN Classic Sports; ESPNews; Fox Movie Channel; Fox Sports World; G4; Golf Channel; GSN; Halogen Network; Music Choice; Nick Jr.; NickToons TV; Outdoor Channel; Versus; WE tv.
Fee: $12.95 monthly.

Digital Pay Service 1
Pay Units: N.A.
Programming (via satellite): Cinemax (multiplexed); Encore (multiplexed); HBO (multiplexed); Showtime (multiplexed); Starz (multiplexed); The Movie Channel (multiplexed).
Fee: $15.00 monthly (TV Asia, TV5, RAI, ART, CCTV, Filipino, TV Russia, or TV Japan), $15.95 monthly (HBO, Cinemax, Showtime, or Starz).

Video-On-Demand: No

Pay-Per-View
iN DEMAND (delivered digitally); Playboy TV (delivered digitally); Fresh (delivered digitally).

Internet Service
Operational: Yes.
Broadband Service: Road Runner.
Fee: $44.95 monthly.

Telephone Service
None
Miles of Plant: 19.0 (coaxial); None (fiber optic). Total homes in franchised area: 1,331. Homes passed included in Owensboro
General Manager: Chris Poynter. Marketing Manager: Doug Rodgers. Technical Operations Director: Don Collins.
Ownership: Time Warner Cable (MSO).

DUNMOR—Windjammer Cable, 4400 PGA Blvd, Ste 902, Palm Beach Gardens, FL 33410. Phones: 877-450-5558; 561-775-1208. Fax: 561-775-7811. Web Site: http://www.windjammercable.com. Also serves Lake Malone, Lewisburg, Muhlenberg County (southern portion) & Penrod. ICA: KY0248.
TV Market Ranking: Below 100 (DUNMOR, Lake Malone, Lewisburg, Muhlenberg County (southern portion), Penrod). Franchise award date: N.A. Franchise expiration date: N.A. Began: N.A.
Channel capacity: N.A. Channels available but not in use: N.A.

Basic Service
Subscribers: N.A. Included in Owensboro
Programming (received off-air): WBKO (ABC, CW) Bowling Green; WEHT (ABC) Evansville; WFIE (NBC) Evansville; WKMA-TV (PBS) Madisonville; WSMV-TV (NBC, TMO) Nashville; WTVF (CBS) Nashville; WZTV (FOX) Nashville.
Programming (via satellite): ABC Family Channel; Arts & Entertainment; CNN; Country Music TV; Discovery Channel; Disney Channel; ESPN; ESPN 2; FX; History Channel; Nickelodeon; Spike TV; TBS Superstation; The Learning Channel; Trinity Broadcasting Network; Turner Network TV; USA Network; WGN America.
Fee: $39.95 installation; $38.15 monthly.

Digital Basic Service
Subscribers: N.A.
Programming (via satellite): American-Life TV Network; BBC America; Bloomberg Television; Discovery Digital Networks; ESPN Classic Sports; ESPNews; FitTV; Fox Sports World; G4; Golf Channel; GSN; INSP; Music Choice; Nick Jr.; Outdoor Channel; Versus; WE tv.
Fee: $52.10 monthly.

Digital Pay Service 1
Pay Units: N.A.
Programming (via satellite): Cinemax (multiplexed); HBO (multiplexed); Showtime (multiplexed); Starz (multiplexed).
Fee: $15.95 monthly (each).

Video-On-Demand: No

Pay-Per-View
HITS 1 (delivered digitally); Playboy TV (delivered digitally); Fresh (delivered digitally).

Internet Service
Operational: No.

Telephone Service
None
Miles of Plant: 16.0 (coaxial); None (fiber optic). Homes passed included in Owensboro
General Manager: Timothy Evard. Operations Director: Belinda Graham. Engineering Director: Mike Earehart. Finance & Accounting Director: Cindy Johnson.
Ownership: Windjammer Communications LLC (MSO).

ELIZABETHTOWN—Comcast Cable, 2919 Ring Rd, Elizabethtown, KY 42701. Phone: 270-765-2731. Fax: 270-737-3379. Web Site: http://www.comcast.com. Also serves Campbellsville, Hodgenville, Larue County (unincorporated areas), Taylor County & Vine Grove. ICA: KY0012.
TV Market Ranking: 38 (Vine Grove); Below 100 (Campbellsville, Hodgenville, Larue County (unincorporated areas), Taylor County); Outside TV Markets (ELIZABETHTOWN). Franchise award date: October 18, 1965. Franchise expiration date: N.A. Began: February 10, 1965.
Channel capacity: N.A. Channels available but not in use: N.A.

Basic Service
Subscribers: 15,418.
Programming (received off-air): WAVE (NBC) Louisville; WBKI-TV (CW) Campbellsville; WBKO (ABC, CW) Bowling Green; WBNA (ION) Louisville; WHAS-TV (ABC) Louisville; WKMJ-TV (PBS) Louisville; WKYT-TV (CBS, CW) Lexington; WKZT-TV (PBS) Elizabethtown; WLKY-TV (CBS) Louisville; WMYO (MNT) Salem; allband FM.
Programming (via satellite): ABC Family Channel; Home Shopping Network; QVC; TBS Superstation; WGN America.
Current originations: Public Access.
Fee: $54.99 installation; $14.35 monthly.

Expanded Basic Service 1
Subscribers: 14,635.
Programming (via satellite): AMC; Animal Planet; Arts & Entertainment; BET Networks; Cartoon Network; CNBC; CNN; Comcast Sports Net Southeast; Comcast/Charter Sports Southeast (CSS); Comedy Central; Country Music TV; C-SPAN; C-SPAN 2; Discovery Channel; Disney Channel; E! Entertainment Television; ESPN; ESPN 2; Eternal Word TV Network; Food Network; Fox News Channel; Fox Sports Net Ohio; FX; G4; Golf Channel; Great American Country; Hallmark Channel; Headline News; HGTV; History Channel; INSP; Lifetime; MTV; Nickelodeon; Outdoor Channel; Speed Channel; Spike TV; Style Network; Syfy; The Learning Channel; Travel Channel; Trinity Broadcasting Network; truTV; Turner Network TV; TV Guide Network; TV Land; USA Network; Versus; VH1; Weather Channel.
Fee: $29.64 monthly.

Digital Basic Service
Subscribers: N.A.
Programming (received off-air): WAVE (NBC) Louisville; WHAS-TV (ABC) Louisville; WKZT-TV (PBS) Elizabethtown; WLKY-TV (CBS) Louisville.
Programming (via satellite): Arts & Entertainment HD; BBC America; Bio; CBS College Sports Network; CMT Pure Country; C-SPAN 3; Current; Discovery Digital Networks; Discovery HD Theater; Encore (multiplexed); ESPN 2 HD; ESPN HD; ESPNews; Flix; Fox College Sports Atlantic; Fox College Sports Central; Fox College Sports Pacific; Fox Reality Channel; Fox Soccer; GAS; Gol TV; GSN; History Channel International; Lifetime Movie Network; MoviePlex; MSNBC; MTV Networks Digital Suite; Music Choice; National Geographic Channel; National Geographic Channel HD Network; NBA TV; NFL Network; Nick Jr.; Nick Too; NickToons TV; Palladia; PBS Kids Sprout; SoapNet; Sundance Channel; Tennis Channel; The Sportsman Channel; Toon Disney; Turner Network TV HD; TV One; TVG Network; Universal HD; Versus HD; WDRB (FOX) Louisville.
Fee: $14.95 monthly.

Pay Service 1
Pay Units: N.A.
Programming (via satellite): HBO.
Fee: $8.69 monthly.

Digital Pay Service 1
Pay Units: N.A.
Programming (via satellite): Cinemax (multiplexed); Cinemax HD; HBO (multiplexed); HBO HD; Showtime (multiplexed); Showtime HD; Starz (multiplexed); Starz HDTV; The Movie Channel (multiplexed).
Fee: $13.05 monthly (each).

Video-On-Demand: Yes

Pay-Per-View
iN DEMAND; iN DEMAND (delivered digitally); Hot Choice (delivered digitally); Playboy TV (delivered digitally).

Internet Service
Operational: Yes.
Broadband Service: Comcast High Speed Internet.
Fee: $42.95 monthly.

Telephone Service
Digital: Operational
Miles of Plant: 406.0 (coaxial); 22.0 (fiber optic). Total homes in franchised area: 16,000.
Technical Operations Director: Bob Tharp. General Manager: Tim Hagan. Marketing Director: Laurie Nicholson.
City fee: 3% of gross.
Ownership: Comcast Cable Communications Inc. (MSO).

ELKHORN CITY—Formerly served by Cebridge Connections. Now served by PIKEVILLE, KY [KY0045]. ICA: KY0059.

ELKTON—Mediacom. Now served by TRENTON, KY [KY0101]. ICA: KY0132.

EOLIA—Charter Communications. Now served by JENKINS, KY [KY0041]. ICA: KY0127.

EVARTS—Evarts TV Inc., PO Box 8, 113 Yocum St, Evarts, KY 40828. Phone: 606-837-2505. Fax: 606-837-3738. Also serves Harlan County (unincorporated areas). ICA: KY0135.
TV Market Ranking: Below 100 (EVARTS, Harlan County (unincorporated areas)). Franchise award date: N.A. Franchise expiration date: N.A. Began: June 1, 1987.
Channel capacity: 42 (not 2-way capable). Channels available but not in use: 6.

Basic Service
Subscribers: 750.
Programming (received off-air): WATE-TV (ABC) Knoxville; WBIR-TV (NBC) Knoxville; WBXX-TV (CW) Crossville; WEMT (FOX) Greeneville; WKYT-TV (CBS, CW) Lexington; WLEX-TV (NBC) Lexington; WLJC-TV (TBN) Beattyville; WTNZ (FOX) Knoxville; WTVQ-DT (ABC) Lexington; WVLT-TV (CBS, MNT) Knoxville; WYMT-TV (CBS, CW) Hazard.
Programming (via satellite): ABC Family Channel; AMC; Cartoon Network; CNN; Country Music TV; Discovery Channel; ESPN; ESPN 2; Fox News Channel; Hallmark Channel; HGTV; History Channel; Home Shopping Network; Lifetime; Lifetime Movie Network; Nickelodeon; Outdoor Channel; Spike TV; Syfy; TBS Superstation; Turner Network TV; TV Land; USA Network; Weather Channel; WGN America.
Current originations: Educational Access.
Fee: $40.00 installation; $25.50 monthly.

Pay Service 1
Pay Units: N.A.
Programming (via satellite): Cinemax; HBO.
Fee: $7.00 monthly (Cinemax), $12.00 monthly (HBO).

Internet Service
Operational: No.

Telephone Service
None
Miles of Plant: 25.0 (coaxial); None (fiber optic).

Manager: Bob Cornett. Chief Technician: John Lutrell.
Ownership: Evarts TV Inc.

FALLSBURG—Inter Mountain Cable Inc., PO Box 159, 20 Laynesville Rd, Harold, KY 41635. Phone: 606-478-9406. Fax: 606-478-1680. Web Site: http://www.imctv.com. ICA: KY0166.
TV Market Ranking: 36 (FALLSBURG). Franchise award date: N.A. Franchise expiration date: N.A. Began: N.A.
Channel capacity: 25 (operating 2-way). Channels available but not in use: 1.
Basic Service
Subscribers: 46.
Programming (received off-air): WCHS-TV (ABC) Charleston; WKMR (PBS) Morehead; WOWK-TV (CBS) Huntington; WSAZ-TV (MNT, NBC) Huntington; WTSF (IND) Ashland; WVAH-TV (FOX) Charleston; WYMT-TV (CBS, CW) Hazard.
Programming (via satellite): ABC Family Channel; AMC; Arts & Entertainment; CNN; Country Music TV; Discovery Channel; Disney Channel; ESPN; Nickelodeon; Spike TV; TBS Superstation; Trinity Broadcasting Network; Turner Network TV; USA Network; WGN America.
Fee: $47.50 installation; $10.95 monthly; $.73 converter.
Pay Service 1
Pay Units: 43.
Programming (via satellite): Cinemax; HBO.
Fee: $7.99 monthly (Cinemax), $11.99 monthly (HBO).
Video-On-Demand: No
Internet Service
Operational: Yes.
Fee: $24.95 monthly.
Telephone Service
Digital: Operational
Fee: $131.93 monthly
Miles of Plant: 24.0 (coaxial); None (fiber optic). Homes passed: 384.
Chief Financial Officer: James Campbell. Manager: Paul Douglas Gearheart. Operations Director: John Schmoldt. Chief Engineer: Jefferson Thacker. Customer Service Manager: Rebecca Walters.
Ownership: Inter-Mountain Cable Inc. (MSO).

FALMOUTH—Insight Communications. Now served by COVINGTON, KY [KY0002]. ICA: KY0087.

FEDSCREEK—Fuller's TV. Now served by HAROLD, KY [KY0006]. ICA: KY0188.

FIVE STAR—Insight Communications. Now served by LOUISVILLE, KY [KY0001]. ICA: KY0162.

FLAT LICK—NewWave Communications, 5026 S Hwy 27, Somerset, KY 42501. Phone: 606-678-9215. Fax: 606-679-7111. Web Site: http://www.newwavecom.com. Also serves Baughman, Bimble, Dewitt, Himyar, Knox County (eastern portion), Salt Gum, Scalf, Turkey Creek & Walker. ICA: KY0078.
TV Market Ranking: Below 100 (Baughman, Bimble, Dewitt, FLAT LICK, Himyar, Knox County (eastern portion), Salt Gum, Scalf, Turkey Creek, Walker). Franchise award date: N.A. Franchise expiration date: N.A. Began: October 1, 1971.
Channel capacity: N.A. Channels available but not in use: N.A.
Basic Service
Subscribers: 1,730.
Programming (received off-air): WAGV (IND) Harlan; WATE-TV (ABC) Knoxville; WBIR-TV (NBC) Knoxville; WBXX-TV (CW) Crossville; WDKY-TV (FOX) Danville; WKSO-TV (PBS) Somerset; WKYT-TV (CBS, CW) Lexington; WLEX-TV (NBC) Lexington; WLJC-TV (TBN) Beattyville; WTVQ-DT (ABC) Lexington; WUPX-TV (ION) Morehead; WVTN-LP Corbin; WYMT-TV (CBS, CW) Hazard.
Programming (via satellite): Home Shopping Network; QVC; ShopNBC; TV Guide Network; WGN America.
Fee: $35.57 installation; $10.95 monthly.
Expanded Basic Service 1
Subscribers: N.A.
Programming (via satellite): ABC Family Channel; AMC; Animal Planet; Arts & Entertainment; Bravo; Cartoon Network; CNBC; CNN; Comcast/Charter Sports Southeast (CSS); Comedy Central; Country Music TV; C-SPAN; C-SPAN 2; Discovery Channel; Disney Channel; E! Entertainment Television; ESPN; ESPN 2; FitTV; Food Network; Fox News Channel; Fox Sports Net Ohio; FX; G4; Golf Channel; Hallmark Channel; Headline News; HGTV; History Channel; INSP; Lifetime; MSNBC; MTV; National Geographic Channel; Nickelodeon; Oxygen; SoapNet; Speed Channel; Spike TV; Style Network; TBS Superstation; The Learning Channel; Toon Disney; Travel Channel; Trinity Broadcasting Network; truTV; Turner Classic Movies; Turner Network TV; TV Land; USA Network; Versus; VH1; WE tv; Weather Channel.
Digital Basic Service
Subscribers: N.A.
Programming (via satellite): BBC America; Bio; Bloomberg Television; Discovery Digital Networks; Do-It-Yourself; ESPN Classic Sports; ESPNews; Fox College Sports Atlantic; Fox College Sports Central; Fox College Sports Pacific; Fox Movie Channel; Fox Soccer; Fuel TV; Fuse; GAS; Great American Country; History Channel International; Independent Film Channel; Jewelry Television; Lifetime Movie Network; Lifetime Real Women; MTV Networks Digital Suite; Music Choice; NFL Network; Nick Jr.; Nick Too; NickToons TV; Sundance Channel; TV Guide Interactive Inc.
Digital Pay Service 1
Pay Units: N.A.
Programming (via satellite): Cinemax (multiplexed); Encore (multiplexed); Flix; HBO (multiplexed); Showtime (multiplexed); Starz (multiplexed); The Movie Channel (multiplexed).
Video-On-Demand: No
Pay-Per-View
iN DEMAND (delivered digitally); NHL Center Ice (delivered digitally); MLB Extra Innings (delivered digitally); Playboy TV (delivered digitally); Fresh (delivered digitally); Shorteez (delivered digitally).
Internet Service
Operational: Yes.
Fee: $40.00 installation; $23.95 monthly.
Telephone Service
None
Miles of Plant: 122.0 (coaxial); None (fiber optic). Homes passed: 2,121. Total homes in franchised area: 2,121.
General Manager: Mark Bookout. Technical Operations Manager: Lynn McMahan.
Ownership: NewWave Communications (MSO).

FLEMINGSBURG—Formerly served by Adelphia Communications. Now served by MOREHEAD, KY [KY0031]. ICA: KY0077.

FORT CAMPBELL—Comcast Cable, PO Box 280570, 660 Mainstream Dr, Nashville, TN 37228-0570. Phone: 615-244-7462. Fax: 615-255-6528. Web Site: http://www.comcast.com. ICA: KY0019.
TV Market Ranking: Outside TV Markets (FORT CAMPBELL). Franchise award date: October 10, 1985. Franchise expiration date: N.A. Began: July 1, 1977.
Channel capacity: N.A. Channels available but not in use: N.A.
Basic Service
Subscribers: 5,642.
Programming (received off-air): WKAG-CA Hopkinsville; WKMA-TV (PBS) Madisonville; WKRN-TV (ABC) Nashville; WNAB (CW) Nashville; WNPT (PBS) Nashville; WSMV-TV (NBC, TMO) Nashville; WTVF (CBS) Nashville; WUXP-TV (MNT) Nashville; WZTV (FOX) Nashville.
Programming (via satellite): ABC Family Channel; AMC; Animal Planet; Arts & Entertainment; BET Networks; Cartoon Network; CNBC; CNN; Comcast/Charter Sports Southeast (CSS); Comedy Central; Country Music TV; C-SPAN; C-SPAN 2; Discovery Channel; Discovery Health Channel; Disney Channel; E! Entertainment Television; ESPN; ESPN 2; Fox News Channel; Fox Sports Net; FX; Golf Channel; Great American Country; Headline News; HGTV; History Channel; Home Shopping Network 2; Lifetime; MTV; Nickelodeon; QVC; Spike TV; Syfy; TBS Superstation; The Learning Channel; truTV; Turner Network TV; TV Guide Network; TV Land; Univision; USA Network; Versus; VH1; Weather Channel; WGN America.
Current originations: Government Access; Educational Access.
Fee: $45.10 installation; $10.75 monthly.
Digital Basic Service
Subscribers: 2,287.
Programming (via satellite): BBC America; C-SPAN 3; Discovery Digital Networks; DMX Music; Encore Action; ESPNews; Flix; GAS; MTV Networks Digital Suite; Nick Jr.; Nick Too; SoapNet; Sundance Channel; Toon Disney; WAM! America's Kidz Network.
Pay Service 1
Pay Units: 880.
Programming (via satellite): Cinemax; HBO; Showtime.
Fee: $10.00 installation; $10.00 monthly (Showtime), $10.50 monthly (Cinemax or HBO).
Digital Pay Service 1
Pay Units: N.A.
Programming (via satellite): Cinemax (multiplexed); HBO (multiplexed); Showtime (multiplexed); Starz (multiplexed); The Movie Channel (multiplexed).
Video-On-Demand: Planned
Pay-Per-View
Addressable homes: 2,287.
iN DEMAND (delivered digitally), Addressable: Yes; Playboy TV (delivered digitally); Fresh (delivered digitally); Shorteez (delivered digitally); Hot Choice (delivered digitally); Pleasure (delivered digitally).
Internet Service
Operational: Yes.
Subscribers: 1,095.
Broadband Service: Comcast High Speed Internet.
Fee: $42.95 monthly.
Telephone Service
Digital: Operational
Homes passed & miles of plant (coax & fiber combined) included in Nashville, TN
Area Vice President & General Manager: John Gauder. Technical Operations Director: Joe Pell. Marketing Director: Marine Mahoney. Marketing Manager: Will Jefferson.
Ownership: Comcast Cable Communications Inc. (MSO).

FRAKES—Suddenlink Communications, 12444 Powerscourt Dr, Saint Louis, MO 63131-3660. Phones: 800-999-6845; 314-965-2020. Fax: 903-561-5485. Web Site: http://www.suddenlink.com. Also serves Chenoa & Davisburg, KY; Claiborne County (portions), Clairfield, Eagan & Hamlin Town, TN. ICA: KY0225.
TV Market Ranking: Below 100 (Chenoa, Claiborne County (portions), Clairfield, Davisburg, Eagan, FRAKES, Hamlin Town). Franchise award date: October 18, 1976. Franchise expiration date: N.A. Began: February 1, 1979.
Channel capacity: 76 (operating 2-way). Channels available but not in use: N.A.
Basic Service
Subscribers: 380.
Programming (received off-air): WAGV (IND) Harlan; WATE-TV (ABC) Knoxville; WBIR-TV (NBC) Knoxville; WBXX-TV (CW) Crossville; WKHA (PBS) Hazard; WTNZ (FOX) Knoxville; WVLR (IND) Tazewell; WVLT-TV (CBS, MNT) Knoxville; WYMT-TV (CBS, CW) Hazard.
Programming (via satellite): Home Shopping Network; QVC; Trinity Broadcasting Network; WGN America.
Current originations: Government Access; Educational Access; Public Access.
Fee: $39.00 installation; $18.95 monthly; $1.63 converter.
Expanded Basic Service 1
Subscribers: N.A.
Programming (via satellite): ABC Family Channel; AMC; Animal Planet; Arts & Entertainment; Cartoon Network; CNN; Comcast Sports Net Southeast; Comedy Central; Country Music TV; C-SPAN; C-SPAN 2; Discovery Channel; Disney Channel; E! Entertainment Television; ESPN; ESPN 2; ESPN Classic Sports; Food Network; Fox News Channel; FX; Hallmark Channel; Headline News; HGTV; History Channel; Lifetime; MTV; Nickelodeon; Spike TV; Syfy; TBS Superstation; The Learning Channel; Turner Classic Movies; Turner Network TV; TV Land; USA Network; VH1; Weather Channel.
Fee: $22.00 monthly.
Digital Basic Service
Subscribers: N.A.
Programming (via satellite): BBC America; Bio; Bloomberg Television; Discovery Digital Networks; DMX Music; ESPNews; Fox

Movie Channel; Fox Soccer; Fuse; G4; GAS; Golf Channel; GSN; History Channel International; Independent Film Channel; Lifetime Movie Network; Military History Channel; MTV2; National Geographic Channel; Nick Jr.; NickToons TV; Outdoor Channel; Science Television; Sleuth; Speed Channel; Toon Disney; Versus; VH1 Classic; VH1 Country; WE tv.
Fee: $12.95 monthly.
Video-On-Demand: No
Pay-Per-View
iN DEMAND (delivered digitally); Playboy TV (delivered digitally); Fresh (delivered digitally).
Internet Service
Operational: Yes. Began: November 1, 2004.
Broadband Service: Cebridge High Speed Cable Internet.
Fee: $49.95 installation; $26.95 monthly.
Telephone Service
None
Miles of Plant: 46.0 (coaxial); None (fiber optic). Homes passed: 613.
Vice President: Robert Herrald. Chief Technician: Jim Thompson.
Ownership: Cequel Communications LLC (MSO).

FRANKFORT—Frankfort Plant Board Cable Service, PO Box 308, 317 W 2nd St, Frankfort, KY 40601-2645. Phones: 888-312-4372; 502-352-4372. Fax: 502-223-4449. Web Site: http://www.fewpb.com. Also serves Graefenburg, Millville & Shelby County. ICA: KY0010.
TV Market Ranking: Below 100 (FRANKFORT, Graefenburg, Millville, Shelby County). Franchise award date: N.A. Franchise expiration date: N.A. Began: October 1, 1952.
Channel capacity: 62 (operating 2-way). Channels available but not in use: None.
Basic Service
Subscribers: 17,600.
Programming (received off-air): KETS (PBS) Little Rock; WAVE (NBC) Louisville; WBKI-TV (CW) Campbellsville; WDKY-TV (FOX) Danville; WDRB (FOX) Louisville; WHAS-TV (ABC) Louisville; WKYT-TV (CBS, CW) Lexington; WLEX-TV (NBC) Lexington; WLKY-TV (CBS) Louisville; WTVQ-DT (ABC) Lexington; WUPX-TV (ION) Morehead; 9 FMs.
Programming (via satellite): CW+; QVC; Weatherscan.
Current originations: Leased Access; Government Access; Educational Access.
Fee: $30.00 installation; $19.00 monthly.
Expanded Basic Service 1
Subscribers: N.A.
Programming (via satellite): ABC Family Channel; AMC; Animal Planet; Arts & Entertainment; BET Networks; Cartoon Network; CNBC; CNN; Comcast Sports Net Southeast; Comedy Central; Country Music TV; C-SPAN; C-SPAN 2; C-SPAN 3; Discovery Channel; E! Entertainment Television; ESPN; ESPN 2; ESPN Classic Sports; Eternal Word TV Network; FitTV; Food Network; Fox News Channel; Hallmark Channel; Headline News; HGTV; History Channel; HorseRacing TV; Lifetime; MTV; NASA TV; National Geographic Channel; Nickelodeon; Outdoor Channel; Spike TV; Syfy; TBS Superstation; The Learning Channel; Travel Channel; Trinity Broadcasting Network; truTV; Turner Classic Movies; Turner Network TV; TV Guide Network; TV Land; USA Network; VH1; Weather Channel.
Fee: $13.70 monthly.
Digital Basic Service
Subscribers: 3,000.
Programming (received off-air): Turner Network TV HD; Universal HD; WAVE (NBC) Louisville; WDRB (FOX) Louisville; WKYT-TV (CBS, CW) Lexington; WTVQ-DT (ABC) Lexington.
Programming (via satellite): AmericanLife TV Network; Arts & Entertainment HD; BBC America; Bio; Bloomberg Television; CMT Pure Country; Current; Discovery HD Theater; Discovery Health Channel; Discovery Home Channel; Discovery Kids Channel; Discovery Military Channel; DMX Music; ESPN 2 HD; ESPN HD; ESPN U; ESPNews; Fox Movie Channel; Fox Soccer; G4; Golf Channel; Great American Country; GSN; Halogen Network; HDNet; HDNet Movies; History Channel International; ID Investigation Discovery; International Television (ITV); KETS (PBS) Little Rock; Lifetime Movie Network; Lifetime Real Women; MTV Hits; MTV2; Nick Jr.; NickToons TV; Outdoor Channel 2 HD; Ovation; PBS Kids Sprout; Science Channel; SoapNet; Speed Channel; Style Network; TeenNick; Toon Disney; VH1 Classic; VH1 Soul; WE tv.
Fee: $12.00 monthly.
Pay Service 1
Pay Units: 1,417.
Programming (via satellite): HBO.
Fee: $8.00 installation; $10.45 monthly.
Digital Pay Service 1
Pay Units: N.A.
Programming (via satellite): Cinemax (multiplexed); Cinemax HD; Encore (multiplexed); HBO (multiplexed); HBO HD; Showtime (multiplexed); Showtime HD; Starz (multiplexed); Starz HDTV; The Movie Channel (multiplexed); The Movie Channel HD.
Fee: $10.45 monthly (HBO, Cinemax, Showtime/TMC or Starz/Encore).
Video-On-Demand: No
Pay-Per-View
Addressable homes: 7,500.
iN DEMAND (delivered digitally), Addressable: Yes.
Internet Service
Operational: Yes. Began: February 1, 2001.
Subscribers: 100.
Broadband Service: FPB ISP.
Fee: $100.00 installation; $29.00 monthly; $7.00 modem lease; $250.00 modem purchase.
Telephone Service
Analog: Not Operational
Digital: Operational
Miles of Plant: 550.0 (coaxial); 200.0 (fiber optic). Homes passed: 20,500. Total homes in franchised area: 22,000.
General Manager: Warner Caines. Chief Technician: Doug Palmer. Marketing & Program Director: Will Bell.
City fee: None.
Ownership: Frankfort Plant Board.

FRANKFORT/STONEWALL—Windjammer Cable, 4400 PGA Blvd, Ste 902, Palm Beach Gardens, FL 33410. Phones: 877-450-5558; 561-775-1208. Fax: 561-775-7811. Web Site: http://www.windjammercable.com. Also serves Frankfort (unincorporated areas) & Stonewall. ICA: KY0284.
TV Market Ranking: Below 100 (Frankfort (unincorporated areas), FRANKFORT/STONEWALL). Franchise award date: N.A. Franchise expiration date: N.A. Began: May 1, 1991.
Channel capacity: 36 (not 2-way capable). Channels available but not in use: 9.
Basic Service
Subscribers: 191.
Programming (received off-air): WAVE (NBC) Louisville; WDKY-TV (FOX) Danville; WHAS-TV (ABC) Louisville; WKLE (PBS) Lexington; WKYT-TV (CBS, CW) Lexington; WLEX-TV (NBC) Lexington; WLKY-TV (CBS) Louisville; WTVQ-DT (ABC) Lexington.
Programming (via satellite): ABC Family Channel; AMC; Arts & Entertainment; CNN; Country Music TV; C-SPAN 2; Discovery Channel; Disney Channel; ESPN; FX; Spike TV; TBS Superstation; The Learning Channel; Trinity Broadcasting Network; Turner Network TV; USA Network; WGN America.
Fee: $39.95 installation; $35.65 monthly.
Digital Basic Service
Subscribers: N.A.
Programming (via satellite): BBC America; Bloomberg Television; Discovery Health Channel; Discovery Kids Channel; ESPN Classic Sports; ESPNews; FitTV; G4; Golf Channel; GSN; Halogen Network; Music Choice; Nick Jr.; NickToons TV; Outdoor Channel; Science Channel; Versus; WE tv.
Fee: $8.45 monthly.
Digital Pay Service 1
Pay Units: N.A.
Programming (via satellite): Cinemax (multiplexed); Encore (multiplexed); HBO (multiplexed); Showtime (multiplexed); Starz (multiplexed); The Movie Channel (multiplexed).
Fee: $15.95 monthly (each).
Video-On-Demand: No
Pay-Per-View
iN DEMAND (delivered digitally); Fresh (delivered digitally).
Internet Service
Operational: No.
Telephone Service
None
Miles of Plant: 17.0 (coaxial); None (fiber optic). Homes passed: 257.
Ownership: Windjammer Communications LLC (MSO).

FRANKLIN—Comcast Cable. Now served by NASHVILLE, TN [TN0002]. ICA: KY0050.

FRENCHBURG—Windjammer Cable, 4400 PGA Blvd, Ste 902, Palm Beach Gardens, FL 33410. Phones: 877-450-5558; 561-775-1208. Fax: 561-775-7811. Web Site: http://www.windjammercable.com. Also serves Ezel & Means. ICA: KY0292.
TV Market Ranking: Below 100 (Ezel, FRENCHBURG, Means). Franchise award date: N.A. Franchise expiration date: N.A. Began: N.A.
Channel capacity: 36 (not 2-way capable). Channels available but not in use: 3.
Basic Service
Subscribers: 855.
Programming (received off-air): WDKY-TV (FOX) Danville; WKMR (PBS) Morehead; WKYT-TV (CBS, CW) Lexington; WLEX-TV (NBC) Lexington; WLJC-TV (TBN) Beattyville; WTVQ-DT (ABC) Lexington; WUPX-TV (ION) Morehead.
Programming (via satellite): C-SPAN; QVC; TBS Superstation; Weather Channel; WGN America.
Fee: $39.95 installation; $19.05 monthly.
Expanded Basic Service 1
Subscribers: 740.
Programming (via satellite): ABC Family Channel; AMC; Arts & Entertainment; CNN; Country Music TV; Discovery Channel; Disney Channel; E! Entertainment Television; ESPN; ESPN 2; FX; Headline News; Lifetime; MSNBC; Nickelodeon; Spike TV; Syfy; The Learning Channel; Turner Network TV; USA Network.
Fee: $26.60 monthly.
Digital Basic Service
Subscribers: N.A.
Programming (via satellite): BBC America; Bio; Black Family Channel; Bloomberg Television; Bravo; Discovery Digital Networks; ESPN Classic Sports; FitTV; Fox Movie Channel; Fox Soccer; G4; GAS; Golf Channel; Great American Country; GSN; HGTV; History Channel; History Channel International; Independent Film Channel; INSP; Lifetime Movie Network; MTV2; National Geographic Channel; Nick Jr.; NickToons TV; Outdoor Channel; Speed Channel; Style Network; The Word Network; Toon Disney; Trinity Broadcasting Network; Turner Classic Movies; Versus; VH1 Classic; VH1 Country; WE tv.
Fee: $54.35 monthly.
Digital Pay Service 1
Pay Units: N.A.
Programming (via satellite): Cinemax (multiplexed); Encore (multiplexed); HBO (multiplexed); Showtime (multiplexed); Starz (multiplexed); The Movie Channel (multiplexed).
Fee: $15.95 monthly (each).
Video-On-Demand: No
Pay-Per-View
HITS 1 (delivered digitally); HITS 2 (delivered digitally); HITS 3 (delivered digitally); HITS 4 (delivered digitally); Playboy TV (delivered digitally); Fresh (delivered digitally).
Internet Service
Operational: No.
Telephone Service
None
Miles of Plant: 72.0 (coaxial); None (fiber optic). Homes passed: 1,379.
General Manager: Timothy Evard. Operations Director: Belinda Graham. Engineering Director: Mike Earehart. Finance & Accounting Director: Cindy Johnson.
Ownership: Windjammer Communications LLC (MSO).

FULTON—NewWave Communications, 906 South 12 St, Belair Shopping Center, Murray, KY 42071. Phone: 888.863.9928 (Customer service). Fax: 270.753.8462. E-mail: info@newwavecom.com. Web Site: http://www.newwavecom.com. Also serves Obion County (portions) & South Fulton. ICA: KY0226.
TV Market Ranking: Below 100 (Obion County (portions) (portions)); Outside TV Markets (FULTON, Obion County (portions) (portions), South Fulton). Franchise award date: N.A. Franchise expiration date: N.A. Began: May 1, 1967.
Channel capacity: 60 (operating 2-way). Channels available but not in use: 18.
Basic Service
Subscribers: 1,218.
Programming (received off-air): KBSI (FOX) Cape Girardeau; KFVS-TV (CBS, CW) Cape Girardeau; WBBJ-TV (ABC) Jackson; WDKA (MNT) Paducah; WKMU (PBS) Murray; WLJT-DT (PBS) Lexington; WPSD-TV (NBC) Paducah; WQWQ-LP (CW) Paducah; WSIL-TV (ABC) Harrisburg; 9 FMs.
Programming (via satellite): C-SPAN; C-SPAN 2; Home Shopping Network; INSP; QVC; ShopNBC; Trinity Broadcasting Network; WGN America.
Current originations: Government Access; Educational Access; Public Access.
Fee: $29.95 installation.

Expanded Basic Service 1
Subscribers: 1,044.
Programming (via satellite): ABC Family Channel; AMC; Animal Planet; Arts & Entertainment; BET Networks; Bravo; Cartoon Network; CNBC; CNN; Comcast Sports Net Southeast; Comedy Central; Country Music TV; Discovery Channel; Disney Channel; E! Entertainment Television; ESPN; ESPN 2; ESPN Classic Sports; Food Network; Fox News Channel; Golf Channel; GSN; Hallmark Channel; Headline News; HGTV; History Channel; Lifetime; MTV; Nickelodeon; Outdoor Channel; SoapNet; Speed Channel; Spike TV; Syfy; TBS Superstation; The Learning Channel; Travel Channel; truTV; Turner Network TV; TV Land; USA Network; VH1; Weather Channel.
Fee: $44.95 monthly.

Digital Basic Service
Subscribers: 197.
Programming (via satellite): BBC America; Bio; Black Family Channel; Bloomberg Television; Discovery Digital Networks; DMX Music; ESPNews; FitTV; Fox Movie Channel; G4; GAS; Great American Country; Halogen Network; History Channel International; Independent Film Channel; Lifetime Movie Network; MTV Networks Digital Suite; Nick Jr.; NickToons TV; Sleuth; Style Network; The Word Network; Toon Disney; Turner Classic Movies; Versus.

Digital Pay Service 1
Pay Units: 386.
Programming (via satellite): Cinemax (multiplexed); Encore (multiplexed); Flix; HBO (multiplexed); Showtime (multiplexed); Starz (multiplexed); The Movie Channel (multiplexed).

Video-On-Demand: No

Pay-Per-View
Hot Choice (delivered digitally); Playboy TV (delivered digitally); Fresh (delivered digitally); Shorteez (delivered digitally); iN DEMAND (delivered digitally).

Internet Service
Operational: Yes.
Subscribers: 258.
Broadband Service: SpeedNet.
Fee: $40.00 installation; $23.95 monthly.

Telephone Service
Digital: Planned

Miles of Plant: 66.0 (coaxial); None (fiber optic). Homes passed: 2,982.
General Manager: Cameron Miller. Technical Operations Manager: Eddie Prior.
City fee: 5% of gross.
Ownership: NewWave Communications (MSO).

GARRARD—NewWave Communications, 5026 S Highway 27, Somerset, KY 42501. Phone: 606-678-9215. Fax: 606-679-7111. Web Site: http://www.newwavecom.com. Also serves Big Creek, Fogertown, Goose Rock, Hima & Oneida. ICA: KY0058.
TV Market Ranking: Below 100 (Big Creek, Fogertown, GARRARD, Goose Rock, Hima, Oneida). Franchise award date: N.A. Franchise expiration date: N.A. Began: December 1, 1955.
Channel capacity: N.A. Channels available but not in use: N.A.

Basic Service
Subscribers: 3,100.
Programming (received off-air): WAGV (IND) Harlan; WATE-TV (ABC) Knoxville; WBIR-TV (NBC) Knoxville; WBXX-TV (CW) Crossville; WDKY-TV (FOX) Danville; WKSO-TV (PBS) Somerset; WKYT-TV (CBS, CW) Lexington; WLEX-TV (NBC) Lexington; WLJC-TV (TBN) Beattyville; WTVQ-DT (ABC) Lexington; WUPX-TV (ION) Morehead; WYMT-TV (CBS, CW) Hazard.
Programming (via satellite): Home Shopping Network; QVC; ShopNBC; TV Guide Network; WGN America.
Fee: $37.79 installation; $5.16 monthly.

Expanded Basic Service 1
Subscribers: N.A.
Programming (via satellite): ABC Family Channel; AMC; Animal Planet; Arts & Entertainment; Bravo; Cartoon Network; CNBC; CNN; Comcast/Charter Sports Southeast (CSS); Comedy Central; Country Music TV; C-SPAN; C-SPAN 2; Discovery Channel; Disney Channel; E! Entertainment Television; ESPN; ESPN 2; FitTV; Food Network; Fox News Channel; Fox Sports Net Ohio; FX; G4; Golf Channel; Hallmark Channel; Headline News; HGTV; History Channel; INSP; Lifetime; MSNBC; MTV; National Geographic Channel; Nickelodeon; Outdoor Channel; Oxygen; SoapNet; Speed Channel; Spike TV; Style Network; Syfy; TBS Superstation; The Learning Channel; Toon Disney; Travel Channel; Trinity Broadcasting Network; truTV; Turner Classic Movies; Turner Network TV; TV Land; USA Network; VH1; WE tv; Weather Channel.
Fee: $19.85 monthly.

Digital Basic Service
Subscribers: N.A.
Programming (via satellite): BBC America; Bio; Bloomberg Television; Discovery Digital Networks; Do-It-Yourself; ESPN Classic Sports; ESPNews; Fox College Sports Atlantic; Fox College Sports Central; Fox College Sports Pacific; Fox Movie Channel; Fox Soccer; Fuel TV; Fuse; GAS; Great American Country; History Channel International; Independent Film Channel; Jewelry Television; Lifetime Movie Network; Lifetime Real Women; MTV Networks Digital Suite; Music Choice; NFL Network; Nick Jr.; Nick Too; Sundance Channel; TV Guide Interactive Inc.

Digital Pay Service 1
Pay Units: N.A.
Programming (via satellite): Cinemax (multiplexed); Encore (multiplexed); HBO (multiplexed); Showtime (multiplexed); Starz (multiplexed); The Movie Channel (multiplexed).

Video-On-Demand: No

Pay-Per-View
iN DEMAND (delivered digitally); NHL Center Ice (delivered digitally); MLB Extra Innings (delivered digitally); Playboy TV (delivered digitally); Fresh (delivered digitally); Shorteez (delivered digitally).

Internet Service
Operational: Yes.
Fee: $40.00 installation; $23.95 monthly.

Telephone Service
None

Miles of Plant: 175.0 (coaxial); None (fiber optic). Homes passed: 3,400. Total homes in franchised area: 3,400.
Technical Operations Manager: Lynn McMahan. General Manager: Mark Bookout.
Ownership: NewWave Communications (MSO).

GARRISON—Formerly served by Adelphia Communications. Now served by VANCEBURG, KY [KY0286]. ICA: KY0125.

GEORGETOWN—Time Warner Cable, 1615 Foxhaven Dr, Richmond, KY 40475. Phones: 859-626-4800; 859-624-9666. Fax: 859-624-0060. Web Site: http://www.timewarnercable.com. Also serves Midway, Paris, Scott County & Stamping Ground. ICA: KY0044.
TV Market Ranking: Below 100 (GEORGETOWN, Midway, Paris, Scott County, Stamping Ground). Franchise award date: N.A. Franchise expiration date: N.A. Began: October 15, 1973.
Channel capacity: N.A. Channels available but not in use: N.A.

Basic Service
Subscribers: 9,079.
Programming (received off-air): WCPO-TV (ABC) Cincinnati; WDKY-TV (FOX) Danville; WKLE (PBS) Lexington; WKRC-TV (CBS, CW) Cincinnati; WKYT-TV (CBS, CW) Lexington; WLEX-TV (NBC) Lexington; WTVQ-DT (ABC) Lexington; WUPX-TV (ION) Morehead; WXIX-TV (FOX) Newport; 2 FMs.
Programming (via satellite): QVC; WGN America.
Fee: $39.95 installation; $12.87 monthly.

Expanded Basic Service 1
Subscribers: 8,776.
Programming (received off-air): WLJC-TV (TBN) Beattyville.
Programming (via satellite): ABC Family Channel; AMC; Animal Planet; Arts & Entertainment; BET Networks; Cartoon Network; CNBC; CNN; Comcast Sports Net Southeast; Comedy Central; Country Music TV; C-SPAN; C-SPAN 2; Discovery Channel; Disney Channel; E! Entertainment Television; ESPN; ESPN 2; Eternal Word TV Network; Food Network; Fox News Channel; Fox Sports Net Ohio; FX; Hallmark Channel; Headline News; HGTV; History Channel; Home Shopping Network; INSP; Lifetime; MSNBC; MTV; Nickelodeon; Oxygen; Product Information Network; Spike TV; Syfy; TBS Superstation; The Learning Channel; Travel Channel; truTV; Turner Network TV; TV Guide Network; TV Land; Univision; USA Network; VH1; Weather Channel.
Fee: $37.48 monthly.

Digital Basic Service
Subscribers: N.A.
Programming (via satellite): AmericanLife TV Network; BBC America; Bio; Black Family Channel; Bloomberg Television; Bravo; Canales N; Discovery Digital Networks; DMX Music; Do-It-Yourself; ESPN Classic Sports; ESPNews; FitTV; Fox College Sports Atlantic; Fox College Sports Central; Fox College Sports Pacific; Fox Movie Channel; Fox Sports World; Fuse; G4; Gaming Entertainment Television; GAS; Golf Channel; Great American Country; GSN; Halogen Network; History Channel International; Independent Film Channel; MTV Networks Digital Suite; Music Choice; National Geographic Channel; Nick Jr.; Nick Too; NickToons TV; Outdoor Channel; ShopNBC; SoapNet; Speed Channel; Style Network; Sundance Channel; The Word Network; Toon Disney; Trinity Broadcasting Network; Turner Classic Movies; Versus; WE tv.
Fee: $6.00 monthly.

Digital Pay Service 1
Pay Units: 429.
Programming (via satellite): Cinemax (multiplexed).
Fee: $12.00 monthly.

Digital Pay Service 2
Pay Units: 536.
Programming (via satellite): HBO (multiplexed).
Fee: $12.00 monthly.

Digital Pay Service 3
Pay Units: 341.
Programming (via satellite): Flix; Showtime (multiplexed); The Movie Channel (multiplexed).
Fee: $12.00 monthly.

Digital Pay Service 4
Pay Units: 315.
Programming (via satellite): Encore (multiplexed); Starz (multiplexed).
Fee: $12.00 monthly.

Digital Pay Service 5
Pay Units: N.A.
Programming (via satellite): ART America; CCTV-4; Filipino Channel; RAI International; Russian Television Network; TV Asia; TV Japan; TV5, La Television International; Zee TV USA; Zhong Tian Channel.
Fee: $15.00 monthly (each).

Video-On-Demand: No

Pay-Per-View
iN DEMAND (delivered digitally); Playboy TV (delivered digitally); Fresh (delivered digitally); Shorteez (delivered digitally); Hot Choice (delivered digitally); Urban Xtra (delivered digitally); Sports PPV (delivered digitally).

Internet Service
Operational: Yes.
Broadband Service: Road Runner.
Fee: $44.95 monthly.

Telephone Service
Digital: Operational
Fee: $44.95 monthly

Miles of Plant: 244.0 (coaxial); 14.0 (fiber optic). Homes passed: 13,297.
Manager: Robert Trott. Technical Operations Manager: Dennis Lester. Marketing Director: Betrina Morse. Government & Public Affairs Manager: Carla Deaton. Office Manager: Laverne Farris.
City fee: 5% of gross.
Ownership: Time Warner Cable (MSO).

GLASGOW—Glasgow Electric Power Board-CATV Division. This cable system has converted to IPTV. See Glasgow, KY [KY5022]. ICA: KY0038.

GRAVES COUNTY—Galaxy Cablevision, 1718 Barlow Rd, Wickliffe, KY 42087-9253. Phones: 270-335-3881; 800-365-6988. Fax: 270-335-5259. Web Site: http://www.galaxycable.com. Also serves Ballard County (portions), Carlisle County (portions), Cunningham, Fancy Farm, Hickory, Lovelaceville, Melber, Sedalia, Symsonia & Wingo. ICA: KY0065.
TV Market Ranking: 69 (Ballard County (portions), Carlisle County (portions), Cunningham, Fancy Farm, GRAVES COUNTY (portions), Hickory, Lovelaceville,

Melber, Sedalia, Symsonia, Wingo); Outside TV Markets (GRAVES COUNTY (portions)). Franchise award date: N.A. Franchise expiration date: N.A. Began: May 1, 1984.
Channel capacity: 54 (operating 2-way). Channels available but not in use: None.
Basic Service
Subscribers: 1,489.
Programming (received off-air): KBSI (FOX) Cape Girardeau; KFVS-TV (CBS, CW) Cape Girardeau; WDKA (MNT) Paducah; WKMU (PBS) Murray; WPSD-TV (NBC) Paducah; WQTV-LP (CW) Murray; WSIL-TV (ABC) Harrisburg; WTCT (IND) Marion.
Programming (via satellite): ABC Family Channel; AMC; Animal Planet; Arts & Entertainment; Cartoon Network; CNBC; CNN; Comedy Central; C-SPAN; Discovery Channel; Disney Channel; E! Entertainment Television; ESPN; ESPN 2; Eternal Word TV Network; Fox News Channel; Fuse; FX; Great American Country; Headline News; HGTV; History Channel; Lifetime; Outdoor Channel; QVC; Syfy; TBS Superstation; The Learning Channel; Turner Network TV; USA Network; Weather Channel; WGN America.
Planned originations: Government Access; Educational Access; Public Access.
Fee: $25.00 installation; $41.70 monthly.
Digital Basic Service
Subscribers: 319.
Programming (via satellite): AmericanLife TV Network; BBC America; Bio; Bloomberg Television; Discovery Digital Networks; DMX Music; ESPN Classic Sports; ESPNews; FitTV; Fox Sports World; G4; Golf Channel; GSN; History Channel International; INSP; National Geographic Channel; Speed Channel; Style Network; Toon Disney; WE tv.
Fee: $12.95 monthly.
Digital Expanded Basic Service
Subscribers: N.A.
Programming (via satellite): DMX Music; Encore; Fox Movie Channel; Lifetime Movie Network; Turner Classic Movies.
Fee: $12.95 monthly.
Pay Service 1
Pay Units: N.A.
Programming (via satellite): Encore; HBO; Showtime.
Fee: $10.00 monthly (Showtime), $11.00 monthly (HBO).
Digital Pay Service 1
Pay Units: N.A.
Programming (via satellite): Cinemax (multiplexed); Flix; HBO (multiplexed); Showtime (multiplexed); The Movie Channel (multiplexed).
Fee: $17.15 monthly.
Video-On-Demand: No
Pay-Per-View
Addressable homes: 459.
ESPN Now (delivered digitally), Addressable: Yes; Movies (delivered digitally); sports (delivered digitally).
Internet Service
Operational: Yes.
Telephone Service
None
Miles of Plant: 190.0 (coaxial); 28.0 (fiber optic). Homes passed: 4,261.
State Manager: Ward Webb. Operations Manager: Treka Hargrove. Technical Manager: Audie Murphy. Customer Service Manager: Malynda Walker.
City fee: 3% of gross.
Ownership: Galaxy Cable Inc. (MSO).

GRAY—Eastern Cable Corp., PO Box 126, Corbin, KY 40702-0126. Phone: 606-528-6400. Fax: 606-523-0427. Also serves Bailey's Switch, Cannon, Girdler & Jarvis. ICA: KY0066.
TV Market Ranking: Below 100 (Bailey's Switch, Cannon, Girdler, GRAY, Jarvis). Franchise award date: April 4, 1972. Franchise expiration date: N.A. Began: April 1, 1981.
Channel capacity: 30 (operating 2-way). Channels available but not in use: None.
Basic Service
Subscribers: 1,770.
Programming (received off-air): WBIR-TV (NBC) Knoxville; WDKY-TV (FOX) Danville; WKYT-TV (CBS, CW) Lexington; WTVQ-DT (ABC) Lexington; WYMT-TV (CBS, CW) Hazard.
Programming (via satellite): ABC Family Channel; Arts & Entertainment; CNN; Country Music TV; Discovery Channel; Disney Channel; ESPN; Home Shopping Network; INSP; Lifetime; Nickelodeon; Spike TV; TBS Superstation; Turner Network TV; USA Network; Weather Channel; WGN America.
Programming (via translator): WKSO-TV (PBS) Somerset.
Current originations: Government Access; Educational Access; Public Access.
Fee: $29.00 installation; $28.50 monthly.
Video-On-Demand: No
Internet Service
Operational: Yes.
Fee: $20.00 installation; $29.95 monthly.
Telephone Service
None
Miles of Plant: 140.0 (coaxial); None (fiber optic). Additional miles planned: 13.0 (coaxial). Homes passed: 2,516. Total homes in franchised area: 2,600.
Manager: Dallas R. Eubanks.
City fee: None.
Ownership: Eastern Cable.

GRAYSON—Suddenlink Communications, 12444 Powerscourt Dr, Saint Louis, MO 63131-3660. Phones: 800-999-6845 (Customer service); 314-965-2020; 314-415-9346. Fax: 903-561-5485. Web Site: http://www.suddenlink.com. Also serves Carter County, Hitchins, Leon & Pactolus. ICA: KY0061.
TV Market Ranking: 36 (GRAYSON, Hitchins, Leon, Pactolus); Below 100 (Carter County (portions)). Franchise award date: N.A. Franchise expiration date: N.A. Began: July 1, 1977.
Channel capacity: N.A. Channels available but not in use: N.A.
Basic Service
Subscribers: 2,505.
Programming (received off-air): WCHS-TV (ABC) Charleston; WKMR (PBS) Morehead; WKYT-TV (CBS, CW) Lexington; WLPX-TV (ION) Charleston; WOWK-TV (CBS) Huntington; WPBY-TV (PBS) Huntington; WQCW (CW) Portsmouth; WSAZ-TV (MNT, NBC) Huntington; WTSF (IND) Ashland; WTVQ-DT (ABC) Lexington; WVAH-TV (FOX) Charleston; allband FM.
Programming (via satellite): ABC Family Channel; AMC; Animal Planet; Arts & Entertainment; Cartoon Network; CNBC; CNN; Comedy Central; Country Music TV; C-SPAN; Discovery Channel; Disney Channel; E! Entertainment Television; ESPN; ESPN 2; Food Network; Fox News Channel; Fox Sports Net Ohio; FX; Hallmark Channel; Headline News; HGTV; History Channel; Lifetime; MTV; National Geographic Channel; Nickelodeon; Outdoor Channel; QVC; Speed Channel; Spike TV; Syfy; TBS Superstation; The Learning Channel; Trinity Broadcasting Network; Turner Network TV; TV Land; USA Network; VH1; Weather Channel; WGN-TV (CW, IND) Chicago.
Fee: $37.45 installation; $39.95 monthly.
Digital Basic Service
Subscribers: N.A.
Programming (via satellite): BBC America; Bio; Bloomberg Television; C-SPAN 3; Discovery Digital Networks; Do-It-Yourself; ESPN Classic Sports; ESPNews; Fox College Sports Atlantic; Fox College Sports Central; Fox College Sports Pacific; Fox Movie Channel; Fuse; G4; GSN; History Channel International; Independent Film Channel; Lifetime Movie Network; Military History Channel; Music Choice; Science Television; SoapNet; Sundance Channel; Toon Disney; WE tv.
Pay Service 1
Pay Units: 183.
Programming (via satellite): HBO.
Fee: $9.95 monthly.
Pay Service 2
Pay Units: 88.
Programming (via satellite): Cinemax.
Fee: $9.95 monthly.
Digital Pay Service 1
Pay Units: N.A.
Programming (via satellite): Cinemax (multiplexed); Flix; HBO (multiplexed); Showtime (multiplexed); Starz (multiplexed); The Movie Channel; The New Encore.
Video-On-Demand: No
Pay-Per-View
iN DEMAND (delivered digitally); Playboy TV (delivered digitally).
Internet Service
Operational: Yes. Began: December 31, 2005.
Broadband Service: Cebridge High Speed Cable Internet.
Fee: $59.95 monthly.
Telephone Service
None
Miles of Plant: 108.0 (coaxial); None (fiber optic). Homes passed: 3,896. Total homes in franchised area: 3,896.
District Manager: Robert Herrald. Manager: Dale Thaxton. Office Manager: Anthony Cochran. Local Manager: Bill Glore.
City fee: 3% of gross.
Ownership: Cequel Communications LLC (MSO).

GREASY CREEK—Suddenlink Communications, 12444 Powerscourt Dr, Saint Louis, MO 63131-3660. Phones: 800-999-6845 (Customer service); 314-965-2020; 314-415-9346. Fax: 903-561-5485. Web Site: http://www.suddenlink.com. Also serves Bell County (southern portion), Ingram, Kayjay & Pathfork. ICA: KY0239.
TV Market Ranking: Below 100 (Bell County (southern portion), GREASY CREEK, Ingram, Kayjay, Pathfork). Franchise award date: December 16, 1983. Franchise expiration date: N.A. Began: January 1, 1977.
Channel capacity: 76 (operating 2-way). Channels available but not in use: N.A.
Basic Service
Subscribers: 1,220.
Programming (received off-air): WAGV (IND) Harlan; WATE-TV (ABC) Knoxville; WBIR-TV (NBC) Knoxville; WBXX-TV (CW) Crossville; WKHA (PBS) Hazard; WTNZ (FOX) Knoxville; WVLR (IND) Tazewell; WVLT-TV (CBS, MNT) Knoxville; WYMT-TV (CBS, CW) Hazard.
Programming (via satellite): Home Shopping Network; QVC; Trinity Broadcasting Network; WGN America.
Fee: $35.00 installation; $18.95 monthly; $1.23 converter.
Expanded Basic Service 1
Subscribers: N.A.
Programming (via satellite): ABC Family Channel; AMC; Animal Planet; Arts & Entertainment; Cartoon Network; Celebrity Shopping Network; CNN; Comcast Sports Net Southeast; Comedy Central; Country Music TV; C-SPAN; C-SPAN 2; Discovery Channel; Disney Channel; E! Entertainment Television; ESPN; ESPN 2; ESPN Classic Sports; Food Network; Fox News Channel; FX; Hallmark Channel; Headline News; HGTV; History Channel; Lifetime; MTV; Nickelodeon; Spike TV; Syfy; TBS Superstation; The Learning Channel; Turner Classic Movies; Turner Network TV; TV Land; USA Network; VH1; Weather Channel.
Fee: $22.00 monthly.
Digital Basic Service
Subscribers: N.A.
Programming (via satellite): BBC America; Bio; Bloomberg Television; Country Music TV; Discovery Digital Networks; DMX Music; ESPNews; Fox Movie Channel; Fox Soccer; Fuse; G4; GAS; Golf Channel; GSN; History Channel International; Independent Film Channel; Lifetime Movie Network; MTV Networks Digital Suite; National Geographic Channel; Nick Jr.; NickToons TV; Outdoor Channel; Sleuth; Speed Channel; Style Network; Toon Disney; Versus; WE tv.
Fee: $12.95 monthly.
Digital Pay Service 1
Pay Units: N.A.
Programming (via satellite): Cinemax (multiplexed); Encore (multiplexed); HBO (multiplexed); Showtime (multiplexed); Starz (multiplexed); The Movie Channel (multiplexed).
Video-On-Demand: No
Pay-Per-View
iN DEMAND (delivered digitally); Playboy TV (delivered digitally); Fresh (delivered digitally).
Internet Service
Operational: Yes.
Broadband Service: Cebridge High Speed Cable Internet.
Fee: $49.95 installation; $26.95 monthly.
Telephone Service
None
Miles of Plant: 54.0 (coaxial); None (fiber optic).
Office Manager: Dena Hoskins. Vice President: Robert Herrald. Chief Technician: Jim Thompson.
Ownership: Cequel Communications LLC (MSO).

GREENSBURG—Access Cable Television Inc., 302 Enterprise Dr, Somerset, KY 42501. Phone: 606-677-2444. Fax: 606-677-2443. E-mail: cable@accesshsd.net. Also serves Green County & Summersville. ICA: KY0110.
TV Market Ranking: Below 100 (Green County, GREENSBURG, Summersville). Franchise award date: September 6, 1982. Franchise expiration date: N.A. Began: March 1, 1955.
Channel capacity: 65 (operating 2-way). Channels available but not in use: None.
Basic Service
Subscribers: 669.
Programming (received off-air): WAVE (NBC) Louisville; WBKI-TV (CW) Campbellsville; WBKO (ABC, CW) Bowling Green; WDKY-TV (FOX) Danville; WDRB (FOX) Louisville; WHAS-TV (ABC) Louisville; WKYT-TV (CBS, CW) Lexington; WKZT-TV (PBS) Elizabethtown; WLEX-TV (NBC) Lexington; WLKY-TV (CBS) Louisville; WNKY (CBS, NBC) Bowling Green; allband FM.

Programming (via satellite): AMC; Arts & Entertainment; CNN; Country Music TV; C-SPAN; C-SPAN 2; Discovery Channel; E! Entertainment Television; ESPN; ESPN 2; Headline News; HGTV; Home Shopping Network; INSP; ION Television; Nickelodeon; QVC; Spike TV; The Learning Channel; Trinity Broadcasting Network; Turner Network TV; VH1; WGN America.
Current originations: Government Access; Educational Access; Public Access.
Fee: $15.00 installation; $18.95 monthly; $3.00 converter; $15.00 additional installation.

Expanded Basic Service 1
Subscribers: 472.
Programming (via satellite): ABC Family Channel; Animal Planet; BET Networks; Cartoon Network; CNBC; Disney Channel; ESPN Classic Sports; Fox News Channel; FX; Gospel Music Channel; Hallmark Channel; History Channel; Lifetime; MSNBC; MTV; Outdoor Channel; Speed Channel; Syfy; TBS Superstation; Travel Channel; TV Land; USA Network; Weather Channel.
Fee: $11.55 monthly.

Pay Service 1
Pay Units: 40.
Programming (via satellite): Cinemax.
Fee: $15.00 installation; $12.95 monthly.

Pay Service 2
Pay Units: 33.
Programming (via satellite): Showtime; The Movie Channel.
Fee: $15.00 installation; $11.95 monthly.

Video-On-Demand: No

Internet Service
Operational: Yes.

Telephone Service
Digital: Operational
Fee: $35.00 installation; $24.95 monthly
Miles of Plant: 92.0 (coaxial); None (fiber optic). Homes passed: 2,098.
President & Manager: Roy Baker.
Ownership: Access Cable Television Inc. (MSO).

GREENUP—Charter Communications. Now served by SOUTH POINT, OH [WV0011]. ICA: KY0195.

GREENVILLE—Comcast Cable, 2919 Ring Rd, Elizabethtown, KY 42701. Phone: 270-737-2731. Fax: 270-737-3379. Web Site: http://www.comcast.com. Also serves Beech Creek, Beechmont, Belton, Browder, Central City, Cleaton, Depoy, Drakesboro, Graham, Powderly & South Carrollton. ICA: KY0023.
TV Market Ranking: Below 100 (Beech Creek, Beechmont, Belton, Browder, Central City, Cleaton, Depoy, Drakesboro, Graham, GREENVILLE, Powderly, South Carrollton). Franchise award date: April 4, 1964. Franchise expiration date: N.A. Began: March 1, 1965.
Channel capacity: 40 (operating 2-way). Channels available but not in use: None.

Basic Service
Subscribers: 5,578.
Programming (received off-air): WAZE-TV (CW) Madisonville; WBKO (ABC, CW) Bowling Green; WEHT (ABC) Evansville; WEVV-TV (CBS, MNT) Evansville; WFIE (NBC) Evansville; WKMA-TV (PBS) Madisonville; WKYU-TV (PBS) Bowling Green; WTVF (CBS) Nashville; WTVW (FOX) Evansville; allband FM.
Programming (via satellite): QVC; WGN America.
Planned originations: Government Access.
Fee: $54.99 installation; $13.08 monthly.

Expanded Basic Service 1
Subscribers: N.A.
Programming (via satellite): ABC Family Channel; AMC; Animal Planet; Arts & Entertainment; BET Networks; Cartoon Network; CNBC; CNN; Comcast Sports Net Southeast; Comcast/Charter Sports Southeast (CSS); Comedy Central; C-SPAN; Discovery Channel; Discovery Health Channel; Disney Channel; E! Entertainment Television; ESPN; ESPN 2; Food Network; Fox News Channel; FX; Golf Channel; Great American Country; GSN; Hallmark Channel; Headline News; HGTV; History Channel; Home Shopping Network; Lifetime; Military History Channel; MSNBC; MTV; National Geographic Channel; Nickelodeon; Outdoor Channel; Speed Channel; Spike TV; Style Network; Syfy; TBS Superstation; The Learning Channel; Travel Channel; Trinity Broadcasting Network; truTV; Turner Network TV; TV Land; USA Network; Versus; VH1; Weather Channel.
Fee: $33.91 monthly.

Digital Basic Service
Subscribers: N.A.
Programming (via satellite): BBC America; CMT Pure Country; C-SPAN 3; Discovery Digital Networks; Encore; ESPNews; Flix; GAS; Lifetime Movie Network; MoviePlex; MTV Networks Digital Suite; NFL Network; Nick Jr.; Nick Too; NickToons TV; PBS Kids Sprout; SoapNet; Sundance Channel; Toon Disney; WAM! America's Kidz Network.
Fee: $14.95 monthly.

Digital Pay Service 1
Pay Units: N.A.
Programming (via satellite): Cinemax (multiplexed); HBO (multiplexed); Showtime (multiplexed); Starz (multiplexed); The Movie Channel (multiplexed).
Fee: $13.05 monthly (each).

Video-On-Demand: No

Pay-Per-View
Playboy TV (delivered digitally); Fresh (delivered digitally); Shorteez (delivered digitally); Pleasure (delivered digitally); Hot Choice (delivered digitally).

Internet Service
Operational: Yes.
Broadband Service: Comcast High Speed Internet.
Fee: $42.95 monthly.

Telephone Service
Digital: Operational
Miles of Plant: 230.0 (coaxial); None (fiber optic). Homes passed: 8,634. Total homes in franchised area: 9,522.
General Manager: Tim Hagan. Marketing Director: Laurie Nicholson. Technical Operations Director: Bob Tharp.
City fee: 3% of gross.
Ownership: Comcast Cable Communications Inc. (MSO).

HARDINSBURG—Windjammer Cable, 4400 PGA Blvd, Ste 902, Palm Beach Gardens, FL 33410. Phones: 877-450-5558; 561-775-1208. Fax: 561-775-7811. Web Site: http://www.windjammercable.com. Also serves Breckinridge County. ICA: KY0098.
TV Market Ranking: Outside TV Markets (Breckinridge County, HARDINSBURG). Franchise award date: March 10, 1987. Franchise expiration date: N.A. Began: June 1, 1982.
Channel capacity: N.A. Channels available but not in use: N.A.

Basic Service
Subscribers: N.A. Included in Owensboro
Programming (received off-air): WAVE (NBC) Louisville; WDRB (FOX) Louisville; WHAS-TV (ABC) Louisville; WKZT-TV (PBS) Elizabethtown; WLKY-TV (CBS) Louisville; WNIN (PBS) Evansville; WTVW (FOX) Evansville.
Programming (via satellite): MTV; QVC; TBS Superstation; WGN America.
Current originations: Government Access; Educational Access; Public Access.
Fee: $39.95 installation; $24.97 monthly; $1.50 converter.

Expanded Basic Service 1
Subscribers: 733.
Programming (via satellite): ABC Family Channel; AMC; CNN; Country Music TV; Discovery Channel; ESPN; Lifetime; Nickelodeon; Spike TV; Turner Network TV; USA Network.
Fee: $15.95 monthly.

Pay Service 1
Pay Units: 113.
Programming (via satellite): Cinemax.
Fee: $15.95 monthly.

Pay Service 2
Pay Units: 145.
Programming (via satellite): HBO.
Fee: $15.95 monthly.

Video-On-Demand: No

Internet Service
Operational: No.

Telephone Service
None
Miles of Plant: 27.0 (coaxial); None (fiber optic). Homes passed included in Owensboro
General Manager: Timothy Evard. Operations Director: Belinda Graham. Engineering Director: Mike Earehart. Finance & Accounting Director: Cindy Johnson.
City fee: 3% of basic.
Ownership: Windjammer Communications LLC (MSO).

HARLAN—Harlan Community TV Inc., PO Box 592, 124 S First St, Harlan, KY 40831. Phone: 606-573-2945. Fax: 606-573-6959. E-mail: hctv@harlanonline.net. Web Site: http://www.harlanonline.net. Also serves Baxter, Cathron's Creek, Grays Knob, Gulston, Harlan County, Keith, Loyall & Yancy. ICA: KY0230.
TV Market Ranking: Below 100 (Baxter, Cathron's Creek, Grays Knob, Gulston, HARLAN, Harlan County, Keith, Loyall, Yancy). Franchise award date: N.A. Franchise expiration date: N.A. Began: January 1, 1953.
Channel capacity: 60 (operating 2-way). Channels available but not in use: 23.

Basic Service
Subscribers: 3,212.
Programming (received off-air): WAGV (IND) Harlan; WATE-TV (ABC) Knoxville; WBIR-TV (NBC) Knoxville; WBXX-TV (CW) Crossville; WDKY-TV (FOX) Danville; WEMT (FOX) Greeneville; WJHL-TV (CBS) Johnson City; WKHA (PBS) Hazard; WKPT-TV (ABC) Kingsport; WKYT-TV (CBS, CW) Lexington; WLEX-TV (NBC) Lexington; WTNZ (FOX) Knoxville; WTVQ-DT (ABC) Lexington; WVLT-TV (CBS, MNT) Knoxville; WYMT-TV (CBS, CW) Hazard; allband FM.
Programming (via satellite): AMC; Animal Planet; Arts & Entertainment; Cartoon Network; CNBC; CNN; Country Music TV; C-SPAN; C-SPAN 2; Discovery Channel; ESPN; ESPN 2; ESPN Classic Sports; Food Network; Fox News Channel; Fox Sports World; FX; Golf Channel; Hallmark Channel; Hallmark Movie Channel; Headline News; HGTV; History Channel; Home Shopping Network; ION Television; Lifetime; MTV; Nickelodeon; Outdoor Channel; Speed Channel; Spike TV; Syfy; TBS Superstation; The Learning Channel; Trinity Broadcasting Network; Turner Classic Movies; Turner Network TV; TV Land; USA Network; VH1; Weather Channel; WGN America; WPIX (CW, IND) New York.
Fee: $40.00 installation; $14.00 monthly.

Pay Service 1
Pay Units: 210.
Programming (via satellite): HBO.
Fee: $10.00 monthly.

Pay Service 2
Pay Units: 50.
Programming (via satellite): Showtime.
Fee: $10.00 monthly.

Pay Service 3
Pay Units: 50.
Programming (via satellite): Cinemax.
Fee: $7.00 monthly.

Video-On-Demand: No

Internet Service
Operational: Yes. Began: April 18, 2000.
Subscribers: 350.
Broadband Service: In-house.
Fee: $39.95 monthly; $9.95 modem lease; $100.00 modem purchase.

Telephone Service
Analog: Not Operational
Digital: Operational
Fee: $41.20 installation; $42.03 monthly
Miles of Plant: 100.0 (coaxial); None (fiber optic).
President & General Manager: Jack B. Hale. Vice President: Mark Lawrence. Office Manager: Joy Taylor.
Ownership: Harlan Community TV Inc.

HAROLD—Inter Mountain Cable Inc., PO Box 159, 20 Laynesville Rd, Harold, KY 41635. Phones: 606-452-2345; 606-478-9406. Fax: 606-478-1680. E-mail: imcable@gearheart.com. Web Site: http://www.imctv.com. Also serves Allen, Argo, Banner, Belfry, Betsy Layne, Bevinsville, Blackberry Creek, Blair Town, Blue River, Boldman, Broad Bottom, Canada, Coal Run, David, Dorton, Dwale, Eastern, Emma, Fedscreek, Floyd County, Freeburn, Galveston, Garrett, Grethel, Hardy, Hi Hat, Hippo, Hite, Hueysville, Hunter, Island Creek, Ivel, Johnson County, Kimper, Knott County (portions), Little Mud Creek, Little Robinson, Magoffin, Majestic, Manton, Martin, Maytown, McCarr, McVeigh, Melvin, Meta, Myra, Peter Fork, Phelps, Phyllis, Pike County, Pikeville, Pinsonfork, Prater Creek, Prater Fork, Prestonsburg, Printer, Pyramid, Ransom, Risner, Robinson Creek, Shelby Gap, Stanville, Stone Coal, Stopover, Teaberry, Toler Creek, Tram, Upper Johns Creek, Watergap, Weeksbury, Wells Addition, West Prestonsburg, Wheelwright & Zebulon, KY; Buchanan County & Hurley, VA; Blackberry City, Hatfield Bottom, Lynn, Matewan,

Mingo County, Newtown, North Matewan, Red Jacket & Thacker, WV. ICA: KY0006.

TV Market Ranking: 36 (Mingo County (portions)); Below 100 (Argo, Belfry, Betsy Layne, Bevinsville, Blackberry City, Blackberry Creek, Blair Town, Blue River, Boldman, Broad Bottom, Buchanan County (portions), Canada, Coal Run, David, Dorton, Eastern, Fedscreek, Floyd County (portions), Freeburn, Galveston, Garrett, Grethel, Hardy, HAROLD, Hatfield Bottom, Hi Hat, Hippo, Hite, Hueysville, Hunter, Hurley, Island Creek, Johnson County (portions), Kimper, Knott County (portions, Little Mud Creek, Little Robinson, Lynn, Magoffin, Majestic, Manton, Martin, Matewan, Maytown, McCarr, McVeigh, Melvin, Meta, Myra, Newtown, North Matewan, Peter Fork, Phelps, Phyllis, Pike County (portions), Pikeville, Pinsonfork, Prater Fork, Printer, Pyramid, Ransom, Red Jacket, Risner, Robinson Creek, Shelby Gap, Stanville, Stopover, Teaberry, Thacker, Weeksbury, Wells Addition, Wheelwright, Zebulon); Outside TV Markets (Allen, Banner, Buchanan County (portions), Dwale, Emma, Floyd County (portions), Ivel, Johnson County (portions), Pike County (portions), Prater Creek, Prestonsburg, Stone Coal, Toler Creek, Tram, Upper Johns Creek, Watergap, West Prestonsburg, Mingo County (portions)). Franchise award date: N.A. Franchise expiration date: N.A. Began: April 1, 1948.

Channel capacity: N.A. Channels available but not in use: N.A.

Basic Service

Subscribers: 21,169.

Programming (received off-air): WCHS-TV (ABC) Charleston; WKPI-TV (PBS) Pikeville; WLJC-TV (TBN) Beattyville; WOWK-TV (CBS) Huntington; WQCW (CW) Portsmouth; WSAZ-TV (MNT, NBC) Huntington; WUPX-TV (ION) Morehead; WVAH-TV (FOX) Charleston; WYMT-TV (CBS, CW) Hazard; allband FM.

Programming (via satellite): QVC; ShopNBC; Syfy; TV Guide Network; Weather Channel; WGN America.

Fee: $40.00 installation; $18.95 monthly.

Expanded Basic Service 1

Subscribers: 18,062.

Programming (via satellite): ABC Family Channel; AMC; Animal Planet; Arts & Entertainment; Boomerang; Bravo; Cartoon Network; CNBC; CNN; Comedy Central; Country Music TV; C-SPAN; Discovery Channel; Disney Channel; E! Entertainment Television; ESPN; ESPN 2; ESPN Classic Sports; Food Network; Fox News Channel; Fox Sports Net; FX; Great American Country; GSN; Hallmark Channel; History Channel; JCTV; Lifetime; MSNBC; MTV; National Geographic Channel; NFL Network; Nickelodeon; Outdoor Channel; SoapNet; Spike TV; TBS Superstation; The Learning Channel; The Sportsman Channel; Travel Channel; truTV; Turner Network TV; TV Land; TVG Network; USA Network; VH1.

Fee: $26.95 monthly.

Digital Basic Service

Subscribers: 962.

Programming (received off-air): WCHS-TV (ABC) Charleston; WVAH-TV (FOX) Charleston.

Programming (via satellite): Anime Network; BBC America; Bloomberg Television; Bravo; Canales N; CBS College Sports Network; Current; Discovery Digital Networks; Discovery HD Theater; DMX Music; ESPN 2; ESPN Classic Sports; ESPNews; Fox College Sports Atlantic; Fox College Sports Central; Fox College Sports Pacific; Fox Movie Channel; Fox Sports Net; Fox Sports World; Fuse; G4; Golf Channel; Great American Country; GSN; HDNet; HDNet Movies; HGTV; Independent Film Channel; Lifetime Movie Network; MTV Networks Digital Suite; Nick Jr.; Outdoor Channel; Ovation; ShopNBC; Speed Channel; Style Network; Syfy; Trinity Broadcasting Network; Trio; Turner Classic Movies; TV One; TVG Network; Universal HD; Versus; WE tv.

Fee: $11.95 monthly; $3.99 converter.

Digital Pay Service 1

Pay Units: 416.

Programming (via satellite): Cinemax (multiplexed).

Fee: $7.95 monthly; $3.99 converter.

Digital Pay Service 2

Pay Units: 453.

Programming (via satellite): HBO (multiplexed).

Fee: $12.95 monthly; $3.99 converter.

Digital Pay Service 3

Pay Units: 144.

Programming (via satellite): Flix; Showtime (multiplexed); Sundance Channel; The Movie Channel.

Fee: $11.95 monthly; $3.99 converter.

Digital Pay Service 4

Pay Units: 407.

Programming (via satellite): Encore (multiplexed); Starz.

Fee: $13.95 monthly; $3.99 converter.

Video-On-Demand: Yes

Pay-Per-View

iN DEMAND (delivered digitally), Addressable: Yes; Hot Choice (delivered digitally); movies (delivered digitally); Fresh (delivered digitally); Shorteez (delivered digitally).

Internet Service

Operational: Yes.

Subscribers: 850.

Fee: $24.95 monthly.

Telephone Service

Analog: Not Operational

Digital: Operational

Fee: $131.93 monthly

Miles of Plant: 11,075.0 (coaxial); None (fiber optic). Homes passed: 26,159.

Manager: Paul Douglas Gearheart. Operations Director: John C. Schmoldt. Chief Engineer: Jefferson Thacker. Business Manager: James O. Campbell. Ad Sales Manager: Wanda Hatfield. Customer Service Supervisor: Rebecca Walters.

City fee: $25.00 flat fee.

Ownership: Inter-Mountain Cable Inc. (MSO).

HARRODSBURG—Time Warner Cable, 1615 Foxhaven Dr, Richmond, KY 40475. Phones: 859-624-9666; 859-626-4800. Fax: 859-624-0060. Web Site: http://www.timewarnercable.com. Also serves Anderson County (eastern portion), Boyle County (portions), Burgin, Danville, Franklin County (southern portion), Junction City, Lancaster, Lawrenceburg, Lincoln County (northern portion), Mercer County, Perryville, Stanford, Versailles & Woodford County (eastern portion). ICA: KY0231.

TV Market Ranking: Below 100 (Anderson County (eastern portion), Boyle County (portions), Burgin, Danville, Franklin County (southern portion), HARRODSBURG, Junction City, Lancaster, Lawrenceburg, Lincoln County (northern portion), Mercer County, Perryville, Stanford, Versailles, Woodford County (eastern portion)). Franchise award date: N.A. Franchise expiration date: N.A. Began: October 1, 1965.

Channel capacity: N.A. Channels available but not in use: N.A.

Basic Service

Subscribers: 20,462.

Programming (received off-air): WAVE (NBC) Louisville; WBKI-TV (CW) Campbellsville; WDKY-TV (FOX) Danville; WDRB (FOX) Louisville; WHAS-TV (ABC) Louisville; WKLE (PBS) Lexington; WKYT-TV (CBS, CW) Lexington; WLEX-TV (NBC) Lexington; WLKY-TV (CBS) Louisville; WTVQ-DT (ABC) Lexington; WUPX-TV (ION) Morehead; 2 FMs.

Programming (via satellite): Country Music TV; C-SPAN; C-SPAN 2; ESPN; ESPN 2; Fox News Channel; Home Shopping Network; QVC; ShopNBC; TV Guide Network; Weather Channel; WGN America.

Current originations: Leased Access; Religious Access; Educational Access; Public Access.

Fee: $39.95 installation; $20.35 monthly; $.59 converter; $19.95 additional installation.

Expanded Basic Service 1

Subscribers: 17,677.

Programming (via satellite): ABC Family Channel; AMC; Animal Planet; Arts & Entertainment; BET Networks; Bravo; Cartoon Network; CNBC; CNN; Comcast Sports Net Southeast; Comedy Central; Discovery Channel; Discovery Health Channel; Disney Channel; E! Entertainment Television; Food Network; Fox Sports Net Ohio; FX; Hallmark Channel; Headline News; HGTV; History Channel; INSP; Lifetime; MSNBC; MTV; Nickelodeon; Oxygen; Spike TV; Syfy; TBS Superstation; The Learning Channel; Travel Channel; Trinity Broadcasting Network; truTV; Turner Network TV; TV Land; USA Network; VH1.

Fee: $30.00 monthly.

Digital Basic Service

Subscribers: N.A.

Programming (via satellite): AmericanLife TV Network; BBC America; Bio; Black Family Channel; Bloomberg Television; Canales N; Discovery Digital Networks; DMX Music; Do-It-Yourself; ESPN Classic Sports; ESPNews; FitTV; Fox College Sports Atlantic; Fox College Sports Central; Fox College Sports Pacific; Fox Sports World; Fuse; G4; GAS; Golf Channel; Great American Country; GSN; Halogen Network; History Channel International; Independent Film Channel; Lifetime Movie Network; MTV Networks Digital Suite; Music Choice; National Geographic Channel; Nick Jr.; Nick Too; NickToons TV; Outdoor Channel; SoapNet; Speed Channel; Style Network; Sundance Channel; The Word Network; Toon Disney; Turner Classic Movies; Versus; WE tv.

Fee: $6.00 monthly (each tier).

Digital Pay Service 1

Pay Units: 3,731.

Programming (via satellite): ART America; CCTV-4; Cinemax (multiplexed); Encore (multiplexed); Filipino Channel; Flix; HBO (multiplexed); RAI International; Russian Television Network; Showtime (multiplexed); Starz (multiplexed); The Movie Channel (multiplexed); TV Asia; TV Japan; TV5, La Television International; Zee TV USA; Zhong Tian Channel.

Fee: $12.00 monthly (HBO, Cinemax, Showtime, TMC or Starz), $15.00 monthly (CCTV, TV Asia, TV5, Filipino, RAI, ART, TV Russia or TV Japan).

Video-On-Demand: No

Pay-Per-View

iN DEMAND (delivered digitally); Playboy TV (delivered digitally); Fresh (delivered digitally); Hot Choice (delivered digitally); Urban Xtra (delivered digitally); Sports PPV (delivered digitally).

Internet Service

Operational: Yes.

Broadband Service: Road Runner.

Fee: $44.95 monthly.

Telephone Service

Digital: Operational

Fee: $49.95 monthly

Miles of Plant: 657.0 (coaxial); None (fiber optic). Homes passed: 23,379. Total homes in franchised area: 23,379.

General Manager: Robert Trott. Technical Operations Manager: Dennis Lester. Marketing Director: Betrina Morse. Government & Public Affairs Manager: Carla Deaton. Office Manager: Laverne Farris.

City fee: 3% of gross.

Ownership: Time Warner Cable (MSO).

HAWESVILLE—Windjammer Cable, 4400 PGA Blvd, Ste 902, Palm Beach Gardens, FL 33410. Phones: 877-450-5558; 561-775-1208. Fax: 561-775-7811. Web Site: http://www.windjammercable.com. ICA: KY0232.

TV Market Ranking: Outside TV Markets (HAWESVILLE). Franchise award date: January 1, 1979. Franchise expiration date: N.A. Began: November 8, 1979.

Channel capacity: N.A. Channels available but not in use: N.A.

Basic Service

Subscribers: N.A. Included in Owensboro

Programming (received off-air): WAVE (NBC) Louisville; WDRB (FOX) Louisville; WEHT (ABC) Evansville; WEVV-TV (CBS, MNT) Evansville; WFIE (NBC) Evansville; WHAS-TV (ABC) Louisville; WKOH (PBS) Owensboro; WLKY-TV (CBS) Louisville; WNIN (PBS) Evansville; WTVW (FOX) Evansville; 2 FMs.

Programming (via satellite): TBS Superstation; USA Network; WGN America.

Current originations: Government Access; Educational Access; Public Access.

Fee: $39.95 installation; $22.84 monthly; $1.98 converter.

Expanded Basic Service 1

Subscribers: N.A.

Programming (via satellite): ABC Family Channel; AMC; Arts & Entertainment; Cartoon Network; CNN; Country Music TV; Discovery Channel; Disney Channel; ESPN; ESPN 2; Headline News; HGTV; History Channel; Lifetime; MTV; Nickelodeon; QVC; Spike TV; The Learning Channel; Turner Classic Movies; Turner Network TV; Weather Channel.

Fee: $17.00 monthly.

Pay Service 1

Pay Units: 78.

Programming (via satellite): HBO.

Fee: $15.95 monthly.

Video-On-Demand: No

Internet Service

Operational: No.

Telephone Service

None

Miles of Plant: 32.0 (coaxial); None (fiber optic). Homes passed included in Owensboro

City fee: 3% of basic.

Ownership: Windjammer Communications LLC (MSO).

HAZARD—Hazard TV Cable Co. Inc., PO Box 929, 143 Gorman Ridge Rd, Hazard, KY 41701. Phone: 606-436-2522. ICA: KY0119.

TV Market Ranking: Below 100 (HAZARD). Franchise award date: N.A. Franchise expiration date: N.A. Began: January 1, 1949.
Channel capacity: 35 (not 2-way capable). Channels available but not in use: N.A.

Basic Service

Subscribers: 750.
Programming (received off-air): WAGV (IND) Harlan; WCYB-TV (CW, NBC) Bristol; WDKY-TV (FOX) Danville; WKHA (PBS) Hazard; WKYT-TV (CBS, CW) Lexington; WLEX-TV (NBC) Lexington; WLJC-TV (TBN) Beattyville; WTVQ-DT (ABC) Lexington; WYMT-TV (CBS, CW) Hazard.
Programming (via satellite): ABC Family Channel; AMC; CNN; Country Music TV; C-SPAN; Discovery Channel; ESPN; ESPN 2; Hallmark Channel; Headline News; Home Shopping Network; ION Television; Nickelodeon; QVC; Spike TV; TBS Superstation; Turner Network TV; TV Land; USA Network; Weather Channel; WGN America.
Current originations: Religious Access.
Fee: $50.00 installation; $27.00 monthly.

Pay Service 1

Pay Units: 61.
Programming (via satellite): HBO.

Pay Service 2

Pay Units: 66.
Programming (via satellite): The Movie Channel.

Internet Service

Operational: No.

Telephone Service

None
Miles of Plant: 75.0 (coaxial); None (fiber optic). Homes passed: 1,000. Total homes in franchised area: 1,000.
Manager: John Earl Edwards Jr.
Ownership: Hazard TV Co. Inc.

HAZEL—Galaxy Cablevision, 1718 Barlow Rd, Wickliffe, KY 42087-9253. Phones: 270-335-3881; 800-365-6988. Fax: 270-335-5259. Web Site: http://www.galaxycable.com. Also serves Puryear. ICA: KY0233.
TV Market Ranking: Outside TV Markets (HAZEL, Puryear). Franchise award date: N.A. Franchise expiration date: N.A. Began: February 1, 1984.
Channel capacity: 36 (operating 2-way). Channels available but not in use: None.

Basic Service

Subscribers: 190.
Programming (received off-air): KBSI (FOX) Cape Girardeau; KFVS-TV (CBS, CW) Cape Girardeau; WBBJ-TV (ABC) Jackson; WDKA (MNT) Paducah; WKMU (PBS) Murray; WPSD-TV (NBC) Paducah; WQTV-LP (CW) Murray.
Programming (via satellite): ABC Family Channel; AMC; Animal Planet; Arts & Entertainment; Cartoon Network; CNBC; CNN; Comedy Central; C-SPAN; Discovery Channel; Disney Channel; E! Entertainment Television; ESPN; ESPN 2; Food Network; Fox News Channel; Fuse; FX; Great American Country; Headline News; HGTV; History Channel; Lifetime; Outdoor Channel; QVC; Syfy; TBS Superstation; The Learning Channel; Turner Classic Movies; Turner Network TV; USA Network; Weather Channel; WGN America.
Fee: $30.00 installation; $41.50 monthly; $3.00 converter.

Digital Basic Service

Subscribers: 51.
Programming (via satellite): BBC America; Bio; Bloomberg Television; Discovery Health Channel; Discovery Kids Channel; Discovery Military Channel; Discovery Planet Green; ESPN Classic Sports; ESPNews; FitTV; Fox Movie Channel; Fox Soccer; Fuse; G4; Golf Channel; GSN; Halogen Network; History Channel International; ID Investigation Discovery; Independent Film Channel; Lifetime Movie Network; National Geographic Channel; PBS Kids Sprout; RFD-TV; Science Channel; Sleuth; Speed Channel; Style Network; WE tv.

Pay Service 1

Pay Units: N.A.
Programming (via satellite): Cinemax; HBO; Showtime.
Fee: $12.00 monthly (each).

Digital Pay Service 1

Pay Units: N.A.
Programming (via satellite): Cinemax (multiplexed); Encore (multiplexed); Flix; HBO (multiplexed); Showtime (multiplexed); Starz (multiplexed); The Movie Channel (multiplexed).

Pay-Per-View

iN DEMAND (delivered digitally); Playboy TV (delivered digitally); Fresh (delivered digitally); Shorteez (delivered digitally); Club Jenna (delivered digitally).

Internet Service

Operational: Yes.
Subscribers: 68.
Fee: $49.95 installation; $44.95 monthly.

Telephone Service

None
Miles of Plant: 15.0 (coaxial); None (fiber optic). Homes passed: 604.
State Manager: Ward Webb. Operations Manager: Treka Hargrove. Technical Manager: Audie Murphy. Customer Service Manager: Malynda Walker.
Ownership: Galaxy Cable Inc. (MSO).

HENDERSON—Now served by EVANSVILLE, IN [IN0006]. ICA: KY0016.

HENDERSON (southern portion)—Mediacom, 90 Main St, Benton, KY 42025-1132. Phones: 417-875-5560 (Springfield regional office); 270-527-9939. Fax: 270-527-0813. Web Site: http://www.mediacomcable.com. Also serves Henderson County (portions). ICA: KY0112.
TV Market Ranking: 86 (HENDERSON, Henderson County (portions)). Franchise award date: April 11, 1989. Franchise expiration date: N.A. Began: January 1, 1989.
Channel capacity: N.A. Channels available but not in use: N.A.

Basic Service

Subscribers: 480.
Programming (received off-air): WAZE-TV (CW) Madisonville; WEHT (ABC) Evansville; WEVV-TV (CBS, MNT) Evansville; WFIE (NBC) Evansville; WKMA-TV (PBS) Madisonville; WNIN (PBS) Evansville; WTVW (FOX) Evansville.
Programming (via satellite): ABC Family Channel; AMC; Animal Planet; Arts & Entertainment; Cartoon Network; CNN; Comedy Central; Country Music TV; Discovery Channel; Disney Channel; E! Entertainment Television; ESPN; ESPN 2; Food Network; Fox News Channel; FX; Great American Country; Headline News; HGTV; History Channel; Lifetime; MSNBC; MTV; National Geographic Channel; Nickelodeon; Outdoor Channel; QVC; Speed Channel; Spike TV; Syfy; TBS Superstation; The Learning Channel; Travel Channel; Trinity Broadcasting Network; truTV; Turner Classic Movies; Turner Network TV; TV Land; USA Network; Weather Channel; WGN America.
Fee: $29.95 installation; $21.95 monthly; $3.95 converter.

Pay Service 1

Pay Units: 82.
Programming (via satellite): Cinemax.
Fee: $10.00 installation; $9.00 monthly.

Pay Service 2

Pay Units: 55.
Programming (via satellite): Encore; Starz.
Fee: $10.00 installation; $7.00 monthly.

Pay Service 3

Pay Units: 101.
Programming (via satellite): HBO.
Fee: $10.00 installation; $10.00 monthly.
Video-On-Demand: No

Internet Service

Operational: No.

Telephone Service

None
Miles of Plant: 35.0 (coaxial); None (fiber optic). Homes passed: 1,036.
Regional Vice President: Bill Copeland. General Manager: Dale Haney. Regional Technical Operations Director: Alan Freedman. Marketing Director: Will Kuebler. Marketing Manager: Melanie Westerman. Technical Operations Manager: Jeff Brown.
Ownership: Mediacom LLC (MSO).

HENDERSON (town)—Now served by OWENSBORO, KY [KY0004]. ICA: KY0306.

HICKMAN—Galaxy Cablevision, 1718 Barlow Rd, Wickliffe, KY 42087-9253. Phones: 270-335-3881; 800-365-6988. Fax: 270-335-5259. Web Site: http://www.galaxycable.com. ICA: KY0234.
TV Market Ranking: Outside TV Markets (HICKMAN). Franchise award date: N.A. Franchise expiration date: N.A. Began: December 1, 1980.
Channel capacity: 78 (operating 2-way). Channels available but not in use: None.

Basic Service

Subscribers: 441.
Programming (received off-air): KBSI (FOX) Cape Girardeau; KFVS-TV (CBS, CW) Cape Girardeau; WBBJ-TV (ABC) Jackson; WKMU (PBS) Murray; WPSD-TV (NBC) Paducah; WSIL-TV (ABC) Harrisburg.
Programming (via satellite): ABC Family Channel; AMC; Animal Planet; Arts & Entertainment; BET Networks; Cartoon Network; CNBC; CNN; Comedy Central; Discovery Channel; Disney Channel; E! Entertainment Television; ESPN; ESPN 2; Food Network; Fox News Channel; Fuse; FX; Great American Country; Headline News; HGTV; History Channel; Home Shopping Network; INSP; Lifetime; Outdoor Channel; Speed Channel; Syfy; TBS Superstation; The Learning Channel; Toon Disney; Turner Classic Movies; Turner Network TV; USA Network; Weather Channel; WGN America.
Fee: $30.00 installation; $42.73 monthly; $3.00 converter.

Digital Basic Service

Subscribers: 96.
Programming (via satellite): AmericanLife TV Network; BBC America; Bio; Bloomberg Television; Discovery Digital Networks; DMX Music; ESPN Classic Sports; ESPNews; FitTV; Fox Sports World; G4; Golf Channel; GSN; Halogen Network; History Channel International; National Geographic Channel; Style Network; Toon Disney; WE tv.
Fee: $13.95 monthly.

Digital Expanded Basic Service

Subscribers: N.A.
Programming (via satellite): Encore (multiplexed); Fox Movie Channel; Lifetime Movie Network.
Fee: $13.95 monthly.

Pay Service 1

Pay Units: N.A.
Programming (via satellite): Cinemax; HBO; Showtime; The Movie Channel.

Digital Pay Service 1

Pay Units: N.A.
Programming (via satellite): Cinemax (multiplexed); Flix; HBO (multiplexed); Showtime (multiplexed); The Movie Channel (multiplexed).
Fee: $14.05 monthly.

Pay-Per-View

Addressable homes: 111.
ESPN Now, Fee: $3.99, Addressable: Yes; Hot Choice (delivered digitally); Playboy TV (delivered digitally); Fresh (delivered digitally); Shorteez (delivered digitally); sports (delivered digitally).

Internet Service

Operational: Yes.
Subscribers: 77.
Broadband Service: Galaxy Cable Internet.
Fee: $49.95 installation; $44.95 monthly.

Telephone Service

None
Miles of Plant: 34.0 (coaxial); 10.0 (fiber optic). Homes passed: 1,385.
State Manager: Ward Webb. Operations Manager: Treka Hargrove. Technical Manager: Audie Murphy. Customer Service Manager: Malynda Walker.
Ownership: Galaxy Cable Inc. (MSO).

HINDMAN—TV Service Inc., PO Box 1410, Hindman, KY 41822-1410. Phones: 606-633-0778; 606-785-3450. Fax: 606-785-3110. E-mail: tvs@tvscable.com. Web Site: http://www.tvscable.com. Also serves Blackey, Bonnyman, Browns Fork, Busy, Chavies, Christopher, Colson, Cowan Creek, Cromona, Cutshin, Dry Fork, Ermine, Estill, Haymond, Isom, Jeff, Jeremiah, Kings Creek, Knott County, Kona, Linefork, Lothair, Maces Creek, Mayking, Millstone, Pippa Passes, Raven, Redfox, Sassafras, Seco, Smilax, Thornton, Topmost, Vicco, Viper & Wayland. ICA: KY0027.
TV Market Ranking: Below 100 (Blackey, Bonnyman, Browns Fork, Busy, Chavies, Christopher, Colson, Cowan Creek, Cromona, Cutshin, Dry Fork, Ermine, Estill, Haymond, HINDMAN, Isom, Jeff, Jeremiah, Kings Creek, Knott County, Kona, Linefork, Lothair, Maces Creek, Mayking, Millstone,

Pippa Passes, Raven, Redfox, Sassafras, Seco, Smilax, Thornton, Topmost, Vicco, Viper, Wayland). Franchise award date: N.A. Franchise expiration date: N.A. Began: April 1, 1966.

Channel capacity: 62 (operating 2-way). Channels available but not in use: N.A.

Basic Service

Subscribers: 12,500.

Programming (received off-air): WCYB-TV (CW, NBC) Bristol; WDKY-TV (FOX) Danville; WKHA (PBS) Hazard; WKYT-TV (CBS, CW) Lexington; WLEX-TV (NBC) Lexington; WLFG (IND) Grundy; WLJC-TV (TBN) Beattyville; WTVQ-DT (ABC) Lexington; WYMT-TV (CBS, CW) Hazard.

Programming (via satellite): CW+; ION Television; WGN America.

Current originations: Educational Access; Public Access; Religious Access.

Fee: $25.00 installation; $19.58 monthly.

Expanded Basic Service 1

Subscribers: 11,950.

Programming (via satellite): ABC Family Channel; Animal Planet; Arts & Entertainment; Bloomberg Television; Boomerang; Cartoon Network; CNN; Comedy Central; Country Music TV; C-SPAN; Discovery Channel; Disney Channel; E! Entertainment Television; ESPN; ESPN 2; ESPN Classic Sports; ESPN U; Food Network; Fox News Channel; Fox Sports Net Ohio; FX; Gospel Music TV; Great American Country; Hallmark Channel; Headline News; HGTV; History Channel; Home Shopping Network; HorseRacing TV; Lifetime; MTV; National Geographic Channel; Nickelodeon; Outdoor Channel; QVC; SoapNet; Spike TV; Syfy; TBS Superstation; The Learning Channel; The Sportsman Channel; Travel Channel; truTV; Turner Classic Movies; Turner Network TV; TV Land; USA Network; VH1; Weather Channel.

Fee: $49.95 monthly.

Digital Basic Service

Subscribers: 850.

Programming (via satellite): AmericanLife TV Network; BBC America; Bio; Black Family Channel; Church Channel; CMT Pure Country; Daystar TV Network; Discovery Health Channel; Discovery Home Channel; Discovery Kids Channel; Discovery Military Channel; Discovery Times Channel; DMX Music; ESPNews; FitTV; Fox College Sports Atlantic; Fox College Sports Central; Fox College Sports Pacific; Fuse; G4; GAS; Golf Channel; GSN; Halogen Network; History Channel International; Independent Film Channel; JCTV; Lifetime Movie Network; MTV Hits; MTV Jams; MTV2; Nick Jr.; NickToons TV; RFD-TV; Science Channel; ShopNBC; Sleuth; Speed Channel; Style Network; The Word Network; Toon Disney; Trinity Broadcasting Network; Versus; VH1 Classic; VH1 Soul; WE tv.

Fee: $11.25 monthly; $3.50 converter.

Digital Pay Service 1

Pay Units: N.A.

Programming (via satellite): Cinemax (multiplexed); Encore (multiplexed); Flix; HBO (multiplexed); Showtime (multiplexed); Starz (multiplexed); Sundance Channel; The Movie Channel (multiplexed).

Fee: $8.50 monthly (Cinemax or TMC), $10.95 monthly (Starz & Encore), $11.50 monthly (HBO or Showtime); $3.50 converter.

Video-On-Demand: No

Pay-Per-View

iN DEMAND (delivered digitally), Fee: $3.99, Addressable: Yes; Playboy TV (delivered digitally); Fresh (delivered digitally); Spice: Xcess (delivered digitally); Club Jenna (delivered digitally).

Internet Service

Operational: Yes. Began: December 1, 2001.

Subscribers: 1,600.

Broadband Service: In-house.

Fee: $89.95 installation; $29.95-$79.95 monthly; $9.95 modem lease.

Telephone Service

Digital: Operational

Miles of Plant: 975.0 (coaxial); 425.0 (fiber optic). Homes passed: 17,615.

General Manager: Archie W. Everage. Assistant Manager: Kenny Salmons. Program Director: Betty Thomas. Chief Technician: Tony Everage.

City fee: None.

Ownership: TV Service Inc. (MSO).

HODGENVILLE—Comcast Cablevision of the South. Now served by ELIZABETHTOWN, KY [KY0012]. ICA: KY0080.

HOPKINSVILLE—NewWave Communications, 530 Noel Avenue, Hopkinsville, KY 42240. Phone: 270-881-9018. Fax: 270-881-9013. Web Site: http://www.newwavecom.com. ICA: KY0014.

TV Market Ranking: Below 100 (HOPKINSVILLE). Franchise award date: N.A. Franchise expiration date: N.A. Began: January 1, 1966.

Channel capacity: 136 (operating 2-way). Channels available but not in use: N.A.

Basic Service

Subscribers: 9,049.

Programming (received off-air): WBKO (ABC, CW) Bowling Green; WKAG-CA Hopkinsville; WKMA-TV (PBS) Madisonville; WKRN-TV (ABC) Nashville; WNAB (CW) Nashville; WNPT (PBS) Nashville; WPGD-TV (IND) Hendersonville; WPSD-TV (NBC) Paducah; WSMV-TV (NBC, TMO) Nashville; WTVF (CBS) Nashville; WUXP-TV (MNT) Nashville; WZTV (FOX) Nashville; 14 FMs.

Programming (via satellite): C-SPAN; C-SPAN 2; Home Shopping Network; INSP; QVC; TV Guide Network; WGN America.

Current originations: Government Access; Educational Access; Religious Access.

Fee: $39.95 installation; $24.00 monthly; $10.00 additional installation.

Expanded Basic Service 1

Subscribers: N.A.

Programming (via satellite): ABC Family Channel; AMC; Animal Planet; Arts & Entertainment; BET Networks; Bravo; Cartoon Network; CNBC; CNN; Comcast Sports Net Southeast; Comcast/Charter Sports Southeast (CSS); Comedy Central; Country Music TV; Discovery Channel; Disney Channel; E! Entertainment Television; ESPN; ESPN 2; ESPN Classic Sports; Food Network; Fox News Channel; FX; G4; Golf Channel; Great American Country; GSN; Hallmark Channel; Hallmark Movie Channel; Headline News; HGTV; History Channel; Lifetime; MSNBC; MTV; National Geographic Channel; Nickelodeon; Outdoor Channel; Oxygen; SoapNet; Speed Channel; Spike TV; Syfy; TBS Superstation; The Learning Channel; Toon Disney; Travel Channel; truTV; Turner Classic Movies; Turner Network TV; TV Land; USA Network; Versus; VH1; Weather Channel.

Digital Basic Service

Subscribers: N.A.

Programming (via satellite): AmericanLife TV Network; BBC America; Bio; CMT Pure Country; CNN en Espanol; College Sports Television; Cooking Channel; Discovery en Espanol; Discovery Health Channel; Discovery Kids Channel; Discovery Military Channel; Discovery Planet Green; Do-It-Yourself; ESPN U; ESPNews; FitTV; Fox Business Channel; Fox College Sports Atlantic; Fox College Sports Central; Fox College Sports Pacific; Fox Movie Channel; Fox Soccer; Fuel TV; Gospel Music Channel; History Channel International; HorseRacing TV; ID Investigation Discovery; Jewelry Television; Lifetime Movie Network; Lifetime Real Women; MTV Hits; MTV Jams; MTV Tres; MTV2; Music Choice; Nick Jr.; Nick Too; NickToons TV; Science Channel; Style Network; TeenNick; Tennis Channel; The Sportsman Channel; VH1 Classic; VH1 Soul.

Digital Pay Service 1

Pay Units: N.A.

Programming (via satellite): Cinemax (multiplexed); Encore (multiplexed); Flix; HBO; Showtime (multiplexed); Starz (multiplexed); The Movie Channel (multiplexed).

Video-On-Demand: Yes

Pay-Per-View

iN DEMAND (delivered digitally); Playboy TV (delivered digitally); Fresh (delivered digitally); Shorteez (delivered digitally); ESPN Gameplan (delivered digitally); Club Jenna (delivered digitally); Spice: Xcess (delivered digitally).

Internet Service

Operational: Yes.

Fee: $40.00 installation; $31.99 monthly.

Telephone Service

None

Miles of Plant: 320.0 (coaxial); None (fiber optic). Homes passed: 18,448. Total homes in franchised area: 13,639.

Technical Operations Manager: Larry Hoyle. Sales & Marketing Manager: Steven Buttram.

City fee: 3% of gross.

Ownership: NewWave Communications (MSO).

HORSE CAVE—Comcast Cable, 2919 Ring Rd, Elizabethtown, KY 42701. Phone: 270-737-2731. Fax: 270-737-3379. Web Site: http://www.comcast.com. Also serves Cave City & Hiseville. ICA: KY0236.

TV Market Ranking: Below 100 (Cave City, Hiseville, HORSE CAVE). Franchise award date: February 3, 1964. Franchise expiration date: N.A. Began: July 1, 1964.

Channel capacity: N.A. Channels available but not in use: N.A.

Basic Service

Subscribers: 2,200.

Programming (received off-air): WAVE (NBC) Louisville; WBKO (ABC, CW) Bowling Green; WDRB (FOX) Louisville; WHAS-TV (ABC) Louisville; WKGB-TV (PBS) Bowling Green; WKYU-TV (PBS) Bowling Green; WLKY-TV (CBS) Louisville; WSMV-TV (NBC, TMO) Nashville; WTVF (CBS) Nashville; WUXP-TV (MNT) Nashville; allband FM.

Programming (via satellite): ABC Family Channel; AMC; Animal Planet; Arts & Entertainment; BET Networks; Cartoon Network; Cinemax; CNBC; CNN; Comcast Sports Net Southeast; Comedy Central; Country Music TV; C-SPAN; Discovery Channel; Disney Channel; E! Entertainment Television; ESPN; ESPN 2; Food Network; Fox News Channel; FX; HBO (multiplexed); Headline News; HGTV; History Channel; Home Shopping Network 2; ION Television; Lifetime; MTV; Nickelodeon; QVC; Showtime; Spike TV; Syfy; TBS Superstation; The Learning Channel; Travel Channel; Trinity Broadcasting Network; Turner Classic Movies; Turner Network TV; TV Land; USA Network; Versus; VH1; Weather Channel; WGN America.

Fee: $36.99 installation; $7.92 monthly.

Digital Basic Service

Subscribers: N.A.

Programming (via satellite): BBC America; C-SPAN 3; Discovery Digital Networks; ESPNews; GAS; MTV Networks Digital Suite; Nick Jr.; Nick Too; SoapNet; Toon Disney; VH1 Classic; VH1 Country; VH1 Soul; WAM! America's Kidz Network.

Fee: $14.95 monthly.

Digital Pay Service 1

Pay Units: N.A.

Programming (via satellite): Cinemax (multiplexed); Encore (multiplexed); Flix; HBO (multiplexed); Showtime (multiplexed); Sundance Channel; The Movie Channel (multiplexed).

Video-On-Demand: No

Pay-Per-View

Hot Choice (delivered digitally).

Internet Service

Operational: Yes.

Broadband Service: Comcast High Speed Internet.

Fee: $42.95 monthly.

Telephone Service

Digital: Operational

Miles of Plant: 97.0 (coaxial); None (fiber optic).

General Manager: Tim Hagan. Marketing Director: Laurie Nicholson. Technical Operations Director: Bob Tharp.

City fee: 3% of gross.

Ownership: Comcast Cable Communications Inc. (MSO).

HUSTONVILLE—Access Cable Television Inc., 302 Enterprise Dr, Somerset, KY 42501. Phones: 606-676-2444; 606-676-0610. Fax: 606-677-2443. E-mail: cable@accesshsd.net. Also serves Moreland. ICA: KY0296.

TV Market Ranking: Below 100 (HUSTONVILLE, Moreland). Franchise award date: N.A. Franchise expiration date: N.A. Began: N.A.

Channel capacity: 35 (not 2-way capable). Channels available but not in use: None.

Basic Service

Subscribers: 65.

Programming (received off-air): WDKY-TV (FOX) Danville; WDRB (FOX) Louisville; WHAS-TV (ABC) Louisville; WKSO-TV (PBS) Somerset; WKYT-TV (CBS, CW) Lexington; WLEX-TV (NBC) Lexington; WTVQ-DT (ABC) Lexington; WUPX-TV (ION) Morehead.

Programming (via satellite): AMC; Arts & Entertainment; CNN; Country Music TV; C-SPAN; Discovery Channel; E! Entertainment Television; ESPN; Headline News; Lifetime; MTV; Nickelodeon; QVC; Syfy; The Learning Channel; Turner Network TV; USA Network; VH1.

Fee: $16.95 monthly.

Expanded Basic Service 1

Subscribers: 48.

Programming (via satellite): ABC Family Channel; Disney Channel; MSNBC; Spike TV; TBS Superstation; WGN America.

Fee: $9.95 monthly.

Pay Service 1

Pay Units: 30.

Programming (via satellite): HBO.

Fee: $11.95 monthly.

Video-On-Demand: No

Internet Service

Operational: No.

Telephone Service
None
Miles of Plant: 44.0 (coaxial); None (fiber optic). Homes passed: 529.
President & Manager: Roy Baker. Chief Technician: Allen Slavin.
Ownership: Access Cable Television Inc. (MSO).

HYDEN—Bowling Corp., PO Box 522, 652 Owls Nest Rd, Hyden, KY 41749-0522. Phone: 606-672-3479. Fax: 606-672-7575. Also serves Leslie County (portions). ICA: KY0238.
TV Market Ranking: Below 100 (HYDEN, Leslie County (portions)). Franchise award date: N.A. Franchise expiration date: N.A. Began: July 1, 1954.
Channel capacity: 48 (not 2-way capable). Channels available but not in use: N.A.
Basic Service
Subscribers: 725.
Programming (received off-air): WATE-TV (ABC) Knoxville; WCYB-TV (CW, NBC) Bristol; WJHL-TV (CBS) Johnson City; WKHA (PBS) Hazard; WKPT-TV (ABC) Kingsport; WKYT-TV (CBS, CW) Lexington; WLOS (ABC) Asheville; WSBN-TV (PBS) Norton; WYMT-TV (CBS, CW) Hazard; allband FM.
Programming (via satellite): ABC Family Channel; CNN; Country Music TV; ESPN; TBS Superstation; Turner Network TV; WGN America; WPIX (CW, IND) New York.
Fee: $75.00 installation; $33.01 monthly.
Pay Service 1
Pay Units: 46.
Programming (via satellite): HBO.
Fee: $11.69 monthly.
Video-On-Demand: No
Internet Service
Operational: No.
Telephone Service
None
Miles of Plant: 30.0 (coaxial); None (fiber optic). Homes passed: 1,100.
Manager: Dan Bowling.
Ownership: Dan Bowling.

INEZ—Charter Communications. Now served by KERMIT, WV [WV0038]. ICA: KY0072.

IRVINE—Irvine Community TV Inc., PO Box 186, 251 Broadway St, Irvine, KY 40336. Phone: 606-723-4240. Fax: 606-723-4723. Also serves Estill County, Ravenna & Wisemantown. ICA: KY0052.
TV Market Ranking: Below 100 (Estill County, IRVINE, Ravenna, Wisemantown). Franchise award date: N.A. Franchise expiration date: N.A. Began: January 1, 1951.
Channel capacity: 60 (operating 2-way). Channels available but not in use: N.A.
Basic Service
Subscribers: 3,767.
Programming (received off-air): Kentucky Educational Television (KET5); WDKY-TV (FOX) Danville; WKYT-TV (CBS, CW) Lexington; WLEX-TV (NBC) Lexington; WLJC-TV (TBN) Beattyville; WTVQ-DT (ABC) Lexington; allband FM.
Programming (via satellite): ABC Family Channel; AMC; Animal Planet; Arts & Entertainment; Cartoon Network; CNN; Comcast Sports Net Southeast; Country Music TV; C-SPAN; Discovery Channel; ESPN; ESPN 2; Fox News Channel; FX; Gospel Music TV; Hallmark Channel; Headline News; HGTV; History Channel; Home Shopping Network; ION Television; Lifetime; MTV; Nickelodeon; QVC; Spike TV; Syfy; TBS Superstation; The Learning Channel; Travel Channel; truTV; Turner Classic Movies; Turner Network TV; TV Guide Network; TV Land; USA Network; VH1; Weather Channel; WGN America.
Fee: $15.00 installation; $28.94 monthly.
Digital Basic Service
Subscribers: N.A.
Programming (via satellite): AmericanLife TV Network; BBC America; Bloomberg Television; Discovery Digital Networks; DMX Music; ESPN Classic Sports; ESPNews; FitTV; Fox Sports World; G4; Golf Channel; GSN; INSP; Outdoor Channel; Si TV; Trinity Broadcasting Network.
Pay Service 1
Pay Units: N.A.
Programming (via satellite): HBO; Showtime.
Fee: $10.50 monthly (each).
Digital Pay Service 1
Pay Units: N.A.
Programming (via satellite): Cinemax (multiplexed); Encore (multiplexed); HBO (multiplexed); Showtime (multiplexed); Starz (multiplexed); The Movie Channel (multiplexed).
Fee: $5.60 monthly (Encore), $8.49 monthly (Cinemax or TMC), $10.00 monthly (Showtime), $10.50 monthly (HBO), $12.95 monthly (Starz/Encore).
Video-On-Demand: No
Pay-Per-View
iN DEMAND (delivered digitally); ESPN (delivered digitally); ESPN Extra (delivered digitally); Sports PPV (delivered digitally); Hot Choice (delivered digitally); Fresh (delivered digitally).
Internet Service
Operational: Yes.
Broadband Service: In-house.
Fee: $22.90 monthly.
Telephone Service
None
Miles of Plant: 134.0 (coaxial); None (fiber optic). Homes passed: 5,500. Total homes in franchised area: 5,500.
Manager: Jim Hays.
City fee: None.
Ownership: Jim Hays.

IRVINGTON—Windjammer Cable, 4400 PGA Blvd, Ste 902, Palm Beach Gardens, FL 33410. Phones: 877-450-5558; 561-775-1208. Fax: 561-775-7811. Web Site: http://www.windjammercable.com. Also serves Irvington (village). ICA: KY0126.
TV Market Ranking: Below 100 (Irvington (village)); Outside TV Markets (IRVINGTON, Irvington (village)). Franchise award date: March 14, 1986. Franchise expiration date: N.A. Began: December 15, 1987.
Channel capacity: N.A. Channels available but not in use: N.A.
Basic Service
Subscribers: N.A. Included in Owensboro
Programming (received off-air): WAVE (NBC) Louisville; WDRB (FOX) Louisville; WHAS-TV (ABC) Louisville; WKPC-TV (PBS) Louisville; WLKY-TV (CBS) Louisville; WMYO (MNT) Salem.
Programming (via satellite): Animal Planet; QVC; TBS Superstation; WGN America.
Current originations: Government Access; Educational Access; Public Access.
Fee: $39.95 installation; $23.72 monthly; $1.50 converter.
Expanded Basic Service 1
Subscribers: N.A.
Programming (via satellite): ABC Family Channel; AMC; CNN; Country Music TV; Discovery Channel; Disney Channel; ESPN; Headline News; Lifetime; Nickelodeon; Spike TV; Turner Network TV; USA Network.
Fee: $16.61 monthly.
Pay Service 1
Pay Units: 80.
Programming (via satellite): HBO.
Fee: $15.95 monthly.
Video-On-Demand: No
Internet Service
Operational: No.
Telephone Service
None
Miles of Plant: 15.0 (coaxial); None (fiber optic). Homes passed included in Owensboro
General Manager: Timothy Evard. Operations Director: Belinda Graham. Engineering Director: Mike Earehart. Finance & Accounting Director: Cindy Johnson.
City fee: 2% of gross.
Ownership: Windjammer Communications LLC (MSO).

ISLAND—Windjammer Cable, 4400 PGA Blvd, Ste 902, Palm Beach Gardens, FL 33410. Phones: 877-450-5558; 561-775-1208. Fax: 561-775-7811. Web Site: http://www.windjammercable.com. ICA: KY0308.
TV Market Ranking: Below 100 (ISLAND). Franchise award date: N.A. Franchise expiration date: N.A. Began: N.A.
Channel capacity: 36 (not 2-way capable). Channels available but not in use: 12.
Basic Service
Subscribers: N.A. Included in Owensboro
Programming (received off-air): WBKO (ABC, CW) Bowling Green; WEHT (ABC) Evansville; WEVV-TV (CBS, MNT) Evansville; WFIE (NBC) Evansville; WKGB-TV (PBS) Bowling Green; WTVW (FOX) Evansville.
Programming (via satellite): ABC Family Channel; Arts & Entertainment; CNN; Country Music TV; Discovery Channel; Disney Channel; ESPN; ESPN 2; History Channel; Nickelodeon; Spike TV; TBS Superstation; The Learning Channel; Trinity Broadcasting Network; Turner Network TV; USA Network; WGN America.
Fee: $39.95 installation; $36.65 monthly.
Digital Basic Service
Subscribers: N.A.
Programming (via satellite): BBC America; Bloomberg Television; Discovery Digital Networks; ESPN Classic Sports; ESPNews; Fox Movie Channel; Fox Soccer; G4; Golf Channel; GSN; Halogen Network; Music Choice; Nick Jr.; NickToons TV; Outdoor Channel; Versus; WE tv.
Fee: $12.95 monthly.
Digital Pay Service 1
Pay Units: N.A.
Programming (via satellite): Cinemax (multiplexed); Encore (multiplexed); HBO (multiplexed); Showtime (multiplexed); Starz (multiplexed); The Movie Channel (multiplexed).
Fee: $15.95 monthly (each).
Video-On-Demand: No
Pay-Per-View
iN DEMAND (delivered digitally); Movies (delivered digitally); Club Jenna (delivered digitally); Playboy TV (delivered digitally); Fresh (delivered digitally).
Internet Service
Operational: No.
Miles of Plant: 8.0 (coaxial); None (fiber optic). Homes passed included in Owensboro
Ownership: Windjammer Communications LLC (MSO).

ISLAND CITY—Formerly served by City TV Cable. No longer in operation. ICA: KY0177.

JACKSON—Windjammer Cable, 4400 PGA Blvd, Ste 902, Palm Beach Gardens, FL 33410. Phones: 877-450-5558; 561-775-1208. Fax: 561-775-7811. Web Site: http://www.windjammercable.com. Also serves Noctor (portions) & Quicksand. ICA: KY0242.
TV Market Ranking: Below 100 (JACKSON (VILLAGE), Noctor (portions), Quicksand). Franchise award date: N.A. Franchise expiration date: N.A. Began: N.A.
Channel capacity: 42 (not 2-way capable). Channels available but not in use: 7.
Basic Service
Subscribers: 1,612.
Programming (received off-air): WDKY-TV (FOX) Danville; WKHA (PBS) Hazard; WKYT-TV (CBS, CW) Lexington; WLEX-TV (NBC) Lexington; WLJC-TV (TBN) Beattyville; WTVQ-DT (ABC) Lexington; WUPX-TV (ION) Morehead; WYMT-TV (CBS, CW) Hazard.
Programming (via satellite): QVC; TBS Superstation; WGN America.
Fee: $39.95 installation; $16.56 monthly; $.73 converter.
Expanded Basic Service 1
Subscribers: 1,440.
Programming (via satellite): ABC Family Channel; AMC; Arts & Entertainment; CNN; Country Music TV; Discovery Channel; Disney Channel; ESPN; ESPN 2; Fox News Channel; FX; Hallmark Channel; Headline News; Lifetime; Nickelodeon; Spike TV; The Learning Channel; Turner Network TV; USA Network; VH1; Weather Channel.
Fee: $28.17 monthly.
Digital Basic Service
Subscribers: N.A.
Programming (via satellite): BBC America; Bio; Black Family Channel; Bloomberg Television; Bravo; Discovery Digital Networks; ESPN Classic Sports; ESPNews; FitTV; Fox College Sports Atlantic; Fox College Sports Central; Fox College Sports Pacific; Fox Movie Channel; Fox Soccer; Fuse; G4; GAS; Golf Channel; Great American Country; GSN; HGTV; History Channel; History Channel International; Independent Film Channel; INSP; Lifetime Movie Network; MTV2; National Geographic Channel; Nick Jr.; NickToons TV; Outdoor Channel; Speed Channel; Style Network; Syfy; The Word Network; Toon Disney; Trinity Broadcasting Network; Turner Classic Movies; Versus; VH1 Classic; VH1 Country; WE tv.
Fee: $56.68 monthly.

Digital Pay Service 1
Pay Units: N.A.
Programming (via satellite): Cinemax (multiplexed); Encore (multiplexed); HBO (multiplexed); Showtime (multiplexed); Starz (multiplexed); The Movie Channel (multiplexed).
Fee: $15.95 monthly (each).
Video-On-Demand: No
Pay-Per-View
HITS 1 (delivered digitally); HITS 2 (delivered digitally); HITS 3 (delivered digitally); HITS 4 (delivered digitally); Playboy TV (delivered digitally); Fresh (delivered digitally).
Internet Service
Operational: No.
Telephone Service
None
Miles of Plant: 83.0 (coaxial); None (fiber optic). Homes passed: 2,243. Total homes in franchised area: 2,631.
General Manager: Timothy Evard. Operations Director: Belinda Graham. Engineering Director: Mike Earehart. Finance & Accounting Director: Cindy Johnson.
Ownership: Windjammer Communications LLC (MSO).

JENKINS—Inter Mountain Cable Inc., PO Box 159, 20 Laynesville Rd, Harold, KY 41635. Phones: 866-917-4688; 606-478-9406. Fax: 606-478-1680. Web Site: http://www.imctv.com. Also serves Bottom, Burdine, Collier Creek, Deane, Eolia, Eversole, Fleming, Gibbo, Jackhorn, Lewis Creek, McRoberts, Neon, Oven Fork, Partridge, Payne Gap, Rado Hollow & Roberts Branch, KY; Pound & Wise County (northern portion), VA. ICA: KY0041.
TV Market Ranking: Below 100 (Bottom, Burdine, Collier Creek, Deane, Eolia, Eversole, Fleming, Gibbo, Jackhorn, JENKINS, Lewis Creek, McRoberts, Neon, Oven Fork, Partridge, Payne Gap, Pound, Rado Hollow, Roberts Branch, Wise County (northern portion)). Franchise award date: N.A. Franchise expiration date: N.A. Began: January 1, 1961.
Channel capacity: 77 (not 2-way capable). Channels available but not in use: 12.
Basic Service
Subscribers: 2,788.
Programming (received off-air): CW+; WCYB-TV (CW, NBC) Bristol; WJHL-TV (CBS) Johnson City; WKPI-TV (PBS) Pikeville; WKPT-TV (ABC) Kingsport; WLFG (IND) Grundy; WSBN-TV (PBS) Norton; WUPX-TV (ION) Morehead; WVAH-TV (FOX) Charleston; WYMT-TV (CBS, CW) Hazard; allband FM.
Programming (via satellite): C-SPAN; Home Shopping Network; QVC; TV Guide Network; Weather Channel; WGN America.
Current originations: Educational Access.
Fee: $47.50 installation; $18.95 monthly; $.73 converter.
Expanded Basic Service 1
Subscribers: N.A.
Programming (via satellite): ABC Family Channel; AMC; Animal Planet; Arts & Entertainment; Boomerang; Cartoon Network; CNBC; CNN; Comcast Sports Net Southeast; Comedy Central; Country Music TV; Discovery Channel; Disney Channel; E! Entertainment Television; ESPN; ESPN 2; Food Network; Fox News Channel; FX; Hallmark Channel; HGTV; History Channel; Lifetime; MSNBC; MTV; MyNetworkTV Inc.; National Geographic Channel; NFL Network; Nickelodeon; ShopNBC; Soap-Net; Spike TV; Syfy; TBS Superstation; The Learning Channel; Travel Channel; truTV; Turner Network TV; TV Land; USA Network; VH1.
Fee: $11.95 monthly.
Digital Basic Service
Subscribers: 643.
Programming (received off-air): WCHS-TV (ABC) Charleston; WSAZ-TV (MNT, NBC) Huntington; WVAH-TV (FOX) Charleston; WYMT-TV (CBS, CW) Hazard.
Programming (via satellite): American-Life TV Network; Anime Network; AZ TV; BBC America; Bio; Blackbelt TV; Bloomberg Television; Bravo; Church Channel; CMT Pure Country; Current; Daystar TV Network; Discovery Digital Networks; Discovery HD Theater; DMX Music; ESPN Classic Sports; ESPN HD; ESPNews; FitTV; Fox College Sports Atlantic; Fox College Sports Central; Fox College Sports Pacific; Fox Movie Channel; Fox Soccer; Fuse; G4; GAS; Golf Channel; Gospel Music Channel; Great American Country; GSN; Halogen Network; HDNet; HDNet Movies; History Channel International; Independent Film Channel; JCTV; Lifetime Movie Network; Military History Channel; MTV Networks Digital Suite; Nick Jr.; NickToons TV; Outdoor Channel; Ovation; Science Television; Sleuth; Speed Channel; Style Network; Sundance Channel; The Word Network; Toon Disney; Trinity Broadcasting Network; Turner Classic Movies; TV One; TVG Network; Universal HD; Versus; WE tv.
Fee: $14.95 monthly.
Pay Service 1
Pay Units: 299.
Programming (via satellite): Flix; Showtime (multiplexed); The Movie Channel (multiplexed).
Fee: $3.95 monthly (Canales), $7.95 monthly (Cinemax), $11.95 monthly (Showtime & TMC), $12.95 monthly (HBO), $13.95 monthly (Starz & Encore).
Digital Pay Service 1
Pay Units: N.A.
Programming (via satellite): Canales N; Cinemax; Encore (multiplexed); Flix; HBO (multiplexed); Showtime (multiplexed); Starz (multiplexed); The Movie Channel (multiplexed).
Fee: $3.95 monthly (Canales), $7.95 monthly (Cinemax), $11.95 monthly (Showtime & TMC), $12.95 monthly (HBO), $13.95 monthly (Starz & Encore).
Video-On-Demand: No
Pay-Per-View
Playboy TV (delivered digitally); Club Jenna (delivered digitally); Hot Choice (delivered digitally); Fresh (delivered digitally); iN DEMAND (delivered digitally).
Internet Service
Operational: Yes.
Fee: $24.95 monthly.
Telephone Service
Digital: Operational
Fee: $131.93 monthly
Miles of Plant: 115.0 (coaxial); 55.0 (fiber optic). Homes passed: 4,350.
Chief Financial Officer: James Campbell. Manager: Paul Douglas Gearheart. Operations Director: John Schmoldt. Chief Engineer: Jefferson Thacker. Customer Service Manager: Rebecca Walters.
City fee: $1,250 annually.
Ownership: Inter-Mountain Cable Inc. (MSO).

KNOX COUNTY/WHITLEY COUNTY—Zito Media, 611 Vader Hill Rd, Coudersport, PA 16915. Phone: 814-260-9575. Web Site: http://www.zitomedia.com. Also serves Bryants Store, Rockholds & Siler. ICA: KY0083.
TV Market Ranking: Below 100 (Bryants Store, KNOX COUNTY, KNOX COUNTY/WHITLEY COUNTY, Rockholds, Siler). Franchise award date: December 1, 1995. Franchise expiration date: N.A. Began: March 1, 1980.
Channel capacity: 60 (2-way capable). Channels available but not in use: 19.
Basic Service
Subscribers: 497.
Programming (received off-air): WATE-TV (ABC) Knoxville; WBIR-TV (NBC) Knoxville; WBXX-TV (CW) Crossville; WDKY-TV (FOX) Danville; WKSO-TV (PBS) Somerset; WKYT-TV (CBS, CW) Lexington; WLEX-TV (NBC) Lexington; WLJC-TV (TBN) Beattyville; WPXK-TV (ION) Jellico; WVLT-TV (CBS, MNT) Knoxville; WYMT-TV (CBS, CW) Hazard; allband FM.
Programming (via satellite): ABC Family Channel; CNN; Country Music TV; C-SPAN; Discovery Channel; Disney Channel; ESPN; ESPN 2; Fox News Channel; Hallmark Channel; Headline News; HGTV; Home Shopping Network; Lifetime; MTV; Nickelodeon; QVC; Spike TV; TBS Superstation; Travel Channel; Trinity Broadcasting Network; Turner Network TV; USA Network; VH1; Weather Channel; WGN America.
Fee: $29.95 installation; $38.00 monthly; $3.95 converter.
Digital Basic Service
Subscribers: N.A.
Programming (via satellite): BBC America; Bio; Bloomberg Television; Discovery Digital Networks; ESPN Classic Sports; ESPNews; Fox Movie Channel; Fox Soccer; Fuse; G4; GAS; Golf Channel; GSN; History Channel International; Independent Film Channel; Lifetime Movie Network; MTV Networks Digital Suite; National Geographic Channel; Nick Jr.; Outdoor Channel; Sleuth; Speed Channel; Style Network; Syfy; Toon Disney; Turner Classic Movies; Versus; WE tv.
Fee: $13.95 monthly.
Digital Pay Service 1
Pay Units: N.A.
Programming (via satellite): Cinemax (multiplexed); Encore (multiplexed); HBO (multiplexed); Showtime (multiplexed); Starz (multiplexed); The Movie Channel (multiplexed).
Video-On-Demand: No
Pay-Per-View
iN DEMAND (delivered digitally); Playboy TV (delivered digitally); Fresh (delivered digitally).
Internet Service
Operational: No.
Telephone Service
None
Miles of Plant: 80.0 (coaxial); None (fiber optic). Additional miles planned: 25.0 (coaxial). Homes passed: 1,300. Total homes in franchised area: 1,800.
Public Relations Manager: Mark Laver.
City fee: None.
Ownership: Zito Media (MSO).

KUTTAWA—Galaxy Cablevision, 1718 Barlow Rd, Wickliffe, KY 42087-9253. Phones: 270-335-3881; 800-365-6988. Fax: 270-335-5259. Web Site: http://www.galaxycable.com. Also serves Eddyville, Grand Rivers, Lake City, Livingston County (portions), Lyon County, Misland & Smithland. ICA: KY0255.
TV Market Ranking: 69 (Eddyville, Grand Rivers, KUTTAWA, Lake City, Livingston County, Lyon County, Misland, Smithland). Franchise award date: N.A. Franchise expiration date: N.A. Began: N.A.
Channel capacity: 54 (not 2-way capable). Channels available but not in use: None.
Basic Service
Subscribers: 974.
Programming (received off-air): KBSI (FOX) Cape Girardeau; KFVS-TV (CBS, CW) Cape Girardeau; WDKA (MNT) Paducah; WKMA-TV (PBS) Madisonville; WPSD-TV (NBC) Paducah; WQWQ-LP (CW) Paducah; WSIL-TV (ABC) Harrisburg; WTCT (IND) Marion.
Programming (via satellite): ABC Family Channel; Animal Planet; Arts & Entertainment; Cartoon Network; CNBC; CNN; C-SPAN; Discovery Channel; Disney Channel; ESPN; ESPN 2; Fox News Channel; Fuse; FX; Great American Country; Headline News; HGTV; History Channel; Home Shopping Network; Lifetime; Outdoor Channel; TBS Superstation; The Learning Channel; Travel Channel; Turner Classic Movies; Turner Network TV; USA Network; Weather Channel; WGN America.
Current originations: Public Access.
Fee: $30.00 installation; $41.10 monthly.
Digital Basic Service
Subscribers: 172.
Programming (via satellite): BBC America; Bio; Bloomberg Television; Discovery Digital Networks; DMX Music; ESPN Classic Sports; ESPNews; FitTV; G4; Golf Channel; GSN; Halogen Network; History Channel International; National Geographic Channel; Speed Channel; Style Network; Toon Disney; WE tv.
Fee: $13.95 monthly.
Digital Expanded Basic Service
Subscribers: N.A.
Programming (via satellite): DMX Music; Encore; Fox Movie Channel; Lifetime Movie Network.
Fee: $13.95 monthly.
Pay Service 1
Pay Units: N.A.
Programming (via satellite): Cinemax; HBO; Showtime; The Movie Channel.
Digital Pay Service 1
Pay Units: 160.
Programming (via satellite): Cinemax (multiplexed); Flix; HBO (multiplexed); Showtime (multiplexed); The Movie Channel (multiplexed).
Fee: $19.55 monthly.
Video-On-Demand: No
Pay-Per-View
Fee: $3.99, Addressable: Yes; Movies (delivered digitally); Playboy TV (delivered digitally); Fresh (delivered digitally).
Internet Service
Operational: No.
Telephone Service
None
Miles of Plant: 75.0 (coaxial); None (fiber optic). Homes passed: 3,356.
State Manager: Ward Webb. Operations Manager: Treka Hargrove. Technical Manager: Audie Murphy. Customer Service Manager: Malynda Walker.
Ownership: Galaxy Cable Inc. (MSO).

LAFAYETTE—Formerly served by Adelphia Communications. No longer in operation. ICA: KY0246.

LAWRENCE COUNTY (southern portion)—Lycom Communications, 305 E Pike St, Louisa, KY 41230. Phone: 606-638-3600. Fax: 606-638-4278. E-mail: info@lycomonline.com. Web Site: http://www.lycomonline.com. Also serves Chapman,

Cherryville, Five Forks & Meads Branch. ICA: KY0251.

TV Market Ranking: 36 (Chapman, Cherryville, Five Forks, LAWRENCE COUNTY (portions), Meads Branch); Below 100 (LAWRENCE COUNTY (portions)). Franchise award date: N.A. Franchise expiration date: N.A. Began: January 1, 1983.

Channel capacity: 60 (operating 2-way). Channels available but not in use: N.A.

Basic Service

Subscribers: 1,032.

Programming (received off-air): WCHS-TV (ABC) Charleston; WKAS (PBS) Ashland; WLPX-TV (ION) Charleston; WOWK-TV (CBS) Huntington; WPBY-TV (PBS) Huntington; WSAZ-TV (MNT, NBC) Huntington; WTSF (IND) Ashland; WVAH-TV (FOX) Charleston; WYMT-TV (CBS, CW) Hazard.

Programming (via satellite): ABC Family Channel; AMC; Animal Planet; Arts & Entertainment; Cartoon Network; CNBC; CNN; Comedy Central; Country Music TV; C-SPAN; C-SPAN 2; CW+; Discovery Channel; Disney Channel; E! Entertainment Television; ESPN; ESPN 2; ESPN Classic Sports; Food Network; Fox News Channel; Fox Sports Net Ohio; FX; Gospel Music Channel; Great American Country; Hallmark Channel; Headline News; Healthy Living Channel; HGTV; History Channel; Home Shopping Network; Lifetime; MTV; National Geographic Channel; Nickelodeon; QVC; RFD-TV; Speed Channel; Spike TV; Syfy; TBS Superstation; The Learning Channel; The Sportsman Channel; Travel Channel; Trinity Broadcasting Network; truTV; Turner Classic Movies; Turner Network TV; TV Guide Network; TV Land; USA Network; VH1; Weather Channel; WGN America.

Current originations: Public Access.

Fee: $45.95 installation; $43.09 monthly; $3.00 converter.

Digital Basic Service

Subscribers: N.A.

Programming (received off-air): WKYT-TV (CBS, CW) Lexington; WSAZ-TV (MNT, NBC) Huntington; WVAH-TV (FOX) Charleston; WYMT-TV (CBS, CW) Hazard.

Programming (via satellite): BBC America; Bloomberg Television; Boomerang; CMT Pure Country; Discovery Health Channel; Discovery Kids Channel; Discovery Military Channel; Discovery Planet Green; DMX Music; Do-It-Yourself; ESPN 2; ESPN Classic Sports; ESPN U; ESPNews; FitTV; Fox Movie Channel; G4; Golf Channel; GSN; ID Investigation Discovery; Independent Film Channel; Nick Jr.; NickToons TV; Science Channel; SoapNet; Speed Channel; Versus; VH1 Classic.

Fee: $11.95 monthly.

Digital Pay Service 1

Pay Units: N.A.

Programming (via satellite): Cinemax (multiplexed); Encore (multiplexed); Flix; HBO (multiplexed); Showtime (multiplexed); Starz (multiplexed); The Movie Channel (multiplexed).

Fee: $11.95 monthly (HBO, CInemax, Showtime/TMC/Flix or Starz/Encore).

Video-On-Demand: No

Internet Service

Operational: Yes.

Broadband Service: Lycom Online.

Fee: $31.95 monthly.

Telephone Service

None

Miles of Plant: 30.0 (coaxial); None (fiber optic).

Manager: Donna Lycans.; Steven Lycans. Chief Technician: Aaron Lycans.

Ownership: Lycom Communications Inc.

LAWRENCEBURG—Now served by HARRODSBURG, KY [KY0231]. ICA: KY0252.

LEBANON—Time Warner Cable, 1615 Foxhaven Dr, Richmond, KY 40475. Phones: 859-626-4800; 859-624-9666. Fax: 859-624-0060. Web Site: http://www.timewarnercable.com. Also serves Loretto, Marion County, Nelson County, New Haven & Springfield. ICA: KY0049.

TV Market Ranking: Below 100 (LEBANON, Loretto, Marion County, Nelson County, New Haven, Springfield). Franchise award date: N.A. Franchise expiration date: N.A. Began: March 9, 1970.

Channel capacity: N.A. Channels available but not in use: N.A.

Basic Service

Subscribers: 3,527.

Programming (received off-air): WAVE (NBC) Louisville; WBKI-TV (CW) Campbellsville; WBNA (ION) Louisville; WDRB (FOX) Louisville; WHAS-TV (ABC) Louisville; WKLE (PBS) Lexington; WKYT-TV (CBS, CW) Lexington; WLEX-TV (NBC) Lexington; WLJC-TV (TBN) Beattyville; WLKY-TV (CBS) Louisville; WMYO (MNT) Salem; WOAY-TV (ABC) Oak Hill; allband FM.

Programming (via satellite): QVC.

Fee: $39.95 installation; $14.80 monthly.

Expanded Basic Service 1

Subscribers: 3,351.

Programming (via satellite): ABC Family Channel; AMC; Animal Planet; Arts & Entertainment; BET Networks; Bravo; Cartoon Network; CNBC; CNN; Comcast Sports Net Southeast; Comedy Central; Country Music TV; C-SPAN; C-SPAN 2; Discovery Channel; Discovery Health Channel; Disney Channel; E! Entertainment Television; ESPN; ESPN 2; Eternal Word TV Network; Food Network; Fox News Channel; Fox Sports Net Ohio; FX; Hallmark Channel; Halogen Network; Headline News; HGTV; History Channel; Home Shopping Network; Lifetime; MSNBC; MTV; Nickelodeon; Oxygen; ShopNBC; Spike TV; Syfy; TBS Superstation; The Learning Channel; Travel Channel; Trinity Broadcasting Network; truTV; Turner Network TV; TV Guide Network; TV Land; USA Network; VH1; Weather Channel; WGN America.

Fee: $32.98 monthly.

Digital Basic Service

Subscribers: N.A.

Programming (received off-air): WKLE (PBS) Lexington; WKYT-TV (CBS, CW) Lexington.

Programming (via satellite): AmericanLife TV Network; BBC America; Bio; Bloomberg Television; Boomerang; Canales N; CBS College Sports Network; CMT Pure Country; Cooking Channel; C-SPAN 3; Current; Daystar TV Network; Discovery Digital Networks; Discovery HD Theater; Do-It-Yourself; Encore (multiplexed); ESPN 2 HD; ESPN Classic Sports; ESPN HD; ESPN U; ESPNews; FamilyNet; Flix; Fox College Sports Atlantic; Fox College Sports Central; Fox College Sports Pacific; Fox Reality Channel; Fox Soccer; Fuel TV; Fuse; G4; GAS; Golf Channel; Gospel Music Channel; Great American Country; GSN; Halogen Network; HDNet; HDNet Movies; History Channel International; Independent Film Channel; Lifetime Movie Network; LOGO; MTV Networks Digital Suite; Music Choice; National Geographic Channel; NBA TV; Nick Jr.; Nick Too; NickToons TV; Outdoor Channel; Ovation; ReelzChannel; Sleuth; SoapNet; Speed Channel; Style Network; Sundance Channel; Tennis Channel; The Sportsman Channel; The Word Network; Toon Disney; Turner Classic Movies; Turner Network TV HD; TVG Network; Universal HD; Versus; WE tv.

Fee: $6.00 monthly (each tier).

Digital Pay Service 1

Pay Units: 482.

Programming (via satellite): Arabic Channel; CCTV-4; Cinemax (multiplexed); Cinemax HD; Filipino Channel; HBO (multiplexed); HBO HD; RAI International; Russian Television Network; Showtime (multiplexed); Showtime HD; Starz (multiplexed); Starz HDTV; The Movie Channel (multiplexed); TV Asia; TV Japan; TV5, La Television International; Zhong Tian Channel.

Fee: $12.00 monthly (HBO, Cinemax, Starz, Showtime or TMC), $15.00 monthly (CCTV, TV Asia, TV5, Filipino, RAI or ART, TV Russia or TV Japan).

Video-On-Demand: No

Pay-Per-View

iN DEMAND (delivered digitally); Fresh (delivered digitally); Hot Choice (delivered digitally); Sports PPV (delivered digitally); Playboy TV (delivered digitally).

Internet Service

Operational: Yes.

Broadband Service: Road Runner.

Fee: $44.95 monthly.

Telephone Service

Digital: Operational

Fee: $44.95 monthly

Miles of Plant: 305.0 (coaxial); None (fiber optic). Homes passed: 5,045.

General Manager: Robert Trott. Technical Operations Manager: Dennis Lester. Marketing Director: Betrina Morse. Government & Public Affairs Manager: Carla Deaton. Office Manager: Laverne Farris.

City fee: 3% of gross.

Ownership: Time Warner Cable (MSO).

LEITCHFIELD—Comcast Cable, 2919 Ring Rd, Elizabethtown, KY 42701. Phone: 270-737-2731. Fax: 270-737-3379. Web Site: http://www.comcast.com. Also serves Clarkson. ICA: KY0067.

TV Market Ranking: Outside TV Markets (Clarkson, LEITCHFIELD). Franchise award date: January 31, 1964. Franchise expiration date: N.A. Began: May 4, 1965.

Channel capacity: N.A. Channels available but not in use: N.A.

Basic Service

Subscribers: 2,196.

Programming (received off-air): WAVE (NBC) Louisville; WBKI-TV (CW) Campbellsville; WBKO (ABC, CW) Bowling Green; WBNA (ION) Louisville; WDRB (FOX) Louisville; WHAS-TV (ABC) Louisville; WKMJ-TV (PBS) Louisville; WKYT-TV (CBS, CW) Lexington; WLKY-TV (CBS) Louisville; WMYO (MNT) Salem; allband FM.

Programming (via satellite): ABC Family Channel; AMC; Animal Planet; Arts & Entertainment; BET Networks; Cartoon Network; CNBC; CNN; Comcast Sports Net Southeast; Comcast/Charter Sports Southeast (CSS); Comedy Central; Country Music TV; C-SPAN; C-SPAN 2; Discovery Channel; Discovery Health Channel; Disney Channel; E! Entertainment Television; ESPN; ESPN 2; Eternal Word TV Network; Food Network; Fox News Channel; Fox Sports Net; FX; Golf Channel; Great American Country; GSN; Hallmark Channel; Headline News; HGTV; History Channel; Home Shopping Network 2; Lifetime; MSNBC; MTV; Nickelodeon; Outdoor Channel; QVC; Speed Channel; Spike TV; Syfy; TBS Superstation; The Learning Channel; Trinity Broadcasting Network; truTV; Turner Network TV; TV Guide Network; TV Land; USA Network; Versus; VH1; Weather Channel; WGN America.

Fee: $54.99 installation; $43.99 monthly.

Digital Basic Service

Subscribers: N.A.

Programming (via satellite): BBC America; C-SPAN 3; Discovery Digital Networks; DMX Music; Encore Action; ESPNews; Flix; G4; GAS; MTV Networks Digital Suite; National Geographic Channel; Nick Jr.; Nick Too; SoapNet; Sundance Channel; Toon Disney; WAM! America's Kidz Network.

Fee: $14.95 monthly.

Digital Pay Service 1

Pay Units: N.A.

Programming (via satellite): Cinemax (multiplexed); HBO (multiplexed); Showtime (multiplexed); Starz (multiplexed); The Movie Channel (multiplexed).

Video-On-Demand: No

Pay-Per-View

iN DEMAND (delivered digitally); Hot Choice (delivered digitally); Sports PPV (delivered digitally); Playboy TV (delivered digitally); Fresh (delivered digitally); iN DEMAND; Shorteez (delivered digitally); Pleasure (delivered digitally).

Internet Service

Operational: Yes.

Broadband Service: Comcast High Speed Internet.

Fee: $42.95 monthly.

Telephone Service

Digital: Operational

Miles of Plant: 82.0 (coaxial); None (fiber optic). Homes passed: 2,502. Total homes in franchised area: 2,502.

General Manager: Tim Hagan. Marketing Director: Laurie Nicholson. Technical Operations Director: Bob Tharp.

City fee: 3% of gross.

Ownership: Comcast Cable Communications Inc. (MSO).

LEROSE—Phil's Cablevision, PO Box 237, Combs, KY 41729. Phone: 606-439-2542. Fax: 606-436-4797. ICA: KY0161.

TV Market Ranking: Below 100 (LEROSE). Franchise award date: January 1, 1976. Franchise expiration date: N.A. Began: N.A.

Channel capacity: 21 (not 2-way capable). Channels available but not in use: N.A.

Basic Service
Subscribers: 165.
Programming (received off-air): WDKY-TV (FOX) Danville; WKLE (PBS) Lexington; WKYT-TV (CBS, CW) Lexington; WLEX-TV (NBC) Lexington; WTVQ-DT (ABC) Lexington; WYMT-TV (CBS, CW) Hazard.
Programming (via satellite): ABC Family Channel; Disney Channel; TBS Superstation; Turner Network TV; USA Network.
Fee: $15.00 installation; $29.95 monthly.
Video-On-Demand: No

Internet Service
Operational: No.

Telephone Service
None
Miles of Plant: 7.0 (coaxial); None (fiber optic).
Manager: James Fields.
Ownership: Booneville Cablevision.

LESLIE COUNTY (northern portion)—Windjammer Cable, 4400 PGA Blvd, Ste 902, Palm Beach Gardens, FL 33410. Phones: 877-450-5558; 561-775-1208. Fax: 561-775-7811. Web Site: http://www.windjammercable.com. Also serves Avawam, Browns Fork, Combs, Hazard & Stinnett (portions). ICA: KY0289.
TV Market Ranking: Below 100 (Avawam, Browns Fork, Combs, Hazard, LESLIE COUNTY (NORTHERN PORTION), Stinnett (portions)). Franchise award date: N.A. Franchise expiration date: N.A. Began: March 1, 1971.
Channel capacity: 36 (not 2-way capable). Channels available but not in use: 3.

Basic Service
Subscribers: 1,496.
Programming (received off-air): WAGV (IND) Harlan; WCYB-TV (CW, NBC) Bristol; WEMT (FOX) Greeneville; WJHL-TV (CBS) Johnson City; WKHA (PBS) Hazard; WKPT-TV (ABC) Kingsport; WYMT-TV (CBS, CW) Hazard.
Programming (via satellite): ABC Family Channel; QVC; Trinity Broadcasting Network; WGN America.
Fee: $39.95 installation; $16.01 monthly.

Expanded Basic Service 1
Subscribers: 1,494.
Programming (via satellite): AMC; Arts & Entertainment; CNN; Country Music TV; C-SPAN; Discovery Channel; Disney Channel; E! Entertainment Television; ESPN; ESPN 2; Fox News Channel; FX; Headline News; INSP; Nickelodeon; Spike TV; TBS Superstation; The Learning Channel; Turner Network TV; USA Network; VH1; Weather Channel.
Fee: $24.52 monthly.

Digital Basic Service
Subscribers: N.A.
Programming (via satellite): BBC America; Bio; Black Family Channel; Bloomberg Television; Bravo; Discovery Digital Networks; ESPN Classic Sports; ESPNews; FitTV; Fox Movie Channel; Fox Sports Net; Fox Sports World; Fuse; G4; GAS; Golf Channel; Great American Country; GSN; Halogen Network; HGTV; History Channel; History Channel International; Independent Film Channel; Lifetime Movie Network; MTV2; National Geographic Channel; Nick Jr.; NickToons TV; Outdoor Channel; Speed Channel; Style Network; Syfy; The Word Network; Toon Disney; Turner Classic Movies; Versus; VH1 Classic; VH1 Country; WE tv.
Fee: $11.31 monthly.

Digital Pay Service 1
Pay Units: N.A.
Programming (via satellite): Cinemax (multiplexed); Encore; HBO; Showtime (multiplexed); The Movie Channel (multiplexed).
Fee: $12.00 monthly (each).
Video-On-Demand: No

Pay-Per-View
Fresh (delivered digitally); Playboy TV (delivered digitally).

Internet Service
Operational: No.

Telephone Service
None
Miles of Plant: 102.0 (coaxial); None (fiber optic). Homes passed: 2,297. Total homes in franchised area: 2,606.
Ownership: Windjammer Communications LLC (MSO).

LEWISPORT—Windjammer Cable, 4400 PGA Blvd, Ste 902, Palm Beach Gardens, FL 33410. Phones: 877-450-5558; 561-775-1208. Fax: 561-775-7811. Web Site: http://www.windjammercable.com. ICA: KY0136.
TV Market Ranking: Outside TV Markets (LEWISPORT).
Channel capacity: N.A. Channels available but not in use: N.A.

Basic Service
Subscribers: N.A. Included in Owensboro
Programming (received off-air): WAVE (NBC) Louisville; WDRB (FOX) Louisville; WEHT (ABC) Evansville; WEVV-TV (CBS, MNT) Evansville; WFIE (NBC) Evansville; WHAS-TV (ABC) Louisville; WKOH (PBS) Owensboro; WLKY-TV (CBS) Louisville; WNIN (PBS) Evansville; WTVW (FOX) Evansville; WWAZ-TV (IND) Fond du Lac [LICENSED & SILENT].
Programming (via satellite): ABC Family Channel; AMC; CNN; Country Music TV; Discovery Channel; Disney Channel; ESPN; ESPN 2; Home Shopping Network; Lifetime; MTV; Nickelodeon; Spike TV; Syfy; TBS Superstation; Trinity Broadcasting Network; Turner Network TV; USA Network; VH1; Weather Channel; WGN America.
Fee: $39.95 installation; $31.19 monthly.

Pay Service 1
Pay Units: 98.
Programming (via satellite): Cinemax; HBO.
Fee: $15.95 monthly.
Video-On-Demand: No

Internet Service
Operational: No.

Telephone Service
None
Miles of Plant: 25.0 (coaxial); None (fiber optic). Homes passed included in Owensboro
General Manager: Timothy Evard. Operations Director: Belinda Graham. Engineering Director: Mike Earehart. Finance & Accounting Director: Cindy Johnson.
Ownership: Windjammer Communications LLC (MSO).

LEXINGTON—Formerly served by Wireless Associates LP. No longer in operation. ICA: KY0303.

LEXINGTON—Insight Communications, 2548 Palumbo Dr, Lexington, KY 40509-1203. Phones: 859-514-1400; 859-514-1439. Fax: 859-514-6990. Web Site: http://www.myinsight.com. Also serves Fayette County & Jessamine County (northern portion). ICA: KY0003.
TV Market Ranking: Below 100 (Fayette County, Jessamine County (northern portion), LEXINGTON). Franchise award date: N.A. Franchise expiration date: N.A. Began: October 1, 1980.
Channel capacity: 74 (operating 2-way). Channels available but not in use: N.A.

Basic Service
Subscribers: 85,932.
Programming (received off-air): KETS (PBS) Little Rock; WBKI-TV (CW) Campbellsville; WDKY-TV (FOX) Danville; WKLE (PBS) Lexington; WKYT-TV (CBS, CW) Lexington; WLEX-TV (NBC) Lexington; WLJC-TV (TBN) Beattyville; WTVQ-DT (ABC) Lexington; WUPX-TV (ION) Morehead.
Programming (via satellite): Discovery Channel; Library Literacy Channel / GHTV; MarketConnect Network; QVC; TBS Superstation; TV Guide Network; Weather Channel; WGN America.
Current originations: Government Access; Educational Access; Public Access.
Fee: $35.00 installation.

Expanded Basic Service 1
Subscribers: 74,714.
Programming (via satellite): ABC Family Channel; AMC; Animal Planet; Arts & Entertainment; BET Networks; Big Ten Network; Bravo; Cartoon Network; CNBC; CNN; Comcast Sports Net Southeast; Comedy Central; Country Music TV; C-SPAN; C-SPAN 2; Disney Channel; E! Entertainment Television; ESPN; ESPN 2; Food Network; Fox News Channel; Fox Sports Net Ohio; FX; G4; Hallmark Channel; Headline News; HGTV; History Channel; Home Shopping Network; Lifetime; MSNBC; MTV; Nickelodeon; Oxygen; SoapNet; Speed Channel; Spike TV; Syfy; Telemundo; The Learning Channel; Travel Channel; truTV; Turner Network TV; TV Land; TVG Network; USA Network; VH1.
Fee: $40.00 monthly.

Digital Basic Service
Subscribers: 28,553.
Programming (received off-air): WDKY-TV (FOX) Danville; WKLE (PBS) Lexington; WKYT-TV (CBS, CW) Lexington; WLEX-TV (NBC) Lexington; WTVQ-DT (ABC) Lexington.
Programming (via satellite): AmericanLife TV Network; BBC America; Bio; Bloomberg Television; Canales N; CBS College Sports Network; Cooking Channel; Discovery Digital Networks; Discovery HD Theater; DMX Music; Do-It-Yourself; Encore (multiplexed); ESPN Classic Sports; ESPN HD; ESPNews; Eternal Word TV Network; Fox College Sports Atlantic; Fox College Sports Central; Fox College Sports Pacific; Fox Movie Channel; Fox Reality Channel; Fox Soccer; Fuse; GAS; Golf Channel; Great American Country; GSN; Halogen Network; HDNet; HDNet Movies; History Channel International; Independent Film Channel; Lifetime Movie Network; MTV Networks Digital Suite; National Geographic Channel; NFL Network; Nick Jr.; Nick Too; NickToons TV; Outdoor Channel; Ovation; PBS Kids Sprout; Style Network; Sundance Channel (multiplexed); Toon Disney; Trinity Broadcasting Network; Turner Classic Movies; Universal HD; Versus; WE tv.
Fee: $17.00 monthly.

Digital Pay Service 1
Pay Units: N.A.
Programming (via satellite): Cinemax (multiplexed); Flix; HBO (multiplexed); HBO HD; Showtime (multiplexed); Showtime HD; Starz (multiplexed); The Movie Channel (multiplexed).
Fee: $10.00 monthly (Cinemax or Starz), $13.00 monthly (HBO or Showtime/TMC).
Video-On-Demand: Yes

Pay-Per-View
Addressable homes: 28,553.
iN DEMAND (delivered digitally), Addressable: Yes; ESPN (delivered digitally); Fresh (delivered digitally); Shorteez (delivered digitally).

Internet Service
Operational: Yes. Began: March 1, 1999.
Subscribers: 14,121.
Broadband Service: InsightBB.com.
Fee: $99.95 installation; $44.95 monthly; $3.00 modem lease; $50.00 modem purchase.

Telephone Service
Digital: Operational
Subscribers: 1,633.
Fee: $40.00 monthly
Miles of Plant: 1,227.0 (coaxial); None (fiber optic). Homes passed: 144,600.
President & Chief Operating Officer: Dinni Jain. Senior Vice President, Operations: John Hutton. Technical Operations Manager: Bob Bennett. Marketing Director: Shannon Likens.
Ownership: Insight Communications Co. (MSO).

LIBERTY—NewWave Communications, 5026 S Hwy 27, Somerset, KY 42501. Phone: 606-678-9215. Fax: 606-679-7111. Web Site: http://www.newwavecom.com. Also serves Casey County, Dunnville, Lincoln County (eastern portion), Middleburg & Yosemite. ICA: KY0082.
TV Market Ranking: Below 100 (Casey County, Dunnville, LIBERTY (VILLAGE), Lincoln County (eastern portion), Middleburg, Yosemite). Franchise award date: January 13, 1986. Franchise expiration date: N.A. Began: August 1, 1953.
Channel capacity: N.A. Channels available but not in use: N.A.

Basic Service
Subscribers: 666.
Programming (received off-air): WAGV (IND) Harlan; WBIR-TV (NBC) Knoxville; WDKY-TV (FOX) Danville; WKSO-TV (PBS) Somerset; WKYT-TV (CBS, CW) Lexington; WLEX-TV (NBC) Lexington; WLJC-TV (TBN) Beattyville; WTVQ-DT (ABC) Lexington; WUPX-TV (ION) Morehead; WYMT-TV (CBS, CW) Hazard.
Programming (via satellite): C-SPAN; CW+; Home Shopping Network; INSP; QVC; ShopNBC; Trinity Broadcasting Network; TV Guide Network; WGN America.
Fee: $20.00 installation; $16.50 monthly; $3.00 converter; $15.00 additional installation.

Expanded Basic Service 1
Subscribers: 465.
Programming (via satellite): ABC Family Channel; AMC; Animal Planet; Arts & Entertainment; BET Networks; Bravo; Cartoon Network; CNBC; CNN; Comcast Sports Net Southeast; Comcast/Charter Sports Southeast (CSS); Comedy Central; Country Music TV; C-SPAN 2; Discovery Channel; Disney Channel; E! Entertainment Television; ESPN; ESPN 2; Food Network; Fox News Channel; FX; G4; Golf Channel; Hallmark Channel; Headline News; HGTV; History Channel; Lifetime; MSNBC; MTV; National Geographic Channel; Nickelodeon; Outdoor Channel; Oxygen; RFD-TV; SoapNet; Speed Channel; Spike TV; Style Network; Syfy; TBS Superstation; The Learning Channel; Toon Disney; Travel Channel; truTV; Turner

Classic Movies; Turner Network TV; TV Land; USA Network; Versus; VH1; Weather Channel.

Digital Basic Service

Subscribers: N.A.

Programming (received off-air): WDKY-TV (FOX) Danville; WKYT-TV (CBS, CW) Lexington; WLEX-TV (NBC) Lexington; WTVQ-DT (ABC) Lexington.

Programming (via satellite): Arts & Entertainment HD; BBC America; Bio; Bloomberg Television; CMT Pure Country; Discovery en Espanol; Discovery HD Theater; Discovery Health Channel; Discovery Kids Channel; Discovery Military Channel; Discovery Planet Green; Do-It-Yourself; ESPN 2 HD; ESPN Classic Sports; ESPN HD; ESPN U; ESPNews; FitTV; Fox College Sports Atlantic; Fox College Sports Central; Fox College Sports Pacific; Fox Movie Channel; Great American Country; HDNet; HDNet Movies; History Channel HD; History Channel International; ID Investigation Discovery; Jewelry Television; Lifetime Movie Network; Lifetime Real Women; MTV Hits; MTV Jams; MTV Tres; MTV2; Music Choice; Nick Jr.; Nick Too; NickToons TV; Palladia; PBS HD; Science Channel; TeenNick; Turner Network TV HD; Universal HD; Versus HD; VH1 Classic; VH1 Soul; Weather Channel HD.

Digital Pay Service 1

Pay Units: N.A.

Programming (via satellite): Cinemax (multiplexed); Cinemax HD; Encore (multiplexed); Flix; HBO (multiplexed); HBO HD; Showtime (multiplexed); Starz (multiplexed); Starz HDTV; The Movie Channel (multiplexed).

Video-On-Demand: No

Pay-Per-View

iN DEMAND (delivered digitally); Penthouse TV (delivered digitally); Ten Clips (delivered digitally); Ten Blue (delivered digitally); Ten Blox (delivered digitally); ESPN Gameplan (delivered digitally).

Internet Service

Operational: No.

Telephone Service

None

Miles of Plant: 72.0 (coaxial); None (fiber optic). Homes passed: 2,400.

General Manager: Mark Bookout.

Franchise fee: 3% of gross.

Ownership: NewWave Communications (MSO).

LINCOLN COUNTY (eastern portion)—Mediacom, 90 Main St, Benton, KY 42025-1132. Phones: 417-875-5560 (Springfield regional office); 270-527-9939. Fax: 270-527-0813. Web Site: http://www.mediacomcable.com. Also serves Brodhead & Rockcastle County (western portion). ICA: KY0253.

TV Market Ranking: Below 100 (Brodhead, LINCOLN COUNTY (EASTERN PORTION), Rockcastle County (western portion)). Franchise award date: March 23, 1989. Franchise expiration date: N.A. Began: March 1, 1990.

Channel capacity: N.A. Channels available but not in use: N.A.

Basic Service

Subscribers: 439.

Programming (received off-air): WBKI-TV (CW) Campbellsville; WDKY-TV (FOX) Danville; WKSO-TV (PBS) Somerset; WKYT-TV (CBS, CW) Lexington; WLEX-TV (NBC) Lexington; WLKY-TV (CBS) Louisville; WTVQ-DT (ABC) Lexington.

Programming (via satellite): ABC Family Channel; CNN; Country Music TV; Discovery Channel; Disney Channel; E! Entertainment Television; ESPN; Fox News Channel; Headline News; History Channel; Lifetime; Nickelodeon; QVC; Spike TV; Syfy; TBS Superstation; Trinity Broadcasting Network; Turner Network TV; USA Network; Weather Channel; WGN America.

Fee: $29.95 installation; $24.95 monthly; $3.95 converter.

Pay Service 1

Pay Units: 61.

Programming (via satellite): HBO.

Fee: $10.00 monthly.

Pay Service 2

Pay Units: N.A.

Programming (via satellite): Cinemax; Encore; Starz.

Video-On-Demand: No

Internet Service

Operational: No.

Telephone Service

None

Miles of Plant: 65.0 (coaxial); None (fiber optic). Homes passed: 780. Total homes in franchised area: 780.

Regional Vice President: Bill Copeland. General Manager: Dale Haney. Regional Technical Operations Director: Alan Freedman. Technical Operations Manager: Jeff Brown. Marketing Director: Will Kuebler. Marketing Manager: Melanie Westerman.

Ownership: Mediacom LLC (MSO).

LIVERMORE—Time Warner Cable, 100 Industrial Dr, Owensboro, KY 42301-8711. Phones: 270-852-2000; 270-685-2991. Fax: 270-688-8228. Web Site: http://www.timewarnercable.com/westernky. Also serves Calhoun, McLean County & Rumsey. ICA: KY0093.

TV Market Ranking: 86 (Calhoun, McLean County (portions)); Below 100 (LIVERMORE, Rumsey, McLean County (portions)). Franchise award date: December 15, 1986. Franchise expiration date: N.A. Began: December 15, 1980.

Channel capacity: N.A. Channels available but not in use: N.A.

Basic Service

Subscribers: N.A. Included in Owensboro

Programming (received off-air): WBKO (ABC, CW) Bowling Green; WEHT (ABC) Evansville; WEVV-TV (CBS, MNT) Evansville; WFIE (NBC) Evansville; WKMA-TV (PBS) Madisonville; WKYU-TV (PBS) Bowling Green; WNIN (PBS) Evansville; WTVF (CBS) Nashville; WTVW (FOX) Evansville.

Programming (via satellite): ABC Family Channel; QVC; TBS Superstation; WGN America.

Current originations: Government Access; Educational Access; Public Access.

Fee: $39.95 installation; $20.66 monthly; $1.50 converter.

Expanded Basic Service 1

Subscribers: N.A.

Programming (via satellite): AMC; CNN; Country Music TV; Discovery Channel; ESPN; Lifetime; MTV; Nickelodeon; Spike TV; Turner Network TV; USA Network.

Fee: $15.25 monthly.

Pay Service 1

Pay Units: 129.

Programming (via satellite): HBO.

Fee: $15.95 monthly.

Pay Service 2

Pay Units: 72.

Programming (via satellite): The Movie Channel.

Fee: $15.95 monthly.

Video-On-Demand: No

Internet Service

Operational: Yes.

Broadband Service: RoadRunner.

Fee: $24.95 monthly.

Telephone Service

Digital: Operational

Fee: $24.95 monthly

Miles of Plant: 32.0 (coaxial); None (fiber optic). Homes passed included in Owensboro

General Manager: Chris Poynter. Marketing Manager: Doug Rodgers. Technical Operations Director: Don Collins.

City fee: 3% of basic.

Ownership: Time Warner Cable (MSO).

LONDON—Time Warner Cable, 1615 Foxhaven Dr, Richmond, KY 40475. Phones: 859-626-4800; 859-624-9666. Fax: 859-624-0060. Web Site: http://www.timewarnercable.com. Also serves Colony, East Bernstadt & Keavy. ICA: KY0015.

TV Market Ranking: Below 100 (East Bernstadt, Keavy); Outside TV Markets (Colony, LONDON). Franchise award date: N.A. Franchise expiration date: N.A. Began: October 1, 1958.

Channel capacity: N.A. Channels available but not in use: N.A.

Basic Service

Subscribers: 8,788.

Programming (received off-air): WDKY-TV (FOX) Danville; WKLE (PBS) Lexington; WKMJ-TV (PBS) Louisville; WKYT-TV (CBS, CW) Lexington; WLEX-TV (NBC) Lexington; WLJC-TV (TBN) Beattyville; WOBZ-LP East Bernstadt, etc.; WTVQ-DT (ABC) Lexington; WUPX-TV (ION) Morehead; WVTN-LP Corbin; WYMT-TV (CBS, CW) Hazard; allband FM.

Programming (via satellite): QVC; WGN America.

Planned originations: Educational Access.

Fee: $39.95 installation; $14.88 monthly.

Expanded Basic Service 1

Subscribers: 8,181.

Programming (via satellite): Animal Planet; Arts & Entertainment; BET Networks; Bravo; Cartoon Network; CNBC; CNN; Comcast Sports Net Southeast; Comedy Central; Country Music TV; C-SPAN; C-SPAN 2; Discovery Channel; Disney Channel; E! Entertainment Television; ESPN; ESPN 2; Eternal Word TV Network; Food Network; Fox News Channel; Fox Sports Net Ohio; FX; Hallmark Channel; Headline News; HGTV; History Channel; Home Shopping Network; INSP; Lifetime; MSNBC; MTV; Nickelodeon; Oxygen; Product Information Network; Spike TV; Syfy; TBS Superstation; The Learning Channel; Travel Channel; truTV; Turner Network TV; TV Guide Network; TV Land; USA Network; VH1; Weather Channel.

Fee: $35.47 monthly.

Digital Basic Service

Subscribers: N.A.

Programming (received off-air): WDKY-TV (FOX) Danville; WKLE (PBS) Lexington; WKYT-TV (CBS, CW) Lexington.

Programming (via satellite): AmericanLife TV Network; BBC America; Bio; Bloomberg Television; Boomerang; Canales N; CBS College Sports Network; CMT Pure Country; Cooking Channel; C-SPAN 3; Current; Daystar TV Network; Discovery Digital Networks; Discovery HD Theater; Do-It-Yourself; Encore (multiplexed); ESPN 2 HD; ESPN Classic Sports; ESPN HD; ESPNews; FamilyNet; Flix (multiplexed); Fox College Sports Atlantic; Fox College Sports Central; Fox College Sports Pacific; Fox Movie Channel; Fox Reality Channel; Fox Soccer; Fuse; G4; GAS; Golf Channel; Gospel Music Channel; Great American Country; GSN; Halogen Network; HDNet; HDNet Movies; History Channel International; Independent Film Channel; Lifetime Movie Network; LOGO; MTV Networks Digital Suite; Music Choice; National Geographic Channel; NBA TV; Nick Jr.; Nick Too; NickToons TV; Outdoor Channel; Ovation; ReelzChannel; ShopNBC; Sleuth; SoapNet; Speed Channel; Style Network; Sundance Channel; Tennis Channel; The Sportsman Channel; The Word Network; Toon Disney; Trinity Broadcasting Network; Turner Classic Movies; Turner Network TV HD; TVG Network; Universal HD; Versus; WE tv.

Fee: $6.00 monthly (each tier).

Digital Pay Service 1

Pay Units: N.A.

Programming (via satellite): Arabic Channel; CCTV-4; Cinemax (multiplexed); Cinemax HD; Filipino Channel; HBO (multiplexed); HBO HD; RAI International; Russian Television Network; Showtime (multiplexed); Showtime HD; Starz (multiplexed); Starz HDTV; The Movie Channel (multiplexed); TV Asia; TV Japan; TV5, La Television International; Zhong Tian Channel.

Fee: $12.00 monthly (HBO, Cinemax, Starz, Showtime or TMC), $15.00 monthly (CCTV, TV Asia, TV 5, Filipino, RAI , ART, Russia or TV Japan).

Video-On-Demand: No

Pay-Per-View

iN DEMAND (delivered digitally); Playboy TV (delivered digitally); Hot Choice (delivered digitally); Sports PPV (delivered digitally); Fresh (delivered digitally).

Internet Service

Operational: Yes.

Broadband Service: Road Runner.

Fee: $44.95 monthly.

Telephone Service

Digital: Operational

Fee: $44.95 monthly

Miles of Plant: 467.0 (coaxial); None (fiber optic). Homes passed: 10,948.

General Manager: Robert Trott. Technical Operations Manager: Dennis Lester. Marketing Director: Betrina Morse. Government & Public Affairs Manager: Carla Deaton. Office Manager: Laverne Farris.

City fee: 3% of gross.

Ownership: Time Warner Cable (MSO).

LOUISA—Lycom Communications, 305 E Pike St, Louisa, KY 41230. Phones: 606-638-3600; 800-489-0640. Fax: 606-638-4278. E-mail: info@lycomonline.com. Web Site: http://www.lycomonline.com. ICA: KY0299.

TV Market Ranking: 36 (LOUISA). Franchise award date: N.A. Franchise expiration date: N.A. Began: January 1, 1991.

Channel capacity: 64 (operating 2-way). Channels available but not in use: 4.

Basic Service

Subscribers: 260.

Programming (received off-air): WCHS-TV (ABC) Charleston; WKAS (PBS) Ashland; WLPX-TV (ION) Charleston; WOWK-TV (CBS) Huntington; WPBY-TV (PBS) Huntington; WSAZ-TV (MNT, NBC) Huntington; WTSF (IND) Ashland; WVAH-TV (FOX) Charleston; WYMT-TV (CBS, CW) Hazard.

Programming (via satellite): ABC Family Channel; AMC; Animal Planet; Arts & Entertainment; Cartoon Network; CNBC; CNN; Comedy Central; Country Music TV; C-SPAN; C-SPAN 2; CW+; Discovery Channel; Disney Channel; E! Entertainment Television; ESPN; ESPN 2; ESPN Classic Sports; Food Network; Fox News Channel; Fox Sports Net Ohio; FX; Gospel Music Channel; Great American Country; Hallmark Channel; Headline News; Healthy Living Channel; HGTV; History Channel; Home Shopping Network; Lifetime; MTV; National Geographic Channel; Nickelodeon; QVC; RFD-TV; Speed Channel; Spike TV; Syfy; TBS Superstation; The Learning Channel; The Sportsman Channel; Travel Channel; Trinity Broadcasting Network; truTV; Turner Classic Movies; Turner Network TV; TV Guide Network; TV Land; USA Network; VH1; Weather Channel; WGN America.

Fee: $45.95 installation; $43.09 monthly.

Digital Basic Service

Subscribers: 65.

Programming (received off-air): WKYT-TV (CBS, CW) Lexington; WSAZ-TV (MNT, NBC) Huntington; WVAH-TV (FOX) Charleston; WYMT-TV (CBS, CW) Hazard.

Programming (via satellite): BBC America; Bloomberg Television; Boomerang; CMT Pure Country; Discovery Health Channel; Discovery Kids Channel; Discovery Military Channel; Discovery Planet Green; DMX Music; Do-It-Yourself; ESPN 2; ESPN Classic Sports; ESPN U; ESPNews; FitTV; Fox Movie Channel; G4; Golf Channel; GSN; ID Investigation Discovery; Independent Film Channel; Nick Jr.; NickToons TV; Science Channel; SoapNet; Speed Channel; Versus; VH1 Classic.

Fee: $11.95 monthly.

Digital Pay Service 1

Pay Units: N.A.

Programming (via satellite): Cinemax (multiplexed); Encore (multiplexed); Flix; HBO (multiplexed); Showtime (multiplexed); Starz (multiplexed); The Movie Channel (multiplexed).

Fee: $11.95 monthly (HBO, Cinemax, Showtime/TMC/Flix or Starz/Encore).

Video-On-Demand: No

Internet Service

Operational: Yes. Began: August 1, 2001.

Subscribers: 140.

Broadband Service: Lycom Online.

Fee: $31.95 monthly.

Telephone Service

None

Miles of Plant: 25.0 (coaxial); None (fiber optic). Homes passed: 1,100.

Manager: Donna Lycans.; Stevan Lycans. Chief Technician: Aaron Lycans.

Ownership: Lycom Communications Inc. (MSO).

LOUISVILLE—Insight Communications, 7810 Preston Hwy, Louisville, KY 40229-2167. Phones: 800-273-0144; 502-357-4400; 502-357-4660. Fax: 502-584-1401. Web Site: http://www.myinsight.com. Also serves Austin, Corydon, Crothersville, Floyd County, Floyds Knobs, Galena, Georgetown, Greenville, Harrison County, Lanesville, Lexington, Little York, New Albany, Pekin, Salem, Scottsburg, Vienna & Washington County, IN; Anchorage, Audubon Park, Bancroft, Barbourmeade, Bedford, Beechwood Village, Bellemeade, Bellewood, Blue Ridge Manor, Borden, Brandenburg, Briarwood, Broeck Pointe, Brownsboro Farm, Brownsboro Village, Buckner, Bullitt County, Cambridge, Campbellsburg, Carrollton, Charlestown, Clarksville, Creekside, Crossgate, Devondale, Douglass Hills, Druid Hills, Eminence, Fincastle, Five Star, Fort Knox, Ghent, Glenview Hills, Glenview Manor, Goose Creek, Graymoor, Green Spring, Hardin County (northern portion), Henry County, Henryville, Hickory Hill, Hills and Dales, Hillview, Hollow Creek, Hollyvilla, Houston Acres, Hunters Hollow, Hurstbourne Acres, Indian Hills, Indian Hills-Cherokee, Jefferson County, Jeffersontown, Jeffersonville, Kingsley, Langdon Place, Lebanon Junction, Lincolnshire, Lyndon, Lynnview, Manor Creek, Maryhill Estates, Meade County (portions), Meadow Vale, Meadowbrook Farm, Meadowview Estates, Middletown, Minor Lane Heights, Mockingbird Valley, Moorland, Mount Washington, Muldraugh, New Castle, New Washington, Norbourne Estates, Northfield, Norwood, Old Brownsboro Place, Otisco, Parkway Village, Pewee Valley, Pioneer Village, Plantation, Pleasureville, Prospect, Radcliff, Richlawn, River Bluff, River Ridge, Riverwood, Rolling Fields, Rolling Hills, Sellersburg, Seneca Gardens, Shelby County, Shelbyville, Shepherdsville, Shively, Simpsonville, South Park View, Spencer County (portions), St. Matthews, St. Regis Park, Strathmoor Manor, Strathmoor Village, Sycamore, Taylorsville, Ten Broeck, Thornhill, Trimble County (eastern portion), Underwood, Utica, Watterson Park, West Buechel, West Point, Wildwood, Windy Hill, Woodland Hills, Woodlawn Park, Worthington Hills & Worthville, KY. ICA: KY0001.

TV Market Ranking: 38 (Anchorage, Audubon Park, Bancroft, Barbourmeade, Bedford, Beechwood Village, Bellemeade, Bellewood, Blue Ridge Manor, Borden, Brandenburg, Briarwood, Broeck Pointe, Brownsboro Farm, Brownsboro Village, Buckner, Bullitt County, Cambridge, Clarksville, Corydon, Creekside, Crossgate, Devondale, Douglass Hills, Druid Hills, Eminence, Fincastle, Five Star, Floyd County, Floyds Knobs, Fort Knox, Galena, Georgetown, Glenview Hills, Glenview Manor, Goose Creek, Graymoor, Green Spring, Greenville, Hardin County (northern portion), Harrison County, Henry County (portions), Henryville, Hickory Hill, Hills and Dales, Hillview, Hollow Creek, Hollyvilla, Houston Acres, Hunters Hollow, Hurstbourne Acres, Indian Hills, Indian Hills-Cherokee, Jefferson County, Jeffersontown, Jeffersonville, Kingsley, Lanesville, Langdon Place, Lebanon Junction, Lexington, Lincolnshire, Little York, LOUISVILLE, Lyndon, Lynnview, Manor Creek, Maryhill Estates, Meade County (portions), Meadow Vale, Meadowbrook Farm, Meadowview Estates, Middletown, Minor Lane Heights, Mockingbird Valley, Moorland, Mount Washington, Muldraugh, New Albany, New Castle, New Washington, Norbourne Estates, Northfield, Norwood, Old Brownsboro Place, Otisco, Palmyra, Parkway Village, Pekin, Pewee Valley, Pioneer Village, Plantation, Pleasureville, Pleasureville, Pleasureville, Prospect, Radcliff, Richlawn, River Bluff, River Ridge, Riverwood, Rolling Fields, Rolling Hills, Salem, Scottsburg, Sellersburg, Seneca Gardens, Shelby County (portions), Shelbyville, Shepherdsville, Shively, Simpsonville, South Park View, Spencer County (portions), St. Matthews, St. Regis Park, Strathmoor Manor, Strathmoor Village, Sycamore, Taylorsville, Ten Broeck, Thornhill, Underwood, Utica, Vienna, Washington County (portions), Watterson Park, West Buechel, West Point, Wildwood, Windy Hill, Woodland Hills, Woodlawn Park, Worthington Hills); Below 100 (Austin, Crothersville, Henry County (portions), Shelby County (portions)); Outside TV Markets (Campbellsburg, Carrollton, Ghent, Trimble County (eastern portion), Worthville, Henry County (portions), Washington County (portions)). Franchise award date: November 26, 1973. Franchise expiration date: N.A. Began: January 15, 1979.

Channel capacity: 72 (operating 2-way). Channels available but not in use: None.

Basic Service

Subscribers: 231,049.

Programming (received off-air): WAVE (NBC) Louisville; WBKI-TV (CW) Campbellsville; WBNA (ION) Louisville; WDRB (FOX) Louisville; WHAS-TV (ABC) Louisville; WKMA-TV (PBS) Madisonville; WKPC-TV (PBS) Louisville; WLKY-TV (CBS) Louisville; WMYO (MNT) Salem; 19 FMs.

Programming (via satellite): C-SPAN; C-SPAN 2; Home Shopping Network; MetroChannels; QVC; TV One; Weather Channel; WGN America.

Current originations: Leased Access; Religious Access; Government Access; Educational Access; Public Access.

Fee: $23.74 installation; $15.92 additional installation.

Expanded Basic Service 1

Subscribers: 218,866.

Programming (via satellite): ABC Family Channel; AMC; Animal Planet; Arts & Entertainment; BET Networks; Bravo; Cartoon Network; CNBC; CNN; Comcast Sports Net Southeast; Comedy Central; Country Music TV; Discovery Channel; Disney Channel; E! Entertainment Television; ESPN; ESPN 2; Food Network; Fox News Channel; Fox Sports Net Ohio; FX; G4; Hallmark Channel; Headline News; HGTV; History Channel; Lifetime; MSNBC; MTV; MTV2; Nickelodeon; Oxygen; SoapNet; Spike TV; Syfy; TBS Superstation; The Learning Channel; Travel Channel; Trinity Broadcasting Network; truTV; Turner Network TV; TV Land; TVG Network; Univision; USA Network; VH1.

Fee: $40.00 monthly.

Digital Basic Service

Subscribers: 50,034.

Programming (received off-air): WAVE (NBC) Louisville; WBKI-TV (CW) Campbellsville; WDRB (FOX) Louisville; WHAS-TV (ABC) Louisville; WKPC-TV (PBS) Louisville; WLKY-TV (CBS) Louisville; WMYO (MNT) Salem.

Programming (via satellite): AmericanLife TV Network; Animal Planet HD; BBC America; Bio; Bloomberg Television; Boomerang; CBS College Sports Network; CMT Pure Country; Cooking Channel; C-SPAN 3; Discovery Channel HD; Discovery HD Theater; Discovery Health Channel; Discovery Kids Channel; Discovery Military Channel; Discovery Planet Green; DMX Music; Do-It-Yourself; Encore (multiplexed); ESPN 2 HD; ESPN Classic Sports; ESPN HD; ESPN U; ESPNews; Eternal Word TV Network; FitTV; Fox Movie Channel; Fox Reality Channel; Fox Soccer; Fuse; Golf Channel; Great American Country; GSN; Halogen Network; HDNet; HDNet Movies; History Channel International; HorseRacing TV; ID Investigation Discovery; Independent Film Channel; Lifetime Movie Network; Lifetime Real Women; LOGO; MTV Hits; MTV Jams; MTV Tres; MTV2; National Geographic Channel; National Geographic Channel HD Network; NFL Network; NFL Network HD; Nick Jr.; Nick Too; NickToons TV; Outdoor Channel; Ovation; Palladia; PBS Kids Sprout; Science Channel; Si TV; Sleuth; Speed Channel; Style Network; Sundance Channel; TBS in HD; TeenNick; Tennis Channel; TLC HD; Toon Disney; Turner Classic Movies; Turner Network TV HD; Universal HD; Versus; VH1 Classic; VH1 Soul; WE tv.

Fee: $17.00 monthly.

Digital Pay Service 1

Pay Units: 157,244.

Programming (via satellite): Cinemax (multiplexed); Cinemax On Demand; Flix; HBO (multiplexed); HBO HD; HBO Latino; HBO On Demand; Showtime (multiplexed); Showtime HD; Showtime On Demand; Starz (multiplexed); The Movie Channel (multiplexed); The Movie Channel On Demand.

Fee: $10.00 monthly (Cinemax or Starz), $13.00 monthly (HBO or Showtime/TMC/Flix).

Video-On-Demand: Yes

Pay-Per-View

Addressable homes: 50,034.

ESPN Now (delivered digitally), Addressable: Yes; iN DEMAND (delivered digitally); Playboy TV (delivered digitally); Fresh (delivered digitally); Shorteez (delivered digitally); sports (delivered digitally).

Internet Service

Operational: Yes.

Subscribers: 12,174.

Broadband Service: InsightBB.com.

Fee: $99.95 installation; $44.95 monthly; $15.00 modem lease; $200.00 modem purchase.

Telephone Service

Digital: Operational

Subscribers: 15,000.

Miles of Plant: 3,500.0 (coaxial); 100.0 (fiber optic). Homes passed: 318,106. Total homes in franchised area: 362,760.

President & Chief Operating Officer: Dinni Jain. Senior Vice President, Operations: John Hutton. District Vice President: Bob Lillie. Regional Marketing Director: Gary P. Dusa. Regional Technical Operations Director: David Brown.

City fee: 3% of gross.

Ownership: Insight Communications Co. (MSO).

LOUISVILLE—No longer in operation. ICA: KY0304.

LOWMANSVILLE—Inter Mountain Cable Inc., PO Box 159, 20 Laynesville Rd, Harold, KY 41635. Phone: 606-478-9406. Fax: 606-478-1680. Web Site: http://www.imctv.com. ICA: KY0318.

TV Market Ranking: Outside TV Markets (LOWMANSVILLE). Franchise award date: N.A. Franchise expiration date: N.A. Began: N.A.

Channel capacity: N.A. Channels available but not in use: N.A.

Basic Service
Subscribers: 53.
Programming (received off-air): WCHS-TV (ABC) Charleston; WKMR (PBS) Morehead; WOWK-TV (CBS) Huntington; WPBY-TV (PBS) Huntington; WSAZ-TV (MNT, NBC) Huntington; WVAH-TV (FOX) Charleston; WYMT-TV (CBS, CW) Hazard.
Programming (via satellite): ABC Family Channel; Arts & Entertainment; CNN; ESPN; ESPN 2; Headline News; History Channel; ION Television; Spike TV; TBS Superstation; The Learning Channel; Turner Network TV; USA Network; WGN America.
Fee: $28.80 monthly.
Pay Service 1
Pay Units: N.A.
Programming (via satellite): Showtime.
Video-On-Demand: No
Pay-Per-View
iN DEMAND (delivered digitally); Hot Choice (delivered digitally); Playboy TV (delivered digitally); Fresh (delivered digitally); Shorteez (delivered digitally).
Internet Service
Operational: Yes.
Fee: $24.95 monthly.
Telephone Service
Digital: Operational
Fee: $131.93 monthly
Chief Financial Officer: James Campbell. Manager: Paul Douglas Gearheart. Operations Director: John Schmoldt. Chief Engineer: Jefferson Thacker.
Ownership: Inter-Mountain Cable Inc. (MSO).

LYNCH—Tri-Star Communications. No longer in operation. ICA: KY0151.

MADISONVILLE—NewWave Communications, 250 Madison Square Dr, Madisonville, KY 42431. Phone: 888.863.9928 (Customer service). Fax: 270.245.2022. Web Site: http://www.newwavecom.com. Also serves Earlington, Hanson, Hopkins County (portions), Mortons Gap & White Plains. ICA: KY0013.
TV Market Ranking: Below 100 (Earlington, Hanson, Hopkins County (portions), MADISONVILLE, Mortons Gap, White Plains). Franchise award date: N.A. Franchise expiration date: N.A. Began: July 1, 1964.
Channel capacity: 118 (operating 2-way). Channels available but not in use: N.A.
Basic Service
Subscribers: 8,682.
Programming (received off-air): WAZE-LP (CW) Evansville; WBKO (ABC, CW) Bowling Green; WEHT (ABC) Evansville; WEVV-TV (CBS, MNT) Evansville; WFIE (NBC) Evansville; WKAG-CA Hopkinsville; WKMA-TV (PBS) Madisonville; WNIN (PBS) Evansville; WPSD-TV (NBC) Paducah; WTVF (CBS) Nashville; WTVW (FOX) Evansville.
Programming (via satellite): C-SPAN; C-SPAN 2; Eternal Word TV Network; Home Shopping Network; INSP; QVC; Trinity Broadcasting Network; TV Guide Network; WGN America.
Fee: $40.00 installation; $7.95 monthly.
Expanded Basic Service 1
Subscribers: N.A.
Programming (via satellite): ABC Family Channel; AMC; Animal Planet; Arts & Entertainment; BET Networks; Bravo; Cartoon Network; CNBC; CNN; Comcast Sports Net Southeast; Comedy Central; Country Music TV; Discovery Channel; Disney Channel; E! Entertainment Television; ESPN; ESPN 2; ESPN Classic Sports; Food Network; Fox News Channel; FX; G4; Golf Channel; Great American Country; GSN; Hallmark Channel; Hallmark Movie Channel; Headline News; HGTV; History Channel; Lifetime; MSNBC; MTV; National Geographic Channel; Nickelodeon; Outdoor Channel; Oxygen; SoapNet; Speed Channel; Spike TV; Syfy; TBS Superstation; The Learning Channel; Toon Disney; Travel Channel; truTV; Turner Classic Movies; Turner Network TV; TV Land; USA Network; Versus; VH1; Weather Channel.
Digital Basic Service
Subscribers: N.A.
Programming (received off-air): WEHT (ABC) Evansville; WEVV-TV (CBS, MNT) Evansville; WFIE (NBC) Evansville; WTVW (FOX) Evansville.
Programming (via satellite): Arts & Entertainment HD; BBC America; Bio; CMT Pure Country; Cooking Channel; Discovery HD Theater; Discovery Health Channel; Discovery Kids Channel; Discovery Military Channel; Discovery Planet Green; Do-It-Yourself; ESPN 2 HD; ESPN HD; ESPN U; ESPNews; FitTV; Fox Movie Channel; FSN HD; Gospel Music Channel; HDNet; HDNet Movies; History Channel HD; History Channel International; HorseRacing TV; ID Investigation Discovery; Jewelry Television; Lifetime Movie Network; Lifetime Real Women; MTV Hits; MTV Jams; MTV2; Music Choice; Nick Jr.; Nick Too; NickToons TV; Palladia; RFD-TV; Science Television; Style Network; TeenNick; Turner Network TV HD; Universal HD; USA Network HD; VH1 Classic; VH1 Soul; Weather Channel HD.
Digital Pay Service 1
Pay Units: N.A.
Programming (via satellite): Cinemax (multiplexed); Cinemax HD; Encore (multiplexed); Flix; HBO (multiplexed); HBO HD; Showtime (multiplexed); Starz (multiplexed); Starz HDTV; The Movie Channel (multiplexed).
Video-On-Demand: Planned
Pay-Per-View
iN DEMAND (delivered digitally); Playboy TV (delivered digitally); Fresh (delivered digitally); Shorteez (delivered digitally); ESPN Gameplan (delivered digitally).
Internet Service
Operational: Yes.
Fee: $40.00 installation; $31.99 monthly.
Telephone Service
None
Miles of Plant: 265.0 (coaxial); 57.0 (fiber optic). Homes passed: 12,912. Total homes in franchised area: 15,807.
General Manager: Mark Boyer. Technical Operations Director: Roy Hibbs.
City fee: 3% of gross.
Ownership: NewWave Communications (MSO).

MALONETON—Time Warner Cable, 1266 Dublin Rd, Columbus, OH 43215-1008. Phones: 888-882-4604; 614-431-1280. Fax: 614-481-5052. Web Site: http://www.timewarnercable.com/midohio. Also serves Greenup County (unincorporated areas) & South Shore. ICA: KY0149.
TV Market Ranking: 36 (Greenup County (unincorporated areas) (portions), MALONETON); Below 100 (South Shore, Greenup County (unincorporated areas) (portions)). Franchise award date: N.A. Franchise expiration date: N.A. Began: May 1, 1989.
Channel capacity: N.A. Channels available but not in use: None.

Basic Service
Subscribers: 451.
Programming (received off-air): WCHS-TV (ABC) Charleston; WKAS (PBS) Ashland; WOWK-TV (CBS) Huntington; WPBO (PBS) Portsmouth; WPBY-TV (PBS) Huntington; WQCW (CW) Portsmouth; WSAZ-TV (MNT, NBC) Huntington; WTSF (IND) Ashland; WVAH-TV (FOX) Charleston.
Programming (via satellite): ABC Family Channel; AMC; Arts & Entertainment; Discovery Channel; Lifetime; QVC; TBS Superstation; Weather Channel; WGN America.
Fee: $29.95 installation; $21.95 monthly; $2.00 converter.
Expanded Basic Service 1
Subscribers: N.A.
Programming (via satellite): CNN; Country Music TV; Disney Channel; ESPN; Headline News; Spike TV; Trinity Broadcasting Network; Turner Network TV; USA Network.
Digital Pay Service 1
Pay Units: N.A.
Programming (via satellite): Cinemax (multiplexed); Encore (multiplexed); HBO (multiplexed); Showtime (multiplexed); Starz (multiplexed); The Movie Channel (multiplexed).
Video-On-Demand: No
Pay-Per-View
Hits Movies & Events (delivered digitally); Playboy TV (delivered digitally).
Internet Service
Operational: Yes.
Broadband Service: RoadRunner.
Fee: $24.95 monthly.
Telephone Service
Digital: Operational
Fee: $24.95 monthly
Miles of Plant: 34.0 (coaxial); None (fiber optic). Homes passed: 548.
President: Rhonda Fraas. Vice President & General Manager: Davie Kreiman. Vice President, Engineering: Randy Hall. Vice President, Government & Public Affairs: Mary Jo Green. Vice President, Marketing: Mark Psigoda. Technical Operations Director: Jim Cavender. Government Affairs Director: Steve Cuckler.
Ownership: Time Warner Cable (MSO).

MANCHESTER—C & W Cable. Now served by ANNVILLE, KY [KY0122]. ICA: KY0211.

MARION—Mediacom, 90 Main St, Benton, KY 42025-1132. Phones: 417-875-5560 (Springfield regional office); 270-527-9939. Fax: 270-527-0813. Web Site: http://www.mediacomcable.com. Also serves Caldwell County, Crittenden County, Fredonia, Princeton & Salem. ICA: KY0071.
TV Market Ranking: 69 (Crittenden County (portions), Fredonia, Salem); Below 100 (Caldwell County (portions), MARION, Princeton, Crittenden County (portions)); Outside TV Markets (Caldwell County (portions)). Franchise award date: N.A. Franchise expiration date: N.A. Began: September 1, 1982.
Channel capacity: N.A. Channels available but not in use: N.A.
Basic Service
Subscribers: 4,547.
Programming (received off-air): KFVS-TV (CBS, CW) Cape Girardeau; WDKA (MNT) Paducah; WEHT (ABC) Evansville; WEVV-TV (CBS, MNT) Evansville; WKAG-CA Hopkinsville; WKMA-TV (PBS) Madisonville; WPSD-TV (NBC) Paducah; WSIL-TV (ABC) Harrisburg; WSMV-TV (NBC, TMO) Nashville; WTVF (CBS) Nashville; WTVW (FOX) Evansville.
Programming (via satellite): TV Guide Network; WGN America.
Fee: $36.95 installation; $18.20 monthly.
Expanded Basic Service 1
Subscribers: N.A.
Programming (via satellite): ABC Family Channel; AMC; Animal Planet; Arts & Entertainment; BET Networks; Bravo; Cartoon Network; CNBC; CNN; Comcast Sports Net Southeast; Comedy Central; Country Music TV; C-SPAN; Discovery Channel; Disney Channel; E! Entertainment Television; ESPN; ESPN 2; FitTV; Food Network; Fox News Channel; FX; GRTV Network; Hallmark Channel; Headline News; HGTV; History Channel; Home Shopping Network; INSP; Lifetime; MSNBC; MTV; Nickelodeon; Outdoor Channel; QVC; SoapNet; Speed Channel; Spike TV; Syfy; TBS Superstation; The Learning Channel; Travel Channel; Trinity Broadcasting Network; Turner Classic Movies; TV Land; Univision; USA Network; VH1; WE tv; Weather Channel.
Digital Basic Service
Subscribers: N.A.
Programming (via satellite): BBC America; Bio; Bloomberg Television; Discovery Digital Networks; Fox Movie Channel; Fox Soccer; Fuse; G4; GAS; Golf Channel; GSN; History Channel International; Independent Film Channel; Lifetime Movie Network; Lime; MTV Networks Digital Suite; Music Choice; National Geographic Channel; Nick Jr.; NickToons TV; Style Network; Turner Classic Movies; Versus.
Digital Pay Service 1
Pay Units: N.A.
Programming (via satellite): Cinemax (multiplexed); Encore (multiplexed); Flix; HBO (multiplexed); Showtime (multiplexed); Starz (multiplexed); Sundance Channel; The Movie Channel (multiplexed).
Video-On-Demand: No
Pay-Per-View
Barker (delivered digitally); Mediacom PPV (delivered digitally); Playboy TV (delivered digitally); TEN Clips (delivered digitally); TEN Blox (delivered digitally).
Internet Service
Operational: Yes, DSL only.
Broadband Service: Mediacom High Speed Internet.
Telephone Service
Digital: Operational
Miles of Plant: 128.0 (coaxial); None (fiber optic).
Regional Vice President: Bill Copeland. General Manager: Dale Haney. Regional Technical Operations Director: Alan Freedman. Technical Operations Manager: Jeff Brown.

Marketing Director: Will Kuebler. Marketing Manager: Melanie Westerman.
City fee: 3% of gross.
Ownership: Mediacom LLC (MSO).

MARSHALL COUNTY—Mediacom, 90 Main St, Benton, KY 42025-1132. Phones: 417-875-5560 (Springfield regional office); 270-527-9939. Fax: 270-527-0813. Web Site: http://www.mediacomcable.com. Also serves Aurora, Gilbertsville & Hardin. ICA: KY0035.
TV Market Ranking: 69 (Aurora, Gilbertsville, Hardin, MARSHALL COUNTY). Franchise award date: N.A. Franchise expiration date: N.A. Began: December 10, 1983.
Channel capacity: N.A. Channels available but not in use: N.A.
Basic Service
Subscribers: 5,289.
Programming (received off-air): KBSI (FOX) Cape Girardeau; KFVS-TV (CBS, CW) Cape Girardeau; WDKA (MNT) Paducah; WKMU (PBS) Murray; WPSD-TV (NBC) Paducah; WSIL-TV (ABC) Harrisburg; WTCT (IND) Marion.
Programming (via satellite): TV Guide Network; WQTV-LP (CW) Murray.
Current originations: Public Access.
Fee: $36.95 installation; $18.43 monthly.
Expanded Basic Service 1
Subscribers: N.A.
Programming (via satellite): ABC Family Channel; AMC; Animal Planet; Arts & Entertainment; Bravo; Cartoon Network; CNBC; CNN; Comcast Sports Net Southeast; Comedy Central; Country Music TV; C-SPAN; Discovery Channel; Disney Channel; E! Entertainment Television; ESPN; ESPN 2; FitTV; Food Network; Fox News Channel; FX; Golf Channel; GRTV Network; Hallmark Channel; Headline News; HGTV; History Channel; Home Shopping Network; INSP; Lifetime; MSNBC; MTV; Nickelodeon; Outdoor Channel; QVC; SoapNet; Speed Channel; Spike TV; Syfy; TBS Superstation; The Learning Channel; Travel Channel; Trinity Broadcasting Network; Turner Network TV; TV Land; Univision; USA Network; VH1; WE tv; Weather Channel; WGN America.
Digital Basic Service
Subscribers: N.A.
Programming (via satellite): BBC America; Bio; Bloomberg Television; Discovery Health Channel; Discovery Home Channel; Discovery Kids Channel; Discovery Times Channel; DMX Music; Fox Movie Channel; Fox Soccer; G4; GAS; GSN; History Channel; Independent Film Channel; Lifetime Movie Network; MTV Networks Digital Suite; National Geographic Channel; Nick Jr.; NickToons TV; Science Television; Style Network; Turner Classic Movies; Versus.
Digital Pay Service 1
Pay Units: N.A.
Programming (via satellite): Cinemax (multiplexed); Encore (multiplexed); Flix (multiplexed); HBO (multiplexed); Showtime (multiplexed); Starz (multiplexed); Sundance Channel (multiplexed); The Movie Channel.
Video-On-Demand: No
Internet Service
Operational: Yes.
Broadband Service: Mediacom High Speed Internet.
Telephone Service
Analog: Not Operational
Digital: Operational
Miles of Plant: 468.0 (coaxial); 23.0 (fiber optic). Homes passed: 5,412. Total homes in franchised area: 7,953.
Regional Vice President: Bill Copeland. General Manager: Dale Haney. Regional Technical Operations Director: Alan Freedman. Technical Operations Manager: Jeff Brown. Marketing Director: Will Kuebler. Marketing Manager: Melanie Westerman.
County fee: 3% of gross.
Ownership: Mediacom LLC (MSO).

MARTINS FORK—Formerly served by Tri-State Cable TV. No longer in operation. ICA: KY0311.

MAYFIELD—NewWave Communications, 906 South 12 St, Belair Shopping Center, Murray, KY 42071. Phone: 573-472-9500. Fax: 270.753.8462. Web Site: http://www.newwavecom.com. Also serves Benton & Calvert City. ICA: KY0037.
TV Market Ranking: 69 (Benton, Calvert City, MAYFIELD). Franchise award date: N.A. Franchise expiration date: N.A. Began: January 1, 1966.
Channel capacity: N.A. Channels available but not in use: N.A.
Basic Service
Subscribers: 6,557.
Programming (received off-air): KBSI (FOX) Cape Girardeau; KFVS-TV (CBS, CW) Cape Girardeau; WBBJ-TV (ABC) Jackson; WDKA (MNT) Paducah; WKMU (PBS) Murray; WKRN-TV (ABC) Nashville; WNPT (PBS) Nashville; WPSD-TV (NBC) Paducah; WQWQ-LP (CW) Paducah; WSIL-TV (ABC) Harrisburg; WSMV-TV (NBC, TMO) Nashville; WTCT (IND) Marion; WTVF (CBS) Nashville; 17 FMs.
Programming (via satellite): INSP; QVC; WGN America.
Current originations: Government Access; Educational Access.
Fee: $40.00 installation; $9.95 monthly; $15.00 additional installation.
Expanded Basic Service 1
Subscribers: N.A.
Programming (via satellite): ABC Family Channel; AMC; Animal Planet; Arts & Entertainment; BET Networks; Cartoon Network; CNBC; CNN; Comcast Sports Net Southeast; Comcast/Charter Sports Southeast (CSS); Comedy Central; Country Music TV; C-SPAN; C-SPAN 2; Discovery Channel; Disney Channel; E! Entertainment Television; ESPN; ESPN 2; ESPN Classic Sports; Eternal Word TV Network; FitTV; Food Network; Fox News Channel; FX; G4; Golf Channel; GSN; Hallmark Channel; Headline News; HGTV; History Channel; Home Shopping Network; ION Television; Lifetime; MSNBC; MTV; National Geographic Channel; Nickelodeon; Outdoor Channel; Oxygen; SoapNet; Speed Channel; Spike TV; Syfy; TBS Superstation; The Learning Channel; Travel Channel; truTV; Turner Classic Movies; Turner Network TV; TV Guide Network; TV Land; USA Network; Versus; VH1; Weather Channel.
Digital Basic Service
Subscribers: N.A.
Programming (received off-air): KBSI (FOX) Cape Girardeau; KFVS-TV (CBS, CW) Cape Girardeau; WKMU (PBS) Murray; WPSD-TV (NBC) Paducah; WSIL-TV (ABC) Harrisburg.
Programming (via satellite): Arts & Entertainment HD; BBC America; Bio; Bloomberg Television; Boomerang; CMT Pure Country; CNN en Espanol; Discovery en Espanol; Discovery HD Theater; Discovery Kids Channel; Discovery Military Channel; Discovery Planet Green; Do-It-Yourself; ESPN 2 HD; ESPN Classic Sports; ESPN HD; ESPN U; ESPNews; FitTV; Fox Movie Channel; FSN HD; Gospel Music Channel; Great American Country; HDNet; HDNet Movies; History Channel HD; History Channel International; HorseRacing TV; ID Investigation Discovery; Lifetime Movie Network; Lifetime Real Women; MTV Hits; MTV Jams; MTV Tres; MTV2; Music Choice; Nick Jr.; Nick Too; NickToons TV; Palladia; Science Television; Sleuth; Style Network; TeenNick; Toon Disney; Turner Network TV HD; Universal HD; Versus HD; VH1 Classic; VH1 Soul; Weather Channel HD.
Digital Pay Service 1
Pay Units: N.A.
Programming (via satellite): Cinemax (multiplexed); Cinemax HD; Encore (multiplexed); Flix; HBO (multiplexed); HBO HD; Showtime (multiplexed); Starz (multiplexed); Starz HDTV; The Movie Channel (multiplexed).
Video-On-Demand: No
Pay-Per-View
iN DEMAND (delivered digitally); Penthouse TV (delivered digitally); Ten Clips (delivered digitally); Ten Blue (delivered digitally); Ten Blox (delivered digitally).
Internet Service
Operational: Yes.
Fee: $40.00 installation; $31.99 monthly.
Telephone Service
Digital: Operational
Fee: $24.99 monthly
Miles of Plant: 141.0 (coaxial); None (fiber optic).
General Manager: Cameron Miller. Technical Operations Manager: Eddie Prior.
City fee: 3% of gross.
Ownership: NewWave Communications (MSO).

MAYSVILLE—Limestone Bracken Cablevision, PO Box 100, 626 Forest Ave, Maysville, KY 41056. Phone: 606-564-9220. Fax: 606-564-4291. E-mail: limestone@maysvilleky.net. Web Site: http://www.limestonecable.com. Also serves Augusta, Brooksville, Germantown, Mason County & Washington. ICA: KY0033.
TV Market Ranking: 17 (Augusta); Outside TV Markets (Brooksville, Germantown, Mason County, MAYSVILLE, Washington). Franchise award date: January 1, 1960. Franchise expiration date: N.A. Began: January 1, 1960.
Channel capacity: 120 (operating 2-way). Channels available but not in use: None.
Basic Service
Subscribers: 5,946.
Programming (received off-air): WCPO-TV (ABC) Cincinnati; WKMR (PBS) Morehead; WKRC-TV (CBS, CW) Cincinnati; WKYT-TV (CBS, CW) Lexington; WLEX-TV (NBC) Lexington; WLWT (NBC) Cincinnati; WSTR-TV (MNT) Cincinnati; WTVQ-DT (ABC) Lexington; WXIX-TV (FOX) Newport; allband FM.
Programming (via satellite): QVC; WGN America.
Fee: $35.00 installation; $16.50 monthly; $35.00 additional installation.
Expanded Basic Service 1
Subscribers: 4,803.
Programming (via satellite): ABC Family Channel; AMC; Animal Planet; Arts & Entertainment; BET Networks; CNBC; CNN; Comcast Sports Net Southeast; Comedy Central; Country Music TV; C-SPAN; Discovery Channel; Disney Channel; E! Entertainment Television; ESPN; ESPN 2; Eternal Word TV Network; Food Network; Fox News Channel; Fox Sports Net Ohio; FX; Great American Country; Headline News; History Channel; Lifetime; Lifetime Movie Network; MTV; National Geographic Channel; Nickelodeon; Outdoor Channel; SoapNet; Speed Channel; Spike TV; Syfy; TBS Superstation; The Learning Channel; Travel Channel; Trinity Broadcasting Network; truTV; Turner Network TV; TV Land; USA Network; VH1; Weather Channel.
Fee: $35.00 installation; $37.30 monthly.
Digital Basic Service
Subscribers: 276.
Programming (via satellite): BBC America; Bio; Bloomberg Television; Bravo; Discovery Digital Networks; DMX Music; Encore (multiplexed); ESPN Classic Sports; ESPNews; FitTV; Fox Movie Channel; Fox Soccer; G4; GAS; Golf Channel; GSN; HGTV; History Channel International; Independent Film Channel; Lime; MTV Networks Digital Suite; Nick Jr.; NickToons TV; Sleuth; Style Network; Toon Disney; Turner Classic Movies.
Fee: $15.65 monthly.
Pay Service 1
Pay Units: 333.
Programming (via satellite): HBO.
Fee: $12.95 monthly.
Pay Service 2
Pay Units: 143.
Programming (via satellite): Showtime.
Fee: $12.95 monthly.
Digital Pay Service 1
Pay Units: N.A.
Programming (via satellite): Cinemax (multiplexed); Flix; HBO (multiplexed); Showtime (multiplexed); Starz (multiplexed); The Movie Channel (multiplexed).
Fee: $12.95 monthly.
Video-On-Demand: No
Pay-Per-View
Addressable homes: 304.
Special events, Addressable: No.
Internet Service
Operational: Yes.
Subscribers: 2,861.
Broadband Service: In-house.
Fee: $21.95-$64.95 monthly.
Telephone Service
None
Miles of Plant: 153.0 (coaxial); 30.0 (fiber optic). Homes passed: 6,500. Total homes in franchised area: 7,500.
Customer Service Manager: Jean Black. Chief Technician: Jeff Mason. Manager: Ron Buerkley. Marketing & Program Director: Jeff Cracraft.
Ownership: Standard Tobacco Co. Inc. (MSO).

McKEE—Peoples Telecom, PO Box 159, US Hwy 421 S, McKee, KY 40447. Phone: 606-287-7101. Fax: 606-287-8332. Web Site: http://www.prtcnet.org. Also serves Bighill, Clover Bottom, Gray Hawk, Jackson County, Morrell, Sandgap & Waneta. ICA: KY0113.
TV Market Ranking: Below 100 (Bighill, Clover Bottom, Gray Hawk, Jackson County, MCKEE, Morrell, Sandgap, Waneta). Franchise award date: N.A. Franchise expiration date: N.A. Began: May 1, 1954.
Channel capacity: N.A. Channels available but not in use: N.A.
Basic Service
Subscribers: 1,400.
Programming (received off-air): WBKI-CA Louisville; WDKY-TV (FOX) Danville; WKLE (PBS) Lexington; WKYT-TV (CBS, CW) Lexington; WLEX-TV (NBC) Lexington; WLJC-TV (TBN) Beattyville; WTVQ-DT (ABC) Lexington; WUPX-TV (ION) Morehead; WYMT-TV (CBS, CW) Hazard; allband FM.

Programming (via satellite): WGN America.
Fee: $15.00 installation; $16.22 monthly.

Expanded Basic Service 1
Subscribers: N.A.
Programming (via satellite): ABC Family Channel; AMC; Animal Planet; Arts & Entertainment; Cartoon Network; CNN; Comcast Sports Net Southeast; Discovery Channel; Disney Channel; ESPN; ESPN 2; Food Network; Fox News Channel; Fox Sports Net Ohio; FX; History Channel; Lifetime; Spike TV; Syfy; TBS Superstation; The Learning Channel; truTV; Turner Classic Movies; Turner Network TV; TV Land; USA Network; VH1; Weather Channel.
Fee: $33.45 monthly.

Digital Basic Service
Subscribers: 500 Includes Booneville.
Programming (via satellite): BBC America; Bio; Bloomberg Television; CMT Pure Country; Discovery Health Channel; Discovery Home Channel; Discovery Kids Channel; Discovery Military Channel; Discovery Times Channel; DMX Music; ESPN 2; ESPN Classic Sports; ESPNews; FitTV; Fox Movie Channel; Fuse; G4; Golf Channel; Halogen Network; HGTV; History Channel; History Channel International; Lifetime Movie Network; MTV Hits; MTV2; Nick Jr.; NickToons TV; Outdoor Channel; Ovation; RFD-TV; Science Channel; SoapNet; Speed Channel; Style Network; TeenNick; Toon Disney; Trinity Broadcasting Network; Turner Classic Movies; VH1 Classic; VH1 Soul.
Fee: $8.35 monthly.

Digital Pay Service 1
Pay Units: N.A.
Programming (via satellite): Cinemax; Encore (multiplexed); Flix; HBO (multiplexed); Showtime (multiplexed); Starz (multiplexed); The Movie Channel (multiplexed).
Fee: $10.95 monthly (Cinemax or Starz/Encore), $12.95 monthly (HBO or Showtime).

Video-On-Demand: No

Internet Service
Operational: No.

Telephone Service
None

Miles of Plant: 82.0 (coaxial); None (fiber optic). Homes passed: 2,100. Miles of plant includes Booneville
General Manager: Keith Gabbard. Chief Technician: Jeff Bingham.
City fee: None.
Ownership: Peoples Rural Telephone Cooperative.

MCKINNEY—NewWave Communications, 5026 S Highway 27, Somerset, KY 42501. Phone: 606-678-9215. Fax: 606-679-7111. Web Site: http://www.newwavecom.com. ICA: KY0297.
TV Market Ranking: Below 100 (MCKINNEY). Franchise award date: N.A. Franchise expiration date: N.A. Began: N.A.
Channel capacity: 54 (not 2-way capable). Channels available but not in use: 1.

Basic Service
Subscribers: 296.
Programming (received off-air): WAGV (IND) Harlan; WBIR-TV (NBC) Knoxville; WBKI-TV (CW) Campbellsville; WDKY-TV (FOX) Danville; WKSO-TV (PBS) Somerset; WKYT-TV (CBS, CW) Lexington; WLEX-TV (NBC) Lexington; WTVQ-DT (ABC) Lexington; WUPX-TV (ION) Morehead; WYMT-TV (CBS, CW) Hazard.
Programming (via satellite): C-SPAN; Home Shopping Network; INSP; QVC; ShopNBC; TV Guide Network; WGN America.
Fee: $18.52 monthly.

Expanded Basic Service 1
Subscribers: 291.
Programming (via satellite): ABC Family Channel; AMC; Animal Planet; Arts & Entertainment; BET Networks; Bravo; Cartoon Network; CNBC; CNN; Comcast Sports Net Southeast; Comcast/Charter Sports Southeast (CSS); Comedy Central; Country Music TV; Court TV; C-SPAN 2; Discovery Channel; Disney Channel; E! Entertainment Television; ESPN; ESPN 2; Food Network; Fox News Channel; Fox Sports Net Ohio; FX; G4; Golf Channel; Hallmark Channel; Headline News; HGTV; History Channel; Lifetime; MSNBC; MTV; National Geographic Channel; Nickelodeon; Outdoor Channel; SoapNet; Speed Channel; Spike TV; Style Network; Syfy; TBS Superstation; The Learning Channel; Toon Disney; Travel Channel; Trinity Broadcasting Network; Turner Classic Movies; Turner Network TV; TV Land; USA Network; Versus; VH1; WE tv; Weather Channel.
Fee: $1.78 monthly.

Digital Basic Service
Subscribers: N.A.
Programming (received off-air): WKYT-TV (CBS, CW) Lexington; WLEX-TV (NBC) Lexington; WTVQ-DT (ABC) Lexington.
Programming (via satellite): BBC America; Bio; Bloomberg Television; CMT Pure Country; Discovery Channel HD; Discovery en Espanol; Discovery Health Channel; Discovery Home Channel; Discovery Kids Channel; Discovery Military Channel; Discovery Times Channel; Do-It-Yourself; ESPN 2 HD; ESPN Classic Sports; ESPN HD; ESPN U; ESPNews; FitTV; Fox College Sports Atlantic; Fox College Sports Central; Fox College Sports Pacific; Fox Movie Channel; GAS; Great American Country; GSN; HDNet; HDNet Movies; History Channel International; Jewelry Television; Lifetime Movie Network; Lifetime Real Women; MTV Hits; MTV Jams; MTV Tres; MTV2; Music Choice; Nick Jr.; Nick Too; NickToons TV; Science Channel; Turner Network TV HD; TV Guide Interactive Inc.; Universal HD; VH1 Classic; VH1 Soul.

Digital Pay Service 1
Pay Units: N.A.
Programming (via satellite): Cinemax (multiplexed); Cinemax HD; Encore; Flix; HBO (multiplexed); HBO HD; Showtime (multiplexed); Starz (multiplexed); Starz HDTV; The Movie Channel (multiplexed).

Video-On-Demand: No

Pay-Per-View
Movies (delivered digitally); Special events (delivered digitally); Ten Clips (delivered digitally); Ten Blue (delivered digitally); Ten Blox (delivered digitally); ESPN Gameplan (delivered digitally).

Internet Service
Operational: No.

Telephone Service
None

Miles of Plant: 19.0 (coaxial); None (fiber optic). Homes passed: 316.
General Manager: Mark Bookout. Technical Operations Manager: Lynn McMahan.
Ownership: NewWave Communications (MSO).

MIDDLESBORO—NewWave Communications, 5026 S Hwy 27, Somerset, KY 42501. Phone: 606.678.9215. Fax: 606.679.7111. Web Site: http://www.newwavecom.com. Also serves Arjay, Bell County (southeastern portion), Calvin, Cubage, Kettle Island, Left Fork, Miracle, Ratford, Stoney Fork & Stray Creek. ICA: KY0034.

TV Market Ranking: Below 100 (Arjay, Bell County (southeastern portion), Calvin, Cubage, Kettle Island, Left Fork, MIDDLESBORO, Miracle, Ratford, Stoney Creek, Stray Creek). Franchise award date: July 20, 1968. Franchise expiration date: N.A. Began: July 20, 1968.
Channel capacity: N.A. Channels available but not in use: N.A.

Basic Service
Subscribers: 3,666.
Programming (received off-air): WAGV (IND) Harlan; WATE-TV (ABC) Knoxville; WBIR-TV (NBC) Knoxville; WBXX-TV (CW) Crossville; WKSO-TV (PBS) Somerset; WPXK-TV (ION) Jellico; WTNZ (FOX) Knoxville; WTVQ-DT (ABC) Lexington; WVLR (IND) Tazewell; WVLT-TV (CBS, MNT) Knoxville; WYMT-TV (CBS, CW) Hazard; allband FM.
Programming (via satellite): C-SPAN; C-SPAN 2; Home Shopping Network; INSP; QVC; ShopNBC; WGN America.
Fee: $35.00 installation; $8.86 monthly; $25.00 additional installation.

Expanded Basic Service 1
Subscribers: N.A.
Programming (via satellite): ABC Family Channel; AMC; Animal Planet; Arts & Entertainment; Bravo; Cartoon Network; CNBC; CNN; Comcast Sports Net Southeast; Comcast/Charter Sports Southeast (CSS); Comedy Central; Country Music TV; Court TV; Discovery Channel; Disney Channel; E! Entertainment Television; ESPN; ESPN 2; Food Network; Fox News Channel; FX; G4; Golf Channel; Hallmark Channel; Headline News; HGTV; History Channel; Lifetime; MSNBC; MTV; National Geographic Channel; Nickelodeon; Oxygen; SoapNet; Speed Channel; Spike TV; Style Network; Syfy; TBS Superstation; The Learning Channel; Toon Disney; Travel Channel; Trinity Broadcasting Network; Turner Classic Movies; Turner Network TV; TV Land; USA Network; Versus; VH1; WE tv; Weather Channel.
Fee: $7.67 monthly.

Digital Basic Service
Subscribers: N.A.
Programming (received off-air): WATE-TV (ABC) Knoxville; WBIR-TV (NBC) Knoxville; WTNZ (FOX) Knoxville; WVLT-TV (CBS, MNT) Knoxville.
Programming (via satellite): BBC America; Bio; CMT Pure Country; Discovery Channel HD; Discovery en Espanol; Discovery Health Channel; Discovery Home Channel; Discovery Kids Channel; Discovery Military Channel; Discovery Times Channel; Do-It-Yourself; ESPN 2 HD; ESPN Classic Sports; ESPN HD; ESPN U; Fox College Sports Atlantic; Fox College Sports Central; Fox College Sports Pacific; Fox Movie Channel; GAS; HDNet; HDNet Movies; History Channel International; Jewelry Television; Lifetime Movie Network; Lifetime Real Women; MTV Jams; MTV Tres; MTV2; Music Choice; Nick Jr.; Nick Too; NickToons TV; Science Channel; Turner Network TV HD; TV Guide Interactive Inc.; Universal HD; VH1 Classic; VH1 Soul.

Digital Pay Service 1
Pay Units: N.A.
Programming (via satellite): Cinemax (multiplexed); Cinemax HD; Encore (multiplexed); Flix; HBO (multiplexed); HBO HD; Showtime (multiplexed); Starz (multiplexed); Starz HDTV; The Movie Channel (multiplexed).

Video-On-Demand: No

Pay-Per-View
iN DEMAND (delivered digitally); Ten Blue (delivered digitally); Ten Clips (delivered digitally); Ten Blox (delivered digitally); ESPN Gameplan (delivered digitally).

Internet Service
Operational: Yes.
Fee: $40.00 installation; $31.99 monthly.

Telephone Service
Digital: Operational
Fee: $24.99 monthly

Miles of Plant: 90.0 (coaxial); None (fiber optic). Homes passed: 5,315. Total homes in franchised area: 5,480.
General Manager: Mark Bookout. Technical Operations Manager: Lynn McMahan.
City fee: 3% of gross.
Ownership: NewWave Communications (MSO).

MIDWAY—Now served by GEORGETOWN, KY [KY0044]. Also serves MIDWAY. ICA: KY0154.

MILLVILLE—Formerly served by Chumley's Antenna Systems Inc. No longer in operation. ICA: KY0196.

MONTICELLO—Community Telecom Services, 514 N Main St, Monticello, KY 42633-1534. Phone: 606-348-8416. Fax: 606-348-6397. Also serves Wayne County. ICA: KY0047.
TV Market Ranking: Below 100 (Wayne County (portions)); Outside TV Markets (MONTICELLO, Wayne County (portions)). Franchise award date: May 12, 1980. Franchise expiration date: N.A. Began: November 1, 1960.
Channel capacity: 37 (operating 2-way). Channels available but not in use: None.

Basic Service
Subscribers: 2,400.
Programming (received off-air): WBIR-TV (NBC) Knoxville; WDKY-TV (FOX) Danville; WKSO-TV (PBS) Somerset; WKYT-TV (CBS, CW) Lexington; WLEX-TV (NBC) Lexington; WTVQ-DT (ABC) Lexington; 3 FMs.
Programming (via satellite): AMC; Arts & Entertainment; Country Music TV; C-SPAN; CW+; Discovery Channel; ESPN; ESPN 2; Fox News Channel; Fox Sports Net Ohio; FX; Headline News; HGTV; History Channel; Home Shopping Network; MTV; Nickelodeon; QVC; Syfy; Trinity Broadcasting Network; TV Land; VH1.
Current originations: Religious Access; Public Access.
Fee: $20.76 monthly.

Expanded Basic Service 1
Subscribers: 2,350.
Programming (via satellite): Lifetime; Turner Network TV; USA Network; Weather Channel.
Fee: $2.58 monthly.
Expanded Basic Service 2
Subscribers: 2,300.
Programming (via satellite): ABC Family Channel; CNN; Disney Channel; Spike TV; TBS Superstation; WGN America.
Fee: $7.12 monthly.
Pay Service 1
Pay Units: 83.
Programming (via satellite): Cinemax.
Fee: $15.00 installation; $10.95 monthly.
Pay Service 2
Pay Units: 154.
Programming (via satellite): HBO.
Fee: $11.95 monthly.
Pay Service 3
Pay Units: 43.
Programming (via satellite): The Movie Channel.
Fee: $10.95 monthly.
Pay Service 4
Pay Units: 41.
Programming (via satellite): Showtime.
Fee: $10.95 monthly.
Video-On-Demand: No
Internet Service
Operational: No.
Telephone Service
None
Miles of Plant: 154.0 (coaxial); None (fiber optic). Homes passed: 4,209.
Manager: Dale Hancock.
Franchise fee: 5% of gross.
Ownership: Community Telecom Services (MSO).

MOREHEAD—Time Warner Cable, 1615 Foxhaven Dr, Richmond, KY 40475. Phones: 859-626-4800; 859-624-9666. Fax: 859-624-0060. Web Site: http://www.timewarnercable.com. Also serves Blue Bank, Burtonville, Carter County (southwestern portion), Cowan, Elizaville, Enterprise, Epworth, Ewing, Fitch, Fleming County, Flemingsburg, Foxport, Globe, Haldeman, Hayward, Hillsboro, Lawton, Limestone, Mount Carmel, Mud Lick, Nepton, Olive Hill, Owingsville, Pine Hill, Poplar Grove, Ribolt, Ringos Mills, Rowan County, Salt Lick, Sharkey, Silica, Soldier, Tollesboro, Triplett, Upper Tygart & Wallingford. ICA: KY0031.
TV Market Ranking: Below 100 (Blue Bank, Burtonville, Carter County (southwestern portion), Cowan, Elizaville, Enterprise, Epworth, Ewing, Fitch, Flemingsburg, Foxport, Globe, Haldeman, Hayward, Hillsboro, Lawton, Limestone, MOREHEAD, Mount Carmel, Nepton, Olive Hill, Owingsville, Poplar Grove, Ribolt, Ringos Mills, Salt Lick, Silica, Soldier, Tollesboro, Triplett, Upper Tygart, Wallingford); Outside TV Markets (Fleming County, Mud Lick, Pine Hill, Rowan County, Sharkey). Franchise award date: January 1, 1958. Franchise expiration date: N.A. Began: January 1, 1958.
Channel capacity: N.A. Channels available but not in use: N.A.
Basic Service
Subscribers: 7,994.
Programming (received off-air): WCHS-TV (ABC) Charleston; WDKY-TV (FOX) Danville; WKMR (PBS) Morehead; WKYT-TV (CBS, CW) Lexington; WLEX-TV (NBC) Lexington; WOWK-TV (CBS) Huntington; WPBO (PBS) Portsmouth; WQCW (CW) Portsmouth; WSAZ-TV (MNT, NBC) Huntington; WTSF (IND) Ashland; WTVQ-DT (ABC) Lexington; WUPX-TV (ION) Morehead; WVAH-TV (FOX) Charleston.
Programming (via satellite): QVC; WGN America.
Fee: $39.95 installation; $12.98 monthly.
Expanded Basic Service 1
Subscribers: 7,875.
Programming (via satellite): ABC Family Channel; AMC; Animal Planet; Arts & Entertainment; BET Networks; CNBC; CNN; Comcast Sports Net Southeast; Comedy Central; Country Music TV; C-SPAN; C-SPAN 2; Discovery Channel; Disney Channel; E! Entertainment Television; ESPN; ESPN 2; Eternal Word TV Network; Food Network; Fox News Channel; Fox Sports Net Ohio; FX; Hallmark Channel; Headline News; HGTV; History Channel; Home Shopping Network; INSP; Lifetime; MSNBC; MTV; Nickelodeon; Oxygen; Product Information Network; ShopNBC; Spike TV; Syfy; TBS Superstation; The Learning Channel; Travel Channel; Trinity Broadcasting Network; truTV; Turner Network TV; TV Guide Network; TV Land; USA Network; VH1; Weather Channel.
Fee: $37.37 monthly.
Digital Basic Service
Subscribers: N.A.
Programming (via satellite): AmericanLife TV Network; BBC America; Bio; Black Family Channel; Bloomberg Television; Bravo; Canales N; Discovery Digital Networks; DMX Music; Do-It-Yourself; ESPN Classic Sports; ESPNews; FitTV; Fox College Sports Atlantic; Fox College Sports Central; Fox College Sports Pacific; Fox Movie Channel; Fox Sports World; Fuse; G4; Gaming Entertainment Television; GAS; Golf Channel; Great American Country; GSN; Halogen Network; History Channel International; Independent Film Channel; Lifetime Movie Network; MTV Networks Digital Suite; Music Choice; National Geographic Channel; Nick Jr.; Nick Too; NickToons TV; Outdoor Channel; Speed Channel; Style Network; Sundance Channel; The Word Network; Turner Classic Movies; Versus; WE tv.
Fee: $6.00 monthly (each tier).
Digital Pay Service 1
Pay Units: 437.
Programming (via satellite): HBO (multiplexed).
Fee: $12.00 monthly.
Digital Pay Service 2
Pay Units: 579.
Programming (via satellite): Encore (multiplexed); Starz (multiplexed).
Fee: $12.00 monthly.
Digital Pay Service 3
Pay Units: 643.
Programming (via satellite): Flix; Showtime (multiplexed); The Movie Channel (multiplexed).
Fee: $12.00 monthly.
Digital Pay Service 4
Pay Units: 290.
Programming (via satellite): Cinemax (multiplexed).
Fee: $12.00 monthly.
Digital Pay Service 5
Pay Units: N.A.
Programming (via satellite): ART America; CCTV-4; Filipino Channel; RAI International; Russian Television Network; TV Asia; TV Japan; TV5, La Television International; Zee TV USA; Zhong Tian Channel.
Fee: $15.00 monthly (each).
Video-On-Demand: Planned
Pay-Per-View
iN DEMAND (delivered digitally); Playboy TV (delivered digitally); Fresh (delivered digitally); Hot Choice (delivered digitally); Urban Xtra (delivered digitally); Sports PPV (delivered digitally).
Internet Service
Operational: Yes.
Broadband Service: Road Runner.
Fee: $42.95 monthly.
Telephone Service
Digital: Planned
Miles of Plant: 585.0 (coaxial); None (fiber optic). Homes passed: 10,351.
General Manager: Robert Trott. Technical Operations Manager: Dennis Lester. Marketing Director: Betrina Morse. Government & Public Affairs Manager: Carla Deaton. Office Manager: Laverne Farris.
City fee: 5% of gross.
Ownership: Time Warner Cable (MSO).

MOREHEAD STATE UNIVERSITY—Morehead State University, 150 University Blvd, Dept. of Communications, Morehead, KY 40351. Phone: 606-783-2675. Fax: 606-783-5078. Web Site: http://www.moreheadstate.edu. ICA: KY0091.
TV Market Ranking: Below 100 (MOREHEAD STATE UNIVERSITY). Franchise award date: N.A. Franchise expiration date: N.A. Began: January 1, 1966.
Channel capacity: 64 (not 2-way capable). Channels available but not in use: 14.
Basic Service
Subscribers: 1,510.
Programming (received off-air): WDKY-TV (FOX) Danville; WKMR (PBS) Morehead; WKYT-TV (CBS, CW) Lexington; WTVQ-DT (ABC) Lexington; WXIX-TV (FOX) Newport; WYMT-TV (CBS, CW) Hazard.
Programming (via satellite): Bloomberg Television; Cartoon Network; CNBC; CNN; CNN International; C-SPAN; C-SPAN 2; FitTV; Headline News; MSNBC; Nickelodeon; The Learning Channel; USA Network; Weather Channel.
Expanded Basic Service 1
Subscribers: 690.
Programming (via satellite): ABC Family Channel; AMC; Animal Planet; Arts & Entertainment; BET Networks; Comedy Central; Country Music TV; Discovery Channel; E! Entertainment Television; ESPN; ESPN 2; ESPN Classic Sports; ESPNews; GSN; History Channel; Lifetime; MTV; MTV2; MuchMusic Network; Spike TV; Syfy; TBS Superstation; truTV; Turner Classic Movies; Turner Network TV; VH1.
Fee: $10.00 monthly.
Video-On-Demand: Planned
Internet Service
Operational: No.
Telephone Service
None
Miles of Plant: 4.0 (coaxial); None (fiber optic). Homes passed: 1,664.
Manager: Mike Hogge. Marketing Director: Taunya Jones. Chief Technician: Jeff Smedley.
Ownership: Morehead State University.

MORGANTOWN—Mediacom, 90 Main St, Benton, KY 42025-1132. Phones: 417-875-5560 (Springfield regional office); 270-527-9939. Fax: 270-527-0813. Web Site: http://www.mediacomcable.com. Also serves Aberdeen, Bee Spring, Brownsville & Edmonson County. ICA: KY0096.
TV Market Ranking: Below 100 (Aberdeen, Bee Spring, Brownsville, Edmonson County, MORGANTOWN). Franchise award date: July 21, 1986. Franchise expiration date: N.A. Began: May 1, 1982.
Channel capacity: N.A. Channels available but not in use: N.A.
Basic Service
Subscribers: 1,492.
Programming (received off-air): WBKO (ABC, CW) Bowling Green; WKGB-TV (PBS) Bowling Green; WKYU-TV (PBS) Bowling Green; WNKY (CBS, NBC) Bowling Green; WPBM-LP Scottsville; WSMV-TV (NBC, TMO) Nashville; WTVF (CBS) Nashville; WZTV (FOX) Nashville.
Programming (via satellite): QVC; WGN America.
Current originations: Government Access; Educational Access; Public Access.
Fee: $46.75 installation; $12.55 monthly.
Expanded Basic Service 1
Subscribers: 672.
Programming (via satellite): ABC Family Channel; AMC; Animal Planet; Arts & Entertainment; Bravo!; Cartoon Network; CNBC; CNN; Comcast Sports Net Southeast; Comedy Central; Country Music TV; C-SPAN; Discovery Channel; Disney Channel; E! Entertainment Television; ESPN; ESPN 2; Food Network; Fox News Channel; FX; Great American Country; Hallmark Channel; Headline News; HGTV; History Channel; INSP; Lifetime; MSNBC; MTV; National Geographic Channel; Nickelodeon; Outdoor Channel; ShopNBC; SoapNet; Speed Channel; Spike TV; Syfy; TBS Superstation; The Learning Channel; Travel Channel; Trinity Broadcasting Network; Turner Classic Movies; Turner Network TV; TV Land; USA Network; VH1; WE tv; Weather Channel.
Fee: $9.75 monthly.
Digital Basic Service
Subscribers: N.A.
Programming (taped): G4.
Programming (via satellite): AmericanLife TV Network; Asian Television Network; BBC America; Bio; Bloomberg Television; Discovery Digital Networks; DMX Music; ESPN Classic Sports; ESPNews; Fox Movie Channel; Fox Soccer; Fuse; GAS; Golf Channel; History Channel International; Independent Film Channel; Lifetime Movie Network; Lime; MTV Networks Digital Suite; National Geographic Channel; Nick Jr.; NickToons TV; Turner Classic Movies; Versus.
Digital Pay Service 1
Pay Units: N.A.
Programming (via satellite): Cinemax (multiplexed); Encore (multiplexed); HBO (multiplexed); Showtime (multiplexed); Starz (multiplexed); The Movie Channel (multiplexed).
Video-On-Demand: No
Pay-Per-View
Barker (delivered digitally); Playboy TV (delivered digitally); Fresh (delivered digitally); Shorteez (delivered digitally).
Internet Service
Operational: Yes.
Broadband Service: Mediacom High Speed Internet.
Telephone Service
None
Miles of Plant: 48.0 (coaxial); None (fiber optic).
Regional Vice President: Bill Copeland. General Manager: Dale Haney. Regional Technical Operations Director: Alan Freedman. Technical Operations Manager: Jeff Brown. Marketing Director: Will Kuebler. Marketing Manager: Melanie Westerman.
City fee: 3% of basic.
Ownership: Mediacom LLC (MSO).

MOUNT OLIVET—Bracken County Cablevision Inc., PO Box 100, 626 Forest Ave, Maysville, KY 41056. Phone: 606-564-9220. Fax: 606-564-4291. E-mail: jcracraft@maysvilleky.net. Web Site: http://www.limestonecable.com. ICA: KY0316.

TV Market Ranking: Outside TV Markets (MOUNT OLIVET). Franchise award date: N.A. Franchise expiration date: N.A. Began: N.A.

Channel capacity: 120 (not 2-way capable). Channels available but not in use: 48.

Basic Service

Subscribers: 120.

Programming (received off-air): WCPO-TV (ABC) Cincinnati; WKRC-TV (CBS, CW) Cincinnati; WKYT-TV (CBS, CW) Lexington; WLEX-TV (NBC) Lexington; WLWT (NBC) Cincinnati; WSTR-TV (MNT) Cincinnati; WTVQ-DT (ABC) Lexington; WXIX-TV (FOX) Newport.

Programming (via satellite): TBS Superstation; WGN America.

Fee: $35.00 installation; $16.50 monthly.

Expanded Basic Service 1

Subscribers: 102.

Programming (via satellite): ABC Family Channel; AMC; Arts & Entertainment; CNN; Country Music TV; C-SPAN; Discovery Channel; ESPN; Fox Sports Net Ohio; MTV; Nickelodeon; QVC; Trinity Broadcasting Network; Turner Network TV; USA Network; VH1; Weather Channel.

Fee: $35.00 installation; $37.30 monthly.

Pay Service 1

Pay Units: 6.

Programming (via satellite): HBO.

Fee: $12.95 monthly.

Pay Service 2

Pay Units: 1.

Programming (via satellite): Showtime.

Fee: $12.95 monthly.

Internet Service

Operational: Yes.

Fee: $21.95-$64.95 monthly.

Telephone Service

None

Miles of Plant: 20.0 (coaxial); None (fiber optic).

Manager: Ron Beurkley. Chief Technician: Jeff Mason. Program & Marketing Director: Jeff Cracraft. Customer Service Manager: Jean Black.

Ownership: Standard Tobacco Co. Inc. (MSO).

MOUNT STERLING—Windjammer Cable, 4400 PGA Blvd, Ste 902, Palm Beach Gardens, FL 33410. Phones: 877-450-5558; 561-775-1208. Fax: 561-775-7811. Web Site: http://www.windjammercable.com. Also serves Bethel, Camargo, Carlisle, Clay City, Jeffersonville, Millersburg, Montgomery County, Nicholas County, North Middletown & Sharpsburg. ICA: KY0046.

TV Market Ranking: Below 100 (Bethel, Camargo, Carlisle, Clay City, Jeffersonville, Millersburg, Montgomery County, MOUNT STERLING, Nicholas County, North Middletown, Sharpsburg). Franchise award date: July 1, 1970. Franchise expiration date: N.A. Began: July 15, 1970.

Channel capacity: N.A. Channels available but not in use: N.A.

Basic Service

Subscribers: 5,139.

Programming (received off-air): WDKY-TV (FOX) Danville; WKLE (PBS) Lexington; WKYT-TV (CBS, CW) Lexington; WLEX-TV (NBC) Lexington; WLJC-TV (TBN) Beattyville; WTVQ-DT (ABC) Lexington; WUPX-TV (ION) Morehead; WXIX-TV (FOX) Newport.

Programming (via satellite): QVC; WGN America.

Current originations: Educational Access; Public Access.

Fee: $39.95 installation; $17.48 monthly.

Expanded Basic Service 1

Subscribers: 4,969.

Programming (via satellite): ABC Family Channel; AMC; Animal Planet; Arts & Entertainment; BET Networks; CNBC; CNN; Comcast Sports Net Southeast; Comedy Network; C-SPAN; C-SPAN 2; Discovery Channel; Disney Channel; ESPN; ESPN 2; Eternal Word TV Network; Food Network; Fox News Channel; Fox Sports Net Ohio; FX; Hallmark Channel; Headline News; History Channel; Home Shopping Network; INSP; Lifetime; MTV; Nickelodeon; Oxygen; Product Information Network; Spike TV; Syfy; TBS Superstation; The Learning Channel; truTV; Turner Network TV; Univision; USA Network; VH1; Weather Channel.

Fee: $32.87 monthly.

Digital Basic Service

Subscribers: N.A.

Programming (via satellite): AmericanLife TV Network; BBC America; Bio; Black Family Channel; Bloomberg Television; Canales N; Discovery Digital Networks; DMX Music; Do-It-Yourself; ESPN Classic Sports; ESPNews; FitTV; Fox College Sports Atlantic; Fox College Sports Central; Fox College Sports Pacific; Fox Movie Channel; Fox Sports World; Fuse; G4; Gaming Entertainment Television; GAS; Golf Channel; Great American Country; GSN; Halogen Network; History Channel International; Independent Film Channel; Lifetime Movie Network; MTV Networks Digital Suite; Music Choice; National Geographic Channel; Nick Jr.; Nick Too; NickToons TV; Outdoor Channel; ShopNBC; SoapNet; Speed Channel; Style Network; Sundance Channel; The Word Network; Toon Disney; Trinity Broadcasting Network; Turner Classic Movies; Versus; WE tv.

Fee: $6.00 monthly (each tier).

Digital Pay Service 1

Pay Units: 195.

Programming (via satellite): Cinemax (multiplexed).

Fee: $12.00 monthly.

Digital Pay Service 2

Pay Units: 285.

Programming (via satellite): HBO (multiplexed).

Fee: $12.00 monthly.

Digital Pay Service 3

Pay Units: 266.

Programming (via satellite): Encore (multiplexed); Starz (multiplexed).

Fee: $12.00 monthly.

Digital Pay Service 4

Pay Units: 235.

Programming (via satellite): Flix; Showtime (multiplexed); The Movie Channel (multiplexed).

Fee: $12.00 monthly.

Digital Pay Service 5

Pay Units: N.A.

Programming (via satellite): ART America; CCTV-4; Filipino Channel; RAI International; Russian Television Network; TV Asia; TV Japan; TV5, La Television International; Zee TV USA.

Fee: $15.00 monthly (each).

Video-On-Demand: No

Pay-Per-View

iN DEMAND (delivered digitally); Playboy TV (delivered digitally); Fresh (delivered digitally); Shorteez (delivered digitally); Hot Choice (delivered digitally); Urban Xtra (delivered digitally); Sports PPV (delivered digitally).

Internet Service

Operational: Yes.

Broadband Service: Road Runner.

Fee: $44.95 monthly.

Telephone Service

Analog: Not Operational

Digital: Operational

Fee: $44.95 monthly

Miles of Plant: 130.0 (coaxial); None (fiber optic). Homes passed: 6,976.

City fee: 4% of gross.

Ownership: Windjammer Communications LLC (MSO).

MOUNT VERNON—Charter Communications. Now served by SOMERSET, KY [KY0021]. ICA: KY0260.

MOZELLE—Windjammer Cable, 4400 PGA Blvd, Ste 902, Palm Beach Gardens, FL 33410. Phones: 877-450-5558; 561-775-1208. Fax: 561-775-7811. Web Site: http://www.windjammercable.com. Also serves Bledsoe & Helton. ICA: KY0261.

TV Market Ranking: Below 100 (Bledsoe, Helton, MOZELLE). Franchise award date: N.A. Franchise expiration date: N.A. Began: N.A.

Channel capacity: 35 (not 2-way capable). Channels available but not in use: 2.

Basic Service

Subscribers: 447.

Programming (received off-air): WAGV (IND) Harlan; WBIR-TV (NBC) Knoxville; WCYB-TV (CW, NBC) Bristol; WEMT (FOX) Greeneville; WJHL-TV (CBS) Johnson City; WKHA (PBS) Hazard; WKPT-TV (ABC) Kingsport; WLEX-TV (NBC) Lexington; WTVQ-DT (ABC) Lexington; WYMT-TV (CBS, CW) Hazard.

Programming (via satellite): INSP; WGN America.

Fee: $29.95 installation; $12.94 monthly; $2.00 converter.

Expanded Basic Service 1

Subscribers: 390.

Programming (via satellite): ABC Family Channel; AMC; Arts & Entertainment; CNN; Country Music TV; Discovery Channel; Disney Channel; ESPN; ESPN 2; FX; Lifetime; Nickelodeon; QVC; Spike TV; TBS Superstation; The Learning Channel; Trinity Broadcasting Network; Turner Network TV; USA Network; VH1.

Fee: $26.65 monthly.

Digital Basic Service

Subscribers: N.A.

Programming (via satellite): BBC America; Bio; Black Family Channel; Bloomberg Television; Bravo; Discovery Digital Networks; ESPN Classic Sports; ESPNews; FitTV; Fox Movie Channel; Fox Sports World; Fuse; G4; GAS; Golf Channel; Great American Country; GSN; Halogen Network; HGTV; History Channel; History Channel International; Independent Film Channel; Lifetime Movie Network; MTV2; National Geographic Channel; Nick Jr.; NickToons TV; Outdoor Channel; Speed Channel; Style Network; Syfy; The Word Network; Toon Disney; Turner Classic Movies; Versus; VH1 Classic; VH1 Country; WE tv.

Fee: $54.54 monthly.

Digital Pay Service 1

Pay Units: N.A.

Programming (via satellite): Cinemax (multiplexed); Encore (multiplexed); HBO (multiplexed); Showtime (multiplexed); Starz (multiplexed); The Movie Channel (multiplexed).

Fee: $15.95 monthly (each).

Video-On-Demand: No

Pay-Per-View

HITS 1 (delivered digitally); HITS 2 (delivered digitally); HITS 3 (delivered digitally); HITS 4 (delivered digitally); Playboy TV (delivered digitally); Fresh (delivered digitally).

Internet Service

Operational: No.

Telephone Service

None

Miles of Plant: 45.0 (coaxial); None (fiber optic). Homes passed: 981.

General Manager: Timothy Evard. Operations Director: Belinda Graham. Engineering Director: Mike Earehart. Finance & Accounting Director: Cindy Johnson.

Ownership: Windjammer Communications LLC (MSO).

MUNFORDVILLE—Mediacom, 90 Main St, Benton, KY 42025-1132. Phones: 417-875-5560 (Springfield regional office); 270-527-9939. Fax: 270-527-0813. Web Site: http://www.mediacomcable.com. Also serves Bonnieville, Hardin County (southeastern portion), Hart County, Larue County (western portion), Sonora & Upton. ICA: KY0086.

TV Market Ranking: Below 100 (Bonnieville, Hardin County (southeastern portion) (portions), Hart County, Larue County (western portion), MUNFORDVILLE, Sonora, Upton); Outside TV Markets (Hardin County (southeastern portion) (portions)). Franchise award date: N.A. Franchise expiration date: N.A. Began: January 1, 1965.

Channel capacity: N.A. Channels available but not in use: N.A.

Basic Service

Subscribers: 1,926.

Programming (received off-air): WAVE (NBC) Louisville; WBKO (ABC, CW) Bowling Green; WDRB (FOX) Louisville; WHAS-TV (ABC) Louisville; WKYU-TV (PBS) Bowling Green; WKZT-TV (PBS) Elizabethtown; WLKY-TV (CBS) Louisville; WNKY (CBS, NBC) Bowling Green; WSMV-TV (NBC, TMO) Nashville; WTVF (CBS) Nashville; allband FM.

Programming (via satellite): TV Guide Network; WGN America.

Fee: $36.95 installation; $19.32 monthly.

Expanded Basic Service 1

Subscribers: N.A.

Programming (via satellite): ABC Family Channel; AMC; AmericanLife TV Network; Animal Planet; Arts & Entertainment; Bravo; Cartoon Network; CNBC; CNN; Comcast Sports Net Southeast; Comedy Central; Country Music TV; C-SPAN; C-SPAN 2; Discovery Channel; Disney Channel; E! Entertainment Television; ESPN; ESPN 2; FitTV; Food Network; Fox News Channel; Fuse; FX; Great American Country; GRTV Network; Hallmark Channel; Headline News; HGTV; History Channel; Home Shopping Network; INSP; ION Television; Lifetime; MSNBC; MTV; National Geographic Channel; Nickelodeon; Outdoor Channel; QVC; RFD-TV; ShopNBC; SoapNet; Speed Channel; Spike TV; Syfy; TBS Superstation; Telemundo; The Learning Channel; Travel Channel; Trinity Broadcasting Network; Turner Network TV; TV Land; USA Network; VH1; WE tv; Weather Channel.

Digital Basic Service

Subscribers: N.A.

Programming (via satellite): Asian Television Network; BBC America; Bio; Bloomberg Television; Discovery Digital Networks; DMX Music; Fox Movie Channel; Fox Soccer; Fuse; G4; GAS; Golf Channel; GSN; History Channel International; Independent Film Channel; Lifetime Movie Network; MTV Networks Digital Suite; Nick Jr.; NickToons TV; Turner Classic Movies; Versus.

Digital Pay Service 1

Pay Units: N.A.

Programming (via satellite): Cinemax (multiplexed); Encore (multiplexed); Flix (multiplexed); HBO (multiplexed); Showtime (multiplexed); Starz (multiplexed); Sundance Channel; The Movie Channel (multiplexed).

Video-On-Demand: No

Pay-Per-View

Barker (delivered digitally); Playboy TV (delivered digitally); TEN Clips (delivered digitally); TEN Blox (delivered digitally); Pleasure (delivered digitally); ESPN Gameplan (delivered digitally).

Internet Service

Operational: Yes.

Broadband Service: Mediacom High Speed Internet.

Telephone Service

None

Miles of Plant: 99.0 (coaxial); None (fiber optic).

Regional Vice President: Bill Copeland. General Manager: Dale Haney. Regional Technical Operations Director: Alan Freedman. Technical Operations Manager: Jeff Brown. Marketing Director: Will Kuebler. Marketing Manager: Melanie Westerman.

City fee: 2% of gross.

Ownership: Mediacom LLC (MSO).

MURRAY—Murray Electric System, PO Box 1095, 401 Olive St, Murray, KY 42071. Phone: 270-753-5312. Fax: 270-761-5781. E-mail: murrayelectric@murray-ky.net. Web Site: http://www2.murray-ky.net. ICA: KY0321. **Note:** This system is an overbuild.

TV Market Ranking: 69 (MURRAY).

Channel capacity: 77 (operating 2-way). Channels available but not in use: N.A.

Basic Service

Subscribers: 2,604.

Programming (received off-air): KBSI (FOX) Cape Girardeau; KFVS-TV (CBS, CW) Cape Girardeau; WBBJ-TV (ABC) Jackson; WDKA (MNT) Paducah; WKMU (PBS) Murray; WKRN-TV (ABC) Nashville; WNPT (PBS) Nashville; WPSD-TV (NBC) Paducah; WQWQ-LP (CW) Paducah; WSIL-TV (ABC) Harrisburg; WSMV-TV (NBC, TMO) Nashville; WTVF (CBS) Nashville.

Current originations: Government Access; Educational Access; Public Access.

Fee: $13.00 monthly.

Expanded Basic Service 1

Subscribers: 2,219.

Programming (via satellite): ABC Family Channel; AMC; Animal Planet; Arts & Entertainment; BET Networks; Boomerang; Cartoon Network; CNBC; CNN; Comcast Sports Net Southeast; Comedy Central; Country Music TV; C-SPAN; C-SPAN 2; Discovery Channel; Disney Channel; E! Entertainment Television; Encore; ESPN; ESPN 2; ESPN Classic Sports; ESPNews; FitTV; Food Network; Fox Movie Channel; Fox News Channel; FX; Golf Channel; Hallmark Channel; Headline News; HGTV; History Channel; Home Shopping Network; INSP; ION Television; Lifetime; MSNBC; MTV; National Geographic Channel; Nickelodeon; Outdoor Channel; Ovation; SoapNet; Speed Channel; Spike TV; Syfy; TBS Superstation; The Learning Channel; Travel Channel; Trinity Broadcasting Network; truTV; Turner Classic Movies; Turner Network TV; TV Guide Network; TV Land; USA Network; VH1; WE tv; Weather Channel; WGN America.

Fee: $40.45 monthly.

Digital Basic Service

Subscribers: N.A.

Programming (via satellite): BBC America; Bio; Bloomberg Television; Bravo; CMT Pure Country; Discovery Digital Networks; DMX Music; Do-It-Yourself; ESPN U; Fox Soccer; Fuse; G4; GAS; Great American Country; GSN; History Channel International; Lifetime Movie Network; MTV Networks Digital Suite; Nick Jr.; NickToons TV; Oxygen; Toon Disney; Versus.

Fee: $15.50 monthly.

Digital Pay Service 1

Pay Units: N.A.

Programming (via satellite): Cinemax (multiplexed); Encore (multiplexed); HBO (multiplexed); Showtime (multiplexed); Starz (multiplexed).

Fee: $8.95 monthly (each).

Video-On-Demand: No

Pay-Per-View

iN DEMAND (delivered digitally); Hot Choice (delivered digitally); Playboy TV (delivered digitally).

Internet Service

Operational: Yes.

Broadband Service: In-house.

Fee: $19.95 monthly.

Telephone Service

None

Miles of Plant: 125.0 (coaxial); 18.0 (fiber optic). Homes passed: 7,100.

General Manager: Tony Thompson. Telecommunications Manager: David Richardson. Chief Technician: Joey Williams.

Ownership: Murray Electric System.

MURRAY—NewWave Communications, 906 South 12 St, Belair Shopping Center, Murray, KY 42071. Phone: 573-472-9500. Fax: 270.753.8462. Web Site: http://www.newwavecom.com. Also serves Calloway County. ICA: KY0025.

TV Market Ranking: 69 (Calloway County (portions)); Outside TV Markets (MURRAY, Calloway County (portions)). Franchise award date: N.A. Franchise expiration date: N.A. Began: May 1, 1965.

Channel capacity: N.A. Channels available but not in use: N.A.

Basic Service

Subscribers: 5,854.

Programming (received off-air): KBSI (FOX) Cape Girardeau; KFVS-TV (CBS, CW) Cape Girardeau; WBBJ-TV (ABC) Jackson; WDKA (MNT) Paducah; WKMU (PBS) Murray; WKRN-TV (ABC) Nashville; WNPT (PBS) Nashville; WPSD-TV (NBC) Paducah; WQWQ-LP (CW) Paducah; WSIL-TV (ABC) Harrisburg; WSMV-TV (NBC, TMO) Nashville; WTCT (IND) Marion; WTVF (CBS) Nashville; 18 FMs.

Programming (via satellite): INSP; QVC; WGN America.

Current originations: Government Access; Educational Access.

Fee: $25.28 installation; $9.30 monthly.

Expanded Basic Service 1

Subscribers: N.A.

Programming (via satellite): ABC Family Channel; AMC; Animal Planet; Arts & Entertainment; BET Networks; Cartoon Network; CNBC; CNN; Comcast Sports Net Southeast; Comcast/Charter Sports Southeast (CSS); Comedy Central; Country Music TV; C-SPAN; C-SPAN 2; Discovery Channel; Disney Channel; E! Entertainment Television; ESPN; ESPN 2; ESPN Classic Sports; Eternal Word TV Network; FitTV; Food Network; Fox News Channel; FX; G4; Golf Channel; GSN; Hallmark Channel; Headline News; HGTV; History Channel; Home Shopping Network; ION Television; Lifetime; MSNBC; MTV; National Geographic Channel; Nickelodeon; Outdoor Channel; Oxygen; SoapNet; Speed Channel; Spike TV; Syfy; TBS Superstation; The Learning Channel; Travel Channel; truTV; Turner Classic Movies; Turner Network TV; TV Guide Network; TV Land; USA Network; Versus; VH1; Weather Channel.

Digital Basic Service

Subscribers: N.A.

Programming (received off-air): KBSI (FOX) Cape Girardeau; KFVS-TV (CBS, CW) Cape Girardeau; WKMU (PBS) Murray; WPSD-TV (NBC) Paducah; WSIL-TV (ABC) Harrisburg.

Programming (via satellite): Arts & Entertainment HD; BBC America; Bio; Bloomberg Television; Boomerang; CMT Pure Country; CNN en Espanol; Discovery en Espanol; Discovery HD Theater; Discovery Health Channel; Discovery Kids Channel; Discovery Military Channel; Discovery Planet Green; Do-It-Yourself; ESPN 2 HD; ESPN Classic Sports; ESPN HD; ESPN U; ESPNews; FitTV; Fox Movie Channel; FSN HD; Gospel Music Channel; Great American Country; HDNet; HDNet Movies; History Channel HD; History Channel International; HorseRacing TV; ID Investigation Discovery; Lifetime Movie Network; Lifetime Real Women; MTV Hits; MTV Jams; MTV Tres; MTV2; Music Choice; Nick Jr.; Nick Too; NickToons TV; Palladia; Science Channel; Sleuth; Style Network; TeenNick; Toon Disney; Turner Network TV HD; Universal HD; Versus HD; VH1 Classic; VH1 Soul; Weather Channel HD.

Digital Pay Service 1

Pay Units: N.A.

Programming (via satellite): Cinemax (multiplexed); Cinemax HD; Encore (multiplexed); Flix; HBO (multiplexed); HBO HD; Showtime (multiplexed); Starz (multiplexed); Starz HDTV; The Movie Channel (multiplexed).

Video-On-Demand: No

Pay-Per-View

iN DEMAND (delivered digitally); Penthouse TV (delivered digitally); Ten Clips (delivered digitally); Ten Blue (delivered digitally); Ten Blox (delivered digitally).

Internet Service

Operational: Yes.

Fee: $40.00 installation; $31.99 monthly.

Telephone Service

Digital: Operational

Fee: $24.99 monthly

Miles of Plant: 65.0 (coaxial); None (fiber optic). Homes passed: 7,600.

General Manager: Cameron Miller. Technical Operations Manager: Eddie Prior.

City fee: 3% of gross.

Ownership: NewWave Communications (MSO).

NEBO—Mediacom, 90 Main St, Benton, KY 42025-1132. Phones: 417-875-5560 (Springfield regional office); 270-527-9939. Fax: 270-527-0813. Web Site: http://www.mediacomcable.com. Also serves Hopkins County. ICA: KY0146.

TV Market Ranking: 86 (Hopkins County (portions)); Below 100 (NEBO, Hopkins County (portions)). Franchise award date: N.A. Franchise expiration date: N.A. Began: January 1, 1984.

Channel capacity: N.A. Channels available but not in use: N.A.

Basic Service

Subscribers: 366.

Programming (received off-air): WEHT (ABC) Evansville; WEVV-TV (CBS, MNT) Evansville; WFIE (NBC) Evansville; WKMA-TV (PBS) Madisonville; WTVW (FOX) Evansville.

Programming (via satellite): ABC Family Channel; CNN; Country Music TV; Discovery Channel; Disney Channel; ESPN; Hallmark Channel; Nickelodeon; QVC; Spike TV; TBS Superstation; Turner Network TV; USA Network; WGN America.

Fee: $36.95 installation; $17.95 monthly.

Pay Service 1

Pay Units: 65.

Programming (via satellite): Cinemax.

Fee: $10.50 monthly.

Pay Service 2

Pay Units: 53.

Programming (via satellite): The Movie Channel.

Pay Service 3

Pay Units: 110.

Programming (via satellite): HBO.

Fee: $10.50 monthly.

Pay Service 4

Pay Units: 73.

Programming (via satellite): Showtime.

Fee: $10.50 monthly.

Video-On-Demand: No

Internet Service

Operational: No.

Telephone Service

None

Miles of Plant: 32.0 (coaxial); None (fiber optic). Homes passed: 600.

Regional Vice President: Bill Copeland. General Manager: Dale Haney. Regional Technical Operations Director: Alan Freedman. Technical Operations Manager: Jeff Brown. Marketing Director: Will Kuebler. Marketing Manager: Melanie Westerman.

City fee: 3% of basic.

Ownership: Mediacom LLC (MSO).

NELSON—Time Warner Cable, 100 Industrial Dr, Owensboro, KY 42301-8711. Phones: 270-852-2000; 270-685-2991. Fax: 270-688-8228. Web Site: http://www.timewarnercable.com/westernky. Also serves Central City (unincorporated areas). ICA: KY0262.

TV Market Ranking: Below 100 (Central City (unincorporated areas), NELSON). Franchise award date: N.A. Franchise expiration date: N.A. Began: N.A.

Channel capacity: 36 (not 2-way capable). Channels available but not in use: 13.

Basic Service

Subscribers: N.A. Included in Owensboro

Programming (received off-air): WBKO (ABC, CW) Bowling Green; WEHT (ABC) Evansville; WEVV-TV (CBS, MNT) Evansville; WFIE (NBC) Evansville; WKGB-TV (PBS) Bowling Green; WTVW (FOX) Evansville.

Programming (via satellite): ABC Family Channel; Arts & Entertainment; CNN; Country Music TV; Discovery Channel; Disney Channel; ESPN; History Channel; Nickelodeon; Spike TV; TBS Superstation; The Learning Channel; Trinity Broadcasting Network; Turner Network TV; USA Network; WGN America.

Fee: $39.95 installation; $36.65 monthly.

Digital Basic Service

Subscribers: N.A.

Programming (via satellite): BBC America; Bloomberg Television; Discovery Digital Networks; ESPN Classic Sports; ESPNews; FitTV; Fox Movie Channel; Fox Soccer; G4; Golf Channel; GSN; Halogen Network; Music Choice; Nick Jr.; NickToons TV; Outdoor Channel; Versus; WE tv.

Fee: $12.95 monthly.

Digital Pay Service 1

Pay Units: N.A.

Programming (via satellite): Cinemax (multiplexed); Encore (multiplexed); HBO (multiplexed); Showtime (multiplexed); Starz (multiplexed); The Movie Channel (multiplexed).

Fee: $15.95 monthly (each).

Video-On-Demand: No

Pay-Per-View

iN DEMAND (delivered digitally); Playboy TV (delivered digitally); Club Jenna (delivered digitally); Fresh (delivered digitally).

Internet Service

Operational: No.

Telephone Service

None

Miles of Plant: 6.0 (coaxial); None (fiber optic). Homes passed included in Owensboro

General Manager: Chris Poynter. Marketing Manager: Doug Rodgers. Technical Operations Director: Don Collins.

Ownership: Time Warner Cable (MSO).

NEW ALBANY—Insight Communications. Now served by LOUISVILLE, KY [KY0001]. ICA: IN0019.

NEW HAVEN—Formerly served by Adelphia Communications. Now served by LEBANON, KY [KY0049]. ICA: KY0137.

NEWPORT—Insight Communications. Now served by COVINGTON, KY [KY0002]. ICA: KY0264.

NICHOLASVILLE—Time Warner Cable, 1615 Foxhaven Dr, Richmond, KY 40475. Phones: 859-626-4800; 859-624-9666. Fax: 859-624-0060. Web Site: http://www.timewarnercable.com. Also serves Jessamine County & Wilmore. ICA: KY0036.

TV Market Ranking: Below 100 (Jessamine County, NICHOLASVILLE, Wilmore). Franchise award date: May 1, 1972. Franchise expiration date: N.A. Began: June 1, 1972.

Channel capacity: N.A. Channels available but not in use: N.A.

Basic Service

Subscribers: 6,160.

Programming (received off-air): WDKY-TV (FOX) Danville; WKLE (PBS) Lexington; WKMU (PBS) Murray; WKYT-TV (CBS, CW) Lexington; WLEX-TV (NBC) Lexington; WTVQ-DT (ABC) Lexington; WUPX-TV (ION) Morehead; 1 FM.

Programming (via satellite): QVC; The Learning Channel; WGN America.

Fee: $39.95 installation; $11.79 monthly; $25.00 additional installation.

Expanded Basic Service 1

Subscribers: 5,829.

Programming (via satellite): ABC Family Channel; AMC; Animal Planet; Arts & Entertainment; BET Networks; Bravo; Cartoon Network; CNBC; CNN; Comcast Sports Net Southeast; Comedy Central; Country Music TV; C-SPAN; C-SPAN 2; Discovery Channel; Disney Channel; E! Entertainment Television; ESPN; ESPN 2; Eternal Word TV Network; Food Network; Fox News Channel; Fox Sports Net Ohio; FX; Hallmark Channel; Headline News; HGTV; History Channel; Home Shopping Network; INSP; Lifetime; MSNBC; MTV; Nickelodeon; Oxygen; Product Information Network; ShopNBC; Spike TV; Syfy; TBS Superstation; The Learning Channel; Travel Channel; Trinity Broadcasting Network; truTV; Turner Network TV; TV Guide Network; TV Land; Univision; USA Network; VH1; Weather Channel.

Fee: $36.71 monthly.

Digital Basic Service

Subscribers: N.A.

Programming (received off-air): WDKY-TV (FOX) Danville; WKLE (PBS) Lexington; WKYT-TV (CBS, CW) Lexington.

Programming (via satellite): AmericanLife TV Network; BBC America; Bio; Bloomberg Television; Boomerang; Canales N; CBS College Sports Network; CMT Pure Country; Cooking Channel; C-SPAN 3; Current; Daystar TV Network; Discovery Digital Networks; Discovery HD Theater; Do-It-Yourself; Encore (multiplexed); ESPN 2 HD; ESPN Classic Sports; ESPN HD; ESPN U; ESPNews; FamilyNet; Flix; Fox College Sports Atlantic; Fox College Sports Central; Fox College Sports Pacific; Fox Movie Channel; Fox Reality Channel; Fox Soccer; Fuel TV; Fuse; G4; GAS; Golf Channel; Gospel Music Channel; Great American Country; GSN; Halogen Network; HDNet; HDNet Movies; History Channel International; Independent Film Channel; Lifetime Movie Network; LOGO; MTV Networks Digital Suite; Music Choice; National Geographic Channel; NBA TV; Nick Jr.; Nick Too; NickToons TV; Outdoor Channel; Ovation; ReelzChannel; Sleuth; SoapNet; Speed Channel; Style Network; Sundance Channel; Tennis Channel; The Sportsman Channel; The Word Network; Toon Disney; Turner Classic Movies; Turner Network TV HD; TVG Network; Universal HD; Versus; WE tv.

Fee: $6.00 monthly (each tier).

Digital Pay Service 1

Pay Units: N.A.

Programming (via satellite): Arabic Channel; CCTV-4; Cinemax (multiplexed); Cinemax HD; Filipino Channel; HBO (multiplexed); HBO HD; RAI International; Russian Television Network; Showtime (multiplexed); Showtime HD; Starz (multiplexed); Starz HDTV; The Movie Channel (multiplexed); TV Asia; TV Japan; TV5, La Television International; Zhong Tian Channel.

Fee: $12.00 monthly (HBO, Cinemax, Showtime/TMC or Starz), $15.00 monthly (CCTV, TV Asia, TV 5, Filipino, RAI or ART, TV Russia orTV Japan).

Video-On-Demand: No

Pay-Per-View

iN DEMAND (delivered digitally); Playboy TV (delivered digitally); Fresh (delivered digitally); Hot Choice (delivered digitally); Sports PPV (delivered digitally).

Internet Service

Operational: Yes.

Broadband Service: Road Runner.

Fee: $44.95 monthly.

Telephone Service

Digital: Operational

Fee: $44.95 monthly

Miles of Plant: 128.0 (coaxial); None (fiber optic). Homes passed: 8,058.

General Manager: Robert Trott. Technical Operations Manager: Dennis Lester. Marketing Director: Betrina Morse. Government & Public Affairs Manager: Carla Deaton. Office Manager: Laverne Farris.

City fee: 4% of gross.

Ownership: Time Warner Cable (MSO).

NORTH MIDDLETOWN—Now served by GEORGETOWN, KY [KY0044]. ICA: KY0169.

NORTONVILLE—Mediacom, 90 Main St, Benton, KY 42025-1132. Phones: 417-875-5560 (Springfield regional office); 270-527-9939. Fax: 270-527-0813. Web Site: http://www.mediacomcable.com. Also serves Christian County, Crofton & Hopkins County (portions). ICA: KY0097.

TV Market Ranking: Below 100 (Christian County (portions), Crofton, Hopkins County (portions), NORTONVILLE); Outside TV Markets (Christian County (portions)). Franchise award date: N.A. Franchise expiration date: N.A. Began: May 1, 1983.

Channel capacity: N.A. Channels available but not in use: N.A.

Basic Service

Subscribers: 1,162.

Programming (received off-air): KFVS-TV (CBS, CW) Cape Girardeau; WAZE-LP (CW) Evansville; WDKA (MNT) Paducah; WEHT (ABC) Evansville; WEVV-TV (CBS, MNT) Evansville; WKAG-CA Hopkinsville; WKMA-TV (PBS) Madisonville; WPSD-TV (NBC) Paducah; WSIL-TV (ABC) Harrisburg; WSMV-TV (NBC, TMO) Nashville; WTVF (CBS) Nashville; WTVW (FOX) Evansville.

Programming (via satellite): TV Guide Network; WFIE (NBC) Evansville; WGN America.

Fee: $36.95 installation; $18.67 monthly.

Expanded Basic Service 1

Subscribers: N.A.

Programming (via satellite): ABC Family Channel; AMC; Animal Planet; Arts & Entertainment; BET Networks; Bravo!; Cartoon Network; CNBC; CNN; Comcast Sports Net Southeast; Comedy Central; Country Music TV; C-SPAN; Discovery Channel; Disney Channel; E! Entertainment Television; ESPN; ESPN 2; FitTV; Food Network; Fox News Channel; FX; GRTV Network; Hallmark Channel; Headline News; HGTV; History Channel; Home Shopping Network; INSP; Lifetime; MSNBC; MTV; Nickelodeon; Outdoor Channel; QVC; SoapNet; Speed Channel; Spike TV; Syfy; TBS Superstation; The Learning Channel; Travel Channel; Trinity Broadcasting Network; Turner Network TV; TV Land; Univision; USA Network; VH1; WE tv; Weather Channel.

Digital Basic Service

Subscribers: N.A.

Programming (via satellite): BBC America; Bio; Bloomberg Television; Discovery Digital Networks; DMX Music; Fox Movie Channel; Fox Soccer; Fuse; G4; GAS; Golf Channel; GSN; History Channel International; Independent Film Channel; Lifetime Movie Network; Lime; MTV Hits; MTV2; National Geographic Channel; Nick Jr.; NickToons TV; Science Television; Turner Classic Movies; Versus; VH1 Classic.

Digital Pay Service 1

Pay Units: N.A.

Programming (via satellite): Cinemax (multiplexed); Encore (multiplexed); Flix (multiplexed); HBO (multiplexed); Showtime (multiplexed); Starz (multiplexed); Sundance Channel (multiplexed); The Movie Channel (multiplexed).

Video-On-Demand: No

Pay-Per-View

Barker (delivered digitally); Playboy TV (delivered digitally); TEN Clips (delivered digitally); TEN Blox (delivered digitally).

Internet Service

Operational: Yes.

Broadband Service: Mediacom High Speed Internet.

Telephone Service

Digital: Operational

Miles of Plant: 50.0 (coaxial); None (fiber optic). Homes passed: 1,474.

Regional Vice President: Bill Copeland. General Manager: Dale Haney. Regional Technical Operations Director: Alan Freedman. Technical Operations Manager: Jeff Brown. Marketing Director: Will Kuebler. Marketing Manager: Melanie Westerman.

City fee: 3% of basic.

Ownership: Mediacom LLC (MSO).

OAK GROVE—Mediacom. Now served by TRENTON, KY [KY0101]. ICA: KY0105.

OLIVE HILL—Now served by MOOREHEAD, KY [KY0031]. ICA: KY0099.

OWENSBORO—Time Warner Cable, 100 Industrial Dr, Owensboro, KY 42301-8711. Phones: 270-685-2991; 270-852-2000. Fax: 270-688-8228. Web Site: http://www.timewarnercable.com/westernky. Also serves Equality, Junction, Old Shawneetown, Ridgway & Shawneetown, IL; Hatfield, Reo, Rockport & Spencer County (portions), IN; Baskett, Beals, Bluff City, Corydon, Daviess County, Grangertown, Hebbardsville, Henderson (town), Henderson County (portions), Morganfield, Reed, Smith Mills Borough, Spottsville, Sturgis, Sullivan, Uniontown, Waverly, Wynn & Zion, KY. ICA: KY0004.

TV Market Ranking: 69 (Equality, Junction, Old Shawneetown, Ridgway, Shawneetown); 86 (Baskett, Beals, Bluff City, Corydon, Daviess County (portions), Grangertown, Hatfield, Hebbardsville,

Henderson (town), Henderson County (portions), Morganfield, OWENSBORO, Reed, Reo, Rockport, Smith Mills Borough, Spencer County (portions), Spottsville, Sturgis, Uniontown, Waverly, Wynn, Zion); Below 100 (Sullivan, Daviess County (portions)); Outside TV Markets (Daviess County (portions)). Franchise award date: N.A. Franchise expiration date: N.A. Began: January 1, 1967.

Channel capacity: N.A. Channels available but not in use: N.A.

Basic Service

Subscribers: 29,000 Includes Newburgh IN, Bremen, Cloverport, Cromwell, Dixon, Dunmor, Hardinsburg, Hawesville, Irvington, Island, Lewisport, Livermore, Nelson, Pleasant Ridge, Rochester, Slaughters & Welchs C.

Programming (received off-air): WAZE-TV (CW) Madisonville; WDRB (FOX) Louisville; WEHT (ABC) Evansville; WEVV-TV (CBS, MNT) Evansville; WFIE (NBC) Evansville; WKMU (PBS) Murray; WNIN (PBS) Evansville; WTVW (FOX) Evansville; WYYW-LP Evansville.

Programming (via satellite): ABC Family Channel; AMC; Animal Planet; Arts & Entertainment; BET Networks; Bravo; Cartoon Network; CNBC; Comcast Sports Net Southeast; Comedy Central; Country Music TV; C-SPAN; C-SPAN 2; Discovery Channel; E! Entertainment Television; ESPN; ESPN 2; Eternal Word TV Network; FX; Golf Channel; Hallmark Channel; Headline News; HGTV; History Channel; Home Shopping Network; Lifetime; MSNBC; MTV; Nickelodeon; Oxygen; Product Information Network; QVC; ShopNBC; Spike TV; Syfy; The Learning Channel; Travel Channel; Trinity Broadcasting Network; truTV; Turner Network TV; TV Guide Network; TV Land; USA Network; VH1; WE tv; Weather Channel; WGN America.

Current originations: Government Access; Educational Access; Public Access.

Fee: $49.95 installation; $36.31 monthly; $1.00 converter.

Expanded Basic Service 1

Subscribers: 22,550.

Programming (via satellite): CNN; Disney Channel; ESPN Classic Sports; Food Network; Fox News Channel; Speed Channel; TBS Superstation; Toon Disney; Versus.

Fee: $12.54 monthly.

Digital Basic Service

Subscribers: 3,178.

Programming (via satellite): AmericanLife TV Network; BBC America; Bio; Black Family Channel; Bloomberg Television; Discovery Digital Networks; Do-It-Yourself; ESPNews; FitTV; Fox Sports World; G4; Great American Country; GSN; History Channel International; INSP; MuchMusic Network; Music Choice; Outdoor Channel; SoapNet.

Fee: $1.10 monthly.

Digital Expanded Basic Service

Subscribers: N.A.

Programming (via satellite): Fox College Sports Atlantic; Fox College Sports Central; Fox College Sports Pacific; Fox Movie Channel; GAS; Independent Film Channel; MTV Networks Digital Suite; National Geographic Channel; Nick Jr.; Nick Too; NickToons TV; Style Network; Sundance Channel; Turner Classic Movies.

Fee: $6.00 monthly (per tier).

Digital Pay Service 1

Pay Units: 2,054.

Programming (via satellite): Arabic Channel; Canales N; CCTV-4; Cinemax (multiplexed); Encore (multiplexed); Filipino Channel; Flix; HBO (multiplexed); RAI International; Russian Television Network; Showtime (multiplexed); Starz (multiplexed); The Movie Channel (multiplexed); TV Asia; TV Japan; TV5, La Television International; Zee TV USA; Zhong Tian Channel.

Fee: $12.00 monthly (HBO, Cinemax, Showtime Unlimited or Starz) $15.00 monthly (CCTV, TV Asia, TV5, Filipino, RAI, ART, TV Russia or TV Japan).

Video-On-Demand: Yes

Pay-Per-View

Addressable homes: 3,178.

Playboy TV (delivered digitally), Addressable: Yes; HITS PPV (delivered digitally); Urban American Television Network (delivered digitally); Hot Choice (delivered digitally); Shorteez (delivered digitally); Fresh (delivered digitally).

Internet Service

Operational: Yes.

Broadband Service: Road Runner.

Fee: $99.95 installation; $44.95 monthly.

Telephone Service

Digital: Operational

Fee: $74.95 installation; $44.95 monthly

Miles of Plant: 1,658.0 (coaxial); None (fiber optic). Homes passed: 80,143. Homes passed includes Newburgh IN, Bremen, Cloverport, Cromwell, Dixon, Dunmor, Hardinsburg, Hawesville, Irvington, Island, Lewisport, Livermore, Nelson, Pleasant Ridge, Rochester, Slaughters & Welchs Creek

General Manager: Chris Poynter. Technical Operations Director: Don Collins. Marketing Manager: Don Rodgers.

City fee: 3% of gross.

Ownership: Time Warner Cable (MSO).

OWINGSVILLE—Now served by MOREHEAD, KY [KY0031]. ICA: KY0139.

PADUCAH—Comcast Cable, 2919 Ring Rd, Elizabethtown, KY 42701. Phone: 270-737-2731. Fax: 270-737-3379. Web Site: http://www.comcast.com. Also serves Brookport, Massac County & Metropolis, IL; Graves County, Kevil, Ledbetter, Livingston County, Marshall County & McCracken County, KY. ICA: KY0005.

TV Market Ranking: 69 (Brookport, Graves County, Kevil, Ledbetter, Livingston County, Marshall County, Massac County, McCracken County, Metropolis, PADUCAH). Franchise award date: N.A. Franchise expiration date: N.A. Began: February 15, 1978.

Channel capacity: N.A. Channels available but not in use: N.A.

Basic Service

Subscribers: 23,965.

Programming (received off-air): WAZE-TV (CW) Madisonville; WDRB (FOX) Louisville; WEHT (ABC) Evansville; WEVV-TV (CBS, MNT) Evansville; WFIE (NBC) Evansville; WKOH (PBS) Owensboro; WNIN (PBS) Evansville; WTVW (FOX) Evansville; 20 FMs.

Programming (via satellite): ABC Family Channel; AMC; Animal Planet; Arts & Entertainment; Cartoon Network; CNBC; CNN; Comcast/Charter Sports Southeast (CSS); Comedy Central; Discovery Channel; Discovery Health Channel; Disney Channel; E! Entertainment Television; ESPN; ESPN 2; Eternal Word TV Network; Food Network; Fox News Channel; Fox Sports Net; FX; Golf Channel; Great American Country; GSN; Headline News; HGTV; History Channel; Home Shopping Network; ION Television; Lifetime; MSNBC; MTV; News Plus; Nickelodeon; QVC; Spike TV; Syfy; TBS Superstation; Turner Network TV; TV Land; USA Network; Versus; VH1; Weather Channel; WGN America.

Current originations: Religious Access; Government Access; Educational Access; Public Access.

Fee: $54.99 installation; $8.70 monthly.

Expanded Basic Service 1

Subscribers: N.A.

Fee: $38.55 monthly.

Digital Basic Service

Subscribers: N.A.

Programming (via satellite): BBC America; C-SPAN 3; Discovery Digital Networks; ESPNews; Fox News Channel; GAS; MTV Networks Digital Suite; Nick Jr.; Nick Too; SoapNet; Syfy; Toon Disney; WAM! America's Kidz Network.

Fee: $14.95 monthly.

Digital Pay Service 1

Pay Units: N.A.

Programming (via satellite): Cinemax (multiplexed); DMX Music; Encore (multiplexed); Flix; HBO (multiplexed); Showtime (multiplexed); Sundance Channel; The Movie Channel (multiplexed).

Fee: $14.95 monthly (each).

Video-On-Demand: Yes

Pay-Per-View

Hot Choice (delivered digitally); iN DEMAND (delivered digitally).

Internet Service

Operational: Yes.

Broadband Service: Comcast High Speed Internet.

Fee: $19.99 installation; $42.95 monthly.

Telephone Service

Digital: Operational

Miles of Plant: 735.0 (coaxial); None (fiber optic). Homes passed: 31,000. Total homes in franchised area: 40,911.

General Manager: Tim Hagan. Marketing Director: Laurie Nicholson. Technical Operations Director: Bob Tharp.

Ownership: Comcast Cable Communications Inc. (MSO).

PADUCAH—Formerly served by NDW II Inc. No longer in operation. ICA: KY0305.

PAINTSVILLE—Charter Communications. Now served by KERMIT, WV [WV0038]. ICA: KY0266.

PARIS—Now served by GEORGETOWN, KY [KY0044]. ICA: KY0043.

PARK CITY—Mediacom, 90 Main St, Benton, KY 42025-1132. Phones: 417-875-5560 (Springfield regional office); 270-527-9939. Fax: 270-527-0813. Web Site: http://www.mediacomcable.com. ICA: KY0324.

TV Market Ranking: Below 100 (PARK CITY).

Channel capacity: N.A. Channels available but not in use: N.A.

Basic Service

Subscribers: N.A.

Programming (received off-air): WBKO (ABC, CW) Bowling Green; WSMV-TV (NBC, TMO) Nashville; WTVF (CBS) Nashville; WZTV (FOX) Nashville.

Programming (via satellite): ABC Family Channel; AMC; Animal Planet; Arts & Entertainment; Cartoon Network; CNBC; CNN; Comedy Central; Country Music TV; C-SPAN; Discovery Channel; Disney Channel; ESPN; ESPN 2; Food Network; Fox News Channel; FX; HBO; Headline News; HGTV; History Channel; INSP; Lifetime; MSNBC; MTV; Nickelodeon; QVC; ShopNBC; Spike TV; Syfy; TBS Superstation; The Learning Channel; Turner Classic Movies; Turner Network TV; USA Network; VH1; W Network; Weather Channel; WGN America; WKGB-TV (PBS) Bowling Green; WKYU-TV (PBS) Bowling Green; WNKY (CBS, NBC) Bowling Green.

Pay Service 1

Pay Units: N.A.

Programming (via satellite): Showtime (multiplexed); The Movie Channel.

Internet Service

Operational: No.

Telephone Service

None

Regional Vice President: Bill Copeland. General Manager: Dale Haney. Regional Technical Operations Director: Alan Freedman. Technical Operations Manager: Jeff Brown. Marketing Director: Will Kuebler. Marketing Manager: Melanie Westerman.

Ownership: Mediacom LLC (MSO).

PARKSVILLE—Formerly served by Charter Communications. No longer in operation. ICA: KY0202.

PATHFORK—Formerly served by Cebridge Connections. Now served by GREASY CREEK, KY [KY0239]. ICA: KY0237.

PERRYVILLE—Now served by HARRODSBURG, KY [KY0231]. ICA: KY0170.

PIKEVILLE—Suddenlink Communications, 2214 S Mayo Trail, Pikeville, KY 41501. Phones: 314-965-2020 (Corporate office); 800-999-6845 (Customer service). Fax: 606-437-6239. Web Site: http://www.suddenlink.com. Also serves Elkhorn City, Pike County (portions) & South Pikeville. ICA: KY0045.

TV Market Ranking: Below 100 (Elkhorn City, Pike County (portions) (portions)); Outside TV Markets (Pike County (portions) (portions), PIKEVILLE, South Pikeville). Franchise award date: December 28, 1987. Franchise expiration date: N.A. Began: September 1, 1951.

Channel capacity: 26 (operating 2-way). Channels available but not in use: 1.

Basic Service

Subscribers: 12,000.

Programming (received off-air): WCHS-TV (ABC) Charleston; WKPI-TV (PBS) Pikeville; WLFG (IND) Grundy; WLPX-TV (ION) Charleston; WOWK-TV (CBS) Huntington; WQCW (CW) Portsmouth; WSAZ-TV (MNT, NBC) Huntington; WVAH-TV (FOX) Charleston; WYMT-TV (CBS, CW) Hazard; allband FM.

Programming (via satellite): C-SPAN; Home Shopping Network; QVC; WGN America.

Fee: $30.25 installation; $17.95 monthly.

Expanded Basic Service 1

Subscribers: 5,851.

Programming (via satellite): ABC Family Channel; AMC; Animal Planet; Arts & Entertainment; Cartoon Network; Celebrity Shopping Network; CNBC; CNN; Comcast Sports Net Southeast; Comedy Central; Country Music TV; Discovery Channel; Disney Channel; E! Entertainment Television; ESPN; ESPN 2; ESPN Classic Sports; Fox News Channel; FX; Headline News; HGTV; History Channel; INSP; Lifetime; MTV; Nickelodeon; Spike TV; Syfy; TBS Superstation; The Learning Channel; Travel Channel; Turner Network TV; TV Land; USA Network; VH1; Weather Channel.

Fee: $21.00 monthly.

Digital Basic Service
Subscribers: N.A.
Programming (via satellite): BBC America; Bio; Bloomberg Television; Country Music TV; Discovery Digital Networks; DMX Music; ESPNews; Fox Movie Channel; Fox Soccer; Fuse; G4; GAS; Golf Channel; GSN; History Channel International; Independent Film Channel; Lifetime Movie Network; MTV2; National Geographic Channel; Nick Jr.; NickToons TV; Outdoor Channel; Sleuth; Speed Channel; Style Network; Toon Disney; Trinity Broadcasting Network; Turner Classic Movies; Versus; VH1 Classic; WE tv.
Fee: $12.95 monthly.

Pay Service 1
Pay Units: 348.
Programming (via satellite): Cinemax.
Fee: $25.00 installation; $10.00 monthly.

Pay Service 2
Pay Units: 414.
Programming (via satellite): HBO.
Fee: $25.00 installation; $10.00 monthly.

Pay Service 3
Pay Units: 134.
Programming (via satellite): The Movie Channel.
Fee: $25.00 installation; $10.00 monthly.

Pay Service 4
Pay Units: N.A.
Programming (via satellite): Showtime (multiplexed).

Digital Pay Service 1
Pay Units: N.A.
Programming (via satellite): Cinemax (multiplexed); Encore (multiplexed); HBO (multiplexed); Showtime (multiplexed); Starz (multiplexed); The Movie Channel (multiplexed).

Video-On-Demand: No

Pay-Per-View
iN DEMAND (delivered digitally); Playboy TV (delivered digitally); Fresh (delivered digitally).

Internet Service
Operational: Yes.
Broadband Service: Cebridge High Speed Cable Internet.
Fee: $49.95 installation; $26.95 monthly.

Telephone Service
None

Miles of Plant: 472.0 (coaxial); 31.0 (fiber optic).
District Manager: Robert Herrald. Manager: Patty Chapman. Chief Technician: David Carte.
City fee: 3% of basic.
Ownership: Cequel Communications LLC (MSO).

PINE HILL—Now served by MOOREHEAD, KY [KY0031]. ICA: KY0271.

PINEVILLE—NewWave Communications, 5026 S Highway 27, Somerset, KY 42501. Phones: 888-863-9928; 606-678-9215. Fax: 606.679.7111. Web Site: http://www.newwavecom.com. Also serves Bell County (portions), Clear Creek, East Pineville, Ferndale, Fourmile, Hulen, Log Mountain & Page. ICA: KY0063.
TV Market Ranking: Below 100 (Bell County (portions), Clear Creek, East Pineville, Ferndale, Fourmile, Hulen, Log Mountain, Page, PINEVILLE). Franchise award date: January 9, 1989. Franchise expiration date: N.A. Began: September 1, 1953.
Channel capacity: N.A. Channels available but not in use: N.A.

Basic Service
Subscribers: 3,021.
Programming (received off-air): WAGV (IND) Harlan; WATE-TV (ABC) Knoxville; WBIR-TV (NBC) Knoxville; WBXX-TV (CW) Crossville; WKHA (PBS) Hazard; WTNZ (FOX) Knoxville; WVLR (IND) Tazewell; WVLT-TV (CBS, MNT) Knoxville; WYMT-TV (CBS, CW) Hazard; allband FM.
Programming (via satellite): Home Shopping Network; QVC; Trinity Broadcasting Network; WGN America.
Current originations: Government Access; Educational Access; Public Access.
Fee: $35.00 installation; $18.95 monthly; $1.10 converter.

Expanded Basic Service 1
Subscribers: N.A.
Programming (via satellite): ABC Family Channel; AMC; Animal Planet; Arts & Entertainment; Cartoon Network; Celebrity Shopping Network; CNN; Comcast Sports Net Southeast; Comedy Central; Country Music TV; C-SPAN; C-SPAN 2; Discovery Channel; Disney Channel; E! Entertainment Television; ESPN; ESPN 2; ESPN Classic Sports; Food Network; Fox News Channel; FX; Hallmark Channel; Headline News; HGTV; History Channel; Lifetime; MTV; Nickelodeon; Spike TV; Syfy; TBS Superstation; The Learning Channel; Turner Classic Movies; Turner Network TV; TV Land; USA Network; VH1; Weather Channel.
Fee: $22.00 monthly.

Digital Basic Service
Subscribers: N.A.
Programming (via satellite): BBC America; Bio; Bloomberg Television; CMT Pure Country; Discovery Health Channel; Discovery Home Channel; Discovery Kids Channel; Discovery Military Channel; Discovery Times Channel; DMX Music; ESPNews; Fox Movie Channel; Fox Soccer; Fuse; G4; GAS; Golf Channel; GSN; History Channel International; Independent Film Channel; Lifetime Movie Network; MTV2; National Geographic Channel; Nick Jr.; NickToons TV; Outdoor Channel; Science Channel; Sleuth; Speed Channel; Toon Disney; Versus; VH1 Classic; WE tv.
Fee: $12.95 monthly.

Digital Pay Service 1
Pay Units: N.A.
Programming (via satellite): Cinemax (multiplexed); Encore (multiplexed); HBO (multiplexed); Showtime (multiplexed); Starz (multiplexed); The Movie Channel (multiplexed).

Video-On-Demand: No

Pay-Per-View
iN DEMAND (delivered digitally); Playboy TV (delivered digitally); Fresh (delivered digitally).

Internet Service
Operational: Yes.
Fee: $40.00 installation; $31.99 monthly.

Telephone Service
Digital: Operational
Fee: $24.99 monthly

Miles of Plant: 243.0 (coaxial); None (fiber optic). Homes passed: 4,970.
General Manager: Mark Bookout. Technical Operations Manager: Lynn McMahan.
City fee: 5% of gross.
Ownership: NewWave Communications (MSO).

PINEVILLE—NewWave Communications. Now served by PINEVILLE, KY [KY0063]. Communities previously served by this system are now served by MIDDLESBORO, KY [KY0034]. ICA: KY0272.

PLEASANT RIDGE—Windjammer Cable, 4400 PGA Blvd, Ste 902, Palm Beach Gardens, FL 33410. Phones: 877-450-5558; 561-775-1208. Fax: 561-775-7811. Web Site: http://www.windjammercable.com. Also serves Philpot, Utica & Whitesville (unincorporated areas). ICA: KY0185.
TV Market Ranking: 86 (Philpot, Utica); Below 100 (PLEASANT RIDGE); Outside TV Markets (Whitesville (unincorporated areas)). Franchise award date: N.A. Franchise expiration date: N.A. Began: N.A.
Channel capacity: N.A. Channels available but not in use: N.A.

Basic Service
Subscribers: N.A. Included in Owensboro
Programming (received off-air): WEHT (ABC) Evansville; WEVV-TV (CBS, MNT) Evansville; WFIE (NBC) Evansville; WKOH (PBS) Owensboro; WNIN (PBS) Evansville; WTVW (FOX) Evansville.
Programming (via satellite): ABC Family Channel; AMC; Arts & Entertainment; CNN; Country Music TV; Discovery Channel; Disney Channel; ESPN; ESPN 2; FX; Nickelodeon; Spike TV; TBS Superstation; The Learning Channel; Trinity Broadcasting Network; Turner Network TV; USA Network; WGN America.
Fee: $39.95 installation; $26.10 monthly.

Digital Pay Service 1
Pay Units: N.A.
Programming (via satellite): Cinemax (multiplexed); Encore (multiplexed); HBO (multiplexed); Showtime (multiplexed); Starz (multiplexed); The Movie Channel (multiplexed).
Fee: $15.95 monthly (each).

Video-On-Demand: No

Pay-Per-View
Club Jenna (delivered digitally); Playboy TV (delivered digitally); Fresh (delivered digitally).

Internet Service
Operational: No.

Telephone Service
None

Miles of Plant: 23.0 (coaxial); None (fiber optic). Homes passed included in Owensboro
General Manager: Timothy Evard. Operations Director: Belinda Graham. Engineering Director: Mike Earehart. Finance & Accounting Director: Cindy Earehart.
Ownership: Windjammer Communications LLC (MSO).

PRESTONSBURG—Suddenlink Communications, Teays Valley Rd, Scott Depot, WV 25560. Phone: 304-757-8001. Fax: 304-757-5807. Web Site: http://www.suddenlink.com. ICA: KY0273.
TV Market Ranking: Below 100 (PRESTONSBURG). Franchise award date: N.A. Franchise expiration date: N.A. Began: May 1, 1951.
Channel capacity: N.A. Channels available but not in use: N.A.

Basic Service
Subscribers: 3,000.
Programming (received off-air): WCHS-TV (ABC) Charleston; WKPI-TV (PBS) Pikeville; WLPX-TV (ION) Charleston; WOWK-TV (CBS) Huntington; WPBY-TV (PBS) Huntington; WQCW (CW) Portsmouth; WSAZ-TV (MNT, NBC) Huntington; WTSF (IND) Ashland; WVAH-TV (FOX) Charleston; WYMT-TV (CBS, CW) Hazard.
Programming (via satellite): C-SPAN; C-SPAN 2; Do-It-Yourself; Home Shopping Network; QVC; ShopNBC; TV Guide Network; WGN America.
Fee: $25.00 installation; $9.00 monthly.

Expanded Basic Service 1
Subscribers: N.A.
Programming (via satellite): ABC Family Channel; AMC; Animal Planet; Arts & Entertainment; BET Networks; Bravo; Cartoon Network; CNBC; CNN; Comedy Central; Country Music TV; Discovery Channel; Disney Channel; E! Entertainment Television; ESPN; ESPN 2; ESPN Classic Sports; Food Network; Fox News Channel; Fox Sports Net Ohio; FX; G4; Golf Channel; GSN; Hallmark Channel; Headline News; HGTV; History Channel; INSP; Lifetime; MSNBC; MTV; National Geographic Channel; Nickelodeon; Outdoor Channel; Oxygen; SoapNet; Speed Channel; Spike TV; Syfy; TBS Superstation; The Learning Channel; Toon Disney; Travel Channel; Trinity Broadcasting Network; truTV; Turner Classic Movies; Turner Network TV; TV Land; USA Network; Versus; VH1; WE tv; Weather Channel.

Digital Basic Service
Subscribers: N.A.
Programming (via satellite): BBC America; Bio; Bloomberg Television; Discovery Digital Networks; Discovery HD Theater; ESPN; ESPNews; Fox College Sports Atlantic; Fox College Sports Central; Fox College Sports Pacific; Fox Movie Channel; Fox Soccer; Fox Sports en Espanol; Fuel TV; Fuse; GAS; Great American Country; History Channel International; Independent Film Channel; Lifetime Movie Network; MTV Networks Digital Suite; Music Choice; NFL Network; Nick Jr.; Nick Too; NickToons TV; Science Television; Sundance Channel; TVG Network.

Pay Service 1
Pay Units: 80.
Programming (via satellite): Encore (multiplexed); Flix; Showtime (multiplexed); The Movie Channel (multiplexed).
Fee: $20.00 installation; $10.00 monthly (Cinemax), $11.00 monthly (HBO).

Digital Pay Service 1
Pay Units: N.A.
Programming (via satellite): Cinemax (multiplexed); HBO (multiplexed); HBO; Showtime; Starz.

Video-On-Demand: Yes

Pay-Per-View
Playboy TV (delivered digitally); Fresh (delivered digitally); Shorteez (delivered digitally).

Internet Service
Operational: Yes. Began: March 1, 2003.
Broadband Service: Cebridge High Speed Cable Internet.
Fee: $49.99 installation; $29.95 monthly.

Telephone Service
Digital: Operational
Fee: $29.95 monthly
Miles of Plant: 29.0 (coaxial); None (fiber optic).
Vice President: David Bach. Marketing Manager: Kenny Phillips. Technical Operations Manager: Dave Andrews.
City fee: 3% of gross.
Ownership: Cequel Communications LLC (MSO).

PRINCETON—Mediacom. Now served by MARION, KY [KY0071]. ICA: KY0274.

PROVIDENCE—Insight Communications, 504 E Main St, Providence, KY 42450. Phone: 270-667-5545. Web Site: http://www.myinsight.com. Also serves Webster County (southern portion). ICA: KY0074.
TV Market Ranking: 86 (Webster County (southern portion) (portions)); Below 100 (PROVIDENCE, Webster County (southern portion) (portions)). Franchise award date: N.A. Franchise expiration date: N.A. Began: December 1, 1967.
Channel capacity: 42 (not 2-way capable). Channels available but not in use: N.A.
Basic Service
Subscribers: 1,412.
Programming (received off-air): WAZE-TV (CW) Madisonville; WEHT (ABC) Evansville; WEVV-TV (CBS, MNT) Evansville; WFIE (NBC) Evansville; WKMA-TV (PBS) Madisonville; WNIN (PBS) Evansville; WPSD-TV (NBC) Paducah; WTVW (FOX) Evansville; allband FM.
Programming (via satellite): Discovery Channel; QVC; TBS Superstation; WGN America.
Fee: $35.00 installation; $13.69 monthly; $2.00 converter.
Expanded Basic Service 1
Subscribers: N.A.
Programming (via satellite): ABC Family Channel; AMC; Animal Planet; Arts & Entertainment; BET Networks; CNBC; CNN; C-SPAN; Disney Channel; ESPN; ESPN 2; Fox News Channel; FX; Headline News; Lifetime; MoviePlex; MTV; Nickelodeon; Spike TV; The Learning Channel; Turner Network TV; USA Network; Weather Channel.
Fee: $21.45 monthly.
Digital Basic Service
Subscribers: N.A.
Programming (via satellite): BBC America; Bloomberg Television; Discovery Health Channel; Discovery Kids Channel; Discovery Military Channel; Discovery Planet Green; FitTV; Fox Movie Channel; Fox Soccer; Halogen Network; ID Investigation Discovery; Independent Film Channel; National Geographic Channel; Outdoor Channel; Science Channel; SoapNet; Speed Channel; Trinity Broadcasting Network; Turner Classic Movies.
Digital Pay Service 1
Pay Units: N.A.
Programming (via satellite): Cinemax (multiplexed); Encore (multiplexed); HBO (multiplexed); Showtime (multiplexed); Starz; The Movie Channel.
Video-On-Demand: No
Pay-Per-View
Playboy TV (delivered digitally); Fresh (delivered digitally).
Internet Service
Operational: No.
Telephone Service
None
Miles of Plant: 44.0 (coaxial); None (fiber optic). Total homes in franchised area: 2,600.
President & Chief Operating Officer: Dinni Jain. Senior Vice President, Operations: John Hutton. District Vice President: Lanae Juffer. Technical Operations Manager: Don Baumholser. Customer Service Manager: Kyle Hamilton.
Ownership: Insight Communications Co. (MSO).

RED BOILING SPRINGS—Celina Cable. Now served by SCOTTSVILLE, KY [KY0073]. ICA: TN0114.

RICHMOND—Time Warner Cable, 1615 Foxhaven Dr, Richmond, KY 40475. Phones: 859-626-4800; 859-624-9666. Fax: 859-624-0060. Web Site: http://www.timewarnercable.com/Central KY/. Also serves Berea, Clark County, Kingston, Kirksville, Madison County, Waco, White Hall & Winchester. ICA: KY0008.
TV Market Ranking: Below 100 (Berea, Clark County, Kingston, Kirksville, Madison County, RICHMOND, Waco, White Hall, Winchester). Franchise award date: N.A. Franchise expiration date: N.A. Began: January 28, 1965.
Channel capacity: N.A. Channels available but not in use: N.A.
Basic Service
Subscribers: 21,262.
Programming (received off-air): WDKY-TV (FOX) Danville; WKLE (PBS) Lexington; WKYT-TV (CBS, CW) Lexington; WLEX-TV (NBC) Lexington; WLJC-TV (TBN) Beattyville; WTVQ-DT (ABC) Lexington; WUPX-TV (ION) Morehead.
Programming (via satellite): QVC; WGN America.
Current originations: Government Access; Educational Access; Public Access; Public Access.
Fee: $39.95 installation; $16.37 monthly; $14.95 additional installation.
Expanded Basic Service 1
Subscribers: 20,479.
Programming (via satellite): ABC Family Channel; AMC; Animal Planet; Arts & Entertainment; BET Networks; Bravo; Cartoon Network; CNBC; CNN; Comcast Sports Net Southeast; Comedy Central; Country Music TV; C-SPAN; C-SPAN 2; Discovery Channel; Disney Channel; E! Entertainment Television; ESPN; ESPN 2; Eternal Word TV Network; Food Network; Fox News Channel; Fox Sports Net Ohio; FX; Hallmark Channel; Headline News; HGTV; History Channel; Home Shopping Network; INSP; Lifetime; MSNBC; MTV; Nickelodeon; Oxygen; Product Information Network; ShopNBC; Spike TV; Syfy; TBS Superstation; The Learning Channel; Travel Channel; Trinity Broadcasting Network; truTV; Turner Network TV; TV Guide Network; TV Land; Univision; USA Network; VH1; Weather Channel.
Fee: $33.98 monthly.
Digital Basic Service
Subscribers: N.A.
Programming (via satellite): AmericanLife TV Network; BBC America; Bio; Black Family Channel; Bloomberg Television; Canales N; Discovery Digital Networks; DMX Music; Do-It-Yourself; ESPN Classic Sports; ESPNews; FitTV; Fox College Sports Atlantic; Fox College Sports Central; Fox College Sports Pacific; Fox Movie Channel; Fox Sports World; Fuse; G4; Gaming Entertainment Television; GAS; Golf Channel; Great American Country; GSN; Halogen Network; History Channel International; Independent Film Channel; Lifetime Movie Network; MTV Networks Digital Suite; Music Choice; National Geographic Channel; Nick Jr.; Nick Too; NickToons TV; Outdoor Channel; SoapNet; Speed Channel; Style Network; Sundance Channel; The Word Network; Toon Disney; Turner Classic Movies; Versus; WE tv.
Fee: $6.00 monthly (each tier).
Digital Pay Service 1
Pay Units: 1,656.
Programming (via satellite): Cinemax (multiplexed).
Fee: $12.00 monthly.
Digital Pay Service 2
Pay Units: 2,165.
Programming (via satellite): HBO (multiplexed).
Fee: $12.00 monthly.
Digital Pay Service 3
Pay Units: 1,348.
Programming (via satellite): Flix; Showtime (multiplexed); The Movie Channel (multiplexed).
Fee: $12.00 monthly.
Digital Pay Service 4
Pay Units: 1,199.
Programming (via satellite): Encore (multiplexed); Starz (multiplexed).
Fee: $12.00 monthly.
Digital Pay Service 5
Pay Units: 766.
Programming (via satellite): ART America; CCTV-4; Filipino Channel; RAI International; Russian Television Network; TV Asia; TV Japan; TV5, La Television International; Zee TV USA; Zhong Tian Channel.
Fee: $15.00 monthly (each).
Video-On-Demand: Yes
Pay-Per-View
iN DEMAND (delivered digitally); Playboy TV (delivered digitally); Fresh (delivered digitally); Shorteez (delivered digitally); Hot Choice (delivered digitally); Urban Xtra (delivered digitally); Sports PPV (delivered digitally).
Internet Service
Operational: Yes.
Broadband Service: Road Runner.
Fee: $44.95 monthly.
Telephone Service
Digital: Operational
Fee: $44.95 monthly
Miles of Plant: 688.0 (coaxial); None (fiber optic). Homes passed: 24,707.
General Manager: Robert Trott. Technical Operations Manager: Dennis Lester. Marketing Director: Betrina Morse. Government & Public Affairs Manager: Carla Deaton. Office Manager: Laverne Farris.
City fee: 3% of gross.
Ownership: Time Warner Cable (MSO).

ROCHESTER—Windjammer Cable, 4400 PGA Blvd, Ste 902, Palm Beach Gardens, FL 33410. Phones: 877-450-5558; 561-775-7811. Fax: 561-775-7811. Web Site: http://www.windjammercable.com. ICA: KY0309.
TV Market Ranking: Below 100 (ROCHESTER). Franchise award date: N.A. Franchise expiration date: N.A. Began: N.A.
Channel capacity: N.A. Channels available but not in use: N.A.
Basic Service
Subscribers: 38.
Programming (received off-air): WBKO (ABC, CW) Bowling Green; WEHT (ABC) Evansville; WEVV-TV (CBS, MNT) Evansville; WFIE (NBC) Evansville; WKGB-TV (PBS) Bowling Green; WTVW (FOX) Evansville.
Programming (via satellite): ABC Family Channel; Animal Planet; Arts & Entertainment; CNN; Country Music TV; Discovery Channel; ESPN; ESPN 2; History Channel; Nickelodeon; Spike TV; TBS Superstation; The Learning Channel; Travel Channel; Trinity Broadcasting Network; Turner Network TV; USA Network; WGN America.
Fee: $39.95 installation; $36.65 monthly.
Digital Basic Service
Subscribers: N.A.
Programming (via satellite): AmericanLife TV Network; BBC America; Bloomberg Television; Discovery Health Channel; Discovery Kids Channel; ESPN Classic Sports; ESPNews; FitTV; Fox Sports World; G4; Golf Channel; GSN; INSP; Music Choice; Nick Jr.; Outdoor Channel; Science Channel; Versus; WE tv.
Fee: $12.95 monthly.
Digital Pay Service 1
Pay Units: N.A.
Programming (via satellite): Cinemax (multiplexed); Encore (multiplexed); HBO (multiplexed); Showtime (multiplexed).
Fee: $15.95 monthly (each).
Video-On-Demand: No
Pay-Per-View
Club Jenna (delivered digitally); Fresh (delivered digitally); Playboy TV (delivered digitally).
Internet Service
Operational: No.
Telephone Service
None
Miles of Plant: 7.0 (coaxial); None (fiber optic). Homes passed: 65.
Ownership: Windjammer Communications LLC (MSO).

ROUGH RIVER DAM—Mediacom. Now served by CANEYVILLE, KY [KY0291]. ICA: KY0276.

RUSSELL COUNTY (unincorporated areas)—Mediacom, 90 Main St, Benton, KY 42025-1132. Phones: 417-875-5560 (Springfield regional office); 270-527-9939. Fax: 270-527-0813. Web Site: http://www.mediacomcable.com. Also serves Casey County (southern portion), Jamestown & Windsor. ICA: KY0114.
TV Market Ranking: Below 100 (Casey County (southern portion), Jamestown, RUSSELL COUNTY (UNINCORPORATED AREAS), Windsor). Franchise award date: April 1, 1988. Franchise expiration date: N.A. Began: May 1, 1989.
Channel capacity: N.A. Channels available but not in use: N.A.
Basic Service
Subscribers: 632.
Programming (received off-air): WBIR-TV (NBC) Knoxville; WBKO (ABC, CW) Bowling Green; WDKY-TV (FOX) Danville; WHAS-TV (ABC) Louisville; WKSO-TV (PBS) Somerset; WKYT-TV (CBS, CW) Lexington; WLEX-TV (NBC) Lexington; WMYT-TV (MNT) Rock Hill; WTVQ-DT (ABC) Lexington.
Programming (via satellite): ABC Family Channel; AMC; Animal Planet; Arts & Entertainment; Cartoon Network; CNBC; CNN; Comedy Central; Country Music TV; C-SPAN 2; Discovery Channel; Disney Channel; E! Entertainment Television; ESPN; ESPN 2; Food Network; Fox News Channel; Fox Sports Net Midwest; FX; Great American Country; Headline News; HGTV; History Channel; Home Shopping Network; INSP; Lifetime; MSNBC; MTV; National Geographic Channel; Nickelodeon; Outdoor Channel; QVC; Speed Channel; Spike TV; Syfy; TBS Superstation; The Learning Channel; Travel Channel; Trinity Broadcasting Network; Turner Net-

work TV; TV Land; USA Network; VH1; Weather Channel; WGN America.
Fee: $29.95 installation; $24.95 monthly; $3.95 converter.
Pay Service 1
Pay Units: 54.
Programming (via satellite): Cinemax.
Fee: $9.00 monthly.
Pay Service 2
Pay Units: 47.
Programming (via satellite): HBO.
Fee: $10.00 monthly.
Pay Service 3
Pay Units: N.A.
Programming (via satellite): Encore; Starz.
Video-On-Demand: No
Internet Service
Operational: No.
Telephone Service
None
Miles of Plant: 70.0 (coaxial); None (fiber optic). Homes passed: 1,050. Total homes in franchised area: 1,050.
Regional Vice President: Bill Copeland. General Manager: Dale Haney. Regional Technical Operations Director: Alan Freedman. Technical Operations Manager: Jeff Brown. Marketing Director: Will Kuebler. Marketing Manager: Melanie Westerman.
Franchise fee: 5% of gross.
Ownership: Mediacom LLC (MSO).

RUSSELL SPRINGS—Duo County Telecom, PO Box 80, 2150 N Main St, Jamestown, KY 42629. Phone: 270-343-3131. Fax: 270-343-3800. E-mail: duotel@duo-county.com. Web Site: http://www.duo-county.com. Also serves Jamestown (portions) & Russell County. ICA: KY0243.
TV Market Ranking: Below 100 (Jamestown (portions), Russell County, RUSSELL SPRINGS). Franchise award date: February 23, 1988. Franchise expiration date: N.A. Began: January 10, 1971.
Channel capacity: N.A. Channels available but not in use: N.A.
Basic Service
Subscribers: 2,950.
Programming (received off-air): WAVE (NBC) Louisville; WBKI-TV (CW) Campbellsville; WBKO (ABC, CW) Bowling Green; WDKY-TV (FOX) Danville; WDRB (FOX) Louisville; WHAS-TV (ABC) Louisville; WKRN-TV (ABC) Nashville; WKYT-TV (CBS, CW) Lexington; WLEX-TV (NBC) Lexington; WLKY-TV (CBS) Louisville; WSMV-TV (NBC, TMO) Nashville; WTVF (CBS) Nashville; WTVQ-DT (ABC) Lexington; 3 FMs.
Programming (via satellite): AMC; Headline News; Home Shopping Network; QVC; WGN America.
Current originations: Public Access.
Fee: $20.00 installation; $23.80 monthly; $15.00 additional installation.
Expanded Basic Service 1
Subscribers: 2,518.
Programming (via satellite): ABC Family Channel; Animal Planet; Arts & Entertainment; BET Networks; Boomerang; Cartoon Network; CNBC; CNN; Comcast Sports Net Southeast; Comedy Central; Country Music TV; C-SPAN; Discovery Channel; Discovery Health Channel; Disney Channel; E! Entertainment Television; ESPN; ESPN 2; ESPN Classic Sports; Food Network; Fox News Channel; FX; G4; Gospel Music Channel; HGTV; History Channel; ION Television; Lifetime; Lifetime Movie Network; Local Cable Weather; MTV; Nickelodeon; Oxygen; RFD-TV; Spike TV; Syfy; The Learning Channel; Travel Channel; Trinity Broadcasting Network; truTV; Turner Network TV; TV Land; USA Network; VH1; Weather Channel.
Fee: $21.15 monthly.
Digital Basic Service
Subscribers: 450.
Programming (via satellite): Bloomberg Television; C-SPAN 2; Do-It-Yourself; ESPNews; Golf Channel; Hallmark Channel; Lifetime Real Women; MSNBC; Music Choice; Outdoor Channel; SoapNet; Speed Channel; Turner Classic Movies; Versus.
Fee: $8.95 monthly.
Digital Pay Service 1
Pay Units: N.A.
Programming (via satellite): Cinemax (multiplexed); Flix; HBO (multiplexed); Showtime; Sundance Channel; The Movie Channel.
Fee: $12.95 monthly (Cinemax, Showtime/TMC/Flix/Sundance or Starz/Encore), $13.95 monthly (HBO).
Video-On-Demand: No
Pay-Per-View
Indemand (delivered digitally), Fee: $3.95-$49.95, Addressable: Yes.
Internet Service
Operational: Yes.
Broadband Service: In-house.
Fee: $21.95 monthly; $40.00 modem purchase.
Telephone Service
None
Miles of Plant: 127.0 (coaxial); None (fiber optic). Homes passed: 5,000.
Vice President, Operations: Mark Henry. Marketing Director: Eric West.
Ownership: Duo County Telephone Cooperative (MSO).

RUSSELLVILLE—Suddenlink Communications, 12444 Powerscourt Dr, Saint Louis, MO 63131-3660. Phones: 800-999-6845 (Customer service); 314-965-2020. Fax: 903-561-5485. Web Site: http://www.suddenlink.com. Also serves Auburn & Logan County. ICA: KY0032.
TV Market Ranking: Below 100 (Auburn, Logan County, RUSSELLVILLE). Franchise award date: March 27, 1986. Franchise expiration date: N.A. Began: April 1, 1980.
Channel capacity: N.A. Channels available but not in use: N.A.
Basic Service
Subscribers: 2,849.
Programming (received off-air): WBKO (ABC, CW) Bowling Green; WKLE (PBS) Lexington; WKYU-TV (PBS) Bowling Green; WNAB (CW) Nashville; WNKY (CBS, NBC) Bowling Green; WNPT (PBS) Nashville; WNPX-TV (ION) Cookeville; WPGD-TV (IND) Hendersonville; WSMV-TV (NBC, TMO) Nashville; WTVF (CBS) Nashville; WUXP-TV (MNT) Nashville; WZTV (FOX) Nashville.
Programming (via satellite): TV Guide Network; WGN America.
Fee: $26.00 installation; $17.95 monthly.
Expanded Basic Service 1
Subscribers: 2,762.
Programming (via satellite): ABC Family Channel; AMC; Animal Planet; Arts & Entertainment; BET Networks; Cartoon Network; CNBC; CNN; Country Music TV; C-SPAN; Discovery Channel; Disney Channel; E! Entertainment Television; ESPN; ESPN 2; ESPN Classic Sports; Food Network; Fox News Channel; FX; Headline News; HGTV; History Channel; Home Shopping Network; Lifetime; MTV; Nickelodeon; QVC; Spike TV; Syfy; TBS Superstation; The Learning Channel; Turner Classic Movies; Turner

Network TV; TV Land; USA Network; VH1; Weather Channel.
Fee: $22.00 monthly.
Digital Basic Service
Subscribers: N.A.
Programming (via satellite): BBC America; Bio; Bloomberg Television; Country Music TV; Discovery Digital Networks; ESPNews; Fox Movie Channel; Fox Soccer; Fuse; G4; GAS; Golf Channel; GSN; History Channel International; Independent Film Channel; Lifetime Movie Network; MTV Networks Digital Suite; National Geographic Channel; Nick Jr.; NickToons TV; Outdoor Channel; Speed Channel; Style Network; Toon Disney; Trinity Broadcasting Network; Versus; WE tv.
Fee: $12.95 monthly.
Digital Pay Service 1
Pay Units: N.A.
Programming (via satellite): Cinemax (multiplexed); Encore (multiplexed); HBO (multiplexed); Showtime (multiplexed); Starz (multiplexed); The Movie Channel (multiplexed).
Fee: $7.95 monthly (Starz & Encore), $18.95 monthly (Cinemax, Showtime or TMC), $20.95 monthly (HBO).
Video-On-Demand: No
Pay-Per-View
iN DEMAND (delivered digitally); Playboy TV (delivered digitally); Fresh (delivered digitally).
Internet Service
Operational: Yes. Began: March 10, 2004.
Broadband Service: Cebridge High Speed Cable Internet.
Fee: $49.95 installation; $26.95 monthly.
Telephone Service
None
Miles of Plant: 96.0 (coaxial); None (fiber optic). Homes passed: 4,689.
President: Tom Kinley. Senior Vice President: Gerald Corman. Vice President: Robert Herald. Chief Technician: Jim Adkins.
City fee: 1% of gross.
Ownership: Cequel Communications LLC (MSO).

SALYERSVILLE—Frank Howard's TV Cable, PO Box 229, 911 E Maple St, Salyersville, KY 41465. Phone: 606-349-3317. Fax: 606-349-3306. Also serves Falcon, Ivyton, Lickburg, Magoffin County & Pleasant Hill. ICA: KY0277.
TV Market Ranking: Below 100 (Ivyton, Magoffin County (portions), SALYERSVILLE); Outside TV Markets (Falcon, Lickburg, Magoffin County (portions), Pleasant Hill). Franchise award date: N.A. Franchise expiration date: N.A. Began: January 1, 1963.
Channel capacity: N.A. Channels available but not in use: N.A.
Basic Service
Subscribers: 1,200.
Programming (received off-air): WCHS-TV (ABC) Charleston; WDKY-TV (FOX) Danville; WFPX-TV (ION) Fayetteville; WKMR (PBS) Morehead; WKYT-TV (CBS, CW) Lexington; WLEX-TV (NBC) Lexington; WLJC-TV (TBN) Beattyville; WOWK-TV (CBS) Huntington; WQCW (CW) Portsmouth; WSAZ-TV (MNT, NBC) Huntington; WTVQ-DT (ABC) Lexington; WYMT-TV (CBS, CW) Hazard.
Programming (via satellite): ABC Family Channel; AMC; Animal Planet; Cartoon Network; CNN; Country Music TV; C-SPAN; C-SPAN 2; Discovery Channel; Disney Channel; E! Entertainment Television; ESPN; ESPN 2; Food Network; FX; G4; Great American Country; Hallmark Channel; Headline News; HGTV; Home Shopping Network; HorseRacing TV; INSP; Lifetime; MTV; Nickelodeon; Outdoor Channel; QVC; Speed Channel; Spike TV; Syfy; TBS Superstation; The Learning Channel; Travel Channel; Trinity Broadcasting Network; Turner Network TV; TV Guide Network; TV Land; USA Network; VH1; WE tv; Weather Channel; WGN America.
Fee: $45.00 installation; $43.08 monthly.
Digital Basic Service
Subscribers: 34.
Programming (via satellite): BBC America; Discovery Digital Networks; Encore (multiplexed); ESPN Classic Sports.
Fee: $13.09 monthly.
Pay Service 1
Pay Units: 50.
Programming (via satellite): Cinemax; HBO.
Fee: $10.00 monthly (Cinemax), $13.00 monthly (HBO).
Digital Pay Service 1
Pay Units: N.A.
Programming (via satellite): HBO (multiplexed); Showtime (multiplexed); Starz (multiplexed); The Movie Channel (multiplexed).
Video-On-Demand: No
Internet Service
Operational: Yes.
Subscribers: 180.
Broadband Service: AT&T.
Fee: $24.95 monthly.
Telephone Service
None
Miles of Plant: 200.0 (coaxial); None (fiber optic). Homes passed: 3,000.
Technical Manager: Rick Howard. Office Manager: Frances Crace. Chief Technician: Greg Bowen.
Ownership: Ruth & Rick Howard.

SANDY HOOK—Windjammer Cable, 4400 PGA Blvd, Ste 902, Palm Beach Gardens, FL 33410. Phones: 877-450-5558; 561-775-1208. Fax: 561-775-7811. Web Site: http://www.windjammercable.com. Also serves Newfoundland & Wrigley. ICA: KY0134.
TV Market Ranking: Below 100 (Newfoundland, SANDY HOOK, Wrigley). Franchise award date: N.A. Franchise expiration date: N.A. Began: June 1, 1958.
Channel capacity: 36 (not 2-way capable). Channels available but not in use: 2.
Basic Service
Subscribers: 501.
Programming (received off-air): WCHS-TV (ABC) Charleston; WKMR (PBS) Morehead; WKYT-TV (CBS, CW) Lexington; WLJC-TV (TBN) Beattyville; WOWK-TV (CBS) Huntington; WPBY-TV (PBS) Hunt-

ington; WSAZ-TV (MNT, NBC) Huntington; WVAH-TV (FOX) Charleston.
Programming (via satellite): C-SPAN; QVC; TBS Superstation; WGN America.
Fee: $39.95 installation; $19.27 monthly; $2.00 converter.

Expanded Basic Service 1
Subscribers: 447.
Programming (via satellite): ABC Family Channel; AMC; Arts & Entertainment; CNBC; CNN; Country Music TV; Discovery Channel; Disney Channel; E! Entertainment Television; ESPN; ESPN 2; Fox News Channel; Headline News; INSP; Lifetime; Nickelodeon; Spike TV; Syfy; The Learning Channel; Turner Network TV; USA Network; Weather Channel.
Fee: $28.14 monthly.

Digital Basic Service
Subscribers: N.A.
Programming (via satellite): BBC America; Bloomberg Television; Bravo; Discovery Digital Networks; ESPN Classic Sports; ESPNews; FitTV; Fox Movie Channel; Fox Soccer; G4; Golf Channel; GSN; Halogen Network; HGTV; History Channel; Independent Film Channel; National Geographic Channel; Nick Jr.; NickToons TV; Outdoor Channel; Speed Channel; Trinity Broadcasting Network; Turner Classic Movies; Versus; VH1 Classic; VH1 Country; WE tv.
Fee: $56.11 monthly.

Digital Pay Service 1
Pay Units: N.A.
Programming (via satellite): Cinemax (multiplexed); Encore; HBO (multiplexed); Showtime (multiplexed); Starz; The Movie Channel (multiplexed).
Fee: $15.95 monthly (each).

Video-On-Demand: No

Pay-Per-View
HITS 1 (delivered digitally); HITS 2 (delivered digitally); HITS 3 (delivered digitally); HITS 4 (delivered digitally); HITS 5 (delivered digitally); HITS 6 (delivered digitally); Playboy TV (delivered digitally); Fresh (delivered digitally).

Internet Service
Operational: No.

Telephone Service
None

Miles of Plant: 40.0 (coaxial); None (fiber optic). Homes passed: 714.
General Manager: Timothy Evard. Operations Director: Belinda Graham. Engineering Director: Mike Earehart. Finance & Accounting Director: Cindy Johnson.
Ownership: Windjammer Communications LLC (MSO).

SCOTTSVILLE—North Central Communications, 872 Hwy 52 Bypass E, PO Box 70, Lafayette, TN 77083. Phone: 615-666-2151. Web Site: http://www.nctc.com. Also serves Lafayette, Red Boiling Springs & Westmoreland. ICA: KY0073.
TV Market Ranking: Below 100 (Lafayette, Red Boiling Springs, SCOTTSVILLE, Westmoreland). Franchise award date: February 1, 1995. Franchise expiration date: N.A. Began: February 1, 1983.
Channel capacity: N.A. Channels available but not in use: N.A.

Digital Basic Service
Subscribers: 3,000.
Programming (received off-air): WBKO (ABC, CW) Bowling Green; WHTN (IND) Murfreesboro; WKRN-TV (ABC) Nashville; WNPT (PBS) Nashville; WPBM-LP Scottsville; WSMV-TV (NBC, TMO) Nashville; WTVF (CBS) Nashville; WUXP-TV (MNT) Nashville; WZTV (FOX) Nashville.
Programming (via satellite): C-SPAN; C-SPAN 2; Home Shopping Network; Local Cable Weather; QVC; Trinity Broadcasting Network; Weather Channel.
Current originations: Government Access; Educational Access; Public Access.
Fee: $19.95 monthly.

Digital Expanded Basic Service
Subscribers: N.A.
Programming (via satellite): ABC Family Channel; AMC; Animal Planet; Arts & Entertainment; BBC America; BET Networks; Bloomberg Television; Boomerang; Bravo; Cartoon Network; CNBC; CNN; Comcast Sports Net Southeast; Comedy Central; Country Music TV; Discovery Channel; Discovery Digital Networks; Discovery Health Channel; Disney Channel; Do-It-Yourself; E! Entertainment Television; ESPN; ESPN 2; ESPN Classic Sports; ESPNews; Food Network; Fox News Channel; FX; G4; Golf Channel; Gospel Music TV; Great American Country; GSN; Hallmark Channel; Headline News; HGTV; History Channel; ION Television; Lifetime; Lifetime Movie Network; Lifetime Real Women; MSNBC; MTV; Music Choice; Nickelodeon; Outdoor Channel; Oxygen; RFD-TV; SoapNet; Speed Channel; Spike TV; Syfy; TBS Superstation; The Learning Channel; Travel Channel; truTV; Turner Classic Movies; Turner Network TV; TV Land; USA Network; Versus; VH1; WGN America.
Fee: $23.00 monthly.

Digital Pay Service 1
Pay Units: N.A.
Programming (via satellite): Cinemax (multiplexed); Encore (multiplexed); Flix; HBO (multiplexed); Showtime (multiplexed); Starz (multiplexed); Sundance Channel; The Movie Channel (multiplexed).

Video-On-Demand: Yes

Pay-Per-View
iN DEMAND (delivered digitally).

Internet Service
Operational: No, DSL & dial-up.

Telephone Service
None

Miles of Plant: 39.0 (coaxial); None (fiber optic). Homes passed: 1,500.
Chief Executive Officer: Tom Rowland. Vice President, Administration: Johnny McClanahan. Vice President, Plant Operations: Ronnie Wilburn.
City fee: 3% of gross.
Ownership: North Central Telephone Cooperative.

SEBREE—NewWave Communications, 250 Madison Square Dr, Madisonville, KY 42431. Phones: 888-863-9928 (Customer service); 270-821-1811. Fax: 270.245.2022. Web Site: http://www.newwavecom.com. ICA: KY0143.
TV Market Ranking: 86 (SEBREE). Franchise award date: December 1, 1980. Franchise expiration date: N.A. Began: August 27, 1981.
Channel capacity: 36 (not 2-way capable). Channels available but not in use: N.A.

Basic Service
Subscribers: 373.
Programming (received off-air): WAZE-LP (CW) Evansville; WEHT (ABC) Evansville; WEVV-TV (CBS, MNT) Evansville; WFIE (NBC) Evansville; WKMA-TV (PBS) Madisonville; WNIN (PBS) Evansville; WPSD-TV (NBC) Paducah; WTVF (CBS) Nashville; WTVW (FOX) Evansville.
Programming (via satellite): Jewelry Television; QVC; WGN America.
Fee: $41.11 installation; $25.20 monthly.

Expanded Basic Service 1
Subscribers: N.A.
Programming (via satellite): ABC Family Channel; American Movie Classics; Animal Planet; Arts & Entertainment; BET Networks; Bravo!; Cartoon Network; CNBC; CNN; Comcast Sports Net Southeast; Comedy Central; Country Music TV; Court TV; C-SPAN; C-SPAN 2; Discovery Channel; Disney Channel; E! Entertainment Television; ESPN; ESPN 2; ESPN Classic Sports; Eternal Word TV Network; Food Network; Fox News Channel; FX; G4; Golf Channel; GSN; Hallmark Channel; Headline News; HGTV; History Channel; Home Shopping Network; INSP; ION Television; Lifetime; MSNBC; MTV; MTV2; National Geographic Channel; Nickelodeon; Outdoor Channel; ShopNBC; SoapNet; Speed Channel; Spike TV; Style Network; Syfy; TBS Superstation; The Learning Channel; Toon Disney; Travel Channel; Trinity Broadcasting Network; Turner Classic Movies; Turner Network TV; TV Guide Network; TV Land; USA Network; Versus; VH1; WE tv; Weather Channel.

Digital Basic Service
Subscribers: N.A.
Programming (received off-air): WEHT (ABC) Evansville; WEVV-TV (CBS, MNT) Evansville; WFIE (NBC) Evansville.
Programming (via satellite): BBC America; Bio; CMT Pure Country; Discovery Channel HD; Discovery Health Channel; Discovery Home Channel; Discovery Kids Channel; Discovery Military Channel; Discovery Times Channel; Do-It-Yourself; ESPN 2 HD; ESPN Classic Sports; ESPN HD; ESPN U; ESPNews; FitTV; GAS; Golf Channel; HDNet; HDNet Movies; History Channel International; Independent Film Channel; Lifetime Movie Network; MTV Jams; MTV Tres; Music Choice; Nick Jr.; Nick Too; NickToons TV; RFD-TV; Science Channel; Turner Network TV HD; Universal HD; VH1 Classic; VH1 Soul; VHUNO.

Digital Pay Service 1
Pay Units: N.A.
Programming (via satellite): Cinemax (multiplexed); Cinemax HD; Encore (multiplexed); Flix; HBO (multiplexed); HBO HD; Showtime (multiplexed); Starz (multiplexed); Starz HDTV; The Movie Channel (multiplexed).

Video-On-Demand: No

Pay-Per-View
Shorteez (delivered digitally); Fresh (delivered digitally); Playboy TV (delivered digitally); Movies (delivered digitally); Special events (delivered digitally); ESPN Gameplan (delivered digitally).

Internet Service
Operational: Yes.
Fee: $40.00 installation; $31.99 monthly.

Telephone Service
Digital: Planned

Miles of Plant: 10.0 (coaxial); None (fiber optic). Homes passed: 609. Total homes in franchised area: 609.
General Manager: Mark Boyer. Technical Operations Director: Roy Hibbs.
City fee: 3% of gross.
Ownership: NewWave Communications (MSO).

SHARPSBURG—Formerly served by Adelphia Communications. Now served by MOUNT STERLING, KY [KY0046]. ICA: KY0279.

SHELBYVILLE—Insight Communications. Now served by LOUISVILLE, KY [KY0001]. ICA: KY0022.

SHEPHERDSVILLE—Inside Connect Cable, 150 Livers Lane, Shepherdsville, KY 40165. Phone: 502-543-7551. Fax: 502-543-7553. E-mail: techsupport@insideconnect.net. Web Site: http://www.insideconnect.net. ICA: KY0327. **Note:** This system is an overbuild.
TV Market Ranking: 38 (SHEPHERDSVILLE). Franchise award date: N.A. Franchise expiration date: N.A. Began: June 1, 1991.
Channel capacity: N.A. Channels available but not in use: N.A.

Basic Service
Subscribers: 1,000.
Programming (received off-air): WAVE (NBC) Louisville; WBKI-TV (CW) Campbellsville; WBNA (ION) Louisville; WDRB (FOX) Louisville; WHAS-TV (ABC) Louisville; WKMJ-TV (PBS) Louisville; WKPC-TV (PBS) Louisville; WLKY-TV (CBS) Louisville; WMYO (MNT) Salem.
Programming (via satellite): ABC Family Channel; AMC; Animal Planet; ART America; Arts & Entertainment; Bloomberg Television; Boomerang; Cartoon Network; CNN; Comedy Central; Cooking Channel; Country Music TV; C-SPAN; C-SPAN 2; Daystar TV Network; Discovery Channel; Disney Channel; Do-It-Yourself; E! Entertainment Television; ESPN; ESPN 2; ESPN Classic Sports; ESPN U; Eternal Word TV Network; Food Network; Fox News Channel; FX; G4; Golf Channel; Great American Country; GSN; Hallmark Channel; Hallmark Movie Channel; Headline News; HGTV; Home Shopping Network; HorseRacing TV; INSP; ION Television; Lifetime; Lifetime Movie Network; MSNBC; MTV; Nickelodeon; Outdoor Channel; Oxygen; Product Information Network; Qubo; QVC; Radar Channel; RFD-TV; ShopNBC; Speed Channel; Style Network; Syfy; TBS Superstation; Tennis Channel; The Learning Channel; The Sportsman Channel; Travel Channel; Trinity Broadcasting Network; truTV; Turner Classic Movies; Turner Network TV; TV Guide Network; TV Land; USA Network; Versus; VH1; Weather Channel; WGN America; Worship Network.
Fee: $45.95 monthly.

Digital Basic Service
Subscribers: N.A.
Programming (received off-air): WAVE (NBC) Louisville; WDRB (FOX) Louisville; WHAS-TV (ABC) Louisville; WLKY-TV (CBS) Louisville.
Programming (via satellite): AmericanLife TV Network; Anime Network; BBC America; Bio; Bravo; Church Channel; CMT Pure Country; Current; Discovery Digital Networks; Discovery HD Theater; DMX Music; ESPN HD; ESPNews; FitTV; Fox College Sports Atlantic; Fox College Sports Central; Fox College Sports Pacific; Fox Movie Channel; Fox Reality Channel; Fox Soccer; Fuse; GAS; GSN; Halogen Network; HGTV; History Channel; History Channel International; Independent Film Channel; JCTV; Military History Channel; MTV Networks Digital Suite; National Geographic Channel; Nick Jr.; NickToons TV; Ovation; PBS Kids Sprout; Sleuth; SoapNet; Style Network; Sundance Channel; The Word Network; Toon Disney; Turner Network TV HD; TVG Network; WE tv.

Digital Pay Service 1
Pay Units: N.A.
Programming (via satellite): Cinemax (multiplexed); Cinemax HD; Encore (multiplexed); Flix; HBO (multiplexed); HBO HD; Showtime (multiplexed); Starz (multiplexed); The Movie Channel (multiplexed).
Fee: $6.00 monthly (Encore), $9.00 monthly (Cinemax or Starz), $12.00 monthly (HBO or Showtime & TMC).

Internet Service
Operational: Yes.
Subscribers: 375.
Fee: $49.95 installation; $29.95 monthly.
Telephone Service
Digital: Operational
Miles of Plant: 115.0 (coaxial); None (fiber optic). Homes passed: 4,500.
Manager & Chief Technician: Rusty Smith. Office Manager: Amy Larison. Network Manager: TJ Scott.
Ownership: Inside Connect Cable LLC.

SITKA—Sitka TV Cable, 109 Depot Rd, Paintsville, KY 41240-1346. Fax: 606-789-3391. ICA: KY0320.
TV Market Ranking: Outside TV Markets (SITKA).
Channel capacity: 27 (not 2-way capable). Channels available but not in use: N.A.
Basic Service
Subscribers: 70.
Programming (received off-air): WCHS-TV (ABC) Charleston; WKPI-TV (PBS) Pikeville; WLPX-TV (ION) Charleston; WOWK-TV (CBS) Huntington; WPBY-TV (PBS) Huntington; WQCW (CW) Portsmouth; WSAZ-TV (MNT, NBC) Huntington; WVAH-TV (FOX) Charleston; WYMT-TV (CBS, CW) Hazard.
Programming (via satellite): ABC Family Channel; Animal Planet; Country Music TV; Discovery Channel; ESPN; HGTV; Home Shopping Network; MSNBC; Spike TV; Syfy; TBS Superstation; Trinity Broadcasting Network; Turner Network TV; TV Land; USA Network; WGN America.
Fee: $23.00 monthly.
Pay Service 1
Pay Units: 12.
Programming (via satellite): The Movie Channel.
Fee: $7.00 monthly.
Video-On-Demand: No
Internet Service
Operational: No.
Telephone Service
None
Miles of Plant: 8.0 (coaxial); None (fiber optic).
Manager: Bart Ward.
Ownership: Sitka TV Cable System.

SLAUGHTERS—Windjammer Cable, 4400 PGA Blvd, Ste 902, Palm Beach Gardens, FL 33410. Phones: 877-450-5558; 561-775-1208. Fax: 561-775-7811. Web Site: http://www.windjammercable.com. ICA: KY0310.
TV Market Ranking: 86 (SLAUGHTERS). Franchise award date: N.A. Franchise expiration date: N.A. Began: N.A.
Channel capacity: 36 (not 2-way capable). Channels available but not in use: 12.
Basic Service
Subscribers: N.A. Included in Owensboro
Programming (received off-air): WEHT (ABC) Evansville; WEVV-TV (CBS, MNT) Evansville; WFIE (NBC) Evansville; WNIN (PBS) Evansville; WTVW (FOX) Evansville.
Programming (via satellite): ABC Family Channel; AMC; Arts & Entertainment; CNN; Country Music TV; Discovery Channel; Disney Channel; ESPN; FX; Nickelodeon; Spike TV; TBS Superstation; The Learning Channel; Trinity Broadcasting Network; Turner Network TV; USA Network; WGN America.
Fee: $39.95 installation; $35.65 monthly.
Digital Basic Service
Subscribers: N.A.
Programming (via satellite): AmericanLife TV Network; BBC America; Bloomberg Television; Discovery Digital Networks; DMX Music; ESPN Classic Sports; ESPNews; FitTV; Fox Movie Channel; Fox Sports World; G4; Golf Channel; GSN; Halogen Network; Music Choice; Nick Jr.; NickToons TV; Outdoor Channel; Versus; WE tv.
Fee: $12.95 monthly.
Digital Pay Service 1
Pay Units: N.A.
Programming (via satellite): Cinemax (multiplexed); Encore (multiplexed); HBO (multiplexed); Showtime (multiplexed); Starz (multiplexed); The Movie Channel (multiplexed).
Fee: $15.95 monthly (each).
Video-On-Demand: No
Pay-Per-View
iN DEMAND (delivered digitally); Playboy TV (delivered digitally); Fresh (delivered digitally).
Internet Service
Operational: No.
Telephone Service
None
Miles of Plant: 3.0 (coaxial); None (fiber optic). Homes passed included in Owensboro
Ownership: Windjammer Communications LLC (MSO).

SOLDIER—Now served by MOOREHEAD, KY [KY0031]. ICA: KY0224.

SOMERSET—NewWave Communications, 5026 S Highway 27, Somerset, KY 42501. Phone: 606-678-9215. Fax: 606-679-7111. Web Site: http://www.newwavecom.com. Also serves Bronston, Burnside, Eubank, Ferguson, Lincoln County, Mount Vernon, Nancy, Pulaski County, Renfro Valley, Rockcastle County, Science Hill, Sloans Valley, Tateville, Waynesburg & Woodson Bend. ICA: KY0021.
TV Market Ranking: Below 100 (Eubank, Lincoln County, Mount Vernon, Pulaski County (portions), Renfro Valley, Rockcastle County, Science Hill, Sloans Valley, Waynesburg, Woodson Bend); Outside TV Markets (Bronston, Burnside, Ferguson, Nancy, Pulaski County (portions), SOMERSET, Tateville). Franchise award date: N.A. Franchise expiration date: N.A. Began: April 1, 1981.
Channel capacity: N.A. Channels available but not in use: N.A.
Basic Service
Subscribers: 8,977.
Programming (received off-air): WAGV (IND) Harlan; WBIR-TV (NBC) Knoxville; WDKY-TV (FOX) Danville; WKSO-TV (PBS) Somerset; WKYT-TV (CBS, CW) Lexington; WLEX-TV (NBC) Lexington; WLJC-TV (TBN) Beattyville; WTVQ-DT (ABC) Lexington; WUPX-TV (ION) Morehead; WYMT-TV (CBS, CW) Hazard.
Programming (via satellite): C-SPAN; Home Shopping Network; INSP; QVC; ShopNBC; Trinity Broadcasting Network; TV Guide Network; WGN America.
Fee: $50.00 installation; $16.94 monthly.
Expanded Basic Service 1
Subscribers: 8,827.
Programming (via satellite): ABC Family Channel; AMC; Animal Planet; Arts & Entertainment; BET Networks; Bravo; Cartoon Network; CNBC; CNN; Comcast Sports Net Southeast; Comcast/Charter Sports Southeast (CSS); Comedy Central; Country Music TV; C-SPAN 2; Discovery Channel; Disney Channel; E! Entertainment Television; ESPN; ESPN 2; Food Network; Fox News Channel; Fox Sports Net Ohio; FX; G4; Golf Channel; Hallmark Channel; Headline News; HGTV; History Channel; Lifetime; MSNBC; MTV; National Geographic Channel; Nickelodeon; Outdoor Channel; Oxygen; SoapNet; Speed Channel; Spike TV; Syfy; TBS Superstation; The Learning Channel; Toon Disney; Travel Channel; truTV; Turner Classic Movies; Turner Network TV; TV Land; USA Network; Versus; VH1; Weather Channel.
Digital Basic Service
Subscribers: N.A.
Programming (received off-air): WDKY-TV (FOX) Danville; WKYT-TV (CBS, CW) Lexington; WLEX-TV (NBC) Lexington; WTVQ-DT (ABC) Lexington.
Programming (via satellite): Arts & Entertainment HD; BBC America; Bio; Bloomberg Television; CMT Pure Country; Discovery en Espanol; Discovery HD Theater; Discovery Health Channel; Discovery Kids Channel; Discovery Military Channel; Discovery Planet Green; Do-It-Yourself; ESPN 2 HD; ESPN Classic Sports; ESPN HD; ESPN U; ESPNews; FitTV; Fox College Sports Atlantic; Fox College Sports Central; Fox College Sports Pacific; Fox Movie Channel; Great American Country; HDNet; HDNet Movies; History Channel HD; History Channel International; ID Investigation Discovery; Jewelry Television; Lifetime Movie Network; Lifetime Real Women; MTV Hits; MTV Jams; MTV Tres; MTV2; Music Choice; Nick Jr.; Nick Too; NickToons TV; Palladia; PBS HD; Science Channel; TeenNick; Turner Network TV HD; Universal HD; Versus HD; VH1 Classic; VH1 Soul; Weather Channel HD.
Digital Pay Service 1
Pay Units: 342.
Programming (via satellite): Cinemax (multiplexed); Cinemax HD; HBO HD; Starz HDTV.
Fee: $7.50 installation; $10.95 monthly.
Digital Pay Service 2
Pay Units: 863.
Programming (via satellite): HBO (multiplexed).
Fee: $11.95 monthly.
Digital Pay Service 3
Pay Units: 649.
Programming (via satellite): Flix; Showtime (multiplexed); The Movie Channel (multiplexed).
Fee: $10.95 monthly.
Digital Pay Service 4
Pay Units: N.A.
Programming (via satellite): Encore (multiplexed); Starz (multiplexed).
Video-On-Demand: No
Pay-Per-View
iN DEMAND (delivered digitally); Penthouse TV (delivered digitally); Ten Clips (delivered digitally); Ten Blue (delivered digitally); Ten Blox (delivered digitally); ESPN Gameplan (delivered digitally).
Internet Service
Operational: Yes.
Fee: $40.00 installation; $31.99 monthly.
Telephone Service
Digital: Operational
Fee: $24.99 monthly
Miles of Plant: 356.0 (coaxial); None (fiber optic). Homes passed: 11,483. Total homes in franchised area: 14,700.
General Manager: Mark Bookout. Technical Operations Manager: Lynn McMahan.
Ownership: NewWave Communications (MSO).

STANFORD—Now served by HARRODSBURG, KY [KY0231]. ICA: KY0283.

STANTON—Windjammer Cable, 4400 PGA Blvd, Ste 902, Palm Beach Gardens, FL 33410. Phones: 877-450-5558; 561-775-1208. Fax: 561-775-7811. Web Site: http://www.windjammercable.com. Also serves Powell County (unincorporated areas). ICA: KY0095.
TV Market Ranking: Below 100 (Powell County (unincorporated areas), STANTON). Franchise award date: N.A. Franchise expiration date: N.A. Began: January 1, 1970.
Channel capacity: 42 (not 2-way capable). Channels available but not in use: 8.
Basic Service
Subscribers: 1,064.
Programming (received off-air): WDKY-TV (FOX) Danville; WKLE (PBS) Lexington; WKYT-TV (CBS, CW) Lexington; WLEX-TV (NBC) Lexington; WLJC-TV (TBN) Beattyville; WTVQ-DT (ABC) Lexington; WUPX-TV (ION) Morehead; WXIX-TV (FOX) Newport.
Programming (via satellite): QVC; TBS Superstation; TV Land; WGN America.
Fee: $39.95 installation; $16.63 monthly.
Expanded Basic Service 1
Subscribers: 1,049.
Programming (via satellite): ABC Family Channel; AMC; Arts & Entertainment; CNN; Country Music TV; C-SPAN; Discovery Channel; Disney Channel; E! Entertainment Television; ESPN; ESPN 2; Fox News Channel; FX; Headline News; Lifetime; MTV; Nickelodeon; Spike TV; Syfy; The Learning Channel; Turner Network TV; USA Network; Weather Channel.
Fee: $23.20 monthly.
Digital Basic Service
Subscribers: N.A.
Programming (via satellite): BBC America; Bio; Bravo; CMT Pure Country; Discovery Digital Networks; ESPN Classic Sports; Fox Soccer; GAS; Golf Channel; GSN; HGTV; History Channel; History Channel International; Independent Film Channel; MTV Networks Digital Suite; National Geographic Channel; Nick Jr.; Speed Channel; Style Network; Turner Classic Movies; Versus; WE tv.
Fee: $10.95 monthly.
Digital Pay Service 1
Pay Units: N.A.
Programming (via satellite): Cinemax (multiplexed); Encore; HBO (multiplexed); Showtime (multiplexed); Starz (multiplexed); The Movie Channel (multiplexed).
Fee: $15.95 monthly (each).
Video-On-Demand: No

Pay-Per-View
iN DEMAND (delivered digitally); Playboy TV (delivered digitally).
Internet Service
Operational: No.
Telephone Service
None
Miles of Plant: 102.0 (coaxial); None (fiber optic). Homes passed: 2,278.
General Manager: Timothy Evard. Operations Director: Belinda Graham. Engineering Director: Mike Earehart. Finance & Accounting Director: Cindy Johnson.
City fee: 3% of gross.
Ownership: Windjammer Communications LLC (MSO).

STURGIS—Now served by OWENSBORO, KY [KY0004]. ICA: KY0102.

SUMMER SHADE—Mediacom, 90 Main St, Benton, KY 42025-1132. Phones: 417-875-5560 (Springfield regional office); 270-527-9939. Fax: 270-527-0813. Web Site: http://www.mediacomcable.com. Also serves Barren County (portions) & Edmonton. ICA: KY0103.
TV Market Ranking: Below 100 (Barren County (portions), EDMONTON); Outside TV Markets (Summer Shade). Franchise award date: N.A. Franchise expiration date: N.A. Began: N.A.
Channel capacity: N.A. Channels available but not in use: N.A.
Basic Service
Subscribers: 1,315.
Programming (received off-air): WAVE (NBC) Louisville; WBKO (ABC, CW) Bowling Green; WDRB (FOX) Louisville; WKSO-TV (PBS) Somerset; WKYU-TV (PBS) Bowling Green; WLKY-TV (CBS) Louisville; WNKY (CBS, NBC) Bowling Green; WPBM-LP Scottsville; WSMV-TV (NBC, TMO) Nashville; WTVF (CBS) Nashville.
Programming (via satellite): Headline News; TV Guide Network; WGN America.
Fee: $36.95 installation; $19.32 monthly.
Expanded Basic Service 1
Subscribers: N.A.
Programming (via satellite): ABC Family Channel; AMC; AmericanLife TV Network; Animal Planet; Arts & Entertainment; Bravo!; Cartoon Network; CNBC; CNN; Comcast Sports Net Southeast; Comedy Central; Country Music TV; C-SPAN; C-SPAN 2; Discovery Channel; Disney Channel; E! Entertainment Television; ESPN; ESPN 2; FitTV; Food Network; Fox News Channel; Fuse; FX; Great American Country; GRTV Network; Hallmark Channel; Headline News; HGTV; History Channel; Home Shopping Network; INSP; ION Television; Lifetime; MSNBC; MTV; National Geographic Channel; Nickelodeon; Outdoor Channel; QVC; RFD-TV; ShopNBC; SoapNet; Speed Channel; Spike TV; Syfy; TBS Superstation; Telemundo; The Learning Channel; Travel Channel; Trinity Broadcasting Network; Turner Network TV; TV Land; USA Network; VH1; WE tv; Weather Channel.
Digital Basic Service
Subscribers: N.A.
Programming (via satellite): BBC America; Bio; Bloomberg Television; Discovery Digital Networks; DMX Music; Fox Movie Channel; Fox Soccer; Fuse; G4; GAS; Golf Channel; GSN; History Channel International; Independent Film Channel; Lifetime Movie Network; Lime; MTV Networks Digital Suite; Nick Jr.; NickToons TV; Turner Classic Movies; Versus.
Pay Service 1
Pay Units: 234.
Programming (via satellite): Cinemax; Flix; HBO (multiplexed); Showtime (multiplexed); Sundance Channel; The Movie Channel.
Fee: $10.50 monthly.
Digital Pay Service 1
Pay Units: N.A.
Programming (via satellite): Cinemax (multiplexed); Encore (multiplexed); Flix (multiplexed); HBO (multiplexed); Showtime (multiplexed); Starz (multiplexed); Sundance Channel (multiplexed); The Movie Channel (multiplexed).
Video-On-Demand: No
Internet Service
Operational: Yes, DSL only.
Broadband Service: Mediacom High Speed Internet.
Telephone Service
Digital: Operational
Miles of Plant: 67.0 (coaxial); None (fiber optic). Homes passed: 1,375.
Regional Vice President: Bill Copeland. General Manager: Dale Haney. Regional Technical Operations Director: Alan Freedman. Technical Operations Manager: Jeff Brown. Marketing Director: Will Kuebler.; Melanie Westerman.
County fee: 3% of gross.
Ownership: Mediacom LLC (MSO).

SUMMERSVILLE—NewWave Communications. Now served by GREENSBURG, KY [KY0110]. ICA: KY0295.

SYCAMORE CREEK—Inter Mountain Cable Inc., PO Box 159, 20 Laynesville Rd, Harold, KY 41635. Phone: 606-478-9406. Fax: 606-478-1680. Web Site: http://www.imctv.com. ICA: KY0194.
TV Market Ranking: Below 100 (SYCAMORE CREEK). Franchise award date: N.A. Franchise expiration date: N.A. Began: July 1, 1977.
Channel capacity: 12 (operating 2-way). Channels available but not in use: N.A.
Basic Service
Subscribers: 20.
Programming (received off-air): WCHS-TV (ABC) Charleston; WKPI-TV (PBS) Pikeville; WOWK-TV (CBS) Huntington; WSAZ-TV (MNT, NBC) Huntington; WUPX-TV (ION) Morehead; WVAH-TV (FOX) Charleston; WYMT-TV (CBS, CW) Hazard.
Programming (via satellite): CNN; ESPN; TBS Superstation; Trinity Broadcasting Network.
Fee: $14.64 monthly.
Internet Service
Operational: Yes.
Fee: $24.95 monthly.
Telephone Service
Digital: Operational
Fee: $131.93 monthly
Homes passed: 75.
Vice President: Paul D Gearheart. Marketing Manager: R. Heath Wiley.
Ownership: Inter-Mountain Cable Inc.

TAYLORSVILLE—Insight Communications. Now served by LOUISVILLE, KY [KY0001]. ICA: KY0140.

TOLLESBORO—Formerly served by Adelphia Communications. Now served by MOREHEAD, KY [KY0031]. ICA: KY0124.

TOMPKINSVILLE—Mediacom, 90 Main St, Benton, KY 42025-1132. Phones: 417-875-5560 (Springfield regional office); 270-527-9939. Fax: 270-527-0813. Web Site: http://www.mediacomcable.com. Also serves Albany, Clinton County (portions), Gamaliel & Monroe County (portions), KY; Pickett County (portions), TN. ICA: KY0092.
TV Market Ranking: Below 100 (Clinton County (portions) (portions), Pickett County (portions) (portions)); Outside TV Markets (Albany, Clinton County (portions) (portions), Gamaliel, Monroe County (portions), Pickett County (portions) (portions), TOMPKINSVILLE). Franchise award date: N.A. Franchise expiration date: N.A. Began: January 1, 1967.
Channel capacity: N.A. Channels available but not in use: N.A.
Basic Service
Subscribers: 3,855.
Programming (received off-air): WBKO (ABC, CW) Bowling Green; WKRN-TV (ABC) Nashville; WKSO-TV (PBS) Somerset; WKYT-TV (CBS, CW) Lexington; WKYU-TV (PBS) Bowling Green; WLKY-TV (CBS) Louisville; WSMV-TV (NBC, TMO) Nashville; WTVF (CBS) Nashville; WUXP-TV (MNT) Nashville; WZTV (FOX) Nashville; allband FM.
Programming (via satellite): ION Television; TV Guide Network; WGN America; WPBM-LP Scottsville.
Fee: $36.95 installation; $19.20 monthly.
Expanded Basic Service 1
Subscribers: N.A.
Programming (via satellite): ABC Family Channel; AMC; AmericanLife TV Network; Animal Planet; Arts & Entertainment; Bravo; Cartoon Network; CNBC; CNN; Comedy Central; Country Music TV; C-SPAN; C-SPAN 2; Discovery Channel; Disney Channel; E! Entertainment Television; ESPN; ESPN 2; FitTV; Food Network; Fox News Channel; Fox Sports Net; Fuse; FX; Great American Country; GRTV Network; Hallmark Channel; Halogen Network; Headline News; HGTV; History Channel; Home Shopping Network; ION Television; Lifetime; MSNBC; MTV; National Geographic Channel; Nickelodeon; Outdoor Channel; QVC; RFD-TV; ShopNBC; SoapNet; Speed Channel; Spike TV; Syfy; TBS Superstation; Telemundo; The Learning Channel; Travel Channel; Trinity Broadcasting Network; truTV; Turner Network TV; TV Land; USA Network; VH1; WE tv; Weather Channel.
Digital Basic Service
Subscribers: N.A.
Programming (via satellite): Barker; BBC America; Bio; Bloomberg Television; CNN HD; Discovery HD Theater; Discovery Health Channel; Discovery Home Channel; Discovery Kids Channel; Discovery Military Channel; ESPN 2 HD; ESPN HD; ESPNews; Fox Movie Channel; Fox Soccer; Fuse; G4; Golf Channel; GSN; HDNet; HDNet Movies; History Channel International; ID Investigation Discovery; Independent Film Channel; Lifetime Movie Network; MTV Hits; MTV2; Nick Jr.; NickToons TV; Science Channel; Sleuth; Style Network; TBS in HD; TeenNick; Turner Classic Movies; Turner Network TV HD; TVG Network; Universal HD; Versus; VH1 Classic.
Digital Pay Service 1
Pay Units: N.A.
Programming (via satellite): Cinemax (multiplexed); Encore (multiplexed); Flix; HBO (multiplexed); Showtime (multiplexed); Showtime HD; Starz (multiplexed); Starz HDTV; Sundance Channel; The Movie Channel (multiplexed).
Video-On-Demand: No
Pay-Per-View
iN DEMAND (delivered digitally); Playgirl TV (delivered digitally); Ten Clips (delivered digitally); Penthouse TV (delivered digitally); Ten Blox.
Internet Service
Operational: Yes.
Broadband Service: Mediacom High Speed Internet.
Telephone Service
Analog: Not Operational
Digital: Operational
Miles of Plant: 79.0 (coaxial); None (fiber optic).
Regional Vice President: Bill Copeland. General Manager: Dale Haney. Regional Technical Operations Director: Alan Freedman. Marketing Director: Will Kuebler. Marketing Manager: Melanie Westerman.
City fee: 5% of gross.
Ownership: Mediacom LLC (MSO).

TRENTON—Mediacom, 90 Main St, Benton, KY 42025-1132. Phone: 270-527-9939. Fax: 270-527-0813. Web Site: http://www.mediacomcable.com. Also serves Christian County, Elkton, Guthrie, Hopkinsville, Oak Grove, Pembroke & Todd County, KY; Dover & Stewart County, TN. ICA: KY0101.
TV Market Ranking: Below 100 (Christian County (portions), Hopkinsville, Todd County (portions)); Outside TV Markets (Christian County (portions), Dover, Elkton, Guthrie, Oak Grove, Pembroke, Stewart County, Todd County (portions), TRENTON). Franchise award date: N.A. Franchise expiration date: N.A. Began: September 1, 1983.
Channel capacity: N.A. Channels available but not in use: N.A.
Basic Service
Subscribers: 3,970.
Programming (received off-air): WBKO (ABC, CW) Bowling Green; WKAG-CA Hopkinsville; WKMA-TV (PBS) Madisonville; WKRN-TV (ABC) Nashville; WNPT (PBS) Nashville; WSMV-TV (NBC, TMO) Nashville; WTVF (CBS) Nashville.
Programming (via satellite): AMC; Home Shopping Network; TV Guide Network; WGN America.
Fee: $36.95 installation; $19.25 monthly.
Expanded Basic Service 1
Subscribers: N.A.
Programming (via satellite): ABC Family Channel; Animal Planet; BET Networks; Cartoon Network; CNBC; CNN; Comedy Central; C-SPAN; Discovery Channel; E! Entertainment Television; ESPN; ESPN 2; ESPN Classic Sports; FitTV; Food Network; Fox News Channel; Fox Sports Net; FX; Hallmark Channel; HGTV; History Channel; INSP; Lifetime; MSNBC; MTV; Nickelodeon; Outdoor Channel; QVC; Speed Channel; Spike TV; Syfy; TBS Superstation; Travel Channel; Trinity Broadcasting Network; Turner Network TV; TV Land; Univision; USA Network; WE tv; Weather Channel.
Digital Basic Service
Subscribers: N.A.
Programming (received off-air): WSIL-TV (ABC) Harrisburg.
Programming (via satellite): BBC America; CCTV-9 (CCTV International); College Sports Television; Discovery Health Channel; Discovery Kids Channel; ESPN 2 HD; ESPN U; ESPNews; Fox Soccer; Golf Channel; GSN; Independent Film Channel; Science Channel; Sleuth; Turner Classic Movies; TVG Network; Versus.

Digital Pay Service 1
Pay Units: N.A.
Programming (via satellite): Cinemax (multiplexed); Encore (multiplexed); HBO (multiplexed); Showtime (multiplexed); Starz (multiplexed); The Movie Channel (multiplexed).
Video-On-Demand: No
Pay-Per-View
Hot Choice (delivered digitally); Playboy TV (delivered digitally); Ten Clips (delivered digitally); Penthouse TV (delivered digitally).
Internet Service
Operational: Yes.
Broadband Service: Mediacom High Speed Internet.
Telephone Service
Analog: Not Operational
Digital: Operational
Miles of Plant: 187.0 (coaxial); None (fiber optic). Homes passed: 4,781.
Regional Vice President: Bill Copeland. General Manager: Dale Haney. Regional Technical Operations Director: Alan Freedman. Marketing Director: Will Kuebler. Marketing Manager: Melanie Westerman.
City fee: 3% of basic.
Ownership: Mediacom LLC (MSO).

TUTOR KEY—P & W TV Cable, 109 Depot Rd, Paintsville, KY 41240-1346. Phone: 606-789-7603. Fax: 606-789-3391. ICA: KY0319.
TV Market Ranking: Outside TV Markets (TUTOR KEY).
Channel capacity: 36 (not 2-way capable). Channels available but not in use: N.A.
Basic Service
Subscribers: 90.
Programming (received off-air): WCHS-TV (ABC) Charleston; WKPI-TV (PBS) Pikeville; WLPX-TV (ION) Charleston; WOWK-TV (CBS) Huntington; WPBY-TV (PBS) Huntington; WQCW (CW) Portsmouth; WSAZ-TV (MNT, NBC) Huntington; WVAH-TV (FOX) Charleston; WYMT-TV (CBS, CW) Hazard.
Programming (via satellite): ABC Family Channel; Animal Planet; Arts & Entertainment; Cartoon Network; CNN; Country Music TV; C-SPAN; Discovery Channel; ESPN; HGTV; Home Shopping Network; Lifetime; Outdoor Channel; Spike TV; Syfy; TBS Superstation; The Learning Channel; Trinity Broadcasting Network; Turner Classic Movies; Turner Network TV; TV Land; USA Network; WGN America.
Fee: $29.00 monthly.
Pay Service 1
Pay Units: N.A.
Programming (via satellite): The Movie Channel.
Fee: $6.00 monthly.
Video-On-Demand: No
Internet Service
Operational: No.
Telephone Service
None
Office Manager: Debbie Burton.
Ownership: P & W TV Cable Systems Inc.

UPTON/SONORA—Mediacom. Now served by MUNFORDVILLE, KY [KY0086]. ICA: KY0048.

VAN LEAR—Big Sandy Broadband, PO Box 586, 510 Rt 302 W, West Van Lear, KY 41268-0586. Phones: 888-789-3455; 606-789-3455. Fax: 606-220-0405. E-mail: info@bigsandybb.com. Web Site: http://www.bigsandybb.com. Also serves Auxier, Boons Camp, Branham Village, Denver, East Point, Hagerhill, Meally, West Van Lear & Williamsport. ICA: KY0070.
TV Market Ranking: Outside TV Markets (Auxier, Boons Camp, Branham Village, Denver, East Point, Hagerhill, Meally, VAN LEAR, West Van Lear, Williamsport). Franchise award date: N.A. Franchise expiration date: N.A. Began: March 5, 1960.
Channel capacity: 52 (operating 2-way). Channels available but not in use: 20.
Basic Service
Subscribers: 2,850.
Programming (received off-air): WCHS-TV (ABC) Charleston; WKPI-TV (PBS) Pikeville; WOWK-TV (CBS) Huntington; WPBY-TV (PBS) Huntington; WQCW (CW) Portsmouth; WSAZ-TV (MNT, NBC) Huntington; WVAH-TV (FOX) Charleston; WYMT-TV (CBS, CW) Hazard.
Programming (via satellite): Home Shopping Network; ION Television; QVC; Trinity Broadcasting Network; WGN America.
Current originations: Leased Access.
Fee: $30.00 installation; $16.95 monthly.
Expanded Basic Service 1
Subscribers: 2,475.
Programming (via satellite): ABC Family Channel; AMC; Animal Planet; Arts & Entertainment; Cartoon Network; CNN; Comedy Central; Country Music TV; C-SPAN; Discovery Channel; Disney Channel; E! Entertainment Television; ESPN; ESPN 2; Food Network; Fox News Channel; Fox Sports Net; FX; G4; Hallmark Channel; HGTV; History Channel; Lifetime; MTV; National Geographic Channel; Nickelodeon; Outdoor Channel; Speed Channel; Spike TV; Syfy; TBS Superstation; The Learning Channel; truTV; Turner Classic Movies; Turner Network TV; TV Guide Network; TV Land; USA Network; VH1; WE tv; Weather Channel.
Fee: $30.00 installation; $41.95 monthly.
Digital Basic Service
Subscribers: 245.
Programming (received off-air): WCHS-TV (ABC) Charleston; WSAZ-TV (MNT, NBC) Huntington; WVAH-TV (FOX) Charleston; WYMT-TV (CBS, CW) Hazard.
Programming (via satellite): BBC America; Discovery Kids Channel; Discovery Military Channel; Discovery Planet Green; DMX Music; ID Investigation Discovery; PBS HD; Science Channel.
Fee: $7.50 installation; $51.95 monthly.
Pay Service 1
Pay Units: 575.
Programming (via satellite): HBO.
Fee: $7.50 installation; $12.75 monthly.
Pay Service 2
Pay Units: N.A.
Programming (via satellite): Encore; Showtime.
Digital Pay Service 1
Pay Units: N.A.
Programming (via satellite): Encore (multiplexed); HBO (multiplexed); Showtime (multiplexed); Starz (multiplexed); The Movie Channel (multiplexed).
Video-On-Demand: No
Pay-Per-View
Addressable homes: 245.
Playboy TV.
Internet Service
Operational: Yes. Began: March 1, 2003.
Subscribers: 1,200.
Broadband Service: In-house.
Fee: $24.95-$54.95 monthly; $4.00 modem lease.
Telephone Service
Analog: Not Operational
Digital: Operational
Subscribers: 250.
Fee: $24.95-$39.95 monthly
Miles of Plant: 120.0 (coaxial); None (fiber optic). Homes passed: 4,000.
Manager: Paul David Butcher. Chief Technician: Marty Wright.
City fee: None.
Ownership: S Corporation.

VANCEBURG—Time Warner Cable, 1266 Dublin Rd, Columbus, OH 43215-1008. Phones: 888-882-4604; 614-431-1280. Fax: 614-481-5052. Web Site: http://www.timewarnercable.com/midohio. Also serves Garrison & Quincy. ICA: KY0286.
TV Market Ranking: Below 100 (Garrison, Quincy, VANCEBURG). Franchise award date: N.A. Franchise expiration date: N.A. Began: January 1, 1965.
Channel capacity: N.A. Channels available but not in use: N.A.
Basic Service
Subscribers: 2,220.
Programming (received off-air): WCPO-TV (ABC) Cincinnati; WKMR (PBS) Morehead; WKYT-TV (CBS, CW) Lexington; WOWK-TV (CBS) Huntington; WQCW (CW) Portsmouth; WSAZ-TV (MNT, NBC) Huntington; WTVQ-DT (ABC) Lexington; WVAH-TV (FOX) Charleston; WXIX-TV (FOX) Newport.
Programming (via satellite): ABC Family Channel; American Movie Classics; Arts & Entertainment; Country Music TV; Discovery Channel; ESPN; ESPN 2; Food Network; Fox News Channel; FX; Headline News; HGTV; Lifetime; Nickelodeon; QVC; Spike TV; Trinity Broadcasting Network; Turner Network TV; USA Network; VH1; Weather Channel; WGN America.
Fee: $23.74 installation; $18.35 monthly.
Expanded Basic Service 1
Subscribers: N.A.
Programming (via satellite): CNN; Disney Channel; TBS Superstation.
Fee: $3.75 monthly.
Pay Service 1
Pay Units: 385.
Programming (via satellite): Cinemax; HBO.
Fee: $11.95 monthly.
Video-On-Demand: No
Internet Service
Operational: Yes.
Broadband Service: RoadRunner.
Fee: $24.95 monthly.
Telephone Service
Digital: Operational
Fee: $24.99 monthly
Miles of Plant: 19.0 (coaxial); None (fiber optic). Homes passed: 4,300. Total homes in franchised area: 4,300.
President: Rhonda Fraas. Vice President & General Manager: David Kreiman. Vice President, Engineering: Randy Hall. Technical Operations Director: Jim Cavender. Vice President, Marketing: Mark Psigoda. Vice President, Government & Public Affairs: Mary Jo Green. Government Affairs Director: Steve Cuckler.
City fee: 3% of gross.
Ownership: Time Warner Cable (MSO).

VANCLEVE—TV Service Inc., PO Box 1410, Hindman, KY 41822-1410. Phones: 606-785-3450; 606-633-0778. Fax: 606-785-3110. E-mail: tvs@tvscable.com. Web Site: http://www.tvscable.com. Also serves Lee City. ICA: KY0325.
TV Market Ranking: Below 100 (Lee City, VANCLEVE).
Channel capacity: 60 (not 2-way capable). Channels available but not in use: N.A.
Basic Service
Subscribers: 225.
Programming (received off-air): WDKY-TV (FOX) Danville; WKPC-TV (PBS) Louisville; WKYT-TV (CBS, CW) Lexington; WLEX-TV (NBC) Lexington; WLFG (IND) Grundy; WLJC-TV (TBN) Beattyville; WTVQ-DT (ABC) Lexington; WUPX-TV (ION) Morehead; WYMT-TV (CBS, CW) Hazard.
Programming (via satellite): WGN America.
Current originations: Educational Access.
Fee: $19.58 monthly.
Expanded Basic Service 1
Subscribers: N.A.
Programming (via satellite): ABC Family Channel; Animal Planet; Arts & Entertainment; Bloomberg Television; Cartoon Network; CNN; Comedy Central; C-SPAN; CW+; Discovery Channel; E! Entertainment Television; ESPN; ESPN 2; Food Network; Fox News Channel; FX; G4; Great American Country; Hallmark Channel; Headline News; HGTV; History Channel; Home Shopping Network; HorseRacing TV; Lifetime; MTV; National Geographic Channel; Nickelodeon; Outdoor Channel; QVC; SoapNet; Speed Channel; Spike TV; Syfy; TBS Superstation; The Learning Channel; Travel Channel; truTV; Turner Classic Movies; Turner Network TV; TV Land; USA Network; VH1; Weather Channel.
Fee: $49.95 monthly.
Digital Basic Service
Subscribers: N.A.
Programming (via satellite): AmericanLife TV Network; BBC America; Bio; Black Family Channel; Church Channel; CMT Pure Country; Daystar TV Network; Discovery Digital Networks; DMX Music; ESPNews; FSN Digital Atlantic; FSN Digital Central; FSN Digital Pacific; Fuse; G4; GAS; Golf Channel; GSN; Halogen Network; History Channel International; Independent Film Channel; JCTV; Lifetime Movie Network; MTV Networks Digital Suite; Nick Jr.; NickToons TV; RFD-TV; ShopNBC; Sleuth; Speed Channel; Style Network; The Word Network; Toon Disney; Trinity Broadcasting Network; Versus; WE tv.
Fee: $11.25 monthly.
Pay Service 1
Pay Units: N.A.
Programming (via satellite): HBO.
Digital Pay Service 1
Pay Units: N.A.
Programming (via satellite): Cinemax (multiplexed); Encore (multiplexed); Flix; HBO (multiplexed); Showtime (multiplexed); Starz (multiplexed); Sundance Channel; The Movie Channel (multiplexed).
Video-On-Demand: No

Pay-Per-View
iN DEMAND (delivered digitally); Playboy TV (delivered digitally); Fresh (delivered digitally).
Internet Service
Operational: Yes.
Fee: $29.95-$79.95 monthly.
Telephone Service
Digital: Operational
Miles of Plant: 28.0 (coaxial); 12.0 (fiber optic).
General Manager: Archie W. Everage. Assistant Manager: Kenny Salmons. Program Director: Betty Thomas. Chief Technician: Tony Everage.
Ownership: TV Service Inc. (MSO).

VARNEY—Inter Mountain Cable Inc., PO Box 159, 20 Laynesville Rd, Harold, KY 41635. Phones: 866-917-4688; 606-478-9406. Fax: 606-478-1680. Web Site: http://www.imctv.com. Also serves Johnny Young Branch, Robinette Knob & Rockhouse. ICA: KY0178.
TV Market Ranking: Below 100 (Rockhouse, VARNEY); Outside TV Markets (Johnny Young Branch, Robinette Knob). Franchise award date: N.A. Franchise expiration date: N.A. Began: N.A.
Channel capacity: 37 (operating 2-way). Channels available but not in use: 4.
Basic Service
Subscribers: 99.
Programming (received off-air): WCHS-TV (ABC) Charleston; WKPI-TV (PBS) Pikeville; WLJC-TV (TBN) Beattyville; WOWK-TV (CBS) Huntington; WQCW (CW) Portsmouth; WSAZ-TV (MNT, NBC) Huntington; WUPX-TV (ION) Morehead; WVAH-TV (FOX) Charleston; WYMT-TV (CBS, CW) Hazard.
Programming (via satellite): QVC; ShopNBC; TV Guide Network; WGN America.
Fee: $27.68 installation; $18.95 monthly; $.73 converter.
Expanded Basic Service 1
Subscribers: N.A.
Programming (via satellite): ABC Family Channel; AMC; Animal Planet; Bravo; Cartoon Network; CNBC; CNN; Comcast Sports Net Southeast; Comedy Central; Country Music TV; C-SPAN; Discovery Channel; Disney Channel; E! Entertainment Television; ESPN; ESPN 2; ESPN Classic Sports; Food Network; Fox News Channel; FX; Great American Country; GSN; Hallmark Channel; HGTV; History Channel; Home Shopping Network; JCTV; Lifetime; MSNBC; MTV; MyNetworkTV Inc.; National Geographic Channel; NFL Network; Nickelodeon; Outdoor Channel; SoapNet; Syfy; TBS Superstation; The Learning Channel; The Sportsman Channel; Travel Channel; truTV; Turner Network TV; TV Land; TVG Network; USA Network; VH1; Weather Channel.
Fee: $11.95 monthly.
Digital Basic Service
Subscribers: N.A.
Programming (received off-air): WCHS-TV (ABC) Charleston; WSAZ-TV (MNT, NBC) Huntington; WVAH-TV (FOX) Charleston; WYMT-TV (CBS, CW) Hazard.
Programming (via satellite): American-Life TV Network; Anime Network; AZ TV; BBC America; Bio; Blackbelt TV; Bloomberg Television; Bravo; Church Channel; CMT Pure Country; Current; Daystar TV Network; Discovery Digital Networks; Discovery HD Theater; DMX Music; ESPN HD; ESPNews; FitTV; Fox College Sports Atlantic; Fox College Sports Central; Fox College Sports Pacific; Fox Movie Channel; Fox Soccer; Fuse; G4; GAS; Golf Channel; Gospel Music Channel; Halogen Network; HDNet; HDNet Movies; History Channel International; Independent Film Channel; Lifetime Movie Network; Military History Channel; MTV Networks Digital Suite; Nick Jr.; NickToons TV; Outdoor Channel; Ovation; Sleuth; Speed Channel; Style Network; The Word Network; Toon Disney; Trinity Broadcasting Network; Turner Classic Movies; TV One; Universal HD; Versus; WE tv.
Fee: $14.95 monthly.
Digital Pay Service 1
Pay Units: N.A.
Programming (via satellite): Canales N; Cinemax (multiplexed); Encore (multiplexed); Flix; HBO (multiplexed); Showtime (multiplexed); Starz (multiplexed); Sundance Channel; The Movie Channel (multiplexed).
Fee: $3.95 monthly (Canales), $7.95monthly (Cinemax), $11.95 monthly (Showtime/TMC), $12.95 monthly (HBO), $13.95 monthly (Starz/ Encore).
Video-On-Demand: No
Pay-Per-View
iN DEMAND (delivered digitally); Hot Choice (delivered digitally); Playboy TV (delivered digitally); Fresh (delivered digitally); Club Jenna (delivered digitally).
Internet Service
Operational: Yes.
Fee: $24.95 monthly.
Telephone Service
Digital: Operational
Fee: $131.93 monthly
Miles of Plant: 15.0 (coaxial); None (fiber optic). Homes passed: 260.
Chief Financial Officer: James Campbell. Manager: Paul Douglas Gearheart. Operations Director: John Schmoldt. Chief Engineer: Jefferson Thacker. Customer Service Manager: Rebecca Walters.
Ownership: Inter-Mountain Cable Inc. (MSO).

VERSAILLES—Now served by HARRODSBURG, KY [KY0231]. ICA: KY0040.

WALKERTOWN—Community TV Inc., 364 Riverview Dr, Hazard, KY 41701-1156. Phone: 606-436-4593. Fax: 606-436-4593. ICA: KY0157.
TV Market Ranking: Below 100 (WALKERTOWN). Franchise award date: N.A. Franchise expiration date: N.A. Began: August 27, 1957.
Channel capacity: N.A. Channels available but not in use: N.A.
Basic Service
Subscribers: 436.
Programming (received off-air): WKMR (PBS) Morehead; WKYT-TV (CBS, CW) Lexington; WLEX-TV (NBC) Lexington; WTVQ-DT (ABC) Lexington; WYMT-TV (CBS, CW) Hazard.
Programming (via satellite): Disney Channel.
Fee: $50.00 installation; $25.00 monthly.
Pay Service 1
Pay Units: 20.
Programming (via satellite): HBO.
Fee: $9.00 monthly.
Pay Service 2
Pay Units: 15.
Programming (via satellite): The Movie Channel.
Fee: $7.50 monthly.
Internet Service
Operational: No.
Telephone Service
None
Miles of Plant: 4.0 (coaxial); None (fiber optic). Homes passed: 500.
Manager: Brenda Caudell. Chief Technician: Roy Godsy.
Ownership: Community TV Inc.

WALLINS CREEK—Zito Media, 611 Vader Hill Rd, Coudersport, PA 16915. Phone: 814-260-9575. Web Site: http://www.zitomedia.com. Also serves Coldiron, Dayhoit & Wallins. ICA: KY0317.
TV Market Ranking: Below 100 (Coldiron, Dayhoit, Wallins, WALLINS CREEK). Franchise award date: N.A. Franchise expiration date: N.A. Began: N.A.
Channel capacity: N.A. Channels available but not in use: N.A.
Basic Service
Subscribers: 1,322.
Programming (received off-air): WAGV (IND) Harlan; WATE-TV (ABC) Knoxville; WBIR-TV (NBC) Knoxville; WBXX-TV (CW) Crossville; WDKY-TV (FOX) Danville; WETP-TV (PBS) Sneedville; WKHA (PBS) Hazard; WKYT-TV (CBS, CW) Lexington; WLEX-TV (NBC) Lexington; WYMT-TV (CBS, CW) Hazard.
Programming (via satellite): Home Shopping Network; WGN America.
Fee: $29.95 installation; $19.95 monthly.
Expanded Basic Service 1
Subscribers: N.A.
Programming (via satellite): ABC Family Channel; AMC; Arts & Entertainment; Cartoon Network; CNBC; CNN; Comedy Central; Country Music TV; C-SPAN; Discovery Channel; Disney Channel; E! Entertainment Television; ESPN; ESPN 2; Fox News Channel; FX; G4; Golf Channel; Headline News; HGTV; History Channel; Lifetime; MTV; Nickelodeon; Oxygen; Speed Channel; Spike TV; Syfy; TBS Superstation; The Learning Channel; Trinity Broadcasting Network; Turner Classic Movies; Turner Network TV; TV Land; USA Network; VH1; Weather Channel.
Fee: $17.48 monthly.
Digital Basic Service
Subscribers: N.A.
Programming (via satellite): BBC America; Bio; Bloomberg Television; Discovery Digital Networks; DMX Music; ESPN Classic Sports; ESPNews; FitTV; Fox Movie Channel; Fox Soccer; Fuse; GAS; GSN; History Channel International; Independent Film Channel; Lifetime Movie Network; MTV Networks Digital Suite; Nick Jr.; Nick Too; NickToons TV; Science Television; Sundance Channel; Toon Disney; TV Guide Interactive Inc.; Versus; WE tv.
Digital Pay Service 1
Pay Units: N.A.
Programming (via satellite): Cinemax (multiplexed); Encore; Flix; HBO (multiplexed); Showtime (multiplexed); Starz (multiplexed); The Movie Channel (multiplexed).
Video-On-Demand: No
Pay-Per-View
iN DEMAND (delivered digitally); The Pleasure Network (delivered digitally); Fresh (delivered digitally); Shorteez (delivered digitally); Playboy TV (delivered digitally).
Internet Service
Operational: No.
Telephone Service
None
Miles of Plant: 43.0 (coaxial); None (fiber optic). Homes passed: 1,547.
Public Relations Manager: Mark Laver.
Ownership: Zito Media (MSO).

WANETA—PRTC, PO Box 159, McKee, KY 40447. Phones: 606-593-5000; 606-287-7101. Web Site: http://www.prtcnet.org. ICA: KY5029.
Channel capacity: N.A. Channels available but not in use: N.A.
Internet Service
Operational: No.
Ownership: Peoples Rural Telephone Cooperative.

WARSAW—Insight Communications, 7906 Dixie Hwy, Florence, KY 41042. Phones: 888-735-0300; 859-431-7766; 859-431-0300 (Customer service). Fax: 859-431-3464. Web Site: http://www.myinsight.com. ICA: KY0148.
TV Market Ranking: 17 (WARSAW). Franchise award date: April 6, 1980. Franchise expiration date: N.A. Began: April 6, 1980.
Channel capacity: 80 (operating 2-way). Channels available but not in use: None.
Basic Service
Subscribers: N.A. Included in Covington
Programming (received off-air): WCET (PBS) Cincinnati; WCPO-TV (ABC) Cincinnati; WCVN-TV (PBS) Covington; WKRC-TV (CBS, CW) Cincinnati; WKYT-TV (CBS, CW) Lexington; WLEX-TV (NBC) Lexington; WLWT (NBC) Cincinnati; WPTO (PBS) Oxford; WSTR-TV (MNT) Cincinnati; WTVQ-DT (ABC) Lexington; WXIX-TV (FOX) Newport.
Programming (via satellite): C-SPAN; C-SPAN 2; CW+; QVC; TV Guide Network; WGN America.
Current originations: Government Access; Educational Access; Public Access.
Fee: $35.00 installation; $.67 converter.
Expanded Basic Service 1
Subscribers: 533.
Programming (via satellite): ABC Family Channel; AMC; Animal Planet; Arts & Entertainment; BET Networks; Cartoon Network; CNBC; CNN; Comcast Sports Net Southeast; Comedy Central; Country Music TV; Discovery Channel; Disney Channel; E! Entertainment Television; ESPN; ESPN 2; Eternal Word TV Network; Food Network; Fox News Channel; Fox Sports Net Ohio; FX; Golf Channel; Hallmark Channel; Headline News; HGTV; History Channel; Home Shopping Network; Lifetime; MSNBC; MTV; Nickelodeon; Oxygen; SoapNet; Spike TV; Style Network; Syfy; TBS Superstation; The Learning Channel; Travel Channel; truTV; Turner Network TV; TV Land; Univision; USA Network; VH1; Weather Channel; Weatherscan.
Fee: $40.00 monthly.
Digital Basic Service
Subscribers: N.A. Included in Covington
Programming (received off-air): WCET (PBS) Cincinnati; WCPO-TV (ABC) Cincinnati; WKRC-TV (CBS, CW) Cincinnati; WLWT (NBC) Cincinnati; WXIX-TV (FOX) Newport.
Programming (via satellite): American-Life TV Network; Animal Planet HD; BBC America; Big Ten Network; Bio; Bloomberg Television; Boomerang; Bravo; CBS College Sports Network; CMT Pure Country; Cooking Channel; C-SPAN 3; Discovery Channel HD; Discovery HD Theater; Discovery Health Channel; Discovery Kids Channel; Discovery Military Channel; Discovery Planet Green; DMX Music; Do-It-Yourself; Encore (multiplexed); ESPN 2 HD; ESPN Classic Sports; ESPN HD; ESPN U; ESPNews; FitTV; Fox Movie Channel; Fox Soccer; Fuse; G4; GAS; Great American Country; GSN; Halogen Network; HDNet; HDNet Movies; History

Channel International; HorseRacing TV; ID Investigation Discovery; Independent Film Channel; ION Television; Lifetime Movie Network; Lifetime Real Women; LOGO; MTV Hits; MTV Jams; MTV Tres; MTV2; mtvU; National Geographic Channel; National Geographic Channel HD Network; NFL Network; NFL Network HD; Nick Jr.; Nick Too; NickToons TV; Outdoor Channel; Ovation; Palladia; PBS Kids Sprout; Science Channel; ShopNBC; Si TV; Speed Channel; Style Network; Sundance Channel; TBS in HD; TeenNick; Tennis Channel; TLC HD; Toon Disney; Trinity Broadcasting Network; Turner Classic Movies; Turner Network TV HD; TVG Network; Universal HD; Versus; VH1 Classic; VH1 Soul; WE tv.
Fee: $17.00 monthly.

Digital Pay Service 1
Pay Units: N.A.
Programming (via satellite): Cinemax (multiplexed); Cinemax On Demand; Flix; HBO (multiplexed); HBO HD; HBO Latino; HBO on Broadband; Showtime (multiplexed); Showtime HD; Showtime On Demand; Starz (multiplexed); The Movie Channel (multiplexed); The Movie Channel On Demand.
Fee: $10.00 monthly (Cinemax or Starz), $13.00 monthly (HBO or Showtime/ TMC).

Video-On-Demand: Yes

Pay-Per-View
iN DEMAND (delivered digitally); Spice: Xcess (delivered digitally); Fresh (delivered digitally); Sports PPV (delivered digitally).

Internet Service
Operational: Yes.
Broadband Service: InsightBB.com.
Fee: $99.95 installation; $44.95 monthly; $10.00 modem lease; $140.00 modem purchase.

Telephone Service
None

Total homes in franchised area: 1,328. Homes passed & miles of plant included in Covington

President & Chief Operating Officer: Dinni Jain. Senior Vice President, Operations: John Hutton. District Vice President: Tim Klinefelter. Technical Operations Director: Bill Arnold. Marketing Coordinator: Maggie Woolf.

Franchise fee: 3% of gross.

Ownership: Insight Communications Co. (MSO).

WELCHS CREEK—Windjammer Cable, 4400 PGA Blvd, Ste 902, Palm Beach Gardens, FL 33410. Phones: 877-450-5558; 561-775-1208. Fax: 561-775-7811. Web Site: http://www.windjammercable.com. ICA: KY0192.

TV Market Ranking: Below 100 (WELCHS CREEK). Franchise award date: N.A. Franchise expiration date: N.A. Began: N.A.

Channel capacity: N.A. Channels available but not in use: N.A.

Basic Service
Subscribers: N.A. Included in Owensboro
Programming (received off-air): WAZE-TV (CW) Madisonville; WDRB (FOX) Louisville; WEHT (ABC) Evansville; WEVV-TV (CBS, MNT) Evansville; WFIE (NBC) Evansville; WKOH (PBS) Owensboro; WNIN (PBS) Evansville; WTVW (FOX) Evansville; WYYW-LP Evansville.
Programming (via satellite): ABC Family Channel; AMC; Animal Planet; Arts & Entertainment; BET Networks; Bravo; Cartoon Network; CNBC; CNN; Comcast Sports Net Southeast; Comedy Central; Country Music TV; C-SPAN; C-SPAN 2; Discovery Channel; Disney Channel; E! Entertainment Television; ESPN; ESPN 2; Eternal Word TV Network; Fox News Channel; FX; Golf Channel; Headline News; HGTV; History Channel; Home Shopping Network; Lifetime; MSNBC; MTV; MTV2; Nickelodeon; Oxygen; Product Information Network; QVC; ShopNBC; Spike TV; Syfy; TBS Superstation; The Learning Channel; Travel Channel; Trinity Broadcasting Network; truTV; Turner Network TV; TV Guide Network; TV Land; USA Network; VH1; Weather Channel; WGN America.
Current originations: Government Access; Educational Access; Public Access; Leased Access.
Fee: $39.95 installation; $35.65 monthly.

Digital Basic Service
Subscribers: N.A.
Programming (via satellite): AmericanLife TV Network; BBC America; Black Family Channel; Bloomberg Television; Canales N; Discovery Digital Networks; Do-It-Yourself; ESPN Classic Sports; ESPN U; ESPNews; FitTV; Fox Movie Channel; Fox Soccer; Fuse; G4; GAS; Great American Country; GSN; Halogen Network; Lifetime Movie Network; MTV Networks Digital Suite; Music Choice; National Geographic Channel; Nick Jr.; Nick Too; NickToons TV; SoapNet; Style Network; The Word Network; Turner Classic Movies; TVG Network; WE tv.
Fee: $12.95 monthly.

Digital Expanded Basic Service
Subscribers: N.A.
Programming (via satellite): Bio; Fox College Sports Atlantic; Fox College Sports Central; Fox College Sports Pacific; Fox Reality Channel; Fuel TV; History Channel International; Independent Film Channel; Outdoor Channel; Sundance Channel.

Digital Expanded Basic Service 2
Subscribers: N.A.
Programming (received off-air): WEHT (ABC) Evansville; WNIN (PBS) Evansville.
Programming (via satellite): Discovery HD Theater; ESPN; HDNet; HDNet Movies; INHD (multiplexed).

Digital Pay Service 1
Pay Units: N.A.
Programming (via satellite): Arabic Channel; CCTV-4; Cinemax (multiplexed); Encore (multiplexed); Filipino Channel; Flix (multiplexed); HBO (multiplexed); RAI International; Russian Television Network; Showtime (multiplexed); Starz (multiplexed); The Movie Channel (multiplexed); TV Asia; TV Japan; TV5, La Television International; Zhong Tian Channel.

Digital Pay Service 2
Pay Units: N.A.
Programming (via satellite): Cinemax; HBO; Showtime; Starz HDTV.

Video-On-Demand: No

Pay-Per-View
Movies (delivered digitally); Playboy TV (delivered digitally); Fresh (delivered digitally); Shorteez (delivered digitally); Hot Choice (delivered digitally); Sports PPV (delivered digitally); NHL Center Ice (delivered digitally); MLB Extra Innings (delivered digitally).

Internet Service
Operational: No.

Telephone Service
None

Miles of Plant: 10.0 (coaxial); None (fiber optic). Homes passed included in Owensboro

Ownership: Windjammer Communications LLC (MSO).

WEST LIBERTY—Windjammer Cable, 4400 PGA Blvd, Ste 902, Palm Beach Gardens, FL 33410. Phones: 877-450-5558; 561-775-1208. Fax: 561-775-7811. Web Site: http://www.windjammercable.com. Also serves Cannel City, Malone & Mize. ICA: KY0090.

TV Market Ranking: Below 100 (Cannel City, Malone, Mize, WEST LIBERTY). Franchise award date: N.A. Franchise expiration date: N.A. Began: August 1, 1952.

Channel capacity: 42 (not 2-way capable). Channels available but not in use: 6.

Basic Service
Subscribers: 1,426.
Programming (received off-air): WDKY-TV (FOX) Danville; WKMR (PBS) Morehead; WKYT-TV (CBS, CW) Lexington; WLEX-TV (NBC) Lexington; WSAZ-TV (MNT, NBC) Huntington; WTVQ-DT (ABC) Lexington; WUPX-TV (ION) Morehead; WYMT-TV (CBS, CW) Hazard.
Programming (via satellite): QVC; TBS Superstation; Weather Channel; WGN America.
Fee: $39.95 installation; $19.30 monthly; $2.00 converter.

Expanded Basic Service 1
Subscribers: 1,236.
Programming (via satellite): ABC Family Channel; AMC; Arts & Entertainment; CNN; Country Music TV; C-SPAN; Discovery Channel; Disney Channel; E! Entertainment Television; ESPN; ESPN 2; Fox News Channel; FX; Headline News; Lifetime; Nickelodeon; Spike TV; Syfy; The Learning Channel; Trinity Broadcasting Network; Turner Network TV; USA Network.
Fee: $27.67 monthly.

Digital Basic Service
Subscribers: N.A.
Programming (via satellite): Bio; Black Family Channel; Bravo; Discovery Digital Networks; DMX Music; ESPN Classic Sports; ESPNews; Fox Sports World; FSN Digital Atlantic; FSN Digital Central; FSN Digital Pacific; Fuse; GAS; Golf Channel; Great American Country; HGTV; History Channel; History Channel International; Independent Film Channel; MTV Networks Digital Suite; National Geographic Channel; Nick Jr.; ShopNBC; Speed Channel; Style Network; The Word Network; Turner Classic Movies; Versus; WE tv.
Fee: $55.67 monthly.

Digital Pay Service 1
Pay Units: N.A.
Programming (via satellite): Cinemax (multiplexed); Encore; HBO (multiplexed); Showtime (multiplexed); The Movie Channel (multiplexed).
Fee: $15.95 monthly (each).

Video-On-Demand: No

Pay-Per-View
Playboy TV (delivered digitally).

Internet Service
Operational: No.

Telephone Service
None

Miles of Plant: 79.0 (coaxial); None (fiber optic). Homes passed: 1,699.

General Manager: Timothy Evard. Operations Director: Belinda Graham. Engineering Director: Mike Earehart. Finance & Accounting Director: Cindy Johnson.

City fee: None.

Ownership: Windjammer Communications LLC (MSO).

WHITESBURG—Comcast Cable, 838 Park Ave NE, Norton, VA 24273-1010. Phones: 423-282-1370 (Gray, TN office); 276-679-4001. Fax: 276-679-3431. Web Site: http://www.comcast.com. Also serves Letcher County (portions). ICA: KY0123.

TV Market Ranking: Below 100 (Letcher County (portions), WHITESBURG). Franchise award date: N.A. Franchise expiration date: N.A. Began: October 1, 1952.

Channel capacity: N.A. Channels available but not in use: N.A.

Basic Service
Subscribers: N.A. Included in Greeneville TN
Programming (received off-air): WAPW-CA Abingdon; WCYB-TV (CW, NBC) Bristol; WDBJ (CBS, MNT) Roanoke; WEMT (FOX) Greeneville; WJHL-TV (CBS) Johnson City; WKPT-TV (ABC) Kingsport; WLFG (IND) Grundy; WSBN-TV (PBS) Norton; WYMT-TV (CBS, CW) Hazard; allband FM.
Programming (via satellite): ABC Family Channel; AMC; Animal Planet; Arts & Entertainment; BET Networks; Cartoon Network; CNBC; CNN; Comcast SportsNet Mid-Atlantic; Comcast/Charter Sports Southeast (CSS); Comedy Central; Country Music TV; C-SPAN; CW Television Network; Discovery Channel; Disney Channel; E! Entertainment Television; ESPN; ESPN 2; Food Network; Fox News Channel; FX; Hallmark Channel; Headline News; HGTV; History Channel; Home Shopping Network; ION Television; Lifetime; MSNBC; MTV; Nickelodeon; QVC; Speed Channel; Spike TV; Syfy; TBS Superstation; The Learning Channel; Travel Channel; Trinity Broadcasting Network; truTV; Turner Network TV; TV Guide Network; TV Land; USA Network; VH1; Weather Channel; WGN America.
Current originations: Government Access; Educational Access; Leased Access.
Fee: $16.39 installation; $19.19 monthly.

Digital Basic Service
Subscribers: N.A.
Programming (received off-air): WCYB-TV (CW, NBC) Bristol; WEMT (FOX) Greeneville; WJHL-TV (CBS) Johnson City; WKPT-TV (ABC) Kingsport.
Programming (via satellite): Animal Planet HD; Arts & Entertainment HD; BBC America; Bio; Bloomberg Television; CMT Pure Country; Cooking Channel; C-SPAN 2; C-SPAN 3; Discovery HD Theater; Discovery Health Channel; Discovery Kids Channel; Discovery Military Channel; Discovery Planet Green; Disney XD; Do-It-Yourself; Encore (multiplexed); ESPN 2 HD; ESPN Classic Sports; ESPN HD; ESPNews; FitTV; Flix; Food Network HD; Fox College Sports Atlantic; Fox College Sports Central; Fox College Sports Pacific; Fox Movie Channel; Fox Soccer; G4; Golf Channel; Gospel Music Channel; Great American Country; GSN; Halogen Network; HGTV HD; His-

tory Channel HD; History Channel International; ID Investigation Discovery; Independent Film Channel; INSP; Lifetime Movie Network; MTV Hits; MTV Jams; MTV Tres; MTV2; Music Choice; National Geographic Channel; National Geographic Channel HD Network; Nick Jr.; Nick Too; NickToons TV; Outdoor Channel; Palladia; PBS Kids Sprout; Science Channel; Starz IndiePlex; Starz RetroPlex; Style Network; TeenNick; The Sportsman Channel; The Word Network; Turner Classic Movies; Turner Network TV HD; Universal HD; Versus; Versus HD; VH1 Classic; VH1 Soul; WAM! America's Kidz Network; WE tv.

Digital Pay Service 1

Pay Units: N.A.

Programming (via satellite): Cinemax (multiplexed); HBO (multiplexed); Showtime (multiplexed); Starz (multiplexed); Starz HDTV; The Movie Channel (multiplexed).

Video-On-Demand: No

Pay-Per-View

Movies (delivered digitally); Playboy TV (delivered digitally); Club Jenna (delivered digitally); Fresh (delivered digitally).

Internet Service

Operational: Yes.

Telephone Service

Digital: Planned

Miles of Plant: 26.0 (coaxial); None (fiber optic). Homes passed: 1,198. Total homes in franchised area: 1,198.

Vice President & General Manager: Dave Sanders. Operations Manager: Larry Matthews. Technical Operations Director: Tim Castor. Marketing Manager: Sandra Munsey. Office Manager: Pam Owens.

Ownership: Comcast Cable Communications Inc. (MSO).

WHITESVILLE—Mediacom, 90 Main St, Benton, KY 42025-1132. Phones: 417-875-5560 (Springfield regional office); 270-527-9939. Fax: 270-527-0813. Web Site: http://www.mediacomcable.com. Also serves Daviess County (portions), Fordsville & Ohio County (portions). ICA: KY0290.

TV Market Ranking: Outside TV Markets (Daviess County (portions), Fordsville, Ohio County (portions), WHITESVILLE). Franchise award date: March 15, 1983. Franchise expiration date: N.A. Began: January 1, 1983.

Channel capacity: N.A. Channels available but not in use: N.A.

Basic Service

Subscribers: 627.

Programming (received off-air): WEHT (ABC) Evansville; WEVV-TV (CBS, MNT) Evansville; WFIE (NBC) Evansville; WKOH (PBS) Owensboro; WNIN (PBS) Evansville; WTVW (FOX) Evansville.

Programming (via satellite): ABC Family Channel; AMC; Animal Planet; Arts & Entertainment; Bravo!; Cartoon Network; CNBC; CNN; Comcast Sports Net Southeast; Comedy Central; Country Music TV; C-SPAN; Discovery Channel; Disney Channel; E! Entertainment Television; ESPN; ESPN 2; Eternal Word TV Network; Food Network; Fox News Channel; FX; Great American Country; Hallmark Channel; Headline News; HGTV; History Channel; Lifetime; MSNBC; MTV; National Geographic Channel; Nickelodeon; Outdoor Channel; QVC; Speed Channel; Spike TV; Syfy; TBS Superstation; The Learning Channel; Travel Channel; Trinity Broadcasting Network; Turner Network TV; TV Land; USA Network; VH1; WE tv; Weather Channel; WGN America.

Fee: $29.95 installation; $24.95 monthly; $3.95 converter.

Pay Service 1

Pay Units: 60.

Programming (via satellite): Cinemax.

Fee: $9.00 monthly.

Pay Service 2

Pay Units: 68.

Programming (via satellite): HBO.

Fee: $10.00 monthly.

Pay Service 3

Pay Units: N.A.

Programming (via satellite): Encore; Starz.

Video-On-Demand: No

Internet Service

Operational: No.

Telephone Service

None

Miles of Plant: 44.0 (coaxial); None (fiber optic). Homes passed: 930.

General Manager: Dale Haney. Marketing Director: Will Kuebler. Marketing Manager: Melanie Westerman. Regional Vice President: Bill Copeland. Regional Technical Operations Director: Alan Freedman. Technical Operations Manager: Jeff Brown.

Ownership: Mediacom LLC (MSO).

WHITLEY CITY—Access Cable Television Inc., 302 Enterprise Dr, Somerset, KY 42501. Phone: 606-677-2444. Fax: 606-677-2443. E-mail: cable@accesshsd.net. Also serves Marshes Siding, Pine Knot, Revelo & Stearns. ICA: KY0055.

TV Market Ranking: Below 100 (Marshes Siding, Pine Knot, Revelo, Stearns, WHITLEY CITY). Franchise award date: January 1, 1976. Franchise expiration date: N.A. Began: January 1, 1976.

Channel capacity: 50 (not 2-way capable). Channels available but not in use: None.

Basic Service

Subscribers: 1,824.

Programming (received off-air): WAGV (IND) Harlan; WATE-TV (ABC) Knoxville; WBXX-TV (CW) Crossville; WDKY-TV (FOX) Danville; WKSO-TV (PBS) Somerset; WKYT-TV (CBS, CW) Lexington; WLEX-TV (NBC) Lexington; WTVQ-DT (ABC) Lexington; WVLT-TV (CBS, MNT) Knoxville; WYMT-TV (CBS, CW) Hazard.

Programming (via satellite): AMC; Country Music TV; C-SPAN; Discovery Channel; ESPN; ESPN 2; Headline News; Home Shopping Network; MTV; Nickelodeon; QVC; Spike TV; Syfy; Trinity Broadcasting Network; Weather Channel; WGN America.

Current originations: Public Access.

Fee: $35.00 installation; $17.95 monthly; $3.00 converter; $15.00 additional installation.

Expanded Basic Service 1

Subscribers: 1,495.

Programming (received off-air): MSNBC.

Programming (via satellite): ABC Family Channel; Animal Planet; Arts & Entertainment; Cartoon Network; CNN; Disney Channel; Food Network; Fox News Channel; FX; Hallmark Channel; HGTV; History Channel; Lifetime; Speed Channel; TBS Superstation; The Learning Channel; Turner Network TV; TV Land; USA Network.

Fee: $9.55 monthly.

Pay Service 1

Pay Units: 210.

Programming (via satellite): Cinemax.

Fee: $10.95 monthly.

Pay Service 2

Pay Units: 93.

Programming (via satellite): The Movie Channel.

Fee: $11.95 monthly.

Video-On-Demand: No

Internet Service

Operational: No.

Telephone Service

None

Miles of Plant: 157.0 (coaxial); None (fiber optic). Homes passed: 3,831.

President & General Manager: Roy Baker. Technical Manager: Allen Slavin.

Ownership: Access Cable Television Inc. (MSO).

WICKLIFFE—Galaxy Cablevision, 1718 Barlow Rd, Wickliffe, KY 42087-9253. Phones: 270-335-3881; 800-365-6988. Fax: 270-335-5259. Web Site: http://www.galaxycable.com. Also serves Arlington, Bardwell, Barlow, Carlisle County, Clinton & La Center. ICA: KY0106.

TV Market Ranking: 69 (Arlington, Bardwell, Barlow, Carlisle County, Clinton, La Center, WICKLIFFE). Franchise award date: N.A. Franchise expiration date: N.A. Began: August 1, 1981.

Channel capacity: 116 (operating 2-way). Channels available but not in use: None.

Basic Service

Subscribers: 1,200.

Programming (received off-air): KBSI (FOX) Cape Girardeau; KFVS-TV (CBS, CW) Cape Girardeau; WDKA (MNT) Paducah; WKPD (PBS) Paducah; WPSD-TV (NBC) Paducah; WQWQ-LP (CW) Paducah; WSIL-TV (ABC) Harrisburg.

Programming (via satellite): ABC Family Channel; AMC; Animal Planet; Arts & Entertainment; BET Networks; Cartoon Network; CNBC; CNN; Comedy Central; C-SPAN; Discovery Channel; Disney Channel; ESPN; ESPN 2; Fox News Channel; Fuse; FX; Great American Country; Hallmark Channel; Headline News; HGTV; History Channel; Home Shopping Network; Lifetime; National Geographic Channel; Outdoor Channel; Syfy; TBS Superstation; The Learning Channel; Toon Disney; Trinity Broadcasting Network; Turner Classic Movies; Turner Network TV; USA Network; Weather Channel; WGN America.

Fee: $30.00 installation; $43.50 monthly.

Digital Basic Service

Subscribers: 500.

Programming (via satellite): AmericanLife TV Network; BBC America; Bio; Bloomberg Television; Discovery Digital Networks; DMX Music; E! Entertainment Television; ESPN Classic Sports; ESPNews; FitTV; Fox Sports World; G4; Golf Channel; GSN; Halogen Network; History Channel International; Speed Channel; Style Network; WE tv.

Fee: $12.99 monthly.

Digital Expanded Basic Service

Subscribers: N.A.

Programming (via satellite): DMX Music; Encore; Fox Movie Channel; Lifetime Movie Network.

Fee: $13.95 monthly.

Pay Service 1

Pay Units: N.A.

Programming (via satellite): Cinemax; Encore; HBO; Showtime; The Movie Channel.

Digital Pay Service 1

Pay Units: N.A.

Programming (via satellite): Cinemax (multiplexed); Flix; HBO (multiplexed); Showtime (multiplexed); The Movie Channel (multiplexed).

Fee: $10.00 monthly (each).

Video-On-Demand: Yes

Pay-Per-View

Addressable homes: 268.

ESPN Now (delivered digitally), Fee: $3.99, Addressable: Yes; Hot Choice (delivered digitally); Movies (delivered digitally); Playboy TV (delivered digitally); Fresh (delivered digitally); Shorteez (delivered digitally); sports (delivered digitally); Urban Xtra (delivered digitally).

Internet Service

Operational: Yes.

Subscribers: 465.

Broadband Service: Galaxy Cable Internet.

Fee: $49.95 installation; $44.95 monthly; $5.00 modem lease.

Telephone Service

Digital: Operational

Miles of Plant: 66.0 (coaxial); 55.0 (fiber optic). Homes passed: 3,144.

State Manager: Ward Webb. Operations Manager: Treka Hargrove. Engineer: John Stewart. Technical Manager: Audie Murphy. Customer Service Manager: Malynda Walker.

City fee: 3% of gross.

Ownership: Galaxy Cable Inc. (MSO).

WILLIAMSBURG—NewWave Communications, 5026 S Highway 27, Somerset, KY 42501. Phone: 606-678-9215. Fax: 606-679-7111. Web Site: http://www.newwavecom.com. Also serves Woodbine. ICA: KY0053.

TV Market Ranking: Below 100 (WILLIAMSBURG, Woodbine). Franchise award date: N.A. Franchise expiration date: N.A. Began: May 15, 1966.

Channel capacity: N.A. Channels available but not in use: N.A.

Basic Service

Subscribers: 2,700.

Programming (received off-air): WAGV (IND) Harlan; WATE-TV (ABC) Knoxville; WBIR-TV (NBC) Knoxville; WBXX-TV (CW) Crossville; WDKY-TV (FOX) Danville; WKSO-TV (PBS) Somerset; WKYT-TV (CBS, CW) Lexington; WLEX-TV (NBC) Lexington; WLJC-TV (TBN) Beattyville; WTVQ-DT (ABC) Lexington; WUPX-TV (ION) Morehead; WVTN-LP Corbin; WYMT-TV (CBS, CW) Hazard; allband FM.

Programming (via satellite): Home Shopping Network; QVC; ShopNBC; TV Guide Network; WGN America.

Fee: $33.85 installation; $8.27 monthly.

Expanded Basic Service 1

Subscribers: N.A.

Programming (via satellite): ABC Family Channel; AMC; Animal Planet; Arts & Entertainment; Bravo; Cartoon Network; CNBC; CNN; Comcast Sports Net Southeast; Comcast/Charter Sports Southeast (CSS); Comedy Central; Country Music TV; C-SPAN; C-SPAN 2; Discovery Channel; Disney Channel; E! Entertainment Television; ESPN; ESPN 2; Food Network; Fox News Channel; FX; G4; Golf Channel; Hallmark Channel; Headline News; HGTV; History Channel; INSP; Lifetime; MSNBC; MTV; National Geographic Channel; Nickelodeon; Outdoor Channel; SoapNet; Speed Channel; Spike TV; Style Network; Syfy; TBS Superstation; The Learning Channel; Toon Disney; Travel Channel; Trinity Broadcasting Network; truTV; Turner Classic Movies; Turner Network TV; TV Land; USA Network; Versus; VH1; WE tv; Weather Channel.

Digital Basic Service

Subscribers: N.A.

Programming (received off-air): WKYT-TV (CBS, CW) Lexington; WLEX-TV (NBC) Lexington; WTVQ-DT (ABC) Lexington.

Programming (via satellite): BBC America; Bio; Bloomberg Television; CMT Pure Country; Discovery Digital Networks; Discovery en Espanol; Discovery HD Theater; Do-It-Yourself; ESPN 2 HD; ESPN Classic Sports; ESPN HD; ESPN U; ESPNews; FitTV; Fox College Sports Atlantic; Fox College Sports Central; Fox College Sports Pacific; Fox Movie Channel; Great American Country; HDNet; HDNet Movies; History Channel International; Jewelry Television; Lifetime Movie Network; Lifetime Real Women; Military History Channel; MTV Networks Digital Suite; MTV Tres; Music Choice; Nick Jr.; Nick Too; NickToons TV; Science Channel; TeenNick; Turner Network TV HD; Universal HD.

Digital Pay Service 1

Pay Units: N.A.

Programming (via satellite): Cinemax (multiplexed); Cinemax HD; Encore (multiplexed); Flix; HBO (multiplexed); HBO HD; Showtime (multiplexed); Starz (multiplexed); Starz HDTV; The Movie Channel (multiplexed).

Video-On-Demand: No

Pay-Per-View

iN DEMAND (delivered digitally); Ten Clips (delivered digitally); Ten Blue (delivered digitally); Ten Blox (delivered digitally); ESPN Gameplan (delivered digitally).

Internet Service

Operational: Yes.

Telephone Service

None

Miles of Plant: 105.0 (coaxial); None (fiber optic). Homes passed: 3,657. Total homes in franchised area: 3,657.

General Manager: Mark Bookout. Technical Operations Manager: Lynn McMahan.

Ownership: NewWave Communications (MSO).

WILLIAMSTOWN—Williamstown Cable, PO Box 147, Williamstown, KY 41097-0147. Phone: 859-824-3633. Fax: 859-824-6320. E-mail: wmtwncable@aol.com. ICA: KY0109.

TV Market Ranking: 17 (WILLIAMSTOWN). Franchise award date: N.A. Franchise expiration date: N.A. Began: November 22, 1984.

Channel capacity: N.A. Channels available but not in use: N.A.

Basic Service

Subscribers: 1,074.

Programming (received off-air): WCET (PBS) Cincinnati; WCPO-TV (ABC) Cincinnati; WDRB (FOX) Louisville; WHAS-TV (ABC) Louisville; WKON (PBS) Owenton; WKRC-TV (CBS, CW) Cincinnati; WKYT-TV (CBS, CW) Lexington; WLEX-TV (NBC) Lexington; WLWT (NBC) Cincinnati; WSTR-TV (MNT) Cincinnati; WXIX-TV (FOX) Newport.

Programming (via satellite): ABC Family Channel; AMC; Animal Planet; Arts & Entertainment; Boomerang; Cartoon Network; CNN; Comedy Central; Country Music TV; C-SPAN; CW+; Discovery Channel; Disney Channel; Do-It-Yourself; E! Entertainment Television; ESPN; ESPN 2; ESPN Classic Sports; Eternal Word TV Network; Food Network; Fox News Channel; Fox Sports Net; FX; Golf Channel; Hallmark Channel; Headline News; HGTV; History Channel; Home Shopping Network; ION Television; Lifetime; MTV; National Geographic Channel; NFL Network; Nickelodeon; Outdoor Channel; Oxygen; QVC; RFD-TV; Speed Channel; Spike TV; Syfy; TBS Superstation; The Learning Channel; Toon Disney; Travel Channel; Trinity Broadcasting Network; truTV; Turner Classic Movies; Turner Network TV; TV Guide Network; TV Land; USA Network; VH1; Weather Channel; WGN America; WTVQ-DT (ABC) Lexington.

Current originations: Public Access.

Fee: $30.00 installation; $21.95 monthly; $5.00 converter.

Digital Basic Service

Subscribers: N.A.

Programming (via satellite): BBC America; Bio; CMT Pure Country; Discovery Health Channel; Discovery Home Channel; Discovery Kids Channel; Discovery Military Channel; Encore; ESPNews; FitTV; Fox College Sports Atlantic; Fox College Sports Central; Fox College Sports Pacific; Fox Movie Channel; Fox Soccer; G4; Great American Country; GSN; History Channel International; ID Investigation Discovery; Independent Film Channel; Nick Jr.; NickToons TV; Science Channel; TeenNick; Versus; VH1 Classic; WE tv.

Digital Pay Service 1

Pay Units: N.A.

Programming (via satellite): Cinemax (multiplexed); Flix; HBO (multiplexed); Showtime (multiplexed); Starz; Sundance Channel; The Movie Channel (multiplexed).

Video-On-Demand: Planned

Internet Service

Operational: Yes.

Subscribers: 160.

Fee: $75.00 installation; $39.95 monthly.

Telephone Service

None

Miles of Plant: 35.0 (coaxial); None (fiber optic). Homes passed: 1,500.

Manager: Chuck Hudson. Assistant Manager & Chief Technician: Roy Osborne. Program Director: Tony Penick.

Ownership: City of Williamstown Cable TV.

WILLISBURG—Windjammer Cable, 4400 PGA Blvd, Ste 902, Palm Beach Gardens, FL 33410. Phones: 877-450-5558; 561-775-1208. Fax: 561-775-7811. Web Site: http://www.windjammercable.com. Also serves Chaplin & Mackville. ICA: KY0322.

TV Market Ranking: Below 100 (Chaplin, Mackville, WILLISBURG).

Channel capacity: 31 (not 2-way capable). Channels available but not in use: None.

Basic Service

Subscribers: N.A.

Programming (received off-air): WAVE (NBC) Louisville; WBKI-TV (CW) Campbellsville; WDKY-TV (FOX) Danville; WDRB (FOX) Louisville; WHAS-TV (ABC) Louisville; WKYT-TV (CBS, CW) Lexington; WKZT-TV (PBS) Elizabethtown; WLEX-TV (NBC) Lexington; WLKY-TV (CBS) Louisville; WMYO (MNT) Salem; WUPX-TV (ION) Morehead.

Programming (via satellite): WGN America.

Fee: $16.42 monthly; $39.95 converter.

Expanded Basic Service 1

Subscribers: N.A.

Programming (via satellite): ABC Family Channel; CNN; Country Music TV; Discovery Channel; Disney Channel; ESPN; ESPN 2; Food Network; Fox News Channel; FX; Headline News; Lifetime; Spike TV; TBS Superstation; TV Land; USA Network.

Fee: $14.33 monthly.

Digital Basic Service

Subscribers: N.A.

Programming (via satellite): BBC America; Bravo; Discovery Digital Networks; DMX Music; ESPN Classic Sports; ESPNews; Golf Channel; GSN; HGTV; History Channel; Independent Film Channel; Lifetime Movie Network; Music Choice; Nick Jr.; NickToons TV; Syfy; Versus; WE tv.

Fee: $7.70 monthly.

Digital Pay Service 1

Pay Units: N.A.

Programming (via satellite): Cinemax (multiplexed); Encore (multiplexed); HBO (multiplexed); Showtime (multiplexed); Starz (multiplexed); The Movie Channel (multiplexed).

Fee: $15.95 monthly (each).

Video-On-Demand: No

Pay-Per-View

iN DEMAND (delivered digitally); Playboy TV (delivered digitally); Fresh (delivered digitally).

Internet Service

Operational: No.

Telephone Service

None

Miles of Plant: 305.0 (coaxial); None (fiber optic). Additional miles planned: 40.0 (coaxial). Miles of plant (coax) includes Elizabeth, IN

Ownership: Windjammer Communications LLC (MSO).

WINCHESTER—Now served by RICHMOND, KY [KY0008]. ICA: KY0018.

LOUISIANA

Total Systems: 104
Total Communities Served: 467
Franchises Not Yet Operating: 0
Applications Pending: 0
Communities with Applications: 0
Number of Basic Subscribers: 1,059,942
Number of Expanded Basic Subscribers: 288,763
Number of Pay Units: 304,959

Top 100 Markets Represented: New Orleans (31); Texarkana, TX-Shreveport, LA (58); Baton Rouge (87); Beaumont-Port Arthur, TX (88); Monroe, LA-El Dorado, AR (99).

For a list of cable communities in this section, see the Cable Community Index located in the back of Cable Volume 2. For explanation of terms used in cable system listings, see p. D-11.

ABBEVILLE—Cox Communications. Now served by BATON ROUGE, LA [LA0003]. ICA: LA0018.

ACADIA PARISH (portions)—Formerly served by Almega Cable. No longer in operation. ICA: LA0236.

ANGOLA—Audubon Cablevision Inc., PO Box 847, Saint Francisville, LA 70775-0847. Phone: 225-635-4275. Fax: 225-635-3637. Also serves Louisiana State Penitentiary & West Feliciana Parish (portions). ICA: LA0224.

TV Market Ranking: 87 (Louisiana State Penitentiary, West Feliciana Parish (portions)); Outside TV Markets (ANGOLA). Franchise award date: N.A. Franchise expiration date: N.A. Began: N.A.

Channel capacity: 38 (not 2-way capable). Channels available but not in use: 1.

Basic Service
Subscribers: 50.
Programming (received off-air): WAFB (CBS) Baton Rouge; WBRZ-TV (ABC) Baton Rouge; WGMB-TV (FOX) Baton Rouge; WVLA-TV (NBC) Baton Rouge.
Programming (via satellite): ABC Family Channel; AMC; Animal Planet; Arts & Entertainment; Cartoon Network; CNN; Cornerstone Television; C-SPAN; Discovery Channel; Discovery Health Channel; ESPN; ESPN 2; Fox News Channel; Headline News; History Channel; Lifetime; Nickelodeon; Spike TV; Syfy; TBS Superstation; The Learning Channel; Travel Channel; Trinity Broadcasting Network; Turner Network TV; TV Land; USA Network; WGN America.
Fee: $25.00 installation; $30.75 monthly.

Pay Service 1
Pay Units: N.A.
Programming (via satellite): Showtime; The Movie Channel.
Fee: $10.00 monthly.

Video-On-Demand: No

Internet Service
Operational: No.

Telephone Service
None

Miles of Plant: 5.0 (coaxial); None (fiber optic). Homes passed: 100. Total homes in franchised area: 100.

Chief Technician: David Daigle. Office Manager: Connie Tillman.

Ownership: Bailey Cable TV Inc. (MSO).

ARCADIA—Rapid Cable, 515 E Longview Dr, Arp, TX 75750. Phone: 903-859-6492. Fax: 903-859-3708. Also serves Bienville Parish (portions). ICA: LA0073.

TV Market Ranking: Below 100 (ARCADIA, Bienville Parish (portions)). Franchise award date: May 23, 1979. Franchise expiration date: N.A. Began: January 1, 1981.

Channel capacity: 54 (not 2-way capable). Channels available but not in use: 15.

Basic Service
Subscribers: 696.
Programming (received off-air): KLTM-TV (PBS) Monroe; KMSS-TV (FOX) Shreveport; KNOE-TV (CBS, CW) Monroe; KSLA (CBS) Shreveport; KTAL-TV (NBC) Texarkana; KTBS-TV (ABC) Shreveport; KTVE (NBC) El Dorado.
Programming (via satellite): ABC Family Channel; AMC; BET Networks; CNN; Discovery Channel; ESPN; Headline News; ION Television; MTV; Nickelodeon; QVC; Spike TV; Syfy; Trinity Broadcasting Network; TV Guide Network; WE tv; Weather Channel.
Fee: $54.95 installation; $20.95 monthly.

Expanded Basic Service 1
Subscribers: 663.
Programming (via satellite): Animal Planet; Comcast Sports Net Southwest; Country Music TV; Disney Channel; ESPN 2; Fox News Channel; History Channel; Home Shopping Network; TBS Superstation; truTV; Turner Network TV; USA Network; WGN America.
Fee: $23.10 monthly.

Digital Basic Service
Subscribers: N.A.
Programming (via satellite): BBC America; Bio; Bloomberg Television; Bravo; CMT Pure Country; Current; Discovery Health Channel; Discovery Kids Channel; Discovery Military Channel; Discovery Planet Green; DMX Music; ESPN Classic Sports; FitTV; Fox Movie Channel; Fuse; G4; Golf Channel; GSN; Halogen Network; HGTV; History Channel International; ID Investigation Discovery; Independent Film Channel; Lifetime Movie Network; MTV Hits; MTV2; Nick Jr.; Outdoor Channel; Science Channel; ShopNBC; Speed Channel; Style Network; TeenNick; Toon Disney; Turner Classic Movies; Versus; VH1 Classic; VH1 Soul.

Digital Pay Service 1
Pay Units: 134.
Programming (via satellite): Cinemax (multiplexed).
Fee: $11.95 monthly.

Digital Pay Service 2
Pay Units: 197.
Programming (via satellite): HBO (multiplexed).
Fee: $11.95 monthly.

Digital Pay Service 3
Pay Units: 98.
Programming (via satellite): Showtime (multiplexed).
Fee: $11.95 monthly.

Digital Pay Service 4
Pay Units: 72.
Programming (via satellite): The Movie Channel (multiplexed).
Fee: $11.95 monthly.

Digital Pay Service 5
Pay Units: 72.
Programming (via satellite): Encore (multiplexed).
Fee: $5.95 monthly.

Digital Pay Service 6
Pay Units: N.A.
Programming (via satellite): Flix; Starz (multiplexed).

Video-On-Demand: No

Pay-Per-View
iN DEMAND (delivered digitally); Hot Choice (delivered digitally); Sports PPV (delivered digitally); ESPN Now (delivered digitally); Playboy TV (delivered digitally).

Internet Service
Operational: No.

Telephone Service
None

Miles of Plant: 36.0 (coaxial); None (fiber optic). Homes passed: 1,572.

Regional Manager: Mike Taylor. Chief Technician: Larry Stafford.

Franchise fee: 3% of gross.

Ownership: Rapid Communications LLC (MSO).

BASILE—Rapid Cable, 515 E Longview Dr, Arp, TX 75750. Phone: 903-859-6492. Fax: 903-859-3708. ICA: LA0094.

TV Market Ranking: Outside TV Markets (BASILE). Franchise award date: December 8, 1981. Franchise expiration date: N.A. Began: July 1, 1982.

Channel capacity: N.A. Channels available but not in use: N.A.

Basic Service
Subscribers: 396.
Programming (received off-air): KADN-TV (FOX) Lafayette; KALB-TV (CBS, NBC) Alexandria; KATC (ABC) Lafayette; KLFY-TV (CBS) Lafayette; KLTL-TV (PBS) Lake Charles; KPLC (NBC) Lake Charles.
Programming (via satellite): Eternal Word TV Network; QVC; TBS Superstation; WGN America.
Fee: $54.95 installation; $20.95 monthly.

Expanded Basic Service 1
Subscribers: N.A.
Programming (via satellite): ABC Family Channel; AMC; Animal Planet; Arts & Entertainment; BET Networks; Cartoon Network; CNBC; CNN; Comedy Central; Country Music TV; C-SPAN; Discovery Channel; Disney Channel; E! Entertainment Television; ESPN; ESPN 2; Fox News Channel; Fox Sports Net; G4; Halogen Network; Headline News; HGTV; History Channel; Lifetime; MTV; Nickelodeon; Outdoor Channel; Oxygen; SoapNet; Spike TV; Style Network; Syfy; The Learning Channel; Toon Disney; Travel Channel; Turner Network TV; TV Land; USA Network; VH1; WE tv; Weather Channel.
Fee: $23.10 monthly.

Digital Basic Service
Subscribers: N.A.
Programming (via satellite): AmericanLife TV Network; BBC America; Bio; Bloomberg Television; Bravo; CMT Pure Country; Discovery Health Channel; Discovery Kids Channel; Discovery Military Channel; Discovery Planet Green; DMX Music; FitTV; Fox Movie Channel; Fox Soccer; Fuse; Golf Channel; GSN; Halogen Network; History Channel International; ID Investigation Discovery; Independent Film Channel; Lifetime Movie Network; MTV Hits; MTV2; Nick Jr.; Science Channel; ShopNBC; Speed Channel; TeenNick; Toon Disney; Trinity Broadcasting Network; Turner Classic Movies; Versus; VH1 Classic; VH1 Soul.

Pay Service 1
Pay Units: 116.
Programming (via satellite): HBO.
Fee: $12.95 monthly.

Pay Service 2
Pay Units: 48.
Programming (via satellite): Cinemax.
Fee: $12.95 monthly.

Digital Pay Service 1
Pay Units: N.A.
Programming (via satellite): Cinemax (multiplexed); Encore (multiplexed); Flix; HBO (multiplexed); Showtime (multiplexed); Starz (multiplexed); The Movie Channel (multiplexed).

Video-On-Demand: No

Pay-Per-View
iN DEMAND (delivered digitally); Hot Choice (delivered digitally); Club Jenna (delivered digitally); Playboy TV (delivered digitally).

Internet Service
Operational: No.

Telephone Service
None

Miles of Plant: 15.0 (coaxial); None (fiber optic). Homes passed: 808.

Regional Manager: Mike Taylor. Chief Technician: Larry Stafford.

City fee: 3% of basic.

Ownership: Rapid Communications LLC (MSO).

BASTROP—Suddenlink Communications, 1611 Park Loop Dr, Bastrop, LA 71220-3474. Phone: 318-281-0094. Fax: 318-283-1094. Web Site: http://www.suddenlink.com. Also serves Mer Rouge & Morehouse Parish (portions). ICA: LA0027.

TV Market Ranking: 99 (BASTROP, Mer Rouge, Morehouse Parish (portions)); Outside TV Markets (Morehouse Parish (portions)). Franchise award date: N.A.

Franchise expiration date: N.A. Began: December 1, 1964.
Channel capacity: 60 (operating 2-way). Channels available but not in use: N.A.

Basic Service
Subscribers: 6,614.
Programming (received off-air): KAQY (ABC) Columbia; KARD (FOX) West Monroe; KLTM-TV (PBS) Monroe; KMCT-TV (IND) West Monroe; KNOE-TV (CBS, CW) Monroe; KTVE (NBC) El Dorado.
Programming (via satellite): BET Networks; CNN; Comcast Sports Net Southwest; C-SPAN; ESPN; Headline News; Home Shopping Network; INSP; QVC; Spike TV; TBS Superstation; TV Guide Network; Weather Channel; WGN America.
Fee: $35.84 installation; $17.30 monthly.

Expanded Basic Service 1
Subscribers: 5,160.
Programming (via satellite): ABC Family Channel; AMC; Animal Planet; Arts & Entertainment; Bravo; Cartoon Network; CNBC; Comedy Central; C-SPAN 2; Discovery Channel; Disney Channel; DMX Music; E! Entertainment Television; ESPN 2; Food Network; Fox News Channel; FX; Great American Country; HGTV; History Channel; Lifetime; MSNBC; MTV; Nickelodeon; Oxygen; Speed Channel; Syfy; The Learning Channel; Travel Channel; Turner Network TV; TV Land; USA Network; Versus; VH1.
Fee: $11.65 monthly.

Digital Basic Service
Subscribers: N.A.
Programming (via satellite): BBC America; Bio; Bloomberg Television; Discovery Digital Networks; Encore Action; ESPN Classic Sports; ESPNews; Fox Sports World; G4; Golf Channel; GSN; Hallmark Channel; History Channel International; Independent Film Channel; Lifetime Movie Network; MuchMusic Network; Outdoor Channel; SoapNet; Sundance Channel; Toon Disney; Trinity Broadcasting Network.

Pay Service 1
Pay Units: 622.
Programming (via satellite): Cinemax; Encore; HBO; Showtime; Starz; The Movie Channel.
Fee: $35.00 installation; $10.00 monthly (Cinemax), $12.00 monthly (HBO), $13.50 monthly (Showtime or Encore).

Digital Pay Service 1
Pay Units: N.A.
Programming (via satellite): Cinemax (multiplexed); HBO (multiplexed); Showtime (multiplexed); Starz (multiplexed); The Movie Channel (multiplexed).

Video-On-Demand: No

Pay-Per-View
Playboy TV (delivered digitally); Fresh (delivered digitally); NBA TV (delivered digitally); ESPN Gameplan (delivered digitally); ESPN Now (delivered digitally); iN DEMAND (delivered digitally).

Internet Service
Operational: Yes.
Broadband Service: Cebridge High Speed Cable Internet.
Fee: $45.00 installation; $29.95 monthly.

Telephone Service
Digital: Operational
Fee: $39.95 monthly
Miles of Plant: 200.0 (coaxial); None (fiber optic). Homes passed: 9,510. Total homes in franchised area: 10,715.
Manager: Ron Watters. Chief Technician: Chris Parrott. District Technician: Robert Ingram.
City fee: 3% of gross.
Ownership: Cequel Communications LLC (MSO).

BATON ROUGE—Cox Communications, 7401 Florida Blvd, Baton Rouge, LA 70806-4131. Phones: 225-237-5000; 225-615-1000. Fax: 225-930-2440. E-mail: sharon.kleinpeter@cox.com. Web Site: http://www.cox.com/batonrouge. Also serves Abbeville, Addis, Ascension Parish, Baker, Baldwin, Bayou Pigeon, Bayou Sorrel, Bayou Vista, Breaux Bridge, Broussard, Brusly, Carencro, Carville, Cecelia, Centerville, Central, Charenton, Crowley, Delcambre, Denham Springs, Donaldsonville, Duplessis, Duson, East Baton Rouge Parish, Erath, Erwinville, Franklin, Garden City, Gonzales, Gramercy, Grosse Tete, Henderson, Iberia Parish, Iberville, Iberville Parish, Jeanerette, Kaplan, Lafayette, Lafayette Parish, Loreauville, Lutcher, Maurice, Milton, New Iberia, Parks, Patterson, Plaquemine, Port Allen, Rayne, Rosedale, Scott, Slaughter, Sorrento, St. Gabriel, St. James Parish, St. Martin Parish, St. Martinville, St. Mary Parish, Sunshine, Verdunville, Vermilion Parish, Walker (portions), Watson, West Baton Rouge Parish, White Castle, Youngsville & Zachary. ICA: LA0003.
TV Market Ranking: 87 (Addis, Ascension Parish, Baker, BATON ROUGE, Bayou Pigeon, Bayou Sorrel, Brusly, Carville, Central, Denham Springs, Donaldsonville, Duplessis, East Baton Rouge Parish, Erwinville, Gonzales, Grosse Tete, Iberia Parish (portions), Iberville, Iberville Parish, Jeanerette, Loreauville, New Iberia, Plaquemine, Port Allen, Rosedale, Slaughter, Sorrento, St. Gabriel, St. Martin Parish (portions), Sunshine, Walker (portions), Watson, West Baton Rouge, White Castle, Zachary); Below 100 (Abbeville, Breaux Bridge, Broussard, Carencro, Cecelia, Crowley, Delcambre, Duson, Erath, Henderson, Kaplan, Lafayette, Lafayette Parish, Maurice, Milton, Parks, Rayne, Scott, St. Martinville, Vermilion Parish, Youngsville, Iberia Parish (portions), St. Martin Parish (portions)); Outside TV Markets (Baldwin, Bayou Vista, Centerville, Charenton, Franklin, Garden City, Gramercy, Lutcher, Patterson, St. James, St. Mary Parish, Verdunville). Franchise award date: January 1, 1974. Franchise expiration date: N.A. Began: April 21, 1975.
Channel capacity: N.A. Channels available but not in use: N.A.

Basic Service
Subscribers: 306,708.
Programming (received off-air): KPBN-LP (IND) Baton Rouge; KZUP-CD (IND) Baton Rouge; WAFB (CBS) Baton Rouge; WBRZ-TV (ABC) Baton Rouge; WGMB-TV (FOX) Baton Rouge; WLFT-CA (IND) Baton Rouge; WLPB-TV (PBS) Baton Rouge; WVLA-TV (NBC) Baton Rouge; 14 FMs.
Programming (via satellite): C-SPAN; C-SPAN 2; Discovery Channel; Eternal Word TV Network; Hallmark Channel; Headline News; QVC; Weather Channel; WGN America.
Current originations: Religious Access; Government Access; Educational Access.
Fee: $54.95 installation; $12.97 monthly; $2.00 converter.

Expanded Basic Service 1
Subscribers: 87,390.
Programming (via satellite): ABC Family Channel; AMC; Animal Planet; Arts & Entertainment; BET Networks; Bravo; Cartoon Network; CNBC; CNN; Comcast Sports Net Southwest; Comedy Central; Country Music TV; Discovery Channel; Disney Channel; E! Entertainment Television; ESPN; ESPN 2; Food Network; Fox News Channel; Fox Sports Net; FX; Golf Channel; Great American Country; HGTV; History Channel; Home Shopping Network; Lifetime; MSNBC; MTV; MTV2; Nickelodeon; Oxygen; ShopNBC; Spike TV; Syfy; TBS Superstation; The Learning Channel; Travel Channel; Trinity Broadcasting Network; truTV; Turner Network TV; TV Guide Network; TV Land; USA Network; VH1.
Fee: $26.02 monthly.

Digital Basic Service
Subscribers: 54,280.
Programming (via satellite): AmericanLife TV Network; BBC America; Bio; Black Family Channel; Bloomberg Television; Discovery Digital Networks; DMX Music; ESPN Classic Sports; Fox Sports en Espanol; Fox Sports World; G4; GSN; Halogen Network; History Channel International; Independent Film Channel; Lifetime Movie Network; MTV Networks Digital Suite; MuchMusic Network; NBA TV; Nick Jr.; Outdoor Channel; Ovation; SoapNet; Speed Channel; Sundance Channel; Toon Disney; Turner Classic Movies; Versus; WE tv.
Fee: $12.00 monthly.

Pay Service 1
Pay Units: 44,720.
Programming (via satellite): Cinemax; Encore; HBO; Showtime; Starz.
Fee: $5.25 installation; $1.75 monthly (Encore), $6.75 monthly (Starz), $11.75 monthly (Cinemax), $12.40 monthly (HBO or Showtime).

Digital Pay Service 1
Pay Units: N.A.
Programming (via satellite): Cinemax (multiplexed); Encore (multiplexed); HBO (multiplexed); Showtime (multiplexed); Starz (multiplexed); The Movie Channel (multiplexed).
Fee: $12.99 monthly (each package).

Video-On-Demand: No

Pay-Per-View
Addressable homes: 41,280.
ESPN Now (delivered digitally), Addressable: Yes; Hot Choice (delivered digitally); iN DEMAND (delivered digitally); Playboy TV (delivered digitally); Fresh (delivered digitally); Shorteez (delivered digitally); Sports PPV (delivered digitally).

Internet Service
Operational: Yes.
Subscribers: 27,200.
Broadband Service: Cox High Speed Internet.
Fee: $99.95 installation; $39.95 monthly; $10.00 modem lease.

Telephone Service
Digital: Operational
Fee: $38.95 monthly
Miles of Plant: 7,588.0 (coaxial); 1,366.0 (fiber optic). Homes passed: 474,509.
Regional Vice President & General Manager: Jacqueline Vines. Vice President, Technical Operations: David Butler. Vice President, Government & Public Affairs: Sharon Kleinpeter. Vice President, Human Resources: Andy Rice. Vice President, Cox Business Services: Leigh King. Vice President, Information Technology: Ramin Rastin. Vice President, Customer Care: Tom Makin.
Baton Rouge fee: 5% of gross.
Ownership: Cox Communications Inc. (MSO).

BAYOU L'OURSE—Allen's TV Cable Service Inc. Now served by MORGAN CITY, LA [LA0188]. ICA: LA0138.

BELLE CHASSE—CMA Cablevision, 8618 Hwy 23, Belle Chasse, LA 70037-2535. Phones: 972-233-9614 (Corporate office); 800-753-2465; 504-392-4060. E-mail: cs@cmaaccess.com. Web Site: http://www.cmaaccess.com. Also serves Bootheville, Buras, Empire, Port Sulphur, Triumph & Venice. ICA: LA0139.
TV Market Ranking: 31 (BELLE CHASSE); Outside TV Markets (Bootheville, Buras, Empire, Port Sulphur, Triumph, Venice). Franchise award date: N.A. Franchise expiration date: N.A. Began: N.A.
Channel capacity: N.A. Channels available but not in use: N.A.

Basic Service
Subscribers: 2,400.
Programming (received off-air): WDSU (NBC) New Orleans; WGNO (ABC) New Orleans; WHNO (IND) New Orleans; WLAE-TV (PBS) New Orleans; WNOL-TV (CW) New Orleans; WPXL-TV (ION) New Orleans; WUPL (MNT) Slidell; WWL-TV (CBS) New Orleans; WYES-TV (PBS) New Orleans.
Programming (via satellite): BET Networks; Home Shopping Network; QVC; TBS Superstation; The Learning Channel; TV Guide Network; WGN America.
Current originations: Public Access.
Fee: $39.95 installation; $17.95 monthly.

Expanded Basic Service 1
Subscribers: N.A.
Programming (via satellite): ABC Family Channel; AMC; Animal Planet; Arts & Entertainment; Bravo; Cartoon Network; CNBC; CNN; Comedy Central; Country Music TV; C-SPAN; Discovery Channel; Disney Channel; E! Entertainment Television; ESPN; ESPN 2; Eternal Word TV Network; Food Network; Fox News Channel; FX; GalaVision; Hallmark Channel; Headline News; History Channel; INSP; Lifetime; MTV; Nickelodeon; Outdoor Channel; SoapNet; Spike TV; Syfy; Travel Channel; Trinity Broadcasting Network; truTV; Turner Classic Movies; Turner Network TV; TV Land; USA Network; VH1; Weather Channel.
Fee: $26.50 monthly.

Digital Basic Service
Subscribers: N.A.
Programming (via satellite): BBC America; Bio; Cox Sports Television; Discovery Digital Networks; Discovery Kids Channel; DMX Music; ESPN Classic Sports; ESPNews; Fox Movie Channel; Fox Sports World; G4; GAS; Golf Channel; GSN; Halogen Network; HGTV; History Channel International; Independent Film Channel; Lifetime Movie Network; MTV2; National Geographic Channel; Nick Jr.; NickToons TV; Speed Channel; Toon Disney; VH1 Classic; VH1 Country; WE tv.
Fee: $12.95 monthly.

Pay Service 1
Pay Units: 1,009.
Programming (via satellite): HBO.
Fee: $14.95 installation; $13.95 monthly.

Digital Pay Service 1
Pay Units: N.A.
Programming (via satellite): Cinemax (multiplexed); Encore (multiplexed); HBO (multiplexed); Showtime (multiplexed); Starz (multiplexed).
Fee: $10.95 monthly (Cinemax or Encore & Starz), $13.95 monthly (HBO or Showtime).

Video-On-Demand: No

Pay-Per-View
iN DEMAND (delivered digitally); Playboy TV (delivered digitally).

Internet Service
Operational: Yes.
Broadband Service: CMA.
Fee: $40.95 monthly; $6.95 modem lease; $149.95 modem purchase.
Telephone Service
Digital: Operational
Fee: $39.95 monthly
Miles of Plant: 300.0 (coaxial); None (fiber optic).
General Manager: Jerry Smith. Marketing Director: Julie Ferguson.
Ownership: Cable Management Assoc. (MSO).

BENTON—Rapid Cable, 515 E Longview Dr, Arp, TX 75750. Phone: 903-859-6492. Fax: 903-859-3708. Also serves Bossier Parish. ICA: LA0214.
TV Market Ranking: 58 (BENTON, Bossier Parish). Franchise award date: N.A. Franchise expiration date: N.A. Began: N.A.
Channel capacity: 37 (not 2-way capable). Channels available but not in use: 4.
Basic Service
Subscribers: 1,163.
Programming (received off-air): KLTS-TV (PBS) Shreveport; KMSS-TV (FOX) Shreveport; KPXJ (CW) Minden; KSHV-TV (MNT) Shreveport; KSLA (CBS) Shreveport; KTAL-TV (NBC) Texarkana; KTBS-TV (ABC) Shreveport.
Programming (via satellite): ABC Family Channel; AMC; BET Networks; Bravo; CNN; Country Music TV; C-SPAN; E! Entertainment Television; ESPN; Halogen Network; Headline News; Home Shopping Network; Lifetime; MTV; Nickelodeon; Weather Channel.
Current originations: Government Access; Educational Access; Public Access.
Fee: $54.95 installation; $20.95 monthly.
Expanded Basic Service 1
Subscribers: 1,140.
Programming (via satellite): Discovery Channel; Disney Channel; Spike TV; Syfy; TBS Superstation; Turner Network TV; USA Network; WGN America.
Fee: $23.10 monthly.
Digital Basic Service
Subscribers: N.A.
Programming (via satellite): AmericanLife TV Network; BBC America; Bio; Bloomberg Television; Bravo; CMT Pure Country; Current; Discovery Health Channel; Discovery Kids Channel; Discovery Military Channel; Discovery Planet Green; DMX Music; ESPN 2; ESPN Classic Sports; FitTV; Fox Movie Channel; Fox Soccer; Fuse; G4; Golf Channel; GSN; Halogen Network; History Channel; History Channel International; ID Investigation Discovery; Independent Film Channel; Lifetime Movie Network; MTV Hits; MTV2; Nick Jr.; Outdoor Channel; Science Channel; ShopNBC; Speed Channel; Style Network; Syfy; TeenNick; Toon Disney; Trinity Broadcasting Network; Turner Classic Movies; Versus; VH1 Classic; VH1 Soul; WE tv.
Pay Service 1
Pay Units: 332.
Programming (via satellite): HBO.
Fee: $12.95 monthly.
Pay Service 2
Pay Units: 149.
Programming (via satellite): Showtime.
Fee: $12.95 monthly.
Pay Service 3
Pay Units: 83.
Programming (via satellite): The Movie Channel.
Fee: $12.95 monthly.
Digital Pay Service 1
Pay Units: N.A.
Programming (via satellite): Cinemax (multiplexed); Encore (multiplexed); Flix; HBO (multiplexed); Showtime (multiplexed); Starz (multiplexed); The Movie Channel (multiplexed).
Video-On-Demand: No
Pay-Per-View
iN DEMAND (delivered digitally); Hot Choice (delivered digitally); Playboy TV (delivered digitally); Fresh (delivered digitally); Shorteez (delivered digitally).
Internet Service
Operational: No.
Telephone Service
None
Miles of Plant: 50.0 (coaxial); None (fiber optic). Homes passed: 1,515.
Regional Manager: Mike Taylor. Chief Technician: Larry Stafford.
Franchise fee: 3% of gross.
Ownership: Rapid Communications LLC (MSO).

BERNICE—Rapid Cable, 515 E Longview Dr, Arp, TX 75750. Phone: 903-859-6492. Fax: 903-859-3708. Also serves Dubach, Lincoln Parish (portions) & Union Parish (portions). ICA: LA0081.
TV Market Ranking: 99 (BERNICE, Lincoln Parish (portions), Union Parish (portions)); Below 100 (Dubach, Lincoln Parish (portions)); Outside TV Markets (Lincoln Parish (portions)). Franchise award date: N.A. Franchise expiration date: N.A. Began: October 1, 1982.
Channel capacity: N.A. Channels available but not in use: N.A.
Basic Service
Subscribers: 390.
Programming (received off-air): KAQY (ABC) Columbia; KARD (FOX) West Monroe; KEJB (MNT)lorado; KKYK-CA (IND) Little Rock; KLTM-TV (PBS) Monroe; KMSS-TV (FOX) Shreveport; KNOE-TV (CBS, CW) Monroe; KPXJ (CW) Minden; KSHV-TV (MNT) Shreveport; KTBS-TV (ABC) Shreveport; KTVE (NBC) El Dorado.
Programming (via satellite): ABC Family Channel; AMC; Animal Planet; Arts & Entertainment; BET Networks; Cartoon Network; CNBC; CNN; Discovery Channel; Disney Channel; E! Entertainment Television; ESPN; ESPN 2; Food Network; Fox News Channel; Fox Sports Net; FX; Great American Country; Headline News; HGTV; Lifetime; MTV; National Geographic Channel; Nickelodeon; Outdoor Channel; QVC; Spike TV; Syfy; TBS Superstation; The Learning Channel; Turner Classic Movies; Turner Network TV; USA Network; Weather Channel.
Fee: $54.95 installation; $44.05 monthly.
Digital Basic Service
Subscribers: N.A.
Programming (via satellite): BBC America; Bio; Bloomberg Television; Discovery Health Channel; Discovery Kids Channel; Discovery Military Channel; Discovery Planet Green; DMX Music; ESPN Classic Sports; ESPNews; Fox College Sports Atlantic; Fox College Sports Central; Fox College Sports Pacific; Fox Soccer; Fuse; G4; Golf Channel; GSN; History Channel; History Channel International; ID Investigation Discovery; Independent Film Channel; Science Channel; ShopNBC; Sleuth; Speed Channel; Style Network; Sundance Channel; Toon Disney; Trinity Broadcasting Network; Versus; WE tv.
Pay Service 1
Pay Units: 46.
Programming (via satellite): HBO.
Fee: $12.95 monthly.
Pay Service 2
Pay Units: 136.
Programming (via satellite): Showtime.
Fee: $12.95 monthly.
Pay Service 3
Pay Units: 18.
Programming (via satellite): The Movie Channel.
Fee: $12.95 monthly.
Digital Pay Service 1
Pay Units: N.A.
Programming (via satellite): Cinemax (multiplexed); Encore (multiplexed); Flix; HBO (multiplexed); Showtime (multiplexed); Starz (multiplexed); The Movie Channel (multiplexed).
Video-On-Demand: No
Pay-Per-View
iN DEMAND (delivered digitally); Playboy TV (delivered digitally); Club Jenna (delivered digitally).
Internet Service
Operational: No.
Telephone Service
None
Miles of Plant: 35.0 (coaxial); None (fiber optic). Homes passed: 1,204.
Regional Manager: Mike Taylor. Chief Technician: Larry Stafford.
Ownership: Rapid Communications LLC (MSO).

BLANCHARD—CMA Cablevision, 4647 Roy Rd Ext, Shreveport, LA 71107. Phones: 800-753-2465; 972-233-9614 (Corporate office); 318-929-3551. Fax: 318-929-0243. Web Site: http://www.cmaaccess.com. Also serves Caddo Parish, Mooringsport, Oil City & Vivian. ICA: LA0038.
TV Market Ranking: 58 (BLANCHARD, Caddo Parish, Mooringsport, Oil City, Vivian). Franchise award date: July 22, 1981. Franchise expiration date: N.A. Began: January 1, 1982.
Channel capacity: N.A. Channels available but not in use: N.A.
Basic Service
Subscribers: 2,475.
Programming (received off-air): KLTS-TV (PBS) Shreveport; KMSS-TV (FOX) Shreveport; KPXJ (CW) Minden; KSHV-TV (MNT) Shreveport; KSLA (CBS) Shreveport; KTAL-TV (NBC) Texarkana; KTBS-TV (ABC) Shreveport; 2 FMs.
Fee: $39.95 installation; $18.45 monthly; $12.95 additional installation.
Expanded Basic Service 1
Subscribers: N.A.
Programming (via satellite): ABC Family Channel; Animal Planet; Arts & Entertainment; BET Networks; Cartoon Network; CNN; Comcast Sports Net Southeast; Comedy Central; Country Music TV; C-SPAN; Discovery Channel; ESPN; ESPN 2; Food Network; Fox News Channel; FX; Hallmark Channel; Headline News; History Channel; Home Shopping Network; Lifetime; MTV; Nick Jr.; Nickelodeon; Outdoor Channel; Spike TV; Syfy; TBS Superstation; The Learning Channel; Travel Channel; Trinity Broadcasting Network; truTV; Turner Classic Movies; Turner Network TV; TV Guide Network; TV Land; USA Network; VH1; Weather Channel; WGN America.
Fee: $22.50 monthly.
Digital Basic Service
Subscribers: N.A.
Programming (via satellite): BBC America; Bio; Bloomberg Television; Discovery Digital Networks; DMX Music; ESPN Classic Sports; ESPNews; Fox Movie Channel; Fox Sports World; GAS; Golf Channel; GSN; HGTV; History Channel International; Independent Film Channel; Lifetime Movie Network; MTV2; NickToons TV; Speed Channel; VH1 Country; WE tv.
Fee: $14.00 monthly.
Pay Service 1
Pay Units: N.A.
Programming (via satellite): HBO; Showtime.
Fee: $14.95 installation; $13.95 monthly (each).
Digital Pay Service 1
Pay Units: N.A.
Programming (via satellite): Cinemax (multiplexed); Encore (multiplexed); HBO (multiplexed); Showtime (multiplexed); Starz (multiplexed).
Fee: $10.95 monthly (Cinemax or Encore & Starz); $13.95 monthly (HBO or Showtime).
Video-On-Demand: No
Pay-Per-View
iN DEMAND (delivered digitally); Playboy TV (delivered digitally).
Internet Service
Operational: Yes. Began: February 1, 2003.
Broadband Service: CMA.
Fee: $39.95 installation; $40.95 monthly; $2.95 modem lease; $149.95 modem purchase.
Telephone Service
Digital: Operational
Fee: $39.95 monthly
Miles of Plant: 124.0 (coaxial); None (fiber optic). Additional miles planned: 5.0 (coaxial). Homes passed: 6,700. Total homes in franchised area: 6,700.
General Manager: Jerry Smith. Marketing Director: Julie Ferguson.
Parish fee: 3% of gross.
Ownership: Cable Management Assoc. (MSO).

BOGALUSA—Charter Communications, 1304 Ridgefield Rd, Thibodaux, LA 70301. Phone: 985-446-4900. Fax: 985-447-9541. Web Site: http://www.charter.com. Also serves Amite, Angle, Franklinton, Sweetwater Creek, Varnado & Washington Parish. ICA: LA0023.
TV Market Ranking: Below 100 (Amite, Franklinton, Sweetwater Creek, Washington Parish (portions)); Outside TV Markets (Angle, BOGALUSA, Varnado, Washington Parish (portions)). Franchise award date: N.A. Franchise expiration date: N.A. Began: October 1, 1966.
Channel capacity: N.A. Channels available but not in use: N.A.
Basic Service
Subscribers: 8,588.
Programming (received off-air): WAFB (CBS) Baton Rouge; WBRZ-TV (ABC) Baton Rouge; WDSU (NBC) New Orleans; WGNO (ABC) New Orleans; WHNO (IND) New Orleans; WLPB-TV (PBS) Baton Rouge; WNOL-TV (CW) New Orleans; WPXL-TV (ION) New Orleans; WSTY-LP (IND) Hammond; WUPL (MNT) Slidell; WVLA-TV (NBC) Baton Rouge; WVUE-DT (FOX) New Orleans; WWL-TV (CBS) New Orleans; WYES-TV (PBS) New Orleans; allband FM.
Programming (via satellite): C-SPAN; Home Shopping Network; TBS Superstation; Trinity Broadcasting Network; TV Guide Network; WGN America.
Fee: $29.99 installation.

Expanded Basic Service 1
Subscribers: N.A.
Programming (via satellite): ABC Family Channel; AMC; Animal Planet; Arts & Entertainment; BET Networks; Cartoon Network; CNBC; CNN; Comcast Sports Net Southwest; Country Music TV; Discovery Channel; Disney Channel; E! Entertainment Television; ESPN; ESPN 2; Eternal Word TV Network; Fox News Channel; FX; Headline News; HGTV; Lifetime; MTV; Nickelodeon; Speed Channel; Spike TV; Syfy; The Learning Channel; Travel Channel; truTV; Turner Classic Movies; Turner Network TV; TV Land; USA Network; VH1; Weather Channel.
Fee: $42.99 monthly.

Digital Basic Service
Subscribers: N.A.
Programming (via satellite): BBC America; Bio; Discovery Digital Networks; Do-It-Yourself; G4; Golf Channel; Great American Country; History Channel International; Independent Film Channel; Lifetime Movie Network; MTV2; Music Choice; Nick Jr.; Science Television; Sundance Channel; Versus; WE tv.

Pay Service 1
Pay Units: N.A.
Programming (via satellite): Encore; Flix; HBO; Showtime (multiplexed); The Movie Channel.
Fee: $9.95 monthly (TMC), $10.95 monthly (HBO or Showtime).

Digital Pay Service 1
Pay Units: N.A.
Programming (via satellite): Cinemax (multiplexed); Starz (multiplexed); The Movie Channel.

Video-On-Demand: No

Internet Service
Operational: Yes.
Broadband Service: Charter Pipeline.

Telephone Service
Digital: Operational

Miles of Plant: 140.0 (coaxial); None (fiber optic). Homes passed: 9,000.
Vice President & General Manager: Kip Kraemer. Operations Manager: Blaine Bercegeay. Technical Operations Director: Gary Savoie. Marketing Director: Lisa Brown. Government Relations Director: Jim Laurent.
City fee: 3% of gross.
Ownership: Charter Communications Inc. (MSO).

BOSSIER CITY—Suddenlink Communications, 725 Benton Rd, Bossier City, LA 71111-3704. Phones: 888-822-5151 (Customer service); 318-747-1666 (Customer service). Fax: 318-746-2186. Web Site: http://www.suddenlink.com. Also serves Barksdale AFB, Bossier Parish, Fillmore, Haughton & Princeton. ICA: LA0008.
TV Market Ranking: 58 (Barksdale AFB, BOSSIER CITY, Bossier Parish, Fillmore, Haughton, Princeton). Franchise award date: August 8, 1979. Franchise expiration date: N.A. Began: August 1, 1978.
Channel capacity: N.A. Channels available but not in use: N.A.

Basic Service
Subscribers: 19,252.
Programming (received off-air): KLTS-TV (PBS) Shreveport; KMSS-TV (FOX) Shreveport; KPXJ (CW) Minden; KSHV-TV (MNT) Shreveport; KSLA (CBS) Shreveport; KTAL-TV (NBC) Texarkana; KTBS-TV (ABC) Shreveport; 12 FMs.
Programming (via satellite): BET Networks; CNN; C-SPAN; Discovery Channel; Eternal Word TV Network; Hallmark Channel; Home Shopping Network; INSP; QVC; Sneak Prevue; TBS Superstation; TV Guide Network; WGN America.
Current originations: Leased Access; Religious Access; Government Access; Public Access.
Planned originations: Educational Access.
Fee: $38.00 installation; $12.80 monthly; $1.10 converter; $24.95 additional installation.

Expanded Basic Service 1
Subscribers: 18,847.
Programming (via satellite): ABC Family Channel; AMC; Animal Planet; Arts & Entertainment; Cartoon Network; CNBC; CNN; Comcast Sports Net Southwest; Comedy Central; C-SPAN 2; Disney Channel; E! Entertainment Television; ESPN; Fox News Channel; FX; Great American Country; Headline News; History Channel; Lifetime; MoviePlex; MTV; Nickelodeon; Spike TV; The Learning Channel; Turner Network TV; USA Network; VH1; Weather Channel.
Fee: $42.00 installation; $15.56 monthly.

Digital Basic Service
Subscribers: N.A.
Programming (via satellite): BBC America; Bravo; Discovery Digital Networks; DMX Music; Encore; ESPN 2; ESPN Classic Sports; Fox Sports World; Golf Channel; GSN; HGTV; Independent Film Channel; MTV Networks Digital Suite; Speed Channel; Syfy; Turner Classic Movies; TV Land; Versus; WE tv.
Fee: $10.00 monthly.

Pay Service 1
Pay Units: 2,990.
Programming (via satellite): Cinemax.
Fee: $9.00 monthly.

Pay Service 2
Pay Units: 1,230.
Programming (via satellite): Starz.
Fee: $6.75 monthly.

Pay Service 3
Pay Units: 6,838.
Programming (via satellite): HBO.
Fee: $10.95 monthly.

Pay Service 4
Pay Units: 1,992.
Programming (via satellite): Showtime.
Fee: $11.50 monthly.

Pay Service 5
Pay Units: 6,901.
Programming (via satellite): Encore.
Fee: $1.75 monthly.

Digital Pay Service 1
Pay Units: N.A.
Programming (via satellite): HBO (multiplexed); Showtime (multiplexed); Starz (multiplexed); The Movie Channel.

Video-On-Demand: No

Pay-Per-View
Addressable homes: 10,806.
iN DEMAND, Addressable: Yes; iN DEMAND (delivered digitally); Spice.

Internet Service
Operational: Yes.
Broadband Service: Cebridge High Speed Cable Internet.
Fee: $45.00 installation; $29.95 monthly.

Telephone Service
Digital: Operational
Fee: $39.95 monthly

Miles of Plant: 526.0 (coaxial); 27.0 (fiber optic). Additional miles planned: 7.0 (coaxial). Homes passed: 33,948. Total homes in franchised area: 34,745.
Manager: Jim Niswender. Marketing Director: Jon Hustmyre. Chief Technician: Lee Anderson.

Franchise fee: 5% of basic gross.
Ownership: Cequel Communications LLC (MSO).

BOURG—Charter Communications, 1304 Ridgefield Rd, Thibodaux, LA 70301. Phone: 985-446-4900. Fax: 985-447-9541. Web Site: http://www.charter.com. Also serves Amelia, Bayou Black, Chauvin, Dulac, Dularge, Gibson, Grand Caillou, Houma, Montegut, Schriever, Terrebonne Parish & Theriot. ICA: LA0013.
TV Market Ranking: Outside TV Markets (Amelia, Bayou Black, BOURG, Chauvin, Dulac, Dularge, Gibson, Grand Caillou, Houma, Montegut, Schriever, Terrebonne Parish, Theriot). Franchise award date: N.A. Franchise expiration date: N.A. Began: November 1, 1979.
Channel capacity: N.A. Channels available but not in use: N.A.

Basic Service
Subscribers: 11,256.
Programming (received off-air): KFOL-CD (IND) Houma; WAFB (CBS) Baton Rouge; WBRZ-TV (ABC) Baton Rouge; WDSU (NBC) New Orleans; WGNO (ABC) New Orleans; WHNO (IND) New Orleans; WLAE-TV (PBS) New Orleans; WNOL-TV (CW) New Orleans; WPXL-TV (ION) New Orleans; WUPL (MNT) Slidell; WVUE-DT (FOX) New Orleans; WWL-TV (CBS) New Orleans; WYES-TV (PBS) New Orleans.
Programming (via satellite): Eternal Word TV Network; Home Shopping Network; QVC; Trinity Broadcasting Network.
Current originations: Government Access; Educational Access; Public Access.
Fee: $29.99 installation.

Expanded Basic Service 1
Subscribers: N.A.
Programming (via satellite): ABC Family Channel; AMC; Animal Planet; Arts & Entertainment; BET Networks; Bravo; Cartoon Network; CNBC; CNN; Comcast Sports Net Southwest; Comedy Central; Country Music TV; C-SPAN; C-SPAN 2; Discovery Channel; Disney Channel; E! Entertainment Television; ESPN; ESPN 2; Food Network; Fox News Channel; FX; G4; Golf Channel; GSN; Hallmark Channel; Headline News; HGTV; History Channel; INSP; Lifetime; MSNBC; MTV; National Geographic Channel; Nickelodeon; Outdoor Channel; Oxygen; Product Information Network; SoapNet; Speed Channel; Spike TV; Syfy; TBS Superstation; Telemundo; The Learning Channel; Toon Disney; Travel Channel; truTV; Turner Classic Movies; Turner Network TV; TV Land; Univision; USA Network; Versus; VH1; WE tv; Weather Channel.
Fee: $42.99 monthly.

Digital Basic Service
Subscribers: N.A.
Programming (received off-air): WDSU (NBC) New Orleans; WWL-TV (CBS) New Orleans.
Programming (via satellite): BBC America; Bio; Bloomberg Television; Discovery Digital Networks; Discovery HD Theater; Do-It-Yourself; ESPN; ESPN Classic Sports; ESPNews; Fox Movie Channel; Fox Soccer; Fuel TV; GAS; Great American Country; HBO; HDNet; HDNet Movies; History Channel International; Independent Film Channel; Lifetime Movie Network; MTV Networks Digital Suite; Music Choice; NFL Network; Nick Jr.; Nick Too; NickToons TV; Showtime; Sundance Channel; TV Guide Interactive Inc.; TVG Network; WealthTV HD.

Digital Pay Service 1
Pay Units: 487.
Programming (via satellite): Cinemax (multiplexed).
Fee: $10.00 installation; $8.95 monthly.

Digital Pay Service 2
Pay Units: 1,516.
Programming (via satellite): HBO (multiplexed).
Fee: $10.00 installation; $10.95 monthly.

Digital Pay Service 3
Pay Units: 1,527.
Programming (via satellite): Showtime (multiplexed).
Fee: $10.00 installation; $8.95 monthly.

Digital Pay Service 4
Pay Units: 1,504.
Programming (via satellite): The Movie Channel (multiplexed).
Fee: $10.00 installation; $8.95 monthly.

Digital Pay Service 5
Pay Units: N.A.
Programming (via satellite): Encore (multiplexed); Flix; Playboy TV; Starz (multiplexed).

Video-On-Demand: Yes

Pay-Per-View
Addressable homes: 3,442.
iN DEMAND (delivered digitally), Addressable: Yes; Playboy TV (delivered digitally); Fresh (delivered digitally); Shorteez (delivered digitally); NASCAR In Car (delivered digitally); NHL Center Ice (delivered digitally); MLB Extra Innings (delivered digitally).

Internet Service
Operational: Yes, DSL only.
Broadband Service: Charter Pipeline.
Fee: $29.99 monthly.

Telephone Service
Digital: Operational
Fee: $29.99 monthly

Miles of Plant: 353.0 (coaxial); 3.0 (fiber optic). Homes passed: 13,792. Total homes in franchised area: 13,792.
Vice President & General Manager: Kip Kraemer. Operations Manager: Ann Danos. Technical Operations Director: Gary Savoie. Marketing Director: Lisa Brown. Government Relations Director: Jim Laurent.
Parish fee: 5% of gross.
Ownership: Charter Communications Inc. (MSO).

BOYCE—Suddenlink Communications, 3250 Donahue Ferry Rd, Pineville, LA 71360. Phone: 314-965-2020. Web Site: http://www.suddenlink.com. Also serves Hotwells & Lake Cotile. ICA: LA0141.
TV Market Ranking: Below 100 (BOYCE, Hotwells, Lake Cotile). Franchise award

date: N.A. Franchise expiration date: N.A. Began: October 1, 1982.

Channel capacity: 54 (operating 2-way). Channels available but not in use: N.A.

Basic Service

Subscribers: 656.

Programming (received off-air): KALB-TV (CBS, NBC) Alexandria; KATC (ABC) Lafayette; KLAX-TV (ABC) Alexandria; KLFY-TV (CBS) Lafayette; KLPA-TV (PBS) Alexandria; KLTM-TV (PBS) Monroe; KNOE-TV (CBS, CW) Monroe.

Programming (via satellite): ABC Family Channel; CNN; ESPN; Nickelodeon; TBS Superstation; USA Network; Weather Channel; WGN America.

Fee: $39.95 installation; $19.95 monthly.

Pay Service 1

Pay Units: 60.

Programming (via satellite): HBO.

Fee: $12.00 monthly.

Pay Service 2

Pay Units: 108.

Programming (via satellite): Showtime.

Fee: $7.00 monthly.

Pay Service 3

Pay Units: 26.

Programming (via satellite): The Movie Channel.

Fee: $10.00 monthly.

Pay Service 4

Pay Units: 123.

Programming (via satellite): Flix.

Fee: $1.95 monthly.

Video-On-Demand: No

Internet Service

Operational: Yes. Began: January 28, 2004.

Broadband Service: Cebridge High Speed Cable Internet.

Fee: $45.00 installation; $29.95 monthly.

Telephone Service

Digital: Operational

Fee: $39.95 monthly

Miles of Plant: 34.0 (coaxial); None (fiber optic). Homes passed: 1,101.

Regional Manager: Todd Cruthird. Area Manager: Mark Hood. Plant Manager: Dion Canaday.

Ownership: Cequel Communications LLC (MSO).

BRAITHWAITE—Formerly served by CMA Cablevision. No longer in operation. ICA: LA0142.

BROUILLETTE—Formerly served by Almega Cable. No longer in operation. ICA: LA0143.

BUNKIE—Charter Communications, 330 Moosa Blvd, Eunice, LA 70535. Phones: 985-446-4900 (Thibodaux office); 318-546-0087. Fax: 318-546-0038. Web Site: http://www.charter.com. Also serves Allen Parish, Elizabeth, Evergreen, Oakdale & Vernon Parish (southeastern portion). ICA: LA0061.

TV Market Ranking: Below 100 (Allen Parish (portions), BUNKIE, Evergreen, Oakdale, Vernon Parish (southeastern portion) (portions)); Outside TV Markets (Allen Parish (portions), Elizabeth, Vernon Parish (southeastern portion) (portions)). Franchise award date: N.A. Franchise expiration date: N.A. Began: January 15, 1968.

Channel capacity: N.A. Channels available but not in use: N.A.

Basic Service

Subscribers: 8,000.

Programming (received off-air): KALB-TV (CBS, NBC) Alexandria; KLAX-TV (ABC) Alexandria; KLFY-TV (CBS) Lafayette; KLPA-TV (PBS) Alexandria; KPLC (NBC) Lake Charles; WAFB (CBS) Baton Rouge; WBRZ-TV (ABC) Baton Rouge; WNTZ-TV (FOX, MNT) Natchez; WPXL-TV (ION) New Orleans; allband FM.

Programming (via satellite): QVC.

Fee: $29.99 installation.

Expanded Basic Service 1

Subscribers: N.A.

Programming (via satellite): ABC Family Channel; AMC; Animal Planet; Arts & Entertainment; BET Networks; Cartoon Network; CNBC; CNN; Comcast Sports Net Southwest; Comedy Central; Country Music TV; C-SPAN; Discovery Channel; Disney Channel; E! Entertainment Television; ESPN; ESPN 2; Eternal Word TV Network; Fox News Channel; Hallmark Channel; Headline News; HGTV; History Channel; Home Shopping Network; Lifetime; MSNBC; MTV; Nickelodeon; Outdoor Channel; Oxygen; Product Information Network; SoapNet; Spike TV; Syfy; TBS Superstation; The Learning Channel; Toon Disney; Travel Channel; Trinity Broadcasting Network; Turner Classic Movies; Turner Network TV; TV Land; USA Network; VH1; WE tv; Weather Channel; WGN America.

Fee: $42.99 monthly.

Pay Service 1

Pay Units: 71.

Programming (via satellite): Cinemax; HBO; Showtime.

Fee: $10.00 installation; $11.50 monthly (each).

Video-On-Demand: No

Internet Service

Operational: Yes.

Broadband Service: Charter Pipeline.

Telephone Service

Digital: Operational

Miles of Plant: 27.0 (coaxial); None (fiber optic).

Vice President & General Manager: Kip Kraemer. Operations Manager: Blane Bercegeay. Technical Operations Director: Gary Savoie. Plant Manager: Joe Semmes. Marketing Director: Lisa Brown.

City fee: 3% of gross.

Ownership: Charter Communications Inc. (MSO).

CALHOUN—CMA Cablevision, 3759 Old Sterlington Rd, Monroe, LA 71203-3086. Phones: 972-233-9614 (Corporate office); 318-345-1010. Fax: 318-343-5255. Web Site: http://www.cmaaccess.com. ICA: LA0104.

TV Market Ranking: 99 (CALHOUN COUNTY (PORTIONS)). Franchise award date: January 12, 1979. Franchise expiration date: N.A. Began: May 1, 1983.

Channel capacity: N.A. Channels available but not in use: N.A.

Basic Service

Subscribers: 230.

Programming (received off-air): KAQY (ABC) Columbia; KARD (FOX) West Monroe; KEJB (MNT)lorado; KLTM-TV (PBS) Monroe; KMCT-TV (IND) West Monroe; KNOE-TV (CBS, CW) Monroe; KTVE (NBC) El Dorado; KWMS-LP West Monroe.

Programming (via satellite): ABC Family Channel; CNN; Discovery Channel; Fox News Channel; Headline News; Home Shopping Network; Nickelodeon; TBS Superstation; The Learning Channel; Weather Channel; WGN America; WPIX (CW, IND) New York.

Current originations: Public Access.

Fee: $39.95 installation; $15.95 monthly; $12.95 additional installation.

Expanded Basic Service 1

Subscribers: N.A.

Programming (via satellite): Animal Planet; Arts & Entertainment; Cartoon Network; Comcast Sports Net Southwest; Country Music TV; E! Entertainment Television; ESPN; ESPN 2; FX; HGTV; History Channel; Lifetime; MTV; Spike TV; Turner Classic Movies; Turner Network TV; TV Land; USA Network; VH1.

Fee: $24.00 monthly.

Digital Basic Service

Subscribers: N.A.

Programming (via satellite): BBC America; Bio; CMT Pure Country; Discovery Health Channel; Discovery Home Channel; Discovery Kids Channel; Discovery Military Channel; Discovery Times Channel; DMX Music; ESPN Classic Sports; ESPNews; Golf Channel; GSN; Halogen Network; History Channel International; Lifetime Movie Network; MTV2; Nick Jr.; Science Channel; Sleuth; Speed Channel; Syfy; TeenNick; VH1 Classic.

Fee: $12.95 monthly.

Pay Service 1

Pay Units: 180.

Programming (via satellite): HBO.

Fee: $14.95 installation; $13.95 monthly.

Digital Pay Service 1

Pay Units: N.A.

Programming (via satellite): Cinemax (multiplexed); Encore (multiplexed); HBO (multiplexed); Showtime (multiplexed); Starz (multiplexed); The Movie Channel (multiplexed).

Fee: $10.95 monthly (Cinemax or Encore/Starz), $13.95 monthly (HBO or Showtime).

Video-On-Demand: No

Pay-Per-View

iN DEMAND (delivered digitally); Playboy TV (delivered digitally); Club Jenna (delivered digitally).

Internet Service

Operational: No.

Telephone Service

None

Miles of Plant: 16.0 (coaxial); None (fiber optic). Homes passed: 600.

General Manager: Jerry Smith. Marketing Director: Julie Ferguson.

Ownership: Cable Management Assoc. (MSO).

CALVIN—Formerly served by Cebridge Connections. No longer in operation. ICA: LA0145.

CAMERON—Formerly served by Charter Communications. No longer in operation. ICA: LA0077.

CAMPTI—Red River Cable TV, PO Box 674, 1813 Bessie St, Coushatta, LA 71019-0674. Phone: 318-932-4991. Fax: 308-932-5123. ICA: LA0111.

TV Market Ranking: Outside TV Markets (CAMPTI). Franchise award date: N.A. Franchise expiration date: N.A. Began: March 1, 1983.

Channel capacity: N.A. Channels available but not in use: N.A.

Basic Service

Subscribers: 318.

Programming (received off-air): KARD (FOX) West Monroe; KLTS-TV (PBS) Shreveport; KMSS-TV (FOX) Shreveport; KNTS-LP (IND) Natchitoches; KSHV-TV (MNT) Shreveport; KSLA (CBS) Shreveport; KTAL-TV (NBC) Texarkana; KTBS-TV (ABC) Shreveport.

Programming (via satellite): American Movie Classics; Animal Planet; Arts & Entertainment; BET Networks; Cartoon Network; CNN; Discovery Channel; ESPN; ESPN 2; Food Network; Fox News Channel; FX; Great American Country; Hallmark Channel; HGTV; History Channel; Home Shopping Network; Lifetime; National Geographic Channel; Outdoor Channel; SoapNet; Speed Channel; Syfy; TBS Superstation; The Learning Channel; Trinity Broadcasting Network; truTV; Turner Classic Movies; Turner Network TV; USA Network; WE tv; Weather Channel; WGN America.

Pay Service 1

Pay Units: N.A.

Programming (via satellite): Cinemax; Encore; HBO.

Video-On-Demand: No

Internet Service

Operational: No.

Telephone Service

None

Miles of Plant: 8.0 (coaxial); None (fiber optic). Homes passed: 550.

Manager: Jimmy Hardy. Secretary: Stephanie Collier.

Ownership: Red River Cable TV (MSO).

CARLYSS—Cameron Communications, PO Box 2237, 153 W Dave Dugas Rd, Sulphur, LA 70663. Phones: 800-737-3900; 337-583-4973. Fax: 337-583-2063. E-mail: meme.reider@camtel.com. Web Site: http://www.camtel.com. Also serves Cameron, Creole, Grand Chenier, Grand Lake, Hackberry & Johnsons Bayou. ICA: LA0063.

TV Market Ranking: 88 (Hackberry, Johnsons Bayou); Below 100 (Cameron, CARLYSS, Creole, Grand Chenier); Outside TV Markets (Grand Lake). Franchise award date: N.A. Franchise expiration date: N.A. Began: N.A.

Channel capacity: 39 (not 2-way capable). Channels available but not in use: None.

Basic Service

Subscribers: 2,137.

Programming (received off-air): KBMT (ABC) Beaumont; KFDM (CBS, CW) Beaumont; KLFY-TV (CBS) Lafayette; KLTL-TV (PBS) Lake Charles; KPLC (NBC) Lake Charles; KVHP (FOX) Lake Charles.

Programming (via satellite): Eternal Word TV Network; QVC.

Current originations: Public Access.

Fee: $9.95 installation; $9.95 monthly.

Expanded Basic Service 1

Subscribers: N.A.

Programming (via satellite): ABC Family Channel; AMC; Animal Planet; Arts & Entertainment; Cartoon Network; CNBC; CNN; Country Music TV; Discovery Channel; Disney Channel; ESPN; Fox News Channel; Fox Sports Net; Headline News; HGTV; History Channel; Lifetime; MTV; Nickelodeon; Spike TV; Syfy; TBS Superstation; The Learning Channel; Toon Disney; Travel Channel; Turner Network TV; USA Network; Weather Channel.

Fee: $31.95 monthly.

Digital Basic Service

Subscribers: N.A.

Programming (via satellite): BBC America; Bloomberg Television; Bravo; Discovery Digital Networks; DMX Music; Encore (multiplexed); ESPN 2; ESPN Classic Sports; ESPNews; Fox Movie Channel; Fox Sports World; G4; Golf Channel; GSN; Halogen Network; Independent Film Channel; Lime; National Geographic Channel; Nick Jr.; NickToons TV; Outdoor Channel;

Speed Channel; Trinity Broadcasting Network; Turner Classic Movies; Versus; VH1 Classic; VH1 Country; WE tv.
Fee: $14.50 monthly.

Digital Pay Service 1
Pay Units: 88.
Programming (via satellite): Cinemax (multiplexed); Flix; HBO (multiplexed); Showtime (multiplexed); Starz (multiplexed); The Movie Channel (multiplexed).
Fee: $7.95 monthly (Starz), $11.95 monthly (Cinemax), $12.95 monthly (Showtime/TMC), $13.95 monthly (HBO).

Video-On-Demand: No

Pay-Per-View
iN DEMAND (delivered digitally).

Internet Service
Operational: No.
Broadband Service: DSL service only.

Telephone Service
None

Miles of Plant: 112.0 (coaxial); None (fiber optic). Homes passed: 2,500.
Manager: George Mack. Marketing Director: Meme Reider. Chief Technician: L. Howard Latiola.
Ownership: Cameron Communications Corp.

CECILIA (northern portion)—Formerly served by Trust Cable. No longer in operation. ICA: LA0147.

CHATHAM—Formerly served by Chatham CATV. No longer in operation. ICA: LA0130.

CHOUDRANT—Formerly served by Almega Cable. No longer in operation. ICA: LA0215.

CLARENCE—Red River Cable TV, PO Box 674, 1813 Bessie St, Coushatta, LA 71019-0674. Phone: 318-932-4991. Fax: 318-932-5123. ICA: LA0133.
TV Market Ranking: Outside TV Markets (CLARENCE). Franchise award date: N.A. Franchise expiration date: N.A. Began: August 1, 1985.
Channel capacity: 12 (not 2-way capable). Channels available but not in use: N.A.

Basic Service
Subscribers: N.A.
Programming (received off-air): KALB-TV (CBS, NBC) Alexandria; KLTM-TV (PBS) Monroe; KNOE-TV (CBS, CW) Monroe; KSLA (CBS) Shreveport; KTAL-TV (NBC) Texarkana; KTBS-TV (ABC) Shreveport.
Programming (via satellite): TBS Superstation; WGN America.

Video-On-Demand: No

Internet Service
Operational: No.

Telephone Service
None

Miles of Plant: 2.0 (coaxial); None (fiber optic). Homes passed: 160.
Manager: Jimmy Hardy. Secretary: Stephanie Collier.
Ownership: Red River Cable TV (MSO).

CLAYTON—Rapid Cable, 515 E Longview Dr, Arp, TX 75750. Phone: 903-859-6492. Fax: 903-859-3708. ICA: LA0123.
TV Market Ranking: Below 100 (CLAYTON (VILLAGE)). Franchise award date: N.A. Franchise expiration date: N.A. Began: March 1, 1983.
Channel capacity: 54 (not 2-way capable). Channels available but not in use: N.A.

Basic Service
Subscribers: 166.
Programming (received off-air): KALB-TV (CBS, NBC) Alexandria; KAQY (ABC) Columbia; KARD (FOX) West Monroe; KLTM-TV (PBS) Monroe; KNOE-TV (CBS, CW) Monroe; WLBT (NBC) Jackson.
Programming (via satellite): ABC Family Channel; Animal Planet; Arts & Entertainment; BET Networks; Cartoon Network; CNN; Discovery Channel; Disney Channel; ESPN; ESPN 2; Fox Sports Net; Great American Country; Headline News; HGTV; Home Shopping Network; Lifetime; MTV; National Geographic Channel; Nickelodeon; Outdoor Channel; Spike TV; TBS Superstation; Trinity Broadcasting Network; Turner Classic Movies; Turner Network TV; USA Network; Weather Channel.
Fee: $54.95 installation; $44.05 monthly.

Pay Service 1
Pay Units: 22.
Programming (via satellite): Cinemax.
Fee: $12.95 monthly.

Pay Service 2
Pay Units: 20.
Programming (via satellite): HBO.
Fee: $12.95 monthly.

Pay Service 3
Pay Units: 23.
Programming (via satellite): Showtime.
Fee: $12.95 monthly.

Video-On-Demand: No

Pay-Per-View
iN DEMAND (delivered digitally); Playboy TV (delivered digitally); Club Jenna (delivered digitally).

Internet Service
Operational: No.

Telephone Service
None

Miles of Plant: 14.0 (coaxial); None (fiber optic). Homes passed: 554.
Regional Manager: Mike Taylor. Chief Technician: Ronnie Stafford.
Ownership: Rapid Communications LLC (MSO).

CLINTON—Trust Cable. Now served by ETHEL, LA [LA0160]. ICA: LA0051.

CLOUTIERVILLE—Formerly served by Almega Cable. No longer in operation. ICA: LA0149.

COLFAX—Rapid Cable, 515 E Longview Dr, Arp, TX 75750. Phone: 903-859-6492. Fax: 903-859-3708. ICA: LA0097.
TV Market Ranking: Below 100 (COLFAX). Franchise award date: N.A. Franchise expiration date: N.A. Began: November 1, 1982.
Channel capacity: 54 (not 2-way capable). Channels available but not in use: N.A.

Basic Service
Subscribers: 342.
Programming (received off-air): KALB-TV (CBS, NBC) Alexandria; KLAX-TV (ABC) Alexandria; KLFY-TV (CBS) Lafayette; KLPA-TV (PBS) Alexandria; KNOE-TV (CBS, CW) Monroe; WNTZ-TV (FOX, MNT) Natchez.
Programming (via satellite): ABC Family Channel; Animal Planet; Arts & Entertainment; BET Networks; Cartoon Network; CNBC; CNN; C-SPAN; Discovery Channel; Disney Channel; ESPN; ESPN 2; Fox Sports Net; FX; Great American Country; Headline News; HGTV; Home Shopping Network; Lifetime; MSNBC; MTV; National Geographic Channel; Nickelodeon; Outdoor Channel; SoapNet; Spike TV; TBS Superstation; Trinity Broadcasting Network; Turner Classic Movies; Turner Network TV; TV Land; USA Network; Weather Channel.
Fee: $54.95 installation; $44.05 monthly.

Digital Basic Service
Subscribers: N.A.
Programming (via satellite): BBC America; Bio; Bloomberg Television; Discovery Health Channel; Discovery Kids Channel; Discovery Military Channel; Discovery Planet Green; DMX Music; ESPN Classic Sports; ESPNews; Fox College Sports Atlantic; Fox College Sports Central; Fox College Sports Pacific; Fox Soccer; Fuse; G4; Golf Channel; GSN; History Channel; History Channel International; ID Investigation Discovery; Independent Film Channel; Science Channel; ShopNBC; Sleuth; Speed Channel; Style Network; Sundance Channel; Toon Disney; Versus; WE tv.

Pay Service 1
Pay Units: 36.
Programming (via satellite): HBO.
Fee: $12.95 monthly.

Pay Service 2
Pay Units: 70.
Programming (via satellite): Showtime.
Fee: $12.95 monthly.

Pay Service 3
Pay Units: 22.
Programming (via satellite): The Movie Channel.
Fee: $12.95 monthly.

Pay Service 4
Pay Units: 97.
Programming (via satellite): Flix.
Fee: $1.95 monthly.

Digital Pay Service 1
Pay Units: N.A.
Programming (via satellite): Cinemax (multiplexed); Encore (multiplexed); Flix; HBO (multiplexed); Showtime (multiplexed); Starz (multiplexed); The Movie Channel (multiplexed).

Video-On-Demand: No

Pay-Per-View
iN DEMAND (delivered digitally); Playboy TV (delivered digitally); Club Jenna (delivered digitally).

Internet Service
Operational: No.

Telephone Service
None

Miles of Plant: 15.0 (coaxial); None (fiber optic). Homes passed: 704.
Regional Manager: Mike Taylor. Chief Technician: Ronnie Stafford.
Ownership: Rapid Communications LLC (MSO).

COLLINSTON—TV Northeast Inc., PO Box 185, 6402 Howell St, Collinston, LA 71229-0185. Phone: 318-874-7011. Fax: 318-874-2041. E-mail: info@northeastnet.net. Web Site: http://www.northeastnet.net. Also serves Bonita & Morehouse Parish (unincorporated areas). ICA: LA0109.
TV Market Ranking: 99 (COLLINSTON, Morehouse Parish (unincorporated areas) (portions)); Outside TV Markets (Bonita, Morehouse Parish (unincorporated areas) (portions)). Franchise award date: N.A. Franchise expiration date: N.A. Began: May 1, 1987.
Channel capacity: 65 (not 2-way capable). Channels available but not in use: N.A.

Basic Service
Subscribers: 300.
Programming (received off-air): KAQY (ABC) Columbia; KARD (FOX) West Monroe; KEJB (MNT)lorado; KLTM-TV (PBS) Monroe; KMCT-TV (IND) West Monroe; KNOE-TV (CBS, CW) Monroe; KTVE (NBC) El Dorado.
Programming (via satellite): ABC Family Channel; Animal Planet; Arts & Entertainment; BET Networks; CNBC; CNN; Country Music TV; C-SPAN; Discovery Channel; Disney Channel; ESPN; ESPN 2; Food Network; Fox News Channel; FX; HGTV; History Channel; Lifetime; Nickelodeon; Outdoor Channel; QVC; Speed Channel; Spike TV; TBS Superstation; The Learning Channel; Travel Channel; Trinity Broadcasting Network; Turner Network TV; TV Land; USA Network; Versus; Weather Channel; WGN America.
Fee: $30.00 installation; $38.95 monthly; $10.00 additional installation.

Pay Service 1
Pay Units: 83.
Programming (via satellite): Cinemax.
Fee: $15.00 installation; $12.00 monthly.

Pay Service 2
Pay Units: 208.
Programming (via satellite): HBO.
Fee: $15.00 installation; $12.00 monthly.

Video-On-Demand: No

Internet Service
Operational: No, DSL only.
Broadband Service: DSL service only.

Telephone Service
None

Miles of Plant: 25.0 (coaxial); None (fiber optic). Homes passed: 600.
Manager: Rector L. Hopgood. Chief Technician: Tim Andrews. Office Manager: Julia Lindsey.
Ownership: Northeast Louisiana Telephone Co. Inc.

COLUMBIA—CMA Cablevision, 3759 Old Sterlington Rd, Monroe, LA 71203-3086. Phones: 972-233-9614 (Corporate office); 318-345-1010. Fax: 318-343-5255. Web Site: http://www.cmaaccess.com. Also serves Banks Springs, Columbia Heights & Grayson. ICA: LA0074.
TV Market Ranking: 99 (Banks Springs, COLUMBIA, Columbia Heights, Grayson). Franchise award date: November 3, 1980. Franchise expiration date: N.A. Began: N.A.
Channel capacity: N.A. Channels available but not in use: N.A.

Basic Service
Subscribers: 500.
Programming (received off-air): KARD (FOX) West Monroe; KEJB (MNT)lorado; KLTM-TV (PBS) Monroe; KMCT-TV (IND) West Monroe; KNOE-TV (CBS, CW) Monroe; KTVE (NBC) El Dorado; KWMS-LP West Monroe.
Programming (via satellite): ABC Family Channel; CNN; ESPN; Fox News Channel; KAQY (ABC) Columbia; TBS Superstation; The Learning Channel; WGN America.
Fee: $39.95 installation; $15.95 monthly; $12.95 additional installation.

Expanded Basic Service 1
Subscribers: 413.
Programming (via satellite): Animal Planet; Arts & Entertainment; BET Networks; Cartoon Network; Country Music TV; Discovery Channel; ESPN 2; FX; HGTV; History Channel; Home Shopping Network; Lifetime; MTV; Nickelodeon; Spike TV; Turner Classic Movies; Turner Network TV; TV Land; USA Network; Weather Channel.
Fee: $24.00 monthly.

Digital Basic Service
Subscribers: N.A.
Programming (via satellite): BBC America; Bio; Discovery Digital Networks; Discovery Kids Channel; ESPN Classic Sports; ESPNews; GAS; Golf Channel; GSN; History Channel International; Lifetime Movie Network; MTV Networks Digital Suite; Music

Choice; National Geographic Channel; Nick Jr.; Science Television.
Fee: $12.95 monthly.
Pay Service 1
Pay Units: 593.
Programming (via satellite): HBO.
Fee: $14.95 installation; $13.95 monthly.
Digital Pay Service 1
Pay Units: N.A.
Programming (via satellite): Cinemax (multiplexed); Encore (multiplexed); HBO (multiplexed); Showtime (multiplexed); Starz (multiplexed); The Movie Channel (multiplexed).
Fee: $10.95 monthly (Cinemax or Starz/Encore), $13.95 monthly (HBO or Showtime).
Video-On-Demand: No
Internet Service
Operational: No.
Telephone Service
None
Miles of Plant: 44.0 (coaxial); None (fiber optic). Homes passed: 1,488.
General Manager: Jerry Smith. Marketing Director: Julie Ferguson.
City fee: 3% of basic gross (Columbia).
Ownership: Cable Management Assoc. (MSO).

COTEAU HOLMES—Formerly served by Trust Cable. No longer in operation. ICA: LA0150.

COTTON VALLEY—Rapid Cable, 515 E Longview Dr, Arp, TX 75750. Phone: 903-859-6492. Fax: 903-859-3708. Also serves Sarepta. ICA: LA0085.
TV Market Ranking: 58 (COTTON VALLEY); Below 100 (Sarepta). Franchise award date: N.A. Franchise expiration date: N.A. Began: December 1, 1982.
Channel capacity: 53 (not 2-way capable). Channels available but not in use: 13.
Basic Service
Subscribers: 247.
Programming (received off-air): KLTS-TV (PBS) Shreveport; KMSS-TV (FOX) Shreveport; KPXJ (CW) Minden; KSHV-TV (MNT) Shreveport; KSLA (CBS) Shreveport; KTAL-TV (NBC) Texarkana; KTBS-TV (ABC) Shreveport.
Programming (via satellite): ABC Family Channel; Animal Planet; Arts & Entertainment; BET Networks; Cartoon Network; CNBC; CNN; Discovery Channel; Disney Channel; ESPN; ESPN 2; FX; Great American Country; Headline News; HGTV; Home Shopping Network; Lifetime; MSNBC; National Geographic Channel; Nickelodeon; Outdoor Channel; Spike TV; TBS Superstation; Trinity Broadcasting Network; Turner Classic Movies; Turner Network TV; USA Network; Weather Channel.
Current originations: Public Access.
Fee: $54.95 installation; $44.05 monthly.
Digital Basic Service
Subscribers: N.A.
Programming (via satellite): BBC America; Bio; Bloomberg Television; Discovery Health Channel; Discovery Kids Channel; Discovery Military Channel; Discovery Planet Green; DMX Music; ESPN Classic Sports; ESPNews; Fox College Sports Atlantic; Fox College Sports Central; Fox College Sports Pacific; Fox Soccer; Fuse; G4; Golf Channel; GSN; History Channel; History Channel International; ID Investigation Discovery; Independent Film Channel; Science Channel; ShopNBC; Sleuth; Speed Channel; Style Network; Sundance Channel; Toon Disney; Versus; WE tv.
Pay Service 1
Pay Units: 43.
Programming (via satellite): HBO.
Fee: $12.95 monthly.
Pay Service 2
Pay Units: 15.
Programming (via satellite): The Movie Channel.
Fee: $12.95 monthly.
Pay Service 3
Pay Units: 71.
Programming (via satellite): Showtime.
Fee: $12.95 monthly.
Pay Service 4
Pay Units: N.A.
Programming (via satellite): Flix.
Digital Pay Service 1
Pay Units: N.A.
Programming (via satellite): Cinemax (multiplexed); Encore (multiplexed); Flix; HBO (multiplexed); Showtime (multiplexed); Starz (multiplexed); The Movie Channel (multiplexed).
Video-On-Demand: No
Pay-Per-View
iN DEMAND (delivered digitally); Playboy TV (delivered digitally); Club Jenna (delivered digitally).
Internet Service
Operational: No.
Telephone Service
None
Miles of Plant: 34.0 (coaxial); None (fiber optic). Homes passed: 1,139.
Regional Manager: Mike Taylor. Chief Technician: Larry Stafford.
Ownership: Rapid Communications LLC (MSO).

COUSHATTA—Red River Cable TV, PO Box 674, 1813 Bessie St, Coushatta, LA 71019-0674. Phone: 318-932-4991. Fax: 318-932-5123. ICA: LA0092.
TV Market Ranking: Outside TV Markets (COUSHATTA). Franchise award date: N.A. Franchise expiration date: N.A. Began: January 1, 1979.
Channel capacity: N.A. Channels available but not in use: N.A.
Basic Service
Subscribers: N.A.
Programming (received off-air): KARD (FOX) West Monroe; KLTS-TV (PBS) Shreveport; KMSS-TV (FOX) Shreveport; KNTS-LP (IND) Natchitoches; KSHV-TV (MNT) Shreveport; KSLA (CBS) Shreveport; KTAL-TV (NBC) Texarkana; KTBS-TV (ABC) Shreveport; truTV.
Programming (via satellite): American Movie Classics; Animal Planet; Arts & Entertainment; BET Networks; Cartoon Network; CNN; Discovery Channel; ESPN; ESPN 2; Food Network; Fox News Channel; FX; Great American Country; Hallmark Channel; HGTV; History Channel; Home Shopping Network; Lifetime; National Geographic Channel; Outdoor Channel; SoapNet; Speed Channel; Syfy; TBS Superstation; The Learning Channel; Trinity Broadcasting Network; Turner Classic Movies; Turner Network TV; USA Network; WE tv; Weather Channel; WGN America.
Fee: $15.00 installation; $32.84 monthly.
Pay Service 1
Pay Units: N.A.
Programming (via satellite): Cinemax; Encore; HBO.
Video-On-Demand: No
Internet Service
Operational: Yes.
Broadband Service: In-house.
Fee: $35.00 monthly; $50.00 modem purchase.
Telephone Service
None
Miles of Plant: 23.0 (coaxial); None (fiber optic). Homes passed: 800.
Manager: Jimmy Hardy. Secretary: Stephanie Collier.
Ownership: Red River Cable TV (MSO).

CROWLEY—Cox Communications. Now served by BATON ROUGE, LA [LA0003]. ICA: LA0152.

DE QUINCY—CommuniComm Services. Now served by VINTON, LA [LA0064]. ICA: LA0047.

DE RIDDER—Suddenlink Communications, 1501 N Pine St, Deridder, LA 70634-2467. Phones: 888-822-5151; 337-463-7728. Fax: 337-463-7728. Web Site: http://www.suddenlink.com. Also serves Beauregard Parish, Rosepine & Vernon Parish. ICA: LA0031.
TV Market Ranking: Below 100 (Beauregard Parish (portions), Vernon Parish (portions)); Outside TV Markets (Beauregard Parish (portions), DE RIDDER, Rosepine, Vernon Parish (portions)). Franchise award date: N.A. Franchise expiration date: N.A. Began: September 1, 1965.
Channel capacity: 35 (operating 2-way). Channels available but not in use: N.A.
Basic Service
Subscribers: N.A.
Programming (received off-air): KALB-TV (CBS, NBC) Alexandria; KBMT (ABC) Beaumont; KLFY-TV (CBS) Lafayette; KLTL-TV (PBS) Lake Charles; KPLC (NBC) Lake Charles; KVHP (FOX) Lake Charles; allband FM.
Programming (via satellite): ABC Family Channel; C-SPAN; C-SPAN 2; Home Shopping Network; INSP; QVC; TBS Superstation; Turner Network TV; WGN America.
Fee: $35.00 installation; $11.98 monthly.
Expanded Basic Service 1
Subscribers: N.A.
Programming (via satellite): AMC; Animal Planet; Arts & Entertainment; BET Networks; Bravo!; Cartoon Network; CNBC; CNN; Comcast Sports Net Southwest; Comedy Central; Discovery Channel; Disney Channel; E! Entertainment Television; ESPN; ESPN 2; Food Network; Fox News Channel; FX; Great American Country; Headline News; HGTV; History Channel; Lifetime; MSNBC; MTV; Nickelodeon; Speed Channel; Spike TV; Syfy; The Learning Channel; Travel Channel; TV Land; USA Network; Versus; VH1; Weather Channel.
Fee: $36.83 monthly.
Digital Basic Service
Subscribers: N.A.
Programming (via satellite): BBC America; Bio; Bloomberg Television; Discovery Digital Networks; Encore Action; ESPN Classic Sports; ESPNews; Fox Sports World; Fuse; G4; GAS; Golf Channel; GSN; Hallmark Channel; History Channel International; Independent Film Channel; Lifetime Movie Network; MTV Networks Digital Suite; NBA TV; NickToons TV; Outdoor Channel; SoapNet; Sundance Channel; Toon Disney; Turner Classic Movies.
Digital Pay Service 1
Pay Units: N.A.
Programming (via satellite): Cinemax (multiplexed); Encore (multiplexed); HBO (multiplexed); Showtime (multiplexed); The Movie Channel.
Video-On-Demand: No
Pay-Per-View
Fresh (delivered digitally); Playboy TV (delivered digitally); sports (delivered digitally); ESPN Gameplan (delivered digitally); iN DEMAND (delivered digitally).
Internet Service
Operational: Yes.
Broadband Service: Cebridge High Speed Cable Internet.
Fee: $45.00 installation; $39.95 monthly.
Telephone Service
Digital: Operational
Fee: $39.95 monthly
Miles of Plant: 96.0 (coaxial); None (fiber optic). Additional miles planned: 4.0 (coaxial). Homes passed: 6,000. Total homes in franchised area: 6,000.
Manager: Mike Stidham. Chief Technician: Steve Shirley.
City fee: 3% of gross.
Ownership: Cequel Communications LLC (MSO).

DELHI—CMA Cablevision, 3759 Old Sterlington Rd, Monroe, LA 71203-3086. Phones: 972-233-9614 (Corporate office); 318-345-1010. Fax: 318-343-5255. Web Site: http://www.cmaaccess.com. Also serves Rayville. ICA: LA0082.
TV Market Ranking: 99 (DELHI, Rayville). Franchise award date: August 14, 1979. Franchise expiration date: N.A. Began: January 1, 1980.
Channel capacity: N.A. Channels available but not in use: N.A.
Basic Service
Subscribers: 1,350.
Programming (received off-air): KAQY (ABC) Columbia; KARD (FOX) West Monroe; KEJB (MNT)lorado; KLTM-TV (PBS) Monroe; KNOE-TV (CBS, CW) Monroe; KTVE (NBC) El Dorado.
Programming (via satellite): CNN; C-SPAN; Fox News Channel; Hallmark Channel; Headline News; Home Shopping Network; INSP; ION Television; QVC; TBS Superstation; Weather Channel; WGN America.
Fee: $39.95 installation; $17.95 monthly; $12.95 additional installation.
Expanded Basic Service 1
Subscribers: N.A.
Programming (via satellite): ABC Family Channel; Animal Planet; Arts & Entertainment; BET Networks; Bravo; Cartoon Network; CNBC; Comcast Sports Net Southwest; Comedy Central; Country Music TV; Discovery Channel; E! Entertainment Television; ESPN; ESPN 2; ESPN Classic Sports; Food Network; FX; Gospel Music Channel; HGTV; History Channel; Lifetime; Lifetime Movie Network; MTV; National Geographic Channel; Nickelodeon; Outdoor Channel; Spike TV; Syfy; The Learning Channel; Travel Channel; Trinity Broadcasting Network; truTV; Turner Classic Movies; Turner Network TV; TV Guide Network; TV Land; USA Network.
Fee: $24.50 monthly.
Digital Basic Service
Subscribers: N.A.
Programming (received off-air): KLTM-TV (PBS) Monroe; KNOE-TV (CBS, CW) Monroe.
Programming (via satellite): BBC America; Bio; Chiller; Discovery Channel HD; Discovery Health Channel; Discovery Home Channel; Discovery Kids Channel; Discovery Military Channel; Discovery Times Channel; DMX Music; ESPN HD; ESPNews; Fox Movie Channel; Fox Soccer; G4; Golf Channel; GSN; Halogen Network; History Channel International; Independent Film Chan-

nel; MTV2; Nick Jr.; NickToons TV; Science Channel; Sleuth; Speed Channel; Style Network; TeenNick; Turner Network TV HD.
Planned programming (via satellite): Universal HD.
Programming (via satellite): VH1 Country; WE tv.
Fee: $12.45 monthly.
Pay Service 1
Pay Units: N.A.
Programming (via satellite): HBO.
Fee: $14.95 installation; $13.95 monthly.
Digital Pay Service 1
Pay Units: N.A.
Programming (via satellite): Cinemax (multiplexed); Cinemax HD; Encore (multiplexed); HBO (multiplexed); HBO HD; Showtime (multiplexed); Showtime HD; Starz (multiplexed); The Movie Channel (multiplexed).
Fee: $10.95 monthly (Cinemax or Encore/ Starz), $13.95 monthly (HBO or Showtime).
Video-On-Demand: No
Pay-Per-View
iN DEMAND (delivered digitally); Spice (delivered digitally); Playboy TV (delivered digitally).
Internet Service
Operational: Yes.
Broadband Service: CMA.
Fee: $39.95 installation; $39.95 monthly; $2.95 modem lease; $39.95 modem purchase.
Telephone Service
Digital: Operational
Fee: $39.95 monthly
Miles of Plant: 43.0 (coaxial); None (fiber optic). Homes passed: 1,650. Total homes in franchised area: 1,650.
General Manager: Jerry Smith. Marketing Director: Julie Ferguson.
Ownership: Cable Management Assoc. (MSO).

DIXIE INN—Formerly served by PC One Cable. No longer in operation. Also serves DIXIE INN. ICA: LA0216.

DODSON—Formerly served by Cebridge Connections. No longer in operation. ICA: LA0153.

DRY PRONG—Rapid Cable, 515 E Longview Dr, Arp, TX 75750. Phone: 903-859-6492. Fax: 903-859-3708. Also serves Bentley & Grant Parish (portions). ICA: LA0090.
TV Market Ranking: Below 100 (Bentley, DRY PRONG, Grant Parish (portions)). Franchise award date: October 28, 1988. Franchise expiration date: N.A. Began: October 28, 1988.
Channel capacity: 40 (not 2-way capable). Channels available but not in use: N.A.
Basic Service
Subscribers: 434.
Programming (received off-air): KALB-TV (CBS, NBC) Alexandria; KLAX-TV (ABC) Alexandria; KLPA-TV (PBS) Alexandria; KNOE-TV (CBS, CW) Monroe; WNTZ-TV (FOX, MNT) Natchez.
Programming (via satellite): ABC Family Channel; Arts & Entertainment; Cartoon Network; CNBC; CNN; Discovery Channel; Disney Channel; E! Entertainment Television; ESPN; ESPN 2; Fox News Channel; Fox Sports Net; Great American Country; Headline News; HGTV; Home Shopping Network; Lifetime; National Geographic Channel; Nickelodeon; Outdoor Channel; SoapNet; Spike TV; Syfy; TBS Superstation; Trinity Broadcasting Network; Turner Classic Movies; Turner Network TV; USA Network; VH1; Weather Channel.
Fee: $54.95 installation; $44.05 monthly.
Digital Basic Service
Subscribers: N.A.
Programming (via satellite): BBC America; Bio; Bloomberg Television; Discovery Health Channel; Discovery Kids Channel; Discovery Military Channel; Discovery Planet Green; DMX Music; ESPN Classic Sports; ESPNews; Fox College Sports Atlantic; Fox College Sports Central; Fox College Sports Pacific; Fox Soccer; Fuse; G4; Golf Channel; GSN; History Channel; History Channel International; ID Investigation Discovery; Independent Film Channel; Science Channel; ShopNBC; Sleuth; Speed Channel; Style Network; Sundance Channel; Toon Disney; Versus; WE tv.
Pay Service 1
Pay Units: 25.
Programming (via satellite): Cinemax.
Fee: $12.95 monthly.
Pay Service 2
Pay Units: 26.
Programming (via satellite): HBO.
Fee: $12.95 monthly.
Pay Service 3
Pay Units: 23.
Programming (via satellite): Showtime.
Fee: $12.95 monthly.
Digital Pay Service 1
Pay Units: N.A.
Programming (via satellite): Cinemax (multiplexed); Encore (multiplexed); Flix; HBO (multiplexed); Showtime (multiplexed); Starz (multiplexed); The Movie Channel (multiplexed).
Video-On-Demand: No
Internet Service
Operational: No.
Telephone Service
None
Miles of Plant: 52.0 (coaxial); None (fiber optic). Homes passed: 838.
Regional Manager: Mike Taylor. Chief Technician: Ronnie Stafford.
Ownership: Rapid Communications LLC (MSO).

EFFIE—Rapid Cable, 515 E Longview Dr, Arp, TX 75750. Phone: 903-859-6492. Fax: 903-859-3708. ICA: LA0156.
TV Market Ranking: Below 100 (EFFIE). Franchise award date: N.A. Franchise expiration date: N.A. Began: N.A.
Channel capacity: 42 (not 2-way capable). Channels available but not in use: N.A.
Basic Service
Subscribers: 168.
Programming (received off-air): KALB-TV (CBS, NBC) Alexandria; KLAX-TV (ABC) Alexandria; KLFY-TV (CBS) Lafayette; KLPA-TV (PBS) Alexandria; WNTZ-TV (FOX, MNT) Natchez.
Programming (via satellite): ABC Family Channel; AMC; Arts & Entertainment; Cartoon Network; CNN; Discovery Channel; Disney Channel; ESPN; Fox Sports Net; Great American Country; Headline News; HGTV; Home Shopping Network; Lifetime; Nickelodeon; Outdoor Channel; Spike TV; TBS Superstation; The Learning Channel; Trinity Broadcasting Network; Turner Network TV; USA Network; VH1; Weather Channel.
Fee: $54.95 installation; $44.05 monthly.
Pay Service 1
Pay Units: 6.
Programming (via satellite): HBO.
Fee: $12.95 monthly.

Pay Service 2
Pay Units: 15.
Programming (via satellite): Showtime.
Fee: $12.95 monthly.
Pay Service 3
Pay Units: 6.
Programming (via satellite): The Movie Channel.
Fee: $12.95 monthly.
Video-On-Demand: No
Internet Service
Operational: No.
Telephone Service
None
Miles of Plant: 21.0 (coaxial); None (fiber optic). Homes passed: 363.
Regional Manager: Mike Taylor. Chief Technician: Ronnie Stafford.
Ownership: Rapid Communications LLC (MSO).

EGAN—Formerly served by Trust Cable. No longer in operation. ICA: LA0157.

ESTHERWOOD—Rapid Cable, 515 E Longview Dr, Arp, TX 75750. Phone: 903-859-6492. Fax: 903-859-3708. Also serves Acadia Parish, Mermentau & Morse. ICA: LA0159.
TV Market Ranking: Below 100 (Acadia Parish, ESTHERWOOD, Mermentau, Morse). Franchise award date: N.A. Franchise expiration date: N.A. Began: October 1, 1988.
Channel capacity: N.A. Channels available but not in use: N.A.
Basic Service
Subscribers: N.A.
Programming (received off-air): KADN-TV (FOX) Lafayette; KAJN-LP (IND) Lafayette; KATC (ABC) Lafayette; KLAF-LP Lafayette; KLFY-TV (CBS) Lafayette; KLTL-TV (PBS) Lake Charles; KPLC (NBC) Lake Charles; KVHP (FOX) Lake Charles.
Programming (via satellite): QVC; Trinity Broadcasting Network; WGN America.
Fee: $54.95 installation; $20.95 monthly.
Expanded Basic Service 1
Subscribers: N.A.
Programming (via satellite): ABC Family Channel; AMC; Arts & Entertainment; BET Networks; Bravo; Cartoon Network; CNBC; CNN; Comcast Sports Net Southwest; Comedy Central; Country Music TV; Discovery Channel; Disney Channel; E! Entertainment Television; ESPN; ESPN 2; Eternal Word TV Network; Fox News Channel; FX; G4; Golf Channel; Headline News; HGTV; History Channel; Lifetime; MTV; Nickelodeon; Outdoor Channel; Oxygen; Speed Channel; Spike TV; Syfy; TBS Superstation; The Learning Channel; Turner Classic Movies; Turner Network TV; TV Land; USA Network; VH1; WE tv; Weather Channel.
Fee: $23.10 monthly.
Digital Basic Service
Subscribers: N.A.
Programming (via satellite): BBC America; Bio; Bloomberg Television; CMT Pure Country; Discovery en Espanol; Discovery Health Channel; Discovery Kids Channel; Discovery Military Channel; Discovery Planet Green; DMX Music; Do-It-Yourself; ESPN Classic Sports; FitTV; Fox Movie Channel; Fox Soccer; Fuse; GSN; History Channel International; ID Investigation Discovery; Independent Film Channel; Lifetime Movie Network; MTV Hits; MTV Jams; MTV Tres; MTV2; Nick Jr.; Nick Too; NickToons TV; Science Channel; Style Network; Sundance Channel; TeenNick; Toon Disney; VH1 Classic; VH1 Soul.
Fee: $12.95 monthly.
Digital Pay Service 1
Pay Units: N.A.
Programming (via satellite): Cinemax (multiplexed); Encore (multiplexed); Flix; HBO (multiplexed); LOGO; Showtime (multiplexed); Starz (multiplexed); The Movie Channel (multiplexed).
Video-On-Demand: No
Pay-Per-View
iN DEMAND (delivered digitally); Club Jenna (delivered digitally); Spice: Xcess (delivered digitally); Playboy TV (delivered digitally).
Internet Service
Operational: No.
Telephone Service
None
Regional Manager: Mike Taylor. Chief Technician: Larry Stafford.
Ownership: Rapid Communications LLC (MSO).

ETHEL—Trust Cable, PO Box 16512, 15 Northtown Dr, Ste L, Jackson, MS 39236. Phone: 601-957-7979. Fax: 601-977-7736. Web Site: http://www.trustcable.com. Also serves Clinton, Jackson, Norwood & Wilson. ICA: LA0160.
TV Market Ranking: 87 (Clinton, ETHEL, Jackson, Wilson); Outside TV Markets (Norwood). Franchise award date: N.A. Franchise expiration date: N.A. Began: N.A.
Channel capacity: N.A. Channels available but not in use: N.A.
Basic Service
Subscribers: 1,375.
Programming (received off-air): KLPB-TV (PBS) Lafayette; WAFB (CBS) Baton Rouge; WBRZ-TV (ABC) Baton Rouge; WGMB-TV (FOX) Baton Rouge; WVLA-TV (NBC) Baton Rouge.
Programming (via satellite): ABC Family Channel; AMC; Animal Planet; Arts & Entertainment; BET Networks; Cartoon Network; CNN; Comedy Central; Country Music TV; Cox Sports Television; C-SPAN; Discovery Channel; Disney Channel; ESPN; ESPN 2; Food Network; Fox News Channel; Fox Sports Net; FX; Golf Channel; Hallmark Channel; HGTV; History Channel; INSP; KTLA (CW) Los Angeles; Lifetime; MTV; Nickelodeon; Outdoor Channel; QVC; SoapNet; Speed Channel; Spike TV; Syfy; TBS Superstation; The Learning Channel; Trinity Broadcasting Network; truTV; Turner Classic Movies; Turner Network TV; TV Land; USA Network; VH1; Weather Channel; WGN America.
Fee: $37.99 monthly.

Pay Service 1
Pay Units: N.A.
Programming (via satellite): Cinemax; HBO (multiplexed).
Fee: $19.95 monthly.
Video-On-Demand: No
Internet Service
Operational: Yes.
Subscribers: 350.
Fee: $29.99 installation; $29.99 monthly; $6.95 modem lease; $69.95 modem purchase.
Telephone Service
None
President: Steven Inzinna.
Ownership: Trust Communications (MSO).

FARMERVILLE—CMA Cablevision, 503 S Main St, Homer, LA 71040-3955. Phones: 972-233-9614 (Corporate office); 800-753-2465; 318-927-2503. Web Site: http://www.cmaaccess.com. ICA: LA0067.
TV Market Ranking: 99 (FARMERVILLE). Franchise award date: N.A. Franchise expiration date: N.A. Began: January 1, 1976.
Channel capacity: N.A. Channels available but not in use: N.A.
Basic Service
Subscribers: 825.
Programming (received off-air): KARD (FOX) West Monroe; KLTM-TV (PBS) Monroe; KNOE-TV (CBS, CW) Monroe; KTVE (NBC) El Dorado.
Programming (via satellite): ABC Family Channel; ESPN; Hallmark Channel; Home Shopping Network; TBS Superstation; WGN America.
Current originations: Public Access.
Fee: $39.95 installation; $14.95 monthly; $12.95 additional installation.
Expanded Basic Service 1
Subscribers: N.A.
Programming (received off-air): KMCT-TV (IND) West Monroe.
Programming (via satellite): Animal Planet; Arts & Entertainment; BET Networks; CNN; Country Music TV; Discovery Channel; ESPN 2; Fox News Channel; HGTV; History Channel; Lifetime; MTV; Nickelodeon; Outdoor Channel; Spike TV; The Learning Channel; Turner Classic Movies; Turner Network TV; TV Land; USA Network; VH1; Weather Channel.
Fee: $25.00 monthly.
Pay Service 1
Pay Units: N.A.
Programming (via satellite): HBO; The Movie Channel.
Fee: $14.95 installation; $13.95 monthly (each).
Video-On-Demand: No
Internet Service
Operational: No.
Telephone Service
None
Miles of Plant: 31.0 (coaxial); None (fiber optic). Homes passed: 1,600. Total homes in franchised area: 1,800.
General Manager: Jerry Smith. Marketing Director: Julie Ferguson.
City fee: 3% of gross.
Ownership: Cable Management Assoc. (MSO).

FERRIDAY—Cable South Media, 301 W 1st Ave, Crossett, AR 71635. Phone: 870-305-1241. Also serves Concordia Parish & Ridgecrest. ICA: LA0233.
TV Market Ranking: Below 100 (Concordia Parish, FERRIDAY, Ridgecrest).
Channel capacity: N.A. Channels available but not in use: N.A.
Basic Service
Subscribers: N.A.
Programming (received off-air): KALB-TV (CBS, NBC) Alexandria; KAQY (ABC) Columbia; KARD (FOX) West Monroe; KLAX-TV (ABC) Alexandria; KLTM-TV (PBS) Monroe; KNOE-TV (CBS, CW) Monroe; WAFB (CBS) Baton Rouge; WNTZ-TV (FOX, MNT) Natchez.
Programming (via satellite): Product Information Network; QVC; TV Guide Network; WGN America.
Current originations: Government Access.
Expanded Basic Service 1
Subscribers: N.A.
Programming (via satellite): ABC Family Channel; AMC; Animal Planet; Arts & Entertainment; BET Networks; Bravo; Cartoon Network; CNBC; CNN; Comcast Sports Net Southwest; Comedy Central; Country Music TV; C-SPAN; C-SPAN 2; Discovery Channel; Disney Channel; E! Entertainment Television; ESPN; ESPN 2; Food Network; Fox News Channel; FX; G4; Hallmark Channel; Headline News; HGTV; History Channel; Home Shopping Network; INSP; ION Television; Lifetime; MSNBC; MTV; National Geographic Channel; Nickelodeon; Outdoor Channel; Oxygen; Product Information Network; SoapNet; Speed Channel; Spike TV; Syfy; TBS Superstation; The Learning Channel; Toon Disney; Travel Channel; Trinity Broadcasting Network; truTV; Turner Classic Movies; Turner Network TV; TV Land; USA Network; Versus; VH1; WE tv; Weather Channel.
Pay Service 1
Pay Units: N.A.
Programming (via satellite): Cinemax; HBO.
Video-On-Demand: No
Internet Service
Operational: No.
Telephone Service
None
Ownership: Cable South Media III LLC (MSO).

FOLSOM—Charter Communications. Now served by SLIDELL (formerly St. Tammany Parish), LA [LA0182]. ICA: LA0161.

FORKED ISLAND—Kaplan Telephone Co. Formerly served by Kaplan, LA [LA0162]. This cable system has converted to IPTV, 118 N Irving Ave, Kaplan, LA 70548. Phones: 866-643-7171; 337-647-7171. Fax: 337-643-6000. E-mail: kaplan@kaplantel.net. Web Site: http://www.ktconline.net. ICA: LA5020.
TV Market Ranking: Below 100 (FORKED ISLAND).
Channel capacity: N.A. Channels available but not in use: N.A.
Internet Service
Operational: Yes.
Telephone Service
Digital: Operational
Ownership: Kaplan Telephone Co. Inc.

FORT POLK—Suddenlink Communications, 12444 Powerscourt Dr, Saint Louis, MO 63131-3660. Phones: 800-999-6845 (Customer service); 314-965-2020. Fax: 903-561-5485. Web Site: http://www.suddenlink.com. Also serves Anacoco. ICA: LA0163.
TV Market Ranking: Outside TV Markets (Anacoco, FORT POLK). Franchise award date: N.A. Franchise expiration date: N.A. Began: July 1, 1978.
Channel capacity: N.A. Channels available but not in use: N.A.
Basic Service
Subscribers: N.A.
Programming (received off-air): KALB-TV (CBS, NBC) Alexandria; KLAX-TV (ABC) Alexandria; KLFY-TV (CBS) Lafayette; WNTZ-TV (FOX, MNT) Natchez.
Programming (via satellite): Eternal Word TV Network; QVC; TV Guide Network.
Fee: $18.95 monthly.
Expanded Basic Service 1
Subscribers: N.A.
Programming (via satellite): ABC Family Channel; AMC; Animal Planet; Arts & Entertainment; BET Networks; Bravo; Cartoon Network; CNBC; CNN; Comcast Sports Net Southwest; Comedy Central; C-SPAN; Discovery Digital Networks; Disney Channel; E! Entertainment Television; ESPN; ESPN 2; ESPN Classic Sports; Food Network; Fox News Channel; FX; Golf Channel; Great American Country; Hallmark Channel; Headline News; HGTV; History Channel; INSP; Lifetime; MSNBC; MTV; National Geographic Channel; Nickelodeon; Outdoor Channel; Shopping Channel; Speed Channel; Spike TV; Syfy; TBS Superstation; Telemundo; The Learning Channel; Turner Classic Movies; Turner Network TV; TV Land; Univision; USA Network; VH1; Weather Channel.
Fee: $10.00 installation; $25.00 monthly.
Digital Basic Service
Subscribers: N.A.
Programming (via satellite): BBC America; Bio; Bloomberg Television; Canales N; C-SPAN 3; Discovery Digital Networks; Do-It-Yourself; ESPNews; Fox College Sports Atlantic; Fox College Sports Central; Fox College Sports Pacific; Fox Movie Channel; Fuse; G4; GSN; History Channel International; Independent Film Channel; Sleuth; SoapNet; Sundance Channel; Toon Disney; Versus; WE tv.
Fee: $3.99 monthly.
Pay Service 1
Pay Units: N.A.
Programming (via satellite): HBO; Showtime; Starz; The Movie Channel.
Digital Pay Service 1
Pay Units: N.A.
Programming (via satellite): Cinemax (multiplexed); Flix; HBO (multiplexed); Showtime (multiplexed); Starz (multiplexed); The Movie Channel (multiplexed).
Video-On-Demand: No
Internet Service
Operational: Yes. Began: October 13, 2004.
Broadband Service: Cebridge High Speed Cable Internet.
Fee: $45.00 installation; $29.95 monthly.
Telephone Service
Digital: Operational
Fee: $39.95 monthly
Miles of Plant: 15.0 (coaxial); None (fiber optic).
Regional Manager: Todd Cruthird.
Ownership: Cequel Communications LLC (MSO).

FOUR CORNERS—Formerly served by CableSouth Inc. No longer in operation. ICA: LA0164.

FRANKLIN—Cox Communications. Now served by BATON ROUGE, LA [LA0003]. ICA: LA0030.

GEORGETOWN—Formerly served by Almega Cable. No longer in operation. ICA: LA0132.

GIBSLAND—Rapid Cable, 515 E Longview Dr, Arp, TX 75750. Phone: 903-859-6492. Fax: 903-859-3708. ICA: LA0115.
TV Market Ranking: Below 100 (GIBSLAND). Franchise award date: N.A. Franchise expiration date: N.A. Began: December 1, 1982.
Channel capacity: 54 (not 2-way capable). Channels available but not in use: N.A.
Basic Service
Subscribers: 125.
Programming (received off-air): KLTS-TV (PBS) Shreveport; KPXJ (CW) Minden; KSHV-TV (MNT) Shreveport; KSLA (CBS) Shreveport; KTAL-TV (NBC) Texarkana; KTBS-TV (ABC) Shreveport.
Programming (via satellite): ABC Family Channel; Arts & Entertainment; BET Networks; Cartoon Network; CNN; Discovery Channel; Disney Channel; ESPN; Great American Country; Halogen Network; Headline News; HGTV; Home Shopping Network; Lifetime; National Geographic Channel; Nickelodeon; Spike TV; TBS Superstation; The Learning Channel; Trinity Broadcasting Network; Turner Classic Movies; Turner Network TV; USA Network; Weather Channel.
Fee: $54.95 installation; $44.05 monthly.
Pay Service 1
Pay Units: 19.
Programming (via satellite): HBO.
Fee: $12.95 monthly.
Pay Service 2
Pay Units: 9.
Programming (via satellite): The Movie Channel.
Fee: $12.95 monthly.
Pay Service 3
Pay Units: 42.
Programming (via satellite): Showtime.
Fee: $12.95 monthly.
Video-On-Demand: No
Internet Service
Operational: No.
Telephone Service
None
Miles of Plant: 10.0 (coaxial); None (fiber optic). Homes passed: 503.
Regional Manager: Mike Taylor. Chief Technician: Larry Stafford.
Ownership: Rapid Communications LLC (MSO).

GOLDEN MEADOW—Vision Communications, 115 West 10th Blvd, Larose, LA 70373. Phones: 800-256-5665; 985-693-4111. Fax: 985-693-3049. Web Site: http://www.viscom.net. Also serves Cut Off, Fourchon, Galliano, Gheens, Grand Isle, Lafourche Parish, Larose, Leeville, Lockport, Mathews & Raceland. ICA: LA0014.
TV Market Ranking: 31 (Lafourche Parish (portions)); Outside TV Markets (Cut Off, Fourchon, Galliano, Gheens, GOLDEN MEADOW, Grand Isle, Larose, Leeville, Lockport, Mathews, Raceland, Lafourche Parish (portions)). Franchise award date: N.A. Franchise expiration date: N.A. Began: April 1, 1969.
Channel capacity: N.A. Channels available but not in use: N.A.
Basic Service
Subscribers: 12,500.
Programming (received off-air): KFOL-CD (IND) Houma; WAFB (CBS) Baton Rouge; WBRZ-TV (ABC) Baton Rouge; WDSU (NBC) New Orleans; WGNO (ABC) New Orleans; WHNO (IND) New Orleans; WNOL-TV (CW) New Orleans; WPXL-TV (ION) New Orleans; WUPL (MNT) Slidell; WVLA-TV (NBC) Baton Rouge; WVUE-DT

(FOX) New Orleans; WWL-TV (CBS) New Orleans; WYES-TV (PBS) New Orleans.

Programming (via satellite): ABC Family Channel; AMC; Animal Planet; Arts & Entertainment; BET Networks; Bravo; Cartoon Network; CNBC; CNN; Comcast Sports Net Southwest; Comedy Central; Country Music TV; Cox Sports Television; C-SPAN; C-SPAN 2; Discovery Channel; Disney Channel; E! Entertainment Television; ESPN; ESPN 2; ESPN Classic Sports; ESPNews; Eternal Word TV Network; Food Network; Fox News Channel; FX; Hallmark Channel; Hallmark Movie Channel; Headline News; HGTV; History Channel; Home Shopping Network; Lifetime; MSNBC; MTV; National Geographic Channel; Nickelodeon; Oxygen; QVC; Spike TV; Syfy; TBS Superstation; Telemundo; The Learning Channel; The Sportsman Channel; Toon Disney; Travel Channel; Trinity Broadcasting Network; truTV; Turner Network TV; TV Guide Network; TV Land; USA Network; VH1; Weather Channel; WGN America; WLAE-TV (PBS) New Orleans.

Fee: $19.99 monthly.

Digital Basic Service

Subscribers: 1,660.

Programming (via satellite): BBC America; Bloomberg Television; Discovery Digital Networks; Fox College Sports Atlantic; Fox College Sports Central; Fox College Sports Pacific; Fox Soccer; G4; Golf Channel; GSN; Halogen Network; MTV Networks Digital Suite; Nick Jr.; Outdoor Channel; Ovation; Speed Channel.

Fee: $8.95 monthly.

Digital Pay Service 1

Pay Units: N.A.

Programming (via satellite): Cinemax (multiplexed); Encore (multiplexed); HBO (multiplexed); Showtime (multiplexed); Starz (multiplexed); Sundance Channel; The Movie Channel (multiplexed).

Fee: $12.95 monthly (HBO, Cinemax, Showtime/TMC or Starz/Encore).

Video-On-Demand: No

Internet Service

Operational: Yes, Dial-up.

Broadband Service: In-house.

Fee: $100.00 installation; $46.99 monthly; $4.99 modem lease; $80.00 modem purchase.

Telephone Service

None

Miles of Plant: 240.0 (coaxial); 30.0 (fiber optic). Homes passed: 15,500. Total homes in franchised area: 15,500.

President: James Callahan. Chief Technician: Danny Landry. Marketing Director: Christie Duet.

City fee: 3% of gross; 2% of gross (Golden Meadow).

Ownership: Vision Communications LLC (Louisiana) (MSO).

GRAMERCY—Cox Communications. Now served by BATON ROUGE, LA [LA0003]. ICA: LA0167.

GRAND CHENIER—CableSouth Inc. Now served by CARLYSS, LA [LA0063]. ICA: LA0168.

GRAND COTEAU—Allen's TV Cable Service Inc., 1580 I-49 N Service Rd, Grand Coteau, LA 70541. Phones: 985-384-8335 (Morgan City office); 337-662-5315. Fax: 985-384-5243. E-mail: info@atvci.net. Web Site: http://www.atvc.net. Also serves Arnaudville, Port Barre, St. Landry Parish (portions), St. Martin Parish (portions) & Sunset. ICA: LA0207.

TV Market Ranking: 87 (St. Martin Parish (portions) (portions)); Below 100 (Arnaudville, GRAND COTEAU, Port Barre, St. Landry Parish (portions), Sunset, St. Martin Parish (portions) (portions)). Franchise award date: N.A. Franchise expiration date: N.A. Began: January 1, 1980.

Channel capacity: N.A. Channels available but not in use: N.A.

Basic Service

Subscribers: 1,157.

Programming (received off-air): KADN-TV (FOX) Lafayette; KALB-TV (CBS, NBC) Alexandria; KATC (ABC) Lafayette; KDCG-CD (ION) Opelousas; KLFY-TV (CBS) Lafayette; KLWB (IND) New Iberia; WAFB (CBS) Baton Rouge; WBRZ-TV (ABC) Baton Rouge; WLPB-TV (PBS) Baton Rouge; WVLA-TV (NBC) Baton Rouge.

Programming (via satellite): C-SPAN; Home Shopping Network; QVC; WGN America.

Fee: $26.95 installation; $15.10 monthly; $3.95 converter; $23.00 additional installation.

Expanded Basic Service 1

Subscribers: N.A.

Programming (via satellite): ABC Family Channel; AMC; Animal Planet; Arts & Entertainment; BET Networks; Bravo; Cartoon Network; CatholicTV; CNBC; CNN; Comcast Sports Net Southwest; Comedy Central; Country Music TV; Cox Sports Television; Discovery Channel; Disney Channel; E! Entertainment Television; ESPN; ESPN 2; ESPN Classic Sports; Eternal Word TV Network; Food Network; Fox News Channel; FX; Headline News; HGTV; History Channel; Lifetime; MSNBC; MTV; Nickelodeon; Outdoor Channel; SoapNet; Spike TV; Syfy; TBS Superstation; The Learning Channel; Travel Channel; Trinity Broadcasting Network; Turner Network TV; TV Land; USA Network; WE tv; Weather Channel.

Fee: $42.50 monthly.

Digital Basic Service

Subscribers: 500.

Programming (via satellite): 3 Angels Broadcasting Network; BBC America; Bio; Bloomberg Television; BYU Television; Church Channel; Classic Arts Showcase; Daystar TV Network; Discovery Channel HD; Discovery en Espanol; Discovery Health Channel; Discovery Home Channel; Discovery Kids Channel (multiplexed); Discovery Military Channel; Discovery Times Channel; Do-It-Yourself; ESPN 2 HD; ESPN HD; ESPNews; FamilyNet; FitTV; Fox Movie Channel; Fox Soccer; FSN Digital Atlantic; FSN Digital Central; FSN Digital Pacific; Fuse; G4; Golden Eagle Broadcasting; Golf Channel; Gospel Music TV; GSN; Hallmark Channel; History Channel International; Independent Film Channel; JCTV; Louisiana Legislative Network; MTV Hits; MTV Jams; MTV Tres; MTV2; National Geographic Channel; National Geographic Channel HD Network; Nick Jr.; Nick Too; NickToons TV; Science Channel; Speed Channel; TeenNick; Tennis Channel; Turner Classic Movies; Turner Network TV HD; Universal HD; Versus; VH1 Classic; VH1 Country; VH1 Soul.

Pay Service 1

Pay Units: N.A.

Programming (via satellite): HBO (multiplexed); Showtime (multiplexed); The Movie Channel (multiplexed).

Digital Pay Service 1

Pay Units: N.A.

Programming (via satellite): Cinemax (multiplexed); Encore (multiplexed); Flix; HBO (multiplexed); Playboy TV; Showtime (multiplexed); Starz (multiplexed); The Movie Channel (multiplexed).

Fee: $7.95 monthly (Encore), $11.50 monthly (Starz or Cinemax), $12.50 monthly (TMC), $12.95 monthly (Playboy), $13.95 monthly (Showtime), $15.25 monthly (HBO).

Video-On-Demand: No

Pay-Per-View

iN DEMAND (delivered digitally); Barker (delivered digitally); Hot Choice (delivered digitally); Playboy TV (delivered digitally); Fresh (delivered digitally); Shorteez (delivered digitally); Spice: Xcess (delivered digitally); Club Jenna (delivered digitally); Tigervision (delivered digitally).

Internet Service

Operational: Yes.

Subscribers: 300.

Broadband Service: atvci.net.

Fee: $34.95 monthly.

Telephone Service

Digital: Operational

Fee: $24.95-$39.95 monthly

Vice President: David C. Price. Chief Executive Officer & General Manager: Greg Price. Chief Technician: Chris A. Price. Office Manager: Cindy LaVergne.

Ownership: Allen's TV Cable Service Inc. (MSO).

GRAND LAKE—CableSouth Inc. Now served by CARLYSS, LA [LA0063]. ICA: LA0169.

GREENSBURG—Formerly served by Almega Cable. No longer in operation. ICA: LA0129.

HACKBERRY—Formerly served by Charter Communications. No longer in operation. ICA: LA0105.

HALL SUMMIT—Formerly served by Red River Cable TV. No longer in operation. ICA: LA0134.

HAMMOND—Charter Communications, 1304 Ridgefield Rd, Thibodaux, LA 70301. Phones: 800-741-4079 (Customer service); 800-888-2954; 985-542-8969. Fax: 985-447-9541. Web Site: http://www.charter.com. Also serves Albany, Amite City, Corbin, French Settlement, Frost, Holden, Independence, Killian, Livingston, Livingston Parish (portions), Lockhart, Ponchatoula, Port Vincent, Roseland, Satsuma, Springfield, Tangipahoa Parish, Tickfaw & Walker. ICA: LA0016.

TV Market Ranking: 31 (Tangipahoa Parish (portions)); 87 (Albany, Corbin, French Settlement, Frost, Holden, Killian, Livingston, Livingston Parish (portions) (portions), Lockhart, Port Vincent, Satsuma, Springfield, Walker); Below 100 (Amite City, HAMMOND, Independence, Ponchatoula, Roseland, Tickfaw, Tangipahoa Parish (portions), Livingston Parish (portions) (portions)). Franchise award date: February 1, 1974. Franchise expiration date: N.A. Began: September 1, 1974.

Channel capacity: N.A. Channels available but not in use: N.A.

Basic Service

Subscribers: 41,080.

Programming (received off-air): WAFB (CBS) Baton Rouge; WBRZ-TV (ABC) Baton Rouge; WDSU (NBC) New Orleans; WGNO (ABC) New Orleans; WHNO (IND) New Orleans; WLPB-TV (PBS) Baton Rouge; WNOL-TV (CW) New Orleans; WPXL-TV (ION) New Orleans; WSTY-LP (IND) Hammond; WUPL (MNT) Slidell; WVLA-TV (NBC) Baton Rouge; WVUE-DT (FOX) New Orleans; WWL-TV (CBS) New Orleans; WYES-TV (PBS) New Orleans; 14 FMs.

Programming (via satellite): Home Shopping Network; INSP; QVC; Trinity Broadcasting Network; WGN America.

Current originations: Leased Access; Government Access; Educational Access; Public Access.

Fee: $29.99 installation.

Expanded Basic Service 1

Subscribers: N.A.

Programming (via satellite): ABC Family Channel; AMC; Animal Planet; Arts & Entertainment; BET Networks; Bravo; Cartoon Network; CNBC; CNN; Comcast Sports Net Southwest; Comedy Central; Country Music TV; C-SPAN; C-SPAN 2; Discovery Channel; Disney Channel; E! Entertainment Television; ESPN; ESPN 2; Eternal Word TV Network; Food Network; Fox News Channel; FX; G4; Golf Channel; GSN; Hallmark Channel; Headline News; HGTV; History Channel; Lifetime; MSNBC; MTV; MTV2; National Geographic Channel; Nickelodeon; Oxygen; Speed Channel; Spike TV; Style Network; Syfy; TBS Superstation; Telemundo; The Learning Channel; Toon Disney; Travel Channel; truTV; Turner Classic Movies; Turner Network TV; TV Land; USA Network; Versus; VH1; WE tv; Weather Channel.

Fee: $42.99 monthly.

Digital Basic Service

Subscribers: N.A.

Programming (received off-air): WAFB (CBS) Baton Rouge; WYES-TV (PBS) New Orleans.

Programming (via satellite): BBC America; Bio; Bloomberg Television; CMT Pure Country; Cooking Channel; Discovery Digital Networks; Discovery HD Theater; Do-It-Yourself; ESPN 2 HD; ESPN Classic Sports; ESPN HD; Fox Movie Channel; Fox Soccer; Fuel TV; GAS; Great American Country; HDNet; HDNet Movies; History Channel International; Independent Film Channel; Lifetime Movie Network; MTV Networks Digital Suite; Music Choice; Nick Jr.; Nick Too; NickToons TV; Palladia; SoapNet; Sundance Channel; Tennis Channel; Turner Network TV HD; TVG Network; Universal HD; WealthTV HD.

Digital Pay Service 1

Pay Units: N.A.

Programming (via satellite): Cinemax (multiplexed); Cinemax HD; Encore (mul-

tiplexed); Flix; HBO (multiplexed); HBO HD; Showtime (multiplexed); Showtime HD; Starz (multiplexed); Starz HDTV; The Movie Channel (multiplexed).
Fee: $10.95 monthly (Starz & Encore), $12.95 monthly (Cinemax, HBO, Showtime or TMC).

Video-On-Demand: Yes

Pay-Per-View

iN DEMAND (delivered digitally); ESPN (delivered digitally); Fresh (delivered digitally); Playboy TV (delivered digitally); Shorteez (delivered digitally).

Internet Service

Operational: Yes.
Broadband Service: Charter Pipeline.
Fee: $29.99 monthly; $9.95 modem lease.

Telephone Service

Digital: Operational
Fee: $29.99 monthly

Miles of Plant: 2,000.0 (coaxial); 751.0 (fiber optic). Homes passed: 64,085.
Vice President & General Manager: Kip Kraemer. Operations Manager: Blaine Bercegeay. Technical Operations Director: Gary Savoie. Marketing Director: Lisa Brown. Government Relations Director: Jim Laurent.
City fee: 2% of gross.
Ownership: Charter Communications Inc. (MSO).

HAUGHTON—Formerly served by Cebridge Connections. No longer in operation. ICA: LA0227.

HAYNESVILLE—CMA Cablevision. Now served by HOMER, LA [LA0062]. ICA: LA0076.

HENRY—Formerly served by CableSouth Inc. No longer in operation. ICA: LA0170.

HOMER—CMA Cablevision, 503 S Main St, Homer, LA 71040-3955. Phones: 972-233-9614 (Corporate office); 800-753-2465; 318-927-2503. Web Site: http://www.cmaaccess.com. Also serves Haynesville. ICA: LA0062.
TV Market Ranking: 99 (Haynesville); Below 100 (HOMER). Franchise award date: N.A. Franchise expiration date: N.A. Began: January 1, 1980.
Channel capacity: 62 (operating 2-way). Channels available but not in use: N.A.

Basic Service

Subscribers: 1,320.
Programming (received off-air): KLTS-TV (PBS) Shreveport; KMSS-TV (FOX) Shreveport; KPXJ (CW) Minden; KSLA (CBS) Shreveport; KTAL-TV (NBC) Texarkana; KTBS-TV (ABC) Shreveport.
Programming (via satellite): BET Networks; CNN; Discovery Channel; Home Shopping Network; Lifetime; QVC; TBS Superstation; The Learning Channel; USA Network; Weather Channel; WGN America.
Fee: $39.95 installation; $18.45 monthly; $12.95 additional installation.

Expanded Basic Service 1

Subscribers: N.A.
Programming (received off-air): KSHV-TV (MNT) Shreveport.
Programming (via satellite): ABC Family Channel; Animal Planet; Arts & Entertainment; Bravo; Cartoon Network; Country Music TV; ESPN; ESPN 2; ESPN Classic Sports; Food Network; Fox News Channel; FX; Hallmark Channel; Headline News; HGTV; History Channel; INSP; ION Television; Local News on Cable; MTV; National Geographic Channel; Nickelodeon; Radar Channel; SoapNet; Spike TV; Syfy; The Sportsman Channel; Travel Channel; Turner Classic Movies; Turner Network TV; TV Land; VH1.
Fee: $21.00 monthly.

Digital Basic Service

Subscribers: N.A.
Programming (via satellite): BBC America; Bio; Bloomberg Television; CMT Pure Country; Discovery Health Channel; Discovery Home Channel; Discovery Kids Channel; Discovery Military Channel; Discovery Times Channel; DMX Music; ESPNews; Fox Movie Channel; Fox Soccer; G4; Golf Channel; GSN; Halogen Network; History Channel International; Independent Film Channel; Lifetime Movie Network; MTV Hits; MTV2; Nick Jr.; NickToons TV; Outdoor Channel; Science Channel; Sleuth; Speed Channel; TeenNick; Trinity Broadcasting Network; VH1 Classic; VH1 Soul; WE tv.
Fee: $12.95 monthly.

Pay Service 1

Pay Units: N.A.
Programming (via satellite): Cinemax; HBO; Showtime.
Fee: $14.95 installation; $10.95 monthly (Cinemax), $13.95 monthly (HBO or Showtime).

Digital Pay Service 1

Pay Units: N.A.
Programming (via satellite): Cinemax (multiplexed); Encore (multiplexed); Flix; HBO (multiplexed); Showtime (multiplexed); Starz (multiplexed); The Movie Channel (multiplexed).
Fee: $10.95 monthly (Cinemax or Encore/Starz), $13.95 monthly (HBO or Showtime).

Video-On-Demand: No

Internet Service

Operational: Yes.
Broadband Service: CMA.
Fee: $34.95 monthly; $2.95 modem lease.

Telephone Service

None

Miles of Plant: 53.0 (coaxial); None (fiber optic). Homes passed: 3,200. Total homes in franchised area: 3,200.
General Manager: Jerry Smith. Marketing Director: Julie Ferguson.
City fee: 3% of gross.
Ownership: Cable Management Assoc. (MSO).

HOSSTON—Comcast Cable, 6529 Quilen Rd, Shreveport, LA 71108-4438. Phone: 318-213-3322. Fax: 318-213-4225. Web Site: http://www.comcast.com. Also serves Belcher & Gilliam. ICA: LA0118.
TV Market Ranking: 58 (Belcher, Gilliam, HOSSTON). Franchise award date: N.A. Franchise expiration date: N.A. Began: October 1, 1990.
Channel capacity: N.A. Channels available but not in use: N.A.

Basic Service

Subscribers: 150.
Programming (received off-air): KLTS-TV (PBS) Shreveport; KMSS-TV (FOX) Shreveport; KSHV-TV (MNT) Shreveport; KSLA (CBS) Shreveport; KTAL-TV (NBC) Texarkana; KTBS-TV (ABC) Shreveport.
Programming (via satellite): C-SPAN; C-SPAN 2; CW+; QVC; WGN America.
Fee: $49.99 installation; $15.66 monthly.

Expanded Basic Service 1

Subscribers: N.A.
Programming (via satellite): ABC Family Channel; AMC; Animal Planet; Arts & Entertainment; BET Networks; Bravo; Cartoon Network; CNBC; CNN; Comcast Sports Net Southwest; Comedy Central; Country Music TV; Discovery Channel; Disney Channel; E! Entertainment Television; ESPN; Fox News Channel; FX; Golf Channel; Hallmark Channel; Halogen Network; Headline News; HGTV; History Channel; Lifetime; MoviePlex; MSNBC; MTV; Nickelodeon; ShopNBC; Speed Channel; Spike TV; Syfy; TBS Superstation; The Learning Channel; Travel Channel; Trinity Broadcasting Network; truTV; Turner Network TV; TV Land; USA Network; Versus; VH1; Weather Channel.
Fee: $34.33 monthly.

Pay Service 1

Pay Units: N.A.
Programming (via satellite): Cinemax; HBO.
Fee: $11.50 monthly (each).

Video-On-Demand: No

Internet Service

Operational: No.

Telephone Service

None

Miles of Plant: 26.0 (coaxial); None (fiber optic). Homes passed: 450. Total homes in franchised area: 602.
General Manager: Fred Fuller.
Ownership: Comcast Cable Communications Inc. (MSO).

HOUMA—Comcast Cable, 104 Lois Rd, Houma, LA 70363-6608. Phone: 985-876-5969. Fax: 985-851-0941. Web Site: http://www.comcast.com. Also serves Bayou Cane, Gray, Lafourche Parish, Schriever & Terrebonne Parish. ICA: LA0010.
TV Market Ranking: 31 (Lafourche Parish (portions)); Outside TV Markets (Bayou Cane, Gray, HOUMA, Schriever, Terrebonne Parish, Lafourche Parish (portions)). Franchise award date: October 1, 1964. Franchise expiration date: N.A. Began: October 1, 1964.
Channel capacity: N.A. Channels available but not in use: N.A.

Basic Service

Subscribers: 33,750.
Programming (received off-air): WAFB (CBS) Baton Rouge; WBRZ-TV (ABC) Baton Rouge; WDSU (NBC) New Orleans; WGNO (ABC) New Orleans; WHNO (IND) New Orleans; WLAE-TV (PBS) New Orleans; WNOL-TV (CW) New Orleans; WUPL (MNT) Slidell; WVUE-DT (FOX) New Orleans; WWL-TV (CBS) New Orleans; WYES-TV (PBS) New Orleans.
Programming (via satellite): Home Shopping Network; ION Television; QVC; ShopNBC; TV Guide Network; WGN America.
Current originations: Leased Access; Government Access; Educational Access.
Fee: $25.41 installation; $8.73 monthly; $2.03 converter.

Expanded Basic Service 1

Subscribers: N.A.
Programming (via satellite): ABC Family Channel; AMC; Animal Planet; Arts & Entertainment; BET Networks; Bravo; Cartoon Network; CNBC; CNN; Comcast Sports Net Southwest; Comedy Central; Country Music TV; C-SPAN; C-SPAN 2; Discovery Channel; Discovery Health Channel; Disney Channel; E! Entertainment Television; ESPN; ESPN 2; ESPN Classic Sports; Eternal Word TV Network; FitTV; Food Network; Fox News Channel; FX; Golf Channel; Hallmark Channel; Headline News; HGTV; History Channel; INSP; Lifetime; Lifetime Movie Network; MSNBC; MTV; Nickelodeon; Oxygen; Spike TV; Syfy; TBS Superstation; The Learning Channel; Travel Channel; Trinity Broadcasting Network; truTV; Turner Classic Movies; Turner Network TV; TV Land; Univision; USA Network; VH1; WE tv; Weather Channel.
Fee: $38.65 monthly.

Digital Basic Service

Subscribers: N.A.
Programming (received off-air): WDSU (NBC) New Orleans; WWL-TV (CBS) New Orleans; WYES-TV (PBS) New Orleans.
Programming (via satellite): AmericanLife TV Network; BBC America; Bio; Bloomberg Television; CBS College Sports Network; Cooking Channel; Cox Sports Television; Current; Discovery Digital Networks; Discovery HD Theater; Do-It-Yourself; Encore (multiplexed); ESPN HD; ESPNews; Fox College Sports Atlantic; Fox College Sports Central; Fox College Sports Pacific; Fox Movie Channel; Fox Soccer; Fuel TV; Fuse; G4; GAS; Great American Country; GSN; Halogen Network; HDNet; HDNet Movies; History Channel International; Independent Film Channel; INHD; MTV Networks Digital Suite; Music Choice; National Geographic Channel; NBA TV; Nick Jr.; NickToons TV; Ovation; Sleuth; Speed Channel; Style Network; Sundance Channel; Tennis Channel; Toon Disney; Turner Network TV HD; Versus.
Fee: $46.95 monthly.

Digital Pay Service 1

Pay Units: N.A.
Programming (via satellite): Cinemax (multiplexed); HBO (multiplexed); HBO HD; Showtime (multiplexed); Showtime HD; Starz (multiplexed); The Movie Channel (multiplexed).
Fee: $12.00 monthly (each package).

Video-On-Demand: Yes

Pay-Per-View

iN DEMAND; Fresh (delivered digitally); Hot Choice (delivered digitally); Playboy TV (delivered digitally); NBA League Pass (delivered digitally); NASCAR In Car (delivered digitally); MLB Extra Innings (delivered digitally); NHL Center Ice (delivered digitally).

Internet Service

Operational: Yes.
Broadband Service: Comcast High Speed Internet.
Fee: $99.95 installation; $42.95 monthly.

Telephone Service

Digital: Operational

Miles of Plant: 379.0 (coaxial); None (fiber optic). Homes passed: 37,000.
General Manager: Jacqui Dugas. Area Chief Technician: Gary Savoie. Marketing Manager: Michelle Pellegrin.
City fee: 5% of basic gross & premium net.
Ownership: Comcast Cable Communications Inc. (MSO).

INNIS—Formerly served by Spillway Communications Inc. No longer in operation. ICA: LA0172.

IOTA—Charter Communications. Now served by ST. LANDRY PARISH, LA [LA0022]. ICA: LA0108.

IOWA—Charter Communications, 330 Moosa Blvd, Eunice, LA 70535. Phones: 337-546-0087; 985-446-4900 (Thibodaux office). Fax: 337-546-0038. Web Site: http://www.charter.com. Also serves Bell City, Hayes, Lacassine & Le Bleu. ICA: LA0060.
TV Market Ranking: Below 100 (Bell City, Hayes, IOWA, Lacassine, Le Bleu). Franchise award date: May 12, 1980. Franchise

expiration date: N.A. Began: September 1, 1981.

Channel capacity: 40 (not 2-way capable). Channels available but not in use: 13.

Basic Service

Subscribers: 1,403.

Programming (received off-air): KATC (ABC) Lafayette; KFDM (CBS, CW) Beaumont; KLFY-TV (CBS) Lafayette; KLTL-TV (PBS) Lake Charles; KPLC (NBC) Lake Charles; KVHP (FOX) Lake Charles.

Programming (via satellite): QVC; WGN America.

Fee: $29.99 installation.

Expanded Basic Service 1

Subscribers: 1,384.

Programming (via satellite): ABC Family Channel; AMC; Animal Planet; Arts & Entertainment; BET Networks; Cartoon Network; CNBC; CNN; Comcast Sports Net Southwest; Country Music TV; C-SPAN; Discovery Channel; Disney Channel; ESPN; ESPN 2; Eternal Word TV Network; Food Network; Fox News Channel; Headline News; HGTV; History Channel; Home Shopping Network; ION Television; Lifetime; MTV; Nickelodeon; Outdoor Channel; SoapNet; Spike TV; Syfy; TBS Superstation; The Learning Channel; Toon Disney; Travel Channel; Trinity Broadcasting Network; Turner Classic Movies; Turner Network TV; TV Land; USA Network; WE tv; Weather Channel.

Fee: $42.99 monthly.

Pay Service 1

Pay Units: 359.

Programming (via satellite): Cinemax; HBO; Showtime.

Fee: $20.00 installation; $10.40 monthly.

Video-On-Demand: No

Internet Service

Operational: No.

Telephone Service

None

Miles of Plant: 82.0 (coaxial); None (fiber optic). Homes passed: 2,012.

Vice President & General Manager: Kip Kraemer. Operations Manager: Blane Bercegeay. Technical Operations Director: Gary Savoie. Plant Manager: Joe Semmes. Marketing Director: Lisa Brown.

City fee: 3% of basic gross.

Ownership: Charter Communications Inc. (MSO).

JENA—Cable South Media, 301 W 1st Ave, Crossett, AR 71635. Phone: 870-305-1241. Also serves Good Pine, La Salle Parish & Midway. ICA: LA0052.

TV Market Ranking: Below 100 (Good Pine, JENA, La Salle Parish, Midway). Franchise award date: N.A. Franchise expiration date: N.A. Began: January 1, 1964.

Channel capacity: N.A. Channels available but not in use: N.A.

Basic Service

Subscribers: 2,122.

Programming (received off-air): KALB-TV (CBS, NBC) Alexandria; KAQY (ABC) Columbia; KARD (FOX) West Monroe; KLAX-TV (ABC) Alexandria; KLTM-TV (PBS) Monroe; KNOE-TV (CBS, CW) Monroe; 3 FMs.

Programming (via satellite): ABC Family Channel; G4; HGTV; Home Shopping Network; INSP; Outdoor Channel; QVC; Syfy; Trinity Broadcasting Network; VH1; Weather Channel; WGN America.

Fee: $22.19 installation; $9.65 monthly; $1.19 converter.

Expanded Basic Service 1

Subscribers: 2,049.

Programming (via satellite): AMC; Animal Planet; Arts & Entertainment; BET Networks; Cartoon Network; CNBC; CNN; Comedy Central; Country Music TV; Discovery Channel; Disney Channel; E! Entertainment Television; ESPN; ESPN 2; Food Network; FX; Hallmark Channel; Headline News; History Channel; Lifetime; MSNBC; MTV; National Geographic Channel; Nickelodeon; Oxygen; Product Information Network; SoapNet; Spike TV; TBS Superstation; The Learning Channel; Toon Disney; Travel Channel; truTV; Turner Network TV; TV Land; USA Network; WE tv.

Fee: $22.19 installation; $12.60 monthly.

Digital Basic Service

Subscribers: N.A.

Programming (via satellite): BBC America; Bio; Bloomberg Television; Bravo; Discovery Digital Networks; ESPN Classic Sports; Fox Movie Channel; Fox Soccer; Fuse; GAS; Golf Channel; GSN; History Channel International; Independent Film Channel; INSP; Lifetime Movie Network; MTV Networks Digital Suite; Music Choice; Nick Jr.; ShopNBC; Speed Channel; Turner Classic Movies; Versus.

Pay Service 1

Pay Units: 146.

Programming (via satellite): HBO; Showtime; The Movie Channel.

Fee: $7.00 monthly.

Digital Pay Service 1

Pay Units: N.A.

Programming (via satellite): Cinemax (multiplexed); Encore (multiplexed); Flix; HBO (multiplexed); Showtime (multiplexed); Starz (multiplexed); The Movie Channel (multiplexed).

Video-On-Demand: No

Pay-Per-View

Hot Choice (delivered digitally); Playboy TV (delivered digitally); Fresh (delivered digitally); Shorteez (delivered digitally).

Internet Service

Operational: No.

Telephone Service

None

Miles of Plant: 97.0 (coaxial); None (fiber optic). Homes passed: 3,385.

City fee: 2% of gross.

Ownership: Cable South Media III LLC (MSO).

JONESBORO—Suddenlink Communications, 1520 S Caraway Rd, Jonesboro, AR 72401-5308. Phones: 888-822-5151; 318-259-4447. Fax: 318-259-4446. Web Site: http://www.suddenlink.com. Also serves East Hodge, Hodge, Jackson Parish (portions), North Hodge & Quitman. ICA: LA0173.

TV Market Ranking: 99 (Jackson Parish (portions)); Below 100 (Jackson Parish (portions)); Outside TV Markets (East Hodge, Hodge, JONESBORO, North Hodge, Quitman, Jackson Parish (portions)). Franchise award date: N.A. Franchise expiration date: N.A. Began: August 1, 1968.

Channel capacity: 42 (not 2-way capable). Channels available but not in use: None.

Basic Service

Subscribers: 2,650.

Programming (received off-air): KAQY (ABC) Columbia; KARD (FOX) West Monroe; KEJB (MNT)lorado; KLTM-TV (PBS) Monroe; KNOE-TV (CBS, CW) Monroe; KSLA (CBS) Shreveport; KTBS-TV (ABC) Shreveport; KTVE (NBC) El Dorado; allband FM.

Programming (via satellite): CNN; C-SPAN; ESPN; Great American Country; Headline News; Home Shopping Network; ION Television; TBS Superstation; Weather Channel.

Fee: $26.93 installation; $13.69 monthly.

Expanded Basic Service 1

Subscribers: N.A.

Programming (via satellite): ABC Family Channel; AMC; Arts & Entertainment; BET Networks; Cartoon Network; Cox Sports Television; Discovery Channel; Disney Channel; ESPN 2; FamilyNet; HGTV; History Channel; Lifetime; Lifetime Movie Network; Nickelodeon; Outdoor Channel; Spike TV; The Learning Channel; Turner Network TV; TV Land; USA Network; VH1.

Fee: $43.72 monthly.

Digital Basic Service

Subscribers: N.A.

Programming (via satellite): BBC America; Bio; Black Family Channel; Bloomberg Television; Discovery Digital Networks; DMX Music; Encore (multiplexed); ESPNews; Fox Soccer; Fuse; G4; Golf Channel; GSN; Halogen Network; History Channel International; Speed Channel; Sundance Channel; The Word Network; Toon Disney; Trinity Broadcasting Network; Versus.

Fee: $13.31 monthly.

Pay Service 1

Pay Units: N.A.

Programming (via satellite): HBO; Showtime; The Movie Channel.

Digital Pay Service 1

Pay Units: N.A.

Programming (via satellite): Cinemax; Encore; HBO (multiplexed); Showtime (multiplexed); Starz (multiplexed); The Movie Channel (multiplexed).

Video-On-Demand: No

Pay-Per-View

ESPN Now (delivered digitally); Action PPV (delivered digitally); ESPN Gameplan (delivered digitally); Shorteez (delivered digitally); Fresh (delivered digitally); Playboy TV (delivered digitally); iN DEMAND (delivered digitally).

Internet Service

Operational: Yes.

Telephone Service

Digital: Operational

Miles of Plant: 73.0 (coaxial); None (fiber optic).

Manager: William R. Rogers. Chief Technician: Richard Woods.

City fee: $50.00 annually.

Ownership: Cequel Communications LLC (MSO).

JONESVILLE—Cable South Media, 301 W 1st Ave, Crossett, AR 71635. Phone: 870-305-1241. ICA: LA0235.

TV Market Ranking: Below 100 (JONESVILLE).

Channel capacity: N.A. Channels available but not in use: N.A.

Basic Service

Subscribers: N.A.

Programming (received off-air): KALB-TV (CBS, NBC) Alexandria; KAQY (ABC) Columbia; KARD (FOX) West Monroe; KLAX-TV (ABC) Alexandria; KLFY-TV (CBS) Lafayette; KNOE-TV (CBS, CW) Monroe; WNTZ-TV (FOX, MNT) Natchez.

Programming (via satellite): Home Shopping Network; KLTM-TV (PBS) Monroe; QVC; WGN America.

Expanded Basic Service 1

Subscribers: N.A.

Programming (via satellite): ABC Family Channel; AMC; Animal Planet; Arts & Entertainment; BET Networks; CNBC; CNN; Country Music TV; C-SPAN; Discovery Channel; Disney Channel; E! Entertainment Television; ESPN; ESPN 2; G4; HGTV; History Channel; Lifetime; MSNBC; MTV; National Geographic Channel; Nickelodeon; Oxygen; SoapNet; Spike TV; Syfy; TBS Superstation; The Learning Channel; Toon Disney; Travel Channel; Trinity Broadcasting Network; Turner Network TV; TV Land; USA Network; Versus; VH1; WE tv; Weather Channel.

Pay Service 1

Pay Units: N.A.

Programming (via satellite): Cinemax; HBO.

Video-On-Demand: No

Internet Service

Operational: No.

Telephone Service

None

Ownership: Cable South Media III LLC (MSO).

KAPLAN—Kaplan Telephone Co. Formery [LA0162]. This cable system has converted to IPTV, 118 N Irving Ave, Kaplan, LA 70548. Phones: 866-643-7171; 337-643-7171. Fax: 337-643-6000. E-mail: kaplan@kaplantel.net. Web Site: http://www.ktconline.net. ICA: LA5021.

TV Market Ranking: Below 100 (KAPLAN). Franchise award date: N.A. Franchise expiration date: N.A. Began: N.A.

Channel capacity: N.A. Channels available but not in use: N.A.

Video-On-Demand: No

Pay-Per-View

Movies (delivered digitally), Fee: $3.95; Adult Programming (delivered digitally), Fee: $9.95.

Internet Service

Operational: Yes.

Telephone Service

Digital: Operational

President: Tony Turnley.

Ownership: Kaplan Telephone Co. Inc. (MSO).

KAPLAN—Kaplan Telephone Co. This cable system has converted to IPTV. See Kaplan, LA [LA5021], LA. ICA: LA0162.

KENTWOOD—Galaxy Cablevision, PO Box 1007, Sikeston, MO 63801-1007. Phones: 573-472-8200; 800-365-6988. Fax: 573-471-0119. Web Site: http://www.galaxycable.com. ICA: LA0098.

TV Market Ranking: Below 100 (KENTWOOD). Franchise award date: N.A. Franchise expiration date: N.A. Began: September 1, 1981.

Channel capacity: 78 (operating 2-way). Channels available but not in use: None.

Basic Service

Subscribers: 344.

Programming (received off-air): WAFB (CBS) Baton Rouge; WBRZ-TV (ABC) Baton Rouge; WDSU (NBC) New Orleans; WGNO (ABC) New Orleans; WLPB-TV (PBS) Baton Rouge; WNOL-TV (CW) New

Orleans; WPXL-TV (ION) New Orleans; WSTY-LP (IND) Hammond; WVLA-TV (NBC) Baton Rouge; WVUE-DT (FOX) New Orleans; WWL-TV (CBS) New Orleans.
Programming (via satellite): ABC Family Channel; Arts & Entertainment; BET Networks; Cartoon Network; CNBC; CNN; Comcast Sports Net Southeast; C-SPAN; Discovery Channel; Disney Channel; ESPN; ESPN 2; Fox News Channel; Fuse; FX; Great American Country; Hallmark Channel; Headline News; HGTV; Lifetime; Outdoor Channel; QVC; TBS Superstation; The Learning Channel; Toon Disney; Travel Channel; Trinity Broadcasting Network; Turner Classic Movies; Turner Network TV; USA Network; Weather Channel; WGN America.
Current originations: Public Access.
Fee: $43.50 monthly.

Digital Basic Service
Subscribers: 107.
Programming (via satellite): BBC America; Bio; Bloomberg Television; Discovery Digital Networks; DMX Music; ESPN Classic Sports; ESPNews; FitTV; Fox College Sports Atlantic; Fox College Sports Central; Fox College Sports Pacific; G4; Golf Channel; GSN; Halogen Network; History Channel; History Channel International; National Geographic Channel; Speed Channel; Style Network; WE tv.
Fee: $13.95 monthly.

Digital Expanded Basic Service
Subscribers: N.A.
Programming (via satellite): DMX Music; Encore; Fox Movie Channel; Lifetime Movie Network.
Fee: $13.95 monthly.

Pay Service 1
Pay Units: 45.
Programming (via satellite): Cinemax; HBO.

Digital Pay Service 1
Pay Units: N.A.
Programming (via satellite): Cinemax (multiplexed); Flix; HBO (multiplexed); Showtime (multiplexed); The Movie Channel (multiplexed).
Fee: $13.26 monthly.

Pay-Per-View
Addressable homes: 92.
ESPN Now (delivered digitally), Fee: $3.99, Addressable: Yes; Hot Choice (delivered digitally); Movies (delivered digitally); Playboy TV (delivered digitally); Fresh (delivered digitally); Shorteez (delivered digitally); sports (delivered digitally); Urban Xtra (delivered digitally).

Internet Service
Operational: Yes.

Telephone Service
None
Miles of Plant: 20.0 (coaxial); None (fiber optic). Homes passed: 905.
State Manager: John Coburn. Technical Manager: Randy Berry.
Ownership: Galaxy Cable Inc. (MSO).

KILBOURNE—Community Communications Co., 1920 Hwy 425 N, Monticello, AR 71655-4463. Phones: 800-272-2191; 870-367-7300. Fax: 870-367-9770. E-mail: generalmanager@ccc-cable.net. Web Site: http://www.ccc-cable.net. ICA: LA0135.
TV Market Ranking: Below 100 (KILBOURNE). Franchise award date: N.A. Franchise expiration date: N.A. Began: May 1, 1982.
Channel capacity: 48 (not 2-way capable). Channels available but not in use: N.A.

Basic Service
Subscribers: 53.
Programming (received off-air): KAQY (ABC) Columbia; KARD (FOX) West Monroe; KARZ-TV (MNT) Little Rock; KEJB (MNT)lorado; KKAP (ETV) Little Rock; KKYK-CA (IND) Little Rock; KLTM-TV (PBS) Monroe; KNOE-TV (CBS, CW) Monroe; KTVE (NBC) El Dorado; WABG-TV (ABC) Greenwood; WXVT (CBS) Greenville.
Programming (via satellite): ABC Family Channel; AMC; CNN; Country Music TV; Discovery Channel; ESPN; ESPN 2; Lifetime; Nickelodeon; Outdoor Channel; QVC; Spike TV; TBS Superstation; Trinity Broadcasting Network; Turner Network TV; USA Network; WGN America.
Fee: $15.00 installation; $28.00 monthly.

Pay Service 1
Pay Units: 30.
Programming (via satellite): HBO.

Video-On-Demand: No

Internet Service
Operational: No.

Telephone Service
None
Miles of Plant: 5.0 (coaxial); None (fiber optic). Homes passed: 120.
Operations Manager: Larry Ivy.
Ownership: Community Communications Co.

KINDER—CommuniComm Services, 2504 Westwood Rd, Westlake, LA 70669. Phone: 337-433-0892. Fax: 337-433-0405. Web Site: http://www.communicomm.com. Also serves Elton & Oberlin. ICA: LA0054.
TV Market Ranking: Below 100 (KINDER); Outside TV Markets (Elton, Oberlin). Franchise award date: N.A. Franchise expiration date: N.A. Began: January 1, 1982.
Channel capacity: N.A. Channels available but not in use: N.A.

Basic Service
Subscribers: N.A.
Programming (received off-air): KADN-TV (FOX) Lafayette; KALB-TV (CBS, NBC) Alexandria; KATC (ABC) Lafayette; KLFY-TV (CBS) Lafayette; KLTL-TV (PBS) Lake Charles; KPLC (NBC) Lake Charles; KVHP (FOX) Lake Charles.
Programming (via satellite): ABC Family Channel; AMC; Animal Planet; Arts & Entertainment; BET Networks; Cartoon Network; CNBC; CNN; Country Music TV; C-SPAN; C-SPAN 2; Discovery Channel; Disney Channel; ESPN; ESPN 2; Eternal Word TV Network; Food Network; Fox Sports Net; Headline News; HGTV; History Channel; INSP; Lifetime; MSNBC; MTV; Nickelodeon; QVC; Spike TV; Syfy; TBS Superstation; The Learning Channel; Turner Network TV; TV Land; USA Network; Versus; VH1; Weather Channel.
Fee: $20.00 installation; $11.95 monthly.

Digital Basic Service
Subscribers: N.A.
Programming (via satellite): American-Life TV Network; BBC America; Bloomberg Television; Bravo; Discovery Digital Networks; DMX Music; Fox Soccer; Fuse; G4; Golf Channel; Halogen Network; Independent Film Channel; Outdoor Channel; Speed Channel; Trinity Broadcasting Network; Turner Classic Movies; WE tv; Weatherscan.
Fee: $26.00 installation; $10.95 monthly.

Pay Service 1
Pay Units: 621.
Programming (via satellite): Cinemax; Encore; HBO (multiplexed); Starz.
Fee: $10.00 installation.

Digital Pay Service 1
Pay Units: N.A.
Programming (via satellite): Cinemax (multiplexed); Encore (multiplexed); HBO (multiplexed); Showtime (multiplexed); Starz (multiplexed); The Movie Channel (multiplexed).

Video-On-Demand: No

Pay-Per-View
Viewer's Choice Canada (delivered digitally); Hot Choice (delivered digitally); Playboy TV (delivered digitally); Fresh (delivered digitally); Shorteez (delivered digitally); Sports PPV (delivered digitally).

Internet Service
Operational: Yes.
Broadband Service: Net Commander.

Telephone Service
None
Miles of Plant: 58.0 (coaxial); None (fiber optic). Homes passed included in Westlake
General Manager: Larry Ivy. Plant Manager: Marcus Edwards.
City fee: 3% of gross.
Ownership: James Cable LLC (MSO).

KROTZ SPRINGS—Rapid Cable, 515 E Longview Dr, Arp, TX 75750. Phone: 903-859-6492. Fax: 903-859-3708. Also serves St. Landry Parish (portions). ICA: LA0112.
TV Market Ranking: Below 100 (KROTZ SPRINGS, St. Landry Parish (portions)). Franchise award date: N.A. Franchise expiration date: N.A. Began: March 1, 1983.
Channel capacity: 54 (not 2-way capable). Channels available but not in use: N.A.

Basic Service
Subscribers: 257.
Programming (received off-air): KALB-TV (CBS, NBC) Alexandria; KATC (ABC) Lafayette; KLFY-TV (CBS) Lafayette; WAFB (CBS) Baton Rouge; WBRZ-TV (ABC) Baton Rouge; WLPB-TV (PBS) Baton Rouge; WVLA-TV (NBC) Baton Rouge.
Programming (via satellite): TBS Superstation; Turner Network TV.
Fee: $54.95 installation; $44.05 monthly.

Pay Service 1
Pay Units: 31.
Programming (via satellite): HBO.
Fee: $12.95 monthly.

Pay Service 2
Pay Units: 29.
Programming (via satellite): The Movie Channel.
Fee: $12.95 monthly.

Pay Service 3
Pay Units: 74.
Programming (via satellite): Showtime.
Fee: $12.95 monthly.

Video-On-Demand: No

Internet Service
Operational: No.

Telephone Service
None
Miles of Plant: 14.0 (coaxial); None (fiber optic). Homes passed: 558.
Regional Manager: Mike Taylor. Chief Technician: Ronnie Stafford.
City fee: 3% of gross.
Ownership: Rapid Communications LLC (MSO).

LA PLACE—Comcast Cable, 136 Farm Rd, La Place, LA 70068-5927. Phone: 985-876-5969. Fax: 985-652-0105. Web Site: http://www.comcast.com. Also serves Edgard, Garyville, Reserve & St. John the Baptist Parish (eastern portion). ICA: LA0021.
TV Market Ranking: 31 (LA PLACE, St. John the Baptist Parish (eastern portion)); Below 100 (Edgard, Garyville, Reserve). Franchise award date: N.A. Franchise expiration date: N.A. Began: May 1, 1980.
Channel capacity: N.A. Channels available but not in use: N.A.

Basic Service
Subscribers: 10,106.
Programming (received off-air): WAFB (CBS) Baton Rouge; WDSU (NBC) New Orleans; WGNO (ABC) New Orleans; WHNO (IND) New Orleans; WLAE-TV (PBS) New Orleans; WLPB-TV (PBS) Baton Rouge; WNOL-TV (CW) New Orleans; WPXL-TV (ION) New Orleans; WUPL (MNT) Slidell; WVUE-DT (FOX) New Orleans; WWL-TV (CBS) New Orleans; WYES-TV (PBS) New Orleans.
Programming (via satellite): ABC Family Channel; AMC; Animal Planet; Arts & Entertainment; BET Networks; Bravo; Cartoon Network; CNBC; CNN; Comcast Sports Net Southwest; Comedy Central; Country Music TV; C-SPAN; Discovery Channel; Disney Channel; E! Entertainment Television; ESPN; ESPN 2; Eternal Word TV Network; Food Network; Fox News Channel; FX; Golf Channel; Hallmark Channel; Headline News; HGTV; History Channel; Home Shopping Network; Lifetime; Lifetime Movie Network; MSNBC; MTV; National Geographic Channel; Nickelodeon; Outdoor Channel; Oxygen; QVC; ShopNBC; SoapNet; Spike TV; Syfy; TBS Superstation; The Learning Channel; Toon Disney; Travel Channel; truTV; Turner Network TV; TV Guide Network; TV Land; USA Network; VH1; WE tv; Weather Channel; WGN America.
Fee: $20.00 installation; $11.67 monthly.

Digital Basic Service
Subscribers: N.A.
Programming (via satellite): American-Life TV Network; BBC America; Bloomberg Television; Discovery Digital Networks; Encore Action; ESPN Classic Sports; ESPNews; FitTV; Fox Movie Channel; Fox Sports World; GAS; GSN; Independent Film Channel; MTV2; MuchMusic Network; Music Choice; Nick Jr.; Ovation; Speed Channel; Style Network; Sundance Channel; Turner Classic Movies; Versus; VH1 Classic.
Fee: $8.00 monthly.

Digital Pay Service 1
Pay Units: N.A.
Programming (via satellite): Cinemax (multiplexed); HBO (multiplexed); Showtime (multiplexed); Starz (multiplexed); The Movie Channel (multiplexed).
Fee: $12.00 monthly (each package).

Video-On-Demand: No

Pay-Per-View
Sports PPV (delivered digitally); iN DEMAND (delivered digitally); Fresh (delivered digitally); Shorteez (delivered digitally); Hot Choice (delivered digitally).
Internet Service
Operational: Yes. Began: July 1, 2002.
Broadband Service: Comcast High Speed Internet.
Fee: $99.95 installation; $44.95 monthly.
Telephone Service
Digital: Operational
Miles of Plant: 173.0 (coaxial); None (fiber optic). Homes passed: 18,000. Total homes in franchised area: 18,000.
General Manager: Jacqui Dugas. Senior Marketing Professional: Laura Anthony. Chief Technician: Dan Matherne.
City fee: 2% of gross.
Ownership: Comcast Cable Communications Inc. (MSO).

LAFAYETTE—Cox Communications. Now served by BATON ROUGE, LA [LA0003]. ICA: LA0176.

LAKE ARTHUR—CommuniComm Services, 2504 Westwood Rd, Westlake, LA 70669. Phone: 337-433-0892. Fax: 337-433-0405. Web Site: http://www.communicomm.com. Also serves Roanoke & Welsh. ICA: LA0078.
TV Market Ranking: Below 100 (LAKE ARTHUR, Roanoke, Welsh). Franchise award date: N.A. Franchise expiration date: N.A. Began: January 1, 1979.
Channel capacity: N.A. Channels available but not in use: N.A.
Basic Service
Subscribers: 1,813.
Programming (received off-air): KADN-TV (FOX) Lafayette; KALB-TV (CBS, NBC) Alexandria; KATC (ABC) Lafayette; KLFY-TV (CBS) Lafayette; KLTL-TV (PBS) Lake Charles; KPLC (NBC) Lake Charles; KVHP (FOX) Lake Charles.
Programming (via satellite): CW+; Eternal Word TV Network; Home Shopping Network.
Fee: $20.00 installation; $11.95 monthly.
Expanded Basic Service 1
Subscribers: N.A.
Programming (via satellite): ABC Family Channel; AMC; Animal Planet; Arts & Entertainment; BET Networks; Bravo; Cartoon Network; CNBC; CNN; Comcast Sports Net Southwest; Comedy Central; Country Music TV; C-SPAN; Discovery Channel; Disney Channel; Do-It-Yourself; E! Entertainment Television; ESPN; ESPN 2; Food Network; Fox Movie Channel; Fox News Channel; FX; Hallmark Channel; Headline News; HGTV; History Channel; INSP; Lifetime; MSNBC; MTV; Nick Jr.; Nickelodeon; QVC; Spike TV; Syfy; TBS Superstation; The Learning Channel; Travel Channel; truTV; Turner Network TV; TV Land; USA Network; Versus; VH1; WE tv; Weather Channel.
Digital Basic Service
Subscribers: N.A.
Programming (via satellite): AmericanLife TV Network; BBC America; Bio; Bloomberg Television; Bravo; CMT Pure Country; Current; Discovery Health Channel; Discovery Kids Channel; Discovery Military Channel; Discovery Planet Green; DMX Music; ESPN 2; ESPN Classic Sports; ESPNews; FitTV; Fox Movie Channel; Fox Soccer; Fuse; G4; Golf Channel; Gospel Music Channel; Great American Country; GSN; Halogen Network; HGTV; History Channel; History Channel International; ID Investigation Discovery; Independent Film Channel; Lifetime Movie Network; MTV Hits; MTV Jams; MTV2; Nick Jr.; NickToons TV; Outdoor Channel; Science Channel; Sleuth; SoapNet; Speed Channel; Style Network; Sundance Channel; Syfy; TeenNick; Trinity Broadcasting Network; Turner Classic Movies; Versus; VH1 Classic; VH1 Soul; WE tv.
Fee: $20.00 installation; $11.95 monthly.
Pay Service 1
Pay Units: N.A.
Programming (via satellite): Cinemax; Encore; HBO (multiplexed); Starz.
Fee: $10.00 installation; $10.95 monthly (Showtime), $11.95 monthly (Cinemax), $12.95 monthly (Starz), $13.95 monthly (HBO).
Digital Pay Service 1
Pay Units: N.A.
Programming (via satellite): Cinemax (multiplexed); Encore (multiplexed); HBO (multiplexed); Showtime (multiplexed); Starz (multiplexed); The Movie Channel (multiplexed).
Fee: $10.00 installation; $11.95 monthly (Cinemax), $12.95 monthly (Starz), $13.95 monthly (HBO).
Video-On-Demand: No
Pay-Per-View
iN DEMAND (delivered digitally); Hot Choice (delivered digitally); Playboy TV (delivered digitally); Fresh (delivered digitally); Shorteez (delivered digitally); Sports PPV (delivered digitally).
Internet Service
Operational: Yes.
Broadband Service: Net Commander.
Fee: $39.95 installation; $51.95 monthly.
Telephone Service
None
Miles of Plant: 25.0 (coaxial); None (fiber optic). Homes passed included in Westlake
General Manager: Larry Ivy. Plant Manager: Marcus Edwards.
City fee: 3% of gross.
Ownership: James Cable LLC (MSO).

LAKE CHARLES—Suddenlink Communications, 1538 E Prien Lake Rd, Lake Charles, LA 70606-0830. Phones: 888-822-5151; 337-477-9674. Fax: 318-474-3436. Web Site: http://www.suddenlink.com. Also serves Calcasieu Parish. ICA: LA0007.
TV Market Ranking: Below 100 (Calcasieu Parish (portions), LAKE CHARLES). Franchise award date: N.A. Franchise expiration date: N.A. Began: September 1, 1967.
Channel capacity: N.A. Channels available but not in use: N.A.
Basic Service
Subscribers: 36,282.
Programming (received off-air): KATC (ABC) Lafayette; KBMT (ABC) Beaumont; KBTV-TV (FOX) Port Arthur; KFAM-LP (IND) Lake Charles; KFDM (CBS, CW) Beaumont; KLFY-TV (CBS) Lafayette; KLTL-TV (PBS) Lake Charles; KPLC (NBC) Lake Charles; KVHP (FOX) Lake Charles; 14 FMs.
Programming (via satellite): BET Networks; Discovery Channel; Eternal Word TV Network; INSP; ION Television; Sneak Prevue; TBS Superstation.
Fee: $60.00 installation; $10.66 monthly; $.77 converter; $25.00 additional installation.
Expanded Basic Service 1
Subscribers: 24,421.
Programming (via satellite): ABC Family Channel; AMC; Animal Planet; Arts & Entertainment; Cartoon Network; CNBC; CNN; Comcast Sports Net Southwest; Comedy Central; C-SPAN; Disney Channel; E! Entertainment Television; ESPN; ESPN 2; ESPN Classic Sports; Food Network; Fox News Channel; FX; G4; Great American Country; Headline News; HGTV; History Channel; Home Shopping Network; Lifetime; MoviePlex; MTV; Nickelodeon; QVC; Spike TV; The Learning Channel; Trinity Broadcasting Network; truTV; Turner Network TV; TV Guide Network; TV Land; USA Network; Weather Channel.
Fee: $10.00 installation; $20.34 monthly.
Digital Basic Service
Subscribers: N.A.
Programming (via satellite): BBC America; Discovery Digital Networks; Fox Sports World; Golf Channel; GSN; Independent Film Channel; Starz; Syfy; Turner Classic Movies; Versus; WE tv.
Fee: $10.00 monthly.
Pay Service 1
Pay Units: 2,098.
Programming (via satellite): Cinemax; HBO; Showtime; Starz.
Fee: $10.00 installation; $1.75 monthly (Encore), $6.75 monthly (Starz), $8.00 monthly (Cinemax), $10.95 monthly (HBO), $11.50 monthly (Showtime).
Digital Pay Service 1
Pay Units: N.A.
Programming (via satellite): Cinemax (multiplexed); HBO (multiplexed); Showtime (multiplexed); Starz (multiplexed); The Movie Channel (multiplexed).
Fee: $6.75 monthly (Starz), $8.00 monthly (Cinemax), $10.95 monthly (HBO), $11.50 monthly (Showtime).
Video-On-Demand: No
Pay-Per-View
Fresh (delivered digitally); movies; Movies (delivered digitally).
Internet Service
Operational: Yes.
Broadband Service: Cebridge High Speed Cable Internet.
Fee: $45.00 installation; $29.95 monthly.
Telephone Service
Digital: Operational
Fee: $39.95 monthly
Miles of Plant: 520.0 (coaxial); 29.0 (fiber optic).
Manager: Mike Ross. Chief Technician: Larry Stehr.
City fee: 4% of gross.
Ownership: Cequel Communications LLC (MSO).

LAKE CLAIBORNE—Formerly served by Almega Cable. No longer in operation. ICA: LA0178.

LAKE PROVIDENCE—CMA Cablevision, 403 Lake St, Lake Providence, LA 71254-2631. Phones: 972-233-9614 (Corporate office); 800-753-2465. Fax: 318-559-5400. Web Site: http://www.cmaaccess.com. Also serves Oak Grove. ICA: LA0053.
TV Market Ranking: Outside TV Markets (LAKE PROVIDENCE, Oak Grove). Franchise award date: November 28, 1979. Franchise expiration date: N.A. Began: January 1, 1980.
Channel capacity: N.A. Channels available but not in use: N.A.
Basic Service
Subscribers: 1,650.
Programming (received off-air): KAQY (ABC) Columbia; KARD (FOX) West Monroe; KEJB (MNT)lorado; KLTM-TV (PBS) Monroe; KNOE-TV (CBS, CW) Monroe; KTVE (NBC) El Dorado.
Programming (via satellite): Eternal Word TV Network; Home Shopping Network; INSP; QVC; TBS Superstation; Weather Channel; WGN America.
Fee: $39.95 installation; $19.95 monthly; $9.95 additional installation.
Expanded Basic Service 1
Subscribers: N.A.
Programming (via satellite): ABC Family Channel; AMC; Animal Planet; Arts & Entertainment; BET Networks; Cartoon Network; CNN; Country Music TV; Discovery Channel; ESPN; ESPN 2; Food Network; Fox News Channel; FX; Hallmark Channel; HGTV; History Channel; ION Television; Lifetime; MTV; Nickelodeon; Outdoor Channel; Spike TV; Syfy; The Learning Channel; Travel Channel; Trinity Broadcasting Network; Turner Classic Movies; Turner Network TV; TV Guide Network; TV Land; USA Network; WABG-TV (ABC) Greenwood.
Fee: $22.50 monthly.
Digital Basic Service
Subscribers: N.A.
Programming (via satellite): Bio; Discovery Digital Networks; DMX Music; ESPN Classic Sports; ESPNews; GAS; Golf Channel; GSN; History Channel International; Lifetime Movie Network; MTV Networks Digital Suite; National Geographic Channel; Nick Jr.; Speed Channel.
Fee: $12.50 monthly.
Pay Service 1
Pay Units: N.A.
Programming (via satellite): HBO; Showtime.
Fee: $14.95 installation; $13.96 monthly (each).
Digital Pay Service 1
Pay Units: N.A.
Programming (via satellite): Cinemax (multiplexed); Encore (multiplexed); HBO (multiplexed); Showtime (multiplexed); Starz (multiplexed); The Movie Channel (multiplexed).
Fee: $13.45 monthly (Cinemax, Showtime or Starz & Encore), $12.95 monthly (HBO).
Video-On-Demand: No
Pay-Per-View
iN DEMAND (delivered digitally); Playboy TV (delivered digitally); Shorteez (delivered digitally).
Internet Service
Operational: No.
Telephone Service
None
Homes passed: 2,400.
General Manager: Jerry Smith. Marketing Director: Julie Ferguson.

Franchise fee: 3% of gross.
Ownership: Cable Management Assoc. (MSO).

LAKE ST. JOHN—Formerly served by Almega Cable. No longer in operation. ICA: LA0131.

LECOMPTE—Suddenlink Communications, 12444 Powerscourt Dr, Saint Louis, MO 63131-3660. Phones: 800-999-6845 (Customer service); 314-965-2020. Fax: 903-561-5485. Web Site: http://www.suddenlink.com. Also serves Cheneyville, Forest Hill, Glenmora, Kolin, McNary, Rapides Parish (portions) & Woodworth. ICA: LA0084.
TV Market Ranking: Below 100 (Cheneyville, Forest Hill, Glenmora, Kolin, LECOMPTE, McNary, Rapides Parish (portions), Woodworth). Franchise award date: N.A. Franchise expiration date: N.A. Began: March 1, 1983.
Channel capacity: 54 (operating 2-way). Channels available but not in use: N.A.
Basic Service
Subscribers: 2,100.
Programming (received off-air): KALB-TV (CBS, NBC) Alexandria; KATC (ABC) Lafayette; KLAX-TV (ABC) Alexandria; KLFY-TV (CBS) Lafayette; KLPA-TV (PBS) Alexandria; KPLC (NBC) Lake Charles.
Programming (via satellite): TBS Superstation; WGN America.
Fee: $39.95 installation; $18.95 monthly.
Pay Service 1
Pay Units: 208.
Programming (via satellite): Cinemax.
Fee: $7.00 monthly.
Pay Service 2
Pay Units: 268.
Programming (via satellite): HBO.
Fee: $12.00 monthly.
Pay Service 3
Pay Units: 301.
Programming (via satellite): Showtime.
Fee: $7.00 monthly.
Pay Service 4
Pay Units: 88.
Programming (via satellite): The Movie Channel.
Fee: $9.00 monthly.
Pay Service 5
Pay Units: 432.
Programming (via satellite): Flix.
Fee: $1.95 monthly.
Video-On-Demand: No
Internet Service
Operational: Yes. Began: January 12, 2005.
Broadband Service: Cebridge High Speed Cable Internet.
Fee: $45.00 installation; $29.95 monthly.
Telephone Service
Digital: Operational
Fee: $39.95 monthly
Miles of Plant: 93.0 (coaxial); None (fiber optic). Homes passed: 2,871.
Regional Manager: Todd Cruthird. Area Manager: Mark Hood. Plant Manager: Dion Canaday.
Ownership: Cequel Communications LLC (MSO).

LEESVILLE—Suddenlink Communications, 12444 Powerscourt Dr, Saint Louis, MO 63131-3660. Phone: 314-965-2020. Web Site: http://www.suddenlink.com. Also serves Newllano & Vernon Parish. ICA: LA0035.
TV Market Ranking: Below 100 (Vernon Parish (portions)); Outside TV Markets (LEESVILLE, Newllano, Vernon Parish (portions)). Franchise award date: N.A. Franchise expiration date: N.A. Began: August 8, 1963.
Channel capacity: 38 (operating 2-way). Channels available but not in use: None.
Basic Service
Subscribers: 2,569.
Programming (received off-air): KALB-TV (CBS, NBC) Alexandria; KLAX-TV (ABC) Alexandria; KLFY-TV (CBS) Lafayette; KLPA-TV (PBS) Alexandria; WNTZ-TV (FOX, MNT) Natchez.
Programming (via satellite): Eternal Word TV Network; QVC; TV Guide Network.
Fee: $39.95 installation; $18.95 monthly; $2.95 converter; $15.00 additional installation.
Expanded Basic Service 1
Subscribers: N.A.
Programming (via satellite): ABC Family Channel; AMC; Animal Planet; Arts & Entertainment; BET Networks; Bravo; Cartoon Network; CNBC; CNN; Comcast Sports Net Southwest; Comedy Central; C-SPAN; Discovery Channel; Disney Channel; E! Entertainment Television; ESPN; ESPN 2; ESPN Classic Sports; Food Network; Fox News Channel; FX; Golf Channel; Great American Country; Hallmark Channel; Headline News; HGTV; History Channel; INSP; Lifetime; MSNBC; MTV; National Geographic Channel; Nickelodeon; Outdoor Channel; Shopping Channel; Speed Channel; Spike TV; Syfy; TBS Superstation; Telemundo; The Learning Channel; Turner Classic Movies; Turner Network TV; TV Land; Univision; USA Network; VH1; Weather Channel.
Digital Basic Service
Subscribers: N.A.
Programming (via satellite): BBC America; Bio; Bloomberg Television; Canales N; C-SPAN 3; Discovery Digital Networks; Do-It-Yourself; ESPNews; Fox College Sports Atlantic; Fox College Sports Central; Fox College Sports Pacific; Fox Movie Channel; Fuse; G4; GSN; History Channel International; Independent Film Channel; Music Choice; Sleuth; SoapNet; Sundance Channel; Toon Disney; Versus; WE tv.
Fee: $3.99 monthly.
Pay Service 1
Pay Units: N.A.
Programming (via satellite): HBO; Showtime; Starz; The Movie Channel.
Fee: $24.95 installation; $10.95 monthly (each).
Digital Pay Service 1
Pay Units: N.A.
Programming (via satellite): Cinemax (multiplexed); Encore (multiplexed); Flix (multiplexed); HBO (multiplexed); Showtime (multiplexed); Starz (multiplexed); The Movie Channel (multiplexed).
Pay-Per-View
iN DEMAND (delivered digitally); Playboy TV (delivered digitally).
Internet Service
Operational: Yes. Began: March 16, 2004.
Broadband Service: Cebridge High Speed Cable Internet.
Fee: $45.00 installation; $29.95 monthly.
Telephone Service
Digital: Operational
Fee: $39.95 monthly
Miles of Plant: 120.0 (coaxial); None (fiber optic). Homes passed: 7,528.
Regional Manager: Todd Cruthird. Technical Manager: Randy Berry. Marketing Director: Beverly Gambell.
City fee: 3% of gross.
Ownership: Cequel Communications LLC (MSO).

LOGANSPORT—CMA Cablevision, 1025-A S Washington St, Mansfield, LA 71052-4215. Phones: 972-233-9614 (Corporate office); 800-753-2465; 318-872-3268. Fax: 318-872-2520. Web Site: http://www.cmaaccess.com. Also serves Stanley, LA; Joaquin, TX. ICA: LA0096.
TV Market Ranking: 58 (Joaquin); Outside TV Markets (LOGANSPORT, Stanley, Joaquin). Franchise award date: N.A. Franchise expiration date: N.A. Began: January 1, 1976.
Channel capacity: 38 (not 2-way capable). Channels available but not in use: N.A.
Basic Service
Subscribers: 300.
Programming (received off-air): KLTS-TV (PBS) Shreveport; KMSS-TV (FOX) Shreveport; KPXJ (CW) Minden; KSHV-TV (MNT) Shreveport; KSLA (CBS) Shreveport; KTAL-TV (NBC) Texarkana; KTBS-TV (ABC) Shreveport.
Programming (via satellite): ABC Family Channel; Arts & Entertainment; BET Networks; Cartoon Network; CNN; Country Music TV; Discovery Channel; Disney Channel; ESPN; ESPN 2; Headline News; HGTV; History Channel; Lifetime; MTV; Nickelodeon; Outdoor Channel; Spike TV; Syfy; TBS Superstation; The Learning Channel; Trinity Broadcasting Network; Turner Classic Movies; Turner Network TV; TV Land; USA Network; VH1; Weather Channel; WGN America.
Fee: $39.95 installation; $37.45 monthly; $12.95 additional installation.
Pay Service 1
Pay Units: 26.
Programming (via satellite): HBO; Showtime.
Fee: $14.95 installation; $13.95 monthly (each).
Video-On-Demand: No
Internet Service
Operational: No.
Telephone Service
None
Miles of Plant: 60.0 (coaxial); None (fiber optic).
General Manager: Jerry Smith. Marketing Director: Julie Ferguson.
City fee: 3% of gross.
Ownership: Cable Management Assoc. (MSO).

MANGHAM—Formerly served by Almega Cable. No longer in operation. ICA: LA0217.

MANSFIELD—CMA Cablevision, 1025-A S Washington St, Mansfield, LA 71052-4215. Phones: 972-233-9614 (Corporate office); 800-753-2465; 318-872-3268. Fax: 318-872-2520. Web Site: http://www.cmaaccess.com. Also serves Grand Cane & South Mansfield. ICA: LA0048.
TV Market Ranking: 58 (Grand Cane, MANSFIELD, South Mansfield). Franchise award date: N.A. Franchise expiration date: N.A. Began: January 1, 1976.
Channel capacity: N.A. Channels available but not in use: N.A.
Basic Service
Subscribers: 1,320.
Programming (received off-air): KLTS-TV (PBS) Shreveport; KMSS-TV (FOX) Shreveport; KPXJ (CW) Minden; KSHV-TV (MNT) Shreveport; KSLA (CBS) Shreveport; KTAL-TV (NBC) Texarkana; KTBS-TV (ABC) Shreveport.
Programming (via satellite): Weather Channel.
Fee: $39.95 installation; $15.95 monthly; $12.95 additional installation.
Expanded Basic Service 1
Subscribers: N.A.
Programming (via satellite): ABC Family Channel; Arts & Entertainment; BET Networks; Bravo!; Cartoon Network; CNN; Comedy Central; Country Music TV; Discovery Channel; ESPN; ESPN 2; ESPN Classic Sports; FamilyNet; Fox News Channel; FX; Hallmark Channel; Headline News; HGTV; History Channel; Home Shopping Network; Lifetime; MTV; Nickelodeon; Outdoor Channel; SoapNet; Spike TV; Syfy; TBS Superstation; The Learning Channel; Trinity Broadcasting Network; truTV; Turner Classic Movies; Turner Network TV; TV Land; USA Network; VH1; WGN America.
Fee: $24.70 monthly.
Digital Basic Service
Subscribers: N.A.
Programming (via satellite): BBC America; Bio; Discovery Digital Networks; DMX Music; ESPNews; Fox Movie Channel; GAS; Golf Channel; GSN; History Channel International; Independent Film Channel; INSP; Lifetime Movie Network; MTV Networks Digital Suite; National Geographic Channel; Nick Jr.; Speed Channel; WE tv.
Fee: $12.00 monthly.
Pay Service 1
Pay Units: 635.
Programming (via satellite): HBO; Showtime.
Fee: $14.95 installation; $12.95 monthly (Showtime), $13.45 monthly (HBO).
Digital Pay Service 1
Pay Units: N.A.
Programming (via satellite): Cinemax (multiplexed); Encore (multiplexed); HBO (multiplexed); Showtime (multiplexed); Starz (multiplexed).
Fee: $10.95 monthly (Cinemax or Starz & Encore), $13.95 monthly (HBO or Showtime).
Video-On-Demand: No
Pay-Per-View
iN DEMAND (delivered digitally); Playboy TV (delivered digitally); Fresh (delivered digitally); Shorteez (delivered digitally).
Internet Service
Operational: Yes.
Broadband Service: CMA.
Fee: $36.95 monthly; $2.95 modem lease.
Telephone Service
None
Miles of Plant: 100.0 (coaxial); None (fiber optic). Homes passed: 3,000. Total homes in franchised area: 3,200.
General Manager: Jerry Smith. Marketing Director: Julie Ferguson.
City fee: 3% of gross.
Ownership: Cable Management Assoc. (MSO).

MANY—Suddenlink Communications, 12444 Powerscourt Dr, Saint Louis, MO 63131-3660. Phone: 314-965-2020. Web Site: http://www.suddenlink.com. Also serves Ebarb, Fisher, Florien, Negreet, Sabine Parish & Zwolle. ICA: LA0183.
TV Market Ranking: Outside TV Markets (Ebarb, Fisher, Florien, MANY, Negreet, Sabine Parish, Zwolle). Franchise award date: N.A. Franchise expiration date: N.A. Began: November 1, 1963.
Channel capacity: N.A. Channels available but not in use: N.A.
Basic Service
Subscribers: N.A.
Programming (received off-air): KALB-TV (CBS, NBC) Alexandria; KLAX-TV (ABC) Alexandria; KLPA-TV (PBS) Alexandria; KMSS-TV (FOX) Shreveport; KNOE-TV (CBS, CW) Monroe; KSHV-TV (MNT)

Shreveport; KSLA (CBS) Shreveport; KTBS-TV (ABC) Shreveport; KTRE (ABC) Lufkin; KYTX (CBS, IND) Nacogdoches; allband FM.
Programming (via satellite): QVC; Weather Channel.
Fee: $5.00 installation; $17.95 monthly.

Expanded Basic Service 1
Subscribers: N.A.
Programming (via satellite): ABC Family Channel; Arts & Entertainment; BET Networks; Cartoon Network; CNN; Comcast Sports Net Southwest; C-SPAN; Discovery Channel; Disney Channel; ESPN; ESPN 2; Eternal Word TV Network; Fox News Channel; Great American Country; Headline News; HGTV; History Channel; Lifetime; Nickelodeon; Outdoor Channel; Spike TV; TBS Superstation; The Learning Channel; Turner Classic Movies; Turner Network TV; TV Guide Network; USA Network; WGN America.
Fee: $19.00 monthly.

Pay Service 1
Pay Units: N.A.
Programming (via satellite): HBO; Showtime.

Internet Service
Operational: Yes. Began: November 2, 2002.
Broadband Service: Cebridge High Speed Cable Internet.
Fee: $45.00 installation; $29.95 monthly.

Telephone Service
Digital: Operational
Fee: $39.95 monthly
Miles of Plant: 54.0 (coaxial); None (fiber optic). Homes passed: 1,662.
Regional Manager: Todd Cruthird.
Ownership: Cequel Communications LLC (MSO).

MARINGOUIN—Spillway Communications Inc., PO Box 337, 10900 Hwy 77, Maringouin, LA 70757. Phones: 800-828-9154; 225-625-2311. Fax: 225-625-3107. E-mail: cs@spillwaycable.com. Web Site: http://www.spillwaycable.com. Also serves Fordoche, Iberville Parish (portions), Livonia & Pointe Coupee Parish. ICA: LA0059.
TV Market Ranking: 87 (Fordoche, Iberville Parish (portions), Livonia, MARINGOUIN, Pointe Coupee Parish (portions)); Outside TV Markets (Pointe Coupee Parish (portions)). Franchise award date: N.A. Franchise expiration date: N.A. Began: N.A.
Channel capacity: N.A. Channels available but not in use: N.A.

Basic Service
Subscribers: 1,628.
Programming (received off-air): KLFY-TV (CBS) Lafayette; WAFB (CBS) Baton Rouge; WBRL-CA (CW) Baton Rouge; WBRZ-TV (ABC) Baton Rouge; WGMB-TV (FOX) Baton Rouge; WLPB-TV (PBS) Baton Rouge; WVLA-TV (NBC) Baton Rouge.
Programming (via satellite): QVC; TBS Superstation.
Current originations: Public Access.
Fee: $50.00 installation; $37.00 monthly.

Expanded Basic Service 1
Subscribers: N.A.
Programming (received off-air): KADN-TV (FOX) Lafayette.
Programming (via satellite): ABC Family Channel; Animal Planet; Arts & Entertainment; BET Networks; Bloomberg Television; CNN; Comedy Central; Country Music TV; Cox Sports Television; Discovery Channel; Disney Channel; Do-It-Yourself; E! Entertainment Television; ESPN; ESPN 2; Eternal Word TV Network; FitTV; Food Network; Fox News Channel; FX; Great American Country; Hallmark Channel; Headline News; HGTV; Home Shopping Network; Lifetime; MTV; National Geographic Channel; Nickelodeon; Outdoor Channel; Shop at Home; SoapNet; Spike TV; Syfy; The Learning Channel; Toon Disney; Travel Channel; Trinity Broadcasting Network; Turner Classic Movies; Turner Network TV; TV Land; USA Network; VH1; Weather Channel; WGN America.

Digital Basic Service
Subscribers: N.A.
Programming (via satellite): AmericanLife TV Network; BBC America; Bio; CMT Pure Country; Current; Discovery Health Channel; Discovery Kids Channel; Discovery Military Channel; Discovery Planet Green; DMX Music; ESPN Classic Sports; ESPNews; Fox Movie Channel; Fox Soccer; Fuse; G4; Golf Channel; GSN; History Channel; History Channel International; ID Investigation Discovery; Independent Film Channel; INSP; International Television (ITV); Lifetime Movie Network; Lime; MBC America; MTV Hits; MTV Jams; MTV2; Nick Jr.; NickToons TV; Ovation; Science Channel; ShopNBC; Speed Channel; Style Network; Sundance Channel; TeenNick; The Word Network; Trio; Versus; VH1 Classic; VH1 Soul; WE tv.

Pay Service 1
Pay Units: 383.
Programming (via satellite): Cinemax; HBO.
Fee: $10.00 monthly.

Digital Pay Service 1
Pay Units: N.A.
Programming (via satellite): Cinemax (multiplexed); Encore (multiplexed); Flix; HBO (multiplexed); Showtime (multiplexed); Starz (multiplexed); The Movie Channel (multiplexed).

Video-On-Demand: No

Pay-Per-View
iN DEMAND (delivered digitally); Hot Choice (delivered digitally); Playboy TV (delivered digitally); Fresh (delivered digitally); Shorteez (delivered digitally); Club Jenna (delivered digitally); ESPN Now (delivered digitally); Sports PPV (delivered digitally).

Internet Service
Operational: Yes.
Broadband Service: In-house.
Fee: $50.00 installation; $32.95-$42.95 monthly.

Telephone Service
None
Miles of Plant: 70.0 (coaxial); None (fiber optic). Homes passed: 2,500.
Manager & Chief Technician: Mark Greene.
City fee: 3% of gross.
Ownership: Spillway Cablevision Inc.

MARION—Bayou Cable TV, PO Box 466, Marion, LA 71260-0466. Phone: 318-292-4774. Fax: 318-292-4775. Web Site: http://www.bayoucable.com. ICA: LA0119.
TV Market Ranking: 99 (MARION). Franchise award date: N.A. Franchise expiration date: N.A. Began: April 1, 1982.
Channel capacity: 50 (not 2-way capable). Channels available but not in use: 6.

Basic Service
Subscribers: 218.
Programming (received off-air): KAQY (ABC) Columbia; KARD (FOX) West Monroe; KLTM-TV (PBS) Monroe; KMCT-TV (IND) West Monroe; KNOE-TV (CBS, CW) Monroe; KTVE (NBC) El Dorado.
Programming (via satellite): AMC; Hallmark Channel; Home Shopping Network; Trinity Broadcasting Network; TV Land.

Current originations: Public Access.
Fee: $30.00 installation; $15.95 monthly.

Expanded Basic Service 1
Subscribers: N.A.
Programming (via satellite): ABC Family Channel; Animal Planet; Arts & Entertainment; BET Networks; CNN; Country Music TV; CW+; Discovery Channel; ESPN; ESPN 2; Food Network; Fox News Channel; FX; HGTV; History Channel; Lifetime; MTV; National Geographic Channel; Nickelodeon; Outdoor Channel; Speed Channel; Spike TV; TBS Superstation; The Learning Channel; Turner Network TV; USA Network; VH1; Weather Channel; WGN America.
Fee: $20.00 monthly.

Pay Service 1
Pay Units: N.A.
Programming (via satellite): Cinemax; HBO.
Fee: $8.95 monthly (Cinemax), $10.95 monthly (HBO).

Video-On-Demand: No

Internet Service
Operational: No.

Telephone Service
None
Miles of Plant: 13.0 (coaxial); None (fiber optic). Homes passed: 450.
Manager: Alan C. Booker. Chief Technician: Mark Andrews.
Ownership: Bayou Cable TV (MSO).

MARKSVILLE—Charter Communications, 330 Moosa Blvd, Eunice, LA 70535. Phone: 337-546-0087 (Eunice office). Fax: 337-546-0038. Web Site: http://www.charter.com. Also serves Hessmer & Mansura. ICA: LA0040.
TV Market Ranking: Below 100 (Hessmer, Mansura, MARKSVILLE). Franchise award date: N.A. Franchise expiration date: N.A. Began: March 1, 1969.
Channel capacity: 42 (not 2-way capable). Channels available but not in use: 2.

Basic Service
Subscribers: 3,154.
Programming (received off-air): KADN-TV (FOX) Lafayette; KALB-TV (CBS, NBC) Alexandria; KLAX-TV (ABC) Alexandria; KLFY-TV (CBS) Lafayette; KPLC (NBC) Lake Charles; WAFB (CBS) Baton Rouge; WBRZ-TV (ABC) Baton Rouge; WLPB-TV (PBS) Baton Rouge; WNTZ-TV (FOX, MNT) Natchez.
Programming (via satellite): QVC; WGN America.
Fee: $29.99 installation.

Expanded Basic Service 1
Subscribers: 2,972.
Programming (via satellite): ABC Family Channel; AMC; Animal Planet; Arts & Entertainment; BET Networks; Cartoon Network; CNBC; CNN; Comcast Sports Net Southwest; Country Music TV; C-SPAN; Discovery Channel; Disney Channel; E! Entertainment Television; ESPN; ESPN 2; Eternal Word TV Network; Food Network; Fox News Channel; FX; Headline News; HGTV; History Channel; Lifetime; MTV; National Geographic Channel; Nickelodeon; Outdoor Channel; Product Information Network; Speed Channel; Spike TV; Syfy; TBS Superstation; The Learning Channel; Toon Disney; Trinity Broadcasting Network; Turner Classic Movies; Turner Network TV; TV Guide Network; TV Land; USA Network; VH1; WE tv; Weather Channel.
Fee: $42.99 monthly.

Digital Basic Service
Subscribers: N.A.
Programming (via satellite): BBC America; Bio; Bloomberg Television; Comcast/Charter Sports Southeast (CSS); Discovery Digital Networks; Do-It-Yourself; Fox Movie Channel; Fox Soccer; Fuel TV; History Channel International; Independent Film Channel; Lifetime Movie Network; MTV2; Music Choice; Nick Jr.; Sundance Channel; TV Guide Interactive Inc.; WealthTV HD.

Digital Pay Service 1
Pay Units: N.A.
Programming (via satellite): Cinemax (multiplexed); Encore (multiplexed); Flix; Starz (multiplexed).

Digital Pay Service 2
Pay Units: 267.
Programming (via satellite): HBO (multiplexed).
Fee: $11.00 monthly.

Digital Pay Service 3
Pay Units: 300.
Programming (via satellite): The Movie Channel (multiplexed).
Fee: $9.00 monthly.

Digital Pay Service 4
Pay Units: 230.
Programming (via satellite): Showtime (multiplexed).
Fee: $9.00 monthly.

Video-On-Demand: Yes

Pay-Per-View
Addressable homes: 900.
iN DEMAND (delivered digitally), Fee: $2.02, Addressable: Yes; Playboy TV (delivered digitally); Fresh (delivered digitally).

Internet Service
Operational: Yes.
Broadband Service: Charter Pipeline.

Telephone Service
Digital: Operational
Miles of Plant: 113.0 (coaxial); None (fiber optic). Homes passed: 4,448.
Vice President & General Manager: Kip Kraemer. Operations Manager: Blane Bercegeay. Technical Operations Director: Gary Savoie. Plant Manager: Joe Semmes. Marketing Director: Lisa Brown.
City fee: 3% of gross.
Ownership: Charter Communications Inc. (MSO).

MARKSVILLE—Rapid Cable, 515 E Longview Dr, Arp, TX 75750. Phone: 903-859-6492. Fax: 903-859-3708. ICA: LA0184.
TV Market Ranking: Below 100 (MARKSVILLE). Franchise award date: N.A. Franchise expiration date: N.A. Began: N.A.
Channel capacity: 42 (not 2-way capable). Channels available but not in use: N.A.

Basic Service
Subscribers: 511.
Programming (received off-air): KALB-TV (CBS, NBC) Alexandria; KBCA (CW) Alexandria; KLAX-TV (ABC) Alexandria; KLFY-TV (CBS) Lafayette; KLPA-TV (PBS) Alexandria; WNTZ-TV (FOX, MNT) Natchez.
Programming (via satellite): ABC Family Channel; AMC; Animal Planet; Arts & Entertainment; Cartoon Network; CNBC; CNN; Comedy Central; Discovery Channel; Disney Channel; E! Entertainment Television; ESPN; ESPN 2; Fox News Channel; FX; Great American Country; Headline News; HGTV; Home Shopping Network; Lifetime; MTV; National Geographic Channel; Nickelodeon; Outdoor Channel; SoapNet; Spike TV; TBS Superstation; The Learning Channel; Trinity Broadcasting Network; Turner Network TV; USA Network; Weather Channel.
Fee: $54.95 installation; $44.05 monthly.

Digital Basic Service
Subscribers: N.A.
Programming (via satellite): AmericanLife TV Network; BBC America; Bio; Bloomberg Television; Discovery Health Channel; Discovery Kids Channel; Discovery Military Channel; Discovery Planet Green; DMX Music; ESPN 2; ESPN Classic Sports; ESPNews; Fox College Sports Atlantic; Fox College Sports Central; Fox College Sports Pacific; Fox Soccer; Fuse; G4; Golf Channel; GSN; Halogen Network; HGTV; History Channel; History Channel International; ID Investigation Discovery; Lifetime Movie Network; Outdoor Channel; Ovation; Science Channel; ShopNBC; Sleuth; Speed Channel; Style Network; Syfy; Trinity Broadcasting Network; Turner Classic Movies; Versus; WE tv.

Pay Service 1
Pay Units: 28.
Programming (via satellite): HBO.
Fee: $12.95 monthly.

Pay Service 2
Pay Units: 20.
Programming (via satellite): The Movie Channel.
Fee: $12.95 monthly.

Pay Service 3
Pay Units: 52.
Programming (via satellite): Showtime.
Fee: $12.95 monthly.

Digital Pay Service 1
Pay Units: N.A.
Programming (via satellite): Cinemax (multiplexed); Encore (multiplexed); Flix; HBO (multiplexed); Showtime (multiplexed); Starz (multiplexed); The Movie Channel (multiplexed).

Video-On-Demand: No

Pay-Per-View
iN DEMAND (delivered digitally); Playboy TV (delivered digitally); Club Jenna (delivered digitally).

Internet Service
Operational: No.

Telephone Service
None

Miles of Plant: 42.0 (coaxial); None (fiber optic). Homes passed: 1,038.
Regional Manager: Mike Taylor. Chief Technician: Ronnie Stafford.
Ownership: Rapid Communications LLC (MSO).

MCINTYRE—Formerly served by Almega Cable. No longer in operation. ICA: LA0226.

MELVILLE—Rapid Cable, 515 E Longview Dr, Arp, TX 75750. Phone: 903-859-6492. Fax: 903-859-3708. ICA: LA0113.
TV Market Ranking: Outside TV Markets (MELVILLE). Franchise award date: N.A. Franchise expiration date: N.A. Began: March 1, 1984.
Channel capacity: 54 (not 2-way capable). Channels available but not in use: N.A.

Basic Service
Subscribers: 223.
Programming (received off-air): KALB-TV (CBS, NBC) Alexandria; KATC (ABC) Lafayette; KLFY-TV (CBS) Lafayette; WAFB (CBS) Baton Rouge; WBRZ-TV (ABC) Baton Rouge; WLPB-TV (PBS) Baton Rouge; WVLA-TV (NBC) Baton Rouge.
Programming (via satellite): Animal Planet; BET Networks; CNN; Country Music TV; Discovery Channel; ESPN; ESPN 2; HGTV; Home Shopping Network; Lifetime; Nickelodeon; Spike TV; TBS Superstation; Trinity Broadcasting Network; Turner Classic Movies; Turner Network TV; USA Network; Versus; Weather Channel; WGN America.
Fee: $54.95 installation; $44.05 monthly.

Pay Service 1
Pay Units: 46.
Programming (via satellite): HBO.
Fee: $12.95 monthly.

Pay Service 2
Pay Units: 27.
Programming (via satellite): The Movie Channel.
Fee: $12.95 monthly.

Pay Service 3
Pay Units: 65.
Programming (via satellite): Showtime.
Fee: $12.95 monthly.

Video-On-Demand: No

Internet Service
Operational: No.

Telephone Service
None

Miles of Plant: 12.0 (coaxial); None (fiber optic). Homes passed: 663.
Regional Manager: Mike Taylor. Chief Technician: Ronnie Stafford.
Ownership: Rapid Communications LLC (MSO).

MERRYVILLE—Rapid Cable, 515 E Longview Dr, Arp, TX 75750. Phone: 903-859-6492. Fax: 903-859-3708. ICA: LA0120.
TV Market Ranking: Outside TV Markets (MERRYVILLE). Franchise award date: March 16, 1984. Franchise expiration date: N.A. Began: August 1, 1986.
Channel capacity: N.A. Channels available but not in use: N.A.

Basic Service
Subscribers: 203.
Programming (received off-air): KBMT (ABC) Beaumont; KBTV-TV (FOX) Port Arthur; KFDM (CBS, CW) Beaumont; KLTL-TV (PBS) Lake Charles; KPLC (NBC) Lake Charles; KVHP (FOX) Lake Charles.
Programming (via satellite): ABC Family Channel; Eternal Word TV Network; QVC; TBS Superstation; WGN America.
Fee: $54.95 installation; $20.95 monthly.

Expanded Basic Service 1
Subscribers: 202.
Programming (via satellite): AMC; Arts & Entertainment; CNBC; CNN; Discovery Channel; Disney Channel; ESPN; ESPN 2; Nickelodeon; Outdoor Channel; SoapNet; Spike TV; Turner Network TV; USA Network; Weather Channel.
Fee: $23.10 monthly.

Digital Basic Service
Subscribers: N.A.
Programming (via satellite): AmericanLife TV Network; BBC America; Bio; Bloomberg Television; Bravo; CMT Pure Country; Discovery Health Channel; Discovery Kids Channel; Discovery Military Channel; Discovery Planet Green; DMX Music; FitTV; Fox Movie Channel; Fox Soccer; Fuse; G4; Golf Channel; GSN; Halogen Network; HGTV; History Channel International; ID Investigation Discovery; Independent Film Channel; Lifetime Movie Network; MTV Hits; MTV2; Nick Jr.; Science Channel; Speed Channel; Style Network; Syfy; TeenNick; Toon Disney; Trinity Broadcasting Network; Turner Classic Movies; Versus; VH1 Classic; VH1 Soul; WE tv.

Pay Service 1
Pay Units: 73.
Programming (via satellite): HBO.
Fee: $12.95 monthly.

Digital Pay Service 1
Pay Units: N.A.
Programming (via satellite): Cinemax (multiplexed); Encore (multiplexed); HBO (multiplexed); Showtime (multiplexed); Starz (multiplexed); The Movie Channel.

Video-On-Demand: No

Pay-Per-View
iN DEMAND (delivered digitally).

Internet Service
Operational: No.

Telephone Service
None

Miles of Plant: 14.0 (coaxial); None (fiber optic). Homes passed: 446.
Regional Manager: Mike Taylor. Chief Technician: Larry Stafford.
City fee: 3% of basic.
Ownership: Rapid Communications LLC (MSO).

MINDEN—Suddenlink Communications, 726 Broadway St, Minden, LA 71055-3307. Phone: 318-377-1978. Web Site: http://www.suddenlink.com. Also serves Webster Parish. ICA: LA0032.
TV Market Ranking: 58 (MINDEN, Webster Parish (portions)); Below 100 (Webster Parish (portions)). Franchise award date: May 1, 1977. Franchise expiration date: N.A. Began: September 1, 1978.
Channel capacity: N.A. Channels available but not in use: N.A.

Basic Service
Subscribers: 4,593.
Programming (received off-air): KLTS-TV (PBS) Shreveport; KMSS-TV (FOX) Shreveport; KPXJ (CW) Minden; KSHV-TV (MNT) Shreveport; KSLA (CBS) Shreveport; KTAL-TV (NBC) Texarkana; KTBS-TV (ABC) Shreveport.
Programming (via satellite): C-SPAN; C-SPAN 2; Home Shopping Network; Jewelry Television; QVC; TBS Superstation; Trinity Broadcasting Network; TV Guide Network; Weather Channel; WGN America.
Fee: $35.00 installation; $21.78 monthly; $10.00 additional installation.

Expanded Basic Service 1
Subscribers: N.A.
Programming (via satellite): ABC Family Channel; AMC; Animal Planet; Arts & Entertainment; BET Networks; Bravo; Cartoon Network; CNBC; CNN; Comcast Sports Net Southwest; Comedy Central; Country Music TV; Cox Sports Television; Discovery Channel; Discovery Health Channel; Disney Channel; ESPN; ESPN 2; Food Network; Fox News Channel; FX; Great American Country; Headline News; HGTV; History Channel; Lifetime; Lifetime Movie Network; MTV; Nickelodeon; Outdoor Channel; Speed Channel; Spike TV; Syfy; The Learning Channel; Travel Channel; truTV; Turner Network TV; TV Land; USA Network; Versus; VH1.
Fee: $10.17 monthly.

Digital Basic Service
Subscribers: N.A.
Programming (via satellite): BBC America; Bio; Bloomberg Television; CBS College Sports Network; CMT Pure Country; Cooking Channel; Discovery en Espanol; Discovery Home Channel; Discovery Kids Channel; Discovery Military Channel; Discovery Times Channel; Do-It-Yourself; Encore (multiplexed); ESPN Classic Sports; ESPNews; Fox Reality Channel; Fox Soccer; Fuel TV; Fuse; G4; Golf Channel; GSN; Hallmark Channel; History Channel International; Independent Film Channel; MTV Hits; MTV Jams; MTV2; Music Choice; National Geographic Channel; Nick Jr.; NickToons TV; Science Channel; SoapNet; Style Network; Sundance Channel; TeenNick; Toon Disney; Turner Classic Movies; TV One; VH1 Classic; VH1 Soul.

Digital Pay Service 1
Pay Units: N.A.
Programming (via satellite): Cinemax (multiplexed); HBO (multiplexed); Showtime (multiplexed); Starz (multiplexed); The Movie Channel (multiplexed).

Video-On-Demand: No

Pay-Per-View
iN DEMAND (delivered digitally); Barker (delivered digitally); Fresh (delivered digitally); Playboy TV (delivered digitally).

Internet Service
Operational: Yes.
Broadband Service: Cebridge High Speed Cable Internet.
Fee: $45.00 installation; $29.95 monthly.

Telephone Service
Digital: Operational
Fee: $39.95 monthly

Miles of Plant: 80.0 (coaxial); None (fiber optic). Homes passed: 5,827. Total homes in franchised area: 5,839.
Manager: Roland Myers. Chief Technician: Brian Garland.
City fee: 3% of gross.
Ownership: Cequel Communications LLC (MSO).

MIRE—Formerly served by Trust Cable. No longer in operation. ICA: LA0185.

MONROE—CMA Cablevision, 3759 Old Sterlington Rd, Monroe, LA 71203-3086. Phones: 972-233-9614 (Corporate office); 318-345-1010. Fax: 318-343-5255. Web Site: http://www.cmaaccess.com. Also serves North Monroe & South Monroe. ICA: LA0049.
TV Market Ranking: 99 (MONROE, South Monroe). Franchise award date: October 3, 1980. Franchise expiration date: N.A. Began: August 1, 1979.
Channel capacity: N.A. Channels available but not in use: N.A.

Basic Service
Subscribers: 1,280.
Programming (received off-air): KAQY (ABC) Columbia; KARD (FOX) West Monroe; KLTM-TV (PBS) Monroe; KMCT-TV (IND) West Monroe; KMNO-LP Monroe; KNOE-TV (CBS, CW) Monroe; KTVE (NBC) El Dorado.
Programming (via satellite): ABC Family Channel; Headline News; Home Shopping Network; ION Television; QVC; TBS Super-

station; TV Guide Network; Weather Channel; WGN America.
Fee: $39.95 installation; $17.95 monthly; $12.95 additional installation.

Expanded Basic Service 1
Subscribers: N.A.
Programming (via satellite): AMC; Animal Planet; Arts & Entertainment; BET Networks; CNBC; CNN; Comcast Sports Net Southwest; Comedy Central; Country Music TV; C-SPAN; Discovery Channel; E! Entertainment Television; ESPN; ESPN 2; Food Network; Fox News Channel; FX; Hallmark Channel; History Channel; Lifetime; MTV; Nickelodeon; Spike TV; Syfy; The Learning Channel; Turner Classic Movies; Turner Network TV; TV Land; USA Network; VH1.
Fee: $24.50 monthly.

Digital Basic Service
Subscribers: N.A.
Programming (via satellite): BBC America; Bio; Bravo!; Discovery Digital Networks; DMX Music; ESPN Classic Sports; ESPNews; Fox Movie Channel; Fox Sports World; G4; GAS; Golf Channel; GSN; HGTV; History Channel International; Independent Film Channel; Lifetime Movie Network; National Geographic Channel; Nick Jr.; Outdoor Channel; Speed Channel; Versus; WE tv.
Fee: $12.45 monthly.

Pay Service 1
Pay Units: N.A.
Programming (via satellite): HBO.
Fee: $14.95 installation; $13.95 monthly.

Digital Pay Service 1
Pay Units: N.A.
Programming (via satellite): Cinemax (multiplexed); Encore (multiplexed); HBO (multiplexed); Showtime (multiplexed); Starz (multiplexed); The Movie Channel (multiplexed).
Fee: $10.95 monthly (Cinemax or Starz/Encore), $13.95 monthly (HBO or Showtime).

Video-On-Demand: No

Pay-Per-View
iN DEMAND (delivered digitally); Playboy TV (delivered digitally); Fresh (delivered digitally).

Internet Service
Operational: Yes.
Broadband Service: CMA.
Fee: $49.95 installation; $39.95 monthly; $9.95 modem lease; $149.95 modem purchase.

Telephone Service
Digital: Operational
Fee: $39.95 monthly

Miles of Plant: 61.0 (coaxial); None (fiber optic). Homes passed: 4,542.
General Manager: Jerry Smith. Marketing Director: Julie Ferguson.
City fee: 3% of gross.
Ownership: Cable Management Assoc. (MSO).

MONTEREY—Formerly served by Almega Cable. No longer in operation. ICA: LA0186.

MONTGOMERY—Rapid Cable, 515 E Longview Dr, Arp, TX 75750. Phone: 903-859-6492. Fax: 903-859-3708. ICA: LA0116.
TV Market Ranking: Outside TV Markets (MONTGOMERY). Franchise award date: April 10, 1983. Franchise expiration date: N.A. Began: July 1, 1985.
Channel capacity: 54 (not 2-way capable). Channels available but not in use: 18.

Basic Service
Subscribers: 133.
Programming (received off-air): KALB-TV (CBS, NBC) Alexandria; KLAX-TV (ABC) Alexandria; KLPA-TV (PBS) Alexandria; KNOE-TV (CBS, CW) Monroe; KNTS-LP (IND) Natchitoches; WNTZ-TV (FOX, MNT) Natchez.
Programming (via satellite): ABC Family Channel; Animal Planet; Arts & Entertainment; Cartoon Network; CNN; C-SPAN; Discovery Channel; Disney Channel; E! Entertainment Television; ESPN; ESPN 2; FX; Great American Country; Headline News; HGTV; Home Shopping Network; Lifetime; National Geographic Channel; Nickelodeon; Outdoor Channel; Spike TV; TBS Superstation; Trinity Broadcasting Network; Turner Classic Movies; Turner Network TV; USA Network; VH1; Weather Channel.
Fee: $54.95 installation; $44.05 monthly.

Pay Service 1
Pay Units: 18.
Programming (via satellite): HBO.
Fee: $12.95 monthly.

Pay Service 2
Pay Units: 9.
Programming (via satellite): The Movie Channel.
Fee: $12.95 monthly.

Pay Service 3
Pay Units: 32.
Programming (via satellite): Showtime.
Fee: $12.95 monthly.

Video-On-Demand: No

Internet Service
Operational: No.

Telephone Service
None

Miles of Plant: 13.0 (coaxial); None (fiber optic). Homes passed: 430.
Regional Manager: Mike Taylor. Chief Technician: Ronnie Stafford.
City fee: 3% of gross.
Ownership: Rapid Communications LLC (MSO).

MOREAUVILLE—Suddenlink Communications, 12444 Powerscourt Dr, Saint Louis, MO 63131-3660. Phones: 800-999-6845 (Customer service); 314-965-2020. Fax: 903-561-5485. Web Site: http://www.suddenlink.com. Also serves Avoyelles Parish, Bordelonville, Cottonport, Echo, Plaucheville, Rapides Parish (portions) & Simmesport. ICA: LA0089.
TV Market Ranking: Below 100 (Avoyelles Parish (portions), Cottonport, Echo, MOREAUVILLE, Rapides Parish (portions)); Outside TV Markets (Avoyelles Parish (portions), Bordelonville, Plaucheville, Simmesport). Franchise award date: N.A. Franchise expiration date: N.A. Began: October 10, 1983.
Channel capacity: 54 (operating 2-way). Channels available but not in use: N.A.

Basic Service
Subscribers: 3,368.
Programming (received off-air): KALB-TV (CBS, NBC) Alexandria; KLAX-TV (ABC) Alexandria; KLFY-TV (CBS) Lafayette; KLPA-TV (PBS) Alexandria; WAFB (CBS) Baton Rouge; WBRZ-TV (ABC) Baton Rouge; WNTZ-TV (FOX, MNT) Natchez.
Programming (via satellite): C-SPAN; Eternal Word TV Network; Home Shopping Network; Trinity Broadcasting Network.
Fee: $39.95 installation; $19.95 monthly.

Expanded Basic Service 1
Subscribers: N.A.
Programming (via satellite): ABC Family Channel; AMC; Animal Planet; Arts & Entertainment; BET Networks; Cartoon Network; CNBC; CNN; Comcast Sports Net Southwest; Discovery Channel; Disney Channel; E! Entertainment Television; ESPN; ESPN 2; Fox News Channel; FX; Great American Country; Headline News; HGTV; History Channel; Lifetime; MSNBC; MTV; National Geographic Channel; Nickelodeon; Outdoor Channel; Spike TV; TBS Superstation; The Learning Channel; Turner Classic Movies; Turner Network TV; TV Land; USA Network; VH1; Weather Channel.
Fee: $24.00 monthly.

Digital Basic Service
Subscribers: N.A.
Programming (via satellite): BBC America; Bio; Discovery Digital Networks; DMX Music; ESPN Classic Sports; ESPNews; Fuse; Golf Channel; GSN; History Channel International; Independent Film Channel; Sleuth; Style Network; Toon Disney; Versus; WE tv.
Fee: $3.99 monthly.

Pay Service 1
Pay Units: 253.
Programming (via satellite): Cinemax.
Fee: $7.00 monthly.

Pay Service 2
Pay Units: 381.
Programming (via satellite): HBO.
Fee: $12.00 monthly.

Pay Service 3
Pay Units: 185.
Programming (via satellite): The Movie Channel.
Fee: $9.00 monthly.

Pay Service 4
Pay Units: 582.
Programming (via satellite): Showtime.
Fee: $7.00 monthly.

Digital Pay Service 1
Pay Units: N.A.
Programming (via satellite): Cinemax (multiplexed); Encore (multiplexed); HBO (multiplexed); Showtime (multiplexed); Starz; The Movie Channel (multiplexed).

Video-On-Demand: No

Pay-Per-View
iN DEMAND (delivered digitally); Playboy TV (delivered digitally).

Internet Service
Operational: Yes. Began: January 5, 2006.
Broadband Service: Cebridge High Speed Cable Internet.
Fee: $45.00 installation; $29.95 monthly.

Telephone Service
Analog: Not Operational
Digital: Operational
Fee: $39.95 monthly

Miles of Plant: 103.0 (coaxial); None (fiber optic). Homes passed: 4,085.
Regional Manager: Todd Cruthird. Area Manager: Mark Hood. Plant Manager: Dion Canaday.
Ownership: Cequel Communications LLC (MSO).

MORGAN CITY—Allen's TV Cable Service Inc., PO Box 2643, 800 Victor II Blvd, Morgan City, LA 70380. Phone: 985-384-8335. Fax: 985-384-5243. E-mail: info@atvci.net. Web Site: http://www.atvc.net. Also serves Bayou L'Ourse, Berwick, Pierre Part, St. Mary Parish & Stephensville. ICA: LA0188.
TV Market Ranking: 87 (Pierre Part); Below 100 (St. Mary Parish (portions)); Outside TV Markets (Bayou L'Ourse, Berwick, MORGAN CITY, St. Mary Parish (portions), Stephensville). Franchise award date: N.A. Franchise expiration date: N.A. Began: January 1, 1960.
Channel capacity: N.A. Channels available but not in use: N.A.

Basic Service
Subscribers: 8,600.
Programming (received off-air): KADN-TV (FOX) Lafayette; KATC (ABC) Lafayette; KLFY-TV (CBS) Lafayette; WAFB (CBS) Baton Rouge; WBRZ-TV (ABC) Baton Rouge; WDSU (NBC) New Orleans; WGMB-TV (FOX) Baton Rouge; WLPB-TV (PBS) Baton Rouge; WPXL-TV (ION) New Orleans; WUPL (MNT) Slidell; WVLA-TV (NBC) Baton Rouge; WVUE-DT (FOX) New Orleans; WWL-TV (CBS) New Orleans; WYES-TV (PBS) New Orleans.
Programming (via satellite): Cox Sports Television; C-SPAN; Home Shopping Network; QVC; SoapNet; WGN America.
Fee: $24.95 installation; $16.50 monthly; $22.00 additional installation.

Expanded Basic Service 1
Subscribers: N.A.
Programming (via satellite): ABC Family Channel; AMC; Animal Planet; Arts & Entertainment; BET Networks; Bravo; Cartoon Network; CNBC; CNN; Comcast Sports Net Southwest; Comedy Central; Country Music TV; Discovery Channel; Disney Channel; E! Entertainment Television; ESPN; ESPN 2; Eternal Word TV Network; Food Network; Fox News Channel; FX; Headline News; HGTV; History Channel; Lifetime; MSNBC; MTV; Nickelodeon; Outdoor Channel; Spike TV; Syfy; TBS Superstation; The Learning Channel; Toon Disney; Travel Channel; Trinity Broadcasting Network; Turner Network TV; TV Land; Univision; USA Network; VH1; WE tv; Weather Channel.
Fee: $29.50 monthly.

Digital Basic Service
Subscribers: 2,100.
Programming (via satellite): BBC America; Bio; Bloomberg Television; Current; Discovery Digital Networks; Do-It-Yourself; ESPNews; Fox College Sports Atlantic; Fox College Sports Central; Fox College Sports Pacific; Fox Movie Channel; Fox Sports World; Fuse; G4; GAS; GSN; Hallmark Channel; History Channel International; Independent Film Channel; MTV Networks Digital Suite; Music Choice; National Geographic Channel; Nick Jr.; Nick Too; NickToons TV; Speed Channel; Style Network; Trio.
Fee: $18.00 monthly; $3.75 converter.

Digital Pay Service 1
Pay Units: N.A.
Programming (via satellite): Cinemax (multiplexed); Encore (multiplexed); HBO (multiplexed); Showtime (multiplexed); Starz (multiplexed); The Movie Channel (multiplexed).
Fee: $3.75 converter.

Video-On-Demand: No

Pay-Per-View
iN DEMAND; Tigervision (delivered digitally); iN DEMAND (delivered digitally); Hot Choice (delivered digitally); Playboy TV (delivered digitally); Fresh (delivered digitally); Shorteez (delivered digitally).
Internet Service
Operational: Yes.
Subscribers: 1,300.
Broadband Service: atvci.net.
Fee: $34.95-$99.95 monthly; $6.75 modem lease; $75.00 modem purchase.
Telephone Service
Digital: Operational
Fee: $24.95-$39.95 monthly
Miles of Plant: 270.0 (coaxial); 60.0 (fiber optic). 750 /860 MHz
President, Chief Executive Officer & General Manager: Greg A. Price. Vice President: David J. Price. Chief Technician: Chris A. Price.
Ownership: Allen's TV Cable Service Inc. (MSO).

NATCHEZ—Rapid Cable, 515 E Longview Dr, Arp, TX 75750. Phone: 903-859-6492. Fax: 903-859-3708. ICA: LA0122.
TV Market Ranking: Outside TV Markets (NATCHEZ). Franchise award date: N.A. Franchise expiration date: N.A. Began: May 1, 1985.
Channel capacity: 54 (not 2-way capable). Channels available but not in use: N.A.
Basic Service
Subscribers: 150.
Programming (received off-air): KALB-TV (CBS, NBC) Alexandria; KARD (FOX) West Monroe; KLAX-TV (ABC) Alexandria; KLPA-TV (PBS) Alexandria; KNOE-TV (CBS, CW) Monroe; KPXJ (CW) Minden.
Programming (via satellite): ABC Family Channel; Arts & Entertainment; BET Networks; Cartoon Network; CNN; Discovery Channel; Disney Channel; ESPN; ESPN 2; Great American Country; Headline News; HGTV; Home Shopping Network; KNTS-LP (IND) Natchitoches; Lifetime; National Geographic Channel; Nickelodeon; Outdoor Channel; SoapNet; Spike TV; TBS Superstation; Trinity Broadcasting Network; Turner Classic Movies; Turner Network TV; USA Network; Weather Channel.
Fee: $54.95 installation; $44.05 monthly.
Digital Basic Service
Subscribers: N.A.
Programming (via satellite): BBC America; Bio; Bloomberg Television; Discovery Health Channel; Discovery Kids Channel; Discovery Military Channel; Discovery Planet Green; DMX Music; ESPN Classic Sports; ESPNews; Fox College Sports Atlantic; Fox College Sports Central; Fox College Sports Pacific; Fox Soccer; Fuse; G4; Golf Channel; GSN; History Channel; ID Investigation Discovery; Lifetime Movie Network; Science Channel; ShopNBC; Sleuth; Speed Channel; Style Network; Syfy; Versus; WE tv.
Pay Service 1
Pay Units: 14.
Programming (via satellite): Cinemax.
Fee: $12.95 monthly.
Pay Service 2
Pay Units: 28.
Programming (via satellite): HBO.
Fee: $12.95 monthly.
Pay Service 3
Pay Units: 40.
Programming (via satellite): Showtime.
Fee: $12.95 monthly.
Digital Pay Service 1
Pay Units: N.A.
Programming (via satellite): Cinemax (multiplexed); Encore (multiplexed); Flix; HBO (multiplexed); Showtime (multiplexed); Starz (multiplexed); The Movie Channel (multiplexed).
Video-On-Demand: No
Pay-Per-View
iN DEMAND (delivered digitally); Playboy TV (delivered digitally); Club Jenna (delivered digitally).
Internet Service
Operational: No.
Telephone Service
None
Miles of Plant: 16.0 (coaxial); None (fiber optic). Homes passed: 415.
Regional Manager: Mike Taylor. Chief Technician: Ronnie Stafford.
Ownership: Rapid Communications LLC (MSO).

NATCHITOCHES—Suddenlink Communications, PO Box 698, 321 Texas St, Natchitoches, LA 71457. Phone: 318-352-5883. Fax: 318-352-4288. Web Site: http://www.suddenlink.com. Also serves Natchitoches Parish. ICA: LA0029.
TV Market Ranking: Below 100 (Natchitoches Parish (portions)); Outside TV Markets (NATCHITOCHES, Natchitoches Parish (portions)). Franchise award date: N.A. Franchise expiration date: N.A. Began: December 1, 1963.
Channel capacity: N.A. Channels available but not in use: N.A.
Basic Service
Subscribers: 8,393.
Programming (received off-air): KALB-TV (CBS, NBC) Alexandria; KLAX-TV (ABC) Alexandria; KLPA-TV (PBS) Alexandria; KMSS-TV (FOX) Shreveport; KNTS-LP (IND) Natchitoches; KPXJ (CW) Minden; KSHV-TV (MNT) Shreveport; KSLA (CBS) Shreveport; KTBS-TV (ABC) Shreveport; allband FM.
Programming (via satellite): ABC Family Channel; CNN; Comcast Sports Net Southwest; C-SPAN; C-SPAN 2; Eternal Word TV Network; Home Shopping Network; QVC; TBS Superstation; TV Guide Network; Weather Channel; WGN America.
Current originations: Educational Access.
Fee: $35.00 installation; $13.95 monthly.
Expanded Basic Service 1
Subscribers: N.A.
Programming (via satellite): AMC; Animal Planet; Arts & Entertainment; BET Networks; Bravo; Cartoon Network; CNBC; Comedy Central; Discovery Channel; Disney Channel; E! Entertainment Television; ESPN; ESPN 2; Food Network; Fox News Channel; FX; Great American Country; Headline News; HGTV; History Channel; Lifetime; MSNBC; MTV; Nickelodeon; Outdoor Life Network (Canada); Oxygen; Speed Channel; Spike TV; Syfy; The Learning Channel; Travel Channel; Turner Network TV; TV Land; USA Network; VH1.
Fee: $14.85 monthly.
Digital Basic Service
Subscribers: N.A.
Programming (via satellite): BBC America; Bio; Bloomberg Television; Discovery Digital Networks; DMX Music; Encore Action (multiplexed); ESPN Classic Sports; ESPNews; Fox Sports World; Fuse; G4; GAS; Golf Channel; GSN; Hallmark Channel; Halogen Network; History Channel International; Independent Film Channel; Lifetime Movie Network; Nick Jr.; NickToons TV; Outdoor Channel; SoapNet; Sundance Channel; Toon Disney; Trinity Broadcasting Network.
Pay Service 1
Pay Units: N.A.
Programming (via satellite): Cinemax; HBO; Showtime; Starz; The Movie Channel.
Fee: $35.00 installation; $7.95 monthly (Starz or Encore), $14.00 monthly (HBO).
Digital Pay Service 1
Pay Units: N.A.
Programming (via satellite): Cinemax (multiplexed); HBO (multiplexed); Showtime (multiplexed); Starz (multiplexed); The Movie Channel (multiplexed).
Video-On-Demand: No
Pay-Per-View
Playboy TV (delivered digitally); Fresh (delivered digitally); NBA TV (delivered digitally); ESPN Gameplan (delivered digitally); ESPN Now (delivered digitally); iN DEMAND (delivered digitally).
Internet Service
Operational: Yes.
Broadband Service: Cebridge High Speed Cable Internet.
Fee: $45.00 installation; $29.95 monthly; $10.00 modem lease.
Telephone Service
Digital: Operational
Fee: $39.95 monthly
Miles of Plant: 141.0 (coaxial); None (fiber optic). Total homes in franchised area: 11,685.
Manager: Ronnie Waters.
Ownership: Cequel Communications LLC (MSO).

NATCHITOCHES (portions)—Rapid Cable. Now served by NATCHEZ, LA [LA0122]. ICA: LA0189.

NEW IBERIA—Cox Communications. Now served by BATON ROUGE, LA [LA0003]. ICA: LA0190.

NEW IBERIA—Suddenlink Communications, 12444 Powerscourt Dr, Saint Louis, MO 63131-3660. Phones: 337-363-0621; 314-965-2020. Fax: 337-363-9171. Web Site: http://www.suddenlink.com. Also serves Iberia Parish (portions), Lydia, St. Martin Parish (portions) & Vermilion Parish (portions). ICA: LA0072.
TV Market Ranking: Below 100 (Iberia Parish (portions), Lydia, NEW IBERIA, St. Martin Parish (portions), Vermilion Parish (portions)). Franchise award date: N.A. Franchise expiration date: N.A. Began: N.A.
Channel capacity: 62 (operating 2-way). Channels available but not in use: 16.
Basic Service
Subscribers: 4,288.
Programming (received off-air): KADN-TV (FOX) Lafayette; KATC (ABC) Lafayette; KLFY-TV (CBS) Lafayette; KLPB-TV (PBS) Lafayette; WVLA-TV (NBC) Baton Rouge.
Programming (via satellite): QVC; TV Guide Network.
Fee: $18.95 monthly; $2.00 converter.
Expanded Basic Service 1
Subscribers: 4,181.
Programming (via satellite): ABC Family Channel; AMC; Animal Planet; Arts & Entertainment; BET Networks; Cartoon Network; CNBC; CNN; Comedy Central; C-SPAN; Discovery Channel; Disney Channel; E! Entertainment Television; ESPN; ESPN 2; Eternal Word TV Network; Food Network; Fox News Channel; FX; Great American Country; Headline News; HGTV; History Channel; Home Shopping Network; Lifetime; MSNBC; MTV; National Geographic Channel; Nickelodeon; Outdoor Channel; Spike TV; Syfy; TBS Superstation; The Learning Channel; Travel Channel; Trinity Broadcasting Network; Turner Classic Movies; Turner Network TV; TV Land; USA Network; VH1; Weather Channel.
Fee: $25.00 monthly.
Digital Basic Service
Subscribers: N.A.
Programming (via satellite): BBC America; Bio; Bloomberg Television; Discovery Digital Networks; DMX Music; ESPN Classic Sports; ESPNews; Fuse; G4; Golf Channel; GSN; History Channel International; Independent Film Channel; Sleuth; Speed Channel; Style Network; Toon Disney; Versus; WE tv.
Fee: $3.99 monthly.
Pay Service 1
Pay Units: 690.
Programming (via satellite): Cinemax.
Fee: $7.95 monthly.
Pay Service 2
Pay Units: 1,051.
Programming (via satellite): HBO.
Fee: $10.95 monthly.
Pay Service 3
Pay Units: 779.
Programming (via satellite): Showtime; The Movie Channel.
Fee: $10.95 monthly (each).
Digital Pay Service 1
Pay Units: N.A.
Programming (via satellite): Cinemax (multiplexed); Encore (multiplexed); HBO (multiplexed); Showtime (multiplexed); Starz (multiplexed); The Movie Channel (multiplexed).
Video-On-Demand: No
Pay-Per-View
iN DEMAND (delivered digitally); Playboy TV (delivered digitally); Fresh (delivered digitally).
Internet Service
Operational: Yes. Began: July 14, 2003.
Broadband Service: Cebridge High Speed Cable Internet.
Fee: $45.00 installation; $29.95 monthly.
Telephone Service
Analog: Not Operational
Digital: Operational
Fee: $39.95 monthly
Miles of Plant: 50.0 (coaxial); 20.0 (fiber optic).
Regional Manager: Todd Cruthird.
Ownership: Cequel Communications LLC (MSO).

NEW ORLEANS—Cox Communications, 2121 Airline Dr, Metairie, LA 70001. Phone: 504-304-7345. Fax: 504-304-2248. Web

Site: http://www.cox.com. Also serves Arabi, Boutte, Chalmette, Destrehan, Gretna, Hahnville, Harahan, Jean Lafitte, Jefferson Parish (portions), Kenner, Luling, Meraux, Montz, Norco, Orleans Parish, St. Bernard Parish, St. Charles Parish (portions), St. Rose, Violet & Westwego. ICA: LA0001.

TV Market Ranking: 31 (Arabi, Boutte, Chalmette, Destrehan, Gretna, Hahnville, Harahan, Jean Lafitte, Jefferson Parish (portions), Kenner, Luling, Meraux, Montz, NEW ORLEANS, Norco, Orleans Parish, St. Bernard Parish, St. Charles Parish (portions), St. Rose, Violet, Westwego). Franchise award date: May 28, 1981. Franchise expiration date: N.A. Began: April 21, 1982.

Channel capacity: N.A. Channels available but not in use: N.A.

Basic Service

Subscribers: 185,000.

Programming (received off-air): WDSU (NBC) New Orleans; WGNO (ABC) New Orleans; WHNO (IND) New Orleans; WLAE-TV (PBS) New Orleans; WNOL-TV (CW) New Orleans; WPXL-TV (ION) New Orleans; WUPL (MNT) Slidell; WVUE-DT (FOX) New Orleans; WWL-TV (CBS) New Orleans; WYES-TV (PBS) New Orleans; allband FM.

Programming (via satellite): BET Networks; C-SPAN 2; Eternal Word TV Network; Headline News; Home Shopping Network; QVC; TBS Superstation; The Learning Channel; Trinity Broadcasting Network; TV Guide Network; Weather Channel; WGN America.

Current originations: Leased Access; Religious Access; Government Access; Educational Access; Public Access.

Fee: $32.99 installation; $15.55 monthly; $15.00 additional installation.

Expanded Basic Service 1

Subscribers: N.A.

Programming (via satellite): ABC Family Channel; AMC; Animal Planet; Arts & Entertainment; Bravo; Cartoon Network; CNBC; CNN; Comcast Sports Net Southwest; Comedy Central; Country Music TV; C-SPAN; Discovery Channel; Disney Channel; E! Entertainment Television; ESPN; ESPN 2; ESPN Classic Sports; Food Network; Fox News Channel; FX; Hallmark Channel; HGTV; History Channel; Lifetime; MSNBC; MTV; MTV2; Nickelodeon; Product Information Network; Sneak Prevue; Speed Channel; Spike TV; Syfy; Travel Channel; truTV; Turner Classic Movies; Turner Network TV; TV Land; USA Network; Versus; VH1.

Fee: $27.44 monthly.

Digital Basic Service

Subscribers: N.A.

Programming (via satellite): BBC America; Bio; Black Family Channel; Bloomberg Television; Canales N; Discovery Digital Networks; Encore Action; ESPNews; Flix; Fox Sports World; G4; Golf Channel; GSN; History Channel International; Lifetime Movie Network; MuchMusic Network; Music Choice; Oxygen; SoapNet; Sundance Channel; The Word Network; Toon Disney.

Fee: $12.58 monthly.

Pay Service 1

Pay Units: 31,867.

Programming (via satellite): Cinemax.

Fee: $11.50 monthly.

Pay Service 2

Pay Units: 7,943.

Programming (via satellite): Independent Film Channel.

Fee: $8.95 monthly.

Pay Service 3

Pay Units: 115,615.

Programming (via satellite): HBO.

Fee: $11.50 monthly.

Pay Service 4

Pay Units: 37,416.

Programming (via satellite): Showtime.

Fee: $11.50 monthly.

Digital Pay Service 1

Pay Units: N.A.

Programming (via satellite): Cinemax (multiplexed); HBO (multiplexed); Showtime (multiplexed); Starz (multiplexed); The Movie Channel (multiplexed).

Fee: $8.30 monthly (Starz & Encore), $12.50 monthly (Cinemax, HBO, Showtime or TMC).

Video-On-Demand: Yes

Pay-Per-View

Addressable homes: 145,251.

Hot Choice; iN DEMAND; iN DEMAND (delivered digitally), Addressable: Yes; Playboy TV (delivered digitally); Fresh (delivered digitally); Shorteez (delivered digitally); sports (delivered digitally).

Internet Service

Operational: Yes.

Broadband Service: Cox High Speed Internet.

Fee: $49.95 installation; $19.99-$53.99 monthly; $15.00 modem lease; $349.00 modem purchase.

Telephone Service

Digital: Operational

Fee: $29.00 installation; $9.95-$39.99 monthly

Miles of Plant: 3,449.0 (coaxial); 643.0 (fiber optic). Homes passed: 500,000.

Vice President & Regional Manager: Greg Bicket. Vice President, Engineering: Mike Latino. Vice President, Marketing: Ellen Lloyd.

City fee: 5% of gross.

Ownership: Cox Communications Inc. (MSO).

NEW ORLEANS—No longer in operation. ICA: LA0231.

NEWELLTON—Rapid Cable, 515 E Longview Dr, Arp, TX 75750. Phone: 903-859-6492. Fax: 903-859-3708. ICA: LA0114.

TV Market Ranking: Below 100 (NEWELLTON). Franchise award date: N.A. Franchise expiration date: N.A. Began: June 1, 1982.

Channel capacity: 54 (not 2-way capable). Channels available but not in use: N.A.

Basic Service

Subscribers: 210.

Programming (received off-air): KAQY (ABC) Columbia; KARD (FOX) West Monroe; KLTM-TV (PBS) Monroe; KNOE-TV (CBS, CW) Monroe; WJTV (CBS) Jackson; WLBT (NBC) Jackson.

Programming (via satellite): ABC Family Channel; Animal Planet; Arts & Entertainment; BET Networks; CNBC; CNN; C-SPAN; Discovery Channel; Disney Channel; ESPN; ESPN 2; Fox News Channel; Fox Sports Net; FX; Golf Channel; Great American Country; Headline News; HGTV; History Channel; Home Shopping Network; Lifetime; MSNBC; MTV; National Geographic Channel; Nickelodeon; Outdoor Channel; Spike TV; TBS Superstation; Trinity Broadcasting Network; Turner Classic Movies; Turner Network TV; USA Network; Weather Channel.

Fee: $54.95 installation; $44.05 monthly.

Digital Basic Service

Subscribers: N.A.

Programming (via satellite): BBC America; Bio; Bloomberg Television; Discovery Health Channel; Discovery Kids Channel; Discovery Military Channel; Discovery Planet Green; DMX Music; ESPN Classic Sports; ESPNews; Fox College Sports Atlantic; Fox College Sports Central; Fox College Sports Pacific; Fox Soccer; Fuse; G4; GSN; History Channel International; ID Investigation Discovery; Independent Film Channel; Science Channel; ShopNBC; Sleuth; Speed Channel; Style Network; Sundance Channel; Toon Disney; Versus; WE tv.

Pay Service 1

Pay Units: 42.

Programming (via satellite): Cinemax.

Fee: $12.95 monthly.

Pay Service 2

Pay Units: 29.

Programming (via satellite): HBO.

Fee: $12.95 monthly.

Pay Service 3

Pay Units: 41.

Programming (via satellite): Showtime.

Fee: $12.95 monthly.

Digital Pay Service 1

Pay Units: N.A.

Programming (via satellite): Cinemax (multiplexed); Encore (multiplexed); Flix; HBO (multiplexed); Showtime (multiplexed); Starz (multiplexed); The Movie Channel (multiplexed).

Video-On-Demand: No

Pay-Per-View

iN DEMAND (delivered digitally); Playboy TV (delivered digitally); Club Jenna (delivered digitally).

Internet Service

Operational: No.

Telephone Service

None

Miles of Plant: 10.0 (coaxial); None (fiber optic). Homes passed: 731.

Regional Manager: Mike Taylor. Chief Technician: Ronnie Stafford.

Ownership: Rapid Communications LLC (MSO).

NORWOOD—Trust Cable. Now served by ETHEL, LA [LA0160]. ICA: LA0191.

OAK GROVE—CMA Cablevision of Lake Providence. Now served by LAKE PROVIDENCE, LA [LA0053]. ICA: LA0086.

OAK RIDGE—Formerly served by Charter Communications. No longer in operation. ICA: LA0218.

OLLA—Rapid Cable, 515 E Longview Dr, Arp, TX 75750. Phone: 903-859-6492. Fax: 903-859-3708. Also serves Tullos & Urania. ICA: LA0238.

TV Market Ranking: Outside TV Markets (OLLA, Tullos, Urania).

Channel capacity: N.A. Channels available but not in use: N.A.

Basic Service

Subscribers: N.A.

Programming (received off-air): KALB-TV (CBS, NBC) Alexandria; KAQY (ABC) Columbia; KARD (FOX) West Monroe; KLAX-TV (ABC) Alexandria; KLTM-TV (PBS) Monroe; KNOE-TV (CBS, CW) Monroe.

Programming (via satellite): ABC Family Channel; American Movie Classics; Animal Planet; Arts & Entertainment; BET Networks; Bravo; Cartoon Network; CNBC; CNN; Comedy Central; Country Music TV; C-SPAN; C-SPAN 2; Discovery Channel; Disney Channel; E! Entertainment Television; ESPN; ESPN 2; Food Network; Fox News Channel; FX; G4; Golf Channel; Hallmark Channel; Headline News; HGTV; History Channel; Home Shopping Network; INSP; ION Television; Lifetime; MSNBC; MTV; National Geographic Channel; Nickelodeon; Outdoor Channel; Oxygen; QVC; ShopNBC; SoapNet; Speed Channel; Spike TV; Syfy; TBS Superstation; The Learning Channel; Toon Disney; Travel Channel; Trinity Broadcasting Network; truTV; Turner Classic Movies; Turner Network TV; TV Land; USA Network; VH1; WE tv; Weather Channel; WGN America.

Digital Basic Service

Subscribers: N.A.

Programming (received off-air): KNOE-TV (CBS, CW) Monroe.

Programming (via satellite): BBC America; Bio; Bloomberg Television; CMT Pure Country; Discovery en Espanol; Discovery Health Channel; Discovery Kids Channel; Discovery Military Channel; Discovery Planet Green; Do-It-Yourself; Fox Movie Channel; Fox Soccer; Fuse; GSN; History Channel International; ID Investigation Discovery; Independent Film Channel; Lifetime Movie Network; MTV Hits; MTV Jams; MTV Tres; MTV2; Music Choice; Nick Jr.; Nick Too; NickToons TV; Science Channel; Style Network; Sundance Channel; TeenNick; VH1 Classic; VH1 Soul.

Digital Pay Service 1

Pay Units: N.A.

Programming (via satellite): Cinemax (multiplexed); Encore; Flix; HBO (multiplexed); LOGO; Showtime (multiplexed); Starz (multiplexed); The Movie Channel (multiplexed).

Pay-Per-View

iN DEMAND (delivered digitally); Playboy TV (delivered digitally).

Internet Service

Operational: No.

Telephone Service

None

Regional Manager: Mike Taylor. Chief Technician: Ronnie Stafford.

Ownership: Rapid Communications LLC (MSO).

PALMETTO—Formerly served by Village Cable Co. No longer in operation.. ICA: LA0136.

PECANIERE—CableSouth Inc. No longer in operation. ICA: LA0192.

PIERRE PART—Allen's TV Cable Service Inc. Now served by MORGAN CITY, LA [LA0188]. ICA: LA0193.

PINE PRAIRIE—Charter Communications, 330 Moosa Blvd, Eunice, LA 70535. Phones: 985-446-4900 (Thibodaux office); 337-546-

0087. Fax: 337-546-0038. Web Site: http://www.charter.com. ICA: LA0127.

TV Market Ranking: Outside TV Markets (PINE PRAIRIE). Franchise award date: May 12, 1983. Franchise expiration date: N.A. Began: December 1, 1983.

Channel capacity: N.A. Channels available but not in use: N.A.

Basic Service

Subscribers: 123.

Programming (received off-air): KADN-TV (FOX) Lafayette; KALB-TV (CBS, NBC) Alexandria; KATC (ABC) Lafayette; KLFY-TV (CBS) Lafayette; KLPA-TV (PBS) Alexandria.

Programming (via satellite): ABC Family Channel; Eternal Word TV Network; QVC; TBS Superstation; WGN America.

Fee: $29.99 installation; $11.85 monthly; $1.30 converter.

Expanded Basic Service 1

Subscribers: 50.

Programming (via satellite): CNN; Discovery Channel; ESPN; Lifetime; Nickelodeon; Spike TV; Turner Network TV; USA Network.

Fee: $9.48 monthly.

Pay Service 1

Pay Units: 7.

Programming (via satellite): Cinemax.

Fee: $10.45 monthly.

Pay Service 2

Pay Units: 21.

Programming (via satellite): HBO.

Fee: $10.45 monthly.

Video-On-Demand: No

Internet Service

Operational: No.

Telephone Service

None

Miles of Plant: 8.0 (coaxial); None (fiber optic). Homes passed: 308. Total homes in franchised area: 325.

Vice President & General Manager: Kip Kraemer. Operations Manager: Blane Bercegeay. Technical Operations Director: Gary Savoie. Plant Manager: Joe Semmes. Marketing Director: Lisa Brown.

City fee: 3% of basic.

Ownership: Charter Communications Inc. (MSO).

PINEVILLE—Suddenlink Communications, 3250 Donahue Ferry Rd, Pineville, LA 71360. Phone: 318-640-2892. Fax: 318-640-6951. Web Site: http://www.suddenlink.com. Also serves Alexandria, Ball, England Authority, Grant Parish, Libuse (portions), Pollock & Rapides Parish. ICA: LA0006.

TV Market Ranking: Below 100 (Alexandria, Ball, England Authority, Grant Parish, Libuse (portions), PINEVILLE, Pollock, Rapides Parish). Franchise award date: August 23, 1957. Franchise expiration date: N.A. Began: October 20, 1958.

Channel capacity: 64 (operating 2-way). Channels available but not in use: 1.

Basic Service

Subscribers: 31,013.

Programming (received off-air): KALB-TV (CBS, NBC) Alexandria; KLAX-TV (ABC) Alexandria; KLFY-TV (CBS) Lafayette; KLPA-TV (PBS) Alexandria; WNTZ-TV (FOX, MNT) Natchez.

Programming (via satellite): ION Television; QVC; TBS Superstation; TV Guide Network; WGN America.

Current originations: Leased Access; Government Access.

Fee: $38.00 installation; $7.73 monthly.

Expanded Basic Service 1

Subscribers: 27,200.

Programming (via satellite): ABC Family Channel; AMC; Animal Planet; Arts & Entertainment; BET Networks; Bravo; Cartoon Network; CNBC; CNN; Comcast Sports Net Southwest; Comedy Central; C-SPAN; C-SPAN 2; Discovery Channel; Disney Channel; E! Entertainment Television; ESPN; ESPN 2; Eternal Word TV Network; Food Network; Fox Movie Channel; Fox News Channel; FX; G4; Great American Country; Headline News; HGTV; History Channel; Home Shopping Network; Lifetime; Lifetime Movie Network; MoviePlex; MSNBC; MTV; Nickelodeon; Outdoor Channel; Speed Channel; Spike TV; Syfy; The Learning Channel; Travel Channel; Trinity Broadcasting Network; truTV; Turner Classic Movies; Turner Network TV; TV Land; USA Network; Versus; VH1; Weather Channel.

Fee: $38.00 installation; $42.67 monthly.

Digital Basic Service

Subscribers: N.A.

Programming (via satellite): BBC America; Bio; Bloomberg Television; Discovery Digital Networks; Encore Action; ESPN Classic Sports; ESPNews; Fox Sports World; Fuse; GAS; Golf Channel; GSN; Hallmark Channel; History Channel International; Independent Film Channel; MTV Networks Digital Suite; Music Choice; NBA TV; Nick Jr.; NickToons TV; SoapNet; Sundance Channel; Toon Disney.

Fee: $19.15 monthly.

Digital Pay Service 1

Pay Units: N.A.

Programming (via satellite): Cinemax (multiplexed); Flix; HBO (multiplexed); Showtime (multiplexed); Starz; The Movie Channel (multiplexed).

Video-On-Demand: No

Pay-Per-View

ESPN Now (delivered digitally); ESPN Gameplan (delivered digitally); NBA TV (delivered digitally); MLB/NHL (delivered digitally); Fresh (delivered digitally); Hot Choice (delivered digitally); Shorteez (delivered digitally); Playboy TV (delivered digitally); iN DEMAND (delivered digitally).

Internet Service

Operational: Yes.

Broadband Service: Cebridge High Speed Cable Internet.

Fee: $45.00 installation; $29.95 monthly.

Telephone Service

Digital: Operational

Fee: $39.95 monthly

Miles of Plant: 900.0 (coaxial); 195.0 (fiber optic). Homes passed: 37,651. Total homes in franchised area: 40,823.

Manager: Diana DeVille. Chief Technician: Stephen Frye.

City fee: 3% of gross.

Ownership: Cequel Communications LLC (MSO).

PLAIN DEALING—Rapid Cable, 515 E Longview Dr, Arp, TX 75750. Phone: 903-859-6492. Fax: 903-859-3708. Also serves Bossier Parish (northern portion). ICA: LA0100.

TV Market Ranking: 58 (Bossier Parish (northern portion), PLAIN DEALING). Franchise award date: September 21, 1982. Franchise expiration date: N.A. Began: May 1, 1983.

Channel capacity: 37 (not 2-way capable). Channels available but not in use: 5.

Basic Service

Subscribers: 104.

Programming (received off-air): KLTS-TV (PBS) Shreveport; KMSS-TV (FOX) Shreveport; KSHV-TV (MNT) Shreveport; KSLA (CBS) Shreveport; KTAL-TV (NBC) Texarkana.

Programming (via satellite): BET Networks; Bravo; Cartoon Network; CNN; Country Music TV; C-SPAN; ESPN; Headline News; HGTV; Lifetime; MTV; Nickelodeon; QVC; Turner Network TV; Weather Channel; WGN America.

Fee: $54.95 installation; $20.95 monthly.

Expanded Basic Service 1

Subscribers: N.A.

Programming (via satellite): ABC Family Channel; Discovery Channel; Disney Channel; Spike TV; Syfy; TBS Superstation; USA Network.

Fee: $23.10 monthly.

Digital Basic Service

Subscribers: N.A.

Programming (via satellite): AmericanLife TV Network; BBC America; Bio; Bloomberg Television; CMT Pure Country; Discovery Health Channel; Discovery Kids Channel; Discovery Military Channel; Discovery Planet Green; DMX Music; FitTV; Fox Movie Channel; Fuse; G4; Golf Channel; GSN; History Channel; History Channel International; ID Investigation Discovery; Independent Film Channel; Lifetime Movie Network; MTV Jams; MTV2; Nick Jr.; Outdoor Channel; Science Channel; Speed Channel; Style Network; TeenNick; Toon Disney; Trinity Broadcasting Network; Turner Classic Movies; Versus; VH1 Classic; VH1 Soul; WE tv.

Pay Service 1

Pay Units: 45.

Programming (via satellite): Cinemax.

Fee: $12.95 monthly.

Pay Service 2

Pay Units: 65.

Programming (via satellite): HBO.

Fee: $12.95 monthly.

Pay Service 3

Pay Units: 34.

Programming (via satellite): Showtime.

Fee: $12.95 monthly.

Digital Pay Service 1

Pay Units: N.A.

Programming (via satellite): Cinemax (multiplexed); Encore (multiplexed); Flix; HBO (multiplexed); Showtime (multiplexed); Starz (multiplexed); The Movie Channel (multiplexed).

Video-On-Demand: No

Pay-Per-View

iN DEMAND (delivered digitally); Hot Choice (delivered digitally); Playboy TV (delivered digitally).

Internet Service

Operational: No.

Telephone Service

None

Miles of Plant: 19.0 (coaxial); None (fiber optic). Homes passed: 513. Total homes in franchised area: 600.

Regional Manager: Mike Taylor. Chief Technician: Larry Stafford.

Franchise fee: 3% of gross.

Ownership: Rapid Communications LLC (MSO).

POINTE A LA HACHE—Formerly served by CMA Cablevision. No longer in operation. ICA: LA0195.

POINTE COUPEE—Charter Communications, 3421 Ewing Dr, New Roads, LA 70760. Phones: 337-546-0087 (Eunice office); 225-638-7632. Fax: 225-638-8360. Web Site: http://www.charter.com. Also serves Morganza, New Roads & Pointe Coupee Parish. ICA: LA0036.

TV Market Ranking: 87 (Morganza, New Roads, POINTE COUPEE, Pointe Coupee Parish (portions)); Below 100 (Pointe Coupee Parish (portions)); Outside TV Markets (Pointe Coupee Parish (portions)). Franchise award date: October 15, 1979. Franchise expiration date: N.A. Began: February 1, 1981.

Channel capacity: N.A. Channels available but not in use: N.A.

Basic Service

Subscribers: 4,446.

Programming (received off-air): KLFY-TV (CBS) Lafayette; WAFB (CBS) Baton Rouge; WBRZ-TV (ABC) Baton Rouge; WGMB-TV (FOX) Baton Rouge; WLPB-TV (PBS) Baton Rouge; WVLA-TV (NBC) Baton Rouge.

Programming (via satellite): Home Shopping Network; QVC; Trinity Broadcasting Network; WGN America.

Current originations: Leased Access; Public Access.

Fee: $29.99 installation; $42.99 monthly.

Digital Basic Service

Subscribers: N.A.

Programming (via satellite): BBC America; Bio; Bloomberg Television; Discovery Digital Networks; Do-It-Yourself; GAS; History Channel International; Independent Film Channel; Lifetime Movie Network; MTV Networks Digital Suite; Music Choice; Nick Jr.; Nick Too; NickToons TV; Style Network; Sundance Channel; WealthTV HD.

Digital Pay Service 1

Pay Units: N.A.

Programming (via satellite): Cinemax (multiplexed); Encore (multiplexed); Flix; HBO (multiplexed); Showtime (multiplexed); Starz (multiplexed); The Movie Channel (multiplexed).

Video-On-Demand: No

Pay-Per-View

iN DEMAND (delivered digitally); Playboy TV (delivered digitally); Fresh (delivered digitally); Shorteez (delivered digitally).

Internet Service

Operational: Yes.

Broadband Service: Charter Pipeline.

Fee: $29.99 monthly.

Telephone Service

Digital: Operational

Miles of Plant: 162.0 (coaxial); None (fiber optic). Homes passed: 5,537. Total homes in franchised area: 11,000.

Vice President & General Manager: Kip Kraemer. Vice President, Government Relations: Jim Laurent. Operations Director: Blane Bercegeay. Technical Operations Director: Gary Savoie. Plant Manager: Joe Semmes. Chief Technician: Jeffrey Venable. Marketing Director: Lisa Brown.

City fee: 3% of gross.

Ownership: Charter Communications Inc. (MSO).

PORT BARRE—Allen's TV Cable Service Inc. Now served by GRAND COTEAU, LA [LA0207]. ICA: LA0197.

RAYVILLE—Formerly served by Cotton Country Cable. No longer in operation. ICA: LA0219.

ROBELINE—Formerly served by MARBAC Communications. No longer in operation. ICA: LA0199.

ROCKY BRANCH—Bayou Cable TV, PO Box 466, Marion, LA 71260-0466. Phone: 318-292-4774. Fax: 318-292-4775. Web Site: http://www.bayoucable.com. ICA: LA0228.

TV Market Ranking: 99 (ROCKY BRANCH). Franchise award date: N.A. Franchise expiration date: N.A. Began: N.A.
Channel capacity: 50 (not 2-way capable). Channels available but not in use: 6.

Basic Service
Subscribers: 139.
Programming (received off-air): KAQY (ABC) Columbia; KARD (FOX) West Monroe; KLTM-TV (PBS) Monroe; KMCT-TV (IND) West Monroe; KNOE-TV (CBS, CW) Monroe; KTVE (NBC) El Dorado.
Programming (via satellite): AMC; Hallmark Channel; Home Shopping Network; QVC; Trinity Broadcasting Network; TV Land.
Fee: $20.00 installation; $15.95 monthly.

Expanded Basic Service 1
Subscribers: N.A.
Programming (via satellite): ABC Family Channel; Animal Planet; Arts & Entertainment; CNN; Country Music TV; CW+; Discovery Channel; ESPN; ESPN 2; FamilyNet; Food Network; Fox News Channel; FX; HGTV; History Channel; Lifetime; MTV; National Geographic Channel; Nickelodeon; Outdoor Channel; Speed Channel; Spike TV; TBS Superstation; The Learning Channel; Turner Network TV; USA Network; VH1; Weather Channel; WGN America.
Fee: $20.00 monthly.

Pay Service 1
Pay Units: N.A.
Programming (via satellite): Cinemax; HBO.
Fee: $8.95 monthly (Cinemax), $10.95 monthly (HBO).

Video-On-Demand: No

Pay-Per-View
Urban American Television Network (delivered digitally); Playboy TV (delivered digitally); Fresh (delivered digitally); Shorteez (delivered digitally).

Internet Service
Operational: No.

Telephone Service
None
Miles of Plant: 15.0 (coaxial); None (fiber optic).
Owner: Alan C. Booker. Chief Technician: Mark Andrews.
Ownership: Bayou Cable TV (MSO).

RODESSA—Formerly served by Almega Cable. No longer in operation. ICA: LA0110.

RUSTON—Suddenlink Communications, 1001 Cooktown Rd, Ruston, LA 71270-3113. Phone: 318-255-6594. Fax: 318-251-2711. Web Site: http://www.suddenlink.com. Also serves Grambling, Lincoln Parish, Simsboro & Vienna. ICA: LA0201.
TV Market Ranking: 99 (Lincoln Parish (portions), RUSTON, Vienna); Below 100 (Grambling, Simsboro, Lincoln Parish (portions)). Franchise award date: N.A. Franchise expiration date: N.A. Began: January 1, 1966.
Channel capacity: N.A. Channels available but not in use: N.A.

Basic Service
Subscribers: N.A.
Programming (received off-air): KAQY (ABC) Columbia; KARD (FOX) West Monroe; KEJB (MNT)lorado; KLTM-TV (PBS) Monroe; KMCT-TV (IND) West Monroe; KNOE-TV (CBS, CW) Monroe; KSLA (CBS) Shreveport; KTBS-TV (ABC) Shreveport; KTVE (NBC) El Dorado; 1 FM.
Programming (via satellite): Comcast Sports Net Southwest; C-SPAN; C-SPAN 2; CW+; Home Shopping Network; INSP; TBS Superstation; Trinity Broadcasting Network; TV Guide Network; Weather Channel; WGN America.
Current originations: Educational Access.
Fee: $7.50 installation; $15.35 monthly.

Expanded Basic Service 1
Subscribers: N.A.
Programming (via satellite): ABC Family Channel; AMC; Animal Planet; Arts & Entertainment; BET Networks; Cartoon Network; CNBC; CNN; Comedy Central; Country Music TV; Cox Sports Television; Discovery Channel; Disney Channel; ESPN; ESPN 2; Food Network; Fox News Channel; FX; Great American Country; Headline News; HGTV; History Channel; Lifetime; MTV; Nickelodeon; Outdoor Channel; Spike TV; Syfy; The Learning Channel; Travel Channel; truTV; Turner Classic Movies; Turner Network TV; TV Land; USA Network; VH1.
Fee: $16.60 monthly.

Digital Basic Service
Subscribers: N.A.
Programming (received off-air): KARD (FOX) West Monroe; KNOE-TV (CBS, CW) Monroe; KTVE (NBC) El Dorado.
Programming (via satellite): BBC America; Bio; Bloomberg Television; Discovery HD Theater; Discovery Health Channel; Discovery Home Channel; Discovery Kids Channel; Discovery Military Channel; Discovery Times Channel; Encore (multiplexed); ESPN HD; ESPNews; Fox Movie Channel; Fox Soccer; Fuse; G4; Golf Channel; GSN; HDNet; HDNet Movies; History Channel International; Lifetime Movie Network; Music Choice; Science Channel; Speed Channel; Toon Disney; Universal HD; Versus; WE tv.

Digital Pay Service 1
Pay Units: N.A.
Programming (via satellite): Cinemax (multiplexed); HBO (multiplexed); HBO HD; Showtime (multiplexed); Showtime HD; Starz (multiplexed); The Movie Channel (multiplexed).

Video-On-Demand: No

Pay-Per-View
ESPN Now (delivered digitally); iN DEMAND (delivered digitally); Playboy TV (delivered digitally); Fresh (delivered digitally).

Internet Service
Operational: Yes.
Broadband Service: Cebridge High Speed Cable Internet.
Fee: $45.00 installation; $29.95 monthly; $10.00 modem lease.

Telephone Service
None
Miles of Plant: 143.0 (coaxial); None (fiber optic).
Manager: J. Rex Holstead. Chief Technician: James C. Jennings.
City fee: 3% of gross.
Ownership: Cequel Communications LLC (MSO).

SHREVEPORT—Comcast Cable, 6529 Quilen Rd, Shreveport, LA 71108-4438. Phone: 318-213-3322. Fax: 318-213-4225. Web Site: http://www.comcast.com. Also serves Bethany, Caddo Parish, De Soto Parish (portions), Greenwood & Stonewall, LA; Waskom, TX. ICA: LA0004.
TV Market Ranking: 58 (Bethany, Caddo Parish, De Soto Parish (portions), Greenwood, SHREVEPORT, Stonewall, Waskom). Franchise award date: January 1, 1974. Franchise expiration date: N.A. Began: October 10, 1976.
Channel capacity: N.A. Channels available but not in use: N.A.

Basic Service
Subscribers: 61,438.
Programming (received off-air): KLTS-TV (PBS) Shreveport; KMSS-TV (FOX) Shreveport; KPXJ (CW) Minden; KSHV-TV (MNT) Shreveport; KSLA (CBS) Shreveport; KTAL-TV (NBC) Texarkana; KTBS-TV (ABC) Shreveport.
Programming (via satellite): QVC; TV Guide Network.
Current originations: Leased Access; Government Access.
Fee: $15.66 monthly.

Expanded Basic Service 1
Subscribers: 55,200.
Programming (via satellite): ABC Family Channel; AMC; Animal Planet; Arts & Entertainment; BET Networks; Bravo; Cartoon Network; CNBC; CNN; Comcast Sports Net Southwest; Comcast/Charter Sports Southeast (CSS); Comedy Central; Country Music TV; C-SPAN; C-SPAN 2; Discovery Channel; Discovery Health Channel; Disney Channel; E! Entertainment Television; ESPN; ESPN 2; FitTV; Food Network; Fox News Channel; FX; Golf Channel; Hallmark Channel; Halogen Network; Headline News; HGTV; History Channel; Home Shopping Network; Lifetime; MSNBC; MTV; National Geographic Channel; Nickelodeon; Oxygen; SoapNet; Speed Channel; Spike TV; Syfy; TBS Superstation; The Learning Channel; Travel Channel; Trinity Broadcasting Network; truTV; Turner Classic Movies; Turner Network TV; TV Land; TV One; Univision; USA Network; Versus; VH1; WE tv; Weather Channel.
Fee: $34.33 monthly.

Digital Basic Service
Subscribers: N.A.
Programming (received off-air): KLTS-TV (PBS) Shreveport; KMSS-TV (FOX) Shreveport; KSLA (CBS) Shreveport; KTAL-TV (NBC) Texarkana; KTBS-TV (ABC) Shreveport.
Programming (via satellite): Arts & Entertainment HD; BBC America; Bio; Bloomberg Television; Boomerang; CBS College Sports Network HD; CMT Pure Country; CNN HD; Cooking Channel; C-SPAN 3; Current; Discovery HD Theater; Discovery Kids Channel; Discovery Military Channel; Discovery Planet Green; Disney Channel; Do-It-Yourself; Encore (multiplexed); ESPN 2 HD; ESPN Classic Sports; ESPN HD; ESPNews; Eternal Word TV Network; Food Network HD; Fox Business Channel; Fox College Sports Atlantic; Fox College Sports Central; Fox College Sports Pacific; Fox Movie Channel; Fox Reality Channel; Fox Soccer; FSN HD; Fuel TV; Fuse; G4; Golf Channel HD; Gospel Music Channel; HGTV HD; History Channel International; ID Investigation Discovery; Independent Film Channel; Jewelry Television; Lifetime Movie Network; MTV Hits; MTV Jams; MTV Tres; MTV2; Music Choice; National Geographic Channel HD Network; NBA TV; NFL Network; NFL Network HD; NHL Network; Nick Jr.; Nick Too; NickToons TV; Outdoor Channel; PBS Kids Sprout; Science Channel; ShopNBC; Style Network; Sundance Channel; TBS in HD; TeenNick; Tennis Channel; The Word Network; Toon Disney; Turner Network TV HD; Universal HD; USA Network HD; Versus HD; VH1 Classic; VH1 Soul; Weatherscan.
Fee: $15.95 monthly.

Digital Pay Service 1
Pay Units: N.A.
Programming (via satellite): Cinemax (multiplexed); Cinemax HD; HBO (multiplexed); HBO HD; MoviePlex; Showtime (multiplexed); Showtime HD; Starz (multiplexed); Starz HDTV; The Movie Channel (multiplexed).
Fee: $11.50 monthly (Cinemax, HBO, Showtime, TMC, or Starz).

Video-On-Demand: Yes

Pay-Per-View
Hot Choice (delivered digitally), Fee: $3.95; iN DEMAND (delivered digitally); MLB Extra Innings (delivered digitally); Spice (delivered digitally), Fee: $6.95; Fresh (delivered digitally); Playboy TV (delivered digitally); Shorteez (delivered digitally); NBA League Pass (delivered digitally); MLS Direct Kick (delivered digitally); ESPN (delivered digitally); NHL Center Ice (delivered digitally).

Internet Service
Operational: Yes.
Broadband Service: Comcast High Speed Internet.
Fee: $99.95 installation; $49.95 monthly.

Telephone Service
Digital: Operational
Fee: $44.95 monthly
Miles of Plant: 1,433.0 (coaxial); 20.0 (fiber optic). Homes passed: 110,000.
Vice President, Government & Community Relations: Annette Hall. General Manager: Fred Fuller.
Ownership: Comcast Cable Communications Inc. (MSO).

SIBLEY—Suddenlink Communications, 12444 Powerscourt Dr, Saint Louis, MO 63131-3660. Phones: 800-999-6845 (Customer service); 314-415-9346; 314-965-2020. Fax: 903-561-5485. Web Site: http://www.suddenlink.com. Also serves Bienville Parish (northwestern portion), Doyline, Dubberly, Heflin, Lake Bistineau, Ringgold & Webster Parish (southern portion). ICA: LA0121.
TV Market Ranking: 58 (Bienville Parish (northwestern portion), Doyline, Dubberly, Heflin, Lake Bistineau, Ringgold, SIBLEY, Webster Parish (southern portion) (portions)); Below 100 (Webster Parish (southern portion) (portions)). Franchise award date: N.A. Franchise expiration date: N.A. Began: October 1, 1982.
Channel capacity: 54 (operating 2-way). Channels available but not in use: N.A.

Basic Service
Subscribers: 1,947.
Programming (received off-air): KLTS-TV (PBS) Shreveport; KNOE-TV (CBS, CW) Monroe; KSLA (CBS) Shreveport; KTAL-TV (NBC) Texarkana; KTBS-TV (ABC) Shreveport; KTVE (NBC) El Dorado.

Programming (via satellite): ABC Family Channel; CNN; Disney Channel; ESPN; Nickelodeon; TBS Superstation; USA Network; Weather Channel; WGN America.
Fee: $39.95 installation; $19.95 monthly.

Pay Service 1
Pay Units: 123.
Programming (via satellite): Cinemax.
Fee: $10.95 monthly.

Pay Service 2
Pay Units: 299.
Programming (via satellite): HBO.
Fee: $10.95 monthly.

Pay Service 3
Pay Units: 136.
Programming (via satellite): The Movie Channel.
Fee: $10.95 monthly.

Pay Service 4
Pay Units: 458.
Programming (via satellite): Showtime.
Fee: $6.00 monthly.

Pay Service 5
Pay Units: 354.
Programming (via satellite): Flix.
Fee: $4.95 monthly.

Video-On-Demand: No

Internet Service
Operational: Yes. Began: May 5, 2005.
Broadband Service: Cebridge High Speed Cable Internet.
Fee: $45.00 installation; $29.95 monthly.

Telephone Service
Digital: Operational
Fee: $39.95 monthly

Miles of Plant: 108.0 (coaxial); None (fiber optic). Homes passed: 3,683.
Area Manager: Russell Gaston. Regional Manager: Todd Cruthird.
Ownership: Cequel Communications LLC (MSO).

SICILY ISLAND—Formerly served by Almega Cable. No longer in operation. ICA: LA0234.

SIMPSON—Rapid Cable, 515 E Longview Dr, Arp, TX 75750. Phone: 903-859-6492. Fax: 903-859-3708. Also serves Slagle. ICA: LA0202.
TV Market Ranking: Outside TV Markets (SIMPSON, Slagle).
Channel capacity: 22 (not 2-way capable). Channels available but not in use: N.A.

Basic Service
Subscribers: N.A.
Programming (received off-air): KALB-TV (CBS, NBC) Alexandria; KLAX-TV (ABC) Alexandria; KLFY-TV (CBS) Lafayette; KLPA-TV (PBS) Alexandria; WNTZ-TV (FOX, MNT) Natchez.
Programming (via satellite): ABC Family Channel; Arts & Entertainment; CNN; Discovery Channel; Disney Channel; ESPN; Fox News Channel; FX; Great American Country; Halogen Network; Headline News; HGTV; Lifetime; National Geographic Channel; Nickelodeon; Outdoor Channel; QVC; Spike TV; Syfy; TBS Superstation; Turner Classic Movies; Turner Network TV; USA Network; Weather Channel.
Fee: $54.95 installation; $44.05 monthly.

Pay Service 1
Pay Units: N.A.
Programming (via satellite): HBO.
Fee: $12.95 monthly.

Internet Service
Operational: No.

Telephone Service
None

Homes passed: 505.
Regional Manager: Mike Taylor.
Ownership: Rapid Communications LLC (MSO).

SLIDELL—Charter Communications, 1304 Ridgefield Rd, Thibodaux, LA 70301. Phone: 985-446-4900. Fax: 985-447-9541. Web Site: http://www.charter.com. Also serves Abita Springs, Covington, Folsom, Lacombe, Madisonville, Mandeville, Pearl River & St. Tammany Parish (unincorporated areas). ICA: LA0182.
TV Market Ranking: 31 (Abita Springs, Covington, Lacombe, Madisonville, Mandeville, Pearl River, SLIDELL, St. Tammany Parish (unincorporated areas) (portions)); Below 100 (Folsom, Abita Springs, St. Tammany Parish (unincorporated areas) (portions)). Franchise award date: November 16, 1978. Franchise expiration date: N.A. Began: June 1, 1979.
Channel capacity: N.A. Channels available but not in use: N.A.

Basic Service
Subscribers: 42,529.
Programming (received off-air): WDSU (NBC) New Orleans; WGNO (ABC) New Orleans; WHNO (IND) New Orleans; WLAE-TV (PBS) New Orleans; WNOL-TV (CW) New Orleans; WPXL-TV (ION) New Orleans; WUPL (MNT) Slidell; WVUE-DT (FOX) New Orleans; WWL-TV (CBS) New Orleans; WYES-TV (PBS) New Orleans.
Programming (via satellite): Home Shopping Network; INSP; QVC; Trinity Broadcasting Network; TV Guide Network; WGN America.
Planned originations: Government Access; Educational Access; Public Access.
Fee: $29.99 installation.

Expanded Basic Service 1
Subscribers: N.A.
Programming (via satellite): ABC Family Channel; AMC; Animal Planet; Arts & Entertainment; BET Networks; Bravo; Cartoon Network; CNBC; CNN; Comcast Sports Net Southwest; Comedy Central; Country Music TV; C-SPAN; C-SPAN 2; Discovery Channel; Disney Channel; E! Entertainment Television; ESPN; ESPN 2; Eternal Word TV Network; Food Network; Fox News Channel; FX; G4; Golf Channel; GSN; Hallmark Channel; Headline News; HGTV; History Channel; Lifetime; MSNBC; MTV; National Geographic Channel; Nickelodeon; Oxygen; Product Information Network; SoapNet; Speed Channel; Spike TV; Style Network; Syfy; TBS Superstation; Telemundo; The Learning Channel; Toon Disney; Travel Channel; truTV; Turner Classic Movies; Turner Network TV; TV Land; USA Network; Versus; VH1; WE tv; Weather Channel.
Fee: $42.99 monthly.

Digital Basic Service
Subscribers: N.A.
Programming (received off-air): WDSU (NBC) New Orleans; WWL-TV (CBS) New Orleans.
Programming (via satellite): BBC America; Bio; Bloomberg Television; Cooking Channel; Discovery Digital Networks; Discovery HD Theater; Do-It-Yourself; ESPN; ESPN Classic Sports; ESPNews; Fox Movie Channel; Fox Soccer; Fuel TV; GAS; Great American Country; HDNet; HDNet Movies; History Channel International; Independent Film Channel; Lifetime Movie Network; MTV Networks Digital Suite; Music Choice; NFL Network; Nick Jr.; Nick Too; NickToons TV; Sundance Channel; TVG Network; WealthTV HD.

Digital Pay Service 1
Pay Units: N.A.
Programming (via satellite): Cinemax (multiplexed); Encore (multiplexed); HBO (multiplexed); Showtime (multiplexed); Starz (multiplexed); The Movie Channel (multiplexed).

Video-On-Demand: Yes

Pay-Per-View
Playboy TV (delivered digitally); Fresh (delivered digitally); Shorteez (delivered digitally).

Internet Service
Operational: Yes.
Broadband Service: Charter Pipeline.
Fee: $29.99 monthly.

Telephone Service
Digital: Operational
Fee: $29.99 monthly

Miles of Plant: 1,341.0 (coaxial); 87.0 (fiber optic).
Vice President & General Manager: Kip Kraemer. Operations Manager: Dave Houghtlin. Technical Operations Director: Gary Savoie. Marketing Director: Lisa Brown. Government Relations Director: Jim Laurent.
City fee: 5% of gross.
Ownership: Charter Communications Inc. (MSO).

SPRINGHILL—CMA Cablevision, 116 S Main St, Springhill, LA 71075-3206. Phones: 972-233-9614 (Corporate office); 800-753-2465; 318-539-9134. Fax: 318-539-9227. Web Site: http://www.cmaaccess.com. Also serves Cullen, Porterville & Webster Parish (unincorporated areas). ICA: LA0204.
TV Market Ranking: 58 (Webster Parish (unincorporated areas) (portions)); Below 100 (Cullen, Porterville, SPRINGHILL, Webster Parish (unincorporated areas) (portions)). Franchise award date: N.A. Franchise expiration date: N.A. Began: N.A.
Channel capacity: N.A. Channels available but not in use: N.A.

Basic Service
Subscribers: 1,695.
Programming (received off-air): KLTS-TV (PBS) Shreveport; KMSS-TV (FOX) Shreveport; KPXJ (CW) Minden; KSHV-TV (MNT) Shreveport; KSLA (CBS) Shreveport; KTAL-TV (NBC) Texarkana; KTBS-TV (ABC) Shreveport; KTVE (NBC) El Dorado.
Programming (via satellite): C-SPAN; Hallmark Channel; Lifetime; QVC; TBS Superstation; Trinity Broadcasting Network; WGN America.
Current originations: Religious Access; Public Access.
Fee: $39.95 installation; $18.95 monthly; $12.95 additional installation.

Expanded Basic Service 1
Subscribers: N.A.
Programming (via satellite): ABC Family Channel; AMC; AmericanLife TV Network; Animal Planet; Arts & Entertainment; BET Networks; Cartoon Network; CNN; Comedy Central; Country Music TV; Discovery Channel; ESPN; ESPN 2; Food Network; Fox News Channel; Headline News; HGTV; History Channel; Home Shopping Network; Nickelodeon; Outdoor Channel; Spike TV; Syfy; The Learning Channel; Travel Channel; Turner Classic Movies; Turner Network TV; TV Guide Network; TV Land; USA Network; VH1; Weather Channel.
Fee: $23.50 monthly.

Digital Basic Service
Subscribers: 210.
Programming (via satellite): BBC America; Bio; Bloomberg Television; Bravo; Discovery Digital Networks; DMX Music; ESPN Classic Sports; ESPNews; Fox Movie Channel; G4; Golf Channel; GSN; Halogen Network; History Channel International; Independent Film Channel; Lifetime Movie Network; MuchMusic Network; Speed Channel; Sundance Channel; Trinity Broadcasting Network; Versus; WE tv.
Fee: $13.95 monthly.

Digital Pay Service 1
Pay Units: N.A.
Programming (via satellite): Cinemax (multiplexed); Encore (multiplexed); HBO (multiplexed); Showtime (multiplexed); Starz (multiplexed).
Fee: $10.95 monthly (Cinemax Encore & Starz); $13.95 monthly (HBO or Showtime).

Video-On-Demand: No

Pay-Per-View
iN DEMAND (delivered digitally); Hot Choice (delivered digitally); Playboy TV (delivered digitally); Fresh (delivered digitally); Shorteez (delivered digitally); ESPN Now (delivered digitally); sports (delivered digitally).

Internet Service
Operational: Yes.
Broadband Service: CMA.
Fee: $40.95 monthly; $2.95 modem lease.

Telephone Service
None

General Manager: Jerry Smith. Marketing Director: Julie Ferguson.
Ownership: Cable Management Assoc. (MSO).

ST. BERNARD PARISH—Cox Communications. Now served by NEW ORLEANS, LA [LA0001]. ICA: LA0009.

ST. FRANCISVILLE—Audubon Cablevision Inc., PO Box 847, Saint Francisville, LA 70775-0847. Phone: 225-635-4275. Fax: 225-635-3637. Also serves West Feliciana Parish. ICA: LA0056.
TV Market Ranking: 87 (ST. FRANCISVILLE, West Feliciana Parish). Franchise award date: N.A. Franchise expiration date: N.A. Began: January 1, 1982.
Channel capacity: 46 (not 2-way capable). Channels available but not in use: 1.

Basic Service
Subscribers: 1,540.
Programming (received off-air): WAFB (CBS) Baton Rouge; WBRZ-TV (ABC) Baton Rouge; WGMB-TV (FOX) Baton Rouge; WVLA-TV (NBC) Baton Rouge.
Programming (via satellite): ABC Family Channel; AMC; Animal Planet; Arts & Entertainment; BET Networks; Cartoon Network; CNN; Country Music TV; C-SPAN; C-SPAN 2; Discovery Channel; Discovery Health Channel; ESPN; ESPN 2; Eternal Word TV Network; Food Network; Fox News Channel; Headline News; HGTV; History Channel; Home Shopping Network; Lifetime; MTV; Nickelodeon; QVC; Spike TV; Syfy; TBS Superstation; The Learning Channel; Travel Channel; Trinity Broadcasting Network; Turner Network TV; TV Land; USA Network; VH1; Weather Channel; WGN America.
Fee: $25.00 installation; $33.41 monthly; $2.00 converter.

Pay Service 1
Pay Units: N.A.
Programming (via satellite): Showtime; The Movie Channel.
Fee: $9.00 monthly (TMC), $10.00 monthly (Showtime).

Video-On-Demand: No

Internet Service
Operational: No.

Telephone Service
None
Miles of Plant: 78.0 (coaxial); 20.0 (fiber optic). Homes passed: 2,247. Total homes in franchised area: 2,247.
Chief Technician: David Daigle. Office Manager: Connie Tillman.
City fee: 3% of gross.
Ownership: Bailey Cable TV Inc. (MSO).

ST. JOSEPH—Suddenlink Communications, 12444 Powerscourt Dr, Saint Louis, MO 63131-3660. Phones: 800-999-6845 (Customer service); 314-965-2020. Web Site: http://www.suddenlink.com. Also serves Lake Bruin & Tensas Parish (portions). ICA: LA0206.
TV Market Ranking: Below 100 (Lake Bruin, ST. JOSEPH, Tensas Parish (portions)). Franchise award date: N.A. Franchise expiration date: N.A. Began: June 1, 1982.
Channel capacity: 54 (operating 2-way). Channels available but not in use: N.A.
Basic Service
Subscribers: 756.
Programming (received off-air): KLTM-TV (PBS) Monroe; KNOE-TV (CBS, CW) Monroe; WAPT (ABC) Jackson; WJTV (CBS) Jackson; WLBT (NBC) Jackson.
Programming (via satellite): ABC Family Channel; CNN; ESPN; Nickelodeon; TBS Superstation; USA Network; Weather Channel; WGN America.
Fee: $39.95 installation; $19.95 monthly.
Pay Service 1
Pay Units: 61.
Programming (via satellite): Cinemax.
Fee: $7.00 monthly.
Pay Service 2
Pay Units: 63.
Programming (via satellite): HBO.
Fee: $12.00 monthly.
Pay Service 3
Pay Units: 77.
Programming (via satellite): Showtime.
Fee: $7.00 monthly.
Video-On-Demand: No
Internet Service
Operational: Yes. Began: April 22, 2004.
Broadband Service: Cebridge High Speed Cable Internet.
Fee: $45.00 installation; $29.95 monthly.
Telephone Service
Digital: Operational
Fee: $39.95 monthly
Miles of Plant: 45.0 (coaxial); None (fiber optic). Homes passed: 971.
Regional Manager: Todd Cruthird. Plant Manager: Dion Canaday.
City fee: 3% of gross.
Ownership: Cequel Communications LLC (MSO).

ST. LANDRY PARISH—Charter Communications, 330 Moosa Blvd, Eunice, LA 70535. Phones: 985-446-4900 (Thibodaux office); 337-546-0087. Fax: 337-546-0038. Web Site: http://www.charter.com. Also serves Chataignier, Church Point, Eunice, Iota, Jennings, Leonville, Opelousas & Washington. ICA: LA0022.
TV Market Ranking: Below 100 (Chataignier, Church Point, Eunice, Iota, Jennings, Leonville, Opelousas, ST. LANDRY PARISH (portions), Washington); Outside TV Markets (ST. LANDRY PARISH (portions)). Franchise award date: N.A. Franchise expiration date: N.A. Began: September 1, 1974.
Channel capacity: N.A. Channels available but not in use: N.A.
Basic Service
Subscribers: 19,500.
Programming (received off-air): KADN-TV (FOX) Lafayette; KALB-TV (CBS, NBC) Alexandria; KATC (ABC) Lafayette; KDCG-CD (ION) Opelousas; KLFY-TV (CBS) Lafayette; KLPB-TV (PBS) Lafayette; WAFB (CBS) Baton Rouge; WBRZ-TV (ABC) Baton Rouge.
Programming (via satellite): QVC.
Current originations: Government Access.
Fee: $29.99 installation.
Expanded Basic Service 1
Subscribers: N.A.
Programming (via satellite): ABC Family Channel; AMC; Animal Planet; Arts & Entertainment; BET Networks; Bravo; Cartoon Network; CNBC; CNN; Comcast Sports Net Southwest; Comedy Central; Country Music TV; C-SPAN; C-SPAN 2; Discovery Channel; Disney Channel; E! Entertainment Television; ESPN; ESPN 2; Eternal Word TV Network; Food Network; Fox News Channel; FX; G4; Golf Channel; GSN; Hallmark Channel; Headline News; HGTV; History Channel; Home Shopping Network; INSP; Lifetime; MSNBC; MTV; National Geographic Channel; Nickelodeon; Outdoor Channel; Oxygen; Product Information Network; SoapNet; Speed Channel; Spike TV; Syfy; TBS Superstation; Telemundo; The Learning Channel; Toon Disney; Travel Channel; Trinity Broadcasting Network; truTV; Turner Classic Movies; Turner Network TV; TV Guide Network; TV Land; USA Network; Versus; VH1; WE tv; Weather Channel.
Fee: $42.99 monthly.
Digital Basic Service
Subscribers: N.A.
Programming (via satellite): BBC America; Bio; Bloomberg Television; Discovery Digital Networks; Discovery HD Theater; Do-It-Yourself; ESPN; ESPN Classic Sports; ESPNews; Fox Movie Channel; Fox Soccer; Fuel TV; GAS; Great American Country; HDNet; HDNet Movies; Independent Film Channel; Lifetime Movie Network; MTV Networks Digital Suite; Music Choice; NFL Network; Nick Jr.; Nick Too; NickToons TV; Sundance Channel; TV Guide Interactive Inc.; TVG Network.
Digital Expanded Basic Service
Subscribers: 8,968.
Fee: $50.00 installation.
Digital Pay Service 1
Pay Units: 1,586.
Programming (via satellite): Cinemax (multiplexed).
Fee: $9.95 monthly.
Digital Pay Service 2
Pay Units: 2,931.
Programming (via satellite): HBO (multiplexed); HBO HD.
Fee: $30.00 installation; $10.95 monthly.
Digital Pay Service 3
Pay Units: 1,451.
Programming (via satellite): Showtime (multiplexed); Showtime HD.
Fee: $30.00 installation; $9.95 monthly.
Digital Pay Service 4
Pay Units: 486.
Programming (via satellite): The Movie Channel (multiplexed).
Fee: $30.00 installation; $10.95 monthly.
Digital Pay Service 5
Pay Units: N.A.
Programming (via satellite): Encore (multiplexed); Flix; Playboy TV; Starz (multiplexed).
Video-On-Demand: Yes

Pay-Per-View
Addressable homes: 3,124.
iN DEMAND (delivered digitally), Addressable: Yes; NASCAR In Car (delivered digitally); Playboy TV (delivered digitally); Fresh (delivered digitally); Shorteez (delivered digitally); NHL Center Ice (delivered digitally); MLB Extra Innings (delivered digitally).
Internet Service
Operational: Yes, DSL only.
Broadband Service: Charter Pipeline.
Fee: $29.99 monthly.
Telephone Service
Digital: Operational
Fee: $29.99 monthly
Miles of Plant: 515.0 (coaxial); None (fiber optic).
Vice President & General Manager: Kip Kraemer. Operations Manager: Blane Bercegeay. Plant Manager: Joe Semmes. Technical Operations Director: Gary Savoie. Marketing Director: Lisa Brown. Government Relations Director: Jim Laurent. Office Manager: Margaretta Frey.
City fee: 3% of gross.
Ownership: Charter Communications Inc. (MSO).

ST. MARTINVILLE—Cox Communications. Now served by BATON ROUGE, LA [LA0003]. ICA: LA0019.

START—Formerly served by Almega Cable. No longer in operation. ICA: LA0126.

STERLINGTON—Bayou Cable TV, PO Box 466, Marion, LA 71260-0466. Phone: 318-292-4774. Fax: 318-292-4775. Web Site: http://www.bayoucable.com. ICA: LA0229.
TV Market Ranking: 99 (STERLINGTON). Franchise award date: N.A. Franchise expiration date: N.A. Began: N.A.
Channel capacity: 50 (operating 2-way). Channels available but not in use: 4.
Basic Service
Subscribers: 558.
Programming (received off-air): KAQY (ABC) Columbia; KARD (FOX) West Monroe; KLTM-TV (PBS) Monroe; KMCT-TV (IND) West Monroe; KNOE-TV (CBS, CW) Monroe; KTVE (NBC) El Dorado.
Programming (via satellite): AMC; Hallmark Channel; Home Shopping Network; QVC; Trinity Broadcasting Network; TV Land.
Fee: $20.00 installation; $15.95 monthly.
Expanded Basic Service 1
Subscribers: N.A.
Programming (via satellite): ABC Family Channel; Animal Planet; Arts & Entertainment; BET Networks; Cartoon Network; CNN; Country Music TV; CW+; Discovery Channel; ESPN; ESPN 2; FamilyNet; Food Network; Fox News Channel; FX; HGTV; History Channel; Lifetime; MTV; National Geographic Channel; Nickelodeon; Outdoor Channel; Speed Channel; Spike TV; TBS Superstation; The Learning Channel; Turner Network TV; USA Network; VH1; Weather Channel; WGN America.
Fee: $20.00 monthly.
Pay Service 1
Pay Units: N.A.
Programming (via satellite): Cinemax; HBO.
Fee: $8.95 monthly (Cinemax), $10.95 monthly (HBO).
Video-On-Demand: No
Pay-Per-View
Urban American Television Network (delivered digitally); Playboy TV (delivered digitally); Fresh (delivered digitally); Shorteez (delivered digitally).
Internet Service
Operational: No.
Telephone Service
None
Miles of Plant: 12.0 (coaxial); None (fiber optic).
Owner: Alan C. Booker. Chief Technician: Mark Andrews.
Ownership: Bayou Cable TV (MSO).

SULPHUR—Suddenlink Communications, 1626 Ruth St, Sulphur, LA 70663-4906. Phone: 337-527-6747. Fax: 337-528-3454. Web Site: http://www.suddenlink.com. Also serves Calcasieu Parish (portions) & Mossville. ICA: LA0024.
TV Market Ranking: 88 (Calcasieu Parish (portions)); Below 100 (Mossville, SULPHUR, Calcasieu Parish (portions)). Franchise award date: December 1, 1976. Franchise expiration date: N.A. Began: January 1, 1975.
Channel capacity: N.A. Channels available but not in use: N.A.
Basic Service
Subscribers: 7,636.
Programming (received off-air): KATC (ABC) Lafayette; KBMT (ABC) Beaumont; KBTV-TV (FOX) Port Arthur; KFAM-LP (IND) Lake Charles; KFDM (CBS, CW) Beaumont; KLFY-TV (CBS) Lafayette; KLTL-TV (PBS) Lake Charles; KPLC (NBC) Lake Charles; KVHP (FOX) Lake Charles.
Programming (via satellite): BET Networks; C-SPAN; Discovery Channel; Eternal Word TV Network; Headline News; INSP; ION Television; TBS Superstation; Trinity Broadcasting Network; Weather Channel.
Current originations: Government Access; Public Access.
Fee: $26.00 installation; $11.31 monthly; $3.00 converter; $10.00 additional installation.
Expanded Basic Service 1
Subscribers: 6,775.
Programming (via satellite): ABC Family Channel; AMC; Animal Planet; Arts & Entertainment; Bravo; Cartoon Network; CNBC; CNN; Comcast Sports Net Southwest; Comedy Central; Country Music TV; Cox Sports Television; C-SPAN 2; Disney Channel; E! Entertainment Television; ESPN; ESPN 2; Food Network; Fox News Channel; FX; G4; HGTV; History Channel; Home Shopping Network; Lifetime; MSNBC; MTV; Nickelodeon; QVC; Spike TV; Syfy; The Learning Channel; Travel Channel; truTV; Turner Network TV; TV Guide Network; TV Land; USA Network; Versus; VH1.
Fee: $40.70 monthly.

Digital Basic Service
Subscribers: N.A.
Programming (received off-air): KLTL-TV (PBS) Lake Charles.
Programming (via satellite): AmericanLife TV Network; BBC America; Bio; Bloomberg Television; Cooking Channel; Discovery Digital Networks; Discovery HD Theater; Do-It-Yourself; Encore (multiplexed); ESPN; ESPN Classic Sports; ESPNews; FamilyNet; Fox Movie Channel; Fox Reality Channel; Fox Soccer; Fuel TV; Fuse; GAS; Golf Channel; Great American Country; GSN; Hallmark Channel; Halogen Network; History Channel International; Independent Film Channel; INHD (multiplexed); Lifetime Movie Network; MTV Networks Digital Suite; Music Choice; National Geographic Channel; NBA TV; Nick Jr.; NickToons TV; Outdoor Channel; SoapNet; Speed Channel; Style Network; Sundance Channel; Tennis Channel; Toon Disney; Turner Classic Movies; TV One; Universal HD; WE tv.
Fee: $10.00 monthly.

Pay Service 1
Pay Units: 581.
Programming (via satellite): Cinemax; Encore; HBO; Showtime; Starz.
Fee: $10.00 installation; $1.75 monthly (Encore), $6.75 monthly (Starz), $9.00 monthly (Cinemax), $10.95 monthly (HBO), $11.50 monthly (Showtime).

Digital Pay Service 1
Pay Units: N.A.
Programming (via satellite): Cinemax (multiplexed); HBO (multiplexed); HBO HD; Showtime (multiplexed); Showtime HD; Starz (multiplexed); Starz HDTV; The Movie Channel.
Fee: $10.95 monthly (HBO), $11.50 monthly (Showtime & TMC).

Video-On-Demand: No

Pay-Per-View
iN DEMAND (delivered digitally), Addressable: Yes.

Internet Service
Operational: Yes.
Broadband Service: Cebridge High Speed Cable Internet.
Fee: $45.00 installation; $29.95 monthly.

Telephone Service
Digital: Operational
Fee: $39.95 monthly

Miles of Plant: 108.0 (coaxial); None (fiber optic). Additional miles planned: 2.0 (coaxial). Homes passed: 8,920. Total homes in franchised area: 9,100.

Manager: Margie Blevins. Marketing Director: Gwen Savoy. Chief Technician: Wade Sherman.

City fee: 3% of gross.

Ownership: Cequel Communications LLC (MSO).

SWEETWATER—Charter Communications. Now served by BOGALUSA, LA [LA0023]. ICA: LA0209.

TALLULAH—CMA Cablevision, 1101A Johnson St, Tallulah, LA 71282. Phones: 800-753-2465; 972-233-9614 (Corporate office). Fax: 318-574-0760. Web Site: http://www.cmaaccess.com. Also serves Madison Parish & Richmond. ICA: LA0042.

TV Market Ranking: Outside TV Markets (Madison Parish, Richmond, TALLULAH). Franchise award date: February 8, 1979. Franchise expiration date: N.A. Began: September 30, 1979.

Channel capacity: N.A. Channels available but not in use: N.A.

Basic Service
Subscribers: 1,650.
Programming (received off-air): KAQY (ABC) Columbia; KARD (FOX) West Monroe; KEJB (MNT)lorado; KLTM-TV (PBS) Monroe; KNOE-TV (CBS, CW) Monroe; KTVE (NBC) El Dorado.
Programming (via satellite): CNN; C-SPAN; Fox News Channel; Hallmark Channel; Headline News; Home Shopping Network; INSP; ION Television; QVC; TBS Superstation; Weather Channel; WGN America.
Fee: $39.95 installation; $17.95 monthly; $12.95 additional installation.

Expanded Basic Service 1
Subscribers: N.A.
Programming (received off-air): WAPT (ABC) Jackson; WLBT (NBC) Jackson; 1 FM.
Programming (via satellite): ABC Family Channel; Animal Planet; Arts & Entertainment; BET Networks; Bravo!; Cartoon Network; CNBC; Comcast Sports Net Southwest; Comedy Central; Country Music TV; Discovery Channel; E! Entertainment Television; ESPN; ESPN 2; ESPN Classic Sports; Food Network; FX; Gospel Music Channel; HGTV; History Channel; Lifetime; Lifetime Movie Network; MTV; National Geographic Channel; Nickelodeon; Outdoor Channel; Spike TV; Syfy; The Learning Channel; Travel Channel; Trinity Broadcasting Network; truTV; Turner Classic Movies; Turner Network TV; TV Guide Network; TV Land; USA Network.
Fee: $24.50 monthly.

Digital Basic Service
Subscribers: N.A.
Programming (received off-air): KLTM-TV (PBS) Monroe; KNOE-TV (CBS, CW) Monroe.
Programming (via satellite): BBC America; Bio; Chiller; CMT Pure Country; Discovery Channel HD; Discovery Health Channel; Discovery Home Channel; Discovery Kids Channel; Discovery Military Channel; Discovery Times Channel; DMX Music; ESPN HD; ESPNews; Fox Movie Channel; Fox Soccer; G4; Golf Channel; GSN; Halogen Network; History Channel International; Independent Film Channel; MTV2; Nick Jr.; NickToons TV; Science Channel; Sleuth; Speed Channel; Style Network; TeenNick; Turner Network TV HD; Universal HD; VH1 Classic; WE tv.
Fee: $12.45 monthly.

Pay Service 1
Pay Units: 270.
Programming (via satellite): HBO.
Fee: $14.95 installation; $13.95 monthly.

Digital Pay Service 1
Pay Units: N.A.
Programming (via satellite): Cinemax (multiplexed); Cinemax HD; Encore (multiplexed); HBO (multiplexed); HBO HD; Showtime (multiplexed); Showtime HD; Starz (multiplexed); The Movie Channel (multiplexed).
Fee: $10.95 monthly (Cinemax or Starz/Encore), $13.95 (HBO or Showtime).

Video-On-Demand: No

Pay-Per-View
iN DEMAND (delivered digitally); Club Jenna (delivered digitally); Playboy TV (delivered digitally); Fresh (delivered digitally).

Internet Service
Operational: Yes.
Fee: $39.95 installation; $39.95 monthly; $2.95 modem lease.

Telephone Service
None

Miles of Plant: 50.0 (coaxial); None (fiber optic). Homes passed: 4,000. Total homes in franchised area: 4,500.

General Manager: Jerry Smith. Marketing Director: Julie Ferguson.

City fee: 2% of gross.

Ownership: Cable Management Assoc. (MSO).

TANGIPAHOA—Formerly served by Almega Cable. No longer in operation. ICA: LA0237.

THIBODAUX—Charter Communications, 1304 Ridgefield Rd, Thibodaux, LA 70301. Phone: 985-446-4900. Fax: 985-447-9541. Web Site: http://www.charter.com. Also serves Assumption Parish (southern portion), Belle Rose (portions), Chackbay, Donaldsonville, Labadieville, Lafourche Parish (western portion), Napoleonville, Paincourtville, Paulina, Raceland, St. James, St. James Parish (southern portion), Supreme & Vacherie. ICA: LA0011.

TV Market Ranking: 87 (Assumption Parish (portions), Belle Rose (portions), Donaldsonville, Paincourtville, St. James Parish (portions)); Outside TV Markets (Chackbay, Labadieville, Lafourche Parish (western portion), Napoleonville, Paulina, Raceland, St. James, Supreme, THIBODAUX, Vacherie, Assumption Parish (portions), St. James Parish (portions)). Franchise award date: April 19, 1966. Franchise expiration date: N.A. Began: April 1, 1970.

Channel capacity: N.A. Channels available but not in use: N.A.

Basic Service
Subscribers: 19,644.
Programming (received off-air): KFOL-CD (IND) Houma; WAFB (CBS) Baton Rouge; WBRZ-TV (ABC) Baton Rouge; WDSU (NBC) New Orleans; WGNO (ABC) New Orleans; WHNO (IND) New Orleans; WLAE-TV (PBS) New Orleans; WLPB-TV (PBS) Baton Rouge; WNOL-TV (CW) New Orleans; WPXL-TV (ION) New Orleans; WUPL (MNT) Slidell; WVLA-TV (NBC) Baton Rouge; WVUE-DT (FOX) New Orleans; WWL-TV (CBS) New Orleans; WYES-TV (PBS) New Orleans.
Programming (via satellite): Eternal Word TV Network; Home Shopping Network; QVC; WGN America.
Fee: $29.99 installation.

Expanded Basic Service 1
Subscribers: 2,506.
Programming (via satellite): ABC Family Channel; AMC; Animal Planet; Arts & Entertainment; BET Networks; Bravo; Cartoon Network; CNN; Comcast Sports Net Southwest; Comedy Central; Country Music TV; C-SPAN; C-SPAN 2; Discovery Channel; Disney Channel; E! Entertainment Television; ESPN; ESPN 2; Food Network; Fox News Channel; FX; G4; Golf Channel; GSN; Hallmark Channel; Halogen Network; Headline News; HGTV; History Channel; Lifetime; MSNBC; MTV; National Geographic Channel; Nickelodeon; Outdoor Channel; Oxygen; Product Information Network; SoapNet; Speed Channel; Spike TV; Syfy; TBS Superstation; Telemundo; The Learning Channel; Toon Disney; Travel Channel; truTV; Turner Classic Movies; Turner Network TV; TV Land; Univision; USA Network; Versus; VH1; WE tv; Weather Channel.
Fee: $42.99 monthly.

Digital Basic Service
Subscribers: N.A.
Programming (received off-air): WDSU (NBC) New Orleans; WWL-TV (CBS) New Orleans.
Programming (via satellite): BBC America; Bio; Bloomberg Television; Discovery Digital Networks; Discovery HD Theater; Do-It-Yourself; ESPN; ESPN Classic Sports; ESPNews; Fox Movie Channel; Fox Soccer; Fuel TV; GAS; Great American Country; HBO; HDNet; HDNet Movies; History Channel International; Independent Film Channel; Lifetime Movie Network; MTV Networks Digital Suite; Music Choice; NFL Network; Nick Jr.; Nick Too; NickToons TV; Showtime; Sundance Channel; TV Guide Interactive Inc.; TVG Network; WealthTV HD.

Digital Pay Service 1
Pay Units: 2,184.
Programming (via satellite): Cinemax (multiplexed).
Fee: $40.00 installation; $9.95 monthly.

Digital Pay Service 2
Pay Units: 5,606.
Programming (via satellite): HBO (multiplexed).
Fee: $40.00 installation; $10.95 monthly.

Digital Pay Service 3
Pay Units: 1,797.
Programming (via satellite): Showtime (multiplexed).
Fee: $40.00 installation; $9.95 monthly.

Digital Pay Service 4
Pay Units: 1,793.
Programming (via satellite): The Movie Channel (multiplexed).
Fee: $40.00 installation; $9.95 monthly.

Digital Pay Service 5
Pay Units: N.A.
Programming (via satellite): Encore (multiplexed); Flix; Playboy TV; Starz (multiplexed).

Video-On-Demand: Yes

Pay-Per-View
Addressable homes: 4,013.
iN DEMAND (delivered digitally), Addressable: Yes; NASCAR In Car (delivered digitally); Playboy TV (delivered digitally); Fresh (delivered digitally); Shorteez (delivered digitally); NHL Center Ice (delivered digitally); MLB Extra Innings (delivered digitally).

Internet Service
Operational: Yes, DSL only.
Broadband Service: Charter Pipeline.
Fee: $29.99 monthly.

Telephone Service
Digital: Operational
Fee: $29.99 monthly

Miles of Plant: 454.0 (coaxial); 228.0 (fiber optic). Homes passed: 23,960. Total homes in franchised area: 27,278.

Vice President & General Manager: Kip Kraemer. Operations Manager: Ann Danos.

Technical Operations Director: Gary Savoie. Marketing Director: Lisa Brown. Government Relations Director: Jim Laurent.
City fee: 5% of gross.
Ownership: Charter Communications Inc. (MSO).

TURKEY CREEK—Rapid Cable, 515 E Longview Dr, Arp, TX 75750. Phone: 903-859-6492. Fax: 903-859-3708. Also serves Evangeline Parish (portions). ICA: LA0095.
TV Market Ranking: Below 100 (Evangeline Parish (portions) (portions), TURKEY CREEK). Franchise award date: October 28, 1988. Franchise expiration date: N.A. Began: October 28, 1988.
Channel capacity: 36 (operating 2-way). Channels available but not in use: N.A.
Basic Service
Subscribers: 182.
Programming (received off-air): KADN-TV (FOX) Lafayette; KALB-TV (CBS, NBC) Alexandria; KLAX-TV (ABC) Alexandria; KLFY-TV (CBS) Lafayette; KLPA-TV (PBS) Alexandria.
Programming (via satellite): ABC Family Channel; Arts & Entertainment; CNN; Discovery Channel; Disney Channel; ESPN; ESPN 2; Fox News Channel; Great American Country; Headline News; HGTV; Home Shopping Network; Lifetime; National Geographic Channel; Nickelodeon; Outdoor Channel; Spike TV; Syfy; TBS Superstation; Trinity Broadcasting Network; Turner Classic Movies; Turner Network TV; TV Land; USA Network; VH1; Weather Channel; WGN America.
Fee: $54.95 installation; $44.05 monthly.
Pay Service 1
Pay Units: 20.
Programming (via satellite): Cinemax.
Fee: $12.95 monthly.
Pay Service 2
Pay Units: 36.
Programming (via satellite): HBO.
Fee: $12.95 monthly.
Pay Service 3
Pay Units: 12.
Programming (via satellite): Showtime.
Fee: $12.95 monthly.
Video-On-Demand: No
Internet Service
Operational: No.
Telephone Service
None
Miles of Plant: 45.0 (coaxial); None (fiber optic). Homes passed: 785.
Regional Manager: Mike Taylor. Chief Technician: Ronnie Stafford.
Ownership: Rapid Communications LLC (MSO).

VARNADO—Charter Communications. Now served by BOGALUSA, LA [LA0023]. ICA: LA0232.

VILLE PLATTE—Suddenlink Communications, 12444 Powerscourt Dr, Saint Louis, MO 63131-3660. Phones: 337-363-0621; 314-965-2020. Web Site: http://www.suddenlink.com. Also serves Evangeline Parish, Mamou, Reddell & Vidrine. ICA: LA0028.
TV Market Ranking: Below 100 (Evangeline Parish (portions)); Outside TV Markets (Evangeline Parish (portions), Mamou, Reddell, Vidrine, VILLE PLATTE). Franchise award date: N.A. Franchise expiration date: N.A. Began: January 1, 1978.
Channel capacity: 62 (operating 2-way). Channels available but not in use: 15.
Basic Service
Subscribers: 5,512.
Programming (received off-air): KADN-TV (FOX) Lafayette; KALB-TV (CBS, NBC) Alexandria; KATC (ABC) Lafayette; KDCG-CD (ION) Opelousas; KLFY-TV (CBS) Lafayette; KLPB-TV (PBS) Lafayette; WBRZ-TV (ABC) Baton Rouge.
Programming (via satellite): TBS Superstation; WGN America.
Current originations: Public Access.
Fee: $32.50 installation; $18.95 monthly; $2.00 converter.
Expanded Basic Service 1
Subscribers: 5,125.
Programming (via satellite): ABC Family Channel; AmericanLife TV Network; Arts & Entertainment; BET Networks; Cartoon Network; CNN; Comcast Sports Net Southwest; Country Music TV; C-SPAN; Discovery Channel; Disney Channel; ESPN; ESPN 2; Eternal Word TV Network; Fox News Channel; Headline News; HGTV; Lifetime; MTV; Nickelodeon; QVC; Spike TV; The Learning Channel; Trinity Broadcasting Network; Turner Classic Movies; Turner Network TV; TV Land; USA Network; Weather Channel.
Fee: $25.00 monthly.
Pay Service 1
Pay Units: 545.
Programming (via satellite): Cinemax.
Fee: $10.00 installation; $7.95 monthly.
Pay Service 2
Pay Units: 688.
Programming (via satellite): HBO.
Fee: $10.00 installation; $10.95 monthly.
Pay Service 3
Pay Units: 710.
Programming (via satellite): Showtime; The Movie Channel.
Fee: $10.00 installation; $10.50 monthly (each).
Internet Service
Operational: Yes. Began: March 24, 2004.
Broadband Service: Cebridge High Speed Cable Internet.
Fee: $45.00 installation; $29.95 monthly.
Telephone Service
Digital: Operational
Fee: $39.95 monthly
Miles of Plant: 143.0 (coaxial); 25.0 (fiber optic). Homes passed: 7,506.
Regional Manager: Todd Cruthird.
Ownership: Cequel Communications LLC (MSO).

VINTON—CommuniComm Services, 2504 Westwood Rd, Westlake, LA 70669. Phone: 337-433-0892. Fax: 337-433-0405. Web Site: http://www.communicomm.com. Also serves De Quincy. ICA: LA0064.
TV Market Ranking: 88 (VINTON); Below 100 (De Quincy). Franchise award date: N.A. Franchise expiration date: N.A. Began: January 1, 1979.
Channel capacity: 30 (operating 2-way). Channels available but not in use: N.A.
Basic Service
Subscribers: N.A.
Programming (received off-air): KATC (ABC) Lafayette; KBMT (ABC) Beaumont; KBTV-TV (FOX) Port Arthur; KFDM (CBS, CW) Beaumont; KLFY-TV (CBS) Lafayette; KPLC (NBC) Lake Charles; KVHP (FOX) Lake Charles; WLPB-TV (PBS) Baton Rouge.
Programming (via satellite): CW+; Eternal Word TV Network; TV Guide Network.
Fee: $20.00 installation; $10.95 monthly.

Expanded Basic Service 1
Subscribers: N.A.
Programming (via satellite): ABC Family Channel; AMC; Animal Planet; Arts & Entertainment; BET Networks; Bravo; Cartoon Network; CNBC; CNN; Comcast Sports Net Southwest; Comedy Central; Country Music TV; C-SPAN; Discovery Channel; Disney Channel; Do-It-Yourself; E! Entertainment Television; ESPN; ESPN 2; Food Network; Fox Movie Channel; Fox News Channel; FX; Hallmark Channel; Headline News; HGTV; History Channel; Lifetime; MSNBC; MTV; Nick Jr.; Nickelodeon; Outdoor Channel; QVC; Spike TV; Syfy; TBS Superstation; The Learning Channel; Travel Channel; truTV; Turner Network TV; TV Land; USA Network; VH1; WE tv; Weather Channel.
Digital Basic Service
Subscribers: N.A.
Programming (via satellite): AmericanLife TV Network; BBC America; Bio; Bloomberg Television; Bravo; Church Channel; CMT Pure Country; Current; Discovery Health Channel; Discovery Kids Channel; Discovery Military Channel; Discovery Planet Green; DMX Music; ESPN 2; ESPN Classic Sports; ESPNews; FitTV; Fox Movie Channel; Fox Soccer; Fuse; G4; Golf Channel; Gospel Music Channel; Great American Country; GSN; Halogen Network; History Channel; History Channel International; ID Investigation Discovery; Independent Film Channel; JCTV; Lifetime Movie Network; MTV Hits; MTV2; National Geographic Channel; NickToons TV; Outdoor Channel; Science Channel; ShopNBC; Sleuth; SoapNet; Speed Channel; Style Network; Sundance Channel; The Word Network; Trinity Broadcasting Network; Turner Classic Movies; Versus; VH1 Classic; WE tv.
Pay Service 1
Pay Units: N.A.
Programming (via satellite): Cinemax; Encore; HBO (multiplexed); Starz.
Fee: $10.00 installation; $10.95 monthly (each).
Digital Pay Service 1
Pay Units: N.A.
Programming (via satellite): Cinemax (multiplexed); Encore (multiplexed); Flix; HBO (multiplexed); Showtime (multiplexed); Starz (multiplexed); The Movie Channel (multiplexed).
Video-On-Demand: No
Pay-Per-View
iN DEMAND (delivered digitally); Hot Choice (delivered digitally); Playboy TV (delivered digitally); Fresh (delivered digitally); Spice: Xcess (delivered digitally); Club Jenna (delivered digitally).
Internet Service
Operational: Yes.
Broadband Service: Net Commander.
Fee: $39.95 installation; $51.95 monthly.
Telephone Service
None
Miles of Plant: 29.0 (coaxial); None (fiber optic). Homes passed included in Westlake
General Manager: Larry Ivy. Plant Manager: Marcus Edwards.
City fee: 3% of gross.
Ownership: James Cable LLC (MSO).

WALLACE RIDGE—Rapid Cable, 515 E Longview Dr, Arp, TX 75750. Phone: 903-859-6492. Fax: 903-859-3708. Also serves Catahoula Parish & Jonesville. ICA: LA0211.
TV Market Ranking: Below 100 (Catahoula Parish, Jonesville, WALLACE RIDGE). Franchise award date: N.A. Franchise expiration date: N.A. Began: N.A.
Channel capacity: 36 (not 2-way capable). Channels available but not in use: N.A.
Basic Service
Subscribers: 111.
Programming (received off-air): KALB-TV (CBS, NBC) Alexandria; KAQY (ABC) Columbia; KARD (FOX) West Monroe; KLAX-TV (ABC) Alexandria; KLPA-TV (PBS) Alexandria; KNOE-TV (CBS, CW) Monroe.
Programming (via satellite): ABC Family Channel; AMC; Animal Planet; Arts & Entertainment; Cartoon Network; CNN; Discovery Channel; Disney Channel; ESPN; ESPN 2; Great American Country; Headline News; HGTV; Lifetime; National Geographic Channel; Nickelodeon; Outdoor Channel; QVC; Spike TV; The Learning Channel; Trinity Broadcasting Network; Turner Network TV; USA Network; VH1; Weather Channel.
Fee: $54.95 installation; $44.05 monthly.
Pay Service 1
Pay Units: 7.
Programming (via satellite): HBO.
Fee: $12.95 monthly.
Pay Service 2
Pay Units: 4.
Programming (via satellite): The Movie Channel.
Fee: $12.95 monthly.
Pay Service 3
Pay Units: 32.
Programming (via satellite): Showtime.
Fee: $12.95 monthly.
Video-On-Demand: No
Internet Service
Operational: No.
Telephone Service
None
Miles of Plant: 24.0 (coaxial); None (fiber optic). Homes passed: 454.
Regional Manager: Mike Taylor. Chief Technician: Ronnie Stafford.
Ownership: Rapid Communications LLC (MSO).

WATERPROOF—Rapid Cable, 515 E Longview Dr, Arp, TX 75750. Phone: 903-859-6492. Fax: 903-859-3708. ICA: LA0212.
TV Market Ranking: Below 100 (WATERPROOF). Franchise award date: N.A. Franchise expiration date: N.A. Began: August 1, 1983.
Channel capacity: 54 (not 2-way capable). Channels available but not in use: N.A.
Basic Service
Subscribers: 109.
Programming (received off-air): KAQY (ABC) Columbia; KARD (FOX) West Monroe; KLTM-TV (PBS) Monroe; KNOE-TV

(CBS, CW) Monroe; WJTV (CBS) Jackson; WLBT (NBC) Jackson.
Programming (via satellite): ABC Family Channel; Animal Planet; Arts & Entertainment; BET Networks; Cartoon Network; CNN; Discovery Channel; Disney Channel; ESPN; ESPN 2; Great American Country; Headline News; HGTV; History Channel; Home Shopping Network; Lifetime; MTV; National Geographic Channel; Nickelodeon; Outdoor Channel; Spike TV; TBS Superstation; Trinity Broadcasting Network; Turner Classic Movies; Turner Network TV; USA Network; Weather Channel.
Fee: $54.95 installation; $44.05 monthly.

Pay Service 1
Pay Units: 31.
Programming (via satellite): Cinemax.
Fee: $12.95 monthly.

Pay Service 2
Pay Units: 15.
Programming (via satellite): HBO.
Fee: $12.95 monthly.

Pay Service 3
Pay Units: 25.
Programming (via satellite): Showtime.
Fee: $12.95 monthly.

Video-On-Demand: No

Internet Service
Operational: No.

Telephone Service
None

Miles of Plant: 10.0 (coaxial); None (fiber optic). Homes passed: 417.
Regional Manager: Mike Taylor. Chief Technician: Ronnie Stafford.
Ownership: Rapid Communications LLC (MSO).

WELSH—CommuniComm Services. Now served by LAKE ARTHUR, LA [LA0078]. ICA: LA0079.

WEST MONROE—Comcast Cable, 5375 Executive Pl, Jackson, MS 39206. Phone: 601-982-1187. Fax: 601-321-3888. Web Site: http://www.comcast.com. Also serves Calhoun, Lakeshore, Monroe, Ouachita Parish (northern portion) & Swartz. ICA: LA0005.
TV Market Ranking: 99 (Calhoun, Lakeshore, Monroe, Ouachita Parish (northern portion), Swartz, WEST MONROE). Franchise award date: N.A. Franchise expiration date: N.A. Began: January 1, 1957.
Channel capacity: N.A. Channels available but not in use: N.A.

Basic Service
Subscribers: 36,000.
Programming (received off-air): KAQY (ABC) Columbia; KARD (FOX) West Monroe; KLTM-TV (PBS) Monroe; KMCT-TV (IND) West Monroe; KNOE-TV (CBS, CW) Monroe; KTVE (NBC) El Dorado.
Programming (via satellite): Discovery Channel; QVC; TBS Superstation; WGN America.
Current originations: Government Access.
Fee: $32.00 installation; $14.42 monthly; $3.00 converter.

Expanded Basic Service 1
Subscribers: 31,139.
Programming (via satellite): ABC Family Channel; AMC; Animal Planet; Arts & Entertainment; BET Networks; Bravo; Cartoon Network; CNBC; CNN; Comcast Sports Net Southwest; Comedy Central; Country Music TV; C-SPAN; C-SPAN 2; Discovery Health Channel; Disney Channel; E! Entertainment Television; ESPN; ESPN 2; ESPN Classic Sports; Food Network; Fox News Channel; Fuse; FX; Golf Channel; Hallmark Channel; Headline News; HGTV; History Channel; Home Shopping Network; ION Television; Lifetime; Lifetime Movie Network; MoviePlex; MSNBC; MTV; National Geographic Channel; Nickelodeon; ShopNBC; SoapNet; Spike TV; Syfy; The Learning Channel; Travel Channel; Trinity Broadcasting Network; truTV; Turner Classic Movies; Turner Network TV; TV Guide Network; TV Land; USA Network; Versus; VH1; WE tv; Weather Channel.
Fee: $31.56 monthly.

Digital Basic Service
Subscribers: N.A.
Programming (received off-air): KNOE-TV (CBS, CW) Monroe.
Programming (via satellite): America's Store; BBC America; Bio; Bloomberg Television; Cooking Channel; C-SPAN 3; Current; Discovery Digital Networks; Discovery HD Theater; Disney Channel; Do-It-Yourself; ESPN HD; ESPNews; Eternal Word TV Network; FamilyNet; FitTV; Fox Movie Channel; Fox Soccer; G4; Great American Country; HDNet; HDNet Movies; History Channel International; Independent Film Channel; INHD; Lifetime Real Women; MTV2; Music Choice; Nick Jr.; Outdoor Channel; Ovation; Speed Channel; Style Network; Sundance Channel; TeenNick; The Word Network; Toon Disney; Turner Network TV HD; TV One; VH1 Classic.
Fee: $12.95 monthly.

Pay Service 1
Pay Units: 2,971.
Programming (via satellite): HBO.
Fee: $9.95 monthly (each).

Digital Pay Service 1
Pay Units: N.A.
Programming (via satellite): Cinemax (multiplexed); Encore (multiplexed); Flix; HBO; HBO HD; Showtime (multiplexed); Showtime HD; Starz (multiplexed); The Movie Channel (multiplexed).
Fee: $11.95 monthly (each).

Video-On-Demand: Yes

Pay-Per-View
iN DEMAND (delivered digitally); Playboy TV (delivered digitally); Fresh (delivered digitally); NBA League Pass (delivered digitally); NHL Center Ice (delivered digitally); MLB Extra Innings (delivered digitally); ESPN Gameplan (delivered digitally); NASCAR In Car (delivered digitally); Sports PPV (delivered digitally).

Internet Service
Operational: Yes.
Broadband Service: Comcast High Speed Internet.
Fee: $30.00 installation; $42.95 monthly.

Telephone Service
Digital: Operational
Fee: $44.95 monthly

Miles of Plant: 627.0 (coaxial); None (fiber optic). Additional miles planned: 30.0 (coaxial); 20.0 (fiber optic). Homes passed included in Jackson
Vice President & General Manager: Ronnie Colvin. Engineering Director: Sandy McKnight. Marketing Director: Wesley Dowling. Customer Care Director: Robert Marsh. Public Affairs Director: Frances Smith.
City fee: 3% of gross.
Ownership: Comcast Cable Communications Inc. (MSO).

WESTLAKE—CommuniComm Services, 2504 Westwood Rd, Westlake, LA 70669. Phone: 337-433-0892. Fax: 337-433-0405. Web Site: http://www.netcommander.com. Also serves Moss Bluff. ICA: LA0025.
TV Market Ranking: Below 100 (Moss Bluff, WESTLAKE). Franchise award date: N.A. Franchise expiration date: N.A. Began: January 1, 1980.
Channel capacity: N.A. Channels available but not in use: N.A.

Basic Service
Subscribers: 8,109.
Programming (received off-air): KATC (ABC) Lafayette; KBMT (ABC) Beaumont; KBTV-TV (FOX) Port Arthur; KFDM (CBS, CW) Beaumont; KLFY-TV (CBS) Lafayette; KPLC (NBC) Lake Charles; WLPB-TV (PBS) Baton Rouge.
Programming (via satellite): TV Guide Network.
Fee: $20.00 installation; $10.25 monthly.

Expanded Basic Service 1
Subscribers: N.A.
Programming (via satellite): ABC Family Channel; AMC; Animal Planet; Arts & Entertainment; BET Networks; Cartoon Network; CNBC; CNN; Country Music TV; C-SPAN; C-SPAN 2; Discovery Channel; Disney Channel; ESPN; ESPN 2; Fox News Channel; Fox Sports Net; FX; Headline News; HGTV; History Channel; Lifetime; MSNBC; MTV; Nickelodeon; Outdoor Channel; QVC; Spike TV; Syfy; TBS Superstation; The Learning Channel; Turner Network TV; TV Land; USA Network; VH1; Weather Channel.
Fee: $20.00 installation; $10.25 monthly.

Digital Basic Service
Subscribers: N.A.
Programming (via satellite): AmericanLife TV Network; BBC America; Bloomberg Television; Bravo; Discovery Health Channel; Discovery Kids Channel; Discovery Military Channel; Discovery Planet Green; DMX Music; Encore (multiplexed); ESPN Classic Sports; ESPNews; Fox Soccer; G4; Golf Channel; GSN; Halogen Network; ID Investigation Discovery; Independent Film Channel; National Geographic Channel; Science Channel; Speed Channel; Trinity Broadcasting Network; Turner Classic Movies; Versus; WE tv; Weatherscan.
Fee: $20.00 installation; $10.25 monthly.

Digital Pay Service 1
Pay Units: N.A.
Programming (via satellite): Cinemax (multiplexed); HBO (multiplexed); Starz (multiplexed).
Fee: $10.00 installation; $11.95 monthly (Cinemax), $12.95 monthly (Starz/Encore), $13.95 monthly (HBO).

Video-On-Demand: No

Pay-Per-View
Movies (delivered digitally).

Internet Service
Operational: Yes.
Broadband Service: Net Commander.
Fee: $39.95 installation; $51.95 monthly.

Telephone Service
None

Miles of Plant: 174.0 (coaxial); None (fiber optic). Additional miles planned: 5.0 (coaxial). Homes passed: 26,000. Homes passed includes Kinder, Lake Arthur, & Vinton
General Manager: Larry Ivy. Plant Manager: Marcus Edwards.
City fee: 3% of gross.
Ownership: James Cable LLC (MSO).

WILSON—CableSouth Inc. Now served by ETHEL, LA [LA0160]. ICA: LA0213.

WINNFIELD—Suddenlink Communications, 701 W Court St, Winnfield, LA 71483-2635. Phone: 318-628-6449. Web Site: http://www.suddenlink.com. Also serves Joyce & Winn Parish. ICA: LA0046.
TV Market Ranking: 99 (Winn Parish (portions)); Below 100 (Joyce, Winn Parish (portions)); Outside TV Markets (WINNFIELD). Franchise award date: April 9, 1963. Franchise expiration date: N.A. Began: April 1, 1964.
Channel capacity: N.A. Channels available but not in use: N.A.

Basic Service
Subscribers: 2,525.
Programming (received off-air): KALB-TV (CBS, NBC) Alexandria; KAQY (ABC) Columbia; KARD (FOX) West Monroe; KCDH-LP Winnfield; KLAX-TV (ABC) Alexandria; KLTM-TV (PBS) Monroe; KNOE-TV (CBS, CW) Monroe; allband FM.
Programming (via satellite): ABC Family Channel; AMC; Animal Planet; Arts & Entertainment; BET Networks; Bravo; Cartoon Network; CNBC; CNN; Comcast Sports Net Southwest; Comedy Central; Country Music TV; Cox Sports Television; C-SPAN; C-SPAN 2; CW+; Discovery Channel; Discovery Health Channel; Disney Channel; E! Entertainment Television; ESPN; ESPN 2; Food Network; Fox News Channel; FX; Great American Country; Headline News; HGTV; History Channel; Home Shopping Network; Jewelry Television; Lifetime; Lifetime Movie Network; MSNBC; MTV; Nickelodeon; Outdoor Channel; Oxygen; QVC; Speed Channel; Spike TV; Syfy; TBS Superstation; The Learning Channel; Travel Channel; Trinity Broadcasting Network; truTV; Turner Classic Movies; Turner Network TV; TV Guide Network; TV Land; USA Network; Versus; VH1; WE tv; Weather Channel.
Fee: $28.59 installation; $29.95 monthly; $2.74 converter.

Digital Basic Service
Subscribers: N.A.
Programming (via satellite): BBC America; Bio; Bloomberg Television; CBS College Sports Network; CMT Pure Country; Cooking Channel; Discovery en Espanol; Discovery Home Channel; Discovery Kids Channel; Discovery Military Channel; Discovery Times Channel; Do-It-Yourself; Encore (multiplexed); ESPN Classic Sports; ESPNews; Fox Reality Channel; Fox Soccer; Fuel TV; Fuse; G4; Golf Channel; GSN; Hallmark Channel; History Channel International; Independent Film Channel; MTV Hits; MTV Jams; MTV2; Music Choice; National Geographic Channel; Nick Jr.; NickToons TV; Science Channel; SoapNet; Style Network; Sundance Channel; TeenNick; Toon Disney; TV One; VH1 Classic; VH1 Soul.

Digital Pay Service 1
Pay Units: N.A.
Programming (via satellite): Cinemax (multiplexed); HBO (multiplexed); Showtime (multiplexed); Starz (multiplexed); The Movie Channel (multiplexed).

Video-On-Demand: No

Pay-Per-View
iN DEMAND (delivered digitally); Barker (delivered digitally); Playboy TV (delivered digitally); Fresh (delivered digitally).

Internet Service
Operational: Yes.
Broadband Service: Cebridge High Speed Cable Internet.

Telephone Service
None

Miles of Plant: 64.0 (coaxial); None (fiber optic). Homes passed: 3,200. Total homes in franchised area: 3,200.
Manager: Ronnie Waters. Chief Technician: Leslie Alexander.
City fee: 2% of gross.
Ownership: Cequel Communications LLC (MSO).

WINNSBORO—Cable South Media, 301 W 1st Ave, Crossett, AR 71635. Phone: 870-305-1241. Also serves Winnsboro Twp. ICA: LA0057.

TV Market Ranking: 99 (WINNSBORO, Winnsboro Twp.). Franchise award date: N.A. Franchise expiration date: N.A. Began: June 1, 1976.

Channel capacity: 37 (not 2-way capable). Channels available but not in use: 4.

Basic Service

Subscribers: 1,600.

Programming (received off-air): KARD (FOX) West Monroe; KLTM-TV (PBS) Monroe; KMCT-TV (IND) West Monroe; KNOE-TV (CBS, CW) Monroe; KTVE (NBC) El Dorado; WJTV (CBS) Jackson; WLBT (NBC) Jackson.

Programming (via satellite): ABC Family Channel; Cartoon Network; WGN America.

Current originations: Religious Access.

Fee: $29.99 installation; $10.30 monthly.

Expanded Basic Service 1

Subscribers: 1,519.

Programming (via satellite): BET Networks; CNN; Country Music TV; C-SPAN; Disney Channel; ESPN; INSP; Lifetime; MTV; Nickelodeon; QVC; Spike TV; Syfy; USA Network; Weather Channel.

Fee: $12.10 monthly.

Expanded Basic Service 2

Subscribers: 1,459.

Programming (via satellite): AMC; Discovery Channel; TBS Superstation; Turner Network TV.

Fee: $21.13 installation; $3.20 monthly.

Pay Service 1

Pay Units: 288.

Programming (via satellite): HBO.

Fee: $10.00 monthly.

Pay Service 2

Pay Units: 283.

Programming (via satellite): Showtime.

Fee: $25.00 installation; $8.00 monthly.

Video-On-Demand: No

Internet Service

Operational: No.

Telephone Service

None

Miles of Plant: 55.0 (coaxial); None (fiber optic). Homes passed: 2,548.

City fee: 3% of gross.

Ownership: Cable South Media III LLC (MSO).

WISNER—CMA Cablevision, 3759 Old Sterlington Rd, Monroe, LA 71203-3086. Phones: 972-233-9614 (Corporate office); 318-345-1010. Fax: 318-343-5255. Web Site: http://www.cmaaccess.com. Also serves Gilbert. ICA: LA0093.

TV Market Ranking: Below 100 (Gilbert, WISNER). Franchise award date: March 11, 1982. Franchise expiration date: N.A. Began: December 1, 1982.

Channel capacity: N.A. Channels available but not in use: N.A.

Basic Service

Subscribers: 180.

Programming (received off-air): KARD (FOX) West Monroe; KLAX-TV (ABC) Alexandria; KLTM-TV (PBS) Monroe; KNOE-TV (CBS, CW) Monroe; KTVE (NBC) El Dorado.

Programming (via satellite): ABC Family Channel; CNN; Country Music TV; Discovery Channel; ESPN; Home Shopping Network; Nickelodeon; Spike TV; TBS Superstation; Turner Classic Movies; Turner Network TV; USA Network; Weather Channel; WGN America.

Fee: $39.95 installation; $38.95 monthly; $9.95 additional installation.

Pay Service 1

Pay Units: N.A.

Programming (via satellite): HBO; Showtime.

Fee: $14.95 installation; $13.95 monthly (each).

Video-On-Demand: No

Internet Service

Operational: No.

Telephone Service

None

Miles of Plant: 23.0 (coaxial); None (fiber optic). Homes passed: 800.

General Manager: Jerry Smith. Marketing Director: Julie Ferguson.

Ownership: Cable Management Assoc. (MSO).

MAINE

Total Systems: **43**
Total Communities Served: **361**
Franchises Not Yet Operating: **0**
Applications Pending: **0**
Communities with Applications: **0**
Number of Basic Subscribers: **325,114**
Number of Expanded Basic Subscribers: **225,086**
Number of Pay Units: **29,562**

Top 100 Markets Represented: Portland-Poland Spring (75).

For a list of cable communities in this section, see the Cable Community Index located in the back of Cable Volume 2.
For explanation of terms used in cable system listings, see p. D-11.

ADDISON—Time Warner Cable, 118 Johnston Rd, Portland, ME 4102. Phones: 207-253-2385; 207-253-2200. Fax: 207-253-2404. Web Site: http://www.timewarnercable.com/NewEngland. Also serves Columbia Falls & Harrington. ICA: ME0044.

TV Market Ranking: Outside TV Markets (ADDISON, Columbia Falls, Harrington). Franchise award date: May 1, 1988. Franchise expiration date: N.A. Began: March 28, 1990.

Channel capacity: N.A. Channels available but not in use: N.A.

Basic Service
Subscribers: 532.
Programming (received off-air): WABI-TV (CBS, CW) Bangor; WLBZ (NBC) Bangor; WMEB-TV (PBS) Orono; WVII-TV (ABC) Bangor.
Programming (via microwave): WSBK-TV (IND) Boston.
Programming (via satellite): C-SPAN; C-SPAN 2; Eternal Word TV Network; Home Shopping Network; ION Television; Product Information Network; QVC; TV Guide Network.
Fee: $56.63 installation; $21.85 monthly.

Expanded Basic Service 1
Subscribers: 487.
Programming (via microwave): New England Cable News.
Programming (via satellite): ABC Family Channel; AMC; Animal Planet; Arts & Entertainment; Bravo; Cartoon Network; CNN; Comcast Sports Net New England; Comedy Central; Country Music TV; Discovery Channel; Disney Channel; E! Entertainment Television; ESPN; ESPN 2; Food Network; Fox News Channel; FX; Hallmark Channel; Headline News; HGTV; History Channel; Lifetime; MSNBC; MTV; Nickelodeon; Oxygen; ShopNBC; Spike TV; Style Network; Syfy; TBS Superstation; The Learning Channel; Travel Channel; truTV; Turner Network TV; TV Land; TV5, La Television International; USA Network; VH1; Weather Channel.

Digital Basic Service
Subscribers: N.A.
Programming (via satellite): BBC America; Bio; Black Family Channel; Bloomberg Television; Discovery Digital Networks; ESPN Classic Sports; ESPNews; Fox College Sports Atlantic (multiplexed); Fox Movie Channel; Fox Soccer; Fuse; G4; GAS; Golf Channel; Great American Country; GSN; History Channel International; Independent Film Channel; INSP; Lifetime Movie Network; MTV Networks Digital Suite; Music Choice; National Geographic Channel; Nick Jr.; Nick Too; NickToons TV; Outdoor Channel; Speed Channel; Style Network; The Word Network; Toon Disney; Trinity Broadcasting Network; Turner Classic Movies; Versus; WE tv.

Digital Pay Service 1
Pay Units: N.A.
Programming (via satellite): Cinemax (multiplexed); Encore (multiplexed); Flix (multiplexed); HBO (multiplexed); Showtime (multiplexed); Starz (multiplexed); The Movie Channel (multiplexed).
Fee: $12.95 monthly (each).

Video-On-Demand: No

Pay-Per-View
Movies (delivered digitally); Playboy TV (delivered digitally); Fresh (delivered digitally).

Internet Service
Operational: Yes.
Broadband Service: RoadRunner.
Fee: $24.95 monthly.

Telephone Service
Digital: Operational
Fee: $24.99 monthly

Miles of Plant: 50.0 (coaxial); None (fiber optic). Homes passed: 1,091.

President: Keith Burkley. Vice President, Marketing & Sales: David Leopold. Vice President, Engineering: Scott Ducott. Vice President, Government & Public Affairs: Melinda Poore.

Ownership: Time Warner Cable (MSO).

AROOSTOOK COUNTY—Time Warner Cable, 118 Johnston Rd, Portland, ME 4102. Phones: 207-253-2200; 207-253-2385. Fax: 207-253-2404. Web Site: http://www.timewarnercable.com/NewEngland. Also serves Ashland, Blaine, Caribou, Castle Hill, Caswell (town), Connor (portions), Easton, Fort Fairfield, Limestone, Mapleton, Mars Hill, New Sweden (portions), Portage, Presque Isle, Washburn, Westfield & Woodland. ICA: ME0008.

TV Market Ranking: Below 100 (AROOSTOOK COUNTY, Ashland, Blaine, Caribou, Castle Hill, Caswell (town), Connor (portions), Easton, Fort Fairfield, Limestone, Mapleton, Mars Hill, New Sweden (portions), Portage, Presque Isle, Washburn, Westfield, Woodland). Franchise award date: N.A. Franchise expiration date: N.A. Began: July 1, 1960.

Channel capacity: N.A. Channels available but not in use: 6.

Basic Service
Subscribers: 9,341.
Programming (received off-air): WAGM-TV (CBS) Presque Isle; WMEM-TV (PBS) Presque Isle.
Programming (via microwave): WLBZ (NBC) Bangor; WVII-TV (ABC) Bangor.
Programming (via satellite): C-SPAN; C-SPAN 2; ION Television; QVC; Shop at Home; TV Guide Network.
Current originations: Public Access; Government Access.
Fee: $56.63 installation; $8.45 monthly; $3.05 converter.

Expanded Basic Service 1
Subscribers: 6,900.
Programming (via satellite): ABC Family Channel; AMC; Animal Planet; Arts & Entertainment; Bravo; Cartoon Network; CNBC; CNN; Comcast Sports Net New England; Comedy Central; Country Music TV; CW+; Discovery Channel; Disney Channel; E! Entertainment Television; ESPN; ESPN 2; ESPN Classic Sports; Eternal Word TV Network; Food Network; Fox News Channel; FX; Golf Channel; GSN; Hallmark Channel; Headline News; HGTV; History Channel; Home Shopping Network; INSP; Lifetime; MSNBC; MTV; National Geographic Channel; New England Sports Network; Nickelodeon; Outdoor Channel; Oxygen; ShopNBC; SoapNet; Speed Channel; Spike TV; Syfy; TBS Superstation; The Learning Channel; Travel Channel; truTV; Turner Classic Movies; Turner Network TV; TV Land; USA Network; Versus; VH1; WE tv; Weather Channel.
Fee: $30.80 monthly.

Digital Basic Service
Subscribers: 119.
Programming (via satellite): American-Life TV Network; America's Store; BBC America; Bio; Bloomberg Television; Boomerang; C-SPAN 3; Discovery Digital Networks; DMX Music; Do-It-Yourself; Encore Action; ESPNews; Fox Movie Channel; Fox Sports World; Fuse; G4; GAS; Great American Country; History Channel International; Independent Film Channel; Lifetime Movie Network; MTV2; Nick Jr.; Ovation; Style Network; Toon Disney; Trinity Broadcasting Network; VH1 Classic.
Fee: $12.99 monthly.

Digital Expanded Basic Service
Subscribers: N.A.
Programming (via satellite): Fox College Sports Atlantic; Fox College Sports Central; Fox College Sports Pacific; Fox Sports en Espanol.
Fee: $2.95 monthly.

Digital Pay Service 1
Pay Units: 217.
Programming (via satellite): Cinemax (multiplexed).
Fee: $12.95 monthly.

Digital Pay Service 2
Pay Units: 728.
Programming (via satellite): HBO (multiplexed).
Fee: $12.95 monthly.

Digital Pay Service 3
Pay Units: 101.
Programming (via satellite): The Movie Channel (multiplexed).
Fee: $12.95 monthly.

Digital Pay Service 4
Pay Units: 157.
Programming (via satellite): Showtime (multiplexed).
Fee: $12.95 monthly.

Digital Pay Service 5
Pay Units: 127.
Programming (via satellite): Starz (multiplexed).
Fee: $12.95 monthly.

Video-On-Demand: Yes

Pay-Per-View
Hot Choice, Addressable: Yes; iN DEMAND; Sports PPV (delivered digitally); Playboy TV (delivered digitally); Fresh; Pleasure; Hot Choice (delivered digitally); iN DEMAND (delivered digitally); Pleasure (delivered digitally); Fresh (delivered digitally); Shorteez (delivered digitally).

Internet Service
Operational: Yes.
Broadband Service: EarthLink, Road Runner.
Fee: $44.95 monthly.

Telephone Service
Analog: Not Operational
Digital: Operational
Fee: $39.99 monthly

Miles of Plant: 384.0 (coaxial); 170.0 (fiber optic). Homes passed: 14,059.

President: Keith Burkley. Vice President, Marketing & Sales: David Leopold. Vice President, Engineering: Scott Ducott. Vice President, Government & Public Affairs: Melinda Poore.

City fee: 3% of gross.

Ownership: Time Warner Cable (MSO).

ASHLAND—Time Warner Cable. Now served by AROOSTOOK COUNTY, ME [ME0008]. ICA: ME0052.

AUGUSTA—Time Warner Cable, 118 Johnston Rd, Portland, ME 4102. Phones: 207-594-2249 (Rockland office); 207-253-2385; 207-253-2200. Fax: 207-253-2404. Web Site: http://www.timewarnercable.com/NewEngland. Also serves Albion, Alna, Auburn, Belgrade (town), Belgrade Lakes, Benton, Boothbay, Boothbay Harbor, Bristol (town), Buckfield (town), Camden, Canton (town), Chelsea, China, Clinton, Cushing (town), Damariscotta, Dixfield, Dresden, East Boothbay, East Dixfield, Edgecomb, Farmingdale, Friendship (town), Gardiner, Greene (town), Hallowell, Hanover (town), Jay, Jefferson (town), Leeds, Lewiston, Lisbon, Lisbon Falls, Litchfield, Livermore, Livermore Falls, Manchester, Mechanic Falls, Mexico, Minot, Monmouth, Mount Vernon (town), New Harbor, Newcastle, Nobleboro, North Monmouth, North Vassalboro, Owls Head, Oxford, Pemaquid, Peru, Pittston, Port Clydge, Portland, Randolph, Readfield (town), Richmond, Rockland, Rockport (town), Rome (town), Round Pond, Roxbury (town), Rumford, Sabattus, Sidney (town), South Bristol (town), South Thomaston (town), Southport (town), Spruce Head, St. George (town), Tenants Harbor, Thomaston, Trevett, Turner, Union (town),

Vassalboro, Vinalhaven, Waldoboro, Wales, Warren (town), Wayne, West Gardiner, West Southport, Westport Isle, Whitefield (town), Windsor (town), Winthrop & Wiscasset. ICA: ME0004.

TV Market Ranking: 75 (Auburn, Boothbay, Boothbay Harbor, Buckfield, Buckfield (town), Canton, Canton (town), Dixfield, Dresden, Farmingdale, Gardiner, Greene (town), Hallowell, Jay, Leeds, Lewiston, Lisbon, Lisbon Falls, Litchfield, Livermore, Livermore Falls, Manchester, Mechanic Falls, Monmouth, North Monmouth, Oxford, Peru, Randolph, Readfield, Readfield (town), Richmond, Sabattus, Southport (town), Trevett, Turner, Wales, Wayne, West Gardiner, Westport Isle, Winthrop, Wiscasset); Below 100 (Alna, AUGUSTA (VILLAGE), Belgrade, Belgrade (town), Belgrade Lakes, Bristol, Bristol (town), Camden, Chelsea, Cushing, Cushing (town), Damariscotta, East Boothbay, Edgecomb, Friendship (town), Jefferson (town), Mount Vernon, Mount Vernon (town), Newcastle, Nobleboro, Owls Head, Pittston, Rockland, Rockport (town), Rome, Rome (town), Sidney (town), South Bristol, South Bristol (town), South Thomaston (town), St. George (town), Thomaston, Union, Union (town), Vinalhaven, Waldoboro, Warren, Warren (town), Whitefield (town), Windsor (town)); Outside TV Markets (Andover, Andover (town), Hanover, Hanover (town), Mexico, Roxbury, Roxbury (town), Rumford). Franchise award date: June 1, 1965. Franchise expiration date: N.A. Began: June 14, 1965.

Channel capacity: 73 (operating 2-way). Channels available but not in use: None.

Basic Service

Subscribers: 35,924.

Programming (received off-air): various Canadian stations; WABI-TV (CBS, CW) Bangor; WCBB (PBS) Augusta; WCSH (NBC) Portland; WGME-TV (CBS) Portland; WMTW (ABC) Poland Spring; WPFO (FOX) Waterville; WPME (MNT) Lewiston; WPXT (CW) Portland.

Programming (via satellite): C-SPAN; C-SPAN 2; Home Shopping Network; ION Television; QVC; ShopNBC; TV Guide Network.

Current originations: Government Access; Educational Access.

Fee: $56.63 installation; $12.00 monthly; $30.00 additional installation.

Expanded Basic Service 1

Subscribers: 32,502.

Programming (via satellite): ABC Family Channel; AMC; Animal Planet; Arts & Entertainment; BET Networks; Bravo; Cartoon Network; CNBC; CNN; Comcast/Charter Sports Southeast (CSS); Comedy Central; Country Music TV; Discovery Channel; Disney Channel; E! Entertainment Television; ESPN; ESPN 2; Eternal Word TV Network; Food Network; Fox News Channel; FX; Great American Country; Hallmark Channel; Headline News; HGTV; History Channel; INSP; Lifetime; MSNBC; MTV; New England Cable News; New England Sports Network; Nickelodeon; Ovation; Oxygen; Product Information Network; Spike TV; Syfy; TBS Superstation; The Learning Channel; Travel Channel; Trinity Broadcasting Network; truTV; Turner Classic Movies; Turner Network TV; TV Land; TV5 USA; USA Network; VH1; Weather Channel.

Fee: $29.00 monthly.

Digital Basic Service

Subscribers: 6,461.

Programming (via satellite): AmericanLife TV Network; BBC America; Bio; Bloomberg Television; Boomerang; Canal 52MX; Cine Latino; CNN en Espanol; CNN International; College Sports Television; Cooking Channel; C-SPAN 3; Current; Discovery en Espanol; Discovery Health Channel; Discovery Home Channel; Discovery Kids Channel; Discovery Military Channel; Disney Channel; Do-It-Yourself; ESPN Classic Sports; ESPN Deportes; ESPN U; ESPNews; FamilyNet; FitTV; Fox Business Channel; Fox Movie Channel; Fox Reality Channel; Fox Soccer; Fox Sports en Espanol; FSN Digital Atlantic; FSN Digital Central; FSN Digital Pacific; Fuel TV; Fuse; G4; Golf Channel; Gospel Music Channel; GSN; Halogen Network; History Channel en Espanol; History Channel International; ID Investigation Discovery; Independent Film Channel; Lifetime Movie Network; LOGO; MTV Hits; MTV Jams; MTV2; Music Choice; National Geographic Channel; NBA TV; NHL Network; Nick Jr.; Nick Too; NickToons TV; Outdoor Channel; PBS Kids Sprout; PBS World; Pentagon Channel; ReelzChannel; Science Channel; SoapNet; Speed Channel; Style Network; Sundance Channel; TeenNick; Tennis Channel; The Sportsman Channel; The Word Network; Toon Disney; Versus; VH1 Classic; WE tv.

Fee: $12.99 monthly.

Digital Pay Service 1

Pay Units: 2,424.

Programming (via satellite): ART America; CCTV-4; Cinemax (multiplexed); Encore (multiplexed); Filipino Channel; Flix; HBO (multiplexed); RAI International; Russian Television Network; Showtime (multiplexed); Starz (multiplexed); The Movie Channel (multiplexed); TV Asia; TV Japan; TV5 USA; Zhong Tian Channel.

Fee: $12.95 monthly (each).

Video-On-Demand: Yes

Pay-Per-View

iN DEMAND (delivered digitally); Penthouse TV (delivered digitally); Playboy TV (delivered digitally); Ten Clips (delivered digitally); Ten Blue (delivered digitally); Ten Blox (delivered digitally).

Internet Service

Operational: Yes.

Broadband Service: Road Runner.

Fee: $42.95 monthly.

Telephone Service

Digital: Planned

Miles of Plant: 1,554.0 (coaxial); None (fiber optic). Homes passed: 53,705.

General Manager: Eileen Martin. Marketing Director: Shanna Allen. Marketing Coordinator: Erica Crosby. Technical Operations Manager: Rockie Marsh. Customer Service Manager: Sue Dwinnal.

City fee: None.

Ownership: Time Warner Cable (MSO).

AVON—Now served by NORTH ANSON, ME [ME0062]. ICA: ME0081.

BANGOR—Time Warner Cable, 83 Anthony Ave, Augusta, ME 04330-7880. Phones: 877-596-5366; 207-623-3685 (Augusta office); 877-500-1055; 207-942-4661 (Bangor office). Fax: 207-623-3407. Web Site: http://www.timewarnercable.com/NewEngland. Also serves Bar Harbor, Bass Harbor, Belfast, Belmont (town), Bernard, Blue Hill (town), Bradley, Brewer, Bucksport, Canaan, Carmel, Castine, Corinna, Corinth (town), Dedham (town), Deer Isle (town), Detroit (town), Dexter, Dover-Foxcroft, Eddington, Ellsworth, Franklin, Franklin (town), Glenburn, Hampden, Hancock, Hartland, Hermon, Holden, Kenduskeag, Lamoine, Levant, Manset, Milford, Mount Desert (town), Newport, Old Town, Orono, Orrington, Palmyra, Pittsfield, Searsport, Sorrento, Southwest Harbor, St. Albans, Stockton Springs, Stonington, Sullivan, Surry, Tremont, Trenton, Veazie, Verona & Winterport. ICA: ME0002.

TV Market Ranking: Below 100 (BANGOR, Belfast, Belmont (town), Blue Hill, Bradley, Brewer, Bucksport, Canaan, Carmel, Castine, Corinna, Corinth (town), Dedham (town), Detroit (town), Dexter, Dover-Foxcroft, Eddington, Ellsworth, Franklin, Franklin (town), Glenburn, Hampden, Hancock, Hartland, Hermon, Holden, Kenduskeag, Lamoine, Levant, Milford, Newport, Old Town, Orono, Orrington, Palmyra, Pittsfield, Searsport, St. Albans, Stockton Springs, Sullivan, Surry, Trenton, Veazie, Verona, Winterport); Outside TV Markets (Bar Harbor, Bass Harbor, Bernard, Deer Isle (town), Manset, Mount Desert (town), Sorrento, Southwest Harbor, Stonington, Tremont). Franchise award date: May 1, 1988. Franchise expiration date: N.A. Began: December 1, 1971.

Channel capacity: 116 (operating 2-way). Channels available but not in use: None.

Basic Service

Subscribers: 39,501.

Programming (received off-air): WABI-TV (CBS, CW) Bangor; WBGR-LP Bangor; WFVX-LP Bangor; WLBZ (NBC) Bangor; WMEB-TV (PBS) Orono; WVII-TV (ABC) Bangor; 10 FMs.

Programming (via microwave): WSBK-TV (IND) Boston.

Programming (via satellite): C-SPAN; C-SPAN 2; CW+; Eternal Word TV Network; Home Shopping Network; Product Information Network; QVC; TV Guide Network; various Canadian stations.

Fee: $29.95 installation; $17.30 monthly.

Expanded Basic Service 1

Subscribers: 33,986.

Programming (via satellite): ABC Family Channel; AMC; Animal Planet; Arts & Entertainment; BET Networks; Bravo; Cartoon Network; CNBC; CNN; Comcast SportsNet Mid-Atlantic; Comedy Central; Country Music TV; Discovery Channel; Disney Channel; E! Entertainment Television; ESPN; ESPN 2; Food Network; Fox News Channel; FX; Great American Country; Hallmark Channel; Headline News; HGTV; History Channel; INSP; Lifetime; MSNBC; MTV; New England Cable News; New England Sports Network; Nickelodeon; Oxygen; ShopNBC; Spike TV; Syfy; TBS Superstation; The Learning Channel; Toon Disney; Travel Channel; truTV; Turner Network TV; TV Land; TV5 USA; USA Network; Versus; VH1; Weather Channel.

Fee: $19.30 monthly.

Digital Basic Service

Subscribers: N.A.

Programming (received off-air): WLBZ (NBC) Bangor; WMEB-TV (PBS) Orono; WVII-TV (ABC) Bangor.

Programming (via satellite): AmericanLife TV Network; Arts & Entertainment HD; BBC America; Bio; Bloomberg Television; Boomerang; Canal 52MX; CBS College Sports Network; Cine Latino; CNN en Espanol; CNN HD; CNN International; Cooking Channel; C-SPAN 3; Current; Discovery en Espanol; Discovery HD Theater; Discovery Health Channel; Discovery Home Channel; Discovery Kids Channel; Discovery Military Channel; Discovery Times Channel; Disney Channel; Do-It-Yourself; Encore (multiplexed); ESPN 2 HD; ESPN Classic Sports; ESPN Deportes; ESPN HD; ESPN U; ESPNews; FamilyNet; FitTV; Flix; Food Network HD; Fox Business Channel; Fox College Sports Atlantic; Fox College Sports Central; Fox College Sports Pacific; Fox HD; Fox Movie Channel; Fox Reality Channel; Fox Soccer; Fox Sports en Espanol; Fuel TV; Fuse; G4; Golf Channel; Gospel Music Channel; GSN; HDNet; HDNet Movies; HGTV HD; History Channel; History Channel en Espanol; History Channel HD; Independent Film Channel; INSP; Lifetime Movie Network; Lifetime Movie Network HD; LOGO; MTV Hits; MTV Jams; MTV2; Music Choice; National Geographic Channel; National Geographic Channel HD Network; NBA TV; NHL Network; NHL Network HD; Nick Jr.; Nick Too; NickToons TV; Outdoor Channel; Ovation; Palladia; Pentagon Channel; ReelzChannel; Science Channel; SoapNet; Speed Channel; Style Network; Sundance Channel; TBS in HD; TeenNick; Tennis Channel; The Sportsman Channel; The Word Network; Trinity Broadcasting Network; Turner Classic Movies; Turner Network TV HD; Universal HD; Versus HD; VH1 Classic; WE tv.

Digital Pay Service 1

Pay Units: 13,137.

Programming (via satellite): ART America; Chinese Television Network; Cinemax (multiplexed); Cinemax HD; Filipino Channel; HBO (multiplexed); HBO HD; RAI International; Russian Television Network; Showtime (multiplexed); Showtime HD; Starz (multiplexed); Starz HDTV; The Movie Channel (multiplexed); TV Asia; TV Japan; Zhong Tian Channel.

Fee: $10.45 monthly (each).

Video-On-Demand: Yes

Pay-Per-View

iN DEMAND (delivered digitally); Playboy TV (delivered digitally); Ten Clips (delivered digitally); Ten Blue (delivered digitally); Ten Blox (delivered digitally); NBA League Pass (delivered digitally); NHL Center Ice (delivered digitally); MLB Extra Innings (delivered digitally); Sports PPV (delivered digitally).

Internet Service

Operational: Yes.

Broadband Service: Road Runner.

Fee: $42.95 monthly.

Telephone Service

None

Miles of Plant: 1,408.0 (coaxial); None (fiber optic). Homes passed: 65,637.

General Manager: Eileen Martin. Chief Technician: Rockie Marsh. Marketing Director: Shanna Allen. Customer Service Manager: Sue Dwinnal.

City fee: 1% of gross.

Ownership: Time Warner Cable (MSO).

BELGRADE—Now served by AUGUSTA, ME [ME0004]. ICA: ME0088.

BETHEL—Formerly served by Adelphia Communications. Now served by SEBAGO (town), ME [ME0107]. ICA: ME0029.

BINGHAM—Moosehead Enterprises, PO Box 526, Greenville, ME 4441. Phone: 207-695-3337. Fax: 207-695-3571. ICA: ME0116.

TV Market Ranking: Outside TV Markets (BINGHAM).

Channel capacity: N.A. Channels available but not in use: N.A.

Basic Service

Subscribers: 482.

Programming (received off-air): WABI-TV (CBS, CW) Bangor; WCSH (NBC) Port-

land; WGME-TV (CBS) Portland; WMEB-TV (PBS) Orono; WMTW (ABC) Poland Spring; WVII-TV (ABC) Bangor.
Programming (via satellite): ABC Family Channel; Arts & Entertainment; CNN; CW+; Discovery Channel; ESPN; ESPN 2; Great American Country; Hallmark Channel; History Channel; Lifetime; Outdoor Channel; QVC; TBS Superstation; Turner Classic Movies; Turner Network TV; USA Network; WGN America; WSBK-TV (IND) Boston.
Fee: $20.50 monthly.
Pay Service 1
Pay Units: 52.
Programming (via satellite): HBO.
Fee: $12.00 monthly.
Video-On-Demand: No
Internet Service
Operational: No.
Telephone Service
None
President: Scott Richardson. Secretary: Sue Richardson.
Ownership: Moosehead Enterprises Inc.

BLUE HILL (town)—Formerly served by Adelphia Communications. Now served by BANGOR, ME [ME0002]. ICA: ME0060.

BOOTHBAY—Formerly served by Adelphia Communications. Now served by AUGUSTA, ME [ME0004]. ICA: ME0034.

BRIDGTON—Now served by SEBAGO (town), ME [ME0107]. ICA: ME0022.

BRISTOL—Now served by AUGUSTA, ME [ME0004]. ICA: ME0039.

BRUNSWICK—Comcast Cable, 676 Island Pond Rd, Manchester, NH 3109. Phone: 603-695-1400. Fax: 603-628-3365. Web Site: http://www.comcast.com. Also serves Bailey Island, Bath, Bowdoin (town), Bowdoinham (town), Durham (town), Freeport (town), Harpswell, Orrs Island, Phippsburg (town), Sebasco Estates, Topsham, West Bath & Woolwich. ICA: ME0010.
TV Market Ranking: 75 (Bailey Island, Bath, Bowdoin (town), Bowdoinham (town), BRUNSWICK, Durham, Freeport (town), Harpswell, Orrs Island, Phippsburg (town), Sebasco Estates, Sebasco Estates, Topsham, West Bath, Woolwich). Franchise award date: N.A. Franchise expiration date: N.A. Began: November 14, 1974.
Channel capacity: N.A. Channels available but not in use: N.A.
Basic Service
Subscribers: N.A. Included in Manchester, NH
Programming (received off-air): WCBB (PBS) Augusta; WCSH (NBC) Portland; WGME-TV (CBS) Portland; WMTW (ABC) Poland Spring; WPME (MNT) Lewiston; WPXT (CW) Portland.
Programming (via satellite): C-SPAN; ShopNBC; TV Guide Network; WPFO (FOX) Waterville.
Current originations: Educational Access; Public Access.
Fee: $43.95 installation; $9.50 monthly.
Expanded Basic Service 1
Subscribers: 17,585.
Programming (via satellite): ABC Family Channel; AMC; Animal Planet; Arts & Entertainment; Bravo; Cartoon Network; CNBC; CNN; Comcast Sports Net New England; Comedy Central; Country Music TV; C-SPAN 2; Discovery Channel; Discovery Health Channel; Disney Channel; E! Entertainment Television; ESPN; ESPN 2; ESPNews; Food Network; Fox News Channel; FX; G4; Hallmark Channel; Headline News; HGTV; History Channel; Home Shopping Network; ION Television; Lifetime; MSNBC; MTV; New England Sports Network; Nickelodeon; QVC; SoapNet; Spike TV; Syfy; TBS Superstation; The Learning Channel; Toon Disney; Travel Channel; truTV; Turner Network TV; TV Land; USA Network; VH1; WE tv; Weather Channel.
Fee: $39.50 monthly.
Digital Basic Service
Subscribers: 5,064.
Programming (received off-air): WCSH (NBC) Portland; WMTW (ABC) Poland Spring.
Programming (via satellite): BBC America; Discovery HD Theater; Discovery Kids Channel; Discovery Military Channel; Discovery Planet Green; ESPN HD; HDNet; HDNet Movies; ID Investigation Discovery; Lifetime Movie Network; MTV Networks Digital Suite; Music Choice; Nick Jr.; Nick Too; NickToons TV; Science Channel; TeenNick.
Fee: $7.95 monthly.
Digital Pay Service 1
Pay Units: N.A.
Programming (via satellite): Cinemax (multiplexed); Cinemax HD; Encore (multiplexed); HBO (multiplexed); HBO HD; Showtime (multiplexed); Showtime HD; Starz (multiplexed); The Movie Channel (multiplexed).
Video-On-Demand: No
Pay-Per-View
ESPN Gameplan (delivered digitally); ESPN Full Court (delivered digitally); Hot Choice (delivered digitally), Addressable: Yes; iN DEMAND (delivered digitally); Playboy TV (delivered digitally); Fresh (delivered digitally); Shorteez (delivered digitally).
Internet Service
Operational: Yes. Began: September 1, 1997.
Subscribers: 10,725.
Broadband Service: Comcast High Speed Internet.
Fee: $42.95 monthly.
Telephone Service
Digital: Operational
Miles of Plant: 1,018.0 (coaxial); None (fiber optic). Homes passed: 31,428.
Regional Vice President: Steve Hackley. Vice President, Technical Operations: Raymond Kowalinski. Sales & Marketing Director: Mark Adamy. Public Relations Director: Marc Goodman.
Franchise fee: 3% -5% of gross.
Ownership: Comcast Cable Communications Inc. (MSO).

BUCKFIELD—Formerly served by Adelphia Communications. Now served by AUGUSTA, ME [ME0004]. ICA: ME0064.

BUXTON—Now served by SEBAGO (town), ME [ME0107]. ICA: ME0011.

CALAIS—Time Warner Cable, 118 Johnston Rd, Portland, ME 4102. Phones: 207-253-2385; 207-253-2200. Fax: 207-253-2404. Web Site: http://www.timewarnercable.com/NewEngland. Also serves Baileyville, Baring, Princeton & Woodland. ICA: ME0024.
TV Market Ranking: Outside TV Markets (Baileyville, Baring, CALAIS, Princeton, Woodland). Franchise award date: December 13, 1962. Franchise expiration date: N.A. Began: September 15, 1963.
Channel capacity: 62 (operating 2-way). Channels available but not in use: N.A.
Basic Service
Subscribers: 2,242.
Programming (received off-air): WABI-TV (CBS, CW) Bangor; WLBZ (NBC) Bangor; WMED-TV (PBS) Calais; WVII-TV (ABC) Bangor; allband FM.
Programming (via satellite): Eternal Word TV Network; ION Television; Product Information Network; QVC; TV Guide Network.
Current originations: Public Access.
Fee: $56.63 installation; $22.21 monthly.
Expanded Basic Service 1
Subscribers: 1,964.
Programming (via satellite): ABC Family Channel; Animal Planet; Arts & Entertainment; Cartoon Network; CNBC; CNN; Comcast Sports Net New England; Country Music TV; C-SPAN; C-SPAN 2; Discovery Channel; Disney Channel; E! Entertainment Television; ESPN; ESPN 2; Food Network; Fox News Channel; FX; HGTV; History Channel; Home Shopping Network; INSP; Lifetime; MSNBC; MTV; New England Sports Network; Nickelodeon; Spike TV; Syfy; TBS Superstation; The Learning Channel; Turner Classic Movies; Turner Network TV; TV Land; USA Network; Versus; VH1; Weather Channel.
Fee: $46.54 monthly.
Digital Basic Service
Subscribers: N.A.
Programming (via satellite): American-Life TV Network; BBC America; Bio; Black Family Channel; Bloomberg Television; Canales N; Discovery Digital Networks; Do-It-Yourself; ESPN Classic Sports; ESPNews; Fox College Sports; Fox Movie Channel; Fox Soccer; Fuse; G4; GAS; Golf Channel; Great American Country; GSN; Hallmark Channel; Halogen Network; History Channel International; Independent Film Channel; Lifetime Movie Network; MTV Networks Digital Suite; Music Choice; National Geographic Channel; Nick Jr.; Nick Too; NickToons TV; Outdoor Channel; SoapNet; Speed Channel; Style Network; Sundance Channel; The Word Network; Toon Disney; Trinity Broadcasting Network; WE tv.
Fee: $12.99 monthly.
Digital Pay Service 1
Pay Units: N.A.
Programming (via satellite): Cinemax (multiplexed); Encore (multiplexed); Flix (multiplexed); HBO (multiplexed); International Television (ITV); Showtime (multiplexed); Starz (multiplexed); The Movie Channel (multiplexed).
Fee: $12.95 monthly (each).
Video-On-Demand: No
Pay-Per-View
Playboy TV (delivered digitally); Fresh (delivered digitally); Hot Choice (delivered digitally); Movies (delivered digitally); MLB Extra Innings (delivered digitally); NHL Center Ice (delivered digitally).
Internet Service
Operational: Yes.
Broadband Service: EarthLink, Road Runner.
Fee: $99.00 installation; $44.95 monthly; $3.00 modem lease.
Telephone Service
None
Miles of Plant: 59.0 (coaxial); 15.0 (fiber optic). Homes passed: 2,984. Total homes in franchised area: 4,400.
President: Keith Burkley. Vice President, Marketing & Sales: David Leopold. Vice President, Engineering: Scott Ducott. Vice President, Government & Public Affairs: Melinda Poore.
Ownership: Time Warner Cable (MSO).

CANTON (town)—Now served by AUGUSTA, ME [ME0004]. ICA: ME0077.

CARRABASSETT VALLEY—Now served by NORTH ANSON, ME [ME0062]. ICA: ME0042.

CASTINE—Formerly served by Adelphia Communications. Now served by BANGOR, ME [ME0002]. ICA: ME0073.

CASTLE HILL—Time Warner Cable. Now served by AROOSTOOK COUNTY, ME [ME0008]. ICA: ME0053.

CHERRYFIELD—Time Warner Cable, 118 Johnston Rd, Portland, ME 4102. Phones: 207-253-2385; 207-253-2200. Fax: 207-253-2404. Web Site: http://www.timewarnercable.com/NewEngland. Also serves Gouldsboro, Milbridge & Winter Harbor. ICA: ME0111.
TV Market Ranking: Outside TV Markets (CHERRYFIELD, Gouldsboro, Milbridge, Winter Harbor). Franchise award date: N.A. Franchise expiration date: N.A. Began: N.A.
Channel capacity: N.A. Channels available but not in use: N.A.
Basic Service
Subscribers: 520.
Programming (received off-air): WABI-TV (CBS, CW) Bangor; WFVX-LP Bangor; WLBZ (NBC) Bangor; WMEB-TV (PBS) Orono; WVII-TV (ABC) Bangor.
Programming (via satellite): C-SPAN; ION Television; National Geographic Channel; QVC.
Fee: $55.63 installation; $37.85 monthly; $25.00 additional installation.
Digital Basic Service
Subscribers: N.A.
Programming (via satellite): AmericanLife TV Network; BBC America; BBC World News; Bio; Bloomberg Television; Bravo; Discovery Health Channel; Discovery Home Channel; Discovery Kids Channel; Discovery Military Channel; ESPN Classic Sports; ESPNews; Fox Movie Channel; Golf Channel; GSN; Healthy Living Channel; HGTV; History Channel International; ID Investigation Discovery; Independent Film Channel; INSP; Lifetime Movie Network; Outdoor Channel; Ovation; Science Channel; Sleuth; Speed Channel; Sundance Channel; TeenNick; Versus; WE tv.
Pay Service 1
Pay Units: 35.
Programming (via satellite): HBO; Showtime; The Movie Channel.
Digital Pay Service 1
Pay Units: N.A.
Programming (via satellite): Cinemax (multiplexed); Encore (multiplexed); HBO (multiplexed); Showtime (multiplexed); Starz (multiplexed); The Movie Channel (multiplexed).
Video-On-Demand: No
Internet Service
Operational: Yes.
Broadband Service: RoadRunner.
Fee: $24.95 monthly.
Telephone Service
Digital: Operational
Fee: $24.99 monthly
President: Keith Burkley. Vice President, Marketing & Sales: David Leopold. Vice President, Engineering: Scott Ducott. Vice Presi-

dent, Government & Public Affairs: Melinda Poore.
Ownership: Time Warner Cable (MSO).

CORNISH (town)—Now served by SEBAGO (town), ME [ME0107]. ICA: ME0041.

DANFORTH—Polaris Cable Services, 34 Military St, Houlton, ME 4730. Phone: 207-532-2579. Fax: 207-532-4025. Web Site: http://www.polariscable.com. Also serves Weston. ICA: ME0090.
TV Market Ranking: Below 100 (Weston); Outside TV Markets (DANFORTH). Franchise award date: January 21, 1978. Franchise expiration date: N.A. Began: January 1, 1984.
Channel capacity: 42 (not 2-way capable). Channels available but not in use: 21.
Basic Service
Subscribers: 91.
Programming (received off-air): WABI-TV (CBS, CW) Bangor; WAGM-TV (CBS) Presque Isle; WLBZ (NBC) Bangor; WMED-TV (PBS) Calais; WPFO (FOX) Waterville; WVII-TV (ABC) Bangor.
Programming (via satellite): ABC Family Channel; AMC; Animal Planet; Arts & Entertainment; CNN; Comedy Central; Country Music TV; Discovery Channel; E! Entertainment Television; ESPN; Food Network; Fox News Channel; Hallmark Channel; Hallmark Movie Channel; Lifetime; New England Sports Network; Nickelodeon; QVC; Spike TV; Syfy; TBS Superstation; The Learning Channel; Trinity Broadcasting Network; truTV; Turner Network TV; USA Network; various Canadian stations; Weather Channel; WGN America.
Fee: $37.40 monthly.
Video-On-Demand: No
Internet Service
Operational: No.
Telephone Service
None
Miles of Plant: 12.0 (coaxial); None (fiber optic). Homes passed: 225. Total homes in franchised area: 400.
General Manager: Gordon Wark. Assistant Manager: Catherine Donovan. Chief Technician: Dana Williamson.
Ownership: NEPSK Inc.

DENMARK—Now served by SEBAGO (town), ME [ME0107]. ICA: ME0085.

EAGLE LAKE—Formerly served by Adelphia Communications. Now served by MADAWASKA, ME [ME0026]. ICA: ME0079.

EAST MACHIAS—Formerly served by Pine Tree Cablevision. No longer in operation. ICA: ME0017.

EASTON—Time Warner Cable. Now served by AROOSTOOK COUNTY, ME [ME0008]. ICA: ME0070.

FORT KENT—Formerly served by Adelphia Communications. Now served by MADAWASKA, ME [ME0026]. ICA: ME0031.

FRANKLIN (town)—Now served by BANGOR, ME [ME0002]. ICA: ME0058.

FRIENDSHIP (town)—Now served by AUGUSTA, ME [ME0004]. ICA: ME0056.

GLENBURN (town)—Now served by BANGOR, ME [ME0002]. ICA: ME0038.

GREENBUSH (town)—Argent Communications, 22 Central Sq, Bristol, NH 3222. Phone: 888-815-0610. Fax: 206-202-1415. Web Site: http://www.argentcommunications.com. Also serves Cardville & Olamon. ICA: ME0061.
TV Market Ranking: Below 100 (Cardville, GREENBUSH (TOWN), Olamon). Franchise award date: N.A. Franchise expiration date: N.A. Began: March 7, 1990.
Channel capacity: 42 (not 2-way capable). Channels available but not in use: 4.
Basic Service
Subscribers: 212.
Programming (received off-air): WABI-TV (CBS, CW) Bangor; WBGR-LP Bangor; WLBZ (NBC) Bangor; WMEB-TV (PBS) Orono; WVII-TV (ABC) Bangor.
Programming (via microwave): WSBK-TV (IND) Boston.
Programming (via satellite): C-SPAN; QVC; Trinity Broadcasting Network.
Current originations: Public Access.
Fee: $56.63 installation; $11.75 monthly.
Expanded Basic Service 1
Subscribers: 202.
Programming (via satellite): ABC Family Channel; AMC; Arts & Entertainment; CNN; Comcast Sports Net New England; Discovery Channel; Disney Channel; ESPN; ESPN 2; FX; Headline News; HGTV; History Channel; MTV; New England Sports Network; Nickelodeon; Spike TV; Syfy; TBS Superstation; The Learning Channel; Turner Network TV; USA Network; Versus; VH1; Weather Channel.
Fee: $13.34 monthly.
Digital Basic Service
Subscribers: N.A.
Programming (via satellite): BBC America; Bloomberg Television; Bravo; Discovery Digital Networks; ESPN Classic Sports; ESPNews; FitTV; Fox Movie Channel; Fox Soccer; G4; Golf Channel; GSN; Halogen Network; Music Choice; Nick Jr.; NickToons TV; Turner Classic Movies; WE tv.
Fee: $62.95 monthly.
Digital Expanded Basic Service
Subscribers: N.A.
Programming (via satellite): Independent Film Channel; Outdoor Channel.
Digital Pay Service 1
Pay Units: N.A.
Programming (via satellite): Cinemax (multiplexed); Encore (multiplexed); HBO (multiplexed); Showtime (multiplexed); Starz (multiplexed); The Movie Channel (multiplexed).
Fee: $12.95 monthly (each).
Video-On-Demand: No
Pay-Per-View
HITS (Headend In The Sky) (delivered digitally); Playboy TV (delivered digitally); Fresh (delivered digitally).
Internet Service
Operational: Yes.
Fee: $20.99-$49.99 monthly.
Telephone Service
Digital: Operational
Fee: $49.95 monthly
Miles of Plant: 32.0 (coaxial); None (fiber optic). Additional miles planned: 2.0 (coaxial). Homes passed: 520.
Manager: Andrew Bauer.; Shawn Bauer.
Ownership: Argent Communications LLC (MSO).

GREENE (town)—Time Warner Cable. Now served by AUGUSTA, ME [ME0004]. ICA: ME0021.

GREENVILLE—Moosehead Enterprises, PO Box 526, Greenville, ME 4441. Phone: 207-695-3337. Fax: 207-695-3571. ICA: ME0113.
TV Market Ranking: Outside TV Markets (GREENVILLE).
Channel capacity: N.A. Channels available but not in use: N.A.
Basic Service
Subscribers: 725.
Programming (received off-air): WABI-TV (CBS, CW) Bangor; WLBZ (NBC) Bangor; WMEB-TV (PBS) Orono; WSBK-TV (IND) Boston; WVII-TV (ABC) Bangor.
Programming (via satellite): ABC Family Channel; Arts & Entertainment; CNN; Discovery Channel; ESPN; ESPN 2; FX; Great American Country; Hallmark Channel; HGTV; History Channel; Lifetime; Outdoor Channel; QVC; TBS Superstation; Turner Classic Movies; Turner Network TV; USA Network; WGN America.
Fee: $20.50 monthly.
Pay Service 1
Pay Units: 80.
Programming (via satellite): HBO.
Fee: $12.00 monthly.
Video-On-Demand: No
Internet Service
Operational: No.
Telephone Service
None
President: Scott Richardson. Secretary: Sue Richardson.
Ownership: Moosehead Enterprises Inc. (MSO).

GUILFORD—Moosehead Enterprises, PO Box 526, Greenville, ME 4441. Phone: 207-695-3337. Fax: 207-695-3571. Also serves Sangerville. ICA: ME0057.
TV Market Ranking: Outside TV Markets (GUILFORD, Sangerville). Franchise award date: N.A. Franchise expiration date: N.A. Began: December 1, 1964.
Channel capacity: 21 (not 2-way capable). Channels available but not in use: 3.
Basic Service
Subscribers: 490.
Programming (received off-air): WABI-TV (CBS, CW) Bangor; WLBZ (NBC) Bangor; WMEB-TV (PBS) Orono; WVII-TV (ABC) Bangor; allband FM.
Programming (via microwave): WSBK-TV (IND) Boston.
Programming (via satellite): Arts & Entertainment; CNN; CW+; Discovery Channel; ESPN; ESPN 2; FX; Great American Country; Hallmark Channel; History Channel; Lifetime; QVC; TBS Superstation; Turner Classic Movies; Turner Network TV; USA Network; WGN America.
Fee: $20.00 installation; $20.50 monthly; $20.00 additional installation.
Pay Service 1
Pay Units: 60.
Programming (via satellite): HBO.
Fee: $10.00 installation; $12.00 monthly.
Video-On-Demand: No
Internet Service
Operational: No.
Telephone Service
None
Miles of Plant: 23.0 (coaxial); None (fiber optic).
President: Scott Richardson. Secretary: Sue Richardson.
Ownership: Moosehead Enterprises Inc. (MSO).

HANCOCK—Now served by BANGOR, ME [ME0002]. ICA: ME0035.

HERMON—Now served by BANGOR, ME [ME0002]. ICA: ME0030.

HOULTON—Polaris Cable Services, 34 Military St, Houlton, ME 4730. Phone: 207-532-2579. Fax: 207-532-4025. Web Site: http://www.polariscable.com. Also serves Hodgdon. ICA: ME0025.
TV Market Ranking: Outside TV Markets (Hodgdon, HOULTON). Franchise award date: N.A. Franchise expiration date: N.A. Began: December 18, 1954.
Channel capacity: 69 (operating 2-way). Channels available but not in use: 18.
Basic Service
Subscribers: 1,685.
Programming (received off-air): WAGM-TV (CBS) Presque Isle; WMEM-TV (PBS) Presque Isle; allband FM.
Programming (via microwave): WABI-TV (CBS, CW) Bangor; WLBZ (NBC) Bangor; WSBK-TV (IND) Boston; WVII-TV (ABC) Bangor.
Programming (via satellite): ABC Family Channel; Animal Planet; Arts & Entertainment; CNN; Country Music TV; C-SPAN; Discovery Channel; Do-It-Yourself; ESPN; Eternal Word TV Network; Fox News Channel; Headline News; History Channel; Home Shopping Network; Lifetime; MTV; National Geographic Channel; New England Sports Network; Nickelodeon; QVC; Spike TV; Syfy; TBS Superstation; The Learning Channel; Travel Channel; Trinity Broadcasting Network; truTV; Turner Classic Movies; Turner Network TV; TV Land; USA Network; VH1; Weather Channel.
Current originations: Educational Access; Public Access.
Fee: $55.00 installation; $41.36 monthly; $25.00 converter; $20.00 additional installation.
Digital Basic Service
Subscribers: 79.
Programming (via satellite): AmericanLife TV Network; BBC America; Bio; Bloomberg Television; Discovery Kids Channel; DMX Music; Encore; ESPN 2; ESPN Classic Sports; ESPNews; Fox Movie Channel; Fox Sports World; G4; GAS; Golf Channel; Great American Country; GSN; Halogen Network; HGTV; History Channel International; Lifetime Movie Network; Lime; MTV Networks Digital Suite; Nick Jr.; NickToons TV; Outdoor Channel; ShopNBC; Speed Channel; Style Network; Toon Disney; Versus; WE tv.
Fee: $14.21 monthly.

Pay Service 1
Pay Units: 53.
Programming (via satellite): HBO.
Fee: $10.00 installation; $14.38 monthly.
Pay Service 2
Pay Units: 12.
Programming (via satellite): Showtime.
Fee: $10.00 installation; $12.38 monthly.
Pay Service 3
Pay Units: 15.
Programming (via satellite): The Movie Channel.
Fee: $10.00 installation; $12.38 monthly.
Pay Service 4
Pay Units: 2.
Programming (via satellite): Cinemax.
Fee: $12.38 monthly.
Pay Service 5
Pay Units: 29.
Programming (via satellite): Starz.
Fee: $12.38 monthly.
Digital Pay Service 1
Pay Units: 130.
Programming (via satellite): Cinemax (multiplexed); Encore (multiplexed); HBO (multiplexed); Showtime (multiplexed); Starz (multiplexed); The Movie Channel (multiplexed).
Fee: $12.40 monthly (HBO, Showtime, or Starz).
Video-On-Demand: No
Pay-Per-View
iN DEMAND (delivered digitally); Hot Choice (delivered digitally); Playboy TV (delivered digitally); Fresh (delivered digitally); Shorteez (delivered digitally); ESPN Now (delivered digitally); Sports PPV (delivered digitally).
Internet Service
Operational: Yes. Began: January 1, 2002.
Subscribers: 328.
Broadband Service: Pioneer Wireless.
Fee: $19.95 monthly.
Telephone Service
None
Miles of Plant: 50.0 (coaxial); None (fiber optic). Homes passed: 2,500. Total homes in franchised area: 3,500.
Manager: Gordon Wark. Assistant Manager: Catherine Donavan. Technical Director: Steve Hardwick. Chief Technician: Dana Williamson. Customer Service: Bonnie Hunt.
Ownership: NEPSK Inc. (MSO).

HOWLAND—Polaris Cable Services, PO Box 610, 72 Main St, Houlton, ME 4730. Phone: 207-532-2579. Fax: 207-532-4025. Web Site: http://www.polariscable.com. Also serves Enfield, Lowell, Passadumkeag & West Enfield. ICA: ME0092.
TV Market Ranking: Below 100 (Enfield, HOWLAND, Lowell, Passadumkeag, West Enfield). Franchise award date: January 1, 1979. Franchise expiration date: N.A. Began: November 1, 1979.
Channel capacity: 42 (not 2-way capable). Channels available but not in use: None.
Basic Service
Subscribers: 646.
Programming (received off-air): WABI-TV (CBS, CW) Bangor; WLBZ (NBC) Bangor; WMEB-TV (PBS) Orono; WVII-TV (ABC) Bangor.
Programming (via microwave): WSBK-TV (IND) Boston.
Programming (via satellite): ABC Family Channel; Animal Planet; Arts & Entertainment; CNBC; CNN; Comedy Central; Country Music TV; C-SPAN; Discovery Channel; Disney Channel; Do-It-Yourself; E! Entertainment Television; ESPN; ESPN 2; Food Network; Fox Movie Channel; Fox News Channel; Hallmark Channel; Hallmark Movie Channel; Headline News; History Channel; Lifetime; MSNBC; MTV; New England Sports Network; Nickelodeon; QVC; Spike TV; Syfy; TBS Superstation; The Learning Channel; Travel Channel; truTV; Turner Network TV; USA Network; VH1; Weather Channel; WGN America; WPIX (CW, IND) New York.
Fee: $55.00 installation; $40.98 monthly; $25.00 converter.
Digital Basic Service
Subscribers: 94.
Programming (via satellite): BBC America; Bio; Bloomberg Television; Country Music TV; Discovery Health Channel; Discovery Home Channel; Discovery Kids Channel; Discovery Military Channel; Discovery Travel & Living (Viajar y Vivir); ESPN 2; ESPN Classic Sports; ESPNews; Fox Movie Channel; G4; GAS; Golf Channel; GSN; HGTV; History Channel International; Lifetime Movie Network; MTV2; National Geographic Channel; NickToons TV; Noggin; Outdoor Channel; Science Channel; Sleuth; Speed Channel; Style Network; Toon Disney; Trinity Broadcasting Network; Turner Classic Movies; VH1 Classic.
Fee: $14.15 monthly.
Digital Pay Service 1
Pay Units: N.A.
Programming (via satellite): Cinemax (multiplexed); Encore (multiplexed); HBO; Showtime (multiplexed); Starz (multiplexed); The Movie Channel (multiplexed).
Video-On-Demand: No
Internet Service
Operational: Yes.
Telephone Service
None
Miles of Plant: 11.0 (coaxial); None (fiber optic). Homes passed: 850. Total homes in franchised area: 1,200.
Manager: Gordon Wark. Assistant Manager: Catherine Donovan.
Ownership: NEPSK Inc.

ISLAND FALLS—Polaris Cable Services, 34 Military St, Houlton, ME 4730. Phone: 207-532-2579. Fax: 207-532-4025. Web Site: http://www.polariscable.com. ICA: ME0108.
TV Market Ranking: Outside TV Markets (ISLAND FALLS). Franchise award date: January 1, 1978. Franchise expiration date: N.A. Began: N.A.
Channel capacity: 42 (not 2-way capable). Channels available but not in use: 12.
Basic Service
Subscribers: 124.
Programming (received off-air): WABI-TV (CBS, CW) Bangor; WAGM-TV (CBS) Presque Isle; WLBZ (NBC) Bangor; WMEM-TV (PBS) Presque Isle; WVII-TV (ABC) Bangor.
Programming (via satellite): ABC Family Channel; Animal Planet; CNN; Country Music TV; C-SPAN; Discovery Channel; Disney Channel; E! Entertainment Television; ESPN; ESPN 2; Food Network; Hallmark Channel; Headline News; History Channel; Lifetime; MTV; New England Sports Network; Nickelodeon; QVC; Spike TV; Syfy; TBS Superstation; The Learning Channel; Travel Channel; Trinity Broadcasting Network; Turner Classic Movies; Turner Network TV; TV Land; USA Network; various Canadian stations; VH1; Weather Channel.
Fee: $55.00 installation; $40.77 monthly; $25.00 converter.
Pay Service 1
Pay Units: 9.
Programming (via satellite): Cinemax; HBO.
Fee: $14.50 monthly (each).
Video-On-Demand: No
Internet Service
Operational: No.
Telephone Service
None
Miles of Plant: 15.0 (coaxial); None (fiber optic). Homes passed: 320. Total homes in franchised area: 600.
Manager: Gordon Wark. Assistant Manager: Catherine Donovan.
Ownership: NEPSK Inc. (MSO).

JACKMAN—Moosehead Enterprises, PO Box 526, Greenville, ME 4441. Phone: 207-695-3337. Fax: 207-695-3571. Also serves Moose River. ICA: ME0065.
TV Market Ranking: Outside TV Markets (JACKMAN, Moose River). Franchise award date: January 1, 1965. Franchise expiration date: N.A. Began: January 1, 1968.
Channel capacity: 21 (not 2-way capable). Channels available but not in use: 3.
Basic Service
Subscribers: 414.
Programming (received off-air): WABI-TV (CBS, CW) Bangor; WCBB (PBS) Augusta; WMTW (ABC) Poland Spring; allband FM.
Programming (via microwave): WSBK-TV (IND) Boston.
Programming (via satellite): ESPN; TBS Superstation; USA Network; WGN America.
Fee: $20.00 installation; $20.50 monthly; $20.00 additional installation.
Pay Service 1
Pay Units: 44.
Programming (via satellite): HBO.
Fee: $10.00 installation; $12.00 monthly.
Video-On-Demand: No
Internet Service
Operational: No.
Telephone Service
None
Miles of Plant: 23.0 (coaxial); None (fiber optic). Homes passed: 450. Total homes in franchised area: 500.
President: Scott Richardson. Manager & Chief Technician: Earl Richardson. Secretary: Sue Richardson.
Ownership: Moosehead Enterprises Inc. (MSO).

JAY—Now served by AUGUSTA, ME [ME0004]. ICA: ME0093.

JONESPORT—Time Warner Cable, 118 Johnston Rd, Portland, ME 4102. Phones: 207-253-2385; 207-253-2200. Fax: 207-253-2404. Web Site: http://www.timewarnercable.com. Also serves Beals. ICA: ME0109.
TV Market Ranking: Outside TV Markets (Beals, JONESPORT). Franchise award date: N.A. Franchise expiration date: N.A. Began: N.A.
Channel capacity: N.A. Channels available but not in use: N.A.
Basic Service
Subscribers: 360.
Programming (received off-air): WABI-TV (CBS, CW) Bangor; WLBZ (NBC) Bangor; WMEB-TV (PBS) Orono; WVII-TV (ABC) Bangor.
Programming (via satellite): ABC Family Channel; Animal Planet; Arts & Entertainment; Cartoon Network; CNN; Country Music TV; C-SPAN; Discovery Channel; Disney Channel; ESPN; G4; Headline News; History Channel; Lifetime; MTV; Nickelodeon; Outdoor Channel; QVC; Spike TV; Syfy; TBS Superstation; The Learning Channel; Travel Channel; Trinity Broadcasting Network; Turner Classic Movies; Turner Network TV; USA Network; VH1; Weather Channel; WGN America.
Fee: $56.63 installation; $34.90 monthly.
Pay Service 1
Pay Units: 20.
Programming (via satellite): Cinemax; HBO; Showtime; The Movie Channel.
Fee: $11.95 monthly (Cinemax or HBO).
Video-On-Demand: No
Internet Service
Operational: Yes.
Broadband Service: RoadRunner.
Fee: $24.95 monthly.
Telephone Service
Digital: Operational
Fee: $24.99 monthly
President: Keith Burkley. Vice President, Marketing & Sales: David Leopold. Vice President, Engineering: Scott Ducott. Vice President, Government & Public Affairs: Melinda Poore.
Ownership: Time Warner Cable (MSO).

KENDUSKEAG—Now served by BANGOR, ME [ME0002]. ICA: ME0040.

KENNEBUNK—Time Warner Cable. Now served by SEBAGO (town), ME [ME0107]. ICA: ME0014.

LEWISTON—Time Warner Cable. Now served by AUGUSTA, ME [ME0004]. ICA: ME0003.

LINCOLN—Time Warner Cable, 118 Johnston Rd, Portland, ME 4102. Phones: 207-253-2385; 207-253-2200. Fax: 207-253-2404. Web Site: http://www.timewarnercable.com/NewEngland. ICA: ME0117.
TV Market Ranking: Below 100 (LINCOLN).
Channel capacity: N.A. Channels available but not in use: N.A.
Basic Service
Subscribers: N.A.
Programming (received off-air): WABI-TV (CBS, CW) Bangor; WBGR-LP Bangor; WLBZ (NBC) Bangor; WMEB-TV (PBS) Orono; WVII-TV (ABC) Bangor.
Programming (via satellite): C-SPAN; C-SPAN 2; Fox Sports Net; Home Shopping Network; MyNetworkTV Inc.; QVC; TV Guide Network.
Fee: $56.63 installation.
Expanded Basic Service 1
Subscribers: N.A.
Programming (via satellite): ABC Family Channel; American Movie Classics; Animal Planet; Arts & Entertainment; Bravo; Cartoon Network; CNBC; CNN; Comcast SportsNet Philly; Comedy Central; Country Music TV; Discovery Channel; Disney Channel; E! Entertainment Television; ESPN; ESPN 2; Food Network; Fox News Channel; FX; Great American Country; Hallmark Channel; Headline News; HGTV; History Channel; INSP; Lifetime; MSNBC; MTV; New England Sports Network; Nickelodeon; ShopNBC; Spike TV; Syfy; TBS Superstation; The Learning Channel; Travel Channel; truTV; Turner Network TV; TV Land; USA Network; VH1; Weather Channel.
Digital Basic Service
Subscribers: N.A.
Programming (via satellite): Arts & Entertainment HD; BBC America; Bio; Bloomberg Television; CNN HD; Current; Discovery Digital Networks; Discovery HD Theater; ESPN 2 HD; ESPN Classic Sports; ESPN HD; ESPNews; FitTV; Food Network HD;

Fox Business Channel; Fox College Sports Atlantic; Fox College Sports Central; Fox College Sports Pacific; Fox Movie Channel; Fox Reality Channel; Fox Soccer; Fuse; G4; Golf Channel; Gospel Music Channel; GSN; Halogen Network; HGTV HD; History Channel HD; History Channel International; Independent Film Channel; Lifetime Movie Network; Lifetime Movie Network HD; LOGO; Military History Channel; MTV Networks Digital Suite; Music Choice; National Geographic Channel; New England Sports Network; Nick Jr.; Nick Too; NickToons TV; Outdoor Channel; Palladia; Speed Channel; Style Network; TBS in HD; TeenNick; The Word Network; Toon Disney; Trinity Broadcasting Network; Turner Classic Movies; Turner Network TV HD; Versus; Versus HD; WE tv.
Fee: $7.50 monthly.

Digital Pay Service 1
Pay Units: N.A.
Programming (via satellite): Cinemax (multiplexed); Encore (multiplexed); HBO (multiplexed); Showtime (multiplexed); Starz (multiplexed); The Movie Channel (multiplexed).

Video-On-Demand: No

Pay-Per-View
iN DEMAND (delivered digitally); Playboy TV (delivered digitally); Club Jenna (delivered digitally); Fresh (delivered digitally).

Internet Service
Operational: Yes.
Broadband Service: EarthLink, Road Runner.
Fee: $38.45 installation; $44.95 monthly.

Telephone Service
None

President: Keith Burkley. Vice President, Marketing & Sales: David Leopold. Vice President, Engineering: Scott Ducott. Vice President, Government & Public Affairs: Melinda Poore.
Ownership: Time Warner Cable (MSO).

LINCOLNVILLE—Lincolnville Communications, PO Box 200, Lincolnville Center, ME 04850-0200. Phones: 800-553-4303; 207-763-9950; 207-763-9900. Fax: 207-763-3028. Also serves Hope (town). ICA: ME0094.
TV Market Ranking: Below 100 (Hope (town)); Outside TV Markets (LINCOLNVILLE). Franchise award date: July 5, 1988. Franchise expiration date: N.A. Began: October 1, 1989.
Channel capacity: 52 (not 2-way capable). Channels available but not in use: N.A.

Basic Service
Subscribers: 896.
Programming (received off-air): WABI-TV (CBS, CW) Bangor; WFVX-LP Bangor; WGME-TV (CBS) Portland; WLBZ (NBC) Bangor; WMEB-TV (PBS) Orono; WPME (MNT) Lewiston; WPXT (CW) Portland; WVII-TV (ABC) Bangor.
Programming (via satellite): ABC Family Channel; American Movie Classics; Animal Planet; Arts & Entertainment; CNBC; CNN; Comcast Sports Net New England; C-SPAN; C-SPAN 2; Discovery Channel; Disney Channel; Do-It-Yourself; ESPN; ESPN 2; Fox News Channel; Great American Country; Headline News; History Channel; Lifetime; MTV; National Geographic Channel; New England Sports Network; Nickelodeon; QVC; Syfy; TBS Superstation; The Learning Channel; Travel Channel; Turner Classic Movies; Turner Network TV; TV Guide Network; USA Network; VH1; Weather Channel.
Current originations: Government Access.
Fee: $35.00 installation; $39.95 monthly.

Digital Basic Service
Subscribers: 215.
Programming (via satellite): BBC America; Bio; Bloomberg Television; CMT Pure Country; Discovery Health Channel; Discovery Home Channel; Discovery Kids Channel; Discovery Times Channel; DMX Music; FitTV; Fox Movie Channel; G4; Golf Channel; GSN; History Channel International; Lifetime Movie Network; Military Channel; MTV2; Nick Jr.; Outdoor Channel; Science Channel; Sleuth; Speed Channel; TeenNick; Toon Disney; Versus; VH1 Classic; WE tv.
Fee: $14.00 monthly.

Digital Pay Service 1
Pay Units: 4.
Fee: $10.00 monthly.

Digital Pay Service 2
Pay Units: 61.
Programming (via satellite): Cinemax (multiplexed); HBO (multiplexed).
Fee: $10.00 monthly.

Digital Pay Service 3
Pay Units: 25.
Programming (via satellite): Encore (multiplexed); Starz (multiplexed).
Fee: $9.00 monthly.

Digital Pay Service 4
Pay Units: 21.
Programming (via satellite): Showtime (multiplexed); The Movie Channel (multiplexed).
Fee: $10.00 monthly.

Video-On-Demand: No

Internet Service
Operational: No.

Telephone Service
None

Miles of Plant: 93.0 (coaxial); None (fiber optic).
Manager: Shirley Manning. Chief Technician: Dave Culbertson.
Ownership: Lincolnville Communications Inc.

LOVELL (town)—Formerly served by Adelphia Communications. Now served by CONWAY, NH [NH0038]. ICA: ME0066.

LUBEC—Formerly served by Pine Tree Cablevision. No longer in operation. ICA: ME0110.

MACHIAS—Formerly served by Pine Tree Cablevision. No longer in operation. ICA: ME0095.

MADAWASKA—Time Warner Cable, 83 Anthony Ave, Augusta, ME 04330-7880. Phones: 877-596-5366; 207-623-3685. Fax: 207-623-3407. Web Site: http://www.timewarnercable.com/NewEngland. Also serves Allagash, Allagash (town), Eagle Lake, Fort Kent, Frenchville, Grand Isle, Hamlin (town), Plantation St. John, St. Agatha, St. Francis, St. Francis Twp., St. John, Van Buren & Wallagrass. ICA: ME0026.
TV Market Ranking: Below 100 (Eagle Lake, Hamlin (town), Van Buren); Outside TV Markets (Allagash, Allagash (town), Fort Kent, Frenchville, Grand Isle, MADAWASKA, Plantation St. John, St. Agatha, St. Francis, St. Francis Twp., St. John, Wallagrass). Franchise award date: December 31, 1986. Franchise expiration date: N.A. Began: June 1, 1957.
Channel capacity: 39 (operating 2-way). Channels available but not in use: None.

Basic Service
Subscribers: 3,324.
Programming (received off-air): WAGM-TV (CBS) Presque Isle; WMEM-TV (PBS) Presque Isle; 6 FMs.
Programming (via microwave): WLBZ (NBC) Bangor; WSBK-TV (IND) Boston; WVII-TV (ABC) Bangor.
Programming (via satellite): CW+; Eternal Word TV Network; Home Shopping Network; QVC; TV Guide Network; WGN America.
Fee: $33.75 installation; $22.95 monthly.

Expanded Basic Service 1
Subscribers: N.A.
Programming (via satellite): ABC Family Channel; AmericanLife TV Network; Animal Planet; Arts & Entertainment; Cartoon Network; CNBC; CNN; Comcast Sports Net New England; Comedy Central; Country Music TV; Discovery Channel; Disney Channel; E! Entertainment Television; ESPN; ESPN 2; Food Network; Fox News Channel; FX; Headline News; HGTV; History Channel; Lifetime; MSNBC; MTV; New England Sports Network; Nickelodeon; Spike TV; Syfy; TBS Superstation; The Learning Channel; Travel Channel; Turner Network TV; TV Land; USA Network; Versus; VH1; Weather Channel.

Digital Basic Service
Subscribers: N.A.
Programming (via satellite): BBC America; Bio; Black Family Channel; Bloomberg Television; Discovery Digital Networks; Do-It-Yourself; ESPN Classic Sports; ESPNews; Fox College Sports (multiplexed); Fox Movie Channel; Fox Soccer; Fuse; G4; GAS; Golf Channel; Great American Country; GSN; Hallmark Channel; Halogen Network; History Channel International; Independent Film Channel; Lifetime Movie Network; MTV Networks Digital Suite; Music Choice; National Geographic Channel; Nick Jr.; Nick Too; NickToons TV; Outdoor Channel; SoapNet; Speed Channel; Style Network; Sundance Channel; The Word Network; Toon Disney; Trinity Broadcasting Network; Turner Classic Movies; WE tv.
Fee: $12.99 monthly.

Digital Pay Service 1
Pay Units: N.A.
Programming (via satellite): Cinemax (multiplexed); Encore (multiplexed); Flix (multiplexed); HBO (multiplexed); Showtime (multiplexed); Starz (multiplexed); The Movie Channel (multiplexed).
Fee: $12.95 monthly (each).

Video-On-Demand: No

Pay-Per-View
Movies (delivered digitally); Fresh (delivered digitally); Playboy TV (delivered digitally).

Internet Service
Operational: Yes.
Broadband Service: Road Runner.
Fee: $99.00 installation; $42.95 monthly; $3.00 modem lease.

Telephone Service
None

Miles of Plant: 85.0 (coaxial); None (fiber optic). Homes passed: 3,871.
General Manager: Eileen Martin. Chief Technician: Rockie Marsh. Marketing Director: Shanna Allen.
City fee: None.
Ownership: Time Warner Cable (MSO).

MADISON—Bee Line Cable TV, PO Box 431, Skowhegan, ME 4976. Phone: 207-474-2727. Fax: 207-474-0966. Also serves Anson, Farmington, Industry, Skowhegan & Wilton. ICA: ME0018.
TV Market Ranking: Below 100 (Anson, Farmington, Industry, MADISON, Skowhegan, Wilton). Franchise award date: N.A. Franchise expiration date: N.A. Began: April 1, 1968.
Channel capacity: 53 (operating 2-way). Channels available but not in use: 5.

Basic Service
Subscribers: 6,624.
Programming (received off-air): WABI-TV (CBS, CW) Bangor; WCBB (PBS) Augusta; WCSH (NBC) Portland; WGME-TV (CBS) Portland; WLBZ (NBC) Bangor; WMTW (ABC) Poland Spring; WPME (MNT) Lewiston; WPXT (CW) Portland; WVII-TV (ABC) Bangor; 6 FMs.
Programming (via satellite): ABC Family Channel; Arts & Entertainment; CNN; C-SPAN; Discovery Channel; Disney Channel; ESPN; Eternal Word TV Network; Headline News; History Channel; Home Shopping Network; Lifetime; MTV; New England Sports Network; Nickelodeon; Spike TV; TBS Superstation; Trinity Broadcasting Network; Turner Network TV; USA Network; VH1.
Fee: $20.00 installation; $45.35 monthly.

Digital Basic Service
Subscribers: 501.
Programming (via satellite): AmericanLife TV Network; Bio; Bloomberg Television; Bravo; DMX Music; ESPN Classic Sports; FitTV; Fox College Sports Atlantic; Fox College Sports Central; Fox College Sports Pacific; Fox Movie Channel; Golf Channel; GSN; History Channel International; Independent Film Channel; National Geographic Channel; Outdoor Channel; Speed Channel; Style Network; WE tv.
Fee: $54.37 monthly.

Pay Service 1
Pay Units: 346.
Programming (via satellite): HBO.
Fee: $11.00 monthly.

Pay Service 2
Pay Units: N.A.
Programming (via satellite): Cinemax; Encore; Showtime; Starz; The Movie Channel.

Digital Pay Service 1
Pay Units: 800.
Programming (via satellite): Cinemax (multiplexed); Encore (multiplexed); HBO (multiplexed); Showtime (multiplexed); Starz (multiplexed); The Movie Channel (multiplexed).
Fee: $8.00 monthly (Cinemax or TMC); $11 monthly (HBO, or Starz & Encore).

Video-On-Demand: No

Pay-Per-View
Playboy TV (delivered digitally); Fresh (delivered digitally); iN DEMAND (delivered digitally); Hot Choice (delivered digitally).
Internet Service
Operational: Yes.
Subscribers: 1,715.
Fee: $34.95 monthly.
Telephone Service
Digital: Operational
Fee: $34.95 monthly
Miles of Plant: 300.0 (coaxial); None (fiber optic).
Manager & Chief Technician: George Allen. Marketing Director: Edythe May.
Franchise fee: None.
Ownership: Bee Line Inc. (MSO).

MARS HILL—Time Warner Cable. Now served by AROOSTOOK COUNTY, ME [ME0008]. ICA: ME0096.

MATTAWAMKEAG (town)—Mattawamkeag Cablevision, PO Box 38, Houlton, ME 04730-0038. Phones: 800-532-4451 (Local only); 207-532-4451. Also serves Mattawamkeag & Winn. ICA: ME0071.
TV Market Ranking: Outside TV Markets (Mattawamkeag, MATTAWAMKEAG (TOWN), Winn). Franchise award date: January 1, 1987. Franchise expiration date: N.A. Began: September 1, 1989.
Channel capacity: 60 (not 2-way capable). Channels available but not in use: N.A.
Basic Service
Subscribers: 275.
Programming (received off-air): WABI-TV (CBS, CW) Bangor; WBGR-LP Bangor; WLBZ (NBC) Bangor; WMEB-TV (PBS) Orono; WVII-TV (ABC) Bangor.
Programming (via satellite): ABC Family Channel; AMC; CNN; Comedy Central; Discovery Channel; ESPN; Great American Country; Lifetime; Nickelodeon; QVC; Spike TV; TBS Superstation; The Learning Channel; Trinity Broadcasting Network; Turner Network TV; TV Land; USA Network; Weather Channel; WGN America; WPIX (CW, IND) New York; WSBK-TV (IND) Boston.
Fee: $25.00 installation; $29.00 monthly; $18.00 converter.
Pay Service 1
Pay Units: 30.
Programming (via satellite): HBO.
Fee: $15.00 installation; $10.95 monthly.
Video-On-Demand: No
Internet Service
Operational: No.
Telephone Service
None
Miles of Plant: 20.0 (coaxial); None (fiber optic). Homes passed: 450. Total homes in franchised area: 450.
Manager: Donald Dee.
Ownership: Donald G. Dee.

MEDWAY—Polaris Cable Services, 34 Military St, Houlton, ME 4730. Phone: 207-532-2579. Fax: 207-532-4025. Web Site: http://www.polariscable.com. ICA: ME0097.
TV Market Ranking: Outside TV Markets (MEDWAY). Franchise award date: January 1, 1978. Franchise expiration date: N.A. Began: November 1, 1979.
Channel capacity: 42 (2-way capable). Channels available but not in use: 13.
Basic Service
Subscribers: 275.
Programming (received off-air): WABI-TV (CBS, CW) Bangor; WAGM-TV (CBS) Presque Isle; WFVX-LP Bangor; WLBZ (NBC) Bangor; WMEM-TV (PBS) Presque Isle; WVII-TV (ABC) Bangor.
Programming (via satellite): ABC Family Channel; Animal Planet; Arts & Entertainment; CNN; Country Music TV; CW+; Discovery Channel; Disney Channel; Do-It-Yourself; E! Entertainment Television; ESPN; ESPN 2; Eternal Word TV Network; Fox News Channel; Headline News; History Channel; Lifetime; MTV; New England Sports Network; Nickelodeon; Spike TV; Syfy; TBS Superstation; The Learning Channel; Travel Channel; Trinity Broadcasting Network; truTV; Turner Network TV; TV Land; USA Network; Weather Channel; WGN America.
Fee: $55.00 installation; $40.98 monthly; $25.00 converter.
Pay Service 1
Pay Units: 9.
Programming (via satellite): HBO.
Fee: $35.00 installation; $14.50 monthly.
Pay Service 2
Pay Units: 3.
Programming (via satellite): Showtime.
Fee: $13.50 monthly.
Video-On-Demand: No
Internet Service
Operational: Yes.
Subscribers: 35.
Fee: $19.95 monthly.
Telephone Service
None
Miles of Plant: 18.0 (coaxial); None (fiber optic). Homes passed: 451. Total homes in franchised area: 560.
Manager: Gordon Wark. Assistant Manager: Catherine Donovan.
Ownership: NEPSK Inc. (MSO).

MILLINOCKET—Bee Line Cable TV, PO Box 431, Skowhegan, ME 4976. Phone: 207-723-4455. Fax: 207-723-2074. Also serves East Millinocket. ICA: ME0015.
TV Market Ranking: Outside TV Markets (East Millinocket, MILLINOCKET). Franchise award date: N.A. Franchise expiration date: N.A. Began: March 4, 1966.
Channel capacity: 53 (not 2-way capable). Channels available but not in use: N.A.
Basic Service
Subscribers: 2,400.
Programming (received off-air): CW11 New York; WABI-TV (CBS, CW) Bangor; WBGR-LP Bangor; WLBZ (NBC) Bangor; WMEB-TV (PBS) Orono; WVII-TV (ABC) Bangor; allband FM.
Programming (via satellite): ABC Family Channel; AMC; Arts & Entertainment; CNBC; CNN; Comcast Sports Net New England; Comedy Central; C-SPAN; Discovery Channel; Disney Channel; ESPN; ESPN 2; Eternal Word TV Network; FX; Great American Country; Headline News; HGTV; History Channel; Home Shopping Network; Lifetime; MTV; New England Sports Network; Nickelodeon; QVC; Spike TV; Syfy; TBS Superstation; The Learning Channel; Toon Disney; Trinity Broadcasting Network; Turner Classic Movies; Turner Network TV; TV Guide Network; TV Land; USA Network; VH1; Weather Channel.
Fee: $20.00 installation; $45.35 monthly.
Digital Basic Service
Subscribers: 400.
Programming (via satellite): AmericanLife TV Network; Bio; Bloomberg Television; Bravo; ESPN Classic Sports; FitTV; Fox College Sports Atlantic; Fox College Sports Central; Fox College Sports Pacific; Fox Movie Channel; Golf Channel; GSN; History Channel International; Independent Film Channel; National Geographic Channel; Outdoor Channel; Speed Channel; Style Network; WE tv.
Fee: $45.63 monthly.
Pay Service 1
Pay Units: N.A.
Programming (via satellite): Cinemax; HBO; The Movie Channel.
Digital Pay Service 1
Pay Units: N.A.
Programming (via satellite): Cinemax (multiplexed); Encore (multiplexed); HBO (multiplexed); Showtime (multiplexed); Starz (multiplexed); The Movie Channel (multiplexed).
Video-On-Demand: No
Pay-Per-View
Hot Choice (delivered digitally); iN DEMAND (delivered digitally); Sports PPV (delivered digitally); Playboy TV (delivered digitally); Fresh (delivered digitally).
Internet Service
Operational: Yes, Dial-up only.
Subscribers: 150.
Fee: $34.95 monthly.
Telephone Service
Digital: Operational
Fee: $34.95 monthly
Miles of Plant: 37.0 (coaxial); None (fiber optic). Homes passed: 4,650.
General Manager & Chief Technician: George Allen. Marketing Director: Edythe May.
Ownership: Bee Line Inc. (MSO).

MILO—Time Warner Cable, 83 Anthony Ave, Augusta, ME 04330-7880. Phones: 877-596-5366; 207-623-3685 (Augusta office); 888-683-1000. Fax: 207-623-3407. Web Site: http://www.timewarnercable.com. Also serves Brownville. ICA: ME0036.
TV Market Ranking: Below 100 (MILO); Outside TV Markets (Brownville). Franchise award date: January 27, 1982. Franchise expiration date: N.A. Began: August 1, 1982.
Channel capacity: N.A. Channels available but not in use: N.A.
Basic Service
Subscribers: 876.
Programming (received off-air): WABI-TV (CBS, CW) Bangor; WLBZ (NBC) Bangor; WMEB-TV (PBS) Orono; WVII-TV (ABC) Bangor.
Programming (via microwave): WSBK-TV (IND) Boston.
Programming (via satellite): C-SPAN; QVC; WGN America.
Fee: $42.43 installation; $21.95 monthly.
Expanded Basic Service 1
Subscribers: N.A.
Programming (via satellite): ABC Family Channel; AMC; AmericanLife TV Network; Animal Planet; Arts & Entertainment; Cartoon Network; CNN; Comcast Sports Net New England; Comedy Central; Country Music TV; C-SPAN 2; Discovery Channel; Disney Channel; E! Entertainment Television; ESPN; ESPN 2; Flix; Food Network; Fox News Channel; FX; Headline News; HGTV; History Channel; Home Shopping Network; Lifetime; MSNBC; MTV; New England Sports Network; Nickelodeon; Spike TV; Syfy; TBS Superstation; The Learning Channel; Travel Channel; Trinity Broadcasting Network; truTV; Turner Network TV; TV Land; USA Network; VH1; Weather Channel.
Fee: $46.54 monthly.
Digital Basic Service
Subscribers: N.A.
Programming (via satellite): BBC America; Black Family Channel; Bloomberg Television; Discovery Digital Networks; ESPN Classic Sports; ESPNews; FitTV; Fox Movie Channel; Fox Soccer; Fuse; G4; GAS; Golf Channel; Great American Country; GSN; Halogen Network; Life Network; MTV Networks Digital Suite; Music Choice; National Geographic Channel; Nick Jr.; Nick Too; NickToons TV; Outdoor Channel; Science Television; Speed Channel; Style Network; The Word Network; Toon Disney; Trinity Broadcasting Network; Turner Classic Movies; WE tv.
Digital Expanded Basic Service
Subscribers: N.A.
Programming (via satellite): Bio; Fox College Sports (multiplexed); History Channel International; Independent Film Channel; Versus.
Pay Service 1
Pay Units: N.A.
Programming (via satellite): Cinemax; Showtime.
Digital Pay Service 1
Pay Units: N.A.
Programming (via satellite): Cinemax (multiplexed); Encore (multiplexed); HBO (multiplexed); Showtime (multiplexed); Starz (multiplexed); The Movie Channel (multiplexed).
Fee: $12.95 monthly (each).
Pay-Per-View
Fresh (delivered digitally); Playboy TV (delivered digitally); Movies (delivered digitally).
Internet Service
Operational: Yes.
Broadband Service: Road Runner.
Fee: $99.00 installation; $42.95 monthly; $3.00 modem lease.
Telephone Service
None
Miles of Plant: 33.0 (coaxial); None (fiber optic). Homes passed: 1,490.
General Manager: Eileen Martin. Marketing Director: Shanna Allen. Chief Technician: Rockie Marsh.
Ownership: Time Warner Cable (MSO).

MONSON—Moosehead Enterprises, PO Box 526, Greenville, ME 4441. Phone: 207-695-3337. Fax: 207-695-3571. ICA: ME0114.
TV Market Ranking: Outside TV Markets (MONSON).
Channel capacity: N.A. Channels available but not in use: N.A.
Basic Service
Subscribers: 115.
Programming (received off-air): WABI-TV (CBS, CW) Bangor; WLBZ (NBC) Bangor; WMEB-TV (PBS) Orono; WSBK-TV (IND) Boston; WVII-TV (ABC) Bangor.
Programming (via satellite): ABC Family Channel; Arts & Entertainment; CNN; CW+; Discovery Channel; ESPN; Great American Country; Hallmark Channel; QVC; TBS Superstation; Turner Classic Movies; Turner Network TV; USA Network; WGN America.
Fee: $19.50 monthly.
Pay Service 1
Pay Units: 15.
Programming (via satellite): HBO.
Fee: $12.00 monthly.
Video-On-Demand: No
Internet Service
Operational: No.
Telephone Service
None
President: Scott Richardson. Secretary: Sue Richardson.
Ownership: Moosehead Enterprises Inc. (MSO).

MONTICELLO (town)—Polaris Cable Services, 34 Military St, Houlton, ME 4730. Phone: 207-532-2579. Fax: 207-532-4025. Web Site: http://www.polariscable.com. Also serves Aroostook County (portions), Bridgewater (town), Littleton (town) & Monticello. ICA: ME0049.

TV Market Ranking: Below 100 (Aroostook County (portions), Bridgewater (town), Littleton (town), Monticello, MONTICELLO (TOWN)); Outside TV Markets (Aroostook County (portions)). Franchise award date: January 1, 1984. Franchise expiration date: N.A. Began: February 1, 1990.

Channel capacity: 42 (operating 2-way). Channels available but not in use: N.A.

Basic Service

Subscribers: 250.

Programming (received off-air): WAGM-TV (CBS) Presque Isle; WLBZ (NBC) Bangor; WMEM-TV (PBS) Presque Isle; WPFO (FOX) Waterville.

Programming (via satellite): ABC Family Channel; AMC; Animal Planet; Arts & Entertainment; Bravo; CNN; Comedy Central; Country Music TV; Discovery Channel; Disney Channel; Do-It-Yourself; E! Entertainment Television; ESPN; ESPN 2; Fox News Channel; Hallmark Channel; Hallmark Movie Channel; Headline News; History Channel; Lifetime; National Geographic Channel; New England Sports Network; Nickelodeon; QVC; Spike TV; Syfy; TBS Superstation; Travel Channel; Trinity Broadcasting Network; truTV; Turner Network TV; USA Network; various Canadian stations; WABC-TV (ABC) New York; Weather Channel; WGN America; WPIX (CW, IND) New York.

Fee: $55.00 installation; $41.14 monthly; $25.00 converter.

Pay Service 1

Pay Units: 8.

Programming (via satellite): HBO.

Fee: $35.00 installation; $14.50 monthly.

Video-On-Demand: No

Internet Service

Operational: Yes.

Subscribers: 73.

Fee: $19.95 monthly.

Telephone Service

None

Miles of Plant: 35.0 (coaxial); None (fiber optic). Homes passed: 450. Total homes in franchised area: 800.

Manager: Gordon Wark. Assistant Manager: Catherine Donovan.

Ownership: NEPSK Inc. (MSO).

MOUNT DESERT (town)—Formerly served by Adelphia Communications. Now served by BANGOR, ME [ME0002]. ICA: ME0069.

NEW SHARON (town)—Argent Communications, 22 Central Sq, Bristol, NH 3222. Phone: 888-815-0610. Fax: 206-202-1415. Web Site: http://www.argentcommunications.com. Also serves Chesterville. ICA: ME0055.

TV Market Ranking: Below 100 (Chesterville, NEW SHARON (TOWN)). Franchise award date: October 1, 1988. Franchise expiration date: N.A. Began: October 5, 1989.

Channel capacity: 42 (not 2-way capable). Channels available but not in use: 4.

Basic Service

Subscribers: 360.

Programming (received off-air): WCBB (PBS) Augusta; WCSH (NBC) Portland; WGME-TV (CBS) Portland; WMTW (ABC) Poland Spring; WPFO (FOX) Waterville; WPME (MNT) Lewiston; WPXT (CW) Portland.

Programming (via satellite): C-SPAN; C-SPAN 2; ION Television; QVC.

Current originations: Public Access.

Fee: $56.63 installation; $33.93 monthly.

Expanded Basic Service 1

Subscribers: N.A.

Programming (via satellite): ABC Family Channel; AMC; Arts & Entertainment; CNN; Comcast Sports Net New England; Discovery Channel; Disney Channel; ESPN; ESPN 2; FX; Headline News; HGTV; History Channel; Lifetime; MTV; New England Sports Network; Nickelodeon; Spike TV; Syfy; TBS Superstation; The Learning Channel; Turner Network TV; USA Network; VH1; Weather Channel.

Digital Basic Service

Subscribers: N.A.

Programming (via satellite): BBC America; Bloomberg Television; Bravo; Discovery Digital Networks; ESPN Classic Sports; ESPNews; FitTV; Fox Movie Channel; Fox Sports World; G4; Golf Channel; GSN; Halogen Network; Independent Film Channel; Outdoor Channel; Trinity Broadcasting Network; Versus; WE tv.

Fee: $62.95 monthly.

Digital Expanded Basic Service

Subscribers: N.A.

Programming (via satellite): Music Choice; Nick Jr.; NickToons TV.

Digital Pay Service 1

Pay Units: N.A.

Programming (via satellite): Cinemax (multiplexed); Encore (multiplexed); HBO (multiplexed); Showtime (multiplexed); Starz (multiplexed); The Movie Channel (multiplexed).

Fee: $12.95 monthly (each).

Video-On-Demand: No

Pay-Per-View

Fresh (delivered digitally); Playboy TV (delivered digitally).

Internet Service

Operational: Yes.

Fee: $20.99-$49.99 monthly.

Telephone Service

Digital: Operational

Fee: $49.95 monthly

Miles of Plant: 44.0 (coaxial); None (fiber optic). Homes passed: 600.

Manager: Andrew Bauer.; Shawn Bauer.

Ownership: Argent Communications LLC (MSO).

NEWCASTLE—Time Warner Cable. Now served by AUGUSTA, ME [ME0004]. ICA: ME0016.

NORTH ANSON—Time Warner Cable, 118 Johnston Rd, Portland, ME 4102. Phone: 207-253-2200. Fax: 207-253-2404. Web Site: http://www.timewarnercable.com/NewEngland. Also serves Avon, Carrabassett Valley, Coplin, Embden, Eustis, Kingfield, New Portland, New Vineyard, Norridgewock, North New Portland, Phillips, Smithfield (town), Solon, Stratton, Strong & Wyman. ICA: ME0062.

TV Market Ranking: Below 100 (Avon, Embden, New Portland, New Vineyard, Norridgewock, NORTH ANSON, North New Portland, Smithfield (town), Solon, Strong, Wyman); Outside TV Markets (Carrabassett Valley, Coplin, Eustis, Kingfield, Phillips, Stratton). Franchise award date: N.A. Franchise expiration date: N.A. Began: N.A.

Channel capacity: 136 (operating 2-way). Channels available but not in use: None.

Basic Service

Subscribers: 3,370.

Programming (received off-air): WABI-TV (CBS, CW) Bangor; WCBB (PBS) Augusta; WCSH (NBC) Portland; WGME-TV (CBS) Portland; WLBZ (NBC) Bangor; WMTW (ABC) Poland Spring; WPFO (FOX) Waterville; WPME (MNT) Lewiston; WPXT (CW) Portland; WVII-TV (ABC) Bangor.

Programming (via satellite): C-SPAN; C-SPAN 2; Eternal Word TV Network; Home Shopping Network; ION Television; QVC; TV Guide Network.

Fee: $56.63 installation; $26.63 monthly.

Expanded Basic Service 1

Subscribers: 3,150.

Programming (via satellite): ABC Family Channel; AMC; Animal Planet; Arts & Entertainment; BET Networks; Bravo; Cartoon Network; CNBC; CNN; Comcast Sports Net New England; Comedy Central; Country Music TV; Discovery Channel; Disney Channel; E! Entertainment Television; ESPN; ESPN 2; Food Network; Fox News Channel; FX; Hallmark Channel; Headline News; HGTV; History Channel; Lifetime; MSNBC; MTV; New England Cable News; New England Sports Network; Nickelodeon; Oxygen; ShopNBC; Spike TV; Syfy; TBS Superstation; The Learning Channel; Toon Disney; Travel Channel; truTV; Turner Classic Movies; Turner Network TV; TV Land; USA Network; Versus; VH1; Weather Channel; WGN America.

Digital Basic Service

Subscribers: N.A.

Programming (via satellite): AmericanLife TV Network; BBC America; Black Family Channel; Bloomberg Television; Discovery Digital Networks; Do-It-Yourself; FitTV; Fox Sports World; G4; Great American Country; GSN; Halogen Network; MuchMusic Network; Outdoor Channel; Trinity Broadcasting Network; WE tv.

Digital Expanded Basic Service

Subscribers: N.A.

Programming (via satellite): Bio; Canales N; ESPN Classic Sports; ESPNews; Fox College Sports Atlantic; Fox College Sports Central; Fox College Sports Pacific; Fox Movie Channel; GAS; Golf Channel; History Channel International; Independent Film Channel; MTV Networks Digital Suite; Music Choice; Nick Jr.; Nick Too; NickToons TV; SoapNet; Speed Channel; Style Network; Sundance Channel.

Digital Pay Service 1

Pay Units: 351.

Programming (via satellite): ART America; CCTV-4; Cinemax (multiplexed); Encore (multiplexed); Filipino Channel; Flix; HBO (multiplexed); RAI International; Russian Television Network; Showtime (multiplexed); Starz (multiplexed); The Movie Channel (multiplexed); TV Asia; TV Japan; TV5, La Television International; Zee TV USA; Zhong Tian Channel.

Fee: $12.95 monthly (each).

Video-On-Demand: Yes

Pay-Per-View

Hot Choice (delivered digitally); Playboy TV (delivered digitally); Fresh (delivered digitally); Urban Extra (delivered digitally); Movies (delivered digitally).

Internet Service

Operational: Yes. Began: August 1, 2002.

Broadband Service: EarthLink, Road Runner.

Fee: $44.95 monthly.

Telephone Service

None

Miles of Plant: 136.0 (coaxial); None (fiber optic). Homes passed: 4,410.

President: Keith Burkley. Vice President, Marketing & Sales: David Leopold. Vice President, Engineering: Scott Ducott. Vice President, Government & Public Affairs: Melinda Poore.

Ownership: Time Warner Cable (MSO).

NORWAY—Now served by SEBAGO (town), ME [ME0107]. ICA: ME0099.

OAKFIELD—Polaris Cable Services, 34 Military St, Houlton, ME 4730. Phone: 207-532-2579. Fax: 207-532-4025. Web Site: http://www.polariscable.com. Also serves Dyer Brook, Merrill & Smyrna. ICA: ME0072.

TV Market Ranking: Outside TV Markets (Dyer Brook, Merrill, OAKFIELD, Smyrna). Franchise award date: January 1, 1976. Franchise expiration date: N.A. Began: January 1, 1978.

Channel capacity: 42 (2-way capable). Channels available but not in use: 16.

Basic Service

Subscribers: 104.

Programming (received off-air): WAGM-TV (CBS) Presque Isle; WLBZ (NBC) Bangor; WMEM-TV (PBS) Presque Isle; WVII-TV (ABC) Bangor.

Programming (via satellite): ABC Family Channel; AMC; Animal Planet; Arts & Entertainment; Bravo; CNN; Comedy Central; Country Music TV; Discovery Channel; Disney Channel; E! Entertainment Television; ESPN; ESPN 2; Fox News Channel; Hallmark Channel; Headline News; History Channel; Lifetime; National Geographic Channel; New England Sports Network; Nickelodeon; QVC; Spike TV; Syfy; TBS Superstation; Travel Channel; Trinity Broadcasting Network; truTV; Turner Network TV; USA Network; various Canadian stations; Weather Channel; WGN America.

Fee: $55.00 installation; $39.11 monthly; $25.00 converter.

Pay Service 1

Pay Units: 6.

Programming (via satellite): HBO.

Fee: $35.00 installation; $14.50 monthly.

Video-On-Demand: No

Internet Service

Operational: No.

Telephone Service

None

Miles of Plant: 15.0 (coaxial); None (fiber optic). Homes passed: 250. Total homes in franchised area: 350.

Manager: Gordon Wark. Assistant Manager: Catherine Donovan.

Ownership: NEPSK Inc. (MSO).

PATTEN—Polaris Cable Services, 34 Military St, Houlton, ME 4730. Phone: 207-532-2579. Fax: 207-532-4025. Web Site: http://www.polariscable.com. ICA: ME0048.

TV Market Ranking: Outside TV Markets (PATTEN). Franchise award date: January 1, 1978. Franchise expiration date: N.A. Began: January 1, 1959.

Channel capacity: 42 (not 2-way capable). Channels available but not in use: 12.

Basic Service

Subscribers: 194.

Programming (received off-air): WABI-TV (CBS, CW) Bangor; WAGM-TV (CBS) Presque Isle; WLBZ (NBC) Bangor; WMEM-TV (PBS) Presque Isle; WVII-TV (ABC) Bangor; 8 FMs.

Programming (via satellite): ABC Family Channel; CNN; C-SPAN; Discovery Channel; ESPN; Headline News; History Channel; Lifetime; MTV; Nickelodeon; Primetime 24; QVC; Spike TV; TBS Superstation;

The Learning Channel; Trinity Broadcasting Network; Turner Classic Movies; Turner Network TV; USA Network; VH1; Weather Channel.
Fee: $55.00 installation; $40.77 monthly; $2.00 converter.
Pay Service 1
Pay Units: 13.
Programming (via satellite): Cinemax; HBO.
Fee: $10.00 installation; $14.50 monthly (each).
Video-On-Demand: No
Internet Service
Operational: No.
Telephone Service
None
Miles of Plant: 20.0 (coaxial); None (fiber optic). Homes passed: 400. Total homes in franchised area: 1,000.
Manager: Gordon Wark. Assistant Manager: Catherine Donovan. Chief Technologist: Donna Williamson.
City fee: None.
Ownership: NEPSK Inc. (MSO).

PEMBROKE—Formerly served by Pine Tree Cablevision. No longer in operation. ICA: ME0100.

PITTSFIELD—Time Warner Cable. Now served by BANGOR, ME [ME0002]. ICA: ME0032.

PLEASANT RIDGE PLANTATION—Formerly served by Pleasant Ridge Cablevision Inc. No longer in operation. ICA: ME0101.

POLAND—Formerly served by Adelphia Communications. No longer in operation. ICA: ME0033.

PORTAGE—Time Warner Cable. Now served by AROOSTOOK COUNTY, ME [ME0008]. ICA: ME0080.

PORTLAND—Time Warner Cable, 118 Johnston Rd, Portland, ME 4102. Phones: 207-253-2200; 207-253-2385. Fax: 207-253-2404. Web Site: http://www.timewarnercable.com/NewEngland. Also serves Cape Elizabeth, Casco, Cumberland, Falmouth, Gorham, Gray (town), New Gloucester (town), North Yarmouth, Peaks Island, Pownal, Raymond, Scarborough, South Portland, Westbrook, Windham & Yarmouth. ICA: ME0001.
TV Market Ranking: 75 (Cape Elizabeth, Casco, Cumberland, Falmouth, Gorham, Gray (town), New Gloucester (town), North Yarmouth, Peaks Island, PORTLAND, Pownal, Raymond, Scarborough, South Portland, Westbrook, Windham, Yarmouth). Franchise award date: June 27, 1974. Franchise expiration date: N.A. Began: February 1, 1975.
Channel capacity: N.A. Channels available but not in use: 1.
Basic Service
Subscribers: 102,700 Includes York.
Programming (received off-air): WCBB (PBS) Augusta; WCSH (NBC) Portland; WENH-TV (PBS) Durham; WGME-TV (CBS) Portland; WMTW (ABC) Poland Spring; WPFO (FOX) Waterville; WPME (MNT) Lewiston; WPXT (CW) Portland.
Programming (via satellite): C-SPAN; QVC; Shop at Home; ShopNBC; TV Guide Network.
Current originations: Leased Access; Government Access; Educational Access; Public Access.
Fee: $56.63 installation; $10.14 monthly.
Expanded Basic Service 1
Subscribers: 56,000.
Programming (via satellite): ABC Family Channel; AMC; Animal Planet; Arts & Entertainment; BET Networks; Bravo; Cartoon Network; CNBC; CNN; Comcast Sports Net New England; Comedy Central; Country Music TV; C-SPAN 2; Discovery Channel; Disney Channel; E! Entertainment Television; ESPN; ESPN 2; Eternal Word TV Network; Food Network; Fox News Channel; FX; Golf Channel; Hallmark Channel; Headline News; HGTV; History Channel; Home Shopping Network; Lifetime; Lifetime Movie Network; MSNBC; MTV; National Geographic Channel; New England Cable News; New England Sports Network; Nickelodeon; Oxygen; SoapNet; Spike TV; Syfy; TBS Superstation; The Learning Channel; Travel Channel; truTV; Turner Network TV; TV Land; USA Network; Versus; VH1; WE tv; Weather Channel.
Fee: $29.11 monthly.
Digital Basic Service
Subscribers: 40,000 Includes York.
Programming (via satellite): AmericanLife TV Network; America's Store; BBC America; Bio; Bloomberg Television; Boomerang; CNN International; Cooking Channel; C-SPAN 3; Discovery Digital Networks; Do-It-Yourself; Encore Action; ESPN Classic Sports; ESPNews; FamilyNet; Fox College Sports Atlantic; Fox College Sports Central; Fox College Sports Pacific; Fox Movie Channel; Fox Sports en Espanol; Fox Sports World; Fuse; G4; GAS; Great American Country; GSN; History Channel International; Lifetime Real Women; MTV2; Music Choice; Nick Jr.; Nick Too; Outdoor Channel; Ovation; Speed Channel; Style Network; Tennis Channel; Toon Disney; Trinity Broadcasting Network; VH1 Classic.
Fee: $12.99 monthly.
Digital Pay Service 1
Pay Units: N.A.
Programming (via satellite): Cinemax (multiplexed); HBO (multiplexed); Showtime (multiplexed); Starz (multiplexed); The Movie Channel (multiplexed); TV5 USA.
Fee: $13.95 monthly (each).
Video-On-Demand: Yes
Pay-Per-View
iN DEMAND, Addressable: Yes; Pleasure; iN DEMAND (delivered digitally); Playboy TV (delivered digitally); Fresh (delivered digitally); Hot Choice (delivered digitally); Pleasure (delivered digitally); Shorteez (delivered digitally); Sports PPV (delivered digitally).
Internet Service
Operational: Yes.
Subscribers: 35,000.
Broadband Service: EarthLink, Road Runner.
Fee: $38.45 installation; $44.95 monthly.
Telephone Service
Analog: Not Operational
Digital: Operational
Subscribers: 70,000.
Fee: $38.45 installation; $39.95 monthly
Miles of Plant: 1,740.0 (coaxial); 542.0 (fiber optic). Homes passed: 74,500. Total homes in franchised area: 83,000.
President: Keith Burkley. Vice President, Marketing & Sales: David Leopold. Vice President, Engineering: Scott Ducott. Vice President, Government & Public Affairs: Melinda Poore.
City fee: 5% of gross.
Ownership: Time Warner Cable (MSO).

RANGELEY (town)—Argent Communications, 22 Central Sq, Bristol, NH 3222. Phone: 888-815-0610. Fax: 206-202-1415. Web Site: http://www.argentcommunications.com. ICA: ME0059.
TV Market Ranking: Outside TV Markets (RANGELEY (TOWN)). Franchise award date: September 1, 1989. Franchise expiration date: N.A. Began: June 17, 1991.
Channel capacity: 42 (not 2-way capable). Channels available but not in use: 6.
Basic Service
Subscribers: 311.
Programming (received off-air): WABI-TV (CBS, CW) Bangor; WCBB (PBS) Augusta; WCSH (NBC) Portland; WMTW (ABC) Poland Spring.
Programming (via microwave): WSBK-TV (IND) Boston.
Programming (via satellite): C-SPAN; C-SPAN 2; QVC; Trinity Broadcasting Network.
Current originations: Educational Access; Public Access.
Fee: $56.63 installation; $22.29 monthly.
Digital Basic Service
Subscribers: N.A.
Programming (via satellite): BBC America; Black Family Channel; Bloomberg Television; Discovery Digital Networks; ESPN Classic Sports; ESPNews; FitTV; Fox Movie Channel; Fox Soccer; Fox Sports World; Fuse; G4; GAS; Golf Channel; Great American Country; GSN; Halogen Network; Lifetime Movie Network; MTV2; National Geographic Channel; Speed Channel; The Word Network; Toon Disney; Turner Classic Movies; VH1 Classic; VH1 Country; WE tv.
Fee: $62.95 monthly.
Digital Expanded Basic Service
Subscribers: N.A.
Programming (via satellite): Bio; DMX Music; Fox College Sports Atlantic; Fox College Sports Central; Fox College Sports Pacific; History Channel International; Independent Film Channel; Nick Jr.; NickToons TV; Outdoor Channel; Versus.
Digital Pay Service 1
Pay Units: N.A.
Programming (via satellite): Cinemax (multiplexed); Encore (multiplexed); HBO (multiplexed); Showtime (multiplexed); Starz (multiplexed); The Movie Channel (multiplexed).
Video-On-Demand: No
Pay-Per-View
HITS (Headend In The Sky) (delivered digitally); Playboy TV (delivered digitally); Fresh (delivered digitally).
Internet Service
Operational: Yes.
Fee: $20.99-$49.99 monthly.
Telephone Service
Digital: Operational
Fee: $49.95 monthly
Miles of Plant: 15.0 (coaxial); None (fiber optic). Additional miles planned: 13.0 (coaxial). Homes passed: 620.
Manager: Andrew Bauer.; Shawn Bauer.
Ownership: Argent Communications LLC (MSO).

ROCKLAND—Time Warner Cable. Now served by AUGUSTA, ME [ME0004]. ICA: ME0005.

ROCKWOOD—Moosehead Enterprises, PO Box 526, Greenville, ME 4441. Phone: 207-695-3337. Fax: 207-695-3571. ICA: ME0115.
TV Market Ranking: Below 100 (ROCKWOOD).
Channel capacity: N.A. Channels available but not in use: N.A.
Basic Service
Subscribers: 135.
Programming (received off-air): WABI-TV (CBS, CW) Bangor; WLBZ (NBC) Bangor; WMEB-TV (PBS) Orono; WVII-TV (ABC) Bangor.
Programming (via satellite): ABC Family Channel; Arts & Entertainment; CNN; Discovery Channel; ESPN; ESPN 2; History Channel; QVC; TBS Superstation; Turner Network TV; USA Network; WGN America; WPIX (CW, IND) New York.
Fee: $19.50 monthly.
Pay Service 1
Pay Units: 9.
Programming (via satellite): HBO.
Fee: $12.00 monthly.
Video-On-Demand: No
Internet Service
Operational: No.
Telephone Service
None
President: Scott Richardson. Secretary: Sue Richardson.
Ownership: Moosehead Enterprises Inc. (MSO).

RUMFORD—Formerly served by Adelphia Communications. Now served by AUGUSTA, ME [ME0004]. ICA: ME0102.

SANFORD—MetroCast Cablevision, 9 Apple Rd, Belmont, NH 03220-3251. Phone: 603-332-8629. Fax: 603-335-4106. Web Site: http://www.metrocastcommunications.com. Also serves Acton, East Lebanon, Shapleigh & Springvale. ICA: ME0012.
TV Market Ranking: 75 (SANFORD, Shapleigh, Springvale); Outside TV Markets (Acton, East Lebanon). Franchise award date: July 5, 1972. Franchise expiration date: N.A. Began: July 1, 1973.
Channel capacity: 78 (operating 2-way). Channels available but not in use: N.A.
Basic Service
Subscribers: 9,300.
Programming (received off-air): WCBB (PBS) Augusta; WCSH (NBC) Portland; WENH-TV (PBS) Durham; WGBH-TV (PBS) Boston; WGME-TV (CBS) Portland; WHDH (NBC) Boston; WMTW (ABC) Poland Spring; WPFO (FOX) Waterville; WPME (MNT) Lewiston; WPXT (CW) Portland.
Programming (via microwave): New England Cable News; WBZ-TV (CBS) Boston; WCVB-TV (ABC) Boston.
Programming (via satellite): C-SPAN; C-SPAN 2; Eternal Word TV Network; Home Shopping Network; QVC; TBS Superstation; various Canadian stations.
Current originations: Leased Access; Religious Access; Government Access; Educational Access; Public Access.
Fee: $30.00 installation; $15.00 monthly.
Expanded Basic Service 1
Subscribers: 8,000.
Programming (via satellite): ABC Family Channel; AMC; Animal Planet; Arts & Entertainment; Bravo; Cartoon Network; CNBC; CNN; Comcast Sports Net New England; Comedy Central; Country Music TV; Discovery Channel; Disney Channel; E! Entertainment Television; ESPN; ESPN 2; ESPN Classic Sports; Food Network; Fox News Channel; FX; Golf Channel; Great American Country; Headline News; HGTV; History Channel; Lifetime; MSNBC; MTV; National Geographic Channel; New England Sports

Network; Nickelodeon; SoapNet; Spike TV; Syfy; The Learning Channel; Travel Channel; Turner Network TV; TV Land; USA Network; VH1; Weather Channel.
Fee: $28.95 monthly.

Digital Basic Service
Subscribers: 2,700.
Programming (received off-air): WCSH (NBC) Portland; WGME-TV (CBS) Portland; WHDH (NBC) Boston; WMTW (ABC) Poland Spring; WMUR-TV (ABC) Manchester.
Programming (via microwave): WBZ-TV (CBS) Boston; WCVB-TV (ABC) Boston.
Programming (via satellite): 3 Angels Broadcasting Network; AmericanLife TV Network; Anime Network; BBC America; Bio; Bloomberg Television; Boomerang; CBS College Sports Network; CMT Pure Country; Cooking Channel; Current; Discovery Digital Networks; Discovery HD Theater; Do-It-Yourself; ESPN 2 HD; ESPN HD; ESPN U; ESPNews; FamilyNet; Fox College Sports Atlantic; Fox College Sports Central; Fox College Sports Pacific; Fox Soccer; Fuel TV; Fuse; G4; GAS; Gospel Music Channel; GSN; Hallmark Channel; Hallmark Movie Channel; HDNet; HDNet Movies; History Channel International; Independent Film Channel; INSP; Lifetime Movie Network; Lifetime Real Women; MTV Networks Digital Suite; Music Choice; National Geographic Channel HD Network; NFL Network; Nick Jr.; NickToons TV; Outdoor Channel; PBS Kids Sprout; ReelzChannel; Speed Channel; Style Network; Toon Disney; Trinity Broadcasting Network; Turner Network TV HD; Universal HD; Versus; WE tv; WealthTV; Weatherscan.
Fee: $6.95 monthly.

Digital Pay Service 1
Pay Units: 2,200.
Programming (via satellite): Cinemax (multiplexed); Cinemax HD; Encore (multiplexed); Flix; HBO (multiplexed); HBO HD; Showtime (multiplexed); Showtime HD; Starz (multiplexed); Starz HDTV; Sundance Channel; The Movie Channel (multiplexed); The Movie Channel HD.
Fee: $12.95 monthly (each).

Video-On-Demand: Yes

Pay-Per-View
Addressable homes: 4,744.
ETC (delivered digitally), Addressable: Yes; Hot Choice (delivered digitally); iN DEMAND; iN DEMAND (delivered digitally); Playboy TV; Playboy TV (delivered digitally); Pleasure (delivered digitally); Fresh (delivered digitally).

Internet Service
Operational: Yes.
Subscribers: 2,900.
Broadband Service: Great Works Internet.
Fee: $99.00 installation; $41.95 monthly; $5.00 modem lease; $149.50 modem purchase.

Telephone Service
None

Miles of Plant: 333.0 (coaxial); 106.0 (fiber optic). Homes passed: 15,966. Total homes in franchised area: 15,966.
Vice President, Operations & General Manager: Steve Murdough. Vice President & Customer Relations Manager: Shirley Clark. Programming Director: Linda Stuchell.
City fee: 3% of gross.
Ownership: Harron Communications LP (MSO).

SEARSMONT—Windjammer Cable, 4400 PGA Blvd, Ste 902, Palm Beach Gardens, FL 33410. Phones: 877-450-5558; 561-775-1208. Fax: 561-775-7811. Web Site: http://www.windjammercable.com. ICA: ME0087.
TV Market Ranking: Below 100 (SEARSMONT). Franchise award date: N.A. Franchise expiration date: N.A. Began: February 6, 1991.
Channel capacity: 42 (not 2-way capable). Channels available but not in use: 6.

Basic Service
Subscribers: 65.
Programming (received off-air): WABI-TV (CBS, CW) Bangor; WLBZ (NBC) Bangor; WMEB-TV (PBS) Orono; WVII-TV (ABC) Bangor.
Programming (via microwave): WSBK-TV (IND) Boston.
Programming (via satellite): C-SPAN; C-SPAN 2; QVC; Trinity Broadcasting Network.
Current originations: Public Access; Government Access; Educational Access.
Fee: $56.63 installation; $31.80 monthly.

Expanded Basic Service 1
Subscribers: 58.
Programming (via satellite): ABC Family Channel; AMC; Arts & Entertainment; CNN; Comcast Sports Net New England; Discovery Channel; Disney Channel; ESPN; FX; Headline News; History Channel; MTV; New England Sports Network; Nickelodeon; Spike TV; Style Network; Syfy; TBS Superstation; The Learning Channel; Turner Network TV; USA Network; VH1; Weather Channel.

Digital Basic Service
Subscribers: N.A.
Programming (via satellite): BBC America; Bloomberg Television; Discovery Digital Networks; ESPN Classic Sports; ESPNews; FitTV; Fox Movie Channel; Fox Soccer; G4; Golf Channel; GSN; Halogen Network; Nick Jr.; NickToons TV; Turner Classic Movies; WE tv.
Fee: $62.95 monthly.

Digital Expanded Basic Service
Subscribers: N.A.
Programming (via satellite): Independent Film Channel; Music Choice; Outdoor Channel; Versus.

Digital Pay Service 1
Pay Units: N.A.
Programming (via satellite): Cinemax (multiplexed); Encore (multiplexed); HBO (multiplexed); Showtime (multiplexed); Starz (multiplexed); The Movie Channel (multiplexed).
Fee: $12.95 monthly (each).

Video-On-Demand: No

Pay-Per-View
HITS (Headend In The Sky) (delivered digitally); Playboy TV (delivered digitally); Fresh (delivered digitally).

Internet Service
Operational: Yes.
Fee: $20.99-$49.99 monthly.

Telephone Service
Digital: Operational
Fee: $49.95 monthly

Miles of Plant: 13.0 (coaxial); None (fiber optic). Additional miles planned: 3.0 (coaxial). Homes passed: 149.
General Manager: Timothy Evard. Operations Director: Belinda Graham. Engineering Director: Mike Earehart. Finance & Accounting Director: Cindy Johnson.
Ownership: Windjammer Communications LLC (MSO).

SEBAGO (town)—Time Warner Cable, 118 Johnston Rd, Portland, ME 4102. Phone: 207-253-2200. Fax: 207-253-2405. Web Site: http://www.timewarnercable.com/NewEngland. Also serves Alfred, Arundel, Baldwin, Bar Mills, Bethel, Bridgton, Bryant Pond, Buxton, Cape Porpoise, Cornish (town), Dayton, Denmark (town), East Baldwin, Greenwood, Harrison, Hiram, Hollis, Kennebunk, Kennebunkport, Kezar Falls, Limerick, Limington, Locke Mills, Lyman, Naples, Newry, Norway, Paris, Parsonfield, Porter, South Paris, Standish, Steep Falls, Waterboro, Waterford (town), West Baldwin, West Paris & Woodstock. ICA: ME0107.
TV Market Ranking: 75 (Alfred, Arundel, Baldwin, Bar Mills, Bethel, Bridgton, Bryant Pond, Buxton, Cape Porpoise, Cornish (town), Dayton, Denmark (town), East Baldwin, Greenwood, Harrison, Hiram, Hollis, Kennebunk, Kennebunkport, Kezar Falls, Limerick, Limington, Locke Mills, Lyman, Naples, Norway, Paris, Porter, SEBAGO (TOWN), South Paris, Standish, Steep Falls, Waterboro, Waterford (town), West Baldwin, West Paris, Woodstock); Outside TV Markets (Newry, Parsonfield). Franchise award date: February 27, 1982. Franchise expiration date: N.A. Began: July 1, 1982.
Channel capacity: N.A. Channels available but not in use: N.A.

Basic Service
Subscribers: 28,446.
Programming (received off-air): WCBB (PBS) Augusta; WCSH (NBC) Portland; WENH-TV (PBS) Durham; WGME-TV (CBS) Portland; WMTW (ABC) Poland Spring; WPFO (FOX) Waterville; WPME (MNT) Lewiston; WPXT (CW) Portland; allband FM.
Programming (via satellite): C-SPAN; C-SPAN 2; Home Shopping Network; QVC; TV Guide Network.
Current originations: Leased Access; Government Access; Educational Access; Public Access.
Fee: $56.63 installation; $9.95 monthly.

Expanded Basic Service 1
Subscribers: 25,424.
Programming (via satellite): ABC Family Channel; AMC; Animal Planet; Arts & Entertainment; BET Networks; Bravo; Cartoon Network; CNBC; CNN; Comcast Sports Net New England; Comedy Central; Country Music TV; Discovery Channel; Disney Channel; E! Entertainment Television; ESPN; ESPN 2; Eternal Word TV Network; Food Network; Fox News Channel; FX; Great American Country; Hallmark Channel; Headline News; HGTV; History Channel; INSP; Lifetime; MSNBC; MTV; New England Cable News; New England Sports Network; Nickelodeon; Ovation; Oxygen; Product Information Network; Spike TV; Syfy; TBS Superstation; The Learning Channel; Travel Channel; Trinity Broadcasting Network; truTV; Turner Classic Movies; Turner Network TV; TV Land; USA Network; VH1; Weather Channel.
Fee: $25.95 monthly.

Digital Basic Service
Subscribers: N.A.
Programming (via satellite): AmericanLife TV Network; BBC America; Bio; Bloomberg Television; Discovery Digital Networks; Do-It-Yourself; ESPN Classic Sports; ESPNews; Fox College Sports Atlantic; Fox College Sports Central; Fox College Sports Pacific; Fox Movie Channel; Fox Sports World; G4; GAS; Golf Channel; GSN; Halogen Network; History Channel; Independent Film Channel; MTV Networks Digital Suite; MuchMusic Network; Music Choice; National Geographic Channel; Nick Jr.; Nick Too; NickToons TV; Outdoor Channel; Speed Channel; Sundance Channel; Versus; WE tv.
Fee: $12.99 monthly.

Digital Pay Service 1
Pay Units: 2,260.
Programming (via satellite): Cinemax (multiplexed); Encore (multiplexed); Flix; HBO (multiplexed); Showtime (multiplexed); Starz (multiplexed); The Movie Channel (multiplexed).
Fee: $15.00 installation; $12.95 monthly (each).

Video-On-Demand: Yes

Pay-Per-View
Hot Choice (delivered digitally); Playboy TV (delivered digitally); Fresh (delivered digitally).

Internet Service
Operational: Yes. Began: January 1, 2002.
Broadband Service: EarthLink, Road Runner.
Fee: $99.00 installation; $44.95 monthly.

Telephone Service
Digital: Operational
Fee: $38.45 installation; $39.95 monthly

Miles of Plant: 1,450.0 (coaxial); None (fiber optic). Homes passed: 50,000.
President: Keith Burkley. Vice President, Marketing & Sales: David Leopold. Vice President, Engineering: Scott Ducott. Vice President, Government & Public Affairs: Melinda Poore.
Ownership: Time Warner Cable (MSO).

SHERMAN—Sherman Cablevision, PO Box 319, West Enfield, ME 4493. Phone: 207-732-3230. Fax: 207-732-3230. Also serves Sherman Mills & Stacyville. ICA: ME0074.
TV Market Ranking: Outside TV Markets (SHERMAN, Sherman Mills, Stacyville). Franchise award date: December 2, 1985. Franchise expiration date: N.A. Began: January 1, 1987.
Channel capacity: 34 (not 2-way capable). Channels available but not in use: 9.

Basic Service
Subscribers: 130.
Programming (received off-air): WABI-TV (CBS, CW) Bangor; WAGM-TV (CBS) Presque Isle; WLBZ (NBC) Bangor; WMEM-TV (PBS) Presque Isle; WVII-TV (ABC) Bangor.
Programming (via microwave): WSBK-TV (IND) Boston.
Programming (via satellite): ABC Family Channel; CNBC; Discovery Channel; ESPN; Lifetime; Nickelodeon; Primetime 24; QVC; Spike TV; TBS Superstation; Trinity Broadcasting Network; Turner Classic Movies; Turner Network TV; USA Network; WGN America; WNBC (NBC) New York; WPIX (CW, IND) New York.
Fee: $50.00 installation; $35.00 monthly; $20.00 additional installation.

Pay Service 1
Pay Units: 18.
Programming (via satellite): HBO.
Fee: $20.00 installation; $11.50 monthly.

Video-On-Demand: No

Internet Service
Operational: No.

Telephone Service
None

Miles of Plant: 15.0 (coaxial); None (fiber optic). Additional miles planned: 1.0 (coaxial). Homes passed: 300. Total homes in franchised area: 450.
Manager: Philomena Lee.; Paul Lee.
Ownership: Sherman Cablevision.

SIDNEY (town)—Now served by AUGUSTA, ME [ME0004]. ICA: ME0045.

SMITHFIELD (town)—Now served by NORTH ANSON, ME [ME0062]. ICA: ME0103.

SORRENTO—Now served by BANGOR, ME [ME0002]. ICA: ME0084.

ST. FRANCIS—Formerly served by Adelphia Communications. Now served by MADAWASKA, ME [ME0026]. ICA: ME0054.

STOCKHOLM (town)—Argent Communications, 22 Central Sq, Bristol, NH 3222. Phone: 888-815-0610. Fax: 206-202-1415. Web Site: http://www.argentcommunications.com. ICA: ME0086.
TV Market Ranking: Below 100 (STOCKHOLM (TOWN)). Franchise award date: May 9, 1989. Franchise expiration date: N.A. Began: June 1, 1990.
Channel capacity: 54 (operating 2-way). Channels available but not in use: 29.
Basic Service
Subscribers: 40.
Programming (received off-air): WAGM-TV (CBS) Presque Isle; WMEM-TV (PBS) Presque Isle.
Programming (via microwave): WLBZ (NBC) Bangor; WVII-TV (ABC) Bangor.
Programming (via satellite): Canadian Learning Television; C-SPAN; C-SPAN 2; QVC; various Canadian stations; WGN America.
Fee: $56.63 installation; $23.70 monthly.
Expanded Basic Service 1
Subscribers: N.A.
Programming (via satellite): ABC Family Channel; CNN; Discovery Channel; ESPN; FX; Lifetime; New England Sports Network; Nickelodeon; Spike TV; TBS Superstation; Turner Network TV; USA Network; VH1.
Digital Basic Service
Subscribers: N.A.
Programming (via satellite): BBC America; Bloomberg Television; Bravo; Discovery Digital Networks; ESPN Classic Sports; ESPNews; FitTV; Fox Movie Channel; Fox Soccer; G4; Golf Channel; GSN; Halogen Network; HGTV; History Channel; Nick Jr.; NickToons TV; Trinity Broadcasting Network; Turner Classic Movies; WE tv.
Fee: $62.95 monthly.
Digital Expanded Basic Service
Subscribers: N.A.
Programming (via satellite): Independent Film Channel; Music Choice; Outdoor Channel; Versus.
Digital Pay Service 1
Pay Units: N.A.
Programming (via satellite): Cinemax (multiplexed); Encore (multiplexed); HBO (multiplexed); Showtime (multiplexed); Starz (multiplexed); The Movie Channel.
Fee: $12.95 monthly (each).
Video-On-Demand: No
Pay-Per-View
iN DEMAND (delivered digitally); Playboy TV (delivered digitally); Club Jenna (delivered digitally).
Internet Service
Operational: Yes.
Fee: $20.99-$49.99 installation.
Telephone Service
Digital: Operational
Fee: $49.95 monthly
Miles of Plant: 6.0 (coaxial); None (fiber optic). Homes passed: 116.
Manager: Andrew Bauer.; Shawn Bauer.
Ownership: Argent Communications LLC (MSO).

STOCKTON SPRINGS—Now served by BANGOR, ME [ME0002]. ICA: ME0068.

STONINGTON—Formerly served by Adelphia Communications. Now served by BANGOR, ME [ME0002]. ICA: ME0046.

TEMPLE (town)—Windjammer Cable, 4400 PGA Blvd, Ste 902, Palm Beach Gardens, FL 33410. Phones: 877-450-5558; 561-775-1208. Fax: 561-775-7811. Web Site: http://www.windjammercable.com. ICA: ME0082.
TV Market Ranking: Below 100 (TEMPLE (TOWN)). Franchise award date: May 10, 1989. Franchise expiration date: N.A. Began: September 25, 1989.
Channel capacity: 42 (not 2-way capable). Channels available but not in use: 6.
Basic Service
Subscribers: 133.
Programming (received off-air): WCBB (PBS) Augusta; WCSH (NBC) Portland; WGME-TV (CBS) Portland; WVII-TV (ABC) Bangor.
Programming (via microwave): WSBK-TV (IND) Boston.
Programming (via satellite): C-SPAN; Home Shopping Network; QVC; Trinity Broadcasting Network.
Current originations: Public Access.
Fee: $56.63 installation; $12.25 monthly; $3.00 converter.
Expanded Basic Service 1
Subscribers: 110.
Programming (via satellite): ABC Family Channel; AMC; Arts & Entertainment; CNN; Comcast Sports Net New England; Discovery Channel; Disney Channel; ESPN; FX; Headline News; HGTV; History Channel; Lifetime; MTV; New England Sports Network; Nickelodeon; Spike TV; Syfy; TBS Superstation; The Learning Channel; Turner Network TV; USA Network; VH1; Weather Channel.
Fee: $20.22 monthly.
Digital Basic Service
Subscribers: N.A.
Programming (via satellite): BBC America; Bloomberg Television; Bravo; Discovery Digital Networks; ESPN Classic Sports; ESPNews; FitTV; Fox Movie Channel; Fox Soccer; G4; Golf Channel; GSN; Halogen Network; Nick Jr.; NickToons TV; Turner Classic Movies; WE tv.
Fee: $62.95 monthly.
Digital Expanded Basic Service
Subscribers: N.A.
Programming (via satellite): Independent Film Channel; Music Choice; Outdoor Channel; Versus.
Digital Pay Service 1
Pay Units: N.A.
Programming (via satellite): Cinemax (multiplexed); Encore (multiplexed); Showtime (multiplexed); Starz (multiplexed); The Movie Channel (multiplexed).
Fee: $12.95 monthly (each).
Video-On-Demand: No
Pay-Per-View
HITS (Headend In The Sky) (delivered digitally); Playboy TV (delivered digitally); Fresh (delivered digitally).
Internet Service
Operational: Yes.
Fee: $20.99-$49.99 installation.
Telephone Service
Digital: Operational
Fee: $49.95 monthly
Miles of Plant: 16.0 (coaxial); None (fiber optic). Homes passed: 223.
General Manager: Timothy Evard. Operations Director: Belinda Graham. Engineering Director: Mike Earehart. Finance & Accounting Director: Cindy Johnson.
Ownership: Windjammer Communications LLC (MSO).

TRENTON—Now served by BANGOR, ME [ME0002]. ICA: ME0063.

UNION (town)—Now served by AUGUSTA, ME [ME0004]. ICA: ME0051.

UNITY—No longer in operation. Also serves UNITY. ICA: ME0043.

VAN BUREN—Time Warner Cable. Now served by MADAWASKA, ME [ME0026]. ICA: ME0037.

VINALHAVEN—Now served by AUGUSTA, ME [ME0004]. ICA: ME0067.

WARREN (town)—Now served by AUGUSTA, ME [ME0004]. ICA: ME0105.

WASHBURN—Time Warner Cable. Now served by AROOSTOOK COUNTY, ME [ME0008]. ICA: ME0050.

WATERVILLE—Time Warner Cable, 118 Johnston Rd, Portland, ME 4102. Phones: 207-253-2385; 207-253-2200. Fax: 207-253-2404. Web Site: http://www.timewarnercable.com/NewEngland. Also serves Albion, Benton, China, Clinton, Fairfield, Hinkley, Oakland, Shawmut, Vassalboro & Winslow. ICA: ME0006.
TV Market Ranking: Below 100 (Albion, Benton, China, Clinton, Fairfield, Hinkley, Oakland, Shawmut, Vassalboro, WATERVILLE, Winslow). Franchise award date: N.A. Franchise expiration date: N.A. Began: April 26, 1971.
Channel capacity: N.A. Channels available but not in use: N.A.
Basic Service
Subscribers: 15,785.
Programming (received off-air): WABI-TV (CBS, CW) Bangor; WCBB (PBS) Augusta; WGME-TV (CBS) Portland; WLBZ (NBC) Bangor; WMTW (ABC) Poland Spring; WPFO (FOX) Waterville; WPME (MNT) Lewiston; WPXT (CW) Portland; allband FM.
Programming (via satellite): C-SPAN; C-SPAN 2; Ovation; TBS Superstation; TV Guide Network.
Current originations: Government Access; Educational Access.
Fee: $56.63 installation; $10.95 monthly; $2.90 converter; $30.00 additional installation.
Expanded Basic Service 1
Subscribers: 14,151.
Programming (via satellite): ABC Family Channel; AMC; Arts & Entertainment; CNBC; CNN; Comcast Sports Net New England; Comedy Central; Country Music TV; Discovery Channel; Disney Channel; Encore; ESPN; ESPN 2; Eternal Word TV Network; Food Network; Fox News Channel; FX; Headline News; HGTV; History Channel; Home Shopping Network; ION Television; Lifetime; MSNBC; MTV; New England Sports Network; Nickelodeon; QVC; Spike TV; Syfy; The Learning Channel; Trinity Broadcasting Network; Turner Classic Movies; Turner Network TV; TV Land; USA Network; VH1; Weather Channel.
Fee: $17.45 monthly.
Digital Basic Service
Subscribers: N.A.
Programming (via satellite): American-Life TV Network; BBC America; Bio; Bloomberg Television; Discovery Digital Networks; Do-It-Yourself; ESPN Classic Sports; ESPNews; Fox Movie Channel; Fox Sports World; G4; Golf Channel; GSN; Halogen Network; History Channel; Independent Film Channel; MTV Networks Digital Suite; MuchMusic Network; Music Choice; National Geographic Channel; Nick Jr.; NickToons TV; Outdoor Channel; Speed Channel; Style Network; Sundance Channel; Toon Disney; truTV; Versus; WE tv.
Fee: $12.99 monthly.
Digital Pay Service 1
Pay Units: 951.
Programming (via satellite): Cinemax (multiplexed); Encore (multiplexed); Flix; HBO (multiplexed); Showtime (multiplexed); Starz (multiplexed); The Movie Channel (multiplexed).
Fee: $12.95 monthly (each).
Video-On-Demand: Yes
Pay-Per-View
Playboy TV (delivered digitally); Fresh (delivered digitally); Movies (delivered digitally).
Internet Service
Operational: Yes.
Broadband Service: EarthLink, Road Runner.
Fee: $49.95 installation; $44.95 monthly.
Telephone Service
Digital: Operational
Fee: $38.45 installation; $39.95 monthly
Miles of Plant: 547.0 (coaxial); None (fiber optic). Additional miles planned: 10.0 (coaxial). Homes passed: 20,522.
President: Keith Burkley. Vice President, Marketing & Sales: David Leopold. Vice President, Engineering: Scott Ducott. Vice President, Government & Public Affairs: Melinda Poore.
City fee: None.
Ownership: Time Warner Cable (MSO).

WELD—Argent Communications, 22 Central Sq, Bristol, NH 3222. Phone: 888-815-0610. Fax: 206-202-1415. Web Site: http://www.argentcommunications.com. ICA: ME0083.
TV Market Ranking: Below 100 (WELD). Franchise award date: N.A. Franchise expiration date: N.A. Began: N.A.
Channel capacity: 40 (not 2-way capable). Channels available but not in use: 7.
Basic Service
Subscribers: 84.
Programming (received off-air): WCBB (PBS) Augusta; WCSH (NBC) Portland; WGME-TV (CBS) Portland; WMTW (ABC) Poland Spring.
Programming (via microwave): WSBK-TV (IND) Boston.
Programming (via satellite): C-SPAN; QVC; Trinity Broadcasting Network.
Current originations: Public Access.
Fee: $45.00 installation; $12.25 monthly.
Expanded Basic Service 1
Subscribers: N.A.
Programming (via satellite): ABC Family Channel; AMC; Arts & Entertainment; CNN; Comcast Sports Net New England; Discovery Channel; Disney Channel; ESPN; FX; Headline News; HGTV; History Channel; MTV; New England Sports Network; Nickelodeon; Spike TV; Syfy; TBS Superstation; The Learning Channel; Turner Network TV; USA Network; VH1; Weather Channel.
Fee: $18.42 monthly.

Digital Basic Service
Subscribers: N.A.
Programming (via satellite): BBC America; Bloomberg Television; Bravo; Discovery Digital Networks; ESPN Classic Sports; ESPNews; FitTV; Fox Movie Channel; Fox Soccer; G4; Golf Channel; GSN; Halogen Network; Nick Jr.; NickToons TV; Turner Classic Movies; WE tv.
Fee: $62.95 monthly.
Digital Expanded Basic Service
Subscribers: N.A.
Programming (via satellite): Independent Film Channel; Music Choice; Outdoor Channel; Versus.
Digital Pay Service 1
Pay Units: N.A.
Programming (via satellite): Cinemax (multiplexed); Encore (multiplexed); HBO (multiplexed); Showtime (multiplexed); Starz (multiplexed); The Movie Channel (multiplexed).
Fee: $12.95 monthly (each).
Video-On-Demand: No
Pay-Per-View
HITS (Headend In The Sky) (delivered digitally); Playboy TV (delivered digitally); Fresh (delivered digitally).
Internet Service
Operational: Yes.
Fee: $20.99-$49.99 installation.
Telephone Service
Digital: Operational
Fee: $49.95 monthly
Miles of Plant: 12.0 (coaxial); None (fiber optic). Homes passed: 201.
Manager: Andrew Bauer.; Shawn Bauer.
Ownership: Argent Communications LLC (MSO).

WILTON/FARMINGTON—Bee Line Cable TV. Now served by MADISON, ME [ME0018]. ICA: ME0028.

WINDHAM—Now served by PORTLAND, ME [ME0001]. ICA: ME0019.

WINTER HARBOR—Pine Tree Cablevision. Now served by CHERRYFIELD, ME [ME0111]. ICA: ME0112.

YORK—Time Warner Cable, 118 Johnston Rd, Portland, ME 4102. Phone: 207-253-2200. Fax: 207-253-2405. E-mail: info@twmaine.com. Web Site: http://www.timewarnercable.com/NewEngland. Also serves Biddeford, Moody, North Berwick, Ogunquit, Old Orchard Beach, Saco & Wells. ICA: ME0009.
TV Market Ranking: 75 (Biddeford, Moody, Ogunquit, Old Orchard Beach, Saco, Wells); Outside TV Markets (North Berwick, YORK). Franchise award date: October 20, 1981. Franchise expiration date: N.A. Began: February 1, 1983.
Channel capacity: N.A. Channels available but not in use: None.
Basic Service
Subscribers: N.A. Included in Portland
Programming (received off-air): WBZ-TV (CBS) Boston; WCBB (PBS) Augusta; WCSH (NBC) Portland; WCVB-TV (ABC) Boston; WENH-TV (PBS) Durham; WGBH-TV (PBS) Boston; WGME-TV (CBS) Portland; WHDH (NBC) Boston; WMTW (ABC) Poland Spring; WPFO (FOX) Waterville; WPME (MNT) Lewiston; WPXT (CW) Portland.
Programming (via satellite): C-SPAN; QVC; ShopNBC; TV Guide Network.
Current originations: Religious Access; Government Access; Educational Access; Public Access.
Fee: $56.63 installation; $11.71 monthly; $1.60 converter.
Expanded Basic Service 1
Subscribers: 24,567.
Programming (via satellite): ABC Family Channel; AMC; AmericanLife TV Network; Animal Planet; Arts & Entertainment; Bravo; Cartoon Network; CNBC; CNN; Comcast Sports Net New England; Comedy Central; Country Music TV; C-SPAN 2; Discovery Channel; Disney Channel; E! Entertainment Television; ESPN; ESPN 2; Eternal Word TV Network; Food Network; Fox News Channel; FX; Golf Channel; Hallmark Channel; Headline News; HGTV; History Channel; Home Shopping Network; Lifetime; Lifetime Movie Network; MoviePlex; MSNBC; MTV; National Geographic Channel; New England Cable News; New England Sports Network; Nickelodeon; Oxygen; Shop at Home; SoapNet; Spike TV; Syfy; TBS Superstation; The Learning Channel; Travel Channel; Turner Classic Movies; Turner Network TV; TV Land; USA Network; Versus; VH1; WE tv; Weather Channel.
Fee: $63.15 installation; $27.54 monthly.
Digital Basic Service
Subscribers: N.A. Included in Portland
Programming (via satellite): America's Store; BBC America; Bio; Bloomberg Television; Boomerang; Cooking Channel; C-SPAN 3; Discovery Digital Networks; Do-It-Yourself; Encore Action; ESPN Classic Sports; ESPNews; FamilyNet; Fox Movie Channel; Fox Sports World; Fuse; G4; GAS; Great American Country; GSN; History Channel International; Independent Film Channel; Lifetime Movie Network; MTV2; Music Choice; Nick Jr.; Nick Too; Outdoor Channel; Ovation; Speed Channel; Style Network; Toon Disney; Trinity Broadcasting Network; truTV; VH1 Classic.
Fee: $12.99 monthly.
Digital Expanded Basic Service
Subscribers: N.A.
Programming (via satellite): Fox College Sports Atlantic; Fox College Sports Central; Fox College Sports Pacific; Fox Sports en Espanol; Tennis Channel.
Fee: $2.95 monthly.
Digital Pay Service 1
Pay Units: 5,000.
Programming (via satellite): Cinemax (multiplexed); HBO (multiplexed); Showtime (multiplexed); Starz (multiplexed); The Movie Channel (multiplexed); TV5, La Television International.
Fee: $12.95 monthly (each).
Video-On-Demand: Yes
Pay-Per-View
Addressable homes: 8,474.
iN DEMAND, Addressable: Yes; Pleasure; Hot Choice (delivered digitally); iN DEMAND (delivered digitally); Playboy TV (delivered digitally); Pleasure (delivered digitally); Fresh (delivered digitally); Shorteez (delivered digitally); sports (delivered digitally).
Internet Service
Operational: Yes.
Broadband Service: EarthLink, Road Runner.
Fee: $79.95 installation; $44.95 monthly.
Telephone Service
Analog: Not Operational
Digital: Operational
Miles of Plant: 779.0 (coaxial); 202.0 (fiber optic). Homes passed: 33,600.
President: Keith Burkley. Vice President, Marketing & Sales: David Leopold. Vice President, Engineering: Scott Ducott. Vice President, Government & Public Affairs: Melinda Poore.
Town fee: 3% of gross.
Ownership: Time Warner Cable (MSO).

MARYLAND

Total Systems: 33
Total Communities Served: 414
Franchises Not Yet Operating: 0
Applications Pending: 0
Communities with Applications: 0
Number of Basic Subscribers: 1,372,603
Number of Expanded Basic Subscribers: 444,711
Number of Pay Units: 177,178

Top 100 Markets Represented: Baltimore (14); Harrisburg-Lancaster-York, PA (57); Washington, DC (9).

**For a list of cable communities in this section, see the Cable Community Index located in the back of Cable Volume 2.
For explanation of terms used in cable system listings, see p. D-11.**

ANNAPOLIS (portions)—Comcast Cable. Now served by ANNE ARUNDEL COUNTY, MD [MD0006]. ICA: MD0013.

ANNE ARUNDEL COUNTY—Comcast Cable, 253 Najoles Rd, Millersville, MD 21108. Phone: 410-729-8000. Fax: 410-729-8001. Web Site: http://www.comcast.com. Also serves Annapolis (portions), Arnold, Brooklyn, Brooklyn Park, Cape St. Claire, Crofton, Crownsville, Davidsonville, Deale, Fort Meade, Galesville, Gambrills, Gibson Island, Glen Burnie, Hanover, Harmans, Harwood, Jessup, Laurel, Linthicum, Linthicum Heights, Lothian, Maryland City, Millersville, Odenton, Pasadena, Riviera Beach, Severn, Severna Park & Sherwood Forest. ICA: MD0006.

TV Market Ranking: 9 (Brooklyn, Brooklyn Park, Deale, Galesville, Harwood, Linthicum, Lothian, Riviera Beach); 9,14 (Annapolis (portions), ANNE ARUNDEL COUNTY (PORTIONS), Arnold, Cape St. Claire, Crofton, Crownsville, Davidsonville, Fort Meade, Gambrills, Gibson Island, Glen Burnie, Hanover, Harmans, Jessup, Laurel, Linthicum Heights, Maryland City, Millersville, Odenton, Pasadena, Severn, Severna Park, Sherwood Forest). Franchise award date: April 2, 1979. Franchise expiration date: N.A. Began: September 1, 1983.

Channel capacity: N.A. Channels available but not in use: N.A.

Basic Service

Subscribers: 74,189.

Programming (received off-air): WBAL-TV (NBC) Baltimore; WBFF (FOX, IND) Baltimore; WETA-TV (PBS) Washington; WFDC-DT (UNV) Arlington; WHUT-TV (PBS) Washington; WJZ-TV (CBS) Baltimore; WMAR-TV (ABC) Baltimore; WMDO-CA (TEL) Washington; WMPT (PBS) Annapolis.

Programming (via satellite): C-SPAN; C-SPAN 2; Home Shopping Network; ION Television; MyNetworkTV Inc.; QVC; WGN America.

Current originations: Government Access; Educational Access.

Fee: $28.95 installation; $16.30 monthly.

Expanded Basic Service 1

Subscribers: 48,717.

Programming (via satellite): ABC Family Channel; AMC; Animal Planet; Arts & Entertainment; BET Networks; Bravo; Cartoon Network; CNBC; CNN; Comcast SportsNet Mid-Atlantic; Comedy Central; Discovery Channel; Discovery Health Channel; Disney Channel; E! Entertainment Television; ESPN; ESPN 2; Eternal Word TV Network; Food Network; Fox News Channel; FX; Golf Channel; GSN; Hallmark Channel; Headline News; HGTV; History Channel; Lifetime; Mid-Atlantic Sports Network; MSNBC; MTV; Nickelodeon; Speed Channel; Spike TV; Style Network; Syfy; TBS Superstation; The Comcast Network; The Learning Channel; Travel Channel; truTV; Turner Classic Movies; Turner Network TV; TV Guide Network; TV Land; TV One; USA Network; Versus; VH1; Weather Channel.

Fee: $50.00 installation; $36.90 monthly.

Digital Basic Service

Subscribers: N.A.

Programming (received off-air): WBAL-TV (NBC) Baltimore; WBFF (FOX, IND) Baltimore; WETA-TV (PBS) Washington; WJLA-TV (ABC) Washington; WJZ-TV (CBS) Baltimore; WMAR-TV (ABC) Baltimore; WNUV (CW) Baltimore; WRC-TV (NBC) Washington; WTTG (FOX) Washington; WUSA (CBS) Washington.

Programming (via satellite): ABC Family HD; Animal Planet HD; Arts & Entertainment HD; Azteca America; BBC America; Big Ten Network; Bio; Bloomberg Television; CBS College Sports Network; Cine Latino; Cine Mexicano; CMT Pure Country; CNN en Espanol; CNN HD; Cooking Channel; Country Music TV; C-SPAN 2; C-SPAN 3; Current; Daystar TV Network; Discovery Channel HD; Discovery en Espanol; Discovery HD Theater; Discovery Kids Channel; Discovery Military Channel; Discovery Planet Green; Disney Channel HD; Disney XD; Do-It-Yourself; Encore (multiplexed); ESPN 2 HD; ESPN Classic Sports; ESPN Deportes; ESPN HD; ESPNews; Flix; Food Network HD; Fox Business Channel; Fox College Sports Atlantic; Fox College Sports Central; Fox College Sports Pacific; Fox News HD; Fox Reality Channel; Fox Soccer; Fox Sports en Espanol; Fuse; FX HD; G4; GalaVision; Gol TV; Golf Channel HD; Gospel Music Channel; Great American Country; HGTV HD; History Channel en Espanol; History Channel HD; History Channel International; ID Investigation Discovery; Independent Film Channel; INSP; ION Life; ION Television; Jewelry Television; Lifetime Real Women; LOGO; MLB Network; MoviePlex; MTV Hits; MTV Jams; MTV Tres; MTV2; mun2 television; Music Choice; National Geographic Channel; National Geographic Channel HD Network; NBA TV; NFL Network; NFL Network HD; NHL Network; Nick Jr.; Nick Too; NickToons TV; Outdoor Channel; Oxygen; Palladia; PBS Kids Sprout; Pentagon Channel; Science Channel; Science Channel HD; ShopNBC; SoapNet; Speed HD; Starz IndiePlex; Starz RetroPlex; Sundance Channel; Syfy HD; TBS in HD; TeenNick; Telefutura; Telemundo; Tennis Channel; TLC HD; Trinity Broadcasting Network; Turner Network TV HD; TV Asia; TVG Network; Universal HD; USA Network HD; VeneMovies; Versus HD; VH1 Classic; VH1 Soul; WAM! America's Kidz Network; Washington Korean TV; WE tv; Weatherscan; Zee TV USA.

Fee: $15.90 monthly.

Digital Pay Service 1

Pay Units: N.A.

Programming (via satellite): Cinemax (multiplexed); Cinemax HD; HBO (multiplexed); HBO HD; Playboy TV; Showtime (multiplexed); Showtime HD; Starz (multiplexed); Starz HDTV; The Movie Channel (multiplexed).

Video-On-Demand: Yes

Pay-Per-View

iN DEMAND (delivered digitally); Playboy TV (delivered digitally); Spice: Xcess (delivered digitally); Penthouse TV (delivered digitally); NBA League Pass (delivered digitally); MLS Direct Kick (delivered digitally); ESPN (delivered digitally); MLB Extra Innings (delivered digitally); NBA (delivered digitally).

Internet Service

Operational: Yes.

Broadband Service: Comcast High Speed Internet.

Fee: $42.95 monthly; $199.00 modem purchase.

Telephone Service

Digital: Operational

Subscribers: 6,000.

Fee: $44.95 monthly

Miles of Plant: 1,675.0 (coaxial); 70.0 (fiber optic). Additional miles planned: 20.0 (coaxial). Homes passed: 98,560. Total homes in franchised area: 180,120.

Vice President & General Manager: Bruce Abbott. Technical Operations Director: Greg Mott. Marketing Manager: Kevin Killen. Community Relations Manager: Sandie Anderson.

Ownership: Comcast Cable Communications Inc. (MSO).

BALTIMORE—Comcast Cable, 8031 Corporate Dr, Nottingham, MD 21236. Phone: 410-931-4600. Fax: 410-336-1619. Web Site: http://www.comcast.com. ICA: MD0001.

TV Market Ranking: 9,14 (BALTIMORE). Franchise award date: December 19, 1984. Franchise expiration date: N.A. Began: July 4, 1986.

Channel capacity: N.A. Channels available but not in use: N.A.

Basic Service

Subscribers: 117,000.

Programming (received off-air): WBAL-TV (NBC) Baltimore; WBFF (FOX, IND) Baltimore; WETA-TV (PBS) Washington; WFDC-DT (UNV) Arlington; WHUT-TV (PBS) Washington; WJZ-TV (CBS) Baltimore; WMAR-TV (ABC) Baltimore; WMPT (PBS) Annapolis; WNUV (CW) Baltimore; WUTB (MNT) Baltimore; allband FM.

Programming (via satellite): C-SPAN; C-SPAN 2; Eternal Word TV Network; Home Shopping Network; ION Television; QVC; ShopNBC; Trinity Broadcasting Network; TV Guide Network; TV Land; WGN America.

Current originations: Leased Access; Educational Access; Government Access; Public Access.

Fee: $44.95 installation.

Expanded Basic Service 1

Subscribers: N.A.

Programming (via satellite): ABC Family Channel; AMC; Animal Planet; Arts & Entertainment; BET Networks; Bravo; Cartoon Network; CNBC; CNN; Comcast SportsNet Mid-Atlantic; Comedy Central; Country Music TV; Discovery Channel; Discovery Health Channel; Disney Channel; E! Entertainment Television; ESPN; ESPN 2; ESPN Classic Sports; ESPNews; Food Network; Fox News Channel; FX; G4; Golf Channel; Hallmark Channel; Headline News; HGTV; History Channel; Lifetime; Mid-Atlantic Sports Network; MSNBC; MTV; Nickelodeon; Spike TV; Style Network; Syfy; TBS Superstation; The Comcast Network; The Learning Channel; Travel Channel; truTV; Turner Classic Movies; Turner Network TV; TV One; USA Network; Versus; VH1; Weather Channel.

Fee: $48.05 monthly.

Digital Basic Service

Subscribers: 25,385.

Programming (received off-air): WBAL-TV (NBC) Baltimore; WBFF (FOX, IND) Baltimore; WJZ-TV (CBS) Baltimore; WMAR-TV (ABC) Baltimore; WMPT (PBS) Annapolis; WNUV (CW) Baltimore.

Programming (via satellite): BBC America; Bio; Black Family Channel; Canales N; CBS College Sports Network; CMT Pure Country; Cooking Channel; C-SPAN 2; C-SPAN 3; Current; Discovery Digital Networks; Discovery HD Theater; Do-It-Yourself; Encore (multiplexed); ESPN 2 HD; ESPN HD; ESPNews; FearNet; Flix; Fox College Sports Atlantic; Fox College Sports Central; Fox College Sports Pacific; Fox Reality Channel; Fox Soccer; GAS; Gol TV; Great American Country; GSN; History Channel International; HorseRacing TV; INHD; INSP; Jewelry Television; Lifetime Movie Network; LOGO; MoviePlex; MTV Networks Digital Suite; Music Choice; National Geographic Channel; National Geographic Channel HD Network; NBA TV; NFL Network; Nick Jr.; Nick Too; NickToons TV; Oxygen; Palladia; PBS Kids Sprout; Russian Television Network; ShopNBC; SoapNet; Speed Channel; Sundance Channel; Tennis Channel; The Word Network; Toon Disney; Trinity Broadcasting Network; Turner Network TV HD; TV Asia; TVG Network; Universal HD; Versus HD; WE tv; Weatherscan; Zee TV USA.

Fee: $18.50 monthly.

Digital Pay Service 1

Pay Units: N.A.

Programming (via satellite): Cinemax (multiplexed); Cinemax HD; HBO (multiplexed); HBO HD; Playboy TV; Showtime (multiplexed); Showtime HD; Starz (multiplexed);

Starz HDTV; The Movie Channel (multiplexed).
Fee: $15.00 monthly (each).
Video-On-Demand: Yes
Pay-Per-View
iN DEMAND (delivered digitally); NBA League Pass (delivered digitally); Playboy TV (delivered digitally); ESPN Gameplan (delivered digitally); MLS Direct Kick (delivered digitally); NHL Center Ice (delivered digitally); MLB Extra Innings (delivered digitally).
Internet Service
Operational: Yes.
Broadband Service: Comcast High Speed Internet.
Fee: $42.95 monthly.
Telephone Service
Digital: Operational
Miles of Plant: 1,138.0 (coaxial); 11.0 (fiber optic). Homes passed: 310,000. Total homes in franchised area: 310,000.
Area Vice President & General Manager: Bryan Lynch. Vice President, Regional Marketing: Mark Watts. Engineering Director: Pete Sarkisian. Marketing Director: Chris Shea. Public Relations Director: John Lamontagne.
City fee: 5% of gross.
Ownership: Comcast Cable Communications Inc. (MSO).

BALTIMORE—Formerly served by Sprint Corp. No longer in operation. ICA: MD0051.

BALTIMORE (Inner Harbor)—Formerly served by Flight Systems Cablevision. No longer in operation. ICA: MD0040.

BALTIMORE COUNTY—Comcast Cable, 8031 Corporate Dr, Nottingham, MD 21236. Phone: 410-931-4600. Fax: 410-336-1619. Web Site: http://www.comcast.com. Also serves Arbutus, Catonsville, Cockeysville, Dundalk, Essex, Lansdowne, Middle River, Owings Mills, Parkville, Perry Hall, Pikesville, Randallstown, Reisterstown, Rosedale, Timonium-Lutherville, Towson & Woodlawn. ICA: MD0003.
TV Market Ranking: 14 (BALTIMORE COUNTY, Cockeysville, Dundalk, Essex, Middle River, Owings Mills, Parkville, Perry Hall, Pikesville, Reisterstown, Rosedale, Timonium-Lutherville); 9,14 (Arbutus, Catonsville, Lansdowne, Randallstown, Towson (portions), Woodlawn). Franchise award date: N.A. Franchise expiration date: N.A. Began: October 1, 1978.
Channel capacity: N.A. Channels available but not in use: N.A.
Basic Service
Subscribers: 218,296.
Programming (received off-air): WBAL-TV (NBC) Baltimore; WBFF (FOX, IND) Baltimore; WETA-TV (PBS) Washington; WFDC-DT (UNV) Arlington; WHUT-TV (PBS) Washington; WJZ-TV (CBS) Baltimore; WMAR-TV (ABC) Baltimore; WMDO-CA (TEL) Washington; WMPB (PBS) Baltimore; WNUV (CW) Baltimore.
Programming (via satellite): ABC Family Channel; AMC; Animal Planet; Arts & Entertainment; BET Networks; Bravo; Cartoon Network; CNBC; CNN; Comcast SportsNet Mid-Atlantic; Comedy Central; Country Music TV; C-SPAN; C-SPAN 2; Discovery Channel; Discovery Health Channel; Disney Channel; E! Entertainment Television; ESPN; ESPN 2; Eternal Word TV Network; Food Network; Fox News Channel; FX; G4; Golf Channel; Hallmark Channel; Headline News; HGTV; History Channel; Home Shopping Network; ION Television; Lifetime; Mid-Atlantic Sports Network; MSNBC; MTV; Nickelodeon; QVC; Speed Channel; Spike TV; Style Network; Syfy; TBS Superstation; The Comcast Network; The Learning Channel; Travel Channel; Trinity Broadcasting Network; truTV; Turner Classic Movies; TV Guide Network; TV Land; TV One; USA Network; Versus; VH1; Weather Channel; WGN America.
Current originations: Leased Access; Government Access; Educational Access; Public Access.
Fee: $44.95 installation; $11.09 monthly; $2.34 converter.
Digital Basic Service
Subscribers: N.A.
Programming (received off-air): WBAL-TV (NBC) Baltimore; WBFF (FOX, IND) Baltimore; WJZ-TV (CBS) Baltimore; WMAR-TV (ABC) Baltimore; WMPB (PBS) Baltimore; WNUV (CW) Baltimore.
Programming (via satellite): ABC Family HD; AMC; Animal Planet HD; Arts & Entertainment HD; BBC America; Big Ten Network; Bio; Bloomberg Television; CBS College Sports Network; Cine Latino; Cine Mexicano; CMT Pure Country; CNN en Espanol; CNN HD; Cooking Channel; Country Music TV; C-SPAN 2; C-SPAN 3; Current; Discovery Channel HD; Discovery en Espanol; Discovery HD Theater; Discovery Kids Channel; Discovery Military Channel; Discovery Planet Green; Disney Channel HD; Disney XD; Do-It-Yourself; Encore (multiplexed); ESPN 2 HD; ESPN Classic Sports; ESPN Deportes; ESPN HD; ESPNews; Flix; Food Network HD; Fox College Sports Atlantic; Fox College Sports Central; Fox College Sports Pacific; Fox Reality Channel; Fox Soccer; Fox Sports en Espanol; Fuse; G4; GalaVision; GAS; Gol TV; Golf Channel HD; Gospel Music Channel; Great American Country; GSN; HGTV HD; History Channel; History Channel en Espanol; History Channel HD; ID Investigation Discovery; Independent Film Channel; ION Life; ION Television; Jewelry Television; Korean Channel; Lifetime Movie Network; LOGO; MLB Network; MoviePlex; MTV Hits; MTV Jams; MTV2; mun2 television; Music Choice; National Geographic Channel; National Geographic Channel HD Network; NBA TV; NFL Network; NFL Network HD; NHL Network; Nick Jr.; Nick Too; NickToons TV; Oxygen; Palladia; PBS Kids Sprout; Russian Television Network; Science Channel; Science Channel HD; SoapNet; Speed HD; Starz IndiePlex; Starz RetroPlex; Style Network; Sundance Channel; Syfy HD; TBS in HD; TeenNick; Telefutura; Telemundo; Tennis Channel; The Word Network; TLC HD; Turner Network TV HD; TV Asia; TVG Network; TVK; Universal HD; USA Network HD; VeneMovies; Versus HD; VH1 Classic; VH1 Soul; WE tv; Weatherscan; Zee TV USA.
Fee: $14.15 monthly.
Digital Pay Service 1
Pay Units: N.A.
Programming (via satellite): Cinemax (multiplexed); Cinemax HD; HBO (multiplexed); HBO HD; HBO On Demand; Playboy TV; Showtime (multiplexed); Showtime HD; Starz (multiplexed); Starz HDTV; The Movie Channel (multiplexed).
Fee: $15.99 monthly (Starz, Cinemax, or Showtime/TMC), $17.99 monthly (HBO).
Video-On-Demand: Yes
Pay-Per-View
iN DEMAND (delivered digitally), Addressable: No; Playboy TV (delivered digitally); NHL Center Ice (delivered digitally); iN DEMAND; MLB Extra Innings (delivered digitally); Fresh (delivered digitally); Spice: Xcess (delivered digitally); NBA League Pass (delivered digitally); ESPN Gameplan (delivered digitally); ESPN Full Court (delivered digitally); NBA TV (delivered digitally).
Internet Service
Operational: Yes.
Broadband Service: Comcast High Speed Internet.
Fee: $42.95 monthly; $199.00 modem purchase.
Telephone Service
Digital: Operational
Fee: $44.95 monthly
Miles of Plant: 3,000.0 (coaxial); None (fiber optic). Homes passed: 320,000. Total homes in franchised area: 341,634.
Area Vice President & General Manager: Bryan Lynch. Engineering Director: Pete Sarkisian. Regional Vice President, Marketing: Mark Watts. Technical Operations Director: Brady Hood. Marketing Director: Chris Shea. Marketing Manager: Lisa Casper.; Michael Cuccurullo.
Ownership: Comcast Cable Communications Inc. (MSO).

BEL AIR—Armstrong Cable Services, 122 S Queen St, Rising Sun, MD 21911. Phones: 410-658-5511; 724-283-0925; 724-283-0925 (Corporate office). Fax: 410-658-4777. E-mail: info@zoominternet.net. Web Site: http://cable.armstrongonewire.com. Also serves Cardiff, Darlington, Fallston, Forest Hill, Harford County (portions), Jarrettsville, Monkton, Pylesville, Street & White Hall. ICA: MD0019. **Note:** This system is an overbuild.
TV Market Ranking: 14 (Fallston); 14,57 (BEL AIR, Cardiff, Darlington, Forest Hill, Harford County (portions), Jarrettsville, Monkton, Pylesville, Street, White Hall). Franchise award date: June 14, 1988. Franchise expiration date: N.A. Began: October 1, 1989.
Channel capacity: 115 (operating 2-way). Channels available but not in use: 56.
Digital Basic Service
Subscribers: N.A.
Programming (received off-air): WBAL-TV (NBC) Baltimore; WBFF (FOX, IND) Baltimore; WGAL (NBC) Lancaster; WJZ-TV (CBS) Baltimore; WMAR-TV (ABC) Baltimore; WMPB (PBS) Baltimore; WNUV (CW) Baltimore; WPMT (FOX) York; WUTB (MNT) Baltimore.
Programming (via satellite): ABC Family Channel; AMC; Animal Planet; Arts & Entertainment; Cartoon Network; CNBC; CNN; Comedy Central; Country Music TV; C-SPAN; Discovery Channel; Disney Channel; E! Entertainment Television; ESPN; ESPN 2; Eternal Word TV Network; Food Network; Fox News Channel; FX; Hallmark Channel; Headline News; HGTV; History Channel; Home Shopping Network; Lifetime; Lifetime Movie Network; Mid-Atlantic Sports Network; MSNBC; MTV; Nickelodeon; QVC; Spike TV; Syfy; TBS Superstation; The Learning Channel; Trinity Broadcasting Network; Turner Classic Movies; Turner Network TV; TV Guide Network; TV Land; USA Network; VH1; Weather Channel.
Current originations: Public Access.
Fee: $51.40 monthly.
Digital Expanded Basic Service
Subscribers: N.A.
Programming (via satellite): AmericanLife TV Network; BBC America; Bio; Bloomberg Television; Boomerang; Chiller; CMT Pure Country; Cooking Channel; Discovery Health Channel; Discovery Kids Channel; Discovery Military Channel; Discovery Planet Green; Do-It-Yourself; ESPN U; ESPNews; FitTV; G4; Golf Channel; Great American Country; GSN; Hallmark Movie Channel; History Channel International; HorseRacing TV; ID Investigation Discovery; Jewelry Television; Lifetime Movie Network; MTV Hits; MTV Jams; MTV Tres; MTV2; mun2 television; Music Choice; National Geographic Channel; NFL Network; Nick Jr.; Nick Too; Outdoor Channel; Oxygen; PBS Kids Sprout; Pentagon Channel; RFD-TV; Science Channel; Sleuth; SoapNet; Speed Channel; TeenNick; Tennis Channel; The Sportsman Channel; Toon Disney; Versus; VH1 Classic; VH1 Soul; WE tv.
Fee: $12.00 monthly.
Digital Expanded Basic Service 2
Subscribers: N.A.
Programming (received off-air): WBAL-TV (NBC) Baltimore; WJZ-TV (CBS) Baltimore; WLYH-TV (CW) Lancaster; WMAR-TV (ABC) Baltimore; WMPB (PBS) Baltimore; WPMT (FOX) York.
Programming (via satellite): Animal Planet HD; Arts & Entertainment HD; CNN HD; Discovery Channel HD; Discovery HD Theater; ESPN 2 HD; ESPN HD; Food Network HD; Fox News HD; FX HD; HGTV HD; History Channel HD; NFL Network HD; NHL Network HD; Syfy HD; TBS in HD; TLC HD; Turner Network TV HD; USA Network HD; WealthTV HD.
Fee: $9.00 monthly.
Digital Pay Service 1
Pay Units: N.A.
Programming (via satellite): Cinemax (multiplexed); Cinemax HD; Encore (multiplexed); Flix; HBO (multiplexed); HBO HD; Showtime (multiplexed); Showtime HD; Starz (multiplexed); Starz HDTV; The Movie Channel (multiplexed).
Fee: $13.95 monthly (HBO, Cinemax, Showtime/TMC/Flix or Starz/Encore).
Video-On-Demand: No
Internet Service
Operational: Yes. Began: February 28, 2003.
Subscribers: 436.
Broadband Service: In-house.
Fee: $30.00 installation; $26.95-$39.95 monthly; $3.49 modem lease.
Telephone Service
Analog: Operational
Fee: $49.95 monthly
Miles of Plant: 350.0 (coaxial); 56.0 (fiber optic). Homes passed: 10,317. Total homes in franchised area: 57,917.
General Manager: James Culver. Technical Operations Director: Ken Goodman. Marketing Director: Jud Stewart.
County fee: 3% of gross.
Ownership: Armstrong Group of Companies (MSO).

BETHESDA—RCN Corp. Formerly [MD0054]. This cable system has converted to IPTV, 196 Van Buren St, Herndon, VA 20170. Phone: 703-434-8200. Web Site: http://www.rcn.com. ICA: MD5097.
TV Market Ranking: 9 (BETHESDA).
Channel capacity: N.A. Channels available but not in use: N.A.
Basic Service
Subscribers: N.A.
Fee: $61.44 monthly.
Expanded Basic Service 1
Subscribers: N.A.
Fee: $76.39 monthly.
Expanded Basic Service 2
Subscribers: N.A.
Fee: $8.99 monthly.

Pay Service 1
Pay Units: N.A.
Fee: $11.95 monthly (Cinemaz or Starz!); $16.95 monthly (Showtime/The Movie Channel); $17.95 monthly (HBO).
Video-On-Demand: Yes
Internet Service
Operational: Yes.
Fee: $38.00 monthly.
Telephone Service
Digital: Operational
Fee: $45.00 monthly
Chairman: Steven J. Simmons. Chief Executive Officer: Jim Holanda.
Ownership: RCN Corp. (MSO).

CAMBRIDGE—Comcast Cable, 5729 W Denneys Rd, Dover, DE 19904-1365. Phone: 302-674-2494. Fax: 302-674-2538. Web Site: http://www.comcast.com. Also serves Bethlehem, Brookview, Caroline County, Church Creek, Denton, Dorchester County (western portion), East New Market, Eldorado, Federalsburg, Galestown, Goldsboro, Greensboro, Harmony, Henderson, Hillsboro, Hurlock, Marydel, Preston, Queen Anne's, Queen Anne's County (portions), Rhodesdale, Ridgely, Secretary, Vienna & Wicomico County (southwestern portion). ICA: MD0025.
TV Market Ranking: Below 100 (Bethlehem, Brookview, CAMBRIDGE, Church Creek, Dorchester County (western portion) (portions), East New Market, Eldorado, Federalsburg, Galestown, Harmony, Hurlock, Preston, Rhodesdale, Secretary, Vienna, Wicomico County (southwestern portion)); Outside TV Markets (Caroline County, Denton, Dorchester County (western portion) (portions), Goldsboro, Greensboro, Henderson, Hillsboro, Marydel, Queen Anne's, Queen Anne's County (portions), Ridgely). Franchise award date: January 1, 1970. Franchise expiration date: N.A. Began: March 1, 1971.
Channel capacity: N.A. Channels available but not in use: N.A.
Basic Service
Subscribers: 17,935.
Programming (received off-air): WBAL-TV (NBC) Baltimore; WBFF (FOX, IND) Baltimore; WBOC-TV (CBS, FOX) Salisbury; WCPB (PBS) Salisbury; WFDC-DT (UNV) Arlington; WJZ-TV (CBS) Baltimore; WMDT (ABC, CW) Salisbury; WRC-TV (NBC) Washington; WUTB (MNT) Baltimore.
Programming (via satellite): C-SPAN; C-SPAN 2; Eternal Word TV Network; Home Shopping Network; ION Television; Mid-Atlantic Sports Network; QVC; The Comcast Network; Trinity Broadcasting Network; TV Guide Network; Weather Channel.
Current originations: Leased Access.
Fee: $44.95 installation; $9.25 monthly.
Expanded Basic Service 1
Subscribers: N.A.
Programming (via satellite): ABC Family Channel; AMC; Animal Planet; Arts & Entertainment; BET Networks; Bravo; Cartoon Network; CNBC; CNN; Comcast SportsNet Mid-Atlantic; Comedy Central; Discovery Channel; Discovery Health Channel; Disney Channel; E! Entertainment Television; ESPN; ESPN 2; Food Network; Fox News Channel; FX; Golf Channel; Hallmark Channel; Headline News; HGTV; History Channel; Jewelry Television; Lifetime; Mid-Atlantic Sports Network; MSNBC; MTV; Nickelodeon; Speed Channel; Spike TV; Style Network; Syfy; TBS Superstation; The Learning Channel; Travel Channel; truTV; Turner Classic Movies; Turner Network TV; TV Guide Network; TV Land; TV One; USA Network; Versus; VH1.
Fee: $37.25 monthly.
Digital Basic Service
Subscribers: N.A.
Programming (received off-air): PBS HD; WBAL-TV (NBC) Baltimore; WBFF (FOX, IND) Baltimore; WBOC-TV (CBS, FOX) Salisbury; WMDT (ABC, CW) Salisbury.
Programming (via satellite): ABC Family HD; Animal Planet HD; Arts & Entertainment HD; BBC America; Big Ten Network; Bio; Bloomberg Television; CBS College Sports Network; Cine Latino; CMT Pure Country; CNN en Espanol; CNN HD; Cooking Channel; Country Music TV; C-SPAN 2; C-SPAN 3; Current; Daystar TV Network; Discovery Channel HD; Discovery en Espanol; Discovery HD Theater; Discovery Kids Channel; Discovery Military Channel; Discovery Planet Green; Disney Channel; Disney Channel HD; Do-It-Yourself; Encore (multiplexed); ESPN 2 HD; ESPN Classic Sports; ESPN Deportes; ESPN HD; ESPNews; FearNet; Flix; Food Network HD; Fox Business Channel; Fox News HD; Fox Reality Channel; Fox Soccer; Fox Sports en Espanol; FSN Digital Atlantic; FSN Digital Central; FSN Digital Pacific; Fuse; FX HD; G4; Gol TV; Golf Channel HD; Great American Country; GSN; here! On Demand; HGTV HD; History Channel en Espanol; History Channel HD; History Channel International; ID Investigation Discovery; Independent Film Channel; ION Television; Jewelry Television; Lifetime Movie Network; LOGO; MLB Network; MoviePlex; MTV Hits; MTV Jams; MTV Tres; MTV2; mun2 television; Music Choice; National Geographic Channel; National Geographic Channel HD Network; NBA TV; NFL Network; NFL Network HD; NHL Network; Nick Jr.; Nick Too; NickToons TV; Outdoor Channel; Palladia; PBS Kids Sprout; Qubo; RFD-TV; Science Channel; Science Channel HD; SoapNet; Speed HD; Starz IndiePlex; Starz RetroPlex; Sundance Channel; Syfy HD; TBS in HD; TeenNick; Telemundo; Tennis Channel; TLC HD; Toon Disney; Turner Network TV HD; TV Guide Network; Universal HD; USA Network HD; VeneMovies; Versus HD; VH1 Classic; VH1 Soul; WAM! America's Kidz Network; WE tv; Weatherscan.
Fee: $19.65 monthly.
Digital Pay Service 1
Pay Units: N.A.
Programming (via satellite): Cinemax (multiplexed); Cinemax HD; Cinemax On Demand; HBO (multiplexed); HBO HD; HBO On Demand; Playboy TV; Showtime (multiplexed); Showtime HD; Showtime On Demand; Starz (multiplexed); Starz HDTV; Starz On Demand; The Movie Channel (multiplexed); The Movie Channel On Demand.
Fee: $12.00 monthly (each).
Video-On-Demand: Yes
Pay-Per-View
iN DEMAND (delivered digitally), Fee: $3.95, Addressable: Yes; Sports PPV (delivered digitally); Spice: Xcess (delivered digitally); Playboy TV (delivered digitally); Penthouse TV (delivered digitally).
Internet Service
Operational: Yes.
Broadband Service: Comcast High Speed Internet.
Fee: $42.95 monthly.
Telephone Service
Digital: Operational
Fee: $44.95 monthly
Miles of plant (coax) included in Dover, DE
Vice President & General Manager: Henry Pearl. Engineering Manager: Cliff Jones. Marketing Director: David Tashjian. Business Operations Director: Cara Dever. Government & Public Affairs Director: Tom Worley.
City fee: 3% of gross.
Ownership: Comcast Cable Communications Inc. (MSO).

CECILTON—Comcast Cable, 5729 W Denneys Rd, Dover, DE 19904-1365. Phone: 302-674-2494. Fax: 302-674-2538. Web Site: http://www.comcast.com. ICA: MD0055.
TV Market Ranking: Below 100 (CECILTON).
Channel capacity: N.A. Channels available but not in use: N.A.
Basic Service
Subscribers: N.A.
Programming (received off-air): KYW-TV (CBS) Philadelphia; WBAL-TV (NBC) Baltimore; WBFF (FOX, IND) Baltimore; WCAU (NBC) Philadelphia; WHYY-TV (PBS) Wilmington; WJZ-TV (CBS) Baltimore; WMAR-TV (ABC) Baltimore; WMPT (PBS) Annapolis; WNUV (CW) Baltimore; WPVI-TV (ABC) Philadelphia; WTXF-TV (FOX) Philadelphia; WUTB (MNT) Baltimore.
Programming (via satellite): C-SPAN; C-SPAN 2; Eternal Word TV Network; Mid-Atlantic Sports Network; QVC; Style Network; TV Guide Network.
Fee: $44.95 installation; $16.25 monthly.
Expanded Basic Service 1
Subscribers: N.A.
Programming (via satellite): ABC Family Channel; Animal Planet; Arts & Entertainment; Cartoon Network; CNBC; CNN; Comcast SportsNet Mid-Atlantic; Comedy Central; Discovery Channel; Disney Channel; E! Entertainment Television; ESPN; ESPN 2; Food Network; Great American Country; Headline News; History Channel; Home Shopping Network; Lifetime; MTV; Nickelodeon; Speed Channel; Spike TV; Syfy; TBS Superstation; The Learning Channel; truTV; Turner Classic Movies; Turner Network TV; TV Land; USA Network; VH1; Weather Channel.
Fee: $25.70 monthly.
Pay Service 1
Pay Units: N.A.
Programming (via satellite): Cinemax; HBO; Showtime.
Fee: $18.00 monthly (each).
Internet Service
Operational: No.
Telephone Service
Digital: Operational
Miles of plant (coax) included in Dover, DE
Vice President & General Manager: Henry Pearl. Area Engineering Manager: Cliff Jones. Marketing Director: David Tashjian. Business Operations Director: Cara Dever. Government & Public Affairs Director: Tom Worley.
Ownership: Comcast Cable Communications Inc. (MSO).

CHARLES COUNTY—Comcast Cable, 253 Najoles Rd, Millersville, MD 21108. Phone: 410-729-8000. Fax: 410-729-8001. Web Site: http://www.comcast.com. Also serves Bel Alton, Benedict, Bryans Road, Bryantown, Cobb Island, Faulkner, Hughesville, Indian Head, Ironsides, Issue, La Plata, Marbury, Marshall Hall, Mount Victoria, Nanjemoy, Newburg, Pisgah, Pomfret, Port Tobacco, Rison, Rock Point, St. Charles, Waldorf, Welcome & White Plains. ICA: MD0012.
TV Market Ranking: 9 (Bel Alton, Benedict, Bryans Road, Bryantown, CHARLES COUNTY (portions), Faulkner, Hughesville, Indian Head, Ironsides, La Plata, Marbury, Marshall Hall, Mount Victoria, Nanjemoy, Pisgah, Pomfret, Port Tobacco, Rison, St. Charles, Waldorf, Welcome, White Plains); Below 100 (Newburg); Outside TV Markets (Cobb Island, Issue, Rock Point, CHARLES COUNTY (portions)). Franchise award date: N.A. Franchise expiration date: N.A. Began: October 10, 1966.
Channel capacity: N.A. Channels available but not in use: N.A.
Basic Service
Subscribers: 29,122.
Programming (received off-air): WDCA (MNT) Washington; WDCW (CW) Washington; WETA-TV (PBS) Washington; WFDC-DT (UNV) Arlington; WHUT-TV (PBS) Washington; WJLA-TV (ABC) Washington; WMDO-CA (TEL) Washington; WMPT (PBS) Annapolis; WPXW-TV (ION) Manassas; WRC-TV (NBC) Washington; WTTG (FOX) Washington; WUSA (CBS) Washington; WZDC-CA (TMO) Washington.
Programming (via satellite): C-SPAN; QVC; WGN America.
Current originations: Leased Access; Leased Access; Educational Access.
Fee: $18.95 installation; $16.30 monthly.
Expanded Basic Service 1
Subscribers: 22,565.
Programming (via satellite): ABC Family Channel; AMC; Animal Planet; Arts & Entertainment; BET Networks; Bravo; Cartoon Network; CNBC; CNN; Comcast SportsNet Mid-Atlantic; Comedy Central; C-SPAN 2; Discovery Channel; Discovery Health Channel; Disney Channel; E! Entertainment Television; ESPN; ESPN 2; Eternal Word TV Network; Food Network; Fox News Channel; FX; Golf Channel; GSN; Hallmark Channel; Headline News; HGTV; History Channel; Home Shopping Network; Lifetime; Mid-Atlantic Sports Network; MSNBC; MTV; Nickelodeon; Speed Channel; Spike TV; Style Network; Syfy; TBS Superstation; The Learning Channel; Travel Channel; Trinity Broadcasting Network; truTV; Turner Network TV; TV Land; USA Network; Versus; VH1; Weather Channel.
Fee: $36.90 monthly.
Digital Basic Service
Subscribers: N.A.
Programming (received off-air): WDCW (CW) Washington; WETA-TV (PBS) Washington; WJLA-TV (ABC) Washington; WMPT (PBS) Annapolis; WRC-TV (NBC) Washington; WTTG (FOX) Washington; WUSA (CBS) Washington.
Programming (via satellite): ABC Family HD; Animal Planet HD; Arts & Entertainment HD; Azteca America; BBC America; Big Ten Network; Bio; Bloomberg Television; CBS College Sports Network; Cine Latino; Cine Mexicano; CMT Pure Country; CNN en Espanol; CNN HD; Cooking Channel; Country Music TV; C-SPAN 2; C-SPAN 3; Current; Daystar TV Network; Discovery Channel HD; Discovery en Espanol; Discovery HD Theater; Discovery Kids Channel; Discovery Military Channel; Discovery Planet Green; Disney Channel HD; Disney XD; Do-It-Yourself; Encore (multiplexed); ESPN 2 HD; ESPN Classic Sports; ESPN Deportes; ESPN HD; ESPNews; Flix; Food Network HD; Fox Business Channel; Fox College Sports Atlantic; Fox College Sports Central; Fox College Sports Pacific; Fox HD; Fox News HD; Fox Reality Channel; Fox Soccer; Fox Sports en Espanol; Fuse; G4; Gol TV; Golf Channel HD; Gospel Music Channel; Great American Country;

HGTV HD; History Channel en Espanol; History Channel HD; History Channel International; ID Investigation Discovery; Independent Film Channel; INSP; Jewelry Television; Lifetime Movie Network; LOGO; MLB Network; MoviePlex; MTV Hits; MTV Jams; MTV Tres; MTV2; mun2 television; Music Choice; National Geographic Channel; National Geographic Channel HD Network; NBA TV; NFL Network; NFL Network HD; NHL Network; Nick Jr.; Nick Too; NickToons TV; Outdoor Channel; Oxygen; Palladia; PBS Kids Sprout; Science Channel; Science Channel HD; ShopNBC; SoapNet; Speed HD; Starz IndiePlex; Starz RetroPlex; Sundance Channel; Syfy HD; TBS in HD; TeenNick; Telemundo; Tennis Channel; The Comcast Network; TLC HD; Trinity Broadcasting Network; Turner Network TV HD; TVG Network; Universal HD; USA Network HD; VeneMovies; Versus HD; VH1 Classic; VH1 Soul; WAM! America's Kidz Network; WE tv; Weatherscan.

Fee: $15.90 monthly.

Digital Pay Service 1

Pay Units: N.A.

Programming (via satellite): Cinemax (multiplexed); Cinemax HD; HBO (multiplexed); HBO HD; Playboy TV; Showtime (multiplexed); Showtime HD; Starz (multiplexed); Starz HDTV; The Movie Channel (multiplexed).

Fee: $14.75 monthly (each).

Video-On-Demand: Yes

Pay-Per-View

iN DEMAND (delivered digitally); Playboy TV (delivered digitally); Spice: Xcess (delivered digitally); Penthouse TV (delivered digitally); Sports PPV (delivered digitally).

Internet Service

Operational: Yes.

Broadband Service: Comcast High Speed Internet.

Fee: $42.95 monthly; $7.00 modem lease.

Telephone Service

Digital: Operational

Fee: $44.95 monthly

Miles of Plant: 601.0 (coaxial); 25.0 (fiber optic). Additional miles planned: 15.0 (coaxial). Homes passed: 31,616. Total homes in franchised area: 49,380.

Vice President & General Manager: Bruce Abbott. Technical Operations Director: Greg Mott. Marketing Manager: Kevin Killen. Government & Public Affairs Manager: Joe Lehan.

City fee: 3% of gross.

Ownership: Comcast Cable Communications Inc. (MSO).

CHESAPEAKE BEACH—Comcast Cable. Now served by PRINCE FREDERICK, MD [MD0016]. ICA: MD0032.

CHEVY CHASE—RCN Corp. Formerly [MD0054]. This cable system has converted to IPTV, 196 Van Buren St, Herndon, VA 20170. Phone: 703-434-8200. Web Site: http://www.rcn.com. ICA: MD5098.

TV Market Ranking: 9 (CHEVY CHASE).

Channel capacity: N.A. Channels available but not in use: N.A.

Internet Service

Operational: Yes.

Fee: $38.00 monthly.

Telephone Service

Digital: Operational

Fee: $45.00 monthly

Chairman: Steven J. Simmons. Chief Executive Officer: Jim Holanda.

Ownership: RCN Corp.

CRISFIELD—Charter Communications, 216 Moore Ave, Suffolk, VA 23434. Phone: 757-539-0713. Fax: 757-539-1057. Web Site: http://www.charter.com. Also serves Somerset County. ICA: MD0031.

TV Market Ranking: Below 100 (CRISFIELD, Somerset County). Franchise award date: N.A. Franchise expiration date: N.A. Began: August 13, 1962.

Channel capacity: N.A. Channels available but not in use: N.A.

Basic Service

Subscribers: 2,147.

Programming (received off-air): WBAL-TV (NBC) Baltimore; WBOC-TV (CBS, FOX) Salisbury; WCPB (PBS) Salisbury; WJZ-TV (CBS) Baltimore; WMAR-TV (ABC) Baltimore; WMDT (ABC, CW) Salisbury; WTTG (FOX) Washington; allband FM.

Programming (via satellite): Home Shopping Network; INSP; QVC.

Fee: $29.99 installation.

Expanded Basic Service 1

Subscribers: 2,033.

Programming (via satellite): ABC Family Channel; AMC; Animal Planet; Arts & Entertainment; BET Networks; Bravo; Cartoon Network; CNBC; CNN; Comcast SportsNet Mid-Atlantic; Comedy Central; Country Music TV; C-SPAN; C-SPAN 2; Discovery Channel; Disney Channel; E! Entertainment Television; ESPN; ESPN 2; Fox News Channel; FX; G4; Golf Channel; Hallmark Channel; Headline News; HGTV; History Channel; Lifetime; MTV; Nickelodeon; Oxygen; Speed Channel; Spike TV; Syfy; TBS Superstation; The Learning Channel; Travel Channel; Turner Classic Movies; Turner Network TV; TV Land; USA Network; VH1; WE tv; Weather Channel.

Fee: $47.99 monthly.

Digital Basic Service

Subscribers: N.A.

Programming (via satellite): BBC America; Bio; Bloomberg Television; Discovery Digital Networks; Do-It-Yourself; ESPN Classic Sports; ESPNews; Fox College Sports Atlantic; Fox College Sports Central; Fox College Sports Pacific; Fox Movie Channel; Fox Soccer; Fuse; GAS; GSN; History Channel International; Independent Film Channel; Lifetime Movie Network; Mid-Atlantic Sports Network; MTV Networks Digital Suite; Music Choice; National Geographic Channel; Nick Jr.; Nick Too; NickToons TV; SoapNet; Sundance Channel; Toon Disney; TV Guide Interactive Inc.

Digital Pay Service 1

Pay Units: 90.

Programming (via satellite): Cinemax (multiplexed).

Fee: $10.95 monthly.

Digital Pay Service 2

Pay Units: 439.

Programming (via satellite): HBO (multiplexed).

Fee: $11.95 monthly.

Digital Pay Service 3

Pay Units: 50.

Programming (via satellite): Showtime (multiplexed).

Fee: $10.95 monthly.

Digital Pay Service 4

Pay Units: 72.

Programming (via satellite): The Movie Channel (multiplexed).

Fee: $10.95 monthly.

Digital Pay Service 5

Pay Units: N.A.

Programming (via satellite): Encore (multiplexed); Flix; Starz (multiplexed).

Video-On-Demand: Yes

Pay-Per-View

iN DEMAND (delivered digitally); Playboy TV (delivered digitally); Fresh (delivered digitally); Shorteez (delivered digitally).

Internet Service

Operational: Yes.

Broadband Service: Charter Pipeline.

Fee: $29.99 monthly.

Telephone Service

Digital: Operational

Miles of Plant: 69.0 (coaxial); None (fiber optic). Homes passed: 2,902.

Vice President & General Manager: Anthony Pope. Operations Manager: Tom Ross. Marketing Director: Brooke Sinclair. Marketing Manager: LaRisa Scales.

Franchise fee: 5% of gross.

Ownership: Charter Communications Inc. (MSO).

CUMBERLAND—Atlantic Broadband, 120 Southmont Blvd, Johnstown, PA 15905. Phones: 888-536-9600; 814-539-8971. Fax: 814-535-7749. E-mail: info@atlanticbb.com. Web Site: http://www.atlanticbb.com. Also serves Allegany County, Corriganville, Cresaptown, Eckhart Mines, Ellerslie, Flintstone, Frostburg, Mount Savage, Pinto & Rawlings, MD; Clearville, Cumberland Valley Twp., Hyndman, Londonderry Twp. (Bedford County) & Southampton Twp. (Bedford County), PA; Carpendale, Davis, Fort Ashby, Hambleton, Hampshire County, Hendricks, Mineral County, Parsons, Ridgeley, Romney, Thomas, Tucker County & Wiley Ford, WV. ICA: MD0014.

TV Market Ranking: Below 100 (Hampshire County (portions), Tucker County (portions)); Outside TV Markets (Allegany County, Carpendale, Clearville, Corriganville, Cresaptown, CUMBERLAND, Cumberland Valley Twp., Davis, Eckhart Mines, Ellerslie, Flintstone, Fort Ashby, Frostburg, Hambleton, Hampshire County (portions), Hendricks, Hyndman, Londonderry Twp. (Bedford County), Mineral County, Mount Savage, Parsons, Pinto, Rawlings, Ridgeley, Romney, Southampton Twp. (Bedford County), Thomas, Tucker County (portions), Wiley Ford). Franchise award date: N.A. Franchise expiration date: N.A. Began: December 1, 1951.

Channel capacity: N.A. Channels available but not in use: N.A.

Basic Service

Subscribers: 20,412.

Programming (received off-air): WDCA (MNT) Washington; WDCW (CW) Washington; WHAG-TV (NBC) Hagerstown; WJAC-TV (NBC) Johnstown; WJAL (IND) Hagerstown; WJLA-TV (ABC) Washington; WJZ-TV (CBS) Baltimore; WNPB-TV (PBS) Morgantown; WTAJ-TV (CBS) Altoona; WTTG (FOX) Washington; WUSA (CBS) Washington; WWCP-TV (FOX) Johnstown; WWPB (PBS) Hagerstown; 25 FMs.

Programming (via satellite): C-SPAN; C-SPAN 2; Eternal Word TV Network; Home Shopping Network; INSP; ION Television; Jewelry Television; QVC; TV Guide Network.

Current originations: Leased Access.

Fee: $46.95 installation; $18.95 monthly; $3.95 converter.

Expanded Basic Service 1

Subscribers: 19,187.

Programming (via satellite): ABC Family Channel; AMC; Animal Planet; Arts & Entertainment; BET Networks; Bravo; Cartoon Network; CNBC; CNN; Comcast SportsNet Mid-Atlantic; Comedy Central; Country Music TV; Discovery Channel; Disney Channel; E! Entertainment Television; ESPN; ESPN 2; Food Network; Fox News Channel; Fox Sports Net Pittsburgh; FX; G4; Golf Channel; GSN; Hallmark Channel; Headline News; HGTV; History Channel; Lifetime; Mid-Atlantic Sports Network; MSNBC; MTV; National Geographic Channel; Nickelodeon; Outdoor Channel; Oxygen; Speed Channel; Spike TV; Syfy; TBS Superstation; The Learning Channel; Toon Disney; Travel Channel; Trinity Broadcasting Network; truTV; Turner Network TV; TV Land; USA Network; Versus; VH1; Weather Channel.

Fee: $36.04 monthly.

Digital Basic Service

Subscribers: 6,200.

Programming (received off-air): WJLA-TV (ABC) Washington; WTTG (FOX) Washington; WUSA (CBS) Washington; WWPB (PBS) Hagerstown.

Programming (via satellite): Animal Planet HD; Arts & Entertainment HD; BBC America; Bio; Bloomberg Television; BlueHighways TV; Boomerang; CCTV-4; Chiller; CMT Pure Country; Discovery Channel HD; Discovery HD Theater; Discovery Health Channel; Discovery Military Channel; Discovery Planet Green; Disney Channel HD; Do-It-Yourself; Encore; ESPN 2 HD; ESPN Classic Sports; ESPN HD; ESPN U; ESPNews; FitTV; Fox News HD; Fox Sports Net Pittsburgh; Fuel TV; Great American Country; History Channel HD; History Channel International; ID Investigation Discovery; Independent Film Channel; Lifetime Movie Network; Lifetime Real Women; MTV Hits; MTV Jams; MTV Latin America; MTV2; Music Choice; NFL Network; NFL Network HD; Nick Jr.; Nick Too; NickToons TV; Outdoor Channel 2 HD; Science Channel; Science Channel HD; SoapNet; Starz; Starz HDTV; Syfy HD; TBS in HD; TeenNick; The Sportsman Channel; TLC HD; Turner Classic Movies; Turner Network TV HD; TVG Network; USA Network HD; VH1 Classic; VH1 Soul; VHUNO; WE tv.

Fee: $18.95 monthly.

Digital Pay Service 1

Pay Units: 1,187.

Programming (via satellite): Cinemax (multiplexed); Cinemax HD.

Fee: $20.00 installation; $15.95 monthly.

Digital Pay Service 2

Pay Units: 3,899.

Programming (via satellite): HBO (multiplexed); HBO HD.

Fee: $20.00 installation; $15.95 monthly.

Digital Pay Service 3

Pay Units: 2,246.

Programming (via satellite): Flix; Showtime (multiplexed); Showtime HD; The Movie Channel (multiplexed).

Fee: $20.00 installation; $15.95 monthly.

Video-On-Demand: Yes

Pay-Per-View

Addressable homes: 6,200.

Club Jenna (delivered digitally), Fee: $8.99-$9.99, Addressable: Yes; Hot Choice (delivered digitally), Fee: $8.99-$9.99; iN DEMAND (delivered digitally); Playboy TV (delivered digitally), Fee: $8.99-$9.99; Fresh (delivered digitally), Fee: $8.99-$9.99; Shorteez (delivered digitally), Fee: $8.99-$9.99; Spice: Xcess (delivered digitally), Fee: $8.99-$9.99.

Internet Service

Operational: Yes.

Broadband Service: Atlantic Broadband High-Speed Internet.

Fee: $24.95-$57.95 monthly.

Telephone Service

Digital: Operational

Fee: $44.95 monthly

Miles of Plant: 509.0 (coaxial); 54.0 (fiber optic). Homes passed: 29,968. Total homes in franchised area: 67,894.
Vice President: David Dane. General Manager: Don Feiertag. Technical Operations Director: Charles Sorchilla. Marketing & Customer Service Director: Dara Leslie. Marketing Manager: Natalie Kurchak.
City fee: 3% of gross.
Ownership: Atlantic Broadband (MSO).

DEEP CREEK LAKE—Comcast Cable, 15 Summit Park Dr, Pittsburgh, PA 15275. Phones: 412-747-6400; 301-895-4375 (Grantsville office). Fax: 412-747-6401. Web Site: http://www.comcast.com. Also serves Accident, Friendsville, Garrett County (unincorporated areas) & McHenry. ICA: MD0044.
TV Market Ranking: Outside TV Markets (Accident, DEEP CREEK LAKE, Friendsville, Garrett County (unincorporated areas), Garrett County (unincorporated areas), McHenry). Franchise award date: N.A. Franchise expiration date: N.A. Began: January 1, 1951.
Channel capacity: N.A. Channels available but not in use: N.A.

Basic Service
Subscribers: N.A.
Programming (received off-air): KDKA-TV (CBS) Pittsburgh; WGPT (PBS) Oakland; WHAG-TV (NBC) Hagerstown; WJAC-TV (NBC) Johnstown; WPCB-TV (IND) Greensburg; WPCW (CW) Jeannette; WPGH-TV (FOX) Pittsburgh; WPMY (MNT) Pittsburgh; WPXI (IND, NBC) Pittsburgh; WQED (PBS) Pittsburgh; WTAE-TV (ABC) Pittsburgh; WWCP-TV (FOX) Johnstown; allband FM.
Programming (via satellite): C-SPAN; C-SPAN 2; Eternal Word TV Network; Hallmark Channel; Headline News; Home Shopping Network; INSP; Product Information Network; QVC; Trinity Broadcasting Network; TV Guide Network; VH1; WGN America.
Current originations: Public Access; Public Access.
Fee: $39.95 installation; $16.74 monthly.

Expanded Basic Service 1
Subscribers: 521.
Programming (via satellite): ABC Family Channel; AMC; Animal Planet; Arts & Entertainment; Bravo; Cartoon Network; CNBC; CNN; Comedy Central; Country Music TV; Discovery Channel; Disney Channel; E! Entertainment Television; ESPN; ESPN 2; Food Network; Fox News Channel; Fox Sports Net Pittsburgh; FX; HGTV; History Channel; ION Television; Lifetime; MSNBC; MTV; Nickelodeon; Outdoor Channel; Oxygen; ShopNBC; Speed Channel; Spike TV; Syfy; TBS Superstation; The Learning Channel; Travel Channel; truTV; Turner Network TV; TV Land; USA Network; Weather Channel.
Fee: $38.00 monthly.

Digital Basic Service
Subscribers: N.A.
Programming (via satellite): AmericanLife TV Network; BBC America; Black Family Channel; Bloomberg Television; Discovery Health Channel; Discovery Home Channel; Discovery Kids Channel; Discovery Military Channel; Discovery Times Channel; Do-It-Yourself; FitTV; Fox Movie Channel; Fox Sports World; Fuse; G4; GAS; Golf Channel; Great American Country; GSN; INSP; MTV Hits; MTV2; National Geographic Channel; Nick Jr.; Nick Too; NickToons TV; Science Channel; SoapNet; The Word Network; Toon Disney; Turner Classic Movies; VH1 Classic; VH1 Country; VH1 Soul; WE tv.
Fee: $15.95 monthly.

Digital Expanded Basic Service
Subscribers: N.A.
Programming (via satellite): Bio; ESPN Classic Sports; ESPNews; Flix; Fox Sports Net Mid-Atlantic; Fox Sports Net West; History Channel International; Independent Film Channel; International Television (ITV); Music Choice; Sundance Channel; Versus.

Digital Pay Service 1
Pay Units: N.A.
Programming (via satellite): Cinemax (multiplexed); Encore (multiplexed); HBO (multiplexed); Showtime (multiplexed).

Video-On-Demand: No

Pay-Per-View
HITS 1 (delivered digitally); Hot Choice (delivered digitally); Playboy TV (delivered digitally); Fresh (delivered digitally); Shorteez (delivered digitally); Sports PPV (delivered digitally).

Internet Service
Operational: Yes. Began: December 1, 2004.
Broadband Service: Comcast High Speed Internet.
Fee: $42.95 monthly.

Telephone Service
Analog: Not Operational
Digital: Operational
Miles of Plant: 189.0 (coaxial); None (fiber optic). Homes passed: 5,326.
Regional Vice President: Linda Hossinger. Manager: Barry Savage. Vice President, Technical Operations: Randy Bender. Vice President, Marketing: Donna Corning. Vice President, Public Affairs: Jody Doherty.
City fee: None.
Ownership: Comcast Cable Communications Inc. (MSO).

EASTON—Easton Cable, PO Box 1189, 201 N Washington St, Easton, MD 21601. Phone: 410-822-6110. Fax: 410-822-4987. E-mail: info@eastonutilities.com. Web Site: http://www.eastonutilities.com. ICA: MD0026.
TV Market Ranking: Outside TV Markets (EASTON). Franchise award date: August 28, 1984. Franchise expiration date: N.A. Began: November 1, 1984.
Channel capacity: 64 (operating 2-way). Channels available but not in use: 10.

Basic Service
Subscribers: 5,899.
Programming (received off-air): WBAL-TV (NBC) Baltimore; WBFF (FOX, IND) Baltimore; WBOC-TV (CBS, FOX) Salisbury; WDCA (MNT) Washington; WETA-TV (PBS) Washington; WJLA-TV (ABC) Washington; WJZ-TV (CBS) Baltimore; WMAR-TV (ABC) Baltimore; WMDT (ABC, CW) Salisbury; WMPT (PBS) Annapolis; WNUV (CW) Baltimore; WRC-TV (NBC) Washington; WUSA (CBS) Washington; WUTB (MNT) Baltimore.
Programming (via satellite): ABC Family Channel; BET Networks; CNN; Country Music TV; C-SPAN; C-SPAN 2; Discovery Channel; Headline News; Home Shopping Network; Lifetime; QVC; TBS Superstation; The Learning Channel; Travel Channel; Trinity Broadcasting Network; Turner Network TV; TV Guide Network; Weather Channel.
Current originations: Religious Access; Educational Access; Public Access.
Fee: $19.95 installation; $12.99 monthly; $10.00 additional installation.

Expanded Basic Service 1
Subscribers: 5,209.
Programming (via satellite): AMC; Animal Planet; Arts & Entertainment; Bravo; Cartoon Network; CNBC; Comcast SportsNet Mid-Atlantic; Comedy Central; Disney Channel; E! Entertainment Television; ESPN; ESPN 2; Food Network; Fox News Channel; FX; G4; Golf Channel; HGTV; History Channel; Mid-Atlantic Sports Network; MSNBC; MTV; Nickelodeon; Speed Channel; Spike TV; Syfy; Turner Classic Movies; TV Land; USA Network; Versus; VH1.
Fee: $39.95 installation; $41.99 monthly.

Digital Basic Service
Subscribers: 782.
Fee: $52.99 monthly.

Digital Pay Service 1
Pay Units: 356.
Programming (via satellite): Cinemax (multiplexed).
Fee: $12.95 monthly.

Digital Pay Service 2
Pay Units: 226.
Programming (via satellite): Encore; Starz.
Fee: $12.95 monthly.

Digital Pay Service 3
Pay Units: 1,300.
Programming (via satellite): HBO (multiplexed).
Fee: $12.95 monthly.

Digital Pay Service 4
Pay Units: 343.
Programming (via satellite): Showtime.
Fee: $12.95 monthly.

Video-On-Demand: No

Pay-Per-View
Addressable homes: 4,856.
iN DEMAND, Fee: $3.95, Addressable: Yes; Hot Choice.

Internet Service
Operational: Yes. Began: December 11, 1998.
Broadband Service: In-house.
Fee: $44.95 installation; $24.95 monthly.

Telephone Service
Digital: Operational
Fee: $34.95 monthly
Miles of Plant: 135.0 (coaxial); None (fiber optic). Homes passed: 6,000. Total homes in franchised area: 8,500.
President & Chief Executive Officer: Hugh Grunden. Vice President, Operations: Geoffrey Oxnam. Manager: William D. Russell.
Ownership: Easton Utilities Commission.

ELKTON—Comcast Cable, 5729 W Denneys Rd, Dover, DE 19904-1365. Phone: 302-674-2494. Fax: 302-674-2538. Web Site: http://www.comcast.com. Also serves Cecil County, Charlestown & North East. ICA: MD0018.
TV Market Ranking: 14,57 (Cecil County (portions)); Below 100 (Charlestown, ELKTON, North East, Cecil County (portions)). Franchise award date: N.A. Franchise expiration date: N.A. Began: August 1, 1971.
Channel capacity: N.A. Channels available but not in use: N.A.

Basic Service
Subscribers: 13,958.
Programming (received off-air): KYW-TV (CBS) Philadelphia; WBAL-TV (NBC) Baltimore; WBFF (FOX, IND) Baltimore; WCAU (NBC) Philadelphia; WJZ-TV (CBS) Baltimore; WMAR-TV (ABC) Baltimore; WMPT (PBS) Annapolis; WNUV (CW) Baltimore; WPVI-TV (ABC) Philadelphia; WTXF-TV (FOX) Philadelphia; WUTB (MNT) Baltimore; 14 FMs.
Programming (via satellite): C-SPAN; Discovery Channel; Eternal Word TV Network; FX; Home Shopping Network; QVC; TBS Superstation; The Comcast Network; Trinity Broadcasting Network; TV Guide Network.
Fee: $44.95 installation; $16.25 monthly; $20.00 additional installation.

Expanded Basic Service 1
Subscribers: 10,505.
Programming (via satellite): ABC Family Channel; AMC; Animal Planet; Arts & Entertainment; BET Networks; Bravo; Cartoon Network; CNBC; CNN; Comcast SportsNet Mid-Atlantic; Comedy Central; C-SPAN 2; Disney Channel; E! Entertainment Television; ESPN; ESPN 2; Food Network; Fox News Channel; Golf Channel; GSN; Headline News; HGTV; History Channel; Lifetime; Mid-Atlantic Sports Network; MSNBC; MTV; Nickelodeon; Oxygen; Speed Channel; Spike TV; Syfy; The Learning Channel; truTV; Turner Classic Movies; Turner Network TV; TV Land; USA Network; Versus; VH1; Weather Channel.
Fee: $30.70 monthly.

Digital Basic Service
Subscribers: N.A.
Programming (via satellite): BBC America; CMT Pure Country; Country Music TV; C-SPAN 2; C-SPAN 3; Discovery Health Channel; Discovery Kids Channel; Discovery Military Channel; Discovery Planet Green; Encore (multiplexed); ESPN Classic Sports; ESPNews; Flix (multiplexed); G4; Great American Country; ID Investigation Discovery; Independent Film Channel; Jewelry Television; MTV Jams; MTV Tres; MTV2; Music Choice; National Geographic Channel; NFL Network; Nick Jr.; Nick Too; Science Channel; SoapNet; Sundance Channel; TeenNick; Tennis Channel; The Sportsman Channel; Toon Disney; TV One; TVG Network; VH1 Classic; VH1 Soul; WE tv.
Fee: $19.15 monthly.

Digital Pay Service 1
Pay Units: N.A.
Programming (via satellite): Cinemax (multiplexed); HBO (multiplexed); Showtime (multiplexed); Starz (multiplexed); The Movie Channel (multiplexed).
Fee: $9.00 monthly (TMC), $12.00 monthly each (HBO, Starz or Showtime).

Video-On-Demand: Planned

Pay-Per-View
Addressable homes: 1,400.
iN DEMAND (delivered digitally), Addressable: Yes; Playboy TV (delivered digitally); Spice (delivered digitally); Club Jenna (delivered digitally).

Internet Service
Operational: Yes.
Broadband Service: Comcast High Speed Internet.
Fee: $42.95 monthly.

Telephone Service
Digital: Operational
Fee: $44.95 monthly
Total homes in franchised area: 20,363. Miles of plant (coax) included in Dover, DE
Vice President & General Manager: Henry Pearl. Area Engineering Manager: Cliff Jones. Marketing Director: David Tashjian. Business Operations Manager: Cara Dever. Government & Public Affairs Director: Tom Worley.
Ownership: Comcast Cable Communications Inc. (MSO).

FREDERICK—Comcast Cable, 11800 Tech Rd, Silver Spring, MD 20904. Phone: 301-625-3500. Fax: 301-625-3474. Web Site: http://www.comcast.com. Also serves Adamstown, Braddock Heights, Brunswick, Burkittsville, Emmitsburg, Fort Detrick, Frederick County, Jefferson, Libertytown, Middletown, Mount Airy, Mount Pleasant, Myersville, New Market, Point of Rocks, Rosemont, Thurmont, Urbana, Walkersville,

Washington County (unincorporated areas) & Woodsboro. ICA: MD0009.

TV Market Ranking: 14 (Libertytown); 9,14 (Frederick County (portions), Mount Airy); Below 100 (Adamstown, Braddock Heights, Brunswick, Burkittsville, Emmitsburg, Fort Detrick, FREDERICK, Jefferson, Middletown, Mount Pleasant, Myersville, New Market, Point of Rocks, Rosemont, Thurmont, Urbana, Walkersville, Washington County (unincorporated areas), Woodsboro, Frederick County (portions)). Franchise award date: N.A. Franchise expiration date: N.A. Began: July 1, 1967.

Channel capacity: N.A. Channels available but not in use: None.

Basic Service

Subscribers: 57,474.

Programming (received off-air): WBAL-TV (NBC) Baltimore; WDCA (MNT) Washington; WDCW (CW) Washington; WETA-TV (PBS) Washington; WHAG-TV (NBC) Hagerstown; WJAL (IND) Hagerstown; WJLA-TV (ABC) Washington; WJZ-TV (CBS) Baltimore; WMAR-TV (ABC) Baltimore; WMPB (PBS) Baltimore; WNVC (ETV) Fairfax; WRC-TV (NBC) Washington; WTTG (FOX) Washington; WUSA (CBS) Washington; WWPX-TV (ION) Martinsburg.

Programming (via microwave): NewsChannel 8.

Programming (via satellite): C-SPAN; Eternal Word TV Network; Hallmark Channel; Halogen Network; Trinity Broadcasting Network; TV Guide Network; Weather Channel.

Current originations: Government Access; Educational Access.

Fee: $12.50 monthly.

Expanded Basic Service 1

Subscribers: 34,249.

Programming (via satellite): ABC Family Channel; AMC; Animal Planet; Arts & Entertainment; BET Networks; CNBC; CNN; Comcast SportsNet Mid-Atlantic; Comedy Central; Discovery Channel; Disney Channel; E! Entertainment Television; ESPN; ESPN 2; Food Network; Fox News Channel; FX; Great American Country; Headline News; HGTV; History Channel; Lifetime; MSNBC; MTV; Nickelodeon; Spike TV; Syfy; TBS Superstation; The Learning Channel; Travel Channel; truTV; Turner Network TV; TV Land; USA Network; VH1.

Fee: $18.49 monthly.

Digital Basic Service

Subscribers: 5,422.

Programming (via satellite): AmericanLife TV Network; BBC America; Bloomberg Television; Bravo; Discovery Digital Networks; DMX Music; ESPN Classic Sports; Fox Sports World; G4; Golf Channel; GSN; Halogen Network; Mid-Atlantic Sports Network; National Geographic Channel; Nick Jr.; Outdoor Channel; Speed Channel; Versus; VH1; VH1 Country; WE tv.

Pay Service 1

Pay Units: 9,552.

Programming (via satellite): Cinemax.

Fee: $8.95 monthly.

Pay Service 2

Pay Units: 30,167.

Programming (via satellite): HBO.

Fee: $10.95 monthly.

Pay Service 3

Pay Units: 1,014.

Programming (via satellite): Showtime.

Fee: $8.95 monthly.

Digital Pay Service 1

Pay Units: N.A.

Programming (via satellite): Cinemax (multiplexed); Encore (multiplexed); Fox Sports en Espanol; HBO (multiplexed); Showtime (multiplexed); Starz (multiplexed); The Movie Channel (multiplexed).

Video-On-Demand: Yes

Pay-Per-View

Addressable homes: 5,422.

Hot Choice (delivered digitally), Addressable: Yes; Fresh (delivered digitally).

Internet Service

Operational: Yes. Began: March 1, 2000.

Subscribers: 720.

Broadband Service: Comcast High Speed Internet.

Fee: $42.95 monthly.

Telephone Service

Digital: Operational

Miles of Plant: 1,688.0 (coaxial); 340.0 (fiber optic). Homes passed: 85,553.

Vice President & General Manager: Sanford Ames, Jr. Technical Operations Director: Tom Kearny. Marketing Director: Kevin Oxedine.

City fee: 3% of gross.

Ownership: Comcast Cable Communications Inc. (MSO).

GAITHERSBURG—RCN Corp. Formerly [MD0054]. This cable system has converted to IPTV, 196 Van Buren St, Herndon, VA 20170. Phone: 703-434-8200. Web Site: http://www.rcn.com. ICA: MD5099.

TV Market Ranking: 9 (GAITHERSBURG (PORTIONS)).

Channel capacity: N.A. Channels available but not in use: N.A.

Internet Service

Operational: Yes.

Fee: $38.00 monthly.

Telephone Service

Digital: Operational

Fee: $45.00 monthly

Chairman: Steven J. Simmons. Chief Executive Officer: Jim Holanda.

Ownership: RCN Corp.

GRANTSVILLE—Comcast Cable, 15 Summit Park Dr, Pittsburgh, PA 15275. Phones: 412-747-6400; 301-895-4375 (Grantsville office). Fax: 412-747-6401. Web Site: http://www.comcast.com. Also serves Boynton, Salisbury & West Salisbury. ICA: MD0045.

TV Market Ranking: Outside TV Markets (Boynton, GRANTSVILLE, Salisbury, West Salisbury). Franchise award date: N.A. Franchise expiration date: N.A. Began: January 1, 1970.

Channel capacity: 42 (not 2-way capable). Channels available but not in use: 3.

Basic Service

Subscribers: N.A.

Programming (received off-air): KDKA-TV (CBS) Pittsburgh; WHAG-TV (NBC) Hagerstown; WJAC-TV (NBC) Johnstown; WPCB-TV (IND) Greensburg; WPCW (CW) Jeannette; WQED (PBS) Pittsburgh; WTAE-TV (ABC) Pittsburgh; WTAJ-TV (CBS) Altoona; WWCP-TV (FOX) Johnstown; allband FM.

Programming (via satellite): Country Music TV; C-SPAN; Home Shopping Network; WGN America.

Fee: $39.95 installation; $14.00 monthly.

Expanded Basic Service 1

Subscribers: 1,126.

Programming (via satellite): ABC Family Channel; Arts & Entertainment; CNN; Discovery Channel; Disney Channel; ESPN; ESPN 2; Fox News Channel; Fox Sports Net Pittsburgh; FX; HGTV; Lifetime; Nickelodeon; Outdoor Channel; Spike TV; TBS Superstation; The Learning Channel; Turner Classic Movies; Turner Network TV; USA Network; VH1; Weather Channel.

Fee: $38.00 monthly.

Pay Service 1

Pay Units: 47.

Programming (via satellite): Cinemax; HBO; Showtime.

Internet Service

Operational: Yes.

Telephone Service

None

Miles of Plant: 110.0 (coaxial); None (fiber optic). Homes passed: 3,940.

Regional Vice President: Linda Hossinger. Manager: Barry Savage. Vice President, Technical Operations: Randy Bender. Vice President, Marketing: Donna Corning. Vice President, Public Affairs: Jody Doherty.

City fee: 3% of gross.

Ownership: Comcast Cable Communications Inc. (MSO).

GRASONVILLE—Atlantic Broadband, 330 Drummer Dr, Grasonville, MD 21638-1204. Phones: 800-559-1746; 410-827-6441. Fax: 410-827-4078. E-mail: info@atlanticbb.com. Web Site: http://www.atlanticbb.com. Also serves Barclay, Betterton, Centreville, Chestertown, Church Hill, Kent County (portions), Millington, Oxford, Queen Anne's County (portions), Queenstown, Rio Vista, Rock Hall, St. Michaels, Stevensville, Sudlersville, Talbot County (portions), Templeville, Trappe & Wye Mills. ICA: MD0050.

TV Market Ranking: 14 (Betterton, Centreville, Chestertown, GRASONVILLE, Kent County (portions), Queen Anne's County (portions), Queenstown, Rock Hall, Stevensville); Below 100 (Talbot County (portions), Trappe, Kent County (portions)); Outside TV Markets (Barclay, Church Hill, Millington, Oxford, Rio Vista, St. Michaels, Sudlersville, Talbot County (portions), Templeville, Wye Mills, Queen Anne's County (portions)). Franchise award date: N.A. Franchise expiration date: N.A. Began: March 15, 1983.

Channel capacity: N.A. Channels available but not in use: N.A.

Basic Service

Subscribers: 15,000.

Programming (received off-air): WBAL-TV (NBC) Baltimore; WBFF (FOX, IND) Baltimore; WBOC-TV (CBS, FOX) Salisbury; WETA-TV (PBS) Washington; WJZ-TV (CBS) Baltimore; WMAR-TV (ABC) Baltimore; WMPT (PBS) Annapolis; WNUV (CW) Baltimore; WTTG (FOX) Washington; WUSA (CBS) Washington; WUTB (MNT) Baltimore.

Programming (via satellite): C-SPAN; C-SPAN 2; Home Shopping Network; Mid-Atlantic Sports Network; QVC.

Current originations: Government Access; Educational Access; Public Access.

Fee: $24.84 monthly.

Expanded Basic Service 1

Subscribers: 12,053.

Programming (via satellite): ABC Family Channel; AMC; Animal Planet; Arts & Entertainment; BET Networks; Bravo; Cartoon Network; CNBC; CNN; Comedy Central; Country Music TV; Discovery Channel; Discovery Health Channel; Disney Channel; E! Entertainment Television; ESPN; ESPN 2; Food Network; Fox News Channel; FX; Headline News; HGTV; History Channel; Lifetime; Lifetime Movie Network; Mid-Atlantic Sports Network; MSNBC; MTV; National Geographic Channel; Nickelodeon; NickToons TV; Speed Channel; Spike TV; Syfy; TBS Superstation; The Learning Channel; Travel Channel; Turner Network TV; TV Land; USA Network; Versus; VH1; Weather Channel.

Fee: $31.45 monthly.

Digital Basic Service

Subscribers: N.A.

Programming (received off-air): WBAL-TV (NBC) Baltimore; WBOC-TV (CBS, FOX) Salisbury; WETA-TV (PBS) Washington; WJZ-TV (CBS) Baltimore; WMAR-TV (ABC) Baltimore; WMPT (PBS) Annapolis; WTTG (FOX) Washington; WUSA (CBS) Washington; WUTB (MNT) Baltimore.

Programming (via satellite): Animal Planet HD; Arts & Entertainment HD; BBC America; Bio; Bloomberg Television; CCTV-4; Cooking Channel; Discovery Channel HD; Discovery en Espanol; Discovery HD Theater; Discovery Kids Channel; Discovery Military Channel; Discovery Planet Green; Do-It-Yourself; Encore; ESPN 2 HD; ESPN Classic Sports; ESPN HD; ESPNews; Eternal Word TV Network; Fuel TV; G4; Golf Channel; Great American Country; GSN; Hallmark Channel; History Channel International; ID Investigation Discovery; Independent Film Channel; Jewelry Television; Lifetime Real Women; LOGO; Mid-Atlantic Sports Network; MTV Hits; MTV Jams; MTV Tres; MTV2; Music Choice; NFL Network; Nick Jr.; Nick Too; Oxygen; Science Channel; SoapNet; Starz; Starz HDTV; Style Network; TBS in HD; TeenNick; The Sportsman Channel; Toon Disney; Trinity Broadcasting Network; Turner Classic Movies; Turner Network TV HD; TVG Network; VH1 Classic; VH1 Country; VH1 Soul; WE tv; Weatherscan.

Fee: $18.95 monthly.

Digital Pay Service 1

Pay Units: 2,121.

Programming (via satellite): Cinemax (multiplexed); Cinemax HD.

Fee: $16.95 monthly.

Digital Pay Service 2

Pay Units: 3,010.

Programming (via satellite): HBO (multiplexed); HBO HD.

Fee: $16.95 monthly.

Digital Pay Service 3

Pay Units: 1,506.

Programming (via satellite): Flix; Showtime (multiplexed); The Movie Channel (multiplexed).

Fee: $16.95 monthly.

Video-On-Demand: Yes

Pay-Per-View

Hot Choice (delivered digitally), Fee: $8.99-$9.99, Addressable: Yes; iN DEMAND (delivered digitally), Fee: $3.99.

Internet Service

Operational: Yes.

Broadband Service: Atlantic Broadband High-Speed Internet.

Fee: $23.95-$57.95 monthly.

Telephone Service
Digital: Operational
Fee: $44.95 monthly
Miles of Plant: 885.0 (coaxial); 285.0 (fiber optic). Homes passed: 32,000.
Vice President & General Manager: Joseph Di Julio. Marketing Director: Sam McGill. Personnel Manager: Susan Gresh. Construction Manager: Rick Hudkins.
Franchise fee: 3% -5% of gross.
Ownership: Atlantic Broadband (MSO).

HAGERSTOWN—Antietam Cable TV, 1000 Willow Cir, Hagerstown, MD 21740-6829. Phones: 301-797-5008 (Technical repair); 301-797-5000 (Customer service). Fax: 301-797-1835. Web Site: http://www.antietamcable.com. Also serves Bolivar, Boonsboro, Clear Spring, Clewsville, Foxville, Funkstown, Halfway, Pinesburg, Smithsburg, Washington County & Williamsport. ICA: MD0011.
TV Market Ranking: Below 100 (Bolivar, Boonsboro, Clear Spring, Clewsville, Foxville, Funkstown, HAGERSTOWN, Halfway, Pinesburg, Smithsburg, Washington County, Williamsport). Franchise award date: August 11, 1966. Franchise expiration date: N.A. Began: February 15, 1967.
Channel capacity: 65 (operating 2-way). Channels available but not in use: N.A.
Basic Service
Subscribers: 39,000.
Programming (received off-air): WDCA (MNT) Washington; WDCW (CW) Washington; WETA-TV (PBS) Washington; WHAG-TV (NBC) Hagerstown; WJAL (IND) Hagerstown; WJLA-TV (ABC) Washington; WJZ-TV (CBS) Baltimore; WMAR-TV (ABC) Baltimore; WRC-TV (NBC) Washington; WTTG (FOX) Washington; WUSA (CBS) Washington; WWPB (PBS) Hagerstown; WWPX-TV (ION) Martinsburg; 28 FMs.
Programming (via satellite): C-SPAN; Eternal Word TV Network; Home Shopping Network; Trinity Broadcasting Network; TV Guide Network.
Current originations: Government Access; Educational Access.
Fee: $59.50 installation; $13.10 monthly; $1.57 converter; $37.90 additional installation.
Expanded Basic Service 1
Subscribers: N.A.
Programming (via satellite): ABC Family Channel; AMC; Animal Planet; Arts & Entertainment; BET Networks; Bravo; Cartoon Network; CNBC; CNN; Comcast SportsNet Mid-Atlantic; Comedy Central; Country Music TV; C-SPAN 2; Discovery Channel; E! Entertainment Television; ESPN; ESPN 2; ESPN Classic Sports; Food Network; Fox News Channel; FX; Hallmark Channel; Headline News; HGTV; History Channel; Lifetime; Mid-Atlantic Sports Network; MSNBC; MTV; National Geographic Channel; Nickelodeon; QVC; ShopNBC; Speed Channel; Spike TV; Syfy; TBS Superstation; The Learning Channel; Travel Channel; truTV; Turner Classic Movies; Turner Network TV; TV Land; USA Network; VH1; Weather Channel.
Fee: $32.65 monthly.
Digital Basic Service
Subscribers: 10,000.
Programming (via satellite): AmericanLife TV Network; BBC America; Bio; Bloomberg Television; Cooking Channel; Discovery Health Channel; Discovery Kids Channel; Discovery Military Channel; Discovery Planet Green; DMX Music; Do-It-Yourself; Encore (multiplexed); ESPNews; Fox College Sports Atlantic; Fox College Sports Central; Fox College Sports Pacific; Fox Movie Channel; Fox Soccer; Fuel TV; G4; Golf Channel; Great American Country; GSN; History Channel International; ID Investigation Discovery; MTV Hits; MTV2; Nick Jr.; NickToons TV; Outdoor Channel; Ovation; Science Channel; Sleuth; SoapNet; TeenNick; Toon Disney; Versus; VH1 Classic.
Fee: $7.98 monthly.
Digital Expanded Basic Service
Subscribers: N.A.
Programming (received off-air): WDCA (MNT) Washington; WJLA-TV (ABC) Washington; WRC-TV (NBC) Washington; WTTG (FOX) Washington; WUSA (CBS) Washington; WWPB (PBS) Hagerstown.
Programming (via satellite): Discovery HD Theater; ESPN HD; Food Network HD; FX HD; HDNet; HDNet Movies; HGTV HD; MGM HD; National Geographic Channel HD Network; Speed HD; Turner Network TV HD; Universal HD.
Fee: $9.95 monthly.
Pay Service 1
Pay Units: 3,102.
Programming (via satellite): Cinemax (multiplexed).
Fee: $20.00 installation; $9.00 monthly.
Pay Service 2
Pay Units: 5,394.
Programming (via satellite): HBO (multiplexed).
Fee: $14.95 monthly.
Pay Service 3
Pay Units: 4,428.
Programming (via satellite): Flix; Showtime.
Fee: $11.25 monthly.
Pay Service 4
Pay Units: 4,176.
Programming (via satellite): Sundance Channel; The Movie Channel.
Fee: $20.00 installation; $11.25 monthly.
Digital Pay Service 1
Pay Units: N.A.
Programming (via satellite): Cinemax (multiplexed); Cinemax HD; Encore (multiplexed); HBO (multiplexed); HBO HD; Showtime (multiplexed); Showtime HD; Starz (multiplexed); The Movie Channel.
Fee: $10.95 monthly (Showtime & TMC or Starz), $16.20 monthly (Cinemax & HBO).
Video-On-Demand: Yes
Pay-Per-View
iN DEMAND (delivered digitally); Playboy TV (delivered digitally); Fresh (delivered digitally); Spice: Xcess (delivered digitally).
Internet Service
Operational: Yes.
Subscribers: 10,000.
Broadband Service: Kiva Networking.
Fee: $40.00 installation; $39.95 monthly.
Telephone Service
Analog: Not Operational
Digital: Operational
Fee: $34.95 monthly
Miles of Plant: 650.0 (coaxial); 200.0 (fiber optic). Homes passed: 40,500. Total homes in franchised area: 45,000.
Manager: Gene Hager. Marketing Director: Cindy Garland. Chief Technician: Gary Davis. Customer Service Manager: Chris Day.
City fee: 3% of gross.
Ownership: Schurz Communications Inc. (MSO).

HANCOCK—Comcast Cable, 3 N Pennsylvania Ave, Hancock, MD 21750-1405. Phones: 434-951-3700 (Charlottesville office); 301-678-6733. Fax: 301-678-7386. Web Site: http://www.comcast.com. Also serves Berkeley, Berkeley Springs, Great Cacapon & Morgan County (portions). ICA: MD0028.
TV Market Ranking: Below 100 (Berkeley, Berkeley Springs, Great Cacapon, HANCOCK, Morgan County (portions)). Franchise award date: N.A. Franchise expiration date: N.A. Began: March 24, 1952.
Channel capacity: 78 (operating 2-way). Channels available but not in use: 22.
Basic Service
Subscribers: 2,921.
Programming (received off-air): WDCA (MNT) Washington; WDCW (CW) Washington; WHAG-TV (NBC) Hagerstown; WJAL (IND) Hagerstown; WJLA-TV (ABC) Washington; WNPB-TV (PBS) Morgantown; WRC-TV (NBC) Washington; WTAJ-TV (CBS) Altoona; WTTG (FOX) Washington; WUSA (CBS) Washington; WWPB (PBS) Hagerstown; WWPX-TV (ION) Martinsburg; allband FM.
Programming (via satellite): Eternal Word TV Network; Headline News; TBS Superstation; Weather Channel.
Current originations: Government Access; Public Access.
Fee: $9.95 monthly.
Expanded Basic Service 1
Subscribers: N.A.
Programming (via satellite): ABC Family Channel; AMC; AmericanLife TV Network; Arts & Entertainment; Cartoon Network; CNBC; CNN; Comcast SportsNet Mid-Atlantic; Comedy Central; Country Music TV; C-SPAN; C-SPAN 2; Discovery Channel; Disney Channel; E! Entertainment Television; ESPN; ESPN 2; FX; Headline News; HGTV; History Channel; Home Shopping Network; Lifetime; MSNBC; MTV; Nickelodeon; Outdoor Channel; QVC; Spike TV; The Learning Channel; Travel Channel; Trinity Broadcasting Network; truTV; Turner Network TV; TV Land; USA Network; VH1.
Fee: $21.95 monthly.
Digital Basic Service
Subscribers: 557.
Programming (via satellite): AmericanLife TV Network; BBC America; Bloomberg Television; Discovery Digital Networks; DMX Music; ESPN Classic Sports; ESPNews; FitTV; Fox Sports World; G4; GSN; INSP; Mid-Atlantic Sports Network; Outdoor Channel; Science Television; Syfy; Trinity Broadcasting Network; Turner Classic Movies; Versus.
Fee: $7.00 monthly.
Digital Expanded Basic Service
Subscribers: N.A.
Programming (via satellite): Bio; GAS; Golf Channel; History Channel International; Lifetime Movie Network; Nick Jr.; WE tv.
Fee: $2.95 monthly.
Pay Service 1
Pay Units: N.A.
Programming (via satellite): Cinemax; HBO; Showtime; The Movie Channel.
Fee: $10.00 monthly (HBO), $9.00 monthly (Cinemax), $11.50 monthly (Showtime, TMC).
Digital Pay Service 1
Pay Units: N.A.
Programming (via satellite): Cinemax (multiplexed); Encore (multiplexed); HBO (multiplexed); Showtime (multiplexed); The Movie Channel (multiplexed).
Fee: $20.95 monthly (HBO), $18.95 monthly (Cinemax, Showtime, TMC or Starz).
Video-On-Demand: No
Pay-Per-View
iN DEMAND (delivered digitally), Fee: $2.99, Addressable: Yes.
Internet Service
Operational: Yes. Began: October 1, 2004.
Subscribers: 200.
Broadband Service: Comcast High Speed Internet.
Fee: $42.95 monthly.
Telephone Service
Digital: Operational
Miles of Plant: 165.0 (coaxial); 109.0 (fiber optic). Homes passed: 4,742.
Vice President & General Manager: Troy Fitzhugh. Technical Operations Director: Tom Jacobs. Chief Technician: John Nichols. Marketing Director: Steve Miles. Office Manager: Penny Miller.
City fee: 5% of gross.
Ownership: Comcast Cable Communications Inc. (MSO).

HARFORD COUNTY—Comcast Cable, 8031 Corporate Dr, Nottingham, MD 21236. Phone: 410-931-4600. Fax: 410-336-1619. Web Site: http://www.comcast.com. Also serves Aberdeen, Abingdon, Bel Air, Belcamp, Churchville, Edgewood Arsenal, Fallston, Forest Hill, Havre de Grace, Joppa & Perryman. ICA: MD0046.
TV Market Ranking: 14 (Aberdeen (portions), Abingdon, Belcamp, Edgewood Arsenal, Fallston, HARFORD COUNTY, Joppa, Perryman); 14,57 (Bel Air, Churchville, Forest Hill, Havre de Grace). Franchise award date: N.A. Franchise expiration date: N.A. Began: November 1, 1971.
Channel capacity: N.A. Channels available but not in use: N.A.
Basic Service
Subscribers: 54,000.
Programming (received off-air): WBAL-TV (NBC) Baltimore; WBFF (FOX, IND) Baltimore; WFDC-DT (UNV) Arlington; WJZ-TV (CBS) Baltimore; WMAR-TV (ABC) Baltimore; WMPB (PBS) Baltimore; WNUV (CW) Baltimore; WTTG (FOX) Washington; WUTB (MNT) Baltimore; allband FM.
Programming (via satellite): ABC Family Channel; AMC; Animal Planet; Arts & Entertainment; BET Networks; Bravo; Cartoon Network; CNBC; CNN; Comcast SportsNet Mid-Atlantic; Comedy Central; Country Music TV; C-SPAN; C-SPAN 2; Discovery Channel; Discovery Health Channel; Disney Channel; E! Entertainment Television; ESPN; ESPN 2; Eternal Word TV Network; Food Network; Fox News Channel; FX; G4; Golf Channel; Great American Country; Hallmark Channel; Headline News; HGTV; History Channel; Home Shopping Network; ION Television; Lifetime; Mid-Atlantic Sports Network; MSNBC; MTV; Nickelodeon; QVC; Speed Channel; Spike TV; Style Network; Syfy; TBS Superstation; The Comcast Network; The Learning Channel; Trinity Broadcasting Network; truTV; Turner Classic Movies; Turner Network TV; TV Guide Network; TV Land; TV One; USA Network; Versus; VH1; Weather Channel; WGN America.
Current originations: Government Access; Educational Access; Leased Access.
Fee: $44.95 installation.
Digital Basic Service
Subscribers: N.A.
Programming (received off-air): WBAL-TV (NBC) Baltimore; WBFF (FOX, IND) Baltimore; WETA-TV (PBS) Washington; WJZ-TV (CBS) Baltimore; WMAR-TV (ABC) Baltimore; WMPB (PBS) Baltimore; WNUV (CW) Baltimore; WTTG (FOX) Washington; WUTB

(MNT) Baltimore; WZDC-CA (TMO) Washington.
Programming (via satellite): ABC Family HD; AMC; Animal Planet HD; Arts & Entertainment HD; BBC America; Big Ten Network; Bio; Bloomberg Television; CBS College Sports Network; Cine Latino; Cine Mexicano; CMT Pure Country; CNN en Espanol; CNN HD; Cooking Channel; Country Music TV; C-SPAN 2; C-SPAN 3; Current; Daystar TV Network; Discovery Channel HD; Discovery en Espanol; Discovery HD Theater; Discovery Kids Channel; Discovery Military Channel; Discovery Planet Green; Disney Channel HD; Disney XD; Do-It-Yourself; Encore (multiplexed); ESPN 2 HD; ESPN Classic Sports; ESPN Deportes; ESPN HD; ESPNews; Exercise TV; Flix; Food Network HD; Fox Business Channel; Fox College Sports Atlantic; Fox College Sports Central; Fox College Sports Pacific; Fox Reality Channel; Fox Soccer (multiplexed); Fox Sports en Espanol; G4; GalaVision; Gol TV; Golf Channel HD; Gospel Music Channel; Great American Country; GSN; HGTV HD; History Channel en Espanol; History Channel HD; History Channel International; Howard TV; ID Investigation Discovery; Independent Film Channel; ION Life; ION Television; Jewelry Television; Lifetime Movie Network; LOGO; MLB Network; MoviePlex; MTV Hits; MTV Jams; MTV Tres; MTV2; mun2 television; Music Choice; National Geographic Channel; National Geographic Channel HD Network; NBA TV; NFL Network; NFL Network HD; NHL Network; Nick Jr.; Nick Too; NickToons TV; Oxygen; Palladia; PBS Kids Sprout; Retirement Living; Science Channel; Science Channel HD; Shalom TV; SoapNet; Speed HD; Starz IndiePlex; Starz RetroPlex; Style Network; Sundance Channel; Syfy HD; TBS in HD; TeenNick; Telefutura; Tennis Channel; The Word Network; TLC HD; Turner Network TV HD; TVG Network; TVK; Universal HD; USA Network HD; VeneMovies; Versus HD; VH1 Classic; VH1 Soul; V-me TV; WE tv; Weatherscan.
Fee: $9.15 monthly.

Digital Pay Service 1
Pay Units: N.A.
Programming (via satellite): Bollywood On Demand; Cinemax (multiplexed); Cinemax HD; HBO (multiplexed); HBO HD; HBO On Demand; Korean Channel; RTV21; Russian Television Network; Showtime (multiplexed); Showtime HD; Starz (multiplexed); Starz HDTV; The Movie Channel (multiplexed); TV Asia; Zee TV USA.
Fee: $15.00 monthly (each).

Video-On-Demand: Yes

Pay-Per-View
iN DEMAND, Fee: $3.99; Spice: Xcess (delivered digitally); iN DEMAND (delivered digitally); Playboy TV (delivered digitally); Sports PPV (delivered digitally); NBA League Pass (delivered digitally); NHL Center Ice (delivered digitally); MLS Direct Kick (delivered digitally); MLB Extra Innings (delivered digitally).

Internet Service
Operational: Yes. Began: January 1, 1999.
Broadband Service: Comcast High Speed Internet.
Fee: $149.00 installation; $42.95 monthly; $7.00 modem lease; $299.00 modem purchase.

Telephone Service
Digital: Operational
Fee: $44.95 monthly

Miles of Plant: 1,077.0 (coaxial); 26.0 (fiber optic). Homes passed: 69,800.

Area Vice President & General Manager: Bryan Lynch. Vice President, Regional Marketing: Mark Watts. Marketing Director: Chris Shea. Technical Operations Director: Brady Hood.
Ownership: Comcast Cable Communications Inc. (MSO).

HOWARD COUNTY—Comcast Cable, 8031 Corporate Dr, Nottingham, MD 21236. Phone: 410-931-4600. Fax: 410-336-1619. Web Site: http://www.comcast.com. Also serves Clarksville, Columbia, Cooksville, Dayton, Ellicott City, Fulton, Glenelg, Glenwood, Highland, Laurel, Lisbon, West Friendship & Woodbine. ICA: MD0008.
TV Market Ranking: 9 (Cooksville, Dayton, Fulton, Glenelg, Glenwood, Highland, HOWARD COUNTY (PORTIONS), Lisbon, West Friendship, Woodbine); 9,14 (Clarksville, Columbia, Ellicott City, Laurel). Franchise award date: February 1, 1974. Franchise expiration date: N.A. Began: January 1, 1977.
Channel capacity: N.A. Channels available but not in use: N.A.

Basic Service
Subscribers: 70,828.
Programming (received off-air): WBAL-TV (NBC) Baltimore; WBFF (FOX, IND) Baltimore; WETA-TV (PBS) Washington; WHUT-TV (PBS) Washington; WJLA-TV (ABC) Washington; WJZ-TV (CBS) Baltimore; WMAR-TV (ABC) Baltimore; WMDO-CA (TEL) Washington; WMPT (PBS) Annapolis; WNUV (CW) Baltimore; WRC-TV (NBC) Washington; WTTG (FOX) Washington; WUSA (CBS) Washington; WUTB (MNT) Baltimore.
Programming (via satellite): ABC Family Channel; Arts & Entertainment; BET Networks; Cartoon Network; CNBC; CNN; C-SPAN; C-SPAN 2; Discovery Channel; E! Entertainment Television; ESPN; ESPN 2; Eternal Word TV Network; Hallmark Channel; Headline News; ION Television; Lifetime; MTV; Nickelodeon; QVC; The Comcast Network; The Learning Channel; Trinity Broadcasting Network; Turner Network TV; TV Guide Network; USA Network; VH1; Weather Channel; WGN America.
Current originations: Government Access; Educational Access; Public Access.
Fee: $44.95 installation; $22.96 monthly.

Expanded Basic Service 1
Subscribers: N.A.
Programming (via satellite): AMC; Animal Planet; Bravo; Comcast SportsNet Philly; Comedy Central; Country Music TV; Discovery Health Channel; ESPN Classic Sports; Food Network; Fox News Channel; FX; Golf Channel; HGTV; History Channel; Home Shopping Network 2; MSNBC; Speed Channel; Spike TV; Style Network; Syfy; TBS Superstation; truTV; TV Land; TV One; Versus.
Fee: $54.95 monthly.

Digital Basic Service
Subscribers: N.A.
Programming (received off-air): WZDC-CA (TMO) Washington.
Programming (via satellite): BBC America; Cooking Channel; C-SPAN 3; Discovery Digital Networks; Do-It-Yourself; ESPNews; G4; GAS; Great American Country; Mid-Atlantic Sports Network; MTV Networks Digital Suite; Music Choice; National Geographic Channel; Nick Jr.; Nick Too; SoapNet; Toon Disney; WAM! America's Kidz Network; Weatherscan.
Fee: $12.30 monthly.

Digital Pay Service 1
Pay Units: N.A.
Programming (via satellite): Canales N; Cinemax (multiplexed); Encore; Flix (multiplexed); HBO (multiplexed); Korean Channel; Russian Television Network; Showtime (multiplexed); Sundance Channel (multiplexed); The Movie Channel (multiplexed); TV Asia; Zee TV USA.
Fee: $16.93 monthly (each).

Video-On-Demand: Yes

Pay-Per-View
Hot Choice (delivered digitally); Playboy TV (delivered digitally); Fresh (delivered digitally); Shorteez (delivered digitally); Pleasure (delivered digitally).

Internet Service
Operational: Yes.
Broadband Service: Comcast High Speed Internet.
Fee: $42.95 monthly; $7.00 modem lease; $199.00 modem purchase.

Telephone Service
Digital: Operational
Fee: $44.95 monthly

Total homes in franchised area: 110,846.
Area Vice President & General Manager: Bryan Lynch. Regional Marketing Manager: Mark Watts. Marketing Director: Chris Shea. Technical Operations Director: Brady Hood.
Ownership: Comcast Cable Communications Inc. (MSO).

HOWARD COUNTY—Mid-Atlantic Communications. Now served by HOWARD COUNTY, MD [MD0008]. ICA: MD0047.

LEXINGTON PARK—GMP Cable TV. Now served by ST. MARYS COUNTY, MD [MD0024]. ICA: MD0022.

LOTHIAN—Comcast Cable. Now served by ANNE ARUNDEL COUNTY, MD [MD0006]. ICA: MD0053.

MILLERSVILLE—Broadstripe, 406 Headquarters Dr, Ste 201, Millersville, MD 21108-2554. Phones: 410-987-9300 (Customer service); 410-987-8400. Fax: 410-987-4890. E-mail: customerservicemd@broadstripe.com. Web Site: http://www.broadstripe.com. Also serves Annapolis Junction, Anne Arundel County (northern portion), Arnold, Brooklyn Park, Gambrills, Glen Burnie, Hanover, Harmans, Jessup, Laurel, Linthicum, Odenton, Pasadena, Severn & Severna Park. ICA: MD0007. **Note:** This system is an overbuild.
TV Market Ranking: 9 (Annapolis Junction, Arnold, Brooklyn Park, Gambrills, Glen Burnie, Hanover, Harmans, Jessup, Laurel, Linthicum, Odenton, Pasadena, Severn, Severna Park); 9,14 (Anne Arundel County (northern portion), MILLERSVILLE). Franchise award date: July 1, 1971. Franchise expiration date: N.A. Began: August 19, 1990.
Channel capacity: 80 (operating 2-way). Channels available but not in use: 8.

Basic Service
Subscribers: 45,000.
Programming (received off-air): WBAL-TV (NBC) Baltimore; WBFF (FOX, IND) Baltimore; WETA-TV (PBS) Washington; WHUT-TV (PBS) Washington; WJLA-TV (ABC) Washington; WJZ-TV (CBS) Baltimore; WMAR-TV (ABC) Baltimore; WMPT (PBS) Annapolis; WNUV (CW) Baltimore; WRC-TV (NBC) Washington; WTTG (FOX) Washington; WUSA (CBS) Washington; WUTB (MNT) Baltimore.
Programming (via satellite): C-SPAN; TV Guide Network.
Current originations: Government Access; Leased Access; Public Access.
Fee: $100.00 installation; $10.00 monthly; $2.00 converter.

Expanded Basic Service 1
Subscribers: N.A.
Programming (via satellite): ABC Family Channel; AMC; Animal Planet; Arts & Entertainment; BET Networks; Bravo; Cartoon Network; CNBC; CNN; Comcast SportsNet Mid-Atlantic; Comedy Central; Cooking Channel; Country Music TV; C-SPAN 2; Discovery Channel; Discovery Health Channel; Disney Channel; E! Entertainment Television; ESPN; ESPN 2; Food Network; Fox News Channel; FX; G4; Golf Channel; GSN; Hallmark Channel; Headline News; HGTV; History Channel; Home Shopping Network; INSP; Lifetime; Mid-Atlantic Sports Network; MSNBC; MTV; National Geographic Channel; Nickelodeon; Oxygen; Paxson Communications Corp.; QVC; ShopNBC; SoapNet; Speed Channel; Spike TV; Syfy; TBS Superstation; The Learning Channel; Toon Disney; Travel Channel; truTV; Turner Classic Movies; Turner Network TV; TV Land; Univision; USA Network; Versus; VH1; WE tv; Weather Channel; WGN America.
Fee: $50.00 installation; $37.65 monthly.

Digital Basic Service
Subscribers: 17,000.
Programming (received off-air): WBAL-TV (NBC) Baltimore; WBFF (FOX, IND) Baltimore; WJZ-TV (CBS) Baltimore; WMAR-TV (ABC) Baltimore; WMPT (PBS) Annapolis; WNUV (CW) Baltimore.
Programming (via satellite): 3 Angels Broadcasting Network; BBC America; Bio; Bloomberg Television; BYU Television; Church Channel; Daystar TV Network; Discovery Digital Networks; Do-It-Yourself; ESPN; Eternal Word TV Network; FamilyNet; GAS; Golden Eagle Broadcasting; Gospel Music Channel; History Channel International; Independent Film Channel; JCTV; Lifetime Movie Network; MTV Networks Digital Suite; Music Choice; Nick Jr.; Nick Too; NickToons TV; Trinity Broadcasting Network.
Fee: $27.90 monthly.

Digital Pay Service 1
Pay Units: N.A.
Programming (via satellite): Cinemax (multiplexed); Cinemax HD; Encore (multiplexed); Flix (multiplexed); HBO (multiplexed); HBO HD; Showtime (multiplexed); Showtime HD; Starz (multiplexed); Starz

HDTV; Sundance Channel (multiplexed); The Movie Channel (multiplexed).
Fee: $12.00 monthly (each).

Video-On-Demand: No

Pay-Per-View

iN DEMAND (delivered digitally); Hot Choice (delivered digitally); Ten Blox (delivered digitally); Ten Blue (delivered digitally); Ten Clips (delivered digitally); Pleasure (delivered digitally).

Internet Service

Operational: Yes.
Subscribers: 17,000.
Broadband Service: Millennium CableSpeed.
Fee: $59.95 installation; $44.95 monthly; $5.00 modem lease; $300.00 modem purchase.

Telephone Service

Digital: Operational
Subscribers: 1,000.
Fee: $29.99 installation; $29.95 monthly

Miles of Plant: 1,200.0 (coaxial); None (fiber optic). Homes passed: 100,000. Total homes in franchised area: 110,000.

President & Chief Executive Officer: Bill Shreffler. Senior Vice President, Programming: Frank Scotello. Vice President, Marketing: Sharon Slotterback. Manager: Richard Oldenburg. Chief Technician: Alan Whitwood. Customer Service Manager: Cindy Stormer.

County fee: 5% of gross.

Ownership: Broadstripe.

MONTGOMERY COUNTY—Comcast Cable, 11800 Tech Rd, Silver Spring, MD 20904. Phone: 301-294-7600. Fax: 301-625-3474. Web Site: http://www.comcast.com. Also serves Barnesville, Bethesda, Boyds, Brookeville, Burtonsville, Cabin John, Chevy Chase, Damascus, Derwood, Gaithersburg, Garrett Park, Germantown, Glen Echo, Kensington, Olney, Poolesville, Potomac, Rockville, Silver Spring, Somerset, Takoma Park, Washington Grove, West Bethesda & Wheaton. ICA: MD0002.

TV Market Ranking: 9 (Barnesville, Boyds, Cabin John, Glen Echo, MONTGOMERY COUNTY (portions), Poolesville, Potomac); 9,14 (Bethesda, Brookeville, Burtonsville, Chevy Chase, Damascus, Derwood, Gaithersburg, Garrett Park, Germantown, Kensington, Olney, Rockville, Silver Spring, Somerset, Takoma Park, Washington Grove, West Bethesda, Wheaton). Franchise award date: May 25, 1983. Franchise expiration date: N.A. Began: September 1, 1984.

Channel capacity: N.A. Channels available but not in use: N.A.

Basic Service

Subscribers: 215,207.
Programming (received off-air): WDCA (MNT) Washington; WDCW (CW) Washington; WETA-TV (PBS) Washington; WFDC-DT (UNV) Arlington; WHUT-TV (PBS) Washington; WJLA-TV (ABC) Washington; WMDO-CA (TEL) Washington; WMPT (PBS) Annapolis; WPXW-TV (ION) Manassas; WRC-TV (NBC) Washington; WTTG (FOX) Washington; WUSA (CBS) Washington.
Programming (via microwave): NewsChannel 8.
Programming (via satellite): C-SPAN; FX; TBS Superstation; The Learning Channel; TV Guide Network; WGN America.
Current originations: Government Access; Educational Access; Public Access.
Fee: $44.99 installation; $14.75 monthly; $13.99 additional installation.

Expanded Basic Service 1

Subscribers: 191,956.
Programming (via satellite): ABC Family Channel; AMC; Animal Planet; Arts & Entertainment; BET Networks; Bravo; Cartoon Network; CNBC; CNN; Comcast SportsNet Mid-Atlantic; Comedy Central; Country Music TV; C-SPAN 2; Discovery Channel; Discovery Health Channel; Disney Channel; E! Entertainment Television; ESPN; ESPN 2; Food Network; Golf Channel; GSN; Headline News; HGTV; History Channel; Home Shopping Network; Lifetime; MSNBC; MTV; Nickelodeon; QVC; Spike TV; Style Network; Syfy; truTV; Turner Classic Movies; Turner Network TV; TV Land; TV One; USA Network; Versus; VH1; Weather Channel.
Fee: $39.40 monthly.

Digital Basic Service

Subscribers: N.A.
Programming (via satellite): BBC America; Cooking Channel; C-SPAN 3; Discovery Digital Networks; Do-It-Yourself; ESPN Classic Sports; ESPNews; G4; GAS; Mid-Atlantic Sports Network; MTV Networks Digital Suite; Music Choice; National Geographic Channel; Nick Jr.; Nick Too; SoapNet; WAM! America's Kidz Network; Weatherscan.
Fee: $14.95 monthly.

Pay Service 1

Pay Units: N.A.
Programming (via satellite): HBO (multiplexed).
Fee: $15.95 monthly.

Digital Pay Service 1

Pay Units: N.A.
Programming (via satellite): Cinemax (multiplexed); Encore; Flix (multiplexed); Flix; HBO (multiplexed); Showtime (multiplexed); Sundance Channel (multiplexed); The Movie Channel (multiplexed).
Fee: $12.95 monthly (Starz, Cinemax, Showtime or TMC), $15.95 monthly (HBO).

Video-On-Demand: Yes

Pay-Per-View

Playboy TV (delivered digitally); Fresh (delivered digitally); Shorteez (delivered digitally); Pleasure (delivered digitally); iN DEMAND (delivered digitally).

Internet Service

Operational: Yes.
Broadband Service: Comcast High Speed Internet.
Fee: $99.00 installation; $42.95 monthly; $3.00 modem lease; $199.00 modem purchase.

Telephone Service

Digital: Operational
Fee: $44.95 monthly

Miles of Plant: 3,900.0 (coaxial); 61.0 (fiber optic). Homes passed: 330,000. Total homes in franchised area: 375,742.

Vice President & General Manager: Sanford Ames, Jr. Technical Operations Director: Tom Kearny. Marketing Director: Kevin Oxedine. Public Relations Manager: Lisa Altman.

County fee: 5% of gross.

Ownership: Comcast Cable Communications Inc. (MSO).

MONTGOMERY COUNTY—RCN Corp. This cable system has converted to IPTV. See Bethesda, MD [MD5097], Chevy Chase, MD [MD5098], Gaithersburg, MD [MD5099] & Takoma Park, MD [MD5102]. ICA: MD0054.

OAKLAND—Suddenlink Communications, 12 South 3rd St, Oakland, MD 21550. Phones: 314-965-2020; 304-472-4193. Fax: 304-472-0756. Web Site: http://www.suddenlink.com. Also serves Crellin, Deep Creek, Deer Park, Kitzmiller, Loch Lynn Heights, Mountain Lake Park & Shallmar, MD; Bayard, Elk Garden & Gormania, WV. ICA: MD0029.

TV Market Ranking: Outside TV Markets (Bayard, Crellin, Deep Creek, Deer Park, Elk Garden, Gormania, Kitzmiller, Loch Lynn Heights, Mountain Lake Park, OAKLAND, Shallmar). Franchise award date: January 1, 1985. Franchise expiration date: N.A. Began: January 1, 1952.

Channel capacity: 78 (operating 2-way). Channels available but not in use: N.A.

Basic Service

Subscribers: 3,282.
Programming (received off-air): KDKA-TV (CBS) Pittsburgh; WBOY-TV (NBC) Clarksburg; WDTV (CBS) Weston; WGPT (PBS) Oakland; WHAG-TV (NBC) Hagerstown; WJAC-TV (NBC) Johnstown; WPCB-TV (IND) Greensburg; WPGH-TV (FOX) Pittsburgh; WPXI (IND, NBC) Pittsburgh; WQED (PBS) Pittsburgh; WTAE-TV (ABC) Pittsburgh.
Programming (via satellite): C-SPAN; Home Shopping Network; Trinity Broadcasting Network; TV Guide Network; Weather Channel; WGN America.
Current originations: Public Access.
Fee: $61.25 installation; $15.98 monthly; $1.24 converter.

Expanded Basic Service 1

Subscribers: 623.
Programming (via satellite): ABC Family Channel; AMC; Animal Planet; Arts & Entertainment; Cartoon Network; CNBC; CNN; Comedy Central; Country Music TV; Discovery Channel; Disney Channel; ESPN; ESPN 2; ESPN Classic Sports; Fox News Channel; Fox Sports Net Pittsburgh; FX; Golf Channel; Great American Country; GSN; Hallmark Channel; Headline News; HGTV; History Channel; Lifetime; MSNBC; MTV; National Geographic Channel; Nickelodeon; Outdoor Channel; SoapNet; Speed Channel; Spike TV; Syfy; TBS Superstation; The Learning Channel; Turner Network TV; TV Land; USA Network; VH1; WE tv.
Fee: $9.96 monthly.

Digital Basic Service

Subscribers: N.A.
Programming (via satellite): BBC America; Bio; Bloomberg Television; Discovery Digital Networks; DMX Music; ESPNews; Fox College Sports Atlantic; Fox College Sports Central; Fox College Sports Pacific; Fox Movie Channel; Fox Soccer; Fuse; G4; History Channel International; Independent Film Channel; Lifetime Movie Network; ShopNBC; Style Network; Toon Disney; Turner Classic Movies; Versus.
Fee: $13.95 monthly.

Pay Service 1

Pay Units: 1,305.
Programming (via satellite): Cinemax; HBO; Showtime.
Fee: $17.50 installation; $7.95 monthly (Cinemax), $11.95 monthly (Showtime), $11.99 monthly (HBO).

Pay Service 2

Pay Units: N.A.
Programming (via satellite): Encore; Starz; The Movie Channel.
Fee: $5.99 monthly (Encore & Starz), $11.95 monthly (TMC).

Digital Pay Service 1

Pay Units: N.A.
Programming (via satellite): Cinemax (multiplexed); Encore (multiplexed); HBO (multiplexed); Showtime (multiplexed); Starz (multiplexed); The Movie Channel.

Video-On-Demand: No

Pay-Per-View

iN DEMAND (delivered digitally); Playboy TV (delivered digitally); Fresh (delivered digitally).

Internet Service

Operational: Yes. Began: June 7, 2004.
Broadband Service: Cebridge High Speed Cable Internet.
Fee: $45.00 installation; $29.95 monthly.

Telephone Service

Analog: Not Operational
Digital: Operational
Fee: $39.95 monthly

Miles of Plant: 125.0 (coaxial); None (fiber optic). Homes passed: 3,964.

Operations Director: Peter Brown.

City fee: 3% of gross; 5% of gross (Bayard, WV).

Ownership: Cequel Communications LLC (MSO).

OCEAN CITY—Comcast Cable, 5729 W Denneys Rd, Dover, DE 19904-1365. Phone: 302-674-2494. Fax: 302-674-2538. Web Site: http://www.comcast.com. Also serves Fenwick Island & Sussex County, DE; Berlin & Worcester County, MD. ICA: MD0010.

TV Market Ranking: Below 100 (Berlin, Fenwick Island, OCEAN CITY, Sussex County, Worcester County). Franchise award date: N.A. Franchise expiration date: N.A. Began: July 1, 1962.

Channel capacity: N.A. Channels available but not in use: N.A.

Basic Service

Subscribers: 31,182.
Programming (received off-air): WBOC-TV (CBS, FOX) Salisbury; WMDT (ABC, CW) Salisbury; WMPT (PBS) Annapolis.
Programming (via microwave): WBAL-TV (NBC) Baltimore; WJZ-TV (CBS) Baltimore; WTTG (FOX) Washington.
Programming (via satellite): C-SPAN; Home Shopping Network; QVC; Trinity Broadcasting Network; TV Guide Network; Weather Channel.
Current originations: Government Access; Educational Access; Public Access.
Fee: $44.95 installation; $15.45 monthly.

Expanded Basic Service 1

Subscribers: N.A.
Programming (via satellite): ABC Family Channel; AMC; America's Store; Animal Planet; Arts & Entertainment; BET Networks; Bravo; Cartoon Network; CNBC; CNN; Comcast SportsNet Mid-Atlantic; Comedy Central; Country Music TV; C-SPAN 2; Discovery Channel; Discovery Health Channel; Disney Channel; E! Entertainment Television; ESPN; ESPN 2; Eternal Word TV Network; Food Network; Fox News Channel; FX; Golf Channel; Great American Country; Headline News; HGTV; History Channel; ION Television; Lifetime; MTV; Nickelodeon; Shop at Home; Spike TV; Syfy; TBS Superstation; The Learning Channel; truTV; Turner Classic Movies; Turner Network TV; TV Land; TV One; USA Network; VH1.
Fee: $26.45 monthly.

Digital Basic Service

Subscribers: N.A.
Programming (via satellite): BBC America; Canales N; C-SPAN 3; Discovery Digital Networks; DMX Music; Encore Action; ESPN Classic Sports; ESPNews; Flix; Fox Sports World; G4; Gaming Entertainment Television; GAS; GSN; Independent Film Channel; Mid-Atlantic Sports Network; MTV

Networks Digital Suite; National Geographic Channel; Nick Jr.; Nick Too; SoapNet; Sundance Channel; Toon Disney; Versus; WE tv; Weatherscan.
Fee: $18.09 monthly.

Pay Service 1
Pay Units: N.A.
Programming (via satellite): Cinemax; HBO; Showtime.
Fee: $18.00 monthly (each).

Digital Pay Service 1
Pay Units: N.A.
Programming (via satellite): Cinemax (multiplexed); HBO (multiplexed); Showtime (multiplexed); Starz (multiplexed); The Movie Channel (multiplexed).
Fee: $16.50 monthly (each).

Video-On-Demand: Yes

Pay-Per-View
Addressable homes: 24,968.
iN DEMAND (delivered digitally), Addressable: Yes; ESPN Now (delivered digitally); ESPN Gameplan (delivered digitally); Sports PPV (delivered digitally).

Internet Service
Operational: Yes. Began: December 31, 2001.
Broadband Service: Comcast High Speed Internet.
Fee: $42.95 monthly.

Telephone Service
Digital: Operational

Miles of Plant: None (coaxial); 11.0 (fiber optic). Homes passed: 37,970. Total homes in franchised area: 45,490. Miles of plant (coax) included in Dover, DE

Vice President & General Manager: Henry Pearl. Area Engineering Manager: Cliff Jones. Marketing Director: David Tashjian. Business Operations Director: Cara Dever. Government & Public Affairs Director: Tom Worley.

City fee: 5% of gross.

Ownership: Comcast Cable Communications Inc. (MSO).

OLDTOWN—Oldtown Community Systems Inc., PO Box 75, 19401 Oldtown Rd SE, Oldtown, MD 21555. Phone: 301-478-5700. Fax: 301-478-5711. Also serves Allegany County (eastern portion), Flintstone & Spring Gap. ICA: MD0035.

TV Market Ranking: Below 100 (Allegany County (portions), Flintstone, OLDTOWN, Spring Gap); Outside TV Markets (Allegany County (portions)). Franchise award date: April 29, 1979. Franchise expiration date: N.A. Began: March 1, 1981.

Channel capacity: 42 (not 2-way capable). Channels available but not in use: 6.

Basic Service
Subscribers: 421.
Programming (received off-air): WDCA (MNT) Washington; WHAG-TV (NBC) Hagerstown; WJLA-TV (ABC) Washington; WMPT (PBS) Annapolis; WTTG (FOX) Washington; WUSA (CBS) Washington.
Programming (via satellite): ABC Family Channel; AMC; Animal Planet; Arts & Entertainment; Cartoon Network; CNN; Comcast SportsNet Mid-Atlantic; Country Music TV; Discovery Channel; Disney Channel; ESPN; ESPN 2; Food Network; FX; GSN; HGTV; History Channel; Lifetime; Nickelodeon; Outdoor Channel; QVC; Spike TV; Syfy; TBS Superstation; The Learning Channel; Trinity Broadcasting Network; Turner Classic Movies; Turner Network TV; TV Land; USA Network; Weather Channel; WGN America.
Current originations: Educational Access; Public Access.
Fee: $25.00 installation; $29.00 monthly.

Pay Service 1
Pay Units: 90.
Programming (via satellite): HBO.
Fee: $10.00 installation; $11.03 monthly.

Video-On-Demand: No

Pay-Per-View
ESPN Now (delivered digitally); iN DEMAND (delivered digitally).

Internet Service
Operational: No.

Telephone Service
None

Miles of Plant: 120.0 (coaxial); None (fiber optic). Homes passed: 900. Total homes in franchised area: 1,500.

Chief Technician: John Wilfong.

Ownership: Oldtown Community Systems Inc.

POCOMOKE—Comcast Cable. Now served by SALISBURY, MD [MD0015]. ICA: MD0052.

PRINCE FREDERICK—Comcast Cable, 1030 Theatre Dr, Prince Frederick, MD 20678-3409. Phones: 800-445-6017 (Customer service); 410-729-8000 (Millersville office); 410-414-9620. Fax: 410-729-8001. Web Site: http://www.comcast.com. Also serves Calvert Beach, Chesapeake Beach, Dunkirk, Huntingtown, Lusby, Mechanicsville, North Beach & Owings. ICA: MD0016.

TV Market Ranking: 9 (Chesapeake Beach, Dunkirk, Huntingtown, Mechanicsville, North Beach, Owings, PRINCE FREDERICK); Below 100 (Mechanicsville); Outside TV Markets (Calvert Beach, Lusby). Franchise award date: January 1, 1984. Franchise expiration date: N.A. Began: February 21, 1985.

Channel capacity: 42 (operating 2-way). Channels available but not in use: None.

Basic Service
Subscribers: 15,981.
Programming (received off-air): WBAL-TV (NBC) Baltimore; WDCA (MNT) Washington; WETA-TV (PBS) Washington; WFDC-DT (UNV) Arlington; WHUT-TV (PBS) Washington; WJLA-TV (ABC) Washington; WJZ-TV (CBS) Baltimore; WMAR-TV (ABC) Baltimore; WMPT (PBS) Annapolis; WPXW-TV (ION) Manassas; WRC-TV (NBC) Washington; WTTG (FOX) Washington; WUSA (CBS) Washington.
Programming (via microwave): NewsChannel 8.
Programming (via satellite): ABC Family Channel; AMC; Animal Planet; Arts & Entertainment; BET Networks; Cartoon Network; CNBC; CNN; Comcast SportsNet Mid-Atlantic; Comedy Central; Country Music TV; C-SPAN 2; Discovery Channel; Discovery Health Channel; Disney Channel; E! Entertainment Television; ESPN; ESPN 2; Eternal Word TV Network; Food Network; Fox News Channel; FX; G4; Golf Channel; GSN; Hallmark Channel; Headline News; HGTV; History Channel; Home Shopping Network; Lifetime; Mid-Atlantic Sports Network; MSNBC; MTV; MyNetworkTV Inc.; National Geographic Channel; Nickelodeon; QVC; Speed Channel; Spike TV; Style Network; Syfy; TBS Superstation; The Comcast Network; The Learning Channel; Travel Channel; Trinity Broadcasting Network; truTV; Turner Classic Movies; Turner Network TV; TV Guide Network; TV Land; TV One; USA Network; Versus; VH1; Weather Channel; WGN America.
Current originations: Government Access; Educational Access; Public Access.
Fee: $25.00 installation; $44.90 monthly; $1.29 converter.

Digital Basic Service
Subscribers: N.A.
Programming (received off-air): WDCW (CW) Washington; WETA-TV (PBS) Washington; WJLA-TV (ABC) Washington; WNVC (ETV) Fairfax; WRC-TV (NBC) Washington; WTTG (FOX) Washington; WUSA (CBS) Washington.
Programming (via satellite): Arts & Entertainment HD; BBC America; Bio; Canales N; CBS College Sports Network; CMT Pure Country; Cooking Channel; Country Music TV; C-SPAN 2; C-SPAN 3; Current; Daystar TV Network; Discovery Digital Networks; Discovery HD Theater; Do-It-Yourself; Encore (multiplexed); ESPN 2; ESPN Classic Sports; ESPN HD; ESPNews; Flix; Fox College Sports Atlantic; Fox College Sports Central; Fox College Sports Pacific; Fox Reality Channel; Fox Soccer; G4; GAS; Gol TV; Great American Country; History Channel International; HorseRacing TV; INSP; Jewelry Television; Lifetime Movie Network; LOGO; MTV Networks Digital Suite; Music Choice; National Geographic Channel HD Network; NBA TV; NFL Network; Nick Jr.; Nick Too; NickToons TV; Outdoor Channel; Oxygen; Palladia; PBS Kids Sprout; SoapNet; Sundance Channel; Tennis Channel; Toon Disney; Trinity Broadcasting Network; Turner Network TV HD; TVG Network; Universal HD; Weatherscan.
Fee: $61.08 monthly.

Digital Pay Service 1
Pay Units: N.A.
Programming (via satellite): Cinemax (multiplexed); Cinemax HD; HBO (multiplexed); HBO HD; Showtime (multiplexed); Showtime HD; Starz (multiplexed); Starz HDTV; The Movie Channel (multiplexed).
Fee: $13.25 monthly (each).

Video-On-Demand: Yes

Pay-Per-View
iN DEMAND (delivered digitally); Fresh (delivered digitally); NBA League Pass (delivered digitally); NHL Center Ice (delivered digitally).

Internet Service
Operational: Yes.
Broadband Service: Comcast High Speed Internet.
Fee: $42.95 monthly; $7.00 modem lease.

Telephone Service
Digital: Operational

Miles of Plant: 663.0 (coaxial); 17.0 (fiber optic). Additional miles planned: 27.0 (coaxial); 31.0 (fiber optic). Homes passed: 23,611.

Technical Operations: Glen Gray. General Manager: Bruce Abbott. Marketing Manager: Chuck Mann. Chief Technician: Greg Mott.

Ownership: Comcast Cable Communications Inc. (MSO).

PRINCE GEORGE'S COUNTY—Comcast Cable, 11800 Tech Rd, Silver Spring, MD 20904. Phone: 301-625-3500. Fax: 301-625-3474. Web Site: http://www.comcast.com. Also serves Accokeek, Andrews AFB, Berwyn Heights, Bladensburg, Bowie, Brandywine, Brentwood, Capitol Heights, Cheverly, Clinton, College Park, Colmar Manor, Cottage City, District Heights, Edmondston, Fairmount Heights, Forest Heights, Forestville, Fort Washington, Glenarden, Greenbelt, Hyattsville, Landover Hills, Largo, Laurel, Montpelier, Morningside, Mount Rainier, New Carrollton, North Brentwood, Oxon Hill, Riverdale, Seat Pleasant, Takoma Park, University Park & Upper Marlboro. ICA: MD0005.

TV Market Ranking: 5 (Mount Rainier); 9 (Accokeek, Andrews AFB, Berwyn Heights, Bladensburg, Bowie, Brandywine, Brentwood, Cheverly, Clinton, College Park, Colmar Manor, Cottage City, Edmondston, Forest Heights, Fort Washington, Glenarden, Greenbelt, Hyattsville, Landover Hills, Laurel, Montpelier, New Carrollton, North Brentwood, Oxon Hill, Riverdale, Takoma Park, University Park, Upper Marlboro); 9,14 (Capitol Heights, District Heights, Fairmount Heights, Forestville, Largo, Morningside, PRINCE GEORGE'S COUNTY (PORTIONS), Seat Pleasant). Franchise award date: January 1, 1982. Franchise expiration date: N.A. Began: January 1, 1982.

Channel capacity: 108 (operating 2-way). Channels available but not in use: N.A.

Basic Service
Subscribers: 177,817.
Programming (received off-air): WBAL-TV (NBC) Baltimore; WDCA (MNT) Washington; WDCW (CW) Washington; WETA-TV (PBS) Washington; WFDC-DT (UNV) Arlington; WHUT-TV (PBS) Washington; WJLA-TV (ABC) Washington; WJZ-TV (CBS) Baltimore; WMAR-TV (ABC) Baltimore; WMPB (PBS) Baltimore; WMPT (PBS) Annapolis; WNUV (CW) Baltimore; WNVC (ETV) Fairfax; WRC-TV (NBC) Washington; WTTG (FOX) Washington; WUSA (CBS) Washington.
Programming (via microwave): NewsChannel 8.
Programming (via satellite): Hallmark Channel; Home Shopping Network; INSP; Sneak Prevue; TBS Superstation; TV Guide Network.
Current originations: Leased Access; Government Access; Educational Access; Public Access.
Fee: $51.34 installation; $13.06 monthly; $17.00 additional installation.

Expanded Basic Service 1
Subscribers: 76,102.
Programming (via satellite): ABC Family Channel; AMC; Animal Planet; Arts & Entertainment; BET Networks; Cartoon Network; CNBC; CNN; Comcast SportsNet Mid-Atlantic; Comedy Central; C-SPAN; Discovery Channel; E! Entertainment Television; ESPN; ESPN 2; Eternal Word TV Network; Fox News Channel; FX; Great American Country; Headline News; HGTV; History Channel; Lifetime; MSNBC; MTV; MTV2; Nickelodeon; Product Information Network; QVC; ShopNBC; Speed Channel; Spike TV; Syfy; The Learning Channel; Travel Channel; Trinity Broadcasting Network; truTV; Turner Network TV; TV Land;

USA Network; Versus; VH1; Weather Channel.
Fee: $37.31 monthly.

Digital Basic Service
Subscribers: N.A.
Programming (via satellite): ABC Family Channel; AMC; Animal Planet; Arts & Entertainment; BET Networks; Cartoon Network; CNBC; CNN; Comcast SportsNet Mid-Atlantic; Comedy Central; C-SPAN; Discovery Channel; Disney Channel; E! Entertainment Television; ESPN; ESPN 2; Eternal Word TV Network; Fox News Channel; FX; Golf Channel; Great American Country; GSN; Headline News; HGTV; History Channel; Home Shopping Network; INSP; Lifetime; Mid-Atlantic Sports Network; MSNBC; MTV; MTV2; Nickelodeon; QVC; ShopNBC; Speed Channel; Style Network; Syfy; TBS Superstation; The Learning Channel; Travel Channel; Trinity Broadcasting Network; truTV; Turner Network TV; USA Network; Versus; VH1; Weather Channel.
Fee: $13.90 monthly.

Pay Service 1
Pay Units: 55,351.
Programming (via satellite): HBO (multiplexed).
Fee: $15.95 monthly.

Pay Service 2
Pay Units: 35,192.
Programming (via satellite): Showtime.
Fee: $12.95 monthly.

Digital Pay Service 1
Pay Units: N.A.
Programming (via satellite): Cinemax (multiplexed); DMX Music; Flix (multiplexed); HBO (multiplexed); Showtime (multiplexed); The Movie Channel (multiplexed).
Fee: $12.95 monthly (Cinemax, Showtime, Starz or TMC), $15.95 monthly (HBO).

Video-On-Demand: Yes

Pay-Per-View
Addressable homes: 61,393.
Hot Choice, Fee: $5.95; iN DEMAND; iN DEMAND (delivered digitally); Playboy TV (delivered digitally); Spice, Fee: $3.95; Fresh (delivered digitally); Spice2, Fee: $5.95; Shorteez (delivered digitally).

Internet Service
Operational: Yes.
Broadband Service: Comcast High Speed Internet.
Fee: $42.95 monthly.

Telephone Service
Digital: Operational
Fee: $44.95 monthly

Miles of Plant: 1,080.0 (coaxial); None (fiber optic). Total homes in franchised area: 355,648.
Vice President & General Manager: Sanford Ames, Jr. Technical Operations Director: Tom Kearny. Marketing Director: Kevin Oxedine.
City fee: 5% of gross.
Ownership: Comcast Cable Communications Inc. (MSO).

PRINCE GEORGE'S COUNTY (northern portion)—Comcast Cable. Now served by PRINCE GEORGE'S COUNTY (formerly southern portion), MD [MD0005]. ICA: MD0004.

SALISBURY—Comcast Cable, 5729 W Denneys Rd, Dover, DE 19904-1365. Phone: 302-674-2494. Fax: 302-674-2539. Web Site: http://www.comcast.com. Also serves Delmar & Sussex County, DE; Chesapeake City, Delmar, Earleville, Fruitland, Galena, Hebron, Mardela Springs, Pocomoke, Princess Anne, Sharptown, Snow Hill, Somerset County, Warwick, Wicomico County & Worcester County, MD. ICA: MD0015.
TV Market Ranking: Below 100 (Chesapeake City, Delmar, Delmar, Earleville, Fruitland, Galena, Hebron, Mardela Springs, Pocomoke, Princess Anne, SALISBURY, Sharptown, Snow Hill, Somerset County, Sussex County, Warwick, Wicomico County, Worcester County). Franchise award date: N.A. Franchise expiration date: N.A. Began: August 27, 1960.
Channel capacity: N.A. Channels available but not in use: N.A.

Basic Service
Subscribers: 22,542.
Programming (received off-air): WBOC-TV (CBS, FOX) Salisbury; WCPB (PBS) Salisbury; WMDT (ABC, CW) Salisbury; 12 FMs.
Programming (via microwave): WBAL-TV (NBC) Baltimore; WJZ-TV (CBS) Baltimore; WRC-TV (NBC) Washington; WTTG (FOX) Washington.
Programming (via satellite): Arts & Entertainment; C-SPAN; C-SPAN 2; Eternal Word TV Network; Home Shopping Network; ION Television; NASA TV; QVC; ShopNBC; The Comcast Network; Trinity Broadcasting Network; TV Guide Network; Univision; Weather Channel.
Fee: $44.95 installation; $19.45 monthly.

Expanded Basic Service 1
Subscribers: N.A.
Programming (via satellite): ABC Family Channel; AMC; America's Store; Animal Planet; BET Networks; Bravo; Cartoon Network; CNBC; CNN; Comcast SportsNet Mid-Atlantic; Comedy Central; Country Music TV; Discovery Channel; Discovery Health Channel; Disney Channel; E! Entertainment Television; ESPN; ESPN 2; Food Network; Fox News Channel; FX; G4; Golf Channel; Great American Country; GSN; Hallmark Channel; Headline News; HGTV; History Channel; Lifetime; MSNBC; MTV; Nickelodeon; Speed Channel; Spike TV; Style Network; Syfy; TBS Superstation; The Learning Channel; Travel Channel; truTV; Turner Classic Movies; Turner Network TV; TV Land; TV One; USA Network; Versus; VH1.
Fee: $34.50 monthly.

Digital Basic Service
Subscribers: N.A.
Programming (received off-air): WBAL-TV (NBC) Baltimore; WBOC-TV (CBS, FOX) Salisbury; WMDT (ABC, CW) Salisbury; WTTG (FOX) Washington.
Programming (via satellite): BBC America; Bio; Canales N; CBS College Sports Network; Cooking Channel; Country Music TV; C-SPAN 3; Current; Discovery Digital Networks; Discovery HD Theater; Disney Channel; Do-It-Yourself; Encore (multiplexed); ESPN 2 HD; ESPN Classic Sports; ESPN HD; ESPNews; FearNet; Flix (multiplexed); Fox College Sports Atlantic; Fox College Sports Central; Fox College Sports Pacific; Fox HD; Fox Reality Channel; Fox Soccer; GAS; Gol TV; History Channel International; HorseRacing TV; Howard TV; INHD; Jewelry Television; Lifetime Movie Network; LOGO; Mid-Atlantic Sports Network; MoviePlex; MTV Networks Digital Suite; Music Choice; National Geographic Channel; NBA TV; NFL Network; Nick Jr.; Nick Too; NickToons TV; Palladia; PBS HD; PBS Kids Sprout; SoapNet; Sundance Channel; Tennis Channel; Toon Disney; Turner Network TV HD; TVG Network; Universal HD; Weatherscan; WWE 24/7.
Fee: $12.00 monthly.

Pay Service 1
Pay Units: 8,185.
Programming (via satellite): HBO.
Fee: $18.00 monthly.

Digital Pay Service 1
Pay Units: N.A.
Programming (via satellite): Cinemax (multiplexed); Cinemax HD; Cinemax On Demand; HBO (multiplexed); HBO HD; HBO On Demand; Showtime (multiplexed); Showtime HD; Showtime On Demand; Starz (multiplexed); Starz HDTV; Starz On Demand; The Movie Channel (multiplexed); The Movie Channel On Demand.
Fee: $11.00 monthly (each).

Video-On-Demand: Yes

Pay-Per-View
iN DEMAND, Addressable: Yes; iN DEMAND (delivered digitally); Playboy TV (delivered digitally); Fresh (delivered digitally); TV Games (delivered digitally); Home Preview Channel (delivered digitally); ESPN (delivered digitally); NBA (delivered digitally).

Internet Service
Operational: Yes.
Broadband Service: Comcast High Speed Internet.
Fee: $42.95 monthly.

Telephone Service
Digital: Operational
Fee: $44.95 monthly

Homes passed: 23,067. Total homes in franchised area: 23,510. Miles of plant (coax) included in Dover, DE
Vice President & General Manager: Henry Pearl. Area Engineering Manager: Cliff Jones. Marketing Director: David Tashjian. Business Operations Director: Cara Dever. Government & Public Affairs Director: Tom Worley.
City fee: 2% of gross.
Ownership: Comcast Cable Communications Inc. (MSO).

ST. MARY'S COUNTY—MetroCast Communications, 43920 Airport View Dr, Hollywood, MD 20636. Phone: 301-373-3201. E-mail: info@metrocastcommunications.com. Web Site: http://www.metrocastcommunications.com. Also serves Abell, Avenue, Bushwood, California, Callaway, Chaptico, Clements, Coltons Point, Compton, Dameron, Dryden, Great Mills, Helen, Hollywood, Leonardtown, Lexington Park, Loveville, Mechanicsville, Morganza, Park Hall, Patuxent Heights, Patuxent River, Piney Point, Ridge, St. Inigoes, Tall Timbers & Valley Lee. ICA: MD0024.
TV Market Ranking: 9 (ST. MARY'S COUNTY (portions)); Outside TV Markets (Abell, Avenue, Bushwood, California, Callaway, Chaptico, Clements, Coltons Point, Compton, Dameron, Dryden, Great Mills, Helen, Hollywood, Leonardtown, Lexington Park, Loveville, Mechanicsville, Morganza, Park Hall, Patuxent Heights, Patuxent River, Piney Point, Ridge, Scotland, St. Inigoes, St. Mary's City, Tall Timbers, Valley Lee, ST. MARY'S COUNTY (portions)). Franchise award date: January 1, 1971. Franchise expiration date: N.A. Began: August 1, 1971.
Channel capacity: 100 (operating 2-way). Channels available but not in use: N.A.

Basic Service
Subscribers: 16,700.
Programming (received off-air): WBAL-TV (NBC) Baltimore; WDCA (MNT) Washington; WDCW (CW) Washington; WETA-TV (PBS) Washington; WJLA-TV (ABC) Washington; WJZ-TV (CBS) Baltimore; WMAR-TV (ABC) Baltimore; WMDO-CA (TEL) Washington; WMPT (PBS) Annapolis; WRC-TV (NBC) Washington; WTTG (FOX) Washington; WUSA (CBS) Washington; allband FM.
Programming (via satellite): Home Shopping Network; QVC.
Current originations: Government Access; Public Access.
Fee: $60.00 installation; $15.55 monthly.

Expanded Basic Service 1
Subscribers: N.A.
Programming (via satellite): ABC Family Channel; AMC; Animal Planet; Arts & Entertainment; BET Networks; Bloomberg Television; Bravo; Cartoon Network; CNBC; CNN; Comcast SportsNet Mid-Atlantic; Comedy Central; Country Music TV; C-SPAN; C-SPAN 2; Discovery Channel; E! Entertainment Television; ESPN; ESPN 2; Eternal Word TV Network; Food Network; Fox Movie Channel; Fox News Channel; FX; G4; Great American Country; Headline News; HGTV; History Channel; Lifetime; Lifetime Movie Network; MSNBC; MTV; National Geographic Channel; Nickelodeon; Outdoor Channel; Pentagon Channel; Speed Channel; Spike TV; Syfy; TBS Superstation; The Learning Channel; Travel Channel; Trinity Broadcasting Network; truTV; Turner Network TV; TV Land; USA Network; Versus; VH1; WE tv; Weather Channel.
Fee: $27.70 monthly.

Digital Basic Service
Subscribers: 15,703.
Programming (received off-air): WBAL-TV (NBC) Baltimore; WETA-TV (PBS) Washington; WJLA-TV (ABC) Washington; WMAR-TV (ABC) Baltimore; WRC-TV (NBC) Washington; WTTG (FOX) Washington; WUSA (CBS) Washington.
Programming (via satellite): BBC America; Bio; Country Music TV; Discovery Digital Networks; Discovery HD Theater; DMX Music; Fuse; GAS; GSN; HDNet; HDNet Movies; History Channel International; MTV Networks Digital Suite; National Geographic Channel HD Network; Nick Jr.; NickToons TV; Outdoor Channel 2 HD; PBS Kids Sprout; Toon Disney; Turner Network TV HD; Universal HD; WealthTV.
Fee: $8.95 monthly.

Digital Expanded Basic Service
Subscribers: 178.
Programming (via satellite): Encore (multiplexed); ESPN Classic Sports; ESPNews; Fox Soccer; Golf Channel; Independent Film Channel; NFL Network; Starz (multiplexed); Turner Classic Movies.
Fee: $9.95 monthly.

Digital Pay Service 1
Pay Units: 1,078.
Programming (via satellite): Cinemax (multiplexed); HBO (multiplexed); Showtime (multiplexed); Showtime HD; Starz HDTV; The Movie Channel (multiplexed).
Fee: $9.95 monthly (Cinemax), $12.95 monthly (HBO or Showtime/TMC).

Video-On-Demand: No

Pay-Per-View
Addressable homes: 1,831.
ESPN Now (delivered digitally), Addressable: Yes; iN DEMAND (delivered digitally); Sports PPV (delivered digitally).

Internet Service
Operational: Yes. Began: January 1, 1998.
Subscribers: 8,464.
Broadband Service: MetroCast Internet.
Fee: $60.00 installation; $41.95 monthly; $2.95 modem lease; $99.00 modem purchase.

Telephone Service
None
Miles of Plant: 709.0 (coaxial); 65.0 (fiber optic). Homes passed: 34,471.
General Manager: Danny Jobe. Programming Director: Linda Stuchell.
City fee: 3% of gross.
Ownership: Harron Communications LP (MSO).

TAKOMA PARK—RCN Corp. Formerly [MD0054]. This cable system has converted to IPTV, 196 Van Buren St, Herndon, VA 20170. Phone: 703-434-8200. Web Site: http://www.rcn.com. ICA: MD5102.
TV Market Ranking: 9 (TAKOMA PARK).
Channel capacity: N.A. Channels available but not in use: N.A.

Internet Service
Operational: Yes.
Fee: $38.00 monthly.

Telephone Service
Digital: Operational
Fee: $45.00 monthly
Chairman: Steven J. Simmons. Chief Executive Officer: Jim Holanda.
Ownership: RCN Corp.

WARWICK—Mid-Atlantic Communications. Now served by SALISBURY, MD [MD0015]. ICA: MD0027.

WESTMINSTER—Comcast Cable, 8031 Corporate Dr, Nottingham, MD 21236. Phone: 410-931-4600. Fax: 410-336-1619. Web Site: http://www.comcast.com. Also serves Carroll County, Hampstead, Manchester, Marriottsville, New Windsor, Sykesville, Taneytown & Union Bridge. ICA: MD0042.
TV Market Ranking: 14 (Manchester); 14,57 (Hampstead, New Windsor, WESTMINSTER); 57 (Taneytown, Westminster); 57,9 (Union Bridge); 9,14 (Carroll County (portions), Marriottsville, Sykesville); Below 100 (Carroll County (portions)). Franchise award date: December 1, 1983. Franchise expiration date: N.A. Began: November 6, 1984.
Channel capacity: N.A. Channels available but not in use: None.

Basic Service
Subscribers: 22,125.
Programming (received off-air): WBAL-TV (NBC) Baltimore; WBFF (FOX, IND) Baltimore; WDCA (MNT) Washington; WETA-TV (PBS) Washington; WJLA-TV (ABC) Washington; WJZ-TV (CBS) Baltimore; WMAR-TV (ABC) Baltimore; WMPT (PBS) Annapolis; WNUV (CW) Baltimore; WRC-TV (NBC) Washington; WUSA (CBS) Washington; WUTB (MNT) Baltimore.
Programming (via satellite): C-SPAN; Home Shopping Network; Product Information Network; QVC; TV Guide Network.
Current originations: Educational Access; Government Access; Public Access.
Fee: $44.95 installation; $10.92 monthly.

Expanded Basic Service 1
Subscribers: 19,687.
Programming (via satellite): ABC Family Channel; AMC; Animal Planet; Arts & Entertainment; BET Networks; Bravo; Cartoon Network; CNBC; CNN; Comcast SportsNet Mid-Atlantic; Comedy Central; Country Music TV; C-SPAN; Discovery Channel; Disney Channel; E! Entertainment Television; ESPN; ESPN 2; Eternal Word TV Network; Food Network; Fox News Channel; FX; G4; GSN; Hallmark Channel; Headline News; HGTV; History Channel; INSP; ION Television; Lifetime; MSNBC; MTV; Nickelodeon; Oxygen; ShopNBC; Speed Channel; Spike TV; Syfy; TBS Superstation; The Learning Channel; Travel Channel; truTV; Turner Classic Movies; Turner Network TV; TV Land; USA Network; VH1; Weather Channel.
Fee: $29.43 monthly.

Digital Basic Service
Subscribers: 3,116.
Programming (via satellite): AmericanLife TV Network; ART America; BBC America; Bio; Black Family Channel; Bloomberg Television; Canales N; CCTV-4; Discovery Digital Networks; DMX Music; Do-It-Yourself; ESPN Classic Sports; ESPNews; Filipino Channel; FitTV; Fox College Sports Atlantic; Fox College Sports Central; Fox College Sports Pacific; Fox Movie Channel; Fox Sports World; Fuse; GAS; Golf Channel; Great American Country; Halogen Network; History Channel International; Independent Film Channel; Mid-Atlantic Sports Network; MTV Networks Digital Suite; Music Choice; National Geographic Channel; Nick Jr.; Nick Too; NickToons TV; Outdoor Channel; RAI International; SoapNet; Style Network; Sundance Channel; The Word Network; Toon Disney; Trinity Broadcasting Network; TV Asia; TV Japan; TV5, La Television International; Versus; WE tv; Zee TV USA; Zhong Tian Channel.

Digital Pay Service 1
Pay Units: 1,252.
Programming (via satellite): Cinemax (multiplexed); Encore (multiplexed); Flix; Showtime (multiplexed); Starz (multiplexed); The Movie Channel (multiplexed).
Fee: $11.50 monthly (each).
Video-On-Demand: Yes

Pay-Per-View
Addressable homes: 3,116.
iN DEMAND (delivered digitally), Addressable: Yes; Playboy TV (delivered digitally); Fresh (delivered digitally); Shorteez (delivered digitally); Hot Choice (delivered digitally); Urban Xtra (delivered digitally); Sports PPV (delivered digitally).

Internet Service
Operational: Yes.
Subscribers: 18,000.
Broadband Service: Comcast High Speed Internet.
Fee: $42.95 monthly.

Telephone Service
Digital: Operational
Miles of Plant: 745.0 (coaxial); None (fiber optic). Additional miles planned: 19.0 (coaxial).
Vice President & General Manager: Bryan Lynch. Vice President, Marketing: Mark Watts. Engineering Director: Pete Sarkisian. Marketing Director: Chris Shea. Technical Operations Director: Brady Hood.
County fee: 3% of gross.
Ownership: Comcast Cable Communications Inc. (MSO).

MASSACHUSETTS

Total Systems: 44
Total Communities Served: 361
Franchises Not Yet Operating: 0
Applications Pending: 0
Communities with Applications: 0
Number of Basic Subscribers: 1,557,180
Number of Expanded Basic Subscribers: 255,340
Number of Pay Units: 106,873

Top 100 Markets Represented: Hartford-New Haven-New Britain-Waterbury-New London, CT (19); Providence, RI-New Bedford, MA (33); Albany-Schenectady-Troy, NY (34); Boston-Cambridge-Worcester-Lawrence (6).

For a list of cable communities in this section, see the Cable Community Index located in the back of Cable Volume 2. For explanation of terms used in cable system listings, see p. D-11.

ALLSTON—RCN Corp. Formerly served by Boston, MA [MA0105]. This cable system has converted to IPTV, 196 Van Buren St, Herndon, VA 20170. Phone: 703-434-8200. Web Site: http://www.rcn.com. ICA: MA5094.
Channel capacity: N.A. Channels available but not in use: N.A.
Internet Service
Operational: Yes.
Chairman: Steven J. Simmons. Chief Executive Officer: Jim Holanda.
Ownership: RCN Corp.

AMESBURY—Formerly served by Comcast Cable. No longer in operation. ICA: MA0052.

AMHERST—Comcast Cable. Now served by SPRINGFIELD, MA [MA0005]. ICA: MA0057.

ANDOVER—Comcast Cable. Now served by WESTFORD, MA [MA0093]. ICA: MA0022.

ARLINGTON—Comcast Cable. Now served by BOSTON, MA [MA0001]. ICA: MA0009.

ARLINGTON—RCN Corp. Formerly served by Boston, MA [MA0105]. This cable system has converted to IPTV, 196 Van Buren St, Herndon, VA 20170. Phone: 703-434-8200. Web Site: http://www.rcn.com. ICA: MA5095.
Channel capacity: N.A. Channels available but not in use: N.A.
Internet Service
Operational: Yes.
Chairman: Steven J. Simmons. Chief Executive Officer: Jim Holanda.
Ownership: RCN Corp.

ATHOL—Time Warner Cable, 1021 Highbridge Rd, Schenectady, NY 12303. Phone: 518-242-8890. Fax: 518-242-8948. Web Site: http://www.timewarnercable.com/albany. Also serves Orange. ICA: MA0062.
TV Market Ranking: 6 (ATHOL, Orange). Franchise award date: January 1, 1954. Franchise expiration date: N.A. Began: November 1, 1954.
Channel capacity: N.A. Channels available but not in use: N.A.
Basic Service
Subscribers: N.A. Included in Albany, NY
Programming (received off-air): WBPX-TV (ION) Boston (multiplexed); WBZ-TV (CBS) Boston; WCVB-TV (ABC) Boston; WEKW-TV (PBS) Keene; WFSB (CBS) Hartford; WFXT (FOX) Boston; WGBH-TV (PBS) Boston; WGBY-TV (PBS) Springfield; WGGB-TV (ABC) Springfield; WHDH (NBC) Boston; WLVI-TV (CW) Cambridge; WMFP (IND) Lawrence; WSBK-TV (IND) Boston; WUNI (UNV) Worcester; WUTF-DT (TEL) Marlborough; WWLP (NBC) Springfield; WYDN (ETV) Worcester; WZMY-TV (MNT) Derry; allband FM.
Programming (via satellite): TBS Superstation.
Current originations: Public Access.
Fee: $38.95 installation; $11.59 monthly; $.49 converter.
Expanded Basic Service 1
Subscribers: N.A.
Programming (via satellite): ABC Family Channel; AMC; Animal Planet; Arts & Entertainment; Cartoon Network; CNBC; CNN; Comcast Sports Net New England; Comedy Central; Country Music TV; C-SPAN; Discovery Channel; Disney Channel; E! Entertainment Television; ESPN; ESPN 2; ESPN Classic Sports; Food Network; Fox News Channel; FX; Golf Channel; Headline News; HGTV; History Channel; Home Shopping Network; Lifetime; MSNBC; MTV; National Geographic Channel; New England Sports Network; Nickelodeon; Oxygen; QVC; ShopNBC; SoapNet; Spike TV; Style Network; Syfy; The Learning Channel; Travel Channel; truTV; Turner Classic Movies; Turner Network TV; TV Land; USA Network; Versus; VH1; WE tv; Weather Channel.
Fee: $25.60 monthly.
Digital Basic Service
Subscribers: N.A. Included in Albany, NY
Programming (via satellite): BBC America; Bloomberg Television; Discovery Digital Networks; ESPNews; Fox Sports World; Fuse; GSN; Independent Film Channel; Lifetime Movie Network; MTV2; Music Choice; Nick Jr.; Speed Channel; Toon Disney; Trinity Broadcasting Network; Trio; Versus.
Fee: $4.95 monthly.
Digital Pay Service 1
Pay Units: N.A.
Programming (via satellite): Cinemax (multiplexed); Encore (multiplexed); HBO (multiplexed); Showtime (multiplexed); Starz (multiplexed); The Movie Channel (multiplexed).
Fee: $14.95 monthly (HBO, Cinemax, Showtime/TMC or Starz/Encore).
Video-On-Demand: Yes
Pay-Per-View
Addressable homes: 1,851.
iN DEMAND (delivered digitally), Addressable: Yes; Playboy TV (delivered digitally); Sports PPV (delivered digitally).
Internet Service
Operational: Yes.
Broadband Service: EarthLink, LocalNet, Road Runner.
Fee: $29.95 installation; $44.95 monthly.
Telephone Service
Analog: Not Operational
Digital: Operational
Fee: $44.95 monthly
Note: Homes passed and miles of plant (coax & fiber) included in Albany, NY
Vice President, Operations: Mark Loreno. Vice President, Engineering: James Marchester. Vice President, Marketing: Tricia Buhr. Vice President, Public Affairs: Peter Taubkin.
City fee: $0.50 per subscriber annually.
Ownership: Time Warner Cable (MSO).; Advance/Newhouse Partnership (MSO).

BELCHERTOWN—Charter Communications, 95 Higgins St, Worcester, MA 1606. Phone: 508-853-1515. Fax: 508-854-5042. Web Site: http://www.charter.com. Also serves Hadley. ICA: MA0069.
TV Market Ranking: 6 (BELCHERTOWN); Below 100 (Hadley). Franchise award date: January 6, 1986. Franchise expiration date: N.A. Began: December 1, 1986.
Channel capacity: N.A. Channels available but not in use: N.A.
Basic Service
Subscribers: 5,200.
Programming (received off-air): WCTX (MNT) New Haven; WDMR-LP (TMO) Springfield; WEDH (PBS) Hartford; WGBY-TV (PBS) Springfield; WGGB-TV (ABC) Springfield; WSHM-LP (CBS) Springfield; WTIC-TV (FOX) Hartford; WVIT (NBC) New Britain; WWLP (NBC) Springfield.
Programming (via satellite): C-SPAN; CW+; INSP; QVC; TV Guide Network.
Current originations: Leased Access; Government Access; Educational Access; Public Access.
Fee: $29.99 installation.
Expanded Basic Service 1
Subscribers: 4,679.
Programming (via microwave): New England Cable News.
Programming (via satellite): ABC Family Channel; AMC; Animal Planet; Arts & Entertainment; Bravo; Cartoon Network; CNBC; CNN; Comcast Sports Net New England; Comedy Central; Country Music TV; C-SPAN 2; Discovery Channel; Disney Channel; E! Entertainment Television; ESPN; ESPN 2; Eternal Word TV Network; FitTV; Food Network; Fox News Channel; FX; G4; Golf Channel; Hallmark Channel; Headline News; HGTV; History Channel; Home Shopping Network; Lifetime; MSNBC; MTV; National Geographic Channel; New England Sports Network; Nickelodeon; Oxygen; Speed Channel; Spike TV; Syfy; TBS Superstation; The Learning Channel; Toon Disney; Travel Channel; truTV; Turner Classic Movies; Turner Network TV; TV Land; Univision; USA Network; Versus; VH1; Weather Channel.
Fee: $53.00 monthly.
Digital Basic Service
Subscribers: N.A.
Programming (via satellite): BBC America; Bio; Bloomberg Television; Discovery Digital Networks; Do-It-Yourself; ESPN Classic Sports; ESPNews; Fox Sports en Espanol; Fox Sports World; FSN Digital Atlantic; FSN Digital Central; FSN Digital Pacific; Fuel TV; Fuse; GAS; Great American Country; History Channel International; Independent Film Channel; International Television (ITV); Lifetime Movie Network; MTV Networks Digital Suite; Music Choice; NFL Network; Nick Jr.; Nick Too; NickToons TV; SoapNet; Sundance Channel; TVG Network; WE tv.
Digital Pay Service 1
Pay Units: 1,400.
Programming (via satellite): Cinemax (multiplexed); Encore (multiplexed); Flix; HBO (multiplexed); Showtime (multiplexed); Starz (multiplexed); The Movie Channel (multiplexed).
Video-On-Demand: Yes
Pay-Per-View
Pleasure (delivered digitally); Playboy TV (delivered digitally); ETC (delivered digitally); Fresh (delivered digitally); NHL Center Ice (delivered digitally); MLB Extra Innings (delivered digitally); iN DEMAND (delivered digitally); NASCAR In Car (delivered digitally).
Internet Service
Operational: Yes. Began: March 1, 2002.
Broadband Service: Charter Pipeline.
Fee: $29.99 monthly.
Telephone Service
Digital: Operational
Fee: $29.99 monthly
Miles of Plant: 150.0 (coaxial); None (fiber optic). Homes passed: 6,048.
Vice President & General Manager: Greg Garabedian. Technical Operations Director: George Duffy. Technical Operations Manager: Beatrice Welch. Marketing Director: Dennis Jerome. Marketing Manager: Paula Cecchetelli.
City fee: $0.50 per subscriber annually.
Ownership: Charter Communications Inc. (MSO).

BERNARDSTON—Comcast Cable. Now served by SPRINGFIELD, MA [MA0005]. ICA: MA0077.

BEVERLY—Comcast Cable. Now served by BOSTON, MA [MA0001]. ICA: MA0020.

BOSTON—Comcast Cable, 55 Concord St, North Reading, MA 1864. Phones: 413-730-4500 (Administrative office); 800-266-2278 (Customer service). Fax: 978-207-2312. Web Site: http://www.comcast.com. Also serves Allston, Arlington, Ashland, Belmont, Beverly, Brighton, Brookline, Burlington, Cambridge, Charlestown, Chelsea, Dedham, Dorchester, Dover, East Boston, Essex, Everett, Framingham, Franklin, Gloucester, Hamilton, Hanscom AFB, Holliston, Hopkinton, Hyde Park, Ipswich, Jamaica Plain, Lexington, Lynn, Lynnfield, Malden, Manchester, Marblehead, Mattapan, Medfield,

Medford, Medway, Melrose, Millis, Nahant, Natick, Needham, Newbury, Newburyport, Newton, North Reading, Norwood, Peabody, Reading, Revere, Rockport, Roslindale, Rowley, Roxbury, Salem, Saugus, Sherborn, Somerville, South Boston, Stoneham, Stow, Swampscott, Wakefield, Waltham, Watertown, Wayland, Wellesley, Wenham, West Newbury, West Roxbury, Weston, Westwood, Wilmington, Winchester, Winthrop & Woburn. ICA: MA0001.

TV Market Ranking: 6 (Allston, Arlington, Ashland, Belmont, Beverly, BOSTON, Brighton, Brookline, Burlington, Cambridge, Charlestown, Chelsea, Dedham, Dorchester, Dover, East Boston, Essex, Everett, Framingham, Franklin, Gloucester, Hamilton, Hanscom AFB, Holliston, Hopkinton, Hyde Park, Ipswich, Jamaica Plain, Lexington, Lynn, Lynnfield, Malden, Manchester, Marblehead, Mattapan, Medfield, Medford, Medway, Melrose, Millis, Nahant, Natick, Needham, Newbury, Newburyport, Newton, North Reading, Norwood, Peabody, Reading, Revere, Rockport, Roslindale, Rowley, Roxbury, Salem, Saugus, Sherborn, Somerville, South Boston, Stoneham, Stow, Swampscott, Wakefield, Waltham, Watertown, Wayland, Wellesley, Wenham, West Newbury, West Roxbury, Weston, Westwood, Wilmington, Winchester, Winthrop, Woburn). Franchise award date: August 12, 1981. Franchise expiration date: N.A. Began: December 29, 1982.

Channel capacity: 104 (operating 2-way). Channels available but not in use: 10.

Basic Service

Subscribers: 600,000.

Programming (received off-air): WBPX-TV (ION) Boston; WBZ-TV (CBS) Boston; WCVB-TV (ABC) Boston; WENH-TV (PBS) Durham; WFXT (FOX) Boston; WGBH-TV (PBS) Boston; WGBX-TV (PBS) Boston; WHDH (NBC) Boston; WLVI-TV (CW) Cambridge; WMFP (IND) Lawrence; WNEU (TMO) Merrimack; WSBK-TV (IND) Boston; WUNI (UNV) Worcester; WUTF-DT (TEL) Marlborough; WWDP (IND) Norwell; WYDN (ETV) Worcester; WZMY-TV (MNT) Derry.

Programming (via satellite): Lifetime; TBS Superstation; The Comcast Network; TV Guide Network.

Current originations: Government Access; Educational Access; Public Access.

Fee: $43.95 installation; $8.63 monthly; $1.21 converter; $34.09 additional installation.

Expanded Basic Service 1

Subscribers: N.A.

Programming (via satellite): ABC Family Channel; AMC; Animal Planet; Arts & Entertainment; BET Networks; Bravo; Cartoon Network; Catholic Television Network; Celtic Vision; Chinese Television Network; CNBC; CNN; Comcast Sports Net New England; Comedy Central; Country Music TV; C-SPAN; C-SPAN 2; Discovery Channel; Disney Channel; E! Entertainment Television; ESPN; ESPN 2; ESPN Classic Sports; Eternal Word TV Network; Flix; Food Network; Fox News Channel; Fox Sports World; Fresh; Fuse; FX; Golf Channel; GSN; Headline News; HGTV; History Channel; Home Shopping Network; Hot Choice; Independent Film Channel; MSNBC; MTV; MTV Latin America; mun2 television; New England Cable News; Nickelodeon; Product Information Network; QVC; RAI USA; Russian Television Network; Spike TV; Syfy; The Learning Channel; Travel Channel; truTV; Turner Classic Movies; Turner Network TV; TV Land; TV5, La Television International; USA Network; VH1; WE tv; Weather Channel.

Fee: $43.92 monthly.

Digital Basic Service

Subscribers: N.A.

Programming (via satellite): BBC America; Bio; Black Family Channel; Bloomberg Television; Celtic Vision; Cooking Channel; Discovery Digital Networks; DMX Music; Do-It-Yourself; ESPNews; Eternal Word TV Network; FitTV; Fox Movie Channel; Fox Sports World; Fuse; G4; GAS; Great American Country; Halogen Network; History Channel International; Independent Film Channel; International Television (ITV); Lifetime Movie Network; Lime; MTV Networks Digital Suite; Music Choice; National Geographic Channel; NBA TV; Nick Jr.; NickToons TV; Outdoor Channel; Oxygen; Science Television; Speed Channel; Style Network; Sundance Channel; The Word Network; Toon Disney; Trinity Broadcasting Network; Turner Classic Movies; Weatherscan.

Fee: $15.50 monthly.

Digital Pay Service 1

Pay Units: N.A.

Programming (via satellite): Cinemax (multiplexed); Encore; Flix; HBO (multiplexed); Showtime (multiplexed); The Movie Channel (multiplexed).

Fee: $14.00 monthly (each).

Video-On-Demand: Yes

Pay-Per-View

iN DEMAND; Barker (delivered digitally); iN DEMAND (delivered digitally); Hot Choice (delivered digitally); Playboy TV (delivered digitally); Fresh (delivered digitally).

Internet Service

Operational: Yes.

Broadband Service: Comcast High Speed Internet.

Fee: $42.95 monthly; $10.00 modem lease.

Telephone Service

Analog: Not Operational

Digital: Operational

Miles of Plant: 806.0 (coaxial); None (fiber optic).

Regional Vice President: Paul D'Arcangelo. Marketing Director: Alan Clairmont. Public Relations Director: Jim Hughes.

City fee: 1% of gross.

Ownership: Comcast Cable Communications Inc. (MSO).

BOSTON—RCN Corp. Formerly [MA0105]. This cable system has converted to IPTV, 196 Van Buren St, Herndon, VA 20170. Phone: 703-434-8200. Web Site: http://www.rcn.com. ICA: MA5096.

Channel capacity: N.A. Channels available but not in use: N.A.

Internet Service

Operational: Yes.

Chairman: Steven J. Simmons. Chief Executive Officer: Jim Holanda.

Ownership: RCN Corp.

BOSTON—RCN Corp. This cable system has converted to IPTV. See Boston, MA [MA5096]. ICA: MA0105.

BRAINTREE—BELD Broadband, 150 Potter Rd, Braintree, MA 02184-1364. Phone: 781-348-2353. Fax: 781-348-1002. E-mail: cservice@beld.com. Web Site: http://www.beld.com. ICA: MA0106. **Note:** This system is an overbuild.

TV Market Ranking: 6 (BRAINTREE). Franchise award date: August 25, 2000. Franchise expiration date: N.A. Began: August 25, 2000.

Channel capacity: 66 (operating 2-way). Channels available but not in use: N.A.

Basic Service

Subscribers: 5,193.

Programming (received off-air): Boston Catholic Television; New England Cable News; QVC; TV Guide Network; WBPX-TV (ION) Boston; WBZ-TV (CBS) Boston; WCVB-TV (ABC) Boston; WFXT (FOX) Boston; WGBH-TV (PBS) Boston; WGBX-TV (PBS) Boston; WHDH (NBC) Boston; WLVI-TV (CW) Cambridge; WMFP (IND) Lawrence; WSBK-TV (IND) Boston; WUNI (UNV) Worcester; WUTF-DT (TEL) Marlborough; WWDP (IND) Norwell; WYDN (ETV) Worcester; WZMY-TV (MNT) Derry.

Programming (via satellite): C-SPAN; C-SPAN 2; QVC; TV Guide Network.

Current originations: Government Access; Educational Access; Public Access.

Fee: $46.00 installation; $53.15 monthly; $24.00 additional installation.

Expanded Basic Service 1

Subscribers: 4,987.

Programming (via satellite): ABC Family Channel; AMC; Animal Planet; Arts & Entertainment; BET Networks; Bravo; Cartoon Network; CMT Pure Country; CNBC; CNN; Comcast Sports Net New England; Comedy Central; Discovery Channel; Disney Channel; E! Entertainment Television; ESPN; Food Network; Fox News Channel; FX; Great American Country; Headline News; HGTV; Home Shopping Network; Lifetime; MSNBC; MTV; New England Sports Network; Nickelodeon; Spike TV; TBS Superstation; The Learning Channel; Travel Channel; truTV; Turner Network TV; TV Land; USA Network; VH1; Weather Channel; WGN.

Fee: $46.00 installation; $43.25 monthly; $24.00 additional installation.

Digital Basic Service

Subscribers: 4,774.

Programming (via satellite): AmericanLife TV Network; BBC America; Bio; Bloomberg Television; Discovery Digital Networks; ESPN 2; ESPN Classic Sports; ESPNews; FitTV; Fox Movie Channel; Fox Soccer; Fuse; G4; GAS; Golf Channel; GSN; History Channel; History Channel International; Independent Film Channel; Lifetime Movie Network; Lifetime Real Women; Military History Channel; MTV Networks Digital Suite; National Geographic Channel; NFL Network; Nick Jr.; NickToons TV; Outdoor Channel; Ovation; Science Television; Speed Channel; Style Network; Syfy; Toon Disney; Trinity Broadcasting Network; Turner Classic Movies; TV Guide Interactive Inc.; Versus; VH1 Classic; VH1 Country; VH1 Soul; WE tv.

Fee: $46.00 installation; $54.00 monthly; $8.00 converter; $24.00 additional installation.

Digital Pay Service 1

Pay Units: N.A.

Programming (via satellite): Cinemax (multiplexed); Encore (multiplexed); Flix; HBO (multiplexed); Showtime (multiplexed); Starz (multiplexed); The Movie Channel (multiplexed).

Video-On-Demand: Yes

Pay-Per-View

iN DEMAND (delivered digitally), Fee: $3.99, Addressable: Yes.

Internet Service

Operational: Yes. Began: December 1, 1999.

Subscribers: 4,052.

Broadband Service: BELD.net.

Fee: $50.00 installation; $43.25 monthly; $7.00 modem lease.

Telephone Service

Digital: Operational

Fee: $48.80 monthly

Miles of Plant: 170.0 (coaxial); None (fiber optic). Homes passed: 11,000.

Acting General Manager: William Bottiggi. Marketing & Programming Director: JoAnn Stak Bregnard. Headend Engineer: Scott Henderson. Broadband Division Manager: Jack Orpen.

Ownership: Braintree Electric Light Department.

BRAINTREE—Comcast Cable. Now served by TAUNTON, MA [MA0033]. ICA: MA0048.

BRIGHTON—RCN Corp. Formerly served by Boston, MA [MA0105]. This cable system has converted to IPTV, 196 Van Buren St, Herndon, VA 20170. Phone: 703-434-8200. Web Site: http://www.rcn.com. ICA: MA5097.

Channel capacity: N.A. Channels available but not in use: N.A.

Internet Service

Operational: Yes.

Chairman: Steven J. Simmons. Chief Executive Officer: Jim Holanda.

Ownership: RCN Corp.

BROCKTON—Comcast Cable. Now served by TAUNTON, MA [MA0033]. ICA: MA0012.

BROOKLINE—RCN Corp. Formerly served by Boston, MA [MA0105]. This cable system has converted to IPTV, 196 Van Buren St, Herndon, VA 20170. Phone: 703-434-8200. Web Site: http://www.rcn.com. ICA: MA5098.

Channel capacity: N.A. Channels available but not in use: N.A.

Internet Service

Operational: Yes.

Chairman: Steven J. Simmons. Chief Executive Officer: Jim Holanda.

Ownership: RCN Corp.

BURLINGTON—RCN Corp. Formerly served by Boston, MA [MA0105]. This cable system has converted to IPTV, 196 Van Buren St, Herndon, VA 20170. Phone: 703-434-8200. Web Site: http://www.rcn.com. ICA: MA5099.

Channel capacity: N.A. Channels available but not in use: N.A.

Internet Service

Operational: Yes.

Chairman: Steven J. Simmons. Chief Executive Officer: Jim Holanda.

Ownership: RCN Corp.

CHARLTON—Charter Communications, 95 Higgins St, Worcester, MA 1606. Phone: 508-853-1515. Fax: 508-854-5042. Web Site: http://www.charter.com. Also serves Brookfield, East Brookfield, East Brookfield (town), North Brookfield & North Brookfield (town). ICA: MA0066.

TV Market Ranking: 6 (Brookfield, CHARLTON, East Brookfield, East Brookfield, North Brookfield, North Brookfield (town)). Franchise award date: December 1, 1988. Franchise expiration date: N.A. Began: December 15, 1988.

Channel capacity: N.A. Channels available but not in use: N.A.

Basic Service

Subscribers: 5,800.

Programming (received off-air): WBPX-TV (ION) Boston; WBZ-TV (CBS) Boston; WCVB-TV (ABC) Boston; WFXT (FOX)

Boston; WGBH-TV (PBS) Boston; WGBX-TV (PBS) Boston; WGBY-TV (PBS) Springfield; WGGB-TV (ABC) Springfield; WHDH (NBC) Boston; WJAR (NBC) Providence; WLVI-TV (CW) Cambridge; WMFP (IND) Lawrence; WSBK-TV (IND) Boston; WUNI (UNV) Worcester; WUTF-DT (TEL) Marlborough; WYDN (ETV) Worcester; WZMY-TV (MNT) Derry.
Programming (via satellite): C-SPAN; C-SPAN 2; Eternal Word TV Network; Home Shopping Network; INSP; MTV2; QVC; TV Guide Network.
Current originations: Government Access; Educational Access; Public Access.
Fee: $29.99 installation.

Expanded Basic Service 1
Subscribers: N.A.
Programming (via microwave): New England Cable News.
Programming (via satellite): ABC Family Channel; AMC; Animal Planet; Arts & Entertainment; Bravo; Cartoon Network; CNBC; CNN; Comcast Sports Net New England; Comedy Central; Discovery Channel; Disney Channel; E! Entertainment Television; ESPN; ESPN 2; Food Network; Fox News Channel; FX; G4; Golf Channel; Hallmark Channel; Headline News; HGTV; History Channel; Lifetime; MSNBC; MTV; New England Sports Network; Nickelodeon; Oxygen; Speed Channel; Spike TV; Syfy; TBS Superstation; The Learning Channel; Toon Disney; Travel Channel; truTV; Turner Classic Movies; Turner Network TV; TV Land; USA Network; Versus; VH1; Weather Channel.
Fee: $55.00 monthly.

Digital Basic Service
Subscribers: N.A.
Programming (received off-air): WCVB-TV (ABC) Boston; WFXT (FOX) Boston; WHDH (NBC) Boston.
Programming (via satellite): BBC America; Bio; Bloomberg Television; CBS College Sports Network; Discovery Digital Networks; Discovery HD Theater; Do-It-Yourself; ESPN Classic Sports; ESPN HD; ESPNews; FitTV; Fox College Sports Atlantic; Fox College Sports Central; Fox College Sports Pacific; Fox Movie Channel; Fox Soccer; Fox Sports en Espanol; Fuel TV; Fuse; GAS; Great American Country; History Channel International; Independent Film Channel; International Television (ITV); Jewelry Television; Lifetime Movie Network; MTV Networks Digital Suite; Music Choice; New England Sports Network; NFL Network; Nick Jr.; Nick Too; NickToons TV; SoapNet; Sundance Channel; TVG Network; WE tv.

Digital Pay Service 1
Pay Units: 164.
Programming (via satellite): Cinemax (multiplexed).
Fee: $6.85 installation; $10.45 monthly.

Digital Pay Service 2
Pay Units: 395.
Programming (via satellite): The Movie Channel (multiplexed).
Fee: $6.85 installation; $9.95 monthly.

Digital Pay Service 3
Pay Units: 462.
Programming (via satellite): HBO (multiplexed); HBO HD.
Fee: $6.85 installation; $12.95 monthly.

Digital Pay Service 4
Pay Units: 384.
Programming (via satellite): Showtime (multiplexed); Showtime HD.
Fee: $6.85 installation; $7.95 monthly.

Digital Pay Service 5
Pay Units: N.A.
Programming (via satellite): Encore (multiplexed); Flix; Starz (multiplexed).
Video-On-Demand: Yes
Pay-Per-View
Addressable homes: 1,700.
iN DEMAND (delivered digitally), Addressable: Yes; Fresh (delivered digitally); Playboy TV (delivered digitally); ETC (delivered digitally); Pleasure (delivered digitally); NHL Center Ice (delivered digitally); MLB Extra Innings (delivered digitally); NASCAR In Car (delivered digitally); iN DEMAND.
Internet Service
Operational: Yes.
Broadband Service: Charter Pipeline.
Fee: $29.99 monthly.
Telephone Service
Digital: Operational
Fee: $29.99 monthly
Miles of Plant: 210.0 (coaxial); None (fiber optic). Homes passed: 6,500. Total homes in franchised area: 7,000.
Vice President & General Manager: Greg Garabedian. Technical Operations Director: Gregg Wood. Technical Operations Manager: Kevin Mailloux. Marketing Director: Dennis Jerome.
City fee: $1.30 per subscriber annually.
Ownership: Charter Communications Inc. (MSO).

CHESTER—Comcast Cable. Now served by SPRINGFIELD, MA [MA0005]. ICA: MA0044.

CHICOPEE—Charter Communications, 95 Higgins St, Worcester, MA 1606. Phone: 508-853-1515. Fax: 508-854-5042. Web Site: http://www.charter.com. Also serves East Longmeadow, Easthampton, Hampden, Ludlow, Southampton & Wilbraham. ICA: MA0082.
TV Market Ranking: 19 (CHICOPEE, East Longmeadow, Hampden, Ludlow, Southampton, Wilbraham); Below 100 (Easthampton). Franchise award date: February 21, 1976. Franchise expiration date: N.A. Began: February 21, 1976.
Channel capacity: N.A. Channels available but not in use: N.A.
Basic Service
Subscribers: 50,919.
Programming (received off-air): WCCT-TV (CW) Waterbury; WCTX (MNT) New Haven; WDMR-LP (TMO) Springfield; WEDH (PBS) Hartford; WGBY-TV (PBS) Springfield; WGGB-TV (ABC) Springfield; WSBK-TV (IND) Boston; WTIC-TV (FOX) Hartford; WVIT (NBC) New Britain; WWLP (NBC) Springfield.
Programming (via satellite): C-SPAN; Portuguese Channel; QVC; Trinity Broadcasting Network; TV Guide Network.
Current originations: Government Access; Educational Access; Public Access.
Fee: $29.99 installation.
Expanded Basic Service 1
Subscribers: 40,937.
Programming (via satellite): ABC Family Channel; AMC; Animal Planet; Arts & Entertainment; Bravo; Cartoon Network; CNBC; CNN; Comedy Central; Country Music TV; C-SPAN 2; Discovery Channel; Disney Channel; E! Entertainment Television; ESPN; ESPN 2; Eternal Word TV Network; FitTV; Food Network; Fox News Channel; FX; G4; Hallmark Channel; Headline News; HGTV; History Channel; Home Shopping Network; Lifetime; MSNBC; MTV; National Geographic Channel; New England Cable News; New England Sports Network; Nickelodeon; Oxygen; Speed Channel; Spike TV; Syfy; TBS Superstation; The Learning Channel; truTV; Turner Network TV; TV Land; Univision; USA Network; Versus; VH1; Weather Channel.
Fee: $53.00 monthly.
Expanded Basic Service 2
Subscribers: 38,025.
Programming (via satellite): Comcast Sports Net New England; Golf Channel; Toon Disney; Travel Channel; Turner Classic Movies.
Fee: $2.25 monthly.
Digital Basic Service
Subscribers: N.A.
Programming (via satellite): BBC America; Bio; Bloomberg Television; Discovery Digital Networks; Do-It-Yourself; ESPN Classic Sports; ESPNews; Fox Sports en Espanol; FSN Digital Atlantic; FSN Digital Central; FSN Digital Pacific; Fuel TV; Fuse; GAS; Great American Country; History Channel International; Independent Film Channel; International Television (ITV); Lifetime Movie Network; MTV Networks Digital Suite; Music Choice; NFL Network; Nick Jr.; Nick Too; NickToons TV; SoapNet; Sundance Channel; TV Guide Interactive Inc.; TVG Network; WE tv.
Digital Pay Service 1
Pay Units: 5,697.
Programming (via satellite): Cinemax (multiplexed).
Fee: $1.99 installation; $9.95 monthly.
Digital Pay Service 2
Pay Units: 11,437.
Programming (via satellite): HBO (multiplexed).
Fee: $1.99 installation; $10.95 monthly.
Digital Pay Service 3
Pay Units: 6,288.
Programming (via satellite): Showtime (multiplexed).
Fee: $1.99 installation; $10.95 monthly.
Digital Pay Service 4
Pay Units: 2,612.
Programming (via satellite): The Movie Channel.
Fee: $1.99 installation; $9.95 monthly.
Digital Pay Service 5
Pay Units: N.A.
Programming (via satellite): Encore (multiplexed); Flix; Starz (multiplexed).
Video-On-Demand: Yes
Pay-Per-View
Addressable homes: 39,845.
iN DEMAND (delivered digitally), Addressable: Yes; Fresh (delivered digitally); Pleasure (delivered digitally); ETC (delivered digitally); Playboy TV (delivered digitally).
Internet Service
Operational: Yes.
Broadband Service: Charter Pipeline.
Fee: $29.99 monthly; $10.00 modem lease; $195.00 modem purchase.
Telephone Service
Digital: Operational
Fee: $29.99 monthly
Miles of Plant: 669.0 (coaxial); None (fiber optic). Homes passed: 51,355.
Vice President & General Manager: Greg Garabedian. Technical Operations Director: George Duffy. Technical Operations Manager: Beatrice Welch. Marketing Director: Dennis Jerome. Marketing Manager: Paula Cecchetilli.
City fee: $0.50 per subscriber annually.
Ownership: Charter Communications Inc. (MSO).

CONWAY—Comcast Cable. Now served by SPRINGFIELD, MA [MA0005]. ICA: MA0073.

DANVERS—Formerly served by Comcast Cable. No longer in operation. ICA: MA0058.

DEDHAM—Comcast Cable. Now served by BOSTON, MA [MA0001]. ICA: MA0061.

DEDHAM—RCN Corp. Formerly served by Boston, MA [MA0105]. This cable system has converted to IPTV, 196 Van Buren St, Herndon, MA 20170. Phone: 703-434-8200. Web Site: http://www.rcn.com. ICA: MA5101.
Channel capacity: N.A. Channels available but not in use: N.A.
Internet Service
Operational: Yes.
Chairman: Steven J. Simmons. Chief Executive Officer: Jim Holanda.
Ownership: RCN Corp.

DORCHESTER—RCN Corp. Formerly served by Boston, MA [MA0105]. This cable system has converted to IPTV, 196 Van Buren St, Herndon, VA 20170. Phone: 703-434-8200. Web Site: http://www.rcn.com. ICA: MA5102.
Channel capacity: N.A. Channels available but not in use: N.A.
Internet Service
Operational: Yes.
Chairman: Steven J. Simmons. Chief Executive Officer: Jim Holanda.
Ownership: RCN Corp.

FAIRHAVEN—Comcast Cable. Now served by TAUNTON, MA [MA0033]. ICA: MA0084.

FORT DEVONS—Formerly served by Americable International. No longer in operation. ICA: MA0072.

FOXBOROUGH—Comcast Cable. Now served by TAUNTON, MA [MA0033]. ICA: MA0004.

FRAMINGHAM—Comcast Cable. Now served by BOSTON, MA [MA0001]. ICA: MA0023.

FRAMINGHAM—RCN Corp. Formerly served by Boston, MA [MA0105]. This cable system has converted to IPTV, 196 Van Buren St, Herndon, VA 20170. Phone: 703-434-8200. Web Site: http://www.rcn.com. ICA: MA5103.
Channel capacity: N.A. Channels available but not in use: N.A.
Internet Service
Operational: Yes.
Chairman: Steven J. Simmons. Chief Executive Officer: Jim Holanda.
Ownership: RCN Corp.

GLOUCESTER—Comcast Cable. Now served by BOSTON, MA [MA0001]. ICA: MA0032.

HAVERHILL—Comcast Cable. Now served by WESTFORD, MA [MA0093]. ICA: MA0085.

HINSDALE—Charter Communications, 95 Higgins St, Worcester, MA 1606. Phone: 508-853-1515. Fax: 508-854-5042. Web Site: http://www.charter.com. ICA: MA0096.
TV Market Ranking: 34 (HINSDALE). Franchise award date: May 16, 1989. Franchise expiration date: N.A. Began: October 1, 1989.
Channel capacity: N.A. Channels available but not in use: N.A.

Basic Service
Subscribers: 411.
Programming (received off-air): WMHT (PBS) Schenectady; WNYA (MNT) Pittsfield; WNYT (NBC) Albany; WRGB (CBS) Schenectady; WSBK-TV (IND) Boston; WTEN (ABC) Albany; WWLP (NBC) Springfield; WXXA-TV (FOX) Albany; WYPX-TV (ION) Amsterdam.
Programming (via satellite): C-SPAN; Home Shopping Network; QVC; TV Guide Network; WPIX (CW, IND) New York.
Current originations: Public Access.
Fee: $15.00 installation; $32.73 monthly; $2.50 converter; $15.00 additional installation.
Expanded Basic Service 1
Subscribers: N.A.
Programming (via satellite): ABC Family Channel; AMC; Animal Planet; Arts & Entertainment; Bravo; Cartoon Network; CNBC; CNN; Comcast Sports Net New England; Comedy Central; Country Music TV; C-SPAN 2; Discovery Channel; Disney Channel; E! Entertainment Television; ESPN; ESPN 2; ESPN Classic Sports; Food Network; Fox News Channel; FX; Headline News; HGTV; History Channel; INSP; Lifetime; MSNBC; MTV; New England Sports Network; Nickelodeon; Speed Channel; Spike TV; Syfy; TBS Superstation; The Learning Channel; Toon Disney; Travel Channel; Turner Network TV; TV Land; USA Network; Versus; VH1; Weather Channel.
Digital Basic Service
Subscribers: N.A.
Programming (via satellite): BBC America; Bio; Discovery Health Channel; Discovery Kids Channel; DMX Music; ESPNews; Fox Soccer; Fuse; GAS; Golf Channel; History Channel International; Independent Film Channel; Lifetime Movie Network; MTV2; Nick Jr.; Science Television; Turner Classic Movies; TV Guide Interactive Inc.; WE tv.
Digital Pay Service 1
Pay Units: 16.
Programming (via satellite): Cinemax (multiplexed).
Fee: $10.45 monthly.
Digital Pay Service 2
Pay Units: 23.
Programming (via satellite): The Movie Channel (multiplexed).
Fee: $9.95 monthly.
Digital Pay Service 3
Pay Units: 32.
Programming (via satellite): HBO (multiplexed).
Fee: $12.95 monthly.
Digital Pay Service 4
Pay Units: 23.
Programming (via satellite): Showtime (multiplexed).
Fee: $10.25 monthly.
Digital Pay Service 5
Pay Units: N.A.
Programming (via satellite): Encore (multiplexed); Flix; Starz (multiplexed).
Video-On-Demand: No
Pay-Per-View
iN DEMAND (delivered digitally); Playboy TV (delivered digitally).
Internet Service
Operational: No.
Telephone Service
None
Miles of Plant: 18.0 (coaxial); None (fiber optic). Homes passed: 706.
Vice President & General Manager: Greg Garabedian. Technical Operations Director: George Duffy. Technical Operations Manager: Beatrice Welch. Marketing Director: Dennis Jerome. Marketing Manager: Paula Cecchetelli.
Ownership: Charter Communications Inc. (MSO).

HOLLAND—Cox Communications, 9 James P. Murphy Hwy, West Warwick, RI 2893. Phones: 401-383-1919 (Administrative office); 401-821-1919 (Customer service). Web Site: http://www.cox.com. ICA: MA0097.
TV Market Ranking: 6 (HOLLAND). Franchise award date: N.A. Franchise expiration date: N.A. Began: N.A.
Channel capacity: N.A. Channels available but not in use: N.A.
Basic Service
Subscribers: 945.
Programming (received off-air): WBZ-TV (CBS) Boston; WCCT-TV (CW) Waterbury; WEDH (PBS) Hartford; WGBH-TV (PBS) Boston; WGBY-TV (PBS) Springfield; WGGB-TV (ABC) Springfield; WSAH (IND) Bridgeport; WSHM-LP (CBS) Springfield; WTIC-TV (FOX) Hartford; WTNH (ABC) New Haven; WUNI (UNV) Worcester; WUVN (UNV) Hartford; WWLP (NBC) Springfield.
Programming (via satellite): Cox Sports Television; C-SPAN; C-SPAN 2; CT-N; MyNetworkTV Inc.; QVC; TBS Superstation; TV Guide Network.
Current originations: Leased Access; Government Access; Educational Access; Public Access.
Fee: $29.99 installation; $29.14 monthly; $2.65 converter; $21.23 additional installation.
Expanded Basic Service 1
Subscribers: N.A.
Programming (via satellite): ABC Family Channel; AMC; Animal Planet; Arts & Entertainment; BET Networks; Bravo; Cartoon Network; CNBC; CNN; Comcast SportsNet Mid-Atlantic; Comedy Central; Discovery Channel; Discovery Health Channel; Disney Channel; E! Entertainment Television; ESPN; ESPN 2; Eternal Word TV Network; Food Network; Fox News Channel; FX; Headline News; HGTV; History Channel; Home Shopping Network; Lifetime; MSNBC; MTV; New England Sports Network; Nickelodeon; ShopNBC; Spike TV; Syfy; The Learning Channel; Travel Channel; truTV; Turner Network TV; TV Land; USA Network; VH1; Weather Channel.
Fee: $21.35 monthly.
Digital Basic Service
Subscribers: N.A.
Programming (received off-air): WCCT-TV (CW) Waterbury; WFSB (CBS) Hartford; WGBY-TV (PBS) Springfield; WGGB-TV (ABC) Springfield; WTIC-TV (FOX) Hartford; WWLP (NBC) Springfield.
Programming (via satellite): AMC HD; Animal Planet HD; Arts & Entertainment HD; Bio; Bio HD; Bloomberg Television; Bravo HD; Cartoon Network HD; CBS College Sports Network; CMT HD; CNBC HD+; CNN HD; CNN International; Comcast SportsNet Mid-Atlantic; Comedy Central; Discovery Channel HD; Discovery HD Theater; Discovery Kids Channel; Discovery Planet Green; Discovery Planet Green HD; E! Entertainment Television HD; ESPN 2 HD; ESPN Classic Sports; ESPN HD; ESPN U; ESPNews; FitTV; Food Network HD; Fox Business Channel; Fox Business Channel HD; Fox News HD; Fox Soccer; Fuel TV; FX HD; G4; Gol TV; Golf Channel; Golf Channel HD; Hallmark Movie Channel HD; HGTV HD; History Channel HD; History Channel International; ID Investigation Discovery; Lifetime Movie Network HD; Lifetime Television HD; Military History Channel; MLB Network; MTV Networks HD; Music Choice; National Geographic Channel; National Geographic Channel HD Network; NBA TV; NBA TV HD; New England Sports Network; NFL Network; NFL Network HD; NHL Network; NHL Network HD; Nick HD; Nick Jr.; Palladia; Science Channel HD; Science Television; Speed Channel; Speed HD; Spike TV HD; Syfy HD; TBS in HD; TLC HD; Travel Channel HD; Turner Network TV HD; Universal HD; USA Network HD; Versus; Versus HD; VH1 HD.
Fee: $55.74 monthly.
Digital Expanded Basic Service
Subscribers: N.A.
Programming (via satellite): BBC America; Boomerang; Chiller; CMT Pure Country; Cooking Channel; Country Music TV; Disney XD; Do-It-Yourself; Fuse; Great American Country; GSN; Hallmark Channel; Halogen Network; Independent Film Channel; INSP; Lifetime Movie Network; LOGO; MTV Hits; MTV Jams; MTV2; mtvU; mun2 television; NickToons TV; Oxygen; PBS Kids Sprout; SoapNet; Sundance Channel; TeenNick; Trinity Broadcasting Network; Turner Classic Movies; TV One; VH1 Classic; WE tv.
Fee: $68.74 monthly.
Digital Expanded Basic Service 2
Subscribers: N.A.
Programming (via satellite): Canal Sur; Cine Latino; CNN en Espanol; De Pelicula; De Pelicula Clasico; Discovery en Espanol; Disney XD en Espanol; ESPN Deportes; Fox Sports en Espanol; GalaVision; History Channel en Espanol; MTV Tres; NickToons en Espanol; RAI International; Ritmoson Latino; Sorpresa; TV Chile; TV Colombia; TV5 USA; WAPA America.
Fee: $9.95 monthly (RAI Italia), $11.95 monthly (TV5), $44.39 monthly (various Spanish channels).
Digital Pay Service 1
Pay Units: N.A.
Programming (via satellite): Cinemax (multiplexed); Cinemax HD; Encore (multiplexed); Flix; HBO (multiplexed); HBO HD; Showtime (multiplexed); Showtime HD; Starz (multiplexed); Starz HDTV; The Movie Channel (multiplexed).
Fee: $13.00 monthly (HBO, Cinemax, Starz/Encore or Shwtime/Flix/TMC).
Video-On-Demand: Yes
Pay-Per-View
iN DEMAND (delivered digitally); Spice: Xcess; Playboy TV (delivered digitally); Shorteez (delivered digitally), Fee: $8.95; Club Jenna (delivered digitally); ESPN Gameplan (delivered digitally); ESPN Full Court (delivered digitally); NBA League Pass; MLS Direct Kick; MLB Extra Innings/NHL Center Ice.
Internet Service
Operational: Yes.
Broadband Service: Cox High Speed Internet.
Fee: $49.95 monthly.
Telephone Service
None
Senior Vice President & General Manager: Paul Cronin. Vice President, Network Services: Allan Gardner. Vice President, Government & Public Affairs: John Wolfe. Vice President, Marketing: Doreen Studley. Residential Product Management Director: Jonathan Leepson. Public Relations Director: Amy Quinn.
Ownership: Cox Communications Inc. (MSO).

HOPKINTON—Comcast Cable. Now served by BOSTON, MA [MA0001]. ICA: MA0074.

HYDE PARK—RCN Corp. Formerly served by Boston, MA [MA0105]. This cable system has converted to IPTV, 196 Van Buren St, Herndon, VA 20170. Phone: 703-434-8200. Web Site: http://www.rcn.com. ICA: MA5105.
Channel capacity: N.A. Channels available but not in use: N.A.
Internet Service
Operational: Yes.
Chairman: Steven J. Simmons. Chief Executive Officer: Jim Holanda.
Ownership: RCN Corp.

LANESBORO—Charter Communications, 95 Higgins St, Worcester, MA 1606. Phone: 508-853-1513. Fax: 508-854-5042. Web Site: http://www.charter.com. ICA: MA0086.
TV Market Ranking: 34 (LANESBORO). Franchise award date: March 23, 1987. Franchise expiration date: N.A. Began: June 1, 1988.
Channel capacity: N.A. Channels available but not in use: N.A.
Basic Service
Subscribers: 830.
Programming (received off-air): WMHT (PBS) Schenectady; WNYT (NBC) Albany; WRGB (CBS) Schenectady; WSBK-TV (IND) Boston; WTEN (ABC) Albany; WWLP (NBC) Springfield; WXXA-TV (FOX) Albany; WYPX-TV (ION) Amsterdam.
Programming (via satellite): Home Shopping Network; INSP; QVC; TV Guide Network; WPIX (CW, IND) New York.
Current originations: Government Access.
Expanded Basic Service 1
Subscribers: N.A.
Programming (via satellite): ABC Family Channel; AMC; Animal Planet; Arts & Entertainment; Bravo; Cartoon Network; CNBC; CNN; Comcast Sports Net New England; Comedy Central; Country Music TV; C-SPAN; C-SPAN 2; Discovery Channel; Disney Channel; E! Entertainment Television; ESPN; ESPN 2; Food Network; Fox News Channel; Headline News; HGTV; History Channel; Lifetime; MSNBC; MTV; New England Sports Network; Nickelodeon; Speed Channel; Spike TV; Syfy; TBS Superstation; The Learning Channel; Toon Disney; Travel Channel; Turner Network TV; TV Land; USA Network; Versus; VH1; Weather Channel.
Fee: $55.00 monthly.
Digital Basic Service
Subscribers: N.A.
Programming (via satellite): BBC America; Bio; Discovery Digital Networks; DMX Mu-

sic; ESPNews; Fox Sports World; Fuse; GAS; Golf Channel; History Channel International; Independent Film Channel; Lifetime Movie Network; MTV2; Nick Jr.; Style Network; Turner Classic Movies; WE tv.

Digital Pay Service 1

Pay Units: N.A.

Programming (via satellite): Cinemax (multiplexed); Encore (multiplexed); HBO (multiplexed); Showtime (multiplexed); Starz; The Movie Channel.

Video-On-Demand: No

Pay-Per-View

Special events, Addressable: Yes.

Internet Service

Operational: No.

Telephone Service

None

Miles of Plant: 44.0 (coaxial); None (fiber optic). Homes passed: 1,050.

Vice President & General Manager: Greg Garabedian. Technical Operations Director: George Duffy. Technical Operations Manager: Beatrice Welch. Marketing Director: Dennis Jerome. Marketing Manager: Paula Cecchetilli.

Ownership: Charter Communications Inc. (MSO).

LAWRENCE—Comcast Cable. Now served by WESTFORD, MA [MA0093]. ICA: MA0015.

LEE—Time Warner Cable. Now served by PITTSFIELD, MA [MA0090]. ICA: MA0059.

LEOMINSTER—Comcast Cable. Now served by WESTFORD, MA [MA0093]. ICA: MA0017.

LEXINGTON—Comcast Cable. Now served by BOSTON, MA [MA0001]. ICA: MA0037.

LEXINGTON—RCN Corp. Formerly served by Boston, MA [MA0105]. This cable system has converted to IPTV, 196 Van Buren St, Herndon, VA 20170. Phone: 703-434-8200. Web Site: http://www.rcn.com. ICA: MA5106.

Channel capacity: N.A. Channels available but not in use: N.A.

Internet Service

Operational: Yes.

Chairman: Steven J. Simmons. Chief Executive Officer: Jim Holanda.

Ownership: RCN Corp.

LONGMEADOW—Comcast Cable. Now served by SPRINGFIELD, MA [MA0005]. ICA: MA0068.

LOWELL—Comcast Cable. Now served by WESTFORD, MA [MA0093]. ICA: MA0008.

MALDEN—Comcast Cable. Now served by BOSTON, MA [MA0001]. ICA: MA0003.

MARION—Comcast Cable. Now served by TAUNTON, MA [MA0033]. ICA: MA0043.

MARLBOROUGH—Comcast Cable. Now served by WESTFORD, MA [MA0093]. ICA: MA0087.

MARSHFIELD—Comcast Cable. Now served by TAUNTON, MA [MA0033]. ICA: MA0088.

MARTHA'S VINEYARD—Comcast Cable. Now served by TAUNTON, MA [MA0033]. ICA: MA0056.

MASHPEE—Comcast Cable. Now served by TAUNTON, MA [MA0033]. ICA: MA0064.

MAYNARD—Comcast Cable. Now served by WESTFORD, MA [MA0093]. ICA: MA0026.

MIDDLEBOROUGH—Comcast Cable. Now served by TAUNTON, MA [MA0033]. ICA: MA0042.

MILFORD—Formerly served by Comcast Cable. No longer in operation. ICA: MA0049.

NANTUCKET—Comcast Cable. Now served by TAUNTON, MA [MA0033]. ICA: MA0067.

NATICK—Comcast Cable. Now served by BOSTON, MA [MA0001]. ICA: MA0045.

NATICK—RCN Corp. Formerly served by Boston, MA [MA0105]. This cable system has converted to IPTV, 196 Van Buren St, Herndon, VA 20170. Phone: 703-434-8200. Web Site: http://www.rcn.com. ICA: MA5108.

Channel capacity: N.A. Channels available but not in use: N.A.

Internet Service

Operational: Yes.

Chairman: Steven J. Simmons. Chief Executive Officer: Jim Holanda.

Ownership: RCN Corp.

NEEDHAM—Comcast Cable. Now served by BOSTON, MA [MA0001]. ICA: MA0010.

NEEDHAM—RCN Corp. Formerly served by Boston, MA [MA0105]. This cable system has converted to IPTV, 196 Van Buren St, Herndon, VA 20170. Phone: 703-434-8200. Web Site: http://www.rcn.com. ICA: MA5109.

Channel capacity: N.A. Channels available but not in use: N.A.

Internet Service

Operational: Yes.

Chairman: Steven J. Simmons. Chief Executive Officer: Jim Holanda.

Ownership: RCN Corp.

NEW BEDFORD—Comcast Cable. Now served by TAUNTON, MA [MA0033]. ICA: MA0013.

NEWBURYPORT—Comcast Cable. Now served by BOSTON, MA [MA0001]. ICA: MA0039.

NEWTON—RCN Corp. Formerly served by Boston, MA [MA0105]. This cable system has converted to IPTV, 196 Van Buren St, Herndon, VA 20170. Phone: 703-434-8200. Web Site: http://www.rcn.com. ICA: MA5110.

Channel capacity: N.A. Channels available but not in use: N.A.

Internet Service

Operational: Yes.

Chairman: Steven J. Simmons. Chief Executive Officer: Jim Holanda.

Ownership: RCN Corp.

NORTH ADAMS—Time Warner Cable. Now served by PITTSFIELD, MA [MA0090]. ICA: MA0036.

NORTH ANDOVER—Comcast Cable. Now served by WESTFORD, MA [MA0093]. ICA: MA0060.

NORWOOD—Comcast Cable. Now served by BOSTON, MA [MA0001]. ICA: MA0040.

ORLEANS—Comcast Cable. Now served by TAUNTON, MA [MA0033]. ICA: MA0030.

PEABODY—Comcast Cable. Now served by BOSTON, MA [MA0001]. ICA: MA0028.

PEMBROKE—Comcast Cable. Now served by TAUNTON, MA [MA0033]. ICA: MA0095.

PEPPERELL—Charter Communications, 95 Higgins St, Worcester, MA 1606. Phone: 508-853-1515. Fax: 508-854-5042. Web Site: http://www.charter.com. Also serves Berlin, Dunstable, Groton & Harvard, MA; Brookline & Hollis, NH. ICA: MA0055.

TV Market Ranking: 6 (Berlin, Brookline, Dunstable, Groton, Harvard, Hollis, PEPPERELL). Franchise award date: January 18, 1985. Franchise expiration date: N.A. Began: February 24, 1986.

Channel capacity: N.A. Channels available but not in use: N.A.

Basic Service

Subscribers: 12,014.

Programming (received off-air): WBPX-TV (ION) Boston; WBZ-TV (CBS) Boston; WCVB-TV (ABC) Boston; WENH-TV (PBS) Durham; WFXT (FOX) Boston; WGBH-TV (PBS) Boston; WGBX-TV (PBS) Boston; WHDH (NBC) Boston; WLVI-TV (CW) Cambridge; WMFP (IND) Lawrence; WMUR-TV (ABC) Manchester; WSBK-TV (IND) Boston; WUNI (UNV) Worcester; WUTF-DT (TEL) Marlborough; WYDN (ETV) Worcester; WZMY-TV (MNT) Derry.

Programming (via satellite): C-SPAN; Eternal Word TV Network; Home Shopping Network; INSP; QVC; TV Guide Network.

Current originations: Government Access; Educational Access; Public Access.

Expanded Basic Service 1

Subscribers: 10,997.

Programming (via satellite): ABC Family Channel; AMC; Animal Planet; Arts & Entertainment; Bravo; Cartoon Network; CNBC; CNN; Comcast Sports Net New England; Comedy Central; Discovery Channel; Disney Channel; E! Entertainment Television; ESPN; ESPN 2; FitTV; Food Network; Fox News Channel; FX; G4; Golf Channel; Hallmark Channel; Headline News; HGTV; History Channel; Lifetime; MSNBC; MTV; National Geographic Channel; New England Cable News; New England Sports Network; Nickelodeon; Oxygen; Speed Channel; Spike TV; Syfy; TBS Superstation; The Learning Channel; Toon Disney; Travel Channel; truTV; Turner Classic Movies; Turner Network TV; TV Land; USA Network; Versus; VH1; Weather Channel.

Fee: $55.00 monthly.

Digital Basic Service

Subscribers: N.A.

Programming (via satellite): BBC America; Bio; Bloomberg Television; Discovery Digital Networks; Do-It-Yourself; ESPN Classic Sports; ESPNews; Fox Sports en Espanol; Fox Sports World; FSN Digital Atlantic; FSN Digital Central; FSN Digital Pacific; Fuel TV; Fuse; GAS; Great American Country; History Channel International; Independent Film Channel; International Television (ITV); Lifetime Movie Network; MTV Networks Digital Suite; Music Choice; NFL Network; Nick Jr.; Nick Too; NickToons TV; SoapNet; Sundance Channel; TVG Network; WE tv.

Digital Pay Service 1

Pay Units: 930.

Programming (via satellite): Cinemax (multiplexed).

Fee: $10.95 monthly.

Digital Pay Service 2

Pay Units: 1,247.

Programming (via satellite): Flix.

Fee: $4.95 monthly.

Digital Pay Service 3

Pay Units: 1,687.

Programming (via satellite): HBO (multiplexed).

Fee: $11.95 monthly.

Digital Pay Service 4

Pay Units: 1,353.

Programming (via satellite): Showtime (multiplexed).

Fee: $10.95 monthly.

Digital Pay Service 5

Pay Units: N.A.

Programming (via satellite): Encore (multiplexed); Starz (multiplexed); The Movie Channel (multiplexed).

Video-On-Demand: Yes

Pay-Per-View

iN DEMAND (delivered digitally), Addressable: Yes; Pleasure (delivered digitally); Playboy TV (delivered digitally); ETC (delivered digitally); Fresh (delivered digitally); NHL Center Ice (delivered digitally); MLB Extra Innings (delivered digitally); NASCAR In Car (delivered digitally).

Internet Service

Operational: Yes.

Broadband Service: Charter Pipeline.

Fee: $29.99 monthly.

Telephone Service

Digital: Operational

Miles of Plant: 492.0 (coaxial); 31.0 (fiber optic).

Vice President & General Manager: Greg Garabedian. Technical Operations Director: George Duffy. Technical Operations Manager: Kevin Mailloux. Marketing Director: Dennis Jerome.

Ownership: Charter Communications Inc. (MSO).

PHILLIPSTON—Comcast Cable. Now served by WESTFORD, MA [MA0093]. ICA: MA0079.

PITTSFIELD—Time Warner Cable, 1021 Highbridge Rd, Schenectady, NY 12303. Phone: 518-242-8890. Fax: 518-242-8948. Web Site: http://www.timewarnercable.com/albany. Also serves Adams, Cheshire, Clarksburg, Dalton, Great Barrington, Housatonic, Lee, Lenox, North Adams, Richmond, Sheffield (town), Stockbridge & Williamstown. ICA: MA0090.

TV Market Ranking: 34 (Adams, Cheshire, Clarksburg, Dalton, Lenox, North Adams, PITTSFIELD, Richmond, Williamstown); Below 100 (Great Barrington, Housatonic, Lee, Sheffield (town), Stockbridge). Franchise award date: January 1, 1956. Franchise expiration date: N.A. Began: November 1, 1956.

Channel capacity: N.A. Channels available but not in use: N.A.

Basic Service

Subscribers: N.A. Included in Albany, NY

Programming (received off-air): WCWN (CW) Schenectady; WFSB (CBS) Hartford; WGBY-TV (PBS) Springfield; WMHT (PBS) Schenectady; WNYT (NBC) Albany; WRGB (CBS) Schenectady; WTEN (ABC) Albany; WWLP (NBC) Springfield; WXXA-TV (FOX) Albany; WYPX-TV (ION) Amsterdam; 23 FMs.

Programming (via microwave): WCVB-TV (ABC) Boston.

Programming (via satellite): C-SPAN 2; TBS Superstation; TV Guide Network.

Current originations: Religious Access; Government Access; Educational Access; Public Access.
Fee: $24.70 installation; $8.97 monthly.

Expanded Basic Service 1
Subscribers: 18,618.
Programming (via satellite): ABC Family Channel; AMC; Animal Planet; Arts & Entertainment; BET Networks; Bravo!; Cartoon Network; CNBC; CNN; Comcast Sports Net New England; Comedy Central; Country Music TV; C-SPAN; Discovery Channel; E! Entertainment Television; ESPN; ESPN 2; ESPN Classic Sports; Eternal Word TV Network; Food Network; Fox News Channel; FX; Golf Channel; Headline News; HGTV; History Channel; Home Shopping Network; Lifetime; Lifetime Movie Network; MSNBC; MTV; National Geographic Channel; New England Cable News; Nickelodeon; Oxygen; QVC; ShopNBC; SoapNet; Spike TV; Style Network; The Learning Channel; Travel Channel; truTV; Turner Classic Movies; Turner Network TV; TV Land; Univision; USA Network; VH1; WE tv; Weather Channel.
Fee: $25.60 monthly.

Digital Basic Service
Subscribers: N.A. Included in Albany, NY
Programming (via satellite): BBC America; Bloomberg Television; Cooking Channel; Country Music TV; C-SPAN 3; Discovery Digital Networks; Disney Channel; DMX Music; Do-It-Yourself; ESPNews; Fox Sports World; FSN Digital Atlantic; FSN Digital Central; FSN Digital Pacific; G4; Great American Country; GSN; Hallmark Channel; History Channel International; Lifetime Real Women; MSG; MSG Plus; MTV Networks Digital Suite; MuchMusic Network; New York 1 News; Nick Jr.; Outdoor Channel; Ovation; Speed Channel; Syfy; Toon Disney; Trinity Broadcasting Network; TV Asia; Versus; Yankees Entertainment & Sports; Zee TV USA.
Fee: $4.95 monthly.

Digital Pay Service 1
Pay Units: N.A.
Programming (via satellite): Cinemax (multiplexed); Encore (multiplexed); Flix; Fox Movie Channel; HBO (multiplexed); Independent Film Channel; Showtime (multiplexed); Starz (multiplexed); Sundance Channel; The Movie Channel (multiplexed).
Fee: $9.95 monthly (RAI, TV Asia, or Zee TV), $14.95 monthly (HBO, Cinemax, Showtime, or Starz).
Video-On-Demand: Yes

Pay-Per-View
Addressable homes: 8,097.
iN DEMAND (delivered digitally), Addressable: Yes; Playboy TV (delivered digitally); Fresh (delivered digitally); Shorteez (delivered digitally); Hot Choice (delivered digitally); Pleasure (delivered digitally); Adult PPV (delivered digitally).

Internet Service
Operational: Yes. Began: January 1, 1999.
Subscribers: 2,500.
Broadband Service: AOL for Broadband; EarthLink; Local.net; Road Runner.
Fee: $29.95 installation; $44.95 monthly.

Telephone Service
Digital: Operational
Note: Homes passed and miles of plant (coax & fiber) included in Albany, NY
Vice President, Operations: Mark Loreno. Vice President, Engineering: James Marchester. Vice President, Marketing: Tricia Buhr. Vice President, Public Affairs: Peter Taubkin. Vice President, Customer Care: Paul Ventosa.
Ownership: Time Warner Cable (MSO).; Advance/Newhouse Partnership (MSO).

PLYMOUTH—Comcast Cable. Now served by TAUNTON, MA [MA0033]. ICA: MA0050.

QUINCY—Comcast Cable. Now served by TAUNTON, MA [MA0033]. ICA: MA0011.

RUSSELL—Russell Municipal Cable TV, PO Box 408, 65 Main St, Russell, MA 01071-0408. Phones: 413-862-6204; 413-862-4707. Fax: 413-862-3103. E-mail: information@russellma.net. Web Site: http://www2.russellma.net. ICA: MA0091.
TV Market Ranking: 19,0 (RUSSELL). Franchise award date: March 10, 1987. Franchise expiration date: N.A. Began: September 1, 1987.
Channel capacity: 150 (2-way capable). Channels available but not in use: N.A.

Basic Service
Subscribers: 470.
Programming (received off-air): WGBY-TV (PBS) Springfield; WGGB-TV (ABC) Springfield; WSHM-LP (CBS) Springfield; WTIC-TV (FOX) Hartford; WWLP (NBC) Springfield.
Programming (via satellite): ABC Family Channel; AMC; Animal Planet; Arts & Entertainment; Cartoon Network; CNN; Comedy Central; Country Music TV; C-SPAN; Discovery Channel; Disney Channel; Do-It-Yourself; E! Entertainment Television; ESPN; ESPN 2; Fox News Channel; Hallmark Channel; Headline News; HGTV; History Channel; Home Shopping Network; Lifetime; MTV; National Geographic Channel; New England Sports Network; Nickelodeon; Spike TV; Syfy; TBS Superstation; The Learning Channel; Travel Channel; truTV; Turner Classic Movies; Turner Network TV; TV Land; USA Network; Versus; VH1; Weather Channel.
Fee: $30.00 installation; $35.50 monthly; $15.00 additional installation.

Pay Service 1
Pay Units: 75.
Programming (via satellite): HBO.
Fee: $12.95 monthly.

Pay Service 2
Pay Units: 27.
Programming (via satellite): The Movie Channel.
Fee: $10.95 monthly.

Pay Service 3
Pay Units: 32.
Programming (via satellite): Showtime.
Fee: $10.95 monthly.
Video-On-Demand: No

Internet Service
Operational: Yes.
Subscribers: 235.
Fee: $75.00 installation; $17.00 monthly.

Telephone Service
Analog: Not Operational
Digital: Planned
Miles of Plant: None (coaxial); 20.0 (fiber optic). Homes passed: 585. Total homes in franchised area: 750. Planning upgrade to 870 MHz
Manager: Susan B. Maxwell. Chief Technician: Richard Trusty.
Ownership: Russell Municipal Cable TV.

RUTLAND (town)—Charter Communications, 95 Higgins St, Worcester, MA 1606. Phone: 508-853-1515. Fax: 508-854-5042. Web Site: http://www.charter.com.

Also serves Barre (town), Hubbardston & Oakham. ICA: MA0071.
TV Market Ranking: 6 (Barre (town), Hubbardston, Oakham, RUTLAND (TOWN)). Franchise award date: December 5, 1988. Franchise expiration date: N.A. Began: May 15, 1989.
Channel capacity: N.A. Channels available but not in use: N.A.

Basic Service
Subscribers: 4,705.
Programming (received off-air): ION Television; WBPX-TV (ION) Boston; WBZ-TV (CBS) Boston; WCVB-TV (ABC) Boston; WFXT (FOX) Boston; WGBH-TV (PBS) Boston; WGBX-TV (PBS) Boston; WGBY-TV (PBS) Springfield; WGGB-TV (ABC) Springfield; WHDH (NBC) Boston; WJAR (NBC) Providence; WLVI-TV (CW) Cambridge; WMFP (IND) Lawrence; WSBK-TV (IND) Boston; WUNI (UNV) Worcester; WUTF-DT (TEL) Marlborough; WYDN (ETV) Worcester; WZMY-TV (MNT) Derry.
Programming (via satellite): C-SPAN; C-SPAN 2; Home Shopping Network; INSP; QVC; TV Guide Network.
Current originations: Government Access; Educational Access; Public Access.
Fee: $29.99 installation.

Expanded Basic Service 1
Subscribers: 4,333.
Programming (via satellite): ABC Family Channel; AMC; Animal Planet; Arts & Entertainment; Bravo; Cartoon Network; CNBC; CNN; Comcast Sports Net New England; Comedy Central; Discovery Channel; Disney Channel; E! Entertainment Television; ESPN; ESPN 2; FitTV; Food Network; Fox News Channel; FX; G4; Golf Channel; Hallmark Channel; Headline News; HGTV; History Channel; Lifetime; MSNBC; MTV; National Geographic Channel; New England Cable News; New England Sports Network; Nickelodeon; Oxygen; Speed Channel; Spike TV; Syfy; TBS Superstation; The Learning Channel; Toon Disney; Travel Channel; truTV; Turner Classic Movies; Turner Network TV; TV Land; USA Network; Versus; VH1; Weather Channel.
Fee: $55.00 monthly.

Digital Basic Service
Subscribers: N.A.
Programming (via satellite): BBC America; Bio; Bloomberg Television; Discovery Digital Networks; Do-It-Yourself; ESPN Classic Sports; ESPNews; Fox Sports en Espanol; Fox Sports World; FSN Digital Atlantic; FSN Digital Central; FSN Digital Pacific; Fuel TV; Fuse; GAS; Great American Country; History Channel International; Independent Film Channel; International Television (ITV); Lifetime Movie Network; MTV Networks Digital Suite; Music Choice; NFL Network; Nick Jr.; Nick Too; NickToons TV; SoapNet; Sundance Channel; TVG Network; WE tv.

Digital Pay Service 1
Pay Units: 315.
Programming (via satellite): Cinemax (multiplexed).
Fee: $10.95 monthly.

Digital Pay Service 2
Pay Units: 420.
Programming (via satellite): Flix.
Fee: $4.95 monthly.

Digital Pay Service 3
Pay Units: 620.
Programming (via satellite): HBO (multiplexed).
Fee: $11.95 monthly.

Digital Pay Service 4
Pay Units: 560.
Programming (via satellite): Showtime (multiplexed).
Fee: $10.95 monthly.

Digital Pay Service 5
Pay Units: N.A.
Programming (via satellite): Encore (multiplexed); Starz (multiplexed); The Movie Channel (multiplexed).
Video-On-Demand: Yes

Pay-Per-View
iN DEMAND (delivered digitally), Addressable: Yes; Pleasure (delivered digitally); Playboy TV (delivered digitally); ETC (delivered digitally); Fresh (delivered digitally); NHL Center Ice (delivered digitally); MLB Extra Innings (delivered digitally); NASCAR In Car (delivered digitally).

Internet Service
Operational: Yes.
Broadband Service: Charter Pipeline.
Fee: $29.99 monthly.

Telephone Service
Digital: Operational
Fee: $29.99 monthly
Miles of Plant: 240.0 (coaxial); 28.0 (fiber optic). Homes passed: 4,990.
Vice President & General Manager: Greg Garabedian. Technical Operations Director: George Duffy. Marketing Director: Dennis Jerome. Technical Operations Manager: Kenny Mailloux.
Ownership: Charter Communications Inc. (MSO).

SAUGUS—Comcast Cable. Now served by BOSTON, MA [MA0001]. ICA: MA0019.

SCITUATE—Comcast Cable. Now served by TAUNTON, MA [MA0033]. ICA: MA0021.

SHREWSBURY—Shrewsbury's Community Cablevision, 100 Maple Ave, Shrewsbury, MA 01545-5347. Phone: 508-841-8500. Fax: 508-842-9419. E-mail: tjosie@ci.shrewsbury.ma.us. Web Site: http://www.shrewsbury-ma.gov/cable. ICA: MA0051.
TV Market Ranking: 6 (SHREWSBURY). Franchise award date: April 1, 1982. Franchise expiration date: N.A. Began: October 9, 1983.
Channel capacity: 80 (operating 2-way). Channels available but not in use: 10.

Basic Service
Subscribers: 11,803.
Programming (received off-air): WBPX-TV (ION) Boston; WBZ-TV (CBS) Boston; WCVB-TV (ABC) Boston; WFXT (FOX) Boston; WGBH-TV (PBS) Boston; WGBX-TV (PBS) Boston; WHDH (NBC) Boston; WJAR (NBC) Providence; WLVI-TV (CW) Cambridge; WNEU (TMO) Merrimack;

WSBE-TV (PBS) Providence; WSBK-TV (IND) Boston; WUNI (UNV) Worcester; WUTF-DT (TEL) Marlborough; WWDP (IND) Norwell; WYDN (ETV) Worcester.
Programming (via satellite): ABC Family Channel; Bravo; Cartoon Network; C-SPAN; C-SPAN 2; Discovery Channel; Eternal Word TV Network; Hallmark Channel; MSNBC; MyNetworkTV Inc.; Shop at Home; ShopNBC; TBS Superstation; Travel Channel; Trinity Broadcasting Network; truTV; TV Guide Network.
Current originations: Religious Access; Government Access; Educational Access; Public Access.
Fee: $50.00 installation; $11.63 monthly; $23.00 additional installation.

Expanded Basic Service 1
Subscribers: 9,901.
Programming (via microwave): New England Cable News.
Programming (via satellite): AMC; Animal Planet; Arts & Entertainment; AZ TV; BET Networks; CNBC; CNN; CNN International; Comcast SportsNet Mid-Atlantic; Comedy Central; Country Music TV; Disney Channel; E! Entertainment Television; ESPN; ESPN 2; ESPN Classic Sports; Food Network; Fox News Channel; FX; Golf Channel; Headline News; HGTV; History Channel; Lifetime; Lifetime Movie Network; MTV; National Geographic Channel; New England Sports Network; Nickelodeon; Spike TV; Syfy; The Learning Channel; Turner Network TV; TV Land; USA Network; VH1; Weather Channel.
Fee: $35.00 installation; $33.55 monthly.

Digital Basic Service
Subscribers: N.A.
Programming (received off-air): WBZ-TV (CBS) Boston; WCVB-TV (ABC) Boston; WFXT (FOX) Boston; WGBH-TV (PBS) Boston; WHDH (NBC) Boston; WLVI-TV (CW) Cambridge; WSBK-TV (IND) Boston.
Programming (via satellite): American Movie Classics; Animal Planet HD; BBC America; Bloomberg Television; Boomerang; Bridges TV; Comcast SportsNet Mid-Atlantic; Cooking Channel; Discovery Channel HD; Discovery HD Theater; Discovery Health Channel; Discovery Home Channel; Discovery Kids Channel; Do-It-Yourself; ESPN 2 HD; ESPN HD; ESPN U; ESPNews; FitTV; Fox Business Channel; Fox Movie Channel; Fox Reality Channel; Fox Soccer; Fuel TV; Fuse; G4; Golf Channel; GSN; HDNet; HDNet Movies; ID Investigation Discovery; Independent Film Channel; Lifetime Real Women; MTV2; National Geographic Channel HD Network; New England Sports Network; NFL Network; NHL Network; Nick Jr.; NickToons TV; Outdoor Channel; Oxygen; PBS Kids Sprout; Science Channel; Science Channel HD; SoapNet; Speed Channel; Style Network; Sundance Channel; TBS in HD; TeenNick; Tennis Channel; The Learning Channel; Toon Disney; Turner Classic Movies; Turner Network TV HD; Universal HD; Versus; Versus HD; VH1 Classic; WE tv.
Fee: $11.95 monthly; $8.95 converter.

Digital Pay Service 1
Pay Units: N.A.
Programming (via satellite): CCTV-4; Cinemax (multiplexed); Cinemax HD; Encore (multiplexed); Flix; HBO (multiplexed); HBO HD; Showtime (multiplexed); Showtime HD; Starz (multiplexed); Starz HDTV; The Movie Channel (multiplexed); The Movie Channel HD; TV Asia; Zee TV USA.
Fee: $10.95 monthly (Cinemax, HBO, Starz & Encore, Zee TV, TV Asia or CCTV-4), $12.95 monthly (Showtime, TMC & Flix), $13.95 monthly (Playboy TV).

Video-On-Demand: Yes

Pay-Per-View
Addressable homes: 9,670.
iN DEMAND (delivered digitally), Fee: $3.95, Addressable: Yes; MLB Extra Innings (delivered digitally); NHL Center Ice (delivered digitally); Playboy TV (delivered digitally).

Internet Service
Operational: Yes.
Subscribers: 5,063.
Broadband Service: In-house.
Fee: $50.00 installation; $19.95-$49.95 monthly.

Telephone Service
Digital: Operational

Miles of Plant: 190.0 (coaxial); 18.0 (fiber optic). Homes passed: 12,343. Total homes in franchised area: 12,343.
Manager: Thomas Josie. Operations Manager: Wayne Cullen. Marketing Manager: Jackie Platt.
City fee: 5% of gross.
Ownership: Shrewsbury's Community Cablevision.

SOMERVILLE—RCN Corp. Formerly served by Boston, MA [MA0105]. This cable system has converted to IPTV, 196 Van Buren St, Herndon, VA 20170. Phone: 703-434-8200. Web Site: http://www.rcn.com. ICA: MA5112.
Channel capacity: N.A. Channels available but not in use: N.A.

Internet Service
Operational: Yes.

Chairman: Steven J. Simmons. Chief Executive Officer: Jim Holanda.
Ownership: RCN Corp.

SOUTH BOSTON—RCN Corp. Formerly served by Boston, MA [MA0105]. This cable system has converted to IPTV, 196 Van Buren St, Herndon, VA 20170. Phone: 703-434-8200. Web Site: http://www.rcn.com. ICA: MA5113.
Channel capacity: N.A. Channels available but not in use: N.A.

Internet Service
Operational: Yes.

Chairman: Steven J. Simmons. Chief Executive Officer: Jim Holanda.
Ownership: RCN Corp.

SOUTH YARMOUTH—Comcast Cable. Now served by TAUNTON, MA [MA0033]. ICA: MA0031.

SPRINGFIELD—Comcast Cable, 3303 Main St, Springfield, MA 1107. Phone: 413-730-4500. Fax: 413-734-9243. Web Site: http://www.comcast.com. Also serves Agawam, Amherst, Bernardston, Bondsville, Buckland, Chester, Conway, Deerfield, Erving, Gilbertville, Gill, Granby, Granville, Greenfield, Hardwick, Holyoke, Huntington, Longmeadow, Millers Falls, Monson, Montague, Northampton, Northfield, Palmer, Pelham, Shelburne, Shelburne Falls, South Deerfield, South Hadley, Southwick, Sunderland, Thorndike, Three Rivers, Turners Falls, Ware, Warren, West Springfield, Westfield, Westhampton & Whately. ICA: MA0005.
TV Market Ranking: 19 (Agawam, Gilbertville, Granville, Holyoke, Huntington, Longmeadow, Southwick, West Springfield); 19,6 (SPRINGFIELD); 6 (Bondsville, Bondsville, Hardwick, Monson, Palmer, Pelham, Thorndike, Three Rivers, Ware, Warren); Below 100 (Amherst, Bernardston, Buckland, Chester, Conway, Deerfield, Erving, Gill, Granby, Greenfield, Millers Falls, Montague, Northampton, Northfield, Shelburne, Shelburne Falls, South Deerfield, South Hadley, Sunderland, Turners Falls, Westhampton, Whately). Franchise award date: September 22, 1981. Franchise expiration date: N.A. Began: January 1, 1981.
Channel capacity: 124 (operating 2-way). Channels available but not in use: N.A.

Basic Service
Subscribers: 132,883.
Programming (received off-air): WBZ-TV (CBS) Boston; WDMR-LP (TMO) Springfield; WEDH (PBS) Hartford; WGBY-TV (PBS) Springfield; WGGB-TV (ABC) Springfield; WSHM-LP (CBS) Springfield; WTNH (ABC) New Haven; WVIT (NBC) New Britain; WWLP (NBC) Springfield.
Programming (via satellite): CW+; WPIX (CW, IND) New York; WSBK-TV (IND) Boston.
Current originations: Religious Access; Government Access; Educational Access; Public Access.
Fee: $45.50 installation; $5.16 monthly.

Expanded Basic Service 1
Subscribers: N.A.
Programming (via satellite): ABC Family Channel; AMC; Animal Planet; Arts & Entertainment; BET Networks; Bravo; Cartoon Network; CNBC; CNN; Comcast Sports Net New England; Comedy Central; Country Music TV; C-SPAN; C-SPAN 2; Discovery Channel; Disney Channel; E! Entertainment Television; ESPN; ESPN 2; ESPN Classic Sports; Eternal Word TV Network; Food Network; Fox News Channel; FX; Great American Country; GSN; Hallmark Channel; Headline News; HGTV; History Channel; Home Shopping Network; INSP; Lifetime; MSNBC; MTV; New England Cable News; New England Sports Network; Nickelodeon; QVC; Spike TV; Syfy; TBS Superstation; The Learning Channel; Travel Channel; truTV; Turner Network TV; TV Guide Network; TV Land; Univision; USA Network; Versus; VH1; WE tv; Weather Channel.
Fee: $47.65 monthly.

Digital Basic Service
Subscribers: N.A.
Programming (via satellite): BBC America; Bio; Black Family Channel; Bloomberg Television; Celtic Vision; Cooking Channel; Discovery Digital Networks; DMX Music; Do-It-Yourself; Encore Action; ESPNews; FitTV; Fox Movie Channel; Fox Sports World; Fuse; G4; GAS; Halogen Network; History Channel International; Independent Film Channel; International Television (ITV); Lifetime Movie Network; Lime; MTV Networks Digital Suite; Music Choice; National Geographic Channel; NBA TV; Nick Jr.; NickToons TV; Outdoor Channel; Oxygen; Speed Channel; Sundance Channel; The Word Network; Toon Disney; Trinity Broadcasting Network; Turner Classic Movies; Weatherscan.
Fee: $13.85 monthly.

Pay Service 1
Pay Units: 48,322.
Programming (via satellite): Cinemax; HBO (multiplexed); Showtime; Starz; The Movie Channel.
Fee: $19.95 installation; $9.95 monthly (each).

Digital Pay Service 1
Pay Units: N.A.
Programming (via satellite): Cinemax (multiplexed); Flix; HBO (multiplexed); Showtime (multiplexed); Starz (multiplexed); The Movie Channel (multiplexed).
Fee: $14.00 monthly (each).

Video-On-Demand: Yes

Pay-Per-View
iN DEMAND (delivered digitally); Barker (delivered digitally); Hot Choice (delivered digitally); Playboy TV (delivered digitally); Fresh (delivered digitally).

Internet Service
Operational: Yes.
Broadband Service: Comcast High Speed Internet.
Fee: $42.95 monthly.

Telephone Service
Digital: Operational
Fee: $44.95 monthly

Miles of Plant: 3,200.0 (coaxial); None (fiber optic). Homes passed: 250,000. Miles of plant (coax) includes miles of plant (fiber)
Regional Vice President: Douglas Guthrie. Vice President & General Manager: Pamela MacKenzie. Technical Operations Director: Jim Jones. Marketing Director: Carolyn Hannan. Marketing Coordinator: Marcia McElroy.
Ownership: Comcast Cable Communications Inc. (MSO).

STERLING—Comcast Cable. Now served by WESTFORD, MA [MA0093]. ICA: MA0053.

STONEHAM—RCN Corp. Formerly served by Boston, MA [MA0105]. This cable system has converted to IPTV, 196 Van Buren St, Herndon, VA 20170. Phone: 703-434-8200. Web Site: http://www.rcn.com. ICA: MA5114.
Channel capacity: N.A. Channels available but not in use: N.A.

Internet Service
Operational: Yes.

Chairman: Steven J. Simmons. Chief Executive Officer: Jim Holanda.
Ownership: RCN Corp.

STOUGHTON—Comcast Cable. Now served by TAUNTON, MA [MA0033]. ICA: MA0025.

TAUNTON—Comcast Cable, 440 Myles Standish Blvd, Taunton, MA 2780. Phone: 413-730-4500. Fax: 313-729-3312. Web Site: http://www.comcast.com. Also serves Abington, Acushnet, Assonet, Attleboro, Avon, Barnstable, Bellingham, Berkley, Blackstone, Bourne, Braintree, Brewster, Bridgewater, Brockton, Canton, Carver, Centerville, Chatham, Chilmark, Cohasset, Cotuit, Dartmouth, Dennis, Dennis Port, Dighton, Duxbury, East Bridgewater, East Dennis, East Falmouth, East Harwich, Eastham, Easton, Edgartown, Fairhaven, Fall River, Falmouth, Foxborough, Franklin, Freetown, Halifax, Hanover, Hanson, Harwich, Harwich Port, Hingham, Holbrook, Hopedale, Hull, Hyannis, Kingston, Lakeville, Mansfield, Marion, Marshfield, Marston Mills, Martha's Vineyard, Mashpee, Mattapoisett, Mendon, Menemsha, Middleborough, Minton, Nantucket, New Bedford, Norfolk, North Attleboro, North Chatham, North Harwich, North Scituate, Norton, Oak Bluffs, Orleans, Osterville, Pembroke, Plainville, Plymouth, Plympton, Provincetown, Quincy, Raynham, Rehoboth, Rochester, Rockland, Rudolph, Sandwich, Scituate, Seekonk, Siasconset, Somerset, South Chatham, South Dennis, South Harwich, South Yarmouth, Stoughton, Swansea, Tisbury, Truro, Vineyard Haven, Walpole, Waquoit, Wareham, Wellfleet, West Barnstable, West Bridgewater, West Chatham, West Dennis, West Harwich, West Tisbury, Weymouth, Whitman, Wrentham, Yarmouth, Yarmouth (port) & Yarmouth (town). ICA: MA0033.

TV Market Ranking: 33 (Acushnet, Assonet, Barnstable, Bourne, Centerville, Chilmark, Cotuit, Dartmouth, Dighton, East Falmouth, Edgartown, Fairhaven, Fall River, Falmouth, Freetown, Hyannis, Marston Mills, Martha's Vineyard, Mashpee, Mattapoisett, Menemsha, New Bedford, Oak Bluffs, Orleans, Osterville, Rehoboth, Rochester, Sandwich, TAUNTON, Tisbury, Vineyard Haven, Waquoit, Wareham, West Barnstable, West Tisbury); 6 (Abington, Avon, Bellingham, Berkley, Blackstone, Braintree, Bridgewater, Brockton, Canton, Carver, Cohasset, Duxbury, East Bridgewater, Easton, Foxborough, Franklin, Halifax, Hanover, Hanson, Hingham, Holbrook, Hopedale, Hull, Kingston, Lakeville, Marion, Marshfield, Mendon, Middleborough, Minton, Norfolk, North Scituate, Pembroke, Plymouth, Plympton, Quincy, Raynham, Rockland, Rudolph, Scituate, Stoughton, Swansea, Walpole, West Bridgewater, Weymouth, Whitman, Wrentham); 6,33 (Attleboro, Mansfield, North Attleboro, Norton, Plainville, Seekonk, Somerset); Below 100 (Brewster, Dennis, Dennis Port, East Dennis, East Harwich, Harwich, Harwich Port, Nantucket, North Harwich, Provincetown, South Chatham, South Dennis, South Harwich, South Yarmouth, West Chatham, West Dennis, West Harwich, Yarmouth, Yarmouth (port), Yarmouth (town)); Outside TV Markets (Chatham, Eastham, North Chatham, Siasconset, Truro, Wellfleet). Franchise award date: July 14, 1981. Franchise expiration date: N.A. Began: December 1, 1981.

Channel capacity: N.A. Channels available but not in use: N.A.

Basic Service

Subscribers: 575,000.

Programming (received off-air): WBZ-TV (CBS) Boston; WCVB-TV (ABC) Boston; WFXT (FOX) Boston; WGBH-TV (PBS) Boston; WGBX-TV (PBS) Boston; WHDH (NBC) Boston; WJAR (NBC) Providence; WLNE-TV (ABC) New Bedford; WLVI-TV (CW) Cambridge; WLWC (CW) New Bedford; WNAC-TV (FOX) Providence; WPRI-TV (CBS) Providence; WPXQ-TV (ION) Block Island; WSBE-TV (PBS) Providence; WSBK-TV (IND) Boston; WUNI (UNV) Worcester; WWDP (IND) Norwell.

Programming (via microwave): Portuguese Channel.

Programming (via satellite): ABC Family Channel; AMC; Animal Planet; Arts & Entertainment; Bravo; Cartoon Network; Catholic Television Network; CNBC; CNN; Comedy Central; C-SPAN; C-SPAN 2; Discovery Channel; Disney Channel; E! Entertainment Television; ESPN; ESPN 2; ESPN Classic Sports; Eternal Word TV Network; Food Network; Fox News Channel; Fox Sports Net; FX; GSN; Hallmark Channel; Headline News; HGTV; History Channel; Home Shopping Network; Lifetime; MSNBC; MTV; New England Cable News; New England Sports Network; Nickelodeon; QVC; Spike TV; Syfy; TBS Superstation; The Comcast Network; The Learning Channel; Travel Channel; truTV; Turner Network TV; TV Land; USA Network; Versus; VH1; WE tv; Weather Channel.

Current originations: Leased Access; Government Access; Educational Access; Public Access.

Fee: $43.95 installation; $13.95 monthly; $1.54 converter; $10.57 additional installation.

Digital Basic Service

Subscribers: N.A.

Programming (via satellite): BBC America; Bio; Black Family Channel; Bloomberg Television; Celtic Vision; Cooking Channel; Discovery Digital Networks; Do-It-Yourself; ESPNews; Eternal Word TV Network; FitTV; Fox Movie Channel; Fox Sports World; Fuse; G4; GAS; Great American Country; Halogen Network; History Channel International; Independent Film Channel; International Television (ITV); Lifetime Movie Network; Lime; MTV Networks Digital Suite; National Geographic Channel; Nick Jr.; NickToons TV; Outdoor Channel; Oxygen; Speed Channel; Style Network; The Word Network; Toon Disney; Trinity Broadcasting Network; Turner Classic Movies; Weatherscan.

Fee: $15.94 monthly.

Digital Pay Service 1

Pay Units: N.A.

Programming (via satellite): Cinemax (multiplexed); Encore; Flix; HBO (multiplexed); Showtime (multiplexed); Sundance Channel; The Movie Channel (multiplexed).

Fee: $15.50 monthly (each).

Video-On-Demand: Yes

Pay-Per-View

Barker (delivered digitally); iN DEMAND (delivered digitally); Hot Choice (delivered digitally); Playboy TV (delivered digitally); Fresh (delivered digitally).

Internet Service

Operational: Yes.

Broadband Service: Comcast High Speed Internet.

Fee: $42.95 monthly; $10.00 modem lease.

Telephone Service

Digital: Operational

Fee: $24.95 monthly

Regional Vice President: Tom Coughlin. Vice President, Technical Operations: Bruce Byorkman. Sales & Marketing Director: Steve Driscoll. Public Relations Director: Jim Hughes.

Franchise fee: $1.30 per subscriber annually.

Ownership: Comcast Cable Communications Inc. (MSO).

UXBRIDGE—Charter Communications, 95 Higgins St, Worcester, MA 1606. Phone: 508-853-1515. Fax: 508-854-5042. Web Site: http://www.charter.com. Also serves Douglas (town), Millville & Sutton. ICA: MA0063.

TV Market Ranking: 6,33 (Douglas (town), Millville, Sutton, UXBRIDGE). Franchise award date: October 7, 1985. Franchise expiration date: N.A. Began: April 1, 1986.

Channel capacity: N.A. Channels available but not in use: N.A.

Basic Service

Subscribers: 8,680.

Programming (received off-air): WBPX-TV (ION) Boston; WBZ-TV (CBS) Boston; WCVB-TV (ABC) Boston; WFXT (FOX) Boston; WGBH-TV (PBS) Boston; WGBX-TV (PBS) Boston; WHDH (NBC) Boston; WJAR (NBC) Providence; WLVI-TV (CW) Cambridge; WMFP (IND) Lawrence; WPRI-TV (CBS) Providence; WSBE-TV (PBS) Providence; WSBK-TV (IND) Boston; WUNI (UNV) Worcester; WUTF-DT (TEL) Marlborough; WYDN (ETV) Worcester; WZMY-TV (MNT) Derry.

Programming (via satellite): C-SPAN; C-SPAN 2; Eternal Word TV Network; Home Shopping Network; INSP; QVC; TV Guide Network.

Current originations: Government Access; Educational Access; Public Access.

Fee: $29.99 installation.

Expanded Basic Service 1

Subscribers: 8,191.

Programming (via satellite): ABC Family Channel; AMC; Animal Planet; Arts & Entertainment; Bravo; Cartoon Network; CNBC; CNN; Comcast Sports Net New England; Comedy Central; Discovery Channel; Disney Channel; E! Entertainment Television; ESPN; ESPN 2; FitTV; Food Network; Fox News Channel; FX; G4; Golf Channel; Hallmark Channel; Headline News; HGTV; History Channel; Lifetime; MSNBC; MTV; National Geographic Channel; New England Cable News; New England Sports Network; Nickelodeon; Oxygen; Speed Channel; Spike TV; Syfy; TBS Superstation; The Learning Channel; Toon Disney; truTV; Turner Classic Movies; Turner Network TV; TV Land; USA Network; Versus; VH1; Weather Channel.

Fee: $55.00 monthly.

Digital Basic Service

Subscribers: N.A.

Programming (via satellite): BBC America; Bio; Bloomberg Television; Discovery Digital Networks; Do-It-Yourself; ESPN Classic Sports; ESPNews; Fox Sports en Espanol; Fox Sports World; FSN Digital Atlantic; FSN Digital Central; FSN Digital Pacific; Fuel TV; Fuse; GAS; Great American Country; History Channel International; Independent Film Channel; International Television (ITV); Lifetime Movie Network; MTV Networks Digital Suite; Music Choice; NFL Network; Nick Jr.; Nick Too; NickToons TV; SoapNet; Sundance Channel; TVG Network; WE tv.

Digital Pay Service 1

Pay Units: 884.

Programming (via satellite): Cinemax (multiplexed).

Fee: $10.95 monthly.

Digital Pay Service 2

Pay Units: 1,002.

Programming (via satellite): Flix.

Fee: $4.95 monthly.

Digital Pay Service 3

Pay Units: 1,474.

Programming (via satellite): HBO (multiplexed).

Fee: $11.95 monthly.

Digital Pay Service 4

Pay Units: 1,139.

Programming (via satellite): Showtime (multiplexed).

Fee: $7.95 monthly.

Digital Pay Service 5

Pay Units: N.A.

Programming (via satellite): Encore (multiplexed); Starz (multiplexed); The Movie Channel (multiplexed).

Video-On-Demand: Yes

Pay-Per-View

iN DEMAND (delivered digitally), Addressable: Yes; Pleasure (delivered digitally); Playboy TV (delivered digitally); ETC (delivered digitally); Fresh (delivered digitally); NHL Center Ice (delivered digitally); MLB Extra Innings (delivered digitally); NASCAR In Car (delivered digitally).

Internet Service

Operational: Yes.

Broadband Service: Charter Pipeline.

Fee: $29.99 monthly.

Telephone Service

Digital: Operational

Fee: $29.99 monthly

Miles of Plant: 255.0 (coaxial); 11.0 (fiber optic).

Vice President & General Manager: Greg Garabedian. Technical Operations Director: George Duffy. Technical Operations Manager: Kevin Mailluox. Marketing Director: Dennis Jerome.

City fee: $1.30 per subscriber annually.

Ownership: Charter Communications Inc. (MSO).

WAKEFIELD—RCN Corp. Formerly served by Boston, MA [MA0105]. This cable system has converted to IPTV, 196 Van Buren St, Herndon, VA 20170. Phone: 703-434-8200. Web Site: http://www.rcn.com. ICA: MA5115.

Channel capacity: N.A. Channels available but not in use: N.A.

Internet Service

Operational: Yes.

Chairman: Steven J. Simmons. Chief Executive Officer: Jim Holanda.

Ownership: RCN Corp.

WALES—Charter Communications, 95 Higgins St, Worcester, MA 1606. Phone: 508-853-1515. Fax: 518-563-2696. Web Site: http://www.charter.com. Also serves Brimfield. ICA: MA0076.

TV Market Ranking: 19 (Brimfield, WALES). Franchise award date: June 26, 1990. Franchise expiration date: N.A. Began: December 1, 1990.

Channel capacity: N.A. Channels available but not in use: N.A.

Basic Service

Subscribers: 1,617.

Programming (received off-air): WCCT-TV (CW) Waterbury; WCTX (MNT) New Haven; WCVB-TV (ABC) Boston; WDMR-LP (TMO) Springfield; WEDH (PBS) Hartford; WGBH-TV (PBS) Boston; WGBY-TV (PBS) Springfield; WGGB-TV (ABC) Springfield; WHDH (NBC) Boston; WSBK-TV (IND) Boston; WSHM-LP (CBS) Springfield; WTIC-TV (FOX) Hartford; WVIT (NBC) New Britain; WWLP (NBC) Springfield.

Programming (via satellite): C-SPAN; INSP; QVC; TV Guide Network.

Current originations: Public Access; Educational Access.

Expanded Basic Service 1

Subscribers: 1,507.

Programming (via satellite): ABC Family Channel; AMC; Animal Planet; Arts & Entertainment; Bravo; Cartoon Network; CNBC; CNN; Comcast Sports Net New England; Comedy Central; Country Music TV; C-SPAN 2; Discovery Channel; Disney Channel; E! Entertainment Television; ESPN; ESPN 2; Eternal Word TV Network; FitTV; Food Network; Fox News Channel; FX; G4; Golf Channel; Hallmark Channel; Headline News; HGTV; History

Channel; Home Shopping Network; Lifetime; MSNBC; MTV; National Geographic Channel; New England Cable News; New England Sports Network; Nickelodeon; Oxygen; Speed Channel; Spike TV; Syfy; TBS Superstation; The Learning Channel; Toon Disney; truTV; Turner Classic Movies; Turner Network TV; TV Land; Univision; USA Network; Versus; VH1; Weather Channel.
Fee: $55.00 monthly.

Digital Basic Service
Subscribers: N.A.
Programming (via satellite): BBC America; Bio; Bloomberg Television; Discovery Digital Networks; Do-It-Yourself; ESPN Classic Sports; ESPNews; Fox Sports en Espanol; Fox Sports World; FSN Digital Atlantic; FSN Digital Central; FSN Digital Pacific; Fuel TV; Fuse; GAS; Great American Country; History Channel International; Independent Film Channel; International Television (ITV); Lifetime Movie Network; MTV Networks Digital Suite; Music Choice; NFL Network; Nick Jr.; Nick Too; SoapNet; Sundance Channel; TVG Network; WE tv.

Digital Pay Service 1
Pay Units: 140.
Programming (via satellite): Cinemax (multiplexed).
Fee: $10.95 monthly.

Digital Pay Service 2
Pay Units: 260.
Programming (via satellite): Flix.
Fee: $4.95 monthly.

Digital Pay Service 3
Pay Units: 172.
Programming (via satellite): HBO (multiplexed).
Fee: $11.95 monthly.

Digital Pay Service 4
Pay Units: 220.
Programming (via satellite): Showtime (multiplexed).
Fee: $7.95 monthly.

Digital Pay Service 5
Pay Units: N.A.
Programming (via satellite): Encore (multiplexed); Starz (multiplexed); The Movie Channel (multiplexed).

Video-On-Demand: Yes

Pay-Per-View
iN DEMAND (delivered digitally), Addressable: Yes; Pleasure (delivered digitally); Playboy TV (delivered digitally); ETC (delivered digitally); Fresh (delivered digitally); NHL Center Ice (delivered digitally); MLB Extra Innings (delivered digitally); NASCAR In Car (delivered digitally).

Internet Service
Operational: Yes.
Broadband Service: Charter Pipeline.
Fee: $29.99 monthly.

Telephone Service
Digital: Operational
Fee: $29.99 monthly

Miles of Plant: 104.0 (coaxial); None (fiber optic). Homes passed: 1,980.
Vice President & General Manager: Greg Garabedian. Technical Operations Director: George Duffy. Technical Operations Manager: Beatrice Welch. Marketing Director: Dennis Jerome. Marketing Manager: Paula Cecchetelli.
Ownership: Charter Communications Inc. (MSO).

WALTHAM—Comcast Cable. Now served by BOSTON, MA [MA0001]. ICA: MA0029.

WALTHAM—RCN Corp. Formerly served by Boston, MA [MA0105]. This cable system has converted to IPTV, 196 Van Buren St, Herndon, VA 20170. Phone: 703-434-8200. Web Site: http://www.rcn.com. ICA: MA5116.
Channel capacity: N.A. Channels available but not in use: N.A.

Internet Service
Operational: Yes.

Chairman: Steven J. Simmons. Chief Executive Officer: Jim Holanda.
Ownership: RCN Corp.

WATERTOWN—Comcast Cable. Now served by BOSTON, MA [MA0001]. ICA: MA0047.

WATERTOWN—RCN Corp. Formerly served by Boston, MA [MA0105]. This cable system has converted to IPTV, 196 Van Buren St, Herndon, VA 20170. Phone: 703-434-8200. Web Site: http://www.rcn.com. ICA: MA5117.
Channel capacity: N.A. Channels available but not in use: N.A.

Internet Service
Operational: Yes.

Chairman: Steven J. Simmons. Chief Executive Officer: Jim Holanda.
Ownership: RCN Corp.

WEST ROXBURY—RCN Corp. Formerly served by Boston, MA [MA0105]. This cable system has converted to IPTV, 196 Van Buren St, Herndon, VA 20170. Phone: 703-434-8200. Web Site: http://www.rcn.com. ICA: MA5118.
Channel capacity: N.A. Channels available but not in use: N.A.

Internet Service
Operational: Yes.

Chairman: Steven J. Simmons. Chief Executive Officer: Jim Holanda.
Ownership: RCN Corp.

WEST STOCKBRIDGE—Charter Communications, 95 Higgins St, Worcester, MA 1606. Phone: 508-853-1515. Fax: 508-854-5042. Web Site: http://www.charter.com. ICA: MA0078.
TV Market Ranking: 34 (WEST STOCKBRIDGE). Franchise award date: April 1, 1989. Franchise expiration date: N.A. Began: May 1, 1989.
Channel capacity: N.A. Channels available but not in use: N.A.

Basic Service
Subscribers: 413.
Programming (received off-air): WMHT (PBS) Schenectady; WNYA (MNT) Pittsfield; WNYT (NBC) Albany; WRGB (CBS) Schenectady; WSBK-TV (IND) Boston; WTEN (ABC) Albany; WWLP (NBC) Springfield; WXXA-TV (FOX) Albany; WYPX-TV (ION) Amsterdam.
Programming (via satellite): C-SPAN; Home Shopping Network; QVC; TV Guide Network; WPIX (CW, IND) New York.
Current originations: Government Access; Public Access.
Fee: $2.50 converter.

Expanded Basic Service 1
Subscribers: N.A.
Programming (via satellite): ABC Family Channel; AMC; Animal Planet; Arts & Entertainment; Bravo; Cartoon Network; CNBC; CNN; Comcast Sports Net New England; Comedy Central; Country Music TV; C-SPAN 2; Discovery Channel; Disney Channel; E! Entertainment Television; ESPN; ESPN 2; ESPN Classic Sports; Food Network; Fox News Channel; FX; Headline News; HGTV; History Channel; INSP; Lifetime; MSNBC; MTV; New England Sports Network; Nickelodeon; Speed Channel; Spike TV; Syfy; TBS Superstation; The Learning Channel; Toon Disney; Travel Channel; Turner Network TV; TV Land; USA Network; Versus; VH1; Weather Channel.
Fee: $55.00 monthly.

Digital Basic Service
Subscribers: N.A.
Programming (via satellite): BBC America; Bio; Discovery Health Channel; Discovery Kids Channel; DMX Music; ESPNews; Fox Soccer; Fuse; GAS; Golf Channel; History Channel International; Independent Film Channel; Lifetime Movie Network; MTV2; Nick Jr.; Science Television; Turner Classic Movies; WE tv.

Pay Service 1
Pay Units: N.A.
Programming (via satellite): Encore (multiplexed); Flix; Showtime (multiplexed); The Movie Channel (multiplexed).

Digital Pay Service 1
Pay Units: 16.
Programming (via satellite): Cinemax (multiplexed); HBO (multiplexed); Starz (multiplexed).
Fee: $10.45 monthly.

Video-On-Demand: No

Pay-Per-View
Addressable homes: 129.
iN DEMAND (delivered digitally), Fee: $24.95-$39.95, Addressable: Yes; Playboy TV (delivered digitally).

Internet Service
Operational: No.

Telephone Service
None

Miles of Plant: 30.0 (coaxial); None (fiber optic). Homes passed: 620.
Vice President & General Manager: Greg Garabedian. Technical Operations Director: George Duffy. Technical Operations Manager: Beatrice Welch. Marketing Director: Dennis Jerome.
Ownership: Charter Communications Inc. (MSO).

WESTFIELD—Comcast Cable. Now served by SPRINGFIELD, MA [MA0005]. ICA: MA0006.

WESTFORD—Comcast Cable, 4 Liberty Way, Westford, MA 1886. Phone: 978-692-1906. Fax: 978-692-9772. Web Site: http://www.comcast.com. Also serves Acton, Andover, Ashburnham, Ashby (town), Ayer, Baldwinville, Bedford, Billerica, Bolton, Boxborough, Boxford, Carlisle (town), Chelmsford, Clinton, Concord, Dracut, East Templeton, Fitchburg, Gardner, Georgetown, Groveland, Haverhill, Hudson, Lancaster, Lawrence, Leominster, Lincoln (town), Littleton (town), Lowell, Lunenburg, Marlborough, Maynard, Merrimac, Methuen, Middleton, North Andover, Otter River, Phillipston, Salisbury, Shirley (town), Sterling, Sudbury, Templeton, Tewksbury, Topsfield, Townsend (town), Tyngsborough, Westminster & Winchendon, MA; South Hampton (town), NH. ICA: MA0093.
TV Market Ranking: 6 (Acton, Andover, Ashburnham, Ashby (town), Ayer, Baldwinville, Bedford, Billerica, Bolton, Boxborough, Boxford, Carlisle (town), Chelmsford, Clinton, Concord, Dracut, East Templeton, Fitchburg, Gardner, Georgetown, Groveland, Haverhill, Hudson, Lancaster, Lawrence, Leominster, Lincoln (town), Littleton (town), Lowell, Lunenburg, Marlborough, Maynard, Merrimac, Methuen, Middleton, North Andover, Otter River, Phillipston, Salisbury, Shirley (town), South Hampton (town), Sterling, Sudbury, Templeton, Tewksbury, Topsfield, Townsend (town), Tyngsborough, WESTFORD, Westminster, Winchendon). Franchise award date: N.A. Franchise expiration date: N.A. Began: December 1, 1983.
Channel capacity: N.A. Channels available but not in use: N.A.

Basic Service
Subscribers: N.A. Included in Manchester, NH
Programming (received off-air): WBPX-TV (ION) Boston; WBZ-TV (CBS) Boston; WCVB-TV (ABC) Boston; WENH-TV (PBS) Durham; WFXT (FOX) Boston; WGBH-TV (PBS) Boston; WGBX-TV (PBS) Boston; WHDH (NBC) Boston; WLVI-TV (CW) Cambridge; WMFP (IND) Lawrence; WNEU (TMO) Merrimack; WSBK-TV (IND) Boston; WUNI (UNV) Worcester; WUTF-DT (TEL) Marlborough; WYDN (ETV) Worcester; WZMY-TV (MNT) Derry.
Programming (via microwave): New England Cable News.
Programming (via satellite): Home Shopping Network; QVC; ShopNBC; The Comcast Network; TV Guide Network.
Current originations: Leased Access; Religious Access; Government Access; Educational Access; Public Access.
Fee: $28.50 installation; $12.12 monthly.

Expanded Basic Service 1
Subscribers: N.A.
Programming (via satellite): ABC Family Channel; AMC; Animal Planet; Arts & Entertainment; BET Networks; Bravo; Cartoon Network; CatholicTV; CNBC; CNN; Comcast Sports Net New England; Comedy Central; Country Music TV; C-SPAN; C-SPAN 2; Discovery Channel; Disney Channel; E! Entertainment Television; ESPN; ESPN 2; ESPN Classic Sports; Eternal Word TV Network; Food Network; Fox News Channel; FX; Golf Channel; GSN; Headline News; HGTV; History Channel; INSP; Lifetime; MSNBC; MTV; National Jewish TV (NJT); New England Sports Network; Nickelodeon; Spike TV; Syfy; TBS Superstation; The Learning Channel; Travel Channel; truTV; Turner Network TV; TV Land; USA Network; Versus; VH1; Weather Channel.
Fee: $39.70 monthly.

Digital Basic Service
Subscribers: N.A.
Programming (received off-air): WBZ-TV (CBS) Boston; WCVB-TV (ABC) Boston; WFXT (FOX) Boston; WGBX-TV (PBS) Boston; WHDH (NBC) Boston; WLVI-TV (CW) Cambridge; WSBK-TV (IND) Boston.
Programming (via satellite): BBC America; Bio; Black Family Channel; Bloomberg Television; CBS College Sports Network; Celtic Vision; Cooking Channel; Country Music TV; Discovery Digital Networks; Discovery HD Theater; Do-It-Yourself; Encore (multiplexed); ESPN HD; ESPNews; Eternal Word TV Network; Flix; Fox College Sports Atlantic; Fox College Sports Central; Fox College Sports Pacific; Fox Movie Channel; Fox Soccer; Fuse; G4; GAS; Great American Country; Halogen Network; History Channel International; Independent Film Channel; INHD (multiplexed); Jewelry Television; Lifetime Movie Network; LOGO; MoviePlex; MTV Networks Digital Suite; Music Choice; National Geographic Channel; NBA TV; NFL Network; Nick Jr.; Nick Too; NickToons TV; Outdoor Channel; Oxygen; PBS Kids Sprout; Speed Channel; Style Network; Sundance Channel; Tennis Channel; The Word Network; Toon Disney; Trinity Broadcasting Network; Turner

Classic Movies; Turner Network TV HD; TV One; TVG Network; WE tv; Weatherscan.
Fee: $11.95 monthly.
Digital Pay Service 1
Pay Units: N.A.
Programming (via satellite): Canales N; Cinemax (multiplexed); Cinemax HD; Encore; Flix; Global Village Network; HBO (multiplexed); HBO HD; RAI International; Russian Television Network; Showtime (multiplexed); Showtime HD; Society of Portuguese Television; Starz (multiplexed); Starz HDTV; The Movie Channel (multiplexed); TV5, La Television International; Zee TV USA; Zhong Tian Channel.
Fee: $9.95 monthly (each foreign language channel).
Video-On-Demand: Yes
Pay-Per-View
Pleasure (delivered digitally); Playboy TV (delivered digitally); Fresh (delivered digitally).
Internet Service
Operational: Yes.
Broadband Service: Comcast High Speed Internet.
Fee: $42.95 monthly.
Telephone Service
Digital: Operational
Fee: $44.95 monthly
Regional Vice President: Steve Hackley. Sales & Marketing Director: Mark Adamy. Public Relations Manager: Marc Goodman.
City fee: $0.50 per subscriber annually.
Ownership: Comcast Cable Communications Inc. (MSO).

WESTPORT—Charter Communications, 95 Higgins St, Worcester, MA 1606. Phone: 508-853-1515. Fax: 508-854-5086. Web Site: http://www.charter.com. ICA: MA0070.
TV Market Ranking: 33 (WESTPORT). Franchise award date: January 14, 1986. Franchise expiration date: N.A. Began: September 1, 1986.
Channel capacity: N.A. Channels available but not in use: N.A.
Basic Service
Subscribers: 4,634.
Programming (received off-air): WBPX-TV (ION) Boston; WBZ-TV (CBS) Boston; WCVB-TV (ABC) Boston; WFXT (FOX) Boston; WGBH-TV (PBS) Boston; WGBX-TV (PBS) Boston; WHDH (NBC) Boston; WJAR (NBC) Providence; WLNE-TV (ABC) New Bedford; WLVI-TV (CW) Cambridge; WNAC-TV (FOX) Providence; WPRI-TV (CBS) Providence; WPXQ-TV (ION) Block Island; WSBE-TV (PBS) Providence; WSBK-TV (IND) Boston; WWDP (IND) Norwell.
Programming (via satellite): C-SPAN; Home Shopping Network; Portuguese Channel; QVC; TV Guide Network; Univision.
Current originations: Government Access; Educational Access; Public Access.
Expanded Basic Service 1
Subscribers: 4,243.
Programming (via satellite): ABC Family Channel; AMC; Animal Planet; Arts & Entertainment; Bravo; CNBC; CNN; Comcast Sports Net New England; Comedy Central; Discovery Channel; Disney Channel; E! Entertainment Television; ESPN; ESPN 2; Food Network; G4; Headline News; HGTV; History Channel; Lifetime; MTV; New England Sports Network; Nickelodeon; Spike TV; Syfy; TBS Superstation; The Learning Channel; Travel Channel; Turner Classic Movies; Turner Network TV; USA Network; VH1; Weather Channel.
Fee: $53.00 monthly.
Digital Basic Service
Subscribers: N.A.
Programming (via satellite): BBC America; Bio; Bloomberg Television; Discovery Digital Networks; Do-It-Yourself; ESPN Classic Sports; ESPNews; Fuse; GAS; GSN; History Channel International; Independent Film Channel; Lifetime Movie Network; MTV Networks Digital Suite; Nick Jr.; Nick Too; NickToons TV; SoapNet; Sundance Channel; Toon Disney; TV Guide Interactive Inc.; WE tv.
Digital Pay Service 1
Pay Units: 409.
Programming (via satellite): Cinemax (multiplexed).
Fee: $10.95 monthly.
Digital Pay Service 2
Pay Units: 457.
Programming (via satellite): Flix.
Fee: $4.95 monthly.
Digital Pay Service 3
Pay Units: 752.
Programming (via satellite): HBO (multiplexed).
Fee: $11.95 monthly.
Digital Pay Service 4
Pay Units: 537.
Programming (via satellite): Showtime (multiplexed).
Fee: $10.95 monthly.
Digital Pay Service 5
Pay Units: N.A.
Programming (via satellite): Encore (multiplexed); Starz (multiplexed); The Movie Channel (multiplexed).
Video-On-Demand: Yes
Pay-Per-View
iN DEMAND (delivered digitally), Addressable: Yes; Playboy TV (delivered digitally); Fresh (delivered digitally); Shorteez (delivered digitally).
Internet Service
Operational: Yes.
Broadband Service: Charter Pipeline.
Fee: $29.99 monthly.
Telephone Service
Digital: Operational
Miles of Plant: 131.0 (coaxial); None (fiber optic). Homes passed: 5,511. Total homes in franchised area: 6,000.
Vice President & General Manager: Greg Garabedian. Technical Manager: Kevin Mailloux. Marketing Director: Dennis Jerome.
City fee: $1.30 per subscriber annually.
Ownership: Charter Communications Inc. (MSO).

WEYMOUTH—Comcast Cable. Now served by TAUNTON, MA [MA0033]. ICA: MA0024.

WINCHENDON—Comcast Cable. Now served by WESTFORD, MA [MA0093]. ICA: MA0075.

WOBURN—Comcast Cable. Now served by BOSTON, MA [MA0001]. ICA: MA0007.

WOBURN—RCN Corp. Formerly served by Boston, MA [MA0105]. This cable system has converted to IPTV, 196 Van Buren St, Herndon, VA 20170. Phone: 703-434-8200. Web Site: http://www.rcn.com. ICA: MA5119.
Channel capacity: N.A. Channels available but not in use: N.A.
Internet Service
Operational: Yes.
Chairman: Steven J. Simmons.
Ownership: RCN Corp.

WORCESTER—Charter Communications, 95 Higgins St, Worcester, MA 1606. Phone: 508-853-1515. Fax: 508-854-5042. Web Site: http://www.charter.com. Also serves Auburn, Boylston, Dudley, Grafton, Holden, Leicester, Millbury, Northborough, Northbridge, Oxford, Paxton, Southborough, Southbridge, Spencer, Sturbridge, Upton, Webster, West Boylston, West Brookfield & Westborough. ICA: MA0002.
TV Market Ranking: 6 (Boylston, Dudley, Holden, Leicester, Northborough, Paxton, Southbridge, Spencer, Sturbridge, West Boylston, West Brookfield); 6,33 (Auburn, Grafton, Millbury, Northbridge, Oxford, Southborough, Upton, Webster, Westborough, WORCESTER TWP.). Franchise award date: January 1, 1972. Franchise expiration date: N.A. Began: May 1, 1969.
Channel capacity: N.A. Channels available but not in use: N.A.
Basic Service
Subscribers: 130,889.
Programming (received off-air): WBPX-TV (ION) Boston; WBZ-TV (CBS) Boston; WCVB-TV (ABC) Boston; WFXT (FOX) Boston; WGBH-TV (PBS) Boston; WGBX-TV (PBS) Boston; WHDH (NBC) Boston; WJAR (NBC) Providence; WLVI-TV (CW) Cambridge; WMFP (IND) Lawrence; WSBK-TV (IND) Boston; WUNI (UNV) Worcester; WUTF-DT (TEL) Marlborough; WYDN (ETV) Worcester; WZMY-TV (MNT) Derry.
Programming (via satellite): C-SPAN; C-SPAN 2; Eternal Word TV Network; Home Shopping Network; INSP; QVC; RAI USA; TV Guide Network.
Current originations: Government Access; Educational Access; Public Access.
Fee: $29.99 installation.
Expanded Basic Service 1
Subscribers: 108,922.
Programming (via microwave): New England Cable News.
Programming (via satellite): ABC Family Channel; AMC; Animal Planet; Arts & Entertainment; BET Networks; Bravo; Cartoon Network; CNBC; CNN; Comcast Sports Net New England; Comedy Central; Discovery Channel; Disney Channel; E! Entertainment Television; ESPN; ESPN 2; FitTV; Food Network; Fox News Channel; FX; G4; Golf Channel; Hallmark Channel; Headline News; HGTV; History Channel; Lifetime; MSNBC; MTV; National Geographic Channel; New England Sports Network; Nickelodeon; Oxygen; Speed Channel; Spike TV; Style Network; Syfy; TBS Superstation; The Learning Channel; Toon Disney; Travel Channel; truTV; Turner Classic Movies; Turner Network TV; TV Land; USA Network; Versus; VH1; Weather Channel.
Fee: $55.00 monthly.
Digital Basic Service
Subscribers: N.A.
Programming (via satellite): BBC America; Bio; Bloomberg Television; Discovery Digital Networks; Do-It-Yourself; ESPN Classic Sports; ESPNews; Fox Sports en Espanol; Fox Sports World; FSN Digital Atlantic; FSN Digital Central; FSN Digital Pacific; Fuel TV; GAS; Great American Country; History Channel International; Independent Film Channel; International Television (ITV); Lifetime Movie Network; MTV Networks Digital Suite; MuchMusic Network; Music Choice; NFL Network; Nick Jr.; Nick Too; NickToons TV; SoapNet; Sundance Channel; TVG Network; WE tv.
Digital Pay Service 1
Pay Units: 14,890.
Programming (via satellite): Cinemax (multiplexed); Encore (multiplexed); Flix; HBO (multiplexed); Showtime (multiplexed); Starz (multiplexed); The Movie Channel (multiplexed).
Video-On-Demand: Yes
Pay-Per-View
Addressable homes: 86,315.
ETC (delivered digitally), Addressable: Yes; iN DEMAND (delivered digitally); Playboy TV (delivered digitally); Pleasure (delivered digitally); Fresh (delivered digitally); NASCAR In Car (delivered digitally); NHL Center Ice (delivered digitally); MLB Extra Innings (delivered digitally).
Internet Service
Operational: Yes.
Broadband Service: Charter Pipeline.
Fee: $29.95 monthly; $10.00 modem lease; $195.00 modem purchase.
Telephone Service
Digital: Operational
Miles of Plant: 1,705.0 (coaxial); 257.0 (fiber optic). Homes passed: 157,098.
Vice President & General Manager: Greg Garabedian. Vice President, Technical Operations: Gregg Wood. Technical Operations Manager: Kevin Mailloux. Marketing Director: Dennis Jerome.
City fee: $0.25 per subscriber annually.
Ownership: Charter Communications Inc. (MSO).

MICHIGAN

Total Systems: 224
Total Communities Served: 1,552
Franchises Not Yet Operating: 0
Applications Pending: 0
Communities with Applications: 0
Number of Basic Subscribers: 2,313,502
Number of Expanded Basic Subscribers: 620,737
Number of Pay Units: 157,622

Top 100 Markets Represented: Kalamazoo-Grand Rapids-Battle Creek (37); Toledo (52); Detroit (5); Flint-Bay City-Saginaw (61); South Bend-Elkhart, IN (80); Lansing-Onondaga (92).

**For a list of cable communities in this section, see the Cable Community Index located in the back of Cable Volume 2.
For explanation of terms used in cable system listings, see p. D-11.**

ADDISON—Comcast Cable, 3500 Patterson Ave SE, Grand Rapids, MI 49512. Phone: 616-977-2200. Fax: 616-977-2224. Web Site: http://www.comcast.com. Also serves Britton, Dover, Dover Twp., Fairfield, Hudson, Madison Twp., Manitou Beach, Palmyra Twp., Raisin Twp., Ridgeway Twp., Rollin, Tecumseh & Woodstock Twp. ICA: MI0124.

TV Market Ranking: 52 (ADDISON, Britton, Dover, Dover Twp., Fairfield, Hudson, Madison Twp., Manitou Beach, Palmyra Twp., Raisin Twp., Ridgeway Twp., Tecumseh, Woodstock Twp.); Below 100 (Rollin). Franchise award date: N.A. Franchise expiration date: N.A. Began: September 1, 1983.

Channel capacity: N.A. Channels available but not in use: N.A.

Basic Service

Subscribers: 1,281.

Programming (received off-air): WHTV (MNT) Jackson; WILX-TV (NBC) Onondaga; WKAR-TV (PBS) East Lansing; WLAJ (ABC, CW) Lansing; WLNS-TV (CBS) Lansing; WSYM-TV (FOX) Lansing; WZPX-TV (ION) Battle Creek.

Programming (via satellite): Comcast Local Detroit; C-SPAN; Home Shopping Network; QVC; TBS Superstation; truTV; various Canadian stations; WGN America.

Current originations: Public Access; Educational Access.

Expanded Basic Service 1

Subscribers: 1,050.

Programming (via satellite): ABC Family Channel; AMC; Animal Planet; Arts & Entertainment; BET Networks; Cartoon Network; CNBC; CNN; Comedy Central; C-SPAN 2; Discovery Channel; Disney Channel; E! Entertainment Television; ESPN; ESPN 2; Food Network; Fox News Channel; Fox Sports Net Detroit; FX; Golf Channel; Headline News; HGTV; History Channel; Lifetime; Michigan Government Television; MSNBC; MTV; Nickelodeon; Spike TV; The Learning Channel; Turner Network TV; TV Guide Network; TV Land; Univision; USA Network; Versus; VH1; Weather Channel.

Fee: $48.99 monthly.

Digital Basic Service

Subscribers: N.A.

Programming (via satellite): BBC America; Bio; Black Family Channel; Bravo; Canales N; Country Music TV; Current; Discovery Digital Networks; Discovery HD Theater; Do-It-Yourself; Encore (multiplexed); ESPN 2 HD; ESPN Classic Sports; ESPN HD; ESPNews; Flix; Fox Reality Channel; Fuse; G4; GAS; Great American Country; GSN; Halogen Network; History Channel; History Channel International; Independent Film Channel; INHD; Lifetime Movie Network; MoviePlex; MTV Networks Digital Suite; Music Choice; National Geographic Channel; NFL Network; Nick Jr.; Nick Too; NickToons TV; Outdoor Channel; Palladia; PBS Kids Sprout; ShopNBC; SoapNet; Style Network; Sundance Channel; Syfy; The Word Network; Toon Disney; Trinity Broadcasting Network; Turner Classic Movies; Versus; WE tv.

Fee: $9.95 monthly.

Digital Pay Service 1

Pay Units: N.A.

Programming (via satellite): Cinemax HD; HBO (multiplexed); HBO HD; Showtime (multiplexed); Showtime HD; Starz (multiplexed); Starz HDTV; The Movie Channel (multiplexed).

Fee: $18.05 monthly (each).

Video-On-Demand: No

Pay-Per-View

iN DEMAND (delivered digitally); Playboy TV (delivered digitally); Fresh (delivered digitally).

Internet Service

Operational: Yes.

Broadband Service: Comcast High Speed Internet.

Fee: $42.95 monthly.

Telephone Service

Digital: Operational

Miles of Plant: 53.0 (coaxial); None (fiber optic). Homes passed: 2,621. Total homes in franchised area: 3,793.

Area Vice President: Larry Williamson. Business Operations Director: Amy Carey. Technical Operations Director: Tom Rice. Sales & Marketing Manager: Rick Finch.

Ownership: Comcast Cable Communications Inc. (MSO).

ADRIAN—Formerly served by Comcast Cable. No longer in operation. ICA: MI0044.

AKRON/FAIRGROVE—Pine River Cable, PO Box 96, McBain, MI 49657. Phone: 888-244-2288. Fax: 231-825-0191. E-mail: info@pinerivercable.com. Web Site: http://www.pinerivercable.com. Also serves Akron (village), Akron Twp., Fairgrove (village) & Fairgrove Twp. ICA: MI0212.

TV Market Ranking: 61 (AKRON, Akron (village), Akron Twp., FAIRGROVE, Fairgrove (village), Fairgrove Twp.). Franchise award date: July 14, 1986. Franchise expiration date: N.A. Began: January 1, 1987.

Channel capacity: 35 (operating 2-way). Channels available but not in use: 6.

Basic Service

Subscribers: 209.

Programming (received off-air): WAQP (IND) Saginaw; WEYI-TV (CW, NBC) Saginaw; WJRT-TV (ABC) Flint; WNEM-TV (CBS, MNT) Bay City; WSMH (FOX) Flint.

Programming (via satellite): ABC Family Channel; CNN; Headline News; Lifetime; MTV; Nickelodeon; QVC; Syfy; Travel Channel; Turner Network TV; VH1; WGN America.

Fee: $50.00 installation; $20.81 monthly.

Expanded Basic Service 1

Subscribers: 204.

Programming (via satellite): Discovery Channel; ESPN; USA Network.

Fee: $4.31 monthly.

Expanded Basic Service 2

Subscribers: 150.

Programming (via satellite): Arts & Entertainment; Disney Channel; Spike TV; TBS Superstation.

Fee: $7.26 monthly.

Pay Service 1

Pay Units: 32.

Programming (via satellite): HBO.

Fee: $11.95 monthly.

Pay Service 2

Pay Units: 40.

Programming (via satellite): Showtime.

Fee: $10.95 monthly.

Internet Service

Operational: No.

Telephone Service

None

Miles of Plant: 14.0 (coaxial); None (fiber optic). Homes passed: 498.

Manager: John Metzler.

Ownership: Pine River Cable (MSO).

ALBA—Charter Communications. Now served by TRAVERSE CITY, MI [MI0026]. ICA: MI0241.

ALLEGAN—Charter Communications, 315 Davis St, Grand Haven, MI 49417-1830. Phone: 231-947-5221. E-mail: dspoelman@chartercom.com. Web Site: http://www.charter.com. Also serves Alamo Twp., Allegan Twp., Cooper Twp., Gobles City, Gunplain Twp., Heath Twp., Hopkins, Manlius Twp., Martin (village), Martin Twp., Otsego City, Overisel Twp., Pine Grove Twp., Plainwell City, Trowbridge Twp., Valley Twp. & Watson Twp. ICA: MI0055.

TV Market Ranking: 37 (Alamo Twp., ALLEGAN, Allegan Twp., Cooper Twp., Gobles City, Gunplain Twp., Heath Twp., Hopkins, Manlius Twp., Martin (village), Martin Twp., Otsego City, Overisel Twp., Pine Grove Twp., Plainwell City, Trowbridge Twp., Valley Twp., Watson Twp.). Franchise award date: January 1, 1968. Franchise expiration date: N.A. Began: April 26, 1968.

Channel capacity: N.A. Channels available but not in use: N.A.

Basic Service

Subscribers: 10,000.

Programming (received off-air): WGVU-TV (PBS) Grand Rapids; WLLA (IND) Kalamazoo; WOOD-TV (NBC) Grand Rapids; WOTV (ABC) Battle Creek; WTLJ (IND) Muskegon; WWMT (CBS, CW) Kalamazoo; WXMI (FOX) Grand Rapids; WXSP-CA (MNT) Grand Rapids; WZPX-TV (ION) Battle Creek; WZZM (ABC) Grand Rapids; allband FM.

Programming (via satellite): C-SPAN; C-SPAN 2; Home Shopping Network; QVC; TBS Superstation; TV Guide Network; WGN America.

Current originations: Leased Access; Public Access; Government Access; Educational Access.

Fee: $29.99 installation; $2.00 converter.

Expanded Basic Service 1

Subscribers: N.A.

Programming (via satellite): ABC Family Channel; AMC; Animal Planet; Arts & Entertainment; Bravo; Cartoon Network; CNBC; CNN; Comedy Central; Country Music TV; Discovery Channel; Disney Channel; E! Entertainment Television; ESPN; ESPN 2; ESPN Classic Sports; ESPNews; Eternal Word TV Network; Food Network; Fox News Channel; Fox Sports Net Detroit; FX; G4; Golf Channel; GSN; Hallmark Channel; Headline News; HGTV; History Channel; INSP; Lifetime; MSNBC; MTV; MTV2; National Geographic Channel; Nickelodeon; Oxygen; SoapNet; Speed Channel; Spike TV; Style Network; Syfy; The Learning Channel; Toon Disney; Travel Channel; Trinity Broadcasting Network; truTV; Turner Classic Movies; Turner Network TV; TV Land; Univision; USA Network; Versus; VH1; WE tv; Weather Channel.

Fee: $47.99 monthly.

Digital Basic Service

Subscribers: N.A.

Programming (received off-air): WGVU-TV (PBS) Grand Rapids; WOOD-TV (NBC) Grand Rapids; WWMT (CBS, CW) Kalamazoo; WXMI (FOX) Grand Rapids; WZZM (ABC) Grand Rapids.

Programming (via satellite): BBC America; Bio; Boomerang; Canales N; CMT Pure Country; Discovery Digital Networks; Discovery HD Theater; Do-It-Yourself; ESPN HD; Fox College Sports Atlantic; Fox College Sports Central; Fox College Sports Pacific; Fox Movie Channel; Fox Soccer; Fuel TV; Fuse; GAS; Great American Country; HDNet; HDNet Movies; History Channel International; Independent Film Channel; Lifetime Movie Network; MTV Networks Digital Suite; Music Choice; Nick Jr.; Nick Too; NickToons TV; Outdoor Channel; Sundance Channel; Turner Network TV HD; Universal HD.

Digital Pay Service 1

Pay Units: N.A.

Programming (via satellite): Cinemax (multiplexed); Cinemax HD; Encore (multiplexed); Flix; HBO (multiplexed); HBO HD; LOGO; Showtime (multiplexed); Showtime HD; Starz (multiplexed); The Movie Channel (multiplexed).

Video-On-Demand: Yes

Pay-Per-View
iN DEMAND (delivered digitally); NHL Center Ice (delivered digitally); MLB Extra Innings (delivered digitally); ESPN (delivered digitally); Playboy TV (delivered digitally); Fresh (delivered digitally); Shorteez (delivered digitally).

Internet Service
Operational: Yes. Began: October 1, 2002.
Broadband Service: Charter Pipeline.
Fee: $49.95 installation; $29.99 monthly.

Telephone Service
Digital: Operational
Miles of Plant: 276.0 (coaxial); None (fiber optic). Homes passed: 12,000.
Vice President & General Manager: Dan Spoelman. Technical Operations Manager: Keith Schiervbeek. Marketing Director: Steve Schuh.
City fee: 4% of gross.
Ownership: Charter Communications Inc. (MSO).

ALLEN (village)—Formerly served by CableDirect. No longer in operation. ICA: MI0256.

ALLENDALE—Charter Communications, 315 Davis St, Grand Haven, MI 49417-1830. Phone: 231-947-5221. Web Site: http://www.charter.com. Also serves Allegan County (portions), Blendon Twp., Coopersville, Country Acres Mobile Home Park, Crockery Twp., Fillmore Twp. (northwest portion), Fruitport Charter Twp. (portions), Fruitport Village, Grand Haven, Holland Twp., Hudsonville, Jamestown Twp. (portions), Laketown Twp., Olive Twp. (Ottawa County), Park Twp. (Ottawa County), Polkton Twp., Port Sheldon Twp., Robinson Twp., Spring Lake, Tallmadge Twp., Wright Twp. (portions) & Zeeland Twp. ICA: MI0094.
TV Market Ranking: 37 (Allegan County (portions), ALLENDALE, Coopersville, Country Acres Mobile Home Park, Crockery Twp., Fillmore Twp. (northwest portion), Fruitport Charter Twp. (portions), Fruitport Village, Grand Haven, Holland Twp., Jamestown Twp. (portions), Laketown Twp., Olive Twp. (Ottawa County), Park Twp. (Ottawa County), Polkton Twp., Port Sheldon Twp., Robinson Twp., Spring Lake, Tallmadge Twp., Wright Twp. (portions), Zeeland Twp.); Below 100 (Blendon Twp., Hudsonville). Franchise award date: December 26, 1980. Franchise expiration date: N.A. Began: August 1, 1981.
Channel capacity: N.A. Channels available but not in use: N.A.

Basic Service
Subscribers: 21,686.
Programming (received off-air): WGVU-TV (PBS) Grand Rapids; WOOD-TV (NBC) Grand Rapids; WOTV (ABC) Battle Creek; WTLJ (IND) Muskegon; WWMT (CBS, CW) Kalamazoo; WXMI (FOX) Grand Rapids; WZPX-TV (ION) Battle Creek; WZZM (ABC) Grand Rapids.
Programming (via satellite): C-SPAN; C-SPAN 2; Home Shopping Network; QVC; TBS Superstation; TV Guide Network; WGN America.
Current originations: Leased Access; Government Access; Educational Access; Public Access.
Fee: $29.99 installation; $12.65 additional installation.

Expanded Basic Service 1
Subscribers: N.A.
Programming (via satellite): ABC Family Channel; AMC; Animal Planet; Arts & Entertainment; Bravo; Cartoon Network; CNBC; CNN; Comedy Central; Country Music TV; Discovery Channel; Disney Channel; E! Entertainment Television; ESPN; ESPN 2; ESPN Classic Sports; ESPNews; Eternal Word TV Network; Food Network; Fox News Channel; Fox Sports Net Detroit; FX; G4; Golf Channel; GSN; Hallmark Channel; Headline News; HGTV; History Channel; INSP; Lifetime; MSNBC; MTV; MTV2; National Geographic Channel; Nickelodeon; Oxygen; SoapNet; Speed Channel; Spike TV; Style Network; Syfy; The Learning Channel; Toon Disney; Travel Channel; Trinity Broadcasting Network; truTV; Turner Classic Movies; Turner Network TV; TV Land; Univision; USA Network; Versus; VH1; WE tv; Weather Channel.
Fee: $47.99 monthly.

Digital Basic Service
Subscribers: N.A.
Programming (received off-air): WGVU-TV (PBS) Grand Rapids; WOOD-TV (NBC) Grand Rapids; WWMT (CBS, CW) Kalamazoo; WXMI (FOX) Grand Rapids; WZZM (ABC) Grand Rapids.
Programming (via satellite): BBC America; Bio; Boomerang; CB Television Michoacan; Cine Mexicano; CMT Pure Country; CNN en Espanol; Discovery en Espanol; Discovery HD Theater; Discovery Health Channel; Discovery Home Channel; Discovery Kids Channel; Discovery Kids en Espanol; Discovery Military Channel; Discovery Times Channel; Do-It-Yourself; ESPN Deportes; ESPN HD; FitTV; Fox College Sports Atlantic; Fox College Sports Central; Fox College Sports Pacific; Fox Movie Channel; Fox Soccer; Fox Sports en Espanol; Fuel TV; Fuse; GalaVision; GAS; Gol TV; Great American Country; HDNet; HDNet Movies; History Channel en Espanol; History Channel International; Independent Film Channel; Lifetime Movie Network; MTV Hits; MTV Jams; MTV Tres; Music Choice; Nick Jr.; Nick Too; NickToons TV; Once Mexico; Outdoor Channel; Science Channel; Sundance Channel; Telefutura; Turner Network TV HD; Universal HD; Univision; VH1 Classic; VH1 Soul; VHUNO; Video Rola.

Digital Pay Service 1
Pay Units: N.A.
Programming (via satellite): Cinemax (multiplexed); Cinemax HD; Encore (multiplexed); Flix; HBO (multiplexed); HBO HD; LOGO; Showtime (multiplexed); Showtime HD; Starz (multiplexed); The Movie Channel (multiplexed).

Video-On-Demand: Yes

Pay-Per-View
iN DEMAND (delivered digitally); NHL Center Ice (delivered digitally); MLB Extra Innings (delivered digitally); ESPN (delivered digitally); Playboy TV (delivered digitally); Fresh (delivered digitally); Shorteez (delivered digitally).

Internet Service
Operational: Yes.
Broadband Service: Charter Pipeline.
Fee: $99.95 installation; $29.99 monthly; $3.95 modem lease.

Telephone Service
Digital: Operational
Fee: $29.99 monthly
Miles of Plant: 293.0 (coaxial); None (fiber optic).
Vice President & General Manager: Dan Spoelman. Technical Operations Manager: Keith Schierbeek. Marketing Director: Steve Schuh.
Ownership: Charter Communications Inc. (MSO).

ALMA—Charter Communications, 2304 S Mission, Mount Pleasant, MI 48858. Phone: 989-775-6846. Fax: 989-772-0350. Web Site: http://www.charter.com. Also serves Arcada Twp., Bethany Twp., Breckenridge, Emerson Twp., Ithaca, Newark Twp., North Star Twp., Pine River Twp., St. Louis, Sumner Twp., Wheeler & Wheeler Twp. ICA: MI0085.
TV Market Ranking: 61 (Breckenridge, Ithaca, North Star Twp., St. Louis, Wheeler, Wheeler Twp.); Below 100 (Arcada Twp.); Outside TV Markets (ALMA, Bethany Twp., Emerson Twp., Newark Twp., Pine River Twp., Sumner Twp.). Franchise award date: N.A. Franchise expiration date: N.A. Began: January 1, 1976.
Channel capacity: N.A. Channels available but not in use: N.A.

Basic Service
Subscribers: 5,625.
Programming (received off-air): WAQP (IND) Saginaw; WBSF (CW) Bay City; WCMU-TV (PBS) Mount Pleasant; WDCQ-TV (PBS) Bad Axe; WEYI-TV (CW, NBC) Saginaw; WFQX-TV (FOX) Cadillac; WJRT-TV (ABC) Flint; WNEM-TV (CBS, MNT) Bay City; WSMH (FOX) Flint; WWTV (CBS) Cadillac; WZZM (ABC) Grand Rapids; allband FM.
Programming (via satellite): CB Television Michoacan; C-SPAN; C-SPAN 2; Eternal Word TV Network; Home Shopping Network; INSP; QVC; TBS Superstation; TV Guide Network; Univision; WGN America.
Current originations: Government Access; Educational Access; Public Access.
Fee: $49.99 installation; $29.99 monthly.

Digital Basic Service
Subscribers: N.A.
Programming (received off-air): WEYI-TV (CW, NBC) Saginaw; WJRT-TV (ABC) Flint; WNEM-TV (CBS, MNT) Bay City; WSMH (FOX) Flint.
Programming (via satellite): BBC America; Bio; CMT Pure Country; Discovery Digital Networks; Do-It-Yourself; ESPN 2 HD; ESPN Classic Sports; ESPN HD; ESPN U; ESPNews; FitTV; Fox Business Channel; Fox College Sports Atlantic; Fox College Sports Central; Fox College Sports Pacific; Fox Movie Channel; Fox Soccer; Fox Sports Net Detroit; Fuel TV; Fuse; GAS; Great American Country; HDNet; HDNet Movies; History Channel International; Independent Film Channel; Lifetime Movie Network; Military History Channel; MTV Networks Digital Suite; Music Choice; Nick Jr.; Nick Too; NickToons TV; Outdoor Channel; ReelzChannel; Sundance Channel; The Sportsman Channel; Turner Network TV HD; Universal HD; WE tv.

Digital Pay Service 1
Pay Units: N.A.
Programming (via satellite): Cinemax (multiplexed); Cinemax HD; Encore (multiplexed); Flix; HBO (multiplexed); HBO HD; LOGO; Showtime (multiplexed); Showtime HD; Starz (multiplexed); Starz HDTV; The Movie Channel (multiplexed).

Video-On-Demand: Yes

Pay-Per-View
iN DEMAND (delivered digitally); ESPN (delivered digitally); NHL Center Ice (delivered digitally); MLB Extra Innings (delivered digitally); Playboy TV (delivered digitally); Club Jenna (delivered digitally); Fresh! (delivered digitally); Fresh (delivered digitally); Shorteez (delivered digitally).

Internet Service
Operational: Yes.
Broadband Service: Charter Pipeline.
Fee: $29.99 monthly.

Telephone Service
Digital: Operational
Fee: $29.99 monthly
Miles of Plant: 68.0 (coaxial); None (fiber optic). Homes passed: 6,104.
Vice President & General Manager: Dan Spoelman. Operations Manager: Ed Bucao. Technology Supervisor: Jason Hannah.
City fee: 3% of gross.
Ownership: Charter Communications Inc. (MSO).

ALMONT—Charter Communications, 7372 Davison Rd, Davison, MI 48423. Phone: 810-652-1400. Web Site: http://www.charter.com. Also serves Almont Twp., Dryden, Dryden Twp., Imlay City, Imlay Twp., Kingston (village), Kingston Twp. & North Branch (village). ICA: MI0257.
TV Market Ranking: 61 (ALMONT, Almont Twp., Dryden, Dryden Twp., Imlay City, Imlay Twp., Kingston (village), Kingston Twp., North Branch (village)). Franchise award date: N.A. Franchise expiration date: N.A. Began: December 1, 1985.
Channel capacity: N.A. Channels available but not in use: N.A.

Basic Service
Subscribers: 1,467.
Programming (received off-air): WADL (IND) Mount Clemens; WDIV-TV (NBC) Detroit; WEYI-TV (CW, NBC) Saginaw; WFUM (PBS) Flint; WJBK (FOX) Detroit; WJRT-TV (ABC) Flint; WKBD-TV (CW) Detroit; WMYD (MNT) Detroit; WNEM-TV (CBS, MNT) Bay City; WPXD-TV (ION) Ann Arbor; WSMH (FOX) Flint; WTVS (PBS) Detroit; WWJ-TV (CBS) Detroit; WXYZ-TV (ABC) Detroit.
Programming (via satellite): QVC; WGN America.
Current originations: Government Access; Educational Access; Public Access.
Fee: $29.99 installation; $13.50 monthly.

Expanded Basic Service 1
Subscribers: N.A.
Programming (via satellite): ABC Family Channel; AMC; Animal Planet; Arts & Entertainment; Bravo; Cartoon Network; CNBC; CNN; Comedy Central; Country Music TV; C-SPAN; Discovery Channel; Disney Channel; E! Entertainment Television; ESPN; ESPN 2; Food Network; Fox News Channel; Fox Sports Net Detroit; FX; G4; Golf Channel; GSN; Hallmark Channel; Headline News; HGTV; History Channel; Home Shopping Network; Lifetime Movie Network; MSNBC; MTV; MTV2; National Geographic Channel; Nickelodeon; Oxygen; SoapNet; Speed Channel; Spike TV; Style Network; Syfy; TBS Superstation; The Learning Channel; Toon Disney; Travel Channel; truTV; Turner Network TV; TV Guide Network; TV Land; Univision; USA Network; Versus; VH1; WE tv; Weather Channel.
Fee: $36.49 monthly.

Digital Basic Service
Subscribers: N.A.
Programming (received off-air): WDIV-TV (NBC) Detroit; WJBK (FOX) Detroit; WTVS (PBS) Detroit; WWJ-TV (CBS) Detroit; WXYZ-TV (ABC) Detroit.
Programming (via satellite): BBC America; Bio; CMT Pure Country; Discovery Digital Networks; Discovery HD Theater; Do-It-Yourself; ESPN Classic Sports; ESPN HD; ESPNews; Fox College Sports Atlantic; Fox College Sports Central; Fox College Sports Pacific; Fox Movie Channel; Fox Soccer; Fuel TV; Fuse; GAS; Great American Country; HDNet; HDNet Movies; History Channel International; Independent Film Chan-

nel; Lifetime Movie Network; MTV Networks Digital Suite; Nick Jr.; Nick Too; NickToons TV; Outdoor Channel; Sundance Channel; Turner Network TV HD; Universal HD.

Digital Pay Service 1

Pay Units: N.A.

Programming (via satellite): Cinemax (multiplexed); Cinemax HD; Encore (multiplexed); Flix; HBO (multiplexed); HBO HD; LOGO; Showtime (multiplexed); Showtime HD; Starz (multiplexed); The Movie Channel (multiplexed).

Video-On-Demand: Yes

Pay-Per-View

iN DEMAND (delivered digitally); ESPN (delivered digitally); NHL Center Ice (delivered digitally); MLB Extra Innings (delivered digitally); Playboy TV (delivered digitally); Fresh (delivered digitally); Shorteez (delivered digitally).

Internet Service

Operational: Yes.

Broadband Service: Charter Pipeline.

Fee: $49.00 installation; $29.99 monthly.

Telephone Service

Digital: Operational

Fee: $29.99 monthly

Vice President & General Manager: Dave Slowick. Technical Operations Director: Lloyd Collins. Marketing Director: Lisa Gayari.

Ownership: Charter Communications Inc. (MSO).

ALPENA—Charter Communications, 2074 M 32 W, Alpena, MI 49707. Phones: 989-356-4503; 231-947-5221 (Traverse City office). Fax: 989-356-3761. Web Site: http://www.charter.com. Also serves Green Twp. (Alpena County), Long Rapids Twp., Maple Ridge Twp. (Alpena County), Ossineke Twp. & Sanborn Twp. ICA: MI0061.

TV Market Ranking: Below 100 (ALPENA, Green Twp. (Alpena County), Long Rapids Twp., Maple Ridge Twp. (Alpena County), Ossineke Twp., Sanborn Twp.). Franchise award date: N.A. Franchise expiration date: N.A. Began: August 1, 1958.

Channel capacity: 77 (operating 2-way). Channels available but not in use: None.

Basic Service

Subscribers: 9,600.

Programming (received off-air): WBKB-TV (CBS, FOX) Alpena; WCML (PBS) Alpena; WKBD-TV (CW) Detroit; WPBN-TV (NBC) Traverse City.

Programming (via microwave): WFQX-TV (FOX) Cadillac; WJRT-TV (ABC) Flint; WTOM-TV (NBC) Cheboygan.

Programming (via satellite): C-SPAN; C-SPAN 2; Eternal Word TV Network; Home Shopping Network; INSP; QVC; TBS Superstation; Trinity Broadcasting Network; TV Guide Network; WGN America.

Current originations: Educational Access.

Fee: $29.99 installation; $13.50 monthly.

Expanded Basic Service 1

Subscribers: N.A.

Programming (via satellite): ABC Family Channel; AMC; Animal Planet; Arts & Entertainment; BET Networks; Bravo; Cartoon Network; CNBC; CNN; Comedy Central; Country Music TV; Discovery Channel; Disney Channel; E! Entertainment Television; ESPN; ESPN 2; FitTV; Food Network; Fox News Channel; Fox Sports Net Detroit; FX; G4; Golf Channel; GSN; Hallmark Channel; Headline News; HGTV; History Channel; Lifetime; MSNBC; MTV; National Geographic Channel; Nickelodeon; Outdoor Channel; Oxygen; SoapNet; Speed Channel; Spike TV; Style Network; Syfy; Telemundo; The Learning Channel; Toon Disney; Travel Channel; truTV; Turner Classic Movies; Turner Network TV; TV Land; Univision; USA Network; Versus; VH1; WE tv; Weather Channel.

Fee: $36.49 monthly.

Digital Basic Service

Subscribers: 2,240.

Programming (via satellite): AmericanLife TV Network; BBC America; Bio; Bloomberg Television; Discovery Digital Networks; DMX Music; Encore Action; ESPN Classic Sports; ESPNews; Fox Movie Channel; Fox Sports World; Fuse; GAS; Halogen Network; History Channel International; Independent Film Channel; Lifetime Movie Network; MTV Networks Digital Suite; Nick Jr.; Sundance Channel.

Fee: $6.95 monthly.

Digital Pay Service 1

Pay Units: 650.

Programming (via satellite): Cinemax (multiplexed).

Fee: $10.00 monthly.

Digital Pay Service 2

Pay Units: 940.

Programming (via satellite): HBO (multiplexed).

Fee: $10.00 monthly.

Digital Pay Service 3

Pay Units: 360.

Programming (via satellite): Showtime (multiplexed); The Movie Channel.

Fee: $10.00 monthly.

Digital Pay Service 4

Pay Units: 650.

Programming (via satellite): Starz (multiplexed).

Fee: $10.00 monthly.

Video-On-Demand: Yes

Pay-Per-View

Addressable homes: 2,240.

ESPN Now (delivered digitally); Hot Choice (delivered digitally); iN DEMAND (delivered digitally), Addressable: Yes; Playboy TV (delivered digitally); Fresh (delivered digitally); Shorteez (delivered digitally).

Internet Service

Operational: Yes.

Broadband Service: Charter Pipeline.

Fee: $49.95 installation; $29.99 monthly; $5.00 modem lease.

Telephone Service

Digital: Operational

Miles of Plant: 365.0 (coaxial); 78.0 (fiber optic). Homes passed: 10,790. Total homes in franchised area: 11,573.

Vice President: Joe Boullion. General Manager: Ed Kavanaugh. Technical Operations Director: Rob Nowak. Marketing Manager: Brenda Auger.

Ownership: Charter Communications Inc. (MSO).

ALPHA (village)—Upper Peninsula Communications, 397 N US Hwy 41, Carney, MI 49812-9757. Phone: 906-639-2194. Fax: 906-639-9936. E-mail: louied@alphacomm.net. ICA: MI0258.

TV Market Ranking: Below 100 (ALPHA (VILLAGE)). Franchise award date: N.A. Franchise expiration date: N.A. Began: August 1, 1990.

Channel capacity: 40 (not 2-way capable). Channels available but not in use: 20.

Basic Service

Subscribers: N.A.

Programming (received off-air): WBKP (ABC) Calumet; WJFW-TV (NBC) Rhinelander; WJMN-TV (CBS) Escanaba; WLUC-TV (NBC) Marquette; WNMU (PBS) Marquette; WZMQ (IND, MNT) Marquette.

Programming (via satellite): ABC Family Channel; AMC; Arts & Entertainment; CNN; Country Music TV; Discovery Channel; Disney Channel; ESPN; ESPN 2; Eternal Word TV Network; Headline News; HGTV; History Channel; ION Television; Lifetime; QVC; Spike TV; TBS Superstation; The Learning Channel; Turner Classic Movies; Turner Network TV; TV Land; USA Network; Weather Channel; WGN America.

Fee: $50.00 installation; $17.00 monthly.

Pay Service 1

Pay Units: N.A.

Programming (via satellite): Showtime.

Video-On-Demand: No

Internet Service

Operational: No.

Telephone Service

None

Miles of Plant: 2.0 (coaxial); None (fiber optic). Homes passed: 114.

Manager & Chief Technician: Louis Dupont.

Ownership: Upper Peninsula Communications Inc. (MSO).

AMASA—Upper Peninsula Communications, 397 N US Hwy 41, Carney, MI 49812-9757. Phone: 906-639-2194. Fax: 906-639-9936. E-mail: louied@alphacomm.net. ICA: MI0259.

TV Market Ranking: Outside TV Markets (AMASA). Franchise award date: N.A. Franchise expiration date: N.A. Began: August 1, 1990.

Channel capacity: 40 (not 2-way capable). Channels available but not in use: 20.

Basic Service

Subscribers: N.A.

Programming (received off-air): WBKP (ABC) Calumet; WJFW-TV (NBC) Rhinelander; WJMN-TV (CBS) Escanaba; WLUC-TV (NBC) Marquette; WNMU (PBS) Marquette; WZMQ (IND, MNT) Marquette.

Programming (via satellite): ABC Family Channel; AMC; Arts & Entertainment; CNN; C-SPAN; Discovery Channel; ESPN; ESPN 2; Headline News; HGTV; History Channel; Home Shopping Network; ION Television; Lifetime; Spike TV; TBS Superstation; The Learning Channel; Trinity Broadcasting Network; Turner Classic Movies; Turner Network TV; TV Land; USA Network; Weather Channel; WGN America.

Fee: $50.00 installation; $24.95 monthly.

Pay Service 1

Pay Units: N.A.

Programming (via satellite): Showtime.

Video-On-Demand: No

Internet Service

Operational: No.

Telephone Service

None

Miles of Plant: 3.0 (coaxial); None (fiber optic). Homes passed: 120.

Manager & Chief Technician: Louis Dupont.

Ownership: Upper Peninsula Communications Inc. (MSO).

AMBOY TWP.—Formerly served by CableDirect. No longer in operation. ICA: MI0260.

ANN ARBOR—Comcast Cable, 29777 Telegraph Rd, Ste 4400B, Southfield, MI 48034. Phones: 248-233-4712; 734-369-3600 (Ann Arbor office). Fax: 248-233-4719. E-mail: mike_cleland@cable.comcast.com. Web Site: http://www.comcast.com. Also serves Barton Hills (village), Brighton, Chelsea, Clinton, Dexter, Genoa Twp., Green Oak Twp., Howell, Lima Twp., Lodi Twp., Manchester, Oceola Twp., Pittsfield Twp., Saline, Scio Twp., Superior Twp. (Washtenaw County), Sylvan Twp., Webster Twp. & Ypsilanti. ICA: MI0006.

TV Market Ranking: 5 (ANN ARBOR, Barton Hills (village), Lima Twp., Lodi Twp., Pittsfield Twp., Superior Twp. (Washtenaw County), Sylvan Twp., Ypsilanti); 61 (Brighton, Genoa Twp., Green Oak Twp., Howell, Oceola Twp.); 92 (Chelsea, Dexter, Webster Twp.); Below 100 (Clinton, Manchester, Saline, Scio Twp.). Franchise award date: January 1, 1972. Franchise expiration date: N.A. Began: August 1, 1972.

Channel capacity: N.A. Channels available but not in use: N.A.

Basic Service

Subscribers: 70,395.

Programming (received off-air): WADL (IND) Mount Clemens; WDIV-TV (NBC) Detroit; WFUM (PBS) Flint; WGTE-TV (PBS) Toledo; WJBK (FOX) Detroit; WKBD-TV (CW) Detroit; WMYD (MNT) Detroit; WPXD-TV (ION) Ann Arbor; WTVS (PBS) Detroit; WUDT-CA Detroit; WWJ-TV (CBS) Detroit; WXYZ-TV (ABC) Detroit; allband FM.

Programming (via satellite): ABC Family Channel; AMC; Animal Planet; Arts & Entertainment; BET Networks; Bravo; Cartoon Network; CNBC; CNN; Comcast Local Detroit; Comedy Central; C-SPAN; C-SPAN 2; CTN: Cambodian Channel; Discovery Channel; Disney Channel; E! Entertainment Television; ESPN; ESPN 2; Food Network; Fox News Channel; Fox Sports Net; FX; G4; Golf Channel; Great American Country; Headline News; HGTV; History Channel; Home Shopping Network; Lifetime; MSNBC; MTV; Nickelodeon; QVC; Speed Channel; Spike TV; Style Network; Syfy; TBS Superstation; The Learning Channel; Travel Channel; truTV; Turner Classic Movies; Turner Network TV; TV Guide Network; TV Land; USA Network; various Canadian stations; Versus; VH1; Weather Channel; WGN America.

Current originations: Leased Access; Government Access; Educational Access; Public Access.

Fee: $25.00 installation; $41.99 monthly; $3.00 converter; $25.00 additional installation.

Digital Basic Service

Subscribers: 17,663.

Programming (via satellite): Arts & Entertainment HD; BBC America; Bio; Black Family Channel; Bloomberg Television; Bridges TV; CMT Pure Country; Cooking Channel; Country Music TV; C-SPAN 3; Current; Daystar TV Network; Discovery Digital Networks; Discovery HD Theater; Do-It-Yourself; Encore (multiplexed); ESPN 2 HD; ESPN Classic Sports; ESPN HD; ESPNews; Eternal Word TV Network; Flix; Food Network HD; Fox College Sports Atlantic; Fox College Sports Central; Fox College Sports Pacific; Fox Movie Channel; Fox Reality Channel; Fox Soccer; Fuse; GAS; Gol TV; Gospel Music Channel; Hallmark Channel; HGTV HD; History Channel International; Independent Film Channel; INHD; INSP; Jewelry Television; Lifetime Movie Network; MTV Networks Digital Suite; Music Choice; National Geographic Channel; NBA TV; NFL Network; Nick Jr.; Nick Too; NickToons TV; Outdoor Channel; Oxygen; Palladia; PBS Kids Sprout; ShopNBC; SoapNet; Sundance Channel; Tennis Channel; The Word Network; Toon Disney; Turner Network TV HD; TV One; Universal HD; Versus HD; WE tv; Weatherscan.

Fee: $15.95 monthly.

Digital Pay Service 1
Pay Units: N.A.
Programming (via satellite): Cinemax (multiplexed); Cinemax HD; HBO (multiplexed); HBO HD; Showtime (multiplexed); Showtime HD; Starz (multiplexed); Starz HDTV; The Movie Channel (multiplexed).
Fee: $9.95 monthly (each).
Video-On-Demand: Yes
Pay-Per-View
Addressable homes: 17,663.
iN DEMAND, Addressable: Yes; NBA TV (delivered digitally); iN DEMAND; Playboy TV (delivered digitally); Fresh (delivered digitally); Movies (delivered digitally); Arabic Channel (delivered digitally); MBC America (delivered digitally); TV Japan (delivered digitally).
Internet Service
Operational: Yes.
Subscribers: 7,874.
Broadband Service: Comcast High Speed Internet.
Fee: $42.95 monthly.
Telephone Service
Digital: Operational
Fee: $44.95 monthly
Miles of Plant: 1,373.0 (coaxial); 25.0 (fiber optic). Homes passed: 117,181.
Area Vice President: Mike Cleland. Vice President, Technical Operations: Steve Thomas. Vice President, Marketing: Tony Lent. Operations Manager: Jeffrey Wack.
City fee: 5% of gross.
Ownership: Comcast Cable Communications Inc. (MSO).

APPLEGATE—Formerly served by Cablevision Systems Corp. No longer in operation. ICA: MI0262.

ARNOLD LAKE—Charter Communications, 2304 S Mission, Mount Pleasant, MI 48858. Phone: 989-775-6846. Fax: 989-772-0350. Web Site: http://www.charter.com. ICA: MI0445.
TV Market Ranking: Outside TV Markets (ARNOLD LAKE).
Channel capacity: N.A. Channels available but not in use: N.A.
Basic Service
Subscribers: N.A.
Programming (received off-air): WAQP (IND) Saginaw; WCMU-TV (PBS) Mount Pleasant; WDCQ-TV (PBS) Bad Axe; WEYI-TV (CW, NBC) Saginaw; WFQX-TV (FOX) Cadillac; WJRT-TV (ABC) Flint; WKBD-TV (CW) Detroit; WNEM-TV (CBS, MNT) Bay City; WSMH (FOX) Flint; WWTV (CBS) Cadillac; WZZM (ABC) Grand Rapids.
Programming (via satellite): C-SPAN; C-SPAN 2; CW+; Eternal Word TV Network; Home Shopping Network; QVC; TBS Superstation; TV Guide Network; Univision; various Canadian stations; WGN America.
Video-On-Demand: No
Internet Service
Operational: No.
Telephone Service
None
Operations Manager: Ed Bucao. Technology Supervisor: Jason Hannah.
Ownership: Charter Communications Inc. (MSO).

ASHLEY—Pine River Cable, PO Box 96, McBain, MI 49657. Phone: 888-244-2288. Fax: 231-825-0191. E-mail: info@pinerivercable.com. Web Site: http://www.pinerivercable.com. ICA: MI0245.
TV Market Ranking: 92 (ASHLEY). Franchise award date: September 1, 1987. Franchise expiration date: N.A. Began: November 1, 1987.
Channel capacity: 36 (not 2-way capable). Channels available but not in use: N.A.
Basic Service
Subscribers: N.A.
Programming (received off-air): WEYI-TV (CW, NBC) Saginaw; WJRT-TV (ABC) Flint; WKAR-TV (PBS) East Lansing; WLNS-TV (CBS) Lansing; WNEM-TV (CBS, MNT) Bay City; WSMH (FOX) Flint; WSYM-TV (FOX) Lansing.
Programming (via satellite): ABC Family Channel; CNN; Discovery Channel; Disney Channel; ESPN; Headline News; TBS Superstation; Turner Network TV; USA Network; WGN America.
Pay Service 1
Pay Units: N.A.
Programming (via satellite): Showtime.
Internet Service
Operational: No.
Telephone Service
None
Miles of Plant: 4.0 (coaxial); None (fiber optic). Homes passed: 188.
Manager: John Metzler.
Ownership: Pine River Cable (MSO).

ATLANTA—Formerly served by Northwoods Cable Inc. No longer in operation. ICA: MI0392.

ATTICA TWP.—Charter Communications. Now served by NORTH BRANCH TWP., MI [MI0337]. ICA: MI0263.

AU GRES—Charter Communications, 2074 M 32 W, Alpena, MI 49707. Phones: 231-947-5221 (Traverse City); 989-356-4503. Fax: 989-356-3761. Web Site: http://www.charter.com. Also serves Sims Twp. & Whitney Twp. ICA: MI0143.
TV Market Ranking: 61 (AU GRES, Sims Twp.); Outside TV Markets (Whitney Twp.). Franchise award date: June 2, 1982. Franchise expiration date: N.A. Began: November 8, 1983.
Channel capacity: N.A. Channels available but not in use: N.A.
Basic Service
Subscribers: 1,481.
Programming (received off-air): WBKB-TV (CBS, FOX) Alpena; WDCQ-TV (PBS) Bad Axe; WEYI-TV (CW, NBC) Saginaw; WJRT-TV (ABC) Flint; WNEM-TV (CBS, MNT) Bay City; WSMH (FOX) Flint; allband FM.
Programming (via satellite): CB Television Michoacan; C-SPAN; C-SPAN 2; CW+; Eternal Word TV Network; Home Shopping Network; INSP; MyNetworkTV Inc.; QVC; TBS Superstation; Trinity Broadcasting Network; TV Guide Network; WGN America.
Current originations: Government Access.
Fee: $29.99 installation; $13.50 monthly; $15.00 additional installation.
Expanded Basic Service 1
Subscribers: 1,400.
Programming (via satellite): ABC Family Channel; AMC; Animal Planet; Arts & Entertainment; BET Networks; Bravo; Cartoon Network; CNBC; CNN; Comedy Central; Country Music TV; Discovery Channel; Disney Channel; E! Entertainment Television; ESPN; ESPN 2; Food Network; Fox News Channel; Fox Sports Net Detroit; FX; G4; Golf Channel; GSN; Hallmark Channel; Headline News; HGTV; History Channel; Lifetime; MSNBC; MTV; MTV2; National Geographic Channel; Nickelodeon; Outdoor Channel; Oxygen; SoapNet; Speed Channel; Spike TV; Syfy; Telemundo; The Learning Channel; Toon Disney; Travel Channel; truTV; Turner Classic Movies; Turner Network TV; TV Land; USA Network; Versus; VH1; WE tv; Weather Channel.
Fee: $36.49 monthly.
Digital Basic Service
Subscribers: N.A.
Programming (received off-air): WEYI-TV (CW, NBC) Saginaw; WJRT-TV (ABC) Flint; WNEM-TV (CBS, MNT) Bay City; WSMH (FOX) Flint.
Programming (via satellite): BBC America; Bio; CMT Pure Country; Discovery Channel HD; Discovery Digital Networks; Do-It-Yourself; ESPN Classic Sports; ESPN HD; ESPNews; FitTV; Fox College Sports Atlantic; Fox College Sports Central; Fox College Sports Pacific; Fox Movie Channel; Fox Soccer; Fox Sports Net Detroit; Fuel TV; Fuse; GAS; Great American Country; HD-Net; HDNet Movies; History Channel International; Independent Film Channel; Lifetime Movie Network; Military History Channel; MTV Networks Digital Suite; Music Choice; Nick Jr.; Nick Too; NickToons TV; Sundance Channel; Turner Network TV HD; Universal HD.
Digital Pay Service 1
Pay Units: N.A.
Programming (via satellite): Cinemax (multiplexed); Cinemax HD; Encore (multiplexed); Flix; HBO (multiplexed); HBO HD; LOGO; Showtime (multiplexed); Showtime HD; Starz (multiplexed); The Movie Channel (multiplexed).
Video-On-Demand: Yes
Pay-Per-View
iN DEMAND (delivered digitally); ESPN (delivered digitally); NHL Center Ice (delivered digitally); MLB Extra Innings (delivered digitally); Playboy TV (delivered digitally); Club Jenna (delivered digitally); Fresh! (delivered digitally); Fresh (delivered digitally); Shorteez (delivered digitally).
Internet Service
Operational: Yes.
Broadband Service: Charter Pipeline.
Fee: $49.95 installation; $29.99 monthly.
Telephone Service
Digital: Operational
Miles of Plant: 73.0 (coaxial); None (fiber optic). Homes passed: 2,928.
Vice President: Joe Boullion. General Manager: Ed Kavanaugh. Technical Operations Director: Rob Nowak. Marketing Manager: Brenda Auger.
Franchise fee: 3% of gross.
Ownership: Charter Communications Inc. (MSO).

BAD AXE—Comcast Cable. Now served by PIGEON, MI [MI0375]. ICA: MI0108.

BALDWIN—Charter Communications, 315 Davis St, Grand Haven, MI 49417-1830. Phone: 616-647-6201. Fax: 616-846-0797. Web Site: http://www.charter.com. Also serves Baldwin (village). ICA: MI0214.
TV Market Ranking: Below 100 (BALDWIN, Baldwin (village)). Franchise award date: N.A. Franchise expiration date: N.A. Began: August 1, 1982.
Channel capacity: 36 (2-way capable). Channels available but not in use: 6.
Basic Service
Subscribers: 215.
Programming (received off-air): WCMV (PBS) Cadillac; WFQX-TV (FOX) Cadillac; WPBN-TV (NBC) Traverse City; WWTV (CBS) Cadillac; WZZM (ABC) Grand Rapids.
Programming (via satellite): ABC Family Channel; C-SPAN; QVC; TBS Superstation; WGN America.
Fee: $38.00 installation; $24.99 monthly; $12.65 additional installation.
Expanded Basic Service 1
Subscribers: N.A.
Programming (via satellite): Arts & Entertainment; Disney Channel; ESPN; Lifetime; MTV; Nickelodeon; Turner Network TV; USA Network; VH1.
Expanded Basic Service 2
Subscribers: N.A.
Programming (via satellite): AMC; CNN; Country Music TV; Discovery Channel; ESPN 2; Food Network; Fox Sports Net Detroit; Headline News; HGTV; Spike TV; The Learning Channel; Weather Channel.
Pay Service 1
Pay Units: 71.
Programming (via satellite): Cinemax; HBO; Starz.
Fee: $6.95 monthly (Starz), $10.95 monthly (Cinemax), $11.95 monthly (HBO).
Video-On-Demand: No
Internet Service
Operational: No.
Telephone Service
None
Miles of Plant: 15.0 (coaxial); None (fiber optic). Homes passed: 524.
Vice President & General Manager: Dan Spoelman. Technical Operations Manager: Keith Schierbeek. Marketing Director: Steve Schuh.
Ownership: Charter Communications Inc. (MSO).

BARRYTON—Pine River Cable, PO Box 96, McBain, MI 49657. Phone: 888-244-2288. Fax: 231-825-0191. E-mail: info@pinerivercable.com. Web Site: http://www.pinerivercable.com. ICA: MI0264.
TV Market Ranking: Outside TV Markets (BARRYTON). Franchise award date: N.A. Franchise expiration date: N.A. Began: May 1, 1988.
Channel capacity: 35 (not 2-way capable). Channels available but not in use: 12.
Basic Service
Subscribers: 58.
Programming (received off-air): WCMU-TV (PBS) Mount Pleasant; WFQX-TV (FOX) Cadillac; WJRT-TV (ABC) Flint; WPBN-TV (NBC) Traverse City; WWTV (CBS) Cadillac; WZZM (ABC) Grand Rapids.
Programming (via satellite): ABC Family Channel; CNN; Country Music TV; Discovery Channel; Disney Channel; ESPN; Head-

line News; TBS Superstation; Turner Network TV; WGN America.
Fee: $50.00 installation; $19.95 monthly.

Pay Service 1
Pay Units: 21.
Programming (via satellite): Showtime.
Fee: $7.00 monthly.

Internet Service
Operational: No.

Telephone Service
None

Miles of Plant: 4.0 (coaxial); None (fiber optic). Homes passed: 200.
Manager: John Metzler.
Ownership: Pine River Cable (MSO).

BARTON CITY—Pine River Cable, PO Box 96, McBain, MI 49657. Phone: 888-244-2288. Fax: 231-825-0191. E-mail: info@pinerivercable.com. Web Site: http://www.pinerivercable.com. Also serves Millen Twp. ICA: MI0265.
TV Market Ranking: Below 100 (BARTON CITY, Millen Twp.). Franchise award date: N.A. Franchise expiration date: N.A. Began: N.A.
Channel capacity: 36 (not 2-way capable). Channels available but not in use: 14.

Basic Service
Subscribers: 62.
Programming (received off-air): WBKB-TV (CBS, FOX) Alpena.
Programming (via microwave): WDIV-TV (NBC) Detroit; WTVS (PBS) Detroit; WXYZ-TV (ABC) Detroit.
Programming (via satellite): ABC Family Channel; Arts & Entertainment; CNN; Discovery Channel; Disney Channel; ESPN; Hallmark Channel; Spike TV; TBS Superstation; The Learning Channel; Trinity Broadcasting Network; Turner Network TV; Weather Channel; WGN America.
Fee: $24.95 monthly.

Pay Service 1
Pay Units: N.A.
Programming (via satellite): Showtime.

Internet Service
Operational: No.

Miles of Plant: 5.0 (coaxial); None (fiber optic). Homes passed: 200.
Manager: John Metzler.
Ownership: Pine River Cable (MSO).

BATTLE CREEK—Comcast Cable, 3500 Patterson Ave SE, Grand Rapids, MI 49512. Phone: 616-977-2200. Fax: 616-977-2224. Web Site: http://www.comcast.com. Also serves Bedford Twp. (Calhoun County), Ceresco, East Leroy, Marshall (portions), Newton Twp., Pennfield Twp. & Springfield. ICA: MI0020.
TV Market Ranking: 37,92 (BATTLE CREEK, Bedford Twp. (Calhoun County), Ceresco, East Leroy, Marshall (portions), Newton Twp., Pennfield Twp., Springfield). Franchise award date: January 1, 1962. Franchise expiration date: N.A. Began: March 1, 1967.
Channel capacity: 78 (operating 2-way). Channels available but not in use: None.

Basic Service
Subscribers: 25,940.
Programming (received off-air): WGVU-TV (PBS) Grand Rapids; WKAR-TV (PBS) East Lansing; WLLA (IND) Kalamazoo; WOOD-TV (NBC) Grand Rapids; WOTV (ABC) Battle Creek; WTLJ (IND) Muskegon; WWMT (CBS, CW) Kalamazoo; WXMI (FOX) Grand Rapids; WZPX-TV (ION) Battle Creek; 1 FM.
Programming (via satellite): Bravo; Discovery Channel; FX; History Channel; Sneak Prevue; Speed Channel; TBS Superstation; VH1; VH1 Country; WGN America.
Current originations: Government Access; Educational Access; Public Access.

Expanded Basic Service 1
Subscribers: 23,621.
Programming (via satellite): ABC Family Channel; AMC; Animal Planet; Arts & Entertainment; BET Networks; Cartoon Network; CNBC; CNN; Country Music TV; C-SPAN; Disney Channel; E! Entertainment Television; ESPN; ESPN 2; Food Network; Fox News Channel; Fox Sports Net Detroit; Hallmark Channel; Headline News; HGTV; Home Shopping Network; Lifetime; MSNBC; MTV; Nickelodeon; QVC; Spike TV; The Learning Channel; truTV; Turner Network TV; TV Guide Network; USA Network; Weather Channel.
Fee: $48.99 monthly.

Digital Basic Service
Subscribers: 4,045.
Programming (via satellite): BBC America; Bravo; Discovery Digital Networks; DMX Music; ESPN Classic Sports; Fox Sports Net; Golf Channel; GSN; History Channel; Independent Film Channel; Nick Jr.; Turner Classic Movies; TV Land; Versus; WE tv.
Fee: $9.95 monthly.

Digital Pay Service 1
Pay Units: N.A.
Programming (via satellite): Cinemax; DMX Music; Encore; HBO; Showtime; Starz; The Movie Channel.
Fee: $18.05 monthly (each).

Video-On-Demand: Planned

Pay-Per-View
iN DEMAND; Playboy TV; Spice.

Internet Service
Operational: Yes. Began: July 1, 1999.
Subscribers: 1,800.
Broadband Service: Comcast High Speed Internet.
Fee: $42.95 monthly.

Telephone Service
Digital: Operational

Miles of Plant: 615.0 (coaxial); 124.0 (fiber optic). Homes passed: 42,742. Total homes in franchised area: 45,354.
Area Vice President: Larry Williamson. Business Operations Director: Amy Carey. Technical Operations Director: Tom Rice. Sales & Marketing Director: Rick Finch. Marketing Coordinator: Megan Martin.
City fee: 5% of gross.
Ownership: Comcast Cable Communications Inc. (MSO).

BAY CITY—Charter Communications, 1480 S Valley Center Dr, Bay City, MI 48706-9754. Phones: 810-652-1400 (Davison office); 989-667-8810. Fax: 989-667-1799. Web Site: http://www.charter.com. Also serves Auburn, Bangor Twp. (Bay County), Beaver Twp., Deep River Twp., Essexville, Frankenlust Twp., Garfield Twp., Hampton Twp., Kawkawlin Twp. (southern portion), Lincoln Twp., Monitor Twp., Pinconning, Pinconning Twp., Portsmouth Twp., Standish, Standish Twp. & Williams Twp. (eastern portion). ICA: MI0018.
TV Market Ranking: 61 (Auburn, Bangor Twp. (Bay County), BAY CITY, Beaver Twp., Deep River Twp., Essexville, Frankenlust Twp., Garfield Twp., Hampton Twp., Kawkawlin Twp. (southern portion), Lincoln Twp., Monitor Twp., Pinconning, Pinconning Twp., Portsmouth Twp., Standish, Standish Twp., Williams Twp. (eastern portion)). Franchise award date: January 1, 1972. Franchise expiration date: N.A. Began: March 1, 1972.
Channel capacity: N.A. Channels available but not in use: N.A.

Basic Service
Subscribers: 28,129.
Programming (received off-air): WAQP (IND) Saginaw; WCMU-TV (PBS) Mount Pleasant; WDCQ-TV (PBS) Bad Axe; WEYI-TV (CW, NBC) Saginaw; WJRT-TV (ABC) Flint; WKBD-TV (CW) Detroit; WNEM-TV (CBS, MNT) Bay City; WSMH (FOX) Flint.
Programming (via satellite): Cornerstone Television; C-SPAN; C-SPAN 2; C-SPAN 3; Eternal Word TV Network; G4; Home Shopping Network; INSP; QVC; TBS Superstation; TV Guide Network; Univision.
Current originations: Public Access; Educational Access; Government Access.
Fee: $38.77 installation; $10.96 monthly; $1.00 converter.

Expanded Basic Service 1
Subscribers: 24,470.
Programming (via satellite): ABC Family Channel; AMC; Animal Planet; Arts & Entertainment; BET Networks; Bravo; Cartoon Network; CNBC; CNN; Comedy Central; Country Music TV; Discovery Channel; Disney Channel; E! Entertainment Television; ESPN; ESPN 2; Food Network; Fox News Channel; Fox Sports Net Detroit; FX; Golf Channel; GSN; Hallmark Channel; Headline News; HGTV; History Channel; Lifetime; MSNBC; MTV; MTV2; National Geographic Channel; Nickelodeon; Outdoor Channel; Oxygen; SoapNet; Speed Channel; Spike TV; Syfy; Telemundo; The Learning Channel; Toon Disney; Travel Channel; truTV; Turner Classic Movies; Turner Network TV; TV Land; USA Network; Versus; VH1; WE tv; Weather Channel.
Fee: $17.72 monthly.

Digital Basic Service
Subscribers: N.A.
Programming (received off-air): WDCQ-TV (PBS) Bad Axe; WEYI-TV (CW, NBC) Saginaw; WJRT-TV (ABC) Flint.
Programming (via satellite): BBC America; Bio; Discovery Digital Networks; Do-It-Yourself; ESPN Classic Sports; ESPN HD; ESPNews; Fox College Sports Atlantic; Fox College Sports Central; Fox College Sports Pacific; Fox Movie Channel; Fox Soccer; Fuel TV; Fuse; GAS; Great American Country; HDNet; HDNet Movies; History Channel International; Independent Film Channel; Lifetime Movie Network; MTV Networks Digital Suite; Music Choice; NFL Network; Nick Jr.; Nick Too; NickToons TV; Sundance Channel; TV Guide Interactive Inc.

Digital Pay Service 1
Pay Units: N.A.
Programming (via satellite): Cinemax (multiplexed); Encore (multiplexed); Flix; HBO (multiplexed); HBO HD; Showtime (multiplexed); Showtime HD; Starz (multiplexed); The Movie Channel (multiplexed).

Video-On-Demand: Yes

Pay-Per-View
iN DEMAND (delivered digitally), Addressable: No; ESPN Sports PPV (delivered digitally); NHL Center Ice/MLB Extra Innings (delivered digitally); Playboy TV (delivered digitally); Fresh (delivered digitally); Shorteez (delivered digitally).

Internet Service
Operational: Yes. Began: October 1, 1998.
Broadband Service: Charter Pipeline.
Fee: $49.95 installation; $29.99 monthly; $10.00 modem lease; $395.00 modem purchase.

Telephone Service
Digital: Operational
Fee: $29.99 monthly

Miles of Plant: 585.0 (coaxial); 111.0 (fiber optic). Homes passed: 42,206.
Vice President & General Manager: Dave Slowick. Technical Operations Director: Lloyd Collins. Marketing Director: Lisa Gayari.
City fee: 5% of gross.
Ownership: Charter Communications Inc. (MSO).

BEAR LAKE—Charter Communications. Now served by TRAVERSE CITY, MI [MI0026]. ICA: MI0149.

BEAVER ISLAND—Pine River Cable, PO Box 96, McBain, MI 49657. Phone: 888-244-2288. Fax: 231-825-0191. E-mail: info@pinerivercable.com. Web Site: http://www.pinerivercable.com. Also serves St. James Twp. ICA: MI0352.
TV Market Ranking: Below 100 (BEAVER ISLAND, St. James Twp.). Franchise award date: N.A. Franchise expiration date: N.A. Began: March 1, 1989.
Channel capacity: 27 (not 2-way capable). Channels available but not in use: N.A.

Basic Service
Subscribers: 70.
Programming (received off-air): WCML (PBS) Alpena; WGTQ (ABC) Sault Ste. Marie; WPBN-TV (NBC) Traverse City; WWTV (CBS) Cadillac.
Programming (via satellite): ABC Family Channel; AMC; Animal Planet; Arts & Entertainment; CNN; Comedy Central; C-SPAN 2; Discovery Channel; Disney Channel; ESPN; Eternal Word TV Network; Fox News Channel; Fox Sports Net; Headline News; HGTV; History Channel; Lifetime; MTV; Nickelodeon; QVC; Spike TV; TBS Superstation; Travel Channel; Turner Network TV; USA Network; Weather Channel; WGN America.
Fee: $50.00 installation; $28.30 monthly.

Pay Service 1
Pay Units: 16.
Programming (via satellite): Encore.
Fee: $11.00 monthly.

Pay Service 2
Pay Units: 25.
Programming (via satellite): HBO.
Fee: $13.00 monthly.

Video-On-Demand: No

Internet Service
Operational: No.

Telephone Service
None

Homes passed: 70. Total homes in franchised area: 225.
Manager: John Metzler.
Ownership: Pine River Cable.

BEAVER TWP. (BAY COUNTY)—Charter Communications. Now served by BAY CITY, MI [MI0018]. ICA: MI0176.

BENTON HARBOR—Comcast Cable, 7720 W 98th St, Hickory Hills, IL 60457. Phones: 574-259-2112 (Mishawaka office); 616-429-3209. Fax: 708-237-3292. Web Site: http://www.comcast.com. Also serves Benton Twp. (Berrien County) & St. Joseph. ICA: MI0045.
TV Market Ranking: 80 (BENTON HARBOR, Benton Twp. (Berrien County), St. Joseph). Franchise award date: May 7, 1976. Franchise expiration date: N.A. Began: July 1, 1977.
Channel capacity: N.A. Channels available but not in use: N.A.

Basic Service
Subscribers: 8,080.
Programming (received off-air): WBBM-TV (CBS) Chicago; WBND-LP South Bend; WGN-TV (CW, IND) Chicago; WHME-TV (IND) South Bend; WLS-TV (ABC) Chicago; WMAQ-TV (NBC) Chicago; WNDU-TV (NBC) South Bend; WNIT (PBS) South Bend; WSBT-TV (CBS, IND) South Bend; WSJV (FOX) Elkhart; WTTW (PBS) Chicago; WWMT (CBS, CW) Kalamazoo.
Programming (via satellite): Hallmark Channel; Home Shopping Network; National Geographic Channel; QVC; Speed Channel; TBS Superstation; TV Guide Network.
Current originations: Government Access; Educational Access.
Fee: $44.99 installation; $16.75 monthly.

Expanded Basic Service 1
Subscribers: N.A.
Programming (via satellite): ABC Family Channel; AMC; Animal Planet; Arts & Entertainment; BET Networks; Bravo; Cartoon Network; CNBC; CNN; Comedy Central; Country Music TV; C-SPAN; C-SPAN 2; Discovery Channel; Disney Channel; E! Entertainment Television; ESPN; ESPN 2; Eternal Word TV Network; Food Network; Fox News Channel; Fox Sports Net Detroit; FX; Golf Channel; Headline News; HGTV; History Channel; ION Television; Lifetime; MSNBC; MTV; Nickelodeon; Spike TV; Syfy; The Learning Channel; truTV; Turner Network TV; TV Land; USA Network; Versus; VH1; Weather Channel.
Fee: $24.24 monthly.

Digital Basic Service
Subscribers: N.A.
Programming (received off-air): WBND-LP South Bend; WNDU-TV (NBC) South Bend; WNIT (PBS) South Bend; WSBT-TV (CBS, IND) South Bend; WSJV (FOX) Elkhart.
Programming (via satellite): BBC America; Bio; Bloomberg Television; Canales N; CMT Pure Country; Cooking Channel; Current; Discovery Digital Networks; Discovery HD Theater; Do-It-Yourself; Encore (multiplexed); ESPN 2 HD; ESPN Classic Sports; ESPN HD; ESPNews; Flix; Fox College Sports Atlantic; Fox College Sports Central; Fox College Sports Pacific; Fox Movie Channel; Fox Reality Channel; Fox Soccer; Fuse; G4; GAS; Gospel Music Channel; Great American Country; GSN; History Channel International; Independent Film Channel; Jewelry Television; Lifetime Movie Network; MTV Networks Digital Suite; Music Choice; NBA TV; NFL Network; Nick Jr.; Nick Too; NickToons TV; Outdoor Channel; Ovation; Oxygen; Palladia; PBS Kids Sprout; ShopNBC; SoapNet; Style Network; Sundance Channel; The Word Network; Toon Disney; Travel Channel; Trinity Broadcasting Network; Turner Classic Movies; Turner Network TV HD; TV One; TVG Network; Versus HD.
Fee: $11.99 monthly.

Digital Pay Service 1
Pay Units: N.A.
Programming (via satellite): Cinemax (multiplexed); Cinemax HD; HBO (multiplexed); HBO HD; Playboy TV; Showtime (multiplexed); Showtime HD; Starz (multiplexed); Starz HDTV; The Movie Channel (multiplexed).
Fee: $10.00 monthly (each).

Video-On-Demand: Yes

Pay-Per-View
iN DEMAND (delivered digitally); Playboy TV (delivered digitally); Fresh (delivered digitally); Shorteez (delivered digitally); ESPN (delivered digitally); NBA League Pass (delivered digitally).

Internet Service
Operational: Yes.

Telephone Service
Digital: Operational

Miles of Plant: 165.0 (coaxial); None (fiber optic). Additional miles planned: 4.0 (coaxial). Homes passed: 16,000. Total homes in franchised area: 17,700.

Area Vice President: Sandy Weicher. Vice President, Technical Operations: Bob Curtis. Vice President, Sales & Marketing: Eric Schaefer. Vice President, Communications: Rich Ruggiero. Technical Operations Manager: John Collucci. Marketing Director: Ron Knutson.

City fee: 4% of gross.

Ownership: Comcast Cable Communications Inc. (MSO).

BERGLAND—Charter Communications. Now served by IRONWOOD, MI [MI0064]. ICA: MI0269.

BERLIN TWP. (St. Clair County)—Charter Communications, 7372 Davison Rd, Davison, MI 48423. Phone: 810-652-1400. Web Site: http://www.charter.com. ICA: MI0270.

TV Market Ranking: Below 100 (BERLIN TWP.). Franchise award date: N.A. Franchise expiration date: N.A. Began: April 1, 1989.

Channel capacity: 40 (not 2-way capable). Channels available but not in use: 20.

Basic Service
Subscribers: 113.
Programming (received off-air): WADL (IND) Mount Clemens; WDIV-TV (NBC) Detroit; WEYI-TV (CW, NBC) Saginaw; WFUM (PBS) Flint; WJBK (FOX) Detroit; WJRT-TV (ABC) Flint; WKBD-TV (CW) Detroit; WMYD (MNT) Detroit; WNEM-TV (CBS, MNT) Bay City; WPXD-TV (ION) Ann Arbor; WSMH (FOX) Flint; WTVS (PBS) Detroit; WWJ-TV (CBS) Detroit; WXYZ-TV (ABC) Detroit.
Programming (via satellite): C-SPAN; QVC; Weather Channel; WGN America.
Current originations: Educational Access; Public Access; Government Access.
Fee: $29.99 installation; $13.50 monthly.

Expanded Basic Service 1
Subscribers: N.A.
Programming (via satellite): ABC Family Channel; AMC; Animal Planet; Arts & Entertainment; Cartoon Network; CNBC; CNN; Comedy Central; Country Music TV; Discovery Channel; Disney Channel; E! Entertainment Television; ESPN; ESPN 2; Fox News Channel; Fox Sports Net Detroit; FX; Headline News; HGTV; History Channel; Home Shopping Network; Lifetime; MTV; Nickelodeon; Spike TV; Syfy; TBS Superstation; The Learning Channel; Travel Channel; Turner Classic Movies; Turner Network TV; Univision; USA Network; VH1.
Fee: $36.49 monthly.

Digital Basic Service
Subscribers: N.A.
Programming (via satellite): BBC America; Discovery Digital Networks; DMX Music; ESPN Classic Sports; ESPNews; Fox Soccer; Golf Channel; GSN; Independent Film Channel; Military History Channel; Speed Channel; Versus; WE tv.

Digital Pay Service 1
Pay Units: N.A.
Programming (via satellite): Cinemax (multiplexed); Encore (multiplexed); HBO (multiplexed); Showtime (multiplexed); Starz (multiplexed); The Movie Channel.

Video-On-Demand: No

Pay-Per-View
iN DEMAND (delivered digitally); Fresh! (delivered digitally).

Internet Service
Operational: No.

Telephone Service
None

Miles of Plant: 13.0 (coaxial); None (fiber optic). Homes passed: 273.

Vice President & General Manager: Dave Slowick. Technical Operations Director: Lloyd Collins. Marketing Director: Lisa Gayari.

Ownership: Charter Communications Inc. (MSO).

BIG PRAIRIE TWP.—Charter Communications, 315 Davis St, Grand Haven, MI 49417-1830. Phone: 616-647-6201. Fax: 616-846-0797. Web Site: http://www.charter.com. ICA: MI0226.

TV Market Ranking: Outside TV Markets (BIG PRAIRIE TWP.). Franchise award date: N.A. Franchise expiration date: N.A. Began: N.A.

Channel capacity: 45 (not 2-way capable). Channels available but not in use: N.A.

Basic Service
Subscribers: 233.
Programming (received off-air): WGVU-TV (PBS) Grand Rapids; WOOD-TV (NBC) Grand Rapids; WTLJ (IND) Muskegon; WWMT (CBS, CW) Kalamazoo; WWTV (CBS) Cadillac; WXMI (FOX) Grand Rapids; WZZM (ABC) Grand Rapids.
Programming (via satellite): QVC; TBS Superstation; WGN America.
Fee: $30.00 installation; $25.45 monthly.

Expanded Basic Service 1
Subscribers: N.A.
Programming (via satellite): ABC Family Channel; AMC; Arts & Entertainment; CNBC; CNN; Country Music TV; C-SPAN; Discovery Channel; Disney Channel; ESPN; ESPN 2; Food Network; Fox Sports Net Detroit; Headline News; HGTV; History Channel; Lifetime; MTV; Nickelodeon; Spike TV; Turner Network TV; USA Network; VH1; Weather Channel.

Pay Service 1
Pay Units: 90.
Programming (via satellite): Cinemax; HBO; Starz.
Fee: $5.95 monthly (Starz), $10.95 monthly (Cinemax), $11.95 monthly (HBO).

Internet Service
Operational: No.

Miles of Plant: 16.0 (coaxial); None (fiber optic). Homes passed: 545.

Vice President & General Manager: Dan Spoelman. Technical Operations Manager: Keith Schierbeek. Marketing Director: Steve Schuh.

Ownership: Charter Communications Inc. (MSO).

BIG RAPIDS—Charter Communications, 315 Davis St, Grand Haven, MI 49417-1830. Phone: 231-947-5221. Web Site: http://www.charter.com. Also serves Green Twp. (Mecosta County) & Paris Twp. ICA: MI0083.

TV Market Ranking: Below 100 (Paris Twp.); Outside TV Markets (BIG RAPIDS, Green Twp. (Mecosta County)). Franchise award date: N.A. Franchise expiration date: N.A. Began: November 1, 1973.

Channel capacity: N.A. Channels available but not in use: N.A.

Basic Service
Subscribers: 3,201.
Programming (received off-air): WCMU-TV (PBS) Mount Pleasant; WFQX-TV (FOX) Cadillac; WGVU-TV (PBS) Grand Rapids; WOOD-TV (NBC) Grand Rapids; WPBN-TV (NBC) Traverse City; WWTV (CBS) Cadillac; WXSP-CA (MNT) Grand Rapids; WZZM (ABC) Grand Rapids; allband FM.
Programming (via satellite): C-SPAN; C-SPAN 2; CW+; Home Shopping Network; QVC; TBS Superstation; TV Guide Network; WGN America.
Current originations: Leased Access; Government Access; Educational Access; Public Access.
Fee: $29.99 installation; $2.00 converter.

Expanded Basic Service 1
Subscribers: 2,857.
Programming (via satellite): ABC Family Channel; AMC; Animal Planet; Arts & Entertainment; Bravo; Cartoon Network; CNBC; CNN; Comedy Central; Country Music TV; Discovery Channel; Disney Channel; E! Entertainment Television; ESPN; ESPN 2; ESPN Classic Sports; ESPNews; Eternal Word TV Network; Food Network; Fox News Channel; Fox Sports Net Detroit; FX; G4; Golf Channel; GSN; Hallmark Channel; Headline News; HGTV; History Channel; INSP; Lifetime; MSNBC; MTV; MTV2; National Geographic Channel; Nickelodeon; Oxygen; SoapNet; Speed Channel; Spike TV; Style Network; Syfy; The Learning Channel; Toon Disney; Travel Channel; Trinity Broadcasting Network; truTV; Turner Classic Movies; Turner Network TV; TV Land; Univision; USA Network; Versus; VH1; WE tv; Weather Channel.
Fee: $47.99 monthly.

Digital Basic Service
Subscribers: N.A.
Programming (received off-air): WFQX-TV (FOX) Cadillac; WGVU-TV (PBS) Grand Rapids; WOOD-TV (NBC) Grand Rapids; WWTV (CBS) Cadillac; WZZM (ABC) Grand Rapids.
Programming (via satellite): BBC America; Bio; Boomerang; Canales N; CMT Pure Country; Discovery Digital Networks; Discovery HD Theater; Do-It-Yourself; ESPN HD; Fox College Sports Atlantic; Fox College Sports Central; Fox College Sports Pacific; Fox Movie Channel; Fox Soccer; Fuel TV; Fuse; GAS; Great American Country; HDNet; HDNet Movies; History Channel International; Independent Film Channel; Lifetime Movie Network; MTV Networks Digital Suite; Music Choice; Nick Jr.; Nick Too; NickToons TV; Outdoor Channel; Sundance Channel; Turner Network TV HD; Universal HD.

Digital Pay Service 1
Pay Units: N.A.
Programming (via satellite): Cinemax (multiplexed); Cinemax HD; Encore (multiplexed); Flix; HBO (multiplexed); HBO HD; LOGO; Showtime (multiplexed); Showtime HD; Starz (multiplexed); The Movie Channel (multiplexed).
Video-On-Demand: Yes
Pay-Per-View
iN DEMAND (delivered digitally); NHL Center Ice (delivered digitally); MLB Extra Innings (delivered digitally); ESPN (delivered digitally); Playboy TV (delivered digitally); Fresh (delivered digitally); Shorteez (delivered digitally).
Internet Service
Operational: Yes. Began: January 1, 2003.
Broadband Service: Charter Pipeline.
Fee: $12.00 installation; $29.99 monthly.
Telephone Service
Digital: Operational
Fee: $29.99 monthly
Miles of Plant: 92.0 (coaxial); None (fiber optic). Homes passed: 6,484. Total homes in franchised area: 22,417.
Vice President & General Manager: Dan Spoelman. Technical Operations Manager: Keith Schierbeck. Marketing Director: Steve Schuh.
City fee: 3% of gross.
Ownership: Charter Communications Inc. (MSO).

BIG STAR LAKE—Charter Communications, 315 Davis St, Grand Haven, MI 49417-1830. Phone: 616-647-6201. Fax: 616-846-0797. Web Site: http://www.charter.com. Also serves Lake Twp. (Lake County) & Star Lake. ICA: MI0173.
TV Market Ranking: Outside TV Markets (BIG STAR LAKE, Lake Twp. (Lake County), Star Lake). Franchise award date: July 5, 1988. Franchise expiration date: N.A. Began: N.A.
Channel capacity: 41 (2-way capable). Channels available but not in use: 11.
Basic Service
Subscribers: 248.
Programming (received off-air): WCMV (PBS) Cadillac; WFQX-TV (FOX) Cadillac; WPBN-TV (NBC) Traverse City; WWTV (CBS) Cadillac; WZZM (ABC) Grand Rapids.
Programming (via satellite): ABC Family Channel; C-SPAN; Lifetime; Nickelodeon; QVC; TBS Superstation; WGN America.
Fee: $38.00 installation; $21.60 monthly.
Expanded Basic Service 1
Subscribers: N.A.
Programming (via satellite): AMC; Arts & Entertainment; CNN; Country Music TV; Discovery Channel; Disney Channel; ESPN 2; Food Network; Fox Sports Net Detroit; Headline News; HGTV; MTV; Spike TV; The Learning Channel; Turner Network TV; USA Network; VH1; Weather Channel.
Pay Service 1
Pay Units: 36.
Programming (via satellite): Cinemax; HBO; Starz.
Fee: $21.00 installation; $6.95 monthly (Starz), $10.95 monthly (Cinemax), $11.95 monthly (HBO).
Internet Service
Operational: No.
Miles of Plant: 27.0 (coaxial); None (fiber optic). Homes passed: 560.
Vice President & General Manager: Dan Spoelman. Technical Operations Manager: Keith Schierbeek. Marketing Director: Steve Schuh.
Ownership: Charter Communications Inc. (MSO).

BILLINGS—Charter Communications, 2074 M 32 W, Alpena, MI 49707. Phones: 231-947-5221 (Traverse City); 989-356-4503. Fax: 989-356-3761. Web Site: http://www.charter.com. Also serves Hay Twp. & Tobacco Twp. ICA: MI0272.
TV Market Ranking: 61 (BILLINGS); Outside TV Markets (Hay Twp., Tobacco Twp.). Franchise award date: N.A. Franchise expiration date: N.A. Began: N.A.
Channel capacity: 54 (not 2-way capable). Channels available but not in use: 16.
Basic Service
Subscribers: 1,534.
Programming (received off-air): WCMU-TV (PBS) Mount Pleasant; WJRT-TV (ABC) Flint; WNEM-TV (CBS, MNT) Bay City; WSMH (FOX) Flint; WWTV (CBS) Cadillac.
Programming (via satellite): ABC Family Channel; Arts & Entertainment; CNN; Country Music TV; C-SPAN; Discovery Channel; ESPN; Headline News; Home Shopping Network; Lifetime; MTV; Nickelodeon; Spike TV; TBS Superstation; USA Network; Weather Channel; WGN America.
Fee: $29.99 installation; $13.50 monthly.
Pay Service 1
Pay Units: 355.
Programming (via satellite): Showtime; The Movie Channel.
Fee: $20.00 installation; $7.00 monthly (each).
Video-On-Demand: No
Internet Service
Operational: No.
Telephone Service
None
Miles of Plant: 60.0 (coaxial); None (fiber optic). Homes passed: 3,332.
Vice President: Joe Boullion. General Manager: Ed Kavanaugh. Technical Operations Director: Rob Nowak. Marketing Manager: Brenda Auger.
Ownership: Charter Communications Inc. (MSO).

BIRMINGHAM—Comcast Cable. Now served by SOUTHFIELD, MI [MI0009]. ICA: MI0022.

BLOOMINGDALE—Bloomingdale Communications Inc., PO Box 187, 101 W. Kalamazoo St., Bloomingdale, MI 49026-0187. Phones: 800-377-3130; 269-521-7300. Fax: 269-521-7373. E-mail: staff@bloomingdalecom.net. Web Site: http://www.bloomingdalecom.net. Also serves Arlington Twp., Bloomingdale Twp. (Van Buren County), Cheshire Twp., Columbia Twp. (Van Buren County), Lee Twp. (Allegan County), Van Buren County (portions) & Waverly Twp. (Van Buren County). ICA: MI0177.
TV Market Ranking: 37 (Arlington Twp., BLOOMINGDALE, Bloomingdale Twp. (Van Buren County), Cheshire Twp., Columbia Twp. (Van Buren County), Lee Twp. (Allegan County), Van Buren County (portions), Waverly Twp. (Van Buren County)). Franchise award date: N.A. Franchise expiration date: N.A. Began: June 1, 1988.
Channel capacity: 40 (not 2-way capable). Channels available but not in use: N.A.
Basic Service
Subscribers: 420.
Programming (received off-air): WGVU-TV (PBS) Grand Rapids; WLLA (IND) Kalamazoo; WOOD-TV (NBC) Grand Rapids; WOTV (ABC) Battle Creek; WSBT-TV (CBS, IND) South Bend; WWMT (CBS, CW) Kalamazoo; WXMI (FOX) Grand Rapids; WZPX-TV (ION) Battle Creek; WZZM (ABC) Grand Rapids.
Programming (via satellite): TBS Superstation; Weather Channel.
Fee: $20.00 installation; $8.95 monthly.
Expanded Basic Service 1
Subscribers: N.A.
Programming (via satellite): ABC Family Channel; AMC; America's Store; Arts & Entertainment; CNBC; CNN; Discovery Channel; Disney Channel; ESPN; ESPN 2; Fox Sports Net; Headline News; History Channel; Nickelodeon; QVC; Spike TV; Syfy; The Learning Channel; Turner Network TV; USA Network; WGN America.
Fee: $20.00 installation; $20.95 monthly (includes Basic Service).
Pay Service 1
Pay Units: 60.
Programming (via satellite): Cinemax; Encore; HBO; The Movie Channel.
Fee: $2.95 monthly (Encore), $8.00 monthly (Cinemax), $8.95 monthly (TMC), $10.00 monthly (HBO).
Video-On-Demand: No
Internet Service
Operational: No, DSL & dialup.
Telephone Service
None
Miles of Plant: 73.0 (coaxial); None (fiber optic). Homes passed: 1,198.
President: Robert Remington. General Manager: Mark Bahnson. Facilities Manager: Dan Key.
Ownership: Bloomingdale Telephone Co. Inc.

BOARDMAN TWP. (southern portion)—Pine River Cable, PO Box 96, McBain, MI 49657. Phone: 888-244-2288. Fax: 231-825-0191. E-mail: info@pinerivercable.com. Web Site: http://www.pinerivercable.com. Also serves Orange Twp. (Kalkaska County). ICA: MI0221.
TV Market Ranking: Below 100 (BOARDMAN TWP. (SOUTHERN PORTION), Orange Twp. (Kalkaska County)). Franchise award date: N.A. Franchise expiration date: N.A. Began: January 15, 1991.
Channel capacity: 54 (not 2-way capable). Channels available but not in use: 30.
Basic Service
Subscribers: 163.
Programming (received off-air): WCML (PBS) Alpena; WFQX-TV (FOX) Cadillac; WGTU (ABC, CW) Traverse City; WPBN-TV (NBC) Traverse City; WWTV (CBS) Cadillac.
Programming (via satellite): TBS Superstation.
Current originations: Public Access.
Fee: $50.00 installation; $8.83 monthly; $1.00 converter.
Expanded Basic Service 1
Subscribers: 143.
Programming (via satellite): ABC Family Channel; Arts & Entertainment; Bravo; CNN; Country Music TV; C-SPAN; Discovery Channel; ESPN; Headline News; HGTV; Spike TV; Turner Network TV; USA Network; Weather Channel.
Fee: $14.10 monthly.
Pay Service 1
Pay Units: 38.
Programming (via satellite): Cinemax.
Fee: $9.95 monthly.
Pay Service 2
Pay Units: 46.
Programming (via satellite): HBO.
Fee: $9.95 monthly.
Internet Service
Operational: No.
Telephone Service
None
Miles of Plant: 18.0 (coaxial); None (fiber optic). Homes passed: 422.
Manager: John Metzler.
Franchise fee: 3% of gross.
Ownership: Pine River Cable (MSO).

BRETHREN—Pine River Cable, PO Box 96, McBain, MI 49657. Phone: 888-244-2288. Fax: 231-825-0191. E-mail: info@pinerivercable.com. Web Site: http://www.pinerivercable.com. Also serves Dickson Twp. ICA: MI0274.
TV Market Ranking: Below 100 (BRETHREN, Dickson Twp.). Franchise award date: N.A. Franchise expiration date: N.A. Began: August 1, 1990.
Channel capacity: 36 (not 2-way capable). Channels available but not in use: 13.
Basic Service
Subscribers: 46.
Programming (received off-air): WJFW-TV (NBC) Rhinelander; WJMN-TV (CBS) Escanaba; WLUC-TV (NBC) Marquette; WNMU (PBS) Marquette.
Programming (via satellite): ABC Family Channel; AMC; Arts & Entertainment; CNN; Country Music TV; Discovery Channel; ESPN; QVC; Showtime; TBS Superstation; The Learning Channel; Turner Network TV; USA Network; WGN America.
Fee: $50.00 installation; $24.95 monthly.
Internet Service
Operational: No.
Miles of Plant: 5.0 (coaxial); None (fiber optic). Homes passed: 199.
Manager: John Metzler.
Ownership: Pine River Cable (MSO).

BRIDGEPORT TWP.—Charter Communications. Now served by SAGINAW, MI [MI0013]. ICA: MI0063.

BRIGHTON—Comcast Cable. Now served by ANN ARBOR, MI [MI0006]. ICA: MI0046.

BRONSON TWP. (portions)—Formerly served by CableDirect. No longer in operation. ICA: MI0329.

BROOKLYN (IRISH HILLS)—Comcast Cable. Now served by JACKSON, MI [MI0039]. ICA: MI0080.

BROOMFIELD VALLEY TRAILER PARK—Charter Communications, 2304 S Mission, Mount Pleasant, MI 48858. Phone: 989-775-6846. Fax: 989-772-0350. Web Site: http://www.charter.com. ICA: MI0275.
TV Market Ranking: Outside TV Markets (BROOMFIELD VALLEY TRAILER PARK). Franchise award date: N.A. Franchise expiration date: N.A. Began: N.A.
Channel capacity: 36 (not 2-way capable). Channels available but not in use: 16.
Basic Service
Subscribers: 55.
Programming (received off-air): WAQP (IND) Saginaw; WCMU-TV (PBS) Mount Pleasant; WJRT-TV (ABC) Flint; WNEM-TV (CBS, MNT) Bay City; WWTV (CBS) Cadillac.
Programming (via satellite): CNN; Discovery Channel; ESPN; Headline News; Spike TV; TBS Superstation; WGN America.
Fee: $30.00 installation; $19.95 monthly.
Pay Service 1
Pay Units: 42.
Programming (via satellite): Showtime; The Movie Channel.
Fee: $20.00 installation; $7.00 monthly (each).
Internet Service
Operational: No.

Telephone Service
None
Miles of Plant: 2.0 (coaxial); None (fiber optic). Homes passed: 1,342.
Vice President & General Manager: Dan Spoelman. Operations Manager: Ed Bucao.
Ownership: Charter Communications Inc. (MSO).

BROWN CITY—Comcast Cable, 1555 Bad Axe Rd, Bad Axe, MI 48413. Phone: 989-269-8927. Fax: 989-269-9125. Web Site: http://www.comcast.com. Also serves Marlette & Marlette Twp. ICA: MI0370.
TV Market Ranking: 61 (Marlette); Outside TV Markets (BROWN CITY, Marlette Twp.). Franchise award date: N.A. Franchise expiration date: N.A. Began: N.A.
Channel capacity: 47 (not 2-way capable). Channels available but not in use: None.
Basic Service
Subscribers: 682.
Programming (received off-air): WADL (IND) Mount Clemens; WDIV-TV (NBC) Detroit; WEYI-TV (CW, NBC) Saginaw; WFUM (PBS) Flint; WJBK (FOX) Detroit; WJRT-TV (ABC) Flint; WKBD-TV (CW) Detroit; WNEM-TV (CBS, MNT) Bay City; WSMH (FOX) Flint; WXYZ-TV (ABC) Detroit.
Programming (via satellite): QVC; TBS Superstation; WGN America.
Fee: $30.00 installation; $11.70 monthly; $2.25 converter.
Expanded Basic Service 1
Subscribers: N.A.
Programming (via satellite): ABC Family Channel; AMC; Arts & Entertainment; CNN; C-SPAN; Discovery Channel; Discovery Health Channel; Disney Channel; ESPN; ESPN 2; Fox Sports Net Detroit; Great American Country; HGTV; History Channel; Lifetime; MTV; Nickelodeon; QVC; Spike TV; Syfy; The Learning Channel; Turner Network TV; USA Network; Weather Channel.
Fee: $43.49 monthly.
Pay Service 1
Pay Units: 83.
Programming (via satellite): Cinemax; HBO; Showtime.
Fee: $10.95 monthly (each).
Internet Service
Operational: No.
Telephone Service
None
Miles of Plant: 32.0 (coaxial); None (fiber optic). Homes passed: 1,275.
General Manager: Thomas J. Lerash. Chief Technician: Marshall Kurschner. Business Manager: Susan McGathy.
Ownership: Comcast Cable Communications Inc. (MSO).

BRUTUS—Pine River Cable, PO Box 96, McBain, MI 49657. Phone: 888-244-2288. Fax: 231-825-0191. Web Site: http://www.pinerivercable.com. ICA: MI0444.
TV Market Ranking: Below 100 (BRUTUS).
Channel capacity: N.A. Channels available but not in use: N.A.
Basic Service
Subscribers: N.A.
Programming (received off-air): WCMV (PBS) Cadillac; WFQX-TV (FOX) Cadillac; WGTU (ABC, CW) Traverse City; WPBN-TV (NBC) Traverse City; WWTV (CBS) Cadillac.
Programming (via satellite): ABC Family Channel; Animal Planet; Arts & Entertainment; CNBC; CNN; Comedy Central; C-SPAN; C-SPAN 2; Discovery Channel; Disney Channel; ESPN; ESPN 2; Food Network; Fox News Channel; Fox Sports Net; FX; Golf Channel; Great American Country; Hallmark Channel; Headline News; HGTV; History Channel; Home Shopping Network; Lifetime; Nickelodeon; QVC; Spike TV; TBS Superstation; The Learning Channel; Trinity Broadcasting Network; Turner Classic Movies; Turner Network TV; TV Land; USA Network; Weather Channel; WGN America.
Pay Service 1
Pay Units: N.A.
Programming (via satellite): Encore (multiplexed); HBO (multiplexed); Showtime.
Internet Service
Operational: No.
Manager: John Metzler.
Ownership: Pine River Cable (MSO).

BURT—Charter Communications. Now served by SAGINAW, MI [MI0013]. ICA: MI0196.

BUTMAN TWP.—Charter Communications, 2074 M 32 W, Alpena, MI 49707. Phones: 231-947-5221 (Traverse City); 989-356-4503. Fax: 989-356-3761. Web Site: http://www.charter.com. Also serves Bourret Twp., Clement Twp. & Secord Twp. ICA: MI0114.
TV Market Ranking: Below 100 (Bourret Twp.); Outside TV Markets (BUTMAN TWP., Clement Twp., Secord Twp.). Franchise award date: September 8, 1988. Franchise expiration date: N.A. Began: June 1, 1990.
Channel capacity: 54 (not 2-way capable). Channels available but not in use: 14.
Basic Service
Subscribers: 1,983.
Programming (received off-air): WAQP (IND) Saginaw; WCMU-TV (PBS) Mount Pleasant; WEYI-TV (CW, NBC) Saginaw; WFQX-TV (FOX) Cadillac; WJRT-TV (ABC) Flint; WNEM-TV (CBS, MNT) Bay City; WSMH (FOX) Flint; WWTV (CBS) Cadillac.
Programming (via satellite): QVC; TBS Superstation.
Fee: $29.99 installation; $13.50 monthly; $1.00 converter.
Expanded Basic Service 1
Subscribers: 1,662.
Programming (via satellite): ABC Family Channel; Arts & Entertainment; CNN; C-SPAN; C-SPAN 2; Discovery Channel; Disney Channel; ESPN; Fox News Channel; Fox Sports Net Detroit; Headline News; HGTV; History Channel; Lifetime; MTV; Nickelodeon; Spike TV; Syfy; The Learning Channel; truTV; Turner Network TV; USA Network; VH1; Weather Channel.
Fee: $36.49 monthly.
Pay Service 1
Pay Units: 173.
Programming (via satellite): Cinemax.
Fee: $9.95 monthly.
Pay Service 2
Pay Units: 242.
Programming (via satellite): HBO.
Fee: $9.95 monthly.
Pay Service 3
Pay Units: 111.
Programming (via satellite): Showtime.
Fee: $9.95 monthly.
Internet Service
Operational: Yes.
Fee: $19.99 monthly.
Telephone Service
Digital: Operational
Fee: $14.99 monthly
Miles of Plant: 105.0 (coaxial); None (fiber optic). Homes passed: 3,393.
Vice President: Joe Boullion. General Manager: Ed Kavanaugh. Technical Operations Director: Rob Nowak. Marketing Manager: Brenda Auger.

Franchise fee: 3% of basic.
Ownership: Charter Communications Inc. (MSO).

CADILLAC—Charter Communications, 701 E South Airport Rd, Traverse City, MI 49686-4861. Phone: 231-947-5221. Fax: 231-947-2004. Web Site: http://www.charter.com. Also serves Cherry Grove Twp., Clam Lake Twp., Haring Twp. & Selma Twp. ICA: MI0082.
TV Market Ranking: Below 100 (CADILLAC, Cherry Grove Twp., Clam Lake Twp., Haring Twp., Selma Twp.). Franchise award date: January 1, 1979. Franchise expiration date: N.A. Began: December 1, 1966.
Channel capacity: N.A. Channels available but not in use: N.A.
Basic Service
Subscribers: 4,334.
Programming (received off-air): WCMV (PBS) Cadillac; WFQX-TV (FOX) Cadillac; WGTU (ABC, CW) Traverse City; WPBN-TV (NBC) Traverse City; WWTV (CBS) Cadillac.
Programming (via satellite): C-SPAN; Michigan Government Television; QVC; TBS Superstation; TV Guide Network; WGN America.
Current originations: Government Access; Educational Access; Public Access.
Fee: $29.99 installation; $13.50 monthly.
Expanded Basic Service 1
Subscribers: N.A.
Programming (via satellite): ABC Family Channel; AMC; Animal Planet; Arts & Entertainment; Bravo; Cartoon Network; CNBC; CNN; Comedy Central; Country Music TV; C-SPAN; C-SPAN 2; Discovery Channel; Disney Channel; E! Entertainment Television; ESPN; ESPN 2; ESPN Classic Sports; Eternal Word TV Network; Food Network; Fox News Channel; Fox Sports Net Detroit; FX; G4; Golf Channel; GSN; Hallmark Channel; HGTV; History Channel; Home Shopping Network; INSP; ION Television; Lifetime; MSNBC; MTV; National Geographic Channel; Nickelodeon; Oxygen; SoapNet; Speed Channel; Spike TV; Style Network; Syfy; The Learning Channel; Toon Disney; Travel Channel; Trinity Broadcasting Network; truTV; Turner Classic Movies; Turner Network TV; TV Land; USA Network; Versus; VH1; WE tv; Weather Channel.
Fee: $36.49 monthly.
Digital Basic Service
Subscribers: N.A.
Programming (via satellite): BBC America; Bio; Boomerang; Discovery Digital Networks; Discovery HD Theater; Do-It-Yourself; ESPN HD; Fox College Sports Atlantic; Fox College Sports Central; Fox College Sports Pacific; Fox Movie Channel; Fox Soccer; Fuel TV; GAS; HDNet; HDNet Movies; History Channel International; Independent Film Channel; Lifetime Movie Network; MTV Networks Digital Suite; Music Choice; NFL Network; Nick Jr.; Nick Too; NickToons TV; Outdoor Channel; Sundance Channel; TV Guide Network.
Digital Pay Service 1
Pay Units: N.A.
Programming (via satellite): Cinemax (multiplexed); Encore (multiplexed); Flix; HBO (multiplexed); HBO HD; Showtime (multiplexed); Showtime HD; Starz (multiplexed); The Movie Channel (multiplexed).
Video-On-Demand: Yes
Pay-Per-View
ESPN (delivered digitally); Playboy TV (delivered digitally); Spice Live (delivered digitally); Spice Platinum (delivered digitally); Hot Net Plus (delivered digitally); Spice Hot (delivered digitally); iN DEMAND (delivered digitally); NASCAR In Car (delivered digitally); NHL Center Ice (delivered digitally); MLB Extra Innings (delivered digitally).
Internet Service
Operational: Yes.
Broadband Service: Charter Pipeline.
Fee: $29.99 monthly.
Telephone Service
Digital: Operational
Fee: $29.99 monthly
Miles of Plant: 113.0 (coaxial); None (fiber optic). Homes passed: 7,346.
Vice President & General Manager: Joe Boullion. Technical Operations Director: Rob Nowak. Marketing Manager: Tammy Reicha.
City fee: 5% of gross.
Ownership: Charter Communications Inc. (MSO).

CAMBRIA TWP.—Formerly served by CableDirect. No longer in operation. ICA: MI0276.

CANADIAN LAKES—Charter Communications, 315 Davis St, Grand Haven, MI 49417-1830. Phone: 616-647-6201. Fax: 616-846-0797. Web Site: http://www.charter.com. Also serves Austin Twp. (Mecosta County), Chippewa Twp. (Mecosta County), Martiny Twp. (southern portion) & Morton Twp. ICA: MI0164.
TV Market Ranking: Outside TV Markets (Austin Twp. (Mecosta County), CANADIAN LAKES, Chippewa Twp. (Mecosta County), Martiny Twp. (southern portion), Morton Twp.). Franchise award date: January 1, 1987. Franchise expiration date: N.A. Began: March 1, 1988.
Channel capacity: 36 (not 2-way capable). Channels available but not in use: 6.
Basic Service
Subscribers: 1,250.
Programming (received off-air): WCMU-TV (PBS) Mount Pleasant; WFQX-TV (FOX) Cadillac; WPBN-TV (NBC) Traverse City; WWTV (CBS) Cadillac; WZZM (ABC) Grand Rapids.
Programming (via satellite): ABC Family Channel; AMC; Animal Planet; Arts & Entertainment; Cartoon Network; CNBC; CNN; C-SPAN; C-SPAN 2; Discovery Channel; Disney Channel; ESPN; Fox News Channel; Fox Sports Net Detroit; FX; Headline News; HGTV; Home Shopping Network; Lifetime; MoviePlex; MTV; Nickelodeon; QVC; Spike TV; TBS Superstation; The Learning Chan-

nel; truTV; Turner Network TV; USA Network; Weather Channel; WGN America.
Fee: $27.02 monthly.
Pay Service 1
Pay Units: 107.
Programming (via satellite): Cinemax; Encore; HBO; Starz.
Fee: $1.71 monthly (Encore), $6.75 monthly (Starz), $11.55 monthly (Cinemax), $12.14 monthly (HBO).
Video-On-Demand: No
Pay-Per-View
iN DEMAND.
Internet Service
Operational: Yes.
Fee: $19.99 monthly.
Telephone Service
None
Miles of Plant: 71.0 (coaxial); None (fiber optic). Homes passed: 1,972. Total homes in franchised area: 5,607.
Vice President & General Manager: Dan Spoelman. Technical Operations Manager: Keith Schierbeek. Marketing Director: Steve Schuh.
Ownership: Charter Communications Inc. (MSO).

CAPAC—Comcast Cable, 1555 Bad Axe Rd, Bad Axe, MI 48413. Phones: 989-269-8927; 800-772-7548. Fax: 989-269-9125. Web Site: http://www.comcast.com. ICA: MI0371.
TV Market Ranking: Below 100 (CAPAC). Franchise award date: N.A. Franchise expiration date: N.A. Began: N.A.
Channel capacity: 42 (not 2-way capable). Channels available but not in use: None.
Basic Service
Subscribers: 266.
Programming (received off-air): WADL (IND) Mount Clemens; WDIV-TV (NBC) Detroit; WJBK (FOX) Detroit; WKBD-TV (CW) Detroit; WMYD (MNT) Detroit; WTVS (PBS) Detroit; WWJ-TV (CBS) Detroit; WXYZ-TV (ABC) Detroit.
Programming (via satellite): C-SPAN; Discovery Health Channel; QVC; TBS Superstation; WGN America.
Fee: $14.50 monthly; $2.25 converter.
Expanded Basic Service 1
Subscribers: N.A.
Programming (via satellite): ABC Family Channel; AMC; Arts & Entertainment; CNN; Disney Channel; ESPN; ESPN 2; Fox Sports Net; Great American Country; Headline News; HGTV; History Channel; Lifetime; MTV; Nickelodeon; Spike TV; Syfy; The Learning Channel; Trinity Broadcasting Network; Turner Network TV; USA Network; Weather Channel.
Fee: $43.49 monthly.
Pay Service 1
Pay Units: N.A.
Programming (via satellite): Cinemax; HBO; Showtime.
Fee: $12.95 monthly (each).
Internet Service
Operational: No.
Telephone Service
None
Miles of Plant: 12.0 (coaxial); None (fiber optic). Homes passed: 680.
General Manager: Thomas J. Lerash. Chief Technician: Marshall Kurschner. Business Manager: Susan McGathy.
Ownership: Comcast Cable Communications Inc. (MSO).

CARO—Charter Communications. Now served by VASSAR, MI [MI0131]. ICA: MI0117.

CARSON CITY—Pine River Cable, PO Box 96, McBain, MI 49657. Phone: 888-244-2288. E-mail: info@pinerivercable.com. Web Site: http://www.pinerivercable.com. Also serves Bloomer Twp. ICA: MI0203.
TV Market Ranking: 92 (Bloomer Twp.); Outside TV Markets (CARSON CITY). Franchise award date: September 1, 1985. Franchise expiration date: N.A. Began: September 1, 1985.
Channel capacity: 46 (not 2-way capable). Channels available but not in use: N.A.
Basic Service
Subscribers: 387.
Programming (received off-air): WILX-TV (NBC) Onondaga; WJRT-TV (ABC) Flint; WKAR-TV (PBS) East Lansing; WLNS-TV (CBS) Lansing; WOOD-TV (NBC) Grand Rapids; WSYM-TV (FOX) Lansing; WWMT (CBS, CW) Kalamazoo; WXMI (FOX) Grand Rapids; WZPX-TV (ION) Battle Creek.
Programming (via satellite): ESPN; QVC; TBS Superstation; WGN America.
Fee: $50.00 installation; $33.49 monthly; $2.00 converter; $35.00 additional installation.
Expanded Basic Service 1
Subscribers: N.A.
Programming (via satellite): ABC Family Channel; AMC; Arts & Entertainment; CNBC; CNN; Comedy Central; Country Music TV; C-SPAN; Discovery Channel; Disney Channel; ESPN 2; Food Network; Fox Sports Net Detroit; Headline News; History Channel; Lifetime; MTV; Nickelodeon; Spike TV; The Learning Channel; Turner Network TV; USA Network; Weather Channel.
Fee: $45.99 monthly.
Pay Service 1
Pay Units: 158.
Programming (via satellite): HBO.
Fee: $11.00 installation; $11.95 monthly.
Pay Service 2
Pay Units: N.A.
Programming (via satellite): Cinemax; Starz.
Video-On-Demand: No
Internet Service
Operational: No.
Telephone Service
None
Miles of Plant: 4.0 (coaxial); None (fiber optic). Homes passed: 665.
Manager: John Metzler.
Ownership: Pine River Cable (MSO).

CASEVILLE—Comcast Cable. Now served by PIGEON, MI [MI0375]. ICA: MI0038.

CASPIAN—Caspian Community TV Corp., PO Box 240, Caspian, MI 49915-0240. Phones: 906-265-3551 (Chief technician); 906-265-4747. Fax: 906-265-6688. Also serves Gaastra & Stambaugh. ICA: MI0163.
TV Market Ranking: Below 100 (CASPIAN, Gaastra, Stambaugh). Franchise award date: January 1, 1955. Franchise expiration date: N.A. Began: June 1, 1955.
Channel capacity: 50 (not 2-way capable). Channels available but not in use: None.
Basic Service
Subscribers: 350.
Programming (received off-air): WFQX-TV (FOX) Cadillac; WJFW-TV (NBC) Rhinelander; WLUC-TV (NBC) Marquette; WNMU (PBS) Marquette; WSAW-TV (CBS, MNT) Wausau; WXYZ-TV (ABC) Detroit; allband FM.
Programming (via microwave): WJMN-TV (CBS) Escanaba; WLUK-TV (FOX) Green Bay.
Programming (via satellite): ABC Family Channel; Animal Planet; Arts & Entertainment; Cartoon Network; CNN; C-SPAN; CW+; Discovery Channel; ESPN; Eternal Word TV Network; Fox Sports Net Detroit; HGTV; History Channel; Lifetime; TBS Superstation; Turner Classic Movies; Turner Network TV; TV Land; USA Network; Weather Channel; WGN America.
Fee: $20.00 installation; $18.00 monthly.
Pay Service 1
Pay Units: 54.
Programming (via satellite): The Movie Channel.
Fee: $20.00 installation; $8.00 monthly.
Internet Service
Operational: No.
Telephone Service
None
Miles of Plant: 27.0 (coaxial); None (fiber optic). Homes passed: 1,530.
Manager: Victor Shepich. Chief Technician: Albert Melchiori.
Ownership: Caspian Community TV Corp.

CASS CITY—Charter Communications. Now served by VASSAR, MI [MI0131]. ICA: MI0179.

CASSOPOLIS—Comcast Cable, 7720 W 98th St, Hickory Hills, IL 60457. Phones: 708-237-3260; 574-259-2112 (Mishawaka office). Fax: 708-237-3292. Web Site: http://www.comcast.com. Also serves Calvin Twp., Dowagiac, Jefferson Twp. (Cass County), LaGrange, Penn Twp., Pokagon Twp. (portions), Silver Creek Twp. (portions), Vandalia (village) & Wayne Twp. ICA: MI0168.
TV Market Ranking: 37 (Calvin Twp., Dowagiac, Penn Twp., Pokagon Twp. (portions), Silver Creek Twp. (portions), Vandalia (village), Wayne Twp.); 37,80 (CASSOPOLIS, Jefferson Twp. (Cass County), LaGrange). Franchise award date: N.A. Franchise expiration date: N.A. Began: September 1, 1983.
Channel capacity: N.A. Channels available but not in use: N.A.
Basic Service
Subscribers: 800.
Programming (received off-air): WHME-TV (IND) South Bend; WNDU-TV (NBC) South Bend; WNIT (PBS) South Bend; WOOD-TV (NBC) Grand Rapids; WOTV (ABC) Battle Creek; WSBT-TV (CBS, IND) South Bend; WSJV (FOX) Elkhart; WWMT (CBS, CW) Kalamazoo.
Programming (via satellite): Discovery Channel; QVC; TBS Superstation; TV Guide Network; WGN America.
Current originations: Government Access; Public Access; Educational Access.
Fee: $48.99 installation; $18.49 monthly.
Expanded Basic Service 1
Subscribers: N.A.
Programming (via satellite): ABC Family Channel; AMC; Animal Planet; Arts & Entertainment; BET Networks; Big Ten Network; Cartoon Network; CNBC; CNN; Comedy Central; C-SPAN; Discovery Channel; Disney Channel; E! Entertainment Television; ESPN; ESPN 2; Food Network; Fox News Channel; Fox Sports Net Detroit; FX; Golf Channel; Headline News; HGTV; History Channel; Lifetime; MSNBC; MTV; Nickelodeon; Spike TV; The Learning Channel; Travel Channel; truTV; Turner Network TV; USA Network; Versus; VH1; Weather Channel.
Fee: $32.00 monthly.
Digital Basic Service
Subscribers: N.A.
Programming (received off-air): WBND-LP South Bend; WNIT (PBS) South Bend; WSBT-TV (CBS, IND) South Bend.
Programming (via satellite): ABC Family HD; Animal Planet HD; Arts & Entertainment HD; BBC America; Big Ten Network; Big Ten Network HD; Bio; Bio HD; Bloomberg Television; Bravo; Bravo HD; CBS College Sports Network; Cine Latino; Cine Mexicano; CMT Pure Country; CNBC HD+; CNN en Espanol; CNN HD; Cooking Channel; Country Music TV; C-SPAN 2; C-SPAN 3; Current; Discovery Channel HD; Discovery en Espanol; Discovery HD Theater; Discovery Health Channel; Discovery Kids Channel; Discovery Military Channel; Discovery Planet Green; Disney Channel HD; Disney XD; Disney XD HD; Do-It-Yourself; Encore (multiplexed); ESPN 2 HD; ESPN Classic Sports; ESPN Deportes; ESPN HD; ESPNews; ESPNews HD; Food Network HD; Fox Business Channel; Fox Business Channel HD; Fox College Sports Atlantic; Fox College Sports Central; Fox College Sports Pacific; Fox Movie Channel; Fox News HD; Fox Reality Channel; Fox Soccer; Fox Sports en Espanol; FSN HD; Fuse; FX HD; G4; Golf Channel HD; Gospel Music Channel; Great American Country; GSN; Hallmark Channel; Hallmark Movie Channel; Hallmark Movie Channel HD; HGTV HD; History Channel en Espanol; History Channel HD; History Channel International; ID Investigation Discovery; Independent Film Channel; ION Life; ION Television; Jewelry Television; Lifetime Movie Network; Lifetime Movie Network HD; MLB Network; MoviePlex; MTV Hits; MTV Jams; MTV Tres; MTV2; mun2 television; Music Choice; National Geographic Channel; National Geographic Channel HD Network; NBA TV; NFL Network; NFL Network HD; Nick Jr.; Nick Too; NickToons TV; Outdoor Channel; Ovation; Oxygen; Palladia; PBS Kids Sprout; Qubo; QVC HD; Science Channel; Science Channel HD; ShopNBC; SoapNet; Speed Channel; Speed HD; Starz IndiePlex; Starz RetroPlex; Style Network; Sundance Channel; Syfy; Syfy HD; TBS in HD; TeenNick; Tennis Channel; The Sportsman Channel; The Word Network; TLC HD; Trinity Broadcasting Network; Turner Classic Movies; Turner Network TV HD; TV Land; TV One; Universal HD; USA Network HD; VeneMovies; Versus HD; VH1 Classic; VH1 Soul; WE tv.
Fee: $11.99 monthly.
Digital Pay Service 1
Pay Units: N.A.
Programming (via satellite): Cinemax (multiplexed); Cinemax HD; Flix; HBO (multiplexed); HBO HD; Playboy TV; Showtime (multiplexed); Showtime HD; Starz (multiplexed); Starz HDTV; The Movie Channel (multiplexed).
Fee: $16.99 monthly (each).
Video-On-Demand: Yes
Pay-Per-View
ESPN (delivered digitally); Sports PPV (delivered digitally); iN DEMAND (delivered digitally); Penthouse TV (delivered digitally); Fresh (delivered digitally); Spice: Xcess (delivered digitally); Playboy TV (delivered digitally); Club Jenna (delivered digitally).
Internet Service
Operational: Yes.
Broadband Service: Comcast High Speed Internet.
Fee: $42.95 monthly.

Telephone Service
Digital: Operational
Miles of Plant: 22.0 (coaxial); None (fiber optic). Homes passed: 1,495. Total homes in franchised area: 1,643.
Area Vice President: Sandy Weicher. Vice President, Technical Operations: Bob Curtis. Vice President, Marketing & Sales: Eric Schaefer. Vice President, Communications: Rich Ruggiero. Technical Operations Manager: John Collucci. Marketing Director: Ron Knutson.
Ownership: Comcast Cable Communications Inc. (MSO).

CHAMPION TWP.—Upper Peninsula Communications, 397 N US Hwy 41, Carney, MI 49812-9757. Phone: 906-639-2194. Fax: 906-639-9936. E-mail: louied@alphacomm.net. Also serves Humboldt Twp. ICA: MI0278.
TV Market Ranking: Below 100 (CHAMPION TWP., Humboldt Twp.). Franchise award date: N.A. Franchise expiration date: N.A. Began: August 1, 1990.
Channel capacity: 40 (not 2-way capable). Channels available but not in use: 20.
Basic Service
Subscribers: N.A.
Programming (received off-air): WBKP (ABC) Calumet; WJMN-TV (CBS) Escanaba; WLUC-TV (NBC) Marquette; WNMU (PBS) Marquette; WSEE-TV (CBS, CW) Erie; WZMQ (IND, MNT) Marquette.
Programming (via satellite): ABC Family Channel; AMC; Arts & Entertainment; CNN; C-SPAN; Discovery Channel; Disney Channel; ESPN; ESPN 2; Headline News; HGTV; History Channel; ION Television; Lifetime; Outdoor Channel; Spike TV; TBS Superstation; The Learning Channel; Trinity Broadcasting Network; Turner Classic Movies; Turner Network TV; TV Land; USA Network; Weather Channel; WGN America.
Fee: $50.00 installation; $24.95 monthly.
Pay Service 1
Pay Units: N.A.
Programming (via satellite): Showtime.
Video-On-Demand: No
Internet Service
Operational: No.
Telephone Service
None
Miles of Plant: 12.0 (coaxial); None (fiber optic). Homes passed: 249.
Manager & Chief Technician: Louis Dupont.
Ownership: Upper Peninsula Communications Inc. (MSO).

CHARLEVOIX—Charter Communications. Now served by TRAVERSE CITY, MI [MI0026]. ICA: MI0115.

CHEBOYGAN—Charter Communications, 701 E South Airport Rd, Traverse City, MI 49686-4861. Phone: 231-947-5221. Fax: 231-947-2004. Web Site: http://www.charter.com. Also serves Aloha Twp., Beaugrand Twp., Benton Twp. (Cheboygan County), Inverness Twp. & Mullet Lake. ICA: MI0101.
TV Market Ranking: Below 100 (Aloha Twp., Beaugrand Twp., Benton Twp. (Cheboygan County), CHEBOYGAN, Inverness Twp., Mullet Lake). Franchise award date: N.A. Franchise expiration date: N.A. Began: October 1, 1968.
Channel capacity: 43 (not 2-way capable). Channels available but not in use: N.A.
Basic Service
Subscribers: 2,473.
Programming (received off-air): WCML (PBS) Alpena; WFQX-TV (FOX) Cadillac; WGTQ (ABC) Sault Ste. Marie; WTOM-TV (NBC) Cheboygan; WWUP-TV (CBS, FOX) Sault Ste. Marie.
Programming (via satellite): C-SPAN; C-SPAN 2; Home Shopping Network; INSP; QVC; TBS Superstation; TV Guide Network; WGN America.
Current originations: Educational Access.
Fee: $29.99 installation; $13.50 monthly; $1.60 converter.
Expanded Basic Service 1
Subscribers: 2,241.
Programming (via satellite): ABC Family Channel; AMC; Animal Planet; Arts & Entertainment; Cartoon Network; CNN; Country Music TV; CW+; Discovery Channel; Disney Channel; E! Entertainment Television; ESPN; ESPN 2; FitTV; Fox News Channel; Fox Sports Net Detroit; FX; Hallmark Channel; Headline News; HGTV; MTV; Nickelodeon; Spike TV; The Learning Channel; Turner Network TV; USA Network; Weather Channel.
Fee: $36.49 monthly.
Digital Basic Service
Subscribers: N.A.
Programming (via satellite): Music Choice.
Digital Pay Service 1
Pay Units: N.A.
Programming (via satellite): Cinemax (multiplexed); Encore (multiplexed); Flix; HBO (multiplexed); Showtime (multiplexed); Starz (multiplexed); The Movie Channel (multiplexed).
Pay-Per-View
iN DEMAND (delivered digitally); Hot Choice (delivered digitally).
Internet Service
Operational: Yes.
Fee: $19.99 monthly.
Telephone Service
Digital: Operational
Fee: $14.99 monthly
Miles of Plant: 112.0 (coaxial); None (fiber optic). Homes passed: 3,687. Total homes in franchised area: 7,131.
Vice President & General Manager: Joe Boullion. Technical Operations Director: Rob Nowak. Marketing Manager: Tammy Reicha.
City fee: 2% of gross.
Ownership: Charter Communications Inc. (MSO).

CHESANING—Charter Communications, 7372 Davison Rd, Davison, MI 48423. Phone: 810-652-1400. Web Site: http://www.charter.com. Also serves Brady Twp. (Saginaw County) & Oakley (village). ICA: MI0160.
TV Market Ranking: 61 (Brady Twp. (Saginaw County), CHESANING, Oakley (village)). Franchise award date: N.A. Franchise expiration date: N.A. Began: January 1, 1982.
Channel capacity: N.A. Channels available but not in use: N.A.
Basic Service
Subscribers: 973.
Programming (received off-air): WAQP (IND) Saginaw; WBSF (CW) Bay City; WDCQ-TV (PBS) Bad Axe; WEYI-TV (CW, NBC) Saginaw; WFUM (PBS) Flint; WJRT-TV (ABC) Flint; WKAR-TV (PBS) East Lansing; WNEM-TV (CBS, MNT) Bay City; WSMH (FOX) Flint.
Programming (via satellite): C-SPAN; C-SPAN 2; Eternal Word TV Network; G4; Home Shopping Network; INSP; MyNetworkTV Inc.; QVC; TBS Superstation; TV Guide Network; Univision; WGN America.

Current originations: Leased Access; Public Access.
Fee: $29.99 installation; $13.50 monthly; $3.50 converter.
Expanded Basic Service 1
Subscribers: 927.
Programming (via satellite): ABC Family Channel; AMC; Animal Planet; Arts & Entertainment; BET Networks; Bravo; Cartoon Network; CNBC; CNN; Comedy Central; Country Music TV; Discovery Channel; Disney Channel; E! Entertainment Television; ESPN; ESPN 2; Food Network; Fox News Channel; Fox Sports Net Detroit; FX; Golf Channel; GSN; Hallmark Channel; Headline News; HGTV; History Channel; Lifetime; MSNBC; MTV; MTV2; National Geographic Channel; Nickelodeon; Outdoor Channel; Oxygen; SoapNet; Speed Channel; Spike TV; Style Network; Syfy; Telemundo; The Learning Channel; Toon Disney; Travel Channel; truTV; Turner Classic Movies; Turner Network TV; TV Land; USA Network; Versus; VH1; WE tv; Weather Channel.
Fee: $36.49 monthly.
Digital Basic Service
Subscribers: N.A.
Programming (received off-air): WDCQ-TV (PBS) Bad Axe; WJRT-TV (ABC) Flint; WNEM-TV (CBS, MNT) Bay City; WSMH (FOX) Flint.
Programming (via satellite): BBC America; Bio; CMT Pure Country; Discovery Digital Networks; Discovery HD Theater; Do-It-Yourself; Do-It-Yourself On Demand; ESPN Classic Sports; ESPN HD; ESPNews; Food Network On Demand; Fox College Sports Atlantic; Fox College Sports Central; Fox College Sports Pacific; Fox Movie Channel; Fox Soccer; Fuel TV; Fuse; GAS; HDNet; HDNet Movies; HGTV On Demand; History Channel International; Howard TV; Independent Film Channel; Lifetime Movie Network; MTV Networks Digital Suite; Music Choice; Nick Jr.; Nick Too; NickToons TV; Sundance Channel; Turner Network TV HD; Universal HD; WEYI-TV (CW, NBC) Saginaw.
Digital Pay Service 1
Pay Units: N.A.
Programming (via satellite): Cinemax (multiplexed); Cinemax HD; Cinemax On Demand; Encore (multiplexed); Flix; HBO (multiplexed); HBO HD; HBO On Demand; LOGO; Showtime (multiplexed); Showtime HD; Showtime On Demand; Starz (multiplexed); Starz On Demand; The Movie Channel (multiplexed).
Video-On-Demand: Yes
Pay-Per-View
iN DEMAND (delivered digitally); ESPN (delivered digitally); NHL Center Ice (delivered digitally); MLB Extra Innings (delivered digitally); Playboy TV (delivered digitally); Fresh (delivered digitally); Shorteez (delivered digitally).
Internet Service
Operational: Yes.
Broadband Service: Charter Pipeline.
Fee: $29.99 monthly.
Telephone Service
Digital: Operational
Miles of Plant: 45.0 (coaxial); None (fiber optic). Homes passed: 1,955. Total homes in franchised area: 2,184.
Vice President & General Manager: Dave Slowick. Technical Operations Director: Lloyd Collins. Marketing Director: Lisa Gayari.
Ownership: Charter Communications Inc.

CHESTER TWP. (Ottawa County)—Charter Communications, 315 Davis St, Grand Haven, MI 49417-1830. Phone: 616-647-6201. Fax: 616-846-0797. Web Site: http://www.charter.com. Also serves Ravenna. ICA: MI0280.
TV Market Ranking: 37 (CHESTER TWP., Ravenna). Franchise award date: N.A. Franchise expiration date: N.A. Began: July 1, 1991.
Channel capacity: 60 (not 2-way capable). Channels available but not in use: 40.
Basic Service
Subscribers: 580.
Programming (received off-air): WGVU-TV (PBS) Grand Rapids; WOOD-TV (NBC) Grand Rapids; WTLJ (IND) Muskegon; WWMT (CBS, CW) Kalamazoo; WXMI (FOX) Grand Rapids; WZZM (ABC) Grand Rapids.
Programming (via satellite): Country Music TV; C-SPAN; QVC; TBS Superstation; WGN America.
Fee: $36.00 installation; $33.49 monthly.
Expanded Basic Service 1
Subscribers: N.A.
Programming (via satellite): ABC Family Channel; AMC; Arts & Entertainment; CNBC; CNN; Comedy Central; Discovery Channel; Disney Channel; ESPN; ESPN 2; Food Network; Fox Sports Net Detroit; Headline News; History Channel; Lifetime; MTV; Nickelodeon; Spike TV; The Learning Channel; Turner Network TV; USA Network; VH1; Weather Channel.
Fee: $45.99 monthly.
Pay Service 1
Pay Units: 191.
Programming (via satellite): Cinemax (multiplexed); Encore; HBO; Showtime; Starz.
Fee: $6.95 monthly (Starz or Encore), $10.95 monthly (Cinemax), $11.95 monthly (HBO), $12.95 monthly (Showtime).
Internet Service
Operational: No.
Telephone Service
None
Homes passed: 873.
Vice President, Operations: Dan Spoelman. Technical Operations Supervisor: Keith Schierbeek. Marketing Director: Steve Schuh. Marketing Coordinator: Tracy Bruce.
Ownership: Charter Communications Inc. (MSO).

CHESTERFIELD—Comcast Cable, 29777 Telegraph Rd, Ste 4400B, Southfield, MI 48034. Phones: 586-883-7000 (Sterling Heights office); 248-233-4712. Fax:

248-233-4719. Web Site: http://www.comcast.com. Also serves Algonac, Armada (village), Armada Twp., Brittany Park, Bruce Twp. (Macomb County), Burtchville Twp., Casco Twp. (St. Clair County), Chesterfield Twp., China Twp., Clay Twp., Clyde Twp. (St. Clair County), Columbus Twp. (St. Clair County), Cottrellville Twp., East China Twp., Fort Gratiot Twp., Harrison Twp., Harsen's Island, Ira Twp., Kimball Twp., Lenox Twp., Marine City, Marysville, Memphis, Metro Towers, New Baltimore, New Haven, New Haven (village), Pinewood Creek, Port Huron, Port Huron Twp., Quail Run, Ray Twp., Richmond, Richmond Twp. (Macomb County), Riley Twp., Romeo, Selfridge AFB, St. Clair, St. Clair Twp. & Washington Twp. (Macomb County). ICA: MI0016.

TV Market Ranking: 5 (Algonac, Armada (village), Armada Twp., Brittany Park, Bruce Twp. (Macomb County), Casco Twp. (St. Clair County), CHESTERFIELD TWP., Chesterfield Twp., Clay Twp., Cottrellville Twp., Harrison Twp., Harsen's Island, Ira Twp., Lenox Twp., Metro Towers, New Baltimore, New Haven, New Haven (village), Ray Twp., Richmond, Richmond Twp. (Macomb County), Romeo, Selfridge AFB, Washington Twp. (Macomb County)); Below 100 (China Twp., Clyde Twp. (St. Clair County), Columbus Twp. (St. Clair County), East China Twp., Kimball Twp., Marine City, Marysville, Memphis, Pinewood Creek, Quail Run, Riley Twp., St. Clair, St. Clair Twp., Richmond Twp. (Macomb County)); Outside TV Markets (Burtchville Twp., Fort Gratiot Twp., Port Huron, Port Huron Twp.). Franchise award date: N.A. Franchise expiration date: N.A. Began: December 1, 1981.

Channel capacity: N.A. Channels available but not in use: N.A.

Basic Service

Subscribers: 61,683.

Programming (received off-air): WADL (IND) Mount Clemens; WDIV-TV (NBC) Detroit; WJBK (FOX) Detroit; WKBD-TV (CW) Detroit; WMYD (MNT) Detroit; WPXD-TV (ION) Ann Arbor; WTVS (PBS) Detroit; WWJ-TV (CBS) Detroit; WXYZ-TV (ABC) Detroit; allband FM.

Programming (via satellite): ABC Family Channel; AMC; Animal Planet; Arts & Entertainment; BET Networks; Big Ten Network; Bravo; Cartoon Network; CNBC; CNN; Comedy Central; C-SPAN; Discovery Channel; Discovery Health Channel; Disney Channel; E! Entertainment Television; ESPN; ESPN 2; Food Network; Fox News Channel; Fox Sports Net Detroit; FX; Golf Channel; Great American Country; Headline News; HGTV; History Channel; Home Shopping Network; Lifetime; MSNBC; MTV; Nickelodeon; QVC; Speed Channel; Spike TV; Style Network; Syfy; TBS Superstation; The Learning Channel; Travel Channel; truTV; Turner Classic Movies; Turner Network TV; TV Land; Univision; USA Network; various Canadian stations; Versus; VH1; Weather Channel; WGN America.

Current originations: Religious Access; Educational Access; Public Access.

Fee: $30.00 installation; $7.00 monthly.

Digital Basic Service

Subscribers: 15,360.

Programming (received off-air): WDIV-TV (NBC) Detroit; WJBK (FOX) Detroit; WKBD-TV (CW) Detroit; WMYD (MNT) Detroit; WTVS (PBS) Detroit; WWJ-TV (CBS) Detroit; WXYZ-TV (ABC) Detroit.

Programming (via satellite): ABC Family HD; Animal Planet HD; ART America; Arts & Entertainment HD; BBC America; Big Ten Network; Bio; Bloomberg Television; Bridges TV; Canal 52MX; Cine Latino; Cine Mexicano; CMT Pure Country; CNN en Espanol; CNN HD; College Sports Television; Cooking Channel; Country Music TV; C-SPAN 2; C-SPAN 3; Current; Daystar TV Network; Discovery Channel HD; Discovery en Espanol; Discovery HD Theater; Discovery Kids Channel; Discovery Military Channel; Discovery Planet Green; Disney Channel HD; Disney XD; Disney XD en Espanol; Do-It-Yourself; Encore (multiplexed); ESPN 2 HD; ESPN Classic Sports; ESPN Deportes; ESPN HD; ESPNews; Eternal Word TV Network; Flix; Food Network HD; Fox Business Channel; Fox College Sports Atlantic; Fox College Sports Central; Fox College Sports Pacific; Fox Reality Channel; Fox Soccer; Fox Sports en Espanol; FSN HD; Fuse; G4; Gol TV; Gospel Music Channel; GSN; Hallmark Channel; HGTV HD; History Channel en Espanol; History Channel HD; History Channel International; ID Investigation Discovery; INSP; Jewelry Television; Lifetime Movie Network; LOGO; Michigan Government Television; Mojo HD; MoviePlex; MTV Hits; MTV Jams; MTV Tres; MTV2; Music Choice; National Geographic Channel; National Geographic Channel HD Network; NBA TV; NFL Network; NFL Network HD; NHL Network; Nick Jr.; Nick Too; NickToons TV; Outdoor Channel; Oxygen; PBS Kids Sprout; Playboy TV; RAI USA; Science Channel; Science Channel HD; ShopNBC; SoapNet; Starz IndiePlex; Starz RetroPlex; Sundance Channel; Syfy HD; TBS in HD; TeenNick; Tennis Channel; The Comcast Network; The Sportsman Channel; The Word Network; TLC HD; Trinity Broadcasting Network; Turner Network TV HD; TV Asia; TV Japan; TV One; Universal HD; USA Network HD; VeneMovies; VH1 Classic; VH1 Soul; WE tv; Weatherscan; Zee TV USA.

Fee: $14.95 monthly.

Digital Pay Service 1

Pay Units: 4,000.

Programming (via satellite): Cinemax (multiplexed); Cinemax HD; HBO (multiplexed); HBO HD; Showtime (multiplexed); Showtime HD; Starz (multiplexed); Starz HDTV; The Movie Channel (multiplexed).

Fee: $9.95 monthly (each).

Video-On-Demand: Yes

Pay-Per-View

Addressable homes: 52,000.

iN DEMAND, Addressable: Yes; ESPN Extra (delivered digitally); ESPN Now (delivered digitally); Hot Choice (delivered digitally); iN DEMAND (delivered digitally); Playboy TV (delivered digitally); Pleasure (delivered digitally); Fresh (delivered digitally); Shorteez (delivered digitally).

Internet Service

Operational: Yes.

Subscribers: 6,847.

Broadband Service: Comcast High Speed Internet.

Fee: $99.00 installation; $42.95 monthly; $10.00 modem lease; $199.00 modem purchase.

Telephone Service

Digital: Operational

Fee: $44.95 monthly

Miles of Plant: 1,900.0 (coaxial); None (fiber optic). Homes passed: 110,800. Total homes in franchised area: 110,800.

Area Vice President: Mike Casillo. Vice President, Technical Operations: Steve Thomas. Vice President, Marketing: Tony Lent. Vice President, Communications: Jerome Espy.

Ownership: Comcast Cable Communications Inc. (MSO).

CHIPPEWA TWP. (Isabella County)—Charter Communications, 2304 S Mission, Mount Pleasant, MI 48858. Phone: 989-775-6846. Fax: 989-772-0350. Web Site: http://www.charter.com. Also serves Denver Twp. (Isabella County), Geneva Twp. (Midland County) & Greendale Twp. ICA: MI0156.

TV Market Ranking: 61 (Geneva Twp. (Midland County), Greendale Twp.); Below 100 (CHIPPEWA TWP., Denver Twp. (Isabella County)); Outside TV Markets (Denver Twp. (Isabella County)). Franchise award date: August 1, 1988. Franchise expiration date: N.A. Began: October 1, 1988.

Channel capacity: N.A. Channels available but not in use: N.A.

Basic Service

Subscribers: 1,118.

Programming (received off-air): WAQP (IND) Saginaw; WCMU-TV (PBS) Mount Pleasant; WDCQ-TV (PBS) Bad Axe; WEYI-TV (CW, NBC) Saginaw; WFQX-TV (FOX) Cadillac; WJRT-TV (ABC) Flint; WNEM-TV (CBS, MNT) Bay City; WSMH (FOX) Flint; WWTV (CBS) Cadillac.

Programming (via satellite): C-SPAN; C-SPAN 2; CW+; Eternal Word TV Network; Home Shopping Network; MyNetworkTV Inc.; QVC; TBS Superstation; TV Guide Network; Univision; various Canadian stations; WGN America.

Current originations: Religious Access; Government Access; Educational Access; Public Access.

Fee: $38.77 installation; $8.42 monthly; $1.00 converter.

Expanded Basic Service 1

Subscribers: 1,078.

Programming (via satellite): ABC Family Channel; AMC; Animal Planet; Arts & Entertainment; BET Networks; Bravo; Cartoon Network; CNBC; CNN; Comedy Central; Country Music TV; Discovery Channel; Disney Channel; E! Entertainment Television; ESPN; ESPN 2; Food Network; Fox News Channel; Fox Sports Net Detroit; FX; G4; Golf Channel; GSN; Hallmark Channel; Headline News; HGTV; History Channel; Lifetime; MSNBC; MTV; MTV2; National Geographic Channel; Nickelodeon; Oxygen; SoapNet; Speed Channel; Spike TV; Syfy; Telemundo; The Learning Channel; Toon Disney; Travel Channel; truTV; Turner Classic Movies; Turner Network TV; TV Land; USA Network; Versus; VH1; Weather Channel.

Fee: $14.52 monthly.

Digital Basic Service

Subscribers: N.A.

Programming (received off-air): WEYI-TV (CW, NBC) Saginaw; WJRT-TV (ABC) Flint; WNEM-TV (CBS, MNT) Bay City; WSMH (FOX) Flint.

Programming (via satellite): BBC America; Bio; CMT Pure Country; Discovery Digital Networks; Discovery HD Theater; Do-It-Yourself; ESPN 2 HD; ESPN Classic Sports; ESPN HD; ESPN U; ESPNews; Food Network On Demand; Fox Business Channel; Fox College Sports Atlantic; Fox College Sports Central; Fox College Sports Pacific; Fox Movie Channel; Fox Soccer; Fuel TV; Fuse; GAS; Great American Country; HDNet; HDNet Movies; HGTV On Demand; History Channel International; Howard TV; Independent Film Channel; Lifetime Movie Network; MTV Networks Digital Suite; Music Choice; Nick Jr.; Nick Too; NickToons TV; Outdoor Channel; ReelzChannel; Starz (multiplexed); Style Network; Sundance Channel; The Sportsman Channel; Turner Network TV HD; TV Guide SPOT; Universal HD; WE tv.

Digital Pay Service 1

Pay Units: N.A.

Programming (via satellite): Cinemax (multiplexed); Cinemax HD; Cinemax On Demand; Encore (multiplexed); Flix; HBO (multiplexed); HBO HD; HBO On Demand; LOGO; Showtime (multiplexed); Showtime HD; Showtime On Demand; Starz HDTV; Starz On Demand; The Movie Channel (multiplexed); The Movie Channel On Demand.

Video-On-Demand: Yes

Pay-Per-View

Movies & Events (delivered digitally); ESPN (delivered digitally); NHL Center Ice (delivered digitally); MLB Extra Innings (delivered digitally); Playboy TV (delivered digitally); Fresh (delivered digitally); Shorteez (delivered digitally).

Internet Service

Operational: Yes.

Broadband Service: Charter Pipeline.

Fee: $29.99 monthly.

Telephone Service

Digital: Operational

Miles of Plant: 75.0 (coaxial); None (fiber optic). Homes passed: 1,824.

Vice President & General Manager: Dan Spoelman. Operations Manager: Ed Bucao. Technology Supervisor: Jason Hannah.

Franchise fee: 3% of gross.

Ownership: Charter Communications Inc. (MSO).

CLARE—Charter Communications. Now served by MOUNT PLEASANT, MI [MI0069]. ICA: MI0355.

CLARK TWP.—Formerly served by Northwoods Cable Inc. No longer in operation. ICA: MI0282.

CLARKSTON—Comcast Cable. Now served by PONTIAC, MI [MI0017]. ICA: MI0283.

CLEON TWP.—Ace Communications Group of Michigan. Formerly served by Thompsonville, MI [MI0230]. This cable system has converted to IPTV, PO Box 69, 5351 N M-37, Houston, MI 49668-0069. Phone: 800-361-8178. Fax: 231-885-9915. E-mail: miinfo@acegroup.cc. Web Site: http://www.acegroup.cc. ICA: MI5024.

TV Market Ranking: Below 100 (Cleon Twp.).

Channel capacity: N.A. Channels available but not in use: N.A.

Video-On-Demand: Yes

Internet Service
Operational: Yes.
Fee: $50.00 installation; $29.95 monthly.
Telephone Service
Digital: Operational
Fee: $21.05 monthly
Chief Executive Officer: Todd Roesler.
Ownership: Ace Communications Group.

CLIMAX TWP.—Climax Telephone Co., 110 N Main St, Climax, MI 49034-9637. Phones: 800-627-5287; 269-746-4411. Fax: 269-746-9914. E-mail: info@ctstelecom.com. Web Site: http://www.ctstelecom.com. Also serves Charleston Twp. (portions), Comstock Twp. (portions), Pavilion Twp. (portions) & Scotts. ICA: MI0285.
TV Market Ranking: 37 (Charleston Twp. (portions), CLIMAX TWP., Comstock Twp. (portions), Pavilion Twp. (portions), Scotts). Franchise award date: N.A. Franchise expiration date: N.A. Began: June 1, 1985.
Channel capacity: 60 (not 2-way capable). Channels available but not in use: 24.
Basic Service
Subscribers: 456.
Programming (received off-air): WGVU-TV (PBS) Grand Rapids; WLLA (IND) Kalamazoo; WOOD-TV (NBC) Grand Rapids; WOTV (ABC) Battle Creek; WTLJ (IND) Muskegon; WWMT (CBS, CW) Kalamazoo; WXMI (FOX) Grand Rapids.
Programming (via satellite): ABC Family Channel; Arts & Entertainment; CNN; Disney Channel; Fox Sports Net Detroit; FX; Home Shopping Network; MTV; Nickelodeon; The Learning Channel; WGN America.
Fee: $15.00 installation; $17.48 monthly.
Expanded Basic Service 1
Subscribers: N.A.
Programming (via satellite): AMC; CNBC; Discovery Channel; ESPN; Food Network; Headline News; HGTV; History Channel; Spike TV; TBS Superstation; Toon Disney; Turner Network TV; USA Network; VH1; Weather Channel.
Fee: $14.71 monthly.
Pay Service 1
Pay Units: 96.
Programming (via satellite): HBO.
Fee: $12.95 monthly.
Pay Service 2
Pay Units: 71.
Programming (via satellite): Showtime.
Fee: $11.95 monthly.
Video-On-Demand: No
Internet Service
Operational: No, DSL only.
Telephone Service
None
Miles of Plant: 6.0 (coaxial); 6.0 (fiber optic). Additional miles planned: 13.0 (coaxial). Homes passed: 800.
Manager: Bob Stewart. Sales Manager: Joe Vernon. Office Manager: Barb Payne.
Ownership: Climax Telephone Co.

COLDWATER—Charter Communications, 7372 Davison Rd, Coldwater, MI 48423. Phone: 810-652-1400. Web Site: http://www.charter.com. Also serves Algansee Twp., Batavia Twp., Bethel Twp., Bronson, Burlington (village), Burr Oak, Colon, Fawn River Twp., Fredonia Twp., Girard Twp., Kinderhook Twp., Litchfield, Ovid Twp., Quincy, Reading, Sturgis, Tekonsha & White Pigeon Twp. (eastern portion). ICA: MI0032.
TV Market Ranking: 37 (Batavia Twp., Bethel Twp., Bronson, Burlington (village), Burr Oak, COLDWATER, Colon, Girard Twp., Ovid Twp., Quincy); 37,80 (Fawn River Twp., Sturgis, Sturgis Twp., White Pigeon Twp. (eastern portion)); 37,92 (Fredonia Twp., Litchfield, Tekonsha); Below 100 (Reading); Outside TV Markets (Algansee Twp., Kinderhook Twp.). Franchise award date: N.A. Franchise expiration date: N.A. Began: July 1, 1966.
Channel capacity: N.A. Channels available but not in use: N.A.
Basic Service
Subscribers: N.A.
Programming (received off-air): WILX-TV (NBC) Onondaga; WKAR-TV (PBS) East Lansing; WLLA (IND) Kalamazoo; WLNS-TV (CBS) Lansing; WOOD-TV (NBC) Grand Rapids; WOTV (ABC) Battle Creek; WSYM-TV (FOX) Lansing; WTLJ (IND) Muskegon; WWMT (CBS, CW) Kalamazoo; WXMI (FOX) Grand Rapids; WXSP-CA (MNT) Grand Rapids; WZPX-TV (ION) Battle Creek.
Programming (via satellite): Eternal Word TV Network; Home Shopping Network; QVC; Toon Disney; TV Guide Network; WGN America.
Current originations: Leased Access; Government Access; Public Access; Educational Access.
Fee: $29.99 installation; $2.50 converter.
Expanded Basic Service 1
Subscribers: N.A.
Programming (via satellite): ABC Family Channel; AMC; AmericanLife TV Network; Animal Planet; Arts & Entertainment; Bravo; Cartoon Network; CNBC; CNN; Comedy Central; Country Music TV; C-SPAN; Discovery Channel; Disney Channel; E! Entertainment Television; ESPN; ESPN 2; ESPN Classic Sports; FitTV; Food Network; Fox News Channel; Fox Sports Net Detroit; FX; G4; Golf Channel; GSN; Hallmark Channel; Headline News; HGTV; History Channel; Lifetime; MSNBC; MTV; National Geographic Channel; Nickelodeon; Oxygen; SoapNet; Speed Channel; Spike TV; Syfy; TBS Superstation; Telemundo; The Learning Channel; Travel Channel; truTV; Turner Classic Movies; Turner Network TV; TV Land; Univision; USA Network; Versus; VH1; WE tv; Weather Channel.
Fee: $47.99 monthly.
Digital Basic Service
Subscribers: N.A.
Programming (via satellite): BBC America; Bio; Bloomberg Television; Discovery Digital Networks; Fox Movie Channel; Fox Sports World; Fuse; GAS; Halogen Network; History Channel International; Independent Film Channel; Lifetime Movie Network; MTV2; Music Choice; Nick Jr.; NickToons TV; TV Guide Interactive Inc.; VH1 Classic; VH1 Country.
Digital Pay Service 1
Pay Units: 6,650.
Programming (via satellite): Cinemax (multiplexed); Encore (multiplexed); HBO (multiplexed); Showtime (multiplexed); Starz (multiplexed); The Movie Channel (multiplexed).
Fee: $25.00 installation.
Video-On-Demand: Yes
Pay-Per-View
iN DEMAND (delivered digitally); Playboy TV (delivered digitally); Fresh (delivered digitally).
Internet Service
Operational: Yes.
Broadband Service: Charter Pipeline.
Fee: $29.99 monthly.
Telephone Service
Digital: Operational
Miles of Plant: 412.0 (coaxial); None (fiber optic). Additional miles planned: 10.0 (coaxial). Homes passed: 21,293.
Vice President & General Manager: Dave Slowick. Technical Operations Manager: Frank Staley. Marketing Director: Steve Schuh.
City fee: 3% of gross.
Ownership: Charter Communications Inc. (MSO).

COLDWATER—CityOne Communications, 1 Grand St, Coldwater, MI 49036-1620. Phone: 517-279-9531. Fax: 517-278-5107. E-mail: cityone@cbpu.com. Web Site: http://www.cbpu.com. ICA: MI0436. **Note:** This system is an overbuild.
TV Market Ranking: 37 (COLDWATER).
Channel capacity: 84 (operating 2-way). Channels available but not in use: N.A.
Basic Service
Subscribers: N.A.
Programming (received off-air): WILX-TV (NBC) Onondaga; WKAR-TV (PBS) East Lansing; WLLA (IND) Kalamazoo; WLNS-TV (CBS) Lansing; WOOD-TV (NBC) Grand Rapids; WOTV (ABC) Battle Creek; WTLJ (IND) Muskegon; WWMT (CBS, CW) Kalamazoo; WXMI (FOX) Grand Rapids; WXSP-CA (MNT) Grand Rapids; WZPX-TV (ION) Battle Creek.
Programming (via satellite): Cartoon Network; Country Music TV; C-SPAN; C-SPAN 2; Discovery Channel; Food Network; Home Shopping Network; INSP; QVC; The Learning Channel; Travel Channel; Weather Channel.
Current originations: Educational Access; Public Access.
Fee: $10.95 monthly.
Expanded Basic Service 1
Subscribers: N.A.
Programming (via satellite): ABC Family Channel; AMC; Animal Planet; Arts & Entertainment; Bravo; CNBC; CNN; Comedy Central; Cooking Channel; Discovery Health Channel; Disney Channel; E! Entertainment Television; ESPN; ESPN 2; ESPN Classic Sports; ESPNews; Eternal Word TV Network; Fox Movie Channel; Fox News Channel; Fox Sports Net Detroit; FX; Golf Channel; Great American Country; GSN; Hallmark Channel; Headline News; Healthy Living Channel; History Channel; Lifetime; MSNBC; MTV; National Geographic Channel; Nickelodeon; Outdoor Channel; SoapNet; Speed Channel; Spike TV; Syfy; TBS Superstation; Telemundo; Toon Disney; truTV; Turner Classic Movies; Turner Network TV; TV Land; USA Network; VH1; WE tv; WGN America.
Fee: $28.25 monthly.
Digital Basic Service
Subscribers: N.A.
Programming (via satellite): BBC America; Bio; Discovery Digital Networks; DMX Music; Do-It-Yourself; Fox Sports World; G4; GAS; History Channel International; Independent Film Channel; International Television (ITV); Lifetime Movie Network; MTV Networks Digital Suite; MuchMusic Network; Nick Jr.; NickToons TV; Science Television; Style Network; Versus.
Fee: $41.20 monthly.
Digital Pay Service 1
Pay Units: N.A.
Programming (via satellite): Cinemax (multiplexed); Encore (multiplexed); Flix; HBO (multiplexed); Showtime (multiplexed); Starz (multiplexed); Sundance Channel; The Movie Channel (multiplexed); WAM! America's Kidz Network.
Fee: $12.00 monthly (Cinemax), $14.25 monthly (HBO, Flix/Showtime/Sundance/TMC, or Starz/Encore).
Video-On-Demand: No
Pay-Per-View
iN DEMAND (delivered digitally).
Internet Service
Operational: Yes.
Broadband Service: In-house.
Fee: $75.00 installation; $36.99 monthly.
Telephone Service
Analog: Not Operational
Digital: Operational
Fee: $39.95 installation; $29.95 monthly
Manager: Linden H. Cox.
Ownership: Coldwater Board of Public Utilities.

COLEMAN—Charter Communications, 315 Davis St, Grand Haven, MI 49417-1830. Phone: 616-647-6201. Fax: 616-846-0797. Web Site: http://www.charter.com. Also serves Warren Twp. ICA: MI0207.
TV Market Ranking: Outside TV Markets (COLEMAN, Warren Twp.). Franchise award date: July 24, 1984. Franchise expiration date: N.A. Began: June 1, 1985.
Channel capacity: N.A. Channels available but not in use: N.A.
Basic Service
Subscribers: 373.
Programming (received off-air): various Canadian stations; WAQP (IND) Saginaw; WBSF (CW) Bay City; WCMU-TV (PBS) Mount Pleasant; WDCQ-TV (PBS) Bad Axe; WEYI-TV (CW, NBC) Saginaw; WJRT-TV (ABC) Flint; WKBD-TV (CW) Detroit; WNEM-TV (CBS, MNT) Bay City; WSMH (FOX) Flint; WWTV (CBS) Cadillac.
Programming (via satellite): Cornerstone Television; C-SPAN; C-SPAN 2; Eternal Word TV Network; G4; Home Shopping Network; INSP; Michigan Government Television; QVC; TBS Superstation; TV Guide Network; Univision; WGN America.
Current originations: Public Access.
Fee: $29.99 installation.
Expanded Basic Service 1
Subscribers: 365.
Programming (via satellite): ABC Family Channel; AMC; Animal Planet; Arts & Entertainment; BET Networks; Bravo; Cartoon Network; CNBC; CNN; Comedy Central; Country Music TV; Discovery Channel; Disney Channel; E! Entertainment Television; ESPN; ESPN 2; Food Network; Fox News Channel; Fox Sports Net Detroit; FX; Golf Channel; GSN; Hallmark Channel; Headline News; HGTV; History Channel; Lifetime; MSNBC; MTV; MTV2; National Geographic Channel; Nickelodeon; Outdoor Channel; Oxygen; SoapNet; Speed Channel; Spike TV; Style Network; Syfy; Telemundo; The Learning Channel; Toon Dis-

ney; Travel Channel; truTV; Turner Classic Movies; Turner Network TV; TV Land; USA Network; Versus; VH1; WE tv; Weather Channel.
Fee: $47.99 monthly.

Digital Basic Service
Subscribers: N.A.
Programming (received off-air): WDCQ-TV (PBS) Bad Axe; WEYI-TV (CW, NBC) Saginaw; WJRT-TV (ABC) Flint.
Programming (via satellite): BBC America; Bio; Discovery Digital Networks; Do-It-Yourself; ESPN; ESPN Classic Sports; ESPNews; FitTV; Fox College Sports Atlantic; Fox College Sports Central; Fox College Sports Pacific; Fox Movie Channel; Fox Soccer; Fuel TV; Fuse; GAS; Great American Country; HDNet; HDNet Movies; History Channel International; Independent Film Channel; Lifetime Movie Network; MTV Networks Digital Suite; Music Choice; NFL Network; Nick Jr.; Nick Too; NickToons TV; Sundance Channel; TV Guide Interactive Inc.; WJRT-TV (ABC) Flint.

Digital Pay Service 1
Pay Units: N.A.
Programming (via satellite): Cinemax (multiplexed); Encore (multiplexed); Flix; HBO (multiplexed); HBO HD; LOGO; Showtime (multiplexed); Showtime HD; Starz (multiplexed); The Movie Channel (multiplexed).

Video-On-Demand: Yes

Pay-Per-View
iN DEMAND (delivered digitally); ESPN (delivered digitally); NHL Center Ice (delivered digitally); MLB Extra Innings (delivered digitally); Playboy TV (delivered digitally); Spice Live (delivered digitally); Spice Platinum (delivered digitally); Hot Net Plus (delivered digitally); Spice Hot (delivered digitally).

Internet Service
Operational: Yes.
Broadband Service: Charter Pipeline.
Fee: $29.99 monthly.

Telephone Service
Digital: Operational
Fee: $29.99 monthly

Miles of Plant: 12.0 (coaxial); None (fiber optic). Homes passed: 649.
Vice President & General Manager: Dan Spoelman. Technical Operations Manager: Keith Schierbeek. Marketing Director: Steve Schuh.
Ownership: Charter Communications Inc. (MSO).

COPEMISH (village)—Ace Communications Group of Michigan. Formerly served by Thompsonville, MI [MI0230]. This cable system has converted to IPTV, PO Box 69, 5351 N M-37, Houston, MI 49668-0069. Phone: 800-361-8178. Fax: 231-885-9915. E-mail: miinfo@acegroup.cc. Web Site: http://www.acegroup.cc. ICA: MI5025.
TV Market Ranking: Below 100 (Copemish).
Channel capacity: N.A. Channels available but not in use: N.A.

Video-On-Demand: Yes

Internet Service
Operational: Yes.
Fee: $50.00 installation; $29.95 monthly.

Telephone Service
Digital: Operational
Fee: $21.05 monthly

Chief Executive Officer: Todd Roesler.
Ownership: Ace Communications Group.

COUNTRY ACRES—Charter Communications. Now served by ALLENDALE, MI [MI0094]. ICA: MI0252.

CRYSTAL FALLS—City of Crystal Falls, 401 Superior Ave, Crystal Falls, MI 49920-1424. Phone: 906-875-3212. Web Site: http://www.crystalfalls.org. ICA: MI0190.
TV Market Ranking: Below 100 (CRYSTAL FALLS). Franchise award date: April 1, 1959. Franchise expiration date: N.A. Began: April 1, 1959.
Channel capacity: 42 (operating 2-way). Channels available but not in use: 22.

Basic Service
Subscribers: 795.
Programming (received off-air): WJMN-TV (CBS) Escanaba; WLUC-TV (NBC) Marquette; WNMU (PBS) Marquette.
Programming (via satellite): Arts & Entertainment; CNN; Discovery Channel; Disney Channel; ESPN; Fox Sports Net Detroit; Hallmark Channel; HGTV; History Channel; Home Shopping Network; Nickelodeon; Spike TV; TBS Superstation; Turner Classic Movies; Turner Network TV; TV Land; USA Network; VH1; Weather Channel; WGN America.
Fee: $30.00 installation; $18.00 monthly.

Pay Service 1
Pay Units: 207.
Programming (via satellite): HBO.
Fee: $20.00 installation; $9.50 monthly.

Internet Service
Operational: No.

Telephone Service
None

Miles of Plant: 20.0 (coaxial); None (fiber optic). Homes passed: 900.
Manager: Charles Nordeman. Chief Technician: Angelo Diqui.
Ownership: City of Crystal Falls.

CRYSTAL TWP.—Great Lakes Communication, PO Box 365, 122 Lake St, Crystal, MI 48818. Phone: 989-235-6100. Fax: 989-235-6247. Web Site: http://www.glccmi.com. ICA: MI0180.
TV Market Ranking: Outside TV Markets (CRYSTAL TWP.). Franchise award date: January 1, 1988. Franchise expiration date: N.A. Began: February 1, 1989.
Channel capacity: 60 (2-way capable). Channels available but not in use: N.A.

Basic Service
Subscribers: 460.
Programming (received off-air): WAQP (IND) Saginaw; WCMU-TV (PBS) Mount Pleasant; WEYI-TV (CW, NBC) Saginaw; WILX-TV (NBC) Onondaga; WJRT-TV (ABC) Flint; WKAR-TV (PBS) East Lansing; WLNS-TV (CBS) Lansing; WOOD-TV (NBC) Grand Rapids; WSMH (FOX) Flint; WWUP-TV (CBS, FOX) Sault Ste. Marie; WXMI (FOX) Grand Rapids.
Programming (via satellite): ABC Family Channel; AMC; Arts & Entertainment; Cartoon Network; CNN; Comedy Central; C-SPAN; Discovery Channel; Disney Channel; ESPN; ESPN 2; Food Network; Fox News Channel; Fox Sports Net; FX; Great American Country; Hallmark Channel; Headline News; HGTV; History Channel; Home Shopping Network; ION Television; MSNBC; MTV; National Geographic Channel; Nickelodeon; Outdoor Channel; QVC; Spike TV; Syfy; TBS Superstation; The Learning Channel; Turner Classic Movies; Turner Network TV; TV Land; USA Network; Versus; VH1; Weather Channel; WGN America.
Fee: $50.00 installation; $29.85 monthly.

Pay Service 1
Pay Units: 45.
Programming (via satellite): Cinemax.
Fee: $11.00 monthly.

Pay Service 2
Pay Units: 64.
Programming (via satellite): HBO.
Fee: $11.00 monthly.

Pay Service 3
Pay Units: N.A.
Programming (via satellite): Encore; Starz.

Video-On-Demand: No

Internet Service
Operational: No.

Telephone Service
None

Miles of Plant: 28.0 (coaxial); None (fiber optic). Additional miles planned: 12.0 (coaxial). Homes passed: 1,142. Total homes in franchised area: 2,000.
Vice President & General Manager: Mark Winslow. Chief Technician: Larry Miller.
Ownership: Crystal Cable TV Inc.

CUSTER—Charter Communications, 315 Davis St, Grand Haven, MI 49417-1830. Phone: 616-647-6201. Fax: 616-846-0797. Web Site: http://www.charter.com. Also serves Branch Twp. (Mason Co.), Fountain, Sherman Twp. (Mason County) & Sweetwater Twp. (Lake County). ICA: MI0167.
TV Market Ranking: Below 100 (Sweetwater Twp. (Lake County)); Outside TV Markets (Branch Twp. (Mason Co.), CUSTER, Fountain, Sherman Twp. (Mason County)). Franchise award date: N.A. Franchise expiration date: N.A. Began: October 19, 1990.
Channel capacity: 61 (2-way capable). Channels available but not in use: 26.

Basic Service
Subscribers: 638.
Programming (received off-air): WCMW (PBS) Manistee; WFQX-TV (FOX) Cadillac; WPBN-TV (NBC) Traverse City; WWTV (CBS) Cadillac; WZZM (ABC) Grand Rapids.
Programming (via satellite): ABC Family Channel; C-SPAN; QVC; TBS Superstation; The Learning Channel; VH1; WGN America.
Fee: $38.00 installation; $24.99 monthly.

Expanded Basic Service 1
Subscribers: N.A.
Programming (via satellite): AMC; Arts & Entertainment; CNBC; CNN; Country Music TV; Discovery Channel; Disney Channel; ESPN; ESPN 2; Food Network; Fox Sports Net Detroit; Headline News; HGTV; Lifetime; MSNBC; MTV; Nickelodeon; Spike TV; truTV; Turner Classic Movies; Turner Network TV; USA Network; Weather Channel.

Pay Service 1
Pay Units: 173.
Programming (via satellite): Cinemax; HBO; Starz.
Fee: $6.95 monthly (Starz), $10.95 monthly (Cinemax), $11.95 monthly (HBO).

Video-On-Demand: No

Internet Service
Operational: No.

Telephone Service
None

Miles of Plant: 52.0 (coaxial); None (fiber optic). Homes passed: 1,546.
Vice President & General Manager: Dan Spoelman. Technical Operations Manager: Keith Schierbeek. Marketing Director: Steve Schuh.
City fee: 5% of basic.
Ownership: Charter Communications Inc. (MSO).

DAVISON—Charter Communications, 7372 Davison Rd, Davison, MI 48423. Phones: 810-652-1400; 810-652-1430. Web Site: http://www.charter.com. Also serves Atlas Twp., Forest Twp. (Genesee County), Goodrich, Oregon Twp., Otisville & Richfield Twp. (Genesee County). ICA: MI0290.
TV Market Ranking: 61 (Atlas Twp., DAVISON, Forest Twp. (Genesee County), Goodrich, Oregon Twp., Otisville, Richfield Twp. (Genesee County)). Franchise award date: N.A. Franchise expiration date: N.A. Began: July 1, 1979.
Channel capacity: N.A. Channels available but not in use: N.A.

Basic Service
Subscribers: 11,281.
Programming (received off-air): Home Shopping Network; WAQP (IND) Saginaw; WBSF (CW) Bay City; WDIV-TV (NBC) Detroit; WEYI-TV (CW, NBC) Saginaw; WFUM (PBS) Flint; WJRT-TV (ABC) Flint; WKAR-TV (PBS) East Lansing; WNEM-TV (CBS, MNT) Bay City; WSMH (FOX) Flint; WTVS (PBS) Detroit; WXYZ-TV (ABC) Detroit.
Programming (via satellite): ION Television; QVC; WGN America.
Current originations: Government Access; Educational Access; Public Access.
Fee: $29.99 installation; $13.50 monthly.

Expanded Basic Service 1
Subscribers: N.A.
Programming (via satellite): ABC Family Channel; AMC; Animal Planet; Arts & Entertainment; Bravo; Cartoon Network; CNBC; CNN; Comedy Central; Country Music TV; C-SPAN; Discovery Channel; Disney Channel; E! Entertainment Television; ESPN; ESPN 2; ESPN Classic Sports; Food Network; Fox News Channel; Fox Sports Net Detroit; FX; G4; Golf Channel; GSN; Hallmark Channel; Headline News; HGTV; History Channel; Lifetime; MSNBC; MTV; MTV2; National Geographic Channel; Nickelodeon; Oxygen; SoapNet; Speed Channel; Spike TV; Style Network; Syfy; TBS Superstation; The Learning Channel; Toon Disney; Travel Channel; truTV; Turner Classic Movies; Turner Network TV; TV Guide Network; TV Land; USA Network; Versus; VH1; WE tv; Weather Channel.
Fee: $36.49 monthly.

Digital Basic Service
Subscribers: N.A.
Programming (received off-air): Turner Network TV HD; WEYI-TV (CW, NBC) Saginaw; WFUM (PBS) Flint; WJRT-TV (ABC) Flint; WNEM-TV (CBS, MNT) Bay City; WSMH (FOX) Flint.
Programming (via satellite): BBC America; Bio; CMT Pure Country; Discovery Digital Networks; Discovery HD Theater; Do-It-Yourself; Do-It-Yourself On Demand; ESPN HD; ESPNews; Food Network On Demand; Fox College Sports Atlantic; Fox College Sports Central; Fox College Sports Pacific; Fox Movie Channel; Fox Soccer; Fuel TV; Fuse; GAS; Great American Country; HDNet; HDNet Movies; HGTV On Demand; History Channel International; Howard TV; Independent Film Channel; Lifetime Movie Network; LOGO; MTV Networks Digital Suite; Music Choice; Nick Jr.; Nick Too; NickToons TV; Outdoor Channel; Sundance Channel; Universal HD; Versus On Demand.

Digital Pay Service 1
Pay Units: N.A.
Programming (via satellite): Cinemax (multiplexed); Cinemax HD; Cinemax On Demand; Encore (multiplexed); Flix; HBO (multiplexed); HBO HD; HBO On Demand; Showtime (multiplexed); Showtime HD; Showtime On Demand; Starz (multiplexed); Starz On Demand; The Movie Channel (multiplexed).

Video-On-Demand: Yes

Pay-Per-View
Events & Movies (delivered digitally); ESPN (delivered digitally); NHL Center Ice (delivered digitally); MLB Extra Innings (delivered digitally); Playboy TV (delivered digitally); Fresh (delivered digitally); Shorteez (delivered digitally).
Internet Service
Operational: Yes.
Broadband Service: Charter Pipeline.
Fee: $29.99 monthly.
Telephone Service
Digital: Operational
Vice President & General Manager: Dave Slowick. Technical Operations Director: Lloyd Collins. Marketing Director: Lisa Gayari.
Ownership: Charter Communications Inc. (MSO).

DE TOUR (village)—Upper Peninsula Communications, 397 N US Hwy 41, Carney, MI 49812-9757. Phone: 906-639-2194. Fax: 906-639-9936. E-mail: louied@alphacomm.net. ICA: MI0291.
TV Market Ranking: Outside TV Markets (DE TOUR (VILLAGE)). Franchise award date: March 1, 1988. Franchise expiration date: N.A. Began: December 12, 1988.
Channel capacity: 36 (not 2-way capable). Channels available but not in use: 18.
Basic Service
Subscribers: N.A.
Programming (received off-air): WCML (PBS) Alpena; WGTQ (ABC) Sault Ste. Marie; WTOM-TV (NBC) Cheboygan; WWUP-TV (CBS, FOX) Sault Ste. Marie.
Programming (via satellite): ABC Family Channel; CNN; Discovery Channel; ESPN; TBS Superstation; Turner Network TV; WGN America.
Fee: $25.00 installation; $14.50 monthly; $1.50 converter.
Pay Service 1
Pay Units: 15.
Programming (via satellite): HBO.
Fee: $9.50 monthly.
Video-On-Demand: No
Internet Service
Operational: No.
Telephone Service
None
Miles of Plant: 5.0 (coaxial); None (fiber optic).
Manager & Chief Technician: Louis Dupont.
Ownership: Upper Peninsula Communications Inc. (MSO).

DEARBORN—Comcast Cable. Now served by PLYMOUTH, MI [MI0012]. ICA: MI0021.

DEARBORN HEIGHTS—Comcast Cable. Now served by PLYMOUTH, MI [MI0012]. ICA: MI0010.

DECKERVILLE—Comcast Cable, 1555 Bad Axe Rd, Bad Axe, MI 48413. Phones: 989-269-8927; 800-772-7548. Fax: 989-269-9125. Web Site: http://www.comcast.com. Also serves Bridgehampton Twp., Carsonville, Port Sanilac & Sanilac Twp. ICA: MI0372.
TV Market Ranking: Outside TV Markets (Bridgehampton Twp., Carsonville, DECKERVILLE, Port Sanilac, Sanilac Twp.). Franchise award date: N.A. Franchise expiration date: N.A. Began: N.A.
Channel capacity: 42 (not 2-way capable). Channels available but not in use: None.
Basic Service
Subscribers: 938.
Programming (received off-air): WDIV-TV (NBC) Detroit; WEYI-TV (CW, NBC) Saginaw; WFUM (PBS) Flint; WJRT-TV (ABC) Flint; WKBD-TV (CW) Detroit; WNEM-TV (CBS, MNT) Bay City; WSMH (FOX) Flint; WXYZ-TV (ABC) Detroit.
Programming (via satellite): QVC; TBS Superstation; WGN America.
Current originations: Public Access.
Fee: $14.50 monthly.
Expanded Basic Service 1
Subscribers: N.A.
Programming (via satellite): ABC Family Channel; AMC; Arts & Entertainment; CNN; Discovery Channel; Discovery Health Channel; Disney Channel; ESPN; ESPN 2; Fox Sports Net; Great American Country; Headline News; HGTV; History Channel; Lifetime; Michigan Government Television; MTV; Nickelodeon; Spike TV; Syfy; The Learning Channel; Trinity Broadcasting Network; Turner Network TV; USA Network; Weather Channel.
Fee: $43.49 monthly.
Pay Service 1
Pay Units: N.A.
Programming (via satellite): Cinemax; HBO; Showtime.
Fee: $10.95 monthly (each).
Internet Service
Operational: No.
Telephone Service
None
Miles of Plant: 58.0 (coaxial); None (fiber optic). Homes passed: 1,721.
General Manager: Thomas J. Lerash. Chief Technician: Marshall Kurschner. Business Manager: Susan McGathy.
Ownership: Comcast Cable Communications Inc. (MSO).

DELTON—Charter Communications, 315 Davis St, Grand Haven, MI 49417-1830. Phone: 616-647-6201. Fax: 616-846-0797. Web Site: http://www.charter.com. Also serves Barry Twp. (portions), Hope Twp. (Barry County), Johnstown Twp. & Prairieville Twp. (portions). ICA: MI0186.
TV Market Ranking: 37 (Barry Twp. (portions), DELTON, Hope Twp. (Barry County), Johnstown Twp., Prairieville Twp. (portions)). Franchise award date: January 1, 1984. Franchise expiration date: N.A. Began: January 1, 1984.
Channel capacity: 45 (not 2-way capable). Channels available but not in use: N.A.
Basic Service
Subscribers: 638.
Programming (received off-air): WGVU-TV (PBS) Grand Rapids; WILX-TV (NBC) Onondaga; WLLA (IND) Kalamazoo; WLNS-TV (CBS) Lansing; WOOD-TV (NBC) Grand Rapids; WOTV (ABC) Battle Creek; WTLJ (IND) Muskegon; WWMT (CBS, CW) Kalamazoo; WXMI (FOX) Grand Rapids; WZPX-TV (ION) Battle Creek; WZZM (ABC) Grand Rapids.
Programming (via satellite): C-SPAN; QVC; TBS Superstation; WGN America.
Fee: $36.00 installation; $33.49 monthly; $10.00 additional installation.
Expanded Basic Service 1
Subscribers: N.A.
Programming (via satellite): ABC Family Channel; AMC; Arts & Entertainment; CNBC; CNN; Country Music TV; Discovery Channel; Disney Channel; ESPN; ESPN 2; Food Network; Fox Sports Net Detroit; History Channel; Lifetime; MTV; Nickelodeon; Spike TV; Turner Network TV; Weather Channel.
Fee: $45.99 monthly.

Pay Service 1
Pay Units: 148.
Programming (via satellite): Cinemax; HBO.
Fee: $10.00 installation; $10.95 monthly (Cinemax), $11.95 monthly (HBO).
Pay Service 2
Pay Units: N.A.
Programming (via satellite): Starz.
Video-On-Demand: No
Internet Service
Operational: No.
Telephone Service
None
Miles of Plant: 25.0 (coaxial); None (fiber optic). Homes passed: 925.
Vice President & General Manager: Dan Spoelman. Marketing Director: Steve Schuh. Technical Operations Manager: Keith Schierbeek.
Ownership: Charter Communications Inc. (MSO).

DETROIT—Comcast Cable, 29777 Telegraph Rd, Ste 4400B, Southfield, MI 48034. Phones: 734-254-1500 (Plymouth office); 248-233-4712. Fax: 248-233-4719. Web Site: http://www.comcast.com. Also serves Hamtramck. ICA: MI0001.
TV Market Ranking: 5 (DETROIT, Hamtramck). Franchise award date: August 31, 1983. Franchise expiration date: N.A. Began: December 18, 1986.
Channel capacity: 117 (operating 2-way). Channels available but not in use: N.A.
Basic Service
Subscribers: 133,647.
Programming (received off-air): various Canadian stations; WADL (IND) Mount Clemens; WDIV-TV (NBC) Detroit; WJBK (FOX) Detroit; WKBD-TV (CW) Detroit; WMYD (MNT) Detroit; WPXD-TV (ION) Ann Arbor; WTVS (PBS) Detroit; WWJ-TV (CBS) Detroit; WXYZ-TV (ABC) Detroit; 20 FMs.
Programming (via satellite): ABC Family Channel; AMC; America's Store; Animal Planet; Arts & Entertainment; BET Networks; Black Family Channel; Bravo; Cartoon Network; CNBC; CNN; Comedy Central; C-SPAN; C-SPAN 2; Discovery Channel; E! Entertainment Television; ESPN; ESPN 2; ESPN Classic Sports; Food Network; Fox News Channel; Golf Channel; GSN; Headline News; HGTV; History Channel; Home Shopping Network; INSP; Lifetime; MSNBC; MTV; Nickelodeon; QVC; Sneak Prevue; Speed Channel; Spike TV; Style Network; Syfy; TBS Superstation; The Learning Channel; Trinity Broadcasting Network; truTV; Turner Classic Movies; Turner Network TV; TV Guide Network; TV Land; Univision; USA Network; VH1; Weather Channel; WGN America.
Current originations: Leased Access; Religious Access; Government Access; Educational Access; Public Access.
Fee: $25.00 installation; $50.99 monthly; $5.00 additional installation.
Digital Basic Service
Subscribers: 33,279.
Programming (via satellite): BBC America; Catholic Television Network; Christian Television Network; C-SPAN 3; Discovery Digital Networks; DMX Music; Encore Action; ESPNews; Flix; G4; GAS; MTV Networks Digital Suite; National Geographic Channel; Nick Jr.; Nick Too; ShopNBC; SoapNet; Sundance Channel; The Word Network; Toon Disney; Weatherscan.
Fee: $14.95 monthly.
Pay Service 1
Pay Units: 47,781.
Programming (via satellite): Cinemax; HBO; Showtime; The Movie Channel.
Fee: $15.00 installation; $9.00 monthly (each).
Digital Pay Service 1
Pay Units: N.A.
Programming (via satellite): Cinemax (multiplexed); HBO (multiplexed); Showtime (multiplexed); Starz (multiplexed); The Movie Channel (multiplexed).
Fee: $9.00 monthly (each).
Video-On-Demand: Yes
Pay-Per-View
Addressable homes: 33,279.
iN DEMAND (delivered digitally), Addressable: Yes; Playboy TV (delivered digitally); Fresh (delivered digitally); Shorteez (delivered digitally); Pleasure (delivered digitally).
Internet Service
Operational: Yes.
Subscribers: 14,835.
Broadband Service: Comcast High Speed Internet.
Fee: $42.95 monthly; $7.00 modem lease; $299.00 modem purchase.
Telephone Service
Analog: Not Operational
Digital: Operational
Fee: $44.95 monthly
Miles of Plant: 2,073.0 (coaxial); 24.0 (fiber optic). Homes passed: 374,057. Total homes in franchised area: 433,000.
Vice President & General Manager: Mike Cleland. Vice President, Technical Operations: Steve Thomas. Vice President, Marketing: Tony Lent. Vice President, Communications: Jerome Espy.
City fee: 5% of gross.
Ownership: Comcast Cable Communications Inc. (MSO).

DETROIT—Formerly served by Sprint Corp. No longer in operation. ICA: MI0387.

DETROIT—WOW! Internet Cable & Phone, 7887 E Belleview Ave, Ste 1000, Englewood, CO 80111. Phones: 720-479-3500; 866-496-9669 (Customer service). Fax: 720-479-3585. Web Site: http://www1.wowway.com. Also serves Allen Park, Berkley, Canton Twp., Center Line, Clawson, Clinton, Dearborn, Dearborn Heights, Eastpointe, Ferndale, Fraser, Garden City, Grosse Ile, Harrison Twp., Hazel Park, Huntington Woods, Lincoln Park, Madison Heights, Melvindale, Mount Clemens, Northville, Northville Twp., Pleasant Ridge, Plymouth, Plymouth Twp., Riverview, Rochester, Rochester Hills, Roseville, Royal Oak, Shelby Twp., Southgate, St. Clair Shores, Sterling Heights, Taylor, Trenton, Troy, Utica, Warren, Wayne, Westland & Woodhaven. ICA: MI0422. **Note:** This system is an overbuild.

TV Market Ranking: 5 (Allen Park, Berkley, Canton Twp., Center Line, Clawson, Clinton, Dearborn, Dearborn Heights, DETROIT, Eastpointe, Ferndale, Fraser, Garden City, Grosse Ile, Harrison Twp., Hazel Park, Huntington Woods, Lincoln Park, Madison Heights, Melvindale, Mount Clemens, Northville, Northville Twp., Pleasant Ridge, Plymouth, Plymouth Twp., Riverview, Rochester, Rochester Hills, Roseville, Royal Oak, Shelby Twp., Southgate, St. Clair Shores, Sterling Heights, Taylor, Trenton, Troy, Utica, Warren, Wayne, Westland, Woodhaven). Franchise award date: June 1, 1995. Franchise expiration date: N.A. Began: N.A.

Channel capacity: N.A. Channels available but not in use: N.A.

Basic Service

Subscribers: N.A. Included in Chicago

Programming (received off-air): various Canadian stations; WADL (IND) Mount Clemens; WDIV-TV (NBC) Detroit; WFUM (PBS) Flint; WJBK (FOX) Detroit; WKBD-TV (CW) Detroit; WMYD (MNT) Detroit; WPXD-TV (ION) Ann Arbor; WTVS (PBS) Detroit; WWJ-TV (CBS) Detroit; WXYZ-TV (ABC) Detroit.

Programming (via satellite): Home Shopping Network; INSP; TBS Superstation; WGN America.

Current originations: Leased Access; Government Access; Educational Access; Public Access.

Fee: $39.99 installation; $16.99 monthly.

Expanded Basic Service 1

Subscribers: N.A.

Programming (via satellite): ABC Family Channel; AMC; Animal Planet; Arts & Entertainment; BET Networks; Big Ten Network; Bravo; Cartoon Network; CNBC; CNN; Comedy Central; Country Music TV; C-SPAN; C-SPAN 2; Discovery Channel; Discovery Health Channel; Disney Channel; E! Entertainment Television; ESPN; ESPN 2; ESPN Classic Sports; Eternal Word TV Network; Food Network; Fox News Channel; Fox Sports Net Detroit; FX; Golf Channel; GSN; Hallmark Channel; Headline News; HGTV; History Channel; Lifetime; MSNBC; MTV; MTV2; National Geographic Channel; Nickelodeon; NickToons TV; QVC; ShopNBC; Speed Channel; Spike TV; Syfy; The Learning Channel; Toon Disney; Travel Channel; truTV; Turner Classic Movies; Turner Network TV; TV Land; USA Network; VH1; Weather Channel.

Fee: $34.76 monthly.

Digital Basic Service

Subscribers: N.A.

Programming (via satellite): ABC News Now; BBC America; Big Ten Network; Bio; Bloomberg Television; Bridges TV; CMT Pure Country; Cooking Channel; Discovery HD Theater; Discovery Kids Channel; Discovery Military Channel; Discovery Planet Green; DMX Music; Do-It-Yourself; Encore (multiplexed); ESPNews; Fox Business Channel; Fox College Sports Atlantic; Fox College Sports Central; Fox College Sports Pacific; Fox Movie Channel; Fox Reality Channel; Fox Soccer; G4; GemsTV; HDNet; HDNet Movies; here! On Demand; History Channel International; ID Investigation Discovery; Jewelry Television; Lifetime Movie Network; Lifetime Real Women; MTV Hits; NFL Network; NFL Network HD; Nick Jr.; Nick Too; Outdoor Channel; Oxygen; PBS Kids Sprout; Retro Television Network; Science Channel; SoapNet; Starz (multiplexed); Style Network; Sundance Channel; TeenNick; Tennis Channel; The Word Network; Trinity Broadcasting Network; Versus; VH1 Classic; WE tv; WealthTV HD; WWE 24/7.

Fee: $25.23 monthly.

Digital Expanded Basic Service

Subscribers: N.A.

Programming (via satellite): Al Jazeera English; Arabic Channel.

Fee: $4.99 monthly.

Digital Pay Service 1

Pay Units: N.A.

Programming (via satellite): Cinemax (multiplexed); Cinemax On Demand; Flix; HBO (multiplexed); HBO On Demand; Showtime (multiplexed); Showtime On Demand; The Movie Channel (multiplexed); The Movie Channel On Demand.

Fee: $15.00 monthly (HBO, Cinemax, Showtime/TMC/Flix or Starz).

Video-On-Demand: Yes

Pay-Per-View

iN DEMAND (delivered digitally); Hot Choice (delivered digitally); Ten Xtsy (delivered digitally).

Internet Service

Operational: Yes.

Broadband Service: WOW! Internet.

Fee: $40.99-$72.99 monthly; $2.50 modem lease.

Telephone Service

Digital: Operational

Total homes in franchised area: 517,500.

Vice President & General Manager: Mark Dineen. Vice President, Sales & Marketing: Cathy Kuo. Chief Technical Officer: Cash Hagen.

Ownership: WideOpenWest LLC (MSO).

DIMONDALE—Broadstripe, 2512 Lansing Rd, Charlotte, MI 48813-8447. Phone: 517-543-1245. Fax: 517-543-8057. E-mail: michigan_contact@broadsripe.com. Web Site: http://www.broadstripe.com. Also serves Alaiedon Twp., Albion, Athens, Aurelius Twp., Bath Twp., Bellevue, Benton Twp. (Eaton County), Boston Twp., Bunker Hill Twp., Burlington Twp., Campbell Twp., Carmel Twp., Charlotte, Clarksville, Concord, Convis Twp., Danby Twp., Dansville (village), Eagle (village), Eagle Twp., Eaton Twp., Eckford Twp., Fowlerville, Fredonia Twp., Grass Lake, Grass Lake Twp., Green Oak Twp., Handy Twp., Hanover, Hastings, Hastings Twp., Henrietta Twp., Homer, Horton, Ingham Twp., Laingsburg, Lake Odessa, Leslie Twp., Liberty Twp., Lyons Twp., Marengo Twp., Marshall, Mason, Morrice, Mulliken, North Plains Twp., Odessa Twp., Olivet, Oneida Charter Twp., Onondaga Twp., Parma, Perry, Pewamo, Pleasant Lake, Portland, Potterville, Pulaski Twp., Roxanne Twp., Saranac, Sciota Twp., Shaftsburg, Sheridan Twp., Sherwood, South Lyon, Spring Arbor Twp., Stockbridge, Sunfield, Union City, Vevay Twp., Victor Twp., Walton Twp., Waterloo Twp., Watertown Twp. (Clinton County), Webberville, Westphalia, Wheatfield Twp., Williamston, Williamstown Twp., Windsor Twp. & Woodhull Twp. ICA: MI0136.

TV Market Ranking: 37 (Albion, Athens, Bellevue, Boston Twp., Burlington Twp., Campbell Twp., Charlotte, Clarksville, Convis Twp., Hastings, Hastings Twp., Marengo Twp., Marshall, Olivet, Saranac, Sheridan Twp., Sherwood, Union City, Walton Twp.); 37,92 (Benton Twp. (Eaton County), Concord, DIMONDALE, Eaton Twp., Hanover, Homer, Horton, Lake Odessa, Liberty Twp., Mulliken, Odessa Twp., Parma, Potterville, Pulaski Twp., Roxanne Twp., Spring Arbor Twp., Sunfield); 5 (Green Oak Twp., South Lyon); 61 (Laingsburg, Morrice, Sciota Twp., Shaftsburg, Williamston); 61,92 (Fowlerville, Handy Twp., Perry, Victor Twp., Webberville, Wheatfield Twp., Williamstown Twp., Woodhull Twp.); 92 (Alaiedon Twp., Aurelius Twp., Bath Twp., Bunker Hill Twp., Carmel Twp., Danby Twp., Dansville (village), Eagle (village), Eagle Twp., Eckford Twp., Fredonia Twp., Grass Lake, Grass Lake Twp., Henrietta Twp., Ingham Twp., Leslie Twp., Lyons Twp., Mason, North Plains Twp., Oneida Charter Twp., Onondaga Twp., Pewamo, Pleasant Lake, Portland, Stockbridge, Vevay Twp., Waterloo Twp., Watertown Twp. (Clinton County), Westphalia, Windsor Twp.). Franchise award date: N.A. Franchise expiration date: N.A. Began: November 1, 1982.

Channel capacity: N.A. Channels available but not in use: N.A.

Basic Service

Subscribers: 38,000 Includes Vermontville.

Programming (received off-air): WADL (IND) Mount Clemens; WDIV-TV (NBC) Detroit; WEYI-TV (CW, NBC) Saginaw; WGVU-TV (PBS) Grand Rapids; WHTV (MNT) Jackson; WILX-TV (NBC) Onondaga; WJBK (FOX) Detroit; WJRT-TV (ABC) Flint; WKAR-TV (PBS) East Lansing; WKBD-TV (CW) Detroit; WLAJ (ABC, CW) Lansing; WLLA (IND) Kalamazoo; WLNS-TV (CBS) Lansing; WMYD (MNT) Detroit; WOOD-TV (NBC) Grand Rapids; WOTV (ABC) Battle Creek; WPXD-TV (ION) Ann Arbor; WSMH (FOX) Flint; WSYM-TV (FOX) Lansing; WTVS (PBS) Detroit; WWJ-TV (CBS) Detroit; WWMT (CBS, CW) Kalamazoo; WXMI (FOX) Grand Rapids; WXYZ-TV (ABC) Detroit; WZPX-TV (ION) Battle Creek; WZZM (ABC) Grand Rapids.

Programming (via satellite): C-SPAN; C-SPAN 2; Home Shopping Network; QVC; ShopNBC; TV Guide Network; WGN America.

Current originations: Government Access; Public Access.

Fee: $29.95 installation; $16.25 monthly.

Expanded Basic Service 1

Subscribers: N.A.

Programming (via satellite): ABC Family Channel; AMC; Animal Planet; Arts & Entertainment; Cartoon Network; CNBC; CNN; Comedy Central; Cooking Channel; Country Music TV; Discovery Channel; Disney Channel; E! Entertainment Television; ESPN; ESPN 2; Food Network; Fox News Channel; Fox Sports Net; Fox Sports Net Detroit; FX; Headline News; HGTV; History Channel; Lifetime; MSNBC; MTV; National Geographic Channel; Nickelodeon; SoapNet; Speed Channel; Spike TV; Syfy; TBS Superstation; The Learning Channel; Toon Disney; Travel Channel; Trinity Broadcasting Network; truTV; Turner Network TV; TV Land; USA Network; VH1; Weather Channel.

Fee: $32.74 monthly.

Digital Basic Service

Subscribers: 10,500.

Programming (via satellite): BBC America; Bio; Bloomberg Television; Bravo; Discovery Digital Networks; Discovery HD Theater; DMX Music; Do-It-Yourself; ESPN Classic Sports; ESPN HD; ESPNews; Fox Movie Channel; Fox Sports World; FSN Digital Atlantic; FSN Digital Central; FSN Digital Pacific; Fuse; G4; GAS; Golf Channel; Great American Country; GSN; Hallmark Channel; History Channel International; Independent Film Channel; INSP; Lifetime Movie Network; MTV Networks Digital Suite; Nick Jr.; NickToons TV; Outdoor Channel; Style Network; Syfy; The Sportsman Channel; Toon Disney; Trinity Broadcasting Network; Turner Classic Movies; WE tv.

Fee: $10.25 monthly.

Digital Pay Service 1

Pay Units: N.A.

Programming (via satellite): Cinemax (multiplexed); Encore (multiplexed); HBO (multiplexed); HBO HD; Playboy TV; Showtime (multiplexed); Starz; Starz HDTV; The Movie Channel (multiplexed).

Fee: $20.00 installation; $6.18 monthly (Starz/Encore), $7.26 monthly (Cinemax or Showtime/TMC), $8.77 monthly (HBO), $14.95 monthly (Playboy).

Video-On-Demand: No

Pay-Per-View

iN DEMAND (delivered digitally), Addressable: Yes.

Internet Service

Operational: Yes. Began: January 1, 1997.

Subscribers: 13,100.

Broadband Service: Millennium Cable-Speed.

Fee: $49.95 installation; $27.95 monthly; $5.00 modem lease.

Telephone Service

Digital: Operational

Fee: $39.99 installation; $49.99 monthly

Miles of Plant: 1,697.0 (coaxial); 320.0 (fiber optic).

President & Chief Executive Officer: Bill Shreffler. Senior Vice President, Programming: Frank Scotello. General Manager: David Harwood. Chief Engineer: Mark Jordan. Chief Technician: Ron Allen. Marketing Director: Suzanne Harwood. Government Relations Director: Rick Clark.

Ownership: Broadstripe (MSO).

DOWAGIAC—Comcast Cable. Now served by CASSOPOLIS, MI [MI0168]. ICA: MI0292.

DRUMMOND ISLAND—Formerly served by Northwoods Cable Inc. No longer in operation. ICA: MI0210.

DURAND—Charter Communications, 7372 Davison Rd, Davison, MI 48423. Phone: 810-652-1400. Web Site: http://www.charter.com. Also serves Bancroft, Burns Twp., Byron, Clayton Twp. (Genesee County), Gaines, Gaines Twp. (Genesee County), Lennon, Shiawassee Twp., Venice Twp., Vernon (village), Vernon Twp. (Shiawassee County) & Woodcreek Manor. ICA: MI0075.

TV Market Ranking: 61,92 (Bancroft, Burns Twp., Byron, Clayton Twp. (Genesee County), DURAND, Gaines, Gaines Twp. (Genesee County), Lennon, Shiawassee Twp., Venice Twp., Vernon (village), Vernon Twp. (Shiawassee County), Woodcreek Manor). Franchise award date: January 1, 1981. Franchise expiration date: N.A. Began: January 20, 1982.

Channel capacity: N.A. Channels available but not in use: N.A.

Basic Service

Subscribers: 5,500.

Programming (received off-air): WAQP (IND) Saginaw; WDIV-TV (NBC) Detroit; WEYI-TV (CW, NBC) Saginaw; WFUM (PBS) Flint; WILX-TV (NBC) Onondaga; WJRT-TV (ABC) Flint; WKAR-TV (PBS) East Lansing; WKBD-TV (CW) Detroit; WLNS-TV (CBS) Lansing; WMYD (MNT) Detroit; WNEM-TV (CBS, MNT) Bay City; WSMH (FOX) Flint; WXYZ-TV (ABC) Detroit.

Programming (via satellite): Home Shopping Network; ION Television; QVC; WGN America.

Current originations: Government Access; Educational Access; Public Access.
Fee: $29.99 installation; $13.50 monthly.

Expanded Basic Service 1
Subscribers: N.A.
Programming (via satellite): ABC Family Channel; AMC; Animal Planet; Arts & Entertainment; Bravo; Cartoon Network; CNBC; CNN; Comedy Central; Country Music TV; C-SPAN; Discovery Channel; Disney Channel; E! Entertainment Television; ESPN; ESPN 2; ESPN Classic Sports; Food Network; Fox News Channel; Fox Sports Net Detroit; FX; G4; Golf Channel; GSN; Hallmark Channel; Headline News; HGTV; History Channel; Lifetime; MSNBC; MTV; MTV2; National Geographic Channel; Nickelodeon; Oxygen; SoapNet; Speed Channel; Spike TV; Style Network; Syfy; TBS Superstation; The Learning Channel; Toon Disney; Travel Channel; truTV; Turner Classic Movies; Turner Network TV; TV Guide Network; TV Land; USA Network; Versus; VH1; WE tv; Weather Channel.
Fee: $36.49 monthly.

Digital Basic Service
Subscribers: N.A.
Programming (via satellite): BBC America; Bio; Discovery Digital Networks; Do-It-Yourself; ESPN; FitTV; Fox College Sports Atlantic; Fox College Sports Central; Fox College Sports Pacific; Fox Movie Channel; Fox Soccer; Fuel TV; Fuse; GAS; Great American Country; HDNet; HDNet Movies; History Channel International; Independent Film Channel; Lifetime Movie Network; MTV Networks Digital Suite; Music Choice; NFL Network; Nick Jr.; Nick Too; NickToons TV; Sundance Channel; TV Guide Interactive Inc.

Digital Pay Service 1
Pay Units: N.A.
Programming (via satellite): Cinemax (multiplexed); Encore (multiplexed); Flix; HBO (multiplexed); HBO HD; Showtime (multiplexed); Showtime HD; Starz (multiplexed); The Movie Channel (multiplexed).

Video-On-Demand: Yes

Pay-Per-View
Playboy TV (delivered digitally); Spice Live (delivered digitally); Hot Net Plus (delivered digitally); Spice Platinum (delivered digitally); Spice Hot (delivered digitally); iN DEMAND (delivered digitally); NASCAR In Car (delivered digitally); ESPN Sports PPV (delivered digitally); NHL Center Ice (delivered digitally); MLB Extra Innings (delivered digitally).

Internet Service
Operational: Yes.
Broadband Service: Charter Pipeline.
Fee: $29.99 monthly.

Telephone Service
Digital: Operational
Fee: $29.99 monthly

Miles of Plant: 210.0 (coaxial); None (fiber optic). Homes passed: 8,590.
Vice President & General Manager: Dave Slowick. Technical Operations Director: Lloyd Collins. Marketing Director: Lisa Gayari.
Ownership: Charter Communications Inc. (MSO).

EAGLE HARBOR TWP.—Cable America Corp., 7822 E Grayrd, Scottsdale, AZ 85260. Phones: 480-315-1818 (Corporate fax); 480-315-1820. Fax: 906-289-4959. E-mail: info@cableaz.com. Web Site: http://www.cableamerica.com. Also serves Agate Harbor. ICA: MI0293.
TV Market Ranking: Below 100 (Agate Harbor, EAGLE HARBOR TWP.). Franchise award date: September 1, 1992. Franchise expiration date: N.A. Began: N.A.
Channel capacity: 62 (not 2-way capable). Channels available but not in use: 8.

Basic Service
Subscribers: 163.
Programming (received off-air): WBKP (ABC) Calumet; WCCO-TV (CBS) Minneapolis; WDIV-TV (NBC) Detroit; WJMN-TV (CBS) Escanaba; WKBD-TV (CW) Detroit; WLUC-TV (NBC) Marquette; WNMU (PBS) Marquette; WTVS (PBS) Detroit; WWJ-TV (CBS) Detroit; WZMQ (IND, MNT) Marquette.
Programming (via satellite): AMC; Animal Planet; Arts & Entertainment; BBC America; Cartoon Network; Classic Arts Showcase; CNBC; CNN; Comedy Central; C-SPAN; C-SPAN 2; Deutsche Welle TV; Discovery Channel; ESPN; ESPN 2; Food Network; Fox News Channel; Fox Sports Net Detroit; FX; G4; Hallmark Channel; Headline News; HGTV; History Channel; Home Shopping Network; ION Television; Lifetime; MSNBC; NASA TV; Nickelodeon; QVC; Speed Channel; Syfy; TBS Superstation; The Learning Channel; truTV; Turner Classic Movies; Turner Network TV; TV Land; USA Network; VH1; Weather Channel; WGN America.
Current originations: Public Access.
Fee: $35.00 installation; $17.00 monthly.

Pay Service 1
Pay Units: 2.
Programming (via satellite): HBO.
Fee: $10.00 monthly.

Video-On-Demand: No

Internet Service
Operational: No.

Telephone Service
None

Miles of Plant: 9.0 (coaxial); None (fiber optic). Homes passed: 350.
Vice President, Engineering: Alan Jackson. Chief Technician: James Grove. Corporate Secretary: Gloria Jackson.
Ownership: CableAmerica Corp. (MSO).

EAST JORDAN—Charter Communications. Now served by TRAVERSE CITY, MI [MI0026]. ICA: MI0095.

EAST LANSING—Comcast Cable, 3500 Patterson Ave SE, Grand Rapids, MI 49512. Phone: 616-977-2200. Fax: 616-977-2224. Web Site: http://www.comcast.com. Also serves Alaiedon Twp. (portions), Haslett, Meridian Twp., Okemos & Wheatfield Twp. (portions). ICA: MI0024.
TV Market Ranking: 92 (Alaiedon Twp. (portions), EAST LANSING, Haslett, Meridian Twp., Okemos, Wheatfield Twp. (portions)). Franchise award date: January 1, 1969. Franchise expiration date: N.A. Began: June 1, 1970.
Channel capacity: 76 (operating 2-way). Channels available but not in use: N.A.

Basic Service
Subscribers: 22,516.
Programming (received off-air): WHTV (MNT) Jackson; WILX-TV (NBC) Onondaga; WKAR-TV (PBS) East Lansing; WLAJ (ABC, CW) Lansing; WLNS-TV (CBS) Lansing; WSYM-TV (FOX) Lansing; WZPX-TV (ION) Battle Creek; 20 FMs.
Programming (via satellite): Comcast Local Detroit; C-SPAN; FX; Home Shopping Network; QVC; TBS Superstation; truTV; various Canadian stations; WGN America.
Current originations: Government Access; Educational Access; Public Access.

Expanded Basic Service 1
Subscribers: N.A.
Programming (via satellite): ABC Family Channel; AMC; Animal Planet; Arts & Entertainment; BET Networks; Cartoon Network; CNBC; CNN; Comedy Central; C-SPAN 2; Discovery Channel; Disney Channel; E! Entertainment Television; ESPN; ESPN 2; Food Network; Fox News Channel; Fox Sports Net Detroit; Golf Channel; Headline News; HGTV; History Channel; Lifetime; Michigan Government Television; MSNBC; MTV; Nickelodeon; Spike TV; The Learning Channel; Turner Network TV; TV Guide Network; TV Land; Univision; USA Network; Versus; VH1; Weather Channel.
Fee: $48.99 monthly.

Digital Basic Service
Subscribers: N.A.
Programming (received off-air): WILX-TV (NBC) Onondaga; WKAR-TV (PBS) East Lansing; WLAJ (ABC, CW) Lansing; WLNS-TV (CBS) Lansing.
Programming (via satellite): BBC America; Bio; Black Family Channel; Bloomberg Television; Bravo; Country Music TV; Current; Discovery HD Theater; Discovery Kids Channel; Discovery Military Channel; Discovery Planet Green; Do-It-Yourself; Encore (multiplexed); ESPN 2 HD; ESPN Classic Sports; ESPN HD; ESPNews; Flix; Fox College Sports Atlantic; Fox College Sports Central; Fox College Sports Pacific; Fox Movie Channel; Fox Reality Channel; Fox Soccer; Fuse; G4; Great American Country; GSN; Halogen Network; History Channel; History Channel International; ID Investigation Discovery; Independent Film Channel; INHD; Lifetime Movie Network; MoviePlex; MTV Networks Digital Suite; Music Choice; National Geographic Channel; NBA TV; NFL Network; Nick Jr.; Nick Too; NickToons TV; Outdoor Channel; Palladia; PBS Kids Sprout; Science Channel; ShopNBC; SoapNet; Speed Channel; Style Network; Sundance Channel; Syfy; TeenNick; The Word Network; Toon Disney; Trinity Broadcasting Network; Turner Classic Movies; Versus; WE tv.
Fee: $9.95 monthly.

Digital Pay Service 1
Pay Units: N.A.
Programming (via satellite): Cinemax (multiplexed); Cinemax HD; HBO (multiplexed); HBO HD; Showtime (multiplexed); Showtime HD; Starz (multiplexed); Starz HDTV; The Movie Channel.
Fee: $18.05 monthly (each).

Video-On-Demand: Yes

Pay-Per-View
iN DEMAND (delivered digitally); Playboy TV (delivered digitally); Fresh (delivered digitally).

Internet Service
Operational: Yes.
Broadband Service: Comcast High Speed Internet.
Fee: $150.00 installation; $42.95 monthly.

Telephone Service
Digital: Operational

Miles of Plant: 320.0 (coaxial); 34.0 (fiber optic). Additional miles planned: 10.0 (coaxial). Homes passed: 30,840. Total homes in franchised area: 30,840.
Area Vice President: Larry Williamson. Business Operations Director: Amy Carey. Technical Operations Director: Tom Rice. Sales & Marketing Director: Rick Finch.
City fee: 5% of gross.
Ownership: Comcast Cable Communications Inc. (MSO).

EATON RAPIDS—Comcast Cable. Now served by LANSING, MI [MI0007]. ICA: MI0138.

EDWARDSBURG—Comcast Cable. Now served by THREE RIVERS, MI [MI0050]. ICA: MI0296.

ELSIE—Charter Communications, 7372 Davison Rd, Davison, MI 48423. Phone: 810-652-1400. Web Site: http://www.charter.com. Also serves Middlebury Twp. & Ovid Village. ICA: MI0373.
TV Market Ranking: 61,92 (ELSIE, Middlebury Twp., Ovid Village). Franchise award date: N.A. Franchise expiration date: N.A. Began: N.A.
Channel capacity: 45 (operating 2-way). Channels available but not in use: N.A.

Basic Service
Subscribers: 791.
Programming (received off-air): WEYI-TV (CW, NBC) Saginaw; WFUM (PBS) Flint; WILX-TV (NBC) Onondaga; WJRT-TV (ABC) Flint; WKAR-TV (PBS) East Lansing; WLNS-TV (CBS) Lansing; WNEM-TV (CBS, MNT) Bay City; WSMH (FOX) Flint; WSYM-TV (FOX) Lansing.
Programming (via satellite): QVC.
Fee: $29.99 installation; $13.50 monthly; $3.50 converter.

Expanded Basic Service 1
Subscribers: 741.
Programming (via satellite): ABC Family Channel; AMC; Arts & Entertainment; CNN; Country Music TV; Discovery Channel; ESPN; Lifetime; MTV; Nickelodeon; Spike TV; TBS Superstation; The Learning Channel; Turner Network TV; USA Network; Weather Channel; WGN America.
Fee: $36.49 monthly.

Pay Service 1
Pay Units: 121.
Programming (via satellite): Cinemax.
Fee: $11.45 monthly.

Pay Service 2
Pay Units: 142.
Programming (via satellite): HBO.
Fee: $11.45 monthly.

Pay Service 3
Pay Units: 38.
Programming (via satellite): Showtime.
Fee: $11.45 monthly.

Pay Service 4
Pay Units: N.A.
Programming (via satellite): Encore.
Fee: $1.75 monthly.

Internet Service
Operational: No.

Telephone Service
None
Homes passed: 1,654. Total homes in franchised area: 1,654.
Vice President & General Manager: Dave Slowick. Technical Operations Director: Lloyd Collins. Marketing Director: Lisa Gayari.
Ownership: Charter Communications Inc. (MSO).

ENGADINE—Upper Peninsula Communications, 397 N US Hwy 41, Carney, MI 49812-9757. Phone: 906-639-2194. Fax: 906-639-9936. E-mail: louied@alphacomm.net. Also serves Naubinway. ICA: MI0297.
TV Market Ranking: Outside TV Markets (ENGADINE, Naubinway). Franchise award date: April 1, 1988. Franchise expiration date: N.A. Began: March 24, 1989.
Channel capacity: 36 (operating 2-way). Channels available but not in use: 14.
Basic Service
Subscribers: N.A.
Programming (received off-air): WCML (PBS) Alpena; WFQX-TV (FOX) Cadillac; WKRN-TV (ABC) Nashville; WTOM-TV (NBC) Cheboygan; WWUP-TV (CBS, FOX) Sault Ste. Marie.
Programming (via satellite): ABC Family Channel; Arts & Entertainment; CNBC; CNN; C-SPAN; Discovery Channel; Disney Channel; ESPN; Eternal Word TV Network; HGTV; History Channel; Home Shopping Network; ION Television; Lifetime; Outdoor Channel; QVC; Spike TV; TBS Superstation; The Learning Channel; Trinity Broadcasting Network; Turner Classic Movies; Turner Network TV; TV Land; USA Network; Weather Channel; WGN America.
Fee: $25.00 installation; $15.50 monthly; $1.50 converter.
Pay Service 1
Pay Units: 36.
Programming (via satellite): Cinemax.
Fee: $7.50 monthly.
Internet Service
Operational: No.
Telephone Service
None
Miles of Plant: 10.0 (coaxial); None (fiber optic).
Manager & Chief Technician: Louis Dupont.
Ownership: Upper Peninsula Communications Inc. (MSO).

ESCANABA—Charter Communications, 359 US 41 East, Negaunee, MI 49866. Phones: 231-947-5221 (Traverse City office); 906-475-0107. Fax: 906-475-7007. Web Site: http://www.charter.com. Also serves Bark River Twp., Brampton Twp., Ford River Twp., Gladstone, Harris Twp., Hiawatha Twp., Manistique, Masonville Twp. (southern portion), Rapid River, Thompson Twp. & Wells Twp. ICA: MI0054.
TV Market Ranking: Below 100 (Brampton Twp., ESCANABA, Ford River Twp., Gladstone, Harris Twp., Masonville Twp. (southern portion), Rapid River, Wells Twp.); Outside TV Markets (Hiawatha Twp., Manistique, Thompson Twp.). Franchise award date: N.A. Franchise expiration date: N.A. Began: January 1, 1960.
Channel capacity: 110 (operating 2-way). Channels available but not in use: 52.
Basic Service
Subscribers: 12,861.
Programming (received off-air): WBKP (ABC) Calumet; WBUP (ABC) Ishpeming; WJMN-TV (CBS) Escanaba; WLUC-TV (NBC) Marquette; WNMU (PBS) Marquette; WZMQ (IND, MNT) Marquette; 4 FMs.
Programming (via microwave): WLUK-TV (FOX) Green Bay.
Programming (via satellite): C-SPAN; C-SPAN 2; C-SPAN 3; Eternal Word TV Network; G4; Home Shopping Network; INSP; QVC; TBS Superstation; TV Guide Network; various Canadian stations; WGN America.
Current originations: Educational Access; Public Access; Government Access.
Fee: $29.99 installation; $13.50 monthly; $.92 converter.
Expanded Basic Service 1
Subscribers: 11,139.
Programming (via satellite): ABC Family Channel; AMC; Animal Planet; Arts & Entertainment; Bravo; Cartoon Network; CNBC; CNN; Comedy Central; Country Music TV; Discovery Channel; Disney Channel; E! Entertainment Television; ESPN; ESPN 2; FitTV; Food Network; Fox News Channel; Fox Sports Net Detroit; FX; Golf Channel; GSN; Hallmark Channel; Headline News; HGTV; History Channel; Lifetime; MSNBC; MTV; National Geographic Channel; Nickelodeon; Oxygen; SoapNet; Speed Channel; Spike TV; Style Network; Syfy; The Learning Channel; Toon Disney; Travel Channel; truTV; Turner Classic Movies; Turner Network TV; TV Land; USA Network; Versus; VH1; WE tv; Weather Channel.
Fee: $36.49 monthly.
Digital Basic Service
Subscribers: N.A.
Programming (received off-air): WJMN-TV (CBS) Escanaba; WLUC-TV (NBC) Marquette; WNMU (PBS) Marquette.
Programming (via satellite): BBC America; Bio; CMT Pure Country; Cooking Channel; Discovery Digital Networks; Discovery HD Theater; Do-It-Yourself; ESPN Classic Sports; ESPN HD; ESPNews; Food Network On Demand; Fox College Sports Atlantic; Fox College Sports Central; Fox College Sports Pacific; Fox Movie Channel; Fox Soccer; Fuel TV; Fuse; GAS; Great American Country; HDNet; HDNet Movies; HGTV On Demand; History Channel International; Howard TV; Independent Film Channel; Lifetime Movie Network; MTV Networks Digital Suite; Music Choice; Nick Jr.; Nick Too; NickToons TV; Outdoor Channel; Sundance Channel; Turner Network TV HD; Universal HD; Versus On Demand.
Digital Pay Service 1
Pay Units: N.A.
Programming (via satellite): Cinemax (multiplexed); Cinemax HD; Cinemax On Demand; Encore (multiplexed); Flix; HBO (multiplexed); HBO HD; HBO On Demand; LOGO; Showtime (multiplexed); Showtime HD; Showtime On Demand; Starz (multiplexed); Starz On Demand; The Movie Channel (multiplexed).
Video-On-Demand: Yes
Pay-Per-View
Movies & Events (delivered digitally); ESPN (delivered digitally); NHL Center Ice (delivered digitally); MLB Extra Innings (delivered digitally); Playboy TV (delivered digitally); Fresh (delivered digitally); Shorteez (delivered digitally).
Internet Service
Operational: Yes.
Broadband Service: Charter Pipeline.
Fee: $49.95 installation; $29.99 monthly.
Telephone Service
Digital: Operational
Fee: $29.99 monthly
Miles of Plant: 318.0 (coaxial); 176.0 (fiber optic). Homes passed: 15,452. Total homes in franchised area: 17,304.
Vice President: Joe Boullion. General Manager: Rex Buettenbach. Technical Operations Director: Rob Nowak. Marketing Manager: Sandy Gottschalk. Government Relations Manager: Don Gladwell.
City fee: None.
Ownership: Charter Communications Inc. (MSO).

EVART—Charter Communications, 315 Davis St, Grand Haven, MI 49417-1830. Phone: 616-647-6201. Fax: 616-846-0797. Web Site: http://www.charter.com. Also serves Osceola Twp. (Osceola County). ICA: MI0187.
TV Market Ranking: Below 100 (EVART, Osceola Twp. (Osceola County)). Franchise award date: February 26, 1981. Franchise expiration date: N.A. Began: N.A.
Channel capacity: 36 (2-way capable). Channels available but not in use: 5.
Basic Service
Subscribers: 501.
Programming (received off-air): WCMU-TV (PBS) Mount Pleasant; WFQX-TV (FOX) Cadillac; WPBN-TV (NBC) Traverse City; WWTV (CBS) Cadillac; WZZM (ABC) Grand Rapids.
Programming (via satellite): ABC Family Channel; Country Music TV; C-SPAN; QVC; TBS Superstation; USA Network; WGN America.
Current originations: Government Access; Educational Access; Public Access.
Fee: $38.00 installation; $21.16 monthly.
Expanded Basic Service 2
Subscribers: N.A.
Programming (via satellite): AMC; Arts & Entertainment; CNBC; CNN; Discovery Channel; Disney Channel; ESPN; ESPN 2; Food Network; Fox Sports Net Detroit; HGTV; Lifetime; MTV; Nickelodeon; Spike TV; The Learning Channel; Turner Network TV; Weather Channel.
Pay Service 1
Pay Units: 104.
Programming (via satellite): Cinemax; HBO; Starz.
Fee: $21.00 installation; $6.95 monthly (Starz), $10.95 monthly (Cinemax), $11.95 monthly (HBO).
Internet Service
Operational: Yes.
Fee: $19.99 monthly.
Telephone Service
Digital: Operational
Fee: $14.99 monthly
Miles of Plant: 13.0 (coaxial); None (fiber optic). Homes passed: 972.
Vice President & General Manager: Dan Spoelman. Technical Operations Manager: Keith Schierbeek. Marketing Director: Steve Schuh.
City fee: 5% of gross.
Ownership: Charter Communications Inc. (MSO).

EWEN—Charter Communications. Now served by IRONWOOD, MI [MI0064]. ICA: MI0298.

FALMOUTH—Pine River Cable, PO Box 96, McBain, MI 49657. Phone: 888-244-2288. Fax: 231-825-0191. Web Site: http://www.pinerivercable.com. ICA: MI0443.
TV Market Ranking: Below 100 (FALMOUTH).
Channel capacity: N.A. Channels available but not in use: N.A.
Basic Service
Subscribers: N.A.
Programming (received off-air): WFQX-TV (FOX) Cadillac; WGN America; WPBN-TV (NBC) Traverse City; WWTV (CBS) Cadillac.
Programming (via satellite): ABC Family Channel; Arts & Entertainment; CNN; Country Music TV; C-SPAN; C-SPAN 2; Discovery Channel; Disney Channel; ESPN; Fox News Channel; Fox Sports Net Detroit; GSN; Hallmark Channel; Headline News; History Channel; Lifetime; Lifetime Movie Network; Nickelodeon; QVC; Spike TV; TBS Superstation; The Learning Channel; Trinity Broadcasting Network; truTV; Turner Network TV; TV Land; USA Network; WCMV (PBS) Cadillac; Weather Channel.
Internet Service
Operational: No.
Manager: John Metzler.
Ownership: Pine River Cable (MSO).

FARMINGTON—Bright House Networks. Now served by LIVONIA, MI [MI0019]. ICA: MI0015.

FENTON—Charter Communications, 7372 Davison Rd, Davison, MI 48423. Phone: 810-652-1400. Fax: 989-792-2982. Web Site: http://www.charter.com. Also serves Argentine Twp., Deerfield, Fenton Twp., Linden & Tyrone Twp. (Livingston County). ICA: MI0035.
TV Market Ranking: 61 (Argentine Twp., Deerfield, FENTON, Fenton Twp., Linden, Tyrone Twp. (Livingston County)). Franchise award date: N.A. Franchise expiration date: N.A. Began: September 1, 1980.
Channel capacity: N.A. Channels available but not in use: N.A.
Basic Service
Subscribers: 11,040.
Programming (received off-air): WAQP (IND) Saginaw; WBSF (CW) Bay City; WDIV-TV (NBC) Detroit; WEYI-TV (CW, NBC) Saginaw; WFUM (PBS) Flint; WJRT-TV (ABC) Flint; WKAR-TV (PBS) East Lansing; WMYD (MNT) Detroit; WNEM-TV (CBS, MNT) Bay City; WSMH (FOX) Flint; WTVS (PBS) Detroit; WXYZ-TV (ABC) Detroit; allband FM.
Programming (via satellite): Home Shopping Network; ION Television; QVC; WGN America.
Current originations: Educational Access; Public Access; Government Access.
Fee: $29.99 installation; $13.50 monthly; $15.00 additional installation.
Expanded Basic Service 1
Subscribers: N.A.
Programming (via satellite): ABC Family Channel; AMC; Animal Planet; Arts & Entertainment; Bravo; Cartoon Network; CNBC; CNN; Comedy Central; Country Music TV; C-SPAN; Discovery Channel; Disney Channel; E! Entertainment Television; ESPN; ESPN 2; Food Network; Fox News Channel; Fox Sports Net Detroit; FX; G4; Golf Channel; GSN; Hallmark Channel; Headline News; HGTV; History Channel; Lifetime; MSNBC; MTV; MTV2; National Geographic Channel; Nickelodeon; Oxygen; SoapNet; Speed Channel; Spike TV; Syfy; TBS Superstation; The Learning Channel; Toon Disney; Travel Channel; truTV; Turner Classic Movies; Turner Network TV; TV Guide Network; TV Land; USA Network; Versus; VH1; Weather Channel.
Fee: $36.49 monthly.
Digital Basic Service
Subscribers: N.A.
Programming (received off-air): WEYI-TV (CW, NBC) Saginaw; WFUM (PBS) Flint; WJRT-TV (ABC) Flint; WNEM-TV (CBS, MNT) Bay City; WSMH (FOX) Flint.
Programming (via satellite): BBC America; Bio; CMT Pure Country; Discovery Digital Networks; Do-It-Yourself; ESPN 2 HD;

ESPN Classic Sports; ESPN HD; ESPN U; ESPNews; FitTV; Fox Business Channel; Fox College Sports Atlantic; Fox College Sports Central; Fox College Sports Pacific; Fox Movie Channel; Fox Soccer; Fox Sports Net Detroit; Fuel TV; Fuse; GAS; Great American Country; HDNet; HDNet Movies; History Channel International; Independent Film Channel; Lifetime Movie Network; Military History Channel; MTV Networks Digital Suite; Music Choice; Nick Jr.; Nick Too; NickToons TV; Outdoor Channel; ReelzChannel; Sundance Channel; The Sportsman Channel; Turner Network TV HD; WE tv.

Digital Pay Service 1

Pay Units: N.A.

Programming (via satellite): Cinemax (multiplexed); Cinemax HD; Encore (multiplexed); Flix; HBO (multiplexed); HBO HD; LOGO; Showtime (multiplexed); Showtime HD; Starz (multiplexed); Starz HDTV; The Movie Channel (multiplexed).

Video-On-Demand: Yes

Pay-Per-View

iN DEMAND (delivered digitally); ESPN (delivered digitally); NHL Center Ice (delivered digitally); MLB Extra Innings (delivered digitally); Playboy TV (delivered digitally); Club Jenna (delivered digitally); Fresh! (delivered digitally); Fresh (delivered digitally); Shorteez (delivered digitally).

Internet Service

Operational: Yes.

Broadband Service: Charter Pipeline.

Fee: $29.99 monthly.

Telephone Service

Digital: Operational

Miles of Plant: 347.0 (coaxial); None (fiber optic). Additional miles planned: 30.0 (coaxial). Homes passed: 20,200.

Vice President & General Manager: Dave Slowick. Technical Operations Director: Lloyd Collins. Marketing Director: Lisa Gayari.

City fee: 3% of basic gross.

Ownership: Charter Communications Inc. (MSO).

FIFE LAKE—Charter Communications. Now served by TRAVERSE CITY, MI [MI0026]. ICA: MI0224.

FINE LAKE—Pine River Cable, PO Box 96, McBain, MI 49657. Phone: 888-244-2288. Fax: 231-825-0191. E-mail: info@pinerivercable.com. Web Site: http://www.pinerivercable.com. ICA: MI0223.

TV Market Ranking: 37 (FINE LAKE). Franchise award date: October 14, 1987. Franchise expiration date: N.A. Began: January 1, 1988.

Channel capacity: 36 (operating 2-way). Channels available but not in use: 12.

Basic Service

Subscribers: 222.

Programming (received off-air): WGVK (PBS) Kalamazoo; WILX-TV (NBC) Onondaga; WOOD-TV (NBC) Grand Rapids; WOTV (ABC) Battle Creek; WSYM-TV (FOX) Lansing; WWMT (CBS, CW) Kalamazoo; WXMI (FOX) Grand Rapids.

Programming (via satellite): Disney Channel.

Fee: $50.00 installation; $19.95 monthly.

Pay Service 1

Pay Units: 50.

Programming (via satellite): Showtime.

Fee: $7.00 monthly.

Internet Service

Operational: No.

Telephone Service

None

Miles of Plant: 6.0 (coaxial); None (fiber optic). Homes passed: 370.

Manager: John Metzler.

Ownership: Pine River Cable (MSO).

FLINT—Comcast Cable, 29777 Telegraph Rd, Ste 4400B, Southfield, MI 48034. Phones: 248-233-4712; 586-883-7000 (Sterling Heights office). Fax: 248-233-4719. Web Site: http://www.comcast.com. Also serves Burton, Clio, Flint Twp., Flushing, Flushing Twp., Genesee Twp., Grand Blanc, Grand Blanc Twp., Holly Village, Mount Morris, Mount Morris Twp., Mundy Twp., Swartz Creek & Vienna Twp. (Genesee County). ICA: MI0004.

TV Market Ranking: 61 (Burton, Clio, FLINT, Flint Twp., Flushing, Flushing Twp., Genesee Twp., Grand Blanc, Grand Blanc Twp., Holly Village, Mount Morris, Mount Morris Twp., Mundy Twp., Swartz Creek, Vienna Twp. (Genesee County)). Franchise award date: N.A. Franchise expiration date: N.A. Began: April 1, 1966.

Channel capacity: N.A. Channels available but not in use: N.A.

Basic Service

Subscribers: 92,232.

Programming (received off-air): WAQP (IND) Saginaw; WBSF (CW) Bay City; WEYI-TV (CW, NBC) Saginaw; WFUM (PBS) Flint; WJBK (FOX) Detroit; WJRT-TV (ABC) Flint; WKAR-TV (PBS) East Lansing; WKBD-TV (CW) Detroit; WNEM-TV (CBS, MNT) Bay City; WPXD-TV (ION) Ann Arbor; WSMH (FOX) Flint; WXYZ-TV (ABC) Detroit.

Programming (via satellite): ABC Family Channel; AMC; Animal Planet; Arts & Entertainment; BET Networks; Big Ten Network; Cartoon Network; CNBC; CNN; Comedy Central; Discovery Channel; Discovery Health Channel; Disney Channel; E! Entertainment Television; ESPN; ESPN 2; Food Network; Fox News Channel; Fox Sports Net Detroit; FX; Golf Channel; Great American Country; Hallmark Channel; Headline News; HGTV; History Channel; Home Shopping Network; Lifetime; MSNBC; MTV; Nickelodeon; QVC; Speed Channel; Spike TV; Style Network; Syfy; TBS Superstation; The Learning Channel; Travel Channel; truTV; Turner Classic Movies; Turner Network TV; TV Land; TV One; Univision; USA Network; various Canadian stations; Versus; VH1; Weather Channel; WGN America.

Current originations: Leased Access; Educational Access; Public Access.

Fee: $25.00 installation; $10.43 monthly.

Digital Basic Service

Subscribers: N.A.

Programming (received off-air): WEYI-TV (CW, NBC) Saginaw; WFUM (PBS) Flint; WJRT-TV (ABC) Flint; WNEM-TV (CBS, MNT) Bay City; WSMH (FOX) Flint.

Programming (via satellite): ABC Family HD; AMC HD; Animal Planet HD; Arts & Entertainment HD; BBC America; Big Ten Network; Big Ten Network HD; Bio; Bloomberg Television; Bridges TV; CMT Pure Country; CNN HD; Cooking Channel; Country Music TV; C-SPAN 2; C-SPAN 3; Current; Daystar TV Network; Discovery Channel HD; Discovery HD Theater; Discovery Kids Channel; Discovery Military Channel; Discovery Planet Green; Discovery Planet Green HD; Disney Channel HD; Disney XD; Do-It-Yourself; Encore (multiplexed); Encore Wam; ESPN 2 HD; ESPN Classic Sports; ESPN HD; ESPNews; Eternal Word TV Network; FearNet; Flix; Fox Business Channel; Fox News HD; Fox Reality Channel; Fox Soccer; FSN HD; Fuse; FX HD; G4; Golf Channel HD; Gospel Music Channel; GSN; HGTV HD; History Channel HD; History Channel International; ID Investigation Discovery; Independent Film Channel; INSP; Lifetime Movie Network; LOGO; MBC America; Michigan Government Television; MoviePlex; MTV Hits; MTV Jams; MTV Tres; MTV2; Music Choice; National Geographic Channel; National Geographic Channel HD Network; NFL Network HD; Nick Jr.; Nick Too; NickToons TV; Oxygen; Palladia; PBS Kids Sprout; Qubo; ReelzChannel; Retirement Living; Science Channel; Science Channel HD; ShopNBC; SoapNet; Speed HD; Starz IndiePlex; Starz RetroPlex; Sundance Channel; Syfy HD; TBS in HD; TeenNick; Telemundo; The Word Network; TLC HD; Trinity Broadcasting Network; Turner Network TV HD; Universal HD; USA Network HD; Versus HD; VH1 Classic; VH1 Soul; WE tv; Weatherscan.

Digital Expanded Basic Service

Subscribers: N.A.

Programming (via satellite): College Sports Television; Fox College Sports Atlantic; Fox College Sports Central; Fox College Sports Pacific; Fox Soccer; Gol TV; NBA TV; NFL Network; NHL Network; Outdoor Channel; Tennis Channel; The Sportsman Channel.

Digital Expanded Basic Service 2

Subscribers: N.A.

Programming (via satellite): Canal 52MX; Cine Latino; Cine Mexicano; CNN en Espanol; Discovery en Espanol; ESPN Deportes; Fox Sports en Espanol; History Channel en Espanol; MTV Tres; VeneMovies.

Digital Pay Service 1

Pay Units: N.A.

Programming (via satellite): Bollywood On Demand; Cinemax (multiplexed); Cinemax HD; Filipino On Demand; HBO (multiplexed); HBO HD; Playboy TV; Showtime (multiplexed); Showtime HD; Starz (multiplexed); Starz HDTV; The Movie Channel (multiplexed); TV Asia; Zee TV USA.

Video-On-Demand: Yes

Pay-Per-View

iN DEMAND; iN DEMAND (delivered digitally); MLB Extra Innings (delivered digitally); Playboy TV (delivered digitally); Pleasure (delivered digitally); Fresh (delivered digitally); NFL Network (delivered digitally); Sports PPV (delivered digitally); NBA League Pass (delivered digitally); NHL Center Ice (delivered digitally).

Internet Service

Operational: Yes.

Broadband Service: Comcast High Speed Internet.

Fee: $149.99 installation; $32.95 monthly; $7.00 modem lease; $199.00 modem purchase.

Telephone Service

Digital: Operational

Fee: $44.95 monthly

Miles of Plant: 1,468.0 (coaxial); 38.0 (fiber optic). Additional miles planned: 107.0 (fiber optic). Total homes in franchised area: 173,811.

Area Vice President: Mike Casillo. Vice President, Technical Operations: Steve Thomas. Vice President, Marketing: Tony Lent. Vice President, Communications: Jerome Espy.

City fee: 3% of gross.

Ownership: Comcast Cable Communications Inc. (MSO).

FORESTER TWP.—Formerly served by Cablevision Systems Corp. No longer in operation. ICA: MI0254.

FORESTVILLE—Formerly served by Cablevision Systems Corp. No longer in operation. ICA: MI0391.

FOWLER—Charter Communications. Now served by ST. JOHNS, MI [MI0353]. ICA: MI0222.

FRASER TWP.—Charter Communications, 7372 Davison Rd, Davison, MI 48423. Phone: 810-652-1400. Web Site: http://www.charter.com. Also serves Kawkawlin Twp. & Linwood. ICA: MI0197.

TV Market Ranking: 61 (FRASER TWP., Kawkawlin Twp., Linwood). Franchise award date: August 13, 1984. Franchise expiration date: N.A. Began: August 1, 1985.

Channel capacity: 35 (not 2-way capable). Channels available but not in use: None.

Basic Service

Subscribers: 670.

Programming (received off-air): various Canadian stations; WAQP (IND) Saginaw; WBSF (CW) Bay City; WCMU-TV (PBS) Mount Pleasant; WDCQ-TV (PBS) Bad Axe; WEYI-TV (CW, NBC) Saginaw; WJRT-TV (ABC) Flint; WKBD-TV (CW) Detroit; WNEM-TV (CBS, MNT) Bay City; WSMH (FOX) Flint; WWTV (CBS) Cadillac.

Programming (via satellite): Cornerstone Television; C-SPAN; C-SPAN 2; Eternal Word TV Network; G4; Home Shopping Network; INSP; Michigan Government Television; QVC; TBS Superstation; TV Guide Network; Univision; WGN America.

Current originations: Public Access.

Fee: $29.99 installation; $13.50 monthly.

Expanded Basic Service 1

Subscribers: 656.

Programming (via satellite): ABC Family Channel; AMC; Animal Planet; Arts & Entertainment; BET Networks; Bravo; Cartoon Network; CNBC; CNN; Comedy Central; Country Music TV; Discovery Channel; Disney Channel; E! Entertainment Television; ESPN; ESPN 2; Food Network; Fox News Channel; Fox Sports Net Detroit; FX; Golf Channel; GSN; Hallmark Channel; Headline News; HGTV; History Channel; Lifetime; MSNBC; MTV; MTV2; National Geographic Channel; Nickelodeon; Outdoor Channel; Oxygen; SoapNet; Speed Channel; Spike TV; Style Network; Syfy; Telemundo; The Learning Channel; Toon Disney; Travel Channel; truTV; Turner Classic Movies; Turner Network TV; TV Land;

USA Network; Versus; VH1; WE tv; Weather Channel.
Fee: $36.49 monthly.
Internet Service
Operational: No.
Telephone Service
Digital: Operational
Miles of Plant: 32.0 (coaxial); None (fiber optic). Homes passed: 1,081.
Vice President & General Manager: Dave Slowick. Technical Operations Director: Lloyd Collins. Marketing Director: Lisa Gayari.
Franchise fee: 5% of gross.
Ownership: Charter Communications Inc. (MSO).

FREDERIC TWP.—Charter Communications, 2074 M 32 W, Alpena, MI 49707. Phones: 231-947-5221 (Traverse City); 989-356-4503. Fax: 989-356-3761. Web Site: http://www.charter.com. ICA: MI0300.
TV Market Ranking: Below 100 (FREDERIC TWP.). Franchise award date: N.A. Franchise expiration date: N.A. Began: N.A.
Channel capacity: 40 (not 2-way capable). Channels available but not in use: 19.
Basic Service
Subscribers: 99.
Programming (received off-air): WCML (PBS) Alpena; WGTU (ABC, CW) Traverse City; WPBN-TV (NBC) Traverse City; WWTV (CBS) Cadillac.
Programming (via satellite): ABC Family Channel; AMC; Arts & Entertainment; CNN; Country Music TV; Discovery Channel; ESPN; Showtime; TBS Superstation; Turner Network TV; USA Network; WGN America.
Fee: $29.99 installation; $49.99 monthly.
Internet Service
Operational: No.
Telephone Service
None
Miles of Plant: 8.0 (coaxial); None (fiber optic). Homes passed: 255.
Vice President: Joe Boullion. General Manager: Ed Kavanaugh. Technical Operations Director: Rob Nowak. Marketing Manager: Brenda Auger.
Ownership: Charter Communications Inc. (MSO).

FREE SOIL—Formerly served by Charter Communications. No longer in operation. ICA: MI0301.

FREEPORT—Lewiston Communications, PO Box 169, 2 E Main St, Fremont, MI 49412-0169. Phones: 231-924-8060; 800-443-0758. Fax: 231-924-6155. Also serves Carlton Twp., Freeport City & Irving Twp. ICA: MI0302.
TV Market Ranking: 37 (Carlton Twp., FREEPORT, Freeport City, Irving Twp.). Franchise award date: N.A. Franchise expiration date: N.A. Began: May 1, 1989.
Channel capacity: 54 (operating 2-way). Channels available but not in use: N.A.
Basic Service
Subscribers: 307.
Programming (received off-air): WGVU-TV (PBS) Grand Rapids; WOOD-TV (NBC) Grand Rapids; WWMT (CBS, CW) Kalamazoo; WXMI (FOX) Grand Rapids; WZPX-TV (ION) Battle Creek; WZZM (ABC) Grand Rapids.
Programming (via satellite): ABC Family Channel; AMC; Animal Planet; Arts & Entertainment; Cartoon Network; CNBC; CNN; Comedy Central; Country Music TV; C-SPAN; Discovery Channel; Discovery Health Channel; E! Entertainment Television; ESPN; ESPN 2; Fox News Channel; Fox Sports Net Detroit; FX; G4; Golf Channel; Hallmark Channel; Headline News; HGTV; History Channel; Lifetime; National Geographic Channel; Nickelodeon; Outdoor Channel; QVC; Speed Channel; Spike TV; Syfy; TBS Superstation; The Learning Channel; Trinity Broadcasting Network; truTV; Turner Classic Movies; Turner Network TV; TV Land; USA Network; VH1; Weather Channel; WGN America.
Fee: $55.00 installation; $38.99 monthly.
Pay Service 1
Pay Units: 6.
Programming (via satellite): HBO; Showtime.
Fee: $11.95 monthly.
Video-On-Demand: No
Internet Service
Operational: No.
Telephone Service
None
Miles of Plant: 29.0 (coaxial); None (fiber optic). Homes passed: 700. Total homes in franchised area: 2,000.
Manager: Charles Lathrop. Chief Technician: Jim Batch.
Ownership: Lewiston Communications (MSO).

FROST TWP.—Charter Communications. Now served by MOUNT PLEASANT, MI [MI0069]. ICA: MI0303.

GAGETOWN—Comcast Cable. Now served by PIGEON, MI [MI0375]. ICA: MI0427.

GARDEN TWP.—Upper Peninsula Communications, 397 N US Hwy 41, Carney, MI 49812-9757. Phone: 906-639-2194. Fax: 906-639-9936. E-mail: louied@alphacomm.net. ICA: MI0305.
TV Market Ranking: Below 100 (GARDEN TWP.). Franchise award date: N.A. Franchise expiration date: N.A. Began: March 1, 1992.
Channel capacity: N.A. Channels available but not in use: N.A.
Basic Service
Subscribers: 127.
Programming (received off-air): WJMN-TV (CBS) Escanaba; WKRN-TV (ABC) Nashville; WLUC-TV (NBC) Marquette; WNMU (PBS) Marquette; WZMQ (IND, MNT) Marquette.
Programming (via satellite): ABC Family Channel; Arts & Entertainment; CNBC; CNN; C-SPAN; Discovery Channel; ESPN; ESPN 2; Eternal Word TV Network; Fox Sports Net; HGTV; History Channel; ION Television; Outdoor Channel; Spike TV; Syfy; TBS Superstation; Trinity Broadcasting Network; Turner Classic Movies; Turner Network TV; USA Network; Weather Channel; WGN America.
Current originations: Public Access.
Fee: $26.00 installation; $14.50 monthly.
Pay Service 1
Pay Units: N.A.
Programming (via satellite): Cinemax.
Fee: $7.50 monthly.
Internet Service
Operational: No.
Telephone Service
None
Manager & Chief Technician: Louis Dupont.
Ownership: Upper Peninsula Communications Inc. (MSO).

GARFIELD TWP. (Clare County)—Charter Communications. Now served by MOUNT PLEASANT, MI [MI0069]. ICA: MI0306.

GAYLORD—Charter Communications. Now served by TRAVERSE CITY, MI [MI0026]. ICA: MI0093.

GERMFASK—Upper Peninsula Communications, 397 N US Hwy 41, Carney, MI 49812-9757. Phone: 906-639-2194. Fax: 906-639-9936. E-mail: louied@alphacomm.net. ICA: MI0307.
TV Market Ranking: Outside TV Markets (GERMFASK). Franchise award date: N.A. Franchise expiration date: N.A. Began: N.A.
Channel capacity: 40 (not 2-way capable). Channels available but not in use: 20.
Basic Service
Subscribers: 76.
Programming (received off-air): WKRN-TV (ABC) Nashville; WZMQ (IND, MNT) Marquette.
Programming (via microwave): WJMN-TV (CBS) Escanaba; WTVS (PBS) Detroit.
Programming (via satellite): AMC; Arts & Entertainment; CNN; C-SPAN; Discovery Channel; ESPN; ESPN 2; Hallmark Channel; HGTV; History Channel; Home Shopping Network; ION Television; Lifetime; Outdoor Channel; Spike TV; TBS Superstation; The Learning Channel; Turner Classic Movies; Turner Network TV; TV Land; USA Network; Weather Channel; WGN America; WNBC (NBC) New York.
Pay Service 1
Pay Units: N.A.
Programming (via satellite): Showtime.
Internet Service
Operational: No.
Telephone Service
None
Miles of Plant: 5.0 (coaxial); None (fiber optic). Homes passed: 114.
Manager & Chief Technician: Louis Dupont.
Ownership: Upper Peninsula Communications Inc. (MSO).

GILEAD—Formerly served by CableDirect. No longer in operation. ICA: MI0308.

GILMORE TWP. (Isabella County)—Charter Communications. Now served by MOUNT PLEASANT, MI [MI0069]. ICA: MI0247.

GLENNIE (village)—Pine River Cable, PO Box 96, McBain, MI 49657. Phone: 888-244-2288. Fax: 231-825-0191. E-mail: info@pinerivercable.com. Web Site: http://www.pinerivercable.com. Also serves Curtisville. ICA: MI0309.
TV Market Ranking: Outside TV Markets (Curtisville, GLENNIE (VILLAGE)). Franchise award date: N.A. Franchise expiration date: N.A. Began: N.A.
Channel capacity: 36 (not 2-way capable). Channels available but not in use: 8.
Basic Service
Subscribers: 298.
Programming (received off-air): WBKB-TV (CBS, FOX) Alpena.
Programming (via microwave): WDIV-TV (NBC) Detroit; WTVS (PBS) Detroit; WXYZ-TV (ABC) Detroit.
Programming (via satellite): ABC Family Channel; AMC; Arts & Entertainment; CNN; Country Music TV; Discovery Channel; ESPN; Showtime; TBS Superstation; Turner Network TV; USA Network; WGN America.
Fee: $50.00 installation; $24.95 monthly.
Internet Service
Operational: No.
Miles of Plant: 32.0 (coaxial); None (fiber optic). Homes passed: 1,063.
Manager: John Metzler.
Ownership: Pine River Cable (MSO).

GOODELLS—Formerly served by Cablevision Systems Corp. No longer in operation. ICA: MI0310.

GRAND LAKE—Charter Communications, 701 E South Airport Rd, Traverse City, MI 49686-4861. Phone: 616-947-5221. Fax: 616-947-2004. Web Site: http://www.charter.com. Also serves Krakow, Presque Isle Twp. & Pulawski Twp. ICA: MI0185.
TV Market Ranking: Below 100 (GRAND LAKE, Krakow, Presque Isle Twp., Pulawski Twp.). Franchise award date: N.A. Franchise expiration date: N.A. Began: N.A.
Channel capacity: 36 (2-way capable). Channels available but not in use: 4.
Basic Service
Subscribers: 487.
Programming (received off-air): WBKB-TV (CBS, FOX) Alpena; WCML (PBS) Alpena; WGTQ (ABC) Sault Ste. Marie; WTOM-TV (NBC) Cheboygan; WWUP-TV (CBS, FOX) Sault Ste. Marie.
Programming (via satellite): ABC Family Channel; C-SPAN; Headline News; QVC; TBS Superstation; Turner Network TV; WGN America.
Fee: $29.99 installation; $13.50 monthly.
Expanded Basic Service 1
Subscribers: N.A.
Programming (via satellite): AMC; Arts & Entertainment; CNBC; CNN; Country Music TV; Discovery Channel; Disney Channel; ESPN; ESPN 2; Food Network; Fox Sports Net Detroit; Lifetime; MTV; Nickelodeon; Spike TV; The Learning Channel; USA Network; VH1; Weather Channel.
Fee: $36.49 monthly.
Pay Service 1
Pay Units: 89.
Programming (via satellite): Cinemax; HBO.
Fee: $10.95 monthly (Cinemax), $11.95 monthly (HBO).
Video-On-Demand: No
Internet Service
Operational: No.
Telephone Service
None
Miles of Plant: 51.0 (coaxial); None (fiber optic). Homes passed: 992.

Vice President & General Manager: Joe Boullion. Marketing Manager: Tammy Reicha. Technical Operations Director: Rob Nowak.
Ownership: Charter Communications Inc. (MSO).

GRAND MARAIS—Cable America Corp., 115 Glenwood Rd, Marquette, MI 49855-9502. Phone: 906-249-1057. ICA: MI0215.
TV Market Ranking: Outside TV Markets (GRAND MARAIS). Franchise award date: N.A. Franchise expiration date: N.A. Began: January 1, 1986.
Channel capacity: 36 (not 2-way capable). Channels available but not in use: 18.

Basic Service
Subscribers: 237.
Programming (received off-air): WJMN-TV (CBS) Escanaba; WLUC-TV (NBC) Marquette; WNMU (PBS) Marquette; WXYZ-TV (ABC) Detroit; WZMQ (IND, MNT) Marquette.
Programming (via satellite): ABC Family Channel; AMC; Arts & Entertainment; Cartoon Network; CNBC; CNN; Discovery Channel; Disney Channel; ESPN; ESPN 2; Fox News Channel; Fox Sports Net; FX; Great American Country; Hallmark Channel; HGTV; History Channel; Home Shopping Network; ION Television; Lifetime; Speed Channel; Syfy; TBS Superstation; The Learning Channel; Travel Channel; truTV; Turner Network TV; TV Land; USA Network; Weather Channel; WGN America.
Current originations: Educational Access.
Fee: $35.00 installation; $17.95 monthly.

Pay Service 1
Pay Units: 56.
Programming (via satellite): Showtime; The Movie Channel.
Fee: $15.00 installation; $6.95 monthly.

Video-On-Demand: No

Internet Service
Operational: No.

Telephone Service
None

Miles of Plant: 13.0 (coaxial); None (fiber optic). Homes passed: 420.
Manager: Robert Grove.
Ownership: Grove Cable Co. (MSO).

GRAND RAPIDS—Comcast Cable, 3500 Patterson Ave SE, Grand Rapids, MI 49512. Phone: 616-977-2200. Fax: 616-977-2224. Web Site: http://www.comcast.com. Also serves Ada, Alpine Twp. (portions), Byron Twp., Caledonia, Cannon Twp., Cascade Twp., Dorr Twp. (portions), East Grand Rapids, Gaines Twp. (Kent County), Georgetown Twp., Grand Rapids Twp., Grandville, Grattan Twp., Jamestown Twp. (portions), Kentwood, Plainfield Twp. (Kent County) (portions), Tallmadge Twp. (portions), Vergennes Twp., Walker, Wright Twp. (Ottawa County) (portions) & Wyoming. ICA: MI0003.
TV Market Ranking: 37 (Ada, Alpine Twp. (portions), Byron Twp., Caledonia, Cannon Twp., Cascade Twp., Dorr Twp. (portions), East Grand Rapids, Gaines Twp. (Kent County), Georgetown Twp., GRAND RAPIDS, Grandville, Grattan Twp., Jamestown Twp. (portions), Kentwood, Plainfield Twp. (Kent County) (portions), Tallmadge Twp. (portions), Vergennes Twp., Walker, Wright Twp. (Ottawa County) (portions), Wyoming). Franchise award date: August 1, 1976. Franchise expiration date: N.A. Began: August 1, 1976.
Channel capacity: 133 (operating 2-way). Channels available but not in use: 42.

Basic Service
Subscribers: 125,165.
Programming (received off-air): WGVU-TV (PBS) Grand Rapids; WLLA (IND) Kalamazoo; WOOD-TV (NBC) Grand Rapids; WOTV (ABC) Battle Creek; WTLJ (IND) Muskegon; WWMT (CBS, CW) Kalamazoo; WXMI (FOX) Grand Rapids; WXSP-CA (MNT) Grand Rapids; WZZM (ABC) Grand Rapids; 18 FMs.
Programming (via satellite): C-SPAN; CW+; Home Shopping Network; ION Television; QVC; TBS Superstation; TV Guide Network; WGN America.
Current originations: Leased Access; Government Access; Educational Access; Public Access.

Expanded Basic Service 1
Subscribers: 117,815.
Programming (via satellite): ABC Family Channel; AMC; Animal Planet; Arts & Entertainment; BET Networks; Cartoon Network; CNBC; CNN; Comedy Central; Country Music TV; Discovery Channel; Disney Channel; E! Entertainment Television; ESPN; ESPN 2; Food Network; Fox News Channel; Fox Sports Net Detroit; FX; GalaVision; Golf Channel; Hallmark Channel; Headline News; History Channel; Lifetime; MSNBC; MTV; Nickelodeon; Spike TV; The Learning Channel; Travel Channel; truTV; Turner Classic Movies; Turner Network TV; TV Land; Univision; USA Network; Versus; VH1; Weather Channel.
Fee: $50.99 monthly.

Digital Basic Service
Subscribers: 25,428.
Programming (via satellite): Animal Planet HD; Arts & Entertainment HD; BBC America; Bio HD; Bloomberg Television; Bravo; CMT Pure Country; Cooking Channel; C-SPAN 2; C-SPAN 3; Current; Discovery Channel HD; Discovery HD Theater; Discovery Health Channel; Discovery Kids Channel; Discovery Military Channel; Discovery Planet Green; Disney XD; Disney XD HD; Do-It-Yourself; Encore (multiplexed); Encore Wam; ESPN 2; ESPN 2 HD; ESPN Classic Sports; ESPN HD; ESPNews HD; Eternal Word TV Network; Exercise TV; FearNet; FitTV; Flix; Food Network HD; Fox Business Channel; Fox News HD; Fox Reality Channel; Fox Soccer; FSN HD; Fuse; FX HD; G4; Golf Channel HD; Gospel Music Channel; Great American Country; GSN; Halogen Network; HGTV; HGTV HD; History Channel HD; History Channel International; ID Investigation Discovery; Independent Film Channel; Jewelry Television; Lifetime Movie Network; Lifetime Movie Network HD; Lifetime Television HD; LOGO; Michigan Government Television; Mojo HD; MTV Hits; MTV Jams; MTV Networks Digital Suite; MTV Tres; MTV2; Music Choice; National Geographic Channel; National Geographic Channel HD Network; NBA TV; Nick HD; Nick Jr.; Nick Too; NickToons TV; Outdoor Channel; Oxygen; Palladia; Science Channel; Science Channel HD; ShopNBC; SoapNet; Spike TV HD; Starz IndiePlex; Starz RetroPlex; Style Network; Sundance Channel; Syfy; Syfy HD; TBS in HD; TeenNick; The Word Network; TLC HD; Travel Channel HD; Trinity Broadcasting Network; Turner Network TV HD; TV One; Universal HD; USA Network HD; Versus HD; VH1 Classic; VH1 Soul; WE tv.
Fee: $25.00 installation; $15.95 monthly; $3.85 converter.

Digital Expanded Basic Service
Subscribers: N.A.
Programming (via satellite): Cine Latino; Cine Mexicano; CNN en Espanol; Discovery en Espanol; ESPN Deportes; Fox Sports en Espanol; History Channel en Espanol; MTV Tres; mun2 television; VeneMovies.

Digital Expanded Basic Service 2
Subscribers: N.A.
Programming (via satellite): CBS College Sports Network; College Sports Television; Fox College Sports Atlantic; Fox College Sports Central; Fox College Sports Pacific; Fox Movie Channel; Fox Soccer; Gol TV; NBA TV; NFL Network; NFL Network HD; NHL Network; Speed Channel; Speed HD; Tennis Channel; The Sportsman Channel.

Digital Pay Service 1
Pay Units: N.A.
Programming (via satellite): Bollywood On Demand; Cinemax (multiplexed); Cinemax HD; HBO (multiplexed); HBO Latino; HBO On Demand; here! On Demand; Howard TV; Playboy TV; Showtime (multiplexed); Showtime HD; Starz (multiplexed); Starz HDTV; The Movie Channel (multiplexed).
Fee: $14.05 monthly (each).

Video-On-Demand: Yes

Pay-Per-View
Addressable homes: 47,846.
ESPN Extra, Addressable: Yes; special events; ESPN Full Court; Fresh; Hot Choice; iN DEMAND; Penthouse TV; Playboy TV; Club Jenna; Spice: Xcess.

Internet Service
Operational: Yes.
Broadband Service: Comcast High Speed Internet.
Fee: $42.95 monthly.

Telephone Service
Digital: Operational
Fee: $44.95 monthly

Miles of Plant: 2,710.0 (coaxial); 396.0 (fiber optic). Homes passed: 205,893. Total homes in franchised area: 211,869.
Area Vice President: Larry Williamson. Technical Operations Director: Tom Rice. Business Operations Director: Amy Carey. Sales & Marketing Director: Rick Finch. Marketing Manager: Meghan Martin.
City fee: of gross ($25,000 minimum).
Ownership: Comcast Cable Communications Inc. (MSO).

GRANT—Charter Communications, 315 Davis St, Grand Haven, MI 49417-1830. Phone: 616-647-6201. Fax: 616-846-0797. Web Site: http://www.charter.com. Also serves Ashland Twp., Brooks Twp. (portions), Casnovia (village), Croton Twp., Everett Twp., Garfield Twp. (Newaygo County), Grant Twp. (Newaygo County) & Newaygo. ICA: MI0105.
TV Market Ranking: 37 (Ashland Twp., Brooks Twp. (portions), Casnovia (village), Croton Twp., Everett Twp., Garfield Twp. (Newaygo County), GRANT, Grant Twp. (Newaygo County), Newaygo). Franchise award date: N.A. Franchise expiration date: N.A. Began: August 1, 1983.
Channel capacity: N.A. Channels available but not in use: N.A.

Basic Service
Subscribers: 1,714.
Programming (received off-air): WGVU-TV (PBS) Grand Rapids; WOOD-TV (NBC) Grand Rapids; WTLJ (IND) Muskegon; WWMT (CBS, CW) Kalamazoo; WWTV (CBS) Cadillac; WXMI (FOX) Grand Rapids; WXSP-CA (MNT) Grand Rapids; WZPX-TV (ION) Battle Creek; WZZM (ABC) Grand Rapids.
Programming (via satellite): C-SPAN 2; Home Shopping Network; QVC; TBS Superstation; TV Guide Network; WGN America.
Current originations: Leased Access; Government Access; Educational Access; Public Access.
Fee: $29.99 installation.

Expanded Basic Service 1
Subscribers: N.A.
Programming (via satellite): ABC Family Channel; AMC; Animal Planet; Arts & Entertainment; Bravo; Cartoon Network; CNBC; CNN; Comedy Central; Country Music TV; C-SPAN; Discovery Channel; Disney Channel; E! Entertainment Television; ESPN; ESPN 2; ESPN Classic Sports; ESPNews; Eternal Word TV Network; Food Network; Fox News Channel; Fox Sports Net Detroit; FX; G4; Golf Channel; GSN; Hallmark Channel; HDNet; HDNet Movies; Headline News; HGTV; History Channel; INSP; Lifetime; MSNBC; MTV; MTV2; National Geographic Channel; Nickelodeon; Oxygen; SoapNet; Speed Channel; Spike TV; Style Network; Syfy; The Learning Channel; Toon Disney; Travel Channel; Trinity Broadcasting Network; truTV; Turner Classic Movies; Turner Network TV; TV Land; Univision; USA Network; Versus; VH1; Weather Channel.
Fee: $47.99 monthly.

Digital Basic Service
Subscribers: N.A.
Programming (received off-air): WOOD-TV (NBC) Grand Rapids.
Programming (via satellite): BBC America; Bio; Boomerang; CNN en Espanol; Discovery Digital Networks; DMX Music; Do-It-Yourself; Fox Movie Channel; Fuse; GAS; Great American Country; History Channel International; Independent Film Channel; Lifetime Movie Network; MTV Networks Digital Suite (multiplexed); Nick Jr.; Nick Too; NickToons TV; Science Television; Sundance Channel; TV Guide Interactive Inc.

Digital Pay Service 1
Pay Units: N.A.
Programming (via satellite): Cinemax (multiplexed); Encore (multiplexed); FitTV; Flix; Fox College Sports Atlantic; Fox College Sports Central; Fox College Sports Pacific; Fox Soccer; Fuel TV; HBO (multiplexed); NFL Network; Outdoor Channel; Showtime (multiplexed); Starz (multiplexed); The Movie Channel (multiplexed).

Video-On-Demand: No

Pay-Per-View
iN DEMAND (delivered digitally); Playboy TV (delivered digitally); Spice Live (delivered digitally); NASCAR In Car (delivered

digitally); Spice Platinum (delivered digitally); Hot Net Plus (delivered digitally); NHL Center Ice/MLB Extra Innings (delivered digitally); Spice Hot (delivered digitally); ESPN Sports (delivered digitally).

Internet Service

Operational: Yes.

Broadband Service: Charter Pipeline.

Fee: $29.99 monthly.

Telephone Service

None

Miles of Plant: 85.0 (coaxial); None (fiber optic). Homes passed: 3,812.

Vice President & General Manager: Dan Spoelman. Technical Operations Manager: Keith Schierbeek. Marketing Director: Steve Schuh.

Ownership: Charter Communications Inc. (MSO).

GRASS LAKE—Millennium Digital Media. Now served by DIMONDALE, MI [MI0136]. ICA: MI0191.

GRAYLING—Charter Communications, 2074 M 32 W, Alpena, MI 49707. Phones: 231-947-5221 (Traverse City office); 989-356-4503. Fax: 989-356-3761. Web Site: http://www.charter.com. Also serves Beaver Creek Twp. ICA: MI0129.

TV Market Ranking: Below 100 (GRAYLING); Outside TV Markets (Beaver Creek Twp.). Franchise award date: N.A. Franchise expiration date: N.A. Began: December 1, 1976.

Channel capacity: 61 (operating 2-way). Channels available but not in use: 7.

Basic Service

Subscribers: 1,773.

Programming (received off-air): WCMU-TV (PBS) Mount Pleasant; WDCQ-TV (PBS) Bad Axe; WFQX-TV (FOX) Cadillac; WGTU (ABC, CW) Traverse City; WPBN-TV (NBC) Traverse City; WWTV (CBS) Cadillac.

Programming (via satellite): C-SPAN; C-SPAN 2; Eternal Word TV Network; Michigan Government Television; MyNetworkTV Inc.; QVC; TBS Superstation; Trinity Broadcasting Network; TV Guide Network; various Canadian stations; WGN America.

Current originations: Government Access; Educational Access; Public Access.

Fee: $29.99 installation; $13.50 monthly.

Expanded Basic Service 1

Subscribers: N.A.

Programming (via satellite): ABC Family Channel; AMC; Animal Planet; Arts & Entertainment; Cartoon Network; CNBC; CNN; Comedy Central; Country Music TV; CW+; Discovery Channel; Disney Channel; E! Entertainment Television; ESPN; ESPN 2; Food Network; Fox News Channel; Fox Sports Net Detroit; FX; Golf Channel; GSN; Headline News; HGTV; History Channel; Lifetime; MSNBC; MTV; MTV2; Nickelodeon; SoapNet; Speed Channel; Spike TV; Style Network; Syfy; The Learning Channel; Toon Disney; Travel Channel; truTV; Turner Classic Movies; Turner Network TV; TV Land; USA Network; Versus; VH1; Weather Channel.

Fee: $36.49 monthly.

Digital Basic Service

Subscribers: N.A.

Programming (via satellite): BBC America; Bio; CMT Pure Country; Do-It-Yourself; ESPN Classic Sports; ESPN U; ESPNews; Fox College Sports Atlantic; Fox College Sports Central; Fox College Sports Pacific; Fox Movie Channel; Fox Soccer; Fuel TV; Fuse; GAS; Great American Country; History Channel International; Independent Film Channel; Lifetime Movie Network; MTV Networks Digital Suite; Music Choice; National Geographic Channel; Nick Jr.; Nick Too; NickToons TV; Outdoor Channel; ReelzChannel; Sundance Channel; The Sportsman Channel; WE tv.

Digital Pay Service 1

Pay Units: N.A.

Programming (via satellite): Cinemax (multiplexed); Encore (multiplexed); Flix; HBO (multiplexed); LOGO; Showtime (multiplexed); Starz (multiplexed); The Movie Channel (multiplexed).

Video-On-Demand: No

Pay-Per-View

iN DEMAND (delivered digitally); Playboy TV (delivered digitally); Fresh (delivered digitally); Shorteez (delivered digitally).

Internet Service

Operational: Yes.

Broadband Service: Charter Pipeline.

Fee: $29.99 monthly.

Telephone Service

None

Miles of Plant: 65.0 (coaxial); 26.0 (fiber optic). Homes passed: 2,731.

Vice President: Joe Boullion. General Manager: Ed Kavanaugh. Technical Operations Director: Rob Novak. Marketing Manager: Brenda Auger.

City fee: 2% of gross.

Ownership: Charter Communications Inc. (MSO).

GREENVILLE—Charter Communications, 315 Davis St, Grand Haven, MI 49417-1830. Phone: 616-647-6201. Fax: 616-846-0797. Web Site: http://www.charter.com. Also serves Belding, Eureka Twp., Montcalm Twp., Orleans Twp. (portions), Otisco Twp. & Spencer Twp. ICA: MI0068.

TV Market Ranking: 37 (Belding, Eureka Twp., GREENVILLE, Montcalm Twp., Orleans Twp. (portions), Otisco Twp., Spencer Twp.). Franchise award date: N.A. Franchise expiration date: N.A. Began: October 4, 1977.

Channel capacity: N.A. Channels available but not in use: N.A.

Basic Service

Subscribers: 6,174.

Programming (received off-air): WGVU-TV (PBS) Grand Rapids; WKAR-TV (PBS) East Lansing; WLLA (IND) Kalamazoo; WOOD-TV (NBC) Grand Rapids; WTLJ (IND) Muskegon; WWMT (CBS, CW) Kalamazoo; WXMI (FOX) Grand Rapids; WXSP-CA (MNT) Grand Rapids; WZPX-TV (ION) Battle Creek; WZZM (ABC) Grand Rapids.

Programming (via satellite): C-SPAN; C-SPAN 2; Home Shopping Network; QVC; TBS Superstation; TV Guide Network; WGN America; WOTV (ABC) Battle Creek.

Current originations: Government Access; Educational Access; Public Access.

Fee: $29.99 installation.

Expanded Basic Service 1

Subscribers: N.A.

Programming (via satellite): ABC Family Channel; AMC; Animal Planet; Arts & Entertainment; Bravo; Cartoon Network; CNBC; CNN; Comedy Central; Country Music TV; Discovery Channel; Disney Channel; E! Entertainment Television; ESPN; ESPN 2; ESPN Classic Sports; ESPNews; Eternal Word TV Network; Food Network; Fox News Channel; Fox Sports Net Detroit; FX; G4; Golf Channel; GSN; Hallmark Channel; Headline News; HGTV; History Channel; INSP; Lifetime; MSNBC; MTV; MTV2; National Geographic Channel; Nickelodeon; Oxygen; SoapNet; Speed Channel; Spike TV; Style Network; Syfy; The Learning Channel; Toon Disney; Travel Channel; Trinity Broadcasting Network; truTV; Turner Classic Movies; Turner Network TV; TV Land; Univision; USA Network; Versus; VH1; WE tv; Weather Channel.

Fee: $47.99 monthly.

Digital Basic Service

Subscribers: N.A.

Programming (received off-air): WOOD-TV (NBC) Grand Rapids; WXMI (FOX) Grand Rapids; WZZM (ABC) Grand Rapids.

Programming (via satellite): BBC America; Bio; Boomerang; CNN en Espanol; Discovery Digital Networks; Discovery HD Theater; Do-It-Yourself; ESPN; Fox College Sports Atlantic; Fox College Sports Central; Fox College Sports Pacific; Fox Movie Channel; Fox Soccer; Fuel TV; GAS; Great American Country; HDNet; HDNet Movies; History Channel International; Independent Film Channel; Lifetime Movie Network; MTV Networks Digital Suite; Music Choice; NFL Network; Nick Jr.; Nick Too; NickToons TV; Outdoor Channel; Sundance Channel.

Digital Pay Service 1

Pay Units: N.A.

Programming (via satellite): Cinemax (multiplexed); Encore; HBO (multiplexed); Showtime (multiplexed); Starz; The Movie Channel.

Video-On-Demand: Yes

Pay-Per-View

Addressable homes: 1,588.

Spice; Playboy TV (delivered digitally).

Internet Service

Operational: Yes.

Broadband Service: Charter Pipeline.

Fee: $29.99 monthly.

Telephone Service

Digital: Operational

Fee: $29.99 monthly

Miles of Plant: 147.0 (coaxial); None (fiber optic). Homes passed: 9,814.

Vice President & General Manager: Dan Spoelman. Technical Operations Manager: Keith Schierbeek. Marketing Director: Steve Schuh.

City fee: 5% of gross.

Ownership: Charter Communications Inc. (MSO).

HALE—Charter Communications, 2074 M 32 W, Alpena, MI 49707. Phones: 231-947-5221 (Traverse City); 989-356-4503. Fax: 989-356-3761. Web Site: http://www.charter.com. Also serves Hill Twp. & Ogemaw County (unincorporated areas). ICA: MI0311.

TV Market Ranking: Outside TV Markets (HALE, Hill Twp., Ogemaw County (unincorporated areas)). Franchise award date: July 12, 1984. Franchise expiration date: N.A. Began: December 1, 1986.

Channel capacity: 35 (not 2-way capable). Channels available but not in use: 8.

Basic Service

Subscribers: 650.

Programming (received off-air): WBKB-TV (CBS, FOX) Alpena; WCML (PBS) Alpena; WEYI-TV (CW, NBC) Saginaw; WJRT-TV (ABC) Flint; WNEM-TV (CBS, MNT) Bay City.

Programming (via satellite): ABC Family Channel; AMC; ESPN; MTV; Nickelodeon; QVC; TBS Superstation; The Learning Channel; Turner Network TV; USA Network; VH1; WGN America.

Fee: $28.50 installation; $20.08 monthly; $15.00 additional installation.

Expanded Basic Service 1

Subscribers: 626.

Programming (via satellite): CNN; Discovery Channel; Disney Channel; Lifetime; Syfy; Turner Network TV.

Fee: $7.41 monthly.

Pay Service 1

Pay Units: 86.

Programming (via satellite): HBO.

Fee: $11.95 monthly.

Pay Service 2

Pay Units: 53.

Programming (via satellite): Showtime.

Fee: $10.95 monthly.

Pay Service 3

Pay Units: 30.

Programming (via satellite): The Movie Channel.

Fee: $10.95 monthly.

Internet Service

Operational: No.

Telephone Service

None

Miles of Plant: 52.0 (coaxial); None (fiber optic). Homes passed: 1,279.

Vice President: Joe Boullion. General Manager: Ed Kavanaugh. Technical Operations Director: Rob Nowak. Marketing Manager: Brenda Auger.

Ownership: Charter Communications Inc. (MSO).

HAMLIN TWP. (Mason County)—Charter Communications, 315 Davis St, Grand Haven, MI 49417-1830. Phone: 616-647-6201. Fax: 616-846-0797. Web Site: http://www.charter.com. ICA: MI0382.

TV Market Ranking: Outside TV Markets (HAMLIN TWP.). Franchise award date: N.A. Franchise expiration date: N.A. Began: July 1, 1991.

Channel capacity: 62 (not 2-way capable). Channels available but not in use: 36.

Basic Service

Subscribers: 200.

Programming (received off-air): WCMV (PBS) Cadillac; WFQX-TV (FOX) Cadillac; WPBN-TV (NBC) Traverse City; WWTV (CBS) Cadillac; WZZM (ABC) Grand Rapids.

Programming (via satellite): ABC Family Channel; Arts & Entertainment; CNN; Country Music TV; C-SPAN; Discovery Channel; Disney Channel; ESPN; Headline News; Lifetime; MTV; Nickelodeon; QVC; TBS Superstation; Turner Classic Movies; Turner Network TV; USA Network; Weather Channel; WGN America.

Fee: $35.00 installation; $18.95 monthly.

Pay Service 1

Pay Units: N.A.

Programming (via satellite): Cinemax; HBO.

Fee: $10.00 monthly (each).

Internet Service

Operational: No.

Telephone Service

None

Miles of Plant: 19.0 (coaxial); None (fiber optic). Homes passed: 440.

Vice President & General Manager: Dan Spoelman. Technical Operations Manager: Keith Schierbeek. Marketing Director: Steve Schuh.

Ownership: Charter Communications Inc. (MSO).

HARBOR BEACH—Comcast Cable. Now served by PIGEON, MI [MI0375]. ICA: MI0428.

HART—Charter Communications, 315 Davis St, Grand Haven, MI 49417-1830. Phone: 616-647-6201. Fax: 616-846-0797. Web

Site: http://www.charter.com. Also serves Benona Twp., Hart Twp. & Shelby (unincorporated areas). ICA: MI0268.
TV Market Ranking: Below 100 (Benona Twp., HART, Hart Twp., Shelby (unincorporated areas)). Franchise award date: N.A. Franchise expiration date: N.A. Began: N.A.
Channel capacity: 40 (2-way capable). Channels available but not in use: 19.

Basic Service
Subscribers: 1,167.
Programming (received off-air): WGVU-TV (PBS) Grand Rapids; WPBN-TV (NBC) Traverse City; WTLJ (IND) Muskegon; WWTV (CBS) Cadillac; WZZM (ABC) Grand Rapids.
Programming (via satellite): ABC Family Channel; AMC; Arts & Entertainment; CNN; Country Music TV; Discovery Channel; ESPN; QVC; Showtime; Spike TV; TBS Superstation; Travel Channel; Turner Network TV; USA Network; WGN America.
Fee: $50.00 installation; $30.00 monthly.

Internet Service
Operational: Yes.
Fee: $19.99 monthly.

Telephone Service
Digital: Operational
Fee: $14.99 monthly
Miles of Plant: 20.0 (coaxial); None (fiber optic).
Vice President & General Manager: Dan Spoelman. Technical Operations Manager: Keith Schierbeek. Marketing Director: Steve Schuh.
Ownership: Charter Communications Inc. (MSO).

HARTLAND—Comcast Cable, 29777 Telegraph Rd, Ste 4400B, Southfield, MI 48034. Phones: 586-883-7000 (Sterling Heights office); 248-233-4712. Fax: 248-233-4719. Web Site: http://www.comcast.com. Also serves Howell Twp. & Oceola Twp. ICA: MI0367.
TV Market Ranking: 61 (HARTLAND, Howell Twp., Oceola Twp.). Franchise award date: N.A. Franchise expiration date: N.A. Began: N.A.
Channel capacity: 58 (operating 2-way). Channels available but not in use: N.A.

Basic Service
Subscribers: 2,578.
Programming (received off-air): WADL (IND) Mount Clemens; WDIV-TV (NBC) Detroit; WFUM (PBS) Flint; WJBK (FOX) Detroit; WJRT-TV (ABC) Flint; WKAR-TV (PBS) East Lansing; WKBD-TV (CW) Detroit; WLNS-TV (CBS) Lansing; WMYD (MNT) Detroit; WPXD-TV (ION) Ann Arbor; WTVS (PBS) Detroit; WWJ-TV (CBS) Detroit; WXYZ-TV (ABC) Detroit.
Programming (via satellite): ABC Family Channel; QVC; TBS Superstation; Trinity Broadcasting Network; TV Guide Network; various Canadian stations; WGN America.
Current originations: Leased Access; Government Access; Educational Access.

Expanded Basic Service 1
Subscribers: N.A.
Programming (via satellite): ABC Family Channel; AMC; Animal Planet; Arts & Entertainment; Big Ten Network; Bravo; Cartoon Network; CNBC; CNN; Comedy Central; C-SPAN; C-SPAN 2; Discovery Channel; Discovery Health Channel; Disney Channel; E! Entertainment Television; ESPN; ESPN 2; Food Network; Fox News Channel; Fox Sports Net Detroit; FX; Golf Channel; Great American Country; Headline News; HGTV; History Channel; Lifetime; MSNBC; MTV; Nickelodeon; Spike TV; Syfy; The Learning Channel; Turner Network TV; TV Land; USA Network; Versus; VH1; Weather Channel.
Fee: $25.00 installation; $48.99 monthly.

Digital Basic Service
Subscribers: 642.
Programming (received off-air): WDIV-TV (NBC) Detroit; WJBK (FOX) Detroit; WKBD-TV (CW) Detroit; WMYD (MNT) Detroit; WTVS (PBS) Detroit; WWJ-TV (CBS) Detroit; WXYZ-TV (ABC) Detroit.
Programming (via satellite): ABC Family HD; Animal Planet HD; Arts & Entertainment HD; BBC America; Big Ten Network; CMT Pure Country; CNN HD; C-SPAN 3; Discovery Channel HD; Discovery HD Theater; Discovery Kids Channel; Discovery Military Channel; Discovery Planet Green; Disney Channel HD; Encore (multiplexed); ESPN 2 HD; ESPN HD; ESPNews; Flix; Food Network; Food Network HD; Fox Business Channel; FSN HD; G4; Golf Channel HD; HGTV HD; History Channel HD; ID Investigation Discovery; Jewelry Television; LOGO; Mojo HD; MTV Hits; MTV Jams; MTV Tres; MTV2; Music Choice; National Geographic Channel; National Geographic Channel HD Network; Nick Jr.; Nick Too; Science Channel; Science Channel HD; ShopNBC; SoapNet; Sundance Channel; Syfy HD; TBS in HD; TeenNick; The Word Network; TLC HD; Toon Disney; Trinity Broadcasting Network; Turner Network TV HD; TV One; Universal HD; USA Network HD; Versus HD; VH1 Classic; VH1 Soul; Weatherscan.
Fee: $15.95 monthly.

Digital Pay Service 1
Pay Units: N.A.
Programming (via satellite): Cinemax (multiplexed); Cinemax HD; HBO (multiplexed); HBO HD; Showtime (multiplexed); Showtime HD; Starz (multiplexed); Starz HDTV; The Movie Channel (multiplexed).

Video-On-Demand: Yes

Pay-Per-View
Addressable homes: 642.
iN DEMAND (delivered digitally), Addressable: Yes; Playboy TV (delivered digitally); Fresh (delivered digitally); Spice: Xcess (delivered digitally); Pleasure (delivered digitally); NBA League Pass (delivered digitally).

Internet Service
Operational: Yes.
Subscribers: 287.
Broadband Service: Comcast High Speed Internet.
Fee: $42.95 monthly.

Telephone Service
Digital: Operational
Fee: $44.95 monthly
Miles of Plant: 204.0 (coaxial); None (fiber optic). Homes passed: 3,544.
Area Vice President: Mike Castillo. Vice President, Technical Operations: Steve Thomas. Vice President, Marketing: Tony Lent. Vice President, Communications: Jerome Espy.
Ownership: Comcast Cable Communications Inc. (MSO).

HAZEL PARK—Comcast Cable. Now served by STERLING HEIGHTS, MI [MI0002]. ICA: MI0079.

HESPERIA—Charter Communications, 315 Davis St, Grand Haven, MI 49417-1830. Phone: 616-647-6201. Fax: 616-846-0797. Web Site: http://www.charter.com. Also serves Newfield Twp. ICA: MI0434.

TV Market Ranking: Below 100 (HESPERIA, Newfield Twp.). Franchise award date: N.A. Franchise expiration date: N.A. Began: N.A.
Channel capacity: 40 (not 2-way capable). Channels available but not in use: N.A.

Basic Service
Subscribers: 356.
Programming (received off-air): WGVU-TV (PBS) Grand Rapids; WOOD-TV (NBC) Grand Rapids; WPBN-TV (NBC) Traverse City; WTLJ (IND) Muskegon; WWTV (CBS) Cadillac; WXMI (FOX) Grand Rapids; WZZM (ABC) Grand Rapids.
Programming (via satellite): TBS Superstation; WGN America.
Fee: $14.00 monthly.

Expanded Basic Service 1
Subscribers: N.A.
Programming (via satellite): ABC Family Channel; AMC; Animal Planet; Arts & Entertainment; CNBC; CNN; Discovery Channel; Disney Channel; ESPN; ESPN 2; Fox News Channel; Fox Sports Net Detroit; FX; Headline News; HGTV; History Channel; Lifetime; MSNBC; MTV; Nickelodeon; QVC; Spike TV; The Learning Channel; Turner Network TV; TV Land; USA Network; Weather Channel.
Fee: $19.95 monthly.

Pay Service 1
Pay Units: N.A.
Programming (via satellite): HBO; The Movie Channel.
Fee: $9.95 monthly (TMC), $10.45 monthly (HBO).

Internet Service
Operational: No.

Telephone Service
None
Vice President & General Manager: Dan Spoelman. Technical Operations Manager: Keith Schierbeek. Marketing Director: Steve Schuh.
Ownership: Charter Communications Inc. (MSO).

HIGGINS LAKE—Charter Communications, 2074 M 32 W, Alpena, MI 49707. Phones: 231-947-5521 (Traverse City office); 989-356-4503. Fax: 989-356-3761. E-mail: jboullion@chartercom.com. Web Site: http://www.charter.com. Also serves Crawford County (portions), Gerrish Twp. (portions), Lake Twp. (Roscommon County) & Lyon Twp. (Roscommon County). ICA: MI0077.
TV Market Ranking: Below 100 (Crawford County (portions)); Outside TV Markets (Gerrish Twp. (portions), HIGGINS LAKE, Lake Twp. (Roscommon County), Lyon Twp. (Roscommon County)). Franchise award date: January 1, 1987. Franchise expiration date: N.A. Began: October 1, 1987.
Channel capacity: 58 (not 2-way capable). Channels available but not in use: 22.

Basic Service
Subscribers: 3,720.
Programming (received off-air): WCMU-TV (PBS) Mount Pleasant; WDCQ-TV (PBS) Bad Axe; WFQX-TV (FOX) Cadillac; WGTU (ABC, CW) Traverse City; WKBD-TV (CW) Detroit; WNEM-TV (CBS, MNT) Bay City; WPBN-TV (NBC) Traverse City; WWTV (CBS) Cadillac.
Programming (via satellite): C-SPAN; Eternal Word TV Network; QVC; TBS Superstation; Trinity Broadcasting Network; TV Guide Network; WGN America.
Fee: $29.99 installation; $13.50 monthly.

Expanded Basic Service 1
Subscribers: N.A.
Programming (via satellite): ABC Family Channel; AMC; Animal Planet; Arts & Entertainment; Cartoon Network; CNBC; CNN; Comedy Central; Country Music TV; Discovery Channel; Disney Channel; E! Entertainment Television; ESPN; ESPN 2; ESPN Classic Sports; Food Network; Fox News Channel; Fox Sports Net Detroit; FX; Golf Channel; GSN; Headline News; HGTV; History Channel; Lifetime; MSNBC; MTV; MTV2; Nickelodeon; Outdoor Channel; SoapNet; Speed Channel; Spike TV; Style Network; Syfy; The Learning Channel; Toon Disney; Travel Channel; truTV; Turner Classic Movies; Turner Network TV; TV Land; USA Network; Versus; VH1; Weather Channel.
Fee: $36.49 monthly.

Digital Basic Service
Subscribers: N.A.
Programming (via satellite): BBC America; Bio; Discovery Digital Networks; Do-It-Yourself; ESPNews; Fox College Sports Atlantic; Fox College Sports Central; Fox College Sports Pacific; Fox Movie Channel; Fox Soccer; Fuel TV; Fuse; GAS; Great American Country; History Channel International; Independent Film Channel; Lifetime Movie Network; MTV Networks Digital Suite; Music Choice; National Geographic Channel; NFL Network; Nick Jr.; Nick Too; NickToons TV; Sundance Channel.

Digital Pay Service 1
Pay Units: N.A.
Programming (via satellite): Cinemax (multiplexed); Flix (multiplexed); HBO (multiplexed); Showtime (multiplexed); Starz (multiplexed); The Movie Channel (multiplexed); The New Encore (multiplexed).

Video-On-Demand: No

Pay-Per-View
iN DEMAND (delivered digitally); Playboy TV (delivered digitally); Fresh (delivered digitally).

Internet Service
Operational: Yes.
Broadband Service: Charter Pipeline.
Fee: $29.99 monthly.

Telephone Service
None
Miles of Plant: 153.0 (coaxial); 1.0 (fiber optic). Additional miles planned: 1.0 (coaxial). Homes passed: 4,859.
Vice President: Joe Boullion. General Manager: Ed Kavanaugh. Technical Operations Director: Rob Nowak. Marketing Manager: Brenda Auger.
Ownership: Charter Communications Inc. (MSO).

HIGHLAND PARK—Charter Communications, 7372 Davison Rd, Davison, MI 48423. Phone: 810-652-1400. Web Site: http://www.charter.com. ICA: MI0066.

TV Market Ranking: 5 (HIGHLAND PARK). Franchise award date: July 12, 1982. Franchise expiration date: N.A. Began: July 13, 1984.

Channel capacity: 52 (not 2-way capable). Channels available but not in use: 14.

Basic Service

Subscribers: 968.

Programming (received off-air): WADL (IND) Mount Clemens; WDIV-TV (NBC) Detroit; WJBK (FOX) Detroit; WKBD-TV (CW) Detroit; WMYD (MNT) Detroit; WTVS (PBS) Detroit; WWJ-TV (CBS) Detroit; WXYZ-TV (ABC) Detroit.

Programming (via satellite): TBS Superstation; WGN America.

Current originations: Government Access; Educational Access; Public Access.

Fee: $29.99 installation; $13.50 monthly.

Expanded Basic Service 1

Subscribers: N.A.

Programming (via satellite): ABC Family Channel; Arts & Entertainment; BET Networks; CNN; C-SPAN; C-SPAN 2; Discovery Channel; Disney Channel; ESPN; Home Shopping Network; Lifetime; Nickelodeon; Turner Network TV; USA Network; Weather Channel.

Fee: $36.49 monthly.

Pay Service 1

Pay Units: N.A.

Programming (via satellite): Cinemax; HBO; Showtime; The Movie Channel.

Fee: $9.50 monthly (each).

Internet Service

Operational: No.

Telephone Service

None

Miles of Plant: 40.0 (coaxial); None (fiber optic). Total homes in franchised area: 7,726.

Vice President & General Manager: Dave Slowick. Technical Operations Director: Lloyd Collins. Marketing Director: Lisa Gayari.

City fee: 5% of gross.

Ownership: Charter Communications Inc. (MSO).

HILLMAN TWP.—Formerly served by Northwoods Cable Inc. No longer in operation. ICA: MI0235.

HILLSDALE—Comcast Cable, 3500 Patterson Ave SE, Grand Rapids, MI 49512. Phone: 616-977-2200. Fax: 616-977-2224. Web Site: http://www.comcast.com. Also serves Adams Twp. (Hillsdale County), Allen, Cambria Twp., Fayette Twp., Jefferson Twp. (Hillsdale County), Jonesville Village, North Adams Village, Pittsford Twp. & Scipio Twp. ICA: MI0070.

TV Market Ranking: 92 (Adams Twp. (Hillsdale County), Allen, Jonesville Village, North Adams Village, Scipio Twp., Waldron Village); Below 100 (Cambria Twp., Fayette Twp., HILLSDALE, Jefferson Twp. (Hillsdale County), Pittsford Twp.). Franchise award date: N.A. Franchise expiration date: N.A. Began: January 1, 1966.

Channel capacity: N.A. Channels available but not in use: N.A.

Basic Service

Subscribers: 6,070.

Programming (received off-air): WILX-TV (NBC) Onondaga; WKAR-TV (PBS) East Lansing; WKBD-TV (CW) Detroit; WLAJ (ABC, CW) Lansing; WLNS-TV (CBS) Lansing; WSYM-TV (FOX) Lansing; WTOL (CBS) Toledo; WTVG (ABC) Toledo.

Programming (via satellite): ABC Family Channel; AMC; Animal Planet; Cartoon Network; Comedy Central; C-SPAN; C-SPAN 2; ESPN; HGTV; ION Television; QVC; TBS Superstation; truTV; Turner Network TV; TV Guide Network; TV Land; Weather Channel; WGN America.

Current originations: Public Access.

Expanded Basic Service 1

Subscribers: 5,079.

Programming (via satellite): Arts & Entertainment; CNBC; CNN; Discovery Channel; Discovery Health Channel; Disney Channel; E! Entertainment Television; ESPN 2; Food Network; Fox News Channel; Fox Sports Net Detroit; FX; G4; Golf Channel; Great American Country; Halogen Network; Headline News; History Channel; Lifetime; MTV; Nickelodeon; Speed Channel; Spike TV; Style Network; Syfy; The Learning Channel; USA Network; Versus; VH1.

Fee: $48.99 monthly.

Digital Basic Service

Subscribers: N.A.

Programming (via satellite): BBC America; CMT Pure Country; Cooking Channel; C-SPAN 3; Discovery Kids Channel; Discovery Military Channel; Discovery Planet Green; Disney XD; Do-It-Yourself; Encore (multiplexed); ESPNews; FearNet; Flix; G4; GSN; ID Investigation Discovery; MTV Hits; MTV Jams; MTV Tres; MTV2; Music Choice; National Geographic Channel; Nick Jr.; Nick Too; Oxygen; PBS Kids Sprout; Science Channel; SoapNet; TeenNick; Trinity Broadcasting Network; VH1 Classic; VH1 Soul.

Fee: $9.95 monthly.

Digital Pay Service 1

Pay Units: N.A.

Programming (via satellite): Cinemax (multiplexed); HBO (multiplexed); HBO On Demand; Playboy TV; Showtime (multiplexed); Starz (multiplexed); The Movie Channel (multiplexed).

Fee: $18.05 monthly (each).

Video-On-Demand: No

Pay-Per-View

iN DEMAND (delivered digitally); Playboy TV; Fresh (delivered digitally); Spice: Xcess (delivered digitally); Hot Choice (delivered digitally).

Internet Service

Operational: Yes.

Broadband Service: Comcast High Speed Internet.

Fee: $42.95 monthly.

Telephone Service

None

Miles of Plant: 200.0 (coaxial); None (fiber optic). Homes passed: 7,200.

Area Vice President: Larry Williamson. Business Operations Director: Amy Carey. Technical Operations Director: Tom Rice. Sales & Marketing Manager: Rick Finch.

Ownership: Comcast Cable Communications Inc. (MSO).

HOLLAND—Comcast Cable, 3500 Patterson Ave SE, Grand Rapids, MI 49512. Phone: 616-977-2200. Fax: 616-977-2224. Web Site: http://www.comcast.com. ICA: MI0056.

TV Market Ranking: 37 (HOLLAND). Franchise award date: October 1, 1973. Franchise expiration date: N.A. Began: March 1, 1976.

Channel capacity: N.A. Channels available but not in use: N.A.

Basic Service

Subscribers: 9,210.

Programming (received off-air): WGVU-TV (PBS) Grand Rapids; WLLA (IND) Kalamazoo; WOOD-TV (NBC) Grand Rapids; WOTV (ABC) Battle Creek; WTLJ (IND) Muskegon; WWMT (CBS, CW) Kalamazoo; WXMI (FOX) Grand Rapids; WXSP-CA (MNT) Grand Rapids; WZPX-TV (ION) Battle Creek; WZZM (ABC) Grand Rapids; 18 FMs.

Programming (via satellite): ABC Family Channel; AMC; Arts & Entertainment; CNBC; CNN; C-SPAN; C-SPAN 2; Discovery Channel; ESPN; Headline News; Home Shopping Network; Lifetime; MTV; Nickelodeon; QVC; Spike TV; TBS Superstation; Travel Channel; Trinity Broadcasting Network; Turner Network TV; TV Guide Network; TV Land; USA Network; VH1; Weather Channel; WGN America.

Current originations: Religious Access; Government Access; Educational Access; Public Access.

Expanded Basic Service 1

Subscribers: N.A.

Programming (via satellite): Animal Planet; BET Networks; Cartoon Network; Comcast Local Detroit; Comedy Central; Country Music TV; Disney Channel; E! Entertainment Television; Food Network; Fox News Channel; Fox Sports Net Detroit; FX; GalaVision; Golf Channel; Hallmark Channel; History Channel; MSNBC; Oxygen; The Learning Channel; truTV; TV Land; Univision.

Fee: $48.99 monthly.

Digital Basic Service

Subscribers: N.A.

Programming (via satellite): AmericanLife TV Network; BBC America; Bio; Bloomberg Television; Bravo; Discovery Kids Channel; Discovery Military Channel; Discovery Planet Green; ESPN 2; ESPN Now; FitTV; Fox Movie Channel; Fox Soccer; FSN Digital Atlantic (multiplexed); FSN Digital Central; FSN Digital Pacific; Fuse; G4; Gospel Music Channel; Great American Country; GSN; Halogen Network; HGTV; History Channel; History Channel International; ID Investigation Discovery; Independent Film Channel; International Television (ITV); Lifetime Movie Network; Lime; MTV Tres; MTV2; Music Choice; National Geographic Channel; Nick Jr.; NickToons TV; Outdoor Channel; Ovation; Science Channel; ShopNBC; Speed Channel; Style Network; Sundance Channel; Syfy; TeenNick; The Word Network; Turner Classic Movies; TV Land; WAM! America's Kidz Network; WE tv.

Fee: $9.95 monthly.

Digital Pay Service 1

Pay Units: N.A.

Programming (via satellite): Canales N; Cinemax (multiplexed); Encore (multiplexed); Flix; HBO (multiplexed); Showtime (multiplexed); The Movie Channel (multiplexed).

Fee: $18.05 monthly (each).

Video-On-Demand: Planned

Pay-Per-View

iN DEMAND (delivered digitally); Barker (delivered digitally); Fresh (delivered digitally); Shorteez (delivered digitally); Playboy TV (delivered digitally); Hot Choice (delivered digitally).

Internet Service

Operational: Yes.

Broadband Service: Comcast High Speed Internet.

Fee: $42.95 monthly.

Telephone Service

Digital: Operational

Miles of Plant: 118.0 (coaxial); None (fiber optic). Homes passed: 12,348.

Area Vice President: Larry Williamson. Technical Operations Director: Tom Rice. Sales & Marketing Director: Rick Finch. Business Operations Director: Amy Carey.

City fee: 3% of gross.

Ownership: Comcast Cable Communications Inc. (MSO).

HOPE TWP. (Midland County)—Charter Communications, 7372 Davison Rd, Davison, MI 48423. Phone: 810-652-1400. Web Site: http://www.charter.com. Also serves Edenville Twp., Garfield Twp. (Bay County) & Mills Twp. (Midland County). ICA: MI0189.

TV Market Ranking: 61 (Edenville Twp., Garfield Twp. (Bay County), HOPE TWP. (MIDLAND COUNTY), Mills Twp. (Midland County)). Franchise award date: December 17, 1988. Franchise expiration date: N.A. Began: June 1, 1990.

Channel capacity: 54 (operating 2-way). Channels available but not in use: N.A.

Basic Service

Subscribers: 619.

Programming (received off-air): various Canadian stations; WAQP (IND) Saginaw; WCMU-TV (PBS) Mount Pleasant; WDCQ-TV (PBS) Bad Axe; WEYI-TV (CW, NBC) Saginaw; WJRT-TV (ABC) Flint; WKBD-TV (CW) Detroit; WNEM-TV (CBS, MNT) Bay City; WSMH (FOX) Flint; WWTV (CBS) Cadillac.

Programming (via satellite): C-SPAN; C-SPAN 2; Eternal Word TV Network; G4; Home Shopping Network; INSP; Michigan Government Television; QVC; TBS Superstation; TV Guide Network; Univision; WGN America.

Current originations: Government Access; Educational Access; Public Access.

Fee: $29.99 installation; $13.50 monthly; $1.00 converter.

Expanded Basic Service 1

Subscribers: 585.

Programming (via satellite): ABC Family Channel; AMC; Animal Planet; Arts & Entertainment; BET Networks; Bravo; Cartoon Network; CNBC; CNN; Comedy Central; Country Music TV; Discovery Channel; Disney Channel; E! Entertainment Television; ESPN; ESPN 2; Food Network; Fox News Channel; Fox Sports Net Detroit; FX; Golf Channel; GSN; Hallmark Channel; Headline News; HGTV; History Channel; Lifetime; MSNBC; MTV; MTV2; National Geographic Channel; Nickelodeon; Outdoor Channel; Oxygen; SoapNet; Speed Channel; Spike TV; Style Network; Syfy; Telemundo; The Learning Channel; Toon Disney; Travel Channel; truTV; Turner Classic Movies; Turner Network TV; TV Land; USA Network; Versus; VH1; WE tv; Weather Channel.

Fee: $36.49 monthly.

Video-On-Demand: No

Pay-Per-View

iN DEMAND (delivered digitally); ESPN (delivered digitally); NHL Center Ice (delivered digitally); MLB Extra Innings (delivered digitally); Playboy TV (delivered digitally); Spice Live (delivered digitally); Spice Platinum (delivered digitally); Hot Net Plus (delivered digitally); Spice Hot (delivered digitally).

Internet Service

Operational: No.

Telephone Service

None

Miles of Plant: 49.0 (coaxial); None (fiber optic). Homes passed: 1,032.

Vice President & General Manager: Dave Slowick. Technical Operations Director: Lloyd Collins. Marketing Director: Lisa Gayari.

Township fee: 3% of gross.
Ownership: Charter Communications Inc. (MSO).

HOUGHTON—Charter Communications, 359 US 41 East, Negaunee, MI 49866. Phones: 231-947-5221 (Traverse City office); 906-475-0107. Fax: 906-475-7007. Web Site: http://www.charter.com. Also serves Adams Twp. (Houghton County), Ahmeek, Allouez Twp., Baraga, Calumet, Chassell Twp., Copper City, Dollar Bay, Hancock, Hubbell, Lake Linden, L'Anse, Laurium, Osceola Twp. (Houghton County), Ripley, South Range & Torch Lake Twp. (Houghton County). ICA: MI0049.
TV Market Ranking: Below 100 (Adams Twp. (Houghton County), Ahmeek, Allouez Twp., Baraga, Calumet, Chassell Twp., Copper City, Dollar Bay, Hancock, HOUGHTON, Hubbell, Lake Linden, L'anse, Laurium, Osceola Twp. (Houghton County), Ripley, South Range, Torch Lake Twp. (Houghton County)). Franchise award date: August 1, 1955. Franchise expiration date: N.A. Began: August 1, 1955.
Channel capacity: N.A. Channels available but not in use: N.A.

Basic Service
Subscribers: 12,000.
Programming (received off-air): WBUP (ABC) Ishpeming; WJMN-TV (CBS) Escanaba; WLUC-TV (NBC) Marquette; WLUK-TV (FOX) Green Bay; WNMU (PBS) Marquette; WZMQ (IND, MNT) Marquette.
Programming (via satellite): C-SPAN; C-SPAN 2; C-SPAN 3; CW+; Eternal Word TV Network; G4; Home Shopping Network; INSP; QVC; TBS Superstation; Trinity Broadcasting Network; TV Guide Network; various Canadian stations; Weather Channel; WGN America.
Current originations: Religious Access; Educational Access; Public Access.
Fee: $29.99 installation; $13.50 monthly.

Expanded Basic Service 1
Subscribers: 9,994.
Programming (via satellite): ABC Family Channel; AMC; Animal Planet; Arts & Entertainment; Bravo; Cartoon Network; CNBC; CNN; Comedy Central; Country Music TV; Discovery Channel; Disney Channel; E! Entertainment Television; ESPN; ESPN 2; FitTV; Food Network; Fox News Channel; Fox Sports Net Detroit; FX; Golf Channel; GSN; Hallmark Channel; Headline News; HGTV; History Channel; Lifetime; MSNBC; MTV; National Geographic Channel; Nickelodeon; Oxygen; SoapNet; Speed Channel; Spike TV; Style Network; Syfy; The Learning Channel; Toon Disney; Travel Channel; truTV; Turner Classic Movies; Turner Network TV; TV Land; USA Network; Versus; VH1; WE tv.
Fee: $36.49 monthly.

Digital Basic Service
Subscribers: N.A.
Programming (received off-air): WJMN-TV (CBS) Escanaba; WLUC-TV (NBC) Marquette; WNMU (PBS) Marquette.
Programming (via satellite): BBC America; Bio; CMT Pure Country; Cooking Channel; Discovery Digital Networks; Discovery HD Theater; Do-It-Yourself; ESPN Classic Sports; ESPN HD; ESPNews; Food Network On Demand; Fox College Sports Atlantic; Fox College Sports Central; Fox College Sports Pacific; Fox Movie Channel; Fox Soccer; Fuel TV; Fuse; GAS; Great American Country; HDNet; HDNet Movies; HGTV On Demand; History Channel International; Howard TV; Independent Film Channel; Lifetime Movie Network; MTV Networks Digital Suite; Nick Jr.; Nick Too; NickToons TV; Outdoor Channel; Sundance Channel; Turner Network TV HD; Universal HD; Versus On Demand.

Digital Pay Service 1
Pay Units: N.A.
Programming (via satellite): Cinemax (multiplexed); Cinemax HD; Cinemax On Demand; Encore (multiplexed); Flix; HBO (multiplexed); HBO HD; HBO On Demand; LOGO; Showtime (multiplexed); Showtime HD; Showtime On Demand; Starz (multiplexed); Starz On Demand; The Movie Channel (multiplexed).

Video-On-Demand: Yes

Pay-Per-View
iN DEMAND (delivered digitally); ESPN (delivered digitally); NHL Center Ice (delivered digitally); MLB Extra Innings (delivered digitally); Playboy TV (delivered digitally); Fresh (delivered digitally); Shorteez (delivered digitally).

Internet Service
Operational: Yes.
Broadband Service: Charter Pipeline.
Fee: $49.95 installation; $29.99 monthly.

Telephone Service
Digital: Operational
Fee: $29.99 monthly

Miles of Plant: 284.0 (coaxial); 129.0 (fiber optic). Homes passed: 14,305. Total homes in franchised area: 18,937.
Vice President: Joe Boulion. General Manager: Rex Buettgenbach. Technical Operations Director: Rob Nowak. Marketing Manager: Sandy Gottschalk. Government Relations Manager: Don Gladwell.
City fee: 3% of basic.
Ownership: Charter Communications Inc. (MSO).

HOUGHTON LAKE—Charter Communications, 2074 M 32 W, Alpena, MI 49707. Phones: 231-947-5221 (Traverse City office); 989-356-4503. Fax: 989-356-3761. E-mail: jboullion@chartercom.com. Web Site: http://www.charter.com. Also serves Backus Twp., Denton Twp. & Markey Twp. ICA: MI0081.
TV Market Ranking: Below 100 (Backus Twp., Denton Twp., HOUGHTON LAKE, Markey Twp.). Franchise award date: N.A. Franchise expiration date: N.A. Began: N.A.
Channel capacity: N.A. Channels available but not in use: N.A.

Basic Service
Subscribers: 4,023.
Programming (received off-air): WCMU-TV (PBS) Mount Pleasant; WDCQ-TV (PBS) Bad Axe; WEYI-TV (CW, NBC) Saginaw; WFQX-TV (FOX) Cadillac; WGTU (ABC, CW) Traverse City; WJRT-TV (ABC) Flint; WKBD-TV (CW) Detroit; WNEM-TV (CBS, MNT) Bay City; WPBN-TV (NBC) Traverse City; WSMH (FOX) Flint; WWTV (CBS) Cadillac.
Programming (via satellite): C-SPAN; C-SPAN 2; Eternal Word TV Network; G4; Home Shopping Network; INSP; QVC; TBS Superstation; Trinity Broadcasting Network; TV Guide Network; WGN America.
Current originations: Government Access; Educational Access; Public Access.
Fee: $29.99 installation; $13.50 monthly.

Expanded Basic Service 1
Subscribers: N.A.
Programming (via satellite): ABC Family Channel; AMC; Animal Planet; Arts & Entertainment; Bravo; Cartoon Network; CNBC; CNN; Comedy Central; Country Music TV; Discovery Channel; Disney Channel; E! Entertainment Television; ESPN; ESPN 2; ESPN Classic Sports; Food Network; Fox News Channel; Fox Sports Net Detroit; FX; Golf Channel; GSN; Hallmark Channel; HDNet; HDNet Movies; Headline News; HGTV; History Channel; Lifetime; MSNBC; MTV; MTV2; National Geographic Channel; Nickelodeon; Outdoor Channel; Oxygen; SoapNet; Speed Channel; Spike TV; Style Network; Syfy; Telemundo; The Learning Channel; Toon Disney; Travel Channel; truTV; Turner Classic Movies; Turner Network TV; TV Land; USA Network; Versus; VH1; Weather Channel.
Fee: $36.49 monthly.

Digital Basic Service
Subscribers: N.A.
Programming (via satellite): BBC America; Bio; Discovery Digital Networks; Do-It-Yourself; ESPNews; Fox College Sports Atlantic; Fox College Sports Central; Fox College Sports Pacific; Fox Movie Channel; Fox Soccer; Fuel TV; Fuse; GAS; Great American Country; History Channel International; Independent Film Channel; Lifetime Movie Network; MTV Networks Digital Suite; Music Choice; NFL Network; Nick Jr.; Nick Too; Nickelodeon; Sundance Channel.

Digital Pay Service 1
Pay Units: N.A.
Programming (via satellite): Cinemax (multiplexed); Encore (multiplexed); Flix; HBO (multiplexed); HBO HD; Showtime (multiplexed); Showtime HD; Starz (multiplexed); The Movie Channel (multiplexed).

Video-On-Demand: Yes

Pay-Per-View
iN DEMAND (delivered digitally); ESPN (delivered digitally); NHL Center Ice (delivered digitally); MLB Extra Innings (delivered digitally); Playboy TV (delivered digitally); Fresh (delivered digitally).

Internet Service
Operational: Yes.
Broadband Service: Charter Pipeline.
Fee: $29.99 monthly.

Telephone Service
Digital: Operational

Miles of Plant: 144.0 (coaxial); 24.0 (fiber optic). Homes passed: 7,157.
Vice President: Joe Boullion. General Manager: Ed Kavanaugh. Technical Operations Director: Rob Nowak. Marketing Manager: Brenda Auger.
Ownership: Charter Communications Inc. (MSO).

HOWARD CITY—Charter Communications, 315 Davis St, Grand Haven, MI 49417-1830. Phone: 616-647-6201. Fax: 616-846-0797. Web Site: http://www.charter.com. Also serves Aetna Twp. (Mecosta County), Austin Twp. (Mecosta County), Deerfield Twp. (Mecosta County), Ensley Twp., Maple Valley Twp. (Montcalm County), Morley, Nelson Twp. (portions), Pierson (village), Pine Twp., Reynolds Twp., Sand Lake, Stanwood & Winfield Twp. ICA: MI0100.
TV Market Ranking: 37 (Ensley Twp., HOWARD CITY, Maple Valley Twp. (Montcalm County), Nelson Twp. (portions), Pierson (village), Pine Twp., Reynolds Twp., Sand Lake); Outside TV Markets (Aetna Twp. (Mecosta County), Austin Twp. (Mecosta County), Deerfield Twp. (Mecosta County), Morley, Stanwood, Winfield Twp.). Franchise award date: July 1, 1985. Franchise expiration date: N.A. Began: August 15, 1985.
Channel capacity: N.A. Channels available but not in use: N.A.

Basic Service
Subscribers: 1,958.
Programming (received off-air): WGVU-TV (PBS) Grand Rapids; WOOD-TV (NBC) Grand Rapids; WOTV (ABC) Battle Creek; WTLJ (IND) Muskegon; WWMT (CBS, CW) Kalamazoo; WWTV (CBS) Cadillac; WXMI (FOX) Grand Rapids; WXSP-CA (MNT) Grand Rapids; WZPX-TV (ION) Battle Creek; WZZM (ABC) Grand Rapids.
Programming (via satellite): C-SPAN; C-SPAN 2; Home Shopping Network; QVC; TBS Superstation; TV Guide Network; WGN America.
Current originations: Government Access; Public Access; Leased Access; Educational Access.
Fee: $29.99 installation.

Expanded Basic Service 1
Subscribers: N.A.
Programming (via satellite): ABC Family Channel; AMC; Animal Planet; Arts & Entertainment; Bravo; Cartoon Network; CNBC; CNN; Comedy Central; Country Music TV; Discovery Channel; Disney Channel; E! Entertainment Television; ESPN; ESPN 2; ESPN Classic Sports; ESPNews; Eternal Word TV Network; Food Network; Fox News Channel; Fox Sports Net Detroit; FX; G4; Golf Channel; GSN; Hallmark Channel; Headline News; HGTV; History Channel; INSP; Lifetime; MSNBC; MTV; MTV2; National Geographic Channel; Nickelodeon; Oxygen; SoapNet; Speed Channel; Spike TV; Style Network; Syfy; The Learning Channel; Toon Disney; Travel Channel; Trinity Broadcasting Network; truTV; Turner Classic Movies; Turner Network TV; TV Land; Univision; USA Network; Versus; VH1; WE tv; Weather Channel.
Fee: $47.99 monthly.

Digital Basic Service
Subscribers: N.A.
Programming (received off-air): WOOD-TV (NBC) Grand Rapids; WWTV (CBS) Cadillac; WXMI (FOX) Grand Rapids; WZZM (ABC) Grand Rapids.
Programming (via satellite): BBC America; Bio; Boomerang; CNN en Espanol; Discovery Digital Networks; Discovery HD Theater; Do-It-Yourself; ESPN; FitTV; Fox College Sports Atlantic; Fox College Sports Central; Fox College Sports Pacific; Fox Movie Channel; Fox Soccer; Fuel TV; Fuse; GAS; Great American Country; HDNet; HDNet Movies; History Channel International; Independent Film Channel; Lifetime Movie Network; LWS Local Weather Station; MTV Networks Digital Suite; Music Choice; NFL Network; Nick Jr.; Nick Too; NickToons TV; Outdoor Channel; Sundance Channel; TV Guide Interactive Inc.

Digital Pay Service 1
Pay Units: N.A.
Programming (via satellite): Cinemax (multiplexed); Encore (multiplexed); Flix; HBO (multiplexed); HBO HD; Showtime (multiplexed); Showtime HD; Starz (multiplexed); The Movie Channel (multiplexed).
Video-On-Demand: Yes
Pay-Per-View
Playboy TV (delivered digitally); Spice Live (delivered digitally); Spice Platinum (delivered digitally); Hot Net Plus (delivered digitally); Spice Hot (delivered digitally); iN DEMAND (delivered digitally); NASCAR In Car (delivered digitally); NHL Center Ice (delivered digitally); MLB Extra Innings (delivered digitally); ESPN (delivered digitally).
Internet Service
Operational: Yes.
Broadband Service: Charter Pipeline.
Fee: $29.99 monthly.
Telephone Service
Digital: Operational
Fee: $29.99 monthly
Miles of Plant: 141.0 (coaxial); None (fiber optic). Homes passed: 3,993.
Vice President & General Manager: Dan Spoelman. Technical Operations Manager: Keith Schierbeek. Marketing Director: Steve Schuh.
City fee: 1% of basic gross.
Ownership: Charter Communications Inc. (MSO).

HUDSON—Comcast Cable, 3500 Patterson Ave SE, Grand Rapids, MI 49512. Phone: 616-977-2200. Fax: 616-977-2224. Web Site: http://www.comcast.com. ICA: MI0182.
TV Market Ranking: Below 100 (HUDSON). Franchise award date: N.A. Franchise expiration date: N.A. Began: May 1, 1973.
Channel capacity: N.A. Channels available but not in use: N.A.
Basic Service
Subscribers: 715.
Programming (received off-air): WILX-TV (NBC) Onondaga; WKAR-TV (PBS) East Lansing; WKBD-TV (CW) Detroit; WLAJ (ABC, CW) Lansing; WLNS-TV (CBS) Lansing; WSYM-TV (FOX) Lansing; WTOL (CBS) Toledo; WTVG (ABC) Toledo; allband FM.
Programming (via satellite): C-SPAN; C-SPAN 2; ION Television; QVC; truTV; TV Guide Network; Weather Channel; WGN America.
Current originations: Public Access.
Expanded Basic Service 1
Subscribers: N.A.
Programming (via satellite): Arts & Entertainment; CNBC; CNN; Discovery Channel; Discovery Health Channel; Disney Channel; E! Entertainment Television; ESPN 2; Food Network; Fox News Channel; Fox Sports Net Detroit; FX; G4; Golf Channel; Great American Country; Halogen Network; Headline News; History Channel; Lifetime; MTV; Nickelodeon; Speed Channel; Spike TV; Style Network; Syfy; The Learning Channel; USA Network; Versus; VH1.
Fee: $48.99 monthly.
Expanded Basic Service 2
Subscribers: N.A.
Programming (via satellite): ABC Family Channel; AMC; Animal Planet; Cartoon Network; Comedy Central; ESPN; HGTV; TBS Superstation; Turner Network TV; TV Land.
Digital Basic Service
Subscribers: N.A.
Programming (via satellite): BBC America; CMT Pure Country; Cooking Channel; C-SPAN 3; Discovery Kids Channel; Discovery Military Channel; Discovery Planet Green; Disney XD; Do-It-Yourself; Encore (multiplexed); ESPNews; FearNet; Flix; G4; GSN; ID Investigation Discovery; MTV Hits; MTV Jams; MTV Tres; MTV2; Music Choice; National Geographic Channel; Nick Jr.; Nick Too; Oxygen; PBS Kids Sprout; Science Channel; SoapNet; TeenNick; Trinity Broadcasting Network; VH1 Classic; VH1 Soul.
Digital Pay Service 1
Pay Units: N.A.
Programming (via satellite): Cinemax (multiplexed); HBO (multiplexed); HBO On Demand; Playboy TV; Showtime (multiplexed); Starz (multiplexed); The Movie Channel (multiplexed).
Pay-Per-View
iN DEMAND (delivered digitally); Playboy TV (delivered digitally); Fresh (delivered digitally); Spice: Xcess (delivered digitally); Hot Choice (delivered digitally).
Internet Service
Operational: Yes.
Telephone Service
Digital: Operational
Miles of Plant: 22.0 (coaxial); None (fiber optic). Homes passed: 1,072.
Area Vice President: Larry Williams. Business Operations Director: Amy Carey. Technical Operations Director: Tom Rice. Sales & Marketing Manager: Rick Finch.
Ownership: Comcast Cable Communications Inc. (MSO).

IMLAY CITY—Charter Communications. Now served by ALMONT, MI [MI0257]. ICA: MI0313.

INDIAN RIVER—Charter Communications, 701 E South Airport Rd, Traverse City, MI 49686-4861. Phone: 231-947-5221. Fax: 231-947-2004. E-mail: jboullion@chartercom.com. Web Site: http://www.charter.com. Also serves Alanson (village), Burt Twp., Littlefield Twp. & Tuscarora Twp. ICA: MI0159.
TV Market Ranking: Below 100 (Alanson (village), Burt Twp., INDIAN RIVER, Littlefield Twp., Tuscarora Twp.). Franchise award date: N.A. Franchise expiration date: N.A. Began: November 14, 1981.
Channel capacity: 40 (2-way capable). Channels available but not in use: 9.
Basic Service
Subscribers: 1,017.
Programming (received off-air): WCML (PBS) Alpena; WFUP (FOX) Vanderbilt; WGTQ (ABC) Sault Ste. Marie; WTOM-TV (NBC) Cheboygan; WWUP-TV (CBS, FOX) Sault Ste. Marie.
Programming (via satellite): Country Music TV; C-SPAN; QVC; TBS Superstation; WGN America.
Current originations: Government Access; Educational Access; Public Access.
Fee: $29.99 installation; $13.50 monthly.
Expanded Basic Service 1
Subscribers: N.A.
Programming (via satellite): ABC Family Channel; AMC; Arts & Entertainment; CNN; Discovery Channel; Disney Channel; ESPN; ESPN 2; Food Network; Fox Sports Net Detroit; Headline News; Lifetime; MTV; Nickelodeon; Spike TV; The Learning Channel; Turner Network TV; USA Network; Weather Channel.
Fee: $36.49 monthly.
Pay Service 1
Pay Units: 307.
Programming (via satellite): Cinemax; HBO; Starz.
Fee: $5.95 monthly (Starz), $10.95 monthly (Cinemax), $11.95 monthly (HBO).
Internet Service
Operational: Yes.
Fee: $19.99 monthly.
Telephone Service
Digital: Operational
Fee: $14.99 monthly
Miles of Plant: 39.0 (coaxial); None (fiber optic). Homes passed: 1,921.
Vice President & General Manager: Joe Boullion. Technical Operations Director: Rob Nowak. Marketing Manager: Tommy Reicha.
Ownership: Charter Communications Inc. (MSO).

IONIA—Charter Communications, 315 Davis St, Grand Haven, MI 49417-1830. Phone: 616-647-6201. Fax: 616-846-0797. Web Site: http://www.charter.com. Also serves Berlin Twp. (Ionia County), Day Twp., Douglass Twp., Easton Twp., Edmore, Evergreen Twp., Home Twp., Ionia Twp., Lyons Twp., Lyons Village, McBrides Village, Montcalm Twp. (northern portion), Muir, Orleans Twp. (portions), Pine Twp., Ronald Twp., Sheridan, Sidney Twp. & Stanton. ICA: MI0091.
TV Market Ranking: 37 (Douglass Twp., Evergreen Twp., Lyons Twp., Lyons Village, McBrides Village, Montcalm Twp. (northern portion), Muir, Orleans Twp. (portions), Ronald Twp., Sheridan, Sidney Twp.); 37,92 (Berlin Twp. (Ionia County), Easton Twp., IONIA, Ionia Twp.); Outside TV Markets (Day Twp., Edmore, Home Twp., Pine Twp., Stanton). Franchise award date: October 23, 1978. Franchise expiration date: N.A. Began: August 1, 1979.
Channel capacity: 46 (not 2-way capable). Channels available but not in use: N.A.
Basic Service
Subscribers: 5,449.
Programming (received off-air): WCMU-TV (PBS) Mount Pleasant; WGVU-TV (PBS) Grand Rapids; WKAR-TV (PBS) East Lansing; WLNS-TV (CBS) Lansing; WOOD-TV (NBC) Grand Rapids; WOTV (ABC) Battle Creek; WSYM-TV (FOX) Lansing; WWMT (CBS, CW) Kalamazoo; WXMI (FOX) Grand Rapids; WXSP-CA (MNT) Grand Rapids; WZPX-TV (ION) Battle Creek; WZZM (ABC) Grand Rapids.
Programming (via satellite): C-SPAN; C-SPAN 2; Home Shopping Network; QVC; TBS Superstation; TV Guide Network; WGN America.
Current originations: Government Access; Educational Access; Public Access.
Fee: $29.99 installation; $10.00 additional installation.
Expanded Basic Service 1
Subscribers: N.A.
Programming (via satellite): ABC Family Channel; AMC; Animal Planet; Arts & Entertainment; Bravo; Cartoon Network; CNBC; CNN; Comedy Central; Country Music TV; Discovery Channel; Disney Channel; E! Entertainment Television; ESPN; ESPN 2; ESPN Classic Sports; ESPNews; Eternal Word TV Network; Food Network; Fox News Channel; Fox Sports Net Detroit; FX; G4; Golf Channel; GSN; Hallmark Channel; Headline News; HGTV; History Channel; INSP; Lifetime; MSNBC; MTV; MTV2; National Geographic Channel; Nickelodeon; Oxygen; SoapNet; Speed Channel; Spike TV; Style Network; Syfy; The Learning Channel; Toon Disney; Travel Channel; Trinity Broadcasting Network; truTV; Turner Classic Movies; Turner Network TV; TV Land; Univision; USA Network; Versus; VH1; WE tv; Weather Channel.
Fee: $47.99 monthly.
Digital Basic Service
Subscribers: N.A.
Programming (received off-air): LWS Local Weather Station; WOOD-TV (NBC) Grand Rapids; WXMI (FOX) Grand Rapids; WZZM (ABC) Grand Rapids.
Programming (via satellite): BBC America; Bio; Boomerang; CNN en Espanol; Discovery Digital Networks; Discovery HD Theater; Do-It-Yourself; ESPN; FitTV; Fox College Sports Atlantic; Fox College Sports Central; Fox College Sports Pacific; Fox Movie Channel; Fox Soccer; Fuel TV; Fuse; GAS; Great American Country; HDNet; HDNet Movies; History Channel International; Independent Film Channel; Lifetime Movie Network; MTV Networks Digital Suite; Music Choice; NFL Network; Nick Jr.; Nick Too; NickToons TV; Outdoor Channel; Sundance Channel; TV Guide Interactive Inc.
Digital Pay Service 1
Pay Units: N.A.
Programming (via satellite): Cinemax (multiplexed); Encore (multiplexed); Flix; HBO (multiplexed); Showtime (multiplexed); Starz (multiplexed); The Movie Channel (multiplexed).
Video-On-Demand: Yes
Pay-Per-View
Playboy TV (delivered digitally); Spice Live (delivered digitally); Spice Platinum (delivered digitally); Hot Net Plus (delivered digitally); Spice Hot (delivered digitally); iN DEMAND (delivered digitally); NASCAR In Car (delivered digitally); NHL Center Ice (delivered digitally); MLB Extra Innings (delivered digitally); ESPN (delivered digitally).
Internet Service
Operational: Yes.
Broadband Service: Charter Pipeline.
Fee: $29.99 monthly.
Telephone Service
Digital: Operational
Fee: $29.99 monthly
Miles of Plant: 225.0 (coaxial); None (fiber optic). Homes passed: 9,683.
Vice President & General Manager: Dan Spoelman. Technical Operations Manager: Keith Schierbeck. Marketing Director: Steve Schuh.
Ownership: Charter Communications Inc. (MSO).

IRON MOUNTAIN—Charter Communications, 359 US 41 East, Negaunee, MI 49866. Phones: 231-947-5221 (Traverse City office); 906-475-0107. Fax: 906-475-7007. Web Site: http://www.charter.com. Also serves Breitung Twp., Hermansville, Kingsford, Meyer Twp., Sagola Twp. & Waucedah Twp., MI; Aurora, Commonwealth & Florence, WI. ICA: MI0067. **Note:** This system is an overbuild.
TV Market Ranking: Below 100 (Aurora, Breitung Twp., Commonwealth, Florence, Hermansville, IRON MOUNTAIN, Kingsford, Meyer Twp., Sagola Twp., Waucedah Twp.). Franchise award date: November 1, 1955. Franchise expiration date: N.A. Began: November 1, 1955.
Channel capacity: 74 (operating 2-way). Channels available but not in use: None.
Basic Service
Subscribers: 8,098.
Programming (received off-air): WBKP (ABC) Calumet; WJMN-TV (CBS) Escan-

aba; WLUC-TV (NBC) Marquette; WNMU (PBS) Marquette; 16 FMs.
Programming (via microwave): WLUK-TV (FOX) Green Bay.
Programming (via satellite): C-SPAN; C-SPAN 2; Eternal Word TV Network; QVC; TBS Superstation; TV Guide Network; Weather Channel; WGN America.
Current originations: Public Access.
Fee: $29.99 installation; $13.50 monthly.

Expanded Basic Service 1
Subscribers: 7,677.
Programming (via satellite): ABC Family Channel; AMC; Animal Planet; Arts & Entertainment; Bravo; Cartoon Network; CNBC; CNN; Comedy Central; Country Music TV; Discovery Channel; Disney Channel; E! Entertainment Television; ESPN; ESPN 2; Food Network; Fox News Channel; Fox Sports Net Detroit; FX; G4; Golf Channel; GSN; Hallmark Channel; Headline News; HGTV; History Channel; Home Shopping Network; INSP; Lifetime; MSNBC; MTV; National Geographic Channel; Nickelodeon; Oxygen; SoapNet; Speed Channel; Spike TV; Syfy; The Learning Channel; Toon Disney; Travel Channel; truTV; Turner Classic Movies; Turner Network TV; TV Land; USA Network; Versus; VH1; WE tv.
Fee: $36.49 monthly.

Digital Basic Service
Subscribers: 110.
Programming (via satellite): BBC America; Bio; Bloomberg Television; Discovery Digital Networks; DMX Music; Do-It-Yourself; ESPN Classic Sports; GAS; History Channel International; Independent Film Channel; Lifetime Movie Network; MTV Networks Digital Suite; MuchMusic Network; Nick Jr.; Style Network; Sundance Channel.
Fee: $2.46 monthly.

Digital Pay Service 1
Pay Units: 4,576.
Programming (via satellite): Cinemax (multiplexed); Encore (multiplexed); Flix; HBO (multiplexed); Showtime (multiplexed); Starz (multiplexed); The Movie Channel (multiplexed).
Fee: $9.65 monthly (each).

Video-On-Demand: Yes

Pay-Per-View
Addressable homes: 110.
Hot Choice (delivered digitally), Addressable: Yes; iN DEMAND (delivered digitally); Playboy TV (delivered digitally); Fresh (delivered digitally); Shorteez (delivered digitally).

Internet Service
Operational: Yes.
Broadband Service: Charter Pipeline.
Fee: $49.95 installation; $29.99 monthly.

Telephone Service
Digital: Operational
Fee: $29.99 monthly

Miles of Plant: 185.0 (coaxial); 5.0 (fiber optic). Additional miles planned: 5.0 (coaxial); 5.0 (fiber optic). Homes passed: 9,825. Total homes in franchised area: 13,590.

Vice President: Joe Boullion. General Manager: Rex Buettgenbach. Technical Operations Director: Rob Nowak. Marketing Manager: Sandy Gottschalk. Government Relations Manager: Don Gladwell.

City fee: None.

Ownership: Charter Communications Inc. (MSO).

IRON MOUNTAIN—Northside T.V. Corp., 521 Vulcan St, Iron Mountain, MI 49801-2333. Phone: 906-774-1351. Fax: 906-774-1393. E-mail: steve@upnorthcable.com. Web Site: http://www.upnorthcable.com. ICA: MI0194.

TV Market Ranking: Below 100 (IRON MOUNTAIN). Franchise award date: N.A. Franchise expiration date: N.A. Began: October 1, 1955.

Channel capacity: 60 (operating 2-way). Channels available but not in use: N.A.

Basic Service
Subscribers: 875.
Programming (received off-air): WGBA-TV (NBC) Green Bay; WJFW-TV (NBC) Rhinelander; WLUC-TV (NBC) Marquette; WNMU (PBS) Marquette; WXYZ-TV (ABC) Detroit; allband FM.
Programming (via microwave): WBAY-TV (ABC, IND) Green Bay; WJMN-TV (CBS) Escanaba; WLUK-TV (FOX) Green Bay.
Programming (via satellite): ABC Family Channel; AMC; Arts & Entertainment; Cartoon Network; CNN; C-SPAN; Discovery Channel; ESPN; Eternal Word TV Network; Fox News Channel; G4; Hallmark Channel; Headline News; HGTV; History Channel; Home Shopping Network; INSP; Lifetime; MTV; National Geographic Channel; Nickelodeon; Spike TV; TBS Superstation; The Learning Channel; Turner Network TV; TV Land; USA Network; VH1; Weather Channel; WGN America.
Fee: $60.00 installation; $33.00 monthly; $20.00 additional installation.

Pay Service 1
Pay Units: 150.
Programming (via satellite): HBO.
Fee: $10.00 monthly.

Internet Service
Operational: Yes.
Broadband Service: In-house.
Fee: $30.00 monthly; $5.00 modem lease.

Telephone Service
Digital: Operational
Fee: $28.00 monthly

Miles of Plant: 14.0 (coaxial); None (fiber optic).

Office Manager: Judy Short.

Ownership: Northside TV Corp.

IRON RIVER—Iron River Cable, 316 N 2nd Ave, Iron River, MI 49935-1418. Phone: 906-265-3810. Fax: 906-265-3020. Web Site: http://www.ironriver.tv. Also serves Bates Twp., Iron River Twp. & Stambaugh Twp. ICA: MI0132.

TV Market Ranking: Below 100 (Bates Twp., IRON RIVER, Iron River Twp., Stambaugh Twp.). Franchise award date: May 27, 1957. Franchise expiration date: N.A. Began: November 1, 1957.

Channel capacity: 60 (operating 2-way). Channels available but not in use: 11.

Basic Service
Subscribers: 1,159.
Programming (received off-air): WBKP (ABC) Calumet; WJMN-TV (CBS) Escanaba; WLUC-TV (NBC) Marquette; WLUK-TV (FOX) Green Bay; WNMU (PBS) Marquette; WYOW (ABC, CW) Eagle River; WZMQ (IND, MNT) Marquette; allband FM.
Programming (via satellite): AMC; Cartoon Network; Country Music TV; C-SPAN; Discovery Channel; Disney Channel; ESPN; ESPN 2; Eternal Word TV Network; FitTV; Food Network; Fox Sports Net Detroit; FX; Golf Channel; HGTV; History Channel; Lifetime; National Geographic Channel; Nickelodeon; Outdoor Channel; QVC; Syfy; TBS Superstation; The Learning Channel; Trinity Broadcasting Network; Turner Classic Movies; Turner Network TV; TV Land; USA Network; various Canadian stations; VH1; Weather Channel; WGN America.
Fee: $50.00 installation; $20.00 monthly; $40.00 additional installation.

Expanded Basic Service 1
Subscribers: 850.
Programming (via satellite): Animal Planet; Arts & Entertainment; CNN; Comedy Central; Fox News Channel; MTV; Speed Channel; Spike TV; Versus.
Fee: $14.00 monthly.

Pay Service 1
Pay Units: 455.
Programming (via satellite): Cinemax; HBO; Showtime.
Fee: $20.00 installation.

Video-On-Demand: No

Internet Service
Operational: No, DSL.

Telephone Service
None

Miles of Plant: 52.0 (coaxial); 8.0 (fiber optic). Homes passed: 2,000. Total homes in franchised area: 2,315.

Chief Technician: Jerry Ward. Office Manager: Syndra Mottes.

Ownership: Iron River Cooperative TV Antenna Corp.

IRONWOOD—Charter Communications, 115 E McLeod Ave, Ironwood, MI 49938-2119. Phones: 231-947-5221 (Traverse City office); 906-475-0107 (Negaunee office). Fax: 906-932-0473. Web Site: http://www.charter.com. Also serves Bergland, Bergland Twp., Bessemer, Carp Lake, Erwin Twp., Ewen, Greenland Twp., Mass City, Ontonagon, Rockland Twp., Stannard Twp., Wakefield, Watersmeet & White Pine, MI; Hurley, Knight (town), Montreal & Pence, WI. ICA: MI0064.

TV Market Ranking: Below 100 (Watersmeet); Outside TV Markets (Bergland, Bergland Twp., Bessemer, Carp Lake, Erwin Twp., Ewen, Greenland Twp., Hurley, IRONWOOD, Knight (town), Mass City, Montreal, Ontonagon, Pence, Rockland Twp., Stannard Twp., Wakefield, White Pine). Franchise award date: January 1, 1958. Franchise expiration date: N.A. Began: January 1, 1958.

Channel capacity: 77 (operating 2-way). Channels available but not in use: 8.

Basic Service
Subscribers: 10,394.
Programming (received off-air): KBJR-TV (MNT, NBC) Superior; KDLH (CBS, CW) Duluth; KQDS-TV (FOX) Duluth; WDIO-DT (ABC) Duluth; WJFW-TV (NBC) Rhinelander; WJMN-TV (CBS) Escanaba; WLEF-TV (PBS) Park Falls; WLUC-TV (NBC) Marquette; WNMU (PBS) Marquette; WZMQ (IND, MNT) Marquette.
Programming (via satellite): C-SPAN; C-SPAN 2; C-SPAN 3; Eternal Word TV Network; G4; Hallmark Channel; Home Shopping Network; QVC; TBS Superstation; The Learning Channel; Travel Channel; TV Guide Network; WGN America.
Current originations: Educational Access; Public Access.
Fee: $29.99 installation; $13.50 monthly.

Expanded Basic Service 1
Subscribers: 6,220.
Programming (via satellite): ABC Family Channel; AMC; Animal Planet; Arts & Entertainment; Bravo; Cartoon Network; CNBC; CNN; Comedy Central; Country Music TV; Discovery Channel; Disney Channel; E! Entertainment Television; ESPN; ESPN 2; FitTV; Food Network; Fox News Channel; Fox Sports Net Detroit; FX; Golf Channel; GSN; Headline News; HGTV; History Channel; INSP; Lifetime; MSNBC; MTV; National Geographic Channel; Nickelodeon; Oxygen; SoapNet; Speed Channel; Spike TV; Style Network; Syfy; Toon Disney; truTV; Turner Classic Movies; Turner Network TV; TV Land; USA Network; Versus; VH1; WE tv; Weather Channel.
Fee: $36.49 monthly.

Digital Basic Service
Subscribers: N.A.
Programming (via satellite): BBC America; Bio; Cooking Channel; Discovery Digital Networks; Do-It-Yourself; ESPN Classic Sports; Fox College Sports Atlantic; Fox College Sports Central; Fox College Sports Pacific; Fox Movie Channel; Fox Soccer; Fuel TV; GAS; Great American Country; History Channel International; Independent Film Channel; Lifetime Movie Network; MTV Networks Digital Suite; NFL Network; Nick Jr.; Nick Too; NickToons TV; Outdoor Channel; Sundance Channel.

Digital Pay Service 1
Pay Units: N.A.
Programming (via microwave): The Movie Channel (multiplexed).
Programming (via satellite): Cinemax (multiplexed); DMX Music; Encore (multiplexed); HBO; Showtime (multiplexed); Starz (multiplexed).

Video-On-Demand: Yes

Pay-Per-View
iN DEMAND; Movies; special events.

Internet Service
Operational: Yes.
Broadband Service: Charter Pipeline.
Fee: $39.99 monthly.

Telephone Service
Digital: Operational

Miles of Plant: 253.0 (coaxial); 115.0 (fiber optic). Homes passed: 12,277.

Vice President: Joe Boullion. General Manager: Rex Buettgenbach. Technical Operations Director: Rob Nowak. Marketing Manager: Sandy Gottschalk. Government Relations Manager: Don Gladwell.

Ironwood City fee: 3% of basic gross.

Ownership: Charter Communications Inc. (MSO).

JACKSON—Comcast Cable, 3500 Patterson Ave SE, Grand Rapids, MI 49512. Phone: 616-977-2200. Fax: 616-977-2224. Web Site: http://www.comcast.com. Also serves Blackman Twp., Brooklyn (Irish Hills), Cambridge Twp., Cement City (village), Columbia Twp., Franklin Twp., Leoni Twp., Liberty Twp. (Jackson County), Napoleon Twp., Norvell Twp., Onsted (village), Rives Twp., Sandstone Twp. (portions), Somerset Twp., Spring Arbor Twp., Summit Twp. (Jackson County) & Summit-Leoni. ICA: MI0039.

TV Market Ranking: 37,92 (Spring Arbor Twp.); 92 (Blackman Twp., Brooklyn (Irish Hills), Cambridge Twp., Cement City (village), Columbia Twp., Franklin Twp., JACKSON (VILLAGE), Leoni Twp., Liberty Twp. (Jackson County), Napoleon Twp., Norvell Twp., Rives Twp., Sandstone Twp. (portions), Somerset Twp., Summit Twp. (Jackson County), Summit-Leoni); Below 100 (Onsted (village)). Franchise award date: January 1, 1965. Franchise expiration date: N.A. Began: January 8, 1967.

Channel capacity: N.A. Channels available but not in use: N.A.

Basic Service

Subscribers: 34,161.

Programming (received off-air): WDIV-TV (NBC) Detroit; WHTV (MNT) Jackson; WILX-TV (NBC) Onondaga; WJBK (FOX) Detroit; WKAR-TV (PBS) East Lansing; WLAJ (ABC, CW) Lansing; WLNS-TV (CBS) Lansing; WSYM-TV (FOX) Lansing; WTVS (PBS) Detroit; WWMT (CBS, CW) Kalamazoo; WXYZ-TV (ABC) Detroit; WZPX-TV (ION) Battle Creek; 26 FMs.

Programming (via satellite): Home Shopping Network; Michigan Government Television; QVC; The Comcast Network; TV Guide Network; WGN America.

Current originations: Government Access; Leased Access; Public Access.

Fee: $10.50 monthly.

Expanded Basic Service 1

Subscribers: N.A.

Programming (via satellite): ABC Family Channel; AMC; Animal Planet; Arts & Entertainment; BET Networks; Big Ten Network; Cartoon Network; CNBC; CNN; Comedy Central; Country Music TV; C-SPAN; C-SPAN 2; Discovery Channel; Disney Channel; E! Entertainment Television; ESPN; ESPN 2; Food Network; Fox News Channel; Fox Sports Net Detroit; FX; Golf Channel; Hallmark Channel; Headline News; HGTV; History Channel; Lifetime; MSNBC; MTV; Nickelodeon; Spike TV; TBS Superstation; The Learning Channel; Travel Channel; truTV; Turner Network TV; TV Land; USA Network; Versus; VH1; Weather Channel.

Fee: $48.99 monthly.

Digital Basic Service

Subscribers: N.A.

Programming (via satellite): BBC America; Bio; Bio HD; Bloomberg Television; Bravo; Cartoon Network HD; CMT Pure Country; College Sports Television; Cooking Channel; C-SPAN 2; C-SPAN 3; Current; Discovery Health Channel; Discovery Kids Channel; Discovery Military Channel; Discovery Planet Green; Discovery Planet Green HD; Disney XD; Disney XD HD; Do-It-Yourself; E! Entertainment Television HD; Encore (multiplexed); ESPN Classic Sports; ESPNews; EWTN; FitTV; Flix; Fox Business Channel; Fox News HD; Fox Reality Channel; Fox Soccer; Fuse; Fuse HD; FX HD; G4; Gol TV; Gospel Music Channel; Great American Country; GSN; Halogen Network; History Channel International; ID Investigation Discovery; Independent Film Channel; Jewelry Television; Lifetime Movie Network; Lifetime Movie Network HD; Lifetime Television HD; LOGO; MGM HD; Michigan Government Television; MTV Hits; MTV Jams; MTV Tres; MTV2; Music Choice; National Geographic Channel; NBA TV; NHL Network; Nick HD; Nick Jr.; Nick Too; NickToons TV; Outdoor Channel; PBS Kids Sprout; Science Channel; ShopNBC; SoapNet; Speed Channel; Spike TV HD; Starz IndiePlex; Starz RetroPlex; Style Network; Sundance Channel; Syfy; TeenNick; The Sportsman Channel; The Word Network; Travel Channel HD; Trinity Broadcasting Network; Turner Classic Movies; TV One; VH1 Classic; VH1 Soul; WE tv.

Fee: $9.95 monthly.

Digital Expanded Basic Service

Subscribers: N.A.

Programming (received off-air): WILX-TV (NBC) Onondaga; WKAR-TV (PBS) East Lansing; WLAJ (ABC, CW) Lansing; WLNS-TV (CBS) Lansing; WSYM-TV (FOX) Lansing.

Programming (via satellite): ABC Family HD; AMC HD; Animal Planet HD; Arts & Entertainment HD; CNN HD; Discovery Channel HD; Discovery HD Theater; Disney Channel HD; ESPN 2 HD; ESPN HD; Food Network HD; FSN HD; Golf Channel HD; HGTV HD; History Channel HD; Mojo HD; National Geographic Channel HD Network; NFL Network HD; Palladia; Science Channel HD; Syfy HD; TBS in HD; TLC HD; Turner Network TV HD; Universal HD; USA Network HD; Versus HD.

Digital Expanded Basic Service 2

Subscribers: N.A.

Programming (via satellite): College Sports Television; Fox College Sports Atlantic; Fox College Sports Central; Fox College Sports Pacific; Fox Movie Channel; Fox Soccer; Gol TV; NBA TV; NFL Network; NHL Network; Speed Channel; Speed HD; The Sportsman Channel.

Digital Pay Service 1

Pay Units: N.A.

Programming (via satellite): Cinemax (multiplexed); Cinemax HD; HBO (multiplexed); HBO HD; Playboy TV; Showtime (multiplexed); Showtime HD; Starz (multiplexed); Starz HDTV; The Movie Channel (multiplexed).

Fee: $18.05 monthly (each).

Video-On-Demand: Yes

Pay-Per-View

iN DEMAND (delivered digitally); Hot Choice (delivered digitally); Playboy TV (delivered digitally); Spice: Xcess (delivered digitally); Fresh (delivered digitally); Club Jenna (delivered digitally); NBA League Pass (delivered digitally); MLS Direct Kick (delivered digitally); NHL Center Ice (delivered digitally).

Internet Service

Operational: Yes.

Broadband Service: Comcast High Speed Internet.

Fee: $42.95 monthly.

Telephone Service

Digital: Operational

Miles of Plant: 387.0 (coaxial); None (fiber optic). Homes passed: 69,044. Total homes in franchised area: 74,713.

Area Vice President: Larry Williamson. Business Operations Director: Amy Carey. Technical Operations Director: Tom Rice. Sales & Marketing Manager: Rick Finch.

City fee: 3% of gross.

Ownership: Comcast Cable Communications Inc. (MSO).

JACKSON—Comcast Cable. Now served by JACKSON, MI [MI0039]. ICA: MI0031.

JACKSON—Formerly served by Wireless Cable Systems Inc. No longer in operation. ICA: MI0390.

JAMESTOWN TWP.—Charter Communications. Now served by ALLENDALE, MI [MI0094]. ICA: MI0109.

JONES—Comcast Cable. Now served by THREE RIVERS, MI [MI0050]. ICA: MI0315.

KALAMAZOO—Charter Communications, 315 Davis St, Grand Haven, MI 49417-1830. Phone: 616-647-6201. Fax: 616-846-0797. Web Site: http://www.charter.com. Also serves Alamo Twp., Comstock Twp., Kalamazoo Twp. (western portion), Oshtemo Twp., Parchment, Pavilion Twp. & Portage (northeastern portion). ICA: MI0011.

TV Market Ranking: 37 (Alamo Twp., Comstock Twp., KALAMAZOO, Kalamazoo Twp. (western portion), Oshtemo Twp., Parchment, Pavilion Twp.); 37,80 (Portage (northeastern portion)). Franchise award date: N.A. Franchise expiration date: N.A. Began: October 1, 1966.

Channel capacity: 78 (operating 2-way). Channels available but not in use: N.A.

Basic Service

Subscribers: 46,076.

Programming (received off-air): WGVU-TV (PBS) Grand Rapids; WLLA (IND) Kalamazoo; WOOD-TV (NBC) Grand Rapids; WOTV (ABC) Battle Creek; WTLJ (IND) Muskegon; WWMT (CBS, CW) Kalamazoo; WXMI (FOX) Grand Rapids; WXSP-CA (MNT) Grand Rapids; WZPX-TV (ION) Battle Creek; WZZM (ABC) Grand Rapids.

Programming (via microwave): WGN-TV (CW, IND) Chicago; WTTW (PBS) Chicago.

Programming (via satellite): C-SPAN; C-SPAN 2; Home Shopping Network; Michigan Government Television; QVC; ShopNBC; TV Guide Network.

Current originations: Government Access; Educational Access; Public Access.

Fee: $29.99 installation.

Expanded Basic Service 1

Subscribers: N.A.

Programming (via satellite): ABC Family Channel; AMC; Animal Planet; Arts & Entertainment; BET Networks; Bravo; Cartoon Network; CNBC; CNN; Comedy Central; Country Music TV; Discovery Channel; Disney Channel; Do-It-Yourself; E! Entertainment Television; ESPN; ESPN 2; ESPN Classic Sports; FitTV; Food Network; Fox News Channel; Fox Sports Net Detroit; FX; G4; Golf Channel; GSN; Hallmark Channel; Headline News; HGTV; History Channel; Lifetime; MSNBC; MTV; National Geographic Channel; Nickelodeon; Oxygen; Product Information Network; SoapNet; Speed Channel; Spike TV; Syfy; TBS Superstation; Telemundo; The Learning Channel; Toon Disney; Travel Channel; truTV; Turner Classic Movies; Turner Network TV; TV Land; USA Network; Versus; VH1; WE tv; Weather Channel.

Fee: $47.99 monthly.

Digital Basic Service

Subscribers: N.A.

Programming (via satellite): BBC America; Bio; Boomerang; CNN en Espanol; CNN International; Discovery Digital Networks; Do-It-Yourself; Fox Sports World; FSN Digital Atlantic; FSN Digital Central; FSN Digital Pacific; Fuel TV; Fuse; GAS; Great American Country; History Channel International; Independent Film Channel; Lifetime Movie Network; LWS Local Weather Station; MTV Networks Digital Suite; Music Choice; NFL Network; Nick Jr.; Nick Too; Outdoor Channel; Sundance Channel; TV Guide Interactive Inc.

Digital Pay Service 1

Pay Units: N.A.

Programming (via satellite): Cinemax (multiplexed); Encore (multiplexed); Flix; HBO (multiplexed); Showtime (multiplexed); Starz (multiplexed); The Movie Channel (multiplexed).

Fee: $11.05 monthly (Cinemax, HBO, Showtime or Flix & TMC), $14.95 monthly (Starz/Encore).

Video-On-Demand: Yes

Pay-Per-View

iN DEMAND (delivered digitally); Playboy TV (delivered digitally); Fresh (delivered digitally); Shorteez (delivered digitally); Sports PPV (delivered digitally); NHL Center Ice (delivered digitally); MLB Extra Innings (delivered digitally); ESPN Now (delivered digitally).

Internet Service

Operational: Yes.

Subscribers: 6,000.

Broadband Service: Charter Pipeline.

Fee: $29.99 monthly; $5.00 modem lease.

Telephone Service

Digital: Operational

Fee: $29.99 monthly

Miles of Plant: 1,031.0 (coaxial); 311.0 (fiber optic). Homes passed: 82,000. Total homes in franchised area: 86,528.

Vice President & General Manager: Dan Spoelman. Technical Operations Manager: Keith Schierbeek. Marketing Director: Steve Schuh.

Ownership: Charter Communications Inc. (MSO).

KALEVA (village)—Pine River Cable, PO Box 96, McBain, MI 49657. Phone: 888-244-2288. Fax: 231-825-0191. E-mail: info@pinerivercable.com. Web Site: http://www.pinerivercable.com. Also serves Kaleva & Maple Grove Twp. (Manistee County). ICA: MI0242.

TV Market Ranking: Below 100 (Kaleva, KALEVA (VILLAGE), Maple Grove Twp. (Manistee County)). Franchise award date: N.A. Franchise expiration date: N.A. Began: June 1, 1989.

Channel capacity: 41 (2-way capable). Channels available but not in use: 11.

Basic Service

Subscribers: 134.

Programming (received off-air): WCMW (PBS) Manistee; WFQX-TV (FOX) Cadillac; WGTU (ABC, CW) Traverse City; WPBN-TV (NBC) Traverse City; WWTV (CBS) Cadillac.

Programming (via satellite): ABC Family Channel; C-SPAN; QVC; TBS Superstation; WGN America.

Current originations: Government Access; Educational Access; Public Access.

Fee: $38.00 installation; $10.80 monthly.

Expanded Basic Service 1
Subscribers: N.A.
Programming (via satellite): AMC; Arts & Entertainment; CNN; Country Music TV; Discovery Channel; Disney Channel; E! Entertainment Television; ESPN; ESPN 2; Food Network; Fox Sports Net Detroit; Headline News; HGTV; Lifetime; MTV; Nickelodeon; Spike TV; The Learning Channel; Turner Network TV; USA Network; VH1; Weather Channel.
Pay Service 1
Pay Units: 41.
Programming (via satellite): Cinemax; HBO.
Fee: $10.95 monthly (Cinemax), $11.95 monthly (HBO).
Internet Service
Operational: No.
Miles of Plant: 5.0 (coaxial); None (fiber optic). Homes passed: 246.
Manager: John Metzler.
Ownership: Pine River Cable (MSO).

KEELER TWP.—Sister Lakes Cable TV, 517 Petrie Ave, Saint Joseph, MI 49085-1927. Phones: 269-424-5737; 269-983-2665. Also serves Silver Creek Twp. & Sister Lakes. ICA: MI0135.
TV Market Ranking: 37,80 (KEELER TWP., Silver Creek Twp., Sister Lakes). Franchise award date: May 1, 1986. Franchise expiration date: N.A. Began: July 1, 1987.
Channel capacity: 41 (not 2-way capable). Channels available but not in use: N.A.
Basic Service
Subscribers: 1,383.
Programming (received off-air): WBND-LP South Bend; WFLD (FOX) Chicago; WGN-TV (CW, IND) Chicago; WHME-TV (IND) South Bend; WNDU-TV (NBC) South Bend; WNIT (PBS) South Bend; WSBT-TV (CBS, IND) South Bend; WSJV (FOX) Elkhart; WTTW (PBS) Chicago; WWMT (CBS, CW) Kalamazoo; WXMI (FOX) Grand Rapids.
Programming (via satellite): AMC; Animal Planet; Arts & Entertainment; Cartoon Network; CNBC; CNN; Comedy Central; Country Music TV; Discovery Channel; ESPN; ESPN 2; Food Network; Fox News Channel; FX; Great American Country; Hallmark Channel; Headline News; HGTV; History Channel; Lifetime; MTV; National Geographic Channel; Nickelodeon; Outdoor Channel; QVC; Spike TV; Syfy; TBS Superstation; The Learning Channel; Travel Channel; Turner Network TV; TV Land; USA Network; VH1; Weather Channel.
Current originations: Educational Access.
Fee: $30.00 installation; $31.00 monthly.
Pay Service 1
Pay Units: 77.
Programming (via satellite): HBO.
Fee: $14.00 monthly.
Pay Service 2
Pay Units: 41.
Programming (via satellite): Showtime.
Fee: $10.00 monthly.
Pay Service 3
Pay Units: 22.
Programming (via satellite): Cinemax.
Fee: $10.00 monthly.
Video-On-Demand: No
Internet Service
Operational: Yes.
Subscribers: 350.
Fee: $40.00 installation; $41.40 monthly.
Telephone Service
None
Miles of Plant: 40.0 (coaxial); None (fiber optic). Homes passed: 2,200.
Chief Technician: Tim Olmstead.
City fee: 3% of basic.
Ownership: Satellite Operations Inc.

KINCHELOE—Charter Communications, 359 US 41 E, Negaumee, MI 49866. Phones: 231-947-5221 (Traverse City office); 906-475-0107. Fax: 906-475-7007. Web Site: http://www.charter.com. Also serves Kinross & Rudyard Twp. ICA: MI0200.
TV Market Ranking: Below 100 (KINCHELOE, Kinross, Rudyard Twp.). Franchise award date: December 30, 1986. Franchise expiration date: N.A. Began: June 1, 1987.
Channel capacity: 52 (not 2-way capable). Channels available but not in use: 17.
Basic Service
Subscribers: 1,055.
Programming (received off-air): WCML (PBS) Alpena; WFQX-TV (FOX) Cadillac; WGTQ (ABC) Sault Ste. Marie; WTOM-TV (NBC) Cheboygan; WWUP-TV (CBS, FOX) Sault Ste. Marie.
Fee: $29.99 installation; $13.50 monthly.
Expanded Basic Service 1
Subscribers: 1,006.
Programming (via satellite): ABC Family Channel; AMC; Arts & Entertainment; CNBC; CNN; Country Music TV; C-SPAN; Discovery Channel; Disney Channel; ESPN; ESPN 2; Fox Sports Net Detroit; Headline News; HGTV; History Channel; Lifetime; MTV; Nickelodeon; Spike TV; TBS Superstation; truTV; Turner Network TV; USA Network; Weather Channel; WGN America.
Fee: $36.49 monthly.
Pay Service 1
Pay Units: 165.
Programming (via satellite): Encore.
Fee: $15.51 installation; $1.50 monthly.
Pay Service 2
Pay Units: 167.
Programming (via satellite): HBO.
Fee: $15.51 installation; $10.00 monthly.
Pay Service 3
Pay Units: 160.
Programming (via satellite): Showtime.
Fee: $15.51 installation; $10.00 monthly.
Pay Service 4
Pay Units: 134.
Programming (via satellite): The Movie Channel.
Fee: $15.51 installation; $10.00 monthly.
Internet Service
Operational: Yes.
Fee: $19.99 monthly.
Telephone Service
None
Miles of Plant: 32.0 (coaxial); None (fiber optic).
Vice President: Joe Boullion. General Manager: Rex Buettgenbach. Manager: John Badenski. Techical Operations Director: Rob Nowak. Chief Technician: John Randazzo. Marketing Manager: Sandy Gottschalk.
Ownership: Charter Communications Inc. (MSO).

KINDERHOOK TWP.—Formerly served by CableDirect. No longer in operation. ICA: MI0232.

KINGSTON TWP.—Charter Communications. Now served by NORTH BRANCH TWP., MI [MI0337]. ICA: MI0318.

LAKE GEORGE—Charter Communications, 2304 S Mission, Mount Pleasant, MI 48858. Phone: 989-775-6846. Fax: 989-772-0350. Web Site: http://www.charter.com. Also serves Freeman Twp. & Lincoln Twp. (Clare County). ICA: MI0319.
TV Market Ranking: Below 100 (Freeman Twp., LAKE GEORGE, Lincoln Twp. (Clare County)). Franchise award date: N.A. Franchise expiration date: N.A. Began: June 1, 1989.
Channel capacity: N.A. Channels available but not in use: N.A.
Basic Service
Subscribers: 399.
Programming (received off-air): WCMU-TV (PBS) Mount Pleasant; WFQX-TV (FOX) Cadillac; WJRT-TV (ABC) Flint; WNEM-TV (CBS, MNT) Bay City; WPBN-TV (NBC) Traverse City; WWTV (CBS) Cadillac; WZZM (ABC) Grand Rapids.
Programming (via satellite): ABC Family Channel; CNN; Country Music TV; Discovery Channel; Disney Channel; ESPN; Headline News; TBS Superstation; Turner Network TV; WGN America.
Fee: $30.00 installation; $19.95 monthly.
Pay Service 1
Pay Units: 27.
Programming (via satellite): Showtime.
Fee: $7.00 monthly.
Internet Service
Operational: No.
Telephone Service
N.A.
Miles of Plant: 26.0 (coaxial); None (fiber optic). Homes passed: 720.
Vice President & General Manager: Dan Spoelman. Operations Manager: Ed Bucao.
Ownership: Charter Communications Inc. (MSO).

LAKEVIEW—Charter Communications, 315 Davis St, Grand Haven, MI 49417-1830. Phone: 616-647-6201. Fax: 616-846-0797. Web Site: http://www.charter.com. Also serves Belvidere Twp., Cato Twp. & Six Lakes. ICA: MI0172.
TV Market Ranking: Outside TV Markets (Belvidere Twp., Cato Twp., LAKEVIEW, Six Lakes). Franchise award date: N.A. Franchise expiration date: N.A. Began: N.A.
Channel capacity: 45 (not 2-way capable). Channels available but not in use: N.A.
Basic Service
Subscribers: 568.
Programming (received off-air): WCMU-TV (PBS) Mount Pleasant; WGVU-TV (PBS) Grand Rapids; WOOD-TV (NBC) Grand Rapids; WTLJ (IND) Muskegon; WWTV (CBS) Cadillac; WXMI (FOX) Grand Rapids; WZPX-TV (ION) Battle Creek; WZZM (ABC) Grand Rapids.
Programming (via satellite): C-SPAN; QVC; TBS Superstation; WGN America.
Fee: $36.00 installation; $25.45 monthly.
Expanded Basic Service 1
Subscribers: N.A.
Programming (via satellite): ABC Family Channel; AMC; Arts & Entertainment; CNBC; CNN; Comedy Central; Discovery Channel; Disney Channel; ESPN; ESPN 2; Food Network; Fox Sports Net Detroit; Headline News; HGTV; History Channel; Lifetime; MTV; Nickelodeon; Spike TV; The Learning Channel; Turner Network TV; USA Network; VH1; Weather Channel.
Pay Service 1
Pay Units: 208.
Programming (via satellite): Cinemax; HBO; Starz.
Fee: $6.95 monthly (Starz), $10.95 monthly (Cinemax).
Internet Service
Operational: No.
Miles of Plant: 34.0 (coaxial); None (fiber optic). Homes passed: 1,347.
Vice President & General Manager: Dan Spoelman. Technical Operations Manager: Keith Schierbeek. Marketing Director: Steve Schuh.
Ownership: Charter Communications Inc. (MSO).

LANSING—Comcast Cable, 3500 Patterson Ave SE, Grand Rapids, MI 49512. Phone: 616-977-2200. Fax: 616-977-2224. Web Site: http://www.comcast.com. Also serves Alaiedon Twp., Clinton County, De Witt, De Witt Twp., Delhi Twp., Delta Twp., Eaton Rapids, Grand Ledge, Hamlin Twp. (portions), Lansing Twp., Oneida Twp., Watertown Twp. (Clinton County) & Windsor Charter Twp. ICA: MI0007.
TV Market Ranking: 92 (Alaiedon Twp., Clinton County, De Witt, De Witt Twp., Delhi Twp., Delta Twp., Eaton Rapids, Grand Ledge, Hamlin Twp. (portions), LANSING, Lansing Twp., Oneida Twp., Watertown Twp. (Clinton County), Windsor Charter Twp.). Franchise award date: April 29, 1974. Franchise expiration date: N.A. Began: April 1, 1976.
Channel capacity: N.A. Channels available but not in use: N.A.
Basic Service
Subscribers: 65,000.
Programming (received off-air): Michigan Government Television; WHTV (MNT) Jackson; WILX-TV (NBC) Onondaga; WKAR-TV (PBS) East Lansing; WKBD-TV (CW) Detroit; WLAJ (ABC, CW) Lansing; WLNS-TV (CBS) Lansing; WSYM-TV (FOX) Lansing; WZPX-TV (ION) Battle Creek.
Programming (via satellite): Comcast Local Detroit; TBS Superstation; WGN America.
Current originations: Religious Access; Government Access; Educational Access; Public Access.
Expanded Basic Service 1
Subscribers: N.A.
Programming (via satellite): ABC Family Channel; AMC; Animal Planet; Arts & Entertainment; BET Networks; Bravo; Cartoon Network; CNBC; CNN; Comedy Central; Country Music TV; C-SPAN; C-SPAN 2; Discovery Channel; Disney Channel; E! Entertainment Television; ESPN; ESPN 2; Food Network; Fox News Channel; Fox Sports Net Detroit; FX; Golf Channel; Headline News; HGTV; History Channel; Home Shopping Network; Lifetime; MSNBC; MTV; Nickelodeon; QVC; Spike TV; The Learning Channel; truTV; Turner Network TV; TV Guide Network; TV Land; Univision; USA Network; Versus; VH1; Weather Channel.
Fee: $48.99 monthly.

Digital Basic Service
Subscribers: N.A.
Programming (received off-air): WILX-TV (NBC) Onondaga; WKAR-TV (PBS) East Lansing; WLAJ (ABC, CW) Lansing; WLNS-TV (CBS) Lansing; WSYM-TV (FOX) Lansing.
Programming (via satellite): ABC Family HD; Animal Planet HD; Arts & Entertainment HD; BBC America; Bio; Bio HD; Bloomberg Television; Bravo; Cartoon Network HD; Cine Latino; Cine Mexicano; CMT Pure Country; CNN en Espanol; CNN HD; Current; Discovery Channel HD; Discovery en Espanol; Discovery Health Channel; Discovery Kids Channel; Discovery Military Channel; Discovery Planet Green; Disney Channel HD; Do-It-Yourself; Encore (multiplexed); ESPN 2 HD; ESPN Classic Sports; ESPN Deportes; ESPN HD; ESPNews; Eternal Word TV Network; Flix; Food Network HD; Fox College Sports Atlantic; Fox College Sports Central; Fox College Sports Pacific; Fox Movie Channel; Fox News HD; Fox Reality Channel; Fox Soccer; Fox Sports en Espanol; FSN HD; Fuse; FX HD; G4; Gospel Music Channel; Great American Country; GSN; Hallmark Channel; Halogen Network; HGTV HD; History Channel en Espanol; History Channel HD; History Channel International; ID Investigation Discovery; Independent Film Channel; INHD; Lifetime Movie Network; Lifetime Movie Network HD; Lifetime Television HD; Lime; MoviePlex; MTV Hits; MTV Tres; MTV2; mun2 television; Music Choice; National Geographic Channel; National Geographic Channel HD Network; NBA TV; NFL Network; Nick HD; Nick Jr.; Nick Too; NickToons TV; Outdoor Channel; Palladia; PBS Kids Sprout; Science Channel; Science Channel HD; ShopNBC; SoapNet; Speed Channel; Speed HD; Spike TV HD; Sundance Channel; Syfy; Syfy HD; TBS in HD; TeenNick; The Word Network; TLC HD; Toon Disney; Trinity Broadcasting Network; Turner Classic Movies; Turner Network TV HD; TV One; USA Network HD; VeneMovies; VH1 Classic; VH1 Soul; WE tv.
Fee: $9.95 monthly.

Digital Pay Service 1
Pay Units: 29,764.
Programming (via satellite): Cinemax (multiplexed); Cinemax HD; HBO (multiplexed); HBO HD; Showtime (multiplexed); Showtime HD; Starz (multiplexed); Starz HDTV; The Movie Channel (multiplexed).
Fee: $15.00 installation; $18.05 monthly (each).

Video-On-Demand: Yes

Pay-Per-View
ESPN (delivered digitally), Addressable: No; iN DEMAND (delivered digitally); NBA League Pass (delivered digitally); MLB Extra Innings (delivered digitally); NHL Center Ice (delivered digitally); Fresh (delivered digitally); Playboy TV (delivered digitally); Hot Choice (delivered digitally).

Internet Service
Operational: Yes.
Broadband Service: Comcast High Speed Internet.
Fee: $42.95 monthly.

Telephone Service
Digital: Operational
Fee: $44.95 monthly

Miles of Plant: 930.0 (coaxial); 10.0 (fiber optic). Homes passed: 90,817. Total homes in franchised area: 91,295.
Area Vice President: Larry Williamson. Business Operations Director: Amy Carey. Technical Operations Director: Tom Rice. Sales & Marketing Manager: Rick Finch.
City fee: 3% of gross.
Ownership: Comcast Cable Communications Inc. (MSO).

LANSING—Formerly served by Sprint Corp. No longer in operation. ICA: MI0394.

LAPEER—Charter Communications, 7372 Davison Rd, Davison, MI 48423. Phone: 810-652-1400. Web Site: http://www.charter.com. Also serves Columbiaville, Deerfield Twp. (Lapeer County), Elba Twp. (Lapeer County), Lapeer Twp., Marathon Twp., Mayfield Twp. (Lapeer County) & Oregon Twp. ICA: MI0073.
TV Market Ranking: 37 (Deerfield Twp. (Lapeer County)); 61 (Columbiaville, Elba Twp. (Lapeer County), LAPEER, Lapeer Twp., Marathon Twp., Mayfield Twp. (Lapeer County), Oregon Twp.). Franchise award date: June 1, 1980. Franchise expiration date: N.A. Began: N.A.
Channel capacity: N.A. Channels available but not in use: N.A.

Basic Service
Subscribers: 6,822.
Programming (received off-air): WADL (IND) Mount Clemens; WDIV-TV (NBC) Detroit; WEYI-TV (CW, NBC) Saginaw; WFUM (PBS) Flint; WJBK (FOX) Detroit; WJRT-TV (ABC) Flint; WKBD-TV (CW) Detroit; WNEM-TV (CBS, MNT) Bay City; WPXD-TV (ION) Ann Arbor; WSMH (FOX) Flint; WWJ-TV (CBS) Detroit; WXYZ-TV (ABC) Detroit.
Programming (via satellite): Home Shopping Network; QVC; WGN America.
Current originations: Government Access; Educational Access; Public Access.
Fee: $29.99 installation; $13.50 monthly.

Expanded Basic Service 1
Subscribers: N.A.
Programming (via satellite): ABC Family Channel; AMC; Animal Planet; Arts & Entertainment; Bravo; Cartoon Network; CNBC; CNN; Comedy Central; Country Music TV; C-SPAN; Discovery Channel; Disney Channel; E! Entertainment Television; ESPN; ESPN 2; ESPN Classic Sports; Eternal Word TV Network; Food Network; Fox News Channel; Fox Sports Net Detroit; FX; G4; Golf Channel; GSN; Hallmark Channel; Headline News; HGTV; History Channel; Lifetime; MSNBC; MTV; MTV2; National Geographic Channel; Nickelodeon; Oxygen; SoapNet; Speed Channel; Spike TV; Syfy; TBS Superstation; The Learning Channel; Toon Disney; Travel Channel; truTV; Turner Classic Movies; Turner Network TV; TV Guide Network; TV Land; USA Network; Versus; VH1; Weather Channel.
Fee: $36.49 monthly.

Digital Basic Service
Subscribers: N.A.
Programming (via satellite): BBC America; Bio; Discovery Digital Networks; Do-It-Yourself; ESPN; Fox College Sports Atlantic; Fox College Sports Central; Fox College Sports Pacific; Fox Movie Channel; Fox Soccer; Fuel TV; Fuse; GAS; Great American Country; HDNet; HDNet Movies; History Channel International; Independent Film Channel; Lifetime Movie Network; MTV Networks Digital Suite; Music Choice; NFL Network; Nick Jr.; Nick Too; NickToons TV; Sundance Channel.

Pay Service 1
Pay Units: 2,279.
Programming (via satellite): Flix; HBO; Showtime (multiplexed); The Movie Channel (multiplexed).
Fee: $20.00 installation; $11.95 monthly (HBO), $15.00 monthly (Cinemax, Showtime or TMC).

Digital Pay Service 1
Pay Units: N.A.
Programming (via satellite): Cinemax (multiplexed); Encore (multiplexed); HBO (multiplexed); Starz (multiplexed).

Video-On-Demand: Yes

Pay-Per-View
Addressable homes: 4,557.
Playboy TV (delivered digitally); Spice (delivered digitally); Spice Live (delivered digitally).

Internet Service
Operational: Yes.
Broadband Service: Charter Pipeline.
Fee: $29.99 monthly.

Telephone Service
Digital: Operational
Fee: $29.99 monthly

Miles of Plant: 222.0 (coaxial); None (fiber optic). Homes passed: 10,188.
Vice President & General Manager: Dave Slowick. Technical Operations Director: Lloyd Collins. Marketing Director: Lisa Gayari.
Ownership: Charter Communications Inc. (MSO).

LAWTON—Comcast Cable, 3500 Patterson Ave SE, Grand Rapids, MI 49512. Phone: 616-977-2200. Fax: 616-977-2224. Web Site: http://www.comcast.com. Also serves Almena Twp., Antwerp Twp., Decatur (village), Lawrence, Lawton (village), Paw Paw (village), Porter Twp. (Van Buren County) & Waverly Twp. (Van Buren County). ICA: MI0322.
TV Market Ranking: 37,80 (Almena Twp., Antwerp Twp., Decatur (village), Lawrence, LAWTON, Lawton (village), Paw Paw (village), Porter Twp. (Van Buren County), Waverly Twp. (Van Buren County)). Franchise award date: N.A. Franchise expiration date: N.A. Began: N.A.
Channel capacity: 78 (operating 2-way). Channels available but not in use: 25.

Basic Service
Subscribers: 4,010.
Programming (received off-air): WGVU-TV (PBS) Grand Rapids; WLLA (IND) Kalamazoo; WOBC-CA Battle Creek; WOOD-TV (NBC) Grand Rapids; WOTV (ABC) Battle Creek; WTLJ (IND) Muskegon; WWMT (CBS, CW) Kalamazoo; WXMI (FOX) Grand Rapids; WZPX-TV (ION) Battle Creek.
Programming (via satellite): QVC; TBS Superstation; WGN America.

Expanded Basic Service 1
Subscribers: 3,900.
Programming (via satellite): ABC Family Channel; AMC; Animal Planet; Arts & Entertainment; Cartoon Network; CNBC; CNN; Comedy Central; Country Music TV; C-SPAN; C-SPAN 2; Discovery Channel; Disney Channel; E! Entertainment Television; ESPN; ESPN 2; Eternal Word TV Network; FitTV; Food Network; Fox News Channel; Fox Sports Net Detroit; FX; Headline News; HGTV; History Channel; Home Shopping Network; Lifetime; MSNBC; MTV; Nickelodeon; Product Information Network; Spike TV; Syfy; The Learning Channel; Travel Channel; Turner Classic Movies; Turner Network TV; TV Land; USA Network; Versus; VH1; Weather Channel.
Fee: $40.00 installation; $48.99 monthly.

Digital Basic Service
Subscribers: N.A.
Programming (via satellite): BBC America; Bio; Bravo; Discovery Digital Networks; DMX Music; ESPN 2; ESPN Classic Sports; ESPNews; Fox Soccer; Fuse; GAS; Golf Channel; GSN; History Channel; History Channel International; Independent Film Channel; International Television (ITV); Lifetime Movie Network; MTV Networks Digital Suite; National Geographic Channel; NBA TV; NFL Network; Nick Jr.; Speed Channel; Style Network; Syfy; Toon Disney; Turner Classic Movies; WE tv.
Fee: $9.95 monthly.

Digital Pay Service 1
Pay Units: N.A.
Programming (via satellite): Cinemax (multiplexed); Encore (multiplexed); HBO (multiplexed); Showtime (multiplexed); Starz (multiplexed); Sundance Channel; The Movie Channel (multiplexed).
Fee: $18.05 monthly (each).

Video-On-Demand: No

Pay-Per-View
iN DEMAND (delivered digitally); Playboy TV (delivered digitally).

Internet Service
Operational: Yes.
Broadband Service: Comcast High Speed Internet.
Fee: $42.95 monthly.

Telephone Service
None

Miles of Plant: 188.0 (coaxial); 12.0 (fiber optic). Additional miles planned: 12.0 (coaxial).
Area Vice President: Larry Williamson. Business Operations Director: Amy Carey. Technical Operations Director: Tom Rice. Sales & Marketing Director: Rick Finch.
Ownership: Comcast Cable Communications Inc. (MSO).

LE ROY (village)—Pine River Cable, PO Box 96, McBain, MI 49657. Phone: 888-244-2288. Fax: 231-825-0191. E-mail: info@pinerivercable.com. Web Site: http://www.pinerivercable.com. Also serves Ashton, Luther (village) & Tustin (village). ICA: MI0198.
TV Market Ranking: Below 100 (Ashton, LE ROY (VILLAGE), Luther (village), Tustin (village)). Franchise award date: N.A. Franchise expiration date: N.A. Began: July 1, 1989.
Channel capacity: 50 (operating 2-way). Channels available but not in use: 15.

Basic Service
Subscribers: 523.
Programming (received off-air): WCMV (PBS) Cadillac; WGTU (ABC, CW) Traverse City; WPBN-TV (NBC) Traverse City; WWTV (CBS) Cadillac; WZZM (ABC) Grand Rapids.
Programming (via satellite): ABC Family Channel; Arts & Entertainment; Cartoon Network; CNN; Comedy Central; Country Music TV; Discovery Channel; Disney Channel; ESPN; Fox Sports Net; Headline News; Home Shopping Network; Lifetime; MTV; Nickelodeon; QVC; Spike TV; Syfy; TBS Superstation; Turner Network TV; USA Network; VH1; WGN America.
Current originations: Educational Access.
Fee: $50.00 installation; $34.60 monthly.

Pay Service 1
Pay Units: 76.
Programming (via satellite): Cinemax (multiplexed).
Fee: $11.00 monthly.

Pay Service 2
Pay Units: 96.
Programming (via satellite): HBO (multiplexed).
Fee: $13.00 monthly.
Video-On-Demand: No
Internet Service
Operational: Yes. Began: April 1, 2003.
Broadband Service: West Michigan Internet Service.
Telephone Service
None
Miles of Plant: 69.0 (coaxial); None (fiber optic). Additional miles planned: 10.0 (coaxial). Homes passed: 885.
Manager: John Metzler.
Ownership: Pine River Cable (MSO).

LENNON—Lennon Telephone Co., PO Box 329, 3095 Sheridan Rd, Lennon, MI 48449-0338. Phones: 888-204-1077; 810-621-3363. Fax: 810-621-9600. E-mail: customerserv@lentel.com. Web Site: http://www.lentel.com. Also serves Clayton Twp. (Genesee County), Corunna, Durand, Gaines Twp. (Genesee County), Hazelton Twp., New Lothrop, Venice Twp. & Vernon Twp. ICA: MI0336. **Note:** This system is an overbuild.
TV Market Ranking: 61 (Clayton Twp. (Genesee County), Corunna, Durand, Gaines Twp. (Genesee County), Hazelton Twp., LENNON, New Lothrop, Venice Twp., Vernon Twp.). Franchise award date: N.A. Franchise expiration date: N.A. Began: June 1, 1989.
Channel capacity: 80 (operating 2-way). Channels available but not in use: N.A.
Basic Service
Subscribers: 1,800.
Programming (received off-air): WAQP (IND) Saginaw; WEYI-TV (CW, NBC) Saginaw; WFUM (PBS) Flint; WILX-TV (NBC) Onondaga; WJRT-TV (ABC) Flint; WKAR-TV (PBS) East Lansing; WLNS-TV (CBS) Lansing; WNEM-TV (CBS, MNT) Bay City; WSMH (FOX) Flint; WXYZ-TV (ABC) Detroit.
Programming (via satellite): CW+; Home Shopping Network; ION Television; MyNetworkTV Inc.; QVC; TV Guide Network; Weather Channel; WGN America.
Current originations: Public Access.
Fee: $20.00 installation; $36.70 monthly.
Expanded Basic Service 1
Subscribers: N.A.
Programming (via satellite): ABC Family Channel; AMC; Animal Planet; Arts & Entertainment; Big Ten Network; Bravo; Cartoon Network; CNBC; CNN; Comedy Central; Country Music TV; Court TV; C-SPAN; Discovery Channel; Disney Channel; Do-It-Yourself; E! Entertainment Television; ESPN; ESPN 2; ESPN Classic Sports; Food Network; Fox News Channel; Fox Sports Net; FX; Golf Channel; Hallmark Channel; Headline News; HGTV; History Channel; Lifetime; MTV; National Geographic Channel; NFL Network; Nickelodeon; Oxygen; RFD-TV; SoapNet; Speed Channel; Spike TV; Syfy; TBS Superstation; The Learning Channel; Toon Disney; Travel Channel; Turner Classic Movies; Turner Network TV; TV Land; USA Network; Versus; VH1; WE tv.
Digital Basic Service
Subscribers: 220.
Programming (received off-air): WEYI-TV (CW, NBC) Saginaw; WFUM (PBS) Flint; WJRT-TV (ABC) Flint; WNEM-TV (CBS, MNT) Bay City.
Programming (via satellite): AmericanLife TV Network; BBC America; Bio; Bloomberg Television; Current; Daystar TV Network; Discovery Health Channel; Discovery Kids Channel; Discovery Military Channel; Discovery Planet Green; DMX Music; ESPNews; FitTV; Fox College Sports Atlantic; Fox College Sports Central; Fox College Sports Pacific; Fox Movie Channel; Fox Soccer; G4; Great American Country; GSN; Halogen Network; History Channel International; ID Investigation Discovery; Independent Film Channel; Lifetime Movie Network; MTV Hits; MTV2; Nick Jr.; NickToons TV; Outdoor Channel; Science Channel; Sleuth; Style Network; TeenNick; TVG Network; VH1 Classic; VH1 Country; VH1 Soul.
Fee: $25.00 installation; $51.70 monthly.
Pay Service 1
Pay Units: N.A.
Programming (via satellite): Cinemax (multiplexed); Encore; HBO (multiplexed).
Fee: $12.00 monthly.
Digital Pay Service 1
Pay Units: N.A.
Programming (via satellite): Cinemax (multiplexed); Encore (multiplexed); HBO (multiplexed); Showtime (multiplexed); Starz (multiplexed); The Movie Channel (multiplexed).
Video-On-Demand: No
Pay-Per-View
Fresh (delivered digitally); Spice: Xcess (delivered digitally); Playboy TV (delivered digitally); Club Jenna (delivered digitally); Hot Choice (delivered digitally); iN DEMAND (delivered digitally).
Internet Service
Operational: Yes.
Subscribers: 950.
Broadband Service: In-house.
Fee: $31.99 monthly.
Telephone Service
None
Homes passed: 5,000.
Office Manager: Sharon Patsey.
Ownership: TVC Inc.

LEVERING—Charter Communications, 701 E South Airport Rd, Traverse City, MI 49686-4861. Phone: 231-947-5221. Fax: 231-947-2004. Web Site: http://www.charter.com. Also serves Carp Lake. ICA: MI0218.
TV Market Ranking: Below 100 (Carp Lake, LEVERING). Franchise award date: September 1, 1992. Franchise expiration date: N.A. Began: April 1, 1992.
Channel capacity: 34 (not 2-way capable). Channels available but not in use: None.
Basic Service
Subscribers: 166.
Programming (received off-air): WCML (PBS) Alpena; WFUP (FOX) Vanderbilt; WGTQ (ABC) Sault Ste. Marie; WPBN-TV (NBC) Traverse City; WWUP-TV (CBS, FOX) Sault Ste. Marie.
Programming (via satellite): ABC Family Channel; Animal Planet; Arts & Entertainment; Cartoon Network; CNN; C-SPAN; Discovery Channel; E! Entertainment Television; ESPN; Fox Sports Net Detroit; Hallmark Channel; HGTV; Lifetime; Nickelodeon; Spike TV; Syfy; TBS Superstation; The Learning Channel; Turner Network TV; USA Network; Weather Channel.
Fee: $29.99 installation; $1.60 converter.
Pay Service 1
Pay Units: 21.
Programming (via satellite): Cinemax.
Fee: $10.50 monthly.
Pay Service 2
Pay Units: 28.
Programming (via satellite): HBO.
Fee: $10.50 monthly.

Pay Service 3
Pay Units: 23.
Programming (via satellite): Encore.
Fee: $1.75 monthly.
Pay Service 4
Pay Units: 23.
Programming (via satellite): Starz.
Fee: $6.75 monthly.
Internet Service
Operational: No.
Telephone Service
None
Miles of Plant: 15.0 (coaxial); None (fiber optic). Homes passed: 470.
Vice President & General Manager: Joe Boullion. Marketing Manager: Tammy Reicha. Technical Operations Director: Rob Nowak.
Ownership: Charter Communications Inc.

LEWISTON—Lewiston Communications, PO Box 169, 2 E Main St, Fremont, MI 49412-0169. Phones: 231-924-8060; 800-443-0758. Fax: 231-924-6155. Also serves Albert Twp., Greenwood Twp. (Oscoda County) & Montmorency County. ICA: MI0323.
TV Market Ranking: Below 100 (Albert Twp., Greenwood Twp. (Oscoda County), LEWISTON, Montmorency County). Franchise award date: N.A. Franchise expiration date: N.A. Began: November 1, 1987.
Channel capacity: 54 (operating 2-way). Channels available but not in use: None.
Basic Service
Subscribers: 1,830.
Programming (received off-air): WBKB-TV (CBS, FOX) Alpena; WCML (PBS) Alpena; WFUP (FOX) Vanderbilt; WGTU (ABC, CW) Traverse City; WTOM-TV (NBC) Cheboygan; WWTV (CBS) Cadillac.
Programming (via satellite): ABC Family Channel; AMC; Animal Planet; Arts & Entertainment; Cartoon Network; CNBC; CNN; Comedy Central; Country Music TV; C-SPAN; Discovery Channel; Discovery Health Channel; E! Entertainment Television; ESPN; ESPN 2; Fox News Channel; Fox Sports Net Detroit; FX; G4; Golf Channel; Hallmark Channel; Headline News; HGTV; History Channel; Lifetime; National Geographic Channel; Nickelodeon; Outdoor Channel; QVC; Speed Channel; Spike TV; Syfy; TBS Superstation; The Learning Channel; Trinity Broadcasting Network; truTV; Turner Classic Movies; Turner Network TV; TV Land; USA Network; Weather Channel; WGN America.
Current originations: Educational Access.
Fee: $55.00 installation; $38.99 monthly.
Pay Service 1
Pay Units: 35.
Programming (via satellite): Cinemax; HBO; Showtime.
Fee: $11.95 monthly (each).
Video-On-Demand: No
Internet Service
Operational: No.
Telephone Service
None
Miles of Plant: 71.0 (coaxial); None (fiber optic). Total homes in franchised area: 2,500.
Manager: Charles Lathrop. Chief Technician: Jim Batch.
Ownership: Lewiston Communications (MSO).

LEXINGTON—Comcast Cable, 1555 Bad Axe Rd, Bad Axe, MI 48413. Phone: 989-269-8927. Fax: 989-269-9125. Web Site: http://www.comcast.com. Also serves Buel Twp., Croswell & Worth Twp. ICA: MI0128.
TV Market Ranking: Outside TV Markets (Buel Twp., Croswell, LEXINGTON, Worth Twp.). Franchise award date: N.A. Franchise expiration date: N.A. Began: N.A.
Channel capacity: 46 (not 2-way capable). Channels available but not in use: N.A.
Basic Service
Subscribers: 2,553.
Programming (received off-air): various Canadian stations; WADL (IND) Mount Clemens; WDIV-TV (NBC) Detroit; WFUM (PBS) Flint; WJBK (FOX) Detroit; WKBD-TV (CW) Detroit; WMYD (MNT) Detroit; WWJ-TV (CBS) Detroit; WXYZ-TV (ABC) Detroit.
Programming (via satellite): Discovery Health Channel; QVC; TBS Superstation; Trinity Broadcasting Network; TV Guide Network.
Current originations: Educational Access.
Fee: $14.50 monthly.
Expanded Basic Service 1
Subscribers: 2,118.
Programming (via satellite): ABC Family Channel; AMC; Arts & Entertainment; CNBC; CNN; C-SPAN; Discovery Channel; Disney Channel; ESPN; ESPN 2; Fox Sports Net Detroit; FX; Great American Country; Headline News; HGTV; History Channel; Lifetime; MTV; Nickelodeon; Spike TV; Syfy; The Learning Channel; truTV; Turner Network TV; TV Land; USA Network; Weather Channel.
Fee: $43.49 monthly.
Digital Basic Service
Subscribers: N.A.
Programming (via satellite): CMT Pure Country; Discovery Kids Channel; Flix; MTV Jams; MTV Tres; MTV2; Music Choice; Nick Jr.; NickToons TV; Science Channel; TeenNick; VH1 Classic; VH1 Soul.
Digital Expanded Basic Service
Subscribers: N.A.
Programming (via satellite): BBC America; Discovery Military Channel; Discovery Planet Green; Encore (multiplexed); ID Investigation Discovery; MTV Hits; Nick Too; Sundance Channel.
Digital Pay Service 1
Pay Units: N.A.
Programming (via satellite): Cinemax (multiplexed); HBO (multiplexed); Showtime (multiplexed); Starz (multiplexed); The Movie Channel (multiplexed).
Fee: $14.99 monthly (each).
Video-On-Demand: No
Pay-Per-View
Hot Choice (delivered digitally).
Internet Service
Operational: No.

Telephone Service
None
Miles of Plant: 105.0 (coaxial); None (fiber optic). Homes passed: 4,378.
General Manager: Thomas J. Lerash. Chief Technician: Marshall Kurschner. Business Manager: Susan McGathy.
Ownership: Comcast Cable Communications Inc. (MSO).

LILLEY TWP.—Charter Communications, 315 Davis St, Grand Haven, MI 49417-1830. Phone: 616-647-6201. Fax: 616-846-0797. Web Site: http://www.charter.com. Also serves Bitely & Brohman. ICA: MI0192.
TV Market Ranking: Outside TV Markets (Bitely, Brohman, LILLEY TWP.). Franchise award date: N.A. Franchise expiration date: N.A. Began: August 1, 1990.
Channel capacity: 36 (not 2-way capable). Channels available but not in use: 10.
Basic Service
Subscribers: 222.
Programming (received off-air): WCMV (PBS) Cadillac; WFQX-TV (FOX) Cadillac; WPBN-TV (NBC) Traverse City; WWTV (CBS) Cadillac; WZZM (ABC) Grand Rapids.
Programming (via satellite): ABC Family Channel; AMC; Arts & Entertainment; CNN; Country Music TV; Discovery Channel; Disney Channel; ESPN; Headline News; Showtime; Spike TV; TBS Superstation; The Learning Channel; Trinity Broadcasting Network; Turner Network TV; USA Network; WGN America.
Fee: $24.95 installation; $28.00 monthly.
Internet Service
Operational: No.
Miles of Plant: 43.0 (coaxial); None (fiber optic). Homes passed: 900.
Vice President & General Manager: Dan Spoelman. Technical Operations Manager: Keith Schierbeek. Marketing Director: Steve Schuh.
Ownership: Charter Communications Inc. (MSO).

LIVINGSTON COUNTY—Charter Communications, 7372 Davison Rd, Davison, MI 48423. Phone: 810-652-1400. Web Site: http://www.charter.com. Also serves Dexter Twp., Green Oak Twp., Hamburg Twp., Marion Twp. (Livingston County), Northfield Twp., Pinckney, Putnam Twp., Salem Twp. (Washtenaw County), Unadilla Twp., Webster Twp. & Whitmore Lake. ICA: MI0036.
TV Market Ranking: 5 (Salem Twp. (Washtenaw County)); 92 (Green Oak Twp., LIVINGSTON COUNTY (portions), Marion Twp. (Livingston County), Northfield Twp., Pinckney, Unadilla Twp., Webster Twp., Whitmore Lake); Below 100 (Dexter Twp., Hamburg Twp., Putnam Twp., LIVINGSTON COUNTY (portions)). Franchise award date: January 1, 1981. Franchise expiration date: N.A. Began: September 1, 1981.
Channel capacity: N.A. Channels available but not in use: N.A.
Basic Service
Subscribers: 16,200.
Programming (received off-air): WADL (IND) Mount Clemens; WDIV-TV (NBC) Detroit; WFUM (PBS) Flint; WJBK (FOX) Detroit; WKAR-TV (PBS) East Lansing; WKBD-TV (CW) Detroit; WLNS-TV (CBS) Lansing; WMYD (MNT) Detroit; WPXD-TV (ION) Ann Arbor; WTVS (PBS) Detroit; WWJ-TV (CBS) Detroit; WXYZ-TV (ABC) Detroit.
Programming (via satellite): C-SPAN; QVC; various Canadian stations; WGN America.
Current originations: Public Access; Government Access; Educational Access.
Fee: $29.99 installation; $13.50 monthly.
Expanded Basic Service 1
Subscribers: 13,310.
Programming (via satellite): ABC Family Channel; AMC; Animal Planet; Arts & Entertainment; Bravo; Cartoon Network; CNBC; CNN; Comedy Central; Country Music TV; Discovery Channel; Disney Channel; E! Entertainment Television; ESPN; ESPN 2; Food Network; Fox News Channel; Fox Sports Net Detroit; FX; G4; Golf Channel; GSN; Hallmark Channel; Headline News; HGTV; History Channel; Home Shopping Network; Lifetime; MSNBC; MTV; MTV2; National Geographic Channel; Nickelodeon; Soap-Net; Speed Channel; Spike TV; Style Network; Syfy; TBS Superstation; The Learning Channel; Toon Disney; Travel Channel; truTV; Turner Classic Movies; Turner Network TV; TV Guide Network; TV Land; USA Network; Versus; VH1; Weather Channel.
Fee: $36.49 monthly.
Digital Basic Service
Subscribers: N.A.
Programming (received off-air): WDIV-TV (NBC) Detroit; WJBK (FOX) Detroit; WTVS (PBS) Detroit; WWJ-TV (CBS) Detroit; WXYZ-TV (ABC) Detroit.
Programming (via satellite): BBC America; Bio; CMT Pure Country; C-SPAN 2; Discovery Digital Networks; Discovery HD Theater; Do-It-Yourself; Do-It-Yourself On Demand; ESPN 2 HD; ESPN Classic Sports; ESPN HD; ESPN U; ESPNews; Eurocinema; Food Network On Demand; Fox Business Channel; Fox College Sports Atlantic; Fox College Sports Central; Fox College Sports Pacific; Fox Movie Channel; Fox Soccer; Fuel TV; Fuse; GAS; Great American Country; HDNet; HDNet Movies; HGTV On Demand; History Channel International; Howard TV; Independent Film Channel; Lifetime Movie Network; MTV Networks Digital Suite; Music Choice; Nick Jr.; Nick Too; NickToons TV; Outdoor Channel; PBS KIDS/PBS KIDS GO!; ReelzChannel; Sundance Channel; The Sportsman Channel; Trinity Broadcasting Network; Turner Network TV HD; Universal HD; Versus On Demand; WE tv.
Digital Pay Service 1
Pay Units: N.A.
Programming (via satellite): Cinemax (multiplexed); Cinemax HD; Cinemax On Demand; Encore (multiplexed); Flix; HBO (multiplexed); HBO HD; HBO On Demand; LOGO; Showtime; Showtime HD; Showtime On Demand; Starz; Starz HDTV; Starz On Demand; The Movie Channel (multiplexed).
Video-On-Demand: Yes
Pay-Per-View
iN DEMAND (delivered digitally); ESPN (delivered digitally); NHL Center Ice (delivered digitally); MLB Extra Innings (delivered digitally); Playboy TV (delivered digitally); Fresh (delivered digitally); Shorteez (delivered digitally).
Internet Service
Operational: Yes.
Broadband Service: Charter Pipeline.
Fee: $49.95 installation; $29.99 monthly; $3.95 modem lease.
Telephone Service
Digital: Operational
Fee: $29.99 monthly
Miles of Plant: 800.0 (coaxial); 40.0 (fiber optic). Homes passed: 21,700. Total homes in franchised area: 24,000.
Vice President: Dave Slowick. Technical Operations Director: Lloyd Collins. Marketing Director: Lisa Gayari.
Ownership: Charter Communications Inc. (MSO).

LIVONIA—Bright House Networks, 14525 Farmington Rd, Livonia, MI 48154-5405. Phones: 734-422-3200 (Customer service); 734-422-2810. Fax: 734-422-2239. E-mail: bob.mccann@mybrighthouse.com. Web Site: http://michigan.brighthouse.com. Also serves Farmington, Farmington Hills, Novi & Redford. ICA: MI0019.
TV Market Ranking: 5 (Farmington, Farmington Hills, LIVONIA, Novi, Redford). Franchise award date: January 1, 1983. Franchise expiration date: N.A. Began: February 6, 1984.
Channel capacity: 62 (operating 2-way). Channels available but not in use: N.A.
Basic Service
Subscribers: 75,140.
Programming (received off-air): various Canadian stations; WADL (IND) Mount Clemens; WDIV-TV (NBC) Detroit; WJBK (FOX) Detroit; WKBD-TV (CW) Detroit; WMYD (MNT) Detroit; WPXD-TV (ION) Ann Arbor; WTVS (PBS) Detroit; WWJ-TV (CBS) Detroit; WXYZ-TV (ABC) Detroit.
Programming (via satellite): ABC Family Channel; AMC; Animal Planet; Arts & Entertainment; BET Networks; Bravo; Cartoon Network; CNBC; CNN; Comedy Central; Country Music TV; C-SPAN; C-SPAN 2; Discovery Channel; Disney Channel; E! Entertainment Television; ESPN; ESPN 2; ESPN Classic Sports; Eternal Word TV Network; Food Network; Fox News Channel; Fox Sports Net Detroit; FX; Golf Channel; Headline News; HGTV; History Channel; Home Shopping Network; Lifetime; MSNBC; MTV; National Geographic Channel; Nickelodeon; Oxygen; QVC; ShopNBC; Speed Channel; Spike TV; Syfy; TBS Superstation; The Learning Channel; Travel Channel; truTV; Turner Classic Movies; Turner Network TV; TV Guide Network; TV Land; USA Network; VH1; WE tv; Weather Channel; WGN America.
Current originations: Leased Access; Government Access; Educational Access; Public Access.
Fee: $28.43 installation; $46.15 monthly; $2.50 converter.
Digital Basic Service
Subscribers: N.A.
Programming (via satellite): AmericanLife TV Network; BBC America; Bloomberg Television; Discovery Digital Networks; DMX Music; ESPN Now; ESPNews; Fox Sports World; G4; GAS; GSN; Lifetime Movie Network; MTV2; MuchMusic Network; Nick Jr.; Outdoor Channel; Ovation; Style Network; Toon Disney; Versus; VH1 Classic; WAM! America's Kidz Network.
Fee: $13.50 monthly.
Digital Expanded Basic Service
Subscribers: N.A.
Programming (via satellite): Encore Action; Fox Movie Channel; Independent Film Channel; Sundance Channel.
Digital Pay Service 1
Pay Units: 3,467.
Programming (via satellite): Cinemax (multiplexed); Flix; HBO (multiplexed); Showtime (multiplexed); Starz (multiplexed); The Movie Channel (multiplexed).
Fee: $11.00 monthly (each).
Video-On-Demand: Yes
Pay-Per-View
sports (delivered digitally); iN DEMAND (delivered digitally); Fresh (delivered digitally); Shorteez (delivered digitally); Pleasure (delivered digitally); Hot Choice (delivered digitally).
Internet Service
Operational: Yes.
Broadband Service: Road Runner; EarthLink; AOL for Broadband.
Fee: $49.95 installation; $44.95 monthly.
Telephone Service
Analog: Not Operational
Digital: Operational
Fee: $39.95 monthly
Miles of Plant: 1,274.0 (coaxial); None (fiber optic). Homes passed: 107,621.
President: Bob McCann. Vice President, Engineering: Armis Baumanis. Vice President, Marketing: Dan Dinsmore. Customer Service Manager: Mary Taylor.
City fee: 3% of gross.
Ownership: Bright House Networks LLC (MSO).

LOWELL—Comcast Cable, 3500 Patterson Ave SE, Grand Rapids, MI 49512. Phones: 866-908-9252; 616-977-2228. Fax: 616-977-2224. Web Site: http://www.comcast.com. Also serves Lowell Twp. & Vergennes Twp. ICA: MI0122.
TV Market Ranking: 37 (LOWELL, Lowell Twp., Vergennes Twp.). Franchise award date: January 1, 1983. Franchise expiration date: N.A. Began: January 1, 1983.
Channel capacity: 54 (operating 2-way). Channels available but not in use: 8.
Basic Service
Subscribers: 1,758.
Programming (received off-air): WGVU-TV (PBS) Grand Rapids; WLLA (IND) Kalamazoo; WOOD-TV (NBC) Grand Rapids; WOTV (ABC) Battle Creek; WTLJ (IND) Muskegon; WWMT (CBS, CW) Kalamazoo; WXMI (FOX) Grand Rapids; WXSP-CA (MNT) Grand Rapids; WZPX-TV (ION) Battle Creek; WZZM (ABC) Grand Rapids.
Programming (via satellite): ABC Family Channel; AMC; Animal Planet; Arts & Entertainment; CNN; Comedy Central; C-SPAN; Discovery Channel; Disney Channel; Disney XD; ESPN; ESPN 2; Eternal Word TV Network; Fox Sports Net; FX; Headline News; HGTV; History Channel; Lifetime; MSNBC; MTV; Nickelodeon; QVC; Spike TV; Syfy; TBS Superstation; The Learning Channel; Travel Channel; Turner Network TV; TV Guide Network; USA Network; VH1; Weather Channel; WGN America.
Current originations: Public Access.
Fee: $25.00 installation; $28.30 monthly.
Digital Basic Service
Subscribers: N.A.
Programming (via satellite): BBC America; Bio; Bravo; CMT Pure Country; Discovery Health Channel; Discovery Kids Channel; Discovery Military Channel; Discovery Planet Green; ESPN 2; ESPN Classic Sports; ESPNews; Fox Soccer; Fuse; Golf Channel; GSN; History Channel International; ID Investigation Discovery; Independent Film Channel; Lifetime Movie Network; MTV2; Music Choice; Nick Jr.; Science Channel; Speed Channel; Style Network; TeenNick; Turner Classic Movies; Versus; VH1 Classic; WE tv.
Pay Service 1
Pay Units: 285.
Programming (via satellite): Cinemax.
Fee: $8.50 monthly.
Pay Service 2
Pay Units: 341.
Programming (via satellite): HBO.
Fee: $11.50 monthly.

Pay Service 3
Pay Units: 170.
Programming (via satellite): Showtime; The Movie Channel.
Fee: $12.95 monthly.

Digital Pay Service 1
Pay Units: N.A.
Programming (via satellite): Cinemax (multiplexed); Encore (multiplexed); HBO (multiplexed); Showtime (multiplexed); Starz (multiplexed); The Movie Channel (multiplexed).

Video-On-Demand: No

Pay-Per-View
iN DEMAND (delivered digitally).

Internet Service
Operational: Yes. Began: November 1, 2001.
Subscribers: 510.
Broadband Service: In-house.
Fee: $50.00 installation; $44.95 monthly; $4.95 modem lease.

Telephone Service
None
Miles of Plant: 60.0 (coaxial); None (fiber optic). Additional miles planned: 3.0 (coaxial). Homes passed: 3,100. Total homes in franchised area: 3,700.
Area Vice President: Larry Williamson.
City fee: 5% of gross.
Ownership: Comcast Cable Communications Inc. (MSO).

LUDINGTON—Charter Communications, 315 Davis St, Grand Haven, MI 49417-1830. Phone: 616-647-6201. Fax: 616-846-0797. Web Site: http://www.charter.com. Also serves Amber Twp., Pere Marquette Twp., Scottville & Summit Twp. (Mason Co.). ICA: MI0324.
TV Market Ranking: Outside TV Markets (Amber Twp., LUDINGTON, Pere Marquette Twp., Scottville, Summit Twp. (Mason Co.)). Franchise award date: N.A. Franchise expiration date: N.A. Began: March 1, 1968.
Channel capacity: N.A. Channels available but not in use: N.A.

Basic Service
Subscribers: 4,951.
Programming (received off-air): WBAY-TV (ABC, IND) Green Bay; WCMU-TV (PBS) Mount Pleasant; WFQX-TV (FOX) Cadillac; WFRV-TV (CBS) Green Bay; WGVU-TV (PBS) Grand Rapids; WLUK-TV (FOX) Green Bay; WPBN-TV (NBC) Traverse City; WWTV (CBS) Cadillac; WXSP-CA (MNT) Grand Rapids; WZZM (ABC) Grand Rapids; allband FM.
Programming (via satellite): C-SPAN; C-SPAN 2; Home Shopping Network; QVC; TBS Superstation; TV Guide Network; WGN America.
Current originations: Leased Access; Government Access; Educational Access; Public Access.
Fee: $29.99 installation.

Expanded Basic Service 1
Subscribers: N.A.
Programming (via satellite): ABC Family Channel; AMC; Animal Planet; Arts & Entertainment; Bravo; Cartoon Network; CNBC; CNN; Comedy Central; Country Music TV; Discovery Channel; Disney Channel; E! Entertainment Television; ESPN; ESPN 2; ESPN Classic Sports; ESPNews; Eternal Word TV Network; Food Network; Fox News Channel; Fox Sports Net Detroit; FX; G4; Golf Channel; GSN; Hallmark Channel; Headline News; HGTV; History Channel; INSP; Lifetime; MSNBC; MTV; MTV2; National Geographic Channel; Nickelodeon; Oxygen; SoapNet; Speed Channel; Spike TV; Style Network; Syfy; The Learning Channel; Toon Disney; Travel Channel; Trinity Broadcasting Network; truTV; Turner Classic Movies; Turner Network TV; TV Land; Univision; USA Network; Versus; VH1; WE tv; Weather Channel.
Fee: $47.99 monthly.

Digital Basic Service
Subscribers: N.A.
Programming (received off-air): WFQX-TV (FOX) Cadillac; WPBN-TV (NBC) Traverse City; WWTV (CBS) Cadillac; WZZM (ABC) Grand Rapids.
Programming (via satellite): BBC America; Bio; Boomerang; Canales N; CMT Pure Country; Discovery Digital Networks; Discovery HD Theater; Do-It-Yourself; ESPN HD; Fox College Sports Atlantic; Fox College Sports Central; Fox College Sports Pacific; Fox Movie Channel; Fox Soccer; Fuel TV; Fuse; GAS; Great American Country; HDNet; HDNet Movies; History Channel International; Independent Film Channel; Lifetime Movie Network; MTV Networks Digital Suite; Music Choice; Nick Jr.; Nick Too; NickToons TV; Outdoor Channel; Sundance Channel; Turner Network TV HD; Universal HD.

Digital Pay Service 1
Pay Units: N.A.
Programming (via satellite): Cinemax (multiplexed); Cinemax HD; Encore (multiplexed); Flix; HBO (multiplexed); HBO HD; LOGO; Showtime (multiplexed); Showtime HD; Starz (multiplexed); The Movie Channel (multiplexed).

Video-On-Demand: No

Pay-Per-View
iN DEMAND (delivered digitally); NHL Center Ice (delivered digitally); MLB Extra Innings (delivered digitally); ESPN (delivered digitally); Playboy TV (delivered digitally); Fresh (delivered digitally); Shorteez (delivered digitally).

Internet Service
Operational: Yes. Began: January 1, 2003.
Broadband Service: Charter Pipeline.
Fee: $29.99 monthly.

Telephone Service
None
Miles of Plant: 220.0 (coaxial); None (fiber optic).
Vice President & General Manager: Dan Spoelman. Technical Operations Manager: Keith Schierbeek. Marketing Director: Steve Schuh.
City fee: 3% of gross.
Ownership: Charter Communications Inc. (MSO).

LUZERNE—Pine River Cable, PO Box 96, McBain, MI 49657. Phone: 888-244-2288. Fax: 231-825-0191. E-mail: info@pinerivercable.com. Web Site: http://www.pinerivercable.com. ICA: MI0325.
TV Market Ranking: Outside TV Markets (LUZERNE). Franchise award date: N.A. Franchise expiration date: N.A. Began: N.A.
Channel capacity: 36 (not 2-way capable). Channels available but not in use: 15.

Basic Service
Subscribers: 52.
Programming (received off-air): WBKB-TV (CBS, FOX) Alpena; WCML (PBS) Alpena; WFUP (FOX) Vanderbilt; WGTU (ABC, CW) Traverse City; WPBN-TV (NBC) Traverse City.
Programming (via satellite): ABC Family Channel; AMC; Arts & Entertainment; CNN; Country Music TV; Discovery Channel; ESPN; Showtime; TBS Superstation; Turner Network TV; USA Network; WGN America.
Fee: $50.00 installation; $24.95 monthly.

Internet Service
Operational: No.
Miles of Plant: 5.0 (coaxial); None (fiber optic). Homes passed: 286.
Manager: John Metzler.
Ownership: Pine River Cable (MSO).

MACKINAC ISLAND—Charter Communications, PO Box 808, 2682 Ashmun St, Sault Sainte Marie, MI 49783. Phones: 231-947-5221 (Traverse City); 906-632-8541. Fax: 906-635-1520. Web Site: http://www.charter.com. ICA: MI0199.
TV Market Ranking: Below 100 (MACKINAC ISLAND). Franchise award date: July 11, 1990. Franchise expiration date: N.A. Began: July 15, 1991.
Channel capacity: 60 (not 2-way capable). Channels available but not in use: 28.

Basic Service
Subscribers: 588.
Programming (received off-air): WCML (PBS) Alpena; WFQX-TV (FOX) Cadillac; WGTQ (ABC) Sault Ste. Marie; WTOM-TV (NBC) Cheboygan; WWUP-TV (CBS, FOX) Sault Ste. Marie.
Programming (via satellite): C-SPAN.
Current originations: Government Access.
Fee: $29.99 installation; $13.50 monthly; $1.21 converter.

Expanded Basic Service 1
Subscribers: 575.
Programming (via satellite): ABC Family Channel; AMC; Arts & Entertainment; CNBC; CNN; Discovery Channel; Disney Channel; ESPN; ESPN 2; Fox Sports Net Detroit; Headline News; HGTV; History Channel; Nickelodeon; QVC; Spike TV; TBS Superstation; Turner Network TV; USA Network; Weather Channel; WGN America.
Fee: $36.49 monthly.

Pay Service 1
Pay Units: 100.
Programming (via satellite): HBO.
Fee: $15.51 installation; $10.00 monthly.

Pay Service 2
Pay Units: 82.
Programming (via satellite): Showtime.
Fee: $15.51 installation; $10.00 monthly.

Pay Service 3
Pay Units: 35.
Programming (via satellite): The Movie Channel.
Fee: $15.51 installation; $10.00 monthly.

Internet Service
Operational: No.
Miles of Plant: 12.0 (coaxial); None (fiber optic). Homes passed: 721. Total homes in franchised area: 741.
Manager: John Badenski. Chief Technician: John Randazzo.
Ownership: Charter Communications Inc. (MSO).

MACKINAW CITY—Charter Communications, 701 E South Airport Rd, Traverse City, MI 49686-4861. Phone: 231-947-5221. Fax: 231-947-2004. E-mail: jboullion@chartercom.com. Web Site: http://www.charter.com. Also serves Mackinaw Twp. & Wawatam Twp. ICA: MI0326.
TV Market Ranking: Below 100 (MACKINAW CITY, Mackinaw Twp., Wawatam Twp.). Franchise award date: N.A. Franchise expiration date: N.A. Began: June 1, 1968.
Channel capacity: 42 (not 2-way capable). Channels available but not in use: None.

Basic Service
Subscribers: 332.
Programming (received off-air): WCML (PBS) Alpena; WFUP (FOX) Vanderbilt; WGTU (ABC, CW) Traverse City; WTOM-TV (NBC) Cheboygan; WWUP-TV (CBS, FOX) Sault Ste. Marie.
Programming (via microwave): WKBD-TV (CW) Detroit.
Programming (via satellite): Discovery Channel; FX; TBS Superstation; WGN America.
Current originations: Educational Access.
Fee: $29.99 installation; $13.50 monthly; $1.60 converter.

Expanded Basic Service 1
Subscribers: 302.
Programming (via satellite): ABC Family Channel; AMC; Animal Planet; Arts & Entertainment; Cartoon Network; CNN; C-SPAN; C-SPAN 2; Disney Channel; ESPN; Fox News Channel; Fox Sports Net Detroit; Hallmark Channel; HGTV; Home Shopping Network; MTV; Nickelodeon; QVC; Spike TV; The Learning Channel; truTV; Turner Network TV; USA Network; Weather Channel.
Fee: $36.49 monthly.

Pay Service 1
Pay Units: 36.
Programming (via satellite): Cinemax.
Fee: $12.85 monthly.

Pay Service 2
Pay Units: 67.
Programming (via satellite): Encore.
Fee: $1.75 monthly.

Pay Service 3
Pay Units: 54.
Programming (via satellite): HBO.
Fee: $13.45 monthly.

Pay Service 4
Pay Units: 38.
Programming (via satellite): Starz.
Fee: $6.75 monthly.

Pay-Per-View
Special events.

Internet Service
Operational: Yes.
Fee: $19.99 monthly.

Telephone Service
Digital: Operational
Fee: $14.99 monthly
Miles of Plant: 14.0 (coaxial); None (fiber optic).
Vice President & General Manager: Joe Boullion. Technical Operations Director: Rob Nowak. Marketing Manager: Tammy Reicha.
Ownership: Charter Communications Inc. (MSO).

MADISON HEIGHTS—Comcast Cable. Now served by STERLING HEIGHTS, MI [MI0002]. ICA: MI0052.

MANCELONA—Charter Communications. Now served by TRAVERSE CITY, MI [MI0026]. Also serves MANCELONA. ICA: MI0087.

MANISTEE—Charter Communications. Now served by TRAVERSE CITY, MI [MI0026]. ICA: MI0089.

MANTON—Charter Communications. Now served by TRAVERSE CITY, MI [MI0026]. ICA: MI0137.

MAPLE RAPIDS—Pine River Cable, PO Box 96, McBain, MI 49657. Phone: 888-244-2288. Fax: 231-825-0191. E-mail: info@pinerivercable.com. Web Site: http://www.pinerivercable.com. ICA: MI0234.
TV Market Ranking: 92 (MAPLE RAPIDS). Franchise award date: April 1, 1987. Fran-

chise expiration date: N.A. Began: September 1, 1987.
Channel capacity: 36 (operating 2-way). Channels available but not in use: 11.

Basic Service
Subscribers: N.A.
Programming (received off-air): WILX-TV (NBC) Onondaga; WJRT-TV (ABC) Flint; WKAR-TV (PBS) East Lansing; WLNS-TV (CBS) Lansing; WOOD-TV (NBC) Grand Rapids; WSYM-TV (FOX) Lansing; WWMT (CBS, CW) Kalamazoo.
Programming (via satellite): ABC Family Channel; CNN; Discovery Channel; Disney Channel; ESPN; Headline News; TBS Superstation; Turner Network TV; USA Network; WGN America.
Fee: $30.00 installation; $19.95 monthly.

Pay Service 1
Pay Units: 51.
Programming (via satellite): Showtime.
Fee: $20.00 installation; $7.00 monthly.

Internet Service
Operational: No.

Telephone Service
None
Miles of Plant: 4.0 (coaxial); None (fiber optic). Homes passed: 269.
Manager: John Metzler.
Ownership: Pine River Cable (MSO).

MARCELLUS—Mediacom, 109 E 5th St, Ste A, Auburn, IN 46706. Phone: 260-927-3015. Fax: 260-347-4433. Web Site: http://www.mediacomcable.com. ICA: MI0431.
TV Market Ranking: 37,80 (MARCELLUS). Franchise award date: N.A. Franchise expiration date: N.A. Began: November 4, 1996.
Channel capacity: 83 (operating 2-way). Channels available but not in use: 37.

Basic Service
Subscribers: 325.
Programming (received off-air): WHME-TV (IND) South Bend; WNDU-TV (NBC) South Bend; WNIT (PBS) South Bend; WOOD-TV (NBC) Grand Rapids; WOTV (ABC) Battle Creek; WSBT-TV (CBS, IND) South Bend; WSJV (FOX) Elkhart; WWMT (CBS, CW) Kalamazoo; WXMI (FOX) Grand Rapids.
Programming (via satellite): WGN America.
Fee: $45.00 installation; $20.95 monthly.

Expanded Basic Service 1
Subscribers: 270.
Programming (via satellite): ABC Family Channel; AMC; Animal Planet; Arts & Entertainment; Cartoon Network; CNN; Comedy Central; Country Music TV; Discovery Channel; Disney Channel; ESPN; ESPN 2; Food Network; Fox Sports Net Detroit; Headline News; HGTV; History Channel; Home Shopping Network; Lifetime; MTV; Nickelodeon; Radar Channel; Spike TV; Syfy; TBS Superstation; The Learning Channel; Travel Channel; Trinity Broadcasting Network; truTV; Turner Network TV; TV Land; USA Network; VH1; Weather Channel.
Fee: $29.00 monthly.

Pay Service 1
Pay Units: 108.
Programming (via satellite): Cinemax; HBO.
Fee: $7.99 monthly (Cinemax), $13.50 monthly (HBO).

Video-On-Demand: No

Internet Service
Operational: No.

Telephone Service
None
Miles of Plant: 14.0 (coaxial); None (fiber optic). Homes passed: 783.
Operations Director: Joe Poffenberger. Technical Operations Manager: Craig Grey.
City fee: 5% of gross.
Ownership: Mediacom LLC (MSO).

MARENISCO TWP.—Upper Peninsula Communications, 397 N US Hwy 41, Carney, MI 49812-9757. Phone: 906-639-2194. Fax: 906-639-9936. E-mail: louied@alphacomm.net. ICA: MI0249.
TV Market Ranking: Outside TV Markets (MARENISCO TWP.). Franchise award date: January 14, 1985. Franchise expiration date: N.A. Began: January 1, 1986.
Channel capacity: 36 (not 2-way capable). Channels available but not in use: 18.

Basic Service
Subscribers: N.A.
Programming (received off-air): KQDS-TV (FOX) Duluth; WBKB-TV (CBS, FOX) Alpena; WJFW-TV (NBC) Rhinelander; WLEF-TV (PBS) Park Falls; WSAW-TV (CBS, MNT) Wausau; WYOW (ABC, CW) Eagle River.
Programming (via satellite): ABC Family Channel; Arts & Entertainment; CNN; C-SPAN; Discovery Channel; Disney Channel; ESPN; ESPN 2; Eternal Word TV Network; HGTV; History Channel; Home Shopping Network; ION Television; Lifetime; Outdoor Channel; Spike TV; TBS Superstation; Turner Classic Movies; Turner Network TV; TV Land; USA Network; Weather Channel; WGN America.
Fee: $39.95 installation; $15.50 monthly; $1.50 converter.

Pay Service 1
Pay Units: 21.
Programming (via satellite): Cinemax; HBO.
Fee: $7.50 monthly (Cinemax), $9.50 monthly (HBO).

Video-On-Demand: No

Internet Service
Operational: No.

Telephone Service
None
Miles of Plant: 3.0 (coaxial); None (fiber optic). Homes passed: 150. Total homes in franchised area: 150.
Manager & Chief Technician: Louis Dupont.
Ownership: Upper Peninsula Communications Inc. (MSO).

MARION—Pine River Cable, PO Box 96, McBain, MI 49657. Phone: 888-244-2288. Fax: 231-825-0191. E-mail: info@pinerivercable.com. Web Site: http://www.pinerivercable.com. Also serves Marion Twp. (Osceola County). ICA: MI0219.
TV Market Ranking: Below 100 (MARION, Marion Twp. (Osceola County)). Franchise award date: April 1, 1984. Franchise expiration date: N.A. Began: April 1, 1984.
Channel capacity: 36 (2-way capable). Channels available but not in use: 6.

Basic Service
Subscribers: 204.
Programming (received off-air): WCMV (PBS) Cadillac; WFQX-TV (FOX) Cadillac; WGTU (ABC, CW) Traverse City; WPBN-TV (NBC) Traverse City; WWTV (CBS) Cadillac.
Programming (via satellite): ABC Family Channel; C-SPAN; QVC; TBS Superstation; WGN America.
Fee: $50.00 installation; $20.35 monthly.

Expanded Basic Service 1
Subscribers: N.A.
Programming (via satellite): AMC; Arts & Entertainment; CNN; Country Music TV; Discovery Channel; Disney Channel; E! Entertainment Television; ESPN; ESPN 2; Food Network; Fox Sports Net Detroit; Headline News; HGTV; Lifetime; MTV; Nickelodeon; Spike TV; The Learning Channel; Turner Network TV; USA Network; VH1; Weather Channel.

Pay Service 1
Pay Units: 33.
Programming (via satellite): Cinemax; HBO.
Fee: $2.00 installation; $10.95 monthly (Cinemax), $11.95 monthly (HBO).

Internet Service
Operational: No.
Miles of Plant: 5.0 (coaxial); None (fiber optic). Homes passed: 431.
Manager: John Metzler.
City fee: 3% on gross.
Ownership: Pine River Cable (MSO).

MARQUETTE—Charter Communications, 359 US 41 East, Negaunee, MI 49866. Phones: 231-947-5221 (Traverse City office); 906-475-0107. Fax: 906-475-7007. E-mail: jboullion@chartercom.com. Web Site: http://www.charter.com. Also serves Au Train Twp., Chatham, Chocolay Twp., Christmas, Eben Junction, Ely Twp., Forsyth Twp., Grand Island Twp., Gwinn, Harvey, Ishpeming, Little Lake, Munising, Negaunee, Palmer, Princeton, Rock River Twp., Sands Twp., Skandia Twp., Tilden Twp. & Wetmore. ICA: MI0033.
TV Market Ranking: Below 100 (Au Train Twp., Chatham, Chocolay Twp., Christmas, Eben Junction, Ely Twp., Forsyth Twp., Grand Island Twp., Gwinn, Harvey, Ishpeming, Little Lake, MARQUETTE, Negaunee, Palmer, Princeton, Rock River Twp., Sands Twp., Skandia Twp., Tilden Twp.); Outside TV Markets (Munising, Wetmore). Franchise award date: October 1, 1960. Franchise expiration date: N.A. Began: October 1, 1960.
Channel capacity: 112 (operating 2-way). Channels available but not in use: 31.

Basic Service
Subscribers: 19,300.
Programming (received off-air): WBKP (ABC) Calumet; WBUP (ABC) Ishpeming; WJMN-TV (CBS) Escanaba; WLUC-TV (NBC) Marquette; WNMU (PBS) Marquette; WZMQ (IND, MNT) Marquette.
Programming (via microwave): WLUK-TV (FOX) Green Bay.
Programming (via satellite): C-SPAN; C-SPAN 2; C-SPAN 3; Eternal Word TV Network; G4; Home Shopping Network; INSP; QVC; TBS Superstation; TV Guide Network; various Canadian stations; Weather Channel; WGN America.
Current originations: Leased Access; Government Access; Educational Access; Public Access.
Fee: $29.99 installation; $13.50 monthly.

Expanded Basic Service 1
Subscribers: 16,486.
Programming (via satellite): ABC Family Channel; AMC; Animal Planet; Arts & Entertainment; Bravo; Cartoon Network; CNBC; CNN; Comedy Central; Country Music TV; Discovery Channel; Disney Channel; E! Entertainment Television; ESPN; ESPN 2; FitTV; Food Network; Fox News Channel; Fox Sports Net Detroit; FX; Golf Channel; GSN; Hallmark Channel; Headline News; HGTV; History Channel; Lifetime; MSNBC; MTV; National Geographic Channel; Nickelodeon; Oxygen; SoapNet; Speed Channel; Spike TV; Style Network; Syfy; The Learning Channel; Toon Disney; Travel Channel; truTV; Turner Classic Movies; Turner Network TV; TV Land; USA Network; Versus; VH1; WE tv.
Fee: $36.49 monthly.

Digital Basic Service
Subscribers: N.A.
Programming (received off-air): WJMN-TV (CBS) Escanaba; WLUC-TV (NBC) Marquette; WNMU (PBS) Marquette.
Programming (via satellite): BBC America; Bio; CMT Pure Country; Cooking Channel; Discovery Digital Networks; Discovery HD Theater; Do-It-Yourself; ESPN Classic Sports; ESPN HD; ESPNews; Food Network On Demand; Fox College Sports Atlantic; Fox College Sports Central; Fox College Sports Pacific; Fox Movie Channel; Fox Soccer; Fuel TV; Fuse; GAS; Great American Country; HDNet; HDNet Movies; HGTV On Demand; History Channel International; Howard TV; Independent Film Channel; Lifetime Movie Network; MTV Networks Digital Suite; Music Choice; Nick Jr.; Nick Too; Outdoor Channel; Sundance Channel; Turner Network TV HD; Universal HD; Versus On Demand.

Digital Pay Service 1
Pay Units: N.A.
Programming (via satellite): Cinemax (multiplexed); Cinemax HD; Cinemax On Demand; Encore (multiplexed); Flix; HBO (multiplexed); HBO HD; HBO On Demand; LOGO; Showtime (multiplexed); Showtime HD; Showtime On Demand; Starz (multiplexed); Starz On Demand; The Movie Channel (multiplexed).

Video-On-Demand: Yes

Pay-Per-View
iN DEMAND (delivered digitally); ESPN (delivered digitally); NHL Center Ice (delivered digitally); MLB Extra Innings (delivered digitally); Playboy TV (delivered digitally); Fresh (delivered digitally); Shorteez (delivered digitally).

Internet Service
Operational: Yes.
Broadband Service: Charter Pipeline.
Fee: $49.95 installation; $29.99 monthly.

Telephone Service
Digital: Operational
Fee: $29.99 monthly
Miles of Plant: 471.0 (coaxial); 231.0 (fiber optic). Homes passed: 29,072. Total homes in franchised area: 34,000.
Vice President: Joe Boullion. General Manager: Rex Buettgenbach. Technical Operations Director: Rob Nowak. Marketing Manager: Sandy Gottschalk. Government Relations Manager: Don Gladwell.
Ownership: Charter Communications Inc. (MSO).

MASS CITY—Charter Communications. Now served by IRONWOOD, MI [MI0064]. ICA: MI0217.

MATTAWAN—Mediacom, 109 E 5th St, Ste A, Auburn, IN 46706. Phone: 260-927-3015. Fax: 260-347-4433. Web Site: http://www.mediacomcable.com. Also serves Almena Twp. & Antwerp Twp. ICA: MI0141.
TV Market Ranking: 37 (Almena Twp., Antwerp Twp., MATTAWAN). Franchise award date: N.A. Franchise expiration date: N.A. Began: April 1, 1974.
Channel capacity: N.A. Channels available but not in use: N.A.

Basic Service
Subscribers: 1,265.
Programming (received off-air): WGVU-TV (PBS) Grand Rapids; WLLA (IND) Kalamazoo; WNDU-TV (NBC) South Bend; WOOD-TV (NBC) Grand Rapids; WOTV (ABC) Battle Creek; WWMT (CBS, CW) Kalamazoo; WXMI (FOX) Grand Rapids; WZPX-TV (ION) Battle Creek.

Programming (via satellite): Trinity Broadcasting Network; WGN America.
Fee: $45.00 installation; $20.95 monthly.

Expanded Basic Service 1
Subscribers: 1,023.
Programming (via satellite): ABC Family Channel; AMC; Animal Planet; Arts & Entertainment; Cartoon Network; CNBC; CNN; Comedy Central; Country Music TV; Discovery Channel; Disney Channel; E! Entertainment Television; ESPN; ESPN 2; ESPN Classic Sports; Eternal Word TV Network; Food Network; Fox Sports Net Detroit; Hallmark Channel; Headline News; HGTV; History Channel; Home Shopping Network; Lifetime; MSNBC; MTV; MTV2; Nickelodeon; QVC; Radar Channel; ShopNBC; Speed Channel; Spike TV; Syfy; TBS Superstation; The Learning Channel; Travel Channel; truTV; Turner Network TV; Univision; USA Network; VH1; Weather Channel.
Fee: $29.00 monthly.

Digital Basic Service
Subscribers: N.A.
Programming (via satellite): AmericanLife TV Network; BBC America; Bio; Bloomberg Television; Discovery Digital Networks; ESPNews; Fox Movie Channel; Fox Soccer; Fuse; G4; Golf Channel; Halogen Network; History Channel International; Independent Film Channel; Lifetime Movie Network; Military History Channel; MTV Hits; Music Choice; National Geographic Channel; Nick Jr.; NickToons TV; Outdoor Channel; Science Channel; Sleuth; Style Network; TeenNick; Turner Classic Movies; TVG Network; Versus; VH1 Classic.
Fee: $9.00 monthly.

Digital Pay Service 1
Pay Units: N.A.
Programming (via satellite): Cinemax (multiplexed); Encore (multiplexed); HBO (multiplexed); Showtime (multiplexed); Starz (multiplexed); The Movie Channel (multiplexed).
Fee: $11.95 monthly (each).

Video-On-Demand: No

Pay-Per-View
Barker (delivered digitally); iN DEMAND (delivered digitally); Club Jenna (delivered digitally); Playboy TV (delivered digitally); Fresh (delivered digitally); Spice: Xcess (delivered digitally).

Internet Service
Operational: No.

Telephone Service
None

Operations Director: Joe Poffenberger. Technical Operations Manager: Craig Grey.
Ownership: Mediacom LLC (MSO).

MAYVILLE—Charter Communications. Now served by NORTH BRANCH TWP., MI [MI0337]. ICA: MI0374.

MCBAIN—Pine River Cable, PO Box 96, McBain, MI 49657. Phone: 888-244-2288. Fax: 231-825-0191. E-mail: info@pinerivercable.com. Web Site: http://www.pinerivercable.com. Also serves Riverside Twp. ICA: MI0240.
TV Market Ranking: Below 100 (MCBAIN, Riverside Twp.). Franchise award date: N.A. Franchise expiration date: N.A. Began: February 1, 1984.
Channel capacity: 36 (2-way capable). Channels available but not in use: 6.

Basic Service
Subscribers: 166.
Programming (received off-air): WCMV (PBS) Cadillac; WFQX-TV (FOX) Cadillac; WGTU (ABC, CW) Traverse City; WPBN-TV (NBC) Traverse City; WWTV (CBS) Cadillac.
Programming (via satellite): ABC Family Channel; C-SPAN; QVC; TBS Superstation; WGN America.
Fee: $50.00 installation; $21.60 monthly.

Expanded Basic Service 1
Subscribers: N.A.
Programming (via satellite): AMC; Arts & Entertainment; CNN; Country Music TV; Discovery Channel; Disney Channel; E! Entertainment Television; ESPN; ESPN 2; Food Network; Fox Sports Net Detroit; Headline News; HGTV; Lifetime; MTV; Nickelodeon; Spike TV; The Learning Channel; Turner Network TV; USA Network; VH1; Weather Channel.

Pay Service 1
Pay Units: 14.
Programming (via satellite): Cinemax; HBO.
Fee: $21.00 installation; $10.95 monthly (Cinemax), $11.95 monthly (HBO).

Internet Service
Operational: No.

Miles of Plant: 6.0 (coaxial); None (fiber optic). Homes passed: 262.
Manager: John Metzler.
City fee: 3% of basic.
Ownership: Pine River Cable (MSO).

MEARS—Lewiston Communications, PO Box 169, 2 E Main St, Fremont, MI 49412-0169. Phones: 231-924-8060; 800-443-0758. Fax: 231-924-6155. Also serves Golden Twp. ICA: MI0395.
TV Market Ranking: Below 100 (Golden Twp., MEARS). Franchise award date: N.A. Franchise expiration date: N.A. Began: N.A.
Channel capacity: N.A. Channels available but not in use: N.A.

Basic Service
Subscribers: 300.
Programming (received off-air): WCMW (PBS) Manistee; WPBN-TV (NBC) Traverse City; WWTV (CBS) Cadillac; WZZM (ABC) Grand Rapids.
Programming (via satellite): ABC Family Channel; AMC; Animal Planet; Arts & Entertainment; Cartoon Network; CNBC; CNN; Comedy Central; Country Music TV; C-SPAN; Discovery Channel; Discovery Health Channel; E! Entertainment Television; ESPN; ESPN 2; Fox News Channel; Fox Sports Net Detroit; FX; G4; Golf Channel; Hallmark Channel; Headline News; HGTV; History Channel; Lifetime; National Geographic Channel; Nickelodeon; Outdoor Channel; QVC; Speed Channel; Spike TV; Syfy; TBS Superstation; The Learning Channel; Trinity Broadcasting Network; truTV; Turner Classic Movies; Turner Network TV; TV Land; USA Network; VH1; Weather Channel; WFQX-TV (FOX) Cadillac; WGN America.
Fee: $55.00 installation; $43.95 monthly.

Pay Service 1
Pay Units: 10.
Programming (via satellite): HBO.
Fee: $11.95 monthly.

Pay Service 2
Pay Units: 6.
Programming (via satellite): Showtime.
Fee: $11.95 monthly.

Video-On-Demand: No

Internet Service
Operational: Yes.
Subscribers: 15.
Broadband Service: In-house.
Fee: $24.95 monthly.

Telephone Service
None

Miles of Plant: 30.0 (coaxial); None (fiber optic). Total homes in franchised area: 860.
Manager: Charles Lathrop. Chief Technician: Jim Batch.
Ownership: Lewiston Communications (MSO).

MECOSTA—Charter Communications, 2304 S Mission, Mount Pleasant, MI 48858. Phone: 989-775-6846. Fax: 989-772-0350. Web Site: http://www.charter.com. Also serves Martiny Twp. ICA: MI0327.
TV Market Ranking: Outside TV Markets (Martiny Twp., MECOSTA). Franchise award date: N.A. Franchise expiration date: N.A. Began: October 1, 1989.
Channel capacity: 36 (not 2-way capable). Channels available but not in use: 12.

Basic Service
Subscribers: 377.
Programming (received off-air): WCMU-TV (PBS) Mount Pleasant; WFQX-TV (FOX) Cadillac; WPBN-TV (NBC) Traverse City; WWTV (CBS) Cadillac; WZZM (ABC) Grand Rapids.
Programming (via satellite): ABC Family Channel; CNN; Country Music TV; Disney Channel; ESPN; Headline News; TBS Superstation; Turner Network TV; USA Network; WGN America.
Fee: $19.95 monthly.

Pay Service 1
Pay Units: N.A.
Programming (via satellite): Showtime.
Fee: $7.00 monthly.

Internet Service
Operational: No.

Telephone Service
None

Miles of Plant: 27.0 (coaxial); None (fiber optic). Homes passed: 1,174.
Vice President & General Manager: Dan Spoelman. Operations Manager: Ed Bucao.
Ownership: Charter Communications Inc. (MSO).

MELLEN TWP.—Packerland Broadband, PO Box 885, 105 Kent St, Iron Mountain, MI 49801. Phones: 906-774-6621; 800-236-8434. Fax: 906-776-2811. E-mail: inquiries@plbb.us. Web Site: http://www.packerlandbroadband.com. ICA: MI0330.
TV Market Ranking: Below 100 (MELLEN TWP.). Franchise award date: N.A. Franchise expiration date: N.A. Began: N.A.
Channel capacity: N.A. Channels available but not in use: N.A.

Basic Service
Subscribers: 148.
Programming (received off-air): WBKP (ABC) Calumet; WJMN-TV (CBS) Escanaba; WLUC-TV (NBC) Marquette; WNMU (PBS) Marquette; WZMQ (IND, MNT) Marquette.
Programming (via satellite): ABC Family Channel; AMC; Arts & Entertainment; CNBC; CNN; C-SPAN; Discovery Channel; Disney Channel; ESPN; ESPN 2; HGTV; History Channel; Home Shopping Network; ION Television; Lifetime; Outdoor Channel; Spike TV; TBS Superstation; The Learning Channel; Trinity Broadcasting Network; Turner Network TV; TV Land; USA Network; Weather Channel; WGN America.
Current originations: Public Access.
Fee: $26.00 installation; $14.50 monthly.

Pay Service 1
Pay Units: N.A.
Programming (via satellite): Showtime.
Fee: $7.50 monthly.

Internet Service
Operational: No.

Telephone Service
None

Homes passed: 240.
General Manager: Dan Plante. Technical Supervisor: Chad Kay.
Ownership: Cable Constructors Inc. (MSO).

MENDON—Mediacom, 109 E 5th St, Ste A, Auburn, IN 46706. Phone: 260-927-3015. Fax: 260-347-4433. Web Site: http://www.mediacomcable.com. ICA: MI0213.
TV Market Ranking: 37,80 (MENDON (VILLAGE)). Franchise award date: N.A. Franchise expiration date: N.A. Began: December 1, 1983.
Channel capacity: 37 (operating 2-way). Channels available but not in use: None.

Basic Service
Subscribers: 306.
Programming (received off-air): WHME-TV (IND) South Bend; WLLA (IND) Kalamazoo; WNDU-TV (NBC) South Bend; WOOD-TV (NBC) Grand Rapids; WOTV (ABC) Battle Creek; WSBT-TV (CBS, IND) South Bend; WSJV (FOX) Elkhart; WWMT (CBS, CW) Kalamazoo; WXMI (FOX) Grand Rapids.
Programming (via satellite): Home Shopping Network; WGN America.
Fee: $45.00 installation; $20.95 monthly.

Expanded Basic Service 1
Subscribers: 248.
Programming (via satellite): ABC Family Channel; AMC; Animal Planet; Arts & Entertainment; Cartoon Network; CNBC; CNN; Country Music TV; C-SPAN; C-SPAN 2; Discovery Channel; Disney Channel; E! Entertainment Television; ESPN; ESPN 2; Food Network; Fox News Channel; Fox Sports Net; Hallmark Channel; Headline News; HGTV; History Channel; Lifetime; MSNBC; MTV; Nickelodeon; Speed Channel; Spike TV; Syfy; TBS Superstation; The Learning Channel; Travel Channel; Trinity Broadcasting Network; truTV; Turner Network TV; TV Land; Univision; USA Network; VH1; Weather Channel.
Fee: $29.00 monthly.

Pay Service 1
Pay Units: 81.
Programming (via satellite): Cinemax; HBO.
Fee: $7.99 monthly (Cinemax), $13.50 monthly (HBO).

Video-On-Demand: No

Internet Service
Operational: No.

Telephone Service
None

Miles of Plant: 16.0 (coaxial); None (fiber optic). Homes passed: 724.
Operations Director: Joe Poffenberger. Technical Operations Manager: Craig Grey.
City fee: 3% of gross.
Ownership: Mediacom LLC (MSO).

MERRITT TWP.—Formerly served by Cablevision Systems Corp. No longer in operation. ICA: MI0384.

MESICK—Pine River Cable, PO Box 96, McBain, MI 49657. Phone: 888-244-2288. Fax: 231-825-0191. E-mail: info@pinerivercable.com. Web Site: http://www.pinerivercable.com. Also serves Springville Twp. ICA: MI0246.
TV Market Ranking: Below 100 (MESICK (VILLAGE), Springville Twp.). Franchise award date: N.A. Franchise expiration date: N.A. Began: October 1, 1988.
Channel capacity: 41 (2-way capable). Channels available but not in use: N.A.

Basic Service
Subscribers: 108.
Programming (received off-air): WCMV (PBS) Cadillac; WFQX-TV (FOX) Cadillac; WGTU (ABC, CW) Traverse City; WPBN-TV (NBC) Traverse City; WWTV (CBS) Cadillac.
Programming (via satellite): ABC Family Channel; C-SPAN; QVC; TBS Superstation; WGN America.
Fee: $38.00 installation; $21.50 monthly.
Expanded Basic Service 2
Subscribers: N.A.
Programming (via satellite): AMC; Arts & Entertainment; CNN; Country Music TV; Discovery Channel; Disney Channel; E! Entertainment Television; ESPN; ESPN 2; Food Network; Fox Sports Net Detroit; Headline News; HGTV; Lifetime; MTV; Nickelodeon; Spike TV; The Learning Channel; Turner Network TV; USA Network; VH1; Weather Channel.
Pay Service 1
Pay Units: 17.
Programming (via satellite): Cinemax; HBO.
Fee: $21.00 installation; $10.95 monthly (Cinemax), $11.95 monthly (HBO).
Internet Service
Operational: No.
Miles of Plant: 5.0 (coaxial); None (fiber optic). Homes passed: 210.
Manager: John Metzler.
Ownership: Pine River Cable (MSO).

MICHIGAMME TWP.—Upper Peninsula Communications, 397 N US Hwy 41, Carney, MI 49812-9757. Phone: 906-639-2194. Fax: 906-639-9936. E-mail: louied@alphacomm.net. ICA: MI0331.
TV Market Ranking: Below 100 (MICHIGAMME TWP.). Franchise award date: N.A. Franchise expiration date: N.A. Began: August 1, 1990.
Channel capacity: 40 (not 2-way capable). Channels available but not in use: 19.
Basic Service
Subscribers: N.A.
Programming (received off-air): WBKP (ABC) Calumet; WJMN-TV (CBS) Escanaba; WLUC-TV (NBC) Marquette; WNMU (PBS) Marquette; WZMQ (IND, MNT) Marquette.
Programming (via satellite): ABC Family Channel; AMC; Arts & Entertainment; CNBC; CNN; C-SPAN; Discovery Channel; Disney Channel; ESPN; ESPN 2; HGTV; History Channel; Home Shopping Network; ION Television; Lifetime; Outdoor Channel; Spike TV; TBS Superstation; The Learning Channel; Trinity Broadcasting Network; Turner Network TV; TV Land; USA Network; Weather Channel; WGN America.
Fee: $50.00 installation; $24.95 monthly.
Pay Service 1
Pay Units: N.A.
Programming (via satellite): Showtime.
Internet Service
Operational: No.
Telephone Service
None
Miles of Plant: 10.0 (coaxial); None (fiber optic). Homes passed: 246.
Manager & Chief Technician: Louis Dupont.
Ownership: Upper Peninsula Communications Inc. (MSO).

MIDDLEVILLE/CALEDONIA—Charter Communications, 315 Davis St, Grand Haven, MI 49417-1830. Phone: 616-647-6201. Fax: 616-846-0797. Web Site: http://www.charter.com. Also serves Bowne Twp., Caledonia Twp. (Kent County), Cascade Twp., Dorr Twp. (portions), Gaines Twp. (Kent County), Leighton Twp., Martin Twp., Moline, Orangeville Twp., Thornapple Twp., Wayland & Yankee Springs Twp. ICA: MI0097.
TV Market Ranking: 37 (Bowne Twp., Caledonia Twp. (Kent County), Cascade Twp., Dorr Twp. (portions), Gaines Twp. (Kent County), Leighton Twp., Martin Twp., MIDDLEVILLE, Moline, Orangeville Twp., Thornapple Twp., Wayland, Yankee Springs Twp.). Franchise award date: November 1, 1982. Franchise expiration date: N.A. Began: N.A.
Channel capacity: N.A. Channels available but not in use: N.A.
Basic Service
Subscribers: 5,967.
Programming (received off-air): WGVU-TV (PBS) Grand Rapids; WOOD-TV (NBC) Grand Rapids; WOTV (ABC) Battle Creek; WTLJ (IND) Muskegon; WWMT (CBS, CW) Kalamazoo; WXMI (FOX) Grand Rapids; WXSP-CA (MNT) Grand Rapids; WZPX-TV (ION) Battle Creek; WZZM (ABC) Grand Rapids.
Programming (via satellite): C-SPAN; C-SPAN 2; CW+; Home Shopping Network; QVC; TBS Superstation; TV Guide Network; WGN America.
Current originations: Leased Access; Government Access; Educational Access; Public Access.
Fee: $29.99 installation.
Expanded Basic Service 1
Subscribers: N.A.
Programming (via satellite): ABC Family Channel; AMC; Animal Planet; Arts & Entertainment; Bravo; Cartoon Network; CNBC; CNN; Comedy Central; Country Music TV; Discovery Channel; Disney Channel; E! Entertainment Television; ESPN; ESPN 2; ESPN Classic Sports; ESPNews; Eternal Word TV Network; Food Network; Fox News Channel; Fox Sports Net Detroit; FX; G4; Golf Channel; GSN; Hallmark Channel; Headline News; HGTV; History Channel; INSP; Lifetime; MSNBC; MTV; MTV2; National Geographic Channel; Nickelodeon; Oxygen; SoapNet; Speed Channel; Spike TV; Style Network; Syfy; The Learning Channel; Toon Disney; Travel Channel; Trinity Broadcasting Network; truTV; Turner Classic Movies; Turner Network TV; TV Land; Univision; USA Network; Versus; VH1; WE tv; Weather Channel.
Fee: $47.99 monthly.
Digital Basic Service
Subscribers: N.A.
Programming (received off-air): WGVU-TV (PBS) Grand Rapids; WOOD-TV (NBC) Grand Rapids; WWMT (CBS, CW) Kalamazoo; WXMI (FOX) Grand Rapids; WZZM (ABC) Grand Rapids.
Programming (via satellite): BBC America; Bio; Boomerang; Canales N; CMT Pure Country; Discovery Digital Networks; Discovery HD Theater; Do-It-Yourself; ESPN HD; Fox College Sports Atlantic; Fox College Sports Central; Fox College Sports Pacific; Fox Movie Channel; Fox Soccer; Fuel TV; Fuse; GAS; Great American Country; HDNet; HDNet Movies; History Channel International; Independent Film Channel; Lifetime Movie Network; MTV Networks Digital Suite; Nick Jr.; Nick Too; NickToons TV; Outdoor Channel; Sundance Channel; Turner Network TV HD; Universal HD.
Digital Pay Service 1
Pay Units: N.A.
Programming (via satellite): Cinemax (multiplexed); Cinemax HD; Encore (multiplexed); Flix; HBO (multiplexed); HBO HD; LOGO; Showtime (multiplexed); Showtime HD; Starz (multiplexed); The Movie Channel (multiplexed).
Video-On-Demand: No
Pay-Per-View
iN DEMAND (delivered digitally); NHL Center Ice (delivered digitally); MLB Extra Innings (delivered digitally); ESPN (delivered digitally); Playboy TV (delivered digitally); Fresh (delivered digitally); Shorteez (delivered digitally).
Internet Service
Operational: Yes.
Broadband Service: Charter Pipeline.
Fee: $29.99 monthly.
Telephone Service
None
Miles of Plant: 173.0 (coaxial); None (fiber optic). Homes passed: 6,725.
Vice President & General Manager: Dan Spoelman. Technical Operations Manager: Keith Schierbeek. Marketing Director: Steve Schuh.
Ownership: Charter Communications Inc. (MSO).

MIDLAND—Charter Communications, 7372 Davison Rd, Davison, MI 48423. Phone: 810-652-1400. Web Site: http://www.charter.com. Also serves Edenville Twp., Ingersoll Twp., Larkin Twp., Lee Twp., Midland Twp., Mount Haley Twp. & Williams Twp. (western portion). ICA: MI0030.
TV Market Ranking: 61 (Edenville Twp., Ingersoll Twp., Larkin Twp., Lee Twp., MIDLAND, Midland Twp., Mount Haley Twp., Williams Twp. (western portion)). Franchise award date: June 1, 1972. Franchise expiration date: N.A. Began: June 1, 1972.
Channel capacity: N.A. Channels available but not in use: N.A.
Basic Service
Subscribers: 19,476.
Programming (received off-air): MyNetworkTV Inc.; WAQP (IND) Saginaw; WBSF (CW) Bay City; WDIV-TV (NBC) Detroit; WEYI-TV (CW, NBC) Saginaw; WFUM (PBS) Flint; WJRT-TV (ABC) Flint; WKAR-TV (PBS) East Lansing; WNEM-TV (CBS, MNT) Bay City; WSMH (FOX) Flint; WTVS (PBS) Detroit; WXYZ-TV (ABC) Detroit.
Programming (via satellite): Home Shopping Network; ION Television; QVC; TBS Superstation; WGN America.
Current originations: Educational Access; Government Access; Public Access.
Fee: $29.99 installation; $13.50 monthly.
Expanded Basic Service 1
Subscribers: 14,274.
Programming (via satellite): ABC Family Channel; AMC; Animal Planet; Arts & Entertainment; Bravo; Cartoon Network; CNBC; CNN; Comedy Central; Country Music TV; C-SPAN; Discovery Channel; Disney Channel; E! Entertainment Television; ESPN; ESPN 2; Food Network; Fox News Channel; Fox Sports Net Detroit; FX; Golf Channel; GSN; Hallmark Channel; Headline News; HGTV; History Channel; Lifetime; MSNBC; MTV; MTV2; National Geographic Channel; Nickelodeon; Oxygen; SoapNet; Speed Channel; Spike TV; Syfy; The Learning Channel; Toon Disney; Travel Channel; truTV; Turner Classic Movies; Turner Network TV; TV Guide Network; TV Land; USA Network; Versus; VH1; Weather Channel.
Fee: $36.49 monthly.
Digital Basic Service
Subscribers: N.A.
Programming (received off-air): CMT Pure Country; WEYI-TV (CW, NBC) Saginaw; WFUM (PBS) Flint; WJRT-TV (ABC) Flint; WNEM-TV (CBS, MNT) Bay City; WSMH (FOX) Flint.
Programming (via satellite): BBC America; Bio; Discovery Digital Networks; Discovery HD Theater; Do-It-Yourself; ESPN 2 HD; ESPN Classic Sports; ESPN HD; ESPN U; ESPNews; Fox Business Channel; Fox College Sports Atlantic; Fox College Sports Central; Fox College Sports Pacific; Fox Movie Channel; Fox Soccer; Fuel TV; Fuse; GAS; Great American Country; HDNet; HDNet Movies; History Channel International; Independent Film Channel; Lifetime Movie Network; MTV Networks Digital Suite; Music Choice; Nick Jr.; Nick Too; NickToons TV; Outdoor Channel; ReelzChannel; Sundance Channel; The Sportsman Channel; Turner Network TV HD; TV Guide Interactive Inc.; Universal HD; WE tv.
Digital Pay Service 1
Pay Units: N.A.
Programming (via satellite): Cinemax (multiplexed); Cinemax HD; Encore (multiplexed); Flix; HBO (multiplexed); HBO HD; LOGO; Showtime (multiplexed); Showtime HD; Starz (multiplexed); Starz HDTV; The Movie Channel (multiplexed).
Video-On-Demand: Yes
Pay-Per-View
iN DEMAND (delivered digitally); ESPN (delivered digitally); NHL Center Ice (delivered digitally); MLB Extra Innings (delivered digitally); Playboy TV (delivered digitally); Shorteez (delivered digitally); Fresh (delivered digitally).
Internet Service
Operational: Yes.
Broadband Service: Charter Pipeline.
Fee: $99.00 installation; $29.99 monthly.
Telephone Service
Digital: Operational
Fee: $29.99 monthly
Miles of Plant: 525.0 (coaxial); 73.0 (fiber optic). Homes passed: 27,883.
Vice President & General Manager: Dave Slowick. Technical Operations Director: Lloyd Collins. Marketing Director: Lisa Gayari.
City fee: 5% of gross.
Ownership: Charter Communications Inc. (MSO).

MIKADO TWP.—Pine River Cable, PO Box 96, McBain, MI 49657. Phone: 888-244-2288. Fax: 231-825-0191. Web Site: http://www.pinerivercable.com. ICA: MI0440.
TV Market Ranking: Below 100 (MIKADO TWP.); Outside TV Markets (MIKADO TWP.).
Channel capacity: N.A. Channels available but not in use: N.A.

Internet Service
Operational: No.
Manager: John Metzler.
Ownership: Pine River Cable (MSO).

MINDEN CITY—Formerly served by Cablevision Systems Corp. No longer in operation. ICA: MI0332.

MIO—Charter Communications, 2074 M 32 W, Alpena, MI 49707. Phones: 231-947-5221 (Traverse City); 989-356-4503. Fax: 989-356-3761. Web Site: http://www.charter.com. Also serves Big Creek Twp., Comins Twp., Elmer Twp., Fairview & Mentor Twp. ICA: MI0430.
TV Market Ranking: Outside TV Markets (Big Creek Twp., Comins Twp., Elmer Twp., Fairview, Mentor Twp., MIO). Franchise award date: N.A. Franchise expiration date: N.A. Began: N.A.
Channel capacity: N.A. Channels available but not in use: N.A.
Basic Service
Subscribers: N.A.
Programming (received off-air): WBKB-TV (CBS, FOX) Alpena; WCML (PBS) Alpena; WFUP (FOX) Vanderbilt; WGTU (ABC, CW) Traverse City; WTOM-TV (NBC) Cheboygan; WWTV (CBS) Cadillac.
Programming (via satellite): ABC Family Channel; Animal Planet; Arts & Entertainment; CNN; Comedy Central; Discovery Channel; Disney Channel; ESPN; Fox News Channel; Lifetime; Nickelodeon; QVC; Spike TV; Syfy; TBS Superstation; Turner Classic Movies; Turner Network TV; USA Network; Weather Channel; WGN America; WNBC (NBC) New York.
Current originations: Public Access.
Fee: $26.25 monthly.
Pay Service 1
Pay Units: N.A.
Programming (via satellite): Cinemax; HBO; Showtime.
Fee: $9.95 monthly (each).
Internet Service
Operational: No.
Telephone Service
None
Vice President: Joe Boullion. General Manager: Ed Kavanaugh. Technical Operations Director: Rob Nowak. Marketing Manager: Brenda Auger.
Ownership: Charter Communications Inc. (MSO).

MISSAUKEE COUNTY (unincorporated areas)—Pine River Cable, PO Box 96, McBain, MI 49657. Phone: 888-244-2288. Fax: 231-825-0191. E-mail: info@pinerivercable.com. Web Site: http://www.pinerivercable.com. ICA: MI0441.
TV Market Ranking: Below 100 (MISSAUKEE COUNTY (UNINCORPORATED AREAS)).
Channel capacity: N.A. Channels available but not in use: N.A.
Basic Service
Subscribers: N.A.
Programming (received off-air): WCMV (PBS) Cadillac; WFQX-TV (FOX) Cadillac; WGTU (ABC, CW) Traverse City; WPBN-TV (NBC) Traverse City; WWTV (CBS) Cadillac.
Programming (via satellite): ABC Family Channel; Arts & Entertainment; Cartoon Network; CNN; Comedy Central; C-SPAN; C-SPAN 2; Discovery Channel; Disney Channel; ESPN; ESPN 2; Food Network; Fox News Channel; Fox Sports Net Detroit; FX; Great American Country; Hallmark Channel; Headline News; HGTV; History Channel; Home Shopping Network; Lifetime; Nickelodeon; Outdoor Channel; QVC; Speed Channel; Spike TV; TBS Superstation; The Learning Channel; Trinity Broadcasting Network; Turner Classic Movies; Turner Network TV; TV Land; USA Network; VH1; Weather Channel; WGN America.
Pay Service 1
Pay Units: N.A.
Programming (via satellite): Encore (multiplexed); HBO (multiplexed); Showtime.
Internet Service
Operational: No.
Manager: John Metzler.
Ownership: Pine River Cable (MSO).

MONROE—Charter Communications, 7372 Davison Rd, Davison, MI 48423. Phone: 810-652-1400. Web Site: http://www.charter.com. Also serves Ash Twp., Berlin Twp. (Monroe County), Blissfield, Blissfield Twp., Carleton (village), Deerfield Twp. (Lenawee County), Dundee Twp., Erie Twp., Estral Beach, Exeter Twp., Frenchtown Twp., Huron Twp. (Wayne County), Ida Twp., La Salle Twp., London Twp., Luna Pier, Maybee, Monroe Twp. (Monroe County), Palmyra Twp., Petersburg, Raisinville Twp., Riga Twp. & Summerfield Twp. (Monroe County). ICA: MI0027.
TV Market Ranking: 5,52 (Ash Twp., Berlin Twp. (Monroe County), Carleton (village), Erie Twp., Estral Beach, Exeter Twp., Frenchtown Twp., Huron Twp. (Wayne County), La Salle Twp., London Twp., Maybee, MONROE, Monroe Twp. (Monroe County), Raisinville Twp.); 52 (Blissfield, Blissfield Twp., Deerfield Twp. (Lenawee County), Dundee Twp., Ida Twp., Luna Pier, Palmyra Twp., Petersburg, Riga Twp., Summerfield Twp. (Monroe County)). Franchise award date: N.A. Franchise expiration date: N.A. Began: December 1, 1982.
Channel capacity: N.A. Channels available but not in use: N.A.
Basic Service
Subscribers: 16,118.
Programming (received off-air): WADL (IND) Mount Clemens; WDIV-TV (NBC) Detroit; WGTE-TV (PBS) Toledo; WJBK (FOX) Detroit; WKBD-TV (CW) Detroit; WLMB (IND) Toledo; WMYD (MNT) Detroit; WNWO-TV (NBC) Toledo; WPXD-TV (ION) Ann Arbor; WTOL (CBS) Toledo; WTVG (ABC) Toledo; WTVS (PBS) Detroit; WUPW (FOX) Toledo; WWJ-TV (CBS) Detroit; WXYZ-TV (ABC) Detroit.
Programming (via satellite): Home Shopping Network; INSP; QVC; TBS Superstation; TV Guide Network; WGN America.
Current originations: Leased Access; Government Access; Educational Access; Public Access.
Fee: $29.99 installation; $13.50 monthly.
Expanded Basic Service 1
Subscribers: 15,754.
Programming (via satellite): ABC Family Channel; AMC; Animal Planet; Arts & Entertainment; BET Networks; Bravo; Cartoon Network; CNBC; CNN; Comedy Central; Country Music TV; C-SPAN; Discovery Channel; Disney Channel; E! Entertainment Television; ESPN; ESPN 2; ESPN Classic Sports; Eternal Word TV Network; FitTV; Food Network; Fox News Channel; Fox Sports Net Detroit; FX; G4; Golf Channel; GSN; Hallmark Channel; Headline News; HGTV; History Channel; Jewelry Television; Lifetime; MSNBC; MTV; National Geographic Channel; Nickelodeon; Oxygen; SoapNet; Speed Channel; Spike TV; Syfy; The Learning Channel; Toon Disney; Travel Channel; truTV; Turner Classic Movies; Turner Network TV; TV Land; Univision; USA Network; Versus; VH1; WE tv; Weather Channel.
Fee: $36.49 monthly.
Digital Basic Service
Subscribers: N.A.
Programming (received off-air): WDIV-TV (NBC) Detroit; WJBK (FOX) Detroit; WTVS (PBS) Detroit; WWJ-TV (CBS) Detroit; WXYZ-TV (ABC) Detroit.
Programming (via microwave): Weatherscan.
Programming (via satellite): BBC America; Bio; Boomerang; CMT Pure Country; CNN en Espanol; Discovery Channel HD; Discovery Digital Networks; Do-It-Yourself; ESPN HD; ESPNews; Fox College Sports Atlantic; Fox College Sports Central; Fox College Sports Pacific; Fox Sports Net Detroit; Fuel TV; GAS; HDNet; HDNet Movies; History Channel International; Independent Film Channel; Lifetime Movie Network; Military History Channel; MTV Networks Digital Suite; Music Choice; Nick Jr.; Nick Too; NickToons TV; Outdoor Channel; PBS Kids Channel; PBS World; Turner Network TV HD; Universal HD.
Digital Pay Service 1
Pay Units: N.A.
Programming (via satellite): Cinemax (multiplexed); Cinemax HD; Encore (multiplexed); Flix; HBO (multiplexed); HBO HD; LOGO; Showtime (multiplexed); Showtime HD; Starz (multiplexed); The Movie Channel (multiplexed).
Video-On-Demand: Yes
Pay-Per-View
iN DEMAND (delivered digitally); NHL Center Ice (delivered digitally); MLB Extra Innings (delivered digitally); Playboy TV (delivered digitally); Club Jenna (delivered digitally); Fresh! (delivered digitally); Fresh (delivered digitally); Shorteez (delivered digitally).
Internet Service
Operational: Yes.
Broadband Service: Charter Pipeline.
Fee: $29.99 monthly.
Telephone Service
Digital: Operational
Fee: $29.99 monthly
Miles of Plant: 601.0 (coaxial); None (fiber optic). Additional miles planned: 7.0 (coaxial). Homes passed: 27,679.
Vice President & General Manager: Dave Slowick. Technical Operations Director: Lloyd Collins. Marketing Director: Lisa Gayari.
Ownership: Charter Communications Inc. (MSO).

MONROE—Comcast Cable. Now served by TAYLOR, MI [MI0008]. ICA: MI0048.

MONTROSE—Charter Communications, 7372 Davison Rd, Davison, MI 48423. Phone: 810-652-1400. Web Site: http://www.charter.com. Also serves Montrose Twp. ICA: MI0130.
TV Market Ranking: 61 (MONTROSE, Montrose Twp.). Franchise award date: N.A. Franchise expiration date: N.A. Began: December 1, 1981.
Channel capacity: N.A. Channels available but not in use: N.A.
Basic Service
Subscribers: 1,334.
Programming (received off-air): WAQP (IND) Saginaw; WBSF (CW) Bay City; WDIV-TV (NBC) Detroit; WEYI-TV (CW, NBC) Saginaw; WFUM (PBS) Flint; WJRT-TV (ABC) Flint; WKAR-TV (PBS) East Lansing; WNEM-TV (CBS, MNT) Bay City; WSMH (FOX) Flint; WTVS (PBS) Detroit; WXYZ-TV (ABC) Detroit.
Programming (via satellite): Home Shopping Network; ION Television; MyNetworkTV Inc.; QVC; WGN America.
Current originations: Educational Access; Public Access; Government Access.
Fee: $29.99 installation; $13.50 monthly; $3.50 converter.
Expanded Basic Service 1
Subscribers: 1,206.
Programming (via satellite): ABC Family Channel; AMC; Animal Planet; Arts & Entertainment; Bravo; Cartoon Network; CNBC; CNN; Comedy Central; Country Music TV; C-SPAN; Discovery Channel; Disney Channel; E! Entertainment Television; ESPN; ESPN 2; Food Network; Fox News Channel; Fox Sports Net Detroit; FX; G4; Golf Channel; GSN; Hallmark Channel; Headline News; HGTV; History Channel; Lifetime; MSNBC; MTV; MTV2; National Geographic Channel; Nickelodeon; Oxygen; SoapNet; Speed Channel; Spike TV; Syfy; TBS Superstation; The Learning Channel; Toon Disney; Travel Channel; truTV; Turner Classic Movies; Turner Network TV; TV Guide Network; TV Land; USA Network; Versus; VH1; Weather Channel.
Fee: $36.49 monthly.
Digital Basic Service
Subscribers: N.A.
Programming (received off-air): WEYI-TV (CW, NBC) Saginaw; WFUM (PBS) Flint; WJRT-TV (ABC) Flint; WNEM-TV (CBS, MNT) Bay City; WSMH (FOX) Flint.
Programming (via satellite): BBC America; Bio; CMT Pure Country; Discovery Digital Networks; Do-It-Yourself; ESPN 2 HD; ESPN Classic Sports; ESPN HD; ESPN U; ESPNews; FitTV; Fox Business Channel; Fox College Sports Atlantic; Fox College Sports Central; Fox College Sports Pacific; Fox Movie Channel; Fox Soccer; Fox Sports Net Detroit; Fuel TV; Fuse; GAS; Great American Country; HDNet; HDNet Movies; History Channel International; Independent Film Channel; Lifetime Movie Network; Military History Channel; MTV Networks Digital Suite; Music Choice; Nick Jr.; Nick Too; NickToons TV; Outdoor Channel; ReelzChannel; Sundance Channel; The Sportsman Channel; Turner Network TV HD; Universal HD; WE tv.
Digital Pay Service 1
Pay Units: N.A.
Programming (via satellite): Cinemax (multiplexed); Cinemax HD; Encore (multiplexed); Flix; HBO (multiplexed); HBO HD; LOGO; Showtime (multiplexed); Showtime HD; Starz (multiplexed); Starz HDTV; The Movie Channel (multiplexed).
Video-On-Demand: Yes
Pay-Per-View
iN DEMAND (delivered digitally); ESPN (delivered digitally); NHL Center Ice (delivered digitally); MLB Extra Innings (delivered digitally); Playboy TV (delivered digitally); Club Jenna (delivered digitally); Fresh! (delivered digitally); Fresh (delivered digitally); Shorteez (delivered digitally).
Internet Service
Operational: Yes.
Broadband Service: Charter Pipeline.
Fee: $29.99 monthly.
Telephone Service
Digital: Operational
Fee: $29.99 monthly

Miles of Plant: 46.0 (coaxial); None (fiber optic). Homes passed: 2,639. Total homes in franchised area: 3,672.
Vice President & General Manager: Dave Slowick. Technical Operations Director: Lloyd Collins. Marketing Director: Lisa Gayari.
Ownership: Charter Communications Inc. (MSO).

MOUNT PLEASANT—Charter Communications, 2304 S Mission, Mount Pleasant, MI 48858. Phone: 989-775-6846. Fax: 989-772-0350. Web Site: http://www.charter.com. Also serves Clare, Coe Twp., Farwell, Frost Twp., Garfield Twp. (Clare County), Gilmore Twp. (Isabella County), Grant Twp. (portions), Harrison, Hatton Twp., Hayes Twp. (Clare County), Isabella Twp., Rosebush, Shepherd, Surrey Twp., Union Twp. (Isabella County), Vernon Twp. & Wise Twp. ICA: MI0069.
TV Market Ranking: 61 (Coe Twp.); Below 100 (Frost Twp., Garfield Twp. (Clare County), Harrison, Hatton Twp., Hayes Twp. (Clare County)); Outside TV Markets (Clare, Farwell, Gilmore Twp. (Isabella County), Grant Twp. (portions), Isabella Twp., MOUNT PLEASANT, Rosebush, Shepherd, Surrey Twp., Union Twp. (Isabella County), Vernon Twp., Wise Twp.). Franchise award date: N.A. Franchise expiration date: N.A. Began: February 1, 1970.
Channel capacity: N.A. Channels available but not in use: N.A.

Basic Service
Subscribers: 9,401.
Programming (received off-air): WAQP (IND) Saginaw; WCMU-TV (PBS) Mount Pleasant; WDCQ-TV (PBS) Bad Axe; WEYI-TV (CW, NBC) Saginaw; WFQX-TV (FOX) Cadillac; WJRT-TV (ABC) Flint; WKBD-TV (CW) Detroit; WNEM-TV (CBS, MNT) Bay City; WSMH (FOX) Flint; WWTV (CBS) Cadillac; WZZM (ABC) Grand Rapids; allband FM.
Programming (via satellite): C-SPAN; C-SPAN 2; CW+; Eternal Word TV Network; Home Shopping Network; QVC; TBS Superstation; TV Guide Network; Univision; various Canadian stations; WGN America.
Current originations: Religious Access; Government Access; Educational Access; Public Access.
Fee: $35.00 installation; $24.95 monthly.

Expanded Basic Service 1
Subscribers: N.A.
Programming (via satellite): ABC Family Channel; AMC; Animal Planet; Arts & Entertainment; BET Networks; Bravo; Cartoon Network; CNBC; CNN; Comedy Central; Country Music TV; Discovery Channel; Disney Channel; E! Entertainment Television; ESPN; ESPN 2; Food Network; Fox News Channel; Fox Sports Net Detroit; FX; G4; Golf Channel; GSN; Hallmark Channel; Headline News; HGTV; History Channel; Lifetime; MSNBC; MTV; MTV2; National Geographic Channel; Nickelodeon; Outdoor Channel; Oxygen; SoapNet; Speed Channel; Spike TV; Syfy; Telemundo; The Learning Channel; Toon Disney; Travel Channel; truTV; Turner Classic Movies; Turner Network TV; TV Land; USA Network; Versus; VH1; WE tv; Weather Channel.

Digital Basic Service
Subscribers: N.A.
Programming (received off-air): WEYI-TV (CW, NBC) Saginaw; WJRT-TV (ABC) Flint; WNEM-TV (CBS, MNT) Bay City; WSMH (FOX) Flint.
Programming (via satellite): BBC America; Bio; CMT Pure Country; Discovery Digital Networks; Discovery HD Theater; Do-It-Yourself; ESPN Classic Sports; ESPN HD; ESPN U; ESPNews; Food Network On Demand; Fox College Sports Atlantic; Fox College Sports Central; Fox College Sports Pacific; Fox Movie Channel; Fox Soccer; Fuel TV; Fuse; GAS; Great American Country; HDNet; HDNet Movies; HGTV On Demand; History Channel International; Howard TV; Independent Film Channel; Lifetime Movie Network; MTV Networks Digital Suite; Music Choice; Nick Jr.; Nick Too; NickToons TV; Style Network; Sundance Channel; Turner Network TV HD; TV Guide SPOT; Universal HD.

Digital Pay Service 1
Pay Units: N.A.
Programming (via satellite): Cinemax (multiplexed); Cinemax HD; Cinemax On Demand; Encore (multiplexed); Flix; HBO (multiplexed); HBO HD; HBO On Demand; LOGO; Showtime (multiplexed); Showtime HD; Showtime On Demand; Starz (multiplexed); Starz On Demand; The Movie Channel (multiplexed).

Video-On-Demand: Yes

Pay-Per-View
movies & events (delivered digitally); ESPN (delivered digitally); NHL Center Ice (delivered digitally); MLB Extra Innings (delivered digitally); Playboy TV (delivered digitally); Fresh (delivered digitally); Shorteez (delivered digitally).

Internet Service
Operational: Yes.
Broadband Service: Charter Pipeline.
Fee: $29.99 monthly.

Telephone Service
Digital: Operational
Fee: $29.99 monthly
Miles of Plant: 210.0 (coaxial); 20.0 (fiber optic). Additional miles planned: 10.0 (coaxial). Homes passed: 12,619.
Vice President & General Manager: Dan Spoelman. Operations Manager: Ed Bucao.
City fee: 3% of gross.
Ownership: Charter Communications Inc. (MSO).

MULLETT TWP.—Formerly served by Northwoods Cable Inc. No longer in operation. ICA: MI0334.

MUSKEGON—Comcast Cable, 3500 Patterson Ave SE, Grand Rapids, MI 49512. Phone: 616-977-2200. Fax: 616-977-2224. Web Site: http://www.comcast.com. Also serves Brooks Twp. (portions), Cedar Creek Twp. (Muskegon County), Dalton Twp., Dayton Twp. (Newaygo County) (portions), Egelston Twp., Ferrysburg, Fremont, Fruitland Twp., Fruitport Charter Twp. (portions), Garfield Twp. (Newaygo County) (portions), Holton Twp., Laketon Twp., Muskegon Heights, Newaygo County, North Muskegon, Norton Shores, Roosevelt Park, Sheridan Twp. (Newaygo County), Sherman Twp. (Newaygo County) & Sullivan Twp. ICA: MI0014.
TV Market Ranking: 37 (Brooks Twp. (portions), Cedar Creek Twp. (Muskegon County), Egelston Twp., Ferrysburg, Fruitport Charter Twp. (portions), Garfield Twp. (Newaygo County) (portions), Laketon Twp., Muskegon Heights, Newaygo County (portions), Norton Shores, Sheridan Twp. (Newaygo County), Sherman Twp. (Newaygo County), Sullivan Twp.); Below 100 (Dalton Twp., Fremont, Fruitland Twp., Holton Twp., MUSKEGON, North Muskegon, Roosevelt Park, Newaygo County (portions)); Outside TV Markets (Newaygo County (portions)). Franchise award date: N.A. Franchise expiration date: N.A. Began: March 3, 1966.
Channel capacity: 78 (operating 2-way). Channels available but not in use: None.

Basic Service
Subscribers: 41,270.
Programming (received off-air): WGVU-TV (PBS) Grand Rapids; WOOD-TV (NBC) Grand Rapids; WOTV (ABC) Battle Creek; WTLJ (IND) Muskegon; WWMT (CBS, CW) Kalamazoo; WXMI (FOX) Grand Rapids; WZPX-TV (ION) Battle Creek; WZZM (ABC) Grand Rapids.
Programming (via satellite): C-SPAN; Home Shopping Network; Michigan Government Television; MSNBC; QVC; TBS Superstation; WGN America.
Current originations: Religious Access; Government Access; Educational Access.

Expanded Basic Service 1
Subscribers: 36,900.
Programming (via satellite): ABC Family Channel; AMC; Animal Planet; Arts & Entertainment; BET Networks; Big Ten Network; Cartoon Network; CNBC; CNN; Comedy Central; Country Music TV; Discovery Channel; Disney Channel; E! Entertainment Television; ESPN; ESPN 2; Food Network; Fox News Channel; Fox Sports Net Detroit; FX; Golf Channel; Headline News; HGTV; History Channel; Lifetime; MTV; Nickelodeon; Spike TV; Syfy; The Learning Channel; Travel Channel; Turner Network TV; TV Land; Univision; USA Network; Versus; VH1; Weather Channel.
Fee: $48.99 monthly.

Digital Basic Service
Subscribers: 6,780.
Programming (via satellite): BBC America; Big Ten Network; Bio; Bloomberg Television; Bravo; CMT Pure Country; Cooking Channel; C-SPAN 2; C-SPAN 3; Current; Discovery Health Channel; Discovery Kids Channel; Discovery Military Channel; Discovery Planet Green; Do-It-Yourself; Encore (multiplexed); ESPN Classic Sports; ESPNews; Eternal Word TV Network; FitTV; Flix; Fox News HD; Fuse; G4; Gospel Music Channel; Great American Country; GSN; Hallmark Channel; Halogen Network; History Channel International; ID Investigation Discovery; Independent Film Channel; Lifetime Movie Network; MLB Network; MTV Hits; MTV Jams; MTV Tres; MTV2; Music Choice; National Geographic Channel; Nick Jr.; Nick Too; NickToons TV; Outdoor Channel; Oxygen; PBS Kids Sprout; Science Channel; ShopNBC; SoapNet; Style Network; Sundance Channel; TeenNick; The Word Network; Toon Disney; truTV; TV Guide Interactive Inc.; VH1 Classic; VH1 Soul; WE tv.
Fee: $9.95 monthly.

Digital Expanded Basic Service
Subscribers: N.A.
Programming (received off-air): WGVU-TV (PBS) Grand Rapids; WOOD-TV (NBC) Grand Rapids; WWMT (CBS, CW) Kalamazoo; WXMI (FOX) Grand Rapids; WZZM (ABC) Grand Rapids.
Programming (via satellite): Discovery HD Theater; ESPN 2 HD; ESPN HD; Mojo HD; Palladia.

Digital Expanded Basic Service 2
Subscribers: N.A.
Programming (via satellite): Fox College Sports Atlantic; Fox College Sports Central; Fox College Sports Pacific; Fox Movie Channel; NBA TV; NFL Network; Speed Channel; Speed HD.

Digital Expanded Basic Service 3
Subscribers: N.A.
Programming (via satellite): Cine Latino; Cine Mexicano; CNN en Espanol; Discovery en Espanol; ESPN Deportes; Fox Sports en Espanol; History Channel en Espanol; MTV Tres; mun2 television; VeneMovies.

Digital Pay Service 1
Pay Units: N.A.
Programming (via satellite): Cinemax (multiplexed); Cinemax HD; HBO (multiplexed); HBO HD; Playboy TV; Showtime (multiplexed); Showtime HD; Starz (multiplexed); Starz HDTV; The Movie Channel (multiplexed).
Fee: $18.05 monthly (each).

Video-On-Demand: Yes

Pay-Per-View
Addressable homes: 10,464.
iN DEMAND, Addressable: Yes; iN DEMAND (delivered digitally); Playboy TV (delivered digitally); Fresh (delivered digitally); Spice: Xcess (delivered digitally); Club Jenna (delivered digitally); MLB Extra Innings (delivered digitally); NHL Center Ice (delivered digitally).

Internet Service
Operational: Yes.
Broadband Service: Comcast High Speed Internet.
Fee: $42.95 monthly.

Telephone Service
Digital: Operational
Miles of Plant: 991.0 (coaxial); 81.0 (fiber optic). Homes passed: 61,700. Total homes in franchised area: 70,700.
Area Vice President: Larry Williamson. Technical Operations Director: Tom Rice. Business Operations Director: Amy Carey. Sales & Marketing Director: Rick Finch. Marketing Coordinator: Megan Martin.
Ownership: Comcast Cable Communications Inc. (MSO).

NASHVILLE—Pine River Cable, PO Box 226, LeRoy, MI 49655. Phone: 888-244-2288. Fax: 231-825-0191. E-mail: info@pinerivercable.com. Web Site: http://www.pinerivercable.com. ICA: MI0211.
TV Market Ranking: 37,92 (NASHVILLE). Franchise award date: N.A. Franchise expiration date: N.A. Began: April 1, 1983.
Channel capacity: 36 (not 2-way capable). Channels available but not in use: N.A.

Basic Service
Subscribers: 152.
Programming (received off-air): WILX-TV (NBC) Onondaga; WKAR-TV (PBS) East Lansing; WLLA (IND) Kalamazoo; WLNS-TV (CBS) Lansing; WOOD-TV (NBC) Grand Rapids; WOTV (ABC) Battle Creek; WSYM-TV (FOX) Lansing; WWMT (CBS, CW) Kalamazoo; WXMI (FOX) Grand Rapids; WZPX-TV (ION) Battle Creek.
Programming (via satellite): QVC; TBS Superstation; WGN America.
Current originations: Government Access.
Fee: $39.99 installation; $15.56 monthly.

Expanded Basic Service 1
Subscribers: N.A.
Programming (received off-air): WTLJ (IND) Muskegon.
Programming (via satellite): ABC Family Channel; AMC; CNBC; CNN; Comedy Central; Country Music TV; C-SPAN; Discovery Channel; Disney Channel; ESPN; ESPN 2; Food Network; Fox Sports Net Detroit; Headline News; Lifetime; MTV; Nickelodeon; Spike TV; Toon Disney; Turner Network TV; USA Network; Weather Channel.
Fee: $21.45 monthly.

Pay Service 1
Pay Units: 159.
Programming (via satellite): Cinemax; HBO; Starz.
Fee: $10.00 installation; $9.95 monthly (Starz), $11.45 monthly (Cinemax), $12.45 monthly (HBO).
Internet Service
Operational: No.
Miles of Plant: 11.0 (coaxial); None (fiber optic). Homes passed: 684.
Manager: John Metzler.
Ownership: Pine River Cable (MSO).

NEGAUNEE—City of Negaunee Cable TV, PO Box 70, 101 Silver St, Negaunee, MI 49866. Phone: 906-475-9991. Fax: 906-475-9994. Web Site: http://www.cityofnegaunee.com. ICA: MI0145. **Note:** This system is an overbuild.
TV Market Ranking: Below 100 (NEGAUNEE). Franchise award date: N.A. Franchise expiration date: N.A. Began: March 1, 1985.
Channel capacity: 54 (not 2-way capable). Channels available but not in use: N.A.
Basic Service
Subscribers: 1,230.
Programming (received off-air): WBKP (ABC) Calumet; WFQX-TV (FOX) Cadillac; WJMN-TV (CBS) Escanaba; WLUC-TV (NBC) Marquette; WNMU (PBS) Marquette.
Programming (via microwave): WLUK-TV (FOX) Green Bay.
Programming (via satellite): ABC Family Channel; AMC; Arts & Entertainment; CNBC; CNN; C-SPAN; Discovery Channel; Disney Channel; ESPN; Eternal Word TV Network; Fox Sports Net Detroit; Hallmark Channel; Headline News; History Channel; Lifetime; MTV; Nickelodeon; QVC; Spike TV; TBS Superstation; The Learning Channel; Turner Network TV; USA Network; VH1; Weather Channel; WGN America.
Current originations: Government Access; Public Access.
Fee: $12.00 installation; $25.75 monthly; $12.00 additional installation.
Pay Service 1
Pay Units: 280.
Programming (via satellite): Cinemax; HBO.
Fee: $8.50 monthly.
Video-On-Demand: No
Internet Service
Operational: No.
Telephone Service
None
Miles of Plant: 27.0 (coaxial); None (fiber optic). Homes passed: 1,600.
Manager: Gerald Peterson. Marketing Director: Linda Nicholls. Chief Technician: Dennis Howe.
Ownership: City of Negaunee Cable TV.

NEWBERRY—Charter Communications, PO Box 808, 2682 Ashmun St, Sault Sainte Marie, MI 49783. Phones: 231-947-5221 (Traverse City); 906-632-8541. Fax: 906-635-1520. E-mail: jboullion@chartercom.com. Web Site: http://www.charter.com. Also serves McMillan Twp. (Luce County) & Pentland Twp. ICA: MI0166.
TV Market Ranking: Outside TV Markets (McMillan Twp. (Luce County), NEWBERRY, Pentland Twp.). Franchise award date: N.A. Franchise expiration date: N.A. Began: March 1, 1966.
Channel capacity: 42 (not 2-way capable). Channels available but not in use: None.
Basic Service
Subscribers: 1,200.
Programming (received off-air): WFQX-TV (FOX) Cadillac; WGTQ (ABC) Sault Ste. Marie; WJMN-TV (CBS) Escanaba; WLUC-TV (NBC) Marquette; WNMU (PBS) Marquette; WTOM-TV (NBC) Cheboygan; WWUP-TV (CBS, FOX) Sault Ste. Marie.
Programming (via satellite): Arts & Entertainment; C-SPAN; C-SPAN 2; Discovery Channel; Eternal Word TV Network; FX; Home Shopping Network; QVC; TBS Superstation; WGN America.
Fee: $29.99 installation; $13.50 monthly; $1.60 converter.
Expanded Basic Service 1
Subscribers: 914.
Programming (via satellite): ABC Family Channel; AMC; Animal Planet; Cartoon Network; CNN; Disney Channel; ESPN; ESPN 2; FitTV; Fox News Channel; Fox Sports Net Detroit; Hallmark Channel; Headline News; HGTV; History Channel; Lifetime; MTV; Nickelodeon; SoapNet; Spike TV; The Learning Channel; Toon Disney; truTV; Turner Network TV; TV Land; USA Network; VH1; Weather Channel.
Fee: $36.49 monthly.
Pay Service 1
Pay Units: 129.
Programming (via satellite): Cinemax.
Fee: $12.85 monthly.
Pay Service 2
Pay Units: 229.
Programming (via satellite): Encore.
Fee: $1.75 monthly.
Pay Service 3
Pay Units: 172.
Programming (via satellite): HBO.
Fee: $13.45 monthly.
Pay Service 4
Pay Units: 117.
Programming (via satellite): Starz.
Fee: $6.75 monthly.
Video-On-Demand: No
Internet Service
Operational: No.
Telephone Service
None
Miles of Plant: 32.0 (coaxial); None (fiber optic). Homes passed: 1,479. Total homes in franchised area: 1,749.
Vice President: Joe Boullion. General Manager: Rex Buettengenbach. Manager: John Badenski. Chief Technician: John Randazzo. Marketing Manager: Sandy Gottschalk.
Ownership: Charter Communications Inc. (MSO).

NILES—Comcast Cable, 7720 W 98th St, Hickory Hills, IL 60457. Phones: 574-259-2112 (Mishawaka office); 708-237-3260. Fax: 708-237-3292. Web Site: http://www.comcast.com. Also serves Bertrand Twp., Buchanan, Howard Twp., Milton Twp. (Cass County) & Niles Twp. ICA: MI0042.
TV Market Ranking: 80 (Bertrand Twp., Buchanan, Howard Twp., Milton Twp. (Cass County), NILES, Niles Twp.). Franchise award date: N.A. Franchise expiration date: N.A. Began: September 1, 1979.
Channel capacity: N.A. Channels available but not in use: N.A.
Basic Service
Subscribers: 9,925.
Programming (received off-air): WBND-LP South Bend; WCWW-LP (CW) South Bend; WHME-TV (IND) South Bend; WLS-TV (ABC) Chicago; WNDU-TV (NBC) South Bend; WNIT (PBS) South Bend; WSBT-TV (CBS, IND) South Bend; WSJV (FOX) Elkhart; WWMT (CBS, CW) Kalamazoo.
Programming (via satellite): Home Shopping Network; QVC; TBS Superstation; TV Guide Network; WGN America.

Current originations: Educational Access; Government Access; Leased Access.
Fee: $48.99 installation; $13.11 monthly.
Expanded Basic Service 1
Subscribers: 9,600.
Programming (via satellite): ABC Family Channel; AMC; Animal Planet; Arts & Entertainment; BET Networks; Big Ten Network; Cartoon Network; CNBC; CNN; Comedy Central; C-SPAN; Discovery Channel; Disney Channel; E! Entertainment Television; ESPN; ESPN 2; Food Network; Fox News Channel; Fox Sports Net Detroit; FX; Golf Channel; Headline News; HGTV; History Channel; Lifetime; MSNBC; MTV; Nickelodeon; Spike TV; The Learning Channel; Travel Channel; truTV; Turner Network TV; USA Network; Versus; VH1; Weather Channel.
Fee: $37.38 monthly.
Digital Basic Service
Subscribers: N.A.
Programming (received off-air): WNDU-TV (NBC) South Bend; WNIT (PBS) South Bend; WSBT-TV (CBS, IND) South Bend; WSJV (FOX) Elkhart.
Programming (via satellite): ABC Family HD; Animal Planet HD; Arts & Entertainment HD; BBC America; Big Ten Network; Big Ten Network HD; Bio; Bio HD; Bloomberg Television; Bravo; Bravo HD; CBS College Sports Network; Cine Latino; Cine Mexicano; CMT Pure Country; CNBC HD+; CNN en Espanol; CNN HD; Cooking Channel; Country Music TV; C-SPAN 2; C-SPAN 3; Current; Discovery Channel HD; Discovery en Espanol; Discovery HD Theater; Discovery Health Channel; Discovery Kids Channel; Discovery Military Channel; Discovery Planet Green; Disney Channel HD; Disney XD; Disney XD HD; Do-It-Yourself; Encore (multiplexed); ESPN 2 HD; ESPN Classic Sports; ESPN Deportes; ESPN HD; ESPNews; ESPNews HD; FitTV; Flix; Food Network HD; Fox Business Channel; Fox Business Channel HD; Fox College Sports Atlantic; Fox College Sports Central; Fox College Sports Pacific; Fox Movie Channel; Fox News HD; Fox Reality Channel; Fox Soccer; Fox Sports en Espanol; FSN HD; Fuse; FX HD; G4; Golf Channel HD; Gospel Music Channel; Great American Country; GSN; Hallmark Channel; Hallmark Movie Channel; Hallmark Movie Channel HD; HGTV HD; History Channel en Espanol; History Channel HD; History Channel International; ID Investigation Discovery; Independent Film Channel; ION Life; ION Television; Jewelry Television; Lifetime Movie Network; Lifetime Movie Network HD; MGM HD; MLB Network; MoviePlex; MTV Hits; MTV Jams; MTV Tres; MTV2; mun2 television; Music Choice; National Geographic Channel; National Geographic Channel HD Network; NBA TV; NFL Network; NFL Network HD; NHL Network; Nick Jr.; Nick Too; NickToons TV; Outdoor Channel; Ovation; Oxygen; Qubo; QVC HD; Science Channel; Science Channel HD; ShopNBC; SoapNet; Speed Channel; Speed HD; Starz IndiePlex; Starz RetroPlex; Style Network; Sundance Channel; Syfy; Syfy HD; TeenNick; Tennis Channel; The Sportsman Channel; The Word Network; TLC HD; Trinity Broadcasting Network; Turner Classic Movies; Turner Network TV HD; TV Land; TV One; Universal HD; USA Network HD; VeneMovies; Versus HD; VH1 Classic; VH1 Soul; WE tv.
Fee: $11.99 monthly.
Digital Pay Service 1
Pay Units: 1,647.
Programming (via satellite): Cinemax (multiplexed); Cinemax HD; HBO (multiplexed); HBO HD; Playboy TV; Showtime (multiplexed); Showtime HD; Starz (multiplexed); Starz HDTV; The Movie Channel (multiplexed).
Fee: $16.99 monthly (each).
Video-On-Demand: Yes
Pay-Per-View
iN DEMAND (delivered digitally); Sports PPV (delivered digitally); Club Jenna (delivered digitally); Fresh (delivered digitally); Spice: Xcess (delivered digitally); Playboy TV (delivered digitally).
Internet Service
Operational: Yes. Began: June 1, 2004.
Broadband Service: Comcast High Speed Internet.
Fee: $42.95 monthly.
Telephone Service
Digital: Operational
Miles of Plant: 321.0 (coaxial); 63.0 (fiber optic). Homes passed: 17,080. Total homes in franchised area: 18,034.
Area Vice President: Sandy Weicher. Vice President, Technical Operations: Bob Curtis. Vice President, Marketing & Sales: Eric Schaefer. Vice President, Communications: Rich Ruggiero. Technical Operations Manager: John Collucci. Marketing Director: Ron Knutson.
Ownership: Comcast Cable Communications Inc. (MSO).

NORTH BRANCH TWP.—Charter Communications, 7372 Davison Rd, Davison, MI 48423. Phone: 810-652-1400. Web Site: http://www.charter.com. Also serves Arcadia Twp. (Lapeer County), Attica Twp., Clifford, Dayton Twp. (Tuscola County), Deerfield Twp. (Lapeer County), Freemont Twp., Kingston Twp., Koylton Twp., Marathon, Mayville, Novesta Twp., Otter Lake & Watertown Twp. (Tuscola County). ICA: MI0337.
TV Market Ranking: 61 (Arcadia Twp., Attica Twp., Clifford, Dayton Twp. (Tuscola County), Deerfield Twp. (Lapeer County), Freemont Twp., Koylton Twp., Koylton Twp., Marathon Twp., Mayville, NORTH BRANCH TWP., Novesta Twp., Novesta Twp., Otter Lake, Watertown Twp.); Outside TV Markets (Kingston Twp.). Franchise award date: N.A. Franchise expiration date: N.A. Began: July 1, 1985.
Channel capacity: N.A. Channels available but not in use: N.A.
Basic Service
Subscribers: N.A.
Programming (received off-air): WADL (IND) Mount Clemens; WDIV-TV (NBC) Detroit; WEYI-TV (CW, NBC) Saginaw; WFUM (PBS) Flint; WJBK (FOX) Detroit; WJRT-

TV (ABC) Flint; WKBD-TV (CW) Detroit; WMYD (MNT) Detroit; WNEM-TV (CBS, MNT) Bay City; WPXD-TV (ION) Ann Arbor; WSMH (FOX) Flint; WTVS (PBS) Detroit; WWJ-TV (CBS) Detroit; WXYZ-TV (ABC) Detroit.

Programming (via satellite): C-SPAN; QVC; Weather Channel; WGN America.

Current originations: Government Access; Educational Access; Public Access.

Fee: $35.00 installation; $14.15 monthly.

Expanded Basic Service 1

Subscribers: N.A.

Programming (via satellite): ABC Family Channel; AMC; Animal Planet; Arts & Entertainment; Cartoon Network; CNBC; CNN; Comedy Central; Country Music TV; Discovery Channel; Disney Channel; E! Entertainment Television; ESPN; ESPN 2; Fox News Channel; Fox Sports Net Detroit; FX; Headline News; HGTV; History Channel; Home Shopping Network; Lifetime; MTV; Nickelodeon; Spike TV; Style Network; Syfy; TBS Superstation; The Learning Channel; Travel Channel; Turner Classic Movies; Turner Network TV; USA Network; VH1.

Digital Basic Service

Subscribers: N.A.

Programming (via satellite): BBC America; Cinemax (multiplexed); Discovery Digital Networks; DMX Music; ESPN Classic Sports; ESPNews; Fox Soccer; Golf Channel; GSN; Independent Film Channel; Speed Channel; Starz (multiplexed); Versus; WE tv.

Digital Pay Service 1

Pay Units: N.A.

Programming (via satellite): Encore (multiplexed); HBO (multiplexed); Showtime (multiplexed); The Movie Channel (multiplexed).

Video-On-Demand: Yes

Pay-Per-View

iN DEMAND (delivered digitally); Fresh (delivered digitally).

Internet Service

Operational: Yes.

Broadband Service: Charter Pipeline.

Telephone Service

Digital: Operational

Vice President & General Manager: Dave Slowick. Technical Operations Director: Lloyd Collins. Marketing Director: Lisa Gayari.

Ownership: Charter Communications Inc. (MSO).

NORWAY—City of Norway CATV, PO Box 99, 915 Main St, Norway, MI 49870. Phone: 906-563-9961. Fax: 906-563-7502. Web Site: http://www.norwaymi.com. Also serves Norway Twp. ICA: MI0161.

TV Market Ranking: Below 100 (NORWAY, Norway Twp.). Franchise award date: N.A. Franchise expiration date: N.A. Began: January 1, 1954.

Channel capacity: 49 (operating 2-way). Channels available but not in use: 1.

Basic Service

Subscribers: 1,558.

Programming (received off-air): WBUP (ABC) Ishpeming; WFQX-TV (FOX) Cadillac; WJMN-TV (CBS) Escanaba; WLUK-TV (FOX) Green Bay; WNMU (PBS) Marquette; allband FM.

Programming (via satellite): ABC Family Channel; Cartoon Network; CNBC; C-SPAN; Eternal Word TV Network; Headline News; HGTV; Home Shopping Network; Syfy; TBS Superstation; The Learning Channel; Travel Channel; TV Guide Network; TV Land; Weather Channel; WGN America; WLUC-TV (NBC) Marquette.

Fee: $35.00 installation; $12.00 monthly.

Expanded Basic Service 1

Subscribers: 1,289.

Programming (via satellite): Animal Planet; Arts & Entertainment; CNN; Comedy Central; Country Music TV; Discovery Channel; Disney Channel; ESPN; ESPN 2; Food Network; Fox News Channel; FX; GSN; Hallmark Channel; History Channel; Lifetime; Nickelodeon; Outdoor Channel; Speed Channel; Spike TV; truTV; Turner Classic Movies; Turner Network TV; USA Network; VH1.

Fee: $14.00 monthly.

Pay Service 1

Pay Units: 197.

Programming (via satellite): HBO.

Fee: $10.50 monthly.

Video-On-Demand: No

Internet Service

Operational: Yes.

Subscribers: 733.

Broadband Service: In-house.

Fee: $50.00 installation; $32.00 monthly.

Telephone Service

None

Miles of Plant: 53.0 (coaxial); None (fiber optic).

Manager: Ray Anderson. Chief Technician: James Bryner.

Ownership: City of Norway CATV.

OLIVE TWP. (Ottawa County)—Charter Communications. Now served by ALLENDALE, MI [MI0094]. ICA: MI0139.

OMER—Charter Communications, 2074 M 32 W, Alpena, MI 49707. Phone: 989-356-4503. Fax: 989-356-3761. E-mail: jboullion@chartercom.com. Web Site: http://www.charter.com. Also serves Arenac Twp., Mason Twp. (Arenac County), Turner Twp., Turner Village & Twining. ICA: MI0209.

TV Market Ranking: 61 (Arenac Twp., Mason Twp. (Arenac County), OMER); Outside TV Markets (Turner Twp., Turner Village, Twining). Franchise award date: July 25, 1988. Franchise expiration date: N.A. Began: April 24, 1989.

Channel capacity: 54 (not 2-way capable). Channels available but not in use: 25.

Basic Service

Subscribers: 285.

Programming (received off-air): WAQP (IND) Saginaw; WBKB-TV (CBS, FOX) Alpena; WEYI-TV (CW, NBC) Saginaw; WJRT-TV (ABC) Flint; WNEM-TV (CBS, MNT) Bay City; WSMH (FOX) Flint.

Programming (via satellite): Home Shopping Network; TBS Superstation.

Fee: $29.99 installation; $13.50 monthly.

Expanded Basic Service 1

Subscribers: 267.

Programming (via satellite): ABC Family Channel; Arts & Entertainment; CNN; Comedy Central; C-SPAN; Discovery Channel; ESPN; Headline News; History Channel; MTV; Nickelodeon; Spike TV; The Learning Channel; Turner Network TV; USA Network; Weather Channel.

Fee: $36.49 monthly.

Pay Service 1

Pay Units: 68.

Programming (via satellite): Cinemax.

Fee: $9.95 monthly.

Pay Service 2

Pay Units: 68.

Programming (via satellite): HBO.

Fee: $9.95 monthly.

Internet Service

Operational: No.

Telephone Service

None

Miles of Plant: 24.0 (coaxial); None (fiber optic). Homes passed: 548.

Vice President: Joe Boullion. General Manager: Ed Kavanaugh. Technical Operations Director: Rob Nowak. Marketing Manager: Brenda Auger.

City fee: 3% of basic.

Ownership: Charter Communications Inc. (MSO).

ONAWAY—Formerly served by Northwoods Cable Inc. No longer in operation. ICA: MI0201.

ONTONAGON—Charter Communications. Now served by IRONWOOD, MI [MI0064]. ICA: MI0181.

OSCODA—Charter Communications, 2074 M 32 W, Alpena, MI 49707. Phones: 989-356-4503; 231-947-5521 (Traverse City). Fax: 989-356-3761. E-mail: jboullion@chartercom.com. Web Site: http://www.charter.com. Also serves Alabaster Twp., Alcona Twp., Au Sable Twp. (Iosco County), Baldwin Twp. (Iosco County), Caledonia Twp., East Tawas, Grant Twp. (Iosco County), Greenbush Twp. (Alcona County), Harrisville, Hawes Twp., Lincoln, Long Lake, Oscoda Twp., Plainfield Twp. (Iosco County), Tawas City, Tawas Twp. & Wilber Twp. ICA: MI0338.

TV Market Ranking: Below 100 (Alcona Twp., Greenbush Twp. (Alcona County), Harrisville, Lincoln); Outside TV Markets (Alabaster Twp., Au Sable Twp. (Iosco County), Baldwin Twp. (Iosco County), Caledonia Twp., East Tawas, Grant Twp. (Iosco County), Hawes Twp., Long Lake, OSCODA, Oscoda Twp., Plainfield Twp. (Iosco County), Tawas City, Tawas Twp., Wilber Twp.). Franchise award date: January 1, 1976. Franchise expiration date: N.A. Began: December 1, 1963.

Channel capacity: N.A. Channels available but not in use: N.A.

Basic Service

Subscribers: 10,402.

Programming (received off-air): WBKB-TV (CBS, FOX) Alpena; WDCQ-TV (PBS) Bad Axe; WEYI-TV (CW, NBC) Saginaw; WJRT-TV (ABC) Flint; WKBD-TV (CW) Detroit; WNEM-TV (CBS, MNT) Bay City; WSMH (FOX) Flint.

Programming (via satellite): CB Television Michoacan; C-SPAN; C-SPAN 2; Eternal Word TV Network; Home Shopping Network; INSP; MyNetworkTV Inc.; QVC; TBS Superstation; Trinity Broadcasting Network; TV Guide Network; WGN America.

Current originations: Government Access; Educational Access; Public Access.

Fee: $32.25 installation; $19.89 monthly; $1.21 converter.

Expanded Basic Service 1

Subscribers: 7,212.

Programming (via microwave): G4.

Programming (via satellite): ABC Family Channel; AMC; Animal Planet; Arts & Entertainment; BET Networks; Bravo; Cartoon Network; CNBC; CNN; Comedy Central; Country Music TV; Discovery Channel; Disney Channel; E! Entertainment Television; ESPN; ESPN 2; Food Network; Fox News Channel; Fox Sports Net Detroit; FX; Golf Channel; GSN; Hallmark Channel; Headline News; HGTV; History Channel; Lifetime; MSNBC; MTV; MTV2; National Geographic Channel; Nickelodeon; Outdoor Channel; Oxygen; SoapNet; Speed Channel; Spike TV; Syfy; Telemundo; The Learning Channel; Toon Disney; Travel Channel; truTV; Turner Classic Movies; Turner Network TV; TV Land; USA Network; Versus; VH1; WE tv; Weather Channel.

Fee: $32.25 installation; $10.00 monthly.

Digital Basic Service

Subscribers: N.A.

Programming (received off-air): WEYI-TV (CW, NBC) Saginaw; WJRT-TV (ABC) Flint; WNEM-TV (CBS, MNT) Bay City; WSMH (FOX) Flint.

Programming (via satellite): BBC America; Bio; CMT Pure Country; Discovery Channel HD; Discovery Digital Networks; Do-It-Yourself; ESPN Classic Sports; ESPN HD; ESPNews; FitTV; Fox College Sports Atlantic; Fox College Sports Central; Fox College Sports Pacific; Fox Movie Channel; Fox Soccer; Fox Sports Net Detroit; Fuel TV; Fuse; GAS; Great American Country; HDNet; HDNet Movies; History Channel International; Independent Film Channel; Lifetime Movie Network; Military History Channel; MTV Networks Digital Suite; Music Choice; Nick Jr.; Nick Too; NickToons TV; Sundance Channel; Turner Network TV HD; Universal HD.

Digital Pay Service 1

Pay Units: N.A.

Programming (via satellite): Cinemax (multiplexed); Cinemax HD; Encore (multiplexed); Flix; HBO (multiplexed); HBO HD; LOGO; Showtime (multiplexed); Showtime HD; Starz (multiplexed); The Movie Channel (multiplexed).

Video-On-Demand: Yes

Pay-Per-View

iN DEMAND (delivered digitally); ESPN (delivered digitally); NHL Center Ice (delivered digitally); MLB Extra Innings (delivered digitally); Playboy TV (delivered digitally); Club Jenna (delivered digitally); Fresh! (delivered digitally); Fresh (delivered digitally); Shorteez (delivered digitally).

Internet Service

Operational: Yes.

Broadband Service: Charter Pipeline.

Fee: $29.99 monthly.

Telephone Service

Digital: Operational

Miles of Plant: 340.0 (coaxial); None (fiber optic). Additional miles planned: 2.0 (coaxial). Homes passed: 16,694.

Vice President: Joe Boullion. General Manager: Ed Kavanaugh. Technical Operations Director: Rob Nowak. Marketing Manager: Brenda Auger.

City fee: None.

Ownership: Charter Communications Inc. (MSO).

OSHTEMO TWP.—Comcast Cable, 3500 Patterson Ave SE, Grand Rapids, MI 49512. Phone: 616-977-2200. Fax: 616-977-2224. Web Site: http://www.comcast.com. Also serves Portage (portions) & Texas Twp. ICA: MI0340.

TV Market Ranking: 37 (OSHTEMO TWP., Portage (portions), Texas Twp.). Franchise award date: N.A. Franchise expiration date: N.A. Began: N.A.

Channel capacity: 78 (operating 2-way). Channels available but not in use: 33.

Basic Service

Subscribers: 2,860.

Programming (received off-air): WGVU-TV (PBS) Grand Rapids; WLLA (IND) Kalamazoo; WOBC-CA Battle Creek; WOOD-TV (NBC) Grand Rapids; WOTV (ABC) Battle Creek; WTLJ (IND) Muskegon; WWMT

(CBS, CW) Kalamazoo; WXMI (FOX) Grand Rapids; WZPX-TV (ION) Battle Creek; 1 FM.
Programming (via satellite): C-SPAN; Eternal Word TV Network; Home Shopping Network; QVC; WGN America.
Current originations: Public Access.
Fee: $10.15 monthly.

Expanded Basic Service 1
Subscribers: 2,800.
Programming (via satellite): ABC Family Channel; AMC; Animal Planet; Arts & Entertainment; Cartoon Network; CNBC; CNN; Comcast Local Detroit; Comedy Central; Country Music TV; C-SPAN 2; Discovery Channel; Disney Channel; E! Entertainment Television; ESPN; ESPN 2; FitTV; Food Network; Fox News Channel; Fox Sports Net Detroit; FX; Golf Channel; Headline News; HGTV; History Channel; Lifetime; MSNBC; MTV; Nickelodeon; Product Information Network; Spike TV; Syfy; TBS Superstation; The Learning Channel; Travel Channel; Turner Classic Movies; Turner Network TV; TV Land; USA Network; Versus; VH1; Weather Channel.
Fee: $48.99 monthly.

Digital Basic Service
Subscribers: N.A.
Programming (via satellite): BBC America; Bio; Bravo; CMT Pure Country; Discovery Kids Channel; Discovery Military Channel; Discovery Planet Green; Do-It-Yourself; Encore (multiplexed); ESPN Classic Sports; ESPNews; Flix; Fox Soccer; Fuse; GSN; Hallmark Channel; History Channel; History Channel International; ID Investigation Discovery; Independent Film Channel; Lifetime Movie Network; MTV Hits; MTV Tres; Music Choice; National Geographic Channel; NBA TV; NFL Network; Nick Jr.; Science Channel; Speed Channel; Style Network; TeenNick; Toon Disney; VH1 Classic; WE tv.
Fee: $9.95 monthly.

Digital Pay Service 1
Pay Units: N.A.
Programming (via satellite): Cinemax (multiplexed); HBO (multiplexed); Showtime (multiplexed); Starz (multiplexed); The Movie Channel (multiplexed).
Fee: $18.05 monthly (each).

Video-On-Demand: No

Pay-Per-View
iN DEMAND (delivered digitally); Playboy TV (delivered digitally).

Internet Service
Operational: Yes.
Broadband Service: Comcast High Speed Internet.
Fee: $42.95 monthly.

Telephone Service
Digital: Operational

Miles of Plant: 121.0 (coaxial); 32.0 (fiber optic).
Area Vice President: Larry Williamson. Business Operations Director: Amy Carey. Technical Operations Director: Tom Rice. Sales & Marketing Director: Rick Finch.
City fee: 3% of gross.
Ownership: Comcast Cable Communications Inc. (MSO).

OWOSSO—Charter Communications, 7372 Davison Rd, Davison, MI 48423. Phone: 810-652-1400. Web Site: http://www.charter.com. Also serves Bennington Twp., Caledonia Twp. (Shiawassee County), Corunna, Owosso Twp. & Rush Twp. ICA: MI0057.
TV Market Ranking: 61,92 (Bennington Twp., Caledonia Twp. (Shiawassee County), Corunna, OWOSSO, Owosso Twp., Rush Twp.). Franchise award date: January 1, 1972. Franchise expiration date: N.A. Began: June 1, 1974.
Channel capacity: 79 (operating 2-way). Channels available but not in use: 6.

Basic Service
Subscribers: 9,600.
Programming (received off-air): WAQP (IND) Saginaw; WBSF (CW) Bay City; WDIV-TV (NBC) Detroit; WEYI-TV (CW, NBC) Saginaw; WFUM (PBS) Flint; WJRT-TV (ABC) Flint; WKAR-TV (PBS) East Lansing; WNEM-TV (CBS, MNT) Bay City; WSMH (FOX) Flint; WTVS (PBS) Detroit; WXYZ-TV (ABC) Detroit; 1 FM.
Programming (via satellite): Home Shopping Network; ION Television; MyNetworkTV Inc.; QVC; WGN America.
Current originations: Government Access; Educational Access; Leased Access; Public Access.
Fee: $29.99 installation; $13.50 monthly; $3.50 converter.

Expanded Basic Service 1
Subscribers: 6,170.
Programming (via satellite): ABC Family Channel; AMC; Animal Planet; Arts & Entertainment; Bravo; Cartoon Network; CNBC; CNN; Comedy Central; Country Music TV; C-SPAN; Discovery Channel; Disney Channel; E! Entertainment Television; ESPN; ESPN 2; Food Network; Fox News Channel; Fox Sports Net Detroit; FX; G4; Golf Channel; GSN; Hallmark Channel; Headline News; HGTV; History Channel; Lifetime; MSNBC; MTV; MTV2; National Geographic Channel; Nickelodeon; Oxygen; SoapNet; Speed Channel; Spike TV; Syfy; TBS Superstation; The Learning Channel; Toon Disney; Travel Channel; Turner Classic Movies; Turner Network TV; TV Guide Network; TV Land; USA Network; Versus; VH1; Weather Channel.
Fee: $36.49 monthly.

Digital Basic Service
Subscribers: N.A.
Programming (received off-air): WEYI-TV (CW, NBC) Saginaw; WFUM (PBS) Flint; WJRT-TV (ABC) Flint; WNEM-TV (CBS, MNT) Bay City; WSMH (FOX) Flint.
Programming (via microwave): Fox College Sports Pacific.
Programming (via satellite): BBC America; Bio; CMT Pure Country; Discovery Digital Networks; Do-It-Yourself; ESPN 2 HD; ESPN Classic Sports; ESPN HD; ESPN U; ESPNews; FitTV; Fox Business Channel; Fox College Sports Atlantic; Fox College Sports Central; Fox Movie Channel; Fox Soccer; Fox Sports Net Detroit; Fuel TV; Fuse; GAS; Great American Country; HD-Net; HDNet Movies; History Channel International; Independent Film Channel; Lifetime Movie Network; Military History Channel; MTV Networks Digital Suite; Music Choice; Nick Jr.; Nick Too; NickToons TV; Outdoor Channel; ReelzChannel; Sundance Channel; The Sportsman Channel; Turner Network TV HD; Universal HD; WE tv.

Digital Pay Service 1
Pay Units: N.A.
Programming (via satellite): Cinemax (multiplexed); Cinemax HD; Encore (multiplexed); Flix; HBO (multiplexed); HBO HD; LOGO; Showtime (multiplexed); Showtime HD; Starz (multiplexed); Starz HDTV; The Movie Channel (multiplexed).

Video-On-Demand: Yes

Pay-Per-View
iN DEMAND (delivered digitally); ESPN (delivered digitally); NHL Center Ice (delivered digitally); MLB Extra Innings (delivered digitally); Playboy TV (delivered digitally); Club Jenna (delivered digitally); Fresh! (delivered digitally); Fresh (delivered digitally); Shorteez (delivered digitally).

Internet Service
Operational: Yes.
Broadband Service: Charter Pipeline.
Fee: $29.99 monthly.

Telephone Service
Digital: Operational
Fee: $29.99 monthly

Miles of Plant: 216.0 (coaxial); None (fiber optic). Homes passed: 11,802. Total homes in franchised area: 13,028.
Vice President & General Manager: Dave Slowick. Technical Operations Director: Lloyd Collins. Marketing Director: Lisa Gayari.
City fee: 3% of gross.
Ownership: Charter Communications Inc. (MSO).

OXFORD—Charter Communications, 7372 Davison Rd, Davison, MI 48423. Phone: 810-652-1400. Web Site: http://www.charter.com. Also serves Addison Twp., Brandon Twp., Hadley Twp., Lakeville, Leonard, Metamora, Metamora Twp., Ortonville, Oxford (village) & Oxford Twp. ICA: MI0059.
TV Market Ranking: 5,61 (Addison Twp., Leonard, OXFORD, Oxford (village), Oxford Twp.); 61 (Brandon Twp., Hadley Twp., Lakeville, Metamora, Metamora Twp., Ortonville). Franchise award date: January 1, 1982. Franchise expiration date: N.A. Began: December 1, 1982.
Channel capacity: N.A. Channels available but not in use: N.A.

Basic Service
Subscribers: 14,830.
Programming (received off-air): WADL (IND) Mount Clemens; WDIV-TV (NBC) Detroit; WEYI-TV (CW, NBC) Saginaw; WFUM (PBS) Flint; WJBK (FOX) Detroit; WJRT-TV (ABC) Flint; WKAR-TV (PBS) East Lansing; WKBD-TV (CW) Detroit; WMYD (MNT) Detroit; WNEM-TV (CBS, MNT) Bay City; WPXD-TV (ION) Ann Arbor; WTVS (PBS) Detroit; WWJ-TV (CBS) Detroit; WXYZ-TV (ABC) Detroit.
Programming (via satellite): C-SPAN; Home Shopping Network; QVC; TV Guide Network; Weather Channel; WGN America.
Fee: $29.99 installation; $13.50 monthly.

Expanded Basic Service 1
Subscribers: N.A.
Programming (via satellite): ABC Family Channel; AMC; Animal Planet; Arts & Entertainment; Cartoon Network; CNBC; CNN; Comedy Central; Country Music TV; Discovery Channel; Disney Channel; E! Entertainment Television; ESPN; ESPN 2; Fox News Channel; Fox Sports Net Detroit; Hallmark Channel; Headline News; HGTV; History Channel; Lifetime; MTV; Nickelodeon; Spike TV; Syfy; TBS Superstation; The Learning Channel; Travel Channel; Turner Classic Movies; Turner Network TV; USA Network; VH1.
Fee: $36.49 monthly.

Digital Basic Service
Subscribers: N.A.
Programming (via satellite): BBC America; Discovery Digital Networks; DMX Music; ESPN 2; ESPN Classic Sports; Fox Sports World; Golf Channel; GSN; HGTV; History Channel; Independent Film Channel; Speed Channel; Syfy; Turner Classic Movies; Versus; WE tv.
Fee: $13.00 monthly.

Digital Pay Service 1
Pay Units: 862.
Programming (via satellite): Cinemax (multiplexed); Encore (multiplexed); HBO (multiplexed); Showtime (multiplexed); Starz (multiplexed); The Movie Channel (multiplexed).
Fee: $25.00 installation; $10.00 monthly (Cinemax, HBO, Showtime/TMC, or Starz/Encore).

Video-On-Demand: Yes

Pay-Per-View
iN DEMAND (delivered digitally), Addressable: Yes; Fresh (delivered digitally).

Internet Service
Operational: Yes.
Broadband Service: Charter Pipeline.
Fee: $50.00 installation; $29.99 monthly.

Telephone Service
Digital: Operational
Fee: $29.99 monthly

Miles of Plant: 535.0 (coaxial); None (fiber optic). Homes passed: 18,884. Total homes in franchised area: 22,884.
Vice President & General Manager: Dave Slowick. Technical Operations Director: Lloyd Collins. Marketing Director: Lisa Gayari.
City fee: 5% of gross.
Ownership: Charter Communications Inc. (MSO).

PELLSTON—Charter Communications, 701 E South Airport Rd, Traverse City, MI 49686-4861. Phone: 231-947-5221. Fax: 231-947-2004. E-mail: jboullion@chartercom.com. Web Site: http://www.charter.com. Also serves McKinley Twp. ICA: MI0236.
TV Market Ranking: Below 100 (McKinley Twp., PELLSTON). Franchise award date: August 17, 1987. Franchise expiration date: N.A. Began: January 1, 1988.
Channel capacity: 61 (2-way capable). Channels available but not in use: 31.

Basic Service
Subscribers: 170.
Programming (received off-air): WCML (PBS) Alpena; WFUP (FOX) Vanderbilt; WGTQ (ABC) Sault Ste. Marie; WTOM-TV (NBC) Cheboygan; WWUP-TV (CBS, FOX) Sault Ste. Marie.
Programming (via satellite): C-SPAN; QVC; TBS Superstation; WGN America.
Current originations: Government Access; Educational Access; Public Access.
Fee: $29.99 installation; $13.50 monthly.

Expanded Basic Service 1
Subscribers: N.A.
Programming (via satellite): ABC Family Channel; AMC; Arts & Entertainment; CNN; Country Music TV; Discovery Channel; Disney Channel; ESPN; ESPN 2; Eter-

nal Word TV Network; Food Network; Fox Sports Net Detroit; Headline News; Lifetime; MTV; Nickelodeon; Spike TV; The Learning Channel; Turner Network TV; USA Network; Weather Channel.
Fee: $36.49 monthly.
Pay Service 1
Pay Units: 48.
Programming (via satellite): Cinemax; HBO; Starz.
Fee: $6.95 monthly (Starz), $10.95 monthly (Cinemax), $11.95 monthly (HBO).
Internet Service
Operational: Yes.
Fee: $19.99 monthly.
Telephone Service
Digital: Operational
Fee: $14.99 monthly
Miles of Plant: 6.0 (coaxial); None (fiber optic). Homes passed: 289.
Vice President & General Manager: Joe Boullion. Technical Operations Director: Rob Nowak. Marketing Manager: Tammy Reicha.
Ownership: Charter Communications Inc. (MSO).

PENTWATER—Charter Communications, 315 Davis St, Grand Haven, MI 49417-1830. Phone: 616-647-6201. Fax: 616-846-0797. Web Site: http://www.charter.com. ICA: MI0158.
TV Market Ranking: Outside TV Markets (PENTWATER). Franchise award date: N.A. Franchise expiration date: N.A. Began: May 1, 1976.
Channel capacity: 36 (2-way capable). Channels available but not in use: 6.
Basic Service
Subscribers: 801.
Programming (received off-air): WCMW (PBS) Manistee; WFQX-TV (FOX) Cadillac; WGVU-TV (PBS) Grand Rapids; WPBN-TV (NBC) Traverse City; WWTV (CBS) Cadillac; WZZM (ABC) Grand Rapids.
Programming (via satellite): ABC Family Channel; Country Music TV; C-SPAN; Lifetime; QVC; TBS Superstation; WGN America.
Fee: $38.00 installation; $22.00 monthly.
Expanded Basic Service 1
Subscribers: N.A.
Programming (via satellite): Arts & Entertainment; CNBC; CNN; Discovery Channel; Disney Channel; ESPN; ESPN 2; Food Network; Fox Sports Net Detroit; HGTV; MTV; Nickelodeon; Spike TV; The Learning Channel; Turner Classic Movies; Turner Network TV; USA Network; Weather Channel.
Pay Service 1
Pay Units: 110.
Programming (via satellite): Cinemax; HBO; Starz.
Fee: $6.95 monthly (Starz), $10.95 monthly (Cinemax), $11.95 monthly (HBO).
Internet Service
Operational: Yes.
Fee: $19.99 monthly.
Telephone Service
Digital: Operational
Fee: $14.99 monthly
Miles of Plant: 39.0 (coaxial); None (fiber optic). Homes passed: 1,832.
Vice President & General Manager: Dan Spoelman. Technical Operations Manager: Keith Schierbeek. Marketing Director: Steve Schuh.
City fee: 5% of gross.
Ownership: Charter Communications Inc. (MSO).

PERRINTON—Pine River Cable, PO Box 96, McBain, MI 49657. Phone: 888-244-2288. Fax: 231-825-0191. E-mail: info@pinerivercable.com. Web Site: http://www.pinerivercable.com. Also serves Middleton. ICA: MI0229.
TV Market Ranking: 92 (Middleton, PERRINTON). Franchise award date: April 6, 1987. Franchise expiration date: N.A. Began: N.A.
Channel capacity: 36 (not 2-way capable). Channels available but not in use: 10.
Basic Service
Subscribers: 146.
Programming (received off-air): WILX-TV (NBC) Onondaga; WJRT-TV (ABC) Flint; WKAR-TV (PBS) East Lansing; WLNS-TV (CBS) Lansing; WOOD-TV (NBC) Grand Rapids; WSMH (FOX) Flint; WSYM-TV (FOX) Lansing.
Programming (via satellite): ABC Family Channel; CNN; Discovery Channel; Disney Channel; ESPN; Headline News; TBS Superstation; Turner Network TV; USA Network; WGN America.
Fee: $50.00 installation; $19.95 monthly.
Pay Service 1
Pay Units: 48.
Programming (via satellite): Showtime.
Fee: $20.00 installation; $7.00 monthly.
Internet Service
Operational: No.
Telephone Service
None
Miles of Plant: 6.0 (coaxial); None (fiber optic). Homes passed: 335.
Manager: John Metzler.
Ownership: Pine River Cable (MSO).

PETERSBURG—D & P Cable, 4200 Teal Rd, Petersburg, MI 49270. Phones: 734-279-1339; 800-311-7340; 734-279-9000. Fax: 734-279-2640. Web Site: http://www.d-pcommunications.com. Also serves Blissfield, Britton, Deerfield, Dundee & Morenci. ICA: MI0437. **Note:** This system is an overbuild.
TV Market Ranking: 52 (Blissfield, Britton, Deerfield, Dundee, Morenci, PETERSBURG).
Channel capacity: 77 (operating 2-way). Channels available but not in use: N.A.
Basic Service
Subscribers: 4,059.
Programming (received off-air): WDIV-TV (NBC) Detroit; WGTE-TV (PBS) Toledo; WJBK (FOX) Detroit; WKBD-TV (CW) Detroit; WLMB (IND) Toledo; WMYD (MNT) Detroit; WNWO-TV (NBC) Toledo; WPXD-TV (ION) Ann Arbor; WTOL (CBS) Toledo; WTVG (ABC) Toledo; WTVS (PBS) Detroit; WUPW (FOX) Toledo; WWJ-TV (CBS) Detroit; WXYZ-TV (ABC) Detroit.
Programming (via satellite): C-SPAN; QVC; TV Guide Network; various Canadian stations; WGN America.
Current originations: Educational Access; Public Access.
Fee: $35.00 installation; $16.00 monthly.
Expanded Basic Service 1
Subscribers: 3,779.
Programming (via satellite): ABC Family Channel; AMC; AmericanLife TV Network; Animal Planet; Arts & Entertainment; Cartoon Network; CNBC; CNN; Comedy Central; Country Music TV; Discovery Channel; Disney Channel; E! Entertainment Television; ESPN; ESPN 2; ESPN Classic Sports; ESPNews; Food Network; Fox News Channel; Fox Sports Net Detroit; FX; Golf Channel; Great American Country; Hallmark Channel; Headline News; HGTV; History Channel; Home Shopping Network; INSP; Lifetime; MSNBC; MTV; National Geographic Channel; Nickelodeon; Outdoor Channel; Oxygen; RFD-TV; ShopNBC; Spike TV; Syfy; TBS Superstation; The Learning Channel; Toon Disney; Travel Channel; Trinity Broadcasting Network; truTV; Turner Classic Movies; Turner Network TV; TV Land; Univision; USA Network; VH1; WE tv; Weather Channel.
Fee: $22.50 monthly.
Digital Basic Service
Subscribers: 889.
Programming (via satellite): BBC America; Bloomberg Television; Bravo; Cooking Channel; Discovery Digital Networks; DMX Music; Fox Movie Channel; Fox Soccer; G4; GAS; GSN; Hallmark Channel; Halogen Network; Lime; MTV Networks Digital Suite; Nick Jr.; NickToons TV; Sleuth; Speed Channel; Style Network; The Sportsman Channel; Versus.
Fee: $12.00 monthly.
Digital Pay Service 1
Pay Units: N.A.
Programming (via satellite): Cinemax (multiplexed); Encore (multiplexed); Flix (multiplexed); HBO (multiplexed); Showtime (multiplexed); Starz (multiplexed); The Movie Channel (multiplexed).
Fee: $12.95 monthly (Cinemax, Showtime/TMC, or Starz/Encore), $13.95 monthly (HBO).
Video-On-Demand: No
Pay-Per-View
iN DEMAND (delivered digitally), Addressable: Yes; Fresh (delivered digitally); Playboy TV (delivered digitally).
Internet Service
Operational: Yes.
Subscribers: 1,752.
Broadband Service: Cassnet.
Fee: $27.45 monthly.
Telephone Service
None
Office Manager: Theresa Holman. Engineering Manager: Shane Bauman. Outside Plant Manager: Jamie LaRocca.
Ownership: D & P Communications Inc.

PETOSKEY—Charter Communications. Now served by TRAVERSE CITY, MI [MI0026]. ICA: MI0071.

PICKFORD TWP.—Sunrise Communications LLC, PO Box 733, 20938 Washington Ave, Onaway, MI 49765. Phones: 877-733-8101; 989-733-8100. Fax: 989-733-8155. E-mail: info@src-mi.com. Web Site: http://www.src-mi.com. ICA: MI0228.
TV Market Ranking: Below 100 (PICKFORD TWP.). Franchise award date: November 23, 1988. Franchise expiration date: N.A. Began: January 1, 1990.
Channel capacity: 57 (not 2-way capable). Channels available but not in use: 20.
Basic Service
Subscribers: 135.
Programming (received off-air): WCML (PBS) Alpena; WFQX-TV (FOX) Cadillac; WGTQ (ABC) Sault Ste. Marie; WTOM-TV (NBC) Cheboygan; WWUP-TV (CBS, FOX) Sault Ste. Marie.
Fee: $39.18 installation; $1.21 converter.
Expanded Basic Service 1
Subscribers: N.A.
Programming (via satellite): ABC Family Channel; AMC; Arts & Entertainment; CNN; Discovery Channel; Disney Channel; ESPN; ESPN 2; Fox Sports Net Detroit; HGTV; History Channel; MTV; Nickelodeon; Spike TV; TBS Superstation; Turner Network TV; USA Network; Weather Channel; WGN America.
Fee: $39.18 installation; $39.95 monthly.
Pay Service 1
Pay Units: N.A.
Programming (via satellite): HBO; Showtime.
Internet Service
Operational: Yes.
Fee: $44.95-$99.95 monthly.
Telephone Service
None
Miles of Plant: 13.0 (coaxial); None (fiber optic). Homes passed: 311.
Manager: Rose Boyce.
Ownership: Sunrise Communications LLC (MSO).

PIGEON—Comcast Cable, 1555 Bad Axe Rd, Bad Axe, MI 48413. Phone: 989-269-8927. Fax: 989-269-9125. Web Site: http://www.comcast.com. Also serves Bad Axe, Bay Port Village, Brookfield Twp., Caseville (village), Colfax Twp. (portions), Dwight Twp., Elkton Village, Elmwood Twp., Fairhaven Twp., Gagetown, Gore Twp., Harbor Beach, Hume Twp., Huron Twp., Kinde, McKinley Twp., Meade Twp., Oliver Twp., Owendale, Pointe aux Barques Twp., Port Austin, Port Hope, Rubicon Twp., Sand Beach Twp., Sebewaing, Ubly, Verona Twp. & Winsor Twp. ICA: MI0375.
TV Market Ranking: 61 (Bay Port Village, Fairhaven Twp., Gagetown, Oliver Twp., Owendale, Sebewaing, Winsor Twp.); Outside TV Markets (Bad Axe, Brookfield Twp., Caseville (village), Colfax Twp. (portions), Dwight Twp., Elkton Village, Elmwood Twp., Gore Twp., Harbor Beach, Hume Twp., Huron Twp., Kinde, McKinley Twp., Meade Twp., PIGEON, Pointe aux Barques Twp., Port Hope, Rubicon Twp., Sand Beach Twp., Ubly, Verona Twp., Gagetown). Franchise award date: N.A. Franchise expiration date: N.A. Began: N.A.
Channel capacity: N.A. Channels available but not in use: N.A.
Basic Service
Subscribers: 8,317.
Programming (received off-air): WAQP (IND) Saginaw; WDCQ-TV (PBS) Bad Axe; WEYI-TV (CW, NBC) Saginaw; WJRT-TV (ABC) Flint; WKBD-TV (CW) Detroit; WNEM-TV (CBS, MNT) Bay City; WSMH (FOX) Flint.
Programming (via satellite): C-SPAN; C-SPAN 2; Discovery Health Channel; Home Shopping Network; QVC; TBS Superstation; TV Guide Network; WGN America.
Current originations: Public Access.
Fee: $14.50 monthly.
Expanded Basic Service 1
Subscribers: N.A.
Programming (via satellite): ABC Family Channel; AMC; Animal Planet; Arts & Entertainment; Cartoon Network; CNBC; CNN; Comedy Central; Country Music TV; Discovery Channel; Disney Channel; E! Entertainment Television; ESPN; ESPN 2; Food Network; Fox News Channel; Fox Sports Net Detroit; FX; Golf Channel; Great American Country; GSN; Hallmark Channel; Headline News; HGTV; History Channel; Lifetime; MSNBC; MTV; Nickelodeon; Speed Channel; Spike TV; Syfy; The Learning Channel; Travel Channel; truTV; Turner Classic Movies; Turner Network TV; TV Land; USA Network; Versus; VH1; Weather Channel.
Fee: $48.99 monthly.
Digital Basic Service
Subscribers: N.A.
Programming (received off-air): WEYI-TV (CW, NBC) Saginaw; WJRT-TV (ABC) Flint; WNEM-TV (CBS, MNT) Bay City.
Programming (via satellite): BBC America; Bio; Country Music TV; C-SPAN 3; Dis-

covery HD Theater; Discovery Kids Channel; Discovery Military Channel; Discovery Planet Green; Encore (multiplexed); ESPN 2 HD; ESPN HD; ESPNews; Flix; G4; History Channel International; ID Investigation Discovery; INHD; INHD2; Lifetime Movie Network; MTV Networks Digital Suite; Music Choice; National Geographic Channel; Nick Jr.; Nick Too; NickToons TV; Oxygen; Science Channel; ShopNBC; Sundance Channel; TeenNick; Toon Disney; Turner Network TV HD; Weatherscan.

Digital Pay Service 1

Pay Units: N.A.

Programming (via satellite): Cinemax (multiplexed); Cinemax HD; HBO (multiplexed); HBO HD; Showtime (multiplexed); Showtime HD; Starz (multiplexed); Starz HDTV; The Movie Channel (multiplexed).

Fee: $12.95 monthly (each).

Video-On-Demand: Planned

Pay-Per-View

Hot Choice (delivered digitally); iN DEMAND (delivered digitally); Playboy TV (delivered digitally); Fresh (delivered digitally); Pleasure (delivered digitally).

Internet Service

Operational: Yes. Began: November 1, 2005.

Subscribers: 840.

Broadband Service: Comcast High Speed Internet.

Fee: $42.95 monthly.

Telephone Service

Digital: Operational

Miles of Plant: 343.0 (coaxial); None (fiber optic). Homes passed: 13,365.

General Manager: Thomas J. Lerash. Chief Technician: Marshall Kurschner. Business Manager: Susan McGathy.

Ownership: Comcast Cable Communications Inc. (MSO).

PLYMOUTH—Comcast Cable, 29777 Telegraph Rd, Ste 4400B, Southfield, MI 48034. Phones: 734-254-1500 (Administrative office); 734-459-7300 (Customer service). Fax: 248-233-4719. Web Site: http://www.comcast.com. Also serves Belleville, Canton Twp., Dearborn, Dearborn Heights, Northville, Romulus, Van Buren, Wayne & Westland. ICA: MI0012.

TV Market Ranking: 5 (Belleville, Canton Twp., Dearborn, Dearborn Heights, Northville, PLYMOUTH (VILLAGE), Romulus, Van Buren, Wayne, Westland). Franchise award date: July 14, 1979. Franchise expiration date: N.A. Began: August 1, 1980.

Channel capacity: N.A. Channels available but not in use: N.A.

Basic Service

Subscribers: 33,321.

Programming (received off-air): WADL (IND) Mount Clemens; WDIV-TV (NBC) Detroit; WFUM (PBS) Flint; WJBK (FOX) Detroit; WKBD-TV (CW) Detroit; WMYD (MNT) Detroit; WPXD-TV (ION) Ann Arbor; WTVS (PBS) Detroit; WWJ-TV (CBS) Detroit; WXYZ-TV (ABC) Detroit.

Programming (via satellite): Home Shopping Network; QVC; TBS Superstation; The Comcast Network; WGN America.

Current originations: Leased Access; Government Access; Educational Access; Public Access.

Fee: $25.00 installation; $9.38 monthly.

Expanded Basic Service 1

Subscribers: 31,617.

Programming (received off-air): various Canadian stations; allband FM.

Programming (via satellite): ABC Family Channel; AMC; Animal Planet; Arts & Entertainment; BET Networks; Big Ten Network; Bravo; Cartoon Network; CNBC; CNN; Comedy Central; C-SPAN; Discovery Channel; Disney Channel; E! Entertainment Television; ESPN; ESPN 2; Food Network; Fox News Channel; Fox Sports Net; FX; Golf Channel; Great American Country; Headline News; HGTV; History Channel; Lifetime; MSNBC; MTV; Nickelodeon; Speed Channel; Spike TV; Style Network; Syfy; The Learning Channel; Travel Channel; truTV; Turner Classic Movies; Turner Network TV; TV Land; USA Network; Versus; VH1; Weather Channel.

Fee: $37.99 monthly.

Digital Basic Service

Subscribers: 8,297.

Programming (received off-air): WDIV-TV (NBC) Detroit; WJBK (FOX) Detroit; WKBD-TV (CW) Detroit; WMYD (MNT) Detroit; WTVS (PBS) Detroit; WWJ-TV (CBS) Detroit; WXYZ-TV (ABC) Detroit.

Programming (via satellite): ABC Family HD; AMC HD; Animal Planet HD; Arts & Entertainment HD; BBC America; Big Ten Network; Bio; Black Family Channel; Bloomberg Television; Bridges TV; CMT Pure Country; CNN HD; College Sports Television; Cooking Channel; Country Music TV; C-SPAN 2; C-SPAN 3; Current; Daystar TV Network; Discovery Channel HD; Discovery HD Theater; Discovery Health Channel; Discovery Kids Channel; Discovery Military Channel; Discovery Planet Green; Disney Channel HD; Do-It-Yourself; Encore; ESPN 2 HD; ESPN Classic Sports; ESPN HD; ESPNews; Eternal Word TV Network; Exercise TV; FearNet; Flix; Food Network HD; Fox Business Channel; Fox Movie Channel; Fox News HD; Fox Reality Channel; Fox Soccer; FSN Digital Atlantic; FSN Digital Central; FSN Digital Pacific; FSN HD; Fuse; FX HD; G4; Gol TV; Golf Channel HD; Gospel Music Channel; GSN; Hallmark Channel; HGTV HD; History Channel HD; History Channel International; ID Investigation Discovery; Independent Film Channel; INSP; Jewelry Television; Lifetime Movie Network; LOGO; MLB Network; Mojo HD; MTV Hits; MTV Jams; MTV Tres; MTV2; Music Choice; National Geographic Channel; National Geographic Channel HD Network; NBA TV; NFL Network; NFL Network HD; Nick Jr.; Nick Too; NickToons TV; Outdoor Channel; Oxygen; PBS Kids Sprout; Science Channel; Science Channel HD; ShopNBC; SoapNet; Speed HD; Starz IndiePlex; Starz RetroPlex; Sundance Channel; Syfy HD; TBS in HD; TeenNick; Telemundo; Tennis Channel; The Sportsman Channel; The Word Network; TLC HD; Toon Disney; Trinity Broadcasting Network; Turner Network TV HD; TV Guide Interactive Inc.; TV One; Universal HD; USA Network HD; Versus HD; VH1 Classic; VH1 Soul; WE tv; Weatherscan.

Fee: $16.95 monthly.

Digital Pay Service 1

Pay Units: 1,362.

Programming (via satellite): ART America; Cinemax (multiplexed); Cinemax HD; HBO (multiplexed); HBO HD; MBC America; Showtime (multiplexed); Showtime HD; Starz (multiplexed); Starz HDTV; The Movie Channel (multiplexed); TV Asia; TV Japan; Zee TV USA.

Fee: $11.05 monthly (each).

Video-On-Demand: Yes

Pay-Per-View

Addressable homes: 8,297.

iN DEMAND, Addressable: Yes; iN DEMAND (delivered digitally); ANA Television Network (delivered digitally); NBA TV (delivered digitally); Sports PPV (delivered digitally); Hot Choice (delivered digitally); Playboy TV (delivered digitally); Fresh (delivered digitally); Shorteez (delivered digitally); Pleasure (delivered digitally); TV Japan (delivered digitally).

Internet Service

Operational: Yes.

Subscribers: 3,699.

Broadband Service: Comcast High Speed Internet.

Fee: $42.95 monthly.

Telephone Service

Analog: Not Operational

Digital: Operational

Fee: $44.95 monthly

Miles of Plant: 1,773.0 (coaxial); None (fiber optic). Homes passed: 172,202.

Vice President & General Manager: Mike Cleland. Vice President, Technical Operations: Steve Thomas. Vice President, Marketing: Tony Lent. Vice President, Communications: Jerome Espy. Marketing Coordinator: Bal Bojanowski. Corporate Affairs: Marie Holmes.

City fee: 3% of gross.

Ownership: Comcast Cable Communications Inc. (MSO).

PONTIAC—Comcast Cable, 29777 Telegraph Rd, Ste 4400B, Southfield, MI 48034. Phones: 248-233-4712; 586-883-7000 (Sterling Heights office). Fax: 248-233-4719. Web Site: http://www.comcast.com. Also serves Clarkston, Groveland Twp., Independence Twp., Lake Angelus, Lake Orion, Orion Twp., Rose Twp. (Oakland County), Springfield Twp. & Waterford Twp. ICA: MI0017.

TV Market Ranking: 5 (Clarkston, Groveland Twp., Independence Twp., Lake Orion, Orion Twp., Rose Twp. (Oakland County), Springfield Twp.); 5,61 (Lake Angelus, PONTIAC, Waterford Twp.). Franchise award date: March 1, 1982. Franchise expiration date: N.A. Began: August 1, 1982.

Channel capacity: N.A. Channels available but not in use: N.A.

Basic Service

Subscribers: 49,347.

Programming (received off-air): WADL (IND) Mount Clemens; WDIV-TV (NBC) Detroit; WFUM (PBS) Flint; WJBK (FOX) Detroit; WKBD-TV (CW) Detroit; WMYD (MNT) Detroit; WPXD-TV (ION) Ann Arbor; WTVS (PBS) Detroit; WWJ-TV (CBS) Detroit; WXYZ-TV (ABC) Detroit.

Programming (via satellite): C-SPAN; C-SPAN 2; ESPN; QVC; TV Guide Network; various Canadian stations; WGN America.

Current originations: Government Access; Educational Access; Public Access.

Fee: $25.00 installation; $9.42 monthly; $2.01 converter.

Expanded Basic Service 1

Subscribers: N.A.

Programming (via satellite): ABC Family Channel; AMC; Animal Planet; Arts & Entertainment; BET Networks; Cartoon Network; CNBC; CNN; Comcast Local Detroit; Comedy Central; Discovery Channel; Discovery Health Channel; Disney Channel; E! Entertainment Television; ESPN 2; Food Network; Fox News Channel; Fox Sports Net; FX; Golf Channel; Great American Country; Headline News; HGTV; History Channel; Home Shopping Network; Lifetime; MSNBC; MTV; Nickelodeon; Speed Channel; Style Network; Syfy; TBS Superstation; The Learning Channel; Travel Channel; truTV; Turner Classic Movies; Turner Network TV; TV Land; Univision; USA Network; Versus; VH1; Weather Channel.

Fee: $41.50 monthly.

Digital Basic Service

Subscribers: 8,298.

Programming (received off-air): WDIV-TV (NBC) Detroit; WDWO-CA Detroit; WJBK (FOX) Detroit; WTVS (PBS) Detroit; WWJ-TV (CBS) Detroit; WXYZ-TV (ABC) Detroit.

Programming (via satellite): Arabic Channel; Black Family Channel; Bloomberg Television; Bridges TV; Canales N; CMT Pure Country; Cooking Channel; Country Music TV; C-SPAN 3; Current; Daystar TV Network; Discovery HD Theater; Discovery Kids Channel; Discovery Military Channel; Discovery Planet Green; Do-It-Yourself; Encore (multiplexed); ESPN 2 HD; ESPN HD; Eternal Word TV Network; Fox College Sports Atlantic; Fox College Sports Central; Fox College Sports Pacific; Fox Soccer; G4; Gol TV; Gospel Music Channel; GSN; Hallmark Channel; ID Investigation Discovery; INHD; LOGO; MBC America; MTV Networks Digital Suite; Music Choice; NBA TV; NFL Network; NickToons TV; Oxygen; Palladia; PBS Kids Sprout; RAI International; Science Channel; TeenNick; Tennis Channel; The Word Network; Trinity Broadcasting Network; Turner Network TV HD; TV Asia; TV One; Versus HD; Weatherscan; Zee TV USA.

Fee: $16.50 monthly.

Digital Pay Service 1

Pay Units: N.A.

Programming (via satellite): Cinemax; Cinemax HD; HBO HD; Showtime HD; Starz (multiplexed); Starz HDTV; The Movie Channel.

Fee: $11.41 monthly (each).

Video-On-Demand: Yes

Pay-Per-View

Addressable homes: 8,298.

iN DEMAND, Addressable: Yes; iN DEMAND (delivered digitally); Playboy TV (delivered digitally); Sports PPV (delivered digitally); Pleasure (delivered digitally); NBA TV (delivered digitally).

Internet Service

Operational: Yes.

Subscribers: 3,699.

Broadband Service: Comcast High Speed Internet.

Fee: $42.95 monthly; $7.00 modem lease; $199.00 modem purchase.

Telephone Service

Digital: Operational

Fee: $44.95 monthly

Miles of Plant: 1,267.0 (coaxial); None (fiber optic). Homes passed: 98,949.

Area Vice President: Mike Cleland. Vice President, Technical Operations: Steve Thomas.

Vice President, Marketing: Tony Lent. Vice President, Communications: Jerome Espy.
City fee: 5% of gross.
Ownership: Comcast Cable Communications Inc. (MSO).

PORT AUSTIN—Comcast Cable. Now served by PIGEON, MI [MI0375]. ICA: MI0376.

PORT HOPE—Comcast Cable. Now served by PIGEON, MI [MI0375]. ICA: MI0377.

PORTAGE TWP.—Upper Peninsula Communications, 397 N US Hwy 41, Carney, MI 49812-9757. Phone: 906-639-2194. Fax: 906-639-9936. E-mail: louied@alphacomm.net. ICA: MI0369.
TV Market Ranking: Outside TV Markets (PORTAGE TWP.). Franchise award date: N.A. Franchise expiration date: N.A. Began: June 21, 1993.
Channel capacity: 50 (not 2-way capable). Channels available but not in use: 35.
Basic Service
Subscribers: N.A.
Programming (received off-air): WDIV-TV (NBC) Detroit; WJMN-TV (CBS) Escanaba; WTVS (PBS) Detroit; WXYZ-TV (ABC) Detroit.
Programming (via satellite): ABC Family Channel; CNN; Discovery Channel; ESPN; Spike TV; TBS Superstation; Turner Network TV; WGN America.
Fee: $26.00 installation; $15.00 monthly.
Internet Service
Operational: No.
Telephone Service
None
Miles of Plant: 12.0 (coaxial); None (fiber optic). Homes passed: 300.
Manager & Chief Technician: Louis Dupont.
Ownership: Upper Peninsula Communications Inc. (MSO).

POSEN—Sunrise Communications LLC, PO Box 733, 20938 Washington Ave, Onaway, MI 49765. Phone: 989-733-8100. Fax: 989-733-8155. E-mail: info@scr-mi.com. Web Site: http://www.src-mi.com. Also serves Pulaski Twp. ICA: MI0250.
TV Market Ranking: Below 100 (POSEN, Pulaski Twp.). Franchise award date: N.A. Franchise expiration date: N.A. Began: November 1, 1985.
Channel capacity: 36 (2-way capable). Channels available but not in use: 4.
Basic Service
Subscribers: 117.
Programming (received off-air): WBKB-TV (CBS, FOX) Alpena; WCML (PBS) Alpena; WGTQ (ABC) Sault Ste. Marie; WTOM-TV (NBC) Cheboygan; WWUP-TV (CBS, FOX) Sault Ste. Marie.
Programming (via satellite): ABC Family Channel; C-SPAN; Headline News; QVC; TBS Superstation; Turner Network TV; WGN America.
Fee: $38.00 installation.
Expanded Basic Service 1
Subscribers: N.A.
Programming (via satellite): AMC; Arts & Entertainment; CNBC; CNN; Country Music TV; Discovery Channel; Disney Channel; ESPN; ESPN 2; Food Network; Fox Sports Net Detroit; Lifetime; MTV; Nickelodeon; Spike TV; The Learning Channel; USA Network; VH1; Weather Channel.
Fee: $36.95 monthly.
Pay Service 1
Pay Units: 32.
Programming (via satellite): Cinemax; HBO.
Fee: $10.95 monthly (Cinemax), $11.95 monthly (HBO).
Internet Service
Operational: No.
Telephone Service
None
Miles of Plant: 5.0 (coaxial); None (fiber optic). Homes passed: 199.
Manager: Rose Boyce.
Ownership: Sunrise Communications LLC (MSO).

POWERS—Upper Peninsula Communications, 397 N US Hwy 41, Carney, MI 49812-9757. Phone: 906-639-2194. Fax: 906-639-9936. E-mail: louied@alphacomm.net. Also serves Carney & Nadeau. ICA: MI0341.
TV Market Ranking: Below 100 (Carney, Nadeau, POWERS). Franchise award date: October 1, 1985. Franchise expiration date: N.A. Began: November 1, 1986.
Channel capacity: 36 (not 2-way capable). Channels available but not in use: 14.
Basic Service
Subscribers: 173.
Programming (received off-air): WBKB-TV (CBS, FOX) Alpena; WJFW-TV (NBC) Rhinelander; WJMN-TV (CBS) Escanaba; WKRN-TV (ABC) Nashville; WLUC-TV (NBC) Marquette; WLUK-TV (FOX) Green Bay; WNMU (PBS) Marquette.
Programming (via satellite): ABC Family Channel; Arts & Entertainment; Cartoon Network; CNN; Country Music TV; C-SPAN; Discovery Channel; Disney Channel; ESPN; ESPN 2; Eternal Word TV Network; Fox Sports Net; G4; Headline News; HGTV; History Channel; Home Shopping Network; INSP; ION Television; Lifetime; MTV; Outdoor Channel; Spike TV; TBS Superstation; Turner Classic Movies; Turner Network TV; TV Land; USA Network; Weather Channel; WGN America.
Fee: $26.00 installation; $16.35 monthly; $1.50 converter.
Pay Service 1
Pay Units: 34.
Programming (via satellite): Cinemax.
Fee: $15.00 installation; $7.50 monthly.
Internet Service
Operational: No.
Telephone Service
None
Miles of Plant: 10.0 (coaxial); None (fiber optic). Total homes in franchised area: 400.
Manager & Chief Technician: Louis Dupont.
Ownership: Upper Peninsula Communications Inc. (MSO).

PRESCOTT (village)—Formerly served by Charter Communications. No longer in operation. ICA: MI0342.

REDFORD—Bright House Networks. Now served by LIVONIA, MI [MI0019]. ICA: MI0034.

REED CITY—Charter Communications, 315 Davis St, Grand Haven, MI 49417-1830. Phone: 616-647-6201. Fax: 616-846-0797. Web Site: http://www.charter.com. Also serves Hersey & Richmond Twp. (Osceola County). ICA: MI0165.
TV Market Ranking: Below 100 (Hersey, REED CITY, Richmond Twp. (Osceola County)). Franchise award date: June 4, 1979. Franchise expiration date: N.A. Began: April 1, 1980.
Channel capacity: 61 (2-way capable). Channels available but not in use: 27.
Basic Service
Subscribers: 898.
Programming (received off-air): WCMU-TV (PBS) Mount Pleasant; WFQX-TV (FOX) Cadillac; WPBN-TV (NBC) Traverse City; WWTV (CBS) Cadillac; WZZM (ABC) Grand Rapids.
Programming (via satellite): ABC Family Channel; C-SPAN; QVC; TBS Superstation; USA Network; WGN America.
Current originations: Government Access; Educational Access; Public Access.
Fee: $38.00 installation; $19.80 monthly; $12.65 additional installation.
Expanded Basic Service 1
Subscribers: N.A.
Programming (via satellite): AMC; Arts & Entertainment; CNBC; CNN; Country Music TV; Discovery Channel; Disney Channel; ESPN; ESPN 2; Food Network; Fox Sports Net Detroit; HGTV; Lifetime; MSNBC; MTV; Nickelodeon; Spike TV; The Learning Channel; Turner Classic Movies; Turner Network TV; Weather Channel.
Pay Service 1
Pay Units: 231.
Programming (via satellite): Cinemax; HBO; Starz.
Fee: $5.95 monthly (Starz), $10.95 monthly (Cinemax), $11.95 monthly (HBO).
Internet Service
Operational: Yes.
Fee: $19.99 monthly.
Telephone Service
Digital: Operational
Fee: $14.99 monthly
Miles of Plant: 31.0 (coaxial); None (fiber optic). Homes passed: 1,580. Total homes in franchised area: 2,500.
Vice President & General Manager: Dan Spoelman. Technical Operations Manager: Keith Schierbeek. Marketing Director: Steve Schuh.
City fee: 5% of gross (not to exceed $300 annually).
Ownership: Charter Communications Inc. (MSO).

REESE—Charter Communications. Now served by SAGINAW, MI [MI0013]. ICA: MI0429.

REMUS—Charter Communications, 2304 S Mission, Mount Pleasant, MI 48858. Phone: 989-775-6846. Fax: 989-772-0350. Web Site: http://www.charter.com. Also serves Wheatland Twp. (Mecosta County). ICA: MI0344.
TV Market Ranking: Outside TV Markets (REMUS, Wheatland Twp. (Mecosta County)). Franchise award date: N.A. Franchise expiration date: N.A. Began: N.A.
Channel capacity: 36 (not 2-way capable). Channels available but not in use: 13.
Basic Service
Subscribers: N.A.
Programming (received off-air): WCMU-TV (PBS) Mount Pleasant; WJRT-TV (ABC) Flint; WNEM-TV (CBS, MNT) Bay City; WPBN-TV (NBC) Traverse City; WWTV (CBS) Cadillac; WXMI (FOX) Grand Rapids; WZZM (ABC) Grand Rapids.
Programming (via satellite): ABC Family Channel; CNN; Country Music TV; Discovery Channel; ESPN; Headline News; TBS Superstation; Turner Network TV; WGN America.
Fee: $30.00 installation; $19.95 monthly.
Pay Service 1
Pay Units: 75.
Programming (via satellite): Showtime; The Movie Channel.
Fee: $20.00 installation; $7.00 monthly (each).
Internet Service
Operational: No.
Telephone Service
None
Miles of Plant: 3.0 (coaxial); None (fiber optic).
Vice President & General Manager: Dan Spoelman. Operations Manager: Ed Bucao.
Ownership: Charter Communications Inc. (MSO).

REPUBLIC TWP.—Cable America Corp., 115 Glenwood Rd, Marquette, MI 49855-9502. Phone: 906-249-1057. ICA: MI0216.
TV Market Ranking: Below 100 (REPUBLIC TWP.). Franchise award date: N.A. Franchise expiration date: N.A. Began: September 1, 1988.
Channel capacity: 36 (not 2-way capable). Channels available but not in use: 16.
Basic Service
Subscribers: 261.
Programming (received off-air): WJFW-TV (NBC) Rhinelander; WJMN-TV (CBS) Escanaba; WLUC-TV (NBC) Marquette; WNMU (PBS) Marquette; WTOM-TV (NBC) Cheboygan; WXYZ-TV (ABC) Detroit.
Programming (via satellite): ABC Family Channel; Arts & Entertainment; CNN; Discovery Channel; ESPN; Spike TV; TBS Superstation; Turner Network TV; USA Network; WDIV-TV (NBC) Detroit; WGN America.
Current originations: Educational Access.
Fee: $35.00 installation; $16.95 monthly.
Pay Service 1
Pay Units: 109.
Programming (via satellite): Showtime.
Fee: $15.00 installation; $6.95 monthly.
Video-On-Demand: No
Internet Service
Operational: No.
Telephone Service
None
Miles of Plant: 13.0 (coaxial); None (fiber optic). Homes passed: 420. Total homes in franchised area: 420.
Manager: Robert L. Grove.
Ownership: Grove Cable Co. (MSO).

RICHLAND—Comcast Cable, 3500 Patterson Ave SE, Grand Rapids, MI 49512. Phone: 616-977-2200. Fax: 616-977-2224. Web Site: http://www.comcast.com. Also serves Augusta, Barry Twp. (portions), Charleston Twp. (portions), Comstock Twp. (portions), Galesburg, Kalamazoo, Prairieville Twp. (portions), Richland Twp. & Ross Twp. ICA: MI0316.
TV Market Ranking: 37 (Augusta, Barry Twp. (portions), Charleston Twp. (portions), Comstock Twp. (portions), Galesburg, Kalamazoo, Oshtemo, Prairieville Twp. (portions), RICHLAND, Richland Twp., Ross Twp.). Franchise award date: N.A. Franchise expiration date: N.A. Began: November 1, 1983.
Channel capacity: N.A. Channels available but not in use: N.A.
Basic Service
Subscribers: 2,590.
Programming (received off-air): WGVU-TV (PBS) Grand Rapids; WLLA (IND) Kalamazoo; WNDU-TV (NBC) South Bend; WOBC-CA Battle Creek; WOOD-TV (NBC) Grand Rapids; WOTV (ABC) Battle Creek; WTLJ

(IND) Muskegon; WWMT (CBS, CW) Kalamazoo; WXMI (FOX) Grand Rapids; WZPX-TV (ION) Battle Creek.
Programming (via satellite): Home Shopping Network; QVC; TBS Superstation; The Comcast Network.
Current originations: Government Access; Educational Access; Public Access.

Expanded Basic Service 1
Subscribers: N.A.
Programming (via satellite): ABC Family Channel; AMC; Animal Planet; Arts & Entertainment; Cartoon Network; CNBC; CNN; Comedy Central; Country Music TV; C-SPAN; C-SPAN 2; Discovery Channel; Disney Channel; E! Entertainment Television; ESPN; ESPN 2; Eternal Word TV Network; FitTV; Food Network; Fox News Channel; Fox Sports Net Detroit; FX; Headline News; HGTV; History Channel; Lifetime; MSNBC; MTV; Nickelodeon; Product Information Network; Spike TV; Syfy; The Learning Channel; Travel Channel; Turner Classic Movies; Turner Network TV; TV Land; USA Network; Versus; VH1; Weather Channel; WGN America.
Fee: $10.00 installation; $48.99 monthly.

Digital Basic Service
Subscribers: N.A.
Programming (via satellite): BBC America; Bio; Bravo; Discovery Digital Networks; DMX Music; ESPN Classic Sports; ESPNews; GAS; Golf Channel; GSN; History Channel; History Channel International; Independent Film Channel; MTV2; National Geographic Channel; NFL Network; Nick Jr.; Style Network; Toon Disney; VH1 Classic; VH1 Country; WE tv.
Fee: $9.95 monthly.

Digital Expanded Basic Service
Subscribers: N.A.
Programming (via satellite): Fox Soccer; Fuse; Lifetime Movie Network; NBA TV; Speed Channel.

Digital Pay Service 1
Pay Units: N.A.
Programming (via satellite): Cinemax (multiplexed); Encore (multiplexed); HBO (multiplexed); Showtime (multiplexed); Starz (multiplexed); The Movie Channel (multiplexed).
Fee: $18.05 monthly (each).

Video-On-Demand: No

Pay-Per-View
iN DEMAND (delivered digitally); Playboy TV (delivered digitally).

Internet Service
Operational: Yes.
Broadband Service: Comcast High Speed Internet.
Fee: $42.95 monthly.

Telephone Service
Digital: Operational

Miles of Plant: 84.0 (coaxial); None (fiber optic). Additional miles planned: 12.0 (coaxial). Total homes in franchised area: 3,693.
Area Vice President: Larry Williamson. Technical Operations Director: Tom Rice. Sales & Marketing Director: Rick Finch. Business Operations Director: Amy Carey.
Ownership: Comcast Cable Communications Inc. (MSO).

RICHLAND TWP.—Comcast Cable. Now served by RICHLAND (formerly Kalamazoo), MI [MI0316]. ICA: MI0439.

RIVERDALE—Charter Communications, 2304 S Mission, Mount Pleasant, MI 48858. Phone: 989-775-6846. Fax: 989-772-0350. Web Site: http://www.charter.com. Also serves Home Twp., Richland Twp. (Montcalm County), Seville Twp. & Sumner Twp. ICA: MI0175.
TV Market Ranking: Outside TV Markets (EAST RIVERDALE, Home Twp., Richland Twp. (Montcalm County), Seville Twp., Sumner Twp.). Franchise award date: N.A. Franchise expiration date: N.A. Began: N.A.
Channel capacity: 36 (not 2-way capable). Channels available but not in use: N.A.

Basic Service
Subscribers: 635.
Programming (received off-air): WCMU-TV (PBS) Mount Pleasant; WEYI-TV (CW, NBC) Saginaw; WJRT-TV (ABC) Flint; WNEM-TV (CBS, MNT) Bay City; WOOD-TV (NBC) Grand Rapids; WSMH (FOX) Flint; WWTV (CBS) Cadillac; WZPX-TV (ION) Battle Creek; WZZM (ABC) Grand Rapids.
Programming (via satellite): ABC Family Channel; Country Music TV; C-SPAN; QVC; TBS Superstation; WGN America.
Fee: $36.00 installation; $25.45 monthly.

Expanded Basic Service 1
Subscribers: N.A.
Programming (via satellite): AMC; Arts & Entertainment; CNBC; CNN; Comedy Central; Discovery Channel; Disney Channel; ESPN; ESPN 2; Food Network; Fox Sports Net Detroit; Headline News; History Channel; Lifetime; MTV; Nickelodeon; Spike TV; Turner Network TV; USA Network; VH1; Weather Channel.

Pay Service 1
Pay Units: 248.
Programming (via satellite): Cinemax; HBO; Starz.
Fee: $5.98 monthly (Starz), $10.95 monthly (Cinemax), $11.95 monthly (HBO).

Internet Service
Operational: No.

Miles of Plant: 31.0 (coaxial); None (fiber optic). Homes passed: 1,243.
Vice President & General Manager: Dan Spoelman. Operations Manager: Ed Bucao.
Ownership: Charter Communications Inc. (MSO).

RIVES JUNCTION—Formerly served by Cablevision Systems Corp. No longer in operation. ICA: MI0345.

ROCKFORD—Charter Communications, 315 Davis St, Grand Haven, MI 49417-1830. Phone: 616-647-6201. Fax: 616-846-0797. Web Site: http://www.charter.com. Also serves Algoma Twp., Alpine Twp., Cannon, Cedar Springs, Courtland Twp., Kent City, Nelson Twp. (portions), Plainfield Twp. (Kent County), Solon Twp. (Kent County), Sparta, Sparta Twp. & Tyrone Twp. (Kent County). ICA: MI0058.
TV Market Ranking: 37 (Algoma Twp., Alpine Twp., Cannon, Cedar Springs, Courtland Twp., Kent City, Nelson Twp. (portions), Plainfield Twp. (Kent County), ROCKFORD, Solon Twp. (Kent County), Sparta, Sparta Twp., Tyrone Twp. (Kent County)). Franchise award date: December 15, 1980. Franchise expiration date: N.A. Began: April 1, 1981.
Channel capacity: N.A. Channels available but not in use: N.A.

Basic Service
Subscribers: 8,962.
Programming (received off-air): WGVU-TV (PBS) Grand Rapids; WOOD-TV (NBC) Grand Rapids; WOTV (ABC) Battle Creek; WTLJ (IND) Muskegon; WWMT (CBS, CW) Kalamazoo; WXMI (FOX) Grand Rapids; WXSP-CA (MNT) Grand Rapids; WZPX-TV (ION) Battle Creek; WZZM (ABC) Grand Rapids.
Programming (via satellite): C-SPAN; C-SPAN 2; Home Shopping Network; QVC; TBS Superstation; TV Guide Network; WGN America.
Current originations: Public Access.
Fee: $29.99 installation.

Expanded Basic Service 1
Subscribers: N.A.
Programming (via satellite): ABC Family Channel; AMC; Animal Planet; Arts & Entertainment; Bravo; Cartoon Network; CNBC; CNN; Comedy Central; Country Music TV; Discovery Channel; Disney Channel; E! Entertainment Television; ESPN; ESPN 2; ESPN Classic Sports; ESPNews; Eternal Word TV Network; Food Network; Fox News Channel; Fox Sports Net Detroit; FX; G4; Golf Channel; GSN; Hallmark Channel; Headline News; HGTV; History Channel; INSP; Lifetime; MSNBC; MTV; MTV2; National Geographic Channel; Nickelodeon; Oxygen; SoapNet; Speed Channel; Spike TV; Style Network; Syfy; The Learning Channel; Toon Disney; Travel Channel; Trinity Broadcasting Network; truTV; Turner Classic Movies; Turner Network TV; TV Land; Univision; USA Network; Versus; VH1; WE tv; Weather Channel.
Fee: $47.99 monthly.

Digital Basic Service
Subscribers: N.A.
Programming (received off-air): WOOD-TV (NBC) Grand Rapids; WXMI (FOX) Grand Rapids; WZZM (ABC) Grand Rapids.
Programming (via satellite): BBC America; Bio; Boomerang; CNN en Espanol; Discovery Digital Networks; Discovery HD Theater; Do-It-Yourself; Fox College Sports Atlantic; Fox College Sports Central; Fox College Sports Pacific; Fox Movie Channel; Fox Soccer; Fuel TV; GAS; Great American Country; HDNet; HDNet Movies; History Channel International; Independent Film Channel; Lifetime Movie Network; MTV Networks Digital Suite; Music Choice; NFL Network; Nick Jr.; Nick Too; NickToons TV; Outdoor Channel; Science Television; Sundance Channel.

Digital Pay Service 1
Pay Units: N.A.
Programming (via satellite): Cinemax (multiplexed); Encore (multiplexed); HBO (multiplexed); Starz (multiplexed).

Video-On-Demand: Yes

Pay-Per-View
Playboy TV (delivered digitally); Spice Live (delivered digitally); Fresh (delivered digitally).

Internet Service
Operational: Yes.
Broadband Service: Charter Pipeline.
Fee: $29.99 monthly.

Telephone Service
Digital: Operational
Fee: $29.99 monthly

Miles of Plant: 200.0 (coaxial); None (fiber optic). Homes passed: 13,807.
Vice President & General Manager: Dan Spoelman. Technical Operations Manager: Keith Schierbeek. Marketing Director: Steve Schuh.
Ownership: Charter Communications Inc. (MSO).

ROGERS CITY—Charter Communications, 2074 M 32 W, Alpena, MI 49707. Phone: 989-356-4503. Fax: 989-356-3761. E-mail: jboullion@chartercom.com. Web Site: http://www.charter.com. Also serves Moltke Twp. & Rogers Twp. ICA: MI0154.
TV Market Ranking: Below 100 (Moltke Twp., ROGERS CITY, Rogers Twp.). Franchise award date: N.A. Franchise expiration date: N.A. Began: April 1, 1972.
Channel capacity: 61 (2-way capable). Channels available but not in use: 23.

Basic Service
Subscribers: 1,266.
Programming (received off-air): WBKB-TV (CBS, FOX) Alpena; WCML (PBS) Alpena; WFQX-TV (FOX) Cadillac; WGTQ (ABC) Sault Ste. Marie; WTOM-TV (NBC) Cheboygan; WWUP-TV (CBS, FOX) Sault Ste. Marie.
Programming (via satellite): ABC Family Channel; C-SPAN; Headline News; QVC; TBS Superstation; Turner Network TV; WGN America.
Fee: $29.99 installation; $13.50 monthly.

Expanded Basic Service 1
Subscribers: N.A.
Programming (via satellite): AMC; Arts & Entertainment; Cartoon Network; CNBC; CNN; Country Music TV; Discovery Channel; Disney Channel; ESPN; ESPN 2; Food Network; Fox Sports Net Detroit; FX; HGTV; History Channel; Lifetime; MSNBC; MTV; Nickelodeon; Spike TV; The Learning Channel; Turner Classic Movies; USA Network; VH1; Weather Channel.
Fee: $36.49 monthly.

Pay Service 1
Pay Units: 194.
Programming (via satellite): Cinemax; HBO; Starz.
Fee: $6.95 monthly (Starz), $10.95 monthly (Cinemax), $11.95 monthly (HBO).

Internet Service
Operational: Yes.
Broadband Service: Charter Pipeline.
Fee: $29.99 monthly.

Telephone Service
None

Miles of Plant: 27.0 (coaxial); None (fiber optic). Homes passed: 1,794.
Vice President: Joe Boullion. General Manager: Ed Kavanaugh. Technical Operations Director: Rob Nowak. Marketing Manager: Brenda Auger.
Ownership: Charter Communications Inc. (MSO).

ROMULUS—Comcast Cable. Now served by PLYMOUTH, MI [MI0012]. ICA: MI0047.

ROSCOMMON—Charter Communications, 2074 M 32 W, Alpena, MI 49707. Phone: 989-356-8812. Fax: 989-356-3761. E-mail: ekavanaugh@chartercom.com. Web Site: http://www.charter.com. Also serves Gerrish Twp. (portions), Higgins Twp., Roscommon (village) & South Branch Twp. ICA: MI0193.
TV Market Ranking: Outside TV Markets (Gerrish Twp. (portions), Higgins Twp., ROSCOMMON, Roscommon (village), South Branch Twp.). Franchise award date: N.A. Franchise expiration date: N.A. Began: N.A.
Channel capacity: 58 (2-way capable). Channels available but not in use: 7.

Basic Service
Subscribers: 720.
Programming (received off-air): WCMU-TV (PBS) Mount Pleasant; WFQX-TV (FOX) Cadillac; WGTU (ABC, CW) Traverse City; WPBN-TV (NBC) Traverse City; WWTV (CBS) Cadillac.
Programming (via satellite): ABC Family Channel; Eternal Word TV Network; QVC; TBS Superstation; Trinity Broadcasting Network; TV Guide Network; WGN America.

Current originations: Government Access; Educational Access; Public Access.
Fee: $38.00 installation; $20.70 monthly.

Expanded Basic Service 1
Subscribers: N.A.
Programming (via satellite): AMC; Arts & Entertainment; Cartoon Network; CNBC; CNN; Comedy Central; Country Music TV; C-SPAN; Discovery Channel; Disney Channel; E! Entertainment Television; ESPN; ESPN 2; Food Network; Fox Sports Net Detroit; FX; Headline News; HGTV; Lifetime; MSNBC; MTV; Nickelodeon; Sneak Prevue; Spike TV; Syfy; The Learning Channel; truTV; Turner Classic Movies; Turner Network TV; USA Network; VH1; Weather Channel.

Pay Service 1
Pay Units: 238.
Programming (via satellite): Cinemax (multiplexed); Encore; HBO (multiplexed); Showtime; Starz.
Fee: $2.00 installation; $4.95 monthly (Encore), $7.95 monthly (Starz & Encore), $10.95 monthly (Cinemax), $11.95 monthly (HBO),.

Pay-Per-View
Addressable homes: 255.
Spice, Addressable: Yes.

Internet Service
Operational: Yes.
Fee: $19.99 monthly.

Telephone Service
Digital: Operational
Fee: $14.99 monthly

Miles of Plant: 46.0 (coaxial); 9.0 (fiber optic). Homes passed: 1,521.
Ownership: Charter Communications Inc. (MSO).

ROSE CITY—Charter Communications, 2074 M 32 W, Alpena, MI 49707. Phone: 989-356-4503. Fax: 989-356-3761. Web Site: http://www.charter.com. Also serves Cumming Twp., Goodar Twp., Hill Twp., Lupton & Rose Twp. (Ogemaw County). ICA: MI0127.
TV Market Ranking: Outside TV Markets (Cumming Twp., Goodar Twp., Hill Twp., Lupton, ROSE CITY, Rose Twp. (Ogemaw County)). Franchise award date: November 1, 1987. Franchise expiration date: N.A. Began: December 15, 1981.
Channel capacity: 61 (not 2-way capable). Channels available but not in use: N.A.

Basic Service
Subscribers: 979.
Programming (received off-air): WBKB-TV (CBS, FOX) Alpena; WCML (PBS) Alpena; WEYI-TV (CW, NBC) Saginaw; WFQX-TV (FOX) Cadillac; WJRT-TV (ABC) Flint; WNEM-TV (CBS, MNT) Bay City; WWTV (CBS) Cadillac.
Programming (via satellite): ABC Family Channel; Animal Planet; Arts & Entertainment; CNN; Comedy Central; Country Music TV; Discovery Channel; Disney Channel; ESPN; Fox News Channel; Headline News; Lifetime; Nickelodeon; QVC; Spike TV; Syfy; TBS Superstation; Turner Classic Movies; Turner Network TV; USA Network; Weather Channel; WGN America.
Current originations: Government Access; Educational Access; Public Access.
Fee: $29.99 installation; $13.50 monthly; $1.25 converter.

Expanded Basic Service 1
Subscribers: N.A.
Programming (via satellite): CNN; Discovery Channel; ESPN; Headline News; Nickelodeon; Syfy; Turner Network TV; Weather Channel.
Fee: $36.49 monthly.

Pay Service 1
Pay Units: N.A.
Programming (via satellite): Cinemax.
Fee: $9.95 monthly.

Pay Service 2
Pay Units: 134.
Programming (via satellite): HBO.
Fee: $9.95 monthly.

Pay Service 3
Pay Units: 73.
Programming (via satellite): Showtime.
Fee: $9.95 monthly.

Internet Service
Operational: No.

Telephone Service
None

Miles of Plant: 73.0 (coaxial); None (fiber optic). Homes passed: 2,500.
Vice President: Joe Boullion. General Manager: Ed Kavanaugh. Technical Operations Director: Rob Nowak. Marketing Manager: Brenda Auger.
Ownership: Charter Communications Inc. (MSO).

ROSEBUSH—Charter Communications. Now served by MOUNT PLEASANT, MI [MI0069]. ICA: MI0231.

ROSEVILLE—Comcast Cable. Now served by STERLING HEIGHTS, MI [MI0002]. ICA: MI0037.

ROYAL OAK—Comcast Cable, 29777 Telegraph Rd, Ste 4400B, Southfield, MI 48034. Phones: 586 883 7000 (Sterling Heights office); 248-233 4712. Fax: 248-233-4719. Web Site: http://www.comcast.com. Also serves Auburn Hills, Berkley, Clawson, Ferndale, Huntington Woods, Oakland Twp., Pleasant Ridge, Rochester, Rochester Hills & Troy. ICA: MI0005.
TV Market Ranking: 5 (Auburn Hills, Berkley, Clawson, Ferndale, Huntington Woods, Oakland Twp., Pleasant Ridge, ROYAL OAK, Troy); 5,61 (Rochester, Rochester Hills). Franchise award date: October 23, 1982. Franchise expiration date: N.A. Began: October 29, 1983.
Channel capacity: 120 (operating 2-way). Channels available but not in use: 30.

Basic Service
Subscribers: 69,263.
Programming (received off-air): WADL (IND) Mount Clemens; WDIV-TV (NBC) Detroit; WFUM (PBS) Flint; WJBK (FOX) Detroit; WKBD-TV (CW) Detroit; WMYD (MNT) Detroit; WPXD-TV (ION) Ann Arbor; WTVS (PBS) Detroit; WXYZ-TV (ABC) Detroit.
Programming (via satellite): Catholic Television Network; CNN; C-SPAN; C-SPAN 2; ESPN; Home Shopping Network 2; QVC; Sneak Prevue; TBS Superstation; TV Guide Network; Univision; Weather Channel; WGN America.
Current originations: Leased Access; Religious Access; Government Access; Educational Access; Public Access.
Fee: $25.00 installation; $10.29 monthly.

Expanded Basic Service 1
Subscribers: 66,877.
Programming (received off-air): various Canadian stations.
Programming (via satellite): ABC Family Channel; AMC; Animal Planet; Arts & Entertainment; BET Networks; Bravo; CNBC; Comcast Local Detroit; Comedy Central; Country Music TV; Discovery Channel; Disney Channel; E! Entertainment Television; ESPN 2; ESPN Classic Sports; Food Network; Fox News Channel; Fox Sports Net; FX; Golf Channel; Headline News; HGTV; History Channel; Lifetime; MSNBC; MTV; Nickelodeon; Speed Channel; Spike TV; Style Network; Syfy; The Learning Channel; Travel Channel; Trinity Broadcasting Network; truTV; Turner Classic Movies; Turner Network TV; TV Land; USA Network; Versus; VH1.
Fee: $40.99 monthly.

Digital Basic Service
Subscribers: 17,247.
Programming (via satellite): BBC America; Bio; C-SPAN 3; Discovery Digital Networks; DMX Music; Encore Action; ESPNews; Flix; Fox Sports World; G4; GAS; GSN; Independent Film Channel; MTV Networks Digital Suite; National Geographic Channel; Nick Jr.; Nick Too; Outdoor Channel; ShopNBC; SoapNet; Sundance Channel; Toon Disney; WE tv; Weatherscan.
Fee: $14.95 monthly.

Pay Service 1
Pay Units: 12,361.
Programming (via satellite): Cinemax; HBO (multiplexed); Showtime (multiplexed); The Movie Channel.
Fee: $9.95 monthly (each).

Digital Pay Service 1
Pay Units: N.A.
Programming (via satellite): Cinemax (multiplexed); HBO (multiplexed); Showtime (multiplexed); Starz (multiplexed); The Movie Channel (multiplexed).
Fee: $9.95 monthly (each).

Video-On-Demand: Yes

Pay-Per-View
Addressable homes: 17,247.
iN DEMAND, Fee: $2.99-$5.95, Addressable: Yes; iN DEMAND (delivered digitally); ESPN Now (delivered digitally); ESPN Extra (delivered digitally); NBA TV (delivered digitally); Hot Choice (delivered digitally); Playboy TV (delivered digitally); Fresh (delivered digitally); Shorteez (delivered digitally); Pleasure (delivered digitally); TV Asia (delivered digitally); Zee TV USA (delivered digitally).

Internet Service
Operational: Yes.
Subscribers: 7,689.
Broadband Service: Comcast High Speed Internet.
Fee: $49.95 installation; $42.95 monthly; $10.00 modem lease.

Telephone Service
Digital: Operational
Fee: $44.95 monthly

Miles of Plant: 1,693.0 (coaxial); 10.0 (fiber optic). Homes passed: 125,245.
Area Vice President: Mike Cleland. Vice President, Technical Operations: Steve Thomas. Vice President, Marketing: Tony Lent. Vice President, Communications: Jerome Espy.
City fee: 5% of gross.
Ownership: Comcast Cable Communications Inc. (MSO).

RUTLAND TWP.—Charter Communications, 315 Davis St, Grand Haven, MI 49417-1830. Phone: 616-647-6201. Fax: 616-846-0797. Web Site: http://www.charter.com. ICA: MI0220.
TV Market Ranking: 37 (RUTLAND TWP.). Franchise award date: N.A. Franchise expiration date: N.A. Began: November 1, 1983.
Channel capacity: 36 (not 2-way capable). Channels available but not in use: N.A.

Basic Service
Subscribers: 297.
Programming (received off-air): WGVU-TV (PBS) Grand Rapids; WILX-TV (NBC) Onondaga; WLLA (IND) Kalamazoo; WLNS-TV (CBS) Lansing; WOOD-TV (NBC) Grand Rapids; WOTV (ABC) Battle Creek; WTLJ (IND) Muskegon; WWMT (CBS, CW) Kalamazoo; WXMI (FOX) Grand Rapids; WZPX-TV (ION) Battle Creek; WZZM (ABC) Grand Rapids.
Programming (via satellite): QVC; TBS Superstation; WGN America.
Fee: $36.00 installation; $25.45 monthly; $10.00 additional installation.

Expanded Basic Service 1
Subscribers: N.A.
Programming (via satellite): ABC Family Channel; AMC; Arts & Entertainment; CNBC; CNN; Country Music TV; C-SPAN; Discovery Channel; Disney Channel; ESPN; ESPN 2; Food Network; Fox Sports Net Detroit; Headline News; Lifetime; Nickelodeon; Spike TV; The Learning Channel; Turner Network TV; USA Network; Weather Channel.

Pay Service 1
Pay Units: 117.
Programming (via satellite): Cinemax; HBO; Starz.
Fee: $10.00 installation; $5.95 monthly (Starz), $10.95 monthly (Cinemax), $11.95 monthly (HBO).

Internet Service
Operational: No.

Miles of Plant: 16.0 (coaxial); None (fiber optic). Homes passed: 589.
Vice President & General Manager: Dan Spoelman. Technical Operations Manager: Keith Schierbeek. Marketing Director: Steve Schuh.
Ownership: Charter Communications Inc. (MSO).

SAGE TWP.—Charter Communications, 2304 S Mission, Mount Pleasant, MI 48858. Phone: 989-775-6846. Fax: 989-772-0350. Web Site: http://www.charter.com. Also serves Grout Twp. & Hamilton Twp. (Clare County). ICA: MI0133.
TV Market Ranking: Below 100 (Hamilton Twp. (Clare County)); Outside TV Markets (Grout Twp., SAGE TWP.). Franchise award date: January 22, 1988. Franchise expiration date: N.A. Began: December 1, 1988.
Channel capacity: 54 (not 2-way capable). Channels available but not in use: 11.

Basic Service
Subscribers: 1,185.
Programming (received off-air): WAQP (IND) Saginaw; WCMU-TV (PBS) Mount Pleasant; WEYI-TV (CW, NBC) Saginaw; WFQX-TV (FOX) Cadillac; WJRT-TV (ABC) Flint; WNEM-TV (CBS, MNT) Bay City; WSMH (FOX) Flint; WWTV (CBS) Cadillac.
Programming (via satellite): Home Shopping Network.
Fee: $38.77 installation; $8.42 monthly; $1.00 converter.

Expanded Basic Service 1
Subscribers: 1,029.
Programming (via satellite): ABC Family Channel; Arts & Entertainment; CNN; Country Music TV; C-SPAN; Discovery Channel; Disney Channel; ESPN; Fox News Channel; Fox Sports Net Detroit; Headline News; HGTV; History Channel; Lifetime; MTV; Nickelodeon; Spike TV; Syfy; TBS Superstation; The Learning Channel; truTV; Turner Network TV; USA Network; Weather Channel; WGN America.
Fee: $14.89 monthly.

Pay Service 1
Pay Units: 172.
Programming (via satellite): Cinemax.
Fee: $9.95 monthly.

Pay Service 2
Pay Units: 180.
Programming (via satellite): HBO.
Fee: $9.95 monthly.
Video-On-Demand: No
Internet Service
Operational: No.
Telephone Service
None
Miles of Plant: 71.0 (coaxial); None (fiber optic). Homes passed: 2,438. Total homes in franchised area: 3,750.
Vice President & General Manager: Dan Spoelman. Operations Manager: Ed Bucao.
Township fee: 3% of gross.
Ownership: Charter Communications Inc. (MSO).

SAGINAW—Charter Communications, 7372 Davison Rd, Davison, MI 48423. Phone: 810-652-1400. Web Site: http://www.charter.com. Also serves Albee Twp., Birch Run, Blumfield Twp., Bridgeport (portions), Bridgeport Charter Twp., Bridgeport Twp., Buena Vista Twp., Burt, Carrollton, Denmark Twp., Frankenmuth, Freeland, Hemlock, James Twp., Jonesfield Twp., Kochville Twp. (portions), Maple Grove Twp., Merrill, Reese, Richland Twp., Saginaw Twp., Spaulding Twp., St. Charles (village), St. Charles Twp., Swan Creek Twp., Taymouth Twp., Thomas Twp., Tittabawassee Twp. & Zilwaukee. ICA: MI0013.
TV Market Ranking: 61 (Albee Twp., Birch Run, Blumfield Twp., Bridgeport (portions), Bridgeport Charter Twp., Bridgeport Twp., Buena Vista Twp., Burt, Carrollton, Denmark Twp., Frankenmuth, Freeland, Hemlock, James Twp., Jonesfield Twp., Kochville Twp. (portions), Maple Grove Twp., Merrill, Reese, Richland Twp., SAGINAW, Saginaw Twp., Spaulding Twp., St. Charles (village), St. Charles Twp., Swan Creek Twp., Taymouth Twp., Thomas Twp., Tittabawassee Twp., Zilwaukee). Franchise award date: January 1, 1971. Franchise expiration date: N.A. Began: May 1, 1973.
Channel capacity: 68 (operating 2-way). Channels available but not in use: None.
Basic Service
Subscribers: 55,949.
Programming (received off-air): WAQP (IND) Saginaw; WBSF (CW) Bay City; WDCQ-TV (PBS) Bad Axe; WEYI-TV (CW, NBC) Saginaw; WFUM (PBS) Flint; WJRT-TV (ABC) Flint; WKAR-TV (PBS) East Lansing; WNEM-TV (CBS, MNT) Bay City; WSMH (FOX) Flint.
Programming (via satellite): C-SPAN; C-SPAN 2; Eternal Word TV Network; G4; Home Shopping Network; INSP; Michigan Government Television; MyNetworkTV Inc.; QVC; TBS Superstation; TV Guide Network; Univision; WGN America.
Current originations: Leased Access; Government Access; Educational Access; Public Access.
Fee: $29.99 installation; $13.50 monthly.
Expanded Basic Service 1
Subscribers: 45,914.
Programming (via satellite): ABC Family Channel; AMC; Animal Planet; Arts & Entertainment; BET Networks; Bravo; Cartoon Network; CNBC; CNN; Comedy Central; Country Music TV; Discovery Channel; Disney Channel; E! Entertainment Television; ESPN; ESPN 2; Food Network; Fox News Channel; Fox Sports Net Detroit; FX; Golf Channel; GSN; Hallmark Channel; Headline News; HGTV; History Channel; Lifetime; MSNBC; MTV; MTV2; National Geographic Channel; Nickelodeon; Outdoor Channel; Oxygen; SoapNet; Speed Channel; Spike TV; Style Network; Syfy; Telemundo; The Learning Channel; Toon Disney; Travel Channel; truTV; Turner Classic Movies; Turner Network TV; TV Land; USA Network; Versus; VH1; WE tv; Weather Channel.
Fee: $36.49 monthly.
Digital Basic Service
Subscribers: N.A.
Programming (received off-air): WDCQ-TV (PBS) Bad Axe; WEYI-TV (CW, NBC) Saginaw; WJRT-TV (ABC) Flint; WNEM-TV (CBS, MNT) Bay City; WSMH (FOX) Flint.
Programming (via satellite): BBC America; Bio; CMT Pure Country; Discovery Digital Networks; Discovery HD Theater; Do-It-Yourself; Do-It-Yourself On Demand; ESPN Classic Sports; ESPN HD; ESPNews; Food Network On Demand; Fox College Sports Atlantic; Fox College Sports Central; Fox College Sports Pacific; Fox Movie Channel; Fox Soccer; Fuel TV; Fuse; GAS; Great American Country; HDNet; HDNet Movies; HGTV On Demand; History Channel International; Howard TV; Independent Film Channel; Lifetime Movie Network; MTV Networks Digital Suite; Music Choice; Nick Jr.; Nick Too; NickToons TV; Sundance Channel; Turner Network TV HD; TV Guide SPOT; Universal HD.
Digital Pay Service 1
Pay Units: N.A.
Programming (via satellite): Cinemax (multiplexed); Cinemax HD; Cinemax On Demand; Encore (multiplexed); Flix; HBO (multiplexed); HBO HD; HBO On Demand; LOGO; Showtime (multiplexed); Showtime HD; Showtime On Demand; Starz (multiplexed); Starz On Demand; The Movie Channel (multiplexed).
Video-On-Demand: Yes
Pay-Per-View
iN DEMAND (delivered digitally); ESPN (delivered digitally); NHL Center Ice (delivered digitally); MLB Extra Innings (delivered digitally); Playboy TV (delivered digitally); Fresh (delivered digitally); Shorteez (delivered digitally).
Internet Service
Operational: Yes.
Broadband Service: Charter Pipeline.
Fee: $29.99 monthly.
Telephone Service
None
Miles of Plant: 1,197.0 (coaxial); 98.0 (fiber optic). Homes passed: 80,602.
Vice President & General Manager: Dave Slowick. Technical Operations Director: Lloyd Collins. Marketing Director: Lisa Gayari.
City & township fee: 5% of gross.
Ownership: Charter Communications Inc. (MSO).

SALINE—Comcast Cable. Now served by ANN ARBOR, MI [MI0006]. ICA: MI0065.

SANDUSKY—Comcast Cable, 1555 Bad Axe Rd, Bad Axe, MI 48413. Phone: 989-269-8927. Fax: 989-269-9125. Web Site: http://www.comcast.com. Also serves Watertown Twp. (Sanilac County). ICA: MI0162.
TV Market Ranking: Outside TV Markets (SANDUSKY, Watertown Twp. (Sanilac County)). Franchise award date: N.A. Franchise expiration date: N.A. Began: December 1, 1981.
Channel capacity: 44 (not 2-way capable). Channels available but not in use: None.
Basic Service
Subscribers: 893.
Programming (received off-air): WDIV-TV (NBC) Detroit; WEYI-TV (CW, NBC) Saginaw; WFUM (PBS) Flint; WJRT-TV (ABC) Flint; WKBD-TV (CW) Detroit; WNEM-TV (CBS, MNT) Bay City; WSMH (FOX) Flint; WXYZ-TV (ABC) Detroit.
Programming (via satellite): QVC; TBS Superstation; various Canadian stations; WGN America.
Current originations: Public Access.
Fee: $14.50 monthly; $2.25 converter.
Expanded Basic Service 1
Subscribers: N.A.
Programming (via satellite): ABC Family Channel; AMC; Arts & Entertainment; CNN; Discovery Channel; Discovery Health Channel; Disney Channel; ESPN; ESPN 2; Fox Sports Net Detroit; Great American Country; Headline News; HGTV; History Channel; Lifetime; MTV; Nickelodeon; Spike TV; Syfy; The Learning Channel; Trinity Broadcasting Network; truTV; Turner Network TV; USA Network; Weather Channel.
Fee: $43.49 monthly.
Pay Service 1
Pay Units: 134.
Programming (via satellite): Cinemax; HBO; Showtime.
Fee: $10.95 monthly (each).
Internet Service
Operational: No.
Telephone Service
None
Miles of Plant: 31.0 (coaxial); None (fiber optic). Homes passed: 1,187. Total homes in franchised area: 1,898.
General Manager: Thomas J. Lerash. Chief Technician: Marshall Kurschner. Business Manager: Susan McGathy.
Ownership: Comcast Cable Communications Inc. (MSO).

SANFORD—Formerly served by Charter Communications. No longer in operation. ICA: MI0088.

SAUGATUCK—Comcast Cable, 3500 Patterson Ave SE, Grand Rapids, MI 49512. Phone: 616-977-2200. Fax: 616-977-2224. Web Site: http://www.comcast.com. Also serves Clyde Twp. (Allegan County), Douglas, Fennville, Ganges Twp. & Manlius Twp. ICA: MI0110.
TV Market Ranking: 37 (Clyde Twp. (Allegan County), Fennville, Manlius Twp., SAUGATUCK); Outside TV Markets (Douglas, Ganges Twp.). Franchise award date: N.A. Franchise expiration date: N.A. Began: March 1, 1981.
Channel capacity: N.A. Channels available but not in use: N.A.
Basic Service
Subscribers: 1,800.
Programming (received off-air): WGVU-TV (PBS) Grand Rapids; WOOD-TV (NBC) Grand Rapids; WWMT (CBS, CW) Kalamazoo; WXMI (FOX) Grand Rapids; WZPX-TV (ION) Battle Creek; WZZM (ABC) Grand Rapids.
Programming (via satellite): ABC Family Channel; Arts & Entertainment; BET Networks; CNN; C-SPAN; Discovery Channel; Headline News; Home Shopping Network 2; Lifetime; MTV; Nickelodeon; QVC; TBS Superstation; Turner Network TV; Weather Channel; WGN America; WLLA (IND) Kalamazoo; WTLJ (IND) Muskegon.
Expanded Basic Service 1
Subscribers: 1,700.
Programming (via satellite): AMC; Animal Planet; Cartoon Network; Comedy Central; C-SPAN 2; Disney Channel; E! Entertainment Television; ESPN; ESPN 2; Food Network; Fox News Channel; Fox Sports Net Detroit; FX; Golf Channel; Hallmark Channel; HGTV; History Channel; MSNBC; Spike TV; Style Network; The Learning Channel; truTV; TV Guide Network; USA Network; Versus; VH1.
Fee: $48.99 monthly.
Digital Basic Service
Subscribers: N.A.
Programming (via satellite): BBC America; Bio; Bravo; Discovery Kids Channel; Discovery Military Channel; Discovery Planet Green; DMX Music; ESPN Classic Sports; ESPN Now; ESPNews; FitTV; Fox Soccer; G4; Gospel Music Channel; Great American Country; GSN; Halogen Network; History Channel International; ID Investigation Discovery; Independent Film Channel; Lime; MTV Hits; MTV2; National Geographic Channel; Nick Jr.; NickToons TV; Science Channel; ShopNBC; Sundance Channel; Syfy; TeenNick; The Word Network; Toon Disney; Trinity Broadcasting Network; Turner Classic Movies; TV Land; VH1 Classic; VH1 Soul; WAM! America's Kidz Network; WE tv.
Fee: $9.95 monthly.
Digital Pay Service 1
Pay Units: N.A.
Programming (via satellite): Cinemax (multiplexed); Encore (multiplexed); Flix; HBO (multiplexed); Showtime (multiplexed); Starz (multiplexed); The Movie Channel (multiplexed).
Fee: $18.05 monthly (each).
Video-On-Demand: No
Pay-Per-View
Sports PPV (delivered digitally); NBA League Pass (delivered digitally); NHL/MLB (delivered digitally); iN DEMAND (delivered digitally); Barker (delivered digitally); Hot Choice (delivered digitally); Fresh (delivered digitally); Playboy TV (delivered digitally).
Internet Service
Operational: Yes.
Broadband Service: Comcast High Speed Internet.
Fee: $42.95 monthly.
Telephone Service
Digital: Operational
Miles of Plant: 68.0 (coaxial); None (fiber optic). Homes passed: 3,700.
Area Vice President: Larry Williamson. Business Operations Director: Amy Carey. Technical Operations Director: Tom Rice. Sales & Marketing Director: Rick Finch.
Ownership: Comcast Cable Communications Inc. (MSO).

SAULT STE. MARIE—Charter Communications, PO Box 808, 2682 Ashmun St, Sault Sainte Marie, MI 49783. Phones: 231-947-5221 (Traverse City); 906-632-8541. Fax: 906-635-1520. E-mail: jboullion@chartercom.com. Web Site: http://www.charter.com. Also serves Bay Mills Twp., Brimley, Dafter Twp., Moran, Soo Twp., St. Ignace, St. Ignace Twp. & Superior Twp. (Chippewa County). ICA: MI0090.
TV Market Ranking: Below 100 (Bay Mills Twp., Brimley, Dafter Twp., Moran, SAULT STE. MARIE, Soo Twp., St. Ignace, St. Ignace Twp., Superior Twp. (Chippewa County)). Franchise award date: N.A.

Franchise expiration date: N.A. Began: April 1, 1961.
Channel capacity: 77 (operating 2-way). Channels available but not in use: 7.
Basic Service
Subscribers: 6,054.
Programming (received off-air): WFQX-TV (FOX) Cadillac; WGTQ (ABC) Sault Ste. Marie; WNMU (PBS) Marquette; WTOM-TV (NBC) Cheboygan; WWUP-TV (CBS, FOX) Sault Ste. Marie.
Programming (via satellite): Michigan Government Television; QVC; TV Guide Network; Weather Channel; WGN America.
Current originations: Government Access.
Fee: $29.99 installation; $13.50 monthly; $1.21 converter.
Expanded Basic Service 1
Subscribers: 5,661.
Programming (via satellite): ABC Family Channel; AMC; Animal Planet; Arts & Entertainment; Bravo; Cartoon Network; CNBC; CNN; Comedy Central; Country Music TV; C-SPAN; C-SPAN 2; Discovery Channel; Disney Channel; E! Entertainment Television; ESPN; ESPN 2; ESPN Classic Sports; Eternal Word TV Network; FitTV; Food Network; Fox News Channel; Fox Sports Net Detroit; FX; G4; Golf Channel; GSN; Hallmark Channel; Headline News; HGTV; History Channel; Home Shopping Network; INSP; ION Television; Lifetime; MSNBC; MTV; National Geographic Channel; Nickelodeon; Oxygen; SoapNet; Speed Channel; Spike TV; Style Network; Syfy; TBS Superstation; The Learning Channel; Toon Disney; Travel Channel; Trinity Broadcasting Network; truTV; Turner Classic Movies; Turner Network TV; TV Land; USA Network; Versus; VH1; WE tv; Weather Channel.
Fee: $36.49 monthly.
Digital Basic Service
Subscribers: N.A.
Programming (via satellite): BBC America; Bio; Boomerang; Discovery Digital Networks; Discovery HD Theater; Do-It-Yourself; ESPN HD; Fox College Sports Atlantic; Fox College Sports Central; Fox College Sports Pacific; Fox Movie Channel; Fox Soccer; Fuel TV; GAS; HDNet; HDNet Movies; History Channel International; Independent Film Channel; Lifetime Movie Network; MTV Networks Digital Suite; Music Choice; NFL Network; Nick Jr.; Nick Too; NickToons TV; Outdoor Channel; Sundance Channel; TV Guide Interactive Inc.
Digital Pay Service 1
Pay Units: N.A.
Programming (via satellite): Cinemax (multiplexed); Encore (multiplexed); Flix; HBO (multiplexed); Showtime (multiplexed); Starz (multiplexed); The Movie Channel (multiplexed).
Video-On-Demand: Yes
Pay-Per-View
Playboy TV (delivered digitally); Spice Live (delivered digitally); Spice Platinum (delivered digitally); Hot Net Plus (delivered digitally); Spice Hot (delivered digitally); iN DEMAND (delivered digitally); NASCAR In Car (delivered digitally); NHL Center Ice (delivered digitally); MLB Extra Innings (delivered digitally); Sports PPV (delivered digitally).
Internet Service
Operational: Yes.
Broadband Service: Charter Pipeline.
Fee: $29.99 monthly.
Telephone Service
Digital: Operational
Miles of Plant: 223.0 (coaxial); 67.0 (fiber optic). Homes passed: 9,247.
Vice President: Joe Boullion. General Manager: Rex Buettgenbach. Manager: John Badenski. Chief Technician: John Randazzo. Marketing Manager: Sandy Gottschalk.
Franchise fee: None.
Ownership: Charter Communications Inc. (MSO).

SEBEWAING—Comcast Cable. Now served by PIGEON, MI [MI0375]. ICA: MI0184.

SENEY TWP.—Cable America Corp., 115 Glenwood Rd, Marquette, MI 49855-9502. Phone: 906-249-1057. ICA: MI0253.
TV Market Ranking: Outside TV Markets (SENEY TWP.). Franchise award date: N.A. Franchise expiration date: N.A. Began: September 1, 1992.
Channel capacity: 36 (not 2-way capable). Channels available but not in use: 21.
Basic Service
Subscribers: 42.
Programming (received off-air): WJMN-TV (CBS) Escanaba; WLUC-TV (NBC) Marquette; WNMU (PBS) Marquette; WZMQ (IND, MNT) Marquette.
Programming (via satellite): ABC Family Channel; AMC; Arts & Entertainment; CNBC; CNN; C-SPAN; Discovery Channel; Disney Channel; ESPN; ESPN 2; Fox Sports Net; FX; Great American Country; Hallmark Channel; HGTV; History Channel; Lifetime; Outdoor Channel; QVC; Syfy; TBS Superstation; The Learning Channel; truTV; Turner Network TV; TV Land; USA Network; WDIV-TV (NBC) Detroit; Weather Channel; WGN America; WXYZ-TV (ABC) Detroit.
Current originations: Government Access; Educational Access; Public Access.
Fee: $35.00 installation; $16.95 monthly.
Video-On-Demand: No
Internet Service
Operational: No.
Telephone Service
None
Miles of Plant: 3.0 (coaxial); None (fiber optic). Homes passed: 96.
Manager: Robert L. Grove.
Ownership: Grove Cable Co.

SHERWOOD TWP.—Formerly served by CableDirect. No longer in operation. ICA: MI0251.

SHINGLETON—Cable America Corp., 115 Glenwood Rd, Marquette, MI 49855-9502. Phones: 800-661-4169; 906-249-1057. ICA: MI0383.
TV Market Ranking: Outside TV Markets (SHINGLETON). Franchise award date: N.A. Franchise expiration date: N.A. Began: January 1, 1992.
Channel capacity: 36 (not 2-way capable). Channels available but not in use: N.A.
Basic Service
Subscribers: 152.
Programming (received off-air): WJMN-TV (CBS) Escanaba; WLUC-TV (NBC) Marquette; WNMU (PBS) Marquette; WXYZ-TV (ABC) Detroit; WZMQ (IND, MNT) Marquette.
Programming (via satellite): ABC Family Channel; AMC; Arts & Entertainment; Cartoon Network; CNBC; CNN; C-SPAN; Discovery Channel; Disney Channel; ESPN; ESPN 2; Fox News Channel; Fox Sports Net; FX; Great American Country; Hallmark Channel; HGTV; History Channel; Home Shopping Network; ION Television; Lifetime; QVC; Speed Channel; Syfy; TBS Superstation; The Learning Channel; Travel Channel; truTV; Turner Network TV; TV Land; USA Network; Weather Channel; WGN America.
Fee: $25.00 installation; $20.95 monthly.
Pay Service 1
Pay Units: N.A.
Programming (via satellite): Showtime; The Movie Channel.
Fee: $6.95 monthly.
Video-On-Demand: No
Internet Service
Operational: No.
Telephone Service
None
Miles of Plant: 2.0 (coaxial); None (fiber optic). Homes passed: 175.
Manager: Robert L. Grove.
Ownership: Grove Cable Co.

SKIDWAY LAKE—Charter Communications, 2074 M 32 W, Alpena, MI 49707. Phones: 231-947-5221 (Traverse City); 989-356-4501. Fax: 989-356-3761. Web Site: http://www.charter.com. Also serves Churchill Twp., Logan Twp. & Mills Twp. (Ogemaw County). ICA: MI0118.
TV Market Ranking: Outside TV Markets (Churchill Twp., Logan Twp., Mills Twp. (Ogemaw County), SKIDWAY LAKE). Franchise award date: N.A. Franchise expiration date: N.A. Began: N.A.
Channel capacity: N.A. Channels available but not in use: N.A.
Basic Service
Subscribers: 1,505.
Programming (received off-air): WBKB-TV (CBS, FOX) Alpena; WDCQ-TV (PBS) Bad Axe; WEYI-TV (CW, NBC) Saginaw; WJRT-TV (ABC) Flint; WNEM-TV (CBS, MNT) Bay City; WSMH (FOX) Flint.
Programming (via satellite): CB Television Michoacan; C-SPAN; C-SPAN 2; CW+; Eternal Word TV Network; Home Shopping Network; INSP; MyNetworkTV Inc.; QVC; TBS Superstation; Trinity Broadcasting Network; TV Guide Network; WGN America.
Current originations: Government Access; Educational Access; Public Access.
Fee: $29.99 installation; $13.50 monthly.
Expanded Basic Service 1
Subscribers: N.A.
Programming (via satellite): ABC Family Channel; AMC; Animal Planet; Arts & Entertainment; BET Networks; Bravo; Cartoon Network; CNBC; CNN; Comedy Central; Country Music TV; Discovery Channel; Disney Channel; E! Entertainment Television; ESPN; ESPN 2; Food Network; Fox News Channel; Fox Sports Net Detroit; FX; G4; Golf Channel; GSN; Hallmark Channel; Headline News; HGTV; History Channel; Lifetime; MSNBC; MTV; MTV2; National Geographic Channel; Nickelodeon; Outdoor Channel; Oxygen; SoapNet; Speed Channel; Spike TV; Syfy; Telemundo; The Learning Channel; Toon Disney; Travel Channel; truTV; Turner Classic Movies; Turner Network TV; TV Land; USA Network; Versus; VH1; WE tv; Weather Channel.
Fee: $36.49 monthly.
Digital Basic Service
Subscribers: N.A.
Programming (received off-air): WEYI-TV (CW, NBC) Saginaw; WJRT-TV (ABC) Flint; WNEM-TV (CBS, MNT) Bay City; WSMH (FOX) Flint.
Programming (via satellite): BBC America; Bio; CMT Pure Country; Discovery Channel HD; Discovery Digital Networks; Do-It-Yourself; ESPN Classic Sports; ESPN HD; ESPNews; FitTV; Fox College Sports Atlantic; Fox College Sports Central; Fox College Sports Pacific; Fox Movie Channel; Fox Soccer; Fox Sports Net Detroit; Fuel TV; Fuse; GAS; Great American Country; HDNet; HDNet Movies; History Channel International; Independent Film Channel; Lifetime Movie Network; Military History Channel; MTV Networks Digital Suite; Music Choice; Nick Jr.; Nick Too; NickToons TV; Sundance Channel; Turner Network TV HD; Universal HD.
Digital Pay Service 1
Pay Units: N.A.
Programming (via satellite): Cinemax (multiplexed); Cinemax HD; Encore (multiplexed); Flix; HBO (multiplexed); HBO HD; LOGO; Showtime (multiplexed); Showtime HD; Starz (multiplexed); The Movie Channel (multiplexed).
Video-On-Demand: Yes
Pay-Per-View
iN DEMAND (delivered digitally); ESPN (delivered digitally); NHL Center Ice (delivered digitally); MLB Extra Innings (delivered digitally); Playboy TV (delivered digitally); Club Jenna (delivered digitally); Fresh! (delivered digitally); Fresh (delivered digitally); Shorteez (delivered digitally).
Internet Service
Operational: Yes.
Broadband Service: Charter Pipeline.
Fee: $29.99 monthly.
Telephone Service
None
Miles of Plant: 58.0 (coaxial); None (fiber optic). Homes passed: 3,250. Total homes in franchised area: 4,000.
Vice President: Joe Boullion. Marketing Manager: Brenda Auger. General Manager: Ed Kavanaugh. Technical Operations Director: Rob Nowak.
City fee: 2% of gross.
Ownership: Charter Communications Inc. (MSO).

SOUTH HAVEN—Comcast Cable, 3500 Patterson Ave SE, Grand Rapids, MI 49512. Phone: 616-977-2200. Fax: 616-977-2224. Web Site: http://www.comcast.com. Also serves Arlington Twp., Bangor, Casco Twp. (Allegan County), Covert Twp., Geneva Twp. (Van Buren County), Glenn, Hartford, Lawrence & South Haven Twp. ICA: MI0086.
TV Market Ranking: 37 (Arlington Twp., Bangor, Casco Twp. (Allegan County), Covert Twp., Geneva Twp. (Van Buren County), Glenn, Hartford, Lawrence); Outside TV Markets (SOUTH HAVEN, South Haven Twp.). Franchise award date: N.A. Franchise expiration date: N.A. Began: August 1, 1967.
Channel capacity: 75 (operating 2-way). Channels available but not in use: 26.
Basic Service
Subscribers: 3,600.
Programming (received off-air): WGVU-TV (PBS) Grand Rapids; WLLA (IND) Kalamazoo; WOOD-TV (NBC) Grand Rapids; WOTV (ABC) Battle Creek; WTLJ (IND) Muskegon; WWMT (CBS, CW) Kalamazoo; WXMI (FOX) Grand Rapids; WZPX-TV (ION) Battle Creek; WZZM (ABC) Grand Rapids.
Programming (via satellite): C-SPAN; Home Shopping Network; QVC; Sneak Prevue; TBS Superstation; TV Guide Network; WGN America.
Current originations: Government Access; Educational Access.
Fee: $12.00 monthly.
Expanded Basic Service 1
Subscribers: 3,350.
Programming (via satellite): ABC Family Channel; AMC; Animal Planet; Arts & Enter-

tainment; BET Networks; Cartoon Network; CNN; Comedy Central; C-SPAN 2; Discovery Channel; Disney Channel; E! Entertainment Television; ESPN; ESPN 2; Food Network; Fox News Channel; Fox Sports Net Detroit; FX; Golf Channel; Hallmark Channel; Headline News; HGTV; History Channel; Lifetime; MSNBC; MTV; Nickelodeon; Outdoor Channel; Oxygen; Spike TV; Style Network; The Learning Channel; truTV; Turner Network TV; USA Network; VH1; Weather Channel.
Fee: $48.99 monthly.

Digital Basic Service
Subscribers: N.A.
Programming (via satellite): American-Life TV Network; BBC America; Bio; Black Family Channel; Bloomberg Television; Bravo; Canales N; Discovery Digital Networks; ESPN Classic Sports; ESPN Now; ESPNews; FitTV; Fox Movie Channel; Fox Sports Net; Fox Sports World; Fuse; G4; GAS; Great American Country; GSN; Halogen Network; History Channel International; Independent Film Channel; International Television (ITV); Lifetime Movie Network; Lime; MTV Networks Digital Suite; MTV2; Music Choice; National Geographic Channel; Nick Jr.; NickToons TV; Outdoor Channel; Ovation; ShopNBC; Speed Channel; Sundance Channel; Syfy; The Word Network; Toon Disney; Trinity Broadcasting Network; Turner Classic Movies; TV Land; WAM! America's Kidz Network; WE tv.
Fee: $9.95 monthly.

Digital Pay Service 1
Pay Units: N.A.
Programming (via satellite): Cinemax (multiplexed); Encore; Flix; HBO (multiplexed); Showtime (multiplexed); The Movie Channel (multiplexed).
Fee: $18.05 monthly (each).

Video-On-Demand: No

Pay-Per-View
iN DEMAND (delivered digitally); Fresh (delivered digitally); Shorteez (delivered digitally); Playboy TV (delivered digitally); Hot Choice (delivered digitally).

Internet Service
Operational: Yes.
Broadband Service: Comcast High Speed Internet.
Fee: $42.95 monthly.

Telephone Service
Digital: Operational

Miles of Plant: 108.0 (coaxial); 55.0 (fiber optic). Homes passed: 5,854. Total homes in franchised area: 9,500.
Area Vice President: Larry Williamson. Business Operations Director: Amy Carey. Technical Operations Director: Tom Rice. Sales & Marketing Director: Rick Finch.
Ownership: Comcast Cable Communications Inc. (MSO).

SOUTHFIELD—Comcast Cable, 29777 Telegraph Rd, Ste 4400B, Southfield, MI 48034. Phones: 248-233-4712; 248-233-4700; 734-254-1500 (Plymouth office). Fax: 248-233-4719. E-mail: mike_cleland@cable.comcast.com. Web Site: http://www.comcast.com. Also serves Beverly Hills, Bingham Farms, Birmingham, Bloomfield Hills, Bloomfield Twp. (Oakland County), Franklin, Lathrup Village, Oak Park & Royal Oak Twp. ICA: MI0009.
TV Market Ranking: 5 (Beverly Hills, Bingham Farms, Birmingham, Bloomfield Hills, Bloomfield Twp. (Oakland County), Franklin, Lathrup Village, Oak Park, Royal Oak Twp., SOUTHFIELD). Franchise award date: October 15, 1981. Franchise expiration date: N.A. Began: March 11, 1982.
Channel capacity: N.A. Channels available but not in use: N.A.

Basic Service
Subscribers: 33,199.
Programming (received off-air): WADL (IND) Mount Clemens; WDIV-TV (NBC) Detroit; WFUM (PBS) Flint; WJBK (FOX) Detroit; WKBD-TV (CW) Detroit; WMYD (MNT) Detroit; WPXD-TV (ION) Ann Arbor; WTVS (PBS) Detroit; WWJ-TV (CBS) Detroit; WXYZ-TV (ABC) Detroit; allband FM.
Programming (via satellite): Catholic Television Network; C-SPAN; C-SPAN 2; ESPN; Home Shopping Network; QVC; WGN America.
Current originations: Leased Access; Government Access; Educational Access; Public Access.
Fee: $25.00 installation; $13.13 monthly.

Expanded Basic Service 1
Subscribers: N.A.
Programming (via satellite): ABC Family Channel; AMC; Animal Planet; Arts & Entertainment; BET Networks; Bravo; Cartoon Network; CNBC; CNN; Comcast Local Detroit; Comedy Central; Discovery Channel; Disney Channel; E! Entertainment Television; ESPN 2; ESPN Classic Sports; Food Network; Fox News Channel; Fox Reality Channel; Fox Sports Net; FX; Golf Channel; Headline News; HGTV; History Channel; Lifetime; MSNBC; MTV; Nickelodeon; Speed Channel; Spike TV; Style Network; Syfy; TBS Superstation; The Learning Channel; Travel Channel; truTV; Turner Classic Movies; Turner Network TV; TV Guide Network; TV Land; TV One; USA Network; Versus; VH1; Weather Channel.
Fee: $42.99 monthly.

Digital Basic Service
Subscribers: 8,267.
Programming (received off-air): WDIV-TV (NBC) Detroit; WJBK (FOX) Detroit; WKBD-TV (CW) Detroit; WLPC-LP Detroit; WMYD (MNT) Detroit; WTVS (PBS) Detroit; WWJ-TV (CBS) Detroit; WXYZ-TV (ABC) Detroit.
Programming (via satellite): Arts & Entertainment HD; BBC America; Bio; Black Family Channel; Bridges TV; Cooking Channel; Country Music TV; C-SPAN 3; Current; Discovery Digital Networks; Discovery HD Theater; Do-It-Yourself; Encore (multiplexed); ESPN HD; ESPNews; Eternal Word TV Network; FearNet; Flix; Fox Movie Channel; Fox Reality Channel; Fuse; G4; GAS; Great American Country; Hallmark Channel; History Channel International; Independent Film Channel; INHD; INSP; Jewelry Television; Lifetime Movie Network; LOGO; MTV Networks Digital Suite; Music Choice; National Geographic Channel; National Geographic Channel HD Network; NBA TV; NFL Network; Nick Jr.; Nick Too; NickToons TV; Oxygen; Palladia; PBS Kids Sprout; ShopNBC; SoapNet; Sundance Channel; The Word Network; Toon Disney; Trinity Broadcasting Network; Turner Network TV HD; Universal HD; Versus HD; WAM! America's Kidz Network; WE tv; Weatherscan.
Fee: $14.95 monthly.

Digital Pay Service 1
Pay Units: N.A.
Programming (via satellite): Cinemax (multiplexed); HBO (multiplexed); Showtime (multiplexed); Starz (multiplexed); The Movie Channel (multiplexed).
Fee: $7.50 monthly (each).

Video-On-Demand: Yes

Pay-Per-View
Addressable homes: 8,267.
iN DEMAND (delivered digitally), Addressable: Yes; iN DEMAND; Playboy TV (delivered digitally); Fresh (delivered digitally); Pleasure (delivered digitally).

Internet Service
Operational: Yes.
Subscribers: 3,686.
Broadband Service: Comcast High Speed Internet.
Fee: $99.95 installation; $42.95 monthly.

Telephone Service
Digital: Operational
Fee: $44.95 monthly

Miles of Plant: 1,156.0 (coaxial); 213.0 (fiber optic). Homes passed: 82,836.
Area Vice President: Mike Cleland. Vice President, Technical Operations: Steve Thomas. Vice President, Marketing: Tony Lent. Vice President, Communications: Jerome Espy.
City fee: 5% of gross.
Ownership: Comcast Cable Communications Inc. (MSO).

SPRINGDALE TWP.—Ace Communications Group of Michigan. Formerly served by Thompsonville, MI [MI0230]. This cable system has converted to IPTV, PO Box 69, 5351 N M-37, Houston, MI 49668-0069. Phone: 800-361-8178. Fax: 231-885-9915. E-mail: miinfo@acegroup.cc. Web Site: http://www.acegroup.cc. ICA: MI5026.
TV Market Ranking: Below 100 (Springdale Twp.).
Channel capacity: N.A. Channels available but not in use: N.A.

Video-On-Demand: Yes

Internet Service
Operational: Yes.
Fee: $50.00 installation; $29.95 monthly.

Telephone Service
Digital: Operational
Fee: $21.05 monthly

Chief Executive Officer: Todd Roesler.
Ownership: Ace Communications Group.

SPRINGFIELD TWP. (Oakland County)—Comcast Cable. Now served by PONTIAC, MI [MI0017]. ICA: MI0107.

SPRINGPORT TWP.—Springport Telephone Co., PO Box 208, 400 E Main St, Springport, MI 49284. Phone: 517-857-3500. Fax: 517-857-3329. E-mail: janet@springcom.com. Web Site: http://www3.springcom.com. Also serves Brookfield Twp. (Eaton County), Clarence Twp., Parma Twp. & Springport (village). ICA: MI0350.
TV Market Ranking: 37,92 (Clarence Twp., Springport (village), SPRINGPORT TWP.); 92 (Brookfield Twp. (Eaton County), Parma Twp.). Franchise award date: N.A. Franchise expiration date: N.A. Began: August 1, 1989.
Channel capacity: 62 (operating 2-way). Channels available but not in use: None.

Basic Service
Subscribers: 850.
Programming (received off-air): WILX-TV (NBC) Onondaga; WKAR-TV (PBS) East Lansing; WLAJ (ABC, CW) Lansing; WLNS-TV (CBS) Lansing; WOOD-TV (NBC) Grand Rapids; WOTV (ABC) Battle Creek; WSYM-TV (FOX) Lansing; WWMT (CBS, CW) Kalamazoo.
Current originations: Public Access.
Fee: $35.00 installation; $13.00 monthly; $40.00 converter.

Expanded Basic Service 1
Subscribers: 800.
Programming (received off-air): WHTV (MNT) Jackson; WXMI (FOX) Grand Rapids.
Programming (via satellite): ABC Family Channel; AMC; Animal Planet; Arts & Entertainment; Cartoon Network; CNBC; CNN; C-SPAN; C-SPAN 2; Discovery Channel; Disney Channel; E! Entertainment Television; ESPN; ESPN 2; Fox News Channel; Fox Sports Net; FX; G4; Golf Channel; Great American Country; HGTV; History Channel; INSP; Lifetime; MTV; Nickelodeon; Outdoor Channel; QVC; Speed Channel; Spike TV; Syfy; TBS Superstation; The Learning Channel; Toon Disney; Travel Channel; Turner Classic Movies; Turner Network TV; TV Land; USA Network; VH1; Weather Channel; WGN America.
Fee: $24.00 monthly.

Pay Service 1
Pay Units: N.A.
Programming (via satellite): Cinemax; Encore; HBO; Showtime.
Fee: $2.00 monthly (Encore), $9.50 monthly (Cinemax), $9.00 monthly (Showtime), $11.70 monthly (HBO).

Video-On-Demand: No

Internet Service
Operational: Yes. Began: December 31, 1999.
Subscribers: 400.
Broadband Service: In-house.
Fee: $60.00 installation; $39.95 monthly.

Telephone Service
None

Miles of Plant: 50.0 (coaxial); None (fiber optic).
General Manager: Janet Beilfuss. Chief Technician: Jerry Riske.
Ownership: Springport Telephone Co.

ST. HELEN—Charter Communications, 2074 M 32 W, Alpena, MI 49707. Phones: 231-947-5221 (Traverse City office); 231-947-5221 (Traverse City office); 989-356-4503. Fax: 989-356-3761. Web Site: http://www.charter.com. Also serves Beaverton, Buckeye Twp., Gladwin, Grout Twp. & Richfield Twp. (Roscommon County). ICA: MI0116.
TV Market Ranking: Outside TV Markets (Beaverton, Buckeye Twp., Gladwin, Grout Twp., Richfield Twp. (Roscommon County), ST. HELEN). Franchise award date: N.A. Franchise expiration date: N.A. Began: N.A.
Channel capacity: N.A. Channels available but not in use: N.A.

Basic Service
Subscribers: 4,000.
Programming (received off-air): WCMU-TV (PBS) Mount Pleasant; WDCQ-TV (PBS) Bad Axe; WEYI-TV (CW, NBC) Saginaw; WFQX-TV (FOX) Cadillac; WGTU (ABC, CW) Traverse City; WJRT-TV (ABC) Flint; WNEM-TV (CBS, MNT) Bay City; WPBN-TV (NBC) Traverse City; WSMH (FOX) Flint; WWTV (CBS) Cadillac.
Programming (via satellite): C-SPAN; C-SPAN 2; Eternal Word TV Network; G4; Home Shopping Network; INSP; QVC; TBS Superstation; Trinity Broadcasting Network; TV Guide Network; WGN America; WKBD-TV (CW) Detroit.
Current originations: Government Access; Educational Access; Public Access.
Fee: $29.99 installation; $13.50 monthly.

Expanded Basic Service 1
Subscribers: N.A.
Programming (via satellite): ABC Family Channel; AMC; Animal Planet; Arts & Entertainment; Bravo; Cartoon Network; CNBC;

CNN; Comedy Central; Country Music TV; Discovery Channel; Disney Channel; E! Entertainment Television; ESPN; ESPN Classic Sports; Food Network; Fox News Channel; Fox Sports Net Detroit; FX; Golf Channel; GSN; Hallmark Channel; Headline News; HGTV; History Channel; Lifetime; MSNBC; MTV; MTV2; National Geographic Channel; Nickelodeon; Outdoor Channel; Oxygen; SoapNet; Speed Channel; Spike TV; Syfy; Telemundo; The Learning Channel; Toon Disney; Travel Channel; truTV; Turner Classic Movies; Turner Network TV; TV Land; USA Network; Versus; VH1; WE tv; Weather Channel.
Fee: $36.49 monthly.

Digital Basic Service
Subscribers: N.A.
Programming (via satellite): BBC America; Bio; Discovery Digital Networks; DMX Music; Do-It-Yourself; ESPNews; Fox College Sports Atlantic; Fox College Sports Central; Fox College Sports Pacific; Fox Movie Channel; Fox Soccer; Fuel TV; Fuse; GAS; Great American Country; HDNet; HDNet Movies; History Channel International; Independent Film Channel; Lifetime Movie Network; MTV Networks Digital Suite; NFL Network; Nick Jr.; Nick Too; NickToons TV; Sundance Channel; TV Guide Network.

Digital Pay Service 1
Pay Units: 1,253.
Programming (via satellite): Cinemax (multiplexed); Encore (multiplexed); Flix; HBO (multiplexed); HBO HD; Showtime (multiplexed); Showtime HD; Starz (multiplexed); The Movie Channel (multiplexed).
Fee: $1.95 installation; $6.95 monthly (Starz), $10.95 monthly (Cinemax), $11.95 monthly (HBO), $12.95 monthly (Showtime).

Video-On-Demand: Yes

Pay-Per-View
iN DEMAND (delivered digitally); NASCAR In Car (delivered digitally); ESPN Sports PPV (delivered digitally); NHL Center Ice/ MLB Extra Innings (delivered digitally); Playboy TV (delivered digitally); Spice Live (delivered digitally); Spice Platinum (delivered digitally); Hot Net Plus (delivered digitally); Spice Hot (delivered digitally).

Internet Service
Operational: Yes.
Broadband Service: Charter Pipeline.
Fee: $29.99 monthly.

Telephone Service
None

Miles of Plant: 168.0 (coaxial); 123.0 (fiber optic). Homes passed: 8,238.

Vice President: Joe Boullion. General Manager: Ed Kavanaugh. Technical Operations Director: Rob Nowak. Marketing Manager: Brenda Auger.

Ownership: Charter Communications Inc. (MSO).

ST. IGNACE—Charter Communications. Now served by SAULT STE. MARIE, MI [MI0090]. ICA: MI0152.

ST. JOHNS—Charter Communications, 7372 Davison Rd, Davison, MI 48423. Phones: 989-667-0611 (Customer service); 989-799-5080 (Administrative office). Fax: 989-799-7829. Web Site: http://www.charter.com. Also serves Bingham Twp. & Fowler. ICA: MI0353.

TV Market Ranking: 92 (Bingham Twp., Fowler, ST. JOHNS). Franchise award date: N.A. Franchise expiration date: N.A. Began: January 1, 1983.

Channel capacity: 78 (operating 2-way). Channels available but not in use: 1.

Basic Service
Subscribers: 2,689.
Programming (received off-air): WAQP (IND) Saginaw; WCMU-TV (PBS) Mount Pleasant; WEYI-TV (CW, NBC) Saginaw; WFUM (PBS) Flint; WILX-TV (NBC) Onondaga; WJRT-TV (ABC) Flint; WKAR-TV (PBS) East Lansing; WKBD-TV (CW) Detroit; WLAJ (ABC, CW) Lansing; WLNS-TV (CBS) Lansing; WNEM-TV (CBS, MNT) Bay City; WOOD-TV (NBC) Grand Rapids; WSYM-TV (FOX) Lansing; WZPX-TV (ION) Battle Creek; 15 FMs.
Programming (via satellite): C-SPAN; C-SPAN 2; Eternal Word TV Network; Home Shopping Network; INSP; ION Television; QVC; TBS Superstation; TV Guide Network; WGN America.
Fee: $29.99 installation; $13.50 monthly.

Expanded Basic Service 1
Subscribers: N.A.
Programming (via satellite): ABC Family Channel; AMC; Animal Planet; Arts & Entertainment; BET Networks; Bravo; Cartoon Network; CNBC; CNN; Comedy Central; Country Music TV; Discovery Channel; Disney Channel; E! Entertainment Television; ESPN; ESPN 2; Food Network; Fox News Channel; Fox Sports Net Detroit; FX; Golf Channel; GSN; Hallmark Channel; Headline News; HGTV; History Channel; Lifetime; MSNBC; MTV; National Geographic Channel; Nickelodeon; Outdoor Channel; Oxygen; SoapNet; Speed Channel; Spike TV; Syfy; Telemundo; The Learning Channel; Toon Disney; Travel Channel; truTV; Turner Classic Movies; Turner Network TV; TV Land; USA Network; Versus; VH1; WE tv; Weather Channel.
Fee: $36.49 monthly.

Digital Basic Service
Subscribers: N.A.
Programming (via satellite): BBC America; Bio; Bloomberg Television; Discovery Digital Networks; Do-It-Yourself; Great American Country; History Channel International; Independent Film Channel; Lifetime Movie Network; MuchMusic Network; Music Choice; Style Network; Sundance Channel.
Fee: $11.45 monthly.

Digital Pay Service 1
Pay Units: N.A.
Programming (via satellite): Cinemax (multiplexed); Encore (multiplexed); Flix; HBO (multiplexed); Showtime (multiplexed); Starz (multiplexed); The Movie Channel (multiplexed).
Fee: $10.00 monthly (Cinemax, HBO, Flix/ Showtime/TMC, or Starz/Encore).

Video-On-Demand: Yes

Pay-Per-View
Hot Choice (delivered digitally), Addressable: Yes; iN DEMAND (delivered digitally); Playboy TV (delivered digitally); Fresh (delivered digitally); Shorteez (delivered digitally); sports.

Internet Service
Operational: Yes.
Broadband Service: Charter Pipeline.
Fee: $29.99 monthly.

Telephone Service
Digital: Operational
Fee: $29.99 monthly

Miles of Plant: 34.0 (coaxial); None (fiber optic).

Vice President & General Manager: Dave Slowick. Technical Operations Director: Lloyd Collins. Marketing Director: Lisa Gayari.

Ownership: Charter Communications Inc. (MSO).

ST. JOSEPH TWP.—Comcast Cable, 7720 W 98th St, Hickory HIlls, IL 60457. Phones: 574-259-2112 (Mishawaka office); 708-237-3260. Fax: 708-237-3292. Web Site: http://www.comcast.com. Also serves La Porte County (portions) & New Carlisle, IN; Bainbridge Twp., Baroda (village), Benton Harbor, Berrien Springs, Berrien Twp., Bridgman, Chikaming Twp., Lake Twp., Lincoln Twp. (Berrien County), Oronoko Twp., Royalton Twp., Shoreham, Sodus Twp., Stevensville, Three Oaks & Weesaw, MI. ICA: MI0051.

TV Market Ranking: 37 (Bainbridge Twp.); 37,80 (Berrien Springs, Berrien Twp., ST. JOSEPH TWP., Stevensville); 80 (Baroda (village), Benton Harbor, Bridgman, Chikaming Twp., La Porte County (portions), Lake Twp., Lincoln Twp. (Berrien County), New Carlisle, Oronoko Twp., Royalton Twp., Shoreham, Sodus Twp., Three Oaks, Weesaw). Franchise award date: N.A. Franchise expiration date: N.A. Began: June 1, 1981.

Channel capacity: N.A. Channels available but not in use: N.A.

Basic Service
Subscribers: 14,538.
Programming (received off-air): WBBM-TV (CBS) Chicago; WBND-LP South Bend; WCWW-LP (CW) South Bend; WHME-TV (IND) South Bend; WLS-TV (ABC) Chicago; WMAQ-TV (NBC) Chicago; WNDU-TV (NBC) South Bend; WNIT (PBS) South Bend; WPWR-TV (MNT) Gary; WSBT-TV (CBS, IND) South Bend; WSJV (FOX) Elkhart; WTTW (PBS) Chicago; WWMT (CBS, CW) Kalamazoo.
Programming (via satellite): ABC Family Channel; Discovery Channel; Home Shopping Network; QVC; TBS Superstation; TV Guide Network; WGN America.
Current originations: Government Access; Educational Access; Public Access.
Fee: $48.99 installation; $16.75 monthly.

Expanded Basic Service 1
Subscribers: 13,995.
Programming (via satellite): AMC; Animal Planet; Arts & Entertainment; BET Networks; Cartoon Network; CNBC; CNN; Comedy Central; Country Music TV; C-SPAN; C-SPAN 2; Disney Channel; E! Entertainment Television; ESPN; ESPN 2; Eternal Word TV Network; Food Network; Fox News Channel; Fox Sports Net Detroit; FX; Golf Channel; Hallmark Channel; Headline News; HGTV; History Channel; ION Television; Lifetime; Michigan Government Television; MSNBC; MTV; Nickelodeon; Spike TV; Style Network; Syfy; Telemundo; The Learning Channel; Travel Channel; truTV; Turner Network TV; TV Land; USA Network; Versus; VH1; Weather Channel.
Fee: $24.24 monthly.

Digital Basic Service
Subscribers: 2,075.
Programming (via satellite): American-Life TV Network; BBC America; Bio; Black Family Channel; Bloomberg Television; Bravo; Canales N; Cooking Channel; Discovery Digital Networks; DMX Music; Do-It-Yourself; Encore Action; ESPN; ESPN Classic Sports; ESPNews; FitTV; Fox College Sports Atlantic; Fox College Sports Central; Fox College Sports Pacific; Fox Movie Channel; Fox Soccer; Fuse; G4; GAS; Great American Country; GSN; Halogen Network; History Channel International; Independent Film Channel; INHD (multiplexed); Jewelry Television; Lifetime Movie Network; Lime; MTV Networks Digital Suite; Music Choice; National Geographic Channel; NFL Network; Nick Jr.; Nick Too; NickToons TV; Outdoor Channel; Ovation; ShopNBC; Speed Channel; Sundance Channel; Syfy; The Word Network; Toon Disney; Trinity Broadcasting Network; Turner Classic Movies; TV Land; WE tv; WNIT (PBS) South Bend; WSBT-TV (CBS, IND) South Bend.
Fee: $11.99 monthly.

Digital Pay Service 1
Pay Units: 1,011.
Programming (via satellite): Cinemax (multiplexed); HBO; Showtime; Starz.
Fee: $12.15 installation; $11.00 monthly.

Digital Pay Service 2
Pay Units: 920.
Programming (via satellite): HBO (multiplexed).
Fee: $12.15 installation; $11.00 monthly.

Digital Pay Service 3
Pay Units: 800.
Programming (via satellite): Showtime (multiplexed).
Fee: $12.15 installation; $11.00 monthly.

Digital Pay Service 4
Pay Units: 3,700.
Programming (via satellite): Flix; The Movie Channel (multiplexed).
Fee: $12.15 installation; $11.00 monthly.

Digital Pay Service 5
Pay Units: 1,200.
Programming (via satellite): Starz (multiplexed).
Fee: $12.15 installation; $4.75 monthly.

Video-On-Demand: Yes

Pay-Per-View
Addressable homes: 2,075.
iN DEMAND (delivered digitally), Addressable: Yes; Sports PPV (delivered digitally); NHL Center Ice (delivered digitally); NBA TV (delivered digitally); MLB Extra Innings (delivered digitally); Fresh (delivered digitally); Shorteez (delivered digitally); Playboy TV (delivered digitally); Hot Choice (delivered digitally); ESPN Sports PPV (delivered digitally).

Internet Service
Operational: Yes.
Broadband Service: Comcast High Speed Internet.
Fee: $42.95 monthly.

Telephone Service
None

Miles of Plant: 537.0 (coaxial); 40.0 (fiber optic). Homes passed: 21,900. Total homes in franchised area: 28,658.

Area Vice President: Sandy Weicher. Vice President, Technical Operations: Bob Curtis. Vice President, Sales & Marketing: Eric Schaefer. Vice President, Communications: Rich Ruggiero. Technical Operations Manager: John Collucci. Marketing Director: Ron Knutson.

Ownership: Comcast Cable Communications Inc. (MSO).

STANDISH—Charter Communications. Now served by BAY CITY, MI [MI0018]. ICA: MI0146.

STANTON—Charter Communications. Now served by IONIA, MI [MI0091]. ICA: MI0112.

STEPHENSON—Howard Cable, PO Box 127, 111 Pine St, Peshtigo, WI 54157. Phones: 800-472-0576; 715-582-1141. Fax: 715-582-1142. E-mail: cableone@new.rr.com. Also serves Daggett. ICA: MI0227.

TV Market Ranking: Below 100 (Daggett, STEPHENSON). Franchise award date: N.A. Franchise expiration date: N.A. Began: February 1, 1985.

Channel capacity: 30 (not 2-way capable). Channels available but not in use: N.A.

Basic Service
Subscribers: 200.
Programming (received off-air): WACY-TV (MNT) Appleton; WBAY-TV (ABC, IND) Green Bay; WFRV-TV (CBS) Green Bay; WGBA-TV (NBC) Green Bay; WIWB (CW) Suring; WLUK-TV (FOX) Green Bay; WNMU (PBS) Marquette; WPNE-TV (PBS) Green Bay.
Fee: $10.00 installation; $9.95 monthly.
Expanded Basic Service 1
Subscribers: N.A.
Programming (via satellite): ABC Family Channel; Eternal Word TV Network; HGTV; Lifetime; Nickelodeon; Spike TV; Turner Network TV; USA Network.
Fee: $10.00 monthly.
Expanded Basic Service 2
Subscribers: N.A.
Programming (via satellite): AMC; Animal Planet; Arts & Entertainment; Bloomberg Television; Bravo; Classic Arts Showcase; CNN; Comedy Central; Country Music TV; Discovery Channel; Disney Channel; Do-It-Yourself; E! Entertainment Television; ESPN; ESPN 2; Food Network; Fox Movie Channel; Fox News Channel; FX; Great American Country; Hallmark Channel; Headline News; History Channel; Home Shopping Network; MTV; National Geographic Channel; Outdoor Channel; QVC; Syfy; TBS Superstation; The Learning Channel; Toon Disney; Travel Channel; Trinity Broadcasting Network; truTV; Turner Classic Movies; TV Land; VH1; WGN America.
Fee: $10.00 monthly.
Pay Service 1
Pay Units: 6.
Programming (via satellite): HBO.
Fee: $5.00 installation; $10.95 monthly.
Video-On-Demand: No
Internet Service
Operational: No.
Telephone Service
None
Miles of Plant: 6.0 (coaxial); None (fiber optic). Homes passed: 320.
Manager & Chief Technician: Howard C. Lock.
City fee: None.
Ownership: Howard Lock.

STEPHENSON—Packerland Broadband, PO Box 885, 105 Kent St, Iron Mountain, MI 49801. Phones: 906-774-6621; 800-236-8434. Fax: 906-776-2811. E-mail: inquiries@plbb.us. Web Site: http://www.packerlandbroadband.com. Also serves Wallace. ICA: MI0433. **Note:** This system is an overbuild.
TV Market Ranking: Below 100 (STEPHENSON); Outside TV Markets (Wallace). Franchise award date: N.A. Franchise expiration date: N.A. Began: N.A.
Channel capacity: N.A. Channels available but not in use: N.A.
Basic Service
Subscribers: 84.
Programming (received off-air): WBAY-TV (ABC, IND) Green Bay; WFRV-TV (CBS) Green Bay; WGBA-TV (NBC) Green Bay; WLUC-TV (NBC) Marquette; WLUK-TV (FOX) Green Bay; WNMU (PBS) Marquette.
Programming (via satellite): ABC Family Channel; CNN; CW+; Discovery Channel; TBS Superstation; Turner Network TV; WGN America.
Fee: $13.50 monthly.
Expanded Basic Service 1
Subscribers: N.A.
Programming (via satellite): Arts & Entertainment; CNBC; C-SPAN; Disney Channel; ESPN; ESPN 2; Eternal Word TV Network; Fox Sports Net Detroit; HGTV; History Channel; Home Shopping Network; ION Television; Lifetime; Nickelodeon; Outdoor Channel; Spike TV; Syfy; The Learning Channel; Trinity Broadcasting Network; Turner Classic Movies; USA Network; Weather Channel.
Pay Service 1
Pay Units: N.A.
Programming (via satellite): Cinemax; HBO.
Internet Service
Operational: Yes.
Fee: $26.95 monthly.
Telephone Service
None
General Manager: Dan Plante. Technical Supervisor: Chad Kay.
Ownership: Cable Constructors Inc. (MSO).

STERLING—Pine River Cable, PO Box 96, McBain, MI 49657. Phone: 888-244-2288. Fax: 231-825-0191. E-mail: info@pinerivercable.com. Web Site: http://www.pinerivercable.com. Also serves Sterling Village. ICA: MI0244.
TV Market Ranking: 61 (STERLING, Sterling Village). Franchise award date: July 10, 1984. Franchise expiration date: N.A. Began: December 1, 1986.
Channel capacity: 35 (not 2-way capable). Channels available but not in use: 13.
Basic Service
Subscribers: 110.
Programming (received off-air): WEYI-TV (CW, NBC) Saginaw; WJRT-TV (ABC) Flint; WNEM-TV (CBS, MNT) Bay City; WWTV (CBS) Cadillac.
Programming (via satellite): ABC Family Channel; ESPN; Lifetime; Nickelodeon; QVC; Spike TV; Syfy; Travel Channel.
Fee: $50.00 installation; $17.64 monthly; $15.00 additional installation.
Expanded Basic Service 1
Subscribers: N.A.
Programming (via satellite): CNN; Headline News; USA Network.
Fee: $2.60 monthly.
Expanded Basic Service 2
Subscribers: 109.
Programming (via satellite): Discovery Channel; TBS Superstation; Turner Network TV; WGN America.
Fee: $4.95 monthly.
Pay Service 1
Pay Units: 29.
Programming (via satellite): HBO.
Fee: $11.95 monthly.
Pay Service 2
Pay Units: 22.
Programming (via satellite): Showtime.
Fee: $10.95 monthly.
Internet Service
Operational: No.
Telephone Service
None
Miles of Plant: 5.0 (coaxial); None (fiber optic). Homes passed: 233.
Manager: John Metzler.
Ownership: Pine River Cable (MSO).

STERLING HEIGHTS—Comcast Cable, 29777 Telegraph Rd, Ste 4400B, Southfield, MI 48034. Phones: 248-233-4712; 586-883-7000 (Macomb office). Fax: 248-233-4719. Web Site: http://www.comcast.com. Also serves Center Line, Clinton Twp., Eastpointe, Fraser, Grosse Pointe, Grosse Pointe Farms, Grosse Pointe Park, Grosse Pointe Shores, Grosse Pointe Woods, Harper Woods, Hazel Park, Macomb Twp., Madison Heights, Mount Clemens, Ray Twp., Roseville, Shelby Twp., St. Clair Shores, Utica & Warren. ICA: MI0002.
TV Market Ranking: 5 (Center Line, Clinton Twp., Eastpointe, Fraser, Grosse Point Shores, Grosse Pointe, Grosse Pointe Farms, Grosse Pointe Park, Grosse Pointe Woods, Harper Woods, Hazel Park, Macomb Twp., Madison Heights, Mount Clemens, Ray Twp., Roseville, Shelby Twp., St. Clair Shores, STERLING HEIGHTS, Utica, Warren). Franchise award date: N.A. Franchise expiration date: N.A. Began: December 1, 1982.
Channel capacity: N.A. Channels available but not in use: N.A.
Basic Service
Subscribers: 295,622.
Programming (received off-air): WADL (IND) Mount Clemens; WDIV-TV (NBC) Detroit; WJBK (FOX) Detroit; WKBD-TV (CW) Detroit; WMYD (MNT) Detroit; WPXD-TV (ION) Ann Arbor; WTVS (PBS) Detroit; WWJ-TV (CBS) Detroit; WXYZ-TV (ABC) Detroit; 12 FMs.
Programming (via satellite): ABC Family Channel; AMC; Animal Planet; Arts & Entertainment; BET Networks; Big Ten Network; Bravo; Cartoon Network; CNBC; CNN; Comedy Central; C-SPAN; Discovery Channel; Discovery Health Channel; Disney Channel; E! Entertainment Television; ESPN; ESPN 2; Food Network; Fox News Channel; Fox Sports Net Detroit; FX; Golf Channel; Great American Country; Headline News; HGTV; History Channel; Home Shopping Network; Lifetime; MSNBC; MTV; Nickelodeon; QVC; Speed Channel; Spike TV; Style Network; Syfy; TBS Superstation; The Learning Channel; Travel Channel; truTV; Turner Classic Movies; Turner Network TV; TV Guide Network; TV Land; USA Network; various Canadian stations; Versus; VH1; Weather Channel; WGN America.
Current originations: Leased Access; Government Access; Educational Access; Public Access.
Fee: $25.00 installation; $36.99 monthly.
Digital Basic Service
Subscribers: 66,381.
Programming (received off-air): WDIV-TV (NBC) Detroit; WJBK (FOX) Detroit; WKBD-TV (CW) Detroit; WMYD (MNT) Detroit; WTVS (PBS) Detroit; WWJ-TV (CBS) Detroit; WXYZ-TV (ABC) Detroit.
Programming (via satellite): ABC Family HD; AMC HD; Arts & Entertainment HD; BBC America; Big Ten Network; Big Ten Network HD; Bio; Bloomberg Television; Canal 52MX; Cine Latino; Cine Mexicano; CMT Pure Country; CNN en Espanol; CNN HD; College Sports Television; Cooking Channel; Country Music TV; C-SPAN 2; C-SPAN 3; Current; Daystar TV Network; Discovery en Espanol; Discovery HD Theater; Discovery Kids Channel; Discovery Military Channel; Discovery Planet Green; Disney Channel HD; Disney XD en Espanol; Do-It-Yourself; Encore (multiplexed); ESPN 2 HD; ESPN Classic Sports; ESPN Deportes; ESPN HD; ESPNews; Eternal Word TV Network; Flix; Food Network HD; Fox Business Channel; Fox College Sports Atlantic; Fox College Sports Central; Fox College Sports Pacific; Fox Reality Channel; Fox Soccer; Fox Sports en Espanol; FSN HD; Fuse; G4; Gol TV; Golf Channel HD; Gospel Music Channel; GSN; Hallmark Channel; HGTV HD; History Channel en Espanol; History Channel HD; History Channel International; ID Investigation Discovery; INSP; Jewelry Television; Lifetime Movie Network; LOGO; Mojo HD; MoviePlex; MTV Hits; MTV Jams; MTV Tres; MTV2; Music Choice; National Geographic Channel; National Geographic Channel HD Network; NBA TV; NFL Network; NFL Network HD; NHL Network; Nick Jr.; Nick Too; NickToons TV; Outdoor Channel; Oxygen; PBS Kids Sprout; Science Channel; Science Channel HD; ShopNBC; SoapNet; Starz IndiePlex; Starz RetroPlex; Sundance Channel; TBS in HD; TeenNick; Telemundo; Tennis Channel; The Sportsman Channel; The Word Network; Toon Disney; Trinity Broadcasting Network; Turner Network TV HD; TV One; Universal HD; USA Network HD; VeneMovies; Versus HD; VH1 Classic; VH1 Soul; WE tv; Weatherscan.
Fee: $14.95 monthly.
Digital Pay Service 1
Pay Units: N.A.
Programming (via satellite): ART America; Bridges TV; Cinemax (multiplexed); Cinemax HD; HBO (multiplexed); HBO HD; RAI International; Showtime (multiplexed); Showtime HD; Starz (multiplexed); Starz HDTV; The Movie Channel (multiplexed); TV Asia; TV Japan; Zee TV USA.
Fee: $11.95 monthly (each).
Video-On-Demand: Yes
Pay-Per-View
Addressable homes: 66,381.
iN DEMAND; ESPN Extra (delivered digitally); ESPN Now (delivered digitally); NBA League Pass (delivered digitally); Playboy TV (delivered digitally); MLS Direct Kick (delivered digitally); NHL Center Ice (delivered digitally); Spice: Xcess (delivered digitally); MLS Direct Kick (delivered digitally).
Internet Service
Operational: Yes.
Subscribers: 29,592.
Broadband Service: Comcast High Speed Internet.
Fee: $149.00 installation; $42.94 monthly; $7.00 modem lease.
Telephone Service
Digital: Operational
Fee: $44.95 monthly
Miles of Plant: 6,109.0 (coaxial); 35.0 (fiber optic). Homes passed: 643,126.
Area Vice President: Mike Casillo. Vice President, Technical Operations: Steve Thomas. Vice President, Marketing: Tony Lent. Vice President, Communications: Jerome Espy. Marketing Coordinator: Kenyatta Scott.
Ownership: Comcast Cable Communications Inc. (MSO).

TAYLOR—Comcast Cable, 29777 Telegraph Rd, Ste 4400B, Southfield, MI 48034. Phones: 734-254-1500 (Plymouth office); 248-233-4712. Fax: 248-233-4719. E-mail: mike_cleland@cable.comcast.com.

Web Site: http://www.comcast.com. Also serves Allen Park, Augusta Twp., Berlin Twp. (Monroe County), Brownstown Twp., Dundee (village), Ecorse, Exeter Twp., Flat Rock, Frenchtown Twp., Garden City, Gibraltar, Grosse Ile, Inkster, Lincoln Park, London Twp., Melvindale, Monroe, Monroe Twp., Raisinville Twp., River Rouge, Riverview, Rockwood, South Rockwood, Southgate, Sumpter Twp., Trenton, Woodhaven & York Twp. ICA: MI0008.

TV Market Ranking: 5 (Allen Park, Augusta Twp., Berlin Twp. (Monroe County), Brownstown Twp., Dundee (village), Ecorse, Exeter Twp., Flat Rock, Frenchtown Twp., Garden City, Gibraltar, Grosse Ile, Inkster, Lincoln Park, London Twp., Melvindale, Monroe, Monroe Twp., Raisinville Twp., River Rouge, Riverview, Rockwood, South Rockwood, Southgate, Sumpter Twp., TAYLOR, Trenton, Woodhaven, York Twp.). Franchise award date: N.A. Franchise expiration date: N.A. Began: October 1, 1980.

Channel capacity: N.A. Channels available but not in use: N.A.

Basic Service

Subscribers: 69,393.

Programming (received off-air): WADL (IND) Mount Clemens; WDIV-TV (NBC) Detroit; WGTE-TV (PBS) Toledo; WJBK (FOX) Detroit; WKBD-TV (CW) Detroit; WMYD (MNT) Detroit; WTVS (PBS) Detroit; WWJ-TV (CBS) Detroit; WXYZ-TV (ABC) Detroit.

Programming (via satellite): C-SPAN; C-SPAN 2; ESPN; GSN; ION Television; Michigan Government Television; QVC; TBS Superstation; TV Guide Network; WGN America.

Current originations: Leased Access; Government Access; Educational Access; Public Access.

Fee: $25.00 installation; $10.89 monthly; $1.99 converter; $15.00 additional installation.

Expanded Basic Service 1

Subscribers: 69,000.

Programming (via satellite): ABC Family Channel; AMC; Animal Planet; Arts & Entertainment; BET Networks; Bravo; Catholic Television Network; CNBC; CNN; Comcast Local Detroit; Comedy Central; Country Music TV; Discovery Channel; E! Entertainment Television; ESPN 2; ESPN Classic Sports; Eternal Word TV Network; Food Network; Fox News Channel; Fox Sports Net Detroit; FX; GAS; Golf Channel; Great American Country; Headline News; HGTV; History Channel; Home Shopping Network; Lifetime; MSNBC; MTV; Nick Jr.; Nickelodeon; Speed Channel; Spike TV; Style Network; Syfy; The Learning Channel; Trinity Broadcasting Network; truTV; Turner Classic Movies; Turner Network TV; TV Land; Univision; USA Network; Versus; VH1; Weather Channel.

Fee: $26.10 monthly.

Digital Basic Service

Subscribers: 17,279.

Programming (via satellite): BBC America; C-SPAN 3; Discovery Digital Networks; Disney Channel; DMX Music; Encore Action; ESPNews; Flix; G4; MTV Networks Digital Suite; National Geographic Channel; Nick Too; ShopNBC; SoapNet; Sundance Channel; The Word Network; Toon Disney; Weatherscan.

Fee: $14.95 monthly.

Digital Pay Service 1

Pay Units: N.A.

Programming (via satellite): Cinemax (multiplexed); HBO (multiplexed); Showtime (multiplexed); Starz (multiplexed); The Movie Channel (multiplexed).

Fee: $9.50 monthly (each).

Video-On-Demand: Yes

Pay-Per-View

Addressable homes: 47,512.

iN DEMAND, Fee: $3.95, Addressable: Yes; iN DEMAND (delivered digitally); NBA TV (delivered digitally); Hot Choice (delivered digitally); TVN Entertainment (delivered digitally); Playboy TV (delivered digitally); Fresh (delivered digitally); Shorteez (delivered digitally); Pleasure (delivered digitally); ESPN Now (delivered digitally); ESPN Extra (delivered digitally).

Internet Service

Operational: Yes.

Subscribers: 7,703.

Broadband Service: Comcast High Speed Internet.

Fee: $149.99 installation; $42.94 monthly; $7.00 modem lease; $199.00 modem purchase.

Telephone Service

Digital: Operational

Fee: $44.95 monthly

Miles of Plant: 1,887.0 (coaxial); 856.0 (fiber optic). Homes passed: 165,330.

Area Vice President: Mike Cleland. Vice President, Technical Operations: Steve Thomas. Vice President, Marketing: Tony Lent. Vice President, Communications: Jerome Espy.

City fee: 5% of gross.

Ownership: Comcast Cable Communications Inc. (MSO).

THETFORD TWP.—Charter Communications, 7372 Davison Rd, Davison, MI 48423. Phone: 810-652-1400. Web Site: http://www.charter.com. Also serves Arbela Twp., Genesee County (portions) & Vienna Twp. (portions). ICA: MI0378.

TV Market Ranking: 61 (Arbela Twp., Genesee County (portions), THETFORD TWP., Vienna Twp. (portions)). Franchise award date: N.A. Franchise expiration date: N.A. Began: May 1, 1982.

Channel capacity: N.A. Channels available but not in use: N.A.

Basic Service

Subscribers: 1,774.

Programming (received off-air): WAQP (IND) Saginaw; WBSF (CW) Bay City; WDIV-TV (NBC) Detroit; WEYI-TV (CW, NBC) Saginaw; WFUM (PBS) Flint; WJRT-TV (ABC) Flint; WKAR-TV (PBS) East Lansing; WNEM-TV (CBS, MNT) Bay City; WSMH (FOX) Flint; WTVS (PBS) Detroit; WXYZ-TV (ABC) Detroit.

Programming (via satellite): Home Shopping Network; ION Television; MyNetworkTV Inc.; QVC; WGN America.

Current originations: Government Access; Educational Access; Public Access.

Fee: $29.99 installation; $13.50 monthly.

Expanded Basic Service 1

Subscribers: 1,669.

Programming (via satellite): ABC Family Channel; AMC; Animal Planet; Arts & Entertainment; Bravo; Cartoon Network; CNBC; CNN; Comedy Central; Country Music TV; C-SPAN; Discovery Channel; Disney Channel; E! Entertainment Television; ESPN; ESPN 2; Food Network; Fox News Channel; Fox Sports Net Detroit; FX; G4; Golf Channel; GSN; Hallmark Channel; Headline News; HGTV; History Channel; Lifetime; MSNBC; MTV; MTV2; National Geographic Channel; Nickelodeon; Oxygen; SoapNet; Speed Channel; Spike TV; Syfy; TBS Superstation; The Learning Channel; Toon Disney; Travel Channel; truTV; Turner Classic Movies; Turner Network TV; TV Guide Network; TV Land; USA Network; Versus; VH1; Weather Channel.

Fee: $39.95 installation; $36.49 monthly.

Digital Basic Service

Subscribers: N.A.

Programming (received off-air): WEYI-TV (CW, NBC) Saginaw; WFUM (PBS) Flint; WJRT-TV (ABC) Flint; WNEM-TV (CBS, MNT) Bay City; WSMH (FOX) Flint.

Programming (via satellite): BBC America; Bio; CMT Pure Country; Discovery Digital Networks; Do-It-Yourself; ESPN 2 HD; ESPN Classic Sports; ESPN HD; ESPN U; ESPNews; FitTV; Fox Business Channel; Fox College Sports Atlantic; Fox College Sports Central; Fox College Sports Pacific; Fox Movie Channel; Fox Soccer; Fox Sports Net Detroit; Fuel TV; Fuse; GAS; Great American Country; HDNet; HDNet Movies; History Channel International; Independent Film Channel; Lifetime Movie Network; Military History Channel; MTV Networks Digital Suite; Music Choice; Nick Jr.; Nick Too; NickToons TV; Outdoor Channel; ReelzChannel; Sundance Channel; The Sportsman Channel; Turner Network TV HD; Universal HD; WE tv.

Digital Pay Service 1

Pay Units: N.A.

Programming (via satellite): Cinemax (multiplexed); Cinemax HD; Encore (multiplexed); Flix; HBO (multiplexed); HBO HD; LOGO; Showtime (multiplexed); Showtime HD; Starz (multiplexed); Starz HDTV; The Movie Channel (multiplexed).

Video-On-Demand: Yes

Pay-Per-View

iN DEMAND (delivered digitally); ESPN (delivered digitally); NHL Center Ice (delivered digitally); MLB Extra Innings (delivered digitally); Playboy TV (delivered digitally); Club Jenna (delivered digitally); Fresh! (delivered digitally); Fresh (delivered digitally); Shorteez (delivered digitally).

Internet Service

Operational: Yes.

Broadband Service: Charter Pipeline.

Fee: $29.99 monthly.

Telephone Service

Digital: Operational

Fee: $29.99 monthly

Miles of Plant: 72.0 (coaxial); None (fiber optic). Homes passed: 3,236. Total homes in franchised area: 9,402.

Vice President & General Manager: Dave Slowick. Technical Operations Director: Lloyd Collins. Marketing Director: Lisa Gayari.

Ownership: Charter Communications Inc. (MSO).

THOMAS TWP.—Charter Communications. Now served by SAGINAW, MI [MI0013]. ICA: MI0072.

THOMPSONVILLE—Ace Communications Group of Michigan. Formerly [MI0230]. This cable system has converted to IPTV, PO Box 69, 5351 N M-37, Houston, MI 49668-0069. Phone: 800-361-8178. Fax: 231-885-9915. E-mail: miinfo@acegroup.cc. Web Site: http://www.acegroup.cc. ICA: MI5027.

TV Market Ranking: Below 100 (THOMPSONVILLE). Franchise award date: N.A. Franchise expiration date: N.A. Began: N.A.

Channel capacity: N.A. Channels available but not in use: N.A.

Video-On-Demand: Yes

Internet Service

Operational: Yes, Both DSL & dial-up.

Telephone Service

Digital: Operational

Fee: $21.05 monthly

Chief Executive Officer: Todd Roesler.

Ownership: Ace Communications Group (MSO).

THOMPSONVILLE—Ace Communications Group. This cable system has converted to IPTV. See Thompsonville, MI [MI5027], MI. ICA: MI0230.

THREE OAKS—Comcast Cable. Now served by ST. JOSEPH TWP., MI [MI0051]. ICA: MI0078.

THREE RIVERS—Comcast Cable, 3500 Patterson Ave SE, Grand Rapids, MI 49512. Phone: 616-977-2200. Fax: 616-977-2224. Web Site: http://www.comcast.com. Also serves Elkhart & Lagrange County, IN; Brady Twp. (Kalamazoo County), Centreville, Constantine, Edwardsburg, Fabius Twp., Flowerfield Twp., Jones, Lockport Twp., Mendon Twp., Mottville Twp., Newberg Twp., Nottawa Twp. (St. Joseph County), Pavilion Twp., Portage (southern portion), Porter Twp., Prairie Ronde, Prairie Ronde Twp., Schoolcraft, Vicksburg, Washington & White Pigeon, MI. ICA: MI0050.

TV Market Ranking: 27 (Prairie Ronde Twp.); 37 (Brady Twp. (Kalamazoo County), Jones, Newberg Twp., Pavilion Twp., Portage (southern portion), Porter Twp., Prairie Ronde, Vicksburg); 37,80 (Centreville, Constantine, Fabius Twp., Flowerfield Twp., Lockport Twp., Mendon Twp., Mottville Twp., Nottawa Twp. (St. Joseph County), Schoolcraft, THREE RIVERS, White Pigeon); 80 (Edwardsburg, Elkhart, Lagrange County, Washington). Franchise award date: N.A. Franchise expiration date: N.A. Began: March 31, 1972.

Channel capacity: N.A. Channels available but not in use: N.A.

Basic Service

Subscribers: 1,631.

Programming (received off-air): WGN-TV (CW, IND) Chicago; WGVK (PBS) Kalamazoo; WHME-TV (IND) South Bend; WNDU-TV (NBC) South Bend; WNIT (PBS) South Bend; WOOD-TV (NBC) Grand Rapids; WOTV (ABC) Battle Creek; WSBT-TV (CBS, IND) South Bend; WSJV (FOX) Elkhart; WWMT (CBS, CW) Kalamazoo; WXMI (FOX) Grand Rapids; WZPX-TV (ION) Battle Creek; allband FM.

Programming (via satellite): Great American Country; Home Shopping Network; QVC; TBS Superstation; WLLA (IND) Kalamazoo.

Current originations: Public Access.

Fee: $45.00 installation; $14.23 monthly; $2.24 converter.

Expanded Basic Service 1

Subscribers: N.A.

Programming (via satellite): ABC Family Channel; AMC; Arts & Entertainment; BET Networks; CNBC; CNN; C-SPAN; C-SPAN 2; Discovery Channel; Disney Channel; ESPN; ESPN 2; Fox Sports Net Detroit; Hallmark Channel; Headline News; History Channel; Lifetime; MSNBC; MTV; Nickelodeon; Spike TV; Syfy; The Learning Channel; Travel Channel; Turner Network TV; USA Network; VH1; Weather Channel.

Fee: $48.99 monthly.

Digital Basic Service

Subscribers: N.A.

Programming (via satellite): BBC America; Bravo!; Discovery Digital Networks; DMX Music; ESPN Classic Sports; ESPNews; Fox Sports Net Arizona; Golf Channel; GSN; HGTV; Independent Film Channel; Nick Jr.;

Turner Classic Movies; TV Land; Versus; WE tv.
Fee: $9.95 monthly.

Digital Pay Service 1
Pay Units: N.A.
Programming (via satellite): Cinemax (multiplexed); HBO (multiplexed); Showtime (multiplexed); Starz (multiplexed); The Movie Channel (multiplexed).
Fee: $18.05 monthly (each).

Video-On-Demand: No

Pay-Per-View
Playboy TV (delivered digitally); iN DEMAND (delivered digitally).

Internet Service
Operational: Yes.
Broadband Service: Comcast High Speed Internet.
Fee: $42.95 monthly.

Telephone Service
Analog: Not Operational
Digital: Operational

Miles of Plant: 811.0 (coaxial); 26.0 (fiber optic). Additional miles planned: 5.0 (coaxial); 38.0 (fiber optic). Homes passed: 26,000.

Area Vice President: Larry Williamson. Technical Operations Director: Tom Rice. Sales & Marketing Director: Rick Finch. Business Operations Director: Amy Carey.

Ownership: Comcast Cable Communications Inc. (MSO).

TRAVERSE CITY—Charter Communications, 701 E South Airport Rd, Traverse City, MI 49686-4861. Phones: 800-545-0994; 231-947-5221. Fax: 231-947-2004. E-mail: jboullion@chartercom.com. Web Site: http://www.charter.com. Also serves Acadia Twp., Acme Twp., Alba, Almira Twp., Bagley Twp., Bay Shore, Bay Twp., Bay View, Bear Creek Twp., Bear Lake, Bellaire (village), Benzie County (portions), Benzonia, Beulah, Bingham Twp. (Leelanau County), Blair Twp., Blue Lake Twp., Boyne City, Boyne Falls, Boyne Valley Twp., Buckley, Caldwell Twp., Cedar Creek Twp., Centerville Twp., Central Lake, Charlevoix, Charlevoix Twp., Chester Twp., Chestonia Twp., Clearwater Twp., Cleveland Twp., Cold Springs Twp., Conway, Corwith Twp., Crystal Lake, East Bay Twp., East Jordan, East Lake, Elberta, Elk Rapids, Elk Rapids (town), Elk Rapids (village), Elk Rapids Twp., Elmira Twp., Elmwood Twp. (Leelanau County), Empire, Empire Twp., Evangeline Twp., Eveline Twp., Excelsior Twp., Fife Lake, Fife Lake Twp., Filer Twp., Forest Home Twp., Forest Twp., Frankfort, Garfield Twp. (Grand Traverse County), Gaylord, Gilmore Twp. (Benzie County), Glen Arbor Twp., Grant Twp. (Grand Traverse County), Green Lake Twp., Hanover Twp., Harbor Springs, Hayes Twp., Helena Twp., Homestead Twp., Honor, Inland Twp., Joyfield Twp., Kalkaska, Kasson Twp., Kearney Twp., Kingsley, Lake Ann, Lake Ann (village), Lake City, Lake Twp., Lake Twp. (Benzie County), Leelanau Twp., Leland Twp., Liberty Twp., Littlefield Twp., Livingston Twp., Long Lake Twp., Mancelona, Mancelona Twp., Manistee, Manistee Twp., Manton, Marion Twp., Mayfield, Mayfield Twp. (Grand Traverse County), Melrose Twp., Milton Twp. (Antrim County), Missaukee County (portions), Northport, Norwood, Oden, Onekama (village), Paradise Twp., Peninsula Twp., Petoskey, Pleasant View Twp., Pleasanton Twp., Rapid River Twp., Reeder Twp., Resort Twp., Solon Twp. (Leelanau County), South Arm Twp., Springfield Twp., Springvale Twp., Star Twp., Stronach Twp., Suttons Bay, Suttons Bay Twp., The Homestead, Torch Lake Twp. (Antrim County), Vanderbilt, West Traverse Twp., Whitewater Twp. & Wilson Twp. ICA: MI0026.

TV Market Ranking: Below 100 (Acme Twp., Alba, Almira Twp., Bagley Twp., Bay Shore, Bay Twp., Bay View, Bear Creek Twp., Bellaire (village), Benzie County (portions), Benzonia, Beulah, Bingham Twp. (Leelanau County), Blair Twp., Blue Lake Twp., Boyne City, Boyne Falls, Boyne Valley Twp., Buckley, Caldwell Twp., Cedar Creek Twp., Centerville Twp., Central Lake, Charlevoix, Charlevoix Twp., Chester Twp., Chestonia Twp., Clearwater Twp., Cleveland Twp., Cold Springs Twp., Conway, Corwith Twp., Crystal Lake, East Bay Twp., East Jordan, Elberta, Elk Rapids, Elk Rapids (town), Elk Rapids (village), Elk Rapids Twp., Elmira Twp., Elmwood Twp. (Leelanau County), Empire, Empire Twp., Evangeline Twp., Eveline Twp., Excelsior Twp., Fife Lake, Fife Lake Twp., Forest Home Twp., Forest Twp., Frankfort, Garfield Twp. (Grand Traverse County), Gaylord, Gilmore Twp. (Benzie County), Glen Arbor Twp., Grant Twp. (Grand Traverse County), Green Lake Twp., Hanover Twp., Harbor Springs, Hayes Twp., Helena Twp., Homestead Twp., Honor, Inland Twp., Joyfield Twp., Kalkaska, Kasson Twp., Kearney Twp., Kingsley, Lake Ann, Lake City, Lake Twp., Lake Twp. (Benzie County), Leelanau Twp., Leland Twp., Liberty Twp., Little Traverse Twp., Littlefield Twp., Livingston Twp., Long Lake Twp., Mancelona, Mancelona Twp., Manton, Marion Twp., Mayfield, Mayfield Twp. (Grand Traverse County), Melrose Twp., Milton Twp. (Antrim County), Missaukee County (portions), Northport, Norwood, Oden, Paradise Twp., Peninsula Twp., Petoskey, Pleasant View Twp., Pleasanton Twp., Rapid River Twp., Reeder Twp., Resort Twp., Solon Twp. (Leelanau County), South Arm Twp., Springfield Twp., Springvale Twp., Star Twp., Suttons Bay, Suttons Bay Twp., The Homestead, Torch Lake Twp. (Antrim County), TRAVERSE CITY, Vanderbilt, West Traverse Twp., Whitewater Twp., Wilson Twp.); Outside TV Markets (Acadia Twp., Bear Lake, East Lake, Filer Twp., Manistee, Manistee Twp., Onekama (village), Stronach Twp.). Franchise award date: January 1, 1965. Franchise expiration date: N.A. Began: January 1, 1966.

Channel capacity: 54 (operating 2-way). Channels available but not in use: N.A.

Basic Service
Subscribers: 65,926.
Programming (received off-air): WCMV (PBS) Cadillac; WFQX-TV (FOX) Cadillac; WGTU (ABC, CW) Traverse City; WPBN-TV (NBC) Traverse City; WWTV (CBS) Cadillac.
Programming (via satellite): C-SPAN; Headline News; Michigan Government Television; QVC; TBS Superstation; TV Guide Network; WGN America.
Current originations: Government Access; Educational Access; Public Access.
Fee: $38.00 installation; $9.11 monthly; $12.65 additional installation.

Expanded Basic Service 1
Subscribers: 17,901.
Programming (via satellite): ABC Family Channel; AMC; Animal Planet; Arts & Entertainment; Bravo!; Cartoon Network; CNBC; CNN; Comedy Central; Country Music TV; C-SPAN; C-SPAN 2; Discovery Channel; Disney Channel; E! Entertainment Television; ESPN; ESPN 2; ESPN Classic Sports; Eternal Word TV Network; Food Network; Fox News Channel; Fox Sports Net Detroit; FX; G4; Golf Channel; GSN; Hallmark Channel; HGTV; History Channel; Home Shopping Network; INSP; ION Television; Lifetime; MSNBC; MTV; National Geographic Channel; Nickelodeon; Oxygen; SoapNet; Speed Channel; Spike TV; Syfy; The Learning Channel; Toon Disney; Travel Channel; Trinity Broadcasting Network; truTV; Turner Classic Movies; Turner Network TV; TV Land; USA Network; Versus; VH1; WE tv; Weather Channel.
Fee: $12.24 monthly.

Digital Basic Service
Subscribers: N.A.
Programming (via satellite): BBC America; Bio; Boomerang; Discovery Digital Networks; Discovery HD Theater; Do-It-Yourself; ESPN HD; Fox College Sports Atlantic; Fox College Sports Central; Fox College Sports Pacific; Fox Movie Channel; Fox Soccer; Fuel TV; GAS; HDNet; HDNet Movies; History Channel International; Independent Film Channel; Lifetime Movie Network; MTV Networks Digital Suite; Music Choice; NFL Network; Nick Jr.; Nick Too; NickToons TV; Outdoor Channel; Sundance Channel.

Digital Pay Service 1
Pay Units: N.A.
Programming (via satellite): Cinemax (multiplexed); Encore (multiplexed); Flix; HBO (multiplexed); Showtime (multiplexed); Starz (multiplexed); The Movie Channel (multiplexed).

Video-On-Demand: Yes

Pay-Per-View
Hot Net Plus (delivered digitally); Playboy TV (delivered digitally); Spice Hot (delivered digitally); Spice Platinum (delivered digitally); Spice Live (delivered digitally); iN DEMAND (delivered digitally); NHL Center Ice/MLB Extra Innings (delivered digitally); ESPN Sports PPV (delivered digitally); NASCAR In Car (delivered digitally).

Internet Service
Operational: Yes.
Broadband Service: Charter Pipeline.
Fee: $99.95 installation; $29.99 monthly; $3.95 modem lease.

Telephone Service
Digital: Operational
Fee: $29.99 monthly

Miles of Plant: 1,677.0 (coaxial); 103.0 (fiber optic). Homes passed: 89,276.

Vice President & General Manager: Joe Boullion. Technical Operations Director: Rob Nowak. Marketing Manager: Tammy Reicha.

City fee: 5% of gross.

Ownership: Charter Communications Inc. (MSO).

UBLY—Comcast Cable. Now served by PIGEON, MI [MI0375]. ICA: MI0379.

UNION CITY—Broadstripe, 2512 Lansing Rd, Charlotte, MI 48813-8447. Phones: 800-444-6997; 517-543-1245. Fax: 517-543-8057. E-mail: michigan_contact@broadstripe.com. Web Site: http://www.broadstripe.com. Also serves Athens, Burlington Twp. (Calhoun County) & Sherwood Twp. ICA: MI0174.

TV Market Ranking: 37 (Athens, Burlington Twp. (Calhoun County), Sherwood Twp., UNION CITY). Franchise award date: N.A. Franchise expiration date: N.A. Began: August 1, 1984.

Channel capacity: 61 (operating 2-way). Channels available but not in use: None.

Basic Service
Subscribers: N.A.
Programming (received off-air): WILX-TV (NBC) Onondaga; WKAR-TV (PBS) East Lansing; WLLA (IND) Kalamazoo; WOOD-TV (NBC) Grand Rapids; WOTV (ABC) Battle Creek; WSYM-TV (FOX) Lansing; WTLJ (IND) Muskegon; WWMT (CBS, CW) Kalamazoo; WXMI (FOX) Grand Rapids; WXSP-CA (MNT) Grand Rapids.
Programming (via satellite): C-SPAN; Home Shopping Network; QVC; Weather Channel; WGN America.
Current originations: Government Access; Public Access.
Fee: $34.95 installation; $16.25 monthly; $14.95 additional installation.

Expanded Basic Service 1
Subscribers: N.A.
Programming (via satellite): ABC Family Channel; AMC; Arts & Entertainment; Cartoon Network; CNBC; CNN; Comedy Central; Country Music TV; Discovery Channel; Disney Channel; E! Entertainment Television; ESPN; ESPN 2; Fox News Channel; Fox Sports Net; Headline News; HGTV; History Channel; Lifetime; MSNBC; MTV; National Geographic Channel; Nickelodeon; Speed Channel; Spike TV; TBS Superstation; The Learning Channel; truTV; Turner Network TV; TV Land; USA Network; Versus; VH1.
Fee: $28.45 monthly.

Digital Basic Service
Subscribers: N.A.
Programming (via satellite): AmericanLife TV Network; BBC America; Bio; Bloomberg Television; Discovery Digital Networks; DMX Music; Fox Movie Channel; Fox Sports World; G4; GAS; Golf Channel; GSN; Halogen Network; History Channel International; Independent Film Channel; Lifetime Movie Network; MTV2; MuchMusic Network; Nick Jr.; Nick Too; Outdoor Channel; Toon Disney; Turner Classic Movies; VH1 Classic; VH1 Country.
Fee: $13.35 monthly; $9.95 converter.

Digital Pay Service 1
Pay Units: N.A.
Programming (via satellite): Cinemax (multiplexed); Encore (multiplexed); HBO (multiplexed); Showtime (multiplexed); Starz (multiplexed); The Movie Channel (multiplexed).
Fee: $14.95 installation; $6.95 monthly (Cinemax, Showtime/TMC, or Starz/Encore), $8.43 monthly (HBO).

Video-On-Demand: No

Pay-Per-View
Addressable: Yes; iN DEMAND (delivered digitally); Playboy TV (delivered digitally); Fresh (delivered digitally).

Internet Service
Operational: Yes.
Fee: $49.95 installation; $27.95 monthly.

Telephone Service
Digital: Operational
Fee: $39.99 installation; $49.99 monthly
Miles of Plant: 29.0 (coaxial); None (fiber optic). Homes passed: 1,299.
President & Chief Executive Officer: Bill Shreffler. Senior Vice President, Programming: Frank Scotello. Manager: David Harwood. Chief Engineer: Mark Jordan. Chief Technician: Ron Allen. Marketing Manager: Suzanne Harwood. Government Relations Director: Rick Clark.
Ownership: Broadstripe (MSO).

UNIONVILLE—Pine River Cable, PO Box 96, McBain, MI 49657. Phone: 888-244-2288. Fax: 231-825-0191. E-mail: info@pinerivercable.com. Web Site: http://www.pinerivercable.com. Also serves Unionville Village. ICA: MI0243.
TV Market Ranking: 61 (UNIONVILLE, Unionville Village). Franchise award date: July 23, 1984. Franchise expiration date: N.A. Began: November 1, 1986.
Channel capacity: 35 (operating 2-way). Channels available but not in use: 13.
Basic Service
Subscribers: 114.
Programming (received off-air): WAQP (IND) Saginaw; WEYI-TV (CW, NBC) Saginaw; WJRT-TV (ABC) Flint; WNEM-TV (CBS, MNT) Bay City; WSMH (FOX) Flint.
Programming (via satellite): ABC Family Channel; ESPN; Lifetime; Nickelodeon; QVC; Syfy; Turner Network TV.
Fee: $50.00 installation; $16.74 monthly.
Expanded Basic Service 1
Subscribers: N.A.
Programming (via satellite): Discovery Channel; Headline News; USA Network.
Pay Service 1
Pay Units: 31.
Programming (via satellite): HBO.
Fee: $11.95 monthly.
Pay Service 2
Pay Units: 20.
Programming (via satellite): Showtime.
Fee: $10.95 monthly.
Internet Service
Operational: No.
Telephone Service
None
Miles of Plant: 5.0 (coaxial); None (fiber optic). Homes passed: 239.
Manager: John Metzler.
Ownership: Pine River Cable (MSO).

VASSAR—Charter Communications, 7372 Davison Rd, Davison, MI 48423. Phone: 810-652-1400. Web Site: http://www.charter.com. Also serves Almer Twp., Caro, Cass City, Elkland Twp., Ellington Twp., Indianfields Twp., Millington, Millington Twp., Tuscola Twp. & Vassar Twp. ICA: MI0131.
TV Market Ranking: 61 (Almer Twp., Caro, Cass City, Elkland Twp., Ellington Twp., Indianfields Twp., Millington, Millington Twp., Tuscola Twp., VASSAR, Vassar Twp.). Franchise award date: N.A. Franchise expiration date: N.A. Began: March 1, 1974.
Channel capacity: N.A. Channels available but not in use: N.A.
Basic Service
Subscribers: 4,592.
Programming (received off-air): WAQP (IND) Saginaw; WBSF (CW) Bay City; WDIV-TV (NBC) Detroit; WEYI-TV (CW, NBC) Saginaw; WFUM (PBS) Flint; WJRT-TV (ABC) Flint; WKAR-TV (PBS) East Lansing; WNEM-TV (CBS, MNT) Bay City; WSMH (FOX) Flint; WTVS (PBS) Detroit; WXYZ-TV (ABC) Detroit; allband FM.
Programming (via satellite): Home Shopping Network; ION Television; MyNetworkTV Inc.; QVC; WGN America.
Current originations: Government Access; Educational Access; Public Access.
Fee: $29.99 installation; $13.50 monthly.
Expanded Basic Service 1
Subscribers: N.A.
Programming (via satellite): ABC Family Channel; AMC; Animal Planet; Arts & Entertainment; Bravo; Cartoon Network; CNBC; CNN; Comedy Central; Country Music TV; C-SPAN; Discovery Channel; Disney Channel; E! Entertainment Television; ESPN; ESPN 2; Food Network; Fox News Channel; Fox Sports Net Detroit; FX; G4; Golf Channel; GSN; Hallmark Channel; Headline News; HGTV; History Channel; Lifetime; MSNBC; MTV; MTV2; National Geographic Channel; Nickelodeon; Oxygen; SoapNet; Speed Channel; Spike TV; Style Network; Syfy; TBS Superstation; The Learning Channel; Toon Disney; Travel Channel; truTV; Turner Classic Movies; Turner Network TV; TV Guide Network; TV Land; USA Network; Versus; VH1; Weather Channel.
Fee: $36.49 monthly.
Digital Basic Service
Subscribers: N.A.
Programming (received off-air): WEYI-TV (CW, NBC) Saginaw; WFUM (PBS) Flint; WJRT-TV (ABC) Flint; WNEM-TV (CBS, MNT) Bay City; WSMH (FOX) Flint.
Programming (via satellite): BBC America; Bio; CMT Pure Country; Discovery Digital Networks; Discovery HD Theater; Do-It-Yourself; ESPN 2 HD; ESPN Classic Sports; ESPN HD; ESPN U; ESPNews; Food Network On Demand; Fox Business Channel; Fox College Sports Atlantic; Fox College Sports Central; Fox College Sports Pacific; Fox Movie Channel; Fox Soccer; Fuel TV; Fuse; GAS; Great American Country; HDNet; HDNet Movies; HGTV On Demand; History Channel International; Howard TV; Independent Film Channel; Lifetime Movie Network; MTV Networks Digital Suite; Music Choice; Nick Jr.; Nick Too; NickToons TV; Outdoor Channel; ReelzChannel; Sundance Channel; The Sportsman Channel; Turner Network TV; Universal HD; WE tv.
Digital Pay Service 1
Pay Units: N.A.
Programming (via satellite): Cinemax (multiplexed); Cinemax HD; Cinemax On Demand; Encore (multiplexed); Flix; HBO (multiplexed); HBO HD; HBO On Demand; LOGO; Showtime (multiplexed); Showtime HD; Showtime On Demand; Starz (multiplexed); Starz HDTV; Starz On Demand; The Movie Channel (multiplexed).
Video-On-Demand: Yes
Pay-Per-View
iN DEMAND (delivered digitally); ESPN (delivered digitally); NHL Center Ice (delivered digitally); MLB Extra Innings (delivered digitally); Playboy TV (delivered digitally); Fresh (delivered digitally); Shorteez (delivered digitally).
Internet Service
Operational: Yes.
Broadband Service: Charter Pipeline.
Fee: $29.99 monthly.
Telephone Service
Digital: Operational
Fee: $29.99 monthly
Miles of Plant: 147.0 (coaxial); None (fiber optic). Homes passed: 7,216.
Vice President & General Manager: Dave Slowick. Technical Operations Director: Lloyd Collins. Marketing Director: Lisa Gayari.
Ownership: Charter Communications Inc. (MSO).

VERMONTVILLE—Broadstripe, 2512 Lansing Rd, Charlotte, MI 48813-8447. Phones: 800-444-6997; 517-543-1245. Fax: 517-543-8057. E-mail: michigan_contact@broadstripe.com. Web Site: http://www.broadstripe.com. ICA: MI0368.
TV Market Ranking: 37,92 (VERMONTVILLE). Franchise award date: N.A. Franchise expiration date: N.A. Began: June 1, 1992.
Channel capacity: 78 (operating 2-way). Channels available but not in use: N.A.
Basic Service
Subscribers: N.A. Included in Dimondale
Programming (received off-air): WHTV (MNT) Jackson; WILX-TV (NBC) Onondaga; WKAR-TV (PBS) East Lansing; WLAJ (ABC, CW) Lansing; WLNS-TV (CBS) Lansing; WOOD-TV (NBC) Grand Rapids; WOTV (ABC) Battle Creek; WSYM-TV (FOX) Lansing; WWMT (CBS, CW) Kalamazoo; WXMI (FOX) Grand Rapids; WZPX-TV (ION) Battle Creek.
Programming (via satellite): WGN America.
Current originations: Government Access; Public Access.
Fee: $29.95 installation; $23.68 monthly; $14.95 additional installation.
Expanded Basic Service 1
Subscribers: N.A.
Programming (via satellite): ABC Family Channel; Arts & Entertainment; Cartoon Network; CNN; Comedy Central; Country Music TV; C-SPAN; Discovery Channel; Disney Channel; E! Entertainment Television; ESPN; ESPN 2; Eternal Word TV Network; Fox Sports Net; Headline News; History Channel; Lifetime; MSNBC; MTV; Nickelodeon; QVC; Spike TV; Syfy; TBS Superstation; Turner Network TV; TV Guide Network; USA Network; VH1; Weather Channel.
Digital Basic Service
Subscribers: N.A.
Programming (via satellite): AmericanLife TV Network; BBC America; Bio; Bloomberg Television; Discovery Digital Networks; DMX Music; Fox Movie Channel; Fox Sports World; G4; GAS; Golf Channel; GSN; Halogen Network; HGTV; History Channel International; Independent Film Channel; Lifetime Movie Network; MTV2; MuchMusic Network; National Geographic Channel; Nick Jr.; NickToons TV; Outdoor Channel; Style Network; Toon Disney; Trinity Broadcasting Network; Turner Classic Movies; VH1 Classic; VH1 Country.
Fee: $13.35 monthly.
Digital Pay Service 1
Pay Units: N.A.
Programming (via satellite): Cinemax (multiplexed); Encore (multiplexed); HBO (multiplexed); Showtime (multiplexed); Starz (multiplexed); The Movie Channel (multiplexed).
Video-On-Demand: No
Pay-Per-View
Addressable: Yes; iN DEMAND (delivered digitally); Playboy TV (delivered digitally); Fresh (delivered digitally).
Internet Service
Operational: Yes.
Telephone Service
None
Miles of Plant: 12.0 (coaxial); None (fiber optic). Homes passed: 300.
President & Chief Executive Officer: Bill Shreffler. Vice President, Programming: Frank Scotello. Manager: David Harwood. Chief Engineer: Mark Jordan. Chief Technician: Ron Allen. Marketing Manager: Suzanne Harwood. Government Relations Director: Rick Clark.
Ownership: Broadstripe (MSO).

WALDRON VILLAGE—Comcast Cable, 3500 Patterson Ave SE, Grand Rapids, MI 49512. Phone: 616-977-2200. Fax: 616-977-2224. Web Site: http://www.comcast.com. ICA: MI0438.
TV Market Ranking: Below 100 (WALDRON VILLAGE).
Channel capacity: N.A. Channels available but not in use: N.A.
Basic Service
Subscribers: 102.
Programming (received off-air): WILX-TV (NBC) Onondaga; WKAR-TV (PBS) East Lansing; WLAJ (ABC, CW) Lansing; WLNS-TV (CBS) Lansing; WSYM-TV (FOX) Lansing; WTOL (CBS) Toledo; WTVG (ABC) Toledo.
Programming (via satellite): ABC Family Channel; AMC; Arts & Entertainment; CNN; C-SPAN; Discovery Channel; Disney Channel; ESPN; Fox Sports Net Detroit; Great American Country; Headline News; History Channel; Lifetime; MTV; Nickelodeon; QVC; Spike TV; TBS Superstation; Trinity Broadcasting Network; Turner Network TV; USA Network; VH1; Weather Channel; WGN America.
Current originations: Public Access.
Fee: $48.99 monthly.
Pay Service 1
Pay Units: N.A.
Programming (via satellite): HBO; Showtime; The Movie Channel.
Internet Service
Operational: Yes.
Telephone Service
Digital: Operational
Homes passed: 303.
Area Vice President: Larry Williamson. Technical Operations Director: Tom Rice. Sales & Marketing Director: Rick Finch. Business Operations Director: Amy Carey.
Ownership: Comcast Cable Communications Inc. (MSO).

WALLED LAKE—Comcast Cable, 29777 Telegraph Rd, Ste 4400B, Southfield, MI 48034. Phones: 734-254-1500 (Plymouth office); 248-233-4712. Fax: 248-233-4719. Web Site: http://www.comcast.com. Also serves Commerce Twp., Highland Twp. (Oakland County), Lyon Twp. (Oakland County), Milford, Milford Twp., White Lake, Wixom & Wolverine Lake. ICA: MI0023.
TV Market Ranking: 5,61 (Commerce Twp., Highland Twp. (Oakland County), Lyon Twp. (Oakland County), Milford, Milford Twp., WALLED LAKE, White Lake, Wixom, Wolverine Lake). Franchise award date: December 29, 1983. Franchise expiration date: N.A. Began: December 6, 1984.
Channel capacity: N.A. Channels available but not in use: N.A.
Basic Service
Subscribers: 24,217.
Programming (received off-air): various Canadian stations; WADL (IND) Mount Clemens; WDIV-TV (NBC) Detroit; WFUM (PBS) Flint; WJBK (FOX) Detroit; WKAR-TV (PBS) East Lansing; WKBD-TV (CW) Detroit; WMYD (MNT) Detroit; WPXD-TV (ION) Ann Arbor; WTVS (PBS) Detroit; WWJ-TV (CBS) Detroit; WXYZ-TV (ABC) Detroit.
Programming (via satellite): ABC Family Channel; AMC; Animal Planet; Arts & En-

tertainment; BET Networks; Bravo; Cartoon Network; CNBC; CNN; Comedy Central; C-SPAN; C-SPAN 2; Discovery Channel; Discovery Health Channel; Disney Channel; E! Entertainment Television; ESPN; ESPN 2; ESPN Classic Sports; Food Network; Fox News Channel; Fox Sports Net Detroit; FX; Golf Channel; Great American Country; GSN; Headline News; HGTV; History Channel; Home Shopping Network; INSP; Lifetime; Michigan Government Television; MSNBC; MTV; Nickelodeon; QVC; SoapNet; Speed Channel; Spike TV; Style Network; Syfy; TBS Superstation; The Learning Channel; Trinity Broadcasting Network; truTV; Turner Classic Movies; Turner Network TV; TV Guide Network; TV Land; USA Network; Versus; VH1; Weather Channel; WGN America.

Current originations: Leased Access; Religious Access; Government Access; Educational Access; Public Access.

Fee: $25.00 installation; $46.25 monthly.

Digital Basic Service

Subscribers: 6,031.

Programming (received off-air): WDIV-TV (NBC) Detroit; WJBK (FOX) Detroit; WTVS (PBS) Detroit; WWJ-TV (CBS) Detroit; WXYZ-TV (ABC) Detroit.

Programming (via satellite): BBC America; Bio; Bridges TV; Cooking Channel; C-SPAN 3; Discovery Channel; Discovery Digital Networks; Do-It-Yourself; Encore Action; ESPN; ESPNews; Flix; Fox Sports World; FSN Digital Atlantic; FSN Digital Central; FSN Digital Pacific; G4; GAS; Gol TV; Hallmark Channel; History Channel International; Independent Film Channel; MTV Networks Digital Suite; Music Choice; National Geographic Channel; NBA TV; NFL Network; Nick Jr.; Nick Too; NickToons TV; Oxygen; ShopNBC; Sundance Channel; The Word Network; Toon Disney; TV Asia; TV One; WE tv; Weatherscan.

Fee: $14.95 monthly.

Digital Pay Service 1

Pay Units: N.A.

Programming (via satellite): Cinemax (multiplexed); Cinemax HD; HBO (multiplexed); HBO HD; Showtime (multiplexed); Showtime HD; Starz (multiplexed); Starz HDTV; The Movie Channel (multiplexed).

Fee: $9.95 monthly (each).

Video-On-Demand: Yes

Pay-Per-View

Addressable homes: 6,031.

Hot Choice (delivered digitally), Addressable: Yes; NASCAR In Car (delivered digitally), Addressable: Yes; Fresh (delivered digitally); iN DEMAND (delivered digitally); Playboy TV (delivered digitally); Shorteez (delivered digitally); Pleasure (delivered digitally); NBA TV (delivered digitally); Sports PPV (delivered digitally).

Internet Service

Operational: Yes.

Subscribers: 2,689.

Broadband Service: Comcast High Speed Internet.

Fee: $42.94 monthly.

Telephone Service

Digital: Operational

Fee: $44.95 monthly

Miles of Plant: 689.0 (coaxial); None (fiber optic). Homes passed: 32,000. Total homes in franchised area: 36,000.

Area Vice President: Mike Cleland. Vice President, Technical Operations: Steve Thomas. Vice President, Marketing: Tony Lent. Vice President, Communications: Jerome Espy.

City fee: 5% of gross.

Ownership: Comcast Cable Communications Inc. (MSO).

WATERSMEET—Charter Communications. Now served by IRONWOOD, MI [MI0064]. ICA: MI0358.

WATERVLIET—Comcast Cable, 7720 W 98th St, Hickory Hills, IL 60457. Phones: 708-237-3260; 574-259-2112 (Mishawaka office). Fax: 708-237-3292. Web Site: http://www.comcast.com. Also serves Coloma, Coloma Twp., Hagar Twp., Hartford Twp. (western portion) & Pipestone Twp. ICA: MI0060.

TV Market Ranking: 37,80 (Hartford Twp. (western portion), WATERVLIET); 80 (Hagar Twp., Pipestone Twp.); Outside TV Markets (Coloma, Coloma Twp.). Franchise award date: October 3, 1974. Franchise expiration date: N.A. Began: October 3, 1974.

Channel capacity: N.A. Channels available but not in use: N.A.

Basic Service

Subscribers: 4,546.

Programming (received off-air): WBND-LP South Bend; WCWW-LP (CW) South Bend; WGVU-TV (PBS) Grand Rapids; WHME-TV (IND) South Bend; WMAQ-TV (NBC) Chicago; WNDU-TV (NBC) South Bend; WNIT (PBS) South Bend; WOOD-TV (NBC) Grand Rapids; WOTV (ABC) Battle Creek; WSBT-TV (CBS, IND) South Bend; WSJV (FOX) Elkhart; WWMT (CBS, CW) Kalamazoo; WXMI (FOX) Grand Rapids; allband FM.

Programming (via satellite): QVC; TBS Superstation; WGN America.

Current originations: Public Access.

Fee: $48.99 installation; $15.93 monthly.

Expanded Basic Service 1

Subscribers: N.A.

Programming (via satellite): ABC Family Channel; AMC; Animal Planet; Arts & Entertainment; BET Networks; Cartoon Network; CNBC; CNN; Comedy Central; Country Music TV; C-SPAN; C-SPAN 2; Discovery Channel; Disney Channel; E! Entertainment Television; ESPN; ESPN 2; Eternal Word TV Network; Food Network; Fox News Channel; Fox Sports Net Detroit; FX; Golf Channel; Hallmark Channel; Headline News; HGTV; History Channel; Home Shopping Network; ION Television; Lifetime; MSNBC; MTV; Nickelodeon; Spike TV; Style Network; Syfy; Telemundo; The Learning Channel; Travel Channel; truTV; Turner Network TV; TV Guide Network; TV Land; USA Network; Versus; VH1; Weather Channel.

Fee: $37.49 monthly.

Digital Basic Service

Subscribers: N.A.

Programming (via satellite): American-Life TV Network; BBC America; Bio; Black Family Channel; Bloomberg Television; Bravo; Cooking Channel; Discovery Digital Networks; DMX Music; Do-It-Yourself; ESPN Classic Sports; ESPNews; FitTV; Fox College Sports Atlantic; Fox College Sports Central; Fox College Sports Pacific; Fox Movie Channel; Fox Soccer; Fuse; G4; GAS; Great American Country; GSN; History Channel International; Independent Film Channel; INSP; International Television (ITV); Jewelry Television; Lifetime Movie Network; Lime; MTV Networks Digital Suite; MTV2; National Geographic Channel; NFL Network; Nick Jr.; Nick Too; NickToons TV; Outdoor Channel; Ovation; Science Television; ShopNBC; Speed Channel; Sundance Channel; Syfy; The Word Network; Toon Disney; Trinity Broadcasting Network; Turner Classic Movies; TV Land; WAM! America's Kidz Network; WE tv.

Fee: $11.99 monthly.

Digital Pay Service 1

Pay Units: N.A.

Programming (via satellite): Cinemax; Encore (multiplexed); Flix; HBO; Showtime; Starz (multiplexed); The Movie Channel.

Fee: $16.99 monthly (each).

Video-On-Demand: Yes

Pay-Per-View

Hot Choice; Fresh; Shorteez; Playboy TV (delivered digitally); iN DEMAND (delivered digitally).

Internet Service

Operational: Yes.

Broadband Service: Comcast High Speed Internet.

Fee: $42.95 monthly.

Telephone Service

None

Miles of Plant: 183.0 (coaxial); None (fiber optic). Additional miles planned: 1.0 (coaxial). Homes passed: 10,872.

Area Vice President: Sandy Weicher. Vice President, Technical Operations: Bob Curtis. Vice President, Marketing & Sales: Eric Schaefer. Vice President, Communications: Rich Ruggiero. Technical Operations Manager: John Collucci. Marketing Director: Ron Knutson.

City fee: 3% of basic gross.

Ownership: Comcast Cable Communications Inc. (MSO).

WAYNE—Comcast Cable. Now served by PLYMOUTH, MI [MI0012]. ICA: MI0084.

WEIDMAN—Charter Communications, 2304 S Mission, Mount Pleasant, MI 48858. Phone: 989-785-6846. Fax: 989-772-0350. Web Site: http://www.charter.com. Also serves Beal City, Broomfield Twp., Nottawa Twp. (Isabella County) & Sherman Twp. (Isabella County). ICA: MI0362.

TV Market Ranking: Outside TV Markets (Beal City, Broomfield Twp., Nottawa Twp. (Isabella County), Sherman Twp. (Isabella County), WEIDMAN). Franchise award date: N.A. Franchise expiration date: N.A. Began: N.A.

Channel capacity: 36 (not 2-way capable). Channels available but not in use: 3.

Basic Service

Subscribers: 1,000.

Programming (received off-air): WCMU-TV (PBS) Mount Pleasant; WEYI-TV (CW, NBC) Saginaw; WFQX-TV (FOX) Cadillac; WJRT-TV (ABC) Flint; WNEM-TV (CBS, MNT) Bay City; WPBN-TV (NBC) Traverse City; WSMH (FOX) Flint; WWTV (CBS) Cadillac; WZZM (ABC) Grand Rapids.

Programming (via satellite): ABC Family Channel; Animal Planet; Arts & Entertainment; CNBC; CNN; Country Music TV; C-SPAN; Discovery Channel; Disney Channel; ESPN; ESPN 2; Fox Sports Net Detroit; Headline News; History Channel; Home Shopping Network; Lifetime; Nickelodeon; QVC; Spike TV; Syfy; TBS Superstation; The Learning Channel; Trinity Broadcasting Network; Turner Network TV; USA Network; Weather Channel; WGN America.

Current originations: Public Access.

Fee: $30.00 installation; $23.45 monthly.

Pay Service 1

Pay Units: 320.

Programming (via satellite): Showtime (multiplexed).

Fee: $20.00 installation; $7.00 monthly.

Internet Service

Operational: No.

Telephone Service

None

Miles of Plant: 31.0 (coaxial); None (fiber optic). Homes passed: 1,735.

Vice President & General Manager: Dan Spoelman. Operations Manager: Ed Bucao.

Ownership: Charter Communications Inc. (MSO).

WELLSTON—Pine River Cable, PO Box 96, McBain, MI 49657. Phone: 888-244-2288. Fax: 231-825-0191. E-mail: info@pinerivercable.com. Web Site: http://www.pinerivercable.com. Also serves Norman Twp. ICA: MI0237.

TV Market Ranking: Below 100 (Norman Twp., WELLSTON). Franchise award date: N.A. Franchise expiration date: N.A. Began: July 1, 1991.

Channel capacity: 36 (not 2-way capable). Channels available but not in use: 14.

Basic Service

Subscribers: 43.

Programming (received off-air): WCMV (PBS) Cadillac; WFQX-TV (FOX) Cadillac; WGTU (ABC, CW) Traverse City; WPBN-TV (NBC) Traverse City; WWTV (CBS) Cadillac.

Programming (via satellite): ABC Family Channel; AMC; Arts & Entertainment; CNN; Country Music TV; Discovery Channel; ESPN; Headline News; Lifetime; QVC; Showtime; Spike TV; TBS Superstation; Trinity Broadcasting Network; Turner Network TV; USA Network; WGN America.

Fee: $50.00 installation; $24.95 monthly.

Internet Service

Operational: No.

Miles of Plant: 8.0 (coaxial); None (fiber optic). Homes passed: 260.

Manager: John Metzler.

Ownership: Pine River Cable (MSO).

WEST BLOOMFIELD TWP.—Comcast Cable, 29777 Telegraph Rd, Ste 4400B, Southfield, MI 48034. Phones: 734-254-1500 (Plymouth office); 248-233-4712. Fax: 248-233-4719. Web Site: http://www.comcast.com. Also serves Keego Harbor, Orchard Lake & Sylvan Lake. ICA: MI0028.

TV Market Ranking: 5 (WEST BLOOMFIELD TWP.); 5,61 (Keego Harbor, Orchard Lake, Sylvan Lake). Franchise award date: N.A. Franchise expiration date: N.A. Began: January 1, 1985.

Channel capacity: 79 (operating 2-way). Channels available but not in use: N.A.

Basic Service

Subscribers: 19,339.

Programming (received off-air): WADL (IND) Mount Clemens; WBTV (CBS) Charlotte; WDIV-TV (NBC) Detroit; WFUM (PBS) Flint; WJBK (FOX) Detroit; WKBD-TV (CW) Detroit; WMYD (MNT) Detroit; WPXD-TV (ION) Ann Arbor; WTVS (PBS) Detroit; WWJ-TV (CBS) Detroit; WXYZ-TV (ABC) Detroit.

Programming (via satellite): Catholic Television Network; C-SPAN; C-SPAN 2; ESPN; Eternal Word TV Network; Michigan Government Television; QVC; TBS Superstation; TV Guide Network; Weather Channel; WGN America.

Current originations: Educational Access.

Fee: $25.00 installation; $16.50 monthly.

Expanded Basic Service 1

Subscribers: N.A.

Programming (via satellite): ABC Family Channel; AMC; Animal Planet; Arts & Entertainment; BET Networks; Bravo; Cartoon Network; CNBC; CNN; Comcast Local Detroit; Comedy Central; Discovery Channel; Disney Channel; E! Entertainment Television; ESPN 2; ESPN Classic Sports; Food Network; Fox News Channel; Fox Sports Net; FX; Golf Channel; GSN; Headline News; HGTV; History Channel; Home Shopping Network 2; Lifetime; MSNBC; MTV; Nickelodeon; SoapNet; Speed Channel; Spike TV; Style Network; Syfy; The Learning Channel; Travel Channel; Trinity Broadcasting Network; truTV; Turner Classic Movies; Turner Network TV; TV Land; USA Network; Versus; VH1; WE tv.

Fee: $42.99 monthly.

Digital Basic Service

Subscribers: 4,816.

Programming (via satellite): BBC America; Bio; Cooking Channel; C-SPAN 3; Discovery Digital Networks; Disney Channel; DMX Music; Do-It-Yourself; Encore Action; ESPNews; Flix; Fox Movie Channel; G4; GAS; History Channel International; Independent Film Channel; International Television (ITV); MTV Networks Digital Suite; National Geographic Channel; Nick Jr.; Nick Too; NickToons TV; Oxygen; Science Television; ShopNBC; SoapNet; Sundance Channel; The Word Network; Toon Disney; WAM! America's Kidz Network; Weatherscan.

Fee: $14.95 monthly.

Pay Service 1

Pay Units: 17,969.

Programming (via satellite): Cinemax; HBO; Showtime; The Movie Channel.

Fee: $9.95 installation; $7.50 monthly (each).

Digital Pay Service 1

Pay Units: N.A.

Programming (via satellite): Cinemax (multiplexed); HBO (multiplexed); Showtime (multiplexed); Starz (multiplexed); The Movie Channel (multiplexed).

Fee: $7.50 monthly (each).

Video-On-Demand: Yes

Pay-Per-View

Addressable homes: 4,816.

iN DEMAND, Addressable: Yes; Sports PPV (delivered digitally); ANA Television Network (delivered digitally); NBA TV (delivered digitally); Hot Choice (delivered digitally); Playboy TV (delivered digitally); Fresh (delivered digitally); Shorteez (delivered digitally); Pleasure (delivered digitally); TV Japan (delivered digitally); EDTV (delivered digitally).

Internet Service

Operational: Yes.

Subscribers: 2,147.

Broadband Service: Comcast High Speed Internet.

Fee: $42.95 monthly.

Telephone Service

Digital: Operational

Fee: $14.95 installation; $44.95 monthly

Miles of Plant: 453.0 (coaxial); 36.0 (fiber optic). Homes passed: 25,437.

Area Vice President: Mike Cleland. Vice President, Technical Operations: Steve Thomas. Vice President, Marketing: Tony Lent. Vice President, Communications: Jerome Espy.

Ownership: Comcast Cable Communications Inc. (MSO).

WEST BRANCH—Pine River Cable, PO Box 96, McBain, MI 49657. Phone: 888-244-2288. Fax: 231-825-0191. E-mail: info@pinerivercable.com. Web Site: http://www.pinerivercable.com. Also serves Clear Lake, Edwards Twp. & Ogemaw Twp. ICA: MI0148.

TV Market Ranking: Outside TV Markets (Clear Lake, Edwards Twp., Ogemaw Twp., WEST BRANCH). Franchise award date: N.A. Franchise expiration date: N.A. Began: N.A.

Channel capacity: N.A. Channels available but not in use: N.A.

Basic Service

Subscribers: 1,311.

Programming (received off-air): WBKB-TV (CBS, FOX) Alpena; WDCQ-TV (PBS) Bad Axe; WEYI-TV (CW, NBC) Saginaw; WJRT-TV (ABC) Flint; WNEM-TV (CBS, MNT) Bay City; WSMH (FOX) Flint.

Programming (via satellite): CB Television Michoacan; C-SPAN; C-SPAN 2; CW+; Eternal Word TV Network; Home Shopping Network; INSP; MyNetworkTV Inc.; QVC; TBS Superstation; Trinity Broadcasting Network; TV Guide Network; WGN America.

Current originations: Government Access; Educational Access; Public Access.

Fee: $50.00 installation; $13.50 monthly.

Expanded Basic Service 1

Subscribers: N.A.

Programming (via satellite): ABC Family Channel; AMC; Animal Planet; Arts & Entertainment; BET Networks; Bravo; Cartoon Network; CNBC; CNN; Comedy Central; Country Music TV; Discovery Channel; Disney Channel; E! Entertainment Television; ESPN; ESPN 2; Food Network; Fox News Channel; Fox Sports Net Detroit; FX; G4; Golf Channel; GSN; Hallmark Channel; Headline News; HGTV; History Channel; Lifetime; MSNBC; MTV; MTV2; National Geographic Channel; Nickelodeon; Outdoor Channel; Oxygen; SoapNet; Speed Channel; Spike TV; Telemundo; The Learning Channel; Toon Disney; Travel Channel; truTV; Turner Classic Movies; Turner Network TV; TV Land; USA Network; Versus; VH1; WE tv; Weather Channel.

Fee: $36.49 monthly.

Digital Basic Service

Subscribers: N.A.

Programming (received off-air): WEYI-TV (CW, NBC) Saginaw; WJRT-TV (ABC) Flint; WNEM-TV (CBS, MNT) Bay City; WSMH (FOX) Flint.

Programming (via satellite): BBC America; Bio; CMT Pure Country; Discovery Channel HD; Discovery Digital Networks; Do-It-Yourself; ESPN Classic Sports; ESPN HD; ESPNews; FitTV; Fox College Sports Atlantic; Fox College Sports Central; Fox College Sports Pacific; Fox Movie Channel; Fox Soccer; Fox Sports Net Detroit; Fuel TV; Fuse; GAS; Great American Country; HDNet; HDNet Movies; History Channel International; Independent Film Channel; Lifetime Movie Network; Military History Channel; MTV Networks Digital Suite; Music Choice; Nick Jr.; Nick Too; NickToons TV; Sundance Channel; Turner Network TV HD; Universal HD.

Digital Pay Service 1

Pay Units: N.A.

Programming (via satellite): Cinemax (multiplexed); Cinemax HD; Encore (multiplexed); Flix; HBO (multiplexed); HBO HD; LOGO; Showtime (multiplexed); Showtime HD; Starz (multiplexed); The Movie Channel (multiplexed).

Video-On-Demand: No

Pay-Per-View

iN DEMAND (delivered digitally); ESPN (delivered digitally); NHL Center Ice (delivered digitally); MLB Extra Innings (delivered digitally); Playboy TV (delivered digitally); Club Jenna (delivered digitally); Fresh! (delivered digitally); Fresh (delivered digitally); Shorteez (delivered digitally).

Internet Service

Operational: No.

Telephone Service

Analog: Not Operational

Digital: Planned

Miles of Plant: 47.0 (coaxial); None (fiber optic). Homes passed: 2,033.

Manager: John Metzler.

Ownership: Pine River Cable (MSO).

WHITE CLOUD—Charter Communications, 315 Davis St, Grand Haven, MI 49417-1830. Phone: 616-647-6201. Fax: 616-846-0797. Web Site: http://www.charter.com. Also serves Wilcox Twp. ICA: MI0435.

TV Market Ranking: Below 100 (WHITE CLOUD, Wilcox Twp.). Franchise award date: N.A. Franchise expiration date: N.A. Began: N.A.

Channel capacity: 40 (not 2-way capable). Channels available but not in use: N.A.

Basic Service

Subscribers: 387.

Programming (received off-air): WGVU-TV (PBS) Grand Rapids; WOOD-TV (NBC) Grand Rapids; WPBN-TV (NBC) Traverse City; WTLJ (IND) Muskegon; WWMT (CBS, CW) Kalamazoo; WWTV (CBS) Cadillac; WXMI (FOX) Grand Rapids; WZZM (ABC) Grand Rapids.

Programming (via satellite): TBS Superstation; WGN America.

Fee: $14.00 monthly.

Expanded Basic Service 1

Subscribers: N.A.

Programming (via satellite): ABC Family Channel; AMC; Animal Planet; Arts & Entertainment; CNBC; CNN; Discovery Channel; Disney Channel; ESPN; ESPN 2; Fox News Channel; Fox Sports Net Detroit; FX; Headline News; HGTV; History Channel; Lifetime; MSNBC; MTV; Nickelodeon; QVC; Spike TV; The Learning Channel; Turner Network TV; TV Land; USA Network; Weather Channel.

Fee: $18.95 monthly.

Pay Service 1

Pay Units: N.A.

Programming (via satellite): HBO; The Movie Channel.

Fee: $9.95 monthly (TMC), $11.45 monthly (HBO).

Internet Service

Operational: No.

Telephone Service

None

Vice President & General Manager: Dan Spoelman. Technical Operations Manager: Keith Schierbeek. Marketing Director: Steve Schuh.

Ownership: Charter Communications Inc. (MSO).

WHITEHALL—Charter Communications, 315 Davis St, Grand Haven, MI 49417-1830. Phone: 616-647-6201. Fax: 616-846-0797. Web Site: http://www.charter.com. Also serves Blue Lake Twp. (Muskegon County), Dalton Twp. (portions), Fruitland, Grant Twp. (Oceana County), Lakewood (village), Montague, New Era (village), Rothbury & White River Twp. ICA: MI0092.

TV Market Ranking: Below 100 (Blue Lake Twp. (Muskegon County), Dalton Twp. (portions), Fruitland, Grant Twp. (Oceana County), Lakewood (village), New Era (village), Rothbury, White River Twp., WHITEHALL). Franchise award date: July 1, 1971. Franchise expiration date: N.A. Began: December 1, 1971.

Channel capacity: N.A. Channels available but not in use: N.A.

Basic Service

Subscribers: 4,596.

Programming (received off-air): WGVU-TV (PBS) Grand Rapids; WOOD-TV (NBC) Grand Rapids; WOTV (ABC) Battle Creek; WTLJ (IND) Muskegon; WVTV (CW) Milwaukee; WWMT (CBS, CW) Kalamazoo; WXMI (FOX) Grand Rapids; WXSP-CA (MNT) Grand Rapids; WZPX-TV (ION) Battle Creek; WZZM (ABC) Grand Rapids.

Programming (via satellite): C-SPAN; C-SPAN 2; Home Shopping Network; QVC; TBS Superstation; TV Guide Network; WGN America.

Current originations: Leased Access; Government Access; Educational Access; Public Access.

Fee: $29.99 installation.

Expanded Basic Service 1

Subscribers: N.A.

Programming (via satellite): ABC Family Channel; AMC; Animal Planet; Arts & Entertainment; Bravo; Cartoon Network; CNBC; CNN; Comedy Central; Country Music TV; Discovery Channel; Disney Channel; E! Entertainment Television; ESPN; ESPN 2; ESPN Classic Sports; ESPNews; Eternal Word TV Network; Food Network; Fox News Channel; Fox Sports Net Detroit; FX; G4; Golf Channel; GSN; Hallmark Channel; Headline News; HGTV; History Channel; INSP; Lifetime; MSNBC; MTV; MTV2; National Geographic Channel; Nickelodeon; Outdoor Channel; Oxygen; SoapNet; Speed Channel; Spike TV; Style Network; Syfy; The Learning Channel; Toon Disney; Travel Channel; truTV; Turner Classic Movies; Turner Network TV; TV Land; Univision; USA Network; Versus; VH1; WE tv; Weather Channel.

Fee: $47.99 monthly.

Digital Basic Service

Subscribers: N.A.

Programming (received off-air): LWS Local Weather Station; WOOD-TV (NBC) Grand Rapids; WXMI (FOX) Grand Rapids; WZZM (ABC) Grand Rapids.

Programming (via satellite): BBC America; Bio; Boomerang; CNN en Espanol; Discovery Digital Networks; Discovery HD Theater; Do-It-Yourself; ESPN; FitTV; Fox College Sports Atlantic; Fox College Sports Central; Fox College Sports Pacific; Fox Movie Channel; Fox Soccer; Fuel TV; Fuse; GAS; Great American Country; HDNet; HDNet Movies; History Channel International; Independent Film Channel; Lifetime Movie Network; MTV Networks Digital Suite; Music Choice; NFL Network; Nick Jr.; Nick Too; NickToons TV; Outdoor Channel; Sundance Channel; TV Guide Interactive Inc.

Digital Pay Service 1
Pay Units: N.A.
Programming (via satellite): Cinemax (multiplexed); Encore (multiplexed); Flix; HBO (multiplexed); Showtime (multiplexed); Starz (multiplexed); The Movie Channel (multiplexed).
Video-On-Demand: No
Pay-Per-View
Playboy TV (delivered digitally); Spice Live (delivered digitally); Spice Platinum (delivered digitally); Hot Net Plus (delivered digitally); Spice Hot (delivered digitally); iN DEMAND (delivered digitally); NASCAR In Car (delivered digitally); NHL Center Ice (delivered digitally); MLB Extra Innings (delivered digitally); ESPN (delivered digitally).
Internet Service
Operational: Yes.
Broadband Service: Charter Pipeline.
Fee: $29.99 monthly.
Telephone Service
None
Miles of Plant: 169.0 (coaxial); None (fiber optic). Homes passed: 5,997.
Vice President & General Manager: Dan Spoelman. Technical Operations Manager: Keith Schierbeek. Marketing Director: Steve Schuh.
City fee: 3% of gross.
Ownership: Charter Communications Inc. (MSO).

WHITTEMORE—Charter Communications, 2074 M 32 W, Alpena, MI 49707. Phone: 989-356-4503. Fax: 989-356-3761. Web Site: http://www.charter.com. Also serves Burleigh Twp. ICA: MI0233.
TV Market Ranking: Outside TV Markets (Burleigh Twp., WHITTEMORE). Franchise award date: June 24, 1988. Franchise expiration date: N.A. Began: June 1, 1989.
Channel capacity: 54 (not 2-way capable). Channels available but not in use: 28.
Basic Service
Subscribers: 168.
Programming (received off-air): WAQP (IND) Saginaw; WBKB-TV (CBS, FOX) Alpena; WEYI-TV (CW, NBC) Saginaw; WJRT-TV (ABC) Flint; WNEM-TV (CBS, MNT) Bay City; WSMH (FOX) Flint.
Programming (via satellite): Home Shopping Network; TBS Superstation.
Fee: $29.99 installation; $13.50 monthly; $1.00 converter.
Expanded Basic Service 1
Subscribers: 162.
Programming (via satellite): ABC Family Channel; Arts & Entertainment; CNN; C-SPAN; Discovery Channel; ESPN; HGTV; Lifetime; Spike TV; Turner Network TV; USA Network; Weather Channel.
Fee: $36.49 monthly.
Pay Service 1
Pay Units: 24.
Programming (via satellite): Cinemax.
Fee: $9.95 monthly.
Pay Service 2
Pay Units: 24.
Programming (via satellite): HBO.
Fee: $9.95 monthly.
Internet Service
Operational: No.
Miles of Plant: 8.0 (coaxial); None (fiber optic). Homes passed: 304.
Vice President: Joe Boullion. General Manager: Ed Kavanaugh. Technical Operations Director: Rob Nowak. Marketing Manager: Brenda Auger.
City fee: 3% of gross.
Ownership: Charter Communications Inc. (MSO).

WISNER (village)—Formerly served by Northwoods Cable Inc. No longer in operation. ICA: MI0363.

WOLF LAKE—Pine River Cable, PO Box 96, McBain, MI 49657. Phone: 888-244-2288. Fax: 231-825-0191. E-mail: info@pinerivercable.com. Web Site: http://www.pinerivercable.com. Also serves Lake County (portions). ICA: MI0442.
TV Market Ranking: Below 100 (Lake County (portions), WOLF LAKE).
Channel capacity: N.A. Channels available but not in use: N.A.
Basic Service
Subscribers: N.A.
Programming (received off-air): WCMV (PBS) Cadillac; WFQX-TV (FOX) Cadillac; WPBN-TV (NBC) Traverse City; WWTV (CBS) Cadillac; WZZM (ABC) Grand Rapids.
Programming (via satellite): ABC Family Channel; AMC; Animal Planet; Arts & Entertainment; Cartoon Network; CNN; Comedy Central; Country Music TV; C-SPAN; C-SPAN 2; Discovery Channel; Disney Channel; ESPN; ESPN 2; Fox News Channel; Fox Sports Net Detroit; FX; G4; Headline News; HGTV; History Channel; Home Shopping Network; Lifetime; MTV; Nickelodeon; Outdoor Channel; QVC; Spike TV; Syfy; TBS Superstation; The Learning Channel; Trinity Broadcasting Network; Turner Network TV; USA Network; VH1; Weather Channel; WGN America.
Pay Service 1
Pay Units: N.A.
Programming (via satellite): Encore (multiplexed); HBO (multiplexed).
Internet Service
Operational: No.
Manager: John Metzler.
Ownership: Pine River Cable (MSO).

WOLVERINE (village)—Upper Peninsula Communications, 397 N US Hwy 41, Carney, MI 49812-9757. Phone: 906-639-2194. Fax: 906-639-9936. E-mail: louied@alphacomm.net. ICA: MI0364.
TV Market Ranking: Below 100 (WOLVERINE (VILLAGE)). Franchise award date: July 1, 1988. Franchise expiration date: N.A. Began: May 1, 1989.
Channel capacity: 36 (not 2-way capable). Channels available but not in use: 18.
Basic Service
Subscribers: N.A.
Programming (received off-air): WCML (PBS) Alpena; WGTQ (ABC) Sault Ste. Marie; WTOM-TV (NBC) Cheboygan; WWUP-TV (CBS, FOX) Sault Ste. Marie.
Programming (via satellite): ABC Family Channel; CNN; Discovery Channel; ESPN; TBS Superstation; Turner Network TV; WGN America.
Fee: $25.00 installation; $14.50 monthly; $1.50 converter.
Pay Service 1
Pay Units: 20.
Programming (via satellite): Cinemax.
Fee: $7.50 monthly.
Internet Service
Operational: No.
Telephone Service
None
Miles of Plant: 4.0 (coaxial); None (fiber optic). Additional miles planned: 5.0 (coaxial).
Manager & Chief Technician: Louis Dupont.
Ownership: Upper Peninsula Communications Inc. (MSO).

WOODHAVEN—Comcast Cable. Now served by TAYLOR, MI [MI0008]. ICA: MI0365.

WOODLAND (village)—Pine River Cable, PO Box 96, McBain, MI 49657. Phones: 800-545-0994; 616-846-6967. Fax: 231-825-0191. E-mail: info@pinerivercable.com. Web Site: http://www.pinerivercable.com. ICA: MI0366.
TV Market Ranking: 37 (WOODLAND (VILLAGE)). Franchise award date: N.A. Franchise expiration date: N.A. Began: July 1, 1989.
Channel capacity: 36 (not 2-way capable). Channels available but not in use: 12.
Basic Service
Subscribers: 94.
Programming (received off-air): WKAR-TV (PBS) East Lansing; WOOD-TV (NBC) Grand Rapids; WOTV (ABC) Battle Creek; WSYM-TV (FOX) Lansing; WWMT (CBS, CW) Kalamazoo; WXMI (FOX) Grand Rapids.
Programming (via satellite): CNN; Country Music TV; Discovery Channel; Disney Channel; ESPN; Headline News; TBS Superstation; Turner Network TV; WGN America.
Fee: $50.00 installation; $19.95 monthly.
Pay Service 1
Pay Units: 25.
Programming (via satellite): Showtime.
Fee: $7.00 monthly.
Internet Service
Operational: No.
Telephone Service
None
Miles of Plant: 3.0 (coaxial); None (fiber optic). Homes passed: 170. Total homes in franchised area: 170.
Manager: John Metzler.
Ownership: Pine River Cable (MSO).

WYANDOTTE—Wyandotte Municipal Services, 3005 Biddle Ave, Wyandotte, MI 48192-5901. Phones: 734-324-7100; 734-324-7190. Fax: 734-324-7119. E-mail: stimco@wyan.org. Web Site: http://www.wyan.org. ICA: MI0053.
TV Market Ranking: 5 (WYANDOTTE). Franchise award date: N.A. Franchise expiration date: N.A. Began: January 4, 1983.
Channel capacity: 65 (operating 2-way). Channels available but not in use: 3.
Basic Service
Subscribers: 9,366.
Programming (received off-air): WADL (IND) Mount Clemens; WDIV-TV (NBC) Detroit; WGTE-TV (PBS) Toledo; WJBK (FOX) Detroit; WKBD-TV (CW) Detroit; WMYD (MNT) Detroit; WTVS (PBS) Detroit; WWJ-TV (CBS) Detroit; WXYZ-TV (ABC) Detroit.
Programming (via satellite): ION Television; TV Guide Network; various Canadian stations; Weather Channel.
Current originations: Leased Access; Government Access; Educational Access; Public Access.
Fee: $39.95 installation; $14.95 monthly; $20.00 additional installation.
Expanded Basic Service 1
Subscribers: N.A.
Programming (via microwave): Catholic Television Network.
Programming (via satellite): ABC Family Channel; AMC; Animal Planet; Arts & Entertainment; Big Ten Network; Bravo; Cartoon Network; CNBC; CNN; Comedy Central; Country Music TV; C-SPAN; C-SPAN 2; Discovery Channel; Disney Channel; Do-It-Yourself; E! Entertainment Television; ESPN; ESPN 2; ESPN Classic Sports; Food Network; Fox Movie Channel; Fox News Channel; Fox Sports Net Detroit; FX; G4; Great American Country; Hallmark Channel; Headline News; HGTV; History Channel; Home Shopping Network; Lifetime; MSNBC; MTV; National Geographic Channel; Nickelodeon; Outdoor Channel; QVC; Speed Channel; Spike TV; Syfy; TBS Superstation; The Learning Channel; Travel Channel; Trinity Broadcasting Network; truTV; Turner Classic Movies; Turner Network TV; TV Land; USA Network; VH1; WE tv; WGN America.
Fee: $20.80 monthly.
Digital Basic Service
Subscribers: 1,187.
Programming (received off-air): WDIV-TV (NBC) Detroit; WJBK (FOX) Detroit; WMYD (MNT) Detroit; WTVS (PBS) Detroit; WXYZ-TV (ABC) Detroit.
Programming (via satellite): Arts & Entertainment HD; BBC America; Big Ten Network HD; Bio; CMT Pure Country; Cooking Channel; Discovery HD Theater; Discovery Health Channel; Discovery Kids Channel; ESPN 2 HD; ESPN HD; ESPN U; ESPNews; Fox Business Channel; Fox Reality Channel; Fox Soccer; FSN HD; Golf Channel; GSN; HDNet; HDNet Movies; History Channel HD; History Channel International; Independent Film Channel; Lifetime Movie Network; MTV; MTV Hits; MTV Jams; MTV2; Music Choice; National Geographic Channel HD Network; Nick Jr.; Nick Too; NickToons TV; Oxygen; PBS Kids Sprout; Science Channel; SoapNet; Style Network; TeenNick; Toon Disney; Turner Network TV HD; Universal HD; Versus; Versus HD; VH1 Classic; VH1 Soul.
Fee: $14.95 monthly.
Pay Service 1
Pay Units: 106.
Programming (via satellite): Cinemax.
Fee: $39.95 installation; $9.45 monthly.
Pay Service 2
Pay Units: 1,209.
Programming (via satellite): HBO.
Fee: $39.95 installation; $12.45 monthly.
Pay Service 3
Pay Units: 560.
Programming (via satellite): Showtime; The Movie Channel.
Fee: $11.45 monthly.
Digital Pay Service 1
Pay Units: N.A.
Programming (via satellite): Cinemax (multiplexed); Cinemax HD; Encore (multiplexed); Flix; HBO (multiplexed); HBO HD; Showtime (multiplexed); Showtime HD; Starz (multiplexed); Sundance Channel; The Movie Channel (multiplexed); The Movie Channel HD.
Fee: $9.45 monthly (Cinemax), $10.45 monthly (Starz/Encore), $11.45 monthly (Showtime/TMC), $12.45 monthly (HBO).
Video-On-Demand: No
Pay-Per-View
Addressable homes: 9,307.
iN DEMAND (delivered digitally), Fee: $3.95, Addressable: Yes; Special events (delivered digitally).
Internet Service
Operational: Yes. Began: December 31, 2000.
Subscribers: 5,002.
Broadband Service: Cable Rocket.
Fee: $24.95-$59.95 monthly.
Telephone Service
Digital: Operational
Subscribers: 871.

Fee: $31.99 monthly
Miles of Plant: 72.0 (coaxial); 25.0 (fiber optic). Homes passed: 12,200. Total homes in franchised area: 12,200.
General Manager: Melanie McCoy. Assistant General Manager: James French. Cable Superintendent: Steve Timco. Program Director: Steve Colwell.
City fee: 5% of gross.
Ownership: Wyandotte Municipal Services.

YALE—Comcast Cable, 1555 Bad Axe Rd, Bad Axe, MI 48413. Phone: 989-269-8927. Fax: 989-269-9125. Web Site: http://www.comcast.com. Also serves Brockway, Elk Twp., Peck & Speaker Twp. ICA: MI0381.
TV Market Ranking: Outside TV Markets (Brockway, Elk Twp., Peck, Speaker Twp., YALE). Franchise award date: N.A. Franchise expiration date: N.A. Began: July 1, 1983.
Channel capacity: 42 (not 2-way capable). Channels available but not in use: N.A.

Basic Service
Subscribers: 515.
Programming (received off-air): WADL (IND) Mount Clemens; WDIV-TV (NBC) Detroit; WEYI-TV (CW, NBC) Saginaw; WJBK (FOX) Detroit; WJRT-TV (ABC) Flint; WKBD-TV (CW) Detroit; WMYD (MNT) Detroit; WNEM-TV (CBS, MNT) Bay City; WTVS (PBS) Detroit; WXYZ-TV (ABC) Detroit.
Programming (via satellite): Discovery Health Channel; QVC; TBS Superstation; WGN America.
Fee: $14.50 monthly; $2.25 converter.

Expanded Basic Service 1
Subscribers: N.A.
Programming (via satellite): ABC Family Channel; AMC; Arts & Entertainment; CNN; Discovery Channel; Disney Channel; ESPN; ESPN 2; Fox Sports Net; Great American Country; HGTV; History Channel; Lifetime; MTV; Nickelodeon; Spike TV; Syfy; The Learning Channel; Trinity Broadcasting Network; Turner Network TV; USA Network; Weather Channel.
Fee: $30.00 installation; $43.49 monthly.

Pay Service 1
Pay Units: N.A.
Programming (via satellite): Cinemax; HBO; Showtime.
Fee: $10.95 monthly (each).

Internet Service
Operational: No.

Telephone Service
None
Miles of Plant: 27.0 (coaxial); None (fiber optic). Homes passed: 959.
General Manager: Thomas J. Lerash. Chief Technician: Marshall Kurschner. Business Manager: Susan McGathy.
Ownership: Comcast Cable Communications Inc. (MSO).

YORK TWP.—Comcast Cable. Now served by TAYLOR, MI [MI0008]. ICA: MI0098.

MINNESOTA

Total Systems: **268**
Total Communities Served: **883**
Franchises Not Yet Operating: **0**
Applications Pending: **0**
Communities with Applications: **0**
Number of Basic Subscribers: **1,335,493**
Number of Expanded Basic Subscribers: **656,475**
Number of Pay Units: **183,983**

Top 100 Markets Represented: Minneapolis-St. Paul (13); Sioux Falls-Mitchell, SD (85); Duluth, MN-Superior, WI (89); Fargo-Valley City, ND (98).

For a list of cable communities in this section, see the Cable Community Index located in the back of Cable Volume 2.
For explanation of terms used in cable system listings, see p. D-11.

ADA—Loretel Cablevision, PO Box 72, 13 East 4th Ave, Ada, MN 56510. Phones: 800-343-2762; 800-242-6111 (Customer service); 218-784-5100; 218-784-7171. Fax: 218-784-2706. E-mail: loretel@loretel.net. Web Site: http://www.hectorcom.com. Also serves Borup, Climax, Felton, Fisher, Halstad, Hendrum & Shelly. ICA: MN0265.

TV Market Ranking: 98 (ADA, Borup, Felton, Halstad, Hendrum); Below 100 (Fisher, Shelly); Outside TV Markets (Climax). Franchise award date: March 1, 1991. Franchise expiration date: N.A. Began: April 1, 1982.

Channel capacity: 36 (operating 2-way). Channels available but not in use: 2.

Basic Service

Subscribers: 1,563.

Programming (received off-air): KCPM (MNT) Grand Forks; KFME (PBS) Fargo; KVLY-TV (NBC) Fargo; KVRR (FOX) Fargo; KXJB-TV (CBS) Valley City; WDAY-TV (ABC, CW) Fargo; WDAZ-TV (ABC, CW) Devils Lake.

Programming (via satellite): ABC Family Channel; Arts & Entertainment; Cartoon Network; CNBC; CNN; Comedy Central; Country Music TV; C-SPAN; Discovery Channel; Disney Channel; E! Entertainment Television; ESPN; Food Network; Fox Sports Net Midwest; FX; Lifetime; MTV; National Geographic Channel; Nickelodeon; QVC; Sneak Prevue; Spike TV; Syfy; TBS Superstation; The Learning Channel; Turner Classic Movies; Turner Network TV; TV Land; USA Network; VH1; Weather Channel; WGN America.

Current originations: Religious Access; Public Access.

Fee: $40.00 installation; $33.00 monthly; $2.50 converter; $15.00 additional installation.

Pay Service 1

Pay Units: 187.

Programming (via satellite): HBO.

Fee: $15.00 installation; $13.00 monthly.

Pay Service 2

Pay Units: 155.

Programming (via satellite): Cinemax.

Fee: $15.00 installation; $10.00 monthly.

Pay Service 3

Pay Units: 224.

Programming (via satellite): Encore.

Fee: $15.00 installation; $2.75 monthly.

Video-On-Demand: No

Pay-Per-View

iN DEMAND (delivered digitally); Playboy TV (delivered digitally).

Internet Service

Operational: No.

Broadband Service: Offers dial-up and DSL only; no cable modem service.

Telephone Service

None

Miles of Plant: 14.0 (coaxial); 29.0 (fiber optic). Homes passed: 1,969. Total homes in franchised area: 1,969.

Manager: Steven W. Katka. Chief Technician: Bruce Rosenfelt.

City fee: 2% of gross.

Ownership: Hector Communications Corp. (MSO).

ADAMS—Now served by CHATFIELD, MN [MN0111]. ICA: MN0197.

ADRIAN—Knology, 709 2nd Ave, Worthington, MN 56187. Phones: 507-449-7830; 605-965-9393. Fax: 507-343-7849. Web Site: http://www.knology.com. Also serves Edgerton, Lake Wilson, Luverne, Pipestone & Worthington. ICA: MN0158. **Note:** This system is an overbuild.

TV Market Ranking: 85 (Luverne); Outside TV Markets (ADRIAN, Edgerton, Lake Wilson, Pipestone, Worthington). Franchise award date: N.A. Franchise expiration date: N.A. Began: November 15, 1984.

Channel capacity: N.A. Channels available but not in use: N.A.

Basic Service

Subscribers: 3,595.

Programming (received off-air): KARE (NBC) Minneapolis; KCAU-TV (ABC) Sioux City; KDLT-TV (NBC) Sioux Falls; KELO-TV (CBS, MNT) Sioux Falls; KSFY-TV (ABC) Sioux Falls; KSIN-TV (PBS) Sioux City; KSMN (PBS) Worthington; KTCA-TV (PBS) St. Paul; KTTW (FOX) Sioux Falls; KUSD-TV (PBS) Vermillion; WCCO-TV (CBS) Minneapolis; WFTC (MNT) Minneapolis.

Programming (via satellite): ABC Family Channel; AMC; Animal Planet; Arts & Entertainment; Bravo; Cartoon Network; CNBC; CNN; Comedy Central; Country Music TV; C-SPAN; C-SPAN 2; Discovery Channel; Disney Channel; E! Entertainment Television; ESPN; ESPN 2; ESPN Classic Sports; Eternal Word TV Network; Food Network; Fox Movie Channel; Fox News Channel; Fox Sports Net North; FX; GalaVision; Golf Channel; Headline News; HGTV; History Channel; ION Television; Lifetime; Lifetime Movie Network; MSNBC; MTV; National Geographic Channel; Nickelodeon; Outdoor Channel; QVC; Speed Channel; Spike TV; Syfy; TBS Superstation; Telemundo; The Learning Channel; Toon Disney; Travel Channel; Trinity Broadcasting Network; truTV; Turner Classic Movies; Turner Network TV; TV Guide Network; TV Land; Univision; USA Network; VH1; Weather Channel; WGN America.

Fee: $25.00 installation; $28.95 monthly.

Digital Basic Service

Subscribers: N.A.

Programming (received off-air): KCSD-TV (PBS) Sioux Falls; KDLT-TV (NBC) Sioux Falls; KELO-TV (CBS, MNT) Sioux Falls; KSFY-TV (ABC) Sioux Falls; KTTW (FOX) Sioux Falls; LWS Local Weather Station.

Programming (via satellite): BBC America; Bio; Bloomberg Television; Cooking Channel; Discovery Digital Networks; Discovery HD Theater; Do-It-Yourself; Encore Wam; ESPN; ESPNews; FitTV; Flix; Fox College Sports Atlantic; Fox College Sports Central; Fox College Sports Pacific; Fox Soccer; Fuse; G4; GAS; GSN; Hallmark Channel; HDNet; HDNet Movies; History Channel International; Independent Film Channel; Lifetime Real Women; Lime; MTV Networks Digital Suite; Music Choice; National Geographic Channel; Nick Jr.; NickToons TV; SoapNet; Style Network; Sundance Channel; WE tv.

Pay Service 1

Pay Units: 165.

Programming (via satellite): HBO; Showtime.

Fee: $10.00 installation; $9.85 monthly.

Digital Pay Service 1

Pay Units: N.A.

Programming (via satellite): Canales N; Cinemax; Cinemax (multiplexed); Encore (multiplexed); HBO; HBO (multiplexed); Showtime; Showtime (multiplexed); Starz (multiplexed); The Movie Channel.

Video-On-Demand: Yes

Pay-Per-View

iN DEMAND (delivered digitally); Hot Choice (delivered digitally).

Internet Service

Operational: Yes.

Broadband Service: Knology.Net.

Telephone Service

Analog: Not Operational

Digital: Operational

Miles of Plant: 21.0 (coaxial); None (fiber optic). Homes passed included in Viborg SD

General Manager: Scott Schroeder. Technical Operations Manager: Daryl Elcock. Marketing Manager: Scott Determan.

City fee: 3% of gross.

Ownership: Knology Inc. (MSO).

AITKIN—Charter Communications. Now served by Brainerd, MN [MN0022]. ICA: MN0103.

ALBANY—Charter Communications, 3380 Northern Valley Pl NE, Rochester, MN 55906-3954. Phones: 320-763-6139 (Local office); 507-289-8372. Fax: 507-285-6162. Web Site: http://www.charter.com. ICA: MN0146.

TV Market Ranking: Below 100 (ALBANY). Franchise award date: N.A. Franchise expiration date: N.A. Began: November 1, 1966.

Channel capacity: N.A. Channels available but not in use: N.A.

Basic Service

Subscribers: 500.

Programming (received off-air): KARE (NBC) Minneapolis; KCCO-TV (CBS) Alexandria; KMSP-TV (FOX) Minneapolis; KPXM-TV (ION) St. Cloud; KSAX (ABC) Alexandria; KSTC-TV (IND) Minneapolis; KTCA-TV (PBS) St. Paul; WFTC (MNT) Minneapolis; allband FM.

Programming (via satellite): C-SPAN; C-SPAN 2; Eternal Word TV Network; QVC; TBS Superstation.

Current originations: Public Access.

Fee: $29.95 installation.

Expanded Basic Service 1

Subscribers: 326.

Programming (received off-air): WCMN-LP St. Cloud-Sartell.

Programming (via satellite): ABC Family Channel; AMC; Animal Planet; Arts & Entertainment; Bravo; Cartoon Network; CNBC; CNN; Comedy Central; Country Music TV; Discovery Channel; Disney Channel; E! Entertainment Television; ESPN; ESPN 2; Food Network; Fox News Channel; Fox Sports Net North; FX; G4; Golf Channel; Hallmark Channel; Headline News; HGTV; History Channel; Home Shopping Network; Lifetime; MSNBC; MTV; MTV2; National Geographic Channel; Nickelodeon; Oxygen; Speed Channel; Spike TV; Syfy; The Learning Channel; Travel Channel; truTV; Turner Classic Movies; Turner Network TV; TV Land; Univision; USA Network; Versus; VH1; WE tv; Weather Channel.

Fee: $47.99 monthly.

Digital Basic Service

Subscribers: N.A.

Programming (received off-air): KARE (NBC) Minneapolis; KMSP-TV (FOX) Minneapolis; WCCO-TV (CBS) Minneapolis.

Programming (via satellite): BBC America; Bio; Bloomberg Television; Boomerang; CBS College Sports Network; CNN en Espanol; CNN International; Discovery Digital Networks; Do-It-Yourself; ESPN; ESPN Classic Sports; ESPNews; FitTV; Fox College Sports Atlantic; Fox College Sports Central; Fox College Sports Pacific; Fox Movie Channel; Fox Soccer; Fuel TV; Fuse; GAS; HDNet; HDNet Movies; History Channel International; Independent Film Channel; Lifetime; MTV Networks Digital Suite; Music Choice; NFL Network; Nick Jr.; Nick Too; NickToons TV; Outdoor Channel; SoapNet; Style Network; Sundance Channel; Toon Disney; TV Guide Interactive Inc.

Digital Pay Service 1

Pay Units: N.A.

Programming (via satellite): Cinemax (multiplexed); Encore (multiplexed); HBO; HBO (multiplexed); Showtime; Starz (multiplexed); The Movie Channel.

Video-On-Demand: Yes

Pay-Per-View

iN DEMAND (delivered digitally); NASCAR In Car (delivered digitally); NHL Center Ice (delivered digitally); MLB Extra Innings (delivered digitally); Playboy TV (delivered digitally); Spice Live (delivered digitally); Spice

Platinum (delivered digitally); Hot Net Plus (delivered digitally); Spice Hot (delivered digitally).

Internet Service

Operational: Yes.

Broadband Service: Charter Pipeline.

Fee: $29.99 monthly.

Telephone Service

Digital: Operational

Fee: $29.99 monthly

Homes passed: 980. Miles of plant (coax) included in St. Cloud/Waite Park

Vice President & General Manager: John Crowley. Operations Director: Craig Stensaas. Technical Operations Director: Mark Abramo. Marketing Director: Bill Haarstad.

City fee: None.

Ownership: Charter Communications Inc. (MSO).

ALBERT LEA—Charter Communications, 2206 E Oakland Ave, Austin, MN 55912-4375. Phones: 507-437-6643 (Austin office); 507-289-8372 (Rochester administrative office). Fax: 507-437-7119. Web Site: http://www.charter.com. ICA: MN0021.

TV Market Ranking: Below 100 (ALBERT LEA). Franchise award date: January 1, 1970. Franchise expiration date: N.A. Began: January 1, 1973.

Channel capacity: N.A. Channels available but not in use: N.A.

Basic Service

Subscribers: 5,400.

Programming (received off-air): KAAL (ABC) Austin; KEYC-TV (CBS, FOX) Mankato; KIMT (CBS, MNT) Mason City; KSMQ-TV (PBS) Austin; KTTC (CW, NBC) Rochester; KXLT-TV (FOX) Rochester; KYIN (PBS) Mason City; WFTC (MNT) Minneapolis.

Programming (via satellite): C-SPAN; C-SPAN 2; Home Shopping Network; Product Information Network; QVC; Trinity Broadcasting Network; TV Guide Network; WGN America.

Current originations: Educational Access.

Fee: $29.99 installation.

Expanded Basic Service 1

Subscribers: 4,940.

Programming (via satellite): ABC Family Channel; AMC; Animal Planet; Arts & Entertainment; BET Networks; Bravo; Cartoon Network; CNBC; CNN; Comedy Central; Country Music TV; Discovery Channel; Disney Channel; E! Entertainment Television; ESPN; ESPN 2; Eternal Word TV Network; Food Network; Fox News Channel; Fox Sports Net North; FX; G4; Golf Channel; GSN; Hallmark Channel; Headline News; HGTV; History Channel; INSP; Lifetime; MSNBC; MTV; MTV2; National Geographic Channel; Nickelodeon; Oxygen; ShopNBC; SoapNet; Speed Channel; Spike TV; Syfy; TBS Superstation; The Learning Channel; Toon Disney; Travel Channel; truTV; Turner Network TV; TV Land; Univision; USA Network; Versus; VH1; WE tv; Weather Channel.

Fee: $47.99 monthly.

Digital Basic Service

Subscribers: N.A.

Programming (received off-air): KTTC (CW, NBC) Rochester; KXLT-TV (FOX) Rochester.

Programming (via satellite): BBC America; Bio; Bloomberg Television; Boomerang; CBS College Sports Network; CNN en Espanol; CNN International; Discovery Digital Networks; Do-It-Yourself; ESPN; ESPN Classic Sports; ESPNews; FitTV; Fox College Sports Atlantic; Fox College Sports Central; Fox College Sports Pacific; Fox Movie Channel; Fox Soccer; Fuel TV; Fuse; GAS; HDNet; HDNet Movies; History Channel International; Independent Film Channel; Lifetime Movie Network; MTV Networks Digital Suite; Music Choice; NFL Network; Nick Jr.; Nick Too; NickToons TV; Outdoor Channel; Style Network; Sundance Channel; Turner Classic Movies; TV Guide Interactive Inc.

Digital Pay Service 1

Pay Units: N.A.

Programming (via satellite): Cinemax (multiplexed); Encore (multiplexed); Flix; HBO (multiplexed); HBO HD; Showtime (multiplexed); Showtime HD; Starz (multiplexed); The Movie Channel (multiplexed).

Video-On-Demand: Yes

Pay-Per-View

iN DEMAND (delivered digitally); NASCAR In Car (delivered digitally); NHL Center Ice (delivered digitally); MLB Extra Innings (delivered digitally); Playboy TV (delivered digitally); Spice Live (delivered digitally); Spice Platinum (delivered digitally); Hot Net Plus (delivered digitally); Spice Hot (delivered digitally).

Internet Service

Operational: Yes.

Broadband Service: Charter Pipeline.

Fee: $29.99 monthly.

Telephone Service

Digital: Operational

Fee: $29.99 monthly

Miles of Plant: 81.0 (coaxial); None (fiber optic). Homes passed: 9,100.

Vice President & General Manager: John Crowley. Operations Director: Craig Stensaas. Technical Operations Director: Darin Helgeson. Chief Technician: Ray Madrigal. Marketing Director: Bill Haarstad. Office Manager: Sherry Brown.

City fee: 5% of gross.

Ownership: Charter Communications Inc. (MSO).

ALDEN—US Cable, 402 Red River Ave N, Unit 5, Cold Spring, MN 56320-1521. Phones: 800-783-2356; 320-685-7113. Fax: 320-685-2816. E-mail: help@mn.uscable.com. Web Site: http://www.uscable.com. Also serves Claremont, Clarks Grove, Ellendale, Elysian, Freeborn, Geneva, Hartland, Hollandale, Le Center, Mapleton, Medford, New Richland, St. Clair & Waterville. ICA: MN0266.

TV Market Ranking: Below 100 (ALDEN, Claremont, Clarks Grove, Ellendale, Elysian, Freeborn, Geneva, Hartland, Hollandale, Le Center, Mapleton, New Richland, St. Clair, Waterville); Outside TV Markets (Medford). Franchise award date: N.A. Franchise expiration date: N.A. Began: March 1, 1985.

Channel capacity: 54 (operating 2-way). Channels available but not in use: N.A.

Basic Service

Subscribers: N.A. Included in Cambridge

Programming (received off-air): KAAL (ABC) Austin; KARE (NBC) Minneapolis; KEYC-TV (CBS, FOX) Mankato; KMSP-TV (FOX) Minneapolis; KSMQ-TV (PBS) Austin; KSTP-TV (ABC) St. Paul; KTCA-TV (PBS) St. Paul; KTTC (CW, NBC) Rochester; WCCO-TV (CBS) Minneapolis; WFTC (MNT) Minneapolis; allband FM.

Programming (via satellite): Food Network; TBS Superstation; Travel Channel.

Fee: $20.99 monthly.

Expanded Basic Service 1

Subscribers: N.A.

Programming (received off-air): KSTC-TV (IND) Minneapolis.

Programming (via satellite): ABC Family Channel; Animal Planet; Arts & Entertainment; Big Ten Network; Cartoon Network; CNBC; CNN; Comedy Central; Country Music TV; C-SPAN; Discovery Channel; Disney Channel; ESPN; ESPN 2; Eternal Word TV Network; Fox Sports Net North; FX; HGTV; History Channel; Home Shopping Network; Lifetime; MTV; Nickelodeon; Outdoor Channel; ShopNBC; Spike TV; Syfy; The Learning Channel; Turner Classic Movies; Turner Network TV; TV Land; USA Network; VH1; Weather Channel.

Fee: $22.95 monthly.

Digital Basic Service

Subscribers: N.A. Included in Cambridge

Programming (via satellite): BBC America; Bloomberg Television; Bravo; Discovery Health Channel; Discovery Kids Channel; DMX Music; ESPN Classic Sports; ESPNews; Fox Soccer; Fuse; G4; Golf Channel; GSN; Independent Film Channel; Lifetime Movie Network; MTV2; Nick Jr.; Science Channel; Sleuth; Speed Channel; Style Network; TeenNick; Toon Disney; Trinity Broadcasting Network; Versus; VH1 Classic; WE tv.

Fee: $8.95 monthly.

Digital Expanded Basic Service

Subscribers: N.A.

Programming (via satellite): Bio; CMT Pure Country; Discovery Home Channel; Discovery Military Channel; Encore (multiplexed); FitTV; Fox Movie Channel; Halogen Network; History Channel International; ID Investigation Discovery.

Fee: $2.95 monthly.

Digital Expanded Basic Service 2

Subscribers: N.A.

Programming (via satellite): NFL Network; Outdoor Channel.

Fee: $3.95 monthly.

Digital Pay Service 1

Pay Units: N.A. Included in Cambridge

Programming (via satellite): HBO (multiplexed).

Fee: $14.95 monthly.

Video-On-Demand: No

Pay-Per-View

iN DEMAND (delivered digitally); Fresh (delivered digitally); Playboy TV (delivered digitally); Club Jenna.

Internet Service

Operational: No.

Telephone Service

None

Homes passed & miles of plant included in Cambridge

General Manager: Steve Johnson. Customer Service Director: Jackie Torborg.

City fee: 3% of basic gross.

Ownership: US Cable Corp. (MSO).; Comcast Cable Communications Inc. (MSO).

ALEXANDRIA—Charter Communications, 1111 Hwy 29 N, Alexandria, MN 56308-5015. Phones: 507-289-8372 (Rochester administrative office); 320-763-6139 (Local office). Fax: 320-763-5194. E-mail: jon.melander@chartercom.com. Web Site: http://www.charter.com. Also serves Carlos, Hudson Twp., La Grand Twp. & Osakis. ICA: MN0031.

TV Market Ranking: Below 100 (ALEXANDRIA, Carlos, Hudson Twp., La Grand Twp., Osakis). Franchise award date: N.A. Franchise expiration date: N.A. Began: May 1, 1966.

Channel capacity: N.A. Channels available but not in use: N.A.

Basic Service

Subscribers: 4,358.

Programming (received off-air): KARE (NBC) Minneapolis; KCCO-TV (CBS) Alexandria; KMSP-TV (FOX) Minneapolis; KSAX (ABC) Alexandria; KSTC-TV (IND) Minneapolis; KTCA-TV (PBS) St. Paul; KVRR (FOX) Fargo; KWCM-TV (PBS) Appleton; WFTC (MNT) Minneapolis; WUCW (CW) Minneapolis.

Programming (via satellite): C-SPAN; C-SPAN 2; Eternal Word TV Network; QVC; TBS Superstation.

Current originations: Public Access; Leased Access.

Fee: $29.99 installation; $19.99 monthly; $39.95 additional installation.

Expanded Basic Service 1

Subscribers: N.A.

Programming (via satellite): ABC Family Channel; AMC; Animal Planet; Arts & Entertainment; Bravo; Cartoon Network; CNBC; CNN; Comedy Central; Country Music TV; Discovery Channel; Disney Channel; E! Entertainment Television; ESPN; ESPN 2; Food Network; Fox News Channel; Fox Sports Net North; FX; G4; Golf Channel; Hallmark Channel; Headline News; HGTV; History Channel; Home Shopping Network; Lifetime; MSNBC; MTV; MTV2; National Geographic Channel; Nickelodeon; Oxygen; SoapNet; Speed Channel; Spike TV; Syfy; The Learning Channel; Toon Disney; Travel Channel; truTV; Turner Classic Movies; Turner Network TV; TV Land; Univision; USA Network; Versus; VH1; WE tv; Weather Channel.

Fee: $47.99 monthly.

Digital Basic Service

Subscribers: N.A.

Programming (received off-air): KARE (NBC) Minneapolis; KMSP-TV (FOX) Minneapolis; WCCO-TV (CBS) Minneapolis.

Programming (via satellite): BBC America; Bio; Bloomberg Television; Boomerang; CBS College Sports Network; CNN en Espanol; CNN International; Discovery Digital Networks; Do-It-Yourself; ESPN; ESPN Classic Sports; ESPNews; FitTV; Fox College Sports Atlantic; Fox College Sports Central; Fox College Sports Pacific; Fox Movie Channel; Fox Soccer; Fuel TV; Fuse; GAS; HDNet; HDNet Movies; History Channel International; Independent Film Channel; Lifetime Movie Network; MTV Networks Digital Suite; Music Choice; NFL Network; Nick Jr.; Nick Too; NickToons TV; Outdoor Channel; Style Network; Sundance Channel; TV Guide Interactive Inc.

Digital Pay Service 1

Pay Units: N.A.

Programming (via satellite): Cinemax (multiplexed); Encore (multiplexed); HBO (multiplexed); HBO HD; Showtime (multiplexed); Showtime HD; Starz (multiplexed); The Movie Channel (multiplexed).

Video-On-Demand: Yes

Pay-Per-View

iN DEMAND (delivered digitally); NASCAR In Car (delivered digitally); NHL Center Ice (delivered digitally); MLB Extra Innings (delivered digitally); Playboy TV (delivered digitally); Spice Live (delivered digitally); Spice Platinum (delivered digitally); Hot Net Plus (delivered digitally); Spice Hot (delivered digitally).

Internet Service

Operational: Yes.

Broadband Service: Charter Pipeline.

Telephone Service

Digital: Operational

Fee: $29.99 monthly

Miles of Plant: 230.0 (coaxial); None (fiber optic). Homes passed: 8,199. Miles of plant includes Glenwood

Vice President & General Manager: John Crowley. Operations Director: Craig Sten-

saas. Office Operations Manager: Jon Melander. Chief Technician: Eric Cox. Marketing Director: Bill Haarstad.
City fee: 3% of gross.
Ownership: Charter Communications Inc. (MSO).

ALEXANDRIA—Formerly served by Viking Vision. No longer in operation. ICA: MN0392.

ALTURA—Midcontinent Communications, PO Box 5010, Sioux Falls, SD 57117. Phones: 800-456-0564; 605-229-1775. Web Site: http://www.midcocomm.com. ICA: MN0395.
TV Market Ranking: Below 100 (ALTURA).
Channel capacity: N.A. Channels available but not in use: N.A.

Basic Service
Subscribers: 103.
Programming (received off-air): KMSP-TV (FOX) Minneapolis; KSTP-TV (ABC) St. Paul; KTCA-TV (PBS) St. Paul; KTTC (CW, NBC) Rochester; WCCO-TV (CBS) Minneapolis; WEAU-TV (NBC) Eau Claire; WHLA-TV (PBS) La Crosse; WKBT-DT (CBS, MNT) La Crosse; WLAX (FOX) La Crosse; WXOW (ABC, CW) La Crosse.
Programming (via satellite): C-SPAN; C-SPAN 2; CW+; Home Shopping Network; MyNetworkTV Inc.; QVC; TV Guide Network; WGN America.
Fee: $50.00 installation; $11.95 monthly.

Expanded Basic Service 1
Subscribers: 87.
Programming (via satellite): ABC Family Channel; AMC; Animal Planet; Arts & Entertainment; BET Networks; Bravo; Cartoon Network; CNBC; CNN; Comedy Central; Country Music TV; Discovery Channel; Disney Channel; E! Entertainment Television; ESPN; ESPN 2; ESPN Classic Sports; Eternal Word TV Network; Food Network; Fox News Channel; Fox Sports Net North; FX; G4; Golf Channel; GSN; Hallmark Channel; Headline News; HGTV; History Channel; INSP; Lifetime; MSNBC; MTV; MTV2; National Geographic Channel; Nickelodeon; Outdoor Channel; Oxygen; ShopNBC; SoapNet; Speed Channel; Spike TV; Syfy; TBS Superstation; The Learning Channel; Travel Channel; truTV; Turner Classic Movies; Turner Network TV; TV Land; USA Network; Versus; VH1; Weather Channel.
Fee: $31.95 monthly.

Digital Basic Service
Subscribers: 4.
Programming (via satellite): AmericanLife TV Network; BBC America; Bio; Bloomberg Television; CMT Pure Country; Current; Discovery Digital Networks; ESPNews; Fox Movie Channel; Fox Soccer; Fuse; GAS; Halogen Network; History Channel International; Independent Film Channel; Lifetime Movie Network; MTV Networks Digital Suite; Music Choice; Nick Jr.; Style Network; Toon Disney; Trinity Broadcasting Network; WE tv.
Fee: $19.25 installation; $9.95 monthly; $7.95 converter.

Digital Pay Service 1
Pay Units: N.A.
Programming (via satellite): Cinemax (multiplexed); Encore (multiplexed); Flix; HBO (multiplexed); Showtime (multiplexed); Starz (multiplexed); The Movie Channel (multiplexed).

Video-On-Demand: No

Pay-Per-View
Movies (delivered digitally), Addressable: Yes; Events (delivered digitally).

Internet Service
Operational: Yes.
Broadband Service: Midcontinent.

Telephone Service
Digital: Operational
Homes passed: 170.
Vice President, Public Policy: Tom Simmons. General Manager: Darrell Wrege.
Ownership: Midcontinent Media Inc. (MSO).

ALVARADO—Stephen Cable TV Inc., PO Box 9, 415 5th St, Stephen, MN 56757-0009. Phone: 218-478-3074. Fax: 218-478-2236. ICA: MN0237.
TV Market Ranking: Below 100 (ALVARADO). Franchise award date: June 1, 1981. Franchise expiration date: N.A. Began: November 1, 1981.
Channel capacity: 40 (not 2-way capable). Channels available but not in use: 2.

Basic Service
Subscribers: 88.
Programming (received off-air): KBRR (FOX) Thief River Falls; KGFE (PBS) Grand Forks; KVLY-TV (NBC) Fargo; KXJB-TV (CBS) Valley City; WDAZ-TV (ABC, CW) Devils Lake.
Programming (via satellite): ABC Family Channel; AMC; Arts & Entertainment; CNBC; CNN; Comedy Central; C-SPAN; Discovery Channel; Disney Channel; ESPN; ESPN 2; Fox Sports Net; Great American Country; Hallmark Channel; HGTV; History Channel; Home Shopping Network; Lifetime; MTV; Nickelodeon; Spike TV; TBS Superstation; The Learning Channel; Trinity Broadcasting Network; Turner Network TV; TV Land; USA Network; VH1; Weather Channel; WGN America.
Current originations: Government Access; Educational Access.
Fee: $20.00 installation; $33.50 monthly.

Pay Service 1
Pay Units: 5.
Programming (via satellite): HBO.
Fee: $10.00 installation; $11.00 monthly.

Video-On-Demand: No

Internet Service
Operational: No.

Telephone Service
None
Miles of Plant: 4.0 (coaxial); None (fiber optic). Homes passed: 120.
Manager: Bryan Wixtrom.
City fee: None.
Ownership: Bryan Wixtrom (MSO).

ANNANDALE—Heart of the Lakes Cable System Inc., PO Box 340, 9938 State Hwy 55 NW, Annandale, MN 55302-0340. Phone: 320-274-5800. Fax: 320-274-7178. E-mail: sysop@lakedalelink.net. Web Site: http://www.annandalecabletv.com. Also serves Corinna Twp. ICA: MN0085.
TV Market Ranking: Below 100 (ANNANDALE, Corinna Twp.). Franchise award date: August 1, 1985. Franchise expiration date: N.A. Began: October 1, 1987.
Channel capacity: 40 (not 2-way capable). Channels available but not in use: 6.

Basic Service
Subscribers: 630.
Programming (received off-air): KARE (NBC) Minneapolis; KCCO-TV (CBS) Alexandria; KMSP-TV (FOX) Minneapolis; KSTP-TV (ABC) St. Paul; KTCA-TV (PBS) St. Paul; KTCI-TV (PBS) St. Paul; WCCO-TV (CBS) Minneapolis; WFTC (MNT) Minneapolis; WUCW (CW) Minneapolis.
Current originations: Government Access; Public Access.
Fee: $25.00 installation; $8.95 monthly.

Expanded Basic Service 1
Subscribers: 600.
Programming (received off-air): KPXM-TV (ION) St. Cloud; KSTC-TV (IND) Minneapolis.
Programming (via satellite): ABC Family Channel; AMC; Animal Planet; Arts & Entertainment; Cartoon Network; CNN; Comedy Central; C-SPAN; Discovery Channel; ESPN; ESPN 2; Fox Sports Net North; Golf Channel; Headline News; HGTV; History Channel; Lifetime; MTV; Nickelodeon; QVC; Spike TV; Syfy; TBS Superstation; The Learning Channel; Trinity Broadcasting Network; Turner Network TV; TV Land; USA Network; VH1; Weather Channel; WGN America.
Fee: $28.50 monthly.

Pay Service 1
Pay Units: 38.
Programming (via satellite): Cinemax.
Fee: $6.25 installation; $10.25 monthly.

Pay Service 2
Pay Units: 70.
Programming (via satellite): HBO.
Fee: $6.25 installation; $10.25 monthly.

Pay Service 3
Pay Units: 38.
Programming (via satellite): The Movie Channel.
Fee: $6.25 installation; $10.25 monthly.

Pay Service 4
Pay Units: 13.
Programming (via satellite): Showtime.
Fee: $6.25 installation; $10.25 monthly.

Video-On-Demand: No

Internet Service
Operational: Yes.
Fee: $27.95-$139.00 monthly.

Telephone Service
Digital: Operational
Fee: $30.95 monthly
Miles of Plant: 270.0 (coaxial); None (fiber optic). Homes passed: 827. Total homes in franchised area: 1,000.
Manager: Gene R. South Sr. Chief Technician & Marketing Director: Jim Kaufman.
City fee: 3% of gross.
Ownership: Heart of the Lakes Cable.

APPLETON—Mediacom, PO Box 110, 1504 2nd St SE, Waseca, MN 56093. Phones: 800-332-0245; 507-835-2356. Fax: 507-835-4567. Web Site: http://www.mediacomcable.com. Also serves Clinton, Dawson, Graceville, Lake Valley, Madison & Wheaton. ICA: MN0106.
TV Market Ranking: Outside TV Markets (APPLETON, Clinton, Dawson, Graceville, Lake Valley, Madison, Wheaton). Franchise award date: N.A. Franchise expiration date: N.A. Began: January 1, 1982.
Channel capacity: N.A. Channels available but not in use: N.A.

Basic Service
Subscribers: 3,101.
Programming (received off-air): KARE (NBC) Minneapolis; KCCO-TV (CBS) Alexandria; KDLO-TV (CBS, MNT) Florence; KMSP-TV (FOX) Minneapolis; KPXM-TV (ION) St. Cloud; KSAX (ABC) Alexandria; KSTC-TV (IND) Minneapolis; KTCI-TV (PBS) St. Paul; KWCM-TV (PBS) Appleton; WFTC (MNT) Minneapolis; WUCW (CW) Minneapolis; allband FM.
Programming (via satellite): C-SPAN; Home Shopping Network; TV Guide Network; Weather Channel; WGN America.
Fee: $52.39 installation; $15.59 monthly; $2.00 converter; $17.45 additional installation.

Expanded Basic Service 1
Subscribers: 2,976.
Programming (via satellite): ABC Family Channel; AMC; Animal Planet; Arts & Entertainment; Bravo; Cartoon Network; CNBC; CNN; Comedy Central; Country Music TV; C-SPAN 2; Discovery Channel; Disney Channel; E! Entertainment Television; ESPN; ESPN 2; Eternal Word TV Network; FitTV; Fox Movie Channel; Fox News Channel; Fox Sports Net North; FX; Hallmark Channel; Headline News; HGTV; History Channel; INSP; ION Television; Lifetime; MSNBC; MTV; Nickelodeon; RFD-TV; SoapNet; Speed Channel; Spike TV; Syfy; TBS Superstation; The Learning Channel; Travel Channel; Trinity Broadcasting Network; truTV; Turner Classic Movies; Turner Network TV; TV Land; Univision; USA Network; VH1; WE tv.
Fee: $22.95 monthly.

Digital Basic Service
Subscribers: N.A.
Programming (via satellite): AmericanLife TV Network; BBC America; Bio; Bloomberg Television; Canal 52MX; CCTV-4; Cine Latino; CNN en Espanol; Discovery en Espanol; Discovery HD Theater; Discovery Health Channel; Discovery Home Channel; Discovery Kids Channel; Discovery Military Channel; ESPN 2 HD; ESPN Deportes; ESPN HD; ESPNews; FitTV; Fox Movie Channel; Fox Reality Channel; Fox Soccer; Fox Sports en Espanol; Fuel TV; Fuse; G4; Golf Channel; GSN; Halogen Network; HDNet; HDNet Movies; History Channel en Espanol; History Channel International; ID Investigation Discovery; Independent Film Channel; Lifetime Movie Network; Lifetime Real Women; MTV Hits; MTV Tres; MTV2; Music Choice; National Geographic Channel; Nick Jr.; NickToons TV; Outdoor Channel; ReelzChannel; Science Channel; Sleuth; Style Network; Teen-Nick; Turner Classic Movies; TVG Network; VeneMovies; VH1 Classic.

Pay Service 1
Pay Units: N.A.
Programming (via satellite): Showtime.

Digital Pay Service 1
Pay Units: 314.
Programming (via satellite): Cinemax (multiplexed).
Fee: $7.00 monthly.

Digital Pay Service 2
Pay Units: 217.
Programming (via satellite): Encore (multiplexed); Starz (multiplexed); Starz HDTV.
Fee: $11.00 monthly.

Digital Pay Service 3
Pay Units: 362.
Programming (via satellite): HBO (multiplexed); HBO HD.
Fee: $11.00 monthly.

Digital Pay Service 4
Pay Units: 402.
Programming (via satellite): Flix; Showtime (multiplexed); Showtime HD; Sundance Channel; The Movie Channel (multiplexed); The Movie Channel HD.
Fee: $11.00 monthly (each).

Video-On-Demand: No

Pay-Per-View
iN DEMAND (delivered digitally); Spice: Xcess (delivered digitally); Pleasure (delivered digitally); Playboy TV (delivered digitally); Penthouse TV (delivered digitally); Fresh (delivered digitally); Ten Clips (delivered digitally).

Internet Service
Operational: Yes.
Broadband Service: Mediacom High Speed Internet.

Telephone Service
Digital: Operational
Miles of Plant: 59.0 (coaxial); None (fiber optic). Homes passed: 3,971. Total homes in franchised area: 4,113.
Vice President: Bill Jensen. Engineering Manager: Kraig Kaiser. Marketing & Sales Director: Lori Huberty.
Ownership: Mediacom LLC (MSO).

ARGYLE—Stephen Cable TV Inc., PO Box 9, 415 5th St, Stephen, MN 56757-0009. Phone: 218-478-3074. Fax: 218-478-2236. Also serves Middle River. ICA: MN0203.
TV Market Ranking: Below 100 (ARGYLE, Middle River). Franchise award date: October 23, 1980. Franchise expiration date: N.A. Began: January 1, 1981.
Channel capacity: 45 (not 2-way capable). Channels available but not in use: 4.
Basic Service
Subscribers: 205.
Programming (received off-air): KBRR (FOX) Thief River Falls; KGFE (PBS) Grand Forks; KVLY-TV (NBC) Fargo; KXJB-TV (CBS) Valley City; WDAZ-TV (ABC, CW) Devils Lake; allband FM.
Programming (via satellite): ABC Family Channel; AMC; Arts & Entertainment; CNBC; CNN; Comedy Central; Country Music TV; C-SPAN; Discovery Channel; Disney Channel; ESPN; ESPN 2; Fox Sports Net; FX; Great American Country; Hallmark Channel; HGTV; History Channel; Home Shopping Network; Lifetime; MTV; Nickelodeon; Outdoor Channel; Speed Channel; Spike TV; TBS Superstation; The Learning Channel; Trinity Broadcasting Network; Turner Network TV; TV Land; USA Network; VH1; Weather Channel; WGN America.
Current originations: Government Access; Educational Access.
Fee: $20.00 installation; $33.50 monthly.
Pay Service 1
Pay Units: 7.
Programming (via satellite): HBO.
Fee: $10.00 installation; $11.00 monthly.
Video-On-Demand: No
Internet Service
Operational: No.
Telephone Service
None
Miles of Plant: 5.0 (coaxial); None (fiber optic). Homes passed: 250. Total homes in franchised area: 273.
Manager: Bryan Wixtrom.
City fee: None.
Ownership: Bryan Wixtrom (MSO).

AUSTIN—Charter Communications, 2206 E Oakland Ave, Austin, MN 55912-4375. Phones: 507-289-8372 (Rochester administrative office); 507-437-6643. Fax: 507-437-7119. Web Site: http://www.charter.com. ICA: MN0019.
TV Market Ranking: Below 100 (AUSTIN). Franchise award date: January 1, 1971. Franchise expiration date: N.A. Began: March 1, 1973.
Channel capacity: N.A. Channels available but not in use: N.A.
Basic Service
Subscribers: 7,300.
Programming (received off-air): KAAL (ABC) Austin; KIMT (CBS, MNT) Mason City; KSMQ-TV (PBS) Austin; KTCA-TV (PBS) St. Paul; KTTC (CW, NBC) Rochester; KXLT-TV (FOX) Rochester; 18 FMs.
Programming (via satellite): C-SPAN; C-SPAN 2; Home Shopping Network; KYIN (PBS) Mason City; Product Information Network; QVC; Trinity Broadcasting Network; TV Guide Network; WGN America.
Current originations: Public Access.
Fee: $29.99 installation.
Expanded Basic Service 1
Subscribers: 5,511.
Programming (received off-air): WFTC (MNT) Minneapolis.
Programming (via satellite): ABC Family Channel; AMC; Animal Planet; Arts & Entertainment; BET Networks; Bravo; Cartoon Network; CNBC; CNN; Comedy Central; Country Music TV; Discovery Channel; Disney Channel; E! Entertainment Television; ESPN; ESPN 2; Eternal Word TV Network; Food Network; Fox News Channel; Fox Sports Net North; FX; G4; Golf Channel; GSN; Hallmark Channel; Headline News; HGTV; History Channel; INSP; Lifetime; MSNBC; MTV; MTV2; National Geographic Channel; Nickelodeon; Oxygen; ShopNBC; SoapNet; Speed Channel; Spike TV; Syfy; TBS Superstation; The Learning Channel; Toon Disney; Travel Channel; truTV; Turner Network TV; TV Land; Univision; USA Network; Versus; VH1; WE tv; Weather Channel.
Fee: $47.99 monthly.
Digital Basic Service
Subscribers: N.A.
Programming (via satellite): BBC America; Bio; Bloomberg Television; Boomerang; CBS College Sports Network; CNN en Espanol; CNN International; Discovery Digital Networks; Do-It-Yourself; ESPN Classic Sports; ESPNews; Fox College Sports Atlantic; Fox College Sports Central; Fox College Sports Pacific; Fox Movie Channel; Fox Soccer; Fuel TV; Fuse; GAS; HDNet; HDNet Movies; History Channel International; Independent Film Channel; Lifetime Movie Network; MTV Networks Digital Suite; Music Choice; NFL Network; Nick Jr.; Nick Too; NickToons TV; Outdoor Channel; Style Network; Sundance Channel; Turner Classic Movies.
Digital Pay Service 1
Pay Units: N.A.
Programming (via satellite): Cinemax (multiplexed); Encore (multiplexed); Flix; HBO (multiplexed); HBO HD; Showtime (multiplexed); Showtime HD; Starz (multiplexed); The Movie Channel.
Fee: $9.95 monthly (Cinemax or HBO), $11.95 monthly (Showtime).
Video-On-Demand: Yes
Pay-Per-View
iN DEMAND (delivered digitally); NASCAR In Car (delivered digitally); NHL Center Ice (delivered digitally); MLB Extra Innings (delivered digitally); Playboy TV (delivered digitally); Spice Live (delivered digitally); Spice Platinum (delivered digitally); Hot Net Plus (delivered digitally); Spice Hot (delivered digitally).
Internet Service
Operational: Yes.
Broadband Service: Charter Pipeline.
Fee: $29.99 monthly.
Telephone Service
Digital: Operational
Fee: $29.99 monthly
Miles of Plant: 106.0 (coaxial); 10.0 (fiber optic). Homes passed: 11,500.
Vice President & General Manager: John Crowley. Operations Director: Craig Stensaas. Technical Operations Director: Darin Helgeson. Technical Supervisor: Ray Madrigal. Marketing Director: Bill Haarstad. Office Manager: Sherry Brown.
City fee: 1% of basic.
Ownership: Charter Communications Inc. (MSO).

AVON—US Cable of Coastal Texas LP. Now served by CAMBRIDGE, MN [MN0016]. ICA: MN0268.

BABBITT—Midcontinent Communications, PO Box 5010, Sioux Falls, SD 57117. Phones: 800-456-0564; 605-229-1775. Web Site: http://www.midcocomm.com. ICA: MN0116.
TV Market Ranking: Outside TV Markets (BABBITT). Franchise award date: N.A. Franchise expiration date: N.A. Began: October 1, 1967.
Channel capacity: N.A. Channels available but not in use: N.A.
Basic Service
Subscribers: 613.
Programming (via microwave): KBJR-TV (MNT, NBC) Superior; KDLH (CBS, CW) Duluth; KQDS-TV (FOX) Duluth; WDIO-DT (ABC) Duluth; WDSE (PBS) Duluth.
Programming (via satellite): C-SPAN; Eternal Word TV Network; INSP; QVC; WGN America.
Fee: $29.99 installation.
Expanded Basic Service 1
Subscribers: 506.
Programming (via satellite): ABC Family Channel; AMC; Animal Planet; Arts & Entertainment; Bravo; Cartoon Network; CNBC; CNN; Comedy Central; Country Music TV; Discovery Channel; Disney Channel; E! Entertainment Television; ESPN; ESPN 2; Fox News Channel; Fox Sports Net North; FX; Hallmark Channel; Headline News; HGTV; History Channel; Lifetime; MSNBC; MTV; Nickelodeon; Oxygen; Speed Channel; Spike TV; Syfy; TBS Superstation; The Learning Channel; truTV; Turner Classic Movies; Turner Network TV; TV Land; USA Network; VH1; Weather Channel.
Fee: $47.99 monthly.
Digital Basic Service
Subscribers: N.A.
Programming (via satellite): BBC America; Bio; Discovery Digital Networks; Do-It-Yourself; Fox College Sports Atlantic; Fox College Sports Central; Fox College Sports Pacific; Fox Movie Channel; Fox Soccer; G4; GAS; History Channel International; Independent Film Channel; MTV Networks Digital Suite; Music Choice; Nick Jr.; Nick Too; NickToons TV; SoapNet; Style Network; Sundance Channel; Toon Disney; TV Guide Interactive Inc.; WE tv.
Digital Pay Service 1
Pay Units: N.A.
Programming (via satellite): Cinemax (multiplexed); Encore; Flix; HBO (multiplexed); Showtime (multiplexed); Starz (multiplexed); The Movie Channel (multiplexed).
Video-On-Demand: No
Pay-Per-View
iN DEMAND (delivered digitally); Hot Choice (delivered digitally).
Internet Service
Operational: Yes.
Broadband Service: Midcontinent.
Fee: $29.99 monthly.
Telephone Service
Analog: Operational
Miles of Plant: 13.0 (coaxial); None (fiber optic). Homes passed: 774. Total homes in franchised area: 774.
Vice President, Public Policy: Tom Simmons. General Manager: Darrell Wraye.
City fee: None.
Ownership: Midcontinent Media Inc. (MSO).

BADGER—Sjoberg's Cable TV Inc., 315 Main Ave N, Thief River Falls, MN 56701-1905. Phones: 800-828-8808; 218-681-3044. Fax: 218-681-6801. E-mail: office1@mncable.net. Web Site: http://local.mncable.net. ICA: MN0269.
TV Market Ranking: Outside TV Markets (BADGER). Franchise award date: January 1, 1990. Franchise expiration date: N.A. Began: January 1, 1990.
Channel capacity: 78 (operating 2-way). Channels available but not in use: 18.
Basic Service
Subscribers: 131.
Programming (received off-air): KAWE (PBS) Bemidji; KCPM (MNT) Grand Forks; KVLY-TV (NBC) Fargo; KXJB-TV (CBS) Valley City; WDAZ-TV (ABC, CW) Devils Lake.
Programming (via satellite): CNN; ESPN; TBS Superstation; various Canadian stations.
Fee: $25.00 installation; $10.00 monthly.
Expanded Basic Service 1
Subscribers: N.A.
Programming (received off-air): KBRR (FOX) Thief River Falls.
Programming (via satellite): ABC Family Channel; Animal Planet; Arts & Entertainment; Cartoon Network; CNBC; Comedy Central; Country Music TV; CW+; Discovery Channel; E! Entertainment Television; ESPN 2; Food Network; Fox News Channel; Fox Sports Net; FX; HGTV; History Channel; Home Shopping Network; Lifetime; MSNBC; MTV; Nickelodeon; Spike TV; Syfy; The Learning Channel; Turner Classic Movies; Turner Network TV; TV Land; USA Network; Weather Channel; WGN America.
Fee: $23.71 monthly.
Digital Basic Service
Subscribers: N.A.
Programming (via satellite): AmericanLife TV Network; Arts & Entertainment HD; BBC America; Bio; Blackbelt TV; Bloomberg Television; Bravo; Chiller; CMT Pure Country; CNN HD; College Sports Television; Cooking Channel; Current; Daystar TV Network; Discovery Channel HD; Discovery Health Channel; Discovery Kids Channel; Discovery Military Channel; Discovery Planet Green; DMX Music; Do-It-Yourself; ESPN 2 HD; ESPN Classic Sports; ESPN HD; ESPN U; ESPNews; Eternal Word TV Network; Food Network HD; Fox Business Channel; Fox College Sports Atlantic; Fox College Sports Central; Fox College Sports Pacific; Fox Movie Channel; Fox Reality Channel; Fox Soccer; FSN HD; G4; Golf Channel; Gospel Music Channel; Great American Country; GSN; Hallmark Channel; HDNet; HDNet Movies; Headline News; HGTV HD; History Channel HD; History Channel International; HorseRacing TV; ID Investigation Discovery; Independent Film Channel; Lifetime Movie Network; MTV Hits; MTV2; National Geographic Channel; Nick Jr.; NickToons TV; Outdoor Channel; Outdoor Channel 2 HD; Ovation; Oxygen; PBS Kids Sprout; RFD-TV; Science Channel; ShopNBC; Sleuth; SoapNet; Speed Channel; Speed HD; Style Network; Sundance Channel; Syfy HD; TBS in HD; TeenNick; Tennis Channel; The Sportsman Channel; The Word Network; Toon Disney; Turner Network TV HD; TVG Network; Universal HD; USA Network HD; Versus; Versus HD; VH1 Classic; VH1 Soul; WE tv.
Fee: $11.00 monthly.
Pay Service 1
Pay Units: 35.
Programming (via satellite): HBO.
Fee: $11.00 monthly.

Digital Pay Service 1
Pay Units: N.A.
Programming (via satellite): Cinemax (multiplexed); Cinemax HD; Encore (multiplexed); HBO (multiplexed); HBO HD; Showtime (multiplexed); Starz (multiplexed); The Movie Channel (multiplexed).
Fee: $8.00 monthly (Starz/Encore), $9.00 monthly (Cinemax or Showtime/TMC), $11.00 monthly (HBO).
Video-On-Demand: No
Internet Service
Operational: No.
Telephone Service
None
Miles of Plant: 4.0 (coaxial); None (fiber optic). Homes passed: 150. Total homes in franchised area: 150.
Manager: Richard J. Sjoberg. Chief Technician: Jerry Seim.
Ownership: Sjoberg's Cable TV Inc. (MSO).

BAGLEY—Bagley Public Utilities, PO Box M, 18 Main Ave S, Bagley, MN 56621. Phone: 218-694-2300. Fax: 218-694-6632. E-mail: vfletcher@bagleymn.us. Web Site: http://www.bagleymn.us. ICA: MN0133.
TV Market Ranking: Below 100 (BAGLEY). Franchise award date: February 1, 1976. Franchise expiration date: N.A. Began: February 1, 1976.
Channel capacity: 35 (not 2-way capable). Channels available but not in use: None.
Basic Service
Subscribers: 535.
Programming (received off-air): KAWE (PBS) Bemidji; KBRR (FOX) Thief River Falls; KCCW-TV (CBS) Walker; KVLY-TV (NBC) Fargo; KVRR (FOX) Fargo; KXJB-TV (CBS) Valley City; WDAY-TV (ABC, CW) Fargo; allband FM.
Programming (via microwave): KMSP-TV (FOX) Minneapolis.
Programming (via satellite): ABC Family Channel; Arts & Entertainment; Bravo; CNN; Country Music TV; Discovery Channel; Disney Channel; Do-It-Yourself; ESPN; Fox Sports Net North; Hallmark Channel; HGTV; History Channel; Lifetime; Outdoor Channel; QVC; Spike TV; TBS Superstation; The Learning Channel; Trinity Broadcasting Network; Turner Classic Movies; Turner Network TV; Weather Channel; WGN America.
Current originations: Public Access.
Fee: $20.00 installation; $25.00 monthly; $10.00 additional installation.
Pay Service 1
Pay Units: 42.
Programming (via satellite): HBO.
Fee: $12.00 monthly.
Internet Service
Operational: No.
Telephone Service
None
Miles of Plant: 15.0 (coaxial); None (fiber optic). Homes passed: 740.
General Manager: Michael Jensen. Business Manager: Vicky Fletcher. Chief Technician: Kraig Fontaine.
City fee: None.
Ownership: Bagley Public Utilities.

BALATON—Midcontinent Communications, PO Box 5010, Sioux Falls, SD 57117. Phones: 800-456-0564; 605-229-1775. Fax: 605-229-0478. E-mail: mccomm@midco.net. Web Site: http://www.midcocomm.com. ICA: MN0386.
TV Market Ranking: Outside TV Markets (BALATON). Franchise award date: N.A. Franchise expiration date: N.A. Began: N.A.
Channel capacity: 54 (not 2-way capable). Channels available but not in use: N.A.
Basic Service
Subscribers: 190.
Programming (received off-air): KARE (NBC) Minneapolis; KELO-TV (CBS, MNT) Sioux Falls; KMSP-TV (FOX) Minneapolis; KRWF (ABC) Redwood Falls; KSFY-TV (ABC) Sioux Falls; KWCM-TV (PBS) Appleton; WCCO-TV (CBS) Minneapolis; WFTC (MNT) Minneapolis; WUCW (CW) Minneapolis.
Programming (via satellite): C-SPAN; C-SPAN 2; Eternal Word TV Network; INSP; QVC; WGN America.
Current originations: Educational Access.
Fee: $29.99 installation; $34.00 additional installation.
Expanded Basic Service 1
Subscribers: N.A.
Programming (via satellite): ABC Family Channel; AMC; Animal Planet; Arts & Entertainment; Bravo; Cartoon Network; CNBC; CNN; Comedy Central; Country Music TV; Discovery Channel; Disney Channel; E! Entertainment Television; ESPN; ESPN 2; Food Network; Fox News Channel; Fox Sports Net North; FX; Great American Country; Headline News; HGTV; History Channel; Lifetime; MSNBC; MTV; Nickelodeon; Oxygen; Spike TV; Syfy; TBS Superstation; The Learning Channel; Travel Channel; Turner Classic Movies; Turner Network TV; TV Land; USA Network; VH1; Weather Channel.
Fee: $47.99 monthly.
Digital Basic Service
Subscribers: N.A.
Programming (via satellite): BBC America; Bio; Bloomberg Television; Discovery Digital Networks; Do-It-Yourself; Fuse; G4; GAS; GSN; History Channel International; Independent Film Channel; MTV Networks Digital Suite; Music Choice; Nick Jr.; Nick Too; NickToons TV; Style Network; Sundance Channel; TV Guide Interactive Inc.; WE tv.
Digital Pay Service 1
Pay Units: N.A.
Programming (via satellite): Cinemax (multiplexed); Encore; HBO (multiplexed); Showtime (multiplexed); Starz (multiplexed); The Movie Channel (multiplexed).
Video-On-Demand: No
Pay-Per-View
iN DEMAND (delivered digitally); Hot Choice (delivered digitally).
Internet Service
Operational: No.
Telephone Service
None
Miles of Plant: 5.0 (coaxial); None (fiber optic). Homes passed: 330.
Ownership: Midcontinent Media Inc. (MSO).

BARNESVILLE—Barnesville Cable TV, PO Box 550, 102 Front St N, Barnesville, MN 56514-0550. Phones: 800-354-2292; 218-354-2292. Fax: 218-354-2472. E-mail: barnesville@bvillemn.net. Web Site: http://www.barnesvillemn.com/moving/cable.html. ICA: MN0107.
TV Market Ranking: 98 (BARNESVILLE). Franchise award date: N.A. Franchise expiration date: N.A. Began: January 1, 1981.
Channel capacity: 77 (operating 2-way). Channels available but not in use: 16.
Basic Service
Subscribers: 762.
Programming (received off-air): KFME (PBS) Fargo; KMSP-TV (FOX) Minneapolis; KVLY-TV (NBC) Fargo; KVRR (FOX) Fargo; KXJB-TV (CBS) Valley City; WDAY-TV (ABC, CW) Fargo.
Programming (via satellite): Animal Planet; Bloomberg Television; Cartoon Network; CNN; Comedy Central; Country Music TV; E! Entertainment Television; ESPN 2; ESPN Classic Sports; ESPNews; Food Network; Fox News Channel; Fox Sports Net North; FX; G4; Golf Channel; GSN; Hallmark Channel; Headline News; HGTV; Home Shopping Network; MSNBC; MTV; Outdoor Channel; QVC; Speed Channel; Spike TV; TBS Superstation; truTV; Turner Classic Movies; TV Land; VH1; WGN America.
Current originations: Public Access.
Fee: $49.95 installation; $11.95 monthly.
Expanded Basic Service 1
Subscribers: 702.
Programming (via satellite): ABC Family Channel; AMC; Arts & Entertainment; Discovery Channel; ESPN; History Channel; Lifetime; Nickelodeon; Syfy; The Learning Channel; Turner Network TV; USA Network; Weather Channel.
Fee: $17.00 monthly.
Pay Service 1
Pay Units: 38.
Programming (via satellite): Cinemax.
Fee: $15.00 installation; $8.00 monthly.
Pay Service 2
Pay Units: 67.
Programming (via satellite): HBO.
Fee: $15.00 installation; $11.00 monthly.
Pay Service 3
Pay Units: 63.
Programming (via satellite): Encore (multiplexed); Starz.
Fee: $15.00 installation; $9.00 monthly.
Video-On-Demand: No
Internet Service
Operational: No.
Broadband Service: DSL Only.
Telephone Service
None
Miles of Plant: 16.0 (coaxial); None (fiber optic). Homes passed: 910. Total homes in franchised area: 910.
General Manager: Guy Swenson. Marketing Director: Karen Lauer. Chief Technician: Mike Pearson. Program Director: Ione Hammer.
City fee: None.
Ownership: City of Barnesville.

BARNESVILLE—Formerly served by Sprint Corp. No longer in operation. ICA: MN0271.

BARNUM—Savage Communications Inc., PO Box 810, 206 Power Ave N, Hinckley, MN 55037. Phone: 320-384-7442. Fax: 320-384-7446. E-mail: rwsavage@comcast.net. Web Site: http://www.scibroadband.com. ICA: MN0225.
TV Market Ranking: 89 (BARNUM). Franchise award date: April 10, 1989. Franchise expiration date: N.A. Began: April 1, 1990.
Channel capacity: 60 (operating 2-way). Channels available but not in use: 5.
Basic Service
Subscribers: 114.
Programming (received off-air): KBJR-TV (MNT, NBC) Superior; KDLH (CBS, CW) Duluth; KQDS-TV (FOX) Duluth; WDIO-DT (ABC) Duluth; WDSE (PBS) Duluth; WPIX (CW, IND) New York.
Programming (via satellite): ABC Family Channel; Animal Planet; Arts & Entertainment; CNBC; CNN; Comedy Central; C-SPAN; Discovery Channel; Disney Channel; E! Entertainment Television; ESPN; ESPN 2; Fox News Channel; Fox Sports Net; Great American Country; Headline News; HGTV; History Channel; Lifetime; MTV; Nickelodeon; QVC; Spike TV; Syfy; TBS Superstation; The Learning Channel; Turner Classic Movies; Turner Network TV; TV Land; USA Network; VH1; Weather Channel; WGN America.
Fee: $39.95 installation; $34.45 monthly.
Digital Basic Service
Subscribers: N.A.
Programming (via satellite): AmericanLife TV Network; BBC America; Bio; Bloomberg Television; Discovery Digital Networks; DMX Music; ESPN Classic Sports; ESPNews; FitTV; Fox Movie Channel; Fox Sports World; Fuse; G4; Golf Channel; History Channel International; INSP; National Geographic Channel; Outdoor Channel; Sleuth; Speed Channel; Style Network; Trinity Broadcasting Network; Versus; WE tv.
Digital Pay Service 1
Pay Units: N.A.
Programming (via satellite): Cinemax (multiplexed); Encore (multiplexed); Flix; HBO (multiplexed); Showtime (multiplexed); Starz (multiplexed); Sundance Channel; The Movie Channel (multiplexed).
Video-On-Demand: No
Pay-Per-View
Movies (delivered digitally); ESPN Now (delivered digitally); Sports PPV (delivered digitally).
Internet Service
Operational: Yes. Began: April 1, 2004.
Broadband Service: SCI Broadband.
Fee: $24.95 monthly.
Telephone Service
None
Miles of Plant: 5.0 (coaxial); None (fiber optic). Homes passed: 258.
Manager: Mike Danielson. Marketing Director: Ron Savage. Chief Technician: Pat McCabe. Customer Service Manager: Donna Erickson.
Ownership: Savage Communications Inc. (MSO).

BARRETT—Runestone Cable TV, 100 Runestone Dr, Hoffman, MN 56339. Phones: 320-986-2013; 800-986-6602. Fax: 320-986-2050. Web Site: http://www.runestone.net. Also serves Cyrus, Donnelly, Elbow Lake, Erdahl, Herman, Hoffman, Kensington, Lowry, Norcross, Tintah & Wendell. ICA: MN0233.
TV Market Ranking: Below 100 (BARRETT, Cyrus, Donnelly, Elbow Lake, Erdahl, Hoffman, Kensington, Lowry, Norcross); Outside TV Markets (Herman, Tintah, Wendell). Franchise award date: N.A. Franchise expiration date: N.A. Began: December 1, 1984.
Channel capacity: 50 (not 2-way capable). Channels available but not in use: N.A.
Basic Service
Subscribers: 1,450.
Programming (received off-air): KARE (NBC) Minneapolis; KCCO-TV (CBS) Alexandria; KMSP-TV (FOX) Minneapolis; KSAX (ABC) Alexandria; KSTC-TV (IND) Minneapolis; KVLY-TV (NBC) Fargo; KWCM-TV (PBS) Appleton; WFTC (MNT) Minneapolis; WUCW (CW) Minneapolis.
Programming (via satellite): C-SPAN; QVC.
Current originations: Public Access.
Fee: $35.00 installation; $14.71 monthly.
Expanded Basic Service 1
Subscribers: N.A.
Programming (via satellite): ABC Family Channel; AMC; Animal Planet; Arts & Entertainment; Cartoon Network; CNN; Com-

edy Central; Country Music TV; Discovery Channel; Disney Channel; ESPN; ESPN 2; Fox Movie Channel; Fox News Channel; Fox Sports Net North; Hallmark Channel; Headline News; HGTV; History Channel; ION Television; Lifetime; MTV; National Geographic Channel; Nickelodeon; Spike TV; Syfy; TBS Superstation; The Learning Channel; Travel Channel; Trinity Broadcasting Network; Turner Network TV; TV Land; USA Network; VH1; Weather Channel; WGN America.
Fee: $33.74 monthly.

Digital Basic Service
Subscribers: N.A.
Programming (via satellite): Bloomberg Television; CMT Pure Country; Discovery Health Channel; Discovery Kids Channel; Discovery Military Channel; Discovery Planet Green; DMX Music; ESPN Classic Sports; ESPNews; FitTV; G4; Golf Channel; GSN; Halogen Network; ID Investigation Discovery; Nick Jr.; NickToons TV; Outdoor Channel; Science Channel; Speed Channel; TeenNick; Turner Classic Movies; Versus; VH1 Classic.
Fee: $7.38 monthly.

Pay Service 1
Pay Units: 17.
Programming (via satellite): Cinemax; HBO; Showtime.
Fee: $15.00 installation; $8.00 monthly (Cinemax), $9.00 monthly (Showtime), $10.00 monthly (HBO).

Digital Pay Service 1
Pay Units: N.A.
Programming (via satellite): Cinemax (multiplexed); Encore (multiplexed); HBO (multiplexed); Showtime (multiplexed); Starz (multiplexed); The Movie Channel (multiplexed).
Fee: $10.95 monthly (Starz & Encore), $12.95 monthly (Showtime & TMC), $13.95 monthly (Cinemax & HBO).

Video-On-Demand: No

Internet Service
Operational: No, DSL & dialup.

Telephone Service
None

Miles of Plant: 36.0 (coaxial); None (fiber optic). Homes passed: 2,032.
Manager: Lee Maier. Plant Manager: Kent Hedstrom. Chief Technician: Dave Redepenning.
Ownership: Runestone Telecom Association (MSO).

BAUDETTE—Sjoberg's Cable TV Inc., 315 Main Ave N, Thief River Falls, MN 56701-1905. Phones: 800-828-8808; 218-681-3044. Fax: 218-681-6801. E-mail: office1@mncable.net. Web Site: http://local.mncable.net. Also serves Guldrid, Spooner, Wabanica & Wheeler. ICA: MN0091.
TV Market Ranking: Outside TV Markets (BAUDETTE, Guldrid, Spooner, Wabanica, Wheeler). Franchise award date: April 1, 1974. Franchise expiration date: N.A. Began: November 11, 1974.
Channel capacity: 78 (operating 2-way). Channels available but not in use: 18.

Basic Service
Subscribers: 739.
Programming (received off-air): KAWE (PBS) Bemidji; KVLY-TV (NBC) Fargo; KXJB-TV (CBS) Valley City; WDAZ-TV (ABC, CW) Devils Lake; allband FM.
Programming (via satellite): ABC Family Channel; CNN; ESPN; TBS Superstation; USA Network; various Canadian stations.
Current originations: Public Access.
Fee: $25.00 installation; $10.00 monthly; $35.00 additional installation.

Expanded Basic Service 1
Subscribers: N.A.
Programming (received off-air): KCPM (MNT) Grand Forks; KVRR (FOX) Fargo.
Programming (via satellite): Animal Planet; Arts & Entertainment; Cartoon Network; CNBC; Comedy Central; Country Music TV; CW+; Discovery Channel; E! Entertainment Television; ESPN 2; Eternal Word TV Network; Food Network; Fox News Channel; Fox Sports Net North; FX; HGTV; History Channel; Home Shopping Network; Lifetime; MSNBC; MTV; Nickelodeon; Spike TV; Syfy; The Learning Channel; Turner Classic Movies; Turner Network TV; TV Land; Weather Channel; WGN America.
Fee: $21.12 monthly.

Digital Basic Service
Subscribers: N.A.
Programming (via satellite): AmericanLife TV Network; BBC America; Bio; Bloomberg Television; Bravo; CMT Pure Country; Current; Daystar TV Network; Discovery Health Channel; Discovery Kids Channel; Discovery Military Channel; Discovery Planet Green; DMX Music; ESPN Classic Sports; ESPNews; FitTV; Fox Business Channel; Fox College Sports Atlantic; Fox College Sports Central; Fox College Sports Pacific; Fox Movie Channel; Fox Reality Channel; G4; Golf Channel; Gospel Music Channel; Great American Country; GSN; Halogen Network; History Channel International; ID Investigation Discovery; Independent Film Channel; Lifetime Movie Network; MTV Hits; MTV2; National Geographic Channel; Nick Jr.; NickToons TV; Outdoor Channel; Ovation; PBS Kids Sprout; RFD-TV; Science Channel; ShopNBC; Sleuth; Speed Channel; Style Network; Sundance Channel; TeenNick; The Word Network; Toon Disney; Trinity Broadcasting Network; TVG Network; Versus; VH1 Classic; VH1 Soul; WE tv.
Fee: $11.00 monthly.

Pay Service 1
Pay Units: 165.
Programming (via satellite): HBO.
Fee: $11.00 monthly.

Digital Pay Service 1
Pay Units: N.A.
Programming (via satellite): Cinemax (multiplexed); Encore (multiplexed); HBO (multiplexed); Showtime (multiplexed); Starz (multiplexed); The Movie Channel (multiplexed).
Fee: $8.00 monthly (Starz/Encore), $9.00 monthly (Cinemax or Showtime/TMC), $11.00 monthly (HBO).

Video-On-Demand: No

Pay-Per-View
iN DEMAND (delivered digitally).

Internet Service
Operational: Yes.
Broadband Service: Sjoberg's Cable TV.
Fee: $19.95 monthly; $10.65 modem lease; $69.99 modem purchase.

Telephone Service
None

Miles of Plant: 24.0 (coaxial); 7.0 (fiber optic). Homes passed: 1,050. Total homes in franchised area: 1,050.
Manager: Richard Sjoberg. Chief Technician: Jerry Seim.
City fee: None.
Ownership: Sjoberg's Cable TV Inc. (MSO).

BELGRADE—Now served by CHOKIO, MN [MN0210]. ICA: MN0176.

BELLE PLAINE—Now served by WASECA, MN [MN0043]. ICA: MN0102.

BELLECHESTER—Sleepy Eye Telephone. Formerly served by Goodhue, MN [MN0208]. This cable system has converted to IPTV, 111 Second Ave, Goodhue, MN 55027. Phones: 888-742-8010; 651-923-5005. Fax: 651-923-4010. E-mail: on-linecustservice@nu-telcom.net. Web Site: http://www.sleepyeyetel.net. ICA: MN5152.
Channel capacity: N.A. Channels available but not in use: N.A.

Internet Service
Operational: Yes.
Fee: $39.95 monthly.

Ownership: Sleepy Eye Telephone Co.

BELVIEW—Clara City Telephone Co., 215 1st St NW, Clara City, MN 56222. Phones: 888-283-7667; 320-847-2114. Fax: 320-847-2114. ICA: MN0238.
TV Market Ranking: Below 100 (BELVIEW). Franchise award date: July 12, 1984. Franchise expiration date: N.A. Began: July 1, 1985.
Channel capacity: 35 (not 2-way capable). Channels available but not in use: 12.

Basic Service
Subscribers: 60.
Programming (received off-air): KARE (NBC) Minneapolis; KEYC-TV (CBS, FOX) Mankato; KMSP-TV (FOX) Minneapolis; KSTP-TV (ABC) St. Paul; KTCA-TV (PBS) St. Paul; KWCM-TV (PBS) Appleton; WCCO-TV (CBS) Minneapolis; WFTC (MNT) Minneapolis; WUCW (CW) Minneapolis; allband FM.
Programming (via satellite): ABC Family Channel; AMC; Arts & Entertainment; CNN; Discovery Channel; ESPN; ESPN 2; Fox Sports Net; Hallmark Channel; History Channel; Lifetime; Nickelodeon; QVC; Spike TV; TBS Superstation; The Learning Channel; Turner Network TV; TV Land; USA Network; VH1; Weather Channel.
Fee: $40.00 installation; $33.80 monthly.

Pay Service 1
Pay Units: 12.
Programming (via satellite): The Movie Channel.
Fee: $10.00 installation; $10.00 monthly.

Internet Service
Operational: No.

Telephone Service
None

Miles of Plant: 4.0 (coaxial); None (fiber optic). Additional miles planned: 4.0 (coaxial). Homes passed: 150. Total homes in franchised area: 150.
Manager: Bruce Hanson.
Ownership: Hanson Communications Inc. (MSO).

BEMIDJI—Midcontinent Communications, PO Box 5010, Sioux Falls, SD 57117. Phones: 800-456-0564; 605-229-1775. Fax: 605-229-0478. E-mail: mccomm@midco.net. Web Site: http://www.midcocomm.com. Also serves Beltrami County, Cass Lake, Turtle River & Wilton. ICA: MN0033.
TV Market Ranking: Below 100 (Beltrami County (portions), BEMIDJI, Cass Lake, Turtle River, Wilton); Outside TV Markets (Beltrami County (portions)). Franchise award date: January 1, 1968. Franchise expiration date: N.A. Began: January 1, 1971.
Channel capacity: N.A. Channels available but not in use: N.A.

Basic Service
Subscribers: 7,200.
Programming (received off-air): KARE (NBC) Minneapolis; KAWE (PBS) Bemidji; KCCW-TV (CBS) Walker; KMSP-TV (FOX) Minneapolis; KSAX (ABC) Alexandria; KSTC-TV (IND) Minneapolis; KVLY-TV (NBC) Fargo; WDIO-DT (ABC) Duluth; WFTC (MNT) Minneapolis.
Programming (via satellite): C-SPAN; Home Shopping Network; INSP; ION Television; QVC; TV Guide Network; WGN America.
Fee: $29.99 installation.

Expanded Basic Service 1
Subscribers: N.A.
Programming (via satellite): ABC Family Channel; AMC; Animal Planet; Arts & Entertainment; Bravo; Cartoon Network; CNBC; CNN; Comedy Central; Country Music TV; C-SPAN 2; Discovery Channel; Disney Channel; E! Entertainment Television; ESPN; ESPN 2; ESPN Classic Sports; Food Network; Fox News Channel; Fox Sports Net North; FX; G4; Golf Channel; GSN; Hallmark Channel; Headline News; HGTV; History Channel; Lifetime; MSNBC; MTV; National Geographic Channel; Nickelodeon; Outdoor Channel; Oxygen; SoapNet; Speed Channel; Spike TV; Syfy; TBS Superstation; The Learning Channel; Toon Disney; Travel Channel; Trinity Broadcasting Network; truTV; Turner Classic Movies; Turner Network TV; TV Land; USA Network; Versus; VH1; WE tv; Weather Channel.
Fee: $47.99 monthly.

Digital Basic Service
Subscribers: N.A.
Programming (via satellite): BBC America; Bio; Bloomberg Television; Boomerang; CNN en Espanol; CNN International; Discovery Digital Networks; Do-It-Yourself; ESPNews; Fox College Sports Atlantic; Fox College Sports Central; Fox College Sports Pacific; Fox Movie Channel; Fox Soccer; Fuel TV; GAS; History Channel International; Independent Film Channel; Lifetime Movie Network; MTV Networks Digital Suite; Music Choice; NFL Network; Nick Jr.; Nick Too; NickToons TV; Style Network; Sundance Channel; TV Guide Interactive Inc.

Digital Pay Service 1
Pay Units: N.A.
Programming (via satellite): Cinemax (multiplexed); Encore (multiplexed); Flix; HBO (multiplexed); Showtime (multiplexed); Starz (multiplexed); The Movie Channel (multiplexed).

Video-On-Demand: No

Pay-Per-View
iN DEMAND (delivered digitally); NASCAR In Car (delivered digitally); Playboy TV (delivered digitally); Spice Live (delivered digitally); Spice Platinum (delivered digitally); Hot Net Plus (delivered digitally); Spice Hot (delivered digitally).

Internet Service
Operational: Yes. Began: March 1, 2002.
Broadband Service: Charter Pipeline.
Fee: $29.99 monthly.

Telephone Service
None

Miles of Plant: 327.0 (coaxial); None (fiber optic). Homes passed: 10,609.
City fee: 5% of basic.
Ownership: Midcontinent Media Inc. (MSO).

BENSON—Charter Communications. Now served by WILLMAR, MN [MN0018]. ICA: MN0074.

BIG FALLS—North American Communications Corp., PO Box 387, 211 Main St S, Hector, MN 55342-0387. Phones: 800-982-8038; 320-848-6781. Fax: 320-848-2323. E-mail: hcc@hcctel.net. Web Site: http://www.hectorcom.com. ICA: MN0219.

TV Market Ranking: Below 100 (BIG FALLS). Franchise award date: March 15, 1990. Franchise expiration date: N.A. Began: October 15, 1990.

Channel capacity: 54 (not 2-way capable). Channels available but not in use: 32.

Basic Service

Subscribers: 31.

Programming (received off-air): KAWE (PBS) Bemidji; KBJR-TV (MNT, NBC) Superior; KDLH (CBS, CW) Duluth; WIRT-DT (ABC) Hibbing.

Programming (via satellite): ABC Family Channel; AMC; Arts & Entertainment; CNN; Country Music TV; Discovery Channel; Disney Channel; ESPN; Fox Sports Net Midwest; Headline News; Lifetime; Nickelodeon; QVC; Spike TV; TBS Superstation; Trinity Broadcasting Network; Turner Network TV; TV Land; USA Network; Weather Channel; WGN America.

Fee: $40.00 installation; $26.95 monthly; $2.95 converter; $25.00 additional installation.

Pay Service 1

Pay Units: 2.

Programming (via satellite): HBO.

Fee: $15.00 installation; $9.45 monthly.

Pay Service 2

Pay Units: 4.

Programming (via satellite): Cinemax.

Fee: $9.95 monthly.

Video-On-Demand: No

Internet Service

Operational: No.

Broadband Service: Offers dial-up and DSL only; no cable modem service.

Telephone Service

None

Miles of Plant: 6.0 (coaxial); None (fiber optic). Homes passed: 175. Total homes in franchised area: 175.

Manager: Matt Sparks. Chief Technician: George Honzay. Customer Service Supervisor: Patty Groshens.

Ownership: Hector Communications Corp. (MSO).

BIGELOW—Formerly served by American Telecasting of America Inc. No longer in operation. ICA: MN0272.

BIGFORK—North American Communications Corp., PO Box 387, 211 Main St S, Hector, MN 55342-0387. Phones: 800-982-8038; 320-848-6781. Fax: 320-848-2323. E-mail: hcc@hcctel.net. Web Site: http://www.hectorcom.com. ICA: MN0220.

TV Market Ranking: Outside TV Markets (BIGFORK). Franchise award date: N.A. Franchise expiration date: N.A. Began: October 15, 1990.

Channel capacity: 54 (not 2-way capable). Channels available but not in use: 30.

Basic Service

Subscribers: 96.

Programming (received off-air): KAWE (PBS) Bemidji; KBJR-TV (MNT, NBC) Superior; KCCW-TV (CBS) Walker; KDLH (CBS, CW) Duluth; KVRR (FOX) Fargo; WDIO-DT (ABC) Duluth; WIRT-DT (ABC) Hibbing.

Programming (via satellite): ABC Family Channel; AMC; Arts & Entertainment; CNN; Discovery Channel; Disney Channel; ESPN; Fox Sports Net Midwest; Headline News; History Channel; Lifetime; Nickelodeon; QVC; Spike TV; TBS Superstation; Trinity Broadcasting Network; Turner Network TV; TV Land; USA Network; Weather Channel; WGN America.

Fee: $40.00 installation; $26.95 monthly; $2.00 converter; $25.00 additional installation.

Pay Service 1

Pay Units: 8.

Programming (via satellite): HBO.

Fee: $9.95 monthly.

Pay Service 2

Pay Units: 4.

Programming (via satellite): Cinemax.

Fee: $9.45 monthly.

Video-On-Demand: No

Internet Service

Operational: No.

Broadband Service: Offers dial-up and DSL only; no cable modem service.

Telephone Service

None

Miles of Plant: 6.0 (coaxial); None (fiber optic). Homes passed: 200. Total homes in franchised area: 200.

Manager: Matt Sparks. Chief Technician: George Honzey. Customer Service Supervisor: Patty Groshens.

Ownership: Hector Communications Corp. (MSO).

BLACKDUCK—Blackduck Cablevision Inc., PO Box 325, 50 Margaret Ave. NE, Blackduck, MN 56630-0325. Phone: 218-835-7890. Fax: 218-835-3299. E-mail: bdtele@blackduck.net. Web Site: http://www.blackduck.net. ICA: MN0164.

TV Market Ranking: Below 100 (BLACKDUCK). Franchise award date: November 1, 1983. Franchise expiration date: N.A. Began: November 15, 1983.

Channel capacity: 40 (operating 2-way). Channels available but not in use: 12.

Basic Service

Subscribers: 370.

Programming (received off-air): KAWE (PBS) Bemidji; WIRT-DT (ABC) Hibbing; 1 FM.

Programming (via satellite): ABC Family Channel; Arts & Entertainment; CNN; Discovery Channel; Disney Channel; ESPN; ESPN 2; Fox News Channel; Fox Sports Net; HGTV; History Channel; Nickelodeon; Outdoor Channel; Spike TV; TBS Superstation; The Learning Channel; Turner Classic Movies; Turner Network TV; TV Land; USA Network; Weather Channel; WGN America.

Programming (via translator): KARE (NBC) Minneapolis; KMSP-TV (FOX) Minneapolis; WCCO-TV (CBS) Minneapolis.

Fee: $25.00 installation; $17.85 monthly; $1.50 converter.

Pay Service 1

Pay Units: 34.

Programming (via satellite): Cinemax.

Fee: $9.95 monthly.

Pay Service 2

Pay Units: 20.

Programming (via satellite): HBO.

Fee: $9.95 monthly.

Video-On-Demand: No

Internet Service

Operational: No, DSL.

Telephone Service

None

Miles of Plant: 10.0 (coaxial); None (fiber optic). Homes passed: 630. Total homes in franchised area: 630.

Manager: Bob Gannon. Chief Technician: Richard Lien.

Ownership: Blackduck Telephone Co.

BLOOMING PRAIRIE—Mediacom. Now served by Dodge Center, MN [MN0093]. Also serves BLOOMING PRAIRIE. ICA: MN0122.

BLOOMINGTON—Time Warner Cable. Now served by MINNEAPOLIS, MN [MN0001]. ICA: MN0273.

BLUE EARTH—Bevcomm Inc., 123 W 7th St, Blue Earth, MN 56013. Phones: 800-342-1019; 506-526-2822. Web Site: http://www.bevcomm.net. Also serves Elmore. ICA: MN0058.

TV Market Ranking: Outside TV Markets (BLUE EARTH, Elmore). Franchise award date: N.A. Franchise expiration date: N.A. Began: December 1, 1973.

Channel capacity: N.A. Channels available but not in use: N.A.

Basic Service

Subscribers: 1,090.

Programming (received off-air): KAAL (ABC) Austin; KARE (NBC) Minneapolis; KEYC-TV (CBS, FOX) Mankato; KTIN (PBS) Fort Dodge; KTTC (CW, NBC) Rochester; WFTC (MNT) Minneapolis; WUCW (CW) Minneapolis; allband FM.

Programming (via microwave): KMSP-TV (FOX) Minneapolis; KSTP-TV (ABC) St. Paul; KTCA-TV (PBS) St. Paul; WCCO-TV (CBS) Minneapolis.

Programming (via satellite): C-SPAN; C-SPAN 2; Eternal Word TV Network; Home Shopping Network; QVC; TBS Superstation; TV Guide Network; WGN America.

Current originations: Government Access; Educational Access; Public Access; Leased Access.

Fee: $29.99 installation.

Expanded Basic Service 1

Subscribers: N.A.

Programming (via satellite): ABC Family Channel; AMC; Animal Planet; Arts & Entertainment; Bravo; Cartoon Network; CNN; Comedy Central; Country Music TV; Discovery Channel; Disney Channel; E! Entertainment Television; ESPN; ESPN 2; Food Network; Fox News Channel; Fox Sports Net North; FX; GSN; Hallmark Channel; HGTV; History Channel; Lifetime; MTV; MTV2; National Geographic Channel; Nickelodeon; SoapNet; Speed Channel; Spike TV; Syfy; The Learning Channel; Toon Disney; Travel Channel; truTV; Turner Classic Movies; Turner Network TV; TV Land; USA Network; Versus; VH1; WE tv; Weather Channel.

Fee: $47.99 monthly.

Digital Basic Service

Subscribers: N.A.

Programming (via satellite): BBC America; Bio; Discovery Digital Networks; Do-It-Yourself; FitTV; Fox College Sports Atlantic; Fox College Sports Central; Fox College Sports Pacific; Fox Movie Channel; Fox Soccer; Fuel TV; History Channel International; Independent Film Channel; Music Choice; Sundance Channel; TV Guide Interactive Inc.

Digital Pay Service 1

Pay Units: N.A.

Programming (via satellite): Cinemax (multiplexed); Encore (multiplexed); Flix; HBO (multiplexed); Showtime (multiplexed); Starz (multiplexed); The Movie Channel (multiplexed).

Video-On-Demand: No

Pay-Per-View

iN DEMAND (delivered digitally); Playboy TV (delivered digitally); Fresh (delivered digitally); Shorteez (delivered digitally).

Internet Service

Operational: Yes.

Broadband Service: Charter Pipeline.

Fee: $29.99 monthly.

Telephone Service

None

Miles of Plant: 41.0 (coaxial); None (fiber optic). Homes passed: 2,080. Total homes in franchised area: 2,080.

City fee: None.

Ownership: BEVCOMM (MSO).

BLUEBERRY TWP.—Formerly served by MENAHGA, MN [MN0118]. West Central Telephone Assn. This cable system has converted to IPTV, 308 Frontage Rd, Sebeka, MN 56477. Phones: 800-945-2163; 218-837-5151. Web Site: http://www.wcta.net. ICA: MN5249.

TV Market Ranking: Below 100 (BLUEBERRY TWP.).

Channel capacity: N.A. Channels available but not in use: N.A.

Internet Service

Operational: Yes.

Telephone Service

Digital: Operational

Ownership: West Central Telephone Association.

BLUFFTON TWP.—ACS Video. Formerly served by Perham, MN [MN0050]. This cable system has converted to IPTV, 150 Second St SW, Perham, MN 56573. Phone: 866-937-4227. E-mail: answers@arvig.com. Web Site: http://www.arvig.com. ICA: MN5236.

TV Market Ranking: Outside TV Markets (BLUFFTON TWP.).

Channel capacity: N.A. Channels available but not in use: N.A.

Internet Service

Operational: Yes.

Telephone Service

Digital: Operational

Ownership: Arvig Communication Systems.

BOVEY—North American Communications Corp., PO Box 387, 211 Main St S, Hector, MN 55342-0387. Phones: 800-982-8038; 320-848-6781. Fax: 320-848-2323. E-mail: hcc@hcctel.net. Web Site: http://www.hectorcom.com. Also serves Coleraine. ICA: MN0112.

TV Market Ranking: Below 100 (BOVEY, Coleraine). Franchise award date: N.A. Franchise expiration date: N.A. Began: July 10, 1965.

Channel capacity: 78 (not 2-way capable). Channels available but not in use: 35.

Basic Service

Subscribers: 224.

Programming (received off-air): KAWE (PBS) Bemidji; KBJR-TV (MNT, NBC) Superior; KCCW-TV (CBS) Walker; KDLH (CBS, CW) Duluth; KMSP-TV (FOX) Minneapolis; KVRR (FOX) Fargo; WDIO-DT (ABC) Duluth; WDSE (PBS) Duluth; WIRT-DT (ABC) Hibbing; 1 FM.

Programming (via satellite): ABC Family Channel; AMC; Animal Planet; Arts & Entertainment; Cartoon Network; CNBC; CNN; Country Music TV; C-SPAN; Discovery Channel; Disney Channel; ESPN; ESPN 2; Eternal Word TV Network; Fox Sports Net Midwest; Hallmark Channel; Headline News; HGTV; History Channel; Lifetime; MTV; Nickelodeon; QVC; Spike TV; Syfy; TBS Superstation; The Learning Channel; Turner Network TV; TV Land; USA Network; VH1; Weather Channel; WGN America.

Current originations: Public Access.

Fee: $40.00 installation; $22.95 monthly; $3.95 converter; $25.00 additional installation.

Pay Service 1

Pay Units: 12.

Programming (via satellite): HBO.

Fee: $10.95 monthly.

Pay Service 2

Pay Units: 8.

Programming (via satellite): Showtime.

Fee: $9.95 monthly.
Video-On-Demand: No
Internet Service
Operational: No.
Broadband Service: Offers dial-up and DSL only; no cable modem service.
Telephone Service
None
Miles of Plant: 4.0 (coaxial); None (fiber optic). Homes passed: 790. Total homes in franchised area: 795.
Manager: Matt Sparks. Chief Technician: George Honzey. Customer Service Supervisor: Patty Groshens.
City fee: None.
Ownership: Hector Communications Corp. (MSO).

BRAINERD—Charter Communications, 3380 Northern Valley Pl NE, Rochester, MN 55906-3954. Phones: 507-289-8372 (Rochester office); 218-829-9015 (Local office). Fax: 507-285-6162. Web Site: http://www.charter.com. Also serves Aitkin, Baxter, Bay Lake, Browerville, Clarissa, Crosby, Crow Wing County (unincorporated areas), Cuyuna, Deerwood, Irondale, Ironton, Lake Shore, Long Prairie, Nisswa, Oak Lawn Twp., Perry Lake Twp., Rabbit Lake Twp., Riverton, Staples & Wolford. ICA: MN0022.
TV Market Ranking: Below 100 (Browerville, Clarissa, Crow Wing County (unincorporated areas) (portions), Long Prairie); Outside TV Markets (Aitkin, Baxter, Bay Lake, BRAINERD, Crosby, Crow Wing County (unincorporated areas) (portions), Cuyuna, Deerwood, Irondale, Ironton, Lake Shore, Nisswa, Oak Lawn Twp., Perry Lake Twp., Rabbit Lake Twp., Riverton, Staples, Wolford). Franchise award date: December 18, 1955. Franchise expiration date: N.A. Began: November 1, 1956.
Channel capacity: 80 (operating 2-way). Channels available but not in use: 17.
Basic Service
Subscribers: 9,026.
Programming (received off-air): KAWB (PBS) Brainerd; KCCW-TV (CBS) Walker; KPXM-TV (ION) St. Cloud; KSAX (ABC) Alexandria.
Programming (via microwave): KARE (NBC) Minneapolis; KMSP-TV (FOX) Minneapolis; KSTC-TV (IND) Minneapolis; KTCA-TV (PBS) St. Paul; WFTC (MNT) Minneapolis; WUCW (CW) Minneapolis.
Programming (via satellite): C-SPAN; C-SPAN 2; Eternal Word TV Network; Home Shopping Network; INSP; QVC; TBS Superstation; Trinity Broadcasting Network; TV Guide Network; Weather Channel; WGN America.
Current originations: Leased Access; Government Access; Educational Access; Public Access.
Fee: $29.99 installation; $1.36 converter.
Expanded Basic Service 1
Subscribers: N.A.
Programming (via satellite): ABC Family Channel; AMC; Animal Planet; Arts & Entertainment; Bravo; Cartoon Network; CNBC; CNN; Comedy Central; Country Music TV; Discovery Channel; Disney Channel; E! Entertainment Television; ESPN; ESPN 2; Food Network; Fox News Channel; Fox Sports Net North; FX; Golf Channel; Headline News; HGTV; History Channel; Lifetime; MSNBC; MTV; Nickelodeon; Outdoor Channel; Speed Channel; Spike TV; Syfy; The Learning Channel; Travel Channel; truTV; Turner Network TV; TV Land; USA Network; Versus; VH1.
Fee: $47.99 monthly.
Digital Basic Service
Subscribers: N.A.
Programming (via satellite): BBC America; Bio; Boomerang; CNN en Espanol; Discovery Health Channel; Discovery Home Channel; Discovery Kids Channel; Discovery Times Channel; Do-It-Yourself; ESPN Classic Sports; ESPNews; Fox College Sports Atlantic; Fox College Sports Central; Fox College Sports Pacific; Fox Soccer; Fuel TV; G4; GAS; History Channel International; Independent Film Channel; Lifetime Movie Network; MTV Networks Digital Suite; Music Choice; NFL Network; Nick Jr.; Nick Too; NickToons TV; Science Television; SoapNet; Sundance Channel; Toon Disney; Turner Classic Movies; WE tv.
Pay Service 1
Pay Units: N.A.
Programming (via satellite): Flix; Showtime (multiplexed); The Movie Channel (multiplexed).
Digital Pay Service 1
Pay Units: N.A.
Programming (via satellite): Cinemax (multiplexed); Encore; HBO (multiplexed); Starz (multiplexed).
Video-On-Demand: Yes
Pay-Per-View
Playboy TV (delivered digitally); Fresh (delivered digitally); Shorteez (delivered digitally).
Internet Service
Operational: Yes.
Broadband Service: Charter Pipeline.
Fee: $29.99 monthly.
Telephone Service
Digital: Operational
Miles of Plant: 635.0 (coaxial); 240.0 (fiber optic). Total homes in franchised area: 27,643.
Vice President & General Manager: John Crowley. Technical Operations Director: Mark Abramo. Operations Director: Craig Stensaas. Marketing Director: Bill Haarstad.
City fee: 3% of gross.
Ownership: Charter Communications Inc. (MSO).

BREWSTER—US Cable, 402 Red River Ave N, Unit 5, Cold Spring, MN 56320-1521. Phones: 800-685-2816; 320-685-7113. Fax: 320-685-2816. E-mail: help@mn.uscable.com. Web Site: http://www.uscable.com. ICA: MN0052.
TV Market Ranking: Outside TV Markets (BREWSTER). Franchise award date: N.A. Franchise expiration date: N.A. Began: September 1, 1983.
Channel capacity: 35 (operating 2-way). Channels available but not in use: N.A.
Basic Service
Subscribers: N.A. Included in Cambridge
Programming (received off-air): KARE (NBC) Minneapolis; KDLT-TV (NBC) Sioux Falls; KELO-TV (CBS, MNT) Sioux Falls; KEYC-TV (CBS, FOX) Mankato; KMSP-TV (FOX) Minneapolis; KSFY-TV (ABC) Sioux Falls; KSMN (PBS) Worthington; KSTP-TV (ABC) St. Paul; WFTC (MNT) Minneapolis.
Programming (via satellite): ABC Family Channel; Arts & Entertainment; CNBC; CNN; Comedy Central; Country Music TV; Discovery Channel; ESPN; ESPN 2; Fox Sports Net North; Hallmark Channel; Headline News; HGTV; History Channel; Home Shopping Network; Lifetime; Nickelodeon; Outdoor Channel; Spike TV; TBS Superstation; The Learning Channel; Turner Classic Movies; Turner Network TV; TV Land; USA Network; VH1; Weather Channel; WGN America.
Fee: $39.95 installation; $37.24 monthly.
Pay Service 1
Pay Units: N.A. Included in Cambridge
Programming (via satellite): HBO.
Fee: $11.95 monthly.
Video-On-Demand: No
Internet Service
Operational: Yes.
Telephone Service
None
Homes passed: Included in Cambridge
General Manager: Steve Johnson. Customer Service Director: Jackie Torberg.
City fee: None.
Ownership: US Cable Corp. (MSO).; Comcast Cable Communications Inc. (MSO).

BRICELYN—Bevcomm Inc., 123 W 7th St, Blue Earth, MN 56013. Phones: 800-753-5113; 507-653-4444. Web Site: http://www.bevcomm.net. Also serves Frost & Kiester. ICA: MN0161.
TV Market Ranking: Outside TV Markets (BRICELYN, Frost, Kiester). Franchise award date: N.A. Franchise expiration date: N.A. Began: November 1, 1986.
Channel capacity: 54 (operating 2-way). Channels available but not in use: N.A.
Basic Service
Subscribers: 430.
Programming (received off-air): KAAL (ABC) Austin; KARE (NBC) Minneapolis; KEYC-TV (CBS, FOX) Mankato; KIMT (CBS, MNT) Mason City; KMSP-TV (FOX) Minneapolis; KSTC-TV (IND) Minneapolis; KSTP-TV (ABC) St. Paul; KTTC (CW, NBC) Rochester; WCCO-TV (CBS) Minneapolis; WFTC (MNT) Minneapolis; WUCW (CW) Minneapolis; allband FM.
Programming (via satellite): ABC Family Channel; AMC; Animal Planet; Arts & Entertainment; CNBC; CNN; Comedy Central; Country Music TV; Discovery Channel; Disney Channel; ESPN; ESPN 2; Food Network; Fox News Channel; Fox Sports Net; FX; Hallmark Channel; HGTV; History Channel; Home Shopping Network; Lifetime; MSNBC; MTV; Nickelodeon; Spike TV; Syfy; TBS Superstation; The Learning Channel; truTV; Turner Classic Movies; Turner Network TV; TV Land; USA Network; Versus; VH1; Weather Channel; WGN America.
Current originations: Public Access.
Fee: $40.00 installation; $34.95 monthly.
Digital Basic Service
Subscribers: N.A.
Programming (via satellite): BBC America; Bio; Bloomberg Television; Bravo; Discovery Digital Networks; DMX Music; ESPN 2; ESPN Classic Sports; ESPNews; Fox Soccer; Fuse; G4; GAS; Golf Channel; GSN; Halogen Network; HGTV; History Channel; History Channel International; Independent Film Channel; MTV Networks Digital Suite; National Geographic Channel; Nick Jr.; NickToons TV; Outdoor Channel; Sleuth; Speed Channel; Style Network; Syfy; Toon Disney; Trinity Broadcasting Network; Turner Classic Movies; Versus; WE tv.
Fee: $8.00 monthly.
Pay Service 1
Pay Units: 58.
Programming (via satellite): Cinemax.
Fee: $7.50 installation; $12.95 monthly.
Pay Service 2
Pay Units: 56.
Programming (via satellite): HBO.
Fee: $7.50 installation; $12.95 monthly.
Digital Pay Service 1
Pay Units: N.A.
Programming (via satellite): Cinemax (multiplexed); Encore (multiplexed); Flix; HBO (multiplexed); Showtime (multiplexed); Starz (multiplexed); The Movie Channel (multiplexed).
Fee: $11.95 monthly (Starz/Encore), $12.95 monthly (Showtime/TMC), $15.95 monthly (HBO/Cinemax).
Video-On-Demand: No
Pay-Per-View
iN DEMAND (delivered digitally); Hot Choice (delivered digitally); Playboy TV (delivered digitally); Fresh (delivered digitally).
Internet Service
Operational: No, DSL only.
Telephone Service
None
Miles of Plant: 14.0 (coaxial); 8.0 (fiber optic). Homes passed: 575. Total homes in franchised area: 575.
Ownership: BEVCOMM (MSO).

BROOKLYN PARK—Comcast Cable. Now served by ST. PAUL (formerly Roseville), MN [MN0002]. ICA: MN0004.

BROOTEN—Now served by CHOKIO, MN [MN0210]. ICA: MN0187.

BROWERVILLE—Charter Communications. Now served by BRAINERD, MN [MN0022]. ICA: MN0276.

BROWNS VALLEY—Midcontinent Communications, PO Box 5010, Sioux Falls, SD 57117. Phones: 800-456-0564; 605-229-1775. Fax: 605-229-0478. Web Site: http://www.midcocomm.com. ICA: MN0169.
TV Market Ranking: Outside TV Markets (BROWNS VALLEY). Franchise award date: N.A. Franchise expiration date: N.A. Began: June 1, 1975.
Channel capacity: 35 (not 2-way capable). Channels available but not in use: N.A.
Basic Service
Subscribers: 250.
Programming (received off-air): KABY-TV (ABC) Aberdeen; KCCO-TV (CBS) Alexandria; KDLO-TV (CBS, MNT) Florence; KVLY-TV (NBC) Fargo; KVRR (FOX) Fargo; KWCM-TV (PBS) Appleton; 1 FM.
Programming (via satellite): ABC Family Channel; AMC; Animal Planet; Cartoon Network; CNN; C-SPAN; Discovery Channel; Disney Channel; ESPN; Lifetime; Nickelodeon; Spike TV; TBS Superstation; Turner Network TV; USA Network; Weather Channel; WGN America.
Fee: $24.95 installation; $24.68 monthly.
Pay Service 1
Pay Units: 82.
Programming (via satellite): Encore.
Fee: $1.75 monthly.
Pay Service 2
Pay Units: 35.
Programming (via satellite): HBO.
Fee: $14.19 monthly.
Pay Service 3
Pay Units: 31.
Programming (via satellite): Starz.
Fee: $6.75 monthly.
Video-On-Demand: No
Internet Service
Operational: No.
Telephone Service
None
Miles of Plant: 9.0 (coaxial); None (fiber optic). Homes passed: 432. Total homes in franchised area: 432.
Manager: Jeff Fritch. Chief Technician: Ray Olson.

City fee: None.
Ownership: Midcontinent Media Inc. (MSO).; Comcast Cable Communications Inc. (MSO).

BROWNSVILLE—Now served by CALEDONIA, MN [MN0086]. ICA: MN0231.

BROWNTON—Mediacom, PO Box 110, 1504 2nd St SE, Waseca, MN 56093. Phones: 800-332-0245; 507-835-2356. Fax: 507-835-4567. Web Site: http://www.mediacomcable.com. Also serves Buffalo Lake, Hector, Hutchinson, Lester Prairie, Litchfield, Silver Lake, Stewart & Winsted. ICA: MN0145.
TV Market Ranking: Below 100 (Buffalo Lake, Hector, Litchfield, Stewart); Outside TV Markets (BROWNTON, Hutchinson, Lester Prairie, Silver Lake, Winsted). Franchise award date: N.A. Franchise expiration date: N.A. Began: November 1, 1985.
Channel capacity: N.A. Channels available but not in use: N.A.
Basic Service
Subscribers: 7,064.
Programming (received off-air): KARE (NBC) Minneapolis; KEYC-TV (CBS, FOX) Mankato; KMSP-TV (FOX) Minneapolis; KPXM-TV (ION) St. Cloud; KSTC-TV (IND) Minneapolis; KSTP-TV (ABC) St. Paul; KTCA-TV (PBS) St. Paul; KTCI-TV (PBS) St. Paul; WCCO-TV (CBS) Minneapolis; WFTC (MNT) Minneapolis; WUCW (CW) Minneapolis.
Programming (via satellite): C-SPAN; Home Shopping Network; QVC; TV Guide Network; Weather Channel; WGN America.
Fee: $9.95 monthly.
Expanded Basic Service 1
Subscribers: 6,693.
Programming (via satellite): ABC Family Channel; AMC; Animal Planet; Arts & Entertainment; BET Networks; Bravo; Cartoon Network; CNBC; CNN; Comedy Central; Country Music TV; Discovery Channel; Disney Channel; E! Entertainment Television; ESPN; ESPN 2; Eternal Word TV Network; Food Network; Fox Movie Channel; Fox News Channel; Fox Sports Net North; FX; Hallmark Channel; Headline News; HGTV; History Channel; INSP; Lifetime; MSNBC; MTV; Nickelodeon; SoapNet; Speed Channel; Spike TV; Syfy; TBS Superstation; The Learning Channel; Travel Channel; Trinity Broadcasting Network; truTV; Turner Classic Movies; Turner Network TV; TV Land; Univision; USA Network; VH1; WE tv.
Fee: $26.18 monthly.
Digital Basic Service
Subscribers: N.A.
Programming (via satellite): AmericanLife TV Network; BBC America; Bio; Bloomberg Television; Canales N; Discovery Digital Networks; DMX Music; Fox Sports World; Fuse; G4; Golf Channel; GSN; Halogen Network; History Channel International; Independent Film Channel; Lifetime Movie Network; Lime; Outdoor Channel; Style Network; Versus.
Digital Pay Service 1
Pay Units: 4,783.
Programming (via satellite): Cinemax (multiplexed); Encore (multiplexed); Flix; HBO (multiplexed); Showtime (multiplexed); Starz (multiplexed); Sundance Channel; The Movie Channel (multiplexed).
Fee: $9.95 monthly (each).
Video-On-Demand: No
Pay-Per-View
TVN Entertainment (delivered digitally); ESPN Now (delivered digitally); Sports PPV (delivered digitally); Urban Xtra (delivered digitally); Fresh (delivered digitally); Shorteez (delivered digitally); Playboy TV (delivered digitally); Pleasure (delivered digitally).
Internet Service
Operational: Yes.
Broadband Service: Mediacom High Speed Internet.
Fee: $99.00 installation; $40.95 monthly.
Telephone Service
Analog: Not Operational
Digital: Operational
Miles of Plant: 169.0 (coaxial); None (fiber optic). Homes passed: 10,663.
Vice President: Bill Jensen. Engineering Manager: Kraig Kaiser. Sales & Marketing Director: Lori Huberty.
Ownership: Mediacom LLC (MSO).

BUFFALO—Charter Communications, 101 6th St, Buffalo, MN 55313. Phones: 507-289-8372 (Rochester administrative office); 763-682-5982 (Local office). Fax: 763-682-1645. Web Site: http://www.charter.com. Also serves Albertville, Big Lake, Cokato, Dassel, Dayton, Delano, Elk River, Hassan Twp., Maple Lake, Monticello, Otsego, Rockford, St. Michael & Watertown. ICA: MN0012.
TV Market Ranking: 13 (Albertville, Big Lake, BUFFALO, Dayton, Delano, Elk River, Hassan Twp., Otsego, Rockford, St. Michael, Watertown); Below 100 (Cokato, Dassel, Maple Lake, Monticello). Franchise award date: September 1, 1984. Franchise expiration date: N.A. Began: December 18, 1984.
Channel capacity: N.A. Channels available but not in use: N.A.
Basic Service
Subscribers: 19,000.
Programming (received off-air): KARE (NBC) Minneapolis; KMSP-TV (FOX) Minneapolis; KPXM-TV (ION) St. Cloud; KSTC-TV (IND) Minneapolis; KSTP-TV (ABC) St. Paul; KTCA-TV (PBS) St. Paul; KTCI-TV (PBS) St. Paul; WCCO-TV (CBS) Minneapolis; WFTC (MNT) Minneapolis; WUCW (CW) Minneapolis; 30 FMs.
Programming (via satellite): C-SPAN 2; Eternal Word TV Network; INSP; QVC; TBS Superstation; TV Guide Network; WGN America.
Current originations: Leased Access; Government Access; Educational Access; Public Access.
Fee: $29.99 installation; $2.00 converter.
Expanded Basic Service 1
Subscribers: 9,515.
Programming (via satellite): ABC Family Channel; AMC; Animal Planet; Arts & Entertainment; Bravo; Cartoon Network; CNBC; CNN; Comedy Central; Country Music TV; C-SPAN; Discovery Channel; Disney Channel; E! Entertainment Television; ESPN; ESPN 2; Food Network; Fox News Channel; Fox Sports Net North; FX; G4; Golf Channel; Great American Country; Hallmark Channel; Headline News; HGTV; History Channel; Home Shopping Network; Lifetime; MSNBC; MTV; MTV2; National Geographic Channel; Nickelodeon; Oxygen; Speed Channel; Spike TV; Syfy; The Learning Channel; Travel Channel; truTV; Turner Classic Movies; Turner Network TV; TV Land; Univision; USA Network; Versus; VH1; WE tv; Weather Channel.
Fee: $36.00 installation; $47.99 monthly.
Digital Basic Service
Subscribers: N.A.
Programming (received off-air): KARE (NBC) Minneapolis; KMSP-TV (FOX) Minneapolis; WCCO-TV (CBS) Minneapolis.
Programming (via satellite): BBC America; Bio; Bloomberg Television; Boomerang; CBS College Sports Network; CNN en Espanol; CNN International; Discovery Digital Networks; Do-It-Yourself; ESPN; ESPN Classic Sports; ESPNews; FitTV; Fox College Sports Atlantic; Fox College Sports Central; Fox College Sports Pacific; Fox Movie Channel; Fox Soccer; Fuel TV; Fuse; GAS; HDNet; HDNet Movies; History Channel International; Independent Film Channel; Lifetime Movie Network; MTV Networks Digital Suite; Music Choice; NFL Network; Nick Jr.; Nick Too; NickToons TV; Outdoor Channel; SoapNet; Style Network; Sundance Channel; Toon Disney; TV Guide Interactive Inc.
Digital Pay Service 1
Pay Units: N.A.
Programming (via satellite): Cinemax (multiplexed); Encore (multiplexed); HBO (multiplexed); HBO HD; Showtime (multiplexed); Showtime HD; Starz (multiplexed); The Movie Channel (multiplexed).
Video-On-Demand: Yes
Pay-Per-View
iN DEMAND (delivered digitally); NASCAR In Car (delivered digitally); NHL Center Ice (delivered digitally); MLB Extra Innings (delivered digitally); Playboy TV (delivered digitally); Spice Live (delivered digitally); Spice Platinum (delivered digitally); Hot Net Plus (delivered digitally); Spice Hot (delivered digitally).
Internet Service
Operational: Yes.
Broadband Service: Charter Pipeline.
Fee: $29.99 monthly.
Telephone Service
Digital: Operational
Fee: $29.99 monthly
Miles of Plant: 459.0 (coaxial); 39.0 (fiber optic). Additional miles planned: 5.0 (coaxial). Homes passed: 41,000.
Vice President & General Manager: John Crowley. Operations Director: Craig Stensaas. Chief Technician: Jason Habiger. Marketing Director: Bill Haarstad. Office Manager: Sue Labelle.
City fee: 5% of gross.
Ownership: Charter Communications Inc. (MSO).

CALEDONIA—Mediacom, 4010 Alexandra Dr, Waterloo, IA 50702. Phone: 319-235-2197. Fax: 319-232-7841. Web Site: http://www.mediacomcable.com. Also serves Brownsville, Canton, Dakota, Dresbach, Hokah, Houston, Lanesboro, Mabel, Peterson & Spring Grove. ICA: MN0086.
TV Market Ranking: Below 100 (Brownsville, CALEDONIA, Dakota, Dresbach, Hokah, Houston, Lanesboro, Mabel, Peterson, Spring Grove); Outside TV Markets (Canton). Franchise award date: September 28, 1981. Franchise expiration date: N.A. Began: January 1, 1982.
Channel capacity: N.A. Channels available but not in use: N.A.
Basic Service
Subscribers: 2,783.
Programming (received off-air): KAAL (ABC) Austin; KIMT (CBS, MNT) Mason City; KPXM-TV (ION) St. Cloud; KTTC (CW, NBC) Rochester; KXLT-TV (FOX) Rochester; WEAU-TV (NBC) Eau Claire; WHLA-TV (PBS) La Crosse; WKBT-DT (CBS, MNT) La Crosse; WLAX (FOX) La Crosse; WXOW (ABC, CW) La Crosse.
Programming (via satellite): C-SPAN; C-SPAN 2; QVC; WGN America.
Current originations: Public Access.
Fee: $45.00 installation; $16.95 monthly.
Expanded Basic Service 1
Subscribers: 1,215.
Programming (via satellite): ABC Family Channel; AMC; Animal Planet; Arts & Entertainment; Bravo; Cartoon Network; CNBC; CNN; Comedy Central; Country Music TV; Discovery Channel; Disney Channel; E! Entertainment Television; ESPN; ESPN 2; Eternal Word TV Network; Food Network; Fox News Channel; Fox Sports Net North; FX; Hallmark Channel; Headline News; HGTV; History Channel; Home Shopping Network; Lifetime; MSNBC; MTV; National Geographic Channel; Nickelodeon; Speed Channel; Spike TV; Syfy; TBS Superstation; The Learning Channel; Travel Channel; Trinity Broadcasting Network; truTV; Turner Classic Movies; Turner Network TV; TV Guide Network; TV Land; Univision; USA Network; Versus; VH1; WE tv; Weather Channel.
Fee: $20.96 monthly.
Digital Basic Service
Subscribers: 2,783.
Programming (received off-air): Bio.
Programming (via satellite): American-Life TV Network; BBC America; Bloomberg Television; CCTV-4; Discovery Digital Networks; DMX Music; ESPN U; Fox Movie Channel; Fox Reality Channel; Fox Sports World; Fuel TV; G4; Golf Channel; GSN; Halogen Network; History Channel International; Independent Film Channel; Lifetime Movie Network; Lifetime Real Women; Lime; MTV Networks Digital Suite; Nick Jr.; NickToons TV; Outdoor Channel; Ovation; Style Network; Toon Disney; Turner Classic Movies.
Fee: $45.00 installation; $14.95 monthly.
Digital Pay Service 1
Pay Units: 465.
Programming (via satellite): Cinemax (multiplexed); Encore (multiplexed); Flix; HBO (multiplexed); Showtime (multiplexed); Starz (multiplexed); Sundance Channel; The Movie Channel (multiplexed).
Fee: $45.00 installation; $10.95 monthly (each).
Video-On-Demand: No
Pay-Per-View
TVN Entertainment (delivered digitally); ESPN Now (delivered digitally); Sports PPV (delivered digitally); Urban Xtra (delivered digitally); Fresh (delivered digitally); Shorteez (delivered digitally); Playboy TV (delivered digitally); Pleasure (delivered digitally).
Internet Service
Operational: Yes.
Broadband Service: Mediacom High Speed Internet.
Fee: $40.00 monthly.
Telephone Service
Digital: Operational
Miles of Plant: 74.0 (coaxial); None (fiber optic). Homes passed: 3,981. Total homes in franchised area: 4,175.
Regional Vice President: Doug Frank. General Manager: Doug Nix. Technical Operations Director: Greg Nank. Marketing Director: Steve Schuh. Marketing Coordinator: Joni Lindauer.
City fee: 3% of gross.
Ownership: Mediacom LLC (MSO).

CAMBRIDGE—US Cable, 402 Red River Ave N, Unit 5, Cold Spring, MN 56320-1521. Phones: 800-783-2356; 320-685-7113. Fax: 320-685-2816. E-mail: help@mn.uscable.com. Web Site: http://www.uscable.com. Also serves Rockville, MI; Avon, Baldwin Twp., Becker, Bethel, Blue Hill Twp., Bradford Twp., Braham, Center City, Chisago City,

Clear Lake, Clearwater, Cold Spring, Columbus Twp., East Bethel, Foley, Forest Lake, Foreston, Harris, Haven Twp., Holdingford, Isanti, Lent Twp., Lindstrom, Linwood, Linwood Twp., Livonia Twp., Marine on the St. Croix, May Twp., Milaca, Mora, Nessel Twp., New Scandia Twp., North Branch, Ogilvie, Palmer Twp., Pierz, Pine City, Princeton, Richmond, Royalton, Rush City, Rush Lake, Scandia, Shafer, St. Augusta, St. Francis, St. Joseph, St. Stephen, St. Wendel Twp., Stacy, Stanford Twp., Taylors Falls, Wakefield Twp, Wyoming & Zimmerman, MN. ICA: MN0016.

TV Market Ranking: 13 (Bethel, Center City, Chisago City, Columbus Twp., East Bethel, Forest Lake, Foreston, Lent Twp., Lindstrom, Linwood, Linwood Twp., Marine on the St. Croix, May Twp., New Scandia Twp., Scandia, St. Francis, Stacy, Stanford Twp., Wyoming); Below 100 (Avon, Baldwin Twp., Becker, Blue Hill Twp., Clear Lake, Clear Lake Twp., Clearwater, Cold Spring, Foley, Freeport, Haven Twp., Holdingford, Livonia Twp., Milaca, Palmer Twp., Pierz, Princeton, Richmond, Rockville, Rockville, Royalton, St. Augusta, St. Joseph, St. Joseph Twp., St. Stephen, St. Wendel Twp., Wakefield Twp, Wakefield Twp., Zimmerman); Outside TV Markets (Bradford Twp., Braham, Branch, CAMBRIDGE, Harris, Isanti, Mora, Nessel Twp., North Branch, Ogilvie, Pine City, Rush City, Rush Lake, Shafer, Taylors Falls). Franchise award date: N.A. Franchise expiration date: N.A. Began: December 1, 1983.

Channel capacity: 135 (operating 2-way). Channels available but not in use: N.A.

Basic Service

Subscribers: 29,000 Includes Alden, Brewster, Ceylon, Dunnell, Glenville, Granada, Heron Lake, Minneota, Northrup, Plainview, Round Lake, Storden, Wabash, Wanamingo, Bay City WI, Ellsworth WI, & Pepin WI.

Programming (received off-air): KARE (NBC) Minneapolis; KMSP-TV (FOX) Minneapolis; KPXM-TV (ION) St. Cloud; KSTC-TV (IND) Minneapolis; KSTP-TV (ABC) St. Paul; KTCA-TV (PBS) St. Paul; KTCI-TV (PBS) St. Paul; WCCO-TV (CBS) Minneapolis; WFTC (MNT) Minneapolis; WUCW (CW) Minneapolis.

Programming (via satellite): Eternal Word TV Network; Home Shopping Network; PBS Kids Channel; QVC; ShopNBC; Trinity Broadcasting Network; TV Guide Network; USA Network; WGN America.

Current originations: Government Access; Educational Access; Public Access.

Fee: $20.99 19.99.

Expanded Basic Service 1

Subscribers: N.A.

Programming (via satellite): ABC Family Channel; AMC; Animal Planet; Arts & Entertainment; Bravo; Cartoon Network; CNBC; CNN; Comedy Central; Country Music TV; C-SPAN; C-SPAN 2; Discovery Channel; Disney Channel; Do-It-Yourself; E! Entertainment Television; ESPN; ESPN 2; ESPNews; Food Network; Fox News Channel; Fox Sports Net North; FX; G4; Great American Country; Hallmark Channel; Headline News; HGTV; History Channel; Lifetime; MSNBC; MTV; National Geographic Channel; Nickelodeon; Outdoor Channel; Oxygen; SoapNet; Speed Channel; Spike TV; Syfy; TBS Superstation; The Learning Channel; Travel Channel; truTV; Turner Classic Movies; Turner Network TV; TV Land; VH1; WE tv; Weather Channel.

Fee: $23.99 monthly.

Digital Basic Service

Subscribers: 6,700 Includes Alden, Glenville, Minneota, Plainview, Wabasha, Bay City WI, Ellsworth WI, & Pepin WI.

Programming (received off-air): KARE (NBC) Minneapolis; KMSP-TV (FOX) Minneapolis; KSTP-TV (ABC) St. Paul; WCCO-TV (CBS) Minneapolis.

Programming (via satellite): AZ TV; BBC America; Bloomberg Television; Current; Discovery Digital Networks; Discovery HD Theater; DMX Music; ESPN Classic Sports; ESPN HD; Fuse; Golf Channel; GSN; Independent Film Channel; Lifetime Movie Network; MTV Networks Digital Suite; Nick Jr.; ReelzChannel; Sleuth; Style Network; TeenNick; Toon Disney; Versus; WB.com; WealthTV.

Fee: $8.95 monthly.

Digital Expanded Basic Service

Subscribers: N.A.

Programming (via satellite): Bio; CMT Pure Country; Encore; FitTV; Fox Movie Channel; Hallmark Movie Channel; Halogen Network; History Channel International; Military History Channel; RFD-TV.

Fee: $2.95 monthly.

Digital Expanded Basic Service 2

Subscribers: N.A.

Programming (via satellite): Fox College Sports Atlantic; Fox College Sports Central; Fox College Sports Pacific; Fox Soccer; NFL Network.

Fee: $2.00 monthly.

Digital Pay Service 1

Pay Units: 4,760 Includes Alden, Brewster, Ceylon, Dunnell, Glenville, Granada, Heron Lake, Minneota, Northrup, Plainview, Round Lake, Storden, Wabash, Wanamingo, Bay City WI, Ellsworth WI, & Pepin WI.

Programming (via satellite): Cinemax (multiplexed); Cinemax HD; HBO (multiplexed); HBO HD; Showtime (multiplexed); Showtime HD; Starz (multiplexed); Starz HDTV; The Movie Channel (multiplexed).

Fee: $6.95 monthly (Starz), $14.95 monthly (HBO, Cinemax, Showtime, or TMC).

Video-On-Demand: No

Pay-Per-View

Addressable homes: 3,564.

iN DEMAND (delivered digitally), Addressable: Yes; Playboy TV (delivered digitally); Fresh (delivered digitally).

Internet Service

Operational: Yes. Began: December 31, 2002.

Subscribers: 11,000.

Broadband Service: Warp Drive Online.

Telephone Service

Digital: Planned

Miles of Plant: 2,061.0 (coaxial); 565.0 (fiber optic). Homes passed: 85,150. Homes passed & miles of plant include Alden, Brewster, Ceylon, Dunnell, Glenville, Granada, Heron Lake, Minneota, Northrup, Plainview, Round Lake, Storden, Wabash, Wanamingo, Bay City WI, Ellsworth WI, & Pepin WI

General Manager: Steve Johnson. Customer Service Director: Jackie Torborg.

Ownership: US Cable Corp. (MSO).; Comcast Cable Communications Inc. (MSO).

CANBY—Midcontinent Communications, PO Box 5010, Sioux Falls, SD 57117. Phones: 800-456-0564; 605-229-1775. Fax: 605-229-0478. E-mail: mccomm@midco.net. Web Site: http://www.midcocomm.com. ICA: MN0384.

TV Market Ranking: Outside TV Markets (CANBY). Franchise award date: N.A. Franchise expiration date: N.A. Began: N.A.

Channel capacity: 54 (not 2-way capable). Channels available but not in use: N.A.

Basic Service

Subscribers: 550.

Programming (received off-air): KARE (NBC) Minneapolis; KELO-TV (CBS, MNT) Sioux Falls; KMSP-TV (FOX) Minneapolis; KRWF (ABC) Redwood Falls; KSFY-TV (ABC) Sioux Falls; KWCM-TV (PBS) Appleton; WCCO-TV (CBS) Minneapolis; WFTC (MNT) Minneapolis; WUCW (CW) Minneapolis.

Programming (via satellite): C-SPAN; C-SPAN 2; Eternal Word TV Network; INSP; QVC; WGN America.

Current originations: Public Access; Educational Access.

Fee: $29.99 installation; $34.00 additional installation.

Expanded Basic Service 1

Subscribers: N.A.

Programming (via satellite): ABC Family Channel; AMC; Animal Planet; Arts & Entertainment; Bravo; Cartoon Network; CNBC; CNN; Comedy Central; Country Music TV; Discovery Channel; Disney Channel; E! Entertainment Television; ESPN; ESPN 2; Food Network; Fox News Channel; Fox Sports Net North; FX; Great American Country; Headline News; HGTV; History Channel; Lifetime; MSNBC; MTV; Nickelodeon; Oxygen; Spike TV; Syfy; TBS Superstation; The Learning Channel; Travel Channel; Turner Classic Movies; Turner Network TV; TV Land; USA Network; VH1; Weather Channel.

Fee: $37.99 monthly.

Digital Basic Service

Subscribers: N.A.

Programming (via satellite): BBC America; Bio; Bloomberg Television; Discovery Digital Networks; Do-It-Yourself; Fuse; G4; GAS; GSN; History Channel International; Independent Film Channel; MTV Networks Digital Suite; Music Choice; Nick Jr.; Nick Too; NickToons TV; Style Network; Sundance Channel; TV Guide Interactive Inc.; WE tv.

Digital Pay Service 1

Pay Units: N.A.

Programming (via satellite): Cinemax (multiplexed); Encore; HBO (multiplexed); Showtime (multiplexed); Starz (multiplexed); The Movie Channel (multiplexed).

Video-On-Demand: No

Pay-Per-View

iN DEMAND (delivered digitally); Hot Choice (delivered digitally).

Internet Service

Operational: No.

Telephone Service

None

Miles of Plant: 13.0 (coaxial); None (fiber optic). Homes passed: 1,000.

Ownership: Midcontinent Media Inc. (MSO).

CANNON FALLS—Mediacom, PO Box 110, 1504 2nd St SE, Waseca, MN 56093. Phone: 507-835-2356. Fax: 507-835-4567. Web Site: http://www.mediacomcable.com. ICA: MN0076.

TV Market Ranking: 13 (CANNON FALLS). Franchise award date: December 18, 1984. Franchise expiration date: N.A. Began: April 1, 1985.

Channel capacity: N.A. Channels available but not in use: N.A.

Basic Service

Subscribers: 1,046.

Programming (received off-air): KAAL (ABC) Austin; KARE (NBC) Minneapolis; KIMT (CBS, MNT) Mason City; KMSP-TV (FOX) Minneapolis; KPXM-TV (ION) St. Cloud; KSMQ-TV (PBS) Austin; KSTC-TV (IND) Minneapolis; KSTP-TV (ABC) St. Paul; KTCA-TV (PBS) St. Paul; KTCI-TV (PBS) St. Paul; KTTC (CW, NBC) Rochester; WCCO-TV (CBS) Minneapolis; WFTC (MNT) Minneapolis.

Programming (via satellite): C-SPAN 2; QVC; WGN America.

Current originations: Public Access.

Fee: $30.00 installation; $16.95 monthly; $2.00 converter; $15.00 additional installation.

Expanded Basic Service 1

Subscribers: 910.

Programming (via satellite): ABC Family Channel; AMC; Animal Planet; Arts & Entertainment; BET Networks; Bravo; CNBC; CNN; Comedy Central; Country Music TV; C-SPAN; Discovery Channel; Disney Channel; E! Entertainment Television; ESPN; ESPN 2; ESPN Classic Sports; Eternal Word TV Network; FitTV; Fox News Channel; Fox Sports Net North; FX; Hallmark Channel; Headline News; HGTV; History Channel; Home Shopping Network; INSP; Lifetime; Lifetime Movie Network; MSNBC; MTV; Nickelodeon; ShopNBC; Speed Channel; Spike TV; Syfy; TBS Superstation; The Learning Channel; Travel Channel; Trinity Broadcasting Network; truTV; Turner Classic Movies; Turner Network TV; TV Guide Network; TV Land; Univision; USA Network; Versus; VH1; WE tv; Weather Channel.

Digital Basic Service

Subscribers: N.A.

Programming (via satellite): AmericanLife TV Network; BBC America; Bio; Bloomberg Television; CCTV-4; Discovery HD Theater; Discovery Health Channel; Discovery Home Channel; Discovery Kids Channel; Discovery Military Channel; ESPN 2 HD; ESPN HD; ESPN U; ESPNews; Fox College Sports Atlantic; Fox College Sports Central; Fox College Sports Pacific; Fox Reality Channel; Fox Soccer; Fuel TV; Fuse; G4; Gol TV; Golf Channel; GSN; Halogen Network; HDNet; HDNet Movies; History Channel International; ID Investigation Discovery; Independent Film Channel; Lifetime Movie Network; Lifetime Real Women; MTV Hits; MTV2; Music Choice; National Geographic Channel; Nick Jr.; NickToons TV; Outdoor Channel; ReelzChannel; Science Television; Sleuth; Style Network; TeenNick; Tennis Channel; The Sportsman Channel; TVG Network; Universal HD; VH1 Classic.

Digital Pay Service 1

Pay Units: 103.

Programming (via satellite): Cinemax (multiplexed); Encore (multiplexed); Flix; HBO (multiplexed); HBO HD; Showtime (multiplexed); Showtime HD; Starz (multiplexed); Starz HDTV; Sundance Channel; The Movie Channel (multiplexed); The Movie Channel HD.

Fee: $15.00 installation; $8.95 monthly (TMC), $9.95 monthly (Cinemax or Showtime), $11.95 monthly (HBO).

Video-On-Demand: Yes

Pay-Per-View

iN DEMAND (delivered digitally); Fresh (delivered digitally); Ten Clips (delivered digitally); Playboy TV (delivered digitally).

Internet Service

Operational: Yes.

Broadband Service: Mediacom High Speed Internet.

Fee: $99.00 installation; $40.00 monthly.

Telephone Service
Digital: Operational
Miles of Plant: 32.0 (coaxial); None (fiber optic). Homes passed: 1,831. Total homes in franchised area: 1,934.
Vice President: Bill Jensen. Engineering Manager: Kraig Kaiser. Marketing & Sales Director: Lori Huberty.
City fee: 3% of gross.
Ownership: Mediacom LLC (MSO).

CANOSIA TWP.—New Century Communications, 3588 Kennebec Dr, Eagan, MN 55122-1001. Phone: 651-688-2623. Fax: 651-688-2624. E-mail: tanderson@cablesystemservices.com. Also serves Duluth (unincorporated areas) & Saginaw. ICA: MN0277.
TV Market Ranking: 89 (CANOSIA TWP., Duluth (unincorporated areas), Saginaw). Franchise award date: N.A. Franchise expiration date: N.A. Began: January 1, 1990.
Channel capacity: 40 (not 2-way capable). Channels available but not in use: 19.
Basic Service
Subscribers: 174.
Programming (received off-air): KBJR-TV (MNT, NBC) Superior; KDLH (CBS, CW) Duluth; KQDS-TV (FOX) Duluth; WDIO-DT (ABC) Duluth; WDSE (PBS) Duluth.
Programming (via satellite): ABC Family Channel; AMC; Animal Planet; Arts & Entertainment; CNN; Country Music TV; Discovery Channel; Disney Channel; ESPN; ESPN 2; Flix; Headline News; History Channel; Lifetime; Nickelodeon; Showtime; Spike TV; Syfy; TBS Superstation; The Learning Channel; Trinity Broadcasting Network; Turner Network TV; TV Land; USA Network; Weather Channel; WGN America.
Fee: $30.00 installation; $33.25 monthly.
Video-On-Demand: No
Internet Service
Operational: No.
Telephone Service
None
Miles of Plant: 43.0 (coaxial); None (fiber optic). Homes passed: 910.
Executive Vice President: Marty Walch. Manager & Chief Technician: Todd Anderson.
Ownership: New Century Communications (MSO).

CANTON—Now served by CALEDONIA, MN [MN0086]. ICA: MN0221.

CARLOS—DVSI Cable Television. Now served by PARKERS PRAIRIE, MN [MN0346]. ICA: MN0246.

CEYLON—US Cable, 402 Red River Ave N, Unit 5, Cold Spring, MN 56320-1521. Phones: 800-783-2356; 320-685-7113. Fax: 320-685-2816. E-mail: help@mn.uscable.com. Web Site: http://www.uscable.com. ICA: MN0222.
TV Market Ranking: Outside TV Markets (CEYLON). Franchise award date: N.A. Franchise expiration date: N.A. Began: November 1, 1980.
Channel capacity: N.A. Channels available but not in use: N.A.
Basic Service
Subscribers: N.A. Included in Cambridge
Programming (received off-air): KAAL (ABC) Austin; KARE (NBC) Minneapolis; KEYC-TV (CBS, FOX) Mankato; KMSP-TV (FOX) Minneapolis; KSMN (PBS) Worthington; KSTC-TV (IND) Minneapolis; KSTP-TV (ABC) St. Paul; KYIN (PBS) Mason City; WCCO-TV (CBS) Minneapolis; WFTC (MNT) Minneapolis.
Programming (via satellite): ABC Family Channel; Arts & Entertainment; CNBC; CNN; Comedy Central; Country Music TV; Discovery Channel; ESPN; ESPN 2; Fox Sports Net; Headline News; HGTV; History Channel; Home Shopping Network; Lifetime; Nickelodeon; Outdoor Channel; Spike TV; TBS Superstation; The Learning Channel; Turner Classic Movies; Turner Network TV; TV Land; USA Network; VH1; Weather Channel; WGN America.
Current originations: Public Access.
Fee: $37.24 monthly.
Pay Service 1
Pay Units: N.A. Included in Cambridge
Programming (via satellite): HBO.
Fee: $11.95 monthly.
Internet Service
Operational: No.
Telephone Service
None
Homes passed: Included in Cambridge
General Manager: Steve Johnson. Customer Service Director: Jackie Torberg.
City fee: None.
Ownership: US Cable Corp. (MSO).; Comcast Cable Communications Inc. (MSO).

CHASKA—Time Warner Cable. Now served by MINNEAPOLIS, MN [MN0001]. ICA: MN0279.

CHATFIELD—Mediacom, 4010 Alexandra Dr, Waterloo, IA 50702. Phone: 319-235-2197. Fax: 319-232-7841. Web Site: http://www.mediacomcable.com. Also serves Adams, Dover, Dover Twp., Le Roy, Preston, Rushford, Rushford Village, Spring Valley & St. Charles. ICA: MN0111.
TV Market Ranking: Below 100 (Adams, CHATFIELD, Dover, Dover Twp., Le Roy, Lyle, Preston, Rushford, Rushford Village, Spring Valley, St. Charles). Franchise award date: N.A. Franchise expiration date: N.A. Began: October 1, 1979.
Channel capacity: N.A. Channels available but not in use: N.A.
Basic Service
Subscribers: 4,353.
Programming (received off-air): KAAL (ABC) Austin; KIMT (CBS, MNT) Mason City; KPXM-TV (ION) St. Cloud; KSMQ-TV (PBS) Austin; KTCA-TV (PBS) St. Paul; KTTC (CW, NBC) Rochester; KXLT-TV (FOX) Rochester; WCCO-TV (CBS) Minneapolis; WKBT-DT (CBS, MNT) La Crosse; WLAX (FOX) La Crosse; WUCW (CW) Minneapolis; allband FM.
Programming (via microwave): KSTP-TV (ABC) St. Paul.
Programming (via satellite): C-SPAN; C-SPAN 2; WGN America.
Fee: $35.16 installation; $8.28 monthly; $1.58 converter; $17.58 additional installation.
Expanded Basic Service 1
Subscribers: N.A.
Programming (via satellite): ABC Family Channel; AMC; Animal Planet; Arts & Entertainment; BET Networks; Bravo; Cartoon Network; CNBC; CNN; Comedy Central; Country Music TV; Discovery Channel; Disney Channel; E! Entertainment Television; ESPN; ESPN 2; Eternal Word TV Network; Food Network; Fox News Channel; Fox Sports Net Midwest; FX; Hallmark Channel; Headline News; HGTV; History Channel; Home Shopping Network; INSP; Lifetime; MTV; National Geographic Channel; Nickelodeon; ShopNBC; Speed Channel; Spike TV; Syfy; TBS Superstation; The Learning Channel; Travel Channel; Trinity Broadcasting Network; truTV; Turner Classic Movies; Turner Network TV; TV Guide Network; TV Land; Univision; USA Network; Versus; VH1; WE tv; Weather Channel.
Fee: $16.22 monthly.
Digital Basic Service
Subscribers: N.A.
Programming (via satellite): AmericanLife TV Network; BBC America; Bio; Bloomberg Television; Discovery Digital Networks; DMX Music; Fox Sports World; Fuse; G4; Golf Channel; GSN; Halogen Network; History Channel International; Independent Film Channel; Lifetime Movie Network; Lime; Outdoor Channel; Style Network.
Digital Pay Service 1
Pay Units: 1,200.
Programming (via satellite): Cinemax (multiplexed); Encore (multiplexed); Flix; HBO (multiplexed); Showtime (multiplexed); Starz (multiplexed); Sundance Channel; The Movie Channel (multiplexed).
Fee: $5.95 monthly (Starz & Encore), $7.95 monthly (Cinemax), $11.95 monthly (HBO, Showtime or TMC).
Video-On-Demand: No
Pay-Per-View
TVN Entertainment (delivered digitally); ESPN Now (delivered digitally); Sports PPV (delivered digitally); Urban Xtra (delivered digitally); Fresh (delivered digitally); Shorteez (delivered digitally); Playboy TV (delivered digitally); Pleasure (delivered digitally).
Internet Service
Operational: Yes.
Broadband Service: Mediacom High Speed Internet.
Fee: $99.00 installation; $40.00 monthly.
Telephone Service
Digital: Operational
Miles of Plant: 95.0 (coaxial); None (fiber optic). Homes passed: 6,156.
Regional Vice President: Doug Frank. General Manager: Doug Nix. Technical Operations Director: Greg Nank. Marketing Director: Steve Schuh. Marketing Coordinator: Joni Lindauer.
City fee: 3% of gross.
Ownership: Mediacom LLC (MSO).

CHISAGO CITY—Now served by CAMBRIDGE, MN [MN0016]. ICA: MN0063.

CHOKIO—Mediacom, PO Box 110, 1504 2nd St SE, Waseca, MN 56093. Phones: 800-332-0245; 507-835-2356. Fax: 507-835-4567. Web Site: http://www.mediacomcable.com. Also serves Belgrade, Brooten, Hancock, Morris & Starbuck. ICA: MN0210.
TV Market Ranking: Below 100 (Belgrade, Brooten, Hancock, Morris, Starbuck); Outside TV Markets (CHOKIO). Franchise award date: N.A. Franchise expiration date: N.A. Began: January 1, 1978.
Channel capacity: N.A. Channels available but not in use: N.A.
Basic Service
Subscribers: 2,735.
Programming (received off-air): KPXM-TV (ION) St. Cloud; KTCA-TV (PBS) St. Paul; KTCI-TV (PBS) St. Paul; allband FM.
Programming (via satellite): C-SPAN; Home Shopping Network; QVC; TV Guide Network; Weather Channel; WGN America.
Programming (via translator): KARE (NBC) Minneapolis; KCCO-TV (CBS) Alexandria; KMSP-TV (FOX) Minneapolis; KSAX (ABC) Alexandria; KSTC-TV (IND) Minneapolis; KWCM-TV (PBS) Appleton; WFTC (MNT) Minneapolis; WUCW (CW) Minneapolis.
Fee: $52.39 installation; $16.16 monthly; $17.48 additional installation.
Expanded Basic Service 1
Subscribers: 2,590.
Programming (via satellite): ABC Family Channel; AMC; Animal Planet; Arts & Entertainment; Bravo; Cartoon Network; CNBC; CNN; Comedy Central; Country Music TV; C-SPAN 2; Discovery Channel; Disney Channel; E! Entertainment Television; ESPN; ESPN 2; Eternal Word TV Network; FitTV; Fox Movie Channel; Fox News Channel; Fox Sports Net North; FX; Hallmark Channel; Headline News; HGTV; History Channel; INSP; ION Television; Lifetime; MSNBC; MTV; Nickelodeon; RFD-TV; SoapNet; Speed Channel; Spike TV; Syfy; TBS Superstation; The Learning Channel; Travel Channel; Trinity Broadcasting Network; truTV; Turner Classic Movies; Turner Network TV; TV Land; Univision; USA Network; VH1; WE tv.
Fee: $16.38 monthly.
Digital Basic Service
Subscribers: N.A.
Programming (via satellite): AmericanLife TV Network; BBC America; Bio; Bloomberg Television; Canal 52MX; CCTV-4; Cine Latino; CNN en Espanol; Discovery en Espanol; Discovery HD Theater; Discovery Health Channel; Discovery Home Channel; Discovery Kids Channel; Discovery Military Channel; ESPN 2 HD; ESPN Deportes; ESPN HD; ESPNews; FitTV; Fox Movie Channel; Fox Reality Channel; Fox Soccer; Fox Sports en Espanol; Fuel TV; Fuse; G4; Golf Channel; GSN; Halogen Network; HDNet; HDNet Movies; History Channel en Espanol; History Channel International; ID Investigation Discovery; Independent Film Channel; Lifetime Movie Network; Lifetime Real Women; MTV Hits; MTV Tres; MTV2; Music Choice; National Geographic Channel; Nick Jr.; Outdoor Channel; ReelzChannel; Science Channel; Sleuth; Style Network; Turner Classic Movies; TVG Network; VeneMovies; VH1 Classic.
Pay Service 1
Pay Units: N.A.
Programming (via satellite): Showtime.
Digital Pay Service 1
Pay Units: 805.
Programming (via satellite): Cinemax (multiplexed); Encore (multiplexed); Flix; HBO (multiplexed); HBO HD; Showtime (multiplexed); Showtime HD; Starz (multiplexed); Starz HDTV; Sundance Channel; The Movie Channel (multiplexed); The Movie Channel HD.
Fee: $11.00 monthly (each).
Video-On-Demand: No
Pay-Per-View
iN DEMAND (delivered digitally); Ten Clips (delivered digitally); Penthouse TV (delivered digitally); Fresh (delivered digitally); Pleasure (delivered digitally); Playboy TV (delivered digitally).
Internet Service
Operational: Yes.
Broadband Service: Mediacom High Speed Internet.
Telephone Service
Digital: Operational
Miles of Plant: 56.0 (coaxial); None (fiber optic). Homes passed: 3,732.
Vice President: Bill Jensen. Engineering Manager: Kraig Kaiser. Marketing & Sales Manager: Lori Huberty.
Ownership: Mediacom LLC (MSO).

CLARA CITY—Mediacom, PO Box 110, 1504 2nd St SE, Waseca, MN 56093. Phone: 507-835-2356. Fax: 507-835-4567. Web Site: http://www.mediacomcable.com. Also serves Atwater, Cosmos, Granite Falls, Grove City, Maynard & Paynesville. ICA: MN0125.

TV Market Ranking: Below 100 (CLARA CITY, Cosmos, Granite Falls, Maynard, Paynesville); Outside TV Markets (Atwater, Grove City). Franchise award date: November 17, 1982. Franchise expiration date: N.A. Began: March 10, 1983.

Channel capacity: N.A. Channels available but not in use: N.A.

Basic Service

Subscribers: 3,135.

Programming (received off-air): KCCO-TV (CBS) Alexandria; KPXM-TV (ION) St. Cloud; KSAX (ABC) Alexandria; KWCM-TV (PBS) Appleton; allband FM.

Programming (via satellite): C-SPAN; Home Shopping Network; QVC; TV Guide Network; Weather Channel; WGN America.

Programming (via translator): KARE (NBC) Minneapolis; KMSP-TV (FOX) Minneapolis; KSTC-TV (IND) Minneapolis; KTCA-TV (PBS) St. Paul; KTCI-TV (PBS) St. Paul; WCCO-TV (CBS) Minneapolis; WFTC (MNT) Minneapolis; WUCW (CW) Minneapolis.

Fee: $52.39 installation; $16.57 monthly; $2.00 converter; $17.48 additional installation.

Expanded Basic Service 1

Subscribers: 3,096.

Programming (via satellite): ABC Family Channel; AMC; Animal Planet; Arts & Entertainment; Bravo; Cartoon Network; CNBC; CNN; Comedy Central; Country Music TV; C-SPAN 2; Discovery Channel; Disney Channel; E! Entertainment Television; ESPN; ESPN 2; Eternal Word TV Network; FitTV; Fox Movie Channel; Fox News Channel; Fox Sports Net North; FX; Hallmark Channel; Headline News; HGTV; History Channel; INSP; ION Television; Lifetime; MSNBC; MTV; Nickelodeon; RFD-TV; SoapNet; Speed Channel; Spike TV; Syfy; TBS Superstation; The Learning Channel; Travel Channel; Trinity Broadcasting Network; truTV; Turner Classic Movies; Turner Network TV; TV Land; Univision; USA Network; VH1; WE tv.

Fee: $17.09 monthly.

Digital Basic Service

Subscribers: N.A.

Programming (via satellite): AmericanLife TV Network; BBC America; Bio; Bloomberg Television; Canal 52MX; CCTV-4; Cine Latino; CNN en Espanol; Discovery en Espanol; Discovery HD Theater; Discovery Health Channel; Discovery Home Channel; Discovery Kids Channel; Discovery Military Channel; ESPN 2 HD; ESPN Deportes; ESPN HD; ESPNews; FitTV; Fox Reality Channel; Fox Soccer; Fox Sports en Espanol; Fuel TV; Fuse; G4; Golf Channel; GSN; Halogen Network; HDNet; HDNet Movies; History Channel en Espanol; History Channel International; ID Investigation Discovery; Independent Film Channel; Lifetime Movie Network; Lifetime Real Women; MTV Hits; MTV Tres; MTV2; Music Choice; National Geographic Channel; Nick Jr.; NickToons TV; Outdoor Channel; ReelzChannel; Science Channel; Sleuth; Style Network; TeenNick; Turner Classic Movies; TVG Network; VeneMovies; VH1 Classic.

Pay Service 1

Pay Units: N.A.

Programming (via satellite): Showtime.

Digital Pay Service 1

Pay Units: 496.

Programming (via satellite): Cinemax (multiplexed).

Fee: $7.00 monthly.

Digital Pay Service 2

Pay Units: 412.

Programming (via satellite): Encore (multiplexed); Starz (multiplexed); Starz HDTV.

Fee: $6.95 monthly.

Digital Pay Service 3

Pay Units: 495.

Programming (via satellite): HBO (multiplexed); HBO HD.

Fee: $11.95 monthly.

Digital Pay Service 4

Pay Units: 566.

Programming (via satellite): Flix; Showtime (multiplexed); Showtime HD; Sundance Channel; The Movie Channel (multiplexed); The Movie Channel HD.

Fee: $12.95 monthly.

Video-On-Demand: No

Pay-Per-View

iN DEMAND (delivered digitally); Fresh (delivered digitally); Pleasure (delivered digitally); Playboy TV (delivered digitally); Ten Clips (delivered digitally); Penthouse TV (delivered digitally).

Internet Service

Operational: Yes.

Broadband Service: Mediacom High Speed Internet.

Fee: $40.00 monthly.

Telephone Service

Analog: Not Operational

Digital: Operational

Miles of Plant: 96.0 (coaxial); None (fiber optic). Homes passed: 4,463.

Vice President: Bill Jensen. Engineering Manager: Kraig Kaiser. Marketing & Sales Director: Lori Huberty.

City fee: 3% of gross.

Ownership: Mediacom LLC (MSO).

CLEARBROOK—Garden Valley Telephone Co., PO Box 259, 201 Ross Ave, Erskine, MN 56535-0259. Phones: 218-687-5251; 800-448-8260. Fax: 218-687-2454. E-mail: gvtc@gvtel.com. Web Site: http://www.gvtel.com. Also serves Gonvick. ICA: MN0280.

TV Market Ranking: Below 100 (CLEARBROOK, Gonvick). Franchise award date: August 1, 1983. Franchise expiration date: N.A. Began: February 1, 1984.

Channel capacity: 35 (2-way capable). Channels available but not in use: 8.

Basic Service

Subscribers: 277.

Programming (received off-air): KAWE (PBS) Bemidji; KBRR (FOX) Thief River Falls; KCCW-TV (CBS) Walker; KCPM (MNT) Grand Forks; KFME (PBS) Fargo; KVLY-TV (NBC) Fargo; KXJB-TV (CBS) Valley City; WDAY-TV (ABC, CW) Fargo; WDAZ-TV (ABC, CW) Devils Lake.

Programming (via satellite): ABC Family Channel; AMC; Arts & Entertainment; CNN; Discovery Channel; Disney Channel; ESPN; ESPN 2; Fox Sports Net; Great American Country; History Channel; Spike TV; TBS Superstation; Turner Network TV; TV Land; USA Network; WGN America.

Fee: $51.75 installation; $25.15 monthly; $1.50 converter.

Pay Service 1

Pay Units: 22.

Programming (via satellite): HBO.

Fee: $10.50 monthly.

Video-On-Demand: No

Internet Service

Operational: No.

Telephone Service

None

Miles of Plant: 28.0 (coaxial); None (fiber optic). Total homes in franchised area: 441.

Manager: George Fish. Operations Manager: Dave Hamre. Facilities Manager: Randy Versdahl. Marketing Supervisor: Julie Dahle.

City fee: None.

Ownership: Garden Valley Telephone Co. (MSO).

CLEMENTS—Clara City Telephone Co., 215 1st St NW, Clara City, MN 56222. Phones: 888-283-7667; 320-847-2114. Fax: 320-847-2114. ICA: MN0393.

TV Market Ranking: Below 100 (CLEMENTS). Franchise award date: May 1, 1995. Franchise expiration date: N.A. Began: November 1, 1995.

Channel capacity: 36 (not 2-way capable). Channels available but not in use: 15.

Basic Service

Subscribers: 35.

Programming (received off-air): KARE (NBC) Minneapolis; KEYC-TV (CBS, FOX) Mankato; KMSP-TV (FOX) Minneapolis; KSMN (PBS) Worthington; KSTP-TV (ABC) St. Paul; WCCO-TV (CBS) Minneapolis; WFTC (MNT) Minneapolis; WUCW (CW) Minneapolis.

Programming (via satellite): ABC Family Channel; AMC; Arts & Entertainment; Discovery Channel; ESPN; History Channel; Lifetime; Nickelodeon; The Learning Channel; Turner Network TV; TV Land; USA Network; VH1.

Fee: $50.00 installation; $33.80 monthly.

Pay Service 1

Pay Units: 4.

Programming (via satellite): Showtime.

Fee: $10.00 monthly.

Internet Service

Operational: No.

Telephone Service

None

Miles of Plant: 3.0 (coaxial); None (fiber optic). Homes passed: 80. Total homes in franchised area: 80.

Manager: Bruce Hanson.

Ownership: Hanson Communications Inc. (MSO).

CLINTON—Now served by APPLETON, MN [MN0106]. ICA: MN0193.

CLOQUET—Mediacom, PO Box 110, 1504 2nd St SE, Waseca, MN 56093. Phone: 507-835-2356. Fax: 507-835-4567. Web Site: http://www.mediacomcable.com. Also serves Carlton, Esko, Hermantown, Midway Twp., Proctor, Scanlon & Thomson. ICA: MN0042.

TV Market Ranking: 89 (Carlton, CLOQUET, Esko, Hermantown, Proctor, Scanlon, Thomson); Below 100 (Midway Twp.). Franchise award date: November 29, 1979. Franchise expiration date: N.A. Began: March 1, 1981.

Channel capacity: N.A. Channels available but not in use: N.A.

Basic Service

Subscribers: 6,774.

Programming (received off-air): KBJR-TV (MNT, NBC) Superior; KDLH (CBS, CW) Duluth; KQDS-TV (FOX) Duluth; WDIO-DT (ABC) Duluth; WDSE (PBS) Duluth; allband FM.

Programming (via satellite): C-SPAN; C-SPAN 2; Eternal Word TV Network; Home Shopping Network; INSP; ION Television; TV Guide Network; WGN America.

Current originations: Educational Access; Public Access.

Fee: $10.00 installation; $16.95 monthly; $2.00 converter; $15.00 additional installation.

Expanded Basic Service 1

Subscribers: N.A.

Programming (via satellite): ABC Family Channel; AMC; Animal Planet; Arts & Entertainment; Bravo; Cartoon Network; CNBC; CNN; Comedy Central; Country Music TV; Discovery Channel; Disney Channel; E! Entertainment Television; ESPN; ESPN 2; Fox Movie Channel; Fox News Channel; Fox Sports Net North; FX; Hallmark Channel; Headline News; HGTV; History Channel; Lifetime; MSNBC; MTV; Nickelodeon; Speed Channel; Spike TV; Syfy; TBS Superstation; The Learning Channel; Travel Channel; truTV; Turner Classic Movies; Turner Network TV; TV Land; USA Network; Versus; VH1; WE tv; Weather Channel.

Digital Basic Service

Subscribers: N.A.

Programming (via satellite): AmericanLife TV Network; BBC America; Bio; Bloomberg Television; Canales N; Discovery Digital Networks; DMX Music; Fox Sports World; Fuse; G4; Golf Channel; GSN; Halogen Network; History Channel International; Independent Film Channel; Lifetime Movie Network; Lime; National Geographic Channel; Outdoor Channel; Style Network.

Digital Pay Service 1

Pay Units: 182.

Programming (via satellite): Cinemax (multiplexed); Encore (multiplexed); Flix; HBO (multiplexed); Showtime (multiplexed); Starz (multiplexed); Sundance Channel; The Movie Channel (multiplexed).

Fee: $15.00 installation; $8.95 monthly (Showtime), $9.95 monthly (Cinemax or TMC), $11.95 monthly (HBO).

Video-On-Demand: No

Pay-Per-View

TVN Entertainment (delivered digitally); ESPN Now (delivered digitally); Sports PPV (delivered digitally); Urban Xtra (delivered digitally); Fresh (delivered digitally); Shorteez (delivered digitally); Playboy TV (delivered digitally); Pleasure (delivered digitally).

Internet Service

Operational: Yes.

Broadband Service: Mediacom High Speed Internet.

Fee: $99.00 installation; $40.00 monthly.

Telephone Service

Analog: Not Operational

Digital: Operational

Miles of Plant: 104.0 (coaxial); None (fiber optic). Total homes in franchised area: 7,326.

Vice President: Bill Jensen. Engineering Manager: Kraig Kaiser. Marketing & Sales Director: Lori Huberty.

City fee: 5% of gross.

Ownership: Mediacom LLC (MSO).

COLERAINE—Coleraine Cable Communications System, PO Box 670, Coleraine, MN 55722. Phone: 218-245-2112. Fax: 218-245-2123. ICA: MN0162.

TV Market Ranking: Below 100 (COLERAINE). Franchise award date: January 1, 1991. Franchise expiration date: N.A. Began: January 1, 1992.

Channel capacity: 65 (not 2-way capable). Channels available but not in use: 10.

Basic Service

Subscribers: 395.

Programming (received off-air): KAWE (PBS) Bemidji; KBJR-TV (MNT, NBC) Su-

perior; KCCO-TV (CBS) Alexandria; KDLH (CBS, CW) Duluth; KMSP-TV (FOX) Minneapolis; WDIO-DT (ABC) Duluth; WDSE (PBS) Duluth.
Programming (via satellite): ABC Family Channel; AMC; Animal Planet; Arts & Entertainment; Cartoon Network; CNBC; CNN; Comedy Central; Country Music TV; C-SPAN; Discovery Channel; Disney Channel; ESPN; ESPN 2; Eternal Word TV Network; Hallmark Channel; Headline News; History Channel; Lifetime; MTV; Nickelodeon; Outdoor Channel; QVC; Spike TV; Syfy; TBS Superstation; The Learning Channel; Travel Channel; Turner Classic Movies; Turner Network TV; USA Network; VH1; Weather Channel; WGN America.
Current originations: Public Access.
Fee: $24.00 monthly.

Pay Service 1
Pay Units: 27.
Programming (via satellite): Cinemax.
Fee: $10.00 monthly.

Pay Service 2
Pay Units: 100.
Programming (via satellite): HBO.
Fee: $10.00 monthly.

Video-On-Demand: No

Internet Service
Operational: Yes.
Fee: $29.00 monthly.

Telephone Service
None

Miles of Plant: 6.0 (coaxial); None (fiber optic). Homes passed: 440. Total homes in franchised area: 440.
Manager: Sandy Bluntach. Chief Technician: Temper Payne.
Ownership: Coleraine Cable TV.

COLOGNE—North American Communications Corp., PO Box 387, 211 Main St S, Hector, MN 55342-0387. Phones: 800-982-8038; 320-848-6781. Fax: 320-848-2323. E-mail: hcc@hcctel.net. Web Site: http://www.hectorcom.com. ICA: MN0282.
TV Market Ranking: 13 (COLOGNE). Franchise award date: N.A. Franchise expiration date: N.A. Began: N.A.
Channel capacity: N.A. Channels available but not in use: N.A.

Basic Service
Subscribers: 149.
Programming (received off-air): KARE (NBC) Minneapolis; KMSP-TV (FOX) Minneapolis; KSTP-TV (ABC) St. Paul; KTCA-TV (PBS) St. Paul; KTCI-TV (PBS) St. Paul; WCCO-TV (CBS) Minneapolis; WFTC (MNT) Minneapolis; WUCW (CW) Minneapolis.
Programming (via satellite): ABC Family Channel; AMC; Arts & Entertainment; CNN; Country Music TV; Discovery Channel; Disney Channel; ESPN; ESPN 2; Fox Sports Net Midwest; ION Television; Lifetime; Nickelodeon; QVC; Spike TV; Syfy; TBS Superstation; The Learning Channel; Trinity Broadcasting Network; Turner Network TV; USA Network; VH1; WGN America.
Fee: $40.00 installation; $25.95 monthly; $2.50 converter; $25.00 additional installation.

Pay Service 1
Pay Units: 1.
Programming (via satellite): Cinemax.
Fee: $10.95 monthly.

Pay Service 2
Pay Units: 16.
Programming (via satellite): HBO.
Fee: $10.95 monthly.

Video-On-Demand: No

Internet Service
Operational: No.
Broadband Service: Offers dial-up and DSL only; no cable modem service.

Telephone Service
None

Miles of Plant: 4.0 (coaxial); None (fiber optic).
Manager: Matt Sparks. Chief Technician: George Honzey. Customer Service Supervisor: Patty Groshens.
Ownership: Hector Communications Corp. (MSO).

COMFREY—Clara City Telephone Co., 215 1st St NW, Clara City, MN 56222. Phones: 888-283-7667; 320-847-2114. Fax: 320-847-2114. ICA: MN0209.
TV Market Ranking: Below 100 (COMFREY). Franchise award date: N.A. Franchise expiration date: N.A. Began: September 1, 1984.
Channel capacity: 35 (not 2-way capable). Channels available but not in use: 10.

Basic Service
Subscribers: 50.
Programming (received off-air): KEYC-TV (CBS, FOX) Mankato; allband FM.
Programming (via satellite): ABC Family Channel; AMC; Arts & Entertainment; CNN; Country Music TV; Discovery Channel; ESPN; ESPN 2; Fox Sports Net; Hallmark Channel; History Channel; Lifetime; MTV; Nickelodeon; Spike TV; TBS Superstation; The Learning Channel; Turner Network TV; TV Land; USA Network; Weather Channel; WGN America.
Programming (via translator): KARE (NBC) Minneapolis; KMSP-TV (FOX) Minneapolis; KSMN (PBS) Worthington; KSTP-TV (ABC) St. Paul; WCCO-TV (CBS) Minneapolis; WFTC (MNT) Minneapolis; WUCW (CW) Minneapolis.
Fee: $40.00 installation; $33.80 monthly; $2.00 converter.

Pay Service 1
Pay Units: 4.
Programming (via satellite): Showtime.
Fee: $10.00 monthly.

Internet Service
Operational: No.

Telephone Service
None

Miles of Plant: 5.0 (coaxial); None (fiber optic). Homes passed: 250. Total homes in franchised area: 250.
Manager: Magdalen Maserek. Chief Technician: Randy Maserek. Engineer: LaVerne Maserek.
City fee: None.
Ownership: Hanson Communications Inc. (MSO).

CONCORD—Mediacom. Now served by Dodge Center, MN [MN0093]. ICA: MN0191.

COOK—Mediacom, PO Box 110, 1504 2nd St SE, Waseca, MN 56093. Phones: 800-332-0245; 507-835-2356. Fax: 507-835-4567. E-mail: bjensen@mediacomcc.com. Web Site: http://www.mediacomcable.com. ICA: MN0283.
TV Market Ranking: Below 100 (COOK). Franchise award date: September 15, 1981. Franchise expiration date: N.A. Began: June 1, 1982.
Channel capacity: 52 (not 2-way capable). Channels available but not in use: 36.

Basic Service
Subscribers: 206.
Programming (received off-air): KBJR-TV (MNT, NBC) Superior; KDLH (CBS, CW) Duluth; WDSE (PBS) Duluth; WIRT-DT (ABC) Hibbing; allband FM.
Programming (via satellite): C-SPAN; C-SPAN 2; ION Television; QVC; WGN America.
Current originations: Public Access.
Fee: $50.00 installation; $19.95 monthly.

Expanded Basic Service 1
Subscribers: N.A.
Programming (via satellite): ABC Family Channel; AMC; Animal Planet; Arts & Entertainment; Bravo; CNN; Comedy Central; Country Music TV; Discovery Channel; Disney Channel; E! Entertainment Television; ESPN; ESPN 2; Food Network; Fox Sports Net North; FX; Hallmark Channel; Headline News; History Channel; INSP; Lifetime; Nickelodeon; Speed Channel; Spike TV; Syfy; TBS Superstation; The Learning Channel; Travel Channel; Turner Network TV; TV Land; USA Network; WE tv; Weather Channel.

Pay Service 1
Pay Units: 49.
Programming (via satellite): HBO.
Fee: $10.95 monthly.

Video-On-Demand: No

Internet Service
Operational: No.

Telephone Service
None

Miles of Plant: 5.0 (coaxial); None (fiber optic). Total homes in franchised area: 409.
Vice President: Bill Jensen. Engineering Manager: Kraig Kaiser. Marketing & Sales Director: Lori Huberty.
City fee: None.
Ownership: Mediacom LLC (MSO).

CORLISS TWP.—ACS Video. Formerly served by Perham, MN [MN0050]. This cable system has converted to IPTV, 150 Second St SW, Perham, MN 56573. Phone: 866-937-4227. E-mail: answers@arvig.com. Web Site: http://www.arvig.com. ICA: MN5188.
TV Market Ranking: Outside TV Markets (CORLISS TWP.).
Channel capacity: N.A. Channels available but not in use: N.A.

Internet Service
Operational: Yes.

Telephone Service
Digital: Operational

Ownership: Arvig Communication Systems.

COSMOS—Now served by CLARA CITY, MN [MN0125]. ICA: MN0284.

COTTONWOOD—Charter Communications, 1108 E College Dr, Marshall, MN 56258-1902. Phones: 507-289-8273 (Rochester administrative office); 507-537-1541. Fax: 507-537-1572. Web Site: http://www.charter.com. ICA: MN0385.
TV Market Ranking: Below 100 (COTTONWOOD). Franchise award date: N.A. Franchise expiration date: N.A. Began: N.A.
Channel capacity: N.A. Channels available but not in use: N.A.

Basic Service
Subscribers: 380.
Programming (received off-air): KARE (NBC) Minneapolis; KELO-TV (CBS, MNT) Sioux Falls; KEYC-TV (CBS, FOX) Mankato; KMSP-TV (FOX) Minneapolis; KRWF (ABC) Redwood Falls; KSFY-TV (ABC) Sioux Falls; KSTC-TV (IND) Minneapolis; KTCA-TV (PBS) St. Paul; KWCM-TV (PBS) Appleton; WCCO-TV (CBS) Minneapolis; WFTC (MNT) Minneapolis; WUCW (CW) Minneapolis.
Programming (via satellite): C-SPAN; C-SPAN 2; INSP; QVC; TBS Superstation; Trinity Broadcasting Network; WGN America.
Current originations: Educational Access; Public Access; Government Access.
Fee: $29.99 installation; $34.00 additional installation.

Expanded Basic Service 1
Subscribers: 352.
Programming (via satellite): ABC Family Channel; AMC; Animal Planet; Arts & Entertainment; BET Networks; Bravo; Cartoon Network; CNBC; CNN; Comedy Central; Country Music TV; Discovery Channel; Disney Channel; E! Entertainment Television; ESPN; ESPN 2; Eternal Word TV Network; Food Network; Fox News Channel; Fox Sports Net North; FX; G4; Golf Channel; GSN; Hallmark Channel; Headline News; HGTV; History Channel; Home Shopping Network; Lifetime; MSNBC; MTV; MTV2; National Geographic Channel; Nickelodeon; Oxygen; Speed Channel; Spike TV; Syfy; The Learning Channel; Travel Channel; truTV; Turner Classic Movies; Turner Network TV; TV Guide Network; TV Land; Univision; USA Network; Versus; VH1; WE tv; Weather Channel.
Fee: $47.99 monthly.

Digital Basic Service
Subscribers: N.A.
Programming (received off-air): KARE (NBC) Minneapolis; KMSP-TV (FOX) Minneapolis; WCCO-TV (CBS) Minneapolis.
Programming (via satellite): BBC America; Bloomberg Television; Boomerang; CBS College Sports Network; CNN International; Discovery Digital Networks; Do-It-Yourself; ESPN; ESPN Classic Sports; ESPNews; FitTV; Fox College Sports Atlantic; Fox College Sports Central; Fox College Sports Pacific; Fox Movie Channel; Fox Soccer; Fuel TV; Fuse; GAS; HDNet; HDNet Movies; History Channel International; Independent Film Channel; Lifetime Movie Network; MTV Networks Digital Suite; Music Choice; NFL Network; Nick Jr.; Nick Too; NickToons TV; Outdoor Channel; SoapNet; Style Network; Sundance Channel; Toon Disney; TV Guide Interactive Inc.

Digital Pay Service 1
Pay Units: N.A.
Programming (via satellite): Cinemax (multiplexed); Encore (multiplexed); HBO (multiplexed); HBO HD; Showtime (multiplexed); Showtime HD; Starz (multiplexed); The Movie Channel (multiplexed).

Video-On-Demand: Yes

Pay-Per-View
iN DEMAND (delivered digitally); NASCAR In Car (delivered digitally); NHL Center Ice (delivered digitally); MLB Extra Innings (delivered digitally); Playboy TV (delivered digitally); Spice Live (delivered digitally); Spice Platinum (delivered digitally); Hot Net Plus (delivered digitally); Spice Hot (delivered digitally).

Internet Service
Operational: Yes.
Broadband Service: Charter Pipeline.
Fee: $29.99 monthly.

Telephone Service
Digital: Operational

Miles of Plant: 7.0 (coaxial); None (fiber optic). Homes passed: 550.
Vice President & General Manager: John Crowley. Operations Director: Craig Stensaas. Technical Operations Director: Mark Abramo. Marketing Director: Bill Haarstad. Office Manager: Sue Olson.
Ownership: Charter Communications Inc. (MSO).

COURTLAND—NU-Telecom. Formerly served by New Ulm, MN [MN0285]. This cable system has converted to IPTV, PO Box 697, 22 S Marshall, Springfield, MN 56087-0697. Phones: 800-893-1856; 507-723-4211. Fax: 507-723-4377. E-mail: on-linecustservice@nu-telecom.net. Web Site: http://www.nutelecom.net. ICA: MN5146.

TV Market Ranking: Below 100 (COURTLAND).

Channel capacity: N.A. Channels available but not in use: N.A.

Internet Service

Operational: Yes.

Telephone Service

Digital: Operational

President & Chief Executive Officer: Bill Otis.

Ownership: NU-Telecom.

CROOKSTON—Midcontinent Communications. Now served by GRAND FORKS, ND [ND0003]. ICA: MN0047.

CROSSLAKE—Crosslake Communications, 35910 County Rd 66, Crosslake, MN 56442. Phone: 218-692-2777. Fax: 218-692-2410. E-mail: dennisl@crosslake.net. Web Site: http://www.crosslake.net. Also serves Manhattan Beach. ICA: MN0069.

TV Market Ranking: Below 100 (Manhattan Beach); Outside TV Markets (CROSSLAKE). Franchise award date: N.A. Franchise expiration date: N.A. Began: January 1, 1985.

Channel capacity: 36 (not 2-way capable). Channels available but not in use: 14.

Basic Service

Subscribers: 2,023.

Programming (received off-air): KCCW-TV (CBS) Walker.

Programming (via satellite): ABC Family Channel; AMC; Arts & Entertainment; CNN; C-SPAN; Discovery Channel; E! Entertainment Television; ESPN; Eternal Word TV Network; HGTV; History Channel; Nickelodeon; Spike TV; TBS Superstation; Travel Channel; Trinity Broadcasting Network; Turner Network TV; USA Network; Weather Channel; WGN America.

Programming (via translator): KARE (NBC) Minneapolis; KMSP-TV (FOX) Minneapolis; KSTP-TV (ABC) St. Paul; KVRR (FOX) Fargo; WFTC (MNT) Minneapolis.

Fee: $14.95 monthly.

Pay Service 1

Pay Units: 12.

Programming (via satellite): Showtime; The Movie Channel.

Fee: $13.00 monthly.

Pay Service 2

Pay Units: 120.

Programming (via satellite): Cinemax; HBO.

Fee: $15.00 monthly.

Pay Service 3

Pay Units: 28.

Programming (via satellite): Encore Action; Starz.

Fee: $10.00 monthly.

Video-On-Demand: No

Internet Service

Operational: No, DSL only.

Telephone Service

None

Miles of Plant: 100.0 (coaxial); None (fiber optic).

General Manager: Dennis Leaser. Operations Manager: Jared Johnson. Marketing Director: Debbie Floerchinger.

City fee: None.

Ownership: Crosslake Communicatons.

DAKOTA—Now served by CALEDONIA, MN [MN0086]. ICA: MN0201.

DAWSON—Now served by APPLETON, MN [MN0106]. ICA: MN0117.

DEER CREEK TWP.—ACS Video. Formerly served by Perham, MN [MN0050]. This cable system has converted to IPTV, 150 Second St SW, Perham, MN 56573. Phone: 866-937-4227. E-mail: answers@arvig.com. Web Site: http://www.arvig.com. ICA: MN5189.

Channel capacity: N.A. Channels available but not in use: N.A.

Internet Service

Operational: Yes.

Telephone Service

Digital: Operational

Ownership: Arvig Communication Systems.

DEER RIVER—Paul Bunyan Television, 1831 Anne St NW, Ste 100, Bemidji, MN 56601. Phones: 844-624-4700; 218-444-7288. Fax: 218-444-6003. E-mail: tv@paulbunyan.net. Web Site: http://www.paulbunyan.net. Also serves Ball Club, Deer River Twp., Morse Twp. & Zemple. ICA: MN0180.

TV Market Ranking: Below 100 (Ball Club); Outside TV Markets (DEER RIVER, Deer River Twp., Morse Twp., Zemple). Franchise award date: N.A. Franchise expiration date: N.A. Began: October 1, 1983.

Channel capacity: N.A. Channels available but not in use: N.A.

Digital Basic Service

Subscribers: N.A.

Programming (received off-air): KAWE (PBS) Bemidji; KBJR-TV (MNT, NBC) Superior; KDLH (CBS, CW) Duluth; KPXM-TV (ION) St. Cloud; KSTC-TV (IND) Minneapolis; KSTP-TV (ABC) St. Paul; KVLY-TV (NBC) Fargo; WCCO-TV (CBS) Minneapolis; WDIO-DT (ABC) Duluth; WFTC (MNT) Minneapolis; WUCW (CW) Minneapolis.

Programming (via satellite): 3 Angels Broadcasting Network; ABC Family Channel; AMC; AmericanLife TV Network; America's Store; Animal Planet; Arts & Entertainment; Boomerang; Bravo; Cartoon Network; CNBC; CNN; Comedy Central; Country Music TV; C-SPAN; C-SPAN 2; Discovery Channel; Discovery Health Channel; Disney Channel; DMX Music; Do-It-Yourself; E! Entertainment Television; ESPN; ESPN 2; ESPN Classic Sports; ESPNews; Eternal Word TV Network; Food Network; Fox Movie Channel; Fox News Channel; Fox Sports Net North; Fuse; FX; G4; Golf Channel; GSN; Hallmark Channel; Headline News; HGTV; History Channel; Independent Film Channel; Lifetime; Lifetime Movie Network; MSNBC; MTV; NASA TV; National Geographic Channel; Nickelodeon; Outdoor Channel; Pentagon Channel; QVC; Radar Channel; Shop at Home; Speed Channel; Spike TV; Syfy; TBS Superstation; The Learning Channel; Travel Channel; Trinity Broadcasting Network; truTV; Turner Classic Movies; Turner Network TV; TV Land; USA Network; VH1; WE tv; Weather Channel; WGN America.

Programming (via translator): KQDS-TV (FOX) Duluth.

Current originations: Leased Access; Government Access; Educational Access; Public Access.

Fee: $54.95 monthly (includes phone service).

Digital Expanded Basic Service

Subscribers: N.A.

Programming (via satellite): Bio; CBS College Sports Network; Cooking Channel; Current; FamilyNet; FitTV; Fox College Sports Atlantic; Fox College Sports Central; Fox College Sports Pacific; Fox Soccer; Fuel TV; GAS; Gol TV; Great American Country; History Channel International; HorseRacing TV; Lifetime Real Women; MTV Networks Digital Suite; NBA TV; Nick Jr.; NickToons TV; RFD-TV; SoapNet; Tennis Channel; The Sportsman Channel; Versus.

Fee: $6.99 monthly (Sports tier), $9.99 monthly (learning, news, kids and entertainment channels).

Digital Pay Service 1

Pay Units: N.A.

Programming (via satellite): Cinemax (multiplexed); Encore (multiplexed); Flix (multiplexed); HBO (multiplexed); Showtime (multiplexed); Starz (multiplexed); Sundance Channel (multiplexed); The Movie Channel (multiplexed).

Fee: $10.95 monthly (HBO or Showtime/TMC), $9.95 monthly (Cinemax), $12.95 monthly (Starz/Encore).

Video-On-Demand: No

Internet Service

Operational: Yes.

Telephone Service

None

Miles of Plant: 9.0 (coaxial); None (fiber optic). Homes passed: 500.

Manager: Paul Freudi. Chief Technician: George Daigle. Marketing Supervisor: Brian Bissonette.

City fee: None.

Ownership: Paul Bunyan Telephone Cooperative.

DELAVAN—North American Communications Corp., PO Box 387, 211 Main St S, Hector, MN 55342-0387. Phones: 800-982-8038; 320-848-6781. Fax: 320-848-2323. E-mail: hcc@hcctel.net. Web Site: http://www.hectorcom.com. ICA: MN0289.

TV Market Ranking: Below 100 (DELAVAN). Franchise award date: N.A. Franchise expiration date: N.A. Began: N.A.

Channel capacity: 54 (not 2-way capable). Channels available but not in use: 28.

Basic Service

Subscribers: 39.

Programming (received off-air): KAAL (ABC) Austin; KARE (NBC) Minneapolis; KEYC-TV (CBS, FOX) Mankato; KMSP-TV (FOX) Minneapolis; KSMN (PBS) Worthington; KSTP-TV (ABC) St. Paul; WCCO-TV (CBS) Minneapolis; WFTC (MNT) Minneapolis; WUCW (CW) Minneapolis.

Programming (via satellite): ABC Family Channel; AMC; Arts & Entertainment; CNN; Discovery Channel; Disney Channel; ESPN; Fox Sports Net Midwest; Lifetime; Nickelodeon; QVC; Spike TV; TBS Superstation; Trinity Broadcasting Network; Turner Network TV; USA Network; WGN America.

Current originations: Leased Access; Government Access; Educational Access; Public Access.

Fee: $40.00 installation; $26.95 monthly; $3.50 converter.

Pay Service 1

Pay Units: 2.

Programming (via satellite): Cinemax.

Fee: $10.95 monthly.

Pay Service 2

Pay Units: 1.

Programming (via satellite): HBO.

Fee: $10.95 monthly.

Video-On-Demand: No

Internet Service

Operational: No.

Broadband Service: Offers dial-up and DSL only; no cable modem service.

Telephone Service

None

Miles of Plant: 4.0 (coaxial); None (fiber optic). Homes passed: 124. Total homes in franchised area: 124.

Manager: Matt Sparks. Chief Technician: George Honzey. Customer Service Supervisor: Patty Groshens.

Ownership: Hector Communications Corp. (MSO).

DEXTER—North American Communications Corp., PO Box 387, 211 Main St S, Hector, MN 55342-0387. Phones: 800-982-8038; 320-848-6781. Fax: 320-848-2323. E-mail: hcc@hcctel.net. Web Site: http://www.hectorcom.com. ICA: MN0290.

TV Market Ranking: Below 100 (DEXTER). Franchise award date: N.A. Franchise expiration date: N.A. Began: N.A.

Channel capacity: 54 (not 2-way capable). Channels available but not in use: 34.

Basic Service

Subscribers: 55.

Programming (received off-air): KAAL (ABC) Austin; KIMT (CBS, MNT) Mason City; KSMQ-TV (PBS) Austin; KYIN (PBS) Mason City.

Programming (via satellite): ABC Family Channel; AMC; Arts & Entertainment; CNN; Country Music TV; Discovery Channel; Disney Channel; ESPN; Fox Sports Net Midwest; Lifetime; Nickelodeon; QVC; Spike TV; TBS Superstation; Trinity Broadcasting Network; Turner Network TV; USA Network; WGN America.

Fee: $40.00 installation; $26.95 monthly; $3.50 converter; $25.00 additional installation.

Pay Service 1

Pay Units: 3.

Programming (via satellite): Cinemax.

Fee: $10.95 monthly.

Pay Service 2

Pay Units: 5.

Programming (via satellite): HBO.

Fee: $10.95 monthly.

Video-On-Demand: No

Internet Service

Operational: No.

Telephone Service

None

Miles of Plant: 4.0 (coaxial); None (fiber optic). Homes passed: 125. Total homes in franchised area: 125.

Manager: Matt Sparks. Chief Technician: George Honzey. Customer Service Supervisor: Patty Groshens.

Ownership: Hector Communications Corp. (MSO).

DODGE CENTER—Mediacom, 4010 Alexandra Dr, Waterloo, IA 50702. Phone: 319-235-2197. Fax: 319-232-7841. Web Site: http://www.mediacomcable.com. Also serves Blooming Prairie, Brownsdale, Concord, Hayfield, Kenyon, Mantorville, Waltham & West Concord. ICA: MN0093.

TV Market Ranking: Below 100 (Blooming Prairie, Brownsdale, Concord, DODGE CENTER, Hayfield, Kenyon, Mantorville, Waltham, West Concord). Franchise award date: N.A. Franchise expiration date: N.A. Began: January 1, 1984.

Channel capacity: 71 (operating 2-way). Channels available but not in use: None.

Basic Service

Subscribers: 2,011.

Programming (received off-air): KAAL (ABC) Austin; KARE (NBC) Minneapolis; KIMT (CBS, MNT) Mason City; KMSP-TV (FOX) Minneapolis; KPXM-TV (ION)

St. Cloud; KSMQ-TV (PBS) Austin; KSTC-TV (IND) Minneapolis; KSTP-TV (ABC) St. Paul; KTCA-TV (PBS) St. Paul; KTTC (CW, NBC) Rochester; KXLT-TV (FOX) Rochester; KYIN (PBS) Mason City; WCCO-TV (CBS) Minneapolis; WFTC (MNT) Minneapolis; WUCW (CW) Minneapolis; allband FM.
Programming (via satellite): C-SPAN; C-SPAN 2; QVC; WGN America.
Current originations: Public Access.
Fee: $20.00 installation; $10.95 monthly.

Expanded Basic Service 1
Subscribers: N.A.
Programming (via satellite): ABC Family Channel; AMC; Animal Planet; Arts & Entertainment; BET Networks; Bravo; Cartoon Network; CNBC; CNN; Comedy Central; Country Music TV; Discovery Channel; Disney Channel; E! Entertainment Television; ESPN; ESPN 2; Eternal Word TV Network; Food Network; Fox News Channel; Fox Sports Net Midwest; FX; Hallmark Channel; Headline News; HGTV; History Channel; Home Shopping Network; INSP; Lifetime; MTV; National Geographic Channel; Nickelodeon; ShopNBC; Speed Channel; Spike TV; Syfy; TBS Superstation; The Learning Channel; Travel Channel; Trinity Broadcasting Network; truTV; Turner Classic Movies; Turner Network TV; TV Guide Network; TV Land; Univision; USA Network; Versus; VH1; WE tv; Weather Channel.

Digital Basic Service
Subscribers: N.A.
Programming (via satellite): AmericanLife TV Network; BBC America; Bio; Bloomberg Television; Discovery Digital Networks; DMX Music; Fox Sports World; Fuse; G4; Golf Channel; GSN; Halogen Network; History Channel International; Independent Film Channel; Lifetime Movie Network; Lime; Outdoor Channel; Style Network.

Digital Pay Service 1
Pay Units: N.A.
Programming (via satellite): Cinemax (multiplexed); Encore (multiplexed); Flix; HBO (multiplexed); Showtime (multiplexed); Starz (multiplexed); Sundance Channel; The Movie Channel (multiplexed).
Fee: $9.95 monthly (HBO or Showtime).

Video-On-Demand: No

Pay-Per-View
TVN Entertainment (delivered digitally); ESPN Now (delivered digitally); Sports PPV (delivered digitally); Urban Xtra (delivered digitally); Fresh (delivered digitally); Shorteez (delivered digitally); Playboy TV (delivered digitally); Pleasure (delivered digitally).

Internet Service
Operational: Yes.
Broadband Service: Mediacom High Speed Internet.
Fee: $99.00 installation; $40.00 monthly.

Telephone Service
Digital: Operational
Miles of Plant: 26.0 (coaxial); None (fiber optic).
Regional Vice President: Doug Frank. Manager: Doug Nix. Technical Operations Director: Greg Nank. Marketing Director: Steve Schuh. Marketing Coordinator: Joni Lindauer.
City fee: 3% of gross.
Ownership: Mediacom LLC (MSO).

DORA TWP.—ACS Video. Formerly served by Perham, MN [MN0050]. This cable system has converted to IPTV, 150 Second St SW, Perham, MN 56573. Phone: 866-937-4227. E-mail: answers@arvig.com. Web Site: http://www.arvig.com. ICA: MN5190.
TV Market Ranking: 98 (DORA TWP.).
Channel capacity: N.A. Channels available but not in use: N.A.

Internet Service
Operational: Yes.

Telephone Service
Digital: Operational
Ownership: Arvig Communication Systems.

DULUTH—Charter Communications, 302 E Superior St, Duluth, MN 55802-2196. Phone: 715-831-8940. Fax: 507-285-6162. Web Site: http://www.charter.com. Also serves Rice Lake Twp., MN; Superior (village), WI. ICA: MN0006.
TV Market Ranking: 89 (DULUTH, Rice Lake Twp., Superior (village)). Franchise award date: June 22, 1968. Franchise expiration date: N.A. Began: August 15, 1973.
Channel capacity: N.A. Channels available but not in use: N.A.

Basic Service
Subscribers: 27,270.
Programming (received off-air): KBJR-TV (MNT, NBC) Superior; KDLH (CBS, CW) Duluth; KQDS-TV (FOX) Duluth; WDIO-DT (ABC) Duluth; WDSE (PBS) Duluth.
Programming (via satellite): C-SPAN; C-SPAN 2; Eternal Word TV Network; Home Shopping Network; INSP; QVC; Trinity Broadcasting Network; TV Guide Network; WGN America.
Current originations: Leased Access; Religious Access; Government Access; Educational Access; Public Access.
Fee: $29.99 installation; $.99 converter.

Expanded Basic Service 1
Subscribers: 25,108.
Programming (via satellite): ABC Family Channel; AMC; Animal Planet; Arts & Entertainment; BET Networks; Bravo; Cartoon Network; CNBC; CNN; Comedy Central; Country Music TV; Discovery Channel; Disney Channel; Do-It-Yourself; E! Entertainment Television; ESPN; ESPN 2; ESPN Classic Sports; Food Network; Fox News Channel; Fox Sports Net North; FX; G4; Golf Channel; GSN; Hallmark Channel; Headline News; HGTV; History Channel; Lifetime; MSNBC; MTV; MTV2; National Geographic Channel; Nickelodeon; Outdoor Channel; Oxygen; ShopNBC; SoapNet; Speed Channel; Spike TV; Syfy; TBS Superstation; The Learning Channel; Toon Disney; Travel Channel; truTV; Turner Classic Movies; Turner Network TV; TV Land; USA Network; Versus; VH1; WE tv; Weather Channel.
Fee: $25.48 installation; $47.99 monthly.

Digital Basic Service
Subscribers: N.A.
Programming (via satellite): BBC America; Bio; Discovery Digital Networks; ESPN; ESPNews; Fox College Sports Atlantic; Fox College Sports Central; Fox College Sports Pacific; Fox Soccer; Fuel TV; Fuse; GAS; Great American Country; HDNet; HDNet Movies; History Channel International; Independent Film Channel; Lifetime Movie Network; MTV Networks Digital Suite; Music Choice; NFL Network; Nick Jr.; Nick Too; NickToons TV; Style Network; Sundance Channel; TV Guide Interactive Inc.

Digital Pay Service 1
Pay Units: N.A.
Programming (via satellite): Cinemax (multiplexed); Encore (multiplexed); HBO (multiplexed); HBO HD; Showtime (multiplexed); Showtime HD; Starz (multiplexed); The Movie Channel (multiplexed).

Video-On-Demand: Yes

Pay-Per-View
iN DEMAND (delivered digitally); NASCAR In Car (delivered digitally); NHL Center Ice (delivered digitally); MLB Extra Innings (delivered digitally); Playboy TV (delivered digitally); Spice Live (delivered digitally); Spice Platinum (delivered digitally); Hot Network Plus (delivered digitally); Spice Hot (delivered digitally).

Internet Service
Operational: Yes.
Broadband Service: Charter Pipeline.
Fee: $29.99 monthly; $3.95 modem lease.

Telephone Service
Digital: Operational
Fee: $29.99 monthly
Miles of Plant: 515.0 (coaxial); 2.0 (fiber optic). Additional miles planned: 14.0 (coaxial); 7.0 (fiber optic). Homes passed: 49,958. Total homes in franchised area: 50,150.
Vice President & General Manager: John Crowley. Technical Operations Manager: Tom Gorsuch. Marketing Director: Bill Haarstad. Government Relations Director: Mike Hill.
City fee: 5% of gross.
Ownership: Charter Communications Inc. (MSO).

DUNDEE—Formerly served by American Telecasting of America Inc. No longer in operation. ICA: MN0291.

DUNNELL—US Cable, 402 Red River Ave N, Unit 5, Cold Spring, MN 56320-1521. Phones: 800-783-2356; 320-685-7113. Fax: 320-685-2816. E-mail: help@mn.uscable.com. Web Site: http://www.uscable.com. ICA: MN0263.
TV Market Ranking: Outside TV Markets (DUNNELL). Franchise award date: N.A. Franchise expiration date: N.A. Began: November 1, 1980.
Channel capacity: N.A. Channels available but not in use: N.A.

Basic Service
Subscribers: N.A. Included in Cambridge
Programming (received off-air): KARE (NBC) Minneapolis; KEYC-TV (CBS, FOX) Mankato; KMSP-TV (FOX) Minneapolis; KSMN (PBS) Worthington; KSTC-TV (IND) Minneapolis; KSTP-TV (ABC) St. Paul; KYIN (PBS) Mason City; WCCO-TV (CBS) Minneapolis; WFTC (MNT) Minneapolis.
Programming (via satellite): ABC Family Channel; Arts & Entertainment; CNN; Comedy Central; Country Music TV; ESPN; ESPN 2; Fox Sports Net; HGTV; History Channel; Lifetime; Nickelodeon; Outdoor Channel; Spike TV; TBS Superstation; The Learning Channel; Turner Classic Movies; Turner Network TV; TV Land; USA Network; Weather Channel; WGN.
Fee: $37.24 monthly.

Pay Service 1
Pay Units: N.A. Included in Cambridge
Programming (via satellite): HBO.
Fee: $11.95 monthly.

Internet Service
Operational: No.

Telephone Service
None
Homes passed: Included in Cambridge
General Manager: Steve Johnson. Customer Service Director: Jackie Torberg.
City fee: None.
Ownership: US Cable Corp. (MSO).; Comcast Cable Communications Inc. (MSO).

EAST GULL LAKE—Savage Communications Inc. Now served by PILLAGER, MN [MN0230]. ICA: MN0151.

EASTON—North American Communications Corp., PO Box 387, 211 Main St S, Hector, MN 55342-0387. Phones: 800-982-8038; 320-848-6781. Fax: 320-848-2323. E-mail: hcc@hcctel.net. Web Site: http://www.hectorcom.com. ICA: MN0292.
TV Market Ranking: Below 100 (EASTON). Franchise award date: N.A. Franchise expiration date: N.A. Began: N.A.
Channel capacity: 54 (not 2-way capable). Channels available but not in use: 28.

Basic Service
Subscribers: 31.
Programming (received off-air): KAAL (ABC) Austin; KARE (NBC) Minneapolis; KEYC-TV (CBS, FOX) Mankato; KMSP-TV (FOX) Minneapolis; KSMN (PBS) Worthington; KSTP-TV (ABC) St. Paul; WCCO-TV (CBS) Minneapolis; WFTC (MNT) Minneapolis; WUCW (CW) Minneapolis.
Programming (via satellite): ABC Family Channel; AMC; Arts & Entertainment; CNN; Country Music TV; Discovery Channel; Disney Channel; ESPN; Fox Sports Net Midwest; Nickelodeon; QVC; Spike TV; TBS Superstation; Trinity Broadcasting Network; Turner Network TV; USA Network; WGN America.
Current originations: Leased Access; Government Access; Educational Access; Public Access.
Fee: $40.00 installation; $26.95 monthly; $3.50 converter; $25.00 additional installation.

Pay Service 1
Pay Units: 3.
Programming (via satellite): Cinemax.
Fee: $10.95 monthly.

Pay Service 2
Pay Units: 3.
Programming (via satellite): HBO.
Fee: $10.95 monthly.

Video-On-Demand: No

Internet Service
Operational: No.
Broadband Service: Offers dial-up and DSL only; no cable modem service.

Telephone Service
None
Miles of Plant: 4.0 (coaxial); None (fiber optic). Homes passed: 104. Total homes in franchised area: 104.
Manager: Matt Sparks. Chief Technician: George Honzay. Customer Service Supervisor: Patty Groshens.
Ownership: Hector Communications Corp. (MSO).

ECHO—Clara City Telephone Co., 215 1st St NW, Clara City, MN 56222. Phone: 507-637-8351. Fax: 320-847-2114. ICA: MN0239.
TV Market Ranking: Below 100 (ECHO). Franchise award date: January 1, 1988. Franchise expiration date: N.A. Began: December 26, 1988.
Channel capacity: 36 (not 2-way capable). Channels available but not in use: 12.

Basic Service
Subscribers: 50.
Programming (received off-air): KEYC-TV (CBS, FOX) Mankato; KSFY-TV (ABC) Sioux Falls; KWCM-TV (PBS) Appleton.
Programming (via satellite): ABC Family Channel; AMC; Arts & Entertainment; CNN; Discovery Channel; ESPN; History Channel; Lifetime; Nickelodeon; Spike TV; The Learning Channel; Turner Network TV; TV Land; USA Network; Weather Channel; WGN America.
Programming (via translator): KARE (NBC) Minneapolis; KMSP-TV (FOX) Minneapolis; KSTP-TV (ABC) St. Paul; KTCA-TV (PBS) St.

Paul; WCCO-TV (CBS) Minneapolis; WFTC (MNT) Minneapolis.
Fee: $40.00 installation; $33.80 monthly; $2.00 converter.
Pay Service 1
Pay Units: 4.
Programming (via satellite): Showtime.
Fee: $10.00 installation; $10.00 monthly.
Internet Service
Operational: No.
Telephone Service
None
Miles of Plant: 3.0 (coaxial); None (fiber optic). Homes passed: 150. Total homes in franchised area: 150.
Manager: Bruce Hanson.
Ownership: Hanson Communications Inc. (MSO).

EDNA TWP.—ACS Video. Formerly served by Perham, MN [MN0050]. This cable system has converted to IPTV, 150 Second St SW, Perham, MN 56573. Phone: 866-937-4227. E-mail: answers@arvig.com. Web Site: http://www.arvig.com. ICA: MN5192.
TV Market Ranking: Outside TV Markets (EDNA TWP.).
Channel capacity: N.A. Channels available but not in use: N.A.
Internet Service
Operational: Yes.
Telephone Service
Digital: Operational
Ownership: Arvig Communication Systems.

EITZEN—Ace Communications Group. Formerly [MN0294]. This cable system has converted to IPTV, PO Box 360, 207 E Cedar St, Houston, MN 55943-0360. Phones: 888-404-4940; 507-896-3192. Fax: 507-896-2149. E-mail: info@acegroup.cc. Web Site: http://www.acegroup.cc. ICA: MN5143.
TV Market Ranking: Below 100 (EITZEN). Franchise award date: N.A. Franchise expiration date: N.A. Began: N.A.
Channel capacity: N.A. Channels available but not in use: N.A.
Video-On-Demand: Yes
Internet Service
Operational: Yes.
Fee: $50.00 installation; $39.95 monthly.
Telephone Service
Digital: Operational
Fee: $10.50 monthly
Chief Executive Officer: Todd Roesler.
Ownership: Ace Communications Group (MSO).

EITZEN—Ace Communications Group. This cable system has converted to IPTV. See Eitzen, MN [MN5143], MN. ICA: MN0294.

ELBOW LAKE—Runestone Cable TV. Now served by BARRETT, MN [MN0233]. ICA: MN0135.

ELKO—Mediacom, PO Box 110, 1504 2nd St SE, Waseca, MN 56093. Phones: 800-332-0245; 507-835-2356. Fax: 507-835-4567. Web Site: http://www.mediacomcable.com. Also serves New Market Twp. & Webster Twp. ICA: MN0295.
TV Market Ranking: 13 (ELKO, New Market Twp., Webster Twp.). Franchise award date: N.A. Franchise expiration date: N.A. Began: May 1, 1989.
Channel capacity: N.A. Channels available but not in use: N.A.
Basic Service
Subscribers: N.A.
Programming (received off-air): KARE (NBC) Minneapolis; KMSP-TV (FOX) Minneapolis; KPXM-TV (ION) St. Cloud; KSTC-TV (IND) Minneapolis; KSTP-TV (ABC) St. Paul; KTCA-TV (PBS) St. Paul; KTCI-TV (PBS) St. Paul; WCCO-TV (CBS) Minneapolis; WFTC (MNT) Minneapolis; WUCW (CW) Minneapolis.
Programming (via satellite): C-SPAN; QVC; Weather Channel; WGN America.
Current originations: Public Access.
Fee: $15.45 monthly.
Expanded Basic Service 1
Subscribers: N.A.
Programming (received off-air): WUMN-CA Minneapolis.
Programming (via satellite): ABC Family Channel; AMC; Animal Planet; Arts & Entertainment; BET Networks; Bravo; Cartoon Network; CNBC; CNN; Comedy Central; Country Music TV; C-SPAN 2; Discovery Channel; Disney Channel; E! Entertainment Television; ESPN; ESPN 2; Eternal Word TV Network; Fox Movie Channel; Fox News Channel; Fox Sports Net North; FX; Hallmark Channel; Headline News; HGTV; History Channel; Home Shopping Network; INSP; Lifetime; MSNBC; MTV; Nickelodeon; SoapNet; Speed Channel; Spike TV; Syfy; TBS Superstation; The Learning Channel; Travel Channel; Trinity Broadcasting Network; truTV; Turner Classic Movies; Turner Network TV; TV Guide Network; TV Land; USA Network; VH1; WE tv; Weather Channel.
Digital Basic Service
Subscribers: N.A.
Programming (received off-air): KARE (NBC) Minneapolis; KMSP-TV (FOX) Minneapolis; KSTP-TV (ABC) St. Paul; KTCA-TV (PBS) St. Paul; WCCO-TV (CBS) Minneapolis.
Programming (via satellite): ABC News Now; AmericanLife TV Network; BBC America; Bio; Bloomberg Television; Canal 52MX; CBS College Sports Network; CCTV-4; Cine Latino; CNN en Espanol; CNN HD; Discovery en Espanol; Discovery HD Theater; Discovery Health Channel; Discovery Home Channel; Discovery Kids Channel; Discovery Military Channel; ESPN 2 HD; ESPN Deportes; ESPN HD; ESPN U; ESPNews; FitTV; Fox College Sports Atlantic; Fox College Sports Central; Fox College Sports Pacific; Fox Reality Channel; Fox Soccer; Fox Sports en Espanol; FSN HD; Fuel TV; Fuse; G4; Gol TV; Golf Channel; GSN; Halogen Network; HDNet; HDNet Movies; History Channel en Espanol; History Channel International; ID Investigation Discovery; Independent Film Channel; ION Life; Lifetime Movie Network; Lifetime Real Women; MTV Hits; MTV Tres; MTV2; Music Choice; National Geographic Channel; Nick Jr.; NickToons TV; Outdoor Channel; Qubo; ReelzChannel; Science Channel; Sleuth; Style Network; TBS in HD; TeenNick; Tennis Channel; The Sportsman Channel; Turner Network TV HD; TVG Network; Universal HD; VeneMovies; Versus; VH1 Classic.
Digital Pay Service 1
Pay Units: N.A.
Programming (via satellite): Cinemax (multiplexed); Encore (multiplexed); Flix; HBO (multiplexed); HBO HD; Showtime (multiplexed); Showtime HD; Starz (multiplexed); Starz HDTV; Sundance Channel; The Movie Channel (multiplexed); The Movie Channel HD.
Fee: $9.95 monthly (each).
Video-On-Demand: Yes
Pay-Per-View
iN DEMAND (delivered digitally); Fresh (delivered digitally); Playboy TV (delivered digitally); Spice: Xcess (delivered digitally); Ten Clips (delivered digitally); Penthouse TV (delivered digitally).
Internet Service
Operational: Yes.
Broadband Service: MSN.
Fee: $99.00 installation; $40.00 monthly.
Telephone Service
Digital: Operational
Miles of Plant: 10.0 (coaxial); None (fiber optic).
Vice President: Bill Jensen. Engineering Manager: Kraig Kaiser. Marketing & Sales Director: Lori Huberty.
Ownership: Mediacom LLC (MSO).

ELLSWORTH—Knology, 5100 S Broadband Ln, Sioux Falls, SD 57108-2207. Phone: 605-965-9393. Fax: 605-965-7867. Web Site: http://www.knology.com. ICA: MN0296.
TV Market Ranking: Outside TV Markets (ELLSWORTH). Franchise award date: December 1, 1983. Franchise expiration date: N.A. Began: N.A.
Channel capacity: N.A. Channels available but not in use: N.A.
Basic Service
Subscribers: N.A. Included in Viborg SD
Programming (received off-air): KARE (NBC) Minneapolis; KAUN-LP Sioux Falls; KCAU-TV (ABC) Sioux City; KCPO-LP Sioux Falls; KDLT-TV (NBC) Sioux Falls; KELO-TV (CBS, MNT) Sioux Falls; KMSP-TV (FOX) Minneapolis; KSFY-TV (ABC) Sioux Falls; KSIN-TV (PBS) Sioux City; KSMN (PBS) Worthington; KTCA-TV (PBS) St. Paul; KTTW (FOX) Sioux Falls; KUSD-TV (PBS) Vermillion; WCCO-TV (CBS) Minneapolis; WFTC (MNT) Minneapolis.
Programming (via satellite): ABC Family Channel; AMC; Animal Planet; Arts & Entertainment; Bravo; Cartoon Network; CNBC; CNN; Comedy Central; Country Music TV; C-SPAN; C-SPAN 2; CW+; Discovery Channel; Disney Channel; E! Entertainment Television; ESPN; ESPN 2; ESPN Classic Sports; Food Network; Fox News Channel; Fox Sports Net; FX; GalaVision; Golf Channel; Hallmark Channel; Headline News; HGTV; History Channel; Lifetime; Lifetime Movie Network; MSNBC; MTV; MyNetworkTV Inc.; National Geographic Channel; NFL Network; Nickelodeon; QVC; Speed Channel; Spike TV; Syfy; TBS Superstation; Telemundo; The Learning Channel; Toon Disney; Travel Channel; Trinity Broadcasting Network; truTV; Turner Classic Movies; Turner Network TV; TV Guide Network; TV Land; Univision; USA Network; VH1; Weather Channel; WGN America.
Fee: $25.00 installation; $22.95 monthly.
Digital Basic Service
Subscribers: N.A.
Programming (received off-air): KDLT-TV (NBC) Sioux Falls; KELO-TV (CBS, MNT) Sioux Falls; KSFY-TV (ABC) Sioux Falls; KTTW (FOX) Sioux Falls; KUSD-TV (PBS) Vermillion.
Programming (via satellite): Adult Swim; BBC America; Bio; Bloomberg Television; Boomerang; CMT Pure Country; Cooking Channel; Discovery HD Theater; Discovery Health Channel; Discovery Kids Channel; Discovery Military Channel; Discovery Planet Green; Do-It-Yourself; ESPN 2 HD; ESPN Deportes On Demand; ESPN HD; ESPN On Demand; ESPN U; ESPN U On Demand; ESPNews; Eternal Word TV Network; FitTV; Flix; Fox College Sports Atlantic; Fox College Sports Central; Fox College Sports Pacific; Fox Movie Channel; Fox Reality Channel; Fox Soccer; Fuse; G4; Gospel Music Channel; GSN; HDNet; HDNet Movies; History Channel International; ID Investigation Discovery; Independent Film Channel; Lifetime Real Women; MTV Hits; MTV Jams; MTV2; Music Choice; National Geographic Channel; National Geographic Channel HD Network; National Geographic Channel On Demand; NFL Network HD; Nick Jr.; NickToons TV; Outdoor Channel; Outdoor Channel 2 HD; Outdoor Channel On Demand; QVC HD; RFD-TV; Science Television; Sleuth; Sleuth On Demand; SoapNet; Speed On Demand; Style Network; Sundance Channel; TBS in HD; TeenNick; Turner Network TV HD; TV Guide SPOT; Universal HD; Versus; Versus HD; Versus On Demand; VH1 Classic; VH1 Soul; WAM! America's Kidz Network; WE tv.
Digital Expanded Basic Service
Subscribers: N.A.
Programming (via satellite): Bandamax; De Pelicula; De Pelicula Clasico; Discovery en Espanol; ESPN Deportes; Fox Sports en Espanol; Ritmoson Latino; Telehit.
Digital Pay Service 1
Pay Units: N.A.
Programming (via satellite): Cinemax (multiplexed); Cinemax HD; Cinemax On Demand; Encore (multiplexed); HBO (multiplexed); HBO HD; HBO On Demand; Showtime (multiplexed); Showtime HD; Showtime On Demand; Starz (multiplexed); Starz On Demand; The Movie Channel (multiplexed); The Movie Channel On Demand.
Video-On-Demand: Yes
Internet Service
Operational: Yes.
Broadband Service: Knology.Net.
Fee: $29.95 installation; $39.95 monthly.
Telephone Service
Analog: Not Operational
Digital: Operational
Miles of Plant: 4.0 (coaxial); None (fiber optic). Total homes in franchised area: 274. Homes passed included in Viborg SD
General Manager: Scott Schroeder. Technical Operations Manager: Daryl Elcock. Marketing Manager: Scott Determan.
Ownership: Knology Inc. (MSO).

ELY—Midcontinent Communications, PO Box 5010, Sioux Falls, SD 57117. Phones: 800-456-0564; 605-229-1775. Fax: 605-229-0478. E-mail: mccomm@midco.net. Web Site: http://www.midcocomm.com. Also serves Winton. ICA: MN0060.
TV Market Ranking: Outside TV Markets (ELY, Winton). Franchise award date: May 1, 1956. Franchise expiration date: N.A. Began: May 1, 1956.
Channel capacity: N.A. Channels available but not in use: N.A.
Basic Service
Subscribers: 1,511.
Programming (via microwave): KBJR-TV (MNT, NBC) Superior; KDLH (CBS, CW) Duluth; KQDS-TV (FOX) Duluth; WDIO-DT (ABC) Duluth; WDSE (PBS) Duluth.
Programming (via satellite): C-SPAN; Eternal Word TV Network; INSP; QVC; WGN America.
Fee: $29.99 installation.
Expanded Basic Service 1
Subscribers: N.A.
Programming (via satellite): ABC Family Channel; AMC; Animal Planet; Arts & Entertainment; Bravo; Cartoon Network; CNBC; CNN; Comedy Central; Country Music TV; Discovery Channel; Disney Channel; E! Entertainment Television; ESPN; ESPN 2; Fox News Channel; Fox Sports Net North; FX; G4; Hallmark Channel; Headline News; HGTV; History Channel; Lifetime; MSNBC; MTV; Nickelodeon; Oxygen; Speed Chan-

nel; Spike TV; Syfy; TBS Superstation; The Learning Channel; Turner Classic Movies; Turner Network TV; TV Land; USA Network; VH1; Weather Channel.
Fee: $47.99 monthly.

Digital Basic Service
Subscribers: N.A.
Programming (via satellite): BBC America; Bio; Discovery Digital Networks; Do-It-Yourself; Fox College Sports Atlantic; Fox College Sports Central; Fox College Sports Pacific; Fox Movie Channel; Fox Soccer; GAS; History Channel International; Independent Film Channel; MTV Networks Digital Suite; Music Choice; Nick Jr.; Nick Too; NickToons TV; SoapNet; Style Network; Sundance Channel; Toon Disney; TV Guide Interactive Inc.; WE tv.

Digital Pay Service 1
Pay Units: N.A.
Programming (via satellite): Cinemax (multiplexed); Encore; Flix; HBO (multiplexed); Showtime (multiplexed); Starz (multiplexed); The Movie Channel (multiplexed).

Video-On-Demand: No

Pay-Per-View
iN DEMAND (delivered digitally); Hot Choice (delivered digitally).

Internet Service
Operational: Yes.
Broadband Service: Charter Pipeline.
Fee: $29.99 monthly.

Telephone Service
None

Miles of Plant: 38.0 (coaxial); None (fiber optic). Homes passed: 1,890. Total homes in franchised area: 1,908.
Ownership: Midcontinent Media Inc. (MSO).

EMILY—Emily Cooperative Telephone Co. CATV Division, PO Box 100, 40040 State Hwy 6, Emily, MN 56447-0100. Phones: 800-450-1036; 218-763-3000. Fax: 218-763-2042. E-mail: emilytel@emily.net. Web Site: http://www.emily.net. Also serves Crooked Lake, Fifty Lakes & Outing. ICA: MN0081.
TV Market Ranking: Below 100 (Crooked Lake, Fifty Lakes, Outing); Outside TV Markets (EMILY). Franchise award date: December 22, 1981. Franchise expiration date: N.A. Began: March 1, 1983.
Channel capacity: 35 (operating 2-way). Channels available but not in use: 15.

Basic Service
Subscribers: 875.
Programming (received off-air): KAWE (PBS) Bemidji; KCCW-TV (CBS) Walker; KSAX (ABC) Alexandria.
Programming (via microwave): KARE (NBC) Minneapolis; KMSP-TV (FOX) Minneapolis; KSTC-TV (IND) Minneapolis; WFTC (MNT) Minneapolis.
Programming (via satellite): Eternal Word TV Network; QVC; Trinity Broadcasting Network; TV Guide Network.
Current originations: Religious Access; Educational Access; Public Access.
Fee: $50.00 installation; $17.50 monthly.

Expanded Basic Service 1
Subscribers: N.A.
Programming (via satellite): ABC Family Channel; AMC; Animal Planet; Arts & Entertainment; CNBC; CNN; Discovery Channel; Disney Channel; E! Entertainment Television; ESPN; ESPN 2; Fox News Channel; Fox Sports Net; HGTV; History Channel; Lifetime; Nickelodeon; Spike TV; TBS Superstation; The Learning Channel; Travel Channel; Turner Network TV; USA Network; Weather Channel.
Fee: $17.45 monthly.

Digital Basic Service
Subscribers: N.A.
Programming (via satellite): Bravo; Discovery Digital Networks; DMX Music; ESPN Classic Sports; ESPNews; Fox Sports World; Golf Channel; GSN; Independent Film Channel; National Geographic Channel; Nick Jr.; Speed Channel; Turner Classic Movies; Versus.
Fee: $11.00 monthly.

Digital Pay Service 1
Pay Units: N.A.
Programming (via satellite): Cinemax (multiplexed); Encore (multiplexed); HBO (multiplexed); Showtime (multiplexed); Starz (multiplexed); The Movie Channel (multiplexed).
Fee: $10.00 monthly (Starz/Encore), $15.00 monthly (Showtime/TMC), $18.50 monthly (HBO and Cinemax).

Video-On-Demand: No

Pay-Per-View
Playboy TV (delivered digitally).

Internet Service
Operational: No, DSL & dialup.

Telephone Service
None

Miles of Plant: 75.0 (coaxial); None (fiber optic). Homes passed: 1,500. Total homes in franchised area: 1,900.
General Manager: Robert Olson.
Ownership: Emily Cooperative Telephone Co.

EMMONS—Heck's TV & Cable, PO Box 517, 601 7th St, Armstrong, IA 50514-0517. Phone: 712-864-3431. Fax: 712-864-3431. ICA: MN0227.
TV Market Ranking: Below 100 (EMMONS). Franchise award date: N.A. Franchise expiration date: N.A. Began: November 1, 1986.
Channel capacity: N.A. Channels available but not in use: N.A.

Basic Service
Subscribers: 145.
Programming (received off-air): KAAL (ABC) Austin; KEYC-TV (CBS, FOX) Mankato; KTTC (CW, NBC) Rochester.
Programming (via satellite): ABC Family Channel; Arts & Entertainment; CNN; Discovery Channel; ESPN; Lifetime; Nickelodeon; Spike TV; TBS Superstation; Turner Network TV; USA Network; WGN America.
Fee: $30.50 installation; $18.00 monthly.

Pay Service 1
Pay Units: N.A.
Programming (via satellite): The Movie Channel.
Fee: $10.00 monthly.

Video-On-Demand: No

Internet Service
Operational: No.

Telephone Service
None

Miles of Plant: 3.0 (coaxial); None (fiber optic). Homes passed: 185.
Manager: Steven Heck.
Ownership: Steven Heck (MSO).

ERIE TWP.—ACS Video. Formerly served by Perham, MN [MN0050]. This cable system has converted to IPTV, 150 Second St SW, Perham, MN 56573. Phone: 866-937-4227. E-mail: answers@arvig.com. Web Site: http://www.arvig.com. ICA: MN5193.
TV Market Ranking: Outside TV Markets (ERIE TWP.).
Channel capacity: N.A. Channels available but not in use: N.A.

Internet Service
Operational: Yes.

Telephone Service
Digital: Operational
Ownership: Arvig Communication Systems.

ERSKINE—Garden Valley Telephone Co., PO Box 259, 201 Ross Ave, Erskine, MN 56535-0259. Phones: 800-448-8260; 218-687-5251. Fax: 218-687-2454. E-mail: gvtc@gvtel.com. Web Site: http://www.gvtel.com. Also serves Badger Twp., Bransvold Twp., Godfrey, Godfrey Twp., Grove Park, Grove Park Twp., Hill River Twp., King Twp., Knute Twp., Lessor Twp., McIntosh, Mentor, Sletten Twp., Winger, Woodside & Woodside Twp. ICA: MN0105.
TV Market Ranking: Below 100 (Badger Twp., ERSKINE, Godfrey, Godfrey Twp., Grove Park, Grove Park Twp., Hill River Twp., Lessor Twp., Mentor, Woodside, Woodside Twp.); Outside TV Markets (Bransvold Twp., King Twp., Knute Twp., McIntosh, Sletten Twp., Winger). Franchise award date: March 12, 1979. Franchise expiration date: N.A. Began: N.A.
Channel capacity: 35 (operating 2-way). Channels available but not in use: 10.

Basic Service
Subscribers: 981.
Programming (received off-air): KAWE (PBS) Bemidji; KBRR (FOX) Thief River Falls; KFME (PBS) Fargo; KVLY-TV (NBC) Fargo; KXJB-TV (CBS) Valley City; WDAY-TV (ABC, CW) Fargo; WDAZ-TV (ABC, CW) Devils Lake.
Programming (via satellite): ABC Family Channel; AMC; Arts & Entertainment; CNN; Discovery Channel; Disney Channel; ESPN; Fox Sports Net; History Channel; Spike TV; TBS Superstation; Turner Network TV; TV Land; USA Network; WGN America.
Programming (via translator): KMSP-TV (FOX) Minneapolis.
Current originations: Public Access.
Fee: $40.90 installation; $23.95 monthly; $.75 converter.

Pay Service 1
Pay Units: 160.
Programming (via satellite): HBO.
Fee: $10.50 monthly.

Video-On-Demand: No

Internet Service
Operational: No, DSL & Dialup.

Telephone Service
None

Miles of Plant: 278.0 (coaxial); None (fiber optic). Homes passed: 1,813. Total homes in franchised area: 1,813.
Manager: George Fish. Operations Manager: Dave Hamre. Facilities Manager: Randy Versdahl. Marketing Supervisor: Julie Dahle.
Franchise fee: None.
Ownership: Garden Valley Telephone Co. (MSO).

ESSING—NU-Telecom. Formerly served by New Ulm, MN [MN0285]. This cable system has converted to IPTV, PO Box 697, 22 S Marshall, Springfield, MN 56087-0697. Phones: 800-893-1856; 507-723-4211. Fax: 507-723-4377. E-mail: on-linecustservice@nu-telecom.net. Web Site: http://www.nutelecom.net. ICA: MN5150.
TV Market Ranking: Below 100 (ESSING).
Channel capacity: N.A. Channels available but not in use: N.A.

Internet Service
Operational: Yes.

Telephone Service
Digital: Operational
President & Chief Executive Officer: Bill Otis.
Ownership: NU-Telecom.

EVELETH—Mediacom, PO Box 110, 1504 2nd St SE, Waseca, MN 56093. Phone: 507-835-2356. Fax: 507-835-4567. Web Site: http://www.mediacomcable.com. Also serves Aurora, Biwabik, Buhl, Chisholm, Fayal Twp., Gilbert, Hoyt Lakes, Kinney, Lake County (western portion), Mountain Iron, Parkville, Virginia & Whyte Twp. ICA: MN0017.
TV Market Ranking: Below 100 (Aurora, Biwabik, Buhl, Chisholm, EVELETH, Fayal Twp., Gilbert, Kinney, Mountain Iron, Parkville, Virginia); Outside TV Markets (Hoyt Lakes, Lake County (western portion), Whyte Twp.). Franchise award date: N.A. Franchise expiration date: N.A. Began: December 1, 1967.
Channel capacity: N.A. Channels available but not in use: N.A.

Basic Service
Subscribers: 8,887.
Programming (received off-air): KBJR-TV (MNT, NBC) Superior; KDLH (CBS, CW) Duluth; KQDS-TV (FOX) Duluth; WDSE (PBS) Duluth; WIRT-DT (ABC) Hibbing; allband FM.
Programming (via microwave): KMSP-TV (FOX) Minneapolis.
Programming (via satellite): C-SPAN; C-SPAN 2; Home Shopping Network; TV Guide Network; Weather Channel; WGN America.
Current originations: Public Access.
Fee: $15.00 installation; $13.50 monthly; $4.00 converter; $15.00 additional installation.

Expanded Basic Service 1
Subscribers: N.A.
Programming (via satellite): ABC Family Channel; AMC; Animal Planet; Arts & Entertainment; Bravo; Cartoon Network; CNBC; CNN; Comedy Central; Country Music TV; Discovery Channel; Disney Channel; E! Entertainment Television; ESPN; ESPN 2; Eternal Word TV Network; Food Network; Fox Sports Net North; FX; Hallmark Channel; Headline News; HGTV; History Channel; ION Television; Lifetime; MSNBC; MTV; Nickelodeon; SoapNet; Spike TV; Syfy; TBS Superstation; The Learning Channel; Travel Channel; Trinity Broadcasting Network; truTV; Turner Network TV; USA Network; VH1; WE tv.
Fee: $26.45 monthly.

Digital Basic Service
Subscribers: N.A.
Programming (via satellite): AmericanLife TV Network; BBC America; Bio; Bloomberg Television; Discovery Digital Networks; Fox Sports World; Fuse; G4; Golf Channel; GSN;

Halogen Network; History Channel International; Independent Film Channel; Lifetime Movie Network; Music Choice; Outdoor Channel; Style Network; WE tv.
Fee: $13.00 monthly.

Digital Pay Service 1
Pay Units: N.A.
Programming (via satellite): Cinemax (multiplexed); Encore (multiplexed); Flix; HBO (multiplexed); Showtime (multiplexed); Starz (multiplexed); The Movie Channel (multiplexed).
Fee: $15.00 installation; $11.00 monthly (Cinemax, HBO, Flix/Showtime/TMC, or Starz/Encore).

Video-On-Demand: No

Pay-Per-View
Playboy TV (delivered digitally), Addressable: Yes; Fresh (delivered digitally); Shorteez (delivered digitally); TVN Entertainment (delivered digitally).

Internet Service
Operational: Yes.
Subscribers: 2,005.
Broadband Service: Mediacom High Speed Internet.
Fee: $69.95 installation; $40.95 monthly; $10.00 modem lease; $239.95 modem purchase.

Telephone Service
Digital: Operational

Miles of Plant: 206.0 (coaxial); 75.0 (fiber optic). Homes passed: 15,580. Total homes in franchised area: 18,073.
Vice President: Bill Jensen. Engineering Manager: Kraig Kaiser. Marketing & Sales Director: Lori Huberty.
City fee: 3% of gross.
Ownership: Mediacom LLC (MSO).

FAIRMONT—Midcontinent Communications, PO Box 5010, Sioux Falls, SD 57117. Phones: 800-456-0564; 605-229-1775. Fax: 605-229-0478. E-mail: mccomm@midco.net. Web Site: http://www.midcocomm.com. Also serves Sherburn. ICA: MN0040.
TV Market Ranking: Outside TV Markets (FAIRMONT, Sherburn). Franchise award date: January 1, 1957. Franchise expiration date: N.A. Began: January 1, 1957.
Channel capacity: N.A. Channels available but not in use: N.A.

Basic Service
Subscribers: 3,500.
Programming (received off-air): KAAL (ABC) Austin; KEYC-TV (CBS, FOX) Mankato; KTIN (PBS) Fort Dodge; KTTC (CW, NBC) Rochester; allband FM.
Programming (via microwave): KARE (NBC) Minneapolis; KMSP-TV (FOX) Minneapolis; KSTP-TV (ABC) St. Paul; KTCA-TV (PBS) St. Paul; WCCO-TV (CBS) Minneapolis; WFTC (MNT) Minneapolis; WUCW (CW) Minneapolis.
Programming (via satellite): C-SPAN; C-SPAN 2; Eternal Word TV Network; Home Shopping Network; QVC; TBS Superstation; TV Guide Network; WGN America.
Current originations: Educational Access; Public Access; Government Access.
Fee: $29.99 installation.

Expanded Basic Service 1
Subscribers: N.A.
Programming (via satellite): ABC Family Channel; AMC; Animal Planet; Arts & Entertainment; Bravo; Cartoon Network; CNBC; CNN; Comedy Central; Country Music TV; Discovery Channel; Disney Channel; E! Entertainment Television; ESPN; ESPN 2; Food Network; Fox News Channel; Fox Sports Net North; FX; G4; Golf Channel; GSN; Hallmark Channel; Headline News; HGTV; History Channel; Lifetime; MSNBC; MTV; MTV2; National Geographic Channel; Nickelodeon; Oxygen; SoapNet; Speed Channel; Spike TV; Syfy; The Learning Channel; Toon Disney; Travel Channel; Trinity Broadcasting Network; truTV; Turner Classic Movies; Turner Network TV; TV Land; USA Network; Versus; VH1; WE tv; Weather Channel.
Fee: $47.99 monthly.

Digital Basic Service
Subscribers: N.A.
Programming (via satellite): BBC America; Bio; Bloomberg Television; Boomerang; CNN en Espanol; CNN International; Discovery Digital Networks; Do-It-Yourself; FitTV; Fox College Sports Atlantic; Fox College Sports Central; Fox College Sports Pacific; Fox Movie Channel; Fox Soccer; Fuel TV; GAS; History Channel International; Independent Film Channel; MTV Networks Digital Suite; Music Choice; Nick Jr.; Nick Too; NickToons TV; Style Network; Sundance Channel; TV Guide Interactive Inc.

Digital Pay Service 1
Pay Units: N.A.
Programming (via satellite): Cinemax (multiplexed); Encore (multiplexed); Flix; HBO (multiplexed); Showtime (multiplexed); Starz (multiplexed); The Movie Channel (multiplexed).

Video-On-Demand: No

Pay-Per-View
iN DEMAND (delivered digitally); NASCAR In Car (delivered digitally); Playboy TV (delivered digitally); Fresh (delivered digitally); Shorteez (delivered digitally).

Internet Service
Operational: Yes.
Broadband Service: Charter Pipeline.
Fee: $29.99 monthly.

Telephone Service
None

Miles of Plant: 99.0 (coaxial); None (fiber optic). Homes passed: 5,200.
City fee: 5% of gross.
Ownership: Midcontinent Media Inc. (MSO).

FARIBAULT—Charter Communications, 3380 Northern Valley Pl NE, Rochester, MN 55906-3954. Phones: 507-334-7248 (Local office); 507-289-8372 (Rochester administrative office). Fax: 507-285-6162. Web Site: http://www.charter.com. Also serves Rice County & Walcott Twp. ICA: MN0026.
TV Market Ranking: 13 (Rice County (portions)); Below 100 (FARIBAULT, Rice County (portions)); Outside TV Markets (Walcott Twp., Rice County (portions)). Franchise award date: August 1, 1969. Franchise expiration date: N.A. Began: January 1, 1970.
Channel capacity: 96 (operating 2-way). Channels available but not in use: 14.

Basic Service
Subscribers: 5,070.
Programming (received off-air): KARE (NBC) Minneapolis; KMSP-TV (FOX) Minneapolis; KPXM-TV (ION) St. Cloud; KSMQ-TV (PBS) Austin; KSTC-TV (IND) Minneapolis; KSTP-TV (ABC) St. Paul; KTCA-TV (PBS) St. Paul; WCCO-TV (CBS) Minneapolis; WFTC (MNT) Minneapolis; WUCW (CW) Minneapolis; 15 FMs.
Programming (via satellite): C-SPAN; C-SPAN 2; Home Shopping Network; Product Information Network; QVC; Trinity Broadcasting Network; TV Guide Network; WGN America.
Current originations: Religious Access; Educational Access; Public Access.
Fee: $29.99 installation.

Expanded Basic Service 1
Subscribers: N.A.
Programming (via satellite): ABC Family Channel; AMC; Animal Planet; Arts & Entertainment; BET Networks; Bravo; Cartoon Network; CNBC; CNN; Comedy Central; Country Music TV; Discovery Channel; Disney Channel; E! Entertainment Television; ESPN; ESPN 2; Eternal Word TV Network; Food Network; Fox News Channel; Fox Sports Net North; FX; G4; Golf Channel; GSN; Hallmark Channel; Headline News; HGTV; History Channel; INSP; Lifetime; MSNBC; MTV; MTV2; National Geographic Channel; Nickelodeon; Oxygen; ShopNBC; SoapNet; Speed Channel; Spike TV; Syfy; TBS Superstation; The Learning Channel; Toon Disney; Travel Channel; truTV; Turner Network TV; TV Land; Univision; USA Network; Versus; VH1; WE tv; Weather Channel.
Fee: $47.99 monthly.

Digital Basic Service
Subscribers: N.A.
Programming (received off-air): KARE (NBC) Minneapolis; KMSP-TV (FOX) Minneapolis; WCCO-TV (CBS) Minneapolis.
Programming (via satellite): BBC America; Bio; Bloomberg Television; Boomerang; CBS College Sports Network; CNN en Espanol; CNN International; Discovery Digital Networks; Do-It-Yourself; ESPN; ESPN Classic Sports; ESPNews; FitTV; Fox College Sports Atlantic; Fox College Sports Central; Fox College Sports Pacific; Fox Movie Channel; Fox Soccer; Fuel TV; Fuse; GAS; HDNet; HDNet Movies; History Channel International; Independent Film Channel; Lifetime Movie Network; MTV Networks Digital Suite; Music Choice; NFL Network; Nick Jr.; Nick Too; NickToons TV; Outdoor Channel; Style Network; Sundance Channel; Turner Classic Movies; TV Guide Interactive Inc.

Digital Pay Service 1
Pay Units: N.A.
Programming (via satellite): Cinemax (multiplexed); Encore (multiplexed); Flix; HBO (multiplexed); HBO HD; Showtime (multiplexed); Showtime HD; Starz (multiplexed); The Movie Channel (multiplexed).

Video-On-Demand: Yes

Pay-Per-View
iN DEMAND (delivered digitally); NASCAR In Car (delivered digitally); NHL Center Ice (delivered digitally); MLB Extra Innings (delivered digitally); Playboy TV (delivered digitally); Spice Live (delivered digitally); Spice Platinum (delivered digitally); Hot Net Plus (delivered digitally); Spice Hot (delivered digitally).

Internet Service
Operational: Yes.
Broadband Service: Charter Pipeline.
Fee: $29.99 monthly.

Telephone Service
Digital: Operational
Fee: $29.99 monthly

Miles of Plant: 96.0 (coaxial); 17.0 (fiber optic). Homes passed: 10,000.
Vice President & General Manager: John Crowley. Operations Director: Craig Stensaas. Technical Operations Director: Darin Helgeson. Technical Supervisor: Ray Madrigal. Marketing Director: Bill Haarstad.
City fee: 2% of gross.
Ownership: Charter Communications Inc. (MSO).

FERGUS FALLS—Charter Communications, 414 W Stanton Ave, Fergus Falls, MN 56537-2506. Phones: 507-289-8372 (Rochester office); 218-739-3464. Fax: 218-736-7008. Web Site: http://www.charter.com. Also serves Aurdal Twp., Buse Twp. & Dane Prairie Twp. ICA: MN0032.
TV Market Ranking: Outside TV Markets (Aurdal Twp., Buse Twp., Dane Prairie Twp., FERGUS FALLS). Franchise award date: December 1, 1964. Franchise expiration date: N.A. Began: January 1, 1964.
Channel capacity: N.A. Channels available but not in use: N.A.

Basic Service
Subscribers: 4,811.
Programming (received off-air): KCCO-TV (CBS) Alexandria; KFME (PBS) Fargo; KSAX (ABC) Alexandria; KVLY-TV (NBC) Fargo; KVRR (FOX) Fargo; KWCM-TV (PBS) Appleton; KXJB-TV (CBS) Valley City; WDAY-TV (ABC, CW) Fargo; allband FM.
Programming (via microwave): KMSP-TV (FOX) Minneapolis; KSTC-TV (IND) Minneapolis.
Programming (via satellite): C-SPAN; C-SPAN 2; Home Shopping Network; INSP; QVC; Trinity Broadcasting Network; TV Guide Network; WGN America.
Current originations: Leased Access; Government Access; Educational Access; Public Access.
Fee: $29.99 installation; $2.00 converter.

Expanded Basic Service 1
Subscribers: 3,722.
Programming (via satellite): ABC Family Channel; AMC; Animal Planet; Arts & Entertainment; Bravo; Cartoon Network; CNBC; CNN; Comedy Central; Country Music TV; Discovery Channel; Disney Channel; E! Entertainment Television; ESPN; ESPN 2; Food Network; Fox News Channel; Fox Sports Net North; FX; G4; Golf Channel; GSN; Hallmark Channel; Headline News; HGTV; History Channel; Lifetime; MSNBC; MTV; National Geographic Channel; Nickelodeon; Outdoor Channel; Oxygen; SoapNet; Speed Channel; Spike TV; Syfy; TBS Superstation; The Learning Channel; Toon Disney; Travel Channel; truTV; Turner Network TV; TV Land; USA Network; Versus; VH1; WE tv; Weather Channel.
Fee: $47.99 monthly.

Digital Basic Service
Subscribers: N.A.
Programming (via satellite): BBC America; Bio; Discovery Digital Networks; Do-It-Yourself; ESPNews; Fox College Sports Atlantic; Fox College Sports Central; Fox College Sports Pacific; Fox Soccer; Fuel TV; GAS; History Channel International; Independent Film Channel; MTV Networks Digital Suite; Music Choice; NFL Network; Nick Jr.; Nick Too; NickToons TV; Sundance Channel; TV Guide Interactive Inc.

Digital Pay Service 1
Pay Units: N.A.
Programming (via satellite): Cinemax (multiplexed); Encore; Flix; HBO (multiplexed); Showtime (multiplexed); Starz (multiplexed); The Movie Channel (multiplexed).

Video-On-Demand: Yes

Pay-Per-View
iN DEMAND; NASCAR In Car (delivered digitally); Playboy TV (delivered digitally); Spice Live (delivered digitally); Spice Platinum (delivered digitally); Hot Net Plus (delivered digitally); Spice Hot (delivered digitally).

Internet Service
Operational: Yes. Began: July 1, 2002.
Broadband Service: Charter Pipeline.
Fee: $29.99 monthly.

Telephone Service
Digital: Operational
Miles of Plant: 104.0 (coaxial); None (fiber optic). Homes passed: 7,316.
Vice President & General Manager: John Crowley. Operations Director: Craig Stensaas. Technical Operations Director: Mark Abramo. Marketing Director: Bill Haarstad.
City fee: None.
Ownership: Charter Communications Inc. (MSO).

FERTILE—Loretel Cablevision, PO Box 72, 13 East 4th Ave, Ada, MN 56510. Phones: 800-343-2762; 218-784-5100; 218-784-5151. Fax: 218-784-2706. E-mail: loretel@loretel.net. Web Site: http://www.hectorcom.com. ICA: MN0297.
TV Market Ranking: Outside TV Markets (FERTILE). Franchise award date: December 1, 1991. Franchise expiration date: N.A. Began: December 1, 1991.
Channel capacity: 36 (not 2-way capable). Channels available but not in use: 4.
Basic Service
Subscribers: 282.
Programming (received off-air): KBRR (FOX) Thief River Falls; KFME (PBS) Fargo; KVLY-TV (NBC) Fargo; KXJB-TV (CBS) Valley City; WDAY-TV (ABC, CW) Fargo; WPCH-TV (IND) Atlanta.
Programming (via satellite): CNN; E! Entertainment Television; Food Network; Lifetime; MTV; QVC; TV Land; WGN America.
Fee: $40.00 installation; $31.00 monthly; $2.00 converter; $15.00 additional installation.
Pay Service 1
Pay Units: 20.
Programming (via satellite): Cinemax.
Fee: $15.00 installation; $10.00 monthly.
Pay Service 2
Pay Units: 27.
Programming (via satellite): HBO.
Fee: $15.00 installation; $13.00 monthly.
Pay Service 3
Pay Units: 46.
Programming (via satellite): Encore.
Fee: $2.75 monthly.
Video-On-Demand: No
Internet Service
Operational: No.
Broadband Service: Offers dial-up and DSL only; no cable modem service.
Telephone Service
None
Miles of Plant: None (coaxial); 11.0 (fiber optic). Homes passed: 487. Total homes in franchised area: 487.
Manager: Steven W. Katka. Chief Technician: Bruce Rosenfelt.
City fee: 3% of gross.
Ownership: Hector Communications Corp. (MSO).

FINLAND—Formerly served by New Century Communications. No longer in operation. ICA: MN0298.

FLOODWOOD—Savage Communications Inc., PO Box 810, 206 Power Ave N, Hinckley, MN 55037. Phone: 320-384-7442. Fax: 320-384-7446. E-mail: rwsavage@scicable.com. Web Site: http://www.scibroadband.com. ICA: MN0175.
TV Market Ranking: Below 100 (FLOODWOOD). Franchise award date: July 28, 1984. Franchise expiration date: N.A. Began: June 1, 1985.
Channel capacity: 77 (2-way capable). Channels available but not in use: 22.
Basic Service
Subscribers: 149.
Programming (received off-air): KBJR-TV (MNT, NBC) Superior; KCCW-TV (CBS) Walker; KDLH (CBS, CW) Duluth; KQDS-TV (FOX) Duluth; WDIO-DT (ABC) Duluth; WDSE (PBS) Duluth; WPIX (CW, IND) New York.
Programming (via satellite): ABC Family Channel; Animal Planet; Arts & Entertainment; CNBC; CNN; Comedy Central; C-SPAN; Discovery Channel; Disney Channel; E! Entertainment Television; ESPN; ESPN 2; Fox News Channel; Fox Sports Net; Great American Country; Headline News; HGTV; History Channel; Lifetime; MTV; Nickelodeon; QVC; Spike TV; Syfy; TBS Superstation; The Learning Channel; Turner Classic Movies; Turner Network TV; TV Land; USA Network; VH1; Weather Channel; WGN America.
Current originations: Public Access.
Planned originations: Leased Access; Government Access; Educational Access.
Fee: $39.95 installation; $33.95 monthly.
Digital Basic Service
Subscribers: N.A.
Programming (via satellite): AmericanLife TV Network; Arts & Entertainment; BBC America; Bloomberg Television; Discovery Digital Networks; DMX Music; ESPN Classic Sports; ESPNews; FitTV; Fox Movie Channel; Fox Sports World; Fuse; G4; Golf Channel; History Channel International; INSP; National Geographic Channel; Outdoor Channel; Sleuth; Speed Channel; Trinity Broadcasting Network; Versus; WE tv.
Digital Pay Service 1
Pay Units: N.A.
Programming (via satellite): Cinemax; Encore; Flix; HBO; Showtime; Starz; Sundance Channel; The Movie Channel.
Video-On-Demand: No
Pay-Per-View
Movies (delivered digitally); ESPN Now (delivered digitally); Sports PPV (delivered digitally).
Internet Service
Operational: Yes.
Broadband Service: SCI Broadband.
Telephone Service
None
Miles of Plant: 4.0 (coaxial); None (fiber optic). Additional miles planned: 2.0 (coaxial). Homes passed: 324. Total homes in franchised area: 324.
Manager: Mike Danielson. Marketing Director: Ron Savage. Chief Technician: Pat McCabe. Customer Service Manager: Donna Erickson.
City fee: 3% of gross.
Ownership: Savage Communications Inc. (MSO).

FOSSTON—City of Fosston Cable TV, 220 1st St E, Fosston, MN 56542-1324. Phones: 218-435-1959; 218-435-1737. Fax: 218-435-1961. E-mail: dave.larson@fosston.com. Web Site: http://www.fosston.com. ICA: MN0123.
TV Market Ranking: Outside TV Markets (FOSSTON). Franchise award date: October 1, 1977. Franchise expiration date: N.A. Began: October 1, 1977.
Channel capacity: 45 (not 2-way capable). Channels available but not in use: 2.
Basic Service
Subscribers: 633.
Programming (received off-air): KAWE (PBS) Bemidji; KBRR (FOX) Thief River Falls; KCCO-TV (CBS) Alexandria; KVLY-TV (NBC) Fargo; KXJB-TV (CBS) Valley City; WDAY-TV (ABC, CW) Fargo.
Programming (via satellite): ABC Family Channel; AMC; Animal Planet; Arts & Entertainment; CNN; Country Music TV; C-SPAN; Discovery Channel; Disney Channel; ESPN; ESPN 2; Fox News Channel; Fox Sports Net; Hallmark Channel; HGTV; History Channel; Lifetime; Nickelodeon; Outdoor Channel; Spike TV; Syfy; TBS Superstation; The Learning Channel; Travel Channel; Turner Classic Movies; Turner Network TV; TV Land; USA Network; VH1; Weather Channel; WGN America.
Fee: $24.00 installation; $25.00 monthly.
Pay Service 1
Pay Units: 90.
Programming (via satellite): HBO.
Fee: $12.50 installation; $11.00 monthly.
Pay Service 2
Pay Units: 30.
Programming (via satellite): Cinemax.
Fee: $12.50 installation; $7.00 monthly.
Video-On-Demand: No
Internet Service
Operational: No.
Telephone Service
None
Miles of Plant: 11.0 (coaxial); None (fiber optic). Homes passed: 720. Total homes in franchised area: 720.
Manager: David Larson. Marketing Director: Laurel Skala. Chief Technician: David K. Larson.
City fee: None.
Ownership: City of Fosston Cable TV.

FOUNTAIN—North American Communications Corp., PO Box 387, 211 Main St S, Hector, MN 55342-0387. Phones: 800-982-8038; 320-848-6781. Fax: 320-848-2323. E-mail: hcc@hcctel.net. Web Site: http://www.hectorcom.com. ICA: MN0299.
TV Market Ranking: Below 100 (FOUNTAIN). Franchise award date: February 1, 1989. Franchise expiration date: N.A. Began: N.A.
Channel capacity: 54 (not 2-way capable). Channels available but not in use: 31.
Basic Service
Subscribers: 62.
Programming (received off-air): KAAL (ABC) Austin; KIMT (CBS, MNT) Mason City; KSMQ-TV (PBS) Austin; KTTC (CW, NBC) Rochester; WLAX (FOX) La Crosse.
Programming (via satellite): ABC Family Channel; AMC; Arts & Entertainment; CNN; Country Music TV; Discovery Channel; Disney Channel; ESPN; Fox Sports Net Midwest; Lifetime; Nickelodeon; QVC; Spike TV; TBS Superstation; Trinity Broadcasting Network; Turner Network TV; USA Network; WGN America.
Fee: $40.00 installation; $26.95 monthly; $3.50 converter; $25.00 additional installation.
Pay Service 1
Pay Units: 5.
Programming (via satellite): Cinemax.
Fee: $10.95 monthly.
Pay Service 2
Pay Units: 3.
Programming (via satellite): HBO.
Fee: $10.95 monthly.
Video-On-Demand: No
Internet Service
Operational: No.
Broadband Service: Offers dial-up and DSL only; no cable modem service.
Telephone Service
None
Miles of Plant: 4.0 (coaxial); None (fiber optic). Homes passed: 141. Total homes in franchised area: 141.
Manager: Matt Sparks. Chief Technician: George Honzay. Customer Service Supervisor: Patty Groshens.
Ownership: Hector Communications Corp. (MSO).

FRENCH RIVER TWP.—Formerly served by New Century Communications. No longer in operation. ICA: MN0300.

FRIDLEY—Time Warner Cable. Now served by MINNEAPOLIS, MN [MN0001]. ICA: MN0005.

FULDA—Now served by PIPESTONE, MN [MN0348]. ICA: MN0142.

GARDEN CITY—North American Communications Corp., PO Box 387, 211 Main St S, Hector, MN 55342-0387. Phones: 800-982-8038; 320-848-6781. Fax: 320-848-2323. E-mail: hcc@hcctel.net. Web Site: http://www.hectorcom.com. ICA: MN0301.
TV Market Ranking: Below 100 (GARDEN CITY). Franchise award date: N.A. Franchise expiration date: N.A. Began: N.A.
Channel capacity: 54 (not 2-way capable). Channels available but not in use: 29.
Basic Service
Subscribers: 33.
Programming (received off-air): KARE (NBC) Minneapolis; KEYC-TV (CBS, FOX) Mankato; KMSP-TV (FOX) Minneapolis; KSMN (PBS) Worthington; KSTP-TV (ABC) St. Paul; WCCO-TV (CBS) Minneapolis; WFTC (MNT) Minneapolis; WUCW (CW) Minneapolis.
Programming (via satellite): ABC Family Channel; AMC; Arts & Entertainment; CNN; Country Music TV; Discovery Channel; Disney Channel; ESPN; Fox Sports Net Midwest; Nickelodeon; QVC; Spike TV; TBS Superstation; Trinity Broadcasting Network; Turner Network TV; USA Network; WGN America.
Current originations: Leased Access; Government Access; Educational Access; Public Access.
Fee: $40.00 installation; $26.95 monthly; $3.50 converter; $25.00 additional installation.
Pay Service 1
Pay Units: 2.
Programming (via satellite): Cinemax.
Fee: $10.95 monthly.
Pay Service 2
Pay Units: 4.
Programming (via satellite): HBO.
Fee: $10.95 monthly.
Video-On-Demand: No

Internet Service
Operational: No.
Broadband Service: Offers dial-up and DSL only; no cable modem service.
Telephone Service
None
Miles of Plant: 4.0 (coaxial); None (fiber optic). Homes passed: 113. Total homes in franchised area: 113.
Manager: Matt Sparks. Chief Technician: George Honzay. Customer Service Supervisor: Patty Groshens.
Ownership: Hector Communications Corp. (MSO).

GARY—Loretel Cablevision, PO Box 72, 13 East 4th Ave, Ada, MN 56510. Phones: 800-343-2762; 218-784-5100; 218-784-5151. Fax: 218-784-2706. E-mail: loretel@loretel.net. Web Site: http://www.hectorcom.com. ICA: MN0264.
TV Market Ranking: Outside TV Markets (GARY). Franchise award date: N.A. Franchise expiration date: N.A. Began: September 1, 1991.
Channel capacity: 30 (not 2-way capable). Channels available but not in use: 6.
Basic Service
Subscribers: 55.
Programming (received off-air): KFME (PBS) Fargo; KVLY-TV (NBC) Fargo; KVRR (FOX) Fargo; KXJB-TV (CBS) Valley City; WDAY-TV (ABC, CW) Fargo; WPCH-TV (IND) Atlanta.
Programming (via satellite): ABC Family Channel; Arts & Entertainment; CNN; Discovery Channel; ESPN; ESPN 2; Fox Sports Net Midwest; Nickelodeon; QVC; Spike TV; Syfy; Turner Network TV; USA Network; Weather Channel; WGN America.
Fee: $40.00 installation; $25.00 monthly; $2.50 converter; $15.00 additional installation.
Pay Service 1
Pay Units: 18.
Programming (via satellite): HBO.
Fee: $12.00 monthly.
Video-On-Demand: No
Internet Service
Operational: No.
Broadband Service: Offers dial-up and DSL only; no cable modem service.
Telephone Service
None
Miles of Plant: 3.0 (coaxial); None (fiber optic). Homes passed: 80.
Manager: Steven W. Katka. Chief Technician: Bruce Rosenfelt.
City fee: None.
Ownership: Hector Communications Corp. (MSO).

GAYLORD—Now served by REDWOOD FALLS, MN [MN0057]. ICA: MN0053.

GIRARD TWP.—ACS Video. Formerly served by Perham, MN [MN0050]. This cable system has converted to IPTV, 150 Second St SW, Perham, MN 56573. Phone: 866-937-4227. E-mail: answers@arvig.com. Web Site: http://www.arvig.com. ICA: MN5196.
TV Market Ranking: Outside TV Markets (GIRARD TWP.).
Channel capacity: N.A. Channels available but not in use: N.A.
Internet Service
Operational: Yes.
Telephone Service
Digital: Operational
Ownership: Arvig Communication Systems.

GLENCOE—Midcontinent Communications, PO Box 5010, Sioux Falls, SD 57117. Phones: 800-456-0564; 605-229-1775. Fax: 605-229-0478. E-mail: mccomm@midco.net. Web Site: http://www.midcocomm.com. ICA: MN0065.
TV Market Ranking: Outside TV Markets (GLENCOE). Franchise award date: July 8, 1982. Franchise expiration date: N.A. Began: March 17, 1983.
Channel capacity: 60 (not 2-way capable). Channels available but not in use: 2.
Basic Service
Subscribers: 1,200.
Programming (received off-air): KARE (NBC) Minneapolis; KEYC-TV (CBS, FOX) Mankato; KMSP-TV (FOX) Minneapolis; KPXM-TV (ION) St. Cloud; KSTC-TV (IND) Minneapolis; KSTP-TV (ABC) St. Paul; KTCA-TV (PBS) St. Paul; WCCO-TV (CBS) Minneapolis; WFTC (MNT) Minneapolis; WUCW (CW) Minneapolis; allband FM.
Programming (via satellite): C-SPAN; Eternal Word TV Network; Home Shopping Network; QVC; TV Guide Network.
Current originations: Religious Access; Government Access; Educational Access; Public Access.
Fee: $29.99 installation.
Expanded Basic Service 1
Subscribers: 728.
Programming (via satellite): ABC Family Channel; AMC; Animal Planet; Arts & Entertainment; Bloomberg Television; Cartoon Network; CNBC; CNN; Comedy Central; Country Music TV; Discovery Channel; Disney Channel; E! Entertainment Television; ESPN; ESPN 2; Fox News Channel; Fox Sports Net North; FX; G4; Headline News; HGTV; History Channel; Lifetime; MSNBC; MTV; National Geographic Channel; Nickelodeon; Oxygen; SoapNet; Spike TV; Syfy; TBS Superstation; The Learning Channel; Toon Disney; Turner Network TV; TV Land; Univision; USA Network; Versus; VH1; WE tv; Weather Channel; WGN America.
Fee: $47.99 monthly.
Digital Basic Service
Subscribers: N.A.
Programming (via satellite): BBC America; Bio; Discovery Digital Networks; Do-It-Yourself; GAS; GSN; History Channel International; Independent Film Channel; MTV Networks Digital Suite; Music Choice; Nick Jr.; Nick Too; NickToons TV; Style Network; Sundance Channel; TV Guide Interactive Inc.
Digital Pay Service 1
Pay Units: N.A.
Programming (via satellite): Cinemax (multiplexed); Encore; Flix; HBO (multiplexed); Showtime (multiplexed); Starz (multiplexed); The Movie Channel (multiplexed).
Video-On-Demand: No
Pay-Per-View
iN DEMAND (delivered digitally); Hot Choice (delivered digitally).
Internet Service
Operational: Yes.
Broadband Service: Charter Pipeline.
Fee: $29.99 monthly.
Telephone Service
None
Miles of Plant: 23.0 (coaxial); 23.0 (fiber optic). Homes passed: 2,400.
City fee: 3% of gross.
Ownership: Midcontinent Media Inc. (MSO).

GLENVILLE—US Cable, 402 Red River Ave N, Unit 5, Cold Spring, MN 56320-1521. Phones: 800-642-5509; 320-685-7113. Fax: 320-685-7134. E-mail: help@mn.uscable.com. Web Site: http://www.uscable.com. ICA: MN0183.
TV Market Ranking: Below 100 (GLENVILLE). Franchise award date: N.A. Franchise expiration date: N.A. Began: March 1, 1985.
Channel capacity: 54 (not 2-way capable). Channels available but not in use: N.A.
Basic Service
Subscribers: N.A. Included in Cambridge
Programming (received off-air): KAAL (ABC) Austin; KARE (NBC) Minneapolis; KEYC-TV (CBS, FOX) Mankato; KMSP-TV (FOX) Minneapolis; KSMQ-TV (PBS) Austin; KSTP-TV (ABC) St. Paul; KTCA-TV (PBS) St. Paul; KTTC (CW, NBC) Rochester; WCCO-TV (CBS) Minneapolis; WFTC (MNT) Minneapolis; allband FM.
Programming (via satellite): Food Network; TBS Superstation; Travel Channel.
Current originations: Government Access; Public Access.
Fee: $20.99 monthly.
Expanded Basic Service 1
Subscribers: N.A.
Programming (received off-air): KSTC-TV (IND) Minneapolis.
Programming (via satellite): ABC Family Channel; Animal Planet; Arts & Entertainment; Cartoon Network; CNBC; CNN; Comedy Central; Country Music TV; C-SPAN; Discovery Channel; Disney Channel; ESPN; ESPN 2; Eternal Word TV Network; Fox Sports Net North; FX; HGTV; History Channel; Home Shopping Network; Lifetime; MTV; Nickelodeon; Outdoor Channel; ShopNBC; Spike TV; Syfy; The Learning Channel; Turner Classic Movies; Turner Network TV; TV Land; USA Network; VH1; Weather Channel.
Fee: $22.95 monthly.
Digital Basic Service
Subscribers: N.A. Included in Cambridge
Programming (via satellite): BBC America; Bio; Bloomberg Television; Bravo; Discovery Digital Networks; DMX Music; Encore; ESPN Classic Sports; ESPNews; FitTV; Fox Movie Channel; Fox Soccer; Fuse; G4; Golf Channel; GSN; Halogen Network; History Channel International; Independent Film Channel; Lifetime Movie Network; Lime; Military History Channel; MTV2; NFL Network; Nick Jr.; Outdoor Channel; Sleuth; Speed Channel; Style Network; TeenNick; Toon Disney; Trinity Broadcasting Network; Versus; VH1 Classic; WE tv.
Digital Pay Service 1
Pay Units: N.A. Included in Cambridge
Programming (via satellite): Cinemax (multiplexed); HBO (multiplexed); Showtime (multiplexed); Starz (multiplexed); The Movie Channel (multiplexed).
Fee: $6.95 monthly (Starz), $14.95 monthly (Cinemax, HBO, Showtime or TMC).
Pay-Per-View
iN DEMAND (delivered digitally); Fresh (delivered digitally); Playboy TV (delivered digitally); Club Jenna (delivered digitally).
Internet Service
Operational: No.
Telephone Service
None
Homes passed: Included in Cambridge
General Manager: Steve Johnson. Customer Service Director: Jackie Torberg.
City fee: 3% of basic gross.
Ownership: US Cable Corp. (MSO).; Comcast Cable Communications Inc. (MSO).

GLENWOOD—Charter Communications, 1111 Hwy 29 N, Alexandria, MN 56308-5015. Phones: 320-763-6139 (Local office); 507-289-8372 (Rochester administrative office). Fax: 320-763-5194. E-mail: jon.melander@chartercom.com. Web Site: http://www.charter.com. Also serves Long Beach. ICA: MN0082.
TV Market Ranking: Below 100 (GLENWOOD, Long Beach). Franchise award date: N.A. Franchise expiration date: N.A. Began: August 1, 1966.
Channel capacity: N.A. Channels available but not in use: N.A.
Basic Service
Subscribers: 974.
Programming (received off-air): KCCO-TV (CBS) Alexandria; KSAX (ABC) Alexandria; KWCM-TV (PBS) Appleton; allband FM.
Programming (via microwave): KARE (NBC) Minneapolis; KMSP-TV (FOX) Minneapolis; KSTC-TV (IND) Minneapolis; KTCA-TV (PBS) St. Paul; WFTC (MNT) Minneapolis.
Programming (via satellite): C-SPAN; C-SPAN 2; Eternal Word TV Network; QVC; TBS Superstation.
Current originations: Government Access.
Fee: $29.99 installation.
Expanded Basic Service 1
Subscribers: 793.
Programming (via satellite): ABC Family Channel; AMC; Animal Planet; Arts & Entertainment; Bravo; Cartoon Network; CNBC; CNN; Comedy Central; Country Music TV; Discovery Channel; Disney Channel; E! Entertainment Television; ESPN; ESPN 2; Food Network; Fox News Channel; Fox Sports Net North; FX; G4; Golf Channel; Hallmark Channel; Headline News; HGTV; History Channel; Home Shopping Network; Lifetime; MSNBC; MTV; MTV2; National Geographic Channel; Nickelodeon; Oxygen; SoapNet; Speed Channel; Spike TV; Syfy; The Learning Channel; Toon Disney; Travel Channel; truTV; Turner Classic Movies; Turner Network TV; TV Land; Univision; USA Network; Versus; VH1; WE tv; Weather Channel.
Fee: $47.99 monthly.
Digital Basic Service
Subscribers: N.A.
Programming (via microwave): KARE (NBC) Minneapolis; KMSP-TV (FOX) Minneapolis; WCCO-TV (CBS) Minneapolis.
Programming (via satellite): BBC America; Bio; Bloomberg Television; Boomerang; CBS College Sports Network; CNN en Espanol; CNN International; Discovery Digital Networks; Do-It-Yourself; ESPN; ESPN Classic Sports; ESPNews; FitTV; Fox College Sports Atlantic; Fox College Sports

Central; Fox College Sports Pacific; Fox Movie Channel; Fox Soccer; Fuel TV; Fuse; GAS; HDNet; HDNet Movies; History Channel International; Independent Film Channel; Lifetime Movie Network; MTV Networks Digital Suite; Music Choice; NFL Network; Nick Jr.; Nick Too; NickToons TV; Outdoor Channel; Style Network; Sundance Channel; TV Guide Interactive Inc.

Digital Pay Service 1
Pay Units: N.A.
Programming (via satellite): Cinemax (multiplexed); Encore (multiplexed); HBO (multiplexed); HBO HD; Showtime (multiplexed); Showtime HD; Starz (multiplexed); The Movie Channel (multiplexed).

Video-On-Demand: Yes

Pay-Per-View
iN DEMAND (delivered digitally); NASCAR In Car (delivered digitally); NHL Center Ice (delivered digitally); MLB Extra Innings (delivered digitally); Playboy TV (delivered digitally); Spice Live (delivered digitally); Spice Platinum (delivered digitally); Hot Net Plus (delivered digitally); Spice Hot (delivered digitally).

Internet Service
Operational: Yes.
Broadband Service: Charter Pipeline.

Telephone Service
Digital: Operational
Fee: $29.99 monthly

Homes passed: 1,700. Miles of plant (coax) included in Alexandrio

Vice President & General Manager: John Crowley. Operations Director: Craig Stensaas. Chief Technician: Eric Cox. Marketing Director: Bill Haarstad. Office Operations Manager: Jon Melander.

City fee: 2% of gross.

Ownership: Charter Communications Inc. (MSO).

GOOD THUNDER—Woodstock LLC, PO Box C, 337 Aetna St, Ruthton, MN 56170. Phones: 800-752-9397; 507-658-3830. Fax: 507-658-3914. Web Site: http://www.woodstocktel.net. Also serves Amboy. ICA: MN0173.

TV Market Ranking: Below 100 (Amboy, GOOD THUNDER). Franchise award date: June 4, 1984. Franchise expiration date: N.A. Began: January 1, 1985.

Channel capacity: 36 (not 2-way capable). Channels available but not in use: 11.

Basic Service
Subscribers: 300.
Programming (received off-air): KARE (NBC) Minneapolis; KEYC-TV (CBS, FOX) Mankato; KMSP-TV (FOX) Minneapolis; KSMN (PBS) Worthington; KSTC-TV (IND) Minneapolis; KSTP-TV (ABC) St. Paul; WCCO-TV (CBS) Minneapolis; WFTC (MNT) Minneapolis; WUCW (CW) Minneapolis; allband FM.
Programming (via satellite): ABC Family Channel; Animal Planet; Arts & Entertainment; CNN; Comedy Central; Discovery Channel; Disney Channel; ESPN; ESPN 2; Fox Sports Net; HGTV; History Channel; Lifetime; Local Cable Weather; Nickelodeon; Spike TV; TBS Superstation; The Learning Channel; Turner Network TV; VH1; WGN America.
Current originations: Public Access.
Fee: $25.00 installation; $20.95 monthly.

Pay Service 1
Pay Units: 21.
Programming (via satellite): Showtime.
Fee: $8.95 monthly.

Pay Service 2
Pay Units: 10.
Programming (via satellite): The Movie Channel.
Fee: $6.95 monthly.

Video-On-Demand: No

Internet Service
Operational: No, DSL & dialup.

Telephone Service
None

Miles of Plant: 4.0 (coaxial); 14.0 (fiber optic).

Chief Technician & Marketing Director: Dave Bukowski. Program Director: Terry Nelson.

City fee: 3% of gross.

Ownership: Woodstock Telephone Co. (MSO).

GOODHUE—Sleepy Eye Telephone. Formerly [MN0208]. This cable system has converted to IPTV, 111 Second Ave, Goodhue, MN 55027. Phones: 888-742-8010; 651-923-5005. Fax: 651-923-4010. E-mail: on-linecustservice@nu-telecom.net. Web Site: http://www.sleepyeyetel.net. ICA: MN5120.

Channel capacity: N.A. Channels available but not in use: N.A.

Internet Service
Operational: Yes.
Fee: $39.95 monthly.

Telephone Service
Digital: Operational

Ownership: Sleepy Eye Telephone Co.

GOODHUE—Sleepy Eye Telephone. This cable system has converted to IPTV. See Goodhue, MN [MN5120]. ICA: MN0208.

GOODVIEW—Hiawatha Broadband. Formerly served by Winona, MN [MN0398]. This cable system has converted to IPTV, 58 Johnson St, Winona, MN 55987. Phone: 888-474-9995. Fax: 507-474-4000. E-mail: info@hbci.com. Web Site: http://www.hbci.com. ICA: MN5174.

Channel capacity: N.A. Channels available but not in use: N.A.

Internet Service
Operational: Yes.

Ownership: Hiawatha Broadband Communications Inc.

GORMAN TWP.—ACS Video. Formerly served by Perham, MN [MN0050]. This cable system has converted to IPTV, 150 Second St SW, Perham, MN 56573. Phone: 866-937-4227. E-mail: answers@arvig.com. Web Site: http://www.arvig.com. ICA: MN5197.

TV Market Ranking: Outside TV Markets (GORMAN TWP.).

Channel capacity: N.A. Channels available but not in use: N.A.

Internet Service
Operational: Yes.

Telephone Service
Digital: Operational

Ownership: Arvig Communication Systems.

GRACEVILLE—Now served by APPLETON, MN [MN0106]. ICA: MN0188.

GRANADA—US Cable, 402 Red River Ave N, Unit 5, Cold Spring, MN 56320-1521. Phones: 800-783-2356; 320-685-7113. Fax: 320-685-2816. E-mail: help@mn.uscable.com. Web Site: http://www.uscable.com. ICA: MN0257.

TV Market Ranking: Outside TV Markets (GRANADA). Franchise award date: N.A. Franchise expiration date: N.A. Began: December 1, 1981.

Channel capacity: N.A. Channels available but not in use: N.A.

Basic Service
Subscribers: N.A. Included in Cambridge
Programming (received off-air): KAAL (ABC) Austin; KEYC-TV (CBS, FOX) Mankato; KYIN (PBS) Mason City.
Programming (via satellite): ABC Family Channel; Arts & Entertainment; CNBC; CNN; Comedy Central; Country Music TV; Discovery Channel; ESPN; ESPN 2; Fox Sports Net; HGTV; History Channel; Nickelodeon; Outdoor Channel; Spike TV; TBS Superstation; The Learning Channel; Trinity Broadcasting Network; Turner Network TV; USA Network; Weather Channel; WGN America.
Programming (via translator): KARE (NBC) Minneapolis; KMSP-TV (FOX) Minneapolis; KSTC-TV (IND) Minneapolis; KSTP-TV (ABC) St. Paul; KTCA-TV (PBS) St. Paul; WCCO-TV (CBS) Minneapolis.
Fee: $37.24 monthly.

Pay Service 1
Pay Units: N.A. Included in Cambridge
Programming (via satellite): HBO.
Fee: $11.95 monthly.

Internet Service
Operational: No.

Telephone Service
None

Homes passed: Included in Cambridge

General Manager: Steve Johnson. Customer Service Director: Jackie Torberg.

City fee: None.

Ownership: US Cable Corp. (MSO).; Comcast Cable Communications Inc. (MSO).

GRAND MARAIS—Mediacom, PO Box 110, 1504 2nd St SE, Waseca, MN 56093. Phones: 800-332-0245; 507-835-2356. Fax: 507-835-4567. E-mail: bjensen@mediacomcc.com. Web Site: http://www.mediacomcable.com. ICA: MN0303.

TV Market Ranking: Outside TV Markets (GRAND MARAIS). Franchise award date: N.A. Franchise expiration date: N.A. Began: August 1, 1984.

Channel capacity: 37 (not 2-way capable). Channels available but not in use: 16.

Basic Service
Subscribers: 391.
Programming (via satellite): C-SPAN; C-SPAN 2; ION Television; QVC; WGN America.
Programming (via translator): KBJR-TV (MNT, NBC) Superior; KDLH (CBS, CW) Duluth; KQDS-TV (FOX) Duluth; WDIO-DT (ABC) Duluth; WDSE (PBS) Duluth.
Fee: $16.95 monthly.

Expanded Basic Service 1
Subscribers: N.A.
Programming (via satellite): ABC Family Channel; AMC; Animal Planet; Arts & Entertainment; Bravo; CNBC; CNN; Comedy Central; Country Music TV; Discovery Channel; Disney Channel; E! Entertainment Television; ESPN; ESPN 2; Food Network; Fox Sports Net North; FX; Headline News; HGTV; History Channel; INSP; Lifetime; MSNBC; MTV; Nickelodeon; Speed Channel; Spike TV; TBS Superstation; The Learning Channel; Travel Channel; truTV; Turner Network TV; TV Land; USA Network; VH1; WE tv; Weather Channel.

Pay Service 1
Pay Units: 21.
Programming (via satellite): HBO; The Movie Channel.
Fee: $10.95 monthly (each).

Video-On-Demand: No

Internet Service
Operational: No.

Telephone Service
None

Miles of Plant: 14.0 (coaxial); None (fiber optic). Total homes in franchised area: 657.

Vice President: Bill Jensen. Engineering Manager: Kraig Kaiser. Marketing & Sales Director: Lori Huberty.

City fee: 5% of gross.

Ownership: Mediacom LLC (MSO).

GRAND MEADOW—Southern Cablevision Inc., PO Box 27, 112 1st Ave NW, Grand Meadow, MN 55936. Phone: 507-754-5117. Fax: 507-754-5114. ICA: MN0168.

TV Market Ranking: Below 100 (GRAND MEADOW). Franchise award date: August 5, 1984. Franchise expiration date: N.A. Began: October 1, 1984.

Channel capacity: 40 (2-way capable). Channels available but not in use: 5.

Basic Service
Subscribers: 360.
Programming (received off-air): KAAL (ABC) Austin; KIMT (CBS, MNT) Mason City; KSMQ-TV (PBS) Austin; KTTC (CW, NBC) Rochester; KXLT-TV (FOX) Rochester; KYIN (PBS) Mason City; WKBT-DT (CBS, MNT) La Crosse.
Programming (via satellite): ABC Family Channel; AMC; Arts & Entertainment; CNN; Comedy Central; Country Music TV; Discovery Channel; Disney Channel; ESPN; ESPN 2; Fox Sports Net Midwest; HGTV; History Channel; Lifetime; Nickelodeon; Spike TV; TBS Superstation; Turner Network TV; USA Network; VH1; WGN America.
Current originations: Public Access.
Fee: $20.00 installation; $21.95 monthly.

Pay Service 1
Pay Units: 80.
Programming (via satellite): HBO.
Fee: $9.95 monthly.

Pay Service 2
Pay Units: 39.
Programming (via satellite): Showtime.
Fee: $9.95 monthly.

Video-On-Demand: No

Internet Service
Operational: No, DSL.

Telephone Service
None

Miles of Plant: 7.0 (coaxial); None (fiber optic). Homes passed: 400. Total homes in franchised area: 405.

Manager & Chief Technician: Reed Cowan.

City fee: 1% of gross basic service revenue.

Ownership: Southern Cablevision Inc. (MSO).

GRAND RAPIDS—Mediacom, PO Box 110, 1504 2nd St SE, Waseca, MN 56093. Phone: 507-835-2356. Fax: 507-835-4567. Web Site: http://www.mediacomcable.com. Also serves Bass Brook Twp., Grand Prairie, Grand Rapids Twp., Harris Twp., Keewatin, La Prairie Twp. & Nashwauk. ICA: MN0038.

TV Market Ranking: Below 100 (Bass Brook Twp., Grand Prairie, GRAND RAPIDS, Grand Rapids Twp., Harris Twp., Keewatin, La Prairie Twp., Nashwauk). Franchise award date: N.A. Franchise expiration date: N.A. Began: March 1, 1965.

Channel capacity: N.A. Channels available but not in use: N.A.

Basic Service

Subscribers: 5,417.

Programming (received off-air): KAWE (PBS) Bemidji; KBJR-TV (MNT, NBC) Superior; KCCW-TV (CBS) Walker; KDLH (CBS, CW) Duluth; KQDS-TV (FOX) Duluth; WDSE (PBS) Duluth; WIRT-DT (ABC) Hibbing; allband FM.

Programming (via satellite): C-SPAN; C-SPAN 2; QVC; TV Guide Network; Weather Channel; WGN America.

Current originations: Government Access; Educational Access; Public Access.

Fee: $15.00 installation; $16.95 monthly; $2.00 converter; $15.00 additional installation.

Expanded Basic Service 1

Subscribers: 1,251.

Programming (via satellite): ABC Family Channel; AMC; Animal Planet; Arts & Entertainment; Bravo; Cartoon Network; CNBC; CNN; Comedy Central; Country Music TV; CW+; Discovery Channel; Disney Channel; E! Entertainment Television; ESPN; ESPN 2; Eternal Word TV Network; Fox News Channel; Fox Sports Net North; FX; Hallmark Channel; Headline News; HGTV; History Channel; Home Shopping Network; INSP; ION Television; Lifetime; MSNBC; MTV; Nickelodeon; Outdoor Channel; SoapNet; Speed Channel; Spike TV; Syfy; TBS Superstation; The Learning Channel; Travel Channel; Trinity Broadcasting Network; truTV; Turner Classic Movies; Turner Network TV; TV Land; USA Network; VH1; WE tv.

Digital Basic Service

Subscribers: N.A.

Programming (received off-air): KBJR-TV (MNT, NBC) Superior; KDLH (CBS, CW) Duluth; WDIO-DT (ABC) Duluth.

Programming (via satellite): AmericanLife TV Network; BBC America; Bio; Bloomberg Television; CMT Pure Country; Discovery HD Theater; Discovery Health Channel; Discovery Home Channel; Discovery Kids Channel; Discovery Military Channel; ESPN 2 HD; ESPN Classic Sports; ESPN HD; ESPNews; FitTV; Fox Movie Channel; Fox Soccer; Fuse; G4; Golf Channel; GSN; Halogen Network; HDNet; HDNet Movies; History Channel International; ID Investigation Discovery; Independent Film Channel; Lifetime Movie Network; MTV Hits; MTV2; Music Choice; National Geographic Channel; Nick Jr.; NickToons TV; Ovation; Science Channel; Sleuth; Style Network; TeenNick; The Sportsman Channel; TVG Network; Universal HD; Versus; VH1 Classic; VH1 Soul.

Digital Pay Service 1

Pay Units: 523.

Programming (via satellite): Cinemax (multiplexed); Encore (multiplexed); Flix; HBO (multiplexed); HBO HD; Showtime (multiplexed); Showtime HD; Starz (multiplexed); Starz HDTV; Sundance Channel; The Movie Channel (multiplexed); The Movie Channel HD.

Fee: $15.00 installation; $8.95 monthly (Showtime), $11.95 monthly (HBO).

Video-On-Demand: No

Pay-Per-View

iN DEMAND (delivered digitally); Spice: Xcess (delivered digitally); Playboy TV (delivered digitally); Penthouse TV (delivered digitally); Fresh (delivered digitally); Ten Clips (delivered digitally).

Internet Service

Operational: Yes.

Broadband Service: Mediacom High Speed Internet.

Fee: $99.00 installation; $40.00 monthly.

Telephone Service

Digital: Operational

Miles of Plant: 147.0 (coaxial); None (fiber optic). Homes passed: 7,106.

Vice President: Bill Jensen. Engineering Manager: Kraig Kaiser. Marketing & Sales Director: Lori Huberty.

City fee: 2% of gross.

Ownership: Mediacom LLC (MSO).

GRANITE FALLS—Now served by CLARA CITY, MN [MN0125]. ICA: MN0070.

GREEN ISLE—North American Communications Corp., PO Box 387, 211 Main St S, Hector, MN 55342-0387. Phones: 800-982-8038; 320-848-6781. Fax: 320-848-2323. E-mail: hcc@hcctel.net. Web Site: http://www.hectorcom.com. ICA: MN0304.

TV Market Ranking: Outside TV Markets (GREEN ISLE). Franchise award date: N.A. Franchise expiration date: N.A. Began: N.A.

Channel capacity: 54 (not 2-way capable). Channels available but not in use: 29.

Basic Service

Subscribers: 44.

Programming (received off-air): KARE (NBC) Minneapolis; KEYC-TV (CBS, FOX) Mankato; KMSP-TV (FOX) Minneapolis; KSTP-TV (ABC) St. Paul; KTCA-TV (PBS) St. Paul; WCCO-TV (CBS) Minneapolis; WFTC (MNT) Minneapolis; WUCW (CW) Minneapolis.

Programming (via satellite): ABC Family Channel; AMC; Arts & Entertainment; CNN; Discovery Channel; Disney Channel; ESPN; Fox Sports Net Midwest; ION Television; Lifetime; Nickelodeon; QVC; Spike TV; TBS Superstation; Trinity Broadcasting Network; Turner Network TV; USA Network; WGN America.

Current originations: Leased Access; Government Access; Educational Access; Public Access.

Fee: $40.00 installation; $26.95 monthly; $3.50 converter; $25.00 additional installation.

Pay Service 1

Pay Units: 3.

Programming (via satellite): Cinemax.

Fee: $10.95 monthly.

Pay Service 2

Pay Units: 4.

Programming (via satellite): HBO.

Fee: $10.95 monthly.

Video-On-Demand: No

Internet Service

Operational: No.

Broadband Service: Offers dial-up and DSL only; no cable modem service.

Telephone Service

None

Miles of Plant: 4.0 (coaxial); None (fiber optic). Homes passed: 138. Total homes in franchised area: 138.

Manager: Matt Sparks. Chief Technician: George Honzay. Customer Service Supervisor: Patty Groshens.

Ownership: Hector Communications Corp. (MSO).

GREENBUSH—Sjoberg's Cable TV Inc., 315 Main Ave N, Thief River Falls, MN 56701-1905. Phones: 800-828-8808; 218-681-3044. Fax: 218-681-6801. E-mail: office1@mncable.net. Web Site: http://local.mncable.net. Also serves Hereim Twp. ICA: MN0186.

TV Market Ranking: Outside TV Markets (GREENBUSH, Hereim Twp.). Franchise award date: N.A. Franchise expiration date: N.A. Began: February 1, 1977.

Channel capacity: 78 (operating 2-way). Channels available but not in use: 18.

Basic Service

Subscribers: 282.

Programming (received off-air): KAWE (PBS) Bemidji; KCPM (MNT) Grand Forks; various Canadian stations; WDAZ-TV (ABC, CW) Devils Lake; allband FM.

Programming (via microwave): KVLY-TV (NBC) Fargo; KXJB-TV (CBS) Valley City.

Programming (via satellite): CNN; ESPN; TBS Superstation.

Fee: $25.00 installation; $10.00 monthly.

Expanded Basic Service 1

Subscribers: N.A.

Programming (received off-air): KBRR (FOX) Thief River Falls.

Programming (via satellite): ABC Family Channel; Animal Planet; Arts & Entertainment; Cartoon Network; CNBC; Comedy Central; Country Music TV; CW+; Discovery Channel; E! Entertainment Television; ESPN 2; Food Network; Fox News Channel; Fox Sports Net; FX; HGTV; History Channel; Home Shopping Network; Lifetime; MSNBC; MTV; Nickelodeon; Spike TV; Syfy; The Learning Channel; Turner Classic Movies; Turner Network TV; TV Land; USA Network; Weather Channel; WGN America.

Fee: $23.71 monthly.

Digital Basic Service

Subscribers: N.A.

Programming (via satellite): AmericanLife TV Network; BBC America; Bio; Blackbelt TV; Bloomberg Television; Bravo; Chiller; CMT Pure Country; College Sports Television; Cooking Channel; Current; Daystar TV Network; Discovery Health Channel; Discovery Kids Channel; Discovery Military Channel; Discovery Planet Green; DMX Music; Do-It-Yourself; ESPN Classic Sports; ESPN U; ESPNews; Eternal Word TV Network; FitTV; Fox Business Channel; Fox College Sports Atlantic; Fox College Sports Central; Fox College Sports Pacific; Fox Movie Channel; Fox Reality Channel; Fox Soccer; G4; Golf Channel; Gospel Music Channel; Great American Country; GSN; Hallmark Channel; Headline News; History Channel International; HorseRacing TV; ID Investigation Discovery; Independent Film Channel; Lifetime Movie Network; MTV Hits; MTV2; National Geographic Channel; Nick Jr.; NickToons TV; Outdoor Channel; Ovation; Oxygen; PBS Kids Sprout; RFD-TV; Science Channel; ShopNBC; Sleuth; SoapNet; Speed Channel; Style Network; Sundance Channel; TeenNick; Tennis Channel; The Sportsman Channel; The Word Network; Toon Disney; TVG Network; Versus; VH1 Classic; VH1 Soul; WE tv.

Fee: $11.00 monthly.

Digital Expanded Basic Service

Subscribers: N.A.

Programming (received off-air): KAWE (PBS) Bemidji; WDAZ-TV (ABC, CW) Devils Lake.

Programming (via satellite): Arts & Entertainment HD; CNN HD; Discovery Channel HD; ESPN 2 HD; ESPN HD; Food Network HD; FSN HD; HDNet; HDNet Movies; HGTV HD; History Channel HD; Outdoor Channel 2 HD; Speed HD; Syfy HD; TBS in HD; Turner Network TV HD; Universal HD; USA Network HD; Versus HD.

Fee: $5.00 monthly.

Pay Service 1

Pay Units: 50.

Programming (via satellite): HBO.

Fee: $11.00 monthly.

Digital Pay Service 1

Pay Units: N.A.

Programming (via satellite): Cinemax (multiplexed); Cinemax HD; Encore (multiplexed); HBO (multiplexed); HBO HD; Showtime (multiplexed); Starz (multiplexed); The Movie Channel (multiplexed).

Fee: $8.00 monthly (Starz/Encore), $9.00 monthly (Cinemax or Showtime/TMC), $11.00 monthly (HBO).

Video-On-Demand: No

Internet Service

Operational: No.

Telephone Service

None

Miles of Plant: 6.0 (coaxial); 17.0 (fiber optic). Additional miles planned: 1.0 (coaxial). Homes passed: 322. Total homes in franchised area: 322.

Manager: Richard J. Sjoberg. Chief Technician: Jerry Seim.

City fee: None.

Ownership: Sjoberg's Cable TV Inc. (MSO).

GREY EAGLE—diversiCOM. Formerly [MN0232]. This cable system has converted to IPTV, 224 E Main St, Melrose, MN 56352. Phone: 320-256-7471. Fax: 320-256-7555. Web Site: http://www.meltel.com. ICA: MN5142.

TV Market Ranking: Below 100 (GREY EAGLE). Franchise award date: N.A. Franchise expiration date: N.A. Began: N.A.

Channel capacity: N.A. Channels available but not in use: N.A.

Video-On-Demand: No

Internet Service

Operational: Yes.

Fee: $32.95 monthly; $4.95 modem lease.

Telephone Service

Digital: Operational

Fee: $13.00 monthly

Ownership: diversiCOM Melrose Telephone Co.

GREY EAGLE—diversiCOM. This cable system has converted to IPTV. See Grey Eagle, MN [MN5142], MN. ICA: MN0232.

GROVE CITY—Now served by CLARA CITY, MN [MN0125]. ICA: MN0121.

GRYGLA—Garden Valley Telephone Co., PO Box 259, 201 Ross Ave, Erskine, MN 56535-0259. Phones: 218-687-5251; 800-448-8260. Fax: 218-687-2454. E-mail: gvtc@gvtel.com. Web Site: http://www.gvtel.com. ICA: MN0305.

TV Market Ranking: Below 100 (GRYGLA). Franchise award date: N.A. Franchise expiration date: N.A. Began: January 1, 1991.

Channel capacity: 35 (operating 2-way). Channels available but not in use: 10.

Basic Service

Subscribers: 111.

Programming (received off-air): KAWE (PBS) Bemidji; KBRR (FOX) Thief River Falls; KCPM (MNT) Grand Forks; KFME (PBS) Fargo; KVLY-TV (NBC) Fargo; KXJB-TV (CBS) Valley City; WDAY-TV (ABC, CW) Fargo; WDAZ-TV (ABC, CW) Devils Lake.

Programming (via satellite): ABC Family Channel; AMC; Arts & Entertainment; CNN; Discovery Channel; Disney Channel; ESPN; ESPN 2; Fox Sports Net; Great American Country; History Channel; Spike TV; TBS Superstation; Turner Network TV; TV Land; USA Network; WGN America.

Fee: $43.90 installation; $25.15 monthly; $1.00 converter; $15.75 additional installation.

Pay Service 1

Pay Units: 20.

Programming (via satellite): HBO.

Fee: $24.15 installation; $10.50 monthly; $1.00 converter; $15.75 additional installation.

Video-On-Demand: No

Internet Service

Operational: No.

Telephone Service

None

Miles of Plant: 8.0 (coaxial); None (fiber optic). Homes passed: 153.

Manager: George Fish. Operations Manager: Dave Hamre. Chief Technician: Randy Versdahl. Marketing Supervisor: Julie Dahle.

Ownership: Garden Valley Telephone Co. (MSO).

HALLOCK—Midcontinent Communications, PO Box 5010, Sioux Falls, SD 57117. Phones: 800-888-1300; 800-456-0564; 605-229-1775. Fax: 605-229-0478. E-mail: mccomm@midco.net. Web Site: http://www.midcocomm.com. ICA: MN0134.

TV Market Ranking: Below 100 (HALLOCK). Franchise award date: May 1, 1990. Franchise expiration date: N.A. Began: May 12, 1973.

Channel capacity: 41 (not 2-way capable). Channels available but not in use: N.A.

Basic Service

Subscribers: 369.

Programming (received off-air): KGFE (PBS) Grand Forks; KNRR (FOX) Pembina; KVLY-TV (NBC) Fargo; KXJB-TV (CBS) Valley City; various Canadian stations; WDAZ-TV (ABC, CW) Devils Lake; allband FM.

Programming (via satellite): ABC Family Channel; AMC; Arts & Entertainment; Cartoon Network; CNBC; CNN; Country Music TV; C-SPAN; Discovery Channel; Disney Channel; ESPN; ESPN 2; Fox Sports Net North; Headline News; HGTV; History Channel; INSP; Lifetime; Nickelodeon; QVC; Spike TV; TBS Superstation; The Learning Channel; Turner Network TV; TV Land; USA Network; VH1; Weather Channel; WGN America.

Fee: $50.00 installation; $23.06 monthly.

Pay Service 1

Pay Units: 27.

Programming (via satellite): HBO.

Fee: $20.00 installation; $10.95 monthly.

Pay Service 2

Pay Units: 25.

Programming (via satellite): Showtime.

Fee: $20.00 installation; $10.95 monthly.

Pay Service 3

Pay Units: N.A.

Programming (via satellite): The Movie Channel.

Video-On-Demand: No

Internet Service

Operational: No.

Telephone Service

None

Miles of Plant: 11.0 (coaxial); None (fiber optic). Homes passed: 616. Total homes in franchised area: 616.

Manager: Darrell Wrege. Marketing Director: Trish McCann. Customer Service Manager: Carol Haselhorst.

City fee: 3% of gross.

Ownership: Midcontinent Media Inc. (MSO).; Comcast Cable Communications Inc. (MSO).

HAMPTON—Cannon Valley Cablevision. Now served by VERMILLION, MN [MN0391]. ICA: MN0307.

HANCOCK—Now served by CHOKIO, MN [MN0210]. ICA: MN0198.

HANLEY FALLS—Farmers Mutual Telephone Co., PO Box 220, Stanton, IA 51573. Phones: 800-469-2111; 717-829-2111. Web Site: http://online.fmtc.com. ICA: MN0308.

TV Market Ranking: Below 100 (HANLEY FALLS). Franchise award date: April 1, 1989. Franchise expiration date: N.A. Began: March 1, 1990.

Channel capacity: 54 (operating 2-way). Channels available but not in use: N.A.

Basic Service

Subscribers: 75.

Programming (received off-air): KARE (NBC) Minneapolis; KCCO-TV (CBS) Alexandria; KMSP-TV (FOX) Minneapolis; KRWF (ABC) Redwood Falls; KSTC-TV (IND) Minneapolis; KWCM-TV (PBS) Appleton; WFTC (MNT) Minneapolis.

Programming (via satellite): ABC Family Channel; AMC; Animal Planet; Arts & Entertainment; Cartoon Network; CNN; Comedy Central; Country Music TV; Discovery Channel; Disney Channel; ESPN; ESPN 2; Food Network; Fox Sports Net North; Hallmark Channel; HGTV; History Channel; Lifetime; MTV; Nickelodeon; QVC; Spike TV; Syfy; TBS Superstation; The Learning Channel; Trinity Broadcasting Network; Turner Network TV; TV Land; Univision; USA Network; VH1; Weather Channel.

Fee: $10.00 installation; $26.95 monthly.

Pay Service 1

Pay Units: 10.

Programming (via satellite): Cinemax; HBO; Showtime.

Fee: $9.95 monthly (Cinemax), $10.95 monthly (Showtime), $11.95 monthly (HBO).

Video-On-Demand: No

Internet Service

Operational: No.

Telephone Service

None

Miles of Plant: 3.0 (coaxial); None (fiber optic). Homes passed: 125. Total homes in franchised area: 125.

General Manager: Kevin Cabbage. Assistant Manager: Dennis Crawford.

Ownership: Farmers Mutual Telephone Co. (MSO).

HANSKA—Formerly served by Clara City Telephone Co. No longer in operation. ICA: MN0309.

HANSKA—Sleepy Eye Telephone. Formerly served by Goodhue, MN [MN0208]. This cable system has converted to IPTV, 121 Second Ave NW, Sleepy Eye, MN 56085. Phones: 800-235-5133; 507-794-3361. Fax: 507-794-2351. E-mail: onlinecustservice@nu-telcom.net. Web Site: http://www.sleepyeyetel.net. ICA: MN5153.

Channel capacity: N.A. Channels available but not in use: N.A.

Internet Service

Operational: Yes.

Fee: $39.95 monthly.

Telephone Service

Digital: Operational

Ownership: Sleepy Eye Telephone Co.

HARMONY—Harmony Cable Inc., PO Box 308, 35 First Ave SE, Harmony, MN 55939. Phone: 507-886-2525. Fax: 507-886-2500. E-mail: info@harmonytel.com. ICA: MN0159.

TV Market Ranking: Outside TV Markets (HARMONY). Franchise award date: May 30, 1983. Franchise expiration date: N.A. Began: December 6, 1983.

Channel capacity: 37 (2-way capable). Channels available but not in use: None.

Basic Service

Subscribers: 421.

Programming (received off-air): KAAL (ABC) Austin; KIMT (CBS, MNT) Mason City; KTTC (CW, NBC) Rochester; KXLT-TV (FOX) Rochester; KYIN (PBS) Mason City; WKBT-DT (CBS, MNT) La Crosse; WLAX (FOX) La Crosse; WXOW (ABC, CW) La Crosse.

Programming (via satellite): ABC Family Channel; AMC; Animal Planet; Arts & Entertainment; Country Music TV; Disney Channel; ESPN; ESPN 2; Fox News Channel; Fox Sports Net; HGTV; History Channel; Trinity Broadcasting Network; TV Land; VH1; Weather Channel; WGN America.

Fee: $20.00 installation; $19.98 monthly.

Pay Service 1

Pay Units: 90.

Programming (via satellite): HBO; Showtime.

Fee: $20.00 installation; $9.00 monthly (each).

Video-On-Demand: No

Internet Service

Operational: No.

Telephone Service

None

Miles of Plant: 12.0 (coaxial); None (fiber optic). Homes passed: 518. Total homes in franchised area: 518.

Manager: J. Fishbaugher.

City fee: 3% of gross.

Ownership: W. E. Communications Inc.

HAWLEY—Loretel Systems, PO Box 72, 13 East 4th Ave, Ada, MN 56510. Phones: 800-343-2762; 218-784-5100. Fax: 218-784-2706. E-mail: loretel@loretel.net. Web Site: http://www.hectorcom.com. ICA: MN0128.

TV Market Ranking: 98 (HAWLEY). Franchise award date: N.A. Franchise expiration date: N.A. Began: September 1, 1981.

Channel capacity: 35 (operating 2-way). Channels available but not in use: 23.

Basic Service

Subscribers: 518.

Programming (received off-air): KCPM (MNT) Grand Forks; KFME (PBS) Fargo; KVLY-TV (NBC) Fargo; KVRR (FOX) Fargo; KXJB-TV (CBS) Valley City; WDAY-TV (ABC, CW) Fargo; allband FM.

Programming (via satellite): ABC Family Channel; Arts & Entertainment; Cartoon Network; CNBC; CNN; Comedy Central; Country Music TV; C-SPAN; Discovery Channel; Disney Channel; E! Entertainment Television; ESPN; ESPN 2; Food Network; Fox News Channel; Fox Sports Net; FX; Headline News; HGTV; History Channel; Lifetime; MTV; National Geographic Channel; Nickelodeon; Outdoor Channel; QVC; Spike TV; Syfy; TBS Superstation; The Learning Channel; truTV; Turner Classic Movies; Turner Network TV; TV Guide Network; TV Land; USA Network; VH1; Weather Channel; WGN America.

Current originations: Public Access.

Fee: $40.00 installation; $34.00 monthly.

Pay Service 1

Pay Units: 186.

Programming (via satellite): Cinemax; Encore; HBO.

Fee: $8.50 installation; $1.75 monthly (Encore), $l2.00 monthly (Cinemax or HBO).

Video-On-Demand: No

Internet Service

Operational: No.

Broadband Service: Offers dial-up and DSL only; no cable modem service.

Telephone Service

None

Miles of Plant: 11.0 (coaxial); None (fiber optic). Homes passed: 650. Total homes in franchised area: 650.

Manager: Steven W. Katka. Chief Technician: Bruce Rosenfelt.

City fee: None.

Ownership: Hector Communications Corp. (MSO).

HAYFIELD—Mediacom. Now served by Dodge Center, MN [MN0093]. ICA: MN0152.

HAYWARD—North American Communications Corp., PO Box 387, 211 Main St S, Hector, MN 55342-0387. Phones: 800-982-8038; 320-848-6781. Fax: 320-848-2323. E-mail: hcc@hcctel.net. Web Site: http://www.hectorcom.com. ICA: MN0310.

TV Market Ranking: Below 100 (HAYWARD). Franchise award date: June 1, 1989. Franchise expiration date: N.A. Began: N.A.

Channel capacity: 54 (not 2-way capable). Channels available but not in use: 30.

Basic Service

Subscribers: 41.

Programming (received off-air): KAAL (ABC) Austin; KEYC-TV (CBS, FOX) Mankato; KIMT (CBS, MNT) Mason City; KSMQ-TV (PBS) Austin; KTTC (CW, NBC) Rochester; KYIN (PBS) Mason City.

Programming (via satellite): ABC Family Channel; AMC; Arts & Entertainment; CNN; Country Music TV; Discovery Channel; Disney Channel; ESPN; Fox Sports Net Midwest; Lifetime; Nickelodeon; QVC; Spike TV; TBS Superstation; Trinity Broadcasting Network; Turner Network TV; USA Network; WGN America.

Fee: $40.00 installation; $26.95 monthly; $3.50 converter; $25.00 additional installation.

Pay Service 1

Pay Units: 3.

Programming (via satellite): Cinemax.

Fee: $10.95 monthly.

Pay Service 2

Pay Units: 4.

Programming (via satellite): HBO.

Fee: $10.95 monthly.

Video-On-Demand: No

Internet Service

Operational: No.

Broadband Service: Offers dial-up and DSL only; no cable modem service.

Telephone Service

None

Miles of Plant: 4.0 (coaxial); None (fiber optic). Homes passed: 113. Total homes in franchised area: 113.

Manager: Matt Sparks. Chief Technician: George Honzay. Customer Service Supervisor: Patty Groshens.

Ownership: Hector Communications Corp. (MSO).

HECTOR—Now served by BROWNTON, MN [MN0145]. ICA: MN0109.

HENDRICKS—Formerly served by US Cable of Coastal Texas LP. No longer in operation. ICA: MN0190.

HENDRICKS—ITC. Formerly served by Clear Lake, SD [SD0047]. This cable system has converted to IPTV, 312 Fourth St W, Clear Lake, SD 57226. Phones: 800-417-8667; 605-874-2181. Fax: 605-874-2014. E-mail: info@itc-web.com. Web Site: http://www.itc-web.com. ICA: MN5251.

Channel capacity: N.A. Channels available but not in use: N.A.

Internet Service

Operational: Yes.

Fee: $39.95 monthly.

Telephone Service

Digital: Operational

General Manager: Jerry Heiberger.

Ownership: Interstate Telecommunications Cooperative Inc.

HENNING TWP.—ACS Video. Formerly served by Perham, MN [MN0050]. This cable system has converted to IPTV, 150 Second St SW, Perham, MN 56573. Phone: 866-937-4227. E-mail: answers@arvig.com. Web Site: http://www.arvig.com. ICA: MN5145.

TV Market Ranking: Below 100 (HENNING TWP.).

Channel capacity: N.A. Channels available but not in use: N.A.

Internet Service

Operational: Yes.

Telephone Service

Digital: Operational

Ownership: Arvig Communication Systems.

HENRIETTA TWP.—ACS Video. Formerly served by Perham, MN [MN0050]. This cable system has converted to IPTV, 150 Second St SW, Perham, MN 56573. Phone: 866-937-4227. E-mail: answers@arvig.com. Web Site: http://www.arvig.com. ICA: MN5199.

TV Market Ranking: Below 100 (HENRIETTA TWP.).

Channel capacity: N.A. Channels available but not in use: N.A.

Internet Service

Operational: Yes.

Telephone Service

Digital: Operational

Ownership: Arvig Communication Systems.

HERON LAKE—US Cable, 402 Red River Ave N, Unit 5, Cold Spring, MN 56320-1521. Phones: 800-783-2356; 320-685-7113. Fax: 320-685-2816. E-mail: help@mn.uscable.com. Web Site: http://www.uscable.com. Also serves Okabena. ICA: MN0195.

TV Market Ranking: Outside TV Markets (HERON LAKE, Okabena). Franchise award date: N.A. Franchise expiration date: N.A. Began: February 1, 1984.

Channel capacity: 35 (not 2-way capable). Channels available but not in use: N.A.

Basic Service

Subscribers: N.A. Included in Cambridge

Programming (received off-air): KELO-TV (CBS, MNT) Sioux Falls; KEYC-TV (CBS, FOX) Mankato; KSFY-TV (ABC) Sioux Falls; KSMN (PBS) Worthington.

Programming (via satellite): ABC Family Channel; Arts & Entertainment; Cartoon Network; CNBC; CNN; Comedy Central; Country Music TV; Discovery Channel; ESPN; ESPN 2; Eternal Word TV Network; Food Network; Fox Sports Net; Headline News; HGTV; History Channel; Home Shopping Network; Lifetime; Nickelodeon; Outdoor Channel; Spike TV; TBS Superstation; The Learning Channel; Turner Classic Movies; Turner Network TV; TV Land; USA Network; VH1; Weather Channel; WGN America.

Programming (via translator): KARE (NBC) Minneapolis; KMSP-TV (FOX) Minneapolis; KSTC-TV (IND) Minneapolis; KSTP-TV (ABC) St. Paul; WCCO-TV (CBS) Minneapolis; WFTC (MNT) Minneapolis.

Current originations: Leased Access.

Fee: $37.24 monthly.

Pay Service 1

Pay Units: N.A. Included in Cambridge

Programming (via satellite): Cinemax; HBO.

Internet Service

Operational: No.

Telephone Service

None

Homes passed: Included in Cambridge

General Manager: Steve Johnson. Customer Service Director: Jackie Torberg.

City fee: None.

Ownership: US Cable Corp. (MSO).; Comcast Cable Communications Inc. (MSO).

HIBBING—Mediacom, PO Box 110, 1504 2nd St SE, Waseca, MN 56093. Phone: 507-835-2356. Fax: 507-835-4567. Web Site: http://www.mediacomcable.com. ICA: MN0027.

TV Market Ranking: Below 100 (HIBBING). Franchise award date: January 1, 1965. Franchise expiration date: N.A. Began: March 10, 1966.

Channel capacity: 66 (operating 2-way). Channels available but not in use: N.A.

Basic Service

Subscribers: 387.

Programming (received off-air): KBJR-TV (MNT, NBC) Superior; KDLH (CBS, CW) Duluth; KQDS-TV (FOX) Duluth; WDIO-DT (ABC) Duluth; WDSE (PBS) Duluth; allband FM.

Programming (via microwave): KMSP-TV (FOX) Minneapolis.

Programming (via satellite): Home Shopping Network; QVC; TBS Superstation; WGN America.

Current originations: Religious Access; Government Access; Educational Access; Public Access.

Fee: $59.75 installation; $15.71 monthly.

Expanded Basic Service 1

Subscribers: N.A.

Programming (via satellite): ABC Family Channel; AMC; Animal Planet; Arts & Entertainment; Cartoon Network; Classic Arts Showcase; CNBC; CNN; Comedy Central; Country Music TV; C-SPAN; C-SPAN 2; Discovery Channel; Disney Channel; ESPN; ESPN 2; Eternal Word TV Network; Food Network; Fox Movie Channel; Fox News Channel; Fox Sports Net Midwest; FX; GSN; Hallmark Channel; Headline News; HGTV; History Channel; ION Television; Lifetime; MTV; Nickelodeon; Outdoor Channel; Spike TV; Syfy; The Learning Channel; Travel Channel; truTV; Turner Network TV; TV Land; USA Network; VH1; Weather Channel.

Fee: $50.00 installation; $48.05 monthly.

Digital Basic Service

Subscribers: 515.

Programming (via satellite): AmericanLife TV Network; BBC America; Bio; Bloomberg Television; Discovery Digital Networks; ESPN Classic Sports; G4; GAS; Golf Channel; History Channel International; Independent Film Channel; Lifetime Movie Network; MTV Networks Digital Suite; Nick Jr.; Ovation; Speed Channel; Trinity Broadcasting Network; Turner Classic Movies; Versus; WE tv.

Digital Pay Service 1

Pay Units: 162.

Programming (via satellite): HBO (multiplexed).

Fee: $11.95 monthly.

Digital Pay Service 2

Pay Units: 119.

Programming (via satellite): Cinemax (multiplexed).

Fee: $7.95 monthly.

Digital Pay Service 3

Pay Units: 82.

Programming (via satellite): Showtime (multiplexed); Sundance Channel (multiplexed); The Movie Channel.

Fee: $10.95 monthly.

Digital Pay Service 4

Pay Units: 131.

Programming (via satellite): Encore (multiplexed); Starz (multiplexed).

Fee: $10.95 monthly.

Video-On-Demand: No

Pay-Per-View

Addressable homes: 515.

iN DEMAND (delivered digitally), Addressable: Yes; Playboy TV (delivered digitally); Fresh (delivered digitally); Shorteez (delivered digitally); special events (delivered digitally).

Internet Service

Operational: Yes.

Subscribers: 1,497.

Broadband Service: Mediacom High Speed Internet.

Fee: $42.50 installation; $30.00 monthly.

Telephone Service

Digital: Operational

Miles of Plant: 90.0 (coaxial); None (fiber optic). Homes passed: 6,100. Total homes in franchised area: 6,200.

Regional Vice President: Bill Jensen. Engineering Manager: Kraig Kaiser. Marketing & Sales Director: Lori Huberty.

City fee: None.

Ownership: Mediacom LLC (MSO).

HILL CITY—Savage Communications Inc., PO Box 810, 206 Power Ave N, Hinckley, MN 55037. Phone: 320-384-7442. Fax: 320-384-7446. E-mail: rwsavage@scicable.com. Web Site: http://www.scibroadband.com. ICA: MN0153.

TV Market Ranking: Outside TV Markets (HILL CITY). Franchise award date: August 1, 1984. Franchise expiration date: N.A. Began: September 9, 1985.

Channel capacity: 54 (2-way capable). Channels available but not in use: 5.

Basic Service

Subscribers: 211.

Programming (received off-air): KAWE (PBS) Bemidji; KBJR-TV (MNT, NBC) Superior; KCCW-TV (CBS) Walker; KDLH (CBS, CW) Duluth; KQDS-TV (FOX) Duluth; WDIO-DT (ABC) Duluth; WDSE (PBS) Duluth; WPIX (CW, IND) New York.

Programming (via satellite): ABC Family Channel; Animal Planet; Arts & Entertainment; CNBC; CNN; Comedy Central; C-SPAN; Discovery Channel; Disney Channel; E! Entertainment Television; ESPN; ESPN 2; Fox News Channel; Fox Sports Net; Great American Country; Headline News; HGTV; History Channel; Lifetime; MTV; Nickelodeon; QVC; Spike TV; Syfy; TBS Superstation; The Learning Channel; Turner Classic Movies; Turner Network TV; TV Land; USA Network; VH1; Weather Channel; WGN America.

Fee: $39.95 installation; $32.95 monthly.

Digital Basic Service

Subscribers: N.A.

Programming (via satellite): AmericanLife TV Network; BBC America; Bio; Bloomberg Television; Discovery Digital Networks; DMX Music; ESPN Classic Sports; ESPNews; FitTV; Fox Movie Channel; Fox Sports World; Fuse; G4; Golf Channel; History Channel International; INSP; National Geographic Channel; Outdoor Channel; Sleuth; Speed Channel; Style Network; Trinity Broadcasting Network; Versus; WE tv.

Digital Pay Service 1

Pay Units: N.A.

Programming (via satellite): Cinemax (multiplexed); Encore (multiplexed); Flix; HBO (multiplexed); Showtime (multiplexed); Starz (multiplexed); Sundance Channel; The Movie Channel (multiplexed).

Video-On-Demand: No

Pay-Per-View

Movies (delivered digitally); ESPN Now (delivered digitally); Sports PPV (delivered digitally).

Internet Service

Operational: Yes.

Broadband Service: SCI Broadband.

Fee: $24.95 monthly.

Telephone Service
None
Miles of Plant: 9.0 (coaxial); None (fiber optic). Homes passed: 290. Total homes in franchised area: 290.
Manager: Mike Danielson. Marketing Director: Ron Savage. Chief Technician: Pat McCabe. Customer Service Manager: Donna Erickson.
City fee: 3% of basic gross.
Ownership: Savage Communications Inc. (MSO).

HILLS—Alliance Communications, PO Box 349, 612 3rd St, Garretson, SD 57030-0349. Phones: 800-701-4980; 605-594-3411. Fax: 605-594-6776. E-mail: email@alliancecom.net. Web Site: http://www.alliancecom.net. ICA: MN0215.
TV Market Ranking: 85 (HILLS). Franchise award date: July 12, 1983. Franchise expiration date: N.A. Began: March 14, 1984.
Channel capacity: 36 (not 2-way capable). Channels available but not in use: 7.
Basic Service
Subscribers: 166.
Programming (received off-air): KCAU-TV (ABC) Sioux City; KDLT-TV (NBC) Sioux Falls; KELO-TV (CBS, MNT) Sioux Falls; KMEG (CBS) Sioux City; KSFY-TV (ABC) Sioux Falls; KSMN (PBS) Worthington; KTIV (CW, NBC) Sioux City; KTTW (FOX) Sioux Falls; KUSD-TV (PBS) Vermillion.
Programming (via satellite): ABC Family Channel; AMC; Animal Planet; Arts & Entertainment; Bloomberg Television; Cartoon Network; CNN; Comedy Central; Country Music TV; C-SPAN; Discovery Channel; Disney Channel; ESPN; ESPN 2; ESPN Classic Sports; Eternal Word TV Network; Food Network; Fox News Channel; Fox Sports Net; FX; Golf Channel; Great American Country; Headline News; HGTV; History Channel; Home Shopping Network; Lifetime; LWS Local Weather Station; MTV; Nickelodeon; Outdoor Channel; QVC; Speed Channel; Spike TV; Syfy; TBS Superstation; The Learning Channel; Travel Channel; truTV; Turner Classic Movies; Turner Network TV; TV Land; Univision; USA Network; VH1; Weather Channel; WGN America.
Fee: $30.00 installation; $26.95 monthly.
Pay Service 1
Pay Units: 38.
Programming (via satellite): HBO.
Fee: $13.00 installation; $9.95 monthly.
Pay Service 2
Pay Units: 9.
Programming (via satellite): Showtime; The Movie Channel.
Fee: $13.00 installation; $9.95 monthly.
Video-On-Demand: No
Internet Service
Operational: No.
Broadband Service: Offers dial-up and DSL only; no cable modem service.
Telephone Service
None
Miles of Plant: 4.0 (coaxial); None (fiber optic). Homes passed: 209. Total homes in franchised area: 264.
Manager: Don Snyders. Marketing Director: Amy Ahlers. Chief Technician: Bob Stiefvater.
City fee: 2% of basic gross.
Ownership: Alliance Communications (MSO).

HOKAH—Now served by CALEDONIA, MN [MN0086]. ICA: MN0192.

HOMER—Hiawatha Broadband. Formerly served by Winona, MN [MN0398]. This cable system has converted to IPTV, 58 Johnson St, Winona, MN 55987. Phone: 888-474-9995. Fax: 507-474-4000. E-mail: info@hbci.com. Web Site: http://www.hbci.com. ICA: MN5172.
Channel capacity: N.A. Channels available but not in use: N.A.
Internet Service
Operational: Yes.
Ownership: Hiawatha Broadband Communications Inc.

HOUSTON—Now served by CALEDONIA, MN [MN0086]. ICA: MN0138.

HOWARD LAKE—Mediacom, PO Box 110, 1504 2nd St SE, Waseca, MN 56093. Phones: 800-332-0245; 507-835-2356. Fax: 507-835-4567. Web Site: http://www.mediacomcable.com. ICA: MN0143.
TV Market Ranking: Below 100 (HOWARD LAKE). Franchise award date: N.A. Franchise expiration date: N.A. Began: January 1, 1985.
Channel capacity: N.A. Channels available but not in use: N.A.
Basic Service
Subscribers: 381.
Programming (received off-air): KARE (NBC) Minneapolis; KEYC-TV (CBS, FOX) Mankato; KMSP-TV (FOX) Minneapolis; KPXM-TV (ION) St. Cloud; KSTC-TV (IND) Minneapolis; KSTP-TV (ABC) St. Paul; KTCA-TV (PBS) St. Paul; KTCI-TV (PBS) St. Paul; WCCO-TV (CBS) Minneapolis; WFTC (MNT) Minneapolis; WUCW (CW) Minneapolis.
Programming (via satellite): C-SPAN; Home Shopping Network; QVC; TV Guide Network; WGN America.
Current originations: Public Access.
Fee: $39.95 installation; $18.01 monthly.
Expanded Basic Service 1
Subscribers: N.A.
Programming (received off-air): WUMN-CA Minneapolis.
Programming (via satellite): ABC Family Channel; AMC; Animal Planet; Arts & Entertainment; BET Networks; Bravo; Cartoon Network; CNBC; CNN; Comedy Central; Country Music TV; Discovery Channel; Disney Channel; E! Entertainment Television; ESPN; ESPN 2; Eternal Word TV Network; Food Network; Fox Movie Channel; Fox News Channel; Fox Sports Net; FX; Hallmark Channel; Headline News; HGTV; History Channel; INSP; Lifetime; MSNBC; MTV; Nickelodeon; Outdoor Channel; SoapNet; Speed Channel; Spike TV; Syfy; TBS Superstation; The Learning Channel; Travel Channel; Trinity Broadcasting Network; truTV; Turner Classic Movies; Turner Network TV; TV Land; USA Network; VH1; WE tv; Weather Channel.
Digital Basic Service
Subscribers: N.A.
Programming (via satellite): AmericanLife TV Network; BBC America; Bio; Bloomberg Television; Canal 52MX; Cine Latino; CNN en Espanol; Discovery en Espanol; Discovery HD Theater; Discovery Health Channel; Discovery Home Channel; Discovery Kids Channel; Discovery Military Channel; ESPN 2 HD; ESPN HD; ESPNews; FitTV; Fox Soccer; Fox Sports en Espanol; Fuse; G4; Golf Channel; Halogen Network; HDNet; HDNet Movies; History Channel en Espanol; History Channel International; ID Investigation Discovery; Independent Film Channel; Lifetime Movie Network; MTV Hits; MTV Tres; MTV2; National Geographic Channel; Nick Jr.; NickToons TV; Outdoor Channel; Science Channel; Sleuth; Style Network; TeenNick; Universal HD; VH1 Classic.
Digital Pay Service 1
Pay Units: N.A.
Programming (via satellite): Cinemax (multiplexed); Encore (multiplexed); HBO (multiplexed); HBO HD; Showtime (multiplexed); Showtime HD; Starz (multiplexed); Starz HDTV; The Movie Channel (multiplexed); The Movie Channel HD.
Video-On-Demand: Yes
Internet Service
Operational: Yes.
Broadband Service: Mediacom High Speed Internet.
Telephone Service
Digital: Operational
Miles of Plant: 7.0 (coaxial); None (fiber optic). Homes passed: 540.
Vice President: Bill Jensen. Engineering Manager: Kraig Kaiser. Marketing & Sales Director: Lori Huberty.
City fee: 3% of gross.
Ownership: Mediacom LLC (MSO).

HUTCHINSON—Now served by BROWNTON, MN [MN0145]. ICA: MN0035.

INTERNATIONAL FALLS—Midcontinent Communications, PO Box 5010, Sioux Falls, SD 57117. Phones: 800-456-0564; 605-229-1775. Fax: 605-229-0478. Web Site: http://www.midcocomm.com. Also serves Jameson, Koochiching County, Ranier & South International Falls. ICA: MN0036.
TV Market Ranking: Below 100 (Jameson, Ranier); Outside TV Markets (INTERNATIONAL FALLS, Koochiching County, South International Falls). Franchise award date: N.A. Franchise expiration date: N.A. Began: October 1, 1957.
Channel capacity: N.A. Channels available but not in use: N.A.
Basic Service
Subscribers: 3,800.
Programming (via microwave): KBJR-TV (MNT, NBC) Superior; KDLH (CBS, CW) Duluth; KQDS-TV (FOX) Duluth; WDIO-DT (ABC) Duluth; WDSE (PBS) Duluth.
Programming (via satellite): C-SPAN; Eternal Word TV Network; Home Shopping Network; INSP; QVC; TBS Superstation; TV Guide Network; WGN America.
Current originations: Public Access.
Fee: $29.99 installation; $2.00 converter.
Expanded Basic Service 1
Subscribers: N.A.
Programming (via satellite): ABC Family Channel; AMC; Animal Planet; Arts & Entertainment; Bravo; Cartoon Network; CNBC; CNN; Comedy Central; Country Music TV; Discovery Channel; Disney Channel; E! Entertainment Television; ESPN; ESPN 2; Food Network; Fox News Channel; FX; G4; Golf Channel; Hallmark Channel; Headline News; HGTV; History Channel; Lifetime; MSNBC; MTV; National Geographic Channel; Nickelodeon; Outdoor Channel; Oxygen; Speed Channel; Spike TV; Syfy; The Learning Channel; Travel Channel; truTV; Turner Network TV; TV Land; USA Network; Versus; VH1; WE tv; Weather Channel.
Fee: $47.99 monthly.
Digital Basic Service
Subscribers: N.A.
Programming (via satellite): BBC America; Bio; Discovery Digital Networks; Do-It-Yourself; Fox Movie Channel; Fox Sports World; GAS; History Channel International; Independent Film Channel; Lifetime Movie Network; MTV Networks Digital Suite; Music Choice; Nick Jr.; Sundance Channel.
Digital Pay Service 1
Pay Units: N.A.
Programming (via satellite): Cinemax (multiplexed); Encore; Flix; HBO (multiplexed); Showtime (multiplexed); Starz (multiplexed); The Movie Channel (multiplexed).
Fee: $25.00 installation; $9.65 monthly (Cinemax or HBO).
Video-On-Demand: No
Pay-Per-View
Hot Choice (delivered digitally); iN DEMAND (delivered digitally); Playboy TV (delivered digitally); Fresh (delivered digitally); Shorteez (delivered digitally); Sports PPV (delivered digitally).
Internet Service
Operational: Yes.
Broadband Service: Charter Pipeline.
Fee: $29.99 monthly.
Telephone Service
None
Miles of Plant: 101.0 (coaxial); None (fiber optic). Homes passed: 4,819. Total homes in franchised area: 4,819.
City fee: $100.00 annually.
Ownership: Midcontinent Media Inc. (MSO).

IONA—Formerly served by American Telecasting of America Inc. No longer in operation. ICA: MN0312.

ISLE—Savage Communications Inc., PO Box 810, 206 Power Ave N, Hinckley, MN 55037. Phones: 800-229-9809; 320-384-7442. Fax: 320-384-7446. E-mail: rwsavage@scicable.com. Web Site: http://www.scibroadband.com. Also serves Isle Harbor, Onamia, South Harbor & Wahkon. ICA: MN0313.
TV Market Ranking: Outside TV Markets (ISLE, Isle Harbor, South Harbor, Wahkon). Franchise award date: October 6, 1987. Franchise expiration date: N.A. Began: N.A.
Channel capacity: 60 (2-way capable). Channels available but not in use: None.
Basic Service
Subscribers: 1,559.
Programming (received off-air): KARE (NBC) Minneapolis; KMSP-TV (FOX) Minneapolis; KPXM-TV (ION) St. Cloud; KSTC-TV (IND) Minneapolis; KSTP-TV (ABC) St. Paul; KTCA-TV (PBS) St. Paul; KTCI-TV (PBS) St. Paul; WCCO-TV (CBS) Minneapolis; WFTC (MNT) Minneapolis; WUCW (CW) Minneapolis.
Programming (via satellite): ABC Family Channel; Animal Planet; Arts & Entertainment; Cartoon Network; CNBC; CNN; Comedy Central; C-SPAN; Discovery Channel; Disney Channel; E! Entertainment Televi-

sion; ESPN; ESPN 2; Eternal Word TV Network; Fox News Channel; Fox Sports Net; Great American Country; Headline News; HGTV; History Channel; Lifetime; MTV; National Geographic Channel; Nickelodeon; QVC; Spike TV; Syfy; TBS Superstation; The Learning Channel; Turner Classic Movies; Turner Network TV; TV Land; USA Network; VH1; Weather Channel; WGN America.
Current originations: Public Access.
Fee: $39.95 installation; $33.95 monthly.

Digital Basic Service
Subscribers: N.A.
Programming (via satellite): AmericanLife TV Network; BBC America; Bio; Bloomberg Television; Discovery Digital Networks; DMX Music; ESPN Classic Sports; ESPNews; FitTV; Fox Movie Channel; Fox Sports World; Fuse; G4; Golf Channel; History Channel International; INSP; National Geographic Channel; Outdoor Channel; Sleuth; Speed Channel; Style Network; Trinity Broadcasting Network; Versus; WE tv.

Pay Service 1
Pay Units: 167.
Programming (via satellite): HBO.
Fee: $10.95 monthly.

Digital Pay Service 1
Pay Units: N.A.
Programming (via satellite): Cinemax (multiplexed); Encore (multiplexed); HBO (multiplexed); Showtime (multiplexed); Starz (multiplexed); The Movie Channel (multiplexed).

Video-On-Demand: No

Pay-Per-View
Movies (delivered digitally); ESPN Now (delivered digitally); Sports PPV (delivered digitally).

Internet Service
Operational: Yes.
Broadband Service: SCI Broadband.
Fee: $19.95 monthly.

Telephone Service
None

Miles of Plant: 97.0 (coaxial); None (fiber optic). Homes passed: 3,492. Total homes in franchised area: 3,492.
Manager: Mike Danielson. Marketing Director: Ron Savage. Chief Technician: Pat McCabe. Customer Service Manager: Donna Erickson.
Ownership: Savage Communications Inc. (MSO).

IVANHOE—Mediacom, PO Box 110, 1504 2nd St SE, Waseca, MN 56093. Phone: 507-835-2356. Fax: 507-835-4567. Web Site: http://www.mediacomcable.com. Also serves Lake Benton & Tyler. ICA: MN0189.
TV Market Ranking: Outside TV Markets (IVANHOE, Lake Benton, Tyler). Franchise award date: October 30, 1975. Franchise expiration date: N.A. Began: December 1, 1976.
Channel capacity: N.A. Channels available but not in use: N.A.

Basic Service
Subscribers: 987.
Programming (received off-air): KARE (NBC) Minneapolis; KCPO-LP Sioux Falls; KDLT-TV (NBC) Sioux Falls; KELO-TV (CBS, MNT) Sioux Falls; KESD-TV (PBS) Brookings; KSFY-TV (ABC) Sioux Falls; KSMN (PBS) Worthington; KTCA-TV (PBS) St. Paul; KTTW (FOX) Sioux Falls; KWSD (CW) Sioux Falls; allband FM.
Programming (via satellite): C-SPAN; C-SPAN 2; TV Guide Network; Weather Channel; WGN America.
Programming (via translator): WCCO-TV (CBS) Minneapolis.
Fee: $52.39 installation; $7.22 monthly; $2.00 converter; $17.48 additional installation.

Expanded Basic Service 1
Subscribers: 952.
Programming (via satellite): ABC Family Channel; AMC; Animal Planet; Arts & Entertainment; Bravo; Cartoon Network; CNBC; CNN; Comedy Central; Country Music TV; Discovery Channel; Disney Channel; E! Entertainment Television; ESPN; ESPN 2; Eternal Word TV Network; Food Network; Fox Movie Channel; Fox News Channel; Fox Sports Net North; FX; GalaVision; Hallmark Channel; Headline News; HGTV; History Channel; Home Shopping Network; INSP; Lifetime; MSNBC; MTV; Nickelodeon; RFD-TV; SoapNet; Speed Channel; Spike TV; Syfy; TBS Superstation; The Learning Channel; Travel Channel; Trinity Broadcasting Network; truTV; Turner Classic Movies; Turner Network TV; TV Land; Univision; USA Network; VH1; WE tv.
Fee: $14.81 monthly.

Digital Basic Service
Subscribers: 186.
Programming (via satellite): AmericanLife TV Network; BBC America; Bio; Bloomberg Television; Discovery Digital Networks; DMX Music; Fox Sports World; Fuse; G4; Golf Channel; GSN; Halogen Network; History Channel International; Independent Film Channel; Lifetime Movie Network; Outdoor Channel; Style Network.

Digital Pay Service 1
Pay Units: 137.
Programming (via satellite): Cinemax (multiplexed).
Fee: $7.00 monthly.

Digital Pay Service 2
Pay Units: 100.
Programming (via satellite): Encore (multiplexed); Starz (multiplexed).
Fee: $5.00 monthly.

Digital Pay Service 3
Pay Units: 118.
Programming (via satellite): HBO (multiplexed).
Fee: $11.00 monthly.

Digital Pay Service 4
Pay Units: 186.
Programming (via satellite): Flix; Showtime (multiplexed); Sundance Channel; The Movie Channel (multiplexed).
Fee: $11.00 monthly (each).

Video-On-Demand: Yes

Pay-Per-View
TVN Entertainment (delivered digitally); Fresh (delivered digitally); Shorteez (delivered digitally); Playboy TV (delivered digitally); Hot Choice (delivered digitally).

Internet Service
Operational: Yes, DSL only.
Broadband Service: Mediacom High Speed Internet.

Telephone Service
Digital: Operational

Miles of Plant: 49.0 (coaxial); None (fiber optic). Homes passed: 1,467.
Vice President: Bill Jensen. Engineering Manager: Kraig Kaiser. Marketing & Sales Manager: Lori Huberty.
City fee: None.
Ownership: Mediacom LLC (MSO).

JACKSON—Jackson Municipal TV System, 80 W Ashley St, Jackson, MN 56143-1669. Phone: 507-847-3225. Fax: 507-847-5586. ICA: MN0314.
TV Market Ranking: Outside TV Markets (JACKSON (VILLAGE)). Franchise award date: June 1, 1957. Franchise expiration date: N.A. Began: July 1, 1957.
Channel capacity: 82 (operating 2-way). Channels available but not in use: 38.

Basic Service
Subscribers: 1,548.
Programming (received off-air): KARE (NBC) Minneapolis; KEYC-TV (CBS, FOX) Mankato; KMSP-TV (FOX) Minneapolis; KSFY-TV (ABC) Sioux Falls; KSMN (PBS) Worthington; KSTC-TV (IND) Minneapolis; KSTP-TV (ABC) St. Paul; KTIN (PBS) Fort Dodge; WCCO-TV (CBS) Minneapolis; WFTC (MNT) Minneapolis; WUCW (CW) Minneapolis; allband FM.
Programming (via satellite): ABC Family Channel; TBS Superstation; The Learning Channel; USA Network; Weather Channel; WGN America.
Current originations: Religious Access; Educational Access; Public Access.
Fee: $15.00 installation; $7.50 monthly.

Expanded Basic Service 1
Subscribers: 1,298.
Programming (via satellite): AMC; Animal Planet; Arts & Entertainment; Cartoon Network; CNN; Comedy Central; Discovery Channel; Disney Channel; Do-It-Yourself; E! Entertainment Television; ESPN; ESPN 2; Food Network; Fox News Channel; Fox Sports Net; FX; Great American Country; Hallmark Channel; Headline News; HGTV; History Channel; Lifetime; MTV; National Geographic Channel; Nickelodeon; Outdoor Channel; Speed Channel; Spike TV; Syfy; Travel Channel; Turner Classic Movies; Turner Network TV; TV Land; VH1.
Fee: $15.00 installation; $10.75 monthly.

Pay Service 1
Pay Units: 269.
Programming (via satellite): HBO.
Fee: $8.95 monthly.

Video-On-Demand: No

Internet Service
Operational: No.

Telephone Service
None

Miles of Plant: 37.0 (coaxial); None (fiber optic). Homes passed: 1,610. Total homes in franchised area: 1,800.
Manager: Curtis G. Egeland. Chief Technician: Steve Jenson.
City fee: None.
Ownership: Jackson Municipal TV System.

JANESVILLE—Now served by WASECA, MN [MN0043]. ICA: MN0124.

JASPER—Knology, 5100 S Broadband Ln, Sioux Falls, SD 57108-2207. Phones: 877-633-4567; 605-965-9393. Fax: 605-965-7867. Web Site: http://www.knology.com. ICA: MN0315.
TV Market Ranking: 85 (JASPER). Franchise award date: October 12, 1982. Franchise expiration date: N.A. Began: June 1, 1983.
Channel capacity: N.A. Channels available but not in use: N.A.

Basic Service
Subscribers: 180.
Programming (received off-air): KARE (NBC) Minneapolis; KAUN-LP Sioux Falls; KCAU-TV (ABC) Sioux City; KCPO-LP Sioux Falls; KDLT-TV (NBC) Sioux Falls; KELO-TV (CBS, MNT) Sioux Falls; KMSP-TV (FOX) Minneapolis; KSFY-TV (ABC) Sioux Falls; KSIN-TV (PBS) Sioux City; KTCA-TV (PBS) St. Paul; KTTW (FOX) Sioux Falls; KUSD-TV (PBS) Vermillion; KWSD (CW) Sioux Falls; WCCO-TV (CBS) Minneapolis; WFTC (MNT) Minneapolis.
Programming (via satellite): ABC Family Channel; AMC; Animal Planet; Arts & Entertainment; Bravo; Cartoon Network; CNBC; CNN; Comedy Central; Country Music TV; C-SPAN; C-SPAN 2; Discovery Channel; Disney Channel; E! Entertainment Television; ESPN; ESPN 2; ESPN Classic Sports; Food Network; Fox News Channel; Fox Sports Net North; FX; GalaVision; Golf Channel; Hallmark Channel; Headline News; HGTV; History Channel; Lifetime; Lifetime Movie Network; MSNBC; MTV; MyNetworkTV Inc.; National Geographic Channel; NFL Network; Nickelodeon; QVC; Speed Channel; Spike TV; Syfy; TBS Superstation; Telemundo; The Learning Channel; Toon Disney; Travel Channel; Trinity Broadcasting Network; truTV; Turner Classic Movies; Turner Network TV; TV Guide Network; TV Land; Univision; USA Network; VH1; Weather Channel; WGN America.
Fee: $25.00 installation; $22.95 monthly.

Digital Basic Service
Subscribers: N.A.
Programming (received off-air): KDLT-TV (NBC) Sioux Falls; KELO-TV (CBS, MNT) Sioux Falls; KSFY-TV (ABC) Sioux Falls; KUSD-TV (PBS) Vermillion.
Programming (via satellite): Bandamax; BBC America; Bio; Bloomberg Television; Boomerang; CMT Pure Country; Cooking Channel; De Pelicula; De Pelicula Clasico; Discovery en Espanol; Discovery HD Theater; Discovery Health Channel; Discovery Kids Channel; Discovery Military Channel; Discovery Planet Green; Do-It-Yourself; Encore Wam; ESPN 2 HD; ESPN Deportes; ESPN Deportes On Demand; ESPN HD; ESPN On Demand; ESPN U; ESPN U On Demand; ESPNews; Eternal Word TV Network; FitTV; Flix; Fox College Sports Atlantic; Fox College Sports Central; Fox College Sports Pacific; Fox Movie Channel; Fox Reality Channel; Fox Soccer; Fox Sports en Espanol; Fuse; G4; Gospel Music Channel; GSN; HDNet; HDNet Movies; History Channel International; ID Investigation Discovery; Independent Film Channel; KTTW (FOX) Sioux Falls; Lifetime Real Women; MTV Hits; MTV Jams; MTV2; Music Choice; National Geographic Channel; National Geographic Channel HD Network; National Geographic Channel On Demand; NFL Network HD; Nick Jr.; NickToons TV; Outdoor Channel; Outdoor Channel 2 HD; Outdoor Channel On Demand; QVC HD; RFD-TV; Ritmoson Latino; Science Channel; Sleuth; Sleuth On Demand; SoapNet; Speed On Demand; Style Network; Sundance Channel; TBS in HD; TeenNick; Telehit; Turner Network TV HD; TV Guide SPOT; Universal HD; Versus; Versus HD; Versus On Demand; VH1 Classic; VH1 Soul; WE tv.

Digital Pay Service 1
Pay Units: N.A.
Programming (via satellite): Cinemax (multiplexed); Cinemax HD; Cinemax On Demand; Encore (multiplexed); HBO (multiplexed); HBO HD; HBO Latino; Showtime (multiplexed); Showtime HD; Showtime On Demand; Starz (multiplexed); Starz On Demand; The Movie Channel (multiplexed); The Movie Channel On Demand.

Video-On-Demand: Yes

Pay-Per-View
iN DEMAND (delivered digitally); Hot Choice (delivered digitally).

Internet Service
Operational: Yes.
Broadband Service: Knology.Net.

Telephone Service
Analog: Not Operational
Digital: Operational

Miles of Plant: 6.0 (coaxial); None (fiber optic). Homes passed included in Viborg SD
General Manager: Scott Schroeder. Technical Operations Manager: Daryl Elcock. Marketing Manager: Scott Determan.
City fee: 3% of gross.
Ownership: Knology Inc. (MSO).

JEFFERS—NU-Telecom. Formerly [MN0316]. This cable system has converted to IPTV, PO Box 697, 27 N Minnesota, New Ulm, MN 56073-0697. Phones: 800-893-1856; 507-723-4211. Fax: 507-723-4377. E-mail: onlinecustservice@nu-telecom.net. Web Site: http://www.nutelecom.net. ICA: MN5116.
TV Market Ranking: Below 100 (JEFFERS). Franchise award date: N.A. Franchise expiration date: N.A. Began: N.A.
Channel capacity: N.A. Channels available but not in use: N.A.
Internet Service
Operational: Yes.
Telephone Service
Digital: Operational
President: Bill Otis.
City fee: 2% of gross.
Ownership: NU-Telecom (MSO).

JEFFERSON—NU-Telecom. This cable system has converted to IPTV. See Jeffers, MN [MN5116], MN. ICA: MN0316.

JORDAN—Time Warner Cable. Now served by MINNEAPOLIS, MN [MN0001]. ICA: MN0317.

KARLSTAD—Sjoberg's Cable TV Inc., 315 Main Ave N, Thief River Falls, MN 56701-1905. Phones: 800-828-8808; 218-681-3044. Fax: 218-681-6801. E-mail: office1@mncable.net. Web Site: http://local.mncable.net. Also serves Deerwood Twp. ICA: MN0179.
TV Market Ranking: Outside TV Markets (Deerwood Twp., KARLSTAD). Franchise award date: N.A. Franchise expiration date: N.A. Began: September 1, 1978.
Channel capacity: 78 (operating 2-way). Channels available but not in use: 18.
Basic Service
Subscribers: 298.
Programming (received off-air): KBRR (FOX) Thief River Falls; KCPM (MNT) Grand Forks; KGFE (PBS) Grand Forks; WDAZ-TV (ABC, CW) Devils Lake; allband FM.
Programming (via microwave): KVLY-TV (NBC) Fargo; KXJB-TV (CBS) Valley City.
Programming (via satellite): CNN; ESPN; TBS Superstation; various Canadian stations.
Current originations: Public Access.
Fee: $25.00 installation; $10.00 monthly.
Expanded Basic Service 1
Subscribers: N.A.
Programming (via satellite): ABC Family Channel; Animal Planet; Arts & Entertainment; Cartoon Network; CNBC; Comedy Central; Country Music TV; C-SPAN; CW+; Discovery Channel; Disney Channel; E! Entertainment Television; ESPN 2; Food Network; Fox News Channel; Fox Sports Net; FX; HGTV; History Channel; Home Shopping Network; Lifetime; MSNBC; MTV; Nickelodeon; Spike TV; Syfy; The Learning Channel; Turner Classic Movies; Turner Network TV; TV Land; USA Network; VH1; Weather Channel; WGN America.
Fee: $23.71 monthly.
Digital Basic Service
Subscribers: N.A.
Programming (via satellite): AmericanLife TV Network; BBC America; Bio; Blackbelt TV; Bloomberg Television; Bravo; Chiller; CMT Pure Country; College Sports Television; Cooking Channel; Current; Daystar TV Network; Discovery Health Channel; Discovery Kids Channel; Discovery Military Channel; Discovery Planet Green; DMX Music; Do-It-Yourself; ESPN Classic Sports; ESPN U; ESPNews; Eternal Word TV Network; FitTV; Fox Business Channel; Fox College Sports Atlantic; Fox College Sports Central; Fox College Sports Pacific; Fox Movie Channel; Fox Reality Channel; Fox Soccer; G4; Golf Channel; Gospel Music Channel; Great American Country; GSN; Hallmark Channel; Halogen Network; Headline News; History Channel International; HorseRacing TV; ID Investigation Discovery; Independent Film Channel; Lifetime Movie Network; MTV Hits; MTV2; National Geographic Channel; Nick Jr.; NickToons TV; Outdoor Channel; Ovation; Oxygen; PBS Kids Sprout; ReelzChannel; RFD-TV; Science Channel; ShopNBC; Sleuth; SoapNet; Speed Channel; Style Network; Sundance Channel; TeenNick; Tennis Channel; The Sportsman Channel; The Word Network; Toon Disney; Trinity Broadcasting Network; TVG Network; Versus; VH1 Classic; VH1 Soul; WE tv.
Fee: $11.00 monthly.
Digital Expanded Basic Service
Subscribers: N.A.
Programming (received off-air): PBS HD; WDAZ-TV (ABC, CW) Devils Lake.
Programming (via satellite): Arts & Entertainment HD; CNN HD; Discovery HD Theater; ESPN 2 HD; ESPN HD; Food Network HD; FSN HD; HDNet; HDNet Movies; HGTV HD; History Channel HD; Outdoor Channel 2 HD; Speed HD; Syfy HD; TBS in HD; Turner Network TV HD; Universal HD; USA Network HD; Versus HD.
Fee: $5.00 monthly.
Pay Service 1
Pay Units: 79.
Programming (via satellite): Cinemax; HBO.
Fee: $9.00 monthly (Cinemax), $11.00 monthly (HBO).
Digital Pay Service 1
Pay Units: N.A.
Programming (via satellite): Cinemax (multiplexed); Cinemax HD; Encore (multiplexed); HBO (multiplexed); HBO HD; Showtime (multiplexed); Starz (multiplexed); The Movie Channel (multiplexed).
Fee: $8.00 monthly (Starz/Encore), $9.00 monthly (Cinemax or Showtime/TMC), $11.00 monthly (HBO).
Video-On-Demand: No
Internet Service
Operational: No.
Telephone Service
None
Miles of Plant: 6.0 (coaxial); 17.0 (fiber optic). Homes passed: 348. Total homes in franchised area: 390.
Manager: Richard J. Sjoberg. Chief Technician: Jerry Seim.
City fee: None.
Ownership: Sjoberg's Cable TV Inc. (MSO).

KEEWATIN—Now served by GRAND RAPIDS, MN [MN0038]. ICA: MN0078.

KEGO TWP.—ACS Video. Formerly served by Perham, MN [MN0050]. This cable system has converted to IPTV, 150 Second St SW, Perham, MN 56573. Phone: 866-937-4227. E-mail: answers@arvig.com. Web Site: http://www.arvig.com. ICA: MN5204.
TV Market Ranking: Below 100 (KEGO TWP.).
Channel capacity: N.A. Channels available but not in use: N.A.
Internet Service
Operational: Yes.
Telephone Service
Digital: Operational
Ownership: Arvig Communication Systems.

KELLIHER—Formerly served by North American Communications Corp. No longer in operation. ICA: MN0318.

KENNEDY—Stephen Cable TV Inc., PO Box 9, 415 5th St, Stephen, MN 56757-0009. Phone: 218-478-3074. Fax: 218-478-2236. ICA: MN0234.
TV Market Ranking: Below 100 (KENNEDY). Franchise award date: June 7, 1982. Franchise expiration date: N.A. Began: November 1, 1982.
Channel capacity: 30 (operating 2-way). Channels available but not in use: 13.
Basic Service
Subscribers: 63.
Programming (received off-air): KBRR (FOX) Thief River Falls; KGFE (PBS) Grand Forks; KVLY-TV (NBC) Fargo; WDAZ-TV (ABC, CW) Devils Lake.
Programming (via satellite): ABC Family Channel; AMC; Arts & Entertainment; CNBC; CNN; Comedy Central; C-SPAN; Discovery Channel; Disney Channel; ESPN; ESPN 2; Food Network; Fox Sports Net; Great American Country; HGTV; History Channel; Lifetime; Nickelodeon; Spike TV; TBS Superstation; The Learning Channel; Trinity Broadcasting Network; Turner Network TV; TV Land; USA Network; various Canadian stations; VH1; Weather Channel; WGN America.
Programming (via translator): KXJB-TV (CBS) Valley City.
Current originations: Government Access; Educational Access; Public Access.
Fee: $20.00 installation; $33.50 monthly.
Pay Service 1
Pay Units: 5.
Programming (via satellite): HBO.
Fee: $10.00 installation; $11.00 monthly.
Video-On-Demand: No
Internet Service
Operational: No.
Telephone Service
None
Miles of Plant: 4.0 (coaxial); None (fiber optic). Homes passed: 141. Total homes in franchised area: 170.
Manager: Bryan Wixtrom.
City fee: None.
Ownership: Bryan Wixtrom (MSO).

KENYON—Now served by DODGE CENTER, MN [MN0093]. Also serves KENYON. ICA: MN0127.

KERKHOVEN—Charter Communications. Now served by WILLMAR, MN [MN0018]. ICA: MN0157.

KNIFE LAKE TWP.—New Century Communications, 3588 Kennebec Dr, Eagan, MN 55122-1001. Phone: 651-688-2623. Fax: 651-688-2624. E-mail: tanderson@cablesystemservices.com. ICA: MN0319.
TV Market Ranking: Outside TV Markets (KNIFE LAKE TWP.). Franchise award date: N.A. Franchise expiration date: N.A. Began: N.A.
Channel capacity: N.A. Channels available but not in use: N.A.
Basic Service
Subscribers: 23.
Programming (received off-air): KARE (NBC) Minneapolis; KMSP-TV (FOX) Minneapolis; KSTP-TV (ABC) St. Paul; KTCA-TV (PBS) St. Paul; WCCO-TV (CBS) Minneapolis; WUCW (CW) Minneapolis.
Programming (via satellite): ABC Family Channel; AMC; Arts & Entertainment; CNN; Country Music TV; Discovery Channel; Disney Channel; ESPN; Lifetime; Showtime; Spike TV; TBS Superstation; The Learning Channel; Trinity Broadcasting Network; Turner Network TV; TV Land; USA Network; WGN America.
Fee: $30.00 installation; $33.85 monthly.
Video-On-Demand: No
Internet Service
Operational: No.
Telephone Service
None
Homes passed: 345.
Executive Vice President: Marty Walch. Manager & Chief Technician: Todd Anderson.
Ownership: New Century Communications (MSO).

KNIFE RIVER—New Century Communications, 3588 Kennebec Dr, Eagan, MN 55122-1001. Phone: 651-688-2623. Fax: 651-688-2624. E-mail: tanderson@cablesystemservices.com. Also serves Two Harbors (unincorporated areas). ICA: MN0320.
TV Market Ranking: 89 (KNIFE RIVER, Two Harbors (unincorporated areas)). Franchise award date: N.A. Franchise expiration date: N.A. Began: N.A.
Channel capacity: 40 (not 2-way capable). Channels available but not in use: 19.
Basic Service
Subscribers: 22.
Programming (received off-air): KBJR-TV (MNT, NBC) Superior; KDLH (CBS, CW) Duluth; KQDS-TV (FOX) Duluth; WDIO-DT (ABC) Duluth; WDSE (PBS) Duluth.
Programming (via satellite): ABC Family Channel; AMC; Arts & Entertainment; CNN; Country Music TV; Discovery Channel; Disney Channel; ESPN; Headline News; Lifetime; Nickelodeon; QVC; Showtime; Spike TV; TBS Superstation; The Learning Channel; Trinity Broadcasting Network; Turner Network TV; TV Land; USA Network; WGN America.
Fee: $30.00 installation; $33.85 monthly.
Video-On-Demand: No
Internet Service
Operational: No.
Telephone Service
None
Miles of Plant: 25.0 (coaxial); None (fiber optic). Homes passed: 500.
Executive Vice President: Marty Walch. Manager & Chief Technician: Todd Anderson.
Ownership: New Century Communications (MSO).

LAFAYETTE—Now served by WASECA, MN [MN0043]. ICA: MN0235.

LAKE BRONSON—Stephen Cable TV Inc., PO Box 9, 415 5th St, Stephen, MN 56757-0009. Phone: 218-478-3074. Fax: 218-478-2236. ICA: MN0240.
TV Market Ranking: Below 100 (LAKE BRONSON). Franchise award date: August 18, 1985. Franchise expiration date: N.A. Began: September 1, 1985.
Channel capacity: 40 (not 2-way capable). Channels available but not in use: 4.
Basic Service
Subscribers: 62.
Programming (received off-air): KGFE (PBS) Grand Forks; KNRR (FOX) Pembina; KVLY-TV (NBC) Fargo; KXJB-TV (CBS)

Valley City; WDAZ-TV (ABC, CW) Devils Lake.
Programming (via satellite): ABC Family Channel; AMC; Arts & Entertainment; CNBC; CNN; Comedy Central; Country Music TV; Discovery Channel; Disney Channel; ESPN; ESPN 2; Fox Sports Net; HGTV; History Channel; Lifetime; Nickelodeon; Spike TV; Syfy; TBS Superstation; The Learning Channel; Trinity Broadcasting Network; Turner Network TV; TV Land; USA Network; various Canadian stations; VH1; Weather Channel; WGN America.
Current originations: Religious Access; Government Access; Educational Access; Public Access.
Fee: $20.00 installation; $32.50 monthly.

Pay Service 1
Pay Units: 3.
Programming (via satellite): HBO.
Fee: $11.00 monthly.
Video-On-Demand: No

Internet Service
Operational: No.

Telephone Service
None
Miles of Plant: 5.0 (coaxial); None (fiber optic). Homes passed: 130. Total homes in franchised area: 150.
Manager: Bryan Wixtrom.
City fee: None.
Ownership: Bryan Wixtrom (MSO).

LAKE CITY—Mediacom, PO Box 110, 1504 2nd St SE, Waseca, MN 56093. Phone: 507-835-2356. Fax: 507-835-4567. Web Site: http://www.mediacomcable.com. Also serves Florence Twp., Frontenac, Lake Twp. & Mount Pleasant Twp. ICA: MN0054.
TV Market Ranking: Below 100 (Florence Twp., Frontenac, LAKE CITY, Lake Twp., Mount Pleasant Twp.). Franchise award date: May 10, 1982. Franchise expiration date: N.A. Began: July 5, 1983.
Channel capacity: N.A. Channels available but not in use: N.A.

Basic Service
Subscribers: 1,239.
Programming (received off-air): KARE (NBC) Minneapolis; KMSP-TV (FOX) Minneapolis; KSTP-TV (ABC) St. Paul; KTCA-TV (PBS) St. Paul; KTCI-TV (PBS) St. Paul; KTTC (CW, NBC) Rochester; WCCO-TV (CBS) Minneapolis; WEAU-TV (NBC) Eau Claire; WFTC (MNT) Minneapolis; WKBT-DT (CBS, MNT) La Crosse; WLAX (FOX) La Crosse; WUCW (CW) Minneapolis; 5 FMs.
Programming (via satellite): WGN America.
Current originations: Educational Access; Public Access.
Fee: $25.00 installation; $16.95 monthly; $2.00 converter.

Expanded Basic Service 1
Subscribers: 84.
Programming (via satellite): ABC Family Channel; AMC; Animal Planet; Arts & Entertainment; Cartoon Network; CNBC; CNN; Comedy Central; Country Music TV; C-SPAN; C-SPAN 2; Discovery Channel; Disney Channel; E! Entertainment Television; ESPN; ESPN 2; Eternal Word TV Network; Food Network; Fox News Channel; Fox Sports Net North; FX; Hallmark Channel; Headline News; HGTV; History Channel; INSP; Lifetime; MSNBC; MTV; Nickelodeon; QVC; Speed Channel; Spike TV; Syfy; TBS Superstation; The Learning Channel; Travel Channel; Turner Network TV; TV Land; USA Network; VH1; WE tv; Weather Channel.

Digital Basic Service
Subscribers: N.A.
Programming (via satellite): AmericanLife TV Network; BBC America; Bio; Bloomberg Television; Discovery Digital Networks; DMX Music; Fox Sports World; Fuse; G4; Golf Channel; GSN; Halogen Network; History Channel International; Independent Film Channel; Lifetime Movie Network; Lime; National Geographic Channel; Outdoor Channel; Style Network.

Digital Pay Service 1
Pay Units: 93.
Programming (via satellite): Cinemax (multiplexed); Encore (multiplexed); Flix; HBO (multiplexed); Showtime (multiplexed); Starz (multiplexed); Sundance Channel; The Movie Channel (multiplexed).
Fee: $15.00 installation; $9.95 monthly (Cinemax, Showtime or TMC), $11.95 monthly (HBO).
Video-On-Demand: No

Pay-Per-View
TVN Entertainment (delivered digitally); ESPN Now (delivered digitally); Sports PPV (delivered digitally); Urban Xtra (delivered digitally); Fresh (delivered digitally); Shorteez (delivered digitally); Playboy TV (delivered digitally); Pleasure (delivered digitally).

Internet Service
Operational: Yes.
Broadband Service: Mediacom High Speed Internet.
Fee: $99.00 installation; $40.00 monthly.

Telephone Service
None
Miles of Plant: 50.0 (coaxial); None (fiber optic). Homes passed: 2,087.
Vice President: Bill Jensen. Engineering Manager: Kraig Kaiser. Marketing & Sales Director: Lori Huberty.
City fee: 3% of basic gross.
Ownership: Mediacom LLC (MSO).

LAKE CRYSTAL—Now served by WASECA, MN [MN0043]. ICA: MN0108.

LAKE LILLIAN—Farmers Mutual Telephone Co., PO Box 220, Stanton, IA 51573. Phones: 800-469-2111; 717-829-2111. Web Site: http://online.fmtc.com. ICA: MN0321.
TV Market Ranking: Below 100 (LAKE LILLIAN). Franchise award date: December 1, 1988. Franchise expiration date: N.A. Began: April 1, 1990.
Channel capacity: 54 (operating 2-way). Channels available but not in use: N.A.

Basic Service
Subscribers: 79.
Programming (received off-air): KARE (NBC) Minneapolis; KCCO-TV (CBS) Alexandria; KMSP-TV (FOX) Minneapolis; KSAX (ABC) Alexandria; KSTC-TV (IND) Minneapolis; KWCM-TV (PBS) Appleton; WFTC (MNT) Minneapolis; WUCW (CW) Minneapolis.
Programming (via satellite): ABC Family Channel; AMC; Animal Planet; Arts & Entertainment; Cartoon Network; CNN; Comedy Central; Country Music TV; Discovery Channel; Disney Channel; ESPN; ESPN 2; Food Network; Fox Sports Net North; Hallmark Channel; HGTV; History Channel; Lifetime; MTV; Nickelodeon; Outdoor Channel; QVC; Spike TV; Syfy; TBS Superstation; The Learning Channel; Trinity Broadcasting Network; Turner Network TV; TV Land; USA Network; VH1; Weather Channel.
Fee: $10.00 installation; $26.95 monthly.

Pay Service 1
Pay Units: 2.
Programming (via satellite): Cinemax; HBO; Showtime.
Fee: $9.95 monthly (Cinemax), $10.95 monthly (Showtime), $11.95 monthly (HBO).
Video-On-Demand: No

Internet Service
Operational: No.

Telephone Service
None
Miles of Plant: 3.0 (coaxial); None (fiber optic). Homes passed: 130. Total homes in franchised area: 130.
Manager: Kevin Cabbage. Assistant Manager: Dennis Crawford.
Ownership: Farmers Mutual Telephone Co. (MSO).

LAKE MINNETONKA—Mediacom, PO Box 110, 1504 2nd St SE, Waseca, MN 56093. Phone: 507-835-2356. Fax: 507-835-4567. Web Site: http://www.mediacomcable.com. Also serves Chanhassen, Deephaven, Excelsior, Greenwood, Long Lake, Loretto, Maple Plain, Medina, Minnetonka Beach, Minnetrista, Mound, Orono, Shorewood, Spring Park, St. Bonifacius, Tonka Bay, Victoria, Waconia, Wayzata & Woodland. ICA: MN0010.
TV Market Ranking: 13 (Chanhassen, Deephaven, Excelsior, Greenwood, LAKE MINNETONKA, Long Lake, Loretto, Maple Plain, Medina, Minnetonka Beach, Minnetrista, Mound, Orono, Shorewood, Spring Park, St. Bonifacius, Tonka Bay, Victoria, Waconia, Wayzata, Woodland). Franchise award date: May 11, 1984. Franchise expiration date: N.A. Began: December 1, 1984.
Channel capacity: N.A. Channels available but not in use: N.A.

Basic Service
Subscribers: 16,487.
Programming (received off-air): KARE (NBC) Minneapolis; KMSP-TV (FOX) Minneapolis; KPXM-TV (ION) St. Cloud; KSTC-TV (IND) Minneapolis; KSTP-TV (ABC) St. Paul; KTCA-TV (PBS) St. Paul; KTCI-TV (PBS) St. Paul; WCCO-TV (CBS) Minneapolis; WFTC (MNT) Minneapolis; WUCW (CW) Minneapolis.
Programming (via satellite): C-SPAN; C-SPAN 2; QVC; Weather Channel; WGN America.
Current originations: Leased Access; Religious Access; Government Access; Educational Access; Public Access.
Fee: $4.95 installation; $13.50 monthly.

Expanded Basic Service 1
Subscribers: 15,492.
Programming (via satellite): ABC Family Channel; AMC; Animal Planet; Arts & Entertainment; BET Networks; Bravo; Cartoon Network; CNBC; CNN; Comedy Central; Country Music TV; Discovery Channel; Disney Channel; E! Entertainment Television; ESPN; ESPN 2; Eternal Word TV Network; Food Network; Fox Movie Channel; Fox News Channel; Fox Sports Net Minnesota; FX; Hallmark Channel; Headline News; HGTV; History Channel; Home Shopping Network; INSP; Lifetime; MSNBC; MTV; Nickelodeon; SoapNet; Speed Channel; Spike TV; Syfy; TBS Superstation; The Learning Channel; Travel Channel; Trinity Broadcasting Network; truTV; Turner Classic Movies; Turner Network TV; TV Guide Network; TV Land; Univision; USA Network; VH1; WE tv.
Fee: $26.45 monthly.

Digital Basic Service
Subscribers: 3,300.
Programming (via satellite): AmericanLife TV Network; BBC America; Bio; Bloomberg Television; Canales N; Discovery Digital Networks; Fox Sports World; Fuse; G4; Golf Channel; GSN; Halogen Network; History Channel International; Independent Film Channel; Lifetime Movie Network; Lime; Music Choice; Outdoor Channel; Style Network; Versus.
Fee: $13.00 monthly.

Digital Pay Service 1
Pay Units: 12,116.
Programming (via satellite): Cinemax (multiplexed); Encore (multiplexed); Flix; HBO (multiplexed); Showtime (multiplexed); Starz (multiplexed); Sundance Channel; The Movie Channel (multiplexed).
Fee: $10.00 monthly (each).
Video-On-Demand: Yes

Pay-Per-View
Addressable homes: 3,300.
Pleasure (delivered digitally); ESPN Now (delivered digitally), Addressable: Yes; ETC (delivered digitally); Playboy TV (delivered digitally); Fresh (delivered digitally); Shorteez (delivered digitally); TVN Entertainment (delivered digitally); Sports PPV (delivered digitally).

Internet Service
Operational: Yes.
Subscribers: 3,000.
Broadband Service: Mediacom High Speed Internet.
Fee: $69.95 installation; $40.95 monthly; $10.00 modem lease; $239.95 modem purchase.

Telephone Service
Analog: Not Operational
Digital: Operational
Miles of Plant: 529.0 (coaxial); None (fiber optic). Homes passed: 26,052.
Vice President: Bill Jensen. Engineering Manager: Kraig Kaiser. Marketing & Sales Director: Lori Huberty.
City fee: 5% of gross.
Ownership: Mediacom LLC (MSO).

LAKEFIELD—Lakefield Cable TV, PO Box 1023, 301 Main St, Lakefield, MN 56150-1023. Phone: 507-662-5457. Fax: 507-662-5990. E-mail: utilities@lakefieldmn.com. ICA: MN0110.
TV Market Ranking: Outside TV Markets (LAKEFIELD). Franchise award date: N.A. Franchise expiration date: N.A. Began: July 1, 1978.
Channel capacity: 43 (not 2-way capable). Channels available but not in use: 1.

Basic Service
Subscribers: 715.
Programming (received off-air): KDLT-TV (NBC) Sioux Falls; KELO-TV (CBS, MNT) Sioux Falls; KEYC-TV (CBS, FOX) Mankato; KSFY-TV (ABC) Sioux Falls; allband FM.
Programming (via satellite): ABC Family Channel; AMC; Arts & Entertainment; CNN; Comedy Central; Country Music TV; Discovery Channel; Disney Channel; ESPN; ESPN 2; Fox Sports Net; Hallmark Channel; Headline News; HGTV; History Channel; Lifetime; MTV; Nickelodeon; Outdoor Channel; QVC; Speed Channel; Spike TV; Syfy; TBS Superstation; The Learning Channel; Turner Network TV; TV Land; USA Network; VH1; Weather Channel; WGN America.
Programming (via translator): KARE (NBC) Minneapolis; KMSP-TV (FOX) Minneapolis; KSTP-TV (ABC) St. Paul; KTCA-TV (PBS) St. Paul; WCCO-TV (CBS) Minneapolis; WFTC (MNT) Minneapolis; WUCW (CW) Minneapolis.

Current originations: Religious Access; Public Access.
Fee: $20.00 installation; $25.00 monthly; $4.00 converter.
Pay Service 1
Pay Units: 55.
Programming (via satellite): The Movie Channel.
Fee: $10.00 monthly.
Video-On-Demand: No
Internet Service
Operational: No.
Telephone Service
None
Miles of Plant: 10.0 (coaxial); None (fiber optic). Homes passed: 820. Total homes in franchised area: 820.
Manager: Joni Hanson. Utility Supervisor: Jim Koep.
City fee: 3% of gross.
Ownership: City of Lakefield Public Utilities.

LAMBERTON—Lamberton TV Cable Co., 749 Des Moines Dr, Windom, MN 56101-1604. Phone: 507-831-4938. Fax: 507-831-4938. ICA: MN0171.
TV Market Ranking: Below 100 (LAMBERTON). Franchise award date: N.A. Franchise expiration date: N.A. Began: November 1, 1971.
Channel capacity: 40 (not 2-way capable). Channels available but not in use: N.A.
Basic Service
Subscribers: 235.
Programming (received off-air): KELO-TV (CBS, MNT) Sioux Falls; KEYC-TV (CBS, FOX) Mankato; KSFY-TV (ABC) Sioux Falls; allband FM.
Programming (via satellite): ABC Family Channel; CNN; Discovery Channel; ESPN; Headline News; Nickelodeon; Spike TV; TBS Superstation; The Learning Channel; Turner Network TV; USA Network; Weather Channel; WGN America.
Programming (via translator): KARE (NBC) Minneapolis; KMSP-TV (FOX) Minneapolis; KSTP-TV (ABC) St. Paul; KTCA-TV (PBS) St. Paul; KWCM-TV (PBS) Appleton; WCCO-TV (CBS) Minneapolis; WFTC (MNT) Minneapolis; WUCW (CW) Minneapolis.
Fee: $15.00 installation; $33.95 monthly.
Pay Service 1
Pay Units: 10.
Programming (via satellite): Showtime.
Fee: $15.00 installation; $15.00 monthly.
Video-On-Demand: No
Internet Service
Operational: No.
Telephone Service
None
Miles of Plant: 16.0 (coaxial); None (fiber optic). Homes passed: 398. Total homes in franchised area: 600.
Manager: Robert E. Turner.
City fee: None.
Ownership: Robert E. Turner (MSO).

LANCASTER—Stephen Cable TV Inc., PO Box 9, 415 5th St, Stephen, MN 56757-0009. Phone: 218-478-3074. Fax: 218-478-2236. ICA: MN0228.
TV Market Ranking: Below 100 (LANCASTER). Franchise award date: June 13, 1984. Franchise expiration date: N.A. Began: August 1, 1984.
Channel capacity: 40 (not 2-way capable). Channels available but not in use: 1.
Basic Service
Subscribers: 113.
Programming (received off-air): KGFE (PBS) Grand Forks; KNRR (FOX) Pembina; KVLY-TV (NBC) Fargo; KXJB-TV (CBS) Valley City; WDAZ-TV (ABC, CW) Devils Lake.
Programming (via satellite): ABC Family Channel; AMC; Arts & Entertainment; CNBC; CNN; Comedy Central; Country Music TV; Discovery Channel; Disney Channel; ESPN; ESPN 2; Fox Sports Net; Hallmark Channel; HGTV; History Channel; Lifetime; MTV; Nickelodeon; Spike TV; Syfy; TBS Superstation; The Learning Channel; Trinity Broadcasting Network; Turner Network TV; TV Land; USA Network; various Canadian stations; VH1; Weather Channel; WGN America.
Current originations: Religious Access; Government Access; Public Access.
Fee: $20.00 installation; $33.50 monthly.
Pay Service 1
Pay Units: 5.
Programming (via satellite): HBO.
Fee: $10.00 installation; $11.00 monthly.
Video-On-Demand: No
Internet Service
Operational: No.
Telephone Service
None
Miles of Plant: 5.0 (coaxial); None (fiber optic). Homes passed: 160.
Manager: Bryan Wixtrom.
City fee: None.
Ownership: Bryan Wixtrom (MSO).

LANESBORO—Now served by CALEDONIA, MN [MN0086]. Also serves LANESBORO. ICA: MN0160.

LE ROY—Mediacom. Now served by CHATFIELD, MN [MN0111]. ICA: MN0174.

LE SUEUR—Now served by WASECA, MN [MN0043]. ICA: MN0068.

LEOTA—Formerly served by American Telecasting of America Inc. No longer in operation. ICA: MN0323.

LESTER PRAIRIE—Now served by BROWNTON, MN [MN0145]. ICA: MN0072.

LEWISVILLE—North American Communications Corp., PO Box 387, 211 Main St S, Hector, MN 55342-0387. Phones: 800-982-8038; 320-848-6781. Fax: 320-848-2323. E-mail: hcc@hcctel.net. Web Site: http://www.hectorcom.com. ICA: MN0325.
TV Market Ranking: Below 100 (LEWISVILLE). Franchise award date: N.A. Franchise expiration date: N.A. Began: N.A.
Channel capacity: 54 (not 2-way capable). Channels available but not in use: 29.
Basic Service
Subscribers: 22.
Programming (received off-air): KARE (NBC) Minneapolis; KEYC-TV (CBS, FOX) Mankato; KMSP-TV (FOX) Minneapolis; KSMN (PBS) Worthington; KSTP-TV (ABC) St. Paul; WCCO-TV (CBS) Minneapolis; WFTC (MNT) Minneapolis; WUCW (CW) Minneapolis.
Programming (via satellite): ABC Family Channel; AMC; Arts & Entertainment; CNN; Country Music TV; Discovery Channel; Disney Channel; ESPN; Fox Sports Net Midwest; Nickelodeon; QVC; Spike TV; TBS Superstation; Trinity Broadcasting Network; Turner Network TV; USA Network; WGN America.
Current originations: Leased Access; Government Access; Educational Access; Public Access.
Fee: $40.00 installation; $26.95 monthly; $3.50 converter; $25.00 additional installation.
Pay Service 1
Pay Units: 1.
Programming (via satellite): HBO.
Fee: $10.95 monthly.
Pay Service 2
Pay Units: N.A.
Programming (via satellite): Cinemax.
Fee: $10.95 monthly.
Video-On-Demand: No
Internet Service
Operational: No.
Broadband Service: Offers dial-up and DSL only; no cable modem service.
Telephone Service
None
Miles of Plant: 4.0 (coaxial); None (fiber optic). Homes passed: 108. Total homes in franchised area: 108.
Manager: Matt Sparks. Chief Technician: George Honzay. Customer Service Supervisor: Patty Groshens.
Ownership: Hector Communications Corp. (MSO).

LISMORE—K-Communications Inc., 337 Aetna St, Ruthton, MN 56170-0018. Phones: 800-752-9397; 507-658-3830. Fax: 507-658-3914. Web Site: http://www.woodstocktel.net. ICA: MN0326.
TV Market Ranking: Outside TV Markets (LISMORE). Franchise award date: September 1, 1988. Franchise expiration date: N.A. Began: N.A.
Channel capacity: 28 (not 2-way capable). Channels available but not in use: None.
Basic Service
Subscribers: 80.
Programming (received off-air): KDLT-TV (NBC) Sioux Falls; KELO-TV (CBS, MNT) Sioux Falls; KSFY-TV (ABC) Sioux Falls; KTTW (FOX) Sioux Falls.
Programming (via microwave): KSTP-TV (ABC) St. Paul.
Programming (via satellite): ABC Family Channel; Animal Planet; Arts & Entertainment; CNN; CW+; Discovery Channel; Disney Channel; ESPN; Fox Sports Net; History Channel; Lifetime; Spike TV; TBS Superstation; The Learning Channel; Trinity Broadcasting Network; Turner Network TV; USA Network; WGN America.
Fee: $25.00 installation; $19.95 monthly.
Pay Service 1
Pay Units: 21.
Programming (via satellite): Showtime.
Fee: $10.50 monthly.
Video-On-Demand: No
Internet Service
Operational: No, DSL only.
Telephone Service
None
Miles of Plant: 3.0 (coaxial); None (fiber optic).
Chief Technician & Marketing Director: Dave Bukowski. Program Director: Terry Nelson.
Ownership: Woodstock Telephone Co. (MSO).

LITCHFIELD—Now served by BROWNTON, MN [MN0145]. ICA: MN0327.

LITTLE FALLS—Charter Communications, 3380 Northern Valley Pl NE, Rochester, MN 55906-3954. Phone: 507-289-8372. Fax: 507-285-6162. Web Site: http://www.charter.com. Also serves Belle Prairie Twp., Green Prairie Twp., Little Falls Twp. & Pike Creek Twp. ICA: MN0044.
TV Market Ranking: Below 100 (Belle Prairie Twp., Green Prairie Twp., LITTLE FALLS, Little Falls Twp., Pike Creek Twp.). Franchise award date: December 1, 1961. Franchise expiration date: N.A. Began: December 1, 1961.
Channel capacity: N.A. Channels available but not in use: N.A.
Basic Service
Subscribers: 2,500.
Programming (received off-air): KAWB (PBS) Brainerd; KCCO-TV (CBS) Alexandria; KPXM-TV (ION) St. Cloud; KSAX (ABC) Alexandria; 23 FMs.
Programming (via microwave): KARE (NBC) Minneapolis; KMSP-TV (FOX) Minneapolis; KSTC-TV (IND) Minneapolis; KTCA-TV (PBS) St. Paul; WFTC (MNT) Minneapolis; WUCW (CW) Minneapolis.
Programming (via satellite): C-SPAN; C-SPAN 2; Eternal Word TV Network; QVC; TBS Superstation; Trinity Broadcasting Network; WGN America.
Current originations: Public Access.
Fee: $29.99 installation; $2.00 converter.
Expanded Basic Service 1
Subscribers: N.A.
Programming (received off-air): WCMN-LP St. Cloud-Sartell.
Programming (via satellite): ABC Family Channel; AMC; Animal Planet; Arts & Entertainment; Bravo; Cartoon Network; CNBC; CNN; Comedy Central; Country Music TV; Discovery Channel; Disney Channel; E! Entertainment Television; ESPN; ESPN 2; Food Network; Fox News Channel; Fox Sports Net North; FX; G4; Golf Channel; Hallmark Channel; Headline News; HGTV; History Channel; Home Shopping Network; Lifetime; MSNBC; MTV; National Geographic Channel; Nickelodeon; Oxygen; Speed Channel; Spike TV; Syfy; The Learning Channel; Travel Channel; truTV; Turner Classic Movies; Turner Network TV; TV Land; Univision; USA Network; Versus; VH1; WE tv; Weather Channel.
Fee: $47.99 monthly.
Digital Basic Service
Subscribers: N.A.
Programming (via satellite): BBC America; Bio; Bloomberg Television; Boomerang; CNN en Espanol; CNN International; Discovery Digital Networks; Do-It-Yourself; ESPN Classic Sports; ESPNews; Fox Movie Channel; Fox Sports World; FSN Digital Atlantic; FSN Digital Central; FSN Digital Pacific; Fuel TV; Fuse; GAS; History Channel International; Independent Film Channel; Lifetime Movie Network; MTV Networks Digital Suite; Music Choice; NFL Network; Nick Jr.; Nick Too; NickToons TV; Outdoor Channel; SoapNet; Sundance Channel; Toon Disney; TV Guide Interactive Inc.
Digital Pay Service 1
Pay Units: 149.
Programming (via satellite): Cinemax (multiplexed); Encore (multiplexed); HBO (multiplexed); Showtime (multiplexed); Starz (multiplexed); The Movie Channel (multiplexed).
Fee: $10.00 installation; $6.95 monthly.
Video-On-Demand: Yes
Pay-Per-View
Playboy TV (delivered digitally); Fresh (delivered digitally); Shorteez (delivered digitally); iN DEMAND (delivered digitally); Sports PPV (delivered digitally).
Internet Service
Operational: Yes.
Broadband Service: Charter Pipeline.
Fee: $29.99 monthly.
Telephone Service
Digital: Operational
Fee: $29.99 monthly
Homes passed: 4,700. Miles of plant (coax) included in St. Cloud/Waite Park

Vice President & General Manager: John Crowley. Operations Director: Craig Stensaas. Technical Operations Director: Mark Abramo. Marketing Director: Bill Haarstad.
City fee: 3% of gross.
Ownership: Charter Communications Inc. (MSO).

LITTLEFORK—Midcontinent Communications, PO Box 5010, Sioux Falls, SD 57117. Phones: 800-456-0564; 218-283-3409. Web Site: http://www.midcocomm.com. ICA: MN0200.
TV Market Ranking: Below 100 (LITTLEFORK). Franchise award date: N.A. Franchise expiration date: N.A. Began: October 1, 1970.
Channel capacity: 26 (not 2-way capable). Channels available but not in use: N.A.
Basic Service
Subscribers: 262.
Programming (via microwave): KBJR-TV (MNT, NBC) Superior; KDLH (CBS, CW) Duluth; WDIO-DT (ABC) Duluth; WDSE (PBS) Duluth.
Programming (via satellite): ABC Family Channel; AMC; Animal Planet; CNN; Discovery Channel; ESPN; Fox News Channel; Fox Sports Net Minnesota; FX; MTV; Nickelodeon; Spike TV; TBS Superstation; The Learning Channel; Turner Network TV; USA Network; VH1.
Fee: $59.95 installation; $22.07 monthly; $39.95 additional installation.
Pay Service 1
Pay Units: N.A.
Programming (via satellite): Encore; HBO; Starz.
Fee: $9.65 monthly (HBO).
Video-On-Demand: No
Internet Service
Operational: No.
Telephone Service
None
Miles of Plant: 9.0 (coaxial); None (fiber optic). Homes passed: 285. Total homes in franchised area: 285.
Ownership: Midcontinent Media Inc. (MSO).

LONG LAKE—New Century Communications, 3588 Kennebec Dr, Eagan, MN 55122-1001. Phone: 651-688-2623. Fax: 651-688-2624. E-mail: tanderson@cablesystemservices.com. ICA: MN0245.
TV Market Ranking: 13 (LONG LAKE). Franchise award date: N.A. Franchise expiration date: N.A. Began: N.A.
Channel capacity: 40 (not 2-way capable). Channels available but not in use: 24.
Basic Service
Subscribers: 25.
Programming (received off-air): KBJR-TV (MNT, NBC) Superior; KDLH (CBS, CW) Duluth; WDSE (PBS) Duluth; WIRT-DT (ABC) Hibbing.
Programming (via satellite): ABC Family Channel; AMC; Arts & Entertainment; CNN; Country Music TV; Discovery Channel; ESPN; Headline News; Showtime; Spike TV; TBS Superstation; Turner Network TV; USA Network; WGN America.
Fee: $33.85 monthly.
Video-On-Demand: No
Internet Service
Operational: No.
Telephone Service
None
Miles of Plant: 5.0 (coaxial); None (fiber optic). Homes passed: 143.
Executive Vice President: Marty Walch. Manager & Chief Technician: Todd Anderson.
Ownership: New Century Communications (MSO).

LONG PRAIRIE—Charter Communications. Now served by BRAINERD, MN [MN0022]. ICA: MN0329.

LOWRY—Lowry Telephone Co. Now served by BARRETT, MN [MN0233]. ICA: MN0330.

LUVERNE—Now served by WORTHINGTON, MN [MN0041]. ICA: MN0059.

LYLE—No longer in operation. ICA: MN0218.

MABEL—Now served by CALEDONIA, MN [MN0086]. ICA: MN0149.

MADELIA—Time Warner Cable. Now served by MINNEAPOLIS, MN [MN0001]. ICA: MN0101.

MADISON—Now served by APPLETON, MN [MN0106]. ICA: MN0096.

MADISON LAKE—North American Communications Corp., PO Box 387, 211 Main St S, Hector, MN 55342-0387. Phones: 800-982-8038; 320-848-6781. Fax: 320-848-2323. E-mail: hcc@hcctel.net. Web Site: http://www.hectorcom.com. Also serves Kasota & Washington Twp. ICA: MN0331.
TV Market Ranking: Below 100 (Kasota, MADISON LAKE, Washington Twp.). Franchise award date: N.A. Franchise expiration date: N.A. Began: January 1, 1988.
Channel capacity: N.A. Channels available but not in use: N.A.
Basic Service
Subscribers: 285.
Programming (received off-air): KAAL (ABC) Austin; KARE (NBC) Minneapolis; KEYC-TV (CBS, FOX) Mankato; KMSP-TV (FOX) Minneapolis; KSTC-TV (IND) Minneapolis; KSTP-TV (ABC) St. Paul; KTCA-TV (PBS) St. Paul; WCCO-TV (CBS) Minneapolis; WFTC (MNT) Minneapolis; WUCW (CW) Minneapolis.
Programming (via satellite): ABC Family Channel; AMC; Arts & Entertainment; CNN; Discovery Channel; Disney Channel; ESPN; ESPN 2; Fox Sports Net North; HGTV; History Channel; Lifetime; Nickelodeon; QVC; Spike TV; TBS Superstation; The Learning Channel; Trinity Broadcasting Network; Turner Network TV; TV Land; USA Network; VH1; Weather Channel; WGN America.
Fee: $40.00 installation; $25.95 monthly; $2.50 converter; $25.00 additional installation.
Pay Service 1
Pay Units: 2.
Programming (via satellite): Cinemax.
Fee: $10.95 monthly.
Pay Service 2
Pay Units: 24.
Programming (via satellite): HBO.
Fee: $10.95 monthly.
Video-On-Demand: No
Internet Service
Operational: No.
Telephone Service
None
Miles of Plant: 7.0 (coaxial); None (fiber optic).
Manager: Matt Sparks. Chief Technician: George Honzay. Customer Service Supervisor: Patty Groshens.
Ownership: Hector Communications Corp. (MSO).

MAGNOLIA—Formerly served by American Telecasting of America Inc. No longer in operation. ICA: MN0332.

MAHNOMEN—Loretel Cablevision, PO Box 72, 13 East 4th Ave, Ada, MN 56510. Phones: 800-343-2762; 218-784-5100; 218-784-5151. Fax: 218-784-2706. E-mail: loretel@loretel.net. Web Site: http://www.hectorcom.com. ICA: MN0144.
TV Market Ranking: Outside TV Markets (MAHNOMEN). Franchise award date: N.A. Franchise expiration date: N.A. Began: July 1, 1982.
Channel capacity: 35 (operating 2-way). Channels available but not in use: N.A.
Basic Service
Subscribers: 402.
Programming (received off-air): KCCW-TV (CBS) Walker; KCPM (MNT) Grand Forks; KFME (PBS) Fargo; KVLY-TV (NBC) Fargo; KVRR (FOX) Fargo; KXJB-TV (CBS) Valley City; WDAY-TV (ABC, CW) Fargo.
Programming (via satellite): ABC Family Channel; AMC; Arts & Entertainment; CNBC; CNN; Country Music TV; C-SPAN; Discovery Channel; Disney Channel; ESPN; ESPN 2; Food Network; Fox Sports Net; Headline News; History Channel; Lifetime; MTV; Nickelodeon; QVC; Spike TV; Syfy; TBS Superstation; The Learning Channel; Turner Network TV; TV Land; USA Network; VH1; Weather Channel; WGN America.
Fee: $25.00 installation; $34.00 monthly.
Pay Service 1
Pay Units: 25.
Programming (via satellite): HBO.
Fee: $12.00 monthly.
Pay Service 2
Pay Units: 7.
Programming (via satellite): Cinemax.
Fee: $12.00 monthly.
Pay Service 3
Pay Units: 13.
Programming (via satellite): Cinemax; HBO.
Fee: $21.00 monthly.
Video-On-Demand: No
Internet Service
Operational: No.
Broadband Service: Offers dial-up and DSL only; no cable modem service.
Telephone Service
None
Miles of Plant: 7.0 (coaxial); None (fiber optic). Homes passed: 540.
Manager: Steven W. Katka. Cable Chief Technician: Bruce Rosefelt.
City fee: None.
Ownership: Hector Communications Corp. (MSO).

MANKATO—Charter Communications, 1724 E Madison Ave, Mankato, MN 56001-5446. Phones: 507-388-3930; 507-289-8372 (Rochester office). Fax: 507-388-4172. E-mail: becky.vigesaa@chartercom.com. Web Site: http://www.charter.com. Also serves Belgrade Twp., Eagle Lake, Lime Twp., Mankato Twp., North Mankato, Skyline & South Bend Twp. ICA: MN0013.
TV Market Ranking: Below 100 (Belgrade Twp., Eagle Lake, Lime Twp., MANKATO, North Mankato, Skyline, South Bend Twp.). Franchise award date: November 1, 1956. Franchise expiration date: N.A. Began: April 1, 1957.
Channel capacity: N.A. Channels available but not in use: N.A.
Basic Service
Subscribers: 16,000.
Programming (received off-air): KAAL (ABC) Austin; KARE (NBC) Minneapolis; KEYC-TV (CBS, FOX) Mankato; KMSP-TV (FOX) Minneapolis; KSMQ-TV (PBS) Austin; KSTP-TV (ABC) St. Paul; KTCA-TV (PBS) St. Paul; WCCO-TV (CBS) Minneapolis; WFTC (MNT) Minneapolis; 22 FMs.
Programming (via satellite): C-SPAN; C-SPAN 2; Eternal Word TV Network; Home Shopping Network; Product Information Network; QVC; Trinity Broadcasting Network; TV Guide Network; WGN America.
Current originations: Educational Access; Government Access; Leased Access; Public Access.
Fee: $29.99 installation.
Expanded Basic Service 1
Subscribers: N.A.
Programming (via satellite): ABC Family Channel; AMC; Animal Planet; Arts & Entertainment; BET Networks; Bravo; Cartoon Network; CNBC; CNN; Comedy Central; Country Music TV; Discovery Channel; Disney Channel; E! Entertainment Television; ESPN; ESPN 2; Food Network; Fox News Channel; Fox Sports Net North; FX; G4; Golf Channel; GSN; Hallmark Channel; Headline News; HGTV; History Channel; Lifetime; MSNBC; MTV; MTV2; National Geographic Channel; Nickelodeon; Oxygen; ShopNBC; SoapNet; Speed Channel; Spike TV; Syfy; TBS Superstation; The Learning Channel; Toon Disney; Travel Channel; truTV; Turner Classic Movies; Turner Network TV; TV Land; Univision; USA Network; Versus; VH1; WE tv; Weather Channel.
Fee: $49.99 monthly.
Digital Basic Service
Subscribers: N.A.
Programming (received off-air): KARE (NBC) Minneapolis; KEYC-TV (CBS, FOX) Mankato; KMSP-TV (FOX) Minneapolis.
Programming (via satellite): BBC America; Bio; Bloomberg Television; Boomerang; CBS College Sports Network; CNN en Espanol; CNN International; Discovery Digital Networks; Do-It-Yourself; ESPN Classic Sports; ESPN HD; ESPNews; Fox College Sports Atlantic; Fox College Sports Central; Fox College Sports Pacific; Fox Movie Channel; Fox Soccer; Fuel TV; Fuse; GAS; HDNet; HDNet Movies; History Channel International; Independent Film Channel; Lifetime Movie Network; MTV Networks Digital Suite; Music Choice; NFL Network; Nick Jr.; Nick Too; NickToons TV; Outdoor Channel; Style Network; Sundance Channel; TV Guide Interactive Inc.
Digital Pay Service 1
Pay Units: N.A.
Programming (via satellite): Cinemax (multiplexed); Encore (multiplexed); Flix; HBO (multiplexed); HBO HD; Showtime (multiplexed); Showtime HD; Starz (multiplexed); The Movie Channel (multiplexed).
Video-On-Demand: Yes
Pay-Per-View
iN DEMAND (delivered digitally); NASCAR In Car (delivered digitally); NHL Center Ice (delivered digitally); MLB Extra Innings (delivered digitally); Playboy TV (delivered digitally); Spice Live (delivered digitally); Spice Platinum (delivered digitally); Hot Net Plus (delivered digitally); Spice Hot (delivered digitally).
Internet Service
Operational: Yes.
Broadband Service: Charter Pipeline.
Telephone Service
Digital: Operational
Fee: $29.99 monthly
Miles of Plant: 203.0 (coaxial); None (fiber optic). Homes passed: 24,000.
Vice President & General Manager: John Crowley. Technical Operations Director: Darin Helgeson. Operations Director: Craig Stensaas. Technical Operations Supervi-

sor: Jason Gruber. Marketing Director: Bill Haarstad. Office Manager: Becky Vigesaa.
City fee: 3% of gross.
Ownership: Charter Communications Inc. (MSO).

MAPLEVIEW—North American Communications Corp., PO Box 387, 211 Main St S, Hector, MN 55342-0387. Phones: 800-982-8038; 320-848-6781. Fax: 320-848-2323. E-mail: hcc@hcctel.net. Web Site: http://www.hectorcom.com. Also serves Lansing. ICA: MN0333.
TV Market Ranking: Below 100 (Lansing, MAPLEVIEW). Franchise award date: N.A. Franchise expiration date: N.A. Began: N.A.
Channel capacity: 54 (not 2-way capable). Channels available but not in use: 31.
Basic Service
Subscribers: 27.
Programming (received off-air): KAAL (ABC) Austin; KIMT (CBS, MNT) Mason City; KSMQ-TV (PBS) Austin; KYIN (PBS) Mason City.
Programming (via satellite): ABC Family Channel; AMC; Arts & Entertainment; CNN; Country Music TV; Discovery Channel; Disney Channel; ESPN; Fox Sports Net Midwest; Lifetime; Nickelodeon; QVC; Spike TV; TBS Superstation; Trinity Broadcasting Network; Turner Network TV; USA Network; WGN America.
Fee: $40.00 installation; $26.95 monthly; $3.50 converter; $25.00 additional installation.
Pay Service 1
Pay Units: 1.
Programming (via satellite): Cinemax.
Fee: $10.95 monthly.
Pay Service 2
Pay Units: 7.
Programming (via satellite): HBO.
Fee: $10.95 monthly.
Video-On-Demand: No
Internet Service
Operational: No.
Telephone Service
None
Miles of Plant: 4.0 (coaxial); None (fiber optic). Homes passed: 385. Total homes in franchised area: 385.
Manager: Matt Sparks. Chief Technician: George Honzay. Customer Service Supervisor: Patty Groshens.
Ownership: Hector Communications Corp. (MSO).

MARBLE—Marble Cable TV Systems, PO Box 38, 302 Alice Ave, Marble, MN 55764-0038. Phones: 218-247-7577; 218-247-7576. Fax: 218-247-7555. Also serves Calumet. ICA: MN0334.
TV Market Ranking: Below 100 (Calumet, MARBLE). Franchise award date: N.A. Franchise expiration date: N.A. Began: March 2, 1983.
Channel capacity: 60 (2-way capable). Channels available but not in use: 27.
Basic Service
Subscribers: 388.
Programming (received off-air): KBJR-TV (MNT, NBC) Superior; KDLH (CBS, CW) Duluth; KQDS-TV (FOX) Duluth; WCCO-TV (CBS) Minneapolis; WDIO-DT (ABC) Duluth; WDSE (PBS) Duluth.
Programming (via satellite): ABC Family Channel; AMC; Arts & Entertainment; Bravo; CNN; C-SPAN; Discovery Channel; Disney Channel; E! Entertainment Television; ESPN; ESPN 2; Food Network; Fox Movie Channel; Fox Sports Net; FX; HGTV; History Channel; Home Shopping Network; Lifetime; Nickelodeon; Outdoor Channel; SoapNet; Spike TV; Syfy; TBS Superstation; The Learning Channel; Toon Disney; truTV; Turner Classic Movies; Turner Network TV; TV Land; USA Network; Weather Channel; WGN America.
Current originations: Public Access.
Fee: $20.00 installation; $15.00 monthly.
Pay Service 1
Pay Units: 111.
Programming (via satellite): Showtime.
Fee: $10.00 monthly.
Video-On-Demand: No
Internet Service
Operational: No.
Telephone Service
None
Miles of Plant: 6.0 (coaxial); 390.0 (fiber optic).
Manager & Program Director: Tom Poore. Chief Technician: Mark Castellano.
Ownership: Marble Cable TV Systems.

MARSHALL—Charter Communications, 1108 E College Dr, Marshall, MN 56258-1902. Phones: 507-289-8372 (Rochester administrative office); 507-537-1541 (Local office). Fax: 507-537-1572. Web Site: http://www.charter.com. ICA: MN0030.
TV Market Ranking: Below 100 (MARSHALL COUNTY (PORTIONS)). Franchise award date: May 21, 1965. Franchise expiration date: N.A. Began: November 1, 1965.
Channel capacity: N.A. Channels available but not in use: N.A.
Basic Service
Subscribers: 2,600.
Programming (received off-air): KELO-TV (CBS, MNT) Sioux Falls; KEYC-TV (CBS, FOX) Mankato; KRWF (ABC) Redwood Falls; KSFY-TV (ABC) Sioux Falls; KWCM-TV (PBS) Appleton.
Programming (via microwave): KARE (NBC) Minneapolis; KMSP-TV (FOX) Minneapolis; KSTC-TV (IND) Minneapolis; KTCA-TV (PBS) St. Paul; WCCO-TV (CBS) Minneapolis; WFTC (MNT) Minneapolis; WUCW (CW) Minneapolis.
Programming (via satellite): C-SPAN; C-SPAN 2; INSP; QVC; TBS Superstation; Trinity Broadcasting Network; WGN America.
Current originations: Government Access; Educational Access; Public Access.
Fee: $29.99 installation.
Expanded Basic Service 1
Subscribers: N.A.
Programming (via satellite): ABC Family Channel; AMC; Animal Planet; Arts & Entertainment; BET Networks; Bravo; Cartoon Network; CNBC; CNN; Comedy Central; Country Music TV; Discovery Channel; Disney Channel; E! Entertainment Television; ESPN; ESPN 2; Eternal Word TV Network; Food Network; Fox News Channel; Fox Sports Net North; FX; G4; Golf Channel; GSN; Hallmark Channel; Headline News; HGTV; History Channel; Home Shopping Network; Lifetime; MSNBC; MTV; MTV2; National Geographic Channel; Nickelodeon; Oxygen; Speed Channel; Spike TV; Syfy; The Learning Channel; Travel Channel; truTV; Turner Classic Movies; Turner Network TV; TV Guide Network; TV Land; Univision; USA Network; Versus; VH1; WE tv; Weather Channel.
Fee: $47.99 monthly.
Digital Basic Service
Subscribers: N.A.
Programming (via microwave): KARE (NBC) Minneapolis; KMSP-TV (FOX) Minneapolis; WCCO-TV (CBS) Minneapolis.
Programming (via satellite): BBC America; Bio; Bloomberg Television; Boomerang; CBS College Sports Network; CNN International; Discovery Digital Networks; Do-It-Yourself; ESPN; ESPN Classic Sports; ESPNews; FitTV; Fox College Sports Atlantic; Fox College Sports Central; Fox College Sports Pacific; Fox Movie Channel; Fox Soccer; Fuel TV; Fuse; GAS; HDNet; HDNet Movies; History Channel International; Independent Film Channel; Lifetime Movie Network; MTV Networks Digital Suite; Music Choice; NFL Network; Nick Jr.; Nick Too; NickToons TV; Outdoor Channel; SoapNet; Style Network; Sundance Channel; Toon Disney; TV Guide Interactive Inc.
Digital Pay Service 1
Pay Units: N.A.
Programming (via satellite): Cinemax (multiplexed); Encore (multiplexed); HBO (multiplexed); HBO HD; Showtime (multiplexed); Showtime HD; Starz (multiplexed); The Movie Channel (multiplexed).
Video-On-Demand: Yes
Pay-Per-View
iN DEMAND (delivered digitally); NASCAR In Car (delivered digitally); NHL Center Ice (delivered digitally); MLB Extra Innings (delivered digitally); Playboy TV (delivered digitally); Spice Live (delivered digitally); Spice Platinum (delivered digitally); Spice Hot (delivered digitally).
Internet Service
Operational: Yes.
Broadband Service: Charter Pipeline.
Fee: $29.99 monthly.
Telephone Service
Digital: Operational
Miles of Plant: 150.0 (coaxial); None (fiber optic). Homes passed: 6,400.
Vice President & General Manager: John Crowley. Operations Director: Craig Stensaas. Technical Operations Director: Mark Abramo. Marketing Director: Bill Haarstad. Office Manager: Sue Olson.
State fee: 1% of gross. City fee: 3% of gross.
Ownership: Charter Communications Inc. (MSO).

MARSHALL—Knology, 5100 S Broadband Ln, Sioux Falls, SD 57108-2207. Phone: 605-965-9393. Fax: 605-965-7867. Web Site: http://www.knology.com. Also serves Currie, Slayton & Tracy. ICA: MN0288. **Note:** This system is an overbuild.
TV Market Ranking: Below 100 (MARSHALL COUNTY (PORTIONS), Tracy); Outside TV Markets (Currie, Slayton). Franchise award date: N.A. Franchise expiration date: N.A. Began: August 1, 1984.
Channel capacity: N.A. Channels available but not in use: N.A.
Basic Service
Subscribers: N.A. Included in Viborg SD
Programming (received off-air): KARE (NBC) Minneapolis; KDLT-TV (NBC) Sioux Falls; KELO-TV (CBS, MNT) Sioux Falls; KEYC-TV (CBS, FOX) Mankato; KMSP-TV (FOX) Minneapolis; KRWF (ABC) Redwood Falls; KSFY-TV (ABC) Sioux Falls; KSTC-TV (IND) Minneapolis; KTCA-TV (PBS) St. Paul; KTTW (FOX) Sioux Falls; KWCM-TV (PBS) Appleton; WCCO-TV (CBS) Minneapolis; WFTC (MNT) Minneapolis.
Programming (via satellite): ABC Family Channel; AMC; Animal Planet; Arts & Entertainment; Bravo; Cartoon Network; CNBC; CNN; Comedy Central; Country Music TV; C-SPAN; C-SPAN 2; CW+; Discovery Channel; Disney Channel; E! Entertainment Television; ESPN; ESPN 2; ESPN Classic Sports; Food Network; Fox News Channel; Fox Sports Net North; FX; Golf Channel; Hallmark Channel; Headline News; HGTV; History Channel; Lifetime; Lifetime Movie Network; MSNBC; MTV; MyNetworkTV Inc.; National Geographic Channel; NFL Network; Nickelodeon; QVC; Speed Channel; Spike TV; Syfy; TBS Superstation; The Learning Channel; Toon Disney; Travel Channel; Trinity Broadcasting Network; truTV; Turner Classic Movies; Turner Network TV; TV Guide Network; TV Land; USA Network; VH1; Weather Channel; WGN America.
Current originations: Government Access; Educational Access.
Fee: $35.00 installation; $20.66 monthly.
Digital Basic Service
Subscribers: N.A.
Programming (received off-air): KDLT-TV (NBC) Sioux Falls; KELO-TV (CBS, MNT) Sioux Falls; KSFY-TV (ABC) Sioux Falls; KTTW (FOX) Sioux Falls; QVC HD.
Programming (via satellite): Bandamax; BBC America; Bio; Bloomberg Television; Boomerang; CMT Pure Country; Cooking Channel; De Pelicula; De Pelicula Clasico; Discovery en Espanol; Discovery HD Theater; Discovery Health Channel; Discovery Kids Channel; Discovery Military Channel; Discovery Planet Green; Do-It-Yourself; ESPN 2 HD; ESPN Deportes; ESPN Deportes On Demand; ESPN HD; ESPN On Demand; ESPN U; ESPN U On Demand; ESPNews; Eternal Word TV Network; FitTV; Flix; Fox College Sports Atlantic; Fox College Sports Central; Fox College Sports Pacific; Fox Movie Channel; Fox Reality Channel; Fox Soccer; Fox Sports en Espanol; Fuse; G4; Gospel Music Channel; GSN; HDNet; HDNet Movies; History Channel International; ID Investigation Discovery; Independent Film Channel; Lifetime Real Women; MTV Hits; MTV Jams; MTV2; Music Choice; National Geographic Channel; National Geographic Channel HD Network; National Geographic Channel On Demand; NFL Network HD; Nick Jr.; NickToons TV; Outdoor Channel; Outdoor Channel 2 HD; Outdoor Channel On Demand; RFD-TV; Ritmoson Latino; Science Channel; Sleuth; Sleuth On Demand; SoapNet; Speed On Demand; Style Network; Sundance Channel; TBS in HD; TeenNick; Telehit; Turner Network TV HD; TV Guide SPOT; Universal HD; Versus; Versus HD; Versus On Demand; VH1 Classic; VH1 Soul; WAM! America's Kidz Network; WE tv.
Pay Service 1
Pay Units: 18.
Programming (via satellite): HBO (multiplexed); Showtime (multiplexed).
Fee: $10.00 installation; $9.95 monthly (each).
Digital Pay Service 1
Pay Units: N.A.
Programming (via satellite): Cinemax (multiplexed); Cinemax HD; Cinemax On Demand; Encore (multiplexed); HBO (multiplexed); HBO HD; HBO on Broadband; Showtime (multiplexed); Showtime HD; Showtime On Demand; Starz (multiplexed); Starz HDTV; Starz On Demand; The Movie Channel (multiplexed); The Movie Channel On Demand.
Video-On-Demand: Yes
Pay-Per-View
iN DEMAND (delivered digitally); Hot Choice (delivered digitally).
Internet Service
Operational: Yes.
Broadband Service: Knology.Net.
Fee: $29.95 installation; $39.95 monthly.
Telephone Service
Analog: Not Operational
Digital: Operational

Miles of Plant: 3.0 (coaxial); None (fiber optic). Homes passed: Included in Viborg SD
General Manager: Scott Schroeder. Technical Operations Manager: Daryl Elcock. Marketing Manager: Scott Determan.
Ownership: Knology Inc. (MSO).

MAYER—North American Communications Corp., PO Box 387, 211 Main St S, Hector, MN 55342-0387. Phones: 800-982-8038; 320-848-6781. Fax: 320-848-2323. E-mail: hcc@hcctel.net. Web Site: http://www.hectorcom.com. Also serves New Germany. ICA: MN0335.
TV Market Ranking: 13 (MAYER, New Germany). Franchise award date: June 1, 1988. Franchise expiration date: N.A. Began: January 1, 1989.
Channel capacity: 54 (not 2-way capable). Channels available but not in use: 28.
Basic Service
Subscribers: 82.
Programming (received off-air): KARE (NBC) Minneapolis; KMSP-TV (FOX) Minneapolis; KSTP-TV (ABC) St. Paul; KTCA-TV (PBS) St. Paul; KTCI-TV (PBS) St. Paul; WCCO-TV (CBS) Minneapolis; WFTC (MNT) Minneapolis; WUCW (CW) Minneapolis.
Programming (via satellite): ABC Family Channel; AMC; Arts & Entertainment; CNN; Country Music TV; Discovery Channel; Disney Channel; ESPN; Fox Sports Net Midwest; Lifetime; Nickelodeon; QVC; Spike TV; TBS Superstation; Trinity Broadcasting Network; Turner Network TV; USA Network; WGN America.
Fee: $40.00 installation; $26.95 monthly; $3.50 converter; $25.00 additional installation.
Pay Service 1
Pay Units: 2.
Programming (via satellite): Cinemax.
Fee: $10.95 monthly.
Pay Service 2
Pay Units: 6.
Programming (via satellite): HBO.
Fee: $10.95 monthly.
Video-On-Demand: No
Internet Service
Operational: No.
Broadband Service: Offers dial-up and DSL only; no cable modem service.
Telephone Service
None
Miles of Plant: 4.0 (coaxial); None (fiber optic). Homes passed: 337. Total homes in franchised area: 337.
Manager: Matt Sparks. Chief Technician: George Honzay. Customer Service Supervisor: Patty Groshens.
Ownership: Hector Communications Corp. (MSO).

MAZEPPA—Formerly served by US Cable of Coastal Texas LP. No longer in operation. ICA: MN0204.

MAZEPPA—Sleepy Eye Telephone. Formerly served by Goodhue, MN [MN0208]. This cable system has converted to IPTV, 111 Second Ave, Goodhue, MN 55027. Fax: 651-923-4010. E-mail: onlinecustservice@nu-telcom.net. Web Site: http://www.sleepyeyetel.net. ICA: MN5151.
Channel capacity: N.A. Channels available but not in use: N.A.
Internet Service
Operational: Yes.
Fee: $39.95 monthly.
Telephone Service
Digital: Operational
Ownership: Sleepy Eye Telephone Co.

MCGREGOR—Savage Communications Inc., PO Box 810, 206 Power Ave N, Hinckley, MN 55037. Phone: 320-384-7442. Fax: 320-384-7446. E-mail: rwsavage@scicable.com. Web Site: http://www.scibroadband.com. ICA: MN0229.
TV Market Ranking: Outside TV Markets (MCGREGOR). Franchise award date: May 31, 1988. Franchise expiration date: N.A. Began: August 1, 1990.
Channel capacity: 60 (2-way capable). Channels available but not in use: 5.
Basic Service
Subscribers: 102.
Programming (received off-air): KBJR-TV (MNT, NBC) Superior; KCCW-TV (CBS) Walker; KDLH (CBS, CW) Duluth; KQDS-TV (FOX) Duluth; WDIO-DT (ABC) Duluth; WDSE (PBS) Duluth; WPIX (CW, IND) New York.
Programming (via satellite): ABC Family Channel; Animal Planet; Arts & Entertainment; CNBC; CNN; Comedy Central; C-SPAN; Discovery Channel; Disney Channel; E! Entertainment Television; ESPN; ESPN 2; Fox News Channel; Fox Sports Net; Great American Country; Headline News; HGTV; History Channel; Lifetime; MTV; Nickelodeon; QVC; Spike TV; Syfy; TBS Superstation; The Learning Channel; Turner Classic Movies; Turner Network TV; TV Land; USA Network; VH1; Weather Channel; WGN America.
Fee: $39.95 installation; $33.95 monthly; $1.00 converter.
Pay Service 1
Pay Units: 12.
Programming (via satellite): Cinemax.
Fee: $9.95 monthly.
Pay Service 2
Pay Units: 14.
Programming (via satellite): HBO.
Fee: $10.95 monthly.
Video-On-Demand: No
Internet Service
Operational: No.
Telephone Service
None
Miles of Plant: 6.0 (coaxial); None (fiber optic). Homes passed: 197. Total homes in franchised area: 197.
Manager: Mike Danielson. Marketing Director: Ron Savage. Chief Technician: Pat McCabe. Customer Service Manager: Donna Erickson.
Ownership: Savage Communications Inc. (MSO).

MELROSE—Charter Communications, 3380 Northern Valley Pl NE, Rochester, MN 55906-3954. Phone: 507-289-8372. Fax: 507-285-6162. Web Site: http://www.charter.com. ICA: MN0095.
TV Market Ranking: Below 100 (MELROSE). Franchise award date: N.A. Franchise expiration date: N.A. Began: February 1, 1967.
Channel capacity: N.A. Channels available but not in use: N.A.
Basic Service
Subscribers: 803.
Programming (received off-air): KCCO-TV (CBS) Alexandria; KPXM-TV (ION) St. Cloud; KSAX (ABC) Alexandria; allband FM.
Programming (via microwave): KARE (NBC) Minneapolis; KMSP-TV (FOX) Minneapolis; KSTC-TV (IND) Minneapolis; KTCA-TV (PBS) St. Paul; WFTC (MNT) Minneapolis.
Programming (via satellite): C-SPAN; C-SPAN 2; Eternal Word TV Network; QVC; TBS Superstation.
Current originations: Public Access.
Fee: $29.99 installation.
Expanded Basic Service 1
Subscribers: 693.
Programming (received off-air): WCMN-LP St. Cloud-Sartell.
Programming (via satellite): ABC Family Channel; AMC; Animal Planet; Arts & Entertainment; Bravo; Cartoon Network; CNBC; CNN; Comedy Central; Country Music TV; Discovery Channel; Disney Channel; E! Entertainment Television; ESPN; ESPN 2; Food Network; Fox News Channel; Fox Sports Net North; FX; G4; Golf Channel; Hallmark Channel; Headline News; HGTV; History Channel; Home Shopping Network; Lifetime; MSNBC; MTV; MTV2; National Geographic Channel; Nickelodeon; Oxygen; Speed Channel; Spike TV; Syfy; The Learning Channel; Travel Channel; truTV; Turner Classic Movies; Turner Network TV; TV Land; Univision; USA Network; Versus; VH1; WE tv; Weather Channel.
Fee: $47.99 monthly.
Digital Basic Service
Subscribers: N.A.
Programming (via microwave): KARE (NBC) Minneapolis; KMSP-TV (FOX) Minneapolis; WCCO-TV (CBS) Minneapolis.
Programming (via satellite): BBC America; Bio; Bloomberg Television; Boomerang; CBS College Sports Network; CNN en Espanol; CNN International; Discovery Digital Networks; Do-It-Yourself; ESPN; ESPN Classic Sports; ESPNews; FitTV; Fox College Sports Atlantic; Fox College Sports Central; Fox College Sports Pacific; Fox Movie Channel; Fox Soccer; Fuel TV; Fuse; GAS; HDNet; HDNet Movies; History Channel International; Independent Film Channel; Lifetime Movie Network; MTV Networks Digital Suite; Music Choice; NFL Network; Nick Jr.; Nick Too; NickToons TV; Outdoor Channel; SoapNet; Style Network; Sundance Channel; Toon Disney; TV Guide Interactive Inc.
Digital Pay Service 1
Pay Units: N.A.
Programming (via satellite): Cinemax (multiplexed); Encore (multiplexed); HBO (multiplexed); HBO HD; Showtime (multiplexed); Showtime HD; Starz (multiplexed); The Movie Channel (multiplexed).
Video-On-Demand: Yes
Pay-Per-View
In Demand Previews (delivered digitally); iN DEMAND (delivered digitally); NASCAR In Car (delivered digitally); NHL Center Ice (delivered digitally); MLB Extra Innings (delivered digitally); Playboy TV (delivered digitally); Spice Live (delivered digitally); Spice Platinum (delivered digitally); Hot Net Plus (delivered digitally); Spice Hot (delivered digitally).
Internet Service
Operational: Yes.
Broadband Service: Charter Pipeline.
Fee: $29.99 monthly.
Telephone Service
Digital: Operational
Homes passed: 1,400. Miles of plant (coax) included in St. Cloud/Waite Park
Vice President & General Manager: John Crowley. Operations Director: Craig Stensaas. Technical Operations Director: Mark Abramo. Marketing Director: Bill Haarstad.
City fee: None.
Ownership: Charter Communications Inc. (MSO).

MENAGHA—West Central Telephone Assn. This cable system has converted to IPTV. See Menagha, MN [MN5130]. ICA: MN0118.

MENAHGA—West Central Telephone Assn. This cable system has converted to IPTV, 308 Frontage Rd, Sebeka, MN 56477. Phones: 800-945-2163; 218-837-5151. Web Site: http://www.wcta.net. ICA: MN5130.
TV Market Ranking: Below 100 (MENAHGA).
Channel capacity: N.A. Channels available but not in use: N.A.
Internet Service
Operational: Yes.
Telephone Service
Digital: Operational
Ownership: West Central Telephone Association.

MIDDLE RIVER—Sjoberg's Cable TV Inc., 315 Main Ave N, Thief River Falls, MN 56701-1905. Phones: 800-828-8808; 218-681-3044. Fax: 218-681-6801. E-mail: office1@mncable.net. Web Site: http://local.mncable.net. Also serves Spruce Valley Twp. ICA: MN0236.
TV Market Ranking: Below 100 (MIDDLE RIVER, Spruce Valley Twp.). Franchise award date: N.A. Franchise expiration date: N.A. Began: February 1, 1979.
Channel capacity: 78 (2-way capable). Channels available but not in use: 18.
Basic Service
Subscribers: 129.
Programming (received off-air): KBRR (FOX) Thief River Falls; KCPM (MNT) Grand Forks; KGFE (PBS) Grand Forks; various Canadian stations; WDAZ-TV (ABC, CW) Devils Lake; allband FM.
Programming (via microwave): KVLY-TV (NBC) Fargo; KXJB-TV (CBS) Valley City.
Programming (via satellite): CNN; ESPN; TBS Superstation.
Current originations: Public Access.
Fee: $25.00 installation; $10.00 monthly.
Expanded Basic Service 1
Subscribers: N.A.
Programming (via satellite): ABC Family Channel; Animal Planet; Arts & Entertainment; Cartoon Network; CNBC; Comedy Central; Country Music TV; C-SPAN; CW+; Discovery Channel; Disney Channel; E! Entertainment Television; ESPN 2; Food Network; Fox News Channel; Fox Sports Net; FX; HGTV; History Channel; Home Shopping Network; Lifetime; MSNBC; MTV; Nickelodeon; Spike TV; Syfy; The Learning Channel; Turner Classic Movies; Turner Network TV; TV Land; USA Network; VH1; Weather Channel; WGN America.
Fee: $23.71 monthly.
Digital Basic Service
Subscribers: N.A.
Programming (via satellite): AmericanLife TV Network; BBC America; Bio; Blackbelt TV; Bloomberg Television; Bravo; Chiller; CMT Pure Country; College Sports Television; Cooking Channel; Current; Daystar TV Network; Discovery Health Channel; Discovery Kids Channel; Discovery Military Channel; Discovery Planet Green; DMX Music; Do-It-Yourself; ESPN Classic Sports; ESPN U; ESPNews; Eternal Word TV Network; FitTV; Fox Business Channel; Fox College Sports Atlantic; Fox College Sports Central; Fox College Sports Pacific; Fox Movie Channel; Fox Reality Channel; Fox Soccer; G4; Golf Channel; Gospel Music Channel; Great American Country; GSN; Hallmark Channel; Halogen Network; Headline News; History Channel International; HorseRacing TV; ID Investigation Discovery; Independent Film Channel; Lifetime Movie Network; MTV Hits; MTV2; National Geographic Channel; Nick Jr.; NickToons

TV; Outdoor Channel; Ovation; Oxygen; PBS Kids Sprout; ReelzChannel; RFD-TV; Science Channel; ShopNBC; Sleuth; SoapNet; Speed Channel; Style Network; Sundance Channel; TBS in HD; TeenNick; Tennis Channel; The Sportsman Channel; The Word Network; Toon Disney; Trinity Broadcasting Network; TVG Network; Versus; VH1 Classic; VH1 Soul; WE tv.
Fee: $11.00 monthly.

Digital Expanded Basic Service
Subscribers: N.A.
Programming (received off-air): WDAZ-TV (ABC, CW) Devils Lake.
Programming (via satellite): Arts & Entertainment HD; CNN HD; Discovery Channel HD; ESPN 2 HD; ESPN HD; Food Network HD; FSN HD; HDNet; HDNet Movies; HGTV HD; History Channel HD; Outdoor Channel 2 HD; PBS HD; Speed HD; Syfy HD; Turner Network TV HD; Universal HD; USA Network HD; Versus HD.
Fee: $5.00 monthly; $5.00 converter.

Pay Service 1
Pay Units: 22.
Programming (via satellite): HBO.
Fee: $11.00 monthly.

Pay Service 2
Pay Units: N.A.
Programming (via satellite): Cinemax.
Fee: $9.00 monthly.

Digital Pay Service 1
Pay Units: N.A.
Programming (via satellite): Cinemax (multiplexed); Cinemax HD; Encore (multiplexed); HBO (multiplexed); HBO HD; Showtime (multiplexed); Starz (multiplexed); The Movie Channel (multiplexed).
Fee: $8.00 monthly (Starz/Encore), $9.00 monthly (Cinemax or Showtime/TMC), $11.00 monthly (HBO).

Video-On-Demand: No

Pay-Per-View
Addressable homes: 2.
iN DEMAND, Addressable: Yes; World Wrestling Entertainment Inc.

Internet Service
Operational: No.

Telephone Service
None

Miles of Plant: 6.0 (coaxial); 11.0 (fiber optic). Homes passed: 159. Total homes in franchised area: 160.
Manager: Richard J. Sjoberg. Chief Technician: Jerry Seim.
City fee: None.
Ownership: Sjoberg's Cable TV Inc. (MSO).

MINNEAPOLIS—Comcast Cable, 10 River Park Plz, St. Paul, MN 55107. Phone: 612-493-5000. Fax: 612-493-5837. Web Site: http://www.comcast.com. Also serves Bloomington, Carver, Carver County (unincorporated areas), Chaska, Eden Prairie, Edina, Fridley, Hopkins, Jordan, Madelia, Minnetonka, Montrose, New Prague, New Ulm, Richfield, Shakopee, St. Louis Park & Waverly. ICA: MN0001.
TV Market Ranking: 13 (Bloomington, Carver, Carver County (unincorporated areas), Chaska, Eden Prairie, Edina, Fridley, Hopkins, Jordan, MINNEAPOLIS, Minnetonka, Montrose, New Prague, Richfield, Shakopee, St. Louis Park); Below 100 (Madelia, New Ulm, Waverly). Franchise award date: January 1, 1982. Franchise expiration date: N.A. Began: December 1, 1983.
Channel capacity: 120 (operating 2-way). Channels available but not in use: N.A.

Basic Service
Subscribers: 230,000.
Programming (received off-air): KARE (NBC) Minneapolis; KMSP-TV (FOX) Minneapolis; KPXM-TV (ION) St. Cloud; KSTC-TV (IND) Minneapolis; KSTP-TV (ABC) St. Paul; KTCI-TV (PBS) St. Paul; WCCO-TV (CBS) Minneapolis; WFTC (MNT) Minneapolis; WUCW (CW) Minneapolis.
Programming (via satellite): CNN; Country Music TV; C-SPAN; C-SPAN 2; Eternal Word TV Network; Home Shopping Network; MTV2; QVC; ShopNBC; TBS Superstation; WGN America.
Current originations: Leased Access; Religious Access; Government Access; Educational Access; Public Access.
Fee: $44.83 installation; $10.57 monthly; $19.99 additional installation.

Expanded Basic Service 1
Subscribers: 140,550.
Programming (via satellite): ABC Family Channel; AMC; Animal Planet; Arts & Entertainment; BET Networks; Bravo; Cartoon Network; CNBC; Comedy Central; Discovery Channel; Disney Channel; E! Entertainment Television; ESPN; ESPN 2; ESPN Classic Sports; FitTV; Food Network; Fox News Channel; Fox Sports Net North; FX; Golf Channel; Hallmark Channel; Headline News; HGTV; History Channel; Lifetime; Lifetime Movie Network; MSNBC; MTV; National Geographic Channel; Nickelodeon; Oxygen; SoapNet; Spike TV; Style Network; Syfy; The Learning Channel; Travel Channel; truTV; Turner Classic Movies; Turner Network TV; TV Land; Univision; USA Network; Versus; VH1; WE tv; Weather Channel.
Fee: $36.38 monthly.

Digital Basic Service
Subscribers: 54,990.
Programming (via satellite): AmericanLife TV Network; America's Store; BBC America; Bio; Black Family Channel; Bloomberg Television; Boomerang; CCTV-4; Cooking Channel; Country Music TV; C-SPAN 3; Discovery Digital Networks; Discovery Kids Channel; Disney Channel; Do-It-Yourself; ESPNews; Fox Sports en Espanol; Fox Sports World; Fuse; G4; GAS; Great American Country; GSN; History Channel International; Independent Film Channel; Lifetime Real Women; Music Choice; Nick Jr.; Outdoor Channel; The Word Network; Toon Disney; VH1 Classic.
Fee: $9.95 monthly.

Digital Expanded Basic Service
Subscribers: 14,000.
Programming (via satellite): Encore Action; Fox Movie Channel; FSN Digital Atlantic; FSN Digital Central; FSN Digital Pacific; Fuel TV; Independent Film Channel; MoviePlex; NBA TV; Ovation; Speed Channel; Sundance Channel; Tennis Channel.
Fee: $8.90 monthly.

Digital Pay Service 1
Pay Units: 10,000.
Programming (via satellite): Cinemax (multiplexed).
Fee: $10.00 installation; $10.95 monthly.

Digital Pay Service 2
Pay Units: 4,200.
Programming (via satellite): Starz (multiplexed).
Fee: $10.00 installation; $10.95 monthly.

Digital Pay Service 3
Pay Units: 10,400.
Programming (via satellite): The Movie Channel (multiplexed).
Fee: $10.00 installation; $10.95 monthly.

Digital Pay Service 4
Pay Units: 11,600.
Programming (via satellite): HBO (multiplexed).
Fee: $10.00 installation; $10.95 monthly.

Digital Pay Service 5
Pay Units: 10,200.
Programming (via satellite): Showtime (multiplexed).
Fee: $10.00 installation; $10.95 monthly.

Digital Pay Service 6
Pay Units: N.A.
Programming (via satellite): Saigon Broadcasting TV Network; TV Asia; Zee TV USA.
Fee: $14.95 monthly (each).

Video-On-Demand: Yes

Pay-Per-View
Addressable homes: 54,990.
iN DEMAND (delivered digitally), Addressable: Yes; sports (delivered digitally); Shorteez (delivered digitally); Fresh (delivered digitally); Pleasure (delivered digitally); Playboy TV (delivered digitally).

Internet Service
Operational: Yes.
Subscribers: 29,309.
Broadband Service: Comcast High Speed Internet.
Fee: $100.00 installation; $42.95 monthly.

Telephone Service
Digital: Operational
Fee: $44.95 monthly

Miles of Plant: 2,828.0 (coaxial); 434.0 (fiber optic). Homes passed: 413,000.
Vice President: Bill Wright. Vice President, Sales & Marketing: Nick Kozel. Vice President, Government & Public Affairs: Kim Roden. Technical Operations Director: Mark Bisenius.
City fee: 5% of gross.
Ownership: Comcast Cable Communications Inc. (MSO).

MINNEOTA—US Cable, 402 Red River Ave N, Unit 5, Cold Spring, MN 56320-1521. Phones: 320-685-7113; 800-783-2356. Fax: 320-685-2816. E-mail: help@mn.uscable.com. Web Site: http://www.uscable.com. Also serves Clarkfield, Ghent, Lynd, Milroy, Morgan, Porter, Renville, Russell, Sacred Heart & Taunton. ICA: MN0336.
TV Market Ranking: Below 100 (Milroy, Morgan, Renville, Sacred Heart); Outside TV Markets (Clarkfield, Ghent, Lynd, MINNEOTA, Porter, Russell, Taunton). Franchise award date: N.A. Franchise expiration date: N.A. Began: February 1, 1973.
Channel capacity: N.A. Channels available but not in use: N.A.

Basic Service
Subscribers: N.A. Included in Cambridge
Programming (received off-air): KEYC-TV (CBS, FOX) Mankato; KSFY-TV (ABC) Sioux Falls; KWCM-TV (PBS) Appleton; allband FM.
Programming (via satellite): ABC Family Channel; Animal Planet; Arts & Entertainment; CNBC; CNN; Country Music TV; C-SPAN; Discovery Channel; ESPN; ESPN 2; Eternal Word TV Network; Food Network; Fox Sports Net; FX; Headline News; HGTV; History Channel; Home Shopping Network; Lifetime; MSNBC; MTV; Nickelodeon; Outdoor Channel; ShopNBC; Spike TV; TBS Superstation; The Learning Channel; Trinity Broadcasting Network; Turner Classic Movies; Turner Network TV; TV Land; USA Network; VH1; Weather Channel; WGN America.
Programming (via translator): KARE (NBC) Minneapolis; KMSP-TV (FOX) Minneapolis; KSTC-TV (IND) Minneapolis; KSTP-TV (ABC) St. Paul; KTCA-TV (PBS) St. Paul; WCCO-TV (CBS) Minneapolis; WFTC (MNT) Minneapolis.
Current originations: Public Access.
Fee: $40.95 monthly.

Digital Basic Service
Subscribers: N.A. Included in Cambridge
Programming (via satellite): BBC America; Bloomberg Television; Bravo; Discovery Digital Networks; DMX Music; ESPN Classic Sports; ESPNews; Fox Soccer; Fuse; G4; Golf Channel; GSN; Independent Film Channel; Lifetime Movie Network; MTV Networks Digital Suite; Nick Jr.; Sleuth; Speed Channel; Style Network; Syfy; TeenNick; Toon Disney; Versus; WE tv.
Fee: $8.95 monthly.

Digital Expanded Basic Service
Subscribers: N.A.
Programming (via satellite): Bio; CMT Pure Country; Encore (multiplexed); FitTV; Fox Movie Channel; Halogen Network; History Channel; Military History Channel.
Fee: $2.95 monthly.

Digital Pay Service 1
Pay Units: N.A. Included in Cambridge
Programming (via satellite): Cinemax (multiplexed); HBO (multiplexed); Showtime (multiplexed); Starz (multiplexed); The Movie Channel (multiplexed).
Fee: $6.95 monthly (Starz), $14.95 monthly (HBO, Cinemax, Showtime or TMC).

Video-On-Demand: No

Pay-Per-View
Fresh (delivered digitally); Playboy TV (delivered digitally); iN DEMAND (delivered digitally).

Internet Service
Operational: No.

Telephone Service
None

Homes passed: Included in Cambridge
General Manager: Steve Johnson. Customer Service Director: Jackie Torberg.
City fee: None.
Ownership: US Cable Corp. (MSO).; Comcast Cable Communications Inc. (MSO).

MINNESOTA CITY—Hiawatha Broadband. Formerly served by Winona, MN [MN0398]. This cable system has converted to IPTV, 58 Johnson St, Winona, MN 55987. Phone: 888-474-9995. Fax: 507-474-4000. E-mail: info@hbci.com. Web Site: http://www.hbci.com. ICA: MN5173.
Channel capacity: N.A. Channels available but not in use: N.A.

Internet Service
Operational: Yes.

Ownership: Hiawatha Broadband Communications Inc.

MINNESOTA LAKE—Bevcomm TV, PO Box 188, 208 Main St N, Minnesota Lake, MN 56068-0188. Phones: 888-846-8177; 507-462-3490. Fax: 507-462-3802. E-mail: info@bevcomm.net. Web Site: http://www.bevcomm.net. Also serves Delavan & Easton. ICA: MN0337.
TV Market Ranking: Below 100 (Delavan, Easton, MINNESOTA LAKE). Franchise award date: N.A. Franchise expiration date: N.A. Began: April 1, 1983.
Channel capacity: 33 (not 2-way capable). Channels available but not in use: 5.

Basic Service
Subscribers: 130.
Programming (received off-air): KAAL (ABC) Austin; KARE (NBC) Minneapolis; KEYC-TV (CBS, FOX) Mankato; KMSP-

TV (FOX) Minneapolis; KSTP-TV (ABC) St. Paul; KTCA-TV (PBS) St. Paul; KTTC (CW, NBC) Rochester; WCCO-TV (CBS) Minneapolis.
Programming (via satellite): ABC Family Channel; AMC; CNN; C-SPAN; Discovery Channel; Disney Channel; ESPN; Fox Sports Net Midwest; Lifetime; MTV; Nickelodeon; Spike TV; Syfy; TBS Superstation; Turner Network TV; USA Network; WGN America.
Current originations: Public Access.
Fee: $27.00 installation; $19.95 monthly; $.50 converter.

Pay Service 1
Pay Units: 87.
Programming (via satellite): HBO.
Fee: $10.00 installation; $9.50 monthly.

Video-On-Demand: No

Internet Service
Operational: No.

Telephone Service
None

Miles of Plant: 17.0 (coaxial); None (fiber optic). Homes passed: 307. Total homes in franchised area: 307.
Manager & Chief Technician: Scott Linde. Sales Manager: John Sonnek.
Ownership: BEVCOMM.

MONTEVIDEO—Charter Communications, 1108 E College Dr, Marshall, MN 56258-1902. Phones: 507-289-8372 (Rochester administrative office); 507-537-1541. Fax: 507-537-1572. Web Site: http://www.charter.com. ICA: MN0051.
TV Market Ranking: Outside TV Markets (MONTEVIDEO). Franchise award date: March 20, 1962. Franchise expiration date: N.A. Began: November 1, 1965.
Channel capacity: N.A. Channels available but not in use: N.A.

Basic Service
Subscribers: 2,000.
Programming (received off-air): KWCM-TV (PBS) Appleton.
Programming (via microwave): KARE (NBC) Minneapolis; KCCO-TV (CBS) Alexandria; KMSP-TV (FOX) Minneapolis; KSAX (ABC) Alexandria; KSTC-TV (IND) Minneapolis; KSTP-TV (ABC) St. Paul; KTCA-TV (PBS) St. Paul; WCCO-TV (CBS) Minneapolis; WFTC (MNT) Minneapolis.
Programming (via satellite): C-SPAN; C-SPAN 2; Eternal Word TV Network; QVC; TBS Superstation; Trinity Broadcasting Network; WGN America.
Current originations: Public Access.
Fee: $29.99 installation.

Expanded Basic Service 1
Subscribers: N.A.
Programming (received off-air): WCMN-LP St. Cloud-Sartell.
Programming (via satellite): ABC Family Channel; AMC; Animal Planet; Arts & Entertainment; Bravo; Cartoon Network; CNBC; CNN; Comedy Central; Country Music TV; Discovery Channel; Disney Channel; E! Entertainment Television; ESPN; ESPN 2; Food Network; Fox News Channel; Fox Sports Net North; FX; G4; Golf Channel; Hallmark Channel; Headline News; HGTV; History Channel; Home Shopping Network; Lifetime; MSNBC; MTV; MTV2; National Geographic Channel; Nickelodeon; Oxygen; Speed Channel; Spike TV; Syfy; The Learning Channel; Travel Channel; truTV; Turner Classic Movies; Turner Network TV; TV Land; Univision; USA Network; Versus; VH1; WE tv; Weather Channel.
Fee: $47.99 monthly.

Digital Basic Service
Subscribers: N.A.
Programming (via microwave): KARE (NBC) Minneapolis; KMSP-TV (FOX) Minneapolis; WCCO-TV (CBS) Minneapolis.
Programming (via satellite): BBC America; Bio; Bloomberg Television; Boomerang; CBS College Sports Network; CNN en Espanol; CNN International; Discovery Digital Networks; Do-It-Yourself; ESPN; ESPN Classic Sports; ESPNews; FitTV; Fox College Sports Atlantic; Fox College Sports Central; Fox College Sports Pacific; Fox Movie Channel; Fox Soccer; Fuel TV; Fuse; GAS; HDNet; HDNet Movies; History Channel International; Independent Film Channel; Lifetime Movie Network; MTV Networks Digital Suite; Music Choice; NFL Network; Nick Jr.; Nick Too; NickToons TV; Outdoor Channel; SoapNet; Style Network; Sundance Channel; Toon Disney; TV Guide Interactive Inc.

Digital Pay Service 1
Pay Units: N.A.
Programming (via satellite): Cinemax (multiplexed); Encore (multiplexed); HBO (multiplexed); HBO HD; Showtime (multiplexed); Showtime HD; Starz (multiplexed); The Movie Channel (multiplexed).

Video-On-Demand: Yes

Pay-Per-View
iN DEMAND (delivered digitally); NASCAR In Car (delivered digitally); NHL Center Ice (delivered digitally); MLB Extra Innings (delivered digitally); Playboy TV (delivered digitally); Spice Live (delivered digitally); Spice Platinum (delivered digitally); Hot Net Plus (delivered digitally); Spice Hot (delivered digitally).

Internet Service
Operational: Yes. Began: December 17, 2002.
Broadband Service: Charter Pipeline.
Fee: $29.99 monthly.

Telephone Service
Digital: Operational

Miles of Plant: 33.0 (coaxial); None (fiber optic). Homes passed: 2,900.
Vice President & General Manager: John Crowley. Operations Director: Craig Stensaas. Technical Operations Director: Mark Abramo. Marketing Director: Bill Haarstad. Office Manager: Sue Olson.
State fee: 1% of gross. City fee: 5% of gross.
Ownership: Charter Communications Inc. (MSO).

MONTGOMERY—Mediacom, PO Box 110, 1504 2nd St SE, Waseca, MN 56093. Phones: 800-332-0245; 507-835-2356. Fax: 507-835-4567. Web Site: http://www.mediacomcable.com. ICA: MN0338.
TV Market Ranking: Below 100 (MONTGOMERY). Franchise award date: N.A. Franchise expiration date: N.A. Began: January 1, 1988.
Channel capacity: 66 (operating 2-way). Channels available but not in use: N.A.

Basic Service
Subscribers: N.A.
Programming (received off-air): KARE (NBC) Minneapolis; KEYC-TV (CBS, FOX) Mankato; KMSP-TV (FOX) Minneapolis; KPXM-TV (ION) St. Cloud; KSTC-TV (IND) Minneapolis; KSTP-TV (ABC) St. Paul; KTCA-TV (PBS) St. Paul; KTCI-TV (PBS) St. Paul; WCCO-TV (CBS) Minneapolis; WFTC (MNT) Minneapolis; WUCW (CW) Minneapolis.
Programming (via satellite): C-SPAN; C-SPAN 2; QVC; TV Guide Network; Weather Channel; WGN America.
Fee: $14.95 monthly.

Expanded Basic Service 1
Subscribers: N.A.
Programming (received off-air): WUMN-CA Minneapolis.
Programming (via satellite): ABC Family Channel; AMC; Animal Planet; Arts & Entertainment; BET Networks; Bravo; Cartoon Network; CNBC; CNN; Comedy Central; Country Music TV; Discovery Channel; Disney Channel; E! Entertainment Television; ESPN; ESPN 2; Eternal Word TV Network; Fox Movie Channel; Fox News Channel; Fox Sports Net North; FX; Hallmark Channel; Headline News; HGTV; History Channel; INSP; Lifetime; MSNBC; MTV; Nickelodeon; SoapNet; Speed Channel; Spike TV; Syfy; TBS Superstation; The Learning Channel; Travel Channel; Trinity Broadcasting Network; truTV; Turner Classic Movies; Turner Network TV; TV Land; USA Network; VH1; WE tv.

Digital Basic Service
Subscribers: N.A.
Programming (received off-air): KARE (NBC) Minneapolis; KSTP-TV (ABC) St. Paul; WCCO-TV (CBS) Minneapolis.
Programming (via satellite): AmericanLife TV Network; BBC America; Bio; Bloomberg Television; Canal 52MX; CCTV-9 (CCTV International); Cine Latino; CNN en Espanol; Discovery en Espanol; Discovery HD Theater; Discovery Health Channel; Discovery Home Channel; Discovery Kids Channel; Discovery Military Channel; ESPN 2 HD; ESPN HD; ESPNews; FitTV; Fox Soccer; Fox Sports en Espanol; Fuse; G4; Golf Channel; GSN; Halogen Network; HDNet; HDNet Movies; History Channel en Espanol; History Channel International; ID Investigation Discovery; Independent Film Channel; Lifetime Movie Network; MTV Hits; MTV Tres; MTV2; Music Choice; National Geographic Channel; Nick Jr.; NickToons TV; Outdoor Channel; Science Channel; Sleuth; Style Network; TeenNick; Toon Disney en Espanol; Universal HD; VH1 Classic.

Digital Pay Service 1
Pay Units: N.A.
Programming (via satellite): Cinemax (multiplexed); Encore (multiplexed); Flix; HBO (multiplexed); HBO HD; Showtime (multiplexed); Showtime HD; Starz (multiplexed); Starz HDTV; Sundance Channel; The Movie Channel (multiplexed); The Movie Channel HD.
Fee: $9.95 monthly (each).

Video-On-Demand: Yes

Pay-Per-View
iN DEMAND (delivered digitally); Pleasure (delivered digitally); Playboy TV (delivered digitally); Penthouse TV (delivered digitally); Ten Clips (delivered digitally).

Internet Service
Operational: Yes.
Broadband Service: Mediacom High Speed Internet.
Fee: $99.00 installation; $40.00 monthly.

Telephone Service
Digital: Operational

Vice President: Bill Jensen. Engineering Manager: Kraig Kaiser. Marketing & Sales Manager: Lori Huberty.
Ownership: Mediacom LLC (MSO).

MONTROSE—Time Warner Cable. Now served by MINNEAPOLIS, MN [MN0001]. ICA: MN0339.

MOOSE LAKE—Mediacom, PO Box 110, 1504 2nd St SE, Waseca, MN 56093. Phone: 507-835-5975. Fax: 507-835-4567. Web Site: http://www.mediacomcable.com. Also serves Moose Lake Twp. & Windermere Twp. ICA: MN0136.
TV Market Ranking: Outside TV Markets (MOOSE LAKE, Moose Lake Twp., Windermere Twp.). Franchise award date: September 16, 1982. Franchise expiration date: N.A. Began: August 1, 1983.
Channel capacity: N.A. Channels available but not in use: N.A.

Basic Service
Subscribers: 407.
Programming (received off-air): KBJR-TV (MNT, NBC) Superior; KDLH (CBS, CW) Duluth; KQDS-TV (FOX) Duluth; WCCO-TV (CBS) Minneapolis; WDIO-DT (ABC) Duluth; WDSE (PBS) Duluth; allband FM.
Programming (via satellite): C-SPAN; C-SPAN 2; CW+; Eternal Word TV Network; Home Shopping Network; INSP; ION Television; MyNetworkTV Inc.; TV Guide Network; WGN America.
Fee: $25.00 installation; $16.95 monthly; $15.00 additional installation.

Expanded Basic Service 1
Subscribers: N.A.
Programming (via satellite): ABC Family Channel; AMC; Animal Planet; Arts & Entertainment; Bravo; Cartoon Network; CNBC; CNN; Comedy Central; Country Music TV; Discovery Channel; Disney Channel; E! Entertainment Television; ESPN; ESPN 2; ESPN Classic Sports; Fox Movie Channel; Fox News Channel; Fox Sports Net North; FX; Hallmark Channel; Headline News; HGTV; History Channel; Lifetime; MSNBC; MTV; Nickelodeon; Outdoor Channel; QVC; Speed Channel; Spike TV; Syfy; TBS Superstation; The Learning Channel; Travel Channel; truTV; Turner Classic Movies; Turner Network TV; TV Land; USA Network; VH1; WE tv; Weather Channel.

Digital Basic Service
Subscribers: N.A.
Programming (received off-air): KBJR-TV (MNT, NBC) Superior; KDLH (CBS, CW) Duluth; WDIO-DT (ABC) Duluth.
Programming (via satellite): AmericanLife TV Network; BBC America; Bio; Bloomberg Television; Discovery HD Theater; Discovery Health Channel; Discovery Home Channel; Discovery Kids Channel; Discovery Military Channel; DMX Music; ESPN 2 HD; ESPN HD; ESPNews; FitTV; Fox Soccer; Fuse; G4; Golf Channel; GSN; Halogen Network; HDNet; HDNet Movies; History Channel International; ID Investigation Discovery; Independent Film Channel; Lifetime Movie Network; MTV Hits; MTV2; National Geographic Channel; Nick Jr.; NickToons TV; Science Channel; Sleuth; Style Network; TeenNick; TVG Network; Universal HD; VH1 Classic.

Digital Pay Service 1
Pay Units: 81.
Programming (via satellite): Cinemax (multiplexed); Encore (multiplexed); Flix; HBO (multiplexed); HBO HD; Showtime (multiplexed); Showtime HD; Starz (multiplexed); Starz HDTV; Sundance Channel; The Movie Channel (multiplexed); The Movie Channel HD.
Fee: $15.00 installation; $8.95 monthly (Showtime), $11.95 monthly (HBO).

Video-On-Demand: No

Pay-Per-View
iN DEMAND (delivered digitally); Spice: Xcess (delivered digitally); Penthouse TV (delivered digitally); Fresh (delivered digitally); Ten Clips (delivered digitally); Playboy TV (delivered digitally).

Internet Service
Operational: Yes.
Broadband Service: Mediacom High Speed Internet.
Fee: $99.00 installation; $40.00 monthly.
Telephone Service
Digital: Operational
Miles of Plant: 15.0 (coaxial); None (fiber optic). Homes passed: 587.
Vice President: Bill Jensen. Engineering Manager: Kraig Kaiser. Marketing & Sales Director: Lori Huberty.
City fee: 3% of basic gross.
Ownership: Mediacom LLC (MSO).

MORRIS—Now served by CHOKIO, MN [MN0210]. ICA: MN0340.

MORRISTOWN—Cannon Valley Cablevision, PO Box 337, 202 N First St, Bricelyn, MN 56014. Phones: 507-653-4444 (Administrative office); 800-390-6562; 507-685-4321. Fax: 507-653-4449. E-mail: cvtel@cvtel.net. Web Site: http://www.cvtel.net. Also serves Warsaw. ICA: MN0167.
TV Market Ranking: Below 100 (MORRISTOWN, Warsaw). Franchise award date: N.A. Franchise expiration date: N.A. Began: August 1, 1984.
Channel capacity: 57 (operating 2-way). Channels available but not in use: 4.
Basic Service
Subscribers: 350.
Programming (received off-air): KARE (NBC) Minneapolis; KEYC-TV (CBS, FOX) Mankato; KMSP-TV (FOX) Minneapolis; KSTC-TV (IND) Minneapolis; KSTP-TV (ABC) St. Paul; KTCA-TV (PBS) St. Paul; WCCO-TV (CBS) Minneapolis; WFTC (MNT) Minneapolis; WUCW (CW) Minneapolis.
Programming (via satellite): ABC Family Channel; AMC; Animal Planet; Arts & Entertainment; CNBC; CNN; Comedy Central; Country Music TV; C-SPAN; Discovery Channel; Disney Channel; ESPN; ESPN 2; ESPN Classic Sports; Food Network; Fox News Channel; Fox Sports Net North; FX; Hallmark Channel; HGTV; History Channel; Home Shopping Network; Lifetime; MSNBC; MTV; Nickelodeon; Spike TV; Syfy; TBS Superstation; The Learning Channel; truTV; Turner Classic Movies; Turner Network TV; TV Land; USA Network; Versus; VH1; Weather Channel; WGN America.
Fee: $40.00 installation; $39.95 monthly; $25.00 additional installation.
Digital Basic Service
Subscribers: N.A.
Programming (via satellite): BBC America; Bio; Bloomberg Television; Bravo; Discovery Digital Networks; DMX Music; ESPN 2; ESPN Classic Sports; ESPNews; Fox Soccer; Fuse; G4; GAS; Golf Channel; GSN; Halogen Network; HGTV; History Channel; History Channel International; Independent Film Channel; MTV Networks Digital Suite; National Geographic Channel; Nick Jr.; NickToons TV; Outdoor Channel; Speed Channel; Style Network; Syfy; Toon Disney; Trinity Broadcasting Network; Trio; Turner Classic Movies; Versus; WE tv.
Fee: $8.00 monthly.
Pay Service 1
Pay Units: 40.
Programming (via satellite): Cinemax.
Fee: $7.50 installation; $12.95 monthly.
Pay Service 2
Pay Units: 62.
Programming (via satellite): HBO.
Fee: $7.50 installation; $12.95 monthly.
Pay Service 3
Pay Units: 37.
Programming (via satellite): Showtime.
Fee: $7.50 installation; $12.95 monthly.
Digital Pay Service 1
Pay Units: N.A.
Programming (via satellite): Cinemax (multiplexed); Encore; Flix; HBO (multiplexed); Showtime (multiplexed); Starz; The Movie Channel (multiplexed).
Fee: $11.95 monthly (Starz/Encore), $12.95 monthly (Showtime/TMC), $15.95 monthly (HBO/Cinemax).
Video-On-Demand: No
Pay-Per-View
Fresh (delivered digitally); Playboy TV (delivered digitally); Hot Choice (delivered digitally); iN DEMAND (delivered digitally).
Internet Service
Operational: Yes, Both DSL & dial-up.
Broadband Service: Cannon Valley.
Fee: $26.95 monthly.
Telephone Service
None
Miles of Plant: 18.0 (coaxial); None (fiber optic). Homes passed: 521. Total homes in franchised area: 521.
President: Scott Johnson. Operations Manager: Aaron Johnson. Office Manager: Loretta Johnson.
City fee: 3% of gross.
Ownership: BEVCOMM (MSO).

MOTLEY—Savage Communications Inc. Now served by PILLAGER, MN [MN0230]. ICA: MN0217.

MOUNTAIN LAKE—Mediacom, PO Box 110, 1504 2nd St SE, Waseca, MN 56093. Phone: 507-835-2356. Fax: 507-835-4597. Web Site: http://www.mediacomcable.com. ICA: MN0126.
TV Market Ranking: Outside TV Markets (MOUNTAIN LAKE). Franchise award date: N.A. Franchise expiration date: N.A. Began: March 1, 1973.
Channel capacity: N.A. Channels available but not in use: N.A.
Basic Service
Subscribers: N.A.
Programming (received off-air): KEYC-TV (CBS, FOX) Mankato; KPXM-TV (ION) St. Cloud; KSTC-TV (IND) Minneapolis; KTCI-TV (PBS) St. Paul; WFTC (MNT) Minneapolis; WUCW (CW) Minneapolis; allband FM.
Programming (via satellite): C-SPAN; C-SPAN 2; TV Guide Network; WGN America.
Programming (via translator): KARE (NBC) Minneapolis; KMSP-TV (FOX) Minneapolis; KSTP-TV (ABC) St. Paul; KTCA-TV (PBS) St. Paul; WCCO-TV (CBS) Minneapolis.
Fee: $27.50 installation; $14.95 monthly.
Expanded Basic Service 1
Subscribers: N.A.
Programming (received off-air): WUMN-CA Minneapolis.
Programming (via satellite): ABC Family Channel; AMC; Animal Planet; Arts & Entertainment; BET Networks; Bravo; Cartoon Network; CNBC; CNN; Comedy Central; Country Music TV; Discovery Channel; Disney Channel; E! Entertainment Television; ESPN; ESPN 2; Eternal Word TV Network; Food Network; Fox Movie Channel; Fox News Channel; Fox Sports Net North; FX; Hallmark Channel; Headline News; HGTV; History Channel; INSP; Lifetime; MSNBC; MTV; Nickelodeon; QVC; SoapNet; Speed Channel; Spike TV; Syfy; TBS Superstation; The Learning Channel; Travel Channel; Trinity Broadcasting Network; truTV; Turner Classic Movies; Turner Network TV; TV Land; USA Network; VH1; WE tv; Weather Channel.
Digital Basic Service
Subscribers: N.A.
Programming (received off-air): KARE (NBC) Minneapolis; KSTP-TV (ABC) St. Paul; KTCI-TV (PBS) St. Paul.
Programming (via satellite): AmericanLife TV Network; BBC America; Bio; Bloomberg Television; Canales N; Discovery Digital Networks; Discovery HD Theater; DMX Music; ESPN; ESPN 2; ESPNews; FitTV; Fox Soccer; Fuse; G4; GAS; Golf Channel; GSN; Halogen Network; HDNet; HDNet Movies; History Channel International; Independent Film Channel; Lifetime Movie Network; Lime; MTV Networks Digital Suite; National Geographic Channel; Nick Jr.; NickToons TV; Outdoor Channel; Sleuth; Style Network; TVG Network; Universal HD.
Digital Pay Service 1
Pay Units: N.A.
Programming (via satellite): Cinemax (multiplexed); Encore (multiplexed); Flix (multiplexed); HBO (multiplexed); HBO; Showtime (multiplexed); Showtime; Starz (multiplexed); Starz HDTV; Sundance Channel (multiplexed); The Movie Channel (multiplexed); The Movie Channel.
Video-On-Demand: Yes
Pay-Per-View
ESPN (delivered digitally); Fresh (delivered digitally); Shorteez (delivered digitally); Playboy TV (delivered digitally); Pleasure (delivered digitally); Ten Clips (delivered digitally).
Internet Service
Operational: Yes.
Broadband Service: Mediacom High Speed Internet.
Telephone Service
Digital: Operational
Miles of Plant: 10.0 (coaxial); None (fiber optic). Homes passed: 700. Total homes in franchised area: 700.
Vice President: Bill Jensen. Engineering Manager: Kraig Kaiser. Marketing & Sales Director: Lori Huberty.
City fee: None.
Ownership: Mediacom LLC (MSO).

NEVIS TWP.—ACS Video. Formerly served by Perham, MN [MN0050]. This cable system has converted to IPTV, 150 Second St SW, Perham, MN 56573. Phone: 866-937-4227. E-mail: answers@arvig.com. Web Site: http://www.arvig.com. ICA: MN5206.
TV Market Ranking: Below 100 (NEVIS TWP.).
Channel capacity: N.A. Channels available but not in use: N.A.
Internet Service
Operational: Yes.
Telephone Service
Digital: Operational
Ownership: Arvig Communication Systems.

NEW AUBURN—North American Communications Corp., PO Box 387, 211 Main St S, Hector, MN 55342-0387. Phones: 800-982-8038; 320-848-6781. Fax: 320-848-2323. E-mail: hcc@hcctel.net. Web Site: http://www.hectorcom.com. ICA: MN0248.
TV Market Ranking: Outside TV Markets (NEW AUBURN). Franchise award date: N.A. Franchise expiration date: N.A. Began: February 1, 1990.
Channel capacity: 54 (not 2-way capable). Channels available but not in use: 29.
Basic Service
Subscribers: 45.
Programming (received off-air): KARE (NBC) Minneapolis; KEYC-TV (CBS, FOX) Mankato; KMSP-TV (FOX) Minneapolis; KSTP-TV (ABC) St. Paul; KTCA-TV (PBS) St. Paul; WCCO-TV (CBS) Minneapolis; WFTC (MNT) Minneapolis; WUCW (CW) Minneapolis.
Programming (via satellite): ABC Family Channel; AMC; Arts & Entertainment; CNN; Country Music TV; Discovery Channel; Disney Channel; ESPN; Fox Sports Net Midwest; ION Television; Nickelodeon; QVC; Spike TV; TBS Superstation; Trinity Broadcasting Network; Turner Network TV; USA Network; WGN America.
Fee: $40.00 installation; $26.95 monthly; $3.50 converter; $25.00 additional installation.
Pay Service 1
Pay Units: 1.
Programming (via satellite): Cinemax.
Fee: $10.95 monthly.
Pay Service 2
Pay Units: 6.
Programming (via satellite): HBO.
Fee: $10.95 monthly.
Video-On-Demand: No
Internet Service
Operational: No.
Telephone Service
None
Miles of Plant: 4.0 (coaxial); None (fiber optic). Homes passed: 141. Total homes in franchised area: 141.
Manager: Matt Sparks. Chief Technician: George Honzay. Customer Service Supervisor: Patty Groshens.
Ownership: Hector Communications Corp. (MSO).

NEW MARKET—North American Communications Corp., PO Box 387, 211 Main St S, Hector, MN 55342-0387. Phones: 800-982-8038; 320-848-6781. Fax: 320-848-2323. E-mail: hcc@hcctel.net. Web Site: http://www.hectorcom.com. ICA: MN0223.
TV Market Ranking: 13 (NEW MARKET). Franchise award date: N.A. Franchise expiration date: N.A. Began: June 1, 1992.
Channel capacity: 36 (not 2-way capable). Channels available but not in use: 8.
Basic Service
Subscribers: 30.
Programming (received off-air): KARE (NBC) Minneapolis; KMSP-TV (FOX) Minneapolis; KSTP-TV (ABC) St. Paul; KTCA-TV (PBS) St. Paul; KTCI-TV (PBS) St. Paul; WCCO-TV (CBS) Minneapolis; WFTC (MNT) Minneapolis; WUCW (CW) Minneapolis.
Programming (via satellite): ABC Family Channel; AMC; Arts & Entertainment; CNN; Country Music TV; Discovery Channel; Disney Channel; ESPN; Fox Sports Net Midwest; ION Television; Lifetime; MTV; Nickelodeon; QVC; Spike TV; TBS Superstation; Trinity Broadcasting Network; Turner Network TV; USA Network; WGN America.
Fee: $40.00 installation; $26.95 monthly; $3.50 converter; $25.00 additional installation.
Pay Service 1
Pay Units: 2.
Programming (via satellite): Cinemax.
Fee: $10.95 monthly.
Pay Service 2
Pay Units: 1.
Programming (via satellite): HBO.
Fee: $10.95 monthly.
Video-On-Demand: No

Internet Service
Operational: No.
Broadband Service: Offers dial-up and DSL only; no cable modem service.
Telephone Service
None
Miles of Plant: 10.0 (coaxial); None (fiber optic). Homes passed: 312. Total homes in franchised area: 312.
Manager: Matt Sparks. Chief Technician: George Honzay. Customer Service Supervisor: Patty Groshens.
Ownership: Hector Communications Corp. (MSO).

NEW PRAGUE—Time Warner Cable. Now served by MINNEAPOLIS, MN [MN0001]. ICA: MN0341.

NEW ULM—NU-Telecom. Formerly [MN0285]. This cable system has converted to IPTV, PO Box 697, 27 N Minnesota, New Ulm, MN 56073-0697. Phones: 800-893-1856; 507-723-4211. Fax: 507-723-4377. E-mail: on-linecustservice@nu-telcom.net. Web Site: http://www.nutelecom.net. ICA: MN5117.
TV Market Ranking: Below 100 (NEW ULM). Franchise award date: N.A. Franchise expiration date: N.A. Began: N.A.
Channel capacity: N.A. Channels available but not in use: N.A.
Video-On-Demand: No
Internet Service
Operational: Yes.
Telephone Service
Digital: Operational
President & Chief Executive Officer: Bill Otis.
Franchise fee: None.
Ownership: NU-Telecom (MSO).

NEW ULM—NU-Telecom. This cable system has converted to IPTV. See New Ulm, MN [MN5117], MN. ICA: MN0285.

NEW ULM—Time Warner Cable. Now served by MINNEAPOLIS, MN [MN0001]. ICA: MN0034.

NEWFOLDEN—Sjoberg's Cable TV Inc., 315 Main Ave N, Thief River Falls, MN 56701-1905. Phones: 800-828-8808; 218-681-3044. Fax: 218-681-6801. Web Site: http://trf.mncable.net. ICA: MN0249.
TV Market Ranking: Below 100 (NEWFOLDEN). Franchise award date: N.A. Franchise expiration date: N.A. Began: N.A.
Channel capacity: 68 (operating 2-way). Channels available but not in use: 8.
Basic Service
Subscribers: 123.
Programming (received off-air): KBRR (FOX) Thief River Falls; KCPM (MNT) Grand Forks; KGFE (PBS) Grand Forks; KVLY-TV (NBC) Fargo; KXJB-TV (CBS) Valley City; WDAZ-TV (ABC, CW) Devils Lake.
Programming (via satellite): CNN; ESPN; TBS Superstation; various Canadian stations.
Current originations: Public Access.
Fee: $25.00 installation; $10.00 monthly.
Expanded Basic Service 1
Subscribers: N.A.
Programming (via satellite): ABC Family Channel; Animal Planet; Arts & Entertainment; Cartoon Network; CNBC; Comedy Central; Country Music TV; C-SPAN; CW+; Discovery Channel; Disney Channel; E! Entertainment Television; ESPN 2; Food Network; Fox News Channel; Fox Sports Net; FX; HGTV; History Channel; Home Shopping Network; Lifetime; MSNBC; MTV; Nickelodeon; Spike TV; Syfy; The Learning Channel; Turner Classic Movies; Turner Network TV; TV Land; USA Network; VH1; Weather Channel; WGN America.
Fee: $23.71 monthly.
Digital Basic Service
Subscribers: N.A.
Programming (via satellite): AmericanLife TV Network; BBC America; Bio; Blackbelt TV; Bloomberg Television; Bravo; CBS College Sports Network; Chiller; CMT Pure Country; Cooking Channel; Current; Daystar TV Network; Discovery Health Channel; Discovery Kids Channel; Discovery Military Channel; Discovery Planet Green; DMX Music; Do-It-Yourself; ESPN Classic Sports; ESPN U; ESPNews; Eternal Word TV Network; FitTV; Fox Business Channel; Fox College Sports Atlantic; Fox College Sports Central; Fox College Sports Pacific; Fox Movie Channel; Fox Reality Channel; Fox Soccer; G4; Golf Channel; Gospel Music TV; Great American Country; GSN; Hallmark Channel; Halogen Network; Headline News; History Channel International; HorseRacing TV; ID Investigation Discovery; Independent Film Channel; Lifetime Movie Network; MTV Hits; MTV2; National Geographic Channel; Nick Jr.; NickToons TV; Outdoor Channel; Ovation; Oxygen; PBS Kids Sprout; ReelzChannel; RFD-TV; Science Channel; ShopNBC; Sleuth; SoapNet; Speed Channel; Style Network; Sundance Channel; TeenNick; Tennis Channel; The Sportsman Channel; The Word Network; Toon Disney; Trinity Broadcasting Network; TVG Network; Versus; VH1 Classic; VH1 Soul; WE tv.
Fee: $11.00 monthly.
Digital Expanded Basic Service
Subscribers: N.A.
Programming (via satellite): Arts & Entertainment HD; CNN HD; Discovery Channel HD; ESPN 2 HD; ESPN HD; Food Network HD; FSN HD; HDNet; HDNet Movies; HGTV HD; History Channel HD; Outdoor Channel 2 HD; PBS HD; Speed HD; Syfy HD; TBS in HD; Turner Network TV HD; Universal HD; USA Network HD; Versus HD.
Fee: $5.00 monthly; $5.00 converter.
Pay Service 1
Pay Units: 23.
Programming (via satellite): Cinemax; HBO.
Fee: $9.00 monthly (Cinemax), $11.00 monthly (HBO).
Digital Pay Service 1
Pay Units: N.A.
Programming (via satellite): Cinemax (multiplexed); Cinemax HD; Encore (multiplexed); HBO (multiplexed); HBO HD; Showtime (multiplexed); Starz (multiplexed); The Movie Channel (multiplexed).
Fee: $8.00 monthly (Starz/Encore), $9.00 monthly (Cinemax or Showtime/TMC), $11.00 monthly (HBO).
Video-On-Demand: No
Pay-Per-View
Addressable homes: 2.
World Wrestling Entertainment Inc., Addressable: Yes.
Internet Service
Operational: No.
Telephone Service
None
Miles of Plant: 4.0 (coaxial); 7.0 (fiber optic). Homes passed: 140. Total homes in franchised area: 140.
Manager: Richard J. Sjoberg. Chief Technician: Jerry Seim.
Ownership: Sjoberg's Cable TV Inc. (MSO).

NEWTON TWP—ACS Video. Formerly served by Perham, MN [MN0050]. This cable system has converted to IPTV, 150 Second St SW, Perham, MN 56573. Phone: 866-937-4227. E-mail: answers@arvig.com. Web Site: http://www.arvig.com. ICA: MN5237.
TV Market Ranking: Outside TV Markets (NEWTON TWP).
Channel capacity: N.A. Channels available but not in use: N.A.
Internet Service
Operational: Yes.
Telephone Service
Digital: Operational
Ownership: Arvig Communication Systems.

NICOLLET—Clara City Telephone Co., 215 1st St NW, Clara City, MN 56222. Phones: 888-283-7667; 320-847-2114. Fax: 320-847-2114. ICA: MN0342.
TV Market Ranking: Below 100 (NICOLLET). Franchise award date: June 1, 1991. Franchise expiration date: N.A. Began: N.A.
Channel capacity: 36 (operating 2-way). Channels available but not in use: 11.
Basic Service
Subscribers: 225.
Programming (received off-air): KARE (NBC) Minneapolis; KEYC-TV (CBS, FOX) Mankato; KMSP-TV (FOX) Minneapolis; KSTP-TV (ABC) St. Paul; KTCA-TV (PBS) St. Paul; KTCI-TV (PBS) St. Paul; WCCO-TV (CBS) Minneapolis; WFTC (MNT) Minneapolis; WUCW (CW) Minneapolis.
Programming (via satellite): ABC Family Channel; AMC; Arts & Entertainment; CNN; Comedy Central; Country Music TV; C-SPAN; Discovery Channel; ESPN; ESPN 2; Eternal Word TV Network; Fox Sports Net; Hallmark Channel; HGTV; History Channel; Lifetime; MTV; Nickelodeon; Spike TV; TBS Superstation; The Learning Channel; Turner Network TV; TV Land; USA Network; Weather Channel; WGN America.
Fee: $40.00 installation; $33.80 monthly; $2.00 converter.
Pay Service 1
Pay Units: 19.
Programming (via satellite): The Movie Channel.
Fee: $10.00 monthly.
Internet Service
Operational: No.
Telephone Service
None
Miles of Plant: 6.0 (coaxial); None (fiber optic).
Manager: Bruce Hanson.
Franchise fee: None.
Ownership: Hanson Communications Inc. (MSO).

NORTHROP—US Cable, 402 Red River Ave N, Unit 5, Cold Spring, MN 56320-1521. Phone: 320-685-7113. Fax: 320-685-2816. Web Site: http://www.uscable.com. ICA: MN0401.
TV Market Ranking: Outside TV Markets (NORTHROP).
Channel capacity: N.A. Channels available but not in use: N.A.
Basic Service
Subscribers: N.A. Included in Cambridge
Programming (received off-air): KAAL (ABC) Austin; KARE (NBC) Minneapolis; KEYC-TV (CBS, FOX) Mankato; KMSP-TV (FOX) Minneapolis; KSTC-TV (IND) Minneapolis; KSTP-TV (ABC) St. Paul; KTCA-TV (PBS) St. Paul; WCCO-TV (CBS) Minneapolis; WFTC (MNT) Minneapolis; WUCW (CW) Minneapolis.
Programming (via satellite): ABC Family Channel; Arts & Entertainment; CNN; Comedy Central; Country Music TV; Discovery Channel; ESPN; ESPN 2; Fox Sports Net North; Hallmark Channel; HGTV; History Channel; Lifetime; Nickelodeon; Outdoor Channel; Spike TV; TBS Superstation; The Learning Channel; Turner Classic Movies; Turner Network TV; TV Land; USA Network; Weather Channel; WGN America.
Fee: $36.24 monthly.
Pay Service 1
Pay Units: N.A. Included in Cambridge
Programming (via satellite): HBO.
Fee: $11.95 monthly.
Internet Service
Operational: No.
Miles of plant & homes passed included in Cambridge.
General Manager: Steve Johnson. Customer Service Director: Jackie Torborg.
Ownership: US Cable Corp. (MSO).

NORWOOD—Mediacom, PO Box 110, 1504 2nd St SE, Waseca, MN 56093. Phone: 507-835-2356. Fax: 507-835-4567. Web Site: http://www.mediacomcable.com. Also serves Hamburg & Young America. ICA: MN0083.
TV Market Ranking: 13 (NORWOOD, Young America); Outside TV Markets (Hamburg). Franchise award date: N.A. Franchise expiration date: N.A. Began: October 1, 1984.
Channel capacity: N.A. Channels available but not in use: N.A.
Basic Service
Subscribers: 811.
Programming (received off-air): KARE (NBC) Minneapolis; KMSP-TV (FOX) Minneapolis; KPXM-TV (ION) St. Cloud; KSTC-TV (IND) Minneapolis; KSTP-TV (ABC) St. Paul; KTCA-TV (PBS) St. Paul; KTCI-TV (PBS) St. Paul; WCCO-TV (CBS) Minneapolis; WFTC (MNT) Minneapolis; WUCW (CW) Minneapolis; allband FM.
Programming (via satellite): C-SPAN; C-SPAN 2; WGN America.
Fee: $39.95 installation; $16.76 monthly.
Expanded Basic Service 1
Subscribers: N.A.
Programming (received off-air): WUMN-CA Minneapolis.
Programming (via satellite): ABC Family Channel; AMC; Animal Planet; Arts & Entertainment; BET Networks; Bravo; Cartoon Network; CNBC; CNN; Comedy Central; Country Music TV; Discovery Channel; Disney Channel; E! Entertainment Television; ESPN; ESPN 2; Eternal Word TV Network; Food Network; Fox Movie Channel; Fox News Channel; Fox Sports Net North; FX; Hallmark Channel; Headline News; HGTV; History Channel; Home Shopping Network; INSP; Lifetime; MSNBC; MTV; Nickelodeon; QVC; SoapNet; Speed Channel; Spike TV; Syfy; TBS Superstation; The Learning Channel; Travel Channel; Trinity Broadcasting Network; truTV; Turner Classic Movies; Turner Network TV; TV Guide Network; TV Land; USA Network; VH1; WE tv; Weather Channel.
Digital Basic Service
Subscribers: N.A.
Programming (received off-air): KARE (NBC) Minneapolis; KSTP-TV (ABC) St. Paul; KTCI-TV (PBS) St. Paul.
Programming (via satellite): AmericanLife TV Network; BBC America; Bio; Bloomberg Television; Canales N; Discovery Digital Networks; Discovery HD Theater; DMX Music; ESPN; ESPN 2; ESPNews; FitTV; Fox Soccer; Fuse; G4; GAS; Golf Channel; GSN; Halogen Network; HDNet;

HDNet Movies; History Channel International; Independent Film Channel; Lifetime Movie Network; Lime; MTV Networks Digital Suite; National Geographic Channel; Nick Jr.; NickToons TV; Outdoor Channel; Sleuth; Style Network; TVG Network; Universal HD.

Digital Pay Service 1

Pay Units: N.A.

Programming (via satellite): Cinemax (multiplexed); Encore (multiplexed); Flix (multiplexed); HBO (multiplexed); HBO; Showtime (multiplexed); Showtime; Starz (multiplexed); Starz HDTV; Sundance Channel (multiplexed); The Movie Channel (multiplexed); The Movie Channel.

Video-On-Demand: Yes

Pay-Per-View

ESPN (delivered digitally); Fresh (delivered digitally); Shorteez (delivered digitally); Playboy TV (delivered digitally); Pleasure (delivered digitally); Ten Clips (delivered digitally).

Internet Service

Operational: Yes.

Broadband Service: Mediacom High Speed Internet.

Telephone Service

Digital: Operational

Miles of Plant: 41.0 (coaxial); None (fiber optic). Homes passed: 1,159.

Vice President: Bill Jensen. Engineering Manager: Kraig Kaiser. Marketing & Sales Director: Lori Huberty.

City fee: 3% of gross.

Ownership: Mediacom LLC (MSO).

OKLEE—Garden Valley Telephone Co., PO Box 259, 201 Ross Ave, Erskine, MN 56535-0259. Phone: 218-687-5251. Fax: 218-687-2454. E-mail: gvtc@gvtel.com. Web Site: http://www.gvtel.com. Also serves Plummer. ICA: MN0344.

TV Market Ranking: Below 100 (OKLEE, Plummer). Franchise award date: September 20, 1983. Franchise expiration date: N.A. Began: April 1, 1984.

Channel capacity: 35 (not 2-way capable). Channels available but not in use: 10.

Basic Service

Subscribers: 254.

Programming (received off-air): KAWE (PBS) Bemidji; KBRR (FOX) Thief River Falls; KCPM (MNT) Grand Forks; KFME (PBS) Fargo; KVLY-TV (NBC) Fargo; KXJB-TV (CBS) Valley City; WDAY-TV (ABC, CW) Fargo; WDAZ-TV (ABC, CW) Devils Lake.

Programming (via satellite): ABC Family Channel; AMC; Arts & Entertainment; CNN; Discovery Channel; Disney Channel; ESPN; ESPN 2; Fox Sports Net; Great American Country; History Channel; Spike TV; TBS Superstation; TV Land; USA Network; WGN America.

Fee: $39.90 installation; $22.95 monthly; $.75 converter.

Pay Service 1

Pay Units: 42.

Programming (via satellite): HBO.

Fee: $10.50 monthly.

Video-On-Demand: No

Internet Service

Operational: No.

Telephone Service

None

Miles of Plant: 17.0 (coaxial); None (fiber optic). Homes passed: 428.

Manager: George Fish. Operations Manager: Dave Hamre. Facilities Manager: Randy Versdahl. Marketing Supervisor: Julie Dahle.

Ownership: Garden Valley Telephone Co. (MSO).

OLIVIA—Mediacom, PO Box 110, 1504 2nd St SE, Waseca, MN 56093. Phones: 800-332-0245; 507-835-2356. Fax: 507-835-4567. Web Site: http://www.mediacomcable.com. Also serves Bird Island & Danube. ICA: MN0062.

TV Market Ranking: Below 100 (Bird Island, Danube, OLIVIA). Franchise award date: January 14, 1982. Franchise expiration date: N.A. Began: April 10, 1983.

Channel capacity: N.A. Channels available but not in use: N.A.

Basic Service

Subscribers: 1,082.

Programming (received off-air): KEYC-TV (CBS, FOX) Mankato; KPXM-TV (ION) St. Cloud; KWCM-TV (PBS) Appleton; allband FM.

Programming (via satellite): C-SPAN; TV Guide Network; WGN America.

Programming (via translator): KARE (NBC) Minneapolis; KMSP-TV (FOX) Minneapolis; KSTC-TV (IND) Minneapolis; KSTP-TV (ABC) St. Paul; KTCA-TV (PBS) St. Paul; KTCI-TV (PBS) St. Paul; WCCO-TV (CBS) Minneapolis; WFTC (MNT) Minneapolis; WUCW (CW) Minneapolis.

Current originations: Educational Access.

Fee: $52.39 installation; $6.48 monthly; $2.00 converter; $17.48 additional installation.

Expanded Basic Service 1

Subscribers: 1,063.

Programming (via satellite): ABC Family Channel; AMC; Animal Planet; Arts & Entertainment; BET Networks; Bravo; Cartoon Network; CNBC; CNN; Comedy Central; Country Music TV; Discovery Channel; Disney Channel; E! Entertainment Television; ESPN; ESPN 2; Eternal Word TV Network; Food Network; Fox Movie Channel; Fox News Channel; Fox Sports Net North; FX; Hallmark Channel; Headline News; HGTV; History Channel; INSP; Lifetime; MSNBC; MTV; Nickelodeon; QVC; SoapNet; Speed Channel; Spike TV; Syfy; TBS Superstation; The Learning Channel; Travel Channel; Trinity Broadcasting Network; Turner Classic Movies; Turner Network TV; TV Land; Univision; USA Network; VH1; WE tv; Weather Channel.

Fee: $16.56 monthly.

Digital Basic Service

Subscribers: 146.

Programming (via satellite): AmericanLife TV Network; BBC America; Bio; Bloomberg Television; Canales N; Discovery Digital Networks; DMX Music; Fox Sports World; Fuse; G4; Golf Channel; GSN; Halogen Network; History Channel International; Independent Film Channel; Lifetime Movie Network; Lime; Outdoor Channel; Style Network; Versus.

Fee: $7.00 monthly.

Digital Pay Service 1

Pay Units: 132.

Programming (via satellite): Cinemax (multiplexed).

Fee: $9.95 monthly.

Digital Pay Service 2

Pay Units: 110.

Programming (via satellite): Encore (multiplexed); Starz (multiplexed).

Fee: $5.00 monthly.

Digital Pay Service 3

Pay Units: 179.

Programming (via satellite): HBO (multiplexed).

Fee: $11.00 monthly.

Digital Pay Service 4

Pay Units: 198.

Programming (via satellite): Flix; Showtime (multiplexed); Sundance Channel; The Movie Channel (multiplexed).

Fee: $11.00 monthly (each).

Video-On-Demand: Yes

Pay-Per-View

TVN Entertainment (delivered digitally); ESPN Now (delivered digitally); Sports PPV (delivered digitally); Urban Xtra (delivered digitally); Fresh (delivered digitally); Shorteez (delivered digitally); Playboy TV (delivered digitally); Pleasure (delivered digitally).

Internet Service

Operational: Yes.

Broadband Service: Mediacom High Speed Internet.

Telephone Service

Digital: Operational

Miles of Plant: 45.0 (coaxial); None (fiber optic). Homes passed: 2,202.

Vice President: Bill Jensen. Engineering Manager: Kraig Kaiser. Marketing & Sales Director: Lori Huberty.

Franchise fee: 3% of gross.

Ownership: Mediacom LLC (MSO).

ONAMIA—Savage Communications Inc. Now served by ISLE, MN [MN0313]. ICA: MN0211.

ORTONVILLE—Midcontinent Communications. Now served by WATERTOWN, SD [SD0004]. ICA: MN0073.

OSAGE TWP.—ACS Video. Formerly served by Perham, MN [MN0050]. This cable system has converted to IPTV, 150 Second St SW, Perham, MN 56573. Phone: 866-937-4227. E-mail: answers@arvig.com. Web Site: http://www.arvig.com. ICA: MN5132.

TV Market Ranking: Below 100 (OSAGE TWP.).

Channel capacity: N.A. Channels available but not in use: N.A.

Internet Service

Operational: Yes.

Telephone Service

Digital: Operational

Ownership: Arvig Communication Systems.

OSAKIS—Charter Communications. Now served by ALEXANDRIA, MN [MN0031]. ICA: MN0155.

OSLO—Midcontinent Communications, PO Box 5010, Sioux Falls, SD 57117. Phones: 800-456-0564; 605-229-1775. Fax: 605-229-1775. E-mail: mccomm@midco.net. Web Site: http://www.midcocomm.com. ICA: MN0252.

TV Market Ranking: Below 100 (OSLO). Franchise award date: May 21, 1984. Franchise expiration date: N.A. Began: January 1, 1987.

Channel capacity: 43 (not 2-way capable). Channels available but not in use: N.A.

Basic Service

Subscribers: 102.

Programming (received off-air): KBRR (FOX) Thief River Falls; KGFE (PBS) Grand Forks; KVLY-TV (NBC) Fargo; KXJB-TV (CBS) Valley City; WDAZ-TV (ABC, CW) Devils Lake.

Programming (via satellite): ABC Family Channel; AMC; Animal Planet; Arts & Entertainment; Cartoon Network; CNBC; CNN; Country Music TV; C-SPAN; Discovery Channel; Discovery Health Channel; Disney Channel; ESPN; ESPN 2; Fox News Channel; Fox Sports Net North; Headline News; HGTV; History Channel; INSP; Lifetime; MSNBC; Nickelodeon; Outdoor Channel; QVC; Spike TV; Syfy; TBS Superstation; The Learning Channel; Turner Network TV; TV Land; USA Network; VH1; WE tv; Weather Channel; WGN America.

Fee: $50.00 installation; $26.50 monthly.

Pay Service 1

Pay Units: 21.

Programming (via satellite): HBO.

Fee: $20.00 installation; $12.00 monthly.

Pay Service 2

Pay Units: 6.

Programming (via satellite): The Movie Channel.

Fee: $20.00 installation; $11.00 monthly.

Pay Service 3

Pay Units: 6.

Programming (via satellite): Showtime.

Fee: $20.00 installation; $11.00 monthly.

Video-On-Demand: No

Internet Service

Operational: No.

Telephone Service

None

Miles of Plant: 3.0 (coaxial); None (fiber optic). Homes passed: 172.

Manager: Darrell Wrege. Marketing Director: Fred Jamieson. Customer Service Manager: Kathy Fuhrmann.

Ownership: Midcontinent Media Inc. (MSO).; Comcast Cable Communications Inc. (MSO).

OSTRANDER—North American Communications Corp., PO Box 387, 211 Main St S, Hector, MN 55342-0387. Phones: 800-982-8038; 320-848-6781. Fax: 320-848-2323. E-mail: hcc@hcctel.net. Web Site: http://www.hectorcom.com. ICA: MN0259.

TV Market Ranking: Below 100 (OSTRANDER). Franchise award date: February 1, 1989. Franchise expiration date: N.A. Began: February 1, 1990.

Channel capacity: 54 (not 2-way capable). Channels available but not in use: 29.

Basic Service

Subscribers: 39.

Programming (received off-air): KAAL (ABC) Austin; KIMT (CBS, MNT) Mason City; KSMQ-TV (PBS) Austin; KYIN (PBS) Mason City; WHLA-TV (PBS) La Crosse; WLAX (FOX) La Crosse.

Programming (via satellite): ABC Family Channel; AMC; Arts & Entertainment; CNN; Country Music TV; Discovery Channel; Disney Channel; ESPN; Fox Sports Net Midwest; Lifetime; Nickelodeon; QVC; Spike

TV; TBS Superstation; Trinity Broadcasting Network; Turner Network TV; USA Network; WGN America.
Fee: $40.00 installation; $26.95 monthly; $3.50 converter; $25.00 additional installation.
Pay Service 1
Pay Units: 1.
Programming (via satellite): Cinemax.
Fee: $10.95 monthly.
Pay Service 2
Pay Units: 1.
Programming (via satellite): HBO.
Fee: $10.95 monthly.
Video-On-Demand: No
Internet Service
Operational: No.
Broadband Service: Offers dial-up and DSL only; no cable modem service.
Telephone Service
None
Miles of Plant: 4.0 (coaxial); None (fiber optic). Homes passed: 114. Total homes in franchised area: 114.
Manager: Matt Sparks. Customer Service Supervisor: Patty Groshens. Chief Technician: George Honzay.
Ownership: Hector Communications Corp. (MSO).

OTTERTAIL TWP.—ACS Video. Formerly served by Perham, MN [MN0050]. This cable system has converted to IPTV, 150 Second St SW, Perham, MN 56573. Phone: 866-937-4227. E-mail: answers@arvig.com. Web Site: http://www.arvig.com. ICA: MN5208.
TV Market Ranking: Outside TV Markets (OTTERTAIL TWP.).
Channel capacity: N.A. Channels available but not in use: N.A.
Internet Service
Operational: Yes.
Telephone Service
Digital: Operational
Ownership: Arvig Communication Systems.

OTTO TWP.—ACS Video. Formerly served by Perham, MN [MN0050]. This cable system has converted to IPTV, 150 Second St SW, Perham, MN 56573. Phone: 866-937-4227. E-mail: answers@arvig.com. Web Site: http://www.arvig.com. ICA: MN5209.
TV Market Ranking: Outside TV Markets (OTTO TWP.).
Channel capacity: N.A. Channels available but not in use: N.A.
Internet Service
Operational: Yes.
Telephone Service
Digital: Operational
Ownership: Arvig Communication Systems.

OWATONNA—Charter Communications, 2206 E Oakland Ave, Austin, MN 55912-4375. Phones: 507-455-2456; 507-289-8372 (Rochester administrative office). Fax: 507-437-7119. Web Site: http://www.charter.com. ICA: MN0023.
TV Market Ranking: Below 100 (OWATONNA). Franchise award date: June 7, 1983. Franchise expiration date: N.A. Began: December 22, 1983.
Channel capacity: 117 (operating 2-way). Channels available but not in use: 56.
Basic Service
Subscribers: 7,500.
Programming (received off-air): KAAL (ABC) Austin; KARE (NBC) Minneapolis; KEYC-TV (CBS, FOX) Mankato; KMSP-TV (FOX) Minneapolis; KPXM-TV (ION) St. Cloud; KSMQ-TV (PBS) Austin; KSTC-TV (IND) Minneapolis; KSTP-TV (ABC) St. Paul; KTCA-TV (PBS) St. Paul; WCCO-TV (CBS) Minneapolis; WFTC (MNT) Minneapolis; 1 FM.
Programming (via satellite): C-SPAN; Home Shopping Network; Product Information Network; QVC; Trinity Broadcasting Network; TV Guide Network; WGN America.
Current originations: Religious Access; Government Access; Educational Access; Public Access.
Fee: $29.99 installation.
Expanded Basic Service 1
Subscribers: 6,833.
Programming (via satellite): ABC Family Channel; AMC; Animal Planet; Arts & Entertainment; BET Networks; Bravo; Cartoon Network; CNBC; CNN; Comedy Central; Country Music TV; Discovery Channel; Disney Channel; E! Entertainment Television; ESPN; ESPN 2; Eternal Word TV Network; Food Network; Fox News Channel; Fox Sports Net North; FX; G4; Golf Channel; GSN; Hallmark Channel; Headline News; HGTV; History Channel; INSP; Lifetime; MSNBC; MTV; MTV2; National Geographic Channel; Nickelodeon; Oxygen; ShopNBC; SoapNet; Speed Channel; Spike TV; Syfy; TBS Superstation; The Learning Channel; Toon Disney; Travel Channel; truTV; Turner Network TV; TV Land; Univision; USA Network; Versus; VH1; WE tv; Weather Channel.
Fee: $47.99 monthly.
Digital Basic Service
Subscribers: N.A.
Programming (received off-air): KARE (NBC) Minneapolis; KMSP-TV (FOX) Minneapolis; WCCO-TV (CBS) Minneapolis.
Programming (via satellite): BBC America; Bio; Bloomberg Television; Boomerang; CBS College Sports Network; CNN en Espanol; CNN International; Discovery Digital Networks; Do-It-Yourself; ESPN; ESPN Classic Sports; ESPNews; Fox College Sports Atlantic; Fox College Sports Central; Fox College Sports Pacific; Fox Movie Channel; Fox Soccer; Fuel TV; Fuse; GAS; HDNet; HDNet Movies; History Channel International; Independent Film Channel; Lifetime Movie Network; MTV Networks Digital Suite; Music Choice; NFL Network; Nick Jr.; Nick Too; NickToons TV; Outdoor Channel; Style Network; Sundance Channel; Turner Classic Movies; TV Guide Interactive Inc.
Digital Pay Service 1
Pay Units: N.A.
Programming (via satellite): Cinemax (multiplexed); Encore; Flix; HBO (multiplexed); HBO HD; Showtime (multiplexed); Showtime HD; Starz; The Movie Channel (multiplexed).
Video-On-Demand: Yes
Pay-Per-View
iN DEMAND (delivered digitally); NASCAR In Car (delivered digitally); NHL Center Ice (delivered digitally); MLB Extra Innings (delivered digitally); Playboy TV (delivered digitally); Spice Live (delivered digitally); Spice Platinum (delivered digitally); Hot Net Plus (delivered digitally); Spice Hot (delivered digitally).
Internet Service
Operational: Yes.
Broadband Service: Charter Pipeline.
Fee: $29.99 monthly.
Telephone Service
Digital: Operational
Fee: $29.99 monthly
Miles of Plant: 124.0 (coaxial); 26.0 (fiber optic). Homes passed: 11,450.
Vice President & General Manager: John Crowley. Operations Director: Craig Stensaas. Technical Operations Director: Darin Helgeson. Chief Technician: Ray Madrigal. Marketing Director: Bill Haarstad. Office Manager: Sherry Brown.
City fee: 5% of gross.
Ownership: Charter Communications Inc. (MSO).

PARK RAPIDS—Charter Communications, 314 3rd St NW, Bemidji, MN 56601-3113. Phones: 507-289-8372 (Rochester administrative office); 218-751-5511. Fax: 218-751-8455. Web Site: http://www.charter.com. ICA: MN0345.
TV Market Ranking: Below 100 (PARK RAPIDS). Franchise award date: N.A. Franchise expiration date: N.A. Began: April 1, 1966.
Channel capacity: N.A. Channels available but not in use: N.A.
Basic Service
Subscribers: 1,246.
Programming (received off-air): KARE (NBC) Minneapolis; KAWB (PBS) Brainerd; KCCW-TV (CBS) Walker; KMSP-TV (FOX) Minneapolis; KPXM-TV (ION) St. Cloud; KSAX (ABC) Alexandria; KSTC-TV (IND) Minneapolis; KTCA-TV (PBS) St. Paul; KVRR (FOX) Fargo; WFTC (MNT) Minneapolis; WUCW (CW) Minneapolis; allband FM.
Programming (via satellite): C-SPAN; C-SPAN 2; Eternal Word TV Network; Home Shopping Network; INSP; QVC; TBS Superstation; Trinity Broadcasting Network; TV Guide Network; Weather Channel; WGN America.
Fee: $29.99 installation; $2.00 converter.
Expanded Basic Service 1
Subscribers: 996.
Programming (via satellite): ABC Family Channel; AMC; Animal Planet; Arts & Entertainment; Bravo; Cartoon Network; CNBC; CNN; Comedy Central; Country Music TV; Discovery Channel; Disney Channel; E! Entertainment Television; ESPN; ESPN 2; Food Network; Fox News Channel; Fox Sports Net North; FX; Golf Channel; Hallmark Channel; Headline News; HGTV; History Channel; Lifetime; MSNBC; MTV; Nickelodeon; Outdoor Channel; Oxygen; Speed Channel; Spike TV; Syfy; The Learning Channel; Travel Channel; truTV; Turner Network TV; TV Land; USA Network; Versus; VH1.
Fee: $47.99 monthly.
Digital Basic Service
Subscribers: N.A.
Programming (via satellite): BBC America; Bio; Boomerang; CNN en Espanol; Discovery Digital Networks; Do-It-Yourself; ESPN Classic Sports; ESPNews; Fox College Sports Atlantic; Fox College Sports Central; Fox College Sports Pacific; Fox Soccer; Fuel TV; G4; GAS; History Channel International; Independent Film Channel; Lifetime Movie Network; MTV Networks Digital Suite; Music Choice; NFL Network; Nick Jr.; Nick Too; NickToons TV; SoapNet; Style Network; Sundance Channel; Toon Disney; Turner Classic Movies; TV Guide Interactive Inc.; WE tv.
Digital Pay Service 1
Pay Units: N.A.
Programming (via satellite): Cinemax (multiplexed); Encore; Flix; HBO (multiplexed); Showtime (multiplexed); Starz (multiplexed); The Movie Channel (multiplexed).
Video-On-Demand: Yes
Pay-Per-View
iN DEMAND (delivered digitally); NASCAR In Car (delivered digitally); NHL Center Ice (delivered digitally); MLB Extra Innings (delivered digitally); Playboy TV (delivered digitally); Spice Live (delivered digitally); Spice Platinum (delivered digitally); Hot Net Plus (delivered digitally); Spice Hot (delivered digitally).
Internet Service
Operational: Yes.
Broadband Service: Charter Pipeline.
Telephone Service
Digital: Operational
Miles of Plant: 44.0 (coaxial); None (fiber optic). Homes passed: 2,086.
Vice President & General Manager: John Crowley. System Manager: Scott Caoutte. Marketing Director: Bill Haarstad.
City fee: 2% of gross.
Ownership: Charter Communications Inc. (MSO).

PARKERS PRAIRIE—ACS Video, 150 Second St SW, Perham, MN 56573. Phones: 218-338-4227; 320-859-2700; 218-338-4000. Fax: 218-338-3297. E-mail: answers@arvig.com. Web Site: http://www.arvig.com. Also serves Carlos, Eagle Bend, Miltona, Parkers Prairie Twp. & Urbank. ICA: MN0346.
TV Market Ranking: Below 100 (Carlos, Eagle Bend, Miltona, PARKERS PRAIRIE, Parkers Prairie Twp., Urbank). Franchise award date: December 1, 1983. Franchise expiration date: N.A. Began: December 1, 1983.
Channel capacity: 35 (2-way capable). Channels available but not in use: 7.
Basic Service
Subscribers: 671.
Programming (received off-air): KARE (NBC) Minneapolis; KMSP-TV (FOX) Minneapolis; KVRR (FOX) Fargo; KWCM-TV (PBS) Appleton; WCCO-TV (CBS) Minneapolis; WFTC (MNT) Minneapolis.
Programming (via microwave): KSAX (ABC) Alexandria.
Programming (via satellite): ABC Family Channel; AMC; Arts & Entertainment; CNN; Country Music TV; Discovery Channel; Disney Channel; ESPN; ESPN 2; Food Network; Fox Movie Channel; Fox News Channel; Fox Sports Net North; Hallmark Channel; HGTV; History Channel; Lifetime; MTV; Nickelodeon; Spike TV; TBS Superstation; Turner Network TV; TV Land; USA Network; VH1; Weather Channel; WGN America.
Current originations: Public Access.
Fee: $40.00 installation; $33.95 monthly.
Pay Service 1
Pay Units: N.A.
Programming (via satellite): HBO.
Fee: $12.95 monthly.

Internet Service
Operational: Yes.
Broadband Service: ACS Networks.
Fee: $69.95-$154.95 monthly.
Telephone Service
None
Miles of Plant: 25.0 (coaxial); None (fiber optic). Homes passed: 1,000. Total homes in franchised area: 1,000.
Manager: Mark Birkholz. Video Services Director: David Pratt. Chief Technician: Bryan Revering.
Ownership: Arvig Communication Systems (MSO).

PAYNESVILLE—Now served by CLARA CITY, MN [MN0125]. ICA: MN0079.

PELICAN LAKE—Loretel Cablevision, PO Box 72, 13 East 4th Ave, Ada, MN 56510. Phones: 218-784-5100; 800-343-2762. Fax: 218-784-2706. E-mail: loretel@loretel.net. Web Site: http://www.hectorcom.com. Also serves Cormorant Lake (eastern portion), Cormorant Twp., Dunn Twp., Lake Lida & Scambler Twp. ICA: MN0347.
TV Market Ranking: Outside TV Markets (Cormorant Lake (eastern portion), Cormorant Twp., Dunn Twp., Lake Lida, PELICAN LAKE, Scambler Twp.). Franchise award date: N.A. Franchise expiration date: N.A. Began: June 1, 1988.
Channel capacity: 35 (operating 2-way). Channels available but not in use: N.A.
Basic Service
Subscribers: 591.
Programming (received off-air): KCPM (MNT) Grand Forks; KFME (PBS) Fargo; KVLY-TV (NBC) Fargo; KVRR (FOX) Fargo; KXJB-TV (CBS) Valley City; WDAY-TV (ABC, CW) Fargo.
Programming (via satellite): ABC Family Channel; Arts & Entertainment; Cartoon Network; CNBC; CNN; Comedy Central; Country Music TV; C-SPAN; Discovery Channel; Disney Channel; E! Entertainment Television; ESPN; ESPN 2; Food Network; Fox News Channel; Fox Sports Net; FX; Headline News; HGTV; History Channel; Lifetime; MTV; National Geographic Channel; Nickelodeon; Outdoor Channel; QVC; Spike TV; Syfy; TBS Superstation; The Learning Channel; truTV; Turner Classic Movies; Turner Network TV; TV Guide Network; TV Land; USA Network; VH1; Weather Channel; WGN America.
Fee: $37.50 monthly.
Pay Service 1
Pay Units: 45.
Programming (via satellite): HBO.
Fee: $13.00 monthly.
Pay Service 2
Pay Units: 12.
Programming (via satellite): Cinemax.
Fee: $12.00 monthly.
Pay Service 3
Pay Units: 36.
Programming (via satellite): Encore.
Fee: $2.75 monthly.
Video-On-Demand: No
Internet Service
Operational: No.
Broadband Service: Offers dial-up and DSL only; no cable modem service.
Telephone Service
None
Miles of Plant: 37.0 (coaxial); None (fiber optic). Homes passed: 1,100.
Manager: Steven W. Katka. Chief Technician: Bruce Rosefelt.
Ownership: Hector Communications Corp. (MSO).

PELICAN RAPIDS—Loretel Systems, PO Box 406, 20 W Mill St, Pelican Rapids, MN 56572. Phones: 218-863-6451 (Customer service); 800-242-6111 (Customer service); 218-784-5100; 800-343-2762; 218-784-5151. Fax: 218-784-2706. E-mail: loretel@loretel.net. Web Site: http://www.hectorcom.com. ICA: MN0120.
TV Market Ranking: Outside TV Markets (PELICAN RAPIDS). Franchise award date: January 3, 1982. Franchise expiration date: N.A. Began: June 15, 1982.
Channel capacity: 35 (operating 2-way). Channels available but not in use: 4.
Basic Service
Subscribers: 539.
Programming (received off-air): KCPM (MNT) Grand Forks; KFME (PBS) Fargo; KVLY-TV (NBC) Fargo; KVRR (FOX) Fargo; KXJB-TV (CBS) Valley City; WDAY-TV (ABC, CW) Fargo; WPCH-TV (IND) Atlanta.
Programming (via satellite): ABC Family Channel; Arts & Entertainment; Cartoon Network; CNBC; CNN; Comedy Central; Country Music TV; C-SPAN; Discovery Channel; Disney Channel; ESPN; ESPN 2; Food Network; Fox News Channel; Fox Sports Net; FX; Headline News; HGTV; History Channel; Lifetime; MTV; National Geographic Channel; Nickelodeon; Outdoor Channel; QVC; Spike TV; Syfy; The Learning Channel; truTV; Turner Classic Movies; Turner Network TV; TV Guide Network; TV Land; USA Network; VH1; Weather Channel; WGN America.
Fee: $20.00 installation; $33.00 monthly.
Pay Service 1
Pay Units: 136.
Programming (via satellite): Encore.
Fee: $2.75 monthly.
Pay Service 2
Pay Units: 19.
Programming (via satellite): Cinemax.
Fee: $10.00 monthly.
Pay Service 3
Pay Units: 22.
Programming (via satellite): HBO.
Fee: $13.00 monthly.
Video-On-Demand: No
Internet Service
Operational: No.
Broadband Service: Offers dial-up and DSL only; no cable modem service.
Telephone Service
None
Miles of Plant: 17.0 (coaxial); None (fiber optic). Homes passed: 800. Total homes in franchised area: 1,015.
Manager: Steven W. Katka. Chief Technicians: Rodney Earckson.; Bruce Rosefelt.
City fee: None.
Ownership: Hector Communications Corp. (MSO).

PENGILLY—Savage Communications Inc., PO Box 810, 206 Power Ave N, Hinckley, MN 55037. Phone: 320-384-7442. Fax: 320-384-7446. E-mail: rwsavage@scicable.com. Web Site: http://www.scibroadband.com. ICA: MN0390.
TV Market Ranking: Below 100 (PENGILLY). Franchise award date: September 5, 1990. Franchise expiration date: N.A. Began: September 5, 1991.
Channel capacity: 60 (2-way capable). Channels available but not in use: 5.
Basic Service
Subscribers: 285.
Programming (received off-air): KBJR-TV (MNT, NBC) Superior; KCCW-TV (CBS) Walker; KDLH (CBS, CW) Duluth; KQDS-TV (FOX) Duluth; WDIO-DT (ABC) Duluth; WDSE (PBS) Duluth; WPIX (CW, IND) New York.
Programming (via satellite): ABC Family Channel; Animal Planet; Arts & Entertainment; CNBC; CNN; Comedy Central; C-SPAN; Discovery Channel; Disney Channel; E! Entertainment Television; ESPN; ESPN 2; Eternal Word TV Network; Fox News Channel; Fox Sports Net; Great American Country; Headline News; HGTV; History Channel; Lifetime; MTV; Nickelodeon; QVC; Spike TV; Syfy; TBS Superstation; The Learning Channel; Turner Classic Movies; Turner Network TV; TV Land; USA Network; VH1; Weather Channel; WGN America.
Fee: $39.95 installation; $39.95 monthly.
Digital Basic Service
Subscribers: N.A.
Programming (via satellite): AmericanLife TV Network; BBC America; Bio; Bloomberg Television; Discovery Digital Networks; DMX Music; ESPN Classic Sports; ESPNews; FitTV; Fox Movie Channel; Fox Sports World; Fuse; G4; Golf Channel; History Channel International; INSP; National Geographic Channel; Outdoor Channel; Sleuth; Speed Channel; Style Network; Trinity Broadcasting Network; Versus; WE tv.
Digital Pay Service 1
Pay Units: N.A.
Programming (via satellite): Cinemax (multiplexed); Encore (multiplexed); Flix; HBO (multiplexed); Showtime (multiplexed); Starz (multiplexed); Sundance Channel; The Movie Channel (multiplexed).
Video-On-Demand: No
Pay-Per-View
Movies (delivered digitally); ESPN Now (delivered digitally); Sports PPV (delivered digitally).
Internet Service
Operational: Yes.
Broadband Service: SCI Broadband.
Fee: $24.95 monthly.
Telephone Service
None
Miles of Plant: 21.0 (coaxial); None (fiber optic). Homes passed: 572. Total homes in franchised area: 572.
Manager: Mike Danielson. Marketing Director: Ron Savage. Chief Technician: Pat McCabe. Customer Service Manager: Donna Erickson.
Ownership: Savage Communications Inc. (MSO).

PEQUOT LAKES—Charter Communications, 3380 Northern Valley Pl NE, Rochester, MN 55906-3954. Phones: 507-289-8372 (Rochester office); 218-829-9015 (Local office). Fax: 507-285-6162. Web Site: http://www.charter.com. Also serves Backus, Barclay Twp., Birch Lake Twp., Breezy Point, Center Twp., Chickamaw Beach, Crow Wing County (northern portion), Fairview Twp., Hackensack, Hiram Twp., Jenkins, Lake Edwards Twp., Loon Lake Twp., Pine River, Powers Twp., Walden Twp. & Wilson Twp. ICA: MN0025.
TV Market Ranking: Below 100 (Backus, Barclay Twp., Birch Lake Twp., Chickamaw Beach, Crow Wing County (portions), Fairview Twp., Hackensack, Hiram Twp., Jenkins, Powers Twp., Walden Twp., Wilson Twp.); Outside TV Markets (Breezy Point, Center Twp., Crow Wing County (portions), Lake Edwards Twp., Loon Lake Twp., PEQUOT LAKES, Pine River). Franchise award date: N.A. Franchise expiration date: N.A. Began: August 1, 1983.
Channel capacity: N.A. Channels available but not in use: N.A.
Basic Service
Subscribers: 6,174.
Programming (received off-air): KARE (NBC) Minneapolis; KCCW-TV (CBS) Walker; KMSP-TV (FOX) Minneapolis; KSAX (ABC) Alexandria; KTCA-TV (PBS) St. Paul; WFTC (MNT) Minneapolis.
Programming (via satellite): C-SPAN; QVC; WGN America.
Current originations: Public Access.
Fee: $29.99 installation; $9.53 additional installation.
Expanded Basic Service 1
Subscribers: 5,082.
Programming (via satellite): ABC Family Channel; AMC; Animal Planet; Arts & Entertainment; CNBC; CNN; Country Music TV; Discovery Channel; Disney Channel; E! Entertainment Television; ESPN; ESPN 2; Eternal Word TV Network; Fox News Channel; Fox Sports Net North; Headline News; HGTV; History Channel; Lifetime; MTV; Nickelodeon; Spike TV; Syfy; TBS Superstation; The Learning Channel; Travel Channel; Turner Classic Movies; Turner Network TV; TV Land; USA Network; Versus; VH1; Weather Channel.
Fee: $47.99 monthly.
Pay Service 1
Pay Units: 161.
Programming (via satellite): Cinemax; HBO; Showtime.
Fee: $10.00 installation; $8.95 monthly (Cinemax); $9.95 monthly (Showtime).
Video-On-Demand: Yes
Internet Service
Operational: Yes.
Broadband Service: Charter Pipeline.
Telephone Service
Digital: Operational
Miles of Plant: 220.0 (coaxial); None (fiber optic).
Vice President & General Manager: John Crowley. Operations Director: Craig Stensaas. Technical Operations Director: Mark Abramo. Marketing Director: Bill Haarstad.
Ownership: Charter Communications Inc. (MSO).

PERHAM—ACS Video, 150 Second St SW, Perham, MN 56573. Phone: 218-346-5500. Fax: 218-346-8829. E-mail: answers@arvig.com. Web Site: http://www.arvig.com. Also serves Akeley, Amor Twp., Audubon, Battle Lake, Bertha, Bluffton (village), Callaway, Clitherall (village), Clitherall Twp., Cormorant Twp., Dead Lake Twp., Deer Creek, Dent, Detroit Lakes, Detroit Twp., Everts Twp., Frazee, Henning, Hewitt, Holmesville Twp., Lake Eunice Twp., Lake Park, Lakeview Twp., Leech Lake Twp., Lida Twp., Longville,

Maine, Mantrap Twp., Nevis, New York Mills, Nidaros Twp., Osage, Ottertail, Perham (village), Richville, Richwood Twp., Shingobee Twp., Staples (village), Sverdrup Twp., Vining (village), Wadena, Walker & Waubun. ICA: MN0050. **Note:** This system is an overbuild.

TV Market Ranking: 98 (Lake Park); Below 100 (Akeley, Battle Lake, Clitherall (village), Clitherall Twp., Henning, Leech Lake Twp., Longville, Mantrap Twp., Nevis, Osage, Shingobee Twp., Vining (village), Walker); Outside TV Markets (Amor Twp., Audubon, Bertha, Bluffton (village), Callaway, Cormorant Twp., Dead Lake Twp., Deer Creek, Dent, Detroit Lakes, Detroit Twp., Everts Twp., Frazee, Holmesville Twp., Lake Eunice Twp., Lakeview Twp., Lida Twp., Maine, New York Mills, Nidaros Twp., Ottertail, PERHAM, Perham (village), Richville, Richwood Twp., Staples (village), Sverdrup Twp., Wadena, Waubun). Franchise award date: September 1, 1973. Franchise expiration date: N.A. Began: March 9, 1996.

Channel capacity: 38 (operating 2-way). Channels available but not in use: N.A.

Basic Service

Subscribers: 11,835.

Programming (received off-air): K49FA Fergus Falls; KCCO-TV (CBS) Alexandria; KCPM (MNT) Grand Forks; KFME (PBS) Fargo; KVLY-TV (NBC) Fargo; KVRR (FOX) Fargo; KXJB-TV (CBS) Valley City; WDAY-TV (ABC, CW) Fargo.

Programming (via satellite): C-SPAN; Home Shopping Network; WGN America.

Current originations: Leased Access; Public Access.

Fee: $40.00 installation; $22.49 monthly.

Expanded Basic Service 1

Subscribers: 11,148.

Programming (via satellite): ABC Family Channel; Arts & Entertainment; CNBC; CNN; Country Music TV; Discovery Channel; ESPN; ESPN 2; Fox News Channel; Fox Sports Net; FX; Hallmark Channel; Lifetime; MTV; Nickelodeon; QVC; Spike TV; TBS Superstation; The Learning Channel; Turner Network TV; USA Network; VH1; Weather Channel.

Fee: $50.00 installation; $36.95 monthly.

Digital Basic Service

Subscribers: 2,201.

Programming (via satellite): AmericanLife TV Network; BBC America; Cooking Channel; Discovery Digital Networks; DMX Music; Do-It-Yourself; ESPN Classic Sports; ESPNews; Fox Movie Channel; G4; Golf Channel; GSN; Halogen Network; HGTV; History Channel; Independent Film Channel; Lifetime Movie Network; National Geographic Channel; Nick Jr.; Outdoor Channel; Speed Channel; Syfy; The Sportsman Channel; Turner Classic Movies; Versus; WE tv.

Fee: $22.00 monthly.

Digital Pay Service 1

Pay Units: 947.

Programming (via satellite): Cinemax (multiplexed); HBO (multiplexed).

Fee: $15.00 installation; $15.95 monthly.

Digital Pay Service 2

Pay Units: 489.

Programming (via satellite): Encore (multiplexed); Showtime (multiplexed); Starz (multiplexed); The Movie Channel (multiplexed).

Fee: $15.00 installation; $10.95 monthly.

Video-On-Demand: Yes

Pay-Per-View

Addressable homes: 2,504.

Fee: $9.95, Addressable: Yes; iN DEMAND (delivered digitally), Fee: $3.95, Addressable: Yes; Playboy TV (delivered digitally), Fee: $8.95, Addressable: Yes.

Internet Service

Operational: Yes.

Subscribers: 1,800.

Broadband Service: In-house.

Fee: $69.95-$154.95 monthly.

Telephone Service

None

Miles of Plant: 844.0 (coaxial); 60.0 (fiber optic). Additional miles planned: 40.0 (coaxial). Homes passed: 24,705. Total homes in franchised area: 24,705.

Video Services Director: David Pratt. Headend Technician: Dennis Kempenich. Video Operations Coordinator: Joel Smith.

City fee: None.

Ownership: Arvig Communication Systems (MSO).

PERHAM TWP.—ACS Video. Formerly served by Perham, MN [MN0050]. This cable system has converted to IPTV, 150 Second St SW, Perham, MN 56573. Phone: 866-937-4227. E-mail: answers@arvig.com. Web Site: http://www.arvig.com. ICA: MN5212.

TV Market Ranking: Outside TV Markets (PERHAM TWP.).

Channel capacity: N.A. Channels available but not in use: N.A.

Internet Service

Operational: Yes.

Telephone Service

Digital: Operational

Ownership: Arvig Communication Systems.

PETERSON—Now served by CALEDONIA, MN [MN0086]. ICA: MN0251.

PILLAGER—Savage Communications Inc., PO Box 810, 206 Power Ave N, Hinckley, MN 55037. Phone: 320-384-7442. Fax: 320-384-7446. Web Site: http://www.scibroadband.com. Also serves East Gull Lake & Motley. ICA: MN0230.

TV Market Ranking: Outside TV Markets (East Gull Lake, Motley, PILLAGER). Franchise award date: April 17, 1985. Franchise expiration date: N.A. Began: December 2, 1985.

Channel capacity: N.A. Channels available but not in use: N.A.

Basic Service

Subscribers: 1,099.

Programming (received off-air): KARE (NBC) Minneapolis; KAWB (PBS) Brainerd; KCCO-TV (CBS) Alexandria; KMSP-TV (FOX) Minneapolis; KSAX (ABC) Alexandria; KSTC-TV (IND) Minneapolis; WFTC (MNT) Minneapolis; WPIX (CW, IND) New York.

Programming (via satellite): ABC Family Channel; Animal Planet; Arts & Entertainment; Cartoon Network; CNBC; CNN; Comedy Central; C-SPAN; Discovery Channel; Disney Channel; E! Entertainment Television; ESPN; ESPN 2; Fox News Channel; Fox Sports Net; Golf Channel; Great American Country; Headline News; HGTV; History Channel; Lifetime; MTV; National Geographic Channel; Nickelodeon; QVC; Spike TV; Syfy; TBS Superstation; The Learning Channel; Turner Classic Movies; Turner Network TV; TV Land; USA Network; VH1; Weather Channel; WGN America.

Current originations: Public Access.

Fee: $50.00 installation; $21.47 monthly.

Digital Basic Service

Subscribers: N.A.

Programming (via satellite): AmericanLife TV Network; BBC America; Bio; Bloomberg Television; Discovery Digital Networks; DMX Music; ESPN Classic Sports; ESPNews; FitTV; Fox Movie Channel; Fox Sports World; Fuse; G4; History Channel International; INSP; National Geographic Channel; Outdoor Channel; Sleuth; Speed Channel; Trinity Broadcasting Network; Versus; WE tv.

Pay Service 1

Pay Units: 78.

Programming (via satellite): HBO.

Fee: $20.00 installation; $12.00 monthly.

Digital Pay Service 1

Pay Units: N.A.

Programming (via satellite): Cinemax; Encore; HBO; Showtime; Starz; The Movie Channel.

Video-On-Demand: No

Pay-Per-View

Movies (delivered digitally); ESPN Now (delivered digitally); Sports PPV (delivered digitally).

Internet Service

Operational: Yes.

Broadband Service: SCI Broadband.

Fee: $39.95 monthly.

Telephone Service

None

Miles of Plant: 66.0 (coaxial); None (fiber optic). Homes passed: 1,921.

Manager: Mike Danielson. Marketing Director: Ron Savage. Chief Technician: Pat McCabe. Customer Service Manager: Donna Erickson.

City fee: None.

Ownership: Savage Communications Inc. (MSO).

PINE ISLAND—Pine Island Telephone Co., PO Box 588, 108 2nd St SW, Pine Island, MN 55963. Phones: 800-992-8857; 507-356-8302. Fax: 507-356-4001. E-mail: rdkpitc@pitel.net. Web Site: http://www.pitel.net. Also serves Oronoco. ICA: MN0089.

TV Market Ranking: Below 100 (Oronoco, PINE ISLAND). Franchise award date: June 12, 1989. Franchise expiration date: N.A. Began: October 28, 1982.

Channel capacity: N.A. Channels available but not in use: N.A.

Digital Basic Service

Subscribers: 1,321.

Programming (received off-air): KAAL (ABC) Austin; KARE (NBC) Minneapolis; KIMT (CBS, MNT) Mason City; KMSP-TV (FOX) Minneapolis; KPXM-TV (ION) St. Cloud; KSTC-TV (IND) Minneapolis; KSTP-TV (ABC) St. Paul; KTTC (CW, NBC) Rochester; KXLT-TV (FOX) Rochester; WCCO-TV (CBS) Minneapolis; WFTC (MNT) Minneapolis; WUCW (CW) Minneapolis; allband FM.

Programming (via satellite): ABC Family Channel; AMC; AmericanLife TV Network; America's Store; Animal Planet; Arts & Entertainment; Boomerang; Bravo; Cartoon Network; CNBC; CNN; Comedy Central; Country Music TV; C-SPAN; C-SPAN 2; Discovery Channel; Discovery Health Channel; Disney Channel; DMX Music; Do-It-Yourself; E! Entertainment Television; ESPN; ESPN 2; ESPN Classic Sports; ESPNews; Eternal Word TV Network; Food Network; Fox Movie Channel; Fox News Channel; Fox Sports Net North; Fuse; FX; G4; Golf Channel; Great American Country; GSN; Hallmark Channel; Headline News; HGTV; History Channel; Independent Film Channel; Lifetime; Lifetime Movie Network; MSNBC; MTV; National Geographic Channel; Nickelodeon; Outdoor Channel; QVC; RFD-TV; SoapNet; Speed Channel; Spike TV; Syfy; TBS Superstation; The Learning Channel; The Sportsman Channel; Toon Disney; Travel Channel; Trinity Broadcasting Network; truTV; Turner Classic Movies; Turner Network TV; TV Land; USA Network; VH1; WE tv; Weather Channel; WGN America.

Current originations: Educational Access; Public Access.

Fee: $80.00 installation; $32.55 monthly; $2.00 converter.

Digital Pay Service 1

Pay Units: 86.

Programming (via satellite): Cinemax.

Fee: $7.95 monthly.

Digital Pay Service 2

Pay Units: 147.

Programming (via satellite): HBO.

Fee: $11.95 monthly.

Digital Pay Service 3

Pay Units: 64.

Programming (via satellite): Flix; Showtime; Sundance Channel; The Movie Channel (multiplexed).

Fee: $12.95 monthly.

Digital Pay Service 4

Pay Units: 94.

Programming (via satellite): Encore (multiplexed); Starz.

Fee: $4.95 monthly.

Digital Pay Service 5

Pay Units: 8.

Programming (via satellite): Playboy TV.

Fee: $11.95 monthly.

Video-On-Demand: No

Internet Service

Operational: No.

Broadband Service: Offers dial-up and DSL only; no cable modem service.

Telephone Service

None

Miles of Plant: 14.0 (coaxial); 7.0 (fiber optic). Homes passed: 1,388. Total homes in franchised area: 1,388.

Manager: Richard D. Keane. Office Manager: Paula Hofstad. Chief Technician: Corey Cordell.

City fee: 3% of gross.

Ownership: Hector Communications Corp. (MSO).

PINE LAKE TWP.—ACS Video. Formerly served by Perham, MN [MN0050]. This cable system has converted to IPTV, 150 Second St SW, Perham, MN 56573. Phone: 866-937-4227. E-mail: answers@arvig.com. Web Site: http://www.arvig.com. ICA: MN5214.

TV Market Ranking: Outside TV Markets (PINE LAKE TWP.).

Channel capacity: N.A. Channels available but not in use: N.A.

Internet Service
Operational: Yes.
Telephone Service
Digital: Operational
Ownership: Arvig Communication Systems.

PIPESTONE—Mediacom, PO Box 110, 1504 2nd St SE, Waseca, MN 56093. Phones: 800-332-0245; 507-835-2356. Fax: 507-835-4567. Web Site: http://www.mediacomcable.com. Also serves Fulda & Slayton. ICA: MN0348.
TV Market Ranking: Outside TV Markets (Fulda, PIPESTONE, Slayton). Franchise award date: N.A. Franchise expiration date: N.A. Began: November 1, 1974.
Channel capacity: N.A. Channels available but not in use: N.A.
Basic Service
Subscribers: 2,736.
Programming (received off-air): KARE (NBC) Minneapolis; KCPO-LP Sioux Falls; KDLT-TV (NBC) Sioux Falls; KELO-TV (CBS, MNT) Sioux Falls; KESD-TV (PBS) Brookings; KSFY-TV (ABC) Sioux Falls; KSMN (PBS) Worthington; KTTW (FOX) Sioux Falls; KWSD (CW) Sioux Falls; allband FM.
Programming (via satellite): C-SPAN; C-SPAN 2; TV Guide Network; Weather Channel; WGN America.
Programming (via translator): KTCA-TV (PBS) St. Paul; WCCO-TV (CBS) Minneapolis.
Fee: $52.39 installation; $16.38 monthly; $17.48 additional installation.
Expanded Basic Service 1
Subscribers: 2,653.
Programming (via satellite): ABC Family Channel; AMC; Animal Planet; Arts & Entertainment; Bravo; Cartoon Network; CNBC; CNN; Comedy Central; Country Music TV; Discovery Channel; Disney Channel; E! Entertainment Television; ESPN; ESPN 2; Eternal Word TV Network; Fox Movie Channel; Fox News Channel; Fox Sports Net North; FX; GalaVision; Hallmark Channel; Headline News; HGTV; History Channel; Home Shopping Network; INSP; Lifetime; MSNBC; MTV; Nickelodeon; RFD-TV; SoapNet; Speed Channel; Spike TV; Syfy; TBS Superstation; The Learning Channel; Travel Channel; Trinity Broadcasting Network; truTV; Turner Classic Movies; Turner Network TV; TV Land; Univision; USA Network; VH1; WE tv.
Fee: $15.69 monthly.
Digital Basic Service
Subscribers: N.A.
Programming (received off-air): KDLT-TV (NBC) Sioux Falls; KELO-TV (CBS, MNT) Sioux Falls; KESD-TV (PBS) Brookings; KSFY-TV (ABC) Sioux Falls; KTTW (FOX) Sioux Falls.
Programming (via satellite): ABC News Now; AmericanLife TV Network; BBC America; Bio; Bloomberg Television; Canal 52MX; CBS College Sports Network; CCTV-9 (CCTV International); Cine Latino; CNN en Espanol; CNN HD; Discovery en Espanol; Discovery HD Theater; Discovery Health Channel; Discovery Home Channel; Discovery Kids Channel; Discovery Military Channel; ESPN 2 HD; ESPN Deportes; ESPN HD; ESPN U; ESPNews; FitTV; Fox College Sports Atlantic; Fox College Sports Pacific; Fox Reality Channel; Fox Soccer; Fox Sports en Espanol; FSN HD; Fuse; G4; Gol TV; Golf Channel; GSN; Halogen Network; HDNet; HDNet Movies; History Channel en Espanol; History Channel International; ID Investigation Discovery; Independent Film Channel; ION Life; Lifetime Movie Network; Lifetime Real Women; MTV Hits; MTV Tres; MTV2; Music Choice; National Geographic Channel; Nick Jr.; NickToons TV; Outdoor Channel; Qubo; ReelzChannel; Science Channel; Sleuth; Style Network; TBS in HD; TeenNick; Tennis Channel; The Sportsman Channel; Turner Network TV HD; TVG Network; Universal HD; VeneMovies; VH1 Classic.
Fee: $6.95 monthly.
Digital Pay Service 1
Pay Units: 325.
Programming (via satellite): Cinemax (multiplexed); HBO HD; Showtime HD; Starz HDTV; The Movie Channel HD.
Fee: $7.00 monthly.
Digital Pay Service 2
Pay Units: 284.
Programming (via satellite): Encore (multiplexed); Starz (multiplexed).
Fee: $5.00 monthly.
Digital Pay Service 3
Pay Units: 349.
Programming (via satellite): HBO (multiplexed).
Fee: $11.00 monthly.
Digital Pay Service 4
Pay Units: 510.
Programming (via satellite): Flix; Showtime (multiplexed); Sundance Channel; The Movie Channel (multiplexed).
Fee: $11.00 monthly (each).
Video-On-Demand: No
Pay-Per-View
iN DEMAND (delivered digitally); Spice: Xcess (delivered digitally); Playboy TV (delivered digitally); Penthouse TV (delivered digitally); Fresh (delivered digitally); Ten Clips (delivered digitally).
Internet Service
Operational: Yes.
Broadband Service: Mediacom High Speed Internet.
Telephone Service
Digital: Operational
Miles of Plant: 57.0 (coaxial); None (fiber optic). Homes passed: 4,432.
Vice President: Bill Jensen. Engineering Manager: Kraig Kaiser. Marketing & Sales Director: Lori Huberty.
Franchise fee: 5% of gross.
Ownership: Mediacom LLC (MSO).

PLAINVIEW—US Cable, 402 Red River Ave N, Unit 5, Cold Spring, MN 56320-1521. Phone: 320-685-7113. Fax: 320-685-2816. E-mail: help@mn.uscable.com. Web Site: http://www.uscable.com. Also serves Elgin. ICA: MN0080.
TV Market Ranking: Below 100 (Elgin, PLAINVIEW). Franchise award date: N.A. Franchise expiration date: N.A. Began: April 15, 1983.
Channel capacity: N.A. Channels available but not in use: N.A.
Basic Service
Subscribers: N.A. Included in Cambridge
Programming (received off-air): KARE (NBC) Minneapolis; KMSP-TV (FOX) Minneapolis; KSTC-TV (IND) Minneapolis; KSTP-TV (ABC) St. Paul; KTCA-TV (PBS) St. Paul; KTTC (CW, NBC) Rochester; WCCO-TV (CBS) Minneapolis; WFTC (MNT) Minneapolis; WKBT-DT (CBS, MNT) La Crosse; WUCW (CW) Minneapolis; WXOW (ABC, CW) La Crosse.
Programming (via satellite): Eternal Word TV Network; HGTV; QVC; Turner Classic Movies; Weather Channel; WGN America.
Current originations: Public Access.
Fee: $20.99 monthly.

Expanded Basic Service 1
Subscribers: N.A.
Programming (via satellite): ABC Family Channel; Animal Planet; Arts & Entertainment; Bravo; Cartoon Network; CNBC; CNN; Comedy Central; Country Music TV; C-SPAN; C-SPAN 2; Discovery Channel; Disney Channel; E! Entertainment Television; ESPN; ESPN 2; Food Network; Fox News Channel; Fox Sports Net; FX; Great American Country; Hallmark Channel; Headline News; History Channel; Lifetime; MTV; National Geographic Channel; Nickelodeon; ShopNBC; SoapNet; Speed Channel; Spike TV; Syfy; TBS Superstation; The Learning Channel; Travel Channel; truTV; Turner Network TV; TV Land; USA Network; VH1.
Fee: $23.08 monthly.
Digital Basic Service
Subscribers: N.A. Included in Cambridge
Programming (via satellite): BBC America; Bio; Bloomberg Television; Discovery Digital Networks; DMX Music; Encore (multiplexed); ESPN Classic Sports; ESPNews; Fox Movie Channel; Fox Soccer; Fuse; G4; GAS; Golf Channel; GSN; Halogen Network; History Channel International; Independent Film Channel; Lifetime Movie Network; Lime; MTV Networks Digital Suite; Nick Jr.; Outdoor Channel; Sleuth; Speed Channel; Style Network; Toon Disney; Trinity Broadcasting Network; Versus; WE tv.
Fee: $8.95 monthly.
Digital Pay Service 1
Pay Units: N.A. Included in Cambridge
Programming (via satellite): Cinemax (multiplexed); HBO (multiplexed); Showtime (multiplexed); Starz (multiplexed); The Movie Channel (multiplexed).
Fee: $6.95 monthly (Starz), $14.95 monthly (HBO, Cinemax, Showtime or TMC).
Video-On-Demand: No
Pay-Per-View
Playboy TV (delivered digitally); Fresh (delivered digitally); iN DEMAND (delivered digitally).
Internet Service
Operational: Yes.
Telephone Service
None
Homes passed: Included in Cambridge
General Manager: Steve Johnson. Customer Service Director: Jackie Torberg.
Ownership: Comcast Cable Communications Inc. (MSO).; US Cable Corp. (MSO).

PLATO—North American Communications Corp., PO Box 387, 211 Main St S, Hector, MN 55342-0387. Phones: 800-982-8038; 320-848-6781. Fax: 320-848-2323. E-mail: hcc@hcctel.net. Web Site: http://www.hectorcom.com. ICA: MN0247.
TV Market Ranking: Outside TV Markets (PLATO). Franchise award date: N.A. Franchise expiration date: N.A. Began: February 1, 1990.
Channel capacity: 36 (not 2-way capable). Channels available but not in use: 12.
Basic Service
Subscribers: 38.
Programming (received off-air): KARE (NBC) Minneapolis; KMSP-TV (FOX) Minneapolis; KSTP-TV (ABC) St. Paul; KTCA-TV (PBS) St. Paul; WCCO-TV (CBS) Minneapolis; WFTC (MNT) Minneapolis; WUCW (CW) Minneapolis.
Programming (via satellite): ABC Family Channel; AMC; Arts & Entertainment; CNN; Discovery Channel; Disney Channel; ESPN; Fox Sports Net Midwest; Lifetime; Nickelodeon; QVC; Spike TV; TBS Superstation; Trinity Broadcasting Network; Turner Network TV; USA Network; WGN America.
Fee: $40.00 installation; $26.95 monthly; $3.50 converter; $25.00 additional installation.
Pay Service 1
Pay Units: N.A.
Programming (via satellite): Cinemax.
Fee: $10.95 monthly.
Pay Service 2
Pay Units: 4.
Programming (via satellite): HBO.
Fee: $10.95 monthly.
Video-On-Demand: No
Internet Service
Operational: No.
Broadband Service: Offers dial-up and DSL only; no cable modem service.
Telephone Service
None
Miles of Plant: 4.0 (coaxial); None (fiber optic). Homes passed: 128. Total homes in franchised area: 128.
Manager: Matt Sparks. Customer Service Supervisor: Patty Groshens. Chief Technician: George Honzay.
Ownership: Hector Communications Corp. (MSO).

PRIOR LAKE—Mediacom, PO Box 110, 1504 2nd St SE, Waseca, MN 56093. Phone: 507-835-2356. Fax: 507-835-4567. Web Site: http://www.mediacomcable.com. Also serves Canterbury Estates, Credit River, Savage & Spring Lake Twp. ICA: MN0039.
TV Market Ranking: 13 (Canterbury Estates, Credit River, PRIOR LAKE, Savage, Spring Lake Twp.). Franchise award date: September 9, 1983. Franchise expiration date: N.A. Began: September 1, 1984.
Channel capacity: 70 (operating 2-way). Channels available but not in use: None.
Basic Service
Subscribers: 5,381.
Programming (received off-air): KARE (NBC) Minneapolis; KMSP-TV (FOX) Minneapolis; KPXM-TV (ION) St. Cloud; KSTC-TV (IND) Minneapolis; KSTP-TV (ABC) St. Paul; KTCA-TV (PBS) St. Paul; KTCI-TV (PBS) St. Paul; WCCO-TV (CBS) Minneapolis; WFTC (MNT) Minneapolis; WUCW (CW) Minneapolis.
Programming (via satellite): C-SPAN; Weather Channel; WGN America.
Current originations: Leased Access; Religious Access; Government Access; Educational Access; Public Access.
Fee: $30.00 installation; $16.95 monthly; $15.00 additional installation.

Expanded Basic Service 1
Subscribers: 799.
Programming (via satellite): ABC Family Channel; AMC; Animal Planet; Arts & Entertainment; BET Networks; Bravo; Cartoon Network; CNBC; CNN; Comedy Central; Country Music TV; C-SPAN 2; Discovery Channel; Disney Channel; E! Entertainment Television; ESPN; ESPN 2; Eternal Word TV Network; Food Network; Fox Movie Channel; Fox News Channel; Fox Sports Net North; FX; Hallmark Channel; Headline News; HGTV; History Channel; Home Shopping Network; INSP; Lifetime; MSNBC; MTV; Nickelodeon; QVC; SoapNet; Speed Channel; Spike TV; Syfy; TBS Superstation; The Learning Channel; Travel Channel; Trinity Broadcasting Network; truTV; Turner Classic Movies; Turner Network TV; TV Guide Network; TV Land; Univision; USA Network; VH1; WE tv.

Digital Basic Service
Subscribers: N.A.
Programming (via satellite): AmericanLife TV Network; BBC America; Bio; Bloomberg Television; Canales N; Discovery Digital Networks; DMX Music; Fox Sports World; Fuse; G4; Golf Channel; GSN; Halogen Network; History Channel International; Independent Film Channel; Lifetime Movie Network; Lime; National Geographic Channel; Outdoor Channel; Style Network.

Digital Pay Service 1
Pay Units: 350.
Programming (via satellite): Cinemax (multiplexed); Encore (multiplexed); Flix; HBO (multiplexed); Showtime (multiplexed); Starz (multiplexed); Sundance Channel; The Movie Channel (multiplexed).
Fee: $15.00 installation; $8.95 monthly (Showtime), $9.95 monthly (Cinemax or TMC), $11.95 monthly (HBO).

Video-On-Demand: Yes

Pay-Per-View
TVN Entertainment (delivered digitally); ESPN Now (delivered digitally); Sports PPV (delivered digitally); Urban Xtra (delivered digitally); Fresh (delivered digitally); Shorteez (delivered digitally); Playboy TV (delivered digitally); Pleasure (delivered digitally).

Internet Service
Operational: Yes.
Broadband Service: Mediacom High Speed Internet.
Fee: $99.00 installation; $40.00 monthly.

Telephone Service
Digital: Operational

Miles of Plant: 133.0 (coaxial); None (fiber optic). Homes passed: 6,238.
Vice President: Bill Jensen. Engineering Manager: Kraig Kaiser. Marketing & Sales Director: Lori Huberty.
City fee: 3% of gross.
Ownership: Mediacom LLC (MSO).

PROCTOR—Now served by CLOQUET, MN [MN0042]. ICA: MN0064.

RACINE—North American Communications Corp., PO Box 387, 211 Main St S, Hector, MN 55342-0387. Phones: 800-982-8038; 320-848-6781. Fax: 320-848-2323. E-mail: hcc@hcctel.net. Web Site: http://www.hectorcom.com. ICA: MN0258.
TV Market Ranking: Below 100 (RACINE). Franchise award date: February 1, 1989. Franchise expiration date: N.A. Began: February 1, 1990.
Channel capacity: 54 (not 2-way capable). Channels available but not in use: 28.

Basic Service
Subscribers: 57.
Programming (received off-air): KAAL (ABC) Austin; KIMT (CBS, MNT) Mason City; KSMQ-TV (PBS) Austin; KYIN (PBS) Mason City; WHLA-TV (PBS) La Crosse; WLAX (FOX) La Crosse.
Programming (via satellite): ABC Family Channel; AMC; Arts & Entertainment; CNN; Country Music TV; Discovery Channel; ESPN; Fox Sports Net Midwest; Lifetime; Nickelodeon; QVC; Spike TV; TBS Superstation; Turner Network TV; USA Network; WGN America.
Fee: $40.00 installation; $26.95 monthly; $3.50 converter; $25.00 additional installation.

Pay Service 1
Pay Units: 5.
Programming (via satellite): HBO.
Fee: $10.95 monthly.

Pay Service 2
Pay Units: N.A.
Programming (via satellite): Cinemax.
Fee: $10.95 monthly.

Video-On-Demand: No

Internet Service
Operational: No.
Broadband Service: Offers dial-up and DSL only; no cable modem service.

Telephone Service
None

Miles of Plant: 4.0 (coaxial); None (fiber optic). Homes passed: 115. Total homes in franchised area: 115.
Manager: Matt Sparks. Chief Technician: George Honzay. Customer Service Supervisor: Patty Groshens.
Ownership: Hector Communications Corp. (MSO).

RANDALL—Consolidated Telecommunications Co. Formerly [MN0202]. This cable system has converted to IPTV, PO Box 972, 1102 Madison St, Brainerd, MN 56401. Phones: 800-753-9104; 218-454-1234. Web Site: http://www.ctctelcom.net. ICA: MN5026.
TV Market Ranking: Outside TV Markets (RANDALL). Franchise award date: N.A. Franchise expiration date: N.A. Began: N.A.
Channel capacity: N.A. Channels available but not in use: N.A.

Internet Service
Operational: Yes.

Telephone Service
Digital: Operational

Ownership: Consolidated Telecommunications Co. (MSO).

RANDALL—Consolidated Telecommunications Co. This cable system has converted to IPTV. See RANDALL, MN [MN5026], MN. ICA: MN0202.

RANDOLPH—Cannon Valley Cablevision. Now served by VERMILLION, MN [MN0391]. ICA: MN0350.

RAVENNA—Cannon Valley Cablevision. Now served by VERMILLION, MN [MN0391]. ICA: MN0351.

RAYMOND—Farmers Mutual Telephone Co., PO Box 220, Stanton, IA 51573. Phones: 800-469-2111; 717-829-2111. Web Site: http://online.fmtc.com. ICA: MN0352.
TV Market Ranking: Below 100 (RAYMOND). Franchise award date: September 1, 1988. Franchise expiration date: N.A. Began: May 1, 1989.
Channel capacity: 54 (operating 2-way). Channels available but not in use: N.A.

Basic Service
Subscribers: 210.
Programming (received off-air): KARE (NBC) Minneapolis; KCCO-TV (CBS) Alexandria; KMSP-TV (FOX) Minneapolis; KSAX (ABC) Alexandria; KSTC-TV (IND) Minneapolis; KWCM-TV (PBS) Appleton; WFTC (MNT) Minneapolis; WUCW (CW) Minneapolis.
Programming (via satellite): ABC Family Channel; AMC; Animal Planet; Arts & Entertainment; Cartoon Network; CNN; Comedy Central; Country Music TV; Discovery Channel; Disney Channel; E! Entertainment Television; ESPN; ESPN 2; Food Network; Fox Sports Net North; Golf Channel; Hallmark Channel; Hallmark Movie Channel; HGTV; History Channel; Lifetime; MTV; Nickelodeon; Outdoor Channel; QVC; Speed Channel; Spike TV; Syfy; TBS Superstation; The Learning Channel; Trinity Broadcasting Network; Turner Network TV; TV Land; USA Network; VH1; Weather Channel; WGN America.
Fee: $10.00 installation; $26.95 monthly.

Pay Service 1
Pay Units: 15.
Programming (via satellite): Cinemax; HBO; Showtime.
Fee: $9.95 monthly (Cinemax), $10.95 monthly (Showtime), $11.95 monthly (HBO).

Video-On-Demand: No

Internet Service
Operational: No.

Telephone Service
None

Miles of Plant: 5.0 (coaxial); None (fiber optic). Homes passed: 300. Total homes in franchised area: 300.
General Manager: Kevin Cabbage. Assistant Manager: Dennis Crawford.
Ownership: Farmers Mutual Telephone Co. (MSO).

READING—Formerly served by American Telecasting of Minnesota Inc. No longer in operation. ICA: MN0353.

RED LAKE FALLS—Sjoberg's Cable TV Inc., 315 Main Ave N, Thief River Falls, MN 56701-1905. Phones: 800-828-8808; 218-681-3044. Fax: 218-681-6801. Web Site: http://trf.mncable.net. Also serves Red Lake Twp. ICA: MN0141.
TV Market Ranking: Below 100 (RED LAKE FALLS, Red Lake Twp.). Franchise award date: N.A. Franchise expiration date: N.A. Began: October 1, 1977.
Channel capacity: 78 (operating 2-way). Channels available but not in use: 18.

Basic Service
Subscribers: 530.
Programming (received off-air): KCPM (MNT) Grand Forks; KGFE (PBS) Grand Forks; KVLY-TV (NBC) Fargo; KXJB-TV (CBS) Valley City; various Canadian stations; WDAZ-TV (ABC, CW) Devils Lake; allband FM.
Programming (via microwave): KBRR (FOX) Thief River Falls.
Programming (via satellite): CNN; ESPN; TBS Superstation.
Current originations: Public Access.
Fee: $25.00 installation; $10.00 monthly.

Expanded Basic Service 1
Subscribers: N.A.
Programming (via satellite): ABC Family Channel; Animal Planet; Arts & Entertainment; Cartoon Network; CNBC; Comedy Central; Country Music TV; C-SPAN; CW+; Discovery Channel; Discovery Channel HD; Disney Channel; E! Entertainment Television; ESPN 2; Food Network; Fox News Channel; Fox Sports Net; FX; HGTV; History Channel; Home Shopping Network; Lifetime; MSNBC; MTV; Nickelodeon; Spike TV; Syfy; The Learning Channel; Turner Classic Movies; Turner Network TV; TV Land; USA Network; VH1; Weather Channel; WGN America.
Fee: $23.71 monthly.

Digital Basic Service
Subscribers: N.A.
Programming (via satellite): AmericanLife TV Network; BBC America; Bio; Blackbelt TV; Bloomberg Television; Bravo; CBS College Sports Network; Chiller; CMT Pure Country; Cooking Channel; Current; Daystar TV Network; Discovery Health Channel; Discovery Kids Channel; Discovery Military Channel; Discovery Planet Green; DMX Music; Do-It-Yourself; ESPN Classic Sports; ESPN U; ESPNews; Eternal Word TV Network; FitTV; Fox Business Channel; Fox College Sports Atlantic; Fox College Sports Central; Fox College Sports Pacific; Fox Movie Channel; Fox Reality Channel; Fox Soccer; G4; Golf Channel; Gospel Music Channel; Great American Country; GSN; Hallmark Channel; Halogen Network; Headline News; History Channel International; HorseRacing TV; ID Investigation Discovery; Independent Film Channel; Lifetime Movie Network; MTV Hits; MTV2; National Geographic Channel; Nick Jr.; NickToons TV; Outdoor Channel; Ovation; Oxygen; PBS Kids Sprout; ReelzChannel; RFD-TV; Science Channel; ShopNBC; Sleuth; SoapNet; Speed Channel; Style Network; Sundance Channel; TeenNick; Tennis Channel; The Sportsman Channel; The Word Network; Toon Disney; Trinity Broadcasting Network; TVG Network; Versus; VH1 Classic; VH1 Soul; WE tv.
Fee: $11.00 monthly.

Digital Expanded Basic Service
Subscribers: N.A.
Programming (via satellite): Arts & Entertainment HD; CNN HD; ESPN 2 HD; ESPN HD; Food Network HD; FSN HD; HDNet; HDNet Movies; HGTV HD; History Channel HD; Outdoor Channel 2 HD; PBS HD; Speed HD; Syfy HD; TBS in HD; Turner Network TV HD; Universal HD; USA Network HD; Versus HD.
Fee: $5.00 monthly; $5.00 converter.

Pay Service 1
Pay Units: 110.
Programming (via satellite): HBO.
Fee: $11.00 monthly.

Pay Service 2
Pay Units: N.A.
Programming (via satellite): Cinemax.
Fee: $9.00 monthly.

Digital Pay Service 1
Pay Units: N.A.
Programming (via satellite): Cinemax (multiplexed); Cinemax HD; Encore (multiplexed); HBO (multiplexed); HBO HD; Showtime (multiplexed); Starz (multiplexed); The Movie Channel (multiplexed).
Fee: $8.00 monthly (Starz/Encore), $9.00 monthly (Cinemax or Showtime/TMC), $11.00 monthly (HBO).

Video-On-Demand: No

Internet Service
Operational: No.

Telephone Service
None

Miles of Plant: 13.0 (coaxial); 19.0 (fiber optic). Homes passed: 555. Total homes in franchised area: 555.
Manager: Richard J. Sjoberg. Chief Technician: Jerry Seim.

City fee: None.
Ownership: Sjoberg's Cable TV Inc. (MSO).

RED ROCK—North American Communications Corp., PO Box 387, 211 Main St S, Hector, MN 55342-0387. Phones: 800-982-8038; 320-848-6781. Fax: 320-848-2323. E-mail: hcc@hcctel.net. Web Site: http://www.hectorcom.com. ICA: MN0354.
TV Market Ranking: Below 100 (RED ROCK). Franchise award date: N.A. Franchise expiration date: N.A. Began: N.A.
Channel capacity: 54 (not 2-way capable). Channels available but not in use: 30.
Basic Service
Subscribers: 38.
Programming (received off-air): KAAL (ABC) Austin; KIMT (CBS, MNT) Mason City; KSMQ-TV (PBS) Austin; KYIN (PBS) Mason City.
Programming (via satellite): ABC Family Channel; AMC; Arts & Entertainment; CNN; Country Music TV; Discovery Channel; ESPN; ESPN 2; Lifetime; Nickelodeon; QVC; Spike TV; TBS Superstation; Turner Network TV; USA Network; WGN America.
Fee: $40.00 installation; $26.95 monthly; $3.50 converter; $25.00 additional installation.
Pay Service 1
Pay Units: 3.
Programming (via satellite): HBO.
Fee: $10.95 monthly.
Pay Service 2
Pay Units: N.A.
Programming (via satellite): Cinemax.
Fee: $10.95 monthly.
Video-On-Demand: No
Internet Service
Operational: No.
Broadband Service: Offers dial-up and DSL only; no cable modem service.
Telephone Service
None
Miles of Plant: 4.0 (coaxial); None (fiber optic). Homes passed: 185. Total homes in franchised area: 185.
Manager: Matt Sparks. Chief Technician: George Honzay. Customer Service Supervisor: Patty Groshens.
Ownership: Hector Communications Corp. (MSO).

RED WING—Charter Communications, 16900 Cedar Ave S, Rosemount, MN 55068-5129. Phones: 507-289-8372 (Rochester administrative office); 952-432-2575. Fax: 952-432-5765. Web Site: http://www.charter.com. ICA: MN0028.
TV Market Ranking: Outside TV Markets (RED WING). Franchise award date: January 26, 1981. Franchise expiration date: N.A. Began: November 1, 1972.
Channel capacity: N.A. Channels available but not in use: N.A.
Basic Service
Subscribers: 4,010.
Programming (received off-air): KARE (NBC) Minneapolis; KMSP-TV (FOX) Minneapolis; KPXM-TV (ION) St. Cloud; KSTC-TV (IND) Minneapolis; KSTP-TV (ABC) St. Paul; KTCA-TV (PBS) St. Paul; KTCI-TV (PBS) St. Paul; WCCO-TV (CBS) Minneapolis; WFTC (MNT) Minneapolis; WKBT-DT (CBS, MNT) La Crosse; WUCW (CW) Minneapolis.
Programming (via satellite): C-SPAN; C-SPAN 2; Home Shopping Network; INSP; QVC; TV Guide Network; WGN America.
Current originations: Government Access; Public Access.
Fee: $29.99 installation; $2.75 converter.
Expanded Basic Service 1
Subscribers: N.A.
Programming (via satellite): ABC Family Channel; AMC; Animal Planet; Arts & Entertainment; BET Networks; Bravo; Cartoon Network; CNBC; CNN; Comedy Central; Country Music TV; Discovery Channel; Disney Channel; E! Entertainment Television; ESPN; ESPN 2; Food Network; Fox News Channel; Fox Sports Net North; FX; G4; Golf Channel; GSN; Hallmark Channel; Headline News; HGTV; History Channel; Lifetime; MSNBC; MTV; MTV2; National Geographic Channel; Nickelodeon; Oxygen; SoapNet; Speed Channel; Spike TV; Style Network; Syfy; TBS Superstation; The Learning Channel; Toon Disney; Travel Channel; truTV; Turner Classic Movies; Turner Network TV; TV Land; Univision; USA Network; Versus; VH1; WE tv; Weather Channel.
Fee: $47.99 monthly.
Digital Basic Service
Subscribers: N.A.
Programming (via satellite): BBC America; Bio; CNN International; Discovery Digital Networks; Do-It-Yourself; FitTV; Fuel TV; Fuse; GAS; History Channel International; Lifetime Movie Network; MTV Networks Digital Suite; Music Choice; Nick Jr.; Nick Too; NickToons TV; Sundance Channel; TV Guide Interactive Inc.
Digital Pay Service 1
Pay Units: N.A.
Programming (via satellite): Cinemax (multiplexed); Encore (multiplexed); Flix; HBO (multiplexed); Showtime (multiplexed); Starz (multiplexed); The Movie Channel (multiplexed).
Video-On-Demand: Yes
Pay-Per-View
iN DEMAND (delivered digitally); NASCAR In Car (delivered digitally); NHL Center Ice (delivered digitally); MLB Extra Innings (delivered digitally); Playboy TV (delivered digitally); Fresh (delivered digitally); Shorteez (delivered digitally).
Internet Service
Operational: Yes.
Broadband Service: Charter Pipeline.
Fee: $29.99 monthly.
Telephone Service
Digital: Operational
Miles of Plant: 92.0 (coaxial); None (fiber optic). Homes passed: 7,800.
Vice President & General Manager: John Crowley. Operations Director: Craig Stensaas. Technical Operations Director: Darin Helgeson. Technical Operations Manager: Mark Harder.; Clayton Snyder. Marketing Director: Bill Haarstad. Office Manager: Linda Lindberg.
City fee: 5% of gross.
Ownership: Charter Communications Inc. (MSO).

REDEYE TWP.—Formerly served by MENAGHA, MN [MN0112]. West Central Telephone Assn. This cable system has converted to IPTV, 308 Frontage Rd, Sebeka, MN 56477. Phones: 800-945-2163; 218-837-5151. Web Site: http://www.wcta.net. ICA: MN5250.
TV Market Ranking: Outside TV Markets (REDEYE TWP.).
Channel capacity: N.A. Channels available but not in use: N.A.
Internet Service
Operational: Yes.
Telephone Service
Digital: Operational
Ownership: West Central Telephone Association.

REDWOOD FALLS—Mediacom, PO Box 110, 1504 2nd St SE, Waseca, MN 56093. Phone: 507-835-2356. Fax: 507-835-4567. Web Site: http://www.mediacomcable.com. Also serves Arlington, Fairfax, Franklin, Gaylord, Gibbon, Lower Sioux, Morton, North Redwood, Sleepy Eye, Springfield & Winthrop. ICA: MN0057.
TV Market Ranking: Below 100 (Arlington, Fairfax, Franklin, Gaylord, Gibbon, Lower Sioux, Morton, North Redwood, REDWOOD FALLS, Sleepy Eye, Springfield, Winthrop). Franchise award date: November 1, 1981. Franchise expiration date: N.A. Began: September 1, 1982.
Channel capacity: N.A. Channels available but not in use: N.A.
Basic Service
Subscribers: 5,628.
Programming (received off-air): KEYC-TV (CBS, FOX) Mankato; KPXM-TV (ION) St. Cloud; KSTC-TV (IND) Minneapolis; KTCI-TV (PBS) St. Paul; KWCM-TV (PBS) Appleton; WUCW (CW) Minneapolis; allband FM.
Programming (via satellite): C-SPAN; TV Guide Network; Weather Channel; WGN America.
Programming (via translator): KARE (NBC) Minneapolis; KMSP-TV (FOX) Minneapolis; KSTP-TV (ABC) St. Paul; KTCA-TV (PBS) St. Paul; WCCO-TV (CBS) Minneapolis; WFTC (MNT) Minneapolis.
Fee: $52.39 installation; $10.91 monthly; $2.00 converter; $17.48 additional installation.
Expanded Basic Service 1
Subscribers: 5,451.
Programming (via satellite): ABC Family Channel; AMC; Animal Planet; Arts & Entertainment; BET Networks; Bravo; Cartoon Network; CNBC; CNN; Comedy Central; Country Music TV; Discovery Channel; Disney Channel; E! Entertainment Television; ESPN; ESPN 2; Eternal Word TV Network; Food Network; Fox Movie Channel; Fox News Channel; Fox Sports Net North; FX; Hallmark Channel; Headline News; HGTV; History Channel; INSP; Lifetime; MSNBC; MTV; Nickelodeon; QVC; SoapNet; Speed Channel; Spike TV; Syfy; TBS Superstation; The Learning Channel; Travel Channel; Trinity Broadcasting Network; Turner Classic Movies; Turner Network TV; TV Land; Univision; USA Network; VH1; WE tv.
Fee: $16.52 monthly.
Digital Basic Service
Subscribers: 481.
Programming (via satellite): AmericanLife TV Network; BBC America; Bio; Bloomberg Television; Canales N; Discovery Digital Networks; DMX Music; Fox Sports World; Fuse; G4; Golf Channel; GSN; Halogen Network; History Channel International; Independent Film Channel; Lifetime Movie Network; Lime; National Geographic Channel; Outdoor Channel; Style Network.
Fee: $7.00 monthly.
Digital Pay Service 1
Pay Units: 733.
Programming (via satellite): Cinemax (multiplexed).
Fee: $9.95 monthly.
Digital Pay Service 2
Pay Units: 670.
Programming (via satellite): Encore (multiplexed); Starz (multiplexed).
Fee: $8.00 monthly.
Digital Pay Service 3
Pay Units: 945.
Programming (via satellite): HBO (multiplexed).
Fee: $11.00 monthly.
Digital Pay Service 4
Pay Units: 896.
Programming (via satellite): Showtime (multiplexed); The Movie Channel (multiplexed).
Fee: $11.00 monthly (each).
Digital Pay Service 5
Pay Units: N.A.
Programming (via satellite): Flix; Sundance Channel.
Video-On-Demand: Yes
Pay-Per-View
Addressable homes: 481.
TVN Entertainment (delivered digitally), Addressable: Yes; ESPN Now (delivered digitally); Sports PPV (delivered digitally); Urban Xtra (delivered digitally); Fresh (delivered digitally); Shorteez (delivered digitally); Playboy TV (delivered digitally); Pleasure (delivered digitally).
Internet Service
Operational: Yes.
Broadband Service: Mediacom High Speed Internet.
Fee: $40.00 monthly.
Telephone Service
Digital: Operational
Miles of Plant: 183.0 (coaxial); None (fiber optic). Homes passed: 9,242.
Vice President: Bill Jensen. Engineering Manager: Kraig Kaiser. Marketing & Sales Director: Lori Huberty.
City fee: 3% of gross.
Ownership: Mediacom LLC (MSO).

REDWOOD FALLS—NU-Telecom. Formerly served by New Ulm, MN [MN0285]. This cable system has converted to IPTV, PO Box 697, 22 S Marshall, Springfield, MN 56087-0697. Phones: 800-893-1856; 507-723-4211. Fax: 507-723-4377. E-mail: onlinecustservice@nu-telecom.net. Web Site: http://www.nutelecom.net. ICA: MN5147.
TV Market Ranking: Below 100 (REDWOOD FALLS).
Channel capacity: N.A. Channels available but not in use: N.A.
Internet Service
Operational: Yes.
Telephone Service
Digital: Operational
President & Chief Executive Officer: Bill Otis.
Ownership: NU-Telecom.

REMER—Eagle Cablevision Inc., PO Box 39, 205 First Ave NE, Remer, MN 56672-0039. Phone: 218-566-2302. Fax: 218-566-2166. Web Site: http://www.jtc-companies.com. ICA: MN0355.
TV Market Ranking: Below 100 (REMER). Franchise award date: N.A. Franchise expiration date: N.A. Began: January 1, 1971.
Channel capacity: 24 (not 2-way capable). Channels available but not in use: N.A.
Basic Service
Subscribers: 188.
Programming (received off-air): KAWE (PBS) Bemidji; KCCW-TV (CBS) Walker; WIRT-DT (ABC) Hibbing; allband FM.
Programming (via satellite): ABC Family Channel; CNN; Discovery Channel; ESPN; TBS Superstation; Turner Network TV; USA Network; WGN America; WNBC (NBC) New York.
Fee: $25.00 installation; $12.00 monthly.
Video-On-Demand: No
Internet Service
Operational: No, DSL & dial-up.
Telephone Service
None
Miles of Plant: 2.0 (coaxial); None (fiber optic). Additional miles planned: 2.0 (coaxial).

President: Conrad Johnson. Manager & Chief Technician: Dwayne Johnson.
Ownership: Eagle Cablevision Inc.

REVERE—Revere TV Cable Co., 749 Des Moines Dr, Windom, MN 56101-1604. Phone: 507-831-4938. Fax: 507-831-4938. E-mail: cabletv@rrcnet.org. ICA: MN0356.
TV Market Ranking: Below 100 (REVERE). Franchise award date: N.A. Franchise expiration date: N.A. Began: January 1, 1972.
Channel capacity: 36 (not 2-way capable). Channels available but not in use: 6.
Basic Service
Subscribers: 20.
Programming (received off-air): KELO-TV (CBS, MNT) Sioux Falls; KEYC-TV (CBS, FOX) Mankato; KSFY-TV (ABC) Sioux Falls; KSMN (PBS) Worthington; KWCM-TV (PBS) Appleton; 1 FM.
Programming (via satellite): ABC Family Channel; CNN; Country Music TV; Discovery Channel; ESPN; FamilyNet; Fox Sports Net; Headline News; HGTV; Lifetime; Nickelodeon; Spike TV; TBS Superstation; The Learning Channel; Turner Classic Movies; Turner Network TV; TV Land; USA Network; Weather Channel; WGN America.
Programming (via translator): KARE (NBC) Minneapolis; KMSP-TV (FOX) Minneapolis; KSTP-TV (ABC) St. Paul; KWCM-TV (PBS) Appleton; WCCO-TV (CBS) Minneapolis; WFTC (MNT) Minneapolis; WUCW (CW) Minneapolis.
Fee: $15.00 installation; $14.95 monthly.
Pay Service 1
Pay Units: N.A.
Programming (via satellite): Showtime.
Video-On-Demand: No
Internet Service
Operational: No.
Telephone Service
None
Miles of Plant: 1.0 (coaxial); None (fiber optic). Homes passed: 45. Total homes in franchised area: 45.
Manager: Kjell Turner.
Ownership: Robert E. Turner (MSO).

ROCHESTER—Charter Communications, 3380 Northern Valley Pl NE, Rochester, MN 55906-3954. Phone: 507-289-8372. Fax: 507-285-6162. Web Site: http://www.charter.com. Also serves Byron, Cascade Twp., Eyota, Haverhill Twp., Kasson, Marion Twp., Oronoco Twp., Stewartville & Zumbrota. ICA: MN0008.
TV Market Ranking: Below 100 (Byron, Cascade Twp., Eyota, Haverhill Twp., Kasson, Marion Twp., Oronoco Twp., ROCHESTER, Stewartville, Zumbrota). Franchise award date: May 19, 1958. Franchise expiration date: N.A. Began: October 1, 1958.
Channel capacity: N.A. Channels available but not in use: N.A.
Basic Service
Subscribers: 31,300.
Programming (received off-air): KAAL (ABC) Austin; KIMT (CBS, MNT) Mason City; KMSP-TV (FOX) Minneapolis; KSMQ-TV (PBS) Austin; KSTP-TV (ABC) St. Paul; KTCA-TV (PBS) St. Paul; KTTC (CW, NBC) Rochester; KXLT-TV (FOX) Rochester; WCCO-TV (CBS) Minneapolis; 17 FMs.
Programming (via satellite): C-SPAN; C-SPAN 2; Home Shopping Network; QVC; Trinity Broadcasting Network; TV Guide Network; WGN America.
Current originations: Government Access; Educational Access; Public Access.
Fee: $29.95 installation; $.76 converter; $19.95 additional installation.
Expanded Basic Service 1
Subscribers: N.A.
Programming (via satellite): ABC Family Channel; AMC; Animal Planet; Arts & Entertainment; BET Networks; Bravo; Cartoon Network; CNBC; CNN; Comedy Central; Country Music TV; Discovery Channel; Disney Channel; E! Entertainment Television; ESPN; ESPN 2; Eternal Word TV Network; FitTV; Food Network; Fox Sports Net North; FX; G4; Golf Channel; GSN; Hallmark Channel; Headline News; HGTV; History Channel; INSP; Lifetime; MSNBC; MTV; National Geographic Channel; Nickelodeon; Oxygen; ShopNBC; SoapNet; Speed Channel; Spike TV; Syfy; TBS Superstation; The Learning Channel; Toon Disney; Travel Channel; truTV; Turner Network TV; TV Land; Univision; USA Network; Versus; VH1; WE tv; Weather Channel.
Fee: $47.99 monthly.
Digital Basic Service
Subscribers: N.A.
Programming (via satellite): BBC America; Bio; Bloomberg Television; Boomerang; CNN en Espanol; CNN International; Discovery Digital Networks; Do-It-Yourself; ESPN Classic Sports; ESPNews; Fox Movie Channel; Fox Sports World; FSN Digital Atlantic; FSN Digital Central; FSN Digital Pacific; Fuel TV; Fuse; GAS; History Channel International; Independent Film Channel; Lifetime Movie Network; MTV Networks Digital Suite; Music Choice; NFL Network; Nick Jr.; Nick Too; NickToons TV; Outdoor Channel; Sundance Channel; Turner Classic Movies; TV Guide Interactive Inc.
Fee: $29.99 monthly.
Digital Pay Service 1
Pay Units: N.A.
Programming (via satellite): Cinemax (multiplexed); Encore (multiplexed); Flix; HBO (multiplexed); Showtime (multiplexed); Starz (multiplexed); The Movie Channel (multiplexed).
Video-On-Demand: Yes
Pay-Per-View
Playboy TV (delivered digitally); Fresh (delivered digitally); Shorteez (delivered digitally); iN DEMAND (delivered digitally); Sports PPV (delivered digitally); iN DEMAND.
Internet Service
Operational: Yes.
Broadband Service: Charter Pipeline.
Fee: $29.99 monthly.
Telephone Service
Digital: Operational
Miles of Plant: 449.0 (coaxial); None (fiber optic). Homes passed: 48,500.
Vice President & General Manager: John Crowley. Operations Director: Craig Stensaas. Technical Operations Director: Darin Helgeson. Marketing Director: Bill Haarstad.
City fee: 3% of gross.
Ownership: Charter Communications Inc. (MSO).

ROLLINGSTONE—Charter Communications. Now served by STOCKTON, MN [MN0369]. ICA: MN0213.

ROSE CREEK—North American Communications Corp., PO Box 387, 211 Main St S, Hector, MN 55342-0387. Phones: 800-982-8038; 320-848-6781. Fax: 320-848-2323. E-mail: hcc@hcctel.net. Web Site: http://www.hectorcom.com. ICA: MN0253.
TV Market Ranking: Below 100 (ROSE CREEK). Franchise award date: February 1, 1989. Franchise expiration date: N.A. Began: February 1, 1990.
Channel capacity: 54 (not 2-way capable). Channels available but not in use: 31.
Basic Service
Subscribers: 63.
Programming (received off-air): KAAL (ABC) Austin; KIMT (CBS, MNT) Mason City; KSMQ-TV (PBS) Austin; KYIN (PBS) Mason City.
Programming (via satellite): ABC Family Channel; AMC; Arts & Entertainment; CNN; Country Music TV; Discovery Channel; Disney Channel; ESPN; Fox Sports Net Midwest; Lifetime; Nickelodeon; QVC; Spike TV; TBS Superstation; Trinity Broadcasting Network; Turner Network TV; USA Network; WGN America.
Fee: $40.00 installation; $26.95 monthly; $3.50 converter; $25.00 additional installation.
Pay Service 1
Pay Units: 1.
Programming (via satellite): HBO.
Fee: $10.95 monthly.
Pay Service 2
Pay Units: N.A.
Programming (via satellite): Cinemax.
Fee: $10.95 monthly.
Video-On-Demand: No
Internet Service
Operational: No.
Broadband Service: Offers dial-up and DSL only; no cable modem service.
Telephone Service
None
Miles of Plant: 4.0 (coaxial); None (fiber optic). Homes passed: 132. Total homes in franchised area: 132.
Manager: Matt Sparks. Chief Technician: George Honzay. Customer Service Supervisor: Patty Groshens.
Ownership: Hector Communications Corp. (MSO).

ROSEAU—Sjoberg's Cable TV Inc., 315 Main Ave N, Thief River Falls, MN 56701-1905. Phones: 800-828-8808; 218-681-3044. Fax: 218-681-6801. Web Site: http://trf.mncable.net. ICA: MN0099.
TV Market Ranking: Outside TV Markets (ROSEAU). Franchise award date: N.A. Franchise expiration date: N.A. Began: August 15, 1967.
Channel capacity: 78 (operating 2-way). Channels available but not in use: 6.
Basic Service
Subscribers: 1,027.
Programming (received off-air): KCPM (MNT) Grand Forks; allband FM.
Programming (via microwave): KAWE (PBS) Bemidji; KVLY-TV (NBC) Fargo; KXJB-TV (CBS) Valley City; WDAZ-TV (ABC, CW) Devils Lake.
Programming (via satellite): CNN; ESPN; TBS Superstation.
Fee: $10.00 monthly.
Expanded Basic Service 1
Subscribers: N.A.
Programming (received off-air): KBRR (FOX) Thief River Falls.
Programming (via satellite): ABC Family Channel; Animal Planet; Arts & Entertainment; Cartoon Network; CNBC; Comedy Central; Country Music TV; CW+; Discovery Channel; E! Entertainment Television; ESPN 2; Food Network; Fox News Channel; Fox Sports Net; FX; HGTV; History Channel; Home Shopping Network; Lifetime; MSNBC; MTV; Nickelodeon; Spike TV; Syfy; The Learning Channel; Turner Classic Movies; Turner Network TV; TV Land; USA Network; Weather Channel; WGN America.
Fee: $23.71 monthly.
Digital Basic Service
Subscribers: N.A.
Programming (via satellite): AmericanLife TV Network; BBC America; Bio; Blackbelt TV; Bloomberg Television; Bravo; Chiller; CMT Pure Country; College Sports Television; Cooking Channel; Current; Daystar TV Network; Discovery Health Channel; Discovery Kids Channel; Discovery Military Channel; Discovery Planet Green; DMX Music; Do-It-Yourself; ESPN Classic Sports; ESPN U; ESPNews; Eternal Word TV Network; FitTV; Fox Business Channel; Fox College Sports Atlantic; Fox College Sports Central; Fox College Sports Pacific; Fox Movie Channel; Fox Reality Channel; Fox Soccer; G4; Golf Channel; Gospel Music Channel; Great American Country; GSN; Hallmark Channel; Headline News; History Channel International; HorseRacing TV; ID Investigation Discovery; Independent Film Channel; Lifetime Movie Network; MTV Hits; MTV2; National Geographic Channel; Nick Jr.; NickToons TV; Outdoor Channel; Ovation; Oxygen; PBS Kids Sprout; RFD-TV; Science Channel; ShopNBC; Sleuth; SoapNet; Speed Channel; Style Network; Sundance Channel; TeenNick; Tennis Channel; The Sportsman Channel; The Word Network; Toon Disney; TVG Network; various Canadian stations; Versus; VH1 Classic; VH1 Soul; WE tv.
Fee: $11.00 monthly.
Digital Expanded Basic Service
Subscribers: N.A.
Programming (via satellite): Arts & Entertainment HD; CNN HD; Discovery Channel HD; ESPN 2 HD; ESPN HD; Food Network HD; FSN HD; HDNet; HDNet Movies; HGTV HD; History Channel HD; Outdoor Channel 2 HD; PBS HD; Speed HD; Syfy HD; TBS in HD; Turner Network TV HD; Universal HD; USA Network HD; Versus HD.
Fee: $5.00 monthly; $5.00 converter.
Pay Service 1
Pay Units: 144.
Programming (via satellite): HBO.
Fee: $11.00 monthly.
Digital Pay Service 1
Pay Units: N.A.
Programming (via satellite): Cinemax (multiplexed); Cinemax HD; Encore (multiplexed); HBO; HBO HD; Showtime (multiplexed); Starz (multiplexed); The Movie Channel (multiplexed).
Fee: $8.00 monthly (Starz/Encore), $9.00 monthly (Cinemax or Showtime/TMC), $11.00 monthly (HBO).
Video-On-Demand: No
Internet Service
Operational: Yes. Began: October 1, 1999.
Subscribers: 150.
Broadband Service: Sjoberg's Cable TV.
Fee: $19.95 monthly; $10.00 modem lease; $129.00 modem purchase.
Telephone Service
None
Miles of Plant: 17.0 (coaxial); 7.0 (fiber optic). Homes passed: 1,100. Total homes in franchised area: 1,100.
Manager: Richard J. Sjoberg. Chief Technician: Jerry Seim.
Ownership: Sjoberg's Cable TV Inc. (MSO).

ROSEMOUNT—Charter Communications, 16900 Cedar Ave S, Rosemount, MN 55068-5129. Phones: 507-289-8372 (Rochester office); 952-432-2575. Fax: 952-432-5765. Web Site: http://www.charter.com. Also serves Apple Valley, Bridgewater Twp., Dundas, Empire Twp., Farmington, Lakeville & Northfield. ICA: MN0009.

TV Market Ranking: 13 (Apple Valley, Empire Twp., Farmington, Lakeville, Northfield, ROSEMOUNT); Outside TV Markets (Bridgewater Twp., Dundas). Franchise award date: N.A. Franchise expiration date: N.A. Began: November 1, 1974.

Channel capacity: N.A. Channels available but not in use: N.A.

Basic Service

Subscribers: 35,000.

Programming (received off-air): KARE (NBC) Minneapolis; KMSP-TV (FOX) Minneapolis; KPXM-TV (ION) St. Cloud; KSTC-TV (IND) Minneapolis; KSTP-TV (ABC) St. Paul; KTCA-TV (PBS) St. Paul; KTCI-TV (PBS) St. Paul; WCCO-TV (CBS) Minneapolis; WFTC (MNT) Minneapolis; WUCW (CW) Minneapolis.

Programming (via satellite): C-SPAN; Home Shopping Network; QVC; TV Guide Network; WGN America.

Current originations: Government Access; Educational Access; Public Access.

Fee: $29.99 installation; $1.80 converter.

Expanded Basic Service 1

Subscribers: 28,818.

Programming (via satellite): ABC Family Channel; AMC; Animal Planet; Arts & Entertainment; BET Networks; Bravo; Cartoon Network; CNBC; CNN; Comedy Central; Country Music TV; Discovery Channel; Disney Channel; E! Entertainment Television; ESPN; ESPN 2; Food Network; Fox News Channel; Fox Sports Net Minnesota; FX; G4; Golf Channel; GSN; Hallmark Channel; Headline News; HGTV; History Channel; INSP; Lifetime; MSNBC; MTV; National Geographic Channel; Nickelodeon; SoapNet; Speed Channel; Spike TV; Syfy; TBS Superstation; The Learning Channel; Toon Disney; Travel Channel; truTV; Turner Classic Movies; Turner Network TV; TV Land; USA Network; Versus; VH1; WE tv; Weather Channel.

Fee: $47.99 monthly.

Digital Basic Service

Subscribers: 1,180.

Programming (via satellite): BBC America; Bio; Discovery Digital Networks; Do-It-Yourself; GAS; History Channel International; Lifetime Movie Network; MTV Networks Digital Suite; MuchMusic Network; Music Choice; Nick Jr.; Style Network; Sundance Channel.

Fee: $6.95 monthly.

Digital Pay Service 1

Pay Units: 620.

Programming (via satellite): Encore (multiplexed); Starz (multiplexed).

Fee: $11.95 monthly.

Digital Pay Service 2

Pay Units: 2,902.

Programming (via satellite): Cinemax (multiplexed).

Fee: $11.25 installation; $11.95 monthly.

Digital Pay Service 3

Pay Units: 3,529.

Programming (via satellite): HBO (multiplexed).

Fee: $12.95 monthly.

Digital Pay Service 4

Pay Units: 2,851.

Programming (via satellite): Showtime (multiplexed).

Fee: $11.95 monthly.

Digital Pay Service 5

Pay Units: 2,689.

Programming (via satellite): Flix; The Movie Channel (multiplexed).

Fee: $11.95 monthly.

Video-On-Demand: Yes

Pay-Per-View

Addressable homes: 1,180.

Addressable: Yes; iN DEMAND (delivered digitally); Playboy TV (delivered digitally); Fresh (delivered digitally); Shorteez (delivered digitally); sports.

Internet Service

Operational: Yes.

Broadband Service: Charter Pipeline.

Fee: $29.99 monthly; $9.95 modem lease.

Telephone Service

Digital: Operational

Miles of Plant: 775.0 (coaxial); 116.0 (fiber optic). Homes passed: 59,000.

Vice President & General Manager: John Crowley. Technical Operations Director: Darin Helgeson. Technical Operations Manager: Clayton Snyder.; Mark Harder. Sales & Marketing Director: Bill Haarstad. Office Manager: Linda Lindberg.

City fee: 5% of gross; 13% of Empire & Farmington.

Ownership: Charter Communications Inc. (MSO).

ROUND LAKE—US Cable, 402 Red River Ave N, Unit 5, Cold Spring, MN 56320-1521. Phones: 320-685-7113; 800-783-2356. Fax: 320-685-2816. E-mail: help@mn.uscable.com. Web Site: http://www.uscable.com. ICA: MN0216.

TV Market Ranking: Outside TV Markets (ROUND LAKE). Franchise award date: N.A. Franchise expiration date: N.A. Began: November 1, 1983.

Channel capacity: 35 (operating 2-way). Channels available but not in use: None.

Basic Service

Subscribers: N.A. Included in Cambridge

Programming (received off-air): KDLT-TV (NBC) Sioux Falls; KELO-TV (CBS, MNT) Sioux Falls; KEYC-TV (CBS, FOX) Mankato; KSFY-TV (ABC) Sioux Falls; KSMN (PBS) Worthington; KTIV (CW, NBC) Sioux City.

Programming (via satellite): ABC Family Channel; Arts & Entertainment; CNBC; CNN; Comedy Central; Country Music TV; Discovery Channel; ESPN; ESPN 2; Fox Sports Net; Headline News; HGTV; History Channel; Home Shopping Network; Lifetime; Nickelodeon; Outdoor Channel; Spike TV; TBS Superstation; The Learning Channel; Turner Classic Movies; Turner Network TV; TV Land; USA Network; VH1; Weather Channel; WGN America.

Programming (via translator): KARE (NBC) Minneapolis; KMSP-TV (FOX) Minneapolis; KSTC-TV (IND) Minneapolis; KSTP-TV (ABC) St. Paul; WFTC (MNT) Minneapolis.

Current originations: Leased Access.

Fee: $37.24 monthly.

Pay Service 1

Pay Units: N.A. Included in Cambridge

Programming (via satellite): HBO.

Fee: $11.95 monthly.

Internet Service

Operational: No.

Homes passed: Included in Cambridge

General Manager: Steve Johnson. Customer Service Director: Jackie Torberg.

Ownership: Comcast Cable Communications Inc. (MSO).; US Cable Corp. (MSO).

ROUND LAKE TWP.—New Century Communications, 3588 Kennebec Dr, Eagan, MN 55122-1001. Phone: 651-688-2623. Fax: 651-688-2624. E-mail: tanderson@cablesystemservices.com. Also serves Haugen Twp. & McGregor (unincorporated areas). ICA: MN0357.

TV Market Ranking: Outside TV Markets (Haugen Twp., McGregor (unincorporated areas), ROUND LAKE TWP.). Franchise award date: N.A. Franchise expiration date: N.A. Began: N.A.

Channel capacity: 40 (not 2-way capable). Channels available but not in use: 19.

Basic Service

Subscribers: 96.

Programming (received off-air): KBJR-TV (MNT, NBC) Superior; KCCW-TV (CBS) Walker; KDLH (CBS, CW) Duluth; KQDS-TV (FOX) Duluth; WDIO-DT (ABC) Duluth; WDSE (PBS) Duluth.

Programming (via satellite): ABC Family Channel; Arts & Entertainment; Country Music TV; Discovery Channel; Disney Channel; ESPN; Fox Sports Net; Headline News; History Channel; Lifetime; Outdoor Channel; QVC; Showtime; Spike TV; TBS Superstation; The Learning Channel; Trinity Broadcasting Network; Turner Network TV; TV Land; USA Network; WGN America.

Fee: $30.00 installation; $33.85 monthly.

Video-On-Demand: No

Internet Service

Operational: No.

Telephone Service

None

Miles of Plant: 29.0 (coaxial); None (fiber optic). Homes passed: 700.

Executive Vice President: Marty Walch. Manager & Chief Technician: Todd Anderson.

Ownership: New Century Communications (MSO).

RUSH LAKE TWP.—ACS Video. Formerly served by Perham, MN [MN0050]. This cable system has converted to IPTV, 150 Second St SW, Perham, MN 56573. Phone: 866-937-4227. E-mail: answers@arvig.com. Web Site: http://www.arvig.com. ICA: MN5217.

TV Market Ranking: Outside TV Markets (RUSH LAKE TWP.).

Channel capacity: N.A. Channels available but not in use: N.A.

Internet Service

Operational: Yes.

Telephone Service

Digital: Operational

Ownership: Arvig Communication Systems.

RUSHMORE—K-Communications Inc., 337 Aetna St, Ruthton, MN 56170-0018. Phones: 800-752-9397; 507-658-3830. Fax: 507-658-3914. Web Site: http://www.woodstocktel.net. ICA: MN0358.

TV Market Ranking: Outside TV Markets (RUSHMORE). Franchise award date: N.A. Franchise expiration date: N.A. Began: N.A.

Channel capacity: 28 (not 2-way capable). Channels available but not in use: None.

Basic Service

Subscribers: 100.

Programming (received off-air): KDLT-TV (NBC) Sioux Falls; KELO-TV (CBS, MNT) Sioux Falls; KSFY-TV (ABC) Sioux Falls; KSMN (PBS) Worthington; KTTW (FOX) Sioux Falls.

Programming (via satellite): ABC Family Channel; Animal Planet; Arts & Entertainment; CNN; CW+; Discovery Channel; Disney Channel; ESPN; ESPN 2; Fox Sports Net; History Channel; Lifetime; Nickelodeon; Spike TV; TBS Superstation; The Learning Channel; Trinity Broadcasting Network; Turner Network TV; WGN America.

Fee: $25.00 installation; $18.82 monthly.

Pay Service 1

Pay Units: 11.

Programming (via satellite): Showtime.

Fee: $10.50 monthly.

Video-On-Demand: No

Internet Service

Operational: No, DSL only.

Telephone Service

None

Miles of Plant: 3.0 (coaxial); None (fiber optic).

Chief Technician & Marketing Director: Dave Bukowski. Program Director: Terry Nelson.

Ownership: Woodstock Telephone Co. (MSO).

RUTHTON—K-Communications Inc., 337 Aetna St, Ruthton, MN 56170-0018. Phones: 800-752-9397; 507-658-3830. Fax: 507-658-3914. E-mail: wtcinfo@woodstocktel.net. Web Site: http://www.woodstocktel.net. Also serves Holland & Woodstock. ICA: MN0359.

TV Market Ranking: Outside TV Markets (Holland, RUTHTON, Woodstock). Franchise award date: N.A. Franchise expiration date: N.A. Began: N.A.

Channel capacity: 28 (not 2-way capable). Channels available but not in use: None.

Basic Service

Subscribers: 237.

Programming (received off-air): KDLT-TV (NBC) Sioux Falls; KELO-TV (CBS, MNT) Sioux Falls; KSFY-TV (ABC) Sioux Falls; KSTP-TV (ABC) St. Paul; KTTW (FOX) Sioux Falls; KWCM-TV (PBS) Appleton.

Programming (via microwave): KSMN (PBS) Worthington.

Programming (via satellite): ABC Family Channel; Arts & Entertainment; Bravo; CNN; Comedy Central; CW+; Discovery Channel; Disney Channel; ESPN; ESPN 2; Food Network; Fox Sports Net; GSN; Hallmark Channel; Hallmark Movie Channel; Headline News; HGTV; History Channel; Spike TV; TBS Superstation; Travel Channel; Trinity Broadcasting Network; Turner Network TV; WGN America.

Fee: $25.00 installation; $25.00 monthly.

Pay Service 1

Pay Units: 51.

Programming (via satellite): Showtime.

Fee: $10.50 monthly.

Video-On-Demand: No

Internet Service

Operational: No.

Telephone Service

None

Miles of Plant: 12.0 (coaxial); None (fiber optic).

Chief Technician & Marketing Director: David Bukowski. Program Director: Terry Nelson.

Ownership: Woodstock Telephone Co. (MSO).

RUTLEDGE (village)—Formerly served by New Century Communications. No longer in operation. ICA: MN0360.

SABIN—Midcontinent Communications, PO Box 5010, Sioux Falls, SD 57117. Phones: 800-888-1300; 605-229-1775. Fax: 605-229-0478. E-mail: mccomm@midco.net. Web Site: http://www.midcocomm.com. Also serves Elmwood Twp. ICA: MN0361.

TV Market Ranking: 98 (Elmwood Twp., SABIN). Franchise award date: April 10, 1990. Franchise expiration date: N.A. Began: December 28, 1982.

Channel capacity: N.A. Channels available but not in use: N.A.

Basic Service

Subscribers: 73.

Programming (received off-air): KFME (PBS) Fargo; KVLY-TV (NBC) Fargo; KVRR

(FOX) Fargo; KXJB-TV (CBS) Valley City; WDAY-TV (ABC, CW) Fargo.
Programming (via satellite): ABC Family Channel; AMC; Animal Planet; Arts & Entertainment; Big Ten Network; Bravo; Cartoon Network; CNBC; CNN; Comedy Central; Country Music TV; C-SPAN; C-SPAN 2; CW+; Discovery Channel; Disney Channel; E! Entertainment Television; ESPN; ESPN 2; Eternal Word TV Network; Food Network; Fox News Channel; Fox Sports Net North; FX; Hallmark Channel; Headline News; HGTV; History Channel; Home Shopping Network; INSP; Lifetime; MSNBC; MTV; Nickelodeon; Oxygen; QVC; Speed Channel; Spike TV; Syfy; TBS Superstation; The Learning Channel; Travel Channel; truTV; Turner Classic Movies; Turner Network TV; TV Guide Network; TV Land; USA Network; VH1; Weather Channel; WGN America.
Fee: $50.00 installation; $26.50 monthly.

Digital Basic Service
Subscribers: N.A.
Programming (received off-air): KFME (PBS) Fargo; KVLY-TV (NBC) Fargo; KXJB-TV (CBS) Valley City; WDAY-TV (ABC, CW) Fargo.
Programming (via satellite): 3 Angels Broadcasting Network; ABC Family HD; AmericanLife TV Network; Animal Planet HD; Arts & Entertainment HD; BBC America; Big Ten Network; Bio; Bloomberg Television; Boomerang; Canal Sur; CBS College Sports Network; Cine Latino; Cine Mexicano; CMT Pure Country; CNN en Espanol; CNN HD; Cooking Channel; C-SPAN 3; Current; Discovery Channel HD; Discovery en Espanol; Discovery HD Theater; Discovery Health Channel; Discovery Kids Channel; Discovery Military Channel; Discovery Planet Green; Disney Channel HD; Do-It-Yourself; ESPN 2 HD; ESPN Classic Sports; ESPN Deportes; ESPN HD; ESPNews; EWTN en Espanol; FitTV; Food Network HD; Fox Business Channel; Fox College Sports Atlantic; Fox College Sports Central; Fox College Sports Pacific; Fox Movie Channel; Fox Soccer; Fox Sports en Espanol; FSN HD; Fuse; G4; Gol TV; Golf Channel; Great American Country; GSN; Halogen Network; HDNet; HDNet Movies; HGTV HD; History Channel en Espanol; History Channel HD; History Channel International; ID Investigation Discovery; Independent Film Channel; ION Life; ION Television; JCTV; Lifetime Movie Network; MTV Hits; MTV Jams; MTV Tres; MTV2; mun2 television; Music Choice; National Geographic Channel; National Geographic Channel HD Network; NFL Network; NHL Network; Nick Jr.; Nick Too; NickToons TV; Outdoor Channel; Palladia; PBS Kids Sprout; Pentagon Channel; Qubo; ReelzChannel; RFD-TV; Science Channel; SoapNet; Style Network; Sundance Channel; Syfy HD; TBS in HD; TeenNick; Telemundo; Tennis Channel; The Sportsman Channel; TLC HD; Toon Disney; Toon Disney en Espanol; Trinity Broadcasting Network; Turner Classic Movies; Turner Network TV HD; TV One; TVE Internacional; TVG Network; Universal HD; USA Network HD; Versus; Versus HD; VH1 Classic; VH1 Soul; WE tv.

Digital Pay Service 1
Pay Units: N.A.
Programming (via satellite): Cinemax (multiplexed); Cinemax HD; Encore (multiplexed); Flix; HBO (multiplexed); HBO HD; HBO Latino; Showtime (multiplexed); Showtime HD; Starz (multiplexed); Starz HDTV; The Movie Channel (multiplexed); The Movie Channel HD.
Video-On-Demand: No
Pay-Per-View
iN DEMAND (delivered digitally); NHL Center Ice (delivered digitally); MLB Extra Innings (delivered digitally); NBA League Pass (delivered digitally); MLS Direct Kick (delivered digitally).
Internet Service
Operational: No.
Telephone Service
None
Miles of Plant: 3.0 (coaxial); None (fiber optic). Homes passed: 157. Total homes in franchised area: 157.
Manager: Darrell Wrege. Marketing Director: Fred Jamieson. Customer Service Manager: Kathy Fuhrmann.
City fee: 3% of gross.
Ownership: Comcast Cable Communications Inc. (MSO).; Midcontinent Media Inc. (MSO).

SANBORN—Formerly served by NU-Telecom. No longer in operation. ICA: MN0163.

SANBORN—NU-Telecom. Formerly served by New Ulm, MN [MN0285]. This cable system has converted to IPTV, PO Box 697, 22 S Marshall, Springfield, MN 56087-0697. Phones: 800-893-1856; 507-723-4211. Fax: 507-723-4377. E-mail: on-linecustservice@nu-telecom.net. Web Site: http://www.nutelecom.net. ICA: MN5149.
TV Market Ranking: Below 100 (SANBORN).
Channel capacity: N.A. Channels available but not in use: N.A.
Internet Service
Operational: Yes.
Telephone Service
Digital: Operational
President & Chief Executive Officer: Bill Otis.
Ownership: NU-Telecom.

SANDSTONE—Savage Communications Inc., PO Box 810, 206 Power Ave N, Hinckley, MN 55037. Phone: 320-384-7442. Fax: 320-384-7446. E-mail: rwsavage@scicable.com. Web Site: http://www.scibroadband.com. Also serves Askov & Hinckley. ICA: MN0166.
TV Market Ranking: Outside TV Markets (Askov, Hinckley, SANDSTONE). Franchise award date: August 1, 1984. Franchise expiration date: N.A. Began: January 1, 1985.
Channel capacity: 60 (2-way capable). Channels available but not in use: None.
Basic Service
Subscribers: 1,110.
Programming (received off-air): KARE (NBC) Minneapolis; KBJR-TV (MNT, NBC) Superior; KDLH (CBS, CW) Duluth; KMSP-TV (FOX) Minneapolis; KPXM-TV (ION) St. Cloud; KSTC-TV (IND) Minneapolis; KSTP-TV (ABC) St. Paul; KTCA-TV (PBS) St. Paul; WCCO-TV (CBS) Minneapolis; WDIO-DT (ABC) Duluth; WDSE (PBS) Duluth; WFTC (MNT) Minneapolis; WUCW (CW) Minneapolis.
Programming (via satellite): ABC Family Channel; Animal Planet; Arts & Entertainment; Cartoon Network; CNBC; CNN; Comedy Central; C-SPAN; Discovery Channel; Disney Channel; E! Entertainment Television; ESPN; ESPN 2; Eternal Word TV Network; Fox News Channel; Fox Sports Net; Great American Country; Headline News; HGTV; History Channel; Lifetime; MTV; National Geographic Channel; Nickelodeon; QVC; Spike TV; Syfy; TBS Superstation; The Learning Channel; Turner Classic Movies; Turner Network TV; TV Land; USA Network; VH1; Weather Channel; WGN America.
Fee: $39.95 installation; $33.95 monthly.
Digital Basic Service
Subscribers: N.A.
Programming (via satellite): AmericanLife TV Network; BBC America; Bio; Bloomberg Television; Discovery Digital Networks; DMX Music; ESPN Classic Sports; ESPNews; FitTV; Fox Movie Channel; Fox Sports World; Fuse; G4; Golf Channel; History Channel International; INSP; National Geographic Channel; Outdoor Channel; Sleuth; Speed Channel; Style Network; Trinity Broadcasting Network; Versus; WE tv.
Pay Service 1
Pay Units: 154.
Programming (via satellite): HBO.
Fee: $10.95 monthly.
Digital Pay Service 1
Pay Units: N.A.
Programming (via satellite): Cinemax (multiplexed); Encore (multiplexed); HBO (multiplexed); Showtime (multiplexed); Starz (multiplexed); The Movie Channel (multiplexed).
Video-On-Demand: No
Pay-Per-View
Movies (delivered digitally); ESPN Now (delivered digitally); Sports PPV (delivered digitally).
Internet Service
Operational: Yes.
Broadband Service: SCI Broadband.
Fee: $19.95 monthly.
Telephone Service
None
Miles of Plant: 65.0 (coaxial); None (fiber optic). Homes passed: 1,609. Total homes in franchised area: 1,609.
Manager: Mike Danielson. Marketing Director: Ron Savage. Chief Technician: Pat McCabe. Customer Service Manager: Donna Erickson.
City fee: 3% of gross.
Ownership: Savage Communications Inc. (MSO).

SAUK CENTRE—Charter Communications, 3380 Northern Valley Pl NE, Rochester, MN 55906-3954. Phone: 507-289-8372. Fax: 507-285-6162. Web Site: http://www.charter.com. Also serves Sauk Centre Twp. ICA: MN0071.
TV Market Ranking: Below 100 (SAUK CENTRE, Sauk Centre Twp.). Franchise award date: N.A. Franchise expiration date: N.A. Began: January 1, 1966.
Channel capacity: N.A. Channels available but not in use: N.A.
Basic Service
Subscribers: 290.
Programming (received off-air): KCCO-TV (CBS) Alexandria; KPXM-TV (ION) St. Cloud; KSAX (ABC) Alexandria; KSTC-TV (IND) Minneapolis; WUCW (CW) Minneapolis; allband FM.
Programming (via microwave): KARE (NBC) Minneapolis; KMSP-TV (FOX) Minneapolis; KTCA-TV (PBS) St. Paul; WFTC (MNT) Minneapolis.
Programming (via satellite): C-SPAN; C-SPAN 2; Eternal Word TV Network; QVC; TBS Superstation; Trinity Broadcasting Network; WGN America.
Current originations: Public Access.
Fee: $29.99 installation.
Expanded Basic Service 1
Subscribers: N.A.
Programming (received off-air): WCMN-LP St. Cloud-Sartell.
Programming (via satellite): ABC Family Channel; AMC; Animal Planet; Arts & Entertainment; Bravo; Cartoon Network; CNBC; CNN; Comedy Central; Country Music TV; Discovery Channel; Disney Channel; E! Entertainment Television; ESPN; ESPN 2; Food Network; Fox News Channel; Fox Sports Net North; FX; G4; Golf Channel; Hallmark Channel; Headline News; HGTV; History Channel; Home Shopping Network; Lifetime; MSNBC; MTV; MTV2; National Geographic Channel; Nickelodeon; Oxygen; Speed Channel; Spike TV; Syfy; The Learning Channel; Travel Channel; truTV; Turner Classic Movies; Turner Network TV; TV Land; Univision; USA Network; Versus; VH1; WE tv; Weather Channel.
Fee: $47.99 monthly.
Digital Basic Service
Subscribers: N.A.
Programming (received off-air): KARE (NBC) Minneapolis; KMSP-TV (FOX) Minneapolis; WCCO-TV (CBS) Minneapolis.
Programming (via satellite): BBC America; Bio; Bloomberg Television; Boomerang; CBS College Sports Network; CNN en Espanol; CNN International; Discovery Digital Networks; Do-It-Yourself; ESPN; ESPN Classic Sports; ESPNews; Fox College Sports Atlantic; Fox College Sports Central; Fox College Sports Pacific; Fox Movie Channel; Fox Soccer; Fuel TV; Fuse; GAS; HDNet; HDNet Movies; History Channel International; Independent Film Channel; Lifetime Movie Network; MTV Networks Digital Suite; Music Choice; NFL Network; Nick Jr.; Nick Too; NickToons TV; Outdoor Channel; SoapNet; Style Network; Sundance Channel; TV Guide Interactive Inc.
Digital Pay Service 1
Pay Units: N.A.
Programming (via satellite): Cinemax (multiplexed); Encore (multiplexed); HBO (multiplexed); Showtime (multiplexed); Starz (multiplexed); The Movie Channel (multiplexed).
Video-On-Demand: Yes
Pay-Per-View
iN DEMAND (delivered digitally); NASCAR In Car (delivered digitally); NHL Center Ice (delivered digitally); MLB Extra Innings (delivered digitally); Playboy TV (delivered digitally); Spice Live (delivered digitally); Spice Platinum (delivered digitally); Hot Net Plus (delivered digitally); Spice Hot (delivered digitally).
Internet Service
Operational: Yes.
Broadband Service: Charter Pipeline.
Fee: $29.99 monthly.
Telephone Service
Digital: Operational
Fee: $29.99 monthly
Homes passed: 1,877. Miles of plant (coax) included in St. Cloud/Waite Park
Vice President & General Manager: John Crowley. Operations Director: Craig Stensaas. Technical Operations Director: Mark Abramo. Marketing Director: Bill Haarstad.
City fee: 2% of basic.
Ownership: Charter Communications Inc. (MSO).

SEARLES—NU-Telecom. Formerly served by New Ulm, MN [MN0285]. This cable system has converted to IPTV, PO Box 697, 22 S Marshall, Springfield, MN 56087-0697. Phones: 800-893-

1856; 507-723-4211. Fax: 507-723-4377. E-mail: on-linecustservice@nu-telecom.net. Web Site: http://www.nutelecom.net. ICA: MN5148.
TV Market Ranking: Below 100 (SEARLES).
Channel capacity: N.A. Channels available but not in use: N.A.
Internet Service
Operational: Yes.
Telephone Service
Digital: Operational
President & Chief Executive Officer: Bill Otis.
Ownership: NU-Telecom.

SEBEKA—Formerly served by MENAGHA, MN [MN0118]. West Central Telephone Assn. This cable system has converted to IPTV, 308 Frontage Rd, Sebeka, MN 56477. Phones: 800-945-2163; 213-837-5151. Web Site: http://www.wcta.net. ICA: MN5136.
TV Market Ranking: Outside TV Markets (SEBEKA).
Channel capacity: N.A. Channels available but not in use: N.A.
Internet Service
Operational: Yes.
Telephone Service
Digital: Operational
Ownership: West Central Telephone Association.

SHAKOPEE—Time Warner Cable. Now served by MINNEAPOLIS, MN [MN0001]. ICA: MN0024.

SHEVLIN—Garden Valley Telephone Co., PO Box 259, 201 Ross Ave, Erskine, MN 56535-0259. Phones: 218-687-5251; 800-448-8260. Fax: 218-687-2454. E-mail: gvtc@gvtel.com. Web Site: http://www.gvtel.com. ICA: MN0363.
TV Market Ranking: Below 100 (SHEVLIN). Franchise award date: April 6, 1990. Franchise expiration date: N.A. Began: January 1, 1991.
Channel capacity: 35 (not 2-way capable). Channels available but not in use: 9.
Basic Service
Subscribers: 49.
Programming (received off-air): KAWE (PBS) Bemidji; KBRR (FOX) Thief River Falls; KCCW-TV (CBS) Walker; KCPM (MNT) Grand Forks; KFME (PBS) Fargo; KVLY-TV (NBC) Fargo; KXJB-TV (CBS) Valley City; WDAY-TV (ABC, CW) Fargo; WDAZ-TV (ABC, CW) Devils Lake.
Programming (via satellite): ABC Family Channel; AMC; Arts & Entertainment; CNN; Discovery Channel; Disney Channel; ESPN; ESPN 2; Fox Sports Net; Great American Country; History Channel; Spike TV; TBS Superstation; Turner Network TV; TV Land; USA Network; WGN America.
Fee: $43.90 installation; $23.95 monthly; $.75 converter; $15.75 additional installation.
Pay Service 1
Pay Units: 12.
Programming (via satellite): HBO.
Fee: $10.50 monthly.
Video-On-Demand: No
Internet Service
Operational: No.
Telephone Service
None
Miles of Plant: 6.0 (coaxial); None (fiber optic). Homes passed: 99.
Manager: George Fish. Operations Manager: Dave Hamre. Facilities Manager: Randy Versdahl. Marketing Supervisor: Julie Dahle.
Ownership: Garden Valley Telephone Co. (MSO).

SHULTZ LAKE TWP.—Formerly served by New Century Communications. No longer in operation. ICA: MN0364.

SILVER BAY—Mediacom, PO Box 110, 1504 2nd St SE, Waseca, MN 56093. Phone: 507-835-2356. Fax: 507-835-4567. Web Site: http://www.mediacomcable.com. Also serves Beaver Bay, Lake County, Silver Creek Twp. & Two Harbors. ICA: MN0084.
TV Market Ranking: 89 (Lake County (portions), Two Harbors); Outside TV Markets (Beaver Bay, SILVER BAY, Silver Creek Twp., Lake County (portions)). Franchise award date: N.A. Franchise expiration date: N.A. Began: December 1, 1980.
Channel capacity: N.A. Channels available but not in use: N.A.
Basic Service
Subscribers: 1,855.
Programming (received off-air): KBJR-TV (MNT, NBC) Superior; KDLH (CBS, CW) Duluth; KQDS-TV (FOX) Duluth; WDIO-DT (ABC) Duluth; WDSE (PBS) Duluth.
Programming (via microwave): KMSP-TV (FOX) Minneapolis.
Programming (via satellite): C-SPAN; C-SPAN 2; Eternal Word TV Network; Home Shopping Network; INSP; ION Television; TV Guide Network; WGN America.
Current originations: Public Access.
Fee: $25.00 installation; $17.95 monthly; $.50 converter.
Expanded Basic Service 1
Subscribers: N.A.
Programming (via satellite): ABC Family Channel; AMC; Animal Planet; Arts & Entertainment; Bravo; Cartoon Network; CNBC; CNN; Comedy Central; Country Music TV; Discovery Channel; Disney Channel; E! Entertainment Television; ESPN; ESPN 2; Food Network; Fox Movie Channel; Fox News Channel; Fox Sports Net North; FX; Hallmark Channel; Headline News; HGTV; History Channel; Lifetime; MSNBC; MTV; Nickelodeon; Outdoor Channel; QVC; Speed Channel; Spike TV; Syfy; TBS Superstation; The Learning Channel; Travel Channel; truTV; Turner Classic Movies; Turner Network TV; TV Land; USA Network; VH1; WE tv; Weather Channel.
Fee: $16.95 monthly.
Digital Basic Service
Subscribers: N.A.
Programming (via satellite): AmericanLife TV Network; BBC America; Bio; Bloomberg Television; Discovery Digital Networks; DMX Music; Fox Sports World; Fuse; G4; Golf Channel; GSN; Halogen Network; History Channel International; Independent Film Channel; Lifetime Movie Network; Lime; National Geographic Channel; Style Network; Versus.
Fee: $8.95 monthly.
Digital Pay Service 1
Pay Units: 128.
Programming (via satellite): Cinemax (multiplexed); Encore (multiplexed); Flix; HBO (multiplexed); Showtime (multiplexed); Starz (multiplexed); Sundance Channel; The Movie Channel (multiplexed).
Fee: $25.00 installation; $9.95 monthly (Showtime), $10.95 monthly (HBO).
Video-On-Demand: No
Pay-Per-View
TVN Entertainment (delivered digitally); ESPN Now (delivered digitally); Sports PPV (delivered digitally); Urban Xtra (delivered digitally); Fresh (delivered digitally); Shorteez (delivered digitally); Playboy TV (delivered digitally); Pleasure (delivered digitally).
Internet Service
Operational: Yes.
Broadband Service: Mediacom High Speed Internet.
Fee: $99.00 installation; $40.00 monthly.
Telephone Service
Digital: Operational
Miles of Plant: 39.0 (coaxial); None (fiber optic). Homes passed: 2,834. Total homes in franchised area: 3,264.
Vice President: Bill Jensen. Engineering Manager: Kraig Kaiser. Marketing & Sales Director: Lori Huberty.
City fee: 1% of basic gross.
Ownership: Mediacom LLC (MSO).

SLAYTON—Now served by PIPESTONE, MN [MN0348]. ICA: MN0092.

SLEEPY EYE—Sleepy Eye Telephone. Formerly served by Goodhue, MN [MN0208]. This cable system has converted to IPTV, 121 Second Ave NW, Sleepy Eye, MN 56085. Phones: 800-235-5133; 507-794-3361. Fax: 507-794-2351. E-mail: on-linecustservice@nu-telcom.net. Web Site: http://www.sleepyeyetel.net. ICA: MN5137.
Channel capacity: N.A. Channels available but not in use: N.A.
Internet Service
Operational: Yes.
Fee: $31.95 monthly.
Telephone Service
Digital: Operational
Ownership: Sleepy Eye Telephone Co.

SPRING GROVE—Now served by CALEDONIA, MN [MN0086]. ICA: MN0137.

SPRINGFIELD—Now served by REDWOOD FALLS, MN [MN0057]. ICA: MN0113.

SPRINGFIELD—NU-Telecom. Formerly [MN0396]. This cable system has converted to IPTV, PO Box 697, 22 S Marshall, Springfield, MN 56087-0697. Phones: 800-893-1856; 507-723-4211. Fax: 507-723-4377. E-mail: on-linecustservice@nu-telcom.net. Web Site: http://www.nutelecom.net. ICA: MN5118.
Channel capacity: N.A. Channels available but not in use: N.A.
Internet Service
Operational: Yes.
Telephone Service
Digital: Operational
President & Chief Executive Officer: Bill Otis.
Ownership: NU-Telecom.

SPRINGFIELD—NU-Telecom. This cable system has converted to IPTV. See Springfield, MN [MN5118], MN. ICA: MN0396.

ST. CHARLES—Hiawatha Broadband. Formerly [MN0397]. This cable system has converted to IPTV, 1242 Whitewater Ave, St. Charles, MN 55972. Phone: 888-474-9995. Fax: 507-454-5878. E-mail: info@hbci.com. Web Site: http://www.hbci.com. ICA: MN5158.
TV Market Ranking: Below 100 (ST. CHARLES).
Channel capacity: N.A. Channels available but not in use: N.A.
Internet Service
Operational: Yes.
Ownership: Hiawatha Broadband Communications Inc.

ST. CHARLES—Hiawatha Broadband. This cable system has converted to IPTV. See St. Charles, MN [MN5158]. ICA: MN0397.

ST. CLOUD—Formerly served by Astound Broadband. No longer in operation. ICA: MN0394.

ST. CLOUD/WAITE PARK—Charter Communications, 3380 Northern Valley Pl NE, Rochester, MN 55906-3954. Phones: 507-289-8372 (Rochester administrative office); 320-252-0943; 800-581-0081. Fax: 507-285-6162. Web Site: http://www.charter.com. Also serves Haven Twp., Le Sauk Twp., Minden Twp., Sartell, Sauk Rapids & Waite Park. ICA: MN0011.
TV Market Ranking: Below 100 (Haven Twp., Le Sauk Twp., Minden Twp., Sartell, Sauk Rapids, ST. CLOUD, Waite Park). Franchise award date: June 12, 1984. Franchise expiration date: N.A. Began: January 1, 1967.
Channel capacity: N.A. Channels available but not in use: N.A.
Basic Service
Subscribers: 13,500.
Programming (received off-air): KARE (NBC) Minneapolis; KMSP-TV (FOX) Minneapolis; KPXM-TV (ION) St. Cloud; KSTP-TV (ABC) St. Paul; KTCA-TV (PBS) St. Paul; WCCO-TV (CBS) Minneapolis; WFTC (MNT) Minneapolis; WUCW (CW) Minneapolis; 14 FMs.
Programming (via satellite): C-SPAN; C-SPAN 2; Eternal Word TV Network; KSTC-TV (IND) Minneapolis; QVC; Trinity Broadcasting Network; WGN America.
Current originations: Leased Access; Government Access; Educational Access; Public Access.
Fee: $29.99 installation; $.76 converter; $19.95 additional installation.
Expanded Basic Service 1
Subscribers: N.A.
Programming (received off-air): WCMN-LP St. Cloud-Sartell.
Programming (via satellite): ABC Family Channel; AMC; Animal Planet; Arts & Entertainment; BET Networks; Bravo; Cartoon Network; CNBC; CNN; Comedy Central; Country Music TV; Discovery Channel; Disney Channel; E! Entertainment Television; ESPN; ESPN 2; Food Network; Fox News Channel; Fox Sports Net North; FX; G4; Golf Channel; Great American Country; GSN; Hallmark Channel; Headline News; HGTV; History Channel; Home Shopping Network; Lifetime; MoviePlex; MSNBC; MTV; MTV2; National Geographic Channel; Nickelodeon; Oxygen; Speed Channel; Spike TV; Syfy; TBS Superstation; The Learning Channel; Toon Disney; Travel Channel; truTV; Turner Classic Movies; Turner Network TV; TV Land; Univision; USA Network; Versus; VH1; WE tv; Weather Channel.
Fee: $47.99 monthly.
Digital Basic Service
Subscribers: N.A.
Programming (received off-air): KARE (NBC) Minneapolis; KMSP-TV (FOX) Minneapolis; WCCO-TV (CBS) Minneapolis.
Programming (via satellite): BBC America; Bio; Bloomberg Television; Boomerang; CBS College Sports Network; CNN en Espanol; CNN International; Discovery Digital Networks; Do-It-Yourself; ESPN; ESPN Classic Sports; ESPNews; FitTV; Fox College Sports Atlantic; Fox College Sports Central; Fox College Sports Pacific; Fox Movie Channel; Fox Soccer; Fuel TV; Fuse; GAS; HDNet; HDNet Movies; History Chan-

nel International; Independent Film Channel; Lifetime Movie Network; MTV Networks Digital Suite; Music Choice; NFL Network; Nick Jr.; Nick Too; NickToons TV; Outdoor Channel; SoapNet; Style Network; Sundance Channel; TV Guide Interactive Inc.

Digital Pay Service 1

Pay Units: N.A.

Programming (via satellite): Cinemax (multiplexed); Encore (multiplexed); HBO (multiplexed); Showtime (multiplexed); Starz (multiplexed); The Movie Channel (multiplexed).

Video-On-Demand: Yes

Pay-Per-View

iN DEMAND (delivered digitally); NASCAR In Car (delivered digitally); NHL Center Ice (delivered digitally); MLB Extra Innings (delivered digitally); Playboy TV (delivered digitally); Spice Live (delivered digitally); Spice Platinum (delivered digitally); Hot Net Plus (delivered digitally); Spice Hot (delivered digitally).

Internet Service

Operational: Yes.

Broadband Service: Charter Pipeline.

Fee: $29.99 monthly.

Telephone Service

Digital: Operational

Fee: $29.99 monthly

Miles of Plant: 600.0 (coaxial); None (fiber optic). Miles of plant (coax) includes Albany, Little Falls, Melrose, & Sauk Centre

Vice President & General Manager: John Crowley. Operations Director: Craig Stensaas. Technical Operations Director: Mark Abramo. Marketing Director: Bill Haarstad. Marketing Manager: Lisa Barton.

City fee: 3% of gross.

Ownership: Charter Communications Inc. (MSO).

ST. CROIX—Comcast Cable. Now served by ST. PAUL (formerly Roseville), MN [MN0002]. ICA: MN0007.

ST. HILAIRE—Garden Valley Telephone Co., PO Box 259, 201 Ross Ave, Erskine, MN 56535-0259. Phone: 218-687-5251. Fax: 218-687-2454. E-mail: gvtc@gvtel.com. Web Site: http://www.gvtel.com. ICA: MN0366.

TV Market Ranking: Below 100 (ST. HILAIRE). Franchise award date: April 9, 1990. Franchise expiration date: N.A. Began: November 1, 1990.

Channel capacity: 35 (not 2-way capable). Channels available but not in use: 9.

Basic Service

Subscribers: 93.

Programming (received off-air): KAWE (PBS) Bemidji; KBRR (FOX) Thief River Falls; KCPM (MNT) Grand Forks; KFME (PBS) Fargo; KVLY-TV (NBC) Fargo; KXJB-TV (CBS) Valley City; WDAY-TV (ABC, CW) Fargo; WDAZ-TV (ABC, CW) Devils Lake.

Programming (via satellite): ABC Family Channel; AMC; Arts & Entertainment; CNN; Discovery Channel; Disney Channel; ESPN; ESPN 2; Fox Sports Net; Great American Country; History Channel; Spike TV; TBS Superstation; Turner Network TV; TV Land; USA Network; WGN America.

Fee: $39.90 installation; $22.95 monthly; $.75 converter.

Pay Service 1

Pay Units: 21.

Programming (via satellite): HBO.

Fee: $10.50 monthly.

Video-On-Demand: No

Internet Service

Operational: No.

Telephone Service

None

Miles of Plant: 10.0 (coaxial); None (fiber optic). Homes passed: 147.

General Manager: George Fish. Operations Manager: Dave Hamre. Facilities Manager: Randy Versdahl. Marketing Supervisor: Julie Dahle.

Ownership: Garden Valley Telephone Co. (MSO).

ST. JAMES—Now served by WASECA, MN [MN0043]. ICA: MN0061.

ST. JOSEPH—Formerly served by Astound Communications. No longer in operation. ICA: MN0199.

ST. LOUIS PARK—Time Warner Cable. Now served by MINNEAPOLIS, MN [MN0001]. ICA: MN0367.

ST. PAUL—Comcast Cable, 10 River Park Plz, St. Paul, MN 55107. Phone: 651-493-5000. Fax: 651-493-5837. Web Site: http://www.comcast.com. Also serves Afton, Andover, Anoka, Arden Hills, Bayport, Birchwood Village, Blaine, Brooklyn Center, Brooklyn Park, Burnsville, Centerville, Champlin, Circle Pines, Columbia Heights, Coon Rapids, Corcoran, Cottage Grove, Crystal, Dakota County (portions), Dellwood, Denmark Twp., Eagan, Falcon Heights, Gem Lake, Golden Valley, Grant Twp., Ham Lake, Hanover, Hastings, Hilltop, Hugo, Inver Grove Heights, Lake Elmo, Lake St. Croix Beach, Lakeland, Lakeland Shores, Landfall, Lauderdale, Lexington, Lilydale, Lino Lakes, Little Canada, Mahtomedi, Maple Grove, Maplewood, Marshan Twp., Medicine Lake, Mendota, Mendota Heights, Mounds View, New Brighton, New Hope, Newport, North Oaks, North St. Paul, Oak Grove, Oak Park Heights, Oakdale, Osseo, Pine Springs, Plymouth, Ramsey, Ramsey County, Robbinsdale, Rogers, Roseville, Shoreview, South St. Paul, Spring Lake Park, St. Anthony, St. Croix, St. Marys Point, St. Paul Park, Stillwater, Sunfish Lake, Vadnais Heights, Washington County (portions), West Lakeland, West St. Paul, White Bear Lake, White Bear Twp., Willernie & Woodbury, MN; Grey Cloud Island, Hudson, North Hudson, Prescott, River Falls & Troy, WI. ICA: MN0002.

TV Market Ranking: 13 (Afton, Andover, Anoka, Arden Hills, Bayport, Birchwood Village, Blaine, Brooklyn Center, Brooklyn Park, Burnsville, Centerville, Champlin, Circle Pines, Columbia Heights, Coon Rapids, Corcoran, Cottage Grove, Crystal, Dakota County (portions), Dellwood, Denmark Twp., Eagan, Falcon Heights, Gem Lake, Golden Valley, Grant Twp., Grey Cloud Island, Ham Lake, Hanover, Hastings, Hilltop, Hudson, Hugo, Inver Grove Heights, Lake Elmo, Lake St. Croix Beach, Lakeland, Lakeland Shores, Landfall, Lauderdale, Lexington, Lilydale, Lino Lakes, Little Canada, Mahtomedi, Maple Grove, Maplewood, Marshan Twp., Medicine Lake, Mendota, Mendota Heights, Mounds View, New Brighton, New Hope, Newport, North Hudson, North Oaks, North St. Paul, Oak Grove, Oak Park Heights, Oakdale, Osseo, Pine Springs, Plymouth, Prescott, Ramsey, Ramsey County, River Falls, Robbinsdale, Rogers, Roseville, Shoreview, South St. Paul, Spring Lake Park, St. Anthony, St. Croix, St. Marys Point, ST. PAUL, St. Paul Park, Stillwater, Sunfish Lake, Troy, Vadnais Heights, Washington County (portions), West Lakeland, West St. Paul, White Bear Lake, White Bear Twp., Willernie, Woodbury). Franchise award date: November 12, 1982. Franchise expiration date: N.A. Began: April 1, 1983.

Channel capacity: N.A. Channels available but not in use: N.A.

Basic Service

Subscribers: 350,000.

Programming (received off-air): KARE (NBC) Minneapolis; KMSP-TV (FOX) Minneapolis; KPXM-TV (ION) St. Cloud; KSTC-TV (IND) Minneapolis; KSTP-TV (ABC) St. Paul; KTCA-TV (PBS) St. Paul; KTCI-TV (PBS) St. Paul; WCCO-TV (CBS) Minneapolis; WFTC (MNT) Minneapolis; WUCW (CW) Minneapolis.

Programming (via satellite): Bravo; GSN; NASA TV; TBS Superstation; TV Guide Network; WGN America.

Current originations: Religious Access; Government Access; Educational Access; Public Access.

Fee: $44.99 installation; $9.50 monthly; $2.10 converter.

Expanded Basic Service 1

Subscribers: 330,000.

Programming (via satellite): ABC Family Channel; AMC; Animal Planet; Arts & Entertainment; BET Networks; Cartoon Network; CNBC; CNN; Comedy Central; C-SPAN; C-SPAN 2; Discovery Channel; Disney Channel; E! Entertainment Television; ESPN; ESPN 2; ESPN Classic Sports; Eternal Word TV Network; Food Network; Fox News Channel; FX; Golf Channel; Great American Country; GSN; Headline News; HGTV; History Channel; INSP; Lifetime; MTV; Nickelodeon; QVC; Sneak Prevue; Speed Channel; Spike TV; Syfy; The Learning Channel; Travel Channel; truTV; Turner Classic Movies; Turner Network TV; TV Land; USA Network; VH1; WE tv; Weather Channel.

Fee: $39.48 monthly.

Digital Basic Service

Subscribers: 250,000.

Programming (via satellite): AmericanLife TV Network; BBC America; Bio; Bloomberg Television; Canales N; Discovery Digital Networks; DMX Music; Encore Action; ESPNews; Fox Movie Channel; Fox Sports World; Fuse; G4; GAS; Halogen Network; History Channel International; Independent Film Channel; Lifetime Movie Network; MTV Networks Digital Suite; National Geographic Channel; Nick Jr.; Outdoor Channel; Ovation; Style Network; Sundance Channel; Toon Disney; Trinity Broadcasting Network; Versus; Weatherscan.

Fee: $9.99 monthly.

Digital Pay Service 1

Pay Units: 68,000.

Programming (via satellite): Cinemax (multiplexed); HBO (multiplexed); Showtime (multiplexed); Starz (multiplexed); The Movie Channel (multiplexed).

Fee: $16.99 monthly (each).

Video-On-Demand: Yes

Pay-Per-View

Addressable homes: 250,000.

Hot Choice; Hot Choice (delivered digitally), Addressable: Yes; iN DEMAND, Fee: $4.95; iN DEMAND (delivered digitally); Playboy TV (delivered digitally); Fresh, Fee: $5.95; Fresh (delivered digitally); Shorteez (delivered digitally).

Internet Service

Operational: Yes. Began: June 1, 1999.

Broadband Service: Comcast High Speed Internet.

Fee: $42.95 monthly.

Telephone Service

Digital: Operational

Fee: $44.95 monthly

Miles of Plant: 7,900.0 (coaxial); 2,362.0 (fiber optic). Homes passed: 681,000.

Area Vice President: Bill Wright. Vice President, Sales & Marketing: Nick Kozel. Technical Operations Director: Mark Bisenieus. Marketing Manager: Liz Statz.; Rachel Meyer.; Jeannie Boldt.

City fee: 5% of gross.

Ownership: Comcast Cable Communications Inc. (MSO).

ST. PAUL—Comcast Cable. Now served by St. PAUL, MN (formerly ROSEVILLE, MN) [MN0002]. ICA: MN0003.

ST. PETER—Now served by WASECA, MN [MN0043]. ICA: MN0049.

STACY—Now served by CAMBRIDGE, MN [MN0016]. ICA: MN0185.

STAPLES—Charter Communications. Now served by BRAINERD, MN [MN0022]. ICA: MN0368.

STAR LAKE TWP.—ACS Video. Formerly served by Perham, MN [MN0050]. This cable system has converted to IPTV, 150 Second St SW, Perham, MN 56573. Phone: 866-937-4227. E-mail: answers@arvig.com. Web Site: http://www.arvig.com. ICA: MN5223.

TV Market Ranking: Outside TV Markets (STAR LAKE TWP.).

Channel capacity: N.A. Channels available but not in use: N.A.

Internet Service

Operational: Yes.

Telephone Service

Digital: Operational

Ownership: Arvig Communication Systems.

STARBUCK—Mediacom. Now served by CHOKIO, MN [MN0210]. ICA: MN0131.

STEPHEN—Stephen Cable TV Inc., PO Box 9, 415 5th St, Stephen, MN 56757-0009. Phone: 218-478-3074. Fax: 218-478-2236. ICA: MN0181.

TV Market Ranking: Outside TV Markets (STEPHEN). Franchise award date: July 6, 1978. Franchise expiration date: N.A. Began: January 1, 1979.

Channel capacity: 78 (2-way capable). Channels available but not in use: 29.

Basic Service

Subscribers: 242.

Programming (received off-air): KBRR (FOX) Thief River Falls; KGFE (PBS) Grand Forks; KVLY-TV (NBC) Fargo; KXJB-TV (CBS) Valley City; WDAZ-TV (ABC, CW) Devils Lake; allband FM.

Programming (via satellite): ABC Family Channel; AMC; Arts & Entertainment; CNBC; CNN; Comedy Central; Country Music TV; C-SPAN; C-SPAN 2; Discovery Channel; Disney Channel; E! Entertainment Television; ESPN; ESPN 2; ESPN Classic Sports; Food Network; Fox News Channel; Fox Sports Net; FX; Golf Channel; Great American Country; Hallmark Channel; HGTV; History Channel; Home Shopping Network; Lifetime; MTV; Nickelodeon; Outdoor Channel; Speed Channel; Spike TV; Syfy; TBS Superstation; The Learning Channel; Trinity Broadcasting Network; Turner Network TV; TV Land; USA Network; various Canadian stations; VH1; Weather Channel; WGN America.

Current originations: Government Access; Educational Access; Public Access.
Fee: $20.00 installation; $33.50 monthly.
Pay Service 1
Pay Units: 11.
Programming (via satellite): HBO.
Fee: $10.00 installation; $11.00 monthly.
Video-On-Demand: No
Internet Service
Operational: No.
Telephone Service
None
Miles of Plant: 5.0 (coaxial); None (fiber optic). Homes passed: 320. Total homes in franchised area: 330.
Manager: Bryan Wixtrom.
Ownership: Bryan Wixtrom (MSO).

STOCKTON—Midcontinent Communications, PO Box 5010, Sioux Falls, SD 57117. Phone: 715-831-8940. Web Site: http://www.midcocomm.com. Also serves Lewiston & Rollingstone. ICA: MN0369.
TV Market Ranking: Below 100 (Lewiston, Rollingstone, STOCKTON). Franchise award date: N.A. Franchise expiration date: N.A. Began: July 10, 1977.
Channel capacity: N.A. Channels available but not in use: N.A.
Basic Service
Subscribers: 1,343.
Programming (received off-air): KMSP-TV (FOX) Minneapolis; KSTP-TV (ABC) St. Paul; KTCA-TV (PBS) St. Paul; KTTC (CW, NBC) Rochester; WCCO-TV (CBS) Minneapolis; WEAU-TV (NBC) Eau Claire; WFTC (MNT) Minneapolis; WHLA-TV (PBS) La Crosse; WKBT-DT (CBS, MNT) La Crosse; WLAX (FOX) La Crosse; WXOW (ABC, CW) La Crosse; allband FM.
Programming (via satellite): C-SPAN; C-SPAN 2; QVC; TV Guide Network; WGN America.
Current originations: Educational Access; Public Access; Leased Access; Government Access.
Fee: $50.00 installation; $11.95 monthly.
Expanded Basic Service 1
Subscribers: 1,169.
Programming (via satellite): ABC Family Channel; AMC; Animal Planet; Arts & Entertainment; BET Networks; Bloomberg Television; Bravo; Cartoon Network; CNBC; CNN; Comedy Central; Country Music TV; Discovery Channel; Discovery Digital Networks; Disney Channel; E! Entertainment Television; ESPN; ESPN 2; ESPN Classic Sports; Eternal Word TV Network; FitTV; Food Network; Fox News Channel; Fox Sports Net North; FX; G4; Golf Channel; GSN; Hallmark Channel; Headline News; HGTV; History Channel; Home Shopping Network; INSP; Lifetime; MSNBC; MTV; National Geographic Channel; Nick Jr.; Nickelodeon; Outdoor Channel; Oxygen; ShopNBC; SoapNet; Speed Channel; Spike TV; Syfy; TBS Superstation; The Learning Channel; Toon Disney; Travel Channel; truTV; Turner Classic Movies; Turner Network TV; TV Land; USA Network; Versus; VH1; WE tv; Weather Channel.
Fee: $31.95 monthly.
Digital Basic Service
Subscribers: 370.
Programming (received off-air): WEAU-TV (NBC) Eau Claire; WKBT-DT (CBS, MNT) La Crosse.
Programming (via satellite): BBC America; Bio; Boomerang; CNN en Espanol; CNN International; C-SPAN 3; Do-It-Yourself; ESPN; ESPNews; Fox College Sports Atlantic; Fox College Sports Central; Fox College Sports Pacific; Fox Movie Channel; Fox Soccer; Fuel TV; Fuse; GAS; HDNet; HDNet Movies; History Channel International; Independent Film Channel; Lifetime Movie Network; MTV Networks Digital Suite; Music Choice; NFL Network; Nick Too; NickToons TV; Style Network; Sundance Channel; TV Guide Interactive Inc.
Fee: $6.05 monthly; $8.95 converter.
Digital Pay Service 1
Pay Units: 144.
Programming (via satellite): Cinemax (multiplexed); Flix; Starz (multiplexed).
Fee: $19.25 installation; $13.95 monthly; $8.95 converter.
Digital Pay Service 2
Pay Units: 181.
Programming (via satellite): HBO.
Fee: $19.25 installation; $13.95 monthly; $8.95 converter.
Digital Pay Service 3
Pay Units: 131.
Programming (via satellite): Showtime.
Fee: $19.25 installation; $13.95 monthly; $8.95 converter.
Digital Pay Service 4
Pay Units: 128.
Programming (via satellite): The Movie Channel.
Fee: $19.25 installation; $13.95 monthly; $8.95 converter.
Digital Pay Service 5
Pay Units: 204.
Programming (via satellite): Encore.
Fee: $19.25 installation; $13.95 monthly; $8.95 converter.
Video-On-Demand: Yes
Pay-Per-View
iN DEMAND (delivered digitally); NASCAR In Car (delivered digitally); NHL Center Ice (delivered digitally); MLB Extra Innings (delivered digitally); Playboy TV (delivered digitally); Spice Live (delivered digitally); Spice Platinum (delivered digitally); Hot Net Plus (delivered digitally); Spice Hot (delivered digitally).
Internet Service
Operational: Yes.
Subscribers: 448.
Broadband Service: Midcontinent.
Fee: $29.99 monthly.
Telephone Service
Digital: Operational
Miles of Plant: 27.0 (coaxial); None (fiber optic). Homes passed: 2,065.
General Manager: Darrell Wraye. Vice President, Public Policy: Tom Simmons.
City fee: None.
Ownership: Midcontinent Media Inc. (MSO).

STORDEN—US Cable, 402 Red River Ave N, Unit 5, Cold Spring, MN 56320-1521. Phones: 320-685-7113; 800-783-2356. Fax: 320-685-2816. E-mail: help@mn.uscable.com. Web Site: http://www.uscable.com. ICA: MN0244.
TV Market Ranking: Outside TV Markets (STORDEN). Franchise award date: N.A. Franchise expiration date: N.A. Began: N.A.
Channel capacity: N.A. Channels available but not in use: N.A.
Basic Service
Subscribers: N.A. Included in Cambridge
Programming (received off-air): KARE (NBC) Minneapolis; KELO-TV (CBS, MNT) Sioux Falls; KEYC-TV (CBS, FOX) Mankato; KMSP-TV (FOX) Minneapolis; KSFY-TV (ABC) Sioux Falls; KSTC-TV (IND) Minneapolis; KSTP-TV (ABC) St. Paul; KTCA-TV (PBS) St. Paul; WCCO-TV (CBS) Minneapolis; WFTC (MNT) Minneapolis; WUCW (CW) Minneapolis.
Programming (via satellite): ABC Family Channel; Arts & Entertainment; CNBC; CNN; Comedy Central; Country Music TV; Discovery Channel; ESPN; ESPN 2; Fox Sports Net North; Headline News; History Channel; Lifetime; Nickelodeon; Outdoor Channel; Spike TV; TBS Superstation; The Learning Channel; Turner Classic Movies; Turner Network TV; USA Network; Weather Channel; WGN America.
Fee: $32.00 monthly.
Pay Service 1
Pay Units: N.A. Included in Cambridge
Programming (via satellite): HBO.
Fee: $11.95 monthly.
Internet Service
Operational: No.
Homes passed: Included in Cambridge
General Manager: Steve Johnson. Customer Service Director: Jackie Torberg.
Ownership: US Cable Corp. (MSO).; Comcast Cable Communications Inc. (MSO).

STOWE PRAIRIE TWP.—ACS Video. Formerly served by Perham, MN [MN0050]. This cable system has converted to IPTV, 150 Second St SW, Perham, MN 56573. Phone: 866-937-4227. E-mail: answers@arvig.com. Web Site: http://www.arvig.com. ICA: MN5225.
TV Market Ranking: Below 100 (STOWE PRAIRIE TWP.).
Channel capacity: N.A. Channels available but not in use: N.A.
Internet Service
Operational: Yes.
Telephone Service
Digital: Operational
Ownership: Arvig Communication Systems.

SWANVILLE—Formerly served by 391 Satellite LLC. No longer in operation. ICA: MN0256.

TACONITE—City of Taconite Cable TV, PO Box 137, Taconite, MN 55786-0137. Phone: 218-245-1831. Fax: 218-245-1831. E-mail: taconite@uslink.net. ICA: MN0370.
TV Market Ranking: Below 100 (TACONITE). Franchise award date: January 1, 1964. Franchise expiration date: N.A. Began: November 1, 1965.
Channel capacity: 23 (not 2-way capable). Channels available but not in use: 2.
Basic Service
Subscribers: 110.
Programming (received off-air): KBJR-TV (MNT, NBC) Superior; KCCO-TV (CBS) Alexandria; KDLH (CBS, CW) Duluth; KQDS-TV (FOX) Duluth; WDIO-DT (ABC) Duluth; WDSE (PBS) Duluth.
Programming (via satellite): ABC Family Channel; CNN; Discovery Channel; Disney Channel; ESPN; ESPN 2; Eternal Word TV Network; Fox Sports Net; Nickelodeon; Outdoor Channel; Spike TV; TBS Superstation; Turner Classic Movies; Turner Network TV; USA Network; WGN America.
Internet Service
Operational: No.
Telephone Service
None
Miles of Plant: 4.0 (coaxial); None (fiber optic). Homes passed: 110. Total homes in franchised area: 110.
Manager: Michael Troumbly. Chief Technician: Lloyd Cogswell.
Franchise fee: None.
Ownership: City of Taconite Cable TV.

TAYLORS FALLS—Now served by CAMBRIDGE, MN [MN0016]. ICA: MN0371.

THIEF RIVER FALLS—Sjoberg's Cable TV Inc., 315 Main Ave N, Thief River Falls, MN 56701-1905. Phones: 800-828-8808; 218-681-3044. Fax: 218-681-6801. E-mail: sjobergs@mncable.net. Web Site: http://trf.mncable.net/community. Also serves Holt & Viking. ICA: MN0045.
TV Market Ranking: Below 100 (Holt, THIEF RIVER FALLS, Viking). Franchise award date: N.A. Franchise expiration date: N.A. Began: October 1, 1962.
Channel capacity: 78 (operating 2-way). Channels available but not in use: 18.
Basic Service
Subscribers: 3,493.
Programming (received off-air): KBRR (FOX) Thief River Falls; KCPM (MNT) Grand Forks; KGFE (PBS) Grand Forks; KVLY-TV (NBC) Fargo; KXJB-TV (CBS) Valley City; WDAZ-TV (ABC, CW) Devils Lake; 14 FMs.
Programming (via satellite): CNN; ESPN; TBS Superstation; various Canadian stations.
Current originations: Public Access.
Fee: $25.00 installation; $10.00 monthly.
Expanded Basic Service 1
Subscribers: N.A.
Programming (via satellite): ABC Family Channel; Animal Planet; Arts & Entertainment; Cartoon Network; CNBC; Comedy Central; Country Music TV; C-SPAN; CW+; Discovery Channel; Disney Channel; E! Entertainment Television; ESPN 2; Food Network; Fox News Channel; Fox Sports Net; FX; HGTV; History Channel; Home Shopping Network; Lifetime; MSNBC; MTV; Nickelodeon; Spike TV; Syfy; The Learning Channel; Turner Classic Movies; Turner Network TV; TV Land; USA Network; VH1; Weather Channel; WGN America.
Fee: $23.71 monthly.
Digital Basic Service
Subscribers: N.A.
Programming (received off-air): PBS HD.
Programming (via satellite): AmericanLife TV Network; Arts & Entertainment HD; BBC America; Bio; Blackbelt TV; Bloomberg Television; Bravo; CBS College Sports Network; Chiller; CMT Pure Country; CNN HD; Cooking Channel; Current; Daystar TV Network; Discovery Channel HD; Discovery Health Channel; Discovery Kids Channel; Discovery Military Channel; Discovery Planet Green; DMX Music; Do-It-Yourself; ESPN 2 HD; ESPN Classic Sports; ESPN HD; ESPN U; ESPNews; Eternal Word TV Network; FitTV; Food Network HD; Fox Business Channel; Fox College Sports Atlantic; Fox College Sports Central; Fox College Sports Pacific; Fox Movie Channel; Fox Reality Channel; Fox Soccer; FSN HD; G4; Golf Channel; Gospel Music Channel; Great American Country; GSN; Hallmark Channel; Halogen Network; HDNet; HDNet Movies; Headline News; HGTV HD; History Channel HD; History Channel International; HorseRacing TV; ID Investigation Discovery; Independent Film Channel; Lifetime Movie Network; MTV Hits; MTV2; National Geographic Channel; Nick Jr.; NickToons TV; Outdoor Channel; Outdoor Channel 2 HD; Ovation; Oxygen; PBS Kids Sprout; ReelzChannel; RFD-TV; Science Channel; ShopNBC; Sleuth; SoapNet; Speed Channel; Speed HD; Style Network; Sundance Channel; Syfy HD; TBS in HD; TeenNick; Tennis Channel; The Sportsman Channel; The Word Network; Toon Disney; Trinity Broadcasting Network; Turner Network TV HD; TVG Network; Universal HD; USA Net-

work HD; Versus; Versus HD; VH1 Classic; VH1 Soul; WE tv.
Fee: $11.00 monthly.

Pay Service 1
Pay Units: 590.
Programming (via satellite): HBO.
Fee: $11.00 monthly.

Pay Service 2
Pay Units: 243.
Programming (via satellite): Cinemax.
Fee: $9.00 monthly.

Digital Pay Service 1
Pay Units: N.A.
Programming (via satellite): Cinemax (multiplexed); Cinemax HD; Encore (multiplexed); HBO (multiplexed); HBO HD; Showtime (multiplexed); Starz (multiplexed); The Movie Channel (multiplexed).
Fee: $8.00 monthly (Starz/Encore), $9.00 monthly (Cinemax or Showtime/TMC), $11.00 monthly (HBO).

Video-On-Demand: No

Pay-Per-View
World Wrestling Entertainment Inc., Fee: $2.99.

Internet Service
Operational: Yes. Began: March 1, 1999.
Subscribers: 934.
Broadband Service: Sjoberg's Cable TV.
Fee: $19.95 monthly; $29.95 modem lease; $129.00 modem purchase.

Telephone Service
None

Miles of Plant: 48.0 (coaxial); 85.0 (fiber optic). Homes passed: 3,516. Total homes in franchised area: 3,550.
Manager: Richard J. Sjoberg. Chief Technician: Jerry Seim.
City fee: 3% of gross.
Ownership: Sjoberg's Cable TV Inc. (MSO).

TOWER—Midcontinent Communications, PO Box 5010, Sioux Falls, SD 57117. Phones: 800-456-0564; 605-229-1775. Web Site: http://www.midcocomm.com. Also serves Soudan. ICA: MN0139.
TV Market Ranking: Outside TV Markets (Soudan, TOWER). Franchise award date: N.A. Franchise expiration date: N.A. Began: November 1, 1970.
Channel capacity: N.A. Channels available but not in use: N.A.

Basic Service
Subscribers: 386.
Programming (via microwave): KBJR-TV (MNT, NBC) Superior; KDLH (CBS, CW) Duluth; KQDS-TV (FOX) Duluth; WDIO-DT (ABC) Duluth; WDSE (PBS) Duluth.
Programming (via satellite): C-SPAN; Eternal Word TV Network; INSP; QVC; WGN America.
Fee: $29.99 installation.

Expanded Basic Service 1
Subscribers: N.A.
Programming (via satellite): ABC Family Channel; AMC; Animal Planet; Arts & Entertainment; Bravo; Cartoon Network; CNBC; CNN; Comedy Central; Country Music TV; Discovery Channel; Disney Channel; E! Entertainment Television; ESPN; ESPN 2; Fox News Channel; Fox Sports Net North; FX; Hallmark Channel; Headline News; HGTV; History Channel; Lifetime; MSNBC; MTV; Nickelodeon; Oxygen; Speed Channel; Spike TV; Syfy; TBS Superstation; The Learning Channel; truTV; Turner Classic Movies; Turner Network TV; TV Land; USA Network; VH1; Weather Channel.
Fee: $47.99 monthly.

Digital Basic Service
Subscribers: N.A.
Programming (via satellite): BBC America; Bio; Discovery Digital Networks; Do-It-Yourself; Fox College Sports Atlantic; Fox College Sports Central; Fox College Sports Pacific; Fox Movie Channel; Fox Soccer; G4; GAS; History Channel International; Independent Film Channel; MTV Networks Digital Suite; Music Choice; Nick Jr.; Nick Too; NickToons TV; SoapNet; Style Network; Sundance Channel; Toon Disney; TV Guide Interactive Inc.; WE tv.

Digital Pay Service 1
Pay Units: N.A.
Programming (via satellite): Cinemax (multiplexed); Encore; Flix; HBO (multiplexed); Showtime (multiplexed); Starz (multiplexed); The Movie Channel (multiplexed).

Video-On-Demand: No

Pay-Per-View
Hot Choice (delivered digitally); iN DEMAND (delivered digitally).

Internet Service
Operational: Yes.
Broadband Service: Midcontinent.
Fee: $29.99 monthly.

Telephone Service
Digital: Operational

Miles of Plant: 10.0 (coaxial); None (fiber optic). Homes passed: 580. Total homes in franchised area: 580.
Vice President, Public Policy: Tom Simmons. General Manager: Darrell Wrege.
City fee: None.
Ownership: Midcontinent Media Inc. (MSO).

TRACY—Charter Communications, 1108 E College Dr, Marshall, MN 56258-1902. Phones: 507-289-8372 (Rochester administrative office); 507-537-1541. Fax: 507-537-1572. Web Site: http://www.charter.com. ICA: MN0056.
TV Market Ranking: Below 100 (TRACY). Franchise award date: N.A. Franchise expiration date: N.A. Began: September 1, 1971.
Channel capacity: N.A. Channels available but not in use: N.A.

Basic Service
Subscribers: 390.
Programming (received off-air): KELO-TV (CBS, MNT) Sioux Falls; KRWF (ABC) Redwood Falls; KSFY-TV (ABC) Sioux Falls; KSMN (PBS) Worthington; WUCW (CW) Minneapolis.
Programming (via microwave): KMSP-TV (FOX) Minneapolis; WCCO-TV (CBS) Minneapolis; WFTC (MNT) Minneapolis.
Programming (via satellite): C-SPAN; C-SPAN 2; Eternal Word TV Network; Home Shopping Network; INSP; QVC; WGN America.
Programming (via translator): KARE (NBC) Minneapolis.
Current originations: Educational Access; Public Access.
Fee: $29.99 installation; $34.00 additional installation.

Expanded Basic Service 1
Subscribers: N.A.
Programming (via satellite): ABC Family Channel; AMC; Animal Planet; Arts & Entertainment; Cartoon Network; CNBC; CNN; Comedy Central; Country Music TV; Discovery Channel; Disney Channel; E! Entertainment Television; ESPN; ESPN 2; Food Network; Fox News Channel; Fox Sports Net North; FX; Great American Country; Hallmark Channel; Headline News; HGTV; History Channel; Lifetime; MSNBC; MTV; Nickelodeon; Outdoor Channel; Oxygen; Spike TV; Syfy; TBS Superstation; The Learning Channel; Toon Disney; Turner Classic Movies; Turner Network TV; TV Land; Univision; USA Network; VH1; Weather Channel.
Fee: $47.99 monthly.

Digital Basic Service
Subscribers: N.A.
Programming (via satellite): BBC America; Bio; Bravo; Discovery Digital Networks; DMX Music; ESPN Classic Sports; ESPNews; Fox Movie Channel; Fox Soccer; G4; GAS; Golf Channel; GSN; History Channel International; Independent Film Channel; Lifetime Movie Network; MTV Networks Digital Suite; National Geographic Channel; Nick Jr.; NickToons TV; Speed Channel; Style Network; Sundance Channel; Trinity Broadcasting Network; TV Guide Interactive Inc.; Versus; WE tv.

Digital Pay Service 1
Pay Units: N.A.
Programming (via satellite): Cinemax (multiplexed); Encore; HBO (multiplexed); Showtime (multiplexed); Starz (multiplexed); The Movie Channel (multiplexed).

Video-On-Demand: Yes

Pay-Per-View
iN DEMAND (delivered digitally).

Internet Service
Operational: Yes.
Broadband Service: Charter Pipeline.
Fee: $29.99 monthly.

Telephone Service
Digital: Operational

Miles of Plant: 15.0 (coaxial); None (fiber optic). Homes passed: 1,100.
Vice President & General Manager: John Crowley. Operations Director: Craig Stensaas. Technical Operations Director: Mark Abramo. Marketing Director: Bill Haarstad. Office Manager: Sue Olson.
City fee: 1% of gross.
Ownership: Charter Communications Inc. (MSO).

TRIMONT—Terril Cable Systems, PO Box 100, Terril, IA 51364-0100. Phone: 712-853-6121. Fax: 712-853-6185. Web Site: http://www.terril.com. ICA: MN0372.
TV Market Ranking: Outside TV Markets (TRIMONT). Franchise award date: N.A. Franchise expiration date: N.A. Began: January 1, 1985.
Channel capacity: 35 (operating 2-way). Channels available but not in use: 19.

Basic Service
Subscribers: 200.
Programming (received off-air): KEYC-TV (CBS, FOX) Mankato; KSTC-TV (IND) Minneapolis; KTCA-TV (PBS) St. Paul; WCCO-TV (CBS) Minneapolis; WFTC (MNT) Minneapolis; WUCW (CW) Minneapolis.
Programming (via satellite): ABC Family Channel; Animal Planet; Arts & Entertainment; CNBC; CNN; Country Music TV; Discovery Channel; Disney Channel; ESPN; ESPN 2; Fox Sports Net North; History Channel; Lifetime; MTV; National Geographic Channel; Nickelodeon; Spike TV; TBS Superstation; The Learning Channel; Turner Classic Movies; Turner Network TV; TV Land; USA Network; VH1; Weather Channel; WGN America.
Programming (via translator): KARE (NBC) Minneapolis; KMSP-TV (FOX) Minneapolis; KSTP-TV (ABC) St. Paul.
Fee: $20.00 installation; $29.51 monthly.

Digital Basic Service
Subscribers: N.A.
Programming (via satellite): Alterna'TV; BBC America; Bio; Black Family Channel; Bloomberg Television; Bravo; CMT Pure Country; Discovery Health Channel; Discovery Home Channel; Discovery Kids Channel; Discovery Military Channel; Discovery Times Channel; ESPN Classic Sports; ESPNews; FitTV; Fox College Sports Atlantic; Fox College Sports Central; Fox College Sports Pacific; Fox Movie Channel; Fox Soccer; Fuse; G4; Golf Channel; Great American Country; GSN; Halogen Network; HGTV; History Channel International; Independent Film Channel; Lime; MTV2; National Geographic Channel; Nick Jr.; NickToons TV; Outdoor Channel; Ovation; Science Channel; ShopNBC; Speed Channel; Style Network; TeenNick; Toon Disney; Trinity Broadcasting Network; Trio; Versus; VH1 Classic; WE tv.
Fee: $7.00 monthly (per package).

Digital Pay Service 1
Pay Units: N.A.
Programming (via satellite): Cinemax (multiplexed); Encore (multiplexed); Flix; HBO (multiplexed); Showtime (multiplexed); Starz (multiplexed); Sundance Channel; The Movie Channel (multiplexed).
Fee: $11.00 monthly (each).

Video-On-Demand: No

Pay-Per-View
iN DEMAND (delivered digitally); Hot Choice (delivered digitally); Spice (delivered digitally); Playboy TV (delivered digitally); Spice 2 (delivered digitally).

Internet Service
Operational: No.

Telephone Service
None

Miles of Plant: 6.0 (coaxial); None (fiber optic). Total homes in franchised area: 350.
Manager: Douglas Nelson.
City fee: 3% of basic gross.
Ownership: Ter Tel Enterprises (MSO).

TRUMAN—Terril Cable Systems, PO Box 100, Terril, IA 51364-0100. Phone: 712-853-6121. Fax: 712-853-6185. Web Site: http://www.terril.com. ICA: MN0148.
TV Market Ranking: Below 100 (TRUMAN). Franchise award date: N.A. Franchise expiration date: N.A. Began: February 1, 1985.
Channel capacity: 35 (operating 2-way). Channels available but not in use: N.A.

Basic Service
Subscribers: 310.
Programming (received off-air): KARE (NBC) Minneapolis; KEYC-TV (CBS, FOX) Mankato; KMSP-TV (FOX) Minneapolis; KSTC-TV (IND) Minneapolis; KSTP-TV (ABC) St. Paul; KTCA-TV (PBS) St. Paul; WCCO-TV (CBS) Minneapolis; WFTC (MNT) Minneapolis; WUCW (CW) Minneapolis.
Programming (via satellite): ABC Family Channel; Animal Planet; Arts & Entertainment; CNBC; CNN; Country Music TV; Discovery Channel; Disney Channel; ESPN; ESPN 2; Fox Sports Net North; History Channel; Lifetime; MTV; National Geographic Channel; Nickelodeon; Spike TV; TBS Superstation; The Learning Channel; Turner Classic Movies; Turner Network TV; TV Land; USA Network; VH1; Weather Channel; WGN America.
Fee: $20.00 installation; $29.51 monthly.

Digital Basic Service
Subscribers: N.A.
Programming (via satellite): Alterna'TV; BBC America; Bio; Black Family Channel; Bloomberg Television; Bravo; CMT Pure Country; Discovery Health Channel; Discovery Home Channel; Discovery Kids Channel; Discovery Military Channel; Discovery Times Channel; ESPN Classic Sports; ESPNews; FitTV; Fox College Sports Atlantic; Fox College Sports

Central; Fox College Sports Pacific; Fox Movie Channel; Fox Soccer; Fuse; G4; Golf Channel; Great American Country; GSN; Halogen Network; HGTV; History Channel International; Independent Film Channel; Lime; MTV2; Nick Jr.; NickToons TV; Outdoor Channel; Ovation; Science Channel; ShopNBC; Speed Channel; Style Network; TeenNick; Toon Disney; Trinity Broadcasting Network; Trio; Versus; VH1 Classic; WE tv.
Fee: $7.00 monthly (per package).

Digital Pay Service 1
Pay Units: N.A.
Programming (via satellite): Cinemax (multiplexed); Encore (multiplexed); Flix; HBO (multiplexed); Showtime (multiplexed); Starz (multiplexed); Sundance Channel; The Movie Channel (multiplexed).
Fee: $11.00 monthly (each).

Video-On-Demand: No

Pay-Per-View
iN DEMAND (delivered digitally); Hot Choice (delivered digitally); Spice (delivered digitally); Playboy TV (delivered digitally); Spice 2 (delivered digitally).

Internet Service
Operational: No.

Telephone Service
None

Miles of Plant: 9.0 (coaxial); None (fiber optic). Homes passed: 510.
Manager: Douglas Nelson.
Ownership: Ter Tel Enterprises (MSO).

TURTLE LAKE TWP.—ACS Video. Formerly served by Perham, MN [MN0050]. This cable system has converted to IPTV, 150 Second St SW, Perham, MN 56573. Phone: 866-937-4227. E-mail: answers@arvig.com. Web Site: http://www.arvig.com. ICA: MN5228.
TV Market Ranking: Below 100 (TURTLE LAKE TWP.).
Channel capacity: N.A. Channels available but not in use: N.A.

Internet Service
Operational: Yes.

Telephone Service
Digital: Operational

Ownership: Arvig Communication Systems.

TWIN VALLEY—ACS Video. Formerly served by Perham, MN [MN0050]. This cable system has converted to IPTV, 150 Second St SW, Perham, MN 56573. Phone: 866-937-4227. E-mail: answers@arvig.com. Web Site: http://www.arvig.com. ICA: MN5139.
TV Market Ranking: Outside TV Markets (TWIN VALLEY).
Channel capacity: N.A. Channels available but not in use: N.A.

Internet Service
Operational: Yes.

Telephone Service
Digital: Operational

Ownership: Arvig Communication Systems.

TWO HARBORS—Now served by SILVER BAY, MN [MN0084]. ICA: MN0067.

ULEN—Loretel Cablevision, PO Box 72, 13 East 4th Ave, Ada, MN 56510. Phones: 218-784-5100; 800-343-2762. Fax: 218-784-2706. E-mail: loretel@loretel.net. Web Site: http://www.hectorcom.com. Also serves Hitterdal. ICA: MN0373.
TV Market Ranking: 98 (Hitterdal, ULEN). Franchise award date: N.A. Franchise expiration date: N.A. Began: November 1, 1983.
Channel capacity: 30 (operating 2-way). Channels available but not in use: 2.

Basic Service
Subscribers: 201.
Programming (received off-air): KFME (PBS) Fargo; KVLY-TV (NBC) Fargo; KVRR (FOX) Fargo; KXJB-TV (CBS) Valley City; WDAY-TV (ABC, CW) Fargo.
Programming (via satellite): ABC Family Channel; Arts & Entertainment; Cartoon Network; CNBC; CNN; Comedy Central; Country Music TV; C-SPAN; Discovery Channel; Disney Channel; ESPN; Food Network; Fox Sports Net; KCPM (MNT) Grand Forks; Lifetime; National Geographic Channel; Nickelodeon; QVC; Sneak Prevue; Spike TV; Syfy; TBS Superstation; The Learning Channel; Turner Classic Movies; Turner Network TV; USA Network; VH1; Weather Channel; WGN America.
Current originations: Public Access.
Fee: $40.00 installation; $29.00 monthly.

Expanded Basic Service 1
Subscribers: N.A.
Programming (via satellite): E! Entertainment Television; FX; MTV; TV Land.

Digital Basic Service
Subscribers: N.A.
Programming (via satellite): BBC America; Bio; Discovery Digital Networks; DMX Music; ESPN 2; ESPN Classic Sports; ESPNews; GAS; Golf Channel; HGTV; History Channel; History Channel International; Independent Film Channel; Lifetime Movie Network; MTV2; Nick Jr.; Speed Channel; Toon Disney; Versus; VH1 Classic; VH1 Country.
Fee: $15.95 monthly.

Pay Service 1
Pay Units: 26.
Programming (via satellite): HBO.
Fee: $12.00 monthly.

Pay Service 2
Pay Units: 18.
Programming (via satellite): Cinemax.
Fee: $1.75 monthly (Encore), $9.00 monthly (Cinemax).

Pay Service 3
Pay Units: 36.
Programming (via satellite): Encore.
Fee: $1.75 monthly.

Digital Pay Service 1
Pay Units: N.A.
Programming (via satellite): Encore (multiplexed); HBO (multiplexed); The Movie Channel.

Video-On-Demand: No

Pay-Per-View
iN DEMAND (delivered digitally); Playboy TV (delivered digitally).

Internet Service
Operational: No.
Broadband Service: Offers dial-up and DSL only; no cable modem service.

Telephone Service
None

Miles of Plant: 4.0 (coaxial); 7.0 (fiber optic). Homes passed: 324. Total homes in franchised area: 324.
Manager: Steven W. Katka. Chief Technician: Bruce Rosenfelt.
City fee: None.
Ownership: Hector Communications Corp. (MSO).

VERMILLION—Cannon Valley Cablevision, PO Box 337, 202 N First St, Bricelyn, MN 56014. Phones: 800-753-5113; 507-653-4444. Fax: 507-653-4449. Web Site: http://www.cvtel.net. Also serves Coates, Hampton, Randolph, Randolph Twp. & Ravenna. ICA: MN0391.
TV Market Ranking: 13 (Coates, Hampton, Randolph, Randolph Twp., Ravenna, VERMILLION). Franchise award date: January 1, 1990. Franchise expiration date: N.A. Began: January 1, 1991.
Channel capacity: 72 (operating 2-way). Channels available but not in use: 14.

Basic Service
Subscribers: 1,100.
Programming (received off-air): KARE (NBC) Minneapolis; KMSP-TV (FOX) Minneapolis; KSTC-TV (IND) Minneapolis; KSTP-TV (ABC) St. Paul; KTCA-TV (PBS) St. Paul; KTCI-TV (PBS) St. Paul; WCCO-TV (CBS) Minneapolis; WFTC (MNT) Minneapolis; WUCW (CW) Minneapolis.
Programming (via satellite): ABC Family Channel; AMC; Animal Planet; Arts & Entertainment; Bravo; Cartoon Network; CNBC; CNN; Comedy Central; Country Music TV; C-SPAN; Discovery Channel; Disney Channel; ESPN; ESPN 2; ESPN Classic Sports; Eternal Word TV Network; Food Network; Fox News Channel; Fox Sports Net North; FX; GSN; Hallmark Channel; HGTV; History Channel; Home Shopping Network; ION Television; Lifetime; MSNBC; MTV; National Geographic Channel; Nickelodeon; QVC; Speed Channel; Spike TV; Syfy; TBS Superstation; The Learning Channel; Travel Channel; truTV; Turner Network TV; TV Land; USA Network; VH1; Weather Channel; WGN America.
Fee: $40.00 installation; $39.95 monthly; $25.00 additional installation.

Digital Basic Service
Subscribers: N.A.
Programming (via satellite): BBC America; Bio; Bloomberg Television; Bravo; Discovery Digital Networks; DMX Music; ESPN 2; ESPN Classic Sports; ESPNews; Fox Soccer; Fuse; G4; GAS; Golf Channel; GSN; Halogen Network; HGTV; History Channel; History Channel International; Independent Film Channel; MTV Networks Digital Suite; National Geographic Channel; Nick Jr.; NickToons TV; Outdoor Channel; Speed Channel; Style Network; Syfy; Toon Disney; Trinity Broadcasting Network; Trio; Turner Classic Movies; Versus; WE tv.
Fee: $7.55 monthly.

Pay Service 1
Pay Units: N.A.
Programming (via satellite): HBO; Showtime.
Fee: $12.95 monthly (each).

Digital Pay Service 1
Pay Units: N.A.
Programming (via satellite): Cinemax (multiplexed); Encore (multiplexed); Flix; HBO (multiplexed); Showtime (multiplexed); Starz (multiplexed); The Movie Channel (multiplexed).
Fee: $7.50 installation; $11.95 monthly (Starz/Encore), $12.95 monthly (Showtime/TMC), $15.95 monthly (HBO/Cinemax).

Video-On-Demand: No

Pay-Per-View
iN DEMAND (delivered digitally); Hot Choice (delivered digitally); Playboy TV (delivered digitally); Fresh (delivered digitally).

Internet Service
Operational: Yes.
Broadband Service: Cannon Valley.
Fee: $26.95 monthly.

Telephone Service
None

Miles of Plant: 38.0 (coaxial); 13.0 (fiber optic).
Manager: Scott Johnson. Operations Manager: Aaron Johnson.
Ownership: BEVCOMM (MSO).

VERNDALE—Savage Communications Inc., PO Box 810, 206 Power Ave N, Hinckley, MN 55037. Phone: 320-384-7442. Fax: 320-384-7446. E-mail: rwsavage@scicable.com. Web Site: http://www.scibroadband.com. ICA: MN0214.
TV Market Ranking: Outside TV Markets (VERNDALE). Franchise award date: July 15, 1985. Franchise expiration date: N.A. Began: July 18, 1985.
Channel capacity: 77 (operating 2-way). Channels available but not in use: 22.

Basic Service
Subscribers: 137.
Programming (received off-air): KARE (NBC) Minneapolis; KAWB (PBS) Brainerd; KCCO-TV (CBS) Alexandria; KMSP-TV (FOX) Minneapolis; KSAX (ABC) Alexandria; KVRR (FOX) Fargo; WPIX (CW, IND) New York.
Programming (via satellite): ABC Family Channel; Animal Planet; Arts & Entertainment; CNBC; CNN; Comedy Central; C-SPAN; Discovery Channel; Disney Channel; E! Entertainment Television; ESPN; ESPN 2; Fox Sports Net; Great American Country; Headline News; HGTV; History Channel; Lifetime; MTV; Nickelodeon; QVC; Spike TV; Syfy; TBS Superstation; The Learning Channel; Turner Classic Movies; Turner Network TV; TV Land; USA Network; VH1; Weather Channel; WGN America.
Fee: $39.95 installation; $38.95 monthly.

Digital Basic Service
Subscribers: N.A.
Programming (via satellite): AmericanLife TV Network; BBC America; Bio; Bloomberg Television; Discovery Digital Networks; DMX Music; ESPN Classic Sports; ESPNews; FitTV; Fox Movie Channel; Fox Sports World; Fuse; G4; Golf Channel; History Channel International; INSP; National Geographic Channel; Outdoor Channel; Sleuth; Speed Channel; Style Network; Trinity Broadcasting Network; Versus; WE tv.

Digital Pay Service 1
Pay Units: N.A.
Programming (via satellite): Cinemax (multiplexed); Encore (multiplexed); Flix; HBO (multiplexed); Showtime (multiplexed); Starz (multiplexed); Sundance Channel; The Movie Channel (multiplexed).

Video-On-Demand: No

Pay-Per-View
Movies (delivered digitally); ESPN Now (delivered digitally); Sports PPV (delivered digitally).

Internet Service
Operational: Yes.
Broadband Service: SCI Broadband.
Fee: $19.95 monthly.

Telephone Service
None

Miles of Plant: 5.0 (coaxial); None (fiber optic). Homes passed: 237. Total homes in franchised area: 237.
Manager: Mike Danielson. Marketing Director: Ron Savage. Chief Technician: Pat McCabe. Customer Service Manager: Donna Erickson.
Ownership: Savage Communications Inc. (MSO).

VERNON CENTER—North American Communications Corp., PO Box 387, 211 Main St S, Hector, MN 55342-0387. Phones: 800-982-8038; 320-848-6781. Fax: 320-848-2323. E-mail: hcc@hcctel.net. Web Site: http://www.hectorcom.com. ICA: MN0374.

TV Market Ranking: Below 100 (VERNON CENTER). Franchise award date: N.A. Franchise expiration date: N.A. Began: N.A.
Channel capacity: 54 (not 2-way capable). Channels available but not in use: 29.

Basic Service
Subscribers: 54.
Programming (received off-air): KARE (NBC) Minneapolis; KEYC-TV (CBS, FOX) Mankato; KMSP-TV (FOX) Minneapolis; KSMN (PBS) Worthington; KSTP-TV (ABC) St. Paul; WCCO-TV (CBS) Minneapolis; WFTC (MNT) Minneapolis.
Programming (via satellite): ABC Family Channel; AMC; Arts & Entertainment; CNN; Discovery Channel; Disney Channel; ESPN; Fox Sports Net Midwest; Lifetime; Nickelodeon; QVC; Spike TV; TBS Superstation; Trinity Broadcasting Network; Turner Network TV; USA Network; WGN America.
Current originations: Leased Access; Government Access; Educational Access; Public Access.
Fee: $40.00 installation; $26.95 monthly; $3.50 converter; $25.00 additional installation.

Pay Service 1
Pay Units: 3.
Programming (via satellite): Cinemax.
Fee: $10.95 monthly.

Pay Service 2
Pay Units: 2.
Programming (via satellite): HBO.
Fee: $10.95 monthly.

Video-On-Demand: No

Internet Service
Operational: No.
Broadband Service: Offers dial-up and DSL only; no cable modem service.

Telephone Service
None

Miles of Plant: 4.0 (coaxial); None (fiber optic). Homes passed: 144. Total homes in franchised area: 144.
Manager: Matt Sparks. Chief Technician: George Honzay. Customer Service Supervisor: Patty Groshens.
Ownership: Hector Communications Corp. (MSO).

WABASHA—Hiawatha Broadband. Formerly [MN0399]. This cable system has converted to IPTV, 329 Hiawatha Dr E, Ste 1, Wabasha, MN 55981. Phone: 888-474-9995. Fax: 507-454-5878. E-mail: info@hbci.com. Web Site: http://www.hbci.com. ICA: MN5160.
TV Market Ranking: Below 100 (WABASHA).
Channel capacity: N.A. Channels available but not in use: N.A.

Internet Service
Operational: Yes.

Ownership: Hiawatha Broadband Communications Inc.

WABASHA—Hiawatha Broadband. This cable system has converted to IPTV. See Wabasha, MN [MN5160]. ICA: MN0399.

WABASHA—US Cable, 402 Red River Ave N, Unit 5, Cold Spring, MN 56320-1521. Phones: 320-685-7113; 800-783-2356. Fax: 320-685-2816. E-mail: help@mn.uscable.com. Web Site: http://www.uscable.com. Also serves Kellogg & Reads Landing. ICA: MN0375.
TV Market Ranking: Below 100 (Kellogg, Reads Landing, WABASHA). Franchise award date: N.A. Franchise expiration date: N.A. Began: January 1, 1968.
Channel capacity: N.A. Channels available but not in use: N.A.

Basic Service
Subscribers: N.A. Included in Cambridge
Programming (received off-air): KARE (NBC) Minneapolis; KMSP-TV (FOX) Minneapolis; KSTC-TV (IND) Minneapolis; KSTP-TV (ABC) St. Paul; KTCA-TV (PBS) St. Paul; KTTC (CW, NBC) Rochester; WCCO-TV (CBS) Minneapolis; WEAU-TV (NBC) Eau Claire; WFTC (MNT) Minneapolis; WKBT-DT (CBS, MNT) La Crosse; WUCW (CW) Minneapolis; WXOW (ABC, CW) La Crosse; allband FM.
Programming (via satellite): Eternal Word TV Network; HGTV; QVC; Turner Classic Movies; Weather Channel; WGN.
Current originations: Public Access.
Fee: $10.95 monthly.

Expanded Basic Service 1
Subscribers: N.A.
Programming (via satellite): ABC Family Channel; Animal Planet; Arts & Entertainment; Big Ten Network; Bravo; Cartoon Network; CNBC; CNN; Comedy Central; Country Music TV; C-SPAN; C-SPAN 2; Discovery Channel; Disney Channel; E! Entertainment Television; ESPN; ESPN 2; Food Network; Fox News Channel; Fox Sports Net North; FX; Great American Country; Hallmark Channel; Headline News; History Channel; Lifetime; MTV; National Geographic Channel; Nickelodeon; ShopNBC; SoapNet; Speed Channel; Spike TV; Syfy; TBS Superstation; The Learning Channel; Travel Channel; truTV; Turner Network TV; TV Land; USA Network; VH1.
Fee: $30.62 monthly.

Digital Basic Service
Subscribers: N.A. Included in Cambridge
Programming (received off-air): KARE (NBC) Minneapolis; KMSP-TV (FOX) Minneapolis; KSTP-TV (ABC) St. Paul; KTCA-TV (PBS) St. Paul; WCCO-TV (CBS) Minneapolis; WFTC (MNT) Minneapolis.
Programming (via satellite): BBC America; Big Ten Network HD; Bloomberg Television; Discovery HD Theater; Discovery Health Channel; Discovery Kids Channel; DMX Music; ESPN Classic Sports; ESPN HD; ESPNews; Fox Soccer; Fuse; G4; Golf Channel; GSN; HDNet; HDNet Movies; Independent Film Channel; Lifetime Movie Network; MTV2; National Geographic Channel HD Network; Nick Jr.; Science Channel; Sleuth; Style Network; TeenNick; Toon Disney; Trinity Broadcasting Network; Universal HD; Versus; VH1 Classic; WE tv; WealthTV HD.
Fee: $8.95 monthly.

Digital Expanded Basic Service
Subscribers: N.A.
Programming (via satellite): Bio; CMT Pure Country; Discovery Home Channel; Discovery Military Channel; Encore (multiplexed); FitTV; Fox Movie Channel; Halogen Network; History Channel International; ID Investigation Discovery.
Fee: $2.95 monthly.

Digital Expanded Basic Service 2
Subscribers: N.A.
Programming (via satellite): NFL Network; Outdoor Channel.
Fee: $3.95 monthly.

Digital Pay Service 1
Pay Units: N.A. Included in Cambridge
Programming (via satellite): Cinemax (multiplexed); HBO (multiplexed); Showtime (multiplexed); Starz (multiplexed); The Movie Channel (multiplexed).

Video-On-Demand: No

Pay-Per-View
iN DEMAND (delivered digitally); Fresh (delivered digitally); Playboy TV (delivered digitally); Club Jenna (delivered digitally).

Internet Service
Operational: Yes.
Broadband Service: Warp Drive Online.
Fee: $27.95 monthly.

Telephone Service
None

Homes passed & miles of plant included in Cambridge
General Manager: Steve Johnson. Customer Service Director: Jackie Torborg.
City fee: 3% of gross.
Ownership: Comcast Cable Communications Inc. (MSO).; US Cable Corp. (MSO).

WABASSO—Clara City Telephone Co., 215 1st St NW, Clara City, MN 56222. Phones: 888-283-7667; 320-847-2114. Fax: 320-847-2114. ICA: MN0224.
TV Market Ranking: Below 100 (WABASSO). Franchise award date: June 1, 1984. Franchise expiration date: N.A. Began: July 1, 1984.
Channel capacity: 35 (operating 2-way). Channels available but not in use: 18.

Basic Service
Subscribers: 165.
Programming (received off-air): KEYC-TV (CBS, FOX) Mankato; KWCM-TV (PBS) Appleton.
Programming (via microwave): KARE (NBC) Minneapolis; KMSP-TV (FOX) Minneapolis; KSTP-TV (ABC) St. Paul; KTCA-TV (PBS) St. Paul; WCCO-TV (CBS) Minneapolis.
Programming (via satellite): ABC Family Channel; CNN; Country Music TV; Discovery Channel; Disney Channel; ESPN; TBS Superstation; Turner Network TV; USA Network; WGN America.
Fee: $25.00 installation; $19.13 monthly.

Pay Service 1
Pay Units: 22.
Programming (via satellite): HBO.
Fee: $25.00 installation; $10.00 monthly.

Internet Service
Operational: No.

Telephone Service
None

Miles of Plant: 6.0 (coaxial); None (fiber optic). Homes passed: 265. Total homes in franchised area: 300.
Manager: Bruce Hanson.
City fee: 5% of gross.
Ownership: Hanson Communications Inc. (MSO).

WABEDO TWP.—ACS Video. Formerly served by Perham, MN [MN0050]. This cable system has converted to IPTV, 150 Second St SW, Perham, MN 56573. Phone: 866-937-4227. E-mail: answers@arvig.com. Web Site: http://www.arvig.com. ICA: MN5231.
TV Market Ranking: Below 100 (WABEDO TWP.).
Channel capacity: N.A. Channels available but not in use: N.A.

Internet Service
Operational: Yes.

Telephone Service
Digital: Operational

Ownership: Arvig Communication Systems.

WADENA—Charter Communications, 3380 Northern Valley Pl NE, Rochester, MN 55906-3954. Phones: 218-829-9015 (Local office); 507-289-8372 (Rochester office). Fax: 507-285-6162. Web Site: http://www.charter.com. ICA: MN0376.
TV Market Ranking: Outside TV Markets (WADENA). Franchise award date: N.A. Franchise expiration date: N.A. Began: March 1, 1967.
Channel capacity: N.A. Channels available but not in use: N.A.

Basic Service
Subscribers: 1,475.
Programming (received off-air): KAWB (PBS) Brainerd; KCCW-TV (CBS) Walker; KPXM-TV (ION) St. Cloud; KSAX (ABC) Alexandria; KVRR (FOX) Fargo; allband FM.
Programming (via microwave): KARE (NBC) Minneapolis; KMSP-TV (FOX) Minneapolis; KSTC-TV (IND) Minneapolis; KTCA-TV (PBS) St. Paul; WFTC (MNT) Minneapolis; WUCW (CW) Minneapolis.
Programming (via satellite): C-SPAN; C-SPAN 2; Eternal Word TV Network; Home Shopping Network; INSP; QVC; TBS Superstation; Trinity Broadcasting Network; TV Guide Network; Weather Channel; WGN America.
Fee: $29.99 installation; $2.00 converter; $39.95 additional installation.

Expanded Basic Service 1
Subscribers: 1,163.
Programming (via satellite): ABC Family Channel; AMC; Animal Planet; Arts & Entertainment; Bravo; Cartoon Network; CNBC; CNN; Country Music TV; Discovery Channel; Disney Channel; E! Entertainment Television; ESPN; ESPN 2; Food Network; Fox News Channel; Fox Sports Net North; FX; Golf Channel; Hallmark Channel; Headline News; HGTV; History Channel; Lifetime; MSNBC; MTV; Nickelodeon; Outdoor Channel; Oxygen; Speed Channel; Spike TV; Syfy; The Learning Channel; Travel Channel; truTV; Turner Network TV; TV Land; USA Network; Versus; VH1.
Fee: $47.99 monthly.

Digital Basic Service
Subscribers: N.A.
Programming (via satellite): BBC America; Bio; Boomerang; CNN en Espanol; Discovery Digital Networks; Do-It-Yourself; ESPN Classic Sports; ESPNews; Fox College Sports Atlantic; Fox College Sports Central; Fox College Sports Pacific; Fox Soccer; Fuel TV; G4; GAS; History Channel International; Independent Film Channel; Lifetime Movie Network; MTV Networks Digital Suite; Music Choice; NFL Network; Nick Jr.; NickToons TV; SoapNet; Style Network; Sundance Channel; Toon Disney; Turner Classic Movies; TV Guide Interactive Inc.; WE tv.

Digital Pay Service 1
Pay Units: N.A.
Programming (via satellite): Cinemax (multiplexed); Encore; Flix; HBO (multiplexed); LOGO; Showtime (multiplexed); Starz (multiplexed); The Movie Channel (multiplexed).

Video-On-Demand: Planned

Pay-Per-View
iN DEMAND (delivered digitally); NASCAR In Car (delivered digitally); NHL Center Ice (delivered digitally); MLB Extra Innings (delivered digitally); Playboy TV (delivered digitally); Spice Live (delivered digitally); Spice Platinum (delivered digitally); Spice Hot (delivered digitally).

Internet Service
Operational: Yes. Began: December 13, 2001.
Broadband Service: Charter Pipeline.
Fee: $29.99 monthly.

Telephone Service
Digital: Operational

Miles of Plant: 635.0 (coaxial); 240.0 (fiber optic). Homes passed: 27,643. Total homes in franchised area: 1,866. Homes passed and miles of plant (coax & fiber) includes Brainard

Vice President & General Manager: John Crowley. Operations Director: Craig Stensaas. Technical Operations Director: Mark Abramo. Marketing Director: Bill Haarstad.
City fee: 3% of gross.
Ownership: Charter Communications Inc. (MSO).

WALDORF—Dynax Communications Inc. Now served by WASECA, MN [MN0043]. ICA: MN0260.

WALNUT GROVE—Walnut Grove Cable TV, 749 Des Moines Dr, Windom, MN 56101-1604. Phone: 507-831-4938. Fax: 507-831-4938. ICA: MN0196.
TV Market Ranking: Below 100 (WALNUT GROVE). Franchise award date: N.A. Franchise expiration date: N.A. Began: April 10, 1973.
Channel capacity: 36 (not 2-way capable). Channels available but not in use: 2.
Basic Service
Subscribers: 200.
Programming (received off-air): KELO-TV (CBS, MNT) Sioux Falls; KEYC-TV (CBS, FOX) Mankato; KSFY-TV (ABC) Sioux Falls; KSMN (PBS) Worthington; allband FM.
Programming (via satellite): ABC Family Channel; CNN; Country Music TV; Discovery Channel; ESPN; FamilyNet; Fox Sports Net; Headline News; HGTV; Lifetime; Nickelodeon; Spike TV; TBS Superstation; The Learning Channel; Turner Classic Movies; Turner Network TV; TV Land; USA Network; Weather Channel; WGN America.
Programming (via translator): KARE (NBC) Minneapolis; KMSP-TV (FOX) Minneapolis; KSTP-TV (ABC) St. Paul; KTCA-TV (PBS) St. Paul; WCCO-TV (CBS) Minneapolis; WFTC (MNT) Minneapolis; WUCW (CW) Minneapolis.
Current originations: Public Access.
Fee: $15.00 installation; $24.95 monthly.
Pay Service 1
Pay Units: N.A.
Programming (via satellite): Showtime.
Video-On-Demand: No
Internet Service
Operational: No.
Telephone Service
None
Miles of Plant: 6.0 (coaxial); None (fiber optic). Homes passed: 300. Total homes in franchised area: 369.
Manager: Robert E. Turner.
State fee: 1% of gross. City fee: None.
Ownership: Robert E. Turner (MSO).

WANAMINGO—US Cable, 402 Red River Ave N, Unit 5, Cold Spring, MN 56320-1521. Phones: 320-685-7113; 800-783-2356. Fax: 320-685-2816. E-mail: help@mn.uscable.com. Web Site: http://www.uscable.com. ICA: MN0182.
TV Market Ranking: Below 100 (WANAMINGO). Franchise award date: N.A. Franchise expiration date: N.A. Began: December 1, 1988.
Channel capacity: 30 (not 2-way capable). Channels available but not in use: N.A.
Basic Service
Subscribers: N.A. Included in Cambridge
Programming (received off-air): KARE (NBC) Minneapolis; KMSP-TV (FOX) Minneapolis; KSTC-TV (IND) Minneapolis; KSTP-TV (ABC) St. Paul; KTCA-TV (PBS) St. Paul; KTCI-TV (PBS) St. Paul; KTTC (CW, NBC) Rochester; WCCO-TV (CBS) Minneapolis; WFTC (MNT) Minneapolis.
Programming (via satellite): ABC Family Channel; Animal Planet; Arts & Entertainment; CNBC; CNN; Comedy Central; Country Music TV; C-SPAN; Discovery Channel; Disney Channel; ESPN; ESPN 2; Food Network; Fox Sports Net; Headline News; History Channel; Home Shopping Network; Lifetime; Nickelodeon; QVC; Syfy; TBS Superstation; The Learning Channel; Travel Channel; Turner Classic Movies; Turner Network TV; TV Land; USA Network; VH1; Weather Channel; WGN America.
Current originations: Educational Access; Leased Access.
Fee: $41.72 monthly.
Pay Service 1
Pay Units: N.A. Included in Cambridge
Programming (via satellite): Cinemax; HBO.
Internet Service
Operational: No.
Telephone Service
None
Homes passed: Included in Cambridge
General Manager: Steve Johnson. Customer Service Director: Jackie Torberg.
Ownership: US Cable Corp. (MSO).; Comcast Cable Communications Inc. (MSO).

WARREN—Sjoberg's Cable TV Inc., 315 Main Ave N, Thief River Falls, MN 56701-1905. Phones: 800-828-8808; 218-681-3044. Fax: 218-681-6801. Web Site: http://trf.mncable.net. ICA: MN0115.
TV Market Ranking: Below 100 (WARREN). Franchise award date: N.A. Franchise expiration date: N.A. Began: December 2, 1973.
Channel capacity: 54 (operating 2-way). Channels available but not in use: 8.
Basic Service
Subscribers: 605.
Programming (received off-air): KBRR (FOX) Thief River Falls; KCPM (MNT) Grand Forks; KGFE (PBS) Grand Forks; KVLY-TV (NBC) Fargo; KXJB-TV (CBS) Valley City; WDAZ-TV (ABC, CW) Devils Lake; 9 FMs.
Programming (via satellite): CNN; ESPN; TBS Superstation; various Canadian stations.
Current originations: Public Access.
Fee: $25.00 installation; $10.00 monthly.
Expanded Basic Service 1
Subscribers: N.A.
Programming (via satellite): ABC Family Channel; Animal Planet; Arts & Entertainment; Cartoon Network; CNBC; Comedy Central; Country Music TV; C-SPAN; CW+; Discovery Channel; Disney Channel; E! Entertainment Television; ESPN 2; Food Network; Fox News Channel; Fox Sports Net; FX; HGTV; History Channel; Home Shopping Network; Lifetime; MSNBC; MTV; Nickelodeon; Spike TV; Syfy; The Learning Channel; Turner Classic Movies; Turner Network TV; TV Land; USA Network; VH1; Weather Channel; WGN America.
Fee: $23.71 monthly.
Digital Basic Service
Subscribers: N.A.
Programming (via satellite): AmericanLife TV Network; BBC America; Bio; Blackbelt TV; Bloomberg Television; Bravo; CBS College Sports Network; Chiller; CMT Pure Country; Cooking Channel; Current; Daystar TV Network; Discovery Health Channel; Discovery Kids Channel; Discovery Military Channel; Discovery Planet Green; DMX Music; Do-It-Yourself; ESPN Classic Sports; ESPN U; ESPNews; Eternal Word TV Network; FitTV; Fox Business Channel; Fox College Sports Atlantic; Fox College Sports Central; Fox College Sports Pacific; Fox Movie Channel; Fox Reality Channel; Fox Soccer; G4; Golf Channel; Gospel Music Channel; Great American Country; GSN; Hallmark Channel; Halogen Network; Headline News; History Channel International; HorseRacing TV; ID Investigation Discovery; Independent Film Channel; Lifetime Movie Network; MTV Hits; MTV2; National Geographic Channel; Nick Jr.; NickToons TV; Outdoor Channel; Ovation; Oxygen; PBS Kids Sprout; ReelzChannel; RFD-TV; Science Channel; ShopNBC; Sleuth; SoapNet; Speed Channel; Style Network; Sundance Channel; TeenNick; Tennis Channel; The Sportsman Channel; The Word Network; Toon Disney; Trinity Broadcasting Network; TVG Network; Versus; VH1 Classic; VH1 Soul; WE tv.
Fee: $11.00 monthly.
Digital Expanded Basic Service
Subscribers: N.A.
Programming (via satellite): Arts & Entertainment HD; CNN HD; Discovery Channel HD; ESPN 2 HD; ESPN HD; Food Network HD; FSN HD; HDNet; HDNet Movies; HGTV HD; History Channel HD; Outdoor Channel 2 HD; PBS HD; Speed HD; Syfy HD; TBS in HD; Turner Network TV HD; Universal HD; USA Network HD; Versus HD.
Fee: $5.00 monthly; $5.00 converter.
Pay Service 1
Pay Units: 108.
Programming (via satellite): HBO.
Fee: $11.00 monthly.
Pay Service 2
Pay Units: N.A.
Programming (via satellite): Cinemax.
Fee: $9.00 monthly.
Digital Pay Service 1
Pay Units: N.A.
Programming (via satellite): Cinemax (multiplexed); Cinemax HD; Encore (multiplexed); HBO (multiplexed); HBO HD; Showtime (multiplexed); Starz (multiplexed); The Movie Channel (multiplexed).
Fee: $8.00 monthly (Starz/Encore), $9.00 monthly (Cinemax or Showtime/TMC), $11.00 monthly (HBO).
Video-On-Demand: No
Internet Service
Operational: Yes. Began: December 31, 1999.
Subscribers: 75.
Broadband Service: Sjoberg's Cable TV.
Fee: $19.95 monthly; $10.00 modem lease; $129.00 modem purchase.
Telephone Service
None
Miles of Plant: 14.0 (coaxial); 2.0 (fiber optic). Homes passed: 784. Total homes in franchised area: 877.
Manager: Richard J. Sjoberg. Chief Technician: Jerry Seim.
City fee: None.
Ownership: Sjoberg's Cable TV Inc. (MSO).

WARROAD—Sjoberg's Cable TV Inc., 315 Main Ave N, Thief River Falls, MN 56701-1905. Phones: 800-828-8808; 216-681-3044. Fax: 218-681-6801. Web Site: http://trf.mncable.net. Also serves Lake Twp. ICA: MN0129.
TV Market Ranking: Outside TV Markets (Lake Twp., WARROAD). Franchise award date: N.A. Franchise expiration date: N.A. Began: February 1, 1972.
Channel capacity: 78 (operating 2-way). Channels available but not in use: N.A.
Basic Service
Subscribers: 780.
Programming (received off-air): KAWE (PBS) Bemidji; KCPM (MNT) Grand Forks; allband FM.
Programming (via microwave): KVLY-TV (NBC) Fargo; KXJB-TV (CBS) Valley City; WDAZ-TV (ABC, CW) Devils Lake.
Programming (via satellite): CNN; ESPN; TBS Superstation; various Canadian stations.
Current originations: Public Access.
Fee: $25.00 installation; $10.00 monthly.
Expanded Basic Service 1
Subscribers: N.A.
Programming (received off-air): KNRR (FOX) Pembina.
Programming (via satellite): ABC Family Channel; Animal Planet; Arts & Entertainment; Cartoon Network; CNBC; Comedy Central; Country Music TV; CW+; Discovery Channel; E! Entertainment Television; ESPN 2; Eternal Word TV Network; Food Network; Fox News Channel; Fox Sports Net North; FX; HGTV; History Channel; Home Shopping Network; Lifetime; MSNBC; MTV; Nickelodeon; Spike TV; Syfy; The Learning Channel; Turner Classic Movies; Turner Network TV; TV Land; USA Network; Weather Channel; WGN America.
Fee: $23.71 monthly.
Digital Basic Service
Subscribers: N.A.
Programming (via satellite): AmericanLife TV Network; BBC America; Bio; Blackbelt TV; Bloomberg Television; Bravo; CBS College Sports Network; Chiller; CMT Pure Country; Cooking Channel; Current; Daystar TV Network; Discovery Health Channel; Discovery Kids Channel; Discovery Military Channel; Discovery Planet Green; DMX Music; Do-It-Yourself; ESPN Classic Sports; ESPN U; ESPNews; Eternal Word TV Network; FitTV; Fox Business Channel; Fox College Sports Atlantic; Fox College Sports Central; Fox College Sports Pacific; Fox Movie Channel; Fox Reality Channel; Fox Soccer; G4; Golf Channel; Gospel Music Channel; Great American Country; GSN; Hallmark Channel; Halogen Network; Headline News; History Channel International; HorseRacing TV; ID Investigation Discovery; Independent Film Channel; Lifetime Movie Network; MTV Hits; MTV2; National Geographic Channel; Nick Jr.; NickToons TV; Outdoor Channel; Ovation; Oxygen; PBS Kids Sprout; RFD-TV; Science Channel; ShopNBC; Sleuth; SoapNet; Speed Channel; Style Network; Sundance Channel; TeenNick; Tennis Channel; The Sportsman Channel; The Word Network; Toon Disney; Trinity Broadcasting Network; TVG Network; Versus; VH1 Classic; VH1 Soul; WE tv.
Fee: $11.00 monthly.
Digital Expanded Basic Service
Subscribers: N.A.
Programming (via satellite): Arts & Entertainment HD; CNN HD; Discovery Channel HD; ESPN 2 HD; ESPN HD; Food Network HD; FSN HD; HDNet; HDNet Movies; HGTV HD; History Channel HD; Outdoor Channel 2 HD; PBS HD; Speed HD; Syfy HD; TBS in HD; Turner Network TV HD; Universal HD; USA Network HD; Versus HD.
Fee: $5.00 monthly; $5.00 converter.
Pay Service 1
Pay Units: 199.
Programming (via satellite): HBO.
Fee: $11.00 monthly.
Digital Pay Service 1
Pay Units: N.A.
Programming (via satellite): Cinemax (multiplexed); Cinemax HD; Encore (multiplexed); HBO (multiplexed); HBO HD; Showtime (multiplexed); Starz (multiplexed); The Movie Channel (multiplexed).

Fee: $8.00 monthly (Starz/Encore), $9.00 monthly (Cinemax or Showtime/TMC), $11.00 monthly (HBO).

Video-On-Demand: No

Internet Service

Operational: Yes. Began: December 31, 1999.

Subscribers: 150.

Broadband Service: Sjoberg's Cable TV.

Fee: $19.95 monthly; $10.00 modem lease; $29.00 modem purchase.

Telephone Service

None

Miles of Plant: 14.0 (coaxial); 3.0 (fiber optic). Homes passed: 800. Total homes in franchised area: 830.

Manager: Richard J. Sjoberg. Chief Technician: Jerry Seim.

City fee: None.

Ownership: Sjoberg's Cable TV Inc. (MSO).

WARSAW—North American Communications Corp., PO Box 387, 211 Main St S, Hector, MN 55342-0387. Phones: 800-982-8038; 320-848-6781. Fax: 320-848-2323. E-mail: hcc@hcctel.net. Web Site: http://www.hectorcom.com. Also serves Wells Twp. ICA: MN0377.

TV Market Ranking: Below 100 (WARSAW, Wells Twp.). Franchise award date: N.A. Franchise expiration date: N.A. Began: October 1, 1991.

Channel capacity: 54 (not 2-way capable). Channels available but not in use: N.A.

Basic Service

Subscribers: 134.

Programming (received off-air): KARE (NBC) Minneapolis; KMSP-TV (FOX) Minneapolis; KSTP-TV (ABC) St. Paul; KTCA-TV (PBS) St. Paul; KTCI-TV (PBS) St. Paul; WCCO-TV (CBS) Minneapolis; WFTC (MNT) Minneapolis; WUCW (CW) Minneapolis.

Programming (via satellite): ABC Family Channel; AMC; Arts & Entertainment; CNN; Discovery Channel; Disney Channel; ESPN; ESPN 2; Fox Sports Net Midwest; Lifetime; Nickelodeon; QVC; Spike TV; TBS Superstation; Trinity Broadcasting Network; Turner Network TV; USA Network; WGN America.

Fee: $40.00 installation; $26.95 monthly; $3.50 converter; $25.00 additional installation.

Pay Service 1

Pay Units: 3.

Programming (via satellite): HBO.

Fee: $10.95 monthly.

Pay Service 2

Pay Units: N.A.

Programming (via satellite): Cinemax.

Fee: $10.95 monthly.

Video-On-Demand: No

Internet Service

Operational: No.

Broadband Service: Offers dial-up and DSL only; no cable modem service.

Telephone Service

None

Miles of Plant: 4.0 (coaxial); None (fiber optic). Homes passed: 312. Total homes in franchised area: 312.

Manager: Matt Sparks. Chief Technician: George Honzay. Customer Service Supervisor: Patty Groshens.

Ownership: Hector Communications Corp. (MSO).

WASECA—Mediacom, PO Box 110, 1504 2nd St SE, Waseca, MN 56093. Phones: 800-332-0245; 507-835-2356. Fax: 507-835-4567. Web Site: http://www.mediacomcable.com. Also serves Belle Plaine, Butterfield, Cleveland, Henderson, Janesville, Kasota, Lafayette, Lake Crystal, Le Sueur, Lonsdale, St. James, St. Peter, Waldorf, Wells & Winnebago. ICA: MN0043.

TV Market Ranking: 13 (Belle Plaine, Lonsdale); Below 100 (Cleveland, Henderson, Janesville, Kasota, Lafayette, Lake Crystal, Le Sueur, St. James, St. Peter, WASECA, Wells, Winnebago); Outside TV Markets (Butterfield). Franchise award date: N.A. Franchise expiration date: N.A. Began: January 1, 1974.

Channel capacity: N.A. Channels available but not in use: N.A.

Basic Service

Subscribers: 11,869.

Programming (received off-air): KARE (NBC) Minneapolis; KEYC-TV (CBS, FOX) Mankato; KMSP-TV (FOX) Minneapolis; KSTC-TV (IND) Minneapolis; KSTP-TV (ABC) St. Paul; KTCA-TV (PBS) St. Paul; KTCI-TV (PBS) St. Paul; WCCO-TV (CBS) Minneapolis; WFTC (MNT) Minneapolis; allband FM.

Programming (via satellite): C-SPAN; C-SPAN 2; TV Guide Network; Weather Channel; WGN America.

Fee: $20.00 installation; $17.95 monthly.

Expanded Basic Service 1

Subscribers: 11,304.

Programming (received off-air): WUCW (CW) Minneapolis.

Programming (via satellite): ABC Family Channel; AMC; Animal Planet; Arts & Entertainment; BET Networks; Bravo; Cartoon Network; CNBC; CNN; Comedy Central; Country Music TV; Discovery Channel; Disney Channel; E! Entertainment Television; ESPN; ESPN 2; Eternal Word TV Network; Food Network; Fox Movie Channel; Fox News Channel; Fox Sports Net North; FX; Hallmark Channel; Headline News; HGTV; History Channel; INSP; KPXM-TV (ION) St. Cloud; Lifetime; MSNBC; MTV; Nickelodeon; QVC; SoapNet; Speed Channel; Spike TV; Syfy; TBS Superstation; The Learning Channel; Travel Channel; Trinity Broadcasting Network; truTV; Turner Classic Movies; Turner Network TV; TV Land; Univision; USA Network; VH1; WE tv.

Fee: $15.06 monthly.

Digital Basic Service

Subscribers: N.A.

Programming (via satellite): AmericanLife TV Network; BBC America; Bio; Bloomberg Television; Canales N; Discovery Digital Networks; DMX Music; Fox Sports World; Fuse; G4; GAS; Golf Channel; GSN; Halogen Network; History Channel International; Independent Film Channel; Lifetime Movie Network; Lime; National Geographic Channel; Nick Jr.; Outdoor Channel; Style Network; Versus.

Digital Pay Service 1

Pay Units: 7,562.

Programming (via satellite): Cinemax (multiplexed); Encore (multiplexed); Flix; HBO (multiplexed); Showtime (multiplexed); Starz (multiplexed); Sundance Channel; The Movie Channel (multiplexed).

Fee: $7.00 monthly (Cinemax or Showtime), $9.00 monthly (HBO).

Video-On-Demand: Yes

Pay-Per-View

TVN Entertainment (delivered digitally); ESPN Now (delivered digitally); Sports PPV (delivered digitally); Urban Xtra (delivered digitally); Fresh (delivered digitally); Shorteez (delivered digitally); Playboy TV (delivered digitally); Pleasure (delivered digitally).

Internet Service

Operational: Yes.

Broadband Service: Mediacom High Speed Internet.

Fee: $99.00 installation; $40.00 monthly.

Telephone Service

Analog: Not Operational

Digital: Operational

Miles of Plant: 250.0 (coaxial); None (fiber optic). Homes passed: 17,158.

Regional Vice President: Bill Jensen. Engineering Manager: Kraig Kaiser. Marketing & Sales Director: Lori Huberty.

City fee: 3% of gross.

Ownership: Mediacom LLC (MSO).

WATSON—Farmers Mutual Telephone Co., PO Box 220, Stanton, IA 51573. Phones: 800-1169-2111; 717-829-2111. Web Site: http://online.fmtc.com. Also serves Milan. ICA: MN0379.

TV Market Ranking: Outside TV Markets (Milan, WATSON). Franchise award date: April 1, 1990. Franchise expiration date: N.A. Began: December 20, 1990.

Channel capacity: 54 (operating 2-way). Channels available but not in use: 12.

Basic Service

Subscribers: 140.

Programming (received off-air): KARE (NBC) Minneapolis; KCCO-TV (CBS) Alexandria; KMSP-TV (FOX) Minneapolis; KSAX (ABC) Alexandria; KSTC-TV (IND) Minneapolis; KWCM-TV (PBS) Appleton; WFTC (MNT) Minneapolis; WUCW (CW) Minneapolis.

Programming (via satellite): ABC Family Channel; AMC; Animal Planet; Arts & Entertainment; Cartoon Network; CNN; Comedy Central; Country Music TV; C-SPAN; Discovery Channel; Disney Channel; ESPN; ESPN 2; Food Network; Fox Sports Net North; Hallmark Channel; Hallmark Movie Channel; HGTV; History Channel; Lifetime; MTV; Nickelodeon; QVC; Speed Channel; Spike TV; Syfy; TBS Superstation; The Learning Channel; Trinity Broadcasting Network; Turner Classic Movies; Turner Network TV; TV Land; USA Network; VH1; Weather Channel; WGN America.

Fee: $10.00 installation; $26.95 monthly.

Pay Service 1

Pay Units: 10.

Programming (via satellite): Cinemax; HBO; Showtime.

Fee: $9.95 monthly (Cinemax), $10.95 monthly (Showtime), $11.95 monthly (HBO).

Video-On-Demand: No

Internet Service

Operational: No.

Telephone Service

None

Miles of Plant: 8.0 (coaxial); 9.0 (fiber optic). Homes passed: 275. Total homes in franchised area: 275.

General Manager: Kevin Cabbage. Assistant Manager: Dennis Crawford.

Ownership: Farmers Mutual Telephone Co. (MSO).

WELCOME—Terril Cable Systems, PO Box 100, Terril, IA 51364-0100. Phone: 712-853-6121. Fax: 712-853-6185. Web Site: http://www.terril.com. ICA: MN0380.

TV Market Ranking: Outside TV Markets (WELCOME). Franchise award date: N.A. Franchise expiration date: N.A. Began: September 1, 1986.

Channel capacity: 35 (operating 2-way). Channels available but not in use: N.A.

Basic Service

Subscribers: 200.

Programming (received off-air): KARE (NBC) Minneapolis; KEYC-TV (CBS, FOX) Mankato; KMSP-TV (FOX) Minneapolis; KSTC-TV (IND) Minneapolis; KSTP-TV (ABC) St. Paul; KTCA-TV (PBS) St. Paul; WCCO-TV (CBS) Minneapolis; WFTC (MNT) Minneapolis; WUCW (CW) Minneapolis.

Programming (via satellite): ABC Family Channel; Animal Planet; Arts & Entertainment; CNBC; CNN; Country Music TV; Discovery Channel; Disney Channel; ESPN; ESPN 2; Fox Sports Net North; History Channel; Lifetime; National Geographic Channel; Nickelodeon; Spike TV; TBS Superstation; The Learning Channel; Turner Classic Movies; Turner Network TV; TV Land; USA Network; VH1; Weather Channel; WGN America.

Fee: $20.00 installation; $29.51 monthly.

Digital Basic Service

Subscribers: N.A.

Programming (via satellite): Alterna'TV; BBC America; Bio; Black Family Channel; Bloomberg Television; Bravo; CMT Pure Country; Discovery Health Channel; Discovery Home Channel; Discovery Kids Channel; Discovery Military Channel; Discovery Times Channel; ESPN 2; ESPN Classic Sports; ESPNews; FitTV; Fox College Sports Atlantic; Fox College Sports Central; Fox College Sports Pacific; Fox Movie Channel; Fox Soccer; Fuse; G4; Golf Channel; Great American Country; GSN; Halogen Network; HGTV; History Channel International; Independent Film Channel; Lime; MTV2; Nick Jr.; NickToons TV; Outdoor Channel; Ovation; Science Channel; ShopNBC; Speed Channel; Style Network; TeenNick; Toon Disney; Trinity Broadcasting Network; Trio; Versus; VH1 Classic; WE tv.

Fee: $7.00 monthly (per package).

Digital Pay Service 1

Pay Units: N.A.

Programming (via satellite): Cinemax (multiplexed); Encore (multiplexed); Flix; HBO (multiplexed); Showtime (multiplexed); Starz (multiplexed); Sundance Channel; The Movie Channel (multiplexed).

Fee: $11.00 monthly (each).

Video-On-Demand: No

Pay-Per-View

iN DEMAND (delivered digitally); Hot Choice (delivered digitally); Spice (delivered digitally); Spice 2 (delivered digitally); Playboy TV (delivered digitally).

Internet Service

Operational: No.

Telephone Service

None

Manager: Douglas Nelson.

Ownership: Ter Tel Enterprises.

WELLS—Now served by WASECA, MN [MN0043]. ICA: MN0088.

WESTBROOK—Formerly served by US Cable of Coastal Texas LP. No longer in operation. ICA: MN0154.

WESTBROOK—Westbrook Public Utilities, PO Box 308, Westbrook, MN 56183. Phone: 507-274-6712. Fax: 507-274-5569. ICA: MN0400.

TV Market Ranking: Outside TV Markets (WESTBROOK). Franchise award date: N.A. Franchise expiration date: N.A. Began: December 31, 1992.

Channel capacity: N.A. Channels available but not in use: N.A.

Basic Service

Subscribers: 380.

Programming (received off-air): KARE (NBC) Minneapolis; KELO-TV (CBS, MNT) Sioux Falls; KEYC-TV (CBS, FOX) Mankato; KMSP-TV (FOX) Minneapolis; KSFY-TV (ABC) Sioux Falls; KSTP-TV (ABC) St. Paul; KTTW (FOX) Sioux Falls; WCCO-TV (CBS) Minneapolis.

Programming (via satellite): ABC Family Channel; Arts & Entertainment; CNN; Country Music TV; Discovery Channel; Disney Channel; ESPN; ESPN 2; Fox Sports Net; Hallmark Channel; HGTV; History Channel; Lifetime; Nickelodeon; Speed Channel; Spike TV; TBS Superstation; The Learning Channel; Turner Classic Movies; Turner Network TV; USA Network; Weather Channel; WGN America.

Pay Service 1

Pay Units: N.A.

Programming (via satellite): HBO.

Internet Service

Operational: No.

Miles of Plant: 7.0 (coaxial); None (fiber optic). Homes passed: 400. Total homes in franchised area: 400.

Superintendent: Dennis Jutting.

Ownership: City of Westbrook.

WHEATON—Now served by APPLETON, MN [MN0106]. ICA: MN0104.

WHITE OAK TWP.—ACS Video. Formerly served by Perham, MN [MN0050]. This cable system has converted to IPTV, 150 Second St SW, Perham, MN 56573. Phone: 866-937-4227. E-mail: answers@arvig.com. Web Site: http://www.arvig.com. ICA: MN5234.

TV Market Ranking: Below 100 (WHITE OAK TWP.).

Channel capacity: N.A. Channels available but not in use: N.A.

Internet Service

Operational: Yes.

Telephone Service

Digital: Operational

Ownership: Arvig Communication Systems.

WILLMAR—Charter Communications, 400 Lakeland Dr NE, Willmar, MN 56201. Phones: 320-235-1535 (Local office); 507-289-8372 (Rochester administrative office). Fax: 320-235-1462. E-mail: jmelander@chartercom.com. Web Site: http://www.charter.com. Also serves Benson, Green Lake Twp., Harrison Twp., Irving Twp., Kandiyohi, Kerkhoven, Merdock, New London, New London Twp., Pennock, Spicer & St. Johns Twp. ICA: MN0018.

TV Market Ranking: Outside TV Markets (Benson, Green Lake Twp., Harrison Twp., Irving Twp., Kandiyohi, Kerkhoven, Merdock, New London, New London Twp., Pennock, Spicer, St. Johns Twp., WILLMAR). Franchise award date: December 1, 1957. Franchise expiration date: N.A. Began: November 1, 1957.

Channel capacity: N.A. Channels available but not in use: N.A.

Basic Service

Subscribers: 6,100.

Programming (received off-air): KPXM-TV (ION) St. Cloud; KSAX (ABC) Alexandria; KWCM-TV (PBS) Appleton; 21 FMs.

Programming (via microwave): KARE (NBC) Minneapolis; KMSP-TV (FOX) Minneapolis; KSTC-TV (IND) Minneapolis; KTCA-TV (PBS) St. Paul; WCCO-TV (CBS) Minneapolis; WFTC (MNT) Minneapolis; WUCW (CW) Minneapolis.

Programming (via satellite): C-SPAN; C-SPAN 2; Eternal Word TV Network; QVC; TBS Superstation; Trinity Broadcasting Network; WGN America.

Current originations: Public Access; Government Access; Educational Access.

Fee: $29.99 installation; $9.79 monthly; $2.00 converter; $19.95 additional installation.

Expanded Basic Service 1

Subscribers: N.A.

Programming (received off-air): WCMN-LP St. Cloud-Sartell.

Programming (via satellite): ABC Family Channel; AMC; Animal Planet; Arts & Entertainment; BET Networks; Bravo; Cartoon Network; CNBC; CNN; Comedy Central; Country Music TV; Discovery Channel; Disney Channel; E! Entertainment Television; ESPN; ESPN 2; Food Network; Fox News Channel; Fox Sports Net North; FX; G4; GalaVision; Golf Channel; GSN; Hallmark Channel; Headline News; HGTV; History Channel; Home Shopping Network; Lifetime; MoviePlex; MSNBC; MTV; MTV2; National Geographic Channel; Nickelodeon; Oxygen; SoapNet; Speed Channel; Spike TV; Syfy; The Learning Channel; Travel Channel; truTV; Turner Classic Movies; Turner Network TV; TV Land; Univision; USA Network; Versus; VH1; WE tv; Weather Channel.

Fee: $47.99 monthly.

Digital Basic Service

Subscribers: N.A.

Programming (via microwave): KARE (NBC) Minneapolis; KMSP-TV (FOX) Minneapolis; WCCO-TV (CBS) Minneapolis.

Programming (via satellite): BBC America; Bio; Bloomberg Television; Boomerang; CBS College Sports Network; CNN en Espanol; CNN International; Discovery Digital Networks; Do-It-Yourself; ESPN; ESPN Classic Sports; ESPNews; FitTV; Fox College Sports Atlantic; Fox College Sports Central; Fox College Sports Pacific; Fox Movie Channel; Fox Soccer; Fuel TV; Fuse; GAS; HDNet; HDNet Movies; History Channel International; Independent Film Channel; Lifetime Movie Network; MTV Networks Digital Suite; Music Choice; NFL Network; Nick Jr.; Nick Too; NickToons TV; Outdoor Channel; Style Network; Sundance Channel; Toon Disney; TV Guide Interactive Inc.

Digital Pay Service 1

Pay Units: N.A.

Programming (via satellite): Cinemax (multiplexed); Encore (multiplexed); HBO (multiplexed); HBO HD; Showtime (multiplexed); Showtime HD; Starz (multiplexed); The Movie Channel (multiplexed).

Video-On-Demand: Yes

Pay-Per-View

iN DEMAND (delivered digitally); NASCAR In Car (delivered digitally); NHL Center Ice (delivered digitally); MLB Extra Innings (delivered digitally); Playboy TV (delivered digitally); Spice Live (delivered digitally); Spice Platinum (delivered digitally); Hot Net Plus (delivered digitally); Spice Hot (delivered digitally).

Internet Service

Operational: Yes.

Broadband Service: Charter Pipeline.

Fee: $29.99 monthly.

Telephone Service

Digital: Operational

Miles of Plant: 250.0 (coaxial); None (fiber optic). Homes passed: 11,750.

Vice President & General Manager: John Crowley. Operations Director: Craig Stensaas. Technical Operations Director: Mark Abramo. Marketing Director: Bill Haarstad. Office Manager: Jon Melander.

City fee: None.

Ownership: Charter Communications Inc. (MSO).

WILLOW RIVER—Formerly served by New Century Communications. No longer in operation. ICA: MN0250.

WILMONT—K-Communications Inc., 337 Aetna St, Ruthton, MN 56170-0018. Phones: 800-752-9397; 507-658-3830. Fax: 507-658-3914. Web Site: http://www.woodstocktel.net. ICA: MN0242.

TV Market Ranking: Outside TV Markets (WILMONT). Franchise award date: November 1, 1988. Franchise expiration date: N.A. Began: N.A.

Channel capacity: 28 (not 2-way capable). Channels available but not in use: None.

Basic Service

Subscribers: 82.

Programming (received off-air): KDLT-TV (NBC) Sioux Falls; KELO-TV (CBS, MNT) Sioux Falls; KSFY-TV (ABC) Sioux Falls; KTTW (FOX) Sioux Falls.

Programming (via microwave): KSMN (PBS) Worthington.

Programming (via satellite): ABC Family Channel; Animal Planet; Arts & Entertainment; CNN; CW+; Discovery Channel; Disney Channel; ESPN; ESPN 2; Fox Sports Net; History Channel; Spike TV; TBS Superstation; The Learning Channel; Trinity Broadcasting Network; Turner Network TV; WGN America.

Fee: $25.00 installation; $18.82 monthly.

Pay Service 1

Pay Units: 20.

Programming (via satellite): Showtime.

Fee: $10.50 monthly.

Video-On-Demand: No

Internet Service

Operational: No, DSL & dialup.

Telephone Service

None

Miles of Plant: 3.0 (coaxial); None (fiber optic). Homes passed: 150.

Chief Technician & Marketing Director: David Bukowski. Program Director: Terry Nelson.

Ownership: Woodstock Telephone Co. (MSO).

WINDOM—Windom Telecommunications. This cable system has converted to IPTV. See Windom, MN [MN5119]. ICA: MN0066.

WINDOM—Windom Telecomunications. Formerly [MN0066]. This cable system has converted to IPTV, 443 10th St, Windom, MN 56101. Phone: 507-831-6129. Fax: 507-832-8000. E-mail: support@windomnet.com. Web Site: http://www.windomnet.com. ICA: MN5119.

Channel capacity: N.A. Channels available but not in use: N.A.

Internet Service

Operational: Yes.

Telephone Service

Digital: Operational

Manager: Dan Olsen.

Ownership: Windom Telecommunications.

WINNEBAGO—Now served by WASECA, MN [MN0043]. ICA: MN0114.

WINONA—Charter Communications, 1201 McCann Dr, Altoona, WI 54720-2561. Phone: 715-831-8940. Fax: 715-831-5862. Web Site: http://www.charter.com. Also serves Goodview, Homer Twp., Minnesota City & Wilson. ICA: MN0014.

TV Market Ranking: Below 100 (Goodview, Homer Twp., Minnesota City, Wilson, WINONA). Franchise award date: October 1, 1958. Franchise expiration date: N.A. Began: October 3, 1958.

Channel capacity: N.A. Channels available but not in use: N.A.

Basic Service

Subscribers: 6,042.

Programming (received off-air): KAAL (ABC) Austin; KSTP-TV (ABC) St. Paul; KTCA-TV (PBS) St. Paul; KTTC (CW, NBC) Rochester; KXLT-TV (FOX) Rochester; WCCO-TV (CBS) Minneapolis; WEAU-TV (NBC) Eau Claire; WHLA-TV (PBS) La Crosse; WKBT-DT (CBS, MNT) La Crosse; WLAX (FOX) La Crosse; WXOW (ABC, CW) La Crosse; 3 FMs.

Programming (via satellite): Discovery Channel; Eternal Word TV Network; QVC; TBS Superstation; Weather Channel; WGN America.

Current originations: Leased Access; Religious Access; Government Access; Educational Access; Public Access.

Fee: $50.00 installation; $12.00 monthly.

Expanded Basic Service 1

Subscribers: 5,306.

Programming (via satellite): ABC Family Channel; AMC; Animal Planet; Arts & Entertainment; Cartoon Network; CNBC; CNN; Comedy Central; C-SPAN; Disney Channel; E! Entertainment Television; ESPN; ESPN 2; Food Network; Fox Movie Channel; Fox News Channel; FX; Golf Channel; Great American Country; GSN; Headline News; HGTV; History Channel; Independent Film Channel; Lifetime; MoviePlex; MSNBC; MTV; Nickelodeon; ShopNBC; Spike TV; Syfy; The Learning Channel; Travel Channel; Turner Classic Movies; Turner Network TV; TV Guide Network; TV Land; USA Network; Versus; VH1.

Fee: $31.95 monthly.

Digital Basic Service

Subscribers: 1,925.

Programming (via satellite): AmericanLife TV Network; BBC America; Bloomberg Television; Discovery Digital Networks; DMX Music; ESPN Classic Sports; Fox Sports World; G4; INSP; Outdoor Channel; Ovation; Speed Channel; Trinity Broadcasting Network; WE tv.

Fee: $6.05 monthly.

Digital Pay Service 1

Pay Units: 1,043.

Programming (via satellite): Cinemax (multiplexed).

Fee: $19.25 installation; $11.15 monthly; $1.00 converter.

Digital Pay Service 2

Pay Units: 1,184.

Programming (via satellite): HBO (multiplexed).

Fee: $19.25 installation; $11.15 monthly; $1.00 converter.

Digital Pay Service 3

Pay Units: 1,031.

Programming (via satellite): Showtime (multiplexed).

Fee: $19.25 installation; $11.15 monthly; $1.00 converter.

Digital Pay Service 4

Pay Units: 1,013.

Programming (via satellite): Encore (multiplexed); The Movie Channel (multiplexed).

Fee: $19.25 installation; $11.15 monthly; $1.00 converter.

Video-On-Demand: Yes

Pay-Per-View
Hot Choice delivered digitally (delivered digitally); Sports PPV delivered digitally (delivered digitally); Movies (delivered digitally), Addressable: Yes; special events.

Internet Service
Operational: Yes.
Subscribers: 1,924.
Broadband Service: Charter Pipeline.
Fee: $29.99 monthly.

Telephone Service
Digital: Operational
Fee: $39.99 monthly

Miles of Plant: 133.0 (coaxial); None (fiber optic). Homes passed: 12,940.
Vice President & General Manager: Lisa Washa. Operations Manager: Shirley Weibel. Engineering Director: Tim Normand. Marketing Director: Traci Loonstra. Sales & Marketing Manager: Chris Putzkey. Government Relations Manager: Mike Hill.
City fee: 5% of gross.
Ownership: Charter Communications Inc. (MSO).

WINONA—Hiawatha Broadband. Formerly Winona, MN [MN0398]. This cable system has converted to IPTV, 58 Johnson St, Winona, MN 55987. Phone: 888-474-9995. Fax: 507-474-4000. E-mail: info@hbci.com. Web Site: http://www.hbci.com. ICA: MN5161.
Channel capacity: N.A. Channels available but not in use: N.A.

Internet Service
Operational: Yes.

Ownership: Hiawatha Broadband Communications Inc.

WINONA—Hiawatha Broadband. This cable system has converted to IPTV. See Winona, MN [MN5161]. ICA: MN0398.
TV Market Ranking: Below 100 (WINONA).

WOOD LAKE—Clara City Telephone Co., 215 1st St NW, Clara City, MN 56222. Phones: 888-283-7667; 320-847-2114. Fax: 320-847-2114. ICA: MN0381.
TV Market Ranking: Below 100 (WOOD LAKE). Franchise award date: N.A. Franchise expiration date: N.A. Began: October 1, 1988.
Channel capacity: 36 (not 2-way capable). Channels available but not in use: 14.

Basic Service
Subscribers: 125.
Programming (received off-air): KEYC-TV (CBS, FOX) Mankato; KSFY-TV (ABC) Sioux Falls; KWCM-TV (PBS) Appleton.
Programming (via satellite): ABC Family Channel; AMC; Arts & Entertainment; CNN; Country Music TV; Discovery Channel; ESPN; ESPN 2; Fox Sports Net; History Channel; Lifetime; Nickelodeon; Spike TV; The Learning Channel; Turner Network TV; TV Land; USA Network; Weather Channel.
Programming (via translator): KARE (NBC) Minneapolis; KMSP-TV (FOX) Minneapolis; KSTP-TV (ABC) St. Paul; KTCA-TV (PBS) St. Paul; WCCO-TV (CBS) Minneapolis; WFTC (MNT) Minneapolis.
Fee: $40.00 installation; $33.80 monthly; $2.00 converter.

Pay Service 1
Pay Units: 29.
Programming (via satellite): The Movie Channel.
Fee: $10.00 monthly.

Internet Service
Operational: No.

Telephone Service
None

Miles of Plant: 4.0 (coaxial); None (fiber optic). Homes passed: 165. Total homes in franchised area: 165.
Manager: Bruce Hanson.
Franchise fee: None.
Ownership: Hanson Communications Inc. (MSO).

WORTHINGTON—Mediacom, PO Box 110, 1504 2nd St SE, Waseca, MN 56093. Phone: 507-835-2356. Fax: 507-835-4567. Web Site: http://www.mediacomcable.com. Also serves Luverne. ICA: MN0041.
TV Market Ranking: 85 (Luverne); Outside TV Markets (WORTHINGTON). Franchise award date: January 26, 1981. Franchise expiration date: N.A. Began: December 1, 1981.
Channel capacity: N.A. Channels available but not in use: N.A.

Basic Service
Subscribers: 4,381.
Programming (received off-air): KCPO-LP Sioux Falls; KDLT-TV (NBC) Sioux Falls; KELO-TV (CBS, MNT) Sioux Falls; KESD-TV (PBS) Brookings; KSFY-TV (ABC) Sioux Falls; KSMN (PBS) Worthington; KTTW (FOX) Sioux Falls; KWSD (CW) Sioux Falls; allband FM.
Programming (via microwave): KARE (NBC) Minneapolis; KTCA-TV (PBS) St. Paul; WCCO-TV (CBS) Minneapolis.
Programming (via satellite): C-SPAN; C-SPAN 2; TV Guide Network; Weather Channel; WGN America.
Fee: $20.00 installation; $24.68 monthly.

Expanded Basic Service 1
Subscribers: N.A.
Programming (via satellite): ABC Family Channel; AMC; Animal Planet; Arts & Entertainment; Bravo; Cartoon Network; CNBC; CNN; Comedy Central; Country Music TV; Discovery Channel; Disney Channel; E! Entertainment Television; ESPN; ESPN 2; Eternal Word TV Network; Fox Movie Channel; Fox News Channel; Fox Sports Net North; FX; GalaVision; Hallmark Channel; Headline News; HGTV; History Channel; Home Shopping Network; INSP; Lifetime; MSNBC; MTV; Nickelodeon; RFD-TV; SoapNet; Speed Channel; Spike TV; Syfy; TBS Superstation; The Learning Channel; Travel Channel; Trinity Broadcasting Network; truTV; Turner Classic Movies; Turner Network TV; TV Land; Univision; USA Network; VH1; WE tv.
Fee: $24.68 monthly.

Digital Basic Service
Subscribers: N.A.
Programming (received off-air): KDLT-TV (NBC) Sioux Falls; KELO-TV (CBS, MNT) Sioux Falls; KESD-TV (PBS) Brookings; KSFY-TV (ABC) Sioux Falls; KTTW (FOX) Sioux Falls.
Programming (via satellite): ABC News Now; AmericanLife TV Network; BBC America; Bio; Bloomberg Television; Canal 52MX; CBS College Sports Network; CCTV-9 (CCTV International); Cine Latino; CNN en Espanol; CNN HD; Discovery en Espanol; Discovery HD Theater; Discovery Health Channel; Discovery Home Channel; Discovery Kids Channel; Discovery Military Channel; ESPN 2 HD; ESPN Deportes; ESPN HD; ESPN U; ESPNews; FitTV; Fox College Sports Atlantic; Fox College Sports Central; Fox College Sports Pacific; Fox Reality Channel; Fox Soccer; Fox Sports en Espanol; FSN HD; Fuel TV; Fuse; G4; Gol TV; Golf Channel; GSN; Halogen Network; HDNet; HDNet Movies; History Channel en Espanol; History Channel International; ID Investigation Discovery; Independent Film Channel; ION Life; Lifetime Movie Network; Lifetime Real Women; MTV Hits; MTV Tres; MTV2; Music Choice; National Geographic Channel; Nick Jr.; NickToons TV; Outdoor Channel; Qubo; ReelzChannel; Science Channel; Sleuth; Style Network; TBS in HD; TeenNick; Tennis Channel; The Sportsman Channel; Turner Network TV HD; TVG Network; Universal HD; VeneMovies; VH1 Classic.
Fee: $9.00 monthly.

Digital Pay Service 1
Pay Units: 418.
Programming (via satellite): Cinemax (multiplexed); Encore (multiplexed); Flix; HBO (multiplexed); HBO HD; Showtime (multiplexed); Showtime HD; Starz (multiplexed); Starz HDTV; Sundance Channel; The Movie Channel (multiplexed); The Movie Channel HD.
Fee: $12.50 installation; $10.00 monthly (each).

Video-On-Demand: No

Pay-Per-View
iN DEMAND (delivered digitally); Playboy TV (delivered digitally); Spice: Xcess (delivered digitally); Fresh (delivered digitally); Penthouse TV (delivered digitally); Ten Clips (delivered digitally).

Internet Service
Operational: Yes.
Broadband Service: Mediacom High Speed Internet.
Fee: $40.00 monthly.

Telephone Service
Digital: Operational

Miles of Plant: 82.0 (coaxial); None (fiber optic). Homes passed: 6,792. Total homes in franchised area: 6,792.
Vice President: Bill Jensen. Engineering Manager: Kraig Kaiser. Marketing & Sales Director: Lori Huberty.
City fee: 3% of gross.
Ownership: Mediacom LLC (MSO).

WRENSHALL—Formerly served by New Century Communications. No longer in operation. ICA: MN0261.

WYKOFF—North American Communications Corp., PO Box 387, 211 Main St S, Hector, MN 55342-0387. Phones: 800-982-8038; 320-848-6781. Fax: 320-848-2323. E-mail: hcc@hcctel.net. Web Site: http://www.hectorcom.com. ICA: MN0383.
TV Market Ranking: Below 100 (WYKOFF). Franchise award date: February 1, 1989. Franchise expiration date: N.A. Began: N.A.
Channel capacity: 54 (not 2-way capable). Channels available but not in use: 31.

Basic Service
Subscribers: 82.
Programming (received off-air): KAAL (ABC) Austin; KIMT (CBS, MNT) Mason City; KSMQ-TV (PBS) Austin; KTTC (CW, NBC) Rochester; WLAX (FOX) La Crosse.
Programming (via satellite): ABC Family Channel; AMC; Arts & Entertainment; CNN; Country Music TV; Discovery Channel; Disney Channel; ESPN; Fox Sports Net Midwest; Lifetime; Nickelodeon; QVC; Spike TV; TBS Superstation; Trinity Broadcasting Network; Turner Network TV; USA Network; WGN America.
Fee: $40.00 installation; $26.95 monthly; $3.50 converter; $25.00 additional installation.

Pay Service 1
Pay Units: 7.
Programming (via satellite): Cinemax.
Fee: $10.95 monthly.

Pay Service 2
Pay Units: 3.
Programming (via satellite): HBO.
Fee: $10.95 monthly.

Video-On-Demand: No

Internet Service
Operational: No.
Broadband Service: Offers dial-up and DSL only; no cable modem service.

Telephone Service
None

Miles of Plant: 4.0 (coaxial); None (fiber optic). Homes passed: 185. Total homes in franchised area: 185.
Manager: Matt Sparks. Chief Technician: George Honzay. Customer Service Supervisor: Patty Groshens.
Ownership: Hector Communications Corp. (MSO).

MISSISSIPPI

Total Systems: **115**
Total Communities Served: **347**
Franchises Not Yet Operating: **0**
Applications Pending: **0**

Communities with Applications: **0**
Number of Basic Subscribers: **552,871**
Number of Expanded Basic Subscribers: **120,911**
Number of Pay Units: **49,542**

Top 100 Markets Represented: Memphis (26); New Orleans (31); Mobile, AL-Pensacola, FL (59); Jackson (77).

For a list of cable communities in this section, see the Cable Community Index located in the back of Cable Volume 2.
For explanation of terms used in cable system listings, see p. D-11.

ABERDEEN—MetroCast Communications, 311 Heritage Dr, Oxford, MS 38852. Phones: 662-234-4711; 662-728-8111. Fax: 662-236-3593. Web Site: http://www.metrocastcommunications.com. ICA: MS0035.

TV Market Ranking: Below 100 (ABERDEEN). Franchise award date: N.A. Franchise expiration date: N.A. Began: August 1, 1965.

Channel capacity: N.A. Channels available but not in use: N.A.

Basic Service
Subscribers: 1,688.
Programming (received off-air): W39CD Fulton; WCBI-TV (CBS, CW, MNT) Columbus; WKDH (ABC) Houston; WLOV-TV (FOX) West Point; WMAE-TV (PBS) Booneville; WMC-TV (NBC) Memphis; WPTY-TV (ABC) Memphis; WTVA (NBC) Tupelo.
Programming (via satellite): CW+; INSP; Nickelodeon; QVC; WGN America.
Current originations: Public Access.
Fee: $49.95 installation; $17.95 monthly; $1.25 converter.

Expanded Basic Service 1
Subscribers: 1,669.
Programming (via satellite): ABC Family Channel; AMC; Animal Planet; Arts & Entertainment; BET Networks; Bravo; Cartoon Network; CNBC; CNN; Comcast Sports Net Southeast; Comedy Central; Cooking Channel; Country Music TV; C-SPAN; C-SPAN 2; Discovery Channel; Disney Channel; Do-It-Yourself; E! Entertainment Television; ESPN; Food Network; Fox News Channel; FX; G4; Golf Channel; Great American Country; Hallmark Channel; Headline News; HGTV; History Channel; Home Shopping Network; Lifetime; MSNBC; MTV; National Geographic Channel; Outdoor Channel; SoapNet; Spike TV; Syfy; TBS Superstation; The Learning Channel; Travel Channel; Trinity Broadcasting Network; Turner Network TV; Turner South; TV Land; USA Network; Versus; VH1; WE tv; Weather Channel.
Fee: $33.00 monthly.

Digital Basic Service
Subscribers: N.A.
Programming (received off-air): WCBI-TV (CBS, CW, MNT) Columbus; WPTY-TV (ABC) Memphis.
Programming (via satellite): AmericanLife TV Network; BBC America; Bio; Bloomberg Television; Discovery Digital Networks; Discovery HD Theater; DMX Music; ESPN Classic Sports; ESPNews; Fox Movie Channel; Fox Soccer; Fuse; GAS; GSN; Halogen Network; History Channel International; Independent Film Channel; Lifetime Movie Network; Lime; MTV Networks Digital Suite; NFL Network; Nick Jr.; NickToons TV; Sleuth; Speed Channel; Style Network; Toon Disney; Turner Classic Movies; Turner Network TV HD; Universal HD; WMC-TV (NBC) Memphis.
Fee: $10.00 monthly.

Digital Pay Service 1
Pay Units: N.A.
Programming (via satellite): Cinemax (multiplexed); Encore (multiplexed); Flix; HBO (multiplexed); Showtime (multiplexed); Starz (multiplexed); Sundance Channel; The Movie Channel (multiplexed).
Fee: $6.00 monthly (Encore), $13.00 monthly (HBO, Cinemax, Showtime/TMC or Starz).

Video-On-Demand: Yes

Pay-Per-View
iN DEMAND (delivered digitally); Fresh (delivered digitally); Hot Choice (delivered digitally); Playboy TV (delivered digitally); ESPN (delivered digitally); MLB Extra Innings (delivered digitally).

Internet Service
Operational: Yes.
Broadband Service: MetroCast Internet.
Fee: $79.99 installation; $43.95 monthly.

Telephone Service
Digital: Operational
Fee: $24.95 installation; $29.95 monthly

Miles of Plant: 50.0 (coaxial); None (fiber optic). Homes passed: 3,052.

General Manager: Rick Ferrall. Technical Operations Manager: Jerry Morris. Marketing Manager: Lee Beck.

City fee: None.

Ownership: Harron Communications LP (MSO).

AMORY—MetroCast Communications, 311 Heritage Dr, Oxford, MS 38852. Phones: 662-234-4711; 662-728-8111. Fax: 662-236-3593. Web Site: http://www.metrocastcommunications.com. Also serves Becker, Hatley & Smithville. ICA: MS0127.

TV Market Ranking: Below 100 (AMORY, Becker, Hatley, Smithville). Franchise award date: N.A. Franchise expiration date: N.A. Began: January 1, 1955.

Channel capacity: N.A. Channels available but not in use: N.A.

Basic Service
Subscribers: 3,002.
Programming (received off-air): W39CD Fulton; WCBI-TV (CBS, CW, MNT) Columbus; WHDH (NBC) Boston; WLOV-TV (FOX) West Point; WMAE-TV (PBS) Booneville; WTVA (NBC) Tupelo; 5 FMs.
Programming (via satellite): C-SPAN; C-SPAN 2; INSP; QVC; TBS Superstation; TV Guide Network; Weatherscan.
Fee: $49.95 installation; $17.95 monthly; $1.25 converter.

Expanded Basic Service 1
Subscribers: N.A.
Programming (via satellite): ABC Family Channel; AMC; Animal Planet; Arts & Entertainment; BET Networks; Bravo; Cartoon Network; CNBC; CNN; Comcast Sports Net Southeast; Comedy Central; Cooking Channel; Country Music TV; Discovery Channel; Disney Channel; Do-It-Yourself; ESPN; ESPN 2; Food Network; Fox News Channel; FX; Golf Channel; Great American Country; Headline News; HGTV; History Channel; Home Shopping Network; Lifetime; MTV; National Geographic Channel; Nickelodeon; Outdoor Channel; SoapNet; Spike TV; The Learning Channel; Turner Network TV; TV Land; USA Network; Versus; VH1; WE tv; Weather Channel; WGN America.
Fee: $33.00 monthly.

Digital Basic Service
Subscribers: N.A.
Programming (via satellite): American-Life TV Network; BBC America; Bio; Bloomberg Television; Discovery Digital Networks; DMX Music; ESPN Classic Sports; ESPNews; Fox Movie Channel; Fox Sports World; Fuse; G4; GAS; GSN; Halogen Network; History Channel International; Independent Film Channel; Lifetime Movie Network; MTV2; Nick Jr.; Nick-Toons TV; Speed Channel; Style Network; Toon Disney; Turner Classic Movies; VH1 Classic.
Fee: $10.00 monthly.

Digital Pay Service 1
Pay Units: N.A.
Programming (via satellite): Cinemax (multiplexed); Encore (multiplexed); Flix (multiplexed); HBO (multiplexed); Showtime (multiplexed); Starz; The Movie Channel (multiplexed).
Fee: $6.00 monthly (Encore), $13.00 monthly each (HBO, Cinemax, Showtime/TMC & Starz).

Video-On-Demand: Yes

Pay-Per-View
ESPN (delivered digitally); ESPN Now (delivered digitally); Playboy TV (delivered digitally); Hot Choice (delivered digitally); Fresh (delivered digitally); iN DEMAND (delivered digitally).

Internet Service
Operational: Yes.
Broadband Service: MetroCast Internet.
Fee: $79.99 installation; $43.95 monthly.

Telephone Service
Digital: Operational
Fee: $24.95 installation; $29.95 monthly

Miles of Plant: 50.0 (coaxial); None (fiber optic).

General Manager: Rick Ferrall. Technical Operations Manager: Jerry Morris. Marketing Manager: Lee Beck.

City fee: Pole rental.

Ownership: Harron Communications LP (MSO).

ANGUILLA—CMA Cablevision, 101 S Deer Creek Dr W, Leland, MS 38756-3126. Phones: 972-233-9614 (Corporate office); 662-686-7823. Fax: 662-686-4100. Web Site: http://www.cmaaccess.com. ICA: MS0128.

TV Market Ranking: Below 100 (ANGUILLA). Franchise award date: N.A. Franchise expiration date: N.A. Began: N.A.

Channel capacity: 35 (not 2-way capable). Channels available but not in use: 7.

Basic Service
Subscribers: 150.
Programming (received off-air): WABG-TV (ABC) Greenwood; WDBD (FOX) Jackson; WJTV (CBS) Jackson; WLBT (NBC) Jackson; WXVT (CBS) Greenville.
Programming (via satellite): ABC Family Channel; BET Networks; Cartoon Network; CNN; Discovery Channel; ESPN; Headline News; INSP; Nickelodeon; ShopNBC; Spike TV; TBS Superstation; Turner Classic Movies; Turner Network TV; TV Land; USA Network; Weather Channel; WGN America.
Fee: $39.95 installation; $26.95 monthly; $9.95 additional installation.

Pay Service 1
Pay Units: N.A.
Programming (via satellite): Cinemax; HBO.
Fee: $14.95 installation; $13.95 monthly (each).

Video-On-Demand: No

Internet Service
Operational: No.

Telephone Service
None

Miles of Plant: 9.0 (coaxial); None (fiber optic). Total homes in franchised area: 400.

General Manager: Jerry Smith. Marketing Director: Julie Ferguson.

Ownership: Cable Management Assoc. (MSO).

ARCOLA—CMA Cablevision, 101 S Deer Creek Dr W, Leland, MS 38756-3126. Phones: 972-233-9614 (Corporate office); 662-686-7823. Fax: 662-686-4100. Web Site: http://www.cmaaccess.com. ICA: MS0129.

TV Market Ranking: Below 100 (ARCOLA). Franchise award date: N.A. Franchise expiration date: N.A. Began: N.A.

Channel capacity: 35 (not 2-way capable). Channels available but not in use: N.A.

Basic Service
Subscribers: 65.
Programming (received off-air): WABG-TV (ABC) Greenwood; WDBD (FOX) Jackson; WLBT (NBC) Jackson; WMAO-TV (PBS) Greenwood; WXVT (CBS) Greenville.
Programming (via satellite): ABC Family Channel; AmericanLife TV Network; Arts & Entertainment; BET Networks; Cartoon Network; CNN; Discovery Channel; ESPN; ShopNBC; Spike TV; Syfy; TBS Superstation; Trinity Broadcasting Network; Turner Classic Movies; Turner Network TV; USA Network; WGN America.
Fee: $39.95 installation; $30.95 monthly; $9.95 additional installation.

Pay Service 1
Pay Units: N.A.
Programming (via satellite): Cinemax; HBO.
Fee: $14.95 installation; $10.95 monthly (Cinemax), $13.95 monthly (HBO).
Video-On-Demand: No
Internet Service
Operational: No.
Telephone Service
None
Miles of Plant: 5.0 (coaxial); None (fiber optic). Homes passed: 200.
General Manager: Jerry Smith. Marketing Director: Julie Ferguson.
Ownership: Cable Management Assoc. (MSO).

ARTESIA—Cable TV Inc., PO Box 2598, 612 Hwy 82 W, Starkville, MS 39760. Phone: 662-324-5121. Fax: 662-324-0233. ICA: MS0119.
TV Market Ranking: Below 100 (ARTESIA). Franchise award date: N.A. Franchise expiration date: N.A. Began: April 1, 1989.
Channel capacity: 35 (not 2-way capable). Channels available but not in use: N.A.
Basic Service
Subscribers: 80.
Programming (received off-air): WCBI-TV (CBS, CW, MNT) Columbus; WLOV-TV (FOX) West Point; WTVA (NBC) Tupelo.
Programming (via satellite): Headline News; TBS Superstation; WGN America.
Fee: $40.00 installation; $28.95 monthly.
Pay Service 1
Pay Units: 31.
Programming (via satellite): HBO.
Fee: $9.21 monthly.
Pay Service 2
Pay Units: 29.
Programming (via satellite): Showtime.
Fee: $9.21 monthly.
Internet Service
Operational: No.
Telephone Service
None
Miles of Plant: 4.0 (coaxial); None (fiber optic). Homes passed: 200.
Manager: Andy Williams.
Ownership: Andy Williams.

ASHLAND—MetroCast Communications, 311 Heritage Dr, Oxford, MS 38852. Phones: 662-234-4711; 662-728-8111. Fax: 662-236-3593. Web Site: http://www.metrocastcommunications.com. Also serves Snow Lake Shores. ICA: MS0078.
TV Market Ranking: Below 100 (ASHLAND, Snow Lake Shores). Franchise award date: N.A. Franchise expiration date: N.A. Began: April 15, 1983.
Channel capacity: N.A. Channels available but not in use: N.A.
Basic Service
Subscribers: 203.
Programming (received off-air): WBUY-TV (TBN) Holly Springs; WHBQ-TV (FOX) Memphis; WKNO (PBS) Memphis; WLMT (CW) Memphis; WMAE-TV (PBS) Booneville; WMC-TV (NBC) Memphis; WPTY-TV (ABC) Memphis; WPXX-TV (ION, MNT) Memphis; WREG-TV (CBS) Memphis; WTVA (NBC) Tupelo.
Programming (via satellite): QVC.
Current originations: Educational Access; Leased Access.
Fee: $49.95 installation; $17.95 monthly; $1.25 converter.
Expanded Basic Service 1
Subscribers: N.A.
Programming (via satellite): ABC Family Channel; AMC; Animal Planet; Arts & Entertainment; BET Networks; Cartoon Network; CNBC; CNN; Comcast Sports Net Southeast (multiplexed); Comedy Central; Cooking Channel; Country Music TV; C-SPAN; C-SPAN 2; Discovery Channel; Disney Channel; Do-It-Yourself; E! Entertainment Television; ESPN; ESPN 2; FitTV; Food Network; Fox News Channel; FX; G4; Golf Channel; Great American Country; Headline News; HGTV; INSP; ION Television; Lifetime; MSNBC; MTV; National Geographic Channel; Nickelodeon; Outdoor Channel; SoapNet; Spike TV; SportSouth; Syfy; TBS Superstation; The Learning Channel; Travel Channel; Turner Network TV; Turner South; TV Land; USA Network; Versus; VH1; WE tv; Weather Channel.
Fee: $33.00 monthly.
Digital Basic Service
Subscribers: 34.
Programming (received off-air): WCBI-TV (CBS, CW, MNT) Columbus; WLMT (CW) Memphis; WMC-TV (NBC) Memphis; WPTY-TV (ABC) Memphis.
Programming (via satellite): AmericanLife TV Network; BBC America; Bio; Bloomberg Television; Discovery Digital Networks; Discovery HD Theater; DMX Music; ESPN 2 HD; ESPN Classic Sports; ESPN HD; ESPNews; Fox Movie Channel; Fox Soccer; Fuse; GAS; GSN; Halogen Network; History Channel; History Channel International; Independent Film Channel; Lifetime Movie Network; MTV Networks Digital Suite; NFL Network; Nick Jr.; NickToons TV; Sleuth; Speed Channel; Style Network; Toon Disney; Turner Classic Movies; Turner Network TV HD; Universal HD.
Fee: $10.00 monthly.
Digital Pay Service 1
Pay Units: N.A.
Programming (via satellite): Cinemax (multiplexed); Cinemax HD; Encore (multiplexed); Flix; HBO (multiplexed); HBO HD; Showtime (multiplexed); Starz (multiplexed); Sundance Channel; The Movie Channel (multiplexed).
Fee: $6.00 monthly (Encore), $13.00 monthly (HBO, Cinemax, Showtime/TMC or Starz).
Video-On-Demand: Yes
Pay-Per-View
iN DEMAND (delivered digitally); Fresh (delivered digitally); Hot Choice (delivered digitally); Playboy TV (delivered digitally); ESPN (delivered digitally).
Internet Service
Operational: Yes.
Broadband Service: MetroCast Internet.
Fee: $79.99 installation; $43.95 monthly.
Telephone Service
Digital: Operational
Fee: $24.95 installation; $29.95 monthly
Miles of Plant: 22.0 (coaxial); None (fiber optic). Additional miles planned: 5.0 (coaxial). Homes passed: 661. Total homes in franchised area: 790.
General Manager: Rick Ferrall. Technical Operations Manager: Jerry Morris. Marketing Manager: Lee Beck.
City fee: 3% of gross.
Ownership: Harron Communications LP (MSO).

BALDWYN—MetroCast Communications, 311 Heritage Dr, Oxford, MS 38852. Phones: 662-234-4711; 662-728-8111. Fax: 662-236-3593. Web Site: http://www.metrocastcommunications.com. Also serves Guntown, Lee County & Saltillo. ICA: MS0037.
TV Market Ranking: Below 100 (BALDWYN, Guntown, Lee County, Saltillo). Franchise award date: N.A. Franchise expiration date: N.A. Began: September 1, 1973.
Channel capacity: N.A. Channels available but not in use: N.A.
Basic Service
Subscribers: 2,105.
Programming (received off-air): W34DV Booneville; WCBI-TV (CBS, CW, MNT) Columbus; WKDH (ABC) Houston; WLOV-TV (FOX) West Point; WMAE-TV (PBS) Booneville; WTVA (NBC) Tupelo.
Programming (via satellite): C-SPAN; QVC; TBS Superstation; Weather Channel; WGN America.
Fee: $49.95 installation; $17.95 monthly; $1.25 converter.
Expanded Basic Service 1
Subscribers: 1,700.
Programming (via satellite): ABC Family Channel; AMC; Animal Planet; Arts & Entertainment; BET Networks; Cartoon Network; CNN; Comcast Sports Net Southeast; Discovery Channel; Disney Channel; E! Entertainment Television; ESPN; ESPN 2; Food Network; Fox News Channel; FX; Great American Country; Headline News; HGTV; History Channel; Lifetime; MTV; National Geographic Channel; Nickelodeon; SoapNet; Spike TV; SportSouth; The Learning Channel; Turner Network TV; TV Guide Network; USA Network; Versus; VH1.
Fee: $33.00 monthly.
Digital Basic Service
Subscribers: N.A.
Programming (via satellite): AmericanLife TV Network; BBC America; Bio; Bloomberg Television; Discovery Digital Networks; DMX Music; ESPN Classic Sports; ESPNews; FitTV; Fox Movie Channel; Fox Sports World; Fuse; G4; GAS; Golf Channel; GSN; Halogen Network; History Channel International; Independent Film Channel; Lifetime Movie Network; MTV2; Nick Jr.; NickToons TV; Outdoor Channel; Speed Channel; Style Network; Toon Disney; Turner Classic Movies; VH1 Classic.
Fee: $10.00 monthly.
Digital Pay Service 1
Pay Units: N.A.
Programming (via satellite): Cinemax (multiplexed); Encore; Flix (multiplexed); HBO (multiplexed); Showtime (multiplexed); Starz; The Movie Channel (multiplexed).
Video-On-Demand: Yes
Pay-Per-View
Playboy TV (delivered digitally); Hot Choice (delivered digitally); Fresh (delivered digitally); iN DEMAND (delivered digitally); ESPN (delivered digitally); ESPN Now (delivered digitally).
Internet Service
Operational: Yes.
Broadband Service: MetroCast Internet.
Fee: $79.99 installation; $43.95 monthly.
Telephone Service
Analog: Not Operational
Digital: Operational
Fee: $24.95 installation; $29.95 monthly
Miles of Plant: 30.0 (coaxial); None (fiber optic). Additional miles planned: 5.0 (coaxial). Homes passed: 2,758.
General Manager: Rick Ferrall. Technical Operations Manager: Jerry Morris. Marketing Manager: Lee Beck.
City fee: 3% of gross.
Ownership: Harron Communications LP (MSO).

BASSFIELD—Galaxy Cablevision, PO Box 308, 214 Main St, Ste C, Monticello, MS 39654-0308. Phone: 601-587-9461. Fax: 601-587-7410. Web Site: http://www.galaxycable.com. ICA: MS0130.
TV Market Ranking: Below 100 (BASSFIELD). Franchise award date: N.A. Franchise expiration date: N.A. Began: April 1, 1982.
Channel capacity: 36 (not 2-way capable). Channels available but not in use: 4.
Basic Service
Subscribers: 67.
Programming (received off-air): WDAM-TV (NBC) Laurel; WHLT (CBS) Hattiesburg; WLOX (ABC) Biloxi; WMAH-TV (PBS) Biloxi; WXXV-TV (FOX, MNT) Gulfport.
Programming (via satellite): ABC Family Channel; AMC; Arts & Entertainment; BET Networks; Cartoon Network; CNN; Discovery Channel; Disney Channel; E! Entertainment Television; ESPN; ESPN 2; Fox News Channel; Great American Country; Headline News; Lifetime; Outdoor Channel; QVC; Speed Channel; TBS Superstation; The Learning Channel; Trinity Broadcasting Network; Turner Network TV; USA Network; Weather Channel; WGN America.
Fee: $39.60 monthly.
Pay Service 1
Pay Units: N.A.
Programming (via satellite): Showtime; The Movie Channel.
Fee: $25.00 installation; $11.95 monthly (each).
Internet Service
Operational: No.
Telephone Service
None
Miles of Plant: 11.0 (coaxial); None (fiber optic). Homes passed: 238.
State Manager: Bill Flowers. Technical Manager & Engineer: Greg Berthaut. Customer Service Representative: Rebecca Nelson.; Parlean Myers.
Ownership: Galaxy Cable Inc. (MSO).

BAY SPRINGS—Video Inc., PO Box 409, 2988 Hwy 15, Bay Springs, MS 39422-0409. Phone: 601-764-2121. Fax: 601-764-2051. E-mail: request@tec.com. Web Site: http://tec.com. Also serves Soso. ICA: MS0063.
TV Market Ranking: Below 100 (BAY SPRINGS, Soso). Franchise award date: N.A. Franchise expiration date: N.A. Began: March 1, 1982.
Channel capacity: N.A. Channels available but not in use: N.A.
Basic Service
Subscribers: 2,030.
Programming (received off-air): WDAM-TV (NBC) Laurel; WHLT (CBS) Hattiesburg; WJTV (CBS) Jackson; WTOK-TV (ABC, CW, FOX, MNT) Meridian; WXXV-TV (FOX, MNT) Gulfport.
Programming (via satellite): QVC; Weather Channel.
Current originations: Educational Access.
Fee: $24.95 installation; $10.95 monthly.
Expanded Basic Service 1
Subscribers: N.A.
Programming (via satellite): ABC Family Channel; AMC; Animal Planet; Arts & Entertainment; Boomerang; Cartoon Network; CNN; Comcast Sports Net Southeast; Country Music TV; Discovery Channel; Disney Channel; ESPN; ESPN 2; Fox News Channel; Hallmark Channel; HGTV; History Channel; Lifetime; MSNBC; National Geographic Channel; Nickelodeon; Outdoor Channel; Spike TV; Syfy; TBS Superstation; The Learning Channel; Travel Channel; Turner Network TV; USA Network; WGN America.
Fee: $32.95 monthly.

Digital Basic Service
Subscribers: N.A.
Programming (via satellite): AmericanLife TV Network; Bio; Bloomberg Television; Bravo; Discovery Kids Channel; DMX Music; ESPNews; Fox Movie Channel; Golf Channel; GSN; Halogen Network; History Channel International; Lifetime Movie Network; Lime; NickToons TV; Sleuth; Speed Channel; Style Network; Trinity Broadcasting Network; Turner Classic Movies; WE tv.
Fee: $21.95 monthly.
Pay Service 1
Pay Units: N.A.
Programming (via satellite): Cinemax; HBO; The Movie Channel.
Digital Pay Service 1
Pay Units: N.A.
Programming (via satellite): Cinemax (multiplexed); Encore (multiplexed); HBO (multiplexed); Showtime (multiplexed); Starz (multiplexed); The Movie Channel (multiplexed).
Fee: $12.00 monthly (HBO, Showtime/TMC, Cinemax, or Starz/Encore)).
Video-On-Demand: No
Pay-Per-View
iN DEMAND (delivered digitally); ESPN Now (delivered digitally).
Internet Service
Operational: No, DSL & dialup.
Telephone Service
None
Miles of Plant: 120.0 (coaxial); None (fiber optic). Homes passed: 3,000.
General Manager: Wayne Buffington. Chief Technician: Larry Bundrum.
City fee: 3% of gross.
Ownership: Video Inc.

BAY ST. LOUIS—Mediacom. Now served by WAVELAND, MS [MS0022]. ICA: MS0152.

BEAUMONT—Mediacom, 760 Middle St, PO Box 1009, Fairhope, AL 36532. Phones: 251-928-0374; 850-934-7700 (Gulf Breeze regional office). Fax: 251-928-3804. Web Site: http://www.mediacomcable.com. ICA: MS0093.
TV Market Ranking: Below 100 (BEAUMONT). Franchise award date: October 1, 1983. Franchise expiration date: N.A. Began: February 1, 1986.
Channel capacity: 38 (not 2-way capable). Channels available but not in use: None.
Basic Service
Subscribers: 182.
Programming (received off-air): WDAM-TV (NBC) Laurel; WHLT (CBS) Hattiesburg; WKRG-TV (CBS) Mobile; WLOX (ABC) Biloxi; WMAH-TV (PBS) Biloxi; WXXV-TV (FOX, MNT) Gulfport.
Programming (via satellite): AMC; Animal Planet; Arts & Entertainment; BET Networks; Cartoon Network; CNBC; CNN; Comcast Sports Net Southeast; Comedy Central; Country Music TV; C-SPAN; CW+; Discovery Channel; Disney Channel; E! Entertainment Television; ESPN; ESPN 2; FitTV; Fox News Channel; FX; Hallmark Channel; Headline News; HGTV; History Channel; Home Shopping Network; INSP; MSNBC; MTV; Nickelodeon; QVC; Speed Channel; Spike TV; SportSouth; Syfy; TBS Superstation; The Learning Channel; Turner Classic Movies; Turner Network TV; TV Land; USA Network; Weather Channel.
Fee: $29.50 installation; $44.95 monthly.
Pay Service 1
Pay Units: 41.
Programming (via satellite): Cinemax.
Fee: $10.45 monthly.
Pay Service 2
Pay Units: 64.
Programming (via satellite): HBO (multiplexed).
Fee: $12.45 monthly.
Pay Service 3
Pay Units: 54.
Programming (via satellite): Showtime.
Fee: $10.45 monthly.
Pay Service 4
Pay Units: 32.
Programming (via satellite): The Movie Channel.
Fee: $10.45 monthly.
Pay Service 5
Pay Units: 55.
Programming (via satellite): Flix.
Fee: $2.95 monthly.
Video-On-Demand: No
Internet Service
Operational: No.
Telephone Service
None
Miles of Plant: 10.0 (coaxial); None (fiber optic). Homes passed: 433. Total homes in franchised area: 455.
Vice President: David Servies. Operations Director: Gene Wuchner. Technical Operations Manager: Mike Sneary. Sales & Marketing Manager: Joey Nagem.
Ownership: Mediacom LLC (MSO).

BELMONT—Formerly served by Almega Cable. No longer in operation. ICA: MS0131.

BELZONI—Cable TV of Belzoni Inc., 102 S Hayden St, Belzoni, MS 39038-3914. Phone: 662-247-1834. Fax: 662-247-3237. E-mail: office@belzonicable.com. Web Site: http://www.belzonicable.com. ICA: MS0073.
TV Market Ranking: Below 100 (BELZONI). Franchise award date: N.A. Franchise expiration date: N.A. Began: December 1, 1970.
Channel capacity: 42 (operating 2-way). Channels available but not in use: N.A.
Basic Service
Subscribers: 625.
Programming (received off-air): WABG-TV (ABC) Greenwood; WAPT (ABC) Jackson; WJTV (CBS) Jackson; WLBT (NBC) Jackson; WXVT (CBS) Greenville.
Programming (via satellite): Animal Planet; Arts & Entertainment; BET Networks; Cartoon Network; CNN; Comedy Central; Country Music TV; C-SPAN; Discovery Channel; Disney Channel; E! Entertainment Television; ESPN; ESPN 2; ESPNews; Food Network; Fox News Channel; Fox Sports World; FX; Hallmark Channel; Headline News; HGTV; History Channel; ION Television; Lifetime; MTV; National Geographic Channel; Nickelodeon; Outdoor Channel; QVC; Speed Channel; SportSouth; Syfy; TBS Superstation; The Learning Channel; The Movie Channel; Trinity Broadcasting Network; Turner Classic Movies; Turner Network TV; TV Land; USA Network; VH1; Weather Channel; WGN America.
Fee: $38.00 installation; $30.98 monthly.
Pay Service 1
Pay Units: N.A.
Programming (via satellite): Cinemax; HBO; Showtime.
Fee: $11.77 monthly (each).
Internet Service
Operational: Yes. Began: January 1, 2002.
Broadband Service: Worldcom.
Fee: $32.00 installation; $32.05 monthly.
Telephone Service
None
Miles of Plant: 31.0 (coaxial); None (fiber optic). Homes passed: 826. Total homes in franchised area: 1,465.
Manager: Del Lott. Technician: Les Vance.
City fee: 2% of gross.
Ownership: Del Lott.

BENOIT—Formerly served by J & L Cable. No longer in operation. ICA: MS0101.

BENTONIA—Comcast Cable, 5375 Executive Pl, Jackson, MS 39206. Phone: 601-982-1187. Fax: 601-321-3888. Web Site: http://www.comcast.com. ICA: MS0132.
TV Market Ranking: 77 (BENTONIA). Franchise award date: N.A. Franchise expiration date: N.A. Began: N.A.
Channel capacity: 36 (not 2-way capable). Channels available but not in use: 10.
Basic Service
Subscribers: 50.
Programming (received off-air): WAPT (ABC) Jackson; WDBD (FOX) Jackson; WJTV (CBS) Jackson; WLBT (NBC) Jackson; WMPN-TV (PBS) Jackson.
Programming (via satellite): ABC Family Channel; Arts & Entertainment; BET Networks; CNN; Disney Channel; E! Entertainment Television; ESPN; Hallmark Channel; HGTV; Lifetime; Outdoor Channel; QVC; SportSouth; TBS Superstation; The Learning Channel; Trinity Broadcasting Network; Turner Classic Movies; Turner Network TV; USA Network.
Fee: $25.00 installation; $29.00 monthly; $10.00 additional installation.
Internet Service
Operational: No.
Telephone Service
None
Miles of Plant: 25.0 (coaxial); None (fiber optic). Homes passed: 171.
Vice President & General Manager: Ronnie Colvin. Engineering Director: Sandy McKnight. Marketing Director: Wesley Downing. Public Affairs Director: Frances Smith.
Ownership: Comcast Cable Communications Inc. (MSO).

BILOXI—Cable One, 786 Dr Martin Luther King Jr Blvd, Biloxi, MS 39530-3836. Phone: 228-374-5900. Fax: 228-436-1032. Web Site: http://www.cableone.net. Also serves D'Iberville, Harrison County, Jackson County, Keesler AFB, Ocean Springs & Van Cleave. ICA: MS0002.
TV Market Ranking: Below 100 (BILOXI, D'Iberville, Harrison County, Jackson County, Keesler AFB, Ocean Springs, Van Cleave). Franchise award date: N.A. Franchise expiration date: N.A. Began: January 1, 1963.
Channel capacity: 78 (operating 2-way). Channels available but not in use: 4.
Basic Service
Subscribers: 30,000.
Programming (received off-air): WALA-TV (FOX) Mobile; WDSU (NBC) New Orleans; WEAR-TV (ABC) Pensacola; WKRG-TV (CBS) Mobile; WLOX (ABC) Biloxi; WMAH-TV (PBS) Biloxi; WNOL-TV (CW) New Orleans; WPMI-TV (NBC) Mobile; WWL-TV (CBS) New Orleans; WXXV-TV (FOX, MNT) Gulfport; WYES-TV (PBS) New Orleans.
Programming (via satellite): ABC Family Channel; AMC; Animal Planet; Arts & Entertainment; BET Networks; Cartoon Network; CNBC; CNN; Comcast Sports Net Southeast; Comedy Central; Country Music TV; C-SPAN; Discovery Channel; Disney Channel; ESPN; ESPN 2; Eternal Word TV Network; Food Network; Fox News Channel; FX; Headline News; HGTV; History Channel; Home Shopping Network; Jewelry Television; Lifetime; MSNBC; MTV; Nickelodeon; QVC; ShopNBC; Spike TV; Syfy; TBS Superstation; The Learning Channel; Turner Classic Movies; Turner Network TV; TV Guide Network; TV Land; USA Network; VH1; Weather Channel; WGN America.
Current originations: Public Access.
Fee: $65.00 installation; $46.00 monthly; $20.00 additional installation.
Digital Basic Service
Subscribers: 13,400.
Programming (received off-air): WLOX (ABC) Biloxi; WXXV-TV (FOX, MNT) Gulfport.
Programming (via satellite): 3 Angels Broadcasting Network; Bio; Boomerang; BYU Television; Canales N; Discovery Digital Networks; DMX Music; ESPN Classic Sports; ESPNews; FamilyNet; Fox College Sports Atlantic; Fox College Sports Central; Fox College Sports Pacific; Fox Movie Channel; Fox Soccer; Fuel TV; G4; Golf Channel; Hallmark Channel; History Channel International; INSP; National Geographic Channel; Outdoor Channel; SoapNet; Speed Channel; Toon Disney; Trinity Broadcasting Network; truTV; Turner Network TV HD; TVG Network; Universal HD.
Fee: $8.95 monthly.
Digital Pay Service 1
Pay Units: 3,000.
Programming (via satellite): Cinemax (multiplexed).
Fee: $13.95 monthly.
Digital Pay Service 2
Pay Units: 5,100.
Programming (via satellite): HBO (multiplexed).
Fee: $13.95 monthly.
Digital Pay Service 3
Pay Units: 2,000.
Programming (via satellite): Flix; Showtime (multiplexed); Showtime HD; The Movie Channel (multiplexed); The Movie Channel HD.
Fee: $13.95 monthly.
Digital Pay Service 4
Pay Units: N.A.
Programming (via satellite): Encore (multiplexed); Starz (multiplexed).
Video-On-Demand: No
Pay-Per-View
Addressable homes: 14,003.
Movies (delivered digitally), Fee: $3.95, Addressable: Yes; sports (delivered digitally).
Internet Service
Operational: Yes.
Subscribers: 14,000.
Broadband Service: CableONE.net.
Fee: $75.00 installation; $43.00 monthly.
Telephone Service
Digital: Operational
Fee: $75.00 installation; $39.95 monthly
Miles of Plant: 845.0 (coaxial); None (fiber optic). Homes passed: 45,168. Total homes in franchised area: 45,168.
Technical Operations Manager: Dave Matthews.
City fee: 3% of gross.
Ownership: Cable One Inc. (MSO).

BOONEVILLE—MetroCast Communications, 311 Heritage Dr, Oxford, MS 38852. Phones: 662-234-4711; 662-728-8111. Fax: 662-236-3593. Web Site: http://www.metrocastcommunications.com. Also serves Jumpertown & Prentiss County. ICA: MS0133.

TV Market Ranking: Below 100 (BOONEVILLE, Jumpertown, Prentiss County (portions)); Outside TV Markets (Prentiss County (portions)). Franchise award date: N.A. Franchise expiration date: N.A. Began: January 1, 1967.
Channel capacity: N.A. Channels available but not in use: N.A.

Basic Service
Subscribers: 3,594.
Programming (received off-air): W34DV Booneville; WCBI-TV (CBS, CW, MNT) Columbus; WKDH (ABC) Houston; WLOV-TV (FOX) West Point; WMAE-TV (PBS) Booneville; WMC-TV (NBC) Memphis; WPTY-TV (ABC) Memphis; WTVA (NBC) Tupelo; allband FM.
Programming (via satellite): CW+; Home Shopping Network; QVC; TV Guide Network; WGN America.
Current originations: Government Access.
Fee: $49.95 installation; $17.95 monthly; $1.25 converter.

Expanded Basic Service 1
Subscribers: 2,877.
Programming (via satellite): ABC Family Channel; AMC; Animal Planet; Arts & Entertainment; BET Networks; Cartoon Network; CNBC; CNN; Comcast Sports Net Southeast; Comedy Central; Cooking Channel; Country Music TV; C-SPAN; C-SPAN 2; Discovery Channel; Disney Channel; Do-It-Yourself; E! Entertainment Television; ESPN; ESPN 2; FitTV; Food Network; Fox News Channel; FX; Great American Country; Hallmark Channel; Headline News; HGTV; History Channel; INSP; Lifetime; MSNBC; MTV; National Geographic Channel; Nickelodeon; Outdoor Channel; SoapNet; Spike TV; SportSouth; Syfy; TBS Superstation; The Learning Channel; Travel Channel; Trinity Broadcasting Network; truTV; Turner Network TV; TV Land; USA Network; Versus; VH1; WE tv; Weather Channel.
Fee: $33.00 monthly.

Digital Basic Service
Subscribers: N.A.
Programming (received off-air): WCBI-TV (CBS, CW, MNT) Columbus; WLMT (CW) Memphis; WLOV-TV (FOX) West Point; WMC-TV (NBC) Memphis; WPTY-TV (ABC) Memphis.
Programming (via satellite): AmericanLife TV Network; BBC America; Bio; Bloomberg Television; Discovery Digital Networks; Discovery HD Theater; DMX Music; ESPN 2 HD; ESPN Classic Sports; ESPN HD; ESPNews; Fox Movie Channel; Fox Soccer; Fuse; G4; GAS; Golf Channel; GSN; Halogen Network; History Channel International; Independent Film Channel; Lifetime Movie Network; MTV Networks Digital Suite; NFL Network; Nick Jr.; NickToons TV; Outdoor Channel; Sleuth; Speed Channel; Style Network; Toon Disney; Turner Classic Movies; Turner Network TV HD; Universal HD.
Fee: $10.00 monthly.

Pay Service 1
Pay Units: 409.
Programming (via satellite): HBO.
Fee: $9.95 monthly.

Digital Pay Service 1
Pay Units: N.A.
Programming (via satellite): Cinemax (multiplexed); Cinemax HD; Encore (multiplexed); Flix; HBO (multiplexed); HBO HD; Showtime (multiplexed); Starz (multiplexed); Sundance Channel; The Movie Channel (multiplexed).
Fee: $6.00 monthly (Encore), $13.00 monthly (HBO, Cinemax, Showtime/TMC or Starz).

Video-On-Demand: Yes

Pay-Per-View
iN DEMAND (delivered digitally); ESPN (delivered digitally); Fresh (delivered digitally); Playboy TV (delivered digitally).

Internet Service
Operational: Yes.
Broadband Service: MetroCast Internet.
Fee: $79.99 installation; $43.95 monthly.

Telephone Service
Digital: Operational
Fee: $24.95 installation; $29.95 monthly

Miles of Plant: 75.0 (coaxial); None (fiber optic). Homes passed: 5,108.
General Manager: Rick Ferrall. Technical Operations Manager: Jerry Morris. Marketing Manager: Lee Beck.
Ownership: Harron Communications LP (MSO).

BROOKHAVEN—Cable One, 208 Hwy 51 S, Ste A, Brookhaven, MS 39601-3307. Phones: 601-833-9199; 601-833-7991. Fax: 601-833-8321. E-mail: jivey@cableone.net. Web Site: http://www.cableone.net. Also serves Fernwood, Lincoln County (portions), Magnolia, McComb, New Sight, Pike County & Summit. ICA: MS0024.
TV Market Ranking: Outside TV Markets (BROOKHAVEN, Fernwood, Lincoln County (portions), Magnolia, McComb, New Sight, Pike County, Summit). Franchise award date: April 1, 1964. Franchise expiration date: N.A. Began: April 1, 1964.
Channel capacity: 62 (operating 2-way). Channels available but not in use: N.A.

Basic Service
Subscribers: 11,841.
Programming (received off-air): WAPT (ABC) Jackson; WBRZ-TV (ABC) Baton Rouge; WDAM-TV (NBC) Laurel; WDBD (FOX) Jackson; WJTV (CBS) Jackson; WLBT (NBC) Jackson; WMAU-TV (PBS) Bude; WRBJ (CW) Magee; WUFX (MNT) Vicksburg; WWL-TV (CBS) New Orleans; allband FM.
Programming (via satellite): ABC Family Channel; AMC; Animal Planet; Arts & Entertainment; BET Networks; Bravo; Cartoon Network; CNBC; CNN; Comcast Sports Net Southeast; Comedy Central; Country Music TV; C-SPAN; C-SPAN 2; Discovery Channel; Disney Channel; ESPN; ESPN 2; Food Network; Fox News Channel; FX; Headline News; HGTV; History Channel; Home Shopping Network; Lifetime; MSNBC; MTV; Nickelodeon; QVC; Spike TV; Syfy; The Learning Channel; Travel Channel; Trinity Broadcasting Network; Turner Classic Movies; Turner Network TV; TV Guide Network; TV Land; USA Network; VH1; Weather Channel; WGN America; WPCH-TV (IND) Atlanta.
Current originations: Leased Access.
Fee: $25.00 installation; $46.00 monthly; $15.00 additional installation.

Digital Basic Service
Subscribers: N.A.
Programming (received off-air): WAPT (ABC) Jackson; WDBD (FOX) Jackson; WJTV (CBS) Jackson; WLBT (NBC) Jackson; WMAU-TV (PBS) Bude; WUFX (MNT) Vicksburg.
Programming (via satellite): 3 Angels Broadcasting Network; Bio; Boomerang; BYU Television; Canales N; Discovery Digital Networks; DMX Music; ESPN Classic Sports; ESPNews; FamilyNet; Fox College Sports Atlantic; Fox College Sports Central; Fox College Sports Pacific; Fox Movie Channel; Fox Soccer; Fuel TV; G4; Golf Channel; Great American Country (multiplexed); Hallmark Channel; History Channel International; INSP; National Geographic Channel; Outdoor Channel; SoapNet; Speed Channel; Toon Disney; Trinity Broadcasting Network; truTV; Turner Network TV HD; TVG Network; Universal HD.
Fee: $5.95 monthly.

Digital Pay Service 1
Pay Units: 3,730.
Programming (via satellite): Cinemax (multiplexed); Encore (multiplexed); Flix; HBO (multiplexed); Showtime (multiplexed); Showtime HD; Starz; Sundance Channel; The Movie Channel (multiplexed); The Movie Channel HD.
Fee: $15.00 monthly (each package).

Video-On-Demand: No

Pay-Per-View
iN DEMAND (delivered digitally); Pleasure (delivered digitally); Ten Clips (delivered digitally); Ten Blox (delivered digitally); Ten Blue (delivered digitally).

Internet Service
Operational: Yes.
Subscribers: 1,800.
Broadband Service: CableONE.net.
Fee: $75.00 installation; $43.00 monthly.

Telephone Service
Digital: Operational
Fee: $75.00 installation; $39.95 monthly

Miles of Plant: 317.0 (coaxial); 6.0 (fiber optic). Additional miles planned: 10.0 (coaxial). Homes passed: 14,322.
General Manager: Bobby McCool. Marketing Director: Jullia Ivey. Technical Operations Manager: John Hilbert.
City fee: 3% of gross.
Ownership: Cable One Inc. (MSO).

BRUCE—MetroCast Communications, 311 Heritage Dr, Oxford, MS 38852. Phones: 662-234-4711; 662-728-8111. Fax: 662-236-3593. Web Site: http://www.metrocastcommunications.com. Also serves Pittsboro. ICA: MS0075.
TV Market Ranking: Below 100 (BRUCE, Pittsboro). Franchise award date: January 7, 1962. Franchise expiration date: N.A. Began: January 1, 1962.
Channel capacity: N.A. Channels available but not in use: N.A.

Basic Service
Subscribers: 775.
Programming (received off-air): W15CG Pontotoc; WCBI-TV (CBS, CW, MNT) Columbus; WHBQ-TV (FOX) Memphis; WLOV-TV (FOX) West Point; WMAV-TV (PBS) Oxford; WMC-TV (NBC) Memphis; WPTY-TV (ABC) Memphis; WREG-TV (CBS) Memphis; WTVA (NBC) Tupelo.
Programming (via satellite): WGN America.
Fee: $49.95 installation; $17.95 monthly.

Expanded Basic Service 1
Subscribers: N.A.
Programming (via satellite): ABC Family Channel; AMC; Animal Planet; Arts & Entertainment; BET Networks; Bravo; Cartoon Network; CNBC; CNN; Comcast Sports Net Southeast; Comedy Central; Country Music TV; C-SPAN; C-SPAN 2; Discovery Channel; Disney Channel; E! Entertainment Television; ESPN; ESPN 2; ESPN Classic Sports; FitTV; Food Network; Fox News Channel; FX; Golf Channel; Great American Country; Hallmark Channel; Headline News; HGTV; History Channel; Home Shopping Network; INSP; ION Television; Lifetime; MSNBC; MTV; Nickelodeon; Outdoor Channel; QVC; Speed Channel; Spike TV; Syfy; TBS Superstation; The Learning Channel; Travel Channel; Trinity Broadcasting Network; Turner Network TV; Turner South; TV Land; USA Network; VH1; WE tv; Weather Channel.
Fee: $29.20 installation; $33.00 monthly.

Digital Basic Service
Subscribers: N.A.
Programming (received off-air): WCBI-TV (CBS, CW, MNT) Columbus; WLMT (CW) Memphis; WMC-TV (NBC) Memphis; WPTY-TV (ABC) Memphis.
Programming (via satellite): AmericanLife TV Network; BBC America; Bio; Bloomberg Television; Discovery Digital Networks; Discovery HD Theater; DMX Music; ESPN Classic Sports; ESPNews; Fox Movie Channel; Fox Soccer; Fuse; G4; Golf Channel; GSN; Halogen Network; History Channel International; Independent Film Channel; Lifetime Movie Network; Lime; MTV Networks Digital Suite; National Geographic Channel; NFL Network; Nick Jr.; Outdoor Channel; Sleuth; Speed Channel; Style Network; Toon Disney; Turner Classic Movies; Turner Network TV HD; Universal HD; Versus.
Fee: $10.00 monthly.

Digital Pay Service 1
Pay Units: N.A.
Programming (via satellite): Cinemax (multiplexed); Encore (multiplexed); Flix; HBO (multiplexed); Showtime (multiplexed); Starz (multiplexed); Sundance Channel; The Movie Channel (multiplexed).

Video-On-Demand: No

Pay-Per-View
iN DEMAND (delivered digitally); Fresh (delivered digitally); Hot Choice (delivered digitally); Playboy TV (delivered digitally); ESPN (delivered digitally); MLB Extra Innings (delivered digitally).

Internet Service
Operational: Yes.
Broadband Service: MetroCast Internet.
Fee: $79.99 installation; $43.95 monthly.

Telephone Service
Digital: Operational
Fee: $24.95 installation; $29.95 monthly

Miles of Plant: 38.0 (coaxial); None (fiber optic). Homes passed: 1,400. Total homes in franchised area: 1,400.
General Manager: Rick Ferrall. Technical Operations Manager: Jerry Morris. Marketing Manager: Lee Beck.
Ownership: Harron Communications LP (MSO).

BUDE—Franklin Telephone Co. Inc. SnapVision. Formerly [MS0069]. This cable system has converted to IPTV, PO Box 168, 304 Main St, New Augusta, MS 39462. Phones: 800-531-0427; 601-964-8311. Web Site: http://www.ftcweb.net. ICA: MS5016.

TV Market Ranking: Below 100 (BUDE).
Channel capacity: N.A. Channels available but not in use: N.A.

Internet Service
Operational: Yes.

Telephone Service
Digital: Operational
Ownership: Delta Telephone.

BURNSVILLE—Formerly served by Almega Cable. No longer in operation. ICA: MS0099.

CALHOUN CITY—MetroCast Communications, 311 Heritage Dr, Oxford, MS 38852. Phones: 662-234-4711; 662-728-8111. Fax: 662-236-3593. Web Site: http://www.metrocastcommunications.com. Also serves Calhoun County, Derma & Vardaman. ICA: MS0025.
TV Market Ranking: Below 100 (CALHOUN CITY, Derma, Vardaman); Outside TV Markets (Calhoun County). Franchise award date: April 6, 1965. Franchise expiration date: N.A. Began: August 1, 1965.
Channel capacity: N.A. Channels available but not in use: N.A.

Basic Service
Subscribers: 957.
Programming (received off-air): W15CG Pontotoc; WCBI-TV (CBS, CW, MNT) Columbus; WHBQ-TV (FOX) Memphis; WKDH (ABC) Houston; WLOV-TV (FOX) West Point; WMAV-TV (PBS) Oxford; WMC-TV (NBC) Memphis; WPTY-TV (ABC) Memphis; WREG-TV (CBS) Memphis; WTVA (NBC) Tupelo; 16 FMs.
Programming (via satellite): WGN America.
Current originations: Public Access.
Fee: $49.95 installation; $17.95 monthly.

Expanded Basic Service 1
Subscribers: N.A.
Programming (via satellite): ABC Family Channel; AMC; Animal Planet; Arts & Entertainment; BET Networks; Bravo; Cartoon Network; CNBC; CNN; Comcast Sports Net Southeast; Comedy Central; Country Music TV; C-SPAN; C-SPAN 2; Discovery Channel; Disney Channel; E! Entertainment Television; ESPN; ESPN 2; ESPN Classic Sports; FitTV; Food Network; Fox News Channel; FX; Golf Channel; Great American Country; Hallmark Channel; Headline News; HGTV; History Channel; Home Shopping Network; INSP; ION Television; Lifetime; MSNBC; MTV; Nickelodeon; Outdoor Channel; QVC; Speed Channel; Spike TV; Syfy; TBS Superstation; The Learning Channel; Travel Channel; Trinity Broadcasting Network; Turner Network TV; Turner South; TV Land; USA Network; VH1; WE tv; Weather Channel.
Fee: $33.00 monthly.

Digital Basic Service
Subscribers: N.A.
Programming (received off-air): WCBI-TV (CBS, CW, MNT) Columbus; WLMT (CW) Memphis; WMC-TV (NBC) Memphis; WPTY-TV (ABC) Memphis.
Programming (via satellite): AmericanLife TV Network; BBC America; Bio; Bloomberg Television; Discovery Digital Networks; Discovery HD Theater; DMX Music; ESPN Classic Sports; ESPNews; Fox Movie Channel; Fox Soccer; Fuse; G4; GAS; Golf Channel; GSN; Halogen Network; History Channel International; Independent Film Channel; Lifetime Movie Network; Lime; MTV Networks Digital Suite; National Geographic Channel; NFL Network; Nick Jr.; NickToons TV; Outdoor Channel; Sleuth; Speed Channel; Style Network; Toon Disney; Turner Classic Movies; Turner Network TV HD; Universal HD; Versus.
Fee: $10.00 monthly.

Digital Pay Service 1
Pay Units: N.A.
Programming (via satellite): Cinemax (multiplexed); Encore (multiplexed); Flix; HBO (multiplexed); Showtime (multiplexed); Starz (multiplexed); Sundance Channel.

Video-On-Demand: Yes

Pay-Per-View
iN DEMAND (delivered digitally); Fresh (delivered digitally); Hot Choice (delivered digitally); Playboy TV (delivered digitally); MLB Extra Innings (delivered digitally).

Internet Service
Operational: Yes.
Broadband Service: MetroCast Internet.
Fee: $79.99 installation; $43.95 monthly.

Telephone Service
Digital: Operational
Miles of Plant: 45.0 (coaxial); None (fiber optic). Homes passed: 1,739.
General Manager: Rick Ferrall. Technical Operations Manager: Jerry Morris. Marketing Manager: Lee Beck.
City fee: 3% of gross.
Ownership: Harron Communications LP (MSO).

CANTON—Comcast Cable, 5375 Executive Pl, Jackson, MS 39206. Phone: 601-982-1187. Fax: 601-321-3888. Web Site: http://www.comcast.com. Also serves Madison County. ICA: MS0026.
TV Market Ranking: 77 (CANTON, Madison County (portions)); Outside TV Markets (Madison County (portions)). Franchise award date: N.A. Franchise expiration date: N.A. Began: August 1, 1977.
Channel capacity: 61 (operating 2-way). Channels available but not in use: 11.

Basic Service
Subscribers: 2,892.
Programming (received off-air): WAPT (ABC) Jackson; WDBD (FOX) Jackson; WJTV (CBS) Jackson; WLBT (NBC) Jackson; WMPN-TV (PBS) Jackson; WRBJ (CW) Magee; WUFX (MNT) Vicksburg; 2 FMs.
Programming (via satellite): C-SPAN; C-SPAN 2; QVC; TV Guide Network; WGN America.
Current originations: Government Access; Educational Access; Public Access; Leased Access.
Fee: $14.42 monthly.

Expanded Basic Service 1
Subscribers: N.A.
Programming (received off-air): WXMS-LP Natchez.
Programming (via satellite): ABC Family Channel; AMC; Animal Planet; Arts & Entertainment; BET Networks; Bravo; Cartoon Network; CNBC; CNN; Comcast Sports Net Southeast; Comedy Central; Country Music TV; Discovery Channel; Discovery Health Channel; Disney Channel; E! Entertainment Television; ESPN; ESPN 2; ESPN Classic Sports; ESPNews; FamilyNet; Food Network; Fox News Channel; FX; Hallmark Channel; Headline News; HGTV; History Channel; INSP; ION Television; Lifetime; MSNBC; MTV; Nickelodeon; ShopNBC; SoapNet; Spike TV; Syfy; TBS Superstation; The Learning Channel; Toon Disney; Travel Channel; Trinity Broadcasting Network; truTV; Turner Network TV; Turner South; TV Land; USA Network; VH1; WE tv; Weather Channel.
Fee: $31.56 monthly.

Digital Basic Service
Subscribers: N.A.
Programming (received off-air): WAPT (ABC) Jackson; WJTV (CBS) Jackson; WMPN-TV (PBS) Jackson.
Programming (via satellite): BBC America; Discovery HD Theater; Discovery Kids Channel; Discovery Military Channel; Discovery Planet Green; ESPN HD; HDNet; HDNet Movies; ID Investigation Discovery; Lifetime Movie Network; MTV Networks Digital Suite; Music Choice; NFL Network; Nick Jr.; Nick Too; NickToons TV; Science Channel; Speed Channel; TeenNick; Universal HD.
Fee: $12.95 monthly.

Pay Service 1
Pay Units: 1,351.
Programming (via satellite): HBO.
Fee: $14.95 monthly.

Digital Pay Service 1
Pay Units: N.A.
Programming (via satellite): Cinemax (multiplexed); Cinemax HD; Encore (multiplexed); HBO (multiplexed); HBO HD; Showtime (multiplexed); Showtime HD; Starz (multiplexed); The Movie Channel (multiplexed).
Fee: $11.95 monthly (each).

Video-On-Demand: No

Internet Service
Operational: Yes.
Broadband Service: Comcast High Speed Internet.
Fee: $42.95 monthly.

Telephone Service
Digital: Operational
Miles of Plant: 64.0 (coaxial); None (fiber optic). Homes passed: 5,774.
Vice President & General Manager: Ronnie Colvin. Engineering Director: Sandy McKnight. Marketing Director: Wesley Dowling. Public Affairs Director: Frances Smith.
Ownership: Comcast Cable Communications Inc. (MSO).

CARRIERRE—Charter Communications. Now served by PICAYUNE, MS [MS0023]. ICA: MS0135.

CARTHAGE—MetroCast Communications, PO Box 669, 625-A E Main St, Philadelphia, MS 39350. Phone: 601-656-5050. Fax: 601-656-3223. Web Site: http://www.metrocastcommunications.com. ICA: MS0054.
TV Market Ranking: Outside TV Markets (CARTHAGE). Franchise award date: March 1, 1978. Franchise expiration date: N.A. Began: November 1, 1979.
Channel capacity: 54 (not 2-way capable). Channels available but not in use: None.

Basic Service
Subscribers: 950.
Programming (received off-air): WAPT (ABC) Jackson; WDBD (FOX) Jackson; WJTV (CBS) Jackson; WLBT (NBC) Jackson; WMPN-TV (PBS) Jackson; WTVA (NBC) Tupelo.
Programming (via satellite): C-SPAN; Hallmark Channel; QVC; Trinity Broadcasting Network; WGN America.
Fee: $55.00 installation; $20.99 monthly.

Expanded Basic Service 1
Subscribers: N.A.
Programming (via satellite): Animal Planet; Arts & Entertainment; BET Networks; Cartoon Network; CNBC; CNN; Comcast Sports Net Southeast; Discovery Channel; ESPN; ESPN 2; Food Network; Fox Movie Channel; Fox News Channel; FX; Great American Country; Headline News; HGTV; History Channel; Lifetime; National Geographic Channel; Nickelodeon; Outdoor Channel; Spike TV; Syfy; TBS Superstation; The Learning Channel; Travel Channel; Turner Classic Movies; Turner Network TV; TV Land; USA Network; VH1; Weather Channel.
Fee: $31.00 monthly.

Digital Basic Service
Subscribers: N.A.
Programming (via satellite): BBC America; Discovery Health Channel; Discovery Home Channel; Discovery Kids Channel; Discovery Military Channel; Discovery Times Channel; DMX Music; ESPNews; FitTV; Fox Soccer; G4; Golf Channel; Lifetime Movie Network; Science Channel; Speed Channel; WE tv.
Fee: $5.95 monthly.

Pay Service 1
Pay Units: 123.
Programming (via satellite): Cinemax; HBO.

Digital Pay Service 1
Pay Units: N.A.
Programming (via satellite): Cinemax (multiplexed); Encore (multiplexed); Flix; HBO (multiplexed); Showtime (multiplexed); Starz (multiplexed); The Movie Channel (multiplexed).
Fee: $10.00 monthly (each).

Video-On-Demand: No

Pay-Per-View
iN DEMAND (delivered digitally); Hot Choice (delivered digitally); Playboy TV (delivered digitally); Fresh (delivered digitally).

Internet Service
Operational: Yes.
Broadband Service: MetroCast Internet.
Fee: $79.99 installation; $35.99 monthly.

Telephone Service
None
Miles of Plant: 26.0 (coaxial); None (fiber optic). Homes passed: 1,510. Total homes in franchised area: 3,500.
General Manager: Rick Ferrall. Chief Technician: Stan Burt. Marketing Manager: Lee Beck. Office Manager: Martha Duvall.
Ownership: Harron Communications LP (MSO).

CARY—Formerly served by J & L Cable. No longer in operation. ICA: MS0110.

CENTREVILLE—Trust Cable, PO Box 16512, 15 Northtown Dr, Ste L, Jackson, MS 39236. Phone: 601-957-7979. Fax: 601-977-7736. Web Site: http://www.trustcable.com. Also serves Gloster, Liberty & Woodville. ICA: MS0048.

TV Market Ranking: Below 100 (Gloster, Woodville); Outside TV Markets (CENTREVILLE, Liberty). Franchise award date: N.A. Franchise expiration date: N.A. Began: February 1, 1982.

Channel capacity: N.A. Channels available but not in use: N.A.

Basic Service

Subscribers: 1,025.

Programming (received off-air): WAFB (CBS) Baton Rouge; WBRZ-TV (ABC) Baton Rouge; WGMB-TV (FOX) Baton Rouge; WJTV (CBS) Jackson; WLBT (NBC) Jackson; WMAU-TV (PBS) Bude; WVLA-TV (NBC) Baton Rouge.

Programming (via satellite): ABC Family Channel; AMC; Animal Planet; Arts & Entertainment; BET Networks; Cartoon Network; CNN; Comedy Central; Country Music TV; C-SPAN; Discovery Channel; ESPN; ESPN 2; ESPN Classic Sports; Food Network; Fox News Channel; Fox Sports Net; Great American Country; Hallmark Channel; Hallmark Movie Channel; Headline News; HGTV; History Channel; Home Shopping Network; INSP; Lifetime; Lifetime Movie Network; MSNBC; Nickelodeon; Outdoor Channel; QVC; RFD-TV; Speed Channel; Spike TV; SportSouth; Syfy; TBS Superstation; The Learning Channel; The Sportsman Channel; Travel Channel; Trinity Broadcasting Network; Turner Classic Movies; Turner Network TV; TV Land; USA Network; VH1; Weather Channel; WGN America.

Fee: $14.95 installation; $39.98 monthly.

Pay Service 1

Pay Units: 285.

Programming (via satellite): Cinemax; HBO (multiplexed).

Fee: $19.95 monthly.

Video-On-Demand: No

Internet Service

Operational: Yes.

Subscribers: 100.

Broadband Service: In-house.

Fee: $29.99 installation; $29.99 monthly; $6.95 modem lease; $69.95 modem purchase.

Telephone Service

None

Miles of Plant: 43.0 (coaxial); None (fiber optic). Homes passed: 1,805.

President: Steven Inzinna.

Ownership: Trust Communications (MSO).

CHARLESTON—Cable One. Now served by WINONA, MS [MS0014]. ICA: MS0053.

CHUNKY—Galaxy Cablevision, PO Box 308, 214 Main St, Ste C, Monticello, MS 39654-0308. Phone: 601-587-9461. Fax: 601-587-7410. Web Site: http://www.galaxycable.com. Also serves Hickory & Newton County (portions). ICA: MS0136.

TV Market Ranking: Below 100 (CHUNKY, Hickory, Newton County (portions)). Franchise award date: N.A. Franchise expiration date: N.A. Began: N.A.

Channel capacity: 41 (operating 2-way). Channels available but not in use: 4.

Basic Service

Subscribers: 87.

Programming (received off-air): WAPT (ABC) Jackson; WDAM-TV (NBC) Laurel; WDBD (FOX) Jackson; WJTV (CBS) Jackson; WLBT (NBC) Jackson; WMPN-TV (PBS) Jackson.

Programming (via satellite): ABC Family Channel; AMC; Arts & Entertainment; BET Networks; Cartoon Network; CNBC; CNN; Comcast Sports Net Southeast; Comedy Central; Discovery Channel; Disney Channel; E! Entertainment Television; ESPN; ESPN 2; Fox News Channel; FX; Great American Country; Hallmark Channel; Headline News; HGTV; History Channel; INSP; Lifetime; Outdoor Channel; QVC; Speed Channel; TBS Superstation; The Learning Channel; Trinity Broadcasting Network; Turner Network TV; USA Network; Weather Channel; WGN America.

Fee: $25.00 installation; $40.60 monthly.

Pay Service 1

Pay Units: 43.

Programming (via satellite): HBO; Showtime.

Fee: $25.00 installation; $11.00 monthly.

Pay-Per-View

Hot Choice (delivered digitally); Playboy TV (delivered digitally); Fresh (delivered digitally); Shorteez (delivered digitally).

Internet Service

Operational: No.

Telephone Service

None

Miles of Plant: 18.0 (coaxial); None (fiber optic). Homes passed: 435.

State Manager: Bill Flowers. Technical Manager & Engineer: Greg Berthaut. Customer Service Representative: Rebecca Nelson.; Parlean Myers.

Ownership: Galaxy Cable Inc. (MSO).

CLARKSDALE—Cable One, PO Box 1195, 119 Court St, Clarksdale, MS 38614. Phone: 662-627-4747. Fax: 662-627-2600. E-mail: sstevenson@cableone.net. Web Site: http://www.cableone.net. Also serves Coahoma County, Duncan & Lyon. ICA: MS0017.

TV Market Ranking: Outside TV Markets (CLARKSDALE, Coahoma County, Duncan, Lyon). Franchise award date: May 7, 1957. Franchise expiration date: N.A. Began: April 1, 1958.

Channel capacity: 72 (operating 2-way). Channels available but not in use: 7.

Basic Service

Subscribers: 6,500.

Programming (received off-air): KATV (ABC) Little Rock; WABG-TV (ABC) Greenwood; WHBQ-TV (FOX) Memphis; WKNO (PBS) Memphis; WLMT (CW) Memphis; WMC-TV (NBC) Memphis; WMPN-TV (PBS) Jackson; WPTY-TV (ABC) Memphis; WREG-TV (CBS) Memphis; WTVA (NBC) Tupelo; WXVT (CBS) Greenville; 6 FMs.

Programming (via satellite): ABC Family Channel; AMC; America One Television; Animal Planet; Arts & Entertainment; BET Networks; Cartoon Network; CNBC; CNN; Comcast Sports Net Southeast; Comedy Central; Country Music TV; C-SPAN; Discovery Channel; Disney Channel; ESPN; ESPN 2; Food Network; Fox News Channel; FX; Headline News; HGTV; History Channel; Home Shopping Network; INSP; Lifetime; MSNBC; MTV; Nickelodeon; QVC; Spike TV; Syfy; The Learning Channel; Turner Classic Movies; Turner Network TV; TV Guide Network; TV Land; USA Network; VH1; Weather Channel; WGN America.

Current originations: Educational Access; Public Access.

Fee: $46.00 monthly.

Digital Basic Service

Subscribers: 2,515.

Programming (received off-air): KATV (ABC) Little Rock.

Programming (via satellite): 3 Angels Broadcasting Network; Bio; Boomerang; BYU Television; Canales N; Discovery Digital Networks; ESPN Classic Sports; ESPN HD; FamilyNet; Fox College Sports Atlantic; Fox College Sports Central; Fox College Sports Pacific; Fox Movie Channel; Fox Soccer; Fuel TV; G4; Golf Channel; Great American Country; GSN; Hallmark Channel; History Channel International; INSP; Music Choice; National Geographic Channel; Outdoor Channel; SoapNet; Speed Channel; Toon Disney; Trinity Broadcasting Network; truTV; Turner Network TV HD; TVG Network; Universal HD; WE tv.

Fee: $9.95 monthly.

Digital Pay Service 1

Pay Units: N.A.

Programming (via satellite): Cinemax (multiplexed); HBO (multiplexed); HBO HD; Showtime; Showtime HD; Starz In Black; Sundance Channel; The Movie Channel (multiplexed); The Movie Channel HD.

Fee: $15.00 monthly (each).

Video-On-Demand: No

Pay-Per-View

Hot Choice, Fee: $8.95; iN DEMAND, Fee: $3.95-$8.95; Playboy TV, Fee: $8.95; Movies, Fee: $3.95; iN DEMAND (delivered digitally); Adult PPV (delivered digitally); Sports PPV (delivered digitally).

Internet Service

Operational: Yes. Began: January 1, 2001.

Subscribers: 800.

Broadband Service: CableONE.net.

Fee: $75.00 installation; $43.00 monthly; $5.00 modem lease.

Telephone Service

Digital: Operational

Fee: $75.00 installation; $39.95 monthly

Miles of Plant: 110.0 (coaxial); None (fiber optic). Homes passed: 8,493. Total homes in franchised area: 8,493.

Manager: John Busby. Marketing Director: Sharon Stevenson. Chief Technician: Elvis Brown.

City fee: 2% of gross.

Ownership: Cable One Inc. (MSO).

CLEVELAND—Cable One, PO Box 1200, 221 S Sharpe Ave, Cleveland, MS 38732. Phone: 662-843-4016. Fax: 662-843-6114. E-mail: pete.peden@cableone.net. Web Site: http://www.cableone.net. Also serves Batesville, Boyle, Courtland, Drew, Grenada, Grenada County, Lambert, Marks, Merigold, Mound Bayou, Pace, Pope, Renova, Ruleville, Shaw (portions), Shelby, Symonds & Yazoo City. ICA: MS0019.

TV Market Ranking: Below 100 (Boyle, CLEVELAND, Drew, Grenada, Grenada County (portions), Pace, Renova, Ruleville, Shaw (portions), Symonds); Outside TV Markets (Batesville, Courtland, Grenada County (portions), Lambert, Marks, Merigold, Mound Bayou, Pope, Shelby, Yazoo City). Franchise award date: September 1, 1987. Franchise expiration date: N.A. Began: January 1, 1957.

Channel capacity: 77 (operating 2-way). Channels available but not in use: None.

Basic Service

Subscribers: 21,000.

Programming (received off-air): KATV (ABC) Little Rock; WABG-TV (ABC) Greenwood; WHCQ-LD (ION) Cleveland; WJTV (CBS) Jackson; WMC-TV (NBC) Memphis; WMPN-TV (PBS) Jackson; WREG-TV (CBS) Memphis; WXVT (CBS) Greenville.

Programming (via satellite): ABC Family Channel; AMC; Animal Planet; Arts & Entertainment; BET Networks; Cartoon Network; CNBC; CNN; Comcast Sports Net Southeast; Comedy Central; Country Music TV; C-SPAN; C-SPAN 2; CW+; Discovery Channel; Disney Channel; E! Entertainment Television; ESPN; ESPN 2; Food Network; Fox News Channel; FX; Headline News; HGTV; History Channel; Home Shopping Network; INSP; Lifetime; MSNBC; MTV; Nickelodeon; QVC; Spike TV; Syfy; TBS Superstation; The Learning Channel; Turner Classic Movies; Turner Network TV; TV Guide Network; TV Land; USA Network; VH1; Weather Channel.

Current originations: Educational Access.

Fee: $75.00 installation; $46.00 monthly.

Digital Basic Service

Subscribers: N.A.

Programming (received off-air): WABG-TV (ABC) Greenwood.

Programming (via satellite): 3 Angels Broadcasting Network; Bio; Boomerang; BYU Television; Canales N; Discovery Digital Networks; ESPN Classic Sports; ESPNews; FamilyNet; Fox College Sports Atlantic; Fox College Sports Central; Fox College Sports Pacific; Fox Movie Channel; Fox Soccer; Fuel TV; G4; Golf Channel; Great American Country; Hallmark Channel; History Channel International; INSP; National Geographic Channel; Outdoor Channel; SoapNet; Speed Channel; Toon Disney; Trinity Broadcasting Network; truTV; Turner Network TV HD; Universal HD.

Fee: $8.95 monthly.

Digital Pay Service 1

Pay Units: N.A.

Programming (via satellite): Cinemax (multiplexed); DMX Music; Encore (multiplexed); Flix; HBO (multiplexed); Showtime (multiplexed); Showtime HD; Starz (multiplexed); Sundance Channel; The Movie Channel (multiplexed); The Movie Channel HD.

Fee: $15.00 monthly (each).

Video-On-Demand: No

Pay-Per-View

iN DEMAND (delivered digitally); Pleasure (delivered digitally); Ten Clips (delivered digitally); Ten Blox (delivered digitally); Ten Blue (delivered digitally).

Internet Service

Operational: Yes. Began: June 1, 2002.

Subscribers: 4,900.

Broadband Service: CableONE.net.

Fee: $75.00 installation; $43.00 monthly.

Telephone Service

Digital: Operational

Fee: $75.00 installation; $39.95 monthly

Miles of Plant: 166.0 (coaxial); 60.0 (fiber optic). Homes passed: 37,000. Total homes in franchised area: 37,000.

General Manager: Pete Peden. Marketing Director: Kay Bullock. Technical Manager: Charlie Marshall.

City fee: 4% of gross.

Ownership: Cable One Inc. (MSO).

COFFEEVILLE—MetroCast Communications, 311 Heritage Dr, Oxford, MS 38852. Phones: 662-234-4711; 662-728-8111. Fax: 662-236-3593. Web Site: http://www.metrocastcommunications.com. Also serves Yalobusha County. ICA: MS0137.

TV Market Ranking: Outside TV Markets (COFFEEVILLE, Yalobusha County (portions)). Franchise award date: August 1, 1970. Franchise expiration date: N.A. Began: January 1, 1972.

Channel capacity: N.A. Channels available but not in use: N.A.

Basic Service

Subscribers: 287.

Programming (received off-air): W15CG Pontotoc; WCBI-TV (CBS, CW, MNT) Columbus; WHBQ-TV (FOX) Memphis; WLOV-TV (FOX) West Point; WMAV-TV (PBS) Oxford; WMC-TV (NBC) Mem-

phis; WPTY-TV (ABC) Memphis; WREG-TV (CBS) Memphis; WTVA (NBC) Tupelo.
Programming (via satellite): WGN America.
Current originations: Public Access.
Fee: $49.95 installation; $17.95 monthly.

Expanded Basic Service 1
Subscribers: N.A.
Programming (received off-air): WKDH (ABC) Houston.
Programming (via satellite): ABC Family Channel; AMC; Animal Planet; Arts & Entertainment; BET Networks; Bravo; Cartoon Network; CNBC; CNN; Comcast Sports Net Southeast; Comedy Central; Country Music TV; C-SPAN; C-SPAN 2; Discovery Channel; Disney Channel; E! Entertainment Television; ESPN; ESPN 2; ESPN Classic Sports; FitTV; Food Network; Fox News Channel; FX; Golf Channel; Great American Country; Hallmark Channel; Headline News; HGTV; History Channel; Home Shopping Network; INSP; ION Television; Lifetime; MSNBC; MTV; Nickelodeon; Outdoor Channel; QVC; Speed Channel; Spike TV; Syfy; TBS Superstation; The Learning Channel; Travel Channel; Trinity Broadcasting Network; Turner Network TV; Turner South; TV Land; USA Network; VH1; WE tv; Weather Channel.
Fee: $33.00 monthly.

Digital Basic Service
Subscribers: N.A.
Programming (received off-air): WCBI-TV (CBS, CW, MNT) Columbus; WLMT (CW) Memphis; WMC-TV (NBC) Memphis; WPTY-TV (ABC) Memphis.
Programming (via satellite): AmericanLife TV Network; BBC America; Bio; Bloomberg Television; Discovery Digital Networks; Discovery HD Theater; DMX Music; ESPN Classic Sports; ESPNews; Fox Movie Channel; Fox Soccer; Fuse; GAS; Golf Channel; GSN; Halogen Network; History Channel International; Independent Film Channel; Lifetime Movie Network; Lime; MTV Networks Digital Suite; National Geographic Channel; NFL Network; Nick Jr.; NickToons TV; Outdoor Channel; Sleuth; Speed Channel; Style Network; Toon Disney; Turner Classic Movies; Turner Network TV HD; Universal HD; Versus.
Fee: $10.00 monthly.

Digital Pay Service 1
Pay Units: N.A.
Programming (via satellite): Cinemax (multiplexed); Encore (multiplexed); Flix; HBO (multiplexed); Showtime (multiplexed); Starz (multiplexed); Sundance Channel; The Movie Channel (multiplexed).

Video-On-Demand: Yes

Pay-Per-View
iN DEMAND (delivered digitally); Spike TV (delivered digitally); Hot Choice (delivered digitally); Playboy TV (delivered digitally); ESPN (delivered digitally); MLB Extra Innings (delivered digitally).

Internet Service
Operational: Yes.
Fee: $79.99 installation; $43.95 monthly.

Telephone Service
Digital: Operational
Fee: $24.95 installation; $29.95 monthly
Miles of Plant: 18.0 (coaxial); None (fiber optic). Homes passed: 760.
General Manager: Rick Ferrall. Technical Operations Manager: Jerry Morris. Marketing Manager: Lee Morris.
Ownership: Harron Communications LP (MSO).

COLES POINT—Formerly served by Foster Communications Inc. No longer in operation. ICA: MS0105.

COLLINS—Collins Communications, PO Box 400, City Hall Bldg, Collins, MS 39428-0400. Phone: 601-765-4491. Fax: 601-765-0050. Also serves Covington County (portions). ICA: MS0076.
TV Market Ranking: Below 100 (COLLINS, Covington County (portions)). Franchise award date: N.A. Franchise expiration date: N.A. Began: February 1, 1982.
Channel capacity: 49 (not 2-way capable). Channels available but not in use: N.A.

Basic Service
Subscribers: 933.
Programming (received off-air): WAPT (ABC) Jackson; WDAM-TV (NBC) Laurel; WHLT (CBS) Hattiesburg; WLOX (ABC) Biloxi; WMAH-TV (PBS) Biloxi; WXXV-TV (FOX, MNT) Gulfport.
Programming (via satellite): ABC Family Channel; Animal Planet; Arts & Entertainment; BET Networks; Cartoon Network; CNBC; CNN; Comedy Central; Country Music TV; C-SPAN; Discovery Channel; Disney Channel; ESPN; ESPN 2; Food Network; Fox News Channel; Fox Sports Net; Hallmark Channel; Headline News; HGTV; History Channel; Home Shopping Network; Lifetime; MTV; Nickelodeon; Spike TV; TBS Superstation; The Learning Channel; Travel Channel; Trinity Broadcasting Network; Turner Classic Movies; Turner Network TV; USA Network; VH1; Weather Channel; WGN America.
Fee: $25.15 monthly.

Pay Service 1
Pay Units: 173.
Programming (via satellite): HBO.
Fee: $11.24 monthly.

Pay Service 2
Pay Units: 43.
Programming (via satellite): The Movie Channel.
Fee: $11.24 monthly.

Internet Service
Operational: No.

Telephone Service
None
Miles of Plant: 25.0 (coaxial); None (fiber optic). Homes passed: 1,200. Total homes in franchised area: 1,200.
Chief Technician: Bryan Russell.
City fee: 3% of gross.
Ownership: City of Collins (MSO).

COLUMBIA—Cable South Media, 301 W 1st Ave, Crossett, AR 71635. Phone: 870-305-1241. Also serves Marion County (portions). ICA: MS0036.
TV Market Ranking: Below 100 (COLUMBIA, Marion County (portions)); Outside TV Markets (Marion County (portions)). Franchise award date: N.A. Franchise expiration date: N.A. Began: March 1, 1959.
Channel capacity: N.A. Channels available but not in use: N.A.

Basic Service
Subscribers: 3,100.
Programming (received off-air): W45AA Columbia; WDAM-TV (NBC) Laurel; WHLT (CBS) Hattiesburg; WLBT (NBC) Jackson; WLOX (ABC) Biloxi; WXXV-TV (FOX, MNT) Gulfport; 1 FM.
Programming (via satellite): C-SPAN; CW+; Home Shopping Network; INSP; ION Television; QVC.
Current originations: Public Access.
Fee: $29.99 installation.

Expanded Basic Service 1
Subscribers: N.A.
Programming (via satellite): ABC Family Channel; AMC; Animal Planet; Arts & Entertainment; BET Networks; Bravo; Cartoon

For more information call **800-771-9202** or visit **www.warren-news.com**

Network; CNBC; CNN; Comcast Sports Net Southeast; Comedy Central; Country Music TV; C-SPAN 2; Discovery Channel; Disney Channel; E! Entertainment Television; ESPN; ESPN 2; Food Network; Fox News Channel; G4; Golf Channel; Hallmark Channel; Headline News; HGTV; History Channel; Lifetime; MSNBC; MTV; National Geographic Channel; Nickelodeon; Outdoor Channel; Oxygen; SoapNet; Spike TV; Syfy; TBS Superstation; The Learning Channel; Toon Disney; Travel Channel; Trinity Broadcasting Network; truTV; Turner Classic Movies; Turner Network TV; TV Land; USA Network; Versus; VH1; WE tv; Weather Channel.
Fee: $42.99 monthly.

Digital Basic Service
Subscribers: N.A.
Programming (via satellite): BBC America; Bio; Bloomberg Television; Discovery Digital Networks; Do-It-Yourself; ESPN Classic Sports; Fuse; GAS; History Channel International; Independent Film Channel; Lifetime Movie Network; MTV Networks Digital Suite; Music Choice; Nick Jr.; Nick Too; NickToons TV; Style Network; Sundance Channel; TV Guide Interactive Inc.

Digital Pay Service 1
Pay Units: N.A.
Programming (via satellite): Cinemax (multiplexed); Encore (multiplexed); Flix; HBO (multiplexed); Showtime (multiplexed); Starz (multiplexed); The Movie Channel (multiplexed).

Pay-Per-View
iN DEMAND (delivered digitally); Playboy TV (delivered digitally); Fresh (delivered digitally); Shorteez (delivered digitally).

Internet Service
Operational: Yes.

Telephone Service
Digital: Operational
Miles of Plant: 81.0 (coaxial); None (fiber optic). Homes passed: 4,304.
Ownership: Cable South Media III LLC (MSO).

COLUMBUS—Cable One, PO Box 1468, 319 College St, Columbus, MS 39703. Phone: 662-328-1781. Fax: 662-329-8484. E-mail: dlusby@cableone.net. Web Site: http://www.cableone.net. Also serves Caledonia, Columbus AFB, Hamilton, Lackey, Lowndes County, New Hope, Rural Hill & Steens. ICA: MS0138.
TV Market Ranking: Below 100 (Caledonia, COLUMBUS, Columbus AFB, Hamilton, Lackey, Lowndes County, New Hope, Rural Hill, Steens). Franchise award date: N.A. Franchise expiration date: N.A. Began: September 1, 1954.
Channel capacity: 86 (operating 2-way). Channels available but not in use: N.A.

Basic Service
Subscribers: 14,318.
Programming (received off-air): WCBI-TV (CBS, CW, MNT) Columbus; WCFT-TV (ABC) Tuscaloosa; WLOV-TV (FOX) West Point; WMAB-TV (PBS) Mississippi State; WTVA (NBC) Tupelo.
Programming (via satellite): ABC Family Channel; AMC; Animal Planet; Arts & Entertainment; BET Networks; Cartoon Network; CNBC; CNN; Comcast Sports Net Southeast; Comedy Central; Country Music TV; C-SPAN; C-SPAN 2; CTV News 1; CW+; Discovery Channel; Disney Channel; ESPN; ESPN 2; Food Network; Fox News Channel; FX; Headline News; HGTV; History Channel; Home Shopping Network; Lifetime; MSNBC; MTV; Nickelodeon; QVC; Spike TV; Syfy; TBS Superstation; The Learning Channel; Travel Channel; Turner Classic Movies; Turner Network TV; Turner South; TV Guide Network; TV Land; USA Network; VH1; Weather Channel; WGN America.
Current originations: Public Access.
Fee: $26.75 installation; $46.00 monthly.

Digital Basic Service
Subscribers: 4,996.
Programming (via satellite): 3 Angels Broadcasting Network; Bio; Boomerang; BYU Television; Discovery Digital Networks; DMX Music; ESPN Classic Sports; ESPNews; FamilyNet; Fox College Sports Atlantic; Fox College Sports Central; Fox College Sports Pacific; Fox Movie Channel; Fox Soccer; Fuel TV; G4; Golf Channel; Hallmark Channel; History Channel International; INSP; National Geographic Channel; Outdoor Channel; SoapNet; Speed Channel; Toon Disney; Trinity Broadcasting Network; truTV; Turner Network TV HD; Universal HD.
Fee: $8.95 monthly.

Digital Pay Service 1
Pay Units: N.A.
Programming (via satellite): Canales N; Cinemax (multiplexed); Encore; Flix; HBO (multiplexed); Showtime (multiplexed); Showtime HD; Starz (multiplexed); Sundance Channel; The Movie Channel (multiplexed); The Movie Channel HD.
Fee: $15.00 monthly (each package).

Video-On-Demand: No

Pay-Per-View
Movies (delivered digitally); Ten Blue (delivered digitally); Pleasure (delivered digitally); Ten Clips (delivered digitally); Ten Blox (delivered digitally).

Internet Service
Operational: Yes. Began: February 1, 2001.
Subscribers: 5,300.
Broadband Service: CableONE.net.
Fee: $75.00 installation; $43.00 monthly.

Telephone Service
Digital: Operational
Fee: $75.00 installation; $39.95 monthly
Miles of Plant: 620.0 (coaxial); None (fiber optic). Homes passed: 25,832. Total homes in franchised area: 25,832.
Manager: David Lusby. Office Manager: Peggy Chittem. Technical Operations Manager: Greg Youngblood.
Ownership: Cable One Inc. (MSO).

CORINTH—Windjammer Cable, 4400 PGA Blvd, Ste 902, Palm Beach Gardens, FL 33410. Phones: 877-450-5558; 561-775-1208. Fax: 561-775-7811. Web Site: http://www.windjammercable.com. Also serves Alcorn County, Biggersville, Glen, Kossuth,

Rienzi, Strickland & Theo, MS; Guys, McNairy County & Michie, TN. ICA: MS0016.
TV Market Ranking: Below 100 (McNairy County (portions)); Outside TV Markets (Alcorn County, Biggersville, CORINTH, Glen, Guys, Kossuth, McNairy County (portions), Michie, Rienzi, Strickland, Theo). Franchise award date: N.A. Franchise expiration date: N.A. Began: March 1, 1962.
Channel capacity: N.A. Channels available but not in use: N.A.

Basic Service
Subscribers: N.A. Included in Greenwood
Programming (received off-air): WBBJ-TV (ABC) Jackson; WCBI-TV (CBS, CW, MNT) Columbus; WHBQ-TV (FOX) Memphis; WKDH (ABC) Houston; WKNO (PBS) Memphis; WLMT (CW) Memphis; WLOV-TV (FOX) West Point; WMAE-TV (PBS) Booneville; WMC-TV (NBC) Memphis; WPTY-TV (ABC) Memphis; WREG-TV (CBS) Memphis; WTVA (NBC) Tupelo.
Programming (via satellite): Comcast/Charter Sports Southeast (CSS); ION Television; QVC; WGN America.
Current originations: Religious Access; Public Access.
Fee: $39.95 installation; $42.87 monthly; $.95 converter.

Expanded Basic Service 1
Subscribers: N.A.
Programming (via satellite): ABC Family Channel; AMC; Animal Planet; Arts & Entertainment; BET Networks; Cartoon Network; CNBC; CNN; Comcast Sports Net Southeast; Country Music TV; C-SPAN; C-SPAN 2; Discovery Channel; Discovery Health Channel; Disney Channel; E! Entertainment Television; ESPN; ESPN 2; Food Network; Fox News Channel; FX; Golf Channel; GSN; Headline News; HGTV; History Channel; Home Shopping Network; INSP; Lifetime; MTV; Nickelodeon; Outdoor Channel; Speed Channel; Spike TV; Style Network; TBS Superstation; The Learning Channel; Trinity Broadcasting Network; Turner Classic Movies; Turner Network TV; TV Guide Network; TV Land; USA Network; Versus; VH1; Weather Channel.
Fee: $10.01 monthly.

Pay Service 1
Pay Units: 2,384.
Programming (via satellite): Cinemax; HBO.
Fee: $30.00 installation; $10.00 monthly (each).

Video-On-Demand: No

Pay-Per-View
Hot Choice (delivered digitally); Playboy TV (delivered digitally); Fresh (delivered digitally); Shorteez (delivered digitally); Pleasure (delivered digitally); iN DEMAND (delivered digitally).

Internet Service
Operational: No.

Telephone Service
None

Miles of Plant: 178.0 (coaxial); None (fiber optic). Homes passed included in Greenwood
General Manager: Timothy Evard. Operations Director: Belinda Graham. Engineering Director: Mike Earehart. Finance & Accounting Director: Cindy Johnson.
City fee: 3% of gross.
Ownership: Windjammer Communications LLC (MSO).

CRAWFORD—Cable TV Inc., PO Box 2598, 612 Hwy 82 W, Starkville, MS 39760. Phone: 662-324-5121. Fax: 662-324-0233. ICA: MS0216.
TV Market Ranking: Below 100 (CRAWFORD).
Channel capacity: N.A. Channels available but not in use: N.A.

Basic Service
Subscribers: 86.
Fee: $70.00 installation; $28.95 monthly.

Pay Service 1
Pay Units: 33.
Programming (via satellite): HBO.
Fee: $9.21 monthly.

Pay Service 2
Pay Units: 30.
Programming (via satellite): Showtime.
Fee: $9.21 monthly.

Internet Service
Operational: No.

Telephone Service
None

General Manager: Andy Williams.
Ownership: Andy Williams (MSO).

CROSBY—Franklin Telephone Co. Inc. SnapVision. Formerly served by MEADVILLE-BUDE, MS [MS0069]. This cable system has converted to IPTV, PO Box 168, 304 Main St, New Augusta, MS 39462. Phones: 800-531-0427; 601-964-8311. Web Site: http://www.ftcweb.net. ICA: MS5022.
TV Market Ranking: Below 100 (CROSBY).
Channel capacity: N.A. Channels available but not in use: N.A.

Internet Service
Operational: Yes.

Telephone Service
Digital: Operational

Ownership: Delta Telephone.

CROSBY—Telepex. No longer in operation. ICA: MS0141.

CROWDER—Alliance Communications, PO Box 960, 290 S Broadview St, Greenbrier, AR 72058-9616. Phone: 501-679-6619. Fax: 501-679-5694. Web Site: http://www.alliancecable.net. ICA: MS0109.
TV Market Ranking: Outside TV Markets (CROWDER). Franchise award date: N.A. Franchise expiration date: N.A. Began: December 1, 1984.
Channel capacity: 85 (not 2-way capable). Channels available but not in use: 49.

Basic Service
Subscribers: 79.
Programming (received off-air): WABG-TV (ABC) Greenwood; WHBQ-TV (FOX) Memphis; WMAV-TV (PBS) Oxford; WMC-TV (NBC) Memphis; WPTY-TV (ABC) Memphis; WXVT (CBS) Greenville.
Programming (via satellite): BET Networks; CNN; Discovery Channel; ESPN; TBS Superstation; Turner Network TV; USA Network; WGN America.
Fee: $25.00 installation; $29.40 monthly.

Pay Service 1
Pay Units: 16.
Programming (via satellite): Showtime.
Fee: $11.95 monthly.

Pay Service 2
Pay Units: 1.
Programming (via satellite): HBO.
Fee: $11.95 monthly.

Pay Service 3
Pay Units: N.A.
Programming (via satellite): Cinemax.
Fee: $11.95 monthly.

Pay Service 4
Pay Units: 1.
Programming (via satellite): The Movie Channel.
Fee: $11.95 monthly.

Internet Service
Operational: No.

Telephone Service
None

Miles of Plant: 5.0 (coaxial); None (fiber optic). Homes passed: 252. Total homes in franchised area: 252.
Vice President: Arl Cope. Operations Manager: Jeff Browers. Programming & Marketing Manager: James Fuller.
Ownership: Buford Media Group LLC (MSO).

CRYSTAL SPRINGS—Bailey Cable TV Inc., 807 Church St, Port Gibson, MS 39150-2413. Phone: 601-892-5249. Fax: 601-892-3015. Also serves Copiah County, Hazlehurst & Terry. ICA: MS0143.
TV Market Ranking: 77 (Copiah County (portions), CRYSTAL SPRINGS, Hazlehurst, Terry); Outside TV Markets (Copiah County (portions)). Franchise award date: N.A. Franchise expiration date: N.A. Began: N.A.
Channel capacity: 38 (not 2-way capable). Channels available but not in use: 5.

Basic Service
Subscribers: 1,200.
Programming (received off-air): WAPT (ABC) Jackson; WDBD (FOX) Jackson; WJTV (CBS) Jackson; WLBT (NBC) Jackson; WMAA (ETV) Columbus.
Programming (via satellite): ABC Family Channel; Arts & Entertainment; Cartoon Network; CNN; Country Music TV; C-SPAN; Discovery Channel; ESPN; ESPN 2; History Channel; MTV; Nickelodeon; QVC; Spike TV; Syfy; TBS Superstation; The Learning Channel; Trinity Broadcasting Network; Turner Network TV; TV Land; USA Network; VH1; Weather Channel; WGN America.
Fee: $20.00 installation; $33.62 monthly.

Pay Service 1
Pay Units: N.A.
Programming (via satellite): Showtime; The Movie Channel.
Fee: $10.08 monthly (each).

Video-On-Demand: No

Internet Service
Operational: No.

Telephone Service
None

Manager: Dwight Bailey. Chief Technician: John Portertaen.
Ownership: Bailey Cable TV Inc. (MSO).

DE KALB—Galaxy Cablevision, PO Box 308, 214 Main St, Ste C, Monticello, MS 39654-0308. Phone: 601-587-9461. Fax: 601-587-7410. Web Site: http://www.galaxycable.com. ICA: MS0144.
TV Market Ranking: Below 100 (DE KALB). Franchise award date: N.A. Franchise expiration date: N.A. Began: January 1, 1987.
Channel capacity: 36 (not 2-way capable). Channels available but not in use: 6.

Basic Service
Subscribers: 140.
Programming (received off-air): WGBC (NBC) Meridian; WMAB-TV (PBS) Mississippi State; WMDN (CBS) Meridian; WTOK-TV (ABC, CW, FOX, MNT) Meridian; WTVA (NBC) Tupelo.
Programming (via satellite): ABC Family Channel; Arts & Entertainment; BET Networks; Cartoon Network; CNN; Comcast Sports Net Southeast; Discovery Channel; Disney Channel; ESPN; Fox News Channel; Great American Country; Hallmark Channel; Headline News; HGTV; Lifetime; Outdoor Channel; QVC; SportSouth; TBS Superstation; Turner Network TV; USA Network; Weather Channel; WGN America.
Fee: $25.00 installation; $22.50 monthly.

Pay Service 1
Pay Units: 23.
Programming (via satellite): HBO.
Fee: $25.00 installation; $11.95 monthly.

Internet Service
Operational: No.

Telephone Service
None

Miles of Plant: 12.0 (coaxial); None (fiber optic). Homes passed: 525.
State Manager: Bill Flowers. Technical Manager & Engineer: Greg Berthaut.
Ownership: Galaxy Cable Inc. (MSO).

DECATUR—Mediacom. Now served by LOUISVILLE, MS [MS0038]. ICA: MS0196.

EAGLE LAKE—Delta Telephone Co. SnapVision. This cable system has converted to IPTV, PO Box 217, Louise, MS 39097. Phones: 877-433-7878; 662-836-5111. Fax: 662-836-5770. Web Site: http://www.dtcweb.net. ICA: MS5023.
TV Market Ranking: Outside TV Markets (EAGLE LAKE).
Channel capacity: N.A. Channels available but not in use: N.A.

Internet Service
Operational: Yes.

Telephone Service
Digital: Operational

Ownership: Delta Telephone.

EAGLE LAKE—Delta Telephone Co. SnapVision. This cable system has converted to IPTV. See Eagle Lake, MS [MS5023]. ICA: MS0211.

EUPORA—Cable TV Inc., PO Box 2598, 612 Hwy 82 W, Starkville, MS 39760. Phone: 662-324-5721. Fax: 662-324-5121. Also serves Webster County. ICA: MS0147.
TV Market Ranking: Below 100 (EUPORA, Webster County); Outside TV Markets (Webster County). Franchise award date: March 16, 1965. Franchise expiration date: N.A. Began: November 1, 1965.
Channel capacity: 41 (not 2-way capable). Channels available but not in use: None.

Basic Service
Subscribers: 507.
Programming (received off-air): WABG-TV (ABC) Greenwood; WCBI-TV (CBS, CW, MNT) Columbus; WKDH (ABC) Houston; WLOV-TV (FOX) West Point; WMAB-TV (PBS) Mississippi State; WTVA (NBC) Tupelo.
Programming (via satellite): ABC Family Channel; AMC; Arts & Entertainment; BET Networks; Cartoon Network; CNBC; CNN; Comcast Sports Net Southeast; C-SPAN; Discovery Channel; Disney Channel; E! Entertainment Television; ESPN; ESPN 2; Fox News Channel; Fuse; FX; Great American Country; GSN; Headline News; HGTV; History Channel; Lifetime; Outdoor Channel; QVC; Speed Channel; TBS Superstation; The Learning Channel; Toon Disney; Trinity Broadcasting Network; Turner Network TV; USA Network; Weather Channel; WGN America.
Current originations: Public Access.
Fee: $40.00 installation; $36.04 monthly.

Pay Service 1
Pay Units: 30.
Programming (via satellite): HBO.
Fee: $14.95 monthly.

Pay Service 2
Pay Units: 30.
Programming (via satellite): Showtime.
Fee: $9.95 monthly.

Internet Service
Operational: No.

Telephone Service
None
Miles of Plant: 23.0 (coaxial); None (fiber optic). Homes passed: 1,393.
General Manager: Andy Williams.
City fee: 3% of basic.
Ownership: Andy Williams (MSO).

EVERGREEN—Formerly served by SouthTel Communications LP. No longer in operation. ICA: MS0111.

FAYETTE—Formerly served by Almega Cable. No longer in operation. ICA: MS0071.

FLORA—Telepak Networks Inc., 467 First St, Flora, MS 39071-9333. Phone: 601-879-3288. Fax: 601-879-8071. ICA: MS0148.
TV Market Ranking: 77 (FLORA). Franchise award date: N.A. Franchise expiration date: N.A. Began: N.A.
Channel capacity: 69 (operating 2-way). Channels available but not in use: N.A.

Basic Service
Subscribers: 225.
Programming (received off-air): WAPT (ABC) Jackson; WDBD (FOX) Jackson; WJTV (CBS) Jackson; WLBT (NBC) Jackson; WMPN-TV (PBS) Jackson.
Programming (via satellite): ABC Family Channel; Arts & Entertainment; BET Networks; CNN; Country Music TV; C-SPAN; Discovery Channel; ESPN; Headline News; Home Shopping Network; Lifetime; MTV; Nickelodeon; QVC; Syfy; TBS Superstation; Turner Classic Movies; Turner Network TV; USA Network; VH1; WGN America.
Current originations: Public Access.
Fee: $20.00 installation; $31.00 monthly.

Pay Service 1
Pay Units: 34.
Programming (via satellite): Cinemax; HBO; Showtime.
Fee: $20.00 installation; $10.00 monthly (each).

Internet Service
Operational: Yes.
Broadband Service: In-house.
Fee: $24.00 monthly.

Telephone Service
None
Miles of Plant: 26.0 (coaxial); None (fiber optic). Additional miles planned: 6.0 (coaxial).
Manager: Terry Taylor. Chief Technician: Wayne Whitehead.
Ownership: Telepak Networks Inc.

FOREST—MetroCast Communications, PO Box 669, 625-A E Main St, Philadelphia, MS 39350. Phone: 601-656-5050. Fax: 601-656-3223. Web Site: http://www.metrocastcommunications.com. Also serves Morton & Scott County (unincorporated areas). ICA: MS0032.
TV Market Ranking: 77 (Morton, Scott County (unincorporated areas) (portions)); Outside TV Markets (FOREST, Scott County (unincorporated areas) (portions)). Franchise award date: January 1, 1969. Franchise expiration date: N.A. Began: December 1, 1970.
Channel capacity: 75 (operating 2-way). Channels available but not in use: None.

Basic Service
Subscribers: 1,720.
Programming (received off-air): WAPT (ABC) Jackson; WDBD (FOX) Jackson; WJTV (CBS) Jackson; WLBT (NBC) Jackson; WMPN-TV (PBS) Jackson; WRBJ (CW) Magee; WTOK-TV (ABC, CW, FOX, MNT) Meridian; WUFX (MNT) Vicksburg.
Programming (via satellite): QVC; Weather Channel; WGN America.
Fee: $55.00 installation; $20.99 monthly.

Expanded Basic Service 1
Subscribers: 1,700.
Programming (via satellite): Animal Planet; Arts & Entertainment; BET Networks; Cartoon Network; CNBC; CNN; Comcast Sports Net Southeast; Comedy Central; C-SPAN; Discovery Channel; ESPN; ESPN 2; Food Network; Fox Movie Channel; Fox News Channel; FX; Great American Country; Hallmark Channel; Headline News; HGTV; History Channel; Lifetime; MTV; Nickelodeon; Outdoor Channel; Spike TV; Syfy; TBS Superstation; The Learning Channel; Travel Channel; Turner Classic Movies; Turner Network TV; TV Land; USA Network; WE tv.
Fee: $30.00 installation; $31.00 monthly.

Digital Basic Service
Subscribers: 186.
Programming (via satellite): BBC America; Canal 52MX; Cine Mexicano; CNN en Espanol; Discovery en Espanol; Discovery Health Channel; Discovery Home Channel; Discovery Kids Channel; Discovery Military Channel; Discovery Times Channel; DMX Music; ESPN Deportes; ESPNews; Fox Soccer; Fox Sports en Espanol; G4; Golf Channel; History Channel en Espanol; Lifetime Movie Network; National Geographic Channel; Science Channel; Speed Channel; Trinity Broadcasting Network.
Fee: $5.95 monthly.

Pay Service 1
Pay Units: 283.
Programming (via satellite): Cinemax; HBO.
Fee: $7.00 monthly (Cinemax), $14.00 monthly (HBO).

Digital Pay Service 1
Pay Units: N.A.
Programming (via satellite): Cinemax (multiplexed); Encore (multiplexed); Flix; HBO (multiplexed); HBO Latino; Showtime (multiplexed); Starz (multiplexed); The Movie Channel (multiplexed).
Fee: $11.00 monthly (HBO, Showtime, or TMC), $14.00 monthly (Cinemax).

Video-On-Demand: No

Pay-Per-View
iN DEMAND (delivered digitally); Hot Choice (delivered digitally); Playboy TV (delivered digitally); Fresh (delivered digitally).

Internet Service
Operational: Yes.
Subscribers: 150.
Broadband Service: MetroCast Internet.
Fee: $79.99 installation; $35.99 monthly.

Telephone Service
None
Miles of Plant: 137.0 (coaxial); None (fiber optic). Homes passed: 3,380. Total homes in franchised area: 7,714.
General Manager: Rick Ferrall. Chief Technician: Stan Burt. Marketing Manager: Lee Beck. Office Manager: Martha Duvall.
City fee: 2% of basic gross.
Ownership: Harron Communications LP (MSO).

FRANKLIN CREEK—Formerly served by CableSouth Inc. No longer in operation. ICA: MS0149.

FULTON—Comcast Cable. Now served by TUPELO, MS [MS0009]. ICA: MS0033.

GLOSTER—Trust Cable. Now served by CENTREVILLE, MS [MS0048]. ICA: MS0219.

GREENVILLE—Suddenlink Communications, 318 Main St, Greenville, MS 38701. Phones: 800-999-6845 (Customer service); 662-332-0518. Web Site: http://www.suddenlink.com. Also serves Metcalfe, Swiftwater & Wayside. ICA: MS0010.
TV Market Ranking: Below 100 (GREENVILLE, Metcalfe, Swiftwater, Wayside). Franchise award date: May 4, 1954. Franchise expiration date: N.A. Began: October 1, 1954.
Channel capacity: 78 (operating 2-way). Channels available but not in use: None.

Basic Service
Subscribers: 13,139.
Programming (received off-air): KATV (ABC) Little Rock; KTVE (NBC) El Dorado; WABG-TV (ABC) Greenwood; WJTV (CBS) Jackson; WLBT (NBC) Jackson; WMAO-TV (PBS) Greenwood; WXVT (CBS) Greenville.
Programming (via satellite): C-SPAN; CW+; INSP; ION Television; TV Guide Network; Weather Channel.
Current originations: Leased Access.
Fee: $35.00 installation; $9.52 monthly.

Expanded Basic Service 1
Subscribers: N.A.
Programming (via satellite): ABC Family Channel; AMC; Arts & Entertainment; BET Networks; CNN; Comcast Sports Net Southeast; C-SPAN 2; Discovery Channel; Disney Channel; E! Entertainment Television; ESPN; Fox News Channel; Great American Country; GSN; Headline News; HGTV; Lifetime; Nickelodeon; Spike TV; The Learning Channel; Turner Network TV; TV Land; USA Network.
Fee: $17.43 monthly.

Expanded Basic Service 2
Subscribers: 720.
Programming (via satellite): Cartoon Network; CNBC; Comedy Central; ESPN 2; History Channel; MoviePlex; MTV; Syfy; Travel Channel; truTV; Turner Classic Movies; VH1.

Expanded Basic Service 3
Subscribers: N.A.
Programming (via satellite): TBS Superstation; WGN America.
Fee: $.65 monthly.

Digital Basic Service
Subscribers: N.A.
Programming (via satellite): BBC America; Bloomberg Television; Discovery Digital Networks; DMX Music; Encore Action; ESPN Classic Sports; ESPNews; Fox Movie Channel; Fox Sports World; G4; Golf Channel; Home Shopping Network; Lifetime Movie Network; MuchMusic Network; Outdoor Channel; Speed Channel; Toon Disney; Trinity Broadcasting Network; Versus; WE tv.

Pay Service 1
Pay Units: 1,275.
Programming (via satellite): Cinemax (multiplexed); Flix; HBO (multiplexed); Showtime (multiplexed); The Movie Channel (multiplexed).
Fee: $9.71 monthly (Cinemax or HBO), $11.60 monthly (Flix, Showtime or TMC).

Digital Pay Service 1
Pay Units: N.A.
Programming (via satellite): Cinemax (multiplexed); HBO (multiplexed); Showtime (multiplexed); Starz (multiplexed); The Movie Channel.

Video-On-Demand: No

Pay-Per-View
iN DEMAND (delivered digitally); Playboy TV (delivered digitally); Fresh (delivered digitally); ESPN Gameplan (delivered digitally); ESPN Now (delivered digitally); iN DEMAND.

Internet Service
Operational: Yes. Began: March 1, 2002.
Broadband Service: Cebridge High Speed Cable Internet.
Fee: $29.95 monthly.

Telephone Service
None
Miles of Plant: 233.0 (coaxial); 50.0 (fiber optic). Additional miles planned: 11.0 (coaxial). Homes passed: 18,500. Total homes in franchised area: 18,500.
Manager: John Marshall. Chief Technician: Steve Bennett.
City fee: 3% of gross.
Ownership: Cequel Communications LLC (MSO).

GREENWOOD—Windjammer Cable, 4400 PGA Blvd, Ste 902, Palm Beach Gardens, FL 33410. Phones: 877-450-5558; 561-775-1208. Fax: 561-775-7811. Web Site: http://www.windjammercable.com. Also serves Indianola, Leflore County, Moorhead, Sidon & Sunflower County. ICA: MS0151.
TV Market Ranking: Below 100 (GREENWOOD, Indianola, Leflore County, Moorhead, Sidon, Sunflower County (portions)); Outside TV Markets (Sunflower County (portions)). Franchise award date: N.A. Franchise expiration date: N.A. Began: October 1, 1955.
Channel capacity: N.A. Channels available but not in use: N.A.

Basic Service
Subscribers: 10,000 Includes Corinth & Pontotoc.
Programming (received off-air): WABG-TV (ABC) Greenwood; WJTV (CBS) Jackson; WLBT (NBC) Jackson; WMAO-TV (PBS) Greenwood; WTVA (NBC) Tupelo; WXVT (CBS) Greenville; 10 FMs.
Programming (via microwave): WMC-TV (NBC) Memphis.
Programming (via satellite): ABC Family Channel; AmericanLife TV Network; Arts & Entertainment; BET Networks; Cartoon Network; CNBC; Comedy Central; Country Music TV; C-SPAN; C-SPAN 2; CW+; Discovery Channel; E! Entertainment Television; ESPN; ESPN Classic Sports; FitTV; Food Network; FX; Golf Channel; Headline News; HGTV; History Channel; Home Shopping Network; INSP; ION Television; Lifetime; MSNBC; MTV; Nickelodeon; QVC; ShopNBC; Spike TV; Syfy; TBS Superstation; The Learning Channel; Travel Channel; Trinity Broadcasting Network; Turner Classic Movies; TV Guide Network; TV Land;

USA Network; VH1; Weather Channel; WGN America.
Current originations: Leased Access.
Fee: $29.95 installation; $45.95 monthly; $.56 converter.
Expanded Basic Service 1
Subscribers: N.A.
Programming (via satellite): AMC; Bravo; CNN; Comcast Sports Net Southeast; Disney Channel; ESPN 2; Fox News Channel; Hallmark Channel; Oxygen; Product Information Network; Style Network; Toon Disney; truTV; Turner Network TV.
Fee: $8.00 monthly.
Digital Basic Service
Subscribers: N.A.
Programming (via satellite): Animal Planet; BBC America; Bio; Bloomberg Television; Discovery Digital Networks; Discovery HD Theater; Do-It-Yourself; ESPN HD; ESPNews; Fox Movie Channel; Fox Soccer; Fuse; G4; GAS; GSN; Halogen Network; HDNet; HDNet Movies; History Channel International; Independent Film Channel; Lifetime Movie Network; LOGO; MTV Networks Digital Suite; Music Choice; National Geographic Channel; Nick Jr.; Nick Too; NickToons TV; Outdoor Channel; SoapNet; Speed Channel; Turner Network TV HD; Turner South; Universal HD; Versus; WE tv.
Fee: $58.99 monthly.
Digital Pay Service 1
Pay Units: N.A.
Programming (via satellite): Cinemax (multiplexed); Encore (multiplexed); HBO (multiplexed); HBO HD; Showtime (multiplexed); Showtime HD; Starz (multiplexed); The Movie Channel (multiplexed).
Fee: $12.00 monthly (each).
Video-On-Demand: Planned
Pay-Per-View
Playboy TV (delivered digitally); Hot Choice (delivered digitally); Fresh (delivered digitally); iN DEMAND (delivered digitally).
Internet Service
Operational: Yes.
Broadband Service: In-house.
Fee: $20.99-$49.99 installation; $44.95 monthly.
Telephone Service
Digital: Operational
Fee: $49.95 monthly
Miles of Plant: 146.0 (coaxial); None (fiber optic). Homes passed: 25,900. Homes passed includes Corinth & Pontotoc
Ownership: Windjammer Communications LLC (MSO).

GRENADA—Cable One. Now served by CLEVELAND, MS [MS0019]. ICA: MS0021.

GUNNISON—Formerly served by J & L Cable. No longer in operation. ICA: MS0108.

HATTIESBURG—Comcast Cable, 2100 Lincoln Rd, Hattiesburg, MS 39402-3114. Phone: 601-579-3960. Fax: 601-268-3956. Web Site: http://www.comcast.com. Also serves Forrest County, Heidelberg, Jasper County (unincorporated areas), Jones County (portions), Lamar County, Oak Grove, Petal, Purvis, Rawls Springs & Sandersville. ICA: MS0005.
TV Market Ranking: Below 100 (Forrest County, HATTIESBURG, Heidelberg, Jasper County (unincorporated areas), Jones County (portions), Lamar County, Oak Grove, Petal, Purvis, Rawls Springs, Sandersville). Franchise award date: N.A. Franchise expiration date: N.A. Began: January 1, 1954.
Channel capacity: N.A. Channels available but not in use: N.A.
Basic Service
Subscribers: 59,134 Includes Laurel, Meridian, & Paulding.
Programming (received off-air): WDAM-TV (NBC) Laurel; WHLT (CBS) Hattiesburg; WLOX (ABC) Biloxi; WMAH-TV (PBS) Biloxi; WXXV-TV (FOX, MNT) Gulfport.
Programming (via satellite): ABC Family Channel; AMC; Animal Planet; Arts & Entertainment; BET Networks; Bravo; Cartoon Network; CNBC; CNN; Comcast Sports Net Southeast; Comcast/Charter Sports Southeast (CSS); Comedy Central; Country Music TV; C-SPAN; C-SPAN 2; CW+; Discovery Channel; Discovery Health Channel; E! Entertainment Television; ESPN; ESPN 2; ESPN Classic Sports; Eternal Word TV Network; Food Network; Fox News Channel; FX; Golf Channel; Great American Country; GSN; Headline News; HGTV; History Channel; Home Shopping Network; INSP; ION Television; Lifetime; MSNBC; MTV; Nickelodeon; Outdoor Channel; QVC; Speed Channel; Spike TV; Style Network; Syfy; TBS Superstation; The Learning Channel; Trinity Broadcasting Network; truTV; Turner Classic Movies; Turner Network TV; TV Guide Network; TV Land; USA Network; Versus; VH1; Weather Channel; WGN America.
Current originations: Religious Access; Educational Access.
Fee: $60.00 installation; $6.15 monthly; $7.50 additional installation.
Digital Basic Service
Subscribers: 28,189 Includes Laurel, Meridian, & Paulding.
Programming (via satellite): BBC America; C-SPAN 3; Discovery Digital Networks; Disney Channel; DMX Music; ESPNews; G4; GAS; MTV Networks Digital Suite; National Geographic Channel; Nick Jr.; Nick Too; Science Television; SoapNet; Toon Disney; WAM! America's Kidz Network; Weatherscan.
Fee: $9.95 monthly.
Pay Service 1
Pay Units: 2,485.
Programming (via satellite): Cinemax; HBO; Showtime.
Fee: $14.50 monthly (each).
Digital Pay Service 1
Pay Units: N.A.
Programming (via satellite): Cinemax (multiplexed); Encore (multiplexed); HBO (multiplexed); Showtime (multiplexed); Starz (multiplexed); Sundance Channel (multiplexed); The Movie Channel (multiplexed).
Fee: $14.50 monthly (each).
Video-On-Demand: Yes
Pay-Per-View
iN DEMAND (delivered digitally); Hot Choice (delivered digitally); Playboy TV (delivered digitally); Fresh (delivered digitally); Shorteez (delivered digitally); Pleasure (delivered digitally).
Internet Service
Operational: Yes.
Subscribers: 2,153.
Broadband Service: Comcast High Speed Internet.
Fee: $42.95 monthly; $5.00 modem lease.
Telephone Service
Digital: Operational
Miles of Plant: 782.0 (coaxial); None (fiber optic). Total homes in franchised area: 47,389.
General Manager: Farrel Ryder. Operations Manager: Mike Boez. Marketing Manager: Dan Carleton.
City fee: 3% of gross.
Ownership: Comcast Cable Communications Inc. (MSO).

HAZLEHURST/TERRY—Bailey Cable TV Inc. Now served by CRYSTAL SPRINGS, MS [MS0143]. ICA: MS0153.

HICKORY FLAT—MetroCast Communications, 311 Heritage Dr, Oxford, MS 38852. Phones: 662-234-4711; 662-728-8111. Fax: 662-236-3593. Web Site: http://www.metrocastcommunications.com. ICA: MS0154.
TV Market Ranking: Below 100 (HICKORY FLAT).
Channel capacity: N.A. Channels available but not in use: N.A.
Basic Service
Subscribers: N.A.
Programming (received off-air): WBII-CD Holly Springs; WBUY-TV (TBN) Holly Springs; WCBI-TV (CBS, CW, MNT) Columbus; WHBQ-TV (FOX) Memphis; WKDH (ABC) Houston; WKNO (PBS) Memphis; WLMT (CW) Memphis; WLOV-TV (FOX) West Point; WMAE-TV (PBS) Booneville; WMC-TV (NBC) Memphis; WPTY-TV (ABC) Memphis; WPXX-TV (ION, MNT) Memphis; WREG-TV (CBS) Memphis; WTVA (NBC) Tupelo.
Programming (via microwave): W34DV Booneville.
Programming (via satellite): CW+; Home Shopping Network; MyNetworkTV Inc.; QVC; TV Guide Network; WGN.
Current originations: Educational Access; Leased Access.
Fee: $49.95 installation; $17.95 monthly.
Expanded Basic Service 1
Subscribers: N.A.
Programming (via satellite): ABC Family Channel; AMC; Animal Planet; Arts & Entertainment; BET Networks; Bravo; Cartoon Network; CNBC; CNN; Comcast/Charter Sports Southeast (CSS); Comedy Central; Country Music TV; C-SPAN; C-SPAN 2; Discovery Channel; Disney Channel; E! Entertainment Television; ESPN; ESPN 2; ESPN Classic Sports; Food Network; Fox News Channel; Fox Sports Net; FX; Golf Channel; Great American Country; Hallmark Channel; Headline News; HGTV; History Channel; INSP; ION Television; Lifetime; MSNBC; MTV; National Geographic Channel; Nickelodeon; Outdoor Channel; SoapNet; Spike TV; SportSouth; Syfy; TBS Superstation; The Learning Channel; TNT; Travel Channel; TV Land; USA Network; Versus; VH1; WE tv; Weather Channel.
Fee: $33.00 monthly.
Digital Basic Service
Subscribers: N.A.
Programming (received off-air): WCBI-TV (CBS, CW, MNT) Columbus; WLOV-TV (FOX) West Point; WMC-TV (NBC) Memphis; WPTY-TV (ABC) Memphis.
Programming (via satellite): American-Life TV Network; Animal Planet HD; Arts & Entertainment HD; BBC America; Bio; Bloomberg Television; Boomerang; Cooking Channel; Discovery Channel HD; Discovery HD Theater; Discovery Health Channel; Discovery Kids Channel; Discovery Military Channel; Discovery Planet Green; DMX Music; Do-It-Yourself; ESPN 2 HD; ESPN HD; ESPN U; ESPNews; FamilyNet; FitTV; Fox College Sports Atlantic; Fox College Sports Central; Fox College Sports Pacific; Fox Movie Channel; Fox Soccer; Fuel TV; Fuse; G4; Gospel Music TV; GSN; Hallmark Movie Channel; Halogen Network; HDNet; HDNet Movies; History Channel HD; History Channel International; ID Investigation Discovery; Independent Film Channel; Lifetime Movie Network; MTV Hits; MTV2; National Geographic Channel HD Network; NFL Network; NFL Network HD; Nick Jr.; NickToons TV; Outdoor Channel 2 HD; PBS Kids Sprout; RFD-TV; Science Channel; Sleuth; Speed Channel; Style Network; TeenNick; The Learning Channel; Toon Disney; Turner Classic Movies; Turner Network TV HD; Universal HD; VH1 Classic; VH1 Soul.
Fee: $10.00 monthly.
Digital Pay Service 1
Pay Units: N.A.
Programming (via satellite): Cinemax (multiplexed); Cinemax HD; Encore (multiplexed); Flix; HBO (multiplexed); HBO HD; Showtime (multiplexed); Starz (multiplexed); Sundance Channel; The Movie Channel (multiplexed).
Video-On-Demand: Yes
Pay-Per-View
iN DEMAND (delivered digitally); ESPN (delivered digitally); Fresh (delivered digitally); Club Jenna (delivered digitally); Playboy TV (delivered digitally).
Telephone Service
Digital: Operational
Fee: $24.95 installation; $29.95 monthly
General Manager: Rick Ferrall. Technical Operations Manager: Jerry Morris. Marketing Manager: Lee Beck.
Ownership: Harron Communications LP (MSO).

HOLLANDALE—CMA Cablevision, 101 S Deer Creek Dr W, Leland, MS 38756-3126. Phones: 972-233-9614 (Corporate office); 662-686-7823. Fax: 662-686-4100. Web Site: http://www.cmaaccess.com. ICA: MS0060.
TV Market Ranking: Below 100 (HOLLANDALE). Franchise award date: August 20, 1974. Franchise expiration date: N.A. Began: January 1, 1976.
Channel capacity: N.A. Channels available but not in use: N.A.
Basic Service
Subscribers: 625.
Programming (received off-air): WABG-TV (ABC) Greenwood; WDBD (FOX) Jackson; WJTV (CBS) Jackson; WLBT (NBC) Jackson; WMAO-TV (PBS) Greenwood; WXVT (CBS) Greenville.
Programming (via satellite): ABC Family Channel; BET Networks; CNN; ESPN; Hallmark Channel; MTV; Spike TV; TBS Superstation; Turner Classic Movies; USA Network; WGN America.
Current originations: Public Access.
Fee: $39.95 installation; $19.45 monthly; $12.95 additional installation.
Expanded Basic Service 1
Subscribers: N.A.
Programming (via satellite): Arts & Entertainment; Comcast Sports Net Southeast; Country Music TV; CW+; Discovery Channel; E! Entertainment Television; ESPN 2; Fox News Channel; Headline News; HGTV; History Channel; Home Shopping Network; Lifetime; Nickelodeon; Syfy; The Learning Channel; Trinity Broadcasting Network; Turner Network TV; TV Land; VH1; Weather Channel.
Fee: $21.00 monthly.
Pay Service 1
Pay Units: 100.
Programming (via satellite): Cinemax; HBO.
Fee: $14.95 installation; $10.95 monthly (Cinemax), $13.95 monthly (HBO).
Video-On-Demand: No

Internet Service
Operational: No.
Telephone Service
None
Miles of Plant: 17.0 (coaxial); None (fiber optic). Homes passed: 1,400. Total homes in franchised area: 1,400.
General Manager: Jerry Smith. Marketing Director: Julie Ferguson.
Ownership: Cable Management Assoc. (MSO).

HOLLY SPRINGS—MetroCast Communications, 311 Heritage Dr, Oxford, MS 38852. Phones: 662-234-4711; 662-728-8111. Fax: 662-236-3593. Web Site: http://www.metrocastcommunications.com. ICA: MS0040.
TV Market Ranking: Below 100 (HOLLY SPRINGS). Franchise award date: N.A. Franchise expiration date: N.A. Began: January 1, 1981.
Channel capacity: N.A. Channels available but not in use: N.A.
Basic Service
Subscribers: 1,367.
Programming (received off-air): W34DV Booneville; WBII-CD Holly Springs; WBUY-TV (TBN) Holly Springs; WCBI-TV (CBS, CW, MNT) Columbus; WHBQ-TV (FOX) Memphis; WKDH (ABC) Houston; WKNO (PBS) Memphis; WLMT (CW) Memphis; WLOV-TV (FOX) West Point; WMAE-TV (PBS) Booneville; WMC-TV (NBC) Memphis; WPTY-TV (ABC) Memphis; WPXX-TV (ION, MNT) Memphis; WREG-TV (CBS) Memphis; WTVA (NBC) Tupelo.
Programming (via satellite): CW+; Home Shopping Network; QVC; TV Guide Network; WGN America.
Current originations: Leased Access; Educational Access.
Fee: $49.95 installation; $17.95 monthly.
Expanded Basic Service 1
Subscribers: 1,029.
Programming (via satellite): ABC Family Channel; AMC; Animal Planet; Arts & Entertainment; BET Networks; Bravo; Cartoon Network; CNBC; CNN; Comcast Sports Net Southeast; Comedy Central; Cooking Channel; Country Music TV; C-SPAN; C-SPAN 2; Discovery Channel; Disney Channel; Do-It-Yourself; E! Entertainment Television; ESPN; ESPN 2; FitTV; Food Network; Fox News Channel; FX; G4; Golf Channel; Great American Country; Hallmark Channel; Headline News; HGTV; History Channel; INSP; ION Television; Lifetime; MSNBC; MTV; National Geographic Channel; Nickelodeon; Outdoor Channel; SoapNet; Spike TV; SportSouth; Syfy; TBS Superstation; The Learning Channel; Travel Channel; Turner Network TV; TV Land; USA Network; Versus; VH1; WE tv; Weather Channel.
Fee: $33.00 monthly.
Digital Basic Service
Subscribers: N.A.
Programming (received off-air): WCBI-TV (CBS, CW, MNT) Columbus; WLMT (CW) Memphis; WMC-TV (NBC) Memphis; WPTY-TV (ABC) Memphis.
Programming (via satellite): AmericanLife TV Network; BBC America; Bio; Bloomberg Television; Discovery Digital Networks; Discovery HD Theater; DMX Music; ESPN 2 HD; ESPN Classic Sports; ESPN HD; ESPNews; Fox Movie Channel; Fox Soccer; Fuse; GAS; GSN; Halogen Network; History Channel International; Independent Film Channel; Lifetime Movie Network; MTV Networks Digital Suite; NFL Network; Nick Jr.; NickToons TV; Sleuth; Speed Channel; Style Network; Toon Disney; Turner Classic Movies; Turner Network TV HD; Universal HD.
Fee: $10.00 monthly.
Digital Pay Service 1
Pay Units: N.A.
Programming (via satellite): Cinemax (multiplexed); Cinemax HD; Encore (multiplexed); Flix; HBO (multiplexed); HBO HD; Showtime (multiplexed); Starz (multiplexed); Sundance Channel; The Movie Channel (multiplexed).
Fee: $6.00 monthly (Encore), $13.00 monthly (HBO, Cinemax, Showtime/TMC or Starz).
Video-On-Demand: Yes; Yes
Pay-Per-View
iN DEMAND (delivered digitally); Fresh (delivered digitally); Playboy TV (delivered digitally); ESPN (delivered digitally).
Internet Service
Operational: Yes.
Broadband Service: MetroCast Internet.
Fee: $79.99 installation; $43.95 monthly; $2.00 modem lease.
Telephone Service
Digital: Operational
Fee: $24.95 installation; $29.95 monthly
Miles of Plant: 34.0 (coaxial); None (fiber optic). Homes passed: 2,578.
General Manager: Rick Ferrall. Technical Operations Manager: Jerry Morris. Marketing Manager: Lee Beck.
Ownership: Harron Communications LP (MSO).

HOUSTON—Mediacom. Now served by PONTOTOC, MS [MS0045]. ICA: MS0044.

HUMPHREYS COUNTY (portions)—Delta Telephone Inc. SnapVision. Formerly served by ISOLA-INVERNESS, MS [MS0080]. This cable system has converted to IPTV, PO Box 217, Louise, MS 39097. Phones: 877-433-7878; 662-836-5111. Fax: 662-836-5770. Web Site: http://www.dtcweb.net. ICA: MS5027.
TV Market Ranking: Below 100 (HUMPHREYS COUNTY (PORTIONS)).
Channel capacity: N.A. Channels available but not in use: N.A.
Internet Service
Operational: Yes.
Telephone Service
Digital: Operational
Ownership: Delta Telephone.

INDIANOLA—Formerly served by Adelphia Communications. Now served by GREENWOOD, MS [MS0151]. ICA: MS0155.

INVERNESS—Telepak Networks. Formerly [MS0080]. This cable system has converted to IPTV, PO Box 429, Meadville, MS 39653. Phone: 877-835-3725. Fax: 601-384-8420. E-mail: questions@telepak.net. Web Site: http://www.telepaknetworks.com. ICA: MS5007.
Channel capacity: N.A. Channels available but not in use: N.A.
Internet Service
Operational: Yes.
Ownership: Delta Telephone.

ISOLA—Delta Telephone Inc. SnapVision. Formerly [MS0080]. This cable system has converted to IPTV, PO Box 217, Louise, MS 38754. Phones: 877-433-7878; 662-836-5111. Fax: 662-836-5770. Web Site: http://www.dtcweb.net. ICA: MS5011.
Channel capacity: N.A. Channels available but not in use: N.A.

Internet Service
Operational: Yes.
Telephone Service
Digital: Operational
Ownership: Delta Telephone.

ISOLA-INVERNESS—Telepak Networks. This cable system has converted to IPTV. See Isola, MS [MS5011] and Inverness, MS [MS5007]. ICA: MS0080.

ITTA BENA—Cable One. Now served by WINONA, MS [MS0014]. ICA: MS0156.

IUKA—MetroCast Communications, 311 Heritage Dr, Oxford, MS 38852. Phones: 662-234-4711; 662-728-8111. Fax: 662-236-3593. Web Site: http://www.metrocastcommunications.com. Also serves Tishomingo County. ICA: MS0043.
TV Market Ranking: Below 100 (IUKA, Tishomingo County). Franchise award date: N.A. Franchise expiration date: N.A. Began: January 1, 1964.
Channel capacity: 116 (operating 2-way). Channels available but not in use: None.
Basic Service
Subscribers: 1,195.
Programming (received off-air): W34DV Booneville; WBBJ-TV (ABC) Jackson; WCBI-TV (CBS, CW, MNT) Columbus; WHDF (CW) Florence; WHNT-TV (CBS) Huntsville; WKDH (ABC) Houston; WLOV-TV (FOX) West Point; WMAE-TV (PBS) Booneville; WTVA (NBC) Tupelo.
Programming (via satellite): Home Shopping Network; QVC; TV Guide Network; WGN America.
Fee: $49.95 installation; $17.95 monthly.
Expanded Basic Service 1
Subscribers: N.A.
Programming (via satellite): ABC Family Channel; AMC; Animal Planet; Arts & Entertainment; BET Networks; Cartoon Network; CNBC; CNN; Comcast Sports Net Southeast; Comedy Central; Cooking Channel; Country Music TV; C-SPAN; C-SPAN 2; CW+; Discovery Channel; Disney Channel; Do-It-Yourself; E! Entertainment Television; ESPN; ESPN 2; FitTV; Food Network; Fox News Channel; FX; Great American Country; Hallmark Channel; Headline News; HGTV; History Channel; INSP; Lifetime; MSNBC; MTV; National Geographic Channel; Nickelodeon; Outdoor Channel; SoapNet; Spike TV; Syfy; TBS Superstation; The Learning Channel; Travel Channel; Trinity Broadcasting Network; truTV; Turner Network TV; Turner South; TV Land; USA Network; Versus; VH1; WE tv; Weather Channel.
Fee: $33.00 monthly.
Digital Basic Service
Subscribers: N.A.
Programming (received off-air): WCBI-TV (CBS, CW, MNT) Columbus.
Programming (via satellite): AmericanLife TV Network; BBC America; Bio; Bloomberg Television; Discovery Digital Networks; Discovery HD Theater; DMX Music; ESPN Classic Sports; ESPNews; Fox Movie Channel; Fox Soccer; Fuse; G4; GAS; Golf Channel; GSN; Halogen Network; History Channel International; Independent Film Channel; Lifetime Movie Network; Lime; MTV Networks Digital Suite; NFL Network; Nick Jr.; NickToons TV; Outdoor Channel; Sleuth; Speed Channel; Style Network; Toon Disney; Turner Classic Movies; Turner Network TV HD; Universal HD.
Fee: $10.00 monthly.
Digital Pay Service 1
Pay Units: N.A.
Programming (via satellite): Cinemax (multiplexed); Encore (multiplexed); Flix; HBO (multiplexed); Showtime (multiplexed); Starz (multiplexed); Sundance Channel; The Movie Channel (multiplexed).
Fee: $6.00 monthly (Encore), $13.00 monthly (HBO, Cinemax, Showtime/TMC, or Starz).
Video-On-Demand: Yes
Pay-Per-View
Fresh (delivered digitally); Hot Choice (delivered digitally); Playboy TV (delivered digitally); ESPN (delivered digitally); MLB Extra Innings (delivered digitally); iN DEMAND (delivered digitally).
Internet Service
Operational: Yes.
Broadband Service: MetroCast Internet.
Fee: $79.99 installation; $43.95 monthly.
Telephone Service
Digital: Operational
Fee: $24.95 installation; $29.95 monthly
Miles of Plant: 77.0 (coaxial); 18.0 (fiber optic). Homes passed: 2,526.
General Manager: Rick Ferrall. Technical Operations Manager: Jerry Morris. Marketing Manager: Lee Beck.
Ownership: Harron Communications LP (MSO).

JACKSON—Comcast Cable, 5375 Executive Pl, Jackson, MS 39206. Phone: 601-982-1187. Fax: 601-321-3888. Web Site: http://www.comcast.com. Also serves Bolton, Clinton, Edwards, Florence, Hinds County, Madison, Madison County, Rankin County, Raymond, Richland & Ridgeland. ICA: MS0001.
TV Market Ranking: 77 (Bolton, Clinton, Edwards, Florence, Hinds County, JACKSON (VILLAGE), Madison, Madison County (portions), Rankin County, Raymond, Richland, Ridgeland); Outside TV Markets (Madison County (portions)). Franchise award date: March 3, 1970. Franchise expiration date: N.A. Began: September 2, 1972.
Channel capacity: N.A. Channels available but not in use: N.A.
Basic Service
Subscribers: 75,000.
Programming (received off-air): W23BC Jackson; WAPT (ABC) Jackson; WDBD (FOX) Jackson; WJTV (CBS) Jackson; WLBT (NBC) Jackson; WMPN-TV (PBS) Jackson; WRBJ (CW) Magee; WUFX (MNT) Vicksburg; WXMS-LP Natchez.
Programming (via satellite): C-SPAN; QVC; The Comcast Network; Weather Channel; WGN America.
Current originations: Leased Access; Educational Access; Government Access.
Fee: $32.00 installation; $14.42 monthly.

Expanded Basic Service 1
Subscribers: 69,000.
Programming (via satellite): ABC Family Channel; AMC; Animal Planet; Arts & Entertainment; BET Networks; Bravo; Cartoon Network; CNBC; CNN; Comcast Sports Net Southeast; Comcast/Charter Sports Southeast (CSS); Comedy Central; Country Music TV; C-SPAN 2; Discovery Channel; Discovery Health Channel; Disney Channel; E! Entertainment Television; ESPN; ESPN 2; Food Network; Fox News Channel; FX; Golf Channel; Hallmark Channel; Headline News; HGTV; History Channel; Home Shopping Network; ION Television; Lifetime; Lifetime Movie Network; MSNBC; MTV; Nickelodeon; SoapNet; Spike TV; SportSouth; Syfy; TBS Superstation; The Learning Channel; Travel Channel; Trinity Broadcasting Network; truTV; Turner Classic Movies; Turner Network TV; TV Guide Network; TV Land; USA Network; Versus; VH1.
Fee: $31.56 monthly.

Digital Basic Service
Subscribers: N.A.
Programming (received off-air): WAPT (ABC) Jackson; WDBD (FOX) Jackson; WJTV (CBS) Jackson; WLBT (NBC) Jackson; WMPN-TV (PBS) Jackson.
Programming (via satellite): ABC Family HD; Animal Planet HD; Arts & Entertainment HD; BBC America; Big Ten Network; Bio; Bloomberg Television; Boomerang; CBS College Sports Network; CMT Pure Country; CNN HD; Cooking Channel; C-SPAN 3; Current; Daystar TV Network; Discovery Channel HD; Discovery HD Theater; Discovery Kids Channel; Discovery Military Channel; Discovery Planet Green; Disney Channel HD; Do-It-Yourself; Encore (multiplexed); ESPN 2 HD; ESPN Classic Sports; ESPN HD; ESPNews; Eternal Word TV Network; FamilyNet; FearNet; FitTV; Flix; Food Network HD; Fox Business Channel; Fox College Sports Atlantic; Fox College Sports Central; Fox College Sports Pacific; Fox Movie Channel; Fox News HD; Fox Reality Channel; Fox Soccer; FSN HD; Fuel TV; Fuse; FX HD; G4; Gol TV; Golf Channel HD; Gospel Music Channel; Great American Country; HGTV HD; History Channel HD; History Channel International; ID Investigation Discovery; Independent Film Channel; INSP; MLB Network; MoviePlex; MTV Hits; MTV Jams; MTV Tres; MTV2; Music Choice; National Geographic Channel; National Geographic Channel HD Network; NBA TV; NFL Network; NFL Network HD; Nick Jr.; Nick Too; NickToons TV; Outdoor Channel; Palladia; PBS Kids Sprout; Retro Television Network; Science Channel; ShopNBC; Speed Channel; Speed HD; Style Network; Sundance Channel; Syfy HD; TBS in HD; TeenNick; Tennis Channel; The Word Network; Toon Disney; Trinity Broadcasting Network; Turner Network TV HD; TV One; Universal HD; Univision; USA Network HD; Versus HD; VH1 Classic; VH1 Soul; WE tv.
Fee: $12.95 monthly.

Digital Pay Service 1
Pay Units: N.A.
Programming (via satellite): Cinemax (multiplexed); Cinemax HD; HBO (multiplexed); HBO HD; MoviePlex; Playboy TV; Showtime (multiplexed); Showtime HD; Starz (multiplexed); Starz HDTV; The Movie Channel (multiplexed).
Fee: $11.95 monthly (each).
Video-On-Demand: Yes

Pay-Per-View
iN DEMAND (delivered digitally); NBA League Pass, Fee: $3.95; MLS Direct Kick (delivered digitally); NHL Center Ice (delivered digitally); MLB Extra Innings (delivered digitally); Sports PPV delivered digitally (delivered digitally); Playboy TV (delivered digitally); Fresh (delivered digitally); Ten Blox (delivered digitally).

Internet Service
Operational: Yes. Began: June 1, 2000.
Subscribers: 6,613.
Broadband Service: Comcast High Speed Internet.
Fee: $79.95 installation; $42.95 monthly.

Telephone Service
Digital: Operational
Fee: $44.95 monthly

Miles of Plant: 1,514.0 (coaxial); None (fiber optic). Homes passed: 215,000. Homes passed includes West Monroe

Vice President & General Manager: Ronnie Colvini. Engineering Director: Sandy McKnight. Chief Technician: Clifton Callahan. Marketing Director: Wesley Dowling. Public Affairs Director: Frances Smith.

City fee: 5% of gross.

Ownership: Comcast Cable Communications Inc. (MSO).

JONESTOWN—Alliance Communications, PO Box 960, 290 S Broadview St, Greenbrier, AR 72058-9616. Phone: 501-679-6619. Fax: 501-679-5694. Web Site: http://www.alliancecable.net. Also serves Friars Point, Lula & Moon Lake. ICA: MS0092.

TV Market Ranking: Outside TV Markets (Friars Point, JONESTOWN, Lula, Moon Lake). Franchise award date: N.A. Franchise expiration date: N.A. Began: December 1, 1984.

Channel capacity: 65 (not 2-way capable). Channels available but not in use: 11.

Basic Service
Subscribers: 533.
Programming (received off-air): KATV (ABC) Little Rock; WABG-TV (ABC) Greenwood; WHBQ-TV (FOX) Memphis; WLMT (CW) Memphis; WMAV-TV (PBS) Oxford; WMC-TV (NBC) Memphis; WPTY-TV (ABC) Memphis; WREG-TV (CBS) Memphis; WXVT (CBS) Greenville.
Programming (via satellite): ABC Family Channel; BET Networks; CNN; ESPN; TBS Superstation; Turner Network TV; USA Network; WGN America.
Fee: $25.00 installation; $19.62 monthly.

Expanded Basic Service 1
Subscribers: 440.
Programming (via satellite): AMC; Animal Planet; Arts & Entertainment; Cartoon Network; C-SPAN; Discovery Channel; ESPN 2; FX; Hallmark Channel; Headline News; History Channel; Home Shopping Network; Lifetime; MTV; Nickelodeon; Outdoor Channel; Spike TV; Syfy; The Learning Channel; Trinity Broadcasting Network; truTV; Turner Classic Movies; TV Land; VH1; Weather Channel.

Digital Basic Service
Subscribers: 46.
Programming (via satellite): BBC America; Bio; Bloomberg Television; Discovery Digital Networks; ESPN Classic Sports; ESPNews; Fox Movie Channel; Fox Sports World; G4; GAS; Golf Channel; GSN; Halogen Network; HGTV; History Channel International; Independent Film Channel; MTV Networks Digital Suite; Music Choice; National Geographic Channel; Nick Jr.; NickToons TV; Ovation; Speed Channel; Sundance Channel; Versus; WE tv.

Pay Service 1
Pay Units: N.A.
Programming (via satellite): Cinemax; HBO.
Fee: $10.95 monthly (each).

Digital Pay Service 1
Pay Units: N.A.
Programming (via satellite): Cinemax (multiplexed); Encore (multiplexed); Flix; HBO (multiplexed); Showtime (multiplexed); Starz (multiplexed); The Movie Channel (multiplexed).

Pay-Per-View
Hot Choice (delivered digitally); Playboy TV (delivered digitally); Fresh (delivered digitally); Shorteez (delivered digitally).

Internet Service
Operational: No.

Telephone Service
None

Miles of Plant: 28.0 (coaxial); None (fiber optic). Homes passed: 1,164.

Vice President: Arl Cope. Operations Manager: Jeff Browers. Programming & Marketing Director: James Fuller.

Ownership: Buford Media Group LLC (MSO).

JUMPERTOWN—Vista III Media. Now served by BOONEVILLE, MS [MS0133]. ICA: MS0114.

KILN—Formerly served by Trust Cable. No longer in operation. ICA: MS0157.

KOSCIUSKO—MetroCast Communications, PO Box 1667, 725 Veterans Memorial Dr, Kosciusko, MS 39090. Phone: 662-289-3281. Fax: 662-289-2910. Web Site: http://www.metrocastcommunications.com. Also serves Attala County (unincorporated areas) & McAdams. ICA: MS0158.

TV Market Ranking: Below 100 (Attala County (unincorporated areas) (portions)); Outside TV Markets (Attala County (unincorporated areas) (portions), KOSCIUSKO, McAdams). Franchise award date: January 1, 1966. Franchise expiration date: N.A. Began: April 1, 1967.

Channel capacity: N.A. Channels available but not in use: N.A.

Basic Service
Subscribers: 1,875.
Programming (received off-air): WABG-TV (ABC) Greenwood; WAPT (ABC) Jackson; WDBD (FOX) Jackson; WJTV (CBS) Jackson; WLBT (NBC) Jackson; WMAB-TV (PBS) Mississippi State; WTVA (NBC) Tupelo.
Programming (via satellite): C-SPAN; QVC; Trinity Broadcasting Network; WGN America.
Fee: $55.00 installation; $20.99 monthly; $2.50 converter.

Expanded Basic Service 1
Subscribers: N.A.
Programming (via satellite): ABC Family Channel; Animal Planet; Arts & Entertainment; BET Networks; Cartoon Network; CNBC; CNN; Comcast Sports Net Southeast; Country Music TV; Discovery Channel; ESPN; ESPN 2; Food Network; Fox Movie Channel; Fox News Channel; FX; Great American Country; Hallmark Channel; Headline News; HGTV; History Channel; Lifetime; National Geographic Channel; Nickelodeon; Outdoor Channel; Speed Channel; Spike TV; Syfy; TBS Superstation; The Learning Channel; Travel Channel; Turner Classic Movies; Turner Network TV; TV Land; USA Network; VH1; Weather Channel.
Fee: $31.00 monthly.

Digital Basic Service
Subscribers: 385.
Programming (received off-air): WABG-TV (ABC) Greenwood; WJTV (CBS) Jackson; WMAB-TV (PBS) Mississippi State.
Programming (via satellite): BBC America; Bravo; Discovery HD Theater; Discovery Home Channel; Discovery Kids Channel; Discovery Military Channel; Discovery Times Channel; DMX Music; ESPN 2 HD; ESPN HD; ESPNews; FitTV; Fox Soccer; G4; Golf Channel; Independent Film Channel; Science Television; Turner Network TV HD; WE tv.
Fee: $5.95 monthly.

Pay Service 1
Pay Units: 249.
Programming (via satellite): Cinemax; HBO.
Fee: $13.50 monthly.

Digital Pay Service 1
Pay Units: N.A.
Programming (via satellite): Cinemax (multiplexed); Encore (multiplexed); Flix; HBO (multiplexed); Showtime (multiplexed); Starz (multiplexed); The Movie Channel (multiplexed).
Fee: $10.00 monthly (each).
Video-On-Demand: No

Pay-Per-View
Addressable homes: 935.
Playboy TV (delivered digitally), Addressable: Yes; iN DEMAND (delivered digitally); Fresh (delivered digitally); Hot Choice (delivered digitally).

Internet Service
Operational: Yes.
Broadband Service: MetroCast Internet.
Fee: $79.99 installation; $35.99 monthly.

Telephone Service
Analog: Not Operational
Digital: Operational
Fee: $30.00 installation; $29.99 monthly

Miles of Plant: 120.0 (coaxial); None (fiber optic).

General Manager: Rick Ferrall. Chief Technician: Eddie Turner. Marketing Manager: Lee Beck. Customer Service Manager: Theresa Fuller.

City fee: 3% of basic gross.

Ownership: Harron Communications LP (MSO).

KOSSUTH—Time Warner Cable. Now served by CORINTH, MS [MS0016]. ICA: MS0046.

LAKE—Galaxy Cablevision, PO Box 308, 214 Main St, Ste C, Monticello, MS 39654-0308. Phone: 601-587-9461. Fax: 601-587-7410. Web Site: http://www.galaxycable.com. Also serves Newton County (portions) & Scott County (portions). ICA: MS0159.

TV Market Ranking: Below 100 (Newton County (portions) (portions)); Outside TV Markets (LAKE, Scott County (portions) (portions)). Franchise award date: N.A. Franchise expiration date: N.A. Began: N.A.

Channel capacity: 36 (not 2-way capable). Channels available but not in use: None.

Basic Service
Subscribers: 203.
Programming (received off-air): WDBD (FOX) Jackson; WGBC (NBC) Meridian; WJTV (CBS) Jackson; WLBT (NBC) Jackson; WMPN-TV (PBS) Jackson; WTOK-TV (ABC, CW, FOX, MNT) Meridian.
Programming (via satellite): ABC Family Channel; AMC; Arts & Entertainment; Cartoon Network; CNBC; CNN; Comcast Sports Net Southeast; Discovery Channel; Disney Channel; ESPN; ESPN 2; Fox News Channel; FX; Great American Coun-

try; Hallmark Channel; Headline News; HGTV; History Channel; Lifetime; Outdoor Channel; QVC; Speed Channel; TBS Superstation; Toon Disney; Trinity Broadcasting Network; Turner Network TV; USA Network; Weather Channel; WGN America.
Current originations: Public Access.
Fee: $25.00 installation; $37.49 monthly.

Pay Service 1
Pay Units: 77.
Programming (via satellite): HBO.
Fee: $11.00 monthly.

Internet Service
Operational: No.

Telephone Service
None

Miles of Plant: 38.0 (coaxial); None (fiber optic). Homes passed: 659.
State Manager: Bill Flowers. Technical Manager & Engineer: Greg Berthaut.
Ownership: Galaxy Cable Inc. (MSO).

LAUDERDALE—Comcast Cable. Now served by MERIDIAN, MS [MS0007]. ICA: MS0160.

LAUREL—Comcast Cable, 2100 Lincoln Rd, Hattiesburg, MS 39402-3114. Phone: 601-579-3960. Fax: 601-268-3956. Web Site: http://www.comcast.com. Also serves Calhoun, Ellisville, Jones County, Pendorff & Shady Grove (portions). ICA: MS0013.
TV Market Ranking: Below 100 (Calhoun, Ellisville, Jones County, LAUREL, Pendorff, Shady Grove (portions)). Franchise award date: N.A. Franchise expiration date: N.A. Began: June 1, 1964.
Channel capacity: N.A. Channels available but not in use: N.A.

Basic Service
Subscribers: N.A. Included in Hattiesburg
Programming (received off-air): WDAM-TV (NBC) Laurel; WHLT (CBS) Hattiesburg; WLOX (ABC) Biloxi; WMAW-TV (PBS) Meridian; WXXV-TV (FOX, MNT) Gulfport.
Programming (via satellite): CNN; ION Television; QVC; Weather Channel.
Fee: $60.00 installation; $6.15 monthly.

Expanded Basic Service 1
Subscribers: 9,543.
Programming (via satellite): ABC Family Channel; AMC; Animal Planet; Arts & Entertainment; BET Networks; Cartoon Network; CNBC; Comcast Sports Net Southeast; Comcast/Charter Sports Southeast (CSS); Comedy Central; Country Music TV; C-SPAN; C-SPAN 2; CW+; Discovery Channel; Discovery Health Channel; E! Entertainment Television; ESPN; ESPN 2; ESPN Classic Sports; Eternal Word TV Network; Food Network; Fox News Channel; FX; Golf Channel; Great American Country; GSN; Hallmark Channel; Headline News; HGTV; History Channel; Home Shopping Network; INSP; Lifetime; MSNBC; MTV; Nickelodeon; Outdoor Channel; Speed Channel; Spike TV; Style Network; Syfy; TBS Superstation; The Learning Channel; Trinity Broadcasting Network; truTV; Turner Classic Movies; Turner Network TV; TV Guide Network; TV Land; USA Network; Versus; VH1; WGN America.
Fee: $41.35 monthly.

Digital Basic Service
Subscribers: N.A. Included in Hattiesburg
Programming (via satellite): BBC America; Country Music TV; C-SPAN 3; Discovery Digital Networks; Discovery HD Theater; Disney Channel; Encore (multiplexed); ESPN HD; ESPNews; Flix; G4; GAS; INHD; INHD2; MTV Networks Digital Suite; Music Choice; National Geographic Channel; NFL Network; Nick Jr.; Nick Too; SoapNet; Sundance Channel; Toon Disney; WAM! America's Kidz Network; Weatherscan.
Fee: $9.95 monthly.

Pay Service 1
Pay Units: 250.
Programming (via satellite): Cinemax; HBO; Showtime.
Fee: $25.00 installation; $14.50 monthly (each).

Digital Pay Service 1
Pay Units: N.A.
Programming (via satellite): Cinemax (multiplexed); Cinemax HD; HBO (multiplexed); HBO HD; Showtime (multiplexed); Showtime HD; Starz (multiplexed); Starz HDTV; The Movie Channel (multiplexed).

Video-On-Demand: Yes

Pay-Per-View
iN DEMAND (delivered digitally); Hot Choice (delivered digitally); Playboy TV (delivered digitally); Fresh (delivered digitally); Shorteez (delivered digitally); Pleasure (delivered digitally).

Internet Service
Operational: Yes.
Broadband Service: Comcast High Speed Internet.
Fee: $42.95 monthly; $5.00 modem lease.

Telephone Service
Digital: Operational

Miles of Plant: 469.0 (coaxial); None (fiber optic). Homes passed: 10,442. Miles of plant (coax) includes miles of plant (fiber)
General Manager: Farrel Ryder. Operations Manager: Mike Boez. Marketing Manager: Dan Carleton.
City fee: 3% of gross.
Ownership: Comcast Cable Communications Inc. (MSO).

LEAKESVILLE—Galaxy Cablevision, PO Box 308, 214 Main St, Ste C, Monticello, MS 39654-0308. Phone: 601-587-9461. Fax: 601-587-7410. Web Site: http://www.galaxycable.com. ICA: MS0095.
TV Market Ranking: Outside TV Markets (LEAKESVILLE). Franchise award date: N.A. Franchise expiration date: N.A. Began: July 14, 1989.
Channel capacity: 41 (not 2-way capable). Channels available but not in use: 6.

Basic Service
Subscribers: 96.
Programming (received off-air): WDAM-TV (NBC) Laurel; WKRG-TV (CBS) Mobile; WLOX (ABC) Biloxi; WMAH-TV (PBS) Biloxi; WXXV-TV (FOX, MNT) Gulfport.
Programming (via satellite): ABC Family Channel; AMC; Arts & Entertainment; Cartoon Network; CNBC; CNN; Comcast Sports Net Southeast; Comedy Central; Discovery Channel; Disney Channel; ESPN; ESPN 2; Fox News Channel; FX; Great American Country; Headline News; Lifetime; Outdoor Channel; QVC; Speed Channel; SportSouth; TBS Superstation; Travel Channel; Trinity Broadcasting Network; Turner Network TV; USA Network; Weather Channel; WGN America.
Fee: $40.10 monthly.

Pay Service 1
Pay Units: N.A.
Programming (via satellite): HBO.
Fee: $9.42 monthly.

Internet Service
Operational: No.

Telephone Service
None

Miles of Plant: 11.0 (coaxial); None (fiber optic). Homes passed: 588.

State Manager: Bill Flowers. Technical Manager & Engineer: Greg Berthaut. Customer Service Representative: Parlean Myers.; Rebecca Nelson.
Ownership: Galaxy Cable Inc. (MSO).

LELAND—CMA Cablevision, 101 S Deer Creek Dr W, Leland, MS 38756-3126. Phones: 972-233-9614 (Corporate office); 800-753-2465; 662-686-7823. Fax: 662-686-4100. Web Site: http://www.cmaaccess.com. Also serves Elizabeth. ICA: MS0039.
TV Market Ranking: Below 100 (Elizabeth, LELAND). Franchise award date: N.A. Franchise expiration date: N.A. Began: February 1, 1957.
Channel capacity: N.A. Channels available but not in use: N.A.

Basic Service
Subscribers: 1,337.
Programming (received off-air): WABG-TV (ABC) Greenwood; WDBD (FOX) Jackson; WJTV (CBS) Jackson; WLBT (NBC) Jackson; WMAO-TV (PBS) Greenwood; WXVT (CBS) Greenville.
Programming (via satellite): C-SPAN; CW+; Fox Sports Net; Home Shopping Network; ION Television; MTV; TBS Superstation; Travel Channel; Trinity Broadcasting Network; Weather Channel; WGN America.
Current originations: Public Access.
Fee: $39.95 installation; $23.95 monthly; $12.95 additional installation.

Expanded Basic Service 1
Subscribers: N.A.
Programming (via satellite): AMC; Animal Planet; Arts & Entertainment; BET Networks; Cartoon Network; CNN; Comcast Sports Net Southeast; Country Music TV; C-SPAN 2; Discovery Channel; E! Entertainment Television; ESPN; ESPN 2; Fox News Channel; FX; Hallmark Channel; HGTV; History Channel; Lifetime; MSNBC; MTV; Nickelodeon; Spike TV; Syfy; The Learning Channel; Turner Classic Movies; Turner Network TV; TV Land; USA Network; VH1.
Fee: $16.50 monthly.

Pay Service 1
Pay Units: 270.
Programming (via satellite): Cinemax; HBO.
Fee: $14.95 installation; $13.95 monthly (each).

Video-On-Demand: No

Internet Service
Operational: No.

Telephone Service
None

Miles of Plant: 25.0 (coaxial); None (fiber optic). Additional miles planned: 5.0 (coaxial). Homes passed: 2,600. Total homes in franchised area: 2,700.
General Manager: Jerry Smith. Marketing Director: Julie Ferguson.
City fee: 1% of gross.
Ownership: Cable Management Assoc. (MSO).

LEXINGTON—CableSouth Media. Now served by WINONA, MS [MS0014]. ICA: MS0161.

LIBERTY—Trust Cable. Now served by CENTREVILLE, MS [MS0048]. ICA: MS0221.

LONG BEACH—Cable One, 19201 Pineville Rd, Long Beach, MS 39560-3315. Phone: 228-864-1506. Fax: 228-867-6992. E-mail: jwhite@cableone.net. Web Site: http://www.cableone.net. Also serves Diamondhead, Gulfport, Hancock County (portions), Harrison County, Pass Christian & Saucier. ICA: MS0008.
TV Market Ranking: Below 100 (Diamondhead, Gulfport, Hancock County (portions), Harrison County (portions), LONG BEACH, Pass Christian, Saucier). Franchise award date: N.A. Franchise expiration date: N.A. Began: February 1, 1968.
Channel capacity: 78 (operating 2-way). Channels available but not in use: None.

Basic Service
Subscribers: 32,202.
Programming (received off-air): WDSU (NBC) New Orleans; WGNO (ABC) New Orleans; WKRG-TV (CBS) Mobile; WLOX (ABC) Biloxi; WMAH-TV (PBS) Biloxi; WNOL-TV (CW) New Orleans; WVUE-DT (FOX) New Orleans; WWL-TV (CBS) New Orleans; WXXV-TV (FOX, MNT) Gulfport; WYES-TV (PBS) New Orleans; 4 FMs.
Programming (via satellite): ABC Family Channel; AMC; Animal Planet; Arts & Entertainment; BET Networks; Cartoon Network; CNBC; CNN; Comcast Sports Net Southeast; Country Music TV; C-SPAN; C-SPAN 2; Discovery Channel; Disney Channel; E! Entertainment Television; ESPN; ESPN 2; Eternal Word TV Network; Food Network; Fox News Channel; FX; Headline News; HGTV; History Channel; Home Shopping Network; Lifetime; MSNBC; MTV; NASA TV; Nickelodeon; Product Information Network; QVC; ShopNBC; Spike TV; Syfy; TBS Superstation; The Learning Channel; Trinity Broadcasting Network; Turner Classic Movies; Turner Network TV; TV Guide Network; TV Land; USA Network; VH1; Weather Channel; WGN America.
Fee: $50.00 installation; $46.00 monthly; $1.50 converter; $15.00 additional installation.

Digital Basic Service
Subscribers: 11,199.
Programming (received off-air): WGNO (ABC) New Orleans; WXXV-TV (FOX, MNT) Gulfport; WYES-TV (PBS) New Orleans.
Programming (via satellite): 3 Angels Broadcasting Network; Bio; Boomerang; BYU Television; Discovery Digital Networks; ESPN Classic Sports; ESPNews; FamilyNet; Fox College Sports Atlantic; Fox College Sports Central; Fox College Sports Pacific; Fox Movie Channel; Fox Soccer; Fuel TV; G4; Golf Channel; Great American Country; Hallmark Channel; History Channel International; INSP; National Geographic Channel; Outdoor Channel; SoapNet; Speed Channel; Telemundo; Toon Disney; Trinity Broadcasting Net-

work; truTV; Turner Network TV HD; TVG Network; Universal HD.
Fee: $8.95 monthly.
Digital Pay Service 1
Pay Units: N.A.
Programming (via satellite): Cinemax; Encore (multiplexed); Showtime HD; Starz (multiplexed); The Movie Channel HD.
Fee: $15.00 monthly (each).
Video-On-Demand: No
Pay-Per-View
Addressable homes: 14,805.
iN DEMAND (delivered digitally), Addressable: Yes; Pleasure (delivered digitally); Ten Clips (delivered digitally); Ten Blox (delivered digitally); Ten Blue (delivered digitally).
Internet Service
Operational: Yes. Began: September 1, 2001.
Subscribers: 14,000.
Broadband Service: CableONE.net.
Fee: $75.00 installation; $43.00 monthly; $170.00 modem purchase.
Telephone Service
Digital: Operational
Fee: $75.00 installation; $39.95 monthly
Miles of Plant: 1,190.0 (coaxial); None (fiber optic). Homes passed: 42,500. Total homes in franchised area: 42,500.
Manager: Jim Perry. Chief Technician: Mike Thompson. Marketing Director: Carol Lucas.
City fee: 3% of gross.
Ownership: Cable One Inc. (MSO).

LOUISE—Delta Telephone Inc. SnapVision. Formerly served by MEADVILLE-BUDE, MS [MS0069]. This cable system has converted to IPTV, PO Box 217, Louise, MS 39097. Phones: 877-433-7878; 662-836-5111. Fax: 662-836-5770. Web Site: http://www.dtcweb.net. ICA: MS5029.
TV Market Ranking: Outside TV Markets (LOUISE).
Channel capacity: N.A. Channels available but not in use: N.A.
Internet Service
Operational: Yes.
Ownership: Delta Telephone.

LOUISE—Formerly Branch Cable Inc. served by MEADVILLE-BUDE, MS [MS0069]. This cable system has converted to IPTV, see Louise, MS [MS5029]. ICA: MS0121.

LUCEDALE—Mediacom, 760 Middle St, PO Box 1009, Fairhope, AL 36532. Phones: 850-934-7700 (Gulf Breeze regional office); 251-928-0374. Fax: 251-928-3804. Web Site: http://www.mediacomcable.com. Also serves George County. ICA: MS0065.
TV Market Ranking: 59 (George County (portions), LUCEDALE); Below 100 (George County (portions)); Outside TV Markets (George County (portions)). Franchise award date: May 20, 1980. Franchise expiration date: N.A. Began: August 1, 1981.
Channel capacity: N.A. Channels available but not in use: N.A.
Basic Service
Subscribers: 599.
Programming (received off-air): WALA-TV (FOX) Mobile; WDAM-TV (NBC) Laurel; WEAR-TV (ABC) Pensacola; WFNA (CW) Gulf Shores; WJTC (IND) Pensacola; WKRG-TV (CBS) Mobile; WLOX (ABC) Biloxi; WMAH-TV (PBS) Biloxi; WMPV-TV (TBN) Mobile; WPMI-TV (NBC) Mobile.
Programming (via satellite): ABC Family Channel; AMC; Animal Planet; Arts & Entertainment; BET Networks; Cartoon Network; CNBC; CNN; Comcast Sports Net Southeast; Comedy Central; Country Music TV; C-SPAN; Discovery Channel; Disney Channel; E! Entertainment Television; ESPN; ESPN 2; Food Network; Fox News Channel; FX; Golf Channel; Hallmark Channel; Headline News; HGTV; History Channel; Home Shopping Network; INSP; ION Television; Lifetime; MSNBC; MTV; Nickelodeon; Outdoor Channel; QVC; Speed Channel; Spike TV; SportSouth; Syfy; TBS Superstation; The Learning Channel; Toon Disney; Travel Channel; truTV; Turner Classic Movies; Turner Network TV; TV Guide Network; TV Land; USA Network; VH1; WE tv; Weather Channel; WGN America.
Fee: $29.50 installation; $44.95 monthly; $3.35 converter; $20.00 additional installation.
Digital Basic Service
Subscribers: N.A.
Programming (via satellite): BBC America; Discovery Digital Networks; DMX Music; Fox Sports World; GSN; Independent Film Channel.
Fee: $7.00 monthly; $5.00 converter.
Digital Pay Service 1
Pay Units: 226.
Programming (via satellite): HBO (multiplexed).
Fee: $11.95 monthly.
Digital Pay Service 2
Pay Units: 123.
Programming (via satellite): Flix; Showtime (multiplexed); Sundance Channel; The Movie Channel (multiplexed).
Fee: $9.95 monthly.
Digital Pay Service 3
Pay Units: 191.
Programming (via satellite): Cinemax (multiplexed).
Fee: $9.95 monthly.
Digital Pay Service 4
Pay Units: N.A.
Programming (via satellite): Encore (multiplexed); Starz (multiplexed).
Fee: $9.95 monthly.
Video-On-Demand: Yes
Pay-Per-View
Movies (delivered digitally); special events (delivered digitally); Sports PPV (delivered digitally).
Internet Service
Operational: Yes.
Broadband Service: Mediacom High Speed Internet.
Fee: $49.95 installation; $40.95 monthly.
Telephone Service
Digital: Operational
Miles of Plant: 22.0 (coaxial); None (fiber optic). Homes passed: 977. Total homes in franchised area: 1,033.
Vice President: David Servies. Operations Director: Gene Wuchner. Technical Operations Manager: Mike Sneary. Sales & Marketing Manager: Joey Nagem.
City fee: 3% of basic gross.
Ownership: Mediacom LLC (MSO).

LUMBERTON—Galaxy Cablevision, PO Box 308, 214 Main St, Ste C, Monticello, MS 39654-0308. Phone: 601-587-9461. Fax: 601-587-7410. Web Site: http://www.galaxycable.com. ICA: MS0055.
TV Market Ranking: Below 100 (LUMBERTON). Franchise award date: April 15, 1980. Franchise expiration date: N.A. Began: January 1, 1981.
Channel capacity: 54 (operating 2-way). Channels available but not in use: None.
Basic Service
Subscribers: 323.
Programming (received off-air): WDAM-TV (NBC) Laurel; WHLT (CBS) Hattiesburg; WLOX (ABC) Biloxi; WMAH-TV (PBS) Biloxi; WXXV-TV (FOX, MNT) Gulfport.
Programming (via satellite): ABC Family Channel; AMC; Arts & Entertainment; BET Networks; Bravo; Cartoon Network; CNBC; CNN; Comcast Sports Net Southeast; Comedy Central; C-SPAN; Discovery Channel; Disney Channel; E! Entertainment Television; ESPN; ESPN 2; Fox News Channel; Fuse; FX; Great American Country; Headline News; HGTV; History Channel; Lifetime; Outdoor Channel; QVC; Speed Channel; TBS Superstation; The Learning Channel; Travel Channel; Trinity Broadcasting Network; Turner Network TV; USA Network; Weather Channel; WGN America.
Fee: $43.50 monthly.
Digital Basic Service
Subscribers: 89.
Pay Service 1
Pay Units: 318.
Programming (via satellite): HBO.
Fee: $25.00 installation; $9.42 monthly.
Pay Service 2
Pay Units: N.A.
Programming (via satellite): Encore; Starz.
Internet Service
Operational: No.
Telephone Service
None
Miles of Plant: 17.0 (coaxial); 3.0 (fiber optic). Homes passed: 896.
State Manager: Bill Flowers. Technical Manager & Engineer: Greg Berthaut. Customer Service Representative: Rebecca Nelson.; Parlean Myers.
Ownership: Galaxy Cable Inc. (MSO).

MABEN—MetroCast Communications, 300.5 S Jackson St, Starkville, MS 39759. Phone: 662-323-1615. Fax: 662-323-1682. Web Site: http://www.metrocastcommunications.com. Also serves Mathiston. ICA: MS0094.
TV Market Ranking: Below 100 (MABEN, Mathiston). Franchise award date: N.A. Franchise expiration date: N.A. Began: May 1, 1980.
Channel capacity: 35 (not 2-way capable). Channels available but not in use: 1.
Basic Service
Subscribers: 310.
Programming (received off-air): WCBI-TV (CBS, CW, MNT) Columbus; WKDH (ABC) Houston; WLOV-TV (FOX) West Point; WMAB-TV (PBS) Mississippi State; WTVA (NBC) Tupelo.
Programming (via satellite): ABC Family Channel; Animal Planet; Arts & Entertainment; BET Networks; Cartoon Network; CNBC; CNN; Comcast Sports Net Southeast; Discovery Channel; ESPN; ESPN 2; Fox Movie Channel; Fox News Channel; FX; Great American Country; Hallmark Channel; HGTV; History Channel; Lifetime; Nickelodeon; Spike TV; TBS Superstation; The Learning Channel; Trinity Broadcasting Network; Turner Network TV; TV Land; USA Network; Weather Channel.
Fee: $55.00 installation; $37.99 monthly; $2.50 converter.
Pay Service 1
Pay Units: 100.
Programming (via satellite): HBO; Showtime.
Fee: $13.50 monthly (each).
Internet Service
Operational: No.
Telephone Service
None
Miles of Plant: 26.0 (coaxial); None (fiber optic). Homes passed: 900. Total homes in franchised area: 950.
Regional Manager: Rick Ferrall. Chief Technician: Mitch Douglas. Marketing Manager: Lee Beck.
Ownership: Harron Communications LP (MSO).

MACEDONIA—Galaxy Cablevision, PO Box 308, 214 Main St, Ste C, Monticello, MS 39654-0308. Phone: 601-587-9461. Fax: 601-587-7410. Web Site: http://www.galaxycable.com. Also serves Forrest County, Perry County, Petal & Runnelstown. ICA: MS0163.
TV Market Ranking: Below 100 (Forrest County, MACEDONIA, Petal, Runnelstown). Franchise award date: N.A. Franchise expiration date: N.A. Began: May 1, 1990.
Channel capacity: 41 (not 2-way capable). Channels available but not in use: 2.
Basic Service
Subscribers: 171.
Programming (received off-air): WDAM-TV (NBC) Laurel; WHLT (CBS) Hattiesburg; WLOX (ABC) Biloxi; WMAH-TV (PBS) Biloxi; WXXV-TV (FOX, MNT) Gulfport.
Programming (via satellite): ABC Family Channel; Animal Planet; Arts & Entertainment; Cartoon Network; CNN; Comcast Sports Net Southeast; C-SPAN; Discovery Channel; Disney Channel; ESPN; ESPN 2; Fox News Channel; Fuse; FX; Great American Country; GSN; Headline News; HGTV; Lifetime; Outdoor Channel; QVC; Speed Channel; SportSouth; Syfy; TBS Superstation; Toon Disney; Trinity Broadcasting Network; Turner Classic Movies; Turner Network TV; USA Network; Weather Channel; WGN America.
Fee: $43.75 installation; $39.60 monthly.
Pay Service 1
Pay Units: 44.
Programming (via satellite): HBO.
Fee: $10.95 monthly.
Pay Service 2
Pay Units: N.A.
Programming (via satellite): Cinemax.
Internet Service
Operational: No.
Telephone Service
None
Miles of Plant: 22.0 (coaxial); None (fiber optic). Homes passed: 685.
State Manager: Bill Flowers. Technical Manager & Engineer: Greg Berthaut. Customer Service Representative: Parlean Myers.; Rebecca Nelson.
Ownership: Galaxy Cable Inc. (MSO).

MACON—Cable TV Inc., PO Box 2598, 612 Hwy 82 W, Starkville, MS 39760. Phone: 662-324-5121. Fax: 662-324-0233. ICA: MS0217.
TV Market Ranking: Below 100 (MACON).
Channel capacity: N.A. Channels available but not in use: N.A.
Basic Service
Subscribers: 813.
Fee: $40.00 installation; $35.95 monthly.
Pay Service 1
Pay Units: 74.
Programming (via satellite): HBO.
Fee: $12.75 monthly.
Pay Service 2
Pay Units: 29.
Programming (via satellite): Showtime.
Fee: $12.29 monthly.
Pay Service 3
Pay Units: 4.
Programming (via satellite): Encore; Starz.
Fee: $9.95 monthly.

Pay Service 4
Pay Units: 64.
Programming (via satellite): Cinemax.
Fee: $12.29 monthly.
Internet Service
Operational: No.
Telephone Service
None
General Manager: Andy Williams.
Ownership: Andy Williams (MSO).

MAGEE—Bailey Cable TV Inc., 807 Church St, Port Gibson, MS 39150-2413. Phones: 601-849-4201; 601-892-5249. Fax: 601-892-3015. Also serves Mize & Mount Olive. ICA: MS0051.
TV Market Ranking: Below 100 (MAGEE, Mize, Mount Olive). Franchise award date: N.A. Franchise expiration date: N.A. Began: July 1, 1981.
Channel capacity: 35 (not 2-way capable). Channels available but not in use: 4.
Basic Service
Subscribers: 700.
Programming (received off-air): WAPT (ABC) Jackson; WDAM-TV (NBC) Laurel; WDBD (FOX) Jackson; WJTV (CBS) Jackson; WLBT (NBC) Jackson; WMAA (ETV) Columbus.
Programming (via satellite): ABC Family Channel; Arts & Entertainment; BET Networks; Cartoon Network; CNN; Country Music TV; C-SPAN; Discovery Channel; ESPN; ESPN 2; History Channel; MTV; Nickelodeon; QVC; Spike TV; Syfy; TBS Superstation; The Learning Channel; Trinity Broadcasting Network; Turner Network TV; TV Land; USA Network; VH1; Weather Channel; WGN America.
Current originations: Public Access.
Fee: $20.00 installation; $33.02 monthly; $2.00 converter.
Pay Service 1
Pay Units: N.A.
Programming (via satellite): Showtime; The Movie Channel.
Fee: $9.63 monthly (each).
Video-On-Demand: No
Internet Service
Operational: No.
Telephone Service
None
Miles of Plant: 40.0 (coaxial); None (fiber optic). Additional miles planned: 6.0 (coaxial). Homes passed: 1,750. Total homes in franchised area: 1,750.
Manager: Dwight Bailey. Chief Technician: Jim Morton.
City fee: 3% of gross.
Ownership: Bailey Cable TV Inc. (MSO).

MAYERSVILLE—Formerly served by J & L Cable. No longer in operation. ICA: MS0122.

MCLAURIN—Home Cable Entertainment, 15600 Springfield Rd, Walker, LA 70785-2716. Phone: 225-665-4997. Fax: 225-667-6293. Also serves Dixie. ICA: MS0165.
TV Market Ranking: Below 100 (Dixie, MCLAURIN). Franchise award date: March 1, 1992. Franchise expiration date: N.A. Began: N.A.
Channel capacity: 48 (not 2-way capable). Channels available but not in use: 5.
Basic Service
Subscribers: 179.
Programming (received off-air): WDAM-TV (NBC) Laurel; WHLT (CBS) Hattiesburg; WLOX (ABC) Biloxi; WMAH-TV (PBS) Biloxi; WXXV-TV (FOX, MNT) Gulfport.
Programming (via satellite): ABC Family Channel; CNN; Discovery Channel; Disney Channel; ESPN; Fox Movie Channel; Fox News Channel; Lifetime; Nickelodeon; QVC; Spike TV; TBS Superstation; Trinity Broadcasting Network; USA Network; VH1; WGN America.
Current originations: Religious Access.
Fee: $29.95 monthly.
Pay Service 1
Pay Units: N.A.
Programming (via satellite): Showtime (multiplexed); The Movie Channel.
Fee: $10.95 monthly (each).
Internet Service
Operational: No.
Telephone Service
None
Miles of Plant: 24.0 (coaxial); None (fiber optic).
Manager: Leland Denison. Chief Technician: Dan Boyd.
Ownership: Denison Communications Inc. (MSO).

MEADVILLE—Franklin Telephone Co. Inc. SnapVision. Formerly [MS0069]. This cable system has converted to IPTV, PO Box 168, 304 Main St, New Augusta, MS 39462. Phones: 800-531-0427; 601-964-8311. Web Site: http://www.ftcweb.net. ICA: MS5012.
Channel capacity: N.A. Channels available but not in use: N.A.
Internet Service
Operational: Yes.
Telephone Service
Digital: Operational
Ownership: Delta Telephone.

MEADVILLE-BUDE—Branch Cable Inc. This cable system has converted to IPTV. See Bude, MS [MS5016] & Meadville, MS [MS5012]. ICA: MS0069.

MENDENHALL—Bailey Cable TV Inc., 807 Church St, Port Gibson, MS 39150-2413. Phones: 601-849-4201; 601-892-5249. Fax: 601-892-3015. Also serves d'Lo & Simpson County. ICA: MS0081.
TV Market Ranking: 77 (d'Lo, MENDENHALL, Simpson County (portions)); Below 100 (Simpson County (portions)); Outside TV Markets (Simpson County (portions)). Franchise award date: N.A. Franchise expiration date: N.A. Began: July 1, 1981.
Channel capacity: 38 (not 2-way capable). Channels available but not in use: 4.
Basic Service
Subscribers: 300.
Programming (received off-air): QVC; WAPT (ABC) Jackson; WDBD (FOX) Jackson; WJTV (CBS) Jackson; WLBT (NBC) Jackson; WMAA (ETV) Columbus.
Programming (via satellite): ABC Family Channel; Arts & Entertainment; BET Networks; Cartoon Network; CNN; Country Music TV; C-SPAN; Discovery Channel; ESPN; ESPN 2; History Channel; MTV; Nickelodeon; Spike TV; Syfy; TBS Superstation; The Learning Channel; Trinity Broadcasting Network; Turner Network TV; TV Land; USA Network; VH1; Weather Channel; WGN America.
Fee: $20.00 installation; $33.02 monthly.
Pay Service 1
Pay Units: N.A.
Programming (via satellite): Showtime; The Movie Channel.
Fee: $10.00 installation; $9.63 monthly (each).
Video-On-Demand: No

Internet Service
Operational: No.
Telephone Service
None
Miles of Plant: 20.0 (coaxial); None (fiber optic). Homes passed: 750.
Manager: Dwight Bailey. Chief Technician: Jim Morton.
Ownership: Bailey Cable TV Inc. (MSO).

MERIDIAN—Comcast Cable, 909 24th Ave, Meridian, MS 39301-5008. Phone: 601-579-3960. Fax: 601-693-2278. Web Site: http://www.comcast.com. Also serves Dalewood, Lauderdale, Lauderdale County, Marion, Russell & Toomsuba. ICA: MS0007.
TV Market Ranking: Below 100 (Dalewood, Lauderdale, Lauderdale County, Marion, MERIDIAN, Russell, Toomsuba). Franchise award date: October 15, 1963. Franchise expiration date: N.A. Began: November 1, 1964.
Channel capacity: N.A. Channels available but not in use: N.A.
Basic Service
Subscribers: N.A. Included in Hattiesburg
Programming (received off-air): WGBC (NBC) Meridian; WMAW-TV (PBS) Meridian; WMDN (CBS) Meridian; WTOK-TV (ABC, CW, FOX, MNT) Meridian; 29 FMs.
Programming (via satellite): ESPN; Home Shopping Network; ION Television; QVC; TBS Superstation; TV Guide Network; WGN America.
Fee: $60.00 installation; $6.15 monthly.
Expanded Basic Service 1
Subscribers: N.A.
Programming (via satellite): ABC Family Channel; AMC; Animal Planet; Arts & Entertainment; BET Networks; Bravo; Cartoon Network; CNBC; CNN; Comcast Sports Net Southeast; Comcast/Charter Sports Southeast (CSS); Comedy Central; Country Music TV; C-SPAN; C-SPAN 2; Discovery Channel; Discovery Health Channel; E! Entertainment Television; ESPN 2; Eternal Word TV Network; Food Network; Fox News Channel; FX; Golf Channel; Great American Country; GSN; Headline News; HGTV; History Channel; INSP; Lifetime; MSNBC; MTV; Nickelodeon; Outdoor Channel; Speed Channel; Spike TV; Style Network; Syfy; The Learning Channel; Trinity Broadcasting Network; truTV; Turner Classic Movies; Turner Network TV; TV Land; USA Network; Versus; VH1; Weather Channel.
Fee: $41.35 monthly.
Digital Basic Service
Subscribers: N.A. Included in Hattiesburg
Programming (via satellite): BBC America; C-SPAN 3; Discovery Digital Networks; Disney Channel; ESPNews; GAS; MTV Networks Digital Suite; Music Choice; Nick Jr.; Nick Too; SoapNet; Toon Disney; WAM! America's Kidz Network; Weatherscan.
Fee: $9.95 monthly.
Pay Service 1
Pay Units: N.A.
Programming (via satellite): Cinemax; HBO; Showtime.
Fee: $29.95 installation; $10.50 monthly (Showtime), $11.00 monthly (Cinemax), $11.50 monthly (HBO).
Digital Pay Service 1
Pay Units: N.A.
Programming (via satellite): Cinemax (multiplexed); Encore (multiplexed); Flix (multiplexed); HBO (multiplexed); Showtime (multiplexed); Sundance Channel (multiplexed); The Movie Channel (multiplexed).
Fee: $13.60 monthly (each).
Video-On-Demand: No
Pay-Per-View
iN DEMAND (delivered digitally); Playboy TV (delivered digitally); Fresh (delivered digitally); Shorteez (delivered digitally); Pleasure (delivered digitally).
Internet Service
Operational: Yes.
Broadband Service: Comcast High Speed Internet.
Fee: $42.95 monthly; $5.00 modem lease.
Telephone Service
Digital: Operational
Miles of Plant: 721.0 (coaxial); None (fiber optic). Homes passed: 19,635. Total homes in franchised area: 20,000. Miles of plant (coax) includes miles of plant (fiber)
General Manager: Farrel Ryder. Operations Manager: Larry Frazier. Marketing Manager: Dan Carleton.
City fee: 4% of gross (Meridian).
Ownership: Comcast Cable Communications Inc. (MSO).

MERIDIAN NAVAL AIR STATION—Galaxy Cablevision, PO Box 308, 214 Main St, Ste C, Monticello, MS 39654-0308. Phone: 601-587-9461. Fax: 601-587-7410. Web Site: http://www.galaxycable.com. ICA: MS0215.
TV Market Ranking: Below 100 (MERIDIAN NAVAL AIR STATION).
Channel capacity: 54 (not 2-way capable). Channels available but not in use: None.
Basic Service
Subscribers: 65.
Programming (received off-air): WGBC (NBC) Meridian; WMAW-TV (PBS) Meridian; WMDN (CBS) Meridian; WTOK-TV (ABC, CW, FOX, MNT) Meridian.
Programming (via satellite): ABC Family Channel; Animal Planet; Arts & Entertainment; BET Networks; Cartoon Network; CNN; Comcast Sports Net Southeast; Comedy Central; C-SPAN; Discovery Channel; Discovery Military Channel; Disney Channel; Do-It-Yourself; E! Entertainment Television; ESPN; ESPN 2; Food Network; Fox News Channel; Fuse; FX; Golf Channel; Great American Country; GSN; Headline News; HGTV; History Channel; INSP; Lifetime; MSNBC; Outdoor Channel; QVC; Speed Channel; Syfy; TBS Superstation; The Learning Channel; Toon Disney; Travel Channel; Turner Classic Movies;

Turner Network TV; USA Network; Weather Channel; WGN America.
Current originations: Public Access.
Fee: $39.60 monthly.

Pay Service 1
Pay Units: N.A.
Programming (via satellite): HBO; Showtime.

Internet Service
Operational: No.

Telephone Service
None

Miles of Plant: 8.0 (coaxial); None (fiber optic). Homes passed: 519.
State Manager: Bill Flowers. Technical Manager & Engineer: Greg Berthaut.
Ownership: Galaxy Cable Inc. (MSO).

MONTICELLO—Galaxy Cablevision, PO Box 308, 214 Main St, Ste C, Monticello, MS 39654-0308. Phone: 601-587-9461. Fax: 601-587-7410. Web Site: http://www.galaxycable.com. ICA: MS0072.
TV Market Ranking: Below 100 (MONTICELLO). Franchise award date: January 1, 1981. Franchise expiration date: N.A. Began: November 1, 1981.
Channel capacity: 41 (not 2-way capable). Channels available but not in use: None.

Basic Service
Subscribers: 324.
Programming (received off-air): WAPT (ABC) Jackson; WDAM-TV (NBC) Laurel; WDBD (FOX) Jackson; WJTV (CBS) Jackson; WLBT (NBC) Jackson; WMPN-TV (PBS) Jackson.
Programming (via satellite): ABC Family Channel; AMC; Arts & Entertainment; BET Networks; Cartoon Network; CNBC; CNN; Comcast Sports Net Southeast; Comedy Central; Discovery Channel; Disney Channel; E! Entertainment Television; ESPN; ESPN 2; Fox News Channel; FX; Great American Country; Hallmark Channel; Headline News; HGTV; History Channel; INSP; Lifetime; Outdoor Channel; QVC; Speed Channel; TBS Superstation; The Learning Channel; Trinity Broadcasting Network; Turner Network TV; USA Network; Weather Channel; WGN America.
Fee: $25.00 installation; $41.60 monthly.

Pay Service 1
Pay Units: 343.
Programming (via satellite): HBO; Showtime.
Fee: $25.00 installation.

Pay-Per-View
ESPN Now (delivered digitally), Fee: $3.99, Addressable: Yes; Hot Choice (delivered digitally); Playboy TV (delivered digitally); Fresh (delivered digitally); Shorteez (delivered digitally); Urban Xtra (delivered digitally); sports (delivered digitally).

Internet Service
Operational: No.

Telephone Service
None

Miles of Plant: 32.0 (coaxial); None (fiber optic). Homes passed: 1,016.
State Manager: Bill Flowers. Technical Manager & Engineer: Greg Berthaut. Customer Service Representative: Rebecca Nelson.; Parlean Myers.
Ownership: Galaxy Cable Inc. (MSO).

MOOREVILLE—Formerly served by Foster Communications Inc. No longer in operation. ICA: MS0085.

MOOREVILLE—Formerly served by SouthTel Communications LP. No longer in operation. ICA: MS0166.

MOUND BAYOU—Galaxy Cablevision. Now served by CLEVELAND, MS [MS0019]. Also serves MOUND BAYOU. ICA: MS0061.

NATCHEZ—Cable One, 107 N Dr. M. L. King St, Natchez, MS 39120. Phone: 601-442-5418. Fax: 601-442-1466. E-mail: jivey@cableone.net. Web Site: http://www.cableone.net. Also serves Concordia Parish (portions) & Vidalia, LA; Adams County, MS. ICA: MS0012.
TV Market Ranking: Below 100 (Adams County, Concordia Parish (portions), NATCHEZ, Vidalia). Franchise award date: September 1, 1958. Franchise expiration date: N.A. Began: September 1, 1958.
Channel capacity: N.A. Channels available but not in use: N.A.

Basic Service
Subscribers: 8,718.
Programming (received off-air): KALB-TV (CBS, NBC) Alexandria; KLAX-TV (ABC) Alexandria; KNOE-TV (CBS, CW) Monroe; WAPT (ABC) Jackson; WBRZ-TV (ABC) Baton Rouge; WJTV (CBS) Jackson; WLBT (NBC) Jackson; WMAU-TV (PBS) Bude; WNTZ-TV (FOX, MNT) Natchez; allband FM.
Programming (via satellite): C-SPAN; CW+; TV Guide Network.
Fee: $70.00 installation; $46.00 monthly; $2.00 converter.

Expanded Basic Service 1
Subscribers: N.A.
Programming (via satellite): ABC Family Channel; AMC; Animal Planet; Arts & Entertainment; BET Networks; Cartoon Network; CNBC; CNN; Comcast Sports Net Southeast; Country Music TV; C-SPAN 2; Discovery Channel; Disney Channel; ESPN; ESPN 2; Food Network; Fox News Channel; FX; Headline News; HGTV; History Channel; Home Shopping Network; INSP; Lifetime; MSNBC; MTV; Nickelodeon; QVC; Spike TV; Syfy; TBS Superstation; The Learning Channel; Travel Channel; Turner Classic Movies; Turner Network TV; TV Land; USA Network; VH1; Weather Channel.

Digital Basic Service
Subscribers: 3,455.
Programming (received off-air): KNOE-TV (CBS, CW) Monroe; WMAU-TV (PBS) Bude.
Programming (via satellite): 3 Angels Broadcasting Network; Arts & Entertainment HD; Bio; Boomerang; Boomerang en Espanol; BYU Television; Cine Mexicano; CNN en Espanol; Discovery HD Theater; Discovery Health Channel; Discovery Kids Channel; Discovery Military Channel; ESPN 2 HD; ESPN Classic Sports; ESPN Deportes; ESPN HD; ESPNews; FamilyNet; Food Network HD; Fox College Sports Atlantic; Fox College Sports Central; Fox College Sports Pacific; Fox Movie Channel; Fox Soccer; Fox Sports en Espanol; Fuel TV; Golf Channel; Great American Country; GSN; Hallmark Channel; HGTV HD; History Channel International; INSP; La Familia Network; Latele Novela Network; mun2 television; Music Choice; National Geographic Channel; National Geographic Channel HD Network; Outdoor Channel; Puma TV; Science Channel; SoapNet; Speed Channel; Telemundo; Toon Disney; Toon Disney en Espanol; Trinity Broadcasting Network; TVG Network; Universal HD; WE tv.
Fee: $9.95 monthly.

Digital Pay Service 1
Pay Units: N.A.
Programming (via satellite): Cinemax (multiplexed); Encore (multiplexed); Flix; HBO (multiplexed); HBO HD; Showtime (multiplexed); Showtime HD; Starz (multiplexed); Sundance Channel; The Movie Channel (multiplexed); The Movie Channel HD.
Fee: $15.00 monthly (HBO, Cinemax, Showtime/TMC/Flix/Sundance or Starz/Encore).

Video-On-Demand: No

Pay-Per-View
Addressable homes: 3,455.
Addressable: Yes; iN DEMAND (delivered digitally); Ten Clips (delivered digitally); Ten Blox (delivered digitally); Ten Blue (delivered digitally).

Internet Service
Operational: Yes.
Subscribers: 250.
Broadband Service: CableONE.net.
Fee: $75.00 installation; $43.00 monthly.

Telephone Service
Digital: Operational
Fee: $75.00 installation; $39.95 monthly

Miles of Plant: 273.0 (coaxial); None (fiber optic). Homes passed: 15,250. Total homes in franchised area: 15,250.
Manager: Bobby McCool. Marketing Director: Jullia Ivey. Chief Technician: Kenny Wright. Office Manager: Dorothy Champion.
City fee: 5% of gross.
Ownership: Cable One Inc. (MSO).

NETTLETON—MetroCast Communications, 311 Heritage Dr, Oxford, MS 38852. Phones: 662-234-4711; 662-728-8111. Fax: 662-236-3593. Web Site: http://www.metrocastcommunications.com. Also serves Lee County (portions) & Shannon. ICA: MS0170.
TV Market Ranking: Below 100 (Lee County (portions), NETTLETON, Shannon). Franchise award date: N.A. Franchise expiration date: N.A. Began: December 1, 1982.
Channel capacity: N.A. Channels available but not in use: N.A.

Basic Service
Subscribers: 1,567.
Programming (received off-air): WCBI-TV (CBS, CW, MNT) Columbus; WLOV-TV (FOX) West Point; WMAE-TV (PBS) Booneville; WMC-TV (NBC) Memphis; WPTY-TV (ABC) Memphis; WTVA (NBC) Tupelo.
Programming (via satellite): INSP; QVC; TBS Superstation; TV Guide Network; W39CD Fulton; Weatherscan; WGN America; WKDH (ABC) Houston.
Fee: $49.95 installation; $17.95 monthly.

Expanded Basic Service 1
Subscribers: N.A.
Programming (received off-air): W07BN (TBN) Bruce.
Programming (via satellite): ABC Family Channel; AMC; Animal Planet; Arts & Entertainment; BET Networks; Bravo; Cartoon Network; CNBC; CNN; Comcast Sports Net Southeast; Comedy Central; Cooking Channel; Country Music TV; C-SPAN; C-SPAN 2; Discovery Channel; Disney Channel; Do-It-Yourself; E! Entertainment Television; ESPN; ESPN 2; Food Network; Fox News Channel; FX; G4; Golf Channel; Great American Country; Hallmark Channel; Headline News; HGTV; History Channel; Home Shopping Network; Lifetime; MSNBC; MTV; National Geographic Channel; Nickelodeon; Outdoor Channel; SoapNet; Spike TV; SportSouth; Syfy; TBS Superstation; The Learning Channel; Toon Disney; Travel Channel; Trinity Broadcasting Network; Turner Network TV; TV Land; USA Network; Versus; VH1; WE tv; Weather Channel.
Fee: $33.00 monthly.

Digital Basic Service
Subscribers: N.A.
Programming (received off-air): WCBI-TV (CBS, CW, MNT) Columbus; WMC-TV (NBC) Memphis; WPTY-TV (ABC) Memphis.
Programming (via satellite): AmericanLife TV Network; BBC America; Bio; Bloomberg Television; Discovery Digital Networks; Discovery HD Theater; DMX Music; ESPN; ESPN Classic Sports; ESPNews; Fox Movie Channel; Fox Soccer; Fuse; GAS; GSN; Halogen Network; History Channel International; Independent Film Channel; Lifetime Movie Network; Lime; MTV Networks Digital Suite; NFL Network; Nick Jr.; NickToons TV; Sleuth; Speed Channel; Style Network; Toon Disney; Turner Classic Movies; Turner Network TV HD; Universal HD.
Fee: $10.00 monthly.

Digital Pay Service 1
Pay Units: N.A.
Programming (via satellite): Cinemax (multiplexed); Cinemax; Encore (multiplexed); Flix; HBO (multiplexed); HBO; Showtime (multiplexed); Starz (multiplexed); Sundance Channel; The Movie Channel (multiplexed).
Fee: $6.00 monthly (Encore), $13.00 monthly (HBO, Cinemax, Showtime/TMC, or Starz).

Video-On-Demand: Yes

Pay-Per-View
iN DEMAND (delivered digitally); Fresh (delivered digitally); Hot Choice (delivered digitally); Playboy TV (delivered digitally); ESPN (delivered digitally).

Internet Service
Operational: Yes.
Broadband Service: MetroCast Internet.
Fee: $79.99 installation; $43.95 monthly.

Telephone Service
Digital: Operational
Fee: $24.95 installation; $29.95 monthly

Miles of Plant: 28.0 (coaxial); None (fiber optic).
General Manager: Rick Ferrall. Technical Operations Manager: Bob Gable. Marketing Manager: Lee Beck.
Ownership: Harron Communications LP (MSO).

NEW ALBANY—MetroCast Communications, 311 Heritage Dr, Oxford, MS 38852. Phones: 662-234-4711; 662-728-8111. Fax: 662-236-3593. Web Site: http://www.metrocastcommunications.com. Also serves Ecru, Ingomar, Myrtle & Union County. ICA: MS0027.
TV Market Ranking: Below 100 (Ecru, Ingomar, Myrtle, NEW ALBANY, Union County (portions)). Franchise award date: N.A. Franchise expiration date: N.A. Began: June 1, 1967.
Channel capacity: N.A. Channels available but not in use: N.A.

Basic Service
Subscribers: 4,417.
Programming (received off-air): WBII-CD Holly Springs; WBUY-TV (TBN) Holly Springs; WCBI-TV (CBS, CW, MNT) Columbus; WHBQ-TV (FOX) Memphis; WKDH (ABC) Houston; WKNO (PBS) Memphis; WLMT (CW) Memphis; WLOV-TV (FOX) West Point; WMAE-TV (PBS) Booneville; WMC-TV (NBC) Memphis; WPTY-TV (ABC) Memphis; WPXX-TV (ION, MNT) Memphis; WREG-TV (CBS) Memphis; WTVA (NBC) Tupelo; allband FM.
Programming (via satellite): CW+; QVC; TV Guide Network; WGN America.

Current originations: Leased Access; Educational Access.
Fee: $49.95 installation; $17.95 monthly.

Expanded Basic Service 1
Subscribers: N.A.
Programming (received off-air): W34DV Booneville.
Programming (via satellite): ABC Family Channel; AMC; Animal Planet; Arts & Entertainment; BET Networks; Cartoon Network; CNBC; CNN; Comcast Sports Net Southeast; Comedy Central; Cooking Channel; Country Music TV; C-SPAN; C-SPAN 2; Discovery Channel; Disney Channel; Do-It-Yourself; E! Entertainment Television; ESPN; ESPN 2; FitTV; Food Network; Fox News Channel; FX; Golf Channel; Great American Country; Hallmark Channel; Headline News; HGTV; History Channel; INSP; ION Television; Lifetime; MSNBC; MTV; National Geographic Channel; Nickelodeon; Outdoor Channel; SoapNet; Spike TV; SportSouth; Syfy; TBS Superstation; The Learning Channel; Travel Channel; Turner Network TV; TV Land; USA Network; Versus; VH1; WE tv; Weather Channel.
Fee: $33.00 monthly.

Digital Basic Service
Subscribers: N.A.
Programming (received off-air): WCBI-TV (CBS, CW, MNT) Columbus; WLMT (CW) Memphis; WMC-TV (NBC) Memphis; WPTY-TV (ABC) Memphis.
Programming (via satellite): AmericanLife TV Network; BBC America; Bio; Bloomberg Television; Bravo; Discovery Digital Networks; Discovery HD Theater; DMX Music; ESPN 2 HD; ESPN Classic Sports; ESPN HD; ESPNews; Fox Movie Channel; Fox Soccer; Fuse; G4; GAS; GSN; Halogen Network; History Channel International; Independent Film Channel; Lifetime Movie Network; MTV Networks Digital Suite; NFL Network; Nick Jr.; NickToons TV; Sleuth; Speed Channel; Style Network; Toon Disney; Turner Classic Movies; Turner Network TV HD; Universal HD.
Fee: $10.00 monthly.

Digital Pay Service 1
Pay Units: N.A.
Programming (via satellite): Cinemax (multiplexed); Cinemax HD; Encore (multiplexed); Flix; HBO (multiplexed); HBO HD; Showtime (multiplexed); Starz (multiplexed); Sundance Channel; The Movie Channel (multiplexed).
Fee: $6.00 monthly (Encore), $13.00 monthly (HBO, Cinemax, Showtime/TMC or Starz).

Video-On-Demand: Yes

Pay-Per-View
iN DEMAND (delivered digitally); ESPN (delivered digitally); Fresh (delivered digitally); Playboy TV (delivered digitally).

Internet Service
Operational: Yes.
Broadband Service: MetroCast Internet.
Fee: $79.99 installation; $43.95 monthly.

Telephone Service
Digital: Operational
Fee: $24.95 installation; $29.95 monthly
Miles of Plant: 75.0 (coaxial); None (fiber optic). Additional miles planned: 10.0 (coaxial). Homes passed: 4,683. Total homes in franchised area: 7,213.
General Manager: Rick Ferrall. Technical Operations Manager: Jerry Morris. Marketing Manager: Lee Beck.
City fee: 3% of gross.
Ownership: Harron Communications LP (MSO).

NEW AUGUSTA—Franklin Telephone Co. Inc. SnapVision. Formerly served by MEADVILLE-BUDE, MS [MS0069]. This cable system has converted to IPTV, PO Box 168, 304 Main St, Ackerman, MS 39462. Phones: 800-531-0427; 601-964-8311. Web Site: http://www.ftcweb.net. ICA: MS5030.
TV Market Ranking: Below 100 (NEW AUGUSTA).
Channel capacity: N.A. Channels available but not in use: N.A.

Internet Service
Operational: Yes.

Telephone Service
Digital: Operational
Ownership: Delta Telephone.

NEW AUGUSTA—Telepex. No longer in operation. ICA: MS0117.
TV Market Ranking: Franchise award date: N.A. Franchise expiration date: N.A. Began: N.A.

NEW HEBRON—Branch Cable Inc. This cable system has converted to IPTV. See New Hebron, MS [MS5014]. ICA: MS0171.

NEW HEBRON—Formerly served by Branch Cable Inc. [MS0171]. This cable system has converted to IPTV, 803 Julia St, Isola, MS 38754. Phone: 662-962-5500. ICA: MS5014.
Channel capacity: N.A. Channels available but not in use: N.A.

Internet Service
Operational: Yes.
Ownership: Delta Telephone.

NEWTON—Mediacom. Now served by LOUISVILLE, MS [MS0038]. ICA: MS0059.

OAKLAND—L & J Cable, PO Box 240, Oakland, MS 38948. Phone: 662-307-0553. ICA: MS0208.
TV Market Ranking: Outside TV Markets (OAKLAND). Franchise award date: N.A. Franchise expiration date: N.A. Began: N.A.
Channel capacity: 16 (not 2-way capable). Channels available but not in use: N.A.

Basic Service
Subscribers: 70.
Programming (received off-air): WABG-TV (ABC) Greenwood; WMAO-TV (PBS) Greenwood; WTVA (NBC) Tupelo; WXVT (CBS) Greenville.
Programming (via satellite): ABC Family Channel; BET Networks; CNN; Discovery Channel; Disney Channel; ESPN; TBS Superstation; Trinity Broadcasting Network; Turner Network TV; USA Network; WGN America.
Fee: $25.00 installation; $27.00 monthly.

Internet Service
Operational: No.

Telephone Service
None
Manager & Chief Technician: James Alford.
Ownership: L & J Cable.

OKTIBBEHA COUNTY—Cable TV Inc., PO Box 2598, 612 Hwy 82 W, Starkville, MS 39760. Phone: 662-324-5121. Fax: 662-324-0233. ICA: MS0218.
TV Market Ranking: Below 100 (OKTIBBEHA COUNTY (portions)); Outside TV Markets (OKTIBBEHA COUNTY (portions)).
Channel capacity: N.A. Channels available but not in use: N.A.

Basic Service
Subscribers: 372.
Fee: $40.00 installation; $33.95 monthly.

For more information call **800-771-9202** or visit **www.warren-news.com**

Internet Service
Operational: No.

Telephone Service
None
General Manager: Andy Williams.
Ownership: Andy Williams (MSO).

OSAGE COUNTY—Formerly served by Galaxy Cablevision. No longer in operation. ICA: MS0169.

OSYKA—Formerly served by Almega Cable. No longer in operation. ICA: MS0120.

OXFORD—MetroCast Communications, 311 Heritage Dr, Oxford, MS 38852. Phones: 662-234-4711; 662-728-8111. Fax: 662-236-3593. Web Site: http://www.metrocastcommunications.com. Also serves Abbeville, Lafayette County & University of Mississippi. ICA: MS0020.
TV Market Ranking: Below 100 (Abbeville, Lafayette County, OXFORD, University of Mississippi). Franchise award date: N.A. Franchise expiration date: N.A. Began: June 1, 1971.
Channel capacity: N.A. Channels available but not in use: N.A.

Basic Service
Subscribers: 9,364.
Programming (received off-air): WBUY-TV (TBN) Holly Springs; WCBI-TV (CBS, CW, MNT) Columbus; WHBQ-TV (FOX) Memphis; WKNO (PBS) Memphis; WLMT (CW) Memphis; WLOV-TV (FOX) West Point; WMAV-TV (PBS) Oxford; WMC-TV (NBC) Memphis; WPTY-TV (ABC) Memphis; WREG-TV (CBS) Memphis; WTVA (NBC) Tupelo.
Current originations: Educational Access.
Fee: $49.95 installation; $17.95 monthly; $1.25 converter.

Expanded Basic Service 1
Subscribers: 5,199.
Programming (via satellite): ABC Family Channel; AMC; Animal Planet; Arts & Entertainment; BET Networks; Bravo; Cartoon Network; CNBC; CNN; Comcast Sports Net Southeast; Comedy Central; Cooking Channel; Country Music TV; C-SPAN; C-SPAN 2; Discovery Channel; Disney Channel; Do-It-Yourself; E! Entertainment Television; ESPN; ESPN 2; Food Network; Fox News Channel; FX; Golf Channel; Great American Country; Hallmark Channel; Headline News; HGTV; History Channel; Home Shopping Network; INSP; Lifetime; MTV; National Geographic Channel; Nickelodeon; QVC; SoapNet; Spike TV; TBS Superstation; The Learning Channel; Travel Channel; truTV; Turner Network TV; TV Guide Network; TV Land; USA Network; Versus; VH1; WE tv; Weather Channel; WGN America; WPXX-TV (ION, MNT) Memphis.
Fee: $33.00 monthly.

Digital Basic Service
Subscribers: 3,400.
Programming (via satellite): BBC America; Bio; Bloomberg Television; Discovery Digital Networks; DMX Music; ESPN Classic Sports; ESPNews; FitTV; Fox Movie Channel; Fox Sports World; Fuse; G4; GAS; GSN; Halogen Network; History Channel International; Independent Film Channel; Lifetime Movie Network; MTV2; Nick Jr.; NickToons TV; Outdoor Channel; Speed Channel; Style Network; Toon Disney; Turner Classic Movies; VH1 Classic.
Fee: $10.00 monthly.

Digital Pay Service 1
Pay Units: N.A.
Programming (via satellite): Cinemax (multiplexed); Encore; Flix (multiplexed); HBO (multiplexed); The Movie Channel (multiplexed).
Fee: $6.00 monthly (Encore), $14.00 monthly (HBO, Cinemax, Starz, or TMC/Flix).

Video-On-Demand: Yes

Pay-Per-View
ESPN (delivered digitally); ESPN Now (delivered digitally); Playboy TV (delivered digitally); Hot Choice (delivered digitally); Fresh (delivered digitally); iN DEMAND (delivered digitally).

Internet Service
Operational: Yes.
Subscribers: 4,400.
Broadband Service: MetroCast Internet.
Fee: $79.99 installation; $43.95 monthly; $2.00 modem lease.

Telephone Service
Digital: Operational
Fee: $24.95 installation; $29.95 monthly
Miles of Plant: 279.0 (coaxial); None (fiber optic). Additional miles planned: 5.0 (coaxial). Homes passed: 14,890. Total homes in franchised area: 15,740. Miles of plant (coax) includes miles of plant (fiber)
General Manager: Rick Ferrall. Technical Operations Manager: Jerry Morris. Marketing Manager: Lee Beck.
Ownership: Harron Communications LP (MSO).

PACHUTA—Formerly served by Galaxy Cablevision. No longer in operation. ICA: MS0173.

PASCAGOULA—Cable One, PO Box 1818, 5100 Macphelah Rd, Pascagoula, MS 39567. Phone: 228-769-1221. Fax: 228-769-6216. Web Site: http://www.cableone.net. Also serves Escatawpa, Gautier, Hurley, Jackson County, Moss Point & Wade. ICA: MS0003.
TV Market Ranking: 59 (Escatawpa, Hurley, Jackson County (portions), Moss Point, PASCAGOULA, Wade); Below 100 (Gautier, Jackson County (portions)). Franchise award date: July 25, 1968. Franchise expiration date: N.A. Began: January 1, 1971.
Channel capacity: 84 (operating 2-way). Channels available but not in use: 1.

Basic Service
Subscribers: 19,000.
Programming (received off-air): WALA-TV (FOX) Mobile; WKRG-TV (CBS) Mobile; WLOX (ABC) Biloxi; WMAH-TV (PBS) Biloxi; WPMI-TV (NBC) Mobile; WXXV-TV (FOX, MNT) Gulfport.
Programming (via satellite): ABC Family Channel; AMC; Animal Planet; Arts & Entertainment; BET Networks; Cartoon Network; CNBC; CNN; Comcast Sports Net South-

east; Country Music TV; C-SPAN; C-SPAN 2; CW+; Discovery Channel; Disney Channel; ESPN; ESPN 2; Eternal Word TV Network; Food Network; Fox News Channel; FX; Headline News; HGTV; History Channel; Home Shopping Network; INSP; Lifetime; MSNBC; MTV; Nickelodeon; QVC; Spike TV; Syfy; TBS Superstation; The Learning Channel; Turner Classic Movies; Turner Network TV; TV Guide Network; TV Land; USA Network; VH1; Weather Channel; WGN America.
Current originations: Leased Access; Public Access.
Fee: $75.00 installation; $46.00 monthly; $2.72 converter.

Digital Basic Service
Subscribers: 8,651.
Programming (received off-air): WALA-TV (FOX) Mobile; WLOX (ABC) Biloxi.
Programming (via satellite): 3 Angels Broadcasting Network; Bio; Boomerang; BYU Television; Canales N; Discovery Digital Networks; DMX Music; ESPN Classic Sports; ESPNews; FamilyNet; Fox College Sports Atlantic; Fox College Sports Central; Fox College Sports Pacific; Fox Movie Channel; Fox Soccer; Fuel TV; G4; Golf Channel; Hallmark Channel; History Channel International; INSP; National Geographic Channel; Outdoor Channel; SoapNet; Speed Channel; Toon Disney; Trinity Broadcasting Network; truTV; Turner Network TV HD; TVG Network; Universal HD.
Fee: $8.95 monthly.

Digital Pay Service 1
Pay Units: 3,077.
Programming (via satellite): Cinemax (multiplexed).
Fee: $2.00 installation; $15.00 monthly.

Digital Pay Service 2
Pay Units: 3,498.
Programming (via satellite): HBO (multiplexed).
Fee: $2.00 installation; $15.00 monthly.

Digital Pay Service 3
Pay Units: 1,727.
Programming (via satellite): Flix; Showtime (multiplexed); Showtime HD; Sundance Channel; The Movie Channel (multiplexed); The Movie Channel HD.
Fee: $2.00 installation; $15.00 monthly.

Digital Pay Service 4
Pay Units: N.A.
Programming (via satellite): Encore (multiplexed); Starz (multiplexed).
Fee: $15.00 monthly.

Video-On-Demand: No

Pay-Per-View
Addressable homes: 8,651.
Addressable: Yes; Movies (delivered digitally); Pleasure (delivered digitally); Ten Clips (delivered digitally); Ten Blox (delivered digitally); Ten Blue (delivered digitally); ESPN (delivered digitally).

Internet Service
Operational: Yes. Began: April 1, 2001.
Subscribers: 5,000.
Broadband Service: CableONE.net.
Fee: $75.00 installation; $43.00 monthly.

Telephone Service
Digital: Operational
Fee: $75.00 installation; $39.95 monthly

Miles of Plant: 695.0 (coaxial); 120.0 (fiber optic). Homes passed: 28,000. Total homes in franchised area: 28,000.
General Manager: Cindy Byrd. Marketing Director: Tanya McMillian. Chief Technician: Dennis Lawson.
City fee: 5% of gross.
Ownership: Cable One Inc. (MSO).

PAULDING—Comcast Cable, 2100 Lincoln Rd, Hattiesburg, MS 39402-3114. Phone: 601-579-3960. Fax: 601-268-3956. Web Site: http://www.comcast.com. ICA: MS0210.
TV Market Ranking: Below 100 (PAULDING).
Channel capacity: N.A. Channels available but not in use: N.A.

Basic Service
Subscribers: N.A. Included in Hattiesburg
Programming (received off-air): WDAM-TV (NBC) Laurel; WJTV (CBS) Jackson; WLBT (NBC) Jackson; WMAW-TV (PBS) Meridian; WTOK-TV (ABC, CW, FOX, MNT) Meridian; WXXV-TV (FOX, MNT) Gulfport.
Programming (via satellite): ABC Family Channel; AMC; Animal Planet; Arts & Entertainment; BET Networks; Cartoon Network; Comcast Sports Net Southeast; Comcast/Charter Sports Southeast (CSS); Country Music TV; C-SPAN; Discovery Channel; Discovery Health Channel; Disney Channel; E! Entertainment Television; ESPN; ESPN 2; Food Network; FX; GSN; Headline News; HGTV; History Channel; Home Shopping Network; INSP; Lifetime; MSNBC; Nickelodeon; QVC; Speed Channel; Spike TV; Style Network; Syfy; TBS Superstation; The Learning Channel; Toon Disney; Trinity Broadcasting Network; truTV; Turner Classic Movies; Turner Network TV; TV Land; USA Network; Versus; Weather Channel; WGN America.
Fee: $60.00 installation; $6.15 monthly.

Digital Basic Service
Subscribers: N.A. Included in Hattiesburg
Programming (via satellite): BBC America; Discovery Digital Networks; DMX Music; Flix; GAS; MTV Networks Digital Suite; Nick Jr.; Nick Too; Sundance Channel.
Fee: $9.95 monthly.

Pay Service 1
Pay Units: N.A.
Programming (via satellite): Cinemax; Encore (multiplexed); HBO (multiplexed).

Digital Pay Service 1
Pay Units: N.A.
Programming (via satellite): Cinemax (multiplexed); HBO (multiplexed); Showtime (multiplexed); The Movie Channel (multiplexed).

Video-On-Demand: No

Pay-Per-View
iN DEMAND (delivered digitally); Hot Choice (delivered digitally); Pleasure (delivered digitally).

Internet Service
Operational: Yes.
Broadband Service: Comcast High Speed Internet.
Fee: $42.95 monthly.

Telephone Service
Digital: Operational

Miles of Plant: 145.0 (coaxial); None (fiber optic).
General Manager: Farrel Ryder. Operations Manager: Larry Frazier. Marketing Manager: Dan Carleton.
Ownership: Comcast Cable Communications Inc. (MSO).

PEARL—Comcast Cable, 5375 Executive Pl, Jackson, MS 39206. Phone: 601-982-1187. Fax: 601-321-3888. Web Site: http://www.comcast.com. Also serves Brandon, Fannin, Florence (portions), Flowood, Pelahatchie, Rankin County (portions) & Star. ICA: MS0006.
TV Market Ranking: 77 (Brandon, Fannin, Florence (portions), Flowood, PEARL, Pelahatchie, Rankin County (portions), Star). Franchise award date: January 1, 1975. Franchise expiration date: N.A. Began: December 27, 1977.
Channel capacity: 62 (operating 2-way). Channels available but not in use: None.

Basic Service
Subscribers: 23,413.
Programming (received off-air): WAPT (ABC) Jackson; WDBD (FOX) Jackson; WJTV (CBS) Jackson; WLBT (NBC) Jackson; WMPN-TV (PBS) Jackson; WRBJ (CW) Magee; WUFX (MNT) Vicksburg.
Programming (via satellite): C-SPAN; C-SPAN 2; QVC; Trinity Broadcasting Network; TV Guide Network; WGN America.
Current originations: Public Access; Government Access; Educational Access; Leased Access.
Fee: $14.42 monthly.

Expanded Basic Service 1
Subscribers: 20,273.
Programming (received off-air): WXMS-LP Natchez.
Programming (via satellite): ABC Family Channel; AMC; Animal Planet; Arts & Entertainment; BET Networks; Bravo; Cartoon Network; CNBC; CNN; Comcast Sports Net Southeast; Comedy Central; Country Music TV; Discovery Channel; Discovery Health Channel; Disney Channel; E! Entertainment Television; ESPN; ESPN 2; ESPN Classic Sports; ESPNews; FamilyNet; Food Network; Fox News Channel; FX; Hallmark Channel; Headline News; HGTV; History Channel; INSP; ION Television; Lifetime; MSNBC; MTV; Nickelodeon; Product Information Network; ShopNBC; SoapNet; Spike TV; Syfy; TBS Superstation; The Learning Channel; Toon Disney; Travel Channel; truTV; Turner Network TV; Turner South; TV Land; USA Network; VH1; WE tv; Weather Channel.
Fee: $31.56 monthly.

Digital Basic Service
Subscribers: 7,323.
Programming (received off-air): WAPT (ABC) Jackson; WJTV (CBS) Jackson; WMPN-TV (PBS) Jackson.
Programming (via satellite): BBC America; Discovery Digital Networks; Discovery HD Theater; ESPN HD; HDNet; HDNet Movies; Lifetime Movie Network; MTV Networks Digital Suite; Music Choice; NFL Network; Nick Jr.; Nick Too; NickToons TV; Speed Channel; TeenNick; Universal HD.
Fee: $12.95 monthly.

Pay Service 1
Pay Units: N.A.
Programming (via satellite): HBO (multiplexed).

Digital Pay Service 1
Pay Units: N.A.
Programming (via satellite): Cinemax (multiplexed); Cinemax HD; Encore (multiplexed); HBO (multiplexed); HBO HD; Showtime (multiplexed); Showtime HD; Starz (multiplexed); The Movie Channel (multiplexed).
Fee: $11.95 monthly (each).

Video-On-Demand: No

Pay-Per-View
ESPN Full Court (delivered digitally), Addressable: Yes; ESPN Gameplan (delivered digitally), Addressable: Yes; Playboy TV (delivered digitally), Addressable: Yes; Fresh (delivered digitally).

Internet Service
Operational: Yes.
Subscribers: 2,416.
Broadband Service: Comcast High Speed Internet.
Fee: $42.95 monthly.

Telephone Service
Digital: Planned

Miles of Plant: 733.0 (coaxial); 57.0 (fiber optic). Homes passed: 48,962.
Vice President & General Manager: Ronnie Colvin. Engineering Director: Sandy McKnight. Marketing Director: Wesley Dowling. Public Affairs Director: Frances Smith.
City fee: 5% of gross.
Ownership: Comcast Cable Communications Inc. (MSO).

PEARLINGTON—Mediacom. Now served by WAVELAND, MS [MS0022]. ICA: MS0088.

PHILADELPHIA—MetroCast Communications, PO Box 669, 625-A E Main St, Philadelphia, MS 39350. Phone: 601-656-5050. Fax: 601-656-3223. Web Site: http://www.metrocastcommunications.com. Also serves Choctaw Indian Reservation & Neshoba County (unincorporated areas). ICA: MS0029.
TV Market Ranking: Below 100 (Neshoba County (unincorporated areas) (portions)); Outside TV Markets (Choctaw Indian Reservation, Neshoba County (unincorporated areas) (portions), PHILADELPHIA). Franchise award date: March 20, 1967. Franchise expiration date: N.A. Began: December 10, 1967.
Channel capacity: 62 (operating 2-way). Channels available but not in use: None.

Basic Service
Subscribers: 3,824.
Programming (received off-air): WGBC (NBC) Meridian; WHTV (MNT) Jackson; WJTV (CBS) Jackson; WMAB-TV (PBS) Mississippi State; WMDN (CBS) Meridian; WTOK-TV (ABC, CW, FOX, MNT) Meridian; WTVA (NBC) Tupelo.
Programming (via satellite): CW+; Hallmark Channel; Trinity Broadcasting Network; WGN America.
Fee: $55.00 installation; $20.99 monthly; $10.00 additional installation.

Expanded Basic Service 1
Subscribers: 3,500.
Programming (via satellite): ABC Family Channel; Arts & Entertainment; BET Networks; Cartoon Network; CNBC; CNN; Comcast Sports Net Southeast; Comcast/Charter Sports Southeast (CSS); Comedy Central; Country Music TV; C-SPAN; Discovery Channel; Disney Channel; ESPN; ESPN 2; Food Network; Fox Movie Chan-

nel; Fox News Channel; FX; Golf Channel; Gospel Music Channel; Great American Country; Headline News; HGTV; History Channel; Lifetime; MTV; National Geographic Channel; Nickelodeon; Outdoor Channel; QVC; RFD-TV; Spike TV; SportSouth; Syfy; TBS Superstation; Travel Channel; Turner Classic Movies; Turner Network TV; TV Land; USA Network; VH1; Weather Channel.
Fee: $30.00 installation; $31.00 monthly.

Digital Basic Service
Subscribers: 1,050.
Programming (received off-air): WGBC (NBC) Meridian; WMAB-TV (PBS) Mississippi State; WMDN (CBS) Meridian; WTOK-TV (ABC, CW, FOX, MNT) Meridian.
Programming (via satellite): Animal Planet HD; BBC America; Bravo; CMT Pure Country; Discovery Channel HD; Discovery HD Theater; Discovery Health Channel; Discovery Kids Channel; Discovery Military Channel; Discovery Planet Green; DMX Music; ESPN 2 HD; ESPN HD; ESPNews; FitTV; Fox Soccer; G4; ID Investigation Discovery; Independent Film Channel; Nick Jr.; NickToons TV; Outdoor Channel 2 HD; Science Channel; Science Channel HD; Speed Channel; TLC HD; Turner Network TV HD; VH1 Classic; WE tv.
Fee: $5.95 monthly.

Digital Pay Service 1
Pay Units: N.A.
Programming (via satellite): Cinemax (multiplexed); Cinemax HD; Encore (multiplexed); Flix; HBO (multiplexed); HBO HD; Showtime; Starz (multiplexed); The Movie Channel.

Video-On-Demand: No

Pay-Per-View
iN DEMAND (delivered digitally); Hot Choice (delivered digitally).

Internet Service
Operational: Yes.
Broadband Service: MetroCast Internet.
Fee: $79.99 installation; $35.99 monthly.

Telephone Service
Analog: Not Operational
Digital: Operational
Fee: $30.00 installation; $29.95 monthly

Miles of Plant: 155.0 (coaxial); 16.0 (fiber optic). Homes passed: 3,975. Total homes in franchised area: 7,986.
General Manager: Rick Ferrall. Chief Technician: Stan Burt. Marketing Manager: Lee Beck. Office Manager: Martha Duvall.
City fee: 3% of basic gross.
Ownership: Harron Communications LP (MSO).

PICAYUNE—Charter Communications, 1304 Ridgefield Rd, Thibodaux, LA 70301. Phone: 985-446-4900. Fax: 985-447-9541. Web Site: http://www.charter.com. Also serves Carrierre, McNeill & Pearl River County. ICA: MS0023.
TV Market Ranking: Below 100 (McNeill, Pearl River County (portions), PICAYUNE); Outside TV Markets (Carrierre, Pearl River County (portions)). Franchise award date: December 1, 1963. Franchise expiration date: N.A. Began: September 1, 1964.
Channel capacity: N.A. Channels available but not in use: N.A.

Basic Service
Subscribers: 6,425.
Programming (received off-air): WAFB (CBS) Baton Rouge; WDAM-TV (NBC) Laurel; WDSU (NBC) New Orleans; WGNO (ABC) New Orleans; WHNO (IND) New Orleans; WLAE-TV (PBS) New Orleans; WLOX (ABC) Biloxi; WMAH-TV (PBS) Biloxi; WNOL-TV (CW) New Orleans; WPXL-TV (ION) New Orleans; WUPL (MNT) Slidell; WVUE-DT (FOX) New Orleans; WWL-TV (CBS) New Orleans; WXXV-TV (FOX, MNT) Gulfport; WYES-TV (PBS) New Orleans.
Programming (via satellite): C-SPAN; Home Shopping Network; INSP; QVC; TV Guide Network; WGN America.
Current originations: Leased Access.
Planned originations: Religious Access.
Fee: $29.99 installation.

Expanded Basic Service 1
Subscribers: N.A.
Programming (via satellite): ABC Family Channel; AMC; Animal Planet; Arts & Entertainment; BET Networks; Bravo; Cartoon Network; CNN; Comcast Sports Net Southeast; Comcast/Charter Sports Southeast (CSS); Comedy Central; Country Music TV; C-SPAN 2; Discovery Channel; Disney Channel; E! Entertainment Television; ESPN; ESPN 2; Eternal Word TV Network; Food Network; Fox News Channel; FX; Golf Channel; Headline News; HGTV; History Channel; Lifetime; MSNBC; MTV; National Geographic Channel; Nickelodeon; Outdoor Channel; Product Information Network; SoapNet; Speed Channel; Spike TV; Syfy; TBS Superstation; The Learning Channel; Toon Disney; Travel Channel; Turner Classic Movies; Turner Network TV; TV Land; USA Network; Versus; VH1; WE tv; Weather Channel.
Fee: $42.99 monthly.

Digital Basic Service
Subscribers: N.A.
Programming (via satellite): BBC America; Bio; Discovery Digital Networks; Do-It-Yourself; GAS; History Channel International; Independent Film Channel; Lifetime Movie Network; MTV Networks Digital Suite; Music Choice; Nick Jr.; Nick Too; NickToons TV; Sundance Channel; TV Guide Interactive Inc.

Digital Pay Service 1
Pay Units: N.A.
Programming (via satellite): Cinemax (multiplexed); Encore; Flix; HBO (multiplexed); Showtime (multiplexed); Starz (multiplexed); The Movie Channel (multiplexed).

Video-On-Demand: Yes

Pay-Per-View
iN DEMAND (delivered digitally); Playboy TV (delivered digitally); Fresh (delivered digitally); Shorteez (delivered digitally).

Internet Service
Operational: Yes.
Broadband Service: Charter Pipeline.
Fee: $29.99 monthly.

Telephone Service
Digital: Operational

Miles of Plant: 220.0 (coaxial); None (fiber optic). Total homes in franchised area: 35,301.
Vice President & General Manager: Kip Kraemer. Operations Manager: Dave Houghtlin. Technical Operations Director: Gary Savoie. Marketing Director: Lisa Brown. Government Relations Director: Jim Laurent.
City fee: 3% of gross.
Ownership: Charter Communications Inc. (MSO).

PONTOTOC—MetroCast Communications, 311 Heritage Dr, Oxford, MS 38852. Phones: 662-234-4711; 662-728-8111. Fax: 662-236-3593. Web Site: http://www.metrocastcommunications.com. Also serves Houston & Water Valley. ICA: MS0045.
TV Market Ranking: Below 100 (Houston, PONTOTOC); Outside TV Markets (Water Valley). Franchise award date: May 10, 1966. Franchise expiration date: N.A. Began: November 1, 1968.
Channel capacity: N.A. Channels available but not in use: N.A.

Basic Service
Subscribers: 2,299.
Programming (received off-air): W15CG Pontotoc; WCBI-TV (CBS, CW, MNT) Columbus; WHBQ-TV (FOX) Memphis; WKDH (ABC) Houston; WLOV-TV (FOX) West Point; WMAV-TV (PBS) Oxford; WMC-TV (NBC) Memphis; WPTY-TV (ABC) Memphis; WREG-TV (CBS) Memphis; WTVA (NBC) Tupelo; allband FM.
Programming (via satellite): WGN America.
Fee: $49.95 installation; $17.95 monthly; $3.35 converter; $20.00 additional installation.

Expanded Basic Service 1
Subscribers: N.A.
Programming (via satellite): ABC Family Channel; AMC; Animal Planet; Arts & Entertainment; BET Networks; Bravo; Cartoon Network; CNBC; CNN; Comcast Sports Net Southeast; Comedy Central; Country Music TV; C-SPAN; C-SPAN 2; Discovery Channel; Disney Channel; E! Entertainment Television; ESPN; ESPN 2; ESPN Classic Sports; FitTV; Food Network; Fox News Channel; FX; Golf Channel; Great American Country; Hallmark Channel; Headline News; HGTV; History Channel; Home Shopping Network; INSP; ION Television; Lifetime; MSNBC; MTV; Nickelodeon; Outdoor Channel; QVC; Speed Channel; Spike TV; Syfy; TBS Superstation; The Learning Channel; Travel Channel; Trinity Broadcasting Network; Turner Network TV; Turner South; TV Land; USA Network; VH1; WE tv; Weather Channel.
Fee: $33.00 monthly; $3.35 converter.

Digital Basic Service
Subscribers: N.A.
Programming (received off-air): WCBI-TV (CBS, CW, MNT) Columbus; WLMT (CW) Memphis; WMC-TV (NBC) Memphis; WPTY-TV (ABC) Memphis.
Programming (via satellite): AmericanLife TV Network; BBC America; Bio; Bloomberg Television; Discovery Digital Networks; Discovery HD Theater; DMX Music; ESPN Classic Sports; ESPNews; Fox Movie Channel; Fox Soccer; Fuse; G4; GAS; Golf Channel; GSN; Halogen Network; History Channel International; Independent Film Channel; Lifetime Movie Network; Lime; MTV Networks Digital Suite; National Geographic Channel; NFL Network; Nick Jr.; NickToons TV; Outdoor Channel; Sleuth; Speed Channel; Style Network; Toon Disney; Turner Classic Movies; Turner Network TV HD; Universal HD; Versus.
Fee: $10.00 monthly; $5.00 converter.

Digital Pay Service 1
Pay Units: 563.
Programming (via satellite): HBO (multiplexed).
Fee: $13.00 monthly.

Digital Pay Service 2
Pay Units: 245.
Programming (via satellite): Flix; Showtime (multiplexed); Sundance Channel; The Movie Channel (multiplexed).
Fee: $13.00 monthly.

Digital Pay Service 3
Pay Units: 285.
Programming (via satellite): Cinemax (multiplexed).
Fee: $13.00 monthly.

Digital Pay Service 4
Pay Units: N.A.
Programming (via satellite): Encore (multiplexed); Starz (multiplexed).
Fee: $6.00 monthly (Encore), $13.00 monthly (Starz).

Video-On-Demand: Yes

Pay-Per-View
Movies (delivered digitally); Fresh (delivered digitally); Hot Choice (delivered digitally); Playboy TV (delivered digitally); ESPN (delivered digitally); MLB Extra Innings (delivered digitally).

Internet Service
Operational: Yes.
Broadband Service: MetroCast Internet.
Fee: $79.99 installation; $43.95 monthly.

Telephone Service
Digital: Operational

Miles of Plant: 91.0 (coaxial); None (fiber optic). Homes passed: 3,218. Total homes in franchised area: 3,218.
General Manager: Rick Ferrall. Technical Operations Manager: Jerry Morris. Marketing Manager: Lee Beck.
City fee: 2% of gross.
Ownership: Harron Communications LP (MSO).

PONTOTOC—Windjammer Cable, 4400 PGA Blvd, Ste 902, Palm Beach Gardens, FL 33410. Phones: 877-450-5558; 561-775-1208. Fax: 561-775-7811. Web Site: http://www.windjammercable.com. Also serves Lee County (unincorporated areas). ICA: MS0041.
TV Market Ranking: Below 100 (Lee County (unincorporated areas), PONTOTOC). Franchise award date: N.A. Franchise expiration date: N.A. Began: September 1, 1989.
Channel capacity: N.A. Channels available but not in use: N.A.

Basic Service
Subscribers: N.A. Included in Greenwood
Programming (received off-air): WCBI-TV (CBS, CW, MNT) Columbus; WHBQ-TV (FOX) Memphis; WLOV-TV (FOX) West Point; WMC-TV (NBC) Memphis; WPTY-TV (ABC) Memphis; WTVA (NBC) Tupelo.
Programming (via satellite): ABC Family Channel; AMC; Animal Planet; Arts & Entertainment; BET Networks; CNBC; CNN; Comcast Sports Net Southeast; Comedy Central; Country Music TV; C-SPAN; C-SPAN 2; Discovery Channel; Disney Channel; E! Entertainment Television; ESPN; ESPN 2; Fox News Channel; Headline News; HGTV; History Channel; Lifetime; MSNBC; MTV; Nickelodeon; QVC; Spike TV; Syfy; TBS Superstation; The

Learning Channel; Trinity Broadcasting Network; Turner Network TV; TV Land; USA Network; VH1; Weather Channel; WGN America.
Current originations: Government Access; Educational Access.
Fee: $39.95 installation; $44.64 monthly.
Pay Service 1
Pay Units: N.A.
Programming (via satellite): Cinemax; HBO; Showtime.
Fee: $11.65 monthly (each).
Video-On-Demand: No
Internet Service
Operational: No.
Telephone Service
None
Miles of Plant: 78.0 (coaxial); None (fiber optic). Homes passed included in Greenwood
General Manager: Timothy Evard. Operations Director: Belinda Graham. Engineering Director: Mike Earehart. Finance & Accounting Director: Cindy Johnson.
Ownership: Windjammer Communications LLC (MSO).

POPLARVILLE—Galaxy Cablevision, PO Box 308, 214 Main St, Ste C, Monticello, MS 39654-0308. Phone: 601-587-9461. Fax: 601-587-7410. Web Site: http://www.galaxycable.com. ICA: MS0068.
TV Market Ranking: Below 100 (POPLARVILLE). Franchise award date: N.A. Franchise expiration date: N.A. Began: January 1, 1981.
Channel capacity: 41 (operating 2-way). Channels available but not in use: None.
Basic Service
Subscribers: 386.
Programming (received off-air): WDAM-TV (NBC) Laurel; WGNO (ABC) New Orleans; WHLT (CBS) Hattiesburg; WLOX (ABC) Biloxi; WMAH-TV (PBS) Biloxi; WWL-TV (CBS) New Orleans; WXXV-TV (FOX, MNT) Gulfport.
Programming (via satellite): ABC Family Channel; AMC; Arts & Entertainment; BET Networks; Cartoon Network; CNBC; CNN; Comcast Sports Net Southeast; Comedy Central; C-SPAN; Discovery Channel; Disney Channel; ESPN; ESPN 2; Fox News Channel; Fuse; FX; Great American Country; Hallmark Channel; Headline News; HGTV; History Channel; Lifetime; Outdoor Channel; QVC; TBS Superstation; The Learning Channel; Trinity Broadcasting Network; Turner Network TV; USA Network; Weather Channel; WGN America.
Current originations: Public Access.
Fee: $43.50 monthly.
Pay Service 1
Pay Units: N.A.
Programming (via satellite): HBO.
Fee: $25.00 installation; $9.42 monthly.
Pay Service 2
Pay Units: N.A.
Programming (via satellite): Encore; Starz.
Internet Service
Operational: No.
Telephone Service
None
Miles of Plant: 43.0 (coaxial); None (fiber optic). Homes passed: 1,048.
State Manager: Bill Flowers. Technical Manager & Engineer: Greg Berthaut. Customer Service Representative: Rebecca Nelson.; Parlean Myers.
Ownership: Galaxy Cable Inc. (MSO).

PORT GIBSON—Bailey Cable TV Inc., 807 Church St, Port Gibson, MS 39150-2413. Phones: 601-437-8300; 601-892-5249. Fax: 601-892-3015. ICA: MS0212.
TV Market Ranking: Below 100 (PORT GIBSON).
Channel capacity: 38 (not 2-way capable). Channels available but not in use: 2.
Basic Service
Subscribers: 300.
Programming (received off-air): WAPT (ABC) Jackson; WDBD (FOX) Jackson; WJTV (CBS) Jackson; WLBT (NBC) Jackson; WMAA (ETV) Columbus.
Programming (via satellite): ABC Family Channel; Arts & Entertainment; BET Networks; Cartoon Network; CNBC; CNN; Country Music TV; C-SPAN; Discovery Channel; ESPN; ESPN 2; G4; History Channel; MTV; Nickelodeon; QVC; Spike TV; Syfy; TBS Superstation; The Learning Channel; The Movie Channel; Trinity Broadcasting Network; Turner Network TV; TV Land; USA Network; VH1; WDBD (FOX) Jackson; Weather Channel; WGN America.
Fee: $20.00 installation; $32.12 monthly.
Pay Service 1
Pay Units: N.A.
Programming (via satellite): Showtime.
Fee: $9.63 monthly.
Video-On-Demand: No
Internet Service
Operational: No.
Telephone Service
None
Manager: Dwight Bailey.
Ownership: Bailey Cable TV Inc.

POTTS CAMP—MetroCast Communications, 311 Heritage Dr, Oxford, MS 38852. Phones: 662-234-4711; 662-728-8111. Fax: 662-236-3593. Web Site: http://www.metrocastcommunications.com. Also serves Marshall County. ICA: MS0214.
TV Market Ranking: 26 (Marshall County); Below 100 (POTTS CAMP, Marshall County).
Channel capacity: N.A. Channels available but not in use: N.A.
Basic Service
Subscribers: 135.
Programming (received off-air): WBII-CD Holly Springs; WBUY-TV (TBN) Holly Springs; WCBI-TV (CBS, CW, MNT) Columbus; WHBQ-TV (FOX) Memphis; WKDH (ABC) Houston; WKNO (PBS) Memphis; WLMT (CW) Memphis; WLOV-TV (FOX) West Point; WMAE-TV (PBS) Booneville; WMC-TV (NBC) Memphis; WPTY-TV (ABC) Memphis; WPXX-TV (ION, MNT) Memphis; WREG-TV (CBS) Memphis; WTVA (NBC) Tupelo.
Programming (via microwave): W34DV Booneville.
Programming (via satellite): CW+; Home Shopping Network; MyNetworkTV Inc.; QVC; TV Guide Network; WGN America.
Current originations: Educational Access; Leased Access.
Fee: $49.95 installation; $17.95 monthly.
Expanded Basic Service 1
Subscribers: N.A.
Programming (via satellite): ABC Family Channel; AMC; Animal Planet; Arts & Entertainment; BET Networks; Bravo; Cartoon Network; CNBC; CNN; Comcast/Charter Sports Southeast (CSS); Comedy Central; Cooking Channel; Country Music TV; C-SPAN; C-SPAN 2; Discovery Channel; Disney Channel; Do-It-Yourself; E! Entertainment Television; ESPN; ESPN 2; FitTV; Food Network; Fox News Channel; Fox Sports Net; FX; G4; Golf Channel; Great American Country; Hallmark Channel; Headline News; HGTV; History Channel; INSP; ION Television; Lifetime; MSNBC; MTV; National Geographic Channel; Nickelodeon; Outdoor Channel; SoapNet; Spike TV; SportSouth; Syfy; TBS Superstation; The Learning Channel; Toon Disney; Travel Channel; Turner Network TV; TV Land; USA Network; Versus; VH1; WE tv; Weather Channel.
Digital Basic Service
Subscribers: N.A.
Programming (received off-air): WCBI-TV (CBS, CW, MNT) Columbus; WLOV-TV (FOX) West Point; WMC-TV (NBC) Memphis; WPTY-TV (ABC) Memphis.
Programming (via satellite): AmericanLife TV Network; BBC America; Bio; Bloomberg Television; Discovery Channel HD; Discovery Health Channel; Discovery Kids Channel; Discovery Military Channel; Discovery Planet Green; DMX Music; ESPN 2 HD; ESPN Classic Sports; ESPN HD; ESPNews; Fox Soccer; Fuse; GSN; Halogen Network; History Channel International; ID Investigation Discovery; Independent Film Channel; Lifetime Movie Network; MTV Hits; MTV2; NFL Network; Nick Jr.; NickToons TV; Science Channel; Sleuth; Speed Channel; Style Network; TeenNick; Turner Classic Movies; Turner Network TV HD; Universal HD; VH1 Classic; VH1 Soul.
Digital Pay Service 1
Pay Units: N.A.
Programming (via satellite): Cinemax (multiplexed); Cinemax HD; Encore (multiplexed); Flix; HBO (multiplexed); HBO HD; Showtime (multiplexed); Starz (multiplexed); Sundance Channel; The Movie Channel (multiplexed).
Video-On-Demand: Yes
Pay-Per-View
iN DEMAND (delivered digitally); ESPN (delivered digitally); Fresh (delivered digitally); Club Jenna (delivered digitally); Playboy TV (delivered digitally).
Internet Service
Operational: Yes.
Broadband Service: MetroCast Internet.
Fee: $49.95 installation; $17.95 monthly.
Telephone Service
Digital: Operational
Fee: $24.95 installation; $29.95 monthly
Miles of Plant: 42.0 (coaxial); None (fiber optic). Homes passed: 1,200.
General Manager: Rick Ferrall. Technical Operations Manager: Bob Gabel. Marketing Manager: Lee Beck.
Ownership: Harron Communications LP (MSO).

PRENTISS—Galaxy Cablevision, PO Box 308, 214 Main St, Ste C, Monticello, MS 39654-0308. Phone: 601-587-9461. Fax: 601-587-7410. Web Site: http://www.galaxycable.com. Also serves Silver Creek. ICA: MS0086.
TV Market Ranking: Below 100 (PRENTISS, Silver Creek). Franchise award date: N.A. Franchise expiration date: N.A. Began: April 1, 1982.
Channel capacity: 41 (not 2-way capable). Channels available but not in use: None.
Basic Service
Subscribers: 176.
Programming (received off-air): WAPT (ABC) Jackson; WDAM-TV (NBC) Laurel; WDBD (FOX) Jackson; WJTV (CBS) Jackson; WLBT (NBC) Jackson; WMPN-TV (PBS) Jackson.
Programming (via satellite): ESPN; QVC; The Learning Channel; Weather Channel.
Fee: $41.60 monthly.
Expanded Basic Service 1
Subscribers: N.A.
Programming (via satellite): ABC Family Channel; AMC; Arts & Entertainment; BET Networks; Cartoon Network; CNBC; CNN; Comcast Sports Net Southeast; Comedy Central; Discovery Channel; Disney Channel; E! Entertainment Television; ESPN 2; Fox News Channel; FX; Great American Country; Hallmark Channel; Headline News; HGTV; History Channel; INSP; Lifetime; Outdoor Channel; Speed Channel; TBS Superstation; Trinity Broadcasting Network; Turner Network TV; USA Network; WGN America.
Pay Service 1
Pay Units: N.A.
Programming (via satellite): HBO; Showtime.
Fee: $25.00 installation; $10.00 monthly (each).
Pay-Per-View
Hot Choice (delivered digitally); Playboy TV (delivered digitally); Fresh (delivered digitally); Shorteez (delivered digitally).
Internet Service
Operational: No.
Telephone Service
None
Miles of Plant: 32.0 (coaxial); None (fiber optic). Homes passed: 1,189.
State Manager: Bill Flowers. Technical Manager & Engineer: Greg Berthaut. Customer Service Representative: Rebecca Nelson.; Parlean Myers.
Ownership: Galaxy Cable Inc. (MSO).

PUCKETT—Comcast Cable, 5375 Executive Pl, Jackson, MS 39206. Phone: 601-982-1187. Fax: 601-321-3888. Web Site: http://www.comcast.com. Also serves Johns. ICA: MS0199.
TV Market Ranking: 77 (Johns, PUCKETT). Franchise award date: January 1, 1975. Franchise expiration date: N.A. Began: N.A.
Channel capacity: 40 (not 2-way capable). Channels available but not in use: 9.
Basic Service
Subscribers: N.A.
Programming (received off-air): WAPT (ABC) Jackson; WDBD (FOX) Jackson; WJTV (CBS) Jackson; WLBT (NBC) Jackson; WMPN-TV (PBS) Jackson.
Programming (via satellite): ABC Family Channel; Animal Planet; Arts & Entertainment; CNN; Country Music TV; Discovery Channel; Disney Channel; ESPN; ESPN 2; Headline News; History Channel; Lifetime; MTV; Nickelodeon; QVC; Spike TV; TBS Superstation; The Learning Channel; Turner Network TV; USA Network; VH1; Weather Channel; WGN America.
Pay Service 1
Pay Units: N.A.
Programming (via satellite): HBO; Showtime.
Internet Service
Operational: No.
Telephone Service
None
Miles of Plant: 20.0 (coaxial); None (fiber optic).
Vice President & General Manager: Ronnie Colvin. Engineering Director: Sandy McKnight. Marketing Director: Wesley Dowling. Public Affairs Director: Frances Smith.
Ownership: Comcast Cable Communications Inc. (MSO).

QUITMAN—CMA Cablevision, 917 Robinson St, Waynesboro, MS 39367. Phones: 972-233-9614 (Corporate office); 800-753-2465. Fax: 601-735-0249. Web Site: http://www.cmaaccess.com. Also serves Enterprise & Stonewall. ICA: MS0176.
TV Market Ranking: Below 100 (Enterprise, QUITMAN, Stonewall). Franchise award

date: July 1, 1987. Franchise expiration date: N.A. Began: July 1, 1967.
Channel capacity: N.A. Channels available but not in use: N.A.
Basic Service
Subscribers: 1,020.
Programming (received off-air): WGBC (NBC) Meridian; WMAW-TV (PBS) Meridian; WMDN (CBS) Meridian; WTOK-TV (ABC, CW, FOX, MNT) Meridian.
Programming (via satellite): C-SPAN; Home Shopping Network.
Current originations: Public Access.
Fee: $39.95 installation; $19.45 monthly; $12.95 additional installation.
Expanded Basic Service 1
Subscribers: N.A.
Programming (via satellite): ABC Family Channel; Animal Planet; Arts & Entertainment; BET Networks; Bravo!; Cartoon Network; CNBC; CNN; Comcast Sports Net Southeast; Comedy Central; Country Music TV; Discovery Channel; E! Entertainment Television; ESPN; ESPN 2; Food Network; Fox News Channel; FX; Gospel Music TV; GSN; Hallmark Channel; Headline News; HGTV; History Channel; INSP; Lifetime; MTV; Nickelodeon; Outdoor Channel; QVC; Spike TV; Syfy; TBS Superstation; The Learning Channel; The Sportsman Channel; Travel Channel; Trinity Broadcasting Network; Turner Classic Movies; Turner Network TV; TV Land; Univision; USA Network; VH1; Weather Channel; WGN America.
Fee: $22.00 monthly.
Digital Basic Service
Subscribers: N.A.
Programming (via satellite): BBC America; Bio; Bloomberg Television; Discovery Digital Networks; Discovery Kids Channel; DMX Music; ESPN Classic Sports; ESPNews; Fox Movie Channel; G4; GAS; Golf Channel; Halogen Network; History Channel International; Independent Film Channel; Lifetime Movie Network; MTV Networks Digital Suite; National Geographic Channel; Nick Jr.; NickToons TV; Speed Channel; WE tv.
Fee: $14.95 monthly.
Pay Service 1
Pay Units: 628.
Programming (via satellite): HBO; Showtime.
Fee: $14.95 installation; $13.95 monthly (each).
Digital Pay Service 1
Pay Units: N.A.
Programming (via satellite): Cinemax (multiplexed); Encore (multiplexed); Flix; HBO (multiplexed); Showtime (multiplexed); Starz (multiplexed); Sundance Channel; The Movie Channel (multiplexed).
Fee: $10.95 monthly (Cinemax or Encore/Starz), $13.95 monthly (HBO or Showtime).
Video-On-Demand: No
Pay-Per-View
iN DEMAND (delivered digitally); Hot Choice (delivered digitally); Playboy TV (delivered digitally); Fresh (delivered digitally); Shorteez (delivered digitally).
Internet Service
Operational: Yes.
Broadband Service: CMA.
Fee: $41.95 monthly.
Telephone Service
None
Miles of Plant: 97.0 (coaxial); None (fiber optic).
Manager: Jerry Smith. Marketing Director: Julie Ferguson.
Ownership: Cable Management Assoc. (MSO).

RALEIGH—MetroCast Communications, PO Box 669, 625-A E Main St, Philadelphia, MS 39350. Phone: 601-656-5050. Fax: 601-656-3223. Web Site: http://www.metrocastcommunications.com. ICA: MS0177.
TV Market Ranking: Below 100 (RALEIGH). Franchise award date: March 1, 1982. Franchise expiration date: N.A. Began: August 1, 1983.
Channel capacity: 36 (not 2-way capable). Channels available but not in use: N.A.
Basic Service
Subscribers: 200.
Programming (received off-air): WAPT (ABC) Jackson; WDAM-TV (NBC) Laurel; WDBD (FOX) Jackson; WJTV (CBS) Jackson; WLBT (NBC) Jackson; WMPN-TV (PBS) Jackson.
Programming (via satellite): ABC Family Channel; Arts & Entertainment; CNN; Country Music TV; Discovery Channel; ESPN; Headline News; Home Shopping Network; TBS Superstation; Turner Network TV; WGN America.
Fee: $55.00 installation; $35.99 monthly.
Pay Service 1
Pay Units: 20.
Programming (via satellite): HBO.
Fee: $13.95 monthly.
Internet Service
Operational: No.
Telephone Service
None
Miles of Plant: 18.0 (coaxial); None (fiber optic).
General Manager: Rick Ferrall. Chief Technician: Stan Burt. Marketing Manager: Lee Beck. Office Manager: Martha Duvall.
City fee: 2% of basic gross.
Ownership: Harron Communications LP (MSO).

RICHTON—Galaxy Cablevision, PO Box 308, 214 Main St, Ste C, Monticello, MS 39654-0308. Phone: 601-587-9461. Fax: 601-587-7410. Web Site: http://www.galaxycable.com. ICA: MS0089.
TV Market Ranking: Below 100 (RICHTON). Franchise award date: N.A. Franchise expiration date: N.A. Began: July 14, 1989.
Channel capacity: 41 (not 2-way capable). Channels available but not in use: 5.
Basic Service
Subscribers: 163.
Programming (received off-air): WDAM-TV (NBC) Laurel; WHLT (CBS) Hattiesburg; WLOX (ABC) Biloxi; WMAH-TV (PBS) Biloxi; WXXV-TV (FOX, MNT) Gulfport.
Programming (via satellite): ABC Family Channel; Arts & Entertainment; BET Networks; Cartoon Network; CNBC; CNN; Comcast Sports Net Southeast; Comedy Central; Discovery Channel; Disney Channel; ESPN; ESPN 2; Fox News Channel; Great American Country; Headline News; HGTV; History Channel; Lifetime; Outdoor Channel; QVC; Speed Channel; TBS Superstation; The Learning Channel; Trinity Broadcasting Network; Turner Network TV; USA Network; Weather Channel; WGN America.
Current originations: Public Access.
Fee: $40.60 monthly.
Pay Service 1
Pay Units: N.A.
Programming (via satellite): Cinemax; HBO.
Fee: $9.42 monthly (HBO).
Internet Service
Operational: No.

Telephone Service
None
Miles of Plant: 11.0 (coaxial); None (fiber optic). Homes passed: 525.
State Manager: Bill Flowers. Technical Manager & Engineer: Greg Berthaut. Customer Service Representative: Rebecca Nelson.; Parlean Myers.
Ownership: Galaxy Cable Inc. (MSO).

RIENZI—Formerly served by Adelphia Communications. Now served by KOSSUTH, MI [MI0046]. ICA: MS0097.

RIPLEY—Ripley Video Cable Co. Inc., PO Box 368, 115 N Main St, Ripley, MS 38663. Phone: 662-837-4881. Web Site: http://www.ripleycable.net. Also serves Blue Mountain, Falkner & Pine Grove. ICA: MS0179.
TV Market Ranking: Below 100 (Blue Mountain, Falkner, Pine Grove, RIPLEY). Franchise award date: June 1, 1969. Franchise expiration date: N.A. Began: January 1, 1969.
Channel capacity: 52 (operating 2-way). Channels available but not in use: 20.
Basic Service
Subscribers: 3,500.
Programming (received off-air): WBII-CD Holly Springs; WCBI-TV (CBS, CW, MNT) Columbus; WFLI-TV (CW) Cleveland; WHBQ-TV (FOX) Memphis; WLMT (CW) Memphis; WMAE-TV (PBS) Booneville; WMC-TV (NBC) Memphis; WPTY-TV (ABC) Memphis; WPXX-TV (ION, MNT) Memphis; WREG-TV (CBS) Memphis; WTVA (NBC) Tupelo.
Programming (via satellite): ABC Family Channel; AMC; Animal Planet; Arts & Entertainment; BET Networks; Boomerang; Cartoon Network; CNN; Comcast/Charter Sports Southeast (CSS); Comedy Central; Country Music TV; C-SPAN; Discovery Channel; Disney Channel; E! Entertainment Television; ESPN; ESPN 2; ESPN Classic Sports; Food Network; Fox Sports Net; FX; Great American Country; Hallmark Channel; Headline News; HGTV; History Channel; Home Shopping Network; Lifetime; MTV; National Geographic Channel; Nickelodeon; Outdoor Channel; Spike TV; SportSouth; Syfy; TBS Superstation; The Learning Channel; truTV; Turner Classic Movies; Turner Network TV; Turner South; TV Guide Network; TV Land; USA Network; VH1; Weather Channel; WGN America.
Current originations: Public Access.
Fee: $50.00 installation; $38.00 monthly.
Digital Basic Service
Subscribers: 250.
Programming (via satellite): BBC America; Bio; Bloomberg Television; Discovery Health Channel; Discovery Home Channel; Discovery Kids Channel; Discovery Times Channel; DMX Music; Encore (multiplexed); ESPN Classic Sports; ESPNews; FitTV; Fox Sports World; G4; Golf Channel; GSN; Halogen Network; History Channel International; Independent Film Channel; Lifetime Movie Network; Military Channel; National Geographic Channel; RFD-TV; Science Channel; SoapNet; Speed Channel; Starz (multiplexed); Trinity Broadcasting Network; Versus; WE tv.
Fee: $12.95 monthly.
Pay Service 1
Pay Units: 650.
Programming (via satellite): HBO.
Fee: $10.95 monthly.
Pay Service 2
Pay Units: N.A.
Programming (via satellite): Cinemax.
Fee: $10.95 monthly.
Digital Pay Service 1
Pay Units: N.A.
Programming (via satellite): Cinemax (multiplexed); HBO (multiplexed); Showtime (multiplexed); The Movie Channel (multiplexed).
Fee: $13.95 monthly (each).
Video-On-Demand: No
Pay-Per-View
iN DEMAND (delivered digitally); Playboy TV (delivered digitally).
Internet Service
Operational: Yes.
Subscribers: 125.
Broadband Service: In-house.
Fee: $50.00 installation; $29.95-$59.95 monthly.
Telephone Service
Digital: Operational
Miles of Plant: 127.0 (coaxial); None (fiber optic). Additional miles planned: 10.0 (fiber optic). Homes passed: 4,250. Total homes in franchised area: 5,000.
Manager: Leon M. Bailey Jr. Chief Technician: Daniel F. Alsup.
Franchise fee: 2% of gross.
Ownership: Leon M. Bailey Jr.

ROLLING FORK—RF Cable LLC, 19999 Hwy 61, Rolling Fork, MS 39159. Phone: 662-873-6983. Fax: 662-873-6090. E-mail: rfcable@msdeltawireless.com. ICA: MS0083.
TV Market Ranking: Below 100 (ROLLING FORK). Franchise award date: N.A. Franchise expiration date: N.A. Began: August 1, 1980.
Channel capacity: 51 (not 2-way capable). Channels available but not in use: None.
Basic Service
Subscribers: 600.
Programming (received off-air): WABG-TV (ABC) Greenwood; WAPT (ABC) Jackson; WJTV (CBS) Jackson; WLBT (NBC) Jackson; WMPN-TV (PBS) Jackson.
Programming (via satellite): ABC Family Channel; CNN; TBS Superstation; WGN America.
Fee: $45.00 installation; $32.00 monthly; $40.00 additional installation.
Pay Service 1
Pay Units: 51.
Programming (via satellite): HBO.
Fee: $45.00 installation; $15.00 monthly.
Internet Service
Operational: No.
Telephone Service
None
Miles of Plant: 12.0 (coaxial); None (fiber optic). Additional miles planned: 1.0 (coaxial). Homes passed: 675. Total homes in franchised area: 675.

Manager: George Martin.
Ownership: RF Cable LLC.

ROSEDALE—Community Communications Co., 1920 Highway 425 N, Monticello, AR 71655-4463. Phones: 800-272-2191; 870-367-7300. Fax: 870-367-9770. E-mail: generalmanager@ccc-cable.net. Web Site: http://www.ccc-cable.net. ICA: MS0052.
TV Market Ranking: Below 100 (ROSEDALE). Franchise award date: N.A. Franchise expiration date: N.A. Began: April 1, 1980.
Channel capacity: 48 (not 2-way capable). Channels available but not in use: N.A.
Basic Service
Subscribers: 300.
Programming (received off-air): KARZ-TV (MNT) Little Rock; KASN (CW) Pine Bluff; KATV (ABC) Little Rock; KKYK-CA (IND) Little Rock; KTVE (NBC) El Dorado; WABG-TV (ABC) Greenwood; WMAO-TV (PBS) Greenwood; WXVT (CBS) Greenville.
Programming (via satellite): ABC Family Channel; AMC; Arts & Entertainment; BET Networks; CNN; Comedy Central; Discovery Channel; Disney Channel; ESPN; ESPN 2; Eternal Word TV Network; Fox Sports Net; Home Shopping Network; Lifetime; National Geographic Channel; Nickelodeon; Outdoor Channel; QVC; Spike TV; Syfy; TBS Superstation; The Learning Channel; Trinity Broadcasting Network; Turner Classic Movies; Turner Network TV; USA Network; VH1; Weather Channel; WGN America.
Fee: $30.00 installation; $32.00 monthly.
Pay Service 1
Pay Units: 130.
Programming (via satellite): Cinemax; HBO; Showtime; The Movie Channel.
Fee: $12.00 monthly (each).
Internet Service
Operational: No.
Telephone Service
None
Miles of Plant: 14.0 (coaxial); None (fiber optic). Homes passed: 585.
Operations Manager: Larry Ivy.
Ownership: Community Communications Co. (MSO).

ROXIE—Delta Telephone Inc. SnapVision. Formerly Branch Cable Inc. served by MEADVILLE-BUDE, MS [MS0069]. This cable system has converted to IPTV, see Roxie, MS [MS5009]. ICA: MS0180.

SANFORD—Home Cable Entertainment, 15600 Springfield Rd, Walker, LA 70785-2716. Phone: 225-665-4997. Fax: 225-667-6293. ICA: MS0118.
TV Market Ranking: Below 100 (SANFORD). Franchise award date: N.A. Franchise expiration date: N.A. Began: January 5, 1993.
Channel capacity: 48 (not 2-way capable). Channels available but not in use: 5.
Basic Service
Subscribers: 118.
Programming (received off-air): WDAM-TV (NBC) Laurel; WHLT (CBS) Hattiesburg; WLOX (ABC) Biloxi; WMAW-TV (PBS) Meridian; WXXV-TV (FOX, MNT) Gulfport.
Programming (via satellite): ABC Family Channel; Animal Planet; Arts & Entertainment; Cartoon Network; CNN; Comcast Sports Net Southeast; Country Music TV; Discovery Channel; Disney Channel; Do-It-Yourself; ESPN; ESPN 2; Food Network; Fox Movie Channel; Fox News Channel; FX; HGTV; History Channel; Lifetime; National Geographic Channel; Nickelodeon; Outdoor Channel; QVC; Speed Channel; Spike TV; Syfy; TBS Superstation; The Learning Channel; Turner Classic Movies; Turner Network TV; TV Land; USA Network; Weather Channel; WGN America.
Current originations: Religious Access.
Fee: $29.95 monthly.
Internet Service
Operational: No.
Telephone Service
None
Miles of Plant: 11.0 (coaxial); None (fiber optic). Homes passed: 200.
Manager: Leland Denison. Chief Technician: Dan Boyd.
Ownership: Denison Communications Inc. (MSO).

SCOOBA—Cable TV Inc., PO Box 2598, 612 Hwy 82 W, Starkville, MS 39760. Phone: 662-324-5121. Fax: 662-324-0233. ICA: MS0213.
TV Market Ranking: Below 100 (SCOOBA).
Channel capacity: N.A. Channels available but not in use: N.A.
Basic Service
Subscribers: 87.
Fee: $40.00 installation; $28.95 monthly.
Pay Service 1
Pay Units: 7.
Programming (via satellite): HBO.
Fee: $10.28 monthly.
Pay Service 2
Pay Units: 4.
Programming (via satellite): Cinemax.
Fee: $10.28 monthly.
Internet Service
Operational: No.
Telephone Service
None
General Manager: Andy Williams.
Ownership: Andy Williams (MSO).

SEMINARY—Home Cable Entertainment, 15600 Springfield Rd, Walker, LA 70785-2716. Phone: 225-665-4997. Fax: 225-667-6293. Also serves Covington County (portions) & Jones County (portions). ICA: MS0183.
TV Market Ranking: Below 100 (Covington County (portions), Jones County (portions), SEMINARY). Franchise award date: January 1, 1992. Franchise expiration date: N.A. Began: N.A.
Channel capacity: 48 (not 2-way capable). Channels available but not in use: N.A.
Basic Service
Subscribers: 108.
Programming (received off-air): WGSA (CW) Baxley; WJCL (ABC) Savannah; WMAH-TV (PBS) Biloxi; WSAV-TV (MNT, NBC) Savannah; WTGS (FOX) Hardeeville; WTOC-TV (CBS) Savannah.
Programming (via satellite): ABC Family Channel; Animal Planet; Arts & Entertainment; BET Networks; CNN; Discovery Channel; Disney Channel; ESPN; History Channel; ION Television; Lifetime; Nickelodeon; Outdoor Channel; Spike TV; TBS Superstation; The Learning Channel; Travel Channel; Turner Network TV; TV Land; USA Network; Weather Channel; WGN America.
Current originations: Religious Access.
Fee: $29.95 monthly.
Pay Service 1
Pay Units: N.A.
Programming (via satellite): HBO.
Internet Service
Operational: No.
Telephone Service
None
Miles of Plant: 10.0 (coaxial); None (fiber optic).
Manager: Leland Denison. Chief Technician: Dan Boyd.
Ownership: Denison Communications Inc. (MSO).

SHELBY—Galaxy Cablevision. Now served by CLEVELAND, MS [MS0019]. ICA: MS0070.

SHUBUTA—Galaxy Cablevision, PO Box 308, 214 Main St, Ste C, Monticello, MS 39654-0308. Phone: 601-587-9461. Fax: 601-587-7410. Web Site: http://www.galaxycable.com. ICA: MS0184.
TV Market Ranking: Below 100 (SHUBUTA). Franchise award date: N.A. Franchise expiration date: N.A. Began: N.A.
Channel capacity: 36 (not 2-way capable). Channels available but not in use: None.
Basic Service
Subscribers: 61.
Programming (received off-air): WDAM-TV (NBC) Laurel; WGBC (NBC) Meridian; WMAW-TV (PBS) Meridian; WMDN (CBS) Meridian; WTOK-TV (ABC, CW, FOX, MNT) Meridian.
Programming (via satellite): ABC Family Channel; AMC; Animal Planet; Arts & Entertainment; BET Networks; Cartoon Network; CNBC; CNN; Comcast Sports Net Southeast; C-SPAN; Discovery Channel; Disney Channel; E! Entertainment Television; ESPN; ESPN 2; FX; Great American Country; Hallmark Channel; Headline News; HGTV; Lifetime; Outdoor Channel; SportSouth; TBS Superstation; The Learning Channel; Turner Network TV; USA Network; Weather Channel; WGN America.
Fee: $25.00 installation; $39.10 monthly.
Pay Service 1
Pay Units: 65.
Programming (via satellite): HBO.
Fee: $25.00 installation; $11.00 monthly.
Internet Service
Operational: No.
Telephone Service
None
Miles of Plant: 8.0 (coaxial); None (fiber optic). Homes passed: 260.
State Manager: Bill Flowers. Technical Manager & Engineer: Greg Berthaut. Customer Service Representative: Rebecca Nelson.; Parlean Myers.
Ownership: Galaxy Cable Inc. (MSO).

ST. ANDREWS—Mediacom, 760 Middle St, PO Box 1009, Fairhope, AL 36532. Phones: 850-934-7700 (Gulf Breeze regional office); 251-928-0374. Fax: 251-928-3804. Web Site: http://www.mediacomcable.com. Also serves Ocean Springs. ICA: MS0100.
TV Market Ranking: Below 100 (Ocean Springs, ST. ANDREWS). Franchise award date: May 13, 1982. Franchise expiration date: N.A. Began: March 1, 1983.
Channel capacity: 30 (not 2-way capable). Channels available but not in use: 6.
Basic Service
Subscribers: 341.
Programming (received off-air): WALA-TV (FOX) Mobile; WKRG-TV (CBS) Mobile; WLOX (ABC) Biloxi; WMAH-TV (PBS) Biloxi; WPMI-TV (NBC) Mobile; WXXV-TV (FOX, MNT) Gulfport.
Programming (via satellite): ABC Family Channel; AMC; Animal Planet; Arts & Entertainment; CNBC; CNN; Comcast Sports Net Southeast; Comedy Central; Country Music TV; CW+; Discovery Channel; Disney Channel; E! Entertainment Television; ESPN; ESPN 2; Fox News Channel; FX; Hallmark Channel; Headline News; HGTV; History Channel; Home Shopping Network; MSNBC; MTV; Nickelodeon; Speed Channel; Spike TV; SportSouth; Syfy; TBS Superstation; The Learning Channel; Turner Classic Movies; Turner Network TV; TV Land; USA Network; VH1; Weather Channel; WGN America.
Fee: $29.50 installation; $44.95 monthly; $3.35 converter.
Pay Service 1
Pay Units: 59.
Programming (via satellite): Cinemax.
Fee: $10.45 monthly.
Pay Service 2
Pay Units: N.A.
Programming (via satellite): Flix.
Fee: $2.95 monthly.
Pay Service 3
Pay Units: 105.
Programming (via satellite): HBO (multiplexed).
Fee: $12.45 monthly.
Pay Service 4
Pay Units: 81.
Programming (via satellite): Showtime.
Fee: $10.45 monthly.
Pay Service 5
Pay Units: 51.
Programming (via satellite): The Movie Channel.
Fee: $10.45 monthly.
Video-On-Demand: No
Internet Service
Operational: No.
Telephone Service
None
Miles of Plant: 16.0 (coaxial); None (fiber optic). Homes passed: 430. Total homes in franchised area: 485.
Vice President: David Servies. Operations Director: Gene Wuchner. Technical Operations Manager: Mike Sneary. Sales & Marketing Manager: Joey Nagem.
Ownership: Mediacom LLC (MSO).

STARKVILLE—MetroCast Communications, 300.5 S Jackson St, Starkville, MS 39759. Phone: 662-323-1615. Fax: 662-323-1682. Web Site: http://www.metrocastcommunications.com. Also serves Mississippi State University & Oktibbeha County (portions). ICA: MS0018.
TV Market Ranking: Below 100 (Mississippi State University, Oktibbeha County (portions), STARKVILLE). Franchise award date: N.A. Franchise expiration date: N.A. Began: May 1, 1963.
Channel capacity: 70 (operating 2-way). Channels available but not in use: None.
Basic Service
Subscribers: 7,148.
Programming (received off-air): WCBI-TV (CBS, CW, MNT) Columbus; WHBQ-TV (FOX) Memphis; WKDH (ABC) Houston; WLOV-TV (FOX) West Point; WMAV-TV (PBS) Oxford; WMC-TV (NBC) Memphis; WPTY-TV (ABC) Memphis; WREG-TV (CBS) Memphis; WTVA (NBC) Tupelo.
Programming (via satellite): CW+; Travel Channel; WGN America.
Fee: $55.00 installation; $20.99 monthly; $2.50 converter.
Expanded Basic Service 1
Subscribers: 3,261.
Programming (via satellite): ABC Family Channel; AMC; Animal Planet; Arts & Entertainment; BET Networks; Cartoon Network; CNBC; CNN; Comcast Sports Net Southeast; Comcast/Charter Sports Southeast (CSS); Comedy Central; Country Music TV; C-SPAN; C-SPAN 2; Discovery Channel; Disney Channel; E! Entertainment Television; ESPN; ESPN 2; ESPN Classic Sports;

Food Network; Fox News Channel; FX; Golf Channel; Great American Country; Hallmark Channel; Headline News; HGTV; History Channel; Home Shopping Network; INSP; ION Television; Lifetime; MSNBC; MTV; National Geographic Channel; Nickelodeon; Outdoor Channel; QVC; Spike TV; SportSouth; Syfy; TBS Superstation; The Learning Channel; Trinity Broadcasting Network; Turner Network TV; TV Land; USA Network; VH1; WE tv; Weather Channel.
Fee: $20.00 installation; $31.00 monthly.

Digital Basic Service
Subscribers: N.A.
Programming (received off-air): WCBI-TV (CBS, CW, MNT) Columbus; WLMT (CW) Memphis; WLOV-TV (FOX) West Point; WMC-TV (NBC) Memphis; WPTY-TV (ABC) Memphis.
Programming (via satellite): Animal Planet HD; Arts & Entertainment HD; BBC America; Bio; Bloomberg Television; Bravo; Cooking Channel; Discovery Channel HD; Discovery HD Theater; Discovery Health Channel; Discovery Kids Channel; Discovery Military Channel; Discovery Planet Green; DMX Music; Do-It-Yourself; ESPN 2 HD; ESPN HD; ESPN U; ESPNews; Fox Movie Channel; Fox Soccer; Fuse; G4; Gospel Music Channel; GSN; Halogen Network; HDNet; HDNet Movies; History Channel HD; History Channel International; ID Investigation Discovery; Lifetime Movie Network; MTV Hits; MTV2; National Geographic Channel HD Network; NFL Network; NFL Network HD; Nick Jr.; NickToons TV; Outdoor Channel 2 HD; PBS Kids Sprout; RFD-TV; Science Channel; Science Channel HD; Sleuth; Speed Channel; TeenNick; TLC HD; Toon Disney; Turner Network TV HD; Universal HD; Versus; VH1 Classic; VH1 Soul.
Fee: $5.95 monthly.

Digital Expanded Basic Service
Subscribers: N.A.
Programming (via satellite): AmericanLife TV Network; Boomerang; FamilyNet; FitTV; Fox College Sports Atlantic; Fox College Sports Central; Fox College Sports Pacific; Fuel TV; Hallmark Movie Channel; Independent Film Channel; Style Network; Turner Classic Movies.

Digital Pay Service 1
Pay Units: 3,281.
Programming (via satellite): Cinemax (multiplexed); Cinemax HD; Encore (multiplexed); Flix; HBO (multiplexed); HBO HD; Showtime (multiplexed); Starz (multiplexed); The Movie Channel (multiplexed).
Fee: $15.00 installation.
Video-On-Demand: No

Pay-Per-View
Playboy TV (delivered digitally); Fresh (delivered digitally); Club Jenna (delivered digitally); ESPN (delivered digitally); iN DEMAND (delivered digitally).

Internet Service
Operational: Yes.
Subscribers: 5,000.
Broadband Service: MetroCast Internet.
Fee: $79.99 installation; $35.99 monthly.

Telephone Service
Digital: Operational
Subscribers: 300.
Fee: $30.00 installation; $29.95 monthly
Miles of Plant: 197.0 (coaxial); 12.0 (fiber optic). Additional miles planned: 3.0 (coaxial). Homes passed: 11,952. Total homes in franchised area: 11,952.
General Manager: Rick Ferrall. Chief Technician: Mitch Douglas. Marketing Manager: Lee Beck.
Ownership: Harron Communications LP (MSO).

STATE LINE—Galaxy Cablevision, PO Box 308, 214 Main St, Ste C, Monticello, MS 39654-0308. Phone: 601-587-9461. Fax: 601-587-7410. Web Site: http://www.galaxycable.com. ICA: MS0186.
TV Market Ranking: Outside TV Markets (STATE LINE). Franchise award date: N.A. Franchise expiration date: N.A. Began: February 1, 1990.
Channel capacity: 41 (not 2-way capable). Channels available but not in use: 18.

Basic Service
Subscribers: 45.
Programming (received off-air): WDAM-TV (NBC) Laurel; WKRG-TV (CBS) Mobile; WLOX (ABC) Biloxi; WMAH-TV (PBS) Biloxi; WXXV-TV (FOX, MNT) Gulfport.
Programming (via satellite): ABC Family Channel; Arts & Entertainment; BET Networks; CNN; Discovery Channel; Disney Channel; ESPN; Headline News; Lifetime; Outdoor Channel; QVC; SportSouth; TBS Superstation; Trinity Broadcasting Network; Turner Network TV; USA Network; Weather Channel.
Fee: $43.75 installation; $26.60 monthly.

Pay Service 1
Pay Units: 44.
Programming (via satellite): HBO.
Fee: $26.25 installation; $10.95 monthly.

Internet Service
Operational: No.

Telephone Service
None
Miles of Plant: 9.0 (coaxial); None (fiber optic). Homes passed: 206.
State Manager: Bill Flowers. Technical Manager: Greg Berthaut. Engineer: Barry Lowery. Customer Service Representative: Rebecca Myers.; Parlean Myers.
Ownership: Galaxy Cable Inc. (MSO).

SUMNER—Cable One. No longer in operation. ICA: MS0066.

SUMRALL—Galaxy Cablevision, PO Box 308, 214 Main St, Ste C, Monticello, MS 39654-0308. Phone: 601-587-9461. Fax: 601-587-7410. Web Site: http://www.galaxycable.com. ICA: MS0098.
TV Market Ranking: Below 100 (SUMRALL). Franchise award date: N.A. Franchise expiration date: N.A. Began: July 14, 1989.
Channel capacity: 41 (not 2-way capable). Channels available but not in use: 8.

Basic Service
Subscribers: 141.
Programming (received off-air): WDAM-TV (NBC) Laurel; WHLT (CBS) Hattiesburg; WLOX (ABC) Biloxi; WMAH-TV (PBS) Biloxi; WXXV-TV (FOX, MNT) Gulfport.
Programming (via satellite): ABC Family Channel; AMC; Arts & Entertainment; BET Networks; CNBC; CNN; Comcast Sports Net Southeast; Comedy Central; Discovery Channel; Disney Channel; ESPN; ESPN 2; Fox News Channel; Great American Country; Lifetime; Outdoor Channel; QVC; Speed Channel; TBS Superstation; Toon Disney; Trinity Broadcasting Network; Turner Network TV; USA Network; Weather Channel; WGN America.
Fee: $39.60 monthly.

Pay Service 1
Pay Units: N.A.
Programming (via satellite): Cinemax; HBO.
Fee: $9.42 monthly (HBO).

Internet Service
Operational: No.

Telephone Service
None
Miles of Plant: 13.0 (coaxial); None (fiber optic). Homes passed: 395.
State Manager: Bill Flowers. Technical Manager & Engineer: Greg Berthaut. Customer Service Representative: Rebecca Nelson.; Parlean Myers.
Ownership: Galaxy Cable Inc. (MSO).

SUNFLOWER—Sledge Cable Co. Inc., PO Box 68, 124 Delta Ave, Sunflower, MS 38778. Phones: 662-569-3700; 888-655-7707; 662-569-3311. Fax: 662-569-3200. E-mail: rsledge@deltaland.net. Web Site: http://www.deltaland.net. ICA: MS0195.
TV Market Ranking: Below 100 (SUNFLOWER). Franchise award date: N.A. Franchise expiration date: N.A. Began: September 1, 1984.
Channel capacity: 35 (not 2-way capable). Channels available but not in use: 11.

Basic Service
Subscribers: 310.
Programming (received off-air): WABG-TV (ABC) Greenwood; WLBT (NBC) Jackson; WMAO-TV (PBS) Greenwood; WTVA (NBC) Tupelo; WXVT (CBS) Greenville.
Programming (via satellite): AMC; Arts & Entertainment; BET Networks; Cartoon Network; CNN; Comedy Central; Country Music TV; C-SPAN; CW+; Discovery Channel; Disney Channel; ESPN; ESPN 2; Food Network; Fox News Channel; Hallmark Channel; Headline News; HGTV; History Channel; Lifetime; Nickelodeon; Outdoor Channel; Spike TV; Syfy; TBS Superstation; Trinity Broadcasting Network; truTV; Turner Classic Movies; Turner Network TV; TV Land; USA Network; Weather Channel; WGN America.
Fee: $20.00 installation; $24.95 monthly.

Pay Service 1
Pay Units: 67.
Programming (via satellite): Cinemax.
Fee: $9.50 monthly.

Pay Service 2
Pay Units: 101.
Programming (via satellite): HBO.
Fee: $10.50 monthly.

Internet Service
Operational: No, dialup.

Telephone Service
None
Manager: Robert Sledge Jr.
Ownership: Sledge Telephone Co.

SUNRISE—Home Cable Entertainment, 15600 Springfield Rd, Walker, LA 70785-2716. Phone: 225-665-4997. Fax: 225-667-6293. ICA: MS0107.
TV Market Ranking: Below 100 (SUNRISE). Franchise award date: January 1, 1992. Franchise expiration date: N.A. Began: July 20, 1992.
Channel capacity: 48 (not 2-way capable). Channels available but not in use: 5.

Basic Service
Subscribers: 178.
Programming (received off-air): WDAM-TV (NBC) Laurel; WHLT (CBS) Hattiesburg; WLOX (ABC) Biloxi; WMAW-TV (PBS) Meridian; WXXV-TV (FOX, MNT) Gulfport.
Programming (via satellite): ABC Family Channel; CNN; Discovery Channel; Disney Channel; ESPN; Lifetime; Nickelodeon; QVC; Spike TV; TBS Superstation; Trinity Broadcasting Network; USA Network; VH1; WGN America.
Current originations: Religious Access.
Fee: $29.95 monthly.

Pay Service 1
Pay Units: N.A.
Programming (via satellite): Showtime (multiplexed); The Movie Channel.
Fee: $10.95 monthly (each).

Internet Service
Operational: No.

Telephone Service
None
Miles of Plant: 15.0 (coaxial); None (fiber optic). Homes passed: 300.
Manager: Leland Denison. Chief Technician: Dan Boyd.
Ownership: Denison Communications Inc. (MSO).

TAYLORSVILLE—Galaxy Cablevision, PO Box 308, 214 Main St, Ste C, Monticello, MS 39654-0308. Phone: 601-587-9461. Fax: 601-587-7410. Web Site: http://www.galaxycable.com. ICA: MS0087.
TV Market Ranking: Below 100 (TAYLORSVILLE). Franchise award date: N.A. Franchise expiration date: N.A. Began: February 1, 1983.
Channel capacity: 36 (operating 2-way). Channels available but not in use: None.

Basic Service
Subscribers: 155.
Programming (received off-air): WAPT (ABC) Jackson; WDAM-TV (NBC) Laurel; WDBD (FOX) Jackson; WJTV (CBS) Jackson; WLBT (NBC) Jackson; WMAW-TV (PBS) Meridian.
Programming (via satellite): ABC Family Channel; AMC; Arts & Entertainment; BET Networks; Cartoon Network; CNN; Comcast Sports Net Southeast; Discovery Channel; Disney Channel; E! Entertainment Television; ESPN; ESPN 2; Fox News Channel; FX; Great American Country; Headline News; HGTV; History Channel; Lifetime; Outdoor Channel; QVC; Speed Channel; Syfy; TBS Superstation; The Learning Channel; Toon Disney; Turner Network TV; USA Network; Weather Channel; WGN America.
Current originations: Public Access.
Fee: $41.10 monthly.

Pay Service 1
Pay Units: 147.
Programming (via satellite): HBO; Showtime.
Fee: $25.00 installation; $9.00 monthly (each).

Internet Service
Operational: No.

Telephone Service
None
Miles of Plant: 34.0 (coaxial); None (fiber optic). Homes passed: 664.
State Manager: Bill Flowers. Technical Manager & Engineer: Greg Berthaut. Customer Service Representative: Rebecca Nelson.; Parlean Myers.
City fee: 3% of gross.
Ownership: Galaxy Cable Inc. (MSO).

TUPELO—Comcast Cable, 353 N Gloster St, Tupelo, MS 38804. Phones: 256-859-7828; 662-844-8694. Fax: 662-844-0940. Web Site: http://www.comcast.com. Also serves Belden, Bissell, Chickasaw, Clay County, Fulton, Lee County, Manatachie, Marietta, Mooreville, Okolona, Plantersville, Pontotoc County (portions), Saltillo, Sherman, Tremont, Union County (portions), Verona & West Point. ICA: MS0009.
TV Market Ranking: Below 100 (Belden, Bissell, Chickasaw, Clay County, Fulton, Lee County, Manatachie, Marietta, Okolona, Plantersville, Pontotoc County (portions), Saltillo, Sherman, Tremont, TUPELO, Union County (portions), Verona, West Point). Franchise award date: N.A. Franchise expiration date: N.A. Began: May 1, 1955.
Channel capacity: N.A. Channels available but not in use: N.A.
Basic Service
Subscribers: 27,500.
Programming (received off-air): WAFF (NBC) Huntsville; WFIQ (PBS) Florence; WHBQ-TV (FOX) Memphis; WHDF (CW) Florence; WHNT-TV (CBS) Huntsville; WKDH (ABC) Houston; WMAE-TV (PBS) Booneville; WMC-TV (NBC) Memphis; WTVA (NBC) Tupelo; allband FM.
Programming (via satellite): AMC; Animal Planet; Arts & Entertainment; BET Networks; Cartoon Network; CNBC; CNN; Comcast/Charter Sports Southeast (CSS); Comedy Central; Country Music TV; Discovery Channel; Discovery Health Channel; Disney Channel; E! Entertainment Television; ESPN; ESPN 2; Food Network; Fox News Channel; FX; Golf Channel; Headline News; HGTV; History Channel; Home Shopping Network; Lifetime; LWS Local Weather Station; MTV; MyNetworkTV Inc.; Nickelodeon; Outdoor Channel; QVC; Speed Channel; Spike TV; Style Network; TBS Superstation; The Learning Channel; Turner Classic Movies; Turner Network TV; TV Land; USA Network; Versus; VH1; Weather Channel.
Current originations: Leased Access.
Fee: $62.99 installation; $10.50 monthly.
Digital Basic Service
Subscribers: N.A.
Programming (received off-air): WCBI-TV (CBS, CW, MNT) Columbus; WMAE-TV (PBS) Booneville.
Programming (via satellite): BBC America; Bio; CMT Pure Country; Cooking Channel; C-SPAN 2; C-SPAN 3; Daystar TV Network; Discovery Channel HD; Discovery Kids Channel; Discovery Military Channel; Discovery Planet Green; Disney Channel; Do-It-Yourself; Encore (multiplexed); ESPN 2 HD; ESPN HD; ESPNews; FearNet; Flix; Fox College Sports Atlantic; Fox College Sports Central; Fox College Sports Pacific; Fox Soccer; G4; Gol TV; GSN; History Channel International; ID Investigation Discovery; Jewelry Television; Lifetime Movie Network; MoviePlex; MTV Jams; MTV Tres; MTV2; Music Choice; National Geographic Channel; NBA TV; NFL Network; Nick Jr.; Nick Too; PBS Kids Sprout; Science Channel; SoapNet; Starz IndiePlex; Starz RetroPlex; Sundance Channel; TeenNick; Toon Disney; Turner Network TV HD; TV Guide Interactive Inc.; VH1 Classic; VH1 Soul; WAM! America's Kidz Network.
Fee: $14.95 monthly.
Digital Pay Service 1
Pay Units: N.A.
Programming (via satellite): Cinemax (multiplexed); Cinemax HD; HBO (multiplexed); HBO HD; Showtime (multiplexed); Showtime HD; Starz (multiplexed); Starz HDTV; The Movie Channel (multiplexed).
Video-On-Demand: Yes
Pay-Per-View
iN DEMAND (delivered digitally); Hot Choice (delivered digitally); Special events (delivered digitally).
Internet Service
Operational: Yes.
Broadband Service: Comcast High Speed Internet.
Fee: $42.95 monthly.
Telephone Service
Digital: Operational
Miles of Plant: 1,375.0 (coaxial); None (fiber optic). Homes passed: 57,000.
Vice President & General Manager: Ellen Rosson. Chief Technician: Frank Newsome. Office Manager: Pete Clark.
Ownership: Comcast Cable Communications Inc. (MSO).

TYLERTOWN—Galaxy Cablevision, PO Box 308, 214 Main St, Ste C, Monticello, MS 39654-0308. Phone: 601-587-9461. Fax: 601-587-9461. Web Site: http://www.galaxycable.com. ICA: MS0077.
TV Market Ranking: Outside TV Markets (TYLERTOWN). Franchise award date: N.A. Franchise expiration date: N.A. Began: February 1, 1974.
Channel capacity: 41 (not 2-way capable). Channels available but not in use: None.
Basic Service
Subscribers: 311.
Programming (received off-air): WAFB (CBS) Baton Rouge; WDAM-TV (NBC) Laurel; WDBD (FOX) Jackson; WJTV (CBS) Jackson; WLBT (NBC) Jackson; WLOX (ABC) Biloxi; WMAU-TV (PBS) Bude; WVUE-DT (FOX) New Orleans; WWL-TV (CBS) New Orleans.
Programming (via satellite): ABC Family Channel; Arts & Entertainment; BET Networks; Cartoon Network; CNBC; CNN; Comedy Central; C-SPAN; C-SPAN 2; Discovery Channel; Disney Channel; ESPN; ESPN 2; Fox News Channel; Fuse; FX; Great American Country; Hallmark Channel; Headline News; INSP; Outdoor Channel; QVC; TBS Superstation; The Learning Channel; Toon Disney; Trinity Broadcasting Network; Turner Classic Movies; Turner Network TV; USA Network; Weather Channel; WGN America.
Fee: $14.00 installation; $43.50 monthly.
Digital Basic Service
Subscribers: 60.
Programming (via satellite): AmericanLife TV Network; BBC America; Bio; Bloomberg Television; Discovery Digital Networks; DMX Music; ESPN Classic Sports; ESPNews; FitTV; Fox Sports World; G4; Golf Channel; GSN; History Channel International; National Geographic Channel; Style Network; WE tv.
Fee: $13.96 monthly.
Digital Expanded Basic Service
Subscribers: N.A.
Programming (via satellite): DMX Music; Encore; Fox Movie Channel; Lifetime Movie Network; Turner Classic Movies.
Fee: $13.96 monthly.
Pay Service 1
Pay Units: N.A.
Programming (via satellite): Cinemax; HBO.
Fee: $25.00 installation.
Digital Pay Service 1
Pay Units: N.A.
Programming (via satellite): Cinemax (multiplexed); Flix; HBO (multiplexed); Showtime (multiplexed); The Movie Channel (multiplexed).
Fee: $15.50 monthly.
Pay-Per-View
Addressable homes: 41.
ESPN Now (delivered digitally), Addressable: Yes; Hot Choice (delivered digitally); Playboy TV (delivered digitally); Fresh (delivered digitally); Shorteez (delivered digitally); Urban Xtra (delivered digitally).
Internet Service
Operational: No.
Telephone Service
None
Miles of Plant: 26.0 (coaxial); None (fiber optic). Homes passed: 849.
State Manager: Bill Flowers. Technical Manager & Engineer: Greg Berthaut. Customer Service Representative: Rebecca Nelson.; Parlean Myers.
Ownership: Galaxy Cable Inc. (MSO).

UNION—Mediacom, 123 Ware Dr NE, Huntsville, AL 35811-1061. Phones: 256-852-7427; 850-934-7700 (Gulf Breeze regional office). Fax: 256-851-7708. Web Site: http://www.mediacomcable.com. Also serves Decatur, Louisville, Newton, Noxapater, Union & Winston County (portions). ICA: MS0038.
TV Market Ranking: Below 100 (Decatur, Newton, UNION); Outside TV Markets (Louisville, Noxapater, Winston County (portions)). Franchise award date: December 3, 1963. Franchise expiration date: N.A. Began: December 1, 1964.
Channel capacity: N.A. Channels available but not in use: N.A.
Basic Service
Subscribers: 4,746.
Programming (received off-air): WCBI-TV (CBS, CW, MNT) Columbus; WDBB (CW) Bessemer; WJTV (CBS) Jackson; WLBT (NBC) Jackson; WLOV-TV (FOX) West Point; WMAB-TV (PBS) Mississippi State; WTOK-TV (ABC, CW, FOX, MNT) Meridian; WTVA (NBC) Tupelo; allband FM.
Programming (via satellite): ABC Family Channel; AMC; AmericanLife TV Network; Animal Planet; Arts & Entertainment; BET Networks; Bravo; Cartoon Network; CNBC; CNN; Comcast Sports Net Southeast; Comedy Central; Country Music TV; C-SPAN; C-SPAN 2; Discovery Channel; Disney Channel; E! Entertainment Television; ESPN; ESPN 2; FitTV; Food Network; Fox News Channel; FX; Hallmark Channel; Headline News; HGTV; History Channel; Home Shopping Network; INSP; ION Television; Lifetime; MSNBC; MTV; Nickelodeon; Outdoor Channel; QVC; Speed Channel; Spike TV; SportSouth; Syfy; TBS Superstation; The Learning Channel; Travel Channel; Trinity Broadcasting Network; truTV; Turner Classic Movies; Turner Network TV; TV Land; USA Network; VH1; Weather Channel; WGN America.
Fee: $29.50 installation; $12.15 monthly; $3.35 converter; $20.00 additional installation.
Digital Basic Service
Subscribers: N.A.
Programming (via satellite): BBC America; Discovery Digital Networks; DMX Music; Fox Sports World; GSN; Independent Film Channel; Turner Classic Movies.
Fee: $7.00 monthly; $5.00 converter.
Digital Pay Service 1
Pay Units: 1,084.
Programming (via satellite): HBO (multiplexed).
Fee: $11.95 monthly.
Digital Pay Service 2
Pay Units: 960.
Programming (via satellite): Flix; Showtime (multiplexed); The Movie Channel (multiplexed).
Fee: $9.95 monthly.
Digital Pay Service 3
Pay Units: 939.
Programming (via satellite): Cinemax (multiplexed).
Fee: $9.95 monthly.
Digital Pay Service 4
Pay Units: N.A.
Programming (via satellite): Encore (multiplexed); Starz (multiplexed).
Fee: $9.95 monthly.
Video-On-Demand: No
Pay-Per-View
Movies (delivered digitally); Fresh (delivered digitally); special events (delivered digitally).
Internet Service
Operational: Yes.
Broadband Service: Mediacom High Speed Internet.
Fee: $49.95 installation; $40.95 monthly.
Telephone Service
None
Miles of Plant: 1,200.0 (coaxial); None (fiber optic). Miles of plant includes Ardmore AL, Big Cove AL, Huntsville AL, & Huntland TN
Vice President: Dave Servies. General Manager: Tommy Hill. Sales & Marketing Manager: Joey Nagem. Technical Operations Supervisor: Mark Darwin. Customer Service Supervisor: Sandy Acklin.
City fee: 3% of gross.
Ownership: Mediacom LLC (MSO).

UNION—Mediacom. Now served by LOUISVILLE, MS [MS0038]. ICA: MS0067.

VICKSBURG—Vicksburg Video Inc., PO Box 1276, 900 Hwy 61 N, Vicksburg, MS 39183. Phone: 601-636-1351. Fax: 601-636-3791. E-mail: vicksburgvideocs@cablelynx.com. Web Site: http://www.vicksburgvideo.com. ICA: MS0011.
TV Market Ranking: Below 100 (VICKSBURG). Franchise award date: June 1, 1965. Franchise expiration date: N.A. Began: February 1, 1971.
Channel capacity: 78 (operating 2-way). Channels available but not in use: None.
Basic Service
Subscribers: 9,500.
Programming (received off-air): WAPT (ABC) Jackson; WDBD (FOX) Jackson; WJTV (CBS) Jackson; WLBT (NBC) Jackson; WMPN-TV (PBS) Jackson; WRBJ (CW) Magee; WUFX (MNT) Vicksburg.
Programming (via satellite): ABC Family Channel; AMC; Animal Planet; Arts & Entertainment; BET Networks; Cartoon Network; CNBC; CNN; Comcast Sports Net Southwest; Country Music TV; C-SPAN; C-SPAN 2; Discovery Channel; Disney Channel; ESPN; ESPN 2; ESPN Classic Sports; Eternal Word TV Network; Food Network; Fox News Channel; FX; Headline News; HGTV; History Channel; Home Shopping Network; ION Television; Lifetime; Lifetime Movie Network; MSNBC; MTV; Nickelodeon; QVC; ShopNBC; Sneak

Prevue; Spike TV; Syfy; TBS Superstation; Telemundo; The Learning Channel; Travel Channel; Trinity Broadcasting Network; truTV; Turner Classic Movies; Turner Network TV; TV Guide Network; TV Land; USA Network; VH1; Weather Channel; WGN America.

Current originations: Government Access; Educational Access; Public Access.

Fee: $40.00 installation; $48.90 monthly.

Digital Basic Service

Subscribers: N.A.

Programming (via satellite): AmericanLife TV Network; BBC America; Bio; CMT Pure Country; Discovery Health Channel; Discovery Kids Channel; Discovery Military Channel; Discovery Planet Green; DMX Music; ESPNews; FitTV; Fox Soccer; FSN Digital Atlantic; FSN Digital Central; FSN Digital Pacific; G4; Golf Channel; Great American Country; GSN; Halogen Network; History Channel International; ID Investigation Discovery; Lifetime Movie Network; MTV Hits; MTV Jams; MTV Tres; MTV2; National Geographic Channel; Nick Jr.; Nick Too; NickToons TV; Outdoor Channel; Science Channel; SoapNet; Speed Channel; Style Network; TeenNick; Toon Disney; VH1 Classic; VH1 Soul; WE tv.

Fee: $10.00 monthly.

Digital Expanded Basic Service

Subscribers: N.A.

Programming (received off-air): WAPT (ABC) Jackson; WJTV (CBS) Jackson; WLBT (NBC) Jackson; WMPN-TV (PBS) Jackson.

Programming (via satellite): CNN HD; Discovery Channel HD; ESPN HD; HDNet; HDNet Movies; Outdoor Channel 2 HD; TBS in HD; Turner Network TV HD.

Fee: $5.00 monthly.

Digital Pay Service 1

Pay Units: N.A.

Programming (via satellite): Cinemax (multiplexed); Cinemax HD; Encore (multiplexed); HBO (multiplexed); HBO HD; Starz (multiplexed); Starz HDTV.

Fee: $12.95 monthly (HBO, Cinemax, or Starz/Encore).

Video-On-Demand: No

Pay-Per-View

iN DEMAND (delivered digitally).

Internet Service

Operational: Yes. Began: December 31, 2000.

Broadband Service: Cablelynx.

Fee: $24.95-$44.95 monthly.

Telephone Service

Analog: Not Operational

Digital: Operational

Fee: $45.70 monthly

Miles of Plant: 389.0 (coaxial); 127.0 (fiber optic). Homes passed: 18,291.

General Manager: Beau Balch. Plant Manager: Henry Harris. Office Manager: Dee Dee Sumner.

Ownership: WEHCO Video Inc. (MSO).

WATER VALLEY—Mediacom. Now served by PONTOTOC, MS [MS0045]. ICA: MS0050.

WAVELAND—Mediacom, 760 Middle St, PO Box 1009, Fairhope, AL 36532. Phones: 251-928-0374; 850-934-7700 (Gulf Breeze regional office). Fax: 251-928-3804. Web Site: http://www.mediacomcable.com. Also serves Bay St. Louis, Hancock County (portions) & Pearlington. ICA: MS0022.

TV Market Ranking: 31 (Hancock County (portions), Pearlington); Below 100 (Bay St. Louis, WAVELAND, Hancock County (portions)). Franchise award date: June 22, 1978. Franchise expiration date: N.A. Began: July 1, 1979.

Channel capacity: N.A. Channels available but not in use: N.A.

Basic Service

Subscribers: 6,472.

Programming (received off-air): WDSU (NBC) New Orleans; WGNO (ABC) New Orleans; WLOX (ABC) Biloxi; WMPN-TV (PBS) Jackson; WNOL-TV (CW) New Orleans; WPXL-TV (ION) New Orleans; WUPL (MNT) Slidell; WVUE-DT (FOX) New Orleans; WWL-TV (CBS) New Orleans; WXXV-TV (FOX, MNT) Gulfport; WYES-TV (PBS) New Orleans.

Programming (via satellite): ABC Family Channel; AMC; AmericanLife TV Network; Animal Planet; Arts & Entertainment; BET Networks; Bravo; Cartoon Network; CNBC; CNN; Comcast Sports Net Southeast; Comedy Central; Country Music TV; C-SPAN; C-SPAN 2; Discovery Channel; Disney Channel; E! Entertainment Television; ESPN; ESPN 2; Eternal Word TV Network; FitTV; Food Network; Fox News Channel; FX; Golf Channel; Hallmark Channel; Halogen Network; Headline News; HGTV; History Channel; Home Shopping Network; Lifetime; MSNBC; MTV; Nickelodeon; Outdoor Channel; QVC; Speed Channel; Spike TV; SportSouth; Syfy; TBS Superstation; The Learning Channel; Travel Channel; Trinity Broadcasting Network; truTV; Turner Classic Movies; Turner Network TV; TV Guide Network; TV Land; USA Network; VH1; WE tv; Weather Channel; WGN America.

Current originations: Public Access.

Fee: $29.50 installation; $44.95 monthly; $3.35 converter; $20.00 additional installation.

Digital Basic Service

Subscribers: N.A.

Programming (via satellite): AmericanLife TV Network; BBC America; Bio; Discovery Health Channel; Discovery Home Channel; Discovery Kids Channel; Discovery Military Channel; DMX Music; ESPNews; Fox Movie Channel; Fox Soccer; Fuse; G4; GSN; Halogen Network; History Channel International; ID Investigation Discovery; Independent Film Channel; Lifetime Movie Network; MTV Hits; MTV2; National Geographic Channel; Nick Jr.; NickToons TV; Science Channel; Sleuth; Style Network; TeenNick; Versus; VH1 Classic.

Fee: $7.00 monthly; $5.00 converter.

Digital Pay Service 1

Pay Units: 1,600.

Programming (via satellite): Cinemax (multiplexed).

Fee: $9.95 monthly.

Digital Pay Service 2

Pay Units: N.A.

Programming (via satellite): Encore (multiplexed); Starz (multiplexed).

Fee: $9.95 monthly.

Digital Pay Service 3

Pay Units: 1,600.

Programming (via satellite): HBO (multiplexed).

Fee: $11.95 monthly.

Digital Pay Service 4

Pay Units: 1,571.

Programming (via satellite): Flix; Showtime (multiplexed); Sundance Channel; The Movie Channel (multiplexed).

Fee: $9.95 monthly.

Video-On-Demand: No

Pay-Per-View

Sports PPV (delivered digitally); Movies (delivered digitally); Urban Xtra (delivered digitally); special events (delivered digitally).

Internet Service

Operational: Yes.

Broadband Service: Mediacom High Speed Internet.

Fee: $49.95 installation; $40.95 monthly.

Telephone Service

None

Miles of Plant: 208.0 (coaxial); None (fiber optic). Homes passed: 7,642.

Vice President: David Servies. Operations Director: Gene Wuchner. Technical Operations Manager: Mike Sneary. Sales & Marketing Manager: Joey Nagem.

Ownership: Mediacom LLC (MSO).

WAYNESBORO—CMA Cablevision, 917 Robinson St, Waynesboro, MS 39367. Phones: 972-233-9614 (Corporate office); 601-735-4662. Fax: 601-735-0249. Web Site: http://www.cmaaccess.com. Also serves Buckatunna & Wayne County. ICA: MS0188.

TV Market Ranking: Below 100 (Wayne County (portions), WAYNESBORO); Outside TV Markets (Buckatunna, Wayne County (portions)). Franchise award date: March 3, 1964. Franchise expiration date: N.A. Began: July 1, 1965.

Channel capacity: N.A. Channels available but not in use: N.A.

Basic Service

Subscribers: 1,780.

Programming (received off-air): WDAM-TV (NBC) Laurel; WHLT (CBS) Hattiesburg; WKRG-TV (CBS) Mobile; WLOX (ABC) Biloxi; WMAW-TV (PBS) Meridian; WTOK-TV (ABC, CW, FOX, MNT) Meridian; WXXV-TV (FOX, MNT) Gulfport; allband FM.

Programming (via satellite): QVC; TBS Superstation.

Current originations: Public Access.

Fee: $39.95 installation; $18.95 monthly; $12.95 additional installation.

Expanded Basic Service 1

Subscribers: N.A.

Programming (via satellite): ABC Family Channel; AMC; Animal Planet; Arts & Entertainment; BET Networks; Bravo!; Cartoon Network; CNBC; CNN; Comcast Sports Net Southeast; Comedy Central; Country Music TV; C-SPAN; CW+; Discovery Channel; E! Entertainment Television; ESPN; ESPN 2; Food Network; Fox News Channel; FX; Gospel Music TV; GSN; Headline News; HGTV; History Channel; Home Shopping Network; INSP; Lifetime; MTV; Nickelodeon; Outdoor Channel; Spike TV; Syfy; The Learning Channel; The Sportsman Channel; Travel Channel; Trinity Broadcasting Network; Turner Network TV; TV Land; Univision; USA Network; VH1; Weather Channel; WGN America.

Fee: $21.00 monthly.

Digital Basic Service

Subscribers: N.A.

Programming (via satellite): BBC America; Bio; Bloomberg Television; Discovery Digital Networks; DMX Music; ESPN Classic Sports; ESPNews; Fox Movie Channel; G4; GAS; Golf Channel; Halogen Network; History Channel International; Independent Film Channel; Lifetime Movie Network; MTV Networks Digital Suite; National Geographic Channel; Nick Jr.; NickToons TV; Speed Channel; WE tv.

Fee: $14.95 monthly.

Pay Service 1

Pay Units: 432.

Programming (via satellite): HBO.

Fee: $9.95 installation; $13.45 monthly.

Pay Service 2

Pay Units: 231.

Programming (via satellite): Showtime.

Fee: $9.95 installation; $12.95 monthly.

Digital Pay Service 1

Pay Units: N.A.

Programming (via satellite): Cinemax (multiplexed); Encore (multiplexed); Flix; HBO (multiplexed); Showtime (multiplexed); Starz (multiplexed); Sundance Channel; The Movie Channel (multiplexed).

Fee: $10.95 monthly (Cinemax or Encore/Starz), $13.95 monthly (HBO or Showtime).

Video-On-Demand: No

Pay-Per-View

iN DEMAND (delivered digitally); Hot Choice (delivered digitally); Playboy TV (delivered digitally); Fresh (delivered digitally); Shorteez (delivered digitally).

Internet Service

Operational: Yes.

Broadband Service: CMA.

Fee: $41.95 monthly.

Telephone Service

None

Miles of Plant: 43.0 (coaxial); None (fiber optic).

General Manager: Jerry Smith. Marketing Director: Julie Ferguson.

City fee: 2% of gross.

Ownership: Cable Management Assoc. (MSO).

WEIR—Delta Telephone Co. SnapVision. Formerly [MS0126]. This cable system has converted to IPTV, PO Box 266, Ackerman, MS 39735. Phones: 877-433-7878; 662-285-6209. Fax: 662-285-6960. Web Site: http://www.dtcweb.net. ICA: MS5013.

Channel capacity: N.A. Channels available but not in use: N.A.

Internet Service

Operational: Yes.

Ownership: Delta Telephone.

WEIR—Delta Telephone Co. SnapVision. This cable system has converted to IPTV. See Weir, MS [MS5013]. ICA: MS0126.

WIGGINS—Mediacom, 760 Middle St, PO Box 1009, Fairhope, AL 36532. Phones: 251-928-0374 (Fairhope office); 850-934-7700 (Gulf Breeze regional office). Fax: 251-928-3804. Web Site: http://www.mediacomcable.

com. Also serves Stone County (portions). ICA: MS0058.

TV Market Ranking: Below 100 (Stone County (portions), WIGGINS). Franchise award date: September 19, 1978. Franchise expiration date: N.A. Began: July 1, 1980.

Channel capacity: N.A. Channels available but not in use: N.A.

Basic Service

Subscribers: 1,340.

Programming (received off-air): WDAM-TV (NBC) Laurel; WHLT (CBS) Hattiesburg; WKRG-TV (CBS) Mobile; WLOX (ABC) Biloxi; WMAH-TV (PBS) Biloxi; WNOL-TV (CW) New Orleans; WWL-TV (CBS) New Orleans; WXXV-TV (FOX, MNT) Gulfport.

Programming (via satellite): ABC Family Channel; AMC; AmericanLife TV Network; Animal Planet; Arts & Entertainment; BET Networks; Bravo; Cartoon Network; CNBC; CNN; Comcast Sports Net Southeast; Comedy Central; Country Music TV; C-SPAN; C-SPAN 2; Discovery Channel; Disney Channel; E! Entertainment Television; ESPN; ESPN 2; Eternal Word TV Network; FitTV; Food Network; Fox News Channel; FX; Golf Channel; Hallmark Channel; Headline News; HGTV; History Channel; Home Shopping Network; INSP; Lifetime; MSNBC; MTV; Nickelodeon; Outdoor Channel; QVC; Speed Channel; Spike TV; SportSouth; Syfy; TBS Superstation; The Learning Channel; Travel Channel; Trinity Broadcasting Network; truTV; Turner Classic Movies; Turner Network TV; TV Guide Network; TV Land; USA Network; VH1; WE tv; Weather Channel; WGN America.

Fee: $29.50 installation; $44.95 monthly; $3.35 converter; $20.00 additional installation.

Digital Basic Service

Subscribers: N.A.

Programming (via satellite): BBC America; Discovery Digital Networks; DMX Music; Fox Sports World; GSN; Independent Film Channel; Turner Classic Movies.

Fee: $7.00 monthly; $5.00 converter.

Digital Pay Service 1

Pay Units: 365.

Programming (via satellite): HBO (multiplexed).

Fee: $11.95 monthly.

Digital Pay Service 2

Pay Units: 46.

Programming (via satellite): Cinemax (multiplexed).

Fee: $9.95 monthly.

Digital Pay Service 3

Pay Units: 178.

Programming (via satellite): Flix; Showtime (multiplexed); The Movie Channel (multiplexed).

Fee: $9.95 monthly.

Digital Pay Service 4

Pay Units: N.A.

Programming (via satellite): Encore (multiplexed); Starz (multiplexed).

Fee: $9.95 monthly.

Video-On-Demand: No

Pay-Per-View

Movies (delivered digitally); Urban Xtra (delivered digitally); special events (delivered digitally).

Internet Service

Operational: Yes.

Broadband Service: Mediacom High Speed Internet.

Fee: $49.95 installation; $40.95 monthly.

Telephone Service

None

Miles of Plant: 42.0 (coaxial); None (fiber optic). Homes passed: 1,571.

Vice President: David Servies. Operations Director: Gene Wuchner. Technical Operations Manager: Mike Sneary. Sales & Marketing Manager: Joey Nagem.

Ownership: Mediacom LLC (MSO).

WINONA—Cable One, 114 Summit St, Winona, MS 38967. Phones: 662-283-1470; 662-283-2437. Fax: 662-283-1547. Web Site: http://www.cableone.net. Also serves Carrollton, Charleston, Duck Hill, Durant, Goodman, Itta Bena, Kilmichael, Leflore County, Lexington, Montgomery County (portions), North Carrollton, Pickens, Tallahatchie County, Tchula, Tutwiler, Vaiden & Webb. ICA: MS0014.

TV Market Ranking: Below 100 (Carrollton, Charleston, Duck Hill, Itta Bena, Leflore County, Lexington, Montgomery County (portions), North Carrollton, Tallahatchie County, Tchula, Vaiden, Webb, WINONA); Outside TV Markets (Durant, Goodman, Kilmichael, Pickens, Tutwiler). Franchise award date: November 11, 1966. Franchise expiration date: N.A. Began: January 1, 1960.

Channel capacity: 116 (operating 2-way). Channels available but not in use: N.A.

Basic Service

Subscribers: 6,600.

Programming (received off-air): WABG-TV (ABC) Greenwood; WJTV (CBS) Jackson; WLBT (NBC) Jackson; WLOV-TV (FOX) West Point; WMAB-TV (PBS) Mississippi State; WTVA (NBC) Tupelo; WXVT (CBS) Greenville.

Programming (via satellite): ABC Family Channel; AMC; Animal Planet; Arts & Entertainment; BET Networks; Cartoon Network; CNBC; CNN; Comcast Sports Net Southeast; Comedy Central; C-SPAN; Discovery Channel; Disney Channel; E! Entertainment Television; ESPN; ESPN 2; Food Network; Fox News Channel; Fuse; FX; Great American Country; Headline News; HGTV; History Channel; INSP; Lifetime; National Geographic Channel; Outdoor Channel; QVC; Speed Channel; Syfy; TBS Superstation; The Learning Channel; Toon Disney; Trinity Broadcasting Network; Turner Classic Movies; Turner Network TV; USA Network; Weather Channel; WGN America.

Fee: $10.00 installation; $46.00 monthly.

Digital Basic Service

Subscribers: 1,500.

Programming (via satellite): AmericanLife TV Network; BBC America; Bio; Bloomberg Television; Discovery Digital Networks; DMX Music; ESPN Classic Sports; ESPNews; FSN Digital Atlantic; FSN Digital Central; FSN Digital Pacific; G4; Golf Channel; GSN; Halogen Network; History Channel International; Outdoor Channel; Style Network; Toon Disney; WE tv.

Fee: $13.95 monthly.

Digital Expanded Basic Service

Subscribers: N.A.

Programming (via satellite): Encore; Fox Movie Channel; Lifetime Movie Network; Turner Classic Movies.

Fee: $5.00 monthly.

Pay Service 1

Pay Units: N.A.

Programming (via satellite): Cinemax; HBO; Showtime; The Movie Channel.

Fee: $25.00 installation; $7.50 monthly (Showtime), $10.00 monthly (Cinemax, HBO or TMC).

Digital Pay Service 1

Pay Units: N.A.

Programming (via satellite): Cinemax (multiplexed); Flix; HBO (multiplexed); Showtime (multiplexed); The Movie Channel (multiplexed).

Fee: $16.00 monthly (each).

Video-On-Demand: No

Pay-Per-View

ESPN Now (delivered digitally); Hot Choice (delivered digitally); Playboy TV (delivered digitally); Fresh (delivered digitally); Movies (delivered digitally); sports (delivered digitally).

Internet Service

Operational: Yes.

Subscribers: 1,000.

Broadband Service: In-house.

Fee: $10.00 installation; $43.00 monthly.

Telephone Service

Digital: Operational

Fee: $20.00 installation; $39.95 monthly

Miles of Plant: 500.0 (coaxial); None (fiber optic). Homes passed: 20,000.

General Manager: Jim Duck. Technical Engineering Manager: Barry Lowery.

Ownership: Cable One Inc. (MSO).

WINSTONVILLE—Formerly served by J & L Cable. No longer in operation. ICA: MS0209.

WOODVILLE—Trust Cable. Now served by WOODVILLE, MS [MS0048]. ICA: MS0220.

MISSOURI

Total Systems: **209**
Total Communities Served: **767**
Franchises Not Yet Operating: **0**
Applications Pending: **0**
Communities with Applications: **0**
Number of Basic Subscribers: **1,529,258**
Number of Expanded Basic Subscribers: **720,512**
Number of Pay Units: **276,841**

Top 100 Markets Represented: St. Louis (11); Kansas City (22); Cape Girardeau, MO-Paducah, KY-Harrisburg, IL (69).

For a list of cable communities in this section, see the Cable Community Index located in the back of Cable Volume 2.
For explanation of terms used in cable system listings, see p. D-11.

ADRIAN—Longview Communications, 12007 Sunrise Valley Dr, Ste 375, Reston, VA 20191. Phones: 866-611-6565 (Customer service); 703-476-9101. Fax: 703-476-9107. Web Site: http://www.longviewcomm.com. ICA: MO0175.

TV Market Ranking: Outside TV Markets (ADRIAN). Franchise award date: N.A. Franchise expiration date: N.A. Began: December 1, 1973.

Channel capacity: N.A. Channels available but not in use: N.A.

Basic Service

Subscribers: 146.

Programming (received off-air): KCPT (PBS) Kansas City; KCTV (CBS) Kansas City; KCWE (CW) Kansas City; KMBC-TV (ABC) Kansas City; KMCI-TV (IND) Lawrence; KPXE-TV (ION) Kansas City; KSHB-TV (NBC) Kansas City; KSMO-TV (MNT) Kansas City; WDAF-TV (FOX) Kansas City; allband FM.

Programming (via satellite): INSP; QVC; Trinity Broadcasting Network.

Fee: $15.00 installation; $19.98 monthly.

Expanded Basic Service 1

Subscribers: N.A.

Programming (via satellite): ABC Family Channel; AMC; Animal Planet; Arts & Entertainment; Cartoon Network; Classic Arts Showcase; CNN; Discovery Channel; Disney Channel; ESPN; ESPN 2; FX; Great American Country; Headline News; HGTV; Lifetime; Nickelodeon; Speed Channel; TBS Superstation; The Learning Channel; Travel Channel; Turner Network TV; USA Network; Weather Channel.

Fee: $17.97 monthly.

Pay Service 1

Pay Units: 39.

Programming (via satellite): Showtime; The Movie Channel.

Fee: $8.95 monthly (TMC), $10.95 monthly (Showtime).

Video-On-Demand: No

Internet Service

Operational: Yes.

Telephone Service

None

Miles of Plant: 13.0 (coaxial); None (fiber optic). Homes passed: 686.

President: John Long. Senior Vice President: Marc W. Cohen. General Manager: Brandon Dickey. Operations Manager: Perry Scarborough.

City fee: 3% of gross.

Ownership: Longview Communications (MSO).

ADVANCE—Formerly served by Cebridge Connections. Now served by MORLEY, MO [MO0171]. ICA: MO0178.

ALBA—Mediacom. Now served by CARL JUNCTION, MO [MO0094]. ICA: MO0237.

ALBANY—Mediacom, 901 N College Ave, Columbia, MO 65201. Phones: 573-442-5531; 573-443-1536; 816-637-4500 (Local office). Fax: 573-449-8492. E-mail: gbaugh@mediacomcc.com. Web Site: http://www.mediacomcable.com. ICA: MO0144.

TV Market Ranking: Outside TV Markets (ALBANY). Franchise award date: August 21, 1973. Franchise expiration date: N.A. Began: N.A.

Channel capacity: N.A. Channels available but not in use: N.A.

Basic Service

Subscribers: 736.

Programming (received off-air): KCPT (PBS) Kansas City; KCTV (CBS) Kansas City; KCWE (CW) Kansas City; KMBC-TV (ABC) Kansas City; KMCI-TV (IND) Lawrence; KPXE-TV (ION) Kansas City; KQTV (ABC) St. Joseph; KSHB-TV (NBC) Kansas City; KSMO-TV (MNT) Kansas City; WDAF-TV (FOX) Kansas City; allband FM.

Programming (via satellite): WGN America.

Current originations: Public Access.

Fee: $35.00 installation; $23.95 monthly.

Expanded Basic Service 1

Subscribers: N.A.

Programming (via satellite): ABC Family Channel; AMC; Animal Planet; Arts & Entertainment; Bravo; Cartoon Network; CNBC; CNN; Comedy Central; Country Music TV; C-SPAN; Discovery Channel; Disney Channel; E! Entertainment Television; ESPN; ESPN 2; Food Network; Fox News Channel; Fox Sports Net Midwest; FX; Hallmark Channel; Headline News; HGTV; History Channel; Home Shopping Network; INSP; Lifetime; MSNBC; MTV; Nickelodeon; Outdoor Channel; QVC; ShopNBC; SoapNet; Speed Channel; Spike TV; Syfy; TBS Superstation; The Learning Channel; Travel Channel; Trinity Broadcasting Network; truTV; Turner Network TV; TV Guide Network; TV Land; USA Network; Weather Channel.

Digital Basic Service

Subscribers: N.A.

Programming (via satellite): BBC America; Bio; Bloomberg Television; Discovery Digital Networks; FitTV; Fox Movie Channel; Fox Soccer; Fuse; G4; GAS; Golf Channel; GSN; History Channel International; Independent Film Channel; Lifetime Movie Network; Lime; MTV Networks Digital Suite; Music Choice; National Geographic Channel; Nick Jr.; NickToons TV; Style Network; Turner Classic Movies; Versus.

Digital Pay Service 1

Pay Units: N.A.

Programming (via satellite): Cinemax (multiplexed); Encore (multiplexed); Flix (multiplexed); HBO (multiplexed); Showtime (multiplexed); Starz (multiplexed); Sundance Channel (multiplexed); The Movie Channel (multiplexed).

Video-On-Demand: No

Pay-Per-View

Mediacom PPV (delivered digitally); Playboy TV (delivered digitally); TEN Clips (delivered digitally); TEN Blox (delivered digitally).

Internet Service

Operational: Yes.

Broadband Service: Mediacom High Speed Internet.

Telephone Service

None

Miles of Plant: 18.0 (coaxial); None (fiber optic). Homes passed: 1,053.

General Manager: Gary Baugh. Marketing Director: Wes Shaver. Technical Operations Manager: Tom Evans.

City fee: 3% of gross.

Ownership: Mediacom LLC (MSO).

ALMA—Longview Communications, 1923 N Main, Higginsville, MO 64037. Phone: 866-611-6565. Fax: 866-329-4790. Web Site: http://www.longviewcomm.com. Also serves Blackburn, Concordia, Corder, Emma, Gilliam, Higginsville, Houstonia, Malta Bend, Slater, Sweet Springs & Waverly. ICA: MO0313.

TV Market Ranking: Below 100 (ALMA, Concordia, Corder, Emma, Houstonia, Sweet Springs); Outside TV Markets (Blackburn, Gilliam, Higginsville, Malta Bend, Slater, Waverly). Franchise award date: N.A. Franchise expiration date: N.A. Began: November 1, 1984.

Channel capacity: 78 (operating 2-way). Channels available but not in use: None.

Basic Service

Subscribers: 3,369.

Programming (received off-air): KCPT (PBS) Kansas City; KCTV (CBS) Kansas City; KCWE (CW) Kansas City; KMBC-TV (ABC) Kansas City; KMCI-TV (IND) Lawrence; KMIZ (ABC) Columbia; KMOS-TV (PBS) Sedalia; KOMU-TV (CW, NBC) Columbia; KPXE-TV (ION) Kansas City; KQFX-LD Columbia; KSHB-TV (NBC) Kansas City; KSMO-TV (MNT) Kansas City; WDAF-TV (FOX) Kansas City.

Programming (via satellite): ABC Family Channel; AMC; Animal Planet; Arts & Entertainment; Boomerang; Cartoon Network; CNN; Comedy Central; Cooking Channel; C-SPAN; Discovery Channel; Disney Channel; E! Entertainment Television; ESPN; ESPN 2; ESPN Classic Sports; Food Network; Fox News Channel; Fox Sports Net Midwest; Fuse; FX; Great American Country; Hallmark Channel; Headline News; HGTV; History Channel; Home Shopping Network; INSP; Lifetime; MSNBC; National Geographic Channel; Outdoor Channel; QVC; ShopNBC; Speed Channel; Syfy; TBS Superstation; The Learning Channel; Toon Disney; Turner Classic Movies; Turner Network TV; TV Guide Network; TV Land; USA Network; Weather Channel; WGN America; XY.tv.

Current originations: Public Access.

Fee: $35.95 installation; $44.35 monthly.

Digital Basic Service

Subscribers: 400.

Programming (via satellite): AmericanLife TV Network; BBC America; Bio; Bloomberg Television; Discovery Digital Networks; DMX Music; ESPN Classic Sports; ESPNews; Fox College Sports Atlantic; Fox College Sports Central; Fox College Sports Pacific; Fox Movie Channel; Fox Soccer; Fuse; G4; Golf Channel; GSN; Halogen Network; History Channel International; Independent Film Channel; Lifetime Movie Network; National Geographic Channel; Outdoor Channel; Sleuth; Speed Channel; Style Network; Turner Classic Movies; WE tv.

Fee: $15.95 monthly.

Pay Service 1

Pay Units: N.A.

Programming (via satellite): Cinemax; HBO; Showtime; The Movie Channel.

Fee: $9.95 monthly (Showtime or TMC), $10.95 monthly (Cinemax), $14.95 monthly (HBO).

Digital Pay Service 1

Pay Units: N.A.

Programming (via satellite): Cinemax (multiplexed); Encore (multiplexed); Flix; HBO (multiplexed); Showtime (multiplexed); Starz (multiplexed); The Movie Channel (multiplexed).

Fee: $9.95 monthly (Showtime or TMC), $10.95 monthly (Cinemax), $14.95 monthly (HBO).

Video-On-Demand: No

Pay-Per-View

iN DEMAND (delivered digitally); Hot Choice (delivered digitally); Playboy TV (delivered digitally); Fresh (delivered digitally).

Internet Service

Operational: Yes.

Subscribers: 599.

Broadband Service: In-house.

Fee: $49.95 installation; $39.95 monthly; $5.00 modem lease.

Telephone Service

None

Miles of Plant: 137.0 (coaxial); None (fiber optic). Homes passed: 6,991.

President: John Long. Senior Vice President: Marc W. Cohen. General Manager: Brandon Dickey. Operations Manager: Perry Scarborough.

Ownership: Longview Communications (MSO).

ALTON—Boycom Cablevision Inc., 3467 Township Line Rd, Poplar Bluff, MO 63901. Phone: 573-686-9101. Fax: 573-686-4722. Web Site: http://www.boycomonline.com. Also serves Howell County. ICA: MO0382.

TV Market Ranking: Outside TV Markets (ALTON, Howell County). Franchise award date: January 1, 1965. Franchise expiration date: N.A. Began: October 15, 1965.
Channel capacity: 37 (not 2-way capable). Channels available but not in use: 6.
Basic Service
Subscribers: 24,000 Includes Birch Tree, Doniphan, Ellington, Ellsinore, Eminence, Marble Hill, Mountain View, Naylor, Van Buren, Winona, & Biggers AR.
Programming (received off-air): KAIT (ABC) Jonesboro; KOLR (CBS) Springfield; KOZK (PBS) Springfield; KSFX-TV (FOX) Springfield; KSPR (ABC) Springfield; KYTV (CW, NBC) Springfield.
Programming (via satellite): AMC; ESPN; QVC; Travel Channel; Trinity Broadcasting Network.
Fee: $29.95 installation; $19.95 monthly; $10.00 additional installation.
Expanded Basic Service 1
Subscribers: 277.
Programming (via satellite): ABC Family Channel; CNN; Country Music TV; Disney Channel; E! Entertainment Television; Hallmark Channel; Lifetime; Spike TV; TBS Superstation; truTV; Turner Network TV; TV Land; USA Network; Weather Channel.
Fee: $20.00 monthly.
Pay Service 1
Pay Units: 38.
Programming (via satellite): Showtime.
Fee: $10.95 monthly.
Pay Service 2
Pay Units: 18.
Programming (via satellite): HBO.
Fee: $11.95 monthly.
Video-On-Demand: No
Pay-Per-View
Playboy TV (delivered digitally); Fresh (delivered digitally); Shorteez (delivered digitally); iN DEMAND (delivered digitally); Urban American Television Network (delivered digitally); ESPN Now (delivered digitally); ESPN (delivered digitally); Hot Choice (delivered digitally).
Internet Service
Operational: Yes.
Telephone Service
None
Miles of Plant: 14.0 (coaxial); None (fiber optic). Homes passed: 402.
President: Steven Boyers. General Manager: Shelly Batton. Chief Technician: Phil Huett.
Ownership: Boycom Cablevision Inc. (MSO).

AMAZONIA—Formerly served by CableDirect. No longer in operation. ICA: MO0356.

AMSTERDAM—Craw-Kan Telephone Co-op. This cable system has converted to IPTV, PO Box 100, 200 N Ozark St, Girard, KS 66743. Phones: 800-362-0316; 620-724-8235. Fax: 620-724-4099. E-mail: webmaster@ckt.net. Web Site: http://www.ckt.net. ICA: MO5189.
Channel capacity: N.A. Channels available but not in use: N.A.
Internet Service
Operational: Yes.
Telephone Service
Digital: Operational
Ownership: Craw-Kan Telephone Cooperative.

AMSTERDAM—Craw-Kan Telephone Co-op. This cable system has converted to IPTV. See Amsterdam, MO [MO5189]. ICA: MO0383.

ANDERSON—Mediacom. Now served by GRANBY, MO [MO0156]. ICA: MO0193.

ANNAPOLIS—Formerly served by Charter Communications. No longer in operation. ICA: MO0432.

APPLETON CITY—Mediacom, 1533 S Enterprise Ave, Springfield, MO 65804. Phone: 417-875-5560. Fax: 417-883-0265. Web Site: http://www.mediacomcable.com. ICA: MO0184.
TV Market Ranking: Outside TV Markets (APPLETON CITY). Franchise award date: June 7, 1973. Franchise expiration date: N.A. Began: June 1, 1975.
Channel capacity: N.A. Channels available but not in use: N.A.
Basic Service
Subscribers: 392.
Programming (received off-air): KCPT (PBS) Kansas City; KCWE (CW) Kansas City; KMBC-TV (ABC) Kansas City; KMOS-TV (PBS) Sedalia; KOAM-TV (CBS) Pittsburg; KODE-TV (ABC) Joplin; KOLR (CBS) Springfield; KPXE-TV (ION) Kansas City; KSHB-TV (NBC) Kansas City; KSNF (NBC) Joplin; WDAF-TV (FOX) Kansas City.
Programming (via satellite): ABC Family Channel; AMC; Arts & Entertainment; CNN; Country Music TV; Disney Channel; ESPN; Headline News; Lifetime; QVC; Spike TV; Syfy; TBS Superstation; The Learning Channel; Turner Network TV; USA Network; Weather Channel; WGN America.
Fee: $35.00 installation; $25.25 monthly.
Pay Service 1
Pay Units: 48.
Programming (via satellite): The Movie Channel.
Fee: $10.50 monthly.
Pay Service 2
Pay Units: 107.
Programming (via satellite): Showtime.
Fee: $10.50 monthly.
Pay Service 3
Pay Units: 104.
Programming (via satellite): HBO.
Fee: $10.50 monthly.
Video-On-Demand: No
Internet Service
Operational: No.
Telephone Service
None
Miles of Plant: 9.0 (coaxial); None (fiber optic). Homes passed: 691.
Regional Vice President: Bill Copeland. Technical Operations Director: Alan Freedman. Marketing Director: Will Kuebler.
City fee: 3% of gross.
Ownership: Mediacom LLC (MSO).

ARCHIE—Mediacom. Now served by BUTLER, MO [MO0097]. ICA: MO0246.

ARGYLE—Formerly served by First Cable of Missouri Inc. No longer in operation. ICA: MO0377.

ARMSTRONG—Formerly served by Cebridge Connections. No longer in operation. ICA: MO0325.

ATLANTA—Formerly served by CableDirect. No longer in operation. ICA: MO0330.

AVA—Mediacom. Now served by SEYMOUR, MO [MO0172]. ICA: MO0116.

BARING—Formerly served by CableDirect. No longer in operation. ICA: MO0440.

BARNARD—Formerly served by CableDirect. No longer in operation. ICA: MO0384.

BARNHART—Charter Communications, 941 Charter Commons Dr, Saint Louis, MO 63017. Phone: 636-207-7044. Fax: 636-230-7034. Web Site: http://www.charter.com. Also serves Byrnes Mills, Cedar Hill, Cedar Hill Lakes, Franklin County (northeastern portion), Gray Summit, High Ridge, House Springs, Jefferson County (unincorporated areas), Kimmswick, Olympian Village, Pacific & Villa Ridge. ICA: MO0385.
TV Market Ranking: 11 (BARNHART, Byrnes Mills, Cedar Hill, Cedar Hill Lakes, Franklin County (northeastern portion), Gray Summit, High Ridge, House Springs, Jefferson County (unincorporated areas) (portions), Kimmswick, Pacific); Outside TV Markets (Olympian Village, Villa Ridge, Jefferson County (unincorporated areas) (portions)). Franchise award date: October 1, 1987. Franchise expiration date: N.A. Began: N.A.
Channel capacity: N.A. Channels available but not in use: N.A.
Basic Service
Subscribers: 14,364.
Programming (received off-air): KDNL-TV (ABC) St. Louis; KETC (PBS) St. Louis; KMOV (CBS) St. Louis; KNLC (IND) St. Louis; KPLR-TV (CW) St. Louis; KSDK (NBC) St. Louis; KTVI (FOX) St. Louis; WPXS (IND) Mount Vernon; WRBU (MNT) East St. Louis.
Programming (via satellite): C-SPAN; C-SPAN 2; Eternal Word TV Network; GRTV Network; Home Shopping Network; INSP; Jewelry Television; QVC; ShopNBC; TBS Superstation; Trinity Broadcasting Network; TV Guide Network; Univision; Weatherscan; WGN America.
Current originations: Government Access; Educational Access; Public Access.
Fee: $29.99 installation.
Expanded Basic Service 1
Subscribers: 12,896.
Programming (via satellite): ABC Family Channel; AMC; Animal Planet; Arts & Entertainment; BET Networks; Bravo; Cartoon Network; CNBC; CNN; Comedy Central; Country Music TV; Discovery Channel; Disney Channel; E! Entertainment Television; ESPN; ESPN 2; Food Network; Fox Movie Channel; Fox News Channel; Fox Sports Net Midwest; FX; G4; Golf Channel; GSN; Hallmark Channel; Headline News; HGTV; History Channel; Lifetime; MSNBC; MTV; National Geographic Channel; Nickelodeon; Oxygen; SoapNet; Speed Channel; Spike TV; Style Network; Syfy; The Learning Channel; Toon Disney; Travel Channel; truTV; Turner Classic Movies; Turner Network TV; TV Land; USA Network; Versus; VH1; WE tv; Weather Channel.
Fee: $49.99 monthly.
Digital Basic Service
Subscribers: 5,616.
Programming (via satellite): BBC America; Bio; Bloomberg Television; Discovery Digital Networks; Do-It-Yourself; Encore Action; ESPN Classic Sports; FitTV; Fox Sports World; FSN Digital Atlantic; FSN Digital Central; FSN Digital Pacific; Fuel TV; Fuse; GAS; Great American Country; History Channel International; Independent Film Channel; International Television (ITV); Lifetime Movie Network; MTV Networks Digital Suite; Music Choice; NFL Network; Nick Jr.; Nick Too; NickToons TV; Sundance Channel.
Digital Pay Service 1
Pay Units: 1,569.
Programming (via satellite): Cinemax (multiplexed).
Fee: $10.00 installation; $11.95 monthly.
Digital Pay Service 2
Pay Units: 852.
Programming (via satellite): Starz (multiplexed).
Fee: $10.00 installation; $7.95 monthly.
Digital Pay Service 3
Pay Units: 2,044.
Programming (via satellite): HBO (multiplexed).
Fee: $11.95 monthly.
Digital Pay Service 4
Pay Units: 1,457.
Programming (via satellite): Showtime (multiplexed).
Fee: $11.95 monthly.
Digital Pay Service 5
Pay Units: 768.
Programming (via satellite): The Movie Channel (multiplexed).
Fee: $11.95 monthly.
Video-On-Demand: Yes
Pay-Per-View
Addressable homes: 4,472.
iN DEMAND (delivered digitally), Fee: $4.95, Addressable: Yes; Sports PPV (delivered digitally); ESPN Now (delivered digitally); Playboy TV (delivered digitally); Fresh (delivered digitally); Shorteez (delivered digitally).
Internet Service
Operational: Yes.
Broadband Service: Charter Pipeline.
Fee: $29.99 monthly.
Telephone Service
Digital: Operational
Fee: $29.99 monthly
Miles of Plant: 778.0 (coaxial); 100.0 (fiber optic). Homes passed: 29,716.
Vice President & General Manager: Steve Trippe. Operations Director: Tom Williams. Technical Operations Manager: John Vichland. Marketing Director: Beverly Wall.
Ownership: Charter Communications Inc. (MSO).

BELL CITY—Semo Communications Corporation. Now served by MORLEY, MO [MO0171]. ICA: MO0311.

BELLE—Formerly served by Almega Cable. No longer in operation. ICA: MO0076.

BENTON—Charter Communications. Now served by CAPE GIRARDEAU, MO [MO0018]. ICA: MO0200.

BERNIE—Formerly served by Cebridge Connections. Now served by DEXTER, MO [MO0039]. ICA: MO0143.

BETHANY—Mediacom, 901 N College Ave, Columbia, MO 65201. Phones: 866-746-7312; 573-443-1513. Fax: 573-449-8492. E-mail: gbaugh@mediacomcc.com. Web Site: http://www.mediacomcable.com. ICA: MO0386.
TV Market Ranking: Outside TV Markets (BETHANY). Franchise award date: N.A. Franchise expiration date: N.A. Began: March 1, 1972.
Channel capacity: N.A. Channels available but not in use: N.A.
Basic Service
Subscribers: 1,222.
Programming (received off-air): KCPT (PBS) Kansas City; KCTV (CBS) Kansas City; KMBC-TV (ABC) Kansas City; KMCI-TV (IND) Lawrence; KPXE-TV (ION) Kansas City; KQTV (ABC) St. Joseph; KSHB-TV (NBC) Kansas City; WDAF-TV (FOX) Kansas City.
Programming (via satellite): WGN America.

Current originations: Public Access.
Fee: $35.00 installation; $27.95 monthly.
Expanded Basic Service 1
Subscribers: N.A.
Programming (via satellite): ABC Family Channel; AMC; Animal Planet; Arts & Entertainment; Bravo; Cartoon Network; CNBC; CNN; Comedy Central; Country Music TV; C-SPAN; Discovery Channel; Disney Channel; E! Entertainment Television; ESPN; ESPN 2; Food Network; Fox News Channel; Fox Sports Net Midwest; FX; Hallmark Channel; Headline News; HGTV; History Channel; Home Shopping Network; INSP; Lifetime; MSNBC; MTV; Nickelodeon; Outdoor Channel; QVC; ShopNBC; SoapNet; Speed Channel; Spike TV; Syfy; TBS Superstation; The Learning Channel; Travel Channel; Trinity Broadcasting Network; truTV; Turner Network TV; TV Guide Network; TV Land; USA Network; VH1; WE tv; Weather Channel.
Fee: $3.95 monthly.
Digital Basic Service
Subscribers: N.A.
Programming (via satellite): BBC America; Bio; Bloomberg Television; Discovery Digital Networks; FitTV; Fox Movie Channel; Fox Soccer; Fuse; G4; GAS; Golf Channel; GSN; History Channel International; Independent Film Channel; Lifetime Movie Network; Lime; MTV Networks Digital Suite; Music Choice; National Geographic Channel; Nick Jr.; NickToons TV; Style Network; Turner Classic Movies; Versus.
Digital Pay Service 1
Pay Units: N.A.
Programming (via satellite): Cinemax (multiplexed); Encore (multiplexed); Flix (multiplexed); HBO (multiplexed); Showtime (multiplexed); Starz (multiplexed); Sundance Channel (multiplexed); The Movie Channel (multiplexed).
Video-On-Demand: No
Pay-Per-View
Mediacom PPV (delivered digitally); Playboy TV (delivered digitally); TEN Clips (delivered digitally); TEN Blox (delivered digitally).
Internet Service
Operational: Yes.
Broadband Service: Mediacom High Speed Internet.
Telephone Service
None
Miles of Plant: 29.0 (coaxial); None (fiber optic). Homes passed: 1,763.
General Manager: Gary Baugh. Marketing Director: Wes Shaver. Technical Operations Manager: Tom Evans.
City fee: 2% of gross.
Ownership: Mediacom LLC (MSO).

BEVIER—Chariton Valley Communications Corp. Now served by MACON, MO [MO0071]. ICA: MO0203.

BILLINGS—Mediacom. Now served by SEYMOUR, MO [MO0126]. Previously served by FORSYTH, MO [MO0126]. ICA: MO0242.

BIRCH TREE—Boycom Cablevision Inc., 3467 Township Line Rd, Poplar Bluff, MO 63901. Phone: 573-686-9101. Fax: 573-686-4722. Web Site: http://www.boycomonline.com. ICA: MO0235.
TV Market Ranking: Outside TV Markets (BIRCH TREE). Franchise award date: February 5, 1970. Franchise expiration date: N.A. Began: N.A.
Channel capacity: N.A. Channels available but not in use: N.A.
Basic Service
Subscribers: N.A. Included in Alton
Programming (received off-air): KAIT (ABC) Jonesboro; KOLR (CBS) Springfield; KOZK (PBS) Springfield; KSFX-TV (FOX) Springfield; KSPR (ABC) Springfield; KYTV (CW, NBC) Springfield.
Programming (via satellite): ABC Family Channel; AMC; Arts & Entertainment; CNN; C-SPAN; Discovery Channel; Disney Channel; ESPN; Fox Sports Net Midwest; FX; Great American Country; Home Shopping Network; Lifetime; Nickelodeon; Speed Channel; Spike TV; TBS Superstation; Trinity Broadcasting Network; Turner Network TV; USA Network; Weather Channel; WGN America.
Fee: $29.95 installation; $39.95 monthly.
Pay Service 1
Pay Units: 35.
Programming (via satellite): Cinemax; HBO.
Fee: $8.99 monthly (Cinemax), $12.99 monthly (HBO).
Video-On-Demand: No
Internet Service
Operational: No.
Telephone Service
None
Miles of Plant: 9.0 (coaxial); None (fiber optic). Homes passed: 362.
President: Steven Boyers. General Manager: Shelly Batton. Chief Technician: Phil Huett.
City fee: None.
Ownership: Boycom Cablevision Inc. (MSO).

BISMARCK—Charter Communications. Now served by FARMINGTON, MO [MO0035]. ICA: MO0174.

BOGARD—Formerly served by CableDirect. No longer in operation. ICA: MO0388.

BOLCKOW—Formerly served by CableDirect. No longer in operation. ICA: MO0363.

BOLIVAR—Windstream, PO Box 180, 1705 S Lillian Ave, Bolivar, MO 65613. Phones: 417-326-1013 (Local office); 800-345-3874; 877-807-9463. Fax: 417-326-8439. Web Site: http://www.windstream.com. Also serves Polk County. ICA: MO0055.
TV Market Ranking: Below 100 (BOLIVAR, Halfway, Polk County (portions)); Outside TV Markets (Polk County (portions)). Franchise award date: May 8, 1980. Franchise expiration date: N.A. Began: November 1, 1981.
Channel capacity: 62 (not 2-way capable). Channels available but not in use: 6.
Basic Service
Subscribers: 2,970.
Programming (received off-air): KOLR (CBS) Springfield; KOZK (PBS) Springfield; KSPR (ABC) Springfield; KWBM (MNT) Harrison [LICENSED & SILENT]; KYTV (CW, NBC) Springfield.
Programming (via satellite): ABC Family Channel; Animal Planet; Arts & Entertainment; CNN; Country Music TV; Discovery Channel; Disney Channel; ESPN; ESPN 2; Fox Movie Channel; Fox News Channel; Fox Sports Net Midwest; FX; Headline News; HGTV; History Channel; Lifetime; National Geographic Channel; Nickelodeon; Odyssey Television Network; Speed Channel; Spike TV; TBS Superstation; The Learning Channel; Trinity Broadcasting Network; Turner Classic Movies; Turner Network TV; USA Network; Weather Channel; WGN America.
Fee: $27.55 monthly.
Pay Service 1
Pay Units: 302.
Programming (via satellite): HBO (multiplexed).
Fee: $12.95 monthly.
Video-On-Demand: No
Internet Service
Operational: No, Both DSL & dial-up.
Broadband Service: Offers dial-up and DSL only; no cable modem service.
Telephone Service
None
Miles of Plant: 75.0 (coaxial); None (fiber optic). Homes passed: 4,000. Total homes in franchised area: 4,000.
President & Chief Executive Officer: Jeff Gardner. Senior Vice President, Network Services: Frank Schueneman. Area Manager: Terry Lockart.
City fee: 3% of gross.
Ownership: Windstream Communications Inc. (MSO).

BOONVILLE—Suddenlink Communications, 1005 Main St, Booneville, MO 65233. Phones: 660-882-7681; 314-965-2020. Fax: 660-880-3183. Web Site: http://www.suddenlink.com. Also serves Cooper County (portions). ICA: MO0062.
TV Market Ranking: Below 100 (BOONVILLE, Cooper County (portions)). Franchise award date: November 5, 1964. Franchise expiration date: N.A. Began: April 1, 1965.
Channel capacity: 61 (operating 2-way). Channels available but not in use: N.A.
Basic Service
Subscribers: 1,954.
Programming (received off-air): KCTV (CBS) Kansas City; KMIZ (ABC) Columbia; KMOS-TV (PBS) Sedalia; KOMU-TV (CW, NBC) Columbia; KQFX-LD Columbia; KRCG (CBS) Jefferson City.
Programming (via satellite): C-SPAN; QVC.
Current originations: Religious Access; Educational Access; Public Access.
Fee: $39.95 installation; $19.95 monthly; $15.00 additional installation.
Expanded Basic Service 1
Subscribers: N.A.
Programming (via satellite): ABC Family Channel; AMC; Animal Planet; Arts & Entertainment; BET Networks; Cartoon Network; CNBC; CNN; Comedy Central; Discovery Channel; Disney Channel; E! Entertainment Television; ESPN; ESPN 2; Food Network; Fox News Channel; Fox Sports Net Midwest; FX; Great American Country; Hallmark Channel; Headline News; HGTV; History Channel; Lifetime; MSNBC; MTV; National Geographic Channel; Nickelodeon; Outdoor Channel; Speed Channel; Spike TV; Syfy; TBS Superstation; The Learning Channel; Travel Channel; Trinity Broadcasting Network; Turner Classic Movies; Turner Network TV; TV Land; USA Network; VH1; Weather Channel.
Fee: $25.00 monthly.
Digital Basic Service
Subscribers: N.A.
Programming (via satellite): BBC America; Bio; Bloomberg Television; Discovery Digital Networks; DMX Music; ESPN Classic Sports; ESPNews; Fox Soccer; Fuse; G4; Golf Channel; GSN; History Channel International; Independent Film Channel; Military History Channel; Science Television; Sleuth; Toon Disney; Versus; WE tv.
Fee: $3.99 monthly.
Pay Service 1
Pay Units: 238.
Programming (via satellite): The Movie Channel.
Fee: $7.95 monthly.
Pay Service 2
Pay Units: 224.
Programming (via satellite): Showtime.
Fee: $9.95 monthly.
Pay Service 3
Pay Units: 506.
Programming (via satellite): HBO.
Fee: $10.95 monthly.
Digital Pay Service 1
Pay Units: N.A.
Programming (via satellite): Cinemax (multiplexed); Encore (multiplexed); HBO (multiplexed); Showtime (multiplexed); Starz; The Movie Channel (multiplexed).
Video-On-Demand: No
Pay-Per-View
iN DEMAND (delivered digitally); Playboy TV (delivered digitally); Fresh (delivered digitally).
Internet Service
Operational: Yes. Began: June 23, 2002.
Broadband Service: Cebridge High Speed Cable Internet.
Fee: $29.95 monthly.
Telephone Service
Analog: Not Operational
Digital: Operational
Fee: $49.95 monthly
Miles of Plant: 45.0 (coaxial); None (fiber optic). Homes passed: 2,988.
Regional Manager: Todd Cruthird. Plant Manager: Brent Lowell. Regional Marketing Manager: Beverly Gambell.
City fee: 2% of gross.
Ownership: Cequel Communications LLC (MSO).

BOSWORTH—Formerly served by CableDirect. No longer in operation. ICA: MO0389.

BOWLING GREEN—Crystal Broadband Networks, PO Box 18036, Chicago, IL 60618. Phone: 817-658-9588. E-mail: info@crystalbn.com. Web Site: http://crystalbn.com. ICA: MO0107.
TV Market Ranking: Below 100 (BOWLING GREEN). Franchise award date: N.A. Franchise expiration date: N.A. Began: March 9, 1983.
Channel capacity: 52 (not 2-way capable). Channels available but not in use: None.
Basic Service
Subscribers: N.A.
Programming (received off-air): KDNL-TV (ABC) St. Louis; KETC (PBS) St. Louis; KHQA-TV (ABC, CBS) Hannibal; KMOV (CBS) St. Louis; KPLR-TV (CW) St. Louis; KSDK (NBC) St. Louis; KTVI (FOX) St. Louis; WGEM-TV (CW, NBC) Quincy; WRBU (MNT) East St. Louis.
Programming (via satellite): C-SPAN; Halogen Network; Home Shopping Network; QVC; WGN America.
Current originations: Public Access.
Fee: $29.95 installation; $19.95 monthly.
Expanded Basic Service 1
Subscribers: N.A.
Programming (via satellite): ABC Family Channel; AMC; Animal Planet; Arts & Entertainment; BET Networks; Cartoon Network; CNBC; CNN; Comedy Central; Country Music TV; Discovery Channel; Disney Channel; E! Entertainment Television; ESPN; ESPN 2; Fox News Channel; Fox Sports Net Midwest; FX; G4; Headline News; HGTV; History Channel; Lifetime; MTV; Nickelodeon; Oxygen; Spike TV; Syfy; TBS Superstation; The Learning Channel; Travel Channel; Turner Network TV; TV Land; USA Network; VH1; Weather Channel.
Fee: $20.00 monthly.

Digital Basic Service
Subscribers: N.A.
Programming (via satellite): BBC America; Bio; Bloomberg Television; Discovery Digital Networks; Do-It-Yourself; ESPN Classic Sports; ESPNews; GAS; GSN; History Channel International; Independent Film Channel; Lifetime Movie Network; MTV Networks Digital Suite; Music Choice; Nick Jr.; Nick Too; NickToons TV; SoapNet; Style Network; Sundance Channel; Toon Disney; WE tv.
Digital Pay Service 1
Pay Units: N.A.
Programming (via satellite): Cinemax (multiplexed); Encore; HBO (multiplexed); Showtime (multiplexed); Starz (multiplexed); The Movie Channel (multiplexed).
Fee: $10.75 monthly (Cinemax, HBO or Showtime).
Video-On-Demand: No
Pay-Per-View
iN DEMAND (delivered digitally); Pleasure (delivered digitally); The Erotic Network (delivered digitally); ETC (delivered digitally).
Internet Service
Operational: Yes.
Telephone Service
Digital: Operational
Miles of Plant: 12.0 (coaxial); None (fiber optic). Homes passed: 1,473.
General Manager: Nidhin Johnson. Program Manager: Shawn Smith.
City fee: 3% of gross.
Ownership: Crystal Broadband Networks (MSO).

BRANSON—Suddenlink Communications, PO Box 1109, 310 Walnut Ext, Branson, MO 65616. Phones: 877-869-7897; 417-334-7897. Fax: 417-335-8262. Web Site: http://www.suddenlink.com. Also serves Branson View Estates, Bull Creek, Compton Ridge, Hollister, Indian Point, Merriam Woods, Rockaway Beach, Taney County (portions) & Venice on the Lake. ICA: MO0038.
TV Market Ranking: Below 100 (BRANSON, Branson View Estates, Bull Creek, Compton Ridge, Hollister, Indian Point, Merriam Woods, Rockaway Beach, Venice on the Lake); Outside TV Markets (Taney County (portions)). Franchise award date: February 28, 1994. Franchise expiration date: N.A. Began: December 1, 1969.
Channel capacity: 40 (2-way capable). Channels available but not in use: 8.
Basic Service
Subscribers: 8,107.
Programming (received off-air): KBNS-CA Branson; KOLR (CBS) Springfield; KOZK (PBS) Springfield; KSFX-TV (FOX) Springfield; KSPR (ABC) Springfield; KWBM (MNT) Harrison [LICENSED & SILENT]; KYTV (CW, NBC) Springfield.
Programming (via satellite): CNN; C-SPAN; C-SPAN 2; Home Shopping Network; QVC; TBS Superstation; Trinity Broadcasting Network; WGN America.
Fee: $29.95 installation; $20.95 monthly; $3.95 converter; $10.00 additional installation.
Expanded Basic Service 1
Subscribers: N.A.
Programming (via satellite): ABC Family Channel; AMC; Animal Planet; Arts & Entertainment; Bravo; Cartoon Network; CNBC; Comedy Central; Country Music TV; Discovery Channel; Disney Channel; E! Entertainment Television; ESPN; ESPN 2; Food Network; Fox News Channel; Fox Sports Net Midwest; FX; Great American Country; Headline News; HGTV; History Channel; INSP; Lifetime; MSNBC; MTV; Nickelodeon; Oxygen; Speed Channel; Spike TV; Syfy; The Learning Channel; Travel Channel; Turner Network TV; TV Guide Network; TV Land; USA Network; Versus; VH1; Weather Channel.
Digital Basic Service
Subscribers: N.A.
Programming (via satellite): BBC America; Bio; Bloomberg Television; Cooking Channel; Discovery Digital Networks; Do-It-Yourself; Encore (multiplexed); ESPN Classic Sports; ESPNews; FitTV; Fox Soccer; Fuel TV; G4; GAS; Golf Channel; GSN; Hallmark Channel; Halogen Network; History Channel International; Independent Film Channel; Lifetime Movie Network; MTV Networks Digital Suite; Music Choice; National Geographic Channel; NBA TV; Nick Jr.; NickToons TV; Outdoor Channel; SoapNet; Sundance Channel; Toon Disney.
Digital Pay Service 1
Pay Units: N.A.
Programming (via satellite): Cinemax (multiplexed); HBO (multiplexed); Showtime (multiplexed); Starz (multiplexed); The Movie Channel (multiplexed).
Video-On-Demand: No
Pay-Per-View
Playboy TV (delivered digitally); Fresh (delivered digitally); ESPN Gameplan (delivered digitally); NBA League Pass (delivered digitally); iN DEMAND (delivered digitally).
Internet Service
Operational: Yes.
Telephone Service
Digital: Operational
Miles of Plant: 304.0 (coaxial); None (fiber optic). Homes passed: 15,098.
Manager: Terrill Bradley. Chief Engineer: Tim Crotti.
City fee: 3% of gross.
Ownership: Cequel Communications LLC (MSO).

BRAYMER—Allegiance Communications, 707 W Saratoga St, Shawnee, OK 74804. Phones: 405-275-6923; 405-395-1131. Web Site: http://www.allegiance.tv. ICA: MO0232.
TV Market Ranking: Outside TV Markets (BRAYMER). Franchise award date: November 1, 1983. Franchise expiration date: N.A. Began: February 1, 1984.
Channel capacity: 41 (not 2-way capable). Channels available but not in use: N.A.
Basic Service
Subscribers: 242.
Programming (received off-air): KCPT (PBS) Kansas City; KCTV (CBS) Kansas City; KCWB-LP Reedley; KCWE (CW) Kansas City; KPXE-TV (ION) Kansas City; KSHB-TV (NBC) Kansas City; KSMO-TV (MNT) Kansas City; WDAF-TV (FOX) Kansas City.
Programming (via satellite): KMBC-TV (ABC) Kansas City; KPXE-TV (ION) Kansas City; Spike TV; TBS Superstation; TV Guide Network; Weather Channel; WGN America.
Current originations: Educational Access.
Fee: $41.11 installation; $28.95 monthly.
Expanded Basic Service 1
Subscribers: N.A.
Programming (via satellite): ABC Family Channel; Animal Planet; Arts & Entertainment; CNN; Country Music TV; Discovery Channel; Disney Channel; ESPN; ESPN 2; Hallmark Channel; History Channel; Lifetime; Nickelodeon; The Learning Channel; Turner Network TV; VH1.
Pay Service 1
Pay Units: 56.
Programming (via satellite): HBO.
Fee: $8.95 monthly (Showtime or TMC), $9.95 monthly (Cinemax), $12.95 monthly (HBO),.
Video-On-Demand: No
Pay-Per-View
iN DEMAND (delivered digitally); ESPN Now (delivered digitally); ESPN Sports PPV (delivered digitally); Hot Choice (delivered digitally); Playboy TV (delivered digitally); Fresh (delivered digitally); Shorteez (delivered digitally); Urban American Television Network (delivered digitally).
Internet Service
Operational: No.
Telephone Service
None
Miles of Plant: 8.0 (coaxial); None (fiber optic). Homes passed: 402. Total homes in franchised area: 402.
Chief Executive Officer: Bill Haggarty. Regional Vice President: Andrew Dearth. Vice President, Marketing: Tracy Bass.
City fee: 3% of gross.
Ownership: Allegiance Communications (MSO).

BROOKFIELD—Suddenlink Communications, 114 N Main St, Brookfield, MO 64628. Phones: 314-965-2020; 660-258-2472. Web Site: http://www.suddenlink.com. Also serves Linn County. ICA: MO0073.
TV Market Ranking: Below 100 (Linn County (portions)); Outside TV Markets (BROOKFIELD, Linn County (portions)). Franchise award date: May 1, 1963. Franchise expiration date: N.A. Began: January 1, 1964.
Channel capacity: 62 (operating 2-way). Channels available but not in use: 1.
Basic Service
Subscribers: 1,752.
Programming (received off-air): KCPT (PBS) Kansas City; KOMU-TV (CW, NBC) Columbia; KSMO-TV (MNT) Kansas City; KTVO (ABC) Kirksville.
Programming (via microwave): KCTV (CBS) Kansas City; KMBC-TV (ABC) Kansas City; KSHB-TV (NBC) Kansas City; WDAF-TV (FOX) Kansas City.
Programming (via satellite): C-SPAN; Home Shopping Network; QVC.
Fee: $45.14 installation; $19.95 monthly; $25.14 additional installation.
Expanded Basic Service 1
Subscribers: N.A.
Programming (via satellite): ABC Family Channel; AMC; Animal Planet; Arts & Entertainment; BET Networks; Cartoon Network; CNBC; CNN; Comedy Central; Discovery Channel; Disney Channel; E! Entertainment Television; ESPN; ESPN 2; Food Network; Fox News Channel; Fox Sports Net Midwest; FX; Great American Country; Hallmark Channel; Headline News; HGTV; History Channel; Lifetime; MSNBC; MTV; National Geographic Channel; Nickelodeon; Spike TV; Syfy; TBS Superstation; The Learning Channel; Travel Channel; Trinity Broadcasting Network; Turner Classic Movies; Turner Network TV; TV Land; USA Network; VH1; Weather Channel.
Fee: $25.00 monthly.
Digital Basic Service
Subscribers: N.A.
Programming (via satellite): BBC America; Bio; Bloomberg Television; Discovery Digital Networks; DMX Music; ESPN Classic Sports; ESPNews; Fox Soccer; Fuse; G4; Golf Channel; GSN; History Channel International; Independent Film Channel; Military History Channel; Outdoor Channel; Science Television; Sleuth; Speed Channel; Toon Disney; Versus; WE tv.
Fee: $3.99 monthly.
Pay Service 1
Pay Units: 252.
Programming (via satellite): Cinemax (multiplexed).
Pay Service 2
Pay Units: 254.
Programming (via satellite): HBO (multiplexed).
Pay Service 3
Pay Units: 141.
Programming (via satellite): Showtime (multiplexed).
Pay Service 4
Pay Units: 141.
Programming (via satellite): The Movie Channel.
Digital Pay Service 1
Pay Units: N.A.
Programming (via satellite): Cinemax (multiplexed); HBO (multiplexed); Showtime (multiplexed); Starz; The Movie Channel (multiplexed); The New Encore (multiplexed).
Video-On-Demand: No
Pay-Per-View
iN DEMAND (delivered digitally); Playboy TV (delivered digitally); Fresh (delivered digitally).
Internet Service
Operational: Yes. Began: January 1, 2003.
Broadband Service: Cebridge High Speed Cable Internet.
Fee: $29.95 monthly.
Telephone Service
None
Miles of Plant: 39.0 (coaxial); 2.0 (fiber optic). Homes passed: 2,600. Total homes in franchised area: 2,600.
Regional Manager: Todd Cruthird.
City fee: 5% of gross.
Ownership: Cequel Communications LLC (MSO).

BROWNING—Formerly served by CableDirect. No longer in operation. ICA: MO0281.

BRUNSWICK—Mediacom. Now served by SALISBURY, MO [MO0155]. ICA: MO0213.

BUFFALO—Longview Communications, 1923 N Main, Higginsville, MO 64037. Phone: 866-611-6565. Fax: 866-329-4790. Web Site: http://www.longviewcomm.com. ICA: MO0127.
TV Market Ranking: Below 100 (BUFFALO). Franchise award date: N.A. Franchise expiration date: N.A. Began: November 1, 1982.
Channel capacity: N.A. Channels available but not in use: N.A.
Basic Service
Subscribers: 322.
Programming (received off-air): KOLR (CBS) Springfield; KOZK (PBS) Springfield; KSFX-TV (FOX) Springfield; KSMO-TV (MNT) Kansas City; KSPR (ABC) Springfield; KYTV (CW, NBC) Springfield.
Programming (via satellite): C-SPAN; ESPN 2; Home Shopping Network; INSP; QVC.
Fee: $35.95 installation; $18.98 monthly; $10.00 additional installation.
Expanded Basic Service 1
Subscribers: N.A.
Programming (via satellite): ABC Family Channel; AMC; Animal Planet; Arts & Entertainment; Bravo; Cartoon Network; CNBC; CNN; College Sports Television;

Comedy Central; Discovery Channel; Disney Channel; E! Entertainment Television; ESPN; Food Network; Fox News Channel; FX; Great American Country; Hallmark Channel; Headline News; HGTV; History Channel; Lifetime; MSNBC; National Geographic Channel; Nickelodeon; Syfy; TBS Superstation; The Learning Channel; Travel Channel; Trinity Broadcasting Network; truTV; Turner Network TV; USA Network; WE tv; Weather Channel; WGN America.
Fee: $19.97 monthly.

Digital Basic Service
Subscribers: 23.
Programming (via satellite): AmericanLife TV Network; BBC America; Bio; Bloomberg Television; Discovery Health Channel; Discovery Home Channel; Discovery Kids Channel; Discovery Military Channel; Discovery Times Channel; Encore (multiplexed); ESPN Classic Sports; ESPNews; FitTV; Fox Movie Channel; G4; Golf Channel; GSN; Halogen Network; History Channel International; Independent Film Channel; Lifetime Movie Network; Outdoor Channel; Science Channel; Speed Channel; Style Network; Toon Disney; Turner Classic Movies.
Fee: $16.00 monthly.

Pay Service 1
Pay Units: 113.
Programming (via satellite): Cinemax; HBO; Showtime; The Movie Channel.
Fee: $8.95 monthly (TMC), $10.95 monthly (Cinemax or Showtime), $12.95 monthly (HBO).

Digital Pay Service 1
Pay Units: N.A.
Programming (via satellite): Cinemax (multiplexed); Flix; HBO (multiplexed); Showtime (multiplexed); Starz (multiplexed); The Movie Channel (multiplexed).
Fee: $8.95 monthly (TMC), $10.95 monthly (Showtime or Cinemax), $12.95 monthly (HBO).

Video-On-Demand: No

Pay-Per-View
iN DEMAND (delivered digitally); Hot Choice (delivered digitally); Playboy TV (delivered digitally); Fresh (delivered digitally); Shorteez (delivered digitally).

Internet Service
Operational: Yes.
Subscribers: 78.
Broadband Service: IBBS.

Telephone Service
None

Miles of Plant: 14.0 (coaxial); None (fiber optic). Homes passed: 1,200.
President: John Long. Senior Vice President: Marc W. Cohen. General Manager: Brandon Dickey. Operations Manager: Perry Scarborough.
Ownership: Longview Communications (MSO).

BUNCETON—Mid-Missouri Telephone Co., PO Box 38, 215 Roe St, Pilot Grove, MO 65276. Phones: 800-892-7073; 660-834-3311. Fax: 660-834-6632. Web Site: http://www.mid-mo.net. ICA: MO0295.
TV Market Ranking: Below 100 (BUNCETON). Franchise award date: December 14, 1982. Franchise expiration date: N.A. Began: January 1, 1984.
Channel capacity: 74 (2-way capable). Channels available but not in use: N.A.

Basic Service
Subscribers: 115.
Programming (received off-air): KCTV (CBS) Kansas City; KCWE (CW) Kansas City; KMCI-TV (IND) Lawrence; KMIZ (ABC) Columbia; KMOS-TV (PBS) Sedalia; KOMU-TV (CW, NBC) Columbia; KPXE-TV (ION) Kansas City; KRCG (CBS) Jefferson City; KSHB-TV (NBC) Kansas City; KSMO-TV (MNT) Kansas City; WDAF-TV (FOX) Kansas City.
Programming (via satellite): ABC Family Channel; AMC; Animal Planet; Arts & Entertainment; Cartoon Network; CNN; Comedy Central; C-SPAN; Discovery Channel; E! Entertainment Television; ESPN; ESPN 2; Food Network; Fox News Channel; Fox Sports Net Midwest; FX; Great American Country; Hallmark Channel; Headline News; HGTV; History Channel; Home Shopping Network; INSP; Lifetime; MSNBC; MTV; National Geographic Channel; Nickelodeon; QVC; Shopping Channel; Spike TV; TBS Superstation; The Learning Channel; Turner Classic Movies; Turner Network TV; TV Guide Network; TV Land; USA Network; VH1; Weather Channel; WGN America.
Fee: $10.00 installation; $11.75 monthly; $1.00 converter.

Digital Basic Service
Subscribers: 1.
Programming (via satellite): AmericanLife TV Network; BBC America; Bio; Bloomberg Television; Discovery Digital Networks; DMX Music; Encore; ESPN Classic Sports; ESPNews; FitTV; Fox Movie Channel; Fox Sports World; Golf Channel; GSN; History Channel International; Independent Film Channel; Life Network; Lifetime Movie Network; MuchMusic Network; Outdoor Channel; Speed Channel; Style Network; Toon Disney; Turner Classic Movies; Weatherscan.
Fee: $15.00 monthly.

Pay Service 1
Pay Units: 12.
Programming (via satellite): Cinemax.
Fee: $9.95 monthly.

Pay Service 2
Pay Units: 2.
Programming (via satellite): HBO.
Fee: $12.95 monthly.

Pay Service 3
Pay Units: 2.
Programming (via satellite): Showtime.
Fee: $8.95 monthly.

Pay Service 4
Pay Units: N.A.
Programming (via satellite): The Movie Channel.
Fee: $9.95 monthly.

Video-On-Demand: No

Internet Service
Operational: No.
Broadband Service: DSL service only.

Telephone Service
None

Miles of Plant: 4.0 (coaxial); None (fiber optic). Homes passed: 220.
Chief Executive Officer: Gary Romig. Chief Technician: Lewis L. Scott Jr.
City fee: 3% of gross.
Ownership: Mid-Missouri Telephone Co. (MSO).

BUNKER—Formerly served by Cebridge Connections. No longer in operation. ICA: MO0278.

BURLINGTON JUNCTION—B & L Technologies LLC, 3329 270th St, Lenox, IA 50851. Phones: 800-798-5488; 641-348-2240. Fax: 641-348-2240. ICA: MO0258.
TV Market Ranking: Outside TV Markets (BURLINGTON JUNCTION). Franchise award date: N.A. Franchise expiration date: N.A. Began: October 1, 1981.
Channel capacity: N.A. Channels available but not in use: N.A.

Basic Service
Subscribers: 60.
Programming (received off-air): KHIN (PBS) Red Oak; KMTV-TV (CBS) Omaha; KPTM (FOX, MNT) Omaha; KQTV (ABC) St. Joseph; WOWT-TV (IND, NBC) Omaha.
Programming (via satellite): ABC Family Channel; CNN; Discovery Channel; ESPN; Headline News; Nickelodeon; Spike TV; TBS Superstation; Turner Network TV; USA Network; WGN America.
Fee: $20.00 installation; $22.95 monthly.

Pay Service 1
Pay Units: 24.
Programming (via satellite): Cinemax; HBO.
Fee: $11.00 monthly (Cinemax), $12.95 monthly (HBO).

Video-On-Demand: No

Internet Service
Operational: No.

Telephone Service
None

Miles of Plant: 7.0 (coaxial); None (fiber optic). Homes passed: 271. Total homes in franchised area: 271.
President & General Manager: Robert Hintz. Office Manager: Linda Hintz.
Ownership: B & L Technologies LLC (MSO).

BUTLER—Mediacom, 901 N College Ave, Columbia, MO 65201. Phones: 417-875-5560 (Springfield regional office); 573-443-1536. Fax: 417-883-0265. Web Site: http://www.mediacomcable.com. Also serves Archie. ICA: MO0097.
TV Market Ranking: Outside TV Markets (Archie, BUTLER). Franchise award date: January 1, 1985. Franchise expiration date: N.A. Began: October 1, 1971.
Channel capacity: N.A. Channels available but not in use: N.A.

Basic Service
Subscribers: 1,637.
Programming (received off-air): KCPT (PBS) Kansas City; KCTV (CBS) Kansas City; KCWE (CW) Kansas City; KMBC-TV (ABC) Kansas City; KOAM-TV (CBS) Pittsburg; KPXE-TV (ION) Kansas City; KSHB-TV (NBC) Kansas City; KSMO-TV (MNT) Kansas City; KSNF (NBC) Joplin; WDAF-TV (FOX) Kansas City.
Programming (via satellite): ABC Family Channel; AMC; Animal Planet; Arts & Entertainment; Cartoon Network; CNBC; CNN; Comedy Central; Country Music TV; C-SPAN; Discovery Channel; Disney Channel; E! Entertainment Television; ESPN; ESPN 2; Food Network; Headline News; HGTV; History Channel; Home Shopping Network; INSP; Lifetime; MSNBC; Nickelodeon; QVC; Speed Channel; Spike TV; Syfy; TBS Superstation; The Learning Channel; Travel Channel; Trinity Broadcasting Network; truTV; Turner Network TV; TV Guide Network; TV Land; USA Network; VH1; WE tv; Weather Channel; WGN America.
Fee: $35.00 installation; $23.95 monthly.

Digital Basic Service
Subscribers: N.A.
Programming (via satellite): AmericanLife TV Network; BBC America; Bio; Bloomberg Television; Discovery Digital Networks; DMX Music; FitTV; Fox Movie Channel; Fox Sports World; Fuse; G4; GAS; Golf Channel; GSN; Halogen Network; History Channel International; Independent Film Channel; Lifetime Movie Network; Lime; MTV Networks Digital Suite; National Geographic Channel; Nick Jr.; NickToons TV; Style Network; Turner Classic Movies; Versus.

Digital Pay Service 1
Pay Units: N.A.
Programming (via satellite): Cinemax (multiplexed); Encore (multiplexed); Flix (multiplexed); HBO (multiplexed); Showtime (multiplexed); Starz (multiplexed); Sundance Channel (multiplexed); The Movie Channel (multiplexed).

Video-On-Demand: No

Pay-Per-View
Urban American Television Network (delivered digitally); Playboy TV (delivered digitally); Ten Clips (delivered digitally); Pleasure (delivered digitally); Hot Body (delivered digitally); Movies (delivered digitally); Events (delivered digitally).

Internet Service
Operational: Yes.
Broadband Service: Mediacom High Speed Internet.

Telephone Service
None

Miles of Plant: 42.0 (coaxial); None (fiber optic). Additional miles planned: 1.0 (coaxial). Homes passed: 2,633.
Regional Vice President: Bill Copeland. Operations Director: Bryan Gann. Regional Technical Operations Manager: Alan Freedman. Technical Operations Manager: Roger Shearer. Marketing Director: Will Kuebler.
City fee: 2% of basic.
Ownership: Mediacom LLC (MSO).

BUTLER COUNTY—Boycom Cablevision Inc., 3467 Township Line Rd, Poplar Bluff, MO 63901. Phone: 573-686-9101. Fax: 573-686-4722. Web Site: http://www.boycomonline.com. ICA: MO0444.
TV Market Ranking: Below 100 (BUTLER COUNTY). Franchise award date: N.A. Franchise expiration date: N.A. Began: May 5, 1993.
Channel capacity: 60 (operating 2-way). Channels available but not in use: 1.

Basic Service
Subscribers: N.A.
Programming (received off-air): KAIT (ABC) Jonesboro; KBSI (FOX) Cape Girardeau; KFVS-TV (CBS, CW) Cape Girardeau; KPOB-TV (ABC) Poplar Bluff; KTEJ (PBS) Jonesboro; WPSD-TV (NBC) Paducah.
Programming (via satellite): 3 Angels Broadcasting Network; ABC Family Channel; AMC; Animal Planet; Arts & Entertainment; Cartoon Network; CNBC; CNN; Comedy Central; C-SPAN; C-SPAN 2; Discovery Channel; Disney Channel; E! Entertainment Television; ESPN; ESPN 2; ESPN Classic Sports; Food Network; Fox News Channel; Fox Sports Net Midwest; Fuse; FX; Golf Channel; Great American Country; Hallmark Channel; Headline News; HGTV; History Channel; Lifetime; MTV; Nickelodeon; Outdoor Channel; QVC; Speed Channel; Spike TV; Syfy; TBS Superstation; The Learning Channel; Travel Channel; Trinity Broadcasting Network; truTV; Turner Network TV; TV Guide Network; TV Land; USA Network; VH1; Weather Channel; WGN America.
Fee: $47.10 monthly.

Digital Basic Service
Subscribers: N.A.
Programming (via satellite): AmericanLife TV Network; BBC America; Bio; Bloomberg Television; Bravo; Discovery Digital Networks; DMX Music; ESPN Classic Sports; ESPNews; Fox Movie Channel; Fox Sports

World; G4; GAS; GSN; Halogen Network; History Channel International; Independent Film Channel; Lifetime Movie Network; MTV Networks Digital Suite; Nick Jr.; Style Network; Toon Disney; Versus; WE tv.
Fee: $1.80 monthly.

Pay Service 1
Pay Units: N.A.
Programming (via satellite): Cinemax; HBO.
Fee: $10.00 monthly (each).

Digital Pay Service 1
Pay Units: N.A.
Programming (via satellite): Cinemax (multiplexed); Encore (multiplexed); Flix; HBO (multiplexed); Showtime (multiplexed); Starz (multiplexed); Sundance Channel; The Movie Channel (multiplexed).
Fee: $10.00 monthly (Cinemax, HBO, Starz/Encore, or Showtime/TMC/Flix/Sundance).

Video-On-Demand: No

Pay-Per-View
iN DEMAND (delivered digitally); ESPN Now (delivered digitally); Sports PPV (delivered digitally).

Internet Service
Operational: Yes. Began: September 1, 2003.
Broadband Service: ParaSun Technologies (ISP & Tech support) and SBC to Net.
Fee: $29.95 monthly.

Telephone Service
None

Miles of Plant: 80.0 (coaxial); None (fiber optic).
President: Steven Boyers. General Manager: Shelly Batton. Chief Technician: Phil Huett.
Ownership: Boycom Cablevision Inc.

CABOOL—Mediacom. Now served by SEYMOUR, MO [MO0172]. ICA: MO0163.

CAINSVILLE—Formerly served by Longview Communications. No longer in operation. ICA: MO0277.

CAIRO—Formerly served by Almega Cable. No longer in operation. ICA: MO0390.

CALIFORNIA—Crystal Broadband Networks, PO Box 180336, Chicago, IL 60618. Phones: 877-319-0328; 630-206-0447. E-mail: info@crystalbn.com. Web Site: http://crystalbn.com. Also serves Moniteau County (portions). ICA: MO0103.
TV Market Ranking: Below 100 (CALIFORNIA, Moniteau County (portions)). Franchise award date: February 4, 1980. Franchise expiration date: N.A. Began: September 1, 1980.
Channel capacity: 41 (not 2-way capable). Channels available but not in use: None.

Basic Service
Subscribers: 1,063.
Programming (received off-air): KMIZ (ABC) Columbia; KMOS-TV (PBS) Sedalia; KNLJ (IND) Jefferson City; KOMU-TV (CW, NBC) Columbia; KRCG (CBS) Jefferson City.
Programming (via satellite): Home Shopping Network; Weather Channel; WGN America.
Fee: $29.95 installation; $19.95 monthly; $20.00 additional installation.

Expanded Basic Service 1
Subscribers: N.A.
Programming (via satellite): ABC Family Channel; AMC; Arts & Entertainment; Bravo; Cartoon Network; CNBC; CNN; Comedy Central; Country Music TV; Discovery Channel; Disney Channel; E! Entertainment Television; ESPN; ESPN 2; Fox News Channel; FX; G4; Headline News; HGTV; History Channel; MTV; Nickelodeon; Oxygen; Spike TV; Syfy; TBS Superstation; The Learning Channel; Turner Network TV; TV Land; USA Network; VH1.
Fee: $20.00 monthly.

Digital Basic Service
Subscribers: 19.
Programming (via satellite): BBC America; Bio; Bloomberg Television; Discovery Digital Networks; Do-It-Yourself; Fuse; GAS; GSN; History Channel International; Independent Film Channel; MTV Networks Digital Suite; Nick Jr.; Nick Too; NickToons TV; SoapNet; Style Network; Sundance Channel; Toon Disney; Trinity Broadcasting Network; WE tv.
Fee: $12.95 monthly.

Digital Pay Service 1
Pay Units: 164.
Programming (via satellite): Cinemax (multiplexed); Encore (multiplexed); HBO (multiplexed); Showtime (multiplexed); Starz (multiplexed); The Movie Channel (multiplexed).

Video-On-Demand: No

Pay-Per-View
Addressable homes: 19.
iN DEMAND (delivered digitally); ETC (delivered digitally); The Erotic Network (delivered digitally); Pleasure (delivered digitally).

Internet Service
Operational: Yes.

Telephone Service
Digital: Operational

Miles of Plant: 22.0 (coaxial); None (fiber optic).
General Manager: Nidhin Johnson. Program Manager: Shawn Smith.
Franchise fee: 5% of gross.
Ownership: Crystal Broadband Networks (MSO).

CAMDEN POINT—Allegiance Communications, 707 W Saratoga St, Shawnee, OK 74804. Phones: 405-275-6923; 405-395-1131. Web Site: http://www.allegiance.tv. Also serves Dearborn & Edgerton. ICA: MO0176.
TV Market Ranking: 22 (CAMDEN POINT, Dearborn, Edgerton). Franchise award date: N.A. Franchise expiration date: N.A. Began: July 1, 1989.
Channel capacity: 60 (not 2-way capable). Channels available but not in use: 21.

Basic Service
Subscribers: 420.
Programming (received off-air): KCPT (PBS) Kansas City; KCTV (CBS) Kansas City; KCWE (CW) Kansas City; KMBC-TV (ABC) Kansas City; KMCI-TV (IND) Lawrence; KPXE-TV (ION) Kansas City; KQTV (ABC) St. Joseph; KSHB-TV (NBC) Kansas City; KSMO-TV (MNT) Kansas City; WDAF-TV (FOX) Kansas City.
Programming (via satellite): TBS Superstation.
Fee: $30.00 installation; $21.95 monthly.

Expanded Basic Service 1
Subscribers: 397.
Programming (via satellite): ABC Family Channel; Animal Planet; Arts & Entertainment; CNN; Comedy Central; Country Music TV; Discovery Channel; Disney Channel; E! Entertainment Television; ESPN; ESPN 2; HGTV; History Channel; Lifetime; Nickelodeon; QVC; SoapNet; Speed Channel; Spike TV; The Learning Channel; Toon Disney; Travel Channel; Turner Classic Movies; Turner Network TV; USA Network; VH1; Weather Channel; WGN America.
Fee: $18.25 monthly.

Video-On-Demand: No

Pay-Per-View
iN DEMAND (delivered digitally); Shorteez (delivered digitally); Fresh (delivered digitally); Playboy TV (delivered digitally); Hot Choice (delivered digitally); ESPN Sports PPV (delivered digitally); iN DEMAND (delivered digitally); Urban American Television Network (delivered digitally); Urban American Television Network (delivered digitally); Shorteez (delivered digitally); Fresh (delivered digitally); Playboy TV (delivered digitally); Hot Choice (delivered digitally); ESPN Sports PPV (delivered digitally); ESPN Now (delivered digitally); ESPN Now (delivered digitally).

Internet Service
Operational: No.

Telephone Service
Digital: Planned

Miles of Plant: 13.0 (coaxial); 24.0 (fiber optic). Homes passed: 650. Total homes in franchised area: 650.
Chief Executive Officer: Bill Haggarty. Regional Vice President: Andrew Dearth. Vice President, Marketing: Tracy Bass.
Ownership: Allegiance Communications (MSO).

CAMERON—Mediacom, 901 N College Ave, Columbia, MO 65201. Phones: 573-443-1536; 816-637-4500 (Local office). Fax: 573-449-8492. E-mail: gbaugh@mediacomcc.com. Web Site: http://www.mediacomcable.com. ICA: MO0089.
TV Market Ranking: Below 100 (CAMERON). Franchise award date: N.A. Franchise expiration date: N.A. Began: May 1, 1981.
Channel capacity: N.A. Channels available but not in use: N.A.

Basic Service
Subscribers: 1,672.
Programming (received off-air): KCPT (PBS) Kansas City; KCTV (CBS) Kansas City; KCWE (CW) Kansas City; KMBC-TV (ABC) Kansas City; KMCI-TV (IND) Lawrence; KPXE-TV (ION) Kansas City; KQTV (ABC) St. Joseph; KSHB-TV (NBC) Kansas City; KSMO-TV (MNT) Kansas City; WDAF-TV (FOX) Kansas City.
Programming (via satellite): ABC Family Channel; AMC; Animal Planet; Arts & Entertainment; CNN; Country Music TV; C-SPAN; Discovery Channel; Disney Channel; ESPN; ESPN 2; Headline News; Lifetime; MTV; Nickelodeon; QVC; Spike TV; TBS Superstation; The Learning Channel; Turner Network TV; TV Land; USA Network; Weather Channel; WGN America.
Fee: $35.00 installation; $23.95 monthly.

Expanded Basic Service 1
Subscribers: N.A.
Programming (via satellite): Bravo; Cartoon Network; CNBC; Comedy Central; E! Entertainment Television; Food Network; Fox News Channel; Fox Sports Net Midwest; FX; Hallmark Channel; HGTV; History Channel; Home Shopping Network; INSP; MSNBC; Outdoor Channel; ShopNBC; SoapNet; Speed Channel; Syfy; Travel Channel; Trinity Broadcasting Network; truTV; TV Guide Network; VH1; WE tv.

Digital Basic Service
Subscribers: N.A.
Programming (via satellite): BBC America; Bio; Bloomberg Television; Discovery Digital Networks; FitTV; Fox Movie Channel; Fox Soccer; Fuse; G4; GAS; Golf Channel; GSN; History Channel International; Independent Film Channel; Lifetime Movie Network; Lime; MTV Networks Digital Suite; Music Choice; National Geographic Channel; Nick Jr.; NickToons TV; Style Network; Turner Classic Movies; Versus.

Digital Pay Service 1
Pay Units: N.A.
Programming (via satellite): Cinemax (multiplexed); Encore (multiplexed); Flix (multiplexed); HBO (multiplexed); Showtime (multiplexed); Starz (multiplexed); Sundance Channel (multiplexed); The Movie Channel (multiplexed).

Video-On-Demand: No

Internet Service
Operational: Yes.
Broadband Service: Mediacom High Speed Internet.

Telephone Service
None

Miles of Plant: 28.0 (coaxial); None (fiber optic). Homes passed: 2,476.
General Manager: Gary Baugh. Marketing Director: Wes Shaver. Technical Operations Manager: Tom Evans.
City fee: 5% of gross.
Ownership: Mediacom LLC (MSO).

CANTON—Formerly served by Westcom. No longer in operation. ICA: MO0391.

CAPE GIRARDEAU—Charter Communications, 3140 W Nash Rd, Scott City, MO 63780. Phones: 573-472-0247 (Sikeston office); 573-335-4424; 606-207-7044 (St Louis office). Fax: 573-334-9265. Web Site: http://www.charter.com. Also serves Benton, Bertrand, Chaffee, Charleston, East Prairie, Illmo, Jackson, Kelso, Lambert, Miner, Mississippi County (central portion), Morehouse, New Hamburg, Oran, Scott City, Scott County & Sikeston. ICA: MO0018.
TV Market Ranking: 69 (Benton, Bertrand, CAPE GIRARDEAU, Chaffee, Charleston, Illmo, Jackson, Kelso, Lambert, Miner, Mississippi County (central portion), Morehouse, New Hamburg, Oran, Scott City, Scott County, Sikeston); Outside TV Markets (East Prairie). Franchise award date: N.A. Franchise expiration date: N.A. Began: December 1, 1978.
Channel capacity: N.A. Channels available but not in use: N.A.

Basic Service
Subscribers: 26,343.
Programming (received off-air): KBSI (FOX) Cape Girardeau; KFVS-TV (CBS, CW) Cape Girardeau; WDKA (MNT) Paducah; WPSD-TV (NBC) Paducah; WQWQ-LP (CW) Paducah; WSIL-TV (ABC) Harrisburg; WSIU-TV (PBS) Carbondale; WTCT (IND) Marion; allband FM.
Programming (via satellite): ABC Family Channel; BET Networks; C-SPAN; C-SPAN 2; Discovery Channel; Eternal Word TV Network; Home Shopping Network; INSP; Jewelry Television; QVC; Syfy; TBS Superstation; TV Guide Network; Weather Channel; WGN America.
Current originations: Government Access; Educational Access; Public Access.
Fee: $29.99 installation.

Expanded Basic Service 1
Subscribers: 24,709.
Programming (via satellite): AMC; Animal Planet; Arts & Entertainment; Bravo; Cartoon Network; CNBC; CNN; Comedy Central; Country Music TV; Disney Channel; E! Entertainment Television; ESPN; ESPN 2; Food Network; Fox News Channel; Fox Sports Net Midwest; FX; G4; Golf Channel; Great American Country; GSN; Hallmark Channel; Headline News; HGTV;

History Channel; Lifetime; MSNBC; MTV; MTV2; Nickelodeon; Outdoor Channel; Oxygen; Product Information Network; SoapNet; Speed Channel; Spike TV; Style Network; The Learning Channel; Travel Channel; truTV; Turner Classic Movies; Turner Network TV; TV Land; USA Network; Versus; VH1.
Fee: $49.99 monthly.

Digital Basic Service
Subscribers: N.A.
Programming (received off-air): KDNL-TV (ABC) St. Louis; KFVS-TV (CBS, CW) Cape Girardeau; WPSD-TV (NBC) Paducah.
Programming (via satellite): Animal Planet HD; Arts & Entertainment HD; BBC America; Bio; Bloomberg Television; CBS College Sports Network; CMT Pure Country; CNN en Espanol; CNN HD; CNN International; Discovery Channel HD; Discovery Health Channel; Discovery Kids Channel; Discovery Military Channel; Discovery Planet Green; Do-It-Yourself; ESPN 2 HD; ESPN Classic Sports; ESPN HD; ESPN U; ESPNews; FitTV; Fox Business Channel; Fox College Sports Atlantic; Fox College Sports Central; Fox College Sports Pacific; Fox Soccer; FSN HD; Fuel TV; HDNet; HDNet Movies; History Channel HD; History Channel International; ID Investigation Discovery; Lifetime Movie Network; LOGO; MTV Hits; MTV Tres; mtvU; Music Choice; National Geographic Channel; Nick Jr.; Nick Too; NickToons TV; Science Channel; Science Channel HD; Sundance Channel; TBS in HD; TeenNick; The Sportsman Channel; TLC HD; Toon Disney; Turner Network TV HD; Versus HD; VH1 Classic; VH1 Soul; WE tv; Weather Channel HD.

Digital Pay Service 1
Pay Units: 4,524.
Programming (via satellite): Cinemax (multiplexed); Encore (multiplexed); Flix; HBO (multiplexed); HBO HD; Showtime (multiplexed); Showtime HD; Starz (multiplexed); The Movie Channel (multiplexed).
Fee: $11.95 monthly (each).

Video-On-Demand: Yes

Pay-Per-View
iN DEMAND (delivered digitally); Playboy TV (delivered digitally); Ten Clips (delivered digitally); Penthouse TV (delivered digitally).

Internet Service
Operational: Yes. Began: March 8, 2002.
Broadband Service: Charter Pipeline.
Fee: $49.95 installation; $29.99 monthly.

Telephone Service
Digital: Operational
Fee: $29.99 monthly

Miles of Plant: 850.0 (coaxial); None (fiber optic). Homes passed: 41,735. Miles of plant include Perryville & New Madrid

Vice President & General Manager: Steve Trippe. Operations Director: Dave Miller. Operations Manager: Dave Huntsman. Plant Manager: Kevin Goetz. Technical Operations Manager: John Vichland. Marketing Director: Beverly Wall.

City fee: 5% of gross.

Ownership: Charter Communications Inc. (MSO).

CARL JUNCTION—Mediacom, 1533 S Enterprise Ave, Springfield, MO 65804. Phone: 417-875-5560. Fax: 417-883-0265. Web Site: http://www.mediacomcable.com. Also serves Galena, KS; Airport Drive Village, Alba, Duenweg, Duquesne, Jasper County, Neck City, Oronogo & Purcell, MO. ICA: MO0094.

TV Market Ranking: Below 100 (Airport Drive Village, Alba, CARL JUNCTION, Duenweg, Duquesne, Galena, Jasper County, Neck City, Oronogo, Purcell). Franchise award date: August 1, 1979. Franchise expiration date: N.A. Began: December 21, 1982.

Channel capacity: N.A. Channels available but not in use: N.A.

Basic Service
Subscribers: 3,352.
Programming (received off-air): KCLJ-CA Joplin-Carthage; KFJX (FOX) Pittsburg; KJPX-LP Joplin; KOAM-TV (CBS) Pittsburg; KODE-TV (ABC) Joplin; KOZJ (PBS) Joplin; KSNF (NBC) Joplin.
Programming (via satellite): CW+; INSP; TV Guide Network; WGN America.
Fee: $35.00 installation; $25.25 monthly.

Expanded Basic Service 1
Subscribers: N.A.
Programming (received off-air): KGCS-LD (IND) Joplin.
Programming (via satellite): ABC Family Channel; AMC; AmericanLife TV Network; Animal Planet; Arts & Entertainment; Bravo; Cartoon Network; CNBC; CNN; Comedy Central; Country Music TV; C-SPAN; Discovery Channel; Disney Channel; ESPN; ESPN 2; FitTV; Food Network; Fox Sports Net Midwest; FX; Hallmark Channel; Headline News; HGTV; History Channel; Home Shopping Network; Lifetime; MSNBC; MTV; Nickelodeon; Outdoor Channel; QVC; ShopNBC; SoapNet; Speed Channel; Spike TV; Syfy; TBS Superstation; The Learning Channel; Travel Channel; truTV; Turner Network TV; TV Land; USA Network; VH1; WE tv; Weather Channel.

Digital Basic Service
Subscribers: N.A.
Programming (via satellite): BBC America; Bio; Bloomberg Television; Discovery Digital Networks; ESPNews; Fox Movie Channel; Fox Soccer; Fuse; G4; GAS; Golf Channel; GSN; History Channel International; Independent Film Channel; Lifetime Movie Network; Lime; MTV Networks Digital Suite; Music Choice; National Geographic Channel; Nick Jr.; NickToons TV; Sleuth; Style Network; Turner Classic Movies; Versus.

Digital Pay Service 1
Pay Units: N.A.
Programming (via satellite): Cinemax (multiplexed); Encore (multiplexed); Flix (multiplexed); HBO (multiplexed); Showtime (multiplexed); Starz (multiplexed); Sundance Channel (multiplexed); The Movie Channel (multiplexed).

Video-On-Demand: Yes

Pay-Per-View
Special events (delivered digitally); Movies (delivered digitally); Playboy TV (delivered digitally); Ten Clips (delivered digitally); Ten Blox (delivered digitally).

Internet Service
Operational: Yes.
Broadband Service: Mediacom High Speed Internet.

Telephone Service
Digital: Operational

Miles of Plant: 86.0 (coaxial); None (fiber optic). Homes passed: 5,903.

Regional Vice President: Bill Copeland. Technical Operations Director: Alan Freedman. Marketing Director: Will Kuebler.

City fee: 3% of gross.

Ownership: Mediacom LLC (MSO).

CARROLLTON—Mediacom, 1533 S Enterprise Ave, Springfield, MO 65804. Phones: 417-875-5560 (Springfield regional office); 816-637-4500 (Excelsior Springs office). Fax: 417-883-0265. Web Site: http://www.mediacomcable.com. ICA: MO0095.

TV Market Ranking: Outside TV Markets (CARROLLTON). Franchise award date: N.A. Franchise expiration date: N.A. Began: December 1, 1976.

Channel capacity: N.A. Channels available but not in use: N.A.

Basic Service
Subscribers: 1,425.
Programming (received off-air): KCTV (CBS) Kansas City; KCWE (CW) Kansas City; KMBC-TV (ABC) Kansas City; KMIZ (ABC) Columbia; KMOS-TV (PBS) Sedalia; KOMU-TV (CW, NBC) Columbia; KPXE-TV (ION) Kansas City; KSHB-TV (NBC) Kansas City; KSMO-TV (MNT) Kansas City; WDAF-TV (FOX) Kansas City; 1 FM.
Programming (via satellite): TV Guide Network; WGN America.
Fee: $35.00 installation; $25.25 monthly.

Expanded Basic Service 1
Subscribers: N.A.
Programming (via satellite): ABC Family Channel; AMC; Animal Planet; Arts & Entertainment; Bravo; Cartoon Network; CNBC; CNN; Comedy Central; Country Music TV; C-SPAN; Discovery Channel; E! Entertainment Television; ESPN; ESPN 2; Food Network; Fox News Channel; Fox Sports Net Midwest; FX; Hallmark Channel; Headline News; HGTV; History Channel; Home Shopping Network; INSP; Lifetime; MSNBC; MTV; Nickelodeon; Outdoor Channel; QVC; ShopNBC; SoapNet; Speed Channel; Spike TV; Syfy; TBS Superstation; The Learning Channel; Travel Channel; Trinity Broadcasting Network; truTV; Turner Network TV; TV Land; USA Network; VH1; WE tv; Weather Channel.
Fee: $3.95 monthly.

Digital Basic Service
Subscribers: N.A.
Programming (via satellite): AmericanLife TV Network; BBC America; Bio; Bloomberg Television; Discovery Digital Networks; FitTV; Fox Movie Channel; Fox Soccer; Fuse; G4; GAS; Golf Channel; GSN; Halogen Network; History Channel International; Independent Film Channel; Lifetime Movie Network; Lime; MTV Networks Digital Suite; Music Choice; National Geographic Channel; Nick Jr.; NickToons TV; Style Network; Turner Classic Movies; Versus.

Digital Pay Service 1
Pay Units: N.A.
Programming (via satellite): Cinemax (multiplexed); Encore (multiplexed); Flix (multiplexed); HBO (multiplexed); Showtime (multiplexed); Starz (multiplexed); Sundance Channel (multiplexed); The Movie Channel (multiplexed).

Video-On-Demand: No

Pay-Per-View
Mediacom PPB & Events PPV (delivered digitally); Playboy TV (delivered digitally); TEN Clips (delivered digitally); Pleasure (delivered digitally); Hot Body (delivered digitally); ESPN Gameplan (delivered digitally).

Internet Service
Operational: Yes.
Broadband Service: Mediacom High Speed Internet.

Telephone Service
Digital: Operational

Miles of Plant: 31.0 (coaxial); None (fiber optic). Homes passed: 2,214.

Regional Vice President: Bill Copeland. Operations Director: Bryan Gann. Regional Technical Operations Director: Alan Freedman. Technical Operations Manager: Roger Shearer. Marketing Director: Will Kuebler.

City fee: 3% of gross.

Ownership: Mediacom LLC (MSO).

CARTHAGE—Suddenlink Communications, 231 E 4th St, Carthage, MO 64836-1629. Phone: 417-358-3002. Fax: 417-359-5373. Web Site: http://www.suddenlink.com. Also serves Brooklyn Heights. ICA: MO0034.

TV Market Ranking: Below 100 (Brooklyn Heights, CARTHAGE). Franchise award date: N.A. Franchise expiration date: N.A. Began: March 1, 1967.

Channel capacity: N.A. Channels available but not in use: N.A.

Basic Service
Subscribers: 4,190.
Programming (received off-air): KFJX (FOX) Pittsburg; KOAM-TV (CBS) Pittsburg; KODE-TV (ABC) Joplin; KOZJ (PBS) Joplin; KSNF (NBC) Joplin; allband FM.
Programming (via satellite): TBS Superstation; WGN America.
Current originations: Government Access.
Fee: $41.08 installation; $8.62 monthly; $1.27 converter.

Expanded Basic Service 1
Subscribers: 3,661.
Programming (via satellite): ABC Family Channel; AMC; Animal Planet; Arts & Entertainment; Cartoon Network; CNBC; CNN; Comedy Central; Country Music TV; C-SPAN; C-SPAN 2; CW+; Discovery Channel; Disney Channel; ESPN; ESPN 2; FitTV; Food Network; Fox News Channel; Fox Sports Net Midwest; FX; Hallmark Channel; Headline News; HGTV; History Channel; Lifetime; Nickelodeon; Outdoor Channel; QVC; Spike TV; Syfy; The Learning Channel; Travel Channel; Turner Network TV; TV Land; Univision; USA Network; VH1; Weather Channel.
Fee: $15.71 monthly.

Digital Basic Service
Subscribers: N.A.
Programming (via satellite): BBC America; Bloomberg Television; Discovery Digital Networks; DMX Music; ESPN Classic Sports; ESPNews; Fox Soccer; G4; Golf Channel; GSN; INSP; Speed Channel; Trinity Broadcasting Network; Turner Classic Movies.

Digital Pay Service 1
Pay Units: N.A.
Programming (via satellite): Canales N; Encore (multiplexed); HBO (multiplexed); Showtime (multiplexed); Starz (multiplexed); Sundance Channel; The Movie Channel (multiplexed).

Pay-Per-View
iN DEMAND (delivered digitally), Addressable: Yes; Fresh (delivered digitally); Playboy TV (delivered digitally); Hot Choice (delivered digitally).

Internet Service
Operational: Yes.
Broadband Service: Cebridge High Speed Cable Internet.
Fee: $29.95 monthly.

Telephone Service
None

Miles of Plant: 121.0 (coaxial); 26.0 (fiber optic). Homes passed: 7,239.

Manager: Terrill Bradley. Chief Engineer: Tim Crotti.

City fee: 3% of gross.

Ownership: Cequel Communications LLC (MSO).

CARUTHERSVILLE—Mediacom, 1533 S Enterprise Ave, Springfield, MO 65804. Phones: 417-875-5560 (Springfield regional office); 573-333-1148 (Caruthersville office). Fax: 417-883-0265. Web Site: http://www.mediacomcable.com. Also serves Hayti & Hayti Heights. ICA: MO0041.

TV Market Ranking: Outside TV Markets (CARUTHERSVILLE, Hayti, Hayti Heights). Franchise award date: May 14, 1964. Franchise expiration date: N.A. Began: January 22, 1966.
Channel capacity: N.A. Channels available but not in use: N.A.

Basic Service

Subscribers: 4,200.
Programming (received off-air): KAIT (ABC) Jonesboro; KBSI (FOX) Cape Girardeau; KFVS-TV (CBS, CW) Cape Girardeau; WDYR-CA Dyersburg; WHBQ-TV (FOX) Memphis; WKNO (PBS) Memphis; WMC-TV (NBC) Memphis; WPTY-TV (ABC) Memphis; WREG-TV (CBS) Memphis.
Programming (via satellite): WGN America.
Current originations: Public Access.
Fee: $40.16 installation; $10.00 monthly; $1.05 converter.

Expanded Basic Service 1

Subscribers: N.A.
Programming (via satellite): ABC Family Channel; AMC; AmericanLife TV Network; Animal Planet; Arts & Entertainment; BET Networks; Bravo; Cartoon Network; CNBC; CNN; Comedy Central; Country Music TV; C-SPAN; C-SPAN 2; Discovery Channel; Disney Channel; E! Entertainment Television; ESPN; ESPN 2; FitTV; Food Network; Fox News Channel; Fox Sports Net Midwest; FX; Hallmark Channel; Headline News; HGTV; History Channel; Home Shopping Network; INSP; Lifetime; MSNBC; MTV; Nickelodeon; Outdoor Channel; QVC; SoapNet; Speed Channel; TBS Superstation; The Learning Channel; Travel Channel; Trinity Broadcasting Network; truTV; Turner Network TV; TV Guide Network; TV Land; USA Network; VH1; Weather Channel.
Fee: $23.37 monthly.

Digital Basic Service

Subscribers: N.A.
Programming (via satellite): AmericanLife TV Network; BBC America; Bloomberg Television; Discovery Digital Networks; DMX Music; Fox Movie Channel; Fox Soccer; Fuse; G4; GAS; Golf Channel; GSN; Independent Film Channel; Lifetime Movie Network; Lime; MTV Hits; MTV2; National Geographic Channel; Nick Jr.; NickToons TV; Science Television; Turner Classic Movies; Versus; VH1 Classic.

Digital Pay Service 1

Pay Units: N.A.
Programming (via satellite): Cinemax (multiplexed); Encore (multiplexed); Flix (multiplexed); HBO (multiplexed); Showtime (multiplexed); Starz (multiplexed); Sundance Channel (multiplexed); The Movie Channel (multiplexed).

Video-On-Demand: No

Pay-Per-View

special events; Barker (delivered digitally); Mediacom PPV (delivered digitally); Playboy TV (delivered digitally); TEN Clips (delivered digitally); TEN (delivered digitally); TEN Blox (delivered digitally).

Internet Service

Operational: Yes.
Broadband Service: Mediacom High Speed Internet.

Telephone Service

None

Miles of Plant: 72.0 (coaxial); 10.0 (fiber optic). Homes passed: 4,721. Total homes in franchised area: 4,750.
Regional Vice President: Bill Copeland. Operations Director: Bryan Gann. Regional Technical Operations Director: Alan Freedman. Technical Operations Director: Roger Shearer. Chief Technician: Randall Waldrop. Marketing Director: Will Kuebler.
City fee: 5% of gross.
Ownership: Mediacom LLC (MSO).

CASS COUNTY—Longview Communications, 1923 N Main, Higginsville, MO 64037. Phone: 866-611-6565. Fax: 866-329-4790. Web Site: http://www.longviewcomm.com. ICA: MO0470.
TV Market Ranking: 22 (CASS COUNTY (portions)); Below 100 (CASS COUNTY (portions)). Franchise award date: December 23, 1997. Franchise expiration date: N.A. Began: N.A.
Channel capacity: N.A. Channels available but not in use: N.A.

Basic Service

Subscribers: 128.
Programming (received off-air): KCPT (PBS) Kansas City; KCTV (CBS) Kansas City; KCWE (CW) Kansas City; KMBC-TV (ABC) Kansas City; KMCI-TV (IND) Lawrence; KPXE-TV (ION) Kansas City; KSHB-TV (NBC) Kansas City; KSMO-TV (MNT) Kansas City; WDAF-TV (FOX) Kansas City.
Programming (via satellite): ABC Family Channel; AMC; Animal Planet; Arts & Entertainment; Cartoon Network; CNN; Discovery Channel; Disney Channel; E! Entertainment Television; ESPN; ESPN 2; Fox News Channel; Fuse; FX; Great American Country; Headline News; Lifetime; Outdoor Channel; TBS Superstation; The Learning Channel; Toon Disney; Turner Network TV; USA Network; Weather Channel; WGN America.
Fee: $35.95 installation; $39.95 monthly.

Pay Service 1

Pay Units: N.A.
Programming (via satellite): Cinemax; HBO.
Fee: $10.95 monthly (Cinemax), $14.95 monthly (HBO).

Internet Service

Operational: No.

Telephone Service

None

Miles of Plant: 31.0 (coaxial); None (fiber optic). Homes passed: 876.
President: John Long. Senior Vice President: Marc W. Cohen. General Manager: Brandon Dickey. Operations Manager: Perry Scarborough.
Ownership: Longview Communications (MSO).

CASS COUNTY (northwestern portion)—Formerly served by Cass County Cable. No longer in operation. ICA: MO0348.

CASSVILLE—Mediacom, 1533 S Enterprise Ave, Springfield, MO 65804. Phone: 417-875-5560. Fax: 417-883-0265. Web Site: http://www.mediacomcable.com. Also serves Exeter & Purdy. ICA: MO0118.
TV Market Ranking: Below 100 (CASSVILLE, Exeter, Purdy). Franchise award date: January 12, 1983. Franchise expiration date: N.A. Began: July 1, 1983.
Channel capacity: N.A. Channels available but not in use: N.A.

Basic Service

Subscribers: 1,628.
Programming (received off-air): KODE-TV (ABC) Joplin; KOLR (CBS) Springfield; KOZK (PBS) Springfield; KSPR (ABC) Springfield; KWBM (MNT) Harrison [LICENSED & SILENT]; KYTV (CW, NBC) Springfield.
Programming (via satellite): ABC Family Channel; AMC; AmericanLife TV Network; Animal Planet; Arts & Entertainment; Bravo; Cartoon Network; CNBC; CNN; Comedy Central; Country Music TV; C-SPAN; Discovery Channel; Disney Channel; ESPN; ESPN 2; FitTV; Food Network; Fox News Channel; Fox Sports Net Midwest; FX; Hallmark Channel; Headline News; HGTV; History Channel; Home Shopping Network; INSP; Lifetime; MSNBC; MTV; Nickelodeon; Outdoor Channel; QVC; ShopNBC; SoapNet; Speed Channel; Spike TV; Syfy; TBS Superstation; The Learning Channel; Travel Channel; Trinity Broadcasting Network; truTV; Turner Network TV; TV Guide Network; TV Land; USA Network; VH1; WE tv; Weather Channel; WGN America.
Fee: $35.00 installation; $23.95 monthly.

Digital Basic Service

Subscribers: N.A.
Programming (via satellite): BBC America; Bio; Bloomberg Television; Discovery Digital Networks; DMX Music; Fox Movie Channel; Fox Sports World; Fuse; G4; GAS; Golf Channel; GSN; History Channel International; Independent Film Channel; Lifetime Movie Network; Lime; MTV Networks Digital Suite; National Geographic Channel; Nick Jr.; NickToons TV; Style Network; Turner Classic Movies; Versus.

Pay Service 1

Pay Units: 212.
Programming (via satellite): Cinemax.
Fee: $10.50 monthly.

Pay Service 2

Pay Units: 461.
Programming (via satellite): HBO (multiplexed).
Fee: $10.50 monthly.

Pay Service 3

Pay Units: 441.
Programming (via satellite): Showtime (multiplexed).
Fee: $10.50 monthly.

Pay Service 4

Pay Units: 179.
Programming (via satellite): The Movie Channel.
Fee: $7.50 monthly.

Pay Service 5

Pay Units: 19.
Programming (via satellite): Flix.
Fee: $2.95 monthly.

Digital Pay Service 1

Pay Units: N.A.
Programming (via satellite): Cinemax (multiplexed); Encore (multiplexed); Flix (multiplexed); HBO (multiplexed); Showtime (multiplexed); Starz (multiplexed); Sundance Channel (multiplexed); The Movie Channel (multiplexed).

Video-On-Demand: Yes

Pay-Per-View

Urban American Television Network (delivered digitally); Playboy TV (delivered digitally); TEN Clips (delivered digitally); Pleasure (delivered digitally); Hot Body (delivered digitally); Events (delivered digitally); Movies (delivered digitally).

Internet Service

Operational: Yes.
Broadband Service: Mediacom High Speed Internet.

Telephone Service

Digital: Operational

Miles of Plant: 45.0 (coaxial); None (fiber optic). Homes passed: 2,787.
Vice President: Bill Copeland. Technical Operations Director: Alan Freedman. Marketing Director: Will Kuebler.
City fee: 3% of basic gross; 0.5% of premium gross.
Ownership: Mediacom LLC (MSO).

CENTERVIEW—Formerly served by CableDirect. No longer in operation. ICA: MO0393.

CENTRALIA—US Cable. Now served by MEXICO, MO [MO0033]. ICA: MO0104.

CHAMOIS—Mid Missouri Broadband, PO Box 3535, Ballwin, MO 63022. Phone: 573-417-4004. Web Site: http://linncityhall.com. ICA: MO0284.
TV Market Ranking: Below 100 (CHAMOIS). Franchise award date: November 7, 1983. Franchise expiration date: N.A. Began: July 1, 1985.
Channel capacity: N.A. Channels available but not in use: N.A.

Basic Service

Subscribers: 125.
Programming (received off-air): KETC (PBS) St. Louis; KMIZ (ABC) Columbia; KNLJ (IND) Jefferson City; KOMU-TV (CW, NBC) Columbia; KPLR-TV (CW) St. Louis; KRCG (CBS) Jefferson City.
Programming (via satellite): Comedy Central; HGTV; QVC; TBS Superstation; WGN America.
Fee: $41.11 installation; $24.20 monthly.

Expanded Basic Service 1

Subscribers: N.A.
Programming (via satellite): ABC Family Channel; AMC; Arts & Entertainment; Cartoon Network; CNN; Country Music TV; Discovery Channel; Disney Channel; ESPN; ESPN 2; Fox News Channel; Fox Sports Net Midwest; FX; Headline News; Lifetime; Nickelodeon; Spike TV; Syfy; truTV; Turner Network TV; TV Land; USA Network; Weather Channel.

Pay Service 1

Pay Units: 25.
Programming (via satellite): Cinemax.
Fee: $10.50 monthly.

Pay Service 2

Pay Units: 25.
Programming (via satellite): HBO.
Fee: $11.00 monthly.

Video-On-Demand: No

Pay-Per-View

Playboy TV (delivered digitally); Fresh (delivered digitally); Shorteez (delivered digitally); Urban American Television Network (delivered digitally); ESPN Now (delivered digitally); ESPN Sports PPV (delivered digitally); Hot Choice (delivered digitally); iN DEMAND (delivered digitally).

Internet Service

Operational: No.

Telephone Service

None

Miles of Plant: 6.0 (coaxial); None (fiber optic). Homes passed: 237. Total homes in franchised area: 237.
Ownership: Mid-Missouri Broadband & Cable LLC (MSO).

CHARLESTON—Charter Communications. Now served by CAPE GIRARDEAU, MO [MO0018]. ICA: MO0043.

CHESTERFIELD—Charter Communications. Now served by OLIVETTE, MO [MO0009]. ICA: MO0015.

CHILHOWEE—Formerly served by National Cable Inc. No longer in operation. ICA: MO0333.

CHILLICOTHE—Windjammer Cable, 4400 PGA Blvd, Ste 902, Palm Beach Gardens, FL 33410. Phones: 561-775-1208; 877-450-5558. Fax: 561-775-7811. Web Site: http://www.windjammercable.com. Also serves Livingston County (portions). ICA: MO0046.

TV Market Ranking: Outside TV Markets (CHILLICOTHE, Livingston County (portions)). Franchise award date: June 4, 1963. Franchise expiration date: N.A. Began: June 4, 1963.
Channel capacity: 79 (operating 2-way). Channels available but not in use: None.

Basic Service
Subscribers: 3,299.
Programming (received off-air): KCPT (PBS) Kansas City; KCTV (CBS) Kansas City; KCWE (CW) Kansas City; KMBC-TV (ABC) Kansas City; KMCI-TV (IND) Lawrence; KPXE-TV (ION) Kansas City; KQTV (ABC) St. Joseph; KSHB-TV (NBC) Kansas City; KSMO-TV (MNT) Kansas City; WDAF-TV (FOX) Kansas City; 23 FMs.
Programming (via satellite): C-SPAN; C-SPAN 2; Home Shopping Network; QVC; ShopNBC; TBS Superstation; Trinity Broadcasting Network; WGN America.
Fee: $35.80 installation; $21.46 monthly; $.57 converter.

Expanded Basic Service 1
Subscribers: 2,963.
Programming (via satellite): ABC Family Channel; AMC; AmericanLife TV Network; Animal Planet; Arts & Entertainment; Bravo; Cartoon Network; CNBC; CNN; Comedy Central; Country Music TV; Discovery Channel; Discovery Health Channel; Disney Channel; E! Entertainment Television; ESPN; ESPN 2; ESPN Classic Sports; Eternal Word TV Network; FitTV; Food Network; Fox News Channel; Fox Sports Net Midwest; FX; Great American Country; Hallmark Channel; Headline News; HGTV; History Channel; INSP; Lifetime; Lifetime Movie Network; MSNBC; MTV; National Geographic Channel; Nickelodeon; Oxygen; Spike TV; Syfy; The Learning Channel; Travel Channel; truTV; Turner Classic Movies; Turner Network TV; TV Land; USA Network; VH1; WE tv; Weather Channel.
Fee: $31.66 monthly.

Digital Basic Service
Subscribers: N.A.
Programming (received off-air): KCPT (PBS) Kansas City; KSHB-TV (NBC) Kansas City.
Programming (via satellite): BBC America; Bio; Bloomberg Television; Discovery Digital Networks; Discovery HD Theater; ESPN; ESPNews; Fox Movie Channel; Fox Sports World; Fuse; G4; GAS; Golf Channel; GSN; Halogen Network; HDNet; HDNet Movies; History Channel International; INHD (multiplexed); MTV Hits; MTV2; Music Choice; Nick Jr.; NickToons TV; Outdoor Channel; Ovation; Speed Channel; Style Network; Sundance Channel; Toon Disney; Turner Network TV; Versus; VH1 Classic.
Fee: $53.99 monthly.

Digital Pay Service 1
Pay Units: N.A.
Programming (via satellite): Cinemax (multiplexed); Encore (multiplexed); HBO; HBO (multiplexed); Independent Film Channel; Showtime; Showtime (multiplexed); Starz (multiplexed); The Movie Channel (multiplexed).
Fee: $12.00 monthly (each).

Video-On-Demand: No

Pay-Per-View
iN DEMAND (delivered digitally); Fresh (delivered digitally); Shorteez (delivered digitally); Playboy TV (delivered digitally); Pleasure (delivered digitally); Hot Choice (delivered digitally); TEN Blue (delivered digitally); TEN Clips (delivered digitally); TEN Blox (delivered digitally).

Internet Service
Operational: Yes.
Broadband Service: In-house.
Fee: $19.95-$49.99 installation; $49.95 monthly.

Telephone Service
Digital: Operational
Fee: $74.95 installation; $49.95 monthly
Miles of Plant: 84.0 (coaxial); None (fiber optic). Total homes in franchised area: 4,914.
General Manager: Timothy Evard. Operations Director: Belinda Graham. Engineering Director: Mike Earehart. Finance & Accounting Director: Cindy Johnson.
City fee: 3% of gross.
Ownership: Windjammer Communications LLC (MSO).

CHULA—Formerly served by CableDirect. No longer in operation. ICA: MO0370.

CLARENCE—Milan Interactive Communications, 312 S Main, PO Box 240, Milan, MO 63556. Phone: 660-265-7174. Fax: 660-256-7174. ICA: MO0394.
TV Market Ranking: Outside TV Markets (CLARENCE). Franchise award date: N.A. Franchise expiration date: N.A. Began: January 1, 1988.
Channel capacity: 36 (not 2-way capable). Channels available but not in use: N.A.

Basic Service
Subscribers: 54.
Programming (received off-air): KHQA-TV (ABC, CBS) Hannibal; KTVO (ABC) Kirksville; WGEM-TV (CW, NBC) Quincy; WTJR (IND) Quincy.
Programming (via satellite): CNN; C-SPAN; Home Shopping Network; TBS Superstation; WGN America.
Fee: $29.95 installation; $40.77 monthly.

Video-On-Demand: No

Pay-Per-View
iN DEMAND (delivered digitally).

Internet Service
Operational: No.

Telephone Service
None
Miles of Plant: 20.0 (coaxial); None (fiber optic). Homes passed: 566. Total homes in franchised area: 566.
President & General Manager: Rick Gardener.
City fee: 3% of basic.
Ownership: Milan Interactive Communications (MSO).

CLARKSBURG—Formerly served by First Cable of Missouri Inc. No longer in operation. ICA: MO0339.

CLARKSDALE—Formerly served by CableDirect. No longer in operation. ICA: MO0355.

CLARKSVILLE—First Cable of Missouri Inc., PO Box 958, 605 Concannon St, Moberly, MO 65270. Phones: 660-263-6300; 800-892-7139. Fax: 660-263-3238. ICA: MO0456.
TV Market Ranking: Below 100 (CLARKSVILLE). Franchise award date: N.A. Franchise expiration date: N.A. Began: June 14, 1995.
Channel capacity: 36 (operating 2-way). Channels available but not in use: 20.

Basic Service
Subscribers: 100.
Programming (received off-air): KDNL-TV (ABC) St. Louis; KETC (PBS) St. Louis; KMOV (CBS) St. Louis; KPLR-TV (CW) St. Louis; KSDK (NBC) St. Louis; KTVI (FOX) St. Louis.

Programming (via satellite): ABC Family Channel; CNN; Discovery Channel; ESPN; Spike TV; TBS Superstation; Turner Network TV; USA Network.
Fee: $35.00 installation; $25.00 monthly; $20.00 additional installation.

Pay Service 1
Pay Units: 50.
Programming (via satellite): Cinemax; HBO.
Fee: $11.00 monthly.

Video-On-Demand: No

Internet Service
Operational: No.
Broadband Service: Offers dial-up and DSL only; no cable modem service.

Telephone Service
None
Miles of Plant: 6.0 (coaxial); None (fiber optic). Homes passed: 294.
Manager: Jesse Wamsley. Chief Technologist: Brian Davis. Accounts Payable: Jessica Wamsley.
Ownership: First Cable of Missouri Inc.

CLARKTON—NewWave Communications, 1311 Business Hwy 60 W, Dexter, MO 63841. Phone: 573-614-4573. Fax: 573-614-4802. Web Site: http://www.newwavecom.com. Also serves Dunklin County, Frisbee, Gibson, Gideon & Holcomb. ICA: MO0110.
TV Market Ranking: Below 100 (CLARKTON, Dunklin County (portions), Gibson, Gideon, Holcomb); Outside TV Markets (Dunklin County (portions), Frisbee). Franchise award date: October 1, 1974. Franchise expiration date: N.A. Began: November 1, 1975.
Channel capacity: 136 (operating 2-way). Channels available but not in use: N.A.

Basic Service
Subscribers: 501.
Programming (received off-air): KAIT (ABC) Jonesboro; KBSI (FOX) Cape Girardeau; KFVS-TV (CBS, CW) Cape Girardeau; KTEJ (PBS) Jonesboro; WPSD-TV (NBC) Paducah; WPTY-TV (ABC) Memphis; allband FM.
Programming (via satellite): ABC Family Channel; AMC; CNN; Discovery Channel; Disney Channel; ESPN; INSP; Lifetime; MTV; Nickelodeon; Spike TV; TBS Superstation; Turner Network TV; USA Network; Weather Channel; WGN America.
Fee: $61.50 installation; $36.95 monthly.

Pay Service 1
Pay Units: N.A.
Programming (via satellite): Cinemax; HBO.
Fee: $17.50 installation; $8.99 monthly (Cinemax), $12.99 monthly (HBO).

Video-On-Demand: No

Internet Service
Operational: Yes.
Fee: $40.00 installation; $31.99 monthly.

Telephone Service
None
Miles of Plant: 66.0 (coaxial); None (fiber optic). Homes passed: 1,421.
General Manager: Ed Gargas. Technical Operations Manager: Jerry Townsend.
City fee: 3% of gross.
Ownership: NewWave Communications (MSO).

CLEARMONT—Formerly served by Longview Communications. No longer in operation. ICA: MO0467.

CLEVER—Suddenlink Communications, 12444 Powerscourt Dr, Saint Louis, MO 63131-3660. Phones: 800-999-6845 (Customer service); 314-965-2020. Fax: 903-561-5485. Web Site: http://www.suddenlink.com. ICA: MO0288.
TV Market Ranking: Below 100 (CLEVER). Franchise award date: N.A. Franchise expiration date: N.A. Began: N.A.
Channel capacity: 42 (not 2-way capable). Channels available but not in use: 16.

Basic Service
Subscribers: 80.
Programming (received off-air): KOLR (CBS) Springfield; KOZK (PBS) Springfield; KSFX-TV (FOX) Springfield; KSPR (ABC) Springfield; KYTV (CW, NBC) Springfield.
Programming (via satellite): ABC Family Channel; Arts & Entertainment; CNN; Country Music TV; Discovery Channel; ESPN; Showtime; TBS Superstation; Turner Network TV; USA Network; WGN America.
Fee: $39.95 installation; $36.45 monthly.

Pay Service 1
Pay Units: 19.
Programming (via satellite): HBO.
Fee: $10.95 monthly.

Pay Service 2
Pay Units: 35.
Programming (via satellite): Showtime.
Fee: $5.95 monthly.

Video-On-Demand: No

Internet Service
Operational: No.

Telephone Service
None
Miles of Plant: 7.0 (coaxial); None (fiber optic). Homes passed: 207.
Regional Manager: Todd Cruthird.
Ownership: Cequel Communications LLC (MSO).

CLINTON—Charter Communications, 210 W 7th St, Sedalia, MO 65301-4217. Phones: 660-826-6520; 636-207-7044 (St Louis office). Fax: 660-826-4583. Web Site: http://www.charter.com. Also serves Henry County. ICA: MO0050.
TV Market Ranking: Outside TV Markets (CLINTON, Henry County). Franchise award date: N.A. Franchise expiration date: N.A. Began: February 1, 1968.
Channel capacity: N.A. Channels available but not in use: N.A.

Basic Service
Subscribers: 3,589.
Programming (received off-air): KCPT (PBS) Kansas City; KCTV (CBS) Kansas City; KCWE (CW) Kansas City; KMBC-TV (ABC) Kansas City; KMCI-TV (IND) Lawrence; KMOS-TV (PBS) Sedalia; KOLR (CBS) Springfield; KPXE-TV (ION) Kansas City; KSHB-TV (NBC) Kansas City; KSMO-TV (MNT) Kansas City; KYTV (CW, NBC) Springfield; WDAF-TV (FOX) Kansas City; 11 FMs.
Programming (via satellite): C-SPAN; QVC; TV Guide Network; WGN America.

Current originations: Government Access.
Fee: $29.99 installation.

Expanded Basic Service 1
Subscribers: 3,317.
Programming (via satellite): ABC Family Channel; AMC; Animal Planet; Arts & Entertainment; BET Networks; Bravo; Cartoon Network; CNBC; CNN; Comedy Central; Country Music TV; C-SPAN 2; Discovery Channel; Disney Channel; E! Entertainment Television; ESPN; ESPN 2; ESPN Classic Sports; FitTV; Food Network; Fox Movie Channel; Fox News Channel; Fox Sports Net; FX; G4; Golf Channel; Great American Country; GSN; Hallmark Channel; Headline News; HGTV; History Channel; Home Shopping Network; INSP; Lifetime; MoviePlex; MSNBC; MTV; Nickelodeon; Oxygen; Speed Channel; Spike TV; Syfy; TBS Superstation; The Learning Channel; Travel Channel; Trinity Broadcasting Network; truTV; Turner Classic Movies; Turner Network TV; TV Land; Univision; USA Network; Versus; VH1; Weather Channel.
Fee: $49.99 monthly.

Digital Basic Service
Subscribers: N.A.
Programming (via satellite): BBC America; Bio; Bloomberg Television; Discovery Digital Networks; Do-It-Yourself; Encore Action; Fox Sports World; FSN Digital Atlantic; FSN Digital Central; FSN Digital Pacific; GAS; History Channel International; Independent Film Channel; MTV Networks Digital Suite; Music Choice; National Geographic Channel; Nick Jr.; Nick Too; Style Network; Sundance Channel; WE tv.
Fee: $10.00 monthly.

Digital Pay Service 1
Pay Units: 285.
Programming (via satellite): Cinemax (multiplexed); HBO (multiplexed); Showtime (multiplexed); Starz (multiplexed); The Movie Channel.

Video-On-Demand: Yes

Pay-Per-View
iN DEMAND (delivered digitally); ETC (delivered digitally); Pleasure (delivered digitally); The Erotic Network (delivered digitally).

Internet Service
Operational: Yes. Began: December 31, 2003.
Broadband Service: Charter Pipeline.
Fee: $29.99 monthly.

Telephone Service
Digital: Operational

Miles of Plant: 59.0 (coaxial); None (fiber optic). Homes passed: 4,008. Total homes in franchised area: 4,032.

Vice President & General Manager: Steve Trippe. Operations Director: Dave Miller. Technical Operations Manager: John Vichland. Marketing Director: Beverly Wall. Office Manager: Vicky Brant.

City fee: 5% of gross.

Ownership: Charter Communications Inc. (MSO).

COFFMAN BEND—Formerly served by Almega Cable. No longer in operation. ICA: MO0124.

COLE CAMP—Longview Communications, 1923 N Main, Higginsville, MO 64037. Phone: 866-611-6565. Fax: 866-329-4790. Web Site: http://www.longviewcomm.com. ICA: MO0201.

TV Market Ranking: Below 100 (COLE CAMP). Franchise award date: N.A. Franchise expiration date: N.A. Began: March 1, 1983.

Channel capacity: N.A. Channels available but not in use: N.A.

Basic Service
Subscribers: 160.
Programming (received off-air): KCWE (CW) Kansas City; KMBC-TV (ABC) Kansas City; KMIZ (ABC) Columbia; KMOS-TV (PBS) Sedalia; KOMU-TV (CW, NBC) Columbia; KRCG (CBS) Jefferson City; KSMO-TV (MNT) Kansas City; WDAF-TV (FOX) Kansas City.
Programming (via satellite): C-SPAN; QVC; Trinity Broadcasting Network.
Fee: $35.95 installation; $15.98 monthly.

Expanded Basic Service 1
Subscribers: N.A.
Programming (via satellite): ABC Family Channel; AMC; Animal Planet; Arts & Entertainment; Cartoon Network; CBS College Sports Network; CNN; Comedy Central; Discovery Channel; Disney Channel; Do-It-Yourself; E! Entertainment Television; ESPN; ESPN 2; ESPN Classic Sports; Food Network; Fox News Channel; FX; Great American Country; Hallmark Channel; Hallmark Movie Channel; Headline News; HGTV; History Channel; Lifetime; MSNBC; Syfy; TBS Superstation; The Learning Channel; Travel Channel; Turner Network TV; USA Network; Weather Channel; WGN America.
Fee: $21.97 monthly.

Digital Basic Service
Subscribers: 14.
Programming (via satellite): AmericanLife TV Network; BBC America; Bio; Bloomberg Television; Discovery Digital Networks; Encore (multiplexed); ESPNews; Fox Movie Channel; Fox Soccer; Fuse; G4; Golf Channel; GSN; Halogen Network; History Channel International; Independent Film Channel; Lifetime Movie Network; Outdoor Channel; Speed Channel; Style Network; Sundance Channel; Toon Disney; Turner Classic Movies; Versus.
Fee: $16.00 monthly.

Pay Service 1
Pay Units: 74.
Programming (via satellite): Cinemax; HBO; Showtime; The Movie Channel.
Fee: $8.95 monthly (TMC), $10.95 monthly (Cinemax or Showtime), $12.95 monthly (HBO).

Digital Pay Service 1
Pay Units: N.A.
Programming (via satellite): Cinemax (multiplexed); Flix; HBO (multiplexed); Showtime (multiplexed); Starz (multiplexed); The Movie Channel (multiplexed).
Fee: $8.95 monthly (TMC), $10.95 monthly (Showtime or Cinemax), $12.95 monthly (HBO).

Video-On-Demand: No

Internet Service
Operational: Yes.
Subscribers: 25.
Broadband Service: IBBS.

Telephone Service
None

Miles of Plant: 6.0 (coaxial); None (fiber optic). Homes passed: 540.

President: John Long. Senior Vice President: Marc W. Cohen. General Manager: Brandon Dickey. Operations Manager: Perry Scarborogh.

Ownership: Longview Communications (MSO).

COLE COUNTY (portions)—Suddenlink Communications, 12444 Powerscourt Dr, Saint Louis, MO 63131-3660. Phone: 314-965-2020. Web Site: http://www.suddenlink.com. Also serves Centertown, Lohman, St. Martins & Wardsville. ICA: MO0060.

TV Market Ranking: Below 100 (Centertown, COLE COUNTY (PORTIONS), Lohman, St. Martins, Wardsville). Franchise award date: July 1, 1986. Franchise expiration date: N.A. Began: October 1, 1986.

Channel capacity: 41 (operating 2-way). Channels available but not in use: N.A.

Basic Service
Subscribers: 2,075.
Programming (received off-air): KMIZ (ABC) Columbia; KMOS-TV (PBS) Sedalia; KNLJ (IND) Jefferson City; KOMU-TV (CW, NBC) Columbia; KRCG (CBS) Jefferson City.
Programming (via satellite): ABC Family Channel; AMC; Arts & Entertainment; Cartoon Network; CNBC; CNN; Country Music TV; C-SPAN; Discovery Channel; Disney Channel; E! Entertainment Television; ESPN; Fox Sports Net Midwest; Headline News; Home Shopping Network; Lifetime; MuchMusic Network; Nickelodeon; QVC; Spike TV; TBS Superstation; Travel Channel; Turner Classic Movies; Turner Network TV; TV Land; USA Network; Weather Channel; WGN America.
Fee: $39.95 installation; $19.95 monthly.

Pay Service 1
Pay Units: 196.
Programming (via satellite): The Movie Channel.
Fee: $5.95 monthly.

Pay Service 2
Pay Units: 172.
Programming (via satellite): Showtime.
Fee: $9.95 monthly.

Pay Service 3
Pay Units: 372.
Programming (via satellite): HBO.
Fee: $10.95 monthly.

Internet Service
Operational: Yes. Began: November 29, 2004.
Broadband Service: Cebridge High Speed Cable Internet.
Fee: $29.95 monthly.

Telephone Service
None

Miles of Plant: 125.0 (coaxial); None (fiber optic). Homes passed: 3,075.

Regional Manager: Todd Cruthird. Regional Marketing Manager: Beverly Gambell.

Ownership: Cequel Communications LLC (MSO).

COLUMBIA—Charter Communications, 1015 Washington Square Shopping Ctr, Washington, MO 63090-5307. Phones: 636-207-7044; 636-239-2197. Fax: 636-239-6865. Web Site: http://www.charter.com. Also serves Ashland, Boone County & Rocheport. ICA: MO0037.

TV Market Ranking: Below 100 (Ashland, Boone County, COLUMBIA, Rocheport). Franchise award date: July 28, 1981. Franchise expiration date: N.A. Began: June 15, 1981.

Channel capacity: N.A. Channels available but not in use: N.A.

Basic Service
Subscribers: 4,087.
Programming (received off-air): KMIZ (ABC) Columbia; KMOS-TV (PBS) Sedalia; KNLJ (IND) Jefferson City; KOMU-TV (CW, NBC) Columbia; KQFX-LD Columbia; KRCG (CBS) Jefferson City.
Programming (via satellite): C-SPAN; Home Shopping Network; INSP; LWS Local Weather Station; QVC; Trinity Broadcasting Network; TV Guide Interactive Inc.; WGN America.
Current originations: Government Access; Educational Access; Public Access.
Fee: $29.99 installation.

Expanded Basic Service 1
Subscribers: 2,500.
Programming (via satellite): ABC Family Channel; AMC; Animal Planet; Arts & Entertainment; BET Networks; Bravo; Cartoon Network; CNBC; CNN; Comedy Central; Country Music TV; Discovery Channel; Disney Channel; E! Entertainment Television; ESPN; ESPN 2; Food Network; Fox News Channel; Fox Sports Net Midwest; FX; G4; GSN; Hallmark Channel; Headline News; HGTV; History Channel; Lifetime; MSNBC; MTV; National Geographic Channel; Nickelodeon; Outdoor Channel; Oxygen; Speed Channel; Spike TV; Syfy; TBS Superstation; The Learning Channel; Travel Channel; truTV; Turner Classic Movies; Turner Network TV; TV Land; USA Network; Versus; VH1; Weather Channel.
Fee: $49.99 monthly.

Digital Basic Service
Subscribers: 293.
Programming (via satellite): BBC America; Bio; Bloomberg Television; Discovery Digital Networks; Do-It-Yourself; ESPN Classic Sports; ESPNews; GAS; History Channel International; Independent Film Channel; Lifetime Movie Network; MTV Networks Digital Suite; Music Choice; Nick Jr.; Nick Too; NickToons TV; SoapNet; Style Network; Sundance Channel; Toon Disney; WE tv.
Fee: $23.49 installation; $10.50 monthly.

Digital Pay Service 1
Pay Units: 271.
Programming (via satellite): Cinemax (multiplexed); Encore (multiplexed); Flix; HBO (multiplexed); Starz (multiplexed); The Movie Channel (multiplexed).

Video-On-Demand: Yes

Pay-Per-View
Addressable homes: 293.
iN DEMAND (delivered digitally), Addressable: Yes; ETC (delivered digitally); Pleasure (delivered digitally).

Internet Service
Operational: Yes.
Broadband Service: Charter Pipeline.
Fee: $29.99 monthly.

Telephone Service
Digital: Operational

Miles of Plant: 175.0 (coaxial); 16.0 (fiber optic). Homes passed: 5,626. Total homes in franchised area: 9,685.

Vice President & General Manager: Steve Trippe. Operations Director: Dave Miller. Technical Operations Manager: John Viehland. Marketing Director: Beverly Wall. Office Manager: Dawn Paul.

City fee: 3% of gross.
Ownership: Charter Communications Inc. (MSO).

COLUMBIA—Mediacom, 901 N College Ave, Columbia, MO 65201. Phones: 573-443-1536; 417-875-5560 (Springfield regional office). Fax: 417-883-0265. Web Site: http://www.mediacomcable.com. Also serves Boone County (portions). ICA: MO0005.
TV Market Ranking: Below 100 (Boone County (portions), COLUMBIA). Franchise award date: July 22, 1977. Franchise expiration date: N.A. Began: July 1, 1977.
Channel capacity: N.A. Channels available but not in use: N.A.
Basic Service
Subscribers: 23,509.
Programming (received off-air): K02NQ Columbia; KETC (PBS) St. Louis; KMIZ (ABC) Columbia; KMOS-TV (PBS) Sedalia; KNLJ (IND) Jefferson City; KOMU-TV (CW, NBC) Columbia; KQFX-LD Columbia; KRCG (CBS) Jefferson City; KSDK (NBC) St. Louis.
Programming (via satellite): C-SPAN 2; Discovery Channel; Home Shopping Network; LWS Local Weather Station; QVC; ShopNBC; TBS Superstation; TV Guide Network; WGN America.
Current originations: Leased Access; Government Access; Educational Access; Public Access.
Fee: $50.00 installation; $10.23 monthly; $1.94 converter; $4.93 additional installation.
Expanded Basic Service 1
Subscribers: 20,000.
Programming (via satellite): ABC Family Channel; AMC; Animal Planet; Arts & Entertainment; BET Networks; Bravo; Cartoon Network; CNBC; CNN; Comedy Central; Country Music TV; C-SPAN; Disney Channel; E! Entertainment Television; ESPN; ESPN 2; Eternal Word TV Network; Food Network; Fox News Channel; Fox Sports Net Midwest; FX; Hallmark Channel; Headline News; HGTV; History Channel; ION Television; Lifetime; MSNBC; MTV; Nickelodeon; Oxygen; Spike TV; Syfy; Telemundo; The Learning Channel; Travel Channel; truTV; Turner Network TV; TV Land; USA Network; VH1; WE tv; Weather Channel.
Fee: $9.85 installation; $16.55 monthly.
Digital Basic Service
Subscribers: N.A.
Programming (received off-air): KMIZ (ABC) Columbia; KMOS-TV (PBS) Sedalia.
Programming (via satellite): AmericanLife TV Network; BBC America; Bio; Bloomberg Television; Discovery Digital Networks; Discovery HD Theater; ESPN; FitTV; Fox Movie Channel; Fox Soccer; Fuse; G4; GAS; Golf Channel; GSN; Halogen Network; HDNet; HDNet Movies; History Channel International; Independent Film Channel; Lifetime Movie Network; Lime; MTV Networks Digital Suite; MTV2; Music Choice; National Geographic Channel; Nick Jr.; NickToons TV; Outdoor Channel; Ovation; Speed Channel; Style Network; Toon Disney; Trinity Broadcasting Network; Turner Classic Movies; Universal HD; Versus.
Digital Pay Service 1
Pay Units: N.A.
Programming (via satellite): Cinemax (multiplexed); Encore (multiplexed); Flix; HBO (multiplexed); Showtime; Starz (multiplexed); Sundance Channel; The Movie Channel (multiplexed).
Video-On-Demand: Yes
Pay-Per-View
ESPN (delivered digitally); Movies (delivered digitally); Fresh (delivered digitally); Shorteez (delivered digitally); Playboy TV (delivered digitally).
Internet Service
Operational: Yes.
Subscribers: 11,299.
Broadband Service: Mediacom High Speed Internet.
Fee: $150.00 installation; $39.95 monthly.
Telephone Service
Digital: Operational
Miles of Plant: 593.0 (coaxial); 50.0 (fiber optic). Additional miles planned: 10.0 (coaxial). Homes passed: 38,701. Total homes in franchised area: 41,870.
Regional Vice President: Bill Copeland. Operations Director: Bryan Gann. Regional Technical Operations Director: Alan Freedman. Technical Operations Manager: Roger Shearer. Marketing Director: Will Kuebler. Marketing Coordinator: Brad Koetters.
City fee: 5% of gross.
Ownership: Mediacom LLC (MSO).

CONCEPTION JUNCTION—B & L Technologies LLC, 3329 270th St, Lenox, IA 50851. Phones: 800-798-5488; 641-348-2240. Fax: 641-348-2240. Also serves Clyde & Conception. ICA: MO0433.
TV Market Ranking: Outside TV Markets (Clyde, Conception, CONCEPTION JUNCTION). Franchise award date: July 31, 1989. Franchise expiration date: N.A. Began: June 1, 1990.
Channel capacity: 36 (not 2-way capable). Channels available but not in use: 6.
Basic Service
Subscribers: 50.
Programming (received off-air): KCTV (CBS) Kansas City; KHIN (PBS) Red Oak; KQTV (ABC) St. Joseph; KSHB-TV (NBC) Kansas City; KSMO-TV (MNT) Kansas City; WDAF-TV (FOX) Kansas City.
Programming (via satellite): ABC Family Channel; Arts & Entertainment; CNN; Discovery Channel; ESPN; Eternal Word TV Network; Nickelodeon; Spike TV; TBS Superstation; Turner Network TV; USA Network; VH1; WGN America.
Fee: $25.00 installation; $30.50 monthly.
Pay Service 1
Pay Units: 3.
Programming (via satellite): HBO.
Fee: $12.00 monthly.
Video-On-Demand: No
Internet Service
Operational: No.
Telephone Service
None
Miles of Plant: 4.0 (coaxial); None (fiber optic). Homes passed: 240.
Manager & Chief Technician: Robert Hintz. Office Manager: Linda Hintz.
Ownership: B & L Technologies LLC (MSO).

CONWAY—Fidelity Communications, 64 N Clark St, Sullivan, MO 63080. Phones: 573-468-8081; 800-392-8070. Fax: 573-468-3834. E-mail: custserv@fidelitycommunications.com. Web Site: http://www.fidelitycommunications.com. ICA: MO0274.
TV Market Ranking: Below 100 (CONWAY). Franchise award date: N.A. Franchise expiration date: N.A. Began: June 1, 1989.
Channel capacity: 42 (not 2-way capable). Channels available but not in use: 20.
Basic Service
Subscribers: 26.
Programming (received off-air): KOLR (CBS) Springfield; KOZK (PBS) Springfield; KSFX-TV (FOX) Springfield; KSPR (ABC) Springfield; KYTV (CW, NBC) Springfield.
Programming (via satellite): ABC Family Channel; CNN; Country Music TV; Discovery Channel; ESPN; Showtime; Spike TV; TBS Superstation; Turner Network TV; USA Network; WGN America.
Current originations: Educational Access.
Planned originations: Religious Access.
Fee: $39.95 installation; $36.75 monthly.
Pay Service 1
Pay Units: 17.
Programming (via satellite): HBO.
Fee: $10.95 monthly.
Pay Service 2
Pay Units: N.A.
Programming (via satellite): Showtime.
Fee: $10.00 monthly.
Internet Service
Operational: No.
Telephone Service
None
Miles of Plant: 9.0 (coaxial); None (fiber optic). Homes passed: 241.
Manager: Andrew B. Davis.
Ownership: Fidelity Communications Co. (MSO).

COWGILL—GH Technologies. Formerly [MO0445]. This cable system has converted to IPTV, PO Box 227, 7926 NE Ste Rte M, Breckenridge, MO 64625. Phones: 800-846-3426; 660-644-5411. Fax: 660-846-3426. E-mail: comments@greenhills.net. Web Site: http://www.greenhills.net. ICA: MO5188.
Channel capacity: N.A. Channels available but not in use: N.A.
Internet Service
Operational: Yes.
Ownership: Green Hills Companies.

COWGILL—GH Technologies. This cable system has converted to IPTV. See Cowgill, MO [MO5188]. ICA: MO0445.

CRAIG—Formerly served by CableDirect. No longer in operation. ICA: MO0397.

CRANE—Mediacom. Now served by SEYMOUR, MO [MO0126]. Previously served by FORSYTH, MO [MO0126].. ICA: MO0198.

CREIGHTON—Formerly served by CableDirect. No longer in operation. ICA: MO0343.

CROCKER—Longview Communications, 12007 Sunrise Valley Dr, Ste 375, Reston, VA 20191. Phones: 866-611-6565 (Customer service); 703-476-9101. Fax: 703-476-9107. Web Site: http://www.longviewcomm.com. ICA: MO0234.
TV Market Ranking: Outside TV Markets (CROCKER). Franchise award date: N.A. Franchise expiration date: N.A. Began: October 1, 1983.
Channel capacity: 41 (not 2-way capable). Channels available but not in use: 7.
Basic Service
Subscribers: 85.
Programming (received off-air): KOLR (CBS) Springfield; KOMU-TV (CW, NBC) Columbia; KOZK (PBS) Springfield; KSFX-TV (FOX) Springfield; KSPR (ABC) Springfield; KYTV (CW, NBC) Springfield.
Programming (via satellite): C-SPAN; C-SPAN 2; Home Shopping Network; ShopNBC; Trinity Broadcasting Network.
Fee: $17.98 monthly.
Expanded Basic Service 1
Subscribers: N.A.
Programming (via satellite): ABC Family Channel; AMC; Animal Planet; Arts & Entertainment; Cartoon Network; CNN; Comedy Central; Discovery Channel; Disney Channel; ESPN; ESPN 2; G4; HGTV; Lifetime; TBS Superstation; Turner Network TV; USA Network; Weather Channel; WGN America.
Fee: $17.97 monthly.
Pay Service 1
Pay Units: 43.
Programming (via satellite): Showtime; The Movie Channel.
Fee: $8.95 monthly (TMC), $10.95 monthly (Showtime).
Video-On-Demand: No
Internet Service
Operational: No.
Telephone Service
None
Miles of Plant: 11.0 (coaxial); None (fiber optic). Homes passed: 500.
President: John Long. Senior Vice President: Marc W. Cohen. General Manager: Brandon Dickey. Operations Manager: Perry Scarborough.
City fee: 3% of gross.
Ownership: Longview Communications (MSO).

CUBA—Formerly served by Charter Communications. No longer in operation. ICA: MO0080.

CURRYVILLE—Formerly served by First Cable of Missouri Inc. No longer in operation. ICA: MO0366.

DE KALB—Formerly served by CableDirect. No longer in operation. ICA: MO0368.

DEXTER—NewWave Communications, 1311 Business Hwy 60 W, Dexter, MO 63841. Phones: 888-863-9928 (Customer service); 573-614-4573 (Dexter office). Fax: 573-614-4802. E-mail: info@newwavecom.com. Web Site: http://www.newwavecom.com. Also serves Bernie, Bloomfield, Campbell, Dunklin County (portions), Essex, Malden & Stoddard County (portions). ICA: MO0039.
TV Market Ranking: 69 (Stoddard County (portions) (portions)); Below 100 (Bernie, Bloomfield, Campbell, DEXTER, Dunklin County (portions), Essex, Malden, Stoddard County (portions) (portions)); Outside TV Markets (Stoddard County (portions) (portions)). Franchise award date: January 1, 1956. Franchise expiration date: N.A. Began: June 1, 1957.
Channel capacity: N.A. Channels available but not in use: N.A.
Basic Service
Subscribers: 5,717.
Programming (received off-air): KAIT (ABC) Jonesboro; KBSI (FOX) Cape Girardeau; KFVS-TV (CBS, CW) Cape Girardeau; KPOB-TV (ABC) Poplar Bluff; WKMU (PBS) Murray; WPSD-TV (NBC) Paducah; WQWQ-LP (CW) Paducah.
Programming (via microwave): WDKA (MNT) Paducah; WTCT (IND) Marion.
Programming (via satellite): C-SPAN; C-SPAN 2; Home Shopping Network; INSP; QVC; ShopNBC; Trinity Broadcasting Network.
Current originations: Public Access.
Fee: $29.95 installation; $17.92 monthly.
Expanded Basic Service 1
Subscribers: 5,242.
Programming (via satellite): ABC Family Channel; AMC; Animal Planet; Arts & Entertainment; Bravo; Cartoon Network; CNBC; CNN; Comedy Central; Country Music TV; Discovery Channel; Disney Channel; E! Entertainment Television; ESPN; ESPN 2; ESPN Classic Sports; Food Network; Fox

News Channel; Fox Sports Net Midwest; FX; Golf Channel; Great American Country; GSN; Hallmark Channel; Headline News; HGTV; History Channel; Jewelry Television; Lifetime; MSNBC; MTV; Nickelodeon; Outdoor Channel; Oxygen; SoapNet; Speed Channel; Spike TV; Syfy; TBS Superstation; The Learning Channel; Travel Channel; truTV; Turner Network TV; TV Land; USA Network; VH1; Weather Channel.
Fee: $42.95 monthly.

Digital Basic Service
Subscribers: 814.
Programming (received off-air): KAIT (ABC) Jonesboro; KBSI (FOX) Cape Girardeau; KFVS-TV (CBS, CW) Cape Girardeau; WPSD-TV (NBC) Paducah.
Programming (via satellite): Arts & Entertainment HD; BBC America; Bio; Bloomberg Television; CMT Pure Country; Discovery HD Theater; Discovery Health Channel; Discovery Kids Channel; Discovery Military Channel; Discovery Planet Green; Do-It-Yourself; ESPN 2 HD; ESPN Classic Sports; ESPN HD; ESPNews; Fox Movie Channel; FSN HD; G4; Halogen Network; HDNet; HDNet Movies; History Channel HD; History Channel International; ID Investigation Discovery; Independent Film Channel; Lifetime Movie Network; MTV Hits; MTV2; Music Choice; Nick Jr.; NickToons TV; Palladia; RFD-TV; Science Channel; Sleuth; Style Network; TeenNick; The Sportsman Channel; Toon Disney; Turner Classic Movies; Turner Network TV HD; USA Network HD; Versus; Versus HD; VH1 Classic; VH1 Soul; Weather Channel HD.

Digital Pay Service 1
Pay Units: 1,298.
Programming (via satellite): Cinemax (multiplexed); Cinemax HD; Encore; Flix; HBO (multiplexed); HBO HD; Showtime (multiplexed); Starz (multiplexed); Starz HDTV; The Movie Channel (multiplexed).

Video-On-Demand: No

Pay-Per-View
iN DEMAND (delivered digitally); Hot Choice (delivered digitally); Playboy TV (delivered digitally); Fresh (delivered digitally); Shorteez (delivered digitally).

Internet Service
Operational: Yes.
Subscribers: 1,844.
Fee: $40.00 installation; $23.95 monthly.

Telephone Service
None

Miles of Plant: 102.0 (coaxial); 10.0 (fiber optic).
General Manager: Ed Gargas. Technical Operations Manager: Jerry Townsend.
Ownership: NewWave Communications (MSO).

DIAMOND—Mediacom. Now served by GRANBY, MO [MO0156]. ICA: MO0266.

DIXON—Cable America Corp. Now served by WAYNESVILLE (formerly ST. ROBERT), MO [MO0023]. ICA: MO0125.

DONIPHAN—Boycom Cablevision Inc., 3467 Township Line Rd, Poplar Bluff, MO 63901. Phone: 573-686-9101. Fax: 573-686-4722. Web Site: http://www.boycomonline.com. ICA: MO0063.
TV Market Ranking: Below 100 (DONIPHAN). Franchise award date: June 6, 1986. Franchise expiration date: N.A. Began: January 1, 1960.
Channel capacity: N.A. Channels available but not in use: N.A.

Basic Service
Subscribers: N.A. Included in Alton
Programming (received off-air): KAIT (ABC) Jonesboro; KFVS-TV (CBS, CW) Cape Girardeau; KTEJ (PBS) Jonesboro; allband FM.
Programming (via satellite): CNN; C-SPAN; CW+; Discovery Channel; Home Shopping Network; TBS Superstation; The Learning Channel; Trinity Broadcasting Network; Turner Network TV; USA Network; WGN America.
Fee: $29.95 installation; $39.95 monthly.

Expanded Basic Service 1
Subscribers: N.A.
Programming (via satellite): ABC Family Channel; AMC; Arts & Entertainment; C-SPAN 2; Disney Channel; E! Entertainment Television; ESPN; ESPN 2; Fox Sports Net Midwest; FX; G4; Great American Country; Headline News; HGTV; History Channel; INSP; Lifetime; MSNBC; National Geographic Channel; Nickelodeon; Outdoor Channel; SoapNet; Spike TV; Syfy; Toon Disney; Turner Classic Movies; TV Land; WE tv; Weather Channel.
Fee: $20.00 monthly.

Pay Service 1
Pay Units: 829.
Programming (via satellite): Cinemax; Encore; HBO; Showtime; Starz; The Movie Channel.
Fee: $8.99 monthly (Cinemax), $12.00 monthly (HBO), $13.99 monthly (Showtime & TMC).

Video-On-Demand: No

Internet Service
Operational: No.

Telephone Service
None

Miles of Plant: 128.0 (coaxial); None (fiber optic). Homes passed: 2,931.
President: Steven Boyers. General Manager: Shelly Batton. Chief Technician: Phil Huett.
City fee: None.
Ownership: Boycom Cablevision Inc. (MSO).

DOOLITTLE—Cable America Corp. Now served by WAYNESVILLE (formerly ST. ROBERT), MO [MO0023]. ICA: MO0265.

DOWNING—Longview Communications, 12007 Sunrise Valley Dr, Ste 375, Reston, VA 20191. Phones: 866-611-6565 (Customer service); 703-476-9101. Fax: 703-476-9107. Web Site: http://www.longviewcomm.com. ICA: MO0398.
TV Market Ranking: Below 100 (DOWNING). Franchise award date: January 1, 1987. Franchise expiration date: N.A. Began: January 1, 1988.
Channel capacity: 36 (not 2-way capable). Channels available but not in use: 7.

Basic Service
Subscribers: 40.
Programming (received off-air): KHQA-TV (ABC, CBS) Hannibal; KTVO (ABC) Kirksville; KYOU-TV (FOX) Ottumwa; WGEM-TV (CW, NBC) Quincy.
Programming (via satellite): ABC Family Channel; AMC; Arts & Entertainment; Classic Arts Showcase; CNN; Country Music TV; C-SPAN; Discovery Channel; Disney Channel; E! Entertainment Television; ESPN; ESPN 2; Headline News; Lifetime; Nickelodeon; QVC; Spike TV; TBS Superstation; The Learning Channel; Trinity Broadcasting Network; Turner Network TV; USA Network; Weather Channel.
Fee: $15.00 installation; $34.95 monthly.

Pay Service 1
Pay Units: 40.
Programming (via satellite): Showtime; The Movie Channel.
Fee: $8.95 monthly (TMC), $10.95 monthly (Showtime).

Video-On-Demand: No

Internet Service
Operational: No.

Telephone Service
None

Miles of Plant: 7.0 (coaxial); None (fiber optic). Homes passed: 225.
President: John Long. Senior Vice President: Marc W. Cohen. General Manager: Brandon Dickey. Operations Director: Perry Scarborough.
Ownership: Longview Communications (MSO).

DREXEL—Formerly served by Almega Cable. No longer in operation. ICA: MO0217.

DUDLEY—Boycom Cablevision Inc., 3467 Township Line Rd, Poplar Bluff, MO 63901. Phone: 573-686-9101. Fax: 573-686-4722. Web Site: http://www.boycomonline.com. ICA: MO0342.
TV Market Ranking: Below 100 (DUDLEY). Franchise award date: March 4, 1984. Franchise expiration date: N.A. Began: November 1, 1985.
Channel capacity: N.A. Channels available but not in use: N.A.

Basic Service
Subscribers: 52.
Programming (received off-air): KBSI (FOX) Cape Girardeau; KFVS-TV (CBS, CW) Cape Girardeau; KPOB-TV (ABC) Poplar Bluff; WPSD-TV (NBC) Paducah.
Programming (via satellite): ABC Family Channel; Animal Planet; Arts & Entertainment; CNN; Country Music TV; Discovery Channel; ESPN; Home Shopping Network; Lifetime; MTV; Nickelodeon; TBS Superstation; The Learning Channel; Trinity Broadcasting Network; Turner Network TV; USA Network; WGN America.
Fee: $61.50 installation; $31.89 monthly.

Pay Service 1
Pay Units: 8.
Programming (via satellite): HBO.
Fee: $13.49 monthly.

Video-On-Demand: No

Internet Service
Operational: Yes.

Telephone Service
None

Miles of Plant: 3.0 (coaxial); None (fiber optic). Homes passed: 116.
President: Steven Boyers. General Manager: Shelly Batton. Chief Technician: Phil Huett.
City fee: 3% of gross.
Ownership: Boycom Cablevision Inc. (MSO).

DUQUESNE—Mediacom. Now served by CARL JUNCTION, MO [MO0094]. ICA: MO0131.

DURHAM—Formerly served by CableDirect. No longer in operation. ICA: MO0439.

EAGLEVILLE—Formerly served by Longview Communications. No longer in operation. ICA: MO0268.

EAST LYNNE—Formerly served by CableDirect. No longer in operation. ICA: MO0364.

EASTON—Formerly served by First Cable of Missouri Inc. No longer in operation. ICA: MO0446.

EDINA—US Cable, 647 Clinic Rd, Hannibal, MO 63401. Phone: 573-581-2404. Fax: 573-581-4053. Web Site: http://www.uscable.com. ICA: MO0189.
TV Market Ranking: Below 100 (EDINA). Franchise award date: N.A. Franchise expiration date: N.A. Began: June 1, 1982.
Channel capacity: N.A. Channels available but not in use: N.A.

Basic Service
Subscribers: N.A. Included in Hannibal
Programming (received off-air): KHQA-TV (ABC, CBS) Hannibal; KTVO (ABC) Kirksville; KYOU-TV (FOX) Ottumwa; WGEM-TV (CW, NBC) Quincy; WTJR (IND) Quincy.
Programming (via satellite): Bravo; Lifetime; TBS Superstation; Turner Network TV; WGN America; WQEC (PBS) Quincy.
Current originations: Public Access.
Fee: $22.09 monthly.

Expanded Basic Service 1
Subscribers: N.A.
Programming (via satellite): ABC Family Channel; Animal Planet; Arts & Entertainment; Cartoon Network; CNBC; CNN; Comedy Central; Country Music TV; Discovery Channel; Disney Channel; E! Entertainment Television; ESPN; ESPN 2; Fox News Channel; Fox Sports Net Midwest; FX; Great American Country; Headline News; History Channel; Home Shopping Network; Nickelodeon; Spike TV; The Learning Channel; TV Land; USA Network; VH1; Weather Channel.
Fee: $19.12 monthly.

Digital Basic Service
Subscribers: N.A. Included in Hannibal
Programming (via satellite): BBC America; Bio; Bloomberg Television; Discovery Digital Networks; Fox Reality Channel; Fuse; G4; GSN; Halogen Network; HGTV; History Channel International; Lime; MTV Networks Digital Suite; Nick Jr.; Sleuth; Style Network; Syfy; Toon Disney; Trinity Broadcasting Network; WealthTV.
Fee: $12.95 monthly; $8.00 converter.

Digital Expanded Basic Service
Subscribers: N.A.
Programming (via satellite): DMX Music; Encore (multiplexed); Fox Movie Channel; Independent Film Channel; Lifetime Movie Network; Turner Classic Movies; WE tv.
Fee: $4.95 monthly.

Digital Expanded Basic Service 2
Subscribers: N.A.
Programming (via satellite): ESPN Classic Sports; ESPNews; Fox Soccer; GAS; Golf Channel; NFL Network; Outdoor Channel; Versus.
Fee: $5.45 monthly.

Pay Service 1
Pay Units: N.A.
Programming (via satellite): Cinemax; HBO.
Fee: $11.95 monthly (each).

Digital Pay Service 1
Pay Units: N.A.
Programming (via satellite): Cinemax (multiplexed); HBO (multiplexed); Showtime (multiplexed); Starz (multiplexed); The Movie Channel.
Fee: $6.95 monthly (Starz), $11.95 monthly (Cinemax, HBO, Showtime or TMX).

Video-On-Demand: No

Pay-Per-View
iN DEMAND (delivered digitally); Fresh (delivered digitally); Playboy TV (delivered digitally).

Internet Service
Operational: Yes.

Telephone Service
None
Homes passed, total homes in franchised area, & miles of plant included in Hannibal
Regional Administrative Director: Rebecca Bramblett. Marketing Director: Rita Watson. Technical Operations Manager: Mark Thake.
Ownership: US Cable Corp. (MSO).; Comcast Cable Communications Inc. (MSO).

EL DORADO SPRINGS—Charter Communications, 210 W 7th St, Sedalia, MO 65301-4217. Phones: 636-207-7044 (St Louis office); 660-826-6520. Fax: 660-826-4583. Web Site: http://www.charter.com. ICA: MO0112.
TV Market Ranking: Outside TV Markets (EL DORADO SPRINGS). Franchise award date: October 1, 1964. Franchise expiration date: N.A. Began: February 1, 1965.
Channel capacity: 49 (not 2-way capable). Channels available but not in use: N.A.

Basic Service
Subscribers: 1,118.
Programming (received off-air): KOAM-TV (CBS) Pittsburg; KODE-TV (ABC) Joplin; KOLR (CBS) Springfield; KOZK (PBS) Springfield; KPXE-TV (ION) Kansas City; KSFX-TV (FOX) Springfield; KSMO-TV (MNT) Kansas City; KSPR (ABC) Springfield; KYTV (CW, NBC) Springfield; WDAF-TV (FOX) Kansas City; allband FM.
Programming (via satellite): Home Shopping Network; INSP; QVC; WGN America.
Fee: $29.99 installation.

Expanded Basic Service 1
Subscribers: 852.
Programming (via satellite): ABC Family Channel; AMC; Arts & Entertainment; Bravo; Cartoon Network; CNBC; CNN; Comedy Central; Country Music TV; Discovery Channel; Disney Channel; E! Entertainment Television; ESPN; ESPN 2; Fox News Channel; FX; G4; Headline News; HGTV; History Channel; Lifetime; MTV; Nickelodeon; Oxygen; Spike TV; Syfy; TBS Superstation; The Learning Channel; Turner Network TV; TV Land; USA Network; VH1; Weather Channel.
Fee: $49.99 monthly.

Digital Basic Service
Subscribers: 68.
Programming (via satellite): BBC America; Bio; Bloomberg Television; Discovery Digital Networks; Do-It-Yourself; GAS; GSN; History Channel International; Independent Film Channel; MTV Networks Digital Suite; Music Choice; Nick Jr.; Nick Too; NickToons TV; Science Television; SoapNet; Style Network; Sundance Channel; Toon Disney; WE tv.
Fee: $16.90 monthly.

Digital Pay Service 1
Pay Units: 243.
Programming (via satellite): Cinemax (multiplexed); Encore (multiplexed); HBO (multiplexed); Showtime (multiplexed); Starz (multiplexed); The Movie Channel (multiplexed).
Fee: $11.95 monthly (each).

Video-On-Demand: No

Pay-Per-View
iN DEMAND (delivered digitally); Pleasure (delivered digitally); ETC (delivered digitally); The Erotic Network (delivered digitally).

Internet Service
Operational: No.

Telephone Service
None
Miles of Plant: 25.0 (coaxial); None (fiber optic). Homes passed: 1,398.
Vice President & General Manager: Steve Trippe. Operations Director: Dave Miller. Technical Operations Manager: Larry Wright. Marketing Director: Beverly Wall. Office Manager: Vicky Brant.
Franchise fee: 3% of gross.
Ownership: Charter Communications Inc. (MSO).

ELDON—Charter Communications. Now served by OSAGE BEACH, MO [MO0017]. ICA: MO0085.

ELLINGTON—Boycom Cablevision Inc., 3467 Township Line Rd, Poplar Bluff, MO 63901. Phone: 573-686-9101. Fax: 573-686-4722. Web Site: http://www.boycomonline.com. Also serves Reynolds County. ICA: MO0164.
TV Market Ranking: Below 100 (Reynolds County (portions)); Outside TV Markets (ELLINGTON, Reynolds County (portions)). Franchise award date: January 1, 1962. Franchise expiration date: N.A. Began: March 20, 1962.
Channel capacity: 21 (not 2-way capable). Channels available but not in use: N.A.

Basic Service
Subscribers: N.A. Included in Alton
Programming (received off-air): KBSI (FOX) Cape Girardeau; KETC (PBS) St. Louis; KFVS-TV (CBS, CW) Cape Girardeau; KPOB-TV (ABC) Poplar Bluff; WPSD-TV (NBC) Paducah; allband FM.
Programming (via satellite): ABC Family Channel; AMC; Arts & Entertainment; CNN; Country Music TV; C-SPAN; Discovery Channel; Disney Channel; ESPN; ESPN 2; Fox News Channel; Fox Sports Net Midwest; FX; Headline News; HGTV; History Channel; Home Shopping Network; INSP; Lifetime; MSNBC; MTV; National Geographic Channel; Nickelodeon; SoapNet; Speed Channel; Spike TV; TBS Superstation; The Learning Channel; Trinity Broadcasting Network; Turner Network TV; TV Land; USA Network; VH1; WE tv; Weather Channel; WGN America; WNBC (NBC) New York.
Fee: $29.95 installation; $39.95 monthly.

Pay Service 1
Pay Units: 72.
Programming (via satellite): Cinemax; HBO.
Fee: $8.99 monthly (Cinemax), $12.99 monthly (HBO).

Video-On-Demand: No

Internet Service
Operational: No.

Telephone Service
None
Miles of Plant: 21.0 (coaxial); None (fiber optic). Homes passed: 689.
President: Steven Boyers. General Manager: Shelly Batton. Chief Technician: Phil Huett.
City fee: 3% of gross.
Ownership: Boycom Cablevision Inc. (MSO).

ELLSINORE—Boycom Cablevision Inc., 3467 Township Line Rd, Poplar Bluff, MO 63901. Phone: 573-686-9101. Fax: 573-686-4722. Web Site: http://www.boycomonline.com. Also serves Grandin. ICA: MO0196.
TV Market Ranking: Below 100 (ELLSINORE, Grandin). Franchise award date: February 2, 1971. Franchise expiration date: N.A. Began: February 1, 1979.
Channel capacity: N.A. Channels available but not in use: N.A.

Basic Service
Subscribers: N.A. Included in Alton
Programming (received off-air): KAIT (ABC) Jonesboro; KBSI (FOX) Cape Girardeau; KFVS-TV (CBS, CW) Cape Girardeau; KTEJ (PBS) Jonesboro; WPSD-TV (NBC) Paducah.
Programming (via satellite): C-SPAN; Home Shopping Network; INSP; Weather Channel; WGN America.
Fee: $29.95 installation; $19.95 monthly.

Expanded Basic Service 1
Subscribers: N.A.
Programming (via satellite): ABC Family Channel; AMC; Animal Planet; Arts & Entertainment; CNN; Country Music TV; Discovery Channel; Disney Channel; ESPN; ESPN 2; Fox News Channel; Fox Sports Net Midwest; FX; Golf Channel; Great American Country; Hallmark Channel; HGTV; History Channel; Lifetime; Lifetime Movie Network; MTV; National Geographic Channel; Nickelodeon; Outdoor Channel; ShopNBC; Speed Channel; Spike TV; Syfy; TBS Superstation; The Learning Channel; Trinity Broadcasting Network; Turner Classic Movies; Turner Network TV; TV Land; USA Network; VH1.
Fee: $20.00 monthly.

Video-On-Demand: No

Internet Service
Operational: No.

Telephone Service
None
Miles of Plant: 28.0 (coaxial); None (fiber optic). Homes passed: 568.
President: Steven Boyers. General Manager: Shelly Batton. Chief Technician: Phil Huett.
City fee: None.
Ownership: Boycom Cablevision Inc. (MSO).

ELMO—Formerly served by CableDirect. No longer in operation. ICA: MO0468.

ELSBERRY—Crystal Broadband Networks, PO Box 180336, Chicago, IL 60618. Phones: 877-319-0328; 630-206-0447. E-mail: info@crystalbn.com. Web Site: http://crystalbn.com. ICA: MO0142.
TV Market Ranking: Outside TV Markets (ELSBERRY). Franchise award date: September 30, 1982. Franchise expiration date: N.A. Began: N.A.
Channel capacity: 61 (not 2-way capable). Channels available but not in use: N.A.

Basic Service
Subscribers: 354.
Programming (received off-air): KDNL-TV (ABC) St. Louis; KETC (PBS) St. Louis; KHQA-TV (ABC, CBS) Hannibal; KMOV (CBS) St. Louis; KPLR-TV (CW) St. Louis; KSDK (NBC) St. Louis; KTVI (FOX) St. Louis; WGEM-TV (CW, NBC) Quincy.
Programming (via satellite): Discovery Channel; INSP; QVC; TV Guide Network; USA Network; VH1; WGN America.
Current originations: Government Access; Educational Access.
Fee: $29.95 installation; $19.95 monthly.

Expanded Basic Service 1
Subscribers: N.A.
Programming (via satellite): ABC Family Channel; AMC; Animal Planet; Arts & Entertainment; CNBC; CNN; Comedy Central; Country Music TV; C-SPAN; Disney Channel; E! Entertainment Television; ESPN; ESPN 2; Fox News Channel; Fox Sports Net Midwest; FX; Headline News; HGTV; History Channel; Lifetime; MTV; Nickelodeon; Spike TV; TBS Superstation; Travel Channel; truTV; Turner Network TV; TV Land; Weather Channel.
Fee: $20.00 monthly.

Pay Service 1
Pay Units: 37.
Programming (via satellite): Cinemax.
Fee: $23.49 installation; $9.95 monthly.

Pay Service 2
Pay Units: 49.
Programming (via satellite): Encore.
Fee: $23.49 installation; $4.95 monthly.

Pay Service 3
Pay Units: 43.
Programming (via satellite): HBO (multiplexed).
Fee: $23.49 installation; $10.50 monthly.

Pay Service 4
Pay Units: 44.
Programming (via satellite): The Movie Channel.
Fee: $23.49 installation; $9.95 monthly.

Pay Service 5
Pay Units: 53.
Programming (via satellite): Showtime.
Fee: $23.49 installation; $10.50 monthly.

Video-On-Demand: No

Pay-Per-View
iN DEMAND.

Internet Service
Operational: Yes.

Telephone Service
Digital: Operational
Miles of Plant: 22.0 (coaxial); None (fiber optic). Homes passed: 931. Total homes in franchised area: 1,202.
General Manager: Nidhin Johnson. Program Manager: Shawn Smith.
City fee: 5% of gross.
Ownership: Crystal Broadband Networks (MSO).

EMINENCE—Boycom Cablevision Inc., 3467 Township Line Rd, Poplar Bluff, MO 63901. Phone: 573-686-9101. Fax: 573-686-4722. Web Site: http://www.boycomonline.com. ICA: MO0195.
TV Market Ranking: Outside TV Markets (EMINENCE). Franchise award date: September 13, 1984. Franchise expiration date: N.A. Began: N.A.
Channel capacity: 54 (operating 2-way). Channels available but not in use: 23.

Basic Service
Subscribers: N.A. Included in Alton
Programming (received off-air): KAIT (ABC) Jonesboro; KFVS-TV (CBS, CW) Cape Girardeau; KOLR (CBS) Springfield; KOZK (PBS) Springfield; KSFX-TV (FOX) Springfield; KSPR (ABC) Springfield; KYTV (CW, NBC) Springfield; WNBC (NBC) New York.
Programming (via satellite): Home Shopping Network; Weather Channel; WGN America.
Fee: $29.95 installation; $19.95 monthly.

Expanded Basic Service 1
Subscribers: N.A.
Programming (via satellite): ABC Family Channel; AMC; Arts & Entertainment; CNN; Discovery Channel; Disney Channel; ESPN; ESPN 2; Fox Sports Net Midwest; FX; Great American Country; History Channel; Lifetime; MTV; Nickelodeon; Speed Channel; Spike TV; TBS Superstation; Toon Disney; Trinity Broadcasting Network; Turner Network TV; TV Land; USA Network; VH1.
Fee: $20.00 monthly.

Pay Service 1
Pay Units: 108.
Programming (via satellite): Cinemax; HBO.
Fee: $17.50 installation; $8.99 monthly (Cinemax), $12.99 monthly (HBO).

Pay Service 2
Pay Units: N.A.
Programming (via satellite): Encore; Showtime; The Movie Channel.

Fee: $3.99 monthly (Encore), $13.99 monthly (Showtime or TMC).
Video-On-Demand: No
Internet Service
Operational: No.
Telephone Service
None
Miles of Plant: 31.0 (coaxial); None (fiber optic). Homes passed: 572.
Regional Manager: Paul Broseman. Plant Manager: Tony Gilbert.
City fee: None.
Ownership: Boycom Cablevision Inc. (MSO).

EOLIA—Formerly served by First Cable of Missouri Inc. No longer in operation. ICA: MO0312.

ESSEX—Formerly served by Cebridge Connections. Now served by DEXTER, MO [MO0039]. ICA: MO0263.

EUGENE—Formerly served by First Cable of Missouri Inc. No longer in operation. ICA: MO0376.

EVERTON—Mediacom, 1533 S Enterprise Ave, Springfield, MO 65804. Phone: 417-875-5560. Fax: 417-883-0265. Web Site: http://www.mediacomcable.com. Also serves Ash Grove, Golden City, Greene County (unincorporated areas), Greenfield, Lockwood, Miller, Mount Vernon, Walnut Grove & Willard. ICA: MO0400.
TV Market Ranking: Below 100 (Ash Grove, EVERTON, Golden City, Greene County (unincorporated areas), Greenfield, Miller, Mount Vernon, Walnut Grove, Willard); Outside TV Markets (Lockwood). Franchise award date: N.A. Franchise expiration date: N.A. Began: N.A.
Channel capacity: N.A. Channels available but not in use: N.A.
Basic Service
Subscribers: 3,719.
Programming (received off-air): K15CZ Springfield; KOLR (CBS) Springfield; KOZK (PBS) Springfield; KSFX-TV (FOX) Springfield; KSNF (NBC) Joplin; KSPR (ABC) Springfield; KWBM (MNT) Harrison [LICENSED & SILENT]; KYTV (CW, NBC) Springfield.
Programming (via satellite): ShopNBC; TV Guide Network; WGN America.
Current originations: Educational Access; Public Access.
Fee: $35.00 installation; $23.95 monthly.
Expanded Basic Service 1
Subscribers: N.A.
Programming (via satellite): ABC Family Channel; AMC; AmericanLife TV Network; Animal Planet; Arts & Entertainment; Bravo; Cartoon Network; CNBC; CNN; Comedy Central; Country Music TV; C-SPAN; Discovery Channel; Disney Channel; E! Entertainment Television; ESPN; ESPN 2; Food Network; Fox Movie Channel; Fox News Channel; Fox Sports Net Midwest; FX; Hallmark Channel; Headline News; HGTV; History Channel; Home Shopping Network; INSP; Lifetime; MSNBC; MTV; Nickelodeon; Outdoor Channel; QVC; SoapNet; Speed Channel; Spike TV; Syfy; TBS Superstation; The Learning Channel; Travel Channel; Trinity Broadcasting Network; truTV; Turner Network TV; TV Land; USA Network; VH1; WE tv; Weather Channel.
Digital Basic Service
Subscribers: N.A.
Programming (received off-air): KSPR (ABC) Springfield; KYTV (CW, NBC) Springfield.
Programming (via satellite): BBC America; Bio; Bloomberg Television; Canales N; Discovery Digital Networks; Discovery HD Theater; ESPN; ESPNews; Fox Soccer; Fuse; G4; GAS; Golf Channel; GSN; HDNet; HDNet Movies; History Channel International; Independent Film Channel; Lifetime Movie Network; Lime; MTV Networks Digital Suite; Music Choice; National Geographic Channel; Nick Jr.; NickToons TV; Sleuth; Style Network; Turner Classic Movies; Universal HD; Versus.
Digital Pay Service 1
Pay Units: N.A.
Programming (via satellite): Cinemax (multiplexed); Encore (multiplexed); Flix (multiplexed); HBO (multiplexed); HBO HD; Showtime (multiplexed); Showtime HD; Starz (multiplexed); Starz HDTV; Sundance Channel (multiplexed); The Movie Channel (multiplexed).
Video-On-Demand: Yes
Pay-Per-View
Special events (delivered digitally); Movies (delivered digitally); Playboy TV (delivered digitally); Ten Clips (delivered digitally); Ten Blox (delivered digitally); ESPN Gameplan (delivered digitally).
Internet Service
Operational: Yes.
Broadband Service: Mediacom High Speed Internet.
Telephone Service
Analog: Not Operational
Digital: Operational
Miles of Plant: 5.0 (coaxial); None (fiber optic).
Regional Vice President: Bill Copeland. Technical Operations Director: Alan Freedman. Marketing Director: Will Kuebler.
Franchise fee: 3% of gross.
Ownership: Mediacom LLC (MSO).

EWING—Formerly served by CableDirect. No longer in operation. ICA: MO0296.

EXCELSIOR SPRINGS—Mediacom, 901 N College Ave, Columbia, MO 65201. Phones: 573-443-1536; 816-637-4500 (Local office). Fax: 573-449-8492. E-mail: gbaugh@mediacomcc.com. Web Site: http://www.mediacomcable.com. Also serves Crystal Lakes, Excelsior Estates, Homestead Village, Lawson & Woods Heights. ICA: MO0040.
TV Market Ranking: 22 (Crystal Lakes, Excelsior Estates, EXCELSIOR SPRINGS, Homestead Village, Lawson, Woods Heights). Franchise award date: February 16, 1981. Franchise expiration date: N.A. Began: January 1, 1982.
Channel capacity: N.A. Channels available but not in use: N.A.
Basic Service
Subscribers: 3,720.
Programming (received off-air): KCPT (PBS) Kansas City; KCTV (CBS) Kansas City; KCWE (CW) Kansas City; KMBC-TV (ABC) Kansas City; KMCI-TV (IND) Lawrence; KPXE-TV (ION) Kansas City; KQTV (ABC) St. Joseph; KSHB-TV (NBC) Kansas City; KSMO-TV (MNT) Kansas City; WDAF-TV (FOX) Kansas City; allband FM.
Programming (via satellite): WGN America.
Current originations: Public Access.
Fee: $35.00 installation; $23.95 monthly; $2.20 converter.
Expanded Basic Service 1
Subscribers: N.A.
Programming (via satellite): ABC Family Channel; AMC; Animal Planet; Arts & Entertainment; Bravo; Cartoon Network; CNBC; CNN; Comedy Central; Country Music TV; C-SPAN; Discovery Channel; Disney Channel; E! Entertainment Television; ESPN; ESPN 2; Food Network; Fox News Channel; Fox Sports Net Midwest; FX; Hallmark Channel; Headline News; HGTV; History Channel; Home Shopping Network; INSP; Lifetime; MSNBC; MTV; Nickelodeon; Outdoor Channel; QVC; ShopNBC; SoapNet; Speed Channel; Spike TV; Syfy; TBS Superstation; The Learning Channel; Travel Channel; Trinity Broadcasting Network; truTV; Turner Network TV; TV Guide Network; TV Land; USA Network; VH1; WE tv; Weather Channel.
Digital Basic Service
Subscribers: N.A.
Programming (via satellite): BBC America; Bio; Bloomberg Television; Discovery Digital Networks; FitTV; Fox Movie Channel; Fox Soccer; Fuse; G4; GAS; Golf Channel; GSN; History Channel International; Independent Film Channel; Lifetime Movie Network; Lime; MTV Networks Digital Suite; Music Choice; National Geographic Channel; Nick Jr.; NickToons TV; Style Network; Turner Classic Movies; Versus.
Digital Pay Service 1
Pay Units: N.A.
Programming (via satellite): Cinemax (multiplexed); Encore (multiplexed); Flix (multiplexed); HBO (multiplexed); Showtime (multiplexed); Starz (multiplexed); Sundance Channel (multiplexed); The Movie Channel (multiplexed).
Video-On-Demand: No
Pay-Per-View
Mediacom PPV (delivered digitally); Playboy TV (delivered digitally); TEN Clips (delivered digitally); TEN Blox (delivered digitally).
Internet Service
Operational: Yes.
Broadband Service: Mediacom High Speed Internet.
Telephone Service
None
Miles of Plant: 94.0 (coaxial); None (fiber optic). Homes passed: 6,074.
General Manager: Gary Baugh. Marketing Director: Wes Shaver. Technical Operations Manager: Tom Evans.
City fee: 3% of gross.
Ownership: Mediacom LLC (MSO).

FAIR GROVE—Fidelity Communications, 64 N Clark St, Sullivan, MO 63080. Phones: 573-468-8081; 800-392-8070. Fax: 573-468-3834. E-mail: custserv@fidelitycommunications.com. Web Site: http://www.fidelitycommunications.com. Also serves Greene County (portions). ICA: MO0461.
TV Market Ranking: Below 100 (FAIR GROVE, Greene County (portions)). Franchise award date: N.A. Franchise expiration date: N.A. Began: N.A.
Channel capacity: 41 (not 2-way capable). Channels available but not in use: N.A.
Basic Service
Subscribers: 88.
Programming (received off-air): KOLR (CBS) Springfield; KOZK (PBS) Springfield; KSFX-TV (FOX) Springfield; KSPR (ABC) Springfield; KYTV (CW, NBC) Springfield.
Programming (via satellite): ABC Family Channel; AMC; AmericanLife TV Network; Arts & Entertainment; CNBC; CNN; Country Music TV; C-SPAN; Discovery Channel; ESPN; Food Network; Headline News; History Channel; Lifetime; Nickelodeon; QVC; Spike TV; Syfy; TBS Superstation; The Learning Channel; Trinity Broadcasting Network; Turner Classic Movies; Turner Network TV; TV Land; USA Network; Weather Channel; WGN America.
Fee: $39.95 installation; $30.95 monthly.
Pay Service 1
Pay Units: 18.
Programming (via satellite): Showtime.
Fee: $9.95 monthly.
Pay Service 2
Pay Units: 48.
Programming (via satellite): HBO.
Fee: $10.95 monthly.
Internet Service
Operational: No.
Telephone Service
Digital: Planned
Miles of Plant: 29.0 (coaxial); None (fiber optic). Homes passed: 416.
Manager: Andrew B. Davis.
Ownership: Fidelity Communications Co. (MSO).

FAIR PLAY—Formerly served by Cebridge Connections. No longer in operation. ICA: MO0286.

FARBER—US Cable. Now served by MEXICO, MO [MO0033]. ICA: MO0109.

FARMINGTON—Charter Communications, 403 E Karsch Blvd, Farmington, MO 63640. Phones: 636-207-7044 (St Louis office); 573-756-5691. Fax: 573-756-0123. Web Site: http://www.charter.com. Also serves Arcadia, Bismarck, Bonne Terre, Cobalt Village, Desloge, Doe Run, East Bonne, Elvins, Esther, Flat River, Frankclay, Fredericktown, Iron City, Iron Mountain Lake, Ironton, Junction City, Leadington, Leadwood, Middlebrook, Park Hills, Pilot Knob, Rivermines & Terre du Lac. ICA: MO0035.
TV Market Ranking: Outside TV Markets (Arcadia, Bismarck, Bonne Terre, Cobalt Village, Desloge, Doe Run, East Bonne, Elvins, Esther, FARMINGTON, Flat River, Frankclay, Fredericktown, Iron City, Iron Mountain Lake, Ironton, Junction City, Leadington, Leadwood, Middlebrook, Park Hills, Pilot Knob, Rivermines, Terre du Lac). Franchise award date: N.A. Franchise expiration date: N.A. Began: August 13, 1980.
Channel capacity: N.A. Channels available but not in use: N.A.
Basic Service
Subscribers: 13,951.
Programming (received off-air): KDNL-TV (ABC) St. Louis; KETC (PBS) St. Louis; KFVS-TV (CBS, CW) Cape Girardeau; KMOV (CBS) St. Louis; KNLC (IND) St. Louis; KPLR-TV (CW) St. Louis; KSDK (NBC) St. Louis; KTVI (FOX) St. Louis; WRBU (MNT) East St. Louis; 1 FM.
Programming (via satellite): C-SPAN; C-SPAN 2; Eternal Word TV Network; Home Shopping Network; INSP; ION Television; QVC; ShopNBC; TV Guide Interactive Inc.; WGN America.
Current originations: Educational Access.
Fee: $29.99 installation.
Expanded Basic Service 1
Subscribers: 13,814.
Programming (via satellite): ABC Family Channel; AMC; Animal Planet; Arts & Entertainment; BET Networks; Bravo; Cartoon Network; CNBC; CNN; Comedy Central; Country Music TV; Discovery Channel; Disney Channel; E! Entertainment Television; ESPN; ESPN 2; ESPN Classic Sports; Food Network; Fox News Channel; Fox Sports Net Midwest; FX; G4; Golf Channel; Great American Country; GSN; Hallmark

Channel; Headline News; HGTV; History Channel; Lifetime; MSNBC; MTV; National Geographic Channel; Nickelodeon; Oxygen; SoapNet; Speed Channel; Spike TV; Style Network; Syfy; TBS Superstation; The Learning Channel; Toon Disney; Travel Channel; Trinity Broadcasting Network; truTV; Turner Classic Movies; Turner Network TV; TV Land; USA Network; Versus; VH1; WE tv; Weather Channel.
Fee: $49.99 monthly.

Digital Basic Service
Subscribers: N.A.
Programming (via satellite): BBC America; Bio; Bloomberg Television; Discovery Digital Networks; Do-It-Yourself; Fox Movie Channel; Fox Sports World; FSN Digital Atlantic; FSN Digital Central; FSN Digital Pacific; GAS; History Channel International; Independent Film Channel; Lifetime Movie Network; MTV Networks Digital Suite; Music Choice; Nick Jr.; Nick Too; NickToons TV; Sundance Channel.
Fee: $15.00 installation; $9.98 monthly.

Digital Pay Service 1
Pay Units: 2,094.
Programming (via satellite): Cinemax (multiplexed); Encore (multiplexed); Flix; HBO (multiplexed); Showtime (multiplexed); Starz (multiplexed); The Movie Channel (multiplexed).
Fee: $15.00 installation; $9.98 monthly (each).

Video-On-Demand: Yes

Pay-Per-View
Barker (delivered digitally); iN DEMAND (delivered digitally); ETC (delivered digitally); Pleasure (delivered digitally).

Internet Service
Operational: Yes.
Broadband Service: Charter Pipeline.
Fee: $29.99 monthly.

Telephone Service
Digital: Operational
Fee: $29.99 monthly

Miles of Plant: 441.0 (coaxial); None (fiber optic). Homes passed: 21,496.

Vice President & General Manager: Steve Trippe. Operations Director: Dave Miller. Operations Manager: Dave Huntsman. Technical Operations Manager: Barry Moore. Plant Manager: Kevin Goetz. Marketing Director: Beverly Wall. Office Manager: Amy Gibbs.

City fee: 3% of gross.

Ownership: Charter Communications Inc. (MSO).

FAUCETT—Formerly served by CableDirect. No longer in operation. ICA: MO0323.

FAYETTE—Suddenlink Communications, 12444 Powerscourt Dr, Saint Louis, MO 63131-3660. Phones: 800-999-6845 (Customer service); 314-965-2020. Web Site: http://www.suddenlink.com. ICA: MO0122.

TV Market Ranking: Below 100 (FAYETTE). Franchise award date: N.A. Franchise expiration date: N.A. Began: December 1, 1978.

Channel capacity: 36 (2-way capable). Channels available but not in use: N.A.

Basic Service
Subscribers: 585.
Programming (received off-air): KCPT (PBS) Kansas City; KMIZ (ABC) Columbia; KMOS-TV (PBS) Sedalia; KOMU-TV (CW, NBC) Columbia; KRCG (CBS) Jefferson City.
Programming (via satellite): ABC Family Channel; AMC; Animal Planet; Arts & Entertainment; BET Networks; CNN; Country Music TV; Discovery Channel; Disney Channel; E! Entertainment Television; ESPN; Fox News Channel; Fox Sports Net Midwest; Headline News; HGTV; History Channel; Nickelodeon; QVC; Spike TV; TBS Superstation; The Learning Channel; Travel Channel; Turner Network TV; TV Land; USA Network; Weather Channel; WGN America.
Current originations: Educational Access.
Fee: $39.95 installation; $19.95 monthly.

Pay Service 1
Pay Units: 128.
Programming (via satellite): HBO.
Fee: $10.95 monthly.

Pay Service 2
Pay Units: 51.
Programming (via satellite): Showtime.
Fee: $9.95 monthly.

Pay Service 3
Pay Units: 56.
Programming (via satellite): The Movie Channel.
Fee: $7.95 monthly.

Video-On-Demand: No

Internet Service
Operational: No.

Telephone Service
None

Miles of Plant: 18.0 (coaxial); None (fiber optic). Homes passed: 1,000.

Regional Manager: Todd Cruthird. Regional Marketing Manager: Beverly Gambell.

Ownership: Cequel Communications LLC (MSO).

FERGUSON—Charter Communications, 941 Charter Commons Dr, Saint Louis, MO 63017. Phone: 636-207-7044. Fax: 636-230-7034. Web Site: http://www.charter.com. Also serves Bellerive, Bel-Nor, Bel-Ridge, Berkeley, Beverly Hills, Calverton Park, Cool Valley, Dellwood, Glen Echo Park, Greendale, Hillsdale, Normandy, Norwood Court, Pagedale, Pasadena Hills, Pasadena Park, Uplands Park, Velda City, Velda Village Hills & Vinita Terrace. ICA: MO0014.

TV Market Ranking: 11 (Bellerive, Bel-Nor, Bel-Ridge, Berkeley, Beverly Hills, Calverton Park, Cool Valley, Dellwood, FERGUSON, Glen Echo Park, Greendale, Hillsdale, Normandy, Norwood Court, Pagedale, Pasadena Hills, Pasadena Park, Uplands Park, Velda City, Velda Village Hills, Vinita Terrace). Franchise award date: N.A. Franchise expiration date: N.A. Began: October 27, 1981.

Channel capacity: 84 (operating 2-way). Channels available but not in use: 3.

Basic Service
Subscribers: 11,875.
Programming (received off-air): KDNL-TV (ABC) St. Louis; KETC (PBS) St. Louis; KMOV (CBS) St. Louis; KNLC (IND) St. Louis; KPLR-TV (CW) St. Louis; KSDK (NBC) St. Louis; KTVI (FOX) St. Louis; WPXS (IND) Mount Vernon; WRBU (MNT) East St. Louis; 9 FMs.
Programming (via satellite): C-SPAN; C-SPAN 2; Eternal Word TV Network; Home Shopping Network; INSP; QVC; ShopNBC; TBS Superstation; Trinity Broadcasting Network; TV Guide Network; Univision; WGN America.
Current originations: Leased Access; Religious Access; Government Access; Educational Access; Public Access.
Fee: $29.99 installation.

Expanded Basic Service 1
Subscribers: N.A.
Programming (via satellite): ABC Family Channel; AMC; Animal Planet; Arts & Entertainment; BET Networks; Bravo; Cartoon Network; CNBC; CNN; Comedy Central; Country Music TV; Discovery Channel; Disney Channel; E! Entertainment Television; ESPN; ESPN 2; Food Network; Fox Movie Channel; Fox News Channel; Fox Sports Net Midwest; FX; G4; Golf Channel; GSN; Hallmark Channel; Headline News; HGTV; History Channel; Lifetime; MSNBC; MTV; National Geographic Channel; Nickelodeon; Oxygen; SoapNet; Speed Channel; Spike TV; Style Network; The Learning Channel; Toon Disney; Travel Channel; truTV; Turner Classic Movies; Turner Network TV; TV Land; USA Network; Versus; VH1; WE tv; Weather Channel.
Fee: $49.99 monthly.

Digital Basic Service
Subscribers: N.A.
Programming (via satellite): BBC America; Bio; Bloomberg Television; Discovery Digital Networks; Do-It-Yourself; Encore Action; ESPN Classic Sports; FitTV; Fox Sports World; FSN Digital Atlantic; FSN Digital Central; FSN Digital Pacific; Fuel TV; Fuse; GAS; Great American Country; History Channel International; Independent Film Channel; International Television (ITV); Lifetime Movie Network; MTV Networks Digital Suite; Music Choice; NFL Network; Nick Jr.; Nick Too; NickToons TV; Sundance Channel.

Digital Pay Service 1
Pay Units: 10,833.
Programming (via satellite): Cinemax (multiplexed); HBO (multiplexed); Showtime (multiplexed); Starz (multiplexed); The Movie Channel (multiplexed).
Fee: $12.02 monthly (Cinemax, HBO or Showtime).

Video-On-Demand: Yes

Pay-Per-View
iN DEMAND (delivered digitally); ESPN Now (delivered digitally); Sports PPV (delivered digitally); Playboy TV (delivered digitally); Fresh (delivered digitally); Shorteez (delivered digitally).

Internet Service
Operational: Yes.
Broadband Service: Charter Pipeline.
Fee: $29.99 monthly.

Telephone Service
Digital: Operational
Fee: $29.99 monthly

Miles of Plant: 253.0 (coaxial); None (fiber optic). Homes passed: 26,032. Total homes in franchised area: 31,000.

Vice President & General Manager: Steve Trippe. Operations Director: Tom Williams. Marketing Director: Beverly Wall.

City fee: 5% of gross.

Ownership: Charter Communications Inc. (MSO).

FISK—Boycom Cablevision Inc., 3467 Township Line Rd, Poplar Bluff, MO 63901. Phone: 573-686-9101. Fax: 573-686-4722. Web Site: http://www.boycomonline.com. ICA: MO0318.

TV Market Ranking: Below 100 (FISK). Franchise award date: N.A. Franchise expiration date: N.A. Began: January 1, 1985.

Channel capacity: N.A. Channels available but not in use: N.A.

Basic Service
Subscribers: 103.
Programming (received off-air): KAIT (ABC) Jonesboro; KBSI (FOX) Cape Girardeau; KFVS-TV (CBS, CW) Cape Girardeau; KPOB-TV (ABC) Poplar Bluff; WPSD-TV (NBC) Paducah.
Programming (via satellite): ABC Family Channel; Discovery Channel; ESPN; Spike TV; TBS Superstation; WGN America.
Fee: $21.95 monthly.

Pay Service 1
Pay Units: N.A.
Programming (via satellite): The Movie Channel.
Fee: $11.95 monthly.

Video-On-Demand: No

Internet Service
Operational: No.

Telephone Service
None

Miles of Plant: 3.0 (coaxial); None (fiber optic).

President: Steven Boyers. General Manager: Shelly Batton. Chief Technician: Phil Huett.

Ownership: Boycom Cablevision Inc. (MSO).

FLAT RIVER—Charter Communications. Now served by FARMINGTON, MO [MO0035]. ICA: MO0026.

FORDLAND—Formerly served by Cebridge Connections. No longer in operation. ICA: MO0289.

FORSYTH—Mediacom, 1533 S Enterprise Ave, Springfield, MO 65804. Phone: 417-875-5560. Fax: 417-883-0265. Web Site: http://www.mediacomcable.com. Also serves Kimberling City & Ozark Beach (portions). ICA: MO0126.

TV Market Ranking: Below 100 (FORSYTH, Kimberling City, Ozark Beach (portions)). Franchise award date: N.A. Franchise expiration date: N.A. Began: November 1, 1982.

Channel capacity: N.A. Channels available but not in use: N.A.

Basic Service
Subscribers: 2,470.
Programming (received off-air): K15CZ Springfield; KOLR (CBS) Springfield; KOZK (PBS) Springfield; KSFX-TV (FOX) Springfield; KSPR (ABC) Springfield; KWBM (MNT) Harrison [LICENSED & SILENT]; KYTV (CW, NBC) Springfield.
Programming (via satellite): ShopNBC; TV Guide Network; WGN America.
Current originations: Educational Access; Public Access.
Fee: $35.00 installation; $25.25 monthly.

Expanded Basic Service 1
Subscribers: N.A.
Programming (via satellite): ABC Family Channel; AMC; AmericanLife TV Network; Animal Planet; Arts & Entertainment; Bravo; Cartoon Network; CNBC; CNN; Comedy Central; Country Music TV; C-SPAN; Discovery Channel; Disney Channel; E! Entertainment Television; ESPN; ESPN 2; Food Network; Fox Movie Channel; Fox News Channel; Fox Sports Net Midwest; FX; Hallmark Channel; Headline News; HGTV; History Channel; Home Shopping Network; INSP; Lifetime; MSNBC; MTV; Nickelodeon; Outdoor Channel; QVC; SoapNet; Speed Channel; Spike TV; Syfy; TBS Superstation; The Learning Channel; Travel Channel; Trinity Broadcasting Network; truTV; Turner Network TV; TV Land; USA Network; VH1; WE tv; Weather Channel.

Digital Basic Service
Subscribers: N.A.
Programming (received off-air): KSPR (ABC) Springfield; KYTV (CW, NBC) Springfield.
Programming (via satellite): BBC America; Bio; Bloomberg Television; Canales N; Discovery Digital Networks; Discovery HD Theater; ESPN; ESPNews; Fox Soccer; Fuse; G4; GAS; Golf Channel; GSN; HDNet; HDNet Movies; History Channel International; Independent Film Channel;

Lifetime Movie Network; Lime; MTV Networks Digital Suite; Music Choice; National Geographic Channel; Nick Jr.; NickToons TV; Sleuth; Style Network; Turner Classic Movies; Universal HD; Versus.

Digital Pay Service 1

Pay Units: N.A.

Programming (via satellite): Cinemax (multiplexed); Encore (multiplexed); Flix (multiplexed); HBO (multiplexed); HBO; Showtime (multiplexed); Showtime; Starz (multiplexed); Starz HDTV; Sundance Channel (multiplexed); The Movie Channel (multiplexed).

Video-On-Demand: Yes

Pay-Per-View

Special events (delivered digitally); Movies (delivered digitally); Playboy TV (delivered digitally); Ten Clips (delivered digitally); Ten Blox (delivered digitally); ESPN Gameplan (delivered digitally).

Internet Service

Operational: Yes.

Broadband Service: Mediacom High Speed Internet.

Telephone Service

Analog: Not Operational

Digital: Operational

Miles of Plant: 74.0 (coaxial); None (fiber optic). Homes passed: 4,117.

Regional Vice President: Bill Copeland. Technical Operations Director: Alan Freedman. Marketing Director: Will Kuebler. Customer Service Manager: Cindy Reese.

City fee: 3% of gross.

Ownership: Mediacom LLC (MSO).

FRANKFORD—Formerly served by Westcom. No longer in operation. ICA: MO0326.

FREDERICKTOWN—Charter Communications. Now served by FARMINGTON, MO [MO0035]. ICA: MO0074.

FREEBURG—Formerly served by CableDirect. No longer in operation. ICA: MO0282.

FREMONT—Formerly served by Cebridge Connections. No longer in operation. ICA: MO0378.

FULTON—Charter Communications, 1015 Washington Square Shopping Ctr, Washington, MO 63090-5307. Phones: 636-207-7044 (St Louis office); 636-239-2197. Fax: 636-239-6865. Web Site: http://www.charter.com. Also serves Auxvasse, Callaway County (portions) & Kingdom City. ICA: MO0045.

TV Market Ranking: Below 100 (Auxvasse, Callaway County (portions), FULTON, Kingdom City). Franchise award date: N.A. Franchise expiration date: N.A. Began: December 1, 1968.

Channel capacity: N.A. Channels available but not in use: N.A.

Basic Service

Subscribers: 3,355.

Programming (received off-air): KMIZ (ABC) Columbia; KMOS-TV (PBS) Sedalia; KNLJ (IND) Jefferson City; KOMU-TV (CW, NBC) Columbia; KPLR-TV (CW) St. Louis; KQFX-LD Columbia; KRCG (CBS) Jefferson City; allband FM.

Programming (via satellite): C-SPAN; C-SPAN 2; GRTV Network; Home Shopping Network; INSP; QVC; ShopNBC; Trinity Broadcasting Network; TV Guide Network; Weather Channel; WGN America.

Current originations: Government Access; Educational Access.

Fee: $29.95 installation.

Expanded Basic Service 1

Subscribers: N.A.

Programming (via satellite): ABC Family Channel; AMC; Animal Planet; Arts & Entertainment; BET Networks; Bravo; Cartoon Network; CNBC; CNN; Comedy Central; Country Music TV; Discovery Channel; Disney Channel; E! Entertainment Television; ESPN; ESPN 2; Food Network; Fox News Channel; Fox Sports Net Midwest; FX; G4; Golf Channel; Great American Country; GSN; Hallmark Channel; Headline News; HGTV; History Channel; ION Television; Lifetime; MSNBC; MTV; Nickelodeon; Outdoor Channel; Oxygen; SoapNet; Speed Channel; Spike TV; Syfy; TBS Superstation; The Learning Channel; Toon Disney; Travel Channel; truTV; Turner Classic Movies; Turner Network TV; TV Land; USA Network; Versus; VH1; WE tv.

Fee: $49.99 monthly.

Digital Basic Service

Subscribers: 1,042.

Programming (via satellite): BBC America; Bio; Bloomberg Television; Discovery Digital Networks; Do-It-Yourself; Fox Movie Channel; FSN Digital Atlantic; FSN Digital Central; FSN Digital Pacific; History Channel International; Independent Film Channel; Lifetime Movie Network; Music Choice; National Geographic Channel; Sundance Channel.

Digital Pay Service 1

Pay Units: 1,811.

Programming (via satellite): Cinemax (multiplexed); Encore (multiplexed); HBO (multiplexed); Showtime (multiplexed); Starz (multiplexed).

Fee: $10.95 monthly (each).

Video-On-Demand: Yes

Pay-Per-View

iN DEMAND (delivered digitally); Hot Choice (delivered digitally); ETC (delivered digitally); Pleasure (delivered digitally); The Erotic Netword (delivered digitally).

Internet Service

Operational: Yes.

Broadband Service: Charter Pipeline.

Fee: $29.99 monthly.

Telephone Service

Digital: Operational

Miles of Plant: 100.0 (coaxial); None (fiber optic). Homes passed: 4,455. Total homes in franchised area: 5,500.

Vice President & General Manager: Steve Trippe. Operations Director: Dave Miller. Technical Operations Manager: John Viehland. Marketing Director: Beverly Wall. Office Manager: Dawn Paul.

City fee: 5% of gross.

Ownership: Charter Communications Inc. (MSO).

GAINESVILLE—Formerly served by Almega Cable. No longer in operation. ICA: MO0229.

GALENA—Formerly served by Almega Cable. No longer in operation. ICA: MO0314.

GALENA—Mediacom. Now served by CARL JUNCTION, MO [MO0094]. ICA: KS0075.

GALLATIN—Longview Communications, 1923 N Main, Higginsville, MO 64037. Phone: 866-611-6565. Fax: 866-329-4790. Web Site: http://www.longviewcomm.com. ICA: MO0147.

TV Market Ranking: Outside TV Markets (GALLATIN). Franchise award date: N.A. Franchise expiration date: N.A. Began: September 1, 1983.

Channel capacity: 78 (operating 2-way). Channels available but not in use: None.

Basic Service

Subscribers: 296.

Programming (received off-air): KCPT (PBS) Kansas City; KCTV (CBS) Kansas City; KCWE (CW) Kansas City; KMBC-TV (ABC) Kansas City; KMCI-TV (IND) Lawrence; KPXE-TV (ION) Kansas City; KQTV (ABC) St. Joseph; KSHB-TV (NBC) Kansas City; KSMO-TV (MNT) Kansas City; WDAF-TV (FOX) Kansas City; allband FM.

Programming (via satellite): ABC Family Channel; AMC; Animal Planet; Arts & Entertainment; Cartoon Network; CNN; Discovery Channel; Disney Channel; E! Entertainment Television; ESPN; ESPN 2; Food Network; Fox News Channel; FX; Great American Country; Headline News; INSP; Lifetime; Outdoor Channel; Oxygen; QVC; ShopNBC; Speed Channel; Syfy; TBS Superstation; The Learning Channel; Toon Disney; Turner Network TV; TV Land; USA Network; Weather Channel; WGN America; XY.tv.

Fee: $35.95 installation; $42.25 monthly.

Digital Basic Service

Subscribers: 56.

Programming (via satellite): AmericanLife TV Network; BBC America; Bio; Bloomberg Television; Discovery Digital Networks; DMX Music; ESPN Classic Sports; ESPNews; Fox Movie Channel; Fuse; G4; Golf Channel; GSN; Halogen Network; HGTV; History Channel; History Channel International; Lifetime Movie Network; National Geographic Channel; Style Network; Trio; Turner Classic Movies; WE tv.

Fee: $15.95 monthly.

Pay Service 1

Pay Units: 11.

Programming (via satellite): Cinemax; HBO; Showtime; Starz; The Movie Channel.

Fee: $9.95 monthly (Showtime, Starz or TMC), $10.95 monthly (Cinemax), $14.95 monthly (HBO).

Digital Pay Service 1

Pay Units: N.A.

Programming (via satellite): Cinemax (multiplexed); Encore (multiplexed); Flix; HBO (multiplexed); Showtime (multiplexed); Starz (multiplexed); The Movie Channel (multiplexed).

Fee: $9.95 monthly (Showtime, TMC or Starz), $10.95 monthly (Cinemax), $14.95 monthly (HBO).

Video-On-Demand: No

Pay-Per-View

Addressable homes: 11.

ESPN Now (delivered digitally), Addressable: Yes; sports (delivered digitally); Urban Xtra (delivered digitally).

Internet Service

Operational: Yes.

Subscribers: 72.

Broadband Service: Longview Broadband.

Telephone Service

None

Miles of Plant: 16.0 (coaxial); None (fiber optic). Homes passed: 921.

President: John Long. Senior Vice President: Marc W. Cohen. General Manager: Brandon Dickey. Operations Manager: Perry Scarborough.

City fee: 3% of gross.

Ownership: Longview Communications (MSO).

GALT—Formerly served by CableDirect. No longer in operation. ICA: MO0402.

GARDEN CITY—Formerly served by Longview Communications. No longer in operation. ICA: MO0211.

GASCONADE—Formerly served by First Cable of Missouri Inc. No longer in operation. ICA: MO0331.

GERALD—Fidelity Communications, 64 N Clark St, Sullivan, MO 63080. Phones: 800-392-8070; 573-468-8081. Web Site: http://www.fidelitycommunications.com. Also serves Rosebud. ICA: MO0206.

TV Market Ranking: Outside TV Markets (GERALD, Rosebud). Franchise award date: November 10, 1983. Franchise expiration date: N.A. Began: N.A.

Channel capacity: N.A. Channels available but not in use: N.A.

Basic Service

Subscribers: 191.

Programming (received off-air): KDNL-TV (ABC) St. Louis; KETC (PBS) St. Louis; KMIZ (ABC) Columbia; KMOV (CBS) St. Louis; KOMU-TV (CW, NBC) Columbia; KPLR-TV (CW) St. Louis; KRCG (CBS) Jefferson City; KSDK (NBC) St. Louis; KTVI (FOX) St. Louis.

Programming (via satellite): QVC; TBS Superstation; WGN America.

Fee: $29.95 installation; $19.95 monthly.

Expanded Basic Service 1

Subscribers: N.A.

Programming (via satellite): ABC Family Channel; AMC; Animal Planet; Arts & Entertainment; Cartoon Network; CNN; Country Music TV; Discovery Channel; ESPN; ESPN 2; Headline News; HGTV; INSP; Lifetime; MTV; Nickelodeon; Spike TV; Syfy; Travel Channel; Turner Network TV; USA Network.

Fee: $20.00 monthly.

Pay Service 1

Pay Units: 59.

Programming (via satellite): Cinemax.

Fee: $10.50 monthly.

Pay Service 2

Pay Units: 56.

Programming (via satellite): HBO.

Fee: $11.00 monthly.

Video-On-Demand: No

Internet Service

Operational: No, DSL.

Telephone Service

None

Miles of Plant: 16.0 (coaxial); None (fiber optic). Homes passed: 510. Total homes in franchised area: 510.

Manager: Andrew Davis.

City fee: 3% of gross.

Ownership: Fidelity Communications Co. (MSO).

GLASGOW—Suddenlink Communications, 12444 Powerscourt Dr, Saint Louis, MO 63131-3660. Phones: 800-999-6845 (Customer service); 314-965-2020. Fax: 903-561-5485. Web Site: http://www.suddenlink.com. ICA: MO0199.

TV Market Ranking: Below 100 (GLASGOW). Franchise award date: N.A. Franchise expiration date: N.A. Began: November 1, 1978.

Channel capacity: 36 (2-way capable). Channels available but not in use: N.A.

Basic Service

Subscribers: 293.

Programming (received off-air): KCPT (PBS) Kansas City; KCTV (CBS) Kansas City; KMIZ (ABC) Columbia; KMOS-TV (PBS) Sedalia; KOMU-TV (CW, NBC) Columbia; KRCG (CBS) Jefferson City; WDAF-TV (FOX) Kansas City.

Programming (via satellite): ABC Family Channel; Arts & Entertainment; CNN; Country Music TV; Discovery Channel; Disney Channel; ESPN; Headline News;

History Channel; Nickelodeon; QVC; Spike TV; TBS Superstation; The Learning Channel; Turner Classic Movies; Turner Network TV; TV Land; USA Network; Weather Channel; WGN America.
Fee: $39.95 installation; $19.95 monthly.
Pay Service 1
Pay Units: 36.
Programming (via satellite): The Movie Channel.
Fee: $7.95 monthly.
Pay Service 2
Pay Units: 31.
Programming (via satellite): Showtime.
Fee: $9.95 monthly.
Pay Service 3
Pay Units: 51.
Programming (via satellite): HBO.
Fee: $10.95 monthly.
Video-On-Demand: No
Internet Service
Operational: No.
Telephone Service
None
Miles of Plant: 11.0 (coaxial); None (fiber optic). Homes passed: 600.
Regional Manager: Todd Cruthird. Regional Marketing Manager: Beverly Gambell.
Ownership: Cequel Communications LLC (MSO).

GOODMAN—Mediacom. Now served by GRANBY, MO [MO0156]. ICA: MO0223.

GOWER—Allegiance Communications, 707 W Saratoga St, Shawnee, OK 74804. Phones: 405-275-6923; 405-395-1131. Web Site: http://www.allegiance.tv. ICA: MO0208.
TV Market Ranking: 22 (GOWER). Franchise award date: September 1, 1981. Franchise expiration date: N.A. Began: June 30, 1982.
Channel capacity: 31 (not 2-way capable). Channels available but not in use: N.A.
Basic Service
Subscribers: 334.
Programming (received off-air): KCPT (PBS) Kansas City; KCTV (CBS) Kansas City; KCWE (CW) Kansas City; KMBC-TV (ABC) Kansas City; KPXE-TV (ION) Kansas City; KQTV (ABC) St. Joseph; KSHB-TV (NBC) Kansas City; KSMO-TV (MNT) Kansas City; WDAF-TV (FOX) Kansas City.
Programming (via satellite): ABC Family Channel; AMC; Arts & Entertainment; Discovery Channel; ESPN; ESPN 2; Headline News; Lifetime; Nickelodeon; QVC; The Learning Channel; Turner Network TV; USA Network; Weather Channel.
Fee: $21.95 monthly.
Expanded Basic Service 1
Subscribers: 302.
Programming (via satellite): CNN; Country Music TV; Disney Channel; Spike TV; TBS Superstation; WGN America.
Fee: $10.01 monthly.
Pay Service 1
Pay Units: 95.
Programming (via satellite): HBO.
Fee: $24.95 installation; $11.95 monthly.
Pay Service 2
Pay Units: 54.
Programming (via satellite): Showtime.
Fee: $11.95 monthly.
Video-On-Demand: No
Pay-Per-View
Addressable homes: 18.
Urban American Television Network (delivered digitally); ESPN Now (delivered digitally); ESPN Sports PPV (delivered digitally); iN DEMAND (delivered digitally); Spice2 (delivered digitally); Spice (delivered digitally); Playboy TV (delivered digitally); Hot Choice (delivered digitally).
Internet Service
Operational: No.
Telephone Service
None
Miles of Plant: 11.0 (coaxial); None (fiber optic). Homes passed: 488.
Chief Executive Officer: Bill Haggarty. Regional Vice President: Andrew Dearth. Vice President, Marketing: Tracy Bass.
Franchise fee: 3% of gross.
Ownership: Allegiance Communications (MSO).

GRANBY—Mediacom, 1533 S Enterprise Ave, Springfield, MO 65804. Phones: 417-875-5588; 417-875-5560. Fax: 417-883-0265. Web Site: http://www.mediacomcable.com. Also serves Anderson, Diamond, Goodman, Jasper, Liberal, Mulberry, Newtonia, Sarcoxie & Stark City. ICA: MO0156.
TV Market Ranking: Below 100 (Anderson, Diamond, Goodman, GRANBY, Jasper, Liberal, Mulberry, Newtonia, Sarcoxie, Stark City). Franchise award date: October 14, 1981. Franchise expiration date: N.A. Began: November 1, 1983.
Channel capacity: N.A. Channels available but not in use: N.A.
Basic Service
Subscribers: 2,404.
Programming (received off-air): KCLJ-CA Joplin-Carthage; KFJX (FOX) Pittsburg; KJPX-LP Joplin; KOAM-TV (CBS) Pittsburg; KODE-TV (ABC) Joplin; KOZK (PBS) Springfield; KSNF (NBC) Joplin.
Programming (via satellite): CW+; TV Guide Network; WGN America.
Fee: $35.00 installation; $25.25 monthly.
Expanded Basic Service 1
Subscribers: N.A.
Programming (received off-air): KGCS-LD (IND) Joplin.
Programming (via satellite): ABC Family Channel; AMC; AmericanLife TV Network; Animal Planet; Arts & Entertainment; Bravo; Cartoon Network; CNBC; CNN; Comedy Central; Country Music TV; C-SPAN; Discovery Channel; Disney Channel; ESPN; ESPN 2; FitTV; Food Network; Fox News Channel; Fox Sports Net Midwest; FX; Hallmark Channel; Headline News; HGTV; History Channel; Home Shopping Network; Lifetime; MSNBC; MTV; Nickelodeon; Outdoor Channel; QVC; ShopNBC; SoapNet; Speed Channel; Spike TV; Syfy; TBS Superstation; The Learning Channel; Travel Channel; truTV; Turner Network TV; TV Land; USA Network; VH1; Weather Channel.
Digital Basic Service
Subscribers: N.A.
Programming (via satellite): BBC America; Bio; Bloomberg Television; Discovery Digital Networks; ESPNews; Fox Movie Channel; Fox Soccer; Fuse; G4; GAS; Golf Channel; GSN; History Channel International; Independent Film Channel; Lifetime Movie Network; Lime; MTV Networks Digital Suite; Music Choice; National Geographic Channel; Nick Jr.; NickToons TV; Sleuth; Style Network; Turner Classic Movies; Versus.
Pay Service 1
Pay Units: 93.
Programming (via satellite): Cinemax.
Fee: $10.00 installation; $9.00 monthly.
Pay Service 2
Pay Units: 153.
Programming (via satellite): HBO.
Fee: $10.00 installation; $9.00 monthly.
Pay Service 3
Pay Units: 144.
Programming (via satellite): Flix; Showtime (multiplexed); The Movie Channel.
Fee: $10.50 monthly.

Digital Pay Service 1
Pay Units: N.A.
Programming (via satellite): Cinemax (multiplexed); Encore (multiplexed); Flix (multiplexed); HBO (multiplexed); Showtime (multiplexed); Starz (multiplexed); Sundance Channel (multiplexed); The Movie Channel (multiplexed).
Video-On-Demand: Yes
Pay-Per-View
Special events (delivered digitally); Movies (delivered digitally); Playboy TV (delivered digitally); Ten Clips (delivered digitally); Ten Blox (delivered digitally).
Internet Service
Operational: Yes.
Broadband Service: Mediacom High Speed Internet.
Telephone Service
Digital: Operational
Miles of Plant: 93.0 (coaxial); None (fiber optic). Homes passed: 4,802.
Vice President: Bill Copeland. Technical Operations Director: Alan Freedman. Marketing Director: Will Kuebler.
City fee: 3% of basic & premium.
Ownership: Mediacom LLC (MSO).

GRANT CITY—B & L Technologies LLC, 3329 270th St, Lenox, IA 50851. Phones: 800-798-5488; 641-348-2240. Fax: 641-348-2240. ICA: MO0204.
TV Market Ranking: Outside TV Markets (GRANT CITY). Franchise award date: N.A. Franchise expiration date: N.A. Began: September 1, 1975.
Channel capacity: 41 (not 2-way capable). Channels available but not in use: 4.
Basic Service
Subscribers: 151.
Programming (received off-air): KCCI (CBS) Des Moines; KCTV (CBS) Kansas City; KHIN (PBS) Red Oak; KQTV (ABC) St. Joseph; KTAJ-TV (TBN) St. Joseph; WDAF-TV (FOX) Kansas City; WHO-DT (NBC) Des Moines; allband FM.
Programming (via satellite): ABC Family Channel; AMC; Arts & Entertainment; CNN; Country Music TV; Discovery Channel; Disney Channel; ESPN; ESPN 2; Headline News; Lifetime; Nickelodeon; QVC; Spike TV; TBS Superstation; The Learning Channel; Turner Network TV; USA Network; Weather Channel; WGN America.
Fee: $10.00 installation; $33.95 monthly.
Pay Service 1
Pay Units: 49.
Programming (via satellite): Encore; Showtime; Starz; The Movie Channel.
Fee: $10.95 monthly (Showtime), $8.95 monthly (TMC or Starz/Encore).
Video-On-Demand: No
Internet Service
Operational: No.
Telephone Service
None
Miles of Plant: 13.0 (coaxial); None (fiber optic). Homes passed: 513.
President & General Manager: Robert Hintz. Office Manager: Linda Hintz.
City fee: 3% of gross.
Ownership: B & L Technologies LLC (MSO).

GRAVOIS MILLS—Lake Communications, TX 76021. Phone: 87-242-3830. Web Site: http://lakecommunicationsonline.com. ICA: MO0087.
TV Market Ranking: Below 100 (GRAVOIS MILLS). Franchise award date: N.A. Franchise expiration date: N.A. Began: N.A.
Channel capacity: 42 (not 2-way capable). Channels available but not in use: 4.
Basic Service
Subscribers: 553.
Programming (received off-air): KOLR (CBS) Springfield; KOMU-TV (CW, NBC) Columbia; KOZK (PBS) Springfield; KSFX-TV (FOX) Springfield; KSPR (ABC) Springfield; KYTV (CW, NBC) Springfield.
Programming (via satellite): ABC Family Channel; AMC; Arts & Entertainment; CNBC; CNN; Country Music TV; C-SPAN; Discovery Channel; ESPN; Hallmark Channel; Headline News; Home Shopping Network; Lifetime; Nickelodeon; Spike TV; TBS Superstation; Turner Network TV; USA Network; Weather Channel; WGN America.
Fee: $29.95 installation; $39.95 monthly.
Pay Service 1
Pay Units: 22.
Programming (via satellite): Cinemax.
Fee: $10.00 monthly.
Pay Service 2
Pay Units: 34.
Programming (via satellite): HBO.
Fee: $10.95 monthly.
Pay Service 3
Pay Units: 106.
Programming (via satellite): Showtime.
Fee: $10.00 monthly.
Video-On-Demand: No
Internet Service
Operational: No.
Telephone Service
None
Miles of Plant: 61.0 (coaxial); None (fiber optic). Homes passed: 2,247.
President & General Manager: Tony Gilbert.
Ownership: Lake Communications (MSO).

GREEN CASTLE—Longview Communications, 12007 Sunrise Valley Dr, Ste 375, Reston, VA 20191. Phones: 866-611-6565 (Customer service); 703-476-9101. Fax: 703-476-9107. Web Site: http://www.longviewcomm.com. Also serves Green City. ICA: MO0324.
TV Market Ranking: Below 100 (GREEN CASTLE, Green City). Franchise award date: N.A. Franchise expiration date: N.A. Began: September 1, 1983.
Channel capacity: 41 (not 2-way capable). Channels available but not in use: 1.
Basic Service
Subscribers: 187.
Programming (received off-air): KCNC-TV (CBS) Denver; KHQA-TV (ABC, CBS) Hannibal; KRMA-TV (PBS) Denver; KTVO (ABC) Kirksville; KUSA (NBC) Denver; KYOU-TV (FOX) Ottumwa; WGEM-TV (CW, NBC) Quincy.
Programming (via satellite): ABC Family Channel; AMC; Animal Planet; Arts & Entertainment; Cartoon Network; CNN; Discovery Channel; Disney Channel; E! En-

tertainment Television; ESPN; ESPN 2; Fox News Channel; FX; Great American Country; Headline News; HGTV; History Channel; Lifetime; Lifetime Movie Network; Outdoor Channel; QVC; Syfy; TBS Superstation; The Learning Channel; Toon Disney; Trinity Broadcasting Network; Turner Network TV; USA Network; Weather Channel; WGN America.
Fee: $30.00 installation; $41.25 monthly.

Pay Service 1
Pay Units: 8.
Programming (via satellite): HBO; Showtime.
Fee: $9.95 monthly (Showtime), $14.95 monthly (HBO).

Video-On-Demand: No

Internet Service
Operational: No.

Telephone Service
None

Miles of Plant: 16.0 (coaxial); None (fiber optic). Homes passed: 543. Total homes in franchised area: 556.
President: John Long. Senior Vice President: Marc W. Cohen. General Manager: Brandon Dickey. Operations Manager: Perry Scarborough.
Ownership: Longview Communications (MSO).

GREEN RIDGE—Formerly served by CableDirect. No longer in operation. ICA: MO0316.

GREENTOP—Longview Communications, 12007 Sunrise Valley Dr, Ste 375, Reston, VA 20191. Phones: 866-611-6565 (Customer service); 703-476-9101. Fax: 703-476-9107. Web Site: http://www.longviewcomm.com. Also serves Queen City. ICA: MO0280.
TV Market Ranking: Below 100 (GREENTOP, Queen City). Franchise award date: N.A. Franchise expiration date: N.A. Began: January 15, 1984.
Channel capacity: 41 (not 2-way capable). Channels available but not in use: 8.

Basic Service
Subscribers: 195.
Programming (received off-air): KHQA-TV (ABC, CBS) Hannibal; KTVO (ABC) Kirksville; KYOU-TV (FOX) Ottumwa; WGEM-TV (CW, NBC) Quincy.
Programming (via satellite): ABC Family Channel; AMC; Animal Planet; Arts & Entertainment; Cartoon Network; CNN; Comedy Central; Discovery Channel; Disney Channel; E! Entertainment Television; ESPN; ESPN 2; Fox News Channel; Great American Country; Headline News; KRMA-TV (PBS) Denver; Lifetime; Outdoor Channel; QVC; TBS Superstation; The Learning Channel; Toon Disney; Turner Network TV; TV Land; USA Network; Weather Channel; WGN America.
Fee: $30.00 installation; $41.75 monthly.

Pay Service 1
Pay Units: N.A.
Programming (via satellite): HBO; Showtime.
Fee: $9.95 monthly (Showtime), $14.95 monthly (HBO).

Video-On-Demand: No

Internet Service
Operational: No.

Telephone Service
None

Miles of Plant: 18.0 (coaxial); None (fiber optic). Homes passed: 564.
President: John Long. Senior Vice President: Marc W. Cohen. General Manager: Brandon Dickey. Operations Manager: Perry Scarborough.
City fee: None.
Ownership: Longview Communications (MSO).

GREENVILLE—Formerly served by Almega Cable. No longer in operation. ICA: MO0247.

HALLSVILLE—Longview Communications, 12007 Sunrise Valley Dr, Ste 375, Reston, VA 20191. Phones: 866-611-6565 (Customer service); 703-476-9101. Fax: 703-476-9107. Web Site: http://www.longviewcomm.com. ICA: MO0255.
TV Market Ranking: Below 100 (HALLSVILLE). Franchise award date: N.A. Franchise expiration date: N.A. Began: February 1, 1985.
Channel capacity: N.A. Channels available but not in use: N.A.

Basic Service
Subscribers: 106.
Programming (received off-air): KMIZ (ABC) Columbia; KMOS-TV (PBS) Sedalia; KNLJ (IND) Jefferson City; KOMU-TV (CW, NBC) Columbia; KQFX-LD Columbia; KRCG (CBS) Jefferson City.
Programming (via satellite): ABC Family Channel; AMC; Animal Planet; Arts & Entertainment; Boomerang; Cartoon Network; Classic Arts Showcase; CNN; Comedy Central; C-SPAN; Discovery Channel; Disney Channel; Do-It-Yourself; E! Entertainment Television; ESPN; ESPN 2; ESPN Classic Sports; Food Network; Fox News Channel; Fuse; FX; Great American Country; Hallmark Channel; Hallmark Movie Channel; Headline News; HGTV; History Channel; Lifetime; MSNBC; National Geographic Channel; Outdoor Channel; Oxygen; QVC; Syfy; TBS Superstation; The Learning Channel; Toon Disney; Travel Channel; Turner Network TV; USA Network; Weather Channel.
Current originations: Public Access.
Fee: $25.00 installation; $41.95 monthly.

Digital Basic Service
Subscribers: N.A.
Programming (via satellite): AmericanLife TV Network; Anime Network; BBC America; Bio; Bloomberg Television; Discovery Health Channel; Discovery Home Channel; Discovery Kids Channel; Discovery Military Channel; Discovery Times Channel; DMX Music; Encore (multiplexed); ESPNews; FitTV; Fox Movie Channel; Fox Soccer; G4; Golf Channel; GSN; Halogen Network; History Channel International; Independent Film Channel; Lifetime Movie Network; PBS Kids Sprout; Science Channel; Sleuth; Speed Channel; Style Network; Turner Classic Movies; Versus.
Fee: $17.00 monthly.

Pay Service 1
Pay Units: 79.
Programming (via satellite): Cinemax; HBO; Showtime; The Movie Channel.
Fee: $9.95 monthly (Showtime or TMC), $10.95 monthly (Cinemax), $14.95 monthly (HBO).

Digital Pay Service 1
Pay Units: N.A.
Programming (via satellite): HBO (multiplexed); Showtime (multiplexed); Starz (multiplexed); The Movie Channel (multiplexed).
Fee: $9.95 monthly (Showtime or TMC), $10.95 monthly (Cinemax), $14.95 monthly (HBO).

Video-On-Demand: No

Pay-Per-View
iN DEMAND (delivered digitally); Hot Choice (delivered digitally); Playboy TV (delivered digitally); Fresh (delivered digitally); Club Jenna (delivered digitally); Spice: Xcess (delivered digitally).

Internet Service
Operational: Yes.

Telephone Service
None

Miles of Plant: 8.0 (coaxial); None (fiber optic). Homes passed: 492.
President: John Long. Senior Vice President: Marc W. Cohen. General Manager: Brandon Dickey. Operations Manager: Perry Scarborough.
City fee: 3% of gross.
Ownership: Longview Communications (MSO).

HAMILTON—Allegiance Communications, 707 W Saratoga St, Shawnee, OK 74804. Phones: 405-275-6923; 405-395-1131. Web Site: http://www.allegiance.tv. ICA: MO0160.
TV Market Ranking: Outside TV Markets (HAMILTON). Franchise award date: August 31, 1981. Franchise expiration date: N.A. Began: April 1, 1982.
Channel capacity: 41 (not 2-way capable). Channels available but not in use: N.A.

Basic Service
Subscribers: 388.
Programming (received off-air): KCPT (PBS) Kansas City; KCTV (CBS) Kansas City; KCWB-LP Reedley; KMBC-TV (ABC) Kansas City; KQTV (ABC) St. Joseph; KSHB-TV (NBC) Kansas City; KSMO-TV (MNT) Kansas City; WDAF-TV (FOX) Kansas City.
Programming (via satellite): TBS Superstation; WGN America.
Fee: $41.11 installation; $23.50 monthly.

Expanded Basic Service 1
Subscribers: N.A.
Programming (via satellite): ABC Family Channel; Animal Planet; Arts & Entertainment; CNN; Discovery Channel; Disney Channel; ESPN; ESPN 2; Fox News Channel; FX; History Channel; Lifetime; Nickelodeon; Spike TV; Syfy; truTV; Turner Network TV; TV Land; USA Network; VH1; Weather Channel.

Pay Service 1
Pay Units: 45.
Programming (via satellite): The Movie Channel.
Fee: $8.95 monthly.

Pay Service 2
Pay Units: 79.
Programming (via satellite): HBO.
Fee: $10.50 monthly.

Pay Service 3
Pay Units: 58.
Programming (via satellite): Showtime.
Fee: $10.50 monthly.

Video-On-Demand: No

Pay-Per-View
Urban American Television Network (delivered digitally); ESPN Now (delivered digitally); ESPN Sports PPV (delivered digitally); Hot Choice (delivered digitally); Playboy TV (delivered digitally); Fresh (delivered digitally); Shorteez (delivered digitally); iN DEMAND (delivered digitally).

Internet Service
Operational: No.

Telephone Service
None

Miles of Plant: 15.0 (coaxial); None (fiber optic). Homes passed: 778. Total homes in franchised area: 778.
Chief Executive Officer: Bill Haggarty. Regional Vice President: Andrew Dearth. Vice President, Marketing: Tracy Bass.
City fee: 4% of gross.
Ownership: Allegiance Communications (MSO).

HANNIBAL—US Cable, 647 Clinic Rd, Hannibal, MO 63401. Phones: 573-581-2404; 660-263-5757. Fax: 573-581-4053. Web Site: http://www.uscable.com. Also serves Monroe City, Palmyra, Paris, Shelbina & Shelbyville. ICA: MO0021.
TV Market Ranking: Below 100 (HANNIBAL, Monroe City, Palmyra, Shelbina); Outside TV Markets (Paris, Shelbyville). Franchise award date: N.A. Franchise expiration date: N.A. Began: December 1, 1968.
Channel capacity: N.A. Channels available but not in use: N.A.

Basic Service
Subscribers: 18,258 Includes Edina, Jonesburg, Louisiana, Madison, Mexico, Moberly, Perry, & Winfield.
Programming (received off-air): KDNL-TV (ABC) St. Louis; KETC (PBS) St. Louis; KHQA-TV (ABC, CBS) Hannibal; KPLR-TV (CW) St. Louis; KTVO (ABC) Kirksville; WGEM-TV (CW, NBC) Quincy; WQEC (PBS) Quincy; WTJR (IND) Quincy; 8 FMs.
Programming (via microwave): KTVI (FOX) St. Louis.
Programming (via satellite): Headline News; Home Shopping Network; Lifetime; Turner Network TV; TV Guide Network; Weather Channel.
Current originations: Leased Access; Public Access.
Fee: $60.00 installation; $17.95 monthly; $1.76 converter; $40.00 additional installation.

Expanded Basic Service 1
Subscribers: 5,879.
Programming (via satellite): ABC Family Channel; AMC; Animal Planet; Arts & Entertainment; BET Networks; Bravo; Cartoon Network; CNBC; CNN; Comedy Central; Country Music TV; C-SPAN; C-SPAN 2; Discovery Channel; Disney Channel; E! Entertainment Television; ESPN; ESPN 2; Eternal Word TV Network; Food Network; Fox News Channel; Fox Sports Net Midwest; FX; Great American Country; Hallmark Channel; HGTV; History Channel; MSNBC; MTV; National Geographic Channel; Nickelodeon; Oxygen; QVC; ShopNBC; SoapNet; Speed Channel; Spike TV; Syfy; TBS Superstation; The Learning Channel; truTV; TV Land; USA Network; VH1.
Fee: $6.70 monthly.

Digital Basic Service
Subscribers: 3,703 Includes Edina, Louisiana, Mexico, Moberly, & Winfield.
Programming (via satellite): BBC America; Bio; Bloomberg Television; Discovery Digital Networks; Fox Reality Channel; Fuse; G4; GSN; Halogen Network; HGTV; History Channel International; Lime; MTV Networks Digital Suite; Nick Jr.; Sleuth; Style Network; Syfy; Toon Disney; Trinity Broadcasting Network; WealthTV.
Fee: $12.95 monthly.

Digital Expanded Basic Service
Subscribers: N.A.
Programming (via satellite): DMX Music; Encore (multiplexed); Fox Movie Channel; Independent Film Channel; Lifetime Movie Network; Turner Classic Movies; WE tv.
Fee: $4.95 monthly.

Digital Expanded Basic Service 2
Subscribers: N.A.
Programming (via satellite): ESPN Classic Sports; ESPNews; Fox Soccer; GAS; Golf Channel; NFL Network; Outdoor Channel; Versus.
Fee: $3.95 monthly.

Pay Service 1
Pay Units: 533.
Programming (via satellite): Cinemax; Encore; HBO; Starz.
Fee: $2.99 monthly (Encore), $9.10 monthly (Starz), $13.40 monthly (Cinemax), $13.90 monthly (HBO).

Digital Pay Service 1
Pay Units: N.A.
Programming (via satellite): Cinemax (multiplexed); HBO (multiplexed); Showtime (multiplexed); Starz (multiplexed); The Movie Channel (multiplexed).
Fee: $6.95 monthly (Starz), $11.95 monthly (HBO, Cinemax, or Showtime/TMC).

Video-On-Demand: No

Pay-Per-View
Playboy TV (delivered digitally); Fresh (delivered digitally); iN DEMAND (delivered digitally).

Internet Service
Operational: Yes.
Subscribers: 4,225.
Broadband Service: Warp Drive Online.
Fee: $14.95 installation; $39.95 monthly.

Telephone Service
Analog: Not Operational
Digital: Operational

Miles of Plant: 686.0 (coaxial); None (fiber optic). Homes passed: 40,450. Total homes in franchised area: 19,500. Homes passed & miles of plant (coax & fiber combined) include Edina, Jonesburg, Louisiana, Madison, Mexico, Moberly, Perry, & Winfield

Technical Operations Manager: Mark Thake. Marketing Director: Rita Watson. Regional Administrative Director: Rebecca Bramblett.

City fee: 7% of gross.

Ownership: US Cable Corp. (MSO).; Comcast Cable Communications Inc. (MSO).

HARRISBURG—Formerly served by First Cable of Missouri Inc. No longer in operation. ICA: MO0338.

HARRISONVILLE—Charter Communications, 210 W 7th St, Sedalia, MO 65301-4217. Phones: 636-207-7044; 660-826-6520. Fax: 660-826-4583. Web Site: http://www.charter.com. ICA: MO0070.

TV Market Ranking: 22 (HARRISONVILLE). Franchise award date: March 5, 1980. Franchise expiration date: N.A. Began: July 19, 1980.

Channel capacity: 65 (not 2-way capable). Channels available but not in use: None.

Basic Service
Subscribers: 1,980.
Programming (received off-air): KCPT (PBS) Kansas City; KCTV (CBS) Kansas City; KCWE (CW) Kansas City; KMBC-TV (ABC) Kansas City; KMCI-TV (IND) Lawrence; KMOS-TV (PBS) Sedalia; KPXE-TV (ION) Kansas City; KSHB-TV (NBC) Kansas City; KSMO-TV (MNT) Kansas City; WDAF-TV (FOX) Kansas City; allband FM.
Programming (via satellite): ABC Family Channel; Arts & Entertainment; CNN; Comedy Central; C-SPAN; E! Entertainment Television; Hallmark Channel; Headline News; Lifetime; MTV; Nickelodeon; QVC; Trinity Broadcasting Network; Turner Network TV; TV Guide Network; USA Network; VH1; WGN America.
Current originations: Government Access; Educational Access.
Fee: $29.99 installation.

Expanded Basic Service 1
Subscribers: 1,576.
Programming (via satellite): AMC; Animal Planet; Bravo; Cartoon Network; CNBC; Country Music TV; Discovery Channel; Disney Channel; ESPN; ESPN 2; FitTV; Food Network; Fox News Channel; Fox Sports Net Midwest; FX; G4; Golf Channel; HGTV; History Channel; Home Shopping Network; MSNBC; National Geographic Channel; Oxygen; SoapNet; Speed Channel; Spike TV; Syfy; TBS Superstation; The Learning Channel; Travel Channel; truTV; Turner Classic Movies; TV Land; Versus; Weather Channel.
Fee: $49.99 monthly.

Digital Basic Service
Subscribers: 94.
Programming (via satellite): BBC America; Bio; Bloomberg Television; Discovery Digital Networks; Do-It-Yourself; GAS; GSN; History Channel International; Independent Film Channel; Lifetime Movie Network; MTV Networks Digital Suite; Music Choice; Nick Jr.; Nick Too; NickToons TV; Style Network; Sundance Channel; Toon Disney; TV Guide Interactive Inc.; WE tv.
Fee: $16.90 monthly.

Digital Pay Service 1
Pay Units: 841.
Programming (via satellite): Cinemax (multiplexed); Encore (multiplexed); Flix; HBO (multiplexed); Showtime (multiplexed); Starz (multiplexed); The Movie Channel (multiplexed).
Fee: $11.95 monthly (each).

Video-On-Demand: Yes

Pay-Per-View
Addressable homes: 94.
iN DEMAND (delivered digitally), Addressable: Yes; ETC (delivered digitally); Pleasure (delivered digitally).

Internet Service
Operational: Yes.
Broadband Service: Charter Pipeline.
Fee: $29.99 monthly.

Telephone Service
Digital: Operational

Miles of Plant: 43.0 (coaxial); None (fiber optic). Homes passed: 2,807. Total homes in franchised area: 2,807.

Vice President & General Manager: Steve Trippe. Operations Director: Dave Miller. Technical Operations Manager: Larry Wright. Marketing Director: Beverly Wall. Office Manager: Vicky Brant.

Franchise fee: 3% of gross.

Ownership: Charter Communications Inc. (MSO).

HARTVILLE—Formerly served by Cebridge Connections. No longer in operation. ICA: MO0279.

HAWK POINT—Formerly served by First Cable of Missouri Inc. No longer in operation. ICA: MO0285.

HERMANN—Mediacom, 901 N College Ave, Columbia, MO 65201. Phones: 573-443-1536; 417-875-5560 (Springfield regional office). Fax: 417-883-0265. Web Site: http://www.mediacomcable.com. ICA: MO0105.

TV Market Ranking: Outside TV Markets (HERMANN). Franchise award date: N.A. Franchise expiration date: N.A. Began: February 1, 1981.

Channel capacity: N.A. Channels available but not in use: N.A.

Basic Service
Subscribers: 1,000.
Programming (received off-air): KDNL-TV (ABC) St. Louis; KETC (PBS) St. Louis; KMIZ (ABC) Columbia; KMOV (CBS) St. Louis; KOMU-TV (CW, NBC) Columbia; KPLR-TV (CW) St. Louis; KRCG (CBS) Jefferson City; KSDK (NBC) St. Louis; KTVI (FOX) St. Louis.
Programming (via satellite): ABC Family Channel; Arts & Entertainment; CNN; C-SPAN; Discovery Channel; Disney Channel; Headline News; Lifetime; MTV; Nickelodeon; QVC; TBS Superstation; Turner Network TV; WGN America.
Current originations: Public Access.
Fee: $60.00 installation; $10.06 monthly; $40.00 additional installation.

Expanded Basic Service 1
Subscribers: 857.
Programming (via satellite): AMC; ESPN; Fox Sports Net; Spike TV; truTV; USA Network.
Fee: $11.27 installation; $2.18 monthly.

Pay Service 1
Pay Units: 40.
Programming (via satellite): Encore; HBO.

Video-On-Demand: No

Internet Service
Operational: Yes.
Broadband Service: Mediacom High Speed Internet.

Telephone Service
None

Miles of Plant: 19.0 (coaxial); None (fiber optic). Homes passed: 1,522. Total homes in franchised area: 1,522.

Regional Vice President: Bill Copeland. Operations Director: Bryan Gann. Regional Technical Operations Director: Alan Freedman. Technical Operations Manager: Roger Shearer. Marketing Director: Will Kuebler.

Ownership: Mediacom LLC (MSO).

HIGBEE—Longview Communications, 12007 Sunrise Valley Dr, Ste 375, Reston, VA 20191. Phones: 866-611-6565 (Customer service); 703-476-9101. Fax: 703-476-9107. Web Site: http://www.longviewcomm.com. ICA: MO0260.

TV Market Ranking: Below 100 (HIGBEE). Franchise award date: N.A. Franchise expiration date: N.A. Began: December 1, 1983.

Channel capacity: 36 (not 2-way capable). Channels available but not in use: 1.

Basic Service
Subscribers: 46.
Programming (received off-air): KMIZ (ABC) Columbia; KMOS-TV (PBS) Sedalia; KNLJ (IND) Jefferson City; KOMU-TV (CW, NBC) Columbia; KRCG (CBS) Jefferson City.
Programming (via satellite): ABC Family Channel; AMC; Animal Planet; Arts & Entertainment; Cartoon Network; CNN; Discovery Channel; Disney Channel; E! Entertainment Television; ESPN; ESPN 2; Great American Country; Headline News; History Channel; Lifetime; MSNBC; Outdoor Channel; QVC; TBS Superstation; The Learning Channel; Turner Network TV; USA Network; Weather Channel; WGN America.
Fee: $39.45 monthly.

Pay Service 1
Pay Units: 57.
Programming (via satellite): Cinemax; HBO; Showtime; Starz; The Movie Channel.
Fee: $9.95 monthly (Showtime, Starz, or TMC), $10.95 monthly (Cinemax), $14.95 monthly (HBO).

Video-On-Demand: No

Internet Service
Operational: No.

Telephone Service
None

Miles of Plant: 6.0 (coaxial); None (fiber optic). Homes passed: 346.

President: John Long. Senior Vice President: Marc W. Cohen. General Manager: Brandon Dickey. Operations Manager: Perry Scarborough.

City fee: 3% of gross.

Ownership: Longview Communications (MSO).

HIGHWAY DD—Formerly served by Cebridge Connections. Now served by NIXA, MO [MO0068]. ICA: MO0092.

HOLDEN—Crystal Broadband Networks, PO Box 180336, Chicago, IL 60618. Phones: 877-319-0328; 630-206-0447. E-mail: info@crystalbn.com. Web Site: http://crystalbn.com. ICA: MO0145.

TV Market Ranking: Outside TV Markets (HOLDEN). Franchise award date: August 10, 1981. Franchise expiration date: N.A. Began: October 1, 1981.

Channel capacity: 31 (not 2-way capable). Channels available but not in use: N.A.

Basic Service
Subscribers: 451.
Programming (received off-air): KCTV (CBS) Kansas City; KMBC-TV (ABC) Kansas City; KMOS-TV (PBS) Sedalia; KPXE-TV (ION) Kansas City; KSHB-TV (NBC) Kansas City; KSMO-TV (MNT) Kansas City; WDAF-TV (FOX) Kansas City.

Programming (via satellite): Bravo; ESPN; MTV; QVC; TBS Superstation; Trinity Broadcasting Network; USA Network; VH1.
Fee: $29.95 installation; $19.95 monthly.
Expanded Basic Service 1
Subscribers: 324.
Programming (via satellite): AMC; CNN; Comedy Central; Country Music TV; Discovery Channel; Disney Channel; Headline News; Lifetime; Spike TV; Turner Network TV.
Fee: $20.00 monthly.
Pay Service 1
Pay Units: 35.
Programming (via satellite): Cinemax.
Fee: $11.95 monthly.
Pay Service 2
Pay Units: 59.
Programming (via satellite): HBO.
Fee: $11.95 monthly.
Pay Service 3
Pay Units: 47.
Programming (via satellite): Showtime.
Fee: $11.95 monthly.
Pay Service 4
Pay Units: 27.
Programming (via satellite): The Movie Channel.
Fee: $11.95 monthly.
Video-On-Demand: No
Pay-Per-View
Addressable homes: 7.
iN DEMAND (delivered digitally), Addressable: Yes; Urban Xtra (delivered digitally); Hot Choice (delivered digitally); ESPN Now (delivered digitally); Playboy TV (delivered digitally); Fresh (delivered digitally); Shorteez (delivered digitally); Sports PPV (delivered digitally).
Internet Service
Operational: Yes.
Telephone Service
None
Miles of Plant: 16.0 (coaxial); None (fiber optic). Homes passed: 866.
General Manager: Nidhin Johnson. Program Manager: Shawn Smith.
Franchise fee: 3% of gross.
Ownership: Crystal Broadband Networks (MSO).

HOLT—Formerly served by CableDirect. No longer in operation. ICA: MO0248.

HOLTS SUMMIT—Mediacom. Now served by JEFFERSON CITY, MO [MO0020]. ICA: MO0108.

HOPKINS—B & L Technologies LLC, 3329 270th St, Lenox, IA 50851. Phones: 800-798-5488; 641-348-2240. Fax: 641-348-2240. ICA: MO0261.
TV Market Ranking: Outside TV Markets (HOPKINS). Franchise award date: N.A. Franchise expiration date: N.A. Began: January 1, 1982.
Channel capacity: 31 (not 2-way capable). Channels available but not in use: 2.
Basic Service
Subscribers: 76.
Programming (received off-air): KHIN (PBS) Red Oak; KMTV-TV (CBS) Omaha; KPTM (FOX, MNT) Omaha; KQTV (ABC) St. Joseph; WOWT-TV (IND, NBC) Omaha.
Programming (via satellite): ABC Family Channel; CNN; Discovery Channel; ESPN; Spike TV; TBS Superstation; Turner Network TV; WGN America.
Fee: $20.00 installation; $23.16 monthly.
Pay Service 1
Pay Units: 50.
Programming (via satellite): Cinemax.
Fee: $11.00 monthly.
Pay Service 2
Pay Units: 44.
Programming (via satellite): HBO.
Fee: $12.95 monthly.
Video-On-Demand: No
Internet Service
Operational: No.
Telephone Service
None
Miles of Plant: 7.0 (coaxial); None (fiber optic). Homes passed: 271. Total homes in franchised area: 300.
President & General Manager: Robert Hintz. Office Manager: Linda Hintz.
Ownership: B & L Technologies LLC (MSO).

HORNERSVILLE—Base Cablevision, PO Box 553, Kennett, MO 63857-0553. Phone: 573-717-1568. ICA: MO0429.
TV Market Ranking: Outside TV Markets (HORNERSVILLE). Franchise award date: N.A. Franchise expiration date: N.A. Began: N.A.
Channel capacity: 31 (not 2-way capable). Channels available but not in use: N.A.
Basic Service
Subscribers: 132.
Programming (received off-air): KAIT (ABC) Jonesboro; KFVS-TV (CBS, CW) Cape Girardeau; WHBQ-TV (FOX) Memphis; WKNO (PBS) Memphis; WLMT (CW) Memphis; WMC-TV (NBC) Memphis; WPTY-TV (ABC) Memphis; WREG-TV (CBS) Memphis.
Programming (via satellite): ABC Family Channel; CNN; ESPN; TBS Superstation; Turner Network TV; Weather Channel; WGN America.
Current originations: Religious Access.
Fee: $15.00 installation; $24.19 monthly.
Pay Service 1
Pay Units: 9.
Programming (via satellite): Showtime.
Fee: $9.95 monthly.
Video-On-Demand: No
Internet Service
Operational: No.
Telephone Service
None
Miles of Plant: 4.0 (coaxial); None (fiber optic). Homes passed: 440.
Manager: Larry Jones. Office Manager: Linda Nixon.
Ownership: Base Cablevision Inc.

HOUSTON—Houston Cable Inc. Now served by WAYNESVILLE, MO [MO0023]. ICA: MO0146.

HUME—Formerly served by Midwest Cable Inc. No longer in operation. ICA: MO0335.

HURDLAND—Formerly served by CableDirect. No longer in operation. ICA: MO0435.

IBERIA—Longview Communications, 12007 Sunrise Valley Dr, Ste 375, Reston, VA 20191. Phones: 866-611-6565 (Customer service); 703-476-9101. Fax: 703-476-9107. Web Site: http://www.longviewcomm.com. ICA: MO0245.
TV Market Ranking: Below 100 (IBERIA). Franchise award date: N.A. Franchise expiration date: N.A. Began: January 1, 1984.
Channel capacity: 41 (not 2-way capable). Channels available but not in use: 2.
Basic Service
Subscribers: 87.
Programming (received off-air): KMIZ (ABC) Columbia; KMOS-TV (PBS) Sedalia; KNLJ (IND) Jefferson City; KOMU-TV (CW, NBC) Columbia; KRCG (CBS) Jefferson City; KSFX-TV (FOX) Springfield.
Programming (via satellite): C-SPAN; C-SPAN 2; Home Shopping Network; QVC; ShopNBC; Trinity Broadcasting Network.
Fee: $17.98 monthly.
Expanded Basic Service 1
Subscribers: N.A.
Programming (via satellite): ABC Family Channel; AMC; Animal Planet; Arts & Entertainment; Cartoon Network; CNN; Discovery Channel; Disney Channel; ESPN; ESPN 2; G4; Headline News; HGTV; History Channel; Lifetime; Nickelodeon; TBS Superstation; Travel Channel; Turner Network TV; USA Network; Weather Channel; WGN America.
Fee: $17.97 monthly.
Pay Service 1
Pay Units: 36.
Programming (via satellite): Showtime; The Movie Channel.
Fee: $8.95 monthly (TMC), $10.95 monthly each (Cinemax & Showtime), $12.95 monthly (HBO).
Video-On-Demand: No
Internet Service
Operational: No.
Telephone Service
None
Miles of Plant: 11.0 (coaxial); None (fiber optic). Homes passed: 425.
President: John Long. Senior Vice President: Marc W. Cohen. General Manager: Brandon Dickey. Operations Manager: Perry Scarborough.
City fee: 3% of gross.
Ownership: Longview Communications (MSO).

IMPERIAL—Charter Communications, 941 Charter Commons Dr, Saint Louis, MO 63017. Phone: 636-207-7044. Fax: 636-230-7034. Web Site: http://www.charter.com. Also serves Arnold, Crystal City, De Soto, Festus, Herculaneum, High Ridge, Hillsboro, Jefferson County & Pevely. ICA: MO0012.
TV Market Ranking: 11 (Arnold, Crystal City, Festus, Herculaneum, High Ridge, Hillsboro, IMPERIAL, Jefferson County (portions), Pevely); Outside TV Markets (De Soto, Jefferson County (portions)). Franchise award date: November 1, 1981. Franchise expiration date: N.A. Began: December 1, 1982.
Channel capacity: N.A. Channels available but not in use: N.A.
Basic Service
Subscribers: 15,668.
Programming (received off-air): KDNL-TV (ABC) St. Louis; KETC (PBS) St. Louis; KMOV (CBS) St. Louis; KNLC (IND) St. Louis; KPLR-TV (CW) St. Louis; KSDK (NBC) St. Louis; KTVI (FOX) St. Louis; WPXS (IND) Mount Vernon; WRBU (MNT) East St. Louis.
Programming (via satellite): AMC; C-SPAN; C-SPAN 2; Eternal Word TV Network; GRTV Network; Home Shopping Network; INSP; QVC; ShopNBC; TBS Superstation; Trinity Broadcasting Network; TV Guide Network; Univision; Weatherscan; WGN America.
Current originations: Educational Access; Public Access.
Fee: $29.99 installation.
Expanded Basic Service 1
Subscribers: 14,943.
Programming (via satellite): ABC Family Channel; AMC; Animal Planet; Arts & Entertainment; BET Networks; Bravo; Cartoon Network; CNBC; CNN; Comedy Central; Country Music TV; Discovery Channel; Disney Channel; E! Entertainment Television; ESPN; ESPN 2; Food Network; Fox Movie Channel; Fox News Channel; Fox Sports Net Midwest; FX; G4; Golf Channel; GSN; Hallmark Channel; Headline News; HGTV; History Channel; Lifetime; MSNBC; MTV; National Geographic Channel; Nickelodeon; Oxygen; SoapNet; Speed Channel; Spike TV; Style Network; Syfy; The Learning Channel; Toon Disney; Travel Channel; truTV; Turner Classic Movies; Turner Network TV; TV Land; USA Network; Versus; VH1; WE tv; Weather Channel.
Fee: $49.99 monthly.
Digital Basic Service
Subscribers: N.A.
Programming (via satellite): BBC America; Bio; Bloomberg Television; Discovery Digital Networks; Do-It-Yourself; Encore Action; ESPN Classic Sports; FitTV; Fox Sports World; FSN Digital Atlantic; FSN Digital Central; FSN Digital Pacific; Fuel TV; Fuse; GAS; Great American Country; History Channel International; Independent Film Channel; International Television (ITV); Lifetime Movie Network; MTV Networks Digital Suite; Music Choice; NFL Network; Nick Jr.; Nick Too; NickToons TV; Sundance Channel.
Digital Pay Service 1
Pay Units: 1,083.
Programming (via satellite): Cinemax (multiplexed); HBO (multiplexed); Showtime (multiplexed); Starz (multiplexed); The Movie Channel (multiplexed).
Video-On-Demand: Yes
Pay-Per-View
iN DEMAND (delivered digitally); Sports PPV (delivered digitally); ESPN Now (delivered digitally); Playboy TV (delivered digitally); Fresh (delivered digitally); Shorteez (delivered digitally).
Internet Service
Operational: Yes.
Broadband Service: Charter Pipeline.
Fee: $29.99 monthly.
Telephone Service
Digital: Operational
Fee: $29.99 monthly
Miles of Plant: 473.0 (coaxial); None (fiber optic). Homes passed: 30,310. Total homes in franchised area: 30,310.
Vice President & General Manager: Steve Trippe. Operations Director: Tom Williams. Marketing Director: Beverly Wall.
Ownership: Charter Communications Inc. (MSO).

INDEPENDENCE—Comcast Cable, PO Box 2000, 4700 Little Blue Pkwy, Independence, MO 64057. Phone: 816-795-8377. Fax: 816-795-0946. Web Site: http://www.comcast.com. Also serves Baldwin Park, Bates City, Blue Springs, Buckner, Grain Valley, Greenwood, Jackson County, Kansas City (portions), Lake Lotawano, Lake Tapawingo, Lake Winnebago, Lees Summit, Oak Grove, Odessa, Peculiar, Pleasant Hill, Raymore, Raytown, Sibley & Sugar Creek. ICA: MO0004.
TV Market Ranking: 22 (Baldwin Park, Bates City, Blue Springs, Buckner, Grain Valley, Greenwood, INDEPENDENCE, Jackson County, Kansas City (portions), Lake Lotawano, Lake Tapawingo, Lake Winnebago, Lees Summit, Oak Grove, Odessa, Peculiar, Pleasant Hill, Raymore, Raytown, Sibley, Sugar Creek). Franchise award date: N.A. Franchise expiration date: N.A. Began: November 1, 1971.
Channel capacity: 110 (operating 2-way). Channels available but not in use: 35.

Basic Service

Subscribers: 75,314.

Programming (received off-air): KCPT (PBS) Kansas City; KCTV (CBS) Kansas City; KCWE (CW) Kansas City; KMBC-TV (ABC) Kansas City; KMCI-TV (IND) Lawrence; KPXE-TV (ION) Kansas City; KSHB-TV (NBC) Kansas City; KSMO-TV (MNT) Kansas City; KUKC-LP Kansas City; WDAF-TV (FOX) Kansas City; allband FM.

Programming (via satellite): C-SPAN; Discovery Health Channel; Home Shopping Network; Product Information Network; QVC; WGN America.

Current originations: Government Access; Educational Access.

Fee: $40.00 installation; $11.95 monthly; $15.00 additional installation.

Expanded Basic Service 1

Subscribers: 62,536.

Programming (via satellite): ABC Family Channel; AMC; Animal Planet; Arts & Entertainment; BET Networks; Bravo; Cartoon Network; CNBC; CNN; Comedy Central; Discovery Channel; Disney Channel; E! Entertainment Television; ESPN; ESPN 2; Food Network; Fox News Channel; Fox Sports Net Kansas City; FX; Golf Channel; Headline News; HGTV; History Channel; Lifetime; MSNBC; MTV; Nickelodeon; Speed Channel; Spike TV; Style Network; Syfy; TBS Superstation; The Learning Channel; Travel Channel; truTV; Turner Classic Movies; Turner Network TV; TV Land; USA Network; VH1; Weather Channel.

Fee: $20.00 installation.

Digital Basic Service

Subscribers: N.A.

Programming (received off-air): KCPT (PBS) Kansas City; KCTV (CBS) Kansas City; KMBC-TV (ABC) Kansas City; KSHB-TV (NBC) Kansas City; WDAF-TV (FOX) Kansas City.

Programming (via satellite): 3 Angels Broadcasting Network; ABC Family HD; Animal Planet HD; Arts & Entertainment HD; BBC America; Big Ten Network; Bio; BYU Television; CBS College Sports Network; Cine Latino; Cine Mexicano; CMT Pure Country; CNN en Espanol; CNN HD; Cooking Channel; C-SPAN 2; C-SPAN 3; Current; Daystar TV Network; Discovery Channel HD; Discovery en Espanol; Discovery HD Theater; Discovery Kids Channel; Discovery Military Channel; Discovery Planet Green; Disney Channel HD; Disney XD; Do-It-Yourself; Encore (multiplexed); ESPN 2 HD; ESPN Classic Sports; ESPN Deportes; ESPN HD; ESPNews; FamilyNet; FearNet; Flix; Food Network HD; Fox Business Channel; Fox College Sports Atlantic; Fox College Sports Central; Fox College Sports Pacific; Fox News HD; Fox Reality Channel; Fox Soccer; Fox Sports en Espanol; FSN HD; Fuse; G4; GalaVision; Gol TV; Golf Channel HD; Great American Country; GSN; Hallmark Movie Channel; Halogen Network; HGTV HD; History Channel en Espanol; History Channel HD; History Channel International; ID Investigation Discovery; Independent Film Channel; INSP; Lifetime Movie Network; LOGO; MLB Network; MTV Hits; MTV Jams; MTV Tres; MTV2; mun2 television; Music Choice; National Geographic Channel; National Geographic Channel HD Network; NBA TV; NFL Network; NFL Network HD; NHL Network; Nick Jr.; Nick Too; NickToons TV; Outdoor Channel; Oxygen; Palladia; PBS Kids Sprout; Retirement Living; Science Channel; Science Channel HD; SoapNet; Starz IndiePlex; Starz RetroPlex; Sundance Channel; Syfy HD; TBS in HD; TeenNick; Telefutura; Tennis Channel; The Sportsman Channel; TLC HD; Trinity Broadcasting Network; Turner Network TV HD; TV Guide Interactive Inc.; TV One; Universal HD; USA Network HD; VeneMovies; Versus HD; VH1 Classic; VH1 Soul; WE tv; Weatherscan.

Fee: $12.96 monthly.

Digital Pay Service 1

Pay Units: N.A.

Programming (via satellite): Cinemax (multiplexed); Cinemax On Demand; HBO (multiplexed); HBO HD; HBO On Demand; Playboy TV; Showtime (multiplexed); Showtime HD; Starz (multiplexed); Starz HDTV; The Movie Channel (multiplexed).

Fee: $9.95 monthly (HBO, Cinemax, Showtime/TMC, Starz, or Playboy).

Video-On-Demand: Yes

Pay-Per-View

Addressable homes: 5,325.

Playboy TV (delivered digitally), Fee: $3.95-$5.95, Addressable: Yes; iN DEMAND (delivered digitally), Fee: $3.95; Penthouse TV (delivered digitally); Spice: Xcess (delivered digitally); iN DEMAND; ESPN Extra (delivered digitally); ESPN Now (delivered digitally); NBA TV (delivered digitally).

Internet Service

Operational: Yes.

Broadband Service: Comcast High Speed Internet.

Fee: $149.00 installation; $42.95 monthly; $7.00 modem lease; $299.00 modem purchase.

Telephone Service

Digital: Operational

Fee: $44.95 monthly

Miles of Plant: 1,629.0 (coaxial); 298.0 (fiber optic). Homes passed: 140,594.

General Manager: Kimberly Wepler. Chief Technician: Ken Covey. Marketing Director: Bill Rougdly. Customer Service Manager: Dana Price.

City fee: 5% of gross.

Ownership: Comcast Cable Communications Inc. (MSO).

IRONTON—Charter Communications. Now served by FARMINGTON, MO [MO0035]. ICA: MO0084.

IVY BEND—Formerly served by Almega Cable. No longer in operation. ICA: MO0169.

JACKSONVILLE—Formerly served by First Cable of Missouri Inc. No longer in operation. ICA: MO0379.

JAMESPORT—Formerly served by CableDirect. No longer in operation. ICA: MO0292.

JASPER—Mediacom. Now served by GRANBY, MO [MO0156]. ICA: MO0218.

JEFFERSON CITY—Mediacom, 901 N College Ave, Columbia, MO 65201. Phones: 573-443-1536; 417-875-5560 (Springfield regional office). Fax: 417-883-0265. Web Site: http://www.mediacomcable.com. Also serves Callaway County, Cole County (portions) & Holts Summit. ICA: MO0020.

TV Market Ranking: Below 100 (Callaway County, Cole County (portions), Holts Summit, JEFFERSON CITY). Franchise award date: April 20, 1971. Franchise expiration date: N.A. Began: May 1, 1970.

Channel capacity: 120 (operating 2-way). Channels available but not in use: N.A.

Basic Service

Subscribers: N.A.

Programming (received off-air): K02NQ Columbia; KMIZ (ABC) Columbia; KMOS-TV (PBS) Sedalia; KNLJ (IND) Jefferson City; KOMU-TV (CW, NBC) Columbia; KRCG (CBS) Jefferson City.

Programming (via microwave): KETC (PBS) St. Louis; KMBC-TV (ABC) Kansas City; KMOV (CBS) St. Louis; KPLR-TV (CW) St. Louis.

Programming (via satellite): C-SPAN 2; Discovery Channel; Home Shopping Network; LWS Local Weather Station; QVC; ShopNBC; TBS Superstation; TV Guide Network; WGN America.

Current originations: Government Access.

Fee: $60.00 installation; $13.25 monthly; $1.18 converter.

Expanded Basic Service 1

Subscribers: N.A.

Programming (via satellite): ABC Family Channel; AMC; Animal Planet; Arts & Entertainment; BET Networks; Bravo; Cartoon Network; CNBC; CNN; Comedy Central; Country Music TV; C-SPAN; Disney Channel; E! Entertainment Television; ESPN; ESPN 2; Eternal Word TV Network; Food Network; Fox News Channel; Fox Sports Net Midwest; FX; Hallmark Channel; Headline News; HGTV; History Channel; ION Television; Lifetime; MSNBC; MTV; Nickelodeon; Oxygen; Spike TV; Syfy; The Learning Channel; Travel Channel; truTV; Turner Network TV; TV Land; USA Network; VH1; WE tv; Weather Channel.

Fee: $45.95 monthly (Family Cable), 55.95 monthly (with Starz & Encore).

Digital Basic Service

Subscribers: N.A.

Programming (received off-air): KMIZ (ABC) Columbia; KMOS-TV (PBS) Sedalia.

Programming (via satellite): AmericanLife TV Network; BBC America; Bio; Bloomberg Television; Current; Discovery Digital Networks; Discovery HD Theater; ESPN; FitTV; Fox Movie Channel; Fox Soccer; Fuse; G4; GAS; Golf Channel; GSN; Halogen Network; HDNet; HDNet Movies; History Channel International; Independent Film Channel; Lifetime Movie Network; Lime; MTV Networks Digital Suite; MTV2; Music Choice; National Geographic Channel; Nick Jr.; NickToons TV; Outdoor Channel; Ovation; Speed Channel; Style Network; Toon Disney; Trinity Broadcasting Network; Turner Classic Movies; Universal HD; Versus.

Digital Pay Service 1

Pay Units: N.A.

Programming (via satellite): Cinemax (multiplexed); Encore (multiplexed); Flix; HBO (multiplexed); Showtime (multiplexed); Starz (multiplexed); Sundance Channel; The Movie Channel (multiplexed).

Video-On-Demand: Yes

Pay-Per-View

ESPN (delivered digitally); Movies (delivered digitally); Fresh (delivered digitally); Shorteez (delivered digitally); Playboy TV (delivered digitally).

Internet Service

Operational: Yes.

Broadband Service: Mediacom High Speed Internet.

Fee: $49.95 monthly.

Telephone Service

Digital: Operational

Miles of Plant: 290.0 (coaxial); 71.0 (fiber optic). Additional miles planned: 13.0 (coaxial).

Regional Vice President: Bill Copeland. Operations Director: Bryan Gann. Regional Technical Operations Director: Alan Freedman. Technical Operations Manager: Roger Shearer. Marketing Director: Will Kuebler.

City fee: 5% of gross.

Ownership: Mediacom LLC (MSO).

JONESBURG—US Cable, 647 Clinic Rd, Hannibal, MO 63401. Phone: 573-581-2404. Fax: 573-581-4053. Web Site: http://www.uscable.com. ICA: MO0463.

TV Market Ranking: Outside TV Markets (JONESBURG). Franchise award date: N.A. Franchise expiration date: N.A. Began: N.A.

Channel capacity: N.A. Channels available but not in use: N.A.

Basic Service

Subscribers: N.A. Included in Hannibal

Programming (received off-air): KDNL-TV (ABC) St. Louis; KETC (PBS) St. Louis; KMOV (CBS) St. Louis; KNLC (IND) St. Louis; KOMU-TV (CW, NBC) Columbia; KPLR-TV (CW) St. Louis; KRCG (CBS) Jefferson City; KSDK (NBC) St. Louis; KTVI (FOX) St. Louis.

Programming (via satellite): Bravo; TBS Superstation; Turner Network TV; WGN America.

Current originations: Public Access.

Fee: $22.09 monthly.

Expanded Basic Service 1

Subscribers: N.A.

Programming (via satellite): ABC Family Channel; Animal Planet; Arts & Entertainment; Cartoon Network; CNN; Comedy Central; Country Music TV; Discovery Channel; Disney Channel; ESPN; ESPN 2; Fox Sports Net Midwest; FX; Headline News; HGTV; History Channel; Home Shopping Network; Lifetime; Nickelodeon; Spike TV; The Learning Channel; Turner Classic Movies; TV Land; USA Network; VH1; Weather Channel.

Fee: $19.12 monthly.

Pay Service 1

Pay Units: 65.

Programming (via satellite): Cinemax.

Fee: $25.00 installation; $11.95 monthly.

Pay Service 2

Pay Units: N.A.

Programming (via satellite): HBO; Showtime.

Fee: $11.95 monthly (each).

Video-On-Demand: No

Internet Service

Operational: No.

Telephone Service

None

Homes passed & total homes in franchised area included in Hannibal

Regional Administrative Director: Rebecca Bramblett. Technical Operations Manager: Roger Young. Marketing Director: Rita Watson.

Ownership: US Cable Corp. (MSO).; Comcast Cable Communications Inc. (MSO).

JOPLIN—Cable One, PO Box 2525, 112 E 32nd St, Joplin, MO 64803. Phone: 417-624-6340. Fax: 417-623-5413. E-mail: webmaster@cableone.net. Web Site: http://www.cableone.net. Also serves Carterville, Cliff Village, Leawood, Newton County, Redings Mill, Saginaw, Shoal Creek Drive, Silver Creek & Webb City. ICA: MO0016.

TV Market Ranking: Below 100 (Carterville, Cliff Village, JOPLIN, Leawood, Redings Mill, Saginaw, Shoal Creek Drive, Silver Creek, Webb City). Franchise award date: N.A. Franchise expiration date: N.A. Began: March 1, 1967.

Channel capacity: 63 (operating 2-way). Channels available but not in use: N.A.

Basic Service

Subscribers: 125,000.

Programming (received off-air): KFJX (FOX) Pittsburg; KOAM-TV (CBS) Pittsburg; KODE-TV (ABC) Joplin; KOZJ (PBS) Joplin; KSNF (NBC) Joplin; 4 FMs.

Programming (via satellite): ABC Family Channel; AMC; Animal Planet; Arts & Entertainment; BET Networks; Bravo; Cartoon Network; CNBC; CNN; Comedy Central; Country Music TV; C-SPAN; C-SPAN 2; CW+; Discovery Channel; Disney Channel; E! Entertainment Television; ESPN; ESPN 2; ESPN Classic Sports; Food Network; Fox News Channel; Fox Sports Net Midwest; FX; Headline News; HGTV; History Channel; Home Shopping Network; ION Television; Lifetime; MSNBC; MTV; Nickelodeon; QVC; ShopNBC; Spike TV; Syfy; TBS Superstation; The Learning Channel; Travel Channel; Trinity Broadcasting Network; Turner Classic Movies; Turner Network TV; TV Guide Network; TV Land; USA Network; VH1; Weather Channel; WGN America.

Current originations: Educational Access; Religious Access; Government Access.

Fee: $30.00 installation; $46.00 monthly.

Digital Basic Service

Subscribers: 3,612.

Programming (received off-air): KOAM-TV (CBS) Pittsburg; KOZJ (PBS) Joplin.

Programming (via satellite): 3 Angels Broadcasting Network; Bio; Boomerang; BYU Television; Canales N; Discovery Digital Networks; ESPN Classic Sports; ESPN HD; ESPNews; FamilyNet; Fox College Sports Atlantic; Fox College Sports Central; Fox College Sports Pacific; Fox Movie Channel; Fox Soccer; Fuel TV; G4; Golf Channel; Great American Country; Hallmark Channel; History Channel International; INSP; Music Choice; National Geographic Channel; Outdoor Channel; SoapNet; Speed Channel; Toon Disney; Trinity Broadcasting Network; truTV; Turner Network TV HD; Universal HD.

Fee: $30.00 installation; $37.50 monthly.

Digital Pay Service 1

Pay Units: N.A.

Programming (via satellite): Cinemax (multiplexed); Encore (multiplexed); Flix; HBO (multiplexed); HBO HD; Showtime (multiplexed); Showtime HD; Starz (multiplexed); Sundance Channel; The Movie Channel (multiplexed); The Movie Channel HD.

Fee: $15.00 monthly (each package).

Video-On-Demand: No

Pay-Per-View

Movies (delivered digitally); Pleasure (delivered digitally); ESPN Now (delivered digitally); Ten Clips (delivered digitally); Ten Blox (delivered digitally); Ten Blue (delivered digitally).

Internet Service

Operational: Yes. Began: September 1, 2002.

Subscribers: 5,686.

Broadband Service: CableONE.net.

Fee: $75.00 installation; $43.00 monthly.

Telephone Service

Digital: Operational

Fee: $75.00 installation; $39.95 monthly

Miles of Plant: 455.0 (coaxial); 315.0 (fiber optic).

General Manager: Charlotte McClure. Plant Manager: Terry Peacock. Marketing Director: Jeff Denefrio.

Ownership: Cable One Inc. (MSO).

JOPLIN (northwest)—Formerly served by Almega Cable. No longer in operation. ICA: MO0205.

KAHOKA—Kahoka Communications Cable Co., 250 N Morgan St, Kahoka, MO 63445-1433. Phone: 660-727-3711. Fax: 660-727-3750. E-mail: sgkahcom@nemr.net. ICA: MO0150.

TV Market Ranking: Outside TV Markets (KAHOKA). Franchise award date: April 1, 1984. Franchise expiration date: N.A. Began: September 1, 1984.

Channel capacity: 80 (not 2-way capable). Channels available but not in use: 17.

Basic Service

Subscribers: 769.

Programming (received off-air): KHQA-TV (ABC, CBS) Hannibal; KTVO (ABC) Kirksville; KYOU-TV (FOX) Ottumwa; WGEM-TV (CW, NBC) Quincy; WTJR (IND) Quincy.

Programming (via satellite): ABC Family Channel; AMC; Animal Planet; Arts & Entertainment; Cartoon Network; CNN; Comedy Central; Country Music TV; C-SPAN; Discovery Channel; Disney Channel; ESPN; ESPN 2; ESPN Classic Sports; Fox Sports Net; FX; G4; Great American Country; Headline News; HGTV; History Channel; Home Shopping Network; INSP; Lifetime; MSNBC; MTV; Nickelodeon; Outdoor Channel; QVC; Shop at Home; Speed Channel; Spike TV; Syfy; TBS Superstation; The Learning Channel; truTV; Turner Classic Movies; Turner Network TV; TV Land; USA Network; VH1; Weather Channel; WGN America.

Current originations: Public Access.

Fee: $20.00 installation; $27.00 monthly.

Pay Service 1

Pay Units: 89.

Programming (via satellite): Cinemax (multiplexed).

Fee: $15.00 installation; $9.95 monthly.

Pay Service 2

Pay Units: 118.

Programming (via satellite): HBO (multiplexed).

Fee: $15.00 installation; $12.95 monthly.

Pay Service 3

Pay Units: 55.

Programming (via satellite): Flix; Showtime; The Movie Channel.

Fee: $15.00 installation; $12.95 monthly (Showtime, TMC, Flix).

Video-On-Demand: No

Internet Service

Operational: Yes.

Fee: $24.95 monthly.

Telephone Service

None

Miles of Plant: 22.0 (coaxial); None (fiber optic). Homes passed: 1,100. Total homes in franchised area: 1,100.

Manager: Sandie Hopp. Chief Technician: Scott Goben.

Ownership: City of Kahoka.

KANSAS CITY—Formerly served by People's Choice TV. No longer in operation. ICA: MO0453.

KANSAS CITY—Time Warner Cable, 6550 Winchester Ave, Kansas City, MO 64133-4660. Phone: 816-358-5360. Fax: 816-358-7987. Web Site: http://www.timewarnercable.com/kansascity. Also serves Bonner Springs, Countryside, De Soto, Edwardsville, Edwardsville Park, Fairway, Fort Leavenworth, Gardner, Johnson County (northeastern portion), Kansas City (south of Kaw River), Lake of the Forest, Lake Quivera, Lansing, Leavenworth, Leavenworth County (portions), Leawood, Lenexa, Merriam, Mission, Mission Hills, Mission Woods, Overland Park, Prairie Village, Roeland Park, Shawnee, Westwood, Westwood Hills & Wyandotte County (portions), KS; Avondale, Belton, Claycomo, Ferrelview, Gladstone, Glenaire, Grandview, Houston Lake, Independence, John Knox Village, Kearney, Lake Quivera, Lake Waukomis, Lee's Summit, Liberty, Lone Jack, North Kansas City, Northmoor, Oaks Village, Oakview, Oakwood, Oakwood Park, Parkville, Platte City, Platte County (portions), Platte Woods, Pleasant Valley, Richards-Gebaur AFB, Riverside, Smithville, Tracy, Trimble, Unity Village, Weatherby Lake & Weston, MO. ICA: MO0001.

TV Market Ranking: 22 (Avondale, Belton, Bonner Springs, Claycomo, Countryside, De Soto, Edwardsville, Edwardsville Park, Fairway, Ferrelview, Fort Leavenworth, Gardner, Gladstone, Glenaire, Grandview, Houston Lake, Independence, John Knox Village, Johnson County (northeastern portion), KANSAS CITY, Kansas City (south of Kaw River), Kearney, Lake of the Forest, Lake Quivira, Lake Waukomis, Lansing, Leavenworth, Leavenworth County (portions), Leawood, Lee's Summit, Lenexa, Liberty, Lone Jack, Merriam, Mission, Mission Hills, Mission Woods, North Kansas City, Northmoor, Oaks Village, Oakview, Oakwood, Oakwood Park, Overland Park, Parkville, Platte City, Platte County (portions), Platte Woods, Pleasant Valley, Prairie Village, Richards-Gebaur AFB, Riverside, Roeland Park, Shawnee, Smithville, Tracy, Trimble, Unity Village, Weatherby Lake, Weston, Westwood, Westwood Hills, Wyandotte County (portions)); Below 100 (Leavenworth County (portions), Platte County (portions)). Franchise award date: January 1, 1979. Franchise expiration date: N.A. Began: May 19, 1980.

Channel capacity: N.A. Channels available but not in use: N.A.

Basic Service

Subscribers: 302,000.

Programming (received off-air): KCPT (PBS) Kansas City; KCTV (CBS) Kansas City; KCWE (CW) Kansas City; KMBC-TV (ABC) Kansas City; KMCI-TV (IND) Lawrence; KPXE-TV (ION) Kansas City; KSHB-TV (NBC) Kansas City; KSMO-TV (MNT) Kansas City; KTWU (PBS) Topeka; WDAF-TV (FOX) Kansas City.

Programming (via satellite): Shop at Home; TBS Superstation; WGN America.

Current originations: Leased Access; Government Access; Educational Access; Public Access.

Fee: $47.21 installation; $10.77 monthly.

Expanded Basic Service 1

Subscribers: 293,000.

Programming (via satellite): ABC Family Channel; AMC; Animal Planet; Arts & Entertainment; BET Networks; Bravo; Cartoon Network; CNBC; CNN; Comedy Central; Country Music TV; C-SPAN; C-SPAN 2; Discovery Channel; Disney Channel; E! Entertainment Television; ESPN; ESPN 2; ESPN Classic Sports; ESPNews; Food Network; Fox News Channel; Fox Sports Net Midwest; FX; Golf Channel; Hallmark Channel; Headline News; HGTV; History Channel; Home Shopping Network; Lifetime; MoviePlex; MSNBC; MTV; National Geographic Channel; Nickelodeon; Oxygen; QVC; ShopNBC; Sneak Prevue; SoapNet; Spike TV; Style Network; Syfy; The Learning Channel; Travel Channel; truTV; Turner Classic Movies; Turner Network TV; TV Guide Network; TV Land; USA Network; Versus; VH1; WE tv; Weather Channel.

Fee: $38.47 monthly.

Digital Basic Service

Subscribers: 195,000.

Programming (via satellite): AmericanLife TV Network; America's Store; ART America; BBC America; Bio; Black Family Channel; Bloomberg Television; Boomerang; Canales N; Cooking Channel; C-SPAN 3; Discovery Digital Networks; Do-It-Yourself; Encore Action; ESPNews; Eternal Word TV Network; Filipino Channel; Flix; Fox Movie Channel; Fox Sports World; FSN Digital Atlantic; FSN Digital Central; FSN Digital Pacific; G4; GAS; Great American Country; GSN; Halogen Network; History Channel International; Independent Film Channel; Lifetime Movie Network; Lifetime Real Women; MTV2; MuchMusic Network; Music Choice; NBA TV; Nick Jr.; Outdoor Channel; Ovation; Russian Television Network; Speed Channel; Sundance Channel; The Word Network; Toon Disney; Trinity Broadcasting Network; TV Asia; TV5 USA; VH1 Classic.

Fee: $16.25 monthly.

Digital Pay Service 1

Pay Units: 116,000.

Programming (via satellite): Cinemax (multiplexed); HBO (multiplexed); Showtime (multiplexed); Starz (multiplexed); The Movie Channel (multiplexed).

Video-On-Demand: Yes

Pay-Per-View
Addressable homes: 158,032.
Hot Choice (delivered digitally), Fee: $3.95, Addressable: Yes; iN DEMAND (delivered digitally); Playboy TV (delivered digitally); Pleasure (delivered digitally); Fresh (delivered digitally); Shorteez (delivered digitally).
Internet Service
Operational: Yes.
Subscribers: 20,500.
Broadband Service: Road Runner.
Fee: $39.95 installation; $44.95 monthly.
Telephone Service
Digital: Operational
Subscribers: 103,000.
Fee: $39.95 monthly
Miles of Plant: 6,296.0 (coaxial); 1,713.0 (fiber optic). Homes passed: 602,000. Total homes in franchised area: 735,000.
President: Roger Ponder. Vice President, Engineering: Bob Porter. Vice President, Marketing: Dennis Narciso. General Manager: Dale Fox. Public Affairs Director: Damon Shelby Porter. Public Affairs Manager: Lori Hanson.
City fee: 3% -5% of gross.
Ownership: Time Warner Cable (MSO).

KANSAS CITY (portions)—Formerly served by Lenexa, KS [KS0462]. SureWest Broadband. This cable system has converted to IPTV, 9647 Lackman Rd, Lenexa, KS 66219. Phones: 913-825-3000; 913-825-2800. Fax: 913-322-9901. Web Site: http://www.surewest.com. ICA: MO5190.
TV Market Ranking: 22 (KANSAS CITY (PORTIONS)).
Channel capacity: N.A. Channels available but not in use: N.A.
Video-On-Demand: Yes
Internet Service
Operational: Yes.
Telephone Service
Digital: Operational
Ownership: SureWest Broadband.

KENNETT—Windjammer Cable, 4400 PGA Blvd, Ste 902, Palm Beach Gardens, FL 33410. Phones: 877-450-5558; 561-775-1208. Fax: 561-775-7811. Web Site: http://www.windjammercable.com. Also serves Dunklin County & Senath. ICA: MO0032.
TV Market Ranking: Below 100 (Dunklin County (portions)); Outside TV Markets (Dunklin County (portions), KENNETT, Senath). Franchise award date: September 17, 1963. Franchise expiration date: N.A. Began: January 1, 1966.
Channel capacity: 136 (operating 2-way). Channels available but not in use: 44.
Basic Service
Subscribers: 4,300.
Programming (received off-air): KAIT (ABC) Jonesboro; KBSI (FOX) Cape Girardeau; KFVS-TV (CBS, CW) Cape Girardeau; KPOB-TV (ABC) Poplar Bluff; KTEJ (PBS) Jonesboro; KVTJ-DT (IND) Jonesboro; WHBQ-TV (FOX) Memphis; WLMT (CW) Memphis; WMC-TV (NBC) Memphis; WREG-TV (CBS) Memphis; 10 FMs.
Programming (via satellite): Arts & Entertainment; TBS Superstation; WGN America.
Current originations: Religious Access.
Fee: $35.80 installation; $16.58 monthly; $7.95 converter.
Expanded Basic Service 1
Subscribers: 3,500.
Programming (via satellite): ABC Family Channel; AMC; Animal Planet; Arts & Entertainment; BET Networks; Bravo; Cartoon Network; CNBC; CNN; Comedy Central; Country Music TV; C-SPAN 2; Discovery Channel; Discovery Health Channel; Disney Channel; E! Entertainment Television; ESPN; ESPN 2; ESPN Classic Sports; FitTV; Food Network; Fox News Channel; Fox Sports Net Midwest; FX; Golf Channel; Great American Country; Hallmark Channel; Headline News; HGTV; History Channel; Home Shopping Network; INSP; Lifetime; Lifetime Movie Network; MSNBC; MTV; National Geographic Channel; Nickelodeon; Outdoor Channel; Oxygen; QVC; ShopNBC; Spike TV; Syfy; The Learning Channel; Travel Channel; Trinity Broadcasting Network; truTV; Turner Classic Movies; Turner Network TV; TV Guide Network; USA Network; VH1; WE tv; Weather Channel.
Fee: $33.68 monthly.
Digital Basic Service
Subscribers: 960.
Programming (received off-air): KAIT (ABC) Jonesboro; KFVS-TV (CBS, CW) Cape Girardeau; KTEJ (PBS) Jonesboro; WLMT (CW) Memphis; WMC-TV (NBC) Memphis.
Programming (via satellite): America Channel; BBC America; Bio; Bloomberg Television; Discovery Channel; Discovery Digital Networks; ESPN; ESPNews; Fox Sports World; Fuse; G4; GAS; GSN; Halogen Network; HBO; HDNet; HDNet Movies; History Channel International; INHD; MTV Hits; MTV2; Music Choice; Nick Jr.; NickToons TV; Ovation; Science Television; Showtime; Speed Channel; Style Network; Toon Disney; Turner Network TV; Versus; VH1 Classic.
Fee: $53.99 monthly.
Digital Pay Service 1
Pay Units: N.A.
Programming (via satellite): Cinemax (multiplexed); Encore; Fox Movie Channel; HBO (multiplexed); Showtime (multiplexed); Starz (multiplexed); Sundance Channel; The Movie Channel (multiplexed); WAM! America's Kidz Network.
Fee: $12.00 monthly (each).
Video-On-Demand: Planned
Pay-Per-View
iN DEMAND (delivered digitally), Addressable: Yes; Shorteez (delivered digitally), Addressable: Yes; Playboy TV (delivered digitally), Addressable: Yes; Hot Choice (delivered digitally), Addressable: Yes; TEN Blue (delivered digitally), Addressable: Yes; TEN Clip (delivered digitally), Addressable: Yes; TEN Blox (delivered digitally), Addressable: Yes; Fresh (delivered digitally), Addressable: Yes.
Internet Service
Operational: Yes. Began: December 15, 2004.
Subscribers: 720.
Broadband Service: In-house.
Fee: $19.95-$49.99 installation; $44.95 monthly.
Telephone Service
Analog: Not Operational
Digital: Operational
Fee: $49.95 monthly
Miles of Plant: 112.0 (coaxial); 42.0 (fiber optic). Homes passed: 6,800.
General Manager: Timothy Evard. Operations Director: Belinda Graham. Engineering Director: Mike Earehart. Finance & Accounting Director: Cindy Johnson.
City fee: 2%-3% of gross.
Ownership: Windjammer Communications LLC (MSO).

KEYTESVILLE—Longview Communications, 12007 Sunrise Valley Dr, Ste 375, Reston, VA 20191. Phones: 866-611-6565 (Customer service); 703-476-9101. Fax: 703-476-9107. Web Site: http://www.longviewcomm.com. ICA: MO0230.
TV Market Ranking: Outside TV Markets (KEYTESVILLE). Franchise award date: N.A. Franchise expiration date: N.A. Began: May 1, 1983.
Channel capacity: 41 (not 2-way capable). Channels available but not in use: N.A.
Basic Service
Subscribers: 91.
Programming (received off-air): KMIZ (ABC) Columbia; KMOS-TV (PBS) Sedalia; KOMU-TV (CW, NBC) Columbia; KQFX-LD Columbia; KRCG (CBS) Jefferson City.
Programming (via satellite): ABC Family Channel; AMC; Animal Planet; Arts & Entertainment; Classic Arts Showcase; CNN; Country Music TV; C-SPAN; Discovery Channel; Disney Channel; E! Entertainment Television; ESPN; ESPN 2; Food Network; Fox News Channel; Hallmark Channel; Headline News; History Channel; Home Shopping Network; Lifetime; MSNBC; Nickelodeon; Speed Channel; Spike TV; TBS Superstation; The Learning Channel; Trinity Broadcasting Network; Turner Network TV; USA Network; Weather Channel.
Fee: $37.95 monthly.
Pay Service 1
Pay Units: 36.
Programming (via satellite): Cinemax; HBO; Showtime; The Movie Channel.
Fee: $8.95 monthly (TMC), $10.95 monthly (Cinemax or Showtime), $12.95 monthly (HBO).
Video-On-Demand: No
Internet Service
Operational: No.
Telephone Service
None
Miles of Plant: 8.0 (coaxial); None (fiber optic). Homes passed: 269.
President: John Long. Senior Vice President: Marc W. Cohen. General Manager: Brandon Dickey. Operations Manager: Perry Scarborough.
City fee: 3% of gross.
Ownership: Longview Communications (MSO).

KIMBERLING CITY—Mediacom. Now served by FORSYTH, MO [MO0126]. ICA: MO0407.

KING CITY—Longview Communications, 1923 N Main, Higginsville, MO 64037. Phone: 866-611-6565. Fax: 866-329-4790. Web Site: http://www.longviewcomm.com. ICA: MO0214.
TV Market Ranking: Below 100 (KING CITY). Franchise award date: N.A. Franchise expiration date: N.A. Began: September 1, 1983.
Channel capacity: 41 (not 2-way capable). Channels available but not in use: 2.
Basic Service
Subscribers: 110.
Programming (received off-air): KCPT (PBS) Kansas City; KCTV (CBS) Kansas City; KCWE (CW) Kansas City; KMBC-TV (ABC) Kansas City; KQTV (ABC) St. Joseph; KSHB-TV (NBC) Kansas City; KSMO-TV (MNT) Kansas City; KTAJ-TV (TBN) St. Joseph; WDAF-TV (FOX) Kansas City; allband FM.
Programming (via satellite): ABC Family Channel; AMC; Arts & Entertainment; CNN; Country Music TV; Discovery Channel; Disney Channel; ESPN; ESPN 2; Nickelodeon; QVC; Spike TV; TBS Superstation; Turner Network TV; USA Network; Weather Channel; WGN America.
Fee: $35.95 installation; $37.95 monthly.
Pay Service 1
Pay Units: 43.
Programming (via satellite): Encore; Showtime; Starz; The Movie Channel.
Fee: $8.95 monthly (TMC), $9.95 monthly (Starz/Encore), $10.95 monthly (Showtime),.
Video-On-Demand: No
Internet Service
Operational: No.
Telephone Service
None
Miles of Plant: 9.0 (coaxial); None (fiber optic). Homes passed: 396.
President: John Long. Senior Vice President: Marc W. Cohen. General Manager: Brandon Dickey. Operations Manager: Perry Scarborough.
City fee: 3% of gross.
Ownership: Longview Communications (MSO).

KINGSTON—Formerly served by First Cable of Missouri Inc. No longer in operation. ICA: MO0334.

KINLOCH—Formerly served by Data Cablevision. No longer in operation. ICA: MO0153.

KIRKSVILLE—Cable One, PO Box D, 402 N Main St, Kirksville, MO 63501. Phone: 660-665-7066. Fax: 660-627-2603. E-mail: jking@cableone.net. Web Site: http://www.cableone.net. Also serves Adair County. ICA: MO0027.
TV Market Ranking: Below 100 (Adair County, KIRKSVILLE). Franchise award date: September 8, 1964. Franchise expiration date: N.A. Began: N.A.
Channel capacity: 74 (operating 2-way). Channels available but not in use: 11.
Basic Service
Subscribers: 5,125.
Programming (received off-air): KHQA-TV (ABC, CBS) Hannibal; KTVO (ABC) Kirksville; KYOU-TV (FOX) Ottumwa; WGEM-TV (CW, NBC) Quincy; 1 FM.
Programming (via microwave): KCPT (PBS) Kansas City; KCTV (CBS) Kansas City; KSHB-TV (NBC) Kansas City.
Programming (via satellite): America's Store; C-SPAN; C-SPAN 2; Home Shopping Network; QVC; TBS Superstation; TV Guide Network; WGN America.

Current originations: Public Access.
Fee: $75.00 installation; $46.00 monthly.
Expanded Basic Service 1
Subscribers: N.A.
Programming (via satellite): ABC Family Channel; AMC; Animal Planet; Arts & Entertainment; BET Networks; Cartoon Network; CNBC; CNN; Comedy Central; Country Music TV; Discovery Channel; Disney Channel; ESPN; ESPN 2; Food Network; Fox News Channel; Fox Sports Net Midwest; FX; Headline News; HGTV; History Channel; Lifetime; MSNBC; MTV; Nickelodeon; Product Information Network; Spike TV; Syfy; The Learning Channel; Turner Classic Movies; Turner Network TV; TV Land; USA Network; VH1; Weather Channel.
Fee: $42.50 monthly.
Digital Basic Service
Subscribers: 2,000.
Programming (received off-air): KTVO (ABC) Kirksville.
Programming (via satellite): 3 Angels Broadcasting Network; Bio; Boomerang; BYU Television; Canales N; Discovery Digital Networks; DMX Music; ESPN Classic Sports; ESPNews; FamilyNet; Fox College Sports Atlantic; Fox College Sports Central; Fox College Sports Pacific; Fox HD; Fox Movie Channel; Fox Soccer; Fuel TV; G4; Golf Channel; Great American Country; Hallmark Channel; History Channel International; INSP; National Geographic Channel; Outdoor Channel; SoapNet; Speed Channel; Toon Disney; Trinity Broadcasting Network; truTV; Turner Network TV HD; TVG Network; Universal HD.
Digital Pay Service 1
Pay Units: N.A.
Programming (via satellite): Cinemax (multiplexed); Encore (multiplexed); Flix; HBO (multiplexed); Showtime (multiplexed); Showtime HD; Starz (multiplexed); Sundance Channel; The Movie Channel (multiplexed); The Movie Channel HD.
Fee: $15.00 monthly (HBO, Cinemax, Showtime/TMC/Flix/Sundance, or Starz/Encore).
Video-On-Demand: No
Pay-Per-View
Addressable homes: 1,882.
iN Demand, Fee: $3.95-$8.95, Addressable: Yes; iN DEMAND (delivered digitally); Pleasure (delivered digitally); Sports PPV (delivered digitally); Ten Clips (delivered digitally); Ten Blox (delivered digitally); Ten Blue (delivered digitally).
Internet Service
Operational: Yes. Began: January 1, 1988.
Subscribers: 2,104.
Broadband Service: CableONE.net.
Fee: $75.00 installation; $43.00 monthly.
Telephone Service
Digital: Operational
Fee: $75.00 installation; $39.95 monthly
Miles of Plant: 130.0 (coaxial); 47.0 (fiber optic). Homes passed: 9,065. Total homes in franchised area: 9,160.
Manager: Joann King. Chief Technician: Martin Stitzer.
City fee: 3% of gross.
Ownership: Cable One Inc. (MSO).

KNOB NOSTER—Charter Communications. Now served by WARRENSBURG, OH [MO0425]. ICA: MO0061.

KNOX CITY—Formerly served by CableDirect. No longer in operation. ICA: MO0408.

LA BELLE—Formerly served by Westcom. No longer in operation. ICA: MO0219.

LA MONTE—Longview Communications, 12007 Sunrise Valley Dr, Ste 375, Reston, VA 20191. Phones: 866-611-6565 (Customer service); 703-476-9101. Fax: 703-476-9107. Web Site: http://www.longviewcomm.com. ICA: MO0224.
TV Market Ranking: Below 100 (LA MONTE). Franchise award date: N.A. Franchise expiration date: N.A. Began: September 1, 1980.
Channel capacity: 41 (not 2-way capable). Channels available but not in use: N.A.
Basic Service
Subscribers: 60.
Programming (received off-air): KCTV (CBS) Kansas City; KCWE (CW) Kansas City; KMBC-TV (ABC) Kansas City; KMOS-TV (PBS) Sedalia; KPXE-TV (ION) Kansas City; KSHB-TV (NBC) Kansas City; KSMO-TV (MNT) Kansas City; WDAF-TV (FOX) Kansas City.
Programming (via satellite): Classic Arts Showcase; C-SPAN; INSP; QVC.
Fee: $19.98 monthly.
Expanded Basic Service 1
Subscribers: N.A.
Programming (via satellite): ABC Family Channel; AMC; Animal Planet; Arts & Entertainment; CNN; Discovery Channel; Disney Channel; E! Entertainment Television; ESPN; ESPN 2; Fox News Channel; Great American Country; Headline News; History Channel; Lifetime; MSNBC; Speed Channel; TBS Superstation; The Learning Channel; Turner Network TV; USA Network; Weather Channel; WGN America.
Fee: $17.97 monthly.
Pay Service 1
Pay Units: 112.
Programming (via satellite): Cinemax; HBO; Showtime; The Movie Channel.
Fee: $8.95 monthly (TMC), $10.95 monthly (Cinemax or Showtime), $12.95 monthly (HBO).
Video-On-Demand: No
Internet Service
Operational: No.
Telephone Service
None
Miles of Plant: 6.0 (coaxial); None (fiber optic). Homes passed: 449.
President: John Long. Senior Vice President: Marc W. Cohen. General Manager: Brandon Dickey. Operations Manager: Perry Scarborough.
Ownership: Longview Communications (MSO).

LA PLATA—Formerly served by Almega Cable. No longer in operation. ICA: MO0162.

LACLEDE—Longview Communications. Now served by MEADVILLE, MO [MO0434]. ICA: MO0307.

LAKE SHERWOOD—St. Charles Broadband, 700 Fountain Lakes Blvd, Ste 100, Saint Charles, MO 63301-4353. Phone: 636-916-3706. Web Site: http://www.c3broadband.com. Also serves Defiance, Marthasville, New Melle, St. Charles County & Warren County. ICA: MO0458.
TV Market Ranking: 11 (Defiance, New Melle, St. Charles County (portions)); Outside TV Markets (LAKE SHERWOOD, Marthasville, Warren County, St. Charles County (portions)). Franchise award date: January 1, 1988. Franchise expiration date: N.A. Began: N.A.
Channel capacity: 40 (not 2-way capable). Channels available but not in use: None.
Basic Service
Subscribers: 500.
Programming (received off-air): KDNL-TV (ABC) St. Louis; KETC (PBS) St. Louis; KMOV (CBS) St. Louis; KNLC (IND) St. Louis; KPLR-TV (CW) St. Louis; KSDK (NBC) St. Louis; KTVI (FOX) St. Louis; WRBU (MNT) East St. Louis.
Programming (via satellite): ABC Family Channel; AMC; Arts & Entertainment; CNN; C-SPAN; Discovery Channel; Disney Channel; ESPN; Headline News; Home Shopping Network; Lifetime; Nickelodeon; Spike TV; Syfy; TBS Superstation; The Learning Channel; Turner Network TV; USA Network; VH1; Weather Channel; WGN America.
Fee: $45.00 installation; $23.50 monthly; $1.55 converter.
Pay Service 1
Pay Units: 128.
Programming (via satellite): Cinemax.
Fee: $11.00 monthly.
Pay Service 2
Pay Units: 219.
Programming (via satellite): HBO.
Fee: $11.00 monthly.
Internet Service
Operational: No.
Telephone Service
None
Miles of Plant: 52.0 (coaxial); None (fiber optic). Additional miles planned: 6.0 (coaxial). Homes passed: 2,500.
Manager: Dan McKay. Chief Technician: Mike McKay.
Ownership: C3 Broadband Integration.

LAKE ST. LOUIS—Charter Communications, 941 Charter Commons Dr, Saint Louis, MO 63017. Phone: 636-207-7044. Fax: 636-230-7034. Web Site: http://www.charter.com. Also serves Dardenne Prairie, Flint Hill, O'Fallon, St. Charles County, St. Paul, Weldon Spring, Weldon Spring Heights & Wentzville. ICA: MO0028.
TV Market Ranking: 11 (Dardenne Prairie, LAKE ST. LOUIS, O'Fallon, St. Charles County (portions), St. Paul, Weldon Spring, Weldon Spring Heights); Outside TV Markets (Flint Hill, Wentzville, St. Charles County (portions)). Franchise award date: N.A. Franchise expiration date: N.A. Began: December 1, 1983.
Channel capacity: N.A. Channels available but not in use: N.A.
Basic Service
Subscribers: 5,508.
Programming (received off-air): KDNL-TV (ABC) St. Louis; KETC (PBS) St. Louis; KMOV (CBS) St. Louis; KNLC (IND) St. Louis; KPLR-TV (CW) St. Louis; KSDK (NBC) St. Louis; KTVI (FOX) St. Louis; WPXS (IND) Mount Vernon; WRBU (MNT) East St. Louis.
Programming (via satellite): C-SPAN; C-SPAN 2; Eternal Word TV Network; Home Shopping Network; INSP; QVC; ShopNBC; TBS Superstation; Trinity Broadcasting Network; TV Guide Network; Univision; Weatherscan; WGN America.
Current originations: Government Access; Educational Access.
Planned originations: Public Access.
Fee: $30.00 installation; $17.95 monthly.
Expanded Basic Service 1
Subscribers: N.A.
Programming (via satellite): ABC Family Channel; AMC; Animal Planet; Arts & Entertainment; BET Networks; Bravo; Cartoon Network; CNBC; CNN; Comedy Central; Country Music TV; Discovery Channel; Disney Channel; E! Entertainment Television; ESPN; ESPN 2; Food Network; Fox Movie Channel; Fox News Channel; Fox Sports Net Midwest; FX; G4; Golf Channel; GSN; Hallmark Channel; Headline News; HGTV; History Channel; Lifetime; MSNBC; MTV; National Geographic Channel; Nickelodeon; Oxygen; SoapNet; Speed Channel; Spike TV; Style Network; Syfy; The Learning Channel; Toon Disney; Travel Channel; truTV; Turner Classic Movies; Turner Network TV; TV Land; USA Network; Versus; VH1; WE tv; Weather Channel.
Digital Basic Service
Subscribers: N.A.
Programming (via satellite): BBC America; Bio; Bloomberg Television; Discovery Digital Networks; Do-It-Yourself; Encore Action; ESPN Classic Sports; FitTV; Fox Sports World; FSN Digital Atlantic; FSN Digital Central; FSN Digital Pacific; Fuel TV; Fuse; GAS; Great American Country; History Channel International; Independent Film Channel; International Television (ITV); Lifetime Movie Network; MTV Networks Digital Suite; Music Choice; NFL Network; Nick Jr.; Nick Too; NickToons TV; Sundance Channel.
Digital Pay Service 1
Pay Units: 5,059.
Programming (via satellite): Cinemax (multiplexed); HBO (multiplexed); Showtime (multiplexed); Starz (multiplexed); The Movie Channel (multiplexed).
Fee: $10.00 installation; $8.95 monthly (each).
Video-On-Demand: Yes
Pay-Per-View
iN DEMAND (delivered digitally); Sports PPV (delivered digitally); ESPN Now (delivered digitally); Playboy TV (delivered digitally); Fresh (delivered digitally); Shorteez (delivered digitally).
Internet Service
Operational: Yes.
Broadband Service: Charter Pipeline.
Fee: $29.99 monthly; $10.00 modem lease.
Telephone Service
Digital: Operational
Fee: $29.99 monthly
Miles of Plant: 231.0 (coaxial); None (fiber optic). Additional miles planned: 58.0 (coaxial). Homes passed: 8,655.
Vice President & General Manager: Steve Trippe. Operations Director: Tom Williams. Marketing Director: Beverly Wall.
City fee: 3% of gross.
Ownership: Charter Communications Inc. (MSO).

LAKE VIKING—Formerly served by First Cable of Missouri Inc. No longer in operation. ICA: MO0447.

LAMAR—Suddenlink Communications, 231 E 4th St, Carthage, MO 64836-1629. Phone: 417-358-3002. Fax: 417-359-5373. Web Site: http://www.suddenlink.com. Also serves Lamar Heights. ICA: MO0086.
TV Market Ranking: Below 100 (LAMAR, Lamar Heights). Franchise award date: July 16, 1979. Franchise expiration date: N.A. Began: June 23, 1980.
Channel capacity: N.A. Channels available but not in use: N.A.
Basic Service
Subscribers: 1,456.
Programming (received off-air): KFJX (FOX) Pittsburg; KOAM-TV (CBS) Pittsburg; KODE-TV (ABC) Joplin; KOZK (PBS) Springfield; KSNF (NBC) Joplin.
Programming (via satellite): C-SPAN; QVC; TBS Superstation; WGN America.
Fee: $49.98 installation; $8.97 monthly.

Expanded Basic Service 1
Subscribers: 1,267.
Programming (via satellite): ABC Family Channel; AMC; Animal Planet; Arts & Entertainment; CNBC; CNN; Comedy Central; Country Music TV; C-SPAN 2; CW+; Discovery Channel; Disney Channel; ESPN; ESPN 2; FitTV; Food Network; Fox News Channel; Fox Sports Net Midwest; FX; Hallmark Channel; Headline News; HGTV; History Channel; Lifetime; Nickelodeon; Outdoor Channel; Spike TV; Syfy; The Learning Channel; Travel Channel; Turner Network TV; TV Land; USA Network; VH1; Weather Channel.
Fee: $15.10 monthly.
Digital Basic Service
Subscribers: N.A.
Programming (via satellite): BBC America; Bloomberg Television; Discovery Digital Networks; DMX Music; Encore (multiplexed); ESPN Classic Sports; ESPNews; Fox Soccer; G4; Golf Channel; Speed Channel; Trinity Broadcasting Network; Turner Classic Movies.
Digital Pay Service 1
Pay Units: N.A.
Programming (via satellite): Cinemax (multiplexed); HBO (multiplexed); Showtime (multiplexed); Starz (multiplexed); Sundance Channel; The Movie Channel (multiplexed).
Video-On-Demand: Yes
Pay-Per-View
iN DEMAND (delivered digitally), Addressable: Yes; Fresh (delivered digitally); Playboy TV (delivered digitally); Hot Choice (delivered digitally).
Internet Service
Operational: Yes.
Fee: $29.95 monthly.
Telephone Service
None
Miles of Plant: 34.0 (coaxial); 2.0 (fiber optic). Homes passed: 2,148. Total homes in franchised area: 2,148.
Manager: Terrill Bradley. Chief Engineer: Tim Crotti.
City fee: 5% of gross.
Ownership: Cequel Communications LLC (MSO).

LAMPE—Crystal Broadband Networks, PO Box 180336, Chicago, IL 60618. Phone: 817-685-9588. E-mail: info@crystalbn.com. Web Site: http://crystalbn.com. Also serves Blue Eye & Oak Grove, AR; Blue Eye & Persimmon Hollow, MO. ICA: MO0133.
TV Market Ranking: Below 100 (Blue Eye, LAMPE, Oak Grove, Persimmon Hollow). Franchise award date: N.A. Franchise expiration date: N.A. Began: N.A.
Channel capacity: 42 (not 2-way capable). Channels available but not in use: 4.
Basic Service
Subscribers: 440.
Programming (received off-air): KOLR (CBS) Springfield; KOZK (PBS) Springfield; KSFX-TV (FOX) Springfield; KSPR (ABC) Springfield; KYTV (CW, NBC) Springfield.
Programming (via satellite): ABC Family Channel; AMC; Arts & Entertainment; CNBC; CNN; Country Music TV; C-SPAN; Discovery Channel; ESPN; Hallmark Channel; Headline News; Home Shopping Network; Lifetime; Nickelodeon; Spike TV; TBS Superstation; Turner Network TV; USA Network; Weather Channel; WGN America.
Fee: $29.95 installation; $39.95 monthly.
Pay Service 1
Pay Units: 14.
Programming (via satellite): Cinemax.
Fee: $10.95 monthly.
Pay Service 2
Pay Units: 39.
Programming (via satellite): HBO.
Fee: $10.95 monthly.
Pay Service 3
Pay Units: 108.
Programming (via satellite): Showtime.
Fee: $10.95 monthly.
Video-On-Demand: No
Internet Service
Operational: Yes.
Telephone Service
Digital: Operational
Miles of Plant: 78.0 (coaxial); None (fiber optic). Homes passed: 2,100.
General Manager: Nidhin Johnson. Program Manager: Shawn Smith.
Ownership: Crystal Broadband Networks (MSO).

LANCASTER—Longview Communications, 12007 Sunrise Valley Dr, Ste 375, Reston, VA 20191. Phones: 866-611-6565 (Customer service); 703-476-9101. Fax: 703-476-9107. Web Site: http://www.longviewcomm.com. Also serves Glenwood. ICA: MO0212.
TV Market Ranking: Below 100 (Glenwood, LANCASTER). Franchise award date: N.A. Franchise expiration date: N.A. Began: March 1, 1984.
Channel capacity: 41 (not 2-way capable). Channels available but not in use: None.
Basic Service
Subscribers: 106.
Programming (received off-air): KHQA-TV (ABC, CBS) Hannibal; KTVO (ABC) Kirksville; KYOU-TV (FOX) Ottumwa; WGEM-TV (CW, NBC) Quincy.
Programming (via satellite): ABC Family Channel; AMC; Animal Planet; Arts & Entertainment; Classic Arts Showcase; CNN; Comedy Central; C-SPAN; Discovery Channel; Disney Channel; E! Entertainment Television; ESPN; ESPN 2; Fox News Channel; FX; G4; Great American Country; Headline News; HGTV; History Channel; KRMA-TV (PBS) Denver; Lifetime; Lifetime Movie Network; Nickelodeon; QVC; Spike TV; Syfy; TBS Superstation; The Learning Channel; Travel Channel; Turner Network TV; USA Network; Weather Channel.
Fee: $30.00 installation; $37.95 monthly.
Pay Service 1
Pay Units: 32.
Programming (via satellite): Showtime; The Movie Channel.
Fee: $8.95 monthly (TMC), $10.95 monthly (Showtime).
Video-On-Demand: No
Internet Service
Operational: No.
Telephone Service
None
Miles of Plant: 12.0 (coaxial); None (fiber optic). Homes passed: 468.
President: John Long. Senior Vice President: Marc W. Cohen. General Manager: Brandon Dickey. Operations Manager: Perry Scarborough.
Ownership: Longview Communications (MSO).

LATHROP—Allegiance Communications, 707 W Saratoga St, Shawnee, OK 74804. Phones: 405-275-6923; 405-395-1131. Web Site: http://www.allegiance.tv. ICA: MO0410.
TV Market Ranking: 22 (LATHROP). Franchise award date: September 8, 1982. Franchise expiration date: N.A. Began: N.A.
Channel capacity: 41 (not 2-way capable). Channels available but not in use: N.A.

Basic Service
Subscribers: 390.
Programming (received off-air): KCPT (PBS) Kansas City; KCTV (CBS) Kansas City; KCWB-LP Reedley; KMBC-TV (ABC) Kansas City; KQTV (ABC) St. Joseph; KSHB-TV (NBC) Kansas City; KSMO-TV (MNT) Kansas City; WDAF-TV (FOX) Kansas City.
Programming (via satellite): TBS Superstation; WGN America.
Fee: $41.11 installation; $23.50 monthly.
Expanded Basic Service 1
Subscribers: N.A.
Programming (via satellite): ABC Family Channel; AMC; Animal Planet; Arts & Entertainment; CNN; Discovery Channel; Disney Channel; ESPN; ESPN 2; Fox News Channel; FX; History Channel; Lifetime; MTV; Nickelodeon; Spike TV; Syfy; truTV; Turner Network TV; TV Land; USA Network; VH1; Weather Channel.
Pay Service 1
Pay Units: 75.
Programming (via satellite): The Movie Channel.
Fee: $23.49 installation; $8.95 monthly.
Pay Service 2
Pay Units: 111.
Programming (via satellite): HBO.
Fee: $23.49 installation; $10.50 monthly.
Pay Service 3
Pay Units: 70.
Programming (via satellite): Showtime.
Fee: $23.49 installation; $10.50 monthly.
Video-On-Demand: No
Pay-Per-View
iN DEMAND (delivered digitally); Urban Xtra (delivered digitally); Sports PPV (delivered digitally); ESPN Now (delivered digitally); Hot Choice (delivered digitally); Playboy TV (delivered digitally); Fresh (delivered digitally); Shorteez (delivered digitally).
Internet Service
Operational: No.
Telephone Service
None
Homes passed: 703. Total homes in franchised area: 703.
Chief Executive Officer: Bill Haggarty. Regional Vice President: Andrew Dearth. Vice President, Marketing: Tracy Bass.
City fee: 5% of gross.
Ownership: Allegiance Communications (MSO).

LEBANON—Fidelity Communications, 840 E. Hwy 32, Lebanon, MO 65536. Phones: 417-588-7841; 573-468-8081. Fax: 573-468-3834. E-mail: custserv@fidelitycommunications.com. Web Site: http://www.fidelitycommunications.com. Also serves Laclede County & Phillipsburg. ICA: MO0051.
TV Market Ranking: Below 100 (Laclede County (portions)); Outside TV Markets (Laclede County (portions), LEBANON, Phillipsburg). Franchise award date: N.A. Franchise expiration date: N.A. Began: November 1, 1966.
Channel capacity: 41 (operating 2-way). Channels available but not in use: N.A.
Basic Service
Subscribers: 2,041.
Programming (received off-air): KOLR (CBS) Springfield; KOZK (PBS) Springfield; KSFX-TV (FOX) Springfield; KSPR (ABC) Springfield; KYTV (CW, NBC) Springfield.
Programming (via satellite): AmericanLife TV Network; C-SPAN; Hallmark Channel; QVC; Syfy; TV Guide Network; WGN America.
Current originations: Public Access.
Fee: $39.95 installation; $17.95 monthly.
Expanded Basic Service 1
Subscribers: N.A.
Programming (via satellite): ABC Family Channel; AMC; Animal Planet; Arts & Entertainment; Bravo; Cartoon Network; CNBC; CNN; Comedy Central; Country Music TV; Discovery Channel; Disney Channel; E! Entertainment Television; ESPN; Food Network; Fox Sports Net Midwest; GSN; Headline News; HGTV; History Channel; Lifetime; MSNBC; MTV; National Geographic Channel; Nickelodeon; Oxygen; SoapNet; Speed Channel; Spike TV; TBS Superstation; The Learning Channel; Trinity Broadcasting Network; Turner Network TV; TV Land; USA Network; VH1; Weather Channel.
Fee: $43.95 monthly.
Digital Basic Service
Subscribers: N.A.
Programming (via satellite): AmericanLife TV Network; BBC America; Bloomberg Television; CMT Pure Country; Discovery Home Channel; Discovery Kids Channel; Discovery Times Channel; Do-It-Yourself; FitTV; Fox Movie Channel; Fox Soccer; G4; Lifetime Movie Network; MTV2; Nick Jr.; Science Channel.
Fee: $3.95 monthly.
Pay Service 1
Pay Units: 331.
Programming (via satellite): The Movie Channel.
Fee: $7.95 monthly.
Pay Service 2
Pay Units: 275.
Programming (via satellite): Showtime.
Fee: $9.95 installation.
Pay Service 3
Pay Units: 426.
Programming (via satellite): HBO.
Fee: $10.95 monthly.
Internet Service
Operational: Yes.
Fee: $34.95 monthly.
Telephone Service
Digital: Planned
Miles of Plant: 86.0 (coaxial); None (fiber optic). Homes passed: 5,023.
General Manager: Alan Holcomb. Manager: Andrew B. Davis. Chief Technician: Rich Abel.
City fee: 3% of gross.
Ownership: Fidelity Communications Co. (MSO).

LEETON—Formerly served by CableDirect. No longer in operation. ICA: MO0309.

LESTERVILLE—Formerly served by Almega Cable. No longer in operation. ICA: MO0231.

LEXINGTON—Suddenlink Communications, 536 S 13th Hwy, Lexington, MO 64067. Phones: 800-999-6845 (Customer service); 314-965-2020. Web Site: http://www.suddenlink.com. Also serves Napoleon & Wellington. ICA: MO0083.

TV Market Ranking: 22 (Napoleon, Wellington); Outside TV Markets (LEXINGTON). Franchise award date: N.A. Franchise expiration date: N.A. Began: May 1, 1974.

Channel capacity: 36 (operating 2-way). Channels available but not in use: N.A.

Basic Service

Subscribers: 1,479.

Programming (received off-air): KCPT (PBS) Kansas City; KCTV (CBS) Kansas City; KCWE (CW) Kansas City; KMBC-TV (ABC) Kansas City; KMOS-TV (PBS) Sedalia; KPXE-TV (ION) Kansas City; KSHB-TV (NBC) Kansas City; KSMO-TV (MNT) Kansas City; WDAF-TV (FOX) Kansas City; allband FM.

Programming (via satellite): QVC; Weather Channel.

Fee: $39.95 installation; $19.95 monthly.

Expanded Basic Service 1

Subscribers: N.A.

Programming (via satellite): ABC Family Channel; AMC; Animal Planet; Arts & Entertainment; BET Networks; Bravo; Cartoon Network; Celebrity Shopping Network; CNBC; CNN; Comedy Central; C-SPAN; Discovery Channel; Disney Channel; E! Entertainment Television; ESPN; ESPN 2; Food Network; Fox News Channel; Fox Sports Net Midwest; FX; Great American Country; Hallmark Channel; Headline News; HGTV; History Channel; Lifetime; MSNBC; MTV; National Geographic Channel; Nickelodeon; Outdoor Channel; Speed Channel; Spike TV; Syfy; TBS Superstation; The Learning Channel; Travel Channel; Turner Classic Movies; Turner Network TV; TV Land; Univision; USA Network; VH1.

Fee: $23.00 monthly.

Digital Basic Service

Subscribers: N.A.

Programming (via satellite): BBC America; Bio; Bloomberg Television; Discovery Digital Networks; DMX Music; ESPN Classic Sports; ESPNews; Fox College Sports Atlantic; Fox College Sports Central; Fox College Sports Pacific; Fox Soccer; Fuse; G4; Golf Channel; GSN; History Channel International; Independent Film Channel; ShopNBC; Sleuth; Style Network; Sundance Channel; Toon Disney; Trinity Broadcasting Network; Versus; WE tv.

Pay Service 1

Pay Units: 259.

Programming (via satellite): HBO.

Fee: $10.95 monthly.

Pay Service 2

Pay Units: 249.

Programming (via satellite): Showtime.

Fee: $9.95 monthly.

Pay Service 3

Pay Units: 246.

Programming (via satellite): The Movie Channel.

Fee: $7.95 monthly.

Digital Pay Service 1

Pay Units: N.A.

Programming (via satellite): Cinemax (multiplexed); Encore (multiplexed); Flix; HBO (multiplexed); Showtime (multiplexed); Starz (multiplexed); The Movie Channel (multiplexed).

Video-On-Demand: No

Pay-Per-View

iN DEMAND (delivered digitally); Playboy TV (delivered digitally); Fresh (delivered digitally); Shorteez (delivered digitally).

Internet Service

Operational: Yes. Began: March 1, 2002.

Broadband Service: Cebridge High Speed Cable Internet.

Fee: $29.95 monthly.

Telephone Service

None

Miles of Plant: 88.0 (coaxial); None (fiber optic). Homes passed: 2,259.

Regional Manager: Todd Cruthird. Regional Marketing Manager: Beverly Gambell.

Ownership: Cequel Communications LLC (MSO).

LIBERAL—Mediacom. Now served by GRANBY, MO [MO0156]. ICA: MO0187.

LICKING—Licking Cable. Now served by WAYNESVILLE, MO [MO0023]. ICA: MO0170.

LINCOLN—Longview Communications, 12007 Sunrise Valley Dr, Ste 375, Reston, VA 20191. Phones: 866-611-6565 (Customer service); 703-476-9101. Fax: 703-476-9107. Web Site: http://www.longviewcomm.com. ICA: MO0221.

TV Market Ranking: Below 100 (LINCOLN). Franchise award date: N.A. Franchise expiration date: N.A. Began: January 1, 1983.

Channel capacity: 37 (not 2-way capable). Channels available but not in use: None.

Basic Service

Subscribers: 93.

Programming (received off-air): KCWE (CW) Kansas City; KMOS-TV (PBS) Sedalia; KOLR (CBS) Springfield; KSFX-TV (FOX) Springfield; KSMO-TV (MNT) Kansas City; KSPR (ABC) Springfield; KYTV (CW, NBC) Springfield.

Programming (via satellite): C-SPAN; C-SPAN 2; QVC; ShopNBC; Trinity Broadcasting Network.

Fee: $17.98 monthly.

Expanded Basic Service 1

Subscribers: N.A.

Programming (via satellite): ABC Family Channel; AMC; Animal Planet; Arts & Entertainment; Cartoon Network; CNN; Discovery Channel; ESPN; G4; Headline News; HGTV; Lifetime; TBS Superstation; The Learning Channel; Travel Channel; Turner Network TV; USA Network; Weather Channel; WGN America.

Fee: $17.97 monthly.

Pay Service 1

Pay Units: 37.

Programming (via satellite): Showtime; The Movie Channel.

Fee: $8.95 monthly (TMC), $10.95 monthly (Showtime).

Video-On-Demand: No

Internet Service

Operational: No.

Telephone Service

None

Miles of Plant: 6.0 (coaxial); None (fiber optic). Homes passed: 594.

President: John Long. Senior Vice President: Marc W. Cohen. General Manager: Brandon Dickey. Operations Manager: Perry Scarborough.

Ownership: Longview Communications (MSO).

LINN—Mid Missouri Broadband, PO Box 3535, Ballwin, MO 63022. Web Site: http://linncityhall.com. ICA: MO0411.

TV Market Ranking: Below 100 (LINN).

Channel capacity: N.A. Channels available but not in use: N.A.

Basic Service

Subscribers: N.A.

Programming (received off-air): KETC (PBS) St. Louis; KMIZ (ABC) Columbia; KNLJ (IND) Jefferson City; KOMU-TV (CW, NBC) Columbia; KPLR-TV (CW) St. Louis; KRCG (CBS) Jefferson City.

Programming (via satellite): Comedy Central; HGTV; QVC; TBS Superstation; WGN America.

Fee: $41.11 installation; $24.20 monthly.

Expanded Basic Service 1

Subscribers: N.A.

Programming (via satellite): ABC Family Channel; AMC; Arts & Entertainment; Cartoon Network; CNN; Country Music TV; Discovery Channel; Disney Channel; ESPN; ESPN 2; Fox News Channel; Fox Sports Net Midwest; FX; Headline News; Lifetime; Nickelodeon; Spike TV; Syfy; truTV; Turner Network TV; TV Land; USA Network; Weather Channel.

Digital Basic Service

Subscribers: N.A.

Programming (via satellite): AmericanLife TV Network; BBC America; Bio; Bloomberg Television; Bravo; Discovery Digital Networks; Discovery Kids Channel; DMX Music; FitTV; Fox Movie Channel; Fuse; G4; GAS; Golf Channel; GSN; Halogen Network; History Channel; History Channel International; Independent Film Channel; Lifetime Movie Network; MTV Networks Digital Suite; Nick Jr.; Outdoor Channel; ShopNBC; Speed Channel; Style Network; Toon Disney; Trinity Broadcasting Network; Turner Classic Movies; Versus; WE tv.

Pay Service 1

Pay Units: N.A.

Programming (via satellite): Cinemax; HBO.

Digital Pay Service 1

Pay Units: N.A.

Programming (via satellite): Cinemax (multiplexed); Encore (multiplexed); HBO (multiplexed); Showtime (multiplexed); Starz (multiplexed); The Movie Channel (multiplexed).

Internet Service

Operational: No.

Telephone Service

None

Ownership: Mid-Missouri Broadband & Cable LLC.

LOOSE CREEK—Mid Missouri Broadband, PO Box 3535, Ballwin, MO 63022. Phone: 573-417-4004. Fax: 636-552-0028. Web Site: http://linncityhall.com. Also serves Osage County (northwestern portion). ICA: MO0303.

TV Market Ranking: Below 100 (LOOSE CREEK, Osage County (northwestern portion)). Franchise award date: December 29, 1988. Franchise expiration date: N.A. Began: November 26, 1990.

Channel capacity: 60 (operating 2-way). Channels available but not in use: 18.

Basic Service

Subscribers: 45.

Programming (received off-air): KMIZ (ABC) Columbia; KNLJ (IND) Jefferson City; KOMU-TV (CW, NBC) Columbia; KRCG (CBS) Jefferson City.

Programming (via satellite): ABC Family Channel; CNN; Discovery Channel; ESPN; Spike TV; TBS Superstation; Turner Network TV; USA Network; WGN America.

Fee: $35.00 installation; $34.95 monthly; $20.00 additional installation.

Pay Service 1

Pay Units: 2.

Programming (via satellite): HBO.

Fee: $10.00 installation; $12.95 monthly.

Video-On-Demand: No

Internet Service

Operational: Yes. Began: December 31, 1995.

Subscribers: 75.

Broadband Service: In-house.

Fee: $75.00 installation; $44.95 monthly.

Telephone Service

None

Miles of Plant: 7.0 (coaxial); None (fiber optic). Homes passed: 264.

Manager: Dick Herlihy.

Ownership: Dick Herlihy (MSO).

LOUISIANA—US Cable, 647 Clinic Rd, Hannibal, MO 63401. Phone: 573-581-2404. Fax: 573-581-4053. Web Site: http://www.uscable.com. ICA: MO0081.

TV Market Ranking: Below 100 (LOUISIANA). Franchise award date: N.A. Franchise expiration date: N.A. Began: April 15, 1985.

Channel capacity: N.A. Channels available but not in use: N.A.

Basic Service

Subscribers: N.A. Included in Hannibal

Programming (received off-air): KDNL-TV (ABC) St. Louis; KETC (PBS) St. Louis; KHQA-TV (ABC, CBS) Hannibal; KMOV (CBS) St. Louis; KPLR-TV (CW) St. Louis; KSDK (NBC) St. Louis; KTVI (FOX) St. Louis; WGEM-TV (CW, NBC) Quincy; allband FM.

Programming (via satellite): C-SPAN; Discovery Channel; Disney Channel; Hallmark Channel; TBS Superstation; Turner Network TV; TV Guide Network; WGN.

Current originations: Public Access.

Fee: $60.00 installation; $17.74 monthly.

Expanded Basic Service 1

Subscribers: 1,272.

Programming (via satellite): ABC Family Channel; AMC; Animal Planet; Arts & Entertainment; BET Networks; Cartoon Network; CNN; Comedy Central; Country Music TV; E! Entertainment Television; ESPN; Food Network; Fox News Channel; Fox Sports Net Midwest; FX; History Channel; Lifetime; MSNBC; MTV; Nickelodeon; Oxygen; QVC; ShopNBC; Spike TV; The Learning Channel; Travel Channel; truTV; TV Land; USA Network; Weather Channel.

Fee: $24.06 monthly.

Digital Basic Service

Subscribers: N.A. Included in Hannibal

Programming (via satellite): BBC America; Bio; Bloomberg Television; Discovery Digital Networks; Encore (multiplexed); Fox Reality Channel; Fuse; G4; GSN; Halogen Network; HGTV; History Channel International;

Lifetime Movie Network; Lime; MTV Networks Digital Suite; Nick Jr.; Sleuth; Style Network; Syfy; Toon Disney; Trinity Broadcasting Network; Trio; WealthTV.
Fee: $12.95 monthly (Family, Sports or Movies); $8.00 converter.

Digital Expanded Basic Service
Subscribers: N.A.
Programming (via satellite): DMX Music; Encore; Fox Movie Channel; Independent Film Channel; Lifetime Movie Network; Turner Classic Movies; WE tv.

Digital Expanded Basic Service 2
Subscribers: N.A.
Programming (via satellite): ESPN Classic Sports; ESPNews; Fox Soccer; GAS; Golf Channel; NFL Network; Outdoor Channel; Versus.

Pay Service 1
Pay Units: 139.
Programming (via satellite): Cinemax.
Fee: $13.40 monthly.

Pay Service 2
Pay Units: N.A.
Programming (via satellite): Cinemax (multiplexed); Encore; HBO; Showtime; Starz.
Fee: $2.99 monthly (Encore), $9.10 monthly (Starz), $13.60 monthly (Cinemax or Showtime), $13.90 monthly (HBO).

Digital Pay Service 1
Pay Units: N.A.
Programming (via satellite): HBO (multiplexed); Showtime (multiplexed); Starz (multiplexed); The Movie Channel (multiplexed).
Fee: $6.95 monthly (Starz), $11.95 monthly (Cinemax, HBO, Showtime or TMC).

Pay-Per-View
iN DEMAND (delivered digitally); Playboy TV (delivered digitally); Fresh (delivered digitally).

Internet Service
Operational: Yes.
Broadband Service: Warp Drive Online.

Telephone Service
None

Homes passed, total homes in franchised area, & miles of plant included in Hannibal
Regional Administrative Director: Rebecca Bramblett. Technical Operations Manager: Mark Thake. Marketing Director: Rita Watson.
City fee: 3% of gross.
Ownership: US Cable Corp. (MSO).; Comcast Cable Communications Inc. (MSO).

LOWRY CITY—Mediacom, 1533 S Enterprise Ave, Springfield, MO 65804. Phone: 417-875-5560. Fax: 417-883-0265. Web Site: http://www.mediacomcable.com. ICA: MO0252.
TV Market Ranking: Outside TV Markets (LOWRY CITY). Franchise award date: N.A. Franchise expiration date: N.A. Began: July 1, 1986.
Channel capacity: 54 (not 2-way capable). Channels available but not in use: N.A.

Basic Service
Subscribers: 178.
Programming (received off-air): KMBC-TV (ABC) Kansas City; KMOS-TV (PBS) Sedalia; KOLR (CBS) Springfield; KPXE-TV (ION) Kansas City; KSHB-TV (NBC) Kansas City; KYTV (CW, NBC) Springfield; WDAF-TV (FOX) Kansas City.
Programming (via satellite): ABC Family Channel; AMC; CNN; Country Music TV; Discovery Channel; ESPN; ESPN 2; Headline News; Lifetime; Nickelodeon; QVC; Spike TV; TBS Superstation; Turner Network TV; USA Network; Weather Channel; WGN America.
Fee: $35.00 installation; $23.95 monthly.

Pay Service 1
Pay Units: 18.
Programming (via satellite): The Movie Channel.
Fee: $10.50 monthly.

Pay Service 2
Pay Units: 23.
Programming (via satellite): Showtime.
Fee: $10.50 monthly.

Video-On-Demand: No

Internet Service
Operational: No.

Telephone Service
None

Miles of Plant: 4.0 (coaxial); None (fiber optic). Homes passed: 348.
Regional Vice President: Bill Copeland. Technical Operations Manager: Alan Freedman. Marketing Director: Will Kuebler.
City fee: 3% of basic.
Ownership: Mediacom LLC (MSO).

MACKS CREEK—Formerly served by Almega Cable. No longer in operation. ICA: MO0361.

MACON—Chariton Valley Cablevision, 109 Butler St, Macon, MO 63552. Phone: 660-395-9600. Fax: 660-395-4403. E-mail: feedback@cvalley.net. Web Site: http://www.charitonvalley.com. Also serves Bevier, Bucklin, Callao & New Cambria. ICA: MO0071.
TV Market Ranking: Below 100 (Bevier, Bucklin, Callao, MACON, New Cambria). Franchise award date: December 1, 1984. Franchise expiration date: N.A. Began: September 1, 1979.
Channel capacity: N.A. Channels available but not in use: N.A.

Basic Service
Subscribers: 2,103.
Programming (received off-air): KHQA-TV (ABC, CBS) Hannibal; KOMU-TV (CW, NBC) Columbia; KTVO (ABC) Kirksville; KYOU-TV (FOX) Ottumwa; WGEM-TV (CW, NBC) Quincy; 10 FMs.
Programming (via satellite): ABC Family Channel; AMC; Animal Planet; Arts & Entertainment; BET Networks; Cartoon Network; CNBC; CNN; Comedy Central; Country Music TV; C-SPAN; C-SPAN 2; Discovery Channel; Discovery Health Channel; Disney Channel; E! Entertainment Television; ESPN; ESPN 2; ESPN Classic Sports; Food Network; Fox News Channel; Fox Sports Net; Golf Channel; Great American Country; Hallmark Channel; Headline News; HGTV; History Channel; Home Shopping Network; ION Television; KRMA-TV (PBS) Denver; Lifetime; MSNBC; MTV; National Geographic Channel; Nickelodeon; QVC; Speed Channel; Spike TV; Syfy; TBS Superstation; The Learning Channel; Travel Channel; Trinity Broadcasting Network; truTV; Turner Classic Movies; Turner Network TV; TV Guide Network; TV Land; USA Network; Versus; VH1; Weather Channel; WGN America.
Fee: $33.07 installation; $38.99 monthly; $24.80 additional installation.

Digital Basic Service
Subscribers: N.A.
Programming (via satellite): AmericanLife TV Network; Bio; Bloomberg Television; Bravo!; DMX Music; Fox Movie Channel; G4; Halogen Network; History Channel International; Lime; Outdoor Channel; WE tv.

Digital Pay Service 1
Pay Units: N.A.
Programming (via satellite): Cinemax; HBO (multiplexed); Showtime; Starz; The Movie Channel; The New Encore.

Video-On-Demand: No

Pay-Per-View
iN DEMAND (delivered digitally); Fresh (delivered digitally); Hot Choice (delivered digitally); ESPN On Demand (delivered digitally); ESPN Now (delivered digitally).

Internet Service
Operational: No.

Telephone Service
None

Miles of Plant: 66.0 (coaxial); 3.0 (fiber optic). Homes passed: 2,600. Total homes in franchised area: 5,100.
General Manager: Jim Simon. Engineering Manager: Jerry Gravel.
City fee: 3% of gross.
Ownership: Chariton Valley Telecom.

MADISON—US Cable, 647 Clinic Rd, Hannibal, MO 63401. Phone: 573-581-2404. Fax: 573-581-4053. Web Site: http://www.uscable.com. ICA: MO0275.
TV Market Ranking: Outside TV Markets (MADISON). Franchise award date: N.A. Franchise expiration date: N.A. Began: December 1, 1983.
Channel capacity: N.A. Channels available but not in use: N.A.

Basic Service
Subscribers: N.A. Included in Hannibal
Programming (received off-air): KHQA-TV (ABC, CBS) Hannibal; KMIZ (ABC) Columbia; KMOS-TV (PBS) Sedalia; KOMU-TV (CW, NBC) Columbia; KQFX-LD Columbia; KRCG (CBS) Jefferson City; KTVO (ABC) Kirksville; WGEM-TV (CW, NBC) Quincy; WTJR (IND) Quincy.
Programming (via satellite): Home Shopping Network; TBS Superstation; Weatherscan.
Fee: $22.09 monthly.

Expanded Basic Service 1
Subscribers: N.A.
Programming (via satellite): ABC Family Channel; Animal Planet; Arts & Entertainment; Bravo; Cartoon Network; CNN; Comedy Central; Country Music TV; Discovery Channel; Disney Channel; ESPN; ESPN 2; Fox News Channel; Fox Sports Net Midwest; FX; Headline News; HGTV; History Channel; MTV; Nickelodeon; Spike TV; The Learning Channel; Turner Classic Movies; Turner Network TV; TV Land; USA Network; VH1; Weather Channel; WGN America.
Fee: $19.12 monthly.

Pay Service 1
Pay Units: N.A.
Programming (via satellite): Cinemax; HBO.
Fee: $11.95 monthly (each).

Internet Service
Operational: No.

Telephone Service
None

Homes passed and miles of plant included in Hannibal
Regional Administrative Director: Rebecca Bramblett. Technical Operations Manager: Roger Young. Marketing Director: Rita Watson.
Ownership: US Cable Corp. (MSO).; Comcast Cable Communications Inc. (MSO).

MAITLAND—Holway Telephone Co., PO Box 112, 208 Ash St, Maitland, MO 64466. Phone: 660-935-2211. Fax: 660-935-2213. E-mail: holwayinfo@abbmissouri.com. Web Site: http://www.holwaytel.net. Also serves Graham & Skidmore. ICA: MO0336.
TV Market Ranking: Below 100 (MAITLAND); Outside TV Markets (Graham, Skidmore). Franchise award date: N.A. Franchise expiration date: N.A. Began: July 1, 1985.
Channel capacity: 42 (not 2-way capable). Channels available but not in use: N.A.

Basic Service
Subscribers: 300.
Programming (received off-air): KCTV (CBS) Kansas City; KHIN (PBS) Red Oak; KQTV (ABC) St. Joseph; KSHB-TV (NBC) Kansas City; WDAF-TV (FOX) Kansas City.
Programming (via satellite): ABC Family Channel; Arts & Entertainment; Cartoon Network; CNN; Country Music TV; Discovery Channel; Disney Channel; ESPN; ESPN 2; HGTV; History Channel; Lifetime; Nickelodeon; Outdoor Channel; QVC; Spike TV; Syfy; TBS Superstation; The Learning Channel; Trinity Broadcasting Network; Turner Classic Movies; Turner Network TV; TV Land; USA Network; VH1; Weather Channel; WGN America.
Fee: $20.00 installation; $27.95 monthly.

Pay Service 1
Pay Units: N.A.
Programming (via satellite): Flix; HBO; Showtime; The Movie Channel.
Fee: $12.95 monthly (HBO or Showtime/TMC/Flix).

Video-On-Demand: No

Internet Service
Operational: No, DSL & dial-up.

Telephone Service
None

Miles of Plant: 3.0 (coaxial); None (fiber optic). System upgrade is planned
Manager: Bruce Copsey. Marketing Manager: Amanda Lyle. Chief Technician: Paul Sanders.
Ownership: Holway Telephone Co.

MAITLAND—N.W. Communications, PO Box 30, 616 E Park, Rich Hill, MO 64779-0030. Phones: 600-935-2211; 417-395-2121. Fax: 417-395-2120. E-mail: tburchell@klmtel.net. Web Site: http://www.klmtel.net. ICA: MO0473.
TV Market Ranking: Below 100 (MAITLAND).
Channel capacity: N.A. Channels available but not in use: N.A.

Basic Service
Subscribers: N.A.
Programming (received off-air): KCPT (PBS) Kansas City; KCTV (CBS) Kansas City; KMCI-TV (IND) Lawrence; KODE-TV (ABC) Joplin; KSHB-TV (NBC) Kansas City; KSMO-TV (MNT) Kansas City; WDAF-TV (FOX) Kansas City.
Programming (via satellite): ABC Family Channel; Arts & Entertainment; CNN; Comedy Central; Discovery Channel; Disney Channel; ESPN; ESPN 2; Great American Country; Hallmark Channel; HGTV; History Channel; KCWE (CW) Kansas City; KMBC-TV (ABC) Kansas City; Lifetime; Nickelodeon; Outdoor Channel; QVC; Spike TV; Syfy; TBS Superstation; The Learning Channel; Travel Channel; Trinity Broadcasting Network; Turner Network TV; TV Land; USA Network; VH1; WGN America.

Pay Service 1
Pay Units: N.A.
Programming (via satellite): Cinemax; HBO.

Internet Service
Operational: No.

Telephone Service
None

Manager & Chief Technician: Reese Copsey.
Ownership: KLM Telephone Co. (MSO).

MALDEN—NewWave Communications. Now served by DEXTER, MO [MO0039]. ICA: MO0053.

MALDEN—No longer in operation. ICA: MO0449.

MANSFIELD—Mediacom. Now served by SEYMOUR, MO [MO0172]. ICA: MO0190.

MARBLE HILL—Boycom Cablevision Inc., 3467 Township Line Rd, Poplar Bluff, MO 63901. Phone: 573-686-9101. Fax: 573-686-4722. Web Site: http://www.boycomonline.com. Also serves Glenallen. ICA: MO0123.

TV Market Ranking: 69 (Glenallen, MARBLE HILL). Franchise award date: N.A. Franchise expiration date: N.A. Began: September 1, 1975.

Channel capacity: 60 (not 2-way capable). Channels available but not in use: 29.

Basic Service

Subscribers: N.A. Included in Alton

Programming (received off-air): KBSI (FOX) Cape Girardeau; KETC (PBS) St. Louis; KFVS-TV (CBS, CW) Cape Girardeau; WPSD-TV (NBC) Paducah; WSIL-TV (ABC) Harrisburg; allband FM.

Programming (via satellite): ABC Family Channel; Arts & Entertainment; Country Music TV; C-SPAN; E! Entertainment Television; ESPN; Home Shopping Network; QVC; Syfy.

Fee: $29.95 installation; $19.95 monthly; $.98 converter.

Expanded Basic Service 1

Subscribers: 478.

Programming (via satellite): CNN; Discovery Channel; ESPN 2; Food Network; Fox News Channel; HGTV; MSNBC; Nickelodeon; Spike TV; TBS Superstation; The Learning Channel; Turner Network TV; TV Land; USA Network; Weather Channel; WGN America.

Fee: $20.00 monthly.

Pay Service 1

Pay Units: 97.

Programming (via satellite): HBO.

Fee: $35.00 installation; $10.50 monthly.

Video-On-Demand: No

Internet Service

Operational: No.

Telephone Service

None

Miles of Plant: 29.0 (coaxial); None (fiber optic). Homes passed: 1,117. Total homes in franchised area: 1,173.

President: Steven Boyers. General Manager: Shelly Batton. Chief Technician: Phil Huett.

Ownership: Boycom Cablevision Inc. (MSO).

MARCELINE—Mediacom, 1533 S Enterprise Ave, Springfield, MO 65804. Phones: 417-875-5560 (Springfield regional office); 816-637-4500 (Excelsior Springs office). Fax: 417-883-0265. Web Site: http://www.mediacomcable.com. ICA: MO0129.

TV Market Ranking: Outside TV Markets (MARCELINE). Franchise award date: November 4, 1980. Franchise expiration date: N.A. Began: January 1, 1976.

Channel capacity: N.A. Channels available but not in use: N.A.

Basic Service

Subscribers: 992.

Programming (received off-air): KCPT (PBS) Kansas City; KCTV (CBS) Kansas City; KCWE (CW) Kansas City; KMBC-TV (ABC) Kansas City; KOMU-TV (CW, NBC) Columbia; KRCG (CBS) Jefferson City; KSHB-TV (NBC) Kansas City; KSMQ-TV (PBS) Austin; KTVO (ABC) Kirksville; WDAF-TV (FOX) Kansas City; allband FM.

Programming (via satellite): TV Guide Network; WGN America.

Fee: $35.00 installation; $25.25 monthly; $1.70 converter.

Expanded Basic Service 1

Subscribers: N.A.

Programming (via satellite): ABC Family Channel; AMC; Animal Planet; Arts & Entertainment; Bravo; Cartoon Network; CNBC; CNN; Comedy Central; Country Music TV; C-SPAN; Discovery Channel; Disney Channel; E! Entertainment Television; ESPN; ESPN 2; Eternal Word TV Network; Food Network; Fox News Channel; Fox Sports Net Midwest; FX; Hallmark Channel; Headline News; HGTV; History Channel; Home Shopping Network; INSP; Lifetime; MSNBC; MTV; Nickelodeon; Outdoor Channel; QVC; ShopNBC; SoapNet; Speed Channel; Spike TV; Syfy; TBS Superstation; The Learning Channel; Travel Channel; Trinity Broadcasting Network; truTV; Turner Network TV; TV Land; USA Network; VH1; WE tv; Weather Channel.

Digital Basic Service

Subscribers: N.A.

Programming (via satellite): AmericanLife TV Network; BBC America; Bio; Bloomberg Television; Discovery Digital Networks; FitTV; Fox Movie Channel; Fox Soccer; Fuse; G4; GAS; Golf Channel; GSN; History Channel International; Independent Film Channel; Lifetime Movie Network; Lime; MTV Networks Digital Suite; Music Choice; National Geographic Channel; Nick Jr.; NickToons TV; Style Network; Turner Classic Movies; Versus.

Digital Pay Service 1

Pay Units: N.A.

Programming (via satellite): Cinemax (multiplexed); Encore (multiplexed); Flix (multiplexed); HBO (multiplexed); Showtime (multiplexed); Starz (multiplexed); Sundance Channel (multiplexed); The Movie Channel (multiplexed).

Video-On-Demand: No

Pay-Per-View

Mediacom PPV & Events PPV (delivered digitally); Playboy TV (delivered digitally); TEN Clips (delivered digitally); Pleasure (delivered digitally); Hot Body (delivered digitally).

Internet Service

Operational: Yes.

Broadband Service: Mediacom High Speed Internet.

Telephone Service

Digital: Operational

Miles of Plant: 25.0 (coaxial); None (fiber optic). Homes passed: 1,522.

Regional Vice President: Bill Copeland. Operations Director: Bryan Gann. Regional Technical Operations Director: Alan Freedman. Technical Operations Manager: Roger Shearer. Marketing Director: Will Kuebler.

City fee: 3% of gross.

Ownership: Mediacom LLC (MSO).

MARSHALL—Windjammer Cable, 4400 PGA Blvd, Ste 902, Palm Beach Gardens, FL 33410. Phones: 561-775-1208; 877-450-5558. Fax: 561-775-7811. Web Site: http://www.windjammercable.com. ICA: MO0036.

TV Market Ranking: Below 100 (MARSHALL COUNTY (PORTIONS)). Franchise award date: April 15, 1963. Franchise expiration date: N.A. Began: September 23, 1965.

Channel capacity: N.A. Channels available but not in use: N.A.

Basic Service

Subscribers: 4,530.

Programming (received off-air): KCPT (PBS) Kansas City; KCTV (CBS) Kansas City; KCWE (CW) Kansas City; KMBC-TV (ABC) Kansas City; KMCI-TV (IND) Lawrence; KMIZ (ABC) Columbia; KMOS-TV (PBS) Sedalia; KOMU-TV (CW, NBC) Columbia; KPXE-TV (ION) Kansas City; KRCG (CBS) Jefferson City; KSHB-TV (NBC) Kansas City; KSMO-TV (MNT) Kansas City; WDAF-TV (FOX) Kansas City; 22 FMs.

Programming (via satellite): C-SPAN; C-SPAN 2; Home Shopping Network; QVC; ShopNBC; TBS Superstation.

Current originations: Public Access.

Fee: $35.89 installation; $21.46 monthly; $.57 converter; $10.05 additional installation.

Expanded Basic Service 1

Subscribers: N.A.

Programming (via satellite): ABC Family Channel; AMC; Animal Planet; Arts & Entertainment; BET Networks; Bravo; Cartoon Network; CNBC; CNN; Comedy Central; Country Music TV; Discovery Channel; Discovery Health Channel; Disney Channel; E! Entertainment Television; ESPN; ESPN 2; ESPN Classic Sports; FitTV; Food Network; Fox News Channel; Fox Sports Net Midwest; FX; Great American Country; Hallmark Channel; Headline News; HGTV; History Channel; INSP; Lifetime; Lifetime Movie Network; MSNBC; MTV; National Geographic Channel; Nickelodeon; Oxygen; Spike TV; Syfy; The Learning Channel; Travel Channel; Trinity Broadcasting Network; truTV; Turner Network TV; TV Land; Univision; USA Network; VH1; WE tv; Weather Channel.

Fee: $34.40 monthly.

Digital Basic Service

Subscribers: N.A.

Programming (received off-air): KCPT (PBS) Kansas City; KCWE (CW) Kansas City; KMBC-TV (ABC) Kansas City; KMOS-TV (PBS) Sedalia; KSHB-TV (NBC) Kansas City.

Programming (via satellite): AmericanLife TV Network; BBC America; Bio; Bloomberg Television; Current; Discovery Digital Networks; Discovery HD Theater; ESPN; ESPNews; Fox Soccer; Fuse; G4; GAS; Golf Channel; GSN; Halogen Network; HDNet; HDNet Movies; History Channel International; INHD (multiplexed); MTV Hits; MTV2; Music Choice; Nick Jr.; NickToons TV; Outdoor Channel; Ovation; Speed Channel; Style Network; Toon Disney; Turner Classic Movies; Turner Network TV HD; Versus; VH1 Classic.

Fee: $53.99 monthly.

Digital Pay Service 1

Pay Units: N.A.

Programming (via satellite): Cinemax (multiplexed); Encore (multiplexed); Fox Movie Channel; HBO; HBO (multiplexed); Independent Film Channel; Showtime; Showtime (multiplexed); Starz (multiplexed); Sundance Channel; The Movie Channel (multiplexed).

Fee: $12.00 monthly (each).

Video-On-Demand: No

Pay-Per-View

iN DEMAND (delivered digitally); Fresh (delivered digitally); Shorteez (delivered digitally); Playboy TV (delivered digitally); Pleasure (delivered digitally); Hot Choice (delivered digitally); TEN, TEN Blue, TEN Clips, TEN Blox (delivered digitally).

Internet Service

Operational: Yes.

Broadband Service: Road Runner.

Fee: $19.99-$49.99 installation; $44.95 monthly.

Telephone Service

Digital: Operational

Fee: $74.95 installation; $49.95 monthly

Miles of Plant: 81.0 (coaxial); None (fiber optic). Homes passed: 6,054.

General Manager: Timothy Evard. Operations Director: Belinda Graham. Engineering Director: Mike Earehart. Finance & Accounting Director: Cindy Johnson.

City fee: 2% of gross.

Ownership: Windjammer Communications LLC (MSO).

MARSHFIELD—Mediacom. Now served by SEYMOUR, MO [MO0172]. ICA: MO0096.

MARYLAND HEIGHTS—Cable America Corp., 229 Millwell Dr, Maryland Heights, MO 63043-2511. Phone: 314-291-1970. Fax: 314-291-0807. Web Site: http://www.cableamerica.com. ICA: MO0464. **Note:** This system is an overbuild.

TV Market Ranking: 11 (MARYLAND HEIGHTS). Franchise award date: October 24, 1995. Franchise expiration date: N.A. Began: January 1, 1997.

Channel capacity: 74 (operating 2-way). Channels available but not in use: N.A.

Basic Service

Subscribers: 2,920.

Programming (received off-air): KDNL-TV (ABC) St. Louis; KETC (PBS) St. Louis; KMOV (CBS) St. Louis; KNLC (IND) St. Louis; KPLR-TV (CW) St. Louis; KSDK (NBC) St. Louis; KTVI (FOX) St. Louis; WRBU (MNT) East St. Louis.

Programming (via satellite): TV Guide Network.

Current originations: Public Access; Government Access; Educational Access.

Fee: $8.45 monthly.

Expanded Basic Service 1

Subscribers: 2,670.

Programming (via satellite): ABC Family Channel; AMC; Animal Planet; Arts & Entertainment; BBC America; BET Networks; Bravo; Cartoon Network; CNBC; CNN; Comedy Central; Country Music TV; C-SPAN; C-SPAN 2; Discovery Channel; Discovery Health Channel; Disney Channel; E! Entertainment Television; ESPN; ESPN 2; ESPN Classic Sports; Eternal Word TV Network; Food Network; Fox News Channel; Fox Sports Net; FX; GalaVision; Golf Channel; Great American Country; GSN; Hallmark Channel; Headline News; HGTV; History Channel; Home Shopping Network; INSP; ION Television; Lifetime; MTV; National Geographic Channel; Nickelodeon; Oxygen; QVC; SoapNet; Speed Channel; Spike TV; Syfy; TBS Superstation; The Learning Channel; Travel Channel; truTV; Turner Classic Movies; Turner Network TV; TV Land; Univision; USA Network; VH1; Weather Channel; WGN America.

Fee: $33.50 monthly.

Digital Basic Service

Subscribers: 756.

Programming (via satellite): Bio; Bloomberg Television; Discovery Digital Networks; DMX Music; Encore (multiplexed); Fox Movie Channel; Fuse; G4; GAS; Halogen Network; History Channel International; Lifetime Movie Network; MTV2; NickToons TV; Outdoor Channel; Style Network; Toon Disney; Trinity Broadcasting Network; Trio.

Fee: $12.00 monthly.

Digital Pay Service 1
Pay Units: 581.
Programming (via satellite): Cinemax (multiplexed); Flix; HBO (multiplexed); Showtime (multiplexed); Starz (multiplexed); Sundance Channel; The Movie Channel (multiplexed).
Fee: $11.95 monthly (HBO, Cinemax, Showtime/TMC/Flix/Sundance, or Starz).
Video-On-Demand: No
Pay-Per-View
Addressable homes: 7,230.
iN DEMAND, Addressable: Yes; adult PPV (delivered digitally); Special events (delivered digitally).
Internet Service
Operational: Yes. Began: March 1, 2000.
Subscribers: 1,058.
Broadband Service: CableAmerica.
Fee: $15.70 installation; $45.95 monthly; $9.95 modem lease; $199.95 modem purchase.
Telephone Service
Digital: Planned
Miles of Plant: 94.0 (coaxial); None (fiber optic). Homes passed: 7,230.
General Manager: Tom Hopfinger. Chief Technician: James Wright. Office Manager: Robin Wilson.
Ownership: CableAmerica Corp. (MSO).

MARYVILLE—Suddenlink Communications, 12444 Powerscourt Dr, Saint Louis, MO 63131-3660. Phones: 800-999-6845 (Customer service); 314-965-2020. Fax: 903-561-5485. Web Site: http://www.suddenlink.com. Also serves Maryville University & Nodaway County (portions). ICA: MO0413.
TV Market Ranking: Below 100 (Nodaway County (portions)); Outside TV Markets (MARYVILLE, Maryville University, Nodaway County (portions)). Franchise award date: N.A. Franchise expiration date: N.A. Began: April 1, 1964.
Channel capacity: 41 (operating 2-way). Channels available but not in use: N.A.
Basic Service
Subscribers: 3,357.
Programming (received off-air): KCPT (PBS) Kansas City; KCTV (CBS) Kansas City; KCWE (CW) Kansas City; KMBC-TV (ABC) Kansas City; KMTV-TV (CBS) Omaha; KQTV (ABC) St. Joseph; KSHB-TV (NBC) Kansas City; KSMO-TV (MNT) Kansas City; KTAJ-TV (TBN) St. Joseph; WDAF-TV (FOX) Kansas City; WOWT-TV (IND, NBC) Omaha.
Programming (via satellite): Arts & Entertainment; INSP; QVC; Shop at Home; TV Guide Network.
Current originations: Educational Access.
Fee: $39.95 installation; $19.95 monthly.
Expanded Basic Service 1
Subscribers: N.A.
Programming (via satellite): ABC Family Channel; AMC; Animal Planet; Arts & Entertainment; BET Networks; Bravo; Cartoon Network; CNBC; CNN; Comedy Central; C-SPAN; Discovery Channel; Disney Channel; E! Entertainment Television; ESPN; ESPN 2; ESPN Classic Sports; Eternal Word TV Network; Food Network; Fox News Channel; Fox Sports Net Midwest; FX; Golf Channel; Great American Country; Hallmark Channel; Headline News; HGTV; History Channel; Lifetime; MSNBC; MTV; National Geographic Channel; Nickelodeon; Outdoor Channel; SoapNet; Speed Channel; Spike TV; Syfy; TBS Superstation; The Learning Channel; Travel Channel; truTV; Turner Classic Movies; Turner Network TV; TV Land; Univision; USA Network; VH1; Weather Channel.
Fee: $23.00 monthly.
Digital Basic Service
Subscribers: N.A.
Programming (via satellite): BBC America; Bio; Bloomberg Television; Discovery Digital Networks; DMX Music; ESPNews; Fox Movie Channel; Fox Soccer; Fuse; G4; GSN; History Channel International; Independent Film Channel; Military History Channel; Science Television; Sleuth; Sundance Channel; Toon Disney; Versus; WE tv.
Fee: $3.99 monthly.
Pay Service 1
Pay Units: 488.
Programming (via satellite): Cinemax; HBO.
Fee: $10.00 installation; $10.95 monthly.
Pay Service 2
Pay Units: 224.
Programming (via satellite): Showtime.
Fee: $9.95 monthly.
Pay Service 3
Pay Units: 246.
Programming (via satellite): The Movie Channel.
Fee: $7.95 monthly.
Digital Pay Service 1
Pay Units: N.A.
Programming (via satellite): Cinemax (multiplexed); HBO (multiplexed); Showtime (multiplexed); Starz (multiplexed); The Movie Channel (multiplexed); The New Encore (multiplexed).
Video-On-Demand: No
Pay-Per-View
iN DEMAND (delivered digitally); Playboy TV (delivered digitally); Fresh (delivered digitally); Shorteez (delivered digitally).
Internet Service
Operational: Yes. Began: June 3, 2004.
Broadband Service: Cebridge High Speed Cable Internet.
Fee: $29.95 monthly.
Telephone Service
None
Miles of Plant: 87.0 (coaxial); None (fiber optic). Homes passed: 4,741.
Regional Manager: Todd Cruthird. Regional Marketing Manager: Beverly Gambell.
City fee: 5% of gross.
Ownership: Cequel Communications LLC (MSO).

MAYSVILLE—Allegiance Communications, 707 W Saratoga St, Shawnee, OK 74804. Phones: 405-275-6923; 405-395-1131. Web Site: http://www.allegiance.tv. ICA: MO0209.
TV Market Ranking: Below 100 (MAYSVILLE). Franchise award date: January 31, 1981. Franchise expiration date: N.A. Began: April 15, 1982.
Channel capacity: 28 (not 2-way capable). Channels available but not in use: N.A.
Basic Service
Subscribers: 268.
Programming (received off-air): KCPT (PBS) Kansas City; KCTV (CBS) Kansas City; KMBC-TV (ABC) Kansas City; KQTV (ABC) St. Joseph; KSHB-TV (NBC) Kansas City; KSMO-TV (MNT) Kansas City; WDAF-TV (FOX) Kansas City.
Programming (via satellite): ABC Family Channel; AMC; ESPN; ESPN 2; History Channel; Nickelodeon; QVC; Syfy; The Learning Channel; Turner Network TV; USA Network.
Fee: $21.95 monthly.
Expanded Basic Service 1
Subscribers: 247.
Programming (via satellite): CNN; Country Music TV; Discovery Channel; Disney Channel; Headline News; Spike TV; TBS Superstation; WGN America.
Fee: $10.00 monthly.
Pay Service 1
Pay Units: 46.
Programming (via satellite): HBO.
Fee: $11.95 monthly.
Pay Service 2
Pay Units: 39.
Programming (via satellite): Showtime.
Fee: $11.95 monthly.
Video-On-Demand: No
Pay-Per-View
iN DEMAND (delivered digitally); ESPN Now (delivered digitally); Hot Choice (delivered digitally); Urban Xtra (delivered digitally); Playboy TV (delivered digitally); Fresh (delivered digitally); Shorteez (delivered digitally); Sports PPV (delivered digitally).
Internet Service
Operational: No.
Telephone Service
None
Miles of Plant: 8.0 (coaxial); None (fiber optic). Homes passed: 501.
Chief Executive Officer: Bill Haggarty. Regional Vice President: Andrew Dearth. Vice President, Marketing: Tracy Bass.
Franchise fee: 3% of gross.
Ownership: Allegiance Communications (MSO).

MAYVIEW—Formerly served by CableDirect. No longer in operation. ICA: MO0353.

MEADVILLE—Longview Communications, 12007 Sunrise Valley Dr, Ste 375, Reston, VA 20191. Phones: 866-611-6565 (Customer service); 703-476-9101. Fax: 703-476-9107. Web Site: http://www.longviewcomm.com. Also serves Laclede & Wheeling. ICA: MO0434.
TV Market Ranking: Outside TV Markets (Laclede, MEADVILLE, Wheeling). Franchise award date: N.A. Franchise expiration date: N.A. Began: N.A.
Channel capacity: 36 (not 2-way capable). Channels available but not in use: 1.
Basic Service
Subscribers: 70.
Programming (received off-air): KCPT (PBS) Kansas City; KCTV (CBS) Kansas City; KMBC-TV (ABC) Kansas City; KPXE-TV (ION) Kansas City; KSHB-TV (NBC) Kansas City; KTVO (ABC) Kirksville; WDAF-TV (FOX) Kansas City.
Programming (via satellite): America's Store; C-SPAN; QVC; Trinity Broadcasting Network.
Fee: $19.98 monthly.
Expanded Basic Service 1
Subscribers: N.A.
Programming (via satellite): ABC Family Channel; AMC; Animal Planet; Arts & Entertainment; Cartoon Network; Classic Arts Showcase; CNN; Comedy Central; Discovery Channel; Disney Channel; ESPN; ESPN 2; Headline News; HGTV; Lifetime; TBS Superstation; The Learning Channel; Travel Channel; Turner Network TV; USA Network; Weather Channel.
Fee: $17.97 monthly.
Pay Service 1
Pay Units: N.A.
Programming (via satellite): Showtime; The Movie Channel.
Fee: $8.95 monthly (TMC), $10.95 monthly (Showtime).
Video-On-Demand: No
Internet Service
Operational: No.
Telephone Service
None
Miles of Plant: 18.0 (coaxial); None (fiber optic). Homes passed: 663.
President: John Long. Senior Vice President: Marc W. Cohen. General Manager: Brandon Dickey. Operations Manager: Perry Scarborough.
Ownership: Longview Communications (MSO).

MEMPHIS—Longview Communications, 1923 N Main, Higginsville, MO 64037. Phone: 866-611-6565. Fax: 866-329-4790. Web Site: http://www.longviewcomm.com. ICA: MO0149.
TV Market Ranking: Below 100 (MEMPHIS). Franchise award date: N.A. Franchise expiration date: N.A. Began: September 15, 1983.
Channel capacity: N.A. Channels available but not in use: N.A.
Basic Service
Subscribers: 383.
Programming (received off-air): KHQA-TV (ABC, CBS) Hannibal; KIIN (PBS) Iowa City; KTVO (ABC) Kirksville; KYOU-TV (FOX) Ottumwa; WGEM-TV (CW, NBC) Quincy.
Programming (via satellite): ABC Family Channel; AMC; Animal Planet; Arts & Entertainment; Cartoon Network; CNN; Discovery Channel; Disney Channel; E! Entertainment Television; ESPN; ESPN 2; Fox News Channel; FX; Great American Country; Hallmark Channel; Headline News; HGTV; History Channel; INSP; Lifetime; MSNBC; Outdoor Channel; Oxygen; QVC; RFD-TV; Speed Channel; Syfy; TBS Superstation; The Learning Channel; Toon Disney; Trinity Broadcasting Network; truTV; Turner Classic Movies; Turner Network TV; USA Network; Weather Channel; WGN America; XY.tv.
Fee: $35.95 installation; $45.95 monthly.
Digital Basic Service
Subscribers: 50.
Programming (via satellite): BBC America; Bio; Bloomberg Television; Discovery Digital Networks; DMX Music; ESPN Classic Sports; ESPNews; Fox Movie Channel; Fuse; G4; Golf Channel; GSN; Halogen Network; History Channel International; Lifetime Movie Network; National Geographic Channel; Speed Channel; Style Network; Trio; WE tv.
Fee: $15.95 monthly.
Digital Pay Service 1
Pay Units: N.A.
Programming (via satellite): Cinemax (multiplexed); Encore (multiplexed); Flix; HBO (multiplexed); Showtime (multiplexed); Starz (multiplexed); The Movie Channel (multiplexed).
Fee: $9.95 monthly (Showtime or TMC), $10.95 monthly (Cinemax), $12.95 monthly (HBO).
Video-On-Demand: No
Pay-Per-View
iN DEMAND (delivered digitally); Hot Choice (delivered digitally); Playboy TV (delivered digitally); Fresh (delivered digitally).
Internet Service
Operational: Yes.
Subscribers: 73.
Broadband Service: Longview Broadband.
Telephone Service
None
Miles of Plant: 19.0 (coaxial); None (fiber optic). Homes passed: 1,082.
President: John Long. Senior Vice President: Marc W. Cohen. General Manager: Brandon Dickey. Operations Manager: Perry Scarborough.

City fee: 3% of basic.
Ownership: Longview Communications (MSO).

MERCER—Formerly served by Telnet South LC. No longer in operation. ICA: MO0271.

META—Formerly served by CableDirect. No longer in operation. ICA: MO0362.

MEXICO—US Cable, 647 Clinic Rd, Hannibal, MO 63401. Phone: 573-581-2404. Fax: 573-581-4053. Web Site: http://www.uscable.com. Also serves Audrain County (portions), Bellflower, Centralia, Farber, Laddonia, Martinsburg, Montgomery City, New Florence, Vandiver & Wellsville. ICA: MO0033.
TV Market Ranking: Below 100 (Audrain County (portions) (portions), Centralia, Farber, MEXICO, Vandiver); Outside TV Markets (Audrain County (portions) (portions), Bellflower, Laddonia, Martinsburg, Montgomery City, New Florence, Wellsville). Franchise award date: N.A. Franchise expiration date: N.A. Began: December 1, 1966.
Channel capacity: N.A. Channels available but not in use: N.A.
Basic Service
Subscribers: N.A. Included in Hannibal
Programming (received off-air): KETC (PBS) St. Louis; KHQA-TV (ABC, CBS) Hannibal; KMIZ (ABC) Columbia; KNLJ (IND) Jefferson City; KOMU-TV (CW, NBC) Columbia; KPLR-TV (CW) St. Louis; KRCG (CBS) Jefferson City; KSDK (NBC) St. Louis; 7 FMs.
Programming (via microwave): KQFX-LD Columbia.
Programming (via satellite): C-SPAN; Discovery Channel; Great American Country; Headline News; Home Shopping Network; Lifetime; TBS Superstation; Travel Channel; Turner Network TV; TV Guide Network.
Fee: $60.00 installation; $15.95 monthly; $2.00 converter.
Expanded Basic Service 1
Subscribers: N.A.
Programming (via satellite): ABC Family Channel; AMC; Animal Planet; Arts & Entertainment; BET Networks; Cartoon Network; CNBC; CNN; Country Music TV; Disney Channel; E! Entertainment Television; ESPN; ESPN 2; Food Network; Fox News Channel; Fox Sports Net Midwest; FX; Hallmark Channel; HGTV; History Channel; MSNBC; MTV; National Geographic Channel; Nickelodeon; QVC; Spike TV; The Learning Channel; truTV; TV Land; USA Network; VH1; Weather Channel.
Fee: $28.07 monthly.
Digital Basic Service
Subscribers: N.A. Included in Hannibal
Programming (via satellite): BBC America; Bio; Bloomberg Television; Bravo; Discovery Digital Networks; DMX Music; ESPN Classic Sports; ESPNews; Fox Reality Channel; Fox Soccer; Fuse; G4; GAS; Golf Channel; GSN; Independent Film Channel; Lifetime Movie Network; MTV Networks Digital Suite; Nick Jr.; Sleuth; Speed Channel; Syfy; Toon Disney; Trinity Broadcasting Network; Turner Classic Movies; Versus; WE tv.
Fee: $4.95 monthly; $8.00 converter.
Digital Expanded Basic Service
Subscribers: N.A.
Programming (via satellite): CMT Pure Country; Encore (multiplexed); FitTV; Fox Movie Channel; Halogen Network; History Channel International; Military History Channel; Style Network.
Fee: $3.95 monthly; $8.00 converter.
Digital Expanded Basic Service 2
Subscribers: N.A.
Programming (via satellite): NFL Network; Outdoor Channel.
Fee: $4.95 monthly; $8.00 converter.
Pay Service 1
Pay Units: N.A.
Programming (via satellite): HBO.
Fee: $12.49 monthly.
Digital Pay Service 1
Pay Units: N.A.
Programming (via satellite): Showtime (multiplexed).
Fee: $6.95 monthly (Starz), $11.95 monthly (Cinemax, HBO, Showtime or TMC).
Video-On-Demand: No
Pay-Per-View
iN DEMAND (delivered digitally); Fresh (delivered digitally); Playboy TV (delivered digitally); Club Jenna (delivered digitally).
Internet Service
Operational: Yes.
Broadband Service: Warp Drive Online.
Telephone Service
None
Homes passed, total homes in franchised area, & miles of plant included in Hannibal
Technical Operations Manager: Roger Young.
City fee: 7% of gross.
Ownership: US Cable Corp. (MSO).; Comcast Cable Communications Inc. (MSO).

MIDDLETOWN—Formerly served by First Cable of Missouri Inc. No longer in operation. ICA: MO0344.

MILAN—Milan Interactive Services, 312 S. Main, PO Box 240, Milan, MO 63556. Phone: 660-265-7174. ICA: MO0148.
TV Market Ranking: Below 100 (MILAN). Franchise award date: March 7, 1985. Franchise expiration date: N.A. Began: June 1, 1965.
Channel capacity: 41 (not 2-way capable). Channels available but not in use: N.A.
Basic Service
Subscribers: 160.
Programming (received off-air): KHQA-TV (ABC, CBS) Hannibal; KMBC-TV (ABC) Kansas City; KTVO (ABC) Kirksville; KYOU-TV (FOX) Ottumwa; WGEM-TV (CW, NBC) Quincy; WTVS (PBS) Detroit.
Programming (via satellite): Home Shopping Network; INSP; QVC; WGN America.
Fee: $29.95 installation; $39.95 monthly.
Video-On-Demand: No
Internet Service
Operational: No.
Telephone Service
None
Miles of Plant: 16.0 (coaxial); None (fiber optic). Homes passed: 880. Total homes in franchised area: 880.
President & General Manager: Rick Gardener.
City fee: 3% of gross.
Ownership: Milan Interactive Communications (MSO).

MINDENMINES—Formerly served by Cebridge Connections. No longer in operation. ICA: MO0329.

MISSIONARY—Crystal Broadcast Networks, Suite 180336, Chicago, IL 60618. Phones: 877-319-0328; 630-206-0447. E-mail: info@crystalbn.com. Web Site: http://crystalbn.com. ICA: MO0180.
TV Market Ranking: Outside TV Markets (MISSIONARY). Franchise award date: N.A. Franchise expiration date: N.A. Began: N.A.
Channel capacity: 42 (not 2-way capable). Channels available but not in use: 4.
Basic Service
Subscribers: 189.
Programming (received off-air): KOLR (CBS) Springfield; KOMU-TV (CW, NBC) Columbia; KOZK (PBS) Springfield; KSFX-TV (FOX) Springfield; KSPR (ABC) Springfield; KYTV (CW, NBC) Springfield.
Programming (via satellite): ABC Family Channel; AMC; Arts & Entertainment; CNBC; CNN; Country Music TV; C-SPAN; Discovery Channel; ESPN; Hallmark Channel; Headline News; Home Shopping Network; Lifetime; Nickelodeon; Spike TV; TBS Superstation; Turner Network TV; USA Network; Weather Channel; WGN America.
Fee: $29.95 installation; $39.95 monthly.
Pay Service 1
Pay Units: 11.
Programming (via satellite): Cinemax.
Fee: $10.00 monthly.
Pay Service 2
Pay Units: 21.
Programming (via satellite): HBO.
Fee: $10.95 monthly.
Pay Service 3
Pay Units: 44.
Programming (via satellite): Showtime.
Fee: $10.00 monthly.
Video-On-Demand: No
Internet Service
Operational: Yes.
Telephone Service
Digital: Operational
Miles of Plant: 32.0 (coaxial); None (fiber optic). Homes passed: 741.
General Manager: Nidhin Johnson. Program Manager: Shawn Smith.
Ownership: Crystal Broadband Networks (MSO).

MOBERLY—US Cable, 647 Clinic Rd, Hannibal, MO 63401. Phone: 573-581-2404. Fax: 573-581-4053. Web Site: http://www.uscable.com. Also serves Huntsville & Randolph County. ICA: MO0031.
TV Market Ranking: Below 100 (MOBERLY, Randolph County (portions)); Outside TV Markets (Huntsville, Randolph County (portions)). Franchise award date: N.A. Franchise expiration date: N.A. Began: January 1, 1969.
Channel capacity: N.A. Channels available but not in use: N.A.
Basic Service
Subscribers: N.A. Included in Hannibal
Programming (received off-air): KMIZ (ABC) Columbia; KMOS-TV (PBS) Sedalia; KOMU-TV (CW, NBC) Columbia; KPLR-TV (CW) St. Louis; KRCG (CBS) Jefferson City; 14 FMs.
Programming (via microwave): KQFX-LD Columbia.
Programming (via satellite): ABC Family Channel; Fox News Channel; Hallmark Channel; QVC; Turner Network TV; TV Guide Network.
Current originations: Government Access.
Fee: $60.00 installation; $17.72 monthly; $2.00 converter.
Expanded Basic Service 1
Subscribers: 3,395.
Programming (via satellite): AMC; Animal Planet; Arts & Entertainment; BET Networks; Cartoon Network; CNBC; CNN; Country Music TV; C-SPAN; C-SPAN 2; Discovery Channel; Disney Channel; E! Entertainment Television; ESPN; Food Network; Fox Sports Net Midwest; FX; Lifetime; MTV; National Geographic Channel; Nickelodeon; Oxygen; Speed Channel; Spike TV; TBS Superstation; The Learning Channel; truTV; TV Land; USA Network; Weather Channel.
Fee: $23.02 monthly.
Digital Basic Service
Subscribers: N.A. Included in Hannibal
Programming (via satellite): BBC America; Bio; Bloomberg Television; Discovery Digital Networks; Fox Reality Channel; Fuse; G4; GSN; Halogen Network; HGTV; History Channel International; Lime; MTV Networks Digital Suite; Nick Jr.; Sleuth; Style Network; Syfy; Toon Disney; Trinity Broadcasting Network; WealthTV.
Fee: $12.95 monthly.
Digital Expanded Basic Service
Subscribers: N.A.
Programming (via satellite): DMX Music; Encore (multiplexed); Fox Movie Channel; Independent Film Channel; Lifetime Movie Network; Turner Classic Movies; WE tv.
Fee: $3.95 monthly.
Digital Expanded Basic Service 2
Subscribers: N.A.
Programming (via satellite): ESPN Classic Sports; ESPNews; Fox Soccer; GAS; Golf Channel; NFL Network; Outdoor Channel; Versus.
Fee: $4.95 monthly.
Pay Service 1
Pay Units: 268.
Programming (via satellite): HBO.
Fee: $13.90 monthly.
Pay Service 2
Pay Units: N.A.
Programming (via satellite): Cinemax; Encore; Starz.
Fee: $2.99 monthly (Encore), $9.10 monthly (Starz), $13.40 monthly (Cinemax).
Digital Pay Service 1
Pay Units: N.A.
Programming (via satellite): Cinemax (multiplexed); HBO (multiplexed); Showtime (multiplexed); Starz (multiplexed); The Movie Channel (multiplexed).
Fee: $6.95 monthly (Starz), $11.95 monthly (Cinemax, HBO, Showtime or TMC).
Video-On-Demand: No
Pay-Per-View
iN DEMAND (delivered digitally); Playboy TV (delivered digitally); Fresh (delivered digitally).
Internet Service
Operational: Yes.
Broadband Service: Warp Drive Online.
Telephone Service
None
Homes passed & total homes in franchised area included in Hannibal
Regional Administrative Director: Rebecca Bramblett. Technical Operations Manager: Roger Young. Marketing Director: Rita Watson.
City fee: 3% of gross.
Ownership: US Cable Corp. (MSO).; Comcast Cable Communications Inc. (MSO).

MOKANE—Formerly served by First Cable of Missouri Inc. No longer in operation. ICA: MO0349.

MONETT—Suddenlink Communications, 304 Madison Ave, Aurora, MO 65605. Phones: 800-743-0285 (Customer service); 417-358-3002. Fax: 417-359-5373. Web Site: http://www.suddenlink.com. Also serves Aurora, Marionville, Pierce City & Verona. ICA: MO0052.

TV Market Ranking: Below 100 (Aurora, Marionville, MONETT, Pierce City, Verona). Franchise award date: April 7, 1981. Franchise expiration date: N.A. Began: July 1, 1982.

Channel capacity: N.A. Channels available but not in use: N.A.

Basic Service

Subscribers: 4,816.

Programming (received off-air): KOAM-TV (CBS) Pittsburg; KODE-TV (ABC) Joplin; KOLR (CBS) Springfield; KOZK (PBS) Springfield; KSFX-TV (FOX) Springfield; KSNF (NBC) Joplin; KSPR (ABC) Springfield; KYTV (CW, NBC) Springfield.

Programming (via satellite): TBS Superstation; WGN America.

Fee: $42.38 installation; $8.15 monthly.

Expanded Basic Service 1

Subscribers: N.A.

Programming (via satellite): ABC Family Channel; Animal Planet; Arts & Entertainment; Cartoon Network; CNBC; CNN; Comedy Central; Country Music TV; C-SPAN; Discovery Channel; Disney Channel; ESPN; Food Network; Fox News Channel; Fox Sports Net Midwest; FX; Hallmark Channel; Headline News; HGTV; History Channel; Lifetime; Nickelodeon; Outdoor Channel; QVC; Spike TV; Syfy; The Learning Channel; Travel Channel; Turner Network TV; TV Land; USA Network; VH1; Weather Channel.

Fee: $16.44 monthly.

Expanded Basic Service 2

Subscribers: N.A.

Programming (via satellite): AMC; ESPN 2; MTV; Turner Classic Movies.

Fee: $3.95 monthly.

Digital Basic Service

Subscribers: N.A.

Programming (via satellite): Bloomberg Television; Discovery Digital Networks; DMX Music; ESPN Classic Sports; Fox Sports World; G4; Golf Channel; INSP; Speed Channel; Trinity Broadcasting Network.

Pay Service 1

Pay Units: 531.

Programming (via satellite): Cinemax.

Fee: $10.60 installation; $8.95 monthly.

Pay Service 2

Pay Units: 766.

Programming (via satellite): HBO.

Fee: $10.60 installation; $10.95 monthly.

Digital Pay Service 1

Pay Units: N.A.

Programming (via satellite): Cinemax (multiplexed); Encore (multiplexed); HBO (multiplexed); Showtime (multiplexed); Starz (multiplexed); Sundance Channel; The Movie Channel (multiplexed).

Video-On-Demand: Yes

Pay-Per-View

iN DEMAND (delivered digitally), Addressable: Yes.

Internet Service

Operational: Yes.

Broadband Service: Cebridge High Speed Cable Internet.

Fee: $39.95 monthly.

Telephone Service

None

Miles of Plant: 114.0 (coaxial); 35.0 (fiber optic). Total homes in franchised area: 10,324.

Manager: Terrill Bradley. Chief Engineer: Tim Crotti.

City fee: 3% of gross.

Ownership: Cequel Communications LLC (MSO).

MONROE CITY—US Cable of Coastal Texas LP. Now served by HANNIBAL, MO [MO0021]. ICA: MO0058.

MONTGOMERY CITY—US Cable. Now served by MEXICO, MO [MO0033]. ICA: MO0057.

MONTICELLO—Formerly served by CableDirect. No longer in operation. ICA: MO0443.

MORLEY—Semo Communications Corporation, PO Box C, 107 Semo Ln, Sikeston, MO 63801-0937. Phones: 573-471-6594; 573-471-6599. Fax: 573-471-6878. E-mail: cableme@semocommunications.com. Web Site: http://www.semocommunications.com. Also serves Advance, Anniston, Bell City, Blodgett, Brownwood, Canalou, Delta, Fruitland, Haywood City, Matthews, Morehouse Colony, New Madrid County (northern portion), Pocahontas, Scott County (southern portion), Vanduser, Wilson City & Wyatt. ICA: MO0171.

TV Market Ranking: 69 (Advance, Bell City, Blodgett, Brownwood, Delta, Fruitland, Haywood City, Morehouse Colony, MORLEY, New Madrid County (northern portion), Pocahontas, Scott County (southern portion), Vanduser, Wilson City, Wyatt); Outside TV Markets (Anniston, Canalou, Matthews). Franchise award date: November 1, 1981. Franchise expiration date: N.A. Began: January 1, 1982.

Channel capacity: 78 (not 2-way capable). Channels available but not in use: 3.

Basic Service

Subscribers: 1,255.

Programming (received off-air): KBSI (FOX) Cape Girardeau; KFVS-TV (CBS, CW) Cape Girardeau; WDKA (MNT) Paducah; WKMU (PBS) Murray; WPSD-TV (NBC) Paducah; WSIL-TV (ABC) Harrisburg; WTCT (IND) Marion.

Programming (via satellite): Home Shopping Network; ION Television; QVC.

Fee: $35.00 installation; $19.95 monthly; $1.00 converter; $25.00 additional installation.

Expanded Basic Service 1

Subscribers: N.A.

Programming (via satellite): ABC Family Channel; AMC; Animal Planet; Arts & Entertainment; BET Networks; Cartoon Network; CNBC; CNN; Comedy Central; Cooking Channel; C-SPAN; C-SPAN 2; CW+; Discovery Channel; Disney Channel; Do-It-Yourself; E! Entertainment Television; ESPN; ESPN 2; ESPN Classic Sports; Food Network; Fox News Channel; Fox Sports Net Midwest; FX; Great American Country; Hallmark Channel; Headline News; HGTV; History Channel; Lifetime; MTV; National Geographic Channel; Nickelodeon; Outdoor Channel; Oxygen; SoapNet; Speed Channel; Spike TV; Syfy; TBS Superstation; The Learning Channel; Travel Channel; truTV; Turner Classic Movies; Turner Network TV; TV Land; USA Network; VH1; Weather Channel; WGN America.

Fee: $47.95 monthly.

Digital Basic Service

Subscribers: N.A.

Programming (received off-air): KFVS-TV (CBS, CW) Cape Girardeau; WPSD-TV (NBC) Paducah; WSIL-TV (ABC) Harrisburg.

Programming (via satellite): AmericanLife TV Network; BBC America; Bio; Black Family Channel; Bloomberg Television; Bravo; CMT Pure Country; Discovery Health Channel; Discovery Home Channel; Discovery Kids Channel; Discovery Military Channel; Discovery Times Channel; DMX Music; Encore; Encore Action; Encore Avenue; Encore Love; Encore Mystery; Encore Wam; Encore Westerns; ESPN HD; ESPNews; FitTV; Fox College Sports Atlantic; Fox College Sports Central; Fox College Sports Pacific; Fox Movie Channel; Fox Soccer; Fuse; G4; Golf Channel; GSN; Halogen Network; History Channel International; Independent Film Channel; Lifetime Movie Network; Lime; MTV2; National Geographic Channel HD Network; Nick Jr.; NickToons TV; Outdoor Channel 2 HD; RFD-TV; Science Channel; ShopNBC; Sleuth; Style Network; TeenNick; Toon Disney; Trinity Broadcasting Network; Turner Network TV HD; TVG Network; Universal HD; Versus; VH1 Classic; VH1 Soul; WE tv; Weatherscan.

Fee: $14.95 monthly.

Digital Pay Service 1

Pay Units: N.A.

Programming (via satellite): Cinemax (multiplexed); Flix; HBO (multiplexed); Showtime (multiplexed); Starz (multiplexed); The Movie Channel (multiplexed).

Video-On-Demand: No

Pay-Per-View

Spice: Xcess (delivered digitally), Addressable: Yes; Hot Choice (delivered digitally); iN DEMAND (delivered digitally); Playboy TV (delivered digitally); Fresh (delivered digitally); Club Jenna (delivered digitally).

Internet Service

Operational: Yes.

Subscribers: 1,576.

Broadband Service: Cable Rocket.

Fee: $29.95 monthly.

Telephone Service

Digital: Operational

Subscribers: 939.

Fee: $29.99 monthly

Miles of Plant: 150.0 (coaxial); 100.0 (fiber optic). Homes passed: 4,197. Total homes in franchised area: 4,197.

President: Tyrone Garrett. Vice President: Shannon Garrett. Chief Technician: Jim Crittenden.

Ownership: Semo Communications Inc.

MOUND CITY—Longview Communications, 1923 N Main, Higginsville, MO 64037. Phone: 866-611-6565. Fax: 866-329-4790. Web Site: http://www.longviewcomm.com. ICA: MO0183.

TV Market Ranking: Below 100 (MOUND CITY). Franchise award date: N.A. Franchise expiration date: N.A. Began: December 1, 1976.

Channel capacity: N.A. Channels available but not in use: N.A.

Basic Service

Subscribers: 400.

Programming (received off-air): KCPT (PBS) Kansas City; KCTV (CBS) Kansas City; KCWE (CW) Kansas City; KMBC-TV (ABC) Kansas City; KQTV (ABC) St. Joseph; KSHB-TV (NBC) Kansas City; KSMO-TV (MNT) Kansas City; KTAJ-TV (TBN) St. Joseph; WDAF-TV (FOX) Kansas City; allband FM.

Programming (via satellite): C-SPAN; Home Shopping Network.

Fee: $35.95 installation; $20.98 monthly.

Expanded Basic Service 1

Subscribers: N.A.

Programming (via satellite): ABC Family Channel; AMC; Animal Planet; Arts & Entertainment; Bravo; Cartoon Network; CBS College Sports Network; CNBC; CNN; Comedy Central; Discovery Channel; Disney Channel; Do-It-Yourself; E! Entertainment Television; ESPN; ESPN 2; Food Network; Fox News Channel; FX; Great American Country; Hallmark Channel; Hallmark Movie Channel; Headline News; HGTV; History Channel; Lifetime; MSNBC; National Geographic Channel; Nickelodeon; Syfy; TBS Superstation; The Learning Channel; Travel Channel; truTV; Turner Network TV; USA Network; WE tv; Weather Channel; WGN America.

Fee: $19.97 monthly.

Digital Basic Service

Subscribers: 84.

Programming (via satellite): AmericanLife TV Network; BBC America; Bio; Bloomberg Television; Discovery Digital Networks; Encore (multiplexed); ESPN Classic Sports; ESPNews; Fox Movie Channel; G4; Golf Channel; GSN; Halogen Network; History Channel International; Independent Film Channel; Lifetime Movie Network; Outdoor Channel; Speed Channel; Style Network; Toon Disney; Turner Classic Movies.

Fee: $18.00 monthly.

Pay Service 1

Pay Units: 90.

Programming (via satellite): Cinemax; HBO; Showtime; The Movie Channel.

Fee: $8.95 monthly (TMC), $10.95 monthly (Cinemax or Showtime), $12.95 monthly (HBO)monthly (TMC).

Digital Pay Service 1

Pay Units: N.A.

Programming (via satellite): Cinemax (multiplexed); Flix; HBO (multiplexed); Showtime (multiplexed); Starz (multiplexed); The Movie Channel (multiplexed).

Fee: $8.95 monthly (TMC), $10.95 monthly (Showtime & Cinemax), $12.95 monthly (HBO).

Video-On-Demand: No

Pay-Per-View

iN DEMAND (delivered digitally); Hot Choice (delivered digitally); Playboy TV (delivered digitally); Fresh (delivered digitally); Shorteez (delivered digitally).

Internet Service

Operational: Yes.

Subscribers: 121.

Broadband Service: IBBS.

Telephone Service

None

Miles of Plant: 14.0 (coaxial); None (fiber optic). Homes passed: 640.

President: John Long. Senior Vice President: Marc W. Cohen. General Manager: Brandon Dickey. Operations Manager: Perry Scarborogh.

City fee: 3% of gross.

Ownership: Longview Communications (MSO).

MOUNTAIN GROVE—Almega Cable. Now served by WAYNESVILLE, MO [MO0023]. ICA: MO0093.

MOUNTAIN VIEW—Boycom Cablevision Inc., 3467 Township Line Rd, Poplar Bluff, MO 63901. Phone: 573-686-9101. Fax: 573-686-4722. Web Site: http://www.boycomonline.com. ICA: MO0128.

TV Market Ranking: Outside TV Markets (MOUNTAIN VIEW). Franchise award date: January 16, 1969. Franchise expiration date: N.A. Began: January 1, 1970.

Channel capacity: 54 (not 2-way capable). Channels available but not in use: 20.

Basic Service
Subscribers: N.A. Included in Alton
Programming (received off-air): K15CZ Springfield; KOLR (CBS) Springfield; KOZK (PBS) Springfield; KSPR (ABC) Springfield; KTVI (FOX) St. Louis; KYTV (CW, NBC) Springfield.
Programming (via satellite): C-SPAN; Home Shopping Network; Trinity Broadcasting Network; Weather Channel; WGN America.
Fee: $29.95 installation; $19.95 monthly.

Expanded Basic Service 1
Subscribers: N.A.
Programming (via satellite): ABC Family Channel; AMC; Arts & Entertainment; CNN; C-SPAN 2; Discovery Channel; Disney Channel; ESPN; ESPN 2; Fox Sports Net Midwest; FX; G4; Great American Country; Lifetime; MSNBC; MTV; Nickelodeon; Speed Channel; Spike TV; TBS Superstation; The Learning Channel; Toon Disney; Turner Network TV; TV Land; USA Network; VH1.
Fee: $20.00 monthly.

Digital Basic Service
Subscribers: N.A.
Programming (via satellite): BBC America; Bio; Bloomberg Television; Discovery Health Channel; Discovery Kids Channel; Discovery Military Channel; Discovery Planet Green; ESPN Classic Sports; ESPNews; Fox College Sports Atlantic; Fox College Sports Central; Fox College Sports Pacific; Fox Movie Channel; Fox Soccer; Golf Channel; Gospel Music Channel; GSN; Halogen Network; HGTV; History Channel; History Channel International; ID Investigation Discovery; Lifetime Movie Network; National Geographic Channel; Outdoor Channel; Science Channel; ShopNBC; Sleuth; Speed Channel; Style Network; Syfy; Turner Classic Movies; Versus; WE tv.

Pay Service 1
Pay Units: 283.
Programming (via satellite): Cinemax; Encore; HBO; Showtime; Starz; The Movie Channel.
Fee: $5.99 monthly (Starz), $8.99 monthly (Cinemax), $12.99 monthly (HBO), $13.99 monthly (Showtime & TMC).

Digital Pay Service 1
Pay Units: N.A.
Programming (via satellite): Cinemax (multiplexed); Encore (multiplexed); Flix; HBO (multiplexed); Showtime (multiplexed); Starz (multiplexed); The Movie Channel (multiplexed).

Video-On-Demand: No

Pay-Per-View
iN DEMAND (delivered digitally); Playboy TV (delivered digitally); Fresh (delivered digitally); Club Jenna (delivered digitally).

Internet Service
Operational: Yes.

Telephone Service
None
Miles of Plant: 30.0 (coaxial); None (fiber optic). Homes passed: 1,127.
President: Steven Boyers. General Manager: Shelly Batton. Chief Technician: Phil Huett.
Ownership: Boycom Cablevision Inc. (MSO).

NAYLOR—Boycom Cablevision Inc., 3467 Township Line Rd, Poplar Bluff, MO 63901. Phone: 573-686-9101. Fax: 573-686-4722. Web Site: http://www.boycomonline.com. Also serves Neelyville. ICA: MO0181.
TV Market Ranking: Below 100 (NAYLOR, Neelyville). Franchise award date: October 5, 1970. Franchise expiration date: N.A. Began: N.A.
Channel capacity: 22 (operating 2-way). Channels available but not in use: 5.

Basic Service
Subscribers: N.A. Included in Alton
Programming (received off-air): KAIT (ABC) Jonesboro; KBSI (FOX) Cape Girardeau; KFVS-TV (CBS, CW) Cape Girardeau; KPOB-TV (ABC) Poplar Bluff; KTEJ (PBS) Jonesboro; KVTJ-DT (IND) Jonesboro; WNBC (NBC) New York.
Programming (via satellite): ABC Family Channel; CNN; Country Music TV; Discovery Channel; ESPN; Fox Sports Net Midwest; Nickelodeon; Spike TV; TBS Superstation; USA Network; WGN America.
Fee: $29.95 installation; $39.95 monthly.

Pay Service 1
Pay Units: 51.
Programming (via satellite): HBO.
Fee: $12.99 monthly.

Video-On-Demand: No

Internet Service
Operational: No.

Telephone Service
None
Miles of Plant: 18.0 (coaxial); None (fiber optic). Homes passed: 642.
President: Steven Boyers. General Manager: Shelly Batton. Chief Technician: Phil Huett.
City fee: None.
Ownership: Boycom Cablevision Inc. (MSO).

NEOSHO—Suddenlink Communications, 12444 Powerscourt Dr, Saint Louis, MO 63131-3660. Phone: 314-965-2020. Web Site: http://www.suddenlink.com. Also serves Newton County (portions). ICA: MO0047.
TV Market Ranking: Below 100 (NEOSHO, Newton County (portions)). Franchise award date: January 28, 1966. Franchise expiration date: N.A. Began: January 28, 1966.
Channel capacity: 41 (operating 2-way). Channels available but not in use: N.A.

Basic Service
Subscribers: 2,537.
Programming (received off-air): KOAM-TV (CBS) Pittsburg; KODE-TV (ABC) Joplin; KOZJ (PBS) Joplin; KSNF (NBC) Joplin; KYTV (CW, NBC) Springfield.
Programming (via satellite): ABC Family Channel; AMC; Animal Planet; Arts & Entertainment; CNBC; CNN; Country Music TV; C-SPAN; Discovery Channel; Disney Channel; ESPN; Fox Sports Net Midwest; Headline News; HGTV; History Channel; Home Shopping Network; Lifetime; Nickelodeon; QVC; Spike TV; Syfy; TBS Superstation; The Learning Channel; Turner Network TV; TV Land; USA Network; Weather Channel; WGN America.
Current originations: Religious Access; Public Access.
Fee: $39.95 installation; $19.95 monthly.

Pay Service 1
Pay Units: 327.
Programming (via satellite): HBO.
Fee: $15.00 installation; $10.95 monthly.

Pay Service 2
Pay Units: 201.
Programming (via satellite): The Movie Channel.
Fee: $15.00 installation; $7.95 monthly.

Pay Service 3
Pay Units: 198.
Programming (via satellite): Showtime.
Fee: $15.00 installation; $9.95 monthly.

Internet Service
Operational: Yes. Began: October 17, 2003.
Broadband Service: Cebridge High Speed Cable Internet.
Fee: $29.95 monthly.

Telephone Service
None
Miles of Plant: 83.0 (coaxial); None (fiber optic).
Regional Manager: Todd Cruthird. Regional Marketing Manager: Beverly Gambell.
City fee: 5% of gross.
Ownership: Cequel Communications LLC (MSO).

NEVADA—Charter Communications, 210 W 7th St, Sedalia, MO 65301-4217. Phones: 636-207-7044 (St Louis office); 660-826-6520. Fax: 660-826-4583. Web Site: http://www.charter.com. ICA: MO0048.
TV Market Ranking: Outside TV Markets (NEVADA). Franchise award date: N.A. Franchise expiration date: N.A. Began: October 1, 1964.
Channel capacity: 55 (not 2-way capable). Channels available but not in use: N.A.

Basic Service
Subscribers: 3,595.
Programming (received off-air): KCPT (PBS) Kansas City; KCTV (CBS) Kansas City; KFJX (FOX) Pittsburg; KOAM-TV (CBS) Pittsburg; KODE-TV (ABC) Joplin; KOLR (CBS) Springfield; KSHB-TV (NBC) Kansas City; KSNF (NBC) Joplin; 14 FMs.
Programming (via satellite): C-SPAN; Home Shopping Network; INSP; QVC; Weather Channel.
Current originations: Educational Access; Public Access; Government Access.
Fee: $59.95 installation; $9.92 monthly; $2.00 converter; $40.00 additional installation.

Expanded Basic Service 1
Subscribers: 3,255.
Programming (via satellite): ABC Family Channel; AMC; Animal Planet; Arts & Entertainment; Cartoon Network; CNBC; CNN; Comedy Central; Country Music TV; Discovery Channel; Disney Channel; E! Entertainment Television; ESPN; ESPN 2; Food Network; Fox News Channel; Fox Sports Net Midwest; FX; G4; Golf Channel; Hallmark Channel; Headline News; HGTV; History Channel; Lifetime; MTV; Nickelodeon; Oxygen; Speed Channel; Spike TV; Syfy; TBS Superstation; The Learning Channel; Travel Channel; truTV; Turner Classic Movies; Turner Network TV; TV Land; USA Network.
Fee: $10.64 installation; $2.20 monthly.

Digital Basic Service
Subscribers: N.A.
Programming (via satellite): BBC America; Bio; Bloomberg Television; Discovery Digital Networks; Do-It-Yourself; GAS; GSN; History Channel International; Independent Film Channel; MTV Networks Digital Suite; Music Choice; Nick Jr.; Nick Too; NickToons TV; SoapNet; Style Network; Sundance Channel; Toon Disney; TV Guide Interactive Inc.; Versus; WE tv.

Digital Pay Service 1
Pay Units: 169.
Programming (via satellite): Cinemax (multiplexed); Encore (multiplexed); Flix; HBO (multiplexed); Showtime (multiplexed); Starz (multiplexed); The Movie Channel (multiplexed).
Fee: $10.00 installation; $11.50 monthly (each).

Video-On-Demand: No

Pay-Per-View
iN DEMAND (delivered digitally); Pleasure (delivered digitally); ETC (delivered digitally).

Internet Service
Operational: Yes.
Broadband Service: Charter Pipeline.

Telephone Service
None
Miles of Plant: 81.0 (coaxial); None (fiber optic). Homes passed: 4,129.
Vice President & General Manager: Steve Trippe. Operations Director: Dave Miller. Technical Operations Manager: Larry Wright. Marketing Director: Beverly Wall. Office Manager: Vicky Brant.
City fee: 3% of gross.
Ownership: Charter Communications Inc. (MSO).

NEW BLOOMFIELD—Longview Communications, 12007 Sunrise Valley Dr, Ste 375, Reston, VA 20191. Phones: 866-611-6565 (Customer service); 703-476-9101. Fax: 703-476-9107. Web Site: http://www.longviewcomm.com. Also serves Lake Mykee Town. ICA: MO0415.
TV Market Ranking: Below 100 (Lake Mykee Town, NEW BLOOMFIELD). Franchise award date: N.A. Franchise expiration date: N.A. Began: March 1, 1984.
Channel capacity: 41 (not 2-way capable). Channels available but not in use: 5.

Basic Service
Subscribers: 55.
Programming (received off-air): KMIZ (ABC) Columbia; KMOS-TV (PBS) Sedalia; KNLJ (IND) Jefferson City; KOMU-TV (CW, NBC) Columbia; KRCG (CBS) Jefferson City.
Programming (via satellite): ABC Family Channel; AMC; Animal Planet; Arts & Entertainment; Cartoon Network; CNN; Discovery Channel; Disney Channel; ESPN; ESPN 2; Fox News Channel; FX; Great American Country; Headline News; History Channel; Lifetime; Outdoor Channel; QVC; TBS Superstation; The Learning Channel; Toon Disney; Turner Network TV; USA Network; Weather Channel; WGN America.
Fee: $39.95 monthly.

Pay Service 1
Pay Units: 42.
Programming (via satellite): Cinemax; HBO; Showtime; Starz; The Movie Channel.
Fee: $9.95 monthly (Starz, Showtime or TMC), $10.95 monthly (Cinemax), $14.95 monthly (HBO).

Video-On-Demand: No

Internet Service
Operational: No.

Telephone Service
None
Miles of Plant: 15.0 (coaxial); None (fiber optic). Homes passed: 425.
President: John Long. Senior Vice President: Marc W. Cohen. General Manager: Brandon Dickey. Operations Manager: Perry Scarborough.
Ownership: Longview Communications (MSO).

NEW CAMBRIA—Chariton Valley Communications Corp. Now served by MACON, MO [MO0071]. ICA: MO0337.

NEW FRANKLIN—Longview Communications, 12007 Sunrise Valley Dr, Ste 375, Reston, VA 20191. Phones: 866-611-6565 (Customer service); 703-476-9101. Fax: 703-476-9107. Web Site: http://www.

longviewcomm.com. Also serves Franklin. ICA: MO0215.
TV Market Ranking: Below 100 (Franklin, NEW FRANKLIN). Franchise award date: N.A. Franchise expiration date: N.A. Began: May 1, 1982.
Channel capacity: 40 (not 2-way capable). Channels available but not in use: N.A.
Basic Service
Subscribers: 63.
Programming (received off-air): KMIZ (ABC) Columbia; KMOS-TV (PBS) Sedalia; KNLJ (IND) Jefferson City; KOMU-TV (CW, NBC) Columbia; KRCG (CBS) Jefferson City.
Programming (via satellite): Classic Arts Showcase; C-SPAN; C-SPAN 2; Home Shopping Network; QVC; Trinity Broadcasting Network.
Fee: $19.98 monthly.
Expanded Basic Service 1
Subscribers: N.A.
Programming (via satellite): ABC Family Channel; AMC; Animal Planet; Arts & Entertainment; CNN; Discovery Channel; Disney Channel; E! Entertainment Television; ESPN; ESPN 2; Fox News Channel; Fox Sports Net Midwest; Great American Country; Headline News; History Channel; Lifetime; MSNBC; Speed Channel; TBS Superstation; The Learning Channel; Turner Network TV; USA Network; Weather Channel.
Fee: $17.97 monthly.
Pay Service 1
Pay Units: 62.
Programming (via satellite): Cinemax; HBO; Showtime; The Movie Channel.
Fee: $8.95 monthly (TMC), $10.95 monthly (Showtime or Cinemax), $12.95 monthly (HBO).
Video-On-Demand: No
Internet Service
Operational: No.
Telephone Service
None
Miles of Plant: 9.0 (coaxial); None (fiber optic). Homes passed: 528.
President: John Long. Senior Vice President: Marc W. Cohen. General Manager: Brandon Dickey. Operations Manager: Perry Scarborough.
Ownership: Longview Communications (MSO).

NEW HAVEN—Fidelity Communications, 64 N Clark St, Sullivan, MO 63080. Phones: 800-392-8070; 573-468-8081. Web Site: http://www.fidelitycommunications.com. ICA: MO0197.
TV Market Ranking: Outside TV Markets (NEW HAVEN (PORTIONS)). Franchise award date: August 9, 1982. Franchise expiration date: N.A. Began: N.A.
Channel capacity: 41 (not 2-way capable). Channels available but not in use: N.A.
Basic Service
Subscribers: 397.
Programming (received off-air): KDNL-TV (ABC) St. Louis; KETC (PBS) St. Louis; KMIZ (ABC) Columbia; KMOV (CBS) St. Louis; KOMU-TV (CW, NBC) Columbia; KPLR-TV (CW) St. Louis; KRCG (CBS) Jefferson City; KSDK (NBC) St. Louis; KTVI (FOX) St. Louis.
Programming (via satellite): ABC Family Channel; QVC; Trinity Broadcasting Network; WGN America.
Fee: $29.95 installation; $19.95 monthly.
Expanded Basic Service 1
Subscribers: N.A.
Programming (via satellite): AMC; Arts & Entertainment; Cartoon Network; CNBC; Comedy Central; Country Music TV; Discovery Channel; Disney Channel; E! Entertainment Television; ESPN; ESPN 2; Fox News Channel; Fox Sports Net Midwest; Headline News; HGTV; History Channel; Lifetime; MTV; Nickelodeon; Spike TV; Syfy; TBS Superstation; The Learning Channel; Turner Network TV; USA Network; Weather Channel.
Fee: $20.00 monthly.
Pay Service 1
Pay Units: 47.
Programming (via satellite): Cinemax.
Fee: $10.50 monthly.
Pay Service 2
Pay Units: 59.
Programming (via satellite): HBO (multiplexed).
Fee: $11.00 monthly.
Video-On-Demand: No
Pay-Per-View
Urban American Television Network (delivered digitally); ESPN Now (delivered digitally); ESPN Gameplan (delivered digitally); Hot Choice (delivered digitally); Fresh (delivered digitally); Shorteez (delivered digitally); Playboy TV (delivered digitally); iN DEMAND (delivered digitally).
Internet Service
Operational: No, DSL.
Telephone Service
None
Miles of Plant: 15.0 (coaxial); None (fiber optic). Homes passed: 566. Total homes in franchised area: 566.
Manager: Andrew Davis.
City fee: 3% of gross.
Ownership: Fidelity Communications Co. (MSO).

NEW MADRID—Charter Communications, 3140 W Nash Rd, Scott City, MO 63780. Phones: 636-207-7044 (St Louis office); 573-335-4424. Fax: 573-334-9265. Web Site: http://www.charter.com. Also serves Howardville, Lilbourn, Marston, New Madrid County & North Lilbourn. ICA: MO0056.
TV Market Ranking: 69 (New Madrid County (portions)); Below 100 (Lilbourn, Marston, NEW MADRID, North Lilbourn, New Madrid County (portions)); Outside TV Markets (Howardville, New Madrid County (portions)). Franchise award date: January 1, 1971. Franchise expiration date: N.A. Began: October 25, 1971.
Channel capacity: N.A. Channels available but not in use: None.
Basic Service
Subscribers: 1,835.
Programming (received off-air): KBSI (FOX) Cape Girardeau; KFVS-TV (CBS, CW) Cape Girardeau; WDKA (MNT) Paducah; WPSD-TV (NBC) Paducah; WQWQ-LP (CW) Paducah; WSIL-TV (ABC) Harrisburg; WSIU-TV (PBS) Carbondale; WTCT (IND) Marion; allband FM.
Programming (via satellite): ABC Family Channel; BET Networks; C-SPAN; C-SPAN 2; Discovery Channel; Eternal Word TV Network; Home Shopping Network; INSP; Jewelry Television; Product Information Network; QVC; ShopNBC; Syfy; TBS Superstation; TV Guide Network; Weather Channel; WGN America.
Current originations: Government Access; Educational Access; Public Access.
Fee: $29.99 installation.
Expanded Basic Service 1
Subscribers: 1,779.
Programming (via satellite): AMC; Animal Planet; Arts & Entertainment; Bravo; Cartoon Network; CNBC; CNN; Comedy

Central; Country Music TV; Disney Channel; E! Entertainment Television; ESPN; Food Network; Fox News Channel; Fox Sports Net Midwest; G4; Golf Channel; Great American Country; GSN; Hallmark Channel; Headline News; HGTV; History Channel; Lifetime; MSNBC; MTV; MTV2; Nickelodeon; Outdoor Channel; Oxygen; SoapNet; Speed Channel; Spike TV; Style Network; The Learning Channel; Travel Channel; truTV; Turner Classic Movies; Turner Network TV; TV Land; USA Network; Versus; VH1.
Fee: $49.99 monthly.
Digital Basic Service
Subscribers: N.A.
Programming (received off-air): KFVS-TV (CBS, CW) Cape Girardeau; WPSD-TV (NBC) Paducah; WSIL-TV (ABC) Harrisburg; WSIU-TV (PBS) Carbondale.
Programming (via satellite): BBC America; Bio; Bloomberg Television; CBS College Sports Network; CNN en Espanol; CNN International; Discovery Digital Networks; Discovery HD Theater; Do-It-Yourself; ESPN; ESPN Classic Sports; ESPNews; FitTV; Fox College Sports Atlantic; Fox College Sports Central; Fox College Sports Pacific; Fox Soccer; Fuel TV; GAS; HDNet; HDNet Movies; History Channel International; Lifetime Movie Network; MTV Networks Digital Suite; Music Choice; National Geographic Channel; Nick Jr.; Nick Too; NickToons TV; Sundance Channel; The Sportsman Channel; Toon Disney; Turner Network TV HD; TV Guide Interactive Inc.; WE tv.
Digital Pay Service 1
Pay Units: 595.
Programming (via satellite): Cinemax (multiplexed); Cinemax HD; Encore (multiplexed); Flix; HBO (multiplexed); HBO HD; LOGO; Showtime (multiplexed); Showtime HD; Starz (multiplexed); The Movie Channel (multiplexed).
Fee: $10.50 monthly (HBO, Cinemax, Showtime/TMC, or Starz/Encore).
Video-On-Demand: No
Pay-Per-View
iN DEMAND (delivered digitally); Playboy TV (delivered digitally); Spice Live (delivered digitally); Spice Platinum (delivered digitally); Spice Hot (delivered digitally); Hot Net Plus (delivered digitally).
Internet Service
Operational: Yes.
Broadband Service: Charter Pipeline.
Fee: $29.99 monthly.
Telephone Service
Digital: Operational
Fee: $29.99 monthly
Homes passed: 3,302. Miles of plant (coax) included in Cape Girardea
Vice President & General Manager: Steve Trippe. Operations Director: Dave Miller. Operations Manager: Dave Huntsman. Technical Operations Manager: Barry Moore. Plant Manager: Kevin Goetz. Marketing Director: Beverly Wall. Office Manager: Sheila Tuschoff.
Franchise fee: 5% of gross.
Ownership: Charter Communications Inc. (MSO).

NEWBURG—Cable America Corp. Now served by WAYNESVILLE (formerly ST. ROBERT), MO [MO0023]. ICA: MO0240.

NEWTON—Formerly served by Midwest Cable Inc. No longer in operation. ICA: MO0357.

NIANGUA—Formerly served by Almega Cable. No longer in operation. ICA: MO0192.

NIANGUA—Formerly served by Cebridge Connections. Now served by PORTER MILL, MO [MO0090]. ICA: MO0310.

NIXA—Suddenlink Communications, 769 North 29th, Ozark, MO 65721. Phones: 800-999-6845 (Customer service); 314-315-9346; 314-965-2020. Web Site: http://www.suddenlink.com. Also serves Aunt's Creek, Branson West, Christian County, Highlandville, Highway DD, Kimberling City, Lakeview, Ozark, Reeds Spring, Stone County (portions) & Table Rock. ICA: MO0068.
TV Market Ranking: Below 100 (Aunt's Creek, Branson West, Christian County, Highlandville, Highway DD, Kimberling City, Lakeview, NIXA, Ozark, Reeds Spring, Stone County (portions)); Outside TV Markets (Table Rock). Franchise award date: December 1, 1981. Franchise expiration date: N.A. Began: November 10, 1982.
Channel capacity: 41 (operating 2-way). Channels available but not in use: N.A.
Basic Service
Subscribers: 9,318.
Programming (received off-air): K15CZ Springfield; KOLR (CBS) Springfield; KOZK (PBS) Springfield; KSFX-TV (FOX) Springfield; KSPR (ABC) Springfield; KWBM (MNT) Harrison [LICENSED & SILENT]; KYTV (CW, NBC) Springfield.
Programming (via satellite): QVC; Trinity Broadcasting Network; Weather Channel.
Fee: $39.95 installation; $19.95 monthly.
Expanded Basic Service 1
Subscribers: N.A.
Programming (via satellite): ABC Family Channel; AMC; Animal Planet; Arts & Entertainment; Bravo; Cartoon Network; CNBC; CNN; Comedy Central; C-SPAN; Discovery Channel; Disney Channel; E! Entertainment Television; ESPN; Food Network; Fox News Channel; Fox Sports Net Midwest; FX; Golf Channel; Great American Country; Hallmark Channel; Headline News; HGTV; History Channel; INSP; Lifetime; MSNBC; MTV; National Geographic Channel; Nickelodeon; Outdoor Channel; Speed Channel; Spike TV; Syfy; TBS Superstation; The Learning Channel; Travel Channel; Turner Classic Movies; Turner Network TV; TV Land; USA Network; VH1.
Digital Basic Service
Subscribers: N.A.
Programming (via satellite): BBC America; Bio; Bloomberg Television; Country Music TV; Discovery Digital Networks; DMX Mu-

sic; ESPN Classic Sports; ESPNews; Fox Soccer; Fuse; G4; GAS; GSN; History Channel International; Independent Film Channel; Lifetime Movie Network; MTV Networks Digital Suite; Nick Jr.; NickToons TV; Sleuth; Style Network; Toon Disney; Versus; WE tv.

Pay Service 1
Pay Units: 745.
Programming (via satellite): The Movie Channel.
Fee: $5.95 monthly.

Pay Service 2
Pay Units: 1,266.
Programming (via satellite): HBO.
Fee: $10.95 monthly.

Pay Service 3
Pay Units: 1,936.
Programming (via satellite): Showtime.
Fee: $9.95 monthly.

Digital Pay Service 1
Pay Units: N.A.
Programming (via satellite): Cinemax (multiplexed); Encore (multiplexed); HBO (multiplexed); Showtime (multiplexed); Starz (multiplexed); The Movie Channel (multiplexed).

Video-On-Demand: No

Pay-Per-View
iN DEMAND (delivered digitally); Playboy TV (delivered digitally); Fresh (delivered digitally).

Internet Service
Operational: Yes. Began: November 29, 2004.
Broadband Service: Cebridge High Speed Cable Internet.
Fee: $29.95 monthly.

Telephone Service
None

Miles of Plant: 523.0 (coaxial); None (fiber optic). Total homes in franchised area: 15,235.

Regional Manager: Todd Cruthird. Regional Marketing Manager: Beverly Gambell.

Ownership: Cequel Communications LLC (MSO).

NOEL—Crystal Broadband Networks, PO Box 180336, Chicago, IL 60618. Phones: 877-319-0328; 630-206-0447. E-mail: info@crystalbn.com. Web Site: http://crystalbn.com. Also serves Sulphur Springs, AR; Lanagan, McDonald County (portions), Pineville & South West City, MO. ICA: MO0416.

TV Market Ranking: Below 100 (Lanagan, McDonald County (portions), NOEL, Pineville, South West City, Sulphur Springs). Franchise award date: N.A. Franchise expiration date: N.A. Began: N.A.

Channel capacity: 41 (2-way capable). Channels available but not in use: N.A.

Basic Service
Subscribers: 416.
Programming (received off-air): KAFT (PBS) Fayetteville; KFTA-TV (FOX) Fort Smith; KHOG-TV (ABC) Fayetteville; KOAM-TV (CBS) Pittsburg; KODE-TV (ABC) Joplin; KPBI-CA (FOX) Fort Smith; KSNF (NBC) Joplin; KTUL (ABC) Tulsa.
Programming (via satellite): ABC Family Channel; AMC; Animal Planet; Arts & Entertainment; CNBC; CNN; Country Music TV; C-SPAN; Discovery Channel; Disney Channel; E! Entertainment Television; ESPN; Food Network; Fox Sports Net Midwest; Headline News; HGTV; INSP; Lifetime; Nickelodeon; QVC; Spike TV; TBS Superstation; The Learning Channel; Turner Network TV; TV Land; USA Network; Weather Channel; WGN America.
Current originations: Public Access.
Fee: $29.95 installation; $39.95 monthly.

Pay Service 1
Pay Units: 75.
Programming (via satellite): Encore; Showtime.
Fee: $9.95 monthly.

Pay Service 2
Pay Units: 86.
Programming (via satellite): The Movie Channel.
Fee: $7.95 monthly.

Video-On-Demand: No

Internet Service
Operational: Yes.

Telephone Service
Digital: Operational

Miles of Plant: 63.0 (coaxial); None (fiber optic). Homes passed: 1,580.

General Manager: Nidhin Johnson. Program manager: Shawn Smith.

Ownership: Crystal Broadband Networks (MSO).

NORBORNE—GH Technologies. Formerly [MO0469]. This cable system has converted to IPTV, PO Box 227, 7926 NE Ste Rte M, Breckenridge, MO 64625. Phones: 800-846-3426; 660-644-5411. Fax: 660-644-5464. E-mail: comments@greenhills.net. Web Site: http://www.greenhills.net. ICA: MO5171.

TV Market Ranking: Outside TV Markets (NORBORNE). Franchise award date: September 27, 2007. Franchise expiration date: N.A. Began: N.A.

Channel capacity: N.A. Channels available but not in use: N.A.

Internet Service
Operational: Yes.
Fee: $15.00 installation; $27.95 monthly.

Telephone Service
Digital: Operational
Fee: $13.15 monthly

Ownership: Green Hills Companies (MSO).

NORBORNE—GH Technologies. This cable system has converted to IPTV. See Norborne, MO [MO5171]. ICA: MO0469.

NORBORNE—Mediacom, 901 N College Ave, Columbia, MO 65201. Phones: 816-637-4500 (Local office); 573-443-1536. Fax: 573-449-8492. Web Site: http://www.mediacomcable.com. ICA: MO0241.

TV Market Ranking: Outside TV Markets (NORBORNE). Franchise award date: N.A. Franchise expiration date: N.A. Began: July 1, 1984.

Channel capacity: N.A. Channels available but not in use: N.A.

Basic Service
Subscribers: 219.
Programming (received off-air): KCPT (PBS) Kansas City; KCTV (CBS) Kansas City; KCWE (CW) Kansas City; KMBC-TV (ABC) Kansas City; KPXE-TV (ION) Kansas City; KQTV (ABC) St. Joseph; KSHB-TV (NBC) Kansas City; KSMO-TV (MNT) Kansas City; WDAF-TV (FOX) Kansas City.
Programming (via satellite): TV Guide Network; WGN America.
Fee: $35.00 installation; $32.95 monthly; $1.70 converter.

Expanded Basic Service 1
Subscribers: N.A.
Programming (via satellite): ABC Family Channel; AMC; Animal Planet; Arts & Entertainment; Bravo; Cartoon Network; CNBC; CNN; Comedy Central; Country Music TV; C-SPAN; Discovery Channel; E! Entertainment Television; ESPN; ESPN 2; Food Network; Fox News Channel; Fox Sports Net Midwest; FX; Hallmark Channel; Headline News; HGTV; History Channel; Home Shopping Network; INSP; Lifetime; MSNBC; Nickelodeon; Outdoor Channel; QVC; ShopNBC; SoapNet; Speed Channel; Spike TV; Syfy; TBS Superstation; The Learning Channel; Travel Channel; Trinity Broadcasting Network; truTV; Turner Network TV; TV Land; USA Network; VH1; WE tv; Weather Channel.

Digital Basic Service
Subscribers: N.A.
Programming (via satellite): American-Life TV Network; BBC America; Bio; Bloomberg Television; Discovery Digital Networks; FitTV; Fox Movie Channel; Fox Soccer; Fuse; G4; GAS; Golf Channel; GSN; Halogen Network; History Channel International; Independent Film Channel; Lifetime Movie Network; Lime; MTV Networks Digital Suite; Music Choice; National Geographic Channel; Nick Jr.; NickToons TV; Style Network; Turner Classic Movies; Versus.

Digital Pay Service 1
Pay Units: N.A.
Programming (via satellite): Cinemax (multiplexed); Encore (multiplexed); Flix (multiplexed); HBO (multiplexed); Showtime (multiplexed); Starz (multiplexed); Sundance Channel (multiplexed); The Movie Channel (multiplexed).

Video-On-Demand: No

Pay-Per-View
Mediacom PPV (delivered digitally); Playboy TV (delivered digitally); TEN Clips (delivered digitally); Pleasure (delivered digitally); Hot Body (delivered digitally).

Internet Service
Operational: Yes.
Broadband Service: Mediacom High Speed Internet.
Fee: $45.95 monthly.

Telephone Service
None

Miles of Plant: 5.0 (coaxial); None (fiber optic). Homes passed: 361.

General Manager: Gary Baugh. Marketing Director: Wes Shaver. Technical Operations Manager: Tom Evans.

City fee: 3% of basic.

Ownership: Mediacom LLC (MSO).

NORTHSHORE—Formerly served by Almega Cable. No longer in operation. ICA: MO0159.

NORWOOD—Formerly served by Cebridge Connections. No longer in operation. ICA: MO0299.

NOVINGER—Longview Communications, 12007 Sunrise Valley Dr, Ste 375, Reston, VA 20191. Phones: 866-611-6565 (Customer service); 703-476-9101. Fax: 703-476-9107. Web Site: http://www.longviewcomm.com. ICA: MO0233.

TV Market Ranking: Below 100 (NOVINGER). Franchise award date: N.A. Franchise expiration date: N.A. Began: November 1, 1983.

Channel capacity: 41 (not 2-way capable). Channels available but not in use: None.

Basic Service
Subscribers: 112.
Programming (received off-air): KCNC-TV (CBS) Denver; KHQA-TV (ABC, CBS) Hannibal; KTVO (ABC) Kirksville; KUSA (NBC) Denver; KYOU-TV (FOX) Ottumwa; WGEM-TV (CW, NBC) Quincy.
Programming (via satellite): ABC Family Channel; AMC; Animal Planet; Arts & Entertainment; Cartoon Network; CNN; Discovery Channel; Disney Channel; ESPN; ESPN 2; Fox News Channel; Great American Country; Lifetime; Outdoor Channel; QVC; TBS Superstation; The Learning Channel; Toon Disney; Turner Network TV; TV Land; USA Network; Weather Channel; WGN America.
Fee: $30.00 installation; $41.45 monthly.

Pay Service 1
Pay Units: 1.
Programming (via satellite): HBO; Showtime.
Fee: $9.95 monthly (Showtime), $14.95 monthly (HBO).

Video-On-Demand: No

Pay-Per-View
iN DEMAND (delivered digitally); Hot Choice (delivered digitally); Playboy TV (delivered digitally); Fresh (delivered digitally); Shorteez (delivered digitally).

Internet Service
Operational: No.

Telephone Service
None

Miles of Plant: 9.0 (coaxial); None (fiber optic). Homes passed: 310.

President: John Long. Senior Vice President: Marc W. Cohen. General Manager: Brandon Dickey. Operations Manager: Perry Scarborough.

City fee: None.

Ownership: Longview Communications (MSO).

OLIVETTE—Charter Communications, 941 Charter Commons Dr, Saint Louis, MO 63017. Phone: 636-207-7044. Fax: 636-230-7034. Web Site: http://www.charter.com. Also serves Affton, Ballwin, Bella Villa, Black Jack, Bridgeton, Bridgeton Terrace, Charlack, Chesterfield, Clarkson Valley, Country Life Acres, Crestwood, Creve Coeur, Crystal Lake Park, Des Peres, Ellisville, Eureka, Fenton, Florissant, Frontenac, Glendale, Grantwood Village, Green Park, Hanley Hills, Hazelwood, Huntleigh, Kirkwood, Ladue, Lakeshire, Lemay, Mackenzie, Manchester, Marlborough, Mehlville, Oakland, Oakville, Richmond Heights, Rock Hill, Sappington, Shrewsbury, Spanish Lake, St. George, St. John, St. Louis County, Sunset Hills, Sycamore Hills, Times Beach, Town & Country, Twins Oaks, Valley Park, Vinita Park, Warson Woods, Webster Groves, Wilbur Park, Wildwood, Winchester & Woodson Terrace. ICA: MO0009.

TV Market Ranking: 11 (Affton, Ballwin, Bella Villa, Black Jack, Bridgeton, Bridgeton Terrace, Charlack, Chesterfield, Clarkson Valley, Country Life Acres, Crestwood, Creve Coeur, Crystal Lake Park, Des Peres, Ellisville, Eureka, Fenton, Florissant, Frontenac, Glendale, Grantwood Village, Green Park, Hanley Hills, Hazelwood, Huntleigh, KIRKWOOD, Ladue, Lakeshire, Lemay, Mackenzie, Manchester, Marlborough, Mehlville, Oakland, Oakville, OLIVETTE, Richmond Heights, Rock Hill, Sappington, Shrewsbury, Spanish Lake, St. George, St. John, St. Louis County, Sunset Hills, Sycamore Hills, Times Beach, Town & Country, Twin Oaks, Valley Park, Vinita Park, Warson Woods, Webster Groves, Wilbur Park, Wildwood, Winchester, Woodson Terrace). Franchise award date: January 1, 1980. Franchise expiration date: N.A. Began: April 1, 1981.

Channel capacity: N.A. Channels available but not in use: N.A.

Basic Service

Subscribers: 46,618.

Programming (received off-air): KDNL-TV (ABC) St. Louis; KETC (PBS) St. Louis; KMOV (CBS) St. Louis; KNLC (IND) St. Louis; KPLR-TV (CW) St. Louis; KSDK (NBC) St. Louis; KTVI (FOX) St. Louis; WPXS (IND) Mount Vernon; WRBU (MNT) East St. Louis; allband FM.

Programming (via satellite): C-SPAN; C-SPAN 2; Eternal Word TV Network; Home Shopping Network; INSP; Jewelry Television; QVC; ShopNBC; TBS Superstation; Trinity Broadcasting Network; TV Guide Network; Univision; Weather Channel; WGN America.

Current originations: Leased Access; Government Access; Educational Access; Public Access.

Fee: $29.95 installation.

Expanded Basic Service 1

Subscribers: N.A.

Programming (via satellite): ABC Family Channel; AMC; Animal Planet; Arts & Entertainment; BET Networks; Bravo; Cartoon Network; CNBC; CNN; Comedy Central; Country Music TV; Discovery Channel; Disney Channel; E! Entertainment Television; ESPN; ESPN 2; Food Network; Fox Movie Channel; Fox News Channel; Fox Sports Net Midwest; FX; G4; Golf Channel; GSN; Hallmark Channel; Headline News; HGTV; History Channel; Lifetime; MSNBC; MTV; MTV2; National Geographic Channel; Nickelodeon; Oxygen; SoapNet; Speed Channel; Spike TV; Style Network; Syfy; The Learning Channel; Toon Disney; Travel Channel; truTV; Turner Classic Movies; Turner Network TV; TV Land; USA Network; Versus; VH1; WE tv.

Fee: $49.99 monthly.

Digital Basic Service

Subscribers: 12,785.

Programming (via satellite): BBC America; Bio; Black Family Channel; Bloomberg Television; Cooking Channel; Discovery Digital Networks; Do-It-Yourself; Encore Action; ESPN Classic Sports; ESPNews; FitTV; Fox Sports World; FSN Digital Atlantic; FSN Digital Central; FSN Digital Pacific; Fuel TV; Fuse; GAS; Great American Country; History Channel International; Independent Film Channel; International Television (ITV); Lifetime Movie Network; Lifetime Real Women; MTV Networks Digital Suite; Music Choice; NFL Network; Nick Jr.; Nick Too; NickToons TV; Outdoor Channel; Showtime (multiplexed); Sundance Channel; The Movie Channel (multiplexed); TV One; Weatherscan.

Digital Pay Service 1

Pay Units: 14,256.

Programming (via satellite): Cinemax (multiplexed); HBO (multiplexed); Playboy TV; Starz (multiplexed).

Fee: $10.00 installation; $11.75 monthly (each).

Video-On-Demand: Yes

Pay-Per-View

Addressable homes: 12,785.

iN DEMAND (delivered digitally), Addressable: Yes; Sports PPV (delivered digitally); ESPN Now (delivered digitally); Playboy TV (delivered digitally); Fresh (delivered digitally); Shorteez (delivered digitally).

Internet Service

Operational: Yes.

Broadband Service: Charter Pipeline.

Fee: $29.99 monthly; $5.00 modem lease.

Telephone Service

Digital: Operational

Fee: $29.99 monthly

Miles of Plant: 1,172.0 (coaxial); 50.0 (fiber optic). Homes passed: 81,744. Total homes in franchised area: 82,143.

Vice President & General Manager: Steve Trippe. Operations Director: Tom Williams. Marketing Director: Beverly Wall.

Ownership: Charter Communications Inc. (MSO).

OREGON—South Holt Cablevision Inc., PO Box 227, Oregon, MO 64473-0227. Phone: 660-446-2900. Fax: 660-446-2800. E-mail: ottman@ofmlive.net. Also serves Forest City. ICA: MO0191.

TV Market Ranking: Below 100 (Forest City, OREGON). Franchise award date: N.A. Franchise expiration date: N.A. Began: September 1, 1982.

Channel capacity: N.A. Channels available but not in use: N.A.

Basic Service

Subscribers: 380.

Programming (received off-air): KCTV (CBS) Kansas City; KCWE (CW) Kansas City; KMBC-TV (ABC) Kansas City; KQTV (ABC) St. Joseph; KSHB-TV (NBC) Kansas City; KSMO-TV (MNT) Kansas City; KTWU (PBS) Topeka; WDAF-TV (FOX) Kansas City; WIBW-TV (CBS, MNT) Topeka.

Programming (via satellite): ABC Family Channel; CNN; Discovery Channel; Disney Channel; ESPN; ESPN 2; Lifetime; MTV; Nickelodeon; Spike TV; TBS Superstation; Turner Network TV; USA Network; VH1; WGN America.

Fee: $27.00 monthly.

Pay Service 1

Pay Units: 182.

Programming (via satellite): HBO.

Fee: $10.00 monthly.

Video-On-Demand: No

Internet Service

Operational: No.

Telephone Service

None

Miles of Plant: 10.0 (coaxial); None (fiber optic). Homes passed: 598. Total homes in franchised area: 598.

Assistant General Manager: Wendy Ottman. Technician: Steve Rogers.

City fee: 3% of gross.

Ownership: South Holt Cablevision Inc.

OSAGE BEACH—Charter Communications, 5151 Hwy 54, Ste B & C, Osage Beach, MO 65065. Phones: 636-207-7044 (St Louis office); 573-302-0326. Fax: 573-348-0268. Web Site: http://www.charter.com. Also serves Bagnell, Camden County, Camdenton, Eldon, Lake Ozark, Lakeland, Laurie, Linn Creek, Miller County (portions), Morgan County (portions), Sunrise Beach & Village of Four Seasons. ICA: MO0017.

TV Market Ranking: Below 100 (Bagnell, Camden County (portions), Eldon, Lakeland, Laurie, Miller County (portions) (portions), Morgan County (portions) (portions)); Outside TV Markets (Camden County (portions), Camdenton, Lake Ozark, Linn Creek, Miller County (portions) (portions), Morgan County (portions) (portions), OSAGE BEACH, Sunrise Beach, Village of Four Seasons). Franchise award date: January 9, 1975. Franchise expiration date: N.A. Began: November 1, 1975.

Channel capacity: N.A. Channels available but not in use: None.

Basic Service

Subscribers: 9,784.

Programming (received off-air): KMIZ (ABC) Columbia; KMOS-TV (PBS) Sedalia; KNLJ (IND) Jefferson City; KOLR (CBS) Springfield; KOMU-TV (CW, NBC) Columbia; KRCG (CBS) Jefferson City; KSFX-TV (FOX) Springfield; KSPR (ABC) Springfield; KWBM (MNT) Harrison [LICENSED & SILENT]; KYTV (CW, NBC) Springfield.

Programming (via satellite): C-SPAN; C-SPAN 2; INSP; ION Television; LWS Local Weather Station; QVC; Telemundo; TV Guide Interactive Inc.; WGN America.

Current originations: Religious Access; Government Access; Educational Access; Public Access.

Fee: $29.99 installation.

Expanded Basic Service 1

Subscribers: 9,525.

Programming (via satellite): ABC Family Channel; AMC; Animal Planet; Arts & Entertainment; BET Networks; Bravo; Cartoon Network; CNBC; CNN; Comedy Central; Country Music TV; Discovery Channel; Disney Channel; E! Entertainment Television; ESPN; ESPN 2; Eternal Word TV Network; Food Network; Fox Movie Channel; Fox News Channel; Fox Sports Net Midwest; FX; G4; Golf Channel; GSN; Hallmark Channel; Headline News; HGTV; History Channel; Lifetime; MSNBC; MTV; National Geographic Channel; Nickelodeon; Oxygen; SoapNet; Speed Channel; Spike TV; Style Network; Syfy; TBS Superstation; The Learning Channel; Toon Disney; Travel Channel; Trinity Broadcasting Network; truTV; Turner Classic Movies; Turner Network TV; TV Land; Univision; USA Network; Versus; VH1; WE tv; Weather Channel.

Fee: $49.99 monthly.

Digital Basic Service

Subscribers: 5,281.

Programming (via satellite): BBC America; Bio; Boomerang; CNN International; Discovery Digital Networks; Do-It-Yourself; Fox Sports World; FSN Digital Atlantic; FSN Digital Central; FSN Digital Pacific; GAS; History Channel International; Independent Film Channel; Lifetime Movie Network; MTV Networks Digital Suite; Music Choice; Nick Jr.; Nick Too; NickToons TV; Sundance Channel.

Fee: $7.95 monthly.

Digital Pay Service 1

Pay Units: 3,348.

Programming (via satellite): Cinemax (multiplexed); Encore (multiplexed); Flix; HBO (multiplexed); Showtime (multiplexed); Starz (multiplexed); The Movie Channel (multiplexed).

Fee: $11.95 monthly (each).

Video-On-Demand: Yes

Pay-Per-View

Addressable homes: 5,230.

iN DEMAND (delivered digitally), Addressable: Yes; ETC (delivered digitally); Pleasure (delivered digitally).

Internet Service

Operational: Yes.

Broadband Service: Charter Pipeline.

Fee: $39.99 monthly.

Telephone Service

Digital: Operational

Miles of Plant: 889.0 (coaxial); 119.0 (fiber optic). Homes passed: 20,187. Total homes in franchised area: 38,337.

Vice President & General Manager: Steve Trippe. Operations Director: Dave Miller.; Dave Huntsman. Technical Operations Manager: Larry Wright. Marketing Director: Beverly Wall. Office Coordinator: Susan Yackle.

Ownership: Charter Communications Inc. (MSO).

OSCEOLA—Mediacom, 1533 S Enterprise Ave, Springfield, MO 65804. Phone: 417-875-5560. Fax: 417-883-0265. Web Site: http://www.mediacomcable.com. ICA: MO0216.

TV Market Ranking: Outside TV Markets (OSCEOLA). Franchise award date: August 1, 1982. Franchise expiration date: N.A. Began: August 1, 1982.

Channel capacity: 57 (not 2-way capable). Channels available but not in use: N.A.

Basic Service

Subscribers: 309.

Programming (received off-air): KMBC-TV (ABC) Kansas City; KMOS-TV (PBS) Sedalia; KOLR (CBS) Springfield; KOZK (PBS) Springfield; KPXE-TV (ION) Kansas City; KSFX-TV (FOX) Springfield; KSHB-TV (NBC) Kansas City; KSPR (ABC) Springfield; KYTV (CW, NBC) Springfield.

Programming (via satellite): ABC Family Channel; AMC; Animal Planet; Arts & Entertainment; Cartoon Network; CNBC; CNN; Comedy Central; Country Music TV; C-SPAN; Discovery Channel; ESPN; ESPN 2; Food Network; FX; Headline News; HGTV; History Channel; Home Shopping Network; INSP; ION Television; Lifetime; MSNBC; Nickelodeon; QVC; Speed Channel; Spike TV; Syfy; TBS Superstation; The Learning Channel; Travel Channel; Trinity Broadcasting Network; truTV; Turner Network TV; TV Land; USA Network; VH1; WE tv; Weather Channel; WGN America.

Fee: $35.00 installation; $45.95 monthly.

Pay Service 1

Pay Units: 33.

Programming (via satellite): The Movie Channel.

Fee: $10.50 monthly.

Pay Service 2

Pay Units: 68.

Programming (via satellite): Showtime.

Fee: $10.50 monthly.

Pay Service 3
Pay Units: 67.
Programming (via satellite): HBO (multiplexed).
Fee: $10.50 monthly.
Pay Service 4
Pay Units: N.A.
Programming (via satellite): Flix.
Video-On-Demand: No
Internet Service
Operational: No.
Telephone Service
None
Miles of Plant: 8.0 (coaxial); None (fiber optic). Homes passed: 679.
Regional Vice President: Bill Copeland. Technical Operations Manager: Alan Freedman. Marketing Director: Will Kuebler.
City fee: 3% of basic.
Ownership: Mediacom LLC (MSO).

OTTERVILLE—Formerly served by CableDirect. No longer in operation. ICA: MO0304.

OVERLAND—Charter Communications, 941 Charter Commons Dr, Saint Louis, MO 63017. Phone: 636-207-7044. Fax: 636-230-7034. Web Site: http://www.charter.com. Also serves Bellefontaine Neighbors, Breckenridge Hills, Brentwood, Chesterfield, Clayton, Country Club Hills, Creve Coeur, Edmundson, Flordell Hills, Jennings, Maplewood, Maryland Heights, Moline Acres, Northwoods, Pine Lawn, Riverview, St. Ann, St. Louis County (northern portions) & University City. ICA: MO0013.
TV Market Ranking: 11 (Bellefontaine Neighbors, Breckenridge Hills, Brentwood, Chesterfield, Clayton, Country Club Hills, Creve Coeur, Edmundson, Flordell Hills, Jennings, Maplewood, Maryland Heights, Moline Acres, Northwoods, OVERLAND, Pine Lawn, Riverview, St. Ann, St. Louis County (northern portions), University City). Franchise award date: N.A. Franchise expiration date: N.A. Began: January 1, 1982.
Channel capacity: 80 (operating 2-way). Channels available but not in use: N.A.
Basic Service
Subscribers: 18,033.
Programming (received off-air): KDNL-TV (ABC) St. Louis; KETC (PBS) St. Louis; KMOV (CBS) St. Louis; KNLC (IND) St. Louis; KPLR-TV (CW) St. Louis; KSDK (NBC) St. Louis; KTVI (FOX) St. Louis; WPXS (IND) Mount Vernon; WRBU (MNT) East St. Louis.
Programming (via satellite): C-SPAN; C-SPAN 2; Eternal Word TV Network; GRTV Network; Home Shopping Network; INSP; QVC; ShopNBC; TBS Superstation; Trinity Broadcasting Network; TV Guide Network; Univision; Weatherscan; WGN America.
Current originations: Government Access; Educational Access.
Fee: $29.99 installation.
Expanded Basic Service 1
Subscribers: N.A.
Programming (via satellite): ABC Family Channel; AMC; Animal Planet; Arts & Entertainment; BET Networks; Bravo; Cartoon Network; CNBC; CNN; Comedy Central; Country Music TV; Discovery Channel; Disney Channel; E! Entertainment Television; ESPN; ESPN 2; Food Network; Fox Movie Channel; Fox News Channel; Fox Sports Net Midwest; FX; G4; Golf Channel; GSN; Hallmark Channel; Headline News; HGTV; History Channel; Lifetime; MSNBC; MTV; National Geographic Channel; Nickelodeon; Oxygen; SoapNet; Speed Channel; Spike TV; Style Network; Syfy; The Learning Channel; Toon Disney; Travel Channel; truTV; Turner Classic Movies; Turner Network TV; TV Land; USA Network; Versus; VH1; WE tv; Weather Channel.
Fee: $49.99 monthly.
Digital Basic Service
Subscribers: N.A.
Programming (via satellite): BBC America; Bio; Bloomberg Television; Discovery Digital Networks; Do-It-Yourself; Encore Action; ESPN Classic Sports; FitTV; Fox Sports World; FSN Digital Atlantic; FSN Digital Central; FSN Digital Pacific; Fuel TV; Fuse; GAS; Great American Country; History Channel International; Independent Film Channel; International Television (ITV); Lifetime Movie Network; MTV Networks Digital Suite; Music Choice; NFL Network; Nick Jr.; Nick Too; NickToons TV; Sundance Channel.
Digital Pay Service 1
Pay Units: 16,891.
Programming (via satellite): Cinemax (multiplexed); HBO (multiplexed); Showtime (multiplexed); Starz (multiplexed); The Movie Channel (multiplexed).
Fee: $24.95 installation; $8.95 monthly (each).
Video-On-Demand: Yes
Pay-Per-View
iN DEMAND (delivered digitally); Sports PPV (delivered digitally); ESPN Now (delivered digitally); Playboy TV (delivered digitally); Fresh (delivered digitally); Shorteez (delivered digitally).
Internet Service
Operational: Yes.
Broadband Service: Charter Pipeline.
Fee: $29.99 monthly; $5.00 modem lease.
Telephone Service
Digital: Operational
Fee: $29.99 monthly
Miles of Plant: 422.0 (coaxial); 16.0 (fiber optic). Additional miles planned: 16.0 (coaxial). Homes passed: 29,446.
Vice President & General Manager: Steve Trippe. Operations Director: Tom Williams. Marketing Director: Beverly Wall.
Ownership: Charter Communications Inc. (MSO).

PACIFIC—Charter Communications. Now served by BARNHART, MO [MO0385]. ICA: MO0078.

PALMYRA—Cass Cable TV Inc. Now served by HANNIBAL, MO [MO0021]. ICA: MO0101.

PARIS—US Cable. Now served by HANNIBAL, MO [MO0021]. ICA: MO0157.

PARMA—NewWave Communications, 1311 Business Hwy 60 W, Dexter, MO 63841. Phones: 573-614-4573; 888-863-9928. Fax: 573-614-4802. Web Site: http://www.newwavecom.com. Also serves Risco & Tallapoosa. ICA: MO0167.
TV Market Ranking: Below 100 (PARMA); Outside TV Markets (Risco, Tallapoosa). Franchise award date: July 11, 1977. Franchise expiration date: N.A. Began: N.A.
Channel capacity: N.A. Channels available but not in use: N.A.
Basic Service
Subscribers: 172.
Programming (received off-air): KAIT (ABC) Jonesboro; KBSI (FOX) Cape Girardeau; KFVS-TV (CBS, CW) Cape Girardeau; KPOB-TV (ABC) Poplar Bluff; WDKA (MNT) Paducah; WKMU (PBS) Murray; WPSD-TV (NBC) Paducah; WQWQ-LP (CW) Paducah; WTCT (IND) Marion.
Programming (via satellite): C-SPAN; C-SPAN 2; Home Shopping Network; INSP; QVC; ShopNBC; Trinity Broadcasting Network; WGN America.
Fee: $61.50 installation; $34.95 monthly.
Expanded Basic Service 1
Subscribers: N.A.
Programming (via satellite): ABC Family Channel; AMC; Animal Planet; Arts & Entertainment; BET Networks; Bravo; Cartoon Network; CNBC; CNN; Comedy Central; Country Music TV; Discovery Channel; Disney Channel; E! Entertainment Television; ESPN; ESPN 2; ESPN Classic Sports; Food Network; Fox News Channel; Fox Sports Net Midwest; FX; Golf Channel; Great American Country; GSN; Hallmark Channel; Headline News; HGTV; History Channel; Jewelry Television; Lifetime; MSNBC; MTV; Nickelodeon; Outdoor Channel; Oxygen; SoapNet; Speed Channel; Spike TV; Syfy; TBS Superstation; The Learning Channel; Travel Channel; truTV; Turner Network TV; TV Land; USA Network; VH1; Weather Channel.
Digital Basic Service
Subscribers: N.A.
Programming (received off-air): KAIT (ABC) Jonesboro; KBSI (FOX) Cape Girardeau; KFVS-TV (CBS, CW) Cape Girardeau; WPSD-TV (NBC) Paducah.
Programming (via satellite): Arts & Entertainment HD; BBC America; Bio; Bloomberg Television; CMT Pure Country; Discovery HD Theater; Discovery Health Channel; Discovery Kids Channel; Discovery Military Channel; Discovery Planet Green; Do-It-Yourself; ESPN 2 HD; ESPN Classic Sports; ESPN HD; ESPNews; FitTV; Fox Movie Channel; FSN HD; G4; Gospel Music Channel; Halogen Network; HDNet; HDNet Movies; History Channel HD; History Channel International; ID Investigation Discovery; Independent Film Channel; Lifetime Movie Network; MTV Hits; MTV2; Music Choice; Nick Jr.; NickToons TV; Palladia; RFD-TV; Science Channel; Sleuth; Style Network; TeenNick; The Sportsman Channel; The Word Network; Toon Disney; Turner Classic Movies; Turner Network TV HD; USA Network HD; Versus; VH1 Classic; VH1 Soul; Weather Channel HD.
Digital Pay Service 1
Pay Units: N.A.
Programming (via satellite): Cinemax (multiplexed); Cinemax HD; Encore (multiplexed); Flix; HBO (multiplexed); HBO HD; Showtime (multiplexed); Starz (multiplexed); Starz HDTV; The Movie Channel (multiplexed).
Video-On-Demand: No
Pay-Per-View
iN DEMAND (delivered digitally); Hot Choice (delivered digitally); Club Jenna (delivered digitally); Playboy TV (delivered digitally); Fresh (delivered digitally); Shorteez (delivered digitally).
Internet Service
Operational: No.
Telephone Service
None
Miles of Plant: 23.0 (coaxial); None (fiber optic). Homes passed: 710.
General Manager: Ed Gargas. Technical Operations Manager: Jerry Townsend.
City fee: 3% of gross.
Ownership: NewWave Communications (MSO).

PARNELL—B & L Technologies LLC, 3329 270th St, Lenox, IA 50851. Phones: 800-798-5488; 641-348-2240. Fax: 641-348-2240. ICA: MO0442.
TV Market Ranking: Outside TV Markets (PARNELL). Franchise award date: August 3, 1990. Franchise expiration date: N.A. Began: January 1, 1991.
Channel capacity: 36 (not 2-way capable). Channels available but not in use: 11.
Basic Service
Subscribers: 17.
Programming (received off-air): KHIN (PBS) Red Oak; KPTM (FOX, MNT) Omaha; KQTV (ABC) St. Joseph.
Programming (via satellite): ABC Family Channel; AMC; Arts & Entertainment; CNN; Discovery Channel; ESPN; Eternal Word TV Network; History Channel; KARE (NBC) Minneapolis; Nickelodeon; Spike TV; TBS Superstation; Turner Network TV; USA Network; VH1; WCCO-TV (CBS) Minneapolis; WGN America.
Fee: $25.00 installation; $30.50 monthly.
Pay Service 1
Pay Units: 3.
Programming (via satellite): HBO.
Fee: $12.00 monthly.
Video-On-Demand: No
Internet Service
Operational: No.
Telephone Service
None
Miles of Plant: 3.0 (coaxial); None (fiber optic). Homes passed: 85.
Manager & Chief Technician: Robert Hintz.
Ownership: B & L Technologies LLC (MSO).

PERRY—US Cable, 647 Clinic Rd, Hannibal, MO 63401. Phone: 573-581-2404. Fax: 573-581-4053. Web Site: http://www.uscable.com. ICA: MO0250.
TV Market Ranking: Below 100 (PERRY). Franchise award date: N.A. Franchise expiration date: N.A. Began: September 1, 1984.
Channel capacity: N.A. Channels available but not in use: N.A.
Basic Service
Subscribers: N.A. Included in Hannibal
Programming (received off-air): KHQA-TV (ABC, CBS) Hannibal; KMIZ (ABC) Columbia; KOMU-TV (CW, NBC) Columbia; KQFX-LD Columbia; KRCG (CBS) Jefferson City; WGEM-TV (CW, NBC) Quincy; WQEC (PBS) Quincy; WTJR (IND) Quincy.
Programming (via satellite): Home Shopping Network; Lifetime; TBS Superstation; VH1; WGN America.
Fee: $22.09 monthly.
Expanded Basic Service 1
Subscribers: N.A.
Programming (via satellite): ABC Family Channel; Animal Planet; Arts & Entertainment; Cartoon Network; CNN; Comedy Central; Country Music TV; Discovery Channel; Disney Channel; ESPN; ESPN 2; Fox News Channel; FX; Headline News; MTV; Nickelodeon; Spike TV; Syfy; Turner Network TV; USA Network.
Fee: $19.12 monthly.
Pay Service 1
Pay Units: N.A.
Programming (via satellite): Cinemax; HBO.
Fee: $11.95 monthly (each).
Internet Service
Operational: Yes.
Telephone Service
None
Homes passed and miles of plant included in Hannibal
Technical Operations Manager: Roger Young. Marketing Director: Rita Watson. Regional Administrative Director: Rebecca Bramblett.
Ownership: US Cable Corp. (MSO).; Comcast Cable Communications Inc. (MSO).

PERRYVILLE—Charter Communications, 3140 W Nash Rd, Scott City, MO 63780. Phones: 636-207-7044 (St Louis office); 573-335-4424. Fax: 573-334-9265. Web Site: http://www.charter.com. Also serves Perry County (portions). ICA: MO0054.

TV Market Ranking: 69 (Perry County (portions), PERRYVILLE). Franchise award date: N.A. Franchise expiration date: N.A. Began: June 1, 1982.

Channel capacity: N.A. Channels available but not in use: None.

Basic Service

Subscribers: 2,364.

Programming (received off-air): KBSI (FOX) Cape Girardeau; KDNL-TV (ABC) St. Louis; KETC (PBS) St. Louis; KFVS-TV (CBS, CW) Cape Girardeau; KMOV (CBS) St. Louis; KSDK (NBC) St. Louis; KTVI (FOX) St. Louis; WDKA (MNT) Paducah; WPSD-TV (NBC) Paducah; WSIL-TV (ABC) Harrisburg; WSIU-TV (PBS) Carbondale; allband FM.

Programming (via satellite): AMC; Country Music TV; C-SPAN; ESPN; Eternal Word TV Network; Home Shopping Network; INSP; MTV; Nickelodeon; QVC; Syfy; Travel Channel; WGN America.

Current originations: Government Access; Educational Access; Public Access.

Fee: $29.99 installation.

Expanded Basic Service 1

Subscribers: 2,272.

Programming (via satellite): ABC Family Channel; Animal Planet; Arts & Entertainment; Bravo; Cartoon Network; CNBC; CNN; Comedy Central; Discovery Channel; Disney Channel; E! Entertainment Television; ESPN 2; Food Network; Fox Movie Channel; Fox News Channel; Fox Sports Net Midwest; FX; G4; Golf Channel; Hallmark Channel; Headline News; HGTV; History Channel; Lifetime; MSNBC; Oxygen; SoapNet; Speed Channel; Spike TV; TBS Superstation; The Learning Channel; Toon Disney; truTV; Turner Classic Movies; Turner Network TV; TV Land; USA Network; Versus; VH1; Weather Channel.

Fee: $49.99 monthly.

Digital Basic Service

Subscribers: N.A.

Programming (via satellite): BBC America; Bio; Discovery Digital Networks; Do-It-Yourself; GAS; History Channel International; Independent Film Channel; MTV Networks Digital Suite; Music Choice; National Geographic Channel; Nick Jr.; Nick Too; NickToons TV; Sundance Channel; TV Guide Interactive Inc.

Fee: $10.50 monthly.

Digital Pay Service 1

Pay Units: 544.

Programming (via satellite): Cinemax (multiplexed); Encore (multiplexed); Flix; Fox Sports Net Direct (multiplexed); HBO (multiplexed); Showtime (multiplexed); Starz (multiplexed); The Movie Channel (multiplexed).

Fee: $12.50 monthly (each).

Video-On-Demand: No

Pay-Per-View

Hot Choice (delivered digitally); ETC (delivered digitally); Pleasure (delivered digitally); iN DEMAND (delivered digitally).

Internet Service

Operational: Yes. Began: July 1, 2002.

Broadband Service: Charter Pipeline.

Fee: $49.95 installation; $29.99 monthly.

Telephone Service

None

Homes passed: 3,667. Mile of plant (coax) included in Cape Girardea

Vice President & General Manager: Steve Trippe. Operations Director: Dave Miller. Operations Manager: Dave Huntsman. Technical Operations Manager: Barry Moore. Plant Manager: Kevin Goetz. Marketing Director: Beverly Wall. Office Manager: Sheila Tuschoff.

Franchise fee: 5% of gross.

Ownership: Charter Communications Inc. (MSO).

PIEDMONT—Boycom Cablevision Inc., 3467 Township Line Rd, Poplar Bluff, MO 63901. Phone: 573-686-9101. Fax: 573-686-4722. Web Site: http://www.boycomonline.com. Also serves Mill Spring, Patterson & Wayne County (portions). ICA: MO0075.

TV Market Ranking: Below 100 (Mill Spring, Patterson, PIEDMONT, Wayne County (portions) (portions)); Outside TV Markets (Wayne County (portions) (portions)). Franchise award date: July 7, 1964. Franchise expiration date: N.A. Began: January 1, 1965.

Channel capacity: 54 (operating 2-way). Channels available but not in use: 17.

Basic Service

Subscribers: 1,261.

Programming (received off-air): KBSI (FOX) Cape Girardeau; KETC (PBS) St. Louis; KFVS-TV (CBS, CW) Cape Girardeau; KMOV (CBS) St. Louis; KPLR-TV (CW) St. Louis; KPOB-TV (ABC) Poplar Bluff; KSDK (NBC) St. Louis; KTVI (FOX) St. Louis; WPSD-TV (NBC) Paducah.

Programming (via satellite): C-SPAN; Home Shopping Network; The Learning Channel; Trinity Broadcasting Network; Turner Network TV; USA Network; Weather Channel; WGN America.

Current originations: Educational Access.

Fee: $61.50 installation; $19.95 monthly.

Expanded Basic Service 1

Subscribers: 920.

Programming (via satellite): ABC Family Channel; AMC; Animal Planet; Arts & Entertainment; Cartoon Network; CNBC; CNN; Comedy Central; Discovery Channel; Disney Channel; E! Entertainment Television; ESPN; ESPN 2; ESPN Classic Sports; Food Network; Fox News Channel; Fox Sports Net Midwest; Great American Country; Hallmark Channel; Headline News; HGTV; History Channel; Lifetime; MSNBC; MTV; Nickelodeon; Outdoor Channel; SoapNet; Speed Channel; Spike TV; Syfy; TBS Superstation; Travel Channel; TV Land; VH1; WE tv.

Fee: $20.00 monthly.

Digital Basic Service

Subscribers: N.A.

Programming (via satellite): BBC America; Bio; Bloomberg Television; C-SPAN 3; Discovery Digital Networks; DMX Music; Do-It-Yourself; ESPNews; Fox College Sports Atlantic; Fox College Sports Central; Fox College Sports Pacific; Fox Movie Channel; Fuse; G4; GSN; History Channel International; Independent Film Channel; Lifetime Movie Network; Style Network; Sundance Channel; Toon Disney.

Pay Service 1

Pay Units: 496.

Programming (via satellite): Cinemax; Encore; HBO; Showtime; The Movie Channel.

Fee: $5.99 monthly (Encore), $8.99 monthly (Cinemax), $12.99 monthly (HBO), $13.99 monthly (Showtime & TMC).

Pay Service 2

Pay Units: N.A.

Programming (via satellite): Starz.

Digital Pay Service 1

Pay Units: N.A.

Programming (via satellite): Cinemax (multiplexed); Encore (multiplexed); Flix; HBO (multiplexed); Showtime (multiplexed); Starz (multiplexed); The Movie Channel (multiplexed).

Video-On-Demand: No

Pay-Per-View

iN DEMAND (delivered digitally); Playboy TV (delivered digitally); Fresh (delivered digitally).

Internet Service

Operational: Yes.

Telephone Service

None

Miles of Plant: 78.0 (coaxial); None (fiber optic). Homes passed: 2,531.

President: Steven Boyers. General Manager: Shelly Batton. Chief Technician: Phil Huett.

City fee: 5% of basic.

Ownership: Boycom Cablevision Inc. (MSO).

PILOT GROVE—Mid-Missouri Telephone Co., PO Box 38, 215 Roe St, Pilot Grove, MO 65276. Phones: 800-892-7073; 660-834-3311. Fax: 660-834-6632. Web Site: http://www.mid-mo.com. ICA: MO0238.

TV Market Ranking: Below 100 (PILOT GROVE). Franchise award date: December 6, 1982. Franchise expiration date: N.A. Began: June 1, 1983.

Channel capacity: 74 (2-way capable). Channels available but not in use: N.A.

Basic Service

Subscribers: 257.

Programming (received off-air): KCTV (CBS) Kansas City; KCWE (CW) Kansas City; KMCI-TV (IND) Lawrence; KMIZ (ABC) Columbia; KMOS-TV (PBS) Sedalia; KOMU-TV (CW, NBC) Columbia; KPXE-TV (ION) Kansas City; KRCG (CBS) Jefferson City; KSHB-TV (NBC) Kansas City; KSMO-TV (MNT) Kansas City; National Geographic Channel; WDAF-TV (FOX) Kansas City.

Programming (via satellite): ABC Family Channel; AMC; Animal Planet; Arts & Entertainment; Cartoon Network; CNN; Comedy Central; C-SPAN; Discovery Channel; E! Entertainment Television; ESPN; ESPN 2; Food Network; Fox News Channel; Fox Sports Net Midwest; FX; Great American Country; Hallmark Channel; Headline News; HGTV; History Channel; Home Shopping Network; INSP; Lifetime; MSNBC; MTV; Nickelodeon; QVC; Shopping Channel; Spike TV; TBS Superstation; The Learning Channel; Turner Classic Movies; Turner Network TV; TV Guide Network; TV Land; USA Network; VH1; Weather Channel; WGN America.

Fee: $10.00 installation; $28.95 monthly.

Digital Basic Service

Subscribers: 7.

Programming (via satellite): AmericanLife TV Network; BBC America; Bio; Bloomberg Television; Discovery Digital Networks; DMX Music; Encore; ESPN Classic Sports; ESPNews; FitTV; Fox Movie Channel; Fox Sports World; Golf Channel; GSN; History Channel International; Independent Film Channel; Life Network; Lifetime Movie Network; MuchMusic Network; Outdoor Channel; Speed Channel; Style Network; Toon Disney; Weatherscan.

Fee: $15.00 monthly.

Pay Service 1

Pay Units: 25.

Programming (via satellite): Cinemax.

Fee: $9.95 monthly.

Pay Service 2

Pay Units: 24.

Programming (via satellite): HBO.

Fee: $12.95 monthly.

Pay Service 3

Pay Units: 7.

Programming (via satellite): Showtime.

Fee: $8.95 monthly.

Pay Service 4

Pay Units: 4.

Programming (via satellite): The Movie Channel.

Fee: $9.95 monthly.

Video-On-Demand: No

Internet Service

Operational: No.

Telephone Service

None

Miles of Plant: 6.0 (coaxial); None (fiber optic). Homes passed: 360. Total homes in franchised area: 360.

Chief Executive Officer: Gary Romig. Chief Technician: Lewis L. Scott Jr.

City fee: 3% of gross.

Ownership: Mid-Missouri Telephone Co. (MSO).

PLATTSBURG—Allegiance Communications, 707 W Saratoga St, Shawnee, OK 74804. Phones: 405-275-6923; 405-395-1131. Web Site: http://www.allegiance.tv. ICA: MO0158.

TV Market Ranking: 22 (PLATTSBURG). Franchise award date: September 21, 1981. Franchise expiration date: N.A. Began: April 1, 1982.

Channel capacity: 32 (not 2-way capable). Channels available but not in use: N.A.

Basic Service

Subscribers: 775.

Programming (received off-air): KCPT (PBS) Kansas City; KCTV (CBS) Kansas City; KMBC-TV (ABC) Kansas City; KQTV (ABC) St. Joseph; KSHB-TV (NBC) Kansas City; KSMO-TV (MNT) Kansas City; WDAF-TV (FOX) Kansas City.

Programming (via satellite): ABC Family Channel; AMC; Arts & Entertainment; Cartoon Network; CNN; Comedy Central; Country Music TV; C-SPAN; Discovery Channel; Disney Channel; E! Entertainment Television; ESPN; ESPN 2; Home Shopping Network; Nickelodeon; QVC; Spike TV; TBS Superstation; Turner Network TV; USA Network; Weather Channel; WGN America.

Current originations: Public Access.

Fee: $21.18 monthly.

Digital Basic Service

Subscribers: 59.

Programming (via satellite): AmericanLife TV Network; BBC America; Bio; Bloomberg Television; Bravo; Discovery Digital Networks; DMX Music; ESPNews; FitTV; Fox Movie Channel; G4; GAS; Golf Channel;

GSN; Halogen Network; HGTV; History Channel; History Channel International; Independent Film Channel; Lifetime Movie Network; MTV Networks Digital Suite; MuchMusic Network; Nick Jr.; Outdoor Channel; ShopNBC; Speed Channel; Style Network; Syfy; Toon Disney; Trinity Broadcasting Network; Turner Classic Movies; Versus; WE tv.
Fee: $16.90 monthly.

Pay Service 1
Pay Units: 151.
Programming (via satellite): HBO (multiplexed).
Fee: $24.95 installation; $11.95 monthly.

Pay Service 2
Pay Units: 105.
Programming (via satellite): Showtime (multiplexed).
Fee: $24.95 installation; $11.95 monthly.

Digital Pay Service 1
Pay Units: 416.
Programming (via satellite): Cinemax (multiplexed); Encore (multiplexed); Flix; HBO (multiplexed); Showtime (multiplexed); Starz (multiplexed); The Movie Channel (multiplexed).

Video-On-Demand: No

Pay-Per-View
Addressable homes: 59.
ESPN Extra, Addressable: Yes; ESPN Now (delivered digitally); Hot Choice (delivered digitally); iN DEMAND (delivered digitally); Playboy TV (delivered digitally); Spice (delivered digitally); Spice2 (delivered digitally); sports (delivered digitally).

Internet Service
Operational: No.

Telephone Service
None

Miles of Plant: 16.0 (coaxial); None (fiber optic).
Chief Executive Officer: Bill Haggarty. Regional Vice President: Andrew Dearth. Vice President, Marketing: Tracy Bass.
Franchise fee: 3% of gross.
Ownership: Allegiance Communications (MSO).

PLEASANT HOPE—Fidelity Communications, 64 N Clark St, Sullivan, MO 63080. Phone: 573-468-8081. Fax: 573-468-3834. E-mail: custserv@fidelitycommunications.com. Web Site: http://www.fidelitycommunications.com. ICA: MO0328.
TV Market Ranking: Below 100 (PLEASANT HOPE). Franchise award date: N.A. Franchise expiration date: N.A. Began: N.A.
Channel capacity: 42 (not 2-way capable). Channels available but not in use: 20.

Basic Service
Subscribers: 19.
Programming (received off-air): KOLR (CBS) Springfield; KOZK (PBS) Springfield; KSFX-TV (FOX) Springfield; KSPR (ABC) Springfield; KYTV (CW, NBC) Springfield.
Programming (via satellite): ABC Family Channel; Arts & Entertainment; CNN; Country Music TV; Discovery Channel; ESPN; Showtime; TBS Superstation; Turner Network TV; USA Network; WGN America.
Fee: $39.95 installation; $36.75 monthly.

Pay Service 1
Pay Units: 13.
Programming (via satellite): HBO.
Fee: $10.95 monthly.

Pay Service 2
Pay Units: N.A.
Programming (via satellite): Showtime.
Fee: $10.00 monthly.

Internet Service
Operational: No.

Telephone Service
None

Miles of Plant: 10.0 (coaxial); None (fiber optic). Homes passed: 200.
Manager: Andrew B. Davis.
Ownership: Fidelity Communications Co. (MSO).

POCAHONTAS—Semo Communications Corporation. Now served by MORLEY, MO [MO0171]. ICA: MO0225.

POMME DE TERRE—American Broadband, 1348 Mathews Twp Pkwy, Mathews, NC 28105. Phone: 704-845-2263. Fax: 704-845-2299. Web Site: http://www.americanbroadband.com. Also serves Hermitage, Hickory County, Humansville, Pittsburg, Weaubleau & Wheatland. ICA: MO0066.
TV Market Ranking: Outside TV Markets (Hermitage, Hickory County, Humansville, Pittsburg, POMME DE TERRE, Weaubleau, Wheatland). Franchise award date: January 14, 1985. Franchise expiration date: N.A. Began: July 1, 1987.
Channel capacity: 55 (operating 2-way). Channels available but not in use: N.A.

Basic Service
Subscribers: 459.
Programming (received off-air): KOLR (CBS) Springfield; KOZK (PBS) Springfield; KSFX-TV (FOX) Springfield; KSPR (ABC) Springfield; KYTV (CW, NBC) Springfield.
Programming (via satellite): C-SPAN; Home Shopping Network; INSP; QVC; WGN America.
Fee: $29.95 installation; $16.95 monthly.

Expanded Basic Service 1
Subscribers: 387.
Programming (via satellite): ABC Family Channel; AMC; Animal Planet; Arts & Entertainment; Cartoon Network; CNN; Comedy Central; Country Music TV; Discovery Channel; Disney Channel; E! Entertainment Television; ESPN; ESPN 2; ESPN Classic Sports; Food Network; Fox News Channel; Golf Channel; Hallmark Channel; Headline News; HGTV; History Channel; Lifetime; MTV; Nickelodeon; Outdoor Channel; Speed Channel; Spike TV; Syfy; TBS Superstation; The Learning Channel; Travel Channel; Trinity Broadcasting Network; truTV; Turner Network TV; TV Land; USA Network; VH1; Weather Channel.
Fee: $39.95 monthly.

Digital Basic Service
Subscribers: 48.
Programming (via satellite): BBC America; Bio; Bloomberg Television; Discovery Digital Networks; DMX Music; ESPNews; Fox Movie Channel; G4; GAS; Great American Country; GSN; Halogen Network; History Channel International; Independent Film Channel; Lifetime Movie Network; MTV Networks Digital Suite; Nick Jr.; NickToons TV; ShopNBC; Sleuth; Toon Disney; Turner Classic Movies; Versus.

Digital Pay Service 1
Pay Units: 153.
Programming (via satellite): Cinemax (multiplexed); Encore (multiplexed); Flix; HBO (multiplexed); Showtime (multiplexed); Starz (multiplexed).
Fee: $11.95 monthly.

Pay-Per-View
Hot Choice (delivered digitally); Shorteez (delivered digitally); Fresh (delivered digitally); Playboy TV (delivered digitally); iN DEMAND (delivered digitally).

Internet Service
Operational: Yes.
Subscribers: 198.
Fee: $40.00 installation; $31.99 monthly.

Telephone Service
None

Miles of Plant: 88.0 (coaxial); None (fiber optic). Homes passed: 3,285.
President: Pat Eudy.
Franchise fee: 3% of gross.
Ownership: American Broadband Communications Inc. (MSO).

POPLAR BLUFF—City Cable, 3000 N Westwood Blvd, Poplar Bluff, MO 63901-2302. Phone: 573-686-8020. Fax: 573-686-8695. E-mail: info@pbutilities.com. Web Site: http://www.mycitycable.com. Also serves Butler County (portions). ICA: MO0024.
TV Market Ranking: Below 100 (Butler County (portions), POPLAR BLUFF). Franchise award date: November 3, 1957. Franchise expiration date: N.A. Began: August 23, 1957.
Channel capacity: 85 (operating 2-way). Channels available but not in use: 6.

Basic Service
Subscribers: 82,000.
Programming (received off-air): KAIT (ABC) Jonesboro; KBSI (FOX) Cape Girardeau; KFVS-TV (CBS, CW) Cape Girardeau; KPOB-TV (ABC) Poplar Bluff; KTEJ (PBS) Jonesboro; WPSD-TV (NBC) Paducah; WQWQ-LP (CW) Paducah.
Programming (via microwave): KMOV (CBS) St. Louis; KSDK (NBC) St. Louis; WDKA (MNT) Paducah.
Programming (via satellite): Headline News; ION Television; TV Guide Network; Weather Channel; WGN America.
Current originations: Government Access; Educational Access; Public Access; Religious Access.
Fee: $65.00 installation; $12.93 monthly; $65.00 additional installation.

Expanded Basic Service 1
Subscribers: 7,750.
Programming (via satellite): ABC Family Channel; AMC; AmericanLife TV Network; Animal Planet; Arts & Entertainment; BET Networks; Cartoon Network; CNBC; CNN; Comedy Central; Country Music TV; C-SPAN; C-SPAN 2; Discovery Channel; Disney Channel; Do-It-Yourself; E! Entertainment Television; ESPN; ESPN 2; ESPN Classic Sports; ESPNews; Food Network; Fox News Channel; Fox Sports Net Midwest; FX; Golf Channel; Gospel Music TV; Great American Country; Hallmark Channel; HGTV; History Channel; Home Shopping Network; INSP; Lifetime; MSNBC; MTV; National Geographic Channel; Nickelodeon; Outdoor Channel; QVC; Speed Channel; Spike TV; Syfy; TBS Superstation; The Learning Channel; Travel Channel; Trinity Broadcasting Network; truTV; Turner Classic Movies; Turner Network TV; TV Land; USA Network; Versus; VH1; WE tv.
Fee: $43.95 monthly.

Digital Basic Service
Subscribers: 1,106.
Programming (received off-air): KAIT (ABC) Jonesboro; KBSI (FOX) Cape Girardeau; KFVS-TV (CBS, CW) Cape Girardeau; WDKA (MNT) Paducah; WPSD-TV (NBC) Paducah.
Programming (via satellite): 3 Angels Broadcasting Network; Arts & Entertainment HD; BBC America; Bio; Bloomberg Television; Boomerang; CNN International; Colours; Discovery Channel HD; Discovery Health Channel; Discovery Kids Channel; Discovery Military Channel; Discovery Planet Green; ESPN 2 HD; ESPN HD; ESPN U; FitTV; Fox Business Channel; Fox Movie Channel; FSN Digital Atlantic; FSN Digital Central; FSN Digital Pacific; FSN HD; Fuse; FX HD; G4; Gospel Music Channel; Hallmark Movie Channel; HDNet; HDNet Movies; History Channel HD; History Channel International; ID Investigation Discovery; Independent Film Channel; Lifetime Movie Network; MTV Hits; MTV2; Music Choice; National Geographic Channel HD Network; Nick Jr.; NickToons TV; Outdoor Channel 2 HD; RFD-TV; Science Channel; SoapNet; Speed HD; TBN Enlace USA; TeenNick; The Sportsman Channel; Toon Disney; Versus HD; VH1 Classic; WealthTV.
Fee: $10.00 monthly.

Digital Expanded Basic Service
Subscribers: N.A.
Programming (via satellite): Cine Latino; ESPN Deportes; La Familia Network; Latele Novela Network; Puma TV; TV Chile; TV Colombia.
Fee: $4.00 monthly.

Pay Service 1
Pay Units: 420.
Programming (via satellite): Cinemax.
Fee: $10.90 monthly.

Pay Service 2
Pay Units: 1,633.
Programming (via satellite): HBO.
Fee: $12.25 monthly.

Pay Service 3
Pay Units: 442.
Programming (via satellite): Showtime.
Fee: $10.00 monthly.

Digital Pay Service 1
Pay Units: 1,107.
Programming (via satellite): Cinemax (multiplexed); Cinemax HD; Encore (multiplexed); Flix; HBO (multiplexed); HBO HD; Showtime (multiplexed); Showtime HD; Starz (multiplexed); Starz HDTV; The Movie Channel (multiplexed); The Movie Channel HD.
Fee: $8.90 monthly (Starz & Encore), $8.95 monthly (Cinemax), $9.95 monthly (Flix, Showtime, Sundance & TMC), $10.95 monthly (HBO).

Video-On-Demand: No

Pay-Per-View
Addressable homes: 1,106.
Hot Choice (delivered digitally), Addressable: Yes; Barker (delivered digitally), Ad-

dressable: No; iN DEMAND (delivered digitally), Addressable: No; ESPN Gameplan (delivered digitally).

Internet Service

Operational: Yes.

Subscribers: 1,106.

Broadband Service: imsinternet.net, semo.net, tcmax.net.

Fee: $29.95 monthly.

Telephone Service

None

Miles of Plant: 230.0 (coaxial); 35.0 (fiber optic).

General Manager: Bill Bach. Technical Manager: Dave Presley. Sales & Marketing Manager: Gary Davis.

Franchise fee: 5% of gross.

Ownership: Poplar Bluff Municipal Utilities.

PORTAGE DES SIOUX—St. Charles Broadband, 700 Fountain Lakes Blvd, Ste 100, Saint Charles, MO 63301-4353. Phone: 636-916-3706. Web Site: http://www.c3broadband.com. Also serves St. Charles County (unincorporated areas). ICA: MO0418.

TV Market Ranking: 11 (PORTAGE DES SIOUX, St. Charles County (unincorporated areas) (portions)); Outside TV Markets (St. Charles County (unincorporated areas) (portions)). Franchise award date: N.A. Franchise expiration date: N.A. Began: N.A.

Channel capacity: 40 (not 2-way capable). Channels available but not in use: None.

Basic Service

Subscribers: 200.

Programming (received off-air): KDNL-TV (ABC) St. Louis; KMOV (CBS) St. Louis; KNLC (IND) St. Louis; KPLR-TV (CW) St. Louis; KSDK (NBC) St. Louis; KTVI (FOX) St. Louis.

Programming (via satellite): TBS Superstation; WGN America.

Fee: $30.95 monthly.

Internet Service

Operational: No.

Telephone Service

None

Manager: Dan McKay. Chief Technician: Mike McKay.

Ownership: C3 Broadband Integration (MSO).

PORTAGEVILLE—NewWave Communications, 1311 Business Hwy 60 W, Dexter, MO 63841. Phones: 888-863-9928; 573-614-4573. Fax: 573-614-4802. Web Site: http://www.newwavecom.com. Also serves New Madrid County & Pemiscot County. ICA: MO0099.

TV Market Ranking: Below 100 (New Madrid County (portions), Pemiscot County (portions)); Outside TV Markets (New Madrid County (portions), Pemiscot County (portions), PORTAGEVILLE). Franchise award date: September 2, 1969. Franchise expiration date: N.A. Began: May 1, 1970.

Channel capacity: N.A. Channels available but not in use: N.A.

Basic Service

Subscribers: 815.

Programming (received off-air): KAIT (ABC) Jonesboro; KBSI (FOX) Cape Girardeau; KFVS-TV (CBS, CW) Cape Girardeau; KPOB-TV (ABC) Poplar Bluff; KTEJ (PBS) Jonesboro; WHBQ-TV (FOX) Memphis; WKMU (PBS) Murray; WPSD-TV (NBC) Paducah; 5 FMs.

Programming (via satellite): C-SPAN; C-SPAN 2; Home Shopping Network; INSP; QVC; ShopNBC; Trinity Broadcasting Network; WGN America.

Fee: $61.50 installation; $37.95 monthly.

Expanded Basic Service 1

Subscribers: N.A.

Programming (via satellite): ABC Family Channel; AMC; Animal Planet; Arts & Entertainment; BET Networks; Bravo; Cartoon Network; CNBC; CNN; Comedy Central; Country Music TV; Discovery Channel; Disney Channel; E! Entertainment Television; ESPN; ESPN 2; ESPN Classic Sports; Food Network; Fox News Channel; Fox Sports Net Midwest; FX; Golf Channel; Great American Country; GSN; Hallmark Channel; Headline News; HGTV; History Channel; Jewelry Television; Lifetime; MSNBC; MTV; Nickelodeon; Outdoor Channel; Oxygen; SoapNet; Speed Channel; Spike TV; Syfy; TBS Superstation; The Learning Channel; Travel Channel; truTV; Turner Network TV; TV Land; USA Network; VH1; Weather Channel.

Digital Basic Service

Subscribers: N.A.

Programming (received off-air): KAIT (ABC) Jonesboro; KBSI (FOX) Cape Girardeau; KFVS-TV (CBS, CW) Cape Girardeau; WPSD-TV (NBC) Paducah.

Programming (via satellite): Arts & Entertainment HD; BBC America; Bio; Bloomberg Television; CMT Pure Country; Discovery HD Theater; Discovery Health Channel; Discovery Kids Channel; Discovery Military Channel; Discovery Planet Green; Do-It-Yourself; ESPN 2 HD; ESPN HD; ESPNews; FitTV; Fox Movie Channel; FSN HD; G4; Gospel Music Channel; Halogen Network; HDNet; HDNet Movies; History Channel HD; History Channel International; ID Investigation Discovery; Independent Film Channel; Lifetime Movie Network; MTV Hits; MTV2; Music Choice; Nick Jr.; NickToons TV; Palladia; RFD-TV; Science Channel; Sleuth; Style Network; TeenNick; The Sportsman Channel; The Word Network; Toon Disney; Turner Classic Movies; Turner Network TV HD; USA Network HD; Versus; Versus HD; VH1 Classic; VH1 Soul; Weather Channel HD.

Fee: $3.95 monthly.

Digital Pay Service 1

Pay Units: N.A.

Programming (via satellite): Cinemax (multiplexed); Cinemax HD; Encore (multiplexed); Flix; HBO (multiplexed); HBO HD; Showtime (multiplexed); Starz (multiplexed); Starz HDTV; The Movie Channel (multiplexed).

Video-On-Demand: Yes

Pay-Per-View

iN DEMAND (delivered digitally); Playboy TV (delivered digitally); Fresh (delivered digitally); Hot Choice (delivered digitally); Club Jenna (delivered digitally); Spice: Xcess (delivered digitally).

Internet Service

Operational: Yes. Began: May 19, 2004.

Fee: $40.00 installation; $31.99 monthly.

Telephone Service

Digital: Operational

Fee: $24.99 monthly

Miles of Plant: 38.0 (coaxial); None (fiber optic). Homes passed: 1,649.

General Manager: Ed Gargas. Technical Operations Manager: Jerry Townsend.

City fee: 5% of gross.

Ownership: NewWave Communications (MSO).

PORTER MILLS—Lake Communications, MO. Phone: 877-242-3830. Web Site: http://lakecommunicationsonline.com. Also serves Camden County (portions), Greenview & Niangua. ICA: MO0090.

TV Market Ranking: Below 100 (Niangua); Outside TV Markets (Camden County (portions), Greenview, PORTER MILLS). Franchise award date: N.A. Franchise expiration date: N.A. Began: N.A.

Channel capacity: 42 (not 2-way capable). Channels available but not in use: 4.

Basic Service

Subscribers: 490.

Programming (received off-air): KOLR (CBS) Springfield; KOMU-TV (CW, NBC) Columbia; KOZK (PBS) Springfield; KSFX-TV (FOX) Springfield; KSPR (ABC) Springfield; KYTV (CW, NBC) Springfield.

Programming (via satellite): ABC Family Channel; AMC; Arts & Entertainment; CNBC; CNN; Country Music TV; C-SPAN; Discovery Channel; ESPN; Hallmark Channel; Headline News; Home Shopping Network; Lifetime; Nickelodeon; Spike TV; TBS Superstation; Turner Network TV; USA Network; Weather Channel; WGN America.

Fee: $29.95 installation; $39.95 monthly.

Pay Service 1

Pay Units: 17.

Programming (via satellite): Cinemax.

Fee: $10.00 monthly.

Pay Service 2

Pay Units: 56.

Programming (via satellite): HBO.

Fee: $10.95 monthly.

Pay Service 3

Pay Units: 124.

Programming (via satellite): Showtime.

Fee: $10.00 monthly.

Video-On-Demand: No

Internet Service

Operational: No.

Telephone Service

None

Miles of Plant: 48.0 (coaxial); None (fiber optic). Homes passed: 1,622.

President & General Manager: Tony Gilbert.

Ownership: Lake Communications (MSO).

POTOSI—Crystal Broadband Networks, PO Box 180336, Chicago, IL 76021. Phones: 877-319-0328; 630-206-0447. E-mail: info@crystalbn.com. Web Site: http://crystalbn.com. ICA: MO0106.

TV Market Ranking: Outside TV Markets (POTOSI). Franchise award date: January 1, 1980. Franchise expiration date: N.A. Began: October 1, 1981.

Channel capacity: 57 (not 2-way capable). Channels available but not in use: 6.

Basic Service

Subscribers: 1,240.

Programming (received off-air): KDNL-TV (ABC) St. Louis; KETC (PBS) St. Louis; KFVS-TV (CBS, CW) Cape Girardeau; KMOV (CBS) St. Louis; KNLC (IND) St. Louis; KPLR-TV (CW) St. Louis; KSDK (NBC) St. Louis; KTVI (FOX) St. Louis.

Programming (via satellite): C-SPAN; QVC; Trinity Broadcasting Network; WGN America.

Current originations: Educational Access; Public Access.

Fee: $29.95 installation; $19.95 monthly; $15.00 additional installation.

Expanded Basic Service 1

Subscribers: 1,193.

Programming (via satellite): ABC Family Channel; AMC; Arts & Entertainment; Cartoon Network; CNBC; CNN; Comedy Central; Country Music TV; Discovery Channel; Disney Channel; E! Entertainment Television; ESPN; ESPN 2; Fox News Channel; Fox Sports Net Midwest; FX; G4; Hallmark Channel; Headline News; HGTV; History Channel; Lifetime; MTV; Nickelodeon; Oxygen; Spike TV; Syfy; TBS Superstation; The Learning Channel; Travel Channel; truTV; Turner Network TV; TV Land; USA Network; VH1; Weather Channel.

Fee: $20.00 monthly.

Digital Basic Service

Subscribers: 1,161.

Programming (via satellite): BBC America; Bio; Bloomberg Television; Discovery Digital Networks; Do-It-Yourself; GAS; GSN; History Channel International; Independent Film Channel; MTV Networks Digital Suite; Music Choice; Nick Jr.; Nick Too; Nick-Toons TV; SoapNet; Style Network; Sundance Channel; Toon Disney; TV Guide Interactive Inc.; WE tv.

Fee: $12.95 monthly.

Digital Pay Service 1

Pay Units: 469.

Programming (via satellite): Cinemax (multiplexed); Encore Action (multiplexed); Flix; HBO (multiplexed); Showtime (multiplexed); Starz (multiplexed); The Movie Channel (multiplexed).

Fee: $10.00 installation; $10.95 monthly (each).

Video-On-Demand: No

Pay-Per-View

iN DEMAND (delivered digitally); Pleasure (delivered digitally); ETC (delivered digitally).

Internet Service

Operational: Yes.

Telephone Service

None

Miles of Plant: 43.0 (coaxial); None (fiber optic). Homes passed: 2,447.

General Manager: Nidhin Johnson. Program Manager: Shawn Smith.

Franchise fee: 3% of gross.

Ownership: Crystal Broadband Networks (MSO).

POWERSITE—Formerly served by Almega Cable. No longer in operation. ICA: MO0452.

PRINCETON—Longview Communications, 12007 Sunrise Valley Dr, Ste 375, Reston, VA 20191. Phones: 866-611-6565 (Customer service); 703-476-9101. Fax: 703-476-9107. Web Site: http://www.longviewcomm.com. ICA: MO0185.

TV Market Ranking: Outside TV Markets (PRINCETON). Franchise award date: N.A. Franchise expiration date: N.A. Began: December 1, 1973.

Channel capacity: 41 (not 2-way capable). Channels available but not in use: 1.

Basic Service

Subscribers: 155.

Programming (received off-air): KCCI (CBS) Des Moines; KCTV (CBS) Kansas City; KDIN-TV (PBS) Des Moines; KMBC-TV (ABC) Kansas City; KQTV (ABC) St. Joseph; KSHB-TV (NBC) Kansas City; KTVO (ABC) Kirksville; WHO-DT (NBC) Des Moines; WOI-DT (ABC) Ames; allband FM.

Programming (via satellite): ABC Family Channel; AMC; Animal Planet; Arts & Entertainment; Cartoon Network; CNN; Discovery Channel; Disney Channel; ESPN; ESPN 2; Food Network; Fox News Channel; FX; Great American Country; HGTV; History Channel; Lifetime; Outdoor Channel; TBS Superstation; The Learning Channel; Toon Disney; Turner Network TV; USA Network; Weather Channel; WGN America.

Fee: $10.00 installation; $41.45 monthly.

Pay Service 1

Pay Units: 38.

Programming (via satellite): Cinemax; HBO; Showtime; Starz; The Movie Channel.

Fee: $9.95 monthly (Starz, Showtime or TMC), $10.95 monthly (Cinemax), $14.95 monthly (HBO).

Video-On-Demand: No

Internet Service

Operational: No.

Telephone Service

None

Miles of Plant: 12.0 (coaxial); None (fiber optic). Homes passed: 623.

President: John Long. Senior Vice President: Marc W. Cohen. General Manager: Brandon Dickey. Operations Manager: Perry Scarborough.

City fee: 3% of gross.

Ownership: Longview Communications (MSO).

PURDY—Mediacom. Now served by CASSVILLE, MO [MO0118]. ICA: MO0227.

PUXICO—Boycom Cablevision Inc., 3467 Township Line Rd, Poplar Bluff, MO 63901. Phone: 573-686-9101. Fax: 573-686-4722. Web Site: http://www.boycomonline.com. ICA: MO0202.

TV Market Ranking: Below 100 (PUXICO). Franchise award date: January 20, 1982. Franchise expiration date: N.A. Began: August 1, 1982.

Channel capacity: N.A. Channels available but not in use: N.A.

Basic Service

Subscribers: 293.

Programming (received off-air): KAIT (ABC) Jonesboro; KBSI (FOX) Cape Girardeau; KFVS-TV (CBS, CW) Cape Girardeau; KTEJ (PBS) Jonesboro; WPSD-TV (NBC) Paducah.

Programming (via satellite): ABC Family Channel; Animal Planet; Arts & Entertainment; CNN; Discovery Channel; Disney Channel; ESPN; Fox Sports Net Midwest; Great American Country; History Channel; Home Shopping Network; Lifetime; MTV; Nickelodeon; Spike TV; TBS Superstation; Trinity Broadcasting Network; Turner Network TV; USA Network; Weather Channel; WGN America.

Fee: $61.50 installation; $41.15 monthly.

Pay Service 1

Pay Units: 94.

Programming (via satellite): Cinemax; HBO; Showtime; The Movie Channel.

Fee: $9.49 monthly (Cinemax), $13.49 monthly (HBO, Showtime or TMC).

Video-On-Demand: No

Internet Service

Operational: Yes.

Telephone Service

None

Miles of Plant: 15.0 (coaxial); None (fiber optic). Homes passed: 526.

President: Steven Boyers. General Manager: Shelly Batton. Chief Technician: Phil Huett.

City fee: 3% of gross.

Ownership: Boycom Cablevision Inc. (MSO).

QULIN—Boycom Cablevision Inc., 3467 Township Line Rd, Poplar Bluff, MO 63901. Phone: 573-686-9101. Fax: 573-686-4722. Web Site: http://www.boycomonline.com. ICA: MO0291.

TV Market Ranking: Below 100 (QULIN). Franchise award date: N.A. Franchise expiration date: N.A. Began: September 1, 1982.

Channel capacity: N.A. Channels available but not in use: N.A.

Basic Service

Subscribers: N.A.

Programming (received off-air): KAIT (ABC) Jonesboro; KBSI (FOX) Cape Girardeau; KFVS-TV (CBS, CW) Cape Girardeau; KPOB-TV (ABC) Poplar Bluff; KTEJ (PBS) Jonesboro; WPSD-TV (NBC) Paducah.

Programming (via satellite): ABC Family Channel; ESPN; Spike TV; TBS Superstation; WGN America.

Fee: $21.95 monthly.

Pay Service 1

Pay Units: N.A.

Programming (via satellite): The Movie Channel.

Fee: $11.95 monthly.

Video-On-Demand: No

Internet Service

Operational: No.

Telephone Service

None

Miles of Plant: 8.0 (coaxial); None (fiber optic).

President: Steven Boyers. General Manager: Shelly Batton. Chief Technician: Phil Huett.

Ownership: Boycom Cablevision Inc. (MSO).

RAVENWOOD—B & L Technologies LLC, 3329 270th St, Lenox, IA 50851. Phones: 800-798-5488; 641-348-2240. Fax: 641-348-2240. ICA: MO0320.

TV Market Ranking: Outside TV Markets (RAVENWOOD). Franchise award date: June 21, 1988. Franchise expiration date: N.A. Began: January 1, 1989.

Channel capacity: 36 (not 2-way capable). Channels available but not in use: 6.

Basic Service

Subscribers: 45.

Programming (received off-air): KHIN (PBS) Red Oak; KMTV-TV (CBS) Omaha; KQTV (ABC) St. Joseph; KSHB-TV (NBC) Kansas City; KTAJ-TV (TBN) St. Joseph; WDAF-TV (FOX) Kansas City.

Programming (via satellite): ABC Family Channel; AMC; Arts & Entertainment; CNN; Discovery Channel; ESPN; History Channel; KARE (NBC) Minneapolis; Nickelodeon; Spike TV; TBS Superstation; Turner Network TV; USA Network; VH1; WCCO-TV (CBS) Minneapolis; WGN America.

Fee: $25.00 installation; $30.50 monthly.

Pay Service 1

Pay Units: 9.

Programming (via satellite): HBO.

Fee: $12.00 monthly.

Video-On-Demand: No

Internet Service

Operational: No.

Telephone Service

None

Miles of Plant: 5.0 (coaxial); None (fiber optic). Homes passed: 175.

Manager & Chief Technician: Robert Hintz. Office Manager: Linda Hintz.

Ownership: B & L Technologies LLC (MSO).

RENICK—Charter Communications. No longer in operation. ICA: MO0419.

RENICK—Milan Interactive Communications, 312 S Main, PO Box 240, Milan, MO 63556. Phone: 660-265-7174. ICA: MO0471.

TV Market Ranking: Below 100 (RENICK).

Channel capacity: N.A. Channels available but not in use: N.A.

Basic Service

Subscribers: 10.

Programming (received off-air): KMIZ (ABC) Columbia; KOMU-TV (CW, NBC) Columbia; KRCG (CBS) Jefferson City.

Programming (via satellite): CNN; Discovery Channel; ESPN; TBS Superstation; Turner Network TV; USA Network; WGN America.

Fee: $29.95 installation; $40.77 monthly.

Video-On-Demand: No

Internet Service

Operational: No.

Telephone Service

None

President & General Manager: Rick Gardener.

Ownership: Milan Interactive Communications (MSO).

REPUBLIC—Cable America Corp., 655 N Hillside, Republic, MO 65738. Phone: 417-732-7242. Fax: 417-732-8882. Web Site: http://www.cableamerica.com. Also serves Clever & Greene County (southwestern portion). ICA: MO0069.

TV Market Ranking: Below 100 (Clever, Greene County (southwestern portion), REPUBLIC). Franchise award date: March 25, 1995. Franchise expiration date: N.A. Began: July 1, 1981.

Channel capacity: 60 (not 2-way capable). Channels available but not in use: N.A.

Basic Service

Subscribers: 1,828.

Programming (received off-air): KETC (PBS) St. Louis; KOLR (CBS) Springfield; KOZK (PBS) Springfield; KSDK (NBC) St. Louis; KSPR (ABC) Springfield; KWBM (MNT) Harrison [LICENSED & SILENT].

Programming (via satellite): C-SPAN; C-SPAN 2; Home Shopping Network; KSFX-TV (FOX) Springfield; TV Guide Network; Weather Channel; WGN America; WRBU (MNT) East St. Louis.

Current originations: Government Access; Public Access.

Fee: $11.00 monthly.

Expanded Basic Service 1

Subscribers: 1,486.

Programming (via satellite): ABC Family Channel; AMC; Animal Planet; Arts & Entertainment; Cartoon Network; CNBC; CNN; Comedy Central; Discovery Channel; Disney Channel; ESPN; ESPN 2; Food Network; Fox News Channel; Fox Sports Net Midwest; FX; Golf Channel; Great American Country; Hallmark Channel; Headline News; HGTV; History Channel; INSP; Lifetime; MTV; Nickelodeon; QVC; Speed Channel; Spike TV; Syfy; TBS Superstation; The Learning Channel; Travel Channel; Trinity Broadcasting Network; truTV; Turner Classic Movies; Turner Network TV; TV Land; USA Network; Versus; VH1; WE tv.

Fee: $30.95 monthly.

Digital Basic Service

Subscribers: 406.

Programming (via satellite): BBC America; Bio; Bloomberg Television; Bravo; Discovery Digital Networks; DMX Music; Encore (multiplexed); ESPN 2; ESPN Classic Sports; ESPNews; Fox Movie Channel; Fox Sports World; Fuse; G4; GAS; Golf Channel; GSN; Halogen Network; HGTV; History Channel; History Channel International; Independent Film Channel; Lifetime Movie Network; Lime; MTV Networks Digital Suite; Nick Jr.; NickToons TV; Speed Channel; Style Network; Syfy; Toon Disney; Trinity Broadcasting Network; Trio; Turner Classic Movies; WE tv.

Fee: $12.00 monthly.

Digital Pay Service 1

Pay Units: N.A.

Programming (via satellite): Cinemax (multiplexed); HBO (multiplexed); Showtime (multiplexed); Starz (multiplexed); The Movie Channel (multiplexed).

Video-On-Demand: No

Internet Service

Operational: Yes.

Subscribers: 962.

Fee: $14.95 installation; $25.95 monthly.

Telephone Service

Digital: Planned

Miles of Plant: 74.0 (coaxial); None (fiber optic). Homes passed: 4,570.

Area Manager: Debbie Mefford. General Manager: Curtis Scott. Chief Technician: Chris Smith.

City fee: 5% of gross.

Ownership: CableAmerica Corp. (MSO).

RICH HILL—N.W. Communications, PO Box 30, 616 E Park, Rich Hill, MO 64779-0030. Phones: 660-935-2211; 417-395-2121 (Business office). Fax: 417-395-2120. E-mail: tburchell@klmtel.net. Web Site: http://www.klmtel.net. ICA: MO0177.

TV Market Ranking: Outside TV Markets (RICH HILL). Franchise award date: N.A. Franchise expiration date: N.A. Began: July 1, 1976.

Channel capacity: 35 (not 2-way capable). Channels available but not in use: 2.

Basic Service

Subscribers: 417.

Programming (received off-air): KCPT (PBS) Kansas City; KCTV (CBS) Kansas City; KCWE (CW) Kansas City; KMBC-TV (ABC) Kansas City; KMCI-TV (IND) Lawrence; KODE-TV (ABC) Joplin; KPXE-TV (ION) Kansas City; KSHB-TV (NBC) Kansas City; KSMO-TV (MNT) Kansas City; WDAF-TV (FOX) Kansas City; allband FM.

Programming (via satellite): ABC Family Channel; Arts & Entertainment; CNN; Comedy Central; Discovery Channel; Disney Channel; ESPN; ESPN 2; Great American Country; Hallmark Channel; HGTV; History Channel; Lifetime; Nickelodeon; Outdoor Channel; QVC; Spike TV; Syfy; TBS Superstation; The Learning Channel; Travel Channel; Trinity Broadcasting Network; Turner Classic Movies; Turner Network TV; TV Land; USA Network; VH1; WGN America.

Fee: $27.50 installation; $24.72 monthly.

Pay Service 1

Pay Units: 92.

Programming (via satellite): Cinemax; Flix; HBO; Showtime; The Movie Channel.

Fee: $12.95 monthly (each).

Internet Service

Operational: Yes.

Fee: $34.95 monthly.

Telephone Service
None
Miles of Plant: 21.0 (coaxial); None (fiber optic). Additional miles planned: 4.0 (coaxial). Homes passed: 629. Total homes in franchised area: 850.
Manager & Chief Technician: Reese Copsey.
City fee: 3% of gross.
Ownership: KLM Telephone Co. (MSO).

RICHLAND—Cable America Corp. Now served by WAYNESVILLE (formerly ST. ROBERT), MO [MO0023] Cable America Corp. Now served by WAYNESVILLE (formerly ST. ROBERT), MO [MO0023] Cable America Corp. Now served by WAYNESVILLE (formerly ST. ROBERT), MO [MO0023]. ICA: MO0139.

RICHMOND—Mediacom, 901 N College Ave, Columbia, MO 65201. Phones: 573-443-1536; 800-234-2157; 816-637-4500 (Local office). Fax: 573-449-8492. E-mail: gbaugh@mediacomcc.com. Web Site: http://www.mediacomcable.com. Also serves Henrietta. ICA: MO0077.
TV Market Ranking: 22 (Henrietta, RICHMOND). Franchise award date: N.A. Franchise expiration date: N.A. Began: October 1, 1979.
Channel capacity: N.A. Channels available but not in use: N.A.

Basic Service
Subscribers: 2,107.
Programming (received off-air): KCPT (PBS) Kansas City; KCTV (CBS) Kansas City; KCWE (CW) Kansas City; KMBC-TV (ABC) Kansas City; KMCI-TV (IND) Lawrence; KPXE-TV (ION) Kansas City; KSHB-TV (NBC) Kansas City; KSMO-TV (MNT) Kansas City; WDAF-TV (FOX) Kansas City.
Programming (via satellite): KQTV (ABC) St. Joseph; WGN America.
Fee: $35.00 installation; $27.95 monthly; $1.70 converter.

Expanded Basic Service 1
Subscribers: N.A.
Programming (via satellite): ABC Family Channel; AMC; Animal Planet; Arts & Entertainment; Bravo; Cartoon Network; CNBC; CNN; Comedy Central; Country Music TV; C-SPAN; Discovery Channel; Disney Channel; E! Entertainment Television; ESPN; ESPN 2; Food Network; Fox News Channel; Fox Sports Net Midwest; FX; Hallmark Channel; Headline News; HGTV; History Channel; Home Shopping Network; INSP; Lifetime; MSNBC; MTV; Nickelodeon; Outdoor Channel; QVC; ShopNBC; Speed Channel; Spike TV; Syfy; TBS Superstation; The Learning Channel; Travel Channel; Trinity Broadcasting Network; truTV; Turner Network TV; TV Guide Network; TV Land; USA Network; VH1; WE tv; Weather Channel.
Fee: $3.95 monthly.

Digital Basic Service
Subscribers: N.A.
Programming (via satellite): BBC America; Bio; Bloomberg Television; Discovery Digital Networks; FitTV; Fox Movie Channel; Fox Soccer; Fuse; G4; GAS; Golf Channel; GSN; History Channel International; Independent Film Channel; Lifetime Movie Network; Lime; MTV Networks Digital Suite; Music Choice; National Geographic Channel; Nick Jr.; NickToons TV; Style Network; Turner Classic Movies; Versus.

Digital Pay Service 1
Pay Units: N.A.
Programming (via satellite): Cinemax (multiplexed); Encore (multiplexed); Flix (multiplexed); HBO (multiplexed); Showtime (multiplexed); Starz (multiplexed); Sundance Channel (multiplexed); The Movie Channel (multiplexed).

Video-On-Demand: No

Pay-Per-View
Mediacom PPV (delivered digitally); Playboy TV (delivered digitally); TEN Clips (delivered digitally); TEN Blox (delivered digitally).

Internet Service
Operational: Yes.
Broadband Service: Mediacom High Speed Internet.
Fee: $45.95 monthly.

Telephone Service
None
Miles of Plant: 49.0 (coaxial); None (fiber optic). Homes passed: 3,077.
General Manager: Gary Baugh. Marketing Director: Wes Shaver. Technical Operations Manager: Tom Evans.
City fee: 3% of basic.
Ownership: Mediacom LLC (MSO).

ROCKAWAY BEACH—Cox Communications. Now served by BRANSON, MO [MO0038]. ICA: MO0420.

ROCKPORT—Rockport Cablevision, 107 W Opp St, Rockport, MO 64482. Phones: 877-202-1764; 660-744-5311. Fax: 660-744-2120. Web Site: http://www.rptel.net. Also serves Atchison County, Fairfax & Tarkio. ICA: MO0186.
TV Market Ranking: Outside TV Markets (Atchison County, Fairfax, ROCKPORT, Tarkio). Franchise award date: March 1, 1984. Franchise expiration date: N.A. Began: November 1, 1984.
Channel capacity: 36 (not 2-way capable). Channels available but not in use: N.A.

Basic Service
Subscribers: 620.
Programming (received off-air): KCTV (CBS) Kansas City; KETV (ABC) Omaha; KMBC-TV (ABC) Kansas City; KMTV-TV (CBS) Omaha; KPTM (FOX, MNT) Omaha; KQTV (ABC) St. Joseph; KSHB-TV (NBC) Kansas City; KXVO (CW) Omaha; KYNE-TV (PBS) Omaha; WDAF-TV (FOX) Kansas City; WOWT-TV (IND, NBC) Omaha.
Programming (via satellite): ABC Family Channel; AMC; Animal Planet; Arts & Entertainment; Cartoon Network; CNBC; CNN; Comedy Central; Country Music TV; C-SPAN; Discovery Channel; Disney Channel; Do-It-Yourself; ESPN; ESPN 2; ESPN Classic Sports; FitTV; Food Network; Fox News Channel; Fox Sports Net; FX; G4; Golf Channel; Great American Country; Hallmark Channel; Headline News; HGTV; History Channel; Home Shopping Network; Lifetime; MoviePlex; MTV; National Geographic Channel; Nickelodeon; Outdoor Channel; QVC; RFD-TV; Speed Channel; Spike TV; TBS Superstation; The Learning Channel; Travel Channel; Trinity Broadcasting Network; Turner Network TV; TV Land; USA Network; VH1; Weather Channel; WGN America.
Fee: $35.00 installation; $26.00 monthly.

Digital Basic Service
Subscribers: 50.
Programming (via satellite): BBC America; Bravo; Discovery Digital Networks; DMX Music; ESPNews; Independent Film Channel; Nick Jr.; Syfy; Turner Classic Movies; Versus; WE tv.
Fee: $35.00 installation; $21.50 monthly.

Pay Service 1
Pay Units: 16.
Programming (via satellite): Cinemax; Encore; HBO; Starz.
Fee: $25.00 installation; $3.50 monthly (Encore), $8.00 monthly (Starz), $9.00 monthly (Cinemax), $11.00 monthly (HBO).

Digital Pay Service 1
Pay Units: N.A.
Programming (via satellite): Encore (multiplexed); HBO (multiplexed); Starz; The Movie Channel.
Fee: $6.50 monthly (HBO or Cinemax), $6.95 monthly (TMC).

Video-On-Demand: No

Pay-Per-View
iN DEMAND (delivered digitally); Playboy TV (delivered digitally).

Internet Service
Operational: No, DSL.

Telephone Service
None
Miles of Plant: 69.0 (coaxial); None (fiber optic). Homes passed: 3,462. Total homes in franchised area: 3,462.
Manager: Raymond Henagan. Chief Technician: Gary McGuire.
City fee: 3% of basic gross.
Ownership: Rock Port Telephone Co.

ROCKVILLE—Formerly served by N.W. Communications. No longer in operation. ICA: MO0358.

ROGERSVILLE—Mediacom. Now served by SEYMOUR, MO [MO0172]. ICA: MO0272.

ROLLA—Phelps County Cable. Now served by WAYNESVILLE, MO [MO0023]. ICA: MO0421.

RUSSELLVILLE—Longview Communications, 12007 Sunrise Valley Dr, Ste 375, Reston, VA 20191. Phones: 866-611-6565 (Customer service); 703-476-9107. Fax: 703-476-9107. Web Site: http://www.longviewcomm.com. ICA: MO0262.
TV Market Ranking: Below 100 (RUSSELLVILLE). Franchise award date: N.A. Franchise expiration date: N.A. Began: September 1, 1985.
Channel capacity: 41 (not 2-way capable). Channels available but not in use: 5.

Basic Service
Subscribers: 41.
Programming (received off-air): KCPT (PBS) Kansas City; KCTV (CBS) Kansas City; KCWE (CW) Kansas City; KMBC-TV (ABC) Kansas City; KMCI-TV (IND) Lawrence; KPXE-TV (ION) Kansas City; KSHB-TV (NBC) Kansas City; KSMO-TV (MNT) Kansas City; WDAF-TV (FOX) Kansas City.
Programming (via satellite): INSP; QVC; Trinity Broadcasting Network.
Fee: $17.98 monthly.

Expanded Basic Service 1
Subscribers: N.A.
Programming (via satellite): ABC Family Channel; AMC; Animal Planet; Arts & Entertainment; Cartoon Network; CNN; Discovery Channel; Disney Channel; ESPN; ESPN 2; Headline News; HGTV; Lifetime; Nickelodeon; TBS Superstation; The Learning Channel; Travel Channel; Turner Network TV; USA Network; Weather Channel; WGN America.
Fee: $17.97 monthly.

Pay Service 1
Pay Units: 38.
Programming (via satellite): Showtime; The Movie Channel.
Fee: $8.95 monthly (TMC), $10.95 monthly (Showtime).

Video-On-Demand: No

Internet Service
Operational: No.

Telephone Service
None
Miles of Plant: 8.0 (coaxial); None (fiber optic). Homes passed: 341.
President: John Long. Senior Vice President: Marc W. Cohen. General Manager: Brandon Dickey. Operations Manager: Perry Scarborough.
Ownership: Longview Communications (MSO).

SALEM—Fidelity Communications, 64 N Clark St, Sullivan, MO 63080. Phones: 573-468-8081; 800-392-8070. Also serves Dent County. ICA: MO0059.
TV Market Ranking: Outside TV Markets (Dent County, SALEM). Franchise award date: December 20, 1985. Franchise expiration date: N.A. Began: January 1, 1967.
Channel capacity: 56 (operating 2-way). Channels available but not in use: 4.

Basic Service
Subscribers: 2,488.
Programming (received off-air): KETC (PBS) St. Louis; KOLR (CBS) Springfield; KPLR-TV (CW) St. Louis; KRCG (CBS) Jefferson City; KSDK (NBC) St. Louis; KSFX-TV (FOX) Springfield; KSPR (ABC) Springfield; KYTV (CW, NBC) Springfield; 2 FMs.
Programming (via satellite): C-SPAN; Home Shopping Network; INSP; Trinity Broadcasting Network; Weather Channel; WGN America.
Fee: $61.50 installation; $17.95 monthly.

Expanded Basic Service 1
Subscribers: 1,955.
Programming (via satellite): ABC Family Channel; AMC; Animal Planet; Arts & Entertainment; Cartoon Network; CNBC; CNN; Comedy Central; Discovery Channel; Disney Channel; E! Entertainment Television; ESPN; ESPN 2; ESPN Classic Sports; Food Network; Fox News Channel; Fox Sports Net Midwest; FX; Great American Country; Hallmark Channel; Headline News; HGTV; History Channel; Lifetime; MSNBC; MTV; Nickelodeon; Outdoor Channel; RFD-TV; SoapNet; Speed Channel; Spike TV; Syfy; TBS Superstation; The Learning Channel; Travel Channel; Turner Classic Movies; Turner Network TV; TV Land; USA Network; Versus; VH1.
Fee: $21.00 monthly.

Digital Basic Service
Subscribers: N.A.
Programming (via satellite): BBC America; Bio; Bloomberg Television; C-SPAN 3; Discovery Digital Networks; Do-It-Yourself; ESPNews; Fox College Sports Atlantic; Fox College Sports Central; Fox College Sports Pacific; Fox Movie Channel; Fuse; G4; GSN; History Channel International; Independent Film Channel; Military History Channel; Music Choice; Science Television; Sundance Channel; Toon Disney; WE tv.
Fee: $3.99 monthly.

Pay Service 1
Pay Units: 1,030.
Programming (via satellite): Cinemax; Encore; HBO; Showtime; Starz; The Movie Channel.
Fee: $5.99 monthly (Encore), $8.99 monthly (Cinemax), $12.99 monthly (HBO), $13.99 monthly (Showtime & TMC).

Digital Pay Service 1
Pay Units: N.A.
Programming (via satellite): Cinemax (multiplexed); Encore (multiplexed); Flix; HBO (multiplexed); Showtime (multiplexed); Starz (multiplexed); The Movie Channel (multiplexed).
Video-On-Demand: No
Pay-Per-View
iN DEMAND (delivered digitally); Playboy TV (delivered digitally).
Internet Service
Operational: Yes. Began: December 31, 2004.
Broadband Service: Cebridge High Speed Cable Internet.
Fee: $29.95 monthly.
Telephone Service
None
Miles of Plant: 79.0 (coaxial); None (fiber optic). Homes passed: 3,463.
Manager: Andrew Davis.
City fee: 5% of gross.
Ownership: Fidelity Communications Co. (MSO).

SALISBURY—Mediacom, 1533 S Enterprise Ave, Springfield, MO 65804. Phones: 417-875-5560 (Springfield regional office); 816-637-4500. Fax: 417-883-0265. Web Site: http://www.mediacomcable.com. Also serves Brunswick. ICA: MO0155.
TV Market Ranking: Outside TV Markets (Brunswick, SALISBURY). Franchise award date: N.A. Franchise expiration date: N.A. Began: June 1, 1976.
Channel capacity: N.A. Channels available but not in use: N.A.
Basic Service
Subscribers: 935.
Programming (received off-air): KCPT (PBS) Kansas City; KCTV (CBS) Kansas City; KCWE (CW) Kansas City; KMBC-TV (ABC) Kansas City; KMCI-TV (IND) Lawrence; KMIZ (ABC) Columbia; KMOS-TV (PBS) Sedalia; KOMU-TV (CW, NBC) Columbia; KRCG (CBS) Jefferson City; KSHB-TV (NBC) Kansas City; WDAF-TV (FOX) Kansas City.
Programming (via satellite): WGN America.
Fee: $35.00 installation; $45.95 monthly; $1.70 converter.
Expanded Basic Service 1
Subscribers: N.A.
Programming (via satellite): ABC Family Channel; AMC; Animal Planet; Arts & Entertainment; Bravo; Cartoon Network; CNBC; CNN; Comedy Central; Country Music TV; C-SPAN; Discovery Channel; Disney Channel; E! Entertainment Television; ESPN; ESPN 2; Eternal Word TV Network; Food Network; Fox News Channel; Fox Sports Net Midwest; FX; Hallmark Channel; Headline News; HGTV; History Channel; Home Shopping Network; INSP; Lifetime; MSNBC; MTV; Nickelodeon; Outdoor Channel; QVC; ShopNBC; SoapNet; Speed Channel; Spike TV; Syfy; TBS Superstation; The Learning Channel; Travel Channel; Trinity Broadcasting Network; truTV; Turner Network TV; TV Guide Network; TV Land; USA Network; VH1; WE tv; Weather Channel.
Digital Basic Service
Subscribers: N.A.
Programming (via satellite): BBC America; Bio; Bloomberg Television; Discovery Digital Networks; FitTV; Fox Movie Channel; Fox Soccer; Fuse; G4; GAS; Golf Channel; GSN; History Channel International; Independent Film Channel; Lifetime Movie Network; Lime; MTV Networks Digital Suite; Music Choice; National Geographic Channel; Nick Jr.; NickToons TV; Style Network; Turner Classic Movies; Versus.
Fee: $9.95 monthly.
Digital Pay Service 1
Pay Units: N.A.
Programming (via satellite): Cinemax (multiplexed); Encore (multiplexed); Flix (multiplexed); HBO (multiplexed); Showtime (multiplexed); Starz (multiplexed); Sundance Channel (multiplexed); The Movie Channel (multiplexed).
Video-On-Demand: No
Pay-Per-View
Mediacom PPV & Evnets PPV (delivered digitally); Playboy TV (delivered digitally); TEN Clips (delivered digitally); Pleasure (delivered digitally); Hot Body (delivered digitally).
Internet Service
Operational: Yes.
Broadband Service: Mediacom High Speed Internet.
Fee: $55.95 monthly.
Telephone Service
Digital: Operational
Miles of Plant: 25.0 (coaxial); None (fiber optic). Homes passed: 1,496.
Regional Vice President: Bill Copeland. Operations Director: Bryan Gann. Regional Technical Operations Director: Alan Freedman. Technical Operations Manager: Roger Shearer. Marketing Director: Will Kuebler.
City fee: 3% of gross.
Ownership: Mediacom LLC (MSO).

SARCOXIE—Mediacom. Now served by GRANBY, MO [MO0156]. ICA: MO0179.

SCHELL CITY—N.W. Communications, PO Box 30, 616 E Park, Rich Hill, MO 64779-0030. Phone: 417-395-2121. Fax: 417-395-2120. E-mail: tburchell@klmtel.net. Web Site: http://www.klmtel.net. ICA: MO0472.
TV Market Ranking: Outside TV Markets (SCHELL CITY).
Channel capacity: N.A. Channels available but not in use: N.A.
Basic Service
Subscribers: N.A.
Programming (received off-air): KCTV (CBS) Kansas City; KCWE (CW) Kansas City; KMBC-TV (ABC) Kansas City; KOAM-TV (CBS) Pittsburg; KOLR (CBS) Springfield; KOZK (PBS) Springfield; KSFX-TV (FOX) Springfield; KSHB-TV (NBC) Kansas City; KSMO-TV (MNT) Kansas City; KSPR (ABC) Springfield; KYTV (CW, NBC) Springfield; WDAF-TV (FOX) Kansas City.
Programming (via satellite): Arts & Entertainment; CNN; Country Music TV; Discovery Channel; Disney Channel; ESPN; ESPN 2; Headline News; HGTV; History Channel; Lifetime; Nickelodeon; Outdoor Channel; Paxson Communications Corp.; QVC; Speed Channel; Spike TV; TBS Superstation; The Learning Channel; The Sportsman Channel; truTV; Turner Classic Movies; Turner Network TV; USA Network.
Pay Service 1
Pay Units: N.A.
Programming (via satellite): Flix; HBO; Showtime; Sundance Channel; The Movie Channel.
Internet Service
Operational: No.
Telephone Service
None
Manager & Chief Technician: Reese Copsey.
Ownership: KLM Telephone Co. (MSO).

SEDALIA—Charter Communications. Now served by WARRENSBURG, MO [MO0425]. ICA: MO0025.

SELIGMAN—Allegiance Communications, 707 W Saratoga St, Shawnee, OK 74804. Phones: 405-275-6923; 405-395-1131. Web Site: http://www.allegiance.tv. Also serves Washburn. ICA: MO0457.
TV Market Ranking: Below 100 (SELIGMAN, Washburn). Franchise award date: N.A. Franchise expiration date: N.A. Began: N.A.
Channel capacity: 30 (not 2-way capable). Channels available but not in use: N.A.
Basic Service
Subscribers: 188.
Programming (received off-air): KAFT (PBS) Fayetteville; KODE-TV (ABC) Joplin; KOLR (CBS) Springfield; KSFX-TV (FOX) Springfield; KSPR (ABC) Springfield; KYTV (CW, NBC) Springfield.
Programming (via satellite): ABC Family Channel; AMC; Arts & Entertainment; CNN; Discovery Channel; Disney Channel; ESPN; ESPN 2; Great American Country; Lifetime; Nickelodeon; QVC; Spike TV; TBS Superstation; The Learning Channel; Turner Network TV; TV Land; USA Network; Weather Channel; WGN America.
Fee: $25.00 installation; $21.95 monthly.
Pay Service 1
Pay Units: 44.
Programming (via satellite): Showtime.
Fee: $10.95 monthly.
Pay Service 2
Pay Units: 13.
Programming (via satellite): HBO.
Fee: $13.00 monthly.
Pay Service 3
Pay Units: 44.
Programming (via satellite): The Movie Channel.
Fee: $10.95 monthly.
Internet Service
Operational: No.
Telephone Service
None
Chief Executive Officer: Bill Haggarty. Regional Vice President: Andrew Dearth. Vice President, Marketing: Tracy Bass.
Ownership: Allegiance Communications (MSO).

SENECA—Crystal Broadband Networks, PO Box 180336, Chicago, IL 60618. Phones: 877-319-0328; 630-206-0447. E-mail: info@crystalbn.com. Web Site: http://crystalbn.com. ICA: MO0152.
TV Market Ranking: Below 100 (SENECA). Franchise award date: N.A. Franchise expiration date: N.A. Began: January 1, 1986.
Channel capacity: 36 (2-way capable). Channels available but not in use: N.A.
Basic Service
Subscribers: 186.
Programming (received off-air): KOAM-TV (CBS) Pittsburg; KODE-TV (ABC) Joplin; KOZJ (PBS) Joplin; KSNF (NBC) Joplin.
Programming (via satellite): ABC Family Channel; AMC; Animal Planet; Arts & Entertainment; Cartoon Network; CNBC; CNN; Country Music TV; C-SPAN; Discovery Channel; Disney Channel; E! Entertainment Television; ESPN; Headline News; HGTV; History Channel; Home Shopping Network; Lifetime; Nickelodeon; QVC; Spike TV; TBS Superstation; The Learning Channel; Trinity Broadcasting Network; Turner Network TV; TV Land; USA Network; Weather Channel; WGN America.
Fee: $29.95 installation; $39.95 monthly.
Pay Service 1
Pay Units: 41.
Programming (via satellite): HBO.
Fee: $10.95 monthly.
Pay Service 2
Pay Units: 12.
Programming (via satellite): The Movie Channel.
Fee: $9.95 monthly.
Pay Service 3
Pay Units: 24.
Programming (via satellite): Showtime.
Fee: $9.95 monthly.
Video-On-Demand: No
Internet Service
Operational: Yes.
Telephone Service
Digital: Operational
Miles of Plant: 18.0 (coaxial); None (fiber optic). Homes passed: 845.
Regional Manager: Paul Broseman. Plant Manager: Tony Gilbert.
Ownership: Crystal Broadband Networks (MSO).

SEYMOUR—Mediacom, 1533 S Enterprise Ave, Springfield, MO 65804. Phone: 417-875-5560. Fax: 417-883-0265. Web Site: http://www.mediacomcable.com. Also serves Ava, Billings, Cabool, Crane, Mansfield, Marshfield, Rogersville & Strafford. ICA: MO0172.
TV Market Ranking: Below 100 (Billings, Crane, Marshfield, Rogersville, SEYMOUR, Strafford); Outside TV Markets (Ava, Cabool, Mansfield). Franchise award date: July 3, 1979. Franchise expiration date: N.A. Began: N.A.
Channel capacity: N.A. Channels available but not in use: N.A.
Basic Service
Subscribers: 3,100.
Programming (received off-air): KOLR (CBS) Springfield; KOZK (PBS) Springfield; KSPR (ABC) Springfield; KYTV (CW, NBC) Springfield.
Programming (via satellite): ABC Family Channel; AMC; Animal Planet; Arts & Entertainment; Bravo; Cartoon Network; CNBC; CNN; Comedy Central; Country Music TV; C-SPAN; Discovery Channel; Disney Channel; E! Entertainment Television; ESPN; ESPN 2; Food Network; Fox Movie Channel; Fox News Channel; Fox Sports Net; FX; Hallmark Channel; Headline News; HGTV; History Channel; Home Shopping Network; INSP; KWBM (MNT) Harrison [LICENSED & SILENT]; Lifetime; MSNBC; MTV; Nickelodeon; Outdoor Channel; QVC; SoapNet; Speed Channel; Spike TV; Syfy; TBN Enlace USA; TBS Superstation; The Learning Channel; Travel Channel; truTV; Turner Network TV; TV Guide Network; TV Land; USA Network; VH1; W Network; Weather Channel; WGN America.
Fee: $35.00 installation; $45.95 monthly.
Digital Basic Service
Subscribers: N.A.
Programming (via satellite): BBC America; Bio; Bloomberg Television; Bravo; Cine Mexicano; CNN en Espanol; Discovery Digital Networks; Discovery HD Theater; ESPN; FitTV; Fox Sports en Espanol; Fox Sports World; Fuse; G4; GAS; Golf Channel; GSN; HDNet; HDNet Movies; History Channel en Espanol; History Channel International; Independent Film Channel; International Television (ITV); Lifetime Movie Network; MTV Hits; MTV Latin America; MTV2; National Geographic Channel; Nick Jr.; Showtime HD; Starz HDTV; Style Network; Toon Dis-

ney; Turner Classic Movies; TVE International; Versus; VH1 Classic; Worship Network.

Digital Pay Service 1

Pay Units: N.A.

Programming (via satellite): Cinemax (multiplexed); HBO (multiplexed); Showtime (multiplexed); Starz (multiplexed).

Video-On-Demand: Yes

Internet Service

Operational: Yes.

Broadband Service: Mediacom High Speed Internet.

Fee: $55.95 monthly.

Telephone Service

Analog: Not Operational

Digital: Operational

Miles of Plant: 110.0 (coaxial); None (fiber optic). Homes passed: 6,912.

Regional Vice President: Bill Copeland. Technical Operations Director: Alan Freedman. Marketing Director: Will Kuebler. Customer Service Manager: Cindy Reese.

City fee: 3% of basic & premium.

Ownership: Mediacom LLC (MSO).

SHELBINA—US Cable. Now served by HANNIBAL, MO [MO0021]. ICA: MO0098.

SHELDON—Formerly served by Cebridge Connections. No longer in operation. ICA: MO0297.

SHERIDAN—B & L Technologies LLC, 3329 270th St, Lenox, IA 50851. Phones: 800-798-5488; 641-348-2240. Fax: 641-348-2240. ICA: MO0354.

TV Market Ranking: Outside TV Markets (SHERIDAN). Franchise award date: May 2, 1989. Franchise expiration date: N.A. Began: December 1, 1989.

Channel capacity: 36 (not 2-way capable). Channels available but not in use: 7.

Basic Service

Subscribers: 37.

Programming (received off-air): KCCI (CBS) Des Moines; KHIN (PBS) Red Oak; KPTM (FOX, MNT) Omaha; KQTV (ABC) St. Joseph; KTAJ-TV (TBN) St. Joseph; KXVO (CW) Omaha; WHO-DT (NBC) Des Moines.

Programming (via satellite): ABC Family Channel; AMC; Arts & Entertainment; CNN; Country Music TV; Discovery Channel; ESPN; History Channel; KARE (NBC) Minneapolis; Nickelodeon; Spike TV; TBS Superstation; Turner Network TV; USA Network; VH1; WCCO-TV (CBS) Minneapolis; WGN America.

Fee: $25.00 installation; $30.50 monthly.

Pay Service 1

Pay Units: 7.

Programming (via satellite): HBO.

Fee: $12.00 monthly.

Video-On-Demand: No

Internet Service

Operational: No.

Telephone Service

None

Miles of Plant: 2.0 (coaxial); None (fiber optic). Homes passed: 120.

Manager & Chief Technician: Robert Hintz. Office Manager: Linda Hintz.

Ownership: B & L Technologies LLC (MSO).

SILEX—Formerly served by First Cable of Missouri Inc. No longer in operation. ICA: MO0373.

SKIDMORE—Holway Telephone Co. Now served by MAITLAND, MO [MO0336]. ICA: MO0350.

SMITHTON—Longview Communications, 12007 Sunrise Valley Dr, Ste 375, Reston, VA 20191. Phones: 703-476-9101; 866-611-6565. Fax: 703-476-9107. Web Site: http://www.longviewcomm.com. Also serves Brooking Park. ICA: MO0298.

TV Market Ranking: Below 100 (Brooking Park, SMITHTON). Franchise award date: N.A. Franchise expiration date: N.A. Began: June 1, 1985.

Channel capacity: 41 (not 2-way capable). Channels available but not in use: 2.

Basic Service

Subscribers: 182.

Programming (received off-air): KMIZ (ABC) Columbia; KMOS-TV (PBS) Sedalia; KOMU-TV (CW, NBC) Columbia; KRCG (CBS) Jefferson City.

Programming (via satellite): ABC Family Channel; AMC; Animal Planet; Arts & Entertainment; Cartoon Network; CNN; C-SPAN; Discovery Channel; Disney Channel; E! Entertainment Television; ESPN; ESPN 2; Fox News Channel; Fuse; FX; Great American Country; Headline News; HGTV; History Channel; Lifetime; Outdoor Channel; TBS Superstation; The Learning Channel; Turner Classic Movies; Turner Network TV; USA Network; Weather Channel; WGN America.

Fee: $40.95 monthly.

Pay Service 1

Pay Units: 34.

Programming (via satellite): Cinemax; Encore; HBO; Showtime; Starz; The Movie Channel.

Fee: $9.95 monthly (Showtime, TMC or Starz/Encore), $10.95 monthly (Cinemax), $14.95 monthly (HBO).

Video-On-Demand: No

Internet Service

Operational: No.

Telephone Service

None

Miles of Plant: 18.0 (coaxial); None (fiber optic). Homes passed: 889.

President: John Long. Senior Vice President: Marc W. Cohen. General Manager: Brandon Dickey. Operations Manager: Perry Scarborough.

Ownership: Longview Communications (MSO).

SPARTA—Formerly served by Almega Cable. No longer in operation. ICA: MO0257.

SPRING CITY—Formerly served by Almega Cable. No longer in operation. ICA: MO0134.

SPRINGFIELD—Mediacom, 1533 S Enterprise Ave, Springfield, MO 65804. Phone: 417-875-5560. Fax: 417-883-0265. Web Site: http://www.mediacomcable.com. Also serves Battlefield, Brookline (portions) & Greene County (portions). ICA: MO0006.

TV Market Ranking: Below 100 (Battlefield, Brookline (portions), Greene County (portions), SPRINGFIELD). Franchise award date: N.A. Franchise expiration date: N.A. Began: December 1, 1979.

Channel capacity: 141 (operating 2-way). Channels available but not in use: N.A.

Basic Service

Subscribers: 48,000.

Programming (received off-air): KOLR (CBS) Springfield; KOZK (PBS) Springfield; KSFX-TV (FOX) Springfield; KSPR (ABC) Springfield; KYTV (CW, NBC) Springfield; allband FM.

Programming (via satellite): C-SPAN; C-SPAN 2; Discovery Channel; TBS Superstation; Weather Channel; WGN America.

Current originations: Government Access; Educational Access; Public Access.

Fee: $39.95 installation; $8.64 monthly; $18.95 additional installation.

Expanded Basic Service 1

Subscribers: 45,000.

Programming (via satellite): ABC Family Channel; AMC; Animal Planet; Arts & Entertainment; BET Networks; Bravo; Cartoon Network; CNBC; CNN; Comedy Central; Country Music TV; Disney Channel; E! Entertainment Television; ESPN; ESPN 2; Eternal Word TV Network; Fox News Channel; Fox Sports Net Midwest; FX; Hallmark Channel; Headline News; ION Television; Lifetime; MSNBC; MTV; Nickelodeon; QVC; Spike TV; Syfy; The Learning Channel; Travel Channel; Trinity Broadcasting Network; truTV; Turner Network TV; TV Guide Network; USA Network; VH1.

Fee: $12.95 installation; $21.84 monthly.

Expanded Basic Service 2

Subscribers: N.A.

Programming (via satellite): Canales N; DMX Music; Fox Sports en Espanol; Toon Disney.

Fee: $6.99 monthly.

Digital Basic Service

Subscribers: 23,000.

Programming (via satellite): AmericanLife TV Network; BBC America; Discovery Digital Networks; ESPN Classic Sports; Fox Sports World; G4; Golf Channel; GSN; Halogen Network; HGTV; History Channel; Independent Film Channel; Nick Jr.; Outdoor Channel; Speed Channel; Turner Classic Movies; TV Land; Versus; VH1 Country; WE tv.

Fee: $10.00 monthly; $3.50 converter.

Pay Service 1

Pay Units: N.A.

Programming (via satellite): Cinemax (multiplexed); Encore; HBO (multiplexed); Showtime (multiplexed); Starz; The Movie Channel.

Fee: $12.95 installation; $1.75 monthly (Encore), $6.75 monthly (Starz), $12.40 monthly (Cinemax, HBO, Showtime or TMC).

Digital Pay Service 1

Pay Units: N.A.

Programming (via satellite): Cinemax (multiplexed); DMX Music; HBO (multiplexed); Showtime (multiplexed); Starz (multiplexed); The Movie Channel (multiplexed).

Fee: $7.95 monthly (DMX).

Video-On-Demand: Yes

Pay-Per-View

ESPN Extra (delivered digitally), Addressable: Yes; Hot Choice (delivered digitally); iN DEMAND; Playboy TV (delivered digitally); Fresh (delivered digitally); Movies (delivered digitally); special events (delivered digitally).

Internet Service

Operational: Yes.

Subscribers: 21,000.

Broadband Service: Mediacom High Speed Internet.

Fee: $99.95 installation; $45.95 monthly.

Telephone Service

Digital: Operational

Miles of Plant: 802.0 (coaxial); None (fiber optic). Homes passed: 100,000.

Regional Vice President: Bill Copeland. Technical Operations Director: Alan Freedman. Senior Government & Community Relations Manager: Randy Hollis. Marketing Director: Will Kuebler. Marketing Coordinator: Brad Koetters. Customer Service Manager: Cindy Reese.

City fee: 3% of gross.

Ownership: Mediacom LLC (MSO).

ST. CHARLES—Charter Communications, 941 Charter Commons Dr, Saint Louis, MO 63017. Phone: 636-207-7044. Fax: 636-230-7034. Web Site: http://www.charter.com. Also serves Cottleville, Dardenne Prairie, Harvester, O'Fallon, St. Charles County, St. Peters & Weldon Spring. ICA: MO0007.

TV Market Ranking: 11 (Cottleville, Dardenne Prairie, Harvester, O'Fallon, ST. CHARLES, St. Charles County (portions), St. Peters, Weldon Spring); Outside TV Markets (St. Charles County (portions)). Franchise award date: January 1, 1979. Franchise expiration date: N.A. Began: February 4, 1980.

Channel capacity: N.A. Channels available but not in use: N.A.

Basic Service

Subscribers: 46,400.

Programming (received off-air): KDNL-TV (ABC) St. Louis; KETC (PBS) St. Louis; KMOV (CBS) St. Louis; KNLC (IND) St. Louis; KPLR-TV (CW) St. Louis; KSDK (NBC) St. Louis; KTVI (FOX) St. Louis; WPXS (IND) Mount Vernon; WRBU (MNT) East St. Louis.

Programming (via satellite): C-SPAN; C-SPAN 2; Eternal Word TV Network; Home Shopping Network; INSP; QVC; ShopNBC; TBS Superstation; Trinity Broadcasting Network; TV Guide Network; Univision; Weatherscan; WGN America.

Current originations: Educational Access; Public Access; Government Access.

Fee: $29.99 installation.

Expanded Basic Service 1

Subscribers: 45,100.

Programming (via satellite): ABC Family Channel; AMC; Animal Planet; Arts & Entertainment; BET Networks; Bravo; Cartoon Network; CNBC; CNN; Comedy Central; Country Music TV; Discovery Channel; Disney Channel; E! Entertainment Television; ESPN; ESPN 2; Food Network; Fox Movie Channel; Fox News Channel; Fox Sports Net Midwest; FX; G4; Golf Channel; GSN; Hallmark Channel; Headline News; History Channel; Lifetime; MSNBC; MTV; National Geographic Channel; Nickelodeon; Oxygen; SoapNet; Speed Channel; Spike TV; Style Network; Syfy; The Learning Channel; Toon Disney; Travel Channel; truTV; Turner Classic Movies; Turner Network TV; TV Land; USA Network; Versus; VH1; WE tv; Weather Channel.

Fee: $49.99 monthly.

Digital Basic Service

Subscribers: N.A.

Programming (via satellite): BBC America; Bio; Bloomberg Television; Discovery Digital Networks; Do-It-Yourself; Encore Action; ESPN Classic Sports; FitTV; Fox Sports World; FSN Digital Atlantic; FSN Digital Central; FSN Digital Pacific; Fuel TV; Fuse; GAS; Great American Country; History Channel International; Independent Film Channel; International Television (ITV); Lifetime Movie Network; MTV Networks Digital Suite; Music Choice; NFL Network; Nick Jr.; Nick Too; NickToons TV; Sundance Channel.

Fee: $9.95 monthly.

Digital Pay Service 1

Pay Units: 3,945.

Programming (via satellite): Cinemax (multiplexed); HBO (multiplexed); Showtime (multiplexed); Starz (multiplexed); The Movie Channel (multiplexed).

Fee: $10.00 installation; $12.60 monthly (each).

Video-On-Demand: Yes

Pay-Per-View
iN DEMAND (delivered digitally), Addressable: Yes; Sports PPV (delivered digitally); ESPN Now (delivered digitally); Playboy TV (delivered digitally); Fresh (delivered digitally); Shorteez (delivered digitally).
Internet Service
Operational: Yes.
Broadband Service: Charter Pipeline.
Fee: $29.99 monthly.
Telephone Service
Digital: Operational
Fee: $29.99 monthly
Miles of Plant: 993.0 (coaxial); 10.0 (fiber optic). Additional miles planned: 65.0 (coaxial). Homes passed: 71,071. Total homes in franchised area: 78,400.
Vice President & General Manager: Steve Trippe. Operations Director: Tom Williams. Marketing Director: Beverly Wall.
City fee: 3% of gross.
Ownership: Charter Communications Inc. (MSO).

ST. CLAIR—Charter Communications. Now served by SULLIVAN (formerly WASHINGTON), MO [MO0030]. ICA: MO0140.

ST. JAMES—Charter Communications. Now served by SULLIVAN (formerly WASHINGTON), MO [MO0030]. ICA: MO0113.

ST. JOSEPH—St. Joseph Cablevision, PO Box 8069, 102 N Woodbine Rd, Saint Joseph, MO 64506. Phone: 816-279-1234 (Customer service). Fax: 816-279-8773. E-mail: bsevern@npgco.com. Web Site: http://www.npgcable.net. Also serves Agency, Country Club Village, Savannah & Union Star. ICA: MO0011.
TV Market Ranking: Below 100 (Agency, Country Club Village, Savannah, ST. JOSEPH, Union Star). Franchise award date: April 1, 1965. Franchise expiration date: N.A. Began: December 21, 1965.
Channel capacity: 85 (operating 2-way). Channels available but not in use: None.
Basic Service
Subscribers: 24,564.
Programming (received off-air): KCPT (PBS) Kansas City; KCTV (CBS) Kansas City; KMBC-TV (ABC) Kansas City; KQTV (ABC) St. Joseph; KSHB-TV (NBC) Kansas City; KTAJ-TV (TBN) St. Joseph; KTWU (PBS) Topeka; WDAF-TV (FOX) Kansas City; 13 FMs.
Programming (via satellite): ABC Family Channel; Animal Planet; BET Networks; CNBC; CNN; Country Music TV; C-SPAN; C-SPAN 2; Discovery Channel; Discovery Health Channel; Disney Channel; E! Entertainment Television; ESPN; ESPN 2; Eternal Word TV Network; Fox News Channel; Fox Sports Net Midwest; Great American Country; Headline News; HGTV; Home Shopping Network; Lifetime; MoviePlex; MTV; National Geographic Channel; Nickelodeon; Paxson Communications Corp.; Product Information Network; QVC; Spike TV; Syfy; TBS Superstation; The Learning Channel; truTV; Turner Network TV; TV Guide Network; TV Land; USA Network; VH1; Weather Channel; WGN America.
Current originations: Government Access; Educational Access.
Fee: $35.00 installation; $39.95 monthly; $3.75 converter; $18.40 additional installation.
Expanded Basic Service 1
Subscribers: 20,405.
Programming (received off-air): KCWE (CW) Kansas City.
Programming (via satellite): Arts & Entertainment; Cartoon Network; Comedy Central; Food Network; Golf Channel; GSN; Hallmark Channel; History Channel; Lifetime Movie Network; MSNBC; Speed Channel; Travel Channel; Turner Classic Movies; Versus.
Fee: $10.00 installation; $4.70 monthly.
Digital Basic Service
Subscribers: 5,714.
Programming (received off-air): KCPT (PBS) Kansas City; KCTV (CBS) Kansas City; KCWE (CW) Kansas City; KMBC-TV (ABC) Kansas City; KSHB-TV (NBC) Kansas City; WDAF-TV (FOX) Kansas City.
Programming (via satellite): AmericanLife TV Network; BBC America; Bio; Bloomberg Television; Boomerang; Discovery Digital Networks; Discovery HD Theater; Do-It-Yourself; ESPN; ESPN Classic Sports; ESPNews; Fuse; G4; GAS; Halogen Network; HDNet; HDNet Movies; History Channel International; Lime; LOGO; MTV Networks Digital Suite; Music Choice; Nick Jr.; Nick Too; NickToons TV; Outdoor Channel; ShopNBC; SoapNet; Style Network; The Sportsman Channel; Trinity Broadcasting Network; Trio; WE tv.
Digital Pay Service 1
Pay Units: 2,663.
Programming (via satellite): HBO (multiplexed).
Fee: $9.00 monthly.
Digital Pay Service 2
Pay Units: 892.
Programming (via satellite): Cinemax.
Fee: $10.20 monthly.
Digital Pay Service 3
Pay Units: 1,976.
Programming (via satellite): Showtime (multiplexed); The Movie Channel (multiplexed).
Fee: $10.20 monthly.
Digital Pay Service 4
Pay Units: 1,977.
Programming (via satellite): Encore (multiplexed); Starz (multiplexed).
Fee: $10.20 monthly.
Digital Pay Service 5
Pay Units: 160.
Programming (via satellite): Playboy TV.
Fee: $8.00 monthly.
Video-On-Demand: No
Pay-Per-View
Hot Choice (delivered digitally); Fresh (delivered digitally).
Internet Service
Operational: Yes.
Broadband Service: In-house.
Fee: $99.00 installation; $39.95 monthly; $5.00 modem lease; $60.00 modem purchase.
Telephone Service
Digital: Operational
Fee: $44.95 monthly
Miles of Plant: 554.0 (coaxial); 139.0 (fiber optic). Additional miles planned: 15.0 (coaxial); 30.0 (fiber optic). Homes passed: 36,000. Total homes in franchised area: 37,000.
General Manager: Bill Severn. Plant Manager: Steve Ward. Marketing Director: Denise Lewis. Program Director: Michelle Fitzpatrick. Customer Service Manager: LeeAnn Smiley. Administrative Assistant: Lori McCrary.
City fee: 5% of gross.
Ownership: News Press & Gazette Co. (MSO).

ST. LOUIS—Charter Communications, 941 Charter Commons Dr, Saint Louis, MO 63017. Phone: 636-207-7044. Fax: 636-230-7034. Web Site: http://www.charter.com. ICA: MO0002.
TV Market Ranking: 11 (ST. LOUIS). Franchise award date: April 1, 1984. Franchise expiration date: N.A. Began: May 15, 1985.
Channel capacity: N.A. Channels available but not in use: N.A.
Basic Service
Subscribers: 56,252.
Programming (received off-air): KDNL-TV (ABC) St. Louis; KETC (PBS) St. Louis; KMOV (CBS) St. Louis; KNLC (IND) St. Louis; KPLR-TV (CW) St. Louis; KSDK (NBC) St. Louis; KTVI (FOX) St. Louis; WPXS (IND) Mount Vernon; WRBU (MNT) East St. Louis.
Programming (via satellite): C-SPAN; C-SPAN 2; Eternal Word TV Network; Home Shopping Network; INSP; QVC; ShopNBC; TBS Superstation; TV Guide Network; Univision; Weatherscan; WGN America.
Current originations: Leased Access; Government Access; Educational Access; Public Access.
Fee: $29.99 installation.
Expanded Basic Service 1
Subscribers: 55,538.
Programming (via satellite): ABC Family Channel; AMC; Animal Planet; Arts & Entertainment; BET Networks; Bravo; Cartoon Network; CNBC; CNN; Comedy Central; Country Music TV; Discovery Channel; Disney Channel; E! Entertainment Television; ESPN; ESPN 2; Food Network; Fox Movie Channel; Fox News Channel; Fox Sports Net Midwest; FX; Golf Channel; GSN; Hallmark Channel; Headline News; HGTV; History Channel; Lifetime; MSNBC; MTV; National Geographic Channel; Nickelodeon; Oxygen; SoapNet; Speed Channel; Spike TV; Style Network; Syfy; The Learning Channel; Toon Disney; Travel Channel; truTV; Turner Classic Movies; Turner Network TV; TV Land; USA Network; Versus; VH1; WE tv; Weather Channel.
Fee: $49.99 monthly.
Digital Basic Service
Subscribers: 38,400.
Programming (via satellite): BBC America; Bio; Bloomberg Television; Discovery Digital Networks; Do-It-Yourself; Encore Action; ESPN Classic Sports; FitTV; Fox Sports World; FSN Digital Atlantic; FSN Digital Central; FSN Digital Pacific; Fuel TV; Fuse; GAS; Great American Country; History Channel International; Independent Film Channel; International Television (ITV); Lifetime Movie Network; MTV Networks Digital Suite; Music Choice; NFL Network; Nick Jr.; Nick Too; NickToons TV; Sundance Channel; The Word Network.
Fee: $12.60 monthly.
Digital Pay Service 1
Pay Units: 37,000.
Programming (via satellite): Cinemax (multiplexed); HBO (multiplexed); Showtime (multiplexed); Starz (multiplexed); The Movie Channel (multiplexed).
Fee: $10.50 monthly (each).
Video-On-Demand: Yes
Pay-Per-View
Addressable homes: 38,400.
iN DEMAND (delivered digitally), Addressable: Yes; Sports PPV (delivered digitally); ESPN Now (delivered digitally); Playboy TV (delivered digitally); Fresh (delivered digitally); Shorteez (delivered digitally).
Internet Service
Operational: Yes.
Subscribers: 36,000.
Broadband Service: Charter Pipeline.
Fee: $29.99 monthly.
Telephone Service
Digital: Operational
Fee: $29.99 monthly
Miles of Plant: 615.0 (coaxial); 46.0 (fiber optic). Homes passed: 158,814. Total homes in franchised area: 158,814.
Vice President & General Manager: Steve Trippe. Operations Director: Tom Williams. Chief Technologist: Gary Lasser. Marketing Director: Beverly Wall. Marketing Manager: Keisha Irving.
City fee: 5% of gross.
Ownership: Charter Communications Inc. (MSO).

ST. LOUIS—Formerly served by Sprint Corp. No longer in operation. ICA: MO0454.

ST. THOMAS—Formerly served by First Cable of Missouri Inc. No longer in operation. ICA: MO0365.

STANBERRY—Longview Communications, 1923 N Main, Higginsville, MO 64037. Phone: 866-611-6565. Fax: 866-329-4790. Web Site: http://www.longviewcomm.com. ICA: MO0173.
TV Market Ranking: Outside TV Markets (STANBERRY). Franchise award date: N.A. Franchise expiration date: N.A. Began: January 1, 1975.
Channel capacity: N.A. Channels available but not in use: N.A.
Basic Service
Subscribers: 215.
Programming (received off-air): KCPT (PBS) Kansas City; KCTV (CBS) Kansas City; KCWE (CW) Kansas City; KMBC-TV (ABC) Kansas City; KQTV (ABC) St. Joseph; KSHB-TV (NBC) Kansas City; KSMO-TV (MNT) Kansas City; KTAJ-TV (TBN) St. Joseph; WDAF-TV (FOX) Kansas City.
Programming (via satellite): ABC Family Channel; AMC; Animal Planet; Arts & Entertainment; Cartoon Network; CNN; Comedy Central; Country Music TV; C-SPAN; Discovery Channel; Disney Channel; E! Entertainment Television; ESPN; ESPN 2; FamilyNet; Food Network; Fox News Channel; Fox Sports Net Midwest; FX; Great American Country; Headline News; HGTV; History Channel; Home Shopping Network; INSP; Lifetime; Nickelodeon; Outdoor Channel; QVC; Spike TV; Syfy; TBS Superstation; The Learning Channel; Travel Channel; Trinity Broadcasting Network; Turner Classic Movies; Turner Network TV; USA Network; Weather Channel; WGN America.
Fee: $35.95 installation; $41.95 monthly.
Digital Basic Service
Subscribers: 13.
Programming (via satellite): AmericanLife TV Network; BBC America; Bio; Bloomberg Television; Discovery Digital Networks; DMX Music; Encore (multiplexed); ESPN Classic Sports; ESPNews; Fox Movie Channel; Fox Soccer; G4; Golf Channel; GSN; Halogen Network; History Channel International; Lifetime Movie Network; Speed Channel; Style Network; Toon Disney; Turner Classic Movies.
Fee: $18.00 monthly.
Pay Service 1
Pay Units: 76.
Programming (via satellite): Cinemax.
Fee: $10.95 monthly.
Pay Service 2
Pay Units: 80.
Programming (via satellite): HBO.
Fee: $12.95 monthly.

Pay Service 3
Pay Units: N.A.
Programming (via satellite): Showtime; The Movie Channel.
Fee: $8.95 monthly (TMC), $10.95 monthly (Showtime).
Digital Pay Service 1
Pay Units: N.A.
Programming (via satellite): Cinemax (multiplexed); Flix; HBO (multiplexed); Showtime (multiplexed); Starz (multiplexed); The Movie Channel (multiplexed).
Fee: $8.95 monthly (TMC), $10.95 monthly (Showtime or Cinemax), $12.95 monthly (HBO).
Video-On-Demand: No
Pay-Per-View
iN DEMAND (delivered digitally); Hot Choice (delivered digitally); Playboy TV (delivered digitally); Fresh (delivered digitally); Shorteez (delivered digitally).
Internet Service
Operational: Yes.
Subscribers: 29.
Broadband Service: IBBS.
Fee: $29.95 monthly.
Telephone Service
None
Miles of Plant: 13.0 (coaxial); None (fiber optic). Homes passed: 1,200.
President: John Long. Senior Vice President: Marc W. Cohen. General Manager: Brandon Dickey. Operations Manager: Perry Scarborough.
City fee: 3% of gross.
Ownership: Longview Communications (MSO).

STE. GENEVIEVE—Charter Communications, 3140 W Nash Rd, Scott City, MO 63780. Phones: 636-207-7044 (St Louis office); 573-335-4424. Fax: 573-334-9265. Web Site: http://www.charter.com. ICA: MO0091.
TV Market Ranking: Outside TV Markets (STE. GENEVIEVE). Franchise award date: N.A. Franchise expiration date: N.A. Began: March 1, 1977.
Channel capacity: N.A. Channels available but not in use: N.A.
Basic Service
Subscribers: 1,364.
Programming (received off-air): KBSI (FOX) Cape Girardeau; KDNL-TV (ABC) St. Louis; KETC (PBS) St. Louis; KFVS-TV (CBS, CW) Cape Girardeau; KMOV (CBS) St. Louis; KPLR-TV (CW) St. Louis; KSDK (NBC) St. Louis; KTVI (FOX) St. Louis; WPSD-TV (NBC) Paducah; WRBU (MNT) East St. Louis; WSIL-TV (ABC) Harrisburg; WSIU-TV (PBS) Carbondale; 14 FMs.
Programming (via satellite): Arts & Entertainment; C-SPAN; Disney Channel; Eternal Word TV Network; Home Shopping Network; INSP; MTV; Nickelodeon; QVC; TBS Superstation; Trinity Broadcasting Network; Turner Network TV; Weather Channel; WGN America.
Current originations: Government Access; Educational Access; Public Access.
Fee: $29.99 installation.
Expanded Basic Service 1
Subscribers: 1,274.
Programming (via satellite): ABC Family Channel; AMC; Animal Planet; Bravo; Cartoon Network; CNBC; CNN; Comedy Central; Country Music TV; Discovery Channel; E! Entertainment Television; ESPN; ESPN 2; Food Network; Fox Movie Channel; Fox News Channel; Fox Sports Net Midwest; FX; G4; Golf Channel; Great American Country; GSN; Hallmark Channel; Headline News; HGTV; History Channel; Lifetime; MSNBC; National Geographic Channel; Oxygen; SoapNet; Spike TV; Style Network; Syfy; The Learning Channel; Travel Channel; truTV; Turner Classic Movies; TV Land; USA Network; VH1.
Fee: $49.99 monthly.
Digital Basic Service
Subscribers: N.A.
Programming (via satellite): BBC America; Bio; Discovery Digital Networks; Do-It-Yourself; Fox Sports World; GAS; History Channel International; Independent Film Channel; Lifetime Movie Network; MTV Networks Digital Suite; Music Choice; Nick Jr.; Nick Too; NickToons TV; Sundance Channel.
Digital Pay Service 1
Pay Units: 297.
Programming (via satellite): Cinemax (multiplexed); Encore (multiplexed); Flix; HBO (multiplexed); Showtime (multiplexed); Starz (multiplexed); The Movie Channel (multiplexed).
Fee: $35.00 installation; $11.45 monthly (each).
Video-On-Demand: Yes
Pay-Per-View
Hot Choice (delivered digitally); ETC; Pleasure (delivered digitally); iN DEMAND (delivered digitally).
Internet Service
Operational: Yes.
Broadband Service: Charter Pipeline.
Fee: $29.99 monthly.
Telephone Service
Digital: Operational
Miles of Plant: 60.0 (coaxial); None (fiber optic). Homes passed: 2,064.
Vice President & General Manager: Steve Trippe. Operations Director: Dave Miller. Operations Manager: Dave Huntsman. Technical Operations Manager: Barry Moore. Plant Manager: Kevin Goetz. Marketing Director: Beverly Wall. Office Manager: Sheila Tuschoff.
Ownership: Charter Communications Inc. (MSO).

STE. GENEVIEVE—Formerly served by Charter Communications. No longer in operation. ICA: MO0422.

STEELE—NewWave Communications, 1311 Business Hwy 60 W, Dexter, MO 63841. Phones: 573-614-4573; 888-863-9928. Fax: 573-614-4802. Web Site: http://www.newwavecom.com. Also serves Pemiscot County. ICA: MO0135.
TV Market Ranking: Below 100 (Pemiscot County (portions)); Outside TV Markets (Pemiscot County (portions), STEELE). Franchise award date: September 6, 1968. Franchise expiration date: N.A. Began: January 1, 1969.
Channel capacity: N.A. Channels available but not in use: N.A.
Basic Service
Subscribers: 509.
Programming (received off-air): KAIT (ABC) Jonesboro; KFVS-TV (CBS, CW) Cape Girardeau; WHBQ-TV (FOX) Memphis; WKNO (PBS) Memphis; WLMT (CW) Memphis; WMC-TV (NBC) Memphis; WPTY-TV (ABC) Memphis; WREG-TV (CBS) Memphis; allband FM.
Programming (via satellite): ABC Family Channel; AMC; Animal Planet; Arts & Entertainment; BET Networks; CNN; Comedy Central; Discovery Channel; Disney Channel; ESPN; ESPN 2; Fox Sports Net Midwest; GSN; Headline News; History Channel; Home Shopping Network; Lifetime; MSNBC; MTV; National Geographic Channel; Nickelodeon; Speed Channel; Spike TV; TBS Superstation; Toon Disney; Trinity Broadcasting Network; Turner Network TV; TV Land; USA Network; Versus; VH1; Weather Channel; WGN America.
Fee: $61.50 installation; $35.95 monthly.
Digital Basic Service
Subscribers: N.A.
Programming (via satellite): BBC America; Bio; Black Family Channel; Bloomberg Television; Discovery Digital Networks; Discovery Kids Channel; DMX Music; ESPN Classic Sports; ESPNews; FitTV; Fox Movie Channel; Fox Sports World; Golf Channel; Great American Country; Halogen Network; HGTV; History Channel International; Independent Film Channel; Lifetime Movie Network; Lime; Outdoor Channel; ShopNBC; Style Network; Turner Classic Movies; WE tv.
Fee: $3.95 monthly.
Pay Service 1
Pay Units: 346.
Programming (via satellite): Cinemax; HBO; Showtime; The Movie Channel.
Fee: $8.99 monthly (Cinemax), $12.99 monthly (HBO), $13.99 monthly (Showtime & TMC).
Digital Pay Service 1
Pay Units: N.A.
Programming (via satellite): Cinemax (multiplexed); Encore (multiplexed); HBO (multiplexed); Showtime (multiplexed); Starz (multiplexed); The Movie Channel (multiplexed).
Video-On-Demand: No
Pay-Per-View
Fresh; Playboy TV; iN DEMAND.
Internet Service
Operational: Yes.
Fee: $40.00 installation; $31.99 monthly.
Telephone Service
Digital: Planned
Miles of Plant: 28.0 (coaxial); None (fiber optic). Homes passed: 1,099.
General Manager: Ed Gargas. Technical Operations Manager: Jerry Townsend.
City fee: 5% of gross.
Ownership: NewWave Communications (MSO).

STEELVILLE—Charter Communications. Now served by SULLIVAN (formerly WASHINGTON), MO [MO0030]. ICA: MO0151.

STOCKTON—Windstream, PO Box 180, 1705 S Lillian Ave, Bolivar, MO 65613. Phones: 877-807-9463; 800-345-3874; 417-326-1013 (Local office). Fax: 417-326-8439. Web Site: http://www.windstream.com. ICA: MO0166.
TV Market Ranking: Outside TV Markets (STOCKTON). Franchise award date: November 9, 1981. Franchise expiration date: N.A. Began: September 1, 1982.
Channel capacity: 62 (not 2-way capable). Channels available but not in use: 6.
Basic Service
Subscribers: 538.
Programming (received off-air): KOLR (CBS) Springfield; KOZK (PBS) Springfield; KSPR (ABC) Springfield; KWBM (MNT) Harrison [LICENSED & SILENT]; KYTV (CW, NBC) Springfield.
Programming (via satellite): ABC Family Channel; Animal Planet; Arts & Entertainment; CNN; Country Music TV; Discovery Channel; Disney Channel; ESPN; ESPN 2; Fox Movie Channel; Fox News Channel; Fox Sports Net Midwest; FX; Headline News; HGTV; History Channel; Lifetime; National Geographic Channel; Nickelodeon; Odyssey Television Network; QVC; Speed Channel; Spike TV; TBS Superstation; The Learning Channel; Trinity Broadcasting Network; Turner Classic Movies; Turner Network TV; USA Network; Weather Channel; WGN America.
Fee: $27.55 monthly.
Pay Service 1
Pay Units: 62.
Programming (via satellite): HBO.
Fee: $12.95 monthly.
Video-On-Demand: No
Internet Service
Operational: No, DSL & dialup.
Telephone Service
None
Miles of Plant: 25.0 (coaxial); None (fiber optic). Homes passed: 1,000.
Area Manager: Terry Lockhart.
City fee: 3% of gross.
Ownership: Windstream Communications Inc. (MSO).

STOTTS CITY—Formerly served by Cebridge Connections. No longer in operation. ICA: MO0367.

STOVER—Longview Communications, 12007 Sunrise Valley Dr, Ste 375, Reston, VA 20191. Phones: 866-611-6565 (Customer service); 703-476-9101. Fax: 703-476-9107. Web Site: http://www.longviewcomm.com. ICA: MO0226.
TV Market Ranking: Below 100 (STOVER). Franchise award date: N.A. Franchise expiration date: N.A. Began: January 1, 1983.
Channel capacity: 36 (not 2-way capable). Channels available but not in use: None.
Basic Service
Subscribers: 116.
Programming (received off-air): KMIZ (ABC) Columbia; KMOS-TV (PBS) Sedalia; KNLJ (IND) Jefferson City; KOMU-TV (CW, NBC) Columbia; KRCG (CBS) Jefferson City.
Programming (via satellite): Classic Arts Showcase; C-SPAN; C-SPAN 2; Home Shopping Network; INSP.
Fee: $17.98 monthly.
Expanded Basic Service 1
Subscribers: N.A.
Programming (via satellite): ABC Family Channel; AMC; Animal Planet; Arts & Entertainment; Cartoon Network; CNN; Comedy Central; Discovery Channel; Disney Channel; ESPN; ESPN 2; Headline News; HGTV; Lifetime; TBS Superstation; The Learning Channel; Travel Channel; Turner Network TV; USA Network; Weather Channel; WGN America.
Fee: $17.97 monthly.
Pay Service 1
Pay Units: 54.
Programming (via satellite): Showtime; The Movie Channel.
Fee: $8.95 monthly (TMC), $10.95 monthly (Showtime).
Video-On-Demand: No
Internet Service
Operational: No.
Telephone Service
None
Miles of Plant: 6.0 (coaxial); None (fiber optic). Homes passed: 529.
President: John Long. Senior Vice President: Marc W. Cohen. General Manager: Brandon Dickey. Operations Manager: Perry Scarborough.
Ownership: Longview Communications (MSO).

STRAFFORD—Mediacom. Now served by SEYMOUR, MO [MO0172]. ICA: MO0222.

STURGEON—Longview Communications, 12007 Sunrise Valley Dr, Ste 375, Reston, VA 20191. Phones: 866-611-6565 (Customer service); 703-476-9101. Fax: 703-476-9107. Web Site: http://www.longviewcomm.com. Also serves Clark. ICA: MO0395.

TV Market Ranking: Below 100 (Clark, STURGEON). Franchise award date: N.A. Franchise expiration date: N.A. Began: September 1, 1984.

Channel capacity: 41 (not 2-way capable). Channels available but not in use: 5.

Basic Service

Subscribers: 78.

Programming (received off-air): KMIZ (ABC) Columbia; KMOS-TV (PBS) Sedalia; KNLJ (IND) Jefferson City; KOMU-TV (CW, NBC) Columbia; KRCG (CBS) Jefferson City.

Programming (via satellite): ABC Family Channel; AMC; Animal Planet; Arts & Entertainment; Cartoon Network; CNN; C-SPAN; Discovery Channel; Disney Channel; ESPN; ESPN 2; Fox News Channel; Fuse; FX; Headline News; Lifetime; MSNBC; Outdoor Channel; QVC; TBS Superstation; The Learning Channel; Toon Disney; Turner Network TV; USA Network; Weather Channel; WGN America.

Fee: $37.45 monthly.

Pay Service 1

Pay Units: 23.

Programming (via satellite): Cinemax; HBO; Showtime; The Movie Channel.

Fee: $9.95 monthly (Showtime or TMC), $10.95 monthly (Cinemax), $14.95 monthly (HBO).

Video-On-Demand: No

Internet Service

Operational: No.

Telephone Service

None

Miles of Plant: 12.0 (coaxial); None (fiber optic). Homes passed: 428.

President: John Long. Senior Vice President: Marc W. Cohen. General Manager: Brandon Dickey. Operations Manager: Perry Scarborough.

Ownership: Longview Communications (MSO).

SULLIVAN—Charter Communications, 1015 Washington Square Shopping Ctr, Washington, MO 63090-5307. Phones: 636-207-7044 (St. Louis office); 636-239-2197. Fax: 636-239-6865. Web Site: http://www.charter.com. Also serves Bourbon, Crawford County, Cuba, Franklin County (southwestern portion), Parkway, Phelps County (portions), St. Clair, St. James, Steelville, Union & Washington. ICA: MO0030.

TV Market Ranking: 11 (Franklin County (southwestern portion) (portions)); Outside TV Markets (Bourbon, Parkway, Phelps County (portions), St. Clair, St. James, Steelville, SULLIVAN, Union, Washington, Franklin County (southwestern portion) (portions)). Franchise award date: April 1, 1981. Franchise expiration date: N.A. Began: August 1, 1982.

Channel capacity: N.A. Channels available but not in use: N.A.

Basic Service

Subscribers: 11,456.

Programming (received off-air): KDNL-TV (ABC) St. Louis; KETC (PBS) St. Louis; KMOV (CBS) St. Louis; KNLC (IND) St. Louis; KPLR-TV (CW) St. Louis; KRCG (CBS) Jefferson City; KSDK (NBC) St. Louis; KTVI (FOX) St. Louis; WPXS (IND) Mount Vernon; WRBU (MNT) East St. Louis; allband FM.

Programming (via satellite): AMC; Arts & Entertainment; CNBC; Comedy Central; Country Music TV; C-SPAN; C-SPAN 2; Disney Channel; Eternal Word TV Network; Home Shopping Network; INSP; Jewelry Television; Lifetime; MTV; Nickelodeon; Product Information Network; QVC; ShopNBC; The Learning Channel; Toon Disney; Trinity Broadcasting Network; Turner Network TV; TV Guide Network; Univision; USA Network; VH1; Weather Channel; WGN America.

Current originations: Leased Access; Government Access; Educational Access; Public Access.

Fee: $29.99 installation; $15.00 additional installation.

Expanded Basic Service 1

Subscribers: 9,902.

Programming (via satellite): ABC Family Channel; Animal Planet; BET Networks; Bravo; Cartoon Network; CNN; Discovery Channel; E! Entertainment Television; ESPN; ESPN 2; Food Network; Fox News Channel; Fox Sports Net Midwest; FX; G4; Golf Channel; GSN; Hallmark Channel; Headline News; HGTV; History Channel; MSNBC; National Geographic Channel; Oxygen; SoapNet; Speed Channel; Spike TV; Syfy; TBS Superstation; Telemundo; Toon Disney; Travel Channel; truTV; Turner Classic Movies; TV Land; Versus; WE tv.

Fee: $49.99 monthly.

Digital Basic Service

Subscribers: 5,000.

Programming (via satellite): BBC America; Bio; CBS College Sports Network; CMT Pure Country; Discovery en Espanol; Discovery Health Channel; Discovery Kids Channel; Discovery Military Channel; Discovery Planet Green; Do-It-Yourself; ESPNews; Fox College Sports Atlantic; Fox College Sports Central; Fox College Sports Pacific; Fox Soccer; Fuel TV; History Channel International; ID Investigation Discovery; Independent Film Channel; LOGO; MTV Hits; MTV Tres; MTV2; Music Choice; National Geographic Channel; Nick Jr.; Nick Too; NickToons TV; Science Channel; Sundance Channel; TeenNick; The Sportsman Channel; VH1 Classic; VH1 Soul.

Fee: $9.29 monthly.

Digital Pay Service 1

Pay Units: 2,955.

Programming (via satellite): Cinemax (multiplexed); Encore (multiplexed); Flix; HBO (multiplexed); Showtime (multiplexed); Starz (multiplexed); The Movie Channel (multiplexed).

Fee: $10.95 monthly (each).

Video-On-Demand: Yes

Pay-Per-View

Addressable homes: 5,000.

iN DEMAND (delivered digitally), Addressable: Yes; Playboy TV (delivered digitally); Fresh (delivered digitally); Spice: Xcess (delivered digitally).

Internet Service

Operational: Yes.

Subscribers: 4,490.

Broadband Service: Charter Pipeline.

Fee: $29.99 monthly.

Telephone Service

Digital: Operational

Fee: $29.99 monthly

Miles of Plant: 550.0 (coaxial); None (fiber optic). Homes passed: 18,953.

Vice President & General Manager: Steve Trippe. Headend Manager: Chuck Prosser. Operations Director: Dave Miller. Technical Operations Manager: John Viehland. Marketing Director: Beverly Wall. Office Manager: Dawn Paul.

Franchise fee: 6% of gross.

Ownership: Charter Communications Inc. (MSO).

SULLIVAN—Charter Communications. Now served by SULLIVAN (formerly WASHINGTON), MO [MO0030]. ICA: MO0072.

SULLIVAN—Fidelity Communications, 64 N Clark St, Sullivan, MO 63080. Phones: 573-426-5000; 573-468-8081; 573-468-1223. Fax: 573-468-3834. E-mail: cabletv@fidnet.com. Web Site: http://www.fidelitycommunications.com. Also serves Rolla. ICA: MO0042.

TV Market Ranking: Outside TV Markets (Rolla, SULLIVAN). Franchise award date: March 13, 1961. Franchise expiration date: N.A. Began: October 1, 1967.

Channel capacity: N.A. Channels available but not in use: N.A.

Basic Service

Subscribers: 5,299.

Programming (received off-air): KDNL-TV (ABC) St. Louis; KETC (PBS) St. Louis; KMOV (CBS) St. Louis; KPLR-TV (CW) St. Louis; KRCG (CBS) Jefferson City; KSDK (NBC) St. Louis; KTVI (FOX) St. Louis.

Programming (via satellite): ABC Family Channel; Bravo; Disney Channel; Home Shopping Network; QVC; TBS Superstation; TV Guide Network; WGN America.

Current originations: Educational Access.

Fee: $49.95 installation; $15.95 monthly; $15.00 additional installation.

Expanded Basic Service 1

Subscribers: N.A.

Programming (received off-air): KNLC (IND) St. Louis; WRBU (MNT) East St. Louis.

Programming (via satellite): AMC; Animal Planet; Arts & Entertainment; Cartoon Network; CNBC; CNN; Comedy Central; Country Music TV; C-SPAN; C-SPAN 2; Discovery Channel; E! Entertainment Television; ESPN; ESPN 2; ESPN Classic Sports; Eternal Word TV Network; Food Network; Fox News Channel; Fox Sports Net Midwest; FX; GSN; Hallmark Channel; Headline News; HGTV; History Channel; Lifetime; MSNBC; MTV; National Geographic Channel; Nickelodeon; Spike TV; Syfy; The Learning Channel; Toon Disney; Travel Channel; Trinity Broadcasting Network; truTV; Turner Network TV; TV Land; USA Network; VH1; Weather Channel.

Fee: $44.95 monthly.

Digital Basic Service

Subscribers: N.A.

Programming (received off-air): KMOV (CBS) St. Louis.

Programming (via satellite): AmericanLife TV Network; BBC America; Bio; Bloomberg Television; Country Music TV; Discovery Digital Networks; Discovery HD Theater; DMX Music; ESPN; ESPNews; Fox Movie Channel; Fox Soccer; G4; GAS; Golf Channel; GSN; HDNet; HDNet Movies; History Channel International; Independent Film Channel; INSP; KSDK (NBC) St. Louis; MTV2; Nick Jr.; NickToons TV; Outdoor Channel; Speed Channel; Trinity Broadcasting Network; Turner Classic Movies; Versus; VH1.

Fee: $39.95 installation; $10.90 monthly.

Digital Pay Service 1

Pay Units: N.A.

Programming (via satellite): Cinemax (multiplexed); Encore (multiplexed); HBO (multiplexed); Showtime (multiplexed); Showtime; Starz (multiplexed); The Movie Channel (multiplexed).

Video-On-Demand: Yes

Pay-Per-View

iN DEMAND (delivered digitally); Fresh (delivered digitally); Playboy TV (delivered digitally).

Internet Service

Operational: Yes. Began: December 31, 2001.

Broadband Service: In-house.

Fee: $34.95 monthly.

Telephone Service

None

Homes passed: 9,996.

Manager: Don Knight. Chief Technician: Rich Abel.

City fee: 5% of gross.

Ownership: Fidelity Communications Co. (MSO).

SUMMERSVILLE—Formerly served by Almega Cable. No longer in operation. ICA: MO0259.

SYRACUSE—Formerly served by First Cable of Missouri Inc. No longer in operation. ICA: MO0374.

TAOS—Formerly served by Longview Communications. No longer in operation. ICA: MO0270.

TERRE DU LAC—Charter Communications. Now served by FARMINGTON, MO [MO0035]. ICA: MO0194.

THAYER—Charter Communications, 312 Washington Ave, West Plains, MO 65775. Phones: 636-207-7044 (St Louis office); 417-256-2785. Web Site: http://www.charter.com. Also serves Mammoth Spring. ICA: MO0423.

TV Market Ranking: Outside TV Markets (Mammoth Spring, THAYER). Franchise award date: N.A. Franchise expiration date: N.A. Began: July 1, 1959.

Channel capacity: 43 (not 2-way capable). Channels available but not in use: None.

Basic Service

Subscribers: 1,253.

Programming (received off-air): KAIT (ABC) Jonesboro; KOLR (CBS) Springfield; KOZK (PBS) Springfield; KPBI (MNT) Eureka Springs; KSFX-TV (FOX) Springfield; KSPR (ABC) Springfield; KYTV (CW, NBC) Springfield.

Programming (via satellite): AMC; Arts & Entertainment; Comedy Central; C-SPAN; Home Shopping Network; Lifetime; MTV; QVC; Syfy; TBS Superstation; The Learning Channel; Travel Channel; Trinity Broadcasting Network; USA Network; VH1; WGN America.

Current originations: Educational Access; Government Access; Public Access.

Fee: $56.00 installation; $22.36 monthly; $3.45 converter.

Expanded Basic Service 1

Subscribers: 1,110.

Programming (via satellite): ABC Family Channel; CNN; Country Music TV; Discovery Channel; Disney Channel; E! Entertainment Television; ESPN; ESPN 2; Headline News; Nickelodeon; Speed Channel; Spike TV; Turner Network TV; Weather Channel.

Fee: $24.53 monthly.

Pay Service 1
Pay Units: 55.
Programming (via satellite): Cinemax.
Fee: $10.95 monthly.
Pay Service 2
Pay Units: 102.
Programming (via satellite): HBO.
Fee: $11.95 monthly.
Pay Service 3
Pay Units: 43.
Programming (via satellite): The Movie Channel.
Fee: $10.95 monthly.
Pay Service 4
Pay Units: 53.
Programming (via satellite): Showtime.
Fee: $10.95 monthly.
Video-On-Demand: No
Pay-Per-View
Addressable homes: 626.
iN DEMAND, Addressable: Yes.
Internet Service
Operational: No.
Telephone Service
None
Miles of Plant: 50.0 (coaxial); None (fiber optic). Homes passed: 2,322.
Vice President & General Manager: Steve Trippe. Operations Director: Dave Miller. Operations Manager: Dave Huntsman. Plant Manager: Kevin Goetz. Chief Technician: Randy Ward. Marketing Director: Beverly Wall.
Ownership: Charter Communications Inc. (MSO).

TINA—GH Technologies. Formerly [MO0375]. This cable system has converted to IPTV, PO Box 227, 7926 NE Ste Rte M, Breckenridge, MO 64625. Phones: 800-846-3426; 660-644-2000. Fax: 660-644-5464. E-mail: comments@greenhills.net. Web Site: http://www.greenhills.net. ICA: MO5178.
TV Market Ranking: Outside TV Markets (TINA). Franchise award date: September 27, 2007. Franchise expiration date: N.A. Began: N.A.
Channel capacity: N.A. Channels available but not in use: N.A.
Internet Service
Operational: Yes.
Fee: $15.00 installation; $27.95 monthly.
Telephone Service
Digital: Operational
Fee: $20.29 monthly
Ownership: Green Hills Companies (MSO).

TINA—GH Technologies. This cable system has converted to IPTV. See Tina, MO [MO5178], MO. ICA: MO0375.

TIPTON—Charter Communications. No longer in operation. ICA: MO0141.

TIPTON—Crystal Broadband Networks, PO Box 180336, Chicago, IL 60618. Phones: 877-319-0328; 630-206-0447. E-mail: info@crystalbn.com. Web Site: http:/crystalbn.com. ICA: MO0474.
TV Market Ranking: Below 100 (TIPTON).
Channel capacity: N.A. Channels available but not in use: N.A.
Basic Service
Subscribers: N.A.
Programming (received off-air): KMIZ (ABC) Columbia; KMOS-TV (PBS) Sedalia; KNLJ (IND) Jefferson City; KOMU-TV (CW, NBC) Columbia; KQFX-LD Columbia; KRCG (CBS) Jefferson City; KSFX-TV (FOX) Springfield.
Programming (via satellite): ABC Family Channel; Arts & Entertainment; CNN; Discovery Channel; Disney Channel; ESPN; ESPN 2; Home Shopping Network; Nickelodeon; Spike TV; TBS Superstation; Turner Network TV; USA Network; Weather Channel; WGN America.
Digital Basic Service
Subscribers: N.A.
Programming (via satellite): AmericanLife TV Network; BBC America; Bio; Bloomberg Television; Bravo; CMT Pure Country; Discovery Digital Networks; ESPNews; Fox Movie Channel; Fox Soccer; Fuse; G4; GAS; Golf Channel; GSN; Halogen Network; HGTV; History Channel; History Channel International; Independent Film Channel; Lifetime Movie Network; MTV Networks Digital Suite; Nick Jr.; Outdoor Channel; ShopNBC; Speed Channel; Style Network; Syfy; Toon Disney; Trinity Broadcasting Network; Turner Classic Movies; Versus; WE tv.
Pay Service 1
Pay Units: N.A.
Programming (via satellite): Showtime; The Movie Channel.
Digital Pay Service 1
Pay Units: N.A.
Programming (via satellite): Cinemax (multiplexed); Encore (multiplexed); Flix; HBO (multiplexed); Showtime (multiplexed); Starz (multiplexed); The Movie Channel (multiplexed).
Internet Service
Operational: Yes.
Telephone Service
None
General Manager: Nidhin Johnson. Plant Manager: Tony Gilbert.
Ownership: Crystal Broadband Networks (MSO).

TRENTON—Suddenlink Communications, 1005 Main St, Trenton, MO 64683. Phones: 660-359-2677; 314-965-2020. Web Site: http://www.suddenlink.com. Also serves Grundy County. ICA: MO0064.
TV Market Ranking: Outside TV Markets (Grundy County, TRENTON). Franchise award date: January 1, 1957. Franchise expiration date: N.A. Began: January 1, 1965.
Channel capacity: 61 (operating 2-way). Channels available but not in use: 6.
Basic Service
Subscribers: 2,700.
Programming (received off-air): KCPT (PBS) Kansas City; KCTV (CBS) Kansas City; KMBC-TV (ABC) Kansas City; KQTV (ABC) St. Joseph; KSHB-TV (NBC) Kansas City; KSMO-TV (MNT) Kansas City; WDAF-TV (FOX) Kansas City.
Programming (via satellite): C-SPAN; QVC; Trinity Broadcasting Network; TV Guide Network.
Fee: $38.50 installation; $19.95 monthly; $15.50 additional installation.
Expanded Basic Service 1
Subscribers: N.A.
Programming (via satellite): ABC Family Channel; AMC; Animal Planet; Arts & Entertainment; BET Networks; Bravo; Cartoon Network; CNBC; CNN; Comedy Central; Discovery Channel; Disney Channel; E! Entertainment Television; ESPN; ESPN 2; Food Network; Fox News Channel; Fox Sports Net Midwest; FX; Great American Country; Hallmark Channel; Headline News; HGTV; History Channel; Lifetime; MSNBC; MTV; National Geographic Channel; Nickelodeon; Spike TV; Syfy; TBS Superstation; The Learning Channel; Travel Channel; Turner Classic Movies; Turner Network TV; TV Land; USA Network; VH1; Weather Channel.
Fee: $24.00 monthly.
Digital Basic Service
Subscribers: N.A.
Programming (via satellite): BBC America; Bio; Bloomberg Television; Discovery Digital Networks; DMX Music; ESPN Classic Sports; ESPNews; Fox Soccer; Fuse; G4; Golf Channel; GSN; History Channel International; Independent Film Channel; Military History Channel; Outdoor Channel; Science Television; Sleuth; Speed Channel; Toon Disney; Versus; WE tv.
Fee: $3.99 monthly.
Pay Service 1
Pay Units: 334.
Programming (via satellite): Cinemax.
Fee: $13.95 monthly.
Pay Service 2
Pay Units: 107.
Programming (via satellite): The Movie Channel.
Fee: $10.95 monthly.
Pay Service 3
Pay Units: 336.
Programming (via satellite): HBO.
Fee: $13.95 monthly.
Pay Service 4
Pay Units: 167.
Programming (via satellite): Showtime.
Fee: $10.00 installation; $10.95 monthly.
Digital Pay Service 1
Pay Units: N.A.
Programming (via satellite): Cinemax (multiplexed); HBO (multiplexed); Showtime (multiplexed); Starz; The Movie Channel (multiplexed); The New Encore (multiplexed).
Video-On-Demand: No
Pay-Per-View
iN DEMAND (delivered digitally); Playboy TV (delivered digitally); Fresh (delivered digitally).
Internet Service
Operational: Yes. Began: June 2, 2006.
Broadband Service: Cebridge High Speed Cable Internet.
Fee: $29.95 monthly.
Telephone Service
Digital: Operational
Miles of Plant: 51.0 (coaxial); None (fiber optic). Homes passed: 2,996. Total homes in franchised area: 2,999.
Regional Manager: Todd Cruthird.
Ownership: Cequel Communications LLC (MSO).

TRIMBLE—Time Warner Cable. Now served by KANSAS CITY, MO [MO0001]. ICA: MO0424.

TROY—Charter Communications. Now served by WARRENTON, MO [MO0065]. ICA: MO0100.

UNIONVILLE—Unionville Missouri CATV, PO Box 255, 1611 Grant St, Unionville, MO 63565. Phone: 660-947-3818. Fax: 660-947-7756. E-mail: catv@nemr.net. ICA: MO0120.
TV Market Ranking: Below 100 (UNIONVILLE). Franchise award date: N.A. Franchise expiration date: N.A. Began: September 1, 1980.
Channel capacity: 50 (2-way capable). Channels available but not in use: 8.
Basic Service
Subscribers: 950.
Programming (received off-air): KCCI (CBS) Des Moines; KDIN-TV (PBS)es Moines; KTVO (ABC) Kirksville; KYOU-TV (FOX) Ottumwa; WHO-DT (NBC) Des Moines; WOI-DT (ABC) Ames; allband FM.
Programming (via satellite): ABC Family Channel; Arts & Entertainment; Cartoon Network; CNN; Country Music TV; Discovery Channel; Disney Channel; ESPN; ESPN 2; Fox News Channel; Fox Sports Net Midwest; Great American Country; HGTV; History Channel; Lifetime; Lifetime Movie Network; Lifetime Real Women; MTV; Nickelodeon; Outdoor Channel; QVC; Spike TV; Syfy; TBS Superstation; The Learning Channel; Trinity Broadcasting Network; Turner Classic Movies; Turner Network TV; TV Land; USA Network; VH1; Weather Channel; WGN America.
Current originations: Educational Access; Public Access.
Fee: $15.00 installation; $21.00 monthly; $10.00 converter; $25.00 additional installation.
Pay Service 1
Pay Units: 135.
Programming (via satellite): Cinemax.
Fee: $15.00 installation; $7.50 monthly.
Pay Service 2
Pay Units: 45.
Programming (via satellite): The Movie Channel.
Fee: $15.00 installation; $7.50 monthly.
Pay Service 3
Pay Units: 183.
Programming (via satellite): Showtime.
Fee: $15.00 installation; $7.50 monthly.
Video-On-Demand: No
Internet Service
Operational: No.
Telephone Service
None
Miles of Plant: 28.0 (coaxial); None (fiber optic). Homes passed: 1,200. Total homes in franchised area: 1,200.
Manager: Jerry Tilden. Cable Clerk: Melinda Haines. Chief Technician: Frank Hendee.
Ownership: City of Unionville Cable TV.

URBANA—Formerly served by Cebridge Connections. No longer in operation. ICA: MO0380.

URICH—Formerly served by CableDirect. No longer in operation. ICA: MO0276.

UTICA—Formerly served by Green Hills Communications Inc. No longer in operation. ICA: MO0448.

VAN BUREN—Boycom Cablevision Inc., 3467 Township Line Rd, Poplar Bluff, MO 63901. Phone: 573-686-9101. Fax: 573-686-4722. Web Site: http://www.boycomonline.com. ICA: MO0165.
TV Market Ranking: Outside TV Markets (VAN BUREN). Franchise award date: February 5, 1987. Franchise expiration date: N.A. Began: N.A.
Channel capacity: 54 (2-way capable). Channels available but not in use: 14.
Basic Service
Subscribers: N.A. Included in Alton
Programming (received off-air): KAIT (ABC) Jonesboro; KBSI (FOX) Cape Girardeau; KFVS-TV (CBS, CW) Cape Girardeau; KTEJ (PBS) Jonesboro; KYTV (CW, NBC) Springfield; WNBC (NBC) New York.
Programming (via satellite): C-SPAN; Home Shopping Network; Trinity Broadcasting Network; Weather Channel; WGN America.
Fee: $29.95 installation; $19.95 monthly.

Expanded Basic Service 1
Subscribers: 377.
Programming (via satellite): ABC Family Channel; AMC; Arts & Entertainment; CNN; Discovery Channel; Disney Channel; ESPN; ESPN 2; Fox Sports Net Midwest; Great American Country; HGTV; History Channel; Lifetime; MTV; National Geographic Channel; Nickelodeon; Spike TV; TBS Superstation; Toon Disney; Turner Network TV; TV Land; USA Network; VH1.
Fee: $20.00 monthly.
Pay Service 1
Pay Units: 146.
Programming (via satellite): Cinemax; HBO; Showtime; The Movie Channel.
Fee: $9.49 monthly (Cinemax), $13.49 monthly (HBO, Showtime, or TMC).
Video-On-Demand: No
Internet Service
Operational: No.
Telephone Service
None
Miles of Plant: 25.0 (coaxial); None (fiber optic). Homes passed: 717.
President: Steven Boyers. General Manager: Shelly Batton. Chief Technician: Phil Huett.
City fee: 2% of gross.
Ownership: Boycom Cablevision Inc. (MSO).

VANDALIA—Crystal Broadband Networks, PO Box 180336, Chicago, IL 60618. Phones: 877-319-0328; 630-206-0447. E-mail: info@crystalbn.com. Web Site: http://crystalbn.com. ICA: MO0114.
TV Market Ranking: Below 100 (VANDALIA). Franchise award date: November 18, 1982. Franchise expiration date: N.A. Began: September 1, 1983.
Channel capacity: 61 (not 2-way capable). Channels available but not in use: N.A.
Basic Service
Subscribers: 884.
Programming (received off-air): KETC (PBS) St. Louis; KHQA-TV (ABC, CBS) Hannibal; KMIZ (ABC) Columbia; KOMU-TV (CW, NBC) Columbia; KPLR-TV (CW) St. Louis; KRCG (CBS) Jefferson City; KSDK (NBC) St. Louis; WGEM-TV (CW, NBC) Quincy.
Programming (via satellite): C-SPAN; FX; QVC; Weather Channel; WGN America.
Current originations: Government Access; Educational Access.
Fee: $29.95 installation; $19.95 monthly.
Expanded Basic Service 1
Subscribers: N.A.
Programming (via satellite): ABC Family Channel; AMC; Animal Planet; Arts & Entertainment; BET Networks; Cartoon Network; CNBC; CNN; Comedy Central; Country Music TV; Discovery Channel; Disney Channel; E! Entertainment Television; ESPN; ESPN 2; Fox News Channel; Fox Sports Net Midwest; FX; G4; Hallmark Channel; Headline News; HGTV; History Channel; Lifetime; MTV; Nickelodeon; Oxygen; Spike TV; Syfy; TBS Superstation; The Learning Channel; Travel Channel; truTV; Turner Network TV; TV Land; USA Network; Versus; VH1; Weather Channel.
Fee: $20.00 monthly.
Digital Basic Service
Subscribers: N.A.
Programming (via satellite): BBC America; Bio; Bloomberg Television; Discovery Digital Networks; Do-It-Yourself; ESPN Classic Sports; ESPNews; GAS; GSN; History Channel International; Independent Film Channel; Lifetime Movie Network; MTV Networks Digital Suite; Music Choice; Nick Jr.; Nick Too; NickToons TV; SoapNet; Sundance Channel; Toon Disney; WE tv.
Fee: $12.95 monthly.
Digital Pay Service 1
Pay Units: 363.
Programming (via satellite): Cinemax (multiplexed); Encore (multiplexed); Flix; HBO (multiplexed); Showtime (multiplexed); Starz (multiplexed); The Movie Channel (multiplexed).
Fee: $10.50 monthly (each).
Video-On-Demand: No
Pay-Per-View
Pleasure (delivered digitally); ETC (Erotic TV Clips) (delivered digitally); iN DEMAND (delivered digitally).
Internet Service
Operational: Yes.
Telephone Service
Digital: Operational
Miles of Plant: 14.0 (coaxial); None (fiber optic). Homes passed: 1,349. Total homes in franchised area: 1,349.
General Manager: Nidhin Johnson. Program Manager: Shawn Smith.
Ownership: Crystal Broadband Networks (MSO).

VERSAILLES—Crystal Broadband Networks, Box 180336, Chicago, IL 60618. Phones: 877-319-0328; 630-206-0447. E-mail: info@crystalbn.com. Web Site: http://crystalbn.com. ICA: MO0132.
TV Market Ranking: Below 100 (VERSAILLES). Franchise award date: June 2, 1981. Franchise expiration date: N.A. Began: April 1, 1981.
Channel capacity: 43 (not 2-way capable). Channels available but not in use: N.A.
Basic Service
Subscribers: 718.
Programming (received off-air): KMIZ (ABC) Columbia; KMOS-TV (PBS) Sedalia; KNLJ (IND) Jefferson City; KOMU-TV (CW, NBC) Columbia; KRCG (CBS) Jefferson City.
Programming (via satellite): Home Shopping Network; Weather Channel; WGN America.
Current originations: Public Access.
Fee: $29.95 installation; $19.95 monthly; $26.50 additional installation.
Expanded Basic Service 1
Subscribers: 340.
Programming (via satellite): ABC Family Channel; AMC; Arts & Entertainment; Cartoon Network; CNBC; CNN; Comedy Central; Country Music TV; Discovery Channel; Disney Channel; E! Entertainment Television; ESPN; ESPN 2; Fox News Channel; FX; G4; Headline News; HGTV; History Channel; Lifetime; MTV; Nickelodeon; Oxygen; Spike TV; Syfy; TBS Superstation; The Learning Channel; Turner Network TV; TV Land; USA Network; VH1; Weather Channel.
Fee: $20.00 monthly.
Digital Basic Service
Subscribers: 33.
Programming (via satellite): BBC America; Bio; Bloomberg Television; Discovery Digital Networks; Do-It-Yourself; GAS; GSN; History Channel International; Independent Film Channel; MTV Networks Digital Suite; Music Choice; Nick Jr.; Nick Too; NickToons TV; SoapNet; Style Network; Sundance Channel; Toon Disney; TV Guide Interactive Inc.; WE tv.
Fee: $12.95 monthly.
Digital Pay Service 1
Pay Units: 186.
Programming (via satellite): Cinemax (multiplexed); Encore; Flix; HBO (multiplexed); Showtime (multiplexed); Starz (multiplexed); The Movie Channel (multiplexed).
Fee: $11.95 monthly (each).
Video-On-Demand: No
Pay-Per-View
Addressable homes: 33.
ETC (Erotic TV Clips) (delivered digitally); The Pleasure Network (delivered digitally); iN DEMAND (delivered digitally).
Internet Service
Operational: Yes.
Telephone Service
Digital: Operational
Miles of Plant: 17.0 (coaxial); None (fiber optic).
General Manager: Nidhin Johnson. Program Manager: Shawn Smith.
Franchise fee: 3% of gross.
Ownership: Crystal Broadband Networks (MSO).

VIBURNUM—Crystal Broadband Networks, PO Box 180336, Chicago, IL 60618. Phones: 877-319-0328; 630-206-0447. E-mail: info@crystalbn.com. Web Site: http://crystalbn.com. ICA: MO0243.
TV Market Ranking: Outside TV Markets (VIBURNUM). Franchise award date: January 2, 1982. Franchise expiration date: N.A. Began: January 1, 1983.
Channel capacity: 41 (not 2-way capable). Channels available but not in use: N.A.
Basic Service
Subscribers: 274.
Programming (received off-air): KDNL-TV (ABC) St. Louis; KETC (PBS) St. Louis; KFVS-TV (CBS, CW) Cape Girardeau; KMOV (CBS) St. Louis; KPLR-TV (CW) St. Louis; KSDK (NBC) St. Louis; KTVI (FOX) St. Louis.
Programming (via satellite): ABC Family Channel; Disney Channel; WGN America.
Fee: $29.95 installation; $19.95 monthly.
Expanded Basic Service 1
Subscribers: N.A.
Programming (via satellite): AMC; Animal Planet; Arts & Entertainment; Cartoon Network; CNBC; CNN; Country Music TV; Discovery Channel; ESPN; ESPN 2; Food Network; HGTV; Home Shopping Network; INSP; Lifetime; MTV; Nickelodeon; QVC; Spike TV; Syfy; TBS Superstation; Travel Channel; Turner Network TV; USA Network.
Fee: $20.00 monthly.
Pay Service 1
Pay Units: 38.
Programming (via satellite): Cinemax.
Fee: $23.49 installation; $10.50 monthly.
Pay Service 2
Pay Units: 36.
Programming (via satellite): HBO.
Fee: $23.49 installation; $10.50 monthly.
Video-On-Demand: No
Pay-Per-View
Playboy TV (delivered digitally); Shorteez (delivered digitally); Fresh (delivered digitally); Hot Choice (delivered digitally); ESPN Full Court (delivered digitally); iN DEMAND (delivered digitally).
Internet Service
Operational: Yes.
Telephone Service
None
Miles of Plant: 9.0 (coaxial); None (fiber optic). Homes passed: 341. Total homes in franchised area: 341.
General Manager: Nidhin Johnson. Program Manager: Shawn Smith.
City fee: 5% of gross.
Ownership: Crystal Broadband Networks (MSO).

VIENNA—Longview Communications, 12007 Sunrise Valley Dr, Ste 375, Reston, VA 20191. Phones: 866-611-6565 (Customer service); 703-476-9101. Fax: 703-476-9107. Web Site: http://www.longviewcomm.com. ICA: MO0317.
TV Market Ranking: Below 100 (BUNCOMBE). Franchise award date: N.A. Franchise expiration date: N.A. Began: February 1, 1984.
Channel capacity: 41 (not 2-way capable). Channels available but not in use: None.
Basic Service
Subscribers: 73.
Programming (received off-air): KETC (PBS) St. Louis; KMIZ (ABC) Columbia; KNLJ (IND) Jefferson City; KOMU-TV (CW, NBC) Columbia; KRCG (CBS) Jefferson City.
Programming (via satellite): C-SPAN; C-SPAN 2; Home Shopping Network; Trinity Broadcasting Network; WGN America.
Fee: $17.98 monthly.
Expanded Basic Service 1
Subscribers: N.A.
Programming (via satellite): ABC Family Channel; AMC; Animal Planet; Arts & Entertainment; CNN; Discovery Channel; Disney Channel; E! Entertainment Television; ESPN; ESPN 2; Fox News Channel; G4; Great American Country; Headline News; History Channel; Lifetime; MSNBC; Speed Channel; TBS Superstation; The Learning Channel; Turner Network TV; USA Network; Weather Channel.
Fee: $17.97 monthly.
Pay Service 1
Pay Units: 24.
Programming (via satellite): Cinemax; HBO; Showtime; The Movie Channel.
Fee: $8.95 monthly (TMC), $10.95 monthly (Showtime or Cinemax), $12.95 monthly (HBO).
Video-On-Demand: No
Internet Service
Operational: No.
Telephone Service
None
Miles of Plant: 6.0 (coaxial); None (fiber optic). Homes passed: 309.
President: John Long. Senior Vice President: Marc W. Cohen. General Manager: Brandon Dickey. Operations Manager: Perry Scarborough.
City fee: 3% of gross.
Ownership: Longview Communications (MSO).

VILLA RIDGE—Charter Communications. Now served by BARNHART, MO [MO0385]. ICA: MO0401.

WAPPAPELLO—Boycom Cablevision Inc., 3467 Township Line Rd, Poplar Bluff, MO 63901. Phone: 573-686-9101. Fax: 573-686-4722. Web Site: http://www.boycomonline.com. Also serves Butler County (northern portion) & Wayne County (southern portion). ICA: MO0332.
TV Market Ranking: Below 100 (Butler County (northern portion), WAPPAPELLO, Wayne County (southern portion)). Franchise award date: N.A. Franchise expiration date: N.A. Began: N.A.
Channel capacity: 45 (not 2-way capable). Channels available but not in use: None.
Basic Service
Subscribers: N.A.
Programming (received off-air): KAIT (ABC) Jonesboro; KBSI (FOX) Cape Girardeau; KFVS-TV (CBS, CW) Cape Girardeau; KPOB-TV (ABC) Poplar Bluff; KTEJ (PBS) Jonesboro; WPSD-TV (NBC) Paducah; WRBU (MNT) East St. Louis.

Programming (via satellite): ABC Family Channel; AMC; Animal Planet; Arts & Entertainment; Cartoon Network; CNBC; CNN; C-SPAN; Discovery Channel; Disney Channel; ESPN; ESPN 2; Fox News Channel; Fox Sports Net Midwest; Fuse; Golf Channel; Great American Country; Hallmark Channel; Headline News; HGTV; History Channel; Lifetime; Nickelodeon; Outdoor Channel; QVC; Spike TV; Syfy; TBS Superstation; The Learning Channel; Travel Channel; Trinity Broadcasting Network; Turner Network TV; TV Land; USA Network; Weather Channel; WGN America.
Fee: $38.75 monthly.

Pay Service 1
Pay Units: N.A.
Programming (via satellite): Cinemax; HBO.
Fee: $10.00 monthly (each).

Video-On-Demand: No

Internet Service
Operational: No.

Telephone Service
None

Miles of Plant: 6.0 (coaxial); None (fiber optic).
Presiden: Steven Boyers. General Manager: Shelly Batton. Chief Technician: Phil Huett.
Ownership: Boycom Cablevision Inc. (MSO).

WARDELL—Formerly served by Almega Cable. No longer in operation. ICA: MO0228.

WARRENSBURG—Charter Communications, 210 W 7th St, Sedalia, MO 65301-4217. Phones: 636-207-7044 (St Louis office); 660-826-6520. Fax: 660-826-4583. Web Site: http://www.charter.com. Also serves Johnson County (portions), Knob Noster, Pettis County, Sedalia, Walnut Hills & Whiteman AFB. ICA: MO0425.
TV Market Ranking: 22 (Johnson County (portions)); Below 100 (Knob Noster, Pettis County, Sedalia, Walnut Hills, WARRENSBURG, Whiteman AFB); Outside TV Markets (WARRENSBURG, Johnson County (portions)). Franchise award date: March 8, 1976. Franchise expiration date: N.A. Began: October 1, 1966.
Channel capacity: N.A. Channels available but not in use: N.A.

Basic Service
Subscribers: 15,829.
Programming (received off-air): KCPT (PBS) Kansas City; KCTV (CBS) Kansas City; KCWE (CW) Kansas City; KMBC-TV (ABC) Kansas City; KMCI-TV (IND) Lawrence; KMIZ (ABC) Columbia; KMOS-TV (PBS) Sedalia; KOMU-TV (CW, NBC) Columbia; KPXE-TV (ION) Kansas City; KSHB-TV (NBC) Kansas City; KSMO-TV (MNT) Kansas City; WDAF-TV (FOX) Kansas City; allband FM.
Programming (via satellite): AMC; Arts & Entertainment; BET Networks; CNBC; Comedy Central; C-SPAN; C-SPAN 2; Eternal Word TV Network; Hallmark Channel; Home Shopping Network; INSP; LWS Local Weather Station; MTV; QVC; TBS Superstation; Trinity Broadcasting Network; TV Guide Interactive Inc.; TV Guide Network; USA Network; VH1; Weather Channel; WGN America.
Current originations: Educational Access.
Fee: $29.99 installation.

Expanded Basic Service 1
Subscribers: 12,963.
Programming (via satellite): ABC Family Channel; Animal Planet; Bravo; Cartoon Network; CNN; Country Music TV; Discovery Channel; Disney Channel; E! Entertainment Television; ESPN; ESPN 2; ESPN Classic Sports; FitTV; Food Network; Fox Movie Channel; Fox News Channel; Fox Sports Net Midwest; FX; G4; Golf Channel; GSN; Headline News; HGTV; History Channel; Lifetime; MSNBC; National Geographic Channel; Nickelodeon; Oxygen; SoapNet; Speed Channel; Spike TV; Style Network; Syfy; The Learning Channel; Travel Channel; truTV; Turner Classic Movies; Turner Network TV; TV Land; Univision; Versus.
Fee: $49.99 monthly.

Digital Basic Service
Subscribers: 5,317.
Programming (via satellite): BBC America; Bio; Bloomberg Television; CNN en Espanol; Discovery Digital Networks; Do-It-Yourself; GAS; History Channel International; Lifetime Movie Network; MTV Networks Digital Suite; Music Choice; Nick Jr.; Nick Too; NickToons TV; Sundance Channel; Toon Disney; WE tv.
Fee: $7.95 monthly.

Digital Pay Service 1
Pay Units: 5,000.
Programming (via satellite): Cinemax (multiplexed); Encore (multiplexed); Flix; HBO (multiplexed); Showtime (multiplexed); Starz (multiplexed); The Movie Channel (multiplexed).
Fee: $11.95 monthly (each).

Video-On-Demand: Yes

Pay-Per-View
Addressable homes: 5,317.
iN DEMAND (delivered digitally), Addressable: Yes; Hot Choice (delivered digitally); ETC (delivered digitally); Pleasure (delivered digitally).

Internet Service
Operational: Yes.
Subscribers: 5,000.
Broadband Service: Charter Pipeline.
Fee: $29.99 monthly.

Telephone Service
Digital: Operational

Miles of Plant: 319.0 (coaxial); None (fiber optic).
Vice President & General Manager: Steve Trippe. Operations Director: Dave Miller. Technical Operations Manager: Larry Wright. Marketing Director: Beverly Wall. Office Manager: Vicky Brant.
Franchise fee: 3% of gross.
Ownership: Charter Communications Inc. (MSO).

WARRENTON—Charter Communications, 1015 Washington Square Shopping Ctr, Washington, MO 63090-5307. Phones: 636-207-7044 (St Louis office); 636-239-2197. Fax: 636-239-6865. Web Site: http://www.charter.com. Also serves Lincoln County, Moscow Mills, Troy, Truesdale & Wright City. ICA: MO0065.
TV Market Ranking: Outside TV Markets (Lincoln County, Moscow Mills, Troy, Truesdale, WARRENTON, Wright City). Franchise award date: N.A. Franchise expiration date: N.A. Began: August 1, 1983.
Channel capacity: 53 (not 2-way capable). Channels available but not in use: None.

Basic Service
Subscribers: 3,110.
Programming (received off-air): KDNL-TV (ABC) St. Louis; KETC (PBS) St. Louis; KMOV (CBS) St. Louis; KPLR-TV (CW) St. Louis; KSDK (NBC) St. Louis; KTVI (FOX) St. Louis; WRBU (MNT) East St. Louis.
Programming (via satellite): C-SPAN; C-SPAN 2; Home Shopping Network; INSP; QVC; TV Guide Interactive Inc.; WGN America.
Fee: $29.99 installation.

Expanded Basic Service 1
Subscribers: 2,580.
Programming (via satellite): ABC Family Channel; AMC; Animal Planet; Arts & Entertainment; Cartoon Network; CNBC; CNN; Comedy Central; Country Music TV; Discovery Channel; Disney Channel; E! Entertainment Television; ESPN; ESPN 2; Food Network; Fox News Channel; Fox Sports Net Midwest; FX; Hallmark Channel; Headline News; HGTV; History Channel; Lifetime; MTV; National Geographic Channel; Nickelodeon; Speed Channel; Spike TV; Syfy; TBS Superstation; The Learning Channel; Travel Channel; truTV; Turner Network TV; TV Land; USA Network; Versus; VH1; Weather Channel.
Fee: $49.99 monthly.

Digital Basic Service
Subscribers: N.A.
Programming (via satellite): BBC America; Discovery Digital Networks; ESPNews; Fox Sports World; Golf Channel; GSN; Independent Film Channel; Music Choice; Nick Jr.; Sundance Channel; Turner Classic Movies.

Digital Pay Service 1
Pay Units: 287.
Programming (via satellite): Cinemax (multiplexed); Encore (multiplexed); Flix; HBO (multiplexed); Showtime (multiplexed); The Movie Channel (multiplexed).
Fee: $10.75 monthly (each).

Video-On-Demand: Yes

Pay-Per-View
iN DEMAND (delivered digitally); Hot Choice (delivered digitally); ETC (delivered digitally); Pleasure (delivered digitally).

Internet Service
Operational: Yes.
Broadband Service: Charter Pipeline.

Telephone Service
Digital: Operational

Miles of Plant: 250.0 (coaxial); None (fiber optic). Homes passed: 4,534.
Vice President & General Manager: Steve Trippe. Operations Director: Dave Miller. Technical Operations Manager: John Viehland. Marketing Director: Beverly Wall. Office Manager: Dawn Paul.
City fee: 3% of gross.
Ownership: Charter Communications Inc. (MSO).

WARSAW—Crystal Broadband Networks, PO Box 180336, Chicago, IL 60618. Phones: 877-319-0328; 630-206-0447. E-mail: info@crystalbn.com. Web Site: http://crystalbn.com. Also serves White Branch. ICA: MO0426.
TV Market Ranking: Below 100 (WARSAW, White Branch). Franchise award date: February 2, 1976. Franchise expiration date: N.A. Began: October 10, 1966.
Channel capacity: 36 (not 2-way capable). Channels available but not in use: N.A.

Basic Service
Subscribers: 887.
Programming (received off-air): KCTV (CBS) Kansas City; KMBC-TV (ABC) Kansas City; KMIZ (ABC) Columbia; KMOS-TV (PBS) Sedalia; KOLR (CBS) Springfield; KOMU-TV (CW, NBC) Columbia; KSHB-TV (NBC) Kansas City; KSMO-TV (MNT) Kansas City; KYTV (CW, NBC) Springfield; WDAF-TV (FOX) Kansas City; allband FM.
Programming (via satellite): Country Music TV; C-SPAN; ESPN; Home Shopping Network; Lifetime; QVC; Turner Network TV; USA Network; Weather Channel.
Fee: $29.95 installation; $19.95 monthly.

Expanded Basic Service 1
Subscribers: 758.
Programming (via satellite): ABC Family Channel; AMC; Arts & Entertainment; CNN; Discovery Channel; Disney Channel; Food Network; Headline News; Spike TV; TBS Superstation.
Fee: $20.00 monthly.

Pay Service 1
Pay Units: 63.
Programming (via satellite): HBO (multiplexed).
Fee: $11.95 monthly.

Pay Service 2
Pay Units: 48.
Programming (via satellite): Showtime (multiplexed).
Fee: $11.95 monthly.

Pay Service 3
Pay Units: 30.
Programming (via satellite): The Movie Channel (multiplexed).
Fee: $6.00 installation; $11.95 monthly.

Video-On-Demand: No

Pay-Per-View
Addressable homes: 29.
ESPN Extra; ESPN Now; Hot Choice; iN DEMAND; Playboy TV; Spice; Spice2; sports.

Internet Service
Operational: Yes.

Telephone Service
Digital: Operational

Miles of Plant: 19.0 (coaxial); None (fiber optic). Homes passed: 1,006.
General Manager: Nidhin Johnson. Program Manager: Shawn Smith.
Franchise fee: 3% of gross.
Ownership: Crystal Broadband Networks (MSO).

WAYNESVILLE—Cable America Corp., 690 Missouri Ave, Ste 13, St. Robert, MO 65584. Phone: 573-336-5284. Fax: 573-336-4556. Web Site: http://www.cableamerica.com. Also serves Dixon, Doolittle, Fort Leonard Wood, Houston, Licking, Mountain Grove, Newburg, Phelps County (portions), Pulaski County (portions), Richland, Rolla, St. Robert & Willow Springs. ICA: MO0023.
TV Market Ranking: Outside TV Markets (Dixon, DOOLITTLE, Fort Leonard Wood, Houston, Licking, Mountain Grove, Mountain Grove, Newburg, Phelps County (portions), Pulaski County (portions), Richland, Rolla, St. Robert, WAYNESVILLE, Willow Springs). Franchise award date: September 18, 1999. Franchise expiration date: N.A. Began: December 1, 1984.
Channel capacity: 130 (operating 2-way). Channels available but not in use: N.A.

Basic Service
Subscribers: 10,225.
Programming (received off-air): K15CZ Springfield; KOLR (CBS) Springfield; KOZK (PBS) Springfield; KRCG (CBS) Jefferson City; KSFX-TV (FOX) Springfield; KSPR (ABC) Springfield; KWBM (MNT) Harrison [LICENSED & SILENT]; KYTV (CW, NBC) Springfield; allband FM.
Programming (via satellite): Home Shopping Network; Pentagon Channel; TV Guide Network; WGN America.
Current originations: Government Access; Public Access.
Fee: $99.95 installation; $18.59 monthly.

Expanded Basic Service 1
Subscribers: 8,025.
Programming (via satellite): ABC Family Channel; AMC; Animal Planet; Arts & Entertainment; BET Networks; Bravo; Cartoon Network; CNBC; CNN; Comedy Central; Country Music TV; C-SPAN; C-SPAN 2;

Discovery Channel; Disney Channel; E! Entertainment Television; ESPN; ESPN 2; ESPN Classic Sports; Food Network; Fox News Channel; Fox Sports Net Midwest; FX; Great American Country; Hallmark Channel; Headline News; HGTV; History Channel; Lifetime; MSNBC; MTV; NFL Network; Nickelodeon; SoapNet; Spike TV; Syfy; TBS Superstation; The Learning Channel; Travel Channel; Trinity Broadcasting Network; truTV; Turner Network TV; TV Land; Univision; USA Network; VH1; Weather Channel.
Fee: $27.70 monthly.

Digital Basic Service
Subscribers: 3,675.
Programming (via satellite): BBC America; Bio; Bloomberg Television; CMT Pure Country; Discovery Health Channel; Discovery Kids Channel; Discovery Military Channel; Discovery Planet Green; Disney XD; Encore (multiplexed); ESPN 2; ESPN U; ESPNews; FitTV; Fox Movie Channel; Fox Soccer; Fuse; G4; Golf Channel; GSN; Halogen Network; History Channel International; ID Investigation Discovery; Independent Film Channel; Lifetime Movie Network; MTV2; Music Choice; Nick Jr.; NickToons TV; Outdoor Channel; Science Channel; Speed Channel; Style Network; TeenNick; Trinity Broadcasting Network; Turner Classic Movies; VH1 Classic.
Fee: $12.00 monthly.

Digital Expanded Basic Service
Subscribers: N.A.
Programming (received off-air): KOLR (CBS) Springfield; KOZK (PBS) Springfield; KSFX-TV (FOX) Springfield; KSPR (ABC) Springfield; KYTV (CW, NBC) Springfield.
Programming (via satellite): Bravo HD; CNBC HD+; Discovery Channel HD; ESPN 2 HD; ESPN HD; HDNet; HDNet Movies; Syfy HD; TBS in HD; Turner Network TV HD; Universal HD; USA Network HD.
Fee: $6.95 monthly.

Digital Pay Service 1
Pay Units: N.A.
Programming (via satellite): Cinemax (multiplexed); Cinemax HD; Flix; HBO (multiplexed); HBO HD; Showtime (multiplexed); Showtime HD; Starz (multiplexed); Starz HDTV; Sundance Channel; The Movie Channel (multiplexed).
Fee: $11.95 monthly (HBO, Cinemax, Starz or Showtime/TMC/Flix/Sundance).

Video-On-Demand: No

Pay-Per-View
Movies, Fee: $3.99; Hot Choice, Fee: $3.99, Addressable: Yes.

Internet Service
Operational: Yes.
Subscribers: 5,025.
Broadband Service: CableAmerica.
Fee: $14.95 installation; $40.95 monthly; $9.95 modem lease; $199.00 modem purchase.

Telephone Service
None

Miles of Plant: 499.0 (coaxial); None (fiber optic). Homes passed: 20,203. Total homes in franchised area: 967.
Manager: Debra Mefford. Chief Technician: Don Crawford.
City fee: 5% of gross.
Ownership: CableAmerica Corp. (MSO).

WELLSTON—Formerly served by Data Cablevision. No longer in operation. ICA: MO0121.

WEST PLAINS—Charter Communications, 312 Washington Ave, West Plains, MO 65775. Phones: 417-256-2785; 636-207-7044 (St Louis office). Web Site: http://www.charter.com. Also serves Howell County. ICA: MO0044.
TV Market Ranking: Outside TV Markets (Howell County, WEST PLAINS). Franchise award date: N.A. Franchise expiration date: N.A. Began: October 1, 1956.
Channel capacity: 56 (not 2-way capable). Channels available but not in use: None.

Basic Service
Subscribers: 3,255.
Programming (received off-air): K15CZ Springfield; K38HE West Plains; KAIT (ABC) Jonesboro; KKYK-CA (IND) Little Rock; KOLR (CBS) Springfield; KOZK (PBS) Springfield; KSFX-TV (FOX) Springfield; KSPR (ABC) Springfield; KWBM (MNT) Harrison [LICENSED & SILENT]; KYTV (CW, NBC) Springfield.
Programming (via satellite): C-SPAN; Home Shopping Network; QVC; Trinity Broadcasting Network; Weather Channel; WGN America.
Fee: $29.99 installation.

Expanded Basic Service 1
Subscribers: 2,839.
Programming (via satellite): ABC Family Channel; AMC; Arts & Entertainment; Cartoon Network; CNBC; CNN; Comedy Central; Country Music TV; Discovery Channel; Disney Channel; E! Entertainment Television; ESPN; ESPN 2; Fox News Channel; Fox Sports Net Midwest; FX; G4; Golf Channel; Hallmark Channel; Headline News; HGTV; History Channel; Lifetime; MTV; Nickelodeon; Outdoor Channel; Oxygen; Speed Channel; Spike TV; Style Network; Syfy; TBS Superstation; The Learning Channel; Travel Channel; Turner Network TV; TV Land; USA Network; VH1.
Fee: $49.99 monthly.

Digital Basic Service
Subscribers: N.A.
Programming (via satellite): BBC America; Bio; Bloomberg Television; CMT Pure Country; Discovery Digital Networks; Discovery Times Channel; Do-It-Yourself; ESPN Classic Sports; ESPNews; GAS; GSN; History Channel International; Independent Film Channel; Lifetime Movie Network; MTV Networks Digital Suite; Music Choice; Nick Jr.; Nick Too; NickToons TV; SoapNet; Sundance Channel; Toon Disney; WE tv.

Digital Pay Service 1
Pay Units: 786.
Programming (via satellite): Cinemax (multiplexed); Encore; Flix; HBO (multiplexed); LOGO; Showtime (multiplexed); Starz (multiplexed); The Movie Channel (multiplexed).
Fee: $10.95 monthly (each).

Video-On-Demand: Yes

Pay-Per-View
iN Demand (delivered digitally), Addressable: Yes; Ten Clips (delivered digitally).

Internet Service
Operational: Yes.
Broadband Service: Charter Pipeline.

Telephone Service
Digital: Operational

Miles of Plant: 125.0 (coaxial); None (fiber optic). Homes passed: 5,831.
Vice President & General Manager: Steve Trippe. Operations Director: Dave Miller. Operations Manager: Dave Huntsman. Plant Manager: Kevin Goetz. Marketing Director: Beverly Wall.
Franchise fee: 5% of gross.
Ownership: Charter Communications Inc. (MSO).

WESTBORO—Formerly served by CableDirect. No longer in operation. ICA: MO0427.

WESTPHALIA—Formerly served by CableDirect. No longer in operation. ICA: MO0340.

WHEELING—Longview Communications. Now served by MEADVILLE, MO [MO0434]. ICA: MO0436.

WILLIAMSVILLE—Formerly served by Almega Cable. No longer in operation. ICA: MO0267.

WILLOW SPRINGS—Almega Cable. Now served by WAYNESVILLE, MO [MO0023]. ICA: MO0154.

WILSON BEND—Formerly served by Almega Cable. No longer in operation. ICA: MO0220.

WINDSOR—Crystal Broadband Networks, PO Box 180336, Chicago, IL 60618. Phone: 817-685-9588. E-mail: info@crystalbn.com. Web Site: http://crystalbn.com. ICA: MO0119.
TV Market Ranking: Below 100 (WINDSOR). Franchise award date: N.A. Franchise expiration date: N.A. Began: July 1, 1967.
Channel capacity: 38 (not 2-way capable). Channels available but not in use: N.A.

Basic Service
Subscribers: 1,037.
Programming (received off-air): KCTV (CBS) Kansas City; KCWE (CW) Kansas City; KMBC-TV (ABC) Kansas City; KMIZ (ABC) Columbia; KMOS-TV (PBS) Sedalia; KOLR (CBS) Springfield; KPXE-TV (ION) Kansas City; KSHB-TV (NBC) Kansas City; KSMO-TV (MNT) Kansas City; WDAF-TV (FOX) Kansas City; allband FM.
Programming (via satellite): ABC Family Channel; Arts & Entertainment; Bravo; C-SPAN; E! Entertainment Television; ESPN; Home Shopping Network; Lifetime; Nickelodeon; QVC; Syfy.
Fee: $29.95 installation; $19.95 monthly.

Expanded Basic Service 1
Subscribers: 905.
Programming (via satellite): AMC; CNN; Discovery Channel; Disney Channel; ESPN 2; Food Network; G4; Headline News; HGTV; Spike TV; TBS Superstation; Turner Network TV; USA Network; WGN America.
Fee: $20.00 monthly.

Pay Service 1
Pay Units: 70.
Programming (via satellite): HBO.
Fee: $13.49 monthly.

Pay Service 2
Pay Units: 53.
Programming (via satellite): Showtime.
Fee: $11.95 monthly.

Pay Service 3
Pay Units: 30.
Programming (via satellite): The Movie Channel.
Fee: $11.95 monthly.

Video-On-Demand: No

Pay-Per-View
Addressable homes: 51.
ESPN Extra; ESPN Now; Hot Choice; iN DEMAND; Playboy TV; Spice; Spice2; sports.

Internet Service
Operational: No.

Telephone Service
Digital: Operational

Miles of Plant: 21.0 (coaxial); None (fiber optic). Homes passed: 1,285.
Program Manager: Shawn Smith. General Manager: Nidhin Johnson.
Franchise fee: 3% of gross.
Ownership: Crystal Broadband Networks (MSO).

WINFIELD—US Cable, 647 Clinic Rd, Hannibal, MO 63401. Phone: 573-581-2404. Fax: 573-581-4053. Web Site: http://www.uscable.com. Also serves Foley, Lincoln County (southeastern portion) & Old Monroe. ICA: MO0115.
TV Market Ranking: 11 (Lincoln County (southeastern portion) (portions), Old Monroe, WINFIELD); Outside TV Markets (Foley, Lincoln County (southeastern portion) (portions)). Franchise award date: N.A. Franchise expiration date: N.A. Began: N.A.
Channel capacity: N.A. Channels available but not in use: N.A.

Basic Service
Subscribers: N.A. Included in Hannibal
Programming (received off-air): KDNL-TV (ABC) St. Louis; KETC (PBS) St. Louis; KMOV (CBS) St. Louis; KNLC (IND) St. Louis; KPLR-TV (CW) St. Louis; KSDK (NBC) St. Louis; KTVI (FOX) St. Louis; WRBU (MNT) East St. Louis.
Programming (via satellite): QVC; WGN America.
Current originations: Public Access.
Fee: $25.00 installation; $22.52 monthly.

Expanded Basic Service 1
Subscribers: N.A.
Programming (via satellite): ABC Family Channel; Animal Planet; Arts & Entertainment; Cartoon Network; CNBC; CNN; Comedy Central; Country Music TV; Discovery Channel; Disney Channel; ESPN; ESPN 2; Fox News Channel; Fox Sports Net Midwest; FX; Headline News; HGTV; History Channel; Lifetime; National Geographic Channel; Nickelodeon; Spike TV; TBS Superstation; The Learning Channel; Trinity Broadcasting Network; Turner Classic Movies; Turner Network TV; TV Land; USA Network; VH1; Weather Channel.
Fee: $20.05 monthly.

Digital Basic Service
Subscribers: N.A. Included in Hannibal
Programming (via satellite): BBC America; Bio; Bloomberg Television; Discovery Digital Networks; Fox Reality Channel; Fuse; G4; GSN; Halogen Network; HGTV; History Channel International; Lime; MTV Networks Digital Suite; Nick Jr.; Sleuth; Style Network; Syfy; Toon Disney; Trinity Broadcasting Network; WealthTV.
Fee: $12.95 monthly (Family, Sports or Movies).

Digital Expanded Basic Service
Subscribers: N.A.
Programming (via satellite): DMX Music; Encore (multiplexed); Fox Movie Channel; Independent Film Channel; Lifetime Movie Network; Turner Classic Movies; WE tv.
Fee: $5.45 monthly.

Digital Expanded Basic Service 2
Subscribers: N.A.
Programming (via satellite): ESPN Classic Sports; ESPNews; Fox Soccer; GAS; Golf Channel; NFL Network; Outdoor Channel; Versus.
Fee: $5.45 monthly.

Pay Service 1
Pay Units: 50.
Programming (via satellite): Cinemax.
Fee: $11.95 monthly.

Digital Pay Service 1
Pay Units: N.A.
Programming (via satellite): Cinemax (multiplexed); HBO (multiplexed); Showtime (multiplexed); Starz (multiplexed); The Movie Channel (multiplexed).

Fee: $6.95 monthly (Starz), $11.95 monthly (Cinemax, HBO, Showtime or TMC).

Video-On-Demand: No

Pay-Per-View

iN DEMAND (delivered digitally); Playboy TV (delivered digitally); Fresh (delivered digitally).

Internet Service

Operational: Yes.

Telephone Service

None

Homes passed, total homes in franchised area, & miles of plant included in Hannibal

Regional Administrative Director: Rebecca Bramblett. Technical Operations Manager: Mark Thake. Marketing Director: Rita Watson.

Ownership: US Cable Corp. (MSO).; Comcast Cable Communications Inc. (MSO).

WINONA—Boycom Cablevision Inc., 3467 Township Line Rd, Poplar Bluff, MO 63901. Phone: 573-686-9101. Fax: 573-686-4722. Web Site: http://www.boycomonline.com. ICA: MO0207.

TV Market Ranking: Outside TV Markets (WINONA). Franchise award date: September 13, 1971. Franchise expiration date: N.A. Began: N.A.

Channel capacity: 54 (not 2-way capable). Channels available but not in use: 21.

Basic Service

Subscribers: N.A. Included in Alton

Programming (received off-air): KAIT (ABC) Jonesboro; KFVS-TV (CBS, CW) Cape Girardeau; KOLR (CBS) Springfield; KOZK (PBS) Springfield; KSFX-TV (FOX) Springfield; KSPR (ABC) Springfield; KYTV (CW, NBC) Springfield; WNBC (NBC) New York.

Programming (via satellite): Home Shopping Network; WGN America.

Fee: $29.95 installation; $19.95 monthly.

Expanded Basic Service 1

Subscribers: N.A.

Programming (via satellite): ABC Family Channel; AMC; CNN; Discovery Channel; Disney Channel; ESPN; ESPN 2; Fox News Channel; Fox Sports Net Midwest; FX; Great American Country; Lifetime; MTV; Nickelodeon; Speed Channel; Spike TV; TBS Superstation; Toon Disney; Trinity Broadcasting Network; Turner Network TV; TV Land; USA Network; VH1; Weather Channel.

Fee: $20.00 monthly.

Pay Service 1

Pay Units: 82.

Programming (via satellite): Cinemax; HBO; Showtime; The Movie Channel.

Fee: $8.99 monthly (Cinemax), $12.99 monthly (HBO), $13.99 monthly (Showtime or TMC).

Video-On-Demand: No

Internet Service

Operational: No.

Telephone Service

None

Miles of Plant: 20.0 (coaxial); None (fiber optic). Homes passed: 508.

President: Steven Boyers. General Manager: Shelly Batton. Chief Technician: Phil Huett.

Ownership: Boycom Cablevision Inc. (MSO).

WYACONDA—Formerly served by CableDirect. No longer in operation. ICA: MO0428.

MONTANA

Total Systems: **91**
Total Communities Served: **154**
Franchises Not Yet Operating: **0**
Applications Pending: **0**
Communities with Applications: **0**
Number of Basic Subscribers: **210,007**
Number of Expanded Basic Subscribers: **121,228**
Number of Pay Units: **6,085**

Top 100 Markets Represented: N.A.

For a list of cable communities in this section, see the Cable Community Index located in the back of Cable Volume 2.
For explanation of terms used in cable system listings, see p. D-11.

ABSAROKEE—Cable Montana, 222 W 1st St, Laurel, MT 59044. Phones: 800-628-6060; 406-628-6336; 308-236-1512 (Kearney, NE corporate office). Fax: 406-628-8181. Web Site: http://www.cablemt.net. ICA: MT0079.

TV Market Ranking: Outside TV Markets (ABSAROKEE). Franchise award date: N.A. Franchise expiration date: N.A. Began: June 1, 1982.

Channel capacity: N.A. Channels available but not in use: N.A.

Basic Service

Subscribers: 161.

Programming (received off-air): KHMT (FOX) Hardin; KTVQ (CBS, CW) Billings; KULR-TV (NBC) Billings; KUSM-TV (PBS) Bozeman; KWBM (MNT) Harrison [LICENSED & SILENT].

Programming (via satellite): ABC Family Channel; C-SPAN; C-SPAN 2; G4; Lifetime; Nickelodeon; QVC; TBS Superstation; TV Guide Network; Weather Channel; WGN America.

Fee: $24.95 installation; $21.95 monthly.

Expanded Basic Service 1

Subscribers: N.A.

Programming (via satellite): Altitude Sports & Entertainment; AMC; Animal Planet; Arts & Entertainment; Cartoon Network; CNBC; CNN; Comedy Central; Country Music TV; Discovery Channel; E! Entertainment Television; ESPN; ESPN 2; ESPN Classic Sports; Food Network; Fox News Channel; Fox Sports Net; FX; Hallmark Channel; Headline News; HGTV; History Channel; MSNBC; MTV; National Geographic Channel; Outdoor Channel; Spike TV; Syfy; The Learning Channel; truTV; Turner Network TV; TV Land; Versus; VH1.

Fee: $18.04 monthly.

Digital Basic Service

Subscribers: N.A.

Programming (via satellite): Alterna'TV; BBC America; Bio; Black Family Channel; Bloomberg Television; CMT Pure Country; Current; Daystar TV Network; Discovery Health Channel; Discovery Kids Channel; Discovery Military Channel; Discovery Planet Green; DMX Music; ESPN 2; ESPN Classic Sports; ESPNews; FitTV; Fox College Sports Atlantic; Fox College Sports Central; Fox College Sports Pacific; Fox Movie Channel; G4; Golf Channel; GSN; Halogen Network; History Channel; History Channel International; ID Investigation Discovery; Lifetime Movie Network; MTV Hits; MTV2; National Geographic Channel; Nick Jr.; Ovation; Science Channel; ShopNBC; Sleuth; Speed Channel; Style Network; TeenNick; Trinity Broadcasting Network; Versus; VH1 Classic; VH1 Soul; WE tv.

Fee: $13.00 monthly.

Digital Pay Service 1

Pay Units: N.A.

Programming (via satellite): Cinemax (multiplexed); Encore (multiplexed); Flix; HBO (multiplexed); Showtime (multiplexed); Starz (multiplexed); The Movie Channel (multiplexed).

Fee: $13.00 monthly (HBO, Cinemax, Showtime/TMC/Flix or Starz/Encore).

Video-On-Demand: No

Pay-Per-View

Hot Choice (delivered digitally); iN DEMAND (delivered digitally); Playboy TV (delivered digitally); Fresh (delivered digitally); Spice: Xcess (delivered digitally); Club Jenna (delivered digitally).

Internet Service

Operational: Yes.

Fee: $35.95 monthly.

Telephone Service

None

Miles of Plant: 4.0 (coaxial); None (fiber optic). Homes passed: 335. Total homes in franchised area: 335.

Manager: Doug Lane. Operations Manager: Stuart Gilbertson.

Ownership: USA Companies (MSO).

ALBERTON—Bresnan Communications, 511 W Mendenhall Rd, Boweman, MT 59715. Phones: 406-586-1837; 406-782-9383. Web Site: http://www.bresnan.com. ICA: MT0100.

TV Market Ranking: Below 100 (ALBERTON).

Channel capacity: N.A. Channels available but not in use: N.A.

Video-On-Demand: Yes

Internet Service

Operational: Yes.

Telephone Service

None

General Manager: Mike Oswald.

Ownership: Bresnan Communications Inc. (MSO).

ANACONDA—Bresnan Communications, 201 E Front St, Butte, MT 59701-5203. Phones: 406-782-9383; 877-273-7626 (Customer service). Fax: 406-782-9020. Web Site: http://www.bresnan.com. Also serves Deer Lodge County. ICA: MT0014.

TV Market Ranking: Below 100 (ANACONDA, Deer Lodge County (portions)); Outside TV Markets (Deer Lodge County (portions)). Franchise award date: N.A. Franchise expiration date: N.A. Began: September 1, 1962.

Channel capacity: N.A. Channels available but not in use: N.A.

Basic Service

Subscribers: 2,019.

Programming (received off-air): KTVM-TV (NBC) Butte; KWYB (ABC, FOX) Butte; KXLF-TV (CBS, CW) Butte.

Programming (via microwave): KUSM-TV (PBS) Bozeman.

Programming (via satellite): C-SPAN; C-SPAN 2; CW+; Eternal Word TV Network; Home Shopping Network; Lifetime; QVC; TBS Superstation; TV Guide Network.

Fee: $39.95 installation; $20.00 monthly; $.61 converter; $40.00 additional installation.

Expanded Basic Service 1

Subscribers: 1,857.

Programming (via satellite): ABC Family Channel; AMC; Animal Planet; Arts & Entertainment; Cartoon Network; CNBC; CNN; Comedy Central; Country Music TV; Discovery Channel; Disney Channel; E! Entertainment Television; ESPN; ESPN 2; Food Network; Fox News Channel; Fox Sports Net Rocky Mountain; FX; Hallmark Channel; Headline News; HGTV; History Channel; INSP; ION Television; MSNBC; MTV; Nickelodeon; Oxygen; Spike TV; Syfy; The Learning Channel; Travel Channel; truTV; Turner Classic Movies; Turner Network TV; TV Land; USA Network; VH1; Weather Channel.

Fee: $28.99 monthly.

Digital Basic Service

Subscribers: 642.

Programming (via satellite): ABC Family HD; AmericanLife TV Network; Animal Planet HD; Arts & Entertainment HD; BBC America; Bio; Bloomberg Television; Bravo; CBS College Sports Network; CMT Pure Country; Cooking Channel; Discovery Channel HD; Discovery HD Theater; Discovery Health Channel; Discovery Kids Channel; Discovery Military Channel; Discovery Planet Green; Disney Channel HD; DMX Music; Do-It-Yourself; ESPN Classic Sports; ESPN HD; ESPNews; FitTV; Food Network HD; Fox College Sports Atlantic; Fox College Sports Central; Fox College Sports Pacific; Fox Movie Channel; Fox Reality Channel; Fox Soccer; Fuse; G4; Golf Channel; Gospel Music Channel; GSN; Halogen Network; HGTV HD; History Channel HD; History Channel International; HorseTV Channel; ID Investigation Discovery; Independent Film Channel; ION Television; Lifetime Movie Network; MTV Hits; MTV Jams; MTV Tres; MTV2; National Geographic Channel; National Geographic Channel HD Network; NFL Network; Nick Jr.; Nick Too; NickToons TV; Outdoor Channel; PBS Kids Sprout; RFD-TV; Science Channel; Science Channel HD; SoapNet; Speed Channel; Style Network; Syfy HD; TeenNick; The Sportsman Channel; Toon Disney; Trinity Broadcasting Network; Universal HD; USA Network HD; Versus; VH1 Classic; VH1 Soul.

Fee: $11.60 monthly.

Digital Pay Service 1

Pay Units: N.A.

Programming (via satellite): Cinemax (multiplexed); Encore (multiplexed); Flix; HBO (multiplexed); HBO HD; Showtime (multiplexed); Starz (multiplexed); Starz HDTV; The Movie Channel (multiplexed).

Video-On-Demand: No

Pay-Per-View

iN DEMAND (delivered digitally).

Internet Service

Operational: Yes.

Subscribers: 279.

Broadband Service: Bresnan OnLine.

Fee: $39.95 monthly; $3.00 modem lease.

Telephone Service

Digital: Operational

Subscribers: 24.

Fee: $49.99 monthly

Miles of Plant: 34.0 (coaxial); 5.0 (fiber optic). Homes passed: 4,007. Total homes in franchised area: 3,255.

General Manager: Mike Oswald. Chief Technician: Todd Hawke.

City fee: $500 annually.

Ownership: Bresnan Communications Inc. (MSO). Sale pends to Cablevision Systems Corp.

ARLEE—Formerly served by Bresnan Communications. No longer in operation. ICA: MT0092.

BAKER—Mid-Rivers Communications, PO Box 280, 904 C Ave, Circle, MT 59215. Phone: 406-485-3301. Fax: 406-485-2924. E-mail: lcedar@midrivers.com. Web Site: http://www.midrivers.com. ICA: MT0041.

TV Market Ranking: Outside TV Markets (BAKER). Franchise award date: September 1, 1976. Franchise expiration date: N.A. Began: November 1, 1977.

Channel capacity: 65 (operating 2-way). Channels available but not in use: 8.

Basic Service

Subscribers: 725.

Programming (received off-air): KEVN-TV (FOX) Rapid City; KOTA-TV (ABC) Rapid City.

Programming (via microwave): KMGH-TV (ABC) Denver; KQCD-TV (NBC) Dickinson; KUSA (NBC) Denver; KUSM-TV (PBS) Bozeman; KXGN-TV (CBS, NBC) Glendive; KXMA-TV (CBS) Dickinson.

Programming (via satellite): ABC Family Channel; AMC; Animal Planet; Arts & Entertainment; Bloomberg Television; Cartoon Network; CNN; Country Music TV; C-SPAN; CW+; Discovery Channel; Disney Channel; E! Entertainment Television; ESPN; ESPN 2; Eternal Word TV Network; Food Network; Fox News Channel; FX; G4; Great American Country; Hallmark Channel; Headline News; HGTV; History Channel; ION Television; Lifetime; MSNBC; MTV; National Geographic Channel; Nickelodeon; Outdoor Channel; RFD-TV; Speed Channel; Spike TV; Syfy; TBS Superstation; Travel Channel; Trinity Broadcasting Network; truTV; Turner Classic Movies; Turner Network TV; TV

Land; USA Network; VH1; WE tv; Weather Channel; WGN America.
Current originations: Religious Access; Government Access; Educational Access; Public Access.
Fee: $15.00 installation; $29.95 monthly.

Digital Basic Service
Subscribers: N.A.
Programming (via satellite): BBC America; Bravo; CMT Pure Country; Discovery Health Channel; Discovery Kids Channel; Discovery Military Channel; Discovery Planet Green; ESPN 2; ESPN Classic Sports; ESPNews; Fox Soccer; Golf Channel; GSN; HGTV; History Channel; ID Investigation Discovery; Independent Film Channel; National Geographic Channel; Nick Jr.; Science Channel; SoapNet; Syfy; Toon Disney; Turner Classic Movies; Versus; VH1 Classic; WE tv.

Pay Service 1
Pay Units: 138.
Programming (via satellite): Cinemax; HBO.
Fee: $12.00 monthly.

Digital Pay Service 1
Pay Units: N.A.
Programming (via satellite): Cinemax (multiplexed); Encore (multiplexed); HBO (multiplexed); Showtime (multiplexed); Starz (multiplexed); The Movie Channel (multiplexed).

Internet Service
Operational: No.

Telephone Service
None

Miles of Plant: 17.0 (coaxial); None (fiber optic). Homes passed: 763. Total homes in franchised area: 763.
General Manager: Gerry Anderson. Chief Technician: Mike Sokoloski. Customer Service Manager: Deb Wagner.
Ownership: Mid-Rivers Telephone Cooperative Inc. (MSO).

BELFRY—Belfry Cable TV, PO Box 687, Cowley, WY 82420-0687. Phone: 307-548-7888. ICA: MT0106.
TV Market Ranking: Outside TV Markets (BELFRY). Franchise award date: N.A. Franchise expiration date: N.A. Began: January 1, 1987.
Channel capacity: 12 (not 2-way capable). Channels available but not in use: N.A.

Basic Service
Subscribers: 25.
Programming (received off-air): KHMT (FOX) Hardin; KSVI (ABC) Billings; KTVQ (CBS, CW) Billings; KULR-TV (NBC) Billings.
Programming (via satellite): CNN; Discovery Channel; Disney Channel; ESPN; Hallmark Channel; History Channel; Spike TV; TBS Superstation; The Learning Channel; Turner Network TV; WGN America.
Fee: $35.00 installation; $21.95 monthly.

Pay Service 1
Pay Units: 2.
Programming (via satellite): HBO.
Fee: $11.95 monthly.

Internet Service
Operational: No.

Telephone Service
None

Miles of Plant: 2.0 (coaxial); None (fiber optic). Homes passed: 90. Total homes in franchised area: 90.
Manager: Jerri Townsend. Chief Technician: Tim Townsend.
Ownership: Cowley Telecable Inc. (MSO).

BELT—KLiP Interactive, 455 Gees Mill Business Court, Conyers, GA 30013. Phones: 800-388-6577; 678-727-7100. Fax: 678-727-7002. E-mail: jsheehan@klipia.com. Web Site: http://www.klipia.com. ICA: MT0073.
TV Market Ranking: Below 100 (BELT). Franchise award date: N.A. Franchise expiration date: N.A. Began: November 23, 1982.
Channel capacity: 40 (not 2-way capable). Channels available but not in use: 14.

Basic Service
Subscribers: 58.
Programming (received off-air): KBGF-LP Great Falls; KFBB-TV (ABC, FOX) Great Falls; KRTV (CBS, CW) Great Falls; KTGF (IND) Great Falls.
Programming (via satellite): ABC Family Channel; Arts & Entertainment; CNN; Comedy Central; Country Music TV; Discovery Channel; Disney Channel; ESPN; ESPN 2; Fox News Channel; Fox Sports Net Rocky Mountain; Headline News; INSP; KDVR (FOX) Denver; Lifetime; MSNBC; Spike TV; TBS Superstation; Turner Classic Movies; Turner Network TV; USA Network; WGN America.
Fee: $29.95 installation; $28.68 monthly.

Pay Service 1
Pay Units: 2.
Programming (via satellite): HBO.
Fee: $10.00 installation; $10.95 monthly.

Pay Service 2
Pay Units: N.A.
Fee: $10.95 monthly (each).

Video-On-Demand: No

Internet Service
Operational: No.

Telephone Service
None

Miles of Plant: 10.0 (coaxial); None (fiber optic). Homes passed: 355.
Chief Executive Officer: Joseph A. Sheehan. General Manager East: Mark Miller. General Manager West: Vance Johnson.
Ownership: KLiP Interactive LLC (MSO).

BIG FLAT—Formerly served by Bresnan Communications. No longer in operation. ICA: MT0093.

BIG SKY—KLiP Interactive, 455 Gees Mill Business Court, Conyers, GA 30013. Phones: 800-388-6577; 678-727-7100. Fax: 678-727-7002. E-mail: jsheehan@klipia.com. Web Site: http://www.klipia.com. ICA: MT0033.
TV Market Ranking: Below 100 (BIG SKY). Franchise award date: N.A. Franchise expiration date: N.A. Began: October 1, 1981.
Channel capacity: 45 (not 2-way capable). Channels available but not in use: 5.

Basic Service
Subscribers: 667.
Programming (received off-air): KCNC-TV (CBS) Denver; KTVM-TV (NBC) Butte; KTVX (ABC) Salt Lake City; KUSM-TV (PBS) Bozeman; KXLF-TV (CBS, CW) Butte.
Programming (via microwave): KWGN-TV (CW) Denver.
Programming (via satellite): ABC Family Channel; AMC; Animal Planet; Arts & Entertainment; CNBC; CNN; Comedy Central; Country Music TV; Discovery Channel; Disney Channel; E! Entertainment Television; ESPN; ESPN 2; Fox News Channel; Fox Sports Net Rocky Mountain; FX; Golf Channel; Headline News; History Channel; KDVR (FOX) Denver; Lifetime; National Geographic Channel; Outdoor Channel; QVC; Spike TV; TBS Superstation; The Learning Channel; truTV; Turner Network TV; TV Guide Network; TV Land; USA Network; Versus; Weather Channel; WGN America.
Fee: $29.95 installation; $39.95 monthly.

Pay Service 1
Pay Units: 20.
Programming (via satellite): Cinemax.
Fee: $10.95 monthly.

Pay Service 2
Pay Units: 40.
Programming (via satellite): HBO.
Fee: $10.95 monthly.

Video-On-Demand: No

Internet Service
Operational: No.

Telephone Service
None

Miles of Plant: 12.0 (coaxial); None (fiber optic). Homes passed: 859. Total homes in franchised area: 1,100.
Chief Executive Officer: Joseph A. Sheehan. General Manager East: Mark Miller. General Manager West: Vance Johnson.
Franchise fee: None.
Ownership: KLiP Interactive LLC (MSO).

BIG TIMBER—Cable Montana, 222 W 1st St, Laurel, MT 59044. Phones: 800-628-6060; 406-628-6336; 308-236-1512 (Kearney, NE corporate office). Fax: 406-628-8181. Web Site: http://www.cablemt.net. ICA: MT0042.
TV Market Ranking: Outside TV Markets (BIG TIMBER). Franchise award date: N.A. Franchise expiration date: N.A. Began: November 1, 1954.
Channel capacity: N.A. Channels available but not in use: N.A.

Basic Service
Subscribers: 591.
Programming (received off-air): KSVI (ABC) Billings; KTVQ (CBS, CW) Billings; KULR-TV (NBC) Billings; KUSM-TV (PBS) Bozeman; KWGN-TV (CW) Denver.
Programming (via satellite): ABC Family Channel; Cartoon Network; C-SPAN; C-SPAN 2; Fox News Channel; Home Shopping Network; INSP; Outdoor Channel; QVC; TBS Superstation; TV Guide Network; Weather Channel; WGN America.
Fee: $24.95 installation; $21.95 monthly; $2.50 converter.

Expanded Basic Service 1
Subscribers: N.A.
Programming (via satellite): Altitude Sports & Entertainment; AMC; Animal Planet; Arts & Entertainment; CNBC; CNN; Comedy Central; Country Music TV; Discovery Channel; Discovery Health Channel; E! Entertainment Television; ESPN; ESPN 2; ESPN Classic Sports; ESPNews; FitTV; Food Network; Fox Sports Net; FX; G4; Golf Channel; Great American Country; Hallmark Channel; Headline News; HGTV; History Channel; Lifetime; MSNBC; MTV; National Geographic Channel; Nickelodeon; Spike TV; Syfy; The Learning Channel; Travel Channel; Turner Network TV; TV Land; USA Network; Versus; VH1; WE tv.
Fee: $18.04 monthly.

Digital Basic Service
Subscribers: N.A.
Programming (via satellite): AmericanLife TV Network; BBC America; Bio; Black Family Channel; Bloomberg Television; CMT Pure Country; Current; Discovery Health Channel; Discovery Kids Channel; Discovery Military Channel; Discovery Planet Green; DMX Music; ESPN 2; ESPN Classic Sports; ESPNews; FitTV; Fox College Sports Atlantic; Fox College Sports Central; Fox College Sports Pacific; Fox Movie Channel; G4; Golf Channel; GSN; Halogen Network; History Channel; History Channel International; ID Investigation Discovery; Lifetime Movie Network; MTV Hits; MTV2; National Geographic Channel; Nick Jr.; Outdoor Channel; Ovation; Science Channel; ShopNBC; Sleuth; Speed Channel; Style Network; TeenNick; Trinity Broadcasting Network; Versus; VH1 Classic; VH1 Soul; WE tv.
Fee: $13.00 monthly.

Digital Pay Service 1
Pay Units: N.A.
Programming (via satellite): Cinemax (multiplexed); Encore (multiplexed); HBO (multiplexed); Showtime (multiplexed); Starz (multiplexed); The Movie Channel (multiplexed).
Fee: $13.00 monthly (HBO, Cinemax, Showtime/TMC/Flix or Starz/Encore).

Video-On-Demand: No

Pay-Per-View
iN DEMAND (delivered digitally); Hot Choice (delivered digitally); Playboy TV (delivered digitally); Fresh (delivered digitally); Shorteez (delivered digitally); Club Jenna (delivered digitally).

Internet Service
Operational: Yes.
Broadband Service: Cable Montana.
Fee: $35.95 monthly.

Telephone Service
None

Miles of Plant: 13.0 (coaxial); None (fiber optic). Homes passed: 750.
Manager: Doug Lane. Operations Manager: Stuart Gilbertson.
City fee: None.
Ownership: USA Companies (MSO).

BILLINGS—Bresnan Communications, 1860 Monad Rd, Billings, MT 59102. Phones: 406-238-7700; 877-273-7626. Fax: 406-238-7777. E-mail: sodonnell@bresnan.com. Web Site: http://www.bresnan.com. Also serves Lockwood & Yellowstone County. ICA: MT0001.
TV Market Ranking: Below 100 (BILLINGS, Lockwood, Yellowstone County (portions)); Outside TV Markets (Yellowstone County (portions)). Franchise award date: N.A. Franchise expiration date: N.A. Began: December 1, 1968.
Channel capacity: N.A. Channels available but not in use: N.A.

Basic Service
Subscribers: 25,915.
Programming (received off-air): KHMT (FOX) Hardin; KSVI (ABC) Billings; KTVQ (CBS, CW) Billings; KULR-TV (NBC) Billings; KUSM-TV (PBS) Bozeman.
Programming (via satellite): BYU Television; C-SPAN; C-SPAN 2; CW+; Discovery Channel; Eternal Word TV Network; QVC; TBS Superstation; Weather Channel; WGN America.
Current originations: Government Access.
Fee: $49.99 installation; $20.00 monthly; $4.05 converter; $19.99 additional installation.

Expanded Basic Service 1
Subscribers: 21,900.
Programming (via satellite): ABC Family Channel; Altitude Sports & Entertainment; AMC; Animal Planet; Arts & Entertainment; Cartoon Network; CNBC; CNN; Comedy Central; Country Music TV; Disney Channel; E! Entertainment Television; ESPN; ESPN 2; Food Network; Fox News Channel; Fox Sports Net Rocky Mountain; FX; Great American Country; Hallmark Channel; Headline News; HGTV; History Channel; Home Shopping Network; ION Television; Lifetime; MSNBC; MTV; Nickelodeon; Oxygen; Spike TV; Syfy; The Learning Channel; Travel Channel; truTV; Turner Classic Movies; Turner Network TV;

TV Guide Network; TV Land; Univision; USA Network; VH1.
Fee: $22.50 installation; $18.99 monthly; $4.05 converter.

Digital Basic Service
Subscribers: 13,380.
Programming (received off-air): KHMT (FOX) Hardin; KTVQ (CBS, CW) Billings; KULR-TV (NBC) Billings.
Programming (via satellite): 3 Angels Broadcasting Network; ABC Family HD; AmericanLife TV Network; Animal Planet HD; Arts & Entertainment HD; BBC America; Bio; Bloomberg Television; Blue-Highways TV; Bravo; CBS College Sports Network; CMT Pure Country; CNN HD; Cooking Channel; C-SPAN 3; Discovery Channel HD; Discovery HD Theater; Discovery Health Channel; Discovery Kids Channel; Discovery Military Channel; Discovery Planet Green; Disney Channel HD; DMX Music; Do-It-Yourself; ESPN 2 HD; ESPN Classic Sports; ESPN HD; ESPNews; FitTV; Food Network HD; Fox College Sports Atlantic; Fox College Sports Central; Fox College Sports Pacific; Fox Movie Channel; Fox Reality Channel; Fox Soccer; Fuse; G4; Golf Channel; Gospel Music Channel; GSN; Halogen Network; HDNet; HDNet Movies; HGTV HD; History Channel HD; History Channel International; ID Investigation Discovery; Independent Film Channel; INSP; ION Television; Lifetime Movie Network; Lifetime Movie Network HD; MTV Hits; MTV2; National Geographic Channel; National Geographic Channel HD Network; NFL Network; NFL Network HD; NHL Network; Nick Jr.; NickToons TV; Outdoor Channel; PBS Kids Sprout; RFD-TV; Science Channel; Science Channel HD; SoapNet; Speed Channel; Style Network; Syfy HD; TBS in HD; TeenNick; The Sportsman Channel; TLC HD; Toon Disney; Trinity Broadcasting Network; Turner Network TV HD; TV Guide SPOT; Universal HD; USA Network HD; Versus; Versus HD; VH1 Classic; VH1 Soul; Weather Channel HD.
Fee: $11.60 monthly; $4.05 converter.

Digital Pay Service 1
Pay Units: N.A.
Programming (via satellite): Cinemax (multiplexed); Cinemax HD; Cinemax On Demand; Encore (multiplexed); Flix; HBO (multiplexed); HBO HD; HBO On Demand; Showtime (multiplexed); Showtime HD; Starz (multiplexed); Starz HDTV; Starz On Demand; The Movie Channel (multiplexed); The Movie Channel HD.
Fee: $11.00 monthly (HBO, Cinemax, Showtime/TMC/Flix or Starz/Encore).

Video-On-Demand: Yes

Pay-Per-View
ESPN Now (delivered digitally), Addressable: Yes; NBA League Pass (delivered digitally); MLS Direct Kick (delivered digitally); iN DEMAND (delivered digitally), Fee: $.99-$3.99, Addressable: Yes; MLB Extra Innings (delivered digitally); NHL Center Ice (delivered digitally).

Internet Service
Operational: Yes. Began: March 1, 2000.
Broadband Service: Bresnan OnLine.
Fee: $99.95 installation; $39.95 monthly; $3.00 modem lease; $59.95 modem purchase.

Telephone Service
Digital: Operational
Fee: $49.99 monthly

Miles of Plant: 596.0 (coaxial); 144.0 (fiber optic). Homes passed: 52,998.
Vice President & General Manager: Sean O'Donnell. Technical Operations Manager: Tom Campbell. Business Operations Manager: Randi Friez. Marketing Director: Jackie Heitman.
City fee: 5% of gross.
Ownership: Bresnan Communications Inc. (MSO). Sale pends to Cablevision Systems Corp.

BILLINGS—Formerly served by USA Digital TV. No longer in operation. ICA: MT0120.

BILLINGS (western portion)—Cable Montana, 222 W 1st St, Laurel, MT 59044. Phone: 406-628-6336. Web Site: http://www.cablemt.net. ICA: MT0067.
TV Market Ranking: Below 100 (BILLINGS). Franchise award date: N.A. Franchise expiration date: N.A. Began: November 1, 1988.
Channel capacity: N.A. Channels available but not in use: N.A.

Basic Service
Subscribers: 52.
Programming (received off-air): KHMT (FOX) Hardin; KSVI (ABC) Billings; KTVQ (CBS, CW) Billings; KULR-TV (NBC) Billings; KUSM-TV (PBS) Bozeman; KWGN-TV (CW) Denver.
Programming (via satellite): ABC Family Channel; Arts & Entertainment; Cartoon Network; CNBC; CNN; Discovery Channel; ESPN; ESPN 2; Fox News Channel; Great American Country; Hallmark Channel; Headline News; HGTV; History Channel; Lifetime; Nickelodeon; Spike TV; Syfy; TBS Superstation; The Learning Channel; Turner Classic Movies; Turner Network TV; TV Guide Network; USA Network; VH1; Weather Channel; WGN America.
Fee: $29.95 installation; $26.45 monthly.

Digital Basic Service
Subscribers: N.A.
Programming (via satellite): AmericanLife TV Network; BBC America; BET Networks; Bio; Bloomberg Television; Bravo; Discovery Health Channel; Discovery Home Channel; Discovery Kids Channel; Discovery Military Channel; FitTV; Fox Soccer; Fuse; G4; Golf Channel; GSN; History Channel International; ID Investigation Discovery; Independent Film Channel; Lifetime Movie Network; Outdoor Channel; Ovation; Science Channel; Speed Channel; Versus; WE tv; Weather Channel.

Pay Service 1
Pay Units: 10.
Programming (via satellite): Showtime.
Fee: $10.95 monthly.

Pay Service 2
Pay Units: 22.
Programming (via satellite): HBO.
Fee: $10.95 monthly.

Digital Pay Service 1
Pay Units: N.A.
Programming (via satellite): Cinemax (multiplexed); Encore (multiplexed); Flix; HBO (multiplexed); Showtime (multiplexed); Starz (multiplexed); The Movie Channel (multiplexed).

Video-On-Demand: No

Pay-Per-View
iN DEMAND (delivered digitally).

Internet Service
Operational: Yes, Dial-up only.

Telephone Service
Analog: Not Operational
Digital: Operational

Miles of Plant: 10.0 (coaxial); None (fiber optic). Homes passed: 380.
Manager: Doug Wayne. Operations Manager: Stuart Gilbertson.
City fee: None.
Ownership: USA Companies (MSO).

BOULDER—Bresnan Communications, PO Box 5509, 951 W Custer Ave, Helena, MT 59604-5509. Phones: 877-273-7626; 406-442-1060. Fax: 406-443-5843. E-mail: moswald@bresnan.com. Web Site: http://www.bresnan.com. ICA: MT0051.
TV Market Ranking: Below 100 (BOULDER). Franchise award date: N.A. Franchise expiration date: N.A. Began: February 1, 1982.
Channel capacity: 40 (not 2-way capable). Channels available but not in use: None.

Basic Service
Subscribers: 129.
Programming (received off-air): KDVR (FOX) Denver; KTVH-DT (NBC) Helena; KTVM-TV (NBC) Butte; KUSM-TV (PBS) Bozeman; KXLF-TV (CBS, CW) Butte.
Programming (via microwave): KMGH-TV (ABC) Denver.
Programming (via satellite): C-SPAN; Discovery Channel; Lifetime; QVC; TBS Superstation.
Current originations: Public Access.
Fee: $60.00 installation; $20.00 monthly; $40.00 additional installation.

Expanded Basic Service 1
Subscribers: N.A.
Programming (via satellite): ABC Family Channel; AMC; Animal Planet; Arts & Entertainment; Cartoon Network; CNBC; CNN; Disney Channel; ESPN; ESPN 2; Fox News Channel; Fox Sports Net Rocky Mountain; HGTV; MoviePlex; Nickelodeon; Spike TV; The Learning Channel; truTV; Turner Network TV; USA Network; Weather Channel.

Pay Service 1
Pay Units: 56.
Programming (via satellite): Encore; HBO; Showtime; Starz.

Video-On-Demand: No

Internet Service
Operational: Yes.
Fee: $39.95 monthly.

Telephone Service
Analog: Not Operational
Digital: Operational
Fee: $49.99 monthly

Miles of Plant: 8.0 (coaxial); None (fiber optic). Homes passed: 678.
Manager: Mike Oswald. Chief Technician: Ed McFadden.
Ownership: Bresnan Communications Inc. (MSO). Sale pends to Cablevision Systems Corp.

BOZEMAN—Bresnan Communications, 511 W Mendenhall, Bozeman, MT 59715. Phones: 406-586-1837; 406-782-9383 (Butte office). Fax: 406-782-9020. Web Site: http://www.bresnan.com. Also serves Belgrade, Gallatin County & Manhattan. ICA: MT0007.
TV Market Ranking: Below 100 (Belgrade, BOZEMAN, Gallatin County (portions), Manhattan); Outside TV Markets (Gallatin County (portions)). Franchise award date: N.A. Franchise expiration date: N.A. Began: June 1, 1954.
Channel capacity: N.A. Channels available but not in use: N.A.

Basic Service
Subscribers: 12,715.
Programming (received off-air): KBZK (CBS) Bozeman; KTVM-TV (NBC) Butte; KUSM-TV (PBS) Bozeman; KWYB (ABC, FOX) Butte.
Programming (via satellite): Arts & Entertainment; C-SPAN; C-SPAN 2; CW+; Eternal Word TV Network; Home Shopping Network; Lifetime; QVC; TBS Superstation; TV Guide Network.
Current originations: Government Access.
Fee: $46.47 installation; $20.00 monthly; $.88 converter; $15.48 additional installation.

Expanded Basic Service 1
Subscribers: 8,143.
Programming (via satellite): ABC Family Channel; Altitude Sports & Entertainment; AMC; Animal Planet; Bravo; Cartoon Network; CNBC; CNN; Comedy Central; Country Music TV; Discovery Channel; Disney Channel; E! Entertainment Television; ESPN; ESPN 2; Food Network; Fox News Channel; Fox Sports Net Rocky Mountain; FX; Hallmark Channel; Headline News; HGTV; History Channel; INSP; ION Television; MSNBC; MTV; Nickelodeon; Oxygen; Spike TV; Syfy; The Learning Channel; Travel Channel; truTV; Turner Classic Movies; Turner Network TV; TV Land; USA Network; VH1; Weather Channel.

Digital Basic Service
Subscribers: 6,061.
Programming (received off-air): KUSM-TV (PBS) Bozeman.
Programming (via satellite): ABC Family HD; AmericanLife TV Network; Animal Planet HD; Arts & Entertainment HD; BBC America; Bio; Bloomberg Television; Blue-Highways TV; Bravo HD; BYU Television; CBS College Sports Network; CMT Pure Country; CNBC HD+; CNN HD; Cooking Channel; C-SPAN 3; Discovery Channel HD; Discovery HD Theater; Discovery Health Channel; Discovery Kids Channel; Discovery Military Channel; Discovery Planet Green; Disney Channel HD; DMX Music; Do-It-Yourself; ESPN 2 HD; ESPN Classic Sports; ESPN HD; ESPNews; FitTV; Food Network HD; Fox College Sports Atlantic; Fox College Sports Central; Fox College Sports Pacific; Fox Movie Channel; Fox Reality Channel; Fox Soccer; Fuse; G4; Golf Channel; Gospel Music Channel; GSN; Halogen Network; HDNet; HDNet Movies; HGTV HD; History Channel HD; History Channel International; HorseRacing TV; ID Investigation Discovery; Independent Film Channel; ION Life; ION Television; KBZK (CBS) Bozeman; Lifetime Movie Network; Lifetime Movie Network HD; MTV Hits; MTV Jams; MTV Tres; MTV2; National Geographic Channel; National Geographic Channel HD Network; NFL Network; NFL Network HD; NHL Network; Nick Jr.; Nick Too; NickToons TV; Outdoor Channel; Outdoor Channel 2 HD; PBS Kids Sprout; Qubo; RFD-TV; Science Channel; Science Channel HD; SoapNet; Speed Channel; Speed HD; Style Network; Syfy HD; TBS in HD; TeenNick; The Sportsman Channel; TLC HD; Toon Disney; Trinity Broadcasting Network; Turner Network TV HD; TV Guide SPOT; Universal HD; USA Network HD; Versus; Versus HD; VH1 Classic; VH1 Soul; Weather Channel HD.

Digital Pay Service 1
Pay Units: N.A.
Programming (via satellite): Cinemax (multiplexed); Cinemax HD; Cinemax On Demand; Encore (multiplexed); Flix; HBO (multiplexed); HBO HD; HBO On Demand; Showtime (multiplexed); Showtime HD; Showtime On Demand; Starz (multiplexed); Starz HDTV; Starz On Demand; The Movie Channel (multiplexed); The Movie Channel HD.

Video-On-Demand: Yes

Pay-Per-View
ESPN (delivered digitally); MLB Extra Innings (delivered digitally); NHL Center Ice (delivered digitally); iN DEMAND (delivered digitally).
Internet Service
Operational: Yes.
Subscribers: 6,384.
Broadband Service: Bresnan OnLine.
Fee: $39.95 monthly; $3.00 modem lease.
Telephone Service
Analog: Not Operational
Digital: Operational
Subscribers: 1,965.
Fee: $39.95 monthly
Miles of Plant: 324.0 (coaxial); 90.0 (fiber optic). Homes passed: 26,820.
General Manager: Mike Oswald. Chief Technician: Scott Riss.
City fee: None.
Ownership: Bresnan Communications Inc. (MSO). Sale pends to Cablevision Systems Corp.

BRIDGER—Bridger Cable TV, PO Box 561, 215 North B St, Bridger, MT 59014. Phone: 406-662-3516. Fax: 406-662-3516. E-mail: randy@brmt.net. Web Site: http://www.brmt.net. ICA: MT0121.
TV Market Ranking: Outside TV Markets (BRIDGER). Franchise award date: N.A. Franchise expiration date: N.A. Began: N.A.
Channel capacity: 35 (not 2-way capable). Channels available but not in use: N.A.
Basic Service
Subscribers: 150.
Programming (received off-air): KHMT (FOX) Hardin; KSVI (ABC) Billings; KTVQ (CBS, CW) Billings; KULR-TV (NBC) Billings; KUSM-TV (PBS) Bozeman.
Programming (via microwave): KWGN-TV (CW) Denver.
Programming (via satellite): ABC Family Channel; Discovery Channel; History Channel; Home Shopping Network; The Learning Channel; Turner Network TV; Weather Channel; WGN America.
Fee: $18.00 monthly.
Expanded Basic Service 1
Subscribers: 146.
Programming (via satellite): AMC; Animal Planet; Arts & Entertainment; CNN; Country Music TV; Disney Channel; ESPN; ESPN 2; Fox News Channel; Fox Sports Net Rocky Mountain; HGTV; Lifetime; MTV; Nickelodeon; Spike TV; Syfy; Toon Disney; TV Land; USA Network; VH1.
Fee: $18.00 monthly.
Pay Service 1
Pay Units: N.A.
Programming (via satellite): Cinemax; Encore; HBO.
Fee: $1.50 monthly (Encore), $12.00 monthly (Cinemax or HBO).
Video-On-Demand: No
Internet Service
Operational: Yes.
Subscribers: 100.
Fee: $30.00 monthly.
Telephone Service
None
Manager: Randy Novakovich. Office Manager: Deb Novakovic.
Ownership: Randy Novakovich (MSO).

BROADUS—Skyview TV Inc., PO Box 445, 105 N. Wilbur, Broadus, MT 59317. Phone: 406-436-2820. Fax: 406-436-2820. ICA: MT0075.
TV Market Ranking: Outside TV Markets (BROADUS). Franchise award date: N.A. Franchise expiration date: N.A. Began: August 1, 1981.
Channel capacity: 45 (not 2-way capable). Channels available but not in use: None.
Basic Service
Subscribers: 245.
Programming (received off-air): KUSM-TV (PBS) Bozeman.
Programming (via satellite): ABC Family Channel; AMC; Animal Planet; Arts & Entertainment; Cartoon Network; CNN; Country Music TV; C-SPAN; C-SPAN 2; Discovery Channel; Disney Channel; ESPN; ESPN 2; Fox News Channel; Fox Sports Net; Hallmark Channel; Headline News; HGTV; History Channel; Home Shopping Network; Lifetime; MTV; Nickelodeon; Outdoor Channel; Spike TV; Syfy; TBS Superstation; The Learning Channel; Trinity Broadcasting Network; Turner Network TV; TV Land; USA Network; VH1; Weather Channel; WGN America.
Programming (via translator): KOTA-TV (ABC) Rapid City; KTVQ (CBS, CW) Billings; KULR-TV (NBC) Billings.
Fee: $20.00 installation; $31.00 monthly.
Pay Service 1
Pay Units: 40.
Programming (via satellite): HBO.
Fee: $10.00 installation; $10.00 monthly.
Internet Service
Operational: No.
Telephone Service
None
Miles of Plant: 7.0 (coaxial); None (fiber optic). Homes passed: 350. Total homes in franchised area: 350.
Manager: Richard Sturtz.
Ownership: Richard Sturtz.; Gali Estate.; Comcast Cable Communications Inc. (MSO).

BUTTE—Bresnan Communications, 201 E Front St, Butte, MT 59701-5203. Phones: 914-641-3300 (Purchase, NY corporate office); 877-273-7626 (Customer service); 406-782-9383 (Butte office). Fax: 406-782-9020. Web Site: http://www.bresnan.com. Also serves Silver Bow County & Walkerville. ICA: MT0005.
TV Market Ranking: Below 100 (BUTTE (VILLAGE), Silver Bow County, Walkerville). Franchise award date: N.A. Franchise expiration date: N.A. Began: June 1, 1962.
Channel capacity: N.A. Channels available but not in use: N.A.
Basic Service
Subscribers: 7,730.
Programming (received off-air): KTVM-TV (NBC) Butte; KWYB (ABC, FOX) Butte; KXLF-TV (CBS, CW) Butte.
Programming (via microwave): KUSM-TV (PBS) Bozeman.
Programming (via satellite): C-SPAN; C-SPAN 2; CW+; Eternal Word TV Network; Headline News; Home Shopping Network; Lifetime; QVC; TV Guide Network.
Fee: $60.00 installation; $20.00 monthly; $.61 converter; $40.00 additional installation.
Expanded Basic Service 1
Subscribers: 7,266.
Programming (via satellite): ABC Family Channel; Altitude Sports & Entertainment; AMC; Animal Planet; Arts & Entertainment; Cartoon Network; CNBC; CNN; Comedy Central; Country Music TV; Discovery Channel; Disney Channel; E! Entertainment Television; ESPN; ESPN 2; Food Network; Fox News Channel; Fox Sports Net Rocky Mountain; FX; Hallmark Channel; HGTV; History Channel; INSP; ION Television; MSNBC; MTV; Nickelodeon; Oxygen; Spike TV; Syfy; TBS Superstation; The Learning Channel; Travel Channel; truTV; Turner Classic Movies; Turner Network TV; TV Land; USA Network; VH1; Weather Channel.
Fee: $28.99 monthly.
Digital Basic Service
Subscribers: 3,670.
Programming (received off-air): KXLF-TV (CBS, CW) Butte.
Programming (via satellite): ABC Family HD; AmericanLife TV Network; Animal Planet HD; Arts & Entertainment HD; BBC America; Bio; Bloomberg Television; Bravo; Bravo HD; CBS College Sports Network; CMT Pure Country; CNBC HD+; CNN HD; Cooking Channel; Discovery Channel HD; Discovery HD Theater; Discovery Health Channel; Discovery Kids Channel; Discovery Planet Green; Disney Channel HD; DMX Music; Do-It-Yourself; ESPN 2 HD; ESPN Classic Sports; ESPN HD; ESPNews; FitTV; Food Network HD; Fox College Sports Atlantic; Fox College Sports Central; Fox College Sports Pacific; Fox Movie Channel; Fox Reality Channel; Fox Soccer; Fuse; G4; Golf Channel; Gospel Music Channel; GSN; Halogen Network; HDNet; HDNet Movies; HGTV HD; History Channel HD; History Channel International; HorseRacing TV; ID Investigation Discovery; Independent Film Channel; ION Life; ION Television; Lifetime Movie Network; Lifetime Movie Network HD; MTV Hits; MTV Jams; MTV Tres; MTV2; National Geographic Channel; National Geographic Channel HD Network; NFL Network; NFL Network HD; NHL Network; Nick Jr.; Nick Too; NickToons TV; Outdoor Channel; Outdoor Channel 2 HD; Palladia; PBS Kids Sprout; Qubo; RFD-TV; Science Channel; Science Channel HD; SoapNet; Speed Channel; Speed HD; Style Network; Syfy HD; TBS in HD; TeenNick; The Sportsman Channel; TLC HD; Toon Disney; Trinity Broadcasting Network; Turner Network TV HD; TV Guide SPOT; Universal HD; USA Network HD; Versus; Versus HD; VH1 Classic; VH1 Soul; Weather Channel HD.
Fee: $18.00 monthly.
Digital Pay Service 1
Pay Units: N.A.
Programming (via satellite): Cinemax (multiplexed); Cinemax HD; Cinemax On Demand; Encore (multiplexed); Flix; HBO (multiplexed); HBO HD; HBO On Demand; Showtime (multiplexed); Showtime HD; Showtime On Demand; Starz (multiplexed); Starz HDTV; Starz On Demand; The Movie Channel (multiplexed); The Movie Channel HD.
Video-On-Demand: Yes
Pay-Per-View
ESPN (delivered digitally); iN DEMAND (delivered digitally); MLB Extra Innings (delivered digitally); NHL Center Ice (delivered digitally).
Internet Service
Operational: Yes.
Subscribers: 2,873.
Broadband Service: Bresnan OnLine.
Fee: $39.95 monthly; $3.00 modem lease.
Telephone Service
Analog: Not Operational
Digital: Operational
Subscribers: 1,705.
Fee: $49.99 monthly
Miles of Plant: 144.0 (coaxial); 84.0 (fiber optic). Homes passed: 16,380.
General Manager: Mike Oswald. Chief Technician: Todd Hawke.
City fee: $500 (Butte), $50 annually (Walkerville).
Ownership: Bresnan Communications Inc. (MSO). Sale pends to Cablevision Systems Corp.

CASCADE—Bresnan Communications, 2910 10th Ave S, Great Falls, MT 59405. Phones: 877-273-7626; 406-727-8881. Fax: 406-727-6433. E-mail: sodonnell@bresnan.com. Web Site: http://www.bresnan.com. ICA: MT0074.
TV Market Ranking: Below 100 (CASCADE). Franchise award date: N.A. Franchise expiration date: N.A. Began: January 1, 1982.
Channel capacity: N.A. Channels available but not in use: N.A.
Basic Service
Subscribers: 108.
Programming (received off-air): KFBB-TV (ABC, FOX) Great Falls; KRTV (CBS, CW) Great Falls; KTGF (IND) Great Falls; KUSA (NBC) Denver; KUSM-TV (PBS) Bozeman.
Programming (via satellite): C-SPAN; Fox News Channel; Lifetime; QVC; TBS Superstation; The Learning Channel; truTV.
Fee: $44.95 installation; $20.00 monthly.
Expanded Basic Service 1
Subscribers: 91.
Programming (via satellite): ABC Family Channel; AMC; Animal Planet; Arts & Entertainment; Cartoon Network; CNBC; CNN; Discovery Channel; Disney Channel; ESPN; ESPN 2; Fox Sports Net Rocky Mountain; HGTV; History Channel; MoviePlex; Nickelodeon; Spike TV; Turner Network TV; USA Network; Weather Channel.
Fee: $18.99 monthly.
Pay Service 1
Pay Units: N.A.
Programming (via satellite): Encore; HBO; Showtime; Starz.
Fee: $6.99 monthly (Starz/Encore), $14.15 monthly (HBO).
Video-On-Demand: No
Internet Service
Operational: Yes.
Fee: $39.95 monthly.
Telephone Service
Digital: Operational
Fee: $49.99 monthly
Miles of Plant: 5.0 (coaxial); None (fiber optic). Homes passed: 380.
Vice President & General Manager: Sean O'Donnell. Manager: Patty Faloon. Technical Operations Manager: Doug Sappington.
Ownership: Bresnan Communications Inc. (MSO). Sale pends to Cablevision Systems Corp.

CHARLO—Formerly served by KLiP Interactive. No longer in operation. ICA: MT0103.

CHESTER—KLiP Interactive, 455 Gees Mill Business Court, Conyers, GA 30013. Phones: 800-388-6577; 678-727-7100. Fax: 678-727-7002. E-mail: jsheehan@klipia.com. Web Site: http://www.klipia.com. ICA: MT0054.
TV Market Ranking: Outside TV Markets (CHESTER). Franchise award date: N.A. Franchise expiration date: N.A. Began: August 1, 1986.
Channel capacity: 45 (not 2-way capable). Channels available but not in use: 17.
Basic Service
Subscribers: 110.
Programming (received off-air): KFBB-TV (ABC, FOX) Great Falls; KRTV (CBS, CW) Great Falls; KTGF (IND) Great Falls; KUSA (NBC) Denver; KUSM-TV (PBS) Bozeman.

Programming (via satellite): ABC Family Channel; AMC; Animal Planet; Arts & Entertainment; Canadian Learning Television; Cartoon Network; CNN; Discovery Channel; Disney Channel; ESPN; ESPN 2; Fox News Channel; Fox Sports Net Rocky Mountain; HGTV; INSP; Lifetime; Nickelodeon; Spike TV; TBS Superstation; The Learning Channel; Turner Classic Movies; Turner Network TV; USA Network; WGN America.
Current originations: Educational Access.
Fee: $29.95 installation; $35.43 monthly.

Pay Service 1
Pay Units: 8.
Programming (via satellite): HBO.
Fee: $15.00 installation; $10.95 monthly.

Pay Service 2
Pay Units: N.A.
Programming (via satellite): Showtime; The Movie Channel.
Fee: $10.95 monthly (each).

Video-On-Demand: No

Internet Service
Operational: No.

Telephone Service
None

Miles of Plant: 8.0 (coaxial); None (fiber optic). Total homes in franchised area: 519.
Chief Executive Officer: Joseph A. Sheehan. General Manager East: Mark Miller. General Manager West: Vance Johnson.
Ownership: KLiP Interactive LLC (MSO).

CHINOOK—Bresnan Communications, PO Box 391, 1770 2nd St W, Havre, MT 59501. Phones: 406-265-2169; 877-273-7626. Fax: 406-265-8517. E-mail: sodonnell@bresnan.com. Web Site: http://www.bresnan.com. Also serves Blaine County (northern portion). ICA: MT0044.
TV Market Ranking: Below 100 (Blaine County (northern portion), CHINOOK). Franchise award date: July 1, 1991. Franchise expiration date: N.A. Began: February 1, 1981.
Channel capacity: N.A. Channels available but not in use: N.A.

Basic Service
Subscribers: 356.
Programming (via microwave): KFBB-TV (ABC, FOX) Great Falls; KHQ-TV (NBC) Spokane; KRTV (CBS, CW) Great Falls; KTGF (IND) Great Falls; KUSM-TV (PBS) Bozeman.
Programming (via satellite): Arts & Entertainment; CNN; C-SPAN; FX; QVC; TBS Superstation; truTV.
Current originations: Public Access.
Fee: $40.95 installation; $20.00 monthly.

Expanded Basic Service 1
Subscribers: N.A.
Programming (via satellite): ABC Family Channel; AMC; Animal Planet; BYU Television; Cartoon Network; CNBC; Country Music TV; Discovery Channel; Disney Channel; ESPN; ESPN 2; Fox News Channel; Fox Sports Net Rocky Mountain; HGTV; History Channel; Lifetime; MoviePlex; Nickelodeon; Spike TV; The Learning Channel; Turner Network TV; USA Network; Weather Channel.

Digital Basic Service
Subscribers: N.A.
Programming (via satellite): AmericanLife TV Network; BBC America; Bio; Bloomberg Television; Bravo; CBS College Sports Network; CMT Pure Country; Cooking Channel; Discovery Health Channel; Discovery Kids Channel; Discovery Military Channel; Discovery Planet Green; ESPN Classic Sports; ESPNews; FitTV; Food Network; Fox Movie Channel; Fox Reality Channel; Fox Soccer; Fuse; G4; Golf Channel; Gospel Music Channel; GSN; Hallmark Channel; Halogen Network; History Channel International; ID Investigation Discovery; Independent Film Channel; Lifetime Movie Network; MTV Hits; MTV2; National Geographic Channel; Nick Jr.; NickToons TV; Outdoor Channel; PBS Kids Sprout; RFD-TV; Science Channel; SoapNet; Speed Channel; Style Network; Syfy; TeenNick; Toon Disney; Trinity Broadcasting Network; Turner Classic Movies; TV Land; Versus; VH1 Classic; VH1 Soul.

Digital Expanded Basic Service
Subscribers: N.A.
Programming (via satellite): Fox College Sports Atlantic; Fox College Sports Central; Fox College Sports Pacific; HorseRacing TV; NFL Network.

Pay Service 1
Pay Units: 113.
Programming (via satellite): HBO.
Fee: $14.95 installation; $14.15 monthly.

Pay Service 2
Pay Units: 167.
Programming (via satellite): Encore.
Fee: $1.75 monthly.

Pay Service 3
Pay Units: 130.
Programming (via satellite): Starz.
Fee: $6.75 monthly.

Pay Service 4
Pay Units: 28.
Programming (via satellite): Showtime.
Fee: $14.15 monthly.

Digital Pay Service 1
Pay Units: N.A.
Programming (via satellite): Cinemax (multiplexed); Encore (multiplexed); Flix; HBO (multiplexed); Showtime (multiplexed); Starz (multiplexed); The Movie Channel (multiplexed).

Video-On-Demand: No

Internet Service
Operational: Yes.
Fee: $39.95 monthly.

Telephone Service
Digital: Operational
Fee: $49.99 monthly

Miles of Plant: 9.0 (coaxial); None (fiber optic). Homes passed: 820. Total homes in franchised area: 820.
Vice President & General Manager: Sean O'Donnell. Manager: Patty Faloon. Chief Technician: Jim Passon.
City fee: 4% of gross.
Ownership: Bresnan Communications Inc. (MSO). Sale pends to Cablevision Systems Corp.

CHOTEAU—3 Rivers Communications, 202 5th St S, PO Box 429, Fairfield, MT 59436. Phones: 800-796-4567; 406-467-2535. Fax: 406-467-3490. E-mail: 3rt@3rivers.net. Web Site: http://www.3rivers.net. Also serves Fairfield & Teton County. ICA: MT0034.
TV Market Ranking: Below 100 (Fairfield, Teton County (portions)); Outside TV Markets (CHOTEAU, Teton County (portions)). Franchise award date: N.A. Franchise expiration date: N.A. Began: July 1, 1979.
Channel capacity: N.A. Channels available but not in use: N.A.

Basic Service
Subscribers: 527.
Programming (received off-air): KFBB-TV (ABC, FOX) Great Falls; KRTV (CBS, CW) Great Falls; KTGF (IND) Great Falls; KUSM-TV (PBS) Bozeman; allband FM.
Programming (via satellite): C-SPAN; C-SPAN 2; FX; Lifetime; QVC; TBS Superstation; The Learning Channel.
Fee: $44.95 installation; $20.00 monthly.

Expanded Basic Service 1
Subscribers: 289.
Programming (via satellite): ABC Family Channel; Altitude Sports & Entertainment; AMC; Animal Planet; Arts & Entertainment; Cartoon Network; CNBC; CNN; Comedy Central; Country Music TV; Discovery Channel; Disney Channel; E! Entertainment Television; ESPN; ESPN 2; Food Network; Fox News Channel; Fox Sports Net Rocky Mountain; Hallmark Channel; Headline News; HGTV; INSP; MoviePlex; MSNBC; MTV; Nickelodeon; Spike TV; Travel Channel; truTV; Turner Network TV; TV Guide Network; USA Network; VH1; Weather Channel.
Fee: $28.99 monthly.

Digital Basic Service
Subscribers: 121.
Programming (via satellite): AmericanLife TV Network; BBC America; BET Networks; Bio; Bloomberg Television; Bravo; CBS College Sports Network; CMT Pure Country; Discovery Health Channel; Discovery Kids Channel; Discovery Military Channel; Discovery Planet Green; DMX Music; ESPN Classic Sports; ESPNews; FitTV; Fox Movie Channel; Fox Soccer; Fuse; G4; Golf Channel; GSN; History Channel; History Channel International; ID Investigation Discovery; Independent Film Channel; Lifetime Movie Network; MTV Hits; MTV2; National Geographic Channel; Nick Jr.; NickToons TV; Outdoor Channel; PBS Kids Sprout; RFD-TV; Science Channel; SoapNet; Speed Channel; Style Network; Syfy; TeenNick; Toon Disney; Trinity Broadcasting Network; Turner Classic Movies; TV Land; Versus; VH1 Classic; VH1 Soul.

Digital Pay Service 1
Pay Units: N.A.
Programming (via satellite): Encore (multiplexed); HBO (multiplexed); Showtime (multiplexed); Starz (multiplexed); The Movie Channel.

Video-On-Demand: No

Internet Service
Operational: No, DSL & dialup.

Telephone Service
None

Miles of Plant: 16.0 (coaxial); None (fiber optic). Homes passed: 1,500.
General Manager: Steven Krogue. Plant & Facilities Director: Mike Henning. Sales & Marketing Director: Terry Noyd. Customer Operations Director: Sandi Oveson.
City fee: None.
Ownership: 3 Rivers Telephone Cooperative Inc. (MSO).

CIRCLE—Mid-Rivers Communications, PO Box 280, 904 C Ave, Circle, MT 59215. Phone: 406-485-3301. Fax: 406-485-2924. E-mail: mrtc@midrivers.com. Web Site: http://www.midrivers.com. ICA: MT0096.
TV Market Ranking: Outside TV Markets (CIRCLE). Franchise award date: N.A. Franchise expiration date: N.A. Began: January 1, 1984.
Channel capacity: N.A. Channels available but not in use: N.A.

Basic Service
Subscribers: 199.
Programming (received off-air): KUMV-TV (NBC) Williston; KWSE (PBS) Williston; KXGN-TV (CBS, NBC) Glendive.
Programming (via microwave): KMGH-TV (ABC) Denver.
Programming (via satellite): ABC Family Channel; AMC; CNN; Country Music TV; Discovery Channel; Disney Channel; ESPN; Headline News; History Channel; Lifetime; Outdoor Channel; QVC; Spike TV; Syfy; TBS Superstation; Travel Channel; Turner Network TV; WGN America.
Fee: $19.50 monthly.

Pay Service 1
Pay Units: 66.
Programming (via satellite): HBO; The Movie Channel.
Fee: $8.00 monthly (The Movie Channel), $10.00 monthly (HBO).

Internet Service
Operational: No.

Telephone Service
None

Miles of Plant: 6.0 (coaxial); None (fiber optic). Homes passed: 250.
General Manager: Gerry Anderson. Chief Technician: Mike Sokolosky. Customer Service Manager: Deb Wagner.
Ownership: Mid-Rivers Telephone Cooperative Inc. (MSO).

COLSTRIP—Cable Montana, 222 W 1st St, Laurel, MT 59044. Phones: 308-236-1412 (Kearney, NE corporate office); 406-628-6336. Fax: 406-628-8181. Web Site: http://www.cablemt.net. ICA: MT0110.
TV Market Ranking: Outside TV Markets (COLSTRIP). Franchise award date: N.A. Franchise expiration date: N.A. Began: January 1, 1981.
Channel capacity: N.A. Channels available but not in use: N.A.

Basic Service
Subscribers: 300.
Programming (received off-air): KBZK (CBS) Bozeman; KSVI (ABC) Billings; KTVQ (CBS, CW) Billings; KULR-TV (NBC) Billings; KUSM-TV (PBS) Bozeman.
Programming (via satellite): ABC Family Channel; AMC; Animal Planet; Arts & Entertainment; Bloomberg Television; CNN; Country Music TV; C-SPAN; Discovery Channel; Disney Channel; ESPN; Home Shopping Network; MTV; Nickelodeon; Outdoor Channel; QVC; TBS Superstation; Turner Classic Movies; Turner Network TV; USA Network; VH1; WGN America.
Fee: $23.00 monthly.

Expanded Basic Service 1
Subscribers: 186.
Programming (via satellite): Headline News; INSP; Spike TV; Syfy; The Learning Channel.
Fee: $30.00 monthly.

Pay Service 1
Pay Units: 20.
Programming (via satellite): HBO.
Fee: $13.00 monthly.

Pay Service 2
Pay Units: 20.
Programming (via satellite): Starz.
Fee: $9.00 monthly.

Video-On-Demand: No

Internet Service
Operational: Yes.
Fee: $24.95 installation; $19.95 monthly.

Telephone Service
Digital: Operational

Miles of Plant: 20.0 (coaxial); None (fiber optic).
Manager: Doug Lane. Operations Manager: Stuart Gilbertson.
Ownership: USA Companies (MSO).

COLUMBUS—Cable Montana. Now served by LAUREL, MT [MT0023]. ICA: MT0048.

CONRAD—3 Rivers Communications, 202 5th St S, PO Box 429, Fairfield, MT 59436. Phones: 800-796-4567; 406-467-2535. Fax: 406-467-3490. E-mail: 3rt@3rivers.net. Web Site: http://www.3rivers.net. Also serves Pondera County. ICA: MT0031.

TV Market Ranking: Outside TV Markets (CONRAD, Pondera County). Franchise award date: N.A. Franchise expiration date: N.A. Began: June 1, 1979.

Channel capacity: N.A. Channels available but not in use: N.A.

Basic Service

Subscribers: 532.

Programming (received off-air): KFBB-TV (ABC, FOX) Great Falls; KRTV (CBS, CW) Great Falls; KTGF (IND) Great Falls; KUSM-TV (PBS) Bozeman.

Programming (via satellite): CW+; Global Village Network; Home Shopping Network; ION Television; Lifetime; QVC; TBS Superstation; TV Guide Network.

Fee: $44.95 installation; $20.00 monthly.

Expanded Basic Service 1

Subscribers: 525.

Programming (via satellite): ABC Family Channel; Altitude Sports & Entertainment; AMC; Animal Planet; Arts & Entertainment; Cartoon Network; CNBC; CNN; Comedy Central; Country Music TV; C-SPAN; Discovery Channel; Disney Channel; E! Entertainment Television; ESPN; ESPN 2; Food Network; Fox News Channel; Fox Sports Net Rocky Mountain; FX; Hallmark Channel; Headline News; HGTV; MSNBC; Nickelodeon; Oxygen; Spike TV; The Learning Channel; The Sportsman Channel; Travel Channel; truTV; Turner Network TV; USA Network; VH1; Weather Channel.

Fee: $28.99 monthly.

Digital Basic Service

Subscribers: 141.

Programming (via satellite): AmericanLife TV Network; BBC America; Bio; Bloomberg Television; Bravo; CBS College Sports Network; CMT Pure Country; Discovery Health Channel; Discovery Kids Channel; Discovery Military Channel; Discovery Planet Green; DMX Music; ESPN Classic Sports; ESPNews; FitTV; Fox Movie Channel; Fox Soccer; Fuse; G4; Golf Channel; GSN; Halogen Network; History Channel; History Channel International; ID Investigation Discovery; Independent Film Channel; ION Television; Lifetime Movie Network; MTV Hits; MTV2; National Geographic Channel; Nick Jr.; NickToons TV; Outdoor Channel; PBS Kids Sprout; RFD-TV; Science Channel; SoapNet; Speed Channel; Style Network; Syfy; TeenNick; Toon Disney; Trinity Broadcasting Network; TV Land; Versus; VH1 Classic; VH1 Soul.

Digital Pay Service 1

Pay Units: N.A.

Programming (via satellite): Cinemax (multiplexed); Encore (multiplexed); Flix; HBO (multiplexed); Showtime (multiplexed); Starz (multiplexed); The Movie Channel (multiplexed).

Video-On-Demand: No

Pay-Per-View

Hot Choice (delivered digitally); iN DEMAND (delivered digitally); Fresh (delivered digitally).

Internet Service

Operational: No.

Telephone Service

None

Miles of Plant: 17.0 (coaxial); None (fiber optic). Homes passed: 1,415.

General Manager: Steven Krogue. Plant & Facilities Director: Mike Henning. Sales & Marketing Director: Terry Noyd. Customer Operations Director: Sandi Oveson.

City fee: $1500 annually.

Ownership: 3 Rivers Telephone Cooperative Inc. (MSO).

CROW AGENCY—Crow Cable TV, 1119 N Custer Ave, Hardin, MT 59034-0338. Phone: 406-855-7056. Also serves Crow Indian Reservation. ICA: MT0097.

TV Market Ranking: Below 100 (CROW AGENCY, Crow Indian Reservation). Franchise award date: N.A. Franchise expiration date: N.A. Began: January 1, 1964.

Channel capacity: 36 (not 2-way capable). Channels available but not in use: 4.

Basic Service

Subscribers: 220.

Programming (received off-air): KHMT (FOX) Hardin; KSVI (ABC) Billings; KTVQ (CBS, CW) Billings; KULR-TV (NBC) Billings.

Programming (via satellite): ABC Family Channel; Arts & Entertainment; CNN; Country Music TV; C-SPAN; Discovery Channel; Disney Channel; ESPN; ESPN 2; Eternal Word TV Network; History Channel; KRMA-TV (PBS) Denver; Lifetime; Nickelodeon; Spike TV; Syfy; TBS Superstation; The Learning Channel; Toon Disney; Trinity Broadcasting Network; Turner Classic Movies; Turner Network TV; USA Network; Weather Channel; WGN America.

Fee: $40.00 installation; $23.00 monthly.

Pay Service 1

Pay Units: 170.

Programming (via satellite): HBO.

Fee: $9.75 monthly.

Pay Service 2

Pay Units: 90.

Programming (via satellite): Cinemax.

Fee: $9.75 monthly.

Internet Service

Operational: No.

Telephone Service

None

Miles of Plant: 5.0 (coaxial); None (fiber optic). Homes passed: 270.

Manager: Tom Zelka.; Rose Marie Zelka.

Ownership: Tom Zelka.

CULBERTSON—KLiP Interactive, 455 Gees Mill Business Court, Conyers, GA 30013. Phones: 800-388-6577; 706-215-1385. Fax: 678-727-7002. E-mail: jsheehan@klipia.com. Web Site: http://www.klipia.com. ICA: MT0072.

TV Market Ranking: Outside TV Markets (CULBERTSON). Franchise award date: N.A. Franchise expiration date: N.A. Began: March 1, 1981.

Channel capacity: 45 (not 2-way capable). Channels available but not in use: 22.

Basic Service

Subscribers: 122.

Programming (received off-air): KUMV-TV (NBC) Williston; KWSE (PBS) Williston; KXGN-TV (CBS, NBC) Glendive; KXMD-TV (CBS) Williston.

Programming (via microwave): KMGH-TV (ABC) Denver.

Programming (via satellite): Arts & Entertainment; Cartoon Network; CNN; Discovery Channel; Disney Channel; ESPN; ESPN 2; Fox News Channel; Fox Sports Net Rocky Mountain; HGTV; INSP; KDVR (FOX) Denver; Spike TV; TBS Superstation; Turner Classic Movies; Turner Network TV; USA Network; WGN America.

Fee: $29.95 installation; $29.69 monthly.

Pay Service 1

Pay Units: 17.

Programming (via satellite): HBO.

Fee: $10.00 installation; $10.95 monthly.

Pay Service 2

Pay Units: N.A.

Programming (via satellite): Showtime; The Movie Channel.

Fee: $10.95 monthly (each).

Video-On-Demand: No

Internet Service

Operational: No.

Telephone Service

None

Miles of Plant: 7.0 (coaxial); None (fiber optic). Homes passed: 361.

Chief Executive Officer: Joseph A. Sheehan. General Manager East: Mark Miller. General Manager West: Vance Johnson.

Franchise fee: 1% of basic.

Ownership: KLiP Interactive LLC (MSO).

CUT BANK—Bresnan Communications, 2910 10th Ave S, Great Falls, MT 59405. Phones: 877-273-7626; 406-727-8881. Fax: 406-727-6433. E-mail: sodonnell@bresnan.com. Web Site: http://www.bresnan.com. Also serves Glacier County & Toole County. ICA: MT0020.

TV Market Ranking: Outside TV Markets (CUT BANK, Glacier County, Toole County). Franchise award date: N.A. Franchise expiration date: N.A. Began: July 1, 1955.

Channel capacity: N.A. Channels available but not in use: N.A.

Basic Service

Subscribers: 965.

Programming (via microwave): KFBB-TV (ABC, FOX) Great Falls; KHQ-TV (NBC) Spokane; KRTV (CBS, CW) Great Falls; KTGF (IND) Great Falls; KUSM-TV (PBS) Bozeman; KXLY-TV (ABC, MNT) Spokane.

Programming (via satellite): C-SPAN; C-SPAN 2; Home Shopping Network; QVC; TBS Superstation; TV Guide Network.

Fee: $44.95 installation; $20.00 monthly.

Expanded Basic Service 1

Subscribers: 485.

Programming (via satellite): ABC Family Channel; Altitude Sports & Entertainment; AMC; Animal Planet; Arts & Entertainment; Cartoon Network; CNBC; CNN; Comedy Central; Country Music TV; CW+; Discovery Channel; Disney Channel; E! Entertainment Television; ESPN; ESPN 2; Food Network; Fox News Channel; Fox Sports Net Rocky Mountain; FX; Hallmark Channel; Headline News; HGTV; History Channel; INSP; ION Television; Lifetime; MSNBC; MTV; Nickelodeon; Oxygen; Spike TV; Syfy; The Learning Channel; The Sportsman Channel; Travel Channel; truTV; Turner Network TV; TV Land; USA Network; VH1; Weather Channel.

Fee: $28.99 monthly.

Digital Basic Service

Subscribers: 350.

Programming (via satellite): AmericanLife TV Network; BBC America; Bio; Bloomberg Television; Bravo; CBS College Sports Network; CMT Pure Country; Discovery Health Channel; Discovery Kids Channel; Discovery Military Channel; Discovery Planet Green; DMX Music; ESPN Classic Sports; ESPNews; FitTV; Fox College Sports Atlantic; Fox College Sports Central; Fox College Sports Pacific; Fox Movie Channel; Fox Reality Channel; Fox Soccer; Fuse; G4; Golf Channel; Gospel Music Channel; Great American Country; GSN; Halogen Network; History Channel International; HorseRacing TV; ID Investigation Discovery; Independent Film Channel; ION Television; Lifetime Movie Network; MTV Hits; MTV2; National Geographic Channel; NFL Network; Nick Jr.; NickToons TV; Outdoor Channel; PBS Kids Sprout; RFD-TV; Science Channel; SoapNet; Speed Channel; Style Network; TeenNick; Toon Disney; Trinity Broadcasting Network; Versus; VH1 Classic; VH1 Soul.

Digital Pay Service 1

Pay Units: N.A.

Programming (via satellite): Cinemax (multiplexed); Encore (multiplexed); Flix; HBO (multiplexed); Showtime (multiplexed); Starz (multiplexed); The Movie Channel (multiplexed).

Video-On-Demand: No

Pay-Per-View

Hot Choice (delivered digitally); iN DEMAND; iN DEMAND (delivered digitally); Fresh (delivered digitally).

Internet Service

Operational: Yes.

Subscribers: 411.

Broadband Service: Bresnan OnLine.

Fee: $39.95 monthly.

Telephone Service

Digital: Operational

Fee: $49.99 monthly

Miles of Plant: 30.0 (coaxial); None (fiber optic). Homes passed: 2,202.

Vice President & General Manager: Sean O'Donnell. Manager: Patty Faloon. Technical Operations Manager: Doug Sappington.

City fee: None.

Ownership: Bresnan Communications Inc. (MSO). Sale pends to Cablevision Systems Corp.

DARBY—KLiP Interactive, 455 Gees Mill Business Court, Conyers, GA 30013. Phones: 800-388-6577; 678-727-7100. Fax: 678-727-7002. E-mail: jsheehan@klipia.com. Web Site: http://www.klipia.com. ICA: MT0085.

TV Market Ranking: Outside TV Markets (DARBY TWP.). Franchise award date: N.A. Franchise expiration date: N.A. Began: November 1, 1981.

Channel capacity: 40 (not 2-way capable). Channels available but not in use: 10.

Basic Service

Subscribers: 60.

Programming (received off-air): KECI-TV (NBC) Missoula; KMGH-TV (ABC) Denver; KPAX-TV (CBS, CW) Missoula.

Programming (via satellite): ABC Family Channel; Animal Planet; Arts & Entertainment; CNN; Discovery Channel; Disney Channel; ESPN; ESPN 2; Fox News Channel; Fox Sports Net Rocky Mountain; Headline News; History Channel; KDVR (FOX) Denver; Lifetime; Nickelodeon; Outdoor Channel; Spike TV; TBS Superstation; The Learning Channel; Turner Classic Movies; Turner Network TV; USA Network; VH1; Weather Channel; WGN America.

Current originations: Educational Access.

Fee: $29.95 installation; $36.49 monthly.

Pay Service 1

Pay Units: 3.

Programming (via satellite): HBO.

Fee: $10.95 monthly.

Pay Service 2

Pay Units: 1.

Programming (via satellite): Showtime.

Fee: $10.95 monthly.

Pay Service 3

Pay Units: N.A.

Programming (via satellite): The Movie Channel.

Fee: $10.95 monthly.

Video-On-Demand: No

Internet Service

Operational: No.

Telephone Service

None

Miles of Plant: 4.0 (coaxial); None (fiber optic). Homes passed: 79.

Chief Executive Officer: Joseph A. Sheehan. General Manager East: Mark Miller. General Manager West: Vance Johnson.
Ownership: KLiP Interactive LLC (MSO).

DEER LODGE—Bresnan Communications, 201 E Front St, Butte, MT 59701-5203. Phones: 406-782-9383; 877-273-7626 (Customer service). Fax: 406-782-9020. Web Site: http://www.bresnan.com. Also serves Powell County. ICA: MT0025.
TV Market Ranking: Below 100 (Powell County (portions)); Outside TV Markets (DEER LODGE, Powell County (portions)). Franchise award date: N.A. Franchise expiration date: N.A. Began: December 1, 1966.
Channel capacity: N.A. Channels available but not in use: N.A.
Basic Service
Subscribers: 974.
Programming (received off-air): KDVR (FOX) Denver; KMGH-TV (ABC) Denver.
Programming (via microwave): KTVM-TV (NBC) Butte; KUSM-TV (PBS) Bozeman; KXLF-TV (CBS, CW) Butte.
Programming (via satellite): C-SPAN; C-SPAN 2; CW+; Eternal Word TV Network; Home Shopping Network; Lifetime; QVC; TBS Superstation; TV Guide Network.
Fee: $60.00 installation; $20.00 monthly; $40.00 additional installation.
Expanded Basic Service 1
Subscribers: 935.
Programming (via satellite): ABC Family Channel; Altitude Sports & Entertainment; AMC; Animal Planet; Arts & Entertainment; Cartoon Network; CNBC; CNN; Comedy Central; Country Music TV; Discovery Channel; Disney Channel; E! Entertainment Television; ESPN; ESPN 2; Food Network; Fox News Channel; Fox Sports Net Rocky Mountain; FX; Hallmark Channel; Headline News; HGTV; History Channel; INSP; ION Television; MSNBC; MTV; Nickelodeon; Oxygen; Spike TV; Syfy; The Learning Channel; Travel Channel; truTV; Turner Classic Movies; Turner Network TV; TV Land; USA Network; VH1; Weather Channel.
Fee: $48.99 monthly.
Digital Basic Service
Subscribers: 312.
Programming (via satellite): AmericanLife TV Network; Animal Planet HD; Arts & Entertainment HD; BBC America; Bio; Bloomberg Television; Bravo; CBS College Sports Network; CMT Pure Country; Cooking Channel; Current; Discovery HD Theater; Discovery Health Channel; Discovery Kids Channel; Discovery Military Channel; Discovery Planet Green; DMX Music; Do-It-Yourself; ESPN Classic Sports; ESPNews; FitTV; Food Network HD; Fox Movie Channel; Fox Reality Channel; Fox Soccer; Fuse; G4; Golf Channel; Gospel Music Channel; GSN; Halogen Network; HGTV HD; History Channel HD; History Channel International; ID Investigation Discovery; Independent Film Channel; Lifetime Movie Network; MTV Hits; MTV Jams; MTV Tres; MTV2; National Geographic Channel; National Geographic Channel HD Network; NFL Network; Nick Jr.; Nick Too; NickToons TV; Outdoor Channel; PBS Kids Sprout; RFD-TV; Science Channel; Science Channel HD; SoapNet; Speed Channel; Style Network; TeenNick; The Sportsman Channel; Toon Disney; Trinity Broadcasting Network; Universal HD; Versus; VH1 Classic; VH1 Soul.
Fee: $66.58 monthly.
Digital Pay Service 1
Pay Units: N.A.
Programming (via satellite): Cinemax (multiplexed); Encore (multiplexed); Flix; HBO (multiplexed); HBO HD; Showtime (multiplexed); Starz (multiplexed); Starz HDTV; The Movie Channel (multiplexed).
Video-On-Demand: No
Pay-Per-View
iN DEMAND (delivered digitally); Fox College Sports Atlantic (delivered digitally); Fox College Sports Central (delivered digitally); Fox College Sports Pacific (delivered digitally); HorseRacing TV (delivered digitally).
Internet Service
Operational: Yes.
Subscribers: 208.
Broadband Service: Bresnan OnLine.
Fee: $39.95 monthly.
Telephone Service
Digital: Operational
Fee: $49.99 monthly
Miles of Plant: 18.0 (coaxial); 2.0 (fiber optic). Homes passed: 1,988.
General Manager: Mike Oswald. Chief Technician: Todd Hawke.
City fee: $80 annually.
Ownership: Bresnan Communications Inc. (MSO). Sale pends to Cablevision Systems Corp.

DILLON—Bresnan Communications, 201 E Front St, Butte, MT 59701-5203. Phones: 877-273-7626 (Customer service); 406-782-9383. Fax: 406-782-9020. Web Site: http://www.bresnan.com. Also serves Beaverhead County (portions). ICA: MT0019.
TV Market Ranking: Below 100 (Beaverhead County (portions)); Outside TV Markets (Beaverhead County (portions), DILLON). Franchise award date: N.A. Franchise expiration date: N.A. Began: January 1, 1961.
Channel capacity: N.A. Channels available but not in use: N.A.
Basic Service
Subscribers: 1,360.
Programming (received off-air): KDVR (FOX) Denver; KMGH-TV (ABC) Denver; KTVM-TV (NBC) Butte; KXLF-TV (CBS, CW) Butte.
Programming (via microwave): KUSM-TV (PBS) Bozeman.
Programming (via satellite): C-SPAN; C-SPAN 2; CW+; Eternal Word TV Network; Home Shopping Network; Lifetime; QVC; TBS Superstation; TV Guide Network.
Fee: $60.00 installation; $20.00 monthly; $1.50 converter; $40.00 additional installation.
Expanded Basic Service 1
Subscribers: 1,305.
Programming (via satellite): ABC Family Channel; Altitude Sports & Entertainment; AMC; Animal Planet; Arts & Entertainment; Cartoon Network; CNBC; CNN; Comedy Central; Country Music TV; Discovery Channel; Disney Channel; E! Entertainment Television; ESPN; ESPN 2; Food Network; Fox News Channel; Fox Sports Net Rocky Mountain; FX; Hallmark Channel; Headline News; HGTV; History Channel; INSP; ION Television; MSNBC; MTV; Nickelodeon; Oxygen; Spike TV; Syfy; The Learning Channel; Travel Channel; truTV; Turner Classic Movies; Turner Network TV; TV Land; USA Network; VH1; Weather Channel.
Fee: $48.99 monthly.
Digital Basic Service
Subscribers: 413.
Programming (via satellite): ABC Family HD; AmericanLife TV Network; Animal Planet HD; Arts & Entertainment HD; BBC America; Bio; Bloomberg Television; Bravo; CBS College Sports Network; CMT Pure Country; Cooking Channel; Discovery Channel HD; Discovery HD Theater; Discovery Health Channel; Discovery Kids Channel; Discovery Planet Green; Disney Channel HD; DMX Music; Do-It-Yourself; ESPN Classic Sports; ESPN HD; ESPNews; FitTV; Food Network HD; Fox Movie Channel; Fox Reality Channel; Fox Soccer; Fuse; G4; Golf Channel; Gospel Music Channel; GSN; Halogen Network; HGTV HD; History Channel HD; History Channel International; ID Investigation Discovery; Independent Film Channel; Lifetime Movie Network; MTV Hits; MTV Jams; MTV Tres; MTV2; National Geographic Channel; National Geographic Channel HD Network; Nick Jr.; Nick Too; NickToons TV; Outdoor Channel; PBS Kids Sprout; RFD-TV; Science Channel; Science Channel HD; SoapNet; Speed Channel; Style Network; Syfy HD; TeenNick; The Sportsman Channel; Toon Disney; Trinity Broadcasting Network; Universal HD; USA Network HD; Versus; VH1 Classic; VH1 Soul.
Fee: $66.58 monthly.
Digital Pay Service 1
Pay Units: N.A.
Programming (via satellite): Cinemax (multiplexed); Encore (multiplexed); Flix; HBO (multiplexed); HBO HD; Showtime (multiplexed); Starz (multiplexed); Starz HDTV; The Movie Channel (multiplexed).
Video-On-Demand: No
Pay-Per-View
iN DEMAND (delivered digitally); NFL Network (delivered digitally); Fox College Sports Atlantic (delivered digitally); Fox College Sports Central (delivered digitally); Fox College Sports Pacific (delivered digitally); HorseRacing TV (delivered digitally).
Internet Service
Operational: Yes.
Subscribers: 301.
Fee: $39.95 monthly.
Telephone Service
Analog: Not Operational
Digital: Operational
Subscribers: 28.
Fee: $49.99 monthly
Miles of Plant: 41.0 (coaxial); 6.0 (fiber optic). Homes passed: 3,004.
General Manager: Mike Oswald. Chief Technician: Todd Hawke.
City fee: None.
Ownership: Bresnan Communications Inc. (MSO). Sale pends to Cablevision Systems Corp.

DRUMMOND—Drummond Cable TV, PO Box 687, Cowley, WY 82420-0687. Phone: 307-548-7888. ICA: MT0107.
TV Market Ranking: Outside TV Markets (DRUMMOND). Franchise award date: N.A. Franchise expiration date: N.A. Began: January 1, 1988.
Channel capacity: 25 (not 2-way capable). Channels available but not in use: N.A.
Basic Service
Subscribers: 45.
Programming (received off-air): KECI-TV (NBC) Missoula; KXLF-TV (CBS, CW) Butte.
Programming (via microwave): WJBK (FOX) Detroit; WTOL (CBS) Toledo; WTVS (PBS) Detroit; WXYZ-TV (ABC) Detroit.
Programming (via satellite): ABC Family Channel; CNN; Discovery Channel; Disney Channel; ESPN; Hallmark Channel; History Channel; Spike TV; TBS Superstation; The Learning Channel; Turner Network TV; USA Network.
Fee: $35.00 installation; $21.95 monthly.
Pay Service 1
Pay Units: 10.
Programming (via satellite): HBO.
Fee: $10.50 monthly.
Internet Service
Operational: No.
Telephone Service
None
Miles of Plant: 2.0 (coaxial); None (fiber optic).
Manager: Jerri Townsend. Chief Technician: Tim Townsend.
Ownership: Cowley Telecable Inc. (MSO).

DUTTON—KLiP Interactive, 455 Gees Mill Business Court, Conyers, GA 30013. Phones: 800-388-6577; 678-727-7100. Fax: 678-727-7002. E-mail: jsheehan@klipia.com. Web Site: http://www.klipia.com. ICA: MT0089.
TV Market Ranking: Below 100 (DUTTON). Franchise award date: N.A. Franchise expiration date: N.A. Began: June 1, 1986.
Channel capacity: 45 (not 2-way capable). Channels available but not in use: 24.
Basic Service
Subscribers: 22.
Programming (received off-air): KFBB-TV (ABC, FOX) Great Falls; KRTV (CBS, CW) Great Falls; KTGF (IND) Great Falls.
Programming (via satellite): ABC Family Channel; Arts & Entertainment; Cartoon Network; CNN; Country Music TV; Discovery Channel; Disney Channel; ESPN; ESPN 2; HGTV; KDVR (FOX) Denver; KUSA (NBC) Denver; Spike TV; TBS Superstation; Travel Channel; Turner Classic Movies; Turner Network TV; USA Network; WGN America.
Fee: $29.95 installation; $31.45 monthly.
Pay Service 1
Pay Units: 1.
Programming (via satellite): HBO; Showtime; The Movie Channel.
Fee: $15.00 installation; $10.95 monthly (each).
Video-On-Demand: No
Internet Service
Operational: No.
Telephone Service
None
Miles of Plant: 4.0 (coaxial); None (fiber optic). Homes passed: 230.
Chief Executive Officer: Joseph A. Sheehan. General Manager East: Mark Miller. General Manager West: Vance Johnson.
City fee: 3% of basic plus $25.00 per year.
Ownership: KLiP Interactive LLC (MSO).

EKALAKA—Mid-Rivers Communications, PO Box 280, 904 C Ave, Circle, MT 59215. Phone: 406-485-3301. Fax: 406-485-2924. E-mail: mrtc@midrivers.com. Web Site: http://www.midrivers.com. ICA: MT0098.
TV Market Ranking: Outside TV Markets (EKALAKA). Franchise award date: N.A. Franchise expiration date: N.A. Began: June 1, 1982.
Channel capacity: N.A. Channels available but not in use: N.A.
Basic Service
Subscribers: 108.
Programming (received off-air): KCNC-TV (CBS) Denver; KEVN-TV (FOX) Rapid City; KOTA-TV (ABC) Rapid City; KUSA (NBC) Denver; KUSM-TV (PBS) Bozeman; KXGN-TV (CBS, NBC) Glendive.
Programming (via microwave): KUSA (NBC) Denver.

Programming (via satellite): ABC Family Channel; AMC; Animal Planet; CNBC; CNN; Country Music TV; C-SPAN; CW+; Discovery Channel; Disney Channel; ESPN; ESPN 2; Fox News Channel; FX; Great American Country; Hallmark Channel; Headline News; HGTV; History Channel; Lifetime; Outdoor Channel; QVC; RFD-TV; Spike TV; Syfy; TBS Superstation; Travel Channel; Turner Network TV; TV Land; Weather Channel; WGN America.
Fee: $20.00 monthly.

Pay Service 1
Pay Units: 16.
Programming (via satellite): Cinemax; HBO.
Fee: $10.00 monthly (HBO), $8.00 monthly (Cinemax).

Internet Service
Operational: No.

Telephone Service
None

Miles of Plant: 6.0 (coaxial); None (fiber optic). Homes passed: 200. Total homes in franchised area: 300.

General Manager: Gerry Anderson. Chief Technician: Michael Sokolosky. Customer Service Manager: Deb Wagner.

Ownership: Mid-Rivers Telephone Cooperative Inc. (MSO).

ENNIS—KLiP Interactive, 455 Gees Mill Business Court, Conyers, GA 30013. Phones: 800-388-6577; 678-727-7100. Fax: 678-727-7002. E-mail: jsheehan@klipia.com. Web Site: http://www.klipia.com. ICA: MT0062.

TV Market Ranking: Outside TV Markets (ENNIS). Franchise award date: N.A. Franchise expiration date: N.A. Began: September 1, 1980.

Channel capacity: 45 (not 2-way capable). Channels available but not in use: 9.

Basic Service
Subscribers: 83.
Programming (received off-air): KTVM-TV (NBC) Butte; KUSM-TV (PBS) Bozeman; KXLF-TV (CBS, CW) Butte.
Programming (via microwave): KCNC-TV (CBS) Denver; KMGH-TV (ABC) Denver; KUSA (NBC) Denver.
Programming (via satellite): ABC Family Channel; Animal Planet; Arts & Entertainment; Cartoon Network; CNN; Discovery Channel; Disney Channel; ESPN; ESPN 2; Fox News Channel; Fox Sports Net Rocky Mountain; Headline News; HGTV; History Channel; KDVR (FOX) Denver; MTV; Nickelodeon; QVC; Spike TV; TBS Superstation; The Learning Channel; Travel Channel; Turner Classic Movies; Turner Network TV; USA Network; Versus; VH1; Weather Channel; WGN America.
Fee: $29.95 installation; $39.95 monthly.

Pay Service 1
Pay Units: 5.
Programming (via satellite): HBO.
Fee: $10.95 monthly.

Pay Service 2
Pay Units: 2.
Programming (via satellite): Showtime.
Fee: $10.95 monthly.

Pay Service 3
Pay Units: N.A.
Programming (via satellite): The Movie Channel.
Fee: $10.95 monthly.

Video-On-Demand: No

Internet Service
Operational: No.

Telephone Service
None

Miles of Plant: 7.0 (coaxial); None (fiber optic). Homes passed: 116. Total homes in franchised area: 116.

Chief Executive Officer: Joseph A. Sheehan. General Manager East: Mark Miller. General Manager West: Vance Johnson.

Ownership: KLiP Interactive LLC (MSO).

EUREKA—Tobacco Valley Communications, 300 Dewey Ave, Eureka, MT 59917-0648. Phones: 406-889-3311; 406-889-3099. Fax: 406-889-3787. ICA: MT0119.

TV Market Ranking: Outside TV Markets (EUREKA). Franchise award date: N.A. Franchise expiration date: N.A. Began: N.A.

Channel capacity: N.A. Channels available but not in use: N.A.

Basic Service
Subscribers: 560.
Programming (received off-air): KAYU-TV (FOX) Spokane; KCFW-TV (NBC) Kalispell; KHQ-TV (NBC) Spokane; KPAX-TV (CBS, CW) Missoula; KREM (CBS) Spokane; KSPS-TV (PBS) Spokane; KXLY-TV (ABC, MNT) Spokane; various Canadian stations; 4 FMs.
Programming (via satellite): ABC Family Channel; Animal Planet; Arts & Entertainment; Boomerang; Cartoon Network; CNBC; CNN; Discovery Channel; ESPN; ESPN 2; FamilyNet; Fox News Channel; Great American Country; Hallmark Channel; Headline News; History Channel; National Geographic Channel; Outdoor Channel; RFD-TV; Syfy; TBS Superstation; The Learning Channel; Turner Network TV; USA Network; WGN America.
Current originations: Government Access; Educational Access; Public Access.
Fee: $25.00 installation; $19.95 monthly.

Digital Basic Service
Subscribers: N.A.
Programming (via satellite): AmericanLife TV Network; Bio; Bloomberg Television; Bravo; Discovery Digital Networks; DMX Music; ESPN 2; ESPN Classic Sports; ESPNews; FitTV; Fox Movie Channel; Fox Soccer; G4; Golf Channel; GSN; Halogen Network; HGTV; History Channel International; Independent Film Channel; Science Channel; Sleuth; Speed Channel; Style Network; Trinity Broadcasting Network; Turner Classic Movies; Versus; WE tv.

Digital Pay Service 1
Pay Units: N.A.
Programming (via satellite): Cinemax (multiplexed); Encore (multiplexed); HBO (multiplexed); Showtime (multiplexed); Starz (multiplexed); The Movie Channel (multiplexed).

Internet Service
Operational: No, DSL only.

Telephone Service
None

Miles of Plant: 15.0 (coaxial); None (fiber optic). Homes passed: 700. Total homes in franchised area: 700.

Manager: Randy Wilson. Chief Technician: Robert Little.

Ownership: InterBel Telephone Cooperative Inc.

FAIRVIEW—Mid-Rivers Communications, PO Box 280, 904 C Ave, Circle, MT 59215. Phone: 406-485-3301. Fax: 406-485-2924. Web Site: http://www.midrivers.com. ICA: MT0059.

TV Market Ranking: Below 100 (FAIRVIEW). Franchise award date: October 12, 1988. Franchise expiration date: N.A. Began: January 1, 1982.

Channel capacity: 77 (operating 2-way). Channels available but not in use: N.A.

Basic Service
Subscribers: 315.
Programming (received off-air): KUMV-TV (NBC) Williston; KWSE (PBS) Williston; KXGN-TV (CBS, NBC) Glendive; KXMD-TV (CBS) Williston.
Programming (via satellite): ABC Family Channel; CNN; Country Music TV; C-SPAN; Disney Channel; Headline News; KMGH-TV (ABC) Denver; QVC; Spike TV; TBS Superstation; Weather Channel; WGN America.
Current originations: Government Access; Educational Access; Public Access.
Fee: $9.90 monthly.

Expanded Basic Service 1
Subscribers: N.A.
Programming (via satellite): AMC; Animal Planet; Arts & Entertainment; Cartoon Network; CNBC; Comedy Central; Discovery Channel; E! Entertainment Television; ESPN; ESPN 2; Eternal Word TV Network; FitTV; Food Network; Fox News Channel; Fox Sports Net Rocky Mountain; FX; HGTV; History Channel; Lifetime; Nickelodeon; Outdoor Channel; Speed Channel; Syfy; The Learning Channel; Travel Channel; Trinity Broadcasting Network; Turner Network TV; TV Land; USA Network; VH1.
Fee: $11.05 monthly.

Digital Basic Service
Subscribers: N.A.
Programming (via satellite): BBC America; Bio; Bloomberg Television; Bravo; Discovery Digital Networks; DMX Music; ESPN Classic Sports; ESPNews; Fox Movie Channel; Fox Soccer; Fuse; G4; GAS; Golf Channel; GSN; History Channel International; Independent Film Channel; Lifetime Movie Network; Lime; MTV Networks Digital Suite; National Geographic Channel; Nick Jr.; NickToons TV; Style Network; Toon Disney; Trinity Broadcasting Network; Versus; WE tv.

Pay Service 1
Pay Units: 68.
Programming (via satellite): Cinemax; HBO; Showtime; The Movie Channel.
Fee: $8.00 monthly (Cinemax, TMC or Showtime), $10.00 monthly (HBO).

Digital Pay Service 1
Pay Units: N.A.
Programming (via satellite): Cinemax (multiplexed); Encore (multiplexed); Flix; HBO (multiplexed); Showtime (multiplexed); Starz (multiplexed); The Movie Channel (multiplexed).

Video-On-Demand: No

Pay-Per-View
NBA League Pass (delivered digitally); iN DEMAND (delivered digitally); Barker (delivered digitally).

Internet Service
Operational: Yes.
Broadband Service: MegaSpeed.
Fee: $25.00 installation; $49.95 monthly; $150.00 modem purchase.

Telephone Service
None

Miles of Plant: 9.0 (coaxial); None (fiber optic). Homes passed: 488.

General Manager: Gerry Anderson. Chief Technician: Mike Sokolosky. Customer Service Manager: Deb Wagner.

Ownership: Mid-Rivers Telephone Cooperative Inc. (MSO).

FORSYTH—Cable Montana, 222 W 1st St, Laurel, MT 59044. Phones: 308-236-1512 (Kearney, NE corporate office); 800-628-6060; 406-628-6336. Fax: 406-628-8181. Web Site: http://www.cablemt.net. ICA: MT0036.

TV Market Ranking: Outside TV Markets (FORSYTH). Franchise award date: N.A. Franchise expiration date: N.A. Began: December 1, 1975.

Channel capacity: N.A. Channels available but not in use: N.A.

Basic Service
Subscribers: 409.
Programming (received off-air): KHMT (FOX) Hardin; KSVI (ABC) Billings; KTVQ (CBS, CW) Billings; KULR-TV (NBC) Billings; KUSM-TV (PBS) Bozeman.
Programming (via satellite): ABC Family Channel; Arts & Entertainment; CNBC; CW+; Outdoor Channel; QVC; Spike TV; TBS Superstation; The Learning Channel; TV Guide Network; Weather Channel; WGN.
Fee: $24.95 installation; $21.95 monthly.

Expanded Basic Service 1
Subscribers: N.A.
Programming (via satellite): Altitude Sports & Entertainment; AMC; Animal Planet; Cartoon Network; CNN; Country Music TV; Discovery Channel; E! Entertainment Television; ESPN; ESPN 2; ESPNews; Food Network; Fox News Channel; Fox Sports Net; FX; Hallmark Channel; Headline News; HGTV; History Channel; Lifetime; MSNBC; MTV; Nickelodeon; Syfy; Turner Network TV; TV Land; USA Network; VH1.
Fee: $18.04 monthly.

Digital Basic Service
Subscribers: N.A.
Programming (via satellite): Alterna'TV; BBC America; Bio; Black Family Channel; Bloomberg Television; CMT Pure Country; Current; Discovery Health Channel; Discovery Kids Channel; Discovery Military Channel; Discovery Planet Green; DMX Music; ESPN 2; ESPN Classic Sports; ESPNews; FitTV; Fox College Sports Atlantic; Fox College Sports Central; Fox College Sports Pacific; Fox Movie Channel; G4; Golf Channel; GSN; Halogen Network; History Channel; History Channel International; ID Investigation Discovery; Lifetime Movie Network; MTV Hits; MTV2; National Geographic Channel; Nick Jr.; Ovation; Science Channel; ShopNBC; Sleuth; Speed Channel; Style Network; TeenNick; Trinity Broadcasting Network; Versus; VH1 Classic; VH1 Soul; WE tv.
Fee: $13.00 monthly.

Digital Pay Service 1
Pay Units: N.A.
Programming (via satellite): Cinemax (multiplexed); Encore (multiplexed); Flix; HBO (multiplexed); Showtime (multiplexed); Starz (multiplexed); The Movie Channel (multiplexed).
Fee: $13.00 monthly (HBO, Cinemax, Starz/Encore or Showtime/TMC/Flix).

Video-On-Demand: No

Pay-Per-View
iN DEMAND (delivered digitally); Hot Choice (delivered digitally); Playboy TV (delivered digitally); Fresh (delivered digitally); Shorteez (delivered digitally); Club Jenna (delivered digitally).

Internet Service
Operational: Yes.
Broadband Service: Cable Montana.
Fee: $35.95 monthly.

Telephone Service
None

Miles of Plant: 20.0 (coaxial); None (fiber optic). Homes passed: 850.

Manager: Doug Lane. Operations Manager: Stuart Gilbertson.
Ownership: USA Companies (MSO).

FORT BENTON—Bresnan Communications, 2910 10th Ave S, Great Falls, MT 59405. Phones: 877-273-7626; 406-727-8881. Fax: 406-727-6433. E-mail: sodonnell@bresnan.com. Web Site: http://www.bresnan.com. ICA: MT0035.
TV Market Ranking: Outside TV Markets (FORT BENTON). Franchise award date: N.A. Franchise expiration date: N.A. Began: March 1, 1980.
Channel capacity: N.A. Channels available but not in use: N.A.
Basic Service
Subscribers: 392.
Programming (received off-air): KFBB-TV (ABC, FOX) Great Falls; KRTV (CBS, CW) Great Falls; KTGF (IND) Great Falls; KUSM-TV (PBS) Bozeman.
Programming (via satellite): C-SPAN; FX; Home Shopping Network; Lifetime; QVC; TBS Superstation; The Learning Channel.
Fee: $44.95 installation; $20.00 monthly.
Expanded Basic Service 1
Subscribers: 390.
Programming (via satellite): ABC Family Channel; AMC; Animal Planet; Arts & Entertainment; Cartoon Network; CNBC; CNN; Comedy Central; Country Music TV; C-SPAN 2; Discovery Channel; Disney Channel; E! Entertainment Television; ESPN; ESPN 2; Food Network; Fox News Channel; Fox Sports Net Rocky Mountain; Hallmark Channel; Headline News; HGTV; History Channel; MSNBC; MTV; Nickelodeon; Oxygen; Spike TV; Travel Channel; truTV; Turner Classic Movies; Turner Network TV; TV Land; USA Network; VH1; Weather Channel.
Fee: $28.99 monthly.
Digital Basic Service
Subscribers: 103.
Programming (via satellite): AmericanLife TV Network; BBC America; Bio; Bloomberg Television; Bravo; CBS College Sports Network; CMT Pure Country; Discovery Health Channel; Discovery Kids Channel; Discovery Military Channel; Discovery Planet Green; DMX Music; ESPN Classic Sports; ESPNews; FitTV; Fox Movie Channel; Fox Soccer; Fuse; G4; Golf Channel; GSN; Halogen Network; History Channel International; ID Investigation Discovery; Independent Film Channel; Lifetime Movie Network; MTV Hits; MTV2; National Geographic Channel; Nick Jr.; NickToons TV; Outdoor Channel; PBS Kids Channel; RFD-TV; Science Channel; SoapNet; Speed Channel; Style Network; Syfy; TeenNick; Toon Disney; Trinity Broadcasting Network; Versus; VH1 Classic; VH1 Soul.
Fee: $66.58 monthly.
Digital Pay Service 1
Pay Units: N.A.
Programming (via satellite): Cinemax (multiplexed); Encore (multiplexed); Flix; HBO (multiplexed); Showtime (multiplexed); Starz (multiplexed); The Movie Channel (multiplexed).
Video-On-Demand: No
Internet Service
Operational: Yes.
Fee: $39.95 monthly.
Telephone Service
Analog: Not Operational
Digital: Operational
Fee: $49.99 monthly
Miles of Plant: 12.0 (coaxial); None (fiber optic). Homes passed: 880. Total homes in franchised area: 880.
Vice President & General Manager: Sean O'Donnell. Manager: Patty Faloon. Technical Operations Manager: Doug Sappington.
City fee: $50 annually.
Ownership: Bresnan Communications Inc. (MSO). Sale pends to Cablevision Systems Corp.

FOUR CORNERS—Formerly served by Northwestern Communications Corp. No longer in operation. ICA: MT0111.

FROMBERG—Cable Montana, 222 W 1st St, Laurel, MT 59044. Phones: 406-628-6336; 308-236-1512 (Kearney, NE corporate office). Fax: 406-628-8181. Web Site: http://www.cablemt.net. ICA: MT0088.
TV Market Ranking: Below 100 (FROMBERG). Franchise award date: January 1, 1983. Franchise expiration date: N.A. Began: January 1, 1983.
Channel capacity: 45 (not 2-way capable). Channels available but not in use: 15.
Basic Service
Subscribers: 78.
Programming (received off-air): KHMT (FOX) Hardin; KSVI (ABC) Billings; KTVQ (CBS, CW) Billings; KULR-TV (NBC) Billings.
Programming (via satellite): ABC Family Channel; Arts & Entertainment; Cartoon Network; CNN; Discovery Channel; Disney Channel; ESPN; HGTV; Spike TV; TBS Superstation; Turner Classic Movies; Turner Network TV; USA Network; WGN America.
Fee: $29.95 installation; $26.45 monthly.
Pay Service 1
Pay Units: 15.
Programming (via satellite): HBO.
Fee: $15.00 installation; $10.95 monthly.
Video-On-Demand: No
Internet Service
Operational: No, Dial-up only.
Telephone Service
None
Miles of Plant: 4.0 (coaxial); None (fiber optic). Homes passed: 199. Total homes in franchised area: 246.
Manager: Doug Lane. Operations Manager: Stuart Gilbertson.
City fee: None.
Ownership: USA Companies (MSO).

GARDINER—Formerly served by North Yellowstone Cable TV. No longer in operation. ICA: MT0112.

GLASGOW—Bresnan Communications, PO Box 391, 1770 2nd St W, Havre, MT 59501. Phone: 406-727-8881. Fax: 406-727-6433. E-mail: sodonnell@bresnan.com. Web Site: http://www.bresnan.com. Also serves Valley County. ICA: MT0022.
TV Market Ranking: Outside TV Markets (GLASGOW, Valley County). Franchise award date: October 1, 1993. Franchise expiration date: N.A. Began: January 1, 1961.
Channel capacity: N.A. Channels available but not in use: N.A.
Basic Service
Subscribers: N.A.
Programming (via microwave): KFBB-TV (ABC, FOX) Great Falls; KRTV (CBS, CW) Great Falls; KTGF (IND) Great Falls; KUSM-TV (PBS) Bozeman.
Programming (via satellite): Arts & Entertainment; C-SPAN; C-SPAN 2; CW+; Home Shopping Network; QVC; TBS Superstation; truTV; TV Guide Network.
Fee: $40.95 installation; $20.00 monthly.
Expanded Basic Service 1
Subscribers: N.A.
Programming (via satellite): ABC Family Channel; Altitude Sports & Entertainment; AMC; Animal Planet; Cartoon Network; CNBC; CNN; Comedy Central; Country Music TV; Discovery Channel; Disney Channel; E! Entertainment Television; ESPN; ESPN 2; Eternal Word TV Network; Food Network; Fox News Channel; Fox Sports Net Rocky Mountain; FX; Hallmark Channel; Headline News; INSP; Lifetime; MSNBC; MTV; Nickelodeon; Oxygen; Spike TV; The Learning Channel; Travel Channel; Turner Network TV; USA Network; VH1; Weather Channel.
Fee: $28.99 monthly.
Digital Basic Service
Subscribers: 264.
Programming (via satellite): AmericanLife TV Network; BBC America; Bio; Bloomberg Television; Bravo; CBS College Sports Network; CMT Pure Country; Discovery Health Channel; Discovery Kids Channel; Discovery Military Channel; Discovery Planet Green; DMX Music; ESPN Classic Sports; ESPNews; FitTV; Fox Movie Channel; Fox Soccer; Fuse; G4; Golf Channel; GSN; Halogen Network; HGTV; History Channel; History Channel International; ID Investigation Discovery; Independent Film Channel; Lifetime Movie Network; MTV Hits; MTV2; National Geographic Channel; Nick Jr.; NickToons TV; Outdoor Channel; PBS Kids Channel; RFD-TV; Science Channel; SoapNet; Speed Channel; Style Network; Syfy; TeenNick; Toon Disney; Trinity Broadcasting Network; Turner Classic Movies; TV Land; Versus; VH1 Classic; VH1 Soul.
Fee: $6.00 monthly.
Digital Pay Service 1
Pay Units: N.A.
Programming (via satellite): Cinemax (multiplexed); Encore (multiplexed); Flix; HBO (multiplexed); Showtime (multiplexed); Starz (multiplexed); The Movie Channel (multiplexed).
Video-On-Demand: No
Pay-Per-View
iN DEMAND (delivered digitally).
Internet Service
Operational: Yes.
Broadband Service: Bresnan OnLine.
Fee: $52.95 monthly.
Telephone Service
Digital: Operational
Fee: $49.99 monthly
Miles of Plant: 24.0 (coaxial); 3.0 (fiber optic).
Vice President & General Manager: Sean O'Donnell. Manager: Patty Faloon. Chief Technician: Jim Passon.
Franchise fee: 3% of gross.
Ownership: Bresnan Communications Inc. (MSO). Sale pends to Cablevision Systems Corp.

GLENDIVE—Mid-Rivers Communications, PO Box 280, 904 C Ave, Circle, MT 59215. Phones: 406-377-3336; 406-238-7700; 406-238-7706. Fax: 406-377-7400. Web Site: http://www.midrivers.com. Also serves Dawson County. ICA: MT0013.
TV Market Ranking: Below 100 (Dawson County (portions), GLENDIVE); Outside TV Markets (Dawson County (portions)). Franchise award date: N.A. Franchise expiration date: N.A. Began: May 1, 1967.
Channel capacity: N.A. Channels available but not in use: N.A.
Basic Service
Subscribers: 2,662.
Programming (received off-air): KMGH-TV (ABC) Denver; KUMV-TV (NBC) Williston; KXGN-TV (CBS, NBC) Glendive.
Programming (via microwave): KDVR (FOX) Denver; KUSM-TV (PBS) Bozeman.
Programming (via satellite): ABC Family Channel; Arts & Entertainment; CNBC; CNN; C-SPAN; CW+; Discovery Channel; Headline News; Lifetime; MTV; Nickelodeon; TBS Superstation; Turner Network TV; Weather Channel; WGN America.
Fee: $60.00 installation; $9.87 monthly; $.64 converter; $40.00 additional installation.
Expanded Basic Service 1
Subscribers: 2,490.
Programming (via satellite): AMC; Animal Planet; Bravo; Cartoon Network; Comedy Central; Country Music TV; C-SPAN 2; Disney Channel; E! Entertainment Television; ESPN; ESPN 2; ESPN Classic Sports; ESPN U; Eternal Word TV Network; FitTV; Food Network; Fox News Channel; Fox Sports Net Rocky Mountain; FX; G4; Great American Country; GSN; Hallmark Channel; HGTV; History Channel; Home Shopping Network; ION Television; MSNBC; National Geographic Channel; Outdoor Channel; Oxygen; RFD-TV; Speed Channel; Spike TV; Syfy; The Learning Channel; Toon Disney; Travel Channel; Trinity Broadcasting Network; truTV; Turner Classic Movies; TV Land; USA Network; VH1.
Fee: $11.39 monthly.
Digital Basic Service
Subscribers: 445.
Programming (via satellite): Arts & Entertainment HD; BBC America; Bio; Bloomberg Television; Bravo; CMT Pure Country; Discovery Channel HD; Discovery Health Channel; Discovery Kids Channel; Discovery Military Channel; Discovery Planet Green; ESPN 2 HD; ESPN Classic Sports; ESPN HD; ESPNews; Food Network HD; Fox Movie Channel; Fox Soccer; Fuse; G4; Golf Channel; GSN; HDNet; HDNet Movies; HGTV HD; History Channel International; ID Investigation Discovery; Independent Film Channel; Lifetime Movie Network; MTV2; National Geographic Channel; National Geographic Channel HD Network; Nick Jr.; NickToons TV; Outdoor Channel 2 HD; Science Channel; Style Network; TeenNick; Toon Disney; Trinity Broadcasting Network; Turner Network TV HD; Universal HD; Versus; VH1 Classic; VH1 Soul; WE tv.
Pay Service 1
Pay Units: N.A.
Programming (via satellite): Cinemax; Encore; HBO; Showtime; Starz; The Movie Channel.
Fee: $11.95 monthly (Cinemax, HBO or Showtime).
Digital Pay Service 1
Pay Units: N.A.
Programming (via satellite): Cinemax (multiplexed); Cinemax HD; Encore (multiplexed); Flix; HBO (multiplexed); HBO HD; Showtime (multiplexed); Starz (multiplexed); The Movie Channel (multiplexed).
Video-On-Demand: No
Pay-Per-View
iN DEMAND (delivered digitally).
Internet Service
Operational: No, Both DSL & dial-up.
Telephone Service
None
Miles of Plant: 43.0 (coaxial); None (fiber optic). Homes passed: 3,339. Total homes in franchised area: 3,339.

General Manager: Gerry Anderson. Chief Technician: Mike Sokoloski. Customer Service Manager: Deb Wagner.
City fee: None.
Ownership: Mid-Rivers Telephone Cooperative Inc. (MSO).

GRANT CREEK—Bresnan Communications. Now served by MISSOULA, MT [MT0002]. ICA: MT0094.

GREAT FALLS—Bresnan Communications, 2910 10th Ave S, Great Falls, MT 59405. Phones: 877-273-7626; 406-727-8881. Fax: 406-727-6433. E-mail: sodonnell@bresnan.com. Web Site: http://www.bresnan.com. Also serves Black Eagle, Cascade County & Malmstrom AFB. ICA: MT0003.
TV Market Ranking: Below 100 (Black Eagle, Cascade County, GREAT FALLS, Malmstrom AFB). Franchise award date: N.A. Franchise expiration date: N.A. Began: June 1, 1958.
Channel capacity: N.A. Channels available but not in use: N.A.

Basic Service
Subscribers: 15,588.
Programming (received off-air): KFBB-TV (ABC, FOX) Great Falls; KRTV (CBS, CW) Great Falls; KTGF (IND) Great Falls; KUSM-TV (PBS) Bozeman; 7 FMs.
Programming (via satellite): C-SPAN; C-SPAN 2; CW+; Eternal Word TV Network; Home Shopping Network; Lifetime; QVC; TBS Superstation; TV Guide Network.
Current originations: Government Access.
Fee: $40.00 installation; $20.00 monthly; $.68 converter.

Expanded Basic Service 1
Subscribers: 15,262.
Programming (via satellite): ABC Family Channel; Altitude Sports & Entertainment; AMC; Animal Planet; Arts & Entertainment; BET Networks; Cartoon Network; CNBC; CNN; Comedy Central; Country Music TV; Discovery Channel; Disney Channel; E! Entertainment Television; ESPN; ESPN 2; ESPN Classic Sports; Food Network; Fox News Channel; Fox Sports Net Rocky Mountain; FX; Hallmark Channel; Headline News; HGTV; History Channel; INSP; ION Television; MSNBC; MTV; Nickelodeon; Oxygen; Spike TV; Syfy; The Learning Channel; Travel Channel; truTV; Turner Classic Movies; Turner Network TV; TV Land; USA Network; VH1; Weather Channel.
Fee: $28.99 monthly.

Digital Basic Service
Subscribers: 8,008.
Programming (received off-air): KRTV (CBS, CW) Great Falls.
Programming (via satellite): ABC Family HD; AmericanLife TV Network; Animal Planet HD; Arts & Entertainment HD; BBC America; Bio; Bloomberg Television; Bravo; BYU Television; CBS College Sports Network; CMT Pure Country; CNN HD; Cooking Channel; C-SPAN 3; Discovery Channel HD; Discovery HD Theater; Discovery Health Channel; Discovery Kids Channel; Discovery Military Channel; Discovery Planet Green; Disney Channel HD; DMX Music; Do-It-Yourself; ESPN 2 HD; ESPN HD; ESPNews; FitTV; Food Network HD; Fox College Sports Atlantic; Fox College Sports Central; Fox College Sports Pacific; Fox Movie Channel; Fox Reality Channel; Fox Soccer; Fuse; G4; Golf Channel; Gospel Music Channel; Great American Country; GSN; Halogen Network; HDNet; HDNet Movies; HGTV HD; History Channel HD; History Channel International; HorseRacing TV; ID Investigation Discovery; Independent Film Channel; ION Life; ION Television; Lifetime Movie Network; Lifetime Movie Network HD; MTV Hits; MTV Jams; MTV Tres; MTV2; National Geographic Channel; National Geographic Channel HD Network; NFL Network; NFL Network HD; NHL Network; Nick Jr.; Nick Too; NickToons TV; Outdoor Channel; Outdoor Channel 2 HD; PBS Kids Sprout; Qubo; RFD-TV; Science Channel; Science Channel HD; SoapNet; Speed Channel; Speed HD; Style Network; Syfy HD; TBS in HD; TeenNick; The Sportsman Channel; TLC HD; Toon Disney; Trinity Broadcasting Network; Turner Network TV HD; Universal HD; USA Network HD; Versus; Versus HD; VH1 Classic; VH1 Soul; Weather Channel HD.
Fee: $8.00 monthly.

Digital Pay Service 1
Pay Units: N.A.
Programming (via satellite): Cinemax (multiplexed); Cinemax HD; Encore (multiplexed); Flix; HBO (multiplexed); HBO HD; HBO On Demand; Showtime (multiplexed); Showtime HD; Showtime On Demand; Starz (multiplexed); Starz HDTV; Starz On Demand; The Movie Channel (multiplexed); The Movie Channel HD.

Video-On-Demand: Yes

Pay-Per-View
Hot Choice (delivered digitally); iN DEMAND (delivered digitally); Playboy TV (delivered digitally); Fresh (delivered digitally); ESPN (delivered digitally); MLB Extra Innings (delivered digitally); NHL Center Ice (delivered digitally).

Internet Service
Operational: Yes. Began: March 1, 2000.
Subscribers: 8,425.
Broadband Service: Bresnan OnLine.
Fee: $99.95 installation; $52.95 monthly; $10.00 modem lease.

Telephone Service
Analog: Not Operational
Digital: Operational
Subscribers: 3,174.
Fee: $49.99 monthly

Miles of Plant: 294.0 (coaxial); 59.0 (fiber optic). Homes passed: 31,585.
Vice President & General Manager: Sean O'Donnell. Manager: Patty Faloon. Technical Operations Manager: Doug Sappington.
City fee: 3% of gross.
Ownership: Bresnan Communications Inc. (MSO). Sale pends to Cablevision Systems Corp.

HAMILTON—Bresnan Communications, 924 S 3rd St W, Missoula, MT 59801-2340. Phone: 877-273-7626. Web Site: http://www.bresnan.com. Also serves Corvallis & Ravalli County. ICA: MT0015.
TV Market Ranking: Below 100 (Ravalli County (portions)); Outside TV Markets (Corvallis, HAMILTON, Ravalli County (portions)). Franchise award date: N.A. Franchise expiration date: N.A. Began: September 1, 1964.
Channel capacity: N.A. Channels available but not in use: N.A.

Basic Service
Subscribers: 1,412.
Programming (received off-air): KECI-TV (NBC) Missoula; KPAX-TV (CBS, CW) Missoula; KTMF (ABC, FOX) Missoula; KUFM-TV (PBS) Missoula.
Programming (via satellite): C-SPAN; C-SPAN 2; CW+; Home Shopping Network; QVC; TBS Superstation; TV Guide Network.

Current originations: Educational Access.
Fee: $44.40 installation; $48.99 monthly.

Expanded Basic Service 1
Subscribers: 1,205.
Programming (via satellite): ABC Family Channel; Altitude Sports & Entertainment; AMC; Animal Planet; Arts & Entertainment; Cartoon Network; CNBC; CNN; Comedy Central; Country Music TV; Discovery Channel; Disney Channel; E! Entertainment Television; ESPN; ESPN 2; Food Network; Fox News Channel; Fox Sports Net Rocky Mountain; FX; Great American Country; Hallmark Channel; Headline News; HGTV; History Channel; INSP; ION Television; Lifetime; MSNBC; MTV; Nickelodeon; Oxygen; Spike TV; Syfy; The Learning Channel; The Sportsman Channel; Travel Channel; truTV; Turner Classic Movies; Turner Network TV; TV Land; USA Network; VH1; Weather Channel.
Fee: $4.00 monthly.

Digital Basic Service
Subscribers: 431.
Programming (via satellite): ABC Family HD; AmericanLife TV Network; Animal Planet HD; Arts & Entertainment HD; BBC America; Bio; Bloomberg Television; Bravo; CMT Pure Country; Discovery Channel HD; Discovery HD Theater; Discovery Health Channel; Discovery Kids Channel; Discovery Military Channel; Discovery Planet Green; Disney Channel HD; DMX Music; ESPN Classic Sports; ESPN HD; ESPNews; FitTV; Food Network HD; Fox College Sports Atlantic; Fox College Sports Central; Fox College Sports Pacific; Fox Movie Channel; Fox Reality Channel; Fox Soccer; Fuse; G4; Golf Channel; Gospel Music Channel; GSN; Halogen Network; HGTV HD; History Channel HD; History Channel International; HorseTV Channel; ID Investigation Discovery; Independent Film Channel; ION Television; Lifetime Movie Network; MTV Hits; MTV2; National Geographic Channel; National Geographic Channel HD Network; NFL Network; Nick Jr.; NickToons TV; Outdoor Channel; PBS Kids Sprout; RFD-TV; Science Channel; Science Channel HD; SoapNet; Speed Channel; Style Network; Syfy HD; TeenNick; Toon Disney; Trinity Broadcasting Network; Universal HD; USA Network HD; Versus; VH1 Classic; VH1 Soul.
Fee: $5.95 monthly.

Digital Pay Service 1
Pay Units: N.A.
Programming (via satellite): Cinemax (multiplexed); Encore (multiplexed); Flix; HBO (multiplexed); HBO HD; Showtime (multiplexed); Starz (multiplexed); Starz HDTV; The Movie Channel (multiplexed).

Video-On-Demand: No

Internet Service
Operational: Yes.
Subscribers: 334.
Broadband Service: Bresnan OnLine.
Fee: $39.95 monthly.

Telephone Service
Digital: Operational
Fee: $49.99 monthly

Miles of Plant: 80.0 (coaxial); 20.0 (fiber optic). Homes passed: 4,593.
General Manager: Mike Oswald. Technical Operations Manager: Alan White.
Franchise fee: 5% of gross.
Ownership: Bresnan Communications Inc. (MSO). Sale pends to Cablevision Systems Corp.

HARDIN—Cable Montana, 222 W 1st St, Laurel, MT 59044. Phones: 800-628-6060; 406-628-6336; 308-236-1512 (Kearney, NE corporate office). Fax: 406-628-8181. Web Site: http://www.cablemt.net. ICA: MT0030.
TV Market Ranking: Below 100 (HARDIN). Franchise award date: N.A. Franchise expiration date: N.A. Began: January 1, 1968.
Channel capacity: N.A. Channels available but not in use: N.A.

Basic Service
Subscribers: 673.
Programming (received off-air): KHMT (FOX) Hardin; KRMA-TV (PBS) Denver; KSVI (ABC) Billings; KTVQ (CBS, CW) Billings; KULR-TV (NBC) Billings; KWBM (MNT) Harrison [LICENSED & SILENT].
Programming (via satellite): 3 Angels Broadcasting Network; ABC Family Channel; Arts & Entertainment; Food Network; Fox Sports Net; Hallmark Channel; Headline News; QVC; TBS Superstation; TV Guide Network; Weather Channel; WGN.
Fee: $24.95 installation; $21.95 monthly.

Expanded Basic Service 1
Subscribers: N.A.
Programming (via satellite): Altitude Sports & Entertainment; AMC; Animal Planet; Cartoon Network; CNBC; CNN; Country Music TV; Discovery Channel; E! Entertainment Television; ESPN; ESPN 2; ESPNews; Fox News Channel; FX; G4; HGTV; History Channel; Lifetime; MSNBC; MTV; Nickelodeon; Outdoor Channel; Spike TV; Syfy; The Learning Channel; Trinity Broadcasting Network; Turner Network TV; TV Land; USA Network; VH1.
Fee: $18.04 monthly.

Digital Basic Service
Subscribers: N.A.
Programming (via satellite): AmericanLife TV Network; BBC America; Bio; Black Family Channel; Bloomberg Television; CMT Pure Country; Current; Daystar TV Network; Discovery Health Channel; Discovery Kids Channel; Discovery Military Channel; Discovery Planet Green; DMX Music; ESPN 2; ESPN Classic Sports; ESPNews; FitTV; Fox College Sports Atlantic; Fox College Sports Central; Fox College Sports Pacific; Fox Movie Channel; G4; Golf Channel; GSN; Halogen Network; History Channel; History Channel International; Lifetime Movie Network; MTV Hits; MTV2; National Geographic Channel; Nick Jr.; Outdoor Channel; Ovation; Science Channel; ShopNBC; Sleuth; Speed Channel; Style Network; TeenNick; Trinity Broadcasting Network; Versus; VH1 Classic; VH1 Soul; WE tv.
Fee: $13.00 monthly.

Digital Pay Service 1
Pay Units: N.A.
Programming (via satellite): Cinemax (multiplexed); Encore (multiplexed); Flix; HBO (multiplexed); Showtime (multiplexed); Starz (multiplexed); The Movie Channel (multiplexed).
Fee: $13.00 monthly (HBO, Cinemax, Showtime/TMC/Flix or Starz/Encore).
Video-On-Demand: No
Internet Service
Operational: Yes.
Broadband Service: Cable Montana.
Fee: $35.95 monthly.
Telephone Service
Digital: Operational
Fee: $39.95 monthly
Miles of Plant: 18.0 (coaxial); None (fiber optic). Additional miles planned: 1.0 (coaxial). Homes passed: 1,326. Total homes in franchised area: 1,326.
Manager: Doug Lane. Operations Manager: Stuart Gilbertson.
City fee: None.
Ownership: USA Companies (MSO).

HARLEM—Bresnan Communications, PO Box 391, 1770 2nd St W, Havre, MT 59501. Phones: 877-273-7626; 406-727-8881. Fax: 406-727-6433. E-mail: sodonnell@bresnan.com. Web Site: http://www.bresnan.com. ICA: MT0071.
TV Market Ranking: Outside TV Markets (HARLEM). Franchise award date: January 1, 1992. Franchise expiration date: N.A. Began: July 1, 1981.
Channel capacity: 38 (operating 2-way). Channels available but not in use: None.
Basic Service
Subscribers: 163.
Programming (via microwave): KFBB-TV (ABC, FOX) Great Falls; KRTV (CBS, CW) Great Falls; KTGF (IND) Great Falls; KUSM-TV (PBS) Bozeman.
Programming (via satellite): Arts & Entertainment; CNN; Country Music TV; C-SPAN; Lifetime; QVC; TBS Superstation; truTV.
Fee: $40.95 installation; $20.00 monthly.
Expanded Basic Service 1
Subscribers: 125.
Programming (via satellite): ABC Family Channel; AMC; Animal Planet; Cartoon Network; CNBC; CNN; Comcast Sports Net Northwest; Discovery Channel; Disney Channel; E! Entertainment Television; ESPN; ESPN 2; Fox News Channel; HGTV; History Channel; Nickelodeon; Spike TV; The Learning Channel; Turner Network TV; USA Network; Weather Channel.
Fee: $28.99 monthly.
Pay Service 1
Pay Units: 73.
Programming (via satellite): HBO.
Fee: $14.15 monthly.
Pay Service 2
Pay Units: 137.
Programming (via satellite): Encore.
Fee: $1.75 monthly.
Pay Service 3
Pay Units: 104.
Programming (via satellite): Starz.
Fee: $6.75 monthly.
Pay Service 4
Pay Units: 29.
Programming (via satellite): Showtime.
Fee: $14.15 monthly.
Video-On-Demand: No
Internet Service
Operational: Yes.
Fee: $52.95 monthly.
Telephone Service
Digital: Operational
Fee: $49.99 monthly
Miles of Plant: 5.0 (coaxial); None (fiber optic). Homes passed: 435. Total homes in franchised area: 521.
Vice President & General Manager: Sean O'Donnell. Manager: Patty Faloon. Chief Technician: Jim Passon.
City fee: 4% of gross.
Ownership: Bresnan Communications Inc. (MSO). Sale pends to Cablevision Systems Corp.

HARLOWTON—Mid-Rivers Communications, PO Box 280, 904 C Ave, Circle, MT 59215. Phone: 406-485-3301. Fax: 406-485-2924. E-mail: lcedar@midrivers.com. Web Site: http://www.midrivers.com. ICA: MT0061.
TV Market Ranking: Outside TV Markets (HARLOWTON). Franchise award date: N.A. Franchise expiration date: N.A. Began: June 1, 1980.
Channel capacity: 65 (not 2-way capable). Channels available but not in use: 20.
Basic Service
Subscribers: 273.
Programming (via satellite): ABC Family Channel; AMC; Animal Planet; Arts & Entertainment; Cartoon Network; CNBC; CNN; Country Music TV; C-SPAN; Discovery Channel; Disney Channel; Do-It-Yourself; E! Entertainment Television; ESPN; ESPN 2; Food Network; Fox News Channel; Fox Sports Net Rocky Mountain; Hallmark Channel; HGTV; History Channel; Home Shopping Network; KWGN-TV (CW) Denver; Lifetime; MTV; Nickelodeon; Outdoor Channel; RFD-TV; Spike TV; Syfy; TBS Superstation; The Learning Channel; Travel Channel; Turner Classic Movies; Turner Network TV; TV Land; USA Network; VH1; WE tv; Weather Channel; WGN America.
Programming (via translator): KSVI (ABC) Billings; KTVQ (CBS, CW) Billings; KULR-TV (NBC) Billings; KUSM-TV (PBS) Bozeman.
Fee: $15.00 installation; $33.45 monthly; $3.00 converter.
Pay Service 1
Pay Units: 99.
Programming (via satellite): HBO; The Movie Channel.
Fee: $15.00 installation; $12.00 monthly.
Internet Service
Operational: No.
Telephone Service
None
Miles of Plant: 11.0 (coaxial); None (fiber optic). Homes passed: 500. Total homes in franchised area: 500.
General Manager: Gerry Anderson. Central Office Supervisor: Mike Sokoloski. Customer Service Manager: Deb Wagner.
Ownership: Mid-Rivers Telephone Cooperative Inc. (MSO).

HAVRE—Bresnan Communications, PO Box 391, 1770 2nd St W, Havre, MT 59501. Phones: 877-273-7626; 406-727-8881. Fax: 406-727-6433. E-mail: sodonnell@bresnan.com. Web Site: http://www.bresnan.com. Also serves Hill County. ICA: MT0008.
TV Market Ranking: Below 100 (HAVRE, Hill County). Franchise award date: October 3, 1988. Franchise expiration date: N.A. Began: January 1, 1954.
Channel capacity: N.A. Channels available but not in use: N.A.
Basic Service
Subscribers: 3,238.
Programming (via microwave): KFBB-TV (ABC, FOX) Great Falls; KHQ-TV (NBC) Spokane; KREM (CBS) Spokane; KRTV (CBS, CW) Great Falls; KTGF (IND) Great Falls; KUSM-TV (PBS) Bozeman; KXLY-TV (ABC, MNT) Spokane.
Programming (via satellite): C-SPAN; C-SPAN 2; CW+; Home Shopping Network; ION Television; QVC; TBS Superstation; TV Guide Network.
Fee: $40.95 installation; $20.00 monthly; $4.05 converter; $18.95 additional installation.
Expanded Basic Service 1
Subscribers: 2,500.
Programming (via satellite): ABC Family Channel; Altitude Sports & Entertainment; AMC; Animal Planet; Arts & Entertainment; Cartoon Network; CNBC; CNN; Comedy Central; Country Music TV; Discovery Channel; Disney Channel; E! Entertainment Television; ESPN; ESPN 2; Eternal Word TV Network; Food Network; Fox News Channel; Fox Sports Net Rocky Mountain; FX; Hallmark Channel; Headline News; HGTV; History Channel; INSP; Lifetime; MSNBC; MTV; Nickelodeon; Oxygen; Spike TV; Syfy; The Learning Channel; truTV; Turner Classic Movies; Turner Network TV; TV Land; USA Network; VH1; Weather Channel.
Fee: $28.99 monthly.
Digital Basic Service
Subscribers: 1,347.
Programming (via satellite): ABC Family HD; AmericanLife TV Network; Animal Planet HD; Arts & Entertainment HD; BBC America; Bio; Bloomberg Television; Bravo; Bravo HD; BYU Television; CBS College Sports Network; CMT Pure Country; CNBC HD+; CNN HD; Cooking Channel; Discovery Channel HD; Discovery HD Theater; Discovery Health Channel; Discovery Kids Channel; Discovery Military Channel; Discovery Planet Green; Disney Channel HD; DMX Music; Do-It-Yourself; ESPN 2 HD; ESPN Classic Sports; ESPN HD; ESPNews; FitTV; Food Network HD; Fox College Sports Atlantic; Fox College Sports Central; Fox College Sports Pacific; Fox Movie Channel; Fox Reality Channel; Fox Soccer; Fuse; G4; Golf Channel; Gospel Music Channel; GSN; Halogen Network; HDNet; HDNet Movies; HGTV HD; History Channel HD; History Channel International; HorseRacing TV; ID Investigation Discovery; Independent Film Channel; ION Television; Lifetime Movie Network; Lifetime Movie Network HD; MTV Hits; MTV Jams; MTV Tres; MTV2; National Geographic Channel; National Geographic Channel HD Network; NFL Network; NFL Network HD; Nick Jr.; Nick Too; NickToons TV; Outdoor Channel; PBS Kids Channel; RFD-TV; Science Channel; Science Channel HD; SoapNet; Speed Channel; Style Network; Syfy HD; TBS in HD; TeenNick; The Sportsman Channel; TLC HD; Toon Disney; Trinity Broadcasting Network; Turner Network TV HD; Universal HD; USA Network HD; Versus; Versus HD; VH1 Classic; VH1 Soul.
Fee: $6.00 monthly; $4.05 converter.
Digital Pay Service 1
Pay Units: N.A.
Programming (via satellite): Cinemax (multiplexed); Cinemax HD; Encore (multiplexed); Flix; HBO (multiplexed); HBO HD; Showtime (multiplexed); Showtime HD; Starz (multiplexed); Starz HDTV; The Movie Channel (multiplexed); The Movie Channel HD.
Video-On-Demand: No
Pay-Per-View
iN DEMAND (delivered digitally), Fee: $3.99; Fresh (delivered digitally), Fee: $8.99.
Internet Service
Operational: Yes.
Subscribers: 804.
Broadband Service: Bresnan OnLine.
Fee: $52.95 monthly.
Telephone Service
Analog: Not Operational
Digital: Operational
Subscribers: 338.
Fee: $49.99 monthly
Miles of Plant: 65.0 (coaxial); 10.0 (fiber optic). Homes passed: 5,593.
Vice President & General Manager: Sean O'Donnell. Manager: Patty Faloon. Chief Technician: Jim Passon.
City fee: 4% of gross.
Ownership: Bresnan Communications Inc. (MSO). Sale pends to Cablevision Systems Corp.

HELENA—Bresnan Communications, PO Box 5509, 951 W Custer Ave, Helena, MT 59604-5509. Phones: 406-442-1060; 877-273-7626. Fax: 406-443-5843. E-mail: moswald@bresnan.com. Web Site: http://www.bresnan.com. Also serves Alhambra, Clancy, East Helena, Helena Valley, Jefferson County (unincorporated areas), Lewis & Clark County & Montana City. ICA: MT0004.
TV Market Ranking: Below 100 (Alhambra, Clancy, East Helena, HELENA, Helena Valley, Jefferson County (unincorporated areas), Lewis & Clark County (portions), Montana City); Outside TV Markets (Lewis & Clark County (portions)). Franchise award date: N.A. Franchise expiration date: N.A. Began: January 1, 1955.
Channel capacity: N.A. Channels available but not in use: N.A.
Basic Service
Subscribers: 13,178.
Programming (received off-air): KDVR (FOX) Denver; KFBB-TV (ABC, FOX) Great Falls; KMTF (CW) Helena; KTVH-DT (NBC) Helena; KXLF-TV (CBS, CW) Butte.
Programming (via microwave): KUSM-TV (PBS) Bozeman.
Programming (via satellite): C-SPAN; C-SPAN 2; Eternal Word TV Network; Home Shopping Network; ION Television; Lifetime; QVC; TBS Superstation; TV Guide Network.
Current originations: Government Access.
Fee: $60.00 installation; $20.00 monthly; $.76 converter; $40.00 additional installation.
Expanded Basic Service 1
Subscribers: 12,888.
Programming (via satellite): ABC Family Channel; Altitude Sports & Entertainment; AMC; Animal Planet; Arts & Entertainment; Cartoon Network; CNBC; CNN; Comedy Central; Country Music TV; Discovery Channel; Disney Channel; E! Entertainment Television; ESPN; ESPN 2; Food Network; Fox News Channel; Fox Sports Net Rocky Mountain; FX; Hallmark Channel; Headline News; HGTV; History Channel; INSP; MSNBC; MTV; Nickelodeon; Oxygen; Spike TV; Syfy; The Learning Channel; Travel Channel; truTV; Turner Network TV; TV Land; USA Network; VH1; Weather Channel.
Fee: $28.99 monthly.
Digital Basic Service
Subscribers: 6,063.
Programming (received off-air): KTVH-DT (NBC) Helena.
Programming (via satellite): ABC Family HD; AmericanLife TV Network; Animal Planet HD; Arts & Entertainment HD; BBC America; Bio; Bloomberg Television;

BlueHighways TV; Bravo; Bravo HD; BYU Television; CBS College Sports Network; CMT Pure Country; CNBC HD+; CNN HD; Cooking Channel; C-SPAN 3; Discovery Channel HD; Discovery HD Theater; Discovery Health Channel; Discovery Kids Channel; Discovery Military Channel; Discovery Planet Green; Disney Channel HD; DMX Music; Do-It-Yourself; ESPN 2 HD; ESPN Classic Sports; ESPN HD; ESPNews; Food Network HD; Fox College Sports Atlantic; Fox College Sports Central; Fox College Sports Pacific; Fox Movie Channel; Fox Reality Channel; Fox Soccer; Fuse; G4; Golf Channel; Gospel Music Channel; Great American Country; GSN; Halogen Network; HDNet; HDNet Movies; HGTV HD; History Channel HD; History Channel International; HorseRacing TV; ID Investigation Discovery; Independent Film Channel; ION Life; ION Television; Lifetime Movie Network; Lifetime Movie Network HD; MTV Hits; MTV2; National Geographic Channel; National Geographic Channel HD Network; NFL Network; NFL Network HD; NHL Network; Nick Jr.; NickToons TV; Outdoor Channel; Outdoor Channel 2 HD; Palladia; PBS Kids Sprout; Qubo; RFD-TV; Science Channel; Science Channel HD; SoapNet; Speed Channel; Speed HD; Style Network; Syfy HD; TBS in HD; TeenNick; The Sportsman Channel; TLC HD; Toon Disney; Trinity Broadcasting Network; Turner Network TV HD; Universal HD; USA Network HD; Versus; Versus HD; VH1 Classic; VH1 Soul; Weather Channel HD.
Fee: $6.00 monthly.

Digital Pay Service 1
Pay Units: N.A.
Programming (via satellite): Cinemax (multiplexed); Cinemax HD; Cinemax On Demand; Encore (multiplexed); Flix; HBO (multiplexed); HBO HD; HBO On Demand; Showtime (multiplexed); Showtime HD; Showtime On Demand; Starz (multiplexed); Starz HDTV; Starz On Demand; The Movie Channel (multiplexed); The Movie Channel HD.

Video-On-Demand: Yes

Pay-Per-View
ESPN Now (delivered digitally); Sports PPV (delivered digitally); iN DEMAND (delivered digitally); Urban Xtra (delivered digitally); Fresh (delivered digitally); Shorteez (delivered digitally); Playboy TV (delivered digitally); Hot Choice (delivered digitally).

Internet Service
Operational: Yes. Began: January 1, 2001.
Subscribers: 5,946.
Broadband Service: Bresnan OnLine.
Fee: $99.95 installation; $52.95 monthly; $10.00 modem lease.

Telephone Service
Analog: Not Operational
Digital: Operational
Subscribers: 2,688.
Fee: $49.99 monthly

Miles of Plant: 335.0 (coaxial); 86.0 (fiber optic). Homes passed: 23,556.
General Manager: Mike Oswald. Chief Technician: Ed McFadden.
City fee: None.
Ownership: Bresnan Communications Inc. (MSO). Sale pends to Cablevision Systems Corp.

HOT SPRINGS—KLiP Interactive, 455 Gees Mill Business Court, Conyers, GA 30013. Phones: 800-388-6577; 678-727-7100. Fax: 678-727-7002. E-mail: jsheehan@klipia.com. Web Site: http://www.klipia.com. ICA: MT0078.
TV Market Ranking: Outside TV Markets (HOT SPRINGS). Franchise award date: N.A. Franchise expiration date: N.A. Began: April 1, 1984.
Channel capacity: 45 (not 2-way capable). Channels available but not in use: 18.

Basic Service
Subscribers: 62.
Programming (received off-air): KECI-TV (NBC) Missoula; KPAX-TV (CBS, CW) Missoula; KTMF (ABC, FOX) Missoula.
Programming (via satellite): ABC Family Channel; Arts & Entertainment; Cartoon Network; CNBC; CNN; Discovery Channel; Disney Channel; ESPN; ESPN 2; History Channel; KDVR (FOX) Denver; Nickelodeon; Outdoor Channel; Spike TV; TBS Superstation; The Learning Channel; Travel Channel; Trinity Broadcasting Network; Turner Classic Movies; Turner Network TV; TV Land; VH1; Weather Channel; WGN America.
Fee: $31.45 installation; $31.47 monthly.

Pay Service 1
Pay Units: 3.
Programming (via satellite): HBO.
Fee: $10.95 monthly.

Pay Service 2
Pay Units: N.A.
Programming (via satellite): Showtime; The Movie Channel.
Fee: $10.95 monthly (each).

Video-On-Demand: No

Internet Service
Operational: No.

Telephone Service
None

Miles of Plant: 3.0 (coaxial); None (fiber optic). Homes passed: 81. Total homes in franchised area: 380.
Chief Executive Officer: Joseph A. Sheehan. General Manager East: Mark Miller. General Manager West: Vance Johnson.
City fee: None.
Ownership: KLiP Interactive LLC (MSO).

HYSHAM—Mid-Rivers Communications, PO Box 280, 904 C Ave, Circle, MT 59215. Phone: 406-485-3301. Fax: 406-485-2924. E-mail: lcedar@midrivers.com. Web Site: http://www.midrivers.com. ICA: MT0086.
TV Market Ranking: Outside TV Markets (HYSHAM). Franchise award date: June 14, 1982. Franchise expiration date: N.A. Began: October 1, 1982.
Channel capacity: 40 (not 2-way capable). Channels available but not in use: 21.

Basic Service
Subscribers: 58.
Programming (received off-air): KHMT (FOX) Hardin; KSVI (ABC) Billings; KTVQ (CBS, CW) Billings; KULR-TV (NBC) Billings.
Programming (via satellite): ABC Family Channel; Cartoon Network; CNN; Discovery Channel; Disney Channel; ESPN; HGTV; Spike TV; TBS Superstation; Turner Classic Movies; Turner Network TV; USA Network; WGN America.
Fee: $15.00 installation; $28.45 monthly.

Pay Service 1
Pay Units: 22.
Programming (via satellite): HBO.
Fee: $15.00 installation; $12.00 monthly.

Internet Service
Operational: No.

Telephone Service
None

Miles of Plant: 5.0 (coaxial); None (fiber optic). Homes passed: 230.
General Manager: Gerry Anderson. Chief Technician: Mike Sokoloski. Customer Service Manager: Deb Wagner.
City fee: None.
Ownership: Mid-Rivers Telephone Cooperative Inc. (MSO).

JOLIET—Cable Montana, 222 W 1st St, Laurel, MT 59044. Phones: 406-628-6336; 308-236-1512 (Kearney, NE corporate office). Fax: 406-628-8181. Web Site: http://www.cablemt.net. ICA: MT0113.
TV Market Ranking: Below 100 (JOLIET). Franchise award date: N.A. Franchise expiration date: N.A. Began: N.A.
Channel capacity: 40 (operating 2-way). Channels available but not in use: 8.

Basic Service
Subscribers: 95.
Programming (received off-air): KHMT (FOX) Hardin; KSVI (ABC) Billings; KTVQ (CBS, CW) Billings; KULR-TV (NBC) Billings; KUSM-TV (PBS) Bozeman.
Programming (via satellite): ABC Family Channel; Altitude Sports & Entertainment; Arts & Entertainment; Cartoon Network; CNN; Comedy Central; Country Music TV; Discovery Channel; E! Entertainment Television; ESPN; ESPN 2; Food Network; HGTV; History Channel; Nickelodeon; Spike TV; Syfy; TBS Superstation; The Learning Channel; truTV; Turner Classic Movies; Turner Network TV; USA Network; WGN America.
Fee: $29.95 installation; $26.45 monthly.

Pay Service 1
Pay Units: 15.
Programming (via satellite): HBO.
Fee: $10.95 monthly.

Video-On-Demand: No

Internet Service
Operational: Yes.
Broadband Service: Cable Montana.

Telephone Service
Digital: Operational

Miles of Plant: 7.0 (coaxial); None (fiber optic). Homes passed: 409.
Manager: Doug Lane. Operations Manager: Stuart Gilbertson.
City fee: None.
Ownership: USA Companies (MSO).

JORDAN—Mid-Rivers Communications, PO Box 280, 904 C Ave, Circle, MT 59215. Phone: 406-485-3301. Fax: 406-485-2924. Web Site: http://www.midrivers.com. ICA: MT0114.
TV Market Ranking: Outside TV Markets (JORDAN). Franchise award date: N.A. Franchise expiration date: N.A. Began: January 1, 1983.
Channel capacity: N.A. Channels available but not in use: N.A.

Basic Service
Subscribers: 158.
Programming (received off-air): KFBB-TV (ABC, FOX) Great Falls; KHMT (FOX) Hardin; KTVQ (CBS, CW) Billings; KULR-TV (NBC) Billings.
Programming (via satellite): ABC Family Channel; AMC; Arts & Entertainment; CNBC; CNN; C-SPAN; Discovery Channel; Disney Channel; Do-It-Yourself; ESPN; ESPN 2; Eternal Word TV Network; Fox Movie Channel; Fox News Channel; Great American Country; Headline News; HGTV; History Channel; ION Television; KUSM-TV (PBS) Bozeman; Lifetime; Nickelodeon; Outdoor Channel; QVC; RFD-TV; Spike TV; Syfy; TBS Superstation; The Learning Channel; Travel Channel; Turner Network TV; TV Land; WE tv; Weather Channel; WGN America.
Fee: $90.00 installation; $19.00 monthly.

Pay Service 1
Pay Units: 47.
Programming (via satellite): HBO; The Movie Channel.
Fee: $8.00 monthly $TMC); $10 monthly (HBO).

Video-On-Demand: No

Internet Service
Operational: Yes.
Broadband Service: MegaSpeed.
Fee: $25.00 installation; $49.95 monthly.

Telephone Service
None

Miles of Plant: 18.0 (coaxial); None (fiber optic). Homes passed: 200.
General Manager: Gerry Anderson. Chief Technician: Mike Sokolosky. Customer Service Manager: Deb Wagner.
Ownership: Mid-Rivers Telephone Cooperative Inc. (MSO).

KALISPELL—Bresnan Communications, 333 First Ave E, Kalispell, MT 59901-4935. Phone: 406-758-2300. Fax: 406-755-7204. E-mail: sodonnell@bresnan.com. Web Site: http://www.bresnan.com. Also serves Bigfork, Columbia Falls, Evergreen, Flathead County & Whitefish. ICA: MT0006.
TV Market Ranking: Below 100 (Bigfork, Columbia Falls, Evergreen, Flathead County (portions), KALISPELL, Whitefish); Outside TV Markets (Flathead County (portions)). Franchise award date: N.A. Franchise expiration date: N.A. Began: May 1, 1983.
Channel capacity: N.A. Channels available but not in use: N.A.

Basic Service
Subscribers: 16,589.
Programming (received off-air): KCFW-TV (NBC) Kalispell; KPAX-TV (CBS, CW) Missoula; KSKN (CW) Spokane; KTMF (ABC, FOX) Missoula; KUFM-TV (PBS) Missoula; 10 FMs.
Programming (via microwave): KREM (CBS) Spokane; KSPS-TV (PBS) Spokane; KXLY-TV (ABC, MNT) Spokane.
Programming (via satellite): C-SPAN; C-SPAN 2; Home Shopping Network; TBS Superstation; TV Guide Network.
Current originations: Leased Access.
Fee: $60.00 installation; $20.00 monthly; $.75 converter; $40.00 additional installation.

Expanded Basic Service 1
Subscribers: 15,872.
Programming (via satellite): ABC Family Channel; Altitude Sports & Entertainment; AMC; Animal Planet; Arts & Entertainment; BYU Television; Cartoon Network; CNBC; CNN; Comcast Sports Net Northwest; Comedy Central; Country Music TV; Discovery Channel; Disney Channel; E! Entertainment Television; ESPN; ESPN 2; Eternal Word TV Network; Food Network; Fox News Channel; FX; Hallmark Channel; Headline News; HGTV; History Channel; INSP; ION Television; Lifetime; MSNBC; MTV; Nickelodeon; Oxygen; QVC; Spike TV; Syfy; The Learning Channel; Travel Channel; truTV; Turner Classic Movies; Turner Network TV; TV Land; USA Network; VH1; Weather Channel.
Fee: $28.99 monthly.

Digital Basic Service
Subscribers: 6,694.
Programming (received off-air): KPAX-TV (CBS, CW) Missoula.
Programming (via satellite): ABC Family HD; AmericanLife TV Network; Animal Planet HD; Arts & Entertainment HD; BBC America; Bio; Bloomberg Television; Bravo; Bravo HD; CBS College Sports Network; CMT Pure Country; CNBC HD+;

CNN HD; Cooking Channel; C-SPAN 3; Discovery Channel HD; Discovery HD Theater; Discovery Health Channel; Discovery Kids Channel; Discovery Military Channel; Discovery Planet Green; Disney Channel HD; DMX Music; Do-It-Yourself; ESPN 2 HD; ESPN Classic Sports; ESPN HD; ESPNews; FitTV; Food Network HD; Fox College Sports Atlantic; Fox College Sports Central; Fox College Sports Pacific; Fox Movie Channel; Fox Reality Channel; Fox Soccer; Fuse; G4; Golf Channel; Gospel Music Channel; GSN; Halogen Network; HDNet; HDNet Movies; HGTV HD; History Channel HD; History Channel International; HorseRacing TV; ID Investigation Discovery; Independent Film Channel; ION Life; ION Television; Lifetime Movie Network; Lifetime Movie Network HD; MTV Hits; MTV Jams; MTV Tres; MTV2; National Geographic Channel; National Geographic Channel HD Network; NFL Network; NFL Network HD; NHL Network; Nick Jr.; Nick Too; NickToons TV; Outdoor Channel; Outdoor Channel 2 HD; Palladia; PBS Kids Sprout; Qubo; RFD-TV; Science Channel; Science Channel HD; SoapNet; Speed Channel; Speed HD; Style Network; Syfy HD; TBS in HD; TeenNick; The Sportsman Channel; TLC HD; Toon Disney; Trinity Broadcasting Network; Turner Network TV HD; Universal HD; USA Network HD; Versus; Versus HD; VH1 Classic; VH1 Soul; Weather Channel HD.
Fee: $6.00 monthly.

Digital Pay Service 1
Pay Units: N.A.
Programming (via satellite): Cinemax (multiplexed); Cinemax HD; Cinemax On Demand; Encore (multiplexed); Flix; HBO (multiplexed); HBO HD; HBO On Demand; Showtime (multiplexed); Showtime HD; Showtime On Demand; Starz (multiplexed); Starz HDTV; Starz On Demand; The Movie Channel (multiplexed).

Video-On-Demand: Yes

Pay-Per-View
iN DEMAND (delivered digitally); ESPN (delivered digitally); MLB Extra Innings (delivered digitally); NHL Center Ice (delivered digitally).

Internet Service
Operational: Yes.
Subscribers: 4,785.
Broadband Service: Bresnan OnLine.
Fee: $52.95 monthly.

Telephone Service
Digital: Operational
Subscribers: 603.
Fee: $49.99 monthly

Miles of Plant: 563.0 (coaxial); 155.0 (fiber optic). Homes passed: 30,289.
Vice President & General Manager: Sean O'Donnell. Chief Technician: Weldon Plympton. Manager: Patty Faloon.
City fee: 3% of gross (Columbia Falls & Whitefish).
Ownership: Bresnan Communications Inc. (MSO). Sale pends to Cablevision Systems Corp.

LAME DEER—Eagle Cablevision Inc., PO Box 469, Lame Deer, MT 59043. Phones: 888-688-2974; 406-477-6232. Fax: 406-477-6232. ICA: MT0058.
TV Market Ranking: Outside TV Markets (LAME DEER). Franchise award date: N.A. Franchise expiration date: N.A. Began: N.A.
Channel capacity: N.A. Channels available but not in use: N.A.

Basic Service
Subscribers: 161 Includes Lodge Grass.
Programming (via microwave): KCNC-TV (CBS) Denver; KMGH-TV (ABC) Denver; KRMA-TV (PBS) Denver; KUSA (NBC) Denver.
Programming (via satellite): ABC Family Channel; CNN; Discovery Channel; ESPN; TBS Superstation; Turner Classic Movies; Turner Network TV; USA Network; WGN America.
Fee: $35.00 installation; $42.00 monthly.

Pay Service 1
Pay Units: N.A.
Programming (via satellite): Cinemax; HBO; Showtime.
Fee: $10.00 monthly (each).

Video-On-Demand: No

Internet Service
Operational: Yes.
Fee: $80.00 installation; $29.00 monthly.

Telephone Service
None

Miles of Plant: 7.0 (coaxial); None (fiber optic). Homes passed: 250.
General Manager: Cliff Schollmeyer. Chief Technician: Adrian Gardener. Office Manager: Evone Stang.
Ownership: Eagle Cablevision (MSO).

LAUREL—Cable Montana, 222 W 1st St, Laurel, MT 59044. Phones: 308-236-1512 (Kearney, NE corporate office); 406-628-6336; 406-628-4290. Fax: 406-628-8181. Web Site: http://www.cablemt.net. Also serves Columbus & Park City. ICA: MT0023.
TV Market Ranking: Below 100 (LAUREL, Park City); Outside TV Markets (Columbus). Franchise award date: N.A. Franchise expiration date: N.A. Began: November 24, 1971.
Channel capacity: N.A. Channels available but not in use: N.A.

Basic Service
Subscribers: 1,823.
Programming (received off-air): KHMT (FOX) Hardin; KSVI (ABC) Billings; KTVQ (CBS, CW) Billings; KULR-TV (NBC) Billings; KUSM-TV (PBS) Bozeman; 2 FMs.
Programming (via satellite): ABC Family Channel; Arts & Entertainment; C-SPAN; C-SPAN 2; G4; KWBM (MNT) Harrison [LICENSED & SILENT]; Lifetime; Nickelodeon; QVC; TBS Superstation; TV Guide Network; Weather Channel; WGN America.
Fee: $21.95 monthly.

Expanded Basic Service 1
Subscribers: N.A.
Programming (via satellite): Altitude Sports & Entertainment; AMC; Animal Planet; Cartoon Network; CNBC; CNN; Comedy Central; Country Music TV; Discovery Channel; E! Entertainment Television; ESPN; ESPN 2; ESPN Classic Sports; Food Network; Fox News Channel; Fox Sports Net; FX; Hallmark Channel; Headline News; HGTV; History Channel; MSNBC; MTV; National Geographic Channel; Outdoor Channel; Spike TV; Syfy; The Learning Channel; truTV; Turner Network TV; TV Land; USA Network; Versus; VH1.
Fee: $18.04 monthly.

Digital Basic Service
Subscribers: N.A.
Programming (via satellite): Alterna'TV; BBC America; Bio; Black Family Channel; Bloomberg Television; CMT Pure Country; Current; Daystar TV Network; Discovery Health Channel; Discovery Kids Channel; Discovery Military Channel; Discovery Planet Green; DMX Music; ESPN 2; ESPN Classic Sports; ESPNews; FitTV; Fox College Sports Atlantic; Fox College Sports Central; Fox College Sports Pacific; Fox Movie Channel; G4; Golf Channel; GSN; Halogen Network; History Channel; History Channel International; ID Investigation Discovery; MTV Hits; MTV2; National Geographic Channel; Nick Jr.; Ovation; Science Channel; ShopNBC; Sleuth; Speed Channel; Style Network; TeenNick; Trinity Broadcasting Network; Versus; VH1 Classic; VH1 Soul; WE tv.
Fee: $13.00 monthly.

Digital Pay Service 1
Pay Units: N.A.
Programming (via satellite): Cinemax (multiplexed); Encore (multiplexed); Flix; Fox Movie Channel; HBO (multiplexed); Lifetime Movie Network; Showtime; Starz (multiplexed); The Movie Channel (multiplexed).
Fee: $13.00 monthly (HBO, Cinemax, Starz/Encore/FMC/Lifetime Movie or Showtime/TMC/Flix).

Video-On-Demand: No

Pay-Per-View
iN DEMAND (delivered digitally); Hot Choice (delivered digitally); Playboy TV (delivered digitally); Fresh (delivered digitally); Spice: Xcess (delivered digitally); Club Jenna (delivered digitally).

Internet Service
Operational: Yes.
Broadband Service: Cable Montana.
Fee: $35.95 monthly.

Telephone Service
Digital: Operational
Fee: $39.95 monthly

Miles of Plant: 31.0 (coaxial); None (fiber optic).
Manager: Doug Lane. Operations Manager: Stuart Gilbertson.
City fee: None.
Ownership: USA Companies (MSO).

LAVINA—Mid-Rivers Communications, PO Box 280, 904 C Ave, Circle, MT 59215. Phone: 406-485-3301. Fax: 406-485-2924. Web Site: http://www.midrivers.com. ICA: MT0109.
TV Market Ranking: Outside TV Markets (LAVINA). Franchise award date: N.A. Franchise expiration date: N.A. Began: January 1, 1984.
Channel capacity: N.A. Channels available but not in use: None.

Basic Service
Subscribers: 47.
Programming (received off-air): KHMT (FOX) Hardin; KSVI (ABC) Billings; KTVQ (CBS, CW) Billings; KULR-TV (NBC) Billings; KUSM-TV (PBS) Bozeman.
Programming (via satellite): ABC Family Channel; CNN; C-SPAN; Discovery Channel; Disney Channel; ESPN; Headline News; INSP; Outdoor Channel; Spike TV; Syfy; TBS Superstation; The Learning Channel; Turner Network TV; WGN America.
Fee: $15.00 monthly.

Expanded Basic Service 1
Subscribers: 41.
Programming (via satellite): Arts & Entertainment; CNBC; ESPN 2; HGTV; Lifetime; Nickelodeon; QVC; Travel Channel; TV Land; WE tv; Weather Channel.
Fee: $11.00 monthly.

Digital Basic Service
Subscribers: N.A.
Programming (via satellite): BBC America; Bravo; Discovery Channel; Discovery Digital Networks; DMX Music; ESPN 2; ESPN Classic Sports; ESPNews; Fox Soccer; Golf Channel; GSN; HGTV; History Channel; Independent Film Channel; National Geographic Channel; Nick Jr.; Syfy; Turner Classic Movies; Versus; VH1 Classic; VH1 Country; WE tv.

Pay Service 1
Pay Units: 2.
Programming (via satellite): Showtime; The Movie Channel.
Fee: $12.00 monthly (each).

Digital Pay Service 1
Pay Units: N.A.
Programming (via satellite): Cinemax (multiplexed); Encore (multiplexed); Flix; HBO (multiplexed); Showtime (multiplexed); Starz (multiplexed); The Movie Channel (multiplexed).

Video-On-Demand: No

Pay-Per-View
iN DEMAND (delivered digitally); ESPN Now (delivered digitally); Sports PPV (delivered digitally).

Internet Service
Operational: No, Both DSL & dial-up.

Telephone Service
None

Miles of Plant: 1.0 (coaxial); None (fiber optic). Homes passed: 60. Total homes in franchised area: 60.
General Manager: Gerry Anderson. Customer Service Representative: Liz Cedar. Chief Technician: Mike Sokolosky. Customer Service Manager: Deb Wagner.
City fee: None.
Ownership: Mid-Rivers Telephone Cooperative Inc. (MSO).

LEWISTOWN—Mid-Rivers Communications, PO Box 280, 904 C Ave, Circle, MT 59215. Phones: 406-485-3301; 406-535-3336. Fax: 406-485-2924. Web Site: http://www.midrivers.com. Also serves Fergus County. ICA: MT0012.
TV Market Ranking: Below 100 (Fergus County, LEWISTOWN). Franchise award date: July 1, 1998. Franchise expiration date: N.A. Began: March 1, 1955.
Channel capacity: N.A. Channels available but not in use: N.A.

Basic Service
Subscribers: 2,082.
Programming (via microwave): KFBB-TV (ABC, FOX) Great Falls; KRTV (CBS, CW) Great Falls; KTGF (IND) Great Falls; KUSM-TV (PBS) Bozeman.
Programming (via satellite): Arts & Entertainment; CNN; C-SPAN; Discovery Channel; FX; Lifetime; QVC; TBS Superstation.
Fee: $40.95 installation; $13.99 monthly; $18.95 additional installation.

Expanded Basic Service 1
Subscribers: 2,080.
Programming (via satellite): ABC Family Channel; AMC; AmericanLife TV Network; Animal Planet; Cartoon Network; CNBC; Discovery Home Channel; Disney Channel; ESPN; Fox News Channel; Fox Sports Net Rocky Mountain; GAS; Hallmark Channel; Halogen Network; Headline News; History Channel; MSNBC; MTV; Nickelodeon; Ovation; Oxygen; Spike TV; The Learning Channel; Toon Disney; Travel Channel; Trinity Broadcasting Network; Turner Network TV; TV Land; USA Network; Weather Channel.
Fee: $16.97 monthly.

Digital Basic Service
Subscribers: 39.
Programming (via satellite): BBC America; Bravo; Discovery Digital Networks; DMX Music; ESPN 2; ESPN Classic Sports; Fox Sports World; Golf Channel; GSN; HGTV; Independent Film Channel; National Geographic Channel; Nick Jr.; Style Network;

Syfy; Turner Classic Movies; Versus; WE tv.
Fee: $12.00 monthly.

Digital Expanded Basic Service
Subscribers: N.A.
Programming (via satellite): Bio; Bloomberg Television; G4; History Channel International; Outdoor Channel; Speed Channel.
Fee: $5.99 monthly.

Pay Service 1
Pay Units: 137.
Programming (via satellite): Cinemax.
Fee: $13.20 monthly.

Pay Service 2
Pay Units: 305.
Programming (via satellite): HBO.
Fee: $14.95 installation; $14.15 monthly.

Pay Service 3
Pay Units: 171.
Programming (via satellite): Showtime.
Fee: $14.15 monthly.

Pay Service 4
Pay Units: 971.
Programming (via satellite): Encore.
Fee: $1.75 monthly.

Pay Service 5
Pay Units: 644.
Programming (via satellite): Starz.
Fee: $6.75 monthly.

Digital Pay Service 1
Pay Units: N.A.
Programming (via satellite): Cinemax (multiplexed); Encore (multiplexed); HBO (multiplexed); Showtime (multiplexed); Starz (multiplexed); The Movie Channel (multiplexed).
Fee: $1.75 monthly (Encore), $6.75 monthly (Starz), $13.20 monthly (Cinemax), $14.15 monthly (HBO, Showtime & TMC).

Video-On-Demand: No

Pay-Per-View
iN DEMAND (delivered digitally), Fee: $3.99; Playboy TV (delivered digitally), Fee: $8.99; Fresh (delivered digitally), Fee: $8.99; Shorteez (delivered digitally), Fee: $8.99, Fee: $11.99.

Internet Service
Operational: No.

Telephone Service
None

Miles of Plant: 46.0 (coaxial); None (fiber optic). Homes passed: 3,512. Total homes in franchised area: 3,616.
General Manager: Gerry Anderson. Chief Technician: Mike Sokolosky. Customer Service Manager: Deb Wagner.
City fee: 5.26% of gross.
Ownership: Mid-Rivers Telephone Cooperative Inc. (MSO).

LIBBY—Windjammer Cable, 4400 PGA Blvd, Ste 902, Palm Beach Gardens, FL 33410. Phones: 877-450-5558; 561-775-1208. Fax: 561-775-7811. Web Site: http://www.windjammercable.com. Also serves Lincoln County. ICA: MT0010.
TV Market Ranking: Below 100 (Lincoln County (portions)); Outside TV Markets (LIBBY, Lincoln County (portions)). Franchise award date: N.A. Franchise expiration date: N.A. Began: March 1, 1981.
Channel capacity: N.A. Channels available but not in use: N.A.

Basic Service
Subscribers: N.A. Included in Coeur d'Alene ID
Programming (received off-air): KPAX-TV (CBS, CW) Missoula; KQUP (IND) Pullman; 7 FMs.
Programming (via microwave): KAYU-TV (FOX) Spokane; KCFW-TV (NBC) Kalispell; KHQ-TV (NBC) Spokane; KREM (CBS) Spokane; KSPS-TV (PBS) Spokane; KXLY-TV (ABC, MNT) Spokane.
Programming (via satellite): C-SPAN; C-SPAN 2; Discovery Channel; Home Shopping Network; MSNBC; Northwest Cable News; QVC; TBS Superstation; WGN America.
Current originations: Leased Access; Religious Access; Government Access; Educational Access; Public Access.
Fee: $39.95 installation; $27.72 monthly; $16.00 additional installation.

Expanded Basic Service 1
Subscribers: N.A. Included in Coeur d'Alene ID
Programming (via satellite): ABC Family Channel; AMC; Animal Planet; Arts & Entertainment; Cartoon Network; CNBC; CNN; Comcast Sports Net Northwest; Comedy Central; Country Music TV; Disney Channel; E! Entertainment Television; ESPN; ESPN 2; Food Network; Fox News Channel; FX; Hallmark Channel; Headline News; HGTV; History Channel; Lifetime; MTV; Nickelodeon; Oxygen; Spike TV; Style Network; Syfy; The Learning Channel; Travel Channel; truTV; Turner Network TV; TV Land; USA Network; VH1; Weather Channel.
Fee: $28.88 monthly.

Digital Basic Service
Subscribers: 375.
Programming (via satellite): AmericanLife TV Network; BBC America; Bio; Bloomberg Television; Bravo; Discovery Digital Networks; FitTV; Fox Movie Channel; Fox Sports World; G4; GAS; Great American Country; GSN; History Channel International; International Television (ITV); Lifetime Movie Network; MBC America; MTV Networks Digital Suite; The Word Network; Toon Disney; Trinity Broadcasting Network; Turner Classic Movies; WE tv.
Fee: $11.99 monthly.

Digital Expanded Basic Service
Subscribers: N.A.
Programming (via satellite): ESPN Classic Sports; ESPNews; Golf Channel; Halogen Network; Independent Film Channel; Music Choice; National Geographic Channel; Nick Jr.; NickToons TV; Outdoor Channel; Speed Channel; Sundance Channel; Versus.
Fee: $12.49 monthly.

Digital Pay Service 1
Pay Units: N.A.
Programming (via satellite): Cinemax (multiplexed); HBO (multiplexed); Showtime (multiplexed); Starz (multiplexed).
Fee: $15.95 monthly (HBO, Showtime, Cinemax or Starz).

Video-On-Demand: No

Pay-Per-View
Shorteez (delivered digitally); Hot Choice (delivered digitally); Urban American Television Network (delivered digitally); Fresh (delivered digitally); Playboy TV (delivered digitally).

Internet Service
Operational: Yes. Began: December 1, 2001.
Subscribers: 300.
Broadband Service: Road Runner.
Fee: $24.95-$46.95 installation; $45.95 monthly.

Telephone Service
None

Homes passed & miles of plant included in Coeur d'Alene ID
General Manager: Timothy Evard. Operations Director: Belinda Graham. Engineering Director: Mike Earehart. Finance & Accounting Director: Cindy Johnson.
City fee: 1% of gross.
Ownership: Windjammer Communications LLC (MSO).

LINCOLN—Lincoln Cable TV, 111 Stemple Pass Rd, Lincoln, MT 59639. Phone: 406-362-4216. Fax: 406-362-4606. E-mail: ltc@linctel.net. Web Site: http://www.linctel.net. ICA: MT0115.
TV Market Ranking: Outside TV Markets (LINCOLN). Franchise award date: N.A. Franchise expiration date: N.A. Began: April 1, 1987.
Channel capacity: 36 (not 2-way capable). Channels available but not in use: 12.

Basic Service
Subscribers: 400.
Programming (received off-air): KTVH-DT (NBC) Helena; KXLF-TV (CBS, CW) Butte.
Programming (via microwave): KRMA-TV (PBS) Denver; KWGN-TV (CW) Denver.
Programming (via satellite): ABC Family Channel; AMC; Arts & Entertainment; CNN; Discovery Channel; ESPN; ESPN 2; Fox Movie Channel; History Channel; Outdoor Channel; Spike TV; TBS Superstation; Turner Network TV; USA Network; Weather Channel; WGN America.
Fee: $20.00 installation; $25.50 monthly; $1.50 converter.

Pay Service 1
Pay Units: 200.
Programming (via satellite): Flix; Showtime; The Movie Channel.
Fee: $11.50 monthly.

Internet Service
Operational: No.

Telephone Service
None

Miles of Plant: 29.0 (coaxial); None (fiber optic). Homes passed: 550. Total homes in franchised area: 1,050.
Manager: Ken Lumpkin. Chief Technician: Arron Daniel.
Franchise fee: None.
Ownership: Lincoln Telephone Co.

LIVINGSTON—Bresnan Communications, 201 E Front St, Butte, MT 59701-5203. Phones: 877-273-7626 (Customer service); 406-782-9383 (Butte office). Web Site: http://www.bresnan.com. Also serves Park County. ICA: MT0011.
TV Market Ranking: Below 100 (LIVINGSTON, Park County (portions)); Outside TV Markets (Park County (portions)). Franchise award date: N.A. Franchise expiration date: N.A. Began: May 1, 1954.
Channel capacity: N.A. Channels available but not in use: N.A.

Basic Service
Subscribers: 2,136.
Programming (received off-air): KHMT (FOX) Hardin; KSVI (ABC) Billings; KTVQ (CBS, CW) Billings; KULR-TV (NBC) Billings.
Programming (via microwave): KUSM-TV (PBS) Bozeman; KWGN-TV (CW) Denver.
Programming (via satellite): C-SPAN; C-SPAN 2; Home Shopping Network; Lifetime; QVC; TBS Superstation; TV Guide Network.
Fee: $46.04 installation; $20.00 monthly; $.79 converter; $7.67 additional installation.

Expanded Basic Service 1
Subscribers: 2,007.
Programming (via satellite): ABC Family Channel; Altitude Sports & Entertainment; AMC; Animal Planet; Arts & Entertainment; Cartoon Network; CNBC; CNN; Comedy Central; Country Music TV; Discovery Channel; Disney Channel; E! Entertainment Television; ESPN; ESPN 2; Food Network; Fox News Channel; Fox Sports Net Rocky Mountain; FX; Hallmark Channel; Headline News; HGTV; History Channel; INSP; ION Television; MSNBC; MTV; Nickelodeon; Oxygen; Spike TV; Syfy; The Learning Channel; Travel Channel; truTV; Turner Classic Movies; Turner Network TV; TV Land; USA Network; VH1; Weather Channel.
Fee: $28.99 monthly.

Digital Basic Service
Subscribers: 712.
Programming (via satellite): ABC Family HD; AmericanLife TV Network; Animal Planet HD; Arts & Entertainment HD; BBC America; Bio; Bloomberg Television; Bravo; CBS College Sports Network; CMT Pure Country; Cooking Channel; Discovery Channel HD; Discovery HD Theater; Discovery Health Channel; Discovery Kids Channel; Discovery Military Channel; Discovery Planet Green; Disney Channel HD; DMX Music; Do-It-Yourself; ESPN Classic Sports; ESPN HD; ESPNews; FitTV; Food Network HD; Fox College Sports Atlantic; Fox College Sports Central; Fox College Sports Pacific; Fox Movie Channel; Fox Reality Channel; Fox Soccer; Fuse; G4; Golf Channel; Gospel Music Channel; GSN; Halogen Network; HGTV HD; History Channel HD; History Channel International; HorseRacing TV; ID Investigation Discovery; Independent Film Channel; ION Television; Lifetime Movie Network; MTV Hits; MTV2; National Geographic Channel; National Geographic Channel HD Network; NFL Network; Nick Jr.; NickToons TV; Outdoor Channel; PBS Kids Sprout; RFD-TV; Science Channel; Science Channel HD; SoapNet; Speed Channel; Style Network; Syfy HD; TeenNick; The Sportsman Channel; Toon Disney; Trinity Broadcasting Network; Universal HD; USA Network HD; Versus; VH1 Classic; VH1 Soul.
Fee: $6.00 monthly.

Digital Pay Service 1
Pay Units: N.A.
Programming (via satellite): Cinemax (multiplexed); Encore (multiplexed); Flix; HBO (multiplexed); HBO HD; Showtime (multiplexed); Starz (multiplexed); Starz HDTV; The Movie Channel (multiplexed).

Video-On-Demand: No

Internet Service
Operational: Yes.
Subscribers: 458.
Fee: $52.95 monthly.

Telephone Service
Analog: Not Operational
Digital: Operational
Subscribers: 2.
Fee: $49.99 monthly

Miles of Plant: 46.0 (coaxial); 8.0 (fiber optic). Homes passed: 4,651.
General Manager: Mike Oswald. Chief Technician: Todd Hawke.
Ownership: Bresnan Communications Inc. (MSO). Sale pends to Cablevision Systems Corp.

LODGE GRASS—Eagle Cablevision Inc., PO Box 610, Lodge Grass, MT 59050. Phones: 888-688-2974; 406-639-2570. Fax: 406-639-2570. ICA: MT0083.
TV Market Ranking: Below 100 (LODGE GRASS). Franchise award date: N.A. Franchise expiration date: N.A. Began: N.A.
Channel capacity: N.A. Channels available but not in use: N.A.

Basic Service
Subscribers: N.A. Included in Lame Deer
Programming (via microwave): KCNC-TV (CBS) Denver; KMGH-TV (ABC) Denver; KRMA-TV (PBS) Denver; KUSA (NBC) Denver.
Programming (via satellite): ABC Family Channel; CNN; Discovery Channel; ESPN; TBS Superstation; Turner Classic Movies; Turner Network TV; USA Network; WGN America.
Fee: $30.00 installation; $40.00 monthly.
Pay Service 1
Pay Units: N.A.
Programming (via satellite): Cinemax; HBO; Showtime.
Fee: $10.00 monthly (each).
Video-On-Demand: No
Internet Service
Operational: Yes.
Fee: $80.00 installation; $29.00 monthly.
Telephone Service
None
Miles of Plant: 5.0 (coaxial); None (fiber optic). Homes passed: 150.
Manager: Cliff Schollmeyer. Office Manager: Joe Doane.
Ownership: Eagle Cablevision (MSO).

LOLO—Bresnan Communications. Now served by MISSOULA, MT [MT0002]. ICA: MT0017.

MALTA—Bresnan Communications, PO Box 391, 1770 2nd St W, Havre, MT 59501. Phones: 877-273-7626; 406-727-8881. Fax: 406-727-6433. E-mail: sodonnell@bresnan.com. Web Site: http://www.bresnan.com. ICA: MT0032.
TV Market Ranking: Outside TV Markets (MALTA). Franchise award date: N.A. Franchise expiration date: N.A. Began: March 1, 1980.
Channel capacity: N.A. Channels available but not in use: N.A.
Basic Service
Subscribers: 489.
Programming (via microwave): KFBB-TV (ABC, FOX) Great Falls; KRTV (CBS, CW) Great Falls; KTGF (IND) Great Falls; KUSM-TV (PBS) Bozeman.
Programming (via satellite): CNN; C-SPAN; C-SPAN 2; CW+; FX; Home Shopping Network; Lifetime; QVC; TBS Superstation; truTV; TV Guide Network.
Fee: $40.95 installation; $20.00 monthly; $1.85 converter; $18.95 additional installation.
Expanded Basic Service 1
Subscribers: 485.
Programming (via satellite): ABC Family Channel; Altitude Sports & Entertainment; AMC; Animal Planet; Arts & Entertainment; Cartoon Network; CNBC; Comedy Central; Country Music TV; Discovery Channel; Disney Channel; E! Entertainment Television; ESPN; ESPN 2; Food Network; Fox News Channel; Fox Sports Net Rocky Mountain; Hallmark Channel; Headline News; History Channel; INSP; MSNBC; MTV; Nickelodeon; Oxygen; Spike TV; The Learning Channel; Travel Channel; Turner Network TV; USA Network; VH1; Weather Channel.
Fee: $28.99 monthly.
Digital Basic Service
Subscribers: N.A.
Programming (via satellite): AmericanLife TV Network; BBC America; Bio; Bloomberg Television; Bravo; CBS College Sports Network; CMT Pure Country; Discovery Health Channel; Discovery Kids Channel; Discovery Military Channel; Discovery Planet Green; DMX Music; ESPN Classic Sports; ESPNews; Fox Movie Channel; Fox Soccer; Fuse; G4; Golf Channel; Gospel Music Channel; GSN; Halogen Network; HGTV; History Channel International; ID Investigation Discovery; Independent Film Channel; Lifetime Movie Network; MTV Hits; MTV2; National Geographic Channel; Nick Jr.; NickToons TV; Outdoor Channel; PBS Kids Sprout; RFD-TV; Science Channel; SoapNet; Speed Channel; Style Network; Syfy; TeenNick; Toon Disney; Trinity Broadcasting Network; Turner Classic Movies; TV Land; Versus; VH1 Classic; VH1 Soul.
Digital Pay Service 1
Pay Units: N.A.
Programming (via satellite): Cinemax (multiplexed); Encore (multiplexed); Flix; HBO (multiplexed); Showtime (multiplexed); Starz (multiplexed); The Movie Channel (multiplexed).
Video-On-Demand: No
Pay-Per-View
iN DEMAND (delivered digitally).
Internet Service
Operational: Yes.
Fee: $52.95 monthly.
Telephone Service
Digital: Operational
Fee: $49.99 monthly
Miles of Plant: 17.0 (coaxial); None (fiber optic). Homes passed: 1,098. Total homes in franchised area: 1,204.
Vice President & General Manager: Sean O'Donnell. Manager: Patty Faloon. Chief Technician: Jim Passon.
City fee: 3% of gross.
Ownership: Bresnan Communications Inc. (MSO). Sale pends to Cablevision Systems Corp.

MANHATTAN—Bresnan Communications. Now served by BOZEMAN, MT [MT0007]. ICA: MT0052.

MARION—Formerly served by Mallard Cablevision. No longer in operation. ICA: MT0101.

MELSTONE—Formerly served by Mel-View Cable TV. No longer in operation. ICA: MT0108.

MILES CITY—Mid-Rivers Communications, PO Box 280, 904 C Ave, Circle, MT 59215. Phone: 406-485-3301. Fax: 406-485-2924. Web Site: http://www.midrivers.com. Also serves Custer County. ICA: MT0009.
TV Market Ranking: Below 100 (Custer County (portions), MILES CITY); Outside TV Markets (Custer County (portions)). Franchise award date: N.A. Franchise expiration date: N.A. Began: June 1, 1962.
Channel capacity: 36 (not 2-way capable). Channels available but not in use: N.A.
Basic Service
Subscribers: 3,396.
Programming (received off-air): KULR-TV (NBC) Billings; KYUS-TV (NBC) Miles City.
Programming (via microwave): KTVQ (CBS, CW) Billings; KUSM-TV (PBS) Bozeman.
Programming (via satellite): ABC Family Channel; Arts & Entertainment; CNBC; CNN; C-SPAN; C-SPAN 2; Discovery Channel; Headline News; Lifetime; MTV; Nickelodeon; QVC; TBS Superstation; Turner Network TV; Weather Channel.
Fee: $60.00 installation; $9.87 monthly; $.69 converter; $40.00 additional installation.
Expanded Basic Service 1
Subscribers: 3,164.
Programming (via satellite): AMC; Disney Channel; ESPN; Fox Sports Net; Spike TV; truTV; USA Network.
Fee: $11.39 monthly.
Digital Basic Service
Subscribers: 1,124.
Pay Service 1
Pay Units: N.A.
Programming (via satellite): Cinemax; Encore; HBO; Showtime; Starz.
Video-On-Demand: No
Internet Service
Operational: No, Both DSL & dial-up.
Telephone Service
None
Miles of Plant: 47.0 (coaxial); None (fiber optic). Homes passed: 4,561. Total homes in franchised area: 4,634.
General Manager: Gerry Anderson. Chief Technician: Mike Sokoloski. Customer Service Manager: Deb Wagner.
City fee: None.
Ownership: Mid-Rivers Telephone Cooperative Inc. (MSO).

MILLTOWN—Bresnan Communications. Now served by MISSOULA, MT [MT0002]. ICA: MT0027.

MISSOULA—Bresnan Communications, 924 S 3rd St W, Missoula, MT 59801-2340. Phone: 406-727-8881. Fax: 406-727-6433. Web Site: http://www.bresnan.com. Also serves Bonner, Clinton, Florence, Grant Creek, Lolo, Milltown, Missoula County, Missoula South, Orchard Homes (portions), Rattlesnake, Rattlesnake Valley & Stevensville. ICA: MT0002.
TV Market Ranking: Below 100 (Bonner, Clinton, Florence, Grant Creek, Lolo, Milltown, MISSOULA, Missoula County (portions), Missoula South, Orchard Homes (portions), Rattlesnake, Rattlesnake Valley, Stevensville); Outside TV Markets (Missoula County (portions)). Franchise award date: N.A. Franchise expiration date: N.A. Began: September 1, 1956.
Channel capacity: N.A. Channels available but not in use: N.A.
Basic Service
Subscribers: 16,301.
Programming (received off-air): KECI-TV (NBC) Missoula; KPAX-TV (CBS, CW) Missoula; KTMF (ABC, FOX) Missoula; KUFM-TV (PBS) Missoula; 3 FMs.
Programming (via microwave): KSPS-TV (PBS) Spokane.
Programming (via satellite): C-SPAN; C-SPAN 2; CW+; Eternal Word TV Network; ION Television; Lifetime; QVC; TBS Superstation; TV Guide Network.
Current originations: Government Access.
Fee: $60.00 installation; $20.00 monthly; $.72 converter; $40.00 additional installation.
Expanded Basic Service 1
Subscribers: 14,142.
Programming (via satellite): ABC Family Channel; Altitude Sports & Entertainment; AMC; Animal Planet; Arts & Entertainment; Bravo; Cartoon Network; CNBC; CNN; Comedy Central; Country Music TV; Discovery Channel; Disney Channel; E! Entertainment Television; ESPN; ESPN 2; Food Network; Fox News Channel; Fox Sports Net Rocky Mountain; FX; Great American Country; Hallmark Channel; Headline News; HGTV; History Channel; Home Shopping Network; INSP; MSNBC; MTV; Nickelodeon; Oxygen; Spike TV; Syfy; The Learning Channel; The Sportsman Channel; Travel Channel; truTV; Turner Classic Movies; Turner Network TV; TV Land; USA Network; VH1; Weather Channel.
Fee: $29.95 installation; $28.99 monthly.
Digital Basic Service
Subscribers: 6,782.
Programming (received off-air): KPAX-TV (CBS, CW) Missoula; KUFM-TV (PBS) Missoula.
Programming (via satellite): ABC Family HD; AmericanLife TV Network; Animal Planet HD; Arts & Entertainment HD; BBC America; Bio; Bloomberg Television; BlueHighways TV; Bravo HD; BYU Television; CBS College Sports Network; CMT Pure Country; CNBC HD+; CNN HD; Cooking Channel; C-SPAN 3; Discovery Channel HD; Discovery HD Theater; Discovery Health Channel; Discovery Military Channel; Discovery Planet Green; Disney Channel HD; DMX Music; Do-It-Yourself; ESPN 2 HD; ESPN Classic Sports; ESPN HD; ESPNews; FitTV; Food Network HD; Fox College Sports Atlantic; Fox College Sports Central; Fox College Sports Pacific; Fox Movie Channel; Fox Reality Channel; Fox Soccer; Fuse; G4; Golf Channel; Gospel Music Channel; GSN; Halogen Network; HDNet; HDNet Movies; HGTV HD; History Channel HD; History Channel International; HorseRacing TV; ID Investigation Discovery; Independent Film Channel; ION Life; ION Television; Lifetime Movie Network; Lifetime Movie Network HD; MTV Hits; MTV Jams; MTV Tres; MTV2; National Geographic Channel; National Geographic Channel HD Network; NFL Network; NFL Network HD; NHL Network; Nick Jr.; Nick Too; NickToons TV; Outdoor Channel; Outdoor Channel 2 HD; Palladia; PBS Kids Sprout; Qubo; RFD-TV; Science Channel; Science Channel HD; SoapNet; Speed Channel; Speed HD; Style Network; Syfy HD; TBS in HD; TeenNick; TLC HD; Toon Disney; Trinity Broadcasting Network; Turner Network TV HD; Universal HD; USA Network HD; Versus; Versus HD; VH1 Classic; VH1 Soul; Weather Channel HD.
Fee: $6.00 monthly.
Digital Pay Service 1
Pay Units: N.A.
Programming (via satellite): Cinemax (multiplexed); Cinemax On Demand; Encore (multiplexed); Flix; HBO (multiplexed); HBO HD; HBO On Demand; Showtime (multiplexed); Showtime HD; Showtime On Demand; Starz (multiplexed); Starz HDTV; Starz On Demand; The Movie Channel (multiplexed); The Movie Channel HD.
Video-On-Demand: Yes
Pay-Per-View
iN DEMAND (delivered digitally); ESPN (delivered digitally); MLB Network (delivered digitally); NHL Center Ice (delivered digitally).
Internet Service
Operational: Yes.
Subscribers: 7,519.
Broadband Service: Bresnan OnLine.
Fee: $52.95 monthly.
Telephone Service
Analog: Not Operational
Digital: Operational
Subscribers: 2,485.
Fee: $49.99 monthly
Miles of Plant: 653.0 (coaxial); 204.0 (fiber optic). Homes passed: 43,586.
General Manager: Mike Oswald. Technical Operations Manager: Alan White.

City fee: $85 annually.
Ownership: Bresnan Communications Inc. (MSO). Sale pends to Cablevision Systems Corp.

MISSOULA—Cable Montana. Now served by MISSOULA, MT [MT0002]. ICA: MT0021.

NINE MILE—Formerly served by Bresnan Communications. No longer in operation. ICA: MT0077.

OPPORTUNITY—Western Cable TV, 201 E Front St, Butte, MT 59701-5203. Phone: 406-723-3362. Fax: 406-782-6541. ICA: MT0076.
TV Market Ranking: Below 100 (OPPORTUNITY). Franchise award date: N.A. Franchise expiration date: N.A. Began: October 1, 1985.
Channel capacity: 33 (not 2-way capable). Channels available but not in use: N.A.
Basic Service
Subscribers: 70.
Programming (received off-air): KTVM-TV (NBC) Butte; KXLF-TV (CBS, CW) Butte.
Programming (via satellite): ABC Family Channel; CNN; Discovery Channel; ESPN; TBS Superstation; Turner Network TV; USA Network; WGN America.
Fee: $30.00 installation; $25.00 monthly.
Pay Service 1
Pay Units: 10.
Programming (via satellite): HBO.
Fee: $10.00 installation; $12.00 monthly.
Internet Service
Operational: No.
Telephone Service
None
Miles of Plant: 12.0 (coaxial); None (fiber optic). Homes passed: 200. Total homes in franchised area: 200.
Manager: Jerry Haynes.
Ownership: Western Cable of Opportunity Inc. (MSO).

PARADISE—KLip Interactive, 455 Gees Mill Business Court, Conyers, GA 30013. Phones: 800-388-6577; 678-727-7100. Fax: 678-727-7002. E-mail: jsheehan@klipia.com. Web Site: http://www.klipia.com. ICA: MT0116.
TV Market Ranking: Outside TV Markets (PARADISE). Franchise award date: N.A. Franchise expiration date: N.A. Began: N.A.
Channel capacity: 40 (not 2-way capable). Channels available but not in use: 23.
Basic Service
Subscribers: 7.
Programming (received off-air): KECI-TV (NBC) Missoula; KPAX-TV (CBS, CW) Missoula; KSPS-TV (PBS) Spokane.
Programming (via satellite): ABC Family Channel; Cartoon Network; CNN; Discovery Channel; Disney Channel; ESPN; ESPN 2; HGTV; Spike TV; TBS Superstation; Trinity Broadcasting Network; Turner Network TV; USA Network.
Programming (via translator): KXLY-TV (ABC, MNT) Spokane.
Fee: $29.95 installation; $31.45 monthly.
Pay Service 1
Pay Units: N.A.
Programming (via satellite): HBO; Showtime; The Movie Channel.
Fee: $10.95 monthly (each).
Video-On-Demand: No
Internet Service
Operational: No.
Telephone Service
None
Miles of Plant: 1.0 (coaxial); None (fiber optic). Homes passed: 10.
Chief Executive Officer: Joseph A. Sheehan. General Manager, West: Vance Johnson. General Manager, East: Mark Miller.
Ownership: KLiP Interactive LLC (MSO).

PARK CITY—Cable Montana. Now served by LAUREL, MT [MT0023]. ICA: MT0091.

PHILIPSBURG—Formerly served by Eagle Cablevision Inc. No longer in operation. ICA: MT0056.

PLAINS—KLiP Interactive, 455 Gees Mill Business Court, Conyers, GA 30013. Phones: 800-388-6577; 678-727-7100. Fax: 678-727-7002. E-mail: jsheehan@klipia.com. Web Site: http://www.klipia.com. ICA: MT0063.
TV Market Ranking: Outside TV Markets (PLAINS). Franchise award date: N.A. Franchise expiration date: N.A. Began: May 1, 1982.
Channel capacity: 65 (2-way capable). Channels available but not in use: 31.
Basic Service
Subscribers: 102.
Programming (received off-air): KDVR (FOX) Denver; KSPS-TV (PBS) Spokane.
Programming (via microwave): KECI-TV (NBC) Missoula; KPAX-TV (CBS, CW) Missoula; KXLY-TV (ABC, MNT) Spokane.
Programming (via satellite): ABC Family Channel; Animal Planet; Arts & Entertainment; Cartoon Network; CNN; Discovery Channel; Disney Channel; E! Entertainment Television; ESPN; ESPN 2; Fox News Channel; Fox Sports Net Rocky Mountain; Headline News; HGTV; History Channel; Nickelodeon; Outdoor Channel; Spike TV; TBS Superstation; The Learning Channel; Trinity Broadcasting Network; Turner Classic Movies; Turner Network TV; USA Network; VH1; Weather Channel; WGN America.
Fee: $32.95 installation; $36.14 monthly.
Pay Service 1
Pay Units: 4.
Programming (via satellite): HBO.
Fee: $10.95 monthly.
Pay Service 2
Pay Units: 3.
Programming (via satellite): Showtime.
Fee: $10.95 monthly.
Pay Service 3
Pay Units: N.A.
Programming (via satellite): The Movie Channel.
Fee: $10.95 monthly.
Video-On-Demand: No
Internet Service
Operational: No.
Telephone Service
None
Miles of Plant: 19.0 (coaxial); None (fiber optic). Homes passed: 134. Total homes in franchised area: 435.
Chief Executive Officer: Joseph A. Sheehan. General Manager East: Mark Miller. General Manager West: Vance Johnson.
City fee: None.
Ownership: KLiP Interactive LLC (MSO).

PLENTYWOOD—KLiP Interactive, 455 Gees Mill Business Court, Conyers, GA 30013. Phones: 800-388-6577; 678-727-7100. Fax: 678-727-7002. E-mail: jsheehan@klipia.com. Web Site: http://www.klipia.com. ICA: MT0039.
TV Market Ranking: Outside TV Markets (PLENTYWOOD). Franchise award date: May 16, 1978. Franchise expiration date: N.A. Began: June 20, 1979.
Channel capacity: 35 (not 2-way capable). Channels available but not in use: 5.
Basic Service
Subscribers: 412.
Programming (received off-air): KUMV-TV (NBC) Williston; KWSE (PBS) Williston; KXGN-TV (CBS, NBC) Glendive; KXMD-TV (CBS) Williston; 1 FM.
Programming (via microwave): KMGH-TV (ABC) Denver.
Programming (via satellite): ABC Family Channel; Arts & Entertainment; CNN; Country Music TV; Discovery Channel; Disney Channel; E! Entertainment Television; ESPN; ESPN 2; Fox News Channel; Fox Sports Net Rocky Mountain; FX; HGTV; History Channel; KDVR (FOX) Denver; Lifetime; National Geographic Channel; Spike TV; TBS Superstation; The Learning Channel; Trinity Broadcasting Network; Turner Classic Movies; Turner Network TV; TV Land; USA Network; Weather Channel; WGN America.
Fee: $31.95 installation; $37.76 monthly.
Pay Service 1
Pay Units: 30.
Programming (via satellite): HBO.
Fee: $10.95 monthly.
Pay Service 2
Pay Units: N.A.
Programming (via satellite): Showtime; The Movie Channel.
Fee: $10.95 monthly (each).
Video-On-Demand: No
Internet Service
Operational: No.
Telephone Service
None
Miles of Plant: 16.0 (coaxial); None (fiber optic). Homes passed: 495. Total homes in franchised area: 800.
Chief Executive Officer: Joseph A. Sheehan. General Manager East: Mark Miller. General Manager West: Vance Johnson.
City fee: None.
Ownership: KLiP Interactive LLC (MSO).

POLSON—Bresnan Communications, 333 First Ave E, Kalispell, MT 59901-4935. Phone: 406-758-2300. Fax: 406-755-7204. E-mail: sodonnell@bresnan.com. Web Site: http://www.bresnan.com. Also serves Lake County, Pablo & Ronan. ICA: MT0016.
TV Market Ranking: Below 100 (Lake County (portions), POLSON); Outside TV Markets (Lake County (portions), Pablo, Ronan). Franchise award date: N.A. Franchise expiration date: N.A. Began: October 1, 1966.
Channel capacity: N.A. Channels available but not in use: N.A.
Basic Service
Subscribers: 2,150.
Programming (received off-air): KECI-TV (NBC) Missoula; KPAX-TV (CBS, CW) Missoula; KTMF (ABC, FOX) Missoula; 6 FMs.
Programming (via microwave): KHQ-TV (NBC) Spokane; KREM (CBS) Spokane; KSPS-TV (PBS) Spokane; KXLY-TV (ABC, MNT) Spokane.
Programming (via satellite): C-SPAN; C-SPAN 2; CW+; Home Shopping Network; KDVR (FOX) Denver; Lifetime; QVC; TBS Superstation.
Fee: $60.00 installation; $20.00 monthly; $40.00 additional installation.
Expanded Basic Service 1
Subscribers: 2,026.
Programming (via satellite): ABC Family Channel; Altitude Sports & Entertainment; AMC; Animal Planet; Arts & Entertainment; Cartoon Network; CNBC; CNN; Comcast Sports Net Northwest; Comedy Central; Country Music TV; Discovery Channel; Disney Channel; E! Entertainment Television; ESPN; ESPN 2; Food Network; Fox News Channel; FX; Hallmark Channel; Headline News; HGTV; History Channel; INSP; ION Television; MSNBC; MTV; Nickelodeon; Oxygen; Spike TV; Syfy; The Learning Channel; Travel Channel; truTV; Turner Classic Movies; Turner Network TV; TV Guide Network; TV Land; USA Network; VH1; Weather Channel.
Fee: $10.95 monthly.
Digital Basic Service
Subscribers: 802.
Programming (received off-air): KPAX-TV (CBS, CW) Missoula.
Programming (via satellite): ABC Family HD; Animal Planet HD; Arts & Entertainment HD; BBC America; Bio; Bloomberg Television; Bravo; Bravo HD; CBS College Sports Network; CMT Pure Country; CNBC HD+; CNN HD; Cooking Channel; Discovery Channel HD; Discovery HD Theater; Discovery Health Channel; Discovery Kids Channel; Discovery Military Channel; Discovery Planet Green; Disney Channel HD; DMX Music; Do-It-Yourself; ESPN 2 HD; ESPN Classic Sports; ESPN HD; ESPNews; FitTV; Food Network HD; Fox College Sports Atlantic; Fox College Sports Central; Fox College Sports Pacific; Fox Movie Channel; Fox Reality Channel; Fox Soccer; Fuse; G4; Golf Channel; Gospel Music Channel; Great American Country; GSN; Halogen Network; HDNet; HDNet Movies; HGTV HD; History Channel HD; History Channel International; HorseRacing TV; ID Investigation Discovery; Independent Film Channel; ION Television; Lifetime Movie Network; Lifetime Movie Network HD; MTV Hits; MTV Jams; MTV Tres; MTV2; National Geographic Channel; National Geographic Channel HD Network; NFL Network; NFL Network HD; Nick Jr.; Nick Too; NickToons TV; Outdoor Channel; Outdoor Channel 2 HD; Palladia; PBS Kids Sprout; RFD-TV; Science Channel; Science Channel HD; SoapNet; Speed Channel; Speed HD; Style Network; Syfy HD; TBS in HD; TeenNick; The Sportsman Channel; TLC HD; Toon Disney; Trinity Broadcasting Network; Turner Network TV HD; Universal HD; USA Network HD; Versus; Versus HD; VH1 Classic; VH1 Soul; Weather Channel HD.
Fee: $24.04 monthly.
Digital Pay Service 1
Pay Units: 710.
Programming (via satellite): Cinemax (multiplexed); Cinemax HD; Encore (multiplexed); Flix; HBO (multiplexed); HBO HD; Showtime (multiplexed); Showtime HD; Starz (multiplexed); Starz HDTV; The Movie Channel (multiplexed); The Movie Channel HD.
Video-On-Demand: No
Pay-Per-View
iN DEMAND (delivered digitally).
Internet Service
Operational: Yes.
Subscribers: 453.
Broadband Service: Bresnan OnLine.
Fee: $52.95 monthly.
Telephone Service
Digital: Operational
Subscribers: 55.
Fee: $49.99 monthly
Miles of Plant: 130.0 (coaxial); 42.0 (fiber optic). Homes passed: 5,492.
Vice President & General Manager: Sean O'Donnell. Manager: Patty Faloon. Chief Technician: Weldon Plympton.
Ownership: Bresnan Communications Inc. (MSO). Sale pends to Cablevision Systems Corp.

POPLAR—KLiP Interactive, 455 Gees Mill Business Court, Conyers, GA 30013. Phones: 800-388-6577; 706-215-1385. Fax: 678-727-7002. E-mail: jsheehan@klipia.com. Web Site: http://www.klipia.com. ICA: MT0040.

TV Market Ranking: Outside TV Markets (POPLAR). Franchise award date: N.A. Franchise expiration date: N.A. Began: October 1, 1982.

Channel capacity: 40 (not 2-way capable). Channels available but not in use: 9.

Basic Service

Subscribers: 203.

Programming (received off-air): KFBB-TV (ABC, FOX) Great Falls; KUMV-TV (NBC) Williston; KWSE (PBS) Williston; KXGN-TV (CBS, NBC) Glendive; KXMD-TV (CBS) Williston.

Programming (via microwave): KMGH-TV (ABC) Denver.

Programming (via satellite): ABC Family Channel; Arts & Entertainment; Cartoon Network; CNN; Comedy Central; Discovery Channel; Disney Channel; ESPN; ESPN 2; Fox News Channel; Fox Sports Net Rocky Mountain; Headline News; HGTV; INSP; KDVR (FOX) Denver; QVC; Spike TV; TBS Superstation; Trinity Broadcasting Network; Turner Classic Movies; Turner Network TV; USA Network; WGN America.

Fee: $29.95 installation; $31.35 monthly.

Pay Service 1

Pay Units: 54.

Programming (via satellite): HBO.

Fee: $10.00 installation; $10.95 monthly.

Pay Service 2

Pay Units: N.A.

Programming (via satellite): Showtime; The Movie Channel.

Fee: $10.95 monthly (each).

Video-On-Demand: No

Internet Service

Operational: No.

Telephone Service

None

Miles of Plant: 14.0 (coaxial); None (fiber optic). Homes passed: 771.

Chief Executive Officer: Joseph A. Sheehan. General Manager, West: Vance Johnson. General Manager, East: Mark Miller.

Ownership: KLiP Interactive LLC (MSO).

RED LODGE—Cable Montana, 222 W 1st St, Laurel, MT 59044. Phones: 800-628-6060; 406-628-6336; 308-236-1512 (Kearney, NE corporate office). Fax: 406-628-8181. Web Site: http://www.cablemt.net. ICA: MT0037.

TV Market Ranking: Outside TV Markets (RED LODGE). Franchise award date: N.A. Franchise expiration date: N.A. Began: July 2, 1984.

Channel capacity: N.A. Channels available but not in use: N.A.

Basic Service

Subscribers: 939.

Programming (received off-air): KHMT (FOX) Hardin; KSVI (ABC) Billings; KTVQ (CBS, CW) Billings; KULR-TV (NBC) Billings; KUSM-TV (PBS) Bozeman; KWBM (MNT) Harrison [LICENSED & SILENT].

Programming (via satellite): ABC Family Channel; Animal Planet; Arts & Entertainment; Eternal Word TV Network; Food Network; Lifetime; QVC; TBS Superstation; The Learning Channel; TV Guide Network; WGN America.

Fee: $24.95 installation; $21.95 monthly.

Expanded Basic Service 1

Subscribers: N.A.

Programming (via satellite): Altitude Sports & Entertainment; AMC; Cartoon Network; CNBC; CNN; Comedy Central; Country Music TV; C-SPAN; Discovery Channel; E! Entertainment Television; ESPN; ESPN 2; ESPN Classic Sports; Fox News Channel; Fox Sports Net Rocky Mountain; FX; G4; Hallmark Channel; Headline News; HGTV; History Channel; MSNBC; MTV; Nickelodeon; Outdoor Channel; Spike TV; Syfy; truTV; Turner Network TV; TV Land; USA Network; VH1; Weather Channel.

Fee: $18.04 monthly.

Digital Basic Service

Subscribers: N.A.

Programming (via satellite): American-Life TV Network; BBC America; Bio; Black Family Channel; Bloomberg Television; CMT Pure Country; Current; Discovery Health Channel; Discovery Kids Channel; Discovery Military Channel; Discovery Planet Green; DMX Music; ESPN Classic Sports; ESPNews; FitTV; Fox College Sports Atlantic; Fox College Sports Central; Fox College Sports Pacific; Fox Movie Channel; G4; Golf Channel; GSN; Halogen Network; History Channel; History Channel International; ID Investigation Discovery; Lifetime Movie Network; MTV Hits; MTV2; National Geographic Channel; Nick Jr.; Outdoor Channel; Ovation; Science Channel; ShopNBC; Sleuth; Speed Channel; Style Network; TeenNick; Trinity Broadcasting Network; Versus; VH1 Classic; VH1 Soul; WE tv.

Fee: $13.00 monthly.

Digital Pay Service 1

Pay Units: N.A.

Programming (via satellite): Cinemax (multiplexed); Encore (multiplexed); Flix; HBO (multiplexed); Showtime (multiplexed); Starz (multiplexed); The Movie Channel (multiplexed).

Fee: $13.00 monthly (HBO, Cinemax, Showtime/TMC/Flix or Starz/Encore).

Video-On-Demand: No

Pay-Per-View

iN DEMAND (delivered digitally); Hot Choice (delivered digitally); Playboy TV (delivered digitally); Fresh (delivered digitally); Shorteez (delivered digitally); Club Jenna (delivered digitally).

Internet Service

Operational: Yes.

Broadband Service: Cable Montana.

Fee: $35.95 monthly.

Telephone Service

Digital: Operational

Fee: $39.95 monthly

Miles of Plant: 14.0 (coaxial); None (fiber optic).

Manager: Doug Lane. Operations Manager: Stuart Gilbertson.

Ownership: USA Companies (MSO).

RICHEY—Mid-Rivers Communications, PO Box 280, 904 C Ave, Circle, MT 59215. Phone: 406-485-3301. Fax: 406-485-2924. E-mail: mrtc@midrivers.com. Web Site: http://www.midrivers.com. ICA: MT0104.

TV Market Ranking: Outside TV Markets (RICHEY). Franchise award date: N.A. Franchise expiration date: N.A. Began: January 1, 1984.

Channel capacity: N.A. Channels available but not in use: N.A.

Basic Service

Subscribers: 93.

Programming (received off-air): KUMV-TV (NBC) Williston; KXGN-TV (CBS, NBC) Glendive; 1 FM.

Programming (via microwave): KMGH-TV (ABC) Denver; KRMA-TV (PBS) Denver.

Programming (via satellite): CNN; C-SPAN; Discovery Channel; Disney Channel; Headline News; QVC; Spike TV; Syfy; TBS Superstation; Weather Channel; WGN America.

Fee: $15.45 monthly.

Expanded Basic Service 1

Subscribers: 81.

Programming (via satellite): ABC Family Channel; AMC; Animal Planet; Arts & Entertainment; Cartoon Network; CNBC; Comedy Central; Country Music TV; C-SPAN 2; E! Entertainment Television; Encore Action; ESPN; ESPN 2; Eternal Word TV Network; FitTV; Food Network; Fox News Channel; Fox Sports Net Rocky Mountain; FX; G4; GSN; Hallmark Channel; HGTV; History Channel; Lifetime; MTV; Nickelodeon; Outdoor Channel; Speed Channel; The Learning Channel; The New Encore; Toon Disney; Travel Channel; truTV; Turner Network TV; TV Land; USA Network; VH1.

Fee: $11.50 monthly.

Pay Service 1

Pay Units: 2.

Programming (via satellite): Cinemax.

Fee: $12.00 monthly.

Pay Service 2

Pay Units: 7.

Programming (via satellite): HBO.

Fee: $12.00 monthly.

Pay Service 3

Pay Units: 2.

Programming (via satellite): Showtime.

Fee: $12.00 monthly.

Pay Service 4

Pay Units: 5.

Programming (via satellite): The Movie Channel.

Fee: $12.00 monthly.

Internet Service

Operational: No, Both DSL & dial-up.

Telephone Service

None

Miles of Plant: 7.0 (coaxial); None (fiber optic). Homes passed: 100.

General Manager: Gerry Anderson. Chief Technician: Mike Sokolosky. Customer Service Manager: Deb Wagner. Customer Service Representative: Liz Cedar.

Ownership: Mid-Rivers Telephone Cooperative Inc. (MSO).

RIVERSIDE GREENS—Formerly served by Northwestern Communications Corp. No longer in operation. ICA: MT0117.

RONAN—Bresnan Communications. Now served by POLSON, MT [MT0016]. ICA: MT0029.

ROUNDUP—Mid-Rivers Communications, PO Box 280, 904 C Ave, Circle, MT 59215. Phone: 406-485-3301. Fax: 406-485-2924. Web Site: http://www.midrivers.com. ICA: MT0043.

TV Market Ranking: Outside TV Markets (ROUNDUP). Franchise award date: N.A. Franchise expiration date: N.A. Began: July 1, 1981.

Channel capacity: N.A. Channels available but not in use: N.A.

Basic Service

Subscribers: 648.

Programming (received off-air): KSVI (ABC) Billings; KTVQ (CBS, CW) Billings; KULR-TV (NBC) Billings.

Programming (via microwave): KUSM-TV (PBS) Bozeman.

Programming (via satellite): ABC Family Channel; Arts & Entertainment; CNBC; CNN; C-SPAN; Discovery Channel; Disney Channel; ESPN; Fox Movie Channel; Headline News; HGTV; History Channel; INSP; Lifetime; Nickelodeon; Outdoor Channel; QVC; Spike TV; Syfy; TBS Superstation; The Learning Channel; Travel Channel; Turner Network TV; TV Land; WE tv; WGN America.

Current originations: Public Access.

Fee: $19.00 monthly.

Expanded Basic Service 1

Subscribers: N.A.

Programming (via satellite): ESPN 2; Weather Channel.

Fee: $2.50 monthly.

Digital Basic Service

Subscribers: N.A.

Programming (via satellite): BBC America; Bravo; Discovery Digital Networks; DMX Music; ESPN 2; ESPN Classic Sports; ESPNews; Fox Soccer; Golf Channel; GSN; HGTV; History Channel; Independent Film Channel; National Geographic Channel; Nick Jr.; Syfy; Turner Classic Movies; Versus; VH1 Classic; VH1 Country; WE tv.

Pay Service 1

Pay Units: 167.

Programming (via satellite): Showtime; The Movie Channel.

Fee: $5.95 monthly (Showtime); $8.00 monthly (TMC).

Digital Pay Service 1

Pay Units: N.A.

Programming (via satellite): Cinemax (multiplexed); Encore (multiplexed); Flix; HBO (multiplexed); Showtime (multiplexed); Starz (multiplexed); The Movie Channel (multiplexed).

Video-On-Demand: No

Pay-Per-View

iN DEMAND (delivered digitally); ESPN Now (delivered digitally); Sports PPV (delivered digitally).

Internet Service

Operational: Yes, DSL only.

Telephone Service

None

Miles of Plant: 13.0 (coaxial); None (fiber optic). Homes passed: 750.

General Manager: Gerry Anderson. Chief Technician: Mike Sokolosky. Customer Service Manager: Deb Wagner.

Ownership: Mid-Rivers Telephone Cooperative Inc. (MSO).

RYEGATE—Mid-Rivers Communications, PO Box 280, 904 C Ave, Circle, MT 59215. Phone: 406-485-3301. Fax: 406-485-2924. E-mail: lcedar@midrivers.com. Web Site: http://www.midrivers.com. ICA: MT0102.

TV Market Ranking: Outside TV Markets (RYEGATE). Franchise award date: May 1, 1983. Franchise expiration date: N.A. Began: September 1, 1983.

Channel capacity: 40 (not 2-way capable). Channels available but not in use: 19.

Basic Service

Subscribers: 42.

Programming (received off-air): KSVI (ABC) Billings; KTVQ (CBS, CW) Billings; KULR-TV (NBC) Billings.

Programming (via satellite): ABC Family Channel; Arts & Entertainment; CNN; Discovery Channel; Disney Channel; E! Entertainment Television; ESPN; History Channel; Lifetime; Spike TV; TBS Superstation; Turner Network TV; TV Land; USA Network; Weather Channel; WGN America.

Current originations: Government Access; Educational Access; Public Access.

Fee: $15.00 installation; $28.45 monthly.

Pay Service 1

Pay Units: 21.

Programming (via satellite): HBO.

Fee: $15.00 installation; $12.00 monthly.

Internet Service

Operational: No.

Telephone Service
None
Miles of Plant: 4.0 (coaxial); None (fiber optic). Homes passed: 118. Total homes in franchised area: 118.
General Manager: Gerry Anderson. Chief Technician: Mike Sokoloski. Customer Service Manager: Deb Wagner.
Ownership: Mid-Rivers Telephone Cooperative Inc. (MSO).

SAVAGE—Mid-Rivers Communications, PO Box 280, 904 C Ave, Circle, MT 59215. Phone: 406-485-3301. Fax: 406-485-2924. E-mail: mrtc@midrivers.com. Web Site: http://www.midrivers.com. ICA: MT0105.
TV Market Ranking: Below 100 (SAVAGE). Franchise award date: N.A. Franchise expiration date: N.A. Began: December 1, 1982.
Channel capacity: 77 (not 2-way capable). Channels available but not in use: N.A.
Basic Service
Subscribers: 83.
Programming (received off-air): KUMV-TV (NBC) Williston; KWSE (PBS) Williston; KXGN-TV (CBS, NBC) Glendive; KXMD-TV (CBS) Williston.
Programming (via microwave): KMGH-TV (ABC) Denver.
Programming (via satellite): CNN; C-SPAN; Disney Channel; Headline News; QVC; Spike TV; TBS Superstation; Weather Channel; WGN America.
Fee: $14.45 monthly.
Expanded Basic Service 1
Subscribers: 80.
Programming (via satellite): ABC Family Channel; AMC; Animal Planet; Arts & Entertainment; Cartoon Network; CNBC; Comedy Central; Country Music TV; C-SPAN 2; Discovery Channel; E! Entertainment Television; ESPN; ESPN 2; Eternal Word TV Network; FitTV; Food Network; Fox News Channel; Fox Sports Net Rocky Mountain; FX; HGTV; History Channel; Lifetime; Nickelodeon; Outdoor Channel; Speed Channel; Syfy; The Learning Channel; The New Encore; Travel Channel; Trinity Broadcasting Network; Turner Network TV; TV Land; USA Network; VH1.
Fee: $10.50 monthly.
Digital Basic Service
Subscribers: N.A.
Programming (via satellite): BBC America; Bravo; Discovery Channel; DMX Music; ESPN 2; ESPN Classic Sports; ESPNews; Fox Soccer; Golf Channel; GSN; HGTV; History Channel; Independent Film Channel; National Geographic Channel; Nick Jr.; Syfy; Turner Classic Movies; Versus; VH1 Classic; VH1 Country; WE tv.
Pay Service 1
Pay Units: 3.
Programming (via satellite): Cinemax; Showtime.
Fee: $12.00 monthly.
Pay Service 2
Pay Units: 11.
Programming (via satellite): HBO.
Fee: $10.00 monthly.
Pay Service 3
Pay Units: 3.
Programming (via satellite): Showtime.
Fee: $12.00 monthly.
Pay Service 4
Pay Units: 3.
Programming (via satellite): The Movie Channel.
Fee: $12.00 monthly.
Digital Pay Service 1
Pay Units: N.A.
Programming (via satellite): Cinemax (multiplexed); Encore (multiplexed); Flix; HBO (multiplexed); Showtime (multiplexed); Starz (multiplexed); The Movie Channel (multiplexed).
Video-On-Demand: No
Pay-Per-View
iN DEMAND (delivered digitally); ESPN Now (delivered digitally); Sports PPV (delivered digitally).
Internet Service
Operational: No.
Telephone Service
None
Miles of Plant: 2.0 (coaxial); None (fiber optic). Homes passed: 100.
General Manager: Gerry Anderson. Chief Technician: Mike Sokolosky. Customer Service Manager: Deb Wagner. Customer Service: Liz Cedar.
Ownership: Mid-Rivers Telephone Cooperative Inc. (MSO).

SCOBEY—KLiP Interactive, 455 Gees Mill Business Court, Conyers, GA 30013. Phones: 800-388-6577; 678-727-7100. Fax: 678-727-7002. E-mail: jsheehan@klipia.com. Web Site: http://www.klipia.com. ICA: MT0047.
TV Market Ranking: Outside TV Markets (SCOBEY). Franchise award date: N.A. Franchise expiration date: N.A. Began: December 1, 1980.
Channel capacity: 40 (not 2-way capable). Channels available but not in use: 15.
Basic Service
Subscribers: 195.
Programming (received off-air): KUMV-TV (NBC) Williston; KXMD-TV (CBS) Williston.
Programming (via microwave): KMGH-TV (ABC) Denver.
Programming (via satellite): ABC Family Channel; Arts & Entertainment; Canadian Learning Television; Cartoon Network; CNN; Discovery Channel; Disney Channel; ESPN; ESPN 2; Fox News Channel; Fox Sports Net Rocky Mountain; HGTV; INSP; KDVR (FOX) Denver; Spike TV; TBS Superstation; Turner Classic Movies; Turner Network TV; USA Network; WGN America.
Current originations: Religious Access.
Fee: $29.95 installation; $31.15 monthly.
Pay Service 1
Pay Units: 20.
Programming (via satellite): HBO.
Fee: $15.00 installation; $10.95 monthly.
Pay Service 2
Pay Units: N.A.
Programming (via satellite): Showtime; The Movie Channel.
Fee: $10.95 monthly (each).
Video-On-Demand: No
Internet Service
Operational: No.
Telephone Service
None
Miles of Plant: 22.0 (coaxial); None (fiber optic). Homes passed: 570.
Chief Executive Officer: Joseph A. Sheehan. General Manager East: Mark Miller. General Manager West: Vance Johnson.
Ownership: KLiP Interactive LLC (MSO).

SEELEY LAKE—Western Montana Community Telephone, 312 Main St SW, Ronan, MT 59864. Phone: 406-676-0788. Fax: 406-467-3490. ICA: MT0060.
TV Market Ranking: Below 100 (SEELEY LAKE). Franchise award date: N.A. Franchise expiration date: N.A. Began: July 1, 1983.
Channel capacity: N.A. Channels available but not in use: N.A.
Basic Service
Subscribers: 95.
Programming (received off-air): KDVR (FOX) Denver; KTVM-TV (NBC) Butte; KXLF-TV (CBS, CW) Butte.
Programming (via microwave): KMGH-TV (ABC) Denver; KRMA-TV (PBS) Denver.
Programming (via satellite): ABC Family Channel; AMC; Animal Planet; Arts & Entertainment; CNN; Country Music TV; Discovery Channel; Disney Channel; ESPN; ESPN 2; Nickelodeon; Spike TV; Syfy; TBS Superstation; Turner Network TV; USA Network; VH1; WGN America.
Fee: $45.00 installation; $29.45 monthly.
Pay Service 1
Pay Units: 56.
Programming (via satellite): Showtime.
Fee: $11.95 monthly.
Pay Service 2
Pay Units: 40.
Programming (via satellite): HBO.
Fee: $11.95 monthly.
Internet Service
Operational: No.
Telephone Service
None
Miles of Plant: 16.0 (coaxial); None (fiber optic). Homes passed: 493.
Ownership: Western Montana Community Telephone (MSO).

SHELBY—3 Rivers Communications, 202 5th St S, PO Box 429, Fairfield, MT 59436. Phones: 800-796-4567; 406-467-2535. Fax: 406-467-3490. E-mail: 3rt@3rivers.net. Web Site: http://www.3rivers.net. ICA: MT0024.
TV Market Ranking: Outside TV Markets (SHELBY). Franchise award date: N.A. Franchise expiration date: N.A. Began: July 1, 1955.
Channel capacity: 62 (operating 2-way). Channels available but not in use: 10.
Basic Service
Subscribers: 646.
Programming (received off-air): KFBB-TV (ABC, FOX) Great Falls; KRTV (CBS, CW) Great Falls; KTGF (IND) Great Falls.
Programming (via microwave): KHQ-TV (NBC) Spokane; KUSM-TV (PBS) Bozeman; KXLY-TV (ABC, MNT) Spokane.
Programming (via satellite): C-SPAN; C-SPAN 2; FX; Lifetime; QVC; TBS Superstation.
Fee: $60.00 installation; $20.00 monthly; $40.00 additional installation.
Expanded Basic Service 1
Subscribers: 485.
Programming (via satellite): ABC Family Channel; Altitude Sports & Entertainment; AMC; Animal Planet; Arts & Entertainment; Cartoon Network; CNBC; CNN; Comedy Central; Country Music TV; Discovery Channel; Disney Channel; ESPN; ESPN 2; Food Network; Fox News Channel; Fox Sports Net Rocky Mountain; Hallmark Channel; Headline News; HGTV; History Channel; Nickelodeon; Oxygen; Spike TV; The Learning Channel; The Sportsman Channel; Travel Channel; truTV; Turner Classic Movies; Turner Network TV; USA Network; Weather Channel.
Fee: $28.99 monthly.
Digital Basic Service
Subscribers: 189.
Programming (via satellite): AmericanLife TV Network; BBC America; Bio; Bloomberg Television; Bravo; CBS College Sports Network; CMT Pure Country; Discovery Health Channel; Discovery Kids Channel; Discovery Military Channel; Discovery Planet Green; DMX Music; ESPN Classic Sports; ESPNews; FitTV; Fox Movie Channel; Fox Soccer; Fuse; G4; Golf Channel; Great American Country; GSN; Halogen Network; History Channel International; ID Investigation Discovery; Independent Film Channel; Lifetime Movie Network; MTV Hits; MTV2; National Geographic Channel; Nick Jr.; NickToons TV; Outdoor Channel; PBS Kids Sprout; RFD-TV; Science Channel; Soapnet; Speed Channel; Style Network; Syfy; TeenNick; Toon Disney; Trinity Broadcasting Network; TV Land; Versus; VH1 Classic; VH1 Soul.
Fee: $6.00 monthly.
Digital Pay Service 1
Pay Units: N.A.
Programming (via satellite): Cinemax (multiplexed); Encore (multiplexed); Flix; HBO (multiplexed); Showtime (multiplexed); Starz (multiplexed); The Movie Channel (multiplexed).
Video-On-Demand: No
Pay-Per-View
Hot Choice (delivered digitally); iN DEMAND; iN DEMAND (delivered digitally); Fresh (delivered digitally).
Internet Service
Operational: No, DSL & dialup.
Telephone Service
None
Miles of Plant: 16.0 (coaxial); None (fiber optic). Homes passed: 1,518. Total homes in franchised area: 1,575.
General Manager: Steven Krogue. Plant & Facilities Director: Mike Henning. Sales & Marketing Director: Terry Noyd. Customer Operations Director: Sandi Oveson.
Ownership: 3 Rivers Telephone Cooperative Inc. (MSO).

SHERIDAN—Formerly served by Ruby Valley Cable Co. Inc. No longer in operation. ICA: MT0084.

SIDNEY—Mid-Rivers Communications, PO Box 280, 904 C Ave, Circle, MT 59215. Phone: 406-485-3301. Fax: 406-485-2924. Web Site: http://www.midrivers.com. ICA: MT0018.
TV Market Ranking: Outside TV Markets (SIDNEY). Franchise award date: N.A. Franchise expiration date: N.A. Began: May 1, 1967.
Channel capacity: 37 (2-way capable). Channels available but not in use: N.A.
Basic Service
Subscribers: 2,282.
Programming (received off-air): KDVR (FOX) Denver; KMGH-TV (ABC) Denver; KUMV-TV (NBC) Williston; KWSE (PBS) Williston; KXMD-TV (CBS) Williston.
Programming (via microwave): KUSM-TV (PBS) Bozeman; KXGN-TV (CBS, NBC) Glendive.
Programming (via satellite): CW+; Headline News; TBS Superstation; WGN America.
Fee: $60.00 installation; $9.95 monthly; $40.00 additional installation.
Expanded Basic Service 1
Subscribers: 2,094.
Programming (via satellite): ABC Family Channel; AMC; Animal Planet; Arts & Entertainment; Bravo; Cartoon Network; CNBC; CNN; Comedy Central; Country Music TV; C-SPAN; C-SPAN 2; Discovery Channel; Disney Channel; E! Entertainment

Television; ESPN; ESPN 2; ESPN Classic Sports; ESPN U; Eternal Word TV Network; FitTV; Food Network; Fox News Channel; Fox Sports Net Rocky Mountain; FX; G4; Great American Country; GSN; Hallmark Channel; HGTV; History Channel; Home Shopping Network; ION Television; Lifetime; MSNBC; MTV; National Geographic Channel; Nickelodeon; Outdoor Channel; Oxygen; RFD-TV; Speed Channel; Spike TV; Syfy; The Learning Channel; Toon Disney; Travel Channel; Trinity Broadcasting Network; truTV; Turner Classic Movies; Turner Network TV; TV Land; USA Network; VH1; Weather Channel.
Fee: $15.00 monthly.

Digital Basic Service
Subscribers: 396.
Programming (received off-air): KXMD-TV (CBS) Williston.
Programming (via satellite): Arts & Entertainment HD; BBC America; Bio; Bloomberg Television; Bravo; CMT Pure Country; Discovery Channel HD; Discovery Health Channel; Discovery Kids Channel; Discovery Military Channel; Discovery Planet Green; ESPN 2 HD; ESPN Classic Sports; ESPN HD; ESPNews; Food Network HD; Fox Movie Channel; Fox Soccer; Fuse; G4; Golf Channel; GSN; HDNet; HDNet Movies; HGTV HD; History Channel International; ID Investigation Discovery; Independent Film Channel; Lifetime Movie Network; MTV2; National Geographic Channel; National Geographic Channel HD Network; Nick Jr.; NickToons TV; Outdoor Channel 2 HD; Science Channel; Style Network; TeenNick; Toon Disney; Trinity Broadcasting Network; Turner Network TV HD; Universal HD; Versus; VH1 Classic; VH1 Soul; WE tv.

Pay Service 1
Pay Units: N.A.
Programming (via satellite): Cinemax; Encore; HBO; Showtime; Starz; The Movie Channel.
Fee: $15.00 installation; $1.75 monthly (Encore), $6.75 monthly (Starz), $10.00 monthly (Cinemax, HBO or Showtime).

Digital Pay Service 1
Pay Units: N.A.
Programming (via satellite): Cinemax (multiplexed); Cinemax HD; Encore (multiplexed); Flix; HBO HD; Showtime (multiplexed); Starz (multiplexed); The Movie Channel (multiplexed).

Video-On-Demand: No

Pay-Per-View
iN DEMAND (delivered digitally).

Internet Service
Operational: No, Both DSL & dial-up.

Telephone Service
None

Miles of Plant: 33.0 (coaxial); None (fiber optic).
General Manager: Gerry Anderson. Chief Technician: Mike Sokoloski. Customer Service Manager: Deb Wagner.
City fee: None.
Ownership: Mid-Rivers Telephone Cooperative Inc. (MSO).

ST. IGNATIUS—KLiP Interactive, 455 Gees Mill Business Court, Conyers, GA 30013. Phones: 800-388-6577; 678-727-7100. Fax: 678-727-7002. E-mail: jsheehan@klipia.com. Web Site: http://www.klipia.com. ICA: MT0055.
TV Market Ranking: Below 100 (ST. IGNATIUS). Franchise award date: N.A. Franchise expiration date: N.A. Began: April 4, 1985.
Channel capacity: 40 (not 2-way capable). Channels available but not in use: 5.

Basic Service
Subscribers: 56.
Programming (received off-air): KECI-TV (NBC) Missoula; KPAX-TV (CBS, CW) Missoula; KTMF (ABC, FOX) Missoula.
Programming (via satellite): ABC Family Channel; Animal Planet; Arts & Entertainment; Cartoon Network; CNN; Discovery Channel; Disney Channel; ESPN; ESPN 2; Fox News Channel; Fox Sports Net Rocky Mountain; Headline News; History Channel; KDVR (FOX) Denver; Lifetime; MTV; Nickelodeon; Outdoor Channel; Spike TV; TBS Superstation; The Learning Channel; Trinity Broadcasting Network; Turner Classic Movies; Turner Network TV; USA Network; VH1; Weather Channel; WGN America.
Fee: $29.95 installation; $37.57 monthly.

Pay Service 1
Pay Units: 9.
Programming (via satellite): HBO.
Fee: $10.95 monthly.

Pay Service 2
Pay Units: 4.
Programming (via satellite): Showtime.
Fee: $10.95 monthly.

Pay Service 3
Pay Units: N.A.
Programming (via satellite): The Movie Channel.
Fee: $10.95 monthly.

Video-On-Demand: No

Internet Service
Operational: No.

Telephone Service
None

Miles of Plant: 4.0 (coaxial); None (fiber optic). Homes passed: 76.
Chief Executive Officer: Joseph A. Sheehan. General Manager East: Mark Miller. General Manager West: Vance Johnson.
Ownership: KLiP Interactive LLC (MSO).

ST. REGIS—KLiP Interactive, 455 Gees Mill Business Court, Conyers, GA 30013. Phones: 800-388-6577; 678-727-7100. Fax: 678-727-7002. E-mail: jsheehan@klipia.com. Web Site: http://www.klipia.com. ICA: MT0090.
TV Market Ranking: Outside TV Markets (ST. REGIS). Franchise award date: N.A. Franchise expiration date: N.A. Began: September 1, 1989.
Channel capacity: 40 (not 2-way capable). Channels available but not in use: 11.

Basic Service
Subscribers: 22.
Programming (received off-air): KECI-TV (NBC) Missoula.
Programming (via microwave): KCNC-TV (CBS) Denver; KXLY-TV (ABC, MNT) Spokane.
Programming (via satellite): ABC Family Channel; Animal Planet; Arts & Entertainment; CNN; Comedy Central; Country Music TV; Discovery Channel; Disney Channel; ESPN; ESPN 2; Headline News; History Channel; KDVR (FOX) Denver; Nickelodeon; Outdoor Channel; Spike TV; TBS Superstation; The Learning Channel; Travel Channel; Turner Classic Movies; Turner Network TV; USA Network; VH1; Weather Channel; WGN America.
Fee: $29.95 installation; $32.95 monthly.

Pay Service 1
Pay Units: N.A.
Programming (via satellite): HBO; Showtime; The Movie Channel.
Fee: $10.95 monthly (each).

Video-On-Demand: No

Internet Service
Operational: No.

Telephone Service
None

Miles of Plant: 4.0 (coaxial); None (fiber optic). Homes passed: 27.
Chief Executive Officer: Joseph A. Sheehan. General Manager East: Mark Miller. General Manager West: Vance Johnson.
Ownership: KLiP Interactive LLC (MSO).

STANFORD—Formerly served by B.E.K. Inc. No longer in operation. ICA: MT0069.

STEVENSVILLE—Bresnan Communications, 924 S 3rd St W, Missoula, MT 59801-2340. Phone: 877-273-7626. Web Site: http://www.bresnan.com. Also serves Ravalli County. ICA: MT0065.
TV Market Ranking: Below 100 (Ravalli County (portions), STEVENSVILLE); Outside TV Markets (Ravalli County (portions)). Franchise award date: N.A. Franchise expiration date: N.A. Began: September 1, 1982.
Channel capacity: 36 (not 2-way capable). Channels available but not in use: None.

Basic Service
Subscribers: 136.
Programming (received off-air): KECI-TV (NBC) Missoula; KPAX-TV (CBS, CW) Missoula; KTMF (ABC, FOX) Missoula.
Programming (via microwave): KSPS-TV (PBS) Spokane.
Programming (via satellite): Altitude Sports & Entertainment; Arts & Entertainment; C-SPAN; CW+; Discovery Channel; Lifetime; QVC; TBS Superstation; truTV.

Expanded Basic Service 1
Subscribers: 131.
Programming (via satellite): ABC Family Channel; AMC; Animal Planet; Cartoon Network; CNBC; CNN; Disney Channel; ESPN; Fox News Channel; Fox Sports Net Rocky Mountain; Headline News; HGTV; Nickelodeon; Spike TV; The Learning Channel; Turner Network TV; USA Network; Weather Channel.
Fee: $47.99 monthly.

Pay Service 1
Pay Units: 35.
Programming (via satellite): Showtime.
Fee: $14.15 monthly.

Pay Service 2
Pay Units: 65.
Programming (via satellite): HBO.
Fee: $14.15 monthly.

Pay Service 3
Pay Units: 179.
Programming (via satellite): Encore.
Fee: $1.75 monthly.

Pay Service 4
Pay Units: 99.
Programming (via satellite): Starz.
Fee: $6.75 monthly.

Video-On-Demand: No

Internet Service
Operational: Yes.
Fee: $36.95 monthly.

Telephone Service
Analog: Not Operational
Digital: Operational
Fee: $46.99 monthly

Miles of Plant: 10.0 (coaxial); None (fiber optic). Homes passed: 1,071.
General Manager: Mike Oswald. Technical Operations Manager: Alan White.
Ownership: Bresnan Communications Inc. (MSO). Sale pends to Cablevision Systems Corp.

SUN PRAIRIE—KLiP Interactive, 455 Gees Mill Business Court, Conyers, GA 30013. Phone: 678-727-7100. Fax: 678-727-7002. E-mail: jsheehan@klipia.com. Web Site: http://www.klipia.com. Also serves Vaughn. ICA: MT0046.
TV Market Ranking: Below 100 (SUN PRAIRIE, Vaughn). Franchise award date: N.A. Franchise expiration date: N.A. Began: December 17, 1981.
Channel capacity: 25 (not 2-way capable). Channels available but not in use: None.

Basic Service
Subscribers: 68.
Programming (received off-air): KBGF-LP Great Falls; KFBB-TV (ABC, FOX) Great Falls; KRTV (CBS, CW) Great Falls; KTGF (IND) Great Falls.
Programming (via satellite): ABC Family Channel; Arts & Entertainment; CNN; Discovery Channel; Disney Channel; ESPN; ESPN 2; Fox News Channel; Fox Sports Net Rocky Mountain; Headline News; HGTV; INSP; KDVR (FOX) Denver; Nickelodeon; Outdoor Channel; Spike TV; TBS Superstation; Turner Classic Movies; Turner Network TV; USA Network; WGN America.
Fee: $29.95 installation; $32.25 monthly.

Pay Service 1
Pay Units: 10.
Programming (via satellite): HBO; Showtime.
Fee: $15.00 installation; $10.95 monthly (each).

Video-On-Demand: No

Internet Service
Operational: No.

Telephone Service
None

Miles of Plant: 30.0 (coaxial); None (fiber optic). Homes passed: 685.
Chief Executive Officer: Joseph A. Sheehan. General Manager East: Mark Miller. General Manager West: Vance Johnson.
City fee: None.
Ownership: KLiP Interactive LLC (MSO).

SUPERIOR—Western Montana Community Telephone, 312 Main St SW, Ronan, MT 59864. Phone: 406-676-0788. ICA: MT0049.
TV Market Ranking: Outside TV Markets (SUPERIOR). Franchise award date: N.A. Franchise expiration date: N.A. Began: March 1, 1963.
Channel capacity: 62 (not 2-way capable). Channels available but not in use: 40.

Basic Service
Subscribers: 127.
Programming (received off-air): KDVR (FOX) Denver; KECI-TV (NBC) Missoula; KMGH-TV (ABC) Denver; KPAX-TV (CBS, CW) Missoula; allband FM.
Programming (via microwave): KRMA-TV (PBS) Denver.
Programming (via satellite): ABC Family Channel; Altitude Sports & Entertainment; AMC; Animal Planet; Arts & Entertainment; CNN; Country Music TV; Discovery Channel; Disney Channel; ESPN; ESPN 2; Headline News; History Channel; Lifetime; Nickelodeon; QVC; Spike TV; TBS Superstation; The Learning Channel; Turner Network TV; TV Land; USA Network; VH1; Weather Channel; WGN America.
Fee: $45.00 installation; $47.99 monthly.

Pay Service 1
Pay Units: 72.
Programming (via satellite): Showtime.
Fee: $11.95 monthly.

Pay Service 2
Pay Units: N.A.
Programming (via satellite): HBO.
Fee: $11.95 monthly.

Video-On-Demand: No

Internet Service
Operational: No.
Telephone Service
None
Miles of Plant: 28.0 (coaxial); None (fiber optic). Homes passed: 807.
General Manager: Mike Oswald. Technical Operations Manager: Alan White.
Ownership: Western Montana Community Telephone (MSO).

TERRY—Mid-Rivers Communications, PO Box 280, 904 C Ave, Circle, MT 59215. Phone: 406-485-3301. Fax: 406-485-2924. E-mail: mrtc@midrivers.com. Web Site: http://www.midrivers.com. Also serves Fallon. ICA: MT0070.
TV Market Ranking: Outside TV Markets (Fallon, TERRY). Franchise award date: July 14, 1981. Franchise expiration date: N.A. Began: March 1, 1982.
Channel capacity: 77 (not 2-way capable). Channels available but not in use: N.A.
Basic Service
Subscribers: 295.
Programming (received off-air): KMGH-TV (ABC) Denver; KXGN-TV (CBS, NBC) Glendive; KYUS-TV (NBC) Miles City.
Programming (via microwave): KRMA-TV (PBS) Denver; KUSA (NBC) Denver.
Programming (via satellite): CNN; C-SPAN; Discovery Channel; Disney Channel; Headline News; QVC; Spike TV; TBS Superstation; WGN America.
Fee: $60.00 installation; $9.25 monthly; $40.00 additional installation.
Expanded Basic Service 1
Subscribers: 252.
Programming (via satellite): ABC Family Channel; AMC; Arts & Entertainment; Cartoon Network; CNBC; Comedy Central; Country Music TV; C-SPAN 2; E! Entertainment Television; Encore; ESPN; ESPN 2; Eternal Word TV Network; FitTV; Food Network; Fox News Channel; G4; Hallmark Channel; HGTV; History Channel; Lifetime; MTV; Nickelodeon; Outdoor Channel; Syfy; The Learning Channel; Toon Disney; Travel Channel; Trinity Broadcasting Network; Turner Network TV; TV Land; USA Network; VH1; Weather Channel.
Fee: $10.50 monthly.
Pay Service 1
Pay Units: 26.
Programming (via satellite): Cinemax; HBO; Showtime; The Movie Channel.
Fee: $10.00 installation; $8.00 monthly (Cinemax, Showtime or TMC), $10.00 monthly (HBO).
Internet Service
Operational: No.
Telephone Service
None
Miles of Plant: 7.0 (coaxial); None (fiber optic). Homes passed: 439.
General Manager: Gerry Anderson. Chief Technician: Mike Sokolosky. Customer Service Manager: Deb Wagner.
Ownership: Mid-Rivers Telephone Cooperative Inc. (MSO).

THOMPSON FALLS—Western Montana Community Telephone, 312 Main St SW, Ronan, MT 59864. Phone: 406-676-0788. ICA: MT0053.
TV Market Ranking: Outside TV Markets (THOMPSON FALLS). Franchise award date: N.A. Franchise expiration date: N.A. Began: July 1, 1982.
Channel capacity: 35 (not 2-way capable). Channels available but not in use: None.
Basic Service
Subscribers: 73.
Programming (received off-air): KDVR (FOX) Denver; KECI-TV (NBC) Missoula; KREM (CBS) Spokane; KUFM-TV (PBS) Missoula; KXLY-TV (ABC, MNT) Spokane.
Programming (via satellite): C-SPAN; Discovery Channel; Lifetime; QVC; TBS Superstation; truTV.
Current originations: Educational Access.
Fee: $43.08 installation; $47.99 monthly.
Expanded Basic Service 1
Subscribers: N.A.
Programming (via satellite): ABC Family Channel; Altitude Sports & Entertainment; AMC; Animal Planet; Cartoon Network; CNBC; CNN; Disney Channel; ESPN; ESPN 2; Fox News Channel; Fox Sports Net Rocky Mountain; Headline News; HGTV; MoviePlex; Spike TV; The Learning Channel; Turner Network TV; USA Network; Weather Channel.
Pay Service 1
Pay Units: N.A.
Programming (via satellite): Encore.
Fee: $1.75 monthly.
Pay Service 2
Pay Units: N.A.
Programming (via satellite): HBO.
Fee: $14.15 monthly.
Pay Service 3
Pay Units: N.A.
Programming (via satellite): Starz.
Fee: $4.75 monthly.
Video-On-Demand: No
Internet Service
Operational: No.
Telephone Service
None
Miles of Plant: 12.0 (coaxial); None (fiber optic). Homes passed: 685.
Ownership: Western Montana Community Telephone (MSO).

TOWNSEND—Bresnan Communications, PO Box 5509, 951 W Custer Ave, Helena, MT 59604-5509. Phones: 877-273-7626; 406-442-1060. Fax: 406-443-5843. E-mail: moswald@bresnan.com. Web Site: http://www.bresnan.com. Also serves Broadwater County. ICA: MT0045.
TV Market Ranking: Below 100 (Broadwater County (portions), TOWNSEND (TOWN)); Outside TV Markets (Broadwater County (portions)). Franchise award date: N.A. Franchise expiration date: N.A. Began: October 1, 1979.
Channel capacity: 32 (not 2-way capable). Channels available but not in use: N.A.
Basic Service
Subscribers: 329.
Programming (received off-air): KDVR (FOX) Denver; KFBB-TV (ABC, FOX) Great Falls; KTVH-DT (NBC) Helena; KXLF-TV (CBS, CW) Butte.
Programming (via microwave): KUSM-TV (PBS) Bozeman.
Programming (via satellite): C-SPAN; Discovery Channel; FX; QVC; TBS Superstation; truTV.
Fee: $60.00 installation; $20.00 monthly; $40.00 additional installation.
Expanded Basic Service 1
Subscribers: 300.
Programming (via satellite): ABC Family Channel; Altitude Sports & Entertainment; AMC; Animal Planet; Arts & Entertainment; Cartoon Network; CNBC; CNN; Disney Channel; ESPN; ESPN 2; Fox News Channel; Fox Sports Net Utah; HGTV; Lifetime; MoviePlex; Nickelodeon; Spike TV; The Learning Channel; Turner Network TV; USA Network; Weather Channel.
Fee: $28.99 monthly.
Digital Basic Service
Subscribers: 121.
Programming (via satellite): BBC America; Bravo; CMT Pure Country; Discovery Health Channel; Discovery Kids Channel; Discovery Military Channel; Discovery Planet Green; DMX Music; ESPN Classic Sports; ESPNews; Fox Soccer; Golf Channel; GSN; History Channel; ID Investigation Discovery; Independent Film Channel; National Geographic Channel; Nick Jr.; Science Channel; SoapNet; Speed Channel; Syfy; Turner Classic Movies; TV Land; Versus; VH1 Classic.
Fee: $6.00 monthly.
Pay Service 1
Pay Units: 76.
Programming (via satellite): Encore; HBO; Showtime; Starz.
Fee: $9.95 monthly.
Digital Pay Service 1
Pay Units: N.A.
Programming (via satellite): Encore (multiplexed); HBO (multiplexed); Showtime Too; Starz Edge; The Movie Channel.
Video-On-Demand: No
Internet Service
Operational: Yes.
Fee: $52.95 monthly.
Telephone Service
Digital: Operational
Fee: $49.99 monthly
Miles of Plant: 12.0 (coaxial); None (fiber optic). Homes passed: 956.
General Manager: Mike Oswald. Chief Technician: Ed McFadden.
City fee: $200 annually.
Ownership: Bresnan Communications Inc. (MSO). Sale pends to Cablevision Systems Corp.

TROY—Windjammer Cable, 4400 PGA Blvd, Ste 902, Palm Beach Gardens, FL 33410. Phones: 877-450-5558; 561-775-1208. Fax: 561-775-7811. Web Site: http://www.windjammercable.com. ICA: MT0122.
TV Market Ranking: Outside TV Markets (TROY).
Channel capacity: N.A. Channels available but not in use: N.A.
Basic Service
Subscribers: N.A. Included in Coeur d'Alene ID
Programming (received off-air): KAYU-TV (FOX) Spokane; KCFW-TV (NBC) Kalispell; KHQ-TV (NBC) Spokane; KQUP (IND) Pullman; KREM (CBS) Spokane; KSPS-TV (PBS) Spokane; KXLY-TV (ABC, MNT) Spokane.
Programming (via satellite): Canadian Learning Television; C-SPAN; C-SPAN 2; Discovery Channel; Home Shopping Network; MSNBC; Northwest Cable News; QVC; TBS Superstation; WGN America.
Fee: $29.95 installation; $27.72 monthly.
Expanded Basic Service 1
Subscribers: N.A. Included in Coeur d'Alene ID
Programming (via satellite): ABC Family Channel; AMC; Animal Planet; Arts & Entertainment; Cartoon Network; CNBC; CNN; Comcast Sports Net Northwest; Comedy Central; Country Music TV; Disney Channel; E! Entertainment Television; ESPN; ESPN 2; Food Network; Fox News Channel; FX; Hallmark Channel; Headline News; HGTV; History Channel; Lifetime; MTV; MTV2; Nickelodeon; Oxygen; Speed Channel; Spike TV; Style Network; Syfy; The Learning Channel; Travel Channel; truTV; Turner Network TV; TV Land; USA Network; VH1; Weather Channel.
Fee: $35.80 installation; $28.88 monthly.
Digital Basic Service
Subscribers: N.A.
Programming (via satellite): BBC America; Bloomberg Television; Bravo; Discovery Digital Networks; ESPN Classic Sports; ESPN Extra; ESPNews; FitTV; Fox Movie Channel; Fox Soccer; G4; Gaming Entertainment Television; GAS; GSN; Halogen Network; Lifetime Movie Network; MTV Networks Digital Suite; Music Choice; National Geographic Channel; Nick Jr.; NickToons TV; Toon Disney; Trinity Broadcasting Network; Turner Classic Movies; WE tv.
Fee: $11.99 monthly.
Digital Expanded Basic Service
Subscribers: N.A.
Programming (via satellite): Bio; Golf Channel; History Channel International; Independent Film Channel; Outdoor Channel; Versus.
Fee: $12.49 monthly.
Digital Pay Service 1
Pay Units: N.A.
Programming (via satellite): Cinemax (multiplexed); Encore (multiplexed); Flix; HBO (multiplexed); Showtime (multiplexed); Starz (multiplexed); The Movie Channel (multiplexed).
Fee: $15.95 monthly (each).
Video-On-Demand: No
Pay-Per-View
HITS (Headend In The Sky) (delivered digitally); Playboy TV (delivered digitally); Fresh (delivered digitally).
Internet Service
Operational: Yes.
Broadband Service: Road Runner.
Fee: $19.95-$24.99 installation; $45.95 monthly; $3.00 modem lease; $99.00 modem purchase.
Telephone Service
None
Homes passed & miles of plant included in Coeur d'Alene ID
General Manager: Timothy Evard. Operations Director: Belinda Graham. Engineering Director: Mike Earehart. Finance & Accounting Director: Cindy Johnson.
Ownership: Windjammer Communications LLC (MSO).

TWIN BRIDGES—Formerly served by Twin Bridges Cable TV Inc. No longer in operation. ICA: MT0118.

VALIER—KLiP Interactive, 455 Gees Mill Business Court, Conyers, GA 30013. Phones: 800-388-6577; 678-727-7100. Fax: 678-727-7002. E-mail: jsheehan@klipia.com. Web Site: http://www.klipia.com. ICA: MT0081.
TV Market Ranking: Outside TV Markets (VALIER). Franchise award date: October 4, 1982. Franchise expiration date: N.A. Began: April 1, 1983.
Channel capacity: 45 (not 2-way capable). Channels available but not in use: 22.
Basic Service
Subscribers: 32.
Programming (received off-air): KFBB-TV (ABC, FOX) Great Falls; KRTV (CBS, CW) Great Falls.
Programming (via satellite): ABC Family Channel; Arts & Entertainment; Canadian Learning Television; Cartoon Network; CNN; Comedy Central; Discovery Channel; Disney Channel; ESPN; ESPN 2; Fox News Channel; Fox Sports Net Rocky Moun-

tain; HGTV; KDVR (FOX) Denver; KUSA (NBC) Denver; Spike TV; TBS Superstation; Turner Classic Movies; Turner Network TV; USA Network; WGN America.
Fee: $29.95 installation; $31.47 monthly.

Pay Service 1
Pay Units: 3.
Programming (via satellite): HBO; Showtime; The Movie Channel.
Fee: $15.00 installation; $10.95 monthly (each).

Video-On-Demand: No

Internet Service
Operational: No.

Telephone Service
None

Miles of Plant: 6.0 (coaxial); None (fiber optic). Homes passed: 307.
Chief Executive Officer: Joseph A. Sheehan. General Manager East: Mark Miller. General Manager West: Vance Johnson.
City fee: None.
Ownership: KLiP Interactive LLC (MSO).

VICTOR—Formerly served by Bresnan Communications. No longer in operation. ICA: MT0082.

WEST YELLOWSTONE—KLiP Interactive, 455 Gees Mill Business Court, Conyers, GA 30013. Phones: 800-388-6577; 678-727-7100. Fax: 678-727-7002. E-mail: jsheehan@klipia.com. Web Site: http://www.klipia.com. ICA: MT0050.
TV Market Ranking: Outside TV Markets (WEST YELLOWSTONE). Franchise award date: N.A. Franchise expiration date: N.A. Began: November 1, 1979.
Channel capacity: 45 (not 2-way capable). Channels available but not in use: 3.

Basic Service
Subscribers: 387.
Programming (received off-air): KISU-TV (PBS) Pocatello; KPVI-DT (NBC) Pocatello; KTVX (ABC) Salt Lake City; KXLF-TV (CBS, CW) Butte.
Programming (via satellite): Arts & Entertainment; CNN; Discovery Channel; Disney Channel; KDVR (FOX) Denver; KSL-TV (NBC) Salt Lake City; KUTV (CBS) Salt Lake City; MTV; QVC; Spike TV; TBS Superstation; Turner Network TV; TV Guide Network; USA Network.
Programming (via translator): KIFI-TV (ABC) Idaho Falls.
Fee: $29.95 installation; $39.95 monthly.

Expanded Basic Service 1
Subscribers: N.A.
Programming (via satellite): ABC Family Channel; Animal Planet; Country Music TV; ESPN; ESPN 2; Fox News Channel; Fox Sports Net Rocky Mountain; Headline News; HGTV; History Channel; Nickelodeon; Outdoor Channel; Syfy; The Learning Channel; Travel Channel; Turner Classic Movies; VH1; Weather Channel; WGN America.
Fee: $16.95 monthly.

Pay Service 1
Pay Units: 22.
Programming (via satellite): HBO.
Fee: $10.95 monthly.

Pay Service 2
Pay Units: 7.
Programming (via satellite): Showtime.
Fee: $10.95 monthly.

Pay Service 3
Pay Units: N.A.
Programming (via satellite): The Movie Channel.
Fee: $10.95 monthly.

Video-On-Demand: No

Internet Service
Operational: No.

Telephone Service
None

Miles of Plant: 10.0 (coaxial); None (fiber optic). Homes passed: 550.
Chief Executive Officer: Joseph A. Sheehan. General Manager East: Mark Miller. General Manager West: Vance Johnson.
City fee: None.
Ownership: KLiP Interactive LLC (MSO).

WHITE SULPHUR SPRINGS—Formerly served by Eagle Cablevision Inc. No longer in operation. ICA: MT0057.

WHITEHALL—Whitehall Cable TV, PO Box 343, 509 First St E, Whitehall, MT 59759-0343. Phone: 866-656-5030. E-mail: herby@in-tch.com. ICA: MT0064.
TV Market Ranking: Below 100 (WHITEHALL). Franchise award date: June 1, 1981. Franchise expiration date: N.A. Began: N.A.
Channel capacity: 35 (not 2-way capable). Channels available but not in use: 2.

Basic Service
Subscribers: 220.
Programming (received off-air): KTVM-TV (NBC) Butte; KWYB (ABC, FOX) Butte; KXLF-TV (CBS, CW) Butte.
Programming (via satellite): ABC Family Channel; Animal Planet; Cartoon Network; CNN; Country Music TV; C-SPAN 2; Discovery Channel; Discovery Travel & Living (Viajar y Vivir); ESPN; ESPN 2; Fox Sports Net Rocky Mountain; Home Shopping Network; MTV; Nickelodeon; Outdoor Channel; QVC; Spike TV; TBS Superstation; The Learning Channel; truTV; Turner Classic Movies; Turner Network TV; TV Land; VH1; Weather Channel; WGN America.
Current originations: Leased Access; Educational Access; Public Access.
Fee: $22.50 installation; $19.00 monthly; $12.50 additional installation.

Pay Service 1
Pay Units: 50.
Programming (via satellite): The Movie Channel.
Fee: $8.50 monthly.

Internet Service
Operational: No.

Telephone Service
None

Miles of Plant: 5.0 (coaxial); None (fiber optic). Homes passed: 425. Total homes in franchised area: 425.
Ownership: Big Sky Communications Inc.

WIBAUX—Mid-Rivers Communications, PO Box 280, 904 C Ave, Circle, MT 59215. Phone: 406-485-3301. Fax: 406-485-2924. E-mail: lcedar@midrivers.com. Web Site: http://www.midrivers.com. ICA: MT0087.
TV Market Ranking: Below 100 (WIBAUX). Franchise award date: N.A. Franchise expiration date: N.A. Began: January 1, 1975.
Channel capacity: N.A. Channels available but not in use: N.A.

Basic Service
Subscribers: 230.
Programming (received off-air): KDSE (PBS) Dickinson; KQCD-TV (NBC) Dickinson; KXGN-TV (CBS, NBC) Glendive.
Programming (via microwave): KMGH-TV (ABC) Denver.
Programming (via satellite): CNN; C-SPAN; C-SPAN 2; Discovery Channel; Disney Channel; Headline News; QVC; Spike TV; TBS Superstation; Weather Channel; WGN America.
Fee: $11.25 monthly.

Expanded Basic Service 1
Subscribers: N.A.
Programming (via satellite): ABC Family Channel; AMC; Animal Planet; Arts & Entertainment; Cartoon Network; CNBC; Comedy Central; Country Music TV; E! Entertainment Television; Encore; ESPN; ESPN 2; Eternal Word TV Network; Food Network; G4; Hallmark Channel; HGTV; History Channel; Lifetime; Nickelodeon; Outdoor Channel; Speed Channel; Syfy; The Learning Channel; Travel Channel; Trinity Broadcasting Network; Turner Network TV; TV Land; USA Network.
Fee: $12.00 monthly.

Pay Service 1
Pay Units: 38.
Programming (via satellite): Cinemax; HBO; Showtime; The Movie Channel.
Fee: $8.00 monthly (Cinemax, Showtime or TMC), $10.00 monthly (HBO).

Internet Service
Operational: No.

Telephone Service
None

Miles of Plant: 7.0 (coaxial); None (fiber optic). Homes passed: 250.
General Manager: Gerry Anderson. Chief Technician: Mike Sokolosky. Customer Service Manager: Deb Wagner.
Ownership: Mid-Rivers Telephone Cooperative Inc. (MSO).

WOLF POINT—Nemont, PO Box 600, 61 Hwy 13 S, Scobey, MT 59263. Phone: 800-636-6680. Fax: 406-783-5283. E-mail: nemont@nemont.coop. Web Site: http://www.nemont.net. Also serves Roosevelt County. ICA: MT0028.
TV Market Ranking: Below 100 (Roosevelt County (portions)); Outside TV Markets (Roosevelt County (portions), WOLF POINT). Franchise award date: February 16, 1981. Franchise expiration date: N.A. Began: June 1, 1979.
Channel capacity: 67 (not 2-way capable). Channels available but not in use: 3.

Basic Service
Subscribers: 722.
Programming (via microwave): KFBB-TV (ABC, FOX) Great Falls; KMGH-TV (ABC) Denver; KUMV-TV (NBC) Williston; KUSA (NBC) Denver; KUSM-TV (PBS) Bozeman; KXMD-TV (CBS) Williston.
Programming (via satellite): C-SPAN; C-SPAN 2; CW+; Home Shopping Network; QVC; TBS Superstation; TV Guide Network; WGN America.
Current originations: Government Access.
Fee: $40.95 installation; $48.99 monthly.

Expanded Basic Service 1
Subscribers: N.A.
Programming (via satellite): ABC Family Channel; Altitude Sports & Entertainment; AMC; Animal Planet; Arts & Entertainment; Cartoon Network; CNBC; CNN; Comedy Central; Country Music TV; Discovery Channel; Disney Channel; E! Entertainment Television; ESPN; ESPN 2; Food Network; Fox News Channel; Fox Sports Net Rocky Mountain; FX; Hallmark Channel; Headline News; HGTV; History Channel; INSP; Lifetime; MSNBC; MTV; Nickelodeon; Oxygen; Spike TV; Syfy; The Learning Channel; Travel Channel; truTV; Turner Classic Movies; Turner Network TV; TV Land; USA Network; VH1; Weather Channel.
Fee: $52.95 monthly.

Digital Basic Service
Subscribers: 347.
Programming (via satellite): AmericanLife TV Network; BBC America; Bio; Bloomberg Television; Bravo; CBS College Sports Network; CMT Pure Country; Discovery Health Channel; Discovery Kids Channel; Discovery Military Channel; Discovery Planet Green; DMX Music; ESPN Classic Sports; ESPNews; Fox Movie Channel; Fox Reality Channel; Fox Soccer; Fuse; G4; Golf Channel; Gospel Music Channel; Great American Country; GSN; Halogen Network; History Channel International; ID Investigation Discovery; Independent Film Channel; Lifetime Movie Network; MTV Hits; MTV2; National Geographic Channel; Nick Jr.; NickToons TV; Outdoor Channel; PBS Kids Sprout; RFD-TV; Science Channel; SoapNet; Speed Channel; Style Network; TeenNick; The Sportsman Channel; Toon Disney; Trinity Broadcasting Network; Versus; VH1 Classic; VH1 Soul.
Fee: $72.95 monthly.

Digital Pay Service 1
Pay Units: N.A.
Programming (via satellite): Cinemax (multiplexed); Encore (multiplexed); Flix; HBO (multiplexed); Showtime (multiplexed); Starz (multiplexed); The Movie Channel (multiplexed).

Video-On-Demand: No

Pay-Per-View
iN DEMAND (delivered digitally); HorseRacing TV (delivered digitally); NFL Network (delivered digitally); Fox College Sports Atlantic (delivered digitally); Fox College Sports Central (delivered digitally); Fox College Sports Pacific (delivered digitally).

Internet Service
Operational: Yes.
Fee: $55.95 monthly.

Telephone Service
Digital: Operational
Fee: $49.99 monthly

Miles of Plant: 18.0 (coaxial); None (fiber optic). Homes passed: 1,617. Total homes in franchised area: 1,690.
City fee: 3% of gross.
Ownership: Nemont Telephone Coop (MSO).

NEBRASKA

Total Systems: **172**
Total Communities Served: **372**
Franchises Not Yet Operating: **0**
Applications Pending: **0**
Communities with Applications: **0**
Number of Basic Subscribers: **571,591**
Number of Expanded Basic Subscribers: **282,932**
Number of Pay Units: **184,139**

Top 100 Markets Represented: Omaha (53); Lincoln-Hastings-Kearney (91).

For a list of cable communities in this section, see the Cable Community Index located in the back of Cable Volume 2.
For explanation of terms used in cable system listings, see p. D-11.

AINSWORTH—Cable Nebraska, 2123 Central Ave, Ste 200, Kearney, NE 68847. Phone: 877-234-0102. Web Site: http://www.cablene.com. Also serves Long Pine & Springview. ICA: NE0049.

TV Market Ranking: Outside TV Markets (AINSWORTH, Long Pine, Springview). Franchise award date: May 14, 1990. Franchise expiration date: N.A. Began: January 1, 1978.

Channel capacity: 56 (not 2-way capable). Channels available but not in use: N.A.

Basic Service
Subscribers: 819.
Programming (received off-air): KMNE-TV (PBS) Bassett; KOLN (CBS, MNT) Lincoln; KPLO-TV (CBS, MNT) Reliance; allband FM.
Programming (via satellite): ABC Family Channel; AMC; Arts & Entertainment; Cartoon Network; CNBC; CNN; Country Music TV; C-SPAN; Discovery Channel; Disney Channel; ESPN; Fox Sports Net Rocky Mountain; Headline News; INSP; KMGH-TV (ABC) Denver; KUSA (NBC) Denver; Lifetime; MTV; Nickelodeon; QVC; Spike TV; TBS Superstation; The Learning Channel; Turner Network TV; TV Guide Network; TV Land; USA Network; VH1; Weather Channel; WGN America.
Current originations: Educational Access.
Fee: $50.00 installation; $26.50 monthly.

Pay Service 1
Pay Units: 29.
Programming (via satellite): Cinemax.
Fee: $20.00 installation; $12.00 monthly.

Pay Service 2
Pay Units: 114.
Programming (via satellite): HBO.
Fee: $20.00 installation; $12.00 monthly.

Pay Service 3
Pay Units: 44.
Programming (via satellite): The Movie Channel.
Fee: $20.00 installation; $12.00 monthly.

Pay Service 4
Pay Units: 38.
Programming (via satellite): Encore.
Fee: $20.00 installation; $12.00 monthly.

Pay Service 5
Pay Units: 50.
Programming (via satellite): Showtime.
Fee: $20.00 installation; $11.00 monthly.

Video-On-Demand: No

Internet Service
Operational: No.

Telephone Service
None

Miles of Plant: 28.0 (coaxial); None (fiber optic). Homes passed: 1,568. Total homes in franchised area: 1,568.
City fee: 3% of gross.
Ownership: USA Companies (MSO).

ALBION—Cable Nebraska, 2123 Central Ave, Ste 200, Kearney, NE 68847. Phone: 308-236-1512. Web Site: http://www.cablene.com. ICA: NE0040.

TV Market Ranking: Outside TV Markets (ALBION). Franchise award date: N.A. Franchise expiration date: N.A. Began: January 1, 1970.

Channel capacity: N.A. Channels available but not in use: N.A.

Basic Service
Subscribers: 550.
Programming (received off-air): KGIN (CBS, MNT) Grand Island; KHAS-TV (NBC) Hastings; KHGI-TV (ABC) Kearney; KHNE-TV (PBS) Hastings; KLKN (ABC) Lincoln; KTVG-TV (FOX) Grand Island.
Programming (via satellite): ABC Family Channel; C-SPAN; C-SPAN 2; Eternal Word TV Network; Hallmark Channel; Headline News; Home Shopping Network; QVC; TBS Superstation; Trinity Broadcasting Network; TV Guide Network; Weather Channel; WGN America.
Current originations: Public Access.
Fee: $35.00 installation; $33.50 monthly.

Expanded Basic Service 1
Subscribers: N.A.
Programming (via satellite): AMC; Animal Planet; Arts & Entertainment; Cartoon Network; CNBC; CNN; Comedy Central; Country Music TV; Discovery Channel; E! Entertainment Television; ESPN; ESPN 2; Food Network; Fox News Channel; Fox Sports Net Midwest; FX; Great American Country; HGTV; History Channel; ION Television; Lifetime; MSNBC; MTV; Nickelodeon; Outdoor Channel; Spike TV; Syfy; The Learning Channel; Travel Channel; truTV; Turner Classic Movies; Turner Network TV; TV Land; Univision; USA Network; VH1.

Digital Basic Service
Subscribers: N.A.
Programming (via satellite): AmericanLife TV Network; BBC America; Bio; Bloomberg Television; Canales N; Current; Discovery Digital Networks; Discovery Kids Channel; DMX Music; ESPN Classic Sports; ESPNews; FitTV; Fox Movie Channel; Fox Sports World; FSN Digital Atlantic; FSN Digital Central; FSN Digital Pacific; G4; GAS; Golf Channel; GSN; Halogen Network; History Channel; History Channel International; International Television (ITV); MBC America; MTV Networks Digital Suite; National Geographic Channel; Nick Jr.; Outdoor Channel; Ovation; ShopNBC; Speed Channel; Style Network; Syfy; Trinity Broadcasting Network; Trio; Versus.

Digital Pay Service 1
Pay Units: N.A.
Programming (via satellite): Cinemax (multiplexed); Encore (multiplexed); Flix; Fox Movie Channel; HBO (multiplexed); Independent Film Channel; Showtime (multiplexed); Starz (multiplexed); Sundance Channel; The Movie Channel (multiplexed); WE tv.

Video-On-Demand: No

Pay-Per-View
iN DEMAND (delivered digitally); Hot Choice (delivered digitally); Playboy TV (delivered digitally); Fresh (delivered digitally); Shorteez (delivered digitally); Urban Xtra (delivered digitally); ESPN Now (delivered digitally); sports (delivered digitally).

Internet Service
Operational: Yes.
Broadband Service: Cable Nebraska.

Telephone Service
None

Miles of Plant: 16.0 (coaxial); None (fiber optic). Homes passed: 1,145.
Operations Manager: Stuart Gilbertson.
City fee: 3% of gross.
Ownership: USA Companies (MSO).

ALEXANDRIA—Comstar Cable TV Inc., PO Box 975, 8358 W Scott Rd, Beatrice, NE 68310-0975. Fax: 402-228-3766. ICA: NE0226.

TV Market Ranking: Outside TV Markets (ALEXANDRIA). Franchise award date: N.A. Franchise expiration date: N.A. Began: June 1, 1989.

Channel capacity: 36 (operating 2-way). Channels available but not in use: N.A.

Basic Service
Subscribers: 33.
Programming (received off-air): KFXL-TV (FOX) Lincoln; KHAS-TV (NBC) Hastings; KHNE-TV (PBS) Hastings; KLKN (ABC) Lincoln; KOLD-TV (CBS) Tucson; KOLN (CBS, MNT) Lincoln.
Programming (via satellite): ABC Family Channel; Arts & Entertainment; CNN; Discovery Channel; ESPN; ESPN 2; Great American Country; HGTV; History Channel; Lifetime; National Geographic Channel; Outdoor Channel; QVC; TBS Superstation; Turner Network TV; USA Network; Weather Channel.
Current originations: Leased Access; Public Access.
Planned originations: Government Access; Educational Access.
Fee: $21.95 monthly.

Pay Service 1
Pay Units: N.A.
Programming (via satellite): HBO.
Fee: $8.40 monthly.

Video-On-Demand: No

Internet Service
Operational: No.

Telephone Service
None

Miles of Plant: 2.0 (coaxial); None (fiber optic). Homes passed: 105.
Manager: Tim Schwarz.
City fee: 5% of gross.
Ownership: Comstar Cable TV Inc. (MSO).

ALLEN—CenCom Inc. This cable system has converted to IPTV. See Allen, NE [NE5002]. ICA: NE0258.

ALLEN (village)—CenCom NNTV. Formerly [NE0258]. This cable system has converted to IPTV, 110 E Elk St, Jackson, NE 68743-0066. Phones: 402-623-4321; 888-397-4321. E-mail: nntc@nntc.net. Web Site: http://www.nntc.net. ICA: NE5002.

Channel capacity: N.A. Channels available but not in use: N.A.

Internet Service
Operational: Yes.

Telephone Service
Digital: Operational

General Manager: Emory Graffis.
Ownership: Northeast Nebraska Telephone Co.

ALLIANCE—Charter Communications, 3380 Northern Valley Pl NE, Rochester, MN 55906. Phones: 308-632-5700 (Scottsbluff office); 507-289-8372 (Rochester administrative office). Fax: 507-285-6162. Web Site: http://www.charter.com. ICA: NE0017.

TV Market Ranking: Outside TV Markets (ALLIANCE).

Channel capacity: N.A. Channels available but not in use: N.A.

Basic Service
Subscribers: N.A.
Programming (received off-air): KCNC-TV (CBS) Denver; KDUH-TV (ABC) Scottsbluff; KDVR (FOX) Denver; KPNE-TV (PBS) North Platte; KSTF (CBS, CW) Scottsbluff; KTNE-TV (PBS) Alliance; KTVD (MNT) Denver; KUSA (NBC) Denver; KWGN-TV (CW) Denver.
Programming (via satellite): C-SPAN; C-SPAN 2; CW+; Eternal Word TV Network; Home Shopping Network; INSP; ION Television; QVC.
Current originations: Public Access; Government Access; Educational Access.

Expanded Basic Service 1
Subscribers: N.A.
Programming (via satellite): ABC Family Channel; Altitude Sports & Entertainment; AMC; Animal Planet; Arts & Entertainment; Bravo; Cartoon Network; CNBC; CNN; Comedy Central; Country Music TV; Discovery Channel; Disney Channel; E! Entertainment Television; ESPN; ESPN 2; Food Network; Fox News Channel; Fox Sports Net Rocky Mountain; FX; GalaVision; Golf Channel; Hallmark Channel; Headline News; HGTV; History Channel; Lifetime; MSNBC; MTV; National Geographic Channel; Nickelodeon; Oxygen; Speed Channel; Spike TV; Style Network; Syfy; TBS Superstation; Telemundo; The Learning Channel; Travel Channel; truTV; Turner Classic Movies; TV Land; Univision; USA Network; Versus; VH1; Weather Channel.
Fee: $44.99 monthly.

Digital Basic Service

Subscribers: N.A.

Programming (via satellite): 3 Angels Broadcasting Network; Arts & Entertainment HD; BBC America; Bio; Bloomberg Television; Boomerang; Bravo; BYU Television; Church Channel; CMT Pure Country; CNN en Espanol; Cooking Channel; Daystar TV Network; Discovery Channel HD; Discovery en Espanol; Discovery HD Theater; Discovery Health Channel; Discovery Kids Channel; Discovery Military Channel; Discovery Planet Green; Disney XD; Do-It-Yourself; ESPN 2 HD; ESPN Classic Sports; ESPN Deportes; ESPN HD; ESPN U; ESPNews; Eternal Word TV Network; FamilyNet; FitTV; Fox Business Channel; Fox College Sports Atlantic; Fox College Sports Central; Fox College Sports Pacific; Fox Movie Channel; Fox Soccer; Fox Sports en Espanol; Fuel TV; Fuse; G4; GalaVision; Golf Channel HD; Great American Country; GSN; Halogen Network; HDNet; HDNet Movies; History Channel HD; History Channel International; ID Investigation Discovery; Independent Film Channel; INSP; JCTV; Lifetime Movie Network; Lifetime Real Women; MLB Network; MTV Hits; MTV Jams; MTV Tres; MTV2; mtvU; mun2 television; Music Choice; NHL Network; Nick Jr.; Nick Too; NickToons TV; Outdoor Channel; Palladia; ReelzChannel; RFD-TV; Science Channel; Smile of a Child; SoapNet; Sundance Channel; TeenNick; Telefutura; Telemundo; Tennis Channel; The Sportsman Channel; TLC HD; Trinity Broadcasting Network; Turner Network TV HD; Universal HD; VH1 Classic; VH1 Soul; WE tv; Weather Channel HD.

Digital Pay Service 1

Pay Units: N.A.

Programming (via satellite): Cinemax (multiplexed); Cinemax HD; Encore (multiplexed); Flix; HBO (multiplexed); HBO HD; Showtime (multiplexed); Showtime HD; Starz (multiplexed); Starz HDTV; The Movie Channel; The Movie Channel HD.

Fee: $14.00 monthly (HBO/Cinemax, Showtime/TMC/Flix, or Starz/Encore).

Pay-Per-View

iN DEMAND (delivered digitally); NHL Center Ice (delivered digitally); MLB Extra Innings (delivered digitally); Playboy TV (delivered digitally); Penthouse TV (delivered digitally).

Vice President & General Manager: John Crowley. Marketing Director: Bill Haarstad. Technical Operations Director: Marty Kovank. Technical Operations Manager: Joel Saunders.

Ownership: Charter Communications Inc. (MSO).

ALMA—Pinpoint Cable TV, PO Box 490, 611 Patterson St, Cambridge, NE 69022-0490. Phones: 888-275-7107; 308-946-9832. Fax: 308-697-3631. E-mail: info@pnpt.com. Web Site: http://www.pnpt.com. ICA: NE0059.

TV Market Ranking: Outside TV Markets (ALMA). Franchise award date: N.A. Franchise expiration date: N.A. Began: N.A.

Channel capacity: 38 (operating 2-way). Channels available but not in use: N.A.

Basic Service

Subscribers: 223.

Programming (received off-air): KGIN (CBS, MNT) Grand Island; KHAS-TV (NBC) Hastings; KHGI-TV (ABC) Kearney; KLNE-TV (PBS) Lexington.

Programming (via satellite): ABC Family Channel; Arts & Entertainment; CNN; Discovery Channel; Disney Channel; ESPN; Eternal Word TV Network; Food Network; Fox News Channel; Fox Sports Net; Fox Sports Net Midwest; Great American Country; Headline News; HGTV; History Channel; INSP; MTV; National Geographic Channel; Nickelodeon; QVC; Spike TV; TBS Superstation; The Learning Channel; Toon Disney; Turner Network TV; TV Land; USA Network; VH1; Weather Channel; WGN America.

Fee: $15.00 installation; $33.95 monthly.

Pay Service 1

Pay Units: 56.

Programming (via satellite): HBO; Showtime; The Movie Channel.

Fee: $11.95 monthly (each).

Video-On-Demand: No

Internet Service

Operational: Yes.

Subscribers: 39.

Fee: $30.00 installation.

Telephone Service

None

Miles of Plant: 10.0 (coaxial); None (fiber optic). Additional miles planned: 1.0 (coaxial). Homes passed: 700.

City fee: 3% of gross.

Ownership: USA Companies (MSO).

ANSLEY—NCTC Cable, PO Box 700, 22 LaBarre St, Gibbon, NE 68840. Phone: 308-468-6341. Fax: 308-468-9929. Web Site: http://www.nctc.net. ICA: NE0150.

TV Market Ranking: Outside TV Markets (ANSLEY). Franchise award date: N.A. Franchise expiration date: N.A. Began: February 1, 1984.

Channel capacity: N.A. Channels available but not in use: N.A.

Basic Service

Subscribers: N.A. Included in Burwell

Programming (received off-air): KGIN (CBS, MNT) Grand Island; KHAS-TV (NBC) Hastings; KHGI-TV (ABC) Kearney; KMNE-TV (PBS) Bassett; KTVG-TV (FOX) Grand Island.

Programming (via satellite): ABC Family Channel; AMC; Animal Planet; Arts & Entertainment; Cartoon Network; CNBC; CNN; Comedy Central; Country Music TV; C-SPAN; CW+; Discovery Channel; E! Entertainment Television; ESPN; ESPN 2; ESPN Classic Sports; Eternal Word TV Network; Food Network; Fox News Channel; Fox Sports Net Rocky Mountain; FX; G4; Great American Country; Hallmark Channel; Headline News; HGTV; History Channel; Home Shopping Network; ION Television; Lifetime; MSNBC; MTV; Nickelodeon; Outdoor Channel; QVC; Spike TV; Syfy; TBS Superstation; The Learning Channel; Travel Channel; Trinity Broadcasting Network; truTV; Turner Classic Movies; Turner Network TV; TV Land; USA Network; Versus; VH1; Weather Channel; WGN America.

Fee: $39.20 monthly.

Digital Basic Service

Subscribers: N.A. Included in Burwell

Programming (via satellite): AmericanLife TV Network; BBC America; Bio; Bloomberg Television; Current; Daystar TV Network; Discovery Digital Networks; DMX Music; ESPNews; FitTV; Fox College Sports Atlantic; Fox College Sports Central; Fox College Sports Pacific; Fox Movie Channel; G4; GAS; Golf Channel; Gospel Music Channel; GSN; Halogen Network; History Channel International; Lifetime Movie Network; MTV Networks Digital Suite; Nick Jr.; Ovation; RFD-TV; ShopNBC; Sleuth; Speed Channel; WE tv.

Fee: $14.00 monthly.

Pay Service 1

Pay Units: 65.

Programming (via satellite): HBO.

Fee: $10.95 monthly.

Digital Pay Service 1

Pay Units: N.A.

Programming (via satellite): Cinemax (multiplexed); Encore (multiplexed); Flix; HBO (multiplexed); Showtime (multiplexed); Starz (multiplexed); The Movie Channel (multiplexed).

Fee: $10.95 monthly (Cinemax), $12.95 monthly (HBO or Showtime, TMC & Flix), $13.95 monthly (Starz & Encore).

Video-On-Demand: No

Internet Service

Operational: No, DSL & dial-up.

Telephone Service

None

Miles of Plant: 4.0 (coaxial); None (fiber optic). Total homes in franchised area: 220. Homes passed included in Burwell

General Manager: Andy Jader. Technical Operations Manager: Nick Jeffres.

City fee: 3% of gross.

Ownership: Nebraska Central Telecom Inc. (MSO).

ARAPAHOE—ACT Communications, PO Box 300, 524 Nebraska Ave, Arapahoe, NE 68922. Phones: 866-222-7873; 308-962-7298. Fax: 308-962-5373. E-mail: atccable@atcjet.net. Web Site: http://www.atcjet.net. Also serves Elwood & Holbrook. ICA: NE0260.

TV Market Ranking: Below 100 (Holbrook); Outside TV Markets (ARAPAHOE, Elwood). Franchise award date: N.A. Franchise expiration date: N.A. Began: January 1, 1983.

Channel capacity: 61 (not 2-way capable). Channels available but not in use: N.A.

Basic Service

Subscribers: 650.

Programming (received off-air): KGIN (CBS, MNT) Grand Island; KHGI-TV (ABC) Kearney; KLNE-TV (PBS) Lexington; KSNK (NBC) McCook.

Programming (taped): Local News on Cable.

Programming (via satellite): ABC Family Channel; Animal Planet; Arts & Entertainment; Cartoon Network; CNN; Comedy Central; Country Music TV; Discovery Channel; Disney Channel; Do-It-Yourself; ESPN; ESPN 2; Food Network; Fox News Channel; Fox Sports Net Midwest; FX; G4; Golf Channel; GSN; Hallmark Channel; HGTV; History Channel; INSP; Nickelodeon; Outdoor Channel; QVC; Speed Channel; Spike TV; Syfy; TBS Superstation; The Learning Channel; The Sportsman Channel; Travel Channel; Turner Classic Movies; Turner Network TV; TV Land; USA Network; VH1; Weather Channel; WGN America.

Fee: $21.00 installation; $21.90 monthly.

Expanded Basic Service 1

Subscribers: 242.

Programming (via satellite): Encore; Encore Action; Encore Love; Encore Mystery; Encore Westerns; Fox Movie Channel; MTV; Starz.

Fee: $20.00 installation; $10.95 monthly.

Pay Service 1

Pay Units: 55.

Programming (via satellite): Cinemax.

Fee: $20.00 installation; $9.95 monthly.

Pay Service 2

Pay Units: 40.

Programming (via satellite): HBO.

Fee: $20.00 installation; $9.95 monthly.

Video-On-Demand: No

Internet Service

Operational: Yes.

Fee: $29.95-$99.95 monthly.

Telephone Service

None

Miles of Plant: None (coaxial); 25.0 (fiber optic). Homes passed: 855.

Manager: John E. Koller. Chief Technician: Michael G Monie.

Ownership: Applied Communications Technology.

ARCADIA—NCTC Cable, PO Box 700, 22 LaBarre St, Gibbon, NE 68840. Phones: 888-873-6282; 308-468-6341. Fax: 308-468-9929. Web Site: http://www.nctc.net. ICA: NE0206.

TV Market Ranking: Outside TV Markets (ARCADIA). Franchise award date: N.A. Franchise expiration date: N.A. Began: N.A.

Channel capacity: N.A. Channels available but not in use: N.A.

Basic Service

Subscribers: N.A. Included in Burwell

Programming (received off-air): KGIN (CBS, MNT) Grand Island; KHAS-TV (NBC) Hastings; KHGI-TV (ABC) Kearney; KMNE-TV (PBS) Bassett; KTVG-TV (FOX) Grand Island.

Programming (via satellite): ABC Family Channel; AMC; Animal Planet; Arts & Entertainment; Cartoon Network; CNBC; CNN; Comedy Central; Country Music TV; C-SPAN; CW+; Discovery Channel; E! Entertainment Television; ESPN; ESPN 2; ESPN Classic Sports; Eternal Word TV Network; Food Network; Fox News Channel; Fox Sports Net Midwest; FX; G4; Great American Country; Hallmark Channel; Headline News; HGTV; History Channel; Home Shopping Network; ION Television; Lifetime; MSNBC; MTV; Nickelodeon; Outdoor Channel; QVC; Spike TV; Syfy; TBS Superstation; The Learning Channel; Travel Channel; Trinity Broadcasting Network; truTV; Turner Classic Movies; Turner Network TV; TV Land; USA Network; Versus; VH1; Weather Channel; WGN America.

Current originations: Public Access.

Fee: $39.20 monthly.

Digital Basic Service

Subscribers: N.A. Included in Burwell

Programming (via satellite): AmericanLife TV Network; BBC America; Bio; Bloomberg Television; Current; Daystar TV Network; Discovery Digital Networks; DMX Music; ESPNews; FitTV; Fox College Sports Atlantic; Fox College Sports Central; Fox College Sports Pacific; Fox Movie Channel; G4; Golf Channel; Gospel Music Channel; GSN; Halogen Network; History Channel International; Lifetime Movie Network; MTV Networks Digital Suite; Nick Jr.; Ovation; RFD-TV; ShopNBC; Sleuth; Speed Channel; TeenNick; WE tv.

Fee: $14.00 monthly.

Pay Service 1

Pay Units: N.A.

Programming (via satellite): HBO.

Fee: $10.95 monthly.

Digital Pay Service 1

Pay Units: N.A.

Programming (via satellite): Cinemax (multiplexed); Encore (multiplexed); Flix; HBO (multiplexed); Showtime (multiplexed); Starz (multiplexed); The Movie Channel (multiplexed).

Fee: $10.95 monthly (Cinemax), $12.95 monthly (HBO or Showtime, TMC & Flix), $13.95 monthly (Starz & Encore).

Video-On-Demand: No

Internet Service

Operational: No, DSL & dial-up.

Telephone Service
None
Miles of Plant: 6.0 (coaxial); None (fiber optic). Homes passed included in Burwell
General Manager: Andy Jader. Technical Operations Manager: Nick Jeffres.
Franchise fee: None.
Ownership: Nebraska Central Telecom Inc. (MSO).

ARNOLD—Great Plains Communications, PO Box 500, 1600 Great Plains Centre, Blair, NE 68008-0500. Phones: 888-343-8014; 402-426-9511. Fax: 402-456-6550. E-mail: lquist@gpcom.com. Web Site: http://www.gpcom.com. Also serves Callaway, Oconto & Stapleton. ICA: NE0114.
TV Market Ranking: Below 100 (Stapleton); Outside TV Markets (ARNOLD, Callaway, Oconto). Franchise award date: N.A. Franchise expiration date: N.A. Began: N.A.
Channel capacity: 80 (operating 2-way). Channels available but not in use: N.A.
Basic Service
Subscribers: 12,454 Includes Bancroft, Bloomfield, Broken Bow, Cortland, Chadron, Chapman, Elgin, Gordon, Grant, Hay Springs, McCook, North Bend, Oshkosh, Ponca, Sutherland, Talmage, & Trenton.
Programming (received off-air): KGIN (CBS, MNT) Grand Island; KNOP-TV (NBC) North Platte; KPNE-TV (PBS) North Platte; KWNB-TV (ABC) Hayes Center.
Programming (via satellite): ABC Family Channel; Animal Planet; Arts & Entertainment; CNBC; CNN; Discovery Channel; Disney Channel; ESPN; Fox News Channel; Fox Sports Net Rocky Mountain; FX; Great American Country; Headline News; KCNC-TV (CBS) Denver; KMGH-TV (ABC) Denver; Lifetime; MTV; Nickelodeon; QVC; Spike TV; TBS Superstation; The Learning Channel; Travel Channel; Turner Network TV; TV Guide Network; TV Land; USA Network; VH1; Weather Channel; WGN America.
Fee: $28.00 installation; $31.50 monthly.
Expanded Basic Service 1
Subscribers: 297.
Programming (via satellite): Cartoon Network; Comedy Central; ESPN 2; HGTV; History Channel; KWGN-TV (CW) Denver; Turner Classic Movies; Versus.
Fee: $6.50 monthly.
Digital Basic Service
Subscribers: 6,000 Includes Bancroft, Bloomfield, Broken Bow, Cortland, Chadron, Chapman, Elgin, Gordon, Grant, Hay Springs, McCook, North Bend, Oshkosh, Ponca, Sutherland, & Talmage.
Programming (via satellite): BBC America; Bio; Bravo; Discovery Digital Networks; DMX Music; ESPN Classic Sports; Fox Sports World; GAS; Golf Channel; History Channel International; Independent Film Channel; Lifetime Movie Network; MTV Networks Digital Suite; National Geographic Channel; Nick Jr.; Outdoor Channel; Speed Channel; Syfy; Turner Classic Movies; WE tv.
Fee: $47.95 monthly.
Pay Service 1
Pay Units: 65.
Programming (via satellite): Cinemax; Flix; HBO; Showtime; Sundance Channel; The Movie Channel.
Fee: $9.95 monthly (Showtime), $10.95 monthly (HBO).
Digital Pay Service 1
Pay Units: N.A.
Programming (via satellite): Cinemax (multiplexed); Encore (multiplexed); HBO (multiplexed); Showtime (multiplexed); The Movie Channel (multiplexed).
Fee: $12.00 monthly.
Video-On-Demand: No
Pay-Per-View
Addressable homes: 45.
iN DEMAND (delivered digitally), Fee: $3.99, Addressable: Yes; Sports PPV.
Internet Service
Operational: Yes, Both DSL & dial-up.
Broadband Service: In-house.
Fee: $49.95 installation; $39.95 monthly.
Telephone Service
None
Miles of Plant: 19.0 (coaxial); None (fiber optic). Homes passed: 21,250. Homes passed includes Bancroft, Bloomfield, Broken Bow, Cortland, Chadron, Chapman, Elgin, Gordon, Grant, Hay Springs, McCook, North Bend, Oshkosh, Ponca, Sutherland, Talmage, & Trenton
Manager: Lee Ann Quist. Chief Technician: Mark Stottler. Marketing Manager: Casey Garrigan.
Franchise fee: None.
Ownership: Great Plains Communications Inc. (MSO).

ASHLAND—Charter Communications. Now served by SPRINGFIELD (formerly Plattsmouth), NE [NE0020]. ICA: NE0047.

ASHTON—NCTC Cable, PO Box 700, 22 LaBarre St, Gibbon, NE 68840. Phone: 308-468-6341. Fax: 308-468-9929. Web Site: http://www.nctc.net. ICA: NE0227.
TV Market Ranking: 91 (ASHTON-SANDY SPRING); Below 100 (ASHTON-SANDY SPRING). Franchise award date: N.A. Franchise expiration date: N.A. Began: May 1, 1989.
Channel capacity: N.A. Channels available but not in use: N.A.
Basic Service
Subscribers: N.A. Included in Burwell
Programming (received off-air): KGIN (CBS, MNT) Grand Island; KHAS-TV (NBC) Hastings; KHGI-TV (ABC) Kearney; KHNE-TV (PBS) Hastings; KTVG-TV (FOX) Grand Island.
Programming (via satellite): ABC Family Channel; American Movie Classics; Animal Planet; Arts & Entertainment; Cartoon Network; CNBC; CNN; Comedy Central; Country Music TV; C-SPAN; CW+; Discovery Channel; E! Entertainment Television; ESPN; ESPN 2; ESPN Classic Sports; Eternal Word TV Network; Food Network; Fox News Channel; Fox Sports Net Rocky Mountain; FX; G4; Great American Country; Hallmark Channel; Headline News; HGTV; History Channel; Home Shopping Network; ION Television; Lifetime; MSNBC; MTV; Nickelodeon; Outdoor Channel; QVC; Spike TV; Syfy; TBS Superstation; The Learning Channel; Travel Channel; Trinity Broadcasting Network; truTV; Turner Classic Movies; Turner Network TV; TV Land; USA Network; Versus; VH1; Weather Channel; WGN America.
Fee: $39.20 monthly.
Digital Basic Service
Subscribers: N.A. Included in Burwell
Programming (via satellite): AmericanLife TV Network; BBC America; Bio; Bloomberg Television; Current; Daystar TV Network; Discovery Health Channel; Discovery Kids Channel; Discovery Military Channel; Discovery Planet Green; DMX Music; ESPN 2; ESPN Classic Sports; ESPNews; FitTV; Fox College Sports Atlantic; Fox College Sports Central; Fox College Sports Pacific; Fox Movie Channel; G4; Golf Channel; GSN; Halogen Network; History Channel; History Channel International; ID Investigation Discovery; Lifetime Movie Network; MTV Hits; MTV2; Nick Jr.; Outdoor Channel; RFD-TV; Science Channel; ShopNBC; Sleuth; SoapNet; Speed Channel; Style Network; Syfy; TeenNick; Toon Disney; Trinity Broadcasting Network; Versus; VH1 Classic; VH1 Country; VH1 Soul; WE tv.
Fee: $14.00 monthly.
Pay Service 1
Pay Units: N.A.
Programming (via satellite): HBO.
Fee: $10.95 monthly.
Digital Pay Service 1
Pay Units: N.A.
Programming (via satellite): Cinemax (multiplexed); Encore (multiplexed); Flix; Fox Movie Channel; HBO (multiplexed); Lifetime Movie Network; Showtime (multiplexed); Starz (multiplexed); The Movie Channel (multiplexed).
Fee: $10.95 monthly (Cinemax), $12.95 monthly (HBO or Showtime/TMC/Flix), $13.95 monthly (Starz/Encore/Fox Movie/Lifetime Movie).
Internet Service
Operational: No, DSL & dial-up.
Telephone Service
None
Miles of Plant: 3.0 (coaxial); None (fiber optic). Homes passed included in Burwell
General Manager: Andy Jader. Technical Operations Manager: Nick Jeffries.
Ownership: Nebraska Central Telecom Inc. (MSO).

ATKINSON—Fort Randall Cable, PO Box 608, 1605 Laurel St, Tyndall, SD 57066. Phones: 888-283-7667; 320-847-2211. Fax: 605-589-3366. ICA: NE0261.
TV Market Ranking: Outside TV Markets (ATKINSON). Franchise award date: N.A. Franchise expiration date: N.A. Began: October 1, 1980.
Channel capacity: 27 (not 2-way capable). Channels available but not in use: N.A.
Basic Service
Subscribers: 277.
Programming (received off-air): KLKN (ABC) Lincoln; KMNE-TV (PBS) Bassett; KOLN (CBS, MNT) Lincoln.
Programming (via satellite): ABC Family Channel; CNN; ESPN; KCNC-TV (CBS) Denver; KDVR (FOX) Denver; KMGH-TV (ABC) Denver; TBS Superstation; Turner Network TV; USA Network; WGN America.
Fee: $29.95 installation; $27.95 monthly.
Pay Service 1
Pay Units: 2.
Programming (via satellite): HBO.
Fee: $11.95 monthly.
Pay Service 2
Pay Units: 1.
Programming (via satellite): Showtime.
Fee: $11.95 monthly.
Pay Service 3
Pay Units: N.A.
Programming (via satellite): Starz.
Fee: $12.95 monthly.
Video-On-Demand: No
Internet Service
Operational: Yes.
Fee: $49.95 monthly.
Telephone Service
None
Miles of Plant: 13.0 (coaxial); None (fiber optic).
Manager: Bruce Hamson.
Ownership: Hanson Communications Inc. (MSO).

AUBURN—Time Warner Cable, 5400 S 16th St, Lincoln, NE 68512-1278. Phone: 402-421-0330. Fax: 402-421-0310. Web Site: http://www.timewarnercable.com/Nebraska. Also serves Nebraska City & Tecumseh. ICA: NE0013.
TV Market Ranking: Outside TV Markets (AUBURN, Nebraska City, Tecumseh). Franchise award date: January 1, 1966. Franchise expiration date: N.A. Began: January 29, 1968.
Channel capacity: N.A. Channels available but not in use: N.A.
Basic Service
Subscribers: N.A. Included in Lincoln
Programming (received off-air): KETV (ABC) Omaha; KMTV-TV (CBS) Omaha; KOLN (CBS, MNT) Lincoln; KPTM (FOX, MNT) Omaha; KUON-TV (PBS) Lincoln; KXVO (CW) Omaha; WOWT-TV (IND, NBC) Omaha.
Programming (via satellite): Shop at Home; Spike TV; Turner Network TV; TV Guide Network; WGN America.
Fee: $40.54 installation; $14.40 monthly; $.69 converter; $18.29 additional installation.
Expanded Basic Service 1
Subscribers: N.A.
Programming (via satellite): ABC Family Channel; AMC; Animal Planet; Arts & Entertainment; BET Networks; Bravo; Cartoon Network; CNBC; CNN; Comedy Central; Country Music TV; C-SPAN; C-SPAN 2; Discovery Channel; Discovery Health Channel; Disney Channel; E! Entertainment Television; ESPN; ESPN 2; ESPN Classic Sports; Eternal Word TV Network; Food Network; Fox News Channel; Fox Sports Net Midwest; FX; Golf Channel; Hallmark Channel; Headline News; HGTV; History Channel; Home Shopping Network; ION Television; Lifetime; Lifetime Movie Network; MSNBC; MTV; National Geographic Channel; Nickelodeon; Oxygen; QVC; ShopNBC; SoapNet; Syfy; TBS Superstation; The Learning Channel; Travel Channel; truTV; Turner Classic Movies; TV Land; Univision; USA Network; VH1; WE tv; Weather Channel.
Fee: $29.50 monthly.
Digital Basic Service
Subscribers: N.A. Included in Lincoln
Programming (via satellite): America's Store; BBC America; Bio; Bloomberg Television; Boomerang; CNN International; Cooking Channel; C-SPAN 3; Discovery Digital Networks; Do-It-Yourself; ESPNews; FitTV; Fox Movie Channel; Fox Sports World; FSN Digital Atlantic; FSN Digital Central; FSN Digital Pacific; Fuse; G4; GAS; Great American Country; GSN;

For more information call **800-771-9202** or visit **www.warren-news.com**

History Channel International; Independent Film Channel; Lifetime Real Women; MTV2; Music Choice; NASA TV; Nick Jr.; NickToons TV; Outdoor Channel; Ovation; Speed Channel; Style Network; Toon Disney; Trinity Broadcasting Network; Versus; VH1 Classic.
Fee: $6.95 monthly.

Digital Pay Service 1
Pay Units: N.A.
Programming (via satellite): Cinemax (multiplexed); HBO (multiplexed); Showtime (multiplexed); Starz (multiplexed); The Movie Channel.
Fee: $9.95 monthly (each).

Video-On-Demand: Yes

Pay-Per-View
Addressable homes: 1,049.
NASCAR In Car (delivered digitally); ESPN Full Court (delivered digitally); NBA League Pass (delivered digitally); NHL Center Ice (delivered digitally); MLB Extra Innings (delivered digitally); Adult PPV (delivered digitally); WNBA Season Pass (delivered digitally); Hot Choice (delivered digitally), Addressable: Yes; iN DEMAND (delivered digitally); Playboy TV (delivered digitally); Pleasure (delivered digitally); Fresh (delivered digitally); Shorteez (delivered digitally); sports (delivered digitally).

Internet Service
Operational: Yes.
Subscribers: 832.
Broadband Service: Road Runner.
Fee: $39.95 installation; $44.95 monthly.

Telephone Service
Digital: Operational
Fee: $39.95 monthly

Miles of Plant: 106.0 (coaxial); None (fiber optic). Homes passed included in Lincoln

President: Beth Scarborough. Vice President, Engineering: John Matejovich. Vice President, Marketing: Brian Cecere. Vice President, Operations: Dick Cassidy. General Manager: Valerie Kramer. Public Affairs Director: Ann Shrewsbury. Technical Operations Manager: Rick Hollman.

City fee: 5% of gross.

Ownership: Time Warner Cable (MSO).; Advance/Newhouse Partnership (MSO).

AURORA—Mid-State Community TV, 1001 12th St, Aurora, NE 68818-2004. Phone: 402-694-4401. Fax: 402-694-2848. E-mail: midstate@midstatetv.com. Web Site: http://www.midstatetv.com. Also serves Doniphan, Giltner, Hampton, Hordville, Marquette & Trumbull. ICA: NE0033.

TV Market Ranking: 91 (AURORA, Doniphan, Giltner, Hampton, Trumbull); Below 100 (Hordville, Marquette). Franchise award date: N.A. Franchise expiration date: N.A. Began: February 1, 1968.

Channel capacity: 60 (not 2-way capable). Channels available but not in use: N.A.

Basic Service
Subscribers: 1,940.
Programming (received off-air): KHAS-TV (NBC) Hastings; KHGI-TV (ABC) Kearney; KHNE-TV (PBS) Hastings; KOLN (CBS, MNT) Lincoln; KTVG-TV (FOX) Grand Island.
Programming (via satellite): ABC Family Channel; AMC; Animal Planet; Arts & Entertainment; Cartoon Network; CNN; Comedy Central; Country Music TV; C-SPAN; Discovery Channel; Disney Channel; Do-It-Yourself; E! Entertainment Television; ESPN; ESPN 2; Food Network; Fox News Channel; Fox Sports Net Midwest; FX; Hallmark Channel; Headline News; ION Television; Lifetime; MSNBC; MTV; National Geographic Channel; Nickelodeon; Oxygen; QVC; Speed Channel; Spike TV; Style Network; TBS Superstation; The Learning Channel; The Sportsman Channel; Travel Channel; truTV; Turner Network TV; TV Guide Network; TV Land; USA Network; VH1; Weather Channel; WGN America; WPIX (CW, IND) New York.
Fee: $20.00 installation; $40.95 monthly; $2.00 converter.

Digital Basic Service
Subscribers: 179.
Programming (via satellite): AmericanLife TV Network; BBC America; Bloomberg Television; Bravo; Discovery Digital Networks; DMX Music; ESPN Classic Sports; ESPNews; FitTV; Fox Movie Channel; Fox Sports World; G4; Golf Channel; GSN; Halogen Network; HGTV; History Channel; Independent Film Channel; Nick Jr.; NickToons TV; Outdoor Channel; Syfy; Trinity Broadcasting Network; Turner Classic Movies; Versus; WE tv.
Fee: $16.90 monthly.

Pay Service 1
Pay Units: 267.
Programming (via satellite): HBO.
Fee: $20.00 installation; $10.50 monthly.

Pay Service 2
Pay Units: 150.
Programming (via satellite): Cinemax.
Fee: $20.00 installation; $7.50 monthly.

Digital Pay Service 1
Pay Units: N.A.
Programming (via satellite): Cinemax (multiplexed); Encore (multiplexed); HBO (multiplexed); Showtime (multiplexed); Starz (multiplexed); The Movie Channel (multiplexed).
Fee: $6.50 monthly (Starz & Encore), $8.50 monthly (Cinemax), $12.50 monthly (HBO), $12.95 monthly (Showtime & TMC).

Video-On-Demand: No

Pay-Per-View
Hot Choice (delivered digitally); ESPN Extra (delivered digitally); ESPN Gameplan (delivered digitally).

Internet Service
Operational: No, DSL & dial-up.

Telephone Service
None

Miles of Plant: 62.0 (coaxial); None (fiber optic). Homes passed: 2,654. Miles of plant (coax) includes miles of plant (fiber)

Manager: Phil C. Nelson. Marketing Director: Tina Hunt. Customer Service Manager: Pat Phillips. Chief Technician: Pat Shaw.

City fee: 3% of gross (Aurora); 3% of basic (Hampton).

Ownership: Mid-State Community TV Inc.

AVOCA—Formerly served by CableDirect. No longer in operation. ICA: NE0123.

BANCROFT—Great Plains Communications, PO Box 500, 1600 Great Plains Centre, Blair, NE 68008-0500. Phones: 888-343-8014; 402-426-9511. Fax: 402-456-6550. Web Site: http://www.gpcom.com. ICA: NE0151.

TV Market Ranking: Outside TV Markets (BANCROFT). Franchise award date: December 1, 1983. Franchise expiration date: N.A. Began: N.A.

Channel capacity: 80 (operating 2-way). Channels available but not in use: N.A.

Basic Service
Subscribers: N.A. Included in Arnold
Programming (received off-air): KCAU-TV (ABC) Sioux City; KETV (ABC) Omaha; KMTV-TV (CBS) Omaha; KPTM (FOX, MNT) Omaha; KTIV (CW, NBC) Sioux City; KXNE-TV (PBS) Norfolk; KXVO (CW) Omaha.
Programming (via satellite): ABC Family Channel; AMC; Animal Planet; Arts & Entertainment; CNN; Discovery Channel; Disney Channel; ESPN; ESPN 2; Fox News Channel; Great American Country; Hallmark Channel; Headline News; HGTV; History Channel; Lifetime; Nickelodeon; QVC; Spike TV; TBS Superstation; The Learning Channel; Travel Channel; Turner Network TV; TV Land; USA Network; Weather Channel; WGN America.
Fee: $28.00 installation; $31.50 monthly.

Digital Basic Service
Subscribers: N.A. Included in Arnold
Programming (via satellite): BBC America; Bio; Bravo; Discovery Digital Networks; DMX Music; ESPN Classic Sports; ESPNews; Fox Sports World; Golf Channel; GSN; History Channel International; Independent Film Channel; Lifetime Movie Network; National Geographic Channel; Outdoor Channel; Speed Channel; Syfy; Trio; Turner Classic Movies; Versus; WE tv.
Fee: $47.95 monthly.

Pay Service 1
Pay Units: 20.
Programming (via satellite): HBO; Showtime.
Fee: $9.95 monthly (Showtime), $10.95 monthly (HBO).

Digital Pay Service 1
Pay Units: 10.
Programming (via satellite): Cinemax (multiplexed); Encore (multiplexed); Flix; HBO (multiplexed); Showtime (multiplexed); The Movie Channel (multiplexed); WAM! America's Kidz Network.
Fee: $12.00 monthly.

Video-On-Demand: No

Pay-Per-View
iN DEMAND (delivered digitally); ESPN (delivered digitally).

Internet Service
Operational: Yes, Both DSL & dial-up.
Broadband Service: In-house.
Fee: $49.95 installation; $39.95 monthly.

Telephone Service
None

Miles of Plant: 4.0 (coaxial); None (fiber optic). Homes passed included in Arnold

General Manager: Lea Ann Quist. Chief Technician: Mark Stottler. Marketing Manager: Casey Carrigan.

Ownership: Great Plains Communications Inc. (MSO).

BASSETT—American Broadband, 1605 Washington St, Blair, NE 68008-0400. Phones: 401-426-6200; 402-533-1000. Fax: 402-533-1111. Web Site: http://www.abbnebraska.com. Also serves Rock County. ICA: NE0094.

TV Market Ranking: Outside TV Markets (BASSETT, Rock County). Franchise award date: N.A. Franchise expiration date: N.A. Began: August 1, 1982.

Channel capacity: 42 (2-way capable). Channels available but not in use: N.A.

Basic Service
Subscribers: N.A. Included in Blair
Programming (received off-air): KLKN (ABC) Lincoln; KMNE-TV (PBS) Bassett; KOLN (CBS, MNT) Lincoln; allband FM.
Programming (via satellite): ABC Family Channel; AMC; Arts & Entertainment; Cartoon Network; CNN; Comedy Central; Country Music TV; C-SPAN; Discovery Channel; E! Entertainment Television; ESPN; ESPN 2; Fox Sports Net Midwest; FX; Headline News; HGTV; History Channel; KUSA (NBC) Denver; Lifetime; Nickelodeon; Spike TV; TBS Superstation; The Learning Channel; Turner Network TV; USA Network; VH1; Weather Channel; WGN America; WTOL (CBS) Toledo.
Fee: $25.00 installation; $30.00 monthly.

Pay Service 1
Pay Units: N.A.
Programming (via satellite): Cinemax.
Fee: $10.00 monthly.

Pay Service 2
Pay Units: 63.
Programming (via satellite): HBO.
Fee: $12.00 monthly.

Pay Service 3
Pay Units: 39.
Programming (via satellite): Showtime.
Fee: $10.00 monthly.

Video-On-Demand: No

Internet Service
Operational: No.

Telephone Service
None

Miles of Plant: 10.0 (coaxial); None (fiber optic). Total homes in area & homes passed included in Blair

State President: Mike Jacobsen. General Manager: Mike Storjohann. Program Director: Kay Peterson.

Ownership: American Broadband Communications Inc. (MSO).

BAYARD—Charter Communications. Now served by SCOTTSBLUFF, NE [NE0008]. ICA: NE0056.

BEATRICE—Charter Communications, PO Box 1448, 809 Central Ave, Kearney, NE 68848-1448. Phones: 507-289-8372 (Rochester administrative office); 308-236-1500. Fax: 308-234-6452. Web Site: http://www.charter.com. ICA: NE0016.

TV Market Ranking: Outside TV Markets (BEATRICE). Franchise award date: N.A. Franchise expiration date: N.A. Began: August 1, 1963.

Channel capacity: N.A. Channels available but not in use: N.A.

Basic Service
Subscribers: 4,918.
Programming (received off-air): KLKN (ABC) Lincoln; KMTV-TV (CBS) Omaha; KOLN (CBS, MNT) Lincoln; KPTM (FOX, MNT) Omaha; KUON-TV (PBS) Lincoln; WIBW-TV (CBS, MNT) Topeka; WOWT-TV (IND, NBC) Omaha.
Programming (via satellite): C-SPAN; C-SPAN 2; Eternal Word TV Network; Home Shopping Network; WGN America.
Current originations: Government Access; Educational Access; Public Access.
Fee: $29.99 installation.

Expanded Basic Service 1
Subscribers: 4,319.
Programming (via satellite): ABC Family Channel; AMC; Animal Planet; Arts & Entertainment; Cartoon Network; CNBC; CNN; Comedy Central; Country Music TV; Discovery Channel; Disney Channel; E! Entertainment Television; ESPN; ESPN 2; Food Network; Fox News Channel; Fox Sports Net; FX; G4; Golf Channel; Hallmark Channel; Headline News; HGTV; History Channel; Lifetime; MSNBC; MTV; Nickelodeon; Oxygen; Speed Channel; Spike TV; TBS Superstation; The Learning Channel; Toon Disney; Travel Channel; truTV; Turner Network TV; TV Land; USA Network; VH1; Weather Channel.
Fee: $47.99 monthly.

Digital Basic Service
Subscribers: N.A.
Programming (via satellite): BBC America; Bio; Bravo; Discovery Health Chan-

nel; Discovery Kids Channel; DMX Music; ESPN Classic Sports; ESPNews; Fox Sports World; GAS; GSN; History Channel International; Independent Film Channel; Lifetime Movie Network; MTV2; Nick Jr.; NickToons TV; Science Television; Syfy; Trinity Broadcasting Network; Turner Classic Movies; TV Guide Interactive Inc.; Versus; WE tv.

Digital Pay Service 1
Pay Units: N.A.
Programming (via satellite): Cinemax (multiplexed); Encore (multiplexed); Flix; HBO (multiplexed); Showtime (multiplexed); Starz (multiplexed); The Movie Channel (multiplexed).

Video-On-Demand: Yes

Pay-Per-View
iN DEMAND (delivered digitally); Playboy TV (delivered digitally); Fresh (delivered digitally); Shorteez (delivered digitally).

Internet Service
Operational: Yes.
Broadband Service: Charter Pipeline.
Fee: $29.99 monthly.

Telephone Service
Digital: Operational

Miles of Plant: 81.0 (coaxial); None (fiber optic). Homes passed: 6,873. Total homes in franchised area: 6,873.

Vice President & General Manager: John Crowley. Technical Operations Director: Marty Kovarik. Technical Operations Manager: Terry Petzoldt. Office Manager: Dawn Harmon.

Ownership: Charter Communications Inc. (MSO).

BEAVER CITY—Pinpoint Cable TV, PO Box 490, 611 Patterson St, Cambridge, NE 69022-0490. Phones: 800-793-2788; 308-697-7678; 308-697-3333. Fax: 308-697-3631. E-mail: info@pnpt.com. Web Site: http://www.pnpt.com. ICA: NE0100.

TV Market Ranking: Outside TV Markets (BEAVER CITY). Franchise award date: N.A. Franchise expiration date: N.A. Began: July 1, 1983.

Channel capacity: N.A. Channels available but not in use: N.A.

Basic Service
Subscribers: 64.
Programming (received off-air): KGIN (CBS, MNT) Grand Island; KHGI-TV (ABC) Kearney; KLNE-TV (PBS) Lexington; KSNK (NBC) McCook.
Programming (via satellite): ABC Family Channel; Arts & Entertainment; CNN; Discovery Channel; Disney Channel; ESPN; Fox Sports Net; FX; Great American Country; Headline News; History Channel; National Geographic Channel; Spike TV; TBS Superstation; The Learning Channel; Trinity Broadcasting Network; TV Land; USA Network; Weather Channel; WGN America.
Fee: $15.00 installation; $33.95 monthly.

Pay Service 1
Pay Units: 3.
Programming (via satellite): HBO; Showtime.
Fee: $11.95 monthly (each).

Video-On-Demand: No

Internet Service
Operational: No.

Telephone Service
None

Miles of Plant: 7.0 (coaxial); None (fiber optic). Homes passed: 400.

General Manager: J. Thomas Shoemaker.

Ownership: PinPoint Communications Inc. (MSO).

BEAVER CROSSING—Galaxy Cablevision, 1928 S Lincoln Ave, Ste 200, York, NE 68467. Phone: 402-362-3332. Fax: 402-362-4890. Web Site: http://www.galaxycable.com. ICA: NE0155.

TV Market Ranking: 91 (BEAVER CROSSING). Franchise award date: N.A. Franchise expiration date: N.A. Began: July 1, 1983.

Channel capacity: 41 (not 2-way capable). Channels available but not in use: 3.

Basic Service
Subscribers: 39.
Programming (received off-air): KETV (ABC) Omaha; KHAS-TV (NBC) Hastings; KHNE-TV (PBS) Hastings; KLKN (ABC) Lincoln; KOLN (CBS, MNT) Lincoln; KPTM (FOX, MNT) Omaha; KXVO (CW) Omaha.
Programming (via satellite): ABC Family Channel; AMC; Animal Planet; Arts & Entertainment; Cartoon Network; CNN; C-SPAN; Discovery Channel; Disney Channel; E! Entertainment Television; ESPN; ESPN 2; Fox Sports Net Midwest; Fuse; Great American Country; Headline News; HGTV; History Channel; Lifetime; Outdoor Channel; QVC; TBS Superstation; The Learning Channel; Turner Classic Movies; Turner Network TV; USA Network; Weather Channel; WGN America.
Fee: $35.00 installation; $42.50 monthly.

Pay Service 1
Pay Units: 10.
Programming (via satellite): Cinemax.
Fee: $9.95 monthly.

Pay Service 2
Pay Units: 17.
Programming (via satellite): HBO.
Fee: $13.95 monthly.

Internet Service
Operational: No.

Telephone Service
None

Miles of Plant: 6.0 (coaxial); None (fiber optic). Homes passed: 222.

State Manager: Cheyenne Wohlford. Technical Manager: Carl Stanley. Sales Manager: Mike Thomas. Customer Service Manager: Donna Bryant.

City fee: 3% of basic.

Ownership: Galaxy Cable Inc. (MSO).

BEAVER LAKE—Our Cable, PO Box 190, 112 E Main St, Breda, IA 51436-0190. Phone: 877-873-8715. E-mail: info@ourcableia.com. Web Site: http://ourcableia.com. ICA: NE0262.

TV Market Ranking: 91 (BEAVER LAKE). Franchise award date: N.A. Franchise expiration date: N.A. Began: N.A.

Channel capacity: N.A. Channels available but not in use: N.A.

Basic Service
Subscribers: N.A. Included in Breda, IA
Programming (received off-air): KETV (ABC) Omaha; KMTV-TV (CBS) Omaha; KPTM (FOX, MNT) Omaha; KUON-TV (PBS) Lincoln; WOWT-TV (IND, NBC) Omaha.
Programming (via satellite): ABC Family Channel; CNN; Discovery Channel; Disney Channel; ESPN; Spike TV; TBS Superstation; Turner Network TV; WGN America.
Fee: $20.00 installation; $31.45 monthly.

Pay Service 1
Pay Units: N.A.
Programming (via satellite): Cinemax; HBO.
Fee: $10.95 monthly (each).

Video-On-Demand: No

Internet Service
Operational: No.

Telephone Service
None

Ownership: Our Cable (MSO).

BEE (village)—Formerly served by TelePartners. No longer in operation. ICA: NE0263.

BEEMER—TelePartners. Now served by NORFOLK, NE [NE0006]. ICA: NE0165.

BELLWOOD—Cable Nebraska, 2123 Central Ave, Ste 200, Kearney, NE 68847. Phone: 308-236-1512. Web Site: http://www.cablene.com. ICA: NE0265.

TV Market Ranking: Outside TV Markets (BELLWOOD). Franchise award date: N.A. Franchise expiration date: N.A. Began: May 1, 1983.

Channel capacity: 41 (not 2-way capable). Channels available but not in use: 6.

Basic Service
Subscribers: 86.
Programming (received off-air): KETV (ABC) Omaha; KLKN (ABC) Lincoln; KMTV-TV (CBS) Omaha; KOLN (CBS, MNT) Lincoln; KPTM (FOX, MNT) Omaha; KUON-TV (PBS) Lincoln; KXVO (CW) Omaha; WOWT-TV (IND, NBC) Omaha.
Programming (via satellite): ABC Family Channel; Arts & Entertainment; CNN; Discovery Channel; ESPN; ESPN 2; Fox Sports Net Midwest; HGTV; Lifetime; Nickelodeon; Outdoor Channel; QVC; TBS Superstation; The Learning Channel; Turner Classic Movies; Turner Network TV; USA Network; Weather Channel; WGN America.
Fee: $35.00 installation; $29.95 monthly.

Pay Service 1
Pay Units: 23.
Programming (via satellite): HBO.
Fee: $13.95 monthly.

Pay Service 2
Pay Units: 9.
Programming (via satellite): Showtime.
Fee: $8.95 monthly.

Pay Service 3
Pay Units: 8.
Programming (via satellite): The Movie Channel.
Fee: $7.95 monthly.

Internet Service
Operational: No.

Miles of Plant: 3.0 (coaxial); None (fiber optic). Homes passed: 192.

Operations Manager: Stuart Gilbertson.

Ownership: USA Companies (MSO).

BENEDICT—Formerly served by Galaxy Cablevision. No longer in operation. ICA: NE0231.

BENKELMAN—BWTelcom, PO Box 645, 607 Chief St, Benkelman, NE 69021. Phones: 800-835-0053; 308-394-6000; 308-423-2000. Fax: 308-423-5618. E-mail: randy@bwtelcom.net. Web Site: http://www.bwtelcom.net. ICA: NE0051.

TV Market Ranking: Outside TV Markets (BENKELMAN). Franchise award date: November 1, 1982. Franchise expiration date: N.A. Began: November 1, 1982.

Channel capacity: 60 (operating 2-way). Channels available but not in use: 7.

Basic Service
Subscribers: 490.
Programming (received off-air): KBSL-DT (CBS) Goodland; KPNE-TV (PBS) North Platte; KSNK (NBC) McCook; KWGN-TV (CW) Denver; KWNB-TV (ABC) Hayes Center.
Programming (via satellite): ABC Family Channel; Arts & Entertainment; CNBC; CNN; Country Music TV; Discovery Channel; ESPN; ESPN 2; ESPN Classic Sports; Fox News Channel; Fox Sports Net Rocky Mountain; FX; KCNC-TV (CBS) Denver; Lifetime; Nickelodeon; Outdoor Channel; Spike TV; Syfy; TBS Superstation; The Learning Channel; Travel Channel; Turner Classic Movies; Turner Network TV; USA Network; VH1; Weather Channel; WGN America.
Fee: $35.00 installation; $19.40 monthly.

Expanded Basic Service 1
Subscribers: N.A.
Programming (via satellite): AMC; Animal Planet; Bloomberg Television; Cartoon Network; Comedy Central; Disney Channel; Food Network; G4; Great American Country; Hallmark Channel; Headline News; HGTV; History Channel; MTV; National Geographic Channel; SoapNet; Speed Channel; TV Land; Versus.
Fee: $45.00 installation; $8.95 monthly.

Pay Service 1
Pay Units: 54.
Programming (via satellite): HBO; Showtime; The Movie Channel.
Fee: $10.43 monthly (Showtime/TMC), $10.95 monthly (HBO).

Video-On-Demand: No

Internet Service
Operational: No, Both DSL & dial-up.

Telephone Service
None

Miles of Plant: 28.0 (coaxial); None (fiber optic). Homes passed: 500.

Manager: Randall Raile. Marketing Director: Loretta Raile.

Ownership: Benkelman Telephone Co. (MSO).

BENNINGTON—Cox Communications. Now served by OMAHA, NE [NE0001]. ICA: NE0110.

BIG SPRINGS—Consolidated Cable Inc., PO Box 6147, 6900 Van Dorn St, Ste 21, Lincoln, NE 68506-0147. Phones: 402-489-2728; 800-742-7464. Fax: 402-489-9034. E-mail: service@consolidatedtelephone.com. Web Site: http://www.nebnet.net. ICA: NE0148.

TV Market Ranking: Outside TV Markets (BIG SPRINGS). Franchise award date: N.A. Franchise expiration date: N.A. Began: January 1, 1989.

Channel capacity: 36 (not 2-way capable). Channels available but not in use: 3.

Basic Service
Subscribers: 102.
Programming (received off-air): KNOP-TV (NBC) North Platte; KPNE-TV (PBS) North Platte.
Programming (via satellite): ABC Family Channel; Arts & Entertainment; CNN;

Country Music TV; Discovery Channel; Disney Channel; ESPN; ESPN 2; Fox News Channel; Fox Sports Net Rocky Mountain; HGTV; History Channel; Home Shopping Network; KCNC-TV (CBS) Denver; KDVR (FOX) Denver; KMGH-TV (ABC) Denver; KWGN-TV (CW) Denver; MTV; Nickelodeon; Spike TV; Syfy; TBS Superstation; Toon Disney; Turner Classic Movies; Turner Network TV; TV Land; USA Network; VH1; Weather Channel; WGN America.
Fee: $28.95 monthly.

Pay Service 1
Pay Units: 7.
Programming (via satellite): HBO.
Fee: $11.00 monthly.

Pay Service 2
Pay Units: 13.
Programming (via satellite): Showtime.
Fee: $9.00 monthly.

Video-On-Demand: No

Internet Service
Operational: No, Both DSL & dial-up.

Telephone Service
None

Miles of Plant: 5.0 (coaxial); None (fiber optic). Homes passed: 211.
Manager: Brian D. Thompson. Chief Technician: Dan Smith.
Ownership: Consolidated Cable Inc. (MSO).

BLAIR—American Broadband, 1605 Washington St, Blair, NE 68008-0400. Phones: 402-426-6200; 402-533-1000. Fax: 402-533-1111. Web Site: http://www.abbnebraska.com. Also serves Arlington, Fort Calhoun, Herman, Kennard & Washington County. ICA: NE0027.
TV Market Ranking: 53 (Arlington, BLAIR, Fort Calhoun, Herman, Kennard, Washington County). Franchise award date: N.A. Franchise expiration date: N.A. Began: November 1, 1980.
Channel capacity: N.A. Channels available but not in use: N.A.

Basic Service
Subscribers: 7,900 Includes Bassett, Laurel, Lyons, Oakland, Tekamah, & Wayne.
Programming (received off-air): KETV (ABC) Omaha; KHIN (PBS) Red Oak; KMTV-TV (CBS) Omaha; KPTM (FOX, MNT) Omaha; KXVO (CW) Omaha; KYNE-TV (PBS) Omaha; WOWT-TV (IND, NBC) Omaha.
Programming (via satellite): C-SPAN; Home Shopping Network; QVC; TV Guide Network; Weather Channel; WGN America.
Current originations: Government Access; Educational Access; Public Access; Leased Access.
Fee: $25.00 installation; $15.53 monthly.

Expanded Basic Service 1
Subscribers: N.A.
Programming (via satellite): ABC Family Channel; AMC; Animal Planet; Arts & Entertainment; CNBC; CNN; Comedy Central; Country Music TV; Discovery Channel; Disney Channel; ESPN; ESPN 2; Food Network; Fox News Channel; Fox Sports Net; FX; Hallmark Channel; Headline News; HGTV; History Channel; Lifetime; MSNBC; MTV; Nickelodeon; Spike TV; Syfy; TBS Superstation; The Learning Channel; truTV; Turner Network TV; USA Network; VH1.
Fee: $19.95 monthly.

Digital Basic Service
Subscribers: 2,300 Includes Lyons, Oakland, Tekamah, & Wayne.
Programming (received off-air): KETV (ABC) Omaha; KMTV-TV (CBS) Omaha; KPTM (FOX, MNT) Omaha; KXVO (CW) Omaha; KYNE-TV (PBS) Omaha; WOWT-TV (IND, NBC) Omaha.
Programming (via satellite): Animal Planet HD; Bio; Discovery Channel HD; Discovery HD Theater; Discovery Health Channel; Discovery Kids Channel; Discovery Military Channel; Discovery Planet Green; DMX Music; ESPN 2 HD; ESPN HD; ESPN U; ESPNews; Eternal Word TV Network; Fox Soccer; FSN Digital Atlantic; FSN Digital Central; FSN Digital Pacific; Fuel TV; Fuse; Golf Channel; GSN; HDNet; HDNet Movies; ID Investigation Discovery; Lifetime Movie Network; MyNetworkTV Inc.; National Geographic Channel; National Geographic Channel HD Network; Outdoor Channel; RFD-TV; Science Channel; Science Channel HD; Sleuth; Speed Channel; Style Network; TLC HD; Toon Disney; Turner Classic Movies; Universal HD; Versus; WE tv.
Fee: $12.94 monthly.

Digital Pay Service 1
Pay Units: N.A.
Programming (via satellite): Cinemax (multiplexed); Cinemax HD; Encore (multiplexed); HBO (multiplexed); HBO HD; Showtime (multiplexed); Showtime HD; Starz (multiplexed); Starz HDTV; The Movie Channel (multiplexed); The Movie Channel HD.
Fee: $11.10 monthly (Cinemax), $12.00 monthly (Starz/Encore or Showtime/TMC), $13.35 monthly (HBO).

Video-On-Demand: No

Pay-Per-View
iN DEMAND (delivered digitally); Playboy TV (delivered digitally); Club Jenna (delivered digitally).

Internet Service
Operational: No.

Telephone Service
None

Miles of Plant: 31.0 (coaxial); None (fiber optic). Homes passed: 10,900. Total homes in franchised area: 10,900. Total homes in area & homes passed includes Bassett, Laurel, Lyons, Oakland, Tekamah, & Wayne
President, State Operations: Mike Jacobsen. General Manager, Cable Television: Mike Storjohann. Programming Manager: Kay Petersen.
City fee: 3% of gross.
Ownership: American Broadband Communications Inc. (MSO).

BLOOMFIELD—Great Plains Communications, PO Box 500, 1600 Great Plains Centre, Blair, NE 68008-0500. Phones: 888-343-8014; 402-426-9511. Fax: 402-456-6550. E-mail: lquist@gpcom.com. Web Site: http://www.gpcom.com. Also serves Center, Creighton, Crofton, Niobrara, Plainview, Verdigre, Wausa & Winnetoon. ICA: NE0065.
TV Market Ranking: Outside TV Markets (BLOOMFIELD, Center, Creighton, Crofton, Niobrara, Plainview, Verdigre, Wausa, Winnetoon). Franchise award date: N.A. Franchise expiration date: N.A. Began: August 1, 1983.
Channel capacity: 80 (operating 2-way). Channels available but not in use: 18.

Basic Service
Subscribers: N.A. Included in Arnold
Programming (received off-air): KCAU-TV (ABC) Sioux City; KELO-TV (CBS, MNT) Sioux Falls; KLKN (ABC) Lincoln; KOLN (CBS, MNT) Lincoln; KPTH (FOX, MNT) Sioux City; KTIV (CW, NBC) Sioux City; KXNE-TV (PBS) Norfolk.
Programming (via satellite): ABC Family Channel; AMC; Animal Planet; Arts & Entertainment; CNBC; CNN; Country Music TV; C-SPAN; Discovery Channel; Disney Channel; ESPN; Fox News Channel; Fox Sports Net Rocky Mountain; Hallmark Channel; Headline News; Lifetime; MTV; Nickelodeon; QVC; Spike TV; Syfy; TBS Superstation; The Learning Channel; Travel Channel; Turner Network TV; TV Guide Network; TV Land; USA Network; VH1; Weather Channel; WGN America.
Fee: $28.00 installation; $31.50 monthly.

Expanded Basic Service 1
Subscribers: N.A.
Programming (via satellite): Cartoon Network; Comedy Central; ESPN 2; Food Network; HGTV; History Channel; Turner Classic Movies; Versus.
Fee: $6.50 monthly.

Digital Basic Service
Subscribers: N.A. Included in Arnold
Programming (via satellite): BBC America; Bio; Bravo; Discovery Digital Networks; DMX Music; ESPN Classic Sports; Fox Sports World; GAS; Golf Channel; History Channel International; Independent Film Channel; Lifetime Movie Network; MTV Networks Digital Suite; Nick Jr.; Speed Channel; Turner Classic Movies; WE tv.
Fee: $47.95 monthly.

Pay Service 1
Pay Units: 90.
Programming (via satellite): Showtime.
Fee: $9.95 monthly.

Pay Service 2
Pay Units: 270.
Programming (via satellite): HBO.
Fee: $10.75 monthly.

Digital Pay Service 1
Pay Units: 195.
Programming (via satellite): Cinemax (multiplexed); Encore (multiplexed); HBO (multiplexed); Showtime (multiplexed); Starz (multiplexed); The Movie Channel (multiplexed).
Fee: $12.00 monthly.

Video-On-Demand: No

Pay-Per-View
Addressable homes: 160.
iN DEMAND (delivered digitally), Fee: $3.49, Addressable: Yes.

Internet Service
Operational: Yes, Both DSL & dial-up.
Broadband Service: In-house.
Fee: $49.95 installation; $39.95 monthly.

Telephone Service
None

Miles of Plant: 18.0 (coaxial); None (fiber optic). Total homes in franchised area: 3,600. Homes passed included in Arnold
General Manager: Lea Ann Quist. Chief Technician: Mark Stottler. Marketing Manager: Casey Garrigan.
Ownership: Great Plains Communications Inc. (MSO).

BLUE HILL—Glenwood Telecommunications, PO Box 97, 510 W Gage St, Blue Hill, NE 68930. Phone: 402-756-3131. Fax: 402-756-3134. E-mail: info@gtmc.net. Web Site: http://www.gtmc.net. Also serves Bladen, Campbell, Funk, Holstein, Lawrence, Lochland, Norman, Roseland & Upland. ICA: NE0093.
TV Market Ranking: 91 (Bladen, BLUE HILL, Campbell, Funk, Holstein, Lawrence, Lochland, Norman, Roseland, Upland). Franchise award date: March 1, 1982. Franchise expiration date: N.A. Began: August 1, 1982.
Channel capacity: 78 (not 2-way capable). Channels available but not in use: 3.

Basic Service
Subscribers: 1,007.
Programming (received off-air): KFXL-TV (FOX) Lincoln; KGIN (CBS, MNT) Grand Island; KHAS-TV (NBC) Hastings; KHGI-TV (ABC) Kearney; KHNE-TV (PBS) Hastings; KTVG-TV (FOX) Grand Island; allband FM.
Programming (via satellite): C-SPAN; Eternal Word TV Network; QVC; Trinity Broadcasting Network; Weather Channel; WGN America.
Fee: $40.00 installation; $14.95 monthly; $1.00 converter.

Expanded Basic Service 1
Subscribers: N.A.
Programming (via satellite): ABC Family Channel; AMC; Animal Planet; Arts & Entertainment; Cartoon Network; CNN; Comedy Central; Country Music TV; Discovery Channel; Disney Channel; Do-It-Yourself; ESPN; ESPN 2; ESPN Classic Sports; ESPN U; Food Network; Fox News Channel; Fox Sports Net Midwest; FX; G4; Golf Channel; Hallmark Channel; Headline News; HGTV; History Channel; Lifetime; MTV; National Geographic Channel; Nickelodeon; Spike TV; Syfy; TBS Superstation; The Learning Channel; The Sportsman Channel; Turner Classic Movies; Turner Network TV; TV Land; USA Network; VH1.
Fee: $17.00 monthly.

Digital Basic Service
Subscribers: 104.
Programming (via satellite): BBC America; Bio; Bloomberg Television; Bravo; CMT Pure Country; Daystar TV Network; Discovery Digital Networks; DMX Music; ESPNews; Fox Movie Channel; FSN Digital Atlantic; FSN Digital Central; FSN Digital Pacific; Fuse; GAS; Great American Country; GSN; Halogen Network; History Channel International; Independent Film Channel; Lifetime Movie Network; MTV Networks Digital Suite; Nick Jr.; NickToons TV; Outdoor Channel; PBS Kids Sprout; RFD-TV; ShopNBC; Sleuth; Speed Channel; Toon Disney; Versus; WE tv.
Fee: $14.95 monthly.

Pay Service 1
Pay Units: 151.
Programming (via satellite): Showtime.
Fee: $10.00 installation; $9.50 monthly.

Pay Service 2
Pay Units: 116.
Programming (via satellite): HBO.
Fee: $10.00 installation; $10.95 monthly.

Digital Pay Service 1
Pay Units: N.A.
Programming (via satellite): Cinemax (multiplexed); Encore (multiplexed); Flix; HBO (multiplexed); Showtime (multiplexed); Starz (multiplexed); The Movie Channel (multiplexed).
Fee: $12.95 monthly (Showtime/TMC or Starz/Encore), $16.95 monthly (HBO/Cinemax).

Video-On-Demand: No

Pay-Per-View
iN DEMAND (delivered digitally); Playboy TV (delivered digitally); Fresh (delivered digitally); Hot Choice (delivered digitally).

Internet Service
Operational: Yes.
Fee: $24.95 monthly.

Telephone Service
None

Miles of Plant: 7.0 (coaxial); None (fiber optic). Total homes in franchised area: 1,158.
General Manager: Stanley Rouse. Chief Technician: Brad Gilbert. Cable TV Supervisor: Ken Kendall.

City fee: 2% of gross.
Ownership: Glenwood Telecommunications (MSO).

BOELUS—NCTC Cable, PO Box 700, 22 LaBarre St, Gibbon, NE 68840. Phones: 888-873-6282; 308-468-6341. Fax: 308-468-9929. Web Site: http://www.nctc.net. ICA: NE0378.
TV Market Ranking: 91 (BOELUS). Franchise award date: N.A. Franchise expiration date: N.A. Began: N.A.
Channel capacity: N.A. Channels available but not in use: N.A.
Basic Service
Subscribers: N.A. Included in Burwell
Programming (received off-air): KGIN (CBS, MNT) Grand Island; KHAS-TV (NBC) Hastings; KHGI-TV (ABC) Kearney; KMNE-TV (PBS) Bassett; KTVG-TV (FOX) Grand Island.
Programming (via satellite): ABC Family Channel; AMC; Animal Planet; Arts & Entertainment; Cartoon Network; CNBC; CNN; Comedy Central; Country Music TV; C-SPAN; CW+; Discovery Channel; E! Entertainment Television; ESPN; ESPN 2; ESPN Classic Sports; Eternal Word TV Network; Food Network; Fox News Channel; Fox Sports Net Midwest; FX; G4; Great American Country; Hallmark Channel; Headline News; HGTV; History Channel; Home Shopping Network; ION Television; Lifetime; MSNBC; MTV; Nickelodeon; Outdoor Channel; QVC; Spike TV; Syfy; TBS Superstation; The Learning Channel; Travel Channel; Trinity Broadcasting Network; truTV; Turner Classic Movies; Turner Network TV; TV Land; USA Network; Versus; VH1; Weather Channel; WGN America.
Fee: $39.20 monthly.
Digital Basic Service
Subscribers: N.A. Included in Burwell
Programming (via satellite): AmericanLife TV Network; BBC America; Bio; Bloomberg Television; Current; Daystar TV Network; Discovery Digital Networks; DMX Music; ESPNews; FitTV; Fox College Sports Atlantic; Fox College Sports Central; Fox College Sports Pacific; Fox Movie Channel; G4; Golf Channel; Gospel Music Channel; GSN; Halogen Network; History Channel International; Lifetime Movie Network; MTV Networks Digital Suite; Nick Jr.; Ovation; RFD-TV; ShopNBC; Sleuth; Speed Channel; TeenNick; WE tv.
Fee: $14.00 monthly.
Pay Service 1
Pay Units: 36.
Programming (via satellite): HBO.
Fee: $10.95 monthly.
Digital Pay Service 1
Pay Units: N.A.
Programming (via satellite): Cinemax (multiplexed); Encore (multiplexed); Flix; HBO (multiplexed); Showtime (multiplexed); Starz (multiplexed); The Movie Channel (multiplexed).
Fee: $10.95 monthly (Cinemax), $12.95 monthly (HBO or Showtime, TMC & Flix), $13.95 monthly (Starz & Encore).
Video-On-Demand: No
Internet Service
Operational: No, DSL & dial-up.
Telephone Service
None
Homes passed included in Burwell
General Manager: Andy Jader. Technical Operations Manager: Nick Jeffres.
Ownership: Nebraska Central Telecom Inc. (MSO).

BRADSHAW—Galaxy Cablevision, 1928 S Lincoln Ave, Ste 200, York, NE 68467. Phone: 402-362-3332. Fax: 402-362-4890. Web Site: http://www.galaxycable.com. ICA: NE0193.
TV Market Ranking: Below 100 (BRADSHAW). Franchise award date: N.A. Franchise expiration date: N.A. Began: September 1, 1984.
Channel capacity: 41 (not 2-way capable). Channels available but not in use: 24.
Basic Service
Subscribers: 13.
Programming (received off-air): KHAS-TV (NBC) Hastings; KHGI-TV (ABC) Kearney; KHNE-TV (PBS) Hastings; KLKN (ABC) Lincoln; KOLN (CBS, MNT) Lincoln.
Programming (via satellite): ABC Family Channel; Cartoon Network; CNN; Disney Channel; ESPN; Lifetime; Outdoor Channel; TBS Superstation; WGN America.
Fee: $35.00 installation; $34.20 monthly.
Pay Service 1
Pay Units: 6.
Programming (via satellite): Cinemax.
Fee: $11.95 monthly.
Pay Service 2
Pay Units: 8.
Programming (via satellite): HBO.
Fee: $12.95 monthly.
Internet Service
Operational: No.
Telephone Service
None
Miles of Plant: 4.0 (coaxial); None (fiber optic). Homes passed: 135.
State Manager: Cheyenne Wohlford. Technical Manager: Carl Stanley. Sales Manager: Mike Thomas. Customer Service Manager: Donna Bryant.
City fee: 1% of basic.
Ownership: Galaxy Cable Inc. (MSO).

BRAINARD—Galaxy Cablevision, 1928 S Lincoln Ave, Ste 200, York, NE 68467. Phone: 402-362-3332. Fax: 402-362-4890. Web Site: http://www.galaxycable.com. ICA: NE0191.
TV Market Ranking: 91 (BRAINARD). Franchise award date: N.A. Franchise expiration date: N.A. Began: September 11, 1989.
Channel capacity: 41 (not 2-way capable). Channels available but not in use: 20.
Basic Service
Subscribers: 11.
Programming (received off-air): KETV (ABC) Omaha; KLKN (ABC) Lincoln; KMTV-TV (CBS) Omaha; KOLN (CBS, MNT) Lincoln; KPTM (FOX, MNT) Omaha; KUON-TV (PBS) Lincoln; KXVO (CW) Omaha; WOWT-TV (IND, NBC) Omaha.
Programming (via satellite): ABC Family Channel; Cartoon Network; CNN; Discovery Channel; Disney Channel; ESPN; Eternal Word TV Network; Outdoor Channel; TBS Superstation; Turner Network TV; WGN America.
Fee: $32.95 monthly.
Pay Service 1
Pay Units: 6.
Programming (via satellite): Cinemax.
Fee: $9.95 monthly.
Pay Service 2
Pay Units: 7.
Programming (via satellite): HBO.
Fee: $13.95 monthly.
Internet Service
Operational: No.
Telephone Service
None
Miles of Plant: 3.0 (coaxial); None (fiber optic). Homes passed: 150.
State Manager: Cheyenne Wohlford. Technical Manager: Carl Stanley. Sales Manager: Mike Thomas. Customer Service Manager: Donna Bryant.
City fee: 3% of basic.
Ownership: Galaxy Cable Inc. (MSO).

BRIDGEPORT—Charter Communications. Now served by SCOTTSBLUFF, NE [NE0008]. ICA: NE0048.

BRISTOW TWP.—Formerly served by Sky Scan Cable Co. No longer in operation. ICA: NE0267.

BROCK—Formerly served by CableDirect. No longer in operation. ICA: NE0245.

BROKEN BOW—Great Plains Communications, PO Box 500, 1600 Great Plains Centre, Blair, NE 68008-0500. Phones: 402-426-9511; 888-343-8014. Fax: 402-456-6550. Web Site: http://www.gpcom.com. ICA: NE0031.
TV Market Ranking: Outside TV Markets (BROKEN BOW). Franchise award date: N.A. Franchise expiration date: N.A. Began: August 1, 1967.
Channel capacity: N.A. Channels available but not in use: N.A.
Basic Service
Subscribers: N.A. Included in Arnold
Programming (received off-air): KGIN (CBS, MNT) Grand Island; KHGI-TV (ABC) Kearney; KMNE-TV (PBS) Bassett; KNOP-TV (NBC) North Platte; 3 FMs.
Programming (via satellite): C-SPAN; C-SPAN 2; Home Shopping Network; QVC; Trinity Broadcasting Network; WGN America.
Current originations: Government Access.
Fee: $25.00 installation; $21.50 monthly; $10.00 additional installation.
Expanded Basic Service 1
Subscribers: N.A.
Programming (via satellite): ABC Family Channel; AMC; Animal Planet; Arts & Entertainment; Bravo; Cartoon Network; CNBC; CNN; Comedy Central; Country Music TV; Discovery Channel; Disney Channel; E! Entertainment Television; ESPN; ESPN 2; FitTV; Food Network; Fox News Channel; Fox Sports Net; Fox Sports Net Midwest; FX; G4; Golf Channel; Great American Country; Hallmark Channel; Headline News; HGTV; History Channel; Lifetime; MSNBC; MTV; National Geographic Channel; Nickelodeon; Oxygen; SoapNet; Speed Channel; Spike TV; Syfy; TBS Superstation; The Learning Channel; Toon Disney; Travel Channel; truTV; Turner Classic Movies; Turner Network TV; TV Land; USA Network; Versus; VH1; Weather Channel.
Fee: $26.25 monthly.
Digital Basic Service
Subscribers: N.A. Included in Arnold
Programming (via satellite): BBC America; Bio; Bloomberg Television; Bravo; Discovery Digital Networks; Do-It-Yourself; Fox Movie Channel; GAS; GSN; History Channel International; Independent Film Channel; Lifetime Movie Network; MTV Networks Digital Suite; Music Choice; Nick Jr.; Nick Too; NickToons TV; Style Network; Sundance Channel; TV Guide Interactive Inc.; WE tv.
Fee: $8.00 monthly.
Digital Pay Service 1
Pay Units: N.A.
Programming (via satellite): Cinemax (multiplexed); Encore; Flix; HBO (multiplexed); Showtime (multiplexed); Starz (multiplexed); The Movie Channel (multiplexed).
Fee: $12.00 monthly (HBO, Cinemax, Starz/Encore or Showtime/TMC/Flix).
Video-On-Demand: No
Pay-Per-View
iN DEMAND delivered digitally (delivered digitally); Pleasure (delivered digitally); The Erotic Network (delivered digitally); Erotic TV Clips (delivered digitally).
Internet Service
Operational: Yes, Both DSL & dial-up.
Broadband Service: In-house.
Fee: $49.95 installation; $39.95 monthly.
Telephone Service
None
Miles of Plant: 27.0 (coaxial); None (fiber optic). Total homes in franchised area: 1,660. Homes passed included in Arnold
General Manager: Lee Ann Quist. Chief Technician: Mark Stottler. Marketing Manager: Casey Garrigan.
City fee: 3% of gross.
Ownership: Great Plains Communications Inc. (MSO).

BRULE—Peregrine Communications, 14818 W 6th Ave, Ste 16A, Golden, CO 80401-6585. Phones: 800-344-5404; 303-278-9660. Web Site: http://www.perecom.com. ICA: NE0174.
TV Market Ranking: Outside TV Markets (BRULE). Franchise award date: N.A. Franchise expiration date: N.A. Began: February 1, 1984.
Channel capacity: N.A. Channels available but not in use: N.A.
Basic Service
Subscribers: 85.
Programming (received off-air): KETV (ABC) Omaha; KNOP-TV (NBC) North Platte; KOLN (CBS, MNT) Lincoln.
Programming (via satellite): ABC Family Channel; CNN; Discovery Channel; Disney Channel; ESPN; KDVR (FOX) Denver; KWGN-TV (CW) Denver; Spike TV; TBS Superstation; Turner Network TV; USA Network; WGN America.
Fee: $30.00 installation; $31.95 monthly.
Pay Service 1
Pay Units: N.A.
Programming (via satellite): HBO.
Fee: $14.00 monthly.
Video-On-Demand: No
Internet Service
Operational: No.
Telephone Service
None
Homes passed: 186.

Manager: Patty Hyyppa. Chief Technician: Don Green.
Ownership: Post Cablevision of Nebraska LP (MSO).

BRUNSWICK—Formerly served by Sky Scan Cable Co. No longer in operation. ICA: NE0268.

BURWELL—NCTC Cable, PO Box 700, 22 LaBarre St, Gibbon, NE 68840. Phones: 888-873-6282; 308-468-6341. Fax: 308-468-9929. Web Site: http://www.nctc.net. ICA: NE0045.
TV Market Ranking: Outside TV Markets (BURWELL). Franchise award date: N.A. Franchise expiration date: N.A. Began: March 1, 1970.
Channel capacity: N.A. Channels available but not in use: N.A.
Basic Service
Subscribers: 800 Includes Ansley, Arcadia, Ashton, Boelus, Dannebrog, Elba, Mason City, North Loup, Sargent, Scotia, & Taylor.
Programming (received off-air): KGIN (CBS, MNT) Grand Island; KHAS-TV (NBC) Hastings; KHGI-TV (ABC) Kearney; KMNE-TV (PBS) Bassett; KTVG-TV (FOX) Grand Island; allband FM.
Programming (via satellite): ABC Family Channel; AMC; Animal Planet; Arts & Entertainment; Cartoon Network; CNBC; CNN; Comedy Central; Country Music TV; C-SPAN; CW+; Discovery Channel; E! Entertainment Television; ESPN; ESPN 2; ESPN Classic Sports; Eternal Word TV Network; Food Network; Fox News Channel; Fox Sports Net Midwest; FX; G4; Great American Country; Hallmark Channel; Headline News; HGTV; History Channel; Home Shopping Network; ION Television; Lifetime; MSNBC; MTV; Nickelodeon; Outdoor Channel; QVC; Spike TV; Syfy; TBS Superstation; The Learning Channel; Travel Channel; Trinity Broadcasting Network; truTV; Turner Classic Movies; Turner Network TV; TV Land; USA Network; Versus; VH1; Weather Channel; WGN America.
Current originations: Public Access.
Fee: $35.00 installation; $39.20 monthly.
Digital Basic Service
Subscribers: 30 Includes Ansley, Arcadia, Ashton, Boelus, Dannebrog, Elba, Mason City, North Loup, Sargent, Scotia, & Taylor.
Programming (via satellite): AmericanLife TV Network; BBC America; Bio; Bloomberg Television; Current; Daystar TV Network; Discovery Digital Networks; DMX Music; ESPNews; FitTV; Fox College Sports Atlantic; Fox College Sports Central; Fox College Sports Pacific; Fox Movie Channel; G4; Golf Channel; Gospel Music Channel; GSN; Halogen Network; History Channel International; Lifetime Movie Network; MTV Networks Digital Suite; Nick Jr.; Ovation; RFD-TV; ShopNBC; Sleuth; Speed Channel; TeenNick; WE tv.
Fee: $14.00 monthly.
Pay Service 1
Pay Units: N.A.
Programming (via satellite): HBO.
Fee: $10.95 monthly.
Digital Pay Service 1
Pay Units: N.A.
Programming (via satellite): Cinemax (multiplexed); Encore (multiplexed); Flix; HBO (multiplexed); Showtime (multiplexed); Starz (multiplexed); The Movie Channel (multiplexed).
Fee: $10.95 monthly (Cinemax), $12.95 monthly (HBO or Showtime, TMC & Flix), $13.95 monthly (Starz & Encore).
Video-On-Demand: No
Internet Service
Operational: No, DSL & dial-up.
Telephone Service
None
Miles of Plant: 13.0 (coaxial); None (fiber optic). Homes passed: 1,600. Homes passed includes Ansley, Arcadia, Ashton, Boelus, Dannebrog, Elba, Mason City, North Loup, Sargent, Scotia, & Taylor
General Manager: Andy Jader. Technical Operations Manager: Nick Jeffres.
City fee: 2% of basic.
Ownership: Nebraska Central Telecom Inc. (MSO).

BUTTE—CenCom Inc. This cable system has converted to IPTV. See Butte (village), NE [NE5005]. ICA: NE0157.

BUTTE (village)—CenCom NNTV. Formerly [NE0157]. This cable system has converted to IPTV, 110 E Elk St, Jackson, NE 68743-0066. Phones: 402-623-4321; 888-397-4321. E-mail: nntc@nntc.net. Web Site: http://www.nntc.net. ICA: NE5005.
Channel capacity: N.A. Channels available but not in use: N.A.
Internet Service
Operational: Yes.
Telephone Service
Digital: Operational
General Manager: Emory Graffis.
Ownership: Northeast Nebraska Telephone Co.

BYRON—Galaxy Cablevision, 1928 S Lincoln Ave, Ste 200, York, NE 68467. Phone: 402-362-3332. Fax: 402-362-4890. Web Site: http://www.galaxycable.com. ICA: NE0249.
TV Market Ranking: Below 100 (BYRON). Franchise award date: N.A. Franchise expiration date: N.A. Began: September 1, 1984.
Channel capacity: 41 (not 2-way capable). Channels available but not in use: 26.
Basic Service
Subscribers: 9.
Programming (received off-air): KHAS-TV (NBC) Hastings; KHNE-TV (PBS) Hastings; KLKN (ABC) Lincoln; KOLN (CBS, MNT) Lincoln.
Programming (via satellite): ABC Family Channel; CNN; ESPN; Outdoor Channel; TBS Superstation; Toon Disney; Turner Network TV; WGN America.
Fee: $35.00 installation; $32.95 monthly.
Pay Service 1
Pay Units: 6.
Programming (via satellite): Cinemax.
Fee: $9.95 monthly.
Pay Service 2
Pay Units: 4.
Programming (via satellite): HBO.
Fee: $13.95 monthly.
Internet Service
Operational: No.
Telephone Service
None
Miles of Plant: 2.0 (coaxial); None (fiber optic). Homes passed: 74.
State Manager: Cheyenne Wohlford. Technical Manager: Carl Stanley. Sales Manager: Mike Thomas. Customer Service Manager: Donna Bryant.
City fee: 3% of basic.
Ownership: Galaxy Cable Inc. (MSO).

CAMBRIDGE—Pinpoint Cable TV, PO Box 490, 611 Patterson St, Cambridge, NE 69022-0490. Phones: 308-697-7678; 800-793-2788; 308-697-3333. Fax: 308-697-3631. E-mail: info@pnpt.com. Web Site: http://www.pnpt.com. Also serves Bartley & Indianola. ICA: NE0269.
TV Market Ranking: Below 100 (Bartley, CAMBRIDGE, Indianola). Franchise award date: N.A. Franchise expiration date: N.A. Began: January 1, 1983.
Channel capacity: 34 (operating 2-way). Channels available but not in use: N.A.
Basic Service
Subscribers: 577.
Programming (received off-air): KGIN (CBS, MNT) Grand Island; KHGI-TV (ABC) Kearney; KLNE-TV (PBS) Lexington; KSNK (NBC) McCook; KTVG-TV (FOX) Grand Island.
Programming (via satellite): ABC Family Channel; Animal Planet; Arts & Entertainment; CNBC; CNN; Country Music TV; Discovery Channel; Disney Channel; ESPN; ESPN 2; Eternal Word TV Network; Fox Sports Net; Golf Channel; HGTV; History Channel; Lifetime; Nickelodeon; Spike TV; TBS Superstation; The Learning Channel; Turner Network TV; USA Network; VH1; Weather Channel; WGN America.
Current originations: Public Access.
Fee: $15.00 installation; $24.95 monthly.
Pay Service 1
Pay Units: 85.
Programming (via satellite): HBO; The Movie Channel.
Fee: $10.95 monthly (each).
Video-On-Demand: No
Internet Service
Operational: Yes. Began: January 1, 2003.
Broadband Service: PinPoint Internet.
Fee: $15.00 installation; $39.95 monthly.
Telephone Service
None
Miles of Plant: 17.0 (coaxial); None (fiber optic). Homes passed: 1,044.
General Manager: J. Thomas Shoemaker. Customer Service Manager: Kim Ervin.
Ownership: PinPoint Communications Inc.

CEDAR BLUFFS—Formerly served by TelePartners. No longer in operation. ICA: NE0175.

CEDAR CREEK—Formerly served by Westcom. No longer in operation. ICA: NE0271.

CEDAR RAPIDS—Cable Nebraska, 2123 Central Ave, Ste 200, Kearney, NE 68847. Phone: 308-236-1512. Web Site: http://www.cablene.com. ICA: NE0154.
TV Market Ranking: Below 100 (CEDAR RAPIDS). Franchise award date: N.A. Franchise expiration date: N.A. Began: January 1, 1985.
Channel capacity: N.A. Channels available but not in use: N.A.
Basic Service
Subscribers: 95.
Programming (received off-air): KGIN (CBS, MNT) Grand Island; KHAS-TV (NBC) Hastings; KHGI-TV (ABC) Kearney; KHNE-TV (PBS) Hastings; KLKN (ABC) Lincoln; KTVG-TV (FOX) Grand Island.
Programming (via satellite): C-SPAN; C-SPAN 2; CW+; Eternal Word TV Network; Home Shopping Network; MyNetworkTV Inc.; QVC; TBS Superstation; Trinity Broadcasting Network; Univision; Weather Channel; WGN America.
Fee: $35.00 installation; $31.20 monthly.
Expanded Basic Service 1
Subscribers: N.A.
Programming (via satellite): ABC Family Channel; AMC; Animal Planet; Arts & Entertainment; Cartoon Network; CNBC; CNN; Comedy Central; Country Music TV; Discovery Channel; E! Entertainment Television; ESPN; ESPN 2; ESPN Classic Sports; Food Network; Fox News Channel; Fox Sports Net Midwest; FX; G4; Great American Country; Hallmark Channel; Headline News; HGTV; History Channel; ION Television; Lifetime; MSNBC; MTV; Nickelodeon; Outdoor Channel; RFD-TV; Spike TV; Syfy; The Learning Channel; Travel Channel; truTV; Turner Classic Movies; Turner Network TV; TV Land; USA Network; Versus; VH1.
Digital Basic Service
Subscribers: N.A.
Programming (via satellite): AmericanLife TV Network; BBC America; Bio; Black Family Channel; Bloomberg Television; Cine Latino; Cine Mexicano; CMT Pure Country; CNN en Espanol; Current; Daystar TV Network; Discovery Channel HD; Discovery en Espanol; Discovery Health Channel; Discovery Kids Channel; Discovery Military Channel; Discovery Planet Green; DMX Music; ESPN 2; ESPN Classic Sports; ESPN Deportes; ESPN HD; ESPNews; FitTV; Fox College Sports Atlantic; Fox College Sports Central; Fox College Sports Pacific; Fox Movie Channel; Fox Sports en Espanol; G4; Golf Channel; GSN; Halogen Network; History Channel; History Channel en Espanol; History Channel International; ID Investigation Discovery; Lifetime Movie Network; MTV Hits; MTV Tres; MTV2; Nick Jr.; Outdoor Channel; Ovation; Science Channel; ShopNBC; Sleuth; Speed Channel; Style Network; Syfy; TBS in HD; TeenNick; Trinity Broadcasting Network; Turner Network TV HD; VeneMovies; Versus; VH1 Classic; VH1 Soul; WE tv.
Digital Pay Service 1
Pay Units: N.A.
Programming (via satellite): Cinemax (multiplexed); Encore (multiplexed); Flix; HBO (multiplexed); HBO Latino; Showtime (multiplexed); Starz (multiplexed); The Movie Channel (multiplexed).
Video-On-Demand: No
Pay-Per-View
iN DEMAND (delivered digitally); Hot Choice (delivered digitally); Playboy TV (delivered digitally); Fresh (delivered digitally); Spice: Xcess (delivered digitally); Club Jenna (delivered digitally).
Internet Service
Operational: Yes.
Broadband Service: Cable Nebraska.
Telephone Service
None
Miles of Plant: 4.0 (coaxial); None (fiber optic). Homes passed: 225.
Operations Manager: Stuart Gilbertson.
City fee: 3% of gross.
Ownership: USA Companies (MSO).

CENTRAL CITY—Cable Nebraska, 2123 Central Ave, Ste 200, Kearney, NE 68847. Phone: 308-236-1512. Fax: 308-946-3749. Web Site: http://www.cablene.com. ICA: NE0044.
TV Market Ranking: Below 100 (CENTRAL CITY). Franchise award date: N.A. Franchise expiration date: N.A. Began: October 12, 1979.
Channel capacity: N.A. Channels available but not in use: N.A.
Basic Service
Subscribers: 403.
Programming (received off-air): KGIN (CBS, MNT) Grand Island; KHAS-TV (NBC) Hastings; KHGI-TV (ABC) Kearney; KHNE-TV (PBS) Hastings; KLKN (ABC) Lincoln; KTVG-TV (FOX) Grand Island.

Programming (via satellite): ABC Family Channel; C-SPAN; C-SPAN 2; Eternal Word TV Network; Hallmark Channel; Headline News; Home Shopping Network; QVC; TBS Superstation; Trinity Broadcasting Network; TV Guide Network; Weather Channel; WGN America.
Current originations: Public Access.
Fee: $35.00 installation; $24.95 monthly.

Expanded Basic Service 1
Subscribers: N.A.
Programming (via satellite): AMC; Animal Planet; Arts & Entertainment; Cartoon Network; CNBC; CNN; Comedy Central; Country Music TV; Discovery Channel; E! Entertainment Television; ESPN; ESPN 2; Food Network; Fox News Channel; Fox Sports Net; FX; Great American Country; HGTV; History Channel; ION Television; Lifetime; MSNBC; MTV; Nickelodeon; Outdoor Channel; Spike TV; Syfy; The Learning Channel; Travel Channel; truTV; Turner Classic Movies; Turner Network TV; TV Land; Univision; USA Network; VH1.

Digital Basic Service
Subscribers: 31.
Programming (via satellite): AmericanLife TV Network; BBC America; Bio; Bloomberg Television; Canales N; Current; Discovery Digital Networks; DMX Music; ESPN 2; ESPN Classic Sports; ESPNews; FitTV; Fox Movie Channel; Fox Sports World; FSN Digital Atlantic; FSN Digital Central; FSN Digital Pacific; G4; GAS; Golf Channel; GSN; History Channel; History Channel International; International Television (ITV); MBC America; MTV Networks Digital Suite; National Geographic Channel; Nick Jr.; Outdoor Channel; Ovation; ShopNBC; Style Network; Trio; Versus.
Fee: $12.95 monthly.

Digital Pay Service 1
Pay Units: N.A.
Programming (via satellite): Cinemax (multiplexed); Daystar TV Network; Flix; Fox Movie Channel; HBO (multiplexed); Independent Film Channel; Lifetime; Showtime (multiplexed); Starz (multiplexed); Sundance Channel; The Movie Channel (multiplexed); WAM! America's Kidz Network; WE tv.
Fee: $5.00 monthly.

Video-On-Demand: No

Pay-Per-View
iN DEMAND (delivered digitally); Hot Choice (delivered digitally); Playboy TV (delivered digitally); Fresh (delivered digitally); Shorteez (delivered digitally); Urban Xtra (delivered digitally).

Internet Service
Operational: Yes.
Broadband Service: Cable Nebraska.

Telephone Service
None
Miles of Plant: 28.0 (coaxial); None (fiber optic). Homes passed: 1,222.
Operations Manager: Stuart Gilbertson.
City fee: 3% of basic.
Ownership: USA Companies (MSO).

CERESCO—Galaxy Cablevision, 1928 S Lincoln Ave, Ste 200, York, NE 68467. Phone: 402-362-3332. Fax: 402-362-4890. Web Site: http://www.galaxycable.com. ICA: NE0116.
TV Market Ranking: 91 (CERESCO). Franchise award date: N.A. Franchise expiration date: N.A. Began: June 1, 1983.
Channel capacity: 41 (not 2-way capable). Channels available but not in use: 11.

Basic Service
Subscribers: 53.
Programming (received off-air): KETV (ABC) Omaha; KMTV-TV (CBS) Omaha; KOLN (CBS, MNT) Lincoln; KPTM (FOX, MNT) Omaha; KUON-TV (PBS) Lincoln; KXVO (CW) Omaha; WOWT-TV (IND, NBC) Omaha.
Programming (via satellite): ABC Family Channel; Cartoon Network; CNN; Discovery Channel; Disney Channel; ESPN; ESPN 2; Fox News Channel; Fox Sports Net Midwest; Headline News; HGTV; Lifetime; Outdoor Channel; TBS Superstation; The Learning Channel; Turner Network TV; USA Network; Weather Channel; WGN America.
Fee: $35.00 installation; $38.95 monthly.

Pay Service 1
Pay Units: 11.
Programming (via satellite): Cinemax.
Fee: $9.95 monthly.

Pay Service 2
Pay Units: 19.
Programming (via satellite): HBO.
Fee: $13.95 monthly.

Pay Service 3
Pay Units: 35.
Programming (via satellite): Showtime.
Fee: $8.95 monthly.

Pay Service 4
Pay Units: 34.
Programming (via satellite): The Movie Channel.
Fee: $7.95 monthly.

Internet Service
Operational: No.

Telephone Service
None
Miles of Plant: 6.0 (coaxial); None (fiber optic). Homes passed: 316.
State Manager: Cheyenne Wohlford. Technical Manager: Carl Stanley. Sales Manager: Mike Thomas. Customer Service Manager: Donna Bryant.
City fee: 3% of basic.
Ownership: Galaxy Cable Inc. (MSO).

CHADRON—Great Plains Communications, PO Box 500, 1600 Great Plains Centre, Blair, NE 68008-0500. Phones: 402-426-9511; 888-343-8014. Fax: 402-426-6550. Web Site: http://www.gpcom.com. ICA: NE0024.
TV Market Ranking: Outside TV Markets (CHADRON). Franchise award date: N.A. Franchise expiration date: N.A. Began: December 1, 1965.
Channel capacity: N.A. Channels available but not in use: N.A.

Basic Service
Subscribers: N.A. Included in Arnold
Programming (received off-air): KDUH-TV (ABC) Scottsbluff; KTNE-TV (PBS) Alliance.
Programming (via microwave): KCNC-TV (CBS) Denver; KDVR (FOX) Denver; KMGH-TV (ABC) Denver; KTVD (MNT) Denver; KUSA (NBC) Denver; KWGN-TV (CW) Denver.
Programming (via satellite): C-SPAN; Home Shopping Network; INSP; QVC; Trinity Broadcasting Network; TV Guide Network; WGN America.
Current originations: Religious Access; Government Access; Educational Access.
Fee: $15.86 installation; $20.10 monthly; $1.13 converter.

Expanded Basic Service 1
Subscribers: N.A.
Programming (via satellite): ABC Family Channel; Altitude Sports & Entertainment; AMC; Animal Planet; Arts & Entertainment; Bravo; Cartoon Network; CNBC;

CNN; Comedy Central; Country Music TV; Discovery Channel; Disney Channel; E! Entertainment Television; ESPN; ESPN 2; ESPN Classic Sports; Food Network; Fox News Channel; Fox Sports Net Rocky Mountain; FX; G4; Golf Channel; Great American Country; Hallmark Channel; Headline News; HGTV; History Channel; Lifetime; Lifetime Movie Network; MSNBC; MTV; National Geographic Channel; Nickelodeon; Outdoor Channel; SoapNet; Speed Channel; Spike TV; Syfy; TBS Superstation; The Learning Channel; Toon Disney; Travel Channel; truTV; Turner Classic Movies; Turner Network TV; TV Land; USA Network; Versus; VH1; Weather Channel.
Fee: $23.89 monthly.

Digital Basic Service
Subscribers: N.A. Included in Arnold
Programming (via satellite): BBC America; Bio; Bloomberg Television; CMT Pure Country; Discovery en Espanol; Discovery Health Channel; Discovery Home Channel; Discovery Kids Channel; Discovery Military Channel; Discovery Times Channel; Do-It-Yourself; FitTV; Fox Movie Channel; GSN; Hallmark Movie Channel; History Channel International; Independent Film Channel; MTV Hits; MTV Jams; MTV Tres; MTV2; Music Choice; Nick Jr.; Nick Too; NickToons TV; RFD-TV; Science Channel; Style Network; TeenNick; VH1 Classic; VH1 Soul; WE tv.

Digital Pay Service 1
Pay Units: N.A.
Programming (via satellite): Cinemax (multiplexed); Encore; Starz (multiplexed).
Fee: $12.00 monthly (Cinemax or Starz/Encore).

Digital Pay Service 2
Pay Units: 274.
Programming (via satellite): HBO (multiplexed).
Fee: $12.00 monthly.

Digital Pay Service 3
Pay Units: 162.
Programming (via satellite): Flix; Showtime (multiplexed); The Movie Channel (multiplexed).
Fee: $12.00 monthly.

Video-On-Demand: No

Pay-Per-View
iN DEMAND (delivered digitally); Pleasure (delivered digitally); ETC (delivered digitally).

Internet Service
Operational: Yes, Both DSL & dial-up.
Subscribers: 480.
Broadband Service: In-house.
Fee: $49.95 installation; $39.95 monthly.

Telephone Service
Analog: Not Operational
Digital: Operational
Miles of Plant: 27.0 (coaxial); None (fiber optic). Homes passed included in Arnold
General Manager: Lea Ann Quist. Chief Technician: Mark Stottler. Marketing Manager: Casey Garrigan.
City fee: 2% of gross.
Ownership: Great Plains Communications Inc. (MSO).

CHAMBERS—Formerly served by Sky Scan Cable Co. No longer in operation. ICA: NE0272.

CHAPMAN—Great Plains Communications, PO Box 500, 1600 Great Plains Centre, Blair, NE 68008-0500. Phones: 888-343-8014; 402-426-9511. Fax: 402-426-6550. Web Site: http://www.gpcom.com. Also serves Wolbach. ICA: NE0273.
TV Market Ranking: 91 (CHAPMAN); Below 100 (Wolbach). Franchise award date: October 1, 1988. Franchise expiration date: N.A. Began: October 1, 1988.
Channel capacity: 80 (operating 2-way). Channels available but not in use: N.A.

Basic Service
Subscribers: N.A. Included in Arnold
Programming (received off-air): KGIN (CBS, MNT) Grand Island; KHAS-TV (NBC) Hastings; KHGI-TV (ABC) Kearney; KHNE-TV (PBS) Hastings; KLKN (ABC) Lincoln; KTVG-TV (FOX) Grand Island.
Programming (via satellite): ABC Family Channel; AMC; Animal Planet; Arts & Entertainment; CNN; Discovery Channel; Disney Channel; ESPN; ESPN 2; Fox News Channel; Fox Sports Net Rocky Mountain; Great American Country; Hallmark Channel; Headline News; HGTV; History Channel; Lifetime; Nickelodeon; QVC; Spike TV; TBS Superstation; The Learning Channel; Travel Channel; Turner Network TV; TV Land; USA Network; Weather Channel; WGN America.
Fee: $45.00 installation; $31.50 monthly.

Digital Basic Service
Subscribers: N.A. Included in Arnold
Programming (via satellite): BBC America; Bio; Bravo; Discovery Digital Networks; DMX Music; ESPN Classic Sports; ESPNews; Fox Sports World; Golf Channel; GSN; History Channel International; Independent Film Channel; Lifetime Movie Network; National Geographic Channel; Outdoor Channel; Speed Channel; Syfy; Trio; Turner Classic Movies; Versus; WE tv.
Fee: $47.95 monthly.

Pay Service 1
Pay Units: 15.
Programming (via satellite): HBO.
Fee: $10.95 monthly.

Pay Service 2
Pay Units: N.A.
Programming (via satellite): Showtime.
Fee: $9.95 monthly.

Digital Pay Service 1
Pay Units: N.A.
Programming (via satellite): Cinemax (multiplexed); Encore (multiplexed); HBO (multiplexed); Showtime (multiplexed); Starz (multiplexed); The Movie Channel (multiplexed).
Fee: $12.00 monthly (HBO, Cinemax, Starz/Encore or Showtime/TMC).

Video-On-Demand: No

Pay-Per-View
iN DEMAND (delivered digitally); ESPN (delivered digitally).

Internet Service
Operational: No, DSL.
Broadband Service: In-house.

Telephone Service
None
Homes passed included in Arnold
General Manager: Lea Ann Quist. Chief Technician: Mark Stottler. Marketing Manager: Casey Garrigan.
City fee: 1% of gross.
Ownership: Great Plains Communications Inc. (MSO).

CHESTER—Galaxy Cablevision, 1928 S Lincoln Ave, Ste 200, York, NE 68467. Phone: 402-362-3332. Fax: 402-362-4890. Web Site: http://www.galaxycable.com. ICA: NE0158.
TV Market Ranking: Below 100 (CHESTER). Franchise award date: N.A. Franchise expiration date: N.A. Began: February 1, 1984.
Channel capacity: 41 (not 2-way capable). Channels available but not in use: 12.
Basic Service
Subscribers: 44.
Programming (received off-air): KHAS-TV (NBC) Hastings; KHNE-TV (PBS) Hastings; KLKN (ABC) Lincoln; KOLN (CBS, MNT) Lincoln.
Programming (via satellite): ABC Family Channel; AMC; Arts & Entertainment; Cartoon Network; CNN; Discovery Channel; Disney Channel; ESPN; Fox Sports Net Midwest; HGTV; History Channel; Lifetime; Outdoor Channel; QVC; TBS Superstation; The Learning Channel; Trinity Broadcasting Network; Turner Classic Movies; Turner Network TV; USA Network; Weather Channel; WGN America.
Fee: $37.20 39.95.
Pay Service 1
Pay Units: 9.
Programming (via satellite): Cinemax.
Fee: $9.95 monthly.
Pay Service 2
Pay Units: 17.
Programming (via satellite): HBO.
Fee: $13.95 monthly.
Internet Service
Operational: No.
Telephone Service
None
Miles of Plant: 5.0 (coaxial); None (fiber optic). Homes passed: 198.
State Manager: Cheyenne Wohlford. Technical Manager: Carl Stanley. Sales Manager: Mike Thomas. Customer Service Manager: Donna Bryant.
City fee: 1% of basic.
Ownership: Galaxy Cable Inc. (MSO).

CLARKS—CenCom Inc. (formerly Clarks Cable TV). This cable system has converted to IPTV. See Clarks (village), NE [NE5006]. ICA: NE0189.

CLARKS (village)—CenCom NNTV. Formerly [NE0189]. This cable system has converted to IPTV, 110 E Elk St, Jackson, NE 68743-0066. Phones: 402-623-4321; 888-397-4321. E-mail: nntc@nntc.net. Web Site: http://www.nntc.net. ICA: NE5006.
Channel capacity: N.A. Channels available but not in use: N.A.
Internet Service
Operational: Yes.
Telephone Service
Digital: Operational
General Manager: Emory Graffis.
Ownership: Northeast Nebraska Telephone Co.

CLARKSON—Formerly served by TelePartners. No longer in operation. ICA: NE0166.

CLAY CENTER—Galaxy Cablevision, 1928 S Lincoln Ave, Ste 200, York, NE 68467. Phone: 402-362-3332. Fax: 402-362-4890. Web Site: http://www.galaxycable.com. Also serves Edgar, Fairfield, Harvard & Sutton. ICA: NE0085.
TV Market Ranking: 91 (CLAY CENTER, Edgar, Fairfield, Harvard, Sutton). Franchise award date: N.A. Franchise expiration date: N.A. Began: June 1, 1982.
Channel capacity: 78 (operating 2-way). Channels available but not in use: None.
Basic Service
Subscribers: 727.
Programming (received off-air): KHAS-TV (NBC) Hastings; KHGI-TV (ABC) Kearney; KHNE-TV (PBS) Hastings; KLKN (ABC) Lincoln; KOLN (CBS, MNT) Lincoln; KPTM (FOX, MNT) Omaha; KXVO (CW) Omaha.
Programming (via satellite): ABC Family Channel; AMC; Animal Planet; Arts & Entertainment; Boomerang; Cartoon Network; CNN; Comedy Central; C-SPAN; Discovery Channel; Disney Channel; E! Entertainment Television; ESPN; ESPN 2; Eternal Word TV Network; Food Network; Fox News Channel; Fox Sports Net Midwest; Fuse; FX; Great American Country; Hallmark Channel; Headline News; HGTV; History Channel; INSP; Lifetime; MSNBC; National Geographic Channel; Outdoor Channel; QVC; Syfy; TBS Superstation; The Learning Channel; Toon Disney; Travel Channel; Trinity Broadcasting Network; Turner Classic Movies; Turner Network TV; TV Guide Network; TV Land; USA Network; Weather Channel; WGN America.
Current originations: Educational Access; Public Access.
Fee: $35.00 installation; $44.75 monthly.
Digital Basic Service
Subscribers: 128.
Programming (via satellite): AmericanLife TV Network; BBC America; Bio; Bloomberg Television; Discovery Digital Networks; DMX Music; ESPN Classic Sports; ESPNews; FitTV; Fox Sports World; FSN Digital Atlantic; FSN Digital Central; FSN Digital Pacific; G4; Golf Channel; GSN; Halogen Network; History Channel International; Outdoor Channel; Speed Channel; Style Network; WE tv.
Fee: $12.95 monthly.
Digital Expanded Basic Service
Subscribers: N.A.
Programming (via satellite): DMX Music; Encore; Fox Movie Channel; Independent Film Channel; Lifetime Movie Network.
Fee: $12.95 monthly.
Pay Service 1
Pay Units: 19.
Programming (via satellite): Cinemax.
Fee: $10.95 monthly.
Pay Service 2
Pay Units: 27.
Programming (via satellite): HBO.
Fee: $13.95 monthly.
Pay Service 3
Pay Units: 44.
Programming (via satellite): Showtime.
Fee: $9.95 monthly.
Pay Service 4
Pay Units: 41.
Programming (via satellite): The Movie Channel.
Fee: $7.95 monthly.
Digital Pay Service 1
Pay Units: N.A.
Programming (via satellite): Cinemax (multiplexed); Flix; HBO (multiplexed); Showtime (multiplexed); The Movie Channel (multiplexed).
Fee: $15.60 monthly.
Pay-Per-View
Addressable homes: 109.
ESPN Now (delivered digitally), Fee: $3.99, Addressable: Yes; Hot Choice (delivered digitally); Movies (delivered digitally); Playboy TV (delivered digitally); Fresh (delivered digitally); sports (delivered digitally).
Internet Service
Operational: Yes.
Subscribers: 134.
Broadband Service: Galaxy Cable Internet.
Fee: $49.95 installation; $44.95 monthly; $5.00 modem lease.
Telephone Service
None
Miles of Plant: 39.0 (coaxial); None (fiber optic). Homes passed: 1,875.
State Manager: Cheyenne Wohlford. Technical Manager: Carl Stanley. Sales Manager: Mike Thomas. Customer Service Manager: Donna Bryant.
City fee: 5% of gross.
Ownership: Galaxy Cable Inc. (MSO).

CLEARWATER—CenCom Inc. This cable system has converted to IPTV. See Clearwater (village), NE [NE5014]. ICA: NE0144.

CLEARWATER (village)—CenCom NNTV. Formerly [NE0144]. This cable system has converted to IPTV, 110 E Elk St, Jackson, NE 68743-0066. Phones: 402-623-4321; 888-397-4321. E-mail: nntc@nntc.net. Web Site: http://www.nntc.net. ICA: NE5014.
Channel capacity: N.A. Channels available but not in use: N.A.
Internet Service
Operational: Yes.
Telephone Service
Digital: Operational
General Manager: Emory Graffis.
Ownership: Northeast Nebraska Telephone Co.

CODY—Midcontinent Communications, PO Box 5010, Sioux Falls, SD 57117. Phones: 800-456-0564; 605-229-1775. Fax: 605-229-0478. E-mail: mccomm@midco.net. Web Site: http://www.midcocomm.com. ICA: NE0274.
TV Market Ranking: Outside TV Markets (CODY). Franchise award date: March 8, 1988. Franchise expiration date: N.A. Began: N.A.
Channel capacity: 37 (not 2-way capable). Channels available but not in use: N.A.
Basic Service
Subscribers: 37.
Programming (received off-air): KRNE-TV (PBS) Merriman.
Programming (via satellite): ABC Family Channel; AMC; Arts & Entertainment; Cartoon Network; CNBC; CNN; Country Music TV; C-SPAN; Discovery Channel; Disney Channel; ESPN; Fox Sports Net Rocky Mountain; FX; Headline News; INSP; KARE (NBC) Minneapolis; KCNC-TV (CBS) Denver; KMGH-TV (ABC) Denver; KWGN-TV (CW) Denver; Lifetime; Nickelodeon; QVC; Spike TV; TBS Superstation; The Learning Channel; Turner Network TV; TV Guide Network; TV Land; USA Network; VH1; Weather Channel; WGN America.
Fee: $50.00 installation; $26.50 monthly.
Pay Service 1
Pay Units: 5.
Programming (via satellite): HBO.
Fee: $20.00 installation; $12.00 monthly.
Pay Service 2
Pay Units: N.A.
Programming (via satellite): Showtime; The Movie Channel.
Fee: $20.00 installation; $11.00 monthly (each).
Video-On-Demand: No
Internet Service
Operational: No.
Telephone Service
None
Miles of Plant: 2.0 (coaxial); None (fiber optic). Homes passed: 79.
Manager: Lonnie Schumacher. Marketing Director: Fred Jamieson. Customer Service Manager: Kathy Fuhrmann.
Ownership: Midcontinent Media Inc. (MSO).; Comcast Cable Communications Inc. (MSO).

COLERIDGE—CenCom Inc. This cable system has converted to IPTV. See Coleridge (village), NE [NE5001]. ICA: NE0113.

COLERIDGE (village)—CenCom NNTV. Formerly [NE0113]. This cable system has converted to IPTV, 110 E Elk St, Jackson, NE 68743-0066. Phones: 402-623-4321; 888-397-4321. E-mail: nntc@nntc.net. Web Site: http://www.nntc.net. ICA: NE5001.
TV Market Ranking: Franchise award date: N.A. Franchise expiration date: N.A. Began: September 1, 2008.
Channel capacity: N.A. Channels available but not in use: N.A.
Internet Service
Operational: Yes.
Telephone Service
Digital: Operational
General Manager: Emory Graffis.
Ownership: Northeast Nebraska Telephone Co.

COLUMBUS—Time Warner Cable, 5400 S 16th St, Lincoln, NE 68512-1278. Phone: 402-421-0330. Fax: 402-421-0310. Web Site: http://www.timewarnercable.com/Nebraska. Also serves David City. ICA: NE0015.
TV Market Ranking: Outside TV Markets (COLUMBUS, David City). Franchise award date: N.A. Franchise expiration date: N.A. Began: January 1, 1964.
Channel capacity: N.A. Channels available but not in use: N.A.
Basic Service
Subscribers: N.A. Included in Lincoln
Programming (received off-air): KETV (ABC) Omaha; KLKN (ABC) Lincoln; KMTV-TV (CBS) Omaha; KOLN (CBS, MNT) Lincoln; KPTM (FOX, MNT) Omaha; KUON-TV (PBS) Lincoln; KXVO (CW) Omaha; WOWT-TV (IND, NBC) Omaha.
Programming (via satellite): Shop at Home; Spike TV; TBS Superstation; TV Guide Network; WGN America.
Current originations: Government Access; Educational Access; Public Access.
Fee: $40.54 installation; $10.53 monthly; $.69 converter; $18.29 additional installation.
Expanded Basic Service 1
Subscribers: N.A.
Programming (via satellite): ABC Family Channel; AMC; Animal Planet; Arts & Entertainment; BET Networks; Bravo; Cartoon Network; CNBC; CNN; Comedy Central; Country Music TV; C-SPAN; C-SPAN 2; Discovery Channel; Discovery Health Channel; Disney Channel; E! Entertainment Television; ESPN; ESPN 2; ESPN Classic Sports; Eternal Word TV Network; Food Network; Fox News Channel; Fox Sports Net Midwest; FX; Golf Channel; Hallmark Channel; Headline News; HGTV; History Channel; Home Shopping Net-

work; ION Television; Lifetime; Lifetime Movie Network; MSNBC; MTV; National Geographic Channel; Nickelodeon; Oxygen; QVC; ShopNBC; SoapNet; Syfy; The Learning Channel; Travel Channel; truTV; Turner Classic Movies; Turner Network TV; TV Land; Univision; USA Network; VH1; WE tv; Weather Channel.
Fee: $36.07 monthly.
Digital Basic Service
Subscribers: N.A. Included in Lincoln
Programming (via satellite): America's Store; BBC America; Bio; Bloomberg Television; Boomerang; Cooking Channel; C-SPAN 3; Discovery Digital Networks; DMX Music; Do-It-Yourself; Encore Action; ESPNews; FitTV; Fox Movie Channel; Fox Sports World; Fuse; G4; Great American Country; GSN; History Channel International; Independent Film Channel; Lifetime Real Women; MTV2; NASA TV; Nick Jr.; Outdoor Channel; Ovation; Speed Channel; Style Network; Toon Disney; Trinity Broadcasting Network; Versus; VH1 Classic.
Fee: $6.95 monthly; $7.65 converter.
Digital Pay Service 1
Pay Units: N.A.
Programming (via satellite): Cinemax (multiplexed); Encore Action (multiplexed); HBO (multiplexed); Showtime (multiplexed); Starz (multiplexed); The Movie Channel (multiplexed).
Fee: $9.95 monthly (each).
Video-On-Demand: Yes
Pay-Per-View
Addressable homes: 2,013.
iN DEMAND (delivered digitally), Addressable: Yes; Fresh (delivered digitally); ESPN Gameplan (delivered digitally); ESPN Full Court (delivered digitally); ESPN Extra (delivered digitally); NBA TV (delivered digitally); Shorteez (delivered digitally); Hot Choice (delivered digitally); Pleasure (delivered digitally); Playboy TV (delivered digitally); ESPN Now (delivered digitally).
Internet Service
Operational: Yes.
Subscribers: 1,151.
Broadband Service: Road Runner.
Fee: $39.95 installation; $44.95 monthly.
Telephone Service
Digital: Operational
Fee: $39.95 monthly
Miles of Plant: 93.0 (coaxial); None (fiber optic). Homes passed included in Lincoln
President: Beth Scarborough. Vice President, Operations: Dick Cassidy. Vice President, Engineering: John Matejovich. Vice President, Marketing: Brian Cecere. General Manager: Valerie Kramer. Public Affairs Director: Ann Shrewsbury. Technical Operations Manager: Rick Hollman.
City fee: 5% of gross.
Ownership: Time Warner Cable (MSO).; Advance/Newhouse Partnership (MSO).

COLUMBUS (portions)—Formerly served by Sky Scan Cable Co. No longer in operation. ICA: NE0275.

COMSTOCK—Formerly served by Consolidated Cable Inc. No longer in operation. ICA: NE0247.

CONCORD (village)—CenCom NNTV. Formerly [NE0385]. This cable system has converted to IPTV, 110 E Elk St, Jackson, NE 68743-0066. Phones: 888-397-4321; 402-623-4321. E-mail: nntc@nntc.net. Web Site: http://www.nntc.net. ICA: NE5013.
Channel capacity: N.A. Channels available but not in use: N.A.
Internet Service
Operational: Yes.
Telephone Service
Digital: Operational
General Manager: Emory Graffis.
Ownership: Northeast Nebraska Telephone Co.

CORTLAND—Great Plains Communications, PO Box 500, 1600 Great Plains Centre, Blair, NE 68008-0500. Phone: 402-426-9511. Fax: 402-456-6550. Web Site: http://www.gpcom.com. Also serves Adams & Firth. ICA: NE0169.
TV Market Ranking: 91 (Adams, CORTLAND, Firth). Franchise award date: December 1, 1982. Franchise expiration date: N.A. Began: January 1, 1984.
Channel capacity: N.A. Channels available but not in use: N.A.
Basic Service
Subscribers: N.A. Included in Arnold
Programming (received off-air): KLKN (ABC) Lincoln; KMTV-TV (CBS) Omaha; KOLN (CBS, MNT) Lincoln; KPTM (FOX, MNT) Omaha; KUON-TV (PBS) Lincoln; WOWT-TV (IND, NBC) Omaha.
Programming (via satellite): ABC Family Channel; Animal Planet; Arts & Entertainment; Cartoon Network; CNN; Country Music TV; Discovery Channel; Disney Channel; E! Entertainment Television; ESPN; ESPN 2; Fox News Channel; FX; History Channel; MTV; Nickelodeon; Spike TV; TBS Superstation; The Learning Channel; Travel Channel; Turner Network TV; TV Land; USA Network; Weather Channel; WGN America.
Fee: $29.99 installation; $47.99 monthly; $1.00 converter.
Digital Basic Service
Subscribers: N.A. Included in Arnold
Programming (via satellite): AmericanLife TV Network; BBC America; Bio; Bloomberg Television; Bravo; Discovery Digital Networks; Encore (multiplexed); ESPN Classic Sports; FitTV; Flix; Fox Movie Channel; Fox Soccer; Fuse; G4; GAS; Golf Channel; GSN; Halogen Network; History Channel International; Independent Film Channel; Lifetime Movie Network; MTV Networks Digital Suite; Music Choice; Nick Jr.; Outdoor Channel; ShopNBC; Showtime (multiplexed); Speed Channel; Style Network; Syfy; The Movie Channel (multiplexed); Toon Disney; Trinity Broadcasting Network; Turner Classic Movies; Versus; WE tv.
Fee: $49.95 installation.
Digital Pay Service 1
Pay Units: N.A.
Programming (via satellite): Cinemax (multiplexed); Encore (multiplexed); HBO (multiplexed); Starz (multiplexed).
Fee: $13.00 monthly (HBO, Cinemax, or Starz/Encore).
Video-On-Demand: No
Pay-Per-View
Movies (delivered digitally), Fee: $3.99; Special events (delivered digitally); Hot Choice (delivered digitally); Playboy TV (delivered digitally); Fresh (delivered digitally); Shorteez (delivered digitally).
Internet Service
Operational: Yes.
Telephone Service
None
Miles of Plant: 13.0 (coaxial); None (fiber optic). Homes passed and Total Homes included in Arnold
General Manager: Lee Ann Quist. Chief Technician: Mark Stottler. Marketing Manager: Kasey Garrigan.

City fee: 0% of gross.
Ownership: Great Plains Communications Inc. (MSO).

COZAD—Charter Communications. Now served by KEARNEY, NE [NE0011]. ICA: NE0029.

CRAWFORD—Mobius Communications Co., PO Box 246, 523 Niobrara Ave, Hemingford, NE 69348. Phone: 308-487-5500. E-mail: info@bbc.net. Web Site: http://www.bbc.net. ICA: NE0042.
TV Market Ranking: Outside TV Markets (CRAWFORD). Franchise award date: N.A. Franchise expiration date: N.A. Began: June 1, 1974.
Channel capacity: N.A. Channels available but not in use: N.A.
Basic Service
Subscribers: 296 Includes Hemingford.
Programming (received off-air): KDUH-TV (ABC) Scottsbluff; KDVR (FOX) Denver; KTNE-TV (PBS) Alliance; 1 FM.
Programming (via microwave): KCNC-TV (CBS) Denver; KMGH-TV (ABC) Denver; KTVD (MNT) Denver; KUSA (NBC) Denver; KWGN-TV (CW) Denver.
Programming (via satellite): WGN America.
Expanded Basic Service 1
Subscribers: 254 Includes Hemingford.
Programming (via satellite): ABC Family Channel; Altitude Sports & Entertainment; AMC; Animal Planet; Arts & Entertainment; Bravo; CNBC; CNN; Comedy Central; Country Music TV; Discovery Channel; Disney Channel; E! Entertainment Television; ESPN; ESPN 2; ESPN Classic Sports; Fox News Channel; Fox Sports Net Rocky Mountain; FX; HGTV; Lifetime; MTV; National Geographic Channel; Nickelodeon; Oxygen; SoapNet; Spike TV; Syfy; TBS Superstation; The Learning Channel; Travel Channel; Turner Network TV; TV Land; USA Network; VH1; Weather Channel.
Digital Basic Service
Subscribers: 12 Includes Hemingford.
Programming (via satellite): AmericanLife TV Network; Arts & Entertainment; BBC America; Bloomberg Television; CMT Pure Country; Current; Discovery Health Channel; Discovery Home Channel; Discovery Kids Channel; Discovery Military Channel; Discovery Times Channel; DMX Music; FitTV; Fox Movie Channel; Fuse; G4; GAS; Golf Channel; GSN; Halogen Network; History Channel; History Channel International; Independent Film Channel; Lifetime Movie Network; MTV Hits; MTV2; Nick Jr.; NickToons TV; Outdoor Channel; Science Channel; Speed Channel; Toon Disney; Trinity Broadcasting Network; Turner Classic Movies; TV Guide Interactive Inc.; Versus; VH1 Classic; VH1 Soul; WE tv.
Pay Service 1
Pay Units: N.A.
Programming (via satellite): HBO.
Fee: $9.50 monthly.
Digital Pay Service 1
Pay Units: N.A.
Programming (via satellite): Cinemax (multiplexed); Encore (multiplexed); Flix; HBO (multiplexed); Showtime (multiplexed); Starz (multiplexed); The Movie Channel (multiplexed).
Video-On-Demand: No
Pay-Per-View
iN DEMAND (delivered digitally); Hot Choice (delivered digitally); Playboy TV (delivered digitally); Fresh (delivered digitally); Shorteez (delivered digitally).
Internet Service
Operational: No.
Broadband Service: Offers dial-up and DSL only; no cable modem service.
Telephone Service
None
Miles of Plant: 15.0 (coaxial); None (fiber optic). Homes passed: 950. Miles of plant & homes passed include Hemingford
General Manager: Theron Jensen. Chief Technician: Randy Dannar.
City fee: 2% of gross.
Ownership: Mobius Communications Co. (MSO).

CRESTON—Formerly served by Sky Scan Cable Co. No longer in operation. ICA: NE0251.

CULBERTSON—Pinpoint Cable TV, PO Box 490, 611 Patterson St, Cambridge, NE 69022-0490. Phones: 800-793-2788; 308-697-7678; 308-697-3333. Fax: 308-697-3631. E-mail: info@pnpt.com. Web Site: http://www.pnpt.com. ICA: NE0120.
TV Market Ranking: Below 100 (CULBERTSON). Franchise award date: N.A. Franchise expiration date: N.A. Began: January 1, 1983.
Channel capacity: N.A. Channels available but not in use: N.A.
Basic Service
Subscribers: 49.
Programming (received off-air): KGIN (CBS, MNT) Grand Island; KLNE-TV (PBS) Lexington; KSNK (NBC) McCook; KWNB-TV (ABC) Hayes Center.
Programming (via satellite): ABC Family Channel; CNN; Discovery Channel; Disney Channel; ESPN; Fox Sports Net; FX; Great American Country; Headline News; HGTV; National Geographic Channel; Nickelodeon; QVC; Spike TV; TBS Superstation; The Learning Channel; TV Land; USA Network; Weather Channel; WGN America.
Fee: $15.00 installation; $33.95 monthly.
Pay Service 1
Pay Units: 8.
Programming (via satellite): HBO; Showtime.
Fee: $11.95 monthly (each).
Video-On-Demand: No
Internet Service
Operational: No, dialup.
Telephone Service
None
Miles of Plant: 5.0 (coaxial); None (fiber optic). Homes passed: 308.
General Manager: J Thomas Shoemaker.
Ownership: PinPoint Communications Inc. (MSO).

CURTIS—Consolidated Cable Inc., PO Box 6147, Lincoln, NE 68506. Phone: 402-489-2728. E-mail: ctelco@curtis-ne.com. Also serves Maywood. ICA: NE0071.

TV Market Ranking: Below 100 (CURTIS, Maywood). Franchise award date: July 1, 1981. Franchise expiration date: N.A. Began: July 1, 1981.

Channel capacity: 100 (operating 2-way). Channels available but not in use: 42.

Basic Service

Subscribers: 470.

Programming (received off-air): KNOP-TV (NBC) North Platte; KOLN (CBS, MNT) Lincoln; KSNK (NBC) McCook; KWGN-TV (CW) Denver; KWNB-TV (ABC) Hayes Center; allband FM.

Programming (via satellite): ABC Family Channel; AMC; Animal Planet; Arts & Entertainment; Cartoon Network; CNBC; CNN; Comedy Central; Country Music TV; Discovery Channel; Disney Channel; Do-It-Yourself; ESPN; ESPN 2; ESPN Classic Sports; Food Network; Fox News Channel; Fox Sports Net Rocky Mountain; FX; Great American Country; Hallmark Channel; Headline News; Healthy Living Channel; History Channel; Home Shopping Network; ION Television; Lifetime; MSNBC; MTV; National Geographic Channel; Network One; Nickelodeon; RFD-TV; SoapNet; Spike TV; Syfy; TBS Superstation; The Learning Channel; Toon Disney; Travel Channel; truTV; Turner Classic Movies; Turner Network TV; TV Land; USA Network; VH1; Weather Channel; WGN America.

Current originations: Educational Access; Public Access.

Fee: $25.95 installation; $31.18 monthly; $15.00 additional installation.

Digital Basic Service

Subscribers: N.A.

Programming (via satellite): AmericanLife TV Network; BBC America; Bio; Church Channel; Daystar TV Network; Discovery Digital Networks; DMX Music; Encore (multiplexed); ESPNews; Fox Soccer; FSN Digital Atlantic; FSN Digital Central; FSN Digital Pacific; Fuse; G4; GAS; Golf Channel; GSN; Halogen Network; HGTV; History Channel International; Independent Film Channel; JCTV; Lifetime Movie Network; Men's Channel; MTV Networks Digital Suite; Nick Jr.; NickToons TV; Outdoor Channel; PBS Kids Sprout; Sleuth; Speed Channel; Starz (multiplexed); Sundance Channel; Trinity Broadcasting Network; Versus; WAM! America's Kidz Network; WE tv.

Fee: $23.00 monthly.

Pay Service 1

Pay Units: 53.

Programming (via satellite): HBO.

Fee: $12.85 monthly.

Digital Pay Service 1

Pay Units: N.A.

Programming (via satellite): Cinemax (multiplexed); Encore (multiplexed); HBO (multiplexed); Starz (multiplexed).

Fee: $8.95 monthly (Cinemax), $12.85 monthly (HBO), $12.95 monthly (Starz/Encore).

Video-On-Demand: No

Pay-Per-View

iN DEMAND (delivered digitally); Hot Choice (delivered digitally).

Internet Service

Operational: No, DSL only.

Telephone Service

None

Miles of Plant: 22.0 (coaxial); 7.0 (fiber optic). Homes passed: 525. Total homes in franchised area: 525.

City fee: 3% of gross.

Ownership: Consolidated Cable Inc.

DALTON—Dalton Telephone Co., PO Box 19048, Colorado City, CO 81019. Phones: 308-377-2222 (Local office); 866-542-6779; 719-676-3301. Web Site: http://www.daltontel.net. Also serves Dix, Gurley, Lodgepole & Potter. ICA: NE0240.

TV Market Ranking: Outside TV Markets (DALTON, Dix, Gurley, Lodgepole, Potter). Franchise award date: N.A. Franchise expiration date: N.A. Began: N.A.

Channel capacity: N.A. Channels available but not in use: N.A.

Basic Service

Subscribers: 214.

Programming (received off-air): KCNC-TV (CBS) Denver; KDUH-TV (ABC) Scottsbluff; KMGH-TV (ABC) Denver; KSTF (CBS, CW) Scottsbluff; KTNE-TV (PBS) Alliance.

Programming (via satellite): ABC Family Channel; AMC; Animal Planet; Arts & Entertainment; Bravo; Cartoon Network; CNBC; CNN; Comedy Central; Country Music TV; C-SPAN; C-SPAN 2; Discovery Channel; Disney Channel; ESPN; ESPN 2; ESPN Classic Sports; Eternal Word TV Network; FitTV; Food Network; Fox News Channel; Fox Sports Net; FX; Great American Country; Hallmark Channel; Headline News; HGTV; INSP; KDVR (FOX) Denver; KUSA (NBC) Denver; Lifetime; MTV; National Geographic Channel; Nickelodeon; QVC; Speed Channel; Spike TV; Syfy; TBS Superstation; The Learning Channel; Travel Channel; truTV; Turner Classic Movies; Turner Network TV; TV Land; USA Network; VH1; Weather Channel; WGN America.

Fee: $19.00 installation; $32.95 monthly.

Digital Basic Service

Subscribers: N.A.

Programming (via satellite): BBC America; Bio; Bravo; Discovery Health Channel; Discovery Home Channel; Discovery Kids Channel; Discovery Military Channel; Discovery Times Channel; DMX Music; Fox Soccer; History Channel; History Channel International; Independent Film Channel; Lifetime Movie Network; MTV Hits; MTV2; Nick Jr.; NickToons TV; Science Channel; Speed Channel; TeenNick; Toon Disney; Versus; VH1 Classic; VH1 Country; VH1 Soul; WE tv.

Fee: $12.94 monthly.

Digital Expanded Basic Service

Subscribers: N.A.

Programming (via satellite): AmericanLife TV Network; Bloomberg Television; ESPNews; Fox College Sports Atlantic; Fox College Sports Central; Fox College Sports Pacific; Fox Movie Channel; Fuse; G4; Golf Channel; GSN; Halogen Network; International Television (ITV); Outdoor Channel; Ovation; Style Network; Trinity Broadcasting Network; Trio.

Fee: $6.00 monthly.

Pay Service 1

Pay Units: N.A.

Programming (via satellite): Cinemax; HBO; Showtime; The Movie Channel.

Fee: $3.00 monthly (TMC), $7.95 monthly (Showtime), $12.95 monthly (HBO or Cinemax).

Digital Pay Service 1

Pay Units: N.A.

Programming (via satellite): Cinemax (multiplexed); Encore (multiplexed); Flix; HBO (multiplexed); Showtime (multiplexed); Starz (multiplexed); The Movie Channel (multiplexed).

Fee: $10.95 monthly (Starz/Encore), $12.95 monthly (HBO, Cinemax, or Showtime/TMC/Flix).

Video-On-Demand: No

Pay-Per-View

iN DEMAND (delivered digitally).

Internet Service

Operational: Yes.

Fee: $35.95 monthly.

Telephone Service

Digital: Operational

Miles of Plant: 15.0 (coaxial); None (fiber optic). Homes passed: 750.

General Manager: David Shipley. Chief Technician: Matt Moore.

Ownership: Southern Kansas Telephone Co.

DANNEBROG—NCTC Cable, PO Box 700, 22 LaBarre St, Gibbon, NE 68840. Phones: 888-873-6282; 308-468-6341. Fax: 308-468-9929. Web Site: http://www.nctc.net. ICA: NE0277.

TV Market Ranking: Below 100 (DANNEBROG). Franchise award date: July 1, 1988. Franchise expiration date: N.A. Began: N.A.

Channel capacity: N.A. Channels available but not in use: N.A.

Basic Service

Subscribers: N.A. Included in Burwell

Programming (received off-air): KGIN (CBS, MNT) Grand Island; KHAS-TV (NBC) Hastings; KHGI-TV (ABC) Kearney; KMNE-TV (PBS) Bassett; KTVG-TV (FOX) Grand Island.

Programming (via satellite): ABC Family Channel; AMC; Animal Planet; Arts & Entertainment; Cartoon Network; CNBC; CNN; Comedy Central; Country Music TV; C-SPAN; CW+; Discovery Channel; E! Entertainment Television; ESPN; ESPN 2; ESPN Classic Sports; Eternal Word TV Network; Food Network; Fox News Channel; Fox Sports Net Midwest; FX; G4; Great American Country; Hallmark Channel; Headline News; HGTV; History Channel; Home Shopping Network; ION Television; Lifetime; MSNBC; MTV; Nickelodeon; Outdoor Channel; QVC; Spike TV; Syfy; TBS Superstation; The Learning Channel; Travel Channel; Trinity Broadcasting Network; truTV; Turner Classic Movies; Turner Network TV; TV Land; USA Network; Versus; VH1; Weather Channel; WGN America.

Fee: $39.20 monthly.

Digital Basic Service

Subscribers: N.A. Included in Burwell

Programming (via satellite): AmericanLife TV Network; BBC America; Bio; Bloomberg Television; Current; Daystar TV Network; Discovery Digital Networks; DMX Music; ESPNews; FitTV; Fox College Sports Atlantic; Fox College Sports Central; Fox College Sports Pacific; Fox Movie Channel; G4; Golf Channel; Gospel Music Channel; GSN; Halogen Network; History Channel International; Lifetime Movie Network; MTV Networks Digital Suite; Nick Jr.; Ovation; RFD-TV; ShopNBC; Sleuth; Speed Channel; TeenNick; WE tv.

Fee: $14.00 monthly.

Pay Service 1

Pay Units: 37.

Programming (via satellite): HBO.

Fee: $10.95 monthly.

Digital Pay Service 1

Pay Units: N.A.

Programming (via satellite): Cinemax (multiplexed); Encore (multiplexed); Flix; HBO (multiplexed); Showtime (multiplexed); Starz (multiplexed); The Movie Channel (multiplexed).

Fee: $10.95 monthly (Cinemax), $12.95 monthly (HBO or Showtime, TMC & Flix), $13.95 monthly (Starz & Encore).

Video-On-Demand: No

Internet Service

Operational: No, DSL & dial-up.

Telephone Service

None

Miles of Plant: 4.0 (coaxial); None (fiber optic). Homes passed included in Burwell

General Manager: Andy Jader. Technical Operations Manager: Nick Jeffres.

City fee: 1% of gross.

Ownership: Nebraska Central Telecom Inc. (MSO).

DAVEY (village)—Formerly served by TelePartners. No longer in operation. ICA: NE0278.

DAVID CITY—Time Warner Cable. Now served by COLUMBUS, NE [NE0015]. ICA: NE0360.

DAWSON—Formerly served by CableDirect. No longer in operation. Also serves DAWSON. ICA: NE0225.

DAYKIN—Comstar Cable TV Inc., PO Box 975, 8358 W Scott Rd, Beatrice, NE 68310-0975. Phone: 402-520-1987. Fax: 402-228-3766. ICA: NE0279.

TV Market Ranking: Outside TV Markets (DAYKIN). Franchise award date: N.A. Franchise expiration date: N.A. Began: December 1, 1989.

Channel capacity: 36 (not 2-way capable). Channels available but not in use: N.A.

Basic Service

Subscribers: 53.

Programming (received off-air): KHNE-TV (PBS) Hastings; KLKN (ABC) Lincoln; KOLN (CBS, MNT) Lincoln; KPTM (FOX, MNT) Omaha; KXVO (CW) Omaha; WOWT-TV (IND, NBC) Omaha.

Programming (via satellite): ABC Family Channel; AMC; Arts & Entertainment; Cartoon Network; CNN; C-SPAN; Discovery Channel; Disney Channel; ESPN; Food Network; Fox Sports Net; FX; Great American Country; Hallmark Channel; Headline News; HGTV; History Channel; Lifetime; QVC; RFD-TV; Syfy; TBS Superstation; The Learning Channel; Turner Network TV; TV Land; USA Network; Weather Channel; WGN America.

Fee: $40.00 installation; $31.95 monthly.

Digital Basic Service

Subscribers: N.A.

Programming (via satellite): Bio; Bloomberg Television; Bravo; Discovery Health Channel; Discovery Military Channel; Discovery Planet Green; Disney XD; ESPN 2; ESPN Classic Sports; ESPNews; Fox Movie Channel; Fuse; G4; Golf Channel; GSN; HGTV; History Channel; History Channel International; ID Investigation Discovery; INSP; National Geographic Channel; Outdoor Channel; Science Channel; Sleuth; SoapNet; Speed Channel; Style Network; Syfy; Trinity Broadcasting Network; Turner Classic Movies; Versus; WE tv.

Pay Service 1

Pay Units: N.A.

Programming (via satellite): HBO.

Fee: $7.50 monthly.

Digital Pay Service 1

Pay Units: N.A.

Programming (via satellite): Encore (multiplexed); HBO (multiplexed); Showtime

(multiplexed); Starz (multiplexed); The Movie Channel (multiplexed).
Video-On-Demand: No
Internet Service
Operational: No.
Telephone Service
None
Miles of Plant: 2.0 (coaxial); None (fiber optic). Homes passed: 100.
Manager: Tim Schwarz.
Ownership: Comstar Cable TV Inc. (MSO).

DECATUR—CenCom Inc. This cable system has converted to IPTV. See Decatur (village), IL [NE5016]. ICA: NE0145.

DECATUR (village)—CenCom NNTV. Formerly [NE0145]. This cable system has converted to IPTV., 110 E Elk St, Jackson, NE 68743-0066. Phones: 402-623-4321; 888-397-4321. E-mail: nntc@nntc.net. Web Site: http://www.nntc.net. ICA: NE5016.
Channel capacity: N.A. Channels available but not in use: N.A.
Internet Service
Operational: Yes.
Telephone Service
Digital: Operational
General Manager: Emory Graffis.
Ownership: Northeast Nebraska Telephone Co.

DESHLER—Galaxy Cablevision, 1928 S Lincoln Ave, Ste 200, York, NE 68467. Phone: 402-362-3332. Fax: 402-362-4890. Web Site: http://www.galaxycable.com. ICA: NE0086.
TV Market Ranking: Below 100 (DESHLER). Franchise award date: N.A. Franchise expiration date: N.A. Began: November 1, 1982.
Channel capacity: 41 (not 2-way capable). Channels available but not in use: 1.
Basic Service
Subscribers: 122.
Programming (received off-air): KHAS-TV (NBC) Hastings; KHNE-TV (PBS) Hastings; KLKN (ABC) Lincoln; KOLN (CBS, MNT) Lincoln.
Programming (via satellite): ABC Family Channel; AMC; Animal Planet; Arts & Entertainment; Cartoon Network; CNN; C-SPAN; Discovery Channel; Disney Channel; E! Entertainment Television; ESPN; ESPN 2; Fox News Channel; Fox Sports Net Midwest; FX; Great American Country; HGTV; History Channel; Lifetime; Outdoor Channel; TBS Superstation; The Learning Channel; Turner Classic Movies; Turner Network TV; USA Network; Weather Channel; WGN America.
Current originations: Public Access.
Fee: $35.00 installation; $41.45 monthly.
Pay Service 1
Pay Units: 13.
Programming (via satellite): Cinemax.
Fee: $9.95 monthly.
Pay Service 2
Pay Units: 18.
Programming (via satellite): HBO.
Fee: $13.95 monthly.
Pay Service 3
Pay Units: 19.
Programming (via satellite): Showtime.
Fee: $8.95 monthly.
Pay Service 4
Pay Units: 4.
Programming (via satellite): The Movie Channel.
Fee: $7.95 monthly.
Pay Service 5
Pay Units: N.A.
Programming (via satellite): Encore.
Internet Service
Operational: No.
Telephone Service
None
Miles of Plant: 6.0 (coaxial); None (fiber optic). Homes passed: 425.
State Manager: Cheyenne Wohlford. Technical Manager: Carl Stanley. Sales Manager: Mike Thomas. Customer Service Manager: Donna Bryant.
City fee: 3% of basic.
Ownership: Galaxy Cable Inc. (MSO).

DILLER—Diode Telecom, Inc, PO Box 236, 300 Commercial St, Diller, NE 68342. Phones: 402-793-2532; 402-793-5125. Fax: 402-793-5139. E-mail: diodedonna@diodecom.net. Web Site: http://www.diodecom.net. Also serves Odell. ICA: NE0137.
TV Market Ranking: Outside TV Markets (DILLER, Odell). Franchise award date: N.A. Franchise expiration date: N.A. Began: January 1, 1983.
Channel capacity: N.A. Channels available but not in use: N.A.
Basic Service
Subscribers: 229.
Programming (received off-air): KLKN (ABC) Lincoln; KOLN (CBS, MNT) Lincoln; KPTM (FOX, MNT) Omaha; KXVO (CW) Omaha.
Programming (via satellite): ABC Family Channel; CNN; Country Music TV; Discovery Channel; ESPN; Fox Sports Net Midwest; FX; Nickelodeon; Outdoor Channel; Spike TV; TBS Superstation; The Learning Channel; Turner Network TV; TV Land; USA Network; Weather Channel; WGN America; WNBC (NBC) New York.
Fee: $19.08 monthly.
Pay Service 1
Pay Units: N.A.
Programming (via satellite): HBO.
Fee: $8.44 monthly.
Video-On-Demand: No
Internet Service
Operational: Yes.
Telephone Service
None
Miles of Plant: 13.0 (coaxial); None (fiber optic). Homes passed: 254.
President: Randy Sandman. Chief Technician: Jeff Nelson. Marketing Director: Danni Stark.
City fee: 6% of gross.
Ownership: Diode Cable Co. Inc. (MSO).

DIX—HunTel Cablevision. Now served by DALTON, NE [NE0240]. ICA: NE0223.

DIXON (village)—CenCom NNTV. Formerly [NE0385]. This cable system has converted to IPTV., 110 E Elk St, Jackson, NE 68743-0066. Phones: 402-623-4321; 888-397-4321. E-mail: nntc@nntc.net. Web Site: http://www.nntc.net. ICA: NE5017.
Channel capacity: N.A. Channels available but not in use: N.A.
Internet Service
Operational: Yes.
Telephone Service
Digital: Operational
General Manager: Emory Graffis.
Ownership: Northeast Nebraska Telephone Co.

DIXON/CONCORD—CenCom Inc. This cable system has converted to IPTV. See Dixon (village), NE [NE5016] & Concord (village), NE [NE5013]. ICA: NE0385.
TV Market Ranking: Below 100 (DIXON).

DODGE—Great Plains Communications. Now served by NORTH BEND, NE [NE0080]. ICA: NE0170.

DONIPHAN—Mid-State Community TV. Now served by AURORA, NE [NE0033]. ICA: NE0108.

DUBOIS—Formerly served by CableDirect. No longer in operation. ICA: NE0244.

DUNCAN—Cable Nebraska, 2123 Central Ave, Ste 200, Kearney, NE 68847. Phone: 308-236-1512. Web Site: http://www.cablene.com. ICA: NE0177.
TV Market Ranking: Outside TV Markets (DUNCAN). Franchise award date: N.A. Franchise expiration date: N.A. Began: March 1, 1985.
Channel capacity: 41 (not 2-way capable). Channels available but not in use: 25.
Basic Service
Subscribers: 31.
Programming (received off-air): KHNE-TV (PBS) Hastings; KLKN (ABC) Lincoln; KOLN (CBS, MNT) Lincoln; KPTM (FOX, MNT) Omaha; KXVO (CW) Omaha; WOWT-TV (IND, NBC) Omaha.
Programming (via satellite): ABC Family Channel; Cartoon Network; CNN; ESPN; Outdoor Channel; TBS Superstation; Turner Network TV; WGN America.
Fee: $35.00 installation; $25.95 monthly.
Pay Service 1
Pay Units: 7.
Programming (via satellite): Cinemax.
Fee: $9.95 monthly.
Pay Service 2
Pay Units: 12.
Programming (via satellite): HBO.
Fee: $13.95 monthly.
Internet Service
Operational: No.
Miles of Plant: 5.0 (coaxial); None (fiber optic). Homes passed: 146.
Operations Manager: Stuart Gilbertson.
City fee: 3% of basic.
Ownership: USA Companies (MSO).

DUNNING—Consolidated Cable Inc., PO Box 6147, 6900 Van Dorn St, Ste 21, Lincoln, NE 68506-0147. Phones: 402-489-2728; 800-742-7464. Fax: 402-489-9034. E-mail: service@consolidatedtelephone.com. Web Site: http://www.nebnet.net. Also serves Anselmo, Halsey, Merna & Thedford. ICA: NE0254.
TV Market Ranking: Outside TV Markets (Anselmo, DUNNING, Halsey, Merna, Thedford). Franchise award date: N.A. Franchise expiration date: N.A. Began: January 17, 1990.
Channel capacity: 42 (not 2-way capable). Channels available but not in use: N.A.
Basic Service
Subscribers: 300.
Programming (received off-air): KGIN (CBS, MNT) Grand Island; KMNE-TV (PBS) Bassett; KNOP-TV (NBC) North Platte; KWNB-TV (ABC) Hayes Center.
Programming (via satellite): ABC Family Channel; Animal Planet; Arts & Entertainment; Cartoon Network; CNBC; CNN; Country Music TV; Discovery Channel; Disney Channel; ESPN; ESPN 2; Fox News Channel; Fox Sports Net Midwest; FX; Hallmark Channel; HGTV; History Television; Home Shopping Network; KTVG-TV (FOX) Grand Island; KWGN-TV (CW) Denver; MTV; Nickelodeon; Spike TV; Syfy; TBS Superstation; The Learning Channel; Turner Classic Movies; Turner Network TV; TV Land; USA Network; Versus; VH1; Weather Channel; WGN America.
Fee: $25.95 installation; $28.95 monthly.
Digital Basic Service
Subscribers: N.A.
Programming (via satellite): AmericanLife TV Network; Bloomberg Television; CMT Pure Country; DMX Music; ESPN Classic Sports; ESPNews; FitTV; Fox College Sports Atlantic; Fox College Sports Central; Fox College Sports Pacific; Fox Movie Channel; G4; GAS; Golf Channel; GSN; Halogen Network; Independent Film Channel; Lifetime Movie Network; MTV Networks Digital Suite; Nick Jr.; NickToons TV; Outdoor Channel; Sleuth; Speed Channel; Style Network; Sundance Channel; Toon Disney; Trinity Broadcasting Network; WE tv.
Fee: $49.95 installation; $12.00 monthly.
Pay Service 1
Pay Units: 43.
Programming (via satellite): HBO.
Fee: $9.00 monthly.
Pay Service 2
Pay Units: N.A.
Programming (via satellite): Showtime.
Fee: $9.00 monthly.
Digital Pay Service 1
Pay Units: N.A.
Programming (via satellite): Cinemax (multiplexed); Encore (multiplexed); Flix; HBO (multiplexed); Showtime (multiplexed); Starz (multiplexed); The Movie Channel (multiplexed).
Fee: $9.00 monthly (each).
Video-On-Demand: No
Pay-Per-View
iN DEMAND (delivered digitally); Hot Choice (delivered digitally); Playboy TV (delivered digitally); Urban American Television Network (delivered digitally); Fresh (delivered digitally).
Internet Service
Operational: No.
Telephone Service
None
Miles of Plant: 6.0 (coaxial); None (fiber optic). Homes passed: 391.
Manager: Brian D. Thompson. Chief Technician: Dan Smith.
Ownership: Consolidated Cable Inc. (MSO).

DWIGHT (village)—Formerly served by TelePartners. No longer in operation. ICA: NE0280.

ELBA—NCTC Cable, PO Box 700, 22 LaBarre St, Gibbon, NE 68840. Phones: 888-873-6282; 308-468-6341. Fax: 308-468-9929. Web Site: http://www.nctc.net. ICA: NE0281.

TV Market Ranking: Below 100 (ELBA). Franchise award date: January 1, 1990. Franchise expiration date: N.A. Began: N.A.
Channel capacity: N.A. Channels available but not in use: N.A.

Basic Service

Subscribers: N.A. Included in Burwell

Programming (received off-air): KGIN (CBS, MNT) Grand Island; KHAS-TV (NBC) Hastings; KHGI-TV (ABC) Kearney; KMNE-TV (PBS) Bassett; KTVG-TV (FOX) Grand Island.

Programming (via satellite): ABC Family Channel; AMC; Animal Planet; Arts & Entertainment; Cartoon Network; CNBC; CNN; Comedy Central; Country Music TV; C-SPAN; CW+; Discovery Channel; E! Entertainment Television; ESPN; ESPN 2; ESPN Classic Sports; Eternal Word TV Network; Food Network; Fox News Channel; Fox Sports Net Midwest; FX; G4; Great American Country; Hallmark Channel; Headline News; HGTV; History Channel; Home Shopping Network; ION Television; Lifetime; MSNBC; MTV; Nickelodeon; Outdoor Channel; QVC; Spike TV; Syfy; TBS Superstation; The Learning Channel; Travel Channel; Trinity Broadcasting Network; truTV; Turner Classic Movies; Turner Network TV; TV Land; USA Network; Versus; VH1; Weather Channel; WGN America.

Fee: $25.48 installation; $39.20 monthly.

Digital Basic Service

Subscribers: N.A. Included in Burwell

Programming (via satellite): AmericanLife TV Network; BBC America; Bio; Bloomberg Television; Current; Daystar TV Network; Discovery Digital Networks; DMX Music; ESPNews; FitTV; Fox College Sports Atlantic; Fox College Sports Central; Fox College Sports Pacific; Fox Movie Channel; G4; Golf Channel; Gospel Music Channel; GSN; Halogen Network; History Channel International; Lifetime Movie Network; MTV Networks Digital Suite; Nick Jr.; Ovation; RFD-TV; ShopNBC; Sleuth; Speed Channel; TeenNick; WE tv.

Fee: $14.00 monthly.

Pay Service 1

Pay Units: 29.

Programming (via satellite): HBO.

Fee: $10.95 monthly.

Digital Pay Service 1

Pay Units: N.A.

Programming (via satellite): Cinemax (multiplexed); Encore (multiplexed); Flix; HBO (multiplexed); Showtime (multiplexed); Starz (multiplexed); The Movie Channel (multiplexed).

Fee: $10.95 monthly (Cinemax), $12.95 monthly (HBO or Showtime, TMC & Flix), $13.95 monthly (Starz & Encore).

Video-On-Demand: No

Internet Service

Operational: No, DSL & dial-up.

Telephone Service

None

Miles of Plant: 4.0 (coaxial); None (fiber optic). Homes passed included in Burwell

General Manager: Andy Jader. Technical Operations Manager: Nick Jeffres.

City fee: 1% of gross.

Ownership: Nebraska Central Telecom Inc. (MSO).

ELGIN—Great Plains Communications, PO Box 500, 1600 Great Plains Centre, Blair, NE 68008-0500. Phones: 888-343-8014; 402-426-9511. Fax: 402-456-6550. Web Site: http://www.gpcom.com. Also serves Ewing, Neligh, Oakdale & Petersburg. ICA: NE0282.

TV Market Ranking: Outside TV Markets (ELGIN, Ewing, Neligh, Oakdale, Petersburg). Franchise award date: January 1, 1983. Franchise expiration date: N.A. Began: March 1, 1984.

Channel capacity: N.A. Channels available but not in use: N.A.

Basic Service

Subscribers: N.A. Included in Arnold

Programming (received off-air): KLKN (ABC) Lincoln; KOLN (CBS, MNT) Lincoln; KTIV (CW, NBC) Sioux City; KUSA (NBC) Denver; KXNE-TV (PBS) Norfolk.

Programming (via satellite): ABC Family Channel; AMC; Animal Planet; Arts & Entertainment; Bravo; Cartoon Network; CNBC; CNN; Comedy Central; Country Music TV; C-SPAN; Discovery Channel; Disney Channel; E! Entertainment Television; ESPN; ESPN 2; Eternal Word TV Network; Fox News Channel; Fox Sports Net Rocky Mountain; Headline News; HGTV; History Channel; Lifetime; MSNBC; MTV; Nickelodeon; QVC; Spike TV; Syfy; TBS Superstation; Travel Channel; Turner Classic Movies; Turner Network TV; TV Guide Network; TV Land; USA Network; Versus; VH1; Weather Channel; WGN America.

Fee: $34.00 installation; $31.50 monthly.

Digital Basic Service

Subscribers: N.A. Included in Arnold

Programming (via satellite): BBC America; Bio; Bravo; Discovery Digital Networks; DMX Music; ESPN Classic Sports; ESPNews; Fox Sports World; GAS; Golf Channel; History Channel International; Independent Film Channel; Lifetime Movie Network; MTV Networks Digital Suite; Nick Jr.; Speed Channel; Trio; Turner Classic Movies; WE tv.

Fee: $47.95 monthly.

Pay Service 1

Pay Units: 200.

Programming (via satellite): Encore; HBO; Showtime.

Fee: $9.95 monthly (Showtime), $10.95 monthly (HBO).

Digital Pay Service 1

Pay Units: N.A.

Programming (via satellite): Cinemax (multiplexed); Encore (multiplexed); HBO (multiplexed); Showtime (multiplexed); Starz (multiplexed); The Movie Channel (multiplexed).

Fee: $12.00 monthly (each).

Video-On-Demand: No

Pay-Per-View

iN DEMAND (delivered digitally), Addressable: Yes.

Internet Service

Operational: Yes, Both DSL & dial-up.

Broadband Service: Netlink.

Fee: $49.95 installation; $39.95 monthly.

Telephone Service

None

Homes passed: Included in Arnold

General Manager: Lee Ann Quist. Chief Technician: Mark Stottler. Marketing Manager: Casey Garrigan.

Ownership: Great Plains Communications Inc. (MSO).

ELSIE—Elsie Communications Inc., PO Box 19048, Colorado City, CO 81019. Phones: 719-676-3301; 308-228-8888 (Local office); 866-542-6780. Web Site: http://www.elsiecomm.net. ICA: NE0257.

TV Market Ranking: Below 100 (ELSIE). Franchise award date: N.A. Franchise expiration date: N.A. Began: N.A.

Channel capacity: 36 (operating 2-way). Channels available but not in use: 22.

Basic Service

Subscribers: 24.

Programming (received off-air): KGIN (CBS, MNT) Grand Island; KNOP-TV (NBC) North Platte; KPNE-TV (PBS) North Platte; KWNB-TV (ABC) Hayes Center.

Programming (via satellite): ABC Family Channel; Animal Planet; Arts & Entertainment; Cartoon Network; CNN; Country Music TV; Discovery Channel; Disney Channel; ESPN; ESPN 2; Fox News Channel; Fox Sports Net Rocky Mountain; FX; HGTV; History Channel; MTV; Nickelodeon; Oxygen; QVC; Spike TV; Syfy; TBS Superstation; The Learning Channel; Turner Classic Movies; Turner Network TV; TV Land; USA Network; VH1; Weather Channel; WGN America.

Pay Service 1

Pay Units: N.A.

Programming (via satellite): HBO; Showtime.

Video-On-Demand: No

Internet Service

Operational: No.

Telephone Service

None

Miles of Plant: 2.0 (coaxial); None (fiber optic). Homes passed: 72.

General Manager: David Shipley. Chief Technician: Scott Hendrickson.

Ownership: American Broadband Communications Inc. (MSO).

ENDICOTT—Formerly served by Westcom. No longer in operation. ICA: NE0211.

EWING—Great Plains Cable TV. Now served by ELGIN, NE [NE0282]. ICA: NE0283.

FAIRBURY—Time Warner Cable, 5400 S 16th St, Lincoln, NE 68512-1278. Phone: 402-421-0330. Fax: 402-421-0310. Web Site: http://www.timewarnercable.com/Nebraska. ICA: NE0018.

TV Market Ranking: Outside TV Markets (FAIRBURY). Franchise award date: January 1, 1966. Franchise expiration date: N.A. Began: August 18, 1963.

Channel capacity: 80 (operating 2-way). Channels available but not in use: None.

Basic Service

Subscribers: N.A. Included in Lincoln

Programming (received off-air): KLKN (ABC) Lincoln; KMTV-TV (CBS) Omaha; KOLN (CBS, MNT) Lincoln; KPTM (FOX, MNT) Omaha; KUON-TV (PBS) Lincoln; KXVO (CW) Omaha; WOWT-TV (IND, NBC) Omaha.

Programming (via satellite): TV Guide Network.

Fee: $40.54 installation; $15.30 monthly; $.69 converter; $18.29 additional installation.

Expanded Basic Service 1

Subscribers: 2,875.

Programming (via satellite): ABC Family Channel; AMC; Animal Planet; Arts & Entertainment; BET Networks; Bravo; Cartoon Network; CNBC; CNN; Comedy Central; Country Music TV; C-SPAN; C-SPAN 2; Discovery Channel; Discovery Health Channel; Disney Channel; E! Entertainment Television; ESPN; ESPN 2; ESPN Classic Sports; Eternal Word TV Network; Food Network; Fox News Channel; Fox Sports Net Midwest; FX; Golf Channel; Hallmark Channel; Headline News; HGTV; History Channel; Home Shopping Network; ION Television; Lifetime; Lifetime Movie Network; MSNBC; MTV; National Geographic Channel; Nickelodeon; Oxygen; QVC; ShopNBC; SoapNet; Spike TV; Syfy; TBS Superstation; The Learning Channel; Travel Channel; truTV; Turner Classic Movies; Turner Network TV; TV Land; Univision; USA Network; VH1; WE tv; Weather Channel; WGN America.

Fee: $28.60 monthly.

Digital Basic Service

Subscribers: N.A. Included in Lincoln

Programming (via satellite): America's Store; BBC America; Bio; Bloomberg Television; Boomerang; Cooking Channel; C-SPAN 3; Discovery Digital Networks; DMX Music; Do-It-Yourself; ESPNews; FitTV; Fox Movie Channel; Fox Sports World; Fuse; G4; Great American Country; GSN; History Channel International; Independent Film Channel; Knowledge Network; Lifetime Real Women; MTV2; NASA TV; Nick Jr.; Outdoor Channel; Ovation; Speed Channel; Style Network; Toon Disney; Trinity Broadcasting Network; Versus; VH1 Classic.

Fee: $6.95 monthly; $7.65 converter.

Digital Pay Service 1

Pay Units: N.A.

Programming (via satellite): Cinemax (multiplexed); Encore Action; HBO (multiplexed); Showtime (multiplexed); Starz (multiplexed); The Movie Channel (multiplexed).

Fee: $9.95 monthly (each).

Video-On-Demand: Yes

Pay-Per-View

Addressable homes: 321.

iN DEMAND (delivered digitally), Addressable: Yes; Fresh (delivered digitally); ESPN Full Court (delivered digitally); ESPN Gameplan (delivered digitally); ESPN Extra (delivered digitally); NBA TV (delivered digitally); Shorteez (delivered digitally); Hot Choice (delivered digitally); Pleasure (delivered digitally); Playboy TV (delivered digitally); ESPN Now (delivered digitally); NHL Center Ice (delivered digitally); MLB Extra Innings (delivered digitally).

Internet Service

Operational: Yes.

Subscribers: 200.

Broadband Service: Road Runner.

Fee: $39.95 installation; $44.95 monthly.

Telephone Service

Digital: Operational

Fee: $39.95 monthly

Miles of Plant: 50.0 (coaxial); None (fiber optic). Total homes in franchised area: 3,800. Homes passed included in Lincoln

President: Beth Scarborough. Vice President, Engineering: John Matejovich. Vice President, Marketing: Brian Cecere. Vice President, Operations: Dick Cassidy. General Manager: Valerie Kramer. Public Affairs Director: Ann Shrewsbury. Technical Operations Manager: Rick Hollman.

City fee: 5% of gross.

Ownership: Time Warner Cable (MSO).; Advance/Newhouse Partnership (MSO).

FALLS CITY—Time Warner Cable, 5400 S 16th St, Lincoln, NE 68512-1278. Phone: 402-421-0330. Fax: 402-421-0310. Web Site: http://www.timewarnercable.com/Nebraska. Also serves Humboldt, Pawnee City & Table Rock. ICA: NE0351.

TV Market Ranking: Outside TV Markets (FALLS CITY, Humbolt, Pawnee City, Table Rock). Franchise award date: N.A. Franchise expiration date: N.A. Began: January 1, 1963.

Channel capacity: N.A. Channels available but not in use: N.A.

Basic Service

Subscribers: N.A. Included in Lincoln

Programming (received off-air): KETV (ABC) Omaha; KMBC-TV (ABC) Kansas

City; KMTV-TV (CBS) Omaha; KOLN (CBS, MNT) Lincoln; KPTM (FOX, MNT) Omaha; KQTV (ABC) St. Joseph; KSHB-TV (NBC) Kansas City; KUON-TV (PBS) Lincoln; KXVO (CW) Omaha; WOWT-TV (IND, NBC) Omaha; allband FM.
Programming (via satellite): Knowledge Network; WGN America.
Fee: $40.54 installation; $14.40 monthly; $.69 converter.

Expanded Basic Service 1
Subscribers: N.A.
Programming (via satellite): ABC Family Channel; AMC; Animal Planet; Arts & Entertainment; BET Networks; Bravo; Cartoon Network; CNBC; CNN; Comedy Central; Country Music TV; C-SPAN; C-SPAN 2; Discovery Channel; Discovery Health Channel; Disney Channel; E! Entertainment Television; ESPN; ESPN 2; ESPN Classic Sports; Eternal Word TV Network; Food Network; Fox News Channel; Fox Sports Net Midwest; FX; Golf Channel; Hallmark Channel; Headline News; HGTV; History Channel; Home Shopping Network; ION Television; Lifetime; Lifetime Movie Network; MSNBC; MTV; National Geographic Channel; Nickelodeon; Oxygen; QVC; ShopNBC; SoapNet; Spike TV; Syfy; TBS Superstation; The Learning Channel; Travel Channel; truTV; Turner Classic Movies; Turner Network TV; TV Guide Network; TV Land; Univision; USA Network; VH1; WE tv; Weather Channel.
Fee: $29.50 monthly.

Digital Basic Service
Subscribers: N.A. Included in Lincoln
Programming (via satellite): America's Store; BBC America; Bio; Bloomberg Television; Boomerang; Canales N; Cooking Channel; C-SPAN 3; Discovery Digital Networks; Do-It-Yourself; ESPNews; FitTV; Fox Movie Channel; Fox Sports World; FSN Digital Atlantic; FSN Digital Central; FSN Digital Pacific; G4; Great American Country; GSN; History Channel International; Independent Film Channel; Knowledge Network; MTV2; Music Choice; NASA TV; NBA TV; Nick Jr.; Outdoor Channel; Ovation; Speed Channel; Style Network; Tennis Channel; Toon Disney; Trinity Broadcasting Network; Versus; VH1 Classic.
Fee: $6.95 monthly.

Digital Pay Service 1
Pay Units: 620.
Programming (via satellite): Cinemax (multiplexed); HBO (multiplexed); Showtime (multiplexed); Starz (multiplexed); The Movie Channel (multiplexed).
Fee: $9.95 monthly (each).

Video-On-Demand: Yes

Pay-Per-View
Addressable homes: 614.
iN DEMAND (delivered digitally), Addressable: Yes; Fresh; Hot Choice (delivered digitally); Pleasure (delivered digitally); Playboy TV (delivered digitally); ESPN Now (delivered digitally); ESPN Gameplan (delivered digitally); ESPN Full Court (delivered digitally); ESPN Extra (delivered digitally); Shorteez (delivered digitally); NBA TV (delivered digitally).

Internet Service
Operational: Yes.
Subscribers: 383.
Broadband Service: Road Runner.
Fee: $39.95 installation; $44.95 monthly.

Telephone Service
Digital: Operational
Fee: $39.95 monthly

Miles of Plant: 60.0 (coaxial); None (fiber optic). Total homes in franchised area: 3,912. Homes passed included in Lincoln

President: Beth Scarborough. Vice President, Engineering: John Matejovich. Vice President, Marketing: Brian Cecere. Vice President, Operations: Dick Cassidy. General Manager: Valerie Kramer. Public Affairs Director: Ann Shrewsbury. Technical Operations Manager: John Koluch.

City fee: 5% of gross.

Ownership: Time Warner Cable (MSO).; Advance/Newhouse Partnership (MSO).

FARNAM—Consolidated Cable Inc., PO Box 6147, 6900 Van Dorn St, Ste 21, Lincoln, NE 68506-0147. Phones: 402-489-2728; 800-742-7464. Fax: 402-489-9034. E-mail: service@consolidatedtelephone.com. Web Site: http://www.nebnet.net. Also serves Eustis. ICA: NE0229.

TV Market Ranking: Outside TV Markets (Eustis, FARNAM). Franchise award date: N.A. Franchise expiration date: N.A. Began: August 1, 1989.

Channel capacity: 78 (2-way capable). Channels available but not in use: 26.

Basic Service
Subscribers: 191.
Programming (received off-air): KGIN (CBS, MNT) Grand Island; KNOP-TV (NBC) North Platte; KPNE-TV (PBS) North Platte; KTVG-TV (FOX) Grand Island; KWNB-TV (ABC) Hayes Center.
Programming (via satellite): ABC Family Channel; AMC; Animal Planet; Arts & Entertainment; Cartoon Network; CNN; Country Music TV; Discovery Channel; Disney Channel; ESPN; ESPN 2; ESPN Classic Sports; Fox Sports Net Midwest; FX; Great American Country; HGTV; History Channel; Home Shopping Network; Lifetime; MTV; Nickelodeon; Spike TV; Syfy; TBS Superstation; The Learning Channel; Turner Network TV; TV Land; USA Network; VH1; Weather Channel; WGN America.
Fee: $25.95 installation; $28.95 monthly.

Digital Basic Service
Subscribers: N.A.
Programming (via satellite): AmericanLife TV Network; Bloomberg Television; CMT Pure Country; DMX Music; ESPN Classic Sports; ESPNews; FitTV; Fox College Sports Atlantic; Fox College Sports Central; Fox College Sports Pacific; Fox Movie Channel; G4; GAS; Golf Channel; GSN; Independent Film Channel; Lifetime Movie Network; MTV Networks Digital Suite; Nick Jr.; NickToons TV; Outdoor Channel; Sleuth; Speed Channel; Style Network; Sundance Channel; Toon Disney; Trinity Broadcasting Network; Versus; WE tv.
Fee: $49.95 installation; $12.00 monthly.

Pay Service 1
Pay Units: 9.
Programming (via satellite): Showtime.
Fee: $9.00 monthly.

Pay Service 2
Pay Units: 18.
Programming (via satellite): Cinemax; Encore; HBO; Starz.
Fee: $9.00 monthly (HBO, Cinemax or Staz/Encore).

Digital Pay Service 1
Pay Units: N.A.
Programming (via satellite): Cinemax (multiplexed); Encore (multiplexed); Flix; HBO (multiplexed); Showtime (multiplexed); Starz (multiplexed); The Movie Channel (multiplexed).
Fee: $9.00 monthly (each).

Video-On-Demand: No

Pay-Per-View
iN DEMAND (delivered digitally); Playboy TV (delivered digitally); Short TV (delivered digitally).

Internet Service
Operational: No, Both DSL & dial-up.

Telephone Service
None

Miles of Plant: 8.0 (coaxial); None (fiber optic). Homes passed: 377.

Manager: Brian D. Thompson. Chief Technician: Dan Smith.

Ownership: Consolidated Cable Inc. (MSO).

FAWN HEIGHTS—Formerly served by TelePartners. No longer in operation. ICA: NE0381.

FILLEY—Comstar Cable TV Inc., PO Box 975, 8358 W Scott Rd, Beatrice, NE 68310-0975. Phone: 402-520-1987 (GM's cell). Fax: 402-228-3766. ICA: NE0284.

TV Market Ranking: Outside TV Markets (FILLEY). Franchise award date: N.A. Franchise expiration date: N.A. Began: October 1, 1988.

Channel capacity: 36 (not 2-way capable). Channels available but not in use: N.A.

Basic Service
Subscribers: 34.
Programming (received off-air): KLKN (ABC) Lincoln; KOLN (CBS, MNT) Lincoln; KPTM (FOX, MNT) Omaha; KUON-TV (PBS) Lincoln; KXVO (CW) Omaha; WOWT-TV (IND, NBC) Omaha.
Programming (via satellite): ABC Family Channel; AMC; Arts & Entertainment; Cartoon Network; CNN; C-SPAN; Discovery Channel; Disney Channel; ESPN; ESPN 2; Food Network; Fox News Channel; Fox Sports Net; FX; Great American Country; Hallmark Channel; HGTV; History Channel; Lifetime; QVC; RFD-TV; Syfy; TBS Superstation; The Learning Channel; Travel Channel; Turner Network TV; USA Network; Weather Channel; WGN America.
Fee: $40.00 installation; $31.95 monthly.

Digital Basic Service
Subscribers: N.A.
Programming (via satellite): AmericanLife TV Network; Bio; Bloomberg Television; Bravo; Discovery Kids Channel; Discovery Military Channel; Discovery Planet Green; Disney XD; ESPN 2; ESPN Classic Sports; ESPNews; FitTV; Fox College Sports Atlantic; Fox College Sports Central; Fox College Sports Pacific; Fox Movie Channel; Fuse; G4; Golf Channel; Great American Country; GSN; HGTV; History Channel; History Channel International; ID Investigation Discovery; INSP; National Geographic Channel; Outdoor Channel; Ovation; RFD-TV; Science Channel; Sleuth; SoapNet; Speed Channel; Trinity Broadcasting Network; Turner Classic Movies; Versus; WE tv.

Pay Service 1
Pay Units: 20.
Programming (via satellite): HBO.
Fee: $7.50 monthly.

Video-On-Demand: No

Internet Service
Operational: No.

Telephone Service
None

Homes passed: 80.

Manager: Tim Schwarz.

Ownership: Comstar Cable TV Inc. (MSO).

FRANKLIN—Formerly served by Pinpoint Cable TV. No longer in operation. ICA: NE0073.

FREMONT—Time Warner Cable, 5400 S 16th St, Lincoln, NE 68512-1278. Phone: 402-421-0330. Fax: 402-421-0310. Web Site: http://www.timewarnercable.com/Nebraska. Also serves Dodge County, Inglewood & Woodcliff Lakes. ICA: NE0007.

TV Market Ranking: 53 (Dodge County (portions), FREMONT, Inglewood); 91 (Woodcliff Lakes); Outside TV Markets (Dodge County (portions)). Franchise award date: N.A. Franchise expiration date: N.A. Began: June 2, 1980.

Channel capacity: N.A. Channels available but not in use: N.A.

Basic Service
Subscribers: N.A. Included in Lincoln
Programming (received off-air): KETV (ABC) Omaha; KMTV-TV (CBS) Omaha; KPTM (FOX, MNT) Omaha; KUON-TV (PBS) Lincoln; KXVO (CW) Omaha; WOWT-TV (IND, NBC) Omaha.
Programming (via satellite): Knowledge Network; Product Information Network; Shop at Home; TV Guide Network.
Current originations: Educational Access; Public Access.
Fee: $40.54 installation; $14.40 monthly; $.69 converter; $18.29 additional installation.

Expanded Basic Service 1
Subscribers: N.A.
Programming (via satellite): ABC Family Channel; AMC; Animal Planet; Arts & Entertainment; BET Networks; Bravo; Cartoon Network; CNBC; CNN; Comedy Central; Country Music TV; C-SPAN; C-SPAN 2; Discovery Channel; Discovery Health Channel; Disney Channel; E! Entertainment Television; ESPN; ESPN 2; ESPN Classic Sports; Eternal Word TV Network; Food Network; Fox News Channel; Fox Sports Net Midwest; FX; Golf Channel; Hallmark Channel; Headline News; HGTV; History Channel; Home Shopping Network; ION Television; Lifetime; Lifetime Movie Network; MSNBC; MTV; National Geographic Channel; Nickelodeon; Oxygen; QVC; ShopNBC; SoapNet; Spike TV; Syfy; TBS Superstation; The Learning Channel; Travel Channel; truTV; Turner Classic Movies; Turner Network TV; TV Land; Univision; USA Network; VH1; WE tv; Weather Channel; WGN America.
Fee: $30.95 monthly.

Digital Basic Service
Subscribers: N.A. Included in Lincoln
Programming (via satellite): America's Store; BBC America; Bio; Bloomberg Television; Boomerang; Canales N; Cooking Channel; C-SPAN 3; Discovery Digital Networks; Do-It-Yourself; ESPNews; FitTV; Fox Movie Channel; Fox Sports World; FSN Digital Atlantic; FSN Digital Central; FSN Digital Pacific; G4; Great American Country; GSN; History Channel International; Independent Film Channel; Knowledge Network; Lifetime Real Women; MTV2; Music

Choice; NASA TV; NBA TV; Nick Jr.; Outdoor Channel; Ovation; Speed Channel; Style Network; Tennis Channel; Toon Disney; Trinity Broadcasting Network; Versus; VH1 Classic.
Fee: $6.95 monthly.

Digital Pay Service 1
Pay Units: 140.
Programming (via satellite): Cinemax (multiplexed); Encore (multiplexed); HBO (multiplexed); Showtime (multiplexed); The Movie Channel.
Fee: $9.95 monthly (each).

Video-On-Demand: Yes

Pay-Per-View
Addressable homes: 91.
NASCAR In Car (delivered digitally); NHL Center Ice (delivered digitally); iN DEMAND (delivered digitally), Addressable: Yes; ESPN Now (delivered digitally); ESPN Full Court (delivered digitally); ESPN Extra (delivered digitally); Fresh (delivered digitally); NBA League Pass (delivered digitally); Shorteez (delivered digitally); Hot Choice (delivered digitally); Pleasure (delivered digitally); Playboy TV (delivered digitally); ESPN Gameplan (delivered digitally).

Internet Service
Operational: Yes.
Subscribers: 52.
Broadband Service: Road Runner, AOL for Broadband, EarthLink.
Fee: $39.95 installation; $44.95 monthly.

Telephone Service
Digital: Operational
Fee: $39.95 monthly

Note: Homes passed included in Lincoln
President: Beth Scarborough. Vice President, Engineering: John Matejovich. Vice President, Marketing: Brian Cecere. Vice President, Operations: Dick Cassidy. General Manager: Valerie Kramer. Public Affairs Director: Ann Shrewsbury. Technical Operations Manager: Rick Hollman.
Ownership: Time Warner Cable (MSO).; Advance/Newhouse Partnership (MSO).

FULLERTON—Cable Nebraska, 2123 Central Ave, Ste 200, Kearney, NE 68847. Phone: 308-236-1512. Web Site: http://www.cablene.com. ICA: NE0058.
TV Market Ranking: Outside TV Markets (FULLERTON). Franchise award date: N.A. Franchise expiration date: N.A. Began: November 1, 1968.
Channel capacity: N.A. Channels available but not in use: N.A.

Basic Service
Subscribers: 268.
Programming (received off-air): KGIN (CBS, MNT) Grand Island; KHAS-TV (NBC) Hastings; KHGI-TV (ABC) Kearney; KHNE-TV (PBS) Hastings; KLKN (ABC) Lincoln; KTVG-TV (FOX) Grand Island; allband FM.
Programming (via satellite): ABC Family Channel; C-SPAN; C-SPAN 2; Eternal Word TV Network; Hallmark Channel; Headline News; Home Shopping Network; QVC; TBS Superstation; Trinity Broadcasting Network; TV Guide Network; Weather Channel; WGN America.
Current originations: Public Access.
Fee: $35.00 installation; $24.95 monthly.

Expanded Basic Service 1
Subscribers: N.A.
Programming (via satellite): AMC; Animal Planet; Arts & Entertainment; Cartoon Network; CNBC; CNN; Comedy Central; Country Music TV; Discovery Channel; E! Entertainment Television; ESPN; ESPN 2; Food Network; Fox News Channel; Fox Sports Net Midwest; FX; Great American Country; HGTV; History Channel; ION Television; Lifetime; MSNBC; Outdoor Channel; Spike TV; Syfy; The Learning Channel; Travel Channel; truTV; Turner Classic Movies; Turner Network TV; TV Land; Univision; USA Network.

Digital Basic Service
Subscribers: 36.
Programming (via satellite): AmericanLife TV Network; BBC America; Bio; Bloomberg Television; Canales N; Current; Discovery Digital Networks; DMX Music; ESPN 2; ESPN Classic Sports; ESPNews; FitTV; Fox Movie Channel; Fox Sports World; FSN Digital Atlantic; FSN Digital Central; FSN Digital Pacific; G4; GAS; Golf Channel; GSN; Halogen Network; History Channel; History Channel International; International Television (ITV); MBC America; MTV; MTV Networks Digital Suite; National Geographic Channel; Nick Jr.; Nickelodeon; Outdoor Channel; Ovation; ShopNBC; Speed Channel; Style Network; Syfy; Trinity Broadcasting Network; Trio; Versus; VH1.
Fee: $12.95 monthly.

Digital Pay Service 1
Pay Units: N.A.
Programming (via satellite): Cinemax (multiplexed); Daystar TV Network; Encore (multiplexed); Flix; Fox Movie Channel; HBO (multiplexed); Independent Film Channel; Lifetime Movie Network; Showtime (multiplexed); Starz (multiplexed); The Movie Channel (multiplexed); WAM! America's Kidz Network; WE tv.
Fee: $15.00 monthly.

Video-On-Demand: No

Pay-Per-View
iN DEMAND (delivered digitally); Playboy TV (delivered digitally).

Internet Service
Operational: Yes.
Broadband Service: Cable Nebraska.

Telephone Service
None

Miles of Plant: 12.0 (coaxial); None (fiber optic). Homes passed: 635.
Operations Manager: Stuart Gilbertson.
City fee: 3% of gross.
Ownership: USA Companies (MSO).

FUNK—Glenwood Telecommunications. Now served by BLUE HILL, NE [NE0093]. ICA: NE0285.

GARLAND—Galaxy Cablevision, 1928 S Lincoln Ave, Ste 200, York, NE 68467. Phone: 402-362-3332. Fax: 402-362-4890. Web Site: http://www.galaxycable.com. ICA: NE0214.
TV Market Ranking: 91 (GARLAND). Franchise award date: N.A. Franchise expiration date: N.A. Began: November 1, 1985.
Channel capacity: 41 (not 2-way capable). Channels available but not in use: 20.

Basic Service
Subscribers: 25.
Programming (received off-air): KETV (ABC) Omaha; KMTV-TV (CBS) Omaha; KOLN (CBS, MNT) Lincoln; KPTM (FOX, MNT) Omaha; KUON-TV (PBS) Lincoln; KXVO (CW) Omaha; WOWT-TV (IND, NBC) Omaha.
Programming (via satellite): ABC Family Channel; Arts & Entertainment; CNN; Discovery Channel; Disney Channel; ESPN; ESPN 2; Outdoor Channel; TBS Superstation; Turner Network TV; USA Network; WGN America.
Fee: $35.00 installation; $33.95 monthly.

Pay Service 1
Pay Units: 6.
Programming (via satellite): Cinemax.
Fee: $9.95 monthly.

Pay Service 2
Pay Units: 12.
Programming (via satellite): HBO.
Fee: $13.95 monthly.

Internet Service
Operational: No.

Telephone Service
None

Miles of Plant: 2.0 (coaxial); None (fiber optic). Homes passed: 90.
State Manager: Cheyenne Wohlford. Technical Manager: Carl Stanley. Sales Manager: Mike Thomas. Customer Service Manager: Donna Bryant.
City fee: 3% of basic.
Ownership: Galaxy Cable Inc. (MSO).

GENEVA—Formerly served by Sprint Corp. No longer in operation. ICA: NE0352.

GENEVA—Galaxy Cablevision, 1928 S Lincoln Ave, Ste 200, York, NE 68467. Phone: 402-362-3332. Fax: 402-362-4890. Web Site: http://www.galaxycable.com. Also serves Bruning, Davenport, Exeter, Fairmont, McCool Junction, Milligan & Shickley. ICA: NE0043.
TV Market Ranking: Below 100 (Bruning, Davenport, Shickley); Outside TV Markets (Exeter, Fairmont, GENEVA, McCool Junction, Milligan). Franchise award date: N.A. Franchise expiration date: N.A. Began: March 1, 1981.
Channel capacity: 78 (operating 2-way). Channels available but not in use: None.

Basic Service
Subscribers: 1,165.
Programming (received off-air): KHAS-TV (NBC) Hastings; KHGI-TV (ABC) Kearney; KHNE-TV (PBS) Hastings; KLKN (ABC) Lincoln; KOLN (CBS, MNT) Lincoln; KPTM (FOX, MNT) Omaha; KXVO (CW) Omaha.
Programming (via satellite): ABC Family Channel; AMC; Animal Planet; Arts & Entertainment; Boomerang; Cartoon Network; CNN; Comedy Central; C-SPAN; Discovery Channel; Disney Channel; E! Entertainment Television; ESPN; ESPN 2; Eternal Word TV Network; Food Network; Fox News Channel; Fox Sports Net Midwest; Fuse; FX; Great American Country; Hallmark Channel; Headline News; HGTV; History Channel; INSP; Lifetime; MSNBC; National Geographic Channel; Outdoor Channel; QVC; Syfy; TBS Superstation; The Learning Channel; Toon Disney; Travel Channel; Trinity Broadcasting Network; Turner Classic Movies; Turner Network TV; TV Guide Network; TV Land; USA Network; Weather Channel; WGN America.
Current originations: Educational Access; Public Access.
Fee: $35.00 installation; $44.75 monthly.

Digital Basic Service
Subscribers: 272.
Programming (via satellite): AmericanLife TV Network; BBC America; Bio; Bloomberg Television; Discovery Digital Networks; DMX Music; ESPN Classic Sports; ESPNews; FitTV; Fox Sports World; FSN Digital Atlantic; FSN Digital Central; FSN Digital Pacific; G4; Golf Channel; GSN; History Channel International; Speed Channel; Style Network; WE tv.
Fee: $12.95 monthly.

Digital Expanded Basic Service
Subscribers: N.A.
Programming (via satellite): DMX Music; Encore; Fox Movie Channel; Independent Film Channel; Lifetime Movie Network.
Fee: $12.95 monthly.

Pay Service 1
Pay Units: 32.
Programming (via satellite): Cinemax.
Fee: $10.95 monthly.

Pay Service 2
Pay Units: 58.
Programming (via satellite): HBO.
Fee: $13.95 monthly.

Pay Service 3
Pay Units: 74.
Programming (via satellite): Showtime.
Fee: $9.95 monthly.

Pay Service 4
Pay Units: 47.
Programming (via satellite): The Movie Channel.
Fee: $7.95 monthly.

Digital Pay Service 1
Pay Units: N.A.
Programming (via satellite): Cinemax (multiplexed); Flix; HBO (multiplexed); Showtime (multiplexed); The Movie Channel (multiplexed).
Fee: $15.60 monthly.

Video-On-Demand: No; No

Pay-Per-View
Addressable homes: 188.
ESPN Now (delivered digitally), Fee: $3.99, Addressable: Yes; Hot Choice (delivered digitally); Movies (delivered digitally); Playboy TV (delivered digitally); Fresh (delivered digitally); sports (delivered digitally).

Internet Service
Operational: Yes.
Subscribers: 292.
Broadband Service: Galaxy Cable Internet.
Fee: $49.95 installation; $44.95 monthly; $5.00 modem lease.

Telephone Service
Digital: Planned

Miles of Plant: 47.0 (coaxial); None (fiber optic). Homes passed: 2,628.
State Manager: Cheyenne Wohlford. Technical Manager: Carl Stanley. Sales Manager: Mike Thomas. Customer Service Manager: Donna Bryant.
City fee: 5% of gross.
Ownership: Galaxy Cable Inc. (MSO).

GENOA—Cable Nebraska, 2123 Central Ave, Ste 200, Kearney, NE 68847. Phone: 308-236-1512. Web Site: http://www.cablene.com. ICA: NE0083.
TV Market Ranking: Outside TV Markets (GENOA). Franchise award date: February 1, 1980. Franchise expiration date: N.A. Began: January 1, 1982.
Channel capacity: N.A. Channels available but not in use: N.A.

Basic Service
Subscribers: 254.
Programming (received off-air): KGIN (CBS, MNT) Grand Island; KHAS-TV (NBC) Hastings; KHGI-TV (ABC) Kearney; KHNE-TV (PBS) Hastings; KLKN (ABC) Lincoln; KTVG-TV (FOX) Grand Island.
Programming (via satellite): C-SPAN; C-SPAN 2; Eternal Word TV Network; Home Shopping Network; MyNetworkTV Inc.; Netlink International; QVC; TBS Superstation; Trinity Broadcasting Network; TV Guide Network; Univision; WB.com; Weather Channel; WGN America.
Current originations: Public Access.
Fee: $35.00 installation; $24.95 monthly.

Expanded Basic Service 1
Subscribers: N.A.
Programming (via satellite): ABC Family Channel; AMC; Animal Planet; Arts & Entertainment; Cartoon Network; CNBC; CNN; Comedy Central; Country Music TV; Discovery Channel; E! Entertainment Television; ESPN; ESPN 2; ESPN Classic Sports; Food Network; Fox News Channel; Fox Sports Net Midwest; FX; G4; Great American Country; Hallmark Channel; Headline News; HGTV; History Channel; ION Television; Lifetime; MSNBC; MTV; Nickelodeon; Outdoor Channel; RFD-TV; Spike TV; Syfy; The Learning Channel; Travel Channel; truTV; Turner Classic Movies; Turner Network TV; TV Land; USA Network; Versus; VH1.
Digital Basic Service
Subscribers: 7.
Programming (via satellite): AmericanLife TV Network; AZ TV; BBC America; Bio; Black Family Channel; Bloomberg Television; Canales N; CMT Pure Country; Current; Discovery Channel HD; Discovery Health Channel; Discovery Home Channel; Discovery Kids Channel; Discovery Military Channel; Discovery Times Channel; DMX Music; ESPN HD; ESPNews; FitTV; Fox College Sports Atlantic; Fox College Sports Central; Fox College Sports Pacific; Fox Movie Channel; GAS; Golf Channel; GSN; Halogen Network; History Channel International; MTV Hits; MTV2; MyNetworkTV Inc.; Netlink International; Nick Jr.; Ovation; Science Channel; ShopNBC; Sleuth; Speed Channel; Style Network; TBS in HD; Turner Network TV HD; VH1 Classic; VH1 Soul; WE tv.
Fee: $13.95 monthly.
Digital Pay Service 1
Pay Units: N.A.
Programming (via satellite): Cinemax (multiplexed); Daystar TV Network; Encore (multiplexed); Flix; HBO (multiplexed); Lifetime Movie Network; Showtime (multiplexed); Starz (multiplexed); The Movie Channel (multiplexed); WAM! America's Kidz Network.
Fee: $10.00 monthly.
Video-On-Demand: No
Pay-Per-View
iN DEMAND (delivered digitally); Playboy TV (delivered digitally); Hot Choice (delivered digitally); Fresh (delivered digitally); Spice: Xcess (delivered digitally); Club Jenna (delivered digitally).
Internet Service
Operational: Yes.
Broadband Service: Cable Nebraska.
Telephone Service
None
Miles of Plant: 8.0 (coaxial); None (fiber optic). Homes passed: 485.
Operations Manager: Stuart Gilbertson.
City fee: 3% of gross.
Ownership: USA Companies (MSO).

GILTNER—Mid-State Community TV. Now served by AURORA, NE [NE0033]. ICA: NE0210.

GINGER COVE—Formerly served by TelePartners. No longer in operation. ICA: NE0362.

GLENVIL—Galaxy Cablevision, 1928 S Lincoln Ave, Ste 200, York, NE 68467. Phone: 402-362-3332. Fax: 402-362-4890. Web Site: http://www.galaxycable.com. ICA: NE0178.
TV Market Ranking: 91 (GLENVIL). Franchise award date: N.A. Franchise expiration date: N.A. Began: March 1, 1984.
Channel capacity: 41 (not 2-way capable). Channels available but not in use: 22.
Basic Service
Subscribers: 13.
Programming (received off-air): KGIN (CBS, MNT) Grand Island; KHAS-TV (NBC) Hastings; KHGI-TV (ABC) Kearney; KHNE-TV (PBS) Hastings; KLKN (ABC) Lincoln.
Programming (via satellite): ABC Family Channel; Arts & Entertainment; Cartoon Network; CNN; Discovery Channel; Disney Channel; ESPN; HBO; Outdoor Channel; TBS Superstation; Turner Network TV; WGN America.
Fee: $35.00 installation; $32.95 monthly.
Pay Service 1
Pay Units: 7.
Programming (via satellite): Cinemax.
Fee: $11.95 monthly.
Internet Service
Operational: No.
Telephone Service
None
Miles of Plant: 3.0 (coaxial); None (fiber optic). Homes passed: 135.
State Manager: Cheyenne Wohlford. Technical Manager: Carl Stanley. Sales Manager: Mike Thomas. Customer Service Manager: Donna Bryant.
City fee: 5% of basic.
Ownership: Galaxy Cable Inc. (MSO).

GOEHNER (village)—Formerly served by TelePartners. No longer in operation. ICA: NE0286.

GORDON—Great Plains Communications, PO Box 500, 1600 Great Plains Centre, Blair, NE 68008-0500. Phone: 402-426-9511. Fax: 402-456-6485. Web Site: http://www.gpcom.com. Also serves Rushville. ICA: NE0287.
TV Market Ranking: Outside TV Markets (GORDON, Rushville). Franchise award date: N.A. Franchise expiration date: N.A. Began: October 3, 1968.
Channel capacity: N.A. Channels available but not in use: N.A.
Basic Service
Subscribers: N.A. Included in Arnold
Programming (received off-air): KDUH-TV (ABC) Scottsbluff; KRNE-TV (PBS) Merriman.
Programming (via microwave): KCNC-TV (CBS) Denver; KTVD (MNT) Denver; KUSA (NBC) Denver; KWGN-TV (CW) Denver.
Programming (via satellite): C-SPAN; Home Shopping Network; INSP; QVC; Trinity Broadcasting Network; WGN America.
Fee: $45.00 installation; $11.00 monthly; $2.00 converter.
Expanded Basic Service 1
Subscribers: N.A.
Programming (via satellite): ABC Family Channel; AMC; Animal Planet; Arts & Entertainment; Bravo; Cartoon Network; CNBC; CNN; Comedy Central; Country Music TV; Discovery Channel; Disney Channel; E! Entertainment Television; ESPN; ESPN 2; Food Network; Fox News Channel; Fox Sports Net Rocky Mountain; FX; G4; Golf Channel; Hallmark Channel; Headline News; HGTV; History Channel; Lifetime; MSNBC; MTV; National Geographic Channel; Nickelodeon; Outdoor Channel; Oxygen; SoapNet; Speed Channel; Spike TV; Syfy; TBS Superstation; The Learning Channel; Toon Disney; Travel Channel; truTV; Turner Classic Movies; Turner Network TV; TV Land; USA Network; Versus; VH1; Weather Channel.
Fee: $45.00 installation; $10.45 monthly.
Digital Basic Service
Subscribers: N.A. Included in Arnold
Programming (via satellite): BBC America; Bio; Bloomberg Television; Discovery Digital Networks; Do-It-Yourself; GAS; GSN; History Channel International; Independent Film Channel; Lifetime Movie Network; MTV Networks Digital Suite; Music Choice; Nick Jr.; Nick Too; Sundance Channel; TV Guide Interactive Inc.; WE tv.
Digital Pay Service 1
Pay Units: 211.
Programming (via satellite): Showtime (multiplexed); The Movie Channel (multiplexed).
Fee: $12.00 monthly.
Digital Pay Service 2
Pay Units: N.A.
Programming (via satellite): Cinemax (multiplexed); Encore (multiplexed); Starz (multiplexed).
Fee: $12.00 monthly (Cinemax or Starz/Encore).
Digital Pay Service 3
Pay Units: 46.
Programming (via satellite): HBO (multiplexed).
Fee: $12.00 monthly.
Video-On-Demand: No
Pay-Per-View
iN DEMAND (delivered digitally); Pleasure (delivered digitally); ETC (delivered digitally).
Internet Service
Operational: Yes.
Fee: $49.95 installation; $39.95 monthly.
Telephone Service
None
Miles of Plant: 29.0 (coaxial); None (fiber optic). Homes passed: Included in Arnold
General Manager: Lea Ann Quist. Chief Technician: Mark Stotler. Marketing Manager: Casey Garrigan.
City fee: 2% of gross.
Ownership: Great Plains Communications Inc. (MSO).

GOTHENBURG—Charter Communications. Now served by KEARNEY, NE [NE0011]. ICA: NE0034.

GRAND ISLAND—Charter Communications, 205 N Webb Rd, Grand Island, NE 68803-4038. Phones: 308-389-4070; 507-289-8372 (Rochester administrative office). Fax: 308-382-2047. Web Site: http://www.charter.com. Also serves Alda, Gibbon, Hall County, Shelton, St. Libory, St. Paul & Wood River. ICA: NE0005.
TV Market Ranking: 91 (Alda, Gibbon, GRAND ISLAND, Hall County, Shelton, Wood River); Below 100 (St. Libory, St. Paul). Franchise award date: February 1, 1978. Franchise expiration date: N.A. Began: February 1, 1992.
Channel capacity: 78 (operating 2-way). Channels available but not in use: 8.
Basic Service
Subscribers: 11,980.
Programming (received off-air): KGIN (CBS, MNT) Grand Island; KHAS-TV (NBC) Hastings; KHGI-TV (ABC) Kearney; KHNE-TV (PBS) Hastings; KLKN (ABC) Lincoln; KTVG-TV (FOX) Grand Island.
Programming (via satellite): C-SPAN; Discovery Channel; Eternal Word TV Network; QVC; TV Guide Network; WGN America.
Current originations: Government Access; Educational Access.
Fee: $29.99 installation; $1.30 converter.
Expanded Basic Service 1
Subscribers: 11,800.
Programming (via satellite): ABC Family Channel; AMC; Animal Planet; Arts & Entertainment; Cartoon Network; CNBC; CNN; Comedy Central; Country Music TV; C-SPAN 2; Disney Channel; E! Entertainment Television; ESPN; ESPN 2; ESPN Classic Sports; Food Network; Fox News Channel; Fox Sports Net Midwest; FX; G4; GalaVision; Golf Channel; GRTV Network; Hallmark Channel; Headline News; HGTV; History Channel; Home Shopping Network; Lifetime; MSNBC; MTV; National Geographic Channel; Nickelodeon; SoapNet; Speed Channel; Spike TV; Syfy; TBS Superstation; The Learning Channel; Toon Disney; Travel Channel; truTV; Turner Network TV; TV Land; USA Network; Versus; VH1; Weather Channel.
Fee: $47.99 monthly.
Digital Basic Service
Subscribers: 2,050.
Programming (via satellite): BBC America; Bio; Bloomberg Television; Bravo; Canales N; Discovery Digital Networks; DMX Music; Fox Sports World; GAS; GSN; Halogen Network; History Channel International; Independent Film Channel; Lifetime Movie Network; MTV Networks Digital Suite; Nick Jr.; Outdoor Channel; Ovation; Style Network; Turner Classic Movies; WE tv.
Digital Pay Service 1
Pay Units: N.A.
Programming (via satellite): Cinemax (multiplexed); Encore (multiplexed); HBO (multiplexed); Showtime (multiplexed); Starz (multiplexed); The Movie Channel.
Video-On-Demand: Yes
Pay-Per-View
Addressable homes: 2,050.
Addressable: Yes; iN DEMAND (delivered digitally); Playboy TV (delivered digitally); Fresh (delivered digitally); Shorteez (delivered digitally).
Internet Service
Operational: Yes.
Broadband Service: Charter Pipeline.
Fee: $29.99 monthly; $9.95 modem lease; $199.95 modem purchase.
Telephone Service
Digital: Operational
Miles of Plant: 288.0 (coaxial); 19.0 (fiber optic). Homes passed: 23,431.
Vice President & General Manager: John Crowley. Technical Operations Director: Marty Kovarik. Technical Operations Manager: Terry Petzoldt. Office Manager: Mary Ivers.

City fee: 5% of gross.
Ownership: Charter Communications Inc. (MSO).

GRAND ISLAND—Galaxy Cablevision, 600 N Grant Ave, York, NE 68467-3043. Phones: 402-362-3332; 800-365-6988. Fax: 402-362-4890. Web Site: http://www.galaxycable.com. ICA: NE0101.
TV Market Ranking: 91 (GRAND ISLAND). Franchise award date: N.A. Franchise expiration date: N.A. Began: March 1, 1988.
Channel capacity: 41 (not 2-way capable). Channels available but not in use: None.
Basic Service
Subscribers: 191.
Programming (received off-air): KGIN (CBS, MNT) Grand Island; KHAS-TV (NBC) Hastings; KHGI-TV (ABC) Kearney; KHNE-TV (PBS) Hastings; KLKN (ABC) Lincoln; KTVG-TV (FOX) Grand Island.
Programming (via satellite): ABC Family Channel; AMC; Animal Planet; Arts & Entertainment; Cartoon Network; CNN; Discovery Channel; Disney Channel; E! Entertainment Television; ESPN; ESPN 2; Fox News Channel; Fox Sports Net Midwest; Fuse; FX; Great American Country; Headline News; HGTV; History Channel; Lifetime; MSNBC; Outdoor Channel; QVC; TBS Superstation; The Learning Channel; Toon Disney; Turner Classic Movies; Turner Network TV; USA Network; Weather Channel; WGN America.
Fee: $35.00 installation; $25.95 monthly.
Pay Service 1
Pay Units: 44.
Programming (via satellite): Cinemax.
Fee: $11.95 monthly.
Pay Service 2
Pay Units: 72.
Programming (via satellite): HBO.
Fee: $12.95 monthly.
Pay Service 3
Pay Units: 46.
Programming (via satellite): Showtime.
Fee: $7.95 monthly.
Pay Service 4
Pay Units: 36.
Programming (via satellite): The Movie Channel.
Fee: $6.95 monthly.
Internet Service
Operational: No.
Telephone Service
None
Miles of Plant: 16.0 (coaxial); None (fiber optic). Homes passed: 712.
State Manager: Cheyenne Wohlford. Technical Manager: Kelly Murphy.
Franchise fee: None.
Ownership: Galaxy Cable Inc. (MSO).

GRANT—Great Plains Communications, PO Box 500, 1600 Great Plains Centre, Blair, NE 68008-0500. Phones: 888-343-8014; 402-426-9511. Fax: 402-456-6550. E-mail: lquist@gpcom.com. Web Site: http://www.gpcom.com. Also serves Hayes Center, Imperial, Palisade & Venango. ICA: NE0070.
TV Market Ranking: Below 100 (Hayes Center, Imperial, Palisade); Outside TV Markets (GRANT, Venango). Franchise award date: N.A. Franchise expiration date: N.A. Began: September 30, 1976.
Channel capacity: N.A. Channels available but not in use: N.A.
Basic Service
Subscribers: N.A. Included in Arnold
Programming (received off-air): KNOP-TV (NBC) North Platte; KOLN (CBS, MNT) Lincoln; KPNE-TV (PBS) North Platte; KWNB-TV (ABC) Hayes Center; allband FM.
Programming (via satellite): ABC Family Channel; AmericanLife TV Network; Animal Planet; Arts & Entertainment; CNBC; CNN; Country Music TV; C-SPAN; Discovery Channel; Disney Channel; E! Entertainment Television; ESPN; Food Network; Fox News Channel; Fox Sports Net Rocky Mountain; FX; Hallmark Channel; Headline News; History Channel; KCNC-TV (CBS) Denver; KUSA (NBC) Denver; KWGN-TV (CW) Denver; Lifetime; MSNBC; QVC; TBS Superstation; The Learning Channel; Travel Channel; Turner Network TV; TV Guide Network; TV Land; USA Network; Weather Channel; WGN America.
Fee: $45.00 installation; $31.50 monthly.
Expanded Basic Service 1
Subscribers: N.A.
Programming (via satellite): AMC; Cartoon Network; Comedy Central; ESPN 2; HGTV; Nickelodeon; Spike TV; VH1.
Fee: $5.95 monthly.
Digital Basic Service
Subscribers: N.A. Included in Arnold
Programming (via satellite): BBC America; Bio; Bravo; Discovery Digital Networks; DMX Music; Encore; ESPN Classic Sports; Fox Sports World; GAS; History Channel International; Independent Film Channel; Lifetime Movie Network; MTV Networks Digital Suite; National Geographic Channel; Nick Jr.; Speed Channel; Syfy; Turner Classic Movies; Versus; WE tv.
Fee: $47.95 monthly.
Pay Service 1
Pay Units: 302.
Programming (via satellite): HBO; Showtime.
Fee: $20.00 installation; $9.00 monthly (each).
Digital Pay Service 1
Pay Units: N.A. Included in analog Pay subs
Programming (via satellite): Cinemax (multiplexed); Encore (multiplexed); HBO (multiplexed); Showtime (multiplexed); Starz (multiplexed); The Movie Channel (multiplexed).
Fee: $12.00 monthly (HBO, Cinemax, Starz/Encore or Showtime/TMC).
Video-On-Demand: No
Pay-Per-View
Addressable homes: 162.
iN DEMAND (delivered digitally), Fee: $3.49, Addressable: Yes; Sports PPV.
Internet Service
Operational: Yes, Both DSL & dial-up.
Subscribers: 511.
Broadband Service: In-house.
Fee: $49.95 installation; $39.95 monthly.
Telephone Service
None
Miles of Plant: 35.0 (coaxial); None (fiber optic). Homes passed included in Arnold
General Manager: Lea Ann Quist. Chief Technician: Mark Stottler. Marketing Manager: Casey Garrigan.
City fee: $25 annually.
Ownership: Great Plains Communications Inc. (MSO).

GREELEY—Center Cable Co., PO Box 117, Greeley, NE 68842-0117. Phones: 308-428-2915 (Office); 308-428-5925 (Home). Fax: 308-428-5585. ICA: NE0179.
TV Market Ranking: Outside TV Markets (GREELEY). Franchise award date: N.A. Franchise expiration date: N.A. Began: April 1, 1982.
Channel capacity: 35 (operating 2-way). Channels available but not in use: None.
Basic Service
Subscribers: 145.
Programming (received off-air): KGIN (CBS, MNT) Grand Island; KHAS-TV (NBC) Hastings; KHGI-TV (ABC) Kearney; KOLN (CBS, MNT) Lincoln.
Programming (via satellite): TBS Superstation; WGN America.
Fee: $33.99 monthly.
Pay Service 1
Pay Units: N.A.
Programming (via satellite): Cinemax; HBO.
Fee: $11.95 monthly (each).
Video-On-Demand: No
Internet Service
Operational: Yes.
Subscribers: 100.
Broadband Service: In-house.
Fee: $24.95-$44.95 monthly.
Telephone Service
None
Miles of Plant: 5.0 (coaxial); None (fiber optic). Homes passed: 180. Total homes in franchised area: 180.
Manager: Martin Callahan.
Ownership: Center Cable TV.

GREENWOOD—Charter Communications. Now served by SPRINGFIELD (formerly Plattsmouth), NE [NE0020]. ICA: NE0159.

GRESHAM—Galaxy Cablevision, 1928 S Lincoln Ave, Ste 200, York, NE 68467. Phone: 402-362-3332. Fax: 402-362-4890. Web Site: http://www.galaxycable.com. ICA: NE0195.
TV Market Ranking: Outside TV Markets (GRESHAM). Franchise award date: N.A. Franchise expiration date: N.A. Began: March 1, 1983.
Channel capacity: 41 (not 2-way capable). Channels available but not in use: 20.
Basic Service
Subscribers: 25.
Programming (received off-air): KHAS-TV (NBC) Hastings; KLKN (ABC) Lincoln; KOLN (CBS, MNT) Lincoln; KPTM (FOX, MNT) Omaha; KUON-TV (PBS) Lincoln.
Programming (via satellite): ABC Family Channel; Arts & Entertainment; CNN; Discovery Channel; Disney Channel; ESPN; Fox Sports Net Midwest; Headline News; Outdoor Channel; TBS Superstation; Turner Classic Movies; Turner Network TV; USA Network; WGN America.
Fee: $35.00 installation; $33.95 monthly.
Pay Service 1
Pay Units: 6.
Programming (via satellite): Cinemax.
Fee: $11.95 monthly.
Pay Service 2
Pay Units: 6.
Programming (via satellite): HBO.
Fee: $12.95 monthly.
Internet Service
Operational: No.
Telephone Service
None
Miles of Plant: 4.0 (coaxial); None (fiber optic). Homes passed: 143.
State Manager: Cheyenne Wohlford. Technical Manager: Carl Stanley. Sales Manager: Mike Thomas. Customer Service Manager: Donna Bryant.
City fee: 1% of basic.
Ownership: Galaxy Cable Inc. (MSO).

GRETNA—Galaxy Cablevision, 1928 S Lincoln Ave, Ste 200, York, NE 68467. Phone: 402-362-3332. Fax: 402-362-4890. Web Site: http://www.galaxycable.com. Also serves Douglas County (portions), Elkhorn, Sarpy County (portions), Valley & Waterloo. ICA: NE0060.
TV Market Ranking: 53,91 (Douglas County (portions), Elkhorn, GRETNA, Sarpy County (portions), Valley, Waterloo). Franchise award date: N.A. Franchise expiration date: N.A. Began: September 1, 1981.
Channel capacity: 41 (not 2-way capable). Channels available but not in use: None.
Basic Service
Subscribers: 505.
Programming (received off-air): KETV (ABC) Omaha; KMTV-TV (CBS) Omaha; KOLN (CBS, MNT) Lincoln; KPTM (FOX, MNT) Omaha; KUON-TV (PBS) Lincoln; KXVO (CW) Omaha; KYNE-TV (PBS) Omaha; WOWT-TV (IND, NBC) Omaha.
Programming (via satellite): ABC Family Channel; AMC; Arts & Entertainment; Cartoon Network; CNBC; CNN; Comedy Central; Discovery Channel; Disney Channel; ESPN; ESPN 2; Fox News Channel; Fox Sports Net Midwest; Fuse; FX; Great American Country; Headline News; History Channel; INSP; Lifetime; Outdoor Channel; QVC; Syfy; TBS Superstation; Toon Disney; Travel Channel; Turner Classic Movies; Turner Network TV; TV Land; USA Network; Weather Channel; WGN America.
Current originations: Public Access.
Fee: $31.45 monthly.
Digital Basic Service
Subscribers: 42.
Programming (via satellite): AmericanLife TV Network; BBC America; Bio; Bloomberg Television; Discovery Digital Networks; DMX Music; ESPN Classic Sports; ESPNews; FitTV; Fox Sports World; FSN Digital Atlantic; FSN Digital Central; FSN Digital Pacific; G4; Golf Channel; GSN; History Channel International; Lime; National Geographic Channel; Speed Channel; Style Network; WE tv.
Fee: $13.95 monthly.
Digital Expanded Basic Service
Subscribers: N.A.
Programming (via satellite): DMX Music; Encore; Fox Movie Channel; Lifetime Movie Network.
Fee: $13.95 monthly.
Pay Service 1
Pay Units: 173.
Programming (via satellite): HBO.
Fee: $12.95 monthly.
Pay Service 2
Pay Units: 55.
Programming (via satellite): Cinemax.
Fee: $11.95 monthly.
Pay Service 3
Pay Units: 41.
Programming (via satellite): Showtime.
Fee: $7.95 monthly.
Pay Service 4
Pay Units: 36.
Programming (via satellite): Encore.
Fee: $3.95 monthly.
Digital Pay Service 1
Pay Units: N.A.
Programming (via satellite): Cinemax (multiplexed); Flix; HBO (multiplexed); Showtime (multiplexed); The Movie Channel (multiplexed).
Fee: $10.00 monthly.
Video-On-Demand: No
Pay-Per-View
Addressable homes: 91.
ESPN Now (delivered digitally), Fee: $3.99, Addressable: Yes; Hot Choice (delivered digitally); Movies (delivered digitally); Playboy TV (delivered digitally); Fresh

(delivered digitally); Shorteez (delivered digitally); sports (delivered digitally); Urban Xtra (delivered digitally).

Internet Service
Operational: No.

Telephone Service
None

Miles of Plant: 51.0 (coaxial); None (fiber optic). Homes passed: 3,662.

State Manager: Cheyenne Wohlford. Technical Manager: Carl Stanley. Sales Manager: Mike Thomas. Customer Service Manager: Donna Bryant.

Ownership: Galaxy Cable Inc. (MSO).

GUIDE ROCK—Glenwood Telecommunications, PO Box 97, 510 W Gage St, Blue Hill, NE 68930. Phone: 402-756-3130. Fax: 402-756-3134. E-mail: info@gtmc.net. Web Site: http://www.gtmc.net. ICA: NE0192.

TV Market Ranking: Below 100 (GUIDE ROCK). Franchise award date: January 1, 1988. Franchise expiration date: N.A. Began: August 1, 1989.

Channel capacity: 42 (operating 2-way). Channels available but not in use: 10.

Basic Service
Subscribers: 57.
Programming (received off-air): KGIN (CBS, MNT) Grand Island; KHAS-TV (NBC) Hastings; KHGI-TV (ABC) Kearney.
Programming (via satellite): ABC Family Channel; Arts & Entertainment; CNN; Country Music TV; Discovery Channel; ESPN; Fox Sports Net; Headline News; History Channel; Network One; Spike TV; TBS Superstation; The Learning Channel; Turner Classic Movies; Turner Network TV; USA Network; Weather Channel; WGN America.
Fee: $40.00 installation; $25.50 monthly.

Pay Service 1
Pay Units: N.A.
Programming (via satellite): HBO.
Fee: $10.00 installation; $12.95 monthly.

Pay Service 2
Pay Units: 4.
Programming (via satellite): Showtime.
Fee: $10.95 monthly.

Video-On-Demand: No

Internet Service
Operational: Yes.
Fee: $24.95 monthly.

Telephone Service
None

Miles of Plant: 3.0 (coaxial); None (fiber optic). Homes passed: 146. Total homes in franchised area: 161.

Manager: Stanley Rouse. Chief Technician: Brad Gilbert.

Ownership: Glenwood Telecommunications (MSO).

HADAR—Sky Scan Cable Co. Now served by NORFOLK, NE [NE0006]. ICA: NE0288.

HAIGLER—BWTelcom, PO Box 645, 607 Chief St, Benkelman, NE 69021. Phones: 800-835-0053; 308-394-6000; 308-423-2000. Fax: 308-423-5818. E-mail: randy@bwtelcom.net. Web Site: http://www.bwtelcom.net. ICA: NE0232.

TV Market Ranking: Outside TV Markets (HAIGLER). Franchise award date: N.A. Franchise expiration date: N.A. Began: September 1, 1989.

Channel capacity: 38 (operating 2-way). Channels available but not in use: 6.

Basic Service
Subscribers: 67.
Programming (received off-air): KBSL-DT (CBS) Goodland; KCNC-TV (CBS) Denver; KWGN-TV (CW) Denver; KWNB-TV (ABC) Hayes Center.
Programming (via satellite): ABC Family Channel; Arts & Entertainment; CNBC; CNN; Country Music TV; Discovery Channel; Disney Channel; ESPN; ESPN 2; Fox Sports Net Rocky Mountain; KPNE-TV (PBS) North Platte; KSNK (NBC) McCook; Lifetime; MTV; Nickelodeon; Outdoor Channel; Spike TV; Syfy; TBS Superstation; The Learning Channel; Turner Network TV; TV Land; USA Network; VH1; Weather Channel; WGN America.
Fee: $45.00 installation; $22.65 monthly.

Pay Service 1
Pay Units: N.A.
Programming (via satellite): HBO; Showtime; The Movie Channel.
Fee: $10.00 installation; $11.95 monthly (Showtime & TMC), $12.49 monthly (HBO).

Video-On-Demand: No

Internet Service
Operational: No, DSL.

Telephone Service
None

Miles of Plant: 3.0 (coaxial); None (fiber optic). Homes passed: 120.

Manager & Chief Technician: Randall Raile. Marketing Director: Loretta Raile.

Ownership: Benkelman Telephone Co. (MSO).

HARDY—Formerly served by Diode Cable Co. No longer in operation. ICA: NE0230.

HARRISON—Windbreak Cable TV, 1140 10th St, Gering, NE 69341-3239. Phone: 308-436-4650. Fax: 308-436-4779. E-mail: bill@intertech.net. Web Site: http://www.windbreak.com/. ICA: NE0380.

TV Market Ranking: Outside TV Markets (HARRISON).

Channel capacity: 36 (operating 2-way). Channels available but not in use: 4.

Basic Service
Subscribers: 51.
Programming (received off-air): KDUH-TV (ABC) Scottsbluff; KSTF (CBS, CW) Scottsbluff; KTNE-TV (PBS) Alliance.
Programming (via satellite): ABC Family Channel; CNN; Discovery Channel; Hallmark Channel; KLWY (FOX) Cheyenne; KUSA (NBC) Denver; KWGN-TV (CW) Denver; Spike TV; TBS Superstation; USA Network; Weather Channel.
Fee: $20.20 installation; $20.30 monthly.

Pay Service 1
Pay Units: 2.
Programming (via satellite): Showtime.
Fee: $20.00 installation; $7.95 monthly.

Pay Service 2
Pay Units: 1.
Programming (via satellite): The Movie Channel.
Fee: $20.00 installation; $7.95 monthly.

Video-On-Demand: No

Internet Service
Operational: Yes. Began: January 1, 1998.
Subscribers: 4.
Broadband Service: In-house.
Fee: $24.95-$39.95 monthly.

Telephone Service
None

Miles of Plant: 32.0 (coaxial); None (fiber optic). Homes passed: 170. Total homes in franchised area: 170.

Manager & Chief Technician: Bill Bauer. Office Manager: Cheryl McLean.

Ownership: WinDBreak Cable (MSO).

HARTINGTON—CedarVision Inc., PO Box 157, 104 W Centre St, Hartington, NE 68739. Phone: 402-254-3933. Fax: 402-254-2453. E-mail: htc@hartel.net. Web Site: http://www.hartel.net. ICA: NE0063.

TV Market Ranking: Outside TV Markets (HARTINGTON). Franchise award date: December 18, 1979. Franchise expiration date: N.A. Began: May 1, 1981.

Channel capacity: 14 (not 2-way capable). Channels available but not in use: None.

Basic Service
Subscribers: 589.
Programming (received off-air): KCAU-TV (ABC) Sioux City; KELO-TV (CBS, MNT) Sioux Falls; KMEG (CBS) Sioux City; KPTH (FOX, MNT) Sioux City; KSFY-TV (ABC) Sioux Falls; KTIV (CW, NBC) Sioux City; KUSD-TV (PBS) Vermillion; KXNE-TV (PBS) Norfolk.
Programming (via satellite): ABC Family Channel; AMC; Animal Planet; Arts & Entertainment; CNN; Comedy Central; Discovery Channel; Disney Channel; ESPN; ESPN 2; Eternal Word TV Network; Great American Country; Hallmark Channel; HGTV; History Channel; Lifetime; Nickelodeon; Spike TV; TBS Superstation; The Learning Channel; Turner Classic Movies; Turner Network TV; USA Network; Weather Channel; WGN America.
Current originations: Public Access.
Fee: $25.00 installation; $18.75 monthly.

Pay Service 1
Pay Units: 80.
Programming (via satellite): HBO.
Fee: $9.50 monthly.

Pay Service 2
Pay Units: 34.
Programming (via satellite): Cinemax.
Fee: $8.00 monthly.

Video-On-Demand: No

Internet Service
Operational: No, DSL.

Telephone Service
None

Miles of Plant: 3.0 (coaxial); None (fiber optic). Homes passed: 688.

Manager: William Dendinger. Marketing Manager: Mike Becker. Chief Technician: Bill Noecker.

Ownership: Hartington Telephone Co.

HASTINGS—Charter Communications, 229 N St Joseph, Hastings, NE 68901. Phones: 308-389-4070 (Grand Island office); 402-462-5153. Fax: 402-462-4350. Web Site: http://www.charter.com. Also serves Adams County & Hastings AFB. ICA: NE0010.

TV Market Ranking: 91 (Adams County, HASTINGS, Hastings AFB). Franchise award date: N.A. Franchise expiration date: N.A. Began: June 1, 1969.

Channel capacity: N.A. Channels available but not in use: N.A.

Basic Service
Subscribers: 6,264.
Programming (received off-air): KGIN (CBS, MNT) Grand Island; KHAS-TV (NBC) Hastings; KHGI-TV (ABC) Kearney; KHNE-TV (PBS) Hastings; KLKN (ABC) Lincoln; KTVG-TV (FOX) Grand Island; 13 FMs.
Programming (via satellite): C-SPAN; C-SPAN 2; Eternal Word TV Network; Home Shopping Network; QVC; TV Guide Network; WGN America.
Current originations: Educational Access; Government Access.
Fee: $29.99 installation; $2.00 converter.

Expanded Basic Service 1
Subscribers: N.A.
Programming (via satellite): ABC Family Channel; AMC; Animal Planet; Arts & Entertainment; Cartoon Network; CNBC; CNN; Comedy Central; Country Music TV; Discovery Channel; Disney Channel; E! Entertainment Television; ESPN; ESPN 2; ESPN Classic Sports; FitTV; Food Network; Fox News Channel; Fox Sports Net Midwest; FX; G4; GalaVision; Golf Channel; Hallmark Channel; Headline News; HGTV; History Channel; Lifetime; MSNBC; MTV; National Geographic Channel; Nickelodeon; Oxygen; SoapNet; Speed Channel; Spike TV; Syfy; TBS Superstation; The Learning Channel; Toon Disney; Travel Channel; truTV; Turner Network TV; TV Land; Univision; USA Network; Versus; VH1; Weather Channel.
Fee: $47.99 monthly.

Digital Basic Service
Subscribers: N.A.
Programming (via satellite): BBC America; Bio; Bloomberg Television; Bravo; Canales N; Discovery Digital Networks; DMX Music; ESPNews; Fox Sports World; GAS; GSN; Halogen Network; History Channel International; Independent Film Channel; Lifetime Movie Network; MTV Networks Digital Suite; Nick Jr.; Outdoor Channel; Sundance Channel; Trinity Broadcasting Network; Turner Classic Movies; TV Guide Interactive Inc.; WE tv.

Digital Pay Service 1
Pay Units: 466.
Programming (via satellite): Encore (multiplexed); HBO (multiplexed); The Movie Channel (multiplexed).
Fee: $11.95 monthly.

Digital Pay Service 2
Pay Units: N.A.
Programming (via satellite): Cinemax (multiplexed); Showtime (multiplexed); Starz (multiplexed).

Video-On-Demand: Yes

Pay-Per-View
iN DEMAND (delivered digitally); Playboy TV (delivered digitally); Fresh (delivered digitally); Shorteez (delivered digitally).

Internet Service
Operational: Yes.
Broadband Service: Charter Pipeline.
Fee: $29.99 monthly.

Telephone Service
Digital: Operational

Miles of Plant: 126.0 (coaxial); None (fiber optic). Homes passed: 9,424. Total homes in franchised area: 9,450.

General Manager: Steve Schirber. Plant Manager: Terry Petzoldt. Office Manager: Mary Ivers.

City fee: 5% of gross.

Ownership: Charter Communications Inc. (MSO).

HAY SPRINGS—Great Plains Communications, PO Box 500, 1600 Great Plains Centre, Blair, NE 68008-0500. Phones: 888-343-8014; 402-426-9511. Fax: 402-456-6550. E-mail: lquist@gpcom.com. Web Site: http://www.gpcom.com. ICA: NE0095.

TV Market Ranking: Outside TV Markets (HAY SPRINGS). Franchise award date: January 1, 1983. Franchise expiration date: N.A. Began: October 1, 1983.

Channel capacity: 80 (operating 2-way). Channels available but not in use: None.

Basic Service

Subscribers: N.A. Included in Arnold

Programming (received off-air): KCNC-TV (CBS) Denver; KDUH-TV (ABC) Scottsbluff; KEVN-TV (FOX) Rapid City; KSTF (CBS, CW) Scottsbluff; KTNE-TV (PBS) Alliance; KUSA (NBC) Denver.

Programming (via satellite): ABC Family Channel; Animal Planet; Arts & Entertainment; CNN; Discovery Channel; Disney Channel; ESPN; ESPN 2; Fox News Channel; Fox Sports Net; Great American Country; Hallmark Channel; Headline News; HGTV; History Channel; KWGN-TV (CW) Denver; Lifetime; MSNBC; Nickelodeon; QVC; Spike TV; TBS Superstation; The Learning Channel; Turner Classic Movies; Turner Network TV; TV Land; USA Network; Weather Channel; WGN America.

Fee: $28.00 installation; $31.50 monthly.

Digital Basic Service

Subscribers: N.A. Included to Arnold

Programming (via satellite): BBC America; Bio; Bravo; Discovery Digital Networks; ESPN Classic Sports; ESPNews; Fox Sports World; Golf Channel; GSN; History Channel International; Independent Film Channel; Lifetime Movie Network; National Geographic Channel; Outdoor Channel; Speed Channel; Syfy; Trio; Versus; WE tv.

Fee: $47.95 monthly.

Digital Pay Service 1

Pay Units: N.A.

Programming (via satellite): Cinemax (multiplexed); Encore (multiplexed); Flix; HBO (multiplexed); Showtime (multiplexed); Starz (multiplexed); The Movie Channel (multiplexed).

Fee: $12.00 monthly (HBO, Cinemax, Starz/Encore or Showtime/TMC).

Video-On-Demand: No

Pay-Per-View

iN DEMAND (delivered digitally); ESPN (delivered digitally).

Internet Service

Operational: Yes, Both DSL & dial-up.

Broadband Service: In-house.

Fee: $49.95 installation; $39.95 monthly.

Telephone Service

None

Miles of Plant: 7.0 (coaxial); None (fiber optic). Homes passed included in Arnold

Manager: Lea Ann Quist. Chief Technician: Mark Stottler. Marketing Manager: Casey Garrigan.

City fee: 3% of gross.

Ownership: Great Plains Communications Inc. (MSO).

HEBRON—Diode Telecom, Inc, PO Box 236, 300 Commercial St, Diller, NE 68342. Phones: 402-793-2532; 402-793-5125. Fax: 402-793-5139. E-mail: diodedonna@diodecom.net. Web Site: http://www.diodecom.net. ICA: NE0068.

TV Market Ranking: Below 100 (HEBRON). Franchise award date: N.A. Franchise expiration date: N.A. Began: December 1, 1980.

Channel capacity: N.A. Channels available but not in use: N.A.

Basic Service

Subscribers: 502.

Programming (received off-air): KHAS-TV (NBC) Hastings; KHNE-TV (PBS) Hastings; KLKN (ABC) Lincoln; KOLN (CBS, MNT) Lincoln.

Programming (via satellite): C-SPAN; Eternal Word TV Network; QVC; Trinity Broadcasting Network; Weather Channel.

Fee: $17.80 monthly.

Expanded Basic Service 1

Subscribers: N.A.

Programming (via satellite): ABC Family Channel; AMC; AmericanLife TV Network; Animal Planet; Arts & Entertainment; Cartoon Network; CNBC; CNN; Comedy Central; Country Music TV; Discovery Channel; Disney Channel; E! Entertainment Television; ESPN; ESPN 2; ESPN Classic Sports; Food Network; Fox News Channel; Fox Sports Net Midwest; FX; Great American Country; GSN; Hallmark Channel; Headline News; HGTV; History Channel; Lifetime; MTV; National Geographic Channel; Nickelodeon; Outdoor Channel; Speed Channel; Spike TV; Syfy; TBS Superstation; The Learning Channel; Travel Channel; truTV; Turner Classic Movies; Turner Network TV; TV Land; USA Network; VH1; WGN America.

Fee: $14.20 monthly.

Digital Basic Service

Subscribers: N.A.

Programming (via satellite): BBC America; Bio; Bloomberg Television; Bravo; Discovery Health Channel; Discovery Home Channel; Discovery Kids Channel; Discovery Military Channel; DMX Music; ESPN Classic Sports; ESPNews; FitTV; Fox Movie Channel; Fox Soccer; Fuse; G4; Golf Channel; Halogen Network; History Channel International; ID Investigation Discovery; Independent Film Channel; Lifetime Movie Network; MTV2; National Geographic Channel; Nick Jr.; NickToons TV; Science Channel; Style Network; TeenNick; Toon Disney; Trio; Versus; VH1 Classic; VH1 Country; WE tv.

Fee: $12.50 monthly.

Pay Service 1

Pay Units: N.A.

Programming (via satellite): Cinemax; HBO.

Fee: $7.50 monthly (Cinemax), $10.25 monthly (HBO).

Digital Pay Service 1

Pay Units: N.A.

Programming (via satellite): Cinemax (multiplexed); HBO (multiplexed); Showtime (multiplexed); Starz (multiplexed).

Video-On-Demand: No

Internet Service

Operational: Yes.

Broadband Service: In-house.

Fee: $24.95 monthly.

Telephone Service

None

Homes passed: 625.

President: Randy Sandman. Chief Technician: Jeff Nelson. Marketing Director: Danni Stark.

Ownership: Diode Cable Co. Inc. (MSO).

HEMINGFORD—Mobius Communications Co., PO Box 246, 523 Niobrara Ave, Hemingford, NE 69348. Phone: 308-487-5500. E-mail: info@bbc.net. Web Site: http://www.bbc.net. ICA: NE0389.

TV Market Ranking: Outside TV Markets (HEMINGFORD).

Channel capacity: N.A. Channels available but not in use: N.A.

Basic Service

Subscribers: N.A. Included in Crawford

Programming (received off-air): KCNC-TV (CBS) Denver; KDVR (FOX) Denver; KMGH-TV (ABC) Denver; KSTF (CBS, CW) Scottsbluff; KTNE-TV (PBS) Alliance; KTVD (MNT) Denver; KUSA (NBC) Denver.

Programming (via satellite): CW+; KDUH-TV (ABC) Scottsbluff; WGN America.

Expanded Basic Service 1

Subscribers: N.A. Included in Crawford

Programming (via satellite): ABC Family Channel; Altitude Sports & Entertainment; Arts & Entertainment; Bravo; CNBC; CNN; Comedy Central; Country Music TV; C-SPAN; Discovery Channel; Disney Channel; E! Entertainment Television; ESPN; ESPN 2; ESPN Classic Sports; Fox News Channel; Fox Sports Net; FX; Headline News; HGTV; History Channel; MSNBC; MTV; National Geographic Channel; Nickelodeon; Oxygen; SoapNet; Spike TV; Syfy; TBS Superstation; The Learning Channel; Travel Channel; Turner Network TV; TV Land; USA Network; VH1; Weather Channel.

Digital Basic Service

Subscribers: N.A. Included in Crawford

Programming (via satellite): AmericanLife TV Network; Arts & Entertainment; BBC America; Bloomberg Television; CMT Pure Country; Current; Discovery Health Channel; Discovery Home Channel; Discovery Kids Channel; Discovery Military Channel; Discovery Times Channel; DMX Music; FitTV; Fox Movie Channel; Fuse; G4; GAS; Golf Channel; GSN; Halogen Network; History Channel; History Channel International; Independent Film Channel; Lifetime Movie Network; MTV Hits; MTV2; Nick Jr.; NickToons TV; Outdoor Channel; Science Channel; Speed Channel; Style Network; Toon Disney; Trinity Broadcasting Network; Turner Classic Movies; Versus; VH1 Classic; VH1 Soul; WE tv.

Pay Service 1

Pay Units: N.A.

Programming (via satellite): HBO.

Digital Pay Service 1

Pay Units: N.A.

Programming (via satellite): Cinemax (multiplexed); Encore (multiplexed); Flix; HBO (multiplexed); Showtime (multiplexed); Starz (multiplexed); The Movie Channel (multiplexed).

Video-On-Demand: No

Internet Service

Operational: No.

Broadband Service: Offers dial-up and DSL only; no cable modem service.

Telephone Service

None

Miles of plant & homes passed included in Crawford

General Manager: Theron Jensen. Chief Technician: Randy Dannar.

Ownership: Mobius Communications Co. (MSO).

HENDERSON—Mainstay Cable TV, PO Box 487, 1000 N Main St, Henderson, NE 68371. Phone: 402-723-4448. Fax: 402-723-4451. E-mail: mainstay@mainstaycomm.net. Web Site: http://www.mainstaycomm.net. ICA: NE0087.

TV Market Ranking: 91 (HENDERSON). Franchise award date: August 9, 1982. Franchise expiration date: N.A. Began: December 1, 1982.

Channel capacity: 35 (operating 2-way). Channels available but not in use: 10.

Basic Service

Subscribers: 390.

Programming (received off-air): KHAS-TV (NBC) Hastings; KHGI-TV (ABC) Kearney; KOLN (CBS, MNT) Lincoln; KUON-TV (PBS) Lincoln.

Programming (via satellite): ABC Family Channel; Arts & Entertainment; Cartoon Network; CNN; Discovery Channel; Disney Channel; ESPN; ESPN 2; Fox News Channel; Fox Sports Net; Hallmark Channel; HGTV; History Channel; INSP; National Geographic Channel; Nickelodeon; Spike TV; TBS Superstation; The Learning Channel; Turner Classic Movies; Turner Network TV; TV Land; USA Network; Weather Channel; WGN America.

Planned originations: Religious Access; Public Access.

Fee: $25.00 installation; $26.00 monthly.

Pay Service 1

Pay Units: 35.

Programming (via satellite): HBO.

Fee: $10.00 monthly.

Video-On-Demand: No

Internet Service

Operational: No, DSL.

Broadband Service: In-house.

Telephone Service

None

Miles of Plant: 13.0 (coaxial); None (fiber optic). Homes passed: 450. Total homes in franchised area: 450.

Manager: Matt Friesen.

City fee: 3% of gross.

Ownership: Mainstay Communications.

HOLDREGE—Charter Communications. Now served by KEARNEY, NE [NE0011]. ICA: NE0028.

HOMER—HunTel Cablevision. Now served by WAYNE, NE [NE0374]. ICA: NE0372.

HOOPER—WesTel Systems, PO Box 330, 012 E 3rd St, Remsen, IA 51050. Phones: 712-786-1181; 800-628-5989; 402-654-3344. Fax: 712-786-2400. E-mail: acctinfo@westelsystems.com. Web Site: http://www.westelsystems.com. Also serves Uehling & Winslow. ICA: NE0131.

TV Market Ranking: Outside TV Markets (HOOPER, Uehling, Winslow). Franchise award date: N.A. Franchise expiration date: N.A. Began: January 1, 1984.

Channel capacity: 40 (not 2-way capable). Channels available but not in use: 1.

Basic Service

Subscribers: 330.

Programming (received off-air): KETV (ABC) Omaha; KLKN (ABC) Lincoln; KMTV-TV (CBS) Omaha; KOLN (CBS, MNT) Lincoln; KPTM (FOX, MNT) Omaha; KUON-TV (PBS) Lincoln; KXVO (CW) Omaha; WOWT-TV (IND, NBC) Omaha.

Programming (via satellite): ABC Family Channel; AMC; Arts & Entertainment; Cartoon Network; CNN; Country Music TV; Discovery Channel; Disney Channel; Do-It-Yourself; ESPN; ESPN 2; Food Network; Fox News Channel; Fox Sports Net; FX; Great American Country; Headline News; HGTV; History Channel; Lifetime; MSNBC; MTV; Nickelodeon; QVC; Speed Channel; Spike TV; Syfy; TBS Superstation; The Learning Channel; Travel Channel; Turner Classic Movies; Turner Network TV; TV Land; USA Network; Versus; VH1; WE tv; Weather Channel; WGN America.

Fee: $30.00 installation; $28.95 monthly.

Digital Basic Service
Subscribers: N.A.
Programming (via satellite): BBC America; Bio; Bloomberg Television; CMT Pure Country; Discovery Health Channel; Discovery Kids Channel; Discovery Military Channel; Discovery Planet Green; DMX Music; ESPN Classic Sports; ESPNews; FitTV; Fox Movie Channel; Fox Soccer; Fuse; Golf Channel; GSN; History Channel International; ID Investigation Discovery; Lifetime Movie Network; MTV Hits; MTV2; Nick Jr.; NickToons TV; Outdoor Channel; RFD-TV; Science Channel; ShopNBC; SoapNet; Style Network; TeenNick; The Word Network; Toon Disney; Trinity Broadcasting Network; Turner Classic Movies; VH1 Classic; VH1 Soul.
Pay Service 1
Pay Units: N.A.
Programming (via satellite): Cinemax; HBO.
Fee: $12.95 monthly.
Digital Pay Service 1
Pay Units: N.A.
Programming (via satellite): Cinemax (multiplexed); Encore (multiplexed); Flix; HBO (multiplexed); Showtime (multiplexed); Starz (multiplexed); The Movie Channel (multiplexed).
Internet Service
Operational: No.
Telephone Service
None
Miles of Plant: 6.0 (coaxial); None (fiber optic). Homes passed: 392.
Manager: Jim Sherburn.
City fee: 4% of basic.
Ownership: West Iowa Telephone Co. (MSO).

HORDVILLE—Mid-State Community TV. Now served by AURORA, NE [NE0033]. ICA: NE0293.

HOWELLS—Formerly served by TelePartners. No longer in operation. ICA: NE0363.

HUBBARD—CenCom Inc. This cable system has converted to IPTV. See Hubbard (village), NE [NE018]. ICA: NE0375.

HUBBARD (village)—CenCom NNTV. Formerly [NE0375]. This cable system has converted to IPTV., 110 E Elk St, Jackson, NE 68743-0066. Phones: 402-623-4321; 888-397-4321. E-mail: nntc@nntc.net. Web Site: http://www.nntc.net. ICA: NE5018.
Channel capacity: N.A. Channels available but not in use: N.A.
Internet Service
Operational: Yes.
Telephone Service
Digital: Operational
General Manager: Emory Graffis.
Ownership: Northeast Nebraska Telephone Co.

HUMPHREY—Cable Nebraska, 2123 Central Ave, Ste 200, Kearney, NE 68847. Phone: 308-236-1512. Web Site: http://www.cablene.com. ICA: NE0142.
TV Market Ranking: Outside TV Markets (HUMPHREY). Franchise award date: N.A. Franchise expiration date: N.A. Began: January 1, 1984.
Channel capacity: 41 (not 2-way capable). Channels available but not in use: None.
Basic Service
Subscribers: 297.
Programming (received off-air): KLKN (ABC) Lincoln; KOLN (CBS, MNT) Lincoln; KPTM (FOX, MNT) Omaha; KXNE-TV (PBS) Norfolk; KXVO (CW) Omaha; WOWT-TV (IND, NBC) Omaha.
Programming (via satellite): ABC Family Channel; AMC; Animal Planet; Arts & Entertainment; Cartoon Network; CNBC; CNN; C-SPAN; Discovery Channel; E! Entertainment Television; ESPN; ESPN 2; Eternal Word TV Network; Food Network; Fox News Channel; Fox Sports Net Midwest; FX; Great American Country; Headline News; HGTV; History Channel; Lifetime; MSNBC; Nickelodeon; Outdoor Channel; QVC; TBS Superstation; The Learning Channel; Turner Network TV; USA Network; VH1; Weather Channel; WGN America.
Fee: $35.00 installation; $29.95 monthly.
Pay Service 1
Pay Units: N.A.
Programming (via satellite): Cinemax; HBO.
Internet Service
Operational: No.
Miles of Plant: 8.0 (coaxial); None (fiber optic). Homes passed: 342.
Operations Manager: Stuart Gilbertson.
City fee: 3% of gross.
Ownership: USA Companies (MSO).

HYANNIS—Consolidated Cable Inc., PO Box 6147, 6900 Van Dorn St, Ste 21, Lincoln, NE 68506-0147. Phones: 402-489-2728; 800-742-7464. Fax: 402-489-9034. E-mail: service@consolidatedtelephone.com. Web Site: http://www.nebnet.net. Also serves Arthur, Grant County (portions) & Mullen. ICA: NE0099.
TV Market Ranking: Outside TV Markets (Arthur, Grant County (portions), HYANNIS, Mullen). Franchise award date: January 1, 1983. Franchise expiration date: N.A. Began: N.A.
Channel capacity: 78 (2-way capable). Channels available but not in use: 35.
Basic Service
Subscribers: 353.
Programming (received off-air): KDUH-TV (ABC) Scottsbluff; KNOP-TV (NBC) North Platte; KRNE-TV (PBS) Merriman.
Programming (via satellite): ABC Family Channel; Animal Planet; Arts & Entertainment; Cartoon Network; CNN; Country Music TV; Discovery Channel; Disney Channel; ESPN; ESPN 2; Fox News Channel; Fox Sports Net Rocky Mountain; Hallmark Channel; Headline News; HGTV; History Channel; Home Shopping Network; KCNC-TV (CBS) Denver; KDVR (FOX) Denver; KWGN-TV (CW) Denver; KWNB-TV (ABC) Hayes Center; MSNBC; MTV; Nickelodeon; Spike TV; Syfy; TBS Superstation; The Learning Channel; Turner Classic Movies; Turner Network TV; TV Land; USA Network; Versus; VH1; Weather Channel; WGN America.
Fee: $25.95 monthly.
Digital Basic Service
Subscribers: N.A.
Programming (via satellite): AmericanLife TV Network; Bloomberg Television; CMT Pure Country; DMX Music; ESPN Classic Sports; ESPNews; FitTV; Fox College Sports Atlantic; Fox College Sports Central; Fox College Sports Pacific; Fox Movie Channel; G4; GAS; Golf Channel; GSN; Halogen Network; Independent Film Channel; Lifetime Movie Network; MTV Networks Digital Suite; Nick Jr.; NickToons TV; Outdoor Channel; Sleuth; Speed Channel; Style Network; Sundance Channel; Toon Disney; Trinity Broadcasting Network; WE tv.
Fee: $24.00 monthly.

Pay Service 1
Pay Units: 46.
Programming (via satellite): HBO.
Fee: $9.00 monthly.
Pay Service 2
Pay Units: 3.
Programming (via satellite): Showtime.
Fee: $9.00 monthly.
Digital Pay Service 1
Pay Units: N.A.
Programming (via satellite): Cinemax (multiplexed); Encore (multiplexed); Flix; HBO (multiplexed); Showtime (multiplexed); Starz (multiplexed); The Movie Channel (multiplexed).
Fee: $9.00 monthly (each).
Video-On-Demand: No
Pay-Per-View
iN DEMAND (delivered digitally); Hot Choice (delivered digitally); Playboy TV (delivered digitally); Urban American Television Network (delivered digitally); Fresh (delivered digitally).
Internet Service
Operational: No, DSL only.
Telephone Service
None
Miles of Plant: 9.0 (coaxial); None (fiber optic). Homes passed: 588. Total homes in franchised area: 588.
Manager: Bryan Thompson. Chief Technician: Dan Smith.
City fee: None.
Ownership: Consolidated Cable Inc. (MSO).

INDIANOLA—Pinpoint Cable TV. Now served by CAMBRIDGE, NE [NE0269]. ICA: NE0109.

JANSEN—Formerly served by Diode Cable Co. No longer in operation. ICA: NE0248.

JOHNSON LAKE—Charter Communications. Now served by KEARNEY, NE [NE0011]. ICA: NE0295.

JUNIATA—Charter Communications, 205 N Webb Rd, Grand Island, NE 68803-4038. Phones: 507-289-8372 (Rochester administrative office); 308-389-4070. Fax: 308-382-2047. Web Site: http://www.charter.com. ICA: NE0125.
TV Market Ranking: 91 (JUNIATA). Franchise award date: N.A. Franchise expiration date: N.A. Began: January 1, 1984.
Channel capacity: 36 (not 2-way capable). Channels available but not in use: N.A.
Basic Service
Subscribers: N.A.
Programming (received off-air): KHAS-TV (NBC) Hastings; KHGI-TV (ABC) Kearney; KHNE-TV (PBS) Hastings; KOLN (CBS, MNT) Lincoln; KTVG-TV (FOX) Grand Island.
Programming (via satellite): ABC Family Channel; AMC; Arts & Entertainment; CNBC; CNN; Discovery Channel; Disney Channel; E! Entertainment Television; ESPN; ESPN 2; Fox Sports Net; Great American Country; History Channel; Home Shopping Network; Lifetime; Nickelodeon; Outdoor Channel; Spike TV; Syfy; TBS Superstation; TLC; Trinity Broadcasting Network; Turner Network TV; TV Land; USA Network; VH1; Weather Channel; WGN America.
Pay Service 1
Pay Units: 39.
Programming (via satellite): Cinemax; HBO.
Fee: $10.45 monthly (each).
Video-On-Demand: No
Internet Service
Operational: Yes.
Fee: $19.99 monthly.
Telephone Service
Digital: Operational
Fee: $14.99 monthly
Miles of Plant: 8.0 (coaxial); None (fiber optic). Homes passed: 300.
Vice President & General Manager: John Crowley. Technical Operations Director: Marty Kovarik. Technical Operations Manager: Terry Petzoldt. Office Manager: Mary Ivers.
Ownership: Charter Communications Inc. (MSO).

KEARNEY—Charter Communications, PO Box 1448, 809 Central Ave, Kearney, NE 68848-1448. Phones: 507-289-8372 (Rochester administrative office); 308-236-1500. Fax: 308-236-1509. Web Site: http://www.charter.com. Also serves Amherst, Axtell, Bertrand, Cairo, Cozad, Dawson County (portions), Elm Creek, Gothenburg, Hildreth, Holdredge, Johnson Lake, Lexington, Litchfield, Loomis, Loup City, Miller (unincorporated areas), Minden, Odessa, Ord, Overton, Phillips, Pleasanton, Ravenna, Riverdale (village), St. Libory, Sumner & Wilcox. ICA: NE0011.
TV Market Ranking: 91 (Amherst, Axtell, Bertrand, Cairo, Elm Creek, Hildreth, Holdredge, KEARNEY, Lexington, Litchfield, Loomis, Miller (unincorporated areas), Minden, Odessa, Overton, Phillips, Pleasanton, Ravenna, Riverdale (village), St. Libory, Sumner, Wilcox); Below 100 (Gothenburg, Lexington (portions)); Outside TV Markets (Cozad, Johnson Lake, Lexington (portions), Loup City, Ord). Franchise award date: N.A. Franchise expiration date: N.A. Began: May 16, 1983.
Channel capacity: N.A. Channels available but not in use: N.A.
Basic Service
Subscribers: 14,642.
Programming (received off-air): KGIN (CBS, MNT) Grand Island; KHAS-TV (NBC) Hastings; KHGI-TV (ABC) Kearney; KHNE-TV (PBS) Hastings; KTVG-TV (FOX) Grand Island; 12 FMs.
Programming (via satellite): C-SPAN; C-SPAN 2; E! Entertainment Television; Eternal Word TV Network; Home Shopping Network; ION Television; QVC; truTV.
Current originations: Religious Access; Educational Access; Public Access.
Planned originations: Government Access.
Fee: $29.99 installation; $1.00 converter.
Expanded Basic Service 1
Subscribers: N.A.
Programming (via satellite): ABC Family Channel; AMC; Animal Planet; Arts & En-

tertainment; Cartoon Network; CNBC; CNN; Comedy Central; Country Music TV; Discovery Channel; Disney Channel; ESPN; ESPN 2; ESPN Classic Sports; FitTV; Food Network; Fox News Channel; Fox Sports Net Midwest; FX; G4; GalaVision; Golf Channel; Hallmark Channel; Headline News; HGTV; History Channel; Lifetime; MSNBC; MTV; National Geographic Channel; Nickelodeon; Oxygen; SoapNet; Speed Channel; Spike TV; Syfy; TBS Superstation; The Learning Channel; Toon Disney; Travel Channel; Trinity Broadcasting Network; Turner Network TV; TV Guide Network; TV Land; USA Network; Versus; VH1; Weather Channel; WGN America.
Fee: $47.99 monthly.

Digital Basic Service
Subscribers: N.A.
Programming (via satellite): BBC America; Bio; Bloomberg Television; Bravo; Discovery Digital Networks; DMX Music; Encore Action; ESPNews; Fox Sports World; GAS; GSN; Halogen Network; History Channel International; Independent Film Channel; Lifetime Movie Network; MTV Networks Digital Suite; Nick Jr.; Outdoor Channel; Style Network; Sundance Channel; Turner Classic Movies; WE tv.

Digital Pay Service 1
Pay Units: 773.
Programming (via satellite): Cinemax (multiplexed); HBO (multiplexed); Showtime (multiplexed); Starz (multiplexed); The Movie Channel.
Fee: $6.00 monthly (Showtime), $7.00 monthly (Cinemax), $10.34 monthly (HBO).

Video-On-Demand: Yes

Pay-Per-View
Addressable: Yes; iN DEMAND (delivered digitally); Fresh (delivered digitally); Shorteez (delivered digitally); Playboy TV (delivered digitally).

Internet Service
Operational: Yes.
Broadband Service: Charter Pipeline.
Fee: $29.99 monthly.

Telephone Service
Digital: Operational

Miles of Plant: 241.0 (coaxial); None (fiber optic).
Vice President & General Manager: John Crowley. Technical Operations Director: Marty Kovarik. Technical Operations Manager: Terry Petzoldt. Marketing Director: Bill Haarstad. Business Manager: Chuck Haase. Office Manager: Dawn Harmon.
City fee: 5% of gross.
Ownership: Charter Communications Inc. (MSO).

KENESAW—Charter Communications, 205 N Webb Rd, Grand Island, NE 68803-4038. Phones: 507-289-8372 (Rochester administrative office); 308-389-4070. Fax: 308-382-2047. Web Site: http://www.charter.com. ICA: NE0379.
TV Market Ranking: 91 (KENESAW). Franchise award date: N.A. Franchise expiration date: N.A. Began: N.A.
Channel capacity: 36 (not 2-way capable). Channels available but not in use: N.A.

Basic Service
Subscribers: 171.
Programming (received off-air): KHAS-TV (NBC) Hastings; KHGI-TV (ABC) Kearney; KHNE-TV (PBS) Hastings; KOLN (CBS, MNT) Lincoln; KTVG-TV (FOX) Grand Island.
Programming (via satellite): ABC Family Channel; AMC; Arts & Entertainment; CNBC; CNN; Discovery Channel; Disney Channel; E! Entertainment Television; ESPN; ESPN 2; Fox Sports Net Midwest; Great American Country; History Channel; Home Shopping Network; Lifetime; Nickelodeon; Outdoor Channel; Spike TV; Syfy; TBS Superstation; The Learning Channel; Trinity Broadcasting Network; Turner Network TV; TV Land; USA Network; VH1; Weather Channel; WGN America.
Fee: $23.55 monthly.

Pay Service 1
Pay Units: 42.
Programming (via satellite): Cinemax (multiplexed); HBO (multiplexed).
Fee: $10.00 monthly (each).

Video-On-Demand: No

Internet Service
Operational: No.

Telephone Service
None

Miles of Plant: 8.0 (coaxial); None (fiber optic). Total homes in franchised area: 327.
Vice President & General Manager: John Crowley. Technical Operations Director: Marty Kovarik. Technical Operations Manager: Terry Petzoldt. Office Manager: Mary Ivers.
Ownership: Charter Communications Inc. (MSO).

KIMBALL—Charter Communications, 3380 Northern Valley Pl NE, Rochester, MN 55906-3954. Phone: 507-289-8372 (Rochester administrative office). Fax: 507-285-6162. Web Site: http://www.charter.com. Also serves Kimball County. ICA: NE0032.
TV Market Ranking: Below 100 (Kimball County (portions)); Outside TV Markets (KIMBALL, Kimball County (portions)). Franchise award date: N.A. Franchise expiration date: N.A. Began: June 1, 1957.
Channel capacity: N.A. Channels available but not in use: N.A.

Basic Service
Subscribers: 1,093.
Programming (received off-air): KDUH-TV (ABC) Scottsbluff; KDVR (FOX) Denver; KSTF (CBS, CW) Scottsbluff; KTNE-TV (PBS) Alliance; KTVD (MNT) Denver; 3 FMs.
Programming (via satellite): C-SPAN; KCNC-TV (CBS) Denver; KMGH-TV (ABC) Denver; KUSA (NBC) Denver; KWGN-TV (CW) Denver; QVC.
Fee: $29.99 installation; $40.00 additional installation.

Expanded Basic Service 1
Subscribers: 1,010.
Programming (via satellite): ABC Family Channel; AMC; Animal Planet; Arts & Entertainment; Cartoon Network; CNBC; CNN; Comedy Central; Country Music TV; Discovery Channel; Disney Channel; E! Entertainment Television; ESPN; ESPN 2; Food Network; Fox News Channel; Fox Sports Net Rocky Mountain; FX; Golf Channel; Great American Country; Hallmark Channel; HGTV; History Channel; Lifetime; MSNBC; MTV; National Geographic Channel; Nickelodeon; Oxygen; SoapNet; Spike TV; Syfy; TBS Superstation; The Learning Channel; Toon Disney; truTV; Turner Classic Movies; Turner Network TV; USA Network; VH1; Weather Channel.
Fee: $47.99 monthly.

Digital Basic Service
Subscribers: N.A.
Programming (via satellite): AmericanLife TV Network; BBC America; Bio; Bloomberg Television; Bravo; Discovery Digital Networks; DMX Music; ESPN Classic Sports; FitTV; Fox Movie Channel; Fox Sports World; Fuse; G4; GAS; GSN; Halogen Network; History Channel International; Independent Film Channel; Lifetime Movie Network; MTV Networks Digital Suite; Nick Jr.; Outdoor Channel; Speed Channel; Trinity Broadcasting Network; TV Guide Interactive Inc.; Versus; WE tv.

Digital Pay Service 1
Pay Units: N.A.
Programming (via satellite): Cinemax (multiplexed); Encore (multiplexed); Flix; HBO (multiplexed); Showtime (multiplexed); Starz (multiplexed); The Movie Channel (multiplexed).

Video-On-Demand: Yes

Pay-Per-View
iN DEMAND (delivered digitally); Hot Choice (delivered digitally); Playboy TV (delivered digitally); Fresh (delivered digitally); Shorteez (delivered digitally).

Internet Service
Operational: Yes.
Broadband Service: Charter Pipeline.
Fee: $29.99 monthly.

Telephone Service
Digital: Operational

Homes passed: 1,639. Total homes in franchised area: 1,639. Miles of plant (coax) included in Sidney
Vice President & General Manager: John Crowley. Technical Operations Director: Marty Kovarik. Technical Operations Manager: Joel Saunders. Marketing Director: Bill Haarstad.
City fee: $1.00-$3.00 per subscriber annually.
Ownership: Charter Communications Inc. (MSO).

LAKE CUNNINGHAM—Formerly served by TelePartners. No longer in operation. ICA: NE0079.

LAKE MALONEY—Charter Communications. Now served by NORTH PLATTE, NE [NE0009]. ICA: NE0297.

LAKE VENTURA—Formerly served by Charter Communications. No longer in operation. ICA: NE0298.

LAKE WACONDA—Formerly served by Westcom. No longer in operation. ICA: NE0343.

LAUREL—American Broadband, 1605 Washington St, Blair, NE 68008-0400. Phones: 402-426-6200; 402-533-1000. Fax: 402-533-1111. Web Site: http://www.abbnebraska.com. ICA: NE0121.
TV Market Ranking: Outside TV Markets (LAUREL). Franchise award date: N.A. Franchise expiration date: N.A. Began: July 1, 1982.
Channel capacity: 41 (operating 2-way). Channels available but not in use: 6.

Basic Service
Subscribers: N.A. Included in Blair
Programming (received off-air): KCAU-TV (ABC) Sioux City; KMEG (CBS) Sioux City; KPTH (FOX, MNT) Sioux City; KSIN-TV (PBS) Sioux City; KTIV (CW, NBC) Sioux City; KXNE-TV (PBS) Norfolk.
Programming (via satellite): ABC Family Channel; AMC; Arts & Entertainment; CNN; Country Music TV; C-SPAN; Discovery Channel; Disney Channel; ESPN; ESPN 2; Fox News Channel; Fox Soccer; FX; Headline News; HGTV; History Channel; Lifetime; MSNBC; MTV; Nickelodeon; QVC; Spike TV; TBS Superstation; Turner Classic Movies; Turner Network TV; TV Land; USA Network; Weather Channel; WGN America.
Current originations: Leased Access.
Fee: $35.00 installation; $29.50 monthly.

Pay Service 1
Pay Units: 50.
Programming (via satellite): HBO.
Fee: $12.95 monthly.

Video-On-Demand: No

Internet Service
Operational: Yes, DSL only.
Broadband Service: In-house.
Fee: $30.00 monthly.

Telephone Service
None

Miles of Plant: 8.0 (coaxial); None (fiber optic). Total homes in area & homes passed included in Blair
Vice President: Rick Plugge.; Karen Aman. General Manager: Mike Jacobsen. Programming Manager: Kay Petersen.
City fee: 5% of gross.
Ownership: American Broadband Communications Inc. (MSO).

LEIGH—Formerly served by TelePartners. No longer in operation. ICA: NE0365.

LEWELLEN—Consolidated Cable Inc., PO Box 6147, 6900 Van Dorn St, Ste 21, Lincoln, NE 68506-0147. Phones: 402-489-2728; 800-742-7464. Fax: 402-489-9034. Web Site: http://www.nebnet.net. ICA: NE0156.
TV Market Ranking: Outside TV Markets (LEWELLEN). Franchise award date: N.A. Franchise expiration date: N.A. Began: February 1, 1989.
Channel capacity: 36 (not 2-way capable). Channels available but not in use: 14.

Basic Service
Subscribers: 27.
Programming (received off-air): KNOP-TV (NBC) North Platte; KPNE-TV (PBS) North Platte; KWNB-TV (ABC) Hayes Center.
Programming (via satellite): ABC Family Channel; Arts & Entertainment; CNN; Country Music TV; Discovery Channel; ESPN; Fox Sports Net Rocky Mountain; Home Shopping Network; KCNC-TV (CBS) Denver; KDVR (FOX) Denver; Nickelodeon; Spike TV; TBS Superstation; Turner Classic Movies; Turner Network TV; USA Network; Weather Channel; WGN America.
Fee: $26.95 monthly.

Pay Service 1
Pay Units: 3.
Programming (via satellite): Showtime.
Fee: $9.00 monthly.

Video-On-Demand: No

Internet Service
Operational: No.

Telephone Service
None

Miles of Plant: 4.0 (coaxial); None (fiber optic). Homes passed: 156.
Manager: Brian D. Thompson. Chief Technician: Dan Smith.
Ownership: Consolidated Cable Inc. (MSO).

LEXINGTON—Charter Communications. Now served by KEARNEY, NE [NE0011]. ICA: NE0022.

LINCOLN—Formerly served by Sprint Corp. No longer in operation. ICA: NE0350.

LINCOLN—Time Warner Cable, 5400 S 16th St, Lincoln, NE 68512-1278. Phones: 402-421-0330; 402-421-0300 (Customer service). Fax: 402-421-0310. Web Site: http://www.timewarnercable.com/Nebraska.

Also serves Crete, Denton, Lancaster County, Seward & Seward County. ICA: NE0002.

TV Market Ranking: 91 (Crete, Denton, Lancaster County, LINCOLN, Seward). Franchise award date: N.A. Franchise expiration date: N.A. Began: September 1, 1968.

Channel capacity: N.A. Channels available but not in use: N.A.

Basic Service

Subscribers: 111,000 Includes Auburn, Columbus, Fairbury, Falls City, Fremont, Superior, & York.

Programming (received off-air): KETV (ABC) Omaha; KLKN (ABC) Lincoln; KMTV-TV (CBS) Omaha; KOLN (CBS, MNT) Lincoln; KPTM (FOX, MNT) Omaha; KUON-TV (PBS) Lincoln; KXVO (CW) Omaha; WOWT-TV (IND, NBC) Omaha.

Programming (via satellite): CNN; C-SPAN; C-SPAN 2; TBS Superstation; The Learning Channel; TV Guide Network; WGN America.

Current originations: Government Access; Educational Access; Public Access.

Fee: $40.54 installation; $14.75 monthly; $.68 converter; $18.29 additional installation.

Expanded Basic Service 1

Subscribers: 75,532.

Programming (via satellite): ABC Family Channel; AMC; Animal Planet; Arts & Entertainment; BET Networks; Bravo; Cartoon Network; CNBC; Comedy Central; Country Music TV; Discovery Channel; Discovery Health Channel; Disney Channel; E! Entertainment Television; ESPN; ESPN 2; ESPN Classic Sports; Eternal Word TV Network; Food Network; Fox News Channel; Fox Sports Net Midwest; FX; Golf Channel; Hallmark Channel; Headline News; HGTV; History Channel; Home Shopping Network; ION Television; Lifetime; Lifetime Movie Network; MSNBC; MTV; National Geographic Channel; Nickelodeon; Oxygen; QVC; ShopNBC; SoapNet; Spike TV; Syfy; Travel Channel; truTV; Turner Classic Movies; Turner Network TV; TV Land; Univision; USA Network; VH1; WE tv; Weather Channel.

Fee: $32.05 monthly.

Digital Basic Service

Subscribers: 46,000 Includes Auburn, Columbus, Fairbury, Falls City, Fremont, & York.

Programming (via satellite): America's Store; BBC America; Bio; Bloomberg Television; Boomerang; Canales N; CNN International; Cooking Channel; C-SPAN 3; Discovery Digital Networks; DMX Music; Do-It-Yourself; ESPNews; FitTV; Fox Movie Channel; Fox Sports World; FSN Digital Atlantic; FSN Digital Central; FSN Digital Pacific; Fuse; G4; GAS; Great American Country; GSN; History Channel International; Independent Film Channel; Lifetime Real Women; MTV2; NASA TV; NBA TV; Nick Jr.; NickToons TV; Outdoor Channel; Ovation; Speed Channel; Style Network; Tennis Channel; Toon Disney; Trinity Broadcasting Network; Versus; VH1 Classic.

Fee: $6.95 monthly.

Digital Pay Service 1

Pay Units: 37,728.

Programming (via satellite): Cinemax (multiplexed); Encore (multiplexed); HBO (multiplexed); Showtime (multiplexed); Starz (multiplexed); The Movie Channel (multiplexed).

Fee: $9.95 monthly (each).

Video-On-Demand: Yes

Pay-Per-View

NASCAR In Car (delivered digitally); NBA League Pass (delivered digitally); WNBA Season Pass; NHL Center Ice (delivered digitally); MLB Extra Innings (delivered digitally); iN DEMAND (delivered digitally); Pleasure (delivered digitally); Playboy TV (delivered digitally); Fresh (delivered digitally); ESPN Full Court (delivered digitally); Shorteez (delivered digitally); NBA TV (delivered digitally); Hot Choice (delivered digitally).

Internet Service

Operational: Yes, DSL only.

Subscribers: 14,040.

Broadband Service: Road Runner.

Fee: $39.95 installation; $44.95 monthly.

Telephone Service

Digital: Operational

Fee: $39.95 monthly

Miles of Plant: 1,028.0 (coaxial); 46.0 (fiber optic). Homes passed: 160,000. Total homes in franchised area: 114,765. Homes passed includes Auburn, Columbus, Fairbury, Falls City, Fremont, Superior, & York

Group Vice President: Beth Scarborough. Vice President, Operations: Dick Cassidy. Senior Engineering Director: John Pokojski. Technical Operations Manager: Rick Hollman. Area Marketing Manager: Sean Heyen. Public Affairs Director: Ann Shrewsbury.

City fee: 5% of gross.

Ownership: Time Warner Cable (MSO).; Advance/Newhouse Partnership (MSO).

LINDSAY—Formerly served by TelePartners. No longer in operation. ICA: NE0366.

LOCHLAND—Glenwood Telecommunications. Now served by BLUE HILL, NE [NE0093]. ICA: NE0384.

LYMAN—Windbreak Cable TV, 1140 10th St, Gering, NE 69341-3239. Phone: 308-436-4650. Fax: 308-436-4779. E-mail: bill@intertech.net. Web Site: http://www.windbreak.com/. ICA: NE0180.

TV Market Ranking: Below 100 (LYMAN). Franchise award date: N.A. Franchise expiration date: N.A. Began: N.A.

Channel capacity: 36 (not 2-way capable). Channels available but not in use: 22.

Basic Service

Subscribers: 25.

Programming (received off-air): KDUH-TV (ABC) Scottsbluff; KGWN-TV (CBS, CW) Cheyenne; KSTF (CBS, CW) Scottsbluff; KTNE-TV (PBS) Alliance.

Programming (via satellite): ABC Family Channel; CNN; C-SPAN; Discovery Channel; Fox News Channel; Hallmark Channel; KUSA (NBC) Denver; Spike TV; TBS Superstation; USA Network; Weather Channel.

Fee: $20.20 installation; $20.30 monthly.

Pay Service 1

Pay Units: 1.

Programming (via satellite): Showtime.

Fee: $20.00 installation; $7.95 monthly.

Pay Service 2

Pay Units: N.A.

Programming (via satellite): The Movie Channel.

Fee: $20.00 installation; $7.95 monthly.

Internet Service

Operational: No.

Telephone Service

None

Miles of Plant: 6.0 (coaxial); None (fiber optic). Homes passed: 190. Total homes in franchised area: 190.

Manager & Chief Technician: Bill Bauer. Office Manager: Cheryl McLean.

City fee: None.

Ownership: WinDBreak Cable.

LYNCH—Formerly served by TelePartners. No longer in operation. ICA: NE0367.

LYONS—American Broadband, 1605 Washington St, Blair, NE 68008-0400. Phones: 888-479-6260; 402-426-6200; 402-533-1000. Fax: 402-375-4077. Web Site: http://www.abbnebraska.com. ICA: NE0112.

TV Market Ranking: Outside TV Markets (LYONS). Franchise award date: N.A. Franchise expiration date: N.A. Began: June 1, 1983.

Channel capacity: N.A. Channels available but not in use: N.A.

Basic Service

Subscribers: N.A. Included in Blair

Programming (received off-air): KCAU-TV (ABC) Sioux City; KETV (ABC) Omaha; KHIN (PBS) Red Oak; KMTV-TV (CBS) Omaha; KPTM (FOX, MNT) Omaha; KTIV (CW, NBC) Sioux City; KXVO (CW) Omaha; WOWT-TV (IND, NBC) Omaha.

Programming (via satellite): C-SPAN; Home Shopping Network; QVC; Weather Channel; WGN America.

Current originations: Public Access.

Fee: $30.00 installation; $15.96 monthly.

Expanded Basic Service 1

Subscribers: N.A.

Programming (via satellite): ABC Family Channel; AMC; Animal Planet; Arts & Entertainment; CNBC; CNN; Comedy Central; Country Music TV; Discovery Channel; ESPN; ESPN 2; Food Network; Fox News Channel; Fox Sports Net Midwest; FX; Hallmark Channel; Headline News; HGTV; History Channel; Lifetime; MSNBC; MTV; Nickelodeon; Spike TV; Syfy; TBS Superstation; The Learning Channel; truTV; Turner Network TV; USA Network; VH1.

Fee: $19.95 monthly.

Digital Basic Service

Subscribers: N.A. Included in Blair

Programming (received off-air): KMTV-TV (CBS) Omaha; KPTM (FOX, MNT) Omaha; KXVO (CW) Omaha; WOWT-TV (IND, NBC) Omaha.

Programming (via satellite): Bio; Discovery Health Channel; Discovery Kids Channel; Discovery Military Channel; Discovery Planet Green; DMX Music; ESPNews; Fox Soccer; Fuse; Golf Channel; GSN; ID Investigation Discovery; KETV (ABC) Omaha; Lifetime Movie Network; Science Channel; Sleuth; Speed Channel; Style Network; Toon Disney; Turner Classic Movies; Versus; WE tv.

Fee: $7.99 monthly; $4.95 converter.

Digital Pay Service 1

Pay Units: N.A.

Programming (via satellite): Cinemax (multiplexed); Encore (multiplexed); HBO (multiplexed); Showtime (multiplexed); Starz (multiplexed); The Movie Channel (multiplexed).

Fee: $11.10 monthly (Cinemax), $12.00 monthly (Starz/Encore or Showtime), $13.35 monthly (HBO).

Video-On-Demand: Yes

Pay-Per-View

iN DEMAND (delivered digitally); Playboy TV (delivered digitally); Club Jenna (delivered digitally).

Internet Service

Operational: Yes.

Broadband Service: In-house.

Fee: $35.00 monthly.

Telephone Service

Digital: Operational

Miles of Plant: 8.0 (coaxial); None (fiber optic). Total homes in area & homes passed included in Blair

President, State Operations: Mike Jacobsen. General Manager, Cable Television: Mike Storjohann. Program Manager: Kay Peterson.

Ownership: American Broadband Communications Inc. (MSO).

MADRID—Consolidated Cable Inc. Now served by WALLACE, NE [NE0336]. ICA: NE0205.

MALCOLM—Galaxy Cablevision, 1928 S Lincoln Ave, Ste 200, York, NE 68467. Phone: 402-362-3332. Fax: 402-362-4890. Web Site: http://www.galaxycable.com. ICA: NE0208.

TV Market Ranking: 91 (MALCOLM). Franchise award date: N.A. Franchise expiration date: N.A. Began: July 1, 1984.

Channel capacity: 41 (not 2-way capable). Channels available but not in use: 14.

Basic Service

Subscribers: 25.

Programming (received off-air): KETV (ABC) Omaha; KLKN (ABC) Lincoln; KMTV-TV (CBS) Omaha; KOLN (CBS, MNT) Lincoln; KPTM (FOX, MNT) Omaha; KUON-TV (PBS) Lincoln; KXVO (CW) Omaha; WOWT-TV (IND, NBC) Omaha.

Programming (via satellite): ABC Family Channel; Animal Planet; Arts & Entertainment; Cartoon Network; CNN; Discovery Channel; Disney Channel; ESPN; Fox Sports Net Midwest; History Channel; Spike TV; TBS Superstation; The Learning Channel; Turner Network TV; USA Network; WGN America.

Current originations: Public Access.

Fee: $35.00 installation; $32.95 monthly.

Pay Service 1

Pay Units: 5.

Programming (via satellite): Cinemax.

Fee: $11.95 monthly.

Pay Service 2

Pay Units: 9.

Programming (via satellite): HBO.

Fee: $12.95 monthly.

Internet Service

Operational: No.

Telephone Service

None

Miles of Plant: 2.0 (coaxial); None (fiber optic). Homes passed: 114.

State Manager: Cheyenne Wohlford. Technical Manager: Carl Stanley. Sales Manager: Mike Thomas. Customer Service Manager: Donna Bryant.

City fee: 1% of basic.

Ownership: Galaxy Cable Inc. (MSO).

MARQUETTE—Mid-State Community TV. Now served by AURORA, NE [NE0033]. ICA: NE0301.

MARTINSBURG—CenCom Inc. This cable system has converted to IPTV. See Martinsburg, NE [NE5022]. ICA: NE0388.

MARTINSBURG (village)—CenCom NNTV. Formerly [NE0388]. This cable system has converted to IPTV, 110 E Elk St, Jackson, NE 68743-0066. Phones: 402-623-4321; 888-397-4321. E-mail: nntc@nntc.net. Web Site: http://www.nntc.net. ICA: NE5022.
Channel capacity: N.A. Channels available but not in use: N.A.
Internet Service
Operational: Yes.
Telephone Service
Digital: Operational
General Manager: Emory Graffis.
Ownership: Northeast Nebraska Telephone Co.

MASKELL (village)—CenCom NNTV. Formerly [NE0387]. This cable system has converted to IPTV, 110 E Elk St, Jackson, NE 68743-0066. Phones: 402-623-4321; 888-397-4321. E-mail: nntc@nntc.net. Web Site: http://www.nntc.net. ICA: NE5023.
Channel capacity: N.A. Channels available but not in use: N.A.
Internet Service
Operational: Yes.
Telephone Service
Digital: Operational
General Manager: Emory Graffis.
Ownership: Northeast Nebraska Telephone Co.

MASON CITY—NCTC Cable, PO Box 700, 22 LaBarre St, Gibbon, NE 68840. Phone: 308-468-6341. Fax: 308-468-9929. Web Site: http://www.nctc.net. ICA: NE0302.
TV Market Ranking: Outside TV Markets (MASON CITY). Franchise award date: N.A. Franchise expiration date: N.A. Began: January 1, 1990.
Channel capacity: N.A. Channels available but not in use: N.A.
Basic Service
Subscribers: N.A. Included in Burwell
Programming (received off-air): KGIN (CBS, MNT) Grand Island; KHAS-TV (NBC) Hastings; KHGI-TV (ABC) Kearney; KMNE-TV (PBS) Bassett; KTVG-TV (FOX) Grand Island.
Programming (via satellite): ABC Family Channel; AMC; Animal Planet; Arts & Entertainment; Cartoon Network; CNBC; CNN; Comedy Central; Country Music TV; C-SPAN; CW+; Discovery Channel; E! Entertainment Television; ESPN; ESPN 2; ESPN Classic Sports; Eternal Word TV Network; Food Network; Fox News Channel; Fox Sports Net Midwest; FX; G4; Great American Country; Hallmark Channel; Headline News; HGTV; History Channel; Home Shopping Network; ION Television; Lifetime; MSNBC; MTV; Nickelodeon; Outdoor Channel; QVC; Spike TV; Syfy; TBS Superstation; The Learning Channel; Travel Channel; Trinity Broadcasting Network; truTV; Turner Classic Movies; Turner Network TV; TV Land; USA Network; Versus; VH1; Weather Channel; WGN America.
Fee: $32.00 installation; $39.20 monthly.
Digital Basic Service
Subscribers: N.A. Included in Burwell
Programming (via satellite): AmericanLife TV Network; BBC America; Bio; Bloomberg Television; Current; Daystar TV Network; Discovery Digital Networks; DMX Music; ESPNews; FitTV; Fox College Sports Atlantic; Fox College Sports Central; Fox College Sports Pacific; Fox Movie Channel; G4; Golf Channel; Gospel Music Channel; GSN; Halogen Network; History Channel International; Lifetime Movie Network; MTV Networks Digital Suite; Nick Jr.; Ovation; RFD-TV; ShopNBC; Sleuth; Speed Channel; TeenNick; WE tv.
Fee: $14.00 monthly.
Pay Service 1
Pay Units: N.A.
Programming (via satellite): HBO.
Fee: $10.95 monthly.
Digital Pay Service 1
Pay Units: N.A.
Programming (via satellite): Cinemax (multiplexed); Encore (multiplexed); Flix; HBO (multiplexed); Showtime (multiplexed); Starz (multiplexed); The Movie Channel (multiplexed).
Fee: $10.95 monthly (Cinemax), $12.95 monthly (HBO or Showtime, TMC & Flix), $13.95 monthly (Starz & Encore).
Video-On-Demand: No
Internet Service
Operational: No, DSL & dial-up.
Telephone Service
None
Miles of Plant: 3.0 (coaxial); None (fiber optic). Homes passed included in Burwell
General Manager: Andy Jader. Technical Operations Manager: Nick Jeffres.
Ownership: Nebraska Central Telecom Inc. (MSO).

MAXWELL—Consolidated Cable Inc., PO Box 6147, 6900 Van Dorn St, Ste 21, Lincoln, NE 68506-0147. Phones: 402-489-2728; 800-742-7464. Fax: 402-489-9034. E-mail: service @consolidatedtelephone.com. Web Site: http://www.nebnet.net. Also serves Brady. ICA: NE0303.
TV Market Ranking: Below 100 (Brady, MAXWELL). Franchise award date: January 1, 1987. Franchise expiration date: N.A. Began: January 1, 1987.
Channel capacity: 78 (not 2-way capable). Channels available but not in use: 24.
Basic Service
Subscribers: 198.
Programming (received off-air): KGIN (CBS, MNT) Grand Island; KNOP-TV (NBC) North Platte; KPNE-TV (PBS) North Platte; KTVG-TV (FOX) Grand Island; KWNB-TV (ABC) Hayes Center.
Programming (via satellite): ABC Family Channel; AMC; Animal Planet; Arts & Entertainment; Cartoon Network; CNN; Comedy Central; Country Music TV; Discovery Channel; Disney Channel; E! Entertainment Television; ESPN; ESPN 2; ESPN Classic Sports; Fox News Channel; Fox Sports Net Midwest; FX; Great American Country; Hallmark Channel; HGTV; History Channel; Home Shopping Network; Lifetime; Nickelodeon; Spike TV; TBS Superstation; The Learning Channel; Turner Network TV; TV Land; USA Network; VH1; Weather Channel; WGN America.
Fee: $29.95 monthly.
Digital Basic Service
Subscribers: N.A.
Programming (via satellite): AmericanLife TV Network; Bloomberg Television; CMT Pure Country; Discovery Times Channel; DMX Music; ESPN Classic Sports; ESPNews; FitTV; Fox College Sports Atlantic; Fox College Sports Central; Fox College Sports Pacific; Fox Movie Channel; G4; GAS; Golf Channel; GSN; Halogen Network; Independent Film Channel; Lifetime Movie Network; MTV Networks Digital Suite; Nick Jr.; NickToons TV; Outdoor Channel; Sleuth; Speed Channel; Style Network; Sundance Channel; Syfy; Toon Disney; Trinity Broadcasting Network; Versus; WE tv.
Fee: $24.00 monthly.
Pay Service 1
Pay Units: 39.
Programming (via satellite): HBO.
Fee: $9.00 monthly.
Digital Pay Service 1
Pay Units: N.A.
Programming (via satellite): Cinemax (multiplexed); Encore (multiplexed); Flix; HBO (multiplexed); Showtime (multiplexed); Starz (multiplexed); The Movie Channel (multiplexed).
Fee: $9.00 monthly (each).
Video-On-Demand: No
Pay-Per-View
iN DEMAND (delivered digitally); Hot Choice (delivered digitally); Playboy TV (delivered digitally); Fresh (delivered digitally); Urban American Television Network (delivered digitally).
Internet Service
Operational: No.
Telephone Service
None
Miles of Plant: 6.0 (coaxial); None (fiber optic). Homes passed: 419. Total homes in franchised area: 419.
Manager: Bryan Thompson. Chief Technician: Dan Smith.
Ownership: Consolidated Cable Inc. (MSO).

McCOOK—Great Plains Communications, PO Box 500, 1600 Great Plains Centre, Blair, NE 68008-0500. Phone: 402-426-9511. Fax: 402-456-6550. Web Site: http://www.gpcom.com. ICA: NE0019.
TV Market Ranking: Below 100 (MCCOOK). Franchise award date: N.A. Franchise expiration date: N.A. Began: November 1, 1970.
Channel capacity: 74 (operating 2-way). Channels available but not in use: N.A.
Basic Service
Subscribers: N.A. Included in Arnold
Programming (received off-air): KGIN (CBS, MNT) Grand Island; KHGI-TV (ABC) Kearney; KLNE-TV (PBS) Lexington; KSNK (NBC) McCook; 4 FMs.
Programming (via satellite): C-SPAN; Discovery Channel; FX; Hallmark Channel; INSP; Lifetime; QVC; TBS Superstation; truTV; TV Guide Network; Weather Channel; WGN America.
Fee: $29.99 installation.
Expanded Basic Service 1
Subscribers: 2,555.
Programming (via satellite): ABC Family Channel; AMC; Animal Planet; Arts & Entertainment; Bravo; Cartoon Network; CNBC; CNN; Country Music TV; Disney Channel; E! Entertainment Television; ESPN; ESPN 2; Eternal Word TV Network; Food Network; Fox News Channel; Fox Sports Net; Fox Sports Net Midwest; G4; Golf Channel; GRTV Network; Headline News; HGTV; Home Shopping Network; MTV; National Geographic Channel; Nickelodeon; Oxygen; SoapNet; Speed Channel; Spike TV; Syfy; The Learning Channel; Toon Disney; Travel Channel; Turner Network TV; USA Network; VH1; WE tv.
Fee: $47.99 monthly.
Digital Basic Service
Subscribers: N.A. Included in Arnold
Programming (via satellite): AmericanLife TV Network; BBC America; Bio; Bloomberg Television; Discovery Digital Networks; DMX Music; Fox Movie Channel; GAS; GSN; Halogen Network; History Channel International; Independent Film Channel; Lifetime Movie Network; MTV Networks Digital Suite; MuchMusic Network; Nick Jr.; Outdoor Channel; ShopNBC; Style Network; Trinity Broadcasting Network; Turner Classic Movies; Versus.
Fee: $12.83 monthly.
Digital Pay Service 1
Pay Units: N.A.
Programming (via satellite): Cinemax (multiplexed); Encore (multiplexed); HBO (multiplexed); Showtime (multiplexed); Starz (multiplexed); The Movie Channel (multiplexed).
Video-On-Demand: No
Pay-Per-View
Hot Choice (delivered digitally), Addressable: Yes; iN DEMAND; iN DEMAND (delivered digitally); Playboy TV (delivered digitally); Fresh (delivered digitally); Shorteez (delivered digitally); sports.
Internet Service
Operational: Yes. Began: February 1, 2003.
Broadband Service: Charter Pipeline.
Fee: $29.99 monthly.
Telephone Service
None
Miles of Plant: 44.0 (coaxial); None (fiber optic). Homes passed: 3,608. Total homes in franchised area: 5,317. Homes passed included in Arnold
General Manager: Lee Ann Quist. Chief Technician: Mark Stottler. Marketing Manager: Casey Garrigan.
City fee: 5% of gross.
Ownership: Great Plains Communications Inc. (MSO).

MEAD—Formerly served by TelePartners. No longer in operation. ICA: NE0185.

MEADOW GROVE—Cable Nebraska, 2123 Central Ave, Ste 200, Kearney, NE 68847. Phone: 308-236-1512. Web Site: http://www.cablene.com. ICA: NE0186.
TV Market Ranking: Outside TV Markets (MEADOW GROVE). Franchise award date: N.A. Franchise expiration date: N.A. Began: December 30, 1987.
Channel capacity: 41 (not 2-way capable). Channels available but not in use: 11.
Basic Service
Subscribers: 77.
Programming (received off-air): KMEG (CBS) Sioux City; KOLN (CBS, MNT) Lincoln; KTIV (CW, NBC) Sioux City; KXNE-TV (PBS) Norfolk.
Programming (via satellite): ABC Family Channel; Animal Planet; Arts & Entertainment; Cartoon Network; CNN; Discovery Channel; ESPN; ESPN 2; Fox Sports Net Midwest; Headline News; History Channel; Lifetime; Nickelodeon; Outdoor Channel; TBS Superstation; The Learning Channel; Turner Network TV; USA Network; Weather Channel; WGN America.
Fee: $35.00 installation; $25.95 monthly.
Pay Service 1
Pay Units: 23.
Programming (via satellite): HBO.
Fee: $20.00 installation; $12.95 monthly.
Pay Service 2
Pay Units: 17.
Programming (via satellite): Showtime.
Fee: $7.95 monthly.
Pay Service 3
Pay Units: 17.
Programming (via satellite): The Movie Channel.
Fee: $6.95 monthly.

Internet Service
Operational: No.
Miles of Plant: 3.0 (coaxial); None (fiber optic). Homes passed: 154. Total homes in franchised area: 163.
Operations Manager: Stuart Gilbertson.
City fee: 5% of gross.
Ownership: USA Companies (MSO).

MINATARE—Charter Communications. Now served by SCOTTSBLUFF, NE [NE0008]. ICA: NE0077.

MINDEN—Charter Communications. Now served by KEARNEY, NE [NE0011]. ICA: NE0037.

MITCHELL—Charter Communications. Now served by SCOTTSBLUFF, NE [NE0008]. ICA: NE0041.

MONROE—Cable Nebraska, 2123 Central Ave, Ste 200, Kearney, NE 68847. Phone: 308-236-1512. Web Site: http://www.cablene.com. ICA: NE0368.
TV Market Ranking: Outside TV Markets (MONROE). Franchise award date: N.A. Franchise expiration date: N.A. Began: N.A.
Channel capacity: N.A. Channels available but not in use: N.A.
Basic Service
Subscribers: 64.
Programming (received off-air): KGIN (CBS, MNT) Grand Island; KHAS-TV (NBC) Hastings; KHGI-TV (ABC) Kearney; KHNE-TV (PBS) Hastings; KLKN (ABC) Lincoln; KTVG-TV (FOX) Grand Island; KUON-TV (PBS) Lincoln.
Programming (via satellite): ABC Family Channel; AMC; Animal Planet; Arts & Entertainment; Cartoon Network; CNBC; CNN; Comedy Central; Country Music TV; C-SPAN; C-SPAN 2; Discovery Channel; E! Entertainment Television; ESPN; ESPN 2; ESPN Classic Sports; Eternal Word TV Network; Food Network; Fox News Channel; Fox Sports Net Rocky Mountain; FX; G4; Great American Country; Hallmark Channel; Headline News; HGTV; History Channel; Lifetime; MSNBC; MTV; Nickelodeon; Outdoor Channel; QVC; Spike TV; Syfy; TBS Superstation; The Learning Channel; Travel Channel; Trinity Broadcasting Network; truTV; Turner Classic Movies; Turner Network TV; TV Land; Univision; USA Network; Versus; VH1; Weather Channel; WGN America.
Fee: $39.00 installation; $27.45 monthly.
Pay Service 1
Pay Units: 16.
Fee: $10.95 monthly.
Video-On-Demand: No
Internet Service
Operational: No.
Telephone Service
None
Miles of Plant: 3.0 (coaxial); None (fiber optic). Homes passed: 122.
Operations Manager: Stuart Gilbertson. Chief Technician: Jeremy Bals.
Ownership: USA Companies (MSO).

MORRILL—Charter Communications. Now served by SCOTTSBLUFF, NE [NE0008]. ICA: NE0076.

NAPER—Cable Nebraska, 2123 Central Ave, Ste 200, Kearney, NE 68847. Phones: 800-456-0564; 605-229-1775. Web Site: http://www.cablene.com. ICA: NE0256.
TV Market Ranking: Outside TV Markets (NAPER). Franchise award date: June 2, 1987. Franchise expiration date: N.A. Began: November 1, 1987.
Channel capacity: 37 (not 2-way capable). Channels available but not in use: N.A.
Basic Service
Subscribers: 30.
Programming (received off-air): KDLV-TV (NBC) Mitchell; KMNE-TV (PBS) Bassett; KPLO-TV (CBS, MNT) Reliance; KPRY-TV (ABC) Pierre.
Programming (via satellite): ABC Family Channel; AMC; Arts & Entertainment; Cartoon Network; CNBC; CNN; Country Music TV; C-SPAN; Discovery Channel; Disney Channel; ESPN; Fox Sports Net Rocky Mountain; FX; Headline News; INSP; Lifetime; Nickelodeon; QVC; Spike TV; TBS Superstation; The Learning Channel; Turner Network TV; TV Guide Network; TV Land; USA Network; VH1; Weather Channel; WGN America.
Fee: $50.00 installation; $26.50 monthly.
Pay Service 1
Pay Units: 1.
Programming (via satellite): HBO.
Fee: $20.00 installation; $12.00 monthly.
Pay Service 2
Pay Units: 1.
Programming (via satellite): Showtime.
Fee: $20.00 installation; $11.00 monthly.
Pay Service 3
Pay Units: 1.
Programming (via satellite): The Movie Channel.
Fee: $20.00 installation; $11.00 monthly.
Video-On-Demand: No
Internet Service
Operational: No.
Telephone Service
None
Miles of Plant: 2.0 (coaxial); None (fiber optic). Homes passed: 78.
Ownership: USA Companies (MSO).

NEHAWKA—Formerly served by Westcom. No longer in operation. ICA: NE0305.

NELSON—Galaxy Cablevision, 1928 S Lincoln Ave, Ste 200, York, NE 68467. Phone: 402-362-3332. Fax: 402-362-4890. Web Site: http://www.galaxycable.com. ICA: NE0306.
TV Market Ranking: 91 (NELSON). Franchise award date: May 1, 1999. Franchise expiration date: N.A. Began: N.A.
Channel capacity: 41 (not 2-way capable). Channels available but not in use: 1.
Basic Service
Subscribers: 74.
Programming (received off-air): KHAS-TV (NBC) Hastings; KHGI-TV (ABC) Kearney; KHNE-TV (PBS) Hastings; KOLN (CBS, MNT) Lincoln.
Programming (via satellite): ABC Family Channel; AMC; Animal Planet; Arts & Entertainment; Cartoon Network; CNBC; CNN; C-SPAN; Discovery Channel; Disney Channel; ESPN; ESPN 2; Fox Sports Net Midwest; Fuse; FX; Great American Country; Headline News; HGTV; History Channel; Home Shopping Network; INSP; Lifetime; Outdoor Channel; QVC; TBS Superstation; The Learning Channel; Turner Network TV; USA Network; Weather Channel; WGN America.
Fee: $40.20 monthly.
Pay Service 1
Pay Units: 57.
Programming (via satellite): Cinemax.
Pay Service 2
Pay Units: 24.
Programming (via satellite): Showtime.

Internet Service
Operational: No.
Telephone Service
None
Miles of Plant: 9.0 (coaxial); None (fiber optic). Homes passed: 250.
State Manager: Cheyenne Wohlford. Technical Manager: Carl Stanley. Sales Manager: Mike Thomas. Customer Service Manager: Donna Bryant.
Ownership: Galaxy Cable Inc. (MSO).

NEWCASTLE—CenCom Inc. This cable system has converted to IPTV. See Newcastle (village), NE [NE5025]. ICA: NE0198.

NEWCASTLE (village)—CenCom NNTV. Formerly [NE0198]. This cable system has converted to IPTV, 110 E Elk St, Jackson, NE 68743-0066. Phones: 402-623-4321; 888-397-4321. E-mail: nntc@nntc.net. Web Site: http://www.nntc.net. ICA: NE5025.
Channel capacity: N.A. Channels available but not in use: N.A.
Internet Service
Operational: Yes.
Telephone Service
Digital: Operational
General Manager: Emory Graffis.
Ownership: Northeast Nebraska Telephone Co.

NEWMAN GROVE—Cable Nebraska, 2123 Central Ave, Ste 200, Kearney, NE 68847. Phone: 308-236-1512. Web Site: http://www.cablene.com. ICA: NE0097.
TV Market Ranking: Outside TV Markets (NEWMAN GROVE). Franchise award date: N.A. Franchise expiration date: N.A. Began: December 1, 1983.
Channel capacity: N.A. Channels available but not in use: N.A.
Basic Service
Subscribers: 214.
Programming (received off-air): KGIN (CBS, MNT) Grand Island; KHAS-TV (NBC) Hastings; KHGI-TV (ABC) Kearney; KHNE-TV (PBS) Hastings; KLKN (ABC) Lincoln; KTVG-TV (FOX) Grand Island.
Programming (via satellite): ABC Family Channel; C-SPAN; C-SPAN 2; Eternal Word TV Network; Hallmark Channel; Headline News; Home Shopping Network; QVC; TBS Superstation; Trinity Broadcasting Network; TV Guide Network; Weather Channel; WGN America.
Current originations: Public Access.
Fee: $35.00 installation; $35.45 monthly.
Expanded Basic Service 1
Subscribers: N.A.
Programming (via satellite): AMC; Animal Planet; Arts & Entertainment; Cartoon Network; CNBC; CNN; Comedy Central; Country Music TV; Discovery Channel; E! Entertainment Television; ESPN; ESPN 2; Food Network; Fox News Channel; Fox Sports Net Midwest; FX; Great American Country; HGTV; History Channel; ION Television; Lifetime; MSNBC; MTV; Nickelodeon; Outdoor Channel; Spike TV; Syfy; The Learning Channel; Travel Channel; truTV; Turner Classic Movies; Turner Network TV; TV Land; Univision; USA Network; VH1; WE tv.
Digital Basic Service
Subscribers: 5.
Programming (via satellite): AmericanLife TV Network; BBC America; Bio; Bloomberg Television; Canales N; Current; Discovery Digital Networks; DMX Music; ESPN Classic Sports; ESPNews; FitTV; Fox Movie Channel; Fox Sports World; FSN Digital Atlantic; FSN Digital Central; FSN Digital Pacific; G4; GAS; Golf Channel; GSN; Halogen Network; History Channel; History Channel International; International Television (ITV); MBC America; MTV Networks Digital Suite; National Geographic Channel; Nick Jr.; Outdoor Channel; Ovation; ShopNBC; Speed Channel; Style Network; Syfy; Trinity Broadcasting Network; Trio; Versus.
Fee: $13.95 monthly.
Digital Pay Service 1
Pay Units: N.A.
Programming (via satellite): Cinemax (multiplexed); Flix; Fox Movie Channel; HBO (multiplexed); Independent Film Channel; Lifetime Movie Network; Showtime (multiplexed); Starz (multiplexed); Sundance Channel; The Movie Channel (multiplexed); WAM! America's Kidz Network.
Fee: $17.00 monthly.
Video-On-Demand: No
Pay-Per-View
Addressable homes: 5.
iN DEMAND (delivered digitally); ESPN Now (delivered digitally), Addressable: Yes; Urban Xtra (delivered digitally); sports (delivered digitally); Hot Choice (delivered digitally); Playboy TV (delivered digitally); Shorteez (delivered digitally).
Internet Service
Operational: Yes.
Broadband Service: Cable Nebraska.
Telephone Service
None
Miles of Plant: 6.0 (coaxial); None (fiber optic). Homes passed: 412.
Operations Manager: Stuart Gilbertson.
City fee: 3% of gross.
Ownership: USA Companies (MSO).

NICKERSON—Formerly served by TelePartners. No longer in operation. ICA: NE0369.

NORFOLK—Cable One, 100 N Victory Rd, Norfolk, NE 68701-6800. Phone: 402-379-2330. Fax: 402-379-4224. E-mail: mdrahota@cableone.net. Web Site: http://www.cableone.net. Also serves Battle Creek, Beemer, Hadar, Hoskins, Madison, Pierce, Pilger, Randolph, Tilden, West Point & Wisner. ICA: NE0006.
TV Market Ranking: Below 100 (Pierce County (portions)); Outside TV Markets (Battle Creek, Beemer, Hadar, Hoskins, Madison, NORFOLK, Pierce, Pierce County (portions), Pilger, Randolph, Tilden, West Point, Wisner). Franchise award date: July 16, 1979. Franchise expiration date: N.A. Began: April 1, 1980.
Channel capacity: 70 (operating 2-way). Channels available but not in use: N.A.

Basic Service

Subscribers: 12,600.

Programming (received off-air): KCAU-TV (ABC) Sioux City; KETV (ABC) Omaha; KMEG (CBS) Sioux City; KMTV-TV (CBS) Omaha; KPTH (FOX, MNT) Sioux City; KTIV (CW, NBC) Sioux City; KXVO (CW) Omaha; KYNE-TV (PBS) Omaha; WOWT-TV (IND, NBC) Omaha; 25 FMs.

Programming (via satellite): C-SPAN; C-SPAN 2; Eternal Word TV Network; Home Shopping Network; QVC; TV Guide Network; WGN America.

Current originations: Leased Access; Educational Access; Public Access.

Fee: $55.00 installation; $46.00 monthly; $16.50 additional installation.

Expanded Basic Service 1

Subscribers: N.A.

Programming (via satellite): ABC Family Channel; AMC; Animal Planet; Arts & Entertainment; Cartoon Network; CNBC; CNN; Comedy Central; Country Music TV; Discovery Channel; Disney Channel; ESPN; ESPN 2; Food Network; Fox News Channel; Fox Sports Net Midwest; FX; Headline News; HGTV; History Channel; Lifetime; MSNBC; MTV; Nickelodeon; Spike TV; Syfy; TBS Superstation; The Learning Channel; Turner Classic Movies; Turner Network TV; TV Land; Univision; USA Network; VH1; Weather Channel.

Digital Basic Service

Subscribers: 4,300.

Programming (received off-air): KCAU-TV (ABC) Sioux City; KMEG (CBS) Sioux City; KPTH (FOX, MNT) Sioux City; KTIV (CW, NBC) Sioux City; KYNE-TV (PBS) Omaha.

Programming (via satellite): 3 Angels Broadcasting Network; Arts & Entertainment HD; Bio; Boomerang; Boomerang en Espanol; BYU Television; Cine Mexicano; CNN en Espanol; Discovery HD Theater; Discovery Health Channel; Discovery Kids Channel; Discovery Military Channel; ESPN 2 HD; ESPN Classic Sports; ESPN Deportes; ESPN HD; ESPNews; FamilyNet; Food Network HD; Fox College Sports Atlantic; Fox College Sports Central; Fox College Sports Pacific; Fox Movie Channel; Fox Soccer; Fox Sports en Espanol; Fuel TV; Golf Channel; Great American Country; GSN; Hallmark Channel; HGTV HD; History Channel International; INSP; La Familia Network; Latele Novela Network; mun2 television; Music Choice; National Geographic Channel; National Geographic Channel HD Network; Outdoor Channel; Science Channel; SoapNet; Speed Channel; TBS in HD; Telemundo; Toon Disney; Toon Disney en Espanol; Trinity Broadcasting Network; Turner Network TV HD; TVG Network; Universal HD; WE tv.

Fee: $9.95 monthly.

Digital Pay Service 1

Pay Units: N.A.

Programming (via satellite): Cinemax (multiplexed); Encore (multiplexed); HBO (multiplexed); HBO HD; Showtime (multiplexed); Showtime HD; Starz; Sundance Channel; The Movie Channel (multiplexed); The Movie Channel HD.

Fee: $7.00 monthly (each).

Video-On-Demand: No

Pay-Per-View

iN DEMAND (delivered digitally); Ten Clips (delivered digitally); Ten Blox; Ten Blue (delivered digitally).

Internet Service

Operational: Yes. Began: July 29, 2003.

Subscribers: 4,100.

Broadband Service: CableONE.net.

Fee: $75.00 installation; $43.00 monthly.

Telephone Service

Digital: Operational

Fee: $75.00 installation; $39.95 monthly

Miles of Plant: 207.0 (coaxial); None (fiber optic). Homes passed: 18,663.

Chief Technician: Scott Owens. General Manager: Mike Drahota.

Franchise fee: 5% of gross.

Ownership: Cable One Inc. (MSO).

NORTH BEND—Great Plains Communications, PO Box 500, 1600 Great Plains Centre, Blair, NE 68008-0500. Phones: 888-343-8014; 402-426-9511. Fax: 402-456-6550. E-mail: lquist@gpcom.com. Web Site: http://www.gpcom.com. Also serves Dodge, Scribner & Snyder. ICA: NE0080.

TV Market Ranking: Outside TV Markets (Dodge, NORTH BEND, Scribner, Snyder). Franchise award date: November 1, 1984. Franchise expiration date: N.A. Began: N.A.

Channel capacity: 80 (operating 2-way). Channels available but not in use: N.A.

Basic Service

Subscribers: N.A. Included in Arnold

Programming (received off-air): KETV (ABC) Omaha; KLKN (ABC) Lincoln; KMTV-TV (CBS) Omaha; KOLN (CBS, MNT) Lincoln; KPTM (FOX, MNT) Omaha; KUON-TV (PBS) Lincoln; KXVO (CW) Omaha; WOWT-TV (IND, NBC) Omaha.

Programming (via satellite): ABC Family Channel; AMC; Animal Planet; Arts & Entertainment; CNN; Country Music TV; Discovery Channel; Disney Channel; ESPN; Fox Sports Net Rocky Mountain; Headline News; Lifetime; Nickelodeon; QVC; Spike TV; Syfy; TBS Superstation; The Learning Channel; Travel Channel; Turner Network TV; TV Land; USA Network; Weather Channel; WGN America.

Current originations: Educational Access; Public Access.

Fee: $45.00 installation; $31.50 monthly.

Expanded Basic Service 1

Subscribers: N.A.

Programming (via satellite): Cartoon Network; Comedy Central; ESPN 2; HGTV; History Channel; Turner Classic Movies; Versus; VH1.

Fee: $6.50 monthly.

Digital Basic Service

Subscribers: N.A. Included in Arnold

Programming (via satellite): BBC America; Bio; Bravo; Discovery Digital Networks; DMX Music; ESPN Classic Sports; Fox Sports World; GAS; Golf Channel; History Channel International; Independent Film Channel; Lifetime Movie Network; MTV Networks Digital Suite; Nick Jr.; Speed Channel; Turner Classic Movies; WE tv.

Fee: $47.95 monthly.

Pay Service 1

Pay Units: N.A.

Programming (via satellite): HBO; Showtime.

Fee: $9.95 monthly (Showtime), $10.95 monthly (HBO).

Digital Pay Service 1

Pay Units: N.A.

Programming (via satellite): Cinemax (multiplexed); Encore (multiplexed); HBO (multiplexed); Showtime (multiplexed); Starz (multiplexed); The Movie Channel (multiplexed).

Fee: $12.00 monthly.

Video-On-Demand: No

Pay-Per-View

iN DEMAND (delivered digitally), Fee: $3.99, Addressable: Yes.

Internet Service

Operational: Yes, Both DSL & dial-up.

Broadband Service: In-house.

Fee: $49.95 installation; $39.95 monthly.

Telephone Service

None

Miles of Plant: 13.0 (coaxial); None (fiber optic). Homes passed included in Arnold

General Manager: Lea Ann Quist. Chief Technician: Mark Stottler. Marketing Manager: Casey Garrigan.

Franchise fee: 3% of basic gross.

Ownership: Great Plains Communications Inc. (MSO).

NORTH LOUP—NCTC Cable, PO Box 700, 22 LaBarre St, Gibbon, NE 68840. Phones: 888-873-6282; 308-468-6341. Fax: 308-468-9929. Web Site: http://www.nctc.net. ICA: NE0209.

TV Market Ranking: Outside TV Markets (NORTH LOUP). Franchise award date: N.A. Franchise expiration date: N.A. Began: N.A.

Channel capacity: N.A. Channels available but not in use: N.A.

Basic Service

Subscribers: N.A. Included in Burwell

Programming (received off-air): KGIN (CBS, MNT) Grand Island; KHAS-TV (NBC) Hastings; KHGI-TV (ABC) Kearney; KMNE-TV (PBS) Bassett; KTVG-TV (FOX) Grand Island.

Programming (via satellite): ABC Family Channel; AMC; Animal Planet; Arts & Entertainment; Cartoon Network; CNBC; CNN; Comedy Central; Country Music TV; C-SPAN; CW+; Discovery Channel; E! Entertainment Television; ESPN; ESPN 2; ESPN Classic Sports; Eternal Word TV Network; Food Network; Fox News Channel; Fox Sports Net; FX; G4; Great American Country; Hallmark Channel; Headline News; HGTV; History Channel; Home Shopping Network; ION Television; Lifetime; MSNBC; MTV; Nickelodeon; Outdoor Channel; QVC; Spike TV; Syfy; TBS Superstation; The Learning Channel; Travel Channel; Trinity Broadcasting Network; truTV; Turner Classic Movies; Turner Network TV; TV Land; USA Network; Versus; VH1; Weather Channel; WGN America.

Fee: $39.20 monthly.

Digital Basic Service

Subscribers: N.A. Included in Burwell

Programming (via satellite): AmericanLife TV Network; BBC America; Bio; Bloomberg Television; Current; Daystar TV Network; Discovery Health Channel; Discovery Kids Channel; Discovery Military Channel; Discovery Planet Green; ESPN 2; ESPN Classic Sports; ESPNews; FitTV; Fox College Sports Atlantic; Fox College Sports Central; Fox College Sports Pacific; Fox Movie Channel; G4; Golf Channel; GSN; Halogen Network; History Channel; History Channel International; ID Investigation Discovery; Lifetime Movie Network; MTV Hits; MTV2; Nick Jr.; Outdoor Channel; RFD-TV; Science Channel; ShopNBC; Sleuth; SoapNet; Speed Channel; Style Network; Syfy; TeenNick; Toon Disney; Trinity Broadcasting Network; Versus; VH1 Classic; VH1 Country; VH1 Soul; WE tv.

Fee: $14.00 monthly.

Pay Service 1

Pay Units: 16.

Programming (via satellite): HBO.

Fee: $10.95 monthly.

Digital Pay Service 1

Pay Units: N.A.

Programming (via satellite): Cinemax (multiplexed); Encore (multiplexed); Flix; Fox Movie Channel; HBO (multiplexed); Lifetime Movie Network; Showtime (multiplexed); Starz (multiplexed); The Movie Channel (multiplexed).

Fee: $10.95 monthly (Cinemax), $12.95 monthly (HBO or Showtime/TMC/Flix), $13.95 monthly (Starz/Encore/Fox Movie/Lifetime Movie).

Video-On-Demand: No

Internet Service

Operational: No, DSL & dial-up.

Telephone Service

None

Miles of Plant: 6.0 (coaxial); None (fiber optic). Homes passed included in Burwell

General Manager: Andy Jader. Technical Operations Manager: Nick Jeffres.

City fee: None.

Ownership: Nebraska Central Telecom Inc. (MSO).

NORTH PLATTE—Charter Communications, 601 E Walker Rd, North Platte, NE 69101. Phones: 308-534-5969; 507-289-8372 (Rochester administrative office). Fax: 308-532-9121. Web Site: http://www.charter.com. Also serves Indian Hills, Lake Maloney & Lincoln County. ICA: NE0009.

TV Market Ranking: 91 (Indian Hills); Below 100 (Lake Maloney, Lincoln County (portions), NORTH PLATTE, Indian Hills); Outside TV Markets (Lincoln County (portions)). Franchise award date: N.A. Franchise expiration date: N.A. Began: August 1, 1970.

Channel capacity: 74 (operating 2-way). Channels available but not in use: N.A.

Basic Service

Subscribers: 7,368.

Programming (received off-air): KGIN (CBS, MNT) Grand Island; KHGI-TV (ABC) Kearney; KNOP-TV (NBC) North Platte; KPNE-TV (PBS) North Platte; 1 FM.

Programming (via satellite): C-SPAN; C-SPAN 2; Discovery Channel; Eternal Word TV Network; Home Shopping Network; ION Television; Oxygen; QVC; WGN America.

Current originations: Government Access.

Fee: $29.99 installation; $2.00 converter.

Expanded Basic Service 1

Subscribers: 7,002.

Programming (via satellite): ABC Family Channel; AMC; Animal Planet; Arts & Entertainment; Cartoon Network; CNBC; CNN; Comedy Central; Country Music TV; Disney Channel; E! Entertainment Television; ESPN; ESPN 2; Food Network; Fox News Channel; Fox Sports Net Midwest; FX; G4; Great American Country; GRTV Network; Hallmark Channel; Headline News; HGTV; INSP; Lifetime; MSNBC; MTV; National Geographic Channel; Nickelodeon; SoapNet; Speed Channel; Spike TV; TBS Superstation; Telemundo; The Learning Channel; Toon Disney; Travel Channel; truTV; Turner Network TV; TV Land; USA Network; Versus; VH1; Weather Channel.

Fee: $47.99 monthly.

Digital Basic Service

Subscribers: 3,300.

Programming (via satellite): AmericanLife TV Network; BBC America; Bio; Bloomberg Television; Bravo; Discovery Digital Networks; DMX Music; ESPN Classic Sports; Fox Movie Channel; Fox Sports World; GAS; Golf Channel; GSN; History Channel; History Channel International; Independent Film Channel; Lifetime Movie Network; MTV Networks Digital Suite; MuchMusic Network; Nick Jr.; Outdoor Channel; Ovation; Style Network; Sundance Channel;

Syfy; Trinity Broadcasting Network; Turner Classic Movies; WE tv.
Fee: $5.93 monthly.

Digital Pay Service 1
Pay Units: 1,201.
Programming (via satellite): Cinemax (multiplexed); Encore (multiplexed); HBO (multiplexed); Showtime (multiplexed); Starz (multiplexed); The Movie Channel (multiplexed).

Video-On-Demand: Yes

Pay-Per-View
Addressable homes: 3,300.
Hot Choice (delivered digitally), Addressable: Yes; iN DEMAND (delivered digitally); Playboy TV (delivered digitally); Fresh (delivered digitally); Shorteez (delivered digitally); sports.

Internet Service
Operational: Yes.
Subscribers: 800.
Broadband Service: Charter Pipeline.
Fee: $29.99 monthly.

Telephone Service
Digital: Operational

Miles of Plant: 114.0 (coaxial); None (fiber optic). Homes passed: 9,892. Total homes in franchised area: 9,896.
Vice President & General Manager: John Crowley. Technical Operations Director: Marty Kovarik. Technical Operations Manager: Joel Saunders. Office Manager: Cathi Wentink.
City fee: 5% of gross.
Ownership: Charter Communications Inc. (MSO).

OAKLAND—American Broadband, 1605 Washington St, Blair, NE 68008-0400. Phones: 402-426-6200; 402-533-1000. Fax: 402-533-1111. Web Site: http://www.abbnebraska.com. ICA: NE0074.
TV Market Ranking: Outside TV Markets (OAKLAND). Franchise award date: N.A. Franchise expiration date: N.A. Began: January 1, 1983.
Channel capacity: N.A. Channels available but not in use: N.A.

Basic Service
Subscribers: N.A. Included in Blair
Programming (received off-air): KETV (ABC) Omaha; KHIN (PBS) Red Oak; KMTV-TV (CBS) Omaha; KPTM (FOX, MNT) Omaha; WOWT-TV (IND, NBC) Omaha.
Programming (via satellite): C-SPAN; Home Shopping Network; KXVO (CW) Omaha; QVC; TV Guide Network; Weather Channel; WGN America.
Current originations: Public Access; Educational Access.
Fee: $15.53 monthly.

Expanded Basic Service 1
Subscribers: N.A.
Programming (via satellite): ABC Family Channel; AMC; Animal Planet; Arts & Entertainment; CNBC; CNN; Comedy Central; Country Music TV; Discovery Channel; Disney Channel; ESPN; ESPN 2; Food Network; Fox News Channel; Fox Sports Net Midwest; FX; Hallmark Channel; Headline News; HGTV; History Channel; Lifetime; MSNBC; MTV; Nickelodeon; Spike TV; Syfy; TBS Superstation; The Learning Channel; truTV; Turner Network TV; USA Network; VH1.
Fee: $19.95 monthly.

Digital Basic Service
Subscribers: N.A.
Programming (received off-air): KETV (ABC) Omaha; KHIN (PBS) Red Oak; KMTV-TV (CBS) Omaha; KPTM (FOX, MNT) Omaha; KXVO (CW) Omaha; WOWT-TV (IND, NBC) Omaha.
Programming (via satellite): Animal Planet HD; Bio; Discovery Channel HD; Discovery HD Theater; Discovery Health Channel; Discovery Kids Channel; Discovery Military Channel; Discovery Planet Green; DMX Music; ESPN 2 HD; ESPN HD; ESPNews; Eternal Word TV Network; Fox Soccer; FSN Digital Atlantic; FSN Digital Central; FSN Digital Pacific; Fuel TV; Fuse; Golf Channel; GSN; HDNet; HDNet Movies; ID Investigation Discovery; Lifetime Movie Network; MyNetworkTV Inc.; National Geographic Channel; National Geographic Channel HD Network; Outdoor Channel; RFD-TV; Science Channel; Science Channel HD; Speed Channel; Style Network; TLC HD; Toon Disney; Turner Classic Movies; Universal HD; Versus; WE tv.
Fee: $12.94 monthly.

Digital Pay Service 1
Pay Units: N.A.
Programming (via satellite): Cinemax (multiplexed); Encore (multiplexed); HBO (multiplexed); Showtime (multiplexed); Starz (multiplexed); The Movie Channel (multiplexed).
Fee: $11.10 monthly (Cinemax), $12.00 monthly (Starz/Encore or Showtime/TMC), $13.35 monthly (HBO).

Video-On-Demand: Yes

Pay-Per-View
iN DEMAND (delivered digitally); Playboy TV (delivered digitally); Club Jenna (delivered digitally).

Internet Service
Operational: Yes, DSL only.
Broadband Service: In-house.
Fee: $35.00 monthly.

Telephone Service
Digital: Operational

Miles of Plant: 12.0 (coaxial); None (fiber optic). Total homes in area & homes passed included in Blair
President, State Operations: Mike Jacobsen. General Manager, Cable Television: Mike Storjohann. Program Director: Kay Peterson.
City fee: 3% of gross.
Ownership: American Broadband Communications Inc. (MSO).

OBERT (village)—CenCom NNTV. Formerly [NE0387]. This cable system has converted to IPTV, 110 E Elk St, Jackson, NE 68743-0066. Phones: 402-623-4321; 888-397-4321. E-mail: nntc@nntc.net. Web Site: http://www.nntc.net. ICA: NE5027.
Channel capacity: N.A. Channels available but not in use: N.A.

Internet Service
Operational: Yes.

Telephone Service
Digital: Operational

General Manager: Emory Graffis.
Ownership: Northeast Nebraska Telephone Co.

OBERT/MASKELL—CenCom Inc. This cable system has converted to IPTV. See Obert, NE [NE5027] & Maskell, NE [NE5023]. ICA: NE0387.
TV Market Ranking: Below 100 (OBERT).

OCONTO—Great Plains Cable TV. Now served by ARNOLD, NE [NE0114]. ICA: NE0309.

OGALLALA—Charter Communications, 3380 Northern Valley Pl NE, Rochester, MN 55906-3954. Phone: 507-289-8372 (Rochester administrative office). Fax: 507-285-6162. Web Site: http://www.charter.com. Also serves Keith County. ICA: NE0025.
TV Market Ranking: Outside TV Markets (Keith County, OGALLALA). Franchise award date: N.A. Franchise expiration date: N.A. Began: January 1, 1965.
Channel capacity: N.A. Channels available but not in use: N.A.

Basic Service
Subscribers: 1,989.
Programming (received off-air): KGIN (CBS, MNT) Grand Island; KHGI-TV (ABC) Kearney; KNOP-TV (NBC) North Platte; KPNE-TV (PBS) North Platte; 1 FM.
Programming (via satellite): C-SPAN 2; Discovery Channel; Eternal Word TV Network; Home Shopping Network; KCNC-TV (CBS) Denver; KDVR (FOX) Denver; KMGH-TV (ABC) Denver; KUSA (NBC) Denver; Lifetime; QVC; WGN America.
Current originations: Educational Access.
Fee: $29.99 installation.

Expanded Basic Service 1
Subscribers: 1,844.
Programming (via satellite): ABC Family Channel; AMC; Animal Planet; Arts & Entertainment; Cartoon Network; CNBC; CNN; Comedy Central; Country Music TV; C-SPAN; Disney Channel; E! Entertainment Television; ESPN; ESPN 2; Food Network; Fox News Channel; Fox Sports Net Rocky Mountain; FX; G4; Great American Country; GRTV Network; Hallmark Channel; Headline News; HGTV; History Channel; ION Television; KWGN-TV (CW) Denver; MSNBC; MTV; National Geographic Channel; Nickelodeon; SoapNet; Speed Channel; Spike TV; TBS Superstation; Telemundo; The Learning Channel; Toon Disney; Travel Channel; truTV; Turner Network TV; TV Land; USA Network; Versus; VH1; Weather Channel.
Fee: $47.99 monthly.

Digital Basic Service
Subscribers: 500.
Programming (via satellite): AmericanLife TV Network; BBC America; Bio; Bloomberg Television; Bravo; Discovery Digital Networks; DMX Music; Fox Movie Channel; Fuse; GAS; Golf Channel; GSN; Halogen Network; History Channel International; Independent Film Channel; Lifetime Movie Network; MTV Networks Digital Suite; Nick Jr.; Outdoor Channel; ShopNBC; Style Network; Syfy; Toon Disney; Trinity Broadcasting Network; Turner Classic Movies; WE tv.
Fee: $11.72 monthly.

Digital Pay Service 1
Pay Units: N.A.
Programming (via satellite): Cinemax (multiplexed); Encore (multiplexed); HBO (multiplexed); Showtime (multiplexed); Starz (multiplexed); The Movie Channel (multiplexed).

Video-On-Demand: Yes

Pay-Per-View
Addressable homes: 500.
Hot Choice (delivered digitally), Addressable: Yes; iN DEMAND (delivered digitally); Playboy TV (delivered digitally); Fresh (delivered digitally); Shorteez (delivered digitally); sports.

Internet Service
Operational: Yes.
Subscribers: 40.
Broadband Service: Charter Pipeline.
Fee: $29.99 monthly.

Telephone Service
Digital: Operational

Miles of Plant: 38.0 (coaxial); None (fiber optic). Homes passed: 2,343. Total homes in franchised area: 2,343.
Vice President & General Manager: John Crowley. Technical Operations Director: Marty Kovarik. Technical Operations Manager: Joel Saunders. Marketing Director: Bill Haarstad.
City fee: 5% of gross.
Ownership: Charter Communications Inc. (MSO).

OMAHA—Cox Communications, 11505 W Dodge Rd, Omaha, NE 68154-2536. Phone: 402-933-2000. Fax: 402-933-0010. Web Site: http://ww2.cox.com/residential/omaha/home.cox. Also serves Carter Lake & Council Bluffs, IA; Bellevue, Bennington, Douglas County, Elkhorn, La Vista, Papillion & Sarpy County (unincorporated areas), NE. ICA: NE0001. **Note:** This system is an overbuild.
TV Market Ranking: 53 (Bellevue, Bennington, Carter Lake, Council Bluffs, Elkhorn, La Vista, OMAHA, Papillion); 53,91 (Douglas County, Sarpy County (unincorporated areas)). Franchise award date: September 4, 1981. Franchise expiration date: N.A. Began: September 4, 1981.
Channel capacity: 115 (operating 2-way). Channels available but not in use: N.A.

Basic Service
Subscribers: 206,000.
Programming (received off-air): KETV (ABC) Omaha; KHIN (PBS) Red Oak; KMTV-TV (CBS) Omaha; KPTM (FOX, MNT) Omaha; KXVO (CW) Omaha; KYNE-TV (PBS) Omaha; News on One - WOWT; WOWT-TV (IND, NBC) Omaha.
Programming (via satellite): Cox Sports Television; C-SPAN; C-SPAN 2; Eternal Word TV Network; Jewelry Television; QVC; TBS Superstation; The Learning Channel; TV Guide Network; Univision; WGN America.
Current originations: Leased Access; Religious Access; Government Access; Educational Access; Public Access.
Fee: $38.95 installation; $16.50 monthly; $21.95 additional installation.

Expanded Basic Service 1
Subscribers: 163,945.
Programming (via satellite): ABC Family Channel; AMC; Animal Planet; Arts & Entertainment; BET Networks; Bravo; Cartoon Network; CNBC; CNN; Comedy Central; Country Music TV; Discovery Channel; Disney Channel; E! Entertainment Television; ESPN; ESPN 2; Food Network; Fox News Channel; Fox Sports Net Rocky Mountain; FX; Golf Channel; Headline News; HGTV; History Channel; Home Shopping Network; ION Televi-

sion; Lifetime; MSNBC; MTV; Nickelodeon; Spike TV; Syfy; Telemundo; Travel Channel; Turner Classic Movies; Turner Network TV; TV Land; USA Network; VH1; Weather Channel.
Fee: $30.79 monthly.

Digital Basic Service
Subscribers: 65,382.
Programming (received off-air): KETV (ABC) Omaha; KMTV-TV (CBS) Omaha; KPTM (FOX, MNT) Omaha; KXVO (CW) Omaha; KYNE-TV (PBS) Omaha; WOWT-TV (IND, NBC) Omaha.
Programming (via satellite): AMC HD; AmericanLife TV Network; Animal Planet HD; Arts & Entertainment HD; Azteca America; Bandamax; BBC America; Bio; Bloomberg Television; Boomerang; Boomerang en Espanol; Bravo HD; Chiller; Cine Latino; CMT HD; CMT Pure Country; CNBC HD+; CNN en Espanol; CNN HD; Cooking Channel; De Pelicula; De Pelicula Clasico; Discovery Channel HD; Discovery en Espanol; Discovery HD Theater; Discovery Health Channel; Discovery Kids Channel; Discovery Planet Green; Discovery Planet Green HD; Do-It-Yourself; Encore; Encore Wam; ESPN 2 HD; ESPN Classic Sports; ESPN Deportes; ESPN HD; ESPN U; ESPNews; EWTN en Espanol; FitTV; Flix; Food Network HD; Fox Reality Channel; Fox Soccer; Fox Sports en Espanol; Fox Sports Net Rocky Mountain; Fuel TV; Fuse; G4; GalaVision; Gol TV; Golf Channel HD; Gospel Music Channel; Great American Country; GSN; Hallmark Channel; Hallmark Movie Channel HD; Halogen Network; HGTV HD; History Channel en Espanol; History Channel HD; History Channel International; ID Investigation Discovery; Independent Film Channel; INSP; Lifetime Movie Network; Lifetime Movie Network HD; Lifetime Television HD; Military Channel; MTV Hits; MTV Jams; MTV Networks HD; MTV Tres; MTV2; mtvU; mun2 television; Music Choice; National Geographic Channel; National Geographic Channel HD Network; NBA TV; NFL Network; NFL Network HD; NHL Network; Nick HD; Nick Jr.; NickToons en Espanol; NickToons TV; Outdoor Channel; Oxygen; Palladia; PBS Kids Sprout; Ritmoson Latino; Science Channel; Science Channel HD; SoapNet; Speed Channel; Spike TV HD; Sundance Channel; Syfy HD; TBS in HD; TeenNick; Telefutura; Telehit; Telemundo; TLC HD; Toon Disney; Travel Channel HD; Trinity Broadcasting Network; truTV; Turner Network TV HD; TV One; Universal HD; USA Network HD; Versus; Versus HD; VH1 Classic; VH1 HD; WGN.
Fee: $15.45 monthly.

Pay Service 1
Pay Units: N.A.
Programming (via satellite): HBO.
Fee: $16.99 monthly.

Digital Pay Service 1
Pay Units: 34,954.
Programming (via satellite): Cinemax (multiplexed); Cinemax HD.
Fee: $8.95 monthly.

Digital Pay Service 2
Pay Units: 13,546.
Programming (via satellite): Starz (multiplexed); Starz HDTV.
Fee: $8.95 monthly.

Digital Pay Service 3
Pay Units: 56,315.
Programming (via satellite): HBO (multiplexed); HBO HD.
Fee: $10.95 monthly.

Digital Pay Service 4
Pay Units: 23,424.
Programming (via satellite): Showtime (multiplexed); Showtime HD.
Fee: $8.95 monthly.

Digital Pay Service 5
Pay Units: 4,921.
Programming (via satellite): The Movie Channel (multiplexed).
Fee: $10.95 monthly.

Video-On-Demand: Yes

Pay-Per-View
Addressable homes: 65,382.
iN DEMAND (delivered digitally), Addressable: Yes; Playboy TV (delivered digitally), Fee: $3.95; Club Jenna (delivered digitally); Spice: Xcess (delivered digitally); Ten Blox (delivered digitally); Ten Clips (delivered digitally).

Internet Service
Operational: Yes. Began: September 1, 1997.
Subscribers: 36,600.
Broadband Service: Cox High Speed Internet.
Fee: $149.95 installation; $29.99-$59.99 monthly; $15.00 modem lease; $219.00 modem purchase.

Telephone Service
Digital: Operational
Fee: $15.89 monthly
Miles of Plant: 3,300.0 (coaxial); 1,100.0 (fiber optic). Total homes in franchised area: 330,000.
Vice President & General Manager: Percy Kirk. Vice President, Network Operations: Joe Seda. Vice President, Public & Government Affairs: Kristin Pec.
City fee: 5% of gross.
Ownership: Cox Communications Inc. (MSO).

OMAHA—Formerly served by Digital Broadcast Corp. No longer in operation. ICA: NE0354.

OMAHA (western portion)—Qwest Choice TV. Formerly [NE0377]. This cable system has converted to IPTV., 1801 California St, Denver, CO 80202. Phones: 800-899-7780; 303-992-1400. Fax: 303-896-8515. Web Site: http://www.qwest.com. ICA: NE5000.
TV Market Ranking: 53 (OMAHA (WESTERN PORTION)). Franchise award date: N.A. Franchise expiration date: N.A. Began: N.A.
Channel capacity: N.A. Channels available but not in use: N.A.

Internet Service
Operational: Yes.
Broadband Service: Choice OnLine.
Fee: $125.00 installation; $49.99 monthly.

Telephone Service
Digital: Operational
Ownership: Qwest Communications International Inc. (MSO).

OMAHA (western portion)—Qwest Choice TV. This cable system has converted to IPTV. See Omaha, NE [NE5000]. ICA: NE0377.

O'NEILL—Cable Nebraska, 2123 Central Ave, Ste 200, Kearney, NE 68847. Phone: 877-234-0102. Web Site: http://www.cablene.com. ICA: NE0030.
TV Market Ranking: Outside TV Markets (O'NEILL). Franchise award date: January 7, 1986. Franchise expiration date: N.A. Began: September 1, 1964.
Channel capacity: 49 (not 2-way capable). Channels available but not in use: N.A.

Basic Service
Subscribers: 1,138.
Programming (received off-air): KELO-TV (CBS, MNT) Sioux Falls; KHGI-LP O'Neill; KMGH-TV (ABC) Denver; KMNE-TV (PBS) Bassett; KOAZ-LP O'Neill; KOLN (CBS, MNT) Lincoln; KTIV (CW, NBC) Sioux City.
Programming (via satellite): ABC Family Channel; AMC; Animal Planet; Arts & Entertainment; Cartoon Network; CNBC; CNN; Comedy Central; Country Music TV; C-SPAN; CW+; Discovery Channel; Disney Channel; ESPN; ESPN 2; ESPNews; Eternal Word TV Network; FitTV; Food Network; Fox News Channel; Fox Sports Net Rocky Mountain; FX; Great American Country; Hallmark Channel; Headline News; HGTV; History Channel; Lifetime; MTV; Nickelodeon; Outdoor Channel; QVC; Speed Channel; Spike TV; Syfy; TBS Superstation; The Learning Channel; Travel Channel; truTV; Turner Network TV; TV Guide Network; TV Land; USA Network; Versus; VH1; WE tv; Weather Channel; WGN America.
Fee: $50.00 installation; $22.83 monthly.

Pay Service 1
Pay Units: 58.
Programming (via satellite): Cinemax.
Fee: $20.00 installation; $11.00 monthly.

Pay Service 2
Pay Units: 190.
Programming (via satellite): HBO.
Fee: $20.00 installation; $12.00 monthly.

Pay Service 3
Pay Units: 115.
Programming (via satellite): Showtime.
Fee: $20.00 installation; $11.00 monthly.

Pay Service 4
Pay Units: 103.
Programming (via satellite): The Movie Channel.
Fee: $20.00 installation; $11.00 monthly.

Video-On-Demand: No

Internet Service
Operational: No.

Telephone Service
None
Miles of Plant: 25.0 (coaxial); None (fiber optic). Homes passed: 2,140.
City fee: 3% of gross.
Ownership: USA Companies (MSO).

ORCHARD—Formerly served by TelePartners. No longer in operation. ICA: NE0370.

ORD—Charter Communications. Now served by KEARNEY, NE [NE0011]. ICA: NE0310.

ORLEANS—Formerly served by Pinpoint Cable TV. No longer in operation. ICA: NE0143.

OSCEOLA—Cable Nebraska, 2123 Central Ave, Ste 200, Kearney, NE 68847. Phone: 308-236-1512. Web Site: http://www.cablene.com. ICA: NE0089.
TV Market Ranking: Outside TV Markets (OSCEOLA). Franchise award date: N.A. Franchise expiration date: N.A. Began: April 1, 1982.
Channel capacity: N.A. Channels available but not in use: N.A.

Basic Service
Subscribers: 238.
Programming (received off-air): KGIN (CBS, MNT) Grand Island; KHAS-TV (NBC) Hastings; KHGI-TV (ABC) Kearney; KHNE-TV (PBS) Hastings; KLKN (ABC) Lincoln; KTVG-TV (FOX) Grand Island.
Programming (via satellite): C-SPAN; C-SPAN 2; CW+; Eternal Word TV Network; Home Shopping Network; MyNetworkTV Inc.; QVC; TBS Superstation; Trinity Broadcasting Network; Univision; Weather Channel; WGN America.
Fee: $35.00 installation; $29.95 monthly.

Expanded Basic Service 1
Subscribers: N.A.
Programming (via satellite): ABC Family Channel; AMC; Animal Planet; Arts & Entertainment; Cartoon Network; CNBC; CNN; Comedy Central; Country Music TV; Discovery Channel; E! Entertainment Television; ESPN; ESPN 2; ESPN Classic Sports; Food Network; Fox News Channel; Fox Sports Net Midwest; FX; G4; Great American Country; Hallmark Channel; Headline News; HGTV; History Channel; ION Television; Lifetime; MSNBC; MTV; Nickelodeon; Outdoor Channel; RFD-TV; Spike TV; Syfy; The Learning Channel; Travel Channel; truTV; Turner Classic Movies; Turner Network TV; TV Land; USA Network; Versus; VH1.

Digital Basic Service
Subscribers: N.A.
Programming (via satellite): AmericanLife TV Network; BBC America; Bio; Black Family Channel; Bloomberg Television; Cine Latino; Cine Mexicano; CMT Pure Country; CNN en Espanol; Current; Daystar TV Network; Discovery Channel HD; Discovery en Espanol; Discovery Health Channel; Discovery Kids Channel; Discovery Military Channel; Discovery Planet Green; DMX Music; ESPN 2; ESPN Classic Sports; ESPN Deportes; ESPN HD; ESPNews; FitTV; Fox College Sports Atlantic; Fox College Sports Central; Fox College Sports Pacific; Fox Movie Channel; Fox Sports en Espanol; G4; Golf Channel; GSN; Halogen Network; History Channel; History Channel en Espanol; History Channel International; ID Investigation Discovery; Lifetime Movie Network; MTV Hits; MTV Tres; MTV2; Nick Jr.; Outdoor Channel; Ovation; Science Channel; ShopNBC; Sleuth; Speed Channel; Style Network; Syfy; TBS in HD; TeenNick; Trinity Broadcasting Network; Turner Network TV HD; VeneMovies; Versus; VH1 Classic; VH1 Soul; WE tv.

Digital Pay Service 1
Pay Units: N.A.
Programming (via satellite): Cinemax (multiplexed); Encore (multiplexed); Flix; HBO (multiplexed); HBO Latino; Showtime (multiplexed); Starz (multiplexed); The Movie Channel (multiplexed).

Video-On-Demand: No

Pay-Per-View
iN DEMAND (delivered digitally); Hot Choice (delivered digitally); Playboy TV (delivered digitally); Fresh (delivered digitally); Spice: Xcess (delivered digitally); Club Jenna (delivered digitally).

Internet Service
Operational: Yes.
Broadband Service: Cable Nebraska.

Telephone Service
None
Miles of Plant: 9.0 (coaxial); None (fiber optic). Homes passed: 429.
Operations Manager: Stuart Gilbertson.
City fee: 3% of basic.
Ownership: USA Companies (MSO).

OSHKOSH—Great Plains Communications, PO Box 500, 1600 Great Plains Centre, Blair, NE 68008-0500. Phone: 402-426-9511. Fax: 402-456-6550. Web Site: http://www.gpcom.com. ICA: NE0090.
TV Market Ranking: Outside TV Markets (OSHKOSH). Franchise award date: N.A.

Franchise expiration date: N.A. Began: January 1, 1968.
Channel capacity: N.A. Channels available but not in use: N.A.

Basic Service
Subscribers: N.A. Included in Arnold
Programming (received off-air): KDUH-TV (ABC) Scottsbluff; KRNE-TV (PBS) Merriman; allband FM.
Programming (via microwave): KCNC-TV (CBS) Denver; KTVD (MNT) Denver; KUSA (NBC) Denver; KWGN-TV (CW) Denver.
Programming (via satellite): C-SPAN; Eternal Word TV Network; Home Shopping Network; INSP; QVC; Trinity Broadcasting Network; WGN America.
Fee: $39.24 installation; $30.95 monthly.

Expanded Basic Service 1
Subscribers: N.A.
Programming (via satellite): ABC Family Channel; AMC; Animal Planet; Arts & Entertainment; Bravo; Cartoon Network; CNBC; CNN; Comedy Central; Country Music TV; Discovery Channel; Disney Channel; E! Entertainment Television; ESPN; ESPN 2; Food Network; Fox News Channel; Fox Sports Net Rocky Mountain; FX; G4; Golf Channel; Hallmark Channel; Headline News; HGTV; History Channel; Lifetime; MSNBC; MTV; National Geographic Channel; Nickelodeon; Outdoor Channel; Oxygen; SoapNet; Speed Channel; Spike TV; Syfy; TBS Superstation; The Learning Channel; Toon Disney; Travel Channel; truTV; Turner Classic Movies; Turner Network TV; TV Land; USA Network; Versus; VH1; Weather Channel.
Fee: $15.86 monthly.

Digital Basic Service
Subscribers: N.A. Included in Arnold
Programming (via satellite): BBC America; Bio; Bloomberg Television; Discovery Digital Networks; Do-It-Yourself; GSN; History Channel International; Independent Film Channel; Lifetime Movie Network; MTV Networks Digital Suite; Music Choice; Nick Jr.; Nick Too; Style Network; Sundance Channel; TeenNick; TV Guide Interactive Inc.; WE tv.

Pay Service 1
Pay Units: 21.
Programming (via satellite): Cinemax; Showtime.
Fee: $3.65 monthly (Encore), $9.70 monthly (Showtime), $11.66 monthly (Cinemax).

Digital Pay Service 1
Pay Units: N.A.
Programming (via satellite): Cinemax (multiplexed); Encore (multiplexed); Flix; HBO (multiplexed); Showtime (multiplexed); Starz (multiplexed); The Movie Channel (multiplexed).

Video-On-Demand: No

Pay-Per-View
iN DEMAND (delivered digitally); Pleasure (delivered digitally); ETC (delivered digitally).

Internet Service
Operational: Yes, Both DSL & dial-up.
Fee: $49.95 installation; $39.95 monthly.

Telephone Service
None
Miles of Plant: 15.0 (coaxial); None (fiber optic). Homes passed: Included in Arnold
General Manager: Lee Ann Quist. Chief Technician: Mark Stottler. Marketing Manager: Casey Garrigan.
City fee: None.
Ownership: Great Plains Communications Inc. (MSO).

OSMOND—HunTel Cablevision. Now served by WAYNE, NE [NE0374]. ICA: NE0119.

OTOE—Formerly served by CableDirect. No longer in operation. ICA: NE0237.

OXFORD—Pinpoint Cable TV, PO Box 490, 611 Patterson St, Cambridge, NE 69022-0490. Phones: 800-793-2788; 308-697-7678; 308-697-3333. Fax: 308-697-3631. E-mail: info@pnpt.com. Web Site: http://www.pnpt.com. ICA: NE0092.
TV Market Ranking: Outside TV Markets (OXFORD). Franchise award date: N.A. Franchise expiration date: N.A. Began: July 1, 1982.
Channel capacity: 36 (not 2-way capable). Channels available but not in use: 2.

Basic Service
Subscribers: 136.
Programming (received off-air): KGIN (CBS, MNT) Grand Island; KHGI-TV (ABC) Kearney; KLNE-TV (PBS) Lexington; KSNK (NBC) McCook; allband FM.
Programming (via satellite): ABC Family Channel; Animal Planet; Arts & Entertainment; Cartoon Network; CNN; Discovery Channel; Disney Channel; ESPN; Fox Sports Net; FX; Great American Country; HGTV; History Channel; Lifetime; National Geographic Channel; Nickelodeon; QVC; Spike TV; TBS Superstation; The Learning Channel; Toon Disney; Trinity Broadcasting Network; Turner Network TV; TV Land; USA Network; Weather Channel; WGN America.
Fee: $15.00 installation; $33.95 monthly.

Pay Service 1
Pay Units: 10.
Programming (via satellite): Showtime.
Fee: $11.95 monthly.

Video-On-Demand: No

Internet Service
Operational: No, DSL.

Telephone Service
None
Miles of Plant: 7.0 (coaxial); None (fiber optic). Homes passed: 442. Total homes in franchised area: 442.
General Manager: J. Thomas Shoemaker.
City fee: 2% of gross.
Ownership: PinPoint Communications Inc. (MSO).

PAGE (village)—Formerly served by Sky Scan Cable Co. No longer in operation. ICA: NE0311.

PALMER—Cable Nebraska, 2123 Central Ave, Ste 200, Kearney, NE 68847. Phone: 308-236-1512. Web Site: http://www.cablene.com. ICA: NE0313.
TV Market Ranking: Below 100 (PALMER). Franchise award date: N.A. Franchise expiration date: N.A. Began: January 1, 1988.
Channel capacity: N.A. Channels available but not in use: N.A.

Basic Service
Subscribers: 87.
Programming (received off-air): KGIN (CBS, MNT) Grand Island; KHAS-TV (NBC) Hastings; KHGI-TV (ABC) Kearney; KHNE-TV (PBS) Hastings; KLKN (ABC) Lincoln; KTVG-TV (FOX) Grand Island.
Programming (via satellite): C-SPAN; C-SPAN 2; Eternal Word TV Network; Home Shopping Network; MyNetworkTV Inc.; QVC; TBS Superstation; Trinity Broadcasting Network; Univision; Weather Channel; WGN America; WPIX (CW, IND) New York.
Fee: $24.95 installation; $19.95 monthly.

Expanded Basic Service 1
Subscribers: N.A.
Programming (via satellite): ABC Family Channel; American Movie Classics; Animal Planet; Arts & Entertainment; Cartoon Network; CNBC; CNN; Comedy Central; Country Music TV; Discovery Channel; E! Entertainment Television; ESPN; ESPN 2; ESPN Classic Sports; Food Network; Fox News Channel; Fox Sports Net; FX; G4; Great American Country; Hallmark Channel; Headline News; HGTV; History Channel; ION Television; Lifetime; MSNBC; MTV; Nickelodeon; Outdoor Channel; RFD-TV; Spike TV; Syfy; The Learning Channel; Travel Channel; truTV; Turner Classic Movies; Turner Network TV; TV Land; USA Network; Versus; VH1.

Digital Basic Service
Subscribers: N.A.
Programming (via satellite): AmericanLife TV Network; BBC America; Bio; Black Family Channel; Bloomberg Television; Cine Latino; Cine Mexicano; CMT Pure Country; CNN en Espanol; Current; Daystar TV Network; Discovery Channel HD; Discovery en Espanol; Discovery Health Channel; Discovery Kids Channel; Discovery Military Channel; Discovery Planet Green; DMX Music; ESPN 2; ESPN Classic Sports; ESPN Deportes; ESPN HD; ESPNews; FitTV; Fox College Sports Atlantic; Fox College Sports Central; Fox College Sports Pacific; Fox Movie Channel; Fox Sports en Espanol; G4; Golf Channel; GSN; Halogen Network; History Channel; History Channel en Espanol; History Channel International; ID Investigation Discovery; Lifetime Movie Network; MTV Hits; MTV Tres; MTV2; Nick Jr.; Outdoor Channel; Ovation; Science Channel; ShopNBC; Sleuth; Speed Channel; Style Network; Syfy; TBS in HD; TeenNick; Trinity Broadcasting Network; Turner Network TV HD; VeneMovies; Versus; VH1 Classic; VH1 Soul; WE tv.

Digital Pay Service 1
Pay Units: N.A.
Programming (via satellite): Cinemax (multiplexed); Encore (multiplexed); Flix; HBO (multiplexed); HBO Latino; Showtime (multiplexed); Starz (multiplexed); The Movie Channel (multiplexed).

Video-On-Demand: No

Pay-Per-View
iN DEMAND (delivered digitally); Hot Choice (delivered digitally); Playboy TV (delivered digitally); Fresh (delivered digitally); Spice: Xcess (delivered digitally); Club Jenna (delivered digitally).

Internet Service
Operational: Yes.
Broadband Service: Cable Nebraska.
Fee: $35.95 monthly.

Telephone Service
None
Operations Manager: Stuart Gilbertson.
Ownership: USA Companies (MSO).

PAXTON—Peregrine Communications, 14818 W 6th Ave, Ste 16A, Golden, CO 80401-6585. Phones: 800-344-5404; 303-278-9660. E-mail: peregrine.info@perecom.com. Web Site: http://www.perecom.com. ICA: NE0162.
TV Market Ranking: Below 100 (PAXTON). Franchise award date: N.A. Franchise expiration date: N.A. Began: February 1, 1985.
Channel capacity: N.A. Channels available but not in use: N.A.

Basic Service
Subscribers: 140.
Programming (received off-air): KETV (ABC) Omaha; KNOP-TV (NBC) North Platte; KOLN (CBS, MNT) Lincoln; KPNE-TV (PBS) North Platte; KWNB-TV (ABC) Hayes Center.
Programming (via satellite): ABC Family Channel; AMC; Arts & Entertainment; CNN; Discovery Channel; Disney Channel; ESPN; Lifetime; QVC; Spike TV; TBS Superstation; Turner Network TV; USA Network; WGN America.
Fee: $30.00 installation; $31.95 monthly.

Pay Service 1
Pay Units: N.A.
Programming (via satellite): HBO.
Fee: $14.00 monthly.

Video-On-Demand: No

Internet Service
Operational: No.

Telephone Service
None
Homes passed: 206.
Manager: Patty Hyyppa. Chief Technician: Don Green. Regional Sales Manager: Marissa Post.
Ownership: Peregrine Communications (MSO).

PENDER—HunTel Cablevision. Now served by WAYNE, NE [NE0374]. ICA: NE0096.

PERU—Galaxy Cablevision, 1928 S Lincoln Ave, Ste 200, York, NE 68467. Phone: 402-362-3332. Fax: 402-362-4890. Web Site: http://www.galaxycable.com. ICA: NE0103.
TV Market Ranking: Outside TV Markets (PERU). Franchise award date: N.A. Franchise expiration date: N.A. Began: N.A.
Channel capacity: 41 (not 2-way capable). Channels available but not in use: 7.

Basic Service
Subscribers: 57.
Programming (received off-air): KETV (ABC) Omaha; KMTV-TV (CBS) Omaha; KOLN (CBS, MNT) Lincoln; KPTM (FOX, MNT) Omaha; KUON-TV (PBS) Lincoln; KXVO (CW) Omaha; WOWT-TV (IND, NBC) Omaha.
Programming (via satellite): ABC Family Channel; Arts & Entertainment; Cartoon Network; CNN; Comedy Central; Discovery Channel; Disney Channel; E! Entertainment Television; ESPN; ESPN 2; Fox News Channel; Fox Sports Net Midwest; Fuse; Great American Country; Headline News; HGTV; Lifetime; Outdoor Channel; TBS Superstation; Toon Disney; Travel Channel; Turner Network TV; USA Network; Weather Channel.
Fee: $40.20 monthly.

Pay Service 1
Pay Units: 34.
Programming (via satellite): Cinemax.
Fee: $11.95 monthly.
Pay Service 2
Pay Units: 39.
Programming (via satellite): HBO.
Fee: $12.95 monthly.
Internet Service
Operational: No.
Telephone Service
None
Miles of Plant: 6.0 (coaxial); None (fiber optic). Homes passed: 320.
State Manager: Cheyenne Wohlford. Technical Manager: Carl Stanley. Sales Manager: Mike Thomas. Customer Service Manager: Donna Bryant.
City fee: 3% of basic.
Ownership: Galaxy Cable Inc. (MSO).

PICKRELL—Comstar Cable TV Inc., PO Box 975, 8358 W Scott Rd, Beatrice, NE 68310-0975. Phone: 402-520-1987 (GM's cell). Fax: 402-228-3766. ICA: NE0315.
TV Market Ranking: 91 (PICKRELL). Franchise award date: N.A. Franchise expiration date: N.A. Began: May 3, 1989.
Channel capacity: 36 (not 2-way capable). Channels available but not in use: N.A.
Basic Service
Subscribers: 46.
Programming (received off-air): KLKN (ABC) Lincoln; KOLN (CBS, MNT) Lincoln; KPTM (FOX, MNT) Omaha; KUON-TV (PBS) Lincoln; KXVO (CW) Omaha; WOWT-TV (IND, NBC) Omaha.
Programming (via satellite): ABC Family Channel; AMC; Arts & Entertainment; Cartoon Network; CNN; C-SPAN; Discovery Channel; Disney Channel; ESPN; ESPN 2; Food Network; Fox News Channel; Fox Sports Net; FX; Great American Country; Hallmark Channel; HGTV; History Channel; Lifetime; QVC; RFD-TV; Syfy; TBS Superstation; The Learning Channel; Travel Channel; Turner Network TV; USA Network; Weather Channel; WGN America.
Fee: $40.00 installation; $31.95 monthly.
Digital Basic Service
Subscribers: N.A.
Programming (via satellite): AmericanLife TV Network; Bio; Bloomberg Television; Bravo; Discovery Kids Channel; Discovery Military Channel; Discovery Planet Green; Disney XD; ESPN 2; ESPN Classic Sports; ESPNews; FitTV; Fox College Sports Atlantic; Fox College Sports Central; Fox College Sports Pacific; Fox Movie Channel; Fuse; G4; Golf Channel; Great American Country; GSN; HGTV; History Channel; History Channel International; ID Investigation Discovery; INSP; National Geographic Channel; Outdoor Channel; Ovation; RFD-TV; Science Channel; Sleuth; SoapNet; Speed Channel; Trinity Broadcasting Network; Turner Classic Movies; Versus; WE tv.
Pay Service 1
Pay Units: N.A.
Programming (via satellite): HBO.
Fee: $7.50 monthly.
Video-On-Demand: No
Internet Service
Operational: No.
Telephone Service
None
Miles of Plant: 2.0 (coaxial); None (fiber optic). Homes passed: 90.
Manager: Tim Schwarz.
Ownership: Comstar Cable TV Inc. (MSO).

PILGER—Sky Scan Cable Co. Now served by NORFOLK, NE [NE0006]. ICA: NE0316.

PLATTE CENTER—Cable Nebraska, 2123 Central Ave, Ste 200, Kearney, NE 68847. Phone: 308-236-1512. Web Site: http://www.cablene.com. ICA: NE0391.
TV Market Ranking: Outside TV Markets (PLATTE CENTER).
Channel capacity: N.A. Channels available but not in use: N.A.
Basic Service
Subscribers: N.A.
Programming (received off-air): KLKN (ABC) Lincoln; KOLN (CBS, MNT) Lincoln; KPTM (FOX, MNT) Omaha; KUON-TV (PBS) Lincoln; KXVO (CW) Omaha; WOWT-TV (IND, NBC) Omaha.
Programming (via satellite): ABC Family Channel; AMC; Arts & Entertainment; Cartoon Network; CNN; Discovery Channel; ESPN; ESPN 2; Fox News Channel; Great American Country; Hallmark Channel; Headline News; HGTV; History Channel; Lifetime; Nickelodeon; Outdoor Channel; QVC; Spike TV; TBS Superstation; The Learning Channel; Turner Network TV; USA Network; Versus; Weather Channel; WGN America.
Pay Service 1
Pay Units: N.A.
Programming (via satellite): HBO.
Internet Service
Operational: No.
Operations Manager: Stuart Gilbertson.
Ownership: USA Companies (MSO).

PLATTE CENTER—Formerly served by TelePartners. No longer in operation. ICA: NE0371.

POLK—Cable Nebraska, 2123 Central Ave, Ste 200, Kearney, NE 68847. Phone: 308-236-1512. Web Site: http://www.cablene.com. ICA: NE0140.
TV Market Ranking: Below 100 (POLK). Franchise award date: N.A. Franchise expiration date: N.A. Began: February 1, 1983.
Channel capacity: N.A. Channels available but not in use: N.A.
Basic Service
Subscribers: 66.
Programming (received off-air): KGIN (CBS, MNT) Grand Island; KHAS-TV (NBC) Hastings; KHGI-TV (ABC) Kearney; KHNE-TV (PBS) Hastings; KLKN (ABC) Lincoln; KTVG-TV (FOX) Grand Island.
Programming (via satellite): C-SPAN; C-SPAN 2; Eternal Word TV Network; Home Shopping Network; MyNetworkTV Inc.; QVC; TBS Superstation; Trinity Broadcasting Network; Univision; Weather Channel; WGN America.
Fee: $35.00 installation; $28.95 monthly.
Expanded Basic Service 1
Subscribers: N.A.
Programming (via satellite): ABC Family Channel; AMC; Animal Planet; Arts & Entertainment; Cartoon Network; CNBC; CNN; Comedy Central; Country Music TV; Court TV; Discovery Channel; E! Entertainment Television; ESPN; ESPN 2; ESPN Classic Sports; Food Network; Fox News Channel; Fox Sports Net Midwest; FX; G4; Great American Country; Hallmark Channel; Headline News; HGTV; History Channel; ION Television; Lifetime; MSNBC; MTV; Nickelodeon; Outdoor Channel; RFD-TV; Spike TV; Syfy; The Learning Channel; Travel Channel; Turner Classic Movies; Turner Network TV; TV Land; USA Network; Versus; VH1.
Digital Basic Service
Subscribers: N.A.
Programming (via satellite): AmericanLife TV Network; BBC America; Bio; Black Family Channel; Bloomberg Television; Cine Latino; Cine Mexicano; CMT Pure Country; CNN en Espanol; Current; Daystar TV Network; Discovery Channel HD; Discovery en Espanol; Discovery Health Channel; Discovery Kids Channel; Discovery Military Channel; Discovery Planet Green; Discovery Times Channel; DMX Music; ESPN 2; ESPN Classic Sports; ESPN Deportes; ESPN HD; ESPNews; FitTV; Fox College Sports Atlantic; Fox College Sports Central; Fox College Sports Pacific; Fox Movie Channel; Fox Sports en Espanol; G4; Golf Channel; GSN; Halogen Network; History Channel; History Channel en Espanol; History Channel International; Lifetime Movie Network; MTV Hits; MTV Tres; MTV2; Nick Jr.; Outdoor Channel; Ovation; Science Channel; ShopNBC; Sleuth; Speed Channel; Style Network; Syfy; TBS in HD; TeenNick; Trinity Broadcasting Network; Turner Network TV HD; VeneMovies; Versus; VH1 Classic; VH1 Soul; WE tv.
Digital Pay Service 1
Pay Units: N.A.
Programming (via satellite): Cinemax (multiplexed); Encore (multiplexed); Flix; HBO (multiplexed); HBO Latino; Showtime (multiplexed); Starz (multiplexed); The Movie Channel.
Video-On-Demand: No
Pay-Per-View
iN DEMAND (delivered digitally); Hot Choice (delivered digitally); Playboy TV (delivered digitally); Fresh (delivered digitally); Spice: Xcess (delivered digitally); Club Jenna (delivered digitally).
Internet Service
Operational: Yes.
Broadband Service: Cable Nebraska.
Telephone Service
None
Miles of Plant: 4.0 (coaxial); None (fiber optic). Homes passed: 194.
Operations Manager: Stuart Gilbertson.
City fee: 1% of basic.
Ownership: USA Companies (MSO).

PONCA—Great Plains Communications, PO Box 500, 1600 Great Plains Centre, Blair, NE 68008-0500. Phones: 888-343-8014; 402-426-9511. Fax: 402-456-6485. E-mail: lquist@gpcom.com. Web Site: http://www.gpcom.com. ICA: NE0318.
TV Market Ranking: Below 100 (PONCA). Franchise award date: March 1, 1984. Franchise expiration date: N.A. Began: N.A.
Channel capacity: 80 (operating 2-way). Channels available but not in use: 30.
Basic Service
Subscribers: 291.
Programming (received off-air): KCAU-TV (ABC) Sioux City; KMEG (CBS) Sioux City; KPTH (FOX, MNT) Sioux City; KSIN-TV (PBS) Sioux City; KTIV (CW, NBC) Sioux City; KXNE-TV (PBS) Norfolk.
Programming (via satellite): ABC Family Channel; AMC; Animal Planet; Arts & Entertainment; CNN; Country Music TV; Discovery Channel; Disney Channel; ESPN; Fox Sports Net; Hallmark Channel; Headline News; Lifetime; MTV; Nickelodeon; QVC; Spike TV; TBS Superstation; The Learning Channel; Travel Channel; Turner Network TV; TV Land; USA Network; VH1; Weather Channel; WGN America.
Fee: $28.00 installation; $31.50 monthly.
Expanded Basic Service 1
Subscribers: 190.
Programming (via satellite): Cartoon Network; Encore; ESPN 2; Golf Channel; HGTV; History Channel; Turner Classic Movies; Versus.
Fee: $6.50 monthly.
Digital Basic Service
Subscribers: 31.
Programming (via satellite): BBC America; Bio; Bravo; Discovery Digital Networks; ESPN Classic Sports; Fox Sports World; GAS; Golf Channel; History Channel International; Independent Film Channel; Lifetime Movie Network; MTV2; National Geographic Channel; Nick Jr.; Outdoor Channel; Speed Channel; Syfy; Turner Classic Movies; VH1 Classic; VH1 Country; WE tv.
Fee: $47.95 monthly.
Pay Service 1
Pay Units: 42.
Programming (via satellite): HBO; Showtime.
Fee: $9.95 monthly (Showtime), $10.95 monthly (HBO).
Video-On-Demand: No
Pay-Per-View
Addressable homes: 30.
ESPN Extra, Addressable: Yes; iN DEMAND, Fee: $3.99.
Internet Service
Operational: Yes, Both DSL & dial-up.
Subscribers: 156.
Broadband Service: Netlink.
Fee: $49.95 installation; $39.95 monthly.
Telephone Service
None
Manager: Lea Ann Quist. Chief Technician: Mark Stottler.
Ownership: Great Plains Communications Inc. (MSO).

PRAGUE—Formerly served by Westcom. No longer in operation. ICA: NE0221.

RAYMOND—Galaxy Cablevision, 1928 S Lincoln Ave, Ste 200, York, NE 68467. Phone: 402-362-3332. Fax: 402-362-4890. Web Site: http://www.galaxycable.com. ICA: NE0250.
TV Market Ranking: 91 (RAYMOND). Franchise award date: N.A. Franchise expiration date: N.A. Began: September 11, 1989.
Channel capacity: 41 (not 2-way capable). Channels available but not in use: 16.
Basic Service
Subscribers: 16.
Programming (received off-air): KLKN (ABC) Lincoln; KOLN (CBS, MNT) Lincoln; KPTM (FOX, MNT) Omaha; KUON-TV (PBS) Lincoln; KXVO (CW) Omaha; WOWT-TV (IND, NBC) Omaha.
Programming (via satellite): ABC Family Channel; Arts & Entertainment; Cartoon Network; CNN; Discovery Channel; ESPN; Fox Sports Net Midwest; Great American Country; Lifetime; Outdoor Channel; TBS Superstation; Toon Disney; Turner Classic Movies; Turner Network TV; USA Network; WGN America.
Fee: $32.95 monthly.
Pay Service 1
Pay Units: 8.
Programming (via satellite): Cinemax.
Fee: $11.95 monthly.
Pay Service 2
Pay Units: 8.
Programming (via satellite): HBO.
Fee: $12.95 monthly.
Internet Service
Operational: No.

Telephone Service
None
Miles of Plant: 2.0 (coaxial); None (fiber optic). Homes passed: 83.
State Manager: Cheyenne Wolhford. Technical Manager: Carl Stanley. Sales Manager: Mike Thomas. Customer Service Manager: Donna Bryant.
City fee: 3% of basic.
Ownership: Galaxy Cable Inc. (MSO).

RED CLOUD—Formerly served by Pinpoint Cable TV. No longer in operation. ICA: NE0321.

REPUBLICAN CITY—Formerly served by Pinpoint Cable TV. No longer in operation. ICA: NE0234.

RICHLAND—Cable Nebraska, 2123 Central Ave, Ste 200, Kearney, NE 68847. Phone: 308-236-1512. Web Site: http://www.cablene.com. Also serves Platte County (portions). ICA: NE0390.
TV Market Ranking: Outside TV Markets (Platte County (portions), RICHLAND).
Channel capacity: N.A. Channels available but not in use: N.A.
Basic Service
Subscribers: N.A.
Programming (received off-air): KETV (ABC) Omaha; KLKN (ABC) Lincoln; KMTV-TV (CBS) Omaha; KOLN (CBS, MNT) Lincoln; KPTM (FOX, MNT) Omaha; KUON-TV (PBS) Lincoln; KXVO (CW) Omaha; WOWT-TV (IND, NBC) Omaha.
Programming (via satellite): Eternal Word TV Network; GalaVision; Home Shopping Network; MTV; QVC; TBS Superstation; Telefutura; Telemundo; Univision; Weather Channel; WGN America; WPIX (CW, IND) New York.
Expanded Basic Service 1
Subscribers: N.A.
Programming (via satellite): ABC Family Channel; AMC; Animal Planet; Arts & Entertainment; Cartoon Network; CNBC; CNN; Comedy Central; Country Music TV; Court TV; Discovery Channel; E! Entertainment Television; ESPN; ESPN 2; ESPN Classic Sports; Food Network; Fox News Channel; Fox Sports Net; FX; G4; Great American Country; Hallmark Channel; Headline News; HGTV; History Channel; ION Television; Lifetime; MSNBC; Nickelodeon; Outdoor Channel; RFD-TV; Spike TV; Syfy; The Learning Channel; Travel Channel; Turner Classic Movies; Turner Network TV; TV Land; USA Network; Versus; VH1.
Digital Basic Service
Subscribers: N.A.
Programming (via satellite): Alterna'TV; BBC America; Bio; Bloomberg Television; Cine Latino; Cine Mexicano; CMT Pure Country; CNN en Espanol; Current; Daystar TV Network; Discovery Channel HD; Discovery en Espanol; Discovery Health Channel; Discovery Kids Channel; Discovery Military Channel; Discovery Planet Green; DMX Music; ESPN 2; ESPN Classic Sports; ESPN Deportes; ESPN HD; ESPNews; FitTV; Fox College Sports Atlantic; Fox College Sports Central; Fox College Sports Pacific; Fox Movie Channel; Fox Sports en Espanol; G4; Golf Channel; GSN; Halogen Network; History Channel; History Channel en Espanol; History Channel International; ID Investigation Discovery; MBC America; MTV Hits; MTV Tres; MTV2; Nick Jr.; Outdoor Channel; Ovation; PBS HD; Science Channel; ShopNBC; Sleuth; Speed Channel; Style Network; Syfy; TBS in HD; TeenNick; Trinity Broadcasting Network; Turner Network TV HD; VeneMovies; Versus; VH1 Classic; VH1 Soul; WE tv.
Pay Service 1
Pay Units: N.A.
Programming (via satellite): HBO Latino.
Digital Pay Service 1
Pay Units: N.A.
Programming (via satellite): Cinemax (multiplexed); Encore (multiplexed); Flix; Fox Movie Channel; HBO (multiplexed); HBO Latino; Lifetime Movie Network; Showtime (multiplexed); Starz (multiplexed); The Movie Channel (multiplexed).
Video-On-Demand: No
Pay-Per-View
iN DEMAND (delivered digitally); Playboy TV (delivered digitally); Hot Choice (delivered digitally); Fresh (delivered digitally); Spice: Xcess (delivered digitally); Club Jenna (delivered digitally).
Internet Service
Operational: Yes.
Broadband Service: Cable Nebraska.
Telephone Service
None
Operations Manager: Stuart Gilbertson.
Ownership: USA Companies (MSO).

RULO—Formerly served by CableDirect. No longer in operation. Also serves RULO. ICA: NE0207.

RUSKIN—Formerly served by Diode Cable Co. No longer in operation. ICA: NE0246.

SALEM—Formerly served by CableDirect. No longer in operation. ICA: NE0242.

SARGENT—NCTC Cable, PO Box 700, 22 LaBarre St, Gibbon, NE 68840. Phones: 888-873-6282; 308-468-6341. Fax: 308-468-9929. Web Site: http://www.nctc.net. ICA: NE0081.
TV Market Ranking: Outside TV Markets (SARGENT). Franchise award date: N.A. Franchise expiration date: N.A. Began: January 1, 1972.
Channel capacity: N.A. Channels available but not in use: N.A.
Basic Service
Subscribers: N.A. Included in Burwell
Programming (received off-air): KGIN (CBS, MNT) Grand Island; KHAS-TV (NBC) Hastings; KHGI-TV (ABC) Kearney; KMNE-TV (PBS) Bassett; KTVG-TV (FOX) Grand Island; allband FM.
Programming (via satellite): ABC Family Channel; AMC; Animal Planet; Arts & Entertainment; Cartoon Network; CNBC; CNN; Comedy Central; Country Music TV; C-SPAN; CW+; Discovery Channel; E! Entertainment Television; ESPN; ESPN 2; ESPN Classic Sports; Eternal Word TV Network; Food Network; Fox News Channel; Fox Sports Net Midwest; FX; G4; Great American Country; Hallmark Channel; Headline News; HGTV; History Channel; Home Shopping Network; ION Television; Lifetime; MSNBC; MTV; Nickelodeon; Outdoor Channel; QVC; Spike TV; Syfy; TBS Superstation; The Learning Channel; Travel Channel; Trinity Broadcasting Network; truTV; Turner Classic Movies; Turner Network TV; TV Land; USA Network; Versus; VH1; Weather Channel; WGN America.
Fee: $39.20 monthly.
Digital Basic Service
Subscribers: N.A. Included in Burwell
Programming (via satellite): AmericanLife TV Network; BBC America; Bio; Bloomberg Television; Current; Daystar TV Network; Discovery Digital Networks; DMX Music; ESPNews; FitTV; Fox College Sports Atlantic; Fox College Sports Central; Fox College Sports Pacific; Fox Movie Channel; G4; GAS; Golf Channel; Gospel Music Channel; GSN; Halogen Network; History Channel International; Lifetime Movie Network; MTV Networks Digital Suite; Nick Jr.; Ovation; RFD-TV; ShopNBC; Sleuth; Speed Channel; WE tv.
Fee: $14.00 monthly.
Pay Service 1
Pay Units: 33.
Programming (via satellite): HBO.
Fee: $10.95 monthly.
Digital Pay Service 1
Pay Units: N.A.
Programming (via satellite): Cinemax (multiplexed); Encore (multiplexed); Flix; HBO (multiplexed); Showtime (multiplexed); Starz (multiplexed); The Movie Channel (multiplexed).
Fee: $10.95 monthly (Cinemax), $12.95 monthly (HBO or Showtime, TMC & Flix), $13.95 monthly (Starz & Encore).
Video-On-Demand: No
Internet Service
Operational: No, DSL & dial-up.
Telephone Service
None
Miles of Plant: 8.0 (coaxial); None (fiber optic). Homes passed included in Burwell
General Manager: Andy Jader. Technical Operations Manager: Nick Jeffres.
City fee: None.
Ownership: Nebraska Central Telecom Inc. (MSO).

SCHUYLER—Cable Nebraska, 2123 Central Ave, Ste 200, Kearney, NE 68847. Phone: 308-236-1512. Fax: 605-229-0478. Web Site: http://www.cablene.com. ICA: NE0039.
TV Market Ranking: Outside TV Markets (SCHUYLER). Franchise award date: N.A. Franchise expiration date: N.A. Began: November 1, 1980.
Channel capacity: N.A. Channels available but not in use: N.A.
Basic Service
Subscribers: 932.
Programming (received off-air): KETV (ABC) Omaha; KLKN (ABC) Lincoln; KMTV-TV (CBS) Omaha; KOLN (CBS, MNT) Lincoln; KPTM (FOX, MNT) Omaha; KUON-TV (PBS) Lincoln; KXVO (CW) Omaha; WOWT-TV (IND, NBC) Omaha.
Programming (via satellite): Eternal Word TV Network; GalaVision; Home Shopping Network; MyNetworkTV Inc.; QVC; TBS Superstation; Telefutura; Telemundo; Univision; Weather Channel; WGN America; WPIX (CW, IND) New York.
Current originations: Public Access.
Fee: $35.00 installation; $36.95 monthly.
Expanded Basic Service 1
Subscribers: N.A.
Programming (via satellite): ABC Family Channel; Animal Planet; Arts & Entertainment; Cartoon Network; CNBC; CNN; Comedy Central; Country Music TV; Discovery Channel; E! Entertainment Television; ESPN; ESPN 2; ESPN Classic Sports; Food Network; Fox News Channel; Fox Sports Net Midwest; FX; G4; Great American Country; Hallmark Channel; Headline News; HGTV; History Channel; ION Television; Lifetime; MSNBC; MTV; Nickelodeon; Outdoor Channel; RFD-TV; Spike TV; Syfy; The Learning Channel; Travel Channel; truTV; Turner Classic Movies; Turner Network TV; TV Land; USA Network; Versus; VH1.
Digital Basic Service
Subscribers: N.A.
Programming (via satellite): Alterna'TV; AZ TV; BBC America; Bio; Bloomberg Television; CMT Pure Country; Current; Daystar TV Network; Discovery Channel HD; Discovery Health Channel; Discovery Home Channel; Discovery Kids Channel; Discovery Times Channel; DMX Music; ESPN HD; ESPNews; FitTV; Fox College Sports Atlantic; Fox College Sports Central; Fox College Sports Pacific; Fox Movie Channel; Golf Channel; GSN; Halogen Network; History Channel International; MBC America; MTV Hits; MTV2; MyNetworkTV Inc.; Netlink International; Nick Jr.; Outdoor Channel; Ovation; Science Channel; ShopNBC; Sleuth; Speed Channel; Style Network; TBS in HD; TeenNick; Trinity Broadcasting Network; Turner Network TV HD; VH1 Classic; VH1 Soul; WE tv.
Fee: $13.00 monthly.
Pay Service 1
Pay Units: N.A.
Programming (via satellite): HBO Latino.
Digital Pay Service 1
Pay Units: N.A.
Programming (via satellite): Cinemax (multiplexed); Encore (multiplexed); Flix; HBO (multiplexed); Lifetime Movie Network; Showtime (multiplexed); Starz (multiplexed); The Movie Channel (multiplexed); WAM! America's Kidz Network.
Fee: $3.00 monthly (Cinemax & HBO), $10.00 monthly (Flix, Showtime, & TMC).
Video-On-Demand: No
Pay-Per-View
iN DEMAND (delivered digitally); Hot Choice (delivered digitally); Playboy TV (delivered digitally); Fresh (delivered digitally); Spice: Xcess (delivered digitally); Club Jenna (delivered digitally).
Internet Service
Operational: Yes.
Broadband Service: Cable Nebraska.
Fee: $42.95 monthly.
Telephone Service
None
Miles of Plant: 32.0 (coaxial); None (fiber optic). Homes passed: 1,778.
Operations Manager: Stuart Gilbertson.
City fee: 3% of basic.
Ownership: USA Companies (MSO).

SCOTIA—NCTC Cable, PO Box 700, 22 LaBarre St, Gibbon, NE 68840. Phones: 888-873-6282; 308-468-6341. Fax: 308-468-9929. Web Site: http://www.nctc.net. ICA: NE0217.

TV Market Ranking: Outside TV Markets (SCOTIA). Franchise award date: N.A. Franchise expiration date: N.A. Began: N.A.
Channel capacity: N.A. Channels available but not in use: N.A.

Basic Service
Subscribers: N.A. Included in Burwell
Programming (received off-air): KGIN (CBS, MNT) Grand Island; KHAS-TV (NBC) Hastings; KHGI-TV (ABC) Kearney; KMNE-TV (PBS) Bassett; KTVG-TV (FOX) Grand Island.
Programming (via satellite): ABC Family Channel; AMC; Arts & Entertainment; Cartoon Network; CNBC; CNN; Comedy Central; Country Music TV; C-SPAN; CW+; Discovery Channel; E! Entertainment Television; ESPN; ESPN 2; ESPN Classic Sports; Eternal Word TV Network; Food Network; Fox News Channel; Fox Sports Net; FX; G4; Great American Country; Hallmark Channel; Headline News; HGTV; History Channel; Home Shopping Network; ION Television; Lifetime; MSNBC; MTV; Nickelodeon; Outdoor Channel; QVC; Spike TV; Syfy; TBS Superstation; The Learning Channel; Travel Channel; Trinity Broadcasting Network; truTV; Turner Classic Movies; Turner Network TV; TV Land; USA Network; Versus; VH1; Weather Channel; WGN America.
Fee: $35.00 installation; $39.20 monthly.

Digital Basic Service
Subscribers: N.A. Included in Burwell
Programming (via satellite): AmericanLife TV Network; BBC America; Bio; Bloomberg Television; Current; Daystar TV Network; Discovery Health Channel; Discovery Kids Channel; Discovery Military Channel; Discovery Planet Green; DMX Music; ESPN 2; ESPN Classic Sports; ESPNews; FitTV; Fox College Sports Atlantic; Fox College Sports Central; Fox College Sports Pacific; Fox Movie Channel; G4; Golf Channel; GSN; Halogen Network; History Channel; History Channel International; ID Investigation Discovery; Lifetime Movie Network; MTV Hits; MTV2; Nick Jr.; Outdoor Channel; RFD-TV; Science Channel; ShopNBC; Sleuth; SoapNet; Speed Channel; Style Network; Syfy; TeenNick; Toon Disney; Trinity Broadcasting Network; Versus; VH1 Classic; VH1 Country; VH1 Soul; WE tv.
Fee: $14.00 monthly.

Pay Service 1
Pay Units: 8.
Programming (via satellite): HBO.
Fee: $10.95 monthly.

Digital Pay Service 1
Pay Units: N.A.
Programming (via satellite): Cinemax (multiplexed); Encore (multiplexed); Flix; Fox Movie Channel; HBO (multiplexed); Lifetime Movie Network; Showtime (multiplexed); Starz (multiplexed); The Movie Channel (multiplexed).
Fee: $10.95 monthly (Cinemax), $12.95 monthly (HBO or Showtime/TMC/Flix), $13.95 monthly (Starz/Encore/Fox Movie/Lifetime Movie).

Video-On-Demand: No

Internet Service
Operational: No, DSL & dial-up.

Telephone Service
None
Miles of Plant: 5.0 (coaxial); None (fiber optic). Homes passed included in Burwell
General Manager: Andy Jader. Technical Operations Manager: Nick Jeffres.
City fee: None.
Ownership: Nebraska Central Telecom Inc. (MSO).

SCOTTSBLUFF—Charter Communications, 3380 Northern Valley Pl NE, Rochester, MN 55906-3954. Phones: 308-632-5700 (Scottsbluff office); 507-289-8372 (Rochester administrative office). Fax: 507-285-6162. Web Site: http://www.charter.com. Also serves Bayard, Box Butte County (portions), Bridgeport, Gering, Melbeta, Minatare, Mitchell, Morrill, Scotts Bluff County & Terrytown. ICA: NE0008.
TV Market Ranking: Below 100 (Bayard, Box Butte County (portions), Bridgeport, Gering, Melbeta, Minatare, Mitchell, Morrill, Scotts Bluff County, SCOTTSBLUFF, Terrytown); Outside TV Markets (Box Butte County (portions)). Franchise award date: N.A. Franchise expiration date: N.A. Began: February 1, 1960.
Channel capacity: N.A. Channels available but not in use: N.A.

Basic Service
Subscribers: 9,443.
Programming (received off-air): KDUH-TV (ABC) Scottsbluff; KLWY (FOX) Cheyenne; KSTF (CBS, CW) Scottsbluff; KTNE-TV (PBS) Alliance; KTVD (MNT) Denver; KUSA (NBC) Denver; KWGN-TV (CW) Denver.
Programming (via satellite): C-SPAN; C-SPAN 2; Eternal Word TV Network; Home Shopping Network; INSP; ION Television; QVC.
Current originations: Government Access; Educational Access.
Fee: $29.99 installation; $2.00 converter.

Expanded Basic Service 1
Subscribers: 7,881.
Programming (via satellite): ABC Family Channel; AMC; Animal Planet; Arts & Entertainment; Bravo; Cartoon Network; CNBC; CNN; Comedy Central; Country Music TV; Discovery Channel; Disney Channel; E! Entertainment Television; ESPN; ESPN 2; Food Network; Fox News Channel; Fox Sports Net Rocky Mountain; FX; G4; GalaVision; Golf Channel; Great American Country; Hallmark Channel; Headline News; HGTV; History Channel; Lifetime; MSNBC; MTV; National Geographic Channel; Nickelodeon; Oxygen; SoapNet; Speed Channel; Spike TV; Syfy; TBS Superstation; Telemundo; The Learning Channel; Travel Channel; truTV; Turner Classic Movies; Turner Network TV; TV Land; Univision; USA Network; Versus; VH1; Weather Channel.
Fee: $47.99 monthly.

Digital Basic Service
Subscribers: N.A.
Programming (via satellite): BBC America; Bio; Bloomberg Television; Discovery Digital Networks; Do-It-Yourself; ESPN Classic Sports; ESPNews; FitTV; Fox Movie Channel; Fox Sports en Espanol; Fox Sports World; Fuel TV; Fuse; GAS; GSN; Halogen Network; History Channel International; Independent Film Channel; Lifetime Movie Network; MTV Networks Digital Suite; Music Choice; Nick Jr.; Nick Too; NickToons TV; Outdoor Channel; Sundance Channel; Toon Disney; Trinity Broadcasting Network; TV Guide Interactive Inc.; WE tv.

Digital Pay Service 1
Pay Units: 636.
Programming (via satellite): Cinemax (multiplexed); Encore (multiplexed); HBO (multiplexed); Showtime (multiplexed).
Fee: $20.00 installation.

Digital Pay Service 2
Pay Units: N.A.
Programming (via satellite): Flix; Starz (multiplexed); The Movie Channel (multiplexed).

Video-On-Demand: Yes

Pay-Per-View
iN DEMAND (delivered digitally); NASCAR In Car (delivered digitally); Hot Choice (delivered digitally); Playboy TV (delivered digitally); Fresh (delivered digitally); Shorteez (delivered digitally).

Internet Service
Operational: Yes.
Broadband Service: Charter Pipeline.
Fee: $29.99 monthly.

Telephone Service
Digital: Operational
Miles of Plant: 233.0 (coaxial); None (fiber optic). Total homes in franchised area: 17,834.
Vice President & General Manager: John Crowley. Technical Operations Director: Marty Kovarik. Technical Operations Manager: Joel Saunders. Marketing Director: Bill Haarstad.
Franchise fee: 3% of gross.
Ownership: Charter Communications Inc. (MSO).

SHELBY—Cable Nebraska, 2123 Central Ave, Ste 200, Kearney, NE 68847. Phone: 308-236-1512. Web Site: http://www.cablene.com. ICA: NE0118.
TV Market Ranking: Outside TV Markets (SHELBY). Franchise award date: N.A. Franchise expiration date: N.A. Began: April 1, 1982.
Channel capacity: N.A. Channels available but not in use: N.A.

Basic Service
Subscribers: 180.
Programming (received off-air): KGIN (CBS, MNT) Grand Island; KHAS-TV (NBC) Hastings; KHGI-TV (ABC) Kearney; KHNE-TV (PBS) Hastings; KLKN (ABC) Lincoln; KTVG-TV (FOX) Grand Island.
Programming (via satellite): C-SPAN; C-SPAN 2; Eternal Word TV Network; Home Shopping Network; MyNetworkTV Inc.; QVC; TBS Superstation; Trinity Broadcasting Network; Univision; Weather Channel; WGN America.
Fee: $35.00 installation; $27.95 monthly.

Expanded Basic Service 1
Subscribers: N.A.
Programming (via satellite): ABC Family Channel; AMC; Animal Planet; Arts & Entertainment; Cartoon Network; CNBC; CNN; Comedy Central; Country Music TV; Discovery Channel; E! Entertainment Television; ESPN; ESPN 2; ESPN Classic Sports; Food Network; Fox News Channel; Fox Sports Net Midwest; FX; G4; Great American Country; Hallmark Channel; Headline News; HGTV; History Channel; ION Television; Lifetime; MSNBC; MTV; Nickelodeon; Outdoor Channel; RFD-TV; Spike TV; Syfy; The Learning Channel; Travel Channel; truTV; Turner Classic Movies; Turner Network TV; TV Land; USA Network; Versus; VH1.

Digital Basic Service
Subscribers: N.A.
Programming (via satellite): AmericanLife TV Network; BBC America; Bio; Black Family Channel; Bloomberg Television; Cine Latino; Cine Mexicano; CMT Pure Country; CNN en Espanol; Current; Daystar TV Network; Discovery Channel HD; Discovery en Espanol; Discovery Health Channel; Discovery Kids Channel; Discovery Military Channel; Discovery Planet Green; DMX Music; ESPN 2; ESPN Classic Sports; ESPN Deportes; ESPN HD; FitTV; Fox College Sports Atlantic; Fox College Sports Central; Fox College Sports Pacific; Fox Movie Channel; Fox Sports en Espanol; G4; Golf Channel; GSN; Halogen Network; History Channel; History Channel en Espanol; History Channel International; ID Investigation Discovery; Lifetime Movie Network; MTV Hits; MTV Tres; MTV2; Nick Jr.; Outdoor Channel; Ovation; Science Channel; ShopNBC; Sleuth; Speed Channel; Style Network; Syfy; TBS in HD; TeenNick; Trinity Broadcasting Network; Turner Network TV HD; VeneMovies; Versus; VH1 Classic; VH1 Soul; WE tv.

Digital Pay Service 1
Pay Units: N.A.
Programming (via satellite): Cinemax (multiplexed); Encore (multiplexed); Flix; HBO (multiplexed); HBO Latino; Showtime (multiplexed); Starz (multiplexed); The Movie Channel (multiplexed).

Video-On-Demand: No

Pay-Per-View
iN DEMAND (delivered digitally); Hot Choice (delivered digitally); Playboy TV (delivered digitally); Fresh (delivered digitally); Spice: Xcess (delivered digitally); Club Jenna (delivered digitally).

Internet Service
Operational: Yes.
Broadband Service: Cable Nebraska.

Telephone Service
None
Miles of Plant: 6.0 (coaxial); None (fiber optic). Homes passed: 325.
Operations Manager: Stuart Gilbertson.
City fee: 1% of basic.
Ownership: USA Companies (MSO).

SHUBERT—Formerly served by CableDirect. No longer in operation. ICA: NE0224.

SIDNEY—Charter Communications, 3380 Northern Valley Pl NE, Rochester, MN 55906-3954. Phone: 507-289-8372 (Rochester administrative office). Fax: 507-285-6162. Web Site: http://www.charter.com. Also serves Cheyenne County. ICA: NE0021.
TV Market Ranking: Below 100 (Cheyenne County (portions), SIDNEY); Outside TV Markets (Cheyenne County (portions)). Franchise award date: N.A. Franchise expiration date: N.A. Began: September 1, 1958.
Channel capacity: N.A. Channels available but not in use: N.A.

Basic Service
Subscribers: 2,000.
Programming (received off-air): KCNC-TV (CBS) Denver; KDUH-TV (ABC) Scottsbluff; KDVR (FOX) Denver; KMGH-TV (ABC) Denver; KSTF (CBS, CW) Scottsbluff; KTNE-TV (PBS) Alliance; KTVD (MNT) Denver; KUSA (NBC) Denver; KWGN-TV (CW) Denver.
Programming (via satellite): C-SPAN; C-SPAN 2; Home Shopping Network; QVC; TV Guide Network.
Current originations: Educational Access; Public Access; Government Access.
Fee: $29.99 installation.

Expanded Basic Service 1
Subscribers: N.A.
Programming (via satellite): ABC Family Channel; AMC; Animal Planet; Arts & Entertainment; Cartoon Network; CNBC; CNN; Comedy Central; Country Music TV; Discovery Channel; Disney Channel; E! Entertainment Television; ESPN; ESPN 2; FitTV; Food Network; Fox News Channel; Fox Sports Net Rocky Mountain; FX; G4; Great American Country; Hallmark Channel; Headline News; HGTV; History Channel; Lifetime; MSNBC; MTV; National Geographic Channel; Nickelodeon; Oxygen; SoapNet; Spike TV; Syfy; TBS Superstation; The Learning Channel; Toon

Disney; Travel Channel; truTV; Turner Network TV; TV Land; USA Network; VH1; Weather Channel.
Fee: $47.99 monthly.

Digital Basic Service
Subscribers: N.A.
Programming (via satellite): AmericanLife TV Network; BBC America; Bio; Bloomberg Television; Bravo; Discovery Digital Networks; DMX Music; ESPN Classic Sports; Fox Movie Channel; Fox Sports World; Fuse; GAS; Golf Channel; GSN; Halogen Network; History Channel International; Independent Film Channel; Lifetime Movie Network; MTV Networks Digital Suite; Nick Jr.; Outdoor Channel; Speed Channel; Trinity Broadcasting Network; Turner Classic Movies; TV Guide Interactive Inc.; Versus; WE tv.

Digital Pay Service 1
Pay Units: N.A.
Programming (via satellite): Cinemax (multiplexed); Encore (multiplexed); Flix; HBO (multiplexed); Showtime (multiplexed); Starz (multiplexed); The Movie Channel (multiplexed).

Video-On-Demand: Yes

Pay-Per-View
iN DEMAND (delivered digitally), Addressable: Yes; Hot Choice (delivered digitally); Playboy TV (delivered digitally); Fresh (delivered digitally); Shorteez (delivered digitally).

Internet Service
Operational: Yes.
Broadband Service: Charter Pipeline.
Fee: $29.99 monthly.

Telephone Service
Digital: Operational

Miles of Plant: 54.0 (coaxial); None (fiber optic). Homes passed: 2,926. Total homes in franchised area: 3,468. Miles of plant (coax) includes Kimball

Vice President & General Manager: John Crowley. Technical Operations Director: Marty Kovarik. Technical Operations Manager: Joel Saunders. Marketing Director: Bill Haarstad.

City fee: 3% of gross.

Ownership: Charter Communications Inc. (MSO).

SILVER CREEK—Cable Nebraska, 2123 Central Ave, Ste 200, Kearney, NE 68847. Phones: 866-638-7877; 877-234-0102. Web Site: http://www.cablene.com. ICA: NE0324.

TV Market Ranking: Outside TV Markets (SILVER CREEK). Franchise award date: N.A. Franchise expiration date: N.A. Began: N.A.

Channel capacity: 41 (not 2-way capable). Channels available but not in use: 10.

Basic Service
Subscribers: 99.
Programming (received off-air): KHAS-TV (NBC) Hastings; KHGI-TV (ABC) Kearney; KHNE-TV (PBS) Hastings; KLKN (ABC) Lincoln; KOLN (CBS, MNT) Lincoln; KPTM (FOX, MNT) Omaha.
Programming (via satellite): ABC Family Channel; AMC; Animal Planet; Arts & Entertainment; Cartoon Network; CNN; Comcast Sports Net Northwest; Discovery Channel; ESPN; Fox Sports Net Midwest; HGTV; History Channel; Lifetime; Nickelodeon; Outdoor Channel; QVC; TBS Superstation; The Learning Channel; Turner Network TV; USA Network; Weather Channel; WGN America.
Fee: $35.00 installation; $27.95 monthly.

Pay Service 1
Pay Units: 26.
Programming (via satellite): HBO.
Fee: $12.95 monthly.

Pay Service 2
Pay Units: 25.
Programming (via satellite): Showtime.
Fee: $7.95 monthly.

Pay Service 3
Pay Units: 23.
Programming (via satellite): The Movie Channel.
Fee: $6.95 monthly.

Internet Service
Operational: No.

Miles of Plant: 4.0 (coaxial); None (fiber optic). Homes passed: 197.

Operations Manager: Stuart Gilbertson.

City fee: 3% of gross.

Ownership: USA Companies (MSO).

SPALDING—Cable Nebraska, 2123 Central Ave, Ste 200, Kearney, NE 68847. Phone: 308-236-1512. Web Site: http://www.cablene.com. ICA: NE0326.

TV Market Ranking: Outside TV Markets (SPALDING). Franchise award date: October 1, 1989. Franchise expiration date: N.A. Began: N.A.

Channel capacity: N.A. Channels available but not in use: N.A.

Basic Service
Subscribers: 160.
Programming (received off-air): KGIN (CBS, MNT) Grand Island; KHAS-TV (NBC) Hastings; KHGI-TV (ABC) Kearney; KHNE-TV (PBS) Hastings; KLKN (ABC) Lincoln.
Programming (via satellite): ABC Family Channel; C-SPAN; C-SPAN 2; Eternal Word TV Network; Hallmark Channel; Headline News; Home Shopping Network; QVC; TBS Superstation; Trinity Broadcasting Network; TV Guide Network; Weather Channel; WGN America.
Current originations: Public Access.
Fee: $24.95 installation; $19.95 monthly.

Expanded Basic Service 1
Subscribers: N.A.
Programming (via satellite): AMC; Animal Planet; Arts & Entertainment; Cartoon Network; CNBC; CNN; Comedy Central; Country Music TV; Discovery Channel; E! Entertainment Television; ESPN; ESPN 2; Fox News Channel; Fox Sports Net; FX; Great American Country; HGTV; History Channel; ION Television; Lifetime; MSNBC; MTV; Nickelodeon; Outdoor Channel; Spike TV; Syfy; The Learning Channel; Travel Channel; truTV; Turner Classic Movies; Turner Network TV; TV Land; Univision; USA Network; VH1.
Fee: $19.25 monthly.

Digital Basic Service
Subscribers: N.A.
Programming (via satellite): AmericanLife TV Network; BBC America; Bio; Bloomberg Television; Canales N; Current; Discovery Digital Networks; DMX Music; ESPN 2; ESPN Classic Sports; ESPNews; FitTV; Fox Movie Channel; Fox Sports World; FSN Digital Atlantic; FSN Digital Central; FSN Digital Pacific; G4; GAS; Golf Channel; GSN; Halogen Network; History Channel; History Channel International; International Television (ITV); MBC America; MTV Networks Digital Suite; National Geographic Channel; Nick Jr.; Outdoor Channel; Ovation; ShopNBC; Speed Channel; Style Network; Syfy; Trinity Broadcasting Network; Trio; Versus.
Fee: $14.00 monthly.

Digital Pay Service 1
Pay Units: N.A.
Programming (via satellite): Cinemax (multiplexed); Encore (multiplexed); Flix; Fox Movie Channel; HBO (multiplexed); Independent Film Channel; Showtime (multiplexed); Starz (multiplexed); Sundance Channel; The Movie Channel (multiplexed); WAM! America's Kidz Network; WE tv.
Fee: $13.00 monthly (each).

Video-On-Demand: No

Pay-Per-View
iN DEMAND (delivered digitally); Hot Choice (delivered digitally); Playboy TV (delivered digitally); Fresh (delivered digitally); Shorteez (delivered digitally); Urban Xtra (delivered digitally); ESPN Now (delivered digitally); Sports PPV (delivered digitally).

Internet Service
Operational: Yes.
Broadband Service: Cable Nebraska.
Fee: $35.95 monthly.

Telephone Service
None

Operations Manager: Stewart Gilbertson.

City fee: 1% of gross.

Ownership: USA Companies (MSO).

SPENCER—CenCom Inc. This cable system has converted to IPTV. See Spencer (village), NE [NE5026]. ICA: NE0147.

SPENCER (village)—CenCom NNTV. Formerly [NE0147]. This cable system has converted to IPTV, 110 E Elk St, Jackson, NE 68743-0066. Phones: 402-623-4321; 888-397-4321. E-mail: nntc@nntc.net. Web Site: http://www.nntc.net. ICA: NE5026.

Channel capacity: N.A. Channels available but not in use: N.A.

Internet Service
Operational: Yes.

Telephone Service
Digital: Operational

General Manager: Emory Graffis.

Ownership: Northeast Nebraska Telephone Co.

SPRINGFIELD—Charter Communications, PO Box 1448, 809 Central Ave, Kearney, NE 68848-1448. Phones: 507-289-8372 (Rochester administrative office); 308-236-1500. Fax: 308-234-6452. Web Site: http://www.charter.com. Also serves Ashland, Cass County, Greenwood, Louisville, Plattsmouth, Wahoo & Waverly. ICA: NE0020.

TV Market Ranking: 53 (Ashland, Greenwood, Louisville, Plattsmouth, Wahoo); 53,91 (Cass County (portions)); 91 (SPRINGFIELD, Waverly). Franchise award date: January 20, 1981. Franchise expiration date: N.A. Began: January 20, 1981.

Channel capacity: 86 (operating 2-way). Channels available but not in use: 36.

Basic Service
Subscribers: 3,106.
Programming (received off-air): KETV (ABC) Omaha; KMTV-TV (CBS) Omaha; KOLN (CBS, MNT) Lincoln; KPTM (FOX, MNT) Omaha; KUON-TV (PBS) Lincoln; KXVO (CW) Omaha; KYNE-TV (PBS) Omaha.
Programming (via satellite): TBS Superstation; WGN America.
Current originations: Educational Access; Public Access.
Fee: $29.99 installation; $1.12 converter.

Expanded Basic Service 1
Subscribers: 3,032.
Programming (via satellite): ABC Family Channel; AMC; Animal Planet; Arts & Entertainment; Cartoon Network; CNBC; CNN; Comedy Central; Discovery Channel; Disney Channel; E! Entertainment Television; ESPN; ESPN 2; Fox Sports Net Midwest; FX; Great American Country; Headline News; HGTV; History Channel; Home Shopping Network; INSP; Lifetime; MSNBC; MTV; Nickelodeon; QVC; Spike TV; Syfy; The Learning Channel; Turner Classic Movies; Turner Network TV; TV Land; USA Network; VH1; Weather Channel.
Fee: $47.99 monthly.

Digital Basic Service
Subscribers: N.A.
Programming (via satellite): BBC America; Bio; Bravo; Discovery Digital Networks; DMX Music; Encore; ESPN Classic Sports; ESPNews; Fox Sports World; Golf Channel; GSN; History Channel International; Independent Film Channel; Lifetime Movie Network; Speed Channel; Versus; WE tv.

Digital Pay Service 1
Pay Units: N.A.
Programming (via satellite): Cinemax (multiplexed); HBO (multiplexed); Showtime (multiplexed); Starz (multiplexed); The Movie Channel (multiplexed).
Fee: $10.50 monthly (each).

Video-On-Demand: Yes

Pay-Per-View
iN DEMAND (delivered digitally); Playboy TV (delivered digitally).

Internet Service
Operational: Yes.
Broadband Service: Charter Pipeline.
Fee: $29.99 monthly.

Telephone Service
Digital: Operational

Miles of Plant: 62.0 (coaxial); 22.0 (fiber optic). Homes passed: 4,608. Total homes in franchised area: 4,608.

Vice President & General Manager: John Crowley. Technical Operations Director: Marty Kovarik. Technical Operations Manager: Terry Petzoldt. Office Manager: Dawn Harmon.

City fee: 3% of gross.

Ownership: Charter Communications Inc. (MSO).

SPRINGFIELD (portions)—Formerly served by TelePartners. No longer in operation. ICA: NE0382.

ST. EDWARD—Cable Nebraska, 2123 Central Ave, Ste 200, Kearney, NE 68847. Phone: 308-236-1512. Web Site: http://www.cablene.com. ICA: NE0104.

TV Market Ranking: Outside TV Markets (ST. EDWARD). Franchise award date: N.A. Franchise expiration date: N.A. Began: September 1, 1983.

Channel capacity: N.A. Channels available but not in use: N.A.

Basic Service
Subscribers: 200.
Programming (received off-air): KGIN (CBS, MNT) Grand Island; KHAS-TV (NBC) Hastings; KHGI-TV (ABC) Kearney; KHNE-TV (PBS) Hastings; KLKN (ABC) Lincoln; KTVG-TV (FOX) Grand Island.
Programming (via satellite): ABC Family Channel; C-SPAN; C-SPAN 2; Eternal Word TV Network; Hallmark Channel; Headline News; Home Shopping Network; QVC; TBS Superstation; Trinity Broadcasting Network; TV Guide Network; Weather Channel; WGN America.
Current originations: Public Access.
Fee: $35.00 installation; $24.95 monthly.
Expanded Basic Service 1
Subscribers: N.A.
Programming (via satellite): AMC; Animal Planet; Arts & Entertainment; Cartoon Network; CNBC; CNN; Comedy Central; Country Music TV; Discovery Channel; E! Entertainment Television; ESPN; ESPN 2; Food Network; Fox News Channel; Fox Sports Net; FX; Great American Country; HGTV; History Channel; ION Television; Lifetime; MSNBC; MTV; Nickelodeon; Outdoor Channel; Spike TV; Syfy; The Learning Channel; Travel Channel; truTV; Turner Classic Movies; Turner Network TV; TV Land; Univision; USA Network; VH1.
Digital Basic Service
Subscribers: N.A.
Programming (via satellite): AmericanLife TV Network; BBC America; Bio; Bloomberg Television; Canales N; Current; Discovery Digital Networks; DMX Music; ESPN 2; ESPN Classic Sports; ESPNews; FitTV; Fox Movie Channel; Fox Sports World; FSN Digital Atlantic; FSN Digital Central; FSN Digital Pacific; G4; GAS; Golf Channel; GSN; Halogen Network; History Channel; History Channel International; International Television (ITV); MBC America; MTV Networks Digital Suite; National Geographic Channel; Nick Jr.; Outdoor Channel; Ovation; ShopNBC; Speed Channel; Style Network; Syfy; Trinity Broadcasting Network; Trio; Versus.
Fee: $13.95 monthly.
Digital Pay Service 1
Pay Units: N.A.
Programming (via satellite): Cinemax (multiplexed); Daystar TV Network; Encore (multiplexed); Flix; Fox Movie Channel; HBO (multiplexed); Independent Film Channel; Lifetime Movie Network; Showtime (multiplexed); Starz (multiplexed); Sundance Channel; The Movie Channel (multiplexed); WAM! America's Kidz Network; WE tv.
Fee: $15.00 monthly.
Video-On-Demand: No
Pay-Per-View
iN DEMAND (delivered digitally); Playboy TV (delivered digitally).
Internet Service
Operational: Yes.
Broadband Service: Cable Nebraska.
Telephone Service
None
Miles of Plant: 8.0 (coaxial); None (fiber optic). Homes passed: 344.
Operations Manager: Stuart Gilbertson.
City fee: 3% of gross.
Ownership: USA Companies (MSO).

STAMFORD—Formerly served by Pinpoint Cable TV. No longer in operation. ICA: NE0239.

STANTON—Stanton Telecom, 1004 Ivy St, Stanton, NE 68779-2341. Phones: 800-411-2264; 402-439-2264; 402-439-5000. Fax: 402-439-7777. E-mail: info@stanton.net. Web Site: http://www.stantontelecom.com. ICA: NE0066.
TV Market Ranking: Outside TV Markets (STANTON). Franchise award date: N.A. Franchise expiration date: N.A. Began: February 15, 1982.
Channel capacity: N.A. Channels available but not in use: N.A.
Basic Service
Subscribers: 532.
Programming (received off-air): KETV (ABC) Omaha; KLKN (ABC) Lincoln; KMEG (CBS) Sioux City; KMTV-TV (CBS) Omaha; KPTM (FOX, MNT) Omaha; KTIV (CW, NBC) Sioux City.
Programming (via satellite): ABC Family Channel; AMC; Animal Planet; Arts & Entertainment; Cartoon Network; CNBC; CNN; Comedy Central; Country Music TV; CW+; Discovery Channel; Disney Channel; ESPN; ESPN 2; ESPN Classic Sports; Food Network; Fox News Channel; Fox Sports Net Midwest; FX; Golf Channel; Great American Country; HGTV; History Channel International; Lifetime; MSNBC; MTV; National Geographic Channel; Network One; Nickelodeon; Outdoor Channel; SoapNet; Spike TV; Syfy; TBS Superstation; The Learning Channel; Travel Channel; Turner Classic Movies; Turner Network TV; TV Land; USA Network; VH1; Weather Channel; WGN America.
Fee: $31.99 installation; $35.99 monthly.
Pay Service 1
Pay Units: 103.
Programming (via satellite): HBO.
Fee: $12.50 installation; $10.50 monthly.
Pay Service 2
Pay Units: 54.
Programming (via satellite): The Movie Channel.
Fee: $12.50 installation; $9.50 monthly.
Video-On-Demand: No
Internet Service
Operational: No, Both DSL & dial-up.
Telephone Service
None
Miles of Plant: 18.0 (coaxial); None (fiber optic). Homes passed: 630. Total homes in franchised area: 630.
Vice President & General Manager: Bob Paden. Outside Plant Manager: Steve Hansen. Marketing & Public Relations Director: Judy Throener. Office Manager: Colleen Paden.
City fee: 3% of basic gross.
Ownership: Cable TV of Stanton.

STAPLEHURST—Galaxy Cablevision, 1928 S Lincoln Ave, Ste 200, York, NE 68467. Phone: 402-362-3332. Fax: 402-362-4890. Web Site: http://www.galaxycable.com. ICA: NE0222.
TV Market Ranking: 91 (STAPLEHURST (VILLAGE)). Franchise award date: N.A. Franchise expiration date: N.A. Began: May 1, 1984.
Channel capacity: 41 (not 2-way capable). Channels available but not in use: 24.
Basic Service
Subscribers: 11.
Programming (received off-air): KETV (ABC) Omaha; KLKN (ABC) Lincoln; KMTV-TV (CBS) Omaha; KOLN (CBS, MNT) Lincoln; KPTM (FOX, MNT) Omaha; KUON-TV (PBS) Lincoln; KXVO (CW) Omaha; WOWT-TV (IND, NBC) Omaha.
Programming (via satellite): ABC Family Channel; CNN; ESPN; Outdoor Channel; TBS Superstation; Turner Network TV; WGN America.
Fee: $35.00 installation; $32.95 monthly.
Pay Service 1
Pay Units: 4.
Programming (via satellite): Cinemax.
Fee: $11.95 monthly.
Pay Service 2
Pay Units: 3.
Programming (via satellite): HBO.
Fee: $12.95 monthly.
Internet Service
Operational: No.
Telephone Service
None
Miles of Plant: 3.0 (coaxial); None (fiber optic). Homes passed: 110.
State Manager: Cheyenne Wohlford. Technical Manager: Carl Stanley. Sales Manager: Mike Thomas. Customer Service Manager: Donna Bryan.
City fee: 1% of basic.
Ownership: Galaxy Cable Inc. (MSO).

STEINAUER—Formerly served by CableDirect. No longer in operation. ICA: NE0376.

STELLA—Formerly served by StellaVision. No longer in operation. ICA: NE0216.

STRATTON—Peregrine Communications, 14818 W 6th Ave, Ste 16A, Golden, CO 80401-6585. Phones: 800-344-5404; 303-278-9660. Fax: 303-278-9685. Web Site: http://www.perecom.com. ICA: NE0328.
TV Market Ranking: Below 100 (STRATTON). Franchise award date: N.A. Franchise expiration date: N.A. Began: July 1, 1985.
Channel capacity: 12 (not 2-way capable). Channels available but not in use: N.A.
Basic Service
Subscribers: 70.
Programming (received off-air): KBSL-DT (CBS) Goodland; KHGI-TV (ABC) Kearney; KLNE-TV (PBS) Lexington; KSNK (NBC) McCook; KWNB-TV (ABC) Hayes Center.
Programming (via satellite): ABC Family Channel; AMC; Arts & Entertainment; CNN; Discovery Channel; Disney Channel; ESPN; Lifetime; Nickelodeon; QVC; Spike TV; TBS Superstation; Turner Network TV; USA Network; WGN America.
Fee: $31.95 monthly.
Pay Service 1
Pay Units: 12.
Programming (via satellite): HBO.
Fee: $14.00 monthly.
Video-On-Demand: No
Internet Service
Operational: No.
Telephone Service
None
Manager: Patty Hyyppa. Chief Technician: Don Green.
Ownership: Peregrine Communications (MSO).

STROMSBURG—Cable Nebraska, 2123 Central Ave, Ste 200, Kearney, NE 68847. Phone: 308-236-1512. Web Site: http://www.cablene.com. ICA: NE0075.
TV Market Ranking: Outside TV Markets (STROMSBURG). Franchise award date: N.A. Franchise expiration date: N.A. Began: April 1, 1981.
Channel capacity: 116 (operating 2-way). Channels available but not in use: None.
Basic Service
Subscribers: 284.
Programming (received off-air): KGIN (CBS, MNT) Grand Island; KHAS-TV (NBC) Hastings; KHGI-TV (ABC) Kearney; KHNE-TV (PBS) Hastings; KLKN (ABC) Lincoln; KTVG-TV (FOX) Grand Island.
Programming (via satellite): C-SPAN; C-SPAN 2; CW+; Eternal Word TV Network; Home Shopping Network; MyNetworkTV Inc.; QVC; TBS Superstation; Trinity Broadcasting Network; Univision; Weather Channel; WGN America.
Fee: $35.00 installation; $37.75 monthly.
Expanded Basic Service 1
Subscribers: N.A.
Programming (via satellite): ABC Family Channel; AMC; Animal Planet; Arts & Entertainment; Cartoon Network; CNBC; CNN; Comedy Central; Country Music TV; Discovery Channel; E! Entertainment Television; ESPN; ESPN 2; ESPN Classic Sports; Food Network; Fox News Channel; Fox Sports Net Midwest; FX; G4; Great American Country; Hallmark Channel; Headline News; HGTV; History Channel; ION Television; Lifetime; MSNBC; MTV; Nickelodeon; Outdoor Channel; RFD-TV; Spike TV; Syfy; The Learning Channel; Travel Channel; truTV; Turner Classic Movies; Turner Network TV; TV Land; USA Network; Versus; VH1.
Digital Basic Service
Subscribers: 39.
Programming (via satellite): AmericanLife TV Network; BBC America; Bio; Black Family Channel; Bloomberg Television; Cine Latino; Cine Mexicano; CMT Pure Country; CNN en Espanol; Current; Daystar TV Network; Discovery Channel HD; Discovery en Espanol; Discovery Health Channel; Discovery Kids Channel; Discovery Military Channel; Discovery Planet Green; DMX Music; ESPN 2; ESPN Classic Sports; ESPN Deportes; ESPN HD; ESPNews; FitTV; Fox College Sports Atlantic; Fox College Sports Central; Fox College Sports Pacific; Fox Movie Channel; Fox Sports en Espanol; G4; Golf Channel; GSN; Halogen Network; History Channel; History Channel en Espanol; History Channel International; ID Investigation Discovery; MTV Hits; MTV Tres; MTV2; Outdoor Channel; Ovation; Science Channel; ShopNBC; Sleuth; Speed Channel; Style Network; Syfy; TBS in HD; TeenNick; Trinity Broadcasting Network; Turner Network TV HD; VeneMovies; Versus; VH1 Classic; VH1 Soul; WE tv.
Fee: $13.95 monthly.
Digital Pay Service 1
Pay Units: N.A.
Programming (via satellite): Cinemax (multiplexed); Encore (multiplexed); Flix; HBO (multiplexed); HBO Latino; Lifetime Movie Network; Showtime (multiplexed); Starz (multiplexed); The Movie Channel (multiplexed).
Video-On-Demand: No
Pay-Per-View
iN DEMAND (delivered digitally); Hot Choice (delivered digitally); Playboy TV (delivered digitally); Fresh (delivered digitally); Club Jenna (delivered digitally); Spice: Xcess (delivered digitally).
Internet Service
Operational: Yes.
Broadband Service: Cable Nebraska.
Telephone Service
None
Miles of Plant: 9.0 (coaxial); None (fiber optic). Homes passed: 530. Total homes in franchised area: 530.
Operations Manager: Stuart Gilbertson.
City fee: 3% of basic.
Ownership: USA Companies (MSO).

STUART—CenCom Inc. This cable system has converted to IPTV. See Stuart (village), NE [NE5030]. ICA: NE0135.

STUART—CenCom NNTV. Formerly [NE0135]. This cable system has converted to IPTV, 110 E Elk St, Jackson, NE 68743-0066. Phones: 402-623-4321; 888-397-4321. E-mail: nntc@nntc.net. Web Site: http://www.nntc.net. ICA: NE5030.
Channel capacity: N.A. Channels available but not in use: N.A.

Internet Service
Operational: Yes.

Telephone Service
Digital: Operational
General Manager: Emory Graffis.
Ownership: Northeast Nebraska Telephone Co.

SUPERIOR—Windjammer Communications, 5400 S 16th St, Lincoln, NE 68512-1278. Phones: 877-450-5558; 561-775-1208. Fax: 402-421-0310. Web Site: http://www.windjammercable.com. ICA: NE0383.
TV Market Ranking: Below 100 (SUPERIOR).
Channel capacity: N.A. Channels available but not in use: N.A.

Basic Service
Subscribers: N.A. Included in Lincoln
Programming (received off-air): KGIN (CBS, MNT) Grand Island; KHAS-TV (NBC) Hastings; KHGI-TV (ABC) Kearney; KLKN (ABC) Lincoln; KUON-TV (PBS) Lincoln.
Programming (via satellite): QVC; TBS Superstation; TV Guide Network; WGN America.
Fee: $40.54 installation; $14.93 monthly.

Expanded Basic Service 1
Subscribers: N.A.
Programming (via satellite): ABC Family Channel; AMC; AmericanLife TV Network; Animal Planet; Arts & Entertainment; BBC America; Boomerang; Cartoon Network; CNBC; CNN; Comedy Central; Country Music TV; C-SPAN; C-SPAN 2; CW+; Discovery Channel; Discovery Health Channel; Disney Channel; E! Entertainment Television; ESPN; ESPN 2; Eternal Word TV Network; Fox Movie Channel; Fox News Channel; Fox Sports Net Midwest; FX; Golf Channel; Great American Country; Hallmark Channel; Headline News; HGTV; History Channel; ION Television; Lifetime; MSNBC; MTV; Nickelodeon; Outdoor Channel; Oxygen; ShopNBC; Spike TV; Syfy; The Learning Channel; Toon Disney; Travel Channel; truTV; Turner Classic Movies; Turner Network TV; TV Land; Univision; USA Network; Versus; VH1; Weather Channel.

Expanded Basic Service 2
Subscribers: N.A.
Programming (via satellite): CBS College Sports Network; ESPN Classic Sports; Flix; Food Network; GSN; Speed Channel.

Pay Service 1
Pay Units: N.A.
Programming (via satellite): Cinemax (multiplexed); Encore; HBO (multiplexed); Showtime (multiplexed).

Video-On-Demand: No

Pay-Per-View
iN DEMAND; Pleasure.

Internet Service
Operational: No.

Telephone Service
None
Note: Homes passed included in Lincoln
Ownership: Windjammer Communications LLC (MSO).

SUTHERLAND—Great Plains Communications, PO Box 500, 1600 Great Plains Centre, Blair, NE 68008-0500. Phones: 888-343-8014; 402-426-9511. Fax: 402-456-6550. Web Site: http://www.gpcom.com. Also serves Hershey. ICA: NE0330.
TV Market Ranking: Below 100 (Hershey, SUTHERLAND). Franchise award date: March 1, 1982. Franchise expiration date: N.A. Began: April 1, 1983.
Channel capacity: 80 (operating 2-way). Channels available but not in use: 25.

Basic Service
Subscribers: N.A. Included in Arnold
Programming (received off-air): KGIN (CBS, MNT) Grand Island; KNOP-TV (NBC) North Platte; KPNE-TV (PBS) North Platte; KWNB-TV (ABC) Hayes Center.
Programming (via satellite): ABC Family Channel; AMC; Animal Planet; Arts & Entertainment; CNN; Discovery Channel; Disney Channel; ESPN; Fox News Channel; Fox Sports Net Rocky Mountain; Great American Country; Headline News; KCNC-TV (CBS) Denver; KMGH-TV (ABC) Denver; Lifetime; Nickelodeon; QVC; Spike TV; TBS Superstation; The Learning Channel; Travel Channel; Turner Network TV; TV Guide Network; USA Network; VH1; Weather Channel; WGN America.
Fee: $45.00 installation; $31.50 monthly.

Expanded Basic Service 1
Subscribers: N.A.
Programming (via satellite): Cartoon Network; Comedy Central; ESPN 2; Food Network; HGTV; History Channel; Turner Classic Movies; TV Land; Versus.
Fee: $6.50 monthly.

Digital Basic Service
Subscribers: N.A. Included in Arnold
Programming (via satellite): BBC America; Bio; Bravo; Discovery Digital Networks; DMX Music; ESPN Classic Sports; Fox Sports World; GAS; Golf Channel; History Channel International; Independent Film Channel; Lifetime Movie Network; MTV Networks Digital Suite; National Geographic Channel; Outdoor Channel; Speed Channel; Syfy; Turner Classic Movies; WE tv.
Fee: $11.50 monthly.

Pay Service 1
Pay Units: 111.
Programming (via satellite): Cinemax; HBO; Showtime (multiplexed).
Fee: $10.00 installation; $9.95 monthly (each).

Pay Service 2
Pay Units: N.A.
Programming (via satellite): Flix; Sundance Channel; The Movie Channel.

Digital Pay Service 1
Pay Units: N.A.
Programming (via satellite): Cinemax (multiplexed); Encore (multiplexed); HBO (multiplexed); Showtime (multiplexed); Starz (multiplexed); The Movie Channel (multiplexed).

Video-On-Demand: No

Pay-Per-View
iN DEMAND (delivered digitally), Fee: $3.99, Addressable: Yes; Sports PPV.

Internet Service
Operational: Yes, Both DSL & dial-up.
Broadband Service: In-house.
Fee: $49.95 installation; $39.95 monthly.

Telephone Service
None
Homes passed included in Arnold
General Manager: Lea Ann Quist. Chief Technician: Mark Stottler. Marketing Manager: Casey Garrigan.
Ownership: Great Plains Communications Inc. (MSO).

SWANTON—Comstar Cable TV Inc., PO Box 975, 8358 W Scott Rd, Beatrice, NE 68310-0975. Phone: 402-520-1987 (GM's cell). Fax: 402-228-3766. ICA: NE0342.
TV Market Ranking: Outside TV Markets (SWANTON). Franchise award date: N.A. Franchise expiration date: N.A. Began: December 1, 1992.
Channel capacity: 36 (not 2-way capable). Channels available but not in use: 22.

Basic Service
Subscribers: 27.
Programming (received off-air): KHNE-TV (PBS) Hastings; KLKN (ABC) Lincoln; KOLN (CBS, MNT) Lincoln; KPTM (FOX, MNT) Omaha; KXVO (CW) Omaha; WOWT-TV (IND, NBC) Omaha.
Programming (via satellite): ABC Family Channel; AMC; Arts & Entertainment; Cartoon Network; CNN; C-SPAN; Discovery Channel; Disney Channel; ESPN; Food Network; FX; Great American Country; Hallmark Channel; Headline News; Lifetime; QVC; RFD-TV; TBS Superstation; The Learning Channel; Turner Network TV; TV Land; USA Network; Weather Channel; WGN America.
Fee: $40.00 installation; $27.95 monthly.

Digital Basic Service
Subscribers: N.A.
Programming (via satellite): Bio; Bloomberg Television; Bravo; Discovery Health Channel; Discovery Military Channel; Discovery Planet Green; Disney XD; ESPN 2; ESPN Classic Sports; ESPNews; Fox Movie Channel; Fuse; G4; Golf Channel; GSN; HGTV; History Channel; History Channel International; ID Investigation Discovery; INSP; National Geographic Channel; Outdoor Channel; Science Channel; Sleuth; SoapNet; Speed Channel; Style Network; Syfy; Trinity Broadcasting Network; Turner Classic Movies; Versus; WE tv.

Pay Service 1
Pay Units: N.A.
Programming (via satellite): HBO.
Fee: $7.50 monthly.

Digital Pay Service 1
Pay Units: N.A.
Programming (via satellite): Encore (multiplexed); HBO (multiplexed); Showtime (multiplexed); Starz (multiplexed); The Movie Channel (multiplexed).

Video-On-Demand: No

Internet Service
Operational: No.

Telephone Service
None
Miles of Plant: 2.0 (coaxial); None (fiber optic). Homes passed: 72.
Manager & Chief Technician: Tim Schwarz.
Ownership: Comstar Cable TV Inc. (MSO).

SYRACUSE—Galaxy Cablevision, 1928 S Lincoln Ave, Ste 200, York, NE 68467. Phone: 402-362-3332. Fax: 402-362-4890. Web Site: http://www.galaxycable.com. Also serves Bennet, Cass County (portions), Cook, Eagle, Elmwood, Johnson, Murdock, Murray, Nemaha County (portions), Palmyra, Sterling, Unadilla & Weeping Water. ICA: NE0053.
TV Market Ranking: 53,91 (Eagle, Elmwood, Murdock, Weeping Water); 91 (Bennet, Cass County (portions), Cook, Murray, Nemaha County (portions), Palmyra, Sterling, SYRACUSE, Unadilla); Outside TV Markets (Johnson). Franchise award date: N.A. Franchise expiration date: N.A. Began: October 1, 1981.
Channel capacity: 78 (operating 2-way). Channels available but not in use: None.

Basic Service
Subscribers: 1,624.
Programming (received off-air): KETV (ABC) Omaha; KLKN (ABC) Lincoln; KMTV-TV (CBS) Omaha; KOLN (CBS, MNT) Lincoln; KPTM (FOX, MNT) Omaha; KUON-TV (PBS) Lincoln; KXVO (CW) Omaha; WOWT-TV (IND, NBC) Omaha.
Programming (via satellite): ABC Family Channel; AMC; Animal Planet; Arts & Entertainment; Boomerang; Cartoon Network; CNN; Comedy Central; C-SPAN; Discovery Channel; Disney Channel; E! Entertainment Television; ESPN; ESPN 2; Eternal Word TV Network; Food Network; Fox News Channel; Fox Sports Net Midwest; Fuse; FX; Great American Country; Hallmark Channel; Headline News; HGTV; History Channel; INSP; Lifetime; MSNBC; National Geographic Channel; Outdoor Channel; QVC; Syfy; TBS Superstation; The Learning Channel; Toon Disney; Travel Channel; Trinity Broadcasting Network; Turner Classic Movies; Turner Network TV; TV Guide Network; TV Land; USA Network; Weather Channel; WGN America.
Current originations: Educational Access; Public Access.
Fee: $35.00 installation; $44.75 monthly.

Digital Basic Service
Subscribers: 455.
Programming (via satellite): AmericanLife TV Network; BBC America; Bio; Bloomberg Television; Discovery Digital Networks; ESPN Classic Sports; ESPNews; FitTV; Fox Sports World; FSN Digital Atlantic; FSN Digital Central; FSN Digital Pacific; G4; Golf Channel; GSN; History Channel International; Style Network; WE tv.
Fee: $12.95 monthly.

Digital Expanded Basic Service
Subscribers: N.A.
Programming (via satellite): DMX Music; Encore; Fox Movie Channel; Independent Film Channel; Lifetime Movie Network.
Fee: $12.95 monthly.

Pay Service 1
Pay Units: 22.
Programming (via satellite): Cinemax.
Fee: $11.95 installation; $11.00 monthly.

Pay Service 2
Pay Units: 46.
Programming (via satellite): HBO.
Fee: $12.95 monthly.

Pay Service 3
Pay Units: 70.
Programming (via satellite): Showtime.
Fee: $7.95 monthly.

Pay Service 4
Pay Units: 67.
Programming (via satellite): The Movie Channel.
Fee: $6.95 monthly.

Digital Pay Service 1
Pay Units: N.A.
Programming (via satellite): Cinemax (multiplexed); Flix; HBO (multiplexed); Showtime (multiplexed); The Movie Channel (multiplexed).
Fee: $15.60 monthly.

Video-On-Demand: No

Pay-Per-View
Addressable homes: 377.
ESPN Now (delivered digitally), Fee: $3.99, Addressable: Yes; Hot Choice (delivered digitally); Movies (delivered digitally); Playboy TV (delivered digitally); Fresh (delivered digitally); sports (delivered digitally).

Internet Service
Operational: Yes.
Subscribers: 449.
Broadband Service: Galaxy Cable Internet.
Fee: $49.95 installation; $44.95 monthly; $5.00 modem lease.

Telephone Service
None

Miles of Plant: 59.0 (coaxial); None (fiber optic). Homes passed: 3,280.
State Manager: Cheyenne Wohlford. Technical Manager: Carl Stanley. Sales Manager: Mike Thomas. Customer Service Manager: Donna Bryant.
City fee: 3% of basic.
Ownership: Galaxy Cable Inc. (MSO).

TALMAGE—Great Plains Communications, PO Box 500, 1600 Great Plains Centre, Blair, NE 68008-0500. Phone: 402-426-9511. Fax: 402-456-6550. Web Site: http://www.gpcom.com. ICA: NE0252.
TV Market Ranking: Outside TV Markets (TALMAGE). Franchise award date: N.A. Franchise expiration date: N.A. Began: January 1, 1989.
Channel capacity: N.A. Channels available but not in use: N.A.

Basic Service
Subscribers: N.A. Included in Arnold
Programming (received off-air): KETV (ABC) Omaha; KMTV-TV (CBS) Omaha; KOLN (CBS, MNT) Lincoln; KPTM (FOX, MNT) Omaha; KUON-TV (PBS) Lincoln; WOWT-TV (IND, NBC) Omaha.
Programming (via satellite): ABC Family Channel; Animal Planet; Cartoon Network; CNN; Country Music TV; Discovery Channel; Disney Channel; E! Entertainment Television; ESPN; ESPN 2; Fox News Channel; FX; History Channel; MTV; Nickelodeon; Spike TV; TBS Superstation; The Learning Channel; Travel Channel; Turner Network TV; TV Land; USA Network; Weather Channel; WGN America.
Current originations: Government Access; Educational Access; Public Access.
Fee: $29.99 installation; $47.99 monthly; $1.20 converter.

Digital Basic Service
Subscribers: N.A. Included in Arnold
Programming (via satellite): AmericanLife TV Network; BBC America; Bio; Bloomberg Television; Bravo; Discovery Digital Networks; Encore; ESPN Classic Sports; Flix; Fox Movie Channel; Fox Soccer; Fuse; G4; GAS; Golf Channel; GSN; Halogen Network; History Channel International; Independent Film Channel; Lifetime Movie Network; MTV Networks Digital Suite; Music Choice; Nick Jr.; Outdoor Channel; ShopNBC; Showtime; Speed Channel; Style Network; Syfy; The Movie Channel; Toon Disney; Trinity Broadcasting Network; Turner Classic Movies; Versus; WE tv.

Digital Pay Service 1
Pay Units: N.A.
Programming (via satellite): Cinemax (multiplexed); Encore (multiplexed); Flix; HBO (multiplexed); Starz (multiplexed).
Fee: $13.00 monthly (HBO/Cinemax or Starz/Encore).

Video-On-Demand: No

Pay-Per-View
iN DEMAND (delivered digitally); Hot Choice (delivered digitally); Playboy TV (delivered digitally); Fresh (delivered digitally); Shorteez (delivered digitally).

Internet Service
Operational: Yes.

Telephone Service
None

Miles of Plant: 2.0 (coaxial); None (fiber optic). Total homes in franchised area: 104. Homes passed included in Arnold
General Manager: Lee Ann Quist. Chief Technician: Mark Stottler. Marketing Manager: Casey Garrigan.
Ownership: Great Plains Communications Inc. (MSO).

TAYLOR—NCTC Cable, PO Box 700, 22 LaBarre St, Gibbon, NE 68840. Phones: 888-873-6282; 308-468-6341. Fax: 308-468-9929. Web Site: http://www.nctc.net. ICA: NE0235.
TV Market Ranking: Outside TV Markets (TAYLOR). Franchise award date: N.A. Franchise expiration date: N.A. Began: N.A.
Channel capacity: N.A. Channels available but not in use: N.A.

Basic Service
Subscribers: N.A. Included in Burwell
Programming (received off-air): KGIN (CBS, MNT) Grand Island; KHAS-TV (NBC) Hastings; KHGI-TV (ABC) Kearney; KMNE-TV (PBS) Bassett; KTVG-TV (FOX) Grand Island.
Programming (via satellite): ABC Family Channel; Animal Planet; Arts & Entertainment; Cartoon Network; CNBC; CNN; Comedy Central; Country Music TV; C-SPAN; CW+; Discovery Channel; E! Entertainment Television; ESPN; ESPN 2; ESPN Classic Sports; Eternal Word TV Network; Food Network; Fox News Channel; Fox Sports Net Midwest; FX; G4; Great American Country; Hallmark Channel; Headline News; HGTV; History Channel; Home Shopping Network; ION Television; Lifetime; MSNBC; MTV; Nickelodeon; Outdoor Channel; QVC; Spike TV; Syfy; TBS Superstation; The Learning Channel; Travel Channel; Trinity Broadcasting Network; truTV; Turner Classic Movies; Turner Network TV; TV Land; USA Network; Versus; VH1; Weather Channel; WGN America.
Fee: $39.20 monthly.

Digital Basic Service
Subscribers: N.A. Included in Burwell
Programming (via satellite): AmericanLife TV Network; BBC America; Bio; Bloomberg Television; Current; Daystar TV Network; Discovery Digital Networks; DMX Music; ESPNews; FitTV; Fox College Sports Atlantic; Fox College Sports Central; Fox College Sports Pacific; Fox Movie Channel; G4; Golf Channel; Gospel Music Channel; GSN; Halogen Network; History Channel International; Lifetime Movie Network; MTV Networks Digital Suite; Nick Jr.; Ovation; RFD-TV; ShopNBC; Sleuth; Speed Channel; TeenNick; WE tv.
Fee: $14.00 monthly.

Pay Service 1
Pay Units: 9.
Programming (via satellite): HBO.
Fee: $10.95 monthly.

Digital Pay Service 1
Pay Units: N.A.
Programming (via satellite): Cinemax (multiplexed); Encore (multiplexed); Flix; HBO (multiplexed); Showtime (multiplexed); Starz (multiplexed); The Movie Channel (multiplexed).
Fee: $10.95 monthly (Cinemax), $12.95 monthly (HBO or Showtime, TMC & Flix), $13.95 monthly (Starz & Encore).

Video-On-Demand: No

Internet Service
Operational: No, DSL & dial-up.

Telephone Service
None

Miles of Plant: 6.0 (coaxial); None (fiber optic). Homes passed included in Burwell
General Manager: Andy Jader. Technical Operations Manager: Nick Jeffres.
City fee: None.
Ownership: Nebraska Central Telecom Inc. (MSO).

TEKAMAH—American Broadband, 1605 Washington St, Blair, NE 68008-0400. Phones: 402-426-6200; 402-533-1000. Fax: 402-533-1111. Web Site: http://www.abbnebraska.com. ICA: NE0061.
TV Market Ranking: Outside TV Markets (TEKAMAH). Franchise award date: N.A. Franchise expiration date: N.A. Began: June 1, 1982.
Channel capacity: N.A. Channels available but not in use: N.A.

Basic Service
Subscribers: N.A. Included in Blair
Programming (received off-air): KETV (ABC) Omaha; KHIN (PBS) Red Oak; KMTV-TV (CBS) Omaha; KPTM (FOX, MNT) Omaha; KXVO (CW) Omaha; WOWT-TV (IND, NBC) Omaha.
Programming (via satellite): C-SPAN; Home Shopping Network; QVC; TV Guide Network; Weather Channel; WGN America.
Current originations: Government Access; Educational Access; Public Access.
Fee: $15.53 monthly.

Expanded Basic Service 1
Subscribers: N.A.
Programming (via satellite): ABC Family Channel; AMC; Animal Planet; Arts & Entertainment; CNBC; CNN; Comedy Central; Country Music TV; Discovery Channel; Disney Channel; ESPN; ESPN 2; Food Network; Fox News Channel; Fox Sports Net Midwest; FX; Hallmark Channel; Headline News; HGTV; History Channel; Lifetime; MSNBC; MTV; Nickelodeon; Spike TV; Syfy; TBS Superstation; The Learning Channel; truTV; Turner Network TV; USA Network; VH1.
Fee: $19.99 monthly.

Digital Basic Service
Subscribers: N.A. Included in Blair
Programming (received off-air): KETV (ABC) Omaha; KMTV-TV (CBS) Omaha; KPTM (FOX, MNT) Omaha; KXVO (CW) Omaha; WOWT-TV (IND, NBC) Omaha.
Programming (via satellite): Animal Planet HD; Bio; Discovery Channel HD; Discovery HD Theater; Discovery Health Channel; Discovery Kids Channel; Discovery Military Channel; Discovery Planet Green; DMX Music; ESPN 2 HD; ESPN HD; ESPN U; ESPNews; Eternal Word TV Network; Fox Soccer; FSN Digital Atlantic; FSN Digital Central; FSN Digital Pacific; Fuel TV; Fuse; Golf Channel; GSN; HDNet; HDNet Movies; ID Investigation Discovery; Lifetime Movie Network; MyNetworkTV Inc.; National Geographic Channel; National Geographic Channel HD Network; Outdoor Channel; RFD-TV; Science Channel; Science Channel HD; Sleuth; Speed Channel; Style Network; Toon Disney; Turner Classic Movies; Universal HD; Versus; WE tv.
Fee: $12.94 monthly.

Digital Pay Service 1
Pay Units: N.A.
Programming (via satellite): Cinemax (multiplexed); Cinemax HD; Encore (multiplexed); HBO (multiplexed); HBO HD; Showtime (multiplexed); Showtime HD; Starz (multiplexed); Starz HDTV; The Movie Channel (multiplexed); The Movie Channel HD.
Fee: $11.10 monthly (Cinemax), $12.00 monthly (Starz/Encore or Showtime/TMC), $13.35 monthly (HBO).

Video-On-Demand: No

Pay-Per-View
iN DEMAND (delivered digitally); Playboy TV (delivered digitally); Club Jenna (delivered digitally).

Internet Service
Operational: Yes, DSL only.
Broadband Service: In-house.
Fee: $35.00 monthly.

Telephone Service
None

Miles of Plant: 15.0 (coaxial); None (fiber optic). Total homes in area & homes passed included in Blair
President, State Operations: Mike Jacobsen. General Manager, Cable Television: Mike Storjohann. Program Director: Kay Peterson.
Ownership: American Broadband Communications Inc. (MSO).

TOBIAS—Formerly served by CableDirect. No longer in operation. ICA: NE0253.

TRENTON—Great Plains Communications, PO Box 500, 1600 Great Plains Centre, Blair, NE 68008-0500. Phone: 402-426-9511. Fax: 402-456-6550. Web Site: http://www.gpcom.com. ICA: NE0141.
TV Market Ranking: Below 100 (TRENTON). Franchise award date: August 17, 1983. Franchise expiration date: N.A. Began: February 1, 1984.
Channel capacity: 62 (not 2-way capable). Channels available but not in use: None.

Basic Service
Subscribers: N.A. Included in Arnold
Programming (received off-air): KBSL-DT (CBS) Goodland; KSNK (NBC) McCook; KWNB-TV (ABC) Hayes Center.
Programming (via satellite): C-SPAN; QVC; WGN America.
Current originations: Educational Access; Public Access.
Fee: $35.83 installation; $21.33 monthly; $.57 converter; $30.18 additional installation.

Expanded Basic Service 1
Subscribers: 154.
Programming (via satellite): ABC Family Channel; AMC; Animal Planet; Arts & Entertainment; Bravo!; Cartoon Network; CNBC; CNN; Comedy Central; Country Music TV; C-SPAN; Discovery Channel; Disney Channel; E! Entertainment Television; ESPN; ESPN 2; Eternal Word TV Network; Food Network; Fox News Channel; Fox Sports Net; FX; Hallmark Channel; Headline News; HGTV; History Channel; Home Shopping Network; Lifetime; Lifetime Movie Network; MSNBC; MTV; Nickelodeon; Oxygen;

ShopNBC; Speed Channel; Spike TV; Syfy; TBS Superstation; The Learning Channel; Travel Channel; Trinity Broadcasting Network; truTV; Turner Classic Movies; Turner Network TV; TV Land; USA Network; VH1; WE tv; Weather Channel.
Fee: $30.18 installation; $22.30 monthly.

Pay Service 1
Pay Units: 11.
Programming (via satellite): Cinemax.
Fee: $10.95 monthly.

Pay Service 2
Pay Units: 27.
Programming (via satellite): HBO.
Fee: $10.95 monthly.

Pay Service 3
Pay Units: 14.
Programming (via satellite): The Movie Channel.
Fee: $11.00 monthly.

Video-On-Demand: No

Pay-Per-View
Hot Choice, Addressable: No.

Internet Service
Operational: No, DSL.

Telephone Service
None

Miles of Plant: 6.0 (coaxial); None (fiber optic). Total homes in franchised area: 250. Homes passed included in Arnold

General Manager: Lee Ann Quist. Chief Technician: Mark Stottler. Marketing Manager: Casey Garrigan.

City fee: 3% of gross.

Ownership: Great Plains Communications Inc. (MSO).

TRUMBULL—Mid-State Community TV. Now served by AURORA, NE [NE0033]. ICA: NE0331.

ULYSSES—Galaxy Cablevision, 1928 S Lincoln Ave, Ste 200, York, NE 68467. Phone: 402-362-3332. Fax: 402-362-4890. Web Site: http://www.galaxycable.com. ICA: NE0183.

TV Market Ranking: 91 (ULYSSES). Franchise award date: N.A. Franchise expiration date: N.A. Began: March 1, 1984.

Channel capacity: 41 (not 2-way capable). Channels available but not in use: 20.

Basic Service
Subscribers: 15.
Programming (received off-air): KETV (ABC) Omaha; KLKN (ABC) Lincoln; KMTV-TV (CBS) Omaha; KOLN (CBS, MNT) Lincoln; KPTM (FOX, MNT) Omaha; KUON-TV (PBS) Lincoln; KXVO (CW) Omaha; WOWT-TV (IND, NBC) Omaha.
Programming (via satellite): ABC Family Channel; CNN; Discovery Channel; Disney Channel; ESPN; Headline News; Lifetime; Outdoor Channel; TBS Superstation; Turner Network TV; WGN America.
Fee: $35.00 installation; $30.20 monthly.

Pay Service 1
Pay Units: 12.
Programming (via satellite): Cinemax.
Fee: $11.95 monthly.

Pay Service 2
Pay Units: 16.
Programming (via satellite): HBO.
Fee: $12.95 monthly.

Internet Service
Operational: No.

Telephone Service
None

Miles of Plant: 4.0 (coaxial); None (fiber optic). Homes passed: 100.

State Manager: Cheyenne Wohlford. Technical Manager: Carl Stanley. Sales Manager: Mike Thomas. Customer Service Manager: Donna Bryant.

City fee: 1% of basic.

Ownership: Galaxy Cable Inc. (MSO).

UNION—Formerly served by Westcom. No longer in operation. ICA: NE0334.

VALENTINE—Cable Nebraska, 2123 Central Ave, Ste 200, Kearney, NE 68847. Phones: 800-456-0564; 605-229-1775. Web Site: http://www.cablene.com. ICA: NE0036.

TV Market Ranking: Outside TV Markets (VALENTINE). Franchise award date: February 25, 1986. Franchise expiration date: N.A. Began: November 30, 1972.

Channel capacity: 62 (not 2-way capable). Channels available but not in use: N.A.

Basic Service
Subscribers: 931.
Programming (received off-air): KMNE-TV (PBS) Bassett; KNOP-TV (NBC) North Platte; KOLN (CBS, MNT) Lincoln; KPLO-TV (CBS, MNT) Reliance; 2 FMs.
Programming (via satellite): ABC Family Channel; Arts & Entertainment; Cartoon Network; CNBC; CNN; Country Music TV; C-SPAN; Discovery Channel; Disney Channel; ESPN; Fox Sports Net; Headline News; KMGH-TV (ABC) Denver; MTV; Nickelodeon; QVC; Spike TV; TBS Superstation; Turner Network TV; TV Guide Network; TV Land; USA Network; VH1; Weather Channel; WGN America.
Fee: $50.00 installation; $22.91 monthly.

Pay Service 1
Pay Units: 51.
Programming (via satellite): Cinemax.
Fee: $20.00 installation; $11.00 monthly.

Pay Service 2
Pay Units: 128.
Programming (via satellite): HBO.
Fee: $20.00 installation; $11.00 monthly.

Pay Service 3
Pay Units: 83.
Programming (via satellite): The Movie Channel.
Fee: $20.00 installation; $11.00 monthly.

Pay Service 4
Pay Units: 86.
Programming (via satellite): Showtime.
Fee: $20.00 installation; $11.00 monthly.

Video-On-Demand: No

Internet Service
Operational: No.

Telephone Service
None

Miles of Plant: 21.0 (coaxial); 3.0 (fiber optic). Homes passed: 1,711.

Franchise fee: 3% of gross.

Ownership: USA Companies (MSO).

VALPARAISO—Galaxy Cablevision, 1928 S Lincoln Ave, Ste 200, York, NE 68467. Phone: 402-362-3332. Fax: 402-362-4890. Web Site: http://www.galaxycable.com. ICA: NE0168.

TV Market Ranking: 91 (VALPARAISO). Franchise award date: N.A. Franchise expiration date: N.A. Began: December 1, 1983.

Channel capacity: 41 (not 2-way capable). Channels available but not in use: 8.

Basic Service
Subscribers: 92.
Programming (received off-air): KETV (ABC) Omaha; KMTV-TV (CBS) Omaha; KOLN (CBS, MNT) Lincoln; KPTM (FOX, MNT) Omaha; KUON-TV (PBS) Lincoln; KXVO (CW) Omaha; WOWT-TV (IND, NBC) Omaha.
Programming (via satellite): ABC Family Channel; Arts & Entertainment; Cartoon Network; CNN; Discovery Channel; Disney Channel; E! Entertainment Television; ESPN; ESPN 2; Eternal Word TV Network; Fox News Channel; Fox Sports Net Midwest; Headline News; History Channel; Lifetime; Outdoor Channel; TBS Superstation; The Learning Channel; Turner Classic Movies; Turner Network TV; USA Network; Weather Channel; WGN America.
Fee: $35.00 installation; $38.95 monthly.

Pay Service 1
Pay Units: 16.
Programming (via satellite): Cinemax.
Fee: $11.95 monthly.

Pay Service 2
Pay Units: 21.
Programming (via satellite): HBO.
Fee: $12.95 monthly.

Internet Service
Operational: No.

Telephone Service
None

Miles of Plant: 5.0 (coaxial); None (fiber optic). Homes passed: 180.

State Manager: Cheyenne Wohlford. Technical Manager: Carl Stanley. Sales Manager: Mike Thomas. Customer Service Manager: Donna Bryant.

City fee: 3% of basic.

Ownership: Galaxy Cable Inc. (MSO).

VERDON—Formerly served by CableDirect. No longer in operation. ICA: NE0218.

WACO—Galaxy Cablevision, 1928 S Lincoln Ave, Ste 200, York, NE 68467. Phone: 402-362-3332. Fax: 402-362-4890. Web Site: http://www.galaxycable.com. Also serves Utica. ICA: NE0212.

TV Market Ranking: 91 (Utica); Outside TV Markets (WACO). Franchise award date: January 8, 1984. Franchise expiration date: N.A. Began: October 1, 1985.

Channel capacity: 41 (not 2-way capable). Channels available but not in use: 3.

Basic Service
Subscribers: 117.
Programming (received off-air): KETV (ABC) Omaha; KHAS-TV (NBC) Hastings; KLKN (ABC) Lincoln; KMTV-TV (CBS) Omaha; KOLN (CBS, MNT) Lincoln; KPTM (FOX, MNT) Omaha; KUON-TV (PBS) Lincoln; KXVO (CW) Omaha; WOWT-TV (IND, NBC) Omaha.
Programming (via satellite): ABC Family Channel; AMC; Arts & Entertainment; Cartoon Network; CNN; C-SPAN; Discovery Channel; Disney Channel; ESPN; Fox News Channel; Fox Sports Net Midwest; Fuse; FX; Headline News; HGTV; Lifetime; Outdoor Channel; QVC; TBS Superstation; Travel Channel; Turner Network TV; USA Network; Weather Channel; WGN America.
Current originations: Public Access.
Fee: $35.00 installation; $41.20 monthly.

Pay Service 1
Pay Units: 2.
Programming (via satellite): Cinemax.
Fee: $9.95 monthly.

Pay Service 2
Pay Units: 3.
Programming (via satellite): HBO.
Fee: $13.95 monthly.

Pay Service 3
Pay Units: N.A.
Programming (via satellite): Showtime; The Movie Channel.
Fee: $7.95 monthly (TMC), $8.95 monthly (Showtime).

Internet Service
Operational: No.

Telephone Service
None

Miles of Plant: 8.0 (coaxial); None (fiber optic). Homes passed: 498.

State Manager: Cheyenne Wohlford. Technical Manager: Carl Stanley. Sales Manager: Mike Thomas. Customer Service Manager: Donna Bryant.

City fee: 1% of basic.

Ownership: Galaxy Cable Inc. (MSO).

WAHOO—Charter Communications. Now served by SPRINGFIELD (formerly Plattsmouth), NE [NE0020]. ICA: NE0035.

WALLACE—Consolidated Cable Inc., PO Box 6147, 6900 Van Dorn St, Ste 21, Lincoln, NE 68506-0147. Phones: 402-489-2728; 800-742-7464. Fax: 402-489-9034. E-mail: service@consolidatedtelephone.com. Web Site: http://www.nebnet.net. Also serves Madrid. ICA: NE0336.

TV Market Ranking: Below 100 (WALLACE); Outside TV Markets (Madrid). Franchise award date: October 7, 1987. Franchise expiration date: N.A. Began: February 1, 1989.

Channel capacity: 37 (not 2-way capable). Channels available but not in use: N.A.

Basic Service
Subscribers: 151.
Programming (received off-air): KGIN (CBS, MNT) Grand Island; KNOP-TV (NBC) North Platte; KPNE-TV (PBS) North Platte; KTVG-TV (FOX) Grand Island; KWNB-TV (ABC) Hayes Center.
Programming (via satellite): ABC Family Channel; Animal Planet; Arts & Entertainment; Cartoon Network; CNN; Country Music TV; Discovery Channel; Disney Channel; ESPN; ESPN 2; Fox News Channel; Fox Sports Net Midwest; FX; HGTV; History Channel; Home Shopping Network; MTV; Nickelodeon; Oxygen; Spike TV; Syfy; TBS Superstation; The Learning Channel; Turner Classic Movies; Turner Network TV; TV Land; USA Network; VH1; Weather Channel; WGN America.
Fee: $25.95 installation; $28.95 monthly.

Digital Basic Service
Subscribers: N.A.
Programming (via satellite): AmericanLife TV Network; Bloomberg Television; CMT Pure Country; DMX Music; ESPN Classic Sports; ESPNews; FitTV; Fox College Sports Atlantic; Fox College Sports Central; Fox College Sports Pacific; Fox Movie Channel; G4; GAS; Golf Channel; GSN; Halogen Network; Independent Film Channel; Lifetime Movie Network; MTV Networks

Digital Suite; Nick Jr.; NickToons TV; Outdoor Channel; Sleuth; Speed Channel; Style Network; Sundance Channel; Toon Disney; Trinity Broadcasting Network; Versus; WE tv.
Fee: $12.00 monthly; $49.95 converter.

Pay Service 1
Pay Units: 27.
Programming (via satellite): HBO.
Fee: $9.00 monthly.

Pay Service 2
Pay Units: 32.
Programming (via satellite): Showtime.
Fee: $9.00 monthly.

Digital Pay Service 1
Pay Units: N.A.
Programming (via satellite): Cinemax (multiplexed); Encore (multiplexed); Flix; HBO (multiplexed); Showtime (multiplexed); Starz (multiplexed); The Movie Channel (multiplexed).
Fee: $9.00 monthly (each).

Video-On-Demand: No

Pay-Per-View
iN DEMAND (delivered digitally); Hot Choice (delivered digitally); Playboy TV (delivered digitally); Urban American Television Network (delivered digitally); Fresh (delivered digitally).

Internet Service
Operational: No.

Telephone Service
None

Miles of Plant: 3.0 (coaxial); 15.0 (fiber optic). Total homes in franchised area: 236.
Manager: Brian D. Thompson. Chief Technician: Dan Smith.
Ownership: Consolidated Cable Inc. (MSO).

WALTHILL—HunTel Cablevision. Now served by WAYNE, NE [NE0374]. ICA: NE0373.

WASHINGTON (village)—Formerly served by TelePartners. No longer in operation. ICA: NE0337.

WAUNETA—BWTelcom, PO Box 645, 607 Chief St, Benkelman, NE 69021. Phones: 800-835-0053; 308-394-6000; 308-423-2000. Fax: 308-423-5818. E-mail: randy@bwtelcom.net. Web Site: http://www.bwtelcom.net. Also serves Chase County. ICA: NE0338.
TV Market Ranking: Below 100 (Chase County, WAUNETA). Franchise award date: N.A. Franchise expiration date: N.A. Began: N.A.
Channel capacity: 60 (operating 2-way). Channels available but not in use: N.A.

Basic Service
Subscribers: 300.
Programming (received off-air): KBSL-DT (CBS) Goodland; KPNE-TV (PBS) North Platte; KSNK (NBC) McCook; KWNB-TV (ABC) Hayes Center.
Programming (via satellite): ABC Family Channel; Arts & Entertainment; CNBC; CNN; Country Music TV; Discovery Channel; ESPN; ESPN 2; ESPN Classic Sports; Fox News Channel; Fox Sports Net Rocky Mountain; FX; Lifetime; Nickelodeon; Outdoor Channel; Spike TV; Syfy; TBS Superstation; The Learning Channel; Travel Channel; Turner Classic Movies; Turner Network TV; USA Network; VH1; Weather Channel; WGN America.
Programming (via translator): KCNC-TV (CBS) Denver; KWGN-TV (CW) Denver.
Current originations: Educational Access.
Fee: $35.00 installation; $19.40 monthly.

Expanded Basic Service 1
Subscribers: N.A.
Programming (via satellite): AMC; Animal Planet; Bloomberg Television; Cartoon Network; Comedy Central; Disney Channel; Food Network; G4; Great American Country; Hallmark Channel; Headline News; HGTV; History Channel; MTV; National Geographic Channel; SoapNet; Speed Channel; TV Land; Versus.
Fee: $8.95 monthly.

Pay Service 1
Pay Units: 26.
Programming (via satellite): HBO; Showtime; The Movie Channel.
Fee: $10.43 monthly (Showtime/TMC), &10.95 monthly (HBO).

Video-On-Demand: No

Internet Service
Operational: No, Both DSL & dial-up.

Telephone Service
None

Manager: Randall Raile. Marketing Director: Loretta Raile.
Ownership: Benkelman Telephone Co. (MSO).

WAYNE—American Broadband, 1605 Washington St, Blair, NE 68008-0400. Phones: 402-375-1120; 402-533-1100. Fax: 402-375-4077. Web Site: http://www.abbnebraska.com. Also serves Belden, Carroll, Emerson, Homer, Osmond, Pender, Wakefield & Walthill. ICA: NE0374.
TV Market Ranking: Below 100 (Emerson, Homer, Pender, Wakefield, Walthill); Outside TV Markets (Belden, Carroll, Osmond, WAYNE). Franchise award date: N.A. Franchise expiration date: N.A. Began: N.A.
Channel capacity: N.A. Channels available but not in use: N.A.

Basic Service
Subscribers: N.A. Included in Blair
Programming (received off-air): KCAU-TV (ABC) Sioux City; KETV (ABC) Omaha; KMEG (CBS) Sioux City; KMTV-TV (CBS) Omaha; KPTH (FOX, MNT) Sioux City; KTIV (CW, NBC) Sioux City; KXNE-TV (PBS) Norfolk; WOWT-TV (IND, NBC) Omaha.
Programming (via satellite): CW+; Eternal Word TV Network; FX; Home Shopping Network; National Geographic Channel; QVC; TV Guide Network; WGN America.
Current originations: Educational Access; Public Access.
Fee: $30.00 installation; $15.95 monthly.

Expanded Basic Service 1
Subscribers: N.A.
Programming (via satellite): ABC Family Channel; AMC; Arts & Entertainment; Cartoon Network; CNBC; CNN; Comedy Central; C-SPAN; Discovery Channel; Disney Channel; E! Entertainment Television; ESPN; ESPN 2; Food Network; Fox News Channel; Fox Sports Net Midwest; Great American Country; HGTV; History Channel; Lifetime; MSNBC; MTV; Nickelodeon; Spike TV; Syfy; TBS Superstation; The Learning Channel; Toon Disney; Turner Network TV; TV Land; USA Network; VH1; Weather Channel.
Fee: $19.99 monthly.

Digital Basic Service
Subscribers: N.A. Included in Blair
Programming (received off-air): KMEG (CBS) Sioux City; KPTH (FOX, MNT) Sioux City.
Programming (via satellite): BBC America; Bloomberg Television; Discovery Health Channel; Discovery Kids Channel; DMX Music; ESPN Classic Sports; ESPNews; FitTV; Fox Movie Channel; Fox Soccer; G4; Golf Channel; GSN; Halogen Network; NickToons TV; Outdoor Channel; Science Channel; Trinity Broadcasting Network; Turner Classic Movies; Versus; WE tv.
Fee: $7.95 monthly.

Pay Service 1
Pay Units: 200.
Programming (via satellite): HBO.
Fee: $13.35 monthly.

Pay Service 2
Pay Units: 90.
Programming (via satellite): Cinemax.
Fee: $11.10 monthly.

Pay Service 3
Pay Units: 80.
Programming (via satellite): Showtime.
Fee: $12.00 monthly.

Digital Pay Service 1
Pay Units: N.A.
Programming (via satellite): Bravo; Cinemax (multiplexed); Encore (multiplexed); HBO (multiplexed); Independent Film Channel; Showtime (multiplexed); Starz (multiplexed); The Movie Channel (multiplexed).
Fee: $11.10 monthly (Cinemax), $12.00 monthly (Starz/Encore/Bravo/IFC or Showtime/TMC), $13.55 monthly (HBO).

Video-On-Demand: No

Pay-Per-View
iN DEMAND (delivered digitally).

Internet Service
Operational: Yes.
Subscribers: 2,200.
Broadband Service: In-house.
Fee: $30.00 monthly; $180.00 modem purchase.

Telephone Service
None

Miles of Plant: 35.0 (coaxial); None (fiber optic). Total homes in area & homes passed included in Blair
President, State Operations: Mike Jacobsen. Cable Manager: Mike Storjohann. General Manager: Joe Jedensky. Programming Manager: Kay Petersen.
Ownership: American Broadband Communications Inc. (MSO).

WESTERN—Galaxy Cablevision, 1928 S Lincoln Ave, Ste 200, York, NE 68467. Phone: 402-362-3332. Fax: 402-362-4890. Web Site: http://www.galaxycable.com. ICA: NE0202.
TV Market Ranking: Outside TV Markets (WESTERN). Franchise award date: N.A. Franchise expiration date: N.A. Began: September 10, 1984.
Channel capacity: 41 (not 2-way capable). Channels available but not in use: 19.

Basic Service
Subscribers: 26.
Programming (received off-air): KHNE-TV (PBS) Hastings; KLKN (ABC) Lincoln; KOLN (CBS, MNT) Lincoln; KPTM (FOX, MNT) Omaha; KUSA (NBC) Denver; KXVO (CW) Omaha.
Programming (via satellite): ABC Family Channel; Cartoon Network; CNN; Discovery Channel; Disney Channel; ESPN; Fox Sports Net Midwest; Outdoor Channel; TBS Superstation; Turner Network TV; USA Network; WGN America.
Fee: $35.00 installation; $32.95 monthly.

Pay Service 1
Pay Units: 8.
Programming (via satellite): Cinemax.
Fee: $11.95 monthly.

Pay Service 2
Pay Units: 11.
Programming (via satellite): HBO.
Fee: $12.95 monthly.

Internet Service
Operational: No.

Telephone Service
None

Miles of Plant: 5.0 (coaxial); None (fiber optic). Homes passed: 168.
State Manager: Cheyenne Wohlford. Technical Manager: Carl Stanley. Engineer: Vance Wewer. Sales Manager: Mike Thomas. Customer Service Manager: Donna Bryant.
City fee: 3% of basic.
Ownership: Galaxy Cable Inc. (MSO).

WESTON—Formerly served by Westcom. No longer in operation. ICA: NE0238.

WILBER—Galaxy Cablevision, 1928 S Lincoln Ave, Ste 200, York, NE 68467. Phone: 402-362-3332. Fax: 402-362-4890. Web Site: http://www.galaxycable.com. Also serves Blue Springs, Clatonia, De Witt, Dorchester, Friend, Hallam, Hickman, Milford, Pleasant Dale, Plymouth & Wymore. ICA: NE0055.
TV Market Ranking: 91 (Clatonia, De Witt, Dorchester, Friend, Hallam, Hickman, Milford, Pleasant Dale, WILBER); Outside TV Markets (Blue Springs, Plymouth, Wymore). Franchise award date: N.A. Franchise expiration date: N.A. Began: June 1, 1981.
Channel capacity: 78 (operating 2-way). Channels available but not in use: None.

Basic Service
Subscribers: 1,950.
Programming (received off-air): KETV (ABC) Omaha; KLKN (ABC) Lincoln; KMTV-TV (CBS) Omaha; KOLN (CBS, MNT) Lincoln; KPTM (FOX, MNT) Omaha; KUON-TV (PBS) Lincoln; KXVO (CW) Omaha; WOWT-TV (IND, NBC) Omaha.
Programming (via satellite): ABC Family Channel; AMC; Animal Planet; Arts & Entertainment; Boomerang; Cartoon Network; CNN; Comedy Central; C-SPAN; Discovery Channel; Disney Channel; E! Entertainment Television; ESPN; ESPN 2; Eternal Word TV Network; Food Network; Fox News Channel; Fox Sports Net Midwest; Fuse; FX; Great American Country; Hallmark Channel; Halogen Network; Headline News; HGTV; History Channel; Lifetime; MSNBC; National Geographic Channel; Outdoor Channel; QVC; Syfy; TBS Superstation; The Learning Channel; Toon Disney; Travel Channel; Trinity Broadcasting Network; Turner Classic Movies; Turner Network TV; TV Guide Network; TV Land; USA Network; Weather Channel; WGN America.
Current originations: Educational Access; Public Access.
Fee: $35.00 installation; $44.75 monthly.

Digital Basic Service
Subscribers: 436.
Programming (via satellite): AmericanLife TV Network; BBC America; Bio; Bloomberg Television; Discovery Digital Networks; ESPN Classic Sports; ESPNews; FitTV; Fox Sports World; FSN Digital Atlantic; FSN Digital Central; FSN Digital Pacific; G4; Golf Channel; GSN; History Channel International; Speed Channel; Style Network; WE tv.
Fee: $12.95 monthly.

Digital Expanded Basic Service
Subscribers: N.A.
Programming (via satellite): DMX Music; Encore; Fox Movie Channel; Independent Film Channel; Lifetime Movie Network.
Fee: $12.95 monthly.

Pay Service 1
Pay Units: 63.
Programming (via satellite): Cinemax.
Fee: $10.95 monthly.

Pay Service 2
Pay Units: 94.
Programming (via satellite): HBO.
Fee: $14.95 monthly.

Pay Service 3
Pay Units: 159.
Programming (via satellite): Showtime.
Fee: $9.95 monthly.

Pay Service 4
Pay Units: 130.
Programming (via satellite): The Movie Channel.
Fee: $7.95 monthly.

Digital Pay Service 1
Pay Units: N.A.
Programming (via satellite): Cinemax (multiplexed); Flix; HBO (multiplexed); Showtime (multiplexed); The Movie Channel (multiplexed).
Fee: $15.60 monthly.

Video-On-Demand: No

Pay-Per-View
Addressable homes: 334.
ESPN Now (delivered digitally), Fee: $3.99, Addressable: Yes; Hot Choice (delivered digitally); Movies (delivered digitally); Playboy TV (delivered digitally); Fresh (delivered digitally); sports (delivered digitally).

Internet Service
Operational: Yes. Began: March 1, 1999.
Subscribers: 527.
Broadband Service: Galaxy Cable Internet.
Fee: $49.95 installation; $44.95 monthly; $5.00 modem lease.

Telephone Service
None

Miles of Plant: 80.0 (coaxial); 1,015.0 (fiber optic). Homes passed: 4,491.
State Manager: Cheyenne Wohlford. Technical Manager: Carl Stanley. Sales Manager: Mike Thomas. Customer Service Manager: Donna Bryant.
City fee: 3% of gross.
Ownership: Galaxy Cable Inc. (MSO).

WINSIDE—CenCom Inc. This cable system has converted to IPTV. See Winside (village), NW [NE5033]. ICA: NE0386.

WINSIDE—Formerly served by Sky Scan Cable Co. No longer in operation. ICA: NE0340.

WINSIDE (village)—CenCom NNTV. Formerly [NE0386]. This cable system has converted to IPTV, 110 E Elk St, Jackson, NE 68743-0066. Phones: 402-623-4321; 888-397-4321. E-mail: nntc@nntc.net. Web Site: http://www.nntc.net. ICA: NE5033.
Channel capacity: N.A. Channels available but not in use: N.A.

Internet Service
Operational: Yes.

Telephone Service
Digital: Operational

General Manager: Emory Graffis.
Ownership: Northeast Nebraska Telephone Co.

WOODCLIFF LAKES—Time Warner Cable. Now served by FREMONT, NE [NE0007]. ICA: NE0364.

WYNOT—CenCom Inc. No longer in operation. ICA: NE0236.

YORK—Time Warner Cable, 5400 S 16th St, Lincoln, NE 68512-1278. Phone: 402-421-0330. Fax: 402-421-0310. Web Site: http://www.timewarnercable.com/Nebraska. ICA: NE0012.
TV Market Ranking: Outside TV Markets (YORK). Franchise award date: January 1, 1966. Franchise expiration date: N.A. Began: January 1, 1964.
Channel capacity: N.A. Channels available but not in use: N.A.

Basic Service
Subscribers: N.A. Included in Lincoln
Programming (received off-air): KETV (ABC) Omaha; KHAS-TV (NBC) Hastings; KHGI-TV (ABC) Kearney; KLKN (ABC) Lincoln; KMTV-TV (CBS) Omaha; KOLN (CBS, MNT) Lincoln; KPTM (FOX, MNT) Omaha; KUON-TV (PBS) Lincoln; KXVO (CW) Omaha; WOWT-TV (IND, NBC) Omaha.
Programming (via satellite): TV Guide Network; WGN America.
Fee: $40.54 installation; $12.73 monthly; $.69 converter; $18.29 additional installation.

Expanded Basic Service 1
Subscribers: N.A.
Programming (via satellite): ABC Family Channel; AMC; Animal Planet; Arts & Entertainment; BET Networks; Bravo; Cartoon Network; CNBC; CNN; Comedy Central; Country Music TV; C-SPAN; C-SPAN 2; Discovery Channel; Discovery Health Channel; Disney Channel; E! Entertainment Television; ESPN; ESPN 2; ESPN Classic Sports; Eternal Word TV Network; Food Network; Fox News Channel; Fox Sports Net Midwest; FX; Golf Channel; Hallmark Channel; Headline News; HGTV; History Channel; Home Shopping Network; ION Television; Lifetime; Lifetime Movie Network; MSNBC; MTV; National Geographic Channel; Nickelodeon; Oxygen; QVC; ShopNBC; SoapNet; Spike TV; Syfy; TBS Superstation; The Learning Channel; Travel Channel; truTV; Turner Classic Movies; Turner Network TV; TV Land; Univision; USA Network; VH1; WE tv; Weather Channel.
Fee: $33.12 monthly.

Digital Basic Service
Subscribers: N.A. Included in Lincoln
Programming (via satellite): America's Store; BBC America; Bio; Bloomberg Television; Boomerang; Canales N; Cooking Channel; C-SPAN 3; Discovery Digital Networks; Do-It-Yourself; ESPNews; FitTV; Fox Movie Channel; Fox Sports World; FSN Digital Atlantic; FSN Digital Central; FSN Digital Pacific; Fuse; G4; Great American Country; GSN; History Channel International; Independent Film Channel; Lifetime Real Women; MTV2; Music Choice; NASA TV; NBA TV; Nick Jr.; Outdoor Channel; Ovation; Speed Channel; Style Network; Tennis Channel; Toon Disney; Trinity Broadcasting Network; Versus; VH1 Classic.
Fee: $6.95 monthly; $7.65 converter.

Digital Pay Service 1
Pay Units: 1,471.
Programming (via satellite): Cinemax (multiplexed); Encore (multiplexed); HBO (multiplexed); Showtime (multiplexed); Starz (multiplexed); The Movie Channel (multiplexed).
Fee: $9.95 monthly (each).

Video-On-Demand: Yes

Pay-Per-View
Addressable homes: 825.
NASCAR In Car (delivered digitally); NBA League Pass (delivered digitally); NHL Center Ice (delivered digitally); Hot Choice (delivered digitally), Addressable: Yes; iN DEMAND (delivered digitally); Playboy TV (delivered digitally); Fresh (delivered digitally); ESPN Full Court (delivered digitally); Shorteez (delivered digitally); Pleasure (delivered digitally).

Internet Service
Operational: Yes.
Subscribers: 590.
Broadband Service: Road Runner.
Fee: $39.95 installation; $44.95 monthly.

Telephone Service
Digital: Operational
Fee: $39.95 monthly

Miles of Plant: 57.0 (coaxial); 5.0 (fiber optic). Total homes in franchised area: 4,408. Homes passed included in Lincoln
President: Beth Scarborough. Vice President, Operations: Dick Cassidy. Vice President, Engineering: John Matejovich. Vice President, Marketing: Brian Cecere. General Manager: Valerie Kramer. Technical Operations Manager: Rick Hollman. Public Affairs Director: Ann Shrewsbury.
Franchise fee: 5% of gross.
Ownership: Time Warner Cable (MSO).; Advance/Newhouse Partnership (MSO).

YUTAN—Formerly served by TelePartners. No longer in operation. ICA: NE0102.

NEVADA

Total Systems: 37
Total Communities Served: 98
Franchises Not Yet Operating: 0
Applications Pending: 0
Communities with Applications: 0
Number of Basic Subscribers: 591,170
Number of Expanded Basic Subscribers: 86,778
Number of Pay Units: 1,628

Top 100 Markets Represented: N.A.

For a list of cable communities in this section, see the Cable Community Index located in the back of Cable Volume 2. For explanation of terms used in cable system listings, see p. D-11.

ALAMO—Rainbow Cable, PO Box 300, 27 Main St, Pioche, NV 89043-0300. Phone: 775-962-5111. Fax: 775-962-5193. ICA: NV0032.
TV Market Ranking: Outside TV Markets (ALAMO). Franchise award date: N.A. Franchise expiration date: N.A. Began: N.A.
Channel capacity: N.A. Channels available but not in use: N.A.
Basic Service
Subscribers: 120.
Programming (via satellite): ABC Family Channel; Country Music TV; Discovery Channel; Disney Channel; ESPN; Headline News; KCNC-TV (CBS) Denver; KMGH-TV (ABC) Denver; KUSA (NBC) Denver; MTV; Nickelodeon; Spike TV; TBS Superstation; The Learning Channel; Turner Network TV; USA Network; WGN America.
Fee: $43.00 installation; $23.25 monthly.
Pay Service 1
Pay Units: N.A.
Programming (via satellite): Cinemax; HBO; Showtime.
Fee: $7.90 monthly (Showtime), $7.95 monthly (Cinemax), $9.95 monthly (HBO).
Video-On-Demand: No
Internet Service
Operational: No.
Telephone Service
None
Manager: Paul Christian. Chief Technician: Paul Donohue. Office Manager: Valinda Woodworth.
Ownership: Christian Enterprises (MSO).

BATTLE MOUNTAIN—Baja Broadband, 1250 Lamoille Hwy, Ste 1150, Elko, NV 89801. Phones: 775-738-1558; 980-235-7600 (Corporate office). Fax: 775-738-8897. E-mail: info@bajabb.tv. Web Site: http://www.bajabroadband.com. ICA: NV0016.
TV Market Ranking: Outside TV Markets (BATTLE MOUNTAIN). Franchise award date: N.A. Franchise expiration date: N.A. Began: January 1, 1987.
Channel capacity: 47 (not 2-way capable). Channels available but not in use: N.A.
Basic Service
Subscribers: 550.
Programming (received off-air): K32CA Battle Mountain; KCWY-DT (NBC) Casper; KOLO-TV (ABC) Reno; KSTU (FOX) Salt Lake City; KTVN (CBS) Reno; KUSA (NBC) Denver.
Programming (via satellite): C-SPAN; C-SPAN 2; CW+; Home Shopping Network; ION Television; KCNC-TV (CBS) Denver; QVC; TV Guide Network.
Fee: $62.00 installation; $15.01 monthly; $15.52 additional installation.
Expanded Basic Service 1
Subscribers: N.A.
Programming (via satellite): ABC Family Channel; AMC; Animal Planet; Arts & Entertainment; Cartoon Network; CNBC; CNN; Comedy Central; Discovery Channel; Disney Channel; E! Entertainment Television; ESPN; ESPN 2; Food Network; Fox News Channel; Fox Sports Net Rocky Mountain; FX; GalaVision; Great American Country; Hallmark Channel; Headline News; HGTV; Lifetime; MSNBC; MTV; Nickelodeon; Spike TV; TBS Superstation; The Learning Channel; the mtn; Travel Channel; Turner Network TV; TV Land; Univision; USA Network; VH1; Weather Channel.
Fee: $24.98 installation; $24.98 monthly.
Digital Basic Service
Subscribers: N.A.
Programming (via satellite): BBC America; Bio; Bloomberg Television; CMT Pure Country; Discovery Health Channel; Discovery Kids Channel; Discovery Military Channel; Discovery Planet Green; DMX Music; FitTV; Fox Movie Channel; Fuse; G4; GSN; Halogen Network; History Channel; History Channel International; ID Investigation Discovery; Independent Film Channel; Lifetime Movie Network; MTV Tres; MTV2; National Geographic Channel; Nick Jr.; NickToons TV; Science Channel; Style Network; Syfy; TeenNick; Toon Disney; Trinity Broadcasting Network; Turner Classic Movies; VH1 Classic; WE tv.
Fee: $11.95 monthly.
Digital Expanded Basic Service
Subscribers: N.A.
Programming (via satellite): ESPN Classic Sports; ESPNews; Fox Soccer; Golf Channel; Outdoor Channel; Speed Channel; Versus.
Digital Pay Service 1
Pay Units: N.A.
Programming (via satellite): Cinemax (multiplexed); Encore (multiplexed); HBO (multiplexed); Showtime (multiplexed); Starz (multiplexed); The Movie Channel (multiplexed).
Video-On-Demand: No
Pay-Per-View
iN DEMAND (delivered digitally); Club Jenna (delivered digitally); Playboy TV (delivered digitally); Fresh (delivered digitally).
Internet Service
Operational: No.
Telephone Service
None
Miles of Plant: 18.0 (coaxial); None (fiber optic). Homes passed: 1,481. Total homes in franchised area: 1,573.
General Manager: Bill Shaw. Technical Operations Manager: Ed Farnum. Office Manager: Deb Hersh.
City fee: 2% of gross.
Ownership: Baja Broadband (MSO).

BEATTY—Eagle West Communications Inc, 1030 S Mesa Dr, Mesa, AZ 85210. Phone: 480-813-8371. Fax: 480-813-4596. ICA: NV0024.
TV Market Ranking: Outside TV Markets (BEATTY). Franchise award date: December 1, 1983. Franchise expiration date: N.A. Began: March 6, 1986.
Channel capacity: 40 (operating 2-way). Channels available but not in use: None.
Basic Service
Subscribers: N.A. Included in East Mesa, AZ
Programming (received off-air): KLAS-TV (CBS) Las Vegas; KSNV-DT (NBC) Las Vegas; KTNV-TV (ABC) Las Vegas; KVMY (MNT) Las Vegas; 1 FM.
Programming (via satellite): ABC Family Channel; Arts & Entertainment; Cartoon Network; CNN; Comedy Central; Country Music TV; C-SPAN; Discovery Channel; E! Entertainment Television; ESPN; Fox Sports Net; Headline News; Home Shopping Network; Lifetime; MTV; Nickelodeon; Spike TV; Syfy; TBS Superstation; The Learning Channel; Trinity Broadcasting Network; truTV; Turner Classic Movies; Turner Network TV; USA Network; Weather Channel; WGN America.
Fee: $26.25 installation; $31.95 monthly; $2.00 converter.
Pay Service 1
Pay Units: 27.
Programming (via satellite): HBO.
Fee: $40.00 installation; $11.95 monthly.
Video-On-Demand: No
Internet Service
Operational: No.
Telephone Service
None
Homes passed & miles of plant included in East Mesa, AZ
General Manager: Ernest McKay.
Ownership: Eagle West Communications (MSO).

BLUE DIAMOND—Formerly served by Eagle West Communications Inc. No longer in operation. ICA: NV0031.

BOULDER CITY (northern portion)—Eagle West Communications Inc, 1030 S Mesa Dr, Mesa, AZ 85210. Phone: 480-813-8371. Fax: 480-813-4596. Also serves Boulder Beach, Hemenway, Lake Mead Base & Lakeview. ICA: NV0033.
TV Market Ranking: Below 100 (Boulder Beach, BOULDER CITY (NORTHERN PORTION), Hemenway, Lake Mead Base, Lakeview). Franchise award date: N.A. Franchise expiration date: N.A. Began: March 15, 1972.
Channel capacity: 48 (not 2-way capable). Channels available but not in use: None.
Basic Service
Subscribers: N.A. Subscribers included in East Mesa, AZ
Programming (received off-air): KLAS-TV (CBS) Las Vegas; KLVX-TV (PBS) Las Vegas; KSNV-DT (NBC) Las Vegas; KTNV-TV (ABC) Las Vegas; KVCW (CW) Las Vegas; KVMY (MNT) Las Vegas; KVVU-TV (FOX) Henderson; allband FM.
Programming (via satellite): ABC Family Channel; Arts & Entertainment; CNN; Discovery Channel; ESPN; Lifetime; Spike TV; TBS Superstation; Turner Network TV; USA Network; WGN America.
Fee: $35.00 installation; $31.95 monthly.
Pay Service 1
Pay Units: N.A.
Programming (via satellite): HBO.
Fee: $12.00 monthly.
Video-On-Demand: No
Internet Service
Operational: No.
Telephone Service
None
Miles of plant & homes passed included in East Mesa, AZ
General Manager: Ernest McKay.
City fee: $100 annually.
Ownership: Eagle West Communications (MSO).

CALIENTE—Rainbow Cable. Now served by PANACA, NV [NV0047]. ICA: NV0035.

CALLVILLE BAY—Formerly served by Eagle West Communications Inc. No longer in operation. ICA: NV0036.

CARLIN—Baja Broadband, 1250 Lamoille Hwy, Ste 1150, Elko, NV 89801. Phone: 775-738-2662. Fax: 775-738-8897. Web Site: http://www.bajabroadband.com. ICA: NV0020.
TV Market Ranking: Below 100 (CARLIN). Franchise award date: July 1, 1986. Franchise expiration date: N.A. Began: November 1, 1986.
Channel capacity: 47 (not 2-way capable). Channels available but not in use: N.A.
Basic Service
Subscribers: 574.
Programming (received off-air): K15EE-D Elko; KENV-DT (NBC) Elko; KSTU (FOX) Salt Lake City; KUCW (CW) Ogden.
Programming (via satellite): C-SPAN; C-SPAN 2; Home Shopping Network; ION Television; QVC.
Programming (via translator): KOLO-TV (ABC) Reno; KTVN (CBS) Reno.
Current originations: Public Access.
Fee: $62.00 installation; $15.01 monthly; $23.21 additional installation.
Expanded Basic Service 1
Subscribers: 543.
Programming (via satellite): ABC Family Channel; AMC; Animal Planet; Arts & Entertainment; Cartoon Network; CNBC; CNN; Comedy Central; Discovery Channel; Disney Channel; E! Entertainment Television; ESPN; ESPN 2; Fox News Channel; Fox Sports Net Rocky Mountain; FX; GalaVision; Great American Country; Hallmark Channel;

Headline News; Lifetime; MSNBC; MTV; Nickelodeon; Spike TV; Style Network; TBS Superstation; The Learning Channel; the mtn; Turner Network TV; TV Land; USA Network; VH1; Weather Channel.
Fee: $13.35 installation; $24.98 monthly.

Digital Basic Service
Subscribers: N.A.
Programming (via satellite): BBC America; Bio; Bloomberg Television; Bravo; CMT Pure Country; Discovery Health Channel; Discovery Kids Channel; Discovery Military Channel; Discovery Planet Green; ESPN Classic Sports; FitTV; Fox Movie Channel; Fuse; G4; GSN; Halogen Network; HGTV; History Channel; History Channel International; ID Investigation Discovery; Independent Film Channel; Lifetime Movie Network; MTV2; Music Choice; National Geographic Channel; Nick Jr.; NickToons TV; Science Channel; Speed Channel; Syfy; TeenNick; Toon Disney; Trinity Broadcasting Network; Turner Classic Movies; VH1 Classic; WE tv.
Fee: $11.95 monthly.

Digital Expanded Basic Service
Subscribers: N.A.
Programming (via satellite): ESPNews; Fox Soccer; Golf Channel; Outdoor Channel; Versus.

Digital Pay Service 1
Pay Units: N.A.
Programming (via satellite): Cinemax (multiplexed); Encore (multiplexed); HBO (multiplexed); Showtime (multiplexed); Starz (multiplexed); The Movie Channel (multiplexed).

Video-On-Demand: No

Pay-Per-View
iN DEMAND (delivered digitally); Playboy TV (delivered digitally); Fresh (delivered digitally); Club Jenna (delivered digitally).

Internet Service
Operational: No.

Telephone Service
None

Miles of Plant: 9.0 (coaxial); None (fiber optic). Homes passed: 763. Total homes in franchised area: 778.
Technical Operations Manager: Ed Farnum.
Ownership: Baja Broadband (MSO).

CARSON CITY—Charter Communications, 9335 Prototype Dr, Reno, NV 89521. Phone: 775-850-1200. Fax: 775-850-1279. Web Site: http://www.charter.com. Also serves Dayton, Lyon County (northwestern portion) & Storey County (southern portion). ICA: NV0004.
TV Market Ranking: Below 100 (CARSON CITY, Dayton, Lyon County (northwestern portion), Storey County (southern portion)). Franchise award date: N.A. Franchise expiration date: N.A. Began: November 1, 1962.
Channel capacity: N.A. Channels available but not in use: N.A.

Basic Service
Subscribers: N.A. Included in Reno
Programming (received off-air): KAME-TV (MNT) Reno; KNPB (PBS) Reno; KNVV-LP Reno; KOLO-TV (ABC) Reno; KREN-TV (CW, UNV) Reno; KRNS-CA (IND) Reno; KRNV-DT (ABC) Reno; KTVN (CBS) Reno; 3 FMs.
Programming (via microwave): KCRA-TV (NBC) Sacramento; KGO-TV (ABC) San Francisco; KRXI-TV (FOX) Reno.
Programming (via satellite): C-SPAN; C-SPAN 2; Hallmark Channel; Home Shopping Network; ION Television; Product Information Network; QVC; TBS Superstation; Weather Channel.
Current originations: Leased Access; Government Access; Educational Access.
Fee: $29.99 installation; $16.66 monthly.

Expanded Basic Service 1
Subscribers: 11,770.
Programming (via satellite): ABC Family Channel; AMC; Animal Planet; Arts & Entertainment; Bravo; Cartoon Network; CNBC; CNN; Comcast Sports Net Bay Area; Comedy Central; Country Music TV; Discovery Channel; Disney Channel; E! Entertainment Television; ESPN; ESPN 2; Food Network; Fox News Channel; FX; G4; GalaVision; Great American Country; Headline News; HGTV; History Channel; Lifetime; MSNBC; MTV; National Geographic Channel; Nickelodeon; Speed Channel; Spike TV; Style Network; The Learning Channel; Travel Channel; truTV; Turner Classic Movies; Turner Network TV; TV Guide Network; TV Land; USA Network; VH1; WE tv.
Fee: $32.58 monthly.

Digital Basic Service
Subscribers: N.A.
Programming (received off-air): KNPB (PBS) Reno; KOLO-TV (ABC) Reno; KRNV-DT (ABC) Reno; KTVN (CBS) Reno.
Programming (via satellite): BBC America; Bio; BYU Television; Canales N; Discovery Digital Networks; Do-It-Yourself; ESPN; ESPN Classic Sports; ESPNews; Fox College Sports Atlantic; Fox College Sports Central; Fox College Sports Pacific; Fox Movie Channel; Fox Soccer; Fuel TV; GAS; Golf Channel; GSN; HDNet; HDNet Movies; History Channel International; Jewelry Television; Lifetime Movie Network; Lifetime Real Women; MTV Networks Digital Suite; Music Choice; NFL Network; Nick Jr.; NickToons TV; SoapNet; Sundance Channel; Syfy; Toon Disney; TV Guide Interactive Inc.; Versus.
Fee: $10.95 monthly.

Digital Pay Service 1
Pay Units: N.A.
Programming (via satellite): Cinemax (multiplexed); Encore; Filipino Channel; HBO (multiplexed); HBO HD; Independent Film Channel; Showtime (multiplexed); Showtime HD; Starz (multiplexed); The Movie Channel (multiplexed).

Video-On-Demand: Yes

Pay-Per-View
Playboy TV (delivered digitally); Pleasure (delivered digitally); ESPN Now (delivered digitally); ESPN Sports PPV (delivered digitally); The Erotic Network (delivered digitally); ETC (delivered digitally); iN DEMAND (delivered digitally); NASCAR In Car (delivered digitally); NHL Center Ice; MLB Extra Innings (delivered digitally).

Internet Service
Operational: Yes.
Broadband Service: Charter Pipeline.
Fee: $29.99 monthly; $10.00 modem lease.

Telephone Service
Digital: Operational

Miles of Plant: 294.0 (coaxial); None (fiber optic). Homes passed: 18,094. Total homes in franchised area: 18,640.
Vice President & General Manager: Manny Martinez. Technical Operations Manager: Carol Eure.
City fee: 2% of gross.
Ownership: Charter Communications Inc. (MSO).

CARSON CITY—Formerly served by Quadravision. No longer in operation. ICA: NV0051.

CRYSTAL BAY—Charter Communications, 9335 Prototype Dr, Reno, NV 89521. Phone: 775-850-1200. Fax: 775-850-1279. Web Site: http://www.charter.com. Also serves Placer County (eastern portion), CA; Washoe County, NV. ICA: NV0005.
TV Market Ranking: Below 100 (CRYSTAL BAY, Placer County (eastern portion) (portions), Washoe County (portions)); Outside TV Markets (Placer County (eastern portion) (portions), Washoe County (portions)). Franchise award date: N.A. Franchise expiration date: N.A. Began: N.A.
Channel capacity: N.A. Channels available but not in use: N.A.

Basic Service
Subscribers: N.A. Included in Reno
Programming (received off-air): KAME-TV (MNT) Reno; KOLO-TV (ABC) Reno; KREN-TV (CW, UNV) Reno; KRNV-DT (ABC) Reno; KTVN (CBS) Reno; KVCJ-LP (PBS) Incline Village.
Programming (via microwave): KCRA-TV (NBC) Sacramento; KGO-TV (ABC) San Francisco; KQED (PBS) San Francisco; KTVU (FOX) Oakland.
Programming (via satellite): ABC Family Channel; CNBC; CNN; C-SPAN; Discovery Channel; Disney Channel; Headline News; Lifetime; MTV; Nickelodeon; QVC; Turner Network TV; Weather Channel.
Fee: $29.99 installation; $16.66 monthly.

Expanded Basic Service 1
Subscribers: 11,205.
Programming (via satellite): AMC; Arts & Entertainment; Comcast Sports Net Bay Area; ESPN; Spike TV; USA Network.
Fee: $32.58 monthly.

Pay Service 1
Pay Units: 677.
Programming (via satellite): Encore; HBO; Showtime; The Movie Channel; TV Japan.

Video-On-Demand: No

Internet Service
Operational: No.

Telephone Service
None

Miles of Plant: 181.0 (coaxial); None (fiber optic). Homes passed: 13,712. Total homes in franchised area: 14,359. 330 MHz (CA side)-550 MHz (NV side)
Vice President & General Manager: Manny Martinez. Technical Operations Manager: Carol Eure.
Ownership: Charter Communications Inc. (MSO).

ELKO—Baja Broadband, 1250 Lamoille Hwy, Ste 1150, Elko, NV 89801. Phones: 775-738-2662; 980-235-7600 (Corporate office). Fax: 775-738-8897. E-mail: info@bajabb.tv. Web Site: http://www.bajabroadband.com. Also serves Elko County (portions) & Spring Creek. ICA: NV0009.
TV Market Ranking: Below 100 (ELKO, Elko County (portions), Spring Creek). Franchise award date: N.A. Franchise expiration date: N.A. Began: October 1, 1956.
Channel capacity: N.A. Channels available but not in use: N.A.

Basic Service
Subscribers: 4,442.
Programming (received off-air): KENV-DT (NBC) Elko; KNPB (PBS) Reno; KTVN (CBS) Reno; KUCW (CW) Ogden.
Programming (via microwave): KSL-TV (NBC) Salt Lake City; KSTU (FOX) Salt Lake City; KTVX (ABC) Salt Lake City; KUED (PBS) Salt Lake City; KUTH-DT (UNV) Provo; KUTV (CBS) Salt Lake City.
Programming (via satellite): C-SPAN; C-SPAN 2; Home Shopping Network; QVC; TV Guide Network.
Fee: $62.00 installation; $15.01 monthly; $.85 converter.

Expanded Basic Service 1
Subscribers: 4,264.
Programming (via satellite): ABC Family Channel; AMC; Animal Planet; Arts & Entertainment; Cartoon Network; CNBC; CNN; Comedy Central; Discovery Channel; Disney Channel; E! Entertainment Television; ESPN; ESPN 2; Food Network; Fox News Channel; Fox Sports Net Rocky Mountain; FX; GalaVision; Great American Country; Hallmark Channel; Headline News; HGTV; History Channel; Lifetime; MSNBC; MTV; Nickelodeon; Spike TV; Style Network; Syfy; TBS Superstation; The Learning Channel; the mtn; Travel Channel; Turner Network TV; TV Land; USA Network; VH1; Weather Channel.
Fee: $25.98 monthly.

Digital Basic Service
Subscribers: N.A.
Programming (via satellite): BBC America; Bio; Bravo; CMT Pure Country; Discovery Health Channel; Discovery Kids Channel; Discovery Military Channel; Discovery Planet Green; DMX Music; FitTV; Fox Movie Channel; Fuse; G4; GSN; Halogen Network; History Channel International; ID Investigation Discovery; Independent Film Channel; Lifetime Movie Network; MTV Tres; MTV2; National Geographic Channel; Nick Jr.; NickToons TV; Science Channel; TeenNick; Toon Disney; Trinity Broadcasting Network; Turner Classic Movies; VH1 Classic; WE tv; WealthTV.

Digital Expanded Basic Service
Subscribers: N.A.
Programming (via satellite): ESPN Classic Sports; ESPN Deportes; ESPNews; Fox Soccer; Golf Channel; Outdoor Channel; Speed Channel; Versus.

Digital Expanded Basic Service 2
Subscribers: N.A.
Programming (via satellite): Cine Latino; CNN en Espanol; Discovery en Espanol; ESPN Deportes; Fox Sports en Espanol; History Channel en Espanol; MTV Tres; mun2 television; VeneMovies.

Digital Pay Service 1
Pay Units: N.A.
Programming (via satellite): Cinemax (multiplexed); Encore (multiplexed); HBO (multiplexed); Showtime (multiplexed); Starz (multiplexed); The Movie Channel (multiplexed).

Video-On-Demand: No

Pay-Per-View
iN DEMAND (delivered digitally); Club Jenna (delivered digitally); Fresh (delivered digitally); Playboy TV (delivered digitally).

Internet Service
Operational: No.

Telephone Service
None

Miles of Plant: 137.0 (coaxial); None (fiber optic).
Chief Executive Officer: William A. Schuler. Chief Operating Officer: Phillip Klein. Technical Operations Manager: Ed Farnum.
City fee: 2% of gross.
Ownership: Baja Broadband (MSO).

ELY—Central Telcom Services, PO Box 7, Fairview, UT 84629. Phone: 435-427-3331. Fax: 435-427-3200. Web Site: http://www.centracom.com. ICA: NV0013.

TV Market Ranking: Below 100 (ELY). Franchise award date: N.A. Franchise expiration date: N.A. Began: August 1, 1983.

Channel capacity: 57 (operating 2-way). Channels available but not in use: 8.

Basic Service

Subscribers: 698.

Programming (received off-air): KBYU-TV (PBS) Provo; KJZZ-TV (MNT) Salt Lake City; KPNZ (IND) Ogden; KSL-TV (NBC) Salt Lake City; KSTU (FOX) Salt Lake City; KTVX (ABC) Salt Lake City; KUCW (CW) Ogden; KUED (PBS) Salt Lake City; KUEN (ETV) Ogden; KUPX-TV (ION) Provo; KUTV (CBS) Salt Lake City; 4 FMs.

Programming (via satellite): Eternal Word TV Network.

Fee: $44.95 installation; $15.88 monthly; $1.50 converter.

Expanded Basic Service 1

Subscribers: N.A.

Programming (received off-air): KLAS-TV (CBS) Las Vegas; KLVX-TV (PBS) Las Vegas; KOLO-TV (ABC) Reno; KSNV-DT (NBC) Las Vegas; KVVU-TV (FOX) Henderson.

Programming (via satellite): ABC Family Channel; AMC; Animal Planet; Arts & Entertainment; Cartoon Network; CNBC; Comedy Central; Country Music TV; Discovery Channel; Disney Channel; ESPN; Fox News Channel; Fox Sports Net Rocky Mountain; FX; GalaVision; Hallmark Channel; Headline News; Lifetime; MTV; Nickelodeon; Outdoor Channel; QVC; Spike TV; TBS Superstation; Telefutura; The Learning Channel; Turner Network TV; TV Land; Univision; USA Network; VH1; Weather Channel; WGN America.

Fee: $26.25 monthly.

Digital Basic Service

Subscribers: 154.

Programming (via satellite): BBC America; Bio; Bravo; Discovery Digital Networks; DMX Music; ESPN 2; ESPN Classic Sports; ESPNews; Fox College Sports Atlantic; Fox College Sports Central; Fox College Sports Pacific; Fox Sports World; Fuse; GAS; Golf Channel; Great American Country; GSN; HGTV; History Channel; History Channel International; Independent Film Channel; Lifetime Movie Network; MTV Networks Digital Suite; National Geographic Channel; Nick Jr.; ShopNBC; Speed Channel; Style Network; The Word Network; Toon Disney; Turner Classic Movies; Versus; WE tv.

Fee: $60.75 monthly.

Video-On-Demand: No

Pay-Per-View

iN DEMAND (delivered digitally); Playboy TV (delivered digitally).

Internet Service

Operational: No.

Telephone Service

None

Miles of Plant: 50.0 (coaxial); None (fiber optic). Homes passed: 2,500. Total homes in franchised area: 2,500.

General Manager: Eddie Cox. CATV Manager: George Lee. Chief Engineer: Kenny Roberts.

Ownership: CentraCom Interactive (MSO).

EMPIRE—United States Gypsum Co., PO Box 130, Hwy 447 N, Empire, NV 89405. Phone: 775-557-2341 (ext. 224). Fax: 775-557-2138. ICA: NV0030.

TV Market Ranking: Outside TV Markets (EMPIRE). Franchise award date: May 1, 1985. Franchise expiration date: N.A. Began: December 1, 1983.

Channel capacity: 30 (not 2-way capable). Channels available but not in use: N.A.

Basic Service

Subscribers: 122.

Programming (received off-air): KOLO-TV (ABC) Reno; KREN-TV (CW, UNV) Reno; KRNV-DT (ABC) Reno; KRXI-TV (FOX) Reno; KTVN (CBS) Reno; WSEE-TV (CBS, CW) Erie; allband FM.

Programming (via satellite): CNN; Country Music TV; Discovery Channel; Disney Channel; ESPN; ESPN 2; History Channel; INSP; Nickelodeon; Outdoor Channel; Spike TV; TBS Superstation; The Learning Channel; Turner Network TV; TV Land; Weather Channel; WGN America; WNBC (NBC) New York; WSEE-TV (CBS, CW) Erie.

Pay Service 1

Pay Units: N.A.

Programming (via satellite): Cinemax; HBO.

Video-On-Demand: No

Internet Service

Operational: No.

Telephone Service

None

Miles of Plant: 4.0 (coaxial); None (fiber optic). Homes passed: 136. Total homes in franchised area: 136.

Manager: Dave Carter. Chief Technician: William Couk. Plant Manager: Ken Samuelson.

Franchise fee: None.

Ownership: United States Gypsum Co.

EUREKA—Central Telcom Services, PO Box 7, Fairview, UT 84629. Phone: 435-427-3331. Fax: 435-427-3200. Web Site: http://www.centracom.com. ICA: NV0027.

TV Market Ranking: Outside TV Markets (EUREKA). Franchise award date: February 1, 1988. Franchise expiration date: N.A. Began: July 25, 1988.

Channel capacity: 40 (not 2-way capable). Channels available but not in use: 4.

Basic Service

Subscribers: 50.

Programming (received off-air): KBYU-TV (PBS) Provo; KJZZ-TV (MNT) Salt Lake City; KPNZ (IND) Ogden; KSTU (FOX) Salt Lake City; KTVX (ABC) Salt Lake City; KUCW (CW) Ogden; KUED (PBS) Salt Lake City; KUEN (ETV) Ogden; 1 FM.

Programming (via satellite): ABC Family Channel; AMC; CNN; Arts & Entertainment; CNN; Comedy Central; Country Music TV; Discovery Channel; Disney Channel; ESPN; Fox News Channel; Fox Sports Net Rocky Mountain; FX; Lifetime; Nickelodeon; QVC; Spike TV; TBS Superstation; The Learning Channel; Turner Network TV; USA Network; Weather Channel; WGN America.

Programming (via translator): KSL-TV (NBC) Salt Lake City; KUTV (CBS) Salt Lake City.

Fee: $29.95 installation; $15.88 monthly; $1.50 converter.

Pay Service 1

Pay Units: 11.

Programming (via satellite): Cinemax.

Fee: $13.95 monthly.

Pay Service 2

Pay Units: 17.

Programming (via satellite): Encore.

Fee: $1.75 monthly.

Pay Service 3

Pay Units: 23.

Programming (via satellite): HBO.

Fee: $13.95 monthly.

Pay Service 4

Pay Units: 5.

Programming (via satellite): Showtime.

Fee: $12.95 monthly.

Pay Service 5

Pay Units: 17.

Programming (via satellite): Starz.

Fee: $13.95 monthly.

Video-On-Demand: No

Internet Service

Operational: No.

Telephone Service

None

Miles of Plant: 7.0 (coaxial); None (fiber optic). Homes passed: 350.

General Manager: Eddie Cox. CATV Manager: George Lee. Chief Engineer: Kenny Roberts.

Ownership: CentraCom Interactive (MSO).

FALLON—Charter Communications, 9335 Prototype Dr, Reno, NV 89521. Phone: 775-850-1200. Fax: 775-850-1279. Web Site: http://www.charter.com. Also serves Churchill County, Fallon Station & Yerington. ICA: NV0008.

TV Market Ranking: Outside TV Markets (Churchill County, FALLON, Fallon Station, Yerington). Franchise award date: N.A. Franchise expiration date: N.A. Began: August 1, 1964.

Channel capacity: N.A. Channels available but not in use: N.A.

Basic Service

Subscribers: N.A. Included in Reno

Programming (received off-air): KAME-TV (MNT) Reno; KNPB (PBS) Reno; KNVV-LP Reno; KOLO-TV (ABC) Reno; KREN-TV (CW, UNV) Reno; KRNS-CA (IND) Reno; KRNV-DT (ABC) Reno; KRXI-TV (FOX) Reno; KTVN (CBS) Reno.

Programming (via satellite): C-SPAN; C-SPAN 2; Eternal Word TV Network; GalaVision; Home Shopping Network; ION Television; Pentagon Channel; QVC; TBS Superstation; Telefutura; TV Guide Network; WGN America.

Current originations: Public Access.

Fee: $29.99 installation; $16.66 monthly; $3.00 converter; $15.00 additional installation.

Expanded Basic Service 1

Subscribers: N.A.

Programming (via satellite): ABC Family Channel; AMC; Animal Planet; Arts & Entertainment; BET Networks; Bravo; Cartoon Network; CNBC; CNN; Comcast Sports Net Bay Area; Comedy Central; Country Music TV; Discovery Channel; Disney Channel; E! Entertainment Television; ESPN; ESPN 2; ESPN Classic Sports; Food Network; Fox Sports en Espanol; FX; G4; Golf Channel; Hallmark Channel; Headline News; HGTV; History Channel; Lifetime; MSNBC; MTV; MTV2; National Geographic Channel; Nickelodeon; Oxygen; Speed Channel; Spike TV; Style Network; Syfy; The Learning Channel; Travel Channel; truTV; Turner Classic Movies; Turner Network TV; TV Land; USA Network; VH1; Weather Channel.

Fee: $32.58 monthly.

Digital Basic Service

Subscribers: N.A.

Programming (received off-air): KNPB (PBS) Reno; KOLO-TV (ABC) Reno; KREN-TV (CW, UNV) Reno; KRNV-DT (ABC) Reno; KRXI-TV (FOX) Reno; KTVN (CBS) Reno.

Programming (via satellite): AmericanLife TV Network; BBC America; Bio; Bloomberg Television; BYU Television; Canales N; CBS College Sports Network; CMT Pure Country; Cooking Channel; Daystar TV Network; Discovery Digital Networks; Discovery HD Theater; Do-It-Yourself; ESPN HD; ESPNews; Fox College Sports Atlantic; Fox College Sports Central; Fox College Sports Pacific; Fox Movie Channel; Fox Soccer; Fuel TV; Fuse; GAS; Gol TV; Great American Country; GSN; Hallmark Movie Channel; Halogen Network; HDNet; HDNet Movies; History Channel International; Howard TV; Independent Film Channel; INSP; Jewelry Television; Lifetime Movie Network; Lifetime Real Women; MTV Networks Digital Suite; Music Choice; Nick Jr.; NickToons TV; Outdoor Channel; Palladia; SoapNet; Sundance Channel; Tennis Channel; Toon Disney; Trinity Broadcasting Network; Turner Network TV HD; Universal HD; Versus; Versus On Demand; WE tv; WealthTV.

Fee: $10.95 monthly.

Digital Pay Service 1

Pay Units: N.A.

Programming (via satellite): Cinemax (multiplexed); Cinemax HD; Cinemax On Demand; Encore (multiplexed); Filipino Channel; HBO (multiplexed); HBO HD; HBO On Demand; Showtime (multiplexed); Showtime HD; Showtime On Demand; Starz (multiplexed); Starz HDTV; Starz On Demand; The Movie Channel (multiplexed).

Video-On-Demand: Yes

Pay-Per-View

iN DEMAND (delivered digitally); NHL Center Ice (delivered digitally); Sports PPV (delivered digitally); Playboy TV (delivered digitally); Ten Clips (delivered digitally); MLB Extra Innings (delivered digitally).

Internet Service

Operational: Yes.

Broadband Service: Charter Pipeline.

Fee: $29.99 monthly; $10.00 modem lease.

Telephone Service

Digital: Operational

Miles of Plant: 49.0 (coaxial); None (fiber optic). Homes passed: 7,266.

Vice President & General Manager: Manny Martinez. Technical Operations Manager: Carol Eure.

City fee: 2% of gross; 3% of gross pay fees.

Ownership: Charter Communications Inc. (MSO).

FERNLEY—Charter Communications, 9335 Prototype Dr, Reno, NV 89521. Phone: 775-850-1200. Fax: 775-850-1279. Web Site: http://www.charter.com. Also serves Lyon County (northern portion), Pyramid Lake & Wadsworth. ICA: NV0012.

TV Market Ranking: Below 100 (FERNLEY, Lyon County (northern portion) (portions), Wadsworth); Outside TV Markets (Lyon County (northern portion) (portions), Pyramid Lake). Franchise award date: N.A. Franchise expiration date: N.A. Began: June 1, 1981.

Channel capacity: N.A. Channels available but not in use: N.A.

Basic Service

Subscribers: N.A. Included in Reno

Programming (received off-air): KAME-TV (MNT) Reno; KNPB (PBS) Reno; KOLO-TV (ABC) Reno; KREN-TV (CW, UNV) Reno; KRNV-DT (ABC) Reno; KTVN (CBS) Reno.

Programming (via satellite): C-SPAN; ION Television; QVC.

Fee: $29.99 installation; $16.66 monthly.

Expanded Basic Service 1

Subscribers: 1,800.

Programming (via satellite): ABC Family Channel; AMC; Animal Planet; Arts & Entertainment; Cartoon Network; CNBC; CNN; Comcast Sports Net Bay Area; Discovery Channel; Disney Channel; E! Entertainment Television; ESPN; ESPN 2; Fox News Channel; FX; GalaVision; Hallmark Channel;

Headline News; History Channel; Lifetime; MSNBC; MTV; Nickelodeon; Spike TV; TBS Superstation; Turner Network TV; TV Land; USA Network; Weather Channel.
Fee: $32.58 monthly.
Digital Basic Service
Subscribers: N.A.
Programming (via satellite): BBC America; Bravo; Discovery Digital Networks; DMX Music; ESPN Classic Sports; GSN; HGTV; Independent Film Channel; Nick Jr.; Syfy; Turner Classic Movies; TV Guide Interactive Inc.; WE tv.
Fee: $10.95 monthly.
Digital Pay Service 1
Pay Units: N.A.
Programming (via satellite): Cinemax (multiplexed); Encore; HBO (multiplexed); Showtime (multiplexed); Starz (multiplexed); The Movie Channel (multiplexed).
Video-On-Demand: Yes
Pay-Per-View
iN DEMAND (delivered digitally); Playboy TV (delivered digitally).
Internet Service
Operational: Yes.
Broadband Service: Charter Pipeline.
Fee: $29.99 monthly.
Telephone Service
Digital: Operational
Miles of Plant: 47.0 (coaxial); None (fiber optic). Homes passed: 2,807.
Vice President & General Manager: Manny Martinez. Technical Operations Manager: Carol Eure.
Ownership: Charter Communications Inc. (MSO).

GARDNERVILLE—Charter Communications, 9335 Prototype Dr, Reno, NV 89521. Phone: 775-850-1200. Fax: 775-850-1279. Web Site: http://www.charter.com. Also serves Centerville, Genoa, Jacks Valley, Minden & Sheridan. ICA: NV0007.
TV Market Ranking: Outside TV Markets (Centerville, GARDNERVILLE, Genoa, Jacks Valley, Minden, Sheridan). Franchise award date: N.A. Franchise expiration date: N.A. Began: January 1, 1975.
Channel capacity: N.A. Channels available but not in use: N.A.
Basic Service
Subscribers: N.A. Included in Reno
Programming (received off-air): KAME-TV (MNT) Reno; KNPB (PBS) Reno; KOLO-TV (ABC) Reno; KREN-TV (CW, UNV) Reno; KRNV-DT (ABC) Reno; KRXI-TV (FOX) Reno; KTVN (CBS) Reno; allband FM.
Programming (via satellite): C-SPAN; C-SPAN 2; Discovery Channel; Hallmark Channel; KTLA (CW) Los Angeles; MTV; TBS Superstation; TV Guide Network; Weather Channel; WPIX (CW, IND) New York.
Current originations: Government Access; Public Access.
Fee: $29.99 installation; $16.66 monthly; $3.00 converter.
Expanded Basic Service 1
Subscribers: N.A.
Programming (via satellite): ABC Family Channel; AMC; America's Store; Animal Planet; Arts & Entertainment; Cartoon Network; CNBC; CNN; Comcast Sports Net Bay Area; Disney Channel; E! Entertainment Television; ESPN; ESPN 2; Fox News Channel; FX; Great American Country; Headline News; HGTV; History Channel; ION Television; Lifetime; MSNBC; Nickelodeon; QVC; Spike TV; Syfy; The Learning Channel; truTV; Turner Network TV; USA Network; VH1.
Fee: $32.58 monthly.
Digital Basic Service
Subscribers: N.A.
Programming (via satellite): Barker; BBC America; Discovery Digital Networks; ESPN Classic Sports; Fox Sports World; Golf Channel; GSN; Independent Film Channel; Turner Classic Movies; TV Land; Versus; WE tv.
Fee: $10.95 monthly.
Digital Pay Service 1
Pay Units: N.A.
Programming (via satellite): Bravo; DMX Music; Encore (multiplexed); HBO (multiplexed); Showtime (multiplexed); Starz (multiplexed).
Video-On-Demand: Yes
Pay-Per-View
Hot Choice (delivered digitally), Addressable: Yes; iN DEMAND (delivered digitally); Fresh (delivered digitally).
Internet Service
Operational: Yes.
Broadband Service: Charter Pipeline.
Fee: $29.99 monthly; $10.00 modem lease.
Telephone Service
Digital: Operational
Miles of Plant: 250.0 (coaxial); 12.0 (fiber optic). Additional miles planned: 10.0 (coaxial). Homes passed: 9,043.
Vice President & General Manager: Manny Martinez. Chief Technician: Carol Eure.
County fee: 5% of gross.
Ownership: Charter Communications Inc. (MSO).

GOLDFIELD—Formerly served by Eagle West Communications Inc. No longer in operation. ICA: NV0039.

HAWTHORNE—Charter Communications, 9335 Prototype Dr, Reno, NV 89521. Phone: 775-850-1200. Fax: 775-850-1279. Web Site: http://www.charter.com. Also serves Babbitt Army Base. ICA: NV0015.
TV Market Ranking: Outside TV Markets (Babbitt Army Base, HAWTHORNE). Franchise award date: N.A. Franchise expiration date: N.A. Began: June 1, 1982.
Channel capacity: 36 (not 2-way capable). Channels available but not in use: N.A.
Basic Service
Subscribers: N.A. Included in Reno
Programming (received off-air): K13WI Hawthorne; KAME-TV (MNT) Reno.
Programming (via microwave): KNPB (PBS) Reno.
Programming (via satellite): C-SPAN; Home Shopping Network; ION Television; QVC.
Programming (via translator): KOLO-TV (ABC) Reno; KRNV-DT (ABC) Reno; KTVN (CBS) Reno.
Fee: $29.99 installation; $16.66 monthly.
Expanded Basic Service 1
Subscribers: N.A.
Programming (via satellite): ABC Family Channel; AMC; Animal Planet; Arts & Entertainment; BET Networks; Cartoon Network; CNBC; CNN; Comcast Sports Net Bay Area; Discovery Channel; Disney Channel; E! Entertainment Television; ESPN; ESPN 2; Fox News Channel; FX; GalaVision; Hallmark Channel; Headline News; HGTV; Lifetime; MoviePlex; MSNBC; MTV; Nickelodeon; Spike TV; TBS Superstation; The Learning Channel; Turner Network TV; USA Network; VH1; Weather Channel.
Fee: $32.58 monthly.
Digital Basic Service
Subscribers: N.A.
Programming (via satellite): BBC America; Bio; Bloomberg Television; Bravo; Discovery Digital Networks; DMX Music; ESPN Classic Sports; FitTV; Fox Movie Channel; Fox Soccer; Fuse; G4; GAS; Golf Channel; GSN; Halogen Network; History Channel; History Channel International; Independent Film Channel; Lifetime Movie Network; MTV Networks Digital Suite; Nick Jr.; Outdoor Channel; Speed Channel; Style Network; Syfy; Toon Disney; Trinity Broadcasting Network; Turner Classic Movies; TV Guide Network; Versus; WE tv.
Digital Pay Service 1
Pay Units: N.A.
Programming (via satellite): Cinemax (multiplexed); Encore; Flix; HBO (multiplexed); Showtime (multiplexed); Starz (multiplexed); The Movie Channel (multiplexed).
Video-On-Demand: No
Pay-Per-View
iN DEMAND (delivered digitally); ESPN Now (delivered digitally); ESPN Sports PPV (delivered digitally); Hot Choice (delivered digitally); Playboy TV (delivered digitally); Fresh (delivered digitally); Shorteez (delivered digitally).
Internet Service
Operational: No.
Telephone Service
None
Miles of Plant: 22.0 (coaxial); None (fiber optic). Homes passed: 1,602. Total homes in franchised area: 1,664.
Vice President & General Manager: Manny Martinez. Technical Operations Manager: Carol Eure.
City fee: $1.25 per subscriber annually.
Ownership: Charter Communications Inc. (MSO).

INDIAN SPRINGS—United Cable Management, PO Box 14375, 2200 Library Circle, Grand Forks, ND 58208. Phone: 701-772-7191. Fax: 701-772-5486. Also serves Creech AFB. ICA: NV0041.
TV Market Ranking: Outside TV Markets (Creech AFB, INDIAN SPRINGS). Franchise award date: N.A. Franchise expiration date: N.A. Began: March 1, 1984.
Channel capacity: 60 (operating 2-way). Channels available but not in use: N.A.
Basic Service
Subscribers: 180.
Programming (received off-air): KLAS-TV (CBS) Las Vegas; KLVX-TV (PBS) Las Vegas; KSNV-DT (NBC) Las Vegas; KTNV-TV (ABC) Las Vegas; KVCW (CW) Las Vegas; KVMY (MNT) Las Vegas; KVVU-TV (FOX) Henderson.
Programming (via satellite): ABC Family Channel; AMC; Animal Planet; Arts & Entertainment; BET Networks; CNBC; CNN; Country Music TV; C-SPAN; Discovery Channel; Disney Channel; ESPN; ESPN 2; Fox News Channel; Headline News; History Channel; Lifetime; MTV; Nickelodeon; QVC; Spike TV; TBS Superstation; Telemundo; The Learning Channel; Trinity Broadcasting Network; Turner Network TV; Univision; USA Network; VH1; Weather Channel; WGN America.
Fee: $25.00 installation; $21.50 monthly.

Pay Service 1
Pay Units: N.A.
Programming (via satellite): HBO; The Movie Channel.
Fee: $8.50 monthly (each).
Video-On-Demand: No
Internet Service
Operational: No.
Telephone Service
None
Miles of Plant: 7.0 (coaxial); None (fiber optic).
Manager & Chief Technician: Pete Sullivan. Technician: Randy Zimney.
Ownership: United Enterprises (MSO).

INDIAN SPRINGS AFB—United Cable Management. No longer in operation. ICA: NV0042.

JACKPOT—Satview Broadband, PO Box 18148, Reno, NV 89511. Phones: 800-225-0605; 775-338-6626. Fax: 775-333-0225. Web Site: http://www.iwantone.tv. ICA: NV0026.
TV Market Ranking: Outside TV Markets (JACKPOT). Franchise award date: January 1, 1974. Franchise expiration date: N.A. Began: January 15, 1976.
Channel capacity: 36 (not 2-way capable). Channels available but not in use: N.A.
Basic Service
Subscribers: 322.
Programming (received off-air): KAID (PBS) Boise; KBOI-TV (CBS) Boise; KIVI-TV (ABC) Nampa; KMVT (CBS) Twin Falls; KSTU (FOX) Salt Lake City; KTVB (NBC) Boise; allband FM.
Programming (via satellite): Arts & Entertainment; CNN; Discovery Channel; Disney Channel; ESPN; ESPN 2; Fox Sports Net Rocky Mountain; GalaVision; History Channel; MTV; Nickelodeon; QVC; Spike TV; Syfy; TBS Superstation; Telefutura; truTV; Turner Classic Movies; Turner Network TV; Univision; USA Network; WGN America.
Current originations: Public Access.
Fee: $30.00 installation; $33.49 monthly.
Pay Service 1
Pay Units: 115.
Programming (via satellite): Cinemax; HBO.
Fee: $8.00 monthly (Cinemax), $9.50 monthly (HBO).
Internet Service
Operational: No.
Miles of Plant: 6.0 (coaxial); None (fiber optic). Additional miles planned: 1.0 (coaxial). Homes passed: 500. Total homes in franchised area: 500.
Chief Executive Officer: Tariq Ahmad.
City fee: None.
Ownership: Satview Broadband Ltd. (MSO).

LAS VEGAS—Cox Communications, 1700 Vegas Dr, Las Vegas, NV 89106. Phones: 702-383-4000 (Customer service); 702-384-8084. Fax: 702-545-2011. Web Site: http://www.cox.com/lasvegas. Also serves Boulder City, Clark County, Green Valley, Henderson & North Las Vegas. ICA: NV0001.
TV Market Ranking: Below 100 (Boulder City, Clark County (portions), Henderson, LAS

VEGAS, North Las Vegas, Winchester); Outside TV Markets (Clark County (portions), Green Valley). Franchise award date: January 1, 1979. Franchise expiration date: N.A. Began: March 1, 1980.

Channel capacity: N.A. Channels available but not in use: N.A.

Basic Service

Subscribers: 430,750.

Programming (received off-air): KBLR (TMO) Paradise; KINC (UNV) Las Vegas; KLAS-TV (CBS) Las Vegas; KLVX-TV (PBS) Las Vegas; KSNV-DT (NBC) Las Vegas; KTNV-TV (ABC) Las Vegas; KTUD-CA (IND) Las Vegas; KVCW (CW) Las Vegas; KVMY (MNT) Las Vegas; KVVU-TV (FOX) Henderson.

Programming (via satellite): Home Shopping Network; QVC; TBS Superstation; WGN; WGN America.

Current originations: Leased Access; Government Access; Educational Access.

Fee: $39.95 installation; $13.00 monthly; $19.95 additional installation.

Expanded Basic Service 1

Subscribers: N.A.

Programming (via satellite): ABC Family Channel; AMC; Animal Planet; Arts & Entertainment; Azteca America; BET Networks; Bravo; Cartoon Network; CNBC; CNN; Comedy Central; Country Music TV; Cox Sports Television; C-SPAN; C-SPAN 2; Discovery Channel; Discovery Health Channel; Disney Channel; E! Entertainment Television; ESPN; ESPN 2; Food Network; Fox News Channel; Fox Sports Net Prime Ticket; Fox Sports Net West; FX; GalaVision; Golf Channel; Hallmark Channel; Headline News; HGTV; History Channel; ION Television; Las Vegas One; Lifetime; MSNBC; MTV; MTV2; Nickelodeon; Spike TV; Syfy; Telefutura; The Learning Channel; Travel Channel; truTV; Turner Classic Movies; Turner Network TV; TV Guide Network; TV Land; USA Network; Versus; VH1; Weather Channel.

Fee: $37.95 monthly.

Digital Basic Service

Subscribers: N.A.

Programming (received off-air): KLAS-TV (CBS) Las Vegas; KLVX-TV (PBS) Las Vegas; KSNV-DT (NBC) Las Vegas; KTNV-TV (ABC) Las Vegas; KVCW (CW) Las Vegas; KVVU-TV (FOX) Henderson.

Programming (via satellite): AMC HD; Animal Planet HD; Arts & Entertainment HD; BBC America; Bio; Bloomberg Television; Boomerang; Bravo HD; BYU Television; Cartoon Network HD; CBS College Sports Network; Chiller; CMT Pure Country; CNBC HD+; CNN HD; Comedy Central; Cooking Channel; Country Music TV; Discovery Channel HD; Discovery HD Theater; Discovery Kids Channel; Discovery Planet Green; Discovery Planet Green HD; Disney XD; Do-It-Yourself; E! Entertainment Television HD; Encore (multiplexed); Encore Wam; ESPN 2 HD; ESPN Classic Sports; ESPN HD; ESPN U; ESPNews; Eternal Word TV Network; FitTV; Food Network HD; Fox Business Channel; Fox College Sports Atlantic; Fox College Sports Central; Fox College Sports Pacific; Fox News HD; Fox Reality Channel; Fox Soccer; Fuel TV; Fuse; FX HD; G4; GemsTV; Golf Channel HD; GSN; Hallmark Movie Channel HD; Halogen Network; HGTV HD; History Channel HD; History Channel International; ID Investigation Discovery; Independent Film Channel; INSP; Jewelry Television; LATV Networks; Lifetime Movie Network; Lifetime Movie Network HD; Lifetime Television HD; LOGO; Mexicanal; Military Channel; MLB Network; MTV Hits; MTV Networks HD; MTV Tres; mtvU; mun2 television; Music Choice; National Geographic Channel; National Geographic Channel HD Network; NBA TV; NFL Network; NFL Network HD; NHL Network; Nick HD; Nick Jr.; NickToons TV; Oxygen; Palladia; PBS Kids Sprout; PBS World; Science Channel; Science Channel HD; Si TV; SoapNet; Speed Channel; Speed HD; Spike TV HD; Sundance Channel; Syfy HD; TBS in HD; TeenNick; Tennis Channel; the mtn; TLC HD; Travel Channel HD; Trinity Broadcasting Network; Turner Network TV HD; TV One; TVG Network; Universal HD; USA Network HD; Versus HD; VH1 Classic; VH1 HD; V-me TV; WE tv; Weatherscan.

Fee: $49.95 installation; $10.45 monthly.

Digital Expanded Basic Service

Subscribers: N.A.

Programming (via satellite): Bandamax; Boomerang en Espanol; Cartoon Network Tambien en Espanol; CNN en Espanol; De Pelicula; De Pelicula Clasico; Discovery en Espanol; ESPN Deportes; EWTN en Espanol; Fox Sports en Espanol; Gol TV; History Channel en Espanol; MTV Tres; NickToons en Espanol; Ritmoson Latino; Telehit; Toon Disney; VeneMovies.

Fee: $4.00 monthly.

Digital Pay Service 1

Pay Units: N.A.

Programming (via satellite): CCTV-4; Cinemax (multiplexed); Cinemax HD; Filipino Channel; Flix; GMA Pinoy TV; HBO (multiplexed); HBO HD; Showtime (multiplexed); Showtime HD; Starz (multiplexed); Starz HDTV; The Movie Channel (multiplexed); TV Japan; Zhong Tian Channel.

Video-On-Demand: Yes

Pay-Per-View

Addressable homes: 165,000.

Playboy TV (delivered digitally), Addressable: Yes; MLB Extra Innings (delivered digitally); NHL Center Ice (delivered digitally); Spice: Xcess (delivered digitally); Club Jenna (delivered digitally); Ten Blox (delivered digitally); Sports PPV (delivered digitally); Ten Clips (delivered digitally); NBA League Pass (delivered digitally); MLS Direct Kick (delivered digitally); special events.

Internet Service

Operational: Yes. Began: August 1, 1997.

Broadband Service: Cox High Speed Internet.

Fee: $99.95 installation; $29.95-$57.99 monthly; $10.00 modem lease; $199.00 modem purchase.

Telephone Service

Digital: Operational

Fee: $10.40 monthly

Miles of Plant: 6,590.0 (coaxial); 1,480.0 (fiber optic). Homes passed: 780,000.

Vice President & General Manager, Cox Business: David Blau. Vice President, Sales & Marketing: Ellen Lloyd. Vice President, Network Development: Henry Schwab. Vice President, Business Operations: Tina Denicole. Vice President, Public Affairs & Government Operations: Steve Schorr.

Franchise fee: 5.45% of gross.

Ownership: Cox Communications Inc. (MSO).

LAS VEGAS—Formerly served by Sprint Corp. No longer in operation. ICA: NV0055.

LAUGHLIN—CMA Cablevision, 3030 Needles Hwy, Ste 1400, Laughlin, NV 89029-0893. Phone: 702-298-3214. Fax: 702-298-3075. Web Site: http://www.cmaaccess.com. Also serves Searchlight. ICA: NV0043.

TV Market Ranking: Below 100 (LAUGHLIN, Searchlight). Franchise award date: January 1, 1985. Franchise expiration date: N.A. Began: April 15, 1985.

Channel capacity: N.A. Channels available but not in use: N.A.

Basic Service

Subscribers: 1,825.

Programming (received off-air): KAET (PBS) Phoenix; KFTR-DT (TEL) Ontario; KINC (UNV) Las Vegas; KLAS-TV (CBS) Las Vegas; KLVX-TV (PBS) Las Vegas; KSNV-DT (NBC) Las Vegas; KTNV-TV (ABC) Las Vegas; KVMY (MNT) Las Vegas; KVVU-TV (FOX) Henderson.

Programming (via satellite): C-SPAN; C-SPAN 2; Home Shopping Network; WGN America.

Current originations: Leased Access; Government Access.

Fee: $39.95 installation; $15.45 monthly; $12.95 additional installation.

Expanded Basic Service 1

Subscribers: N.A.

Programming (via satellite): ABC Family Channel; AMC; Animal Planet; Arts & Entertainment; Bravo!; CNBC; CNN; Comedy Central; Country Music TV; Discovery Channel; E! Entertainment Television; ESPN; ESPN 2; ESPNews; Fox News Channel; FX; Headline News; History Channel; Lifetime; MTV; Nickelodeon; QVC; Spike TV; Syfy; TBS Superstation; The Learning Channel; Toon Disney; Travel Channel; Trinity Broadcasting Network; truTV; Turner Classic Movies; Turner Network TV; TV Guide Network; TV Land; USA Network; VH1; Weather Channel.

Fee: $28.00 monthly.

Digital Basic Service

Subscribers: N.A.

Programming (via satellite): BBC America; Bio; Bravo!; Discovery Digital Networks; ESPN Classic Sports; Fox Sports World; Golf Channel; GSN; HGTV; History Channel International; Independent Film Channel; Lifetime Movie Network; National Geographic Channel; Speed Channel; Style Network; Versus; WE tv.

Fee: $13.95 monthly.

Digital Pay Service 1

Pay Units: N.A.

Programming (via satellite): Cinemax (multiplexed); DMX Music; Encore (multiplexed); HBO (multiplexed); Showtime (multiplexed); Starz (multiplexed); The Movie Channel (multiplexed).

Fee: $12.95 monthly (HBO), $13.95 monthly (Showtime, Cinemax, or Starz & Encore).

Video-On-Demand: No

Pay-Per-View

Addressable homes: 1,500.

Hot Choice, Fee: $3.99, Addressable: Yes; iN DEMAND, Fee: $3.99; Playboy TV, Fee: $5.95; Spice, Fee: $7.95.

Internet Service

Operational: Yes.

Subscribers: 845.

Broadband Service: CMA.

Fee: $39.95 installation; $44.95 monthly; $2.95 modem lease; $39.95 modem purchase.

Telephone Service

Digital: Operational

Fee: $39.95 monthly

Miles of Plant: 32.0 (coaxial); None (fiber optic). Homes passed: 4,282. Total homes in franchised area: 4,282.

General Manager: Jerry Smith. Marketing Director: Julie Ferguson. Chief Technician: Daniel Coenen.

County fee: 3% of gross.

Ownership: Cable Management Assoc. (MSO).

LOCKWOOD—Charter Communications. Now served by RENO, NV [NV0002]. ICA: NV0028.

LOGANDALE—Baja Broadband, 111 W 700 S, Saint George, UT 84770-3550. Phone: 435-628-3681. Fax: 435-674-4225. Web Site: http://www.bajabroadband.com. Also serves Overton. ICA: NV0046.

TV Market Ranking: Outside TV Markets (LOGANDALE, Overton). Franchise award date: N.A. Franchise expiration date: N.A. Began: N.A.

Channel capacity: 54 (not 2-way capable). Channels available but not in use: N.A.

Basic Service

Subscribers: 582.

Programming (received off-air): KBLR (TMO) Paradise; KLAS-TV (CBS) Las Vegas; KLVX-TV (PBS) Las Vegas; KSNV-DT (NBC) Las Vegas; KTNV-TV (ABC) Las Vegas; KVVU-TV (FOX) Henderson.

Programming (via microwave): KSL-TV (NBC) Salt Lake City.

Programming (via satellite): ABC Family Channel; AMC; Animal Planet; Arts & Entertainment; Bravo; Cartoon Network; Comedy Central; Country Music TV; Discovery Channel; Disney Channel; ESPN; Food Network; Headline News; Home Shopping Network; Lifetime; MSNBC; Nickelodeon; Spike TV; Syfy; The Learning Channel; Travel Channel; Turner Network TV; USA Network; WGN America.

Fee: $26.50 installation; $20.99 monthly.

Expanded Basic Service 1

Subscribers: 559.

Programming (via satellite): CNN; TBS Superstation.

Fee: $3.50 monthly.

Pay Service 1

Pay Units: 105.

Programming (via satellite): Cinemax.

Fee: $10.45 monthly.

Pay Service 2

Pay Units: 126.

Programming (via satellite): HBO.

Fee: $10.45 monthly.

Video-On-Demand: No

Pay-Per-View

iN DEMAND (delivered digitally); Hot Choice (delivered digitally); Playboy TV (delivered digitally); Fresh (delivered digitally); Shorteez (delivered digitally).

Internet Service

Operational: No.

Telephone Service

None

Miles of Plant: 27.0 (coaxial); None (fiber optic). Homes passed: 960.

Technical Operations Manager: Ed Farnum. Office Manager: Missy Snow.

Franchise fee: 3% of gross.

Ownership: Baja Broadband (MSO).

LOVELOCK—Lovelock Cable TV, PO Box 1077, Lovelock, NV 89419-1077. Phone: 775-273-2968. Fax: 775-273-7542. ICA: NV0044.

TV Market Ranking: Outside TV Markets (LOVELOCK). Franchise award date: N.A. Franchise expiration date: N.A. Began: September 1, 1983.

Channel capacity: 41 (not 2-way capable). Channels available but not in use: 11.

Basic Service

Subscribers: 380.

Programming (received off-air): KAME-TV (MNT) Reno; KOLO-TV (ABC) Reno; KRNV-DT (ABC) Reno; KTVN (CBS) Reno.

Programming (via satellite): ABC Family Channel; CNN; Country Music TV; C-SPAN; Discovery Channel; ESPN; GalaVision; Headline News; Nickelodeon; Spike TV; TBS Superstation; Turner Network TV; USA Network; WGN America.
Fee: $20.00 installation; $28.56 monthly.

Pay Service 1
Pay Units: 150.
Programming (via satellite): HBO; Showtime; Turner Classic Movies.
Fee: $6.00 monthly (TCM), $11.00 monthly (Showtime), $13.00 monthly (HBO).

Video-On-Demand: No

Internet Service
Operational: No.

Telephone Service
None

Miles of Plant: 10.0 (coaxial); None (fiber optic).
General Manager: Larry Gordon. Marketing Director: Joan Duncan.
Ownership: UNEV Communications Inc. (MSO).

MCGILL—Central Telcom Services, PO Box 7, Fairview, UT 84629. Phone: 435-427-3331. Fax: 435-427-3200. Web Site: http://www.centracom.com. ICA: NV0021.
TV Market Ranking: Below 100 (MCGILL). Franchise award date: February 1, 1988. Franchise expiration date: N.A. Began: May 23, 1988.
Channel capacity: 40 (not 2-way capable). Channels available but not in use: 3.

Basic Service
Subscribers: 74.
Programming (via translator): KBYU-TV (PBS) Provo; KJZZ-TV (MNT) Salt Lake City; KPNZ (IND) Ogden; KSL-TV (NBC) Salt Lake City; KSTU (FOX) Salt Lake City; KTVX (ABC) Salt Lake City; KUCW (CW) Ogden; KUED (PBS) Salt Lake City; KUEN (ETV) Ogden; KUPX-TV (ION) Provo; KUTV (CBS) Salt Lake City.
Current originations: Government Access; Educational Access.
Fee: $49.95 installation; $15.88 monthly; $21.95 additional installation.

Expanded Basic Service 1
Subscribers: N.A.
Programming (received off-air): KLAS-TV (CBS) Las Vegas.
Programming (via satellite): ABC Family Channel; AMC; Animal Planet; Arts & Entertainment; CNN; Comedy Central; Country Music TV; Discovery Channel; Disney Channel; ESPN; Fox News Channel; Fox Sports Net Rocky Mountain; FX; Lifetime; Nickelodeon; QVC; Spike TV; TBS Superstation; The Learning Channel; Turner Network TV; USA Network; Weather Channel; WGN America.
Fee: $25.00 monthly.

Digital Basic Service
Subscribers: 17.
Programming (via satellite): BBC America; Bio; Black Family Channel; Bravo; Discovery Digital Networks; DMX Music; ESPN 2; ESPN Classic Sports; ESPNews; Fox College Sports Atlantic; Fox College Sports Central; Fox College Sports Pacific; Fox Soccer; Fuse; Golf Channel; Great American Country; GSN; HGTV; History Channel; History Channel International; Independent Film Channel; Lifetime Movie Network; National Geographic Channel; ShopNBC; Speed Channel; Style Network; The Word Network; Toon Disney; Trio; Turner Classic Movies; Versus; WE tv.
Fee: $59.75 monthly.

Digital Pay Service 1
Pay Units: N.A.
Programming (via satellite): Cinemax (multiplexed); Encore (multiplexed); Flix; HBO (multiplexed); Showtime (multiplexed); Starz (multiplexed); The Movie Channel (multiplexed).
Fee: $12.95 monthly (HBO, Cinemax, Showtime/TMC/Flix or Starz/Encore).

Video-On-Demand: No

Pay-Per-View
iN DEMAND (delivered digitally); Playboy TV (delivered digitally).

Internet Service
Operational: No.

Telephone Service
None

Miles of Plant: 12.0 (coaxial); None (fiber optic). Homes passed: 500. Total homes in franchised area: 500.
General Manager: Eddie Cox. CATV Manager: George Lee. Chief Engineer: Kenny Roberts.
Ownership: CentraCom Interactive (MSO).

MESQUITE—Baja Broadband, 111 W 700 S, Saint George, UT 84770-3550. Phone: 435-628-3681. Fax: 435-674-4225. Web Site: http://www.bajabroadband.com. Also serves Desert Skies RV Park, AZ; Bunkerville, NV. ICA: NV0045.
TV Market Ranking: Below 100 (MESQUITE, Mohave County (portions)); Outside TV Markets (Desert Skies RV Park, Mohave County (portions)). Franchise award date: July 28, 1986. Franchise expiration date: N.A. Began: December 31, 1986.
Channel capacity: N.A. Channels available but not in use: N.A.

Basic Service
Subscribers: 1,000.
Programming (received off-air): KLAS-TV (CBS) Las Vegas; KLVX-TV (PBS) Las Vegas; KSNV-DT (NBC) Las Vegas; KTNV-TV (ABC) Las Vegas; KVVU-TV (FOX) Henderson.
Programming (via microwave): KBYU-TV (PBS) Provo; KJZZ-TV (MNT) Salt Lake City; KSL-TV (NBC) Salt Lake City; KSTU (FOX) Salt Lake City.
Programming (via satellite): BYU Television; C-SPAN; C-SPAN 2; Home Shopping Network; Product Information Network; QVC; TV Guide Network; Univision; WGN America.
Current originations: Leased Access.
Fee: $53.00 installation; $16.50 monthly.

Expanded Basic Service 1
Subscribers: 697.
Programming (via satellite): ABC Family Channel; AMC; Animal Planet; Arts & Entertainment; Bravo; Cartoon Network; CNBC; CNN; Comedy Central; Country Music TV; Discovery Channel; Disney Channel; E! Entertainment Television; ESPN; ESPN 2; ESPN Classic Sports; Eternal Word TV Network; FitTV; Food Network; Fox Movie Channel; Fox News Channel; Fox Sports Net Rocky Mountain; FX; G4; GalaVision; Golf Channel; GSN; Hallmark Channel; Headline News; HGTV; History Channel; INSP; Lifetime; Lifetime Movie Network; MSNBC; MTV; National Geographic Channel; Nickelodeon; SoapNet; Speed Channel; Spike TV; Syfy; TBS Superstation; The Learning Channel; the mtn; Toon Disney; Travel Channel; truTV; Turner Classic Movies; Turner Network TV; TV Land; USA Network; Versus; VH1; WE tv; Weather Channel.
Fee: $18.45 monthly.

Digital Basic Service
Subscribers: N.A.
Programming (via satellite): BBC America; Bio; Bloomberg Television; CMT Pure Country; Discovery en Espanol; Discovery Health Channel; Discovery Kids Channel; Discovery Military Channel; Do-It-Yourself; Fox Business Channel; Fox Reality Channel; Fuel TV; History Channel International; ID Investigation Discovery; Independent Film Channel; Lifetime Real Women; MTV Hits; MTV Jams; MTV Tres; MTV2; Music Choice; Nick Jr.; Nick Too; NickToons TV; Science Channel; Style Network; Sundance Channel; TeenNick; VH1 Classic; VH1 Soul; VHUNO.
Fee: $11.95 monthly.

Digital Expanded Basic Service
Subscribers: N.A.
Programming (via satellite): CBS College Sports Network; ESPNews; Fox College Sports Atlantic; Fox College Sports Central; Fox College Sports Pacific; Fox Soccer; Fuel TV; MavTV; Outdoor Channel.

Digital Expanded Basic Service 2
Subscribers: N.A.
Programming (received off-air): KSL-TV (NBC) Salt Lake City; KSTU (FOX) Salt Lake City.
Programming (via satellite): Arts & Entertainment HD; ESPN HD; Food Network HD; FSN HD; FX HD; Golf Channel HD; HGTV HD; History Channel HD; National Geographic Channel HD Network; Speed HD; TBS in HD; Turner Network TV HD; Versus HD.

Digital Expanded Basic Service 3
Subscribers: N.A.
Programming (via satellite): HDNet; HDNet Movies; Universal HD.

Digital Pay Service 1
Pay Units: N.A.
Programming (via satellite): Cinemax (multiplexed); Cinemax HD; Encore (multiplexed); Flix; HBO (multiplexed); HBO HD; Showtime (multiplexed); Showtime HD; Starz (multiplexed); Starz HDTV; The Movie Channel (multiplexed); The Movie Channel HD.

Video-On-Demand: No

Pay-Per-View
iN DEMAND (delivered digitally); Spice: Xcess (delivered digitally); Playboy TV (delivered digitally); Fresh (delivered digitally).

Internet Service
Operational: Yes.
Fee: $49.99 installation; $39.99 monthly; $5.00 modem lease; $69.99 modem purchase.

Telephone Service
None

Miles of Plant: 40.0 (coaxial); None (fiber optic). Homes passed: 2,216.
Technical Operations Manager: Ed Farnum. Office Manager: Misty Snow.
Franchise fee: 3% of gross.
Ownership: Baja Broadband (MSO).

NELLIS AFB—Bluebird Communications, 199 Stafford Dr, Las Vegas, NV 89115-2173. Phone: 702-644-2400. Fax: 702-644-7245. Web Site: http://www.bluebirdcommunications.com. ICA: NV0011.
TV Market Ranking: Below 100 (NELLIS AFB). Franchise award date: N.A. Franchise expiration date: N.A. Began: January 1, 1985.
Channel capacity: 36 (not 2-way capable). Channels available but not in use: N.A.

Basic Service
Subscribers: 1,470.
Programming (received off-air): KAME-TV (MNT) Reno; KEEN-CA Las Vegas; KLAS-TV (CBS) Las Vegas; KLVX-TV (PBS) Las Vegas; KSNV-DT (NBC) Las Vegas; KTNV-TV (ABC) Las Vegas; KVCW (CW) Las Vegas; KVMY (MNT) Las Vegas; KVVU-TV (FOX) Henderson.
Programming (via satellite): Telemundo; TV Guide Network; Univision; Weather Channel.
Fee: $35.00 installation; $10.15 monthly.

Digital Basic Service
Subscribers: N.A.
Programming (via satellite): ABC Family Channel; AMC; Animal Planet; Arts & Entertainment; BET Networks; Bravo; Cartoon Network; CNBC; CNN; Comedy Central; Country Music TV; C-SPAN; Discovery Channel; Discovery Health Channel; Disney Channel; DMX Music; E! Entertainment Television; ESPN; ESPN 2; ESPN Classic Sports; Food Network; Fox News Channel; Fox Sports en Espanol; Fox Sports Net West; Fox Sports World; FX; GalaVision; GSN; Hallmark Channel; Headline News; HGTV; History Channel; Lifetime; MSNBC; MTV; NFL Network; Nickelodeon; Oxygen; QVC; ShopNBC; Spike TV; Syfy; TBS Superstation; The Learning Channel; Toon Disney; Travel Channel; truTV; Turner Classic Movies; Turner Network TV; TV Guide Interactive Inc.; TV Land; USA Network; Versus; VH1; Weatherscan; WGN America.
Fee: $42.50 monthly.

Digital Expanded Basic Service
Subscribers: N.A.
Programming (via satellite): AmericanLife TV Network; BBC America; Bio; Blackbelt TV; Bloomberg Television; CMT Pure Country; Current; Daystar TV Network; Discovery Kids Channel; Discovery Military Channel; Discovery Planet Green; ESPNews; FitTV; Fox College Sports Atlantic; Fox College Sports Central; Fox College Sports Pacific; Fox Movie Channel; Fuse; G4; Golf Channel; Gospel Music Channel; Great American Country; Halogen Network; ID Investigation Discovery; Independent Film Channel; Lifetime Movie Network; Lime; MTV Hits; MTV2; National Geographic Channel; Nick Jr.; NickToons TV; Outdoor Channel; Science Channel; Sleuth; SoapNet; Speed Channel; Style Network; Sundance Channel; TeenNick; The Word Network; Trinity Broadcasting Network; TVG Network; VH1 Classic; VH1 Soul; WE tv.
Fee: $19.50 monthly.

Digital Pay Service 1
Pay Units: N.A.
Programming (via satellite): Cinemax (multiplexed); Encore (multiplexed); Flix; HBO (multiplexed); Showtime (multiplexed);

Starz (multiplexed); The Movie Channel (multiplexed).
Fee: $11.95 monthly (Cinemax or Showtime/TMC/Flix), $12.95 monthly (HBO), $15.95 monthly (Starz/Encore).

Video-On-Demand: No

Pay-Per-View

Movies (delivered digitally); Special events (delivered digitally); Playboy TV (delivered digitally).

Internet Service

Operational: Yes.
Subscribers: 511.
Fee: $49.00 installation; $39.95 monthly; $10.00 modem lease; $50.00 modem purchase.

Telephone Service

None

Miles of Plant: 33.0 (coaxial); None (fiber optic). Homes passed: 3,195.
Manager: Pete Sullivan. Chief Technician: Randy Zimney.
Ownership: United Enterprises (MSO).

PAHRUMP—CMA Cablevision, 3030 Needles Hwy, Ste 1400, Laughlin, NV 89029-0893. Phone: 702-298-3214. Fax: 702-298-3075. Web Site: http://www.cmaaccess.com. ICA: NV0014.
TV Market Ranking: Outside TV Markets (PAHRUMP). Franchise award date: January 1, 1989. Franchise expiration date: N.A. Began: January 1, 1985.
Channel capacity: N.A. Channels available but not in use: N.A.

Basic Service

Subscribers: 1,375.
Programming (received off-air): KINC (UNV) Las Vegas; KLAS-TV (CBS) Las Vegas; KLVX-TV (PBS) Las Vegas; KPVM-LP (ION) Pahrump; KSNV-DT (NBC) Las Vegas; KTNV-TV (ABC) Las Vegas; KVMY (MNT) Las Vegas; KVVU-TV (FOX) Henderson.
Programming (via satellite): Animal Planet; CNN; C-SPAN; ESPN; Fox News Channel; FX; Lifetime; Nickelodeon; TBS Superstation; Turner Network TV; TV Land; USA Network; Weather Channel; WGN America.
Fee: $39.95 installation; $21.45 monthly; $12.95 additional installation.

Expanded Basic Service 1

Subscribers: N.A.
Programming (received off-air): KHMP-LD Las Vegas; KPVT-LP Pahrump.
Programming (via satellite): ABC Family Channel; AMC; Arts & Entertainment; Cartoon Network; Comedy Central; Country Music TV; C-SPAN 2; Discovery Channel; E! Entertainment Television; ESPN 2; ESPN Classic Sports; Eternal Word TV Network; Food Network; Fox Sports Net West; GSN; Hallmark Channel; Headline News; HGTV; History Channel; Home Shopping Network; INSP; MSNBC; MTV; National Geographic Channel; QVC; Spike TV; Syfy; The Learning Channel; Travel Channel; Trinity Broadcasting Network; Turner Classic Movies; TV Guide Network; VH1.
Fee: $18.50 monthly.

Digital Basic Service

Subscribers: N.A.
Programming (via satellite): Bio; Discovery Digital Networks; ESPNews; Fox Movie Channel; Fox Sports World; G4; GAS; Golf Channel; History Channel International; Independent Film Channel; Lifetime Movie Network; MTV2; Nick Jr.; NickToons TV; Outdoor Channel; Speed Channel; VH1 Classic; VH1 Country.
Fee: $12.00 monthly.

Digital Pay Service 1

Pay Units: N.A.
Programming (via satellite): Cinemax (multiplexed); DMX Music; Encore (multiplexed); HBO (multiplexed); Showtime (multiplexed); Starz (multiplexed); The Movie Channel (multiplexed).
Fee: $10.95 monthly (Cinemax or Starz/Encore), $13.95 monthly (HBO or Showtime).

Pay-Per-View

Hot Network (delivered digitally); Spice (delivered digitally); movies (delivered digitally); special events (delivered digitally).

Internet Service

Operational: Yes.
Subscribers: 250.
Broadband Service: CMA.
Fee: $39.95 installation; $37.95 monthly; $2.95 modem lease; $39.95 modem purchase.

Telephone Service

Digital: Operational
Fee: $39.95 monthly

Miles of Plant: 270.0 (coaxial); None (fiber optic). Homes passed: 2,000. Total homes in franchised area: 2,258.
General Manager: Jerry Smith. Chief Technician: Greg Petras. Marketing Director: Julie Ferguson.
Ownership: Cable Management Assoc. (MSO).

PANACA—Rainbow Cable, PO Box 300, 27 Main St, Pioche, NV 89043-0300. Phone: 775-962-5111. Fax: 775-962-5193. Also serves Caliente & Pioche. ICA: NV0047.
TV Market Ranking: Outside TV Markets (Caliente, PANACA, Pioche). Franchise award date: N.A. Franchise expiration date: N.A. Began: N.A.
Channel capacity: N.A. Channels available but not in use: N.A.

Basic Service

Subscribers: 632.
Programming (via satellite): ABC Family Channel; Country Music TV; Discovery Channel; Disney Channel; ESPN; Headline News; KCNC-TV (CBS) Denver; KMGH-TV (ABC) Denver; KUSA (NBC) Denver; MTV; Nickelodeon; Spike TV; TBS Superstation; The Learning Channel; Turner Network TV; USA Network; WGN America.
Fee: $43.00 installation; $23.25 monthly.

Pay Service 1

Pay Units: N.A.
Programming (via satellite): Cinemax; HBO; Showtime.
Fee: $7.90 monthly (Showtime), $7.95 monthly (Cinemax), $9.95 monthly (HBO).

Video-On-Demand: No

Internet Service

Operational: No.

Telephone Service

None

Manager: Paul Christian. Chief Technician: Paul Donohue. Office Manager: Valinda Woodworth.
Ownership: Christian Enterprises (MSO).

PIOCHE—Rainbow Cable. Now served by PANACA, NV [NV0047]. ICA: NV0048.

RENO—Charter Communications, 9335 Prototype Dr, Reno, NV 89521. Phone: 775-850-1200. Fax: 775-850-1279. Web Site: http://www.charter.com. Also serves Peavine, CA; Cold Springs, Golden Valley, Hidden Valley, Lemmon Valley, Lockwood, Mogul, Panther Valley, Red Rock, Reno Cascade, Sierra, Spanish Springs, Sparks, Steamboat, Sun Valley, Verdi & Washoe County, NV. ICA: NV0002.
TV Market Ranking: Below 100 (Cold Springs, Golden Valley, Hidden Valley, Lemmon Valley, Lockwood, Mogul, Panther Valley, Peavine, Red Rock, RENO, Reno Cascade, Sierra, Spanish Springs, Sparks, Steamboat, Sun Valley, Verdi, Washoe County). Franchise award date: N.A. Franchise expiration date: N.A. Began: September 1, 1953.
Channel capacity: N.A. Channels available but not in use: N.A.

Basic Service

Subscribers: 141,900 Includes Carson City, Crystal Bay, Fallon, Fernley, Gardnerville, Hawthorne, Silver Springs, Meyers CA, & Northstar CA.
Programming (received off-air): KAME-TV (MNT) Reno; KNPB (PBS) Reno; KOLO-TV (ABC) Reno; KREN-TV (CW, UNV) Reno; KRNV-DT (ABC) Reno; KRXI-TV (FOX) Reno; KTVN (CBS) Reno; 13 FMs.
Programming (via satellite): ABC Family Channel; C-SPAN; C-SPAN 2; Discovery Channel; Eternal Word TV Network; QVC; Sneak Prevue; TBS Superstation; TV Guide Network; Weather Channel.
Current originations: Leased Access; Government Access.
Fee: $29.00 installation; $16.29 monthly.

Expanded Basic Service 1

Subscribers: 54,558.
Programming (via satellite): AMC; Animal Planet; Arts & Entertainment; BET Networks; Cartoon Network; CNBC; CNN; Comcast Sports Net Bay Area; Comedy Central; Disney Channel; E! Entertainment Television; ESPN; ESPN 2; Food Network; Fox News Channel; FX; GalaVision; Great American Country; Hallmark Channel; Headline News; HGTV; Home Shopping Network; ION Television; Lifetime; MSNBC; MTV; mun2 television; Nickelodeon; Product Information Network; Spike TV; Syfy; The Learning Channel; Turner Network TV; TV Land; USA Network; VH1.
Fee: $30.30 monthly.

Digital Basic Service

Subscribers: N.A.
Programming (via satellite): Barker; BBC America; Bravo; Discovery Digital Networks; DMX Music; ESPN Classic Sports; Fox Sports World; Golf Channel; GSN; History Channel; Independent Film Channel; Turner Classic Movies; Versus; WE tv.
Fee: $8.40 monthly.

Pay Service 1

Pay Units: N.A.
Programming (via satellite): Cinemax; Encore; HBO; Showtime; Starz.
Fee: $24.95 installation; $1.75 monthly (Encore), $4.95 monthly (Starz), $12.95 monthly (Cinemax), $14.19 monthly (HBO).

Digital Pay Service 1

Pay Units: N.A.
Programming (via satellite): Cinemax (multiplexed); Encore (multiplexed); HBO (multiplexed); Showtime (multiplexed); Starz (multiplexed); The Movie Channel (multiplexed).

Video-On-Demand: Yes

Pay-Per-View

Hot Choice (delivered digitally); iN DEMAND; iN DEMAND (delivered digitally); Fresh (delivered digitally); Shorteez (delivered digitally).

Internet Service

Operational: Yes. Began: November 1, 2000.
Broadband Service: Charter Pipeline.
Fee: $29.99 monthly; $10.00 modem lease; $300.00 modem purchase.

Telephone Service

Analog: Not Operational
Digital: Operational
Fee: $34.99 monthly

Miles of Plant: 1,076.0 (coaxial); 125.0 (fiber optic). Homes passed: 224,043.
Vice President & General Manager: Manny Martinez. Technical Operations Manager: Carol Eure.
City fee: 3% of gross.
Ownership: Charter Communications Inc. (MSO).

RENO—Formerly served by Quadravision. No longer in operation. ICA: NV0053.

RUTH—Central Telcom Services, PO Box 7, Fairview, UT 84629. Phone: 435-427-3331. Fax: 435-427-3200. Web Site: http://www.centracom.com. ICA: NV0029.
TV Market Ranking: Below 100 (RUTH). Franchise award date: February 1, 1990. Franchise expiration date: N.A. Began: January 1, 1990.
Channel capacity: 40 (operating 2-way). Channels available but not in use: 4.

Basic Service

Subscribers: 16.
Programming (received off-air): KLAS-TV (CBS) Las Vegas; KSL-TV (NBC) Salt Lake City; KSTU (FOX) Salt Lake City; KTVX (ABC) Salt Lake City; KUTV (CBS) Salt Lake City.
Programming (via satellite): ABC Family Channel; AMC; Arts & Entertainment; CNN; Country Music TV; C-SPAN; Discovery Channel; Disney Channel; ESPN; ESPN 2; Headline News; HGTV; Lifetime; MTV; Nickelodeon; QVC; Spike TV; Syfy; TBS Superstation; The Learning Channel; Trinity Broadcasting Network; Turner Network TV; TV Land; USA Network; Weather Channel; WGN America.
Fee: $44.95 installation; $15.88 monthly.

Expanded Basic Service 1

Subscribers: 16.

Pay Service 1

Pay Units: 14.
Programming (via satellite): Cinemax.
Fee: $12.95 monthly.

Pay Service 2

Pay Units: 15.
Programming (via satellite): HBO.
Fee: $12.95 monthly.

Pay Service 3

Pay Units: 19.
Programming (via satellite): Starz.
Fee: $6.75 monthly.

Pay Service 4

Pay Units: 23.
Programming (via satellite): Encore; Showtime.
Fee: $12.95 monthly.

Video-On-Demand: No

Internet Service

Operational: No.

Telephone Service

None

Miles of Plant: 5.0 (coaxial); None (fiber optic). Homes passed: 150.
General Manager: Eddie Cox. CATV Manager: George Lee. Chief Engineer: Kenny Roberts.
Ownership: CentraCom Interactive (MSO).

SILVER SPRINGS—Charter Communications, 9335 Prototype Dr, Reno, NV 89521. Phone: 775-850-1200. Fax: 775-850-1279. Web Site: http://www.charter.com. Also serves Stagecoach. ICA: NV0017.

TV Market Ranking: Below 100 (SILVER SPRINGS, Stagecoach). Franchise award date: October 22, 1987. Franchise expiration date: N.A. Began: September 10, 1988.

Channel capacity: 35 (not 2-way capable). Channels available but not in use: 3.

Basic Service

Subscribers: N.A. Included in Reno

Programming (received off-air): KAME-TV (MNT) Reno; KNPB (PBS) Reno; KOLO-TV (ABC) Reno; KREN-TV (CW, UNV) Reno; KRNV-DT (ABC) Reno; KTVN (CBS) Reno.

Programming (via satellite): C-SPAN; Hallmark Channel; ION Television; QVC.

Fee: $29.99 installation; $16.66 monthly.

Expanded Basic Service 1

Subscribers: 701.

Programming (via satellite): ABC Family Channel; AMC; Animal Planet; Arts & Entertainment; Cartoon Network; CNBC; CNN; Comcast Sports Net Bay Area; Discovery Channel; Disney Channel; ESPN; ESPN 2; Fox News Channel; FX; GalaVision; Great American Country; Headline News; Lifetime; MSNBC; MTV; Nickelodeon; Spike TV; TBS Superstation; Turner Network TV; USA Network; Weather Channel.

Fee: $32.58 monthly.

Digital Basic Service

Subscribers: N.A.

Programming (via satellite): BBC America; Bravo; Discovery Digital Networks; DMX Music; ESPN Classic Sports; ESPNews; Fox Soccer; Golf Channel; GSN; HGTV; History Channel; Independent Film Channel; Nick Jr.; Syfy; Turner Classic Movies; TV Guide Interactive Inc.; TV Land; Versus; WE tv.

Fee: $10.95 monthly.

Digital Pay Service 1

Pay Units: N.A.

Programming (via satellite): Cinemax (multiplexed); Encore (multiplexed); HBO (multiplexed); Showtime (multiplexed); Starz (multiplexed); The Movie Channel (multiplexed).

Video-On-Demand: No

Pay-Per-View

iN DEMAND (delivered digitally); Playboy TV (delivered digitally).

Internet Service

Operational: No.

Telephone Service

None

Miles of Plant: 61.0 (coaxial); None (fiber optic). Total homes in franchised area: 9,577.

Vice President & General Manager: Manny Martinez. Technical Operations Manager: Carol Eure.

Ownership: Charter Communications Inc. (MSO).

TONOPAH—Eagle West Communications Inc, 1030 S Mesa Dr, Mesa, AZ 85210. Phones: 480-813-8371 (Mesa office); 775-482-3492. Fax: 480-813-4596. Also serves Esmeralda County (portions). ICA: NV0050.

TV Market Ranking: Below 100 (TONOPAH); Outside TV Markets (Esmeralda County (portions)). Franchise award date: N.A. Franchise expiration date: N.A. Began: September 23, 1955.

Channel capacity: 49 (not 2-way capable). Channels available but not in use: None.

Basic Service

Subscribers: N.A. Included in East Mesa, AZ

Programming (received off-air): KNPB (PBS) Reno; KOLO-TV (ABC) Reno; KRNV-DT (ABC) Reno; KRXI-TV (FOX) Reno; KTVN (CBS) Reno.

Programming (via satellite): 3 Angels Broadcasting Network; AMC; Animal Planet; Arts & Entertainment; BET Networks; CNN; Comedy Central; Country Music TV; C-SPAN; Discovery Channel; ESPN; ESPN 2; ESPNews; Eternal Word TV Network; Fox Sports Net; G4; Hallmark Channel; Headline News; HGTV; History Channel; Home Shopping Network; ION Television; KCNC-TV (CBS) Denver; KUSA (NBC) Denver; Lifetime; MTV; Nickelodeon; Outdoor Channel; QVC; Spike TV; Syfy; TBS Superstation; The Learning Channel; Travel Channel; Turner Network TV; TV Land; USA Network; VH1; Weather Channel; WGN America.

Fee: $10.00 installation; $31.95 monthly.

Pay Service 1

Pay Units: N.A.

Programming (via satellite): Cinemax; HBO.

Fee: $10.00 monthly.

Video-On-Demand: No

Internet Service

Operational: No.

Telephone Service

None

Homes passed & miles of plant included in East Mesa, AZ

General Manager: Ernest McKay. Manager: Linda Schneider. Chief Technician: John Harness.

Ownership: Eagle West Communications (MSO).

TOPAZ LAKE—Satview Broadband, PO Box 18148, Reno, NV 89511. Phones: 775-338-6626; 800-225-0605. Fax: 775-333-0225. Web Site: http://www.iwantone.tv. Also serves Walker, CA; Holbrook Junction & Topaz Ranch Estates, NV. ICA: NV0019.

TV Market Ranking: Outside TV Markets (Holbrook Junction, TOPAZ LAKE, Topaz Ranch Estates, Walker). Franchise award date: March 1, 1980. Franchise expiration date: N.A. Began: June 5, 1979.

Channel capacity: N.A. Channels available but not in use: N.A.

Basic Service

Subscribers: 200.

Programming (received off-air): KAME-TV (MNT) Reno; KOLO-TV (ABC) Reno; KREN-TV (CW, UNV) Reno; KRNS-CA (IND) Reno; KRNV-DT (ABC) Reno; KRXI-TV (FOX) Reno; KTVN (CBS) Reno; Univision; allband FM.

Programming (via satellite): ABC Family Channel; AMC; Animal Planet; Arts & Entertainment; Cartoon Network; CNBC; CNN; Comcast SportsNet West; Country Music TV; C-SPAN; Discovery Channel; Disney Channel; E! Entertainment Television; ESPN; ESPN 2; Food Network; Fox News Channel; FX; Hallmark Channel; Headline News; HGTV; History Channel; Home Shopping Network; ION Television; KNPB (PBS) Reno; Lifetime; MSNBC; MTV; National Geographic Channel; Nickelodeon; QVC; Speed Channel; Spike TV; Style Network; TBS Superstation; The Learning Channel; Travel Channel; truTV; Turner Classic Movies; Turner Network TV; USA Network; VH1; Weather Channel.

Current originations: Leased Access; Government Access; Educational Access; Public Access.

Fee: $40.00 installation; $26.25 monthly.

Digital Basic Service

Subscribers: N.A.

Programming (received off-air): KNPB (PBS) Reno; KOLO-TV (ABC) Reno; KRNV-DT (ABC) Reno; KRXI-TV (FOX) Reno; KTVN (CBS) Reno.

Programming (via satellite): American-Life TV Network; Arts & Entertainment HD; AYM Sports; Bandamax; BBC America; Bio; Bloomberg Television; Bravo; BYU Television; Cartoon Network; CBS College Sports Network; Cine Latino; CMT Pure Country; CNN en Espanol; Comedy Central; Cooking Channel; C-SPAN 2; Daystar TV Network; Discovery en Espanol; Discovery Familia; Discovery HD Theater; Discovery Health Channel; Discovery Home Channel; Discovery Kids Channel; Discovery Military Channel; Do-It-Yourself; Encore (multiplexed); ESPN 2 HD; ESPN Classic Sports; ESPN Deportes; ESPN HD; ESPN U; ESPNews; FitTV; Fox Business Channel; Fox College Sports Atlantic; Fox College Sports Central; Fox College Sports Pacific; Fox Movie Channel; Fox Soccer; Fox Sports en Espanol; Fuse; G4; Gol TV; Golf Channel; Gospel Music Channel; Great American Country; GSN; Hallmark Movie Channel; Halogen Network; HDNet; HDNet Movies; History Channel en Espanol; History Channel International; HITN; ID Investigation Discovery; Independent Film Channel; Infinito; Jewelry Television; Latin Television (LTV); Lifetime Movie Network; Lifetime Real Women; MTV Hits; MTV Jams; MTV Tres; MTV2; mun2 television; Nick Jr.; Outdoor Channel; Palladia; Science Channel; SoapNet; Sorpresa; Sundance Channel; Syfy; TeenNick; Tennis Channel; The Sportsman Channel; Toon Disney; Trinity Broadcasting Network; Turner Network TV HD; TV Guide Network; TV Land; TVN Entertainment; Versus; VH1 Classic; VH1 Soul; Video Rola; WE tv; WealthTV.

Digital Pay Service 1

Pay Units: N.A.

Programming (via satellite): Cinemax (multiplexed); Cinemax HD; HBO (multiplexed); HBO HD; Showtime (multiplexed); Showtime HD; Starz (multiplexed); Starz HDTV; The Movie Channel.

Internet Service

Operational: No.

Telephone Service

None

Miles of Plant: 30.0 (coaxial); None (fiber optic). Homes passed: 3,000. Total homes in franchised area included in Coleville, CA

Chief Executive Officer: Tariq Ahmad.

County fee: 5% of gross.

Ownership: Satview Broadband Ltd.

VERDI—Suddenlink Communications, 12444 Powerscourt Dr, Saint Louis, MO 63131-3660. Phone: 530-587-6100. Fax: 530-587-1468. Web Site: http://www.suddenlink.com. ICA: NV0056.

TV Market Ranking: Below 100 (VERDI).

Channel capacity: N.A. Channels available but not in use: N.A.

Basic Service

Subscribers: 100.

Programming (received off-air): KAME-TV (MNT) Reno; KCRA-TV (NBC) Sacramento; KGO-TV (ABC) San Francisco; KNPB (PBS) Reno; KOLO-TV (ABC) Reno; KOVR (CBS) Stockton; KQED (PBS) San Francisco; KRNV-DT (ABC) Reno; KRXI-TV (FOX) Reno; KTVN (CBS) Reno; KTXL (FOX) Sacramento.

Programming (via satellite): 3 Angels Broadcasting Network; Cartoon Network; Discovery Channel; Nickelodeon; QVC; TBS Superstation; Weather Channel; WGN America.

Fee: $19.95 monthly.

Expanded Basic Service 1

Subscribers: N.A.

Programming (via satellite): ABC Family Channel; AMC; Arts & Entertainment; CNBC; CNN; Comcast Sports Net Bay Area; C-SPAN; Disney Channel; ESPN; ESPN 2; Food Network; Great American Country; Headline News; History Channel; Lifetime; MTV; Spike TV; The Learning Channel; Travel Channel; Turner Network TV; TV Land; USA Network; VH1.

Fee: $10.04 monthly.

Pay Service 1

Pay Units: N.A.

Programming (via satellite): Cinemax; HBO; Showtime; The Movie Channel.

Internet Service

Operational: No.

Telephone Service

None

Marketing Director: Jason Oelkers.

Ownership: Cequel Communications LLC (MSO).

VIRGINIA CITY—Comstock Community TV Inc., PO Box 9, Virginia City, NV 89440-0009. Phone: 775-847-0572. Also serves Gold Hill. ICA: NV0025.

TV Market Ranking: Below 100 (Gold Hill, VIRGINIA CITY). Franchise award date: N.A. Franchise expiration date: N.A. Began: November 1, 1957.

Channel capacity: 27 (not 2-way capable). Channels available but not in use: 2.

Basic Service

Subscribers: 390.

Programming (received off-air): KAME-TV (MNT) Reno; KNPB (PBS) Reno; KOLO-TV (ABC) Reno; KREN-TV (CW, UNV) Reno; KRNV-DT (ABC) Reno; KRXI-TV (FOX) Reno; KTVN (CBS) Reno.

Programming (via satellite): Animal Planet; Arts & Entertainment; CNN; Comedy Central; Discovery Channel; ESPN; Food Network; Fox Movie Channel; Fox News Channel; Hallmark Channel; Headline News; HGTV; History Channel; Lifetime; National Geographic Channel; Outdoor Channel; QVC; Spike TV; Syfy; TBS Superstation; The Learning Channel; Travel Channel; Turner Classic Movies; Turner Network TV; WGN America.

Fee: $65.00 installation; $15.00 monthly.

Video-On-Demand: No

Internet Service

Operational: No.

Telephone Service
None
Miles of Plant: 5.0 (coaxial); None (fiber optic). Additional miles planned: 2.0 (coaxial).
Manager & Program Director: Barbara Bowers. Chief Technician: Gary Greenlund.
Ownership: Comstock Community TV Inc.

WELLINGTON—Satview Broadband, 3550 Barron Way, Ste 13A, Reno, NV 89511. Phones: 775-338-6626; 800-225-0605. Fax: 775-333-0225. Web Site: http://www.iwantone.tv. ICA: NV0057.
TV Market Ranking: Outside TV Markets (WELLINGTON).
Channel capacity: N.A. Channels available but not in use: N.A.
Digital Basic Service
Subscribers: N.A.
Programming (received off-air): KAME-TV (MNT) Reno; KNPB (PBS) Reno; KOLO-TV (ABC) Reno; KRNV-DT (ABC) Reno; KRXI-TV (FOX) Reno; KTVN (CBS) Reno.
Programming (via satellite): ABC Family Channel; American Movie Classics; AmericanLife TV Network; Arts & Entertainment; BBC America; Bio; Bloomberg Television; Bravo; Classic Arts Showcase; Discovery Channel; Discovery Health Channel; Discovery Kids Channel; Discovery Military Channel; Discovery Planet Green; Disney Channel; ESPN; ESPN 2; FitTV; Fox Movie Channel; Fox News Channel; G4; Golf Channel; Great American Country; HGTV; History Channel; Home Shopping Network; ID Investigation Discovery; MSNBC; Nickelodeon; Outdoor Channel; QVC; Science Channel; Speed Channel; Spike TV; Style Network; Syfy; TBS Superstation; Trinity Broadcasting Network; Turner Classic Movies; Turner Network TV; Univision; USA Network; WE tv; WGN America.
Fee: $38.00 monthly.
Digital Pay Service 1
Pay Units: N.A.
Programming (via satellite): Cinemax (multiplexed); Encore (multiplexed); HBO (multiplexed); Starz (multiplexed); The Movie Channel.
Pay-Per-View
Ten Xtsy (delivered digitally).
Internet Service
Operational: No.
Telephone Service
None
Chief Executive Officer: Tariq Ahmad.
Ownership: Satview Broadband Ltd. (MSO).

WELLS—Satview Broadband, PO Box 18148, Reno, NV 89511. Phones: 800-225-0605; 775-333-6626. Fax: 775-333-0225. Web Site: http://www.iwantone.tv. ICA: NV0023.
TV Market Ranking: Outside TV Markets (WELLS). Franchise award date: N.A. Franchise expiration date: N.A. Began: April 1, 1957.
Channel capacity: N.A. Channels available but not in use: N.A.
Basic Service
Subscribers: 395.
Programming (received off-air): KENV-DT (NBC) Elko; KTVN (CBS) Reno; 2 FMs.
Programming (via microwave): KSL-TV (NBC) Salt Lake City; KSTU (FOX) Salt Lake City; KTVX (ABC) Salt Lake City; KUCW (CW) Ogden; KUED (PBS) Salt Lake City; KUTV (CBS) Salt Lake City.
Programming (via satellite): C-SPAN; Hallmark Channel; Home Shopping Network; QVC.
Current originations: Public Access.
Fee: $45.47 installation; $11.11 monthly; $22.73 additional installation.
Expanded Basic Service 1
Subscribers: N.A.
Programming (via satellite): ABC Family Channel; AMC; Animal Planet; Arts & Entertainment; Cartoon Network; CNBC; CNN; Comedy Central; Discovery Channel; Disney Channel; E! Entertainment Television; ESPN; ESPN 2; Fox News Channel; Fox Sports Net; FX; GalaVision; Headline News; Lifetime; MSNBC; MTV; Nickelodeon; Spike TV; TBS Superstation; The Learning Channel; Turner Network TV; TV Land; USA Network; VH1; Weather Channel.
Fee: $12.67 installation; $1.91 monthly.
Digital Basic Service
Subscribers: N.A.
Programming (via satellite): AmericanLife TV Network; BBC America; Bio; Bloomberg Television; Bravo; Discovery Digital Networks; DMX Music; ESPN Classic Sports; ESPNews; FitTV; Fox Movie Channel; Fox Soccer; Fuse; G4; GAS; Golf Channel; GSN; Halogen Network; HGTV; History Channel; History Channel International; Independent Film Channel; Lifetime Movie Network; MTV Networks Digital Suite; Nick Jr.; Outdoor Channel; Speed Channel; Style Network; Syfy; Toon Disney; Trinity Broadcasting Network; Turner Classic Movies; Versus; WE tv.
Digital Pay Service 1
Pay Units: N.A.
Programming (via satellite): Cinemax (multiplexed); Encore (multiplexed); Flix; HBO (multiplexed); Showtime (multiplexed); Starz (multiplexed); The Movie Channel (multiplexed).
Video-On-Demand: No
Pay-Per-View
iN DEMAND (delivered digitally); ESPN Now (delivered digitally); Sports PPV (delivered digitally); Hot Choice (delivered digitally); Playboy TV (delivered digitally); Fresh (delivered digitally); Shorteez (delivered digitally).
Internet Service
Operational: No.
Telephone Service
None
Miles of Plant: 14.0 (coaxial); None (fiber optic). Homes passed: 534. Total homes in franchised area: 548.
Chief Executive Officer: Tariq Ahmad.
Ownership: Satview Broadband Ltd. (MSO).

WENDOVER—Central Telcom Services, PO Box 7, Fairview, UT 84629. Phone: 435-427-3331. Fax: 435-427-3200. Web Site: http://www.centracom.com. Also serves Wendover. ICA: NV0054.
TV Market Ranking: Outside TV Markets (Wendover, WENDOVER). Franchise award date: N.A. Franchise expiration date: N.A. Began: N.A.
Channel capacity: 60 (not 2-way capable). Channels available but not in use: 11.
Basic Service
Subscribers: 670.
Programming (received off-air): KJZZ-TV (MNT) Salt Lake City; KSL-TV (NBC) Salt Lake City; KSTU (FOX) Salt Lake City; KTVX (ABC) Salt Lake City; KUED (PBS) Salt Lake City; KUTV (CBS) Salt Lake City.
Programming (via satellite): ABC Family Channel; AMC; Animal Planet; Arts & Entertainment; CNBC; CNN; Country Music TV; C-SPAN; Discovery Channel; Disney Channel; ESPN; ESPN 2; Fox Sports Net; GalaVision; HGTV; Lifetime; MTV; Nickelodeon; QVC; Spike TV; Syfy; TBS Superstation; Turner Classic Movies; Turner Network TV; TV Guide Network; TV Land; USA Network; Weather Channel; WGN America.
Current originations: Public Access.
Fee: $44.95 installation; $15.88 monthly.
Expanded Basic Service 1
Subscribers: 665.
Fee: $41.84 monthly.
Digital Basic Service
Subscribers: 52.
Fee: $60.75 monthly.
Pay Service 1
Pay Units: 45.
Programming (via satellite): Cinemax.
Fee: $12.95 monthly.
Pay Service 2
Pay Units: 101.
Programming (via satellite): HBO.
Fee: $12.95 monthly.
Pay Service 3
Pay Units: 49.
Programming (via satellite): Showtime.
Fee: $12.95 monthly.
Pay Service 4
Pay Units: 89.
Programming (via satellite): Encore; Starz.
Fee: $12.95 monthly (Starz).
Video-On-Demand: No
Internet Service
Operational: No.
Telephone Service
None
Miles of Plant: 44.0 (coaxial); None (fiber optic). Homes passed: 1,900. Total homes in franchised area: 2,000.
General Manager: Eddie Cox. CATV Manager: George Lee. Chief Engineer: Kenny Roberts.
Franchise fee: 5% gross.
Ownership: CentraCom Interactive (MSO).

WINNEMUCCA—CalNeva Broadband, 485 W Haskel St, Winnemucca, NV 89445. Phones: 775-625-1138; 775-625-1120. Also serves Humboldt County (portions). ICA: NV0010.
TV Market Ranking: Below 100 (Humboldt County (portions), WINNEMUCCA); Outside TV Markets (Humboldt County (portions)). Franchise award date: March 1, 1982. Franchise expiration date: N.A. Began: August 6, 1982.
Channel capacity: 81 (operating 2-way). Channels available but not in use: 18.
Basic Service
Subscribers: 2,130.
Programming (received off-air): KAME-TV (MNT) Reno; KNPB (PBS) Reno; KOLO-TV (ABC) Reno; KREN-TV (CW, UNV) Reno; KRNV-DT (ABC) Reno; KRXI-TV (FOX) Reno; KTVN (CBS) Reno; KTVX (ABC) Salt Lake City; KUTV (CBS) Salt Lake City.
Programming (via satellite): Home Shopping Network; ION Television; NASA TV; Product Information Network; QVC; WGN America.
Fee: $29.95 installation; $20.00 monthly.
Expanded Basic Service 1
Subscribers: N.A.
Programming (via satellite): 3 Angels Broadcasting Network; ABC Family Channel; AMC; Animal Planet; Arts & Entertainment; Boomerang; Cartoon Network; CNBC; CNN; Comcast Sports Net Bay Area; Comedy Central; Country Music TV; C-SPAN; C-SPAN 2; Discovery Channel; Do-It-Yourself; E! Entertainment Television; ESPN; ESPN 2; ESPN Classic Sports; Food Network; Fox News Channel; FX; GalaVision; Great American Country; Hallmark Channel; Headline News; HGTV; History Channel; Lifetime; MSNBC; MTV; National Geographic Channel; Nickelodeon; Outdoor Channel; Speed Channel; Spike TV; Syfy; TBS Superstation; The Learning Channel; Travel Channel; truTV; Turner Classic Movies; Turner Network TV; TV Guide Network; TV Land; Univision; USA Network; VH1; Weather Channel.
Fee: $19.00 monthly.
Digital Basic Service
Subscribers: N.A.
Programming (via satellite): BBC America; Bio; Bloomberg Television; CMT Pure Country; Current; Discovery Health Channel; Discovery Kids Channel; Discovery Military Channel; Discovery Planet Green; DMX Music; ESPNews; Fox Soccer; G4; Golf Channel; GSN; History Channel International; ID Investigation Discovery; Lifetime Movie Network; MTV Jams; MTV2; Nick Jr.; NickToons TV; Outdoor Channel; Ovation; Science Channel; Speed Channel; Style Network; TeenNick; VH1 Classic; VH1 Soul.
Fee: $12.95 monthly.
Digital Expanded Basic Service
Subscribers: N.A.
Programming (via satellite): Fox Movie Channel; Sundance Channel.
Fee: $4.65 monthly.
Pay Service 1
Pay Units: N.A.
Programming (via satellite): HBO.
Digital Pay Service 1
Pay Units: N.A.
Programming (via satellite): Cinemax (multiplexed); Encore (multiplexed); HBO (multiplexed); Showtime (multiplexed); Starz (multiplexed); The Movie Channel (multiplexed).
Fee: $8.35 monthly (Starz), $13.00 monthly (HBO or Cinemax), $20.30 monthly (Showtime/TMC).
Video-On-Demand: No
Pay-Per-View
Pay-per-view 1 (delivered digitally); Pay-per-view 2 (delivered digitally); Pay-per-view 3 (delivered digitally); Pay-per-view 4 (delivered digitally).
Internet Service
Operational: Yes.
Broadband Service: Rapid High Speed Internet.
Fee: $29.95 installation; $24.95 monthly.
Telephone Service
None
Miles of Plant: 89.0 (coaxial); None (fiber optic). Homes passed: 3,703. Total homes in franchised area: 4,500.
Manager: Tom Gelardi.
Ownership: CalNeva Broadband LLC (MSO).

NEW HAMPSHIRE

Total Systems: 17
Total Communities Served: 206
Franchises Not Yet Operating: 0
Applications Pending: 0
Communities with Applications: 0
Number of Basic Subscribers: 830,274
Number of Expanded Basic Subscribers: 120,767
Number of Pay Units: 25,928

Top 100 Markets Represented: Boston-Cambridge-Worcester-Lawrence (6); Portland-Poland Spring (75).

For a list of cable communities in this section, see the Cable Community Index located in the back of Cable Volume 2.
For explanation of terms used in cable system listings, see p. D-11.

ALSTEAD—Formerly served by Adelphia Communications. Now served by MANCHESTER, NH [NH0048]. ICA: NH0025.

ANDOVER (town)—Formerly served by Adelphia Communications. Now served by BURLINGTON, VT [VT0001]. ICA: NH0028.

BATH (village)—Formerly served by Adelphia Communications. Now served by LITTLETON, NH [NH0020]. ICA: NH0035.

BELMONT—MetroCast Cablevision, 9 Apple Rd, Belmont, NH 03220-3251. Phones: 603-524-4425 (Customer service); 603-524-3767 (Administrative office). Fax: 603-524-5190. Web Site: http://www.metrocastcommunications.com. Also serves Alexandria, Alton, Barnstead, Bridgewater, Bristol, Center Harbor, Deerfield, Epsom, Franklin, Gilford, Gilmanton, Hebron, Laconia, Meredith, New Durham, New Hampton, Northfield, Northfield (town), Northwood, Pittsfield, Sanbornton (town), Strafford (town-portions), Tilton & Wolfeboro. ICA: NH0044.

TV Market Ranking: 6 (Alton, Barnstead, Deerfield, Epsom, Franklin, Gilmanton, Laconia, New Durham, Northfield, Northwood, Pittsfield, Strafford (town-portions), Tilton, Wolfeboro); Below 100 (Alexandria, BELMONT, Bridgewater, Bristol, Center Harbor, Gilford, Hebron, Meredith, New Hampton, Northfield, Sanbornton (town), Alton, Barnstead, Epsom, Franklin, Gilmanton, Laconia, New Durham, Northfield, Pittsfield, Strafford (town-portions), Tilton, Wolfeboro). Franchise award date: N.A. Franchise expiration date: N.A. Began: July 1, 1952.

Channel capacity: 78 (operating 2-way). Channels available but not in use: None.

Basic Service
Subscribers: 36,613.
Programming (received off-air): WCSH (NBC) Portland; WENH-TV (PBS) Durham; WGME-TV (CBS) Portland; WMFP (IND) Lawrence; WMTW (ABC) Poland Spring; WMUR-TV (ABC) Manchester; WNEU (TMO) Merrimack; WPXG-TV (ION) Concord; WZMY-TV (MNT) Derry; allband FM.
Programming (via microwave): New England Cable News; WBZ-TV (CBS) Boston; WCVB-TV (ABC) Boston; WFXT (FOX) Boston; WGBH-TV (PBS) Boston; WHDH (NBC) Boston; WLVI-TV (CW) Cambridge; WSBK-TV (IND) Boston.
Programming (via satellite): C-SPAN; TBS Superstation; TV Guide Network.
Current originations: Leased Access; Government Access; Educational Access; Public Access.
Fee: $30.00 installation; $15.00 monthly.

Expanded Basic Service 1
Subscribers: 31,000.
Programming (via satellite): ABC Family Channel; AMC; Animal Planet; Arts & Entertainment; Bravo; Cartoon Network; CNBC; CNN; Comedy Central; C-SPAN; Discovery Channel; Disney Channel; E! Entertainment Television; ESPN; ESPN 2; Eternal Word TV Network; Fox News Channel; FX; Golf Channel; Headline News; HGTV; History Channel; Home Shopping Network; Lifetime; MSNBC; MTV; New England Sports Network; Nickelodeon; QVC; SoapNet; Spike TV; Syfy; The Learning Channel; Turner Network TV; USA Network; VH1; Weather Channel.
Fee: $28.95 monthly.

Digital Basic Service
Subscribers: 12,827.
Programming (via satellite): AmericanLife TV Network; BBC America; Bio; Bloomberg Television; Boomerang; Discovery Digital Networks; Do-It-Yourself; ESPN Classic Sports; Fox Movie Channel; Fox Sports World; G4; GSN; Halogen Network; History Channel International; Independent Film Channel; Lifetime Movie Network; Music Choice; Nick Jr.; Outdoor Channel; Ovation; Speed Channel; Style Network; truTV; Turner Classic Movies; Versus; WE tv.
Fee: $6.95 monthly.

Digital Pay Service 1
Pay Units: 10,000.
Programming (via satellite): Cinemax (multiplexed); HBO (multiplexed); Showtime (multiplexed); Starz (multiplexed); The Movie Channel (multiplexed).
Fee: $12.95 monthly (each).

Video-On-Demand: Yes

Pay-Per-View
Addressable homes: 13,708.
iN DEMAND, Addressable: Yes; iN DEMAND (delivered digitally); ETC; Pleasure (delivered digitally); TEN-The Erotic Network.

Internet Service
Operational: Yes. Began: January 1, 2001.
Subscribers: 12,500.
Broadband Service: Great Works Internet.
Fee: $99.00 installation; $41.95 monthly; $5.00 modem lease; $149.50 modem purchase.

Telephone Service
Digital: Planned

Miles of Plant: 1,800.0 (coaxial); None (fiber optic). Homes passed: 57,675.
Vice President, Operations & General Manager: Steve Murdough. Vice President & Customer Relations Manager: Shirley Clark. Programming Director: Linda Stuchell.
City fee: None.
Ownership: Harron Communications LP (MSO).

BERLIN—Time Warner Cable, 118 Johnston Rd, Portland, ME 4102. Phone: 207-253-2200. Fax: 207-253-2405. Web Site: http://www.timewarnercable.com/NewEngland. Also serves Dalton, Gorham, Groveton, Lancaster, Northumberland (town), Randolph & Whitefield. ICA: NH0012.

TV Market Ranking: Outside TV Markets (BERLIN, Dalton, Gorham, Groveton, Lancaster, Northumberland (town), Randolph, Whitefield). Franchise award date: N.A. Franchise expiration date: N.A. Began: December 4, 1954.

Channel capacity: 175 (operating 2-way). Channels available but not in use: N.A.

Basic Service
Subscribers: 7,147.
Programming (received off-air): W27BL Berlin; WCAX-TV (CBS) Burlington; WCBB (PBS) Augusta; WCSH (NBC) Portland; WGME-TV (CBS) Portland; WLED-TV (PBS) Littleton; WMTW (ABC) Poland Spring; 16 FMs.
Programming (via microwave): WSBK-TV (IND) Boston.
Programming (via satellite): C-SPAN; C-SPAN 2; Home Shopping Network; Jewelry Television; QVC; TBS Superstation; TV Guide Network.
Fee: $56.63 installation; $15.39 monthly.

Expanded Basic Service 1
Subscribers: 486.
Programming (via satellite): ABC Family Channel; AMC; Animal Planet; Arts & Entertainment; BBC America; Bravo; Cartoon Network; CNBC; CNN; Comedy Central; Country Music TV; Discovery Channel; Discovery Health Channel; Disney Channel; E! Entertainment Television; ESPN; ESPN 2; Eternal Word TV Network; FitTV; Food Network; Fox News Channel; FX; Great American Country; Hallmark Channel; Headline News; HGTV; History Channel; INSP; ION Television; Lifetime; Lifetime Movie Network; MSNBC; MTV; National Geographic Channel; New England Sports Network; Nickelodeon; Oxygen; ShopNBC; SoapNet; Speed Channel; Spike TV; Syfy; The Learning Channel; Travel Channel; truTV; Turner Network TV; TV Land; USA Network; VH1; WE tv; Weather Channel.
Fee: $15.00 installation; $41.82 monthly.

Digital Basic Service
Subscribers: N.A.
Programming (via satellite): AmericanLife TV Network; America's Store; Bloomberg Television; Boomerang; CNN International; C-SPAN 3; Discovery Digital Networks; DMX Music; Do-It-Yourself; ESPN Classic Sports; ESPNews; FamilyNet; Fox Sports World; Fuse; G4; GAS; Golf Channel; GSN; Halogen Network; Independent Film Channel; MTV2; Nick Jr.; NickToons TV; Outdoor Channel; Ovation; Style Network; Toon Disney; Trinity Broadcasting Network; Turner Classic Movies; Versus; VH1 Classic.
Fee: $26.74 monthly.

Digital Expanded Basic Service
Subscribers: N.A.
Programming (via satellite): FSN Digital Atlantic; FSN Digital Central; FSN Digital Pacific; Fuel TV; NBA TV; Tennis Channel.
Fee: $7.00 monthly.

Digital Pay Service 1
Pay Units: N.A.
Programming (via satellite): Cinemax (multiplexed); HBO (multiplexed); Showtime (multiplexed); Starz (multiplexed); The Movie Channel (multiplexed).
Fee: $12.00 monthly.

Video-On-Demand: No

Pay-Per-View
iN DEMAND (delivered digitally); NASCAR In Car (delivered digitally); MLB Extra Innings (delivered digitally); TeN Clips (delivered digitally); TeN Blue (delivered digitally).

Internet Service
Operational: Yes.
Broadband Service: EarthLink, Road Runner.
Fee: $99.95 installation; $44.95 monthly.

Telephone Service
Analog: Not Operational
Digital: Operational
Fee: $39.95 monthly

Miles of Plant: 180.0 (coaxial); 48.0 (fiber optic). Homes passed: 8,551. Total homes in franchised area: 9,101.
President: Keith Burkley. Vice President, Marketing & Sales: David Leopold. Vice President, Engineering: Scott Ducott. Vice President, Government & Public Affairs: Melinda Poore.
City fee: None.
Ownership: Time Warner Cable (MSO).

CAMPTON—Formerly served by Adelphia Communications. Now served by PLYMOUTH, NH [NH0055]. ICA: NH0036.

CARROLL—Formerly served by Adelphia Communications. Now served by LITTLETON, NH [NH0020]. ICA: NH0037.

CLAREMONT—Comcast Cable. Now served by BURLINGTON, VT [VT0001]. ICA: NH0011.

CONCORD—Comcast Cable. Now served by MANCHESTER, NH [NH0048]. ICA: NH0001.

CONWAY—Time Warner Cable, 118 Johnston Rd, Portland, ME 4102. Phone: 207-253-2200. Fax: 207-253-2405. Web Site: http://www.timewarnercable.com. Also serves Acton (town), Fryeburg & Lovell (town), ME; Albany, Bartlett, Brookfield (town), Center Ossipee, Eaton (town), Effingham, Freedom (town), Glen, Jackson, Jefferson (town), Kearsarge, Madison (town), Middleton (town), Moultonborough (town), North Conway, Ossipee (town), Sanbornville, Tamworth (town), Tuftonboro (town) & Wakefield (town), NH. ICA: NH0038.

TV Market Ranking: 75 (Effingham, Freedom (town), Fryeburg, Lovell (town)); Below 100 (Brookfield (town), Middleton (town), Sanbornville, Wakefield (town)); Outside TV Markets (Acton (town), Albany, Bartlett, Center Ossipee, CONWAY, Eaton (town), Glen, Jackson, Jefferson (town), Kearsarge, Madison (town), Moultonborough (town), North Conway, Ossipee (town), Tamworth (town), Tuftonboro (town)). Franchise award date: July 1, 1973. Franchise expiration date: N.A. Began: December 1, 1974.

Channel capacity: N.A. Channels available but not in use: N.A.

Basic Service

Subscribers: 14,000.

Programming (received off-air): WBZ-TV (CBS) Boston; WCBB (PBS) Augusta; WCSH (NBC) Portland; WENH-TV (PBS) Durham; WGME-TV (CBS) Portland; WHDH (NBC) Boston; WMTW (ABC) Poland Spring; WMUR-TV (ABC) Manchester; WPFO (FOX) Waterville; WPXT (CW) Portland.

Programming (via satellite): C-SPAN; C-SPAN 2; Home Shopping Network; ION Television; MyNetworkTV Inc.; New England Cable News; QVC.

Current originations: Leased Access; Government Access; Educational Access; Public Access.

Fee: $56.63 installation; $12.00 monthly.

Expanded Basic Service 1

Subscribers: 13,800.

Programming (via satellite): ABC Family Channel; AMC; Animal Planet; Arts & Entertainment; Bravo; Cartoon Network; CNBC; CNN; Comcast Sports Net New England; Comedy Central; Country Music TV; Discovery Channel; Disney Channel; E! Entertainment Television; ESPN; ESPN 2; Eternal Word TV Network; Food Network; Fox News Channel; FX; Great American Country; Hallmark Channel; HGTV; History Channel; Lifetime; MSNBC; MTV; New England Sports Network; Nickelodeon; Oxygen; Speed Channel; Spike TV; Syfy; TBS Superstation; The Learning Channel; Travel Channel; truTV; Turner Classic Movies; Turner Network TV; TV Guide Network; TV Land; USA Network; VH1; Weather Channel.

Fee: $17.85 monthly.

Digital Basic Service

Subscribers: 853.

Programming (received off-air): WCSH (NBC) Portland; WENH-TV (PBS) Durham; WHDH (NBC) Boston; WMTW (ABC) Poland Spring; WMUR-TV (ABC) Manchester; WPFO (FOX) Waterville.

Programming (via satellite): AmericanLife TV Network; Arts & Entertainment HD; BBC America; BBC America On Demand; Black Family Channel; Bloomberg Television; Canales N; Discovery Digital Networks; Discovery HD Theater; Do-It-Yourself; ESPN 2 HD; ESPN Classic Sports; ESPN HD; ESPNews; Exercise TV; Fox Movie Channel; Fox Soccer; Fuse; G4; GAS; Golf Channel; Great American Country; Great American Country On Demand; GSN; Halogen Network; HDNet; HDNet Movies; Howard TV; Lifetime Movie Network; LOGO; MTV Networks Digital Suite; Music Choice; National Geographic Channel; National Geographic Channel On Demand; Nick Jr.; Nick Too; NickToons TV; Outdoor Channel; Palladia; PBS Kids Sprout; SoapNet; Speed Channel; Speed On Demand; Style Network; The Word Network; Toon Disney; Trinity Broadcasting Network; Turner Network TV HD; Versus; WE tv.

Digital Expanded Basic Service

Subscribers: N.A.

Programming (via satellite): Bio; CBS College Sports Network; Cooking Channel; Fox Reality Channel; FSN Digital Atlantic; FSN Digital Central; FSN Digital Pacific; Fuel TV; History Channel International; Independent Film Channel; Sundance Channel; The Sportsman Channel.

Digital Pay Service 1

Pay Units: 1,371.

Programming (via satellite): ART America; Chinese Television Network; Cinemax (multiplexed); Cinemax HD; Cinemax On Demand; Encore (multiplexed); Filipino Channel; Flix (multiplexed); HBO (multiplexed); HBO HD; HBO On Demand; RAI International; Russian Television Network; Showtime (multiplexed); Showtime HD; Showtime On Demand; Starz (multiplexed); Starz HDTV; Starz On Demand; The Movie Channel (multiplexed); The Movie Channel On Demand; TV Asia; TV Japan; TV5, La Television International.

Fee: $12.95 monthly (each).

Video-On-Demand: Yes

Pay-Per-View

Addressable homes: 853.

Playboy TV (delivered digitally); Hot Choice (delivered digitally), Addressable: Yes; Sports PPV (delivered digitally); MLB Extra Innings (delivered digitally); NHL Center Ice (delivered digitally).

Internet Service

Operational: Yes.

Broadband Service: EarthLink, Road Runner.

Fee: $44.95 monthly.

Telephone Service

Digital: Operational

Fee: $39.95 monthly

Miles of Plant: 861.0 (coaxial); None (fiber optic). Homes passed: 22,000.

President: Keith Burkley. Vice President, Marketing & Sales: David Leopold. Vice President, Engineering: Scott Ducott. Vice President, Government & Public Affairs: Melinda Poore.

City fee: 3% of gross.

Ownership: Time Warner Cable (MSO).

CORNISH—Formerly served by Adelphia Communications. Now served by BURLINGTON, VT [VT0001]. Also serves CORNISH. ICA: NH0065.

DERRY—Comcast Cable. Now served by MANCHESTER, NH [NH0048]. ICA: NH0005.

FREEDOM (town)—Formerly served by Adelphia Communications. Now served by CONWAY, NH [NH0038]. ICA: NH0024.

GRANTHAM—Formerly served by Adelphia Communications. Now served by BURLINGTON, VT [VT0001]. ICA: NH0066.

GREENVILLE—Formerly served by Adelphia Communications. Now served by MANCHESTER, NH [NH0048]. ICA: NH0064.

HILL (town)—Formerly served by Adelphia Communications. Now served by BURLINGTON, VT [VT0001]. ICA: NH0042.

HINSDALE—Formerly served by Adelphia Communications. No longer in operation. ICA: NH0019.

KEENE—Time Warner Cable, 118 Johnston Rd, Portland, ME 4102. Phone: 207-253-2200. Fax: 207-253-2404. Web Site: http://www.timewarnercable.com/NewEngland. Also serves Marlborough, Richmond (town), Roxbury (town), Surry & Swanzey. ICA: NH0009.

TV Market Ranking: Outside TV Markets (KEENE, Marlborough, Richmond (town), Roxbury (town), Surry, Swanzey). Franchise award date: N.A. Franchise expiration date: N.A. Began: December 1, 1955.

Channel capacity: N.A. Channels available but not in use: 12.

Basic Service

Subscribers: 12,190.

Programming (received off-air): WBZ-TV (CBS) Boston; WCVB-TV (ABC) Boston; WEKW-TV (PBS) Keene; WFXT (FOX) Boston; WGBH-TV (PBS) Boston; WHDH (NBC) Boston; WMUR-TV (ABC) Manchester; WNNE (NBC) Hartford; WSBK-TV (IND) Boston; WVTA (PBS) Windsor; WZMY-TV (MNT) Derry; 30 FMs.

Programming (via satellite): C-SPAN; C-SPAN 2; ION Television; Telemundo; TV Guide Network; WLVI-TV (CW) Cambridge.

Current originations: Educational Access; Public Access.

Fee: $56.63 installation; $16.56 monthly.

Expanded Basic Service 1

Subscribers: N.A.

Programming (via satellite): ABC Family Channel; AMC; Animal Planet; Arts & Entertainment; BBC America; Bravo; CNBC; CNN; Comcast Sports Net New England; Country Music TV; Discovery Channel; Discovery Health Channel; Disney Channel; E! Entertainment Television; ESPN; Eternal Word TV Network; FitTV; Food Network; Fox News Channel; FX; Great American Country; Hallmark Channel; Headline News; Home Shopping Network; INSP; Jewelry Television; Lifetime; MSNBC; MTV; New England Sports Network; Nickelodeon; Oxygen; QVC; Shop at Home; ShopNBC; Spike TV; TBS Superstation; The Learning Channel; Travel Channel; truTV; Turner Network TV; TV Land; USA Network; VH1; WE tv; Weather Channel.

Fee: $46.29 monthly.

Expanded Basic Service 2

Subscribers: N.A.

Programming (via satellite): Cartoon Network; Comedy Central; ESPN 2; HGTV; History Channel; Syfy.

Fee: $6.95 monthly.

Digital Basic Service

Subscribers: N.A.

Programming (via satellite): AmericanLife TV Network; America's Store; BBC America; Bloomberg Television; Boomerang; CNN International; C-SPAN 3; Discovery Digital Networks; DMX Music; ESPN Classic Sports; ESPNews; FamilyNet; Fox Sports World; G4; GAS; Golf Channel; GSN; Halogen Network; Independent Film Channel; MTV2; Nick Jr.; NickToons TV; Outdoor Channel; Ovation; Speed Channel; Style Network; Toon Disney; Trinity Broadcasting Network; Turner Classic Movies; Versus; VH1 Classic.

Fee: $44.35 monthly.

Digital Pay Service 1

Pay Units: 5,400.

Programming (via satellite): Cinemax; HBO (multiplexed); Showtime (multiplexed); Starz (multiplexed); The Movie Channel (multiplexed).

Fee: $12.95 monthly (each).

Video-On-Demand: No

Pay-Per-View

MLB Extra Innings (delivered digitally); NASCAR In Car (delivered digitally); iN DEMAND, Addressable: Yes.

Internet Service

Operational: Yes.

Broadband Service: EarthLink, Road Runner.

Fee: $99.95 installation; $44.95 monthly.

Telephone Service

Analog: Not Operational

Digital: Operational

Fee: $39.95 monthly

Miles of Plant: 249.0 (coaxial); 47.0 (fiber optic). Homes passed: 12,300. Total homes in franchised area: 14,829.

President: Keith Burkley. Vice President, Engineering: Scott Ducott. Vice President, Marketing & Sales: David Leopold. Vice President, Government & Public Affairs: Melinda Poore.

Ownership: Time Warner Cable (MSO).

LEBANON—Comcast Cable. Now served by BURLINGTON, VT [VT0001]. ICA: NH0045.

LINCOLN—Formerly served by Adelphia Communications. Now served by PLYMOUTH, NH [NH0055]. ICA: NH0046.

LITTLETON—Time Warner Cable, 118 Johnston Rd, Portland, ME 4102. Phones: 207-253-2385; 207-253-2200. Fax: 207-253-2404. Web Site: http://www.timewarnercable.com. Also serves Bath (village), Bethlehem (town), Carroll, Franconia, Lisbon, Monroe (town) & Sugar Hill (town). ICA: NH0020.

TV Market Ranking: Outside TV Markets (Bath (village), Bethlehem (town), Carroll, Franconia, Lisbon, LITTLETON, Monroe (town), Sugar Hill (town)). Franchise award date: March 1, 1964. Franchise expiration date: N.A. Began: October 7, 1964.

Channel capacity: N.A. Channels available but not in use: N.A.

Basic Service

Subscribers: 4,000.

Programming (received off-air): WCAX-TV (CBS) Burlington; WFFF-TV (CW, FOX) Burlington; WGME-TV (CBS) Portland; WLED-TV (PBS) Littleton; WMUR-TV (ABC) Manchester; WNNE (NBC) Hartford; WVNY (ABC) Burlington; allband FM.

Programming (via satellite): C-SPAN; C-SPAN 2; Home Shopping Network; ION Television; MyNetworkTV Inc.; New England Cable News; QVC; TV Guide Network; WETK (PBS) Burlington.

Current originations: Educational Access.

Fee: $56.63 installation; $12.00 monthly.

Expanded Basic Service 1

Subscribers: 3,549.

Programming (via satellite): ABC Family Channel; AMC; Animal Planet; Arts & Entertainment; Bravo; Cartoon Network; CNBC; CNN; Comcast Sports Net New England; Comedy Central; Country Music TV; Discovery Channel; Disney Channel; E! Entertainment Television; ESPN; ESPN 2; Eternal Word TV Network; Food Network; Fox News Channel; FX; Great American Country; Hallmark Channel; HGTV; History Channel; Lifetime; MSNBC; MTV; New England Sports Network; Nickelodeon; Oxygen; Speed Channel; Spike TV; Syfy; TBS Superstation; The Learning Channel; Travel Channel; truTV; Turner Classic Movies; Turner Network TV; TV Land; USA Network; VH1; Weather Channel.

Fee: $18.69 monthly.

Digital Basic Service
Subscribers: N.A.
Programming (received off-air): WCAX-TV (CBS) Burlington; WENH-TV (PBS) Durham; WMUR-TV (ABC) Manchester.
Programming (via satellite): AmericanLife TV Network; BBC America; BBC America On Demand; Black Family Channel; Bloomberg Television; Canales N; Discovery Digital Networks; Discovery HD Theater; DMX Music; ESPN 2 HD; ESPN Classic Sports; ESPN HD; ESPNews; Exercise TV; Fox Movie Channel; Fox Soccer; Fuse; G4; Golf Channel; Great American Country; Great American Country On Demand; GSN; Halogen Network; HDNet; HDNet Movies; Howard TV; Lifetime Movie Network; LOGO; MTV Networks Digital Suite; National Geographic Channel On Demand; Outdoor Channel; SoapNet; Speed Channel; Speed On Demand; The Word Network; Toon Disney; Trinity Broadcasting Network; Turner Network TV HD; Versus; WE tv; WETK (PBS) Burlington.

Digital Expanded Basic Service
Subscribers: N.A.
Programming (via satellite): Bio; CBS College Sports Network; Cooking Channel; Fox Reality Channel; FSN Digital Atlantic; FSN Digital Central; FSN Digital Pacific; Fuel TV; GAS; History Channel International; Independent Film Channel; National Geographic Channel; Nick Jr.; Nick Too; NickToons TV; Style Network; Sundance Channel; The Sportsman Channel.

Digital Pay Service 1
Pay Units: 352.
Programming (via satellite): ART America; CCTV-4; Cinemax (multiplexed); Cinemax HD; Cinemax On Demand; Encore (multiplexed); Filipino Channel; Flix (multiplexed); HBO (multiplexed); HBO HD; HBO On Demand; RAI USA; Russian Television Network; Showtime (multiplexed); Showtime HD; Showtime On Demand; Starz (multiplexed); Starz HDTV; Starz On Demand; The Movie Channel (multiplexed); The Movie Channel On Demand; TV Asia; TV Japan; TV5, La Television International.
Fee: $12.95 monthly (each).

Video-On-Demand: Yes

Pay-Per-View
Hot Choice (delivered digitally), Addressable: Yes; Playboy TV (delivered digitally); Sports PPV (delivered digitally); NHL Center Ice (delivered digitally); MLB Extra Innings (delivered digitally).

Internet Service
Operational: Yes. Began: January 1, 2000.
Broadband Service: EarthLink, Road Runner.
Fee: $44.95 monthly.

Telephone Service
Digital: Operational
Fee: $44.95 monthly
Miles of Plant: 203.0 (coaxial); None (fiber optic). Homes passed: 5,870. Total homes in franchised area: 5,870.
President: Keith Burkley. Vice President, Marketing & Sales: David Leopold. Vice President, Engineering: Scott Ducott. Vice President, Government & Public Affairs: Melinda Poore.
City fee: 3% of gross.
Ownership: Time Warner Cable (MSO).

LONDONDERRY—Comcast Cable. Now served by MANCHESTER, NH [NH0048]. ICA: NH0008.

MADISON (town)—Formerly served by Adelphia Communications. Now served by CONWAY, NH [NH0038]. ICA: NH0047.

MANCHESTER—Comcast Cable, 676 Island Pond Rd, Manchester, NH 3109. Phone: 603-695-1400. Fax: 603-628-3365. Web Site: http://www.comcast.com. Also serves Allenstown, Alstead, Alstead (town), Alstead Center, Amherst, Antrim, Atkinson, Auburn, Bedford, Bennington, Boscawen, Bow, Brentwood, Candia, Canterbury, Chester, Chester (town), Chesterfield, Chichester (town), Concord, Danville, Deering, Derry, Drewsville, East Kingston, Epping, Exeter, Francestown, Fremont, Fremont (town), Goffstown, Greenland, Greenville, Hampstead, Hampton, Hampton Falls, Hancock, Henniker, Hillsborough, Hillsborough County, Hooksett, Hopkinton, Hudson, Kensington, Kingston, Langdon, Litchfield, Londonderry, Loudon (town), Merrimack, Milford, Mount Vernon, Nashua, New Boston, New Boston (town), New Castle, New Ipswich, Newfields, Newington (town), Newmarket, Newton, North Hampton, North Walpole, Nottingham, Nottingham (town), Pelham, Pembroke, Peterborough, Plaistow, Portsmouth, Raymond, Rye, Salem (town), Sandown, Seabrook, South Charlestown, Stratham, Temple, Walpole, Weare, Webster, West Chesterfield, Wilton & Windham. ICA: NH0048.
TV Market Ranking: 6 (Amherst, Atkinson, Auburn, Bedford, Brentwood, Candia, Chester, Chester (town), Danville, Derry, East Kingston, Epping, Exeter, Fremont, Fremont (town), Goffstown, Greenland, Greenville, Hampstead, Hampton, Hampton Falls, Hillsborough County, Hooksett, Hudson, Kensington, Kingston, Litchfield, Londonderry, MANCHESTER, Merrimack, Milford, Mount Vernon, Nashua, New Boston, New Boston (town), New Castle, New Ipswich, Newfields, Newington (town), Newmarket, Newton, North Hampton, Nottingham, Nottingham (town), Pelham, Plaistow, Portsmouth, Raymond, Rye, Salem (town), Sandown, Seabrook, Stratham, Wilton, Windham); Below 100 (Allenstown, Alstead, Alstead (town), Alstead Center, Antrim, Bennington, Boscawen, Bow, Canterbury, Chesterfield, Chichester (town), Concord, Deering, Drewsville, Francestown, Hancock, Henniker, Hillsborough, Hopkinton, Langdon, Loudon (town), Pembroke, Peterborough, South Charlestown, Temple, Weare, Webster, West Chesterfield); Outside TV Markets (North Walpole, Walpole). Franchise award date: N.A. Franchise expiration date: N.A. Began: January 1, 1966.
Channel capacity: N.A. Channels available but not in use: N.A.

Basic Service
Subscribers: 700,000 Includes Brunsick ME, Westford MA, Bennington VT, & Burlington VT.
Programming (received off-air): WBZ-TV (CBS) Boston; WCVB-TV (ABC) Boston; WENH-TV (PBS) Durham; WFXT (FOX) Boston; WGBH-TV (PBS) Boston; WHDH (NBC) Boston; WLVI-TV (CW) Cambridge; WMFP (IND) Lawrence; WMUR-TV (ABC) Manchester; WNEU (TMO) Merrimack; WSBK-TV (IND) Boston; WUNI (UNV) Worcester; WUTF-DT (TEL) Marlborough; WWDP (IND) Norwell; WYDN (ETV) Worcester; WZMY-TV (MNT) Derry; allband FM.
Programming (via satellite): Disney Channel; TBS Superstation; The Comcast Network; truTV.
Fee: $45.50 installation; $14.38 monthly.

Expanded Basic Service 1
Subscribers: 44,403.
Programming (via satellite): ABC Family Channel; AMC; Animal Planet; Arts & Entertainment; Bravo; Cartoon Network; CNBC; CNN; Comedy Central; C-SPAN; C-SPAN 2; Discovery Channel; E! Entertainment Television; ESPN; ESPN 2; ESPN Classic Sports; Eternal Word TV Network; Food Network; Fox News Channel; FX; GSN; Halogen Network; Headline News; HGTV; History Channel; Home Shopping Network; Lifetime; MSNBC; MTV; New England Sports Network; Nickelodeon; Product Information Network; QVC; Spike TV; Syfy; The Learning Channel; Travel Channel; Turner Network TV; TV Land; USA Network; Versus; VH1; WE tv; Weather Channel.
Fee: $37.20 monthly.

Digital Basic Service
Subscribers: N.A.
Programming (via satellite): BBC America; Bio; Bloomberg Television; Celtic Vision; Cooking Channel; Discovery Digital Networks; Do-It-Yourself; ESPNews; Eternal Word TV Network; FitTV; Fox Movie Channel; Fox Sports World; Fuse; G4; GAS; Great American Country; Halogen Network; History Channel International; Independent Film Channel; International Television (ITV); Lifetime Movie Network; Lime; MTV Networks Digital Suite; Music Choice; National Geographic Channel; Nick Jr.; NickToons TV; Outdoor Channel; Oxygen; Speed Channel; Style Network; The Word Network; Toon Disney; Trinity Broadcasting Network; Turner Classic Movies; Weatherscan.
Fee: $15.45 monthly.

Digital Pay Service 1
Pay Units: N.A.
Programming (via satellite): Canales N; Cinemax (multiplexed); Encore; Flix; HBO (multiplexed); Russian Television Network; Showtime (multiplexed); Starz; Sundance Channel; The Movie Channel (multiplexed); Zee TV USA; Zhong Tian Channel.
Fee: $15.50 monthly (each).

Video-On-Demand: Yes

Pay-Per-View
Hot Choice (delivered digitally); Playboy TV (delivered digitally); iN DEMAND (delivered digitally).

Internet Service
Operational: Yes.
Broadband Service: Comcast High Speed Internet.
Fee: $42.95 monthly; $29.95 modem lease; $200.00 modem purchase.

Telephone Service
Digital: Operational
Fee: $44.95 monthly
Miles of Plant: 5,937.0 (coaxial); 402.0 (fiber optic). Homes passed: 396,769.
Area Vice President: Mary McLaughlin. Regional Vice President: Steve Hackley. Vice President, Technical Operations: Raymond Kowalinski. Sales & Marketing Director: Mark Adamy. Public Relations Director: Marc Goodman.
City fee: 2% of gross.
Ownership: Comcast Cable Communications Inc. (MSO).

MERRIMACK—Formerly served by Adelphia Communications. Now served by MANCHESTER, NH [NH0048]. ICA: NH0049.

MILAN (town)—Argent Communications, 22 Central Sq, Bristol, NH 3222. Phone: 888-815-0610. Fax: 206-202-1415. Web Site: http://www.argentcommunications.com. ICA: NH0029.
TV Market Ranking: Outside TV Markets (MILAN (TOWN)). Franchise award date: June 26, 1989. Franchise expiration date: N.A. Began: November 5, 1990.
Channel capacity: 42 (not 2-way capable). Channels available but not in use: 10.

Basic Service
Subscribers: 268.
Programming (received off-air): W27BL Berlin; WCBB (PBS) Augusta; WCSH (NBC) Portland; WENH-TV (PBS) Durham; WGME-TV (CBS) Portland; WMTW (ABC) Poland Spring; WMUR-TV (ABC) Manchester; WSBK-TV (IND) Boston.
Programming (via satellite): ABC Family Channel; Animal Planet; Arts & Entertainment; Country Music TV; C-SPAN; Home Shopping Network; ION Television; QVC; TBS Superstation; Travel Channel.
Current originations: Government Access; Educational Access; Public Access.
Fee: $56.63 installation; $28.77 monthly; $.89 converter.

Expanded Basic Service 1
Subscribers: N.A.
Programming (via satellite): CNN; Comcast Sports Net New England; Discovery Channel; Disney Channel; ESPN; ESPN 2; Headline News; Lifetime; MTV; New England Sports Network; Nickelodeon; Turner Network TV; USA Network; Weather Channel.

Digital Basic Service
Subscribers: N.A.
Programming (via satellite): BBC America; Bloomberg Television; Bravo; Discovery Digital Networks; ESPN Classic Sports; FitTV; Fox Movie Channel; Fox Sports World; G4; Golf Channel; GSN; Halogen Network; Independent Film Channel; National Geographic Channel; Outdoor Channel; Speed Channel; Trinity Broadcasting Network; Versus; VH1 Country; WE tv.

Digital Expanded Basic Service
Subscribers: N.A.
Programming (via satellite): Music Choice; Nick Jr.

Digital Pay Service 1
Pay Units: N.A.
Programming (via satellite): Encore (multiplexed); HBO (multiplexed); Showtime (multiplexed); Starz (multiplexed); The Movie Channel (multiplexed).
Fee: $12.95 monthly (each).

Video-On-Demand: No

Pay-Per-View
Fresh (delivered digitally); Playboy TV (delivered digitally).

Internet Service
Operational: No.
Telephone Service
None
Miles of Plant: 43.0 (coaxial); None (fiber optic). Additional miles planned: 27.0 (coaxial). Homes passed: 648.
Managers: Andrew Bauer.; Shawn Bauer.
Ownership: Argent Communications LLC (MSO).

MONROE (town)—Formerly served by Adelphia Communications. Now served by LITTLETON, NH [NH0020]. ICA: NH0050.

MOULTONBOROUGH (town)—Formerly served by Adelphia Communications. Now served by CONWAY, NH [NH0038]. ICA: NH0015.

NASHUA—Comcast Cable. Now served by MANCHESTER, NH [NH0048]. ICA: NH0002.

NELSON (town)—Argent Communications, 22 Central Sq, Bristol, NH 3222. Phone: 888-815-0610. Fax: 206-202-1415. Web Site: http://www.argentcommunications.com. Also serves Harrisville (town) & Sullivan (town). ICA: NH0032.
TV Market Ranking: Below 100 (Harrisville (town), NELSON (TOWN), Sullivan (town)). Franchise award date: February 22, 1990. Franchise expiration date: N.A. Began: August 22, 1990.
Channel capacity: 36 (not 2-way capable). Channels available but not in use: 9.
Basic Service
Subscribers: 290.
Programming (received off-air): WBPX-TV (ION) Boston; WBZ-TV (CBS) Boston; WCVB-TV (ABC) Boston; WENH-TV (PBS) Durham; WFXT (FOX) Boston; WGBH-TV (PBS) Boston; WHDH (NBC) Boston; WLVI-TV (CW) Cambridge; WMUR-TV (ABC) Manchester; WNNE (NBC) Hartford; WSBK-TV (IND) Boston; WZMY-TV (MNT) Derry.
Programming (via satellite): ABC Family Channel; Animal Planet; Arts & Entertainment; Cartoon Network; CNBC; CNN; C-SPAN; Discovery Channel; Disney Channel; ESPN; ESPN 2; Headline News; History Channel; Lifetime; MTV; Nickelodeon; QVC; ShopNBC; Spike TV; Syfy; TBS Superstation; The Learning Channel; Travel Channel; Trinity Broadcasting Network; Turner Classic Movies; Turner Network TV; USA Network; Weather Channel.
Fee: $50.00 installation; $34.95 monthly; $25.00 additional installation.
Pay Service 1
Pay Units: 15.
Programming (via satellite): Cinemax; HBO; Showtime; The Movie Channel.
Fee: $15.00 installation; $11.95 monthly (Cinemax), $12.95 monthly (HBO), $14.95 monthly (Showtime & TMC).
Video-On-Demand: No
Internet Service
Operational: Yes.
Fee: $21.00 monthly.
Telephone Service
None
Miles of Plant: 5.0 (coaxial); None (fiber optic).
Managers: Andrew Bauer.; Shawn Bauer.
City fee: 3% of basic gross.
Ownership: Argent Communications LLC (MSO).

NEW BOSTON—Formerly served by Adelphia Communications. Now served by MANCHESTER, NH [NH0048]. ICA: NH0051.

NEW LONDON—Formerly served by Adelphia Communications. Now served by BURLINGTON, VT [VT0001]. ICA: NH0023.

NEWPORT—Formerly served by Adelphia Communications. Now served by BURLINGTON, VT [VT0001]. ICA: NH0017.

PETERBOROUGH—Formerly served by Adelphia Communications. Now served by MANCHESTER, NH [NH0048]. ICA: NH0013.

PLAINFIELD (town)—Formerly served by Adelphia Communications. Now served by BURLINGTON, VT [VT0001]. ICA: NH0054.

PLYMOUTH—Time Warner Cable, 118 Johnston Rd, Portland, ME 4102. Phone: 207-253-2200. Fax: 207-253-2405. Web Site: http://www.timewarnercable.com/NewEngland. Also serves Ashland, Campton, Dorchester (town), Groton (town), Holderness (portions), Lincoln, North Woodstock, Rumney (town), Thornton, Warren (town), Wentworth (town) & Woodstock. ICA: NH0055.
TV Market Ranking: Below 100 (Ashland, Dorchester (town), Groton (town), PLYMOUTH (VILLAGE), Rumney (town), Warren (town), Wentworth (town)); Outside TV Markets (Campton, Holderness (portions), Lincoln, North Woodstock, Thornton, Woodstock). Franchise award date: January 1, 1965. Franchise expiration date: N.A. Began: June 1, 1967.
Channel capacity: N.A. Channels available but not in use: N.A.
Basic Service
Subscribers: 10,000.
Programming (received off-air): WCAX-TV (CBS) Burlington; WENH-TV (PBS) Durham; WMUR-TV (ABC) Manchester; WNNE (NBC) Hartford; WVNY (ABC) Burlington; WVTA (PBS) Windsor; allband FM.
Programming (via microwave): WBZ-TV (CBS) Boston; WCVB-TV (ABC) Boston; WFXT (FOX) Boston; WHDH (NBC) Boston; WSBK-TV (IND) Boston.
Programming (via satellite): C-SPAN 2; Home Shopping Network; ION Television; New England Cable News; QVC; TBS Superstation.
Current originations: Government Access; Educational Access; Leased Access; Public Access.
Fee: $56.63 installation; $12.00 monthly; $2.90 converter.
Expanded Basic Service 1
Subscribers: 9,266.
Programming (via satellite): ABC Family Channel; AMC; Animal Planet; Arts & Entertainment; Bravo; Cartoon Network; CNBC; CNN; Comcast Sports Net New England; Comedy Central; Country Music TV; Discovery Channel; Disney Channel; E! Entertainment Television; ESPN; ESPN 2; Eternal Word TV Network; Food Network; Fox News Channel; FX; Great American Country; Hallmark Channel; Headline News; HGTV; History Channel; Lifetime; MSNBC; MTV; New England Sports Network; Nickelodeon; Oxygen; Spike TV; Syfy; The Learning Channel; Travel Channel; truTV; Turner Classic Movies; Turner Network TV; TV Guide Network; TV Land; USA Network; VH1; Weather Channel.
Fee: $19.61 monthly.
Digital Basic Service
Subscribers: 485.
Programming (via satellite): BBC America; Black Family Channel; Bloomberg Television; Discovery Digital Networks; ESPN Classic Sports; ESPNews; FitTV; Fox Sports World; Fuse; G4; Golf Channel; Great American Country; GSN; Halogen Network; Outdoor Channel; Trinity Broadcasting Network; WE tv.
Digital Expanded Basic Service
Subscribers: N.A.
Programming (via satellite): Bio; Canales N; Do-It-Yourself; Fox Sports Net; FSN Digital Atlantic; FSN Digital Central; FSN Digital Pacific; GAS; History Channel International; Independent Film Channel; MTV Networks Digital Suite; Music Choice; National Geographic Channel; Nick Jr.; Nick Too; NickToons TV; SoapNet; Speed Channel; Style Network; Sundance Channel; Toon Disney; Versus.
Digital Pay Service 1
Pay Units: 1,561.
Programming (via satellite): ART America; Asian Television Network; CCTV-4; Cinemax; Encore (multiplexed); Filipino Channel; Flix; HBO (multiplexed); RAI International; Russian Television Network; Showtime (multiplexed); Starz (multiplexed); The Movie Channel (multiplexed); TV Japan; TV5, La Television International; Zee TV USA.
Fee: $12.95 monthly (each).
Video-On-Demand: Yes
Pay-Per-View
Addressable homes: 485.
Hot Choice (delivered digitally), Addressable: Yes; Playboy TV (delivered digitally); Fresh (delivered digitally).
Internet Service
Operational: Yes.
Broadband Service: EarthLink, Road Runner.
Fee: $44.95 monthly.
Telephone Service
Digital: Operational
Fee: $39.95 monthly
Miles of Plant: 254.0 (coaxial); None (fiber optic). Homes passed: 12,000.
President: Keith Burkley. Vice President, Marketing & Sales: David Leopold. Vice President, Engineering: Scott Ducott. Vice President, Government & Public Affairs: Melinda Poore.
City fee: 3% of gross.
Ownership: Time Warner Cable (MSO).

PORTSMOUTH—Comcast Cable. Now served by MANCHESTER, NH [NH0048]. ICA: NH0003.

ROCHESTER—MetroCast Cablevision, 21 Jarvis Ave, Rochester, NH 3868. Phone: 603-332-8629. Fax: 603-335-4106. Web Site: http://www.metrocastcommunications.com. Also serves Lebanon (portions), ME; Barrington, East Rochester, Farmington, Gonic, Milton, Milton Mills & Strafford (town-portions), NH. ICA: NH0007.
TV Market Ranking: Below 100 (Barrington, East Rochester, Farmington, Gonic, ROCHESTER, Strafford (town-portions)); Outside TV Markets (Lebanon (portions), Milton). Franchise award date: April 1, 1979. Franchise expiration date: N.A. Began: November 1, 1980.
Channel capacity: 78 (operating 2-way). Channels available but not in use: None.
Basic Service
Subscribers: 19,000.
Programming (received off-air): WBZ-TV (CBS) Boston; WCSH (NBC) Portland; WCVB-TV (ABC) Boston; WENH-TV (PBS) Durham; WFXT (FOX) Boston; WGME-TV (CBS) Portland; WHDH (NBC) Boston; WLVI-TV (CW) Cambridge; WMEA-TV (PBS) Biddeford; WMFP (IND) Lawrence; WMTW (ABC) Poland Spring; WMUR-TV (ABC) Manchester; WNEU (TMO) Merrimack; WPXG-TV (ION) Concord; WSBK-TV (IND) Boston; WZMY-TV (MNT) Derry; allband FM.
Programming (via satellite): C-SPAN; Home Shopping Network; QVC.
Current originations: Leased Access; Government Access; Educational Access; Public Access.
Fee: $30.00 installation; $15.00 monthly.
Expanded Basic Service 1
Subscribers: 17,500.
Programming (via microwave): New England Cable News.
Programming (via satellite): ABC Family Channel; AMC; Animal Planet; Arts & Entertainment; Cartoon Network; CNBC; CNN; Comcast Sports Net New England; Comedy Central; Discovery Channel; Disney Channel; E! Entertainment Television; Encore; ESPN; ESPN 2; Eternal Word TV Network; Fox News Channel; FX; Great American Country; Headline News; HGTV; History Channel; Lifetime; MSNBC; MTV; New England Sports Network; Nickelodeon; Spike TV; Syfy; TBS Superstation; The Learning Channel; Toon Disney; Trinity Broadcasting Network; truTV; Turner Network TV; TV Guide Network; USA Network; Versus; VH1; Weather Channel.
Fee: $28.95 monthly.
Digital Basic Service
Subscribers: 7,000.
Programming (via satellite): BBC America; Bio; Bloomberg Television; Boomerang; Discovery Digital Networks; Do-It-Yourself; ESPN Classic Sports; FamilyNet; Fox Movie Channel; Fox Sports World; G4; GSN; Halogen Network; History Channel International; Independent Film Channel; Lifetime Movie Network; Music Choice; National Geographic Channel; Nick Jr.; Outdoor Channel; Ovation; Speed Channel; Style Network; truTV; Turner Classic Movies; Versus; WE tv.
Fee: $6.95 monthly; $4.00 converter.
Digital Pay Service 1
Pay Units: 6,300.
Programming (via satellite): Cinemax (multiplexed); HBO (multiplexed); Showtime (multiplexed); Starz (multiplexed); The Movie Channel (multiplexed).
Fee: $12.95 monthly (each).
Video-On-Demand: Yes
Pay-Per-View
Addressable homes: 7,948.
Hot Choice (delivered digitally), Addressable: Yes; iN DEMAND; iN DEMAND (delivered digitally); Playboy TV; Playboy TV (delivered digitally); Fresh (delivered digitally).
Internet Service
Operational: Yes.
Subscribers: 7,000.
Broadband Service: Great Works Internet.
Fee: $99.00 installation; $41.95 monthly; $5.00 modem lease; $149.50 modem purchase.
Telephone Service
Digital: Planned
Miles of Plant: 556.0 (coaxial); 178.0 (fiber optic). Homes passed: 26,611.

Vice President, Operations & General Manager: Steve Murdough. Vice President & Customer Relations Manager: Shirley Clark. Program Director: Linda Stuchell.
City fee: 3% of gross.
Ownership: Harron Communications LP (MSO).

SPOFFORD—Argent Communications, 22 Central Sq, Bristol, NH 3222. Phone: 888-815-0610. Fax: 206-202-1415. Web Site: http://www.argentcommunications.com. Also serves Chesterfield, East Westmoreland, West Chesterfield & Westmoreland. ICA: NH0057.
TV Market Ranking: Outside TV Markets (Chesterfield, East Westmoreland, SPOFFORD, West Chesterfield, Westmoreland). Franchise award date: October 1, 1971. Franchise expiration date: N.A. Began: November 1, 1971.
Channel capacity: 33 (operating 2-way). Channels available but not in use: 2.
Basic Service
Subscribers: 685.
Programming (received off-air): WBZ-TV (CBS) Boston; WCVB-TV (ABC) Boston; WENH-TV (PBS) Durham; WFXT (FOX) Boston; WHDH (NBC) Boston; WLVI-TV (CW) Cambridge; WMUR-TV (ABC) Manchester; WNNE (NBC) Hartford; WSBK-TV (IND) Boston; allband FM.
Programming (via satellite): ABC Family Channel; Animal Planet; Arts & Entertainment; Cartoon Network; CNBC; CNN; Comcast SportsNet Philly; C-SPAN; Discovery Channel; Disney Channel; ESPN; ESPN 2; Headline News; History Channel; Home Shopping Network; ION Television; Lifetime; MTV; Nickelodeon; ShopNBC; Spike TV; Syfy; TBS Superstation; The Learning Channel; Travel Channel; Trinity Broadcasting Network; Turner Classic Movies; Turner Network TV; USA Network; Weather Channel.
Current originations: Public Access.
Fee: $37.50 installation; $37.85 monthly; $2.50 converter.
Pay Service 1
Pay Units: 87.
Programming (via satellite): Showtime; The Movie Channel.
Pay Service 2
Pay Units: 234.
Programming (via satellite): HBO.
Fee: $17.50 installation; $10.00 monthly.
Video-On-Demand: No
Internet Service
Operational: Yes. Began: January 1, 2003.
Subscribers: 100.
Fee: $21.00 monthly.
Telephone Service
None
Miles of Plant: 32.0 (coaxial); None (fiber optic). Additional miles planned: 2.0 (coaxial).
Managers: Andrew Bauer.; Shawn Bauer.
City fee: $200 annually.
Ownership: Argent Communications LLC (MSO).

STODDARD—Argent Communications, 22 Central Sq, Bristol, NH 3222. Phone: 888-815-0610. Fax: 206-202-1415. Web Site: http://www.argentcommunications.com. Also serves Marlow. ICA: NH0067.
TV Market Ranking: Below 100 (Marlow, STODDARD). Franchise award date: N.A. Franchise expiration date: N.A. Began: N.A.
Channel capacity: N.A. Channels available but not in use: N.A.
Basic Service
Subscribers: 115.
Programming (received off-air): WBPX-TV (ION) Boston; WBZ-TV (CBS) Boston; WCVB-TV (ABC) Boston; WENH-TV (PBS) Durham; WFXT (FOX) Boston; WGBH-TV (PBS) Boston; WHDH (NBC) Boston; WLVI-TV (CW) Cambridge; WMUR-TV (ABC) Manchester; WSBK-TV (IND) Boston; WZMY-TV (MNT) Derry.
Programming (via satellite): ABC Family Channel; Animal Planet; Arts & Entertainment; Cartoon Network; CNBC; CNN; C-SPAN; Discovery Channel; Disney Channel; ESPN; ESPN 2; Headline News; History Channel; Lifetime; MTV; Nickelodeon; ShopNBC; Spike TV; Syfy; TBS Superstation; The Learning Channel; Travel Channel; Trinity Broadcasting Network; Turner Classic Movies; Turner Network TV; USA Network; Weather Channel.
Fee: $50.00 installation; $35.95 monthly; $25.00 additional installation.
Pay Service 1
Pay Units: N.A.
Programming (via satellite): Cinemax; HBO; Showtime; The Movie Channel.
Fee: $15.00 installation; $11.95 monthly (Cinemax), $12.95 monthly (HBO), $14.95 monthly (Showtime & TMC).
Video-On-Demand: No
Internet Service
Operational: No.
Telephone Service
None
Managers: Andrew Bauer.; Shawn Bauer.
Ownership: Argent Communications LLC (MSO).

STRATFORD (town)—Argent Communications, 22 Central Sq, Bristol, NH 3222. Phone: 888-815-0610. Fax: 206-202-1415. Web Site: http://www.argentcommunications.com. Also serves Groveton. ICA: NH0058.
TV Market Ranking: Outside TV Markets (Groveton, STRATFORD (TOWN)). Franchise award date: June 8, 1989. Franchise expiration date: N.A. Began: January 1, 1990.
Channel capacity: 42 (not 2-way capable). Channels available but not in use: 10.
Basic Service
Subscribers: 150.
Programming (received off-air): WCAX-TV (CBS) Burlington; WPFO (FOX) Waterville; WVTB (PBS) St. Johnsbury.
Programming (via satellite): ABC Family Channel; AMC; Arts & Entertainment; CNN; Comcast Sports Net New England; C-SPAN; Discovery Channel; Disney Channel; ESPN; ESPN 2; Fox News Channel; HGTV; History Channel; Home Shopping Network; ION Television; Lifetime; MSNBC; MTV; MyNetworkTV Inc.; New England Sports Network; Nickelodeon; Spike TV; Style Network; Syfy; TBS Superstation; The Learning Channel; Turner Network TV; USA Network; VH1; Weather Channel; WMUR-TV (ABC) Manchester; WNBC (NBC) New York.
Fee: $56.63 installation; $27.07 monthly.
Digital Basic Service
Subscribers: N.A.
Programming (via satellite): BBC America; Bio; Black Family Channel; Bloomberg Television; Bravo; Country Music TV; Discovery Digital Networks; DMX Music; ESPN Classic Sports; ESPNews; Fox College Sports Atlantic; Fox College Sports Central; Fox College Sports Pacific; Fox Movie Channel; Fox Soccer; Fuse; G4; GAS; Golf Channel; Great American Country; Halogen Network; History Channel International; Independent Film Channel; Lifetime Movie Network; MTV Networks Digital Suite; National Geographic Channel; Nick Jr.; NickToons TV; Outdoor Channel; Speed Channel; Style Network; The Word Network; Toon Disney; Trinity Broadcasting Network; Versus; WE tv.
Digital Pay Service 1
Pay Units: N.A.
Programming (via satellite): Cinemax (multiplexed); Encore (multiplexed); HBO (multiplexed); Showtime (multiplexed); Starz (multiplexed); The Movie Channel (multiplexed).
Fee: $12.95 monthly (each).
Video-On-Demand: No
Pay-Per-View
Hits Movies & Events (delivered digitally); Fresh (delivered digitally); Playboy TV (delivered digitally).
Internet Service
Operational: No.
Telephone Service
None
Miles of Plant: 20.0 (coaxial); None (fiber optic). Homes passed: 342.
Managers: Andrew Bauer.; Shawn Bauer.
Ownership: Argent Communications LLC (MSO).

SUGAR HILL (town)—Formerly served by Adelphia Communications. Now served by LITTLETON, NH [NH0020]. ICA: NH0059.

TROY—Argent Communications, 22 Central Sq, Bristol, NH 3222. Phone: 888-815-0610. Fax: 206-202-1415. Web Site: http://www.argentcommunications.com. Also serves Fitzwilliam & Rindge. ICA: NH0060.
TV Market Ranking: Below 100 (Fitzwilliam, Rindge, TROY). Franchise award date: July 21, 1984. Franchise expiration date: N.A. Began: February 28, 1985.
Channel capacity: N.A. Channels available but not in use: N.A.
Basic Service
Subscribers: 1,025.
Programming (received off-air): WBZ-TV (CBS) Boston; WCVB-TV (ABC) Boston; WENH-TV (PBS) Durham; WFXT (FOX) Boston; WGBH-TV (PBS) Boston; WHDH (NBC) Boston; WLVI-TV (CW) Cambridge; WMUR-TV (ABC) Manchester; WSBK-TV (IND) Boston; allband FM.
Programming (via satellite): ABC Family Channel; Animal Planet; Arts & Entertainment; Cartoon Network; CNBC; CNN; Comcast Sports Net New England; C-SPAN; C-SPAN 2; C-SPAN 3; Discovery Channel; Disney Channel; ESPN; ESPN 2; Fox News Channel; FX; G4; Great American Country; Headline News; History Channel; Home Shopping Network; ION Television; Lifetime; MTV; National Geographic Channel; New England Sports Network; Nickelodeon; ShopNBC; Spike TV; Syfy; TBS Superstation; The Learning Channel; Travel Channel; Trinity Broadcasting Network; Turner Classic Movies; Turner Network TV; TV Guide Network; TV Land; USA Network; Weather Channel.
Current originations: Public Access.
Fee: $50.00 installation; $34.90 monthly.
Digital Basic Service
Subscribers: N.A.
Programming (via satellite): Bio; Bloomberg Television; Bravo; CNN International; Discovery Health Channel; Discovery Kids Channel; Discovery Military Channel; Discovery Planet Green; ESPN Classic Sports; ESPNews; FitTV; Fox Movie Channel; Fox Soccer; Golf Channel; GSN; Halogen Network; HGTV; History Channel; ID Investigation Discovery; Independent Film Channel; Lifetime Movie Network; Nick Jr.; Outdoor Channel; Ovation; Science Channel; Speed Channel; Style Network; Sundance Channel; Trio; Turner Classic Movies; WE tv.
Fee: $18.95 monthly.
Pay Service 1
Pay Units: N.A.
Programming (via satellite): HBO.
Fee: $12.95 monthly.
Digital Pay Service 1
Pay Units: N.A.
Programming (via satellite): Cinemax (multiplexed); Encore (multiplexed); HBO (multiplexed); Showtime (multiplexed); Starz (multiplexed); The Movie Channel (multiplexed).
Fee: $9.95 monthly (Starz/Encore), $11.95 monthly (Cinemax), $12.95 monthly (HBO), $14.95 monthly (Showtime/TMC),.
Video-On-Demand: No
Pay-Per-View
Movies (delivered digitally); Special events (delivered digitally); Pleasure (delivered digitally); Fresh (delivered digitally); Shorteez (delivered digitally); Playboy TV (delivered digitally).
Internet Service
Operational: Yes. Began: September 1, 2002.
Subscribers: 165.
Fee: $21.00 monthly; $4.00 modem lease; $50.00 modem purchase.
Telephone Service
None
Miles of Plant: 35.0 (coaxial); None (fiber optic). Additional miles planned: 5.0 (coaxial).
Managers: Andrew Bauer.; Shawn Bauer.
City fee: 3% of gross.
Ownership: Argent Communications LLC (MSO).

WAKEFIELD (town)—Formerly served by Adelphia Communications. Now served by CONWAY, NH [NH0038]. ICA: NH0030.

WARNER TWP.—TDS Telecom, 11 Kearsarge Ave, Contoocook, NH 3229. Phone: 603-746-9911. Fax: 603-746-3567. Web Site: http://www.tdstelecom.com. Also serves Bradford, Newbury & Sutton (town). ICA: NH0018.
TV Market Ranking: Below 100 (Bradford, Newbury, Sutton (town), WARNER TWP.). Franchise award date: June 2, 1984. Fran-

chise expiration date: N.A. Began: November 1, 1984.

Channel capacity: 54 (not 2-way capable). Channels available but not in use: N.A.

Basic Service

Subscribers: 1,903.

Programming (received off-air): WBZ-TV (CBS) Boston; WCVB-TV (ABC) Boston; WENH-TV (PBS) Durham; WFXT (FOX) Boston; WGBH-TV (PBS) Boston; WHDH (NBC) Boston; WLVI-TV (CW) Cambridge; WMTW (ABC) Poland Spring; WMUR-TV (ABC) Manchester; WNEU (TMO) Merrimack; WNNE (NBC) Hartford; WPXG-TV (ION) Concord; WSBK-TV (IND) Boston; WVTA (PBS) Windsor; WZMY-TV (MNT) Derry; allband FM.

Programming (via satellite): ABC Family Channel; AMC; Arts & Entertainment; CNBC; CNN; C-SPAN; Discovery Channel; Disney Channel; ESPN; ESPN 2; FX; Headline News; HGTV; History Channel; Lifetime; MTV; New England Sports Network; Nickelodeon; Spike TV; TBS Superstation; Turner Network TV; TV Guide Network; USA Network; VH1; Weather Channel; WGN America.

Current originations: Leased Access.

Fee: $29.00 installation; $29.95 monthly.

Pay Service 1

Pay Units: 77.

Programming (via satellite): Cinemax.

Fee: $9.95 monthly.

Pay Service 2

Pay Units: 208.

Programming (via satellite): HBO.

Fee: $9.95 monthly.

Pay Service 3

Pay Units: 60.

Programming (via satellite): Showtime.

Fee: $9.95 monthly.

Video-On-Demand: No

Internet Service

Operational: No.

Telephone Service

None

Miles of Plant: 150.0 (coaxial); None (fiber optic). Homes passed: 3,100. Total homes in franchised area: 3,100.

Manager: Marc Violette. Chief Technician: Pete Goodson.

City fee: 3% of basic gross.

Ownership: TDS Telecom.

WATERVILLE VALLEY—SkiSat Cable TV, PO Box 465, Waterville Valley, NH 03215-0465. Phone: 603-236-4850. Fax: 603-236-3661. Also serves Waterville Valley (town). ICA: NH0061.

TV Market Ranking: Outside TV Markets (WATERVILLE VALLEY, Waterville Valley (town)). Franchise award date: January 1, 1983. Franchise expiration date: N.A. Began: January 1, 1983.

Channel capacity: 54 (operating 2-way). Channels available but not in use: 5.

Basic Service

Subscribers: 780.

Programming (received off-air): WBZ-TV (CBS) Boston; WCVB-TV (ABC) Boston; WENH-TV (PBS) Durham; WFXT (FOX) Boston; WGBH-TV (PBS) Boston; WGME-TV (CBS) Portland; WHDH (NBC) Boston; WLVI-TV (CW) Cambridge; WMUR-TV (ABC) Manchester; WNNE (NBC) Hartford; WSBK-TV (IND) Boston; WZMY-TV (MNT) Derry; allband FM.

Programming (via satellite): C-SPAN; ION Television; TV Guide Network.

Current originations: Government Access.

Fee: $60.00 installation; $26.95 monthly; $15.00 additional installation.

Expanded Basic Service 1

Subscribers: 763.

Programming (via satellite): ABC Family Channel; AMC; Arts & Entertainment; Cartoon Network; CNBC; CNN; Comcast Sports Net New England; Comedy Central; Discovery Channel; Disney Channel; ESPN; ESPN 2; Food Network; Fox News Channel; Headline News; HGTV; History Channel; Lifetime; MSNBC; MTV; National Geographic Channel; New England Sports Network; Nickelodeon; TBS Superstation; The Learning Channel; Travel Channel; Turner Network TV; USA Network; Versus; VH1; Weather Channel.

Fee: $60.00 installation; $23.00 monthly.

Pay Service 1

Pay Units: 121.

Programming (via satellite): HBO.

Fee: $15.00 installation; $13.95 monthly.

Video-On-Demand: No

Internet Service

Operational: Yes. Began: January 1, 2003.

Subscribers: 76.

Broadband Service: In-house.

Fee: $40.00 installation; $30.45 monthly; $139.00 modem purchase.

Telephone Service

None

Miles of Plant: 30.0 (coaxial); None (fiber optic). Homes passed: 1,250. Total homes in franchised area: 1,250.

Manager & Chief Technician: Jack Ebert.

Ownership: SkiSat.

WENTWORTH (town)—Formerly served by Adelphia Communications. Now served by PLYMOUTH, NH [NH0055]. ICA: NH0062.

WEST STEWARTSTOWN—White Mountain Cablevision, PO Box 66, Colebrook, NH 03576-0066. Phone: 603-237-5573. Fax: 603-237-8256. Also serves Colebrook, Columbia, Pittsburg & Stewartstown, NH; Canaan & Lemington, VT. ICA: NH0021.

TV Market Ranking: Outside TV Markets (Canaan, Colebrook, Columbia, Lemington, Pittsburg, Stewartstown, WEST STEWARTSTOWN). Franchise award date: N.A. Franchise expiration date: N.A. Began: January 15, 1956.

Channel capacity: 35 (not 2-way capable). Channels available but not in use: 5.

Basic Service

Subscribers: 943.

Programming (received off-air): various Canadian stations; WCAX-TV (CBS) Burlington; WENH-TV (PBS) Durham; WETK (PBS) Burlington; WMTW (ABC) Poland Spring; WMUR-TV (ABC) Manchester; WPFO (FOX) Waterville; allband FM.

Programming (via satellite): ABC Family Channel; Arts & Entertainment; CNN; Comedy Central; Country Music TV; C-SPAN; Discovery Channel; ESPN; ESPN 2; FX; Headline News; HGTV; History Channel; Lifetime; MTV; Nickelodeon; Spike TV; Syfy; TBS Superstation; Turner Network TV; TV Land; USA Network; VH1; WNBC (NBC) New York.

Current originations: Public Access.

Fee: $22.75 installation; $29.50 monthly; $3.00 converter; $20.00 additional installation.

Pay Service 1

Pay Units: 142.

Programming (via satellite): Cinemax; HBO.

Fee: $10.00 monthly (Cinemax), $12.00 monthly (HBO).

Video-On-Demand: No

Internet Service

Operational: No.

Telephone Service

None

Miles of Plant: 62.0 (coaxial); None (fiber optic). Additional miles planned: 2.0 (coaxial). Homes passed: 1,935.

Manager: James Fenney. Chief Technician: Gregory Pinto.

City fee: None.

Ownership: White Mountain Cablevision.

NEW JERSEY

Total Systems: **37**
Total Communities Served: **635**
Franchises Not Yet Operating: **0**
Applications Pending: **0**
Communities with Applications: **0**
Number of Basic Subscribers: **2,779,077**
Number of Expanded Basic Subscribers: **678,028**
Number of Pay Units: **1,230,978**

Top 100 Markets Represented: New York, NY-Linden-Paterson-Newark, NJ (1); Philadelphia, PA-Burlington, NJ (4).

For a list of cable communities in this section, see the Cable Community Index located in the back of Cable Volume 2.
For explanation of terms used in cable system listings, see p. D-11.

ALLAMUCHY TWP.—Cablevision Systems Corp. Now served by DOVER, NJ [NJ0005]. ICA: NJ0046.

ATLANTIC CITY—Formerly served by Orion-Vision. No longer in operation. ICA: NJ0064.

AVALON—Comcast Cable, 401 White Horse Rd, Voorhees, NJ 8043. Phone: 856-821-6100. Fax: 856-821-6108. Web Site: http://www.comcast.com. Also serves Middle Twp., Rio Grande, Sea Isle City, Stone Harbor, Strathmere, Swainton, Upper Twp. & Villas. ICA: NJ0018.

TV Market Ranking: Below 100 (AVALON, Middle Twp., Rio Grande, Sea Isle City, Stone Harbor, Strathmere, Swainton, Upper Twp., Villas). Franchise award date: N.A. Franchise expiration date: N.A. Began: June 2, 1962.

Channel capacity: N.A. Channels available but not in use: N.A.

Basic Service

Subscribers: 13,289.

Programming (received off-air): WGTW-TV (IND) Burlington; WHYY-TV (PBS) Wilmington; WMCN-TV (IND) Atlantic City; WMGM-TV (NBC) Wildwood; WNJS (PBS) Camden; WPHL-TV (MNT) Philadelphia; WPPX-TV (ION) Wilmington; WPSG (CW) Philadelphia; WTXF-TV (FOX) Philadelphia; WUVP-DT (UNV) Vineland; WWSI (TMO) Atlantic City; 16 FMs.

Programming (via microwave): KYW-TV (CBS) Philadelphia; WCAU (NBC) Philadelphia; WPVI-TV (ABC) Philadelphia.

Programming (via satellite): C-SPAN; C-SPAN 2; Eternal Word TV Network; QVC; The Comcast Network; TV Guide Network.

Current originations: Leased Access; Government Access; Educational Access; Public Access.

Fee: $10.70 monthly.

Expanded Basic Service 1

Subscribers: 12,968.

Programming (via satellite): ABC Family Channel; AMC; Animal Planet; Arts & Entertainment; BET Networks; Bravo; Cartoon Network; CNBC; CNN; Comcast SportsNet Philly; Comedy Central; Discovery Channel; Discovery Health Channel; Disney Channel; E! Entertainment Television; ESPN; ESPN 2; Food Network; Fox News Channel; FX; Golf Channel; GSN; Headline News; HGTV; History Channel; Home Shopping Network; Lifetime; MSNBC; MTV; Nickelodeon; Speed Channel; Spike TV; Style Network; Syfy; TBS Superstation; The Learning Channel; truTV; Turner Classic Movies; Turner Network TV; TV Guide Network; TV Land; USA Network; Versus; VH1; Weather Channel.

Fee: $44.30 monthly.

Digital Basic Service

Subscribers: 17,455.

Programming (received off-air): KYW-TV (CBS) Philadelphia; WCAU (NBC) Philadelphia; WHYY-TV (PBS) Wilmington; WPHL-TV (MNT) Philadelphia; WPVI-TV (ABC) Philadelphia; WTXF-TV (FOX) Philadelphia.

Programming (via satellite): BBC America; Bio; Bloomberg Television; Canales N; CBS College Sports Network; Cooking Channel; Country Music TV; C-SPAN 3; Current; Discovery Digital Networks; Discovery HD Theater; Do-It-Yourself; Encore (multiplexed); ESPN 2 HD; ESPN Classic Sports; ESPN HD; ESPNews; FearNet; Flix; Fox College Sports Atlantic; Fox College Sports Central; Fox College Sports Pacific; Fox Reality Channel; Fox Soccer; G4; GAS; Gol TV; Great American Country; Hallmark Channel; History Channel International; INHD; Jewelry Television; Lifetime Movie Network; LOGO; MoviePlex; MTV Networks Digital Suite; Music Choice; National Geographic Channel; NBA TV; NFL Network; Nick Jr.; Nick Too; NickToons TV; Oxygen; Palladia; PBS Kids Sprout; ShopNBC; SoapNet; Sundance Channel; Telefutura; Tennis Channel; Toon Disney; Travel Channel; Turner Network TV HD; TV One; Universal HD; Versus HD; WAM! America's Kidz Network; Weatherscan.

Fee: $14.95 monthly.

Digital Pay Service 1

Pay Units: 1,227.

Programming (via satellite): Cinemax (multiplexed); Cinemax HD; HBO (multiplexed); HBO HD; Showtime (multiplexed); Showtime HD; Starz (multiplexed); Starz HDTV; The Movie Channel (multiplexed).

Fee: $12.00 monthly (each).

Video-On-Demand: Yes

Pay-Per-View

Addressable homes: 17,455.

iN DEMAND, Addressable: Yes; iN DEMAND (delivered digitally); Playboy TV (delivered digitally); Fresh (delivered digitally); Sports PPV (delivered digitally).

Internet Service

Operational: Yes.

Subscribers: 8,931.

Broadband Service: Comcast High Speed Internet.

Fee: $42.95 monthly; $7.00 modem lease; $199.00 modem purchase.

Telephone Service

Digital: Operational

Fee: $44.95 monthly

Miles of Plant: 108.0 (coaxial); None (fiber optic). Homes passed: 18,200.

Area Vice President: John Del Viscio. Vice President, Technical Operations: Mike Taylor. Vice President, Engineering: John Cody. Marketing Director: Aaron Geisel. Public Relations Director: Fred DeAndrea.

City fee: 2% of Basic. State fee: 2% of Basic.

Ownership: Comcast Cable Communications Inc. (MSO).

AVALON—Comcast Cable. Now served by AVALON (formerly Rio Grande), NJ [NJ0018]. ICA: NJ0033.

BAYONNE—Cablevision Systems Corp., 40 Potash Rd, Oakland, NJ 07436-3100. Phones: 201-651-4000; 516-803-2300 (Corporate office). Fax: 516-803-1183. Web Site: http://www.cablevision.com. ICA: NJ0028.

TV Market Ranking: 1 (BAYONNE). Franchise award date: October 24, 1979. Franchise expiration date: N.A. Began: January 1, 1980.

Channel capacity: 87 (operating 2-way). Channels available but not in use: None.

Basic Service

Subscribers: 16,577.

Programming (received off-air): WABC-TV (ABC) New York; WFUT-DT (TEL) Newark; WLIW (PBS) Garden City; WMBC-TV (IND) Newton; WNBC (NBC) New York; WNET (PBS) Newark; WNJN (PBS) Montclair; WNJU (TMO) Linden; WNYW (FOX) New York; WPIX (CW, IND) New York; WPXN-TV (ION) New York; WWOR-TV (MNT) Secaucus; WXTV-DT (UNV) Paterson.

Programming (via microwave): News 12 New Jersey.

Programming (via satellite): Home Shopping Network; QVC; WCBS-TV (CBS) New York.

Current originations: Leased Access; Religious Access; Government Access; Educational Access; Public Access.

Fee: $49.95 installation; $12.79 monthly.

Expanded Basic Service 1

Subscribers: N.A.

Programming (via satellite): ABC Family Channel; AMC; Animal Planet; Arts & Entertainment; BET Networks; Bravo; Cartoon Network; CNBC; Comedy Central; Country Music TV; C-SPAN; C-SPAN 2; Discovery Channel; E! Entertainment Television; ESPN; ESPN 2; FitTV; Food Network; Fox News Channel; FX; GSN; Headline News; HGTV; History Channel; Lifetime; MSNBC; MTV; MTV2; MuchMusic Network; News 12 Traffic & Weather; Nickelodeon; Speed Channel; Spike TV; Syfy; TBS Superstation; The Learning Channel; Travel Channel; truTV; Turner Network TV; TV Land; USA Network; VH1; WE tv; Weather Channel.

Fee: $37.16 monthly.

Digital Basic Service

Subscribers: N.A.

Programming (via satellite): Bio; Bloomberg Television; Country Music TV; C-SPAN 3; Discovery Digital Networks; Disney Channel; ESPN Classic Sports; ESPNews; EuroNews; Flix; Fox Movie Channel; Fox Sports World; G4; GAS; Hallmark Channel; History Channel International; Independent Film Channel; MSG; MSG Plus; MTV; mun2 television; Music Choice; National Geographic Channel; Nick Jr.; NickToons TV; Oxygen; Science Television; Toon Disney; VH1 Classic.

Fee: $10.95 monthly.

Digital Pay Service 1

Pay Units: N.A.

Programming (via satellite): Cinemax (multiplexed); Encore; HBO (multiplexed); Showtime (multiplexed); Starz; The Movie Channel (multiplexed).

Video-On-Demand: Yes

Pay-Per-View

Addressable homes: 3,573.

Special events, Fee: $2.00-$4.00, Addressable: Yes.

Internet Service

Operational: Yes.

Broadband Service: Optimum Online.

Fee: $46.95 installation; $34.95 monthly.

Telephone Service

Digital: Operational

Fee: $46.95 installation; $34.95 monthly

Miles of Plant: 92.0 (coaxial); None (fiber optic). Homes passed: 24,203. Total homes in franchised area: 25,000.

Vice President, Field Operations: Christopher Fulton.

Ownership: Cablevision Systems Corp. (MSO).

BERGENFIELD—Cablevision Systems Corp., 40 Potash Rd, Oakland, NJ 07436-3100. Phones: 516-803-2300 (Corporate office); 201-651-4000. Fax: 516-803-1183. Web Site: http://www.cablevision.com. Also serves Closter, Cresskill, Demarest, Dumont, Emerson, Fair Lawn, Harrington Park, Haworth, Hillsdale, New Milford, Northvale, Norwood, Old Tappan, Oradell, Paramus, River Vale Twp., Rockleigh, Saddle River, Tenafly & Woodcliff Lake. ICA: NJ0013.

TV Market Ranking: 1 (BERGENFIELD, Closter, Cresskill, Dumont, Emerson, Fair Lawn, Harrington Park, Haworth, Hillsdale, New Milford, Northvale, Norwood, Old Tappan, Oradell, Paramus, River Vale Twp., Rockleigh, Saddle River, Tenafly, Woodcliff Lake); 7 (Demarest). Franchise award date: July 18, 1974. Franchise expiration date: N.A. Began: November 1, 1976.

Channel capacity: N.A. Channels available but not in use: N.A.

Basic Service

Subscribers: 57,221.

Programming (received off-air): WABC-TV (ABC) New York; WCBS-TV (CBS) New York; WFME-TV (ETV) West Milford; WFUT-DT (TEL) Newark; WLIW (PBS) Garden City; WLNY-TV (IND) Riverhead; WMBC-TV (IND) Newton; WNBC (NBC) New York; WNET (PBS) Newark; WNJN (PBS) Montclair; WNJU (TMO) Linden; WNYW (FOX) New York; WPIX (CW, IND) New York; WPXN-TV (ION) New York; WRNN-TV (IND) Kingston; WWOR-TV (MNT) Secaucus; WXTV-DT (UNV) Paterson.

Programming (via satellite): Home Shopping Network; News 12 New Jersey.
Current originations: Leased Access; Government Access; Educational Access; Public Access.
Fee: $49.95 installation; $15.52 monthly; $2.72 converter.

Expanded Basic Service 1
Subscribers: N.A.
Programming (via satellite): ABC Family Channel; AMC; Animal Planet; Arts & Entertainment; BET Networks; Bravo; Cartoon Network; CNBC; CNN; Comedy Central; C-SPAN; C-SPAN 2; Discovery Channel; Disney Channel; DMX Music; E! Entertainment Television; ESPN; ESPN 2; Food Network; Fox News Channel; Fuse; FX; Golf Channel; GSN; Headline News; HGTV; History Channel; Independent Film Channel; Lifetime; MSG; MSG Plus; MSNBC; MTV; MTV2; News 12 Traffic & Weather; Nickelodeon; QVC; ShopNBC; SoapNet; Speed Channel; Spike TV; SportsNet New York; Syfy; TBS Superstation; The Comcast Network; The Learning Channel; Travel Channel; truTV; Turner Classic Movies; Turner Network TV; TV Land; USA Network; VH1; WE tv; Weather Channel; Yankees Entertainment & Sports.
Fee: $34.43 monthly.

Digital Basic Service
Subscribers: N.A.
Programming (received off-air): WABC-TV (ABC) New York; WCBS-TV (CBS) New York; WLIW (PBS) Garden City; WNBC (NBC) New York; WPIX (CW, IND) New York; WWOR-TV (MNT) Secaucus.
Programming (via satellite): Azteca America; Bio; Bloomberg Television; Canales N; Channel One; Chinese Television Network; Country Music TV; C-SPAN 3; Discovery Digital Networks; ESPN Classic Sports; ESPN HD; ESPNews; EuroNews; Fox College Sports Atlantic; Fox College Sports Central; Fox College Sports Pacific; Fox HD; Fox Movie Channel; Fox Soccer; Fuel TV; G4; GAS; Gol TV; Golf Channel; Hallmark Channel; History Channel International; Howard TV; INHD; Jewelry Television; Korean Channel; LOGO; MBC America; MSG; MTV Networks Digital Suite; Music Choice; National Geographic Channel; NBA TV; Nick Jr.; NickToons TV; Outdoor Channel; Oxygen; Portuguese Channel; RAI International; Russian Television Network; Sundance Channel; Toon Disney; Turner Network TV HD; TV Asia; TV Japan; TV Polonia; TVG Network; Universal HD; Versus; Zee TV USA.
Fee: $10.95 monthly, $9.95-$14.95 monthly (International Channels).

Pay Service 1
Pay Units: N.A.
Programming (via satellite): Cinemax; Encore; Flix; HBO (multiplexed); Showtime (multiplexed); Starz; The Movie Channel.

Digital Pay Service 1
Pay Units: 109,130.
Programming (via satellite): Cinemax (multiplexed); Cinemax HD; Cinemax On Demand; Encore (multiplexed); HBO (multiplexed); HBO HD; HBO On Demand; Showtime (multiplexed); Showtime HD; Showtime On Demand; Starz (multiplexed); Starz HDTV; The Movie Channel (multiplexed); The Movie Channel HD.
Fee: $9.95 monthly (Showtime/TMC, Cinemax, or Starz/Encore), $11.95 monthly (HBO).

Video-On-Demand: Yes

Pay-Per-View
Pleasure (delivered digitally); Playboy TV (delivered digitally), Fee: $4.95; Fresh (delivered digitally); iN DEMAND (delivered digitally); ESPN Now (delivered digitally); NBA (delivered digitally); NHL/MLB (delivered digitally).

Internet Service
Operational: Yes.
Subscribers: 6,605.
Broadband Service: Optimum Online.
Fee: $46.95 installation; $34.95 monthly; $299.00 modem purchase.

Telephone Service
Digital: Operational
Fee: $46.95 installation; $34.95 monthly
Miles of Plant: 914.0 (coaxial); 115.0 (fiber optic). Homes passed: 85,400.
Vice President, Field Operations: Christopher Fulton.
City fee: 2% of basic.
Ownership: Cablevision Systems Corp. (MSO).

BURLINGTON COUNTY—Comcast Cable, 401 White Horse Rd, Voorhees, NJ 8043. Phone: 856-821-6100. Fax: 856-821-6108. Web Site: http://www.comcast.com. Also serves Beverly, Bordentown, Bordentown Twp., Burlington City, Burlington Twp., Cinnaminson Twp., Delanco Twp., Delran Twp., Edgewater Park Twp., Palmyra, Riverside Twp., Riverton, Westampton Twp. & Willingboro Twp. ICA: NJ0017.
TV Market Ranking: 4 (Beverly, Bordentown, Bordentown Twp., Burlington City, BURLINGTON COUNTY, Burlington Twp., Cinnaminson Twp., Delanco Twp., Delran Twp., Edgewater Park Twp., Palmyra, Riverside Twp., Riverton, Westampton Twp., Willingboro Twp.). Franchise award date: N.A. Franchise expiration date: N.A. Began: December 1, 1967.
Channel capacity: N.A. Channels available but not in use: N.A.

Basic Service
Subscribers: 42,330.
Programming (received off-air): KYW-TV (CBS) Philadelphia; WCAU (NBC) Philadelphia; WFMZ-TV (IND) Allentown; WGTW-TV (IND) Burlington; WHYY-TV (PBS) Wilmington; WMCN-TV (IND) Atlantic City; WNJT (PBS) Trenton; WPHL-TV (MNT) Philadelphia; WPPX-TV (ION) Wilmington; WPSG (CW) Philadelphia; WPVI-TV (ABC) Philadelphia; WTXF-TV (FOX) Philadelphia; WUVP-DT (UNV) Vineland; WWSI (TMO) Atlantic City; WYBE (ETV) Philadelphia.
Programming (via satellite): BET Networks; CNBC; CNN; Comcast SportsNet Mid-Atlantic; C-SPAN; ESPN; ESPN 2; Fox News Channel; Headline News; Lifetime; Nickelodeon; QVC; ShopNBC; TBS Superstation; The Comcast Network; The Learning Channel; Weather Channel; WGN America.
Current originations: Leased Access; Religious Access; Government Access; Educational Access; Public Access.
Fee: $14.05 monthly.

Expanded Basic Service 1
Subscribers: N.A.
Programming (via satellite): ABC Family Channel; AMC; Animal Planet; Bravo; Cartoon Network; Comedy Central; Discovery Channel; Discovery Health Channel; E! Entertainment Television; Eternal Word TV Network; Food Network; FX; G4; Golf Channel; Headline News; HGTV; History Channel; INSP; MSNBC; MTV; Speed Channel; Spike TV; Style Network; Syfy; Turner Classic Movies; Turner Network TV; TV Guide Network; TV Land; USA Network; Versus; VH1.
Fee: $41.55 monthly.

Digital Basic Service
Subscribers: 137,000 Includes Gloucester County, Maple Shade, & Voorhees.
Programming (received off-air): KYW-TV (CBS) Philadelphia; WCAU (NBC) Philadelphia; WHYY-TV (PBS) Wilmington; WNJT (PBS) Trenton; WPHL-TV (MNT) Philadelphia; WPSG (CW) Philadelphia; WTXF-TV (FOX) Philadelphia.
Programming (via satellite): ABC Family HD; Animal Planet HD; Arts & Entertainment HD; BBC America; Big Ten Network; Bio; Bloomberg Television; CBS College Sports Network; Cine Latino; Cine Mexicano; CMT Pure Country; CNN en Espanol; CNN HD; Cooking Channel; Country Music TV; C-SPAN 2; C-SPAN 3; Current; Discovery Channel HD; Discovery en Espanol; Discovery HD Theater; Discovery Kids Channel; Discovery Military Channel; Discovery Planet Green; Disney Channel; Disney Channel HD; Do-It-Yourself; Encore (multiplexed); ESPN 2 HD; ESPN Deportes; ESPN HD; ESPNews; FearNet; Flix; Food Network HD; Fox Business Channel; Fox College Sports Atlantic; Fox College Sports Central; Fox College Sports Pacific; Fox Soccer; Fox Sports en Espanol; Fuse; G4; Gol TV; Gospel Music Channel; Great American Country; GSN; Hallmark Channel; HGTV HD; History Channel en Espanol; History Channel HD; History Channel International; ID Investigation Discovery; Independent Film Channel; Jewelry Television; Lifetime Movie Network; LOGO; MLB Network; Mojo HD; MoviePlex; MTV Hits; MTV Jams; MTV Tres; MTV2; mun2 television; Music Choice; National Geographic Channel; National Geographic Channel HD Network; NFL Network; NFL Network HD; Nick Jr.; Nick Too; NickToons TV; Oxygen; PBS Kids Sprout; ReelzChannel; Science Channel; Science Channel HD; ShopNBC; SoapNet; Starz IndiePlex; Starz RetroPlex; Sundance Channel; Syfy HD; TBS in HD; TeenNick; Telefutura; Tennis Channel; TLC HD; Toon Disney; Travel Channel; truTV; Turner Network TV HD; TV One; TVG Network; Universal HD; USA Network HD; VeneMovies; Versus HD; VH1 Classic; VH1 Soul; WAPA America; WE tv; Weatherscan.
Fee: $14.95 monthly.

Digital Pay Service 1
Pay Units: 16,908.
Programming (via satellite): Cinemax (multiplexed); Cinemax HD; HBO (multiplexed); HBO HD; HBO On Demand; Playboy TV; Showtime (multiplexed); Showtime HD; Showtime On Demand; Starz (multiplexed); Starz HDTV; The Movie Channel (multiplexed); The Movie Channel On Demand.
Fee: $19.10 monthly (each).

Video-On-Demand: Yes

Pay-Per-View
Addressable homes: 18,931.
iN DEMAND, Addressable: Yes; iN DEMAND (delivered digitally); ESPN Now (delivered digitally); Spice: Xcess (delivered digitally); Ten Blox (delivered digitally); Sports PPV (delivered digitally).

Internet Service
Operational: Yes.
Subscribers: 116,000.
Broadband Service: Comcast High Speed Internet.
Fee: $42.95 monthly; $7.00 modem lease; $199.00 modem purchase.

Telephone Service
Digital: Operational
Fee: $44.95 monthly
Miles of Plant: 651.0 (coaxial); 23.0 (fiber optic). Homes passed: 59,620.
Area Vice President: John Del Viscio. Vice President, Technical Operations: Mike Taylor. Vice President, Engineering: John Cody. Marketing Director: Aaron Geisel. Public Relations Director: Fred DeAndrea.
City fee: of gross. State fee: 2% of gross.
Ownership: Comcast Cable Communications Inc. (MSO).

CARLSTADT BOROUGH—Comcast Cable, 800 Rahway Ave, Union, NJ 7083. Phone: 732-602-7444. Fax: 908-851-8888. Web Site: http://www.comcast.com. Also serves East Newark Borough, East Rutherford Borough, Kearny, Lyndhurst Twp., North Arlington Borough, Rutherford Borough & Wallington Borough. ICA: NJ0019.
TV Market Ranking: 1 (CARLSTADT BOROUGH, East Newark Borough, East Rutherford Borough, Kearny, Lyndhurst Twp., North Arlington Borough, Rutherford Borough, Wallington Borough). Franchise award date: N.A. Franchise expiration date: N.A. Began: August 1, 1979.
Channel capacity: N.A. Channels available but not in use: N.A.

Basic Service
Subscribers: 31,310.
Programming (received off-air): WABC-TV (ABC) New York; WCBS-TV (CBS) New York; WFUT-DT (TEL) Newark; WLIW (PBS) Garden City; WMBC-TV (IND) Newton; WNBC (NBC) New York; WNET (PBS) Newark; WNJU (TMO) Linden; WNYE-TV (PBS) New York; WNYW (FOX) New York; WPIX (CW, IND) New York; WPXN-TV (ION) New York; WWOR-TV (MNT) Secaucus; WXTV-DT (UNV) Paterson; 20 FMs.
Programming (via satellite): CNBC; C-SPAN; C-SPAN 2; Eternal Word TV Network; Home Shopping Network; Product Information Network; QVC; The Comcast Network; TV Guide Network; WGN America.
Current originations: Religious Access; Government Access; Educational Access; Public Access.
Fee: $11.15 monthly.

Expanded Basic Service 1
Subscribers: N.A.
Programming (received off-air): WNJN (PBS) Montclair.
Programming (via satellite): ABC Family Channel; AMC; Animal Planet; Arts & Entertainment; BET Networks; Bravo; Cartoon Network; CNN; Comedy Central; Country Music TV; Discovery Channel; Discovery Health Channel; E! Entertainment Television; ESPN; ESPN 2; ESPN Classic Sports; Food Network; Fox News Channel; FX; GalaVision; Golf Channel; GSN; Headline News; HGTV; History Channel; Lifetime; MSG; MSG Plus; MSNBC; MTV; Nickelodeon; ShopNBC; Speed Channel; Spike TV; Style Network; Syfy; TBS Superstation; The Learning Channel; truTV; Turner Classic Movies; Turner Network TV; TV Land; USA Network; Versus; VH1; Weather Channel; Yankees Entertainment & Sports.
Fee: $41.70 monthly.

Digital Basic Service
Subscribers: N.A.
Programming (received off-air): WABC-TV (ABC) New York; WCBS-TV (CBS) New York; WNBC (NBC) New York; WNET (PBS) Newark; WNYW (FOX) New York; WPIX (CW, IND) New York.
Programming (via satellite): BBC America; Bio; Canales N; CBS College Sports Network; Cooking Channel; C-SPAN 3; Discovery Digital Networks; Discovery HD Theater; Disney Channel; Do-It-Yourself; Encore (multiplexed); ESPN 2 HD; ESPN HD;

ESPNews; Flix; Fox College Sports Atlantic; Fox College Sports Central; Fox College Sports Pacific; G4; GAS; Gol TV; History Channel International; INHD; Jewelry Television; LOGO; MTV Networks Digital Suite; National Geographic Channel; NBA TV; NFL Network; Nick Jr.; Nick Too; NickToons TV; Palladia; SoapNet; Sundance Channel (multiplexed); Tennis Channel; Toon Disney; Weatherscan.
Fee: $14.95 monthly.

Digital Pay Service 1
Pay Units: 11,990.
Programming (via satellite): Cinemax (multiplexed); Cinemax HD; Cinemax On Demand; HBO (multiplexed); HBO HD; HBO On Demand; Showtime (multiplexed); Showtime HD; Showtime On Demand; Starz HDTV; Starz On Demand; The Movie Channel (multiplexed); The Movie Channel On Demand.
Fee: $16.20 monthly (each).

Video-On-Demand: Yes

Pay-Per-View
iN DEMAND (delivered digitally); Playboy TV (delivered digitally); Fresh (delivered digitally); Pleasure (delivered digitally); ESPN (delivered digitally); NBA (delivered digitally); NHL/MLB (delivered digitally).

Internet Service
Operational: Yes.
Subscribers: 8,997.
Broadband Service: Comcast High Speed Internet.
Fee: $42.95 monthly; $7.00 modem lease; $299.00 modem purchase.

Telephone Service
Digital: Operational
Fee: $44.95 monthly

Miles of Plant: 201.0 (coaxial); None (fiber optic). Homes passed: 49,700.
Area Vice President: Keith Delviscio. Vice President, Technical Operations: Bob Kennedy. Vice President, Marketing: Marge Jackson. Public Relations Director: Fred DeAndrea.
Ownership: Comcast Cable Communications Inc. (MSO).

DOVER—Cablevision Systems Corp., 683 Route 10 E, Randolph, NJ 7869. Phones: 973-659-2200; 516-803-2300 (Corporate office); 973-361-2969. Fax: 973-659-2266. Web Site: http://www.cablevision.com. Also serves Allamuchy Twp., Boonton, Boonton Twp., Chatham, Denville, East Hanover Twp., Florham Park, Hanover Twp., Hopatcong, Jefferson Twp., Madison, Mine Hill Twp., Montville Twp., Morris Plains, Morris Twp., Morristown, Mount Arlington, Mount Olive Twp., Mountain Lakes, Netcong, Parsippany, Parsippany-Troy Hills Twp., Picatinny Arsenal, Randolph Twp., Rockaway, Rockaway Twp., Roxbury Twp., Stanhope, Victory Gardens & Wharton. ICA: NJ0005.
TV Market Ranking: 1 (Allamuchy Twp. (portions), Boonton, Boonton, Chatham, Denville, DOVER, East Hanover Twp., Florham Park, Hanover Twp., Hopatcong, Jefferson Twp., Madison, Mine Hill Twp., Montville Twp., Morris Plains, Morris Twp., Morristown, Mount Arlington, Mount Olive Twp., Mountain Lakes, Netcong, Parsippany, Parsippany-Troy Hills Twp., Picatinny Arsenal, Randolph Twp., Rockaway, Rockaway Twp., Roxbury Twp., Stanhope, Victory Gardens, Wharton); Below 100 (Allamuchy Twp. (portions)). Franchise award date: February 1, 1972. Franchise expiration date: N.A. Began: February 1, 1972.
Channel capacity: N.A. Channels available but not in use: N.A.

Basic Service
Subscribers: 127,059.
Programming (received off-air): WABC-TV (ABC) New York; WCBS-TV (CBS) New York; WFME-TV (ETV) West Milford; WFUT-DT (TEL) Newark; WMBC-TV (IND) Newton; WNBC (NBC) New York; WNET (PBS) Newark; WNJN (PBS) Montclair; WNJU (TMO) Linden; WNYW (FOX) New York; WPIX (CW, IND) New York; WPXN-TV (ION) New York; WRNN-TV (IND) Kingston; WWOR-TV (MNT) Secaucus; WXTV-DT (UNV) Paterson.
Programming (via microwave): News 12 New Jersey; WLNY-TV (IND) Riverhead.
Programming (via satellite): Home Shopping Network; QVC.
Current originations: Leased Access; Government Access; Educational Access; Public Access.
Fee: $49.95 installation; $11.89 monthly; $1.50 converter.

Expanded Basic Service 1
Subscribers: 109,225.
Programming (via satellite): ABC Family Channel; AMC; Animal Planet; Arts & Entertainment; BET Networks; Bravo; Cartoon Network; CNBC; CNN; Comedy Central; C-SPAN; C-SPAN 2; Discovery Channel; Disney Channel; E! Entertainment Television; ESPN; ESPN 2; Food Network; Fox News Channel; Fuse; FX; GSN; Headline News; HGTV; History Channel; Lifetime; MSG; MSG Plus; MSNBC; MTV; MTV2; News 12 Traffic & Weather; Nickelodeon; SoapNet; Speed Channel; Spike TV; SportsNet New York; Syfy; TBS Superstation; The Learning Channel; Travel Channel; truTV; Turner Network TV; TV Land; USA Network; VH1; WE tv; Weather Channel; Yankees Entertainment & Sports.
Fee: $38.06 monthly.

Digital Basic Service
Subscribers: N.A.
Programming (received off-air): WABC-TV (ABC) New York; WCBS-TV (CBS) New York; WNBC (NBC) New York; WNYW (FOX) New York; WPIX (CW, IND) New York; WWOR-TV (MNT) Secaucus.
Programming (via satellite): Azteca America; BBC World News; Bio; Bloomberg Television; Canal Sur; Caracol; Cartoon Network Tambien en Espanol; Cine Latino; CNN en Espanol; CNN HD; Country Music TV; C-SPAN 3; Discovery en Espanol; Discovery HD Theater; Discovery Home Channel; Discovery Kids Channel; Discovery Military Channel; Docu TVE; Ecuavisia Internacional; ESPN 2 HD; ESPN Classic Sports; ESPN Deportes; ESPN HD; ESPNews; EuroNews; EWTN en Espanol; Food Network HD; Fox College Sports Atlantic; Fox College Sports Central; Fox College Sports Pacific; Fox Movie Channel; Fox Soccer; Fox Sports en Espanol; Fuel TV; G4; GameHD; Gol TV; Golf Channel; Great American Country; Hallmark Channel; here! On Demand; HGTV HD; History Channel en Espanol; History Channel International; Howard TV; HTV Musica; ID Investigation Discovery; Infinito; Jewelry Television; La Familia Network; Latele Novela Network; LOGO; Maria+Vision; Momentum TV; MTV Hits; MTV Tres; mun2 television; Music Choice; National Geographic Channel; National Geographic Channel HD Network; NBA TV; NHL Network; Nick Jr.; NickToons TV; Outdoor Channel; Oxygen; Science Channel; ShopNBC; Sorpresa; Sundance Channel; Supercanal Caribe; TBS in HD; TeenNick; Telefe International; Toon Disney; Toon Disney en Espanol; Turner Network TV HD; TV Chile; TV Colombia; TVE Internacional; TVG Network; Universal HD; Utilisima; VeneMovies; Versus; Versus HD; VH1 Classic; VH1 Soul; V-me TV; WAPA America; World Cinema HD; YES HD.
Fee: $10.95 monthly; $2.95 converter.

Pay Service 1
Pay Units: N.A.
Programming (via satellite): Cinemax; Flix; HBO (multiplexed); Independent Film Channel; Showtime (multiplexed); The Movie Channel; Turner Classic Movies.

Digital Pay Service 1
Pay Units: 51,295.
Programming (via satellite): CCTV-4; Channel One; Cinemax (multiplexed); Cinemax HD; Cinemax On Demand; Encore (multiplexed); HBO (multiplexed); HBO HD; HBO On Demand; International Television (ITV); Korean Channel; MBC America; Playboy TV; RAI International; Russian Television Network; Showtime (multiplexed); Showtime HD; Showtime On Demand; Society of Portuguese Television; Starz (multiplexed); Starz HDTV; The Movie Channel (multiplexed); The Movie Channel HD; TV Asia; TV Japan; TV Polonia; TV5, La Television International; Zee TV USA.
Fee: $9.95 monthly (Showtime, Cinemax, TMC, Starz/Encore, Playboy, RAI, SPT, TV5, or TV Polonia), $11.95 monthly (HBO), $24.95 monthly (TV Japan).

Video-On-Demand: Yes

Pay-Per-View
Addressable homes: 54,128.
Hot Choice, Addressable: Yes; iN DEMAND; Spice; special events.

Internet Service
Operational: Yes.
Broadband Service: Optimum Online.
Fee: $46.95 installation; $34.95 monthly; $299.00 modem purchase.

Telephone Service
Digital: Operational
Fee: $46.95 installation; $34.95 monthly

Miles of Plant: 2,284.0 (coaxial); 106.0 (fiber optic). Homes passed: 167,182.
Vice President, Field Operations: Frank Dagliere. Vice President, Government Affairs: Adam Falk.
City fee: 2% of basic. State fee: 1% of basic.
Ownership: Cablevision Systems Corp. (MSO).

EAST WINDSOR—Comcast Cable, 50 Millstone Rd, Building 300, Ste 200, East Windsor, NJ 8520. Phones: 732-602-7444 (Union office); 732-542-8107. Fax: 732-935-5572. Web Site: http://www.comcast.com. Also serves Cranbury Twp., East Brunswick, East Brunswick Twp., East Windsor Twp., Helmetta, Hightstown, Jamesburg, Monroe Twp., Plainsboro Twp., Princeton Junction, Roosevelt, South Brunswick Twp., Spotswood & West Windsor Twp. ICA: NJ0051.
TV Market Ranking: 1 (East Windsor Twp.); 1,4 (Cranbury Twp., East Brunswick, East Brunswick Twp., EAST WINDSOR, Helmetta, Hightstown, Jamesburg, Monroe Twp., Plainsboro Twp., Princeton Junction, Roosevelt, South Brunswick Twp., Spotswood, West Windsor Twp.). Franchise award date: August 1, 1979. Franchise expiration date: N.A. Began: May 1, 1980.
Channel capacity: N.A. Channels available but not in use: N.A.

Basic Service
Subscribers: 68,463.
Programming (received off-air): WABC-TV (ABC) New York; WCAU (NBC) Philadelphia; WCBS-TV (CBS) New York; WFUT-DT (TEL) Newark; WHYY-TV (PBS) Wilmington; WMBC-TV (IND) Newton; WNBC (NBC) New York; WNET (PBS) Newark; WNJU (TMO) Linden; WNYE-TV (PBS) New York; WNYW (FOX) New York; WPHL-TV (MNT) Philadelphia; WPIX (CW, IND) New York; WPVI-TV (ABC) Philadelphia; WTXF-TV (FOX) Philadelphia; WUVP-DT (UNV) Vineland; WWOR-TV (MNT) Secaucus; WXTV-DT (UNV) Paterson.
Programming (via satellite): C-SPAN; C-SPAN 2; Eternal Word TV Network; ION Television; QVC; TBS Superstation; The Comcast Network; TV Guide Network; WNJT (PBS) Trenton.
Current originations: Government Access; Educational Access; Public Access.
Fee: $15.80 monthly.

Expanded Basic Service 1
Subscribers: N.A.
Programming (via satellite): ABC Family Channel; AMC; Animal Planet; Arts & Entertainment; BET Networks; Bravo; Cartoon Network; CNBC; CNN; Comcast SportsNet Mid-Atlantic; Comedy Central; Discovery Channel; Discovery Health Channel; Disney Channel; E! Entertainment Television; ESPN; ESPN 2; Food Network; Fox News Channel; FX; Golf Channel; Headline News; HGTV; History Channel; Home Shopping Network; Lifetime; MSG; MSG Plus; MSNBC; MTV; News 12 New Jersey; Nickelodeon; Speed Channel; Spike TV; Style Network; Syfy; The Learning Channel; truTV; Turner Classic Movies; Turner Network TV; TV Land; USA Network; Versus; VH1; Weather Channel; Yankees Entertainment & Sports.
Fee: $42.95 monthly.

Digital Basic Service
Subscribers: N.A.
Programming (received off-air): WABC-TV (ABC) New York; WCBS-TV (CBS) New York; WNBC (NBC) New York; WNET (PBS) Newark; WNYW (FOX) New York; WPIX (CW, IND) New York.
Programming (via satellite): BBC America; Bio; Canales N; Cooking Channel; Country Music TV; C-SPAN 3; Current; Discovery Digital Networks; Discovery HD Theater; Disney Channel; Do-It-Yourself; Encore (multiplexed); ESPN 2 HD; ESPN HD; ESPNews; Flix; G4; GAS; Great American Country; GSN; History Channel International; INHD; Jewelry Television; Lifetime Movie Network; LOGO; MTV Networks Digital Suite; Music Choice; National Geographic Channel; NFL Network; Nick Jr.; Nick Too; NickToons TV; Oxygen; Palladia; PBS Kids Sprout; SoapNet; Sundance Channel; The Word Network; Toon Disney; Travel Channel; Trinity Broadcasting

Network; Turner Network TV HD; TV One; Weatherscan.
Fee: $14.95 monthly.

Digital Pay Service 1
Pay Units: 21,786.
Programming (via satellite): Cinemax (multiplexed); Cinemax HD; HBO (multiplexed); HBO HD; Showtime (multiplexed); Showtime HD; Starz (multiplexed); Starz HDTV; The Movie Channel (multiplexed).
Fee: $16.25 monthly (each).

Video-On-Demand: Yes

Pay-Per-View
iN DEMAND (delivered digitally); Playboy TV (delivered digitally); Spice Hot (delivered digitally).

Internet Service
Operational: Yes.
Broadband Service: Comcast High Speed Internet.
Fee: $42.95 monthly; $7.00 modem lease; $199.00 modem purchase.

Telephone Service
Digital: Operational
Fee: $44.95 monthly

Miles of Plant: 1,370.0 (coaxial); None (fiber optic). Homes passed: 93,785.

Regional Senior Vice President: Greg Arnold. Vice President: Keith Taub. Vice President, Technical Operations: Bob Kennedy. Vice President, Marketing: Marge Jackson. Public Relations Director: Fred DeAndrea.

City fee: 2% of gross. State fee: 2% of gross.

Ownership: Comcast Cable Communications Inc. (MSO).

ELIZABETH—Cablevision Systems Corp., 40 Potash Rd, Oakland, NJ 07436-3100. Phones: 516-803-2300 (Corporate office); 201-651-4000. Fax: 516-803-1183. Web Site: http://www.cablevision.com. ICA: NJ0023.

TV Market Ranking: 1 (ELIZABETH). Franchise award date: N.A. Franchise expiration date: N.A. Began: March 31, 1972.

Channel capacity: 116 (operating 2-way). Channels available but not in use: 24.

Basic Service
Subscribers: 24,357.
Programming (received off-air): WABC-TV (ABC) New York; WCBS-TV (CBS) New York; WFME-TV (ETV) West Milford; WFUT-DT (TEL) Newark; WLIW (PBS) Garden City; WMBC-TV (IND) Newton; WNBC (NBC) New York; WNET (PBS) Newark; WNJN (PBS) Montclair; WNJU (TMO) Linden; WNYW (FOX) New York; WPIX (CW, IND) New York; WPXN-TV (ION) New York; WWOR-TV (MNT) Secaucus; WXTV-DT (UNV) Paterson; 27 FMs.
Programming (via satellite): Home Shopping Network; News 12 New Jersey; QVC.
Current originations: Religious Access; Government Access; Public Access.
Fee: $49.95 installation; $12.25 monthly.

Expanded Basic Service 1
Subscribers: 22,200.
Programming (via satellite): ABC Family Channel; AMC; Animal Planet; Arts & Entertainment; BET Networks; Bravo; Cartoon Network; CNBC; CNN; Comedy Central; C-SPAN; C-SPAN 2; Discovery Channel; Disney Channel; E! Entertainment Television; ESPN; ESPN 2; Food Network; Fox News Channel; Fuse; FX; GalaVision; GSN; Headline News; HGTV; History Channel; Independent Film Channel; Lifetime; Madison Square Garden Network; MSNBC; MTV; MTV2; mun2 television; News 12 Traffic & Weather; Nickelodeon; ShopNBC; SoapNet; Speed Channel; Spike TV; SportsNet New York; Syfy; TBS Superstation; The Comcast Network; The Learning Channel; Travel Channel; truTV; Turner Classic Movies; Turner Network TV; TV Land; USA Network; VH1; WE tv; Weather Channel; Yankees Entertainment & Sports.
Fee: $37.70 monthly.

Digital Basic Service
Subscribers: N.A.
Programming (received off-air): WABC-TV (ABC) New York; WCBS-TV (CBS) New York; WNBC (NBC) New York; WNYW (FOX) New York; WPIX (CW, IND) New York; WWOR-TV (MNT) Secaucus.
Programming (via satellite): Azteca America; BBC World News; Bio; Bloomberg Television; Canal Sur; Caracol; Cartoon Network Tambien en Espanol; Cine Latino; CNN en Espanol; CNN HD; Country Music TV; C-SPAN 3; Discovery en Espanol; Discovery HD Theater; Discovery Home Channel; Discovery Kids Channel; Discovery Military Channel; Docu TVE; Ecuavisia Internacional; ESPN 2 HD; ESPN Classic Sports; ESPN Deportes; ESPN HD; ESPNews; EuroNews; EWTN en Espanol; Food Network HD; Fox College Sports Atlantic; Fox College Sports Central; Fox College Sports Pacific; Fox Movie Channel; Fox Soccer; Fox Sports en Espanol; Fuel TV; G4; GameHD; Gol TV; Golf Channel; Great American Country; Hallmark Channel; here! On Demand; HGTV HD; History Channel en Espanol; History Channel International; Howard TV; HTV Musica; ID Investigation Discovery; Infinito; Jewelry Television; La Familia Network; Latele Novela Network; LOGO; Maria+Vision; Momentum TV; MTV Hits; MTV Tres; mun2 television; Music Choice; National Geographic Channel; National Geographic Channel HD Network; NBA TV; NHL Network; Nick Jr.; NickToons TV; Outdoor Channel; Oxygen; Science Channel; Sorpresa; Sundance Channel; Supercanal Caribe; TBS in HD; TeenNick; Telefe International; Toon Disney; Toon Disney en Espanol; Turner Network TV HD; TV Chile; TV Colombia; TVE Internacional; TVG Network; Universal HD; Utilisima; VeneMovies; Versus; Versus HD; VH1 Classic; VH1 Soul; V-me TV; WAPA America; World Cinema HD; YES HD.
Fee: $10.95 monthly.

Pay Service 1
Pay Units: N.A.
Programming (via satellite): Cinemax; Flix; HBO (multiplexed); Portuguese Channel; Showtime (multiplexed); The Movie Channel.

Digital Pay Service 1
Pay Units: 3,274.
Programming (via satellite): Cinemax (multiplexed); Cinemax HD; Cinemax On Demand.
Fee: $9.95 monthly.

Digital Pay Service 2
Pay Units: 10,741.
Programming (via satellite): HBO (multiplexed); HBO On Demand.
Fee: $11.95 monthly.

Digital Pay Service 3
Pay Units: 468.
Programming (via satellite): Encore (multiplexed); Starz (multiplexed); Starz HDTV.
Fee: $9.95 monthly.

Digital Pay Service 4
Pay Units: 2,875.
Programming (via satellite): Showtime (multiplexed); Showtime HD; Showtime On Demand.
Fee: $9.95 monthly.

Digital Pay Service 5
Pay Units: 2,630.
Programming (via satellite): The Movie Channel (multiplexed); The Movie Channel HD.
Fee: $9.95 monthly.

Digital Pay Service 6
Pay Units: N.A.
Programming (via satellite): CCTV-4; Channel One; Korean Channel; Playboy TV; Portuguese Channel; RAI International; Russian Television Network; TV Asia; TV Japan; TV Polonia; TV5, La Television International; Zee Gold.
Fee: $9.95 monthly (RAI, SPT, TV5, TV Polonia or Playboy), $24.95 monthly (TV Japan).

Video-On-Demand: Yes

Pay-Per-View
Addressable homes: 23,700.
Addressable: Yes; Movies; special events; Playboy TV, Addressable: Yes; Spice2, Fee: $24.95, Addressable: Yes.

Internet Service
Operational: Yes.
Broadband Service: Optimum Online.
Fee: $34.95 monthly; $299.00 modem purchase.

Telephone Service
Digital: Operational
Fee: $46.95 installation; $34.95 monthly

Miles of Plant: 182.0 (coaxial); 173.0 (fiber optic). Homes passed: 64,934.

Vice President, Field Operations: Christopher Fulton.

City fee: 2% of gross. State fee: 1.5% of gross.

Ownership: Cablevision Systems Corp. (MSO).

FREEHOLD—Cablevision Systems Corp. Now served by MAMMOTH, NJ [NJ0012]. ICA: NJ0063.

GLOUCESTER COUNTY—Comcast Cable, 401 White Horse Rd, Voorhees, NJ 8043. Phone: 856-821-6100. Fax: 856-821-6108. Web Site: http://www.comcast.com. Also serves Clayton, Deptford Twp., East Greenwich Twp., Glassboro, Greenwich Twp., Mantua Twp., National Park, Paulsboro, Wenonah, West Deptford Twp., Westville, Woodbury & Woodbury Heights. ICA: NJ0022.

TV Market Ranking: 4 (Clayton, Deptford Twp., East Greenwich Twp., Glassboro, GLOUCESTER COUNTY, Greenwich Twp., Mantua Twp., National Park, Paulsboro, Wenonah, West Deptford Twp., Westville, Woodbury, Woodbury Heights). Franchise award date: N.A. Franchise expiration date: N.A. Began: January 1, 1980.

Channel capacity: N.A. Channels available but not in use: N.A.

Basic Service
Subscribers: 41,649.
Programming (received off-air): KYW-TV (CBS) Philadelphia; WCAU (NBC) Philadelphia; WFMZ-TV (IND) Allentown; WGTW-TV (IND) Burlington; WHYY-TV (PBS) Wilmington; WMCN-TV (IND) Atlantic City; WNJS (PBS) Camden; WPHL-TV (MNT) Philadelphia; WPPX-TV (ION) Wilmington; WPSG (CW) Philadelphia; WPVI-TV (ABC) Philadelphia; WTXF-TV (FOX) Philadelphia; WUVP-DT (UNV) Vineland; WWSI (TMO) Atlantic City; WYBE (ETV) Philadelphia.
Programming (via satellite): AMC; C-SPAN; Discovery Channel; Eternal Word TV Network; History Channel; ShopNBC; TBS Superstation; The Comcast Network; Turner Classic Movies; Turner Network TV; TV Land; Weather Channel.
Current originations: Leased Access; Government Access; Educational Access; Public Access.
Fee: $13.85 monthly.

Expanded Basic Service 1
Subscribers: N.A.
Programming (via satellite): ABC Family Channel; Animal Planet; Arts & Entertainment; BET Networks; Bravo; Cartoon Network; CNBC; CNN; Comcast SportsNet Philly; Comedy Central; Discovery Health Channel; E! Entertainment Television; ESPN; ESPN 2; Food Network; Fox News Channel; FX; G4; Golf Channel; GSN; Headline News; HGTV; Home Shopping Network; Lifetime; MSNBC; MTV; Nickelodeon; QVC; Speed Channel; Spike TV; Style Network; Syfy; The Learning Channel; truTV; TV Guide Network; USA Network; Versus; VH1.
Fee: $40.65 monthly.

Digital Basic Service
Subscribers: N.A. included in Burlington County
Programming (received off-air): KYW-TV (CBS) Philadelphia; WCAU (NBC) Philadelphia; WHYY-TV (PBS) Wilmington; WPHL-TV (MNT) Philadelphia; WPSG (CW) Philadelphia; WPVI-TV (ABC) Philadelphia; WTXF-TV (FOX) Philadelphia.
Programming (via satellite): BBC America; Bio; Bloomberg Television; Canales N; Cooking Channel; Country Music TV; C-SPAN 3; Current; Discovery Digital Networks; Discovery HD Theater; Disney Channel; Do-It-Yourself; Encore; ESPN 2 HD; ESPN HD; ESPNews; Flix; Fox College Sports Atlantic; Fox College Sports Central; Fox College Sports Pacific; Fox Reality Channel; Fox Soccer; G4; GAS; Gol TV; Great American Country; Hallmark Channel; History Channel International; INHD; Jewelry Television; Lifetime Movie Network; LOGO; MTV Networks Digital Suite; Music Choice; National Geographic Channel; NBA TV; NFL Network; Nick Jr.; Nick Too; NickToons TV; Oxygen; Palladia; ShopNBC; SoapNet; Sundance Channel; Telefutura; Tennis Channel; Toon Disney; Travel Channel; Turner Network TV HD; TV One; Universal HD; Versus HD; WAM! America's Kidz Network; Weatherscan.
Fee: $14.95 monthly.

Digital Pay Service 1
Pay Units: 14,404.
Programming (via satellite): Cinemax (multiplexed); Cinemax HD; Cinemax On Demand; HBO (multiplexed); HBO HD; HBO On Demand; Showtime (multiplexed); Showtime HD; Showtime On Demand; Starz (multiplexed); Starz HDTV; Starz On Demand; The Movie Channel (multiplexed); The Movie Channel On Demand.
Fee: $17.50 monthly (each).

Video-On-Demand: Yes

Pay-Per-View
Addressable homes: 16,017.
iN DEMAND, Fee: $3.95, Addressable: Yes; iN DEMAND (delivered digitally); Playboy TV (delivered digitally); Fresh (delivered digitally); CBS College Sports Network (delivered digitally); ESPN Now (delivered digitally); Sports PPV (delivered digitally).

Internet Service
Operational: Yes.
Broadband Service: Comcast High Speed Internet.
Fee: $42.95 monthly; $7.00 modem lease; $199.00 modem purchase.

Telephone Service
Digital: Operational
Fee: $44.95 monthly

Miles of Plant: 719.0 (coaxial); None (fiber optic). Homes passed: 55,530.
Area Vice President: John Del Viscio. Vice President, Technical Operations: Mike Taylor. Vice President, Engineering: John Cody. Marketing Director: Aaron Geisel. Public Relations Director: Fred DeAndrea.
Ownership: Comcast Cable Communications Inc. (MSO).

HAMILTON TWP. (Mercer County)—Cablevision Systems Corp., 683 Route 10 E, Randolph, NJ 7869. Phones: 516-803-2300 (Corporate office); 973-659-2200. Fax: 973-659-2266. Web Site: http://www.cablevision.com. Also serves Allentown, Robbinsville, Washington Twp. (Mercer County) & Yardville. ICA: NJ0024.
TV Market Ranking: 4 (Allentown, HAMILTON TWP. (MERCER COUNTY), Robbinsville, Washington Twp. (Mercer County), Yardville). Franchise award date: October 1, 1980. Franchise expiration date: N.A. Began: December 31, 1980.
Channel capacity: N.A. Channels available but not in use: N.A.

Basic Service
Subscribers: 33,112.
Programming (received off-air): KYW-TV (CBS) Philadelphia; WABC-TV (ABC) New York; WCAU (NBC) Philadelphia; WCBS-TV (CBS) New York; WFMZ-TV (IND) Allentown; WFUT-DT (TEL) Newark; WGTW-TV (IND) Burlington; WHYY-TV (PBS) Wilmington; WNBC (NBC) New York; WNET (PBS) Newark; WNJT (PBS) Trenton; WNYW (FOX) New York; WPHL-TV (MNT) Philadelphia; WPIX (CW, IND) New York; WPPX-TV (ION) Wilmington; WPSG (CW) Philadelphia; WPVI-TV (ABC) Philadelphia; WPXN-TV (ION) New York; WTXF-TV (FOX) Philadelphia; WUVP-DT (UNV) Vineland; WWOR-TV (MNT) Secaucus; WXTV-DT (UNV) Paterson; WYBE (ETV) Philadelphia.
Programming (via microwave): News 12 New Jersey.
Current originations: Leased Access; Religious Access; Government Access; Educational Access; Public Access.
Fee: $49.95 installation; $16.72 monthly; $1.75 converter.

Expanded Basic Service 1
Subscribers: N.A.
Programming (via satellite): ABC Family Channel; AMC; Animal Planet; Arts & Entertainment; BET Networks; Bravo; Cartoon Network; CNBC; CNN; Comcast SportsNet Mid-Atlantic; Comedy Central; C-SPAN; C-SPAN 2; Discovery Channel; Disney Channel; E! Entertainment Television; ESPN; ESPN 2; Food Network; Fox News Channel; Fuse; FX; Headline News; HGTV; History Channel; Home Shopping Network; Independent Film Channel; Lifetime; MSG; MSG Plus; MSNBC; MTV; MTV2; News 12 Traffic & Weather; Nickelodeon; QVC; SoapNet; Speed Channel; Spike TV; SportsNet New York; Syfy; TBS Superstation; The Learning Channel; Travel Channel; truTV; Turner Classic Movies; Turner Network TV; TV Land; USA Network; VH1; WE tv; Weather Channel; Yankees Entertainment & Sports.
Fee: $33.23 monthly.

Digital Basic Service
Subscribers: N.A.
Programming (received off-air): WCAU (NBC) Philadelphia; WNYW (FOX) New York; WPSG (CW) Philadelphia; WPVI-TV (ABC) Philadelphia; WWOR-TV (MNT) Secaucus.
Programming (via satellite): Azteca America; BBC World News; Bio; Bloomberg Television; Canal Sur; Caracol; Cartoon Network; Cine Latino; CNN en Espanol; CNN HD; Country Music TV; C-SPAN 3; Discovery en Espanol; Discovery HD Theater; Discovery Home Channel; Discovery Kids Channel; Discovery Military Channel; Docu TVE; Ecuavisia Internacional; ESPN 2 HD; ESPN Classic Sports; ESPN Deportes; ESPN HD; ESPNews; EuroNews; EWTN en Espanol; Food Network HD; Fox College Sports Atlantic; Fox College Sports Central; Fox College Sports Pacific; Fox Movie Channel; Fox Soccer; Fox Sports en Espanol; Fuel TV; G4; GameHD; Gol TV; Golf Channel; Great American Country; Hallmark Channel; here! On Demand; HGTV HD; History Channel en Espanol; History Channel International; Howard TV; HTV Musica; ID Investigation Discovery; Infinito; Jewelry Television; La Familia Network; Latele Novela Network; LOGO; Maria+Vision; Momentum TV; MTV Hits; MTV Tres; mun2 television; Music Choice; National Geographic Channel; National Geographic Channel HD Network; NBA TV; NHL Network; Nick Jr.; NickToons TV; Outdoor Channel; Oxygen; Science Channel; ShopNBC; Sorpresa; Sundance Channel; Supercanal Caribe; TBS in HD; TeenNick; Telefe International; Toon Disney; Toon Disney en Espanol; Turner Network TV HD; TV Chile; TV Colombia; TVE Internacional; TVG Network; Universal HD; Utilisima; VeneMovies; Versus; Versus HD; VH1 Classic; VH1 Soul; V-me TV; WAPA America; WCBS-TV (CBS) New York; World Cinema HD; YES HD.
Fee: $10.95 monthly.

Pay Service 1
Pay Units: N.A.
Programming (via satellite): Cinemax; Flix; HBO (multiplexed); Showtime (multiplexed); The Movie Channel.

Digital Pay Service 1
Pay Units: 15,529.
Programming (via satellite): CCTV-4; Cinemax (multiplexed); Cinemax HD; Cinemax On Demand; Encore (multiplexed); HBO (multiplexed); HBO HD; HBO On Demand; Korean Channel; MBC America; Portuguese Channel; RAI International; Russian Television Network; Showtime (multiplexed); Showtime HD; Showtime On Demand; Starz (multiplexed); Starz HDTV; The Movie Channel (multiplexed); The Movie Channel HD; TV Asia; TV Japan; TV Polonia; TV5, La Television International; Zee Gold.
Fee: $9.95 monthly (Showtime, Cinemax, TMC, Starz/Encore, Playboy, RAI, SPT, TV5 or TV Polonia), $11.95 monthly (HBO), $24.95 monthly (TV Japan).

Video-On-Demand: Yes

Pay-Per-View
Fresh (delivered digitally), Addressable: Yes; Movies (delivered digitally); special events (delivered digitally).

Internet Service
Operational: Yes.
Subscribers: 4,000.
Broadband Service: Optimum Online.
Fee: $46.95 installation; $34.95 monthly; $299.00 modem purchase.

Telephone Service
Digital: Operational
Fee: $46.95 installation; $34.95 monthly
Miles of Plant: 580.0 (coaxial); None (fiber optic). Homes passed: 39,047. Total homes in franchised area: 39,047.
Vice President, Field Operations: Frank Dagliere. Vice President, Government Affairs: Adam Falk.
City fee: 2% of gross. State fee: 2% of gross.
Ownership: Cablevision Systems Corp. (MSO).

HILLSBOROUGH—Comcast Cable, 800 Rahway Ave, Union, NJ 7083. Phone: 973-736-7444. Web Site: http://www.comcast.com. Also serves Annandale, Belle Mead, Bethlehem Twp., Blawenburg, Branchburg Twp., Clinton, Clinton Twp., Delaware Twp., East Amwell Twp., Flagtown, Flemington, Franklin Park, Kingston, Lebanon Borough, Millstone, Montgomery Twp., Neshanic Station, North Branch, Raritan Twp., Readington Twp., Rocky Hill, Skillman, Somerset, South Branch, Tewksbury Twp., Three Bridges, Union Twp. & White House Station. ICA: NJ0025.
TV Market Ranking: 1 (North Branch, Somerset, Tewksbury Twp.); 1,4 (Annandale, Belle Mead, Bethlehem Twp., Blawenburg, Branchburg Twp., Delaware Twp., East Amwell Twp., Flagtown, Flemington, Franklin Park, HILLSBOROUGH, Kingston, Lebanon Borough, Millstone, Montgomery Twp., Neshanic Station, Raritan Twp., Readington Twp., Rocky Hill, Skillman, South Branch, Three Bridges, Union Twp., White House Station); Below 100 (Clinton, Clinton Twp.). Franchise award date: June 19, 1980. Franchise expiration date: N.A. Began: January 2, 1981.
Channel capacity: N.A. Channels available but not in use: N.A.

Basic Service
Subscribers: 81,562 Includes Long Hill Twp. & Princeton.
Programming (received off-air): WABC-TV (ABC) New York; WCBS-TV (CBS) New York; WFUT-DT (TEL) Newark; WHYY-TV (PBS) Wilmington; WMBC-TV (IND) Newton; WNBC (NBC) New York; WNET (PBS) Newark; WNJU (TMO) Linden; WNYE-TV (PBS) New York; WNYW (FOX) New York; WPIX (CW, IND) New York; WPSG (CW) Philadelphia; WPXN-TV (ION) New York; WTXF-TV (FOX) Philadelphia; WWOR-TV (MNT) Secaucus; WXTV-DT (UNV) Paterson.
Programming (via satellite): ABC News; Cable TV Network of New Jersey; C-SPAN; C-SPAN 2; Gavel to Gavel; Home Shopping Network; Jewelry Television; QVC; ShopNBC; The Comcast Network; TV Guide Network; V-me TV; WGN America.
Current originations: Leased Access; Educational Access; Public Access.
Fee: $41.65 installation; $14.80 monthly; $2.00 converter.

Expanded Basic Service 1
Subscribers: N.A.
Programming (via satellite): ABC Family Channel; AMC; Animal Planet; Arts & Entertainment; BET Networks; Bravo; Cartoon Network; CNBC; CNN; Comedy Central; Country Music TV; Discovery Channel; Disney Channel; E! Entertainment Television; ESPN; ESPN 2; ESPN Classic Sports; Eternal Word TV Network; Food Network; Fox News Channel; FX; G4; GSN; Hallmark Channel; Headline News; HGTV; History Channel; Lifetime; MSG; MSG Plus; MSNBC; MTV; MTV2; National Geographic Channel; Nickelodeon; Oxygen; Speed Channel; Spike TV; SportsNet New York; Syfy; TBS Superstation; The Learning Channel; Travel Channel; truTV; Turner Classic Movies; Turner Network TV; TV Land; USA Network; VH1; WE tv; Weather Channel; Yankees Entertainment & Sports.
Fee: $35.19 monthly.

Digital Basic Service
Subscribers: 34,233 Includes Long Hill Twp. & Princeton.
Programming (received off-air): WABC-TV (ABC) New York; WCBS-TV (CBS) New York; WNBC (NBC) New York; WPIX (CW, IND) New York; WWOR-TV (MNT) Secaucus.
Programming (via satellite): Arts & Entertainment HD; BBC America; Big Ten Network; Bio; Bloomberg Television; Boomerang; CBS College Sports Network; CMT Pure Country; CNBC World; CNN HD; Cooking Channel; Current; Daystar TV Network; Discovery HD Theater; Discovery Health Channel; Discovery Kids Channel; Discovery Military Channel; Discovery Planet Green; Do-It-Yourself; Encore (multiplexed); ESPN 2 HD; ESPN HD; ESPNews; Fox Business Channel; Fox College Sports Atlantic; Fox College Sports Central; Fox College Sports Pacific; Fox HD; Fox Movie Channel; Fox Reality Channel; Fox Soccer; Fox Sports en Espanol; Fuel; Fuse; G4; Golf Channel; Golf Channel HD; Hallmark Movie Channel; HDNet; HDNet Movies; History Channel International; ID Investigation Discovery; ImaginAsian TV; Independent Film Channel; MLB Network; MoviePlex; MTV Hits; MTV Jams; MTV Tres; Music Choice; National Geographic Channel HD Network; NBA TV; NFL Network; NFL Network HD; NHL Network; Nick Jr.; Nick Too; NickToons TV; Outdoor Channel; Palladia; PBS Kids Sprout; ReelzChannel; Science Channel; SoapNet; Starz IndiePlex; Starz RetroPlex; Style Network; Sundance Channel; TBS in HD; TeenNick; Tennis Channel; Toon Disney; Turner Network TV HD; TV Guide Network; TV One; Universal HD; Universal Sports; USA Network HD; Versus; Versus HD; VH1 Classic; VH1 Soul; WE tv; WealthTV HD; YES HD.
Fee: $11.10 monthly.

Digital Pay Service 1
Pay Units: N.A.
Programming (via satellite): CCTV-4; Chinese Television Network; Cinemax (multiplexed); Cinemax HD; Filipino Channel; Flix; HBO (multiplexed); HBO HD; RAI International; Showtime (multiplexed); Showtime HD; Starz (multiplexed); Starz HDTV; The Movie Channel (multiplexed); TV Asia; TV5, La Television International; Zee TV USA.

Video-On-Demand: Yes

Pay-Per-View
iN DEMAND; Penthouse TV (delivered digitally); Playboy TV (delivered digitally); Sports PPV (delivered digitally); iN DEMAND (delivered digitally); Spice: Xcess (delivered digitally).

Internet Service
Operational: Yes.
Subscribers: 49,251.
Broadband Service: Comcast High Speed Internet.
Fee: $99.00 installation; $53.95 monthly; $2.00 modem lease.

Telephone Service
Digital: Operational
Subscribers: 5,710.
Homes passed: 118,432. Total homes in franchised area: 2,838. Homes passed includes Long Hill Twp. & Princeton
Area Vice President: Keith Taub.
Ownership: Comcast Cable Communications Inc. (MSO).

HOBOKEN—Cablevision Systems Corp., 40 Potash Rd, Oakland, NJ 07436-3100. Phones: 516-803-2300 (Corporate office); 201-651-4000. Fax: 516-803-1183. Web Site: http://www.cablevision.com.

Also serves North Bergen, Union City, Weehawken & West New York. ICA: NJ0008.

TV Market Ranking: 1 (HOBOKEN, North Bergen, Union City, Weehawken, West New York). Franchise award date: N.A. Franchise expiration date: N.A. Began: September 1, 1970.

Channel capacity: N.A. Channels available but not in use: N.A.

Basic Service

Subscribers: 62,208.

Programming (received off-air): News 12 New Jersey; WABC-TV (ABC) New York; WCBS-TV (CBS) New York; WFME-TV (ETV) West Milford; WFUT-DT (TEL) Newark; WLIW (PBS) Garden City; WMBC-TV (IND) Newton; WNBC (NBC) New York; WNET (PBS) Newark; WNJN (PBS) Montclair; WNJU (TMO) Linden; WNYW (FOX) New York; WPIX (CW, IND) New York; WPXN-TV (ION) New York; WWOR-TV (MNT) Secaucus; WXTV-DT (UNV) Paterson.

Programming (via satellite): Home Shopping Network; QVC.

Current originations: Religious Access; Leased Access; Government Access; Educational Access; Public Access.

Fee: $49.95 installation; $13.26 monthly; $1.76 converter.

Expanded Basic Service 1

Subscribers: N.A.

Programming (via satellite): ABC Family Channel; AMC; Animal Planet; Arts & Entertainment; BET Networks; Bravo; Cartoon Network; CNBC; CNN; Comedy Central; C-SPAN; C-SPAN 2; Discovery Channel; Disney Channel; E! Entertainment Television; ESPN; ESPN 2; Food Network; Fox News Channel; Fuse; FX; GalaVision; GSN; Headline News; HGTV; History Channel; Lifetime; MSNBC; MTV; MTV2; mun2 television; News 12 Traffic & Weather; Nickelodeon; SoapNet; Speed Channel; Spike TV; Syfy; TBS Superstation; The Comcast Network; The Learning Channel; Travel Channel; truTV; Turner Network TV; TV Land; USA Network; VH1; WE tv; Weather Channel.

Fee: $36.69 monthly.

Digital Basic Service

Subscribers: N.A.

Programming (received off-air): WABC-TV (ABC) New York; WCBS-TV (CBS) New York; WNBC (NBC) New York; WNYW (FOX) New York; WPIX (CW, IND) New York; WWOR-TV (MNT) Secaucus.

Programming (via satellite): Azteca America; BBC World News; Bio; Bloomberg Television; Canal Sur; Caracol; Cartoon Network Tambien en Espanol; Cine Latino; CNN en Espanol; CNN HD; Country Music TV; C-SPAN 3; Discovery en Espanol; Discovery HD Theater; Discovery Home Channel; Discovery Kids Channel; Discovery Military Channel; Docu TVE; Ecuavisia Internacional; ESPN 2 HD; ESPN Classic Sports; ESPN Deportes; ESPN HD; ESPNews; EuroNews; EWTN en Espanol; Food Network HD; Fox College Sports Atlantic; Fox College Sports Central; Fox College Sports Pacific; Fox Movie Channel; Fox Soccer; Fox Sports en Espanol; Fuel TV; G4; GameHD; Gol TV; Golf Channel; Great American Country; Hallmark Channel; here! On Demand; HGTV HD; History Channel en Espanol; History Channel International; Howard TV; HTV Musica; ID Investigation Discovery; Infinito; Jewelry Television; La Familia Network; Latele Novela Network; LOGO; Maria+Vision; Momentum TV; MTV Hits; MTV Tres; mun2 television; Music Choice; National Geographic Channel; National Geographic Channel HD Network; NBA TV; NHL Network; Nick Jr.; NickToons TV; Outdoor Channel; Oxygen; Science Channel; ShopNBC; Sorpresa; Sundance Channel; Supercanal Caribe; TBS in HD; TeenNick; Telefe International; The Word Network; Toon Disney; Toon Disney en Espanol; Turner Network TV HD; TV Chile; TV Colombia; TVE Internacional; TVG Network; Universal HD; Utilisima; VeneMovies; Versus; Versus HD; VH1 Classic; VH1 Soul; WAPA America; World Cinema HD; YES HD.

Fee: $10.95 monthly.

Pay Service 1

Pay Units: 25,806.

Programming (via satellite): Cinemax; Flix; HBO (multiplexed); Independent Film Channel; MSG; MSG Plus; Playboy TV; Showtime (multiplexed); The Movie Channel; Turner Classic Movies; Yankees Entertainment & Sports.

Fee: $20.00 installation; $9.95 monthly (Cinemax or TMC), $11.95 monthly (Showtime).

Digital Pay Service 1

Pay Units: N.A.

Programming (via satellite): CCTV-4; Channel One; Cinemax (multiplexed); Cinemax HD; Cinemax On Demand; Encore; HBO (multiplexed); HBO HD; HBO On Demand; International Television (ITV); Korean Channel; MBC America; Playboy TV; Portuguese Channel; RAI International; Russian Television Network; Showtime (multiplexed); Showtime HD; Showtime On Demand; Starz (multiplexed); Starz HDTV; The Movie Channel (multiplexed); The Movie Channel HD; TV Asia; TV Japan; TV Polonia; TV5, La Television International; Zee TV USA.

Fee: $9.95 monthly (Showtime, Cinemax, TMC, Starz/Encore, Playboy, RAI, SPT, TV5, or TV Polonia), $11.95 monthly (HBO), $24.95 monthly (TV Japan).

Video-On-Demand: Yes

Pay-Per-View

Anime Network (delivered digitally); Disney Channel (delivered digitally); iN DEMAND (delivered digitally); NBA TV (delivered digitally); Sports PPV (delivered digitally); Playboy TV; iN DEMAND (delivered digitally); Playboy TV (delivered digitally).

Internet Service

Operational: Yes.

Broadband Service: Optimum Online.

Fee: $46.95 installation; $34.95 monthly; $299.00 modem purchase.

Telephone Service

Digital: Operational

Fee: $46.95 installation; $34.95 monthly

Miles of Plant: 266.0 (coaxial); None (fiber optic). Homes passed: 113,105.

Vice President, Field Operations: Christopher Fulton.

City fee: 2% of gross. State fee: 2% of gross.

Ownership: Cablevision Systems Corp. (MSO).

HUNTERDON COUNTY—Service Electric Cable TV of Hunterdon Inc., 2260 Ave A, Bethlehem, PA 18017-2170. Phones: 800-225-9102; 610-865-9100. Fax: 610-865-5031. E-mail: lillya@sectv.com. Web Site: http://www.sectv.com. Also serves Alexandria Twp., Alpha Boro, Bloomsbury, Frenchtown Boro, Greenwich Twp., Harmony Twp., Holland Twp., Kingwood Twp., Lopatcong Twp., Milford Boro, Phillipsburg & Pohatcong Twp. ICA: NJ0067.

TV Market Ranking: 4 (Alexandria Twp., Holland Twp., HUNTERDON COUNTY, Kingwood Twp.); Below 100 (Alpha, Bloomsbury, Frenchtown Boro, Greenwich Twp., Harmony Twp., Lopatcong Twp., Milford Boro, PHILLIPSBURG, Pohatcong Twp.).

Channel capacity: 90 (operating 2-way). Channels available but not in use: N.A.

Basic Service

Subscribers: 11,339.

Programming (received off-air): KYW-TV (CBS) Philadelphia; WABC-TV (ABC) New York; WBPH-TV (IND) Bethlehem; WCAU (NBC) Philadelphia; WCBS-TV (CBS) New York; WFMZ-TV (IND) Allentown; WHYY-TV (PBS) Wilmington; WLVT-TV (PBS) Allentown; WMBC-TV (IND) Newton; WNBC (NBC) New York; WNJT (PBS) Trenton; WNYW (FOX) New York; WPHL-TV (MNT) Philadelphia; WPIX (CW, IND) New York; WPSG (CW) Philadelphia; WPVI-TV (ABC) Philadelphia; WPXN-TV (ION) New York; WTXF-TV (FOX) Philadelphia; WWOR-TV (MNT) Secaucus.

Programming (via satellite): Eternal Word TV Network; Home Shopping Network; INSP; QVC; ShopNBC; TV Guide Network; Univision.

Current originations: Government Access; Educational Access; Public Access.

Fee: $49.95 installation; $19.49 monthly; $4.95 converter; $29.95 additional installation.

Expanded Basic Service 1

Subscribers: 10,934.

Programming (via satellite): ABC Family Channel; AMC; AmericanLife TV Network; Animal Planet; Arts & Entertainment; BBC America; BET Networks; Bravo; Cartoon Network; CNBC; CNN; Comcast SportsNet Philly; Comedy Central; Country Music TV; C-SPAN; C-SPAN 2; Discovery Channel; Disney Channel; E! Entertainment Television; ESPN; ESPN 2; ESPNews; Food Network; Fox News Channel; FX; Golf Channel; GSN; Hallmark Channel; Headline News; HGTV; History Channel; Lifetime; MSG; MSNBC; MTV; Nickelodeon; Outdoor Channel; Oxygen; Portuguese Channel; Speed Channel; Spike TV; Syfy; TBS Superstation; The Learning Channel; Toon Disney; Travel Channel; truTV; Turner Classic Movies; Turner Network TV; TV Land; USA Network; Versus; VH1; WE tv; Weather Channel; Yankees Entertainment & Sports.

Fee: $49.95 installation; $24.95 additional installation.

Digital Expanded Basic Service

Subscribers: 4,545.

Programming (via satellite): Bio; Boomerang; Discovery Digital Networks; Do-It-Yourself; Fox Movie Channel; Fox Sports World; FSN Digital Atlantic; FSN Digital Central; FSN Digital Pacific; G4; GAS; History Channel International; Independent Film Channel; Lifetime Movie Network; MTV Networks Digital Suite; Music Choice; NASA TV; National Geographic Channel; Nick Jr.; NickToons TV.

Fee: $8.99 monthly; $4.95 converter.

Digital Pay Service 1

Pay Units: 1,174.

Programming (via satellite): Cinemax (multiplexed); Encore (multiplexed); Filipino Channel; Flix; HBO (multiplexed); Playboy TV; Portuguese Channel; RAI International; RTP-USA; Showtime (multiplexed); Starz (multiplexed); The Movie Channel (multiplexed); Zee TV USA.

Fee: $10.49 monthly (Portuguese Channel & RAI), $12.45 monthly (Filipino), $12.99 monthly (Cinemax), $13.49 (monthly) Encore & Starz, $13.99 monthly (Playboy), $14.99 monthly (HBO), $15.49 monthly (Showtime & TMC or Zee TV).

Video-On-Demand: No

Pay-Per-View

Movies, Special Events (delivered digitally), Addressable: Yes.

Internet Service

Operational: Yes. Began: January 1, 1995.

Subscribers: 2,022.

Broadband Service: ProLog Express.

Fee: $39.95 installation; $29.95-$39.95 monthly.

Telephone Service

None

Miles of Plant: 480.0 (coaxial); None (fiber optic).

General Manager: John Capparell. Chief Engineer: Jeff Kelly. Program Director: Andy Himmelwright. Marketing Director: Steve Salash. Regulatory Affairs Director: Arlean Lilly. Customer Service Manager: John Ritter.

Ownership: Service Electric Cable TV Inc. (MSO).

JERSEY CITY—Comcast Cable, 800 Rahway Ave, Union, NJ 7083. Phone: 732-602-7444. Fax: 908-851-8888. Web Site: http://www.comcast.com. ICA: NJ0007.

TV Market Ranking: 1 (JERSEY CITY). Franchise award date: March 5, 1986. Franchise expiration date: N.A. Began: January 17, 1987.

Channel capacity: N.A. Channels available but not in use: N.A.

Basic Service

Subscribers: 48,876.

Programming (received off-air): WABC-TV (ABC) New York; WCBS-TV (CBS) New York; WFUT-DT (TEL) Newark; WLIW (PBS) Garden City; WMBC-TV (IND) Newton; WNBC (NBC) New York; WNET (PBS) Newark; WNJN (PBS) Montclair; WNJU (TMO) Linden; WNYE-TV (PBS) New York; WNYW (FOX) New York; WPIX (CW, IND) New York; WPXN-TV (ION) New York; WWOR-TV (MNT) Secaucus; WXTV-DT (UNV) Paterson.

Programming (via microwave): News 12 New Jersey.

Programming (via satellite): ABC Family Channel; AMC; Animal Planet; Arts & Entertainment; BET Networks; Bravo!; Cartoon Network; CNN; Comedy Central; C-SPAN; Discovery Channel; Discovery Health Channel; E! Entertainment Television; ESPN; ESPN 2; Eternal Word TV Network; Food Network; Fox News Channel; FX; GalaVision; Golf Channel; Headline News; HGTV; History Channel; Home Shopping Network; Lifetime; MoviePlex; MSG; MSG Plus; MSNBC; MTV; Nickelodeon; QVC; Speed Channel; Spike TV; SportsNet New York; Style Network; Syfy; TBS Superstation; The Comcast Network; The Learning Channel; truTV; Turner Classic Movies; Turner Network TV; TV Guide Network; TV Land; USA Network; Versus; VH1; Weather Channel; WGN America; Yankees Entertainment & Sports.

Current originations: Leased Access; Public Access.

Fee: $29.70 installation; $36.20 monthly.

Digital Basic Service

Subscribers: N.A.

Programming (received off-air): WABC-TV (ABC) New York; WCBS-TV (CBS) New York; WNBC (NBC) New York; WNET (PBS) Newark; WNYW (FOX) New York; WPIX (CW, IND) New York.

Programming (via satellite): BBC America; Bio; Canales N; CBS College Sports Network; Cooking Channel; C-SPAN 2; C-SPAN 3; Discovery Digital Networks; Discovery HD Theater; Disney Channel; Do-It-Yourself; Encore (multiplexed); ESPN 2 HD; ESPN Classic Sports; ESPN HD; ESPNews; Flix; Fox College Sports Atlantic; Fox College Sports Central; Fox College Sports Pacific; Fox Soccer; G4; GAS; Gol TV; Great American Country; GSN; Hallmark Channel; History Channel International; INHD; Jewelry Television; Lifetime Movie Network; LOGO; MTV Networks Digital Suite; mun2 television; Music Choice; National Geographic Channel; NBA TV; NFL Network; Nick Jr.; Nick Too; NickToons TV; Oxygen; Palladia; PBS Kids Sprout; ShopNBC; SoapNet; Sundance Channel; Tennis Channel; The Word Network; Toon Disney; Travel Channel; Trinity Broadcasting Network; Turner Network TV HD; TV One; WAM! America's Kidz Network; Weatherscan.

Fee: $15.25 monthly.

Pay Service 1

Pay Units: 25,861.

Programming (via satellite): Cinemax; Showtime.

Digital Pay Service 1

Pay Units: 25,861.

Programming (via satellite): ART America; Cinemax (multiplexed); Cinemax HD; Filipino Channel; HBO (multiplexed); HBO HD; Showtime (multiplexed); Showtime HD; Starz (multiplexed); Starz HDTV; The Movie Channel (multiplexed); TV Asia; Zee TV USA.

Fee: $21.35 monthly (each).

Video-On-Demand: Yes

Pay-Per-View

iN DEMAND (delivered digitally); Spice Hot (delivered digitally), Fee: $5.95; Playboy TV (delivered digitally); Sports PPV (delivered digitally).

Internet Service

Operational: Yes.

Subscribers: 14,549.

Broadband Service: Comcast High Speed Internet.

Fee: $42.95 monthly; $7.00 modem lease; $299.00 modem purchase.

Telephone Service

Digital: Operational

Fee: $44.95 monthly

Miles of Plant: 163.0 (coaxial); 35.0 (fiber optic). Homes passed: 103,991.

Area Vice President: Keith Taub. Vice President, Technical Operations: Bob Kennedy. Vice President, Marketing: Marge Jackson. Public Relations Director: Fred DeAndrea.

City fee: 2% of gross. State fee: 2% of gross.

Ownership: Comcast Cable Communications Inc. (MSO).

LAMBERTVILLE—Comcast Cable, 401 White Horse Rd, Voorhees, NJ 8043. Phone: 856-821-6100. Fax: 856-821-6108. Web Site: http://www.comcast.com. Also serves Delaware Twp. (portions), Hopewell Twp. (Mercer County), Stockton, Titusville & West Amwell Twp. ICA: NJ0042.

TV Market Ranking: 1,4 (Hopewell Twp. (Mercer County)); 4 (Delaware Twp., LAMBERTVILLE, Stockton, Titusville, West Amwell Twp.); Below 100 (Delaware Twp.). Franchise award date: January 1, 1968. Franchise expiration date: N.A. Began: January 1, 1968.

Channel capacity: N.A. Channels available but not in use: N.A.

Basic Service

Subscribers: 7,696.

Programming (received off-air): KYW-TV (CBS) Philadelphia; WABC-TV (ABC) New York; WCAU (NBC) Philadelphia; WCBS-TV (CBS) New York; WFMZ-TV (IND) Allentown; WGTW-TV (IND) Burlington; WHYY-TV (PBS) Wilmington; WLVT-TV (PBS) Allentown; WNBC (NBC) New York; WNET (PBS) Newark; WNJN (PBS) Montclair; WNYW (FOX) New York; WPHL-TV (MNT) Philadelphia; WPIX (CW, IND) New York; WPSG (CW) Philadelphia; WPVI-TV (ABC) Philadelphia; WPXN-TV (ION) New York; WTXF-TV (FOX) Philadelphia; WUVP-DT (UNV) Vineland; WWOR-TV (MNT) Secaucus; WWSI (TMO) Atlantic City; WYBE (ETV) Philadelphia; allband FM.

Programming (via satellite): ABC Family Channel; AMC; Arts & Entertainment; Bravo; Cartoon Network; CNBC; CNN; Comedy Central; C-SPAN; C-SPAN 2; Discovery Channel; E! Entertainment Television; ESPN; ESPN 2; Food Network; Headline News; Home Shopping Network; Lifetime; MTV; Nickelodeon; QVC; Spike TV; Syfy; TBS Superstation; The Comcast Network; The Learning Channel; truTV; Turner Network TV; USA Network; VH1; Weather Channel.

Current originations: Educational Access; Public Access.

Fee: $13.25 monthly.

Expanded Basic Service 1

Subscribers: N.A.

Programming (via satellite): Animal Planet; BET Networks; Comcast SportsNet Philly; Discovery Health Channel; Disney Channel; ESPN Classic Sports; Eternal Word TV Network; Fox News Channel; FX; Golf Channel; HGTV; History Channel; MSG; MSNBC; Speed Channel; Style Network; TV Land; Versus; Yankees Entertainment & Sports.

Fee: $32.90 monthly.

Digital Basic Service

Subscribers: N.A.

Programming (via satellite): BBC America; Bio; Cooking Channel; C-SPAN 3; Discovery Digital Networks; Do-It-Yourself; ESPNews; G4; GAS; History Channel International; MTV Networks Digital Suite; Music Choice; National Geographic Channel; NFL Network; Nick Jr.; Nick Too; SoapNet; Toon Disney; WAM! America's Kidz Network; Weatherscan.

Fee: $19.95 monthly.

Digital Pay Service 1

Pay Units: 1,454.

Programming (via satellite): Cinemax (multiplexed); Encore; Flix (multiplexed); HBO (multiplexed); Showtime (multiplexed); Sundance Channel (multiplexed); The Movie Channel (multiplexed).

Fee: $17.55 monthly (each).

Video-On-Demand: Yes

Pay-Per-View

iN DEMAND (delivered digitally); Playboy TV (delivered digitally); Fresh (delivered digitally); Shorteez (delivered digitally); Pleasure (delivered digitally).

Internet Service

Operational: Yes.

Broadband Service: Comcast High Speed Internet.

Fee: $42.95 monthly.

Telephone Service

Digital: Operational

Fee: $44.95 monthly

Miles of Plant: 402.0 (coaxial); None (fiber optic). Homes passed: 10,125.

Area Vice President: John Del Viscio. Vice President, Technical Operations: Mike Taylor. Vice President, Engineering: John Cody. Marketing Director: Aaron Geisel. Public Relations Director: Fred DeAndrea.

City fee: 2% of gross. State fee: 2% of gross.

Ownership: Comcast Cable Communications Inc. (MSO).

LONG BEACH TWP.—Comcast Cable, 800 Rahway Ave, Union, NJ 7083. Phone: 732-602-7444. Fax: 908-851-8888. Web Site: http://www.comcast.com. Also serves Barnegat Light, Beach Haven, Harvey Cedars, Ship Bottom & Surf City. ICA: NJ0030.

TV Market Ranking: Below 100 (Barnegat Light, Beach Haven, Harvey Cedars, LONG BEACH TWP., Ship Bottom, Surf City). Franchise award date: March 1, 1965. Franchise expiration date: N.A. Began: March 22, 1965.

Channel capacity: N.A. Channels available but not in use: N.A.

Basic Service

Subscribers: 15,486.

Programming (received off-air): KYW-TV (CBS) Philadelphia; WABC-TV (ABC) New York; WCAU (NBC) Philadelphia; WCBS-TV (CBS) New York; WFUT-DT (TEL) Newark; WHYY-TV (PBS) Wilmington; WMCN-TV (IND) Atlantic City; WNBC (NBC) New York; WNET (PBS) Newark; WNJN (PBS) Montclair; WNJU (TMO) Linden; WNYW (FOX) New York; WPHL-TV (MNT) Philadelphia; WPIX (CW, IND) New York; WPSG (CW) Philadelphia; WPVI-TV (ABC) Philadelphia; WPXN-TV (ION) New York; WTXF-TV (FOX) Philadelphia; WWOR-TV (MNT) Secaucus; allband FM.

Programming (via satellite): C-SPAN; C-SPAN 2; Discovery Health Channel; Eternal Word TV Network; Home Shopping Network; QVC; TBS Superstation; The Comcast Network.

Current originations: Leased Access; Government Access; Public Access; Educational Access.

Fee: $11.15 monthly.

Expanded Basic Service 1

Subscribers: N.A.

Programming (via satellite): ABC Family Channel; AMC; Animal Planet; Arts & Entertainment; BET Networks; Bravo; Cartoon Network; CNBC; CNN; Comcast SportsNet Philly; Comedy Central; Discovery Channel; Disney Channel; E! Entertainment Television; ESPN; ESPN 2; ESPN Classic Sports; Food Network; Fox News Channel; FX; Golf Channel; Headline News; HGTV; History Channel; INSP; Lifetime; MSG; MSG Plus; MSNBC; MTV; News 12 New Jersey; Nickelodeon; Speed Channel; Spike TV; SportsNet New York; Style Network; Syfy; The Learning Channel; truTV; Turner Classic Movies; Turner Network TV; TV Land; USA Network; Versus; VH1; Weather Channel; Yankees Entertainment & Sports.

Fee: $41.65 monthly.

Digital Basic Service

Subscribers: 1,600.

Programming (received off-air): WABC-TV (ABC) New York; WCBS-TV (CBS) New York; WNBC (NBC) New York; WNET (PBS) Newark; WNYW (FOX) New York; WPIX (CW, IND) New York.

Programming (via satellite): BBC America; Bio; Bloomberg Television; Canal 52MX; CBS College Sports Network; CMT Pure Country; Cooking Channel; Country Music TV; C-SPAN 3; Current; Discovery Digital Networks; Discovery HD Theater; Disney Channel; Do-It-Yourself; Encore; ESPN 2 HD; ESPN HD; ESPNews; FearNet; Flix; Fox College Sports Atlantic; Fox College Sports Central; Fox College Sports Pacific; Fox Reality Channel; Fox Soccer; G4; GAS; Gol TV; Great American Country; GSN; Hallmark Channel; History Channel International; Howard TV; INHD; Jewelry Television; Lifetime Movie Network; LOGO; MTV Networks Digital Suite; Music Choice; National Geographic Channel; NBA TV; NFL Network; Nick Jr.; Nick Too; NickToons TV; Palladia; PBS Kids Sprout; ShopNBC; SoapNet; Sundance Channel; Tennis Channel; Toon Disney; Travel Channel; Trinity Broadcasting Network; Turner Network TV HD; TV One; Universal HD; Versus HD; Weatherscan.

Fee: $14.95 monthly.

Digital Pay Service 1

Pay Units: 1,007.

Programming (via satellite): Cinemax (multiplexed); Cinemax HD; Encore (multiplexed); HBO (multiplexed); HBO HD; Showtime (multiplexed); Showtime HD; Starz HDTV; The Movie Channel (multiplexed).

Fee: $16.20 monthly (each).

Video-On-Demand: Yes

Pay-Per-View

Addressable homes: 8,009.

iN DEMAND (delivered digitally), Addressable: Yes; Sports PPV (delivered digitally); Playboy TV (delivered digitally); Spice Hot (delivered digitally).

Internet Service

Operational: Yes.

Broadband Service: Comcast High Speed Internet.

Fee: $42.95 monthly.

Telephone Service

Digital: Operational

Fee: $44.95 monthly

Miles of Plant: 182.0 (coaxial); None (fiber optic). Homes passed: 22,443.

Area Vice President: Keith Taub. Vice President, Technical Operations: Bob Kennedy.

Vice President, Marketing: Marge Jackson. Public Relations Director: Fred DeAndrea.
City fee: 2% of gross. State fee: 2% of gross.
Ownership: Comcast Cable Communications Inc. (MSO).

LONG HILL TWP.—Comcast Cable, 90 Lake Dr, East Windsor, NJ 8520. Phone: 609-443-1970. Web Site: http://www.comcast.com. Also serves Bedminster, Bedminster Twp., Bernardsville, Chatham Twp., Chester Borough, Chester Twp., Far Hills Borough, Gillette, Harding Twp., Mendham, Millington, Peapack-Gladstone & Stirling. ICA: NJ0036.

TV Market Ranking: 1 (Bedminster, Bedminster Twp., Bernardsville, Chatham Twp., Chester Borough, Chester Twp., Gillette, Harding Twp., LONG HILL TWP., Mendham, Millington, Peapack-Gladstone, Stirling); 4 (Far Hills Borough). Franchise award date: July 7, 1982. Franchise expiration date: N.A. Began: July 1, 1985.

Channel capacity: N.A. Channels available but not in use: N.A.

Basic Service

Subscribers: N.A. Included in Hillsborough

Programming (received off-air): WABC-TV (ABC) New York; WCBS-TV (CBS) New York; WFUT-DT (TEL) Newark; WLIW (PBS) Garden City; WMBC-TV (IND) Newton; WNBC (NBC) New York; WNET (PBS) Newark; WNJN (PBS) Montclair; WNJU (TMO) Linden; WNYE-TV (PBS) New York; WNYW (FOX) New York; WPIX (CW, IND) New York; WPXN-TV (ION) New York; WWOR-TV (MNT) Secaucus; WXTV-DT (UNV) Paterson.

Programming (via satellite): C-SPAN; C-SPAN 2; Home Shopping Network; QVC; ShopNBC; TV Guide Network; WGN America.

Current originations: Educational Access; Leased Access.

Fee: $41.65 installation; $14.80 monthly; $2.00 converter.

Expanded Basic Service 1

Subscribers: 16,200.

Programming (via satellite): ABC Family Channel; AMC; Animal Planet; Arts & Entertainment; BET Networks; Bravo; Cartoon Network; CNBC; CNN; Comedy Central; Country Music TV; Discovery Channel; Disney Channel; E! Entertainment Television; ESPN; ESPN 2; Eternal Word TV Network; Food Network; Fox News Channel; FX; GSN; Headline News; HGTV; History Channel; Jewelry Television; Lifetime; MSG; MSG Plus; MSNBC; MTV; Nickelodeon; Oxygen; Speed Channel; Spike TV; Syfy; TBS Superstation; The Learning Channel; Travel Channel; truTV; Turner Classic Movies; Turner Network TV; TV Land; USA Network; VH1; Weather Channel; Yankees Entertainment & Sports.

Fee: $35.19 monthly.

Digital Basic Service

Subscribers: N.A. Included in Hillsborough

Programming (via satellite): BBC America; Bio; Boomerang; Cooking Channel; Discovery Digital Networks; Do-It-Yourself; ESPN Classic Sports; ESPNews; Fox Movie Channel; Fox Sports en Espanol; Fox Sports World; FSN Digital Atlantic; FSN Digital Central; FSN Digital Pacific; G4; GAS; Golf Channel; History Channel International; Independent Film Channel; Lifetime Movie Network; MTV Networks Digital Suite; Music Choice; National Geographic Channel; Nick Jr.; Nick Too; Outdoor Channel; Style Network; Sundance Channel; Toon Disney; WE tv.

Pay Service 1

Pay Units: N.A.

Programming (via satellite): Cinemax; HBO (multiplexed); Showtime; The Movie Channel.

Digital Pay Service 1

Pay Units: N.A.

Programming (via satellite): CCTV-4; Chinese Television Network; Cinemax (multiplexed); Encore (multiplexed); Filipino Channel; Flix; HBO (multiplexed); RAI International; Showtime (multiplexed); Starz (multiplexed); The Movie Channel (multiplexed); TV Asia; TV5, La Television International; Zee TV USA.

Fee: $9.95 monthly (RAI or TV5), $11.95 monthly (Filipino), $13.95 monthly (Cinemax, Showtime/TMC/Flix, or Starz/Encore), $14.95 monthly (HBO, TV Asia, Zee TV, or CCTV-4/CTN).

Video-On-Demand: Yes

Pay-Per-View

iN DEMAND (delivered digitally), Addressable: Yes; ETC (delivered digitally); Sports PPV (delivered digitally); iN DEMAND (delivered digitally).

Internet Service

Operational: Yes.

Broadband Service: Comcast High Speed Internet.

Fee: $99.00 installation; $53.95 monthly; $2.00 modem lease.

Telephone Service

Digital: Operational

Homes passed & miles of plant included in Hillsborough

Area Vice President: Keith Taub.

Ownership: Comcast Cable Communications Inc. (MSO).

MAPLE SHADE—Comcast Cable, 401 White Horse Rd, Voorhees, NJ 8043. Phones: 856-779-0771 (Customer service); 800-266-2278; 856-821-6100 (Administrative office). Fax: 856-821-6108. Web Site: http://www.comcast.com. Also serves Brooklawn, Gloucester, Maple Shade Twp. & Mount Ephraim. ICA: NJ0041.

TV Market Ranking: 4 (Brooklawn, Gloucester, MAPLE SHADE, Maple Shade Twp., Mount Ephraim). Franchise award date: October 1, 1978. Franchise expiration date: N.A. Began: March 1, 1975.

Channel capacity: N.A. Channels available but not in use: N.A.

Basic Service

Subscribers: 12,694.

Programming (received off-air): KYW-TV (CBS) Philadelphia; WCAU (NBC) Philadelphia; WFMZ-TV (IND) Allentown; WGTW-TV (IND) Burlington; WHYY-TV (PBS) Wilmington; WMCN-TV (IND) Atlantic City; WNJS (PBS) Camden; WPHL-TV (MNT) Philadelphia; WPPX-TV (ION) Wilmington; WPSG (CW) Philadelphia; WPVI-TV (ABC) Philadelphia; WTXF-TV (FOX) Philadelphia; WUVP-DT (UNV) Vineland; WWSI (TMO) Atlantic City; WYBE (ETV) Philadelphia; 1 FM.

Programming (via satellite): C-SPAN; C-SPAN 2; Eternal Word TV Network; ShopNBC; The Comcast Network.

Current originations: Government Access; Educational Access; Public Access.

Fee: $10.00 monthly.

Expanded Basic Service 1

Subscribers: 10,735.

Programming (via satellite): ABC Family Channel; AMC; Animal Planet; Arts & Entertainment; BET Networks; Bravo; Cartoon Network; CNBC; CNN; Comcast SportsNet Philly; Comedy Central; Discovery Channel; Discovery Health Channel; Disney Channel; E! Entertainment Television; ESPN; ESPN 2; FearNet; Food Network; Fox News Channel; FX; Golf Channel; GSN; Headline News; HGTV; History Channel; Home Shopping Network; Lifetime; MSNBC; MTV; Nickelodeon; QVC; Speed Channel; Spike TV; Style Network; Syfy; TBS Superstation; The Learning Channel; truTV; Turner Classic Movies; Turner Network TV; TV Land; USA Network; Versus; VH1; Weather Channel.

Fee: $42.20 monthly.

Digital Basic Service

Subscribers: N.A. Included in Burlington County

Programming (received off-air): KYW-TV (CBS) Philadelphia; WCAU (NBC) Philadelphia; WHYY-TV (PBS) Wilmington; WPHL-TV (MNT) Philadelphia; WPSG (CW) Philadelphia; WPVI-TV (ABC) Philadelphia; WTXF-TV (FOX) Philadelphia.

Programming (via satellite): BBC America; Bio; Bloomberg Television; Canales N; Cooking Channel; Country Music TV; C-SPAN 3; Current; Discovery Digital Networks; Discovery HD Theater; Do-It-Yourself; Encore (multiplexed); ESPN 2 HD; ESPN Classic Sports; ESPN HD; ESPNews; Flix; Fox College Sports Atlantic; Fox College Sports Central; Fox College Sports Pacific; Fox Reality Channel; Fox Soccer; G4; GAS; Gol TV; Great American Country; Hallmark Channel; History Channel International; INHD; Jewelry Television; Lifetime Movie Network; MTV Networks Digital Suite; Music Choice; National Geographic Channel; NBA TV; NFL Network; Nick Jr.; Nick Too; NickToons TV; Oxygen; Palladia; PBS Kids Sprout; SoapNet; Sundance Channel; Telefutura; Tennis Channel; Toon Disney; Travel Channel; Turner Network TV HD; TV One; Universal HD; Versus HD; WAM! America's Kidz Network; Weatherscan.

Fee: $14.95 monthly.

Digital Pay Service 1

Pay Units: 4,968.

Programming (via satellite): Cinemax (multiplexed); Cinemax HD; Cinemax On Demand; HBO (multiplexed); HBO HD; HBO On Demand; Showtime (multiplexed); Showtime HD; Showtime On Demand; Starz (multiplexed); Starz HDTV; Starz On Demand; The Movie Channel (multiplexed); The Movie Channel On Demand.

Fee: $19.50 monthly (each).

Video-On-Demand: Yes

Pay-Per-View

Addressable homes: 5,295.

iN DEMAND, Addressable: Yes; iN DEMAND (delivered digitally); Playboy TV (delivered digitally); Fresh (delivered digitally); Canal 52MX (delivered digitally); ESPN Now (delivered digitally); Sports PPV (delivered digitally).

Internet Service

Operational: Yes.

Broadband Service: Comcast High Speed Internet.

Fee: $42.95 monthly.

Telephone Service

Digital: Operational

Fee: $44.95 monthly

Miles of Plant: 110.0 (coaxial); None (fiber optic). Homes passed: 17,390.

Area Vice President: John Del Viscio. Vice President, Technical Operations: Mike Taylor. Vice President, Engineering: John Cody. Marketing Director: Aaron Geisel. Public Relations Director: Fred DeAndrea.

City fee: 2% of gross.

Ownership: Comcast Cable Communications Inc. (MSO).

MILLSTONE TWP.—Cablevision Systems Corp. Now served by MONMOUTH, NJ [NJ0012]. ICA: NJ0047.

MONMOUTH COUNTY—Cablevision Systems Corp., 683 Route 10 E, Randolph, NJ 7869. Phones: 516-803-2300 (Corporate office); 973-659-2200. Fax: 973-659-2266. Web Site: http://www.cablevision.com. Also serves Asbury Park, Avon-by-the-Sea, Belmar, Berkley Twp., Bradley Beach, Brielle, Chadwick Beach, Clarksburg, Colts Neck, Dover Twp. (portions), Englishtown, Farmingdale, Freehold, Freehold Twp., Howell, Howell Twp., Interlaken, Jackson, Jackson Twp., Lake Como, Lakewood, Lakewood Twp., Lavallette, Manalapan Twp., Manasquan, Marlboro Twp., Millstone Twp., Neptune, Neptune Twp., Normandy Beach, Ocean Beach, Ocean Twp., Ortley Beach, Pelican Island, Perrineville, Robbinsville, Sea Girt, Seaside Heights, Seaside Park, South Seaside Park, Spring Lake, Spring Lake Heights, Upper Freehold Twp., Wall & Wall Twp. ICA: NJ0012.

TV Market Ranking: 1 (Asbury Park, Avon-by-the-Sea, Belmar, Berkley Twp., Bradley Beach, Clarksburg, Colts Neck, Englishtown, Farmingdale, Freehold, Howell, Interlaken, Jackson, Lake Como, Lakewood, Manalapan Twp., Marlboro Twp., Millstone Twp., Neptune, Ocean Twp., Perrineville, Robbinsville, Spring Lake, Spring Lake Heights, Upper Freehold Twp.NEW JERSEY); 1,4 (Freehold Twp., MONMOUTH COUNTY (portions), Wall); 4 (Howell Twp., Jackson Twp., Lakewood Twp.); Outside TV Markets (Brielle, Chadwick Beach, Dover Twp. (portions) (portions), Lavallette, Manasquan, Normandy Beach, Ocean Beach, Ortley Beach, Pelican Island, Sea Girt, Seaside Heights, Seaside Park, South Seaside Park, MONMOUTH COUNTY (portions), Wall). Franchise award date: N.A. Franchise expiration date: N.A. Began: November 1, 1979.

Channel capacity: N.A. Channels available but not in use: N.A.

Basic Service

Subscribers: 164,956.

Programming (received off-air): WABC-TV (ABC) New York; WCAU (NBC) Philadelphia; WCBS-TV (CBS) New York; WFUT-DT (TEL) Newark; WHYY-TV (PBS) Wilmington; WNBC (NBC) New York; WNET (PBS) Newark; WNJT (PBS) Trenton; WNJU (TMO) Linden; WNYW (FOX) New York; WPHL-TV (MNT) Philadelphia; WPIX (CW, IND) New York; WPVI-TV (ABC) Philadelphia; WPXN-TV (ION) New York; WTXF-TV (FOX) Philadelphia; WWOR-TV (MNT) Secaucus; WXTV-DT (UNV) Paterson.

Programming (via microwave): News 12 New Jersey.

Programming (via satellite): Home Shopping Network; Weather Channel.

Current originations: Leased Access; Religious Access; Government Access; Educational Access; Public Access.

Fee: $49.95 installation; $12.92 monthly; $2.28 converter.

Expanded Basic Service 1

Subscribers: 121,967.

Programming (via satellite): ABC Family Channel; AMC; Animal Planet; Arts & Entertainment; BET Networks; Bravo; Cartoon Network; CNBC; CNN; Comedy Central; C-SPAN; C-SPAN 2; Discovery Channel; Disney Channel; E! Entertainment Television; ESPN; ESPN 2; Flix; Food Network; Fox News Channel; Fuse; FX; GSN; Headline News; HGTV; History Channel; Independent Film Channel; Lifetime; MSG; MSG Plus; MSNBC; MTV; MTV2; News 12 Traffic & Weather; Nickelodeon; QVC; ShopNBC; SoapNet; Speed Channel; Spike TV; SportsNet New York; Syfy; TBS Superstation; The Learning Channel; Travel Channel; truTV; Turner Classic Movies; Turner Network TV; TV Land; USA Network; VH1; WE tv; Yankees Entertainment & Sports.

Fee: $37.03 monthly.

Digital Basic Service

Subscribers: N.A.

Programming (received off-air): WABC-TV (ABC) New York; WCBS-TV (CBS) New York; WNBC (NBC) New York; WNYW (FOX) New York; WPIX (CW, IND) New York.

Programming (via satellite): Azteca America; BBC World News; Bio; Bloomberg Television; Canal Sur; Caracol; Cartoon Network Tambien en Espanol; Cine Latino; CNN en Espanol; CNN HD; Country Music TV; C-SPAN 3; Discovery en Espanol; Discovery HD Theater; Discovery Home Channel; Discovery Kids Channel; Discovery Military Channel; Docu TVE; Ecuavisia Internacional; ESPN 2 HD; ESPN Classic Sports; ESPN Deportes; ESPN HD; ESPNews; EuroNews; EWTN en Espanol; Food Network HD; Fox College Sports Atlantic; Fox College Sports Central; Fox College Sports Pacific; Fox Movie Channel; Fox Soccer; Fox Sports en Espanol; Fuel TV; G4; GameHD; Gol TV; Golf Channel; Great American Country; Hallmark Channel; here! On Demand; HGTV HD; History Channel en Espanol; History Channel International; Howard TV; HTV Musica; ID Investigation Discovery; Infinito; Jewelry Television; La Familia Network; Latele Novela Network; LOGO; Maria+Vision; Momentum TV; MTV Hits; MTV Tres; mun2 television; Music Choice; National Geographic Channel; National Geographic Channel HD Network; NBA TV; NHL Network; Nick Jr.; NickToons TV; Outdoor Channel; Oxygen; Science Channel; Sorpresa; Sundance Channel; Supercanal Caribe; TBS in HD; TeenNick; Telefe International; Toon Disney; Toon Disney en Espanol; Turner Network TV HD; TV Chile; TV Colombia; TVE Internacional; TVG Network; Universal HD; Utilisima; VeneMovies; Versus; Versus HD; VH1 Classic; VH1 Soul; V-me TV; WAPA America; World Cinema HD; YES HD.

Fee: $10.95 monthly.

Pay Service 1

Pay Units: N.A.

Programming (via satellite): Cinemax; HBO (multiplexed); Showtime (multiplexed); The Movie Channel.

Digital Pay Service 1

Pay Units: 74,887.

Programming (via satellite): CCTV-4; Channel One; Cinemax (multiplexed); Cinemax HD; Cinemax On Demand; Encore (multiplexed); HBO (multiplexed); HBO HD; HBO On Demand; International Television (ITV); Korean Channel; MBC America; Playboy TV; Portuguese Channel; RAI International; Russian Television Network; Showtime (multiplexed); Showtime HD; Showtime On Demand; Starz; Starz HDTV; The Movie Channel (multiplexed); The Movie Channel HD; TV Asia; TV Japan; TV Polonia; TV5, La Television International; Zee TV USA.

Fee: $10.00 installation; $9.95 monthly (Showtime, Cinemax, TMC, Starz/Encore, Playboy, RAI, SPT, TV5 or TV Polonia), $11.95 monthly (HBO), $24.95 monthly (TV Japan).

Video-On-Demand: Yes

Internet Service

Operational: Yes.

Broadband Service: Optimum Online.

Fee: $46.95 installation; $34.95 monthly; $299.00 modem purchase.

Telephone Service

Digital: Operational

Fee: $46.95 installation; $34.95 monthly

Miles of Plant: 3,582.0 (coaxial); 399.0 (fiber optic). Homes passed: 203,565.

Vice President, Field Operations: Frank Dagliere. Vice President, Government Affairs: Adam Falk.

City fee: 2% of gross. State fee: 2% of gross.

Ownership: Cablevision Systems Corp. (MSO).

MONMOUTH COUNTY—Comcast Cable, 403 South St, Eatontown, NJ 07724-1878. Phones: 732-602-7444 (Union office); 732-542-8107. Fax: 732-935-5572. Web Site: http://www.comcast.com. Also serves Allenhurst, Atlantic Highlands, Deal, Eatontown, Fair Haven, Fort Monmouth, Freehold, Hazlet Twp., Highlands, Holmdel Twp., Little Silver, Loch Arbour, Long Branch, Middletown Twp., Monmouth Beach, Oceanport, Red Bank, Rumson, Sea Bright, Shrewsbury, Shrewsbury Twp., Tinton Falls & West Long Branch. ICA: NJ0009.

TV Market Ranking: 1 (Allenhurst, Atlantic Highlands, Deal, Eatontown, Fair Haven, Fort Monmouth, Hazlet Twp., Highlands, Holmdel Twp., Little Silver, Loch Arbour, Long Branch, Middletown Twp., Monmouth Beach, MONMOUTH COUNTY, Oceanport, Red Bank, Rumson, Sea Bright, Shrewsbury, Shrewsbury Twp., Tinton Falls, West Long Branch); 1,4 (Freehold). Franchise award date: N.A. Franchise expiration date: N.A. Began: March 1, 1972.

Channel capacity: N.A. Channels available but not in use: N.A.

Basic Service

Subscribers: 75,460.

Programming (received off-air): WABC-TV (ABC) New York; WCAU (NBC) Philadelphia; WCBS-TV (CBS) New York; WFUT-DT (TEL) Newark; WMBC-TV (IND) Newton; WNBC (NBC) New York; WNET (PBS) Newark; WNJN (PBS) Montclair; WNJU (TMO) Linden; WNYE-TV (PBS) New York; WNYW (FOX) New York; WPIX (CW, IND) New York; WPXN-TV (ION) New York; WWOR-TV (MNT) Secaucus; WXTV-DT (UNV) Paterson.

Programming (via satellite): AMC; Cartoon Network; C-SPAN; Eternal Word TV Network; Fox News Channel; QVC; Syfy; TBS Superstation; The Comcast Network; Turner Network TV; WGN America.

Current originations: Educational Access; Public Access.

Fee: $14.50 monthly.

Expanded Basic Service 1

Subscribers: N.A.

Programming (via satellite): ABC Family Channel; Animal Planet; Arts & Entertainment; BET Networks; Bravo; CNBC; CNN; Comedy Central; Country Music TV; C-SPAN 2; Discovery Channel; Discovery Health Channel; E! Entertainment Television; ESPN; ESPN 2; Food Network; FX; Golf Channel; Headline News; HGTV; History Channel; Home Shopping Network; Lifetime; MoviePlex; MSG; MSG Plus; MSNBC; MTV; News 12 New Jersey; Nickelodeon; Speed Channel; Spike TV; SportsNet New York; Style Network; The Learning Channel; truTV; Turner Classic Movies; TV Guide Network; TV Land; USA Network; Versus; VH1; Weather Channel; Yankees Entertainment & Sports.

Fee: $44.25 monthly.

Digital Basic Service

Subscribers: N.A.

Programming (received off-air): WABC-TV (ABC) New York; WCBS-TV (CBS) New York; WNBC (NBC) New York; WNET (PBS) Newark; WNYW (FOX) New York; WPIX (CW, IND) New York.

Programming (via satellite): BBC America; Bio; Bloomberg Television; Canales N; CBS College Sports Network; Cooking Channel; C-SPAN 3; Current; Discovery Digital Networks; Discovery HD Theater; Disney Channel; Do-It-Yourself; Encore (multiplexed); ESPN 2 HD; ESPN Classic Sports; ESPN HD; ESPNews; Flix; Fox College Sports Atlantic; Fox College Sports Central; Fox College Sports Pacific; Fox Reality Channel; Fox Soccer; G4; GAS; Gol TV; Great American Country; GSN; Hallmark Channel; History Channel International; INHD; Jewelry Television; Lifetime Movie Network; MTV Networks Digital Suite; Music Choice; National Geographic Channel; NBA TV; NFL Network; Nick Jr.; Nick Too; NickToons TV; Oxygen; Palladia; PBS Kids Sprout; ShopNBC; SoapNet; Sundance Channel; Tennis Channel; Travel Channel; Trinity Broadcasting Network; Turner Network TV HD; TV Guide Network; TV One; Universal HD; Versus HD; WAM! America's Kidz Network; Weatherscan.

Fee: $14.95 monthly.

Digital Pay Service 1

Pay Units: 30,703.

Programming (via satellite): Cinemax (multiplexed); Cinemax HD; Cinemax On Demand; HBO (multiplexed); HBO HD; HBO On Demand; Showtime (multiplexed); Showtime HD; Showtime On Demand; Starz (multiplexed); Starz HDTV; Starz On Demand; The Movie Channel (multiplexed); The Movie Channel On Demand.

Fee: $16.25 monthly (each).

Video-On-Demand: Yes

Pay-Per-View

Fresh (delivered digitally); Sports PPV (delivered digitally); iN DEMAND (delivered digitally); Playgirl TV (delivered digitally); ESPN (delivered digitally).

Internet Service

Operational: Yes.

Subscribers: 19,231.

Broadband Service: Comcast High Speed Internet.

Fee: $42.95 monthly; $7.00 modem lease; $299.00 modem purchase.

Telephone Service

Digital: Operational

Miles of Plant: 1,292.0 (coaxial); None (fiber optic). Homes passed: 100,613.

Area Vice President: Keith Taub. Vice President, Technical Operations: Bob Kennedy. Vice President, Marketing: Marge Jackson. Public Relations Director: Fred DeAndrea.

City fee: 2% of gross. State fee: 2% of gross.

Ownership: Comcast Cable Communications Inc. (MSO).

NEWARK—Cablevision Systems Corp., 40 Potash Rd, Oakland, NJ 07436-3100. Phones: 516-803-2300 (Corporate office); 201-651-4000. Fax: 518-803-1183. Web Site: http://www.cablevision.com. Also serves South Orange. ICA: NJ0011.

TV Market Ranking: 1 (NEWARK, South Orange). Franchise award date: N.A. Franchise expiration date: N.A. Began: June 19, 1982.

Channel capacity: N.A. Channels available but not in use: N.A.

Basic Service

Subscribers: 54,271.

Programming (received off-air): WABC-TV (ABC) New York; WCBS-TV (CBS) New York; WFME-TV (ETV) West Milford; WFUT-DT (TEL) Newark; WLIW (PBS) Garden City; WMBC-TV (IND) Newton; WNBC (NBC) New York; WNET (PBS) Newark; WNJN (PBS) Montclair; WNJU (TMO) Linden; WNYW (FOX) New York; WPIX (CW, IND) New York; WPXN-TV (ION) New York; WWOR-TV (MNT) Secaucus; WXTV-DT (UNV) Paterson; 2 FMs.

Programming (via microwave): News 12 New Jersey.

Programming (via satellite): Home Shopping Network.

Current originations: Leased Access; Government Access; Educational Access; Public Access.

Fee: $49.95 installation; $9.32 monthly; $2.80 converter.

Expanded Basic Service 1

Subscribers: N.A.

Programming (via satellite): ABC Family Channel; AMC; Animal Planet; Arts & Entertainment; BET Networks; Bravo; Cartoon Network; CNBC; CNN; Comedy Central; C-SPAN; C-SPAN 2; Discovery Channel; Disney Channel; E! Entertainment Television; ESPN; ESPN 2; Food Network; Fox News Channel; Fuse; FX; GalaVision; GSN; Headline News; HGTV; History Channel; Lifetime; MSNBC; MTV; MTV2; mun2 television; News 12 Traffic & Weather; Nickelodeon; QVC; ShopNBC; SoapNet; Speed Channel; Spike TV; SportsNet New York; Syfy; TBS Superstation; The Learning Channel; Travel Channel; truTV; Turner Network TV; TV Land; USA Network; VH1; WE tv; Weather Channel.

Fee: $40.63 monthly.

Digital Basic Service

Subscribers: N.A.

Programming (received off-air): CNN HD; WABC-TV (ABC) New York; WNBC (NBC) New York; WNYW (FOX) New York; WPIX (CW, IND) New York; WWOR-TV (MNT) Secaucus.

Programming (via satellite): Azteca America; BBC World News; Bio; Bloomberg Television; Canal Sur; Caracol; Cartoon Network Tambien en Espanol; Cine Latino; CNN en Espanol; Country Music TV; C-SPAN 3; Discovery en Espanol; Discovery HD Theater; Discovery Home Channel; Discovery Kids Channel; Discovery Military Channel; Docu TVE; Ecuavisia Internacional; ESPN 2 HD; ESPN Classic Sports; ESPN Deportes; ESPN HD; ESPNews; EuroNews; EWTN en

Espanol; Food Network HD; Fox College Sports Atlantic; Fox College Sports Central; Fox College Sports Pacific; Fox Movie Channel; Fox Soccer; Fox Sports en Espanol; Fuel TV; G4; GameHD; Gol TV; Golf Channel; Great American Country; Hallmark Channel; here! On Demand; HGTV HD; History Channel en Espanol; History Channel International; Howard TV; HTV Musica; ID Investigation Discovery; Infinito; Jewelry Television; La Familia Network; Latele Novela Network; LOGO; Maria+Vision; Momentum TV; MSG Plus; MTV Hits; MTV Tres; mun2 television; Music Choice; National Geographic Channel; National Geographic Channel HD Network; NBA TV; NHL Network; Nick Jr.; NickToons TV; Outdoor Channel; Oxygen; Science Channel; Sorpresa; Sundance Channel; Supercanal Caribe; TBS in HD; TeenNick; Telefe International; The Word Network; Toon Disney; Toon Disney en Espanol; Turner Network TV HD; TV Chile; TV Colombia; TVE Internacional; TVG Network; Universal HD; Utilisima; VeneMovies; Versus; Versus HD; VH1 Classic; VH1 Soul; V-me TV; WAPA America; WCBS-TV (CBS) New York; World Cinema HD; YES HD.

Fee: $10.95 monthly.

Pay Service 1

Pay Units: 28,889.

Programming (via satellite): Cinemax; Flix; HBO (multiplexed); Independent Film Channel; MSG; MSG Plus; Playboy TV; Portuguese Channel; Showtime (multiplexed); The Movie Channel; Turner Classic Movies; Yankees Entertainment & Sports.

Digital Pay Service 1

Pay Units: N.A.

Programming (via satellite): CCTV-4; Channel One; Cinemax (multiplexed); Cinemax HD; Cinemax On Demand; Encore (multiplexed); HBO (multiplexed); HBO HD; HBO On Demand; International Television (ITV); Korean Channel; MBC America; Playboy TV; Portuguese Channel; RAI USA; Russian Television Network; Showtime (multiplexed); Showtime HD; Showtime On Demand; Starz (multiplexed); Starz HDTV; The Movie Channel (multiplexed); The Movie Channel HD; TV Asia; TV Japan; TV Polonia; Zee TV USA.

Fee: $9.95 monthly (Showtime, Cinemax, TMC, Starz/Encore, Playboy, RAI, SPT, TV5, or TV Polonia), $11.95 monthly (HBO), $24.95 monthly (TV Japan).

Video-On-Demand: Yes

Pay-Per-View

Addressable homes: 49,000.

Playboy TV (delivered digitally); iN DEMAND (delivered digitally); NBA TV (delivered digitally); Sports PPV (delivered digitally); Playboy TV, Addressable: Yes.

Internet Service

Operational: Yes.

Broadband Service: Optimum Online.

Fee: $46.95 installation; $34.95 monthly; $299.00 modem purchase.

Telephone Service

Digital: Operational

Fee: $46.95 installation; $34.95 monthly

Miles of Plant: 385.0 (coaxial); None (fiber optic). Homes passed: 129,216.

Vice President, Field Operations: Christopher Fulton.

City fee: 3% of gross. State fee: 2% of gross.

Ownership: Cablevision Systems Corp. (MSO).

OAKLAND—Cablevision Systems Corp., 40 Potash Rd, Oakland, NJ 07436-3100. Phones: 516-803-2300 (Corporate office); 201-651-4000. Fax: 516-803-1183. Web Site: http://www.cablevision.com. Also serves Allendale, Alpine, Bloomingdale, Bogota, Butler, Cedar Grove Twp., Clifton, Elmwood Park, Franklin Lakes, Garfield, Glen Rock, Hackensack, Haledon, Hasbrouck Heights, Hawthorne, Ho-Ho-Kus, Kinnelon, Lincoln Park, Little Falls Twp., Lodi, Maywood, Midland Park, Montville Twp. (northeastern portion), North Caldwell, North Haledon, Nutley Twp., Park Ridge, Passaic, Pequannock Twp., Pompton Lakes, Prospect Park, Ramsey, Ridgewood, Ringwood, River Edge, Riverdale, Rochelle Park, Saddle Brook Twp., South Hackensack Twp., Teaneck, Totowa, Upper Saddle River, Waldwick, Wanaque, Washington Twp. (Bergen County), Wayne, West Paterson, Westwood, Wood-Ridge & Wyckoff. ICA: NJ0002.

TV Market Ranking: 1 (Allendale, Alpine, Bloomingdale, Bogota, Butler, Cedar Grove Twp., Clifton, Elmwood Park, Franklin Lakes, Garfield, Glen Rock, Hackensack, Haledon, Hasbrouck Heights, Hawthorne, Ho-Ho-Kus, Kinnelon, Lincoln Park, Little Falls Twp., Lodi, Maywood, Midland Park, Montville Twp. (northeastern portion), North Caldwell, North Haledon, Nutley Twp., OAKLAND, Park Ridge, Passaic, Pequannock Twp., Pompton Lakes, Prospect Park, Ramsey, Ridgewood, Ringwood, River Edge, Riverdale, Rochelle Park, Saddle Brook Twp., South Hackensack Twp., Teaneck, Totowa, Upper Saddle River, Waldwick, Wanaque, Washington Twp. (Bergen County), Wayne, West Paterson, Westwood, Wood-Ridge, Wyckoff). Franchise award date: N.A. Franchise expiration date: N.A. Began: September 1, 1966.

Channel capacity: N.A. Channels available but not in use: N.A.

Basic Service

Subscribers: 221,209.

Programming (received off-air): WABC-TV (ABC) New York; WCBS-TV (CBS) New York; WFME-TV (ETV) West Milford; WFUT-DT (TEL) Newark; WLIW (PBS) Garden City; WLNY-TV (IND) Riverhead; WMBC-TV (IND) Newton; WNBC (NBC) New York; WNET (PBS) Newark; WNJN (PBS) Montclair; WNJU (TMO) Linden; WNYW (FOX) New York; WPIX (CW, IND) New York; WPXN-TV (ION) New York; WRNN-TV (IND) Kingston; WWOR-TV (MNT) Secaucus; WXTV-DT (UNV) Paterson; 15 FMs.

Programming (via microwave): News 12 New Jersey.

Programming (via satellite): Home Shopping Network; QVC.

Current originations: Religious Access; Public Access.

Fee: $49.95 installation; $12.18 monthly; $1.00 converter.

Expanded Basic Service 1

Subscribers: N.A.

Programming (via satellite): ABC Family Channel; AMC; Animal Planet; Arts & Entertainment; BET Networks; Bravo; Cartoon Network; CNBC; CNN; Comedy Central; C-SPAN; C-SPAN 2; Discovery Channel; Disney Channel; E! Entertainment Television; ESPN; ESPN 2; Food Network; Fox News Channel; Fuse; FX; GSN; Headline News; HGTV; History Channel; Lifetime; MSG; MSG Plus; MSNBC; MTV; MTV2; News 12 Traffic & Weather; Nickelodeon; ShopNBC; SoapNet; Speed Channel; Spike TV; SportsNet New York; Syfy; TBS Superstation; The Comcast Network; The Learning Channel; Travel Channel; truTV; Turner Classic Movies; Turner Network TV; TV Land; USA Network; VH1; WE tv; Weather Channel; Yankees Entertainment & Sports.

Fee: $37.77 monthly.

Digital Basic Service

Subscribers: N.A.

Programming (received off-air): WABC-TV (ABC) New York; WCBS-TV (CBS) New York; WNBC (NBC) New York; WNYW (FOX) New York; WPIX (CW, IND) New York; WWOR-TV (MNT) Secaucus.

Programming (via satellite): Azteca America; BBC World News; Bio; Bloomberg Television; Canal Sur; Caracol; Cartoon Network Tambien en Espanol; Cine Latino; CNN en Espanol; CNN HD; Country Music TV; C-SPAN 3; Discovery en Espanol; Discovery HD Theater; Discovery Home Channel; Discovery Military Channel; Docu TVE; Ecuavisia Internacional; ESPN 2 HD; ESPN Classic Sports; ESPN Deportes; ESPN HD; ESPNews; EuroNews; EWTN en Espanol; Food Network HD; Fox College Sports Atlantic; Fox College Sports Central; Fox College Sports Pacific; Fox Movie Channel; Fox Soccer; Fox Sports en Espanol; Fuel TV; G4; GameHD; Gol TV; Golf Channel; Great American Country; Hallmark Channel; here! On Demand; HGTV HD; History Channel en Espanol; History Channel International; Howard TV; HTV Musica; ID Investigation Discovery; Infinito; Jewelry Television; La Familia Network; Latele Novela Network; LOGO; Maria+Vision; Momentum TV; MTV Hits; MTV Tres; mun2 television; Music Choice; National Geographic Channel; National Geographic Channel HD Network; NBA TV; NHL Network; Nick Jr.; NickToons TV; Outdoor Channel; Oxygen; Science Channel; Sorpresa; Sundance Channel; Supercanal Caribe; TBS in HD; TeenNick; Telefe International; Toon Disney; Toon Disney en Espanol; Turner Network TV HD; TV Chile; TV Colombia; TVE Internacional; TVG Network; Universal HD; Utilisima; VeneMovies; Versus; Versus HD; VH1 Classic; VH1 Soul; V-me TV; WAPA America; World Cinema HD; YES HD.

Fee: $10.95 monthly.

Pay Service 1

Pay Units: N.A.

Programming (via satellite): Cinemax; Flix; HBO (multiplexed); Independent Film Channel; Showtime (multiplexed); The Movie Channel.

Digital Pay Service 1

Pay Units: 109,130.

Programming (via satellite): CCTV-4; Channel One; Cinemax (multiplexed); Cinemax HD; Cinemax On Demand; Encore (multiplexed); HBO (multiplexed); HBO HD; HBO On Demand; International Television (ITV); Korean Channel; MBC America; Playboy TV; RAI USA; Russian Television Network; Showtime (multiplexed); Showtime HD; Showtime On Demand; Society of Portuguese Television; Starz; Starz HDTV; The Movie Channel (multiplexed); The Movie Channel HD; TV Asia; TV Japan; TV Polonia; TV5, La Television International; Zee TV USA.

Fee: $9.95 monthly (Showtime, Cinemax, TMC, Starz/Encore, Playboy, RAI, SPT, TV5 or TV Polonia), $11.95 monthly (HBO), $24.95 monthly (TV Japan).

Video-On-Demand: Yes

Pay-Per-View

iN DEMAND; Playboy TV; Fresh; Shorteez.

Internet Service

Operational: Yes.

Broadband Service: Optimum Online.

Fee: $46.95 installation; $34.95 monthly; $299.00 modem purchase.

Telephone Service

Digital: Operational

Fee: $46.95 installation; $34.95 monthly

Miles of Plant: 2,937.0 (coaxial); None (fiber optic). Homes passed: 320,639. Total homes in franchised area: 322,639.

Vice President, Field Operations: Christopher Fulton. Government Affairs Manager: Gary Shaw.

City fee: 2% of basic gross. State fee: 0.55% of basi.

Ownership: Cablevision Systems Corp. (MSO).

OCEAN COUNTY—Comcast Cable, 800 Rahway Ave, Union, NJ 7083. Phone: 732-602-7444. Fax: 908-851-8888. Web Site: http://www.comcast.com. Also serves Bay Head, Brick Twp., Mantoloking, Point Pleasant & Point Pleasant Beach. ICA: NJ0020.

TV Market Ranking: Outside TV Markets (Bay Head, Brick Twp., Mantoloking, OCEAN COUNTY, Point Pleasant, Point Pleasant Beach). Franchise award date: N.A. Franchise expiration date: N.A. Began: March 1, 1968.

Channel capacity: N.A. Channels available but not in use: N.A.

Basic Service

Subscribers: 39,269.

Programming (received off-air): KYW-TV (CBS) Philadelphia; WABC-TV (ABC) New York; WCBS-TV (CBS) New York; WFUT-DT (TEL) Newark; WNBC (NBC) New York; WNET (PBS) Newark; WNJN (PBS) Montclair; WNYE-TV (PBS) New York; WNYW (FOX) New York; WPHL-TV (MNT) Philadelphia; WPIX (CW, IND) New York; WPVI-TV (ABC) Philadelphia; WPXN-TV (ION) New York; WTXF-TV (FOX) Philadelphia; WWOR-TV (MNT) Secaucus; WXTV-DT (UNV) Paterson.

Programming (via satellite): AMC; Cartoon Network; C-SPAN; C-SPAN 2; Discovery Channel; Eternal Word TV Network; Fox News Channel; QVC; Syfy; TBS Superstation; The Comcast Network; Trinity Broadcasting Network; Turner Network TV.

Current originations: Government Access.

Fee: $15.15 monthly; $25.00 additional installation.

Expanded Basic Service 1

Subscribers: N.A.

Programming (via satellite): ABC Family Channel; Animal Planet; Arts & Entertainment; Bravo; CNBC; CNN; Comcast SportsNet Philly; Comedy Central; C-SPAN 2; Discovery Health Channel; E! Entertainment Television; ESPN; ESPN 2; Food Network; FX; Golf Channel; Headline News; HGTV; History Channel; Home Shopping Network; Lifetime; MSG; MSNBC; MTV; News 12 New Jersey; Nickelodeon; SoapNet; Speed Channel; Spike TV; SportsNet New York; Style Network; The Learning Channel; truTV; Turner Classic Movies; TV Guide Network; TV Land; USA Network; Versus; VH1; Weather Channel; Yankees Entertainment & Sports.

Fee: $43.60 monthly.

Digital Basic Service

Subscribers: N.A.

Programming (received off-air): WABC-TV (ABC) New York; WCAU (NBC) Philadelphia; WCBS-TV (CBS) New York; WNBC (NBC) New York; WNET (PBS) Newark; WNYW (FOX) New York.

Programming (via satellite): BBC America; Bio; Bloomberg Television; Canales N; CBS College Sports Network; Cooking Channel; C-SPAN 3; Discovery Digital Networks; Disney Channel; Do-It-Yourself; En-

core (multiplexed); ESPN 2 HD; ESPN Classic Sports; ESPN HD; ESPNews; Flix; Fox College Sports Atlantic; Fox College Sports Central; Fox College Sports Pacific; Fox Reality Channel; Fox Sports World; G4; GAS; Gol TV; Great American Country; GSN; Hallmark Channel; History Channel International; INHD; Jewelry Television; MTV Networks Digital Suite; Music Choice; National Geographic Channel; NBA TV; NFL Network; Nick Jr.; Nick Too; NickToons TV; Oxygen; Palladia; PBS Kids Sprout; ShopNBC; SoapNet; Sundance Channel; Toon Disney; Travel Channel; Trinity Broadcasting Network; Turner Network TV; TV One; Universal HD; Versus HD; WAM! America's Kidz Network; Weatherscan.
Fee: $14.95 monthly.

Digital Pay Service 1
Pay Units: 12,284.
Programming (via satellite): Cinemax (multiplexed); Cinemax HD; HBO (multiplexed); HBO HD; Showtime (multiplexed); Showtime HD; Starz (multiplexed); Starz HDTV; The Movie Channel (multiplexed).
Fee: $16.25 monthly (each).

Video-On-Demand: Yes

Pay-Per-View
Spice Hot (delivered digitally); iN DEMAND (delivered digitally); Playboy TV (delivered digitally); Movies (delivered digitally); Sports PPV (delivered digitally); ESPN (delivered digitally).

Internet Service
Operational: Yes.
Broadband Service: Comcast High Speed Internet.
Fee: $42.95 monthly; $7.00 modem lease; $299.00 modem purchase.

Telephone Service
Digital: Operational
Fee: $44.95 monthly

Miles of Plant: 500.0 (coaxial); None (fiber optic). Homes passed: 79,086.
Area Vice President: Keith Taub. Vice President & Operations Manager: Bob Kennedy. Vice President, Marketing: Marge Jackson. Public Relations Director: Fred DeAndrea.
City fee: 2% of gross. State fee: 2% of gross.
Ownership: Comcast Cable Communications Inc. (MSO).

PALISADES PARK—Time Warner Cable, 120 E 23rd St, New York, NY 10010. Phone: 201-598-7200. Fax: 212-420-4803. Web Site: http://www.timewarnercable.com. Also serves Cliffside Park, Edgewater, Englewood, Englewood Cliffs, Fairview, Fort Lee, Guttenberg, Leonia, Little Ferry, Moonachie, Ridgefield, Ridgefield Park & Teterboro. ICA: NJ0010.
TV Market Ranking: 1 (Cliffside Park, Edgewater, Englewood, Englewood Cliffs, Fairview, Fort Lee, Guttenberg, Leonia, Little Ferry, Moonachie, PALISADES PARK, Ridgefield, Ridgefield Park, Teterboro). Franchise award date: N.A. Franchise expiration date: N.A. Began: November 1, 1971.
Channel capacity: N.A. Channels available but not in use: N.A.

Basic Service
Subscribers: N.A. Included in New York, NY
Programming (received off-air): WABC-TV (ABC) New York; WCBS-TV (CBS) New York; WFUT-DT (TEL) Newark; WLIW (PBS) Garden City; WMBC-TV (IND) Newton; WNBC (NBC) New York; WNET (PBS) Newark; WNJB (PBS) New Brunswick; WNJU (TMO) Linden; WNYE-TV (PBS) New York; WNYW (FOX) New York; WPIX (CW, IND) New York; WPXN-TV (ION) New York; WWOR-TV (MNT) Secaucus; WXTV-DT (UNV) Paterson; 28 FMs.
Programming (via microwave): News 12 New Jersey.
Current originations: Leased Access; Public Access.
Fee: $40.00 installation; $9.86 monthly; $19.00 additional installation.

Expanded Basic Service 1
Subscribers: N.A. Included in New York, NY
Programming (via microwave): New York 1 News.
Programming (via satellite): ABC Family Channel; AMC; Animal Planet; Arts & Entertainment; BET Networks; Bravo; Cartoon Network; CNBC; CNN; Comedy Central; C-SPAN; C-SPAN 2; Discovery Channel; Disney Channel; E! Entertainment Television; ESPN; ESPN 2; ESPN Classic Sports; Eternal Word TV Network; Food Network; Fox News Channel; FX; GalaVision; Golf Channel; GSN; Headline News; HGTV; History Channel; Home Shopping Network; Independent Film Channel; Lifetime; MSG; MSG Plus; MSNBC; MTV; National Geographic Channel; Nickelodeon; Oxygen; QVC; ShopNBC; Spike TV; Syfy; TBS Superstation; The Learning Channel; Travel Channel; truTV; Turner Classic Movies; Turner Network TV; TV Guide Network; TV Land; USA Network; VH1; WE tv; Weather Channel; Yesterday USA.
Fee: $37.08 monthly.

Digital Basic Service
Subscribers: N.A. Included in New York, NY
Programming (via satellite): BBC America; Bloomberg Television; Boomerang; Country Music TV; Discovery Digital Networks; Fox Sports en Espanol; Fox Sports World; Fuse; G4; GAS; Great American Country; Hallmark Channel; Lifetime Movie Network; MTV2; mun2 television; Nick Jr.; SoapNet; Speed Channel; Style Network; Sundance Channel; Toon Disney; Versus; VH1 Classic.
Fee: $9.95 monthly.

Digital Pay Service 1
Pay Units: 38,193.
Programming (via satellite): CCTV-4; Cinemax (multiplexed); Deutsche Welle TV; Encore (multiplexed); HBO (multiplexed); National Greek Television; RAI International; Russian Television Network; Showtime (multiplexed); Starz (multiplexed); The Movie Channel (multiplexed); TV Asia; TV Japan; TV Polonia; TV5, La Television International; Zee TV USA.
Fee: $9.95 monthly (CCTV, RTN, RAI, Deutsche Welle or TV5), $12.95 monthly (HBO, Showtime, Cinemax, TMC, Starz or Encore), $14.95 monthly (TV Asia, Antenna or Zee TV), $17.95 monthly (TV Polonia), $24.95 monthly (TV Japan).

Video-On-Demand: Yes

Pay-Per-View
ESPN Extra (delivered digitally), Addressable: Yes; ESPN Now (delivered digitally); Hot Choice (delivered digitally); iN DEMAND; iN DEMAND (delivered digitally); Playboy TV (delivered digitally); Fresh (delivered digitally); Shorteez (delivered digitally); Sports PPV (delivered digitally).

Internet Service
Operational: Yes. Began: March 1, 2001.
Broadband Service: EarthLink, LocalNet, Road Runner.
Fee: $30.50 installation; $44.95 monthly.

Telephone Service
Digital: Operational
Fee: $39.95 monthly

Total homes in franchised area: 82,016. Homes passed & miles of plant included in New York, NY

President: Howard Szarfarc. Vice President, Engineering: Larry Pestana. Vice President, Technical Operations: Norberto Rivera. Vice President, Marketing: David Goldberg. Vice President, Sales: Ken Fluger. Vice President, Public Affairs: Harriet Novet. General Manager: Brien Kelly.
City fee: 2% of gross. State fee: 2% of gross.
Ownership: Time Warner Cable (MSO).

PARAMUS—US Cable of Paramus-Hillsdale, 590 Valley Health Plz, Paramus, NJ 07652-3605. Phones: 201-930-9000 (customer service); 201-576-9292. Fax: 201-930-9232. E-mail: uscable@nj.uscable.com. Web Site: http://www.uscable.com. Also serves Hillsdale. ICA: NJ0066. **Note:** This system is an overbuild.
TV Market Ranking: 1 (HILLSDALE, PARAMUS). Franchise award date: N.A. Franchise expiration date: N.A. Began: N.A.
Channel capacity: N.A. Channels available but not in use: N.A.

Basic Service
Subscribers: 4,884.
Programming (received off-air): WABC-TV (ABC) New York; WCBS-TV (CBS) New York; WFUT-DT (TEL) Newark; WLIW (PBS) Garden City; WLNY-TV (IND) Riverhead; WMBC-TV (IND) Newton; WNBC (NBC) New York; WNET (PBS) Newark; WNJN (PBS) Montclair; WNJU (TMO) Linden; WNYW (FOX) New York; WPIX (CW, IND) New York; WPXN-TV (ION) New York; WWOR-TV (MNT) Secaucus; WXTV-DT (UNV) Paterson.
Programming (via satellite): C-SPAN; C-SPAN 2; QVC; TBS Superstation; TV Guide Network.
Current originations: Public Access; Government Access.
Fee: $14.99 monthly.

Expanded Basic Service 1
Subscribers: N.A.
Programming (via satellite): ABC Family Channel; AMC; Animal Planet; Arts & Entertainment; BET Networks; Bravo; Cartoon Network; CNBC; CNN; Comedy Central; Discovery Channel; Disney Channel; E! Entertainment Television; ESPN; ESPN 2; Eternal Word TV Network; Food Network; Fox News Channel; Fox Sports Net; FX; Headline News; HGTV; History Channel; Home Shopping Network; Lifetime; MSG; MSNBC; MTV; Nickelodeon; ShopNBC; SoapNet; Speed Channel; Spike TV; Syfy; The Learning Channel; Travel Channel; truTV; Turner Network TV; TV Land; USA Network; VH1; Weather Channel; Yankees Entertainment & Sports.
Fee: $34.96 monthly.

Expanded Basic Service 2
Subscribers: N.A.
Programming (via satellite): Encore (multiplexed).

Digital Basic Service
Subscribers: 1,177.
Programming (via satellite): AZ TV; BBC America; Bloomberg Television; CCTV-4; Discovery Digital Networks; DMX Music; FitTV; Fuse; G4; GSN; Halogen Network; History Channel International; MTV Networks Digital Suite; Nick Jr.; NickToons TV; Style Network; Toon Disney; Trinity Broadcasting Network; WealthTV.
Fee: $8.00 monthly.

Digital Expanded Basic Service
Subscribers: N.A.
Programming (via satellite): Bio; Fox Movie Channel; Independent Film Channel; Lifetime Movie Network; Trio; Turner Classic Movies; WE tv.

Pay Service 1
Pay Units: 1,570 Includes digital subs.
Programming (via satellite): Encore; HBO; Starz.

Digital Pay Service 1
Pay Units: N.A. Included in analog subs
Programming (via satellite): Cinemax (multiplexed); Encore (multiplexed); HBO (multiplexed); Showtime (multiplexed); Starz (multiplexed); The Movie Channel (multiplexed).

Video-On-Demand: No

Pay-Per-View
Shorteez; iN DEMAND; Playboy TV (delivered digitally); Fresh (delivered digitally).

Internet Service
Operational: Yes.
Subscribers: 1,366.
Broadband Service: Warp Drive Online.
Fee: $49.95 installation; $49.95 monthly; $10.00 modem lease; $299.00 modem purchase.

Telephone Service
None

Miles of Plant: 165.0 (coaxial); None (fiber optic). Homes passed: 13,169.
Vice President, Operations: Joseph Appio. Manager: David White. Corporate Marketing Director: Gary MacGregor.
Ownership: US Cable Corp. (MSO).

PATERSON—Cablevision Systems Corp., 40 Potash Rd, Oakland, NJ 07436-3100. Phones: 516-803-2300 (Corporate office); 201-651-4000. Fax: 516-803-1183. Web Site: http://www.cablevision.com. ICA: NJ0059.
TV Market Ranking: 1 (PATERSON). Franchise award date: May 16, 1986. Franchise expiration date: N.A. Began: March 16, 1987.
Channel capacity: N.A. Channels available but not in use: N.A.

Basic Service
Subscribers: 25,722.
Programming (received off-air): WABC-TV (ABC) New York; WCBS-TV (CBS) New York; WFME-TV (ETV) West Milford; WFUT-DT (TEL) Newark; WLIW (PBS) Garden City; WLNY-TV (IND) Riverhead; WMBC-TV (IND) Newton; WNBC (NBC) New York; WNET (PBS) Newark; WNJN (PBS) Montclair; WNJU (TMO) Linden; WNYW (FOX) New York; WPIX (CW, IND) New York; WPXN-TV (ION) New York; WRNN-TV (IND) Kingston; WWOR-TV (MNT) Secaucus; WXTV-DT (UNV) Paterson.
Programming (via microwave): News 12 New Jersey.
Programming (via satellite): Home Shopping Network; QVC.

Current originations: Leased Access; Government Access; Educational Access; Public Access.
Fee: $49.95 installation; $12.18 monthly.

Expanded Basic Service 1
Subscribers: N.A.
Programming (via satellite): ABC Family Channel; AMC; Animal Planet; Arts & Entertainment; BET Networks; Bravo; Cartoon Network; CNBC; CNN; Comedy Central; C-SPAN; C-SPAN 2; Discovery Channel; Disney Channel; E! Entertainment Television; ESPN; ESPN 2; Food Network; Fox News Channel; Fuse; FX; GalaVision; GSN; Headline News; HGTV; History Channel; INSP; Lifetime; MSG; MSG Plus; MSNBC; MTV; MTV2; News 12 Traffic & Weather; Nickelodeon; ShopNBC; SoapNet; Speed Channel; Spike TV; SportsNet New York; Syfy; TBS Superstation; The Comcast Network; The Learning Channel; Travel Channel; Trinity Broadcasting Network; truTV; Turner Classic Movies; Turner Network TV; TV Land; USA Network; VH1; WE tv; Weather Channel; Yankees Entertainment & Sports.
Fee: $37.77 monthly.

Digital Basic Service
Subscribers: N.A.
Programming (received off-air): WABC-TV (ABC) New York; WCBS-TV (CBS) New York; WNBC (NBC) New York; WPIX (CW, IND) New York; WWOR-TV (MNT) Secaucus.
Programming (via satellite): Azteca America; BBC World News; Bio; Bloomberg Television; Canal Sur; Caracol; Cartoon Network Tambien en Espanol; Cine Latino; CNN en Espanol; CNN HD; Country Music TV; C-SPAN 3; Discovery en Espanol; Discovery HD Theater; Discovery Home Channel; Discovery Kids Channel; Discovery Military Channel; Docu TVE; Ecuavisia Internacional; ESPN 2 HD; ESPN Classic Sports; ESPN Deportes; ESPN HD; ESPNews; EuroNews; EWTN en Espanol; Food Network HD; Fox College Sports Atlantic; Fox College Sports Central; Fox College Sports Pacific; Fox Movie Channel; Fox Soccer; Fox Sports en Espanol; Fuel TV; G4; GameHD; Gol TV; Golf Channel; Great American Country; Hallmark Channel; here! On Demand; HGTV HD; History Channel en Espanol; History Channel International; Howard TV; HTV Musica; ID Investigation Discovery; Infinito; Jewelry Television; La Familia Network; Latele Novela Network; LOGO; Maria+Vision; Momentum TV; MTV Hits; MTV Tres; mun2 television; Music Choice; National Geographic Channel; National Geographic Channel HD Network; NBA TV; NHL Network; Nick Jr.; NickToons TV; Outdoor Channel; Oxygen; Science Channel; ShopNBC; Sorpresa; Sundance Channel; Supercanal Caribe; TBS in HD; TeenNick; Telefe International; Toon Disney; Toon Disney en Espanol; Turner Network TV HD; TV Chile; TV Colombia; TVE Internacional; TVG Network; Universal HD; Utilisima; VeneMovies; Versus; Versus HD; VH1 Classic; VH1 Soul; V-me TV; WAPA America; WNYW (FOX) New York; World Cinema HD; YES HD.
Fee: $10.95 monthly.

Pay Service 1
Pay Units: 12,133.
Programming (via satellite): Cinemax; Flix; HBO (multiplexed); Independent Film Channel; Showtime (multiplexed); The Movie Channel.

Digital Pay Service 1
Pay Units: N.A.
Programming (via satellite): CCTV-4; Channel One; Cinemax (multiplexed); Cinemax HD; Cinemax On Demand; Encore (multiplexed); HBO (multiplexed); HBO HD; HBO On Demand; International Television (ITV); Korean Channel; MBC America; Playboy TV; RAI USA; Russian Television Network; Showtime (multiplexed); Showtime HD; Showtime On Demand; Society of Portuguese Television; Starz (multiplexed); Starz HDTV; The Movie Channel (multiplexed); The Movie Channel HD; TV Asia; TV Japan; TV Polonia; TV5, La Television International; Zee TV USA.
Fee: $9.95 monthly (Showtime, Cinemax, TMC, Starz/Encore, Playboy, RAI, SPT, TV5 or TV Polonia), $11.95 monthly (HBO), $24.95 monthly (TV Japan).

Video-On-Demand: Yes

Pay-Per-View
Playboy TV (delivered digitally); Sports PPV (delivered digitally); NBA TV (delivered digitally); iN DEMAND (delivered digitally).

Internet Service
Operational: Yes.
Broadband Service: Optimum Online.
Fee: $46.95 installation; $34.95 monthly; $299.00 modem purchase.

Telephone Service
Digital: Operational
Fee: $46.95 installation; $34.95 monthly
Miles of Plant: 164.0 (coaxial); None (fiber optic). Total homes in franchised area: 50,000.
Vice President, Field Operations: Christoper Fulton.
City fee: 2% of basic gross.
Ownership: Cablevision Systems Corp. (MSO).

PHILLIPSBURG—Service Electric Cable TV of Hunterdon Inc. Now served by HUNTERDON COUNTY, NJ [NJ0067]. ICA: NJ0065.

PLAINFIELD—Comcast Cable, 800 Rahway Ave, Union, NJ 7083. Phone: 732-602-7444. Fax: 908-851-8888. Web Site: http://www.comcast.com. Also serves North Plainfield & South Plainfield. ICA: NJ0026.
TV Market Ranking: 1 (North Plainfield, PLAINFIELD, South Plainfield). Franchise award date: December 1, 1969. Franchise expiration date: N.A. Began: March 30, 1972.
Channel capacity: N.A. Channels available but not in use: N.A.

Basic Service
Subscribers: 22,740.
Programming (received off-air): WABC-TV (ABC) New York; WCBS-TV (CBS) New York; WFUT-DT (TEL) Newark; WMBC-TV (IND) Newton; WNBC (NBC) New York; WNET (PBS) Newark; WNJN (PBS) Montclair; WNJU (TMO) Linden; WNYE-TV (PBS) New York; WNYW (FOX) New York; WPIX (CW, IND) New York; WPXN-TV (ION) New York; WWOR-TV (MNT) Secaucus; WXTV-DT (UNV) Paterson; allband FM.
Programming (via satellite): ABC Family Channel; AMC; Cartoon Network; CNBC; C-SPAN; Discovery Channel; Home Shopping Network; QVC; TBS Superstation; The Comcast Network; Turner Network TV; WGN America.
Current originations: Leased Access; Religious Access; Government Access; Educational Access; Public Access.
Fee: $13.80 monthly.

Expanded Basic Service 1
Subscribers: N.A.
Programming (via satellite): Animal Planet; Arts & Entertainment; BET Networks; Bravo; CNN; Comedy Central; Discovery Health Channel; E! Entertainment Television; ESPN; ESPN 2; Food Network; Fox News Channel; FX; GalaVision; Golf Channel; Headline News; HGTV; History Channel; Lifetime; MoviePlex; MSG; MSG Plus; MSNBC; MTV; News 12 New Jersey; Nickelodeon; Speed Channel; SportsNet New York; Style Network; Syfy; The Learning Channel; truTV; TV Guide Network; TV Land; USA Network; Versus; VH1; Weather Channel; Yankees Entertainment & Sports.
Fee: $43.05 monthly.

Digital Basic Service
Subscribers: N.A.
Programming (received off-air): WABC-TV (ABC) New York; WCBS-TV (CBS) New York; WNBC (NBC) New York; WNET (PBS) Newark; WNYW (FOX) New York; WPIX (CW, IND) New York.
Programming (via satellite): BBC America; Bio; Canales N; CBS College Sports Network; Cooking Channel; Country Music TV; C-SPAN 2; C-SPAN 3; Discovery Digital Networks; Discovery HD Theater; Do-It-Yourself; Encore (multiplexed); ESPN 2 HD; ESPN Classic Sports; ESPN HD; ESPNews; Flix; Fox College Sports Atlantic; Fox College Sports Central; Fox College Sports Pacific; Fox Soccer; G4; GAS; Gol TV; Great American Country; GSN; Hallmark Channel; History Channel International; INHD; Jewelry Television; Lifetime Movie Network; LOGO; MTV Networks Digital Suite; Music Choice; National Geographic Channel; NBA TV; NFL Network; Nick Jr.; Nick Too; NickToons TV; Oxygen; Palladia; PBS Kids Sprout; ShopNBC; SoapNet; Sundance Channel; Tennis Channel; The Word Network; Toon Disney; Travel Channel; Trinity Broadcasting Network; Turner Network TV HD; TV One; Universal HD; WAM! America's Kidz Network; Weatherscan.
Fee: $14.95 monthly.

Pay Service 1
Pay Units: 9,681.
Programming (via satellite): Cinemax; Showtime.
Fee: $11.00 monthly (each).

Digital Pay Service 1
Pay Units: 9,681.
Programming (via satellite): Cinemax (multiplexed); Cinemax HD; Cinemax On Demand; HBO (multiplexed); HBO HD; HBO On Demand; Showtime (multiplexed); Showtime HD; Showtime On Demand; Starz; Starz HDTV; Starz On Demand; The Movie Channel (multiplexed); The Movie Channel On Demand; TV Asia.
Fee: $18.15 monthly (each).

Video-On-Demand: Yes

Pay-Per-View
iN DEMAND (delivered digitally); Playboy TV (delivered digitally); Sports PPV (delivered digitally).

Internet Service
Operational: Yes.
Subscribers: 6,728.
Broadband Service: Comcast High Speed Internet.
Fee: $42.95 monthly; $7.00 modem lease; $299.00 modem purchase.

Telephone Service
Digital: Operational
Fee: $44.95 monthly
Miles of Plant: 240.0 (coaxial); None (fiber optic). Homes passed: 33,440.
Area Vice President: Keith Taub. Vice President, Technical Operations: Bob Kennedy. Vice President, Marketing: Marge Jackson. Public Relations Director: Fred DeAndrea.
City fee: 2% of gross. State fee: 2% of gross.
Ownership: Comcast Cable Communications Inc. (MSO).

PLEASANTVILLE—Comcast Cable. Now served by VINELAND, NJ [NJ0034]. ICA: NJ0006.

PORT MURRAY—Comcast Cable, 800 Rahway Ave, Union, NJ 7083. Phone: 732-602-7444. Fax: 908-851-8888. Web Site: http://www.comcast.com. Also serves Belvidere, Califon, Franklin Twp., Glen Gardner, Hackettstown, Hampton, High Bridge, Independence Twp., Lebanon Twp., Liberty Twp., Mansfield Twp., Mount Olive Twp., Oxford Twp., Washington, Washington Twp. (Morris County), Washington Twp. (Warren County) & White Twp. ICA: NJ0027.
TV Market Ranking: 1 (Califon, Hackettstown, High Bridge, Lebanon Twp., Mount Olive Twp., Washington Twp. (Morris County)); Below 100 (Belvidere, Franklin Twp., Glen Gardner, Hampton, Independence Twp., Liberty Twp., Mansfield Twp., Oxford Twp., PORT MURRAY, Washington, Washington Twp. (Warren County), White Twp.). Franchise award date: N.A. Franchise expiration date: N.A. Began: June 1, 1984.
Channel capacity: N.A. Channels available but not in use: N.A.

Basic Service
Subscribers: 24,390.
Programming (received off-air): WABC-TV (ABC) New York; WCBS-TV (CBS) New York; WFMZ-TV (IND) Allentown; WLVT-TV (PBS) Allentown; WMBC-TV (IND) Newton; WNBC (NBC) New York; WNET (PBS) Newark; WNJN (PBS) Montclair; WNYW (FOX) New York; WPIX (CW, IND) New York; WPXN-TV (ION) New York; WTXF-TV (FOX) Philadelphia; WWOR-TV (MNT) Secaucus; WXTV-DT (UNV) Paterson; allband FM.
Programming (via satellite): AMC; Cartoon Network; CNBC; C-SPAN; Discovery Channel; Fox News Channel; Home Shopping Network; QVC; Syfy; TBS Superstation; The Comcast Network; Turner Network TV; TV Guide Network.
Current originations: Religious Access; Government Access; Educational Access; Public Access.
Fee: $12.80 monthly.

Expanded Basic Service 1
Subscribers: N.A.
Programming (via satellite): ABC Family Channel; Animal Planet; Arts & Entertainment; BET Networks; CNN; Comedy Central; Country Music TV; Discovery Health Channel; E! Entertainment Television; ESPN; ESPN 2; ESPN Classic Sports; Eternal Word TV Network; Food Network; FX; Golf Channel; GSN; Headline News; HGTV; History Channel; Lifetime; MSG; MSG Plus; MSNBC; MTV; News 12 New Jersey; Nickelodeon; Speed Channel; Spike TV; Style Network; The Learning Channel; truTV; TV Land; USA Network; Versus; VH1; Weather Channel; Yankees Entertainment & Sports.
Fee: $43.65 monthly.

Digital Basic Service
Subscribers: N.A.
Programming (received off-air): WABC-TV (ABC) New York; WCBS-TV (CBS) New York; WNBC (NBC) New York; WNET (PBS) Newark; WNYW (FOX) New York.
Programming (via satellite): BBC America; Bio; CBS College Sports Network; Cooking Channel; Country Music TV; C-SPAN 2; C-SPAN 3; Discovery Digital Networks; Discovery HD Theater; Disney Channel; Do-It-Yourself; Encore (multiplexed); ESPN Classic Sports; ESPN HD; ESPNews; Flix; Fox College Sports Atlantic; Fox College Sports Central; Fox College Sports Pacific; Fox Soccer; G4; GAS; Gol TV; Great Ameri-

can Country; GSN; History Channel International; INHD; Jewelry Television; MTV Networks Digital Suite; Music Choice; National Geographic Channel; NFL Network; Nick Jr.; Nick Too; NickToons TV; Oxygen; Palladia; SoapNet; Sundance Channel; Toon Disney; Travel Channel; Trinity Broadcasting Network; Turner Network TV HD; WAM! America's Kidz Network.
Fee: $14.95 monthly.

Pay Service 1
Pay Units: 6,943.
Programming (via satellite): HBO.
Fee: $10.50 monthly (each).

Digital Pay Service 1
Pay Units: 6,943.
Programming (via satellite): Cinemax (multiplexed); Cinemax HD; Cinemax On Demand; HBO (multiplexed); HBO HD; HBO On Demand; Playboy TV; Showtime (multiplexed); Showtime HD; Showtime On Demand; Starz (multiplexed); Starz HDTV; Starz On Demand; The Movie Channel (multiplexed); The Movie Channel On Demand.
Fee: $17.55 monthly (each).

Video-On-Demand: Yes

Pay-Per-View
Fresh; iN DEMAND (delivered digitally); Playboy TV (delivered digitally); FearNet (delivered digitally).

Internet Service
Operational: Yes.
Broadband Service: Comcast High Speed Internet.
Fee: $42.95 monthly; $7.00 modem lease; $199.00 modem purchase.

Telephone Service
Digital: Operational
Fee: $44.95 monthly

Miles of Plant: 807.0 (coaxial); None (fiber optic). Homes passed: 36,400.
Area Vice President: Keith Taub. Vice President, Technical Operations: Bob Kennedy. Vice President, Marketing: Marge Jackson. Public Relations Director: Fred DeAndrea.
City fee: 2% of basic.
Ownership: Comcast Cable Communications Inc. (MSO).

PRINCETON—Comcast Cable, 90 Lake Dr, East Windsor, NJ 8520. Phone: 609-443-1970. Web Site: http://www.comcast.com. Also serves Princeton Twp. ICA: NJ0040.
TV Market Ranking: 1,4 (PRINCETON, Princeton Twp.). Franchise award date: June 19, 1980. Franchise expiration date: N.A. Began: February 1, 1981.
Channel capacity: 100 (operating 2-way). Channels available but not in use: N.A.

Basic Service
Subscribers: N.A. Included in Hillsborough
Programming (received off-air): KYW-TV (CBS) Philadelphia; WABC-TV (ABC) New York; WBPH-TV (IND) Bethlehem; WCAU (NBC) Philadelphia; WCBS-TV (CBS) New York; WFMZ-TV (IND) Allentown; WFUT-DT (TEL) Newark; WGTW-TV (IND) Burlington; WHYY-TV (PBS) Wilmington; WLVT-TV (PBS) Allentown; WMBC-TV (IND) Newton; WNBC (NBC) New York; WNET (PBS) Newark; WNJN (PBS) Montclair; WNJU (TMO) Linden; WNYE-TV (PBS) New York; WNYW (FOX) New York; WPHL-TV (MNT) Philadelphia; WPIX (CW, IND) New York; WPSG (CW) Philadelphia; WPVI-TV (ABC) Philadelphia; WPXN-TV (ION) New York; WTXF-TV (FOX) Philadelphia; WWOR-TV (MNT) Secaucus; WXTV-DT (UNV) Paterson; WYBE (ETV) Philadelphia.
Programming (via satellite): C-SPAN; C-SPAN, 2; Home Shopping Network; QVC; ShopNBC; TV Guide Network; WGN America.
Current originations: Leased Access; Government Access; Educational Access; Public Access.
Fee: $41.65 installation; $14.80 monthly; $2.00 converter.

Expanded Basic Service 1
Subscribers: 6,578.
Programming (via satellite): ABC Family Channel; AMC; Animal Planet; Arts & Entertainment; BET Networks; Bravo; Cartoon Network; CNBC; CNN; Comedy Central; Country Music TV; Discovery Channel; Disney Channel; E! Entertainment Television; ESPN; ESPN 2; Eternal Word TV Network; Food Network; Fox News Channel; FX; GSN; Headline News; HGTV; History Channel; Jewelry Television; Lifetime; MSG; MSG Plus; MSNBC; MTV; Nickelodeon; Oxygen; Speed Channel; Spike TV; Syfy; TBS Superstation; The Learning Channel; Travel Channel; truTV; Turner Classic Movies; Turner Network TV; TV Land; USA Network; VH1; Weather Channel; Yankees Entertainment & Sports.
Fee: $35.19 monthly.

Digital Basic Service
Subscribers: N.A. Included in Hillsborough
Programming (via satellite): BBC America; Bio; Bloomberg Television; Boomerang; Cooking Channel; Discovery Digital Networks; Do-It-Yourself; ESPN Classic Sports; ESPNews; Fox Movie Channel; Fox Sports en Espanol; Fox Sports World; FSN Digital Atlantic; FSN Digital Central; FSN Digital Pacific; G4; GAS; Golf Channel; History Channel International; Independent Film Channel; Lifetime Movie Network; MTV Networks Digital Suite; Music Choice; National Geographic Channel; Nick Jr.; Nick Too; Outdoor Channel; Style Network; Sundance Channel; Toon Disney; WE tv.
Fee: $11.10 monthly.

Pay Service 1
Pay Units: 2,864.
Programming (via satellite): Cinemax; HBO (multiplexed); Showtime; The Movie Channel.
Fee: $15.00 installation; $13.95 monthly (Cinemax or Showtime & TMC), $14.95 monthly (HBO).

Digital Pay Service 1
Pay Units: N.A.
Programming (via satellite): CCTV-4; Chinese Television Network; Cinemax (multiplexed); Encore (multiplexed); Filipino Channel; Flix; HBO (multiplexed); RAI International; Showtime (multiplexed); Starz (multiplexed); The Movie Channel (multiplexed); TV Asia; TV5, La Television International; Zee TV USA.
Fee: $9.95 monthly (RAI or TV5), $11.95 monthly (Filipino), $13.95 monthly (Cinemax, Showtime/TMC/Flix, or Starz/Encore), $14.95 monthly (HBO, TV Asia, Zee TV or CCTV-4/CTN).

Video-On-Demand: Yes

Pay-Per-View
ETC (delivered digitally); iN DEMAND (delivered digitally); Sports PPV (delivered digitally).

Internet Service
Operational: Yes.
Broadband Service: Comcast High Speed Internet.
Fee: $99.00 installation; $53.95 monthly; $2.00 modem lease.

Telephone Service
Digital: Operational
Fee: $29.95 installation; $39.95 monthly

Homes passed & miles of plant Included in Hillsborough
Area Vice President: Keith Taub.
State fee: 2% of basic.
Ownership: Comcast Cable Communications Inc. (MSO).

RARITAN—Cablevision Systems Corp., 683 Route 10 E, Randolph, NJ 7869. Phones: 973-659-2200; 516-803-2300 (Corporate office). Fax: 973-659-2266. Web Site: http://www.cablevision.com. Also serves Aberdeen Twp., Bedminster (portions), Bernards Twp., Bound Brook, Bridgewater, Cliffwood, Cliffwood Beach, Dunellen, Edison, Green Brook, Highland Park, Keansburg, Keyport, Manville, Matawan, Metuchen, Middlesex, Milltown, New Brunswick, North Brunswick Twp., Old Bridge, Parlin, Piscataway, Sayreville, Somerville, South Amboy, South Bound Brook, Union Beach, Warren Twp. & Watchung. ICA: NJ0004.
TV Market Ranking: 1 (Aberdeen Twp., Bedminster (portions), Bernards Twp., Bound Brook, Bridgewater, Cliffwood, Cliffwood Beach, Dunellen, Edison, Green Brook, Highland Park, Keansburg, Keyport, Manville, Matawan, Metuchen, Middlesex, Milltown, New Brunswick, North Brunswick Twp., Old Bridge, Parlin, Piscataway, RARITAN, Sayreville, Somerville, South Amboy, South Bound Brook, Union Beach, Warren Twp., Watchung). Franchise award date: N.A. Franchise expiration date: N.A. Began: August 12, 1977.
Channel capacity: N.A. Channels available but not in use: N.A.

Basic Service
Subscribers: 168,323.
Programming (received off-air): WABC-TV (ABC) New York; WCAU (NBC) Philadelphia; WCBS-TV (CBS) New York; WFUT-DT (TEL) Newark; WHYY-TV (PBS) Wilmington; WNBC (NBC) New York; WNET (PBS) Newark; WNJT (PBS) Trenton; WNJU (TMO) Linden; WNYW (FOX) New York; WPHL-TV (MNT) Philadelphia; WPIX (CW, IND) New York; WPVI-TV (ABC) Philadelphia; WPXN-TV (ION) New York; WTXF-TV (FOX) Philadelphia; WWOR-TV (MNT) Secaucus; WXTV-DT (UNV) Paterson.
Programming (via satellite): Home Shopping Network; News 12 New Jersey.
Current originations: Leased Access; Religious Access; Government Access; Educational Access; Public Access.
Fee: $49.95 installation; $17.29 monthly.

Expanded Basic Service 1
Subscribers: N.A.
Programming (via microwave): News 12 Traffic & Weather.
Programming (via satellite): ABC Family Channel; AMC; Animal Planet; Arts & Entertainment; BET Networks; Bravo; Cartoon Network; CNBC; CNN; Comedy Central; C-SPAN; C-SPAN 2; Discovery Channel; Disney Channel; E! Entertainment Television; ESPN; ESPN 2; Food Network; Fox News Channel; Fuse; FX; GSN; Headline News; HGTV; History Channel; Independent Film Channel; Lifetime; MSG; MSG Plus; MSNBC; MTV; MTV2; Nickelodeon; QVC; SoapNet; Speed Channel; Spike TV; SportsNet New York; Syfy; TBS Superstation; The Comcast Network; The Learning Channel; Travel Channel; truTV; Turner Network TV; TV Land; USA Network; VH1; WE tv; Weather Channel; Yankees Entertainment & Sports.
Fee: $32.66 monthly.

Digital Basic Service
Subscribers: N.A.
Programming (received off-air): WABC-TV (ABC) New York; WCBS-TV (CBS) New York; WNBC (NBC) New York; WNYW (FOX) New York; WPIX (CW, IND) New York; WWOR-TV (MNT) Secaucus.
Programming (via satellite): Azteca America; BBC World News; Bio; Bloomberg Television; Canal Sur; Caracol; Cartoon Network Tambien en Espanol; Cine Latino; CNN en Espanol; CNN HD; Country Music TV; C-SPAN 3; Discovery en Espanol; Discovery HD Theater; Discovery Home Channel; Discovery Kids Channel; Discovery Military Channel; Docu TVE; Ecuavisia Internacional; ESPN 2 HD; ESPN Classic Sports; ESPN Deportes; ESPN HD; ESPNews; EuroNews; EWTN en Espanol; Food Network HD; Fox College Sports Atlantic; Fox College Sports Central; Fox College Sports Pacific; Fox Movie Channel; Fox Soccer; Fox Sports en Espanol; Fuel TV; G4; GameHD; Gol TV; Golf Channel; Great American Country; Hallmark Channel; here! On Demand; HGTV HD; History Channel en Espanol; History Channel International; Howard TV; HTV Musica; ID Investigation Discovery; Infinito; Jewelry Television; La Familia Network; Latele Novela Network; LOGO; Maria+Vision; Momentum TV; MTV Hits; MTV Tres; mun2 television; Music Choice; National Geographic Channel; National Geographic Channel HD Network; NBA TV; NHL Network; Nick Jr.; NickToons TV; Outdoor Channel; Oxygen; Science Channel; ShopNBC; Sorpresa; Sundance Channel; Supercanal Caribe; TBS in HD; TeenNick; Telefe International; Toon Disney; Toon Disney en Espanol; Turner Classic Movies; Turner Network TV HD; TV Chile; TV Colombia; TVE Internacional; TVG Network; Universal HD; Utilisima; VeneMovies; Versus; Versus HD; VH1 Classic; VH1 Soul; V-me TV; WAPA America; World Cinema HD; YES HD.
Fee: $10.95 monthly.

Pay Service 1
Pay Units: N.A.
Programming (via satellite): Cinemax; Flix; HBO (multiplexed); Showtime (multiplexed); The Movie Channel.

Digital Pay Service 1
Pay Units: 83,439.
Programming (via satellite): CCTV-4; Channel One; Cinemax (multiplexed); Cinemax HD; Cinemax On Demand; Encore (multiplexed); HBO (multiplexed); HBO HD; HBO On Demand; International Television (ITV); Korean Channel; MBC America; RAI International; Russian Television Network; Showtime (multiplexed); Showtime HD; Showtime On Demand; Society of Portuguese Television; Starz; Starz HDTV; The Movie Channel (multiplexed); The Movie Channel HD; TV Asia; TV Japan; TV Polonia; TV5, La Television International; Zee TV USA.
Fee: $9.95 monthly (Showtime, Cinemax, TMC, Starz/Encore, Playboy, RAI, SPT, TV5, or TV Polonia), $11.95 monthly (HBO), $24.95 monthly (TV Japan).

Video-On-Demand: Yes

Pay-Per-View
Hot Choice; Fresh, Fee: $5.95; Shorteez; Playboy TV.

Internet Service
Operational: Yes.
Broadband Service: Optimum Online.
Fee: $46.95 installation; $34.95 monthly; $299.00 modem purchase.

Telephone Service
Digital: Operational
Fee: $46.95 installation; $34.95 monthly

Miles of Plant: 3,307.0 (coaxial); 198.0 (fiber optic). Homes passed: 237,075.

Vice President, Field Operations: Frank Dagliere. Vice President, Government Affairs: Adam Falk.
City fee: 2% of gross. State fee: 2% of basic gross.
Ownership: Cablevision Systems Corp. (MSO).

SPARTA—Service Electric Cable Company, PO Box 853, 320 Sparta Ave, Sparta, NJ 7871. Phones: 800-992-0132 (Customer service); 973-729-7642; 973-729-7653 (Administrative office). Fax: 973-729-5635. E-mail: seconj@ptd.net. Web Site: http://www.secable.com/sparta. Also serves Andover Borough, Andover Twp., Blairstown Twp., Branchville, Byram Twp., Frankford Twp., Franklin, Fredon, Frelinghyusen Twp., Green Twp., Hamburg, Hampton Twp., Hardwick Twp., Hardyston Twp., Hope, Jefferson Twp., Knowlton, Lafayette Twp., Newton, Ogdensburg, Sandyston Twp., Sparta Twp., Stillwater Twp., Sussex, Vernon Twp. & Wantage Twp. ICA: NJ0061.
TV Market Ranking: 1 (Andover Borough, Andover Twp., Branchville, Byram Twp., Frankford Twp., Franklin, Fredon, Green Twp., Hamburg, Hampton Twp., Hardyston Twp., Jefferson Twp., Lafayette Twp., Newton, Ogdensburg, SPARTA, Sparta Twp., Sussex, Vernon Twp., Wantage Twp.); Below 100 (Blairstown Twp., Frelinghyusen Twp., Hardwick Twp., Hope, Sandyston Twp., Stillwater Twp., Knowlton). Franchise award date: N.A. Franchise expiration date: N.A. Began: January 1, 1963.
Channel capacity: N.A. Channels available but not in use: N.A.

Basic Service
Subscribers: 33,400.
Programming (received off-air): WABC-TV (ABC) New York; WCBS-TV (CBS) New York; WMBC-TV (IND) Newton; WNBC (NBC) New York; WNET (PBS) Newark; WNJN (PBS) Montclair; WNYE-TV (PBS) New York; WNYW (FOX) New York; WPIX (CW, IND) New York; WPXN-TV (ION) New York; WTBY-TV (TBN) Poughkeepsie; WWOR-TV (MNT) Secaucus; WXTV-DT (UNV) Paterson; allband FM.
Programming (via satellite): C-SPAN; Eternal Word TV Network; News 12 New Jersey; QVC; TV Guide Network; WGN America.
Current originations: Leased Access; Educational Access; Public Access.
Fee: $36.00 installation; $19.99 monthly.

Expanded Basic Service 1
Subscribers: N.A.
Programming (via satellite): ABC Family Channel; AMC; AmericanLife TV Network; Animal Planet; Arts & Entertainment; Cartoon Network; CNBC; CNN; Comedy Central; Country Music TV; Discovery Channel; E! Entertainment Television; ESPN; ESPN 2; ESPN Classic Sports; FitTV; Food Network; Fox Movie Channel; Fox News Channel; FX; Hallmark Channel; Headline News; HGTV; History Channel; Home Shopping Network; Lifetime; MSG; MSG Plus; MSNBC; MTV; National Geographic Channel; NFL Network; Nickelodeon; ShopNBC; SoapNet; Speed Channel; Spike TV; SportsNet New York; Syfy; TBS Superstation; The Learning Channel; Travel Channel; truTV; Turner Classic Movies; Turner Network TV; TV Land; USA Network; Versus; VH1; WE tv; Weather Channel; Yankees Entertainment & Sports.
Fee: $33.13 monthly.

Digital Basic Service
Subscribers: 27,000.
Programming (received off-air): WABC-TV (ABC) New York; WCBS-TV (CBS) New York; WNBC (NBC) New York; WNYW (FOX) New York.
Programming (via satellite): BBC America; Bio; Boomerang; Bravo; Country Music TV; C-SPAN 2; Discovery Digital Networks; Discovery HD Theater; Do-It-Yourself; ESPN U; ESPNews; Fox Sports World; FSN Digital Atlantic; FSN Digital Central; FSN Digital Pacific; Fuel TV; G4; GAS; Golf Channel; Hallmark Channel; HDNet; HDNet Movies; History Channel International; Independent Film Channel; Lifetime Movie Network; MTV Networks Digital Suite; Music Choice; NASA TV; Nick Jr.; Nick Too; Outdoor Channel; PBS Kids Sprout; Turner Network TV HD; TVG Network; WALN Cable Radio.
Fee: $5.99 monthly.

Digital Pay Service 1
Pay Units: N.A.
Programming (via satellite): Cinemax (multiplexed); Encore (multiplexed); HBO (multiplexed); Showtime (multiplexed); Showtime HD; Starz (multiplexed); Starz HDTV; The Movie Channel (multiplexed); The Movie Channel HD.
Fee: $13.00 monthly (HBO), $11.00 monthly (Cinemax).

Video-On-Demand: Planned

Pay-Per-View
Addressable homes: 18,523.
iN DEMAND, Addressable: Yes.

Internet Service
Operational: Yes. Began: January 1, 1996.
Subscribers: 12,000.
Broadband Service: ProLog Express.
Fee: $50.00 installation; $21.95-$89.95 monthly; $9.95 modem lease; $100.00 modem purchase.

Telephone Service
None
Miles of Plant: 1,700.0 (coaxial); 1,700.0 (fiber optic). Homes passed: 45,000. Total homes in franchised area: 62,000.
Manager: William Brayford. Chief Technician: Robert Jais. Regulatory Affairs Director: Arlean Lilly.
State fee: 2% of gross.
Ownership: Service Electric Cable TV Inc. (MSO).

TOMS RIVER—Comcast Cable, 800 Rahway Ave, Union, NJ 7083. Phone: 732-602-7444. Fax: 908-851-8888. Web Site: http://www.comcast.com. Also serves Barnegat Twp., Beachwood, Berkeley Twp., Crestwood Village, Dover Twp. (portions), Eagleswood Twp., Island Heights, Lacey Twp., Lakehurst, Little Egg Harbor Twp., Manahawkin, Manchester Twp., Ocean Gate, Ocean Twp., Pine Beach, South Toms River, Stafford Twp., Tuckerton & Waretown. ICA: NJ0049.
TV Market Ranking: 4 (Berkeley Twp., Crestwood Village, Lakehurst, Manchester Twp., South Toms River); Below 100 (Barnegat Twp., Lacey Twp., Little Egg Harbor Twp., Manahawkin, Ocean Twp., Stafford Twp., Tuckerton, Waretown); Outside TV Markets (Beachwood, Dover Twp. (portions), Eagleswood Twp., Island Heights, Ocean Gate, Pine Beach, TOMS RIVER). Franchise award date: N.A. Franchise expiration date: N.A. Began: September 1, 1971.
Channel capacity: 110 (operating 2-way). Channels available but not in use: N.A.

Basic Service
Subscribers: 119,783.
Programming (received off-air): KYW-TV (CBS) Philadelphia; WABC-TV (ABC) New York; WCAU (NBC) Philadelphia; WCBS-TV (CBS) New York; WFUT-DT (TEL) Newark; WHYY-TV (PBS) Wilmington; WNBC (NBC) New York; WNET (PBS) Newark; WNJT (PBS) Trenton; WNJU (TMO) Linden; WNYW (FOX) New York; WPHL-TV (MNT) Philadelphia; WPIX (CW, IND) New York; WPSG (CW) Philadelphia; WPVI-TV (ABC) Philadelphia; WPXN-TV (ION) New York; WTXF-TV (FOX) Philadelphia; WWOR-TV (MNT) Secaucus; allband FM.
Programming (via microwave): News 12 New Jersey.
Programming (via satellite): Home Shopping Network; Product Information Network; QVC; The Comcast Network.
Current originations: Leased Access; Government Access; Educational Access; Public Access.
Fee: $15.95 monthly.

Expanded Basic Service 1
Subscribers: N.A.
Programming (via satellite): ABC Family Channel; AMC; Animal Planet; Arts & Entertainment; BET Networks; Bravo; Cartoon Network; CNBC; CNN; Comcast SportsNet Philly; Comedy Central; Country Music TV; C-SPAN; Discovery Channel; Discovery Health Channel; Disney Channel; E! Entertainment Television; ESPN; ESPN 2; ESPN Classic Sports; Eternal Word TV Network; Food Network; Fox News Channel; FX; Golf Channel; GSN; Headline News; HGTV; History Channel; INSP; Lifetime; MSG; MSG Plus; MSNBC; MTV; Nickelodeon; Speed Channel; Spike TV; Style Network; Syfy; TBS Superstation; The Learning Channel; truTV; Turner Classic Movies; Turner Network TV; TV Land; USA Network; Versus; VH1; Weather Channel; Yankees Entertainment & Sports.
Fee: $36.85 monthly.

Digital Basic Service
Subscribers: 36,875.
Programming (via satellite): BBC America; Bio; C-SPAN 3; Discovery Digital Networks; Disney Channel; DMX Music; Do-It-Yourself; ESPNews; Flix; G4; GAS; History Channel International; MTV Networks Digital Suite; National Geographic Channel; Nick Jr.; Nick Too; Science Television; ShopNBC; SoapNet; Sundance Channel; Toon Disney; WAM! America's Kidz Network; Weatherscan.
Fee: $14.95 monthly.

Pay Service 1
Pay Units: N.A.
Programming (via satellite): HBO (multiplexed).
Fee: $10.00 monthly.

Digital Pay Service 1
Pay Units: 43,661.
Programming (via satellite): Cinemax (multiplexed); Encore (multiplexed); HBO (multiplexed); Showtime (multiplexed); The Movie Channel (multiplexed).
Fee: $16.20 monthly (each).

Video-On-Demand: Yes

Pay-Per-View
Addressable homes: 30,000.
ESPN Now (delivered digitally); iN DEMAND (delivered digitally); Playboy TV (delivered digitally); Pleasure (delivered digitally); Fresh (delivered digitally); Shorteez (delivered digitally); sports (delivered digitally).

Internet Service
Operational: Yes. Began: June 4, 2004.
Subscribers: 30,774.
Broadband Service: Comcast High Speed Internet.
Fee: $42.95 monthly.

Telephone Service
Digital: Operational
Fee: $44.95 monthly
Miles of Plant: 1,844.0 (coaxial); 450.0 (fiber optic). Homes passed: 142,600.
Area Vice President: Keith Taub. Vice President, Technical Operations: Bob Kennedy. Vice President, Marketing: Marge Jackson. Public Relations Director: Fred DeAndrea.
City fee: 2% of gross.
Ownership: Comcast Cable Communications Inc. (MSO).

TRENTON—Comcast Cable, 401 White Horse Rd, Voorhees, NJ 8043. Phone: 856-821-6100. Fax: 856-821-6108. Web Site: http://www.comcast.com. Also serves Ewing Twp., Hopewell Borough, Lawrence Twp., Lawrenceville, Pennington Borough & West Trenton. ICA: NJ0015.
TV Market Ranking: 1,4 (Hopewell Borough, Lawrence Twp., Lawrenceville); 4 (Ewing Twp., Pennington Borough, TRENTON, West Trenton). Franchise award date: N.A. Franchise expiration date: N.A. Began: March 2, 1981.
Channel capacity: N.A. Channels available but not in use: N.A.

Basic Service
Subscribers: 42,048.
Programming (received off-air): KYW-TV (CBS) Philadelphia; WABC-TV (ABC) New York; WBPH-TV (IND) Bethlehem; WCAU (NBC) Philadelphia; WCBS-TV (CBS) New York; WFMZ-TV (IND) Allentown; WGTW-TV (IND) Burlington; WHYY-TV (PBS) Wilmington; WNBC (NBC) New York; WNET (PBS) Newark; WNJT (PBS) Trenton; WNYW (FOX) New York; WPHL-TV (MNT) Philadelphia; WPPX-TV (ION) Wilmington; WPSG (CW) Philadelphia; WPVI-TV (ABC) Philadelphia; WPXN-TV (ION) New York; WTXF-TV (FOX) Philadelphia; WUVP-DT (UNV) Vineland; WWOR-TV (MNT) Secaucus; WYBE (ETV) Philadelphia.
Programming (via satellite): AMC; Bloomberg Television; Cartoon Network; C-SPAN; C-SPAN 2; Eternal Word TV Network; GSN; QVC; Spike TV; TBS Superstation; The Comcast Network; Turner Network TV; TV Land; WMCN-TV (IND) Atlantic City; WWSI (TMO) Atlantic City.
Current originations: Leased Access; Religious Access; Government Access; Educational Access; Public Access.
Fee: $12.10 monthly.

Expanded Basic Service 1
Subscribers: 41,714.
Programming (received off-air): WPIX (CW, IND) New York.
Programming (via satellite): ABC Family Channel; Animal Planet; Arts & Entertainment; BET Networks; Bravo; CNBC; CNN; Comcast SportsNet Philly; Comedy Central; Discovery Channel; Discovery Health Channel; E! Entertainment Television; ESPN; ESPN 2; Food Network; Fox News Channel; FX; Golf Channel; Headline News; HGTV; History Channel; Home Shopping Network; Lifetime; MSG; MSNBC; MTV; News 12 New Jersey; Nickelodeon; Speed Channel; SportsNet New York; Style Network; Syfy; The Learning Channel; truTV; USA Network; Versus; VH1; Weather Channel; Yankees Entertainment & Sports.
Fee: $43.65 monthly.

Digital Basic Service
Subscribers: N.A.
Programming (received off-air): KYW-TV (CBS) Philadelphia; WCAU (NBC) Philadelphia; WHYY-TV (PBS) Wilmington; WPHL-TV (MNT) Philadelphia; WPSG (CW)

Philadelphia; WPVI-TV (ABC) Philadelphia; WTXF-TV (FOX) Philadelphia.

Programming (via satellite): BBC America; Bio; CMT Pure Country; Cooking Channel; C-SPAN 3; Current; Discovery Digital Networks; Discovery HD Theater; Disney Channel; Do-It-Yourself; Encore (multiplexed); ESPN 2 HD; ESPN Classic Sports; ESPNews; ESPNews HD; Flix; Fox College Sports Atlantic; Fox College Sports Central; Fox College Sports Pacific; Fox Reality Channel; Fox Sports World; G4; GAS; Gol TV; Great American Country; History Channel International; INHD; Jewelry Television; Lifetime Movie Network; LOGO; MoviePlex; MTV Networks Digital Suite; National Geographic Channel On Demand; NBA TV; Nick Jr.; Nick Too; NickToons TV; Palladia; PBS Kids Sprout; SoapNet; Sundance Channel; Toon Disney; Turner Network TV HD; TV One; Versus HD; Weatherscan.

Fee: $14.95 monthly.

Digital Pay Service 1

Pay Units: 19,310.

Programming (via satellite): Cinemax (multiplexed); Cinemax HD; Cinemax On Demand; HBO (multiplexed); HBO HD; HBO On Demand; Showtime (multiplexed); Showtime HD; Showtime On Demand; Starz (multiplexed); Starz HDTV; Starz On Demand; The Movie Channel (multiplexed); The Movie Channel On Demand.

Fee: $19.25 monthly (each).

Video-On-Demand: Yes

Pay-Per-View

Addressable homes: 12,000.

Playboy TV, Addressable: Yes; movies.

Internet Service

Operational: Yes.

Subscribers: 3,735.

Broadband Service: Comcast High Speed Internet.

Fee: $42.95 monthly; $7.00 modem lease; $299.00 modem purchase.

Telephone Service

Digital: Operational

Fee: $44.95 monthly

Miles of Plant: 511.0 (coaxial); 20.0 (fiber optic). Homes passed: 64,690.

Vice President & General Manager: John Del Viscio. Vice President, Technical Operations: Mike Taylor. Vice President, Engineering: John Cody. Marketing Director: Aaron Geisel. Public Relations Director: Fred DeAndrea.

City fee: 2% of gross. State fee: 2% of gross.

Ownership: Comcast Cable Communications Inc. (MSO).

UNION—Comcast Cable, 800 Rahway Ave, Union, NJ 7083. Phone: 732-602-7444. Fax: 908-851-8888. Web Site: http://www.comcast.com. Also serves Belleville Twp., Berkeley Heights Twp., Bloomfield Twp., Caldwell, Carteret, Clark Twp., Cranford Twp., East Orange, Essex Fells, Fairfield Twp., Fanwood, Garwood, Glen Ridge Twp., Harrison, Hillside Twp., Irvington Twp., Kenilworth, Linden, Livingston Twp., Maplewood Twp., Millburn Twp., Montclair Twp., Mountainside, New Providence, Orange, Perth Amboy, Rahway, Roseland, Roselle, Roselle Park, Scotch Plains Twp., Secaucus, Short Hills, South River, Springfield Twp., Summit, Union Twp., Verona Twp., West Caldwell Twp., West Orange, Westfield, Winfield Twp. & Woodbridge Twp. ICA: NJ0001.

TV Market Ranking: 1 (Belleville Twp., Berkeley Heights Twp., Bloomfield Twp., Caldwell, Carteret, Clark Twp., Cranford Twp., East Orange, Essex Fells, Fairfield Twp., Fanwood, Garwood, Glen Ridge Twp., Harrison, Hillside Twp., Irvington Twp., Kenilworth, Linden, Livingston Twp., Maplewood Twp., Millburn Twp., Montclair Twp., Mountainside, New Providence, Orange, Perth Amboy, Rahway, Roseland, Roselle, Roselle Park, Scotch Plains Twp., Secaucus, Short Hills, South River, Springfield Twp., Summit, UNION, Union Twp., Verona Twp., West Caldwell Twp., West Orange, Westfield, Winfield Twp., Woodbridge Twp.). Franchise award date: N.A. Franchise expiration date: N.A. Began: September 1, 1975.

Channel capacity: N.A. Channels available but not in use: N.A.

Basic Service

Subscribers: 276,830.

Programming (received off-air): WABC-TV (ABC) New York; WCBS-TV (CBS) New York; WFUT-DT (TEL) Newark; WLIW (PBS) Garden City; WLNY-TV (IND) Riverhead; WMBC-TV (IND) Newton; WNBC (NBC) New York; WNET (PBS) Newark; WNJN (PBS) Montclair; WNJU (TMO) Linden; WNYE-TV (PBS) New York; WNYW (FOX) New York; WPIX (CW, IND) New York; WPXN-TV (ION) New York; WRNN-LD Nyack; WWOR-TV (MNT) Secaucus; WXTV-DT (UNV) Paterson.

Programming (via satellite): C-SPAN; Eternal Word TV Network; Home Shopping Network; MSG Plus; QVC; TBS Superstation; The Comcast Network; TV Guide Network; WGN America; WMBC-TV (IND) Newton.

Current originations: Leased Access; Government Access; Educational Access; Public Access.

Fee: $13.80 monthly.

Expanded Basic Service 1

Subscribers: N.A.

Programming (via microwave): News 12 New Jersey.

Programming (via satellite): ABC Family Channel; AMC; Animal Planet; Arts & Entertainment; BET Networks; Cartoon Network; CNBC; CNN; Comedy Central; Discovery Channel; Discovery Health Channel; E! Entertainment Television; ESPN; ESPN 2; Food Network; Fox News Channel; FX; Golf Channel; Headline News; HGTV; History Channel; Lifetime; MSG; MSNBC; MTV; Nickelodeon; Speed Channel; Spike TV; SportsNet New York; Style Network; Syfy; The Learning Channel; truTV; Turner Classic Movies; Turner Network TV; TV Land; USA Network; Versus; VH1; Weather Channel; Yankees Entertainment & Sports.

Fee: $19.40 monthly.

Digital Basic Service

Subscribers: N.A.

Programming (received off-air): WABC-TV (ABC) New York; WCBS-TV (CBS) New York; WNBC (NBC) New York; WNET (PBS) Newark; WNYW (FOX) New York; WPIX (CW, IND) New York.

Programming (via satellite): BBC America; Bio; Canales N; CBS College Sports Network; Cooking Channel; Country Music TV; C-SPAN 3; Current; Discovery Digital Networks; Discovery HD Theater; Disney Channel; Do-It-Yourself; Encore (multiplexed); ESPN 2 HD; ESPN HD; ESPNews; FearNet; Flix; Fox College Sports Atlantic; Fox College Sports Central; Fox College Sports Pacific; Fox Soccer; G4; GAS; Gol TV; Great American Country; GSN; Hallmark Channel; History Channel International; INHD; Jewelry Television; Lifetime Movie Network; LOGO; MoviePlex; MTV Networks Digital Suite; Music Choice; National Geographic Channel; NBA TV; NFL Network; Nick Jr.; Nick Too; NickToons TV; Oxygen; Palladia; PBS Kids Sprout; SoapNet; Sundance Channel; Tennis Channel; The Word Network; Toon Disney; Travel Channel; Trinity Broadcasting Network; Turner Network TV HD; TV One; Weatherscan.

Fee: $14.95 monthly.

Pay Service 1

Pay Units: 162,434.

Programming (via satellite): HBO.

Fee: $12.00 installation; $11.00 monthly.

Digital Pay Service 1

Pay Units: 162,434.

Programming (via satellite): ART America; CCTV-4; Cinemax (multiplexed); Cinemax HD; Filipino Channel; HBO (multiplexed); HBO HD; RAI International; Showtime (multiplexed); Showtime HD; Starz (multiplexed); Starz HDTV; The Movie Channel (multiplexed); TV Asia; TV Polonia; TV5, La Television International; Zee TV USA; Zhong Tian Channel.

Fee: $20.25 monthly (each).

Video-On-Demand: Yes

Pay-Per-View

Addressable homes: 101,000.

iN DEMAND (delivered digitally), Fee: $3.95, Addressable: Yes; Playboy TV (delivered digitally), Fee: $4.95; Fresh (delivered digitally); Pleasure (delivered digitally); ESPN (delivered digitally); NBA (delivered digitally); NHL/MLB (delivered digitally).

Internet Service

Operational: Yes.

Subscribers: 93,841.

Broadband Service: Comcast High Speed Internet.

Fee: $42.95 monthly; $7.00 modem lease; $299.00 modem purchase.

Telephone Service

Digital: Operational

Fee: $44.95 monthly

Miles of Plant: 2,554.0 (coaxial); 110.0 (fiber optic). Homes passed: 425,892.

Area Vice President: Keith Taub. Vice President, Technical Operations: Bob Kennedy. Vice President, Marketing: Marge Jackson. Public Relations Director: Fred DeAndrea.

City fee: 2% of gross. State fee: 2% of gross.

Ownership: Comcast Cable Communications Inc. (MSO).

VINELAND—Comcast Cable, 401 White Horse Rd, Voorhees, NJ 8043. Phone: 856-821-6100. Fax: 856-821-6108. Web Site: http://www.comcast.com. Also serves Absecon, Alloway Twp., Atlantic City, Bass River Twp., Bridgeton, Brigantine, Buena, Buena Vista Twp., Carneys Point Twp., Chesilhurst, Commercial Twp., Corbin City, Deerfield Twp., Dennis Twp., Downe Twp., Egg Harbor City, Egg Harbor Twp., Elk Twp., Elmer, Elsinboro Twp., Fairfield Twp. (Cumberland County), Folsom, Franklin Twp. (Gloucester County), Franklinville, Galloway Twp., Hamilton Twp., Hammonton, Harrison Twp. (Gloucester County), Hopewell Twp. (Cumberland County), Laurel Lake, Lawrence Twp. (Cumberland County), Linwood, Logan Twp., Longport, Lower Alloways Creek Twp., Mannington Twp., Margate City, Maurice River Twp., Mays Landing, Millville, Monroe Twp. (Gloucester County), Mullica Twp. (Atlantic County), Newfield, Northfield, Ocean City, Oldmans Twp., Penns Grove, Pennsville Twp., Pilesgrove Twp., Pinehurst, Pittsgrove Twp., Pleasantville, Port Republic, Quinton Twp., Salem, Shiloh, Somers Point, South Harrison Twp., Swedesboro, Turnersville, Upper Deerfield Twp., Upper Pittsgrove Twp., Upper Twp., Ventnor City, Washington Twp. (Gloucester County), Waterford Twp., Weymouth City, Winslow Twp., Woodbine, Woodstown, Woolwich Borough (Gloucester County) & Woolwich Twp. ICA: NJ0034.

TV Market Ranking: 4 (Alloway Twp., Buena, Buena Vista Twp., Chesilhurst, Deerfield Twp., Elk Twp., Elmer, Elsinboro Twp., Folsom, Franklin Twp. (Gloucester County), Franklinville, Hammonton, Harrison Twp. (Gloucester County), Logan Twp., Lower Alloways Creek Twp., Monroe Twp. (Gloucester County), Newfield, Oldmans Twp., Penns Grove, Pennsville Twp., Pilesgrove Twp., Pittsgrove Twp., South Harrison Twp., Swedesboro, Turnersville, Upper Pittsgrove Twp., Washington Twp. (Gloucester County), Waterford Twp., Winslow Twp., Woodstown, Woolwich Twp.); Below 100 (Absecon, Atlantic City, Bridgeton, Brigantine, Commercial Twp., Corbin City, Dennis Twp., Downe Twp., Egg Harbor City, Egg Harbor Twp., Fairfield Twp. (Cumberland County), Galloway Twp., Hamilton Twp., Hopewell Twp. (Cumberland County), Laurel Lake, Lawrence Twp. (Cumberland County), Linwood, Longport, Mannington Twp., Margate City, Maurice River Twp., Mays Landing, Millville, Mullica Twp. (Atlantic County), Northfield, Ocean City, Pinehurst, Pleasantville, Port Republic, Quinton Twp., Salem, Shiloh, Somers Point, Upper Deerfield Twp., Upper Twp., Ventnor City, VINELAND, Weymouth Twp. (Atlantic County), Woodbine). Franchise award date: N.A. Franchise expiration date: N.A. Began: January 1, 1982.

Channel capacity: 78 (operating 2-way). Channels available but not in use: None.

Basic Service

Subscribers: 239,919.

Programming (received off-air): KYW-TV (CBS) Philadelphia; WCAU (NBC) Philadelphia; WGTW-TV (IND) Burlington; WHYY-TV (PBS) Wilmington; WMCN-TV (IND) Atlantic City; WNJN (PBS) Montclair; WPHL-TV (MNT) Philadelphia; WPPX-TV (ION) Wilmington; WPSG (CW) Philadelphia; WPVI-TV (ABC) Philadelphia; WTVE (IND) Reading; WTXF-TV (FOX) Philadelphia; WUVP-DT (UNV) Vineland; WWSI (TMO) Atlantic City; WYBE (ETV) Philadelphia.

Programming (via satellite): Animal Planet; C-SPAN; C-SPAN 2; INSP; QVC; The Comcast Network; TV Guide Network.

Current originations: Leased Access; Government Access.

Fee: $33.00 installation; $12.35 monthly.

Expanded Basic Service 1

Subscribers: 109,543.

Programming (via satellite): ABC Family Channel; AMC; Arts & Entertainment; BET Networks; Bravo; Cartoon Network; CNBC; CNN; Comcast SportsNet Philly; Comedy Central; Discovery Channel; Discovery Health Channel; Disney Channel; E! Entertainment Television; ESPN; ESPN 2; Eternal Word TV Network; Food Network; Fox News Channel; FX; Golf Channel; GSN; Headline News; HGTV; History Channel; Home Shopping Network; Lifetime; MSNBC; MTV; Nickelodeon; Speed Channel; Spike TV; Style Network; Syfy; TBS Superstation; The Learning Channel; truTV; Turner Classic Movies; Turner Network TV; TV Land; USA Network; Versus; VH1; Weather Channel.

Fee: $10.00 installation; $38.75 monthly.

Digital Basic Service

Subscribers: 49,358.

Programming (received off-air): KYW-TV (CBS) Philadelphia; WCAU (NBC) Philadelphia; WHYY-TV (PBS) Wilmington; WPHL-TV (MNT) Philadelphia; WPSG (CW)

Philadelphia; WPVI-TV (ABC) Philadelphia; WTXF-TV (FOX) Philadelphia.

Programming (via satellite): BBC America; Bio; Canales N; CBS College Sports Network; Cooking Channel; Country Music TV; C-SPAN 3; Current; Discovery Digital Networks; Discovery HD Theater; Do-It-Yourself; Encore (multiplexed); ESPN 2 HD; ESPN Classic Sports; ESPN HD; ESPNews; FearNet; Flix; Fox College Sports Atlantic; Fox College Sports Central; Fox College Sports Pacific; Fox Reality Channel; Fox Soccer; G4; GAS; Gol TV; Great American Country; Hallmark Channel; History Channel International; INHD; Jewelry Television; Lifetime Movie Network; LOGO; MTV Networks Digital Suite; Music Choice; National Geographic Channel; NBA TV; NFL Network; Nick Jr.; Nick Too; NickToons TV; Oxygen; Palladia; PBS Kids Sprout; ShopNBC; SoapNet; Sundance Channel; Telefutura; Tennis Channel; Toon Disney; Travel Channel; Turner Network TV HD; TV One; Universal HD; WAM! America's Kidz Network; Weatherscan.

Fee: $15.00 monthly.

Digital Pay Service 1

Pay Units: 67,411.

Programming (via satellite): Cinemax (multiplexed); HBO (multiplexed); Showtime (multiplexed); Starz (multiplexed); The Movie Channel (multiplexed).

Fee: $19.90 monthly (each).

Video-On-Demand: Yes

Pay-Per-View

iN DEMAND, Fee: $3.95; iN DEMAND (delivered digitally); Playboy TV (delivered digitally); Fresh (delivered digitally); Sports PPV (delivered digitally).

Internet Service

Operational: Yes.

Subscribers: 25,253.

Broadband Service: Comcast High Speed Internet.

Fee: $42.95 monthly; $7.00 modem lease; $199.00 modem purchase.

Telephone Service

Digital: Operational

Fee: $44.95 monthly

Miles of Plant: 5,242.0 (coaxial); 142.0 (fiber optic). Homes passed: 333,220.

Area Vice President & General Manager: John DelViscio. Vice President, Technical Operations: Mike Taylor. Vice President, Engineering: John Cody. Marketing Director: Aaron Geisel. Public Relations Director: Fred DeAndrea.

City fee: 2% of gross.

Ownership: Comcast Cable Communications Inc. (MSO).

VOORHEES—Comcast Cable, 401 White Horse Rd, Voorhees, NJ 8043. Phone: 856-821-6100. Fax: 856-821-6108. Web Site: http://www.comcast.com. Also serves Audubon, Audubon Park, Barrington, Bellmawr, Berlin, Berlin Twp., Browns Mills, Camden, Cherry Hill, Chesterfield Twp., Clementon, Collingswood, Eastampton Twp., Evesham Twp., Fieldsboro, Florence Twp., Fort Dix, Gibbsboro, Gloucester Twp., Haddon Heights, Haddon Twp., Haddonfield, Hainesport Twp., Hi-Nella, Laurel Springs, Lawnside, Lindenwold, Lumberton, Magnolia, Mansfield Twp. (Burlington County), McGuire AFB, Medford Lakes, Medford Twp., Merchantville, Moorestown Twp., Mount HollyTwp., Mount Laurel Twp., New Hanover Twp., North Hanover Twp., Oaklyn, Pemberton, Pemberton Twp., Pennsauken Twp., Pine Hill, Pitman, Plumsted Twp., Runnemede, Shamong Twp., Somerdale, Southampton Twp., Springfield Twp., Stratford, Tabernacle Twp., Tavistock, Voorhees Twp., West Berlin, Westampton Twp., Woodland Twp., Woodlynne & Wrightstown. ICA: NJ0003.

TV Market Ranking: 4 (Audubon, Audubon Park, Barrington, Bellmawr, Berlin, Berlin Twp., Browns Mills, Camden, Cherry Hill, Chesterfield Twp., Clementon, Collingswood, Eastampton Twp., Evesham Twp., Fieldsboro, Florence Twp., Fort Dix, Gibbsboro, Gloucester Twp., Haddon Heights, Haddon Twp., Haddonfield, Hainesport Twp., Hi-Nella, Laurel Springs, Lawnside, Lindenwold, Lumberton, Magnolia, Mansfield Twp. (Burlington County), McGuire AFB, Medford Lakes, Medford Twp., Merchantville, Moorestown Twp., Mount Holly Twp., Mount Laurel Twp., New Hanover Twp., North Hanover Twp., Oaklyn, Pemberton, Pemberton Twp., Pennsauken Twp., Pine Hill, Pitman, Plumsted Twp., Runnemede, Shamong Twp., Somerdale, Southampton Twp., Springfield Twp., Stratford, Tabernacle Twp., Tavistock, VOORHEES, Voorhees Twp., West Berlin, Westampton Twp., Woodland Twp., Woodlynne, Wrightstown). Franchise award date: March 21, 1975. Franchise expiration date: N.A. Began: April 15, 1975.

Channel capacity: N.A. Channels available but not in use: N.A.

Basic Service

Subscribers: 229,096.

Programming (received off-air): KYW-TV (CBS) Philadelphia; WCAU (NBC) Philadelphia; WFMZ-TV (IND) Allentown; WGTW-TV (IND) Burlington; WHYY-TV (PBS) Wilmington; WNJS (PBS) Camden; WPHL-TV (MNT) Philadelphia; WPPX-TV (ION) Wilmington; WPSG (CW) Philadelphia; WPVI-TV (ABC) Philadelphia; WTXF-TV (FOX) Philadelphia; WUVP-DT (UNV) Vineland; WWSI (TMO) Atlantic City; WYBE (ETV) Philadelphia; 5 FMs.

Programming (via satellite): C-SPAN; C-SPAN 2; MarketConnect Network; QVC; The Comcast Network.

Current originations: Government Access; Educational Access; Public Access.

Fee: $10.50 monthly.

Expanded Basic Service 1

Subscribers: 211,419.

Programming (via satellite): ABC Family Channel; AMC; Animal Planet; Arts & Entertainment; BET Networks; Bravo; Cartoon Network; CNBC; CNN; Comcast SportsNet Philly; Comedy Central; Country Music TV; Discovery Channel; Discovery Health Channel; E! Entertainment Television; ESPN; ESPN 2; Eternal Word TV Network; Food Network; Fox News Channel; FX; Golf Channel; GSN; Hallmark Channel; Headline News; HGTV; History Channel; Home Shopping Network; Lifetime; MSNBC; MTV; Nickelodeon; ShopNBC; Sneak Prevue; Speed Channel; Spike TV; Style Network; Syfy; TBS Superstation; The Learning Channel; truTV; Turner Classic Movies; Turner Network TV; TV Land; USA Network; Versus; VH1; Weather Channel.

Fee: $23.45 monthly.

Digital Basic Service

Subscribers: N.A. Included in Burlington County

Programming (via satellite): BBC America; Bio; Canales N; Cooking Channel; C-SPAN 3; Discovery Digital Networks; Disney Channel; Do-It-Yourself; Encore Action; ESPNews; Flix; G4; GAS; History Channel International; MTV Networks Digital Suite; Music Choice; National Geographic Channel; Nick Jr.; Nick Too; SoapNet; Sundance Channel; Toon Disney; Weatherscan.

Fee: $14.95 monthly.

Pay Service 1

Pay Units: N.A.

Programming (via satellite): HBO (multiplexed).

Fee: $21.00 installation; $15.00 monthly.

Digital Pay Service 1

Pay Units: N.A.

Programming (via satellite): Cinemax (multiplexed); HBO (multiplexed); Showtime (multiplexed); Starz (multiplexed); The Movie Channel (multiplexed).

Fee: $18.05 monthly (each).

Video-On-Demand: Yes

Pay-Per-View

Sports PPV (delivered digitally); ESPN Now (delivered digitally); iN DEMAND; iN DEMAND (delivered digitally); Playboy TV (delivered digitally); Fresh (delivered digitally); Shorteez (delivered digitally); Pleasure (delivered digitally).

Internet Service

Operational: Yes.

Broadband Service: Comcast High Speed Internet.

Fee: $42.95 monthly; $10.00 modem lease; $290.00 modem purchase.

Telephone Service

Digital: Operational

Miles of Plant: 3,715.0 (coaxial); 2,336.0 (fiber optic). Homes passed: 322,670.

Regional Senior Vice President: Greg Arnold. Area Vice President: John Del Viscio. Vice President, Technical Operations: Mike Taylor. Vice President, Engineering: John Cody. Marketing Director: Aaron Geisel. Public Relations Director: Fred DeAndrea. Government Affairs Director: Kathy Farinaccio.

City fee: 2% of gross. State fee: 2% of gross.

Ownership: Comcast Cable Communications Inc. (MSO).

WILDWOOD—Comcast Cable, 401 White Horse Rd, Voorhees, NJ 8043. Phone: 856-821-6100. Fax: 856-821-6108. Web Site: http://www.comcast.com. Also serves Cape May, Cape May Point, Lower Twp., Middle Twp., North Wildwood, West Cape May, West Wildwood & Wildwood Crest. ICA: NJ0068.

TV Market Ranking: Below 100 (Cape May, Cape May Point, Lower Twp., Middle Twp., North Wildwood, West Cape May, West Wildwood, WILDWOOD, Wildwood Crest).

Channel capacity: N.A. Channels available but not in use: N.A.

Basic Service

Subscribers: 36,851.

Programming (received off-air): KYW-TV (CBS) Philadelphia; WCAU (NBC) Philadelphia; WGTW-TV (IND) Burlington; WHYY-TV (PBS) Wilmington; WMCN-TV (IND) Atlantic City; WMGM-TV (NBC) Wildwood; WNJS (PBS) Camden; WPHL-TV (MNT) Philadelphia; WPPX-TV (ION) Wilmington; WPSG (CW) Philadelphia; WPVI-TV (ABC) Philadelphia; WTXF-TV (FOX) Philadelphia; WUVP-DT (UNV) Vineland; WWSI (TMO) Atlantic City.

Programming (via satellite): C-SPAN; C-SPAN 2; Eternal Word TV Network; QVC; The Comcast Network; TV Guide Network.

Fee: $11.85 monthly.

Expanded Basic Service 1

Subscribers: N.A.

Programming (via satellite): ABC Family Channel; AMC; Animal Planet; Arts & Entertainment; BET Networks; Bravo; Cartoon Network; CNBC; CNN; Comcast SportsNet Mid-Atlantic; Comedy Central; Discovery Channel; Discovery Health Channel; Disney Channel; E! Entertainment Television; ESPN; ESPN 2; Food Network; Fox News Channel; FX; Golf Channel; GSN; Headline News; HGTV; History Channel; Home Shopping Network; Lifetime; MSNBC; MTV; Nickelodeon; Speed Channel; Spike TV; Style Network; Syfy; TBS Superstation; The Learning Channel; truTV; Turner Classic Movies; Turner Network TV; TV Guide Network; TV Land; USA Network; Versus; VH1; Weather Channel.

Fee: $41.50 monthly.

Digital Basic Service

Subscribers: N.A.

Programming (received off-air): KYW-TV (CBS) Philadelphia; WCAU (NBC) Philadelphia; WHYY-TV (PBS) Wilmington; WPHL-TV (MNT) Philadelphia; WPVI-TV (ABC) Philadelphia; WTXF-TV (FOX) Philadelphia.

Programming (via satellite): BBC America; Bio; Bloomberg Television; CBS College Sports Network; CMT Pure Country; Cooking Channel; Country Music TV; C-SPAN 3; Current; Discovery Digital Networks; Discovery HD Theater; Do-It-Yourself; Encore (multiplexed); ESPN 2 HD; ESPN Classic Sports; ESPN HD; ESPNews; Flix; Fox College Sports Atlantic; Fox College Sports Central; Fox College Sports Pacific; Fox Reality Channel; Fox Soccer; G4; GAS; Gol TV; Great American Country; Hallmark Channel; History Channel International; INHD; Jewelry Television; Lifetime Movie Network; LOGO; MTV Networks Digital Suite; Music Choice; National Geographic Channel; NBA TV; NFL Network; Nick Jr.; Nick Too; NickToons TV; Oxygen; Palladia; PBS Kids Sprout; ShopNBC; SoapNet; Sundance Channel; Telefutura; Tennis Channel; Toon Disney; Travel Channel; Turner Network TV HD; TV One; Universal HD; Versus HD; Weatherscan.

Fee: $14.95 monthly.

Digital Pay Service 1

Pay Units: N.A.

Programming (via satellite): Cinemax (multiplexed); Cinemax HD; HBO (multiplexed); HBO HD; Showtime (multiplexed); Showtime HD; Starz (multiplexed); Starz HDTV; The Movie Channel (multiplexed).

Fee: $19.95 monthly (each).

Pay-Per-View

iN DEMAND; iN DEMAND (delivered digitally); Sports PPV (delivered digitally); Playboy TV (delivered digitally); Fresh (delivered digitally).

Internet Service

Operational: Yes.

Broadband Service: Comcast High Speed Internet.

Telephone Service

Digital: Operational

Miles of Plant: 487.0 (coaxial); None (fiber optic). Homes passed: 56,700.

Area Vice President: John DelViscio. Vice President, Technical Operations: Mike Taylor. Vice President, Engineering: John Cody. Marketing Director: Aaron Geisel. Public Relations Director: Fred DeAndrea.

Ownership: Comcast Cable Communications Inc. (MSO).

NEW MEXICO

Total Systems: 53
Total Communities Served: 146
Franchises Not Yet Operating: 0
Applications Pending: 0
Communities with Applications: 0
Number of Basic Subscribers: 321,728
Number of Expanded Basic Subscribers: 198,741
Number of Pay Units: 32,109

Top 100 Markets Represented: Albuquerque (81).

For a list of cable communities in this section, see the Cable Community Index located in the back of Cable Volume 2.
For explanation of terms used in cable system listings, see p. D-11.

ALAMOGORDO—Baja Broadband, 510 24th St, Alamogordo, NM 88310. Phone: 575-437-3101. Fax: 575-344-3439. E-mail: info@bajabroadband.com. Web Site: http://www.bajabroadband.com. Also serves Boles Acres, Holloman AFB, La Luz & Tularosa. ICA: NM0076.

TV Market Ranking: Outside TV Markets (ALAMOGORDO, Boles Acres, Holloman AFB, La Luz, Tularosa). Franchise award date: January 1, 1964. Franchise expiration date: N.A. Began: June 1, 1964.

Channel capacity: 79 (operating 2-way). Channels available but not in use: 8.

Basic Service

Subscribers: 7,453.

Programming (received off-air): KDBC-TV (CBS, MNT) El Paso; KFOX-TV (FOX) El Paso; KRWG-TV (PBS) Las Cruces; KTEL-TV (TMO) Carlsbad; KVBA-LP Alamogordo; KVIA-TV (ABC, CW) El Paso; 15 FMs.

Programming (via microwave): KASA-TV (FOX) Santa Fe; KASY-TV (MNT) Albuquerque; KBIM-TV (CBS) Roswell; KCHF (IND) Santa Fe; KLUZ-TV (UNV) Albuquerque; KOAT-TV (ABC) Albuquerque; KOBR (NBC) Roswell; KRPV-DT (IND) Roswell; KWBQ (CW) Santa Fe.

Programming (via satellite): C-SPAN; C-SPAN 2; Home Shopping Network; QVC; TBS Superstation; TV Guide Network; Weather Channel; WGN America.

Fee: $54.95 installation; $22.00 monthly; $3.43 converter.

Expanded Basic Service 1

Subscribers: N.A.

Programming (via satellite): ABC Family Channel; AMC; Animal Planet; Arts & Entertainment; BET Networks; Bravo; Cartoon Network; CNBC; CNN; Comedy Central; Country Music TV; Discovery Channel; Disney Channel; E! Entertainment Television; ESPN; ESPN 2; FitTV; Food Network; Fox News Channel; Fox Soccer; Fox Sports Net Arizona; FX; G4; GalaVision; Golf Channel; Great American Country; GSN; Hallmark Channel; Headline News; HGTV; History Channel; Lifetime; MSNBC; MTV; National Geographic Channel; Nickelodeon; Speed Channel; Spike TV; Syfy; The Learning Channel; Travel Channel; Turner Network TV; TV Land; USA Network; Versus; VH1; WE tv.

Fee: $27.85 monthly.

Digital Basic Service

Subscribers: N.A.

Programming (via satellite): BBC America; Bio; Bloomberg Television; CMT Pure Country; Discovery en Espanol; Discovery Health Channel; Discovery Kids Channel; Discovery Military Channel; Discovery Planet Green; Do-It-Yourself; ESPN Classic Sports; Fox Business Channel; Fox College Sports Atlantic; Fox College Sports Central; Fox College Sports Pacific; Fox Reality Channel; History Channel International; ID Investigation Discovery; Independent Film Channel; Lifetime Movie Network; Lifetime Real Women; LOGO; MTV Hits; MTV Jams; MTV Tres; MTV2; Music Choice; Nick Jr.; Nick Too; NickToons TV; Science Channel; SoapNet; Style Network; TeenNick; the mtn; Toon Disney; VH1 Classic; VH1 Soul.

Fee: $7.95 monthly.

Digital Expanded Basic Service

Subscribers: N.A.

Programming (received off-air): KDBC-TV (CBS, MNT) El Paso; KFOX-TV (FOX) El Paso; KVIA-TV (ABC, CW) El Paso.

Programming (via microwave): KWGN-TV (CW) Denver.

Programming (via satellite): Arts & Entertainment HD; ESPN HD; Food Network HD; FSN HD; FX HD; Golf Channel HD; HGTV HD; History Channel HD; National Geographic Channel HD Network; Speed HD; TBS in HD; Turner Network TV HD; Versus HD.

Digital Expanded Basic Service 2

Subscribers: N.A.

Programming (via satellite): HDNet; HDNet Movies; Universal HD.

Digital Pay Service 1

Pay Units: N.A.

Programming (via satellite): Cinemax (multiplexed); Cinemax HD; Deutsche Welle TV; Encore (multiplexed); Flix; HBO (multiplexed); HBO HD; Showtime (multiplexed); Showtime HD; Starz (multiplexed); Starz HDTV; The Movie Channel (multiplexed); The Movie Channel HD.

Fee: $4.00 monthly (Encore), $5.00 monthly (Deutsche Welle), $7.00 monthly (Cinemax), $8.00 monthly (Starz), $13.00 monthly (HBO or Showtime).

Video-On-Demand: No

Pay-Per-View

iN DEMAND (delivered digitally); Playboy TV (delivered digitally); Spice: Xcess (delivered digitally); Club Jenna (delivered digitally); Hot Choice (delivered digitally); Fresh (delivered digitally); Shorteez (delivered digitally).

Internet Service

Operational: Yes.

Broadband Service: In-house.

Fee: $49.95 installation; $34.99 monthly; $4.96 modem lease; $69.95 modem purchase.

Telephone Service

Digital: Operational

Miles of Plant: 298.0 (coaxial); 31.0 (fiber optic). Homes passed: 23,650.

Chief Executive Officer: William A. Schuler. Area Vice President & General Manager: Tom Jaskiewicz. Chief Operating Officer: Phillip Klein. Technical Operations Manager: Harold Vilas. Office Manager: Barbara Mick.

City fee: 3% of gross.

Ownership: Baja Broadband (MSO).

ALBUQUERQUE—Comcast Cable, 4611 Montbel Pl NE, Albuquerque, NM 87107-6821. Phone: 505-761-6200. Fax: 505-334-7301. Web Site: http://www.comcast.com. Also serves Bernalillo, Bernalillo County (portion), Bosque Farms, Corrales, Edgewood, Isleta, Kirtland AFB, Los Ranchos de Albuquerque, Moriarty, Peralta, Placitas, Sandia Knoll, Sandoval County (portions), Santa Fe County & Tijeras. ICA: NM0001.

TV Market Ranking: 81 (ALBUQUERQUE, Bernadillo County (portions), Bernalillo, Bosque Farms, Corrales, Edgewood, Isleta, Kirtland AFB, Los Ranchos de Albuquerque, Moriarty, Peralta, Placitas, Sandia Knolls, Sandoval County (portions), Santa Fe County, Tijeras). Franchise award date: September 1, 1977. Franchise expiration date: N.A. Began: June 1, 1978.

Channel capacity: N.A. Channels available but not in use: N.A.

Basic Service

Subscribers: 137,000.

Programming (received off-air): KASA-TV (FOX) Santa Fe; KASY-TV (MNT) Albuquerque; KAZQ (ETV) Albuquerque; KCHF (IND) Santa Fe; KLUZ-TV (UNV) Albuquerque; KNAT-TV (TBN) Albuquerque; KNME-TV (PBS) Albuquerque; KOAT-TV (ABC) Albuquerque; KOB (NBC) Albuquerque; KRQE (CBS) Albuquerque; KWBQ (CW) Santa Fe; 8 FMs.

Programming (via satellite): C-SPAN; Eternal Word TV Network; GalaVision; Home Shopping Network; ION Television; National Geographic Channel; Product Information Network; QVC; Telemundo; TV Guide Network; Versus; WGN America.

Current originations: Leased Access; Government Access; Educational Access; Public Access.

Fee: $48.00 installation; $10.45 monthly; $3.40 converter.

Expanded Basic Service 1

Subscribers: 122,000.

Programming (via satellite): ABC Family Channel; AMC; Animal Planet; Arts & Entertainment; BET Networks; Bravo; Cartoon Network; CNBC; CNN; Comcast Sports Net Southwest; Comedy Central; Country Music TV; C-SPAN 2; Discovery Channel; Discovery Health Channel; Disney Channel; E! Entertainment Television; ESPN; ESPN 2; Food Network; Fox News Channel; FX; Golf Channel; Great American Country; Hallmark Channel; Headline News; HGTV; History Channel; Lifetime; MSNBC; MTV; Nickelodeon; Speed Channel; Spike TV; Style Network; Syfy; TBS Superstation; The Learning Channel; truTV; Turner Classic Movies; Turner Network TV; TV Land; USA Network; VH1; Weather Channel.

Fee: $39.09 monthly.

Digital Basic Service

Subscribers: N.A.

Programming (via satellite): BBC America; Canales N; C-SPAN 3; Discovery Digital Networks; DMX Music; Encore (multiplexed); ESPNews; G4; GAS; MTV Networks Digital Suite; Nick Jr.; Nick Too; Science Television; SoapNet; Toon Disney; WAM! America's Kidz Network; Weatherscan.

Fee: $10.95 monthly.

Digital Pay Service 1

Pay Units: 6,223.

Programming (via satellite): Cinemax (multiplexed); HBO (multiplexed); Showtime (multiplexed); Starz (multiplexed); The Movie Channel (multiplexed).

Fee: $15.95 monthly (Cinemax, Showtime, TMC or Starz), $16.95 monthly (HBO).

Video-On-Demand: Yes

Pay-Per-View

Addressable homes: 36,000.

iN DEMAND, Fee: $3.95, Addressable: Yes; Barker (delivered digitally); Hot Choice (delivered digitally); ShopNBC (delivered digitally); ESPN Extra (delivered digitally); ESPN Now (delivered digitally); iN DEMAND (delivered digitally); Playboy TV (delivered digitally); Pleasure (delivered digitally); Fresh (delivered digitally); Shorteez (delivered digitally); sports (delivered digitally).

Internet Service

Operational: Yes. Began: December 1, 2000.

Subscribers: 13,970.

Broadband Service: Comcast High Speed Internet.

Fee: $150.00 installation; $42.95 monthly; $5.00 modem lease.

Telephone Service

Digital: Operational

Miles of Plant: 3,100.0 (coaxial); 100.0 (fiber optic). Homes passed: 206,058. Total homes in franchised area: 209,828.

Area Vice President: Scott Westerman. Vice President & General Manager: Chris Dunkeson. Engineering Director: Ken Hamilton. Marketing Director: Richard Brehm. Marketing Coordinator: P.J. Ruble. Public Relations Director: Eilene Vaughn-Pickrell.

City fee: 5% of gross.

Ownership: Comcast Cable Communications Inc. (MSO).

ALBUQUERQUE—Formerly served by Multimedia Development Corp. No longer in operation. ICA: NM0100.

ANGEL FIRE—Comcast Cable, PO Box 1854, 1546 Paseo Del Pueblo Sur, Taos, NM 87571-1854. Phones: 505-758-3569; 505-758-3207. Fax: 505-758-4441. Web Site: http://www.comcast.com. ICA: NM0048.

TV Market Ranking: Outside TV Markets (ANGEL FIRE). Franchise award date: January

1, 1980. Franchise expiration date: N.A. Began: January 1, 1981.
Channel capacity: 41 (operating 2-way). Channels available but not in use: N.A.

Basic Service
Subscribers: 421.
Programming (received off-air): KASA-TV (FOX) Santa Fe; KNME-TV (PBS) Albuquerque; KOAT-TV (ABC) Albuquerque; KOB (NBC) Albuquerque; KRQE (CBS) Albuquerque.
Programming (via satellite): ABC Family Channel; AMC; Arts & Entertainment; CNBC; Comcast Sports Net Southwest; Country Music TV; C-SPAN; Disney Channel; E! Entertainment Television; ESPN; ESPN 2; ESPN Classic Sports; Fox News Channel; Golf Channel; Headline News; HGTV; History Channel; Home Shopping Network; Lifetime; MTV; Nickelodeon; The Learning Channel; Turner Classic Movies; TV Land; USA Network; Weather Channel; WGN America.
Programming (via translator): KASY-TV (MNT) Albuquerque; KRPV-DT (IND) Roswell; KWBQ (CW) Santa Fe.
Fee: $30.47 installation; $32.95 monthly.

Expanded Basic Service 1
Subscribers: 83.
Programming (via satellite): CNN; Comedy Central; Discovery Channel; Outdoor Channel; QVC; TBS Superstation; Turner Network TV; VH1.
Fee: $10.55 monthly.

Pay Service 1
Pay Units: 43.
Programming (via satellite): Cinemax; HBO (multiplexed).
Fee: $10.45 monthly (each).

Pay-Per-View
Movies, Addressable: Yes; special events.

Telephone Service
Digital: Operational
Miles of Plant: 20.0 (coaxial); None (fiber optic).
Vice President & General Manager: Chris Dunkesen. Operations Manager: David Quintana.
City fee: 3% of gross.
Ownership: Comcast Cable Communications Inc. (MSO).

ARTESIA—PVT, 4011 W Main St, Artesia, NM 88210-9566. Phone: 505-748-1241. Fax: 505-746-4142. E-mail: pvt@pvt.com. Web Site: http://www.pvt.com. Also serves Cloudcroft, Dexter, Eddy County (portions), Hagerman & Twin Forks. ICA: NM0016.
TV Market Ranking: Below 100 (ARTESIA, Dexter, Eddy County (portions), Hagerman); Outside TV Markets (Cloudcroft, Eddy County (portions), Twin Forks). Franchise award date: September 1, 1993. Franchise expiration date: N.A. Began: March 1, 1961.
Channel capacity: N.A. Channels available but not in use: N.A.

Basic Service
Subscribers: 4,304.
Programming (received off-air): KBIM-TV (CBS) Roswell; KENW (PBS) Portales; KLUZ-TV (UNV) Albuquerque; KOAT-TV (ABC) Albuquerque; KOBR (NBC) Roswell; KRPV-DT (IND) Roswell; KTEL-TV (TMO) Carlsbad.
Programming (via microwave): KASA-TV (FOX) Santa Fe.
Programming (via satellite): C-SPAN; C-SPAN 2; Eternal Word TV Network; GalaVision; Home Shopping Network; KWBQ (CW) Santa Fe; QVC; ShopNBC; TV Guide Network; Weather Channel; WGN America.
Fee: $37.05 installation; $17.15 monthly; $.66 converter; $18.52 additional installation.

Expanded Basic Service 1
Subscribers: 3,938.
Programming (via satellite): ABC Family Channel; AMC; Animal Planet; Arts & Entertainment; Boomerang; Cartoon Network; CNBC; CNN; Comedy Central; Country Music TV; Discovery Channel; Disney Channel; E! Entertainment Television; Encore; ESPN; ESPN 2; ESPN Classic Sports; Food Network; Fox News Channel; Fox Sports Net; FX; Hallmark Channel; Headline News; Lifetime; MTV; National Geographic Channel; Nickelodeon; RFD-TV; Spike TV; Syfy; TBS Superstation; The Learning Channel; Travel Channel; truTV; Turner Classic Movies; Turner Network TV; TV Land; USA Network; VH1.
Fee: $22.00 monthly.

Digital Basic Service
Subscribers: 274 Includes Elephant Butte.
Programming (via satellite): BBC America; Bio; Bloomberg Television; Canales N; Daystar TV Network; Discovery Health Channel; Discovery Kids Channel; Discovery Military Channel; Discovery Planet Green; DMX Music; FitTV; Fuse; G4; Great American Country; GSN; Halogen Network; HGTV; History Channel; History Channel International; ID Investigation Discovery; Lime; MTV2; Nick Jr.; NickToons TV; Science Channel; Sleuth; Style Network; Syfy; Toon Disney; Trinity Broadcasting Network; VH1 Classic; VH1 Country.
Fee: $8.35 monthly.

Digital Expanded Basic Service
Subscribers: 49.
Programming (via satellite): Bravo; E! Entertainment Television; Encore (multiplexed); Fox Movie Channel; Independent Film Channel; Lifetime Movie Network; Turner Classic Movies; WE tv.
Fee: $11.43 monthly.

Digital Expanded Basic Service 2
Subscribers: 58.
Programming (via satellite): ESPNews; Fox College Sports Atlantic; Fox College Sports Central; Fox College Sports Pacific; Fox Soccer; Golf Channel; Outdoor Channel; Speed Channel; TeenNick; Versus.
Fee: $9.38 monthly.

Digital Pay Service 1
Pay Units: 393 Includes Elephant Butte.
Programming (via satellite): Cinemax (multiplexed); HBO (multiplexed); Showtime (multiplexed); Starz (multiplexed); The Movie Channel (multiplexed).

Video-On-Demand: No

Pay-Per-View
Playboy TV (delivered digitally); Fresh (delivered digitally); iN DEMAND (delivered digitally).

Internet Service
Operational: Yes.
Subscribers: 2,121.
Broadband Service: In-house.
Fee: $99.95 installation; $31.95 monthly.

Telephone Service
Analog: Not Operational
Digital: Operational
Subscribers: 1,910.
Fee: $40.00 installation; $21.95 monthly
Miles of Plant: 182.0 (coaxial); 75.0 (fiber optic). Homes passed: 6,300. Total homes in franchised area: 6,300. Miles of plant (fiber) includes Elephant Butte
Chief Executive Officer: Glenn Lovelace. Vice President, Plant & Operations: Sammy Reno. Vice President, Marketing & Sales: Terry Mullins.
City fee: 4% of gross.
Ownership: Penasco Valley Telecommunications (MSO).

BRAZOS—Formerly served by US Cable of Coastal Texas LP. No longer in operation. ICA: NM0073.

CARLSBAD—US Cable of Coastal Texas LP, 611 W Ave A, Seminole, TX 79360. Phones: 800-996-8788; 505-885-4147. Fax: 432-758-3379. E-mail: uscable@tx.uscable.com. Web Site: http://www.uscable.com. Also serves Eddy County & Loving. ICA: NM0008.
TV Market Ranking: Below 100 (CARLSBAD, Eddy County (portions), Loving); Outside TV Markets (Eddy County (portions)). Franchise award date: February 10, 1992. Franchise expiration date: N.A. Began: March 1, 1961.
Channel capacity: 40 (operating 2-way). Channels available but not in use: None.

Basic Service
Subscribers: N.A. Included in Seminole, TX
Programming (received off-air): KBIM-TV (CBS) Roswell; KOBR (NBC) Roswell; KRPV-DT (IND) Roswell; KTEL-TV (TMO) Carlsbad.
Programming (via microwave): KASA-TV (FOX) Santa Fe; KASY-TV (MNT) Albuquerque; KCHF (IND) Santa Fe; KENW (PBS) Portales; KLUZ-TV (UNV) Albuquerque; KOAT-TV (ABC) Albuquerque; KWBQ (CW) Santa Fe.
Programming (via satellite): C-SPAN; Discovery Channel; Hallmark Channel; QVC; Turner Network TV; TV Guide Network; Weather Channel.
Current originations: Public Access.
Fee: $28.84 installation; $20.69 monthly; $.46 converter; $14.43 additional installation.

Expanded Basic Service 1
Subscribers: N.A. Included in Seminole, TX
Programming (via satellite): ABC Family Channel; AMC; Animal Planet; Arts & Entertainment; Boomerang; Cartoon Network; CNBC; CNN; Comedy Central; Country Music TV; C-SPAN 2; Disney Channel; E! Entertainment Television; ESPN; ESPN 2; Eternal Word TV Network; Food Network; Fox News Channel; Fox Sports Net Arizona; FX; GalaVision; Great American Country; Headline News; History Channel; INSP; MTV; mun2 television; National Geographic Channel; Nickelodeon; Oxygen; Speed Channel; Spike TV; Syfy; TBS Superstation; Telefutura; The Learning Channel; truTV; TV Land; USA Network; VH1.
Fee: $23.19 monthly.

Digital Basic Service
Subscribers: N.A.
Programming (via satellite): BBC America; Bio; Bloomberg Television; Bravo; CMT Pure Country; Discovery Health Channel; Discovery Kids Channel; Discovery Military Channel; Discovery Planet Green; DMX Music; Encore (multiplexed); ESPN Classic Sports; ESPNews; FitTV; Fox College Sports Atlantic; Fox College Sports Central; Fox College Sports Pacific; Fox Movie Channel; Fox Reality Channel; Fox Soccer; Fuse; G4; Golf Channel; GSN; Halogen Network; HGTV; History Channel International; ID Investigation Discovery; Independent Film Channel; Lifetime Movie Network; MTV2; NFL Network; Nick Jr.; Outdoor Channel; Science Channel; Sleuth; Speed Channel; Style Network; Syfy; TeenNick; Toon Disney; Trinity Broadcasting Network; Turner Classic Movies; Versus; VH1 Classic; WE tv; WealthTV.
Fee: $17.85 monthly; $8.00 converter.

Digital Expanded Basic Service
Subscribers: N.A.
Programming (via satellite): Cine Latino; Cine Mexicano; CNN en Espanol; Discovery en Espanol; ESPN Deportes; Fox Sports en Espanol; History Channel en Espanol; MTV Tres; mun2 television; VeneMovies.
Fee: $4.95 monthly.

Digital Expanded Basic Service 2
Subscribers: N.A.
Programming (via satellite): Animal Planet HD; Arts & Entertainment HD; Discovery Channel HD; Discovery HD Theater; ESPN HD; Food Network HD; FSN HD; HDNet; HDNet Movies; HGTV HD; History Channel HD; National Geographic Channel HD Network; Syfy HD; Universal HD; USA Network HD; WealthTV HD.
Fee: $16.95 monthly.

Pay Service 1
Pay Units: 669.
Programming (via satellite): Cinemax; Encore; HBO.
Fee: $14.50 monthly.

Digital Pay Service 1
Pay Units: N.A.
Programming (via satellite): Cinemax (multiplexed); HBO (multiplexed); Showtime (multiplexed); Starz (multiplexed); The Movie Channel (multiplexed).
Fee: $11.95 monthly.

Video-On-Demand: No

Pay-Per-View
Addressable homes: 2,000.
iN DEMAND (delivered digitally), Addressable: No; Fresh (delivered digitally); Playboy TV (delivered digitally); Club Jenna.

Internet Service
Operational: Yes.
Broadband Service: Warp Drive Online.
Fee: $14.95 installation; $39.95 monthly.

Telephone Service
None
Homes passed & miles of plant included in Seminole, TX
Manager: Robert Wheeler. Chief Technician: Steve Worthington.
City fee: 4% of gross.
Ownership: US Cable Corp. (MSO).; Comcast Cable Communications Inc. (MSO).

CARRIZOZO—Baja Broadband, 510 24th St, Alamogordo, NM 88310. Phone: 575-437-3101. Fax: 575-344-3439. Web Site: http://www.bajabroadband.com. ICA: NM0051.
TV Market Ranking: Outside TV Markets (CARRIZOZO). Franchise award date: N.A. Franchise expiration date: N.A. Began: January 1, 1977.
Channel capacity: 36 (not 2-way capable). Channels available but not in use: N.A.

Basic Service
Subscribers: 262.
Programming (via satellite): ABC Family Channel; G4; Home Shopping Network; Spike TV; TBS Superstation; Univision; WGN America.
Programming (via translator): KASA-TV (FOX) Santa Fe; KNME-TV (PBS) Albuquerque; KOAT-TV (ABC) Albuquerque; KOB (NBC) Albuquerque; KRQE (CBS) Albuquerque.
Fee: $54.95 installation; $15.49 monthly.

Expanded Basic Service 1
Subscribers: 232.
Programming (received off-air): KRPV-DT (IND) Roswell; KTEL-TV (TMO) Carlsbad.

Programming (via satellite): AMC; Animal Planet; Arts & Entertainment; CNN; Country Music TV; Discovery Channel; E! Entertainment Television; ESPN; Fox News Channel; Headline News; HGTV; Lifetime; Nickelodeon; Speed Channel; Syfy; The Learning Channel; Travel Channel; Turner Network TV; TV Land; USA Network; WE tv.
Fee: $20.00 monthly.
Video-On-Demand: No
Internet Service
Operational: No.
Telephone Service
None
Miles of Plant: 12.0 (coaxial); None (fiber optic). Homes passed: 557.
General Manager: Gary Massaglia. Technical Operations Manager: Harold Vilas. Office Manager: Barbara Mick.
City fee: 2% of gross.
Ownership: Baja Broadband (MSO).

CHAMA—US Cable of Coastal Texas LP, 603 E Pueblo Dr, Espanola, NM 87532-2565. Phones: 505-753-4246; 800-996-8788. Fax: 505-753-9286. E-mail: uscable@tx.uscable.com. Web Site: http://www.uscable.com. Also serves Rio Arriba County. ICA: NM0055.
TV Market Ranking: Below 100 (Rio Arriba County (portions)); Outside TV Markets (CHAMA, Rio Arriba County (portions)). Franchise award date: N.A. Franchise expiration date: N.A. Began: April 1, 1965.
Channel capacity: N.A. Channels available but not in use: N.A.
Basic Service
Subscribers: N.A. Included in Seminole TX
Programming (received off-air): KASA-TV (FOX) Santa Fe; KASY-TV (MNT) Albuquerque; KLUZ-TV (UNV) Albuquerque; KMGH-TV (ABC) Denver; KNME-TV (PBS) Albuquerque; KOAT-TV (ABC) Albuquerque; KOB (NBC) Albuquerque; KRQE (CBS) Albuquerque.
Programming (via satellite): ABC Family Channel; Animal Planet; Arts & Entertainment; CNN; Country Music TV; C-SPAN; Discovery Channel; Disney Channel; E! Entertainment Television; ESPN; Eternal Word TV Network; Food Network; Fox News Channel; Headline News; HGTV; History Channel; Home Shopping Network; KTEL-TV (TMO) Carlsbad; Lifetime; MTV; Nickelodeon; Outdoor Channel; Spike TV; Syfy; TBS Superstation; Telefutura; The Learning Channel; Turner Classic Movies; Turner Network TV; TV Land; USA Network; VH1; Weather Channel; WGN America.
Current originations: Public Access.
Fee: $25.00 installation; $37.91 monthly.
Digital Basic Service
Subscribers: N.A. Included in Seminole TX
Programming (via satellite): AmericanLife TV Network; BBC America; Bio; Black Family Channel; Bloomberg Television; Bravo; Current; Discovery Digital Networks; Encore (multiplexed); ESPN Classic Sports; ESPNews; Fox College Sports Atlantic; Fox College Sports Central; Fox College Sports Pacific; Fox Movie Channel; Fox Sports World; Fuse; G4; GAS; Golf Channel; Great American Country; GSN; Halogen Network; History Channel International; Independent Film Channel; International Television (ITV); Lifetime Movie Network; Lime; MTV Networks Digital Suite; Nick Jr.; Ovation; Sleuth; Speed Channel; Style Network; Sundance Channel; The Word Network; Toon Disney; Trinity Broadcasting Network; Versus; WE tv.
Fee: $5.45 monthly (family, movies or sports); $8.00 converter.
Pay Service 1
Pay Units: N.A.
Programming (via satellite): HBO.
Fee: $11.95 monthly.
Digital Pay Service 1
Pay Units: N.A.
Programming (via satellite): Cinemax (multiplexed); HBO (multiplexed); Showtime (multiplexed); Starz (multiplexed); The Movie Channel (multiplexed).
Fee: $6.95 monthly (Starz), $11.95 monthly (HBO, Cinemax, Showtime or TMC).
Pay-Per-View
Shorteez (delivered digitally); Fresh (delivered digitally); Playboy TV (delivered digitally); iN DEMAND (delivered digitally).
Internet Service
Operational: No.
Telephone Service
None
Homes passed & miles of plant included in Seminole TX
Manager: Roberta Martinez. Chief Technician: John Jelen.
City fee: 3% of gross.
Ownership: US Cable Corp. (MSO).; Comcast Cable Communications Inc. (MSO).

CIMARRON—Comcast Cable, 1026 S 2nd St, Raton, NM 87740. Phone: 575-445-5553. Fax: 575-445-2835. Web Site: http://www.comcast.com. ICA: NM0058.
TV Market Ranking: Outside TV Markets (CIMARRON). Franchise award date: N.A. Franchise expiration date: N.A. Began: May 1, 1982.
Channel capacity: 35 (operating 2-way). Channels available but not in use: 4.
Basic Service
Subscribers: 174.
Programming (via satellite): ABC Family Channel; Animal Planet; Cartoon Network; CNBC; CNN; Country Music TV; Discovery Channel; Disney Channel; E! Entertainment Television; ESPN; ESPN 2; Eternal Word TV Network; Food Network; Hallmark Channel; HGTV; Lifetime; MTV; Nickelodeon; QVC; Spike TV; TBS Superstation; The Learning Channel; Turner Network TV; Univision; USA Network; Versus; VH1.
Programming (via translator): KASA-TV (FOX) Santa Fe; KASY-TV (MNT) Albuquerque; KNME-TV (PBS) Albuquerque; KOAT-TV (ABC) Albuquerque; KOB (NBC) Albuquerque; KRQE (CBS) Albuquerque; KWBQ (CW) Santa Fe.
Fee: $28.44 installation; $34.95 monthly.
Pay Service 1
Pay Units: 36.
Programming (via satellite): Cinemax; Encore; HBO.
Video-On-Demand: No
Internet Service
Operational: Yes.
Telephone Service
None
Miles of Plant: 6.0 (coaxial); None (fiber optic). Homes passed: 321. Total homes in franchised area: 331.
Vice President & General Manager: Chris Dunkeson. Operations Manager: Ricky Armijo. Office Manager: Tammy Trujillo.
Ownership: Comcast Cable Communications Inc. (MSO).

CLAYTON—Baja Broadband, 510 24th St, Alamogordo, NM 88310. Phone: 575-437-3101. Fax: 575-434-3439. Web Site: http://www.bajabroadband.com. ICA: NM0027.
TV Market Ranking: Outside TV Markets (CLAYTON (VILLAGE)). Franchise award date: N.A. Franchise expiration date: N.A. Began: April 1, 1958.
Channel capacity: N.A. Channels available but not in use: N.A.
Basic Service
Subscribers: 1,111.
Programming (via microwave): KAMR-TV (NBC) Amarillo; KCIT (FOX) Amarillo; KETA-TV (PBS) Oklahoma City; KFDA-TV (CBS) Amarillo; KLUZ-TV (UNV) Albuquerque; KNME-TV (PBS) Albuquerque; KPTF-DT (IND) Farwell; KVII-TV (ABC, CW) Amarillo.
Programming (via satellite): Home Shopping Network; QVC; Trinity Broadcasting Network; Univision; Weather Channel; WGN America.
Current originations: Public Access.
Fee: $54.95 installation; $21.99 monthly.
Expanded Basic Service 1
Subscribers: N.A.
Programming (via satellite): ABC Family Channel; AMC; Animal Planet; Arts & Entertainment; Bravo; Cartoon Network; CNBC; CNN; Comedy Central; Country Music TV; Discovery Channel; Disney Channel; E! Entertainment Television; ESPN; ESPN 2; Fox News Channel; FX; G4; Golf Channel; Headline News; HGTV; History Channel; Lifetime; MTV; Nickelodeon; Speed Channel; Spike TV; Syfy; TBS Superstation; The Learning Channel; Travel Channel; Turner Classic Movies; Turner Network TV; TV Land; USA Network; Versus; VH1.
Fee: $20.00 monthly.
Digital Basic Service
Subscribers: N.A.
Programming (via satellite): BBC America; Bio; Bloomberg Television; CMT Pure Country; Discovery en Espanol; Discovery Health Channel; Discovery Kids Channel; Discovery Military Channel; Discovery Planet Green; Do-It-Yourself; ESPN Classic Sports; FitTV; Fox Business Channel; Fuse; GSN; History Channel International; ID Investigation Discovery; Independent Film Channel; Lifetime Movie Network; LOGO; MTV Hits; MTV Jams; MTV Tres; MTV2; Music Choice; Nick Jr.; Nick Too; NickToons TV; Science Channel; SoapNet; Style Network; Sundance Channel; TeenNick; Toon Disney; VH1 Classic; VH1 Soul; WE tv.
Digital Pay Service 1
Pay Units: N.A.
Programming (via satellite): Cinemax (multiplexed); Encore; Flix; HBO (multiplexed); Showtime (multiplexed); Starz (multiplexed); The Movie Channel (multiplexed).
Video-On-Demand: No
Pay-Per-View
iN DEMAND (delivered digitally); Ten Clips (delivered digitally).
Internet Service
Operational: No.
Telephone Service
None
Miles of Plant: 34.0 (coaxial); None (fiber optic). Homes passed: 1,385.
Vice President & General Manager: Tom Jaskiewicz. Technical Operations Manager: Harold Vilas. Office Manager: Barbara Mick.
City fee: None.
Ownership: Baja Broadband (MSO).

CLOUDCROFT—PVTV Cable Services. Now served by ARTESIA, NM [NM0016]. ICA: NM0038.

CLOVIS—Suddenlink Communications, 1106 N Main St, Clovis, NM 88101-5935. Phone: 505-763-4411. Fax: 505-769-3140. Web Site: http://www.suddenlink.com. Also serves Cannon AFB & Texico, NM; Farwell, TX. ICA: NM0007.
TV Market Ranking: Below 100 (Cannon AFB, CLOVIS, Farwell, Texico). Franchise award date: February 1, 1954. Franchise expiration date: N.A. Began: November 9, 1954.
Channel capacity: 41 (operating 2-way). Channels available but not in use: None.
Basic Service
Subscribers: 10,072.
Programming (received off-air): KAMR-TV (NBC) Amarillo; KBIM-TV (CBS) Roswell; KCIT (FOX) Amarillo; KENW (PBS) Portales; KFDA-TV (CBS) Amarillo; KOBR (NBC) Roswell; KVIH-TV (ABC) Clovis; 16 FMs.
Programming (via satellite): ABC Family Channel; CNBC; C-SPAN; C-SPAN 2; Headline News; Home Shopping Network; TBS Superstation; The Learning Channel; Trinity Broadcasting Network; Turner Network TV; TV Guide Network; Weather Channel.
Current originations: Educational Access.
Fee: $38.00 installation; $26.45 monthly; $2.25 converter.
Expanded Basic Service 1
Subscribers: 9,600.
Programming (via satellite): AMC; Animal Planet; Arts & Entertainment; BET Networks; Cartoon Network; CNN; Comcast Sports Net Southwest; Comedy Central; Country Music TV; Discovery Channel; Discovery Health Channel; Disney Channel; E! Entertainment Television; ESPN; ESPN 2; Food Network; Fox News Channel; FX; GalaVision; HGTV; History Channel; Lifetime; MSNBC; MTV; Nickelodeon; Speed Channel; Spike TV; Syfy; Telemundo; Travel Channel; truTV; TV Land; Univision; USA Network; Versus; VH1.
Fee: $26.45 monthly.
Digital Basic Service
Subscribers: N.A.
Programming (via satellite): BBC America; Bio; Bloomberg Television; Canales N; Discovery Digital Networks; DMX Music; Encore Action; ESPN Classic Sports; ESPNews; Eternal Word TV Network; Fox Sports World; Fuse; G4; Golf Channel; Great American Country; GSN; Hallmark Channel; Halogen Network; History Channel International; Independent Film Channel; Lifetime Movie Network; Outdoor Channel; Oxygen; SoapNet; Sundance Channel; Toon Disney.
Pay Service 1
Pay Units: 1,000.
Programming (via satellite): Cinemax; HBO; Showtime; Starz.
Fee: $30.00 installation; $10.95 monthly (each).
Digital Pay Service 1
Pay Units: N.A.
Programming (via satellite): Cinemax (multiplexed); HBO (multiplexed); Showtime (multiplexed); Starz (multiplexed); The Movie Channel (multiplexed).
Video-On-Demand: No
Pay-Per-View
Sports PPV (delivered digitally); iN DEMAND (delivered digitally); ESPN Now (delivered digitally); NBA TV (delivered digitally).
Internet Service
Operational: Yes.
Broadband Service: Cebridge High Speed Cable Internet.
Fee: $100.00 installation; $24.95 monthly.
Telephone Service
Digital: Operational
Fee: $49.95 monthly
Miles of Plant: 200.0 (coaxial); None (fiber optic). Additional miles planned: 80.0 (coax-

ial). Homes passed: 16,161. Total homes in franchised area: 16,300.

Manager: Gordon Smith. Chief Technician: Bob Baker.

City fee: 3% of gross.

Ownership: Cequel Communications LLC (MSO).

CROWNPOINT—Formerly served by Crownpoint Cable TV Inc. No longer in operation. ICA: NM0054.

CUBA—Formerly served by Sun Valley Cable Inc. No longer in operation. ICA: NM0094.

DEMING—Comcast Cable, 109 N Silver Ave, Deming, NM 88030-3711. Phone: 575-546-7909. Fax: 575-546-6718. E-mail: manny_orquiz@cable.comcast.com. Web Site: http://www.comcast.com. ICA: NM0077.

TV Market Ranking: Outside TV Markets (DEMING). Franchise award date: N.A. Franchise expiration date: N.A. Began: February 1, 1967.

Channel capacity: 45 (operating 2-way). Channels available but not in use: N.A.

Basic Service

Subscribers: 3,661.

Programming (via microwave): KASA-TV (FOX) Santa Fe; KASY-TV (MNT) Albuquerque; KCHF (IND) Santa Fe; KLUZ-TV (UNV) Albuquerque; KOAT-TV (ABC) Albuquerque; KOB (NBC) Albuquerque; KRPV-DT (IND) Roswell; KRQE (CBS) Albuquerque; KRWG-TV (PBS) Las Cruces; KTSM-TV (NBC) El Paso; KVIA-TV (ABC, CW) El Paso; KWBQ (CW) Santa Fe.

Programming (via satellite): ABC Family Channel; AMC; Animal Planet; Arts & Entertainment; Cartoon Network; CNBC; CNN; Comedy Central; C-SPAN; Discovery Channel; Discovery Health Channel; Disney Channel; E! Entertainment Television; ESPN; ESPN 2; Fox News Channel; Fox Sports Net West; FX; GalaVision; Golf Channel; HGTV; History Channel; Home Shopping Network 2; Lifetime; MTV; Nickelodeon; QVC; Spike TV; TBS Superstation; Telemundo; The Learning Channel; Trinity Broadcasting Network; Turner Network TV; TV Land; USA Network; Versus; VH1; Weather Channel; WGN America.

Current originations: Public Access.

Fee: $29.75 monthly.

Digital Basic Service

Subscribers: 180.

Programming (via satellite): BBC America; Bio; CBS College Sports Network; Cine Latino; Cine Mexicano; CMT Pure Country; CNN en Espanol; Country Music TV; C-SPAN 3; Discovery en Espanol; Discovery Kids Channel; Discovery Military Channel; Discovery Planet Green; Disney XD; Encore (multiplexed); ESPN Deportes; ESPNews; Eternal Word TV Network; Flix; Food Network; Fox Sports en Espanol; GSN; Hallmark Channel; History Channel en Espanol; History Channel International; ID Investigation Discovery; Lifetime Movie Network; LOGO; MoviePlex; MTV Hits; MTV Jams; MTV Tres; MTV2; mun2 television; Music Choice; National Geographic Channel; NFL Network; Nick Jr.; Nick Too; PBS Kids Sprout; Science Channel; SoapNet; Sundance Channel; Syfy; TeenNick; Travel Channel; truTV; Turner Classic Movies; VeneMovies; VH1 Classic; VH1 Soul.

Fee: $11.95 monthly.

Digital Pay Service 1

Pay Units: 380.

Programming (via satellite): Cinemax (multiplexed); HBO (multiplexed); Showtime (multiplexed); Starz (multiplexed); The Movie Channel (multiplexed).

Fee: $14.95 monthly (each).

Pay-Per-View

Addressable homes: 180.

iN DEMAND (delivered digitally), Addressable: Yes; Hot Choice (delivered digitally); Playboy TV (delivered digitally); Fresh (delivered digitally); Spice: Xcess (delivered digitally).

Internet Service

Operational: Yes.

Telephone Service

None

Miles of Plant: 80.0 (coaxial); None (fiber optic).

Area Vice President: John Christopher. General Manager: Manny Orquiz. Chief Technician: Donnie Hall. Office Manager: Amelia Munoz.

City fee: 3% of gross.

Ownership: Comcast Cable Communications Inc. (MSO).

DIXON—US Cable of Coastal Texas LP, 603 E Pueblo Dr, Espanola, NM 87532-2565. Phones: 505-753-4246; 800-996-8788. Fax: 505-753-9286. Web Site: http://www.uscable.com. ICA: NM0063.

TV Market Ranking: Outside TV Markets (DIXON (VILLAGE)). Franchise award date: N.A. Franchise expiration date: N.A. Began: N.A.

Channel capacity: 20 (not 2-way capable). Channels available but not in use: None.

Basic Service

Subscribers: N.A. Included in Seminole TX

Programming (received off-air): KASA-TV (FOX) Santa Fe; KASY-TV (MNT) Albuquerque; KLUZ-TV (UNV) Albuquerque; KMGH-TV (ABC) Denver; KNME-TV (PBS) Albuquerque; KOAT-TV (ABC) Albuquerque; KOB (NBC) Albuquerque; KRQE (CBS) Albuquerque; KTEL-TV (TMO) Carlsbad.

Programming (via satellite): ABC Family Channel; Animal Planet; Arts & Entertainment; CNN; Country Music TV; C-SPAN; Discovery Channel; Disney Channel; E! Entertainment Television; ESPN; Eternal Word TV Network; Food Network; Fox News Channel; Headline News; HGTV; History Channel; Lifetime; MTV; Nickelodeon; Outdoor Channel; Spike TV; Syfy; TBS Superstation; Telefutura; The Learning Channel; Turner Classic Movies; Turner Network TV; TV Land; USA Network; VH1; Weather Channel; WGN America.

Fee: $19.00 installation; $36.35 monthly.

Digital Basic Service

Subscribers: N.A.

Programming (via satellite): AmericanLife TV Network; BBC America; Bio; Black Family Channel; Bloomberg Television; Bravo; Current; Discovery Digital Networks; DMX Music; Encore (multiplexed); ESPN Classic Sports; ESPNews; Fox College Sports Atlantic; Fox College Sports Central; Fox College Sports Pacific; Fox Movie Channel; Fox Sports World; Fuse; G4; GAS; Golf Channel; Great American Country; GSN; Halogen Network; History Channel International; Independent Film Channel; Lifetime Movie Network; Lime; MTV Networks Digital Suite; Nick Jr.; Ovation; Sleuth; Speed Channel; Style Network; Sundance Channel; The Word Network; Toon Disney; Trinity Broadcasting Network; Versus; WE tv.

Fee: $8.00 converter.

Pay Service 1

Pay Units: N.A.

Programming (via satellite): HBO.

Fee: $11.95 monthly.

Digital Pay Service 1

Pay Units: N.A.

Programming (via satellite): Cinemax (multiplexed); HBO (multiplexed); Showtime (multiplexed); Starz (multiplexed); The Movie Channel (multiplexed).

Fee: $6.95 monthly (Starz), $11.95 monthly (HBO, Cinemax, Showtime, or TMC).

Pay-Per-View

Shorteez (delivered digitally); Fresh (delivered digitally); Playboy TV (delivered digitally); iN DEMAND (delivered digitally).

Internet Service

Operational: No.

Telephone Service

None

Homes passed & miles of plant included in Seminole TX

Manager: Roberta Martinez. Chief Technician: John Jelen.

Ownership: US Cable Corp. (MSO).; Comcast Cable Communications Inc. (MSO).

ELEPHANT BUTTE—PVT, 4011 W Main St, Artesia, NM 88210-9566. Phone: 505-748-1241. Fax: 505-746-4142. Web Site: http://www.pvt.com. ICA: NM0049.

TV Market Ranking: Outside TV Markets (ELEPHANT BUTTE). Franchise award date: N.A. Franchise expiration date: N.A. Began: June 1, 1988.

Channel capacity: N.A. Channels available but not in use: N.A.

Basic Service

Subscribers: 203.

Programming (via satellite): ABC Family Channel; AMC; Arts & Entertainment; CNBC; CNN; Comedy Central; Country Music TV; Discovery Channel; Disney Channel; E! Entertainment Television; ESPN; ESPN 2; Fox News Channel; Fox Sports Net; FX; G4; Headline News; HGTV; History Channel; Home Shopping Network; INSP; Lifetime; Outdoor Channel; Spike TV; TBS Superstation; The Learning Channel; Travel Channel; Turner Network TV; TV Land; USA Network; Weather Channel; WGN America.

Programming (via translator): KASA-TV (FOX) Santa Fe; KLUZ-TV (UNV) Albuquerque; KOAT-TV (ABC) Albuquerque; KOBR (NBC) Roswell; KRQE (CBS) Albuquerque; KRWG-TV (PBS) Las Cruces.

Fee: $25.00 installation; $36.00 monthly.

Digital Basic Service

Subscribers: N.A. Included in Artesia

Programming (via satellite): DMX Music; ESPNews; Fox Sports World; FSN Digital Atlantic; FSN Digital Central; FSN Digital Pacific; Golf Channel; Lifetime Movie Network; Speed Channel; Style Network; Toon Disney; Turner Classic Movies; Versus; WE tv.

Fee: $12.00 monthly.

Pay Service 1

Pay Units: N.A.

Programming (via satellite): HBO.

Fee: $11.00 monthly.

Digital Pay Service 1

Pay Units: N.A. Included in Artesia

Programming (via satellite): Cinemax (multiplexed); Encore (multiplexed); HBO (multiplexed); Showtime (multiplexed); Starz.

Fee: $10.00 monthly (Cinemax, Starz/Encore, or Showtime/TMC), $11.00 monthly (HBO).

Video-On-Demand: No

Internet Service

Operational: No.

Telephone Service

None

Miles of plant included in Artesia

Chief Executive Officer: Glenn Lovelace. Vice President, Plant & Operations: Sammy Reno. Vice President, Sales & Marketing: Terry Mullins.

Ownership: Penasco Valley Telecommunications (MSO).

ESPANOLA—US Cable of Coastal Texas LP, 603 E Pueblo Dr, Espanola, NM 87532-2565. Phones: 505-753-4246; 800-996-8788. Fax: 505-753-9286. E-mail: uscable@tx.uscable.com. Web Site: http://www.uscable.com. ICA: NM0014.

TV Market Ranking: Below 100 (ESPANOLA). Franchise award date: N.A. Franchise expiration date: N.A. Began: August 1, 1978.

Channel capacity: 34 (not 2-way capable). Channels available but not in use: None.

Basic Service

Subscribers: N.A. Included in Seminole TX

Programming (received off-air): KASA-TV (FOX) Santa Fe; KASY-TV (MNT) Albuquerque; KCHF (IND) Santa Fe; KLUZ-TV (UNV) Albuquerque; KNAT-TV (TBN) Albuquerque; KNME-TV (PBS) Albuquerque; KOAT-TV (ABC) Albuquerque; KOB (NBC) Albuquerque; KRPV-DT (IND) Roswell; KRQE (CBS) Albuquerque; KTEL-TV (TMO) Carlsbad; KWBQ (CW) Santa Fe; allband FM.

Programming (via satellite): CNBC; CNN; Comedy Central; C-SPAN; ESPN Deportes; Food Network; Fox Sports en Espanol; Fox Sports Net Rocky Mountain; HGTV; Lifetime; National Geographic Channel; Turner Network TV; TV Guide Network; USA Network; WGN America.

Current originations: Public Access; Government Access.

Fee: $16.90 installation; $31.13 monthly.

Expanded Basic Service 1

Subscribers: N.A. Included in Seminole TX

Programming (via satellite): ABC Family Channel; Animal Planet; Arts & Entertainment; Cartoon Network; Country Music TV; C-SPAN 2; Discovery Channel; Disney Channel; E! Entertainment Television; ESPN; ESPN 2; Eternal Word TV Network; Fox News Channel; FX; Great American Country; Headline News; History Channel; Home Shopping Network; MTV; Nickelodeon; Outdoor Channel; QVC; ShopNBC; Speed Channel; Spike TV; Syfy; TBS Superstation; Telefutura; The Learning Channel; Travel Channel; truTV; Turner Classic Movies; TV Land; VH1; Weather Channel.

Fee: $10.36 monthly.

Digital Basic Service

Subscribers: N.A.

Programming (via satellite): BBC America; Bio; Bloomberg Television; Bravo; Canales N; Discovery Digital Networks; Encore (multiplexed); ESPN Classic Sports; ESPNews; Fox Sports World; Fuse; G4; GAS; Golf Channel; GSN; Halogen Network; History Channel International; Independent Film Channel; Lifetime Movie Network; Lime; MTV Networks Digital Suite; Nick Jr.; Sleuth; Speed Channel; Style Network; Toon Disney; Trinity Broadcasting Network; Versus; WE tv.

Fee: $8.00 converter.

Digital Pay Service 1

Pay Units: N.A.

Programming (via satellite): Cinemax (multiplexed); DMX Music; HBO (multiplexed); Showtime (multiplexed); Starz (multiplexed); The Movie Channel (multiplexed).

Video-On-Demand: No

Pay-Per-View

Playboy TV (delivered digitally); Fresh (delivered digitally); iN DEMAND (delivered digitally).

Internet Service
Operational: No.
Telephone Service
None
Homes passed & miles of plant included in Seminole TX
Manager: Roberta Martinez. Chief Technician: John Jelen.
Ownership: US Cable Corp. (MSO).; Comcast Cable Communications Inc. (MSO).

ESTANCIA—Formerly served by Chamisa Futurevision. No longer in operation. ICA: NM0052.

EUNICE—US Cable of Coastal Texas LP, 611 W Ave A, Seminole, TX 79360. Phone: 800-996-8788. Fax: 432-758-3379. Web Site: http://www.uscable.com. ICA: NM0033.
TV Market Ranking: Below 100 (EUNICE). Franchise award date: N.A. Franchise expiration date: N.A. Began: May 1, 1978.
Channel capacity: N.A. Channels available but not in use: N.A.
Basic Service
Subscribers: N.A. Included in Seminole TX
Programming (received off-air): KASY-TV (MNT) Albuquerque; KBIM-TV (CBS) Roswell; KCHF (IND) Santa Fe; KENW (PBS) Portales; KJTV-TV (FOX) Lubbock; KMID (ABC) Midland; KOAT-TV (ABC) Albuquerque; KOBR (NBC) Roswell; KOSA-TV (CBS, MNT) Odessa; KPEJ-TV (FOX) Odessa; KRPV-DT (IND) Roswell; KTEL-TV (TMO) Carlsbad; KUPB (UNV) Midland; KUPT (MNT) Hobbs; KWBQ (CW) Santa Fe; KWES-TV (NBC) Odessa.
Programming (via satellite): C-SPAN; TBS Superstation; TV Guide Network.
Current originations: Educational Access.
Fee: $35.34 installation; $17.52 monthly.
Expanded Basic Service 1
Subscribers: N.A.
Programming (via satellite): ABC Family Channel; AMC; Animal Planet; Arts & Entertainment; BET Networks; Cartoon Network; CNBC; CNN; Comcast Sports Net Southwest; Comedy Central; Country Music TV; Discovery Channel; Disney Channel; E! Entertainment Television; ESPN; ESPN 2; Eternal Word TV Network; Food Network; Fox News Channel; FX; Hallmark Channel; Headline News; History Channel; Home Shopping Network; Lifetime; MoviePlex; MSNBC; MTV; National Geographic Channel; Nickelodeon; Oxygen; SoapNet; Speed Channel; Spike TV; The Learning Channel; Turner Network TV; TV Land; USA Network; VH1; Weather Channel.
Fee: $24.94 monthly.
Digital Basic Service
Subscribers: N.A. Included in Seminole TX
Programming (via satellite): BBC America; Bio; Bloomberg Television; Bravo; CMT Pure Country; Discovery Health Channel; Discovery Kids Channel; Discovery Military Channel; Discovery Planet Green; DMX Music; Encore (multiplexed); ESPN Classic Sports; ESPNews; FitTV; Fox Reality Channel; Fox Soccer; Fuse; G4; Golf Channel; GSN; Halogen Network; HGTV; History Channel International; ID Investigation Discovery; Independent Film Channel; Lifetime Movie Network; MTV2; mun2 television; NFL Network; Nick Jr.; Outdoor Channel; Science Channel; Sleuth; Speed Channel; Style Network; Syfy; TeenNick; Toon Disney; Trinity Broadcasting Network; Turner Classic Movies; Versus; VH1 Classic; WE tv.
Fee: $17.85 monthly; $8.00 converter.
Digital Expanded Basic Service
Subscribers: N.A.
Programming (via satellite): Cine Latino; Cine Mexicano; CNN en Espanol; Discovery en Espanol; ESPN Deportes; Fox Sports en Espanol; History Channel en Espanol; MTV Tres; mun2 television; VeneMovies.
Fee: $4.95 monthly.
Digital Expanded Basic Service 2
Subscribers: N.A.
Programming (via satellite): Animal Planet HD; Arts & Entertainment HD; Discovery Channel HD; Discovery HD Theater; ESPN HD; Food Network HD; FSN HD; HDNet; HD-Net Movies; HGTV HD; History Channel HD; National Geographic Channel HD Network; Syfy HD; Universal HD; USA Network HD; WealthTV HD.
Fee: $16.95 monthly.
Pay Service 1
Pay Units: 96.
Programming (via satellite): Cinemax; Encore; HBO.
Fee: $3.00 monthly (Encore), $14.50 monthly (HBO or Cinemax).
Digital Pay Service 1
Pay Units: N.A.
Programming (via satellite): Cinemax (multiplexed); HBO (multiplexed); Showtime (multiplexed); Starz (multiplexed); The Movie Channel (multiplexed).
Fee: $8.95 monthly (Starz), $11.95 monthly (HBO, Cinemax, Showtime or TMC).
Video-On-Demand: No
Pay-Per-View
iN DEMAND (delivered digitally); Fresh (delivered digitally); Playboy TV (delivered digitally); Club Jenna (delivered digitally).
Internet Service
Operational: No.
Telephone Service
None
Homes passed & miles of plant included in Seminole TX
General Manager: Daryl Koedyker. Office Manager: Betrilla Wright. Chief Technician: Kendall Galyean.
Ownership: US Cable Corp. (MSO).; Comcast Cable Communications Inc. (MSO).

FARMINGTON—Comcast Cable, 1911 N Butler Ave, Farmington, NM 87401-6334. Phones: 505-863-9334 (Gallop office); 505-327-6143. Fax: 505-326-6606. Web Site: http://www.comcast.com. Also serves Aztec, Bloomfield & Kirtland. ICA: NM0004.
TV Market Ranking: Below 100 (Aztec, Bloomfield, FARMINGTON, Kirtland). Franchise award date: N.A. Franchise expiration date: N.A. Began: May 1, 1954.
Channel capacity: 42 (operating 2-way). Channels available but not in use: N.A.
Basic Service
Subscribers: 17,929.
Programming (received off-air): KOBF (NBC) Farmington; allband FM.
Programming (via microwave): KASA-TV (FOX) Santa Fe; KASY-TV (MNT) Albuquerque; KCHF (IND) Santa Fe; KLUZ-TV (UNV) Albuquerque; KNME-TV (PBS) Albuquerque; KOAT-TV (ABC) Albuquerque; KREZ-TV (CBS) Durango; KTEL-TV (TMO) Carlsbad; KWBQ (CW) Santa Fe.
Programming (via satellite): Cartoon Network; Comedy Central; Headline News; QVC.
Current originations: Educational Access.
Fee: $46.95 installation; $13.95 monthly.
Expanded Basic Service 1
Subscribers: 16,267.
Programming (via satellite): ABC Family Channel; AMC; Animal Planet; Arts & Entertainment; CNBC; CNN; Country Music TV; C-SPAN; C-SPAN 2; Discovery Channel; Disney Channel; E! Entertainment Television; ESPN; Food Network; Fox News Channel; Fox Sports Net Rocky Mountain; FX; Hallmark Channel; INSP; Lifetime; MTV; Nickelodeon; Spike TV; TBS Superstation; The Learning Channel; Turner Network TV; TV Guide Network; USA Network; VH1; Weather Channel.
Fee: $22.00 monthly.
Digital Basic Service
Subscribers: 845.
Programming (via satellite): BBC America; Bio; Bravo; Discovery Digital Networks; DMX Music; ESPN 2; ESPN Classic Sports; ESPNews; Fox Movie Channel; Fox Soccer; Fuse; G4; GAS; Golf Channel; GSN; Halogen Network; HGTV; History Channel; History Channel International; Independent Film Channel; Lifetime Movie Network; MTV2; National Geographic Channel; Nick Jr.; NickToons TV; Outdoor Channel; Speed Channel; Style Network; Syfy; Toon Disney; Trinity Broadcasting Network; Turner Classic Movies; TV Land; Versus; VH1 Classic; VH1 Country; WE tv.
Fee: $15.61 monthly.
Digital Pay Service 1
Pay Units: N.A.
Programming (via satellite): Cinemax (multiplexed); Encore (multiplexed); HBO (multiplexed); Showtime (multiplexed); Starz (multiplexed); The Movie Channel (multiplexed).
Fee: $14.95 monthly (each).
Video-On-Demand: No
Pay-Per-View
Addressable homes: 845.
iN DEMAND (delivered digitally); Fresh (delivered digitally), Fee: $4.99, Addressable: Yes; Playboy TV (delivered digitally).
Internet Service
Operational: Yes.
Telephone Service
None
Miles of Plant: 284.0 (coaxial); None (fiber optic). Homes passed: 39,550.
Vice President & General Manager: Chris Dunkeson. Operations Manager: Mark Johnson.
City fee: 4% of gross.
Ownership: Comcast Cable Communications Inc. (MSO).

FORT SUMNER—Rapid Cable, 230 S Main St, Muleshoe, TX 79347. Phone: 800-763-4984. Fax: 806-272-7507. ICA: NM0040.
TV Market Ranking: Outside TV Markets (FORT SUMNER). Franchise award date: September 12, 1988. Franchise expiration date: N.A. Began: December 1, 1979.
Channel capacity: N.A. Channels available but not in use: N.A.
Basic Service
Subscribers: 88.
Programming (received off-air): KASA-TV (FOX) Santa Fe; KBIM-TV (CBS) Roswell; KENW (PBS) Portales; KLUZ-TV (UNV) Albuquerque; KOAT-TV (ABC) Albuquerque; KOBR (NBC) Roswell; KTEL-TV (TMO) Carlsbad.
Programming (via satellite): ABC Family Channel; Animal Planet; CNN; C-SPAN; Discovery Channel; Disney Channel; ESPN; GalaVision; Great American Country; National Geographic Channel; Nickelodeon; QVC; Spike TV; TBS Superstation; Turner Network TV; USA Network; VH1; Weather Channel.
Fee: $29.95 installation; $38.00 monthly.
Pay Service 1
Pay Units: N.A.
Programming (via satellite): HBO.
Fee: $11.72 monthly.
Video-On-Demand: No
Internet Service
Operational: No.
Telephone Service
None
Miles of Plant: 17.0 (coaxial); None (fiber optic). Homes passed: 610. Total homes in franchised area: 900.
Regional Manager: Kerry Stratton. Regional Engineer: Rick Elmore. Office Manager: Debi Stratton.
Ownership: Rapid Communications LLC (MSO).

FOUR HILLS—Formerly served by JRC Telecommunications. No longer in operation. ICA: NM0032.

GALLUP—Comcast Cable, 201 S 1st St, Gallup, NM 87301-6209. Phone: 505-863-9334. Fax: 505-722-7327. Web Site: http://www.comcast.com. Also serves Gamerco. ICA: NM0010.
TV Market Ranking: Outside TV Markets (GALLUP, Gamerco). Franchise award date: January 1, 1954. Franchise expiration date: N.A. Began: June 1, 1954.
Channel capacity: 56 (operating 2-way). Channels available but not in use: N.A.
Basic Service
Subscribers: 6,036.
Programming (via microwave): KASA-TV (FOX) Santa Fe; KASY-TV (MNT) Albuquerque; KCHF (IND) Santa Fe; KLUZ-TV (UNV) Albuquerque; KNAT-TV (TBN) Albuquerque; KNME-TV (PBS) Albuquerque; KOAT-TV (ABC) Albuquerque; KOBF (NBC) Farmington; KRQE (CBS) Albuquerque; KTEL-TV (TMO) Carlsbad; KWBQ (CW) Santa Fe.
Programming (via satellite): C-SPAN; C-SPAN 2; Discovery Channel; QVC; TBS Superstation; TV Guide Network; Weather Channel; WGN America.
Fee: $29.95 installation; $14.37 monthly.
Expanded Basic Service 1
Subscribers: N.A.
Programming (via satellite): ABC Family Channel; AMC; Animal Planet; Arts & Entertainment; Cartoon Network; CNBC; CNN; Comedy Central; Country Music TV; Discovery Health Channel; Disney Channel; E! Entertainment Television; ESPN; ESPN 2; Eternal Word TV Network; Food Network; Fox News Channel; Fox Sports Net Rocky Mountain; FX; Golf Channel; Hallmark Channel; Headline News; HGTV; History Channel; Home Shopping Network; Lifetime; MTV; Nickelodeon; Spike TV; Syfy;

The Learning Channel; truTV; Turner Network TV; TV Land; USA Network; Versus; VH1.
Fee: $29.53 monthly.
Digital Basic Service
Subscribers: 300.
Programming (via satellite): BBC America; Bio; Bravo; Dallas Cowboys Channel; Discovery Digital Networks; DMX Music; ESPN Classic Sports; ESPNews; Fox Movie Channel; Fox Soccer; Fuse; G4; GAS; GSN; Halogen Network; History Channel International; Independent Film Channel; Lifetime Movie Network; MTV2; National Geographic Channel; NFL Network; Nick Jr.; Outdoor Channel; Speed Channel; Style Network; Toon Disney; Turner Classic Movies; VH1 Classic; VH1 Country; WE tv.
Fee: $10.20 monthly.
Digital Pay Service 1
Pay Units: N.A.
Programming (via satellite): Cinemax (multiplexed); Encore (multiplexed); HBO (multiplexed); Showtime (multiplexed); Starz (multiplexed); The Movie Channel (multiplexed).
Fee: $10.74 monthly (each).
Video-On-Demand: No
Pay-Per-View
iN DEMAND (delivered digitally), Addressable: Yes; Fresh (delivered digitally); Playboy TV (delivered digitally); Shorteez (delivered digitally); Pleasure (delivered digitally).
Internet Service
Operational: Yes.
Telephone Service
None
Miles of Plant: 111.0 (coaxial); None (fiber optic). Homes passed: 19,600.
Vice President & General Manager: Chris Dunkeson. Operations Manager: Mark Johnson. Chief Technician: Pat Gonzales. Office Manager: Mary Gonzales.
City fee: 3% of gross.
Ownership: Comcast Cable Communications Inc. (MSO).

GRANTS—Comcast Cable, 216 N 2nd St, Grants, NM 87020-2504. Phone: 505-287-9451. Fax: 505-287-7474. Web Site: http://www.comcast.com. Also serves Anaconda, Bluewater, McKinley County (south central portion), Milan, San Rafael & Valencia County (portions). ICA: NM0012.
TV Market Ranking: 81 (Valencia County (portions)); Outside TV Markets (Anaconda, Bluewater, GRANTS, McKinley County (south central portion), Milan, San Rafael, Valencia County (portions)). Franchise award date: N.A. Franchise expiration date: N.A. Began: September 1, 1972.
Channel capacity: N.A. Channels available but not in use: N.A.
Basic Service
Subscribers: 3,499.
Programming (received off-air): KASA-TV (FOX) Santa Fe; KASY-TV (MNT) Albuquerque; KCHF (IND) Santa Fe; KLUZ-TV (UNV) Albuquerque; KNME-TV (PBS) Albuquerque; KOAT-TV (ABC) Albuquerque; KOB (NBC) Albuquerque; KRQE (CBS) Albuquerque; KTEL-LP Albuquerque; KWBQ (CW) Santa Fe; 1 FM.
Programming (via satellite): ABC Family Channel; AMC; Animal Planet; Arts & Entertainment; Cartoon Network; CNBC; CNN; Comedy Central; Discovery Channel; Disney Channel; E! Entertainment Television; ESPN; Eternal Word TV Network; Food Network; Fox News Channel; Fox Sports Net; GalaVision; Golf Channel; Great American Country; Hallmark Channel; HGTV; History Channel; Home Shopping Network; Lifetime; MSNBC; MTV; Nickelodeon; Outdoor Channel; QVC; Spike TV; TBS Superstation; The Learning Channel; Trinity Broadcasting Network; Turner Network TV; TV Guide Network; USA Network; Versus; VH1; Weather Channel; WGN America.
Current originations: Educational Access.
Fee: $19.95 installation; $43.50 monthly.
Digital Basic Service
Subscribers: 250 Includes Socorro.
Programming (via satellite): BBC America; Bio; CBS College Sports Network; CMT Pure Country; C-SPAN 3; Discovery Kids Channel; Discovery Military Channel; Discovery Planet Green; Disney XD; Encore (multiplexed); ESPNews; Flix; History Channel International; ID Investigation Discovery; MTV Jams; MTV Tres; MTV2; Music Choice; National Geographic Channel; Nick Jr.; Nick Too; Science Channel; SoapNet; Sundance Channel; TeenNick; the mtn; TV One; VH1 Classic; VH1 Soul; WAM! America's Kidz Network.
Fee: $11.95 monthly.
Digital Pay Service 1
Pay Units: N.A.
Programming (via satellite): Cinemax (multiplexed); HBO (multiplexed); Showtime (multiplexed); Starz (multiplexed); The Movie Channel (multiplexed).
Fee: $14.95 monthly (each).
Video-On-Demand: No
Pay-Per-View
iN DEMAND (delivered digitally); Hot Choice (delivered digitally); Playboy TV (delivered digitally); Fresh (delivered digitally); Pleasure (delivered digitally).
Internet Service
Operational: Yes.
Telephone Service
None
Miles of Plant: 110.0 (coaxial); None (fiber optic). Homes passed: 7,060. Total homes in franchised area: 11,000.
Vice President & General Manager: Chris Dunkeson. Operations Manager: Earl Chavez. Chief Technician: Tommy Chavez.
City fee: 3% of gross.
Ownership: Comcast Cable Communications Inc. (MSO).

HATCH—Comcast Cable, 109 N Silver Ave, Deming, NM 88030-3711. Phones: 505-546-0417; 505-546-7909. Fax: 505-546-6718. E-mail: manny_orquiz@cable.comcast.com. Web Site: http://www.comcast.com. Also serves Placitas & Rodey. ICA: NM0078.
TV Market Ranking: Below 100 (HATCH, Rodey); Outside TV Markets (Placitas). Franchise award date: N.A. Franchise expiration date: N.A. Began: March 1, 1965.
Channel capacity: 46 (operating 2-way). Channels available but not in use: N.A.
Basic Service
Subscribers: 571.
Programming (received off-air): KASA-TV (FOX) Santa Fe; KOAT-TV (ABC) Albuquerque; KOB (NBC) Albuquerque; KRPV-DT (IND) Roswell; KRQE (CBS) Albuquerque; KRWG-TV (PBS) Las Cruces; KTEL-LP Albuquerque; KTSM-TV (NBC) El Paso; KVIA-TV (ABC, CW) El Paso; various Mexican stations; allband FM.
Programming (via satellite): ABC Family Channel; Animal Planet; Arts & Entertainment; Cartoon Network; CNBC; CNN; Comcast Sports Net Southwest; Comedy Central; Country Music TV; C-SPAN; Discovery Channel; Discovery Health Channel; Disney Channel; E! Entertainment Television; ESPN; Food Network; Fox News Channel; GalaVision; Hallmark Channel; HGTV; History Channel; Home Shopping Network; Lifetime; MTV; Nickelodeon; Outdoor Channel; QVC; Spike TV; Syfy; TBS Superstation; The Learning Channel; Trinity Broadcasting Network; truTV; Turner Classic Movies; Turner Network TV; TV Land; Univision; USA Network; Versus; Weather Channel; WGN America.
Fee: $44.50 monthly.
Pay Service 1
Pay Units: 186.
Programming (via satellite): HBO.
Fee: $15.00 installation; $9.00 monthly.
Internet Service
Operational: Yes.
Telephone Service
None
Miles of Plant: 28.0 (coaxial); None (fiber optic).
Vice President: John Christopher. General Manager: Manny Orquiz. Chief Technician: Donnie Hall. Office Manager: Amelia Munoz.
City fee: None.
Ownership: Comcast Cable Communications Inc. (MSO).

HIGH ROLLS MOUNTAIN PARK—Baja Broadband, 510 24th St, Alamogordo, NM 88310. Phone: 575-437-3101. Fax: 575-434-3439. Web Site: http://www.bajabroadband.com. ICA: NM0079.
TV Market Ranking: Outside TV Markets (HIGH ROLLS MOUNTAIN PARK). Franchise award date: N.A. Franchise expiration date: N.A. Began: July 1, 1980.
Channel capacity: 42 (not 2-way capable). Channels available but not in use: 12.
Basic Service
Subscribers: 179.
Programming (received off-air): KASA-TV (FOX) Santa Fe; KRQE (CBS) Albuquerque.
Programming (via satellite): ESPN; QVC; Spike TV; TBS Superstation; WGN America.
Programming (via translator): KOAT-TV (ABC) Albuquerque; KOB (NBC) Albuquerque.
Fee: $54.95 installation; $16.49 monthly.
Expanded Basic Service 1
Subscribers: 163.
Programming (received off-air): KCOS (PBS) El Paso; KTEL-TV (TMO) Carlsbad.
Programming (via satellite): ABC Family Channel; AMC; Animal Planet; Arts & Entertainment; CNBC; CNN; Country Music TV; Discovery Channel; Disney Channel; E! Entertainment Television; ESPN 2; Hallmark Channel; Lifetime; Nickelodeon; The Learning Channel; Turner Network TV; TV Land; USA Network.
Fee: $29.95 installation; $19.00 monthly.
Video-On-Demand: No
Internet Service
Operational: No.
Telephone Service
None
Miles of Plant: 12.0 (coaxial); None (fiber optic). Homes passed: 285.
Vice President & General Manager: Tom Jaskiewicz. Technical Operations Manager: Harold Vilas. Office Manager: Barbara Mick.
Ownership: Baja Broadband (MSO).

HOBBS—US Cable of Coastal Texas LP, 611 W Ave A, Seminole, TX 79360. Phone: 800-996-8788. Fax: 432-758-3379. E-mail: uscable@tx.uscable.com. Web Site: http://www.uscable.com. Also serves Lea County. ICA: NM0006.
TV Market Ranking: Below 100 (HOBBS, Lea County (portions)); Outside TV Markets (Lea County (portions)). Franchise award date: N.A. Franchise expiration date: N.A. Began: January 1, 1955.
Channel capacity: N.A. Channels available but not in use: N.A.
Basic Service
Subscribers: N.A. Included in Seminole TX
Programming (via micorwave): KWBQ (CW) Santa Fe.
Programming (via microwave): KASA-TV (FOX) Santa Fe; KASY-TV (MNT) Albuquerque; KBIM-TV (CBS) Roswell; KCHF (IND) Santa Fe; KENW (PBS) Portales; KJTV-TV (FOX) Lubbock; KLUZ-TV (UNV) Albuquerque; KMID (ABC) Midland; KOAT-TV (ABC) Albuquerque; KOBR (NBC) Roswell; KOSA-TV (CBS, MNT) Odessa; KRPV-DT (IND) Roswell; KTEL-TV (TMO) Carlsbad; KWES-TV (NBC) Odessa.
Programming (via satellite): C-SPAN; QVC; ShopNBC; TBS Superstation; TV Guide Network.
Current originations: Educational Access.
Fee: $35.34 installation; $17.52 monthly; $.58 converter.
Expanded Basic Service 1
Subscribers: N.A. Included in Seminole TX
Programming (via satellite): ABC Family Channel; AMC; Animal Planet; Arts & Entertainment; BET Networks; Cartoon Network; CNBC; CNN; Comcast Sports Net Southwest; Comedy Central; Country Music TV; Discovery Channel; Disney Channel; E! Entertainment Television; ESPN; ESPN 2; Eternal Word TV Network; Food Network; Fox News Channel; FX; Hallmark Channel; Headline News; History Channel; Home Shopping Network; Lifetime; MoviePlex; MSNBC; MTV; National Geographic Channel; Nickelodeon; Oxygen; SoapNet; Speed Channel; Spike TV; The Learning Channel; Turner Network TV; TV Land; USA Network; VH1; Weather Channel.
Fee: $24.94 monthly.
Digital Basic Service
Subscribers: N.A.
Programming (via satellite): BBC America; Bio; Bloomberg Television; Bravo; CMT Pure Country; Discovery Health Channel; Discovery Kids Channel; Discovery Military Channel; Discovery Planet Green; DMX Music; Encore (multiplexed); ESPN Classic Sports; ESPNews; FitTV; Fox Reality Channel; Fox Soccer; Fuse; G4; Golf Channel; GSN; Halogen Network; HGTV; History Channel International; ID Investigation Discovery; Independent Film Channel; Lifetime Movie Network; MTV2; mun2 television; Nick Jr.; Outdoor Channel; Science Channel; Sleuth; Speed Channel; Style Network; Syfy; TeenNick; Toon Disney; Trinity Broadcasting Network; Turner Classic Movies; Versus; VH1 Classic; WE tv.
Fee: $17.85 monthly; $8.00 converter.
Digital Expanded Basic Service
Subscribers: N.A.
Programming (via satellite): Cine Latino; Cine Mexicano; CNN en Espanol; Discovery en Espanol; ESPN Deportes; Fox Sports en Espanol; History Channel en Espanol; MTV Tres; mun2 television; VeneMovies.
Fee: $4.99 monthly.
Digital Expanded Basic Service 2
Subscribers: N.A.
Programming (via satellite): Animal Planet HD; Arts & Entertainment HD; Discovery Channel HD; Discovery HD Theater; ESPN HD; Food Network HD; FSN HD; HDNet; HD-

Net Movies; HGTV HD; History Channel HD; National Geographic Channel HD Network; PBS HD; Syfy HD; Universal HD; USA Network HD; WealthTV HD.
Fee: $16.95 monthly.

Pay Service 1
Pay Units: N.A.
Programming (via satellite): Cinemax; Encore; HBO.
Fee: $3.00 monthly (Encore), $14.50 monthy (HBO & Cinemax).

Digital Pay Service 1
Pay Units: N.A.
Programming (via satellite): Cinemax (multiplexed); HBO (multiplexed); Showtime (multiplexed); Starz (multiplexed); The Movie Channel (multiplexed).
Fee: $8.95 monthly (Starz), $11.95 monthly (HBO, Cinemax, Showtime or TMC).

Video-On-Demand: No

Pay-Per-View
iN DEMAND (delivered digitally); Fresh (delivered digitally); Playboy TV (delivered digitally); Club Jenna (delivered digitally).

Internet Service
Operational: Yes.
Broadband Service: Warp Drive Online.
Fee: $27.95 monthly.

Telephone Service
None

Homes passed & miles of plant included in Seminole TX

General Manager: Daryl Koedyker. Chief Technician: Kendall Galyean. Office Manager: Betrilla Wright.

City fee: 3% of gross.

Ownership: US Cable Corp. (MSO).; Comcast Cable Communications Inc. (MSO).

JAL—US Cable of Coastal Texas LP, 611 W Ave A, Seminole, TX 79360. Phone: 800-996-8788. Fax: 432-758-3379. E-mail: uscable@tx.uscable.com. Web Site: http://www.uscable.com. ICA: NM0037.

TV Market Ranking: Outside TV Markets (JAL). Franchise award date: N.A. Franchise expiration date: N.A. Began: February 1, 1978.

Channel capacity: 35 (not 2-way capable). Channels available but not in use: 7.

Basic Service
Subscribers: N.A. Included in Seminole TX
Programming (received off-air): KENW (PBS) Portales; KMID (ABC) Midland; KMLM-DT (IND) Odessa; KOSA-TV (CBS, MNT) Odessa; KPEJ-TV (FOX) Odessa; KRQE (CBS) Albuquerque; KUPB (UNV) Midland; KWES-TV (NBC) Odessa.
Programming (via satellite): ABC Family Channel; AMC; Animal Planet; Arts & Entertainment; Cartoon Network; CNBC; CNN; Comedy Central; Country Music TV; C-SPAN; Discovery Channel; Disney Channel; E! Entertainment Television; ESPN; ESPN 2; Food Network; Fox News Channel; Fox Sports Net; FX; Hallmark Channel; Headline News; KTLA (CW) Los Angeles; Lifetime; MoviePlex; MTV; National Geographic Channel; Nickelodeon; QVC; ShopNBC; Spike TV; TBS Superstation; Telefutura; The Learning Channel; truTV; Turner Network TV; TV Land; USA Network; VH1; Weather Channel; WGN America.
Current originations: Educational Access.
Fee: $35.34 installation; $38.05 monthly; $17.66 additional installation.

Digital Basic Service
Subscribers: N.A.
Programming (via satellite): BBC America; Bio; Bloomberg Television; Bravo; Canales N; CMT Pure Country; Discovery Health Channel; Discovery Home Channel; Discovery Kids Channel; Discovery Military Channel; Discovery Times Channel; DMX Music; Encore; ESPN Classic Sports; ESPNews; FitTV; Fox Movie Channel; Fox Soccer; Fox Sports World; Fuse; G4; Golf Channel; GSN; Halogen Network; HGTV; History Channel; History Channel International; Independent Film Channel; Lifetime Movie Network; MTV2; NFL Network; Nick Jr.; Outdoor Channel; Science Channel; Sleuth; Speed Channel; Style Network; Syfy; TeenNick; Toon Disney; Trinity Broadcasting Network; Turner Classic Movies; Versus; VH1 Classic; WE tv.
Fee: $5.45 monthly (family, movies or sports); $8.00 converter.

Pay Service 1
Pay Units: N.A.
Programming (via satellite): Encore; HBO; Starz.

Digital Pay Service 1
Pay Units: N.A.
Programming (via satellite): Cinemax; HBO (multiplexed); Showtime (multiplexed); Starz (multiplexed); The Movie Channel (multiplexed).
Fee: $6.95 monthly (Starz), $11.95 monthly (HBO, Cinemax, Showtime or TMC).

Video-On-Demand: No

Pay-Per-View
iN DEMAND (delivered digitally); Playboy TV (delivered digitally); Fresh (delivered digitally); Club Jenna (delivered digitally).

Internet Service
Operational: Yes.

Telephone Service
None

Homes passed & miles of plant included in Seminole TX

Manager: Larry Taylor. Chief Technician: Alan Springer.

City fee: 1% of gross.

Ownership: US Cable Corp. (MSO).; Comcast Cable Communications Inc. (MSO).

LA MESA—Windjammer Cable, 4400 PGA Blvd, Ste 902, Palm Beach Gardens, FL 33410. Phones: 877-450-5558; 561-775-1208. Fax: 561-775-7811. Web Site: http://www.windjammercable.com. Also serves Del Cerro Estates, Mesquite, San Miguel & Vado. ICA: NM0102.

TV Market Ranking: Below 100 (Del Cerro Estates, LA MESA, Mesquite, San Miguel, Vado).

Channel capacity: N.A. Channels available but not in use: N.A.

Basic Service
Subscribers: N.A. Included in El Paso, TX
Programming (received off-air): KCOS (PBS) El Paso; KDBC-TV (CBS, MNT) El Paso; KFOX-TV (FOX) El Paso; KINT-TV (UNV) El Paso; KRWG-TV (PBS) Las Cruces; KSCE (ETV) El Paso; KTFN (TEL) El Paso; KTSM-TV (NBC) El Paso; KVIA-TV (ABC, CW) El Paso; various Mexican stations.
Programming (via satellite): CNBC; C-SPAN; QVC.
Fee: $50.51 installation; $9.70 monthly; $19.99 additional installation.

Expanded Basic Service 1
Subscribers: N.A.
Programming (via satellite): ABC Family Channel; CNN; Comcast Sports Net Southwest; Comedy Central; Discovery Channel; Disney Channel; ESPN; ESPN 2; Headline News; Lifetime; MTV; Nickelodeon; TBS Superstation; The Learning Channel; Turner Network TV; USA Network; VH1; Weather Channel.
Fee: $31.29 monthly.

Pay Service 1
Pay Units: N.A.
Programming (via satellite): Cinemax; HBO; Showtime; The Movie Channel.
Fee: $12.95 monthly (each).

Internet Service
Operational: No.

Miles of plant & homes passed included in El Paso, TX

Ownership: Windjammer Communications LLC (MSO).

LAS CRUCES—Comcast Cable, 110 Idaho Ave, Ste A, Las Cruces, NM 88005-3253. Phone: 505-523-2536. Fax: 505-523-7208. Web Site: http://www.comcast.com. Also serves Dona Ana, Dona Ana County (portions), Mesilla & White Sands. ICA: NM0002.

TV Market Ranking: Below 100 (Dona Ana, Dona Ana County (portions), LAS CRUCES, Mesilla, White Sands); Outside TV Markets (Dona Ana County (portions)). Franchise award date: February 7, 1966. Franchise expiration date: N.A. Began: August 13, 1991.

Channel capacity: N.A. Channels available but not in use: N.A.

Basic Service
Subscribers: 28,000.
Programming (received off-air): KCOS (PBS) El Paso; KDBC-TV (CBS, MNT) El Paso; KFOX-TV (FOX) El Paso; KINT-TV (UNV) El Paso; KOAT-TV (ABC) Albuquerque; KRWG-TV (PBS) Las Cruces; KSCE (ETV) El Paso; KTDO (TMO) Las Cruces; KTFN (TEL) El Paso; KTSM-TV (NBC) El Paso; KVIA-TV (ABC, CW) El Paso; 23 FMs.
Programming (via satellite): C-SPAN; C-SPAN 2; Eternal Word TV Network; Home Shopping Network; QVC; ShopNBC; TV Guide Network; WGN America.
Current originations: Government Access.
Fee: $24.99 installation; $13.39 monthly; $3.50 converter; $18.75 additional installation.

Expanded Basic Service 1
Subscribers: 23,904.
Programming (via satellite): ABC Family Channel; AMC; Animal Planet; Arts & Entertainment; BET Networks; Cartoon Network; CNBC; CNN; Comcast Sports Net Southwest; Comedy Central; Country Music TV; Discovery Channel; Discovery Health Channel; Disney Channel; E! Entertainment Television; ESPN; ESPN 2; Food Network; Fox News Channel; FX; G4; GalaVision; Golf Channel; GSN; Hallmark Channel; Headline News; HGTV; History Channel; Lifetime; MSNBC; MTV; Nickelodeon; Spike TV; Style Network; Syfy; TBS Superstation; The Learning Channel; Travel Channel; truTV; Turner Network TV; TV Land; TV One; USA Network; Versus; VH1; Weather Channel.
Fee: $13.82 monthly.

Digital Basic Service
Subscribers: 1,227.
Programming (received off-air): KDBC-TV (CBS, MNT) El Paso; KFOX-TV (FOX) El Paso; KRWG-TV (PBS) Las Cruces; KTSM-TV (NBC) El Paso; KVIA-TV (ABC, CW) El Paso.
Programming (via satellite): Arts & Entertainment HD; BBC America; Bio; Bravo; Canales N; CBS College Sports Network; CMT Pure Country; Cooking Channel; C-SPAN 3; Current; Discovery Digital Networks; Discovery HD Theater; DMX Music; Do-It-Yourself; Encore (multiplexed); ESPN 2 HD; ESPN Classic Sports; ESPN HD; ESPNews; Flix; Fox College Sports Atlantic; Fox College Sports Central; Fox College Sports Pacific; Fox Reality Channel; Fox Soccer; GAS; Gol TV; Great American Country; Halogen Network; History Channel International; Independent Film Channel; Lifetime Movie Network; LOGO; MoviePlex; MTV Networks Digital Suite; Music Choice; National Geographic Channel; National Geographic Channel HD Network; NBA TV; NFL Network; Nick Jr.; Nick Too; NickToons TV; Outdoor Channel; Palladia; PBS Kids Sprout; SoapNet; Speed Channel; Sundance Channel; Tennis Channel; The Sportsman Channel; Toon Disney; Trinity Broadcasting Network; Turner Classic Movies; Turner Network TV HD; TVG Network; Universal HD; Versus HD; WE tv; Weatherscan.
Fee: $9.21 monthly.

Digital Pay Service 1
Pay Units: 1,661.
Programming (via satellite): Cinemax (multiplexed); Cinemax HD.
Fee: $10.75 installation; $10.00 monthly.

Digital Pay Service 2
Pay Units: 6,340.
Programming (via satellite): HBO (multiplexed); HBO HD.
Fee: $10.75 installation; $10.00 monthly.

Digital Pay Service 3
Pay Units: 3,442.
Programming (via satellite): Showtime (multiplexed); Showtime HD; The Movie Channel (multiplexed).
Fee: $10.75 installation; $10.00 monthly.

Digital Pay Service 4
Pay Units: N.A.
Programming (via satellite): Starz (multiplexed); Starz HDTV.
Fee: $10.00 monthly.

Video-On-Demand: Planned

Pay-Per-View
MLS Direct Kick (delivered digitally); iN DEMAND (delivered digitally); Hot Choice (delivered digitally); Playboy TV (delivered digitally); NBA League Pass (delivered digitally); ESPN Gameplan (delivered digitally); NHL Center Ice (delivered digitally); MLB Extra Innings (delivered digitally).

Internet Service
Operational: Yes.
Broadband Service: Comcast High Speed Internet.
Fee: $42.95 monthly; $5.00 modem lease.

Telephone Service
Digital: Operational

Miles of Plant: 604.0 (coaxial); None (fiber optic). Additional miles planned: 13.0 (coaxial). Homes passed: 40,828. Total homes in franchised area: 40,828.

Vice President & General Manager: John Christopher. Technical Operations Manager: Mark Beaubien. Marketing Manager: Melissa Turner.
City fee: 3% of gross.
Ownership: Comcast Cable Communications Inc. (MSO).

LAS CRUCES—Formerly served by Santa Fe Wireless Cable TV. No longer in operation. ICA: NM0097.

LAS VEGAS—Comcast Cable, 2530 Hot Springs Blvd, Las Vegas, NM 87701-3739. Phone: 505-425-7531. Fax: 505-425-6822. Web Site: http://www.comcast.com. Also serves San Miguel County. ICA: NM0080.
TV Market Ranking: Below 100 (San Miguel County (portions)); Outside TV Markets (LAS VEGAS, San Miguel County (portions)). Franchise award date: N.A. Franchise expiration date: N.A. Began: May 7, 1967.
Channel capacity: 64 (not 2-way capable). Channels available but not in use: N.A.
Basic Service
Subscribers: 3,411.
Programming (received off-air): KASA-TV (FOX) Santa Fe; KASY-TV (MNT) Albuquerque; KCHF (IND) Santa Fe; KLUZ-TV (UNV) Albuquerque; KNME-TV (PBS) Albuquerque; KOAT-TV (ABC) Albuquerque; KOB (NBC) Albuquerque; KRPV-DT (IND) Roswell; KRQE (CBS) Albuquerque; KTEL-TV (TMO) Carlsbad; KWBQ (CW) Santa Fe; 10 FMs.
Programming (via satellite): ABC Family Channel; AMC; Arts & Entertainment; Bravo; Comcast Sports Net Southwest; C-SPAN; Disney Channel; E! Entertainment Television; ESPN; Eternal Word TV Network; Fox News Channel; Home Shopping Network; MTV; Nickelodeon; QVC; Spike TV; TBS Superstation; Telefutura; Turner Network TV; USA Network; Weather Channel; WGN America.
Current originations: Educational Access; Public Access.
Fee: $29.87 installation; $33.95 monthly.
Expanded Basic Service 1
Subscribers: N.A.
Programming (via satellite): Animal Planet; Cartoon Network; CNBC; CNN; Comedy Central; Country Music TV; Discovery Channel; Discovery Health Channel; ESPN 2; Food Network; G4; Golf Channel; Hallmark Channel; HGTV; History Channel; Lifetime; Style Network; Syfy; The Learning Channel; Travel Channel; TV Land; Versus; VH1; Weather Channel.
Fee: $12.55 monthly.
Digital Basic Service
Subscribers: 904.
Programming (via satellite): BBC America; Bio; CBS College Sports Network; CMT Pure Country; C-SPAN 3; Discovery Kids Channel; Discovery Military Channel; Discovery Planet Green; Encore (multiplexed); ESPNews; Flix; History Channel International; ID Investigation Discovery; Lifetime Movie Network; LOGO; MoviePlex; MTV Jams; MTV Tres; MTV2; Music Choice; National Geographic Channel; NFL Network; Nick Jr.; Nick Too; PBS Kids Sprout; RFD-TV; Science Channel; SoapNet; Sundance Channel; TeenNick; the mtn; The Sportsman Channel; Toon Disney; TV One; VH1 Classic; VH1 Soul.
Fee: $10.20 monthly.
Digital Pay Service 1
Pay Units: N.A.
Programming (via satellite): Cinemax (multiplexed); HBO (multiplexed); Showtime (multiplexed); Starz (multiplexed); The Movie Channel (multiplexed).
Fee: $11.49 monthly (each).
Video-On-Demand: No
Pay-Per-View
Addressable homes: 167.
iN DEMAND (delivered digitally), Addressable: Yes; Playboy TV (delivered digitally); Fresh (delivered digitally); Spice: Xcess (delivered digitally); Hot Choice (delivered digitally).
Internet Service
Operational: Yes.
Telephone Service
None
Miles of Plant: 125.0 (coaxial); None (fiber optic). Homes passed: 6,000. Total homes in franchised area: 6,000.
Vice President & General Manager: Chris Dunkeson. Operations Manager: Ricky Armijo. Chief Technician: Henry Garcia.
City fee: 4% of gross.
Ownership: Comcast Cable Communications Inc. (MSO).

LOGAN—Baja Broadband, 510 24th St, Alamogordo, NM 88310. Phone: 575-437-3101. Fax: 575-434-3439. Web Site: http://www.bajabroadband.com. ICA: NM0053.
TV Market Ranking: Outside TV Markets (LOGAN). Franchise award date: N.A. Franchise expiration date: N.A. Began: January 1, 1975.
Channel capacity: 60 (not 2-way capable). Channels available but not in use: 18.
Basic Service
Subscribers: 367.
Programming (received off-air): KAMR-TV (NBC) Amarillo; KCIT (FOX) Amarillo; KFDA-TV (CBS) Amarillo; KVII-TV (ABC, CW) Amarillo.
Programming (via satellite): ABC Family Channel; AMC; Animal Planet; Arts & Entertainment; CNBC; CNN; Country Music TV; Discovery Channel; Disney Channel; ESPN; ESPN 2; Headline News; HGTV; History Channel; Home Shopping Network; Lifetime; Nickelodeon; Speed Channel; Spike TV; Syfy; TBS Superstation; The Learning Channel; Travel Channel; Turner Network TV; TV Land; Univision; USA Network; VH1; Weather Channel; WGN America.
Programming (via translator): KENW (PBS) Portales; KOAT-TV (ABC) Albuquerque; KOB (NBC) Albuquerque; KRPV-DT (IND) Roswell; KRQE (CBS) Albuquerque.
Fee: $54.95 installation; $36.99 monthly.
Digital Basic Service
Subscribers: N.A.
Programming (via satellite): BBC America; Bio; Bloomberg Television; CMT Pure Country; Discovery Health Channel; Discovery Kids Channel; Discovery Military Channel; Discovery Planet Green; FitTV; Fox Movie Channel; Fuse; G4; GSN; Halogen Network; History Channel International; ID Investigation Discovery; Independent Film Channel; Lifetime Movie Network; MTV2; Music Choice; National Geographic Channel; Nick Jr.; NickToons TV; Science Channel; Style Network; TeenNick; Toon Disney; Trinity Broadcasting Network; Turner Classic Movies; VH1 Classic; WE tv.
Digital Expanded Basic Service
Subscribers: N.A.
Programming (via satellite): ESPNews; Fox Soccer; Golf Channel; Outdoor Channel; Versus.
Digital Pay Service 1
Pay Units: N.A.
Programming (via satellite): Cinemax (multiplexed); Encore (multiplexed); HBO (multiplexed); Showtime (multiplexed); Starz; The Movie Channel (multiplexed).
Video-On-Demand: No
Pay-Per-View
iN DEMAND (delivered digitally); Club Jenna (delivered digitally); Playboy TV (delivered digitally); Fresh (delivered digitally).
Internet Service
Operational: No.
Telephone Service
None
Miles of Plant: 20.0 (coaxial); None (fiber optic). Homes passed: 871.
Area Vice President & General Manager: Tom Jaskiewicz. Technical Operations Manager: Harold Vilas. Office Manager: Barbara Mick.
City fee: 3% of gross.
Ownership: Baja Broadband (MSO).

LORDSBURG—City TV Cable Service. No longer in operation. ICA: NM0024.

LOS ALAMOS—Comcast Cable, 2534 Camino Entrada, Santa Fe, NM 87507-4807. Phone: 505-474-7886. Fax: 505-474-7986. Web Site: http://www.comcast.com. Also serves Los Alamos County & White Rock. ICA: NM0015.
TV Market Ranking: Below 100 (LOS ALAMOS, Los Alamos County, White Rock). Franchise award date: N.A. Franchise expiration date: N.A. Began: March 1, 1980.
Channel capacity: N.A. Channels available but not in use: N.A.
Basic Service
Subscribers: 3,310.
Programming (received off-air): KASA-TV (FOX) Santa Fe; KASY-TV (MNT) Albuquerque; KCHF (IND) Santa Fe; KLUZ-TV (UNV) Albuquerque; KNAT-TV (TBN) Albuquerque; KNME-TV (PBS) Albuquerque; KOAT-TV (ABC) Albuquerque; KOB (NBC) Albuquerque; KPAX-TV (CBS, CW) Missoula; KRQE (CBS) Albuquerque; KWBQ (CW) Santa Fe; allband FM.
Programming (via satellite): ABC Family Channel; Nickelodeon; QVC; Spike TV; Telemundo; TV Land; WGN America.
Current originations: Government Access; Educational Access; Public Access.
Fee: $15.00 installation; $31.95 monthly.
Expanded Basic Service 1
Subscribers: 1,400.
Programming (via satellite): AMC; Animal Planet; Arts & Entertainment; Bravo; Cartoon Network; CNBC; CNN; Comcast Sports Net Southwest; Comedy Central; Country Music TV; C-SPAN; C-SPAN 2; Discovery Channel; Discovery Health Channel; Disney Channel; E! Entertainment Television; ESPN; ESPN 2; Eternal Word TV Network; Food Network; Fox News Channel; FX; Golf Channel; Great American Country; Hallmark Channel; Headline News; HGTV; History Channel; Home Shopping Network; Lifetime; MSNBC; MTV; Speed Channel; Style Network; Syfy; TBS Superstation; The Learning Channel; truTV; Turner Network TV; USA Network; Versus; VH1; Weather Channel.
Fee: $6.04 monthly.
Digital Basic Service
Subscribers: 603.
Programming (via satellite): BBC America; C-SPAN 3; Discovery Digital Networks; DMX Music; Encore Action; ESPNews; Flix; GAS; MTV Networks Digital Suite; Nick Jr.; Nick Too; SoapNet; Sundance Channel; Toon Disney.
Fee: $18.58 monthly.
Digital Pay Service 1
Pay Units: N.A.
Programming (via satellite): Cinemax (multiplexed); HBO (multiplexed); Showtime (multiplexed); Starz; The Movie Channel (multiplexed).
Fee: $14.95 monthly (each).
Video-On-Demand: No
Pay-Per-View
iN DEMAND (delivered digitally); Playboy TV (delivered digitally); Fresh (delivered digitally); Shorteez (delivered digitally).
Internet Service
Operational: Yes.
Subscribers: 1,514.
Broadband Service: Comcast High Speed Internet.
Fee: $42.95 monthly; $5.00 modem lease.
Telephone Service
Digital: Operational
Miles of Plant: 129.0 (coaxial); 32.0 (fiber optic). Homes passed: 7,521.
Vice President & General Manager: Chris Dunkeson. Operations Director: Carmen Valadez. Chief Technician: Chris Ciak.
City fee: 3% of gross.
Ownership: Comcast Cable Communications Inc. (MSO).

LOS LUNAS—Comcast Cable, 4611 Montbel Pl NE, Albuquerque, NM 87107-6821. Phone: 505-761-6200. Fax: 505-344-7301. Web Site: http://www.comcast.com. Also serves Belen, Los Chavez & Valencia County (portions). ICA: NM0013.
TV Market Ranking: 81 (Belen, Los Chavez, LOS LUNAS, Valencia County (portions)); Outside TV Markets (Valencia County (portions)). Franchise award date: N.A. Franchise expiration date: N.A. Began: February 1, 1980.
Channel capacity: N.A. Channels available but not in use: N.A.
Basic Service
Subscribers: 4,400.
Programming (received off-air): KASA-TV (FOX) Santa Fe; KASY-TV (MNT) Albuquerque; KAZQ (ETV) Albuquerque; KCHF (IND) Santa Fe; KLUZ-TV (UNV) Albuquerque; KNAT-TV (TBN) Albuquerque; KNME-TV (PBS) Albuquerque; KOAT-TV (ABC) Albuquerque; KOB (NBC) Albuquerque; KRQE (CBS) Albuquerque; KWBQ (CW) Santa Fe.
Programming (via satellite): CNN; C-SPAN; ESPN; Eternal Word TV Network; Home Shopping Network; ION Television; QVC; Telemundo; Turner Network TV; TV Guide Network; Univision; WGN America.
Current originations: Educational Access; Leased Access; Government Access; Public Access.
Fee: $45.00 installation; $10.45 monthly.
Expanded Basic Service 1
Subscribers: 4,275.
Programming (via satellite): ABC Family Channel; AMC; Animal Planet; Arts & Entertainment; BET Networks; Bravo; Cartoon Network; CNBC; Comedy Central; Country Music TV; C-SPAN 2; Discovery Channel; Discovery Health Channel; Disney Channel; E! Entertainment Television; ESPN 2; Food Network; Fox News Channel; Fox Sports Net; FX; GalaVision; Golf Channel; Great American Country; Headline News; HGTV; History Channel; Lifetime; MSNBC; MTV; National Geographic Channel; Nickelodeon; Product Information Network; Speed Channel; Spike TV; Style Network; Syfy; TBS Superstation; The Learning Channel; truTV; Turner Classic Movies; TV Land; USA Network; Versus; VH1; Weather Channel.
Fee: $39.09 monthly.

Digital Basic Service
Subscribers: 216.
Programming (via satellite): BBC America; Canales N; C-SPAN 3; Discovery Digital Networks; DMX Music; Encore Action; ESPNews; Flix; G4; GAS; MTV Networks Digital Suite; Nick Jr.; Nick Too; ShopNBC; SoapNet; Sundance Channel; Toon Disney; Weatherscan.
Fee: $10.95 monthly.
Digital Pay Service 1
Pay Units: N.A.
Programming (via satellite): Cinemax (multiplexed); HBO (multiplexed); Showtime (multiplexed); Starz (multiplexed); The Movie Channel (multiplexed).
Fee: $14.20 monthly (each).
Video-On-Demand: Yes
Pay-Per-View
Addressable homes: 447.
iN DEMAND, Addressable: Yes; ESPN Now (delivered digitally); Shorteez (delivered digitally); Pleasure (delivered digitally); Sports PPV (delivered digitally); ESPN Extra (delivered digitally); NBA TV (delivered digitally); iN DEMAND (delivered digitally); Barker (delivered digitally); Playboy TV (delivered digitally); Fresh (delivered digitally).
Internet Service
Operational: Yes.
Subscribers: 484.
Broadband Service: Comcast High Speed Internet.
Fee: $42.95 monthly; $5.00 modem lease.
Telephone Service
Digital: Operational
Miles of Plant: 281.0 (coaxial); None (fiber optic). Additional miles planned: 20.0 (coaxial). Homes passed: 12,679.
General Manager: Chris Dunkenson. Engineering Director: Bafar Daud. Marketing Director: Sherry Skinner.
City fee: 5% of gross.
Ownership: Comcast Cable Communications Inc.

LOS OJOS—Formerly served by US Cable of Coastal Texas LP. No longer in operation. ICA: NM0081.

LOVINGTON—Comcast Cable, 400 W Polk Ave, Lovington, NM 88260-2791. Phones: 505-396-5426; 505-396-5871. Fax: 505-396-5006. Web Site: http://www.comcast.com. Also serves Lea County. ICA: NM0020.
TV Market Ranking: Below 100 (Lea County (portions), LOVINGTON); Outside TV Markets (Lea County (portions)). Franchise award date: N.A. Franchise expiration date: N.A. Began: December 1, 1954.
Channel capacity: 52 (operating 2-way). Channels available but not in use: N.A.
Basic Service
Subscribers: 2,830.
Programming (received off-air): KASA-TV (FOX) Santa Fe; KASY-TV (MNT) Albuquerque; KBIM-TV (CBS) Roswell; KENW (PBS) Portales; KJTV-TV (FOX) Lubbock; KLUZ-TV (UNV) Albuquerque; KOBR (NBC) Roswell; KRPV-DT (IND) Roswell; KUPT (MNT) Hobbs [Licensed & silent]; KWBQ (CW) Santa Fe; KWES-TV (NBC) Odessa; 1 FM.
Programming (via satellite): CNBC; CNN; Comcast Sports Net Southwest; C-SPAN; C-SPAN 2; ESPN; ESPN 2; GalaVision; Headline News; MSNBC; QVC; Spike TV; Telemundo; Weather Channel.
Programming (via translator): KOAT-TV (ABC) Albuquerque.
Current originations: Public Access.
Fee: $32.00 installation; $15.44 monthly; $.73 converter.
Expanded Basic Service 1
Subscribers: N.A.
Programming (via satellite): ABC Family Channel; AMC; Animal Planet; Arts & Entertainment; BET Networks; Cartoon Network; Country Music TV; Discovery Channel; Discovery Health Channel; Disney Channel; E! Entertainment Television; Fox News Channel; Golf Channel; HGTV; History Channel; Lifetime; MTV; Nickelodeon; Outdoor Channel; Syfy; TBS Superstation; The Learning Channel; Turner Network TV; USA Network; VH1; WGN America.
Fee: $9.30 monthly.
Digital Basic Service
Subscribers: 139.
Programming (via satellite): BBC America; Bio; Canales N; CMT Pure Country; C-SPAN 3; Discovery Digital Networks; Encore (multiplexed); ESPNews; Flix; GAS; History Channel International; Lifetime Movie Network; LOGO; MoviePlex; MTV Networks Digital Suite; Music Choice; National Geographic Channel; NFL Network; Nick Jr.; Nick Too; PBS Kids Sprout; SoapNet; Sundance Channel; Toon Disney; TV One.
Fee: $11.20 monthly.
Digital Pay Service 1
Pay Units: N.A.
Programming (via satellite): Cinemax (multiplexed); HBO (multiplexed); Showtime (multiplexed); Starz (multiplexed); The Movie Channel (multiplexed).
Fee: $10.22 monthly (each).
Video-On-Demand: No
Pay-Per-View
Addressable homes: 139.
iN DEMAND (delivered digitally), Addressable: Yes; Hot Choice (delivered digitally); Playboy TV (delivered digitally).
Internet Service
Operational: Yes.
Telephone Service
None
Miles of Plant: 51.0 (coaxial); None (fiber optic). Homes passed: 3,410.
Area Vice President: John Christopher. General Manager: Dennis Jones. Chief Technician: Spencer DeBord. Office Manager: Carmen Luebano.
City fee: 4% of gross.
Ownership: Comcast Cable Communications Inc. (MSO).

MAXWELL—Formerly served by Rocky Mountain Cable. No longer in operation. ICA: NM0070.

MELROSE—Rapid Cable, 230 S Main St, Muleshoe, TX 79347. Phone: 800-963-4984. Fax: 806-272-7507. ICA: NM0061.
TV Market Ranking: Below 100 (MELROSE). Franchise award date: September 13, 1990. Franchise expiration date: N.A. Began: January 1, 1980.
Channel capacity: N.A. Channels available but not in use: N.A.
Basic Service
Subscribers: 109.
Programming (received off-air): KBIM-TV (CBS) Roswell; KCIT (FOX) Amarillo; KENW (PBS) Portales; KFDA-TV (CBS) Amarillo; KOBR (NBC) Roswell; KVIH-TV (ABC) Clovis.
Programming (via satellite): ABC Family Channel; Animal Planet; CNN; Discovery Channel; Disney Channel; ESPN; Great American Country; Headline News; Lifetime; National Geographic Channel; QVC; Spike TV; TBS Superstation; The Learning Channel; Trinity Broadcasting Network; Turner Network TV; TV Land; USA Network; VH1; Weather Channel.
Programming (via translator): KVDA (TMO) San Antonio.
Fee: $29.95 installation; $38.00 monthly.
Pay Service 1
Pay Units: 27.
Programming (via satellite): Showtime.
Fee: $10.95 monthly.
Video-On-Demand: No
Internet Service
Operational: No.
Telephone Service
None
Miles of Plant: 6.0 (coaxial); None (fiber optic). Homes passed: 262.
Regional Manager: Kerry Stratton. Regional Engineer: Rick Elmore. Office Manager: Debi Stratton.
Ownership: Rapid Communications LLC (MSO).

MORA—Formerly served by Rocky Mountain Cable. No longer in operation. ICA: NM0050.

MOUNTAINAIR—Formerly served by Chamisa Futurevision. No longer in operation. ICA: NM0046.

NAVAJO—Formerly served by Frontier Communications. No longer in operation. ICA: NM0083.

PECOS—Comcast Cable, 2534 Camino Entrada, Santa Fe, NM 87507-4807. Phone: 505-474-7886. Fax: 505-474-7986. Web Site: http://www.comcast.com. ICA: NM0042.
TV Market Ranking: Below 100 (PECOS). Franchise award date: July 14, 1981. Franchise expiration date: N.A. Began: April 1, 1983.
Channel capacity: 47 (not 2-way capable). Channels available but not in use: N.A.
Basic Service
Subscribers: N.A. Included in Santa Fe
Programming (received off-air): KASA-TV (FOX) Santa Fe; KASY-TV (MNT) Albuquerque; KLUZ-TV (UNV) Albuquerque; KNME-TV (PBS) Albuquerque; KOAT-TV (ABC) Albuquerque; KOB (NBC) Albuquerque; KRPV-DT (IND) Roswell; KRQE (CBS) Albuquerque; KTEL-TV (TMO) Carlsbad; KWBQ (CW) Santa Fe.
Programming (via satellite): ABC Family Channel; AMC; Arts & Entertainment; Bravo; Comcast Sports Net Southwest; C-SPAN; Disney Channel; E! Entertainment Television; ESPN; ESPN 2; Eternal Word TV Network; Fox News Channel; GalaVision; Great American Country; HGTV; Home Shopping Network; MTV; Nickelodeon; QVC; Spike TV; Syfy; TBS Superstation; The Learning Channel; Turner Classic Movies; TV Land; USA Network; Versus; Weather Channel; WGN America.
Fee: $16.80 installation; $30.95 monthly.

Expanded Basic Service 1
Subscribers: N.A.
Programming (via satellite): Cartoon Network; CNN; Comedy Central; Country Music TV; Discovery Channel; Turner Network TV.
Fee: $10.20 monthly.
Pay Service 1
Pay Units: 220.
Programming (via satellite): Cinemax; HBO (multiplexed).
Fee: $16.80 installation; $8.44 monthly (each).
Internet Service
Operational: Yes.
Telephone Service
None
Miles of Plant: 16.0 (coaxial); None (fiber optic). Homes passed: 506. Total homes in franchised area: 768.
Vice President & General Manager: Chris Dunkeson. Operations Director: Carmen Valadez. Chief Technician: Chris Ciak.
City fee: 2% of gross.
Ownership: Comcast Cable Communications Inc. (MSO).

PENASCO—US Cable of Coastal Texas LP, 611 W Ave A, Seminole, TX 79360. Phone: 432-758-9221. Fax: 432-758-3379. E-mail: uscable@tx.uscable.com. Web Site: http://www.uscable.com. Also serves Picuris. ICA: NM0105.
TV Market Ranking: Outside TV Markets (PENASCO, Picuris).
Channel capacity: N.A. Channels available but not in use: N.A.
Basic Service
Subscribers: N.A. Included in Seminole TX
Programming (received off-air): KASA-TV (FOX) Santa Fe; KASY-TV (MNT) Albuquerque; KCHF (IND) Santa Fe; KLUZ-TV (UNV) Albuquerque; KNME-TV (PBS) Albuquerque; KOAT-TV (ABC) Albuquerque; KOB (NBC) Albuquerque; KRQE (CBS) Albuquerque; KTEL-TV (TMO) Carlsbad; KWBQ (CW) Santa Fe.
Programming (via satellite): ABC Family Channel; Animal Planet; Arts & Entertainment; CNN; Country Music TV; C-SPAN; Discovery Channel; Disney Channel; ESPN; Eternal Word TV Network; Food Network; Fox News Channel; Headline News; HGTV; History Channel; Home Shopping Network; Lifetime; MTV; Nickelodeon; Spike TV; Syfy; TBS Superstation; Telefutura; The Learning Channel; Turner Classic Movies; Turner Network TV; TV Land; USA Network; VH1; Weather Channel; WGN America.
Fee: $37.45 monthly.
Digital Basic Service
Subscribers: N.A.
Programming (via satellite): AmericanLife TV Network; BBC America; Bloomberg Television; Bravo; Current; Discovery Health Channel; Discovery Kids Channel; Encore; ESPN Classic Sports; ESPNews; Fox College Sports Atlantic; Fox College Sports Central; Fox College Sports Pacific; Fox Soccer; Fuse; G4; GAS; Golf Channel; Great American Country; GSN; Independent Film Channel; Lifetime Movie Network; MTV2;

Nick Jr.; Science Channel; Sleuth; Speed Channel; Style Network; The Word Network; Toon Disney; Trinity Broadcasting Network; Versus; VH1 Classic; VH1 Soul; WE tv.
Fee: $12.95 monthly.

Digital Expanded Basic Service
Subscribers: N.A.
Programming (via satellite): Bio; CMT Pure Country; Discovery Home Channel; Discovery Military Channel; Discovery Times Channel; Encore (multiplexed); FitTV; Fox Movie Channel; Halogen Network; History Channel International; MTV Hits; Ovation.
Fee: $4.95 monthly.

Pay Service 1
Pay Units: N.A.
Programming (via satellite): HBO.
Fee: $11.95 monthly.

Digital Pay Service 1
Pay Units: N.A.
Programming (via satellite): Cinemax (multiplexed); HBO (multiplexed); Showtime (multiplexed); Starz (multiplexed).

Pay-Per-View
iN DEMAND (delivered digitally); Playboy TV (delivered digitally); Fresh (delivered digitally).

Internet Service
Operational: No.
Homes passed & miles of plant included in Seminole TX
Regional Manager: Daryl Koedyker. Technical Operations Director: Jess Webb. Marketing Director: Chandra Davis. Office Manager: Kim Harris.
Ownership: Comcast Cable Communications Inc. (MSO).; US Cable Corp. (MSO).

PLAYAS—Formerly served by Playas CATV. No longer in operation. ICA: NM0084.

POJOAQUE—Comcast Cable, 2534 Camino Entrada, Santa Fe, NM 87507-4807. Phone: 505-474-7886. Fax: 505-474-7986. Web Site: http://www.comcast.com. Also serves Nambe & San Ildefonso Pueblo. ICA: NM0104.
TV Market Ranking: Below 100 (Nambe, POJOAQUE, San Ildefonso Pueblo).
Channel capacity: N.A. Channels available but not in use: N.A.

Basic Service
Subscribers: N.A. Included in Santa Fe
Programming (received off-air): KASA-TV (FOX) Santa Fe; KASY-TV (MNT) Albuquerque; KAZQ (ETV) Albuquerque; KCHF (IND) Santa Fe; KLUZ-TV (UNV) Albuquerque; KNAT-TV (TBN) Albuquerque; KNME-TV (PBS) Albuquerque; KOAT-TV (ABC) Albuquerque; KOB (NBC) Albuquerque; KQDF-LP Albuquerque; KRQE (CBS) Albuquerque; KTEL-TV (TMO) Carlsbad; KTFQ-DT (TEL) Albuquerque; KWBQ (CW) Santa Fe.
Programming (via satellite): BET Networks; Bravo; Comcast Sports Net Southwest; C-SPAN; C-SPAN 2; ESPN; ESPN 2; Eternal Word TV Network; Home Shopping Network; MTV; QVC; The Comcast Network; TV Guide Network; VH1.
Current originations: Leased Access; Government Access.
Fee: $34.95 monthly.

Expanded Basic Service 1
Subscribers: N.A.
Programming (via satellite): ABC Family Channel; AMC; Animal Planet; Arts & Entertainment; Bravo; Cartoon Network; CNBC; CNN; Comedy Central; Country Music TV; Discovery Channel; Discovery Health Channel; Disney Channel; E! Entertainment Television; Food Network; Fox News Channel; FX; G4; GalaVision; Golf Channel; Headline News; HGTV; History Channel; Lifetime; MSNBC; Nickelodeon; Speed Channel; Spike TV; Style Network; TBS Superstation; The Learning Channel; Travel Channel; truTV; Turner Network TV; TV Land; USA Network; Versus; Weather Channel.
Fee: $13.20 monthly.

Digital Basic Service
Subscribers: N.A.
Programming (received off-air): KASA-TV (FOX) Santa Fe; KASY-TV (MNT) Albuquerque; KNME-TV (PBS) Albuquerque; KOAT-TV (ABC) Albuquerque; KOB (NBC) Albuquerque; KRQE (CBS) Albuquerque; KWBQ (CW) Santa Fe.
Programming (via satellite): ABC Family HD; Animal Planet HD; Arts & Entertainment HD; BBC America; Big Ten Network; Bio; Bloomberg Television; CBS College Sports Network; CMT Pure Country; CNN HD; C-SPAN 3; Current; Discovery Channel HD; Discovery HD Theater; Discovery Kids Channel; Discovery Military Channel; Discovery Planet Green; Disney Channel HD; Encore (multiplexed); ESPN 2 HD; ESPN Classic Sports; ESPN HD; ESPNews; Flix; Food Network HD; Fox Business Channel; Fox College Sports Atlantic; Fox College Sports Central; Fox College Sports Pacific; Fox News HD; Fox Reality Channel; Fox Soccer; FSN HD; Fuse; FX HD; Gol TV; Great American Country; GSN; Hallmark Channel; HGTV HD; History Channel HD; History Channel International; ID Investigation Discovery; Independent Film Channel; Lifetime Movie Network; LOGO; Mojo HD; MoviePlex; MTV Hits; MTV Jams; MTV Tres; MTV2; Music Choice; National Geographic Channel; National Geographic Channel HD Network; NBA TV; NFL Network; NFL Network HD; Nick Jr.; Nick Too; NickToons TV; Outdoor Channel; Oxygen; Palladia; PBS Kids Sprout; Science Channel; Science Channel HD; ShopNBC; SoapNet; Speed HD; Starz IndiePlex; Starz RetroPlex; Sundance Channel; Syfy; Syfy HD; TeenNick; Tennis Channel; the mtn; The Sportsman Channel; TLC HD; Toon Disney; Turner Classic Movies; Turner Network TV HD; TV One; TVG Network; Universal HD; USA Network HD; Versus HD; VH1 Classic; VH1 Soul; V-me TV; WE tv.

Digital Pay Service 1
Pay Units: N.A.
Programming (via satellite): Cinemax (multiplexed); Cinemax HD; HBO (multiplexed); HBO HD; Showtime (multiplexed); Showtime HD; Starz (multiplexed); Starz HDTV; The Movie Channel (multiplexed).

Pay-Per-View
Movies (delivered digitally); Special events (delivered digitally); Hot Choice (delivered digitally); Spice: Xcess (delivered digitally); Club Jenna (delivered digitally); Playboy TV (delivered digitally); Fresh (delivered digitally).

Internet Service
Operational: Yes.

Telephone Service
Digital: Operational
Miles of Plant: 42.0 (coaxial); None (fiber optic). Homes passed: 2,500.
Vice President & General Manager: Chris Dunkeson. Operations Director: Carmen Valadez. Chief Technician: Chris Ciak.
Ownership: Comcast Cable Communications Inc. (MSO).

PORTALES—Comcast Cable, 708 E 2nd St, Portales, NM 88130-6006. Phones: 505-356-4222; 505-356-8571. Fax: 505-359-0958. Web Site: http://www.comcast.com. Also serves Roosevelt County. ICA: NM0018.
TV Market Ranking: Below 100 (PORTALES, Roosevelt County (portions)); Outside TV Markets (Roosevelt County (portions)). Franchise award date: N.A. Franchise expiration date: N.A. Began: January 1, 1963.
Channel capacity: 62 (not 2-way capable). Channels available but not in use: N.A.

Basic Service
Subscribers: 2,809.
Programming (received off-air): KAMR-TV (NBC) Amarillo; KASA-TV (FOX) Santa Fe; KCIT (FOX) Amarillo; KENW (PBS) Portales; KFDA-TV (CBS) Amarillo; KVII-TV (ABC, CW) Amarillo; 5 FMs.
Programming (via microwave): KOAT-TV (ABC) Albuquerque.
Programming (via satellite): ABC Family Channel; Disney Channel; ESPN 2; Halogen Network; Spike TV.
Programming (via translator): KBIM-TV (CBS) Roswell; KOBR (NBC) Roswell; KRPV-DT (IND) Roswell.
Current originations: Government Access.
Fee: $24.95 installation; $34.50 monthly; $.81 converter.

Expanded Basic Service 1
Subscribers: N.A.
Programming (via satellite): AMC; Animal Planet; Arts & Entertainment; BET Networks; Cartoon Network; CNBC; CNN; Comcast Sports Net Southwest; Comedy Central; Country Music TV; C-SPAN; C-SPAN 2; Discovery Channel; Discovery Health Channel; E! Entertainment Television; ESPN; Food Network; Fox News Channel; FX; G4; GalaVision; Golf Channel; Hallmark Channel; Headline News; HGTV; History Channel; Home Shopping Network; Lifetime; MSNBC; MTV; Nickelodeon; Outdoor Channel; QVC; Style Network; Syfy; TBS Superstation; Telemundo; The Learning Channel; Travel Channel; Trinity Broadcasting Network; truTV; Turner Network TV; TV Land; Univision; USA Network; Versus; VH1; Weather Channel.
Fee: $5.45 monthly.

Digital Basic Service
Subscribers: 138.
Programming (via satellite): BBC America; Bio; CMT Pure Country; C-SPAN 3; Current; Discovery Digital Networks; Encore (multiplexed); ESPNews; Flix; Fox Reality Channel; GAS; History Channel International; Lifetime Movie Network; LOGO; MTV Networks Digital Suite; Music Choice; National Geographic Channel; NFL Network; Nick Jr.; Nick Too; NickToons TV; PBS Kids Sprout; SoapNet; Sundance Channel; Toon Disney; TV One.
Fee: $11.20 monthly.

Digital Pay Service 1
Pay Units: 450.
Programming (via satellite): Cinemax (multiplexed); HBO (multiplexed); Showtime (multiplexed); Starz (multiplexed); The Movie Channel (multiplexed).
Fee: $5.00 installation; $9.95 monthly (each).

Video-On-Demand: No

Pay-Per-View
Addressable homes: 138.
iN DEMAND (delivered digitally), Addressable: Yes; Hot Choice (delivered digitally); Playboy TV (delivered digitally).

Internet Service
Operational: Yes.

Telephone Service
None
Miles of Plant: 55.0 (coaxial); None (fiber optic). Additional miles planned: 1.0 (coaxial). Homes passed: 4,196. Total homes in franchised area: 4,228.
Area Vice President: John Christopher. General Manager: Dennis Jones. Chief Technician: Spencer DeBord. Office Manager: Frederick Dominguez.
City fee: 3% of gross.
Ownership: Comcast Cable Communications Inc. (MSO).

QUESTA—Comcast Cable, PO Box 1854, 1546 Paseo Del Pueblo Sur, Taos, NM 87571-1854. Phones: 505-758-3569; 505-758-3207. Fax: 505-758-4441. Web Site: http://www.comcast.com. Also serves Cerro. ICA: NM0047.
TV Market Ranking: Outside TV Markets (Cerro, QUESTA). Franchise award date: January 1, 2001. Franchise expiration date: N.A. Began: June 1, 1981.
Channel capacity: 61 (operating 2-way). Channels available but not in use: 12.

Basic Service
Subscribers: 276.
Programming (received off-air): KLUZ-TV (UNV) Albuquerque; KNME-TV (PBS) Albuquerque; KOAT-TV (ABC) Albuquerque; KOB (NBC) Albuquerque; KRQE (CBS) Albuquerque.
Programming (via satellite): ABC Family Channel; AMC; Arts & Entertainment; CNN; Comcast Sports Net Southwest; Comedy Central; Country Music TV; C-SPAN; Discovery Channel; Disney Channel; ESPN; ESPN 2; Eternal Word TV Network; Food Network; Fox News Channel; Fox Sports Net; FX; GalaVision; Headline News; History Channel; Home Shopping Network 2; Lifetime; MSNBC; MTV; Nickelodeon; The Learning Channel; Turner Network TV; TV Land; USA Network; Versus; Weather Channel; WGN America.
Fee: $30.47 installation; $27.62 monthly.

Expanded Basic Service 1
Subscribers: 116.
Programming (via satellite): Cartoon Network; E! Entertainment Television; Golf Channel; QVC; Spike TV; Syfy; TBS Superstation; VH1.
Fee: $14.43 monthly.

Pay Service 1
Pay Units: 68.
Programming (via satellite): Cinemax; HBO (multiplexed).
Fee: $16.00 installation; $10.45 monthly (each).

Pay-Per-View
Movies, Addressable: Yes; special events.

Internet Service
Operational: Yes.

Telephone Service
None
Miles of Plant: 43.0 (coaxial); None (fiber optic).
Vice President & General Manager: Chris Dunkeson. Operations Manager: David Quintana.
City fee: 3% of gross.
Ownership: Comcast Cable Communications Inc. (MSO).

RAMAH—Formerly served by Navajo Communications. No longer in operation. ICA: NM0085.

RATON—Comcast Cable, 1026 S 2nd St, Raton, NM 87740. Phone: 505-445-5553. Fax: 505-445-2835. Web Site: http://www.comcast.com. ICA: NM0019.

TV Market Ranking: Outside TV Markets (RATON). Franchise award date: N.A. Franchise expiration date: N.A. Began: November 1, 1954.
Channel capacity: 49 (not 2-way capable). Channels available but not in use: N.A.

Basic Service
Subscribers: 2,225.
Programming (received off-air): KASA-TV (FOX) Santa Fe; KLUZ-TV (UNV) Albuquerque; KRDO-TV (ABC) Colorado Springs; 1 FM.
Programming (via satellite): Discovery Channel; Hallmark Channel; QVC; TBS Superstation; Telemundo; Weather Channel.
Programming (via translator): KNME-TV (PBS) Albuquerque; KOAT-TV (ABC) Albuquerque; KOB (NBC) Albuquerque; KRQE (CBS) Albuquerque.
Fee: $28.65 installation; $14.37 monthly; $3.00 converter.

Expanded Basic Service 1
Subscribers: N.A.
Programming (via satellite): ABC Family Channel; AMC; Animal Planet; Arts & Entertainment; Cartoon Network; CNBC; CNN; Comedy Central; Country Music TV; Discovery Health Channel; Disney Channel; E! Entertainment Television; ESPN; ESPN 2; Eternal Word TV Network; Fox News Channel; Fox Sports Net Rocky Mountain; FX; Golf Channel; Headline News; HGTV; History Channel; Lifetime; MTV; Nickelodeon; Outdoor Channel; Spike TV; The Learning Channel; Turner Network TV; TV Land; USA Network; Versus; VH1.
Fee: $26.86 monthly.

Digital Basic Service
Subscribers: 708.
Programming (via satellite): BBC America; Bravo; Discovery Digital Networks; DMX Music; ESPN Classic Sports; ESPNews; Fox Sports World; GSN; Independent Film Channel; Nick Jr.; Speed Channel; Syfy; Turner Classic Movies; VH1 Classic; VH1 Country; WE tv.
Fee: $14.95 monthly.

Pay Service 1
Pay Units: 250.
Programming (via satellite): Cinemax; HBO; Showtime.

Digital Pay Service 1
Pay Units: N.A.
Programming (via satellite): Cinemax (multiplexed); Encore (multiplexed); HBO (multiplexed); Showtime (multiplexed); Starz (multiplexed); The Movie Channel (multiplexed).
Fee: $11.03 monthly (each).

Video-On-Demand: No

Pay-Per-View
Addressable homes: 140.
iN DEMAND (delivered digitally), Addressable: Yes; Playboy TV (delivered digitally); Fresh (delivered digitally); Shorteez (delivered digitally).

Internet Service
Operational: Yes.

Telephone Service
None

Miles of Plant: 68.0 (coaxial); None (fiber optic). Homes passed: 3,666. Total homes in franchised area: 3,666.
Vice President & General Manager: Chris Dunkeson. Operations Manager: Ricky Armijo. Office Manager: Tammy Trujillo.
City fee: 2% of gross.
Ownership: Comcast Cable Communications Inc. (MSO).

RED RIVER—Comcast Cable, PO Box 1854, 1546 Paseo Del Pueblo Sur, Taos, NM 87571-1854. Phones: 505-758-3569; 505-758-3207. Fax: 505-758-4441. Web Site: http://www.comcast.com. Also serves Taos County (portions). ICA: NM0086.
TV Market Ranking: Below 100 (Taos County (portions)); Outside TV Markets (RED RIVER, Taos County (portions)). Franchise award date: N.A. Franchise expiration date: N.A. Began: February 1, 1968.
Channel capacity: 32 (not 2-way capable). Channels available but not in use: N.A.

Basic Service
Subscribers: 540.
Programming (received off-air): KASA-TV (FOX) Santa Fe; KNME-TV (PBS) Albuquerque; KOAT-TV (ABC) Albuquerque; KOB (NBC) Albuquerque; KRQE (CBS) Albuquerque; 1 FM.
Programming (via satellite): ABC Family Channel; Animal Planet; Arts & Entertainment; Cartoon Network; CNBC; CNN; Country Music TV; C-SPAN; Discovery Channel; Disney Channel; E! Entertainment Television; ESPN; ESPN 2; HGTV; Lifetime; MTV; Nickelodeon; QVC; Spike TV; TBS Superstation; The Learning Channel; Turner Network TV; USA Network; VH1; Weather Channel.
Fee: $40.00 installation; $42.00 monthly.

Pay Service 1
Pay Units: 171.
Programming (via satellite): HBO.
Fee: $13.68 monthly.

Internet Service
Operational: Yes.

Telephone Service
None

Miles of Plant: 11.0 (coaxial); None (fiber optic).
Vice President & General Manager: Chris Dunkeson. Operations Manager: David Quintana.
Ownership: Comcast Cable Communications Inc. (MSO).

RESERVE—Formerly served by Eagle West Communications Inc. No longer in operation. ICA: NM0065.

RIO RANCHO—Cable One, 7501 Nita Pl, Rio Rancho, NM 87124. Phone: 505-892-5114. Fax: 505-892-0748. E-mail: joan.gunn@cableone.net. Web Site: http://www.cableone.net. ICA: NM0009.
TV Market Ranking: 81 (RIO RANCHO). Franchise award date: N.A. Franchise expiration date: N.A. Began: March 15, 1981.
Channel capacity: 53 (operating 2-way). Channels available but not in use: None.

Basic Service
Subscribers: 8,096.
Programming (received off-air): KASA-TV (FOX) Santa Fe; KASY-TV (MNT) Albuquerque; KAZQ (ETV) Albuquerque; KCHF (IND) Santa Fe; KLUZ-TV (UNV) Albuquerque; KNAT-TV (TBN) Albuquerque; KNME-TV (PBS) Albuquerque; KOAT-TV (ABC) Albuquerque; KOB (NBC) Albuquerque; KRQE (CBS) Albuquerque; KWBQ (CW) Santa Fe; 2 FMs.
Programming (via satellite): Home Shopping Network; QVC; Telefutura; Telemundo; TV Guide Network; WGN America.
Current originations: Public Access.
Fee: $46.00 monthly; $45.62 converter.

Expanded Basic Service 1
Subscribers: N.A.
Programming (via satellite): ABC Family Channel; AMC; Animal Planet; Arts & Entertainment; Cartoon Network; CNBC; CNN; Comedy Central; Country Music TV; C-SPAN; C-SPAN 2; Discovery Channel; Disney Channel; ESPN; ESPN 2; Eternal Word TV Network; Food Network; Fox News Channel; Fox Sports Net Midwest; FX; Headline News; HGTV; History Channel; Lifetime; MSNBC; MTV; Nickelodeon; Spike TV; Syfy; TBS Superstation; The Learning Channel; Travel Channel; Turner Classic Movies; Turner Network TV; TV Land; USA Network; VH1; Weather Channel.

Digital Basic Service
Subscribers: 5,182.
Programming (received off-air): KASA-TV (FOX) Santa Fe; KOAT-TV (ABC) Albuquerque; KOB (NBC) Albuquerque; KRQE (CBS) Albuquerque.
Programming (via satellite): 3 Angels Broadcasting Network; Arts & Entertainment HD; Bio; Boomerang; Boomerang en Espanol; BYU Television; Cine Mexicano; CNN en Espanol; Discovery HD Theater; Discovery Health Channel; Discovery Kids Channel; Discovery Military Channel; ESPN Classic Sports; ESPN Deportes; ESPN HD; ESPNews; FamilyNet; Food Network HD; Fox College Sports Atlantic; Fox College Sports Central; Fox College Sports Pacific; Fox Movie Channel; Fox Soccer; Fox Sports en Espanol; Fuel TV; Golf Channel; Great American Country; GSN; Hallmark Channel; HGTV HD; History Channel International; INSP; La Familia Network; Latele Novela Network; Music Choice; National Geographic Channel; National Geographic Channel HD Network; Outdoor Channel; Science Channel; SoapNet; Speed Channel; TBS in HD; the mtn; Toon Disney; Toon Disney en Espanol; Trinity Broadcasting Network; Turner Network TV HD; TVG Network; Universal HD; WE tv.
Fee: $39.25 monthly.

Digital Pay Service 1
Pay Units: 2,475.
Programming (via satellite): HBO (multiplexed); HBO HD.
Fee: $9.95 installation; $13.95 monthly.

Digital Pay Service 2
Pay Units: 2,228.
Programming (via satellite): Cinemax (multiplexed).
Fee: $9.95 installation; $13.95 monthly.

Digital Pay Service 3
Pay Units: 386.
Programming (via satellite): Flix; Showtime (multiplexed); Showtime HD; Sundance Channel; The Movie Channel; The Movie Channel HD.
Fee: $9.95 installation; $13.95 monthly.

Digital Pay Service 4
Pay Units: N.A.
Programming (via satellite): Encore (multiplexed); Starz (multiplexed).

Video-On-Demand: No

Pay-Per-View
iN DEMAND (delivered digitally); Ten Clips (delivered digitally); Ten Blox (delivered digitally); Ten Blue (delivered digitally).

Internet Service
Operational: Yes.
Broadband Service: CableONE.net.
Fee: $75.00 installation; $43.00 monthly.

Telephone Service
Digital: Operational
Fee: $75.00 installation; $39.95 monthly

Miles of Plant: 250.0 (coaxial); 16.0 (fiber optic). Additional miles planned: 20.0 (coaxial). Homes passed: 17,645. Total homes in franchised area: 18,500.
Manager: Dan Hernandez. Customer Service Manager: Sarah Schuetz. Marketing Director: Joan Gunn.
City fee: 3% of basic.
Ownership: Cable One Inc. (MSO).

ROSWELL—Cable One, 2005 S Main St, Roswell, NM 88203-2508. Phone: 505-623-2391. Fax: 505-624-9569. E-mail: cindilucero@cableone.net. Web Site: http://www.cableone.net. Also serves Chaves County. ICA: NM0005.
TV Market Ranking: Below 100 (Chaves County (portions), ROSWELL); Outside TV Markets (Chaves County (portions)). Franchise award date: N.A. Franchise expiration date: N.A. Began: January 1, 1958.
Channel capacity: 78 (operating 2-way). Channels available but not in use: 10.

Basic Service
Subscribers: 11,556.
Programming (received off-air): KASA-TV (FOX) Santa Fe; KASY-TV (MNT) Albuquerque; KBIM-TV (CBS) Roswell; KENW (PBS) Portales; KLUZ-TV (UNV) Albuquerque; KOAT-TV (ABC) Albuquerque; KOBR (NBC) Roswell; KRPV-DT (IND) Roswell; KTEL-TV (TMO) Carlsbad; KWBQ (CW) Santa Fe; 3 FMs.
Programming (via satellite): ABC Family Channel; AMC; Animal Planet; Arts & Entertainment; BET Networks; Bravo!; Cartoon Network; CNBC; CNN; Country Music TV; C-SPAN; C-SPAN 2; Discovery Channel; Disney Channel; E! Entertainment Television; ESPN; ESPN 2; ESPN Classic Sports; Eternal Word TV Network; Food Network; Fox News Channel; Fox Sports Net Arizona; FX; Headline News; HGTV; History Channel; Home Shopping Network; Lifetime; MSNBC; MTV; Nickelodeon; Product Information Network; QVC; ShopNBC; Spike TV; Syfy; TBS Superstation; The Learning Channel; Turner Classic Movies; Turner Network TV; TV Guide Network; TV Land; USA Network; VH1; Weather Channel.
Current originations: Leased Access; Public Access.
Fee: $90.00 installation; $46.00 monthly; $10.00 converter.

Digital Basic Service
Subscribers: 3,610.
Programming (via satellite): 3 Angels Broadcasting Network; Bio; Boomerang; BYU Television; Canales N; Discovery Digital Networks; ESPN Classic Sports; ESPNews; FamilyNet; Fox College Sports Atlantic; Fox College Sports Central; Fox College Sports Pacific; Fox Movie Channel; Fox Soccer; Fuel TV; G4; Golf Channel; Hallmark Channel; History Channel International; INSP; Music Choice; National Geographic Channel; Outdoor Channel; SoapNet; Speed Channel; Toon Disney;

Trinity Broadcasting Network; truTV; Turner Network TV HD; TVG Network; Universal HD.

Digital Pay Service 1

Pay Units: 3,171.

Programming (via satellite): Cinemax (multiplexed); Encore (multiplexed); Flix; HBO (multiplexed); Showtime (multiplexed); Showtime HD; Sundance Channel; The Movie Channel (multiplexed); The Movie Channel HD.

Fee: $16.00 monthly (each).

Video-On-Demand: No

Pay-Per-View

Pleasure (delivered digitally), Fee: $8.95, Addressable: Yes, Fee: $8.95; Ten Clips (delivered digitally); Ten Blox (delivered digitally); Ten Blue (delivered digitally); Movies (delivered digitally).

Internet Service

Operational: Yes.

Subscribers: 3,003.

Broadband Service: CableONE.net.

Fee: $75.00 installation; $43.00 monthly.

Telephone Service

Digital: Operational

Fee: $75.00 installation; $39.95 monthly

Miles of Plant: 328.0 (coaxial); None (fiber optic). Homes passed: 23,000. Total homes in franchised area: 23,450.

General Manager: David Gonzalez. Technical Operations Manager: Dave Ashlyn. Marketing Manager: Cindi Lucero. Office Manager: April Avitia.

City fee: 5% of gross.

Ownership: Cable One Inc. (MSO).

ROSWELL—Formerly served by Microwave Communication Services. No longer in operation. ICA: NM0098.

RUIDOSO—Baja Broadband, 510 24th St, Alamogordo, NM 88310. Phone: 575-437-3101. Fax: 575-434-3439. Web Site: http://www.bajabroadband.com. Also serves Alto, Capitan, Mescalero Apache Indian Reservation (portions) & Ruidoso Downs. ICA: NM0011.

TV Market Ranking: Outside TV Markets (Alto, Capitan, Mescalero Apache Indian Reservation (portions), RUIDOSO, Ruidoso Downs). Franchise award date: N.A. Franchise expiration date: N.A. Began: January 1, 1965.

Channel capacity: N.A. Channels available but not in use: N.A.

Basic Service

Subscribers: 4,989.

Programming (received off-air): KASA-TV (FOX) Santa Fe; KASY-TV (MNT) Albuquerque; KBIM-TV (CBS) Roswell; KCHF (IND) Santa Fe; KENW (PBS) Portales; KFOX-TV (FOX) El Paso; KLUZ-TV (UNV) Albuquerque; KOAT-TV (ABC) Albuquerque; KOBR (NBC) Roswell; KRPV-DT (IND) Roswell; KTEL-TV (TMO) Carlsbad; KVBA-LP Alamogordo; KVIA-TV (ABC, CW) El Paso.

Programming (via satellite): C-SPAN; C-SPAN 2; Home Shopping Network; QVC; TV Guide Network; Weather Channel; WGN America.

Current originations: Educational Access; Public Access.

Fee: $54.95 installation; $22.00 monthly; $12.74 additional installation.

Expanded Basic Service 1

Subscribers: N.A.

Programming (via satellite): ABC Family Channel; AMC; Animal Planet; Arts & Entertainment; Bravo; Cartoon Network; CNBC; CNN; Comedy Central; Country Music TV; Discovery Channel; Disney Channel; E! Entertainment Television; ESPN; ESPN 2; ESPN Classic Sports; Food Network; Fox News Channel; Fox Sports Net Arizona; FX; G4; Golf Channel; Great American Country; GSN; Hallmark Channel; Headline News; HGTV; History Channel; Lifetime; Lifetime Movie Network; MSNBC; MTV; National Geographic Channel; Nickelodeon; SoapNet; Speed Channel; Spike TV; Style Network; Syfy; TBS Superstation; The Learning Channel; Toon Disney; Travel Channel; truTV; Turner Classic Movies; Turner Network TV; TV Land; USA Network; Versus; VH1.

Digital Basic Service

Subscribers: N.A.

Programming (via satellite): BBC America; Bio; Bloomberg Television; CMT Pure Country; Discovery en Espanol; Discovery Health Channel; Discovery Kids Channel; Discovery Military Channel; Discovery Planet Green; Do-It-Yourself; FitTV; Fox Business Channel; Fox College Sports Atlantic; Fox College Sports Central; Fox College Sports Pacific; Fox Soccer; History Channel International; ID Investigation Discovery; Independent Film Channel; Lifetime Real Women; LOGO; MTV Hits; MTV Jams; MTV Tres; MTV2; Music Choice; Nick Jr.; Nick Too; NickToons TV; Science Channel; Sundance Channel; TeenNick; the mtn; VH1 Classic; VH1 Soul; WE tv.

Fee: $7.95 monthly.

Digital Expanded Basic Service

Subscribers: N.A.

Programming (via satellite): Arts & Entertainment HD; ESPN HD; Food Network HD; FSN HD; FX HD; Golf Channel HD; HGTV HD; History Channel HD; National Geographic Channel HD Network; Speed HD; TBS in HD; Turner Network TV HD; Versus HD.

Digital Expanded Basic Service 2

Subscribers: N.A.

Programming (via satellite): HDNet; HDNet Movies; Universal HD.

Digital Pay Service 1

Pay Units: N.A.

Programming (via satellite): Cinemax (multiplexed); Cinemax HD; Encore (multiplexed); Flix; HBO (multiplexed); HBO HD; Showtime (multiplexed); Showtime HD; Starz (multiplexed); Starz HDTV; The Movie Channel (multiplexed); The Movie Channel HD.

Video-On-Demand: No

Pay-Per-View

iN DEMAND (delivered digitally); Hot Choice (delivered digitally); Fresh (delivered digitally); Shorteez (delivered digitally); Playboy TV (delivered digitally); Club Jenna (delivered digitally); Spice: Xcess (delivered digitally).

Internet Service

Operational: Yes.

Broadband Service: In-house.

Fee: $49.99 installation; $34.99 monthly; $4.95 modem lease; $65.95 modem purchase.

Telephone Service

None

Miles of Plant: 350.0 (coaxial); None (fiber optic). Total homes in franchised area: 14,288.

Area Vice President & General Manager: Tom Jaskiewicz. Technical Operations Manager: Harold Vilas. Office Manager: Barbara Mick.

Ownership: Baja Broadband (MSO).

SAN ANTONIO—Formerly served by Sun Valley Cable Inc. No longer in operation. ICA: NM0095.

SAN JON—Elk River TV Cable Co., PO Box 154, 411 S Main St, Troy, ID 83871. Phones: 877-874-4900; 208-835-5654. Fax: 207-835-5573. Web Site: http://www.elkrivertv.net. ICA: NM0103.

TV Market Ranking: Outside TV Markets (SAN JON).

Channel capacity: 25 (not 2-way capable). Channels available but not in use: N.A.

Basic Service

Subscribers: 550 Includes Cactus TX, Miami TX, Nazareth TX, & Turkey TX.

Programming (received off-air): KACV-TV (PBS) Amarillo; KAMR-TV (NBC) Amarillo; KCIT (FOX) Amarillo; KFDA-TV (CBS) Amarillo; KVII-TV (ABC, CW) Amarillo.

Programming (via satellite): ABC Family Channel; Arts & Entertainment; CNN; Discovery Channel; Disney Channel; ESPN; ESPN 2; History Channel; Lifetime; Spike TV; Syfy; TBS Superstation; The Learning Channel; Turner Network TV; USA Network; WGN America.

Pay Service 1

Pay Units: N.A.

Programming (via satellite): HBO; Showtime.

Video-On-Demand: No

Internet Service

Operational: No.

Telephone Service

None

Manager: Dave & Leslie McGraw. Chief Technician: Justin McGraw.

Ownership: Elk River TV Cable Co. (MSO).

SANTA BARBARA—Formerly served by JRC Telecommunications. No longer in operation. ICA: NM0072.

SANTA CLARA INDIAN RESERVATION—US Cable of Coastal Texas LP, 603 E Pueblo Dr, Espanola, NM 87532-2565. Phones: 800-996-8788; 505-753-4246. Fax: 505-753-9286. E-mail: uscable@tx.uscable.com. Web Site: http://www.uscable.com. Also serves Rio Arriba County (southeastern portion), San Juan Pueblo & Santa Fe County (northern portion). ICA: NM0087.

TV Market Ranking: Below 100 (Rio Arriba County (southeastern portion), San Juan Pueblo, SANTA CLARA INDIAN RESERVATION, Santa Fe County (northern portion)). Franchise award date: N.A. Franchise expiration date: N.A. Began: N.A.

Channel capacity: N.A. Channels available but not in use: N.A.

Basic Service

Subscribers: N.A. Included in Seminole TX

Programming (received off-air): KASA-TV (FOX) Santa Fe; KASY-TV (MNT) Albuquerque; KCHF (IND) Santa Fe; KLUZ-TV (UNV) Albuquerque; KNAT-TV (TBN) Albuquerque; KNME-TV (PBS) Albuquerque; KOAT-TV (ABC) Albuquerque; KOB (NBC) Albuquerque; KRPV-DT (IND) Roswell; KRQE (CBS) Albuquerque; KTEL-TV (TMO) Carlsbad; KWBQ (CW) Santa Fe.

Programming (via satellite): CNBC; CNN; C-SPAN; ESPN Deportes; Food Network; Fox News Channel; Fox Sports Net Rocky Mountain; HGTV; Lifetime; National Geographic Channel; Turner Network TV; TV Guide Network; USA Network; WGN America.

Current originations: Government Access; Public Access.

Fee: $31.13 monthly.

Expanded Basic Service 1

Subscribers: N.A. Included in Seminole TX

Programming (via satellite): ABC Family Channel; Animal Planet; Arts & Entertainment; Cartoon Network; Comedy Central; Country Music TV; C-SPAN 2; Discovery Channel; Disney Channel; E! Entertainment Television; ESPN; ESPN 2; Eternal Word TV Network; Fox Sports en Espanol; FX; Great American Country; Headline News; History Channel; Home Shopping Network; MTV; Nickelodeon; Outdoor Channel; QVC; ShopNBC; Speed Channel; Spike TV; Syfy; TBS Superstation; Telefutura; The Learning Channel; Travel Channel; truTV; Turner Classic Movies; TV Land; VH1; Weather Channel.

Fee: $10.36 monthly.

Digital Basic Service

Subscribers: N.A.

Programming (via satellite): BBC America; Bio; Bloomberg Television; Bravo; Canales N; CMT Pure Country; Discovery Health Channel; Discovery Home Channel; Discovery Kids Channel; Discovery Military Channel; Discovery Times Channel; DMX Music; Encore (multiplexed); ESPN Classic Sports; ESPNews; FitTV; Fox Movie Channel; Fox Soccer; Fox Sports World; Fuse; G4; GAS; Golf Channel; GSN; Halogen Network; History Channel International; Independent Film Channel; Lifetime Movie Network; MTV2; NFL Network; Nick Jr.; Outdoor Channel; Science Channel; Sleuth; Style Network; Toon Disney; Trinity Broadcasting Network; Versus; VH1 Classic; WE tv.

Fee: $5.45 monthly (family, movies or sports); $8.00 converter.

Digital Pay Service 1

Pay Units: N.A.

Programming (via satellite): Cinemax (multiplexed); HBO (multiplexed); Showtime (multiplexed); Starz (multiplexed); The Movie Channel (multiplexed).

Fee: $6.95 monthly (Starz), $11.95 monthly (HBO, Cinemax, Showtime or TMC).

Pay-Per-View

iN DEMAND (delivered digitally); Fresh (delivered digitally); Playboy TV (delivered digitally).

Internet Service

Operational: No.

Telephone Service

None

Homes passed & miles of plant included in Seminole TX

Manager: Phil Griffin. Chief Technician: John Jelen.

Ownership: US Cable Corp. (MSO).; Comcast Cable Communications Inc. (MSO).

SANTA FE—Comcast Cable, 2534 Camino Entrada, Santa Fe, NM 87507-4807. Phone: 505-474-7886. Fax: 505-474-7986. Web Site: http://www.comcast.com. Also serves Eldorado, Santa Fe County, Tesuque & Tesuque Pueblo. ICA: NM0003.

TV Market Ranking: 81 (Santa Fe County (portions)); Below 100 (Eldorado, SANTA FE, Tesuque, Tesuque Pueblo, Santa Fe County (portions)). Franchise award date: N.A. Franchise expiration date: N.A. Began: September 1, 1970.

Channel capacity: N.A. Channels available but not in use: N.A.

Basic Service

Subscribers: 19,754 Includes Pecos & Pojoaque.

Programming (received off-air): KASA-TV (FOX) Santa Fe; KASY-TV (MNT) Albuquerque; KAZQ (ETV) Albuquerque; KCHF (IND) Santa Fe; KLUZ-TV (UNV) Albuquerque; KNAT-TV (TBN) Albuquerque; KNME-TV (PBS) Albuquerque; KOAT-TV (ABC) Albuquerque; KOB (NBC) Albuquerque; KQDF-LP Albuquerque; KRQE (CBS) Albuquerque; KTEL-TV (TMO) Carlsbad; KTFQ-DT (TEL) Albuquerque; KWBQ (CW) Santa Fe; 9 FMs.

Programming (via satellite): C-SPAN; C-SPAN 2; Eternal Word TV Network; Home Shopping Network; QVC; TV Guide Network; Versus.

Current originations: Government Access; Public Access.

Fee: $60.00 installation; $34.95 monthly.

Expanded Basic Service 1

Subscribers: 13,996.

Programming (via satellite): ABC Family Channel; AMC; Animal Planet; Arts & Entertainment; Bravo; Cartoon Network; CNBC; CNN; Comedy Central; Discovery Channel; Discovery Health Channel; Disney Channel; E! Entertainment Television; ESPN; ESPN 2; Fox News Channel; Fox Sports Net Midwest; FX; G4; GalaVision; Golf Channel; GSN; Hallmark Channel; Headline News; History Channel; MSNBC; MTV; Nickelodeon; Speed Channel; Spike TV; TBS Superstation; The Learning Channel; Travel Channel; truTV; Turner Network TV; TV Land; USA Network; Weather Channel.

Fee: $7.26 monthly.

Digital Basic Service

Subscribers: 7,221.

Programming (via satellite): BBC America; C-SPAN 3; Discovery Digital Networks; DMX Music; Encore Action; ESPN Classic Sports; ESPNews; Flix; Fox Sports World; G4; GAS; GSN; Independent Film Channel; MTV Networks Digital Suite; Nick Jr.; Nick Too; SoapNet; Sundance Channel; Syfy; Toon Disney; Turner Classic Movies; WE tv.

Fee: $10.95 monthly.

Digital Pay Service 1

Pay Units: N.A.

Programming (via satellite): Cinemax (multiplexed); HBO (multiplexed); Showtime (multiplexed); Starz (multiplexed); The Movie Channel (multiplexed).

Fee: $14.95 monthly (each).

Video-On-Demand: No

Pay-Per-View

Addressable homes: 810.

iN DEMAND (delivered digitally), Fee: $.99-$4.99, Addressable: Yes; Hot Choice (delivered digitally); Playboy TV (delivered digitally); Fresh (delivered digitally); Shorteez (delivered digitally); Pleasure (delivered digitally).

Internet Service

Operational: Yes.

Subscribers: 8,646.

Broadband Service: Comcast High Speed Internet.

Fee: $42.95 monthly; $5.00 modem lease.

Telephone Service

Digital: Operational

Miles of Plant: 739.0 (coaxial); 184.0 (fiber optic). Homes passed: 51,512.

Vice President & General Manager: Chris Donkeson. Operations Director: Carmen Valadez. Chief Technician: Chris Ciak.

City fee: 4% of gross.

Ownership: Comcast Cable Communications Inc. (MSO).

SANTA FE—Formerly served by Santa Fe Wireless Cable TV. No longer in operation. ICA: NM0099.

SANTA ROSA—Rapid Cable, 230 S Main St, Muleshoe, TX 79347. Phone: 800-963-4984. Fax: 806-272-7507. ICA: NM0030.

TV Market Ranking: Outside TV Markets (SANTA ROSA). Franchise award date: March 11, 1980. Franchise expiration date: N.A. Began: January 1, 1981.

Channel capacity: N.A. Channels available but not in use: N.A.

Basic Service

Subscribers: 145.

Programming (received off-air): KASA-TV (FOX) Santa Fe; KLUZ-TV (UNV) Albuquerque; KNME-TV (PBS) Albuquerque; KOAT-TV (ABC) Albuquerque; KOB (NBC) Albuquerque; KRPV-DT (IND) Roswell; KRQE (CBS) Albuquerque; KTEL-TV (TMO) Carlsbad.

Programming (via satellite): ABC Family Channel; AmericanLife TV Network; Animal Planet; Arts & Entertainment; Cartoon Network; CNN; C-SPAN; Discovery Channel; Disney Channel; ESPN; ESPN 2; Eternal Word TV Network; Fox News Channel; Fox Sports Net; Fox Sports Net Rocky Mountain; FX; GalaVision; Great American Country; Headline News; History Channel; Home Shopping Network; Lifetime; National Geographic Channel; Nickelodeon; QVC; Spike TV; TBS Superstation; The Learning Channel; Turner Classic Movies; Turner Network TV; TV Land; USA Network; VH1; Weather Channel.

Fee: $35.00 installation; $19.95 monthly.

Digital Basic Service

Subscribers: N.A.

Programming (via satellite): BBC America; Bio; Bloomberg Television; Discovery Health Channel; Discovery Kids Channel; Discovery Military Channel; Discovery Planet Green; DMX Music; ESPN 2; ESPN Classic Sports; ESPNews; Fox College Sports Atlantic; Fox College Sports Central; Fox College Sports Pacific; Fox Soccer; Fuse; G4; Golf Channel; GSN; HGTV; History Channel International; ID Investigation Discovery; Independent Film Channel; Outdoor Channel; Science Channel; ShopNBC; Sleuth; Speed Channel; Style Network; Sundance Channel; Toon Disney; Versus; WE tv.

Pay Service 1

Pay Units: 36.

Programming (via satellite): The Movie Channel.

Fee: $5.95 monthly.

Pay Service 2

Pay Units: 71.

Programming (via satellite): Showtime.

Fee: $9.95 monthly.

Pay Service 3

Pay Units: 106.

Programming (via satellite): HBO.

Fee: $10.95 monthly.

Digital Pay Service 1

Pay Units: N.A.

Programming (via satellite): Cinemax (multiplexed); Encore (multiplexed); Flix; HBO (multiplexed); Showtime (multiplexed); Starz (multiplexed); The Movie Channel (multiplexed).

Video-On-Demand: No

Pay-Per-View

iN DEMAND (delivered digitally); Playboy TV (delivered digitally).

Internet Service

Operational: No.

Telephone Service

None

Miles of Plant: 17.0 (coaxial); None (fiber optic). Homes passed: 1,130.

Regional Manager: Kerry Stratton. Regional Engineer: Rick Elmore. Office Manager: Debi Stratton.

Ownership: Rapid Communications LLC (MSO).

SHIPROCK—Formerly served by Frontier Communications. No longer in operation. ICA: NM0101.

SILVER CITY—Comcast Cable, 1014 N Pope St, Silver City, NM 88061-5148. Phones: 505-388-4744; 505-538-3701. Fax: 505-388-4929. E-mail: manny_orquiz@cable.comcast.com. Web Site: http://www.comcast.com. Also serves Arenas Valley, Bayard, Fort Bayard, Grant County (portions), Hurley, Santa Clara, Tyrone & Vanadium (unincorporated areas). ICA: NM0017.

TV Market Ranking: Below 100 (Arenas Valley, Bayard, Fort Bayard, Grant County (portions), Hurley, Santa Clara, SILVER CITY, Tyrone, Vanadium (unincorporated areas)); Outside TV Markets (Grant County (portions)). Franchise award date: N.A. Franchise expiration date: N.A. Began: September 1, 1956.

Channel capacity: 116 (2-way capable). Channels available but not in use: N.A.

Basic Service

Subscribers: 4,800.

Programming (via satellite): ABC Family Channel; Arts & Entertainment; Bravo; CNBC; CNN; Country Music TV; C-SPAN; Discovery Channel; Disney Channel; ESPN; Fox Sports Net West; GalaVision; Hallmark Channel; Headline News; History Channel; Home Shopping Network; Lifetime; MTV; Nickelodeon; QVC; Telemundo; The Learning Channel; Trinity Broadcasting Network; Univision; USA Network; VH1; Weather Channel; WGN America.

Programming (via translator): KASA-TV (FOX) Santa Fe; KOAT-TV (ABC) Albuquerque; KOB (NBC) Albuquerque; KRQE (CBS) Albuquerque; KRWG-TV (PBS) Las Cruces.

Fee: $29.95 installation; $29.75 monthly; $24.95 additional installation.

Expanded Basic Service 1

Subscribers: N.A.

Programming (via satellite): AMC; Animal Planet; Cartoon Network; Comedy Central; Discovery Health Channel; E! Entertainment Television; ESPN 2; Food Network; Fox News Channel; Golf Channel; MSNBC; Speed Channel; Spike TV; Style Network; Syfy; TBS Superstation; Turner Network TV; TV Land; Versus.

Fee: $12.54 monthly.

Digital Basic Service

Subscribers: 294.

Programming (via satellite): C-SPAN 3; DMX Music; ESPNews; Flix; GAS; Nick Jr.; SoapNet; Toon Disney.

Fee: $11.95 monthly.

Digital Pay Service 1

Pay Units: 205.

Programming (via satellite): Cinemax (multiplexed); HBO (multiplexed); Showtime (multiplexed); Starz (multiplexed); The Movie Channel (multiplexed).

Fee: $14.95 monthly (each).

Video-On-Demand: No

Pay-Per-View

Addressable homes: 294.

iN DEMAND (delivered digitally), Addressable: No; Playboy TV (delivered digitally), Addressable: No; Fresh (delivered digitally), Addressable: No; Shorteez (delivered digitally), Addressable: No; Hot Choice (delivered digitally), Addressable: No.

Internet Service

Operational: Yes.

Telephone Service

None

Miles of Plant: 215.0 (coaxial); 36.0 (fiber optic). Homes passed: 10,000. Total homes in franchised area: 10,000.

Area Vice President: John Christopher. General Manager: Manny Orquiz. Chief Technician: Don Hall. Office Manager: Ameilia Munoz.

City fee: 5% of gross.

Ownership: Comcast Cable Communications Inc. (MSO).

SOCORRO—Comcast Cable, 223 Fisher Ave, Socorro, NM 87801-4526. Phone: 505-835-2424. Fax: 505-835-3539. Web Site: http://www.comcast.com. ICA: NM0023.

TV Market Ranking: Outside TV Markets (SOCORRO). Franchise award date: N.A. Franchise expiration date: N.A. Began: January 1, 1977.

Channel capacity: N.A. Channels available but not in use: N.A.

Basic Service

Subscribers: 2,235.

Programming (received off-air): KASA-TV (FOX) Santa Fe; KNAT-TV (TBN) Albuquerque; KNME-TV (PBS) Albuquerque; KOAT-TV (ABC) Albuquerque; KOB (NBC) Albuquerque; KRQE (CBS) Albuquerque.

Programming (via satellite): ABC Family Channel; AMC; Animal Planet; Arts & Entertainment; Cartoon Network; CNN; Comcast Sports Net Southwest; Comedy Central; C-SPAN; Discovery Channel; Discovery Health Channel; Disney Channel; E! Entertainment Television; ESPN; ESPN 2; Eternal Word TV Network; GalaVision; Golf Channel; Great American Country; Hallmark Channel; HGTV; History Channel; Home Shopping Network; MSNBC; MTV; Product Information Network; QVC; Spike TV; Syfy; TBS Superstation; Turner Network TV; TV Land; USA Network; Weather Channel; WGN America.

Fee: $29.95 installation; $35.94 monthly.

Digital Basic Service

Subscribers: N.A. Included in Grants

Programming (via satellite): BBC America; C-SPAN 3; Discovery Digital Networks; DMX Music; Encore Action; ESPNews; Flix; GAS; MTV Networks Digital Suite; Nick Jr.; Nick Too; SoapNet; Sundance Channel; Toon Disney; WAM! America's Kidz Network.

Fee: $12.95 monthly.

Pay Service 1
Pay Units: 981.
Programming (via satellite): Cinemax; HBO (multiplexed); Showtime.
Fee: $10.00 installation; $8.00 monthly (Cinemax), $9.95 monthly (HBO, Showtime or TMC).
Digital Pay Service 1
Pay Units: N.A.
Programming (via satellite): Cinemax (multiplexed); HBO (multiplexed); Showtime (multiplexed); Starz (multiplexed); The Movie Channel (multiplexed).
Fee: $15.00 monthly (each).
Video-On-Demand: No
Pay-Per-View
Addressable homes: 110.
iN DEMAND (delivered digitally), Addressable: Yes; Playboy TV (delivered digitally); Fresh (delivered digitally); Shorteez (delivered digitally); Pleasure (delivered digitally).
Internet Service
Operational: Yes.
Telephone Service
None
Miles of Plant: 31.0 (coaxial); None (fiber optic). Additional miles planned: 2.0 (coaxial). Homes passed: 2,300. Total homes in franchised area: 2,300.
Vice President & General Manager: Chris Dunkeson. Operations Manager: Earl Chavez. Chief Technician: Rick Gallegos. Office Manager: Juanita Romero.
City fee: 3% of gross.
Ownership: Comcast Cable Communications Inc. (MSO).

SPRINGER—Comcast Cable, 2530 Hot Springs Blvd, Las Vegas, NM 87701-3739. Phone: 505-425-7531. Fax: 505-445-6822. Web Site: http://www.comcast.com. ICA: NM0039.
TV Market Ranking: Outside TV Markets (SPRINGER). Franchise award date: N.A. Franchise expiration date: N.A. Began: May 1, 1976.
Channel capacity: 35 (not 2-way capable). Channels available but not in use: 4.
Basic Service
Subscribers: 200.
Programming (received off-air): KASA-TV (FOX) Santa Fe; 1 FM.
Programming (via satellite): ABC Family Channel; Animal Planet; Cartoon Network; CNBC; CNN; Country Music TV; Discovery Channel; Disney Channel; E! Entertainment Television; ESPN; ESPN 2; HGTV; Lifetime; MTV; Nickelodeon; QVC; Spike TV; TBS Superstation; The Learning Channel; Turner Network TV; Univision; USA Network; VH1; Weather Channel.
Programming (via translator): KNME-TV (PBS) Albuquerque; KOAT-TV (ABC) Albuquerque; KOB (NBC) Albuquerque; KRQE (CBS) Albuquerque.
Fee: $29.90 installation; $32.35 monthly.
Pay Service 1
Pay Units: 238.
Programming (via satellite): Encore; HBO.
Video-On-Demand: No
Internet Service
Operational: Yes.
Telephone Service
None
Miles of Plant: 9.0 (coaxial); None (fiber optic). Homes passed: 641. Total homes in franchised area: 654.
Vice President & General Manager: Chris Dunkeson. Operations Manager: Ricky Armijo. Chief Technician: Henry Garcia.
Ownership: Comcast Cable Communications Inc. (MSO).

TAOS—Comcast Cable, PO Box 1854, 1546 Paseo Del Pueblo Sur, Taos, NM 87571-1854. Phones: 505-758-3207; 505-758-3569. Fax: 505-758-4441. Web Site: http://www.comcast.com. Also serves Canon, El Prado, Llano, Ranchos de Taos & Talpa. ICA: NM0090.
TV Market Ranking: Outside TV Markets (Canon, El Prado, Llano, Ranchos de Taos, Talpa, TAOS). Franchise award date: January 1, 1972. Franchise expiration date: N.A. Began: August 1, 1972.
Channel capacity: N.A. Channels available but not in use: N.A.
Basic Service
Subscribers: 1,983.
Programming (received off-air): KASA-TV (FOX) Santa Fe; KASY-TV (MNT) Albuquerque; KCHF (IND) Santa Fe; KLUZ-TV (UNV) Albuquerque; KNME-TV (PBS) Albuquerque; KOAT-TV (ABC) Albuquerque; KOB (NBC) Albuquerque; KRPV-DT (IND) Roswell; KRQE (CBS) Albuquerque; KTEL-TV (TMO) Carlsbad; KWBQ (CW) Santa Fe; 13 FMs.
Programming (via satellite): ABC Family Channel; AMC; Cartoon Network; Comcast Sports Net Southwest; Country Music TV; C-SPAN; C-SPAN 2; Disney Channel; Eternal Word TV Network; Fox News Channel; FX; Hallmark Channel; Headline News; History Channel; Home Shopping Network; Lifetime; MTV; Nickelodeon; QVC; Spike TV; Sundance Channel; The Learning Channel; TV Land; Weather Channel; WGN America.
Current originations: Government Access; Public Access.
Fee: $30.47 installation; $.62 converter.
Expanded Basic Service 1
Subscribers: 845.
Programming (via satellite): Animal Planet; Arts & Entertainment; Bravo; CNBC; CNN; Comedy Central; Discovery Channel; Discovery Health Channel; E! Entertainment Television; ESPN; ESPN 2; Food Network; Golf Channel; HGTV; Speed Channel; Style Network; TBS Superstation; Travel Channel; truTV; Turner Network TV; USA Network.
Fee: $14.43 monthly.
Digital Basic Service
Subscribers: N.A.
Programming (via satellite): BBC America; Bio; Canales N; CBS College Sports Network; CMT Pure Country; C-SPAN 3; Current; Discovery Digital Networks; Encore (multiplexed); ESPNews; Flix; Fox Reality Channel; GAS; History Channel International; Lifetime Movie Network; LOGO; MoviePlex; MTV Networks Digital Suite; Music Choice; National Geographic Channel; NFL Network; Nick Jr.; Nick Too; NickToons TV; PBS Kids Sprout; SoapNet; Syfy; the mtn; Toon Disney; TV One.
Fee: $11.95 monthly.
Digital Pay Service 1
Pay Units: N.A.
Programming (via satellite): Cinemax (multiplexed); HBO (multiplexed); Showtime (multiplexed); Starz (multiplexed).
Fee: $12.87 monthly (each).
Video-On-Demand: No
Pay-Per-View
iN DEMAND; iN DEMAND (delivered digitally); Playboy TV (delivered digitally); Hot Choice (delivered digitally).
Internet Service
Operational: Yes.
Telephone Service
None
Miles of Plant: 90.0 (coaxial); 25.0 (fiber optic).
Vice President & General Manager: Chris Dunkeson. Operations Manager: David Quintana.
Town fee: 5% of gross.
Ownership: Comcast Cable Communications Inc. (MSO).

TATUM—Rapid Cable, 230 S Main St, Muleshoe, TX 79347. Phone: 800-963-4984. Fax: 806-272-7507. ICA: NM0057.
TV Market Ranking: Outside TV Markets (TATUM). Franchise award date: February 26, 1979. Franchise expiration date: N.A. Began: December 1, 1979.
Channel capacity: N.A. Channels available but not in use: N.A.
Basic Service
Subscribers: 49.
Programming (received off-air): KAMC (ABC) Lubbock; KASA-TV (FOX) Santa Fe; KBIM-TV (CBS) Roswell; KENW (PBS) Portales; KLUZ-TV (UNV) Albuquerque; KOAT-TV (ABC) Albuquerque; KOBR (NBC) Roswell; KTEL-LP Albuquerque.
Programming (via satellite): ABC Family Channel; CNN; C-SPAN; Discovery Channel; Disney Channel; ESPN; Fox Sports Net; Great American Country; Lifetime; Nickelodeon; Spike TV; TBS Superstation; The Learning Channel; Trinity Broadcasting Network; Turner Classic Movies; Turner Network TV; TV Land; USA Network; VH1; Weather Channel.
Fee: $29.95 installation; $38.00 monthly.
Pay Service 1
Pay Units: 10.
Programming (via satellite): Showtime.
Fee: $9.95 monthly.
Pay Service 2
Pay Units: 27.
Programming (via satellite): HBO.
Fee: $11.72 monthly.
Video-On-Demand: No
Internet Service
Operational: No.
Telephone Service
None
Miles of Plant: 11.0 (coaxial); None (fiber optic). Homes passed: 348.
Regional Manager: Kerry Stratton. Regional Engineer: Rick Elmore. Office Manager: Debi Stratton.
Ownership: Rapid Communications LLC (MSO).

THOREAU—Comcast Cable, 216 N 2nd St, Grants, NM 87020-2504. Phone: 505-287-9451. Fax: 505-287-7474. Web Site: http://www.comcast.com. Also serves McKinley County (portions). ICA: NM0060.
TV Market Ranking: Outside TV Markets (McKinley County (portions), THOREAU). Franchise award date: N.A. Franchise expiration date: N.A. Began: March 1, 1982.
Channel capacity: N.A. Channels available but not in use: N.A.
Basic Service
Subscribers: 235.
Programming (received off-air): KASA-TV (FOX) Santa Fe; KNME-TV (PBS) Albuquerque; KOAT-TV (ABC) Albuquerque; KOB (NBC) Albuquerque; KRQE (CBS) Albuquerque.
Programming (via satellite): ABC Family Channel; Animal Planet; Arts & Entertainment; CNN; Discovery Channel; Disney Channel; E! Entertainment Television; ESPN; ESPN 2; Eternal Word TV Network; Great American Country; History Channel; Lifetime; Nickelodeon; Spike TV; TBS Superstation; Turner Classic Movies; Turner Network TV; USA Network; Weather Channel; WGN America.
Fee: $19.95 installation; $41.23 monthly.
Pay Service 1
Pay Units: N.A.
Programming (via satellite): Cinemax; HBO.
Fee: $7.00 monthly (Cinemax), $10.00 monthly (HBO).
Video-On-Demand: No
Internet Service
Operational: Yes.
Telephone Service
None
Miles of Plant: 12.0 (coaxial); None (fiber optic). Homes passed: 298. Total homes in franchised area: 298.
Vice President & General Manager: Chris Dunkeson. Operations Manager: Earl Chavez. Chief Technician: Tommy Chavez.
Ownership: Comcast Cable Communications Inc. (MSO).

TOHATCHI—Formerly served by Frontier Communications. No longer in operation. ICA: NM0066.

TRUTH OR CONSEQUENCES—Baja Broadband, 510 24th St, Alamogordo, NM 88310. Phone: 575-437-3101. Fax: 575-434-3439. Web Site: http://www.bajabroadband.com. Also serves Sierra County (unincorporated areas) & Williamsburg. ICA: NM0022.
TV Market Ranking: Below 100 (Sierra County (unincorporated areas) (portions)); Outside TV Markets (Sierra County (unincorporated areas) (portions), TRUTH OR CONSEQUENCES, Williamsburg). Franchise award date: July 1, 1974. Franchise expiration date: N.A. Began: July 1, 1974.
Channel capacity: N.A. Channels available but not in use: N.A.
Basic Service
Subscribers: 2,007.
Programming (via microwave): KASA-TV (FOX) Santa Fe; KASY-TV (MNT) Albuquerque; KFOX-TV (FOX) El Paso; KLUZ-TV (UNV) Albuquerque; KOAT-TV (ABC) Albuquerque; KOB (NBC) Albuquerque; KRPV-DT (IND) Roswell; KRQE (CBS) Albuquerque; KRWG-TV (PBS) Las Cruces; KTEL-TV (TMO) Carlsbad.
Programming (via satellite): Home Shopping Network; QVC; TBS Superstation; Trinity Broadcasting Network; TV Guide Network; Weather Channel; WGN America.
Programming (via translator): KNME-TV (PBS) Albuquerque.
Fee: $54.95 installation; $22.00 monthly.
Expanded Basic Service 1
Subscribers: 1,815.
Programming (via satellite): ABC Family Channel; AMC; Animal Planet; Arts & Entertainment; Cartoon Network; CNBC; CNN; Comedy Central; Country Music TV; Discovery Channel; Disney Channel; Do-It-Yourself; E! Entertainment Television; ESPN; ESPN 2; Food Network; Fox News Channel; FX; G4; Great American Country; GSN; Hallmark Channel; Headline News; History Channel; Lifetime; MSNBC; MTV; Nickelodeon; SoapNet; Spike TV; Style Network; Syfy; The Learning Channel; Travel Channel; truTV; Turner Network TV; TV Land; USA Network; VH1.
Fee: $27.95 monthly.
Digital Basic Service
Subscribers: N.A.
Programming (via satellite): BBC America; Bio; Bloomberg Television; Bravo; CMT Pure Country; Discovery Health Channel; Discovery Kids Channel; Discovery Military

Channel; Discovery Planet Green; ESPN Classic Sports; FitTV; Fox Movie Channel; Fox Soccer; Fuse; Golf Channel; HGTV; History Channel International; ID Investigation Discovery; Independent Film Channel; Lifetime Movie Network; Lifetime Real Women; MTV Hits; MTV2; Music Choice; Nick Jr.; Outdoor Channel; Science Channel; Speed Channel; TeenNick; the mtn; Toon Disney; Turner Classic Movies; Versus; VH1 Classic; VH1 Soul; WE tv.
Fee: $9.95 monthly.

Digital Expanded Basic Service
Subscribers: N.A.
Programming (via satellite): Arts & Entertainment HD; ESPN HD; Food Network HD; HGTV HD; History Channel HD; TBS in HD; Turner Network TV HD.

Digital Expanded Basic Service 2
Subscribers: N.A.
Programming (via satellite): HDNet; HDNet Movies; Universal HD.

Digital Pay Service 1
Pay Units: N.A.
Programming (via satellite): Cinemax (multiplexed); Cinemax HD; Encore (multiplexed); Flix; HBO (multiplexed); HBO HD; Showtime (multiplexed); Showtime HD; Starz (multiplexed); Starz HDTV; The Movie Channel (multiplexed); The Movie Channel HD.

Video-On-Demand: No

Pay-Per-View
iN DEMAND (delivered digitally); Hot Choice (delivered digitally); Playboy TV (delivered digitally); Fresh (delivered digitally); Spice: Xcess (delivered digitally); Ten Clips (delivered digitally); Ten Blox (delivered digitally); Ten Xtsy (delivered digitally).

Internet Service
Operational: Yes. Began: August 1, 2003.
Broadband Service: In-house.
Fee: $49.99 installation; $34.99 monthly; $4.95 modem lease; $69.95 modem purchase.

Telephone Service
None

Miles of Plant: 49.0 (coaxial); None (fiber optic). Homes passed: 3,397.
General Manager: Tom Jaskiewicz. Technical Operations Manager: Harold Vilas. Office Manager: Barbara Mick.
City fee: 3% of gross.
Ownership: Baja Broadband (MSO).

TUCUMCARI—Comcast Cable, 1808 S 1st St, Tucumcari, NM 88401-3506. Phones: 505-461-4410; 505-461-3160. Fax: 505-461-0116. Web Site: http://www.comcast.com. Also serves Quay County. ICA: NM0021.
TV Market Ranking: Below 100 (Quay County (portions)); Outside TV Markets (Quay County (portions), TUCUMCARI). Franchise award date: January 1, 1956. Franchise expiration date: N.A. Began: October 1, 1956.
Channel capacity: 37 (not 2-way capable). Channels available but not in use: 1.

Basic Service
Subscribers: 1,798.
Programming (via satellite): ABC Family Channel; AMC; Arts & Entertainment; Cartoon Network; CNBC; CNN; Comcast Sports Net Southwest; Country Music TV; C-SPAN; CW+; Discovery Channel; Disney Channel; E! Entertainment Television; ESPN; Eternal Word TV Network; GalaVision; Hallmark Channel; Headline News; History Channel; Home Shopping Network; Lifetime; MSNBC; MTV; Nickelodeon; QVC; Spike TV; Syfy; TBS Superstation; The Learning Channel; Trinity Broadcasting Network; Turner Network TV; Univision; USA Network; Versus; VH1; Weather Channel; WGN America.
Programming (via translator): KAMR-TV (NBC) Amarillo; KASA-TV (FOX) Santa Fe; KCIT (FOX) Amarillo; KENW (PBS) Portales; KFDA-TV (CBS) Amarillo; KOAT-TV (ABC) Albuquerque; KOB (NBC) Albuquerque; KRQE (CBS) Albuquerque; KVII-TV (ABC, CW) Amarillo.
Current originations: Educational Access.
Fee: $60.00 installation; $29.95 monthly.

Pay Service 1
Pay Units: 520.
Programming (via satellite): Cinemax; HBO.
Fee: $19.95 installation; $9.00 monthly (Cinemax), $12.95 monthly (HBO).

Video-On-Demand: No

Internet Service
Operational: Yes.

Telephone Service
None

Miles of Plant: 55.0 (coaxial); None (fiber optic). Homes passed: 3,200. Total homes in franchised area: 3,400.
Area Vice President: John Christopher. General Manager: Dennis Jones. Chief Technician: Spencer DeBord. Office Manager: Frederick Dominguez.
City fee: 2% of gross.
Ownership: Comcast Cable Communications Inc. (MSO).

TWIN FORKS—PVTV Cable Services. Now served by ARTESIA, NM [NM0016]. ICA: NM0056.

VAUGHN—Formerly served by Cebridge Connections. No longer in operation. ICA: NM0062.

WAGON MOUND—Formerly served by Rocky Mountain Cable. No longer in operation. ICA: NM0071.

YAH-TA-HEY—Formerly served by Frontier Communications. No longer in operation. ICA: NM0092.

ZUNI—Formerly served by Frontier Communications. No longer in operation. ICA: NM0093.

TELEVISION & CABLE

Factbook Online

Continuously Updated • Easy Internet Access • Fully Searchable

Now you can access the entire contents of the *Television & Cable Factbook* database instantly on your desktop or any Internet connection.

Your subscription to the *Television & Cable Factbook: Online* will provide you with access to over 930,000 detailed records. Best of all, the database is continuously updated to ensure you always have the most current industry intelligence.

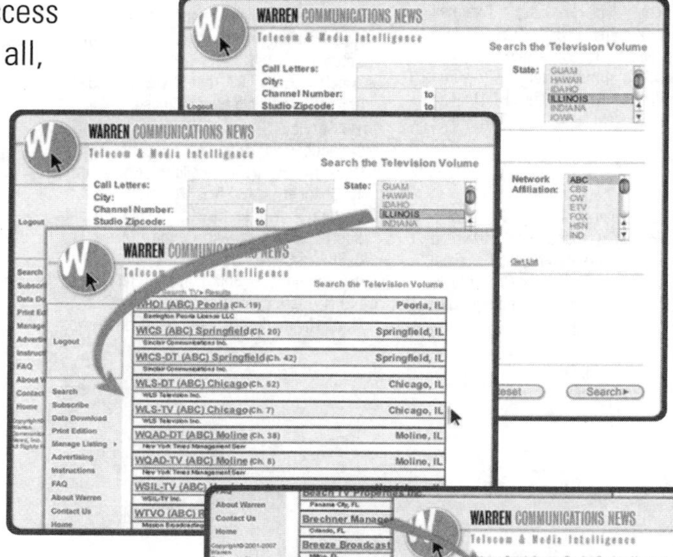

The user-friendly query interface allows you to perform fully customized data searches—so you can retrieve data in a number of ways, tailored to your precise needs. The search options are extensive and flexible, and will save you hours and hours of cumbersome research time.

You'll <u>recover your subscription cost after just a few searches</u> and continue to save enormous amounts of time, money and effort with every search.

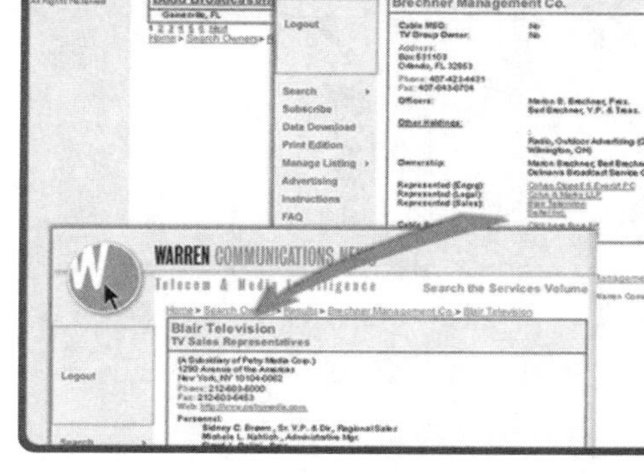

See for yourself why the Factbook: Online is an indispensible tool for you and your business. Sign up for your **no-risk, no obligation** trial today.

Take a FREE 7-day trial at
www.warren-news.com/factbook.htm

You have **nothing to lose** and **lots of time and money to save.**

Alphabetical Listing of TV Markets – 2010

Nielsen DMA TV Households Ranking

Market	Rank
Abilene-Sweetwater, TX	165
Albany, GA	147
Albany-Schenectady-Troy, NY	58
Albuquerque-Santa Fe, NM	46
Alexandria, LA	178
Alpena, MI	208
Amarillo, TX	131
Anchorage, AK	150
Atlanta, GA	8
Augusta, GA-Aiken, SC	114
Austin, TX	44
Bakersfield, CA	125
Baltimore, MD	26
Bangor, ME	154
Baton Rouge, LA	94
Beaumont-Port Arthur, TX	141
Bend, OR	189
Billings, MT	170
Biloxi-Gulfport, MS	163
Binghamton, NY	158
Birmingham (Anniston & Tuscaloosa), AL	40
Bluefield-Beckley-Oak Hill, WV	155
Boise, ID	113
Boston, MA (Manchester, NH)	7
Bowling Green, KY	181
Buffalo, NY	51
Burlington, VT-Plattsburgh, NY	95
Butte-Bozeman, MT	191
Casper-Riverton, WY	195
Cedar Rapids-Waterloo-Iowa City & Dubuque, IA	88
Champaign & Springfield-Decatur, IL	84
Charleston, SC	98
Charleston-Huntington, WV	64
Charlotte, NC	23
Charlottesville, VA	183
Chattanooga, TN	86
Cheyenne, WY-Scottsbluff, NE	197
Chicago, IL	3
Chico-Redding, CA	130
Cincinnati, OH	33
Clarksburg-Weston, WV	168
Cleveland-Akron (Canton), OH	18
Colorado Springs-Pueblo, CO	92
Columbia, SC	78
Columbia-Jefferson City, MO	137
Columbus, GA (Opelika, AL)	127
Columbus, OH	34
Columbus-Tupelo-West Point-Houston, MS	133
Corpus Christi, TX	129
Dallas-Fort Worth, TX	5
Davenport, IA-Rock Island-Moline, IL	99
Dayton, OH	62
Denver, CO	17
Des Moines-Ames, IA	73
Detroit, MI	11
Dothan, AL	169
Duluth, MN-Superior, WI	139
El Paso, TX (Las Cruces, NM)	97
Elmira (Corning), NY	174
Erie, PA	144
Eugene, OR	118
Eureka, CA	194
Evansville, IN	103
Fairbanks, AK	202
Fargo-Valley City, ND	120
Flint-Saginaw-Bay City, MI	69
Fort Myers-Naples, FL	65
Fort Smith-Fayetteville-Springdale-Rogers, AR	100
Fort Wayne, IN	107
Fresno-Visalia, CA	55
Gainesville, FL	160
Glendive, MT	210
Grand Junction-Montrose, CO	184
Grand Rapids-Kalamazoo-Battle Creek, MI	41
Great Falls, MT	190
Green Bay-Appleton, WI	71
Greensboro-High Point-Winston Salem, NC	47
Greenville-New Bern-Washington, NC	101
Greenville-Spartanburg-Anderson, SC-Asheville, NC	36
Greenwood-Greenville, MS	187
Harlingen-Weslaco-Brownsville-McAllen, TX	87
Harrisburg-Lancaster-Lebanon-York, PA	39
Harrisonburg, VA	177
Hartford & New Haven, CT	30
Hattiesburg-Laurel, MS	167
Helena, MT	206
Honolulu, HI	72
Houston, TX	10
Huntsville-Decatur (Florence), AL	79
Idaho Falls-Pocatello, ID (Jackson, WY)	162
Indianapolis, IN	27
Jackson, MS	90
Jackson, TN	182
Jacksonville, FL	49
Johnstown-Altoona-State College, PA	102
Jonesboro, AR	180
Joplin, MO-Pittsburg, KS	148
Juneau, AK	207
Kansas City, MO	31
Knoxville, TN	59
La Crosse-Eau Claire, WI	128
Lafayette, IN	188
Lafayette, LA	123
Lake Charles, LA	175
Lansing, MI	115
Laredo, TX	186
Las Vegas, NV	42
Lexington, KY	63
Lima, OH	201
Lincoln & Hastings-Kearney, NE	106
Little Rock-Pine Bluff, AR	56
Los Angeles, CA	2
Louisville, KY	50
Lubbock, TX	142
Macon, GA	121
Madison, WI	85
Mankato, MN	198
Marquette, MI	179
Medford-Klamath Falls, OR	140
Memphis, TN	48
Meridian, MS	185
Miami-Fort Lauderdale, FL	16
Milwaukee, WI	35
Minneapolis-St. Paul, MN	15
Minot-Bismarck-Dickinson (Williston), ND	157
Missoula, MT	166
Mobile, AL-Pensacola (Fort Walton Beach), FL	60
Monroe, LA-El Dorado, AR	138
Monterey-Salinas, CA	124
Montgomery-Selma, AL	117
Myrtle Beach-Florence, SC	104
Nashville, TN	29
New Orleans, LA	52
New York, NY	1
Norfolk-Portsmouth-Newport News, VA	43
North Platte, NE	209
Odessa-Midland, TX	151
Oklahoma City, OK	45
Omaha, NE	76
Orlando-Daytona Beach-Melbourne, FL	19
Ottumwa, IA-Kirksville, MO	199
Paducah, KY-Cape Girardeau, MO-Harrisburg, IL	80
Palm Springs, CA	145
Panama City, FL	156
Parkersburg, WV	193
Peoria-Bloomington, IL	116
Philadelphia, PA	4
Phoenix (Prescott), AZ	12
Pittsburgh, PA	24
Portland, OR	22
Portland-Auburn, ME	77
Presque Isle, ME	205
Providence, RI-New Bedford, MA	53
Quincy, IL-Hannibal, MO-Keokuk, IA	172
Raleigh-Durham (Fayetteville), NC	25
Rapid City, SD	173
Reno, NV	108
Richmond-Petersburg, VA	57
Roanoke-Lynchburg, VA	66
Rochester, MN-Mason City, IA-Austin, MN	153
Rochester, NY	81
Rockford, IL	134
Sacramento-Stockton-Modesto, CA	20
Salisbury, MD	143
Salt Lake City, UT	32
San Angelo, TX	196
San Antonio, TX	37
San Diego, CA	28
San Francisco-Oakland-San Jose, CA	6
Santa Barbara-Santa Maria-San Luis Obispo, CA	122
Savannah, GA	96
Seattle-Tacoma, WA	13
Sherman, TX-Ada, OK	161
Shreveport, LA	83

Alpha List of TV Markets

U.S. CABLE PENETRATION STATE BY STATE

(As of October 2010)

Note: Figures reflect information supplied by system operators and do not include wireless cable systems.

* Basic subscribers, Expanded Basic subscriber, and Pay Unit totals include analog and digital subscribers. Some cable systems have converted to IPTV.

State	Systems	Basic Subscribers*	Expanded Basic Subscribers*	Pay Units*	Miles of Plant	Homes Passed
Alabama	149	1,149,987	303,124	160,540	32,247	1,282,304
Alaska	30	199,227	129,467	95,845	3,292	240,908
Arizona	64	1,517,365	149,964	255,759	29,033	826,141
Arkansas	171	422,438	91,693	83,986	17,103	827,280
California	180	8,105,648	1,980,713	1,065,342	97,036	13,596,787
Colorado	109	1,385,455	64,360	15,810	21,073	1,989,363
Connecticut	24	1,159,226	288,253	78,812	23,784	1,504,067
Delaware	5	118,752	156,027	12,363	4,854	213,101
District of Columbia	20	176,000	---	---	1,225	325,000
Florida	150	6,654,664	787,708	539,754	97,530	5,830,403
Georgia	216	1,415,962	871,839	272,063	63,235	2,014,006
Hawaii	6	350,115	---	---	4,902	563,120
Idaho	38	284,174	66,460	15,240	8,262	247,226
Illinois	279	2,609,853	601,856	312,275	43,081	4,052,105
Indiana	143	1,422,829	373,353	101,499	34,107	1,765,703
Iowa	245	696,880	349,108	151,223	21,788	956,375
Kansas	203	650,750	295,029	78,936	8,050	803,073
Kentucky	152	1,017,578	570,241	198,356	38,847	1,272,789
Louisiana	104	1,059,942	288,763	304,959	28,732	1,502,064
Maine	43	325,114	225,086	29,562	11,436	386,988
Maryland	33	1,372,603	444,711	177,178	22,113	1,605,207
Massachusetts	44	1,557,180	255,340	106,873	8,779	509,786
Michigan	225	2,314,939	621,564	157,622	55,715	3,537,660
Minnesota	268	1,335,493	656,475	183,983	29,896	1,800,745
Mississippi	115	552,871	120,911	49,542	16,608	771,134
Missouri	209	1,529,258	720,512	276,841	30,189	1,808,487
Montana	91	210,007	121,228	6,085	5,189	299,897
Nebraska	172	571,591	282,932	184,139	9,835	342,833
Nevada	37	591,170	86,778	1,628	11,036	1,084,737
New Hampshire	17	830,274	120,767	25,928	11,092	549,051
New Jersey	37	2,779,077	678,028	1,230,978	43,943	3,587,062
New Mexico	53	321,777	198,692	32,109	8,600	517,447
New York	87	6,514,830	2,688,409	570,850	58,782	8,363,884
North Carolina	108	2,308,435	818,134	234,416	70,867	2,310,437
North Dakota	68	189,526	36,187	15,711	3,783	273,559
Ohio	170	3,423,895	548,354	368,823	67,091	4,633,510
Oklahoma	230	730,761	456,313	213,468	19,448	753,318
Oregon	86	1,087,270	425,128	133,041	25,655	994,256
Pennsylvania	278	3,901,520	1,350,957	136,694	77,434	3,835,640
Rhode Island	3	317,024	272,375	7,000	4,290	21,929
South Carolina	47	1,147,580	628,522	131,195	32,946	1,400,518
South Dakota	125	211,438	650	34,167	5,274	361,679
Tennessee	102	1,721,878	613,451	352,683	45,113	2,203,923
Texas	430	4,929,241	1,726,334	964,000	117,728	5,903,366
Utah	52	324,133	143,077	16,852	11,454	821,459
Vermont	12	37,038	73,931	1,180	5,899	258,918
Virginia	107	1,975,256	417,601	390,794	33,945	1,424,255
Washington	101	1,543,179	552,753	216,556	24,650	1,099,966
West Virginia	132	489,302	212,227	48,594	17,130	599,130
Wisconsin	179	1,630,944	827,680	174,187	26,607	1,878,713
Wyoming	59	122,838	80,657	18,323	3,448	183,155
Cuba	1	976	---	858	40	3,000
Guam	1	48,646	---	2,631	806	53,043
Marianas Islands	1	6,500	---	440	110	10,000
Puerto Rico	3	339,550	102,000	48,334	9,242	983,250
Virgin Islands	2	42,923	22,622	16,845	871	60,549
TOTAL	**6,016**	**77,732,882**	**23,898,344**	**10,302,872**	**1,505,225**	**95,044,306**

U.S. CABLE SYSTEM TOTALS STATE BY STATE

(As of October 2010)

Note: All data is as reported by cable operators or individual cable systems. Not all cable systems or operators report complete data.
* Basic subscriber totals include analog and digital subscribers. Some systems have converted to IPTV.

State	Systems	Communities Served	Franchises Not Yet Operating	Applications Pending	Communities with Applications	Total Basic Subscribers*
Alabama	149	630	0	0	0	1,149,987
Alaska	30	55	0	0	0	199,227
Arizona	64	212	0	0	0	1,517,365
Arkansas	171	510	0	0	0	422,438
California	180	1,172	0	0	0	8,105,648
Colorado	109	339	0	0	0	1,385,455
Connecticut	24	204	0	0	0	1,159,226
Delaware	5	80	0	0	0	118,752
District of Columbia	20	22	0	0	0	176,000
Florida	150	837	0	0	0	6,654,664
Georgia	216	841	0	0	0	1,415,962
Hawaii	6	128	0	0	0	350,115
Idaho	38	189	0	0	0	284,174
Illinois	279	1,300	0	0	0	2,609,853
Indiana	143	727	0	0	0	1,422,829
Iowa	245	756	0	0	0	696,880
Kansas	203	462	0	0	0	650,750
Kentucky	152	1,001	0	0	0	1,017,578
Louisiana	104	467	0	0	0	1,059,942
Maine	43	361	0	0	0	325,114
Maryland	33	414	0	0	0	1,372,603
Massachusetts	44	361	0	0	0	1,557,180
Michigan	225	1,553	0	0	0	2,314,939
Minnesota	268	883	0	0	0	1,335,493
Mississippi	115	347	0	0	0	552,871
Missouri	209	767	0	0	0	1,529,258
Montana	91	154	0	0	0	210,007
Nebraska	172	372	0	0	0	571,591
Nevada	37	98	0	0	0	591,170
New Hampshire	17	206	0	0	0	830,274
New Jersey	37	635	0	0	0	2,779,077
New Mexico	53	146	0	0	0	321,777
New York	87	1,568	0	0	0	6,514,830
North Carolina	108	882	0	0	0	2,308,435
North Dakota	68	233	0	0	0	189,526
Ohio	170	1,815	0	0	0	3,423,895
Oklahoma	230	412	0	0	0	730,761
Oregon	86	379	0	0	0	1,087,270
Pennsylvania	278	2,581	0	0	0	3,901,520
Rhode Island	3	45	0	0	0	317,024
South Carolina	47	368	0	0	0	1,147,580
South Dakota	125	246	0	0	0	211,438
Tennessee	102	542	0	0	0	1,721,878
Texas	430	1,399	0	0	0	4,929,241
Utah	52	210	0	0	0	324,133
Vermont	12	236	0	0	0	37,038
Virginia	107	570	0	0	0	1,975,256
Washington	101	462	0	0	0	1,543,179
West Virginia	132	1,019	0	0	0	489,302
Wisconsin	179	907	0	0	0	1,630,944
Wyoming	59	115	0	0	0	122,838
Cuba	1	1	0	0	0	976
Guam	1	20	0	0	0	48,646
Marianas Islands	1	3	3	0	0	6,500
Puerto Rico	3	87	0	0	0	339,550
Virgin Islands	2	3	0	0	0	42,923
TOTAL	**6,016**	**30,332**	**3**	**0**	**0**	**77,732,882**

Index to Sections
Television & Cable Factbook No. 79

TV STATIONS VOLUME

Section A

Section B

Section C – Charts

CABLE SYSTEMS VOLUME

Section D

Section E

Section F – Charts

Cable Systems State Index